Beckett® RACING Collectibles Price Guide

Number 14

Founder & Advisor: Dr. James Beckett III

Edited By
Tim Trout
with the staff of
BECKETT RACING

Beckett Media LP - Dallas, Texas

Manufactured in the United States of America

Published by Beckett Media LP, an Apprise Media Company

Beckett Media LP
4635 McEwen RD
Dallas, TX 75244
(972) 991-6657
www.beckett.com

Apprise Media LLC
450 Park Avenue
New York, NY 10022
(212) 751-3182
www.apprisemedia.com

First Printing
ISBN 1-930692-76-5

Table of Contents

How To Use 4

History of Racing Cards 9

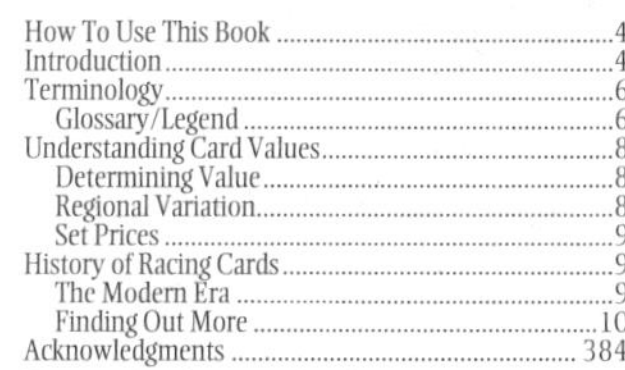

How To Use This Book ... 4
Introduction ... 4
Terminology ... 6
Glossary/Legend ... 6
Understanding Card Values ... 8
Determining Value ... 8
Regional Variation ... 8
Set Prices ... 9
History of Racing Cards ... 9
The Modern Era ... 9
Finding Out More ... 10
Acknowledgments ... 384

Racing Cards Price Guide

2007 AAA Limited Edition ... 11
1990 AC Racing Proven Winners ... 11
1992 Action Packed Allison Family ... 11
1997 Alka-Seltzer Terry Labonte ... 14
1993-94 Alliance Robert Pressley/Dennis Setzer ... 15
1992 Arena Joe Gibbs Racing ... 15
1995 Assets ... 15
1996 Autographed Racing ... 15
2004 Bass Pro Shops Racing ... 16
1986 Big League Cards Alan Kulwicki Quincy's ... 16
1992 Bikers of the Racing Scene ... 17
2004 Blue Bonnet Bobby Labonte ... 17
1998 Burger King Dale Earnhardt ... 17
1992 Card Dynamics Davey Allison ... 17
1996 Classic ... 17
1992 Clevite Engine Builders ... 18
1991 CM Handsome Harry ... 18
1999 Coca-Cola Racing Family ... 18
2006 Press Pass Coca Cola AutoZone ... 18
1993-96 Collector's Advantage Phone Cards ... 18
1992 Coyote Rookies ... 19
1995 Crown Jewels Promos ... 19
1992 Dayco Series 1 ... 20
1955-56 Diamond Matchbooks Indy ... 20
1992 Erin Maxx Trans-Am ... 20
1994 Ernie Irvan Fan Club ... 20
2003 eTopps ... 20
1993 Finish Line Promos ... 21
2000 Firestone Checkered Flag ... 24
1996 Flair ... 24
1992 Food Lion Richard Petty ... 24
1991 Galfield Press Pioneers of Racing ... 25
1992 Hilton G. Hill Gold True Legend ... 25
1991 Hickory Motor Speedway ... 25
1994 High Gear Promos ... 25
1994-95 Highland Mint/VIP ... 25
1993 Hi-Tech Tire Test ... 25
1992 Hooters Alan Kulwicki ... 25
1993 Hoyle Playing Cards ... 26
1995 Images ... 26
1994 IMS Indianapolis 500 Champions Collection ... 26
1991 IROC ... 26
1997 Jurassic Park ... 26
1992 Just Racing Larry Caudill ... 26
2006 Kellogg's Racing ... 26
1996 KnightQuest ... 26
1991 Langenberg ARCA/Hot Stuff ... 27
1992 Limited Editions Promos ... 28
1995 Lipton Tea Johnny Benson Jr. ... 28
2006 Little Debbie ... 28
1992 Mac Tools Winner's Cup ... 28
1993 Maxwell House ... 28
1988 Maxx Charlotte ... 28
1998 Maxximum ... 42
1995 Metallic Impressions Classic Dale Earnhardt 21-Card Tin ... 43
1996 M-Force ... 43
1992 Miller Genuine Draft Rusty Wallace ... 43
1991 Motorcraft Racing ... 43
1994 MW Windows ... 43
2005 NAPA ... 43
2004 National Trading Card Day * ... 43
2003 Nilla Wafers Team Nabisco ... 44
1992 Pace American Canadian Tour ... 44
1992 Pepsi Richard Petty ... 44
1996 Pinnacle ... 44
1991-92 Pioneers of Stock Car Racing ... 46
2004 Post Cereal ... 46
1994 Power ... 46
1997 Predator Promos ... 47
1993 Press Pass Davey Allison ... 47
1991 Pro Set Prototypes ... 91
1994 Quality Care Glidden/Speed ... 93
1996 Racer's Choice ... 93
1997 Race Sharks ... 93
1991 Racing Concepts Shawna Robinson ... 94
1992 Redline Graphics Short Track ... 94
1992 RSS Motorsports Haulers ... 94
1997 SB Motorsports ... 94
1996 Score Board Dale Earnhardt ... 95
1995 Select Promos ... 95
1994 SkyBox ... 95
1992 Slim Jim Bobby Labonte ... 96
1995 SP ... 96
1996 SPx ... 98
1996 Speedflix ... 98
1997 SportsCom FanScan ... 99
1985 SportStars Photo-Graphics Stickers ... 100
2006 Stanley Tools Promo ... 100
1993 Stove Top ... 100
1972 STP ... 100
1991 Sunbelt Racing Legends ... 100
1991 Superior Racing Metals ... 100
2001 Super Shots Hendrick Motorsports ... 101
1991 Texas World Speedway ... 101
1989-90 TG Racing Masters of Racing ... 101
1991 TG Racing Tiny Lund ... 101
1991-92 TG Racing Masters of Racing Update ... 102
1994 Tide Ricky Rudd ... 102
1991 Tiger Tom Pistone ... 102
1991 Track Pack Yesterday's Heroes ... 102
2006 TRAKS ... 107
1996 Ultra ... 108
1983 UNO Racing ... 110
1995 Upper Deck ... 110
1995 US Air Greg Sacks ... 116
2007 Valvoline Racing ... 117
2002 Velveeta Jeff Burton ... 117
1994 VIP ... 117
1996 Viper Promos ... 123
1992 Wheels Kyle Petty ... 124
1991 Winner's Choice New England Drivers ... 137
1995 Western Steer Earnhardt Next Generation ... 138
1995 Zenith ... 138

Drag Racing Card Price Guide

1986 Ace Drag ... 139
1994 Action Packed NHRA ... 139
1993 Advanced Images Quick Eight Racing ... 139
1990 Big Time Drag ... 139
1994 Card Dynamics Joe Amato ... 139
1989 Checkered Flag IHRA ... 139
1965 Donruss Spec Sheet ... 140
1993 Finish Line NHRA Prototypes ... 140
1970 Fleer Dragstrips ... 140
1997 Hi-Tech NHRA ... 141
1993-97 Kustom Kards Bunny Burkett ... 141
1989 Mega Drag ... 141
2007 NHRA Powerade Countdown to the Championship ... 141
2005 Press Pass NHRA ... 141
1991 Pro Set NHRA ... 141
1965 Topps Hot Rods ... 142

Indy/F1 Card Price Guide

1983 A and S Racing Indy ... 142
1986 Ace Formula One ... 143
1990 Action Packed Indy Prototypes ... 143
1991 All World Indy ... 143
1911 American Tobacco Auto Drivers ... 143
1980 Avalon Hill USAC Race Game ... 143
1986 BOSCH Indy ... 144
1991 Carms Formula One ... 144
1997 CART Schedule Cards ... 144
1939 Churchman's Kings of Speed ... 144
1992 Collect-A-Card Andretti Racing ... 144
1987 Formula One Italian ... 144
1992 Golden Era Grand Prix The Early Years ... 144
1978-79 Grand Prix ... 144
1992 Grid Formula One ... 145
1960 Hawes Wax Indy ... 145
1992 Hi-Tech Indy Prototypes ... 145
1988 Heraclio Fournier Formula One ... 146
2002 Indianapolis 500 ... 146
1991 K-Mart ... 146
1991 Langenberg American IndyCar Series ... 146
1991 Legends of Indy ... 146
1992 Limited Appeal Formula One ... 147
1962 Marhoefer Indy ... 147
1993 Maxx Williams Racing ... 147
1971 Mobil The Story of Grand Prix Motor Racing ... 147
1973 Nabisco Sugar Daddy Speedway Collection ... 147
1931 Ogden's Motor Races ... 147
1962 Petpro Limited Grand Prix Racing Cars ... 148
1991 Pro Tracs Formula One ... 148
2007 Rittenhouse IRL ... 148
1970 Shell Racing Cars of the World ... 148
1995 SkyBox Indy 500 ... 148
1926 Sport Company of America Racing ... 149
1954 Stark and Wetzel Indy Winners ... 149
1966 Strombecker ... 149
1911 Turkey Red Automobile Series ... 149
1930 Wills' Cigarettes ... 149

Dirt/Sprint Card Price Guide

1991 Bull Ring ... 149
2002 Choice Rising Stars ... 150
1992 Corter Selinsgrove and Clinton County Speedways ... 150
1991 Dirt Trax ... 150
1991 DK IMCA Dirt Track ... 150
1991 Hav-A-Tampa ... 151
1991 JAGS ... 151
1995 JSK Iceman ... 152
1990 K and W Dirt Track ... 152
1990 Langenberg Rockford Speedway/Hot Stuff ... 152
1992 Racing Legends Sprints ... 153
1992 STARS Modifieds ... 153
1992 Traks Dirt ... 153
1992 Volunteer Racing East Alabama Speedway ... 153
1991 Winner's Choice Modifieds ... 153
1987 World of Outlaws ... 153

Multi-Sport Card Price Guide

1968 American Oil Winners Circle * ... 154
1994-95 Assets * ... 155
1995 Classic Five-Sport Previews * ... 155
1996 Clear Assets * ... 156
1972-83 Dimanche/Derniere Heure * ... 156
1937 Kellogg's Pep Stamps * ... 156
1976 Nabisco Sugar Daddy 1 * ... 156
1996 No Fear * ... 156
1991 Pro Set Pro Files * ... 156
1994 Score Board National Promos * ... 156
1989-91 Sports Illustrated for Kids * ... 156
1996 Visions * ... 156
2004 SportCoins ... 156

Die-Cast Price Guide

2000-01 Action Racing Collectables Ceramic 1:12 ... 157
2008 RCCA Club 1:24 ... 179
1998-01 Action Racing Collectables 1:32 ... 180
1997-99 Brookfield 1:24 ... 189
2007 Checkered Flag Sports Champions 1:24 ... 189
1992 Ertl 1:18 ... 190
1992 Funstuf Pit Row 1:43 ... 191
2002-04 General Mills Petty Promos 1:64 ... 191
2003 GreenLight 1:24 ... 191
2002 Hot Wheels Thunder Series Motorcycles 1:18 191
1998 Johnny Lightning Stock Car Legends 1:64 ... 199
1997 Lindberg ARCA 1:64 ... 199
1990-92 Matchbox White Rose Super Stars 1:64 ... 199
1996 Miscellaneous Promos 1:24 ... 200
2006 Motorsports Authentics Steel 1:16 ... 200
1991-92 Pole Position 1:64 ... 204
1996 Press Pass Sets 1:24/64 ... 204
1997 Race Image 1:43 ... 204
1992-97 Raceway Replicas 1:24 ... 204
1995 Racing Champions Premier 1:18 ... 204
1997 Revell Club 1:18 ... 231
1992 Road Champs 1:43 ... 236
2004 Team Caliber Pit Stop 1:18 ... 237
2002 Winner's Circle 1:18 ... 245
1994 Action/RCCA Dually Trucks 1:2 ... 254
1993-95 Brookfield Dually with Car and Show Trailer 1:25 255
1993-95 Corgi Race Image Transporters 1:64 ... 257
1992 Ertl Founding Fathers Transporters 1:43 ... 257
1997-99 Hartoy American Racing Scene Transporters 1:64 257
1998 Hot Wheels Transporters 1:64 ... 257
1990-93 Matchbox White Rose Team Convoys 1:64 257
2007 Motorsports Authentics/RCCA Transporters Bank 1:24 ... 258
1996-01 Peachstate/GMP Transporters 1:64 ... 258
1993 Racing Champions Transporters 1:43 ... 258
1997 Revell Transporters 1:64 ... 262
1992 Road Champs Transporters 1:64 ... 263
1996-98 Scaleworks Transporters 1:24 ... 263
2003 Team Caliber Owners Series Transporters 1:64 ... 263
1998 Winner's Circle Race 'N' Play Transporters 1:64 ... 263
1987-90 Winross Transporters 1:64 ... 264

Transporters Die-Cast Price Guide

1994 Action/RCCA Dually Trucks 1:24 ... 246
1993-95 Brookfield Dually with Car and Show Trailer 1:25 ... 247
1993-95 Corgi Race Image Transporters 1:64 ... 249
1992 Ertl Founding Fathers Transporters 1:43 ... 249
1997-99 Hartoy American Racing Scene Transporters 1:64 ... 249
1998 Hot Wheels Transporters 1:64 ... 249
1990-93 Matchbox White Rose Team Convoys 1:64 ... 249
2007 Motorsports Authentics/RCCA Transporters Bank 1:24 ... 250
1996-01 Peachstate/GMP Transporters 1:64 ... 250
1993 Racing Champions Transporters 1:43 ... 250
1997 Revell Transporters 1:64 ... 254
1992 Road Champs Transporters 1:64 ... 254
1996-98 Scaleworks Transporters 1:24 ... 255
2003 Team Caliber Owners Series Transporters 1:64 ... 255
1998 Winner's Circle Race 'N' Play Transporters 1:64 ... 255
1987-90 Winross Transporters 1:64 ... 255

Drag Racing Die-Cast Price Guide

1995 Action/RCCA Dragsters 1:24 ... 264
1999 Brookfield NHRA Dually with Trailer 1:24 ... 268
2004 Classic Garage/Ertl Vintage Pro Stock 1:18 ... 268
2002 Ertl American Muscle Arnie Beswick 1:18 ... 268
2002-03 GMP Vintage Dragsters 1:18 ... 268
2004 Hot Wheels Dragsters Promos 1:64 ... 268
1996 Johnny Lightning Top Fuel Legends Dragsters 1:64 ... 268
2003 Lane/Ertl Vintage Pro Stock 1:18 ... 268
2003 Ertl Chevy Legends Pro Stock 1:18 ... 268
2003 Milestone Development Dragsters 1:16 ... 268
2003 PMC Dragsters 1:24 ... 268
2000 Racing Champions Authentics NHRA 1:24 ... 269
1998 Revell Dragsters 1:24 ... 271
2003 RSC Collectibles Vintage Pro Stock 1:24 ... 271
1999-03 Supercar/Ertl Vintage Pro Stock 1:18 ... 271
2002 Team Caliber Dragsters 1:24 ... 271
2001 Thirteen-Twenty Fuelers Dragsters 1:24 ... 271
1997 Winner's Circle Dragsters 1:24 ... 272

Indy /F1 Die-Cast Price Guide

1999 Action Indy Cars 1:18 ... 272
2000-04 Carousel 1 Vintage Indy 1:18 ... 272
1996 EPI Indy 1:24 ... 272
1985 Ertl Motorized Pullback Indy Cars 1:43 ... 272
2004 GreenLight IRL 1:18 ... 272
1993 Hot Wheels Pro Circuit Indy 1:64 ... 273
1970 Johnny Lightning Indy 500 1:64 ... 273
1998 Maisto Indy Racing 1:18 ... 273
1991 Matchbox Indy 500 Coins/Die-Cast 1:55 ... 273
1993 MiniChamps Indy Road Course 1:18 ... 274
1993 Onyx Indy 1:24 ... 274
1994-95 Racing Champions Indy Banks 1:24 ... 274
1997 UT Models Indy 1:18 ... 276
1998 Hot Wheels Racing F1 1:18 ... 276
1988-92 MiniChamps F1 1:18 ... 276
1995 Onyx F1 1:18 ... 278
2005 Quartzo F1 1:18 ... 279
1992-93 Tamiya F1 Collector's Club 1:20 ... 279

Dirt/Sprint/Modified Die-Cast Price Guide

1994 Action/RCCA Dirt Cars 1:24 ... 279
2003 ADC Dirt Late Model Cars 1:24 ... 279
1993 Ertl/Nutmeg Modified Legends 1:64 ... 280
1990 Matchbox Modifieds Series 1 1:64 ... 280
2003 Nutmeg Modified Legends 1:25 ... 280
1998-01 Action/RCCA Sprint 1:18 ... 280
1995 Ertl/Nutmeg Sprint Cars 1:55 ... 281
2002 GMP Vintage Sprint Cars 1:12 ... 281
1991 Matchbox Sprint Cars 1:55 ... 282
1993-94 Racing Champions Sprint Cars 1:24 ... 282

Miscellaneous Die-Cast Price Guide

2005 Action/Funline Muscle Machines 1:18 ... 283
2005 Brookfield Dually and Tailgate Set 1:24 ... 284
2005 GreenLight Pace Cars 1:24 ... 284
2003 Action Racing Collectables MLB 1:24 ... 284
2005 Ertl Collectibles World Series Champions MLB 1:18 ... 284
2002 Fleer Collectibles BMW X-5 MLB 1:24 ... 284
2005-06 Ertl Collectibles Choppers Series NBA 1:10 ... 284
2003-04 Fleer H2 w/Ultra card NBA 1:64 ... 285
2005-06 Upper Deck Cadillac Escalade w/UD card NBA 1:64 ... 285
2003 Action Performance NFL 1:24 ... 285
2005 Ertl Collectibles Chopper Series NFL 1:10 ... 285
2003 Fleer Collectibles Monster Trucks NFL 1:32 ... 285
2003 Action Performance NFL 1:64 ... 285
2005 Ertl Collectibles Classic Rides NFL 1:64 ... 285
2001 Fleer Collectibles PT Cruiser w/Ultra Card NFL 1:64 ... 285
1993 White Rose Transporters NFL 1:80 ... 286
2007 Ertl Collectibles Transporters NFL 1:87 ... 286
2004 Action Performance Blisters Zamboni NHL 1:50 286
2005 Ertl Collectibles Choppers Series NHL 1:18 ... 286
2002 Fleer Collectibles Zamboni NHL 1:50 ... 286
2006 Upper Deck Zamboni w/card NHL 1:50 ... 286

Alphabetical Card Checklist.......287 to 358

Alphabetical Die-Cast Checklist.359 to 383

How To Use This Book

Isn't it great? A book that is geared toward every type of racing collector. From the individual driver collectors to the set collectors to the die-cast collectors this book has something for each to enjoy. This Edition of *Beckett Racing Price Guide and Alphabetical Checklist* has been arranged to fit the collector's needs with the inclusion of a comprehensive card Price Guide, die-cast Price Guide and an alphabetical checklist. The cards and die-cast you collect, who appears on them, what they look like, where they are from, and (most important to most of you) what their current values are enumerated within. Many of the features contained in the other Beckett Price Guides have been incorporated into this volume since condition grading, terminology, and many other aspects of collecting are common to the card hobby in general. We hope you find the book both interesting and useful in your collecting pursuits.

The Beckett Guide has been successful where other attempts have failed because it is complete, current, and valid. This Price Guide contains two prices by condition for all the racing cards listed. Since the condition that most die-cast pieces are commonly sold in is Near Mint-Mint, the die-cast price guide has been arranged to provide two pricing columns. The prices for each piece reflects the current selling range for that piece. The HI column generally represents full retail selling price. The LO column generally represents the lowest price one could expect to find with extensive shopping. The prices for both the cards and die-cast were added to the listings just prior to printing and reflect not the author's opinions or desires but the going retail prices for each card or die-cast, based on the marketplace (racing shows and events, sports card shops, ads from racing publications, current mail-order catalogs, local club meetings, auction results, on-line networks, and other firsthand reportings of actually realized prices).

What is the best price guide available on the market today? Of course, card sellers prefer the price guide with the highest prices, while card buyers naturally prefer the one with the lowest prices. Accuracy, however, is the true test. Use the price guide trusted by more collectors and dealers than all the others combined. Look for the Beckett® namewhich stands for accuracy and integrity.

To facilitate your use of this book, read the complete introductory section on the following pages before going to the pricing pages. Every collectible field has its own terminology; we've tried to capture most of these terms and definitions in our glossary. Please read carefully the section on grading and the condition of your cards, as you cannot determine which price column is appropriate for a given card without first knowing its condition.

Introduction

Did you know that monthly updates are available in the pages of *Beckett Sports Card Mothly*. You can also find daily updates on www.beckett.com. Pricing changes along with new listings for the latest releases in cards and die-casts are there as well.

Inside the pages of *BSCM*, you can find news about the latest and greatest cards and die-casts to hit the market. We also answer questions from other collectors like yourself. Another section that collectors find useful is the MarketWatch and Cards & Die-Casts That Matter Most, where we cover what's hot and what's not and we explain why the secondary market reacted the way it did. Another section that can be very helpful is the individual driver Price Guides. Each month we take a few drivers and break down their collectibles into manageable listings with updated pricing.

You can also head over to www.beckett.com to get daily updates on pricing via the Online Price Guides (OPG) and the latest collectible news on the frontpage.

We are not exclusive to racing collectibles, you can also find information about baseball, basketball, football, golf, hockey, soccer, tennis and wrestling collectibles on www.beckett.com.

We also publish specific sports titles for *Beckett Baseball*, *Beckett Basketball*, *Beckett Football* and *Beckett Hockey* six times a year.

So collecting racing cards — while still pursued as a hobby with youthful exuberance by kids in the neighborhood — has also taken on the trappings of an industry, with thousands of full- and part-time card dealers, as well as vendors of supplies, clubs and conventions. In fact, each year since 1980 thousands of hobbyists have assembled for a National Sports Collectors Convention, at which hundreds of dealers have displayed their wares, seminars have been conducted, autographs penned by sports notables, and millions of cards changed hands. The Beckett Guide is the best annual guide available to the exciting world of racing cards and die-cast. Read it and use it. May your enjoyment and your card collection increase in the coming months and years.

Terminology

Each hobby has its own language to describe its area of interest. With racing being relatively new to the card collecting hobby it has adapted many of the terms and phrases used in other areas of sports card collecting. Most sets are usually referred to by year, by maker, and sometimes by title or theme of the set.

Glossary/Legend

Our glossary defines terms used in the card and die-cast collecting hobby and in this book. Many of these terms are also common to other types of sports memorabilia collecting. Some terms may have several meanings depending on use and context.

ACETATE - A transparent plastic.
ACR- AC Racing.
AM - American Miniatures.
ANN - Announcer.
AP - All-Pro.
ART - Art card.
AUTO - Autograph.
AW - Award Winners.
B - Brothers.
BB - Back to Back.
BC - Busch Clash.
BD - Burning Desire
BF - Buck Fever.
BGN - Busch Grand National.
BL - Blister Pack.
BLISTER - A type of packaging that uses a plastic section adhered to a cardboard backing.
BR - Braille.
BRICK - A group of 50 or more cards having common characteristics that is intended to be bought, sold or traded as a unit.
BT - Breaking Through.
BX - Boxed.
BY - Brickyard 400.
BYS - Brickyard Special.
C - Classics, Conquerors.
CC - Cup Contenders.
CHECKLIST - A list of the cards contained in a particular set. The list is always in numerical order if the cards are numbered. Some unnumbered sets are artificially numbered in alphabetical order, by team and alphabetically within the team, or by uniform number for convenience.
CJT - Crown Jewel Times.
CL - Checklist card. A card that lists in order the cards and drivers in the set or series.
CLAMSHELL - Similar to a blister pack, but uses two sections of plastic affixed to each other.
CLEARCHROME - A method of card manufacturing technology patented by MAXX. It involves the production of a card using an acetate material.
CO - Club Only.
COIN - A small disc of metal or plastic portraying a player in its center.
COLLECTOR ISSUE - A set produced for the sake of the card itself with no product or service sponsor. It derives its name from the fact that most of these sets are produced for sale directly to the hobby market.
COMMON CARD - A typical card of any set; it has no premium value accruing from subject matter, numerical scarcity, popular demand, or anomaly.
COMMON DRIVER - A typical driver card of any set; it has no premium value accruing from subject matter, numerical scarcity, popular demand, or anomaly.
CONVENTION - A gathering of dealers and collectors at a single location for the purpose of buying, selling, and trading sports memorabilia items. Conventions are open to the public and sometimes feature autograph guests, door prizes, contests, seminars, etc. They are frequently referred to simply as "shows."
COR - Corrected card.
COUPON - See Tab.
CPC - Championship Pit Crew.
DB - Daytona Beach.
DD - Double Duty, Driving with Dale.
DEALER - A person who engages in buying, selling, and trading sports collectibles or supplies. A dealer may also be a collector, but as a dealer, his main goal is to earn a profit.
DEI - Dale Earnhardt Inc.
DIE - CUT - A card with part of its stock partially cut, allowing one or more parts to be folded or removed. After removal or appropriate folding, the remaining part of the card can frequently be made to stand up.
DISPLAY CARD - A sheet, usually containing three to nine cards, that is printed and used by the manufacturer to advertise and/or display the packages containing his products and cards. The backs of display cards are blank or contain advertisements.
DOY - Driver of the Year.
DP - Double Print (a card that was printed in double the quantity compared to the other cards in the same series).
DR - Daytona Review, Delco Remy.
DT - Double Trouble.
DUFEX - A method of card manufacturing technology patented by Pinnacle Brands, Inc. It involves a refractive quality to a card with a foil coating.
DW - Daytona Winner.
DYK - Did You Know.
D93 - Daytona 1993.
EMBOSSED - A raised surface; features of a card that are projected from a flat background. (i.e. Action Packed cards).
EOD - End of the Day.
ERR - Error card. A card with erroneous information, spelling, or depiction on either side of the card. Most errors are not corrected by the producing card company.
ETCHED - Impressions within the surface of a card.
EY - Early Years
FB - Fastback.
FCS - Future Cup Stars.
FF - Fan Favorite.
FOIL - Foil embossed stamp on card.
FOLD - Foldout.
F.Q.S. - Fastest Qualifying Speed.
FS - Father/son card.
FULL BLEED - A borderless card; a card containing a photo that encompasses the entire card.
FULL SHEET - A complete sheet of cards that has not been cut up into individual cards by the manufacturer. Also called an uncut sheet.
GLOSS - A card with luster; a shiny finish as in a card with UV coating.
GMP - Georgia Marketing and Promotions.
HB - History Book.
HG - Hot Guns.
HO - Hood Open.
HOLO - Hologram.
HOLOGRAM - A three-dimensional photographic image.
HR - Heroes of Racing.
HV - Heavenly Views
I - Idols.
IB - In the Blood.

IMHOF - International Motorsports Hall of Fame.

INSERT - A card of a different type or any other sports collectible (typically a poster or sticker) contained and sold in the same package along with a card or cards of a major set. An insert card is either unnumbered or not numbered in the same sequence as the major set. Sometimes the inserts are randomly distributed and are not found in every pack.

INTERACTIVE - A concept that involves collector participation.

IROC - International Race of Champions

ISSUE - Synonymous with set, but usually used in conjunction with a manufacturer, e.g., a MAXX issue.

K - Knights.

KARAT - A unit of measure for the fineness of gold; i.e. 24K.

LAYERING - The separation or peeling of one or more layers of the card stock, usually at the corner of the card.

LUM - Lumina.

MAJOR SET - A set produced by a national manufacturer of cards containing a large number of cards. Usually 50 or more different cards comprise a major set.

MB - Matchbox.

MC - Monte Carlo.

MEM - Memorial card. For example 1993 Finish Line NNO Alan Kulwicki.

METALLIC - A glossy design method that enhances card features.

MM - Memorable Moment.

MO - Members Only

MRO- Motor Racing Outreach.

MT - Mac Tools.

MULTI-DRIVER CARD - A single card depicting two or more drivers.

NASCAR - The National Association for Stock Car Auto Racing.

NB - Notchback.

NDA - No Driver Associated.

NL - Next in Line.

NM - Newsmakers.

NNO - No Number on Card.

NITROKROME - A method of card manufacturing technology patented by Press Pass. It involves the use of etched technology to bring out color in the card.

NON-SPORT CARD - A card from a set whose major theme is a subject other than a sports subject. A card of a sports figure or event that is part of a non-sport set is still a non-sport card.

NOTCHING - The grooving of the card, usually caused by fingernails, rubber bands, or bumping card edges against other objects.

NP - NASCAR Properties on Stand.

NS - No Sponsor.

NTB - New Thunderbird Mold for 1995.

OC - Out of the Chute.

OTM - On the mark

OWN - Owner.

P - Promo or Prototype.

PACKS - A means with which cards are issued in terms of pack type (wax, cello, foil, rack, blister, etc.) and channels of distributi on (hobby, retail, etc.).

PARALLEL- A card that is similar in design to its counterpart from the basic set, but offers a distinguishing quality.

PB - Petty Back.

PBC - Polybag.

PLASTIC SHEET - A clear, plastic page that is punched for insertion into a binder (with standard three-ring spacing) containing pockets for displaying cards. Many different styles of sheets exist with pockets of varying sizes to hold the many differing card formats. Also called a display sheet or storage sheet.

PLATINUM - A metallic element used in the process of creating a glossy card.

PLS - Platinum Series.

PO - Power Owners.

PP - Power Prospects, Precision Performers, Past & Present.

PPGC - PPG Champs.

PR - Personal Rides.

PRE - Preview.

PREMIUM - A card, sometimes on photographic stock, that is purchased or obtained in conjunction with, or redemption for another card or product. the premium is not packaged in the same unit as the primary item.

PRISMATIC/PRISM - A glossy or bright design that refracts or disperses light.

PROMO/PROTOTYPE - A card or die-cast issued to preview a set or a release in special association with a racing sponsor. Promo cards are usually issued to the dealers purchasing the cards.

PS - Pole Sitters, Peachstate.

PVC - Polyvinyl Chloride, a substance used to make many of the popular card display protective sheets. It is also used by some die-cast manufacturers to form small boxes to house die-cast collectibles.

PW - Pole Winner, Power Winner.

RARE - A card or series of cards of very limited availability . Unfortunately, "rare" is a subjective term frequently used indiscriminately to hype value. "Rare" cards are harder to obtain than "scarce" cards.

RCCA - Racing Collectibles Club of America.

RCI - Racing Collectibles, Inc.

REDEMPTION- A program established by multiple card manufacturers that allows collectors to mail in a special card (usually a random insert) in return for special cards, sets or other prizes not available through conventional channels.

REGIONAL - A card or set of cards issued and distributed only in a limited geographical area of the country.

REPLICA - An identical copy or reproduction.

REV - Revell.

RET - Retro

ROY - Rookie of the Year.

RQ - Rookie Qualifier.

RR - Race Review

RS - Riding Shotgun.

RW - Race Winner.

S - SportsKings, Shades, Shattered.

SASE - Self-Addressed, Stamped Envelope.

SB - Scrapbook.

SCARCE - A card or series of cards of limited availability. This subjective term is sometimes used indiscriminately to hype value. "Scarce" cards are not as difficult to obtain as "rare" cards.

SD - Season Debut.

SET - One each of the entire run of cards of the same type produced by a particular manufacturer during a single year.

SI - Sports Image. A licensing body for some drivers.

SKIP-NUMBERED - A set that has many unissued card numbers between the lowest number in the set and the highest number in the set; e.g., the 1987 World of Outlaw set. A major set in which a few numbers were not printed is not considered to be skip-numbered.

SL - Stat Leaders.

SM - Speed Machines

SP - Single or Short Print (a card which was printed in lesser quantity compared to the other cards in the same series; see also DP and TP).

SPECIAL CARD - A card that portrays something other than a single driver or team; for example, a card that portrays the previous year's winner of the Daytona 500.

SR - Star Rookie.

SS - Split Shift.

SSA - Super Star Awards.

ST - Small Town. Saturday Night

STANDARD SIZE - Most modern sports cards measure 2-1/2 by 3-1/2 inches. Exceptions are noted in card descriptions throughout this book.

STICKER - A card with removable layer that can be affixed to (stuck on) another surface.

STC - Seven-Time Champion

STO - SuperTruck Owner.

STOCK - The cardboard or paper on which the card is printed.

SUPERIMPOSED - To be affixed on top of something, i.e., a driver photo over a solid background.

T - Tribute

T4 - Turn Four

T10 - Top Ten.

TA - The Allisons.

TB - Thunderbird.

TC - Trophy Case.

TD - Track Dominators.

TEST SET - A set, usually containing a small number of cards, issued by a national card producer and distributed in a limited section or sections of the country. Presumably, the purpose of a test set is to test market appeal for a particular type of card.

THREE-DIMENSIONAL (3D) - A visual image that provides an illusion of depth and perspective.

TOPICAL - a subset or group of cards that have a common theme.

TP - Triple Print (a card that was printed in triple the quantity compared to the other cards in the same series.).

TRAN - Transporter or transparent.

TRANSPARENT - Clear, see through.

TRIMMED - A card cut down from its original size. Trimmed cards are undesirable to most collectors.

TT - Texas Tornado

TT - Top Team.

TTM - To the Maxx.

TW - Team Work.

UER - Uncorrected Error.

UV - Ultraviolet, a glossy coating used in producing cards.

VAR - Variation card. One of two or more cards from the same series with the same number (or player with identical pose if the series is unnumbered) differing from one another by some aspect, the different feature stemming from the printing or stock of the card. This can be caused when the manufacturer of the cards notices an error in one or more of the cards, makes the changes, and then resumes the print run. In this case there will be two versions or variations of the same card. Sometimes one of the variations is relatively scarce.

VL - Victory Lane.

VT - Valvoline Team.

WC - Winston Cup, Winner's Circle.

WCA - Wives, Camera, Action

WCC - Winston Cup Champion.

WCS - Winston Cup Scene.

WD - Winston Decal.

WIN - Winner Insert, Winners.

WP - War Paint

WRC - White Rose Collectibles.

WS - Winston Select.

YB - Yellow & Black Box.

YBH - Yellow Box Hobby Only.

YG - Young Guns.

YR - Year in Review.

YS - Young Stars.

Understanding Values

Determining Value

Why are some items more valuable than others? Obviously, the economic laws of supply and demand are applicable to card collecting just as they are to any other field where a commodity is bought, sold or traded in a free, unregulated market.

Supply (the number of cards available on the market) is less than the total number of cards originally produced since attrition diminishes that original quantity. Each year a percentage of cards is typically thrown away, destroyed or otherwise lost to collectors. This percentage is much, much smaller today than it was in the past because more and more people have become increasingly aware of the value of their cards.

For those who collect only Mint condition cards, the supply of older cards can be quite small indeed. Until recently, collectors were not so conscious of the need to preserve the condition of their cards. For this reason, it is difficult to know exactly how many 1972 STP cards are currently available, Mint or otherwise. It is generally accepted that there are fewer 1972 STP cards available than 1988 Maxx. If demand were equal for each of these sets, the law of supply and demand would increase the price for the least available set. Demand, however, is never equal for all sets, so price correlations can be complicated. The demand for a card is influenced by many factors. These include: (1) the age of the card; (2) the number of cards printed; (3) the driver(s) portrayed on the card; (4) the attractiveness and popularity of the set; and (5) the physical condition of the card.

In general, (1) the older the card, (2) the fewer the number of the cards printed, (3) the more famous, popular and talented the driver, (4) the more attractive and popular the set, and (5) the better the condition of the card, the higher the value of the card will be. There are exceptions to all but one of these factors: the condition of the card. Given two cards similar in all respects except condition, the one in the best condition will always be valued higher.

While those guidelines help to establish the value of a card, the countless exceptions and peculiarities make any simple, direct mathematical formula to determine card values impossible.

Regional Variation

Since the market varies from region to region, card prices of local drivers may be higher. This is known as a regional premium. How significant the premium is — and if there is any premium at all — depends on the local popularity of the driver.

The largest regional premiums usually do not apply to superstars, who often are so well-known nationwide that the prices of their key cards are too high for local dealers to realize a premium.

Lesser stars often command the strongest premiums. Their popularity is concentrated in their home region, creating local demand that greatly exceeds overall demand.

Regional premiums can apply to popular retired drivers and sometimes can be found in the areas where the drivers grew up or started racing.

A regional discount is the converse of a regional premium. Regional discounts occur when a driver has been so popular in his region for so long that local collectors and dealers have accumulated quantities of his key cards. The abundant supply may make the cards available in that area at the lowest prices anywhere.

Set Prices

A somewhat paradoxical situation exists in the price of a complete set vs. the combined cost of the individual cards in the set. In nearly every case, the sum of the prices for the individual cards is higher than the cost for the complete set. This is prevalent especially in the cards of the last few years. The reasons for this apparent anomaly stem from the habits of collectors and from the carrying costs to dealers. Today, each card in a set normally is produced in the same quantity as all other cards in its set.

Many collectors pick up only stars, superstars and particular teams. As a result, the dealer is left with a shortage of certain driver cards and an abundance of others. He therefore incurs an expense in simply "carrying" these less desirable cards in stock. On the other hand, if he sells a complete set, he gets rid of large numbers of cards at one time. For this reason, he generally is willing to receive less money for a complete set. By doing this, he recovers all of his costs and also makes a profit.

The disparity between the price of the complete set and the sum of the individual cards also has been influenced by the fact that some of the major manufacturers now are precollating card sets. Since "pulling" individual cards from the sets involves a specific type of labor (and cost), the singles or star card market is not affected significantly by pre-collation.

Set prices also do not include rare card varieties, unless specifically stated. Of course, the prices for sets do include one example of each type for the given set, but this is the least expensive variety.

History of Racing Cards

The history of racing cards is not an extensive story like with the other major sports. For the modern era of the racing card market only began in 1988. Before that time there were only a few sets produced and the majority of those sets were about forms of racing other than NASCAR. The early cards, 1960-1980, mainly paid tribute to Indy and Drag Racing. While the racing card market may have lagged behind the other sports in early history, it has more than kept up with them in terms of growth since 1988. In just a few short years racing cards have grown from plain photos on plain cardboard to colorful, high-tech works of art.

One of the earliest known racing card set that features racing drivers is the 1911 American Auto Drivers set. The cards were produced for the American Tobacco Company and were inserted in packs of cigarettes. Each of the 25 cards was available with a small ad for either Hassan or Mecca Cigarettes on the cardback. The unnumbered cards feature top race car drivers of the day from both North America and Europe. They represented all types of auto racing events.

There were also a few other racing or automobile focused sets produced during the first half of this century. Sets like the 1911 Turkey Reds and the 1931 Ogden's Motor Races featured the cars and events of that time period. The drivers of the cars were secondary. Other sets issued in Europe like the 1939 Churchman's King of Speed and the Will's Cigarette set featured a few racing cards but those cards were only part of multisport set. These few sets represent the trend for the majority of automobile related issues prior to World War II.

It wasn't until the post World War II era that more driver focused racing sets were introduced to the market. From 1954-1966 racing saw the production of only a few sets. Three of the sets, 1954 Stark and Wetzel Meats, 1960 Hawes Wax and the 1962 Marhoefer Meats, focused on the most popular form of racing at the time, Indy Car. As you can see from the set names, each was a promotional type set. The cards of the two meat products sets were distributed in various meat products. This makes it difficult to find Near Mint or better copies of these cards. The Hawes set was made for the Hawes Furniture Wax company by Canadian card manufacturer Parkhurst. This is the same company that produced the majority of Hockey cards issued during the 50's and early 60's. Topps and Donruss also issued a set each focused on Hot Rods and Drag racing in 1965. Donruss' issue of the 1965 Spec Sheet set comes well before the beginning of their regular production of baseball cards in 1981.

The decade of the 70's saw the production of primarily drag racing sets. More than half of the few racing sets produced during that time had a drag racing theme. All the drag racing sets were produced by Fleer and each focused on drivers of the American Hot Rod Association.

The first NASCAR related set was produced in 1972. The eleven card STP set featured full-bleed photos and unnumbered card backs that contained some biographical information on each of the drivers and the STP name and address. This set was a promotion of the STP corporation and features some of the top names in NASCAR at that time. The cards are tough to come by and usually are found in conditions less than Near Mint. This set is the only full NASCAR card set until the 1983 UNO set and the 1986 SportStars Photo-Graphics set.

From 1980 to the beginning of the modern racing card collecting era (1988), IndyCar sets dominated the market. This was primarily due to the introduction of the A & S Racing Collectables company. This manufacturer produced IndyCar sets from 1983-87. Another form of open-wheel racing also saw its first regular issued set, the 1987 World of Outlaw set. This set features the first card of NASCAR superstar Jeff Gordon.

The Modern Era

In 1988, the racing card market changed. The J.R. Maxx company decided to produce a 100-card racing set that focused on the drivers and cars of NASCAR racing. It was just part of the evolution that NASCAR was going through. The sport itself was growing in popularity and it made common sense for there to be trading cards of these growing heroes of racing. The set was to be the first mass marketed NASCAR trading card set ever issued. Maxx also signed an agreement to be the only licensed card of NASCAR. The issue of this set is considered to be the start of the modern era of racing cards. Through the marketing of these cards, racing fans became aware that there were now racing cards available of their favorite drivers.

During the period of time from 1988-1991, other forms of racing were also flourishing from a card standpoint. There were a couple drag racing sets each of those years, a regular manufacturer of World of Outlaw cards, All World Indy began producing Indy sets and local small tracks started seeing the sale of racing cards that featured the drivers that were racing in that region.

Maxx was the only major producer of NASCAR cards from 1988-90. They were not only making a base set of cards, but were also contracting with companies like Crisco and Holly Farms to make promotional sets that featured those companies logos.

In 1991, the NASCAR card market saw the introduction to two new companies Traks and Pro Set. Pro Set was a major sports card manufacturer of the time but Traks was just getting started. Traks first set in 1991 would include the first NASCAR card of a young driver named Jeff Gordon. They would also go on to produce two promotional Dale Earnhardt sets, a Kyle Petty set and a Richard Petty set that year. Pro Set entered the racing card market from two ways NASCAR and NHRA. They produced full sets for each form of racing.

In 1993, the market would see a dramatic expansion with five new card companies coming jumping into hobby. Action Packed, Finish Line, Hi-Tech, Press Pass, and Wheels all started issuing racing sets in 1993. Action Packed not only brought its embossed printing process to racing cards but also brought the first high end retail product that racing had seen. Prior to this time boxes were generally retailed for $10-$20, but Action Packed's cost was nearly double the highest retail box prices. This did not discourage fans and collectors who were willing to purchase this new high end product. That year also saw the introduction of the parallel insert cards. The 1993 Finish Line set had a silver foil parallel version for each card. This silver parallel set was one of the most sought after and very few collectors were not working on the set at the time.

With greater competition, companies were looking for that edge that would separate their products from the rest. Many new innovations in racing cards hit the market in 1994. Finish Line introduced Phone Cards to racing collectors through inserts in their Finish Line Gold product. Press Pass introduced the first interactive game, with their Cup Chase insert cards. SkyBox introduced the first single race interactive game with their Brickyard winner redemption card. Press Pass with its VIP brand introduced signature redemption cards with its 24K Gold exchange cards. Maxx introduced the first ClearChrome cards with the 20-card subset in their Maxx Medallion product. So from nearly every manufacturer, the collectors were getting something new and different than they had ever seen before.

The market continued to grow in 1996. The hobby saw a total of 30 base brand products produced from nine different manufacturers. The market also saw the lose of Maxx in 1996. The grandfather of the modern racing card era filed bankruptcy and went out of business in the summer. Parallel inserts, Phone Cards and interactive games and race used equipment inserts were also the trend. There were very few products issued in 1996 that didn't include at least one of those four types of cards.

The year of 1997 in racing collectibles was one of both growth and decline. The die cast market exhibited growth while trying to reach more collectors with product and product line variations. The big 3 (Action/RCCA, Racing Champions and Revell) each debuted new premium lines. Action, in conjunction with Hasbro, started its Winner's Circle line to establish a presence in the mass market, Revelll also established its Revell Racing line to serve the same function. Racing Champions, through its merger with Wheels, that established a foundation that has helped to launch a new premium line in conjunction with the 50th anniversary of NASCAR.

The card market exhibited slight growth in 1997. Maxx rejoined the market after being resurrected by Upper Deck. Press Pass was bought by Wheels. Finish Line shut its doors and shutdown it's phone cards. An emphasis was placed again on high-end inserts whether it be autographed cards or cards containing "race-used" items.

Since 1997, the racing card market has seen two manufacturers depart from producing cards. In 1998, Pinnacle declared bankruptcy while in 2000 Upper Deck made the decision to cease racing card production. These actions left Press Pass as the only company producing racing cards.

Press Pass, which created the first "memorabilia" cards, continued to be innovative in their usage of both autographs and memorabilia on cards. To their credit, considering their current monopoly in producing cards, they continue to search for new ways to bring the racing experience to the collector

In addition, both Winner's Circle and Racing Champion have produced die-cast pieces with "memorabilia" cards as part of the whole package.

An important collector shift has occurred in the last few years as the older drivers, while still popular, are making way for a new generation of drivers. Such young drivers as Tony Stewart, Matt Kenseth, Dale Earnhardt Jr, Ryan Newman, Jimmie Johnson and Kevin Harvick have quickly become fan and collector favorites.

Finding Out More

The above has been a thumbnail sketch of racing card collecting from its inception to the present. It is difficult to tell the whole story in just a few pages. Serious collectors should subscribe to at least one of the excellent hobby periodicals. We also suggest that collectors visit their local card shop(s), attend local racing shows or events in their area and sign up for any dealer's catalogs that are available. Card collecting is still a young and informal hobby. You can learn more about it at shops and shows and reading periodicals and catalogs. After all, smart dealers realize that spending a few minutes to teach and educate the beginners about the hobby often pays off in the long run.

2007 AAA Limited Edition

AAA distributed the individual event cards at each NASCAR race during the 2007 season. Each card is serial numbered to 5,000. The set includes one card for each of the 38 NEXTEL Cup events of 2007. Each card is a hard laminated plastic and measures approximately 4' x 8". This full-season set comes in a very nice full-color collector's box, which is hand-numbered on the outside. The outside serial number matches the serial numbers on the cards inside.

COMPLETE SET (38)	50.00	100.00
COMP.FACT.SET (38)	75.00	150.00
COMMON RAGAN	2.00	5.00
1 David Ragan Daytona 2-10	2.00	5.00
2 David Ragan Daytona 2-18	2.00	5.00
3 David Ragan California 2-25	2.00	5.00
4 David Ragan Las Vegas 3-15	2.00	5.00
5 David Ragan Atlanta 3-18	2.00	5.00
6 David Ragan Bristol 3-25	2.00	5.00
7 David Ragan Martinsville 4-1	2.00	5.00
8 David Ragan Texas 4-15	2.00	5.00
9 David Ragan Phoenix 4-21	2.00	5.00
10 David Ragan Talladega 4-29	2.00	5.00
11 David Ragan Richmond 5-6	2.00	5.00
12 David Ragan Darlington 5-13	2.00	5.00
13 David Ragan Charlotte 5-19	2.00	5.00
14 David Ragan Charlotte 5-27	2.00	5.00
15 David Ragan Dover 6-3	2.00	5.00
16 David Ragan Pocono 6-10	2.00	5.00
17 David Ragan Michigan 6-17	2.00	5.00
18 David Ragan Infineon 6-24	2.00	5.00
19 David Ragan New Hampshire 7-1	2.00	5.00
20 David Ragan Daytona 7-7	2.00	5.00
21 David Ragan Chicagoland 7-15	2.00	5.00
22 David Ragan Brickyard 7-29	2.00	5.00
23 David Ragan Pocono 8-5	2.00	5.00
24 David Ragan Watkins Glen 8-12	2.00	5.00
25 David Ragan Michigan 8-21	2.00	5.00
26 David Ragan Bristol 8-25	2.00	5.00
27 David Ragan California 9-2	2.00	5.00
28 David Ragan Richmond 9-8	2.00	5.00
29 David Ragan New Hampshire 9-16	2.00	5.00
30 David Ragan Dover 9-23	2.00	5.00
31 David Ragan Kansas 9-30	2.00	5.00
32 David Ragan Talladega 10-7	2.00	5.00
33 David Ragan Charlotte 10-13	2.00	5.00
34 David Ragan Martinsville 10-21	2.00	5.00
35 David Ragan Atlanta 10-28	2.00	5.00
36 David Ragan Texas 11-4	2.00	5.00
37 David Ragan Phoenix 11-11	2.00	5.00
38 David Ragan Miami-Homestead 11-18	2.00	5.00

1990 AC Racing Proven Winners

This 7-card black-bordered set features drivers sponsored by the AC Racing team. The cards were given away as complete sets and include six top drivers and one unnumbered checklist card. The Proven Winners name is included on the back of the checklist card. The cards were distributed as a promotion given out at many of NASCAR speedways.

COMPLETE SET (7)	25.00	60.00
1 Rusty Wallace	5.00	12.00
2 Darrell Waltrip	3.00	8.00
3 Dale Earnhardt	12.00	30.00
4 Ken Schrader	3.00	8.00
5 Ricky Rudd	3.00	8.00
6 Bobby Hillin	1.50	4.00
NNO Cover/Checklist Card	.75	2.00

1991 AC Racing

This 10-card set was given away as a promotion at many NASCAR speedways. The cards feature some of the top names in racing that carried the AC Racing logo on their cars.

COMPLETE SET (10)	12.50	30.00
1 Dale Earnhardt	5.00	12.00
2 Rusty Wallace	2.00	5.00
3 Darrell Waltrip	1.25	3.00
4 Ernie Irvan	1.25	3.00
5 Ricky Rudd	1.25	3.00
6 Ken Schrader	.75	2.00
7 Kyle Petty	1.50	4.00
8 Rick Wilson	.50	1.25
9 Hut Stricklin	.50	1.25
NNO Cover Card Checklist	.30	.75

1992 AC-Delco

This 10-card set was produced and distributed by AC-Delco and GM Service Parts in 1992. The cards feature a blue bordered design and include drivers of the 1992 AC Race Team.

COMPLETE SET (10)	2.50	6.00
1 Rusty Wallace	1.25	3.00
2 Ricky Rudd	.75	2.00
3 Kyle Petty	1.00	2.50
4 Darrell Waltrip	.75	2.00
5 Ernie Irvan	.75	2.00
6 Ken Schrader	.50	1.25
7 Dave Marcis	.50	1.25
8 Hut Stricklin	.30	.75
9 AC Delco 500 Race	.20	.50
10 Cover/Checklist Card	.20	.50

1992 AC Racing Postcards

This 8-card set was produced and distributed by AC Racing in 1992. The unnumbered cards are postcard sized (approximately 3-3/4" by 5-1/4") and feature an artist's rendering of a top AC Racing sponsored driver on the front. Backs are primarily black in color and include the AC Racing logo. The cards were sold as a complete set packaged in a black wrap-around cardboard package. They were also given away at the AC suite at Michigan Speedway.

COMPLETE SET (8)	4.00	15.00
1 Dale Earnhardt	3.00	8.00
2 Ernie Irvan	.60	1.50
3 Kyle Petty	.75	2.00
4 Ricky Rudd	.60	1.50
5 Ken Schrader	.40	1.00
6 Hut Stricklin	.25	.60
7 Rusty Wallace	1.00	2.50
8 Darrell Waltrip	.60	1.50

1993 AC Racing Foldouts

This 10-card set features drivers sponsored by the AC Racing team. The cards are bi-fold and measure approximately 3-1/2" by 4-5/8" when fully unfolded. Numbering was done according to the driver's car number. The cards were sold as complete sets and packaging included a gray AC Racing 1:64 scale die cast car as well.

COMPLETE SET (10)	4.00	10.00
2 Rusty Wallace	.75	2.00
3 Dale Earnhardt	2.50	6.00
4 Ernie Irvan	.30	.75
17 Darrell Waltrip	.30	.75
24 Jeff Gordon	1.25	3.00
25 Ken Schrader	.20	.50
40 Kenny Wallace	.20	.50
41 Phil Parsons	.20	.50
42 Kyle Petty	.30	.75
NNO Cover/Checklist Card	.10	.30

1992 Action Packed Allison Family

Produced by Action Packed to honor the career of the late Clifford Allison, this set was distributed in factory set form. The cards included Clifford's father Bobby and brother Davey and were sold packaged in a black folding binder with proceeds going to help The Children of Clifford Allison Trust Fund. Production was limited to 5000 numbered sets. The sets were donated by Action Packed to the Allison family. Also, there was one set of 24K gold cards produced.

COMPLETE SET (3)	16.00	40.00
NNO Bobby Allison	4.00	10.00
NNO Clifford Allison	4.00	10.00
NNO Davey Allison	8.00	20.00

1992 Action Packed Kyle Petty Prototypes

Action Packed released this three-card Kyle Petty set as a preview to its initial 1993 NASCAR set. The card numbering begins at 101 and each is clearly marked "prototype" on the cardback.

COMPLETE SET (3)	20.00	35.00
101 Kyle Petty's Car	2.50	6.00
102 Kyle Petty	6.00	15.00
103 Kyle Petty's Car	2.50	6.00

1992 Action Packed Richard Petty

This 3-card set was issued to commemorate the career of Richard Petty. The first two cards were issued together in a cello wrapper with the third card being issued separately.

COMMON CARD (RP1-RP3)	1.50	4.00
RP1 Richard Petty/100,000	2.50	6.00
RP2 Richard Petty's Car/100,000	1.00	2.50
RP3 Richard Petty/50,000	4.00	10.00

1993 Action Packed Prototypes

Action Packed produced these cards to preview its 1993 release. The cards are similar to regular issue 1993 cards, but contain the words "1993 Prototype" on the cardback along with different card numbering. The cards were released together and are often sold as a complete set.

COMPLETE SET (5)	50.00	120.00
AK1 Alan Kulwicki	12.50	30.00
BA1 Bobby Allison	6.00	15.00
DE1 Dale Earnhardt	15.00	40.00
DJ1 Dale Jarrett	6.00	15.00
JG1 Jeff Gordon	15.00	40.00

1993 Action Packed

This is the first Action Packed racing release, issued in three separate series, and features the now standard raised embossed printing process. Twenty-four pack boxes with seven cards per pack housed the first series, while series two and three contained six cards per pack. The series one set was released in early 1993 and includes five different subsets: 92 Race Winners, 92 Pole Winners, Top Ten Points, Young Guns, and King Richard Petty. Series two, released in mid-1993, is highlighted by the first Dale Earnhardt Action Packed cards. A four card sub-set of Dale Earnhardt featured braille on the back of the cards. The series two includes six different subsets: Daytona '93 (90-95), Back in Black (120-123), Back in Black Brail (124-127), The Allisons (140-149), Young Guns (150-156), and Brothers (161-164). Fall 1993 saw the release of series three featuring Rusty Wallace and Race Week in Charlotte subsets, along with six card memorial insert sets of both Davey Allison and Alan Kulwicki. 24K Gold insert cards were also distributed throughout packs of all three series.

COMPLETE SET (207)	25.00	60.00
COMP.SERIES 1 SET (84)	10.00	25.00
COMP.SERIES 2 SET (84)	8.00	20.00
COMP.SERIES 3 SET (39)	8.00	20.00
1 Alan Kulwicki WIN	2.00	5.00
2 Kyle Petty WIN Pattie Petty	.40	1.00
3 Darrell Waltrip's Car WIN	.25	.60
4 Geoff Bodine WIN	.25	.60
5 Davey Allison WIN	1.25	3.00
6 Rusty Wallace WIN	1.00	2.50
7 Harry Gant WIN	.25	.60
8 Ernie Irvan WIN	.40	1.00
9 Mark Martin WIN	1.25	3.00
10 Richard Petty Braille	1.00	2.50
11 Terry Labonte's Car	.40	1.00
12 Bobby Labonte	1.00	2.50
13 Kyle Petty's Car	.25	.60
14 Kyle Petty	.40	1.00
15 Dale Jarrett	1.00	2.50
16 Darrell Waltrip	.40	1.00
17 Darrell Waltrip's Car	.25	.60
18 Ken Schrader's Car	.10	.30
19 Ken Schrader	.25	.60
20 Ken Schrader PW	.25	.60
21 Davey Allison PW	1.25	3.00
22 Mark Martin PW	1.25	3.00
23 Kyle Petty PW	.40	1.00
24 Darrell Waltrip PW	.40	1.00
25 Ernie Irvan PW	.40	1.00
26 Alan Kulwicki PW	.60	1.50
27 Brett Bodine PW	.25	.60
28 Rusty Wallace PW	1.00	2.50
29 Rick Mast PW	.25	.60
30 Sterling Marlin's Car PW	.25	.60
31 Richard Petty's Car Braille	.40	1.00
32 Jeff Gordon	2.50	6.00
33 Ernie Irvan's Car	.25	.60
34 Ernie Irvan	.40	1.00
35 Kenny Wallace	.25	.60
36 Terry Labonte	.75	2.00
37 Geoff Bodine's Car	.10	.30
38 Geoff Bodine	.25	.60
39 Geoff Bodine	.25	.60
40 Alan Kulwicki T10	.60	1.50
41 Darrell Waltrip T10	.40	1.00
42 Kyle Petty T10	.40	1.00
43 Davey Allison T10	1.25	3.00
44 Mark Martin T10	1.00	2.50
45 Harry Gant T10	.25	.60
46 Terry Labonte T10	.40	1.00
47 Sterling Marlin T10	.25	.60
48 Rick Mast	.25	.60
49 Rick Mast w/Car	.25	.60
50 Richard Petty's Car KR	.40	1.00
51 Richard Petty KR Lynda Petty	.40	1.00
52 Richard Petty KR	.40	1.00
53 Richard Petty KR	.40	1.00
54 Richard Petty KR	.40	1.00
55 Sterling Marlin	1.00	2.50
56 Sterling Marlin's Car	.25	.60
57 Brett Bodine	.25	.60
58 Morgan Shepherd	.25	.60
59 Morgan Shepherd's Car	.10	.30
60 Kenny Wallace YG	.25	.60
61 Jeff Gordon YG	1.50	4.00
62 Bobby Labonte YG	1.00	2.50
63 Jeff Gordon YG Kenny Wallace Bobby Labonte	1.50	4.00
64 Alan Kulwicki	.60	1.50
65 Wally Dallenbach Jr.'s Car	.10	.30
66 Wally Dallenbach Jr.	.25	.60
67 Michael Waltrip	.40	1.00
68 Michael Waltrip's Car	.25	.60
69 Hut Stricklin	.25	.60
70 Richard Petty's Car Braille	.40	1.00
71 Richard Petty Braille	.40	1.00
72 Richard Petty Braille	.40	1.00
73 Harry Gant	.25	.60
74 Harry Gant's Car	.10	.30
75 Richard Petty Braille	.40	1.00
76 Richard Petty Braille	.40	1.00
77 Mark Martin	1.00	2.50
78 Mark Martin's Car	.40	1.00
79 Davey Allison's Car	.40	1.00
80 Davey Allison	1.25	3.00
81 Richard Petty	.75	2.00
82 Richard Petty's Car	.25	.60
83 Rusty Wallace	1.25	3.00
84 Rusty Wallace's Car	.40	1.00
85 Alan Kulwicki	.50	1.25
86 Jeff Gordon CRC	2.00	4.00
87 Jeff Gordon's Car	1.25	3.00
88 Dale Earnhardt	2.50	6.00
89 Dale Earnhardt's Car	1.00	2.50
90 Dale Jarrett D93	.30	.75
91 Kyle Petty D93	.15	.40
92 Richard Petty D93	.30	.75
93 Jeff Gordon D93	2.00	4.00
94 Dale Earnhardt D93	1.25	3.00
95 Dale Earnhardt D93	1.25	3.00
96 Brett Bodine	.15	.40
97 Davey Allison	1.25	2.50
98 Davey Allison's Car	.30	.75
99 Kyle Petty	.30	.75
100 Kyle Petty's Car	.15	.40
101 Kenny Wallace	.15	.40
102 Kenny Wallace's Car	.07	.20
103 Darrell Waltrip	.30	.75
104 Darrell Waltrip's Car	.15	.40
105 Rick Mast	.15	.40
106 Rick Mast's Car	.07	.20
107 Rusty Wallace	1.00	2.50
108 Rusty Wallace's Car	.30	.75
109 Mark Martin	1.50	3.00
110 Mark Martin's Car	.30	.75
111 Geoff Bodine	.15	.40
112 Geoff Bodine's Car	.07	.20
113 Wally Dallenbach Jr.	.15	.40
114 Wally Dallenbach Jr.'s Car	.07	.20
115 Dale Jarrett	.75	2.00
116 Morgan Shepherd	.15	.40
117 Morgan Shepherd's Car	.07	.20
118 Rick Wilson	.15	.40
119 Rick Wilson's Car	.07	.20
120 Dale Earnhardt BB	.75	2.00
121 Dale Earnhardt BB	.75	2.00
122 Dale Earnhardt BB	.75	2.00
123 Dale Earnhardt BB	.75	2.00
124 Dale Earnhardt Braille	.75	2.00
125 Dale Earnhardt Braille	.75	2.00
126 Dale Earnhardt Braille	.75	2.00
127 Dale Earnhardt Braille	.75	2.00
128 Ernie Irvan	.30	.75
129 Ernie Irvan's Car	.15	.40
130 Sterling Marlin	.75	2.00
131 Sterling Marlin's Car	.15	.40
132 Jimmy Spencer	.15	.40
133 Jimmy Spencer's Car	.07	.20
134 Ken Schrader	.15	.40
135 Ken Schrader's Car	.07	.20
136 Michael Waltrip	.30	.75
137 Michael Waltrip's Car	.15	.40
138 Dale Earnhardt PW	1.25	3.00
139 Dale Earnhardt WIN with Dale Earnhardt Jr. and Kerry Earnhardt	6.00	15.00
140 Bobby Allison TA Davey Allison Liz Allison Katherine Patton Allison	.75	2.00
141 Donnie Allison TA	.15	.40
142 Clifford Allison TA	.15	.40
143 Donnie Allison TA Bobby Allison	.15	.40
144 Davey Allison TA Liz Allison Robbie Allison Krista Allison	.75	2.00
145 Donnie Allison TA Kenny Allison Donald Allison Ronald Allison	.15	.40
146 Davey Allison TA Clifford Allison Bobby Allison	.75	2.00
147 Bobby Allison TA Judy Allison	.15	.40
148 Donnie Allison TA Pat Allison	.15	.40
149 Hut Stricklin TA Pam Stricklin Taylor Stricklin	.15	.40
150 Jeff Gordon YG	2.00	4.00
151 Kenny Wallace YG	.15	.40
152 Bobby Labonte YG	.75	2.00
153 Jeff Gordon YG	2.00	4.00
154 Kenny Wallace YG	.15	.40
155 Bobby Labonte YG	.75	2.00
156 Jeff Gordon YG Kenny Wallace Bobby Labonte	3.00	6.00
157 Harry Gant	.15	.40
158 Harry Gant's Car	.07	.20
159 Hut Stricklin	.15	.40
160 Richard Petty Kyle Petty	.30	.75
161 Geoff Bodine B Brett Bodine	.15	.40
162 Terry Labonte B Bobby Labonte	.50	1.25
163 Rusty Wallace B Kenny Wallace	.60	1.50
164 Michael Waltrip B Darrell Waltrip	.30	.75
165 Ned Jarrett (Dale Jarrett	.30	.75
166 Bobby Labonte	.75	2.00
167 Terry Labonte	.60	1.50
168 Terry Labonte's Car	.30	.75
169 Geoff Bodine	.07	.20
170 Wally Dallenbach Jr.	.07	.20
171 Dale Earnhardt	1.50	4.00
172 Harry Gant	.07	.20
173 Jeff Gordon	1.50	3.00
174 Bobby Hillin	.07	.20
175 Sterling Marlin	.50	1.25
176 Mark Martin	.75	2.00
177 Morgan Shepherd	.07	.20
178 Kenny Wallace	.07	.20
179 Michael Waltrip	.15	.40
180 Brett Bodine	.07	.20
181 Derrike Cope	.07	.20
182 Ernie Irvan	.15	.40
183 Dale Jarrett	.60	1.50
184 Bobby Labonte	.60	1.50
185 Terry Labonte	.40	1.00
186 Kyle Petty	.15	.40
187 Ken Schrader	.07	.20
188 Jimmy Spencer	.07	.20
189 Hut Stricklin	.07	.20
190 Darrell Waltrip	.15	.40
191 Rusty Wallace RW	.30	1.00
192 Rusty Wallace RW	.30	1.00
193 Rusty Wallace RW	.30	1.00
194 Rusty Wallace's Car RW	.07	.20
195 Rusty Wallace's Car RW	.07	.20
196 Rusty Wallace in Pits RW	.07	.20
197 Rusty Wallace RW	.30	1.00
198 Dale Earnhardt WIN	.75	2.00
199 Ernie Irvan WIN	.15	.40
200 Rick Mast WIN	.07	.20
201 Ernie Irvan PS	.15	.40
202 Dale Earnhardt WIN	.75	2.00
203 Ken Schrader PS	.07	.20
204 Sterling Marlin WIN	.50	1.25
205 Jeff Gordon PS	1.00	2.50
206 Michael Waltrip WIN	.15	.40
207 Dale Earnhardt WIN	.75	2.00
KP1 Kyle Petty's Car Promo	1.25	3.00
KP2 Kyle Petty Promo	1.25	3.00
AKDA Alan Kulwicki Davey Allison	7.50	20.00
AKDAG Alan Kulwicki Davey Allison 24K Gold	12.50	30.00

1993 Action Packed 24K Gold

These insert cards were randomly distributed in all three series of 1993 Action Packed cards. They are distinguishable from the regular issue cards by the "G" suffix on the card numbers as well as the 24Kt. Gold logo on the card fronts.

COMP. SET (72)	1200.00	2400.00
COMP.SERIES 1 (17)	600.00	1200.00
COMP.SERIES 2 (21)	300.00	600.00
COMP.SERIES 3 (34)	300.00	600.00
1G Alan Kulwicki T10	20.00	50.00
2G Darrell Waltrip T10	8.00	20.00
3G Kyle Petty T10	8.00	20.00
4G Davey Allison T10	20.00	50.00
5G Mark Martin T10	15.00	40.00
6G Harry Gant T10	5.00	12.00
7G Terry Labonte T10	10.00	25.00
8G Sterling Marlin T10	10.00	25.00
9G Kenny Wallace YG	5.00	12.00
10G Jeff Gordon YG	20.00	50.00
11G Bobby Labonte YG	12.50	30.00
12G Jeff Gordon YG Kenny Wallace YG Bobby Labonte YG	25.00	60.00
13G Richard Petty KR	10.00	25.00
14G Richard Petty KR	10.00	25.00
15G Richard Petty KR	10.00	25.00
16G Richard Petty KR	10.00	25.00
17G Richard Petty KR	10.00	25.00
18G Dale Earnhardt BB	12.50	30.00
19G Dale Earnhardt BB	12.50	30.00
20G Dale Earnhardt BB	12.50	30.00
21G Dale Earnhardt BB	12.50	30.00
22G Dale Earnhardt BB Braille	12.50	30.00
23G Dale Earnhardt BB Braille	12.50	30.00
24G Dale Earnhardt BB Braille	12.50	30.00
25G Dale Earnhardt BB Braille	12.50	30.00
26G Jeff Gordon YG	20.00	50.00
27G Kenny Wallace YG	4.00	10.00
28G Bobby Labonte YG	12.50	30.00
29G Jeff Gordon YG	20.00	50.00
30G Kenny Wallace YG	4.00	10.00
31G Bobby Labonte YG	12.50	30.00
32G Jeff Gordon YG Kenny Wallace YG Bobby Labonte YG	20.00	50.00
33G Dale Jarrett D93	10.00	25.00
34G Kyle Petty D93	6.00	15.00
35G Richard Petty D93	8.00	20.00
36G Jeff Gordon D93	20.00	50.00
37G Dale Earnhardt D93	15.00	40.00
38G Dale Earnhardt D93	15.00	40.00
39G Alan Kulwicki	10.00	25.00
40G Alan Kulwicki	10.00	25.00
41G Alan Kulwicki	10.00	25.00
42G Alan Kulwicki	10.00	25.00
43G Alan Kulwicki	10.00	25.00
44G Alan Kulwicki	10.00	25.00
45G Davey Allison	12.50	30.00
46G Davey Allison	12.50	30.00
47G Davey Allison	12.50	30.00
48G Davey Allison	12.50	30.00
49G Davey Allison	12.50	30.00
50G Davey Allison	12.50	30.00
51G Geoff Bodine	3.00	8.00
52G Wally Dallenbach Jr.	3.00	8.00
53G Dale Earnhardt	15.00	40.00
54G Harry Gant	3.00	8.00
55G Jeff Gordon	20.00	50.00
56G Bobby Hillin	3.00	8.00
57G Sterling Marlin	10.00	25.00
58G Mark Martin	12.50	30.00
59G Morgan Shepherd	3.00	8.00
60G Kenny Wallace	3.00	8.00
61G Michael Waltrip	5.00	12.00
62G Brett Bodine	3.00	8.00
63G Derrike Cope	3.00	8.00
64G Ernie Irvan	5.00	12.00
65G Dale Jarrett	10.00	25.00
66G Bobby Labonte	10.00	25.00
67G Terry Labonte	10.00	25.00
68G Kyle Petty	5.00	12.00
69G Ken Schrader	3.00	8.00
70G Jimmy Spencer	3.00	8.00
71G Hut Stricklin	3.00	8.00
72G Darrell Waltrip	5.00	12.00

1993 Action Packed Davey Allison

A special insert set devoted to the life of the late Davey Allison. The cards were randomly inserted in series three packs of 1993 Action Packed.

COMPLETE SET (6)	3.00	8.00
COMMON CARD (DA1-DA6)	.75	1.50

1993 Action Packed Alan Kulwicki

A special insert set devoted to the life of the late Alan Kulwicki. The cards were randomly inserted in series three packs of 1993 Action Packed.

COMPLETE SET (6)	3.00	8.00
COMMON CARD (AK1-AK6)	.75	1.50

1994 Action Packed Prototypes

Action Packed released several prototype cards throughout the 1994 year. Two Kyle Petty cards were released for series one, five individual driver cards for series two, and four more for series three. Two prototype 24K Gold cards were also issued, but are not considered part of the basic 11-card set.

COMPLETE SET (11)	25.00	60.00
2R941 Dale Earnhardt	10.00	25.00
2R942 Jeff Gordon	7.50	20.00
2R942G Jeff Gordon 24K Gold	40.00	100.00
2R943 Kyle Petty	2.00	5.00
2R943G Kyle Petty 24K Gold	25.00	60.00
2R944 Dale Jarrett	2.50	6.00
2R945 Rusty Wallace's Car	3.00	8.00
3R941 Ricky Rudd Linda Rudd	2.00	5.00
3R942 Richard Childress	1.25	3.00
3R944 Mark Martin	4.00	10.00
3R94S Jeff Gordon	6.00	15.00

KP1 Kyle Petty's Car	1.25	3.00
KP2 Kyle Petty	2.00	5.00

1994 Action Packed

The 1994 Action Packed set was released in three series with each pack containing six cards. Wax boxes contained 24-packs per box and color photos of popular drivers were featured on the wrapper fronts. The standard Action Packed 24K Gold insert was distributed throughout all three series with series three also including a Richard Childress Racing insert. Series one is highlighted by Race Winners, Top Ten, Young Guns, Two Timers and Pit Crew Champs subsets. Series two features Neil Bonnett and Kyle Petty subsets along with a Daytona Review. A special Kyle Petty Diamond card (#92D) was also inserted in series two, at a rate of approximatey 1:1,650, that features an authentic diamond embedded in the card front. The diamond earring Kyle Petty card is numbered of 1000. The third series is highlighted by a Rest and Relaxation subset (139-167) and a Winner subset (179-193).

COMPLETE SET (209)	20.00	50.00
COMP.SERIES 1 (66)	10.00	25.00
COMP.SERIES 2 (72)	10.00	25.00
COMP.SERIES 3 (71)	10.00	25.00
WAX BOX SERIES 1	15.00	40.00
WAX BOX SERIES 2	15.00	40.00
WAX BOX SERIES 3	20.00	50.00
1 Dale Earnhardt	2.00	5.00
2 Rusty Wallace	.75	2.00
3 Mark Martin	.75	2.00
4 Dale Jarrett	.75	2.00
5 Kyle Petty	.25	.60
6 Ernie Irvan	.25	.60
7 Morgan Shepherd	.10	.30
8 Dale Earnhardt	2.00	5.00
Winston Cup Champion		
9 Ken Schrader	.10	.30
10 Ricky Rudd	.40	1.00
11 Harry Gant	.25	.60
12 Jimmy Spencer	.10	.30
13 Darrell Waltrip	.25	.60
Sarah Waltrip		
14 Jeff Gordon	1.25	3.00
15 Sterling Marlin	.40	1.00
16 Geoff Bodine	.10	.30
17 Michael Waltrip	.25	.60
18 Terry Labonte	.40	1.00
19 Bobby Labonte	.60	1.50
20 Brett Bodine	.10	.30
21 Rick Mast	.10	.30
22 Wally Dallenbach Jr.	.10	.30
23 Kenny Wallace	.10	.30
24 Hut Stricklin	.10	.30
25 Derrike Cope	.10	.30
26 Bobby Hillin	.10	.30
27 Rick Wilson	.10	.30
28 Lake Speed	.10	.30
29 Alan Kulwicki	.50	1.25
30 Jeff Gordon	1.25	3.00
Rookie of the Year		
31 Rusty Wallace's Car WIN	.25	.60
32 Dale Earnhardt WIN	2.00	5.00
33 Mark Martin WIN	.75	2.00
34 Ernie Irvan w/Crew WIN	.25	.60
35 Dale Jarrett WIN	.60	1.50
Joe Gibbs		
36 Morgan Shepherd WIN	.10	.30
37 Kyle Petty WIN	.25	.60
38 Ricky Rudd WIN	.40	1.00
39 Geoff Bodine WIN	.10	.30
40 Davey Allison WIN	.60	1.50
41 Dale Earnhardt's Car	.75	2.00
42 Rusty Wallace's Car	.40	1.00
43 Mark Martin's Car	.40	1.00
44 Dale Jarrett	.40	1.00
Kyle Petty with Car		
45 Kyle Petty's Car	.10	.30
46 Ernie Irvan's Car	.25	.60
47 Morgan Shepherd's Car	.05	.15
48 Bill Elliott's Car	.40	1.00
49 Ken Schrader's Car	.05	.15
50 Ricky Rudd's Car	.10	.30
51 John Andretti R RC	.10	.30
52 Ward Burton R	.25	.60
53 Steve Grissom R	.10	.30
54 Joe Nemechek R	.10	.30
55 Jeff Burton R	.40	1.00
56 Loy Allen Jr. R	.10	.30
57 Lake Speed TC	.10	.30
58 Ernie Irvan with Car TC	.25	.60
59 Geoff Bodine TC	.10	.30
60 Dick Trickle TC	.10	.30
61 Jimmy Hensley TC	.10	.30
62 Buddy Parrott	.05	.15
63 Donnie Richeson	.05	.15
64 Steve Hmiel	.05	.15
65 Mike Hill	.05	.15
66 Doug Hewitt	.05	.15
67 Rusty Wallace	.75	2.00
68 Dale Earnhardt	2.00	5.00
69 Mark Martin	.75	2.00
70 Darrell Waltrip	.25	.60
71 Dale Jarrett	.60	1.50
72 Morgan Shepherd	.10	.30
73 Jeff Gordon	1.25	3.00
74 Ken Schrader	.10	.30
75 Brett Bodine	.10	.30
76 Harry Gant	.25	.60
77 Sterling Marlin	.40	1.00
78 Terry Labonte	.40	1.00
79 Ricky Rudd	.40	1.00
80 Geoff Bodine	.10	.30
81 Ernie Irvan	.25	.60
82 Kyle Petty	.25	.60
83 Jimmy Spencer	.10	.30
84 Hut Stricklin	.10	.30
85 Bobby Labonte	.60	1.50
86 Derrike Cope	.10	.30
87 Loy Allen Jr.	.10	.30
88 Michael Waltrip	.25	.60
89 Ted Musgrave	.10	.30
90 Lake Speed	.10	.30
91 Todd Bodine	.10	.30
92 Kyle Petty KPS	.25	.60
92D Kyle Petty/1000	25.00	60.00
(Diamond Earring)		
93 Kyle Petty BR KPS	.25	.60
94 Kyle Petty KPS	.25	.60
95 Kyle Petty KPS	.25	.60
Aerosmith		
96 Kyle Petty KPS	.25	.60
Pattie Petty		
Austin Petty		
Montgomery Petty		
97 Kyle Petty KPS	.25	.60
Michael Waltrip		
98 Neil Bonnett	.25	.60
David Bonnett		
99 Neil Bonnett	2.00	5.00
Dale Earnhardt		
100 Neil Bonnett	.25	.60
Darrell Waltrip		
101 Neil Bonnett	.40	1.00
102 Neil Bonnett	.40	1.00
103 Jeff Gordon DR	1.25	3.00
104 Dale Earnhardt DR	2.00	5.00
105 Ernie Irvan DR	.25	.60
Kim Irvan		
Jordan Irvan		
106 Loy Allen Jr. DR	.10	.30
107 Sterling Marlin DR	.40	1.00
108 Rusty Wallace's Car	.40	1.00
109 Sterling Marlin's Car	.10	.30
110 Terry Labonte's Car	.25	.60
111 Geoff Bodine's Car	.05	.15
112 Ricky Rudd's Car	.10	.30
113 Lake Speed's Car	.05	.15
114 Ted Musgrave's Car	.05	.15
115 Mark Martin's Car	.40	1.00
116 Hut Stricklin's Car	.05	.15
117 Ken Schrader's Car	.05	.15
118 Jimmy Spencer's Car	.05	.15
119 Kyle Petty's Car	.10	.30
120 Wally Dallenbach Jr.'s Car	.05	.15
121 John Andretti's Car	.05	.15
122 Steve Grissom's Car	.05	.15
123 Ward Burton's Car	.05	.15
124 Joe Nemechek's Car	.05	.15
125 Jeff Burton's Car	.05	.15
126 Dale Earnhardt's Car	.75	2.00
127 Michael Waltrip's Car	.10	.30
128 Dale Jarrett's Car	.40	1.00
129 Morgan Shepherd's Car	.05	.15
130 Bobby Labonte's Car	.10	.30
131 Jeff Gordon's Car	.50	1.25
132 Brett Bodine's Car	.05	.15
133 Michael Waltrip's Car	.10	.30
134 Todd Bodine's Car	.05	.15
135 Ernie Irvan's Car	.25	.60
136 Harry Gant's Car	.10	.30
137 Rick Mast's Car	.05	.15
138 Bill Elliott's Car	.40	1.00
139 Brett Bodine RR	.05	.15
Diane Bodine		
140 Geoff Bodine RR	.10	.30
141 Todd Bodine RR	.05	.15
142 Jeff Burton RR	.10	.30
143 Derrike Cope RR	.10	.30
144 Wally Dallenbach Jr. RR	.10	.30
145 Harry Gant RR	.10	.30
146 Jeff Gordon RR	1.25	3.00
147 Steve Grissom RR	.10	.30
Kyle Grissom		
148 Ernie Irvan RR	.25	.60
149 Dale Jarrett RR	.60	1.50
150 Bobby Labonte RR	.60	1.50
151 Terry Labonte RR	.40	1.00
Justin Labonte		
152 Sterling Marlin RR	.40	1.00
153 Mark Martin RR	.75	2.00
154 Rick Mast RR	.10	.30
Ricky Mast		
155 Ted Musgrave RR	.10	.30
Brittany Musgrave		
156 Joe Nemechek RR	.10	.30
157 Kyle Petty RR	.10	.30
158 Ricky Rudd RR	.40	1.00
Linda Rudd		
159 Greg Sacks RR	.10	.30
160 Ken Schrader RR	.10	.30
161 Morgan Shepherd RR	.10	.30
162 Lake Speed RR	.10	.30
163 Jimmy Spencer RR	.10	.30
164 Hut Stricklin RR	.10	.30
165 Mike Wallace RR	.10	.30
166 Darrell Waltrip RR	.25	.60
Stevie Waltrip		
Jessica Waltrip		
Sarah Waltrip		
167 Michael Waltrip RR	.25	.60
168 Roger Penske	.05	.15
Don Miller		
169 Junior Johnson	.10	.30
170 Robert Yates	.05	.15
171 Joe Gibbs	.25	.60
172 Ricky Rudd	.40	1.00
173 Glen Wood	.05	.15
Len Wood		
Eddie Wood		
Kim Wood		
174 Jack Roush	.05	.15
175 Joe Hendrick(Papa)	.05	.15
Rick Hendrick		
176 Felix Sabates	.05	.15
177 Richard Childress	.25	.60
178 Richard Petty	.40	1.00
179 Dale Earnhardt WIN	2.00	5.00
180 Dale Earnhardt WIN	2.00	5.00
181 Ernie Irvan WIN	.10	.30
182 Ernie Irvan WIN	.10	.30
183 Rusty Wallace WIN	.75	2.00
184 Terry Labonte WIN	.40	1.00
185 Sterling Marlin WIN	.40	1.00
186 Rusty Wallace WIN	.75	2.00
187 Dale Earnhardt WIN	2.00	5.00
188 Ernie Irvan WIN	.25	.60
189 Jeff Gordon WIN	1.25	3.00
190 Rusty Wallace WIN	.75	2.00
191 Rusty Wallace WIN	.75	2.00
192 Rusty Wallace WIN	.75	2.00
193 Jimmy Spencer WIN	.10	.30
194 Ernie Irvan	.25	.60
Kim Irvan		
Jordan Irvan		
195 Ernie Irvan	.25	.60
196 Ernie Irvan	.25	.60
197 Ernie Irvan	.25	.60
198 Ernie Irvan	.25	.60
199 Mark Martin	.75	2.00
200 Mark Martin	.75	2.00
201 Mark Martin	.75	2.00
202 Mark Martin	.75	2.00
203 Mark Martin	.75	2.00
204 Rusty Wallace	.50	1.25
Kenny Wallace		
Mike Wallace		
205 Todd Bodine	.10	.30
Brett Bodine		
Geoff Bodine		
206 Rusty Wallace WS	.50	1.25
207 Geoff Bodine WS	.10	.30
208 Joe Nemechek WS	.10	.30
209 Jeff Gordon WS	1.25	3.00

1994 Action Packed 24K Gold

Randomly inserted in packs over all three 1994 Action Packed series, each card includes the 24Kt. Gold logo on the card front. There were 1,000 of the Jeff Gordon card (#189G) inserted in series three. The only way the card came was autographed and the card is not included in the complete set price. Many cards in the set were also used in subsets in the regular issue. Wrapper stated odds for pulling a 24K Gold card are 1:96 packs.

COMPLETE SET (59)	600.00	1200.00
COMP.SERIES 1 (20)	250.00	500.00
COMP.SERIES 2 (25)	250.00	500.00
COMP.SERIES 3 (14)	250.00	500.00
1G Rusty Wallace WIN	10.00	25.00
2G Dale Earnhardt WIN	25.00	60.00
3G Mark Martin WIN	10.00	25.00
4G Ernie Irvan with Crew WIN	3.00	8.00
5G Dale Jarrett WIN	8.00	20.00
6G Morgan Shepherd WIN	1.50	4.00
7G Kyle Petty WIN	3.00	8.00
8G Ricky Rudd WIN	5.00	12.00
9G Geoff Bodine WIN	1.50	4.00
10G Davey Allison WIN	8.00	20.00
11G Dale Earnhardt's Car	10.00	25.00
12G Rusty Wallace's Car	5.00	12.00
13G Mark Martin's Car	5.00	12.00
14G Dale Jarrett	10.00	25.00
Kyle Petty with Car		
15G Kyle Petty's Car	1.50	4.00
16G Ernie Irvan's Car	3.00	8.00
17G Morgan Shepherd's Car	.75	2.00
18G Bill Elliott's Car	5.00	12.00
19G Ken Schrader's Car	.75	2.00
20G Ricky Rudd's Car	1.50	4.00
21G Rusty Wallace	10.00	25.00
22G Dale Earnhardt	25.00	60.00
23G Mark Martin	10.00	25.00
24G Darrell Waltrip	3.00	8.00
25G Dale Jarrett	10.00	25.00
26G Morgan Shepherd	1.50	4.00
27G Jeff Gordon	15.00	40.00
28G Ken Schrader	1.50	4.00
29G Brett Bodine	1.50	4.00
30G Harry Gant	3.00	8.00
31G Sterling Marlin	5.00	12.00
32G Terry Labonte	5.00	12.00
33G Ricky Rudd	5.00	12.00
34G Geoff Bodine	1.50	4.00
35G Ernie Irvan	3.00	8.00
36G Kyle Petty	3.00	8.00
37G Jimmy Spencer	1.50	4.00
38G Hut Stricklin	1.50	4.00
39G Bobby Labonte	8.00	20.00
40G Derrike Cope	1.50	4.00
41G Loy Allen Jr.	1.50	4.00
42G Michael Waltrip	3.00	8.00
43G Ted Musgrave	1.50	4.00
44G Lake Speed	1.50	4.00
45G Todd Bodine	1.50	4.00
179G Dale Earnhardt WIN	25.00	60.00
180G Dale Earnhardt WIN	25.00	60.00
181G Ernie Irvan WIN	1.50	4.00
182G Ernie Irvan WIN	1.50	4.00
183G Rusty Wallace WIN	10.00	25.00
184G Terry Labonte WIN	5.00	12.00
185G Sterling Marlin WIN	5.00	12.00
186G Rusty Wallace WIN	10.00	25.00
187G Dale Earnhardt WIN	25.00	60.00
188G Ernie Irvan WIN	1.50	4.00
189G Jeff Gordon WIN AUTO	40.00	80.00
190G Rusty Wallace WIN	10.00	25.00
191G Rusty Wallace WIN	10.00	25.00
192G Rusty Wallace WIN	10.00	25.00
193G Jimmy Spencer WIN	1.50	4.00

1994 Action Packed Mint

This set was issued as an upgraded parallel to the basic issue Action Packed release. Each card was serial numbered of 500 and printed with an all-24K Gold cardfront. The cards were packaged separately from the base set release.

*MINT CARDS: 2X TO 5X BASIC CARDS

1994 Action Packed Champ and Challenger

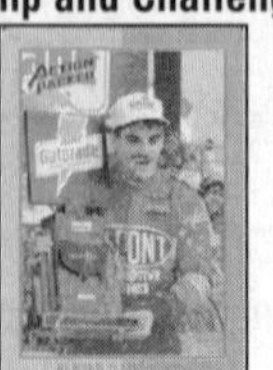

Action Packed issued this special set to highlight the careers of two of NASCAR's most popular drivers of 1994 -- the 1993 "Champ" Dale Earnhardt and "Challenger" Jeff Gordon. The cards were distributed in 6-card packs with 24 packs per box. Cards #1-20 have green and red borders and focus on Gordon, while cards #21-40 feature black and white borders and highlight Earnhardt's 1993 Championship season. The last two cards (#41-42) featured both Gordon and Earnhardt. Complete factory sets were sold through both the Action Packed dealer network and the Action Packed Club.

COMPLETE SET (42)	10.00	25.00
COMPLETE FACT. SET (42)	12.00	30.00
1 Jeff Gordon	.30	.75
2 Ray Evernham	.15	.40
3 Jeff Gordon	.30	.75
4 Jeff Gordon	.30	.75
5 Jeff Gordon	.30	.75
6 Jeff Gordon	.30	.75
7 Jeff Gordon in Pits	.30	.75
8 Jeff Gordon in Pits	.30	.75
9 Jeff Gordon	.30	.75
10 Jeff Gordon	.30	.75
11 Jeff Gordon	.30	.75
12 Jimmy Johnson	.15	.40
13 Jeff Gordon	.30	.75
14 Jeff Gordon	.30	.75
15 Jeff Gordon	.30	.75
16 Jeff Gordon's Car	.15	.40
17 Jeff Gordon's Car	.15	.40
18 Jeff Gordon	.30	.75
19 Jeff Gordon	.30	.75
20 Jeff Gordon	.30	.75
21 Dale Earnhardt	.60	1.50
22 Dale Earnhardt	.60	1.50
23 Dale Earnhardt	.60	1.50
24 Dale Earnhardt	.60	1.50
25 Dale Earnhardt	.60	1.50
26 Dale Earnhardt	.60	1.50
27 Dale Earnhardt	.60	1.50
28 Dale Earnhardt	.60	1.50
29 Dale Earnhardt	.60	1.50
30 Dale Earnhardt	.60	1.50
31 Dale Earnhardt	.60	1.50
Neil Bonnett		
32 Dale Earnhardt's Car	.15	.40
33 Dale Earnhardt's Car	.15	.40
34 Dale Earnhardt	.60	1.50
Alan Kulwicki Cars		
35 Dale Earnhardt's Car	.15	.40
36 Dale Earnhardt's Car	.15	.40
37 Dale Earnhardt	.60	1.50
Rusty Wallace Cars		
38 Dale Earnhardt	.60	1.50
39 Dale Earnhardt	.60	1.50
40 Dale Earnhardt	.60	1.50
41 Dale Earnhardt	.15	.40
Jeff Gordon Cars		
42 Dale Earnhardt	.60	1.50
Jeff Gordon		

1994 Action Packed Champ and Challenger 24K Gold

This insert set is basically a parallel to 12-cards from the regular issue 1994 Action Packed Champ and Challenger issue. As with all Action Packed Gold cards, the 24Kt. Gold stamp appears on the card fronts, while the backs include a "G" suffix on the card numbers. Wrapper stated odds for pulling one of the popular inserts is 1:96.

COMPLETE SET (12)	200.00	400.00
1G Jeff Gordon	15.00	40.00
5G Jeff Gordon	15.00	40.00
9G Jeff Gordon	15.00	40.00
17G Jeff Gordon's Car	15.00	40.00
20G Jeff Gordon	15.00	40.00
22G Dale Earnhardt	15.00	40.00
28G Dale Earnhardt	15.00	40.00
30G Dale Earnhardt	15.00	40.00
32G Dale Earnhardt's Car	15.00	40.00
39G Dale Earnhardt	15.00	40.00
41G Dale Earnhardt's Car	15.00	40.00
Jeff Gordon's Car		
42G Dale Earnhardt	15.00	40.00
Jeff Gordon		

1994 Action Packed Richard Childress Racing

Richard Childress, Dale Earnhardt and the Goodwrench Racing Team are the focus of this insert set from series three packs of 1994 Action Packed. The cards were issued in the same pack ratio as the regular series cards, except cards #18 and #20 which are considered tougher to find than the rest of the set.

COMPLETE SET (20)	12.00	30.00
RCR1 Richard Childress	.15	.40
RCR2 Dale Earnhardt's Car	.75	1.50
RCR3 Dale Earnhardt	1.25	3.00
RCR4 Dale Earnhardt	1.25	3.00
RCR5 Dale Earnhardt's Car	.75	1.50
RCR6 Dale Earnhardt's Car	.75	1.50
RCR7 Andy Petree	.15	.40
RCR8 Eddie Lanier	.15	.40
RCR9 David Smith	.15	.40
RCR10 Jimmy Elledge	.15	.40
RCR11 Cecil Gordon	.15	.40
RCR12 Danny Lawrence	.15	.40
RCR13 Danny Myers	.15	.40
RCR14 Joe Dan Bailey	.15	.40
RCR15 Gene DeHart	.15	.40
RCR16 John Mulloy	.15	.40
RCR17 Hank Jones	.15	.40
RCR18 Craig Donley SP	1.50	3.00
RCR19 Jim Baldwin	.15	.40
RCR20 Don Hawk SP	1.50	3.00

1994 Action Packed Badge of Honor Pins

This set of Badge of Honor Pins was issued one pin at a time as promos mailed directly to dealers and other card retailers. Each pin features a color photo of the driver mounted on a bronze colored solid-metal stick pin. The year of issue is noted below the player photo.

COMPLETE SET (4)	5.00	12.00
1 Jeff Gordon	2.50	6.00
2 Terry Labonte	1.00	2.50
3 Kyle Petty	.75	2.00
4 Rusty Wallace	1.50	4.00

1994 Action Packed Coastars

Action Packed produced these cards in 1994 as 6-card panels ready to be punched-out from their backing. The cards were intended to be used as drink coasters and feature the driver's photo on front and his car on back. They are most often found intact in the original 6-card form. The cards were distributed through the Action Packed dealer network and were also made available to Action Packed Club members.

COMPLETE SET (18)	6.00	15.00
1 Geoff Bodine	.20	.50
2 Dale Earnhardt	1.50	4.00
3 Bill Elliott	.40	1.00
4 Harry Gant	.20	.50
5 Jeff Gordon	.75	2.00
6 Ernie Irvan	.30	.75
7 Dale Jarrett	.50	1.25
8 Bobby Labonte	.50	1.25
9 Terry Labonte	.40	1.00
10 Sterling Marlin	.30	.75
11 Mark Martin	.60	1.50
12 Joe Nemechek	.20	.50
13 Kyle Petty	.30	.75
14 Ricky Rudd	.30	.75
15 Ken Schrader	.20	.50
16 Rusty Wallace	.60	1.50
17 Darrell Waltrip	.30	.75
18 Michael Waltrip	.30	.75

1994 Action Packed Mammoth

These oversized cards (roughly 7 1/2" x 10 1/2") are essentially a super-sized parallel version of the driver's basic issue 1994 Action Packed card. Each was sold separately, primarily through mass market retailers.

COMPLETE SET (5)	7.50	20.00
2 Rusty Wallace	2.00	5.00
3 Mark Martin	2.00	5.00
11 Harry Gant	.75	2.00
14 Jeff Gordon	3.00	8.00
18 Terry Labonte	1.25	3.00

1994 Action Packed Mint Collection Jeff Gordon

This four-card set was originally done fo[r] distribution through the Home Shopping Network. Two of the cards are regular cards from the 1994 Action Packed Champ and Challenger set. The othe[r] two cards were produced with a gold leaf coating. The sets are numbered of 1,000 and come in a black slip cover case.

11 Jeff Gordon Gold Leaf	5.00	12.00
11 Jeff Gordon	2.00	5.00
19 Jeff Gordon Gold Leaf	5.00	12.00
19 Jeff Gordon	2.00	5.00

1994 Action Packed Select 24K Gold

This 10-card set was produced by Action Packed and was distributed through the Winston Cup Catalog in a separate black card display box with each card wrapped in black felt. It focuses on the 1985-1994 winners of the Winston Select. It features the first Action Packed card of Bill Elliott. Some cards reportedly made their way into packs.

COMPLETE SET (10)	30.00	80.00
W1 Darrell Waltrip	1.00	2.50
W2 Bill Elliott	1.00	2.50
W3 Dale Earnhardt	8.00	20.00
W4 Terry Labonte	1.50	4.00
W5 Rusty Wallace	3.00	8.00
W6 Dale Earnhardt	8.00	20.00
W7 Davey Allison	2.50	6.00
W8 Davey Allison	2.50	6.00
W9 Dale Earnhardt	8.00	20.00
W10 Geoff Bodine	.50	1.25

1994 Action Packed Smokin' Joe's

This 13-card set was produced by Action Packed and was distributed through the Winston Cup Catalog. It features members of the Smokin' Joe's racing teams in the NASCAR, NHRA, and AMA circuits. The set includes a 24K Gold checklist.

COMPLETE SET (13)	6.00	15.00
1 Hut Stricklin	.75	2.00
2 Hut Stricklin's Car	.60	1.50
3 Jim Head	.60	1.50
4 Jim Head's Car	.40	1.00
5 Gordie Bonin	.60	1.50
6 Gordie Bonin's Car	.40	1.00
7 Mike Hale	.60	1.50
8 Mike Hale's Bike	.40	1.00
9 Kevin Magee	.60	1.50
10 Kevin Magee's Bike	.40	1.00
11 Mike Smith	.60	1.50
12 Mike Smith's Bike	.40	1.00
13 Checklist Card	.60	1.50

1995 Action Packed Country

Action Packed's third Winston Cup card release fo[r] 1995 was entitled Winston Cup Country and was produced by Pinnacle Brands. The set is comprised of several series of subsets: Riding Shotgun (1-10), Shades (11-20), Motor Racing Outreach (21-25), Now and Then (26-43), Winners (44-56), Crew Chiefs (57-61), Drivers (62-85), SuperTruck Drivers (86-91), SuperTrucks (92-98) and SuperTruck Owners (99-101). The embossed cards were packed 24-foil packs to a box with 6-cards per pack and distributed to both hobby and retail outlets. Insert sets include: Silver Speed parallel, 24KT Team, 2nd Career Choice, and Team Rainbow.

COMPLETE SET (101)	12.00	30.00
1 Bobby Labonte RS	.25	.60
2 Jeremy Mayfield RS	.07	.20
3 Bill Elliott RS	.25	.60
4 Darrell Waltrip RS	.15	.40
5 Dale Earnhardt RS	.60	1.50
6 Jeff Gordon RS	.40	1.00
7 Ricky Rudd RS	.15	.40
8 John Andretti RS	.07	.20
9 Kenny Wallace RS	.07	.20
10 Sterling Marlin RS	.15	.40
11 Dale Earnhardt S	.60	1.50

Rusty Wallace S	.30	.75
Dale Jarrett S	.25	.60
Jeff Gordon S	.40	1.00
Sterling Marlin S	.15	.40
Ricky Rudd S	.15	.40
Dale Earnhardt	.60	1.50
Taylor Nicole Earnhardt S		
Darrell Waltrip S	.15	.40
Terry Labonte S	.25	.60
Richard Petty S	.25	.60
Stevie Waltrip	.15	.40
Darrell Waltrip MRO		
Jeff Gordon	.40	1.00
Brooke Gordon MRO		
Rice Speed	.07	.20
Lake Speed MRO		
Bill Elliott	.25	.60
Cindy Elliott MRO		
Dale Earnhardt	.60	1.50
Teresa Earnhardt		
Max Helton		
Dale Earnhardt NT	.60	1.50
Dale Earnhardt NT	.60	1.50
Dale Earnhardt NT	.60	1.50
Dale Earnhardt NT	.60	1.50
Dale Earnhardt NT	.60	1.50
Dale Earnhardt NT	.60	1.50
Darrell Waltrip NT	.15	.40
Darrell Waltrip NT	.15	.40
Darrell Waltrip NT	.15	.40
Darrell Waltrip NT	.15	.40
Darrell Waltrip NT	.15	.40
Darrell Waltrip NT	.15	.40
Rusty Wallace NT	.30	.75
Rusty Wallace NT	.30	.75
Rusty Wallace NT	.30	.75
Rusty Wallace NT	.30	.75
Rusty Wallace NT	.30	.75
Rusty Wallace NT	.30	.75
Mark Martin WIN	.30	.75
Dale Earnhardt WIN	.60	1.50
Teresa Earnhardt		
Bobby Labonte WIN	.25	.60
Kyle Petty WIN	.15	.40
Terry Labonte WIN	.25	.60
Bobby Labonte WIN	.25	.60
Jeff Gordon WIN	.40	1.00
Jeff Gordon WIN	.40	1.00
Dale Jarrett WIN	.25	.60
Sterling Marlin WIN	.15	.40
Dale Earnhardt WIN	.60	1.50
Mark Martin WIN	.30	.75
Bobby Labonte WIN	.25	.60
Joe Gibbs		
Andy Petree	.02	.10
Steve Hmiel	.02	.10
Ray Evernham	.02	.10
Tony Glover	.02	.10
Robin Pemberton	.02	.10
Dale Earnhardt	1.25	3.00
Jeff Gordon	.75	2.00
Ted Musgrave	.07	.20
Dale Jarrett	.50	1.25
Bobby Hamilton	.07	.20
Morgan Shepherd	.07	.20
Bobby Labonte	.50	1.25
Michael Waltrip	.15	.40
Ricky Rudd	.25	.60
Ken Schrader	.07	.20
Bill Elliott	.30	.75
Steve Grissom	.07	.20
Derrike Cope	.07	.20
Brett Bodine	.07	.20
John Andretti	.07	.20
Rick Mast	.07	.20
Dick Trickle	.07	.20
Ricky Craven	.15	.40
Todd Bodine	.07	.20
Robert Pressley	.07	.20
Kenny Wallace	.07	.20
Jeff Burton	.25	.60
Jimmy Spencer	.07	.20
Geoff Bodine	.07	.20
Ron Hornaday Jr. STD RC	.07	.20
Butch Miller STD	.02	.10
Ken Schrader STD	.07	.20
Tobey Butler STD	.02	.10
Rick Carelli STD	.02	.10
Scott Lagasse STD	.07	.20
Sammy Swindell's SuperTruck	.02	.10
Scott Lagasse's SuperTruck	.02	.10
Mike Bliss' SuperTruck	.02	.10
Mike Chase's SuperTruck	.02	.10
Geoff Bodine's SuperTruck	.02	.10
Ken Schrader's SuperTruck	.02	.10
Ron Hornaday Jr.'s SuperTruck	.02	.10
Jeff Gordon	.40	1.00
Rick Hendrick STO		
0 Jim Venable STO	.02	.10
1 Ken Schrader STO	.07	.20
Jeff Gordon Promo	2.00	5.00
Magic Motion		
6 Bobby Labonte Promo	1.00	2.50

1995 Action Packed Country Silver Speed

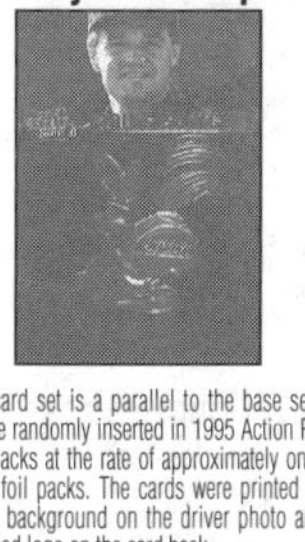

is 84-card set is a parallel to the base set. The ds were randomly inserted in 1995 Action Packed untry packs at the rate of approximately one card ery six foil packs. The cards were printed with a ver foil background on the driver photo and the ver Speed logo on the card back.

OMPLETE SET (84)	75.00	150.00
ILVER SPEEDS: 3X TO 6X BASIC CARDS		

1995 Action Packed Country 24K Team

The 24KT, Micro-Etched cards feature 10 of Winston Cup's best drivers in this 14-card set. Three Dale Earnhardt and three Jeff Gordon cards highlighted a new design for Action Packed's 24K insert line. The cards were seeded at a rate of one per 72 packs.

COMPLETE SET (14)	175.00	350.00
1 Jeff Gordon	12.50	30.00
2 Jeff Gordon	12.50	30.00
3 Jeff Gordon	12.50	30.00
4 Mark Martin	10.00	25.00
5 Dale Earnhardt	20.00	50.00
6 Dale Earnhardt	20.00	50.00
7 Dale Earnhardt	20.00	50.00
8 Rusty Wallace	10.00	25.00
9 Sterling Marlin	5.00	12.00
10 Bobby Labonte	8.00	20.00
11 Bill Elliott	8.00	20.00
12 Ricky Rudd	5.00	12.00
13 Ken Schrader	2.50	6.00
14 Ted Musgrave	2.50	6.00

1995 Action Packed Country 2nd Career Choice

This 9-card insert set features some of the top Winston Cup drivers reviling what they would be doing if they weren't racing. The cards utilize holographic gold-foil printing technology. The cards were seeded at a rate of one per 24 packs.

COMPLETE SET (9)	25.00	60.00
1 Bobby Hillin	.75	2.00
2 Kenny Wallace	.75	2.00
3 Rusty Wallace	6.00	15.00
4 Dale Jarrett	5.00	12.00
5 Derrike Cope	.75	2.00
6 Dale Earnhardt	15.00	40.00
7 Bobby Labonte	5.00	12.00
8 Sterling Marlin	2.00	5.00
9 Terry Labonte	3.00	8.00

1995 Action Packed Country Team Rainbow

This 12-card insert set takes a look at Jeff Gordon and the DuPont Rainbow Warrior team. The cards use lenticular printing technology to bring them to life. The cards were randomly inserted in hobby packs only at a rate of one per 36 packs.

COMPLETE SET (12)	75.00	150.00
1 Jeff Gordon	12.50	25.00
Brooke Gordon		
2 Jeff Gordon's Car	6.00	12.00
3 Jeff Gordon w/Crew	12.50	25.00
Refuse To Lose		
4 Ray Evernham	6.00	12.00
5 Jeff Gordon	12.50	25.00
Brooke Gordon		
6 Pit Stop	6.00	12.00
7 Jeff Gordon's Car	6.00	12.00
8 Jeff Gordon	12.50	25.00
Ray Evernham		
Rick Hendrick		
9 Jeff Gordon's Helmet	6.00	12.00
10 Victory Shout	12.50	25.00
11 Interview	12.50	25.00
12 Jeff Gordon	12.50	25.00
Ray Evernham		
P1 Jeff Gordon Promo #1	3.00	6.00

1995 Action Packed Badge of Honor Pins

This set of Badge of Honor Pins was issued through both hobby and mass market retailers. Each pin features a color photo of the driver mounted on a bronze colored solid-metal stick pin which was attached to a thin pink colored backer board the size of a standard trading card. The year of issue is noted below the player photo.

COMPLETE SET (9)	6.00	15.00
1 Bill Elliott	.75	2.00
2 Jeff Gordon	2.00	5.00
3 Dale Jarrett	1.00	2.50
4 Steve Kinser	.50	1.25
5 Terry Labonte	.75	2.00
6 Mark Martin	1.25	3.00
7 Robert Pressley	.50	1.25
8 Ricky Rudd	.75	2.00
9 Rusty Wallace	1.25	3.00

1995 Action Packed Hendrick Motorsports

This eight-card set was distributed through Hendrick Motorsport's merchandising trailers, as well as some Rick Hendrick's car dealerships.

COMPLETE SET (8)	2.00	5.00
1 Jeff Gordon	.75	2.00
2 Ken Schrader	.20	.50
3 Terry Labonte	.30	.75
4 Scott Lagasse	.20	.50
5 Ricky Hendrick Jr.	.20	.50
6 Rick Hendrick/Cover Card	.10	.30
7 Papa Joe Hendrick	.10	.30
8 Jimmy Johnson	.10	.30

1995 Action Packed Mammoth

This six-card set features the top names in NASCAR. The cards are approximately 7.5" X 10.5" in size. They were distributed through Action Packed dealer network. The cards came in clear poly bag packs with each pack having one card.

COMPLETE SET (6)	10.00	25.00
MM1 Dale Earnhardt	4.00	8.00
MM2 Bill Elliott	.75	2.00
MM3 Rusty Wallace	1.25	3.00
MM4 Jeff Gordon	1.50	4.00
MM5 Mark Martin	1.25	3.00
MM6 Dale Earnhardt	4.00	8.00

1995 Action Packed McDonald's Bill Elliott

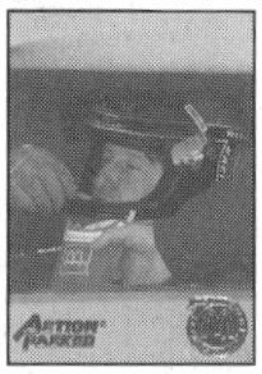

Originally offered during 1995 Speedweeks at Daytona, these cards were distributed through participating Florida and North Carolina area McDonald's restaurants. Three-card cello packs, as well as 21-card factory sets were produced. The set features Bill Elliott's life in and away from racing. Approximately one autograph certificate was distributed per case witch was redeemable for a signed Bill Elliott card.

COMPLETE SET (21)	8.00	16.00
COMPLETE FACT. SET (21)	10.00	20.00
MC1 Bill Elliott	.50	1.00
MC2 Ernie Elliott	.50	1.00
MC3 Bill Elliott	.50	1.00
MC4 Bill Elliott	.50	1.00
MC5 Bill Elliott	.50	1.00
MC6 Bill Elliott's Car	.50	1.00
MC7 Bill Elliott	.50	1.00
MC8 Bill Elliott's Car	.50	1.00
MC9 Bill Elliott in Car	.50	1.00
MC10 Bill Elliott	.50	1.00
MC11 Bill Elliott	.50	1.00
MC12 Bill Elliott	.50	1.00
MC13 Bill Elliott	.50	1.00
MC14 Bill Elliott	.50	1.00
MC15 Bill Elliott	.50	1.00
MC16 Bill Elliott w/ Car	.50	1.00
MC17 Bill Elliott	.50	1.00
MC18 Bill Elliott in Car	.50	1.00
MG19 Bill Elliott	.50	1.00
MG20 Bill Elliott's Transporter	.50	1.00
MG21 Bill Elliott	.50	1.00

1995 Action Packed Preview Promos 24K Gold

This 3-card issue promotes the 1995 Action Packed Preview set. Each of the three cards is numbered and utilizes the 24K Gold technology.

COMPLETE SET (3)	20.00	35.00
P2 Ricky Craven Promo	4.00	10.00
P3 Steve Kinser Promo	4.00	10.00
P4 Bill Elliott Promo	8.00	20.00

1995 Action Packed Preview

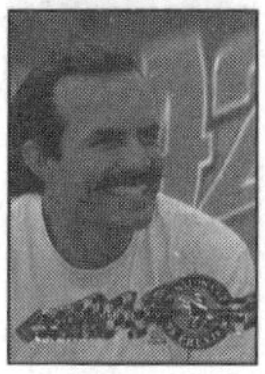

Action Packed's first racing issue for 1995 is also commonly called Action Packed Winston Cup Preview as the wrapper states. The cards were packaged in 6-card packs with 24 packs per box. A new Driving With Dale subset was included featuring popular drivers discussing what it's like to race against Earnhardt. The now standard Action Packed subsets of Race Winners, Pole Winners and Top Ten were also part of the regular issue. This set marks the first regular issue Bill Elliott Action Packed card. There was also a Dale Earnhardt Big Picture redemption card randomly inserted in packs. The card folds out to make a big picture of Dale Earnhardt. There were reportedly 2,500 cards produced.

COMPLETE SET (78)	10.00	25.00
1 John Andretti	.07	.20
2 Brett Bodine	.07	.20
3 Geoff Bodine	.07	.20
4 Todd Bodine	.07	.20
5 Jeff Burton	.25	.60
6 Derrike Cope	.07	.20
7 Dale Earnhardt	1.25	3.00
8 Bill Elliott	.30	.75
9 Jeff Gordon	.75	2.00
10 Steve Grissom	.07	.20
11 Dale Jarrett	.50	1.25
12 Steve Kinser	.07	.20
13 Bobby Labonte	.50	1.25
14 Terry Labonte	.25	.60
15 Mark Martin	.60	1.50
16 Kyle Petty	.15	.40
17 Ricky Rudd	.25	.60
18 Ken Schrader	.07	.20
19 Jimmy Spencer	.07	.20
20 Dick Trickle	.07	.20
21 Kenny Wallace	.07	.20
22 Mike Wallace	.07	.20
23 Rusty Wallace	.60	1.50
24 Darrell Waltrip	.15	.40
25 Michael Waltrip	.15	.40
26 Ricky Craven	.07	.20
27 Steve Kinser	.07	.20
28 Robert Pressley	.07	.20
29 Loy Allen Jr. PW	.02	.10
30 Geoff Bodine PW	.02	.10
31 Chuck Bown PW	.02	.10
32 Ward Burton PW	.02	.10
33 Dale Earnhardt PW	.60	1.50
34 Bill Elliott PW	.25	.60
35 Harry Gant PW	.07	.20
36 Jeff Gordon PW	.40	1.00
37 David Green PW	.02	.10
38 Ernie Irvan PW	.07	.20
39 Sterling Marlin PW	.15	.40
40 Mark Martin PW	.30	.75
41 Rick Mast PW	.02	.10
42 Ted Musgrave PW	.02	.10
43 Ricky Rudd PW	.15	.40
44 Greg Sacks PW	.02	.10
45 Jimmy Spencer PW	.02	.10
46 Rusty Wallace PW	.30	.75
47 Geoff Bodine WIN	.02	.10
48 Dale Earnhardt WIN	.60	1.50
49 Bill Elliott WIN	.25	.60
50 Jeff Gordon WIN	.40	1.00
51 Ernie Irvan WIN	.07	.20
52 Dale Jarrett WIN	.25	.60
53 Terry Labonte WIN	.25	.60
54 Sterling Marlin WIN	.15	.40
55 Mark Martin WIN	.30	.75
56 Ricky Rudd WIN	.15	.40
57 Jimmy Spencer WIN	.02	.10
58 Rusty Wallace WIN	.30	.75
59 Dale Earnhardt WC Champ	.60	1.50
60 Mark Martin T10	.30	.75
61 Rusty Wallace T10	.30	.75
62 Ken Schrader T10	.02	.10
63 Ricky Rudd T10	.15	.40
64 Morgan Shepherd T10	.02	.10
65 Terry Labonte T10	.25	.60
66 Jeff Gordon T10	.40	1.00
67 Darrell Waltrip T10	.07	.20
68 Bill Elliott T10	.25	.60
69 Bill Elliott DD	.25	.60
70 Jeff Gordon DD	.40	1.00
71 Ernie Irvan DD	.07	.20
72 Mark Martin DD	.30	.75
73 Richard Petty DD	.25	.60
74 Robert Pressley DD	.02	.10
75 Ricky Rudd DD	.15	.40
76 Ken Schrader DD	.02	.10
77 Rusty Wallace DD	.30	.75
78 Darrell Waltrip DD	.07	.20
BP1 Dale Earnhardt	12.50	30.00

1995 Action Packed Preview 24K Gold

Randomly inserted in 1995 Action Packed Preview packs, each card includes the now standard 24Kt. Gold logo on the card front. These Gold cards are essentially parallel versions of the corresponding driver's Driving With Dale subset card. Wrapper stated odds for pulling a 24K Gold card are 1:96.

COMPLETE SET (10)	100.00	200.00
1G Bill Elliott	10.00	25.00
2G Jeff Gordon	25.00	60.00
3G Ernie Irvan	2.50	6.00
4G Mark Martin	20.00	50.00
5G Richard Petty	8.00	20.00
6G Robert Pressley	2.50	6.00
7G Ricky Rudd	8.00	20.00
8G Ken Schrader	2.50	6.00
9G Rusty Wallace	20.00	50.00
10G Darrell Waltrip	5.00	12.00

1995 Action Packed Preview Bill Elliott

Action Packed added Bill Elliott to its stable of featured drivers in 1995. This special 6-card insert was distributed in 1995 Action Packed foil packs and includes cards of Elliott's life away from auto racing. There was also a Bill Elliott promo card issued through the Elliott Fan Club.

COMPLETE SET (6)	3.00	8.00
COMMON CARD (BE1-BE6)	.60	1.50

1995 Action Packed Stars

Action Packed's second Winston Cup card release for 1995 was entitled Winston Cup Stars and was Pinnacle Brands' first NASCAR release after acquiring the rights to the Action Packed name. The set is comprised of several series of subsets: Out of the Chute (1-30), Mean Rides (31-45), Race Winners (46-53), Picture Perfect (54-59), Settles In (60-65), Cope With It (66-70), On The Other Side (71-75), Winning The War (76-81), and McDonald's Bill Elliott (82-86) featuring two cards using Pinnacle's patented lenticular printing technology. These two cards (84-85) showing Bill Elliott "morphing" into the Batman logo and the Thunderbat race car, were produced in fewer numbers than the other regular issue cards. Cards were packed 24-foil packs to a box with 6-cards per pack and distributed to both hobby and retail outlets. Insert sets include: Silver Speed parallel, 24K Gold, Dale Earnhardt Race For Eight, and Trucks That Haul (hobby pack exclusive).

COMPLETE SET (86)	10.00	25.00
COMP.SHORT SET (84)	8.00	20.00
HOBBY WAX BOX	20.00	40.00
RETAIL WAX BOX	20.00	40.00
1 Sterling Marlin OC	.15	.40
2 Terry Labonte OC	.25	.60
3 Mark Martin OC	.60	1.50
4 Geoff Bodine OC	.07	.20
5 Jeff Burton OC	.25	.60
6 Ricky Rudd OC	.25	.60
7 Brett Bodine OC	.07	.20
8 Derrike Cope OC	.07	.20
9 Ted Musgrave OC	.07	.20
10 Darrell Waltrip OC	.15	.40
11 Bobby Labonte OC	.50	1.25
12 Morgan Shepherd OC	.07	.20
13 Jimmy Spencer OC	.07	.20
14 Ken Schrader OC	.07	.20
15 Dale Jarrett OC	.50	1.25
16 Kyle Petty OC	.15	.40
17 Michael Waltrip OC	.15	.40
18 Robert Pressley OC	.07	.20
19 John Andretti OC	.07	.20
20 Todd Bodine OC	.07	.20
21 Joe Nemechek OC	.07	.20
22 Bill Elliott OC	.30	.75
23 Dale Earnhardt OC	1.25	3.00
24 Jeff Gordon OC	.75	2.00
25 Rusty Wallace OC	.60	1.50
26 Rick Mast OC	.07	.20
27 Dick Trickle OC	.07	.20
28 Randy LaJoie OC	.07	.20
29 Steve Grissom OC	.07	.20
30 Ricky Craven OC	.07	.20
31 Dale Earnhardt's Car	.50	1.25
32 Rusty Wallace's Car	.25	.60
33 Sterling Marlin's Car	.07	.20
34 Terry Labonte's Car	.15	.40
35 Mark Martin's Car	.25	.60
36 Bill Elliott's Car	.15	.40
37 Ricky Rudd's Car	.07	.20
38 Joe Nemechek's Car	.02	.10
39 Darrell Waltrip's Car	.07	.20
40 Jeff Gordon's Car	.40	1.00
41 Jimmy Spencer's Car	.02	.10
42 Ken Schrader's Car	.02	.10
43 Dale Jarrett's Car	.15	.40
44 Steve Kinser's Car	.02	.10
45 Bobby Hamilton's Car	.02	.10
46 Sterling Marlin RW	.15	.40
47 Jeff Gordon RW	.75	2.00
48 Terry Labonte RW	.25	.60
49 Jeff Gordon RW	.75	2.00
50 Sterling Marlin RW	.15	.40
51 Jeff Gordon RW	.75	2.00
52 Dale Earnhardt RW	1.25	3.00
53 Rusty Wallace RW	.60	1.50
54 Sterling Marlin OC	.15	.40
55 Sterling Marlin OC	.15	.40
56 Sterling Marlin OC	.15	.40
57 Sterling Marlin OC	.15	.40
58 Sterling Marlin OC	.15	.40
59 Sterling Marlin OC	.15	.40
60 Jeff Gordon PP	.40	1.00
61 Jeff Gordon PP	.40	1.00
62 Jeff Gordon PP	.40	1.00
63 Jeff Gordon PP	.40	1.00
64 Jeff Gordon PP	.40	1.00
65 Jeff Gordon PP	.40	1.00
66 Derrike Cope CWI	.07	.20
67 Derrike Cope CWI	.07	.20
68 Derrike Cope CWI	.07	.20
69 Derrike Cope CWI	.07	.20
70 Derrike Cope CWI	.07	.20
71 Ernie Irvan OOS	.15	.40
72 Ernie Irvan OOS	.15	.40
73 Ernie Irvan OOS	.15	.40
74 Ernie Irvan OOS	.15	.40
75 Ernie Irvan OOS	.15	.40
76 Rusty Wallace WW	.30	.75
77 Rusty Wallace WW	.30	.75
78 Rusty Wallace WW	.30	.75
79 Rusty Wallace WW	.30	.75
80 Rusty Wallace WW	.30	.75
81 Rusty Wallace WW	.30	.75
82 Bill Elliott's Thunderbat Car	.15	.40
83 Bill Elliott's Car	.15	.40
84 Bill Elliott Magic Motion SP	2.50	6.00
85 Bill Elliott Magic Motion SP	2.50	6.00
86 Jeff Gordon	.60	1.50
Bobby Labonte		
Terry Labonte		
NNO Dale Earnhardt Brick. 400	3.00	8.00

1995 Action Packed Stars Silver Speed

With the change to Pinnacle Brands, Action Packed changed to include its first full parallel set -- Silver Speed. The cards were inserted in 1995 Action Packed Stars packs at the rate of approximately one card every six foil packs. The cards were printed with a silver foil background on the driver photo and a Silver Speed logo on the card back. Only 84 of 86 of the regular cards were produced with the two Bill Elliott lenticular cards (84-85) being left out.

COMPLETE SET (84)	60.00	125.00
*SILVER SPEEDS: 3X TO 8X BASIC CARDS		

1995 Action Packed Stars 24K Gold

Randomly inserted in 1995 Action Packed Stars packs, each card includes the now standard 24Kt. Gold logo on the card front. These Gold cards are essentially parallel versions of the corresponding driver's regular cards with an emphasis on Jeff Gordon and Dale Earnhardt. Wrapper stated odds for pulling a 24K Gold card are 1:72.

COMPLETE SET (21)	400.00	1000.00
1G Sterling Marlin	3.00	8.00
2G Jeff Gordon	15.00	40.00
3G Terry Labonte	5.00	12.00
4G Jeff Gordon	15.00	40.00
5G Sterling Marlin	3.00	8.00
6G Jeff Gordon	15.00	40.00
7G Dale Earnhardt	25.00	60.00
8G Rusty Wallace	12.50	30.00
9G Dale Earnhardt	25.00	60.00
10G Dale Earnhardt	25.00	60.00
11G Dale Earnhardt	25.00	60.00
12G Dale Earnhardt	25.00	60.00
13G Dale Earnhardt	25.00	60.00
14G Dale Earnhardt	25.00	60.00
15G Dale Earnhardt	25.00	60.00
16G Dale Earnhardt	25.00	60.00
17G Rusty Wallace	12.50	30.00
18G Rusty Wallace	12.50	30.00
19G Jeff Gordon	15.00	40.00
20G Jeff Gordon	15.00	40.00
21G Ernie Irvan	3.00	8.00

1995 Action Packed Stars Dale Earnhardt Race for Eight

Using Pinnacle Brands' micro-etching printing technology, Action Packed produced this 8-card Dale Earnhardt insert set distributed through 1995 Action Packed Stars packs. The cards were inserted at the ratio of 1:24 packs.

COMPLETE SET (8)	25.00	60.00
DE1 Dale Earnhardt	5.00	12.00
DE2 Dale Earnhardt	5.00	12.00
DE3 Dale Earnhardt	5.00	12.00
DE4 Dale Earnhardt	5.00	12.00
DE5 Dale Earnhardt	5.00	12.00
Teresa Earnhardt		
DE6 Dale Earnhardt	5.00	12.00
DE7 Dale Earnhardt	5.00	12.00
DE8 Dale Earnhardt's Car	5.00	12.00

1995 Action Packed Stars Dale Earnhardt Silver Salute

The set consists of four oversized (approximately 5" by 7") cards distributed in both 1995 Action Packed Stars (1,3) and Action Packed Country (2,4). The cards commemorate Earnhardt's silver car used in the 1995 Winston Select. Two cards (1,2) were inserted at the rate of one per box, with the other two (3,4) inserted about one per case.

COMPLETE SET (4)	80.00	200.00
1 Dale Earnhardt w/Silver Car	8.00	20.00
2 Dale Earnhardt Richard Childress	8.00	20.00
3 Dale Earnhardt's Silver Car	50.00	120.00
4 Dale Earnhardt Teresa Earnhardt	40.00	70.00

1995 Action Packed Stars Trucks That Haul

NASCAR's SuperTrucks is the feature of this hobby only insert in 1995 Action Packed Stars foil packs. The cards use Pinnacle's micro-etching printing process and were inserted at the average rate of 1:36 packs.

COMPLETE SET (6)	30.00	50.00
1 Jeff Gordon and Rick Hendrick's Truck	8.00	20.00
2 Teresa Earnhardt's Truck	4.00	10.00
3 Frank Vessels' Truck	2.00	5.00
4 Geoff Bodine's Truck	2.00	5.00
5 Richard Childress' Truck	2.00	5.00
6 Ken Schrader's Truck	2.00	5.00

1995 Action Packed Sundrop Dale Earnhardt

One card was inserted in each specially marked 12-pack of Sundrop citrus soda. Five hundred signed copies of each of the three cards were also randomly inserted in the soft drink packages. However, the autographed cards were not certified in any way and are otherwise indistinguishable from the unsigned regular cards.

COMPLETE SET (3)	12.50	30.00
SD1 Dale Earnhardt	3.00	8.00
SD2 Dale Earnhardt	3.00	8.00
SD3 Dale Earnhardt Kelly Earnhardt Kerry Earnhardt Dale Earnhardt Jr.	6.00	15.00

1996 Action Packed Credentials

This 105-card set was released by Pinnacle Brands. It was the first Action Packed regular issue set to feature square corners, instead of the normal rounded corners. The cards still featured the embossed technology that Action Packed is known for. The set features nine topical subsets; Jeff Gordon Defending Champion (1-5), Dale Earnhardt Seven-Time Champion (6-10), Mark Martin On the Mark (11-15), Daytona Winners (16-19), Drivers (20-54), Speed Machines (55-64), Crew Chiefs (65-69), Owners (70-83), Behind the Scenes (84-93), and Wives, Camera, Action (94-101). Cards were distributed in six card packs with 24 packs per box and 10 boxes per case. The packs carried a suggested retail price of $2.99.

COMPLETE SET (105)	10.00	25.00
1 Jeff Gordon DC	.40	1.00
2 Jeff Gordon DC	.40	1.00
3 Jeff Gordon DC	.40	1.00
4 Jeff Gordon DC	.40	1.00
5 Jeff Gordon DC	.40	1.00
6 Dale Earnhardt STC	.60	1.50
7 Dale Earnhardt STC	.60	1.50
8 Dale Earnhardt STC	.60	1.50
9 Dale Earnhardt STC	.60	1.50
10 Dale Earnhardt STC	.60	1.50
11 Mark Martin OTM	.30	.75
12 Mark Martin OTM	.30	.75
13 Mark Martin OTM	.30	.75
14 Mark Martin OTM	.30	.75
15 Mark Martin OTM	.30	.75
16 Dale Jarrett DW	.25	.60
17 Dale Earnhardt DW	.60	1.50
18 Ernie Irvan DW	.07	.20
19 Dale Jarrett DW	.25	.60
20 Jeff Gordon	.75	2.00
21 Dale Earnhardt	1.25	3.00
22 Sterling Marlin	.25	.60
23 Mark Martin	.60	1.50
24 Rusty Wallace	.60	1.50
25 Terry Labonte	.25	.60
26 Ted Musgrave	.07	.20
27 Bill Elliott	.30	.75
28 Ricky Rudd	.25	.60
29 Bobby Labonte	.50	1.25
30 Morgan Shepherd	.07	.20
31 Michael Waltrip	.15	.40
32 Dale Jarrett	.50	1.25
33 Bobby Hamilton	.07	.20
34 Derrike Cope	.07	.20
35 Ernie Irvan	.15	.40
36 Ken Schrader	.15	.40
37 John Andretti	.07	.20
38 Darrell Waltrip	.15	.40
39 Brett Bodine	.07	.20
40 Rick Mast	.07	.20
41 Ward Burton	.15	.40
42 Lake Speed	.07	.20
43 Loy Allen	.07	.20
44 Hut Stricklin	.07	.20
45 Jimmy Spencer	.07	.20
46 Mike Wallace	.07	.20
47 Joe Nemechek	.07	.20
48 Robert Pressley	.07	.20
49 Geoff Bodine	.07	.20
50 Jeremy Mayfield	.15	.40
51 Jeff Burton	.25	.60
52 Kenny Wallace	.07	.20
53 Bobby Hillin	.07	.20
54 Johnny Benson	.15	.40
55 Rusty Wallace SM	.30	.75
56 Terry Labonte SM	.15	.40
57 Dale Earnhardt SM	.60	1.50
58 Michael Waltrip SM	.15	.40
59 Bobby Hamilton SM	.02	.10
60 Bobby Labonte SM	.25	.60
61 Darrell Waltrip SM	.07	.20
62 Mark Martin SM	.30	.75
63 Richard Childress SM	.15	.40
64 Ken Schrader SM	.07	.20
65 David Smith	.02	.10
66 Ray Evernham	.15	.40
67 Jimmy Makar	.02	.10
68 Larry McReynolds	.02	.10
69 Todd Parrott	.02	.10
70 Roger Penske Don Miller OWN	.02	.10
71 Richard Childress OWN	.15	.40
72 Larry McClure OWN	.02	.10
73 Rick Hendrick OWN	.02	.10
74 Jack Roush OWN	.02	.10
75 Cale Yarborough OWN	.02	.10
76 Ricky Rudd OWN	.15	.40
77 Bobby Allison OWN	.07	.20
78 Richard Petty OWN	.25	.60
79 Darrell Waltrip OWN	.07	.20
80 Joe Gibbs OWN	.15	.40
81 Bill Elliott Charles Hardy OWN	.15	.40
82 Robert Yates OWN	.02	.10
83 Michael Kranefuss Carl Haas OWN	.02	.10
84 Andrea Nemechek BTS	.02	.10
85 Kim Wallace BTS	.02	.10
86 Buffy Waltrip BTS	.02	.10
87 Kim Irvan BTS	.02	.10
88 Kim Burton Paige Burton BTS	.02	.10
89 Rice Speed BTS	.02	.10
90 Stevie Waltrip Darrell Waltrip BTS	.15	.40
91 Cindy Elliott Bill Elliott BTS	.15	.40
92 Brooke Gordon BTS	.25	.60
93 Donna Labonte BTS	.07	.20
94 Darrell Waltrip WCA	.07	.20
95 Sterling Marlin WCA	.15	.40
96 Michael Waltrip WCA	.15	.40
97 Kenny Wallace with Brandy Brittany Brooke WCA	.07	.20
98 Bobby Labonte WCA	.25	.60
99 Jeff Gordon WCA	.40	1.00
100 Jeremy Mayfield WCA	.07	.20
101 Bill Elliott WCA	.15	.40
102 Johnny Benson	.15	.40
103 Ricky Craven Travis Roy	.15	.40
104 Dale Earnhardt CL	.60	1.50
105 Jeff Gordon CL	.30	.75

1996 Action Packed Credentials Silver Speed

This 42-card set is a partial parallel to the Credentials base set. The Silver Speed cards are a selection of cards from the 105 card set printed on silver holographic stock. The cards were randomly inserted in packs at a ratio of 1:6.

COMPLETE SET (42)	40.00	100.00

*SILVER SPEED: 3X TO 6X BASE CARD

1996 Action Packed Credentials Fan Scan

This 9-card insert set allowed collectors to go inside a race car during a NASCAR race. Each card back included a 1-800 phone number along with a personal identification number. During selected

NASCAR races, the collector could phone the number, enter the PIN, and listen to the sounds the driver is hearing inside his helmet. Advanced broadcast electronics made the technology possible. The cards were seeded one in 72 packs.

COMPLETE SET (9)	100.00	250.00
1 Dale Earnhardt	30.00	80.00
2 Dale Earnhardt's Car	15.00	40.00
3 Mark Martin	15.00	40.00
4 Jeff Gordon	20.00	50.00
5 Ted Musgrave	2.00	5.00
6 Ernie Irvan	4.00	10.00
7 Bobby Hamilton	2.00	5.00
8 Dale Jarrett	12.50	30.00
9 Jeff Burton	6.00	15.00

1996 Action Packed Credentials Leaders of the Pack

This 10-card insert set features the top Winston Cup drivers. The cards were printed on rainbow holographic foil with holographic and gold foil stamping. The cards were available in hobby only packs at a rate of one in 35.

COMPLETE SET (10)	75.00	150.00
1 Dale Earnhardt	10.00	25.00
2 Dale Earnhardt	10.00	25.00
3 Dale Earnhardt	10.00	25.00
4 Dale Earnhardt	10.00	25.00
5 Jeff Gordon	6.00	15.00
6 Jeff Gordon	6.00	15.00
7 Jeff Gordon	6.00	15.00
8 Jeff Gordon	6.00	15.00
9 Sterling Marlin	2.00	5.00
10 Sterling Marlin	2.00	5.00

1996 Action Packed Credentials Jumbos

This four-card series feature the top drivers in Winston Cup. The cards measure 5" X 7" and were available one per special retail box.

COMPLETE SET (4)	6.00	15.00
1 Dale Earnhardt	3.00	8.00
2 Jeff Gordon	2.00	5.00
3 Dale Jarrett	1.25	3.00
4 Bill Elliott	.75	2.00

1996 Action Packed McDonald's

For the second year, McDonald's distributed a small card set produced by Action Packed. The 1996 set features square corners instead of Action Packed's traditional rounded ones. While the set has a strong Bill Elliott focus, like the 1995 issue, it also includes cards of other top Winston Cup drivers and their rides. The set was distributed through 4-card packs with one unnumbered checklist card per pack. Packs originally sold for 99-cents from participating McDonald's stores.

COMPLETE SET (29)	6.00	15.00
1 Bill Elliott	.30	.75
2 Dale Earnhardt	1.50	4.00
3 Jeff Gordon	1.00	2.50
6 Bobby Labonte	.60	1.50
7 Terry Labonte	.25	.60
8 Ernie Irvan	.10	.30
9 Kenny Wallace	.08	.25
10 Dale Jarrett	.50	1.25
11 Bill Elliott's Car	.08	.25
12 Dale Earnhardt's Car	.60	1.50
13 Jeff Gordon's Car	.40	1.00
14 Sterling Marlin's Car	.08	.25
15 Mark Martin's Car	.25	.60
16 Bobby Labonte's Car	.10	.30
17 Terry Labonte's Car	.08	.25
18 Ernie Irvan's Car	.07	.15
19 Kenny Wallace's Car	.07	.15
20 Dale Jarrett's Car	.08	.25
21 Bill Elliott	.25	.60
22 Bill Elliott	.25	.60
23 Bill Elliott	.25	.60
24 Bill Elliott	.25	.60
25 Bill Elliott	.25	.60
26 Bill Elliott	.25	.60
27 Bill Elliott	.25	.60
28 Bill Elliott	.25	.60
NNO Bill Elliott Checklist Card DP	.08	.25

1997 Action Packed

This 86-card set was released by Pinnacle Brands. The cards still feature the embossed technology that Action Packed is known for. The set features three topical subsets; Championship Drive (53-56), 1996 A Look Back (57-68), and Orient Express (71-84). Cards were distributed in six card packs with 24 packs per box and 10 boxes per case. The packs carried a suggested retail price of $2.99.

COMPLETE SET (86)	10.00	25.00
1 Bobby Hamilton	.07	.20
2 Rusty Wallace	.60	1.50
3 Dale Earnhardt	1.25	3.00
4 Sterling Marlin	.25	.60
5 Terry Labonte	.25	.60
6 Mark Martin	.60	1.50
7 Jeremy Mayfield	.15	.40
8 Jeff Gordon	.75	2.00
9 Ernie Irvan	.15	.40
10 Ricky Rudd	.25	.60
11 Bill Elliott	.30	.75
12 Jimmy Spencer	.07	.20
13 Dale Jarrett	.50	1.25
14 Ward Burton	.15	.40
15 Michael Waltrip	.15	.40
16 Ted Musgrave	.07	.20
17 Darrell Waltrip	.15	.40
18 Bobby Labonte	.50	1.25
19 John Andretti	.07	.20
20 Robert Pressley	.07	.20
21 Chad Little	.15	.40
22 Geoff Bodine	.07	.20
23 Morgan Shepherd	.07	.20
24 Mike Skinner	.07	.20
25 Ricky Craven	.07	.20
26 Robby Gordon RC	.25	.60
27 Mark Martin's Car	.25	.60
28 Jeremy Mayfield's Car	.02	.10
29 Jeff Gordon's Car	.30	.75
30 Ernie Irvan's Car	.07	.20
31 Ricky Rudd's Car	.07	.20
32 Bill Elliott's Car	.15	.40
33 Jimmy Spencer's Car	.02	.10
34 Dale Jarrett's Car	.15	.40
35 Ward Burton's Car	.02	.10
36 Michael Waltrip's Car	.07	.20
37 Ted Musgrave's Car	.02	.10
38 Darrell Waltrip's Car	.07	.20
39 Bobby Labonte's Car	.15	.40
40 John Andretti's Car	.02	.10
41 Robert Pressley's Car	.02	.10
42 Chad Little's Car	.02	.10
43 Morgan Shepherd's Car	.02	.10
44 Rusty Wallace's Car	.25	.60
45 Dale Earnhardt's Car	.50	1.25
46 Sterling Marlin's Car	.07	.20
47 Terry Labonte's Car	.15	.40
48 Geoff Bodine's Car	.02	.10
49 Bobby Hamilton's Car	.02	.10
50 Mike Skinner's Car	.02	.10
51 Ricky Craven's Car	.02	.10
52 Robby Gordon's Car	.15	.40
53 Terry Labonte	.25	.60
54 Dale Jarrett	.50	1.25
55 Randy LaJoie	.07	.20
56 David Green	.07	.20
57 Randy LaJoie	.07	.20
58 Bill Elliott	.30	.75
59 Michael Waltrip	.15	.40
60 Hut Stricklin	.07	.20
61 Johnny Benson	.07	.20
62 Carl Hill	.07	.20
63 Dale Jarrett	.50	1.25
64 Bill Elliott	.30	.75
65 Elmo Langley	.07	.20
66 Harry Hyde	.02	.10
67 Richard Petty	.25	.60
68 Johnny Benson	.07	.20
69 Rusty Wallace	.60	1.50
70 David Green	.07	.20
71 Michael Waltrip	.15	.40
72 Dale Jarrett	.50	1.25
73 Rusty Wallace's Car	.25	.60
74 Michael Waltrip's Car	.07	.20
75 Robby Gordon's Car	.15	.40
76 Sterling Marlin's Car	.07	.20
77 Ernie Irvan's Car	.07	.20
78 Dale Jarrett's Car	.15	.40
79 David Green	.07	.20
80 Ernie Irvan	.15	.40
81 Johnny Benson's Car	.02	.10
82 Robin Pemberton	.02	.10
83 Terry Labonte's Car	.15	.40
84 Dale Earnhardt's Car	.50	1.25
85 Darrell Waltrip CL	.07	.20
86 Bobby Hamilton CL	.02	.10
P8 Jeff Gordon Promo	1.00	2.50

1997 Action Packed First Impressions

This 86-card set is a parallel to the base set. These cards are marked on the backs by a sillouette First Impressions logo. The cards were randomly inserted in packs at a ratio of 1:7.

COMPLETE SET (86)	25.00	60.00

*FIRST IMPRESS: 1.2X TO 3X BASE CARDS

1997 Action Packed 24K Gold

Each card from this 14-card set is marked with the now standard 24Kt. Gold logo on the card front. The cards were randomly inserted in hobby packs at a ratio of 1:71 and inserted in retail packs at a ratio of 1:86.

COMPLETE SET (14)	150.00	300.00
1 Rusty Wallace	10.00	25.00
2 Dale Earnhardt	20.00	50.00
3 Jeff Gordon	12.50	30.00
4 Ernie Irvan	2.50	6.00
5 Terry Labonte	4.00	10.00
6 Johnny Benson	1.25	3.00
7 David Green	1.25	3.00
8 Dale Jarrett	8.00	20.00
9 Sterling Marlin	4.00	10.00
10 Michael Waltrip	2.50	6.00
11 Mark Martin	10.00	25.00
12 Bobby Hamilton	1.25	3.00
13 Ted Musgrave	1.25	3.00
14 Randy LaJoie	1.25	3.00

1997 Action Packed Chevy Madness

This 6-card set is actually the beginning of a 15-card set that was distributed in 1997 Pinnacle(13-15) and 1997 Racer's Choice(7-12). The cards feature the top Chevy drivers from the Winston Cup Series. The cards were randomly inserted into hobby packs at a ratio of 1:10 and inserted into retail packs at a ratio of 1:12.

COMPLETE SET (6)	10.00	40.00
1 Dale Earnhardt's Car	8.00	20.00
2 Darrell Waltrip's Car	1.00	2.50
3 Dave Marcis' Car	.50	1.25
4 Jeff Gordon's Car	5.00	12.00
5 Sterling Marlin's Car	1.50	4.00
6 Steve Grissom's Car	.50	1.25

1997 Action Packed Fifth Anniversary

This 12-card set celebrates five years of NASCAR card production by Action Packed. The set includes current and retired NASCAR stars. The cards were randomly inserted into hobby packs at a ratio of 1:128 and inserted into retail packs at a ratio of 1:153.

COMPLETE SET (12)	150.00	300.00
1 Richard Petty	6.00	15.00
2 Cale Yarborough	4.00	10.00
3 Bobby Allison	4.00	10.00
4 Ned Jarrett	4.00	10.00
5 Benny Parsons	4.00	10.00
6 Dale Earnhardt	30.00	80.00
7 Rusty Wallace	15.00	40.00
8 Jeff Gordon	20.00	50.00
9 Terry Labonte	6.00	15.00
10 Dale Jarrett	12.50	30.00
11 Mark Martin	15.00	40.00
12 Bill Elliott	8.00	20.00

1997 Action Packed Fifth Anniversary Autographs

This 5-card set is a partial parallel to the Fifth Anniversary set. It contains the first five cards from that set featuring autographs from retired NASCAR legends. The cards were randomly inserted into hobby packs at a ratio of 1:165 and inserted into retail packs at a ratio of 1;198.

COMPLETE SET (5)	75.00	150.00
1 Richard Petty	30.00	60.00
2 Cale Yarborough	6.00	15.00
3 Bobby Allison	6.00	15.00
4 Ned Jarrett	6.00	15.00
5 Benny Parsons	30.00	60.00

1997 Action Packed Ironman Champion

This 2-card set highlights Terry Labonte's run for 1997 Winston Cup Points Championship. The ca were randomly inserted into hobby packs at a ratio 1:192 and inserted into retail packs at a ratio 1:230.

COMPLETE SET (2)	30.00	80.0
1 Terry Labonte	15.00	40.0
2 Terry Labonte Bobby Labonte	15.00	40.0

1997 Action Packed Rolling Thunder

This 14-card set features some of the top stars fr NASCAR. The cards were randomly inserted i hobby packs at a ratio of 1:23 and inserted into re packs at a ratio of 1:28.

COMPLETE SET (14)	60.00	125.0
1 Mark Martin	8.00	20.0
2 Dale Earnhardt	15.00	40.0
3 Jeff Gordon	10.00	25.0
4 Ernie Irvan	2.00	5.0
5 Terry Labonte	3.00	8.0
6 Kyle Petty	2.00	5.0
7 Darrell Waltrip	2.00	5.0
8 Mike Skinner	1.00	2.5
9 Ricky Craven	1.00	2.5
10 Dale Jarrett	6.00	15.0
11 Sterling Marlin	3.00	8.0
12 Steve Grissom	1.00	2.5
13 Bill Elliott	4.00	10.0
14 Ricky Rudd	3.00	8.0

1997 ActionVision

This 12-card set utilizes Kodak's KODAMOTI technology to provide race action replay cards. T product marks the first time that NASCAR trad cards have been marketed in this fashion. Ca were distributed in one card packs with 18 packs box and 20 boxes per case.

COMPLETE SET (12)	12.50	30.0
1 Terry Labonte	1.50	4.0
2 Jeff Gordon Victory Lane	2.50	6.0
3 Dale Earnhardt Qualifying	4.00	10.0
4 Dale Jarrett Victory Lane	2.50	6.0
5 Jeff Gordon Rusty Wallace Terry Labonte	2.50	6.0
6 Jeff Gordon Terry Labonte Ricky Craven	2.50	6.0
7 Rusty Wallace Pit Stop	2.00	5.
8 Dale Earnhardt Pit Stop	4.00	10.0
9 Terry Labonte Pit Stop	1.25	3.
10 Jeff Gordon Pit Stop	2.50	6.0
11 Dale Jarrett Pit Stop	2.00	5.0
12 Bill Elliott Talladega Crash	1.50	4.
P1 Bobby Labonte Promo	3.00	8.0

1997 ActionVision Precious Metal

This 4-card series is the last section of a 9-card that was started in 1997 VIP. The cards from this contain a piece of sheet metal along with a picture the driver and the car which is encased i polyurethane card. Cards with multi-colored pie of sheet metal often carry a premium over those t do not. Each of the four cards inserted i ActionVision was limited in production to 350. cards were randomly inserted into packs at a ratio 1:160.

COMPLETE SET (4)	200.00	400.
*MULTI-COLOR METAL: .75X TO 1.25X		
6 Dale Earnhardt	60.00	150.
7 Dale Jarrett	30.00	80.
8 Ernie Irvan	20.00	50.
9 Mark Martin	40.00	100.

1997 Alka-Seltzer Terr Labonte

This three card Terry Labonte set was availa through a mail-in offer from Alka-Seltzer. The o was posted on Alka-Seltzer's home page on internet. The collector had to fill out a form on-l and in return would receive a free sample of cherry

ored Alka-Seltzer along with one Terry Labonte ing card.

MPLETE SET (3)	2.50	6.00
MMON DRIVER (1-3)	.75	2.00

993-94 Alliance Robert 'ressley/Dennis Setzer

Alliance Racing Team set was released two secutive years by D and D Racing Images. The s in both sets are identical except for the driver #11. The 1993 release features Robert Pressley A), while the 1994 set includes Dennis Setzer B). Either set carries the same value.

MPLETE SET (12)	4.00	6.00
arbara Welch	.20	.50
icky Pearson	.20	.50
icky Case	.20	.50
eff Fender	.20	.50
ick Boles	.20	.50
hris McPherson	.20	.50
larence Ogle	.20	.50
ddie Pearson	.20	.50
wen Edwards	.20	.50
Dennis McCarson	.20	.50
Robert Pressley	.40	1.00
Dennis Setzer	.40	1.00
0 Alliance Transporter	.20	.50
Checklist back		

1992 Arena Joe Gibbs Racing

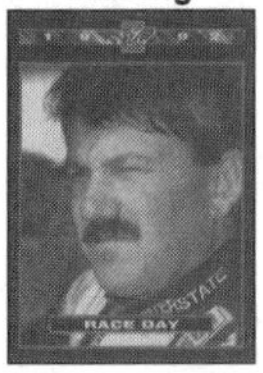

na Trading Cards Inc. produced this set honoring Interstate Batteries Joe Gibbs Racing Team. The s were sold in complete set form and included a ogram card featuring Dale Jarrett's Interstate teries car along with an unnumbered er/checklist card

MPLETE SET (12)	1.25	3.00
oe Gibbs	.15	.40
ale Jarrett	.25	.60
mmy Makar	.05	.15
ale Jarrett's Crew	.25	.60
ale Jarrett's Car	.10	.25
ale Jarrett's Car	.10	.25
ale Jarrett	.25	.60
Jimmy Makar Teamwork		
ale Jarrett Race Day	.25	.60
oe Gibbs Jimmy Makar	.15	.40
Dale Jarrett's Transporter	.10	.25
Cover Card Checklist	.05	.10
0 Dale Jarrett's Car HOLO	1.00	2.50

1995 Assets

50-card set features the top names in racing in ssic's first racing issue under the Assets brand. cards are printed on 18pt. stock and use full- ed printing. There are three topical subsets; ers (1-28),Winners (29-44), and Cars (45-50). cards came six cards per pack, 18 packs per box 16 boxes per case.

MPLETE SET (50)	6.00	15.00
ale Earnhardt	1.00	2.50
usty Wallace	.40	1.00
eff Gordon	.60	1.50
yle Petty	.10	.30
ett Bodine	.05	.15
erling Marlin	.20	.50
arrell Waltrip	.10	.30
erling Marlin	.20	.50
eoff Bodine	.05	.15
Ricky Craven	.05	.15
Robert Pressley	.05	.15
Bobby Labonte	.30	.75
Dale Jarrett	.30	.75
Dick Trickle	.05	.15
Jeff Burton	.20	.50
John Andretti	.05	.15
Ken Schrader	.05	.15
Ernie Irvan	.10	.30
Michael Waltrip	.10	.30
Morgan Shepherd	.05	.15
Ricky Rudd	.20	.50
Steve Kinser	.05	.15
Ted Musgrave	.05	.15
24 Terry Labonte	.20	.50
25 Todd Bodine	.05	.15
26 Ward Burton	.10	.30
27 Mark Martin	.40	1.00
28 Bobby Hamilton	.05	.15
29 Dale Earnhardt	1.00	2.50
30 Rusty Wallace	.40	1.00
31 Jeff Gordon	.60	1.50
32 Kyle Petty	.10	.30
33 Geoff Bodine	.05	.15
34 Sterling Marlin	.20	.50
35 Darrell Waltrip	.10	.30
36 Dale Jarrett	.30	.75
37 Ken Schrader	.05	.15
38 Ernie Irvan	.10	.30
39 Ricky Rudd	.20	.50
40 Terry Labonte	.20	.50
41 Mark Martin	.40	1.00
42 Morgan Shepherd	.05	.15
43 Ward Burton	.10	.30
44 Dale Earnhardt	1.00	2.50
45 Morgan Shepherd's Car	.02	.10
46 Dale Earnhardt's Car	.40	1.00
47 Rusty Wallace's Car	.20	.50
48 Mark Martin's Car	.20	.50
49 Jeff Gordon's Car	.30	.75
50 Checklist	.02	.10
P1 Dale Earnhardt Promo invalid $1000 Phone Card	15.00	30.00

1995 Assets Gold Signature

This 50-card set is a parallel version of the base set. Each card features a gold facsimile signature across the front of the card to differentiate them from the base cards. The odds of pulling a gold signature card were one per 10 packs. Complete sets were also one of the prize levels offered in the Assets Coca-Cola 600 Die Cut redemption game.

COMPLETE SET (50)	30.00	80.00
*GOLD SIG: 2.5X TO 6X BASIC CARDS		

1995 Assets 1-Minute Phone Cards

This 20-card insert set features Winston Cup personalities on 1-minute phone cards. The cards were inserted at a rate of one per pack. The cards expired 12/31/1995. There were three parallel versions of the 1-minute set: the 1-minute gold signature, $2 phone cards and $2 gold signature phone cards. The cards in the 1-minute gold signature set expired on 12/31/1995 and were inserted at a rate of one per 26 packs. The cards in both the $2 set and the $2 signature set expired on 5/1/96. The $2 cards were inserted one per six packs, while the $2 signature cards were inserted one per 58 packs.

COMPLETE 1-MIN.SET (20)	4.00	10.00
COMP.1-MIN GOLD SIG.(20)	12.00	30.00
*1 MIN.GOLD SIG.: 1.2X TO 3X BASIC INSERTS		
COMP.$2 CARD SET (20)	7.50	20.00
*$2.00 CARDS: .8X TO 2X BASIC INSERTS		
COMP.$2 GOLD SIG.(20)	20.00	50.00
*$2 GOLD SIG.: 2X TO 5X BASIC INSERTS		
1 Dick Trickle	.05	.15
2 Bobby Labonte	.30	.75
3 Brett Bodine	.05	.15
4 Dale Earnhardt	1.00	2.50
5 Dale Jarrett	.30	.75
6 Darrell Waltrip	.10	.30
7 Ernie Irvan	.10	.30
8 Geoff Bodine	.05	.15
9 Jeff Gordon	.60	1.50
10 John Andretti	.05	.15
11 Ken Schrader	.05	.15
12 Kyle Petty	.10	.30
13 Mark Martin	.40	1.00
14 Michael Waltrip	.10	.30
15 Morgan Shepherd	.05	.15
16 Ward Burton	.10	.30
17 Ricky Rudd	.20	.50
18 Rusty Wallace	.40	1.00
19 Sterling Marlin	.20	.50
20 Terry Labonte	.20	.50

1995 Assets $5 Phone Cards

This 10-card insert set features the top Winston Cup personalities on $5 phone cards. Each card was worth $5 of phone time. The expiration date of the cards was 5/1/96 and the odds of pulling one from a pack were one in 18. There is also a $25 denomination that was a parallel to the $5 set. The $25 denomination also expired on 5/1/96 and they were randomly inserted at a rate of one per 288 packs.

COMPLETE $5 SET (10)	10.00	25.00
COMPLETE $25 SET (10)	25.00	60.00
*$25 CARDS: 1X TO 2.5X $5.00 CARDS		
*PIN NUMBER REVEALED: HALF VALUE		
1 Sterling Marlin	.60	1.50
2 Dale Earnhardt	3.00	8.00
3 Darrell Waltrip	.40	1.00
4 Jeff Gordon	2.00	5.00
5 Ken Schrader	.20	.50
6 Kyle Petty	.40	1.00
7 Mark Martin	1.25	3.00
8 Richard Petty	.40	1.00
9 Rusty Wallace	1.25	3.00
10 Terry Labonte	.60	1.50

1995 Assets $100 Phone Cards

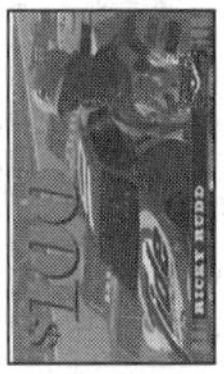

This 5-card insert set features five of the top Winston Cup personalities on $100 phone cards. The cards were inserted at a rate of one per 3200 packs. Each card has a covered pin number on the back that must be revealed to use the card. The cards have an expiration date of 5/1/96. There is also a 5-card parallel version of this set in the amount of $1000. The cards are identical to the $100 except for the dollar denomination. The odds of finding a $1000 card were one per 28,800 packs. There was a $1000 Dale Earnhardt promo phone card that was distributed to dealers and the media. The card is identical to the regular issue except that it doesn't have a pin number in order to make it invalid.

COMPLETE $100 SET (5)	40.00	100.00
*$1000 CARDS: 1.5X TO 4X $100 CARDS		
*USED CARDS: .1X TO .3X BASIC INSERTS		
1 Ricky Rudd	3.00	8.00
2 Dale Earnhardt	15.00	40.00
3 Jeff Gordon	10.00	25.00
4 Mark Martin	6.00	15.00
5 Rusty Wallace	6.00	15.00

1995 Assets Coca-Cola 600 Die Cut Phone Cards

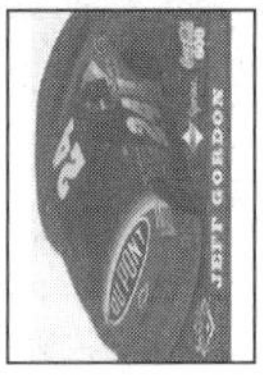

This 10-card insert set was an interactive game for the 1995 Coca-Cola 600 race. The cards were die cut phone cards and if you held the winner of the race, Bobby Labonte you could then call the 1-800 number on the back of the card and enter that card's pin number for a chance to win a prize. The grand prize was a trip for two to the 1996 Coca-Cola 600. There were 3000 special 10-card winner sets produced and numerous bonus prizes offered. The expiration for the game was 12/1/1995.

COMPLETE SET (10)	10.00	25.00
*PIN NUMBER REVEALED: HALF VALUE		
1 Dale Earnhardt	4.00	10.00
2 Rusty Wallace	1.50	4.00
3 Jeff Gordon	2.50	6.00
4 Bobby Labonte	1.25	3.00
5 Terry Labonte	.75	2.00
6 Geoff Bodine	.25	.60
7 Dale Jarrett	1.25	3.00
8 Mark Martin	1.50	4.00
9 Ricky Rudd	.75	2.00
10 Field Card	.15	.40

1995 Assets Images Previews

This 5-card insert set was a preview for Classic's Images racing product. The cards feature micro-foil technolgoy and could be found at a rate of one per 18 Assets packs.

COMPLETE SET (5)	6.00	15.00
RI1 Dale Earnhardt	3.00	8.00
RI2 Al Unser Jr.	.40	1.00
RI3 Rick Mears	.20	.50
RI4 Jeff Gordon	2.00	5.00
RI5 John Force	.40	1.00

1996 Assets Racing

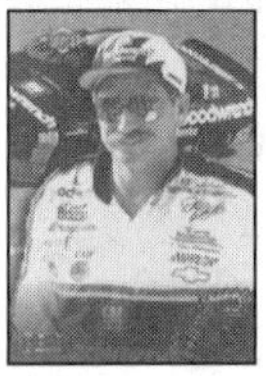

This 50-card set was produced by Classic. The cards were printed on 18-point stock and each card front features foil stamping and dual photos. The cards were distributed via six card packs (5 regular cards and 1 phone card) with 18-packs per box and 12-boxes per case.

COMPLETE SET (50)	6.00	15.00
1 Dale Earnhardt	1.00	2.50
2 Jeff Gordon	.60	1.50
3 Ricky Rudd	.20	.50
4 Geoff Bodine	.05	.15
5 Ernie Irvan	.10	.30
6 John Andretti	.05	.15
7 Kyle Petty	.10	.30
8 Darrell Waltrip	.10	.30
9 Dale Jarrett	.40	1.00
10 Sterling Marlin	.20	.50
11 Jimmy Spencer	.05	.15
12 Loy Allen Jr.	.05	.15
13 Richard Childress	.10	.30
14 Ken Schrader	.05	.15
15 Ned Jarrett	.05	.15
16 Ward Burton	.10	.30
17 Todd Bodine	.05	.15
18 Mark Martin	.50	1.25
19 Morgan Shepherd	.05	.15
20 Bobby Labonte	.40	1.00
21 Robert Pressley	.05	.15
22 Hut Stricklin	.05	.15
23 Jerry Punch	.02	.10
24 Ricky Rudd	.20	.50
25 Ward Burton	.10	.30
26 Bobby Hamilton	.05	.15
27 Johnny Benson	.10	.30
28 Michael Waltrip	.10	.30
29 Mark Martin	.50	1.25
30 Andy Petree	.02	.10
31 Ted Musgrave	.05	.15
32 Mike Wallace	.05	.15
33 Ernie Irvan	.10	.30
34 Jeff Burton	.20	.50
35 Robert Yates	.02	.10
36 Dick Trickle	.05	.15
37 Kenny Wallace	.05	.15
38 Dale Earnhardt	1.00	2.50
39 Brett Bodine	.05	.15
40 Ricky Craven	.05	.15
41 Kyle Petty	.10	.30
42 Dale Jarrett	.40	1.00
43 Darrell Waltrip	.10	.30
44 Dale Earnhardt	1.00	2.50
45 John Andretti	.05	.15
46 Terry Labonte	.20	.50
47 Richard Petty	.20	.50
48 Ernie Irvan	.10	.30
49 Mark Martin	.50	1.25
50 Ricky Rudd	.20	.50
P1 Dale Earnhardt Promo	2.50	6.00
P2 Dale Earnhardt Promo invalid $1000 Phone Card	15.00	30.00

1996 Assets Racing $2 Phone Cards

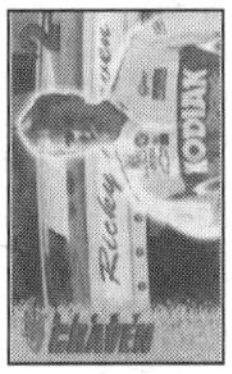

This 25-card set features top drivers on $2 phone cards. Each horizontally designed card featured a driver or car photo on the front and usage instruction on the back. The expiration date for the use of the cards was 11/30/97. The cards were inserted one per pack.

COMPLETE SET (25)	5.00	12.00
1 Dale Earnhardt	1.00	2.50
2 Ward Burton	.10	.30
3 Jimmy Spencer	.05	.15
4 Geoff Bodine	.05	.15
5 Dale Jarrett	.40	1.00
6 Ernie Irvan	.10	.30
7 Ken Schrader	.05	.15
8 Ricky Craven	.05	.15
9 Mark Martin	.50	1.25
10 Dale Earnhardt's Car	.50	1.25
11 Darrell Waltrip	.10	.30
12 Sterling Marlin	.20	.50
13 Ricky Rudd	.20	.50
14 Bill Elliott	.30	.75
15 Rusty Wallace's Car	.10	.30
16 John Andretti	.05	.15
17 Ernie Irvan	.10	.30
18 Michael Waltrip	.10	.30
19 Kyle Petty	.10	.30
20 Mike Wallace	.05	.15
21 Bobby Hamilton	.05	.15
22 Dale Jarrett's Car	.20	.50
23 Ted Musgrave	.05	.15
24 Jeremy Mayfield	.10	.30
25 Ernie Irvan's Car	.05	.15

1996 Assets Racing $5 Phone Cards

This 15-card set features top drivers from the Winston Cup series. Each card carried $5 in phone time. The cards feature a horizontal design on the front and dialing instructions on the back. The phone time expired 11/30/97. The cards were seeded one in five packs.

COMPLETE SET (15)	6.00	15.00
1 Ricky Rudd	.40	1.00
2 Jeff Burton	.40	1.00
3 Mark Martin	1.00	2.50
4 Darrell Waltrip	.25	.60
5 Bill Elliott	.60	1.50
6 Dale Earnhardt	2.00	5.00
7 Brett Bodine	.10	.30
8 Ted Musgrave	.10	.30
9 Michael Waltrip	.25	.60
10 Ernie Irvan	.25	.60
11 Dale Earnhardt's Car	1.00	2.50
12 Kyle Petty	.25	.60
13 Jimmy Spencer	.10	.30
14 Robert Pressley	.10	.30
15 John Andretti	.10	.30

1996 Assets Racing $10 Phone Cards

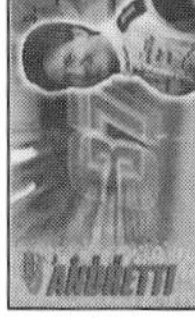

Each card in the 10-card insert set features $10 in phone time. The cards carry a horizontal design on the front and dialing instructions on the back. The phone time expired 11/30/1997. The cards were inserted one in 15 packs.

COMPLETE SET (10)	6.00	15.00
1 John Andretti	.15	.40
2 Bobby Hamilton	.15	.40
3 Robert Pressley	.15	.40
4 Dale Earnhardt	2.50	6.00
5 Ernie Irvan	.30	.75
6 Jimmy Spencer	.15	.40
7 Kyle Petty	.30	.75
8 Mark Martin	1.25	3.00
9 Dale Earnhardt's Car	1.25	3.00
10 Ricky Rudd	.50	1.25

1996 Assets Racing $100 Cup Champion Interactive Phone Cards

This 20-card set was an interactive game. Each card from this set carried a minimum $5 phone time value. Because the game rewarded the card that featured the 1996 Winston Cup Champion and Terry Labonte was not on a regular card in the set, the field card was the winning card in the set. The field card was activated for an additional $95 worth of phone time. The phone cards were randomly seeded one in 15 packs. The phone time on each of the cards expired 11/30/1997.

COMPLETE SET (20)	25.00	60.00
1 Dale Earnhardt	4.00	10.00
2 Jeff Gordon	2.50	6.00
3 Jeff Burton	.75	2.00
4 Dale Jarrett	1.50	4.00
5 Kyle Petty	.50	1.25
6 Darrell Waltrip	.50	1.25
7 Ernie Irvan	.50	1.25
8 Sterling Marlin	.75	2.00
9 Ricky Rudd	.75	2.00
10 Rusty Wallace's Car	.50	1.25
11 Mark Martin	2.00	5.00
12 Ken Schrader	.25	.60
13 Ted Musgrave	.25	.60
14 Michael Waltrip	.50	1.25
15 Ward Burton	.50	1.25
16 Bobby Labonte	1.50	4.00
17 Kenny Wallace	.25	.60
18 Ricky Craven	.25	.60
19 Bobby Hamilton	.25	.60
20 Field Card WIN	2.00	5.00

1996 Assets Racing $1000 Cup Champion Interactive Phone Cards

This 20-card set was an interactive game. Each card from this set carried a minimum $10 phone time value. Because the game rewarded the card that featured the 1996 Winston Cup Champion and Terry Labonte was not on a regular card in the set, the field card was the winning card in the set. The field card was activated for an additional $990 worth of phone time. The $1000 phone cards were randomly seeded one in 432 packs. The phone time on each of the cards expired 11/30/1997.

COMPLETE SET (20)	50.00	120.00
1 Dale Earnhardt	8.00	20.00
2 Rick Mast	.30	.75
3 Ricky Craven	.50	1.25
4 Ward Burton	1.00	2.50
5 Ricky Rudd	1.50	4.00
6 Dale Jarrett	3.00	8.00
7 Michael Waltrip	1.00	2.50
8 Jeff Burton	1.50	4.00
9 Ken Schrader	.50	1.25
10 Mark Martin	4.00	10.00
11 Darrell Waltrip	1.00	2.50
12 Kyle Petty	1.00	2.50
13 Ernie Irvan	1.00	2.50
14 Bobby Hamilton	.50	1.25
15 Ted Musgrave	.50	1.25
16 Kenny Wallace	.50	1.25
17 Rusty Wallace's Car	1.00	2.50
18 Bobby Labonte	3.00	8.00
19 Sterling Marlin	1.50	4.00
20 Field Card WIN	12.00	30.00

1996 Assets Racing Competitor's License

Each card from this 20-card insert set features a custom holographic overlay and simulates a driver's license. The cards were randomly inserted one in 15 packs.

COMPLETE SET (20)	30.00	80.00
CL1 Ernie Irvan	1.25	3.00
CL2 Kyle Petty	1.25	3.00
CL3 Mark Martin	5.00	12.00
CL4 Dale Earnhardt	10.00	25.00
CL5 Brett Bodine	.60	1.50
CL6 Ward Burton	1.25	3.00
CL7 Sterling Marlin	2.00	5.00
CL8 Ricky Craven	.60	1.50
CL9 Ted Musgrave	.60	1.50
CL10 Darrell Waltrip	1.25	3.00
CL11 Ricky Rudd	2.00	5.00
CL12 Dale Jarrett	4.00	10.00
CL13 Geoff Bodine	.60	1.50
CL14 Michael Waltrip	1.25	3.00
CL15 Ken Schrader	.60	1.50
CL16 Bobby Hamilton	.60	1.50
CL17 Bobby Labonte	4.00	10.00
CL18 Jimmy Spencer	.60	1.50
CL19 Jeff Burton	2.00	5.00
CL20 Terry Labonte	2.00	5.00

1996 Assets Racing Race Day

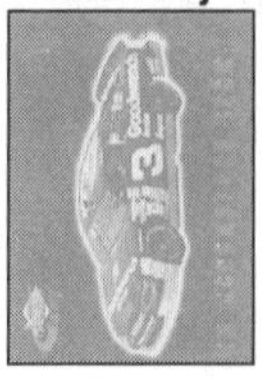

Randomly inserted one in 40 packs are these Race Day insert cards. The 10-card set features topics such as a typical day for a crew chief to an in-depth look at the superstitions and strategies behind 10 top racing teams. These cards are textured to give them a road-surface look and feel.

COMPLETE SET (10)	20.00	50.00
RD1 Morgan Shepherd's Car	.50	1.25
RD2 Rusty Wallace's Car	4.00	10.00
RD3 Dale Earnhardt's Car	8.00	20.00
RD4 Sterling Marlin's Car	1.50	4.00
RD5 Bobby Labonte's Car	3.00	8.00
RD6 Mark Martin's Car	4.00	10.00
RD7 Ernie Irvan's Car	1.00	2.50
RD8 Dale Jarrett's Car	3.00	8.00
RD9 Michael Waltrip's Car	1.00	2.50
RD10 Ricky Rudd's Car	1.50	4.00

1996 Autographed Racing

This 50-card set was the first issue by Score Board of the Autographed Racing brand. The product was packaged 5-cards per pack, 24 packs per box and 12 boxes per case. Original suggested retail on the packs was $4.99 each. The complete set consists of the top drivers on both the Winston Cup and Busch circuits. Also included were special redemption cards for officially licensed racing memorabilia at a rate of one per box.

COMPLETE SET (50)	10.00	20.00
1 Dale Earnhardt	1.00	2.50
2 Jeff Gordon	.60	1.50
3 Kyle Petty	.10	.30
4 Rick Mast	.05	.15

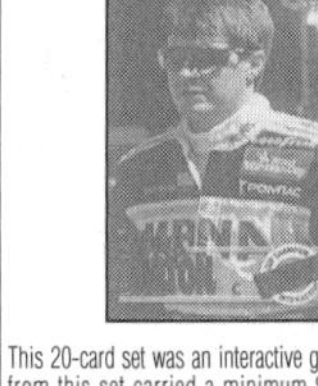

5 Richard Childress	.10	.30
6 Terry Labonte	.20	.50
7 Rusty Wallace's Car	.20	.50
8 Ken Schrader	.05	.15
9 Geoff Bodine	.05	.15
10 Richard Petty	.20	.50
11 Mike Skinner	.05	.15
12 Kenny Wallace	.05	.15
13 Sterling Marlin	.20	.50
14 Robert Pressley	.05	.15
15 Dale Jarrett	.40	1.00
16 Ted Musgrave	.05	.15
17 Ricky Rudd	.20	.50
18 Joe Gibbs	.10	.30
19 Morgan Shepherd	.05	.15
20 Mark Martin's Car	.20	.50
21 Hut Stricklin	.05	.15
22 Larry McReynolds	.02	.10
23 Brett Bodine	.05	.15
24 Mark Martin	.50	1.25
25 Dale Earnhardt's Car	.40	1.00
26 Elton Sawyer	.05	.15
27 Jeff Burton	.20	.50
28 Wood Brothers	.02	.10
29 David Smith	.02	.10
30 Ernie Irvan	.10	.30
31 Steve Hmiel	.02	.10
32 Mike Wallace	.05	.15
33 Dave Marcis	.10	.30
34 Michael Waltrip	.10	.30
35 Darrell Waltrip	.10	.30
36 Robin Pemberton	.02	.10
37 Loy Allen Jr.	.05	.15
38 Dick Trickle	.05	.15
39 Robert Yates	.02	.10
40 Randy LaJoie	.05	.15
41 John Andretti	.05	.15
42 Larry McClure	.02	.10
43 Bobby Labonte	.40	1.00
44 Ward Burton	.10	.30
45 Jeremy Mayfield	.10	.30
46 Ricky Craven	.05	.15
47 Jimmy Spencer	.05	.15
48 Todd Bodine	.05	.15
49 Jack Roush	.02	.10
50 Bobby Hamilton	.05	.15

1996 Autographed Racing Autographs

This 65-card insert set features hand-signed cards of the top names in racing. The cards were inserted at a rate of one in 12 packs. The cards featured red foil on the front along with the autograph. The backs carry the statement, "Congratulations. You've received an authentic 1996 Autographed Racing Autographed Card."

COMPLETE SET (65)	600.00	1000.00
1 Loy Allen Jr.	5.00	12.00
2 John Andretti	5.00	12.00
3 Paul Andrews	3.00	8.00
4 Johnny Benson	5.00	12.00
5 Brett Bodine	5.00	12.00
6 Geoff Bodine	5.00	12.00
7 Todd Bodine	5.00	12.00
8 Jeff Burton	8.00	20.00
9 Ward Burton	8.00	20.00
10 Richard Childress	10.00	25.00
11 Ricky Craven	5.00	12.00
12 Barry Dodson	3.00	8.00
13 Dale Earnhardt's Car	100.00	200.00
14 Joe Gibbs	15.00	30.00
15 Tony Glover	3.00	8.00
16 Jeff Gordon	60.00	120.00
17 David Green	5.00	12.00
18 Bobby Hamilton	10.00	25.00
19 Doug Hewitt	3.00	8.00
20 Steve Hmiel	3.00	8.00
21 Ernie Irvan	10.00	25.00
22 Dale Jarrett	12.50	30.00
23 Ned Jarrett	10.00	25.00
24 Jason Keller	5.00	12.00
25 Bobby Labonte	12.50	30.00
26 Terry Labonte	12.50	30.00
27 Randy LaJoie	5.00	12.00
28 Jimmy Makar	3.00	8.00
29 Dave Marcis	10.00	25.00
30 Sterling Marlin	12.50	30.00
31 Mark Martin	15.00	40.00
32 Rick Mast	5.00	12.00
33 Jeremy Mayfield	10.00	25.00
34 Larry McClure	3.00	8.00
35 Mike McLaughlin	5.00	12.00
36 Larry McReynolds	5.00	12.00
37 Patty Moise	5.00	12.00
38 Brad Parrott	3.00	8.00
39 Buddy Parrott	3.00	8.00
40 Todd Parrott	3.00	8.00
41 Robin Pemberton	3.00	8.00
42 Runt Pittman	3.00	8.00
43 Charley Pressley	3.00	8.00
44 Robert Pressley	5.00	12.00
45 Dr. Jerry Punch	3.00	8.00
46 Chuck Rider	3.00	8.00
47 Jack Roush	10.00	25.00
48 Ricky Rudd	12.50	30.00
49 Elton Sawyer	5.00	12.00
50 Ken Schrader	10.00	25.00
51 Morgan Shepherd	5.00	12.00
52 Mike Skinner	5.00	12.00
53 David Smith	3.00	8.00
54 Jimmy Spencer	10.00	25.00
55 Hut Stricklin	5.00	12.00
56 Dick Trickle	5.00	12.00
57 Kenny Wallace	5.00	12.00
58 Mike Wallace	5.00	12.00
59 Darrell Waltrip	15.00	30.00
60 Michael Waltrip	8.00	20.00
61 Eddie Wood	3.00	8.00
62 Glen Wood	3.00	8.00
63 Kim Wood	3.00	8.00
64 Len Wood	3.00	8.00
65 Robert Yates	3.00	8.00

1996 Autographed Racing Autographs Certified Golds

This is a "Certified" parallel version to the 65-card Autograph set. Each card features gold foil stamping on the front instead of silver and each autographed card is serial numbered. The backs of the Certified cards feature the same statement as the regular autographs. Certified Gold autographs were inserted in packs at a rate of one in 24 packs.

*CERT.GOLDS: .5X TO 1.2X BASIC AUTOS

1 Loy Allen Jr.	6.00	15.00
2 John Andretti	6.00	15.00
3 Paul Andrews	4.00	10.00
4 Johnny Benson	6.00	15.00
5 Brett Bodine	6.00	15.00
6 Geoff Bodine	6.00	15.00
7 Todd Bodine	6.00	15.00
8 Jeff Burton	12.50	30.00
9 Ward Burton	12.50	30.00
10 Richard Childress	12.50	30.00
11 Ricky Craven	6.00	15.00
12 Barry Dodson	4.00	10.00
13 Dale Earnhardt's Car	150.00	300.00
14 Joe Gibbs	15.00	40.00
15 Tony Glover	4.00	10.00
16 Jeff Gordon	60.00	150.00
17 David Green	6.00	15.00
18 Bobby Hamilton	12.50	30.00
19 Doug Hewitt	4.00	10.00
20 Steve Hmiel	4.00	10.00
21 Ernie Irvan	12.50	30.00
22 Dale Jarrett	15.00	40.00
23 Ned Jarrett	12.50	30.00
24 Jason Keller	6.00	15.00
25 Bobby Labonte	12.50	30.00
26 Terry Labonte	20.00	50.00
27 Randy LaJoie	6.00	15.00
28 Jimmy Makar	4.00	10.00
29 Dave Marcis	12.50	30.00
30 Sterling Marlin	15.00	40.00
31 Mark Martin	20.00	50.00
32 Rick Mast	6.00	15.00
33 Jeremy Mayfield	12.50	30.00
34 Larry McClure	4.00	10.00
35 Mike McLaughlin	6.00	15.00
36 Larry McReynolds	6.00	15.00
37 Patty Moise	6.00	15.00
38 Brad Parrott	4.00	10.00
39 Buddy Parrott	4.00	10.00
40 Todd Parrott	4.00	10.00
41 Robin Pemberton	4.00	10.00
42 Runt Pittman	4.00	10.00
43 Charley Pressley	4.00	10.00
44 Robert Pressley	6.00	15.00
45 Dr. Jerry Punch	4.00	10.00
46 Chuck Rider	4.00	10.00
47 Jack Roush	12.50	30.00
48 Ricky Rudd	15.00	40.00
49 Elton Sawyer	6.00	15.00
50 Ken Schrader	12.50	30.00
51 Morgan Shepherd	6.00	15.00
52 Mike Skinner	6.00	15.00
53 David Smith	4.00	10.00
54 Jimmy Spencer	12.50	30.00
55 Hut Stricklin	6.00	15.00
56 Dick Trickle	6.00	15.00
57 Kenny Wallace	6.00	15.00
58 Mike Wallace	6.00	15.00
59 Darrell Waltrip	15.00	40.00
60 Michael Waltrip	12.50	30.00
61 Eddie Wood	4.00	10.00
62 Glen Wood	4.00	10.00
63 Kim Wood	4.00	10.00
64 Len Wood	4.00	10.00
65 Robert Yates	4.00	10.00

1996 Autographed Racing Front Runners

This 89-card set features a double-front design. Each card has basically two front sides. The Front Runners logo on each side is stamped in silver foil. The cards are unnumbered and checklisted below in alphabetical order. Odds of finding a Front Runners card was one every two packs.

COMPLETE SET (89)	15.00	30.00
1 Paul Andrews	.05	.15
Geoff Bodine		
2 Brett Bodine	.05	.15
Geoff Bodine		
3 Brett Bodine	.05	.15
Todd Bodine		
4 Geoff Bodine	.05	.15
Todd Bodine		
5 Jeff Burton	.20	.50
Jeff Burton's Car		
6 Jeff Burton	.20	.50
Ward Burton		
7 Jeff Burton	.50	1.25
Mark Martin with hat		
8 Jeff Burton	.50	1.25
Mark Martin no hat		
9 Jeff Burton's Car	.10	.30
Mark Martin's Car		
10 Jeff Burton	.20	.50
Ted Musgrave		
11 Jeff Burton	.20	.50
Jack Roush		
12 Jeff Burton's Car	.10	.30
Jack Roush		
13 Richard Childress	1.00	2.50
Dale Earnhardt		
wearing helmet		
14 Richard Childress	.40	1.00
Dale Earnhardt's Car		
15 Richard Childress	.20	.50
Richard Petty		
16 Ricky Craven	.05	.15
Ricky Craven		
17 Ricky Craven	.05	.15
Charley Pressley		
18 Ricky Craven DuPont	.05	.15
Charley Pressley		
19 Dale Earnhardt	1.00	2.50
wearing helmet		
Dale Earnhardt celebrating		
20 Dale Earnhardt	1.00	2.50
wearing helmet		
Dale Earnhardt's Car		
21 Dale Earnhardt	1.00	2.50
wearing helmet		
Dale Earnhardt's Olympic car		
22 Dale Earnhardt	1.00	2.50
wearing helmet		
Richard Petty		
23 Joe Gibbs	.40	1.00
Bobby Labonte shades		
24 Joe Gibbs	.40	1.00
Bobby Labonte w/o shades		
25 Joe Gibbs	.10	.30
Bobby Labonte's Car		
26 Tony Glover	.20	.50
Sterling Marlin shades		
27 Tony Glover	.20	.50
Sterling Marlin w/o shades		
28 Tony Glover	.05	.15
Sterling Marlin's Car		
29 Bobby Hamilton	.20	.50
Richard Petty		
30 Bobby Hamilton profile	.20	.50
Richard Petty		
31 Steve Hmiel	.50	1.25
Mark Martin with hat		
32 Steve Hmiel	.50	1.25
Mark Martin no hat		
33 Ernie Irvan profile	.10	.30
Ernie Irvan facing front		
34 Ernie Irvan facing front	.10	.30
Ernie Irvan's car		
35 Ernie Irvan profile	.10	.30
Ernie Irvan's car		
36 Ernie Irvan profile shot	.40	1.00
Dale Jarrett		
Victory Lane at Daytona		
37 Ernie Irvan profile shot	.40	1.00
Dale Jarrett with shades		
38 Ernie Irvan facing front	.40	1.00
Dale Jarrett shades		
39 Ernie Irvan front shot	.40	1.00
Dale Jarrett		
Victory Lane at Daytona		
40 Ernie Irvan's Car	.10	.30
Dale Jarrett's Car		
41 Ernie Irvan facing front	.10	.30
Larry McReynolds		
42 Ernie Irvan profile shot	.10	.30
Larry McReynolds		
43 Ernie Irvan profile shot	.10	.30
Robert Yates		
44 Ernie Irvan facing front	.10	.30
Robert Yates		
45 Ernie Irvan's car	.05	.15
Robert Yates		
46 Dale Jarrett Victory Lane	.40	1.00
Dale Jarrett shades		
47 Dale Jarrett Victory Lane	.40	1.00
Dale Jarrett's car		
48 Dale Jarrett shades	.40	1.00
Dale Jarrett's Car		
49 Dale Jarrett Victory Lane	.40	1.00
Ned Jarrett		
50 Dale Jarrett Victory Lane	.40	1.00
Todd Parrott		
51 Dale Jarrett Victory Lane	.40	1.00
Robert Yates		
52 Dale Jarrett shades	.40	1.00
Robert Yates		
53 Dale Jarrett's Car	.10	.30
Robert Yates		
54 Bobby Labonte shades	.40	1.00
Bobby Labonte w/o shades		
55 Bobby Labonte shades	.40	1.00
Bobby Labonte's Car		
56 Bobby Labonte no shades	.40	1.00
Bobby Labonte's Car		
57 Bobby Labonte shades	.40	1.00
Jimmy Makar		
58 Bobby Labonte no shades	.40	1.00
Jimmy Makar		
59 Sterling Marlin no shades	.20	.50
Sterling Marlin shades		
60 Sterling Marlin no shades	.20	.50
Sterling Marlin's car		
61 Sterling Marlin shades	.20	.50
Sterling Marlin's Car		
62 Sterling Marlin shades	.20	.50
Larry McClure		
63 Sterling Marlin no shades	.20	.50
Larry McClure		
65 Sterling Marlin shades	.20	.50
Runt Pittman		
66 Sterling Marlin w/o shades	.20	.50
Runt Pittman		
66 Sterling Marlin's Car	.05	.15
Runt Pittman		
67 Mark Martin with hat	.50	1.25
Mark Martin no hat		
68 Mark Martin with hat	.50	1.25
Mark Martin's Car		
69 Mark Martin no hat	.50	1.25
Mark Martin's Car		
70 Mark Martin with hat	.50	1.25
Ted Musgrave		
71 Mark Martin no hat	.50	1.25
Ted Musgrave		
72 Mark Martin with hat	.50	1.25
Jack Roush		
73 Mark Martin no hat	.50	1.25
Jack Roush		
74 Mark Martin's Car	.20	.50
Jack Roush		
75 Patty Moise	.05	.15
Elton Sawyer		
76 Ted Musgrave	.05	.15
Jack Roush		
77 Robin Pemberton	.20	.50
Rusty Wallace's Car		
78 Kyle Petty	.20	.50
Richard Petty		
79 Charley Pressley	.05	.15
Robert Pressley		
80 Kenny Wallace	.05	.15
Mike Wallace		
81 Darrell Waltrip with helmet	.10	.30
Darrell Waltrip no helmet		
82 Darrell Waltrip with helmet	.10	.30
Michael Waltrip shades		
83 Darrell Waltrip with helmet	.10	.30
Michael Waltrip		
84 Darrell Waltrip no helmet	.10	.30
Michael Waltrip shades		
85 Darrell Waltrip no helmet	.10	.30
Michael Waltrip		
86 Michael Waltrip	.10	.30
Michael Waltrip shades		
87 Michael Waltrip	.10	.30
Michael Waltrip's car		
88 Michael Waltrip	.10	.30
Wood Brothers		
89 Michael Waltrip's Car	.10	.30
Wood Brothers		

1996 Autographed Racing High Performance

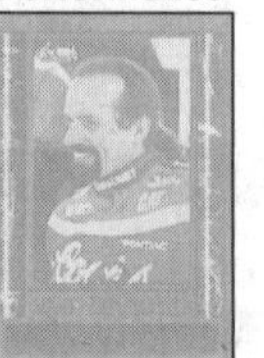

This 20-card insert set includes the top names in racing on foil-stamped cards. The card fronts feature a driver's photo framed by a wood and marble design. The cards were inserted at a rate of one in eight packs.

COMPLETE SET (20)	20.00	50.00
HP1 Dale Earnhardt	6.00	15.00
HP2 Kyle Petty	.75	2.00
HP3 Jeremy Mayfield	.75	2.00
HP4 Sterling Marlin	1.25	3.00
HP5 Ward Burton	.75	2.00
HP6 Mark Martin	3.00	8.00
HP7 Bobby Labonte	2.50	6.00
HP8 Ricky Craven	.40	1.00
HP9 Michael Waltrip	.75	2.00
HP10 Ricky Rudd	1.25	3.00
HP11 Ted Musgrave	.40	1.00
HP12 Ken Schrader	.40	1.00
HP13 Dale Jarrett	2.50	6.00
HP14 Brett Bodine	.40	1.00
HP15 Jimmy Spencer	.40	1.00
HP16 Bobby Hamilton	.40	1.00
HP17 Darrell Waltrip	.75	2.00
HP18 Robert Pressley	.40	1.00
HP19 Ernie Irvan	.75	2.00
HP20 Geoff Bodine	.40	1.00

1996 Autographed Racing Kings of the Circuit $5 Phone Cards

This 10-card insert set highlights the careers of racing legends. Each card carries a $5 phone time value. The cards are printed on silver foil board. The backs feature dialing instructions for the phone time. The phone time on the cards expired 2/28/98. Odds of finding a Kings of the Circuit card are one in 30 packs.

COMPLETE SET (10)	12.00	30.00
KC1 Dale Jarrett	1.50	4.00
KC2 Mark Martin	2.00	5.00
KC3 Sterling Marlin	.75	2.00
KC4 Bill Elliott	1.25	3.00
KC5 Ernie Irvan	.50	1.25
KC6 Dale Earnhardt	4.00	10.00
KC7 Bill Elliott	1.25	3.00
KC8 Dale Earnhardt's Car	1.50	4.00
KC9 Rusty Wallace's Car	.75	2.00
KC10 Dale Earnhardt	4.00	10.00

1997 Autographed Racing

This 50-card set was the second issue by Score Board of the Autographed Racing brand. The product was packaged 5 cards per pack, 24 packs per box, and 10 boxes per case. The complete set consists of drivers from the Winston Cup and Busch circuits.

COMPLETE SET (50)	6.00	15.00
1 Dale Earnhardt	1.00	2.50
2 Kyle Petty	.10	.30
3 Terry Labonte	.20	.50
4 Jeff Gordon	.60	1.50
5 Michael Waltrip	.10	.30
6 Dale Jarrett	.40	1.00
7 Lake Speed	.05	.15
8 Bobby Labonte	.40	1.00
9 Robby Gordon RC	.20	.50
10 Rick Mast	.05	.15
11 Geoff Bodine	.05	.15
12 Sterling Marlin	.20	.50
13 Jeff Burton	.20	.50
14 Steve Park RC	1.00	2.00
15 Darrell Waltrip	.10	.30
16 Randy LaJoie	.05	.15
17 Mark Martin	.50	1.25
18 Bobby Hamilton	.05	.15
19 Ernie Irvan	.10	.30
20 Steve Grissom	.05	.15
21 Ted Musgrave	.05	.15
22 Jeremy Mayfield	.10	.30
23 Ricky Rudd	.20	.50
24 Ricky Craven	.05	.15
25 Hut Stricklin	.05	.15
26 Morgan Shepherd	.05	.15
27 Brett Bodine	.05	.15
28 John Andretti	.05	.15
29 Robert Pressley	.05	.15
30 Dick Trickle	.05	.15
31 Ernie Irvan's Car	.05	.15
32 Robby Gordon's Car	.10	.30
33 Bobby Hamilton's Car	.02	.10
34 Dale Jarrett's Car	.10	.30
35 Rusty Wallace's Car	.20	.50
36 Dale Earnhardt's Car	.60	1.50
37 Sterling Marlin's Car	.05	.15
38 Mark Martin's Car	.20	.50
39 Bobby Labonte's Car	.10	.30
40 Michael Waltrip's Car	.05	.15
41 Dale Earnhardt	1.25	3.00
Jeff Gordon		
42 Dale Jarrett	.30	.75
Ernie Irvan		
43 Jeff Burton	.10	.30
Ricky Craven		
44 Mark Martin	.50	1.25
Sterling Marlin		
45 Micahel Waltrip	.30	.75
Bobby Labonte		
46 Bobby Hamilton	.10	.30
Kyle Petty		
47 Dale Earnhardt	2.00	5.00
Dale Jarrett		
48 Darrell Waltrip	.10	.30
Geoff Bodine		
49 Dale Earnhardt's Car	.60	1.50
Rusty Wallace's Car		
50 Bobby Labonte	.40	1.00
Terry Labonte		

1997 Autographed Racing Autographs

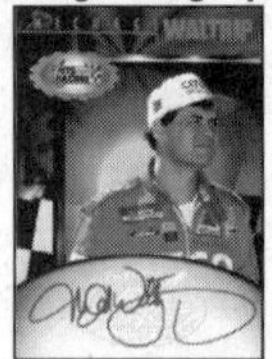

This insert set features hand-signed cards from the top names in racing. It is important to note that the 56-card checklist presented below may not be complete. Some of the autographed cards distributed in packs were in the form of redemption cards or cards from the 1996 Autographed Racing product. Signed cards were randomly inserted into packs at an overall rate of 5:24.

1 John Andretti	7.50	15.00
2 Tommy Baldwin	2.00	5.00
3 Brett Bodine	3.00	8.00
4 Geoff Bodine	3.00	8.00
5 Todd Bodine	3.00	8.00
6 Jeff Burton	8.00	20.00
7 Richard Childress	7.50	15.00
8 Ricky Craven	7.50	15.00
9 Wally Dallenbach Jr.	3.00	8.00
10 Gary DeHart	2.00	5.00
11 Randy Dorton	7.50	15.00
12 Dale Earnhardt	200.00	350.00
13 Ray Evernham	7.50	15.00
14 Joe Gibbs	15.00	30.00
15 Tony Glover	2.00	5.00
16 Jeff Gordon	50.00	100.00
17 Robby Gordon	10.00	25.00
18 Andy Graves	2.00	5.00
19 Steve Grissom	3.00	8.00
20 Bobby Hamilton	10.00	25.00
21 Rick Hendrick	15.00	40.00
22 Steve Hmiel	2.00	5.00
23 Ron Hornaday Jr.	3.00	8.00
24 Ernie Irvan	10.00	25
25 Dale Jarrett	12.50	30
26 Jimmy Johnson	3.00	8
27 Terry Labonte	12.50	30
28 Bobby Labonte	12.50	30
29 Randy LaJoie	3.00	8
30 Jimmy Makar	2.00	5
31 Sterling Marlin	10.00	25
32 Dave Marcis	7.50	15
33 Mark Martin	15.00	40
34 Rick Mast	3.00	8
35 Jeremy Mayfield	7.50	15
36 Kenny Mayne	2.00	5
37 Larry McReynolds	7.50	15
38 Ted Musgrave	3.00	8
39 Buddy Parrott	2.00	5
40 Todd Parrott	2.00	5
41 Robin Pemberton	2.00	5
42 Kyle Petty	7.50	15
43 Shelton Pittman	2.00	5
44 Robert Pressley	3.00	8
45 Dr. Jerry Punch	2.00	5
46 Harry Raimer	2.00	5
47 Dave Rezendes	3.00	8
48 Greg Sacks	3.00	8
49 Morgan Shepherd	3.00	8
50 Hut Stricklin	3.00	8
51 Dick Trickle	3.00	8
52 Kenny Wallace	4.00	10
53 Mike Wallace	7.50	15
54 Darrell Waltrip	12.50	30
55 Michael Waltrip	7.50	15
56 Wood Brothers	2.00	5

1997 Autographed Racing Mayne Street

This 30-card insert set is named for ESPN anno Kenny Mayne. The card backs features commentary on each driver. The cards v randomly inserted into hobby packs at a ratio of

COMPLETE SET (30)	20.00	75
KM1 Dale Earnhardt	8.00	20
KM2 Kyle Petty	1.00	2
KM3 Terry Labonte	1.50	4
KM4 Jeff Gordon	5.00	12
KM5 Michael Waltrip	1.00	2
KM6 Dale Jarrett	3.00	8
KM7 Lake Speed	.50	1
KM8 Bobby Labonte	3.00	8
KM9 Robby Gordon	1.50	4
KM10 Rick Mast	.50	1
KM11 Geoff Bodine	.50	1
KM12 Sterling Marlin	1.50	4
KM13 Jeff Burton	1.50	4
KM14 Steve Park	6.00	15
KM15 Darrell Waltrip	1.00	2
KM16 Randy LaJoie	.50	1
KM17 Mark Martin	4.00	10
KM18 Bobby Hamilton	.50	1
KM19 Ernie Irvan	1.00	2
KM20 Steve Grissom	.50	1
KM21 Ted Musgrave	.50	1
KM22 Jeremy Mayfield	1.00	2
KM23 Ricky Rudd	1.50	4
KM24 Ricky Craven	.50	1
KM25 Hut Stricklin	.50	1
KM26 Morgan Shepherd	.50	1
KM27 Brett Bodine	.50	1
KM28 John Andretti	.50	1
KM29 Robert Pressley	.50	1
KM30 Dick Trickle	.50	1

1997 Autographed Racing Take the Checkered Flag

The 2-card set features hand-numbered c commemorating the winner of each leg of Winston Million. Each card contains a portion real checkered flag. The cards were rando inserted into hobby packs at a ratio of 1:240.

TF1 Jeff Gordon/325	20.00	50
TF2 Mark Martin	15.00	40

2004 Bass Pro Shops Racing

1 Dale Earnhardt Jr.		
2 Martin Truex Jr.	3.00	6
3 Dale Earnhardt Jr.	5.00	10
Martin Truex Jr.		

1986 Big League Card Alan Kulwicki Quincy'

This card was produced by Big League Cards fo Quincy's Steakhouse Racing Team and driver Kulwicki. It features a color image of Kulwicki o front along with the Big League Cards name a the photo and the year and Quincy's title below light blue colored cardback has contact inform for the Steakhouse at the top and a brief bi

Kulwicki followed by a description of his chase for 1986 NASCAR Rookie of the Year honors. A 1985 copyright line appears on the back as well. The card was issued at the 1986 Daytona 500 primarily to media members in their media information kits.

NNO Alan Kulwicki	25.00	60.00

1998 Big League Cards Creative Images

This 10-card promotional set was produced by Big League Cards and distributed by Creative Images of Vermont. Each card was produced in the typical Big League Cards design along with a local Vermont sponsor logo in the lower right corner of the cardfront. Most of these cards were produced earlier than 1998 and often include a copyright date other than 1998. The Creative Images name, address, and phone number are included on the cardback at the bottom edge. Reportedly, only 3,000 sets were produced and they were intially offered in a mail-order advertisement for $29.95 per set.

COMPLETE SET (10)	12.00	30.00
7 Darrell Waltrip	1.50	4.00
8 Ernie Irvan	1.50	4.00
9 Mark Martin	2.50	6.00
10 Dale Jarrett	2.00	5.00
11 Bill Elliott	2.00	5.00
12 Terry Labonte	2.00	5.00
13 Ricky Rudd	1.50	4.00
13 Rusty Wallace	2.50	6.00
29 Dale Earnhardt	6.00	15.00
30 Jeff Gordon	3.00	8.00

1992 Bikers of the Racing Scene

Eagle Productions produced this set featuring participants and other personalities associated with the First Annual Winston Cup Harley Ride in September 1992. The cards feature the Winston Cup personality with their favorite Harley motorcyle. Each checklist card carries the set production number which was limited to 90,000.

COMPLETE SET (34)	3.20	8.00
1 Richard Petty The King	.40	1.00
2 Pre-Dawn	.05	.10
3 Richard Childress	.12	.30
4 Spook Caspers	.07	.20
5 Kirk Shelmerdine	.07	.20
6 Danny Myers	.07	.20
7 Paul Andrews	.07	.20
8 Will Lind	.07	.20
9 Jerry Huskins Randy Butner	.07	.20
10 Jimmy Cox	.07	.20
11 Danny Culler	.07	.20
12 Dennis Dawson	.07	.20
13 Bryan Dorsey	.07	.20
14 Dan Gatewood	.07	.20
15 Kevin Youngblood	.07	.20
16 John Hall	.07	.20
17 Jimmy Means	.07	.20
18 Robin Metdepenningen	.07	.20
19 Gary Nelson	.07	.20
20 Tommy Rigsbee	.07	.20
21 Jimmy Shore	.07	.20
22 Marty Tharpe	.07	.20
23 Danny West	.07	.20
24 Mike McQueen Darren Jolly	.07	.20
25 Kyle Petty	.25	.60
26 Waddell Wilson	.07	.20
27 Steve Barkdoll	.12	.30
28 Dick Brooks	.07	.20
29 Tracy Leslie	.07	.20
30 Michael Waltrip	.15	.40
31 Beth Bruce Michael Waltrip Rick Wilson Richard Childress Danny Culler Don Tilley	.12	.30
32 Rick Wilson	.07	.20
33 Harry Gant	.20	.50
34 Checklist Card	.05	.10
P1 Rick Wilson Promo 1993 Card	.07	.20

2004 Blue Bonnet Bobby Labonte

This 4-card set was issued on packages of Blue Bonnet in late 2004. The 4 cards all feature Bobby Labonte with different accomplishments throughout his career. The cards were meant to be cut off of the box.

COMPLETE SET (4)	2.50	6.00
1 Bobby Labonte 21 wins	.60	1.50
2 Bobby Labonte '00 Champion	.60	1.50
3 Bobby Labonte 26 Top 10s	.60	1.50
4 Bobby Labonte career winnings	.60	1.50

1998 Burger King Dale Earnhardt

This four card set was distributed at participating Burger King's in the Southeast section of the country.

COMPLETE SET (4)	8.00	20.00
1 Dale Earnhardt's Car	1.50	4.00
2 Dale Earnhardt	3.00	8.00
3 Dale Earnhardt's Car	1.50	4.00
4 Dale Earnhardt	3.00	8.00

1992 Card Dynamics Davey Allison

This five-card set was issued in a display box and has five polished aluminum cards that feature Davey Allison. The sets were distributed by Card Dynamics and 4,000 sets were produced. There is a numbered certificate of authenticity that comes with each set.

COMP.FACT SET (5)	35.00	70.00
COMMON CARD (1-5)	6.00	15.00

1992 Card Dynamics Harry Gant

This five-card set was issued in a display box and has five polished aluminum cards that feature Harry Gant. The sets were distributed by Card Dynamics and 4,000 sets were reportedly produced. There is a numbered certificate of authenticity that comes with each set. The set was not produced in the original quantities stated on the certificate.

COMP. FACT SET (5)	10.00	25.00
COMMON CARD (1-5)	2.00	5.00

1992 Card Dynamics Gant Oil

The 1992 Gant Oil cards were produced as promotional advertising for Gant Oil Company. The cards could be purchased for $6.00 when you bought gas at one of the 28 participating Gant Oil stations through out North Carolina. There was one driver available every month over the course of the 10 month long NASCAR season (February to November). Each card has a production serial number and is made of polished aluminum. Cards are unnumbered but have been numbered below in order of release with number of cards produced following each driver's name.

COMPLETE SET (10)	120.00	300.00
1 Darrell Waltrip/4000	15.00	40.00
2 Harry Gant/4000	15.00	40.00
3 Sterling Marlin/4000	15.00	40.00
4 Rusty Wallace/4000	25.00	60.00
5 Davey Allison/5000	25.00	60.00
6 Mark Martin/4000	30.00	80.00
7 Ernie Irvan/4000	15.00	40.00
8 Kyle Petty/4000	20.00	50.00
9 Bill Elliott/5000	20.00	50.00
10 Alan Kulwicki/5000	20.00	50.00

1992 Card Dynamics Jerry Glanville

This five-card set was issued in a display box and has five polished aluminum cards that feature Jerry Glanville. The sets were distributed by Card Dynamics and 5,000 sets were reportedly produced. There is a numbered certificate of authenticity that comes with each set.

COMP. FACT SET (5)	10.00	25.00
COMMON CARD (1-5)	2.00	5.00

1992 Card Dynamics Ernie Irvan

This five-card set was issued in a display box and has five polished aluminum cards that feature Ernie Irvan. The sets were distributed by Card Dynamics and 2,000 sets were reportedly produced. There is a numbered certificate of authenticity that comes with each set. The set was not produced in the original quantities stated on the certificate.

COMP. FACT SET (5)	20.00	50.00
COMMON CARD (1-5)	4.00	10.00

1992 Card Dynamics Alan Kulwicki

This five-card set was issued in a display box and has five polished aluminum cards that feature Alan Kulwicki. The sets were distributed by Card Dynamics and 4,000 sets were reportedly produced. There is a numbered certificate of authenticity that comes with each set. The set was not produced in the original quantities stated on the certificate.

COMP. FACT SET (5)	30.00	75.00
COMMON CARD (1-5)	6.00	15.00

1992 Card Dynamics Kyle Petty

This five-card set was issued in a display box and has five polished aluminum cards that feature Kyle Petty. The sets were distributed by Card Dynamics and 4,000 sets were reportedly produced. There is a numbered certificate of authenticity that comes with each set. The set was not produced in the original quantities stated on the certificate.

COMP. FACT SET (5)	12.50	30.00
COMMON CARD (1-5)	2.50	6.00

1992 Card Dynamics Ricky Rudd

This five-card set was issued in a display box and has five polished aluminum cards that feature Ricky Rudd. The sets were distributed by Card Dynamics and 4,000 sets were reportedly produced. There is a numbered certificate of authenticity that comes with each set. The set was not produced in the original quantities stated on the certificate.

COMP. FACT SET (5)	12.50	30.00
COMMON CARD (1-5)	2.50	6.00

1992 Card Dynamics Rusty Wallace

This five-card set was issued in a display box and has five polished aluminum cards that feature Rusty Wallace. The sets were distributed by Card Dynamics and 2,000 sets were reportedly produced. There is a numbered certificate of authenticity that comes with each set. The set was not produced in the original quantities stated on the certificate.

COMP. FACT SET (5)	20.00	50.00
COMMON CARD (1-5)	4.00	10.00

1992 Card Dynamics Darrell Waltrip

This five-card set was issued in a display box and has five polished aluminum cards that feature Darrell Waltrip. The sets were distributed by Card Dynamics and 4,000 sets were reportedly produced. There is a numbered certificate of authenticity that comes with each set.

COMP.FACT SET (5)	12.50	30.00
COMMON CARD (1-5)	2.50	6.00

1992 Card Dynamics Michael Waltrip

This five-card set was issued in a display box and has five polished aluminum cards that feature Michael Waltrip. The sets were distributed by Card Dynamics and 2,000 sets were reportedly produced. There is a numbered certificate of authenticity that comes with each set. The sets were not produced in the original quantities (15,000) stated on the certificate.

COMP. FACT SET (5)	10.00	25.00
COMMON CARD (1-5)	2.00	5.00

1994 Card Dynamics Black Top Busch Series

This 10-card set was made exclusively for Black Top Racing in King, North Carolina. The set features some of the best NASCAR Winston Cup drivers to race in the Busch series. 5,000 of each card was made. The cards are unnumbered and are listed below in alphabetical order.

COMPLETE SET (10)	32.00	80.00
1 Dale Earnhardt	12.50	30.00
2 Harry Gant	2.50	6.00
3 Jeff Gordon	6.00	15.00
4 Steve Grissom	2.00	5.00
5 Ernie Irvan	2.50	6.00
6 Alan Kulwicki	3.00	8.00
7 Bobby Labonte	4.00	10.00
8 Terry Labonte	3.00	8.00
9 Mark Martin	5.00	12.00
10 Robert Pressley	2.00	5.00

1993 Card Dynamics Alliance Racing Daytona

This three-card set was sold to dealers who attended the Alliance Racing dealers meeting at Daytona Beach on February 11, 1993, during SpeedWeek. There were 999 of the sets produced with each one coming in a blue display box. There was a sequentially numbered certificate in each set. The promo cards were given away as door prizes at the meeting. Only 99 promo sets were produced.

COMPLETE SET (3)	24.00	60.00
1 Robert Pressley	10.00	25.00
2 Robert Pressley's Car	7.50	20.00
3 Ricky Pearson	10.00	25.00

1993-95 Card Dynamics Double Eagle Postcards

This nine-card postcard size set was released in separate series. The first series consisted of five cards and was released in 1993, the second series consisted of two cards and was released in 1994. The third series consisted of two cards and was released in 1995. Each card was produced in quantities of 500 each. The cards were made exclusively for Double Eagle Racing of Asheboro, North Carolina. The cards are unnumbered and are in order of release below. Cards 1-5 are series one cards, 6 and 7 are series two and cards 8 and 9 are series three.

COMPLETE SET (9)	200.00	500.00
1 Jeff Gordon Baby Ruth	40.00	100.00
2 Rusty Wallace	30.00	80.00
3 Dale Earnhardt	75.00	150.00
4 Alan Kulwicki	25.00	60.00
5 Ernie Irvan	20.00	50.00
6 Harry Gant	12.50	30.00
7 Jeff Gordon DuPont	40.00	100.00
8 Mark Martin	30.00	80.00
9 Geoff Bodine	12.50	30.00

1993 Card Dynamics Gant Oil

The 1993 Gant Oil cards were produced as promotional advertising for Gant Oil Company. The cards could be purchased for $8.00 when you bought gas at one of the participating Gant Oil stations throughout North Carolina. There was one driver available every month over the course of the 10 month long NASCAR season (February to November). Each card has a production serial number and is made of polished aluminum. There were 6,000 of each card produced.

COMPLETE SET (10)	60.00	110.00
1 Richard Petty	4.00	10.00
2 Bill Elliott	4.00	10.00
3 Rusty Wallace	5.00	12.00
4 Geoff Bodine	2.40	6.00
5 Harry Gant	3.20	8.00
6 Jeff Gordon	7.50	20.00
7 Kyle Petty	3.20	8.00
8 Dale Earnhardt	15.00	40.00
9 Dale Jarrett	4.00	10.00
10 Alan Kulwicki	5.00	12.00

1993-95 Card Dynamics North State Chevrolet

This three-card set was issued over three consecutive years, 1993-1995. The cards were made specifically for North State Chevrolet in Greensboro, North Carolina. The Dale Earnhardt card was produced in shorter quantities due to distribution through a competitior of Dale Earnhardt Chevrolet. There are 2,000 of each of the Ernie Irvan and Harry Gant. There are 650 of the Dale Earnhardt card. The cards are unnumbered, but are numbered and listed below in the order of year they were released.

COMPLETE SET (3)	125.00	250.00
1 Ernie Irvan	18.00	40.00
2 Dale Earnhardt	100.00	175.00
3 Harry Gant	18.00	40.00

1993 Card Dynamics Robert Pressley

This one-card and die-cast combination piece was sold to Alliance Fan Club members. There were 2,759 sets produced. Each piece comes in a display box and with a certificate of authenticity.

1 Robert Pressley with die-cast car	6.00	15.00

1993 Card Dynamics Robert Pressley Postcard

This postcard was sold to Alliance Fan Club members at an open house meeting in Arden, North Carolina. There were 500 produced.

1 Robert Pressley	10.00	25.00

1993 Card Dynamics Quik Chek

The 1993 Quik Chek cards were produced as promotional advertising for Quik Chek Food and Gas Marts. The cards could be purchased for $6.00 when you bought gas at a Quik Chek. There was one driver available every month over the course of the 10 month long NASCAR season (February to November). Each card has a production serial number and was made on polished aluminum. Cards are unnumbered, but have been numbered below in order of release with number of cards produced following each drivers name.

COMPLETE SET (10)	50.00	100.00
1 Alan Kulwicki/7000	4.00	10.00
2 Harry Gant/5000	3.00	8.00
3 Richard Petty/5000	4.00	10.00
4 Bill Elliott/5000	5.00	12.00
5 Rusty Wallace/5000	6.00	15.00
6 Geoff Bodine/5000	2.50	6.00
7 Kyle Petty/5000	3.00	8.00
8 Dale Earnhardt/7000	20.00	40.00
9 Jeff Gordon/7000	10.00	20.00
10 Mark Martin/5000	6.00	15.00

1994 Card Dynamics Double Eagle Dale Earnhardt

This six-card set was made by Card Dynamics exclusively for Double Eagle Racing in Asheboro, North Carolina. The set features Dale's career from his 1979 Rookie of the Year award to his 1991 Winston Cup title. There were 5,000 of each polished aluminum card made. The cards are unnumbered but arranged below in order of the year they feature.

COMPLETE SET (6)	35.00	75.00
COMMON CARD	6.00	15.00

1994 Card Dynamics Gant Oil

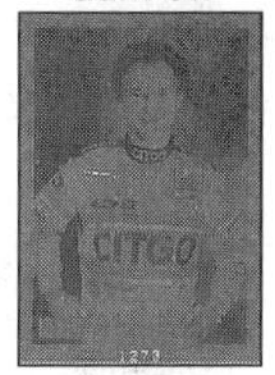

The 1994 Gant Oil cards were produced as promotional advertising for Gant Oil Company. The cards could be purchased for $8.00 when you bought gas at one of the participating Gant Oil stations throughout North Carolina. There was one driver available every month over the course of the 10 month long NASCAR season (February to November). Each card has a production serial number and is made of polished aluminum. There were 6,000 of each card produced. Cards are unnumbered, but have been numbered below in order of release.

COMPLETE SET (10)	40.00	80.00
1 Harry Gant	2.50	6.00
2 Rusty Wallace	6.00	15.00
3 Ernie Irvan	3.00	8.00
4 Jeff Gordon	7.50	20.00
5 Hut Stricklin	2.50	6.00
6 Darrell Waltrip	3.00	8.00
7 Morgan Shepherd	2.50	6.00
8 Mark Martin	6.00	15.00
9 Bobby Labonte	5.00	12.00
10 Ken Schrader	2.50	6.00

1994 Card Dynamics Jeff Gordon Fan Club

This three-card set features Jeff's younger years. The three cards are made of polished aluminum and come in a display box. There were 1,200 sets made and they were sold by the Jeff Gordon Fan Club.

COMP. FACT SET (3)	20.00	50.00
COMMON CARD	7.50	20.00

1994 Card Dynamics Montgomery Motors

This six-card set was available through Montgomery Motors located in Troy, North Carolina. The cards were given away free to any person who test drove a new Ford, Lincoln or Mercury. You could also purchase the cards for $30.00 from the dealership. There were 1,000 silver leaf versions of each card made. A gold leaf parallel version of each card was also made. There were 200 of each of these and they were signed by the drivers.

COMPLETE SET (3)	40.00	100.00
1 Ernie Irvan	12.50	30.00
2 Mark Martin	15.00	40.00
3 Rusty Wallace	12.50	30.00

1994 Card Dynamics Texas Pete Joe Nemechek

This one-card and die-cast combination piece was produced in a quantity of 15,000. The pieces were available to those who sent in labels from cans of Texas Pete's Chili No Beans. The item comes in a white display box with each box sequentially numbered of 15,000 on the front. A letter of authenticity also accompanies the piece and can be found inside the box.

1 Joe Nemechek with die-cast car	4.80	12.00

1995 Card Dynamics Allsports Postcards

These two postcards were issued through the featured driver's fan club. Your club membership was free when you ordered the postcard. There were 500 of each postcard produced. Each card was hand signed and individually numbered.

1 Steve Grissom	15.00	30.00
2 Shawna Robinson	25.00	50.00

1996 Classic

This 60-card set features the top drivers and crew members and contains many of the car and sponsor changes for the 1996 season. The first 50 cards in the set were packaged like a regular set would be. The last 10 cards in the set (51-60) were more like

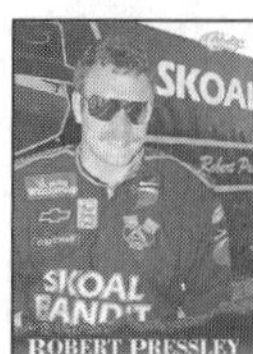

inserts. The SP cards were reported to come anywhere from one every 9 packs to one every 36 packs. There were no stated odds on the SP cards. The set is commonly sold without the final 10 cards in the set due to the difficulty in finding those short printed cards. There were 10 cards in each pack, 36 packs per box and 12 boxes per case. There were also Hot Boxes of Classic produced. A Hot Box yielded at least 5 inserts per pack.

COMPLETE SET (60)	15.00	40.00
COMP.SET w/o SP's (50)	5.00	12.00
COMP.SP SET (10)	10.00	30.00
1 Sterling Marlin	.25	.60
2 Todd Bodine	.07	.20
3 Ted Musgrave	.07	.20
4 Dick Trickle	.07	.20
5 Jack Roush	.02	.10
6 Ricky Rudd	.25	.60
7 Mike Wallace	.07	.20
8 Dave Marcis	.15	.40
9 Robert Pressley	.07	.20
10 Ned Jarrett	.07	.20
11 Jeremy Mayfield	.15	.40
12 Richard Petty	.25	.60
13 Kyle Petty	.15	.40
14 Mark Martin	.40	1.00
15 Steve Hmiel	.02	.10
16 Kenny Wallace	.07	.20
17 Elton Sawyer	.07	.20
18 Jason Keller	.07	.20
19 Larry McClure	.02	.10
20 Ward Burton	.15	.40
21 Shelton Pittman	.02	.10
22 Larry McReynolds	.02	.10
23 Robert Yates	.02	.10
24 Darrell Waltrip	.15	.40
25 Tony Glover	.02	.10
26 Michael Waltrip	.15	.40
27 Len Wood Glen Wood	.02	.10
28 Morgan Shepherd	.07	.20
29 Brett Bodine	.07	.20
30 Mark Martin's Car	.25	.60
31 Sterling Marlin's Car	.07	.20
32 Dale Earnhardt's Car	.60	1.50
33 Dale Jarrett's Car	.15	.40
34 Bobby Hamilton's Car	.02	.10
35 Michael Waltrip's Car	.07	.20
36 Rusty Wallace's Car	.15	.40
37 Ernie Irvan	.15	.40
38 Rick Mast	.07	.20
39 David Green	.07	.20
40 Joe Gibbs	.15	.40
41 Michael Waltrip	.15	.40
42 Ted Musgrave	.07	.20
43 Bobby Labonte	.30	.75
44 Ward Burton	.15	.40
45 Ricky Craven	.07	.20
46 Ken Schrader	.07	.20
47 Geoff Bodine	.07	.20
48 Johnny Benson	.15	.40
49 Dale Jarrett	.30	.75
50 Robin Pemberton	.02	.10
51 Mark Martin SP	2.00	5.00
52 Sterling Marlin SP	1.25	3.00
53 Dale Earnhardt SP	6.00	15.00
54 Michael Waltrip SP	.15	.40
55 Ricky Rudd SP	1.00	2.50
56 Ernie Irvan SP	.15	.40
57 Dale Jarrett SP	2.00	5.00
58 Bobby Labonte SP	2.00	5.00
59 Kyle Petty SP	.15	.40
60 Darrell Waltrip SP	.15	.40
HP96 Dale Earnhardt Promo (Daytona Race Chase hobby)	2.00	5.00
RP96 Dale Earnhardt Promo (Daytona Race Chase retail)	2.50	6.00

1996 Classic Printer's Proof

This 50-card set is a parallel to the base set. Each card features a red foil "Printers Proof 1 of 498" logo on the front to differentiate them from the base cards. The cards are inserted one per 60 packs.

COMPLETE SET (50)	75.00	150.00

*SINGLES: 8X TO 20X BASE CARDS

1996 Classic Silver

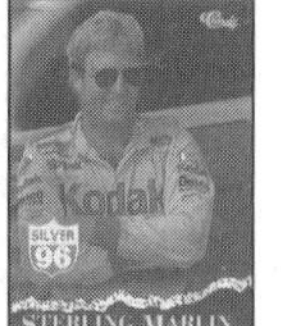

This 50-card set is a parallel to the base brand. The cards feature a "Silver 96" logo on the front that differentiates them from the base cards. The cards were inserted one per pack.

COMPLETE SET (50)	6.00	15.00
*STARS: .6X TO 1.5X BASIC CARDS		

1996 Classic Images Preview

This five-card set is a preview of the '96 Images set. The cards feature top names in racing in micro-foil printing. The odds of pulling a Images Preview card was one per 30 Classic packs.

COMPLETE SET (5)	20.00	50.00
RP1 Sterling Marlin	2.50	6.00
RP2 Mark Martin	3.00	8.00
RP3 Bobby Labonte	3.00	8.00
RP4 Ricky Rudd	3.00	8.00
RP5 Dale Earnhardt's Car Richard Childress	8.00	20.00

1996 Classic Innerview

This 15-card insert set gives fans a look at the top drivers. The double foil stamped cards feature a gold facsimile signature of each driver on the front of their card. The backs feature a driver's answer to a specific question to give the fan more insight to what goes on behind-the-scenes. The cards are randomly inserted in packs at a rate of one per 50 packs.

COMPLETE SET (15)	35.00	75.00
IV1 Mark Martin	3.00	8.00
IV2 Ted Musgrave	.60	1.50
IV3 Dale Earnhardt	8.00	20.00
IV4 Sterling Marlin	2.00	5.00
IV5 Kyle Petty	1.25	3.00
IV6 Mark Martin	3.00	8.00
IV7 Dale Earnhardt	8.00	20.00
IV8 Brett Bodine	.60	1.50
IV9 Geoff Bodine	.60	1.50
IV10 Ricky Rudd	2.00	5.00
IV11 Sterling Marlin	2.00	5.00
IV12 Bobby Labonte	3.00	8.00
IV13 Morgan Shepherd	.60	1.50
IV14 Robert Pressley	.60	1.50
IV15 Michael Waltrip	1.25	3.00

1996 Classic Mark Martin's Challengers

This 10-card set features some of Mark's toughest competitors. Each card has Mark's comments on the back telling what makes each driver a good competitor. The cards feature micro-foil technology and were inserted in packs at a rate of one per 15 packs.

COMPLETE SET (10)	6.00	15.00
MC1 Ted Musgrave	.30	.75
MC2 Michael Waltrip	.60	1.50
MC3 Dale Earnhardt's Car	2.50	6.00
MC4 Dale Jarrett	1.50	4.00
MC5 Sterling Marlin	2.00	2.50
MC6 Ken Schrader	.30	.75
MC7 Geoff Bodine	.30	.75
MC8 Rusty Wallace's Car	.60	1.50
MC9 Bobby Labonte	1.50	4.00
MC10 Mark Martin	1.50	4.00

1996 Classic Race Chase

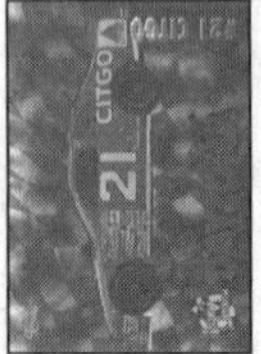

This 20-card insert set was an interactive game for two specific races in the 1996 season. The set is divided into subsets; cards 1-10 were for the '96 Daytona 500 and cards 11-20 were for the '96 TranSouth Financial 400. If you held the winning card for either of those two races, Dale Jarrett and Jeff Gordon respectively, you could redeem that card for a 10-card foil stamped set of the related race. You could also redeem the winning card along with a regular Classic drivers card for each of the second through tenth place finishers for a $50 phone card of a top driver and the 10-card foil stamped set. Since the winners of each of the two races were not represented in the set, the Field Card was the winner in both interactive race games. The expiration for the redemption cards was June 30, 1996.

COMPLETE SET (20)	15.00	40.00
RC1 Michael Waltrip's Car	.75	2.00
RC2 Rusty Wallace's Car	1.50	4.00
RC3 Dale Earnhardt's Car	3.00	8.00
RC4 Sterling Marlin's Car	1.00	2.50
RC5 Ricky Rudd's Car	1.00	2.50
RC6 Mark Martin's Car	1.50	4.00
RC7 Bobby Labonte's Car	1.25	3.00
RC8 Ernie Irvan's Car	.75	2.00
RC9 Morgan Shepherd's Car	.40	1.00
RC10 Field Card WIN	.40	1.00
RC11 Michael Waltrip's Car	.75	2.00
RC12 Rusty Wallace's Car	1.50	4.00
RC13 Dale Earnhardt's Car	3.00	8.00
RC14 Sterling Marlin's Car	1.00	2.50
RC15 Darrell Waltrip's Car	.75	2.00
RC16 Mark Martin's Car	1.50	4.00
RC17 Bobby Labonte's Car	1.25	3.00
RC18 Ernie Irvan's Car	.75	2.00
RC19 Johnny Benson's Car	.40	1.00
RC20 Field Card WIN	.40	1.00

1992 Clevite Engine Builders

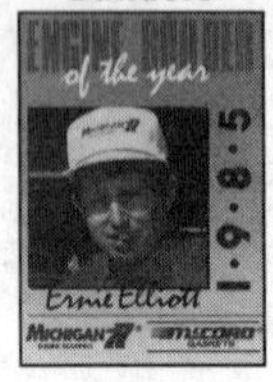

This 12-card promotional set features the top Winston Cup engine builders from 1985-91. The Engine Builder Award is given out each year to the engine builder who has accumulated the most points over the year. The cards are silver bordered and have a color photo on the front. Starting with Ernie Elliott in 1985, the cards are in order of the year that engine builder won the award.

COMPLETE SET (12)	6.00	15.00
1 A.E.Clevite Co.	.40	1.00
2 A.E.Clevite Co.	.40	1.00
3 Michigan Bearings	.40	1.00
4 McCord Gaskets	.40	1.00
5 A.E.Clevite Timing	.40	1.00
6 Ernie Elliott	.60	1.50
7 Randy Dorton	.60	1.50
8 Lou LaRosa	.60	1.50
9 David Evans	.60	1.50
10 Rick Wetzel	.60	1.50
11 Eddie Lanier	.60	1.50
12 Shelton Pittman	.60	1.50

1991 CM Handsome Harry

This 14-card set features one of the most popular drivers in Winston Cup history, Harry Gant. The cards feature a combination of shots of Harry in his early days and at home. Reportedly there were 25,000 sets produced. Also included is a Harry Gant promo card. The card is a cartoon and has the word PROMO in the upper right corner of the front of the card.

COMPLETE SET (14)	1.50	4.00
COMMON CARD (1-14)	.15	.40
P1 Harry Gant Promo	.75	2.00

1999 Coca-Cola Racing Family

These jumbo sized cards (measuring roughly 5 1/2" by 8") were issued in 1999 to promote the Coca-Cola Family of drivers. Each unnumbered card features the driver standing in front of his car along with a facsimile autograph printed across the front.

COMPLETE SET (6)	6.00	15.00
1 Jeff Burton	.60	1.50
2 Dale Earnhardt	4.00	10.00
3 Bill Elliott	.60	1.50
4 Dale Jarrett	.75	2.00
5 Kyle Petty	.40	1.00
6 Ricky Rudd	.50	1.25

2000 Coca-Cola Racing Family

These cards were available as two and four card perforated sheets sold with 16oz and 12 packs of Coca-Cola. They feature the drivers of the Coca-Cola Driving Family. Prices below reflect that of single cards. Uncut sections of cards are valued at the sum of its singles.

COMPLETE SET (16)	12.50	30.00
1 Jeff Burton	.50	1.25
2 Jeff Burton 1999 Coke 600 Win	.50	1.25
3 Dale Earnhardt	3.00	8.00
4 Dale Earnhardt 7 Time Champ	3.00	8.00
5 Bill Elliott	.60	1.50
6 Dale Jarrett	1.00	2.50
7 Dale Jarrett 1999 Cup Champion	1.00	2.50
8 Bobby Labonte	1.00	2.50
9 Bobby Labonte 1999 NAPA 500 Win	1.00	2.50
10 Steve Park	.50	1.25
11 Adam Petty	3.00	8.00
12 Kyle Petty	.60	1.50
13 Adam Petty Kyle Petty	3.00	8.00
14 Tony Stewart	1.25	3.00
15 Tony Stewart 1999 Rookie of the Year	1.25	3.00
16 Coca-Cola Racing Family	2.50	6.00

2001 Coca-Cola Econo Lodge

This set was released in 2001 and sponsored by Coke and Econo Lodge. Each card includes a scratch-off coupon on the back with a color driver photo on the front. The cards measure larger than standard size at roughly 3 1/2" by 5". Prices below reflect that of unscratched cards.

COMPLETE SET (4)	3.00	6.00
1 John Andretti	.50	1.25
2 Dale Jarrett	1.00	2.50
3 Kyle Petty	.60	1.50
4 John Andretti Dale Jarrett Kyle Petty	.75	2.00

2005 Coca-Cola Racing Family AutoZone

COMPLETE SET (8)	10.00	20.00
1 Kurt Busch	1.50	4.00
2 Justin Diercks	1.50	4.00
3 Jeff Fultz	.60	1.50
4 Kevin Harvick	2.50	6.00
5 Jeff Jefferson	.60	1.50
6 Jim Pettit	.60	1.50
7 Kyle Petty	1.00	2.50
8 Tony Stewart	2.50	6.00

2006 Press Pass Coca Cola AutoZone

COMPLETE SET (4)	6.00	15.00
DJ Dale Jarrett	2.00	5.00
GB Greg Biffle	1.25	3.00
MM Mark Martin	2.50	6.00
TS Tony Stewart	3.00	8.00

1993-96 Collector's Advantage Phone Cards

Collector's Advantage was the distributing agent for many different phone card companies, such as Planet Telecom, InterNet, Mecury Marketing, and Speed Call. Each card was produced as a promotion piece for a race day event. The cards were not numbered, nor part of a set, therefore we've cataloged them below in alphabetical order with the serial numbering and year of issue noted.

1 All-Pro Bumper to Bumper 300/4000 $6 1995	8.00	14.00
2 All-Pro Bumper to Bumper 300 Jumbo/400 $6 1995	50.00	70.00
3 Busch Lite 300/4000 $10 1996	10.00	18.00
4 Coca-Cola 600/4000 $6 1995	9.00	15.00
5 Coca-Cola 600 Jumbo/400 $6 1995	60.00	90.00
6 Goodwrench 200 and 400/4000 $5 1996	8.00	14.00
7 Goodwrench 200&400 Jumbo/50 $5 1996		
8 Hoosier 300/4000 $6 1996	9.00	15.00
9 Hoosier 300 Jumbo/50 $6 1996		
10 Hooters 500/1000 $5 1993	30.00	45.00
11 LugNut/4000 $6 1995	8.00	14.00
12 LugNut Jumbo/400 $6 1995		
13 NAPA 500/4000 $5 1995	8.00	14.00
14 NAPA 500 Jumbo/50 $5 1995		
15 Purolator 500/2500 $6 1995	8.00	14.00
16 Red Dog 300 Inaugural/4000 $6 1995	9.00	15.00
17 Red Dog 300 Inaugural Jumbo/400 $6 1995	50.00	80.00
18 UAW-GM 500/4000 $6 1995	8.00	14.00
19 UAW-GM 500 Jumbo/400 $6 1995	50.00	70.00

1997 Collector's Choice

The 1997 Collector's Choice set was issued in one series totalling 155 cards and featured the top names in NASCAR. The set contains the subsets: Drivers (1-50), Maximum MPH (51-100), Speedway Challenge (101-126), Team 3 (127-144) and Transitions (145-153). The cards were packaged 10 cards per pack, 36 packs per box and 12 boxes per case. Suggested retail price on a pack was 99 cents. This was the premiere issue of the Collector's Choice brand in racing by Upper Deck. Also included as an

insert in packs (1:4 packs) was a game piece for Upper Deck's Meet the Stars promotion. Each game piece was a multiple choice trivia card about racing. The collector would scratch of the box next to the answer that they felt best matched the question to determine if they won. Instant win game pieces were also inserted one in 72 packs. Winning game pieces could be sent into Upper Deck for a prize drawing. The Grand Prize was a chance to meet Jeff Gordon. Prizes for 2nd through 4th were for Upper Deck Authenticated shopping sprees. The 5th prize was two special Jeff Gordon Meet the Stars cards. The blank back cards measure 5" X 7"and are titled Dynamic Debut and Magic Memories. These two cards are priced at the bottom of the base set.

COMPLETE SET (155)	5.00	12.00
1 Rick Mast	.05	.15
2 Rusty Wallace	.50	1.25
3 Dale Earnhardt	1.00	2.50
4 Sterling Marlin	.20	.50
5 Terry Labonte	.20	.50
6 Mark Martin	.50	1.25
7 Geoff Bodine	.05	.15
8 Hut Stricklin	.05	.15
9 Lake Speed	.05	.15
10 Ricky Rudd	.20	.50
11 Brett Bodine	.05	.15
12 Derrike Cope	.05	.15
13 Bill Elliott	.25	.60
14 Bobby Hamilton	.05	.15
15 Wally Dallenbach	.05	.15
16 Ted Musgrave	.05	.15
17 Darrell Waltrip	.10	.30
18 Bobby Labonte	.40	1.00
19 Loy Allen	.05	.15
20 Morgan Shepherd	.05	.15
21 Michael Waltrip	.10	.30
22 Ward Burton	.10	.30
23 Jimmy Spencer	.05	.15
24 Jeff Gordon	.60	1.50
25 Ken Schrader	.05	.15
26 Kyle Petty	.10	.30
27 Bobby Hillin	.05	.15
28 Ernie Irvan	.10	.30
29 Jeff Purvis	.05	.15
30 Johnny Benson	.10	.30
31 Dave Marcis	.10	.30
32 Jeremy Mayfield	.10	.30
33 Robert Pressley	.05	.15
34 Jeff Burton	.10	.30
35 Joe Nemechek	.05	.15
36 Dale Jarrett	.40	1.00
37 John Andretti	.05	.15
38 Kenny Wallace	.05	.15
39 Elton Sawyer	.05	.15
40 Dick Trickle	.05	.15
41 Ricky Craven	.05	.15
42 Chad Little	.05	.15
43 Todd Bodine	.05	.15
44 David Green	.05	.15
45 Randy LaJoie	.05	.15
46 Larry Pearson	.05	.15
47 Jason Keller	.05	.15
48 Hermie Sadler	.05	.15
49 Mike McLaughlin	.05	.15
50 Tim Fedewa	.05	.15
51 Rick Mast's Car MM	.02	.10
52 Rusty Wallace's Car MM	.10	.30
53 Ricky Craven's Car MM	.02	.10
54 Sterling Marlin's Car MM	.05	.15
55 Terry Labonte's Car MM	.10	.30
56 Mark Martin's Car MM	.10	.30
57 Geoff Bodine's Car MM	.02	.10
58 Hut Stricklin's Car MM	.02	.10
59 Lake Speed's Car MM	.02	.10
60 Ricky Rudd's Car MM	.05	.15
61 Brett Bodine's Car MM	.02	.10
62 Derrike Cope's Car MM	.02	.10
63 Bill Elliott's Car MM	.10	.30
64 Bobby Hamilton's Car MM	.02	.10
65 Wally Dallenbach's Car MM	.02	.10
66 Ted Musgrave's Car MM	.02	.10
67 Darrell Waltrip's Car MM	.05	.15
68 Bobby Labonte's Car MM	.10	.30
69 Loy Allen's Car MM	.02	.10
70 Morgan Shepherd's Car MM	.02	.10
71 Michael Waltrip's Car MM	.05	.15
72 Ward Burton's Car MM	.02	.10
73 Jimmy Spencer's Car MM	.02	.10
74 Jeff Gordon's Car MM	.25	.60
75 Ken Schrader's Car MM	.02	.10
76 Kyle Petty's Car MM	.05	.15
77 Bobby Hillin's Car MM	.02	.10
78 Ernie Irvan's Car MM	.05	.15
79 Jeff Purvis's Car MM	.02	.10
80 Johnny Benson's Car MM	.02	.10
81 Dave Marcis's Car MM	.05	.15
82 Jeremy Mayfield's Car MM	.05	.15
83 Robert Pressley's Car MM	.02	.10
84 Jeff Burton's Car MM	.05	.15
85 Joe Nemechek's Car MM	.02	.10
86 Dale Jarrett's Car MM	.10	.30
87 John Andretti's Car MM	.02	.10
88 Kenny Wallace's Car MM	.02	.10
89 Elton Sawyer's Car MM	.02	.10
90 Dick Trickle's Car MM	.02	.10
91 Chad Little's Car MM	.02	.10
92 Todd Bodine's Car MM	.02	.10
93 David Green's Car MM	.02	.10
94 Randy LaJoie's Car MM	.02	.10
95 Larry Pearson's Car MM	.02	.10
96 Jason Keller's Car MM	.02	.10
97 Hermie Sadler's Car MM	.02	.10
98 Mike McLaughlin's Car MM	.02	.10
99 Tim Fedewa's Car MM	.02	.10
100 Patty Moise's Car MM	.02	.10
101 Jeff Gordon SC	.30	.75
102 Rusty Wallace SC	.25	.60
103 Sterling Marlin SC	.10	.30
104 Terry Labonte SC	.10	.30
105 Mark Martin SC	.25	.60
106 Ricky Rudd SC	.10	.30
107 Ted Musgrave SC	.02	.10
108 Michael Waltrip SC	.10	.30
109 Dale Jarrett SC	.20	.50
110 Ernie Irvan SC	.05	.15
111 Bill Elliott SC	.10	.30
112 Ken Schrader SC	.02	.10
113 Bobby Labonte SC	.20	.50
114 Kyle Petty SC	.05	.15
115 Ricky Craven SC	.02	.10
116 Bobby Hamilton SC	.02	.10
117 Johnny Benson SC	.10	.30
118 Jeremy Mayfield SC	.10	.30
119 Darrell Waltrip SC	.05	.15
120 Junior Johnson SC	.02	.10
121 Glen Wood SC	.02	.10
122 Benny Parsons SC	.05	.15
123 Bobby Allison SC	.05	.15
124 Ned Jarrett SC	.05	.15
125 Cale Yarborough SC	.05	.15
126 Richard Petty SC	.20	.50
127 Jeff Gordon T3	.30	.75
128 Jeff Gordon T3	.30	.75
129 Jeff Gordon's Car T3	.25	.60
130 Terry Labonte T3	.10	.30
131 Terry Labonte T3	.10	.30
132 Terry Labonte's Car T3	.10	.30
133 Ken Schrader T3	.02	.10
134 Ken Schrader T3	.02	.10
135 Ken Schrader's Car T3	.02	.10
136 Mark Martin T3	.25	.60
137 Mark Martin T3	.25	.60
138 Mark Martin's Car T3	.10	.30
139 Ted Musgrave T3	.02	.10
140 Ted Musgrave T3	.02	.10
141 Ted Musgrave's Car T3	.02	.10
142 Jeff Burton T3	.05	.15
143 Jeff Burton T3	.05	.15
144 Jeff Burton's Car T3	.02	.10
145 Rusty Wallace TRA	.25	.60
146 Ricky Craven TRA	.02	.10
147 Ricky Rudd TRA	.10	.30
148 Bill Elliott TRA	.10	.30
149 Joe Nemechek TRA	.02	.10
150 Brett Bodine TRA	.02	.10
151 Darrell Waltrip TRA	.05	.15
152 Geoff Bodine TRA	.02	.10
153 Dave Marcis TRA	.05	.15
154 Jeff Gordon CL	.25	.60
155 Rusty Wallace CL	.10	.30
NNO Jeff Gordon 5X7 DD	2.00	5.00
NNO Jeff Gordon 5X7 MM	2.00	5.00

1997 Collector's Choice Speedecals

This 48-card insert set features driver's cars on stickers. The stickers were randomly inserted one in three packs.

COMPLETE SET (48)	10.00	20.00
S1 Rick Mast's Car	.10	.25
S2 Joe Nemechek's Car	.10	.25
S3 Rusty Wallace's Car	.75	2.00
S4 Rusty Wallace's Helmet	.75	2.00
S5 Bill Elliott's Car	.40	1.00
S6 Bill Elliott's Helmet	.40	1.00
S7 Sterling Marlin's Car	.30	.75
S8 Sterling Marlin's Helmet	.30	.75
S9 Terry Labonte's Car	.30	.75
S10 Terry Labonte's Helmet	.30	.75
S11 Mark Martin's Car	.75	2.00
S12 Mark Martin's Helmet	.75	2.00
S13 Bobby Hamilton's Car	.10	.25
S14 Derrike Cope's Car	.10	.25
S15 Ricky Craven's Car	.10	.25
S16 Ricky Craven's Helmet	.10	.25
S17 Lake Speed's Car	.10	.25
S18 Morgan Shepherd's Car	.10	.25
S19 Ricky Rudd's Car	.30	.75
S20 Ricky Rudd's Helmet	.30	.75
S21 Kyle Petty's Car	.20	.50
S22 Kyle Petty's Helmet	.20	.50
S23 Johnny Benson's Car	.20	.50
S24 Johnny Benson's Helmet	.20	.50
S25 Ernie Irvan's Car	.20	.50
S26 Kenny Wallace's Car	.10	.25
S27 Jeff Burton's Car	.20	.50
S28 Jeff Burton's Helmet	.20	.50
S29 Ken Schrader's Car	.10	.25
S30 Dave Marcis's Car	.20	.50
S31 Ted Musgrave's Car	.10	.25
S32 Ted Musgrave's Helmet	.10	.25
S33 Darrell Waltrip's Car	.20	.50
S34 Darrell Waltrip's Helmet	.20	.50
S35 Bobby Labonte's Car	.60	1.50
S36 Bobby Labonte's Helmet	.60	1.50
S37 Dale Jarrett's Car	.60	1.50
S38 Dale Jarrett's Helmet	.60	1.50
S39 Jeremy Mayfield's Car	.20	.50
S40 Jeremy Mayfield's Car	.20	.50
S41 Michael Waltrip's Car	.20	.50
S42 Michael Waltrip's Helmet	.20	.50
S43 Ward Burton's Car	.20	.50
S44 Wally Dallenbach's Car	.10	.25
S45 Wally Dallenbach's Helmet	.10	.25
S46 Jimmy Spencer's Car	.10	.25
S47 Jeff Gordon's Car	1.00	2.50
S48 Jeff Gordon's Helmet	1.00	2.50

1997 Collector's Choice Triple Force

This 30-card insert set features 10 groups of three cards. Each group of three cards was given a letter designation. Taking each of the three interlocking die-cut cards a collector could put them together like a puzzle. The cards together formed a photo across all three cards. The odds of pulling a Triple Force card were one in eleven packs.

COMPLETE SET (30)	30.00	80.00
A1 Dale Jarrett	3.00	8.00
A2 Ernie Irvan	1.00	2.50
A3 Dale Jarrett	3.00	8.00
B1 Ted Musgrave	.50	1.25
B2 Jeff Burton	1.00	2.50
B3 Mark Martin	4.00	10.00
C1 Johnny Benson	1.00	2.50
C2 Ricky Craven	.50	1.25
C3 Jeremy Mayfield	1.00	2.50
D1 Terry Labonte	1.50	4.00
D2 Terry Labonte	1.50	4.00
D3 Terry Labonte	1.50	4.00
E1 Jimmy Spencer	.50	1.25
E2 Dale Jarrett	3.00	8.00
E3 Michael Waltrip	1.00	2.50
F1 Jeff Gordon	5.00	12.00
F2 Terry Labonte	1.50	4.00
F3 Ken Schrader	.50	1.25
G1 Terry Labonte	1.50	4.00
G2 Jeff Gordon	5.00	12.00
G3 Jeff Gordon	5.00	12.00
H1 Bobby Hamilton	.50	1.25
H2 Rusty Wallace	4.00	10.00
H3 Geoff Bodine	.50	1.25
I1 Ricky Craven	.50	1.25
I2 Ernie Irvan	1.00	2.50
I3 Dale Jarrett	3.00	8.00
J1 Mark Martin	4.00	10.00
J2 Rusty Wallace	4.00	10.00
J3 Johnny Benson	1.00	2.50

1997 Collector's Choice Upper Deck 500

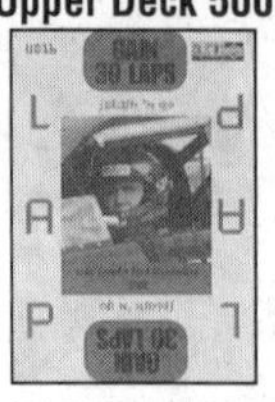

The cards from this 90-card insert set make up pieces to a game. The cards carry driver or car photos. Each card is given a value of laps, track position, or penalty. Similar to a card game the collector plays their cards until one player has accumulated 500 laps. The cards were inserted one per pack.

COMPLETE SET (90)	8.00	20.00
UD1 Dale Earnhardt	1.00	2.50
UD2 Rusty Wallace	.50	1.25
UD3 Rusty Wallace's Car	.10	.30
UD4 Robin Pemberton	.05	.10
UD5 Sterling Marlin	.20	.50
UD6 Sterling Marlin's Car	.05	.15
UD7 Terry Labonte	.20	.50
UD8 Terry Labonte's Car	.10	.30
UD9 Mark Martin	.50	1.25
UD10 Mark Martin's Car	.10	.30
UD11 Steve Hmiel	.05	.10
UD12 Geoff Bodine	.05	.15
UD13 Geoff Bodine's Car	.05	.10
UD14 Hut Stricklin	.05	.15
UD15 Hut Stricklin's Car	.05	.10
UD16 Lake Speed	.05	.15
UD17 Lake Speed's Car	.05	.10
UD18 Ricky Rudd	.20	.50
UD19 Ricky Rudd's Car	.05	.15
UD20 Brett Bodine	.05	.15
UD21 Brett Bodine's Car	.05	.10
UD22 Derrike Cope	.05	.15
UD23 Derrike Cope's Car	.05	.10
UD24 Bobby Allison	.05	.15
UD25 Bill Elliott	.25	.60
UD26 Bill Elliott's Car	.10	.30
UD27 Bobby Hamilton	.05	.15
UD28 Bobby Hamilton's Car	.05	.10
UD29 Richard Petty	.20	.50
UD30 Wally Dallenbach	.05	.15
UD31 Wally Dallenbach's Car	.05	.10
UD32 Ted Musgrave	.05	.15
UD33 Ted Musgrave's Car	.05	.10
UD34 Darrell Waltrip	.10	.30
UD35 Darrell Waltrip's Car	.05	.15
UD36 Bobby Labonte	.40	1.00
UD37 Bobby Labonte's Car	.10	.30
UD38 Loy Allen	.05	.15
UD39 Loy Allen's Car	.05	.10
UD40 Morgan Shepherd	.05	.15
UD41 Morgan Shepherd's Car	.05	.10
UD42 Michael Waltrip	.10	.30
UD43 Michael Waltrip's Car	.05	.15
UD44 Ward Burton	.10	.30
UD45 Ward Burton's Car	.05	.10
UD46 Jimmy Spencer	.05	.15
UD47 Jimmy Spencer's Car	.05	.10
UD48 Jeff Gordon	.60	1.50
UD49 Jeff Gordon's Car	.25	.60
UD50 Ray Evernham	.05	.15
UD51 Rick Hendrick	.05	.10

D52 Ken Schrader	.05	.15
D53 Ken Schrader's Car	.05	.10
D54 Kyle Petty	.10	.30
D55 Kyle Petty's Car	.05	.15
D56 Bobby Hillin	.05	.15
D57 Bobby Hillin's Car	.05	.10
D58 Ernie Irvan	.10	.30
D59 Ernie Irvan's Car	.05	.15
D60 Jeff Purvis	.05	.15
D61 Jeff Purvis's Car	.05	.10
D62 Johnny Benson	.10	.30
D63 Johnny Benson's Car	.05	.10
D64 Dave Marcis	.10	.30
D65 Dave Marcis's Car	.05	.15
D66 Jeremy Mayfield	.10	.30
D67 Jeremy Mayfield's Car	.05	.15
D68 Cale Yarborough	.05	.15
D69 Robert Pressley	.05	.15
D70 Robert Pressley's Car	.05	.10
D71 Jeff Burton	.10	.30
D72 Jeff Burton's Car	.05	.15
D73 Joe Nemechek	.05	.15
D74 Joe Nemechek's Car	.05	.10
D75 Dale Jarrett	.40	1.00
D76 Dale Jarrett's Car	.10	.30
D77 John Andretti	.05	.15
D78 John Andretti's Car	.05	.10
D79 Kenny Wallace	.05	.15
D80 Kenny Wallace's Car	.05	.10
D81 Elton Sawyer	.05	.15
D82 Elton Sawyer's Car	.05	.10
D83 Dick Trickle	.05	.15
D84 Dick Trickle's Car	.05	.10
D85 Ricky Craven	.05	.15
D86 Ricky Craven's Car	.05	.10
D87 Chad Little	.05	.15
D88 Chad Little's Car	.05	.10
D89 Rick Mast	.05	.15
D90 Rick Mast's Car	.05	.10

1997 Collector's Choice Victory Circle

he top 10 active career victory leaders was the cus of this 10-card insert set. The cards feature red il stamping on the front and were inserted one in fty packs.

OMPLETE SET (10)	50.00	120.00
C1 Darrell Waltrip	2.00	5.00
C2 Dale Earnhardt	15.00	40.00
C3 Rusty Wallace	8.00	20.00
C4 Bill Elliott	4.00	10.00
C5 Mark Martin	8.00	20.00
C6 Geoff Bodine	1.00	2.50
C7 Terry Labonte	3.00	8.00
C8 Ricky Rudd	3.00	8.00
C9 Jeff Gordon	10.00	25.00
C10 Ernie Irvan	2.00	5.00

1998 Collector's Choice

he 1998 Collector's Choice set was issued in one eries totalling 117 cards and featured the top names NASCAR. The set consists of five topical subsets: peed Merchants (1-36), Rollin' Thunder (37-72), uture Stock (73-87), Perils of the Pits (88-98), and rophy Dash (99-112). The cards were packaged 14 ards per pack and 36 packs per box. Suggested tail price on a pack was $1.29.

OMPLETE SET (117)	5.00	12.00
OBBY BOX	20.00	50.00
ETAIL BOX	15.00	40.00
Morgan Shepherd	.05	.15
Rusty Wallace	.40	1.00
Dale Earnhardt	.75	2.00
Sterling Marlin	.15	.40
Terry Labonte	.15	.40
Mark Martin	.40	1.00
Geoff Bodine	.05	.15
Hut Stricklin	.05	.15
Lake Speed	.05	.15
0 Ricky Rudd	.15	.40
1 Brett Bodine	.05	.15
2 Dale Jarrett	.30	.75
3 Bill Elliott	.20	.50
4 Bobby Hamilton	.05	.15
5 Wally Dallenbach	.05	.15
6 Ted Musgrave	.05	.15
7 Darrell Waltrip	.08	.25
8 Bobby Labonte	.30	.75
9 Steve Grissom	.05	.15
0 Rick Mast	.05	.15
1 Michael Waltrip	.08	.25
2 Ward Burton	.08	.25
3 Jimmy Spencer	.05	.15
4 Jeff Gordon	.50	1.25
5 Ricky Craven	.05	.15
6 Kyle Petty	.08	.25
7 Kenny Wallace	.05	.15
8 Ernie Irvan	.08	.25
9 David Green	.05	.15
0 Johnny Benson	.08	.25
1 Mike Skinner	.05	.15
2 Jeremy Mayfield	.08	.25
3 Ken Schrader	.05	.15
34 Jeff Burton	.15	.40
35 Robby Gordon	.05	.15
36 Derrike Cope	.05	.15
37 Morgan Shepherd's Car	.05	.15
38 Rusty Wallace's Car	.15	.40
39 Dale Earnhardt's Car	.30	.75
40 Sterling Marlin's Car	.05	.15
41 Terry Labonte's Car	.05	.15
42 Mark Martin's Car	.15	.40
43 Geoff Bodine's Car	.01	.05
44 Hut Stricklin's Car	.01	.05
45 Lake Speed's Car	.01	.05
46 Ricky Rudd's Car	.05	.15
47 Brett Bodine's Car	.01	.05
48 Dale Jarrett's Car	.08	.25
49 Bill Elliott's Car	.05	.15
50 Bobby Hamilton's Car	.01	.05
51 Wally Dallenbach's Car	.01	.05
52 Ted Musgrave's Car	.01	.05
53 Darrell Waltrip's Car	.05	.15
54 Bobby Labonte's Car	.08	.25
55 Steve Grissom's Car	.01	.05
56 Rick Mast's Car	.01	.05
57 Michael Waltrip's Car	.05	.15
58 Ward Burton's Car	.05	.15
59 Jimmy Spencer's Car	.01	.05
60 Jeff Gordon's Car	.20	.50
61 Ricky Craven's Car	.01	.05
62 Kyle Petty's Car	.05	.15
63 Kenny Wallace's Car	.01	.05
64 Ernie Irvan's Car	.05	.15
65 David Green's Car	.01	.05
66 Johnny Benson's Car	.01	.05
67 Mike Skinner's Car	.01	.05
68 Jeremy Mayfield's Car	.05	.15
69 Ken Schrader's Car	.01	.05
70 Jeff Burton's Car	.05	.15
71 Robby Gordon's Car	.01	.05
72 Derrike Cope's Car	.01	.05
73 Jeff Burton FS	.08	.25
74 Robby Gordon FS	.01	.05
75 Mike Skinner FS	.01	.05
76 Johnny Benson FS	.01	.05
77 Ricky Craven FS	.01	.05
78 Ward Burton FS	.05	.15
79 Jeremy Mayfield FS	.05	.15
80 Steve Grissom FS	.01	.05
81 John Andretti FS	.01	.05
82 David Green FS	.01	.05
83 Bobby Labonte FS	.15	.40
84 Kenny Wallace FS	.01	.05
85 Mike Wallace FS	.01	.05
86 Joe Nemechek FS	.01	.05
87 Chad Little FS	.05	.15
88 Jeff Gordon PP	.25	.60
89 Terry Labonte PP	.08	.25
90 Ricky Craven PP	.01	.05
91 Kyle Petty PP	.05	.15
92 Dale Jarrett PP	.15	.40
93 Rusty Wallace PP	.20	.50
94 Ricky Rudd PP	.08	.25
95 Bobby Labonte PP	.15	.40
96 Bobby Hamilton PP	.01	.05
97 Mark Martin PP	.20	.50
98 Jeff Gordon TD	.25	.60
99 Mark Martin TD	.20	.50
100 Terry Labonte TD	.08	.25
101 Dale Jarrett TD	.15	.40
102 Jeff Burton TD	.08	.25
103 Dale Earnhardt TD	.40	1.00
104 Bobby Hamilton TD	.01	.05
105 Ricky Rudd TD	.08	.25
106 Michael Waltrip TD	.05	.15
107 Jeremy Mayfield TD	.05	.15
108 Ted Musgrave TD	.01	.05
109 Bill Elliott TD	.08	.25
110 Johnny Benson TD	.05	.15
111 Rusty Wallace TD	.20	.50
112 Darrell Waltrip TD	.05	.15
113 Checklist	.01	.05
114 Checklist	.01	.05
115 Checklist	.01	.05
116 Checklist	.01	.05
117 Checklist	.01	.05

1998 Collector's Choice Star Quest

This 50-card set is a four-tier insert set that features autographed cards in its fourth tier. The Qualifier Tier (first) cards were inserted into packs at a ratio of 1:3. The Pole Tier (second) cards were inserted into packs at a ratio of 1:11. The Win Tier (third) cards were inserted into packs at a ratio of 1:71. The Championship Tier (fourth) autographed cards were inserted into packs at a ratio of 1:250.

COMP.1-STAR SET (20)	7.50	15.00
SQ1 Brett Bodine	.20	.50
SQ2 Jimmy Spencer's Car	.08	.25
SQ3 Mike Wallace	.20	.50
SQ4 Bobby Labonte	1.25	3.00
SQ5 Morgan Shepherd	.20	.50
SQ6 Derrike Cope's Car	.08	.25
SQ7 Kenny Wallace	.20	.50
SQ8 Chad Little	.20	.50
SQ9 Hut Stricklin	.20	.50
SQ10 Lake Speed's Car	.08	.25
SQ11 Ricky Craven	.40	1.00
SQ12 Steve Grissom	.20	.50
SQ13 Dick Trickle's Car	.08	.25
SQ14 Rick Mast	.20	.50
SQ15 David Green's Car	.08	.25
SQ16 Wally Dallenbach	.20	.50
SQ17 Joe Nemechek	.20	.50
SQ18 Ken Schrader's Car	.08	.25
SQ19 Geoff Bodine's Car	.08	.25
SQ20 Bobby Hamilton's Car	.08	.25
SQ21 Mike Skinner	.50	1.25
SQ22 Michael Waltrip	1.00	2.50
SQ23 Johnny Benson	1.00	2.50
SQ24 Ward Burton	1.00	2.50
SQ25 Robby Gordon's Car	.25	.60
SQ26 Dale Earnhardt	10.00	25.00
SQ27 Ted Musgrave's Car	.25	.60
SQ28 Jeremy Mayfield's Car	.50	1.25
SQ29 Mark Martin's Car	2.00	5.00
SQ30 Sterling Marlin	1.50	4.00
SQ31 Ernie Irvan	4.00	10.00
SQ32 Ricky Rudd	6.00	15.00
SQ33 Jeff Burton	6.00	15.00
SQ34 Rusty Wallace	12.00	30.00
SQ35 Darrell Waltrip	4.00	10.00
SQ36 Jeff Gordon	20.00	50.00
SQ37 Terry Labonte	8.00	20.00
SQ38 Bill Elliott	8.00	20.00
SQ39 Dale Jarrett	10.00	25.00
SQ40 Kyle Petty	4.00	10.00
SQ41 Jeff Gordon AUTO	75.00	150.00
SQ42 Bill Elliott AUTO	30.00	60.00
SQ43 Dale Jarrett AUTO	20.00	50.00
SQ44 Kyle Petty AUTO	20.00	40.00
SQ45 Bobby Labonte AUTO	20.00	50.00
SQ46 Mark Martin AUTO	15.00	40.00
SQ47 Geoff Bodine AUTO	15.00	30.00
SQ48 Rusty Wallace AUTO	30.00	60.00
SQ49 Robby Gordon AUTO	15.00	30.00
SQ50 Ted Musgrave AUTO	15.00	30.00

1998 Collector's Choice CC600

The cards from this 90-card insert set make up pieces to a game. The cards carry driver or car photos. Each card is given a value of laps, track position, or penalty. Similar to a card game the collector plays their cards until one player has accumulated 600 laps. The cards were inserted one per pack.

COMPLETE SET (90)	5.00	12.00
CC1 Play Card	.01	.05
CC2 Play Card	.01	.05
CC3 Play Card	.01	.05
CC4 Play Card	.01	.05
CC5 Play Card	.01	.05
CC6 Morgan Shepherd	.05	.15
CC7 Rusty Wallace	.40	1.00
CC8 Sterling Marlin	.15	.40
CC9 Terry Labonte	.15	.40
CC10 Mark Martin	.40	1.00
CC11 Geoff Bodine	.05	.15
CC12 Hut Stricklin	.05	.15
CC13 Lake Speed	.05	.15
CC14 Ricky Rudd	.15	.40
CC15 Brett Bodine	.05	.15
CC16 Dale Jarrett	.30	.75
CC17 Bill Elliott	.20	.50
CC18 Bobby Hamilton	.05	.15
CC19 Wally Dallenbach	.05	.15
CC20 Ted Musgrave	.05	.15
CC21 Darrell Waltrip	.10	.25
CC22 Bobby Labonte	.30	.75
CC23 Steve Grissom	.05	.15
CC24 Rick Mast	.05	.15
CC25 Michael Waltrip	.10	.25
CC26 Ward Burton	.10	.25
CC27 Jimmy Spencer	.05	.15
CC28 Ricky Craven	.05	.15
CC29 Kyle Petty	.10	.25
CC30 Kenny Wallace	.05	.15
CC31 Ernie Irvan	.10	.25
CC32 David Green	.05	.15
CC33 Johnny Benson	.10	.25
CC34 Mike Skinner	.05	.15
CC35 Jeremy Mayfield	.10	.25
CC36 Ken Schrader	.05	.15
CC37 Jeff Burton	.15	.40
CC38 Robby Gordon	.05	.15
CC39 Derrike Cope	.05	.15
CC40 Morgan Shepherd's Car	.01	.05
CC41 Rusty Wallace's Car	.15	.40
CC42 Sterling Marlin	.15	.40
CC43 Mark Martin	.40	1.00
CC44 Geoff Bodine	.05	.15
CC45 Hut Stricklin	.05	.15
CC46 Lake Speed's Car	.01	.05
CC47 Ricky Rudd's Car	.05	.15
CC48 Brett Bodine	.05	.15
CC49 Dale Jarrett's Car	.10	.25
CC50 Bill Elliott's Car	.10	.25
CC51 Bobby Hamilton	.05	.15
CC52 Wally Dallenbach	.05	.15
CC53 Ted Musgrave's Car	.01	.05
CC54 Darrell Waltrip	.10	.25
CC55 Bobby Labonte's Car	.10	.25
CC56 Steve Grissom's Car	.01	.05
CC57 Rick Mast's Car	.01	.05
CC58 Michael Waltrip	.10	.25
CC59 Ward Burton	.10	.25
CC60 Jimmy Spencer's Car	.01	.05
CC61 Ricky Craven's Car	.01	.05
CC62 Kyle Petty	.10	.25
CC63 Kenny Wallace	.05	.15
CC64 Ernie Irvan's Car	.05	.15
CC65 David Green's Car	.01	.05
CC66 Johnny Benson's Car	.01	.05
CC67 Mike Skinner	.05	.15
CC68 Jeremy Mayfield's Car	.05	.15
CC69 Ken Schrader's Car	.01	.05
CC70 Jeff Burton's Car	.05	.15
CC71 Robby Gordon	.05	.15
CC72 Derrike Cope	.05	.15
CC73 Morgan Shepherd	.05	.15
CC74 Rusty Wallace's Car	.15	.40
CC75 Sterling Marlin's Car	.05	.15
CC76 Mark Martin	.40	1.00
CC77 Geoff Bodine's Car	.01	.05
CC78 Hut Stricklin	.05	.15
CC79 Lake Speed	.05	.15
CC80 Ricky Rudd's Car	.05	.15
CC81 Brett Bodine	.05	.15
CC82 Dale Jarrett	.30	.75
CC83 Bill Elliott's Car	.05	.15
CC84 Bobby Hamilton	.05	.15
CC85 Wally Dallenbach	.05	.15
CC86 Ted Musgrave's Car	.01	.05
CC87 Darrell Waltrip	.10	.25
CC88 Bobby Labonte's Car	.10	.25
CC89 Steve Grissom	.05	.15
CC90 Rick Mast	.05	.15

1992 Coyote Rookies

This 14-card set features Winston Cup Rookies of the Year from 1980-1991. The first card is a checklist, then the next 12 cards are in order of ROY winner starting with Jody Ridley in 1980 and finishing with Bobby Hamilton in 1991. The final card in the set is a promo/checklist card with Jody Ridley on the front.

COMPLETE SET (14)	3.00	8.00
1 Checklist Card	.10	.25
2 Jody Ridley	.15	.40
3 Ron Bouchard	.15	.40
4 Geoff Bodine	.15	.40
5 Sterling Marlin	.40	1.00
6 Rusty Wallace	.60	1.50
7 Ken Schrader	.25	.60
8 Alan Kulwicki	.50	1.25
9 Davey Allison	.60	1.50
10 Ken Bouchard	.15	.40
11 Dick Trickle	.15	.40
12 Rob Moroso	.15	.40
13 Bobby Hamilton	.25	.60
14 Jody Ridley Promo/CL	.15	.40

1995 Crown Jewels Promos

These Promo cards were issued to preview the 1995 Crown Jewels release. The cards are unnumbered and each was serial numbered as noted below.

PD1 Jeff Gordon Diamond/3000	15.00	35.00
PE1 Jeff Gordon Emerald/6000	10.00	25.00
PR1 Jeff Gordon Ruby/12,000	4.00	10.00

1995 Crown Jewels

The 80-card Ruby base set is Wheels Race Cards inaugural Crown Jewels brand issue. The cards, printed on 24 pt. paper stock, came five cards per pack, 24 packs per box and 12 boxes per case. There were two methods of distribution of the product; a hobby only version, that was limited to 2200 cases and a special retail version. The set includes subsets of Winston Cup Drivers (1-30), Winston Cup Driver/Owners (31-35), Winston Cup Crew Chiefs (36-40), Winston Cup Cars (41-53), Busch Drivers (54-63), Headliners (64-73) and Win Cards (74-80). Three redemption programs were included as inserts. All three, the Gemstone game cards, the Dual Jewels redemption game and the E-Race to Win cards expired 12/31/95. There were also three individual inserts randomly seeded in packs. Sterling Marlin Back-to-Back Daytona winner could be found one in 288 packs. The Chad Little Goody's 300 winner autographed card was seeded one in 576. Finally a two sided card that featured Jeff Gordon on one side and Terry Labonte on the other was randomly inserted at a rate of one in 288 packs.

COMPLETE RUBY SET (80)	8.00	20.00
COMP.E-RACE TO WIN SET (10)	.25	.50
DUAL JEWELS REDEMP.CARDS	.02	.10
1 Dale Earnhardt	1.25	3.00
2 Jeff Gordon	.75	2.00
3 Mark Martin	.60	1.50
4 Rusty Wallace	.60	1.50
5 Ricky Rudd	.25	.60
6 Terry Labonte	.25	.60
7 Bobby Labonte	.50	1.25
8 Ken Schrader	.07	.20
9 Sterling Marlin	.25	.60
10 Darrell Waltrip	.15	.40
11 Geoff Bodine	.07	.20
12 Kyle Petty	.15	.40
13 Dale Jarrett	.50	1.25
14 Ernie Irvan	.15	.40
15 Bill Elliott	.30	.75
16 Morgan Shepherd	.07	.20
17 Michael Waltrip	.15	.40
18 Ted Musgrave	.07	.20
19 Lake Speed	.07	.20
20 Jimmy Spencer	.07	.20
21 Brett Bodine	.07	.20
22 Joe Nemechek	.07	.20
23 Steve Grissom	.07	.20
24 Derrike Cope	.07	.20
25 John Andretti	.07	.20
26 Kenny Bernstein	.07	.20
27 Joe Gibbs	.15	.40
28 Larry McClure	.02	.10
29 Travis Carter	.02	.10
30 Junior Johnson	.07	.20
31 Geoff Bodine	.07	.20
32 Ricky Rudd	.25	.60
33 Darrell Waltrip	.15	.40
34 Joe Nemechek	.07	.20
35 Bill Elliott	.30	.75
36 Robin Pemberton	.02	.10
37 Jimmy Makar	.02	.10
38 Bill Ingle	.02	.10
39 Robbie Loomis	.02	.10
40 Buddy Parrott	.02	.10
41 Ken Schrader's Car	.02	.10
42 Bobby Labonte's Car	.15	.40
43 Joe Nemechek's Car	.02	.10
44 Derrike Cope's Car	.02	.10
45 Brett Bodine's Car	.02	.10
46 Kyle Petty's Car	.07	.20
47 Hut Stricklin's Car	.02	.10
48 Jimmy Spencer's Car	.02	.10
49 Ricky Rudd's Transporter	.02	.10
50 Kyle Petty's Transporter	.02	.10
51 Darrell Waltrip's Transporter	.02	.10
52 Terry Labonte's Transporter	.07	.20
53 Geoff Bodine's Transporter	.02	.10
54 David Green	.07	.20
55 Tommy Houston	.07	.20
56 Johnny Benson	.15	.40
57 Chad Little	.07	.20
58 Kenny Wallace	.07	.20
59 Hermie Sadler	.07	.20
60 Jason Keller	.07	.20
61 Bobby Dotter	.07	.20
62 Stevie Reeves	.07	.20
63 Mike McLaughlin	.07	.20
64 Dale Earnhardt's Car	.60	1.50
Darrell Waltrip's Cars CJT		
65 Bill Elliott w/Car CJT	.15	.40
66 Sterling Marlin CJT	.15	.40
67 Chad Little CJT	.07	.20
Mark Rypien		
68 Jeff Gordon CJT	.40	1.00
Terry Labonte		
69 Ernie Irvan CJT	.07	.20
70 Dale Jarrett CJT	.25	.60
71 Bobby Labonte CJT	.25	.60
72 Kyle Petty CJT	.07	.20
73 Jeff Gordon CJT	.30	.75
Terry Labonte's Car		
74 Sterling Marlin RW	.15	.40
75 Jeff Gordon RW	.40	1.00
76 Terry Labonte RW	.15	.40
77 Jeff Gordon RW	.40	1.00
78 Sterling Marlin RW	.15	.40
79 Checklist (1-73)	.02	.10
80 Checklist (74-80/Inserts)	.02	.10
DT1 Jeff Gordon DT	15.00	40.00
Terry Labonte DT		
GS1 Chad Little AUTO	15.00	40.00
SM1 Sterling Marlin BB	15.00	40.00

1995 Crown Jewels Diamond

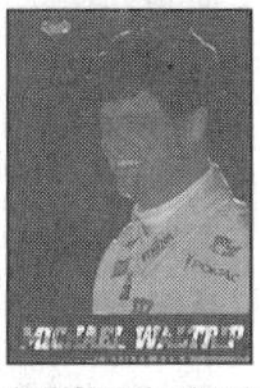

The Crown Jewels Diamond cards are a parallel of the 80-card Ruby base set. These cards were randomly inserted at a rate of one per 13 hobby packs. The cards are sequentially numbered to 599 and feature all-foil and embossed technology.

COMPLETE SET (80)	150.00	300.00
*DIAMOND: 5X TO 12X RUBYS		

1995 Crown Jewels Emerald

The Crown Jewels Emerald cards are a parallel of the 80-card Ruby base set. The cards were randomly inserted at a rate of one per 9 packs of Crown Jewels. The cards are sequentially numbered to 1199 and feature all-foil technology.

COMPLETE SET (80)	125.00	250.00
*EMERALD: 4X TO 10X RUBYS		

1995 Crown Jewels Sapphire

The Crown Jewels Sapphire cards are an embossed parallel of the 80-card Ruby base set. Sapphire sets were available through the Gemstones interactive redemption game. Collectors who found the 11 letters that spelled C-R-O-W-N J-E-W-E-L-S were able to send those letters in for one of the 2,500 Sapphire sets. Each Sapphire set came in a felt-lined black "Jewel" box. The game expired March 31, 1996.

COMPLETE SET (80)	15.00	40.00
*SAPPHIRE: 2X TO 4X RUBYS		

1995 Crown Jewels Dual Jewels

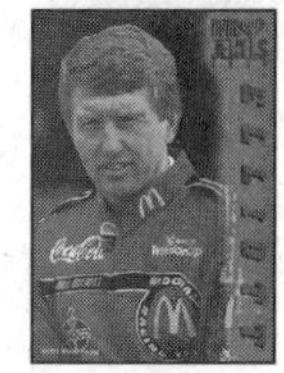

The six-card Ruby insert set features double-sided pairings of the top Winston Cup drivers. The Ruby Dual Jewel cards were inserted one per 48 packs in Crown Jewels. Emerald and Diamond parallels were produced as well and randomly inserted in packs. There was also Dual Jewels redemption game. If you had 2 Ruby, 2 Emerald, and 2 Diamond Dual Jewels redemption cards, you could redeem them for an uncut sheet of the six Dual Jewels cards in Sapphire foil stamping. The expiration of the cards was 12/31/95.

COMPLETE RUBY SET (6)	30.00	80.00
*EMERALDS: .4X TO 1X BASIC INSERTS		
*DIAMONDS: .6X TO 1.5X BASIC INSERTS		
UNCUT SAPPHIRE SHEET	60.00	150.00
DJ1 Dale Earnhardt	10.00	25.00
Jeff Gordon		
DJ2 Rusty Wallace	6.00	15.00
Dale Jarrett		
DJ3 Bill Elliott	6.00	15.00
Terry Labonte		
DJ4 Mark Martin	6.00	15.00
Ernie Irvan		
DJ5 Kyle Petty	3.00	8.00
Ricky Rudd		
DJ6 Dale Earnhardt	10.00	25.00
Dave Marcis		

1995 Crown Jewels Signature Gems

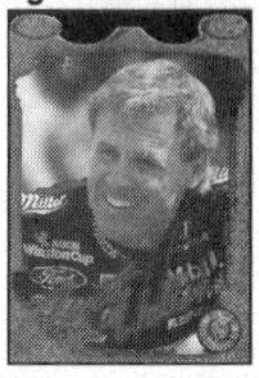

Each of the seven die-cut, micro-etched insert cards feature a top Winston Cup star. The Signature Gems cards were inserted at a rate of one per 48 packs in Crown Jewels.

COMPLETE SET (7)	30.00	80.00
UNCUT SIG.SERIES SHEET	30.00	60.00
SG1 Jeff Gordon	5.00	12.00
SG2 Rusty Wallace	4.00	10.00
SG3 Dale Earnhardt	8.00	20.00
SG4 Ernie Irvan	1.00	2.50
SG5 Ricky Rudd	1.50	4.00
SG6 Mark Martin	4.00	10.00
SG7 Bill Elliott	2.00	5.00

1996 Crown Jewels Elite Promos

These Promo cards were issued to preview the 1995 Crown Jewels release. The cards are unnumbered but have been assigned card numbers below according to its foil color.

PC1 Bobby Labonte Citrine	2.00	5.00
PD1 Bobby Labonte Diamond	2.00	5.00
PE1 Bobby Labonte Emerald	2.00	5.00
PS1 Bobby Labonte Sapphire	2.00	5.00

1996 Crown Jewels Elite

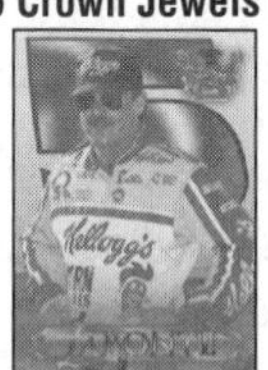

The 1996 Crown Jewels Elite set was issued in one series totalling 78 cards. The set contains the following subsets: Winston Cup Drivers (1-25), Victories (26-34), Owners (35-39), Crew Chiefs (40-47), Driver/Crew Chief (48-56), Car/Hauler (57-66) and BGN Drivers (67-76). Each card is printed on 24-point paper and comes with a red metallic foil stamping. There were 1125 hobby cases produced with 16-boxes per case, 24-packs per box and 5-cards per pack. Finally, a special card was made to commemorate Dale Earnhardt's seven Winston Cup Championships which featured seven different gemstones on one card: amethyst, citrine, emerald, peridot, ruby, sapphire, and topaz. The card was available in base elite boxes at a rate of one in 384 packs and Treasure Chest and Diamond Tribute versions were also made. The Diamond Tribute cards feature seven pieces of real diamond.

COMPLETE RUBY SET (78)	10.00	25.00
WAX BOX HOBBY	25.00	60.00
1 Dale Earnhardt	1.25	3.00
2 Jeff Gordon	.75	2.00
3 Terry Labonte	.25	.60
4 Mark Martin	.60	1.50
5 Sterling Marlin	.25	.60
6 Rusty Wallace	.60	1.50
7 Bill Elliott	.30	.75
8 Bobby Labonte	.50	1.25
9 Dale Jarrett	.50	1.25

10 Bobby Hamilton	.07	.20
11 Ted Musgrave	.07	.20
12 Darrell Waltrip	.15	.40
13 Kyle Petty	.15	.40
14 Ken Schrader	.07	.20
15 Michael Waltrip	.15	.40
16 Derrike Cope	.07	.20
17 Jeff Burton	.25	.60
18 Ricky Craven	.07	.20
19 Steve Grissom	.07	.20
20 Robert Pressley	.07	.20
21 Joe Nemechek	.07	.20
22 Brett Bodine	.07	.20
23 Jimmy Spencer	.07	.20
24 Ward Burton	.15	.40
25 Jeremy Mayfield	.15	.40
26 Dale Jarrett	.50	1.25
27 Dale Earnhardt	1.25	3.00
28 Jeff Gordon	.75	2.00
29 Jeff Gordon	.75	2.00
30 Jeff Gordon	.75	2.00
31 Terry Labonte	.25	.60
32 Rusty Wallace	.60	1.50
33 Sterling Marlin	.25	.60
34 Rusty Wallace	.60	1.50
35 Travis Carter	.02	.10
36 Bobby Allison	.02	.10
37 Robert Yates	.02	.10
38 Larry Hedrick	.02	.10
39 Cale Yarborough	.02	.10
40 Bill Ingle	.02	.10
41 David Smith	.02	.10
42 Todd Parrott	.02	.10
43 Charlie Pressley	.02	.10
44 Donnie Wingo	.02	.10
45 Eddie Wood	.02	.10
46 Len Wood	.02	.10
47 Donnie Richeson	.02	.10
48 Joe Nemechek	.02	.10
Jeff Buice		
49 Charley Pressley	.02	.10
Ricky Craven		
50 Donnie Richeson	.02	.10
Brett Bodine		
51 Jimmy Fennig	.02	.10
Derrike Cope		
52 Todd Parrott	.07	.20
Dale Jarrett		
53 Steve Hmiel	.30	.75
Mark Martin		
54 Robin Pemberton	.60	1.50
Rusty Wallace		
55 Bobby Labonte	.07	.20
Jimmy Makar		
56 David Smith	.60	1.50
Dale Earnhardt		
57 Dale Earnhardt's Transporter	.50	1.25
58 Kyle Petty's Transporter	.07	.20
59 Derrike Cope's Transporter	.02	.10
60 Rusty Wallace's Transporter	.15	.40
61 Bill Elliott's Transporter	.15	.40
62 Dale Jarrett's Transporter	.15	.40
63 Terry Labonte's Transporter	.15	.40
64 Bobby Labonte's Transporter	.15	.40
65 Joe Nemechek's Transporter	.02	.10
66 Steve Grissom's Transporter	.02	.10
67 David Green BGN	.07	.20
68 Randy LaJoie BGN	.07	.20
69 Curtis Markham BGN	.07	.20
70 Phil Parsons BGN	.07	.20
71 Chad Little BGN	.07	.20
72 Jason Keller BGN	.07	.20
73 Jeff Green BGN	.07	.20
74 Mark Martin BGN	.60	1.50
75 Steve Grissom BGN	.07	.20
76 Bobby Labonte BGN	.50	1.25
77 Checklist	.02	.10
78 Checklist	.02	.10
SD1 Dale Earnhardt	100.00	200.00
7 Diamonds/300		
SG1 Dale Earnhardt	25.00	60.00
7 Gems/1500		
SGTC1 Dale Earnhardt	25.00	60.00
7 Gems Treasure Chest/1500		

1996 Crown Jewels Elite Diamond Tribute

The Diamond Tribute parallel was from a special 300-case press run that was sold only through the Wheels distributor network.

COMPLETE SET (78)	10.00	25.00
*DIAM.TRIBUTE: .5X TO 1.2X BASE CARDS		

1996 Crown Jewels Elite Treasure Chest

This set is a parallel of the Crown Jewels set. These cards feature a foil stamped "Treasure Chest" on the cardfronts and 375 cases were produced.

COMPLETE SET (78)	10.00	25.00
*TREAS.CHEST: .5X TO 1.2X BASE CARDS		

1996 Crown Jewels Elite Emerald

This 78-card set is a parallel version of the base Elite set. The cards carry an emerald (green) colored foil stamping that differentiates them from the base Elite cards. The cards were randomly inserted 1 in 13 packs in regular Elite packs.

COMPLETE SET (78)	100.00	200.00
*EMERALDS: 3X TO 8X BASE ELITE CARDS		

1996 Crown Jewels Elite Emerald Treasure Chest

This set is a parallel to the Crown Jewels set. This version is only available in Treasure Chest boxes at a rate of 1 in 13 packs. These cards carry a green foil stamped treasure chest on the front.

COMPLETE SET (78)	125.00	250.00
*EMERALD TCs: .5X TO 1.2X BASE EMERALD		

1996 Crown Jewels Elite Sapphire

This 78-card set is a parallel version of the base Elite set. The cards carry a sapphire (blue) colored foil stamping that differentiates them from the base Elite cards. The cards were randomly inserted one in seven packs in the regular Elite product.

COMPLETE SET (78)	40.00	100.00
*SAPPHIRE CARDS: 2.5X TO 6X BASE ELITE CARDS		

1996 Crown Jewels Elite Diamond Tribute Citrine

This set is a parallel to the Crown Jewels set. These cards carry a yellow foil stamping and were available in Diamond Tribute packs at a rate of one in seven.

COMPLETE SET (78)	75.00	150.00
*DIAM.TRIB.CITRINE: .4X TO 1X BASE SAPP.		

1996 Crown Jewels Elite Sapphire Treasure Chest

This set is another parallel of the Crown Jewels set. This version is only available in Treasure Chest boxes at a rate of one in seven packs. These cards carry a blue foil stamped treasure chest on the front and have been priced with a multiplier below.

COMPLETE SET (78)	75.00	150.00
*SAPPHIRE TCs: .4X TO 1X BASE SAPPHIRE		

1996 Crown Jewels Elite Birthstones of the Champions

Randomly inserted in packs at a rate of one in 192, this six-card set features the active Winston Cup Champions. Each card carries the actual birthstone for that driver. The cards were seeded in packs of the regular Elite product (1:192 packs) with 375 of each card made.

COMPLETE SET (6)	125.00	250.00
COMP.DIAM.TRIBUTE (6)	125.00	250.00
*DIAM.TRIBUTE: .4X TO 1X BASIC INSERTS		
COMP. TREAS.CHEST (6)	150.00	300.00
*TC CARDS: .5X TO 1.2X BASIC INSERTS		
BC1 Dale Earnhardt	30.00	80.00
BC2 Jeff Gordon	20.00	50.00
BC3 Rusty Wallace	15.00	40.00
BC4 Darrell Waltrip	4.00	10.00
BC5 Bill Elliott	8.00	20.00
BC6 Terry Labonte	6.00	15.00

1996 Crown Jewels Elite Dual Jewels Amethyst

Randomly inserted in packs at a rate of one in 96, this eight-card set features the top NASCAR drivers on dual sided cards. Each card has basically two front sides. The cards carry an amethyst or purple color foil stamping.

COMPLETE SET (8)	30.00	80.00
COMP.DIAM.TRIBUTE (8)	30.00	80.00
*DIAMOND TRIB: .4X TO 1X BASIC INSERTS		
COMP.T.CHEST SET (8)	40.00	100.00
*TREAS.CHEST: .5X TO 1.2X BASIC INSERTS		
DJ1 Dale Earnhardt	30.00	60.00
Jeff Gordon		
DJ2 Dale Jarrett	6.00	15.00
Sterling Marlin		
DJ3 Terry Labonte	5.00	12.00
Bobby Labonte		
DJ4 Bill Elliott	6.00	15.00
Mark Martin		
DJ5 Darrell Waltrip	2.50	6.00
Michael Waltrip		
DJ6 Bobby Hamilton	2.50	6.00
Kyle Petty		
DJ7 Rusty Wallace	6.00	15.00
Kenny Wallace		
DJ8 Ward Burton	2.50	6.00
Jeff Burton		

1996 Crown Jewels Elite Dual Jewels Garnet

Randomly inserted in packs at a rate of one in 48, this eight-card set features the top NASCAR drivers on dual sided cards. Each card has basically two front sides. The cards carry a garnet or reddish brown color foil stamping.

COMPLETE SET (8)	25.00	60.00
COMP. DIAMOND TRIB. (8)	25.00	60.00
*DIAMOND TRIB: .4X TO 1X BASIC INSERTS		
COMP.T.CHEST SET (8)	30.00	80.00
*TREAS.CHEST: .5X TO 1.2X BASIC INSERTS		
DJ1 Dale Earnhardt	15.00	40.00
Jeff Gordon		
DJ2 Dale Jarrett	4.00	10.00
Sterling Marlin		
DJ3 Terry Labonte	3.00	8.00
Bobby Labonte		
DJ4 Bill Elliott	4.00	10.00
Mark Martin		
DJ5 Darrell Waltrip	2.00	6.00
Michael Waltrip		
DJ6 Bobby Hamilton	1.50	4.00
Kyle Petty		
DJ7 Rusty Wallace	4.00	10.00
Kenny Wallace		
DJ8 Ward Burton	1.50	4.00
Jeff Burton		

1996 Crown Jewels Elite Dual Jewels Sapphire

Randomly inserted in packs at a rate of one in 192, this eight-card set features the top NASCAR drivers on dual sided cards. Each card has basically two front sides. The cards carry a sapphire or deep blue color foil stamping. There was also a Treasure Chest parallel version of each card. The parallels have a treasure chest logo on them to differentiate them from the base dual jewels cards. These cards were seeded one in 192 Treasure Chest packs.

COMPLETE SET (8)	60.00	150.00
COMP.T. CHEST SET (8)	75.00	200.00
*TREAS.CHEST: .5X TO 1.2X BASIC INSERTS		
DJ1 Dale Earnhardt	40.00	100.00
Jeff Gordon		
DJ2 Dale Jarrett	10.00	25.00
Sterling Marlin		
DJ3 Terry Labonte	8.00	20.00
Bobby Labonte		
DJ4 Bill Elliott	10.00	25.00
Mark Martin		
DJ5 Darrell Waltrip	4.00	10.00
Michael Waltrip		
DJ6 Bobby Hamilton	4.00	10.00
Kyle Petty		
DJ7 Rusty Wallace	10.00	25.00
Kenny Wallace		
DJ8 Ward Burton	4.00	10.00
Jeff Burton		

1996 Crown Jewels Elite Crown Signature Amethyst

This 10-card set features the top Winston Cup drivers. The cards carry a facsimile signature across the front and carry an amethyst or purple logo. There were 480 of each card available only in Diamond Tribute boxes at a rate of one in 24 packs.

COMPLETE SET (10)	40.00	100.00
COMP.GARNET SET (10)	20.00	50.00
*GARNETS: .25X TO .6X BASIC INSERTS		
COMP.PERIDOT SET (10)	20.00	50.00
*PERIDOT: .25X TO .6X BASIC INSERTS		
CS1 Dale Earnhardt	12.50	30.00
CS2 Jeff Gordon	8.00	20.00
CS3 Rusty Wallace	6.00	15.00
CS4 Bill Elliott	3.00	8.00
CS5 Terry Labonte	2.50	6.00
CS6 Bobby Labonte	5.00	12.00
CS7 Ricky Craven	.75	2.00
CS8 Sterling Marlin	2.50	6.00
CS9 Dale Jarrett	5.00	12.00
CS10 Mark Martin	6.00	15.00

1996 Crown Jewels Elite Diamonds in the Rough Sapphire

This five-card set pays tribute to some of the best up and coming young drivers on the Winston Cup circuit. The cards were available in Diamond Tribute boxes only at a rate of one in 48 packs.

COMPLETE SAPPHIRE SET (5)	6.00	15.00
COMP.CITRINE SET (5)	4.00	10.00
*CITRINES: .25X TO .6X BASIC INSERTS		
COMP.RUBY SET (5)	4.00	10.00
*RUBYS: .25X TO .6X BASIC INSERTS		
DR1 Jeff Burton	2.50	6.00
DR2 Steve Grissom	1.25	3.00
DR3 Ricky Craven	1.25	3.00
DR4 Robert Pressley	1.25	3.00
DR5 Jeremy Mayfield	2.50	6.00

1992 Dayco Series 1

The 1992 set was the first of three releases sponsored by Dayco. The cards in each set are numbered consecutively, although they are most often sold as separate series. The 1992 release features nine drivers pictured with their cars at Daytona. An unnumbered checklist/cover card rounds out the set as the tenth card.

COMPLETE SET (10)	4.00	10.00
1 Davey Allison	.60	1.50
2 Rusty Wallace	.60	1.50
3 Derrike Cope	.25	.60
4 Ernie Irvan	.40	1.00
5 Dale Jarrett	.60	1.50
6 Hut Stricklin	.15	.40
7 Sterling Marlin	.40	1.00
8 Morgan Shepherd	.25	.60
9 Bobby Hamilton	.25	.60
NNO Cover Card	.10	.25
Checklist		

1993 Dayco Series 2 Rusty Wallace

The 1993 Dayco set highlights the career of Rusty Wallace. The cards are numbered as a continuation of the 1992 Dayco release. Two foil cards are included as well as a checklist on the back of card #11.

COMPLETE SET (15)	3.00	8.00
11 Rusty Wallace	.30	.75
checklist back		
12 Rusty Wallace's Car	.30	.75
Dale Earnhardt's Car		
13 Rusty Wallace's Car	.30	.75
Rick Mears' Car		
14 Rusty Wallace	.30	.75
Roger Penske		
15 Rusty Wallace	.30	.75
16 Mike Wallace	.30	.75
Kenny Wallace		
Rusty Wallace		
17 Rusty Wallace	.30	.75
18 Rusty Wallace	.30	.75
19 Rusty Wallace	.30	.75
20 Rusty Wallace in Pits	.30	.75
21 Rusty Wallace	.30	.75
Buddy Parrott		
22 Rusty Wallace	.30	.75
23 Rusty Wallace	.30	.75
Buddy Parrott		
Don Miller		
24 Rusty Wallace FOIL	.30	.75
25 Rusty Wallace's Car FOIL	.30	.75

1994 Dayco Series 3

The 1994 set was the last of three releases sponsored by Dayco. The cards are numbered consecutively from series two, although they are most often sold as a separate set. The 1994 release is very similar in design to the 1992 first series and features 14-drivers pictured with their cars at Daytona. Neil Bonnett's card begins the set and includes a checklist cardback.

COMPLETE SET (15)	4.00	10.00
26 Neil Bonnett CL	.40	1.00
27 Rusty Wallace	.75	2.00
28 Sterling Marlin	.40	1.00
29 Geoff Bodine	.30	.75
30 Jeff Burton	.50	1.25
31 Chuck Bown	.30	.75
32 Loy Allen Jr.	.30	.75
33 Harry Gant	.40	1.00
34 Bobby Labonte	.60	1.50
35 Hut Stricklin	.30	.75
36 Ward Burton	.50	1.25
37 Rick Mast	.30	.75
38 Jeremy Mayfield	.30	.75
39 Derrike Cope	.30	.75
40 Dave Marcis	.30	.75

1955-56 Diamond Matchbooks Indy

The Diamond Match Co. produced these matchbook covers featuring Indy 500 drivers. They measure approximately 1 1/2" by 4 1/2" (when completely folded out). We've listed the drivers alphabetically. Each of the covers was produced with black and red ink with a black and white image of the driver in his car. The driver's name appears above the image and the notation "Indianapolis 500" along with the year is printed below the image. A Champion Spark Plugs ad can be found in the middle of the cover and a sponsorship logo or ad is usually found on the back. Most of the drivers are current participants for the 1955 and 1956 races while others feature recent past race winners. Complete covers with matches intact are valued at approximately 1 1/2 times the prices listed below.

COMPLETE SET (7)	100.00	175.00
1 Freddie Agabashian 1955	6.00	12.00
3 Duane Carter 1955	6.00	12.00
8 Jack McGrath 1955	6.00	12.00
9 Pat O'Connor 1955	6.00	12.00
10 Johnnie Parsons 1955	6.00	12.00
13 Jimmy Reece 1955	6.00	12.00
14 Bob Sweikert 1955 Winner	6.00	12.00

1955 Diamond Matchbooks Stock Cars

The Diamond Match Co. produced these matchbook covers featuring Stock Car drivers of various circuits. They measure approximately 1 1/2" by 4 1/2" (when completely folded out). We've listed the drivers alphabetically. Each of the covers was produced with black ink on the text. Complete covers with matches intact are valued at approximately 1 1/2 times the prices listed below.

COMPLETE SET (3)	30.00	60.00
1 Ray Crawford	6.00	12.00
Enrique Iglesias		
2 Tim Flock	7.50	15.00
(1955 Daytona Champion)		
3 Lee Petty	12.50	25.00
(1954 NASCAR Champion)		

1992 Erin Maxx Trans-Am

This 100-card set was produced by Erin Maxx and features top drivers and cars of SCCA Trans-Am racing. The cards feature color photos of the driver or car on the cardfront with a small driver photo on the cardback.

COMPLETE SET (100)	6.00	15.00
1 Wayne Akers' Car	.05	.15
2 Wayne Akers	.08	.25
3 Bobby Archer's Car	.05	.15
4 Bobby Archer	.08	.25
5 Tommy Archer's Car	.05	.15
6 Tommy Archer	.08	.25
7 Jack Baldwin's Car	.08	.25
8 Jack Baldwin	.20	.50
9 Jerry Clinton's Car	.05	.15
10 Jerry Clinton	.08	.25
11 Jim Derhaag's Car	.05	.15
12 Jim Derhaag	.08	.25
13 Michael Dingman's Car	.05	.15
14 Michael Dingman	.08	.25
15 Ron Fellows' Car	.08	.25
16 Ron Fellows	.20	.50
17 Paul Gentilozzi's Car	.08	.25
18 Paul Gentilozzi	.20	.50
19 Scott Sharp's Car	.08	.25
20 Scott Sharp	.20	.50
21 Stuart Hayner's Car	.05	.15
22 Stuart Hayner	.08	.25
23 Phil Mahre's Car	.05	.15
24 Phil Mahre	.08	.25
25 Steve Mahre's Car	.05	.15
26 Steve Mahre	.08	.25
27 Deborah Gregg's Car	.05	.15
28 Deborah Gregg	.08	.25
29 Greg Pickett's Car	.05	.15
30 Greg Pickett	.08	.25
31 George Robinson's Car	.05	.15
32 George Robinson	.08	.25
33 Randy Ruhlman's Car	.05	.15
34 Randy Ruhlman	.08	.25
35 Trois-Rivieres	.05	.15
36 Trois-Rivieres Winners	.05	.15
37 R.J. Valentine's Car	.05	.15
38 R.J. Valentine	.08	.25
39 Tech Inspection	.05	.15
40 Scott Sharp's Car	.08	.25
Wet Racing		
41 Tech Pix	.05	.15
42 Scott Sharp's Car	.08	.25
Series Champion		
43 Wally Owens' Car	.05	.15
44 Kenwood's Tour De Force	.05	.15
45 Glenn Fox's Car	.05	.15
46 Glenn Fox	.08	.25
47 Courtney Smith's Car	.05	.15
48 Courtney Smith	.08	.25
49 Checklist 1-50	.05	.15
50 Checklist 51-100	.05	.15
51 John Anderson's Car	.05	.15
52 Glenn Andrew's Car	.05	.15
53 Jeff Davis' Car	.05	.15
54 Peter De Man's Car	.05	.15
55 Rick Dittman's Car	.05	.15
56 Mike Downs' Car	.05	.15
57 Bill Gray's Car	.05	.15
58 Ed Hinchliff's Car	.05	.15
59 Steve Anderson's Car	.05	.15
60 Les Lindley's Car	.05	.15
61 Bruce Nesbitt's Car	.05	.15
62 Frank Panzarella's Car	.05	.15
63 Bob Patch's Car	.05	.15
64 Mark Pielsticker's Car	.05	.15
65 Andy Porterfield's Car	.05	.15
66 Brian Richards' Car	.05	.15
67 Don Sak's Car	.05	.15
68 Craig Shafer's Car	.05	.15
69 Jerry Simmons' Car	.05	.15
70 Rich Sloma's Car	.05	.15
73 Scott Sharp	.05	.15
Ron Fellows		
Greg Pickett		
Mexico Winners		
74 Irv Hoerr	.05	.15
Darin Brassfield		
Greg Pickett		
Dallas Winners		
75 Scott Sharp	.05	.15
Paul Gentilozzi		
Irv Hoerr		
George Robinson		
Les Lindley		
Dallas Fast Five		
76 Scott Sharp	.05	.1
Greg Pickett		
Paul Gentilozzi		
Detroit Winners		
77 Scott Sharp	.05	.1
Irv Hoerr		
Jack Baldwin		
George Robinson		
Tom Gloy		
Detroit Fast Five		
78 Irv Hoerr	.05	.1
Scott Sharp		
Stuart Hayner		
Portland Winners		
79 Irv Hoerr	.05	.1
Stuart Hayner		
Paul Gentilozzi		
Phil Mahre		
Jack Baldwin		
Portland Fast Five		
80 Darin Brassfield	.05	.1
Scott Sharp		
Jack Baldwin		
Cleveland Winners		
81 Darin Brassfield	.05	.1
Ron Fellows		
Irv Hoerr		
Scott Sharp		
Jack Baldwin		
Cleveland Fast Five		
82 George Robinson	.05	.1
Jack Baldwin		
Les Lindley		
Des Moines Winners		
83 Scott Sharp	.05	.1
Jack Baldwin		
Irv Hoerr		
Ron Fellows		
Darin Brassfield		
Des Moines Fast Five		
84 Scott Sharp	.05	.1
Jack Baldwin		
Les Lindley		
Watkins Glen Winners		
85 Scott Sharp	.05	.1
Darin Brassfield		
Jack Baldwin		
Paul Gentilozzi		
Scott Pruett		
Watkins Glen Fast Five		
86 Scott Sharp	.05	.1
Les Lindley		
Darin Brassfield		
Mosport Winners		
87 Will Moody	.05	.1
88 Darin Brassfield	.05	.1
Paul Gentilozzi		
Scott Sharp		
Mid Ohio Winners		
89 Scott Sharp	.05	.1
Ron Fellows		
Paul Gentilozzi		
Jack Baldwin		
Irv Hoerr		
Denver Fast Five		
90 Scott Sharp	.05	.1
Chris Kneifel		
Irv Hoerr		
R.A. Winners		
91 Scott Sharp	.05	.1
Chris Kneifel		
Bob Sobey		
Les Lindley		
Darin Brassfield		
R.A. Fast Five		
92 Jack Baldwin	.05	.1
Ron Fellows		
Scott Sharp		
Texas World Winners		
93 Paul Gentilozzi	.05	.1
Steve Petty		
Scott Sharp		
Darin Brassfield		
Irv Hoerr		
Texas World Fast Five		
94 Fast Five Alumni	.05	.1
95 Scott Sharp	.05	.1
Ron Fellows		
Jack Baldwin		
Fast Five Shootout		
96 Buz McCall	.05	.1
97 '92 Class Picture	.05	.1
98 '92 Grid	.05	.1
99 '92 Long Beach Start	.05	.1
100 Scott Sharp's Car	.05	.1
Mosport Win		

1994 Ernie Irvan Fan Club

This five card set was distributed exclusively members of the Ernie Irvan Fan Club. The blac bordered cards feature Irvan and family and we sold for $5.00 each through the Club in complete s form. Each card back contains either statistical biographical information and are unnumbered.

COMPLETE SET (5)	2.50	6.0
1 Ernie Irvan	.60	1.5
2 Ernie Irvan	.60	1.5
3 Ernie Irvan	.60	1.5
4 Ernie Irvan	.60	1.5
5 Ernie Irvan's Car	.60	1.5

2003 eTopps

COMPLETE SET (27)	75.00	150.0
PRINT RUNS STATED BELOW		
PROVIDED BY TOPPS		

ony Stewart/3194 5.00 12.00
lark Martin/3403 4.00 10.00
Mark Martin AU/100 30.00 60.00
amie McMurray/3000 4.00 10.00
eff Gordon/6000 6.00 15.00
immie Johnson/2945 5.00 12.00
yan Newman/4000 5.00 12.00
usty Wallace/3126 4.00 10.00
lliott Sadler/2648 3.00 8.00
Ricky Rudd/2164 4.00 10.00
Matt Kenseth/5000 5.00 12.00
Jeff Burton/1682 4.00 10.00
Bill Elliott/2392 6.00 15.00
Casey Mears/2389 3.00 8.00
Ricky Craven/1709 4.00 10.00
Bobby Labonte/2249 3.00 8.00
Sterling Marlin/2186 3.00 8.00
Greg Biffle/2802 3.00 8.00
Robby Gordon/1937 4.00 10.00
Kevin Harvick/4000 5.00 12.00
Kyle Petty/3000 4.00 10.00
Jerry Nadeau/3000 3.00 8.00
Terry Labonte2283 4.00 10.00
Richard Petty/3065 5.00 12.00
Jeremy Mayfield/2216 3.00 8.00
Johnny Benson/3000 3.00 8.00
Joe Nemechek/1910 4.00 10.00
Kurt Busch/3000 3.00 8.00

005 eTopps Autographs

ʌ1 Mark Martin
2003 eTopps/100

993 Finish Line Promos

ish Line released this four-card set in its own o wrapper. Therefore, the promo cards are often d in complete set form.

MPLETE SET (4) 12.50 25.00
Davey Allison 5.00 10.00
Jeff Gordon 6.00 15.00
Terry Labonte 4.00 8.00
Bobby Labonte
Cover Card .20 .50

1993 Finish Line

Set produced this 180-card set for Finish Line. set features star drivers, cars and crew members the top Winston Cup teams from the previous son. Cards were packaged 12 per foil pack with packs per box and in 23-card jumbo packs. erts included a Silver parallel set (one per foil k/two per jumbo), an unnumbered Alan Kulwicki morial card, as well as a 15-card Davey Allison (jumbo packs only). A special hologram card turing Davey Allison (numbered of 5000) was also duced and randomly distributed through foil ks. A factory set was also available through the sh Line Racing Club. Each factory set came with a ish Line binder and sheets and the Davey Allison was also included.

MPLETE SET (180) 8.00 20.00
X BOX 15.00 40.00
lan Kulwicki .25 .60
arry Gant .15 .40
icky Rudd .25 .60
arrell Waltrip .15 .40
usty Wallace .60 1.50
rett Bodine .07 .20
ed Musgrave .07 .20
ick Mast .07 .20
ut Stricklin .07 .20
Todd Bodine .07 .20
Bobby Hillin .07 .20
Mark Martin's Car .25 .60
Wally Dallenbach Jr.'s Car .02 .10
Jeff Gordon's Car .40 1.00
Michael Waltrip's Car .07 .20
Richard Jackson .02 .10
Jack Roush .02 .10
Junior Johnson .07 .20
Glen Wood .02 .10
Leo Jackson .02 .10
George Bradshaw .02 .10
Rick Mast's Car .02 .10
Ken Wilson .02 .10
Don Miller .02 .10
Donnie Richeson .02 .10
Doug Richert .02 .10
Terry Labonte .30 .75
Bobby Labonte
28 Robert Pressley .07 .20
29 Jeff Burton .25 .60
30 Chuck Bown .07 .20
31 Mike Wallace .07 .20
32 Derrike Cope's Car .02 .10
33 Gary Nelson .02 .10
34 Winston Kelley .02 .10
Dick Brooks
Jim Phillips
35 Danny Myers .02 .10
36 Waddell Wilson .02 .10
37 Alan Kulwicki .25 .60
38 Kyle Petty .15 .40
39 Terry Labonte .30 .75
40 Ernie Irvan .15 .40
41 Geoff Bodine .07 .20
42 Dale Jarrett .50 1.25
43 Wally Dallenbach Jr. .07 .20
44 Jimmy Means .07 .20
45 Rusty Wallace's Car .25 .60
46 Sterling Marlin's Car .07 .20
47 Morgan Shepherd's Car .02 .10
48 Davey Allison's Car .15 .40
49 Phil Parsons .07 .20
50 Bill Stavola .02 .10
51 Darrell Waltrip .15 .40
52 Chuck Rider .02 .10
53 Junie Donlavey .02 .10
54 Gary DeHart .02 .10
55 Donnie Wingo .02 .10
56 Ken Howes .02 .10
57 Robin Pemberton .02 .10
58 Jeff Hammond .02 .10
59 Butch Miller .07 .20
60 Ricky Craven .15 .40
61 Richard Petty .30 .75
62 Joey Knuckles .02 .10
63 Donnie Allison .07 .20
64 Joe Moore .02 .10
Allen Bestwick
65 Jim Bown .02 .10
66 Davey Allison .40 1.00
67 Ricky Rudd .25 .60
68 Ernie Irvan .15 .40
69 Geoff Bodine .07 .20
70 Dick Trickle .07 .20
71 Dave Marcis .07 .20
72 Rick Wilson .07 .20
73 Jimmy Spencer's Car .02 .10
74 Ken Schrader's Car .02 .10
75 Rick Wilson's Car .02 .10
76 Alan Kulwicki .25 .60
77 Joe Gibbs .15 .40
78 Felix Sabates .02 .10
79 Buddy Parrott .02 .10
80 Mike Beam .02 .10
81 Mike Hill .02 .10
82 David Green .07 .20
83 Jeff Gordon CRC 1.00 2.50
84 Tom Peck .07 .20
85 Richard Petty .30 .75
86 Dale Inman .02 .10
87 Barney Hall .02 .10
Eli Gold
88 Pete Wright .02 .10
89 Davey Allison .30 .75
90 Terry Labonte .30 .75
91 Morgan Shepherd .07 .20
92 Ted Musgrave .07 .20
93 Jimmy Hensley .07 .20
94 Geoff Bodine's Bobsled .02 .10
95 Darrell Waltrip's Car .07 .20
96 Harry Gant's Car .02 .10
97 Rick Hendrick .02 .10
98 Bill Davis .02 .10
99 Cale Yarborough .07 .20
100 Paul Andrews .02 .10
101 Ray Evernham .02 .10
102 David Fuge .02 .10
103 Ward Burton .15 .40
104 Jimmy Spencer .07 .20
105 Danny Glad .02 .10
106 David Smith .02 .10
107 Darrell Waltrip .15 .40
108 Brett Bodine .07 .20
109 Michael Waltrip .15 .40
110 Jeff Gordon 1.00 2.50
111 Dale Jarrett's Car .15 .40
112 Kenny Wallace's Car .02 .10
113 Bobby Allison .07 .20
114 Richard Petty .25 .60
115 Barry Dodson .02 .10
116 Doug Hewitt .02 .10
117 Bobby Labonte .50 1.25
118 Bobby Dotter .02 .10
119 Neil Bonnett .25 .60
120 Jimmy Fennig .02 .10
121 Kyle Petty .15 .40
122 Rusty Wallace .60 1.50
123 Michael Waltrip .15 .40
124 Ernie Irvan's Car .15 .40
125 Brett Bodine's Car .02 .10
126 Bobby Hamilton's Car .02 .10
127 Larry Hedrick .02 .10
128 Howard Comstock .02 .10
129 Robbie Loomis .02 .10
130 Steve Grissom .07 .20
131 Shelton Pittman .02 .10
132 Jimmy Johnson .02 .10
133 Mark Martin .60 1.50
134 Ken Schrader .07 .20
135 Bobby Labonte .50 1.25
136 Hut Stricklin's Car .02 .10
137 Walter Bud Moore .02 .10
138 Tony Glover .02 .10
139 Troy Beebe .02 .10
140 Tracy Leslie .02 .10
141 Will Lind .02 .10
142 Harry Gant .15 .40
143 Ken Schrader .07 .20
144 Ricky Rudd's Car .07 .20
145 Bobby Hillin's Car .02 .10
146 Billy Hagan .02 .10
147 Larry McReynolds .02 .10
148 Richard Lasater .02 .10
149 Eddie Wood .02 .10
150 Sterling Marlin .30 .75
151 Kenny Wallace .07 .20
152 Larry McClure .02 .10
153 Steve Hmiel .02 .10
154 Kenny Wallace .07 .20
155 Andy Petree .02 .10
156 Morgan Shepherd .07 .20
157 Geoff Bodine's Car .02 .10
158 Robert Yates .02 .10
159 Joe Nemechek .07 .20
160 Jack Sprague .02 .10
161 Kenny Bernstein .07 .20
162 Glen Wood Family .02 .10
163 Tommy Houston .07 .20
164 Mark Martin .60 1.50
165 Bobby Labonte's Car .07 .20
166 Leonard Wood .02 .10
167 Ted Musgrave's Car .02 .10
168 Sterling Marlin .30 .75
169 Dale Jarrett .50 1.25
170 Alan Kulwicki's Car .15 .40
171 Kyle Petty's Car .07 .20
172 Junior Johnson .07 .20
173 Joe Gibbs .30 .75
Dale Jarrett
174 Jimmy Makar .02 .10
175 Tim Brewer .02 .10
176 Len Wood .02 .10
177 Ned Jarrett .07 .20
178 Roger Penske .02 .10
179 Doug Williams .02 .10
180 Hut Stricklin .07 .20
NNO Alan Kulwicki Memorial 1.50 4.00
NNO Davey Allison HOLO/5000 15.00 40.00

1993 Finish Line Silver

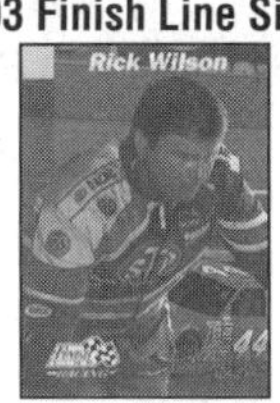

A parallel set to the regular issue 1993 Finish Line set, these cards feature a "Silver Series '93" logo on the front. Cards were packaged one per foil pack and two per jumbo pack.

COMPLETE SET (180) 15.00 40.00
*STARS: 1.2X TO 3X BASIC CARDS

1993 Finish Line Davey Allison

Pro Set produced this 15-card set for Finish Line to honor the 1992 Driver of the Year, Davey Allison. The cards were packaged one per 1993 Finish Line jumbo pack.

COMPLETE SET (15) 4.00 10.00
1 Davey Allison w/car .40 1.00
2 Davey Allison .40 1.00
3 Davey Allison w/car .40 1.00
4 Davey Allison's Car .40 1.00
Bobby Allison's Car
5 Davey Allison .40 1.00
Bobby Allison
6 Davey Allison w/car .40 1.00
7 Davey Allison w/car .40 1.00
8 Davey Allison w/daughter .40 1.00
9 Davey Allison w/car .40 1.00
10 Davey Allison .40 1.00
Donnie Allison
Bobby Allison
Neil Bonnett
Hut Stricklin
Mickey Gibbs
11 Davey Allison w/family .40 1.00
12 Davey Allison .40 1.00
13 Davey Allison w/car .40 1.00
14 Davey Allison w/son .40 1.00
15 Davey Allison .40 1.00

1993 Finish Line Commemorative Sheets

Produced by Pro Set for Finish Line Racing Club, this 30-sheet, blank backed set features the fronts of six 1993 Finish Line cards. The sheets measure approximately 8-1/2" by 11" and include the Finish Line logo along with sheet number. Although the sheets are individually numbered of 10,000, reportedly less than 2500 sets were actually distributed.

COMPLETE SET 30.00 75.00
1 Daytona .75 2.00
Dale Jarrett/Joe Gibbs
Dale Jarrett's Car
Jim Phillips/Dick Brooks/Winston Kelley
Jeff Burton
Jimmy Makar
Mike Wallace
2 Rockingham 1.50 4.00
Rusty Wallace
Barney Hall/Eli Gold
Ernie Irvan UER
misspelled Irvin
Ward Burton
Tony Glover
Ray Evernham
3 Richmond 1.50 4.00
Davey Allison
Ken Schrader's Car
Tom Peck
Paul Andrews
Ken Schrader
Neil Bonnett
4 Atlanta .75 2.00
Morgan Shepherd
Ricky Rudd's Car
Junior Johnson
Barry Dodson
Glen Wood Family
Robert Pressley
5 Darlington .75 2.00
Dave Marcis
Dave Marcis' Car
Jimmy Hensley
Jack Roush
Mark Martin
Billy Hagan
6 Bristol 1.00 2.50
Alan Kulwicki
Sterling Marlin's Car
Joey Knuckles
Gary Nelson
Roger Penske
Chuck Rider
7 North Wilkesboro 1.00 2.50
Donnie Richeson
Rick Mast's Car
Butch Miller
Ricky Rudd
Brett Bodine
Don Miller
8 Martinsville 1.00 2.50
Geoff Bodine
Davey Allison's Car
Doug Hewitt
Bill Davis
Darrell Waltrip
Howard Comstock
9 Talladega 1.00 2.50
Harry Gant
Rusty Wallace's Car
Todd Bodine
Bobby Hillin Jr.
Bobby Hillin Jr.'s Car
Walter Bud Moore
10 Sonoma 1.50 4.00
Dave Fuge
Wally Dallenbach Jr.'s Car
Jeff Gordon
Wally Dallenbach Jr.
Bobby Hamilton's Car
Danny Myers
11 Charlotte .75 2.00
Mark Martin's Car
Chuck Bown
Jeff Gordon's Car
Terry Labonte
Bill Stavola
Rick Mast
12 Dover 1.00 2.50
Richard Petty
Jimmy Spencer's Car
Steve Grissom
Dale Inman
David Smith
Jimmy Spencer
13 Pocono 1.00 2.50
Dale Jarrett
Michael Waltrip's Car
Gary DeHart
Dick Trickle
Michael Waltrip
Ted Musgrave
14 Michigan 1.50 4.00
Kyle Petty
Alan Kulwicki's Car
Junie Donlavey
Robin Pemberton
Alan Kulwicki
Mike Beam
15 Daytona .75 2.00
Felix Sabates
Kenny Wallace's Car
Mike Hill
Joe Gibbs
Joe Moore/Allen Bestwick
Hut Stricklin
16 New Hampshire 1.00 2.50
Ricky Craven
Morgan Shepherd
Bobby Labonte
Glen Wood
Jimmy Means
Bobby Labonte's Car
17 Pocono 1.00 2.50
Kenny Wallace
Troy Beebe
Junior Johnson
Richard Jackson
Will Lind
Ricky Rudd
18 Talladega .75 2.00
Darrell Waltrip
Leonard Wood
Ken Schrader
Tim Brewer
Geoff Bodine's Car
Ned Jarrett
19 Watkins Glen 1.00 2.50
George Bradshaw
Bobby Labonte/Terry Labonte
Robbie Loomis
Waddell Wilson
Rick Wilson's Car
Sterling Marlin
20 Michigan 1.50 4.00
Phil Parsons
Derrike Cope's Car
Bobby Allison
Larry McClure
Andy Petree
Davey Allison
21 Bristol 1.50 4.00
Brett Bodine
Brett Bodine's Car
Rusty Wallace
Buddy Parrott
Jimmy Johnson
Tracy Leslie
22 Darlington 1.00 2.50
Kyle Petty
Kyle Petty's Car
Cale Yarborough
Pete Wright
Jeff Hammond
Danny Glad
23 Richmond 1.50 4.00
Robert Yates
Jeff Gordon
Shelton Pittman
Michael Waltrip
Kenny Bernstein
Ken Wilson
24 Dover 1.00 2.50
Ernie Irvan
Ernie Irvan's Car
Donnie Allison
David Green
Leo Jackson
Bobby Dotter
25 Martinsville .75 2.00
Ted Musgrave
Geoff Bodine
Len Wood
Donnie Wingo
Geoff Bodine's Bobsled
Morgan Shepherd
26 North Wilkesboro 1.00 2.50
Harry Gant
Harry Gant's Car
Jack Sprague
Richard Lasater
Sterling Marlin
Larry McReynolds
27 Charlotte .75 2.00
Steve Hmiel
Mark Martin
Richard Petty
Eddie Wood
Larry Hedrick
Joe Nemechek
28 Rockingham 1.00 2.50
Terry Labonte
Hut Stricklin's Car
Dale Jarrett
Bobby Labonte
Hut Stricklin
Doug Williams
29 Phoenix 1.00 2.50
Richard Petty
Rick Wilson
Ken Howes
Jim Bown
Jimmy Fennig
Kenny Wallace
30 Atlanta 1.50 4.00
Alan Kulwicki
Darrell Waltrip's Car
Rick Hendrick
Darrell Waltrip
Doug Richert
Tommy Houston

1994 Finish Line Promos

Finish Line produced four promo cards to preview the 1994 Finish Line release. The cards were packaged in a cello wrapper and are often sold as a complete set.

COMPLETE SET (4) 3.00 8.00
P1 Harry Gant .75 2.00
P2 Mark Martin 1.25 3.00
P3 Rusty Wallace 1.25 3.00
P4 Cover Card .20 .50

1994 Finish Line

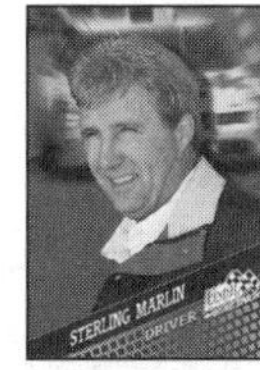

For the first time Finish Line produced their own NASCAR set in 1994. The 150-card set was packaged in 12-card hobby and retail foil packs and 23-card jumbo packs. Inserts included a Silver parallel set, along with six other sets. Finish Line once again included unnumbered tribute cards that featured Jeff Gordon, Hermie Sadler, Harry Gant and a large (5" by 7") Sterling Marlin card.

COMPLETE SET (150) 6.00 15.00
WAX BOX 12.50 30.00
1 Harry Gant .15 .40
2 Rick Mast .07 .20
3 Wally Dallenbach Jr.'s Car .02 .10
4 Geoff Bodine's Car .02 .10
5 Buddy Parrott .02 .10
6 Barney Hall .02 .10
7 Mark Martin .60 1.50
8 Travis Carter .02 .10
9 Ned Jarrett .02 .10
10 Ernie Irvan .15 .40
11 Kyle Petty .15 .40
12 Hut Stricklin .07 .20
13 Jimmy Makar .02 .10
14 John Andretti RC .07 .20
15 Bobby Hillin .07 .20
16 Jimmy Hensley .07 .20
17 Terry Labonte's Car .15 .40
18 Kenny Wallace .07 .20
19 Ted Musgrave's Car .02 .10
20 Dale Jarrett .50 1.25
21 Sterling Marlin .25 .60
22 Eli Gold .02 .10
23 Dave Marcis .15 .40
24 Lake Speed .07 .20
25 Gary DeHart .02 .10
26 Bobby Labonte .50 1.25
27 Ken Schrader .07 .20
28 Kyle Petty's Car .07 .20
29 Rusty Wallace .60 1.50
30 Steve Grissom .07 .20
31 Ernie Irvan .15 .40
32 Michael Waltrip .15 .40
33 Doug Hewitt .02 .10
34 Jimmy Means .07 .20
35 Hut Stricklin .07 .20
36 Jeff Gordon .75 2.00
37 Morgan Shepherd's Car .02 .10
38 Terry Labonte .25 .60
39 Geoff Bodine .07 .20
40 Darrell Waltrip's Car .07 .20
41 Pete Wright .02 .10
42 Morgan Shepherd .07 .20
43 Michael Waltrip's Car .07 .20
44 Bobby Hillin .07 .20
45 Jeff Burton's Car .07 .20
46 Ken Wilson .02 .10
47 Donnie Wingo .02 .10
48 Greg Sacks .07 .20
49 Junior Johnson .07 .20
50 Rick Mast .07 .20
51 Lake Speed's Car .02 .10
52 Ernie Irvan's Car .07 .20
53 Rick Hendrick .02 .10
54 Leo Jackson .02 .10
55 Ray Evernham .15 .40
56 Ken Schrader's Car .02 .10
57 Neil Bonnett .25 .60
58 Richard Petty OWN .25 .60
59 Chuck Rider .02 .10
60 Kyle Petty .15 .40
61 Brett Bodine .07 .20
62 Jimmy Spencer .07 .20
63 Bobby Labonte's Car .25 .60
64 Richard Petty .25 .60
65 Ricky Rudd .25 .60
66 Steve Hmiel .02 .10
67 Dale Jarrett .50 1.25
68 Brett Bodine's Car .02 .10
69 Lake Speed .07 .20
70 Kenny Bernstein .07 .20
71 Larry McReynolds .02 .10
72 Robin Pemberton .02 .10
73 Ricky Rudd .25 .60
74 Rusty Wallace .60 1.50
75 Jeff Gordon .75 2.00
76 Loy Allen Jr. .07 .20
77 Loy Allen Jr.'s Car .02 .10
78 Dale Jarrett .50 1.25
79 Harry Gant .15 .40
80 Morgan Shepherd .07 .20
81 Mike Beam .02 .10
82 Sterling Marlin's Car .07 .20
83 Glen Wood .02 .10
84 Kyle Petty .15 .40
85 Mark Martin .60 1.50
86 Joe Nemechek .07 .20
87 Mike Wallace .07 .20
88 Barry Dodson .02 .10
89 Wally Dallenbach Jr. .07 .20
90 Rusty Wallace .60 1.50
91 Ricky Rudd's Car .07 .20
92 Jack Roush .02 .10
93 Ken Schrader .07 .20
94 Len Wood .02 .10
Eddie Wood
95 Dale Inman .02 .10
96 Roger Penske .02 .10
97 Donnie Richeson .02 .10
98 Mike Hill .02 .10
99 Mark Martin's Car .25 .60
100 Jerry Punch .02 .10
101 Jimmy Hensley .07 .20
102 Darrell Waltrip .15 .40
103 Brett Bodine .07 .20
104 Rusty Wallace's Car .25 .60
105 Tony Glover .02 .10
106 Ward Burton's Car .02 .10
107 Ted Musgrave .07 .20
108 Todd Bodine .07 .20
109 Dale Jarrett's Car .25 .60
110 Leonard Wood .02 .10
111 Jimmy Spencer .07 .20
112 Ernie Irvan .15 .40
113 Jeff Burton .25 .60
114 Jeff Hammond .02 .10
115 Ward Burton .15 .40
116 Ken Schrader .07 .20
117 Butch Mock .02 .10
118 Derrike Cope .07 .20
119 Robert Yates .02 .10
120 Benny Parsons .02 .10
121 Jimmy Spencer's Car .02 .10
122 Morgan Shepherd .07 .20
123 Jeff Gordon 's Car .40 1.00
124 Terry Labonte .25 .60
125 Joe Gibbs .15 .40
126 Mark Martin .60 1.50
127 Hut Stricklin's Car .02 .10
128 Bobby Labonte .50 1.25
129 Darrell Waltrip .15 .40
130 Walter Bud Moore .02 .10
131 Robbie Loomis .07 .20
132 Bobby Allison .15 .40
133 Ken Howes .02 .10
134 Michael Waltrip .15 .40
135 Ricky Rudd .25 .60
136 Jimmy Johnson .02 .10
137 Jimmy Spencer .07 .20
138 Harry Gant .15 .40
139 Jimmy Fennig .02 .10
140 Derrike Cope .07 .20
141 Geoff Bodine .07 .20
142 Felix Sabates .02 .10
143 Cale Yarborough .07 .20
144 Junie Donlavey .02 .10
145 Sterling Marlin .25 .60
146 Richard Broome .02 .10
147 Chuck Bown .07 .20
148 Larry McClure .02 .10
149 Ted Musgrave .07 .20
150 Wally Dallenbach Jr. .07 .20
NNO Jeff Gordon ROY 2.00 5.00
NNO Hermie Sadler ROY .75 2.00

NNO Harry Gant Last Ride	1.00	3.00
NNO Sterling Marlin 5X7	2.00	5.00

1994 Finish Line Silver

A parallel set to the regular issue 1994 Finish Line set, these cards feature a "94 Silver" logo on the front printed in silver foil. Cards were packaged one per foil pack and two per jumbo pack.

COMPLETE SET (150) 12.00 30.00
*SILVERS: 1X TO 2.5X BASIC CARDS

1994 Finish Line Neil Bonnett

Neil Bonnett is the focus of this five-card tribute set randomly inserted in 1994 Finish Line retail packs. All five cards are unnumbered.

COMPLETE SET (5)	3.00	6.00
COMMON CARD	.75	1.50

1994 Finish Line Busch Grand National

Finish Line produced this 15-card insert set that focuses on up-and-coming drivers from Busch Series racing. The cards were randomly packed in all types of 1994 Finish Line racing packs. The odds of pulling a BGN card from a regular pack or a jumbo pack was one in eight packs.

COMPLETE SET (15)	5.00	12.00
BGN1 David Green	.30	.75
BGN2 Jeff Burton	.60	1.50
BGN3 Bobby Dotter	.30	.75
BGN4 Todd Bodine	.30	.75
BGN5 Hermie Sadler	.30	.75
BGN6 Tom Peck	.30	.75
BGN7 Tracy Leslie	.30	.75
BGN8 Ricky Craven	.50	1.25
BGN9 Chuck Bown	.30	.75
BGN10 Steve Grissom	.50	1.25
BGN11 Joe Nemechek	.50	1.25
BGN12 Robert Pressley	.50	1.25
BGN13 Rodney Combs	.30	.75
BGN14 Ward Burton	.50	1.25
BGN15 Mike Wallace	.30	.75

1994 Finish Line Down Home

This 10-card set was produced by Finish Line for insertion in its 1994 racing product. The cards focus on drivers from small towns with information about the driver as well as their hometown. The cards were randomly inserted in all types of 1994 Finish Line racing packs. The cards were seeded in packs at a rate of one in eight packs.

COMPLETE SET (10)	5.00	12.00
1 Harry Gant	.50	1.25
2 Ernie Irvan	.50	1.25
3 Dale Jarrett	1.50	4.00
4 Mark Martin	2.00	5.00
5 Kyle Petty	.50	1.25
6 Ricky Rudd	.75	2.00
7 Ken Schrader	.25	.60
8 Morgan Shepherd	.25	.60
9 Jimmy Spencer	.25	.60
10 Rusty Wallace	2.00	5.00

1994 Finish Line Gold Signature

Gold foil signatures adorn the fronts of these 5 cards randomly inserted in 1994 Finish Line hobby packs. Backs feature a short driver bio and the set title "Gold Signature Series." Odds of finding a Gold Signature card was one in 20 packs. The cards are unnumbered and have been listed below in

alphabetical order.

COMPLETE SET (5)	10.00	25.00
1 Ernie Irvan	1.25	3.00
2 Dale Jarrett	4.00	10.00
3 Mark Martin	5.00	12.00
4 Kyle Petty	1.25	3.00
5 Rusty Wallace	5.00	12.00

1994 Finish Line New Stars on the Horizon

Finish Line produced this eight-card insert set that focuses on 1994 Winston Cup rookies. The cards were randomly packed in all types of 1994 Finish Line racing packs. The cards could be pulled at a rate of one in eight packs.

COMPLETE SET (8)	3.00	8.00
1 John Andretti	.60	1.50
2 Todd Bodine	.30	.75
3 Chuck Bown	.30	.75
4 Jeff Burton	.75	2.00
5 Ward Burton	.60	1.50
6 Steve Grissom	.60	1.50
7 Joe Nemechek	.60	1.50
8 Loy Allen Jr.	.30	.75

1994 Finish Line Victory Lane

Finish Line produced this 18-card insert set that focuses on 1993 race winners. The cards were inserted one per 1994 Finish Line special retail jumbo pack and one every eight regular packs. The cards were printed on silver foil card stock.

COMPLETE SET (18)	12.50	30.00
VL1 Davey Allison VL	1.50	4.00
VL2 Geoff Bodine	.40	1.00
VL3 Ernie Irvan VL	.75	2.00
VL4 Dale Jarrett	2.50	6.00
VL5 Mark Martin VL	3.00	8.00
VL6 Kyle Petty	.75	2.00
VL7 Morgan Shepherd	.40	1.00
VL8 Ricky Rudd	1.25	3.00
VL9 Rusty Wallace VL	3.00	8.00
VL10 Rusty Wallace	3.00	8.00
VL11 Ricky Rudd	1.25	3.00
VL12 Morgan Shepherd	.40	1.00
VL13 Kyle Petty	.75	2.00
VL14 Mark Martin	3.00	8.00
VL15 Dale Jarrett	2.50	6.00
VL16 Davey Allison	1.50	4.00
VL17 Geoff Bodine	.40	1.00
VL18 Ernie Irvan	.75	2.00

1994 Finish Line Gold Promos

Finish Line produced these promo cards to preview the 1994 Finish Line Gold release. The unnumbered cards were packaged in a cello wrapper and are often sold as a complete set.

COMPLETE SET (3)	3.00	8.00
P1 Jeff Gordon's Car Promo	2.50	6.00
P2 Terry Labonte Promo	1.50	4.00
P3 Cover Card Promo	.20	.50

1994 Finish Line Gold

Finish Line produced their first premium NASCAR set in 1994 -- Finish Line Gold. The 100-card set was packaged in 8-card packs with 32 packs per box in 2,500 numbered 12 box cases. Inserts included an Autograph series, Calling Cards and a Teamwork set. Finish Line produced a special Ernie Irvan hologram card (number of 3000) randomly inserted in packs. Three promo cards came packaged in together in a cello pack. They were distributed to dealers and members of the media.

COMPLETE SET (100)	8.00	20.00
WAX BOX	20.00	50.00
1 Joe Gibbs	.15	.40
2 Hut Stricklin's Car	.02	.10
3 Ricky Rudd's Car	.07	.20
4 Sterling Marlin	.25	.60
5 Hut Stricklin	.07	.20
6 Lake Speed	.07	.20
7 Kyle Petty	.15	.40
8 Ernie Irvan	.15	.40
9 Dale Jarrett	.50	1.25
10 Rusty Wallace	.60	1.50
11 Jeff Gordon	.75	2.00
12 Michael Waltrip	.15	.40
13 Darrell Waltrip	.15	.40
14 Mark Martin	.60	1.50
15 Morgan Shepherd	.07	.20
16 Rusty Wallace's Car	.25	.60
17 Robert Pressley	.07	.20
18 Ted Musgrave	.07	.20
19 Ken Schrader	.07	.20
20 Wally Dallenbach Jr.'s Car	.02	.10
21 Geoff Bodine	.07	.20
22 Kyle Petty	.15	.40
23 Brett Bodine's Car	.02	.10
24 Rusty Wallace	.60	1.50
25 Brett Bodine	.07	.20
26 Robert Yates	.02	.10
27 Morgan Shepherd	.07	.20
28 Jeff Gordon	.75	2.00
29 Terry Labonte	.25	.60
30 Darrell Waltrip's Car	.07	.20
31 Darrell Waltrip	.15	.40
32 Bobby Labonte's Car	.15	.40
33 Terry Labonte	.25	.60
34 Ricky Rudd	.25	.60
35 Ken Schrader	.07	.20
36 Harry Gant	.15	.40
37 Kenny Wallace	.07	.20
38 Dale Jarrett	.50	1.25
39 Geoff Bodine	.07	.20
40 Morgan Shepherd's Car	.02	.10
41 Harry Gant	.15	.40
42 Jimmy Spencer	.07	.20
43 Ernie Irvan	.15	.40
44 Ricky Craven	.15	.40
45 Lake Speed	.07	.20
46 Ernie Irvan's Car	.07	.20
47 Terry Labonte's Car	.15	.40
48 Mark Martin	.60	1.50
49 Ricky Rudd	.25	.60
50 Ted Musgrave	.07	.20
51 Sterling Marlin's Car	.07	.20
52 Harry Gant	.15	.40
53 Jimmy Spencer	.07	.20
54 Geoff Bodine	.07	.20
55 Ted Musgrave	.07	.20
56 Felix Sabates Chany Sabates	.02	.10
57 Ricky Rudd	.25	.60
58 Kyle Petty's Car	.07	.20
59 Rusty Wallace	.60	1.50
60 Jeff Gordon	.75	2.00
61 Jack Roush	.02	.10
62 Michael Waltrip	.15	.40
63 Geoff Bodine's Car	.02	.10
64 Darrell Waltrip	.15	.40
65 Jeff Gordon 's Car	.40	1.00
66 Darrell Waltrip	.15	.40
67 Hut Stricklin	.07	.20
68 Rusty Wallace	.60	1.50
69 Morgan Shepherd	.07	.20
70 Sterling Marlin	.25	.60
71 Kyle Petty	.15	.40
72 Mark Martin	.60	1.50
73 Hut Stricklin	.07	.20
74 Michael Waltrip's Car	.07	.20
75 Dale Jarrett	.50	1.25
76 Ken Schrader	.07	.20
77 Terry Labonte	.25	.60
78 Hermie Sadler	.07	.20
79 Mark Martin's Car	.25	.60
80 Ernie Irvan	.15	.40
81 Mark Martin	.60	1.50
82 Brett Bodine	.07	.20
83 Richard Petty	.25	.60
84 Michael Waltrip	.15	.40
85 Kyle Petty	.15	.40
86 Lake Speed's Car	.02	.10
87 Ken Schrader's Car	.02	.10
88 Jeff Gordon	.75	2.00
89 Dale Jarrett	.50	1.25
90 Jimmy Spencer	.07	.20
91 Harry Gant	.15	.40
92 David Green	.07	.20
93 Ernie Irvan	.15	.40
94 Ricky Rudd	.25	.60
95 Dale Jarrett's Car	.15	.40
96 Lake Speed	.07	.20
97 Jimmy Spencer's Car	.02	.10
98 Morgan Shepherd	.07	.20
99 Brett Bodine	.07	.20
100 Sterling Marlin	.25	.60
NNO Ernie Irvan Hologram numbered of 3000	20.00	50.00

1994 Finish Line Gold Autographs

Nineteen drivers and crew members signed copies of their regular 1994 Finish Line Gold cards to be randomly inserted into packs (approximately one per box). The autographs were signed using a gold paint pen and limited to less than 2000 copies of each card.

COMPLETE SET (19)	150.00	300.00
6 Lake Speed	7.50	15.00
15 Morgan Shepherd	7.50	15.00
16 Buddy Parrott	4.00	8.00
17 Robert Pressley	7.50	15.00
33 Terry Labonte	12.50	30.00
37 Kenny Wallace	7.50	15.00
38 Dale Jarrett	25.00	50.00
44 Ricky Craven	10.00	25.00
51 Tony Glover	4.00	8.00
65 Ray Evernham	10.00	25.00
76 Ken Schrader	10.00	25.00
78 Hermie Sadler	7.50	15.00
80 Ernie Irvan	10.00	25.00
81 Mark Martin	15.00	40.00
84 Michael Waltrip	8.00	20.00
92 David Green	7.50	15.00
94 Ricky Rudd	15.00	30.00
95 Jimmy Makar	4.00	8.00
99 Brett Bodine	7.50	15.00

1994 Finish Line Gold Phone Cards

For the first time in racing, prepaid calling cards were inserted in card packs with this set. Each card had a phone value of $2.50 and was printed on the usual plastic stock similar to a credit card. The cards are numbered of 3,000 and carried an expiration date of 12/31/95. Phone cards with the pin number revealed are generally worth half of Mint unscratched cards.

COMPLETE SET (9)	5.00	12.00
1 Geoff Bodine	.10	.30
2 Jeff Gordon	1.25	3.00
3 Ernie Irvan	.25	.60
4 Dale Jarrett	.75	2.00
5 Mark Martin	1.00	2.50
6 Kyle Petty	.25	.60
7 Ricky Rudd	.40	1.00
8 Rusty Wallace	1.00	2.50
9 Darrell Waltrip	.25	.60

1994 Finish Line Gold Teamwork

Teamwork cards were randomly inserted in 1994 Finish Line Gold at a rate of one per eight packs. Each card features a top Winston Cup NASCAR driver along with their crew chief and were printed on gold foil stock.

COMPLETE SET (10)	8.00	20.00
TG1 Rusty Wallace Buddy Parrott	2.50	6.00
TG2 Mark Martin Steve Hmiel	2.50	6.00
TG3 Ricky Rudd Bill Ingle	1.00	2.50
TG4 Dale Jarrett Jimmy Makar	2.00	5.00
TG5 Morgan Shepherd Leonard Wood	.30	.75
TG6 Jeff Gordon Ray Evernham	3.00	8.00
TG7 Ernie Irvan Larry McReynolds	.60	1.50
TG8 Brett Bodine Donnie Richeson	.30	.75
TG9 Geoff Bodine Paul Andrews	.30	.75
TG10 Darrell Waltrip Barry Dodson	.60	1.50

1994 Finish Line Phone Cards

These cards were issued in clear envelopes and sold through major retail outlets. They were the first phone cards released by Finish Line. There were 5000 of each series one card (1-5) produced and 1800 of each series two card (6-10). Finish Line made available a gold version of the Bill Elliott and the Ernie Irvan cards.

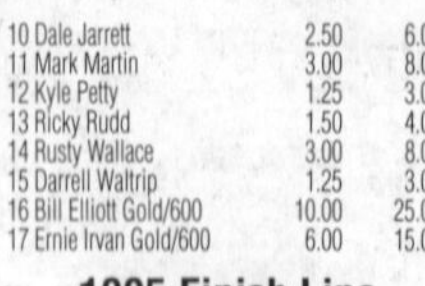

COMPLETE SET (15)	25.00	60.00
1 Bill Elliott	2.00	5.00
2 Jeff Gordon	4.00	10.00
3 Bobby Labonte	2.50	6.00
4 Sterling Marlin	1.50	4.00
5 Rusty Wallace	3.00	8.00
6 Geoff Bodine	1.25	3.00
7 Bill Elliott	2.00	5.00
8 Jeff Gordon	4.00	10.00
9 Ernie Irvan	1.25	3.00
10 Dale Jarrett	2.50	6.00
11 Mark Martin	3.00	8.00
12 Kyle Petty	1.25	3.00
13 Ricky Rudd	1.50	4.00
14 Rusty Wallace	3.00	8.00
15 Darrell Waltrip	1.25	3.00
16 Bill Elliott Gold/600	10.00	25.00
17 Ernie Irvan Gold/600	6.00	15.00

1995 Finish Line

Classic produced this 1995 set for Finish Line. The 120-card set was packaged in 10-card hobby and 10-card retail foil packs with 36-packs per box. Hobby cases were numbered sequentially to 1995. Inserts included Silver foil and Printer's Proof parallel sets, along with four others. Hobby and retail pack versions differed according to which inserts could be found. Two different Dale Earnhardt autographed cards, one for hobby and one for retail packs, were also randomly inserted. Each signed card was numbered of 250. Other than the signature the cards are the same as card #89 in the set. There was also another Dale Eanhardt certified autograph card similar to #111 in the basic set that was also serial numbered to 250, but there were no foil markings or nameplate on the front of the card.

COMPLETE SET (120)	6.00	15.00
1 Dale Earnhardt	1.25	3.00
2 Rusty Wallace	.60	1.50
3 Darrell Waltrip	.15	.40
4 Sterling Marlin	.25	.60
5 Terry Labonte	.25	.60
6 Mark Martin	.60	1.50
7 Geoff Bodine	.07	.20
8 Jeff Burton	.25	.60
9 Jimmy Spencer	.07	.20
10 Ricky Rudd	.25	.60
11 Brett Bodine	.07	.20
12 Bobby Allison	.07	.20
13 John Andretti Nancy Andretti	.07	.20
14 Rick Hendrick	.02	.10
15 Robert Gee	.02	.10
16 Ted Musgrave	.07	.20
17 Darrell Waltrip	.15	.40
18 Dale Jarrett	.50	1.25
19 Kenny Wallace	.07	.20
20 David Green	.07	.20
21 Morgan Shepherd	.07	.20
22 Rick Mast	.07	.20
23 Chad Little	.07	.20
24 Jeff Gordon Brooke Sealy	.75	2.00
25 Ken Schrader	.07	.20
26 Steve Kinser Kenny Bernstein	.07	.20
27 Sterling Marlin	.25	.60
28 Ernie Irvan		
29 Geoff Bodine	.07	.20
30 Michael Waltrip Elizabeth Waltrip	.15	.40
31 Ward Burton	.15	.40
32 Jeremy Mayfield	.15	.40
33 Robert Pressley	.07	.20
34 Rusty Wallace	.50	1.50
35 Todd Bodine	.07	.20
36 Paul Andrews	.02	.10
37 Dale Jarrett	.50	1.25
38 Morgan Shepherd	.07	.20
39 Joe Nemechek Andrea Nemechek	.07	.20
40 Felix Sabates	.02	.10
41 Ricky Craven	.15	.40
42 Kyle Petty	.15	.40
43 Richard Petty	.25	.60
44 Robert Yates	.02	.10
45 Hermie Sadler	.07	.20
46 Johnny Benson	.15	.40
47 Ken Schrader	.07	.20
48 Steve Grissom	.07	.20
49 Bobby Dotter	.07	.20
50 Dick Trickle	.07	.20
51 Ernie Irvan Jordan Irvan	.15	.40
52 Kyle Petty	.15	.40
53 Jeff Gordon	.75	2.00
54 Mark Martin	.60	1.50
55 Morgan Shepherd	.07	.20
56 Ward Burton	.15	.40
57 Jimmy Makar	.02	.10
58 Darrell Waltrip	.15	.40
59 Walter Bud Moore	.02	.10
60 Rick Mast	.07	.20
61 Michael Waltrip	.15	.40
62 Derrike Cope	.07	.20
63 Buddy Parrott	.02	.10
64 Lake Speed	.07	.20
65 Ray Evernham	.02	.10
66 Steve Hmiel	.02	.10
67 Jeff Gordon Ray Evernham	.60	1.50
68 Brett Bodine	.07	.20
69 Terry Labonte	.25	.60
70 Rusty Wallace	.60	1.50
71 Larry Pearson	.02	.10
72 Ted Musgrave	.07	.20
73 Kyle Petty	.15	.40
74 John Andretti	.07	.20
75 Todd Bodine Lynn Bodine	.07	.20
76 Joe Nemechek	.07	.20
77 Jimmy Spencer	.07	.20
78 Brett Bodine	.07	.20
79 Mark Martin	.60	1.50
80 Harry Gant	.15	.40
81 Lake Speed	.07	.20
82 Larry McReynolds	.02	.10
83 Ricky Rudd	.25	.
84 Loy Allen Jr.	.07	.
85 Travis Carter	.02	.
86 Mike Wallace	.07	.
87 Geoff Bodine	.07	.
88 Dennis Setzer	.07	.
89 Dale Earnhardt	1.25	3.
90 Mike Wallace	.07	.
91 Bobby Labonte	.50	1.
92 Ernie Irvan	.15	.
93 Jeff Burton	.25	.
94 Sterling Marlin	.25	.
95 Michael Waltrip	.15	.
96 Tim Fedewa	.07	.
97 Terry Labonte	.25	.
98 Jeremy Mayfield	.15	.
99 Bill Ingle	.02	.
100 Ken Schrader	.07	.
101 Tony Glover	.02	.
102 Todd Bodine	.07	.
103 Bobby Labonte	.50	1.
104 Richard Petty	.25	.
105 Jeff Gordon	.75	2.
106 Ricky Rudd	.25	.
107 A.G. Dillard	.02	.
108 Junior Johnson	.07	.
109 Steve Grissom	.07	.
110 Dale Jarrett	.50	1.
111 Dale Earnhardt	1.25	3.
112 Kenny Wallace	.07	.
113 Jimmy Johnson	.02	.
114 Dave Marcis	.07	.
115 Kenny Bernstein	.07	.
116 Bobby Hamilton	.07	.
117 Steve Kinser	.07	.
118 John Andretti	.07	.
119 Derrike Cope	.07	.
120 Ricky Craven	.15	.
CE1 Dale Earnhardt Club Promo	3.00	8.
HP1 Dale Earnhardt Promo (hobby version)	2.50	6.
RP1 Dale Earnhardt Promo (retail version)	2.50	6.
89AUH Dale Earnhardt AU/250 Red Hobby	100.00	200.
89AUR Dale Earnhardt AU/250 Blue Retail	100.00	200.
111AU Dale Earnhardt AU/250	100.00	200.

1995 Finish Line Printer's Proof

A parallel to the regular 1995 Finish Line set, th cards feature a red foil "Printer's Proof" logo on cardfront along with the numbering "One of 3 The cards were inserted in hobby packs only w wrapper stated odds of 1:18 packs.

COMPLETE SET (120) 100.00 200.
*PRINT.PROOFS: 3X TO 8X BASIC CARDS

1995 Finish Line Silve

A parallel set to the regular issue 1995 Finish set, these cards feature a "95 Silver" logo on front printed in silver foil. Cards were packaged per foil pack in both hobby and retail versions.

COMPLETE SET (120) 12.00 30.
*SILVERS: 1X TO 2X BASIC CARDS

1995 Finish Line Dale Earnhardt

Randomly inserted in 1995 Finish Line packs, th 10 cards feaured Dale Earnhardt and were prir using Classic's micro-lined printing technolc Wrapper stated odds for pulling one of the cards 1:18.

COMPLETE SET (10)	25.00	50.
COMMON CARD (DE1-DE10)	3.00	8.

1995 Finish Line Gold Signature

Cards from this 16-card set were randomly inse in 1995 Finish Line retail packs. Each card numbered one of 1995. The cards could be foun a rate of one per nine retail packs.

COMPLETE SET (16)	50.00	120.
GS1 Jeff Gordon	8.00	20.
GS2 Rusty Wallace	6.00	15.
GS3 Dale Earnhardt	12.50	30.

GS4 Sterling Marlin	2.50	6.00
GS5 Terry Labonte	2.50	6.00
GS6 Mark Martin	6.00	15.00
GS7 Geoff Bodine	.75	2.00
GS8 Ken Schrader	.75	2.00
GS9 Kyle Petty	1.50	4.00
GS10 Ricky Rudd	2.50	6.00
GS11 Michael Waltrip	1.50	4.00
GS12 Darrell Waltrip	1.50	4.00
GS13 Dale Jarrett	5.00	12.00
GS14 Morgan Shepherd	.75	2.00
GS15 Lake Speed	.75	2.00
GS16 Ted Musgrave	.75	2.00

1995 Finish Line Standout Cars

Randomly inserted in hobby only packs, these 10 cards feature top driver's cars in a "Standout" format. The card's background could actually be folded to allow the card to stand-up by itself. Wrapper stated odds for pulling one of the cards is 1:9 packs.

COMPLETE SET (10)	10.00	25.00
SC1 Dale Earnhardt's Car	4.00	10.00
SC2 Mark Martin's Car	2.00	5.00
SC3 Rusty Wallace's Car	2.00	5.00
SC4 Ricky Rudd's Car	.75	2.00
SC5 Morgan Shepherd's Car	.25	.60
SC6 Terry Labonte's Car	.75	2.00
SC7 Jeff Gordon's Car	2.50	6.00
SC8 Darrell Waltrip's Car	.50	1.25
SC9 Geoff Bodine's Car	.25	.60
SC10 Michael Waltrip's Car	.50	1.25

1995 Finish Line Standout Drivers

Randomly inserted in retail only packs, these 10-cards feature top drivers in a "Standout" format. The card background could actually be folded to allow the card to stand-up by itself. The same ten drivers were used for both the Standout Cars and Standout Drivers insert sets. Wrapper stated odds for pulling one of the cards is 1:9 packs.

COMPLETE SET (10)	15.00	40.00
SD1 Dale Earnhardt	6.00	15.00
SD2 Mark Martin	3.00	8.00
SD3 Rusty Wallace	3.00	8.00
SD4 Ricky Rudd	1.25	3.00
SD5 Morgan Shepherd	.40	1.00
SD6 Terry Labonte	1.25	3.00
SD7 Jeff Gordon	4.00	10.00
SD8 Darrell Waltrip	.75	2.00
SD9 Geoff Bodine	.40	1.00
SD10 Michael Waltrip	.75	2.00

1995 Finish Line Coca-Cola 600

Although packaged and distributed separately, the Coca-Cola 600 set is simply a parallel version of the 50-card 1995 Assets racing release. Each card features special red foil lettering on the cardfront commemorating the 1995 Speed Street Festival in conjunction with the Coca-Cola 600 in Charlotte. The cards were packaged in factory set form only. Two insert sets were also included in each factory set: Die Cuts and Coca-Cola 600 race Winners. The sets were sold during the Speed Street Festival and on a live QVC broadcast from the festival.

COMPLETE SET (50)	3.00	8.00
COMP.FACT.SET (65)	6.00	15.00
*SINGLES: .2X TO .5X BASE ASSETS		

1995 Finish Line Coca-Cola 600 Die Cuts

These cards were packaged one complete set per 1995 Finish Line Coca-Cola 600 factory set. They are essentially a parallel to the 1995 Assets Coca-Cola 600 Die Cuts insert issue except for a different cardback and smaller number of cards -- five instead of ten.

COMPLETE SET (5)	1.25	3.00
C1 Dale Earnhardt	.50	1.25
C2 Rusty Wallace	.20	.50
C3 Jeff Gordon	.30	.75
C4 Dale Jarrett	.15	.40
C5 Mark Martin	.20	.50

1995 Finish Line Coca-Cola 600 Winners

One complete set was included in each 1995 Finish Line Coca-Cola 600 factory set. The ten cards feature former winners of the Coca-Cola 600 printed on reflective foil card stock.

COMPLETE SET (10)	2.00	5.00
CC1 Darrell Waltrip	.05	.15
CC2 Dale Earnhardt	.50	1.25
CC3 Kyle Petty	.05	.15
CC4 Darrell Waltrip	.05	.15
CC5 Darrell Waltrip	.05	.15
CC6 Rusty Wallace	.20	.50
CC7 Davey Allison's Car	.05	.15
CC8 Dale Earnhardt	.50	1.25
CC9 Dale Earnhardt	.50	1.25
CC10 Jeff Gordon	.30	.75

1995 Finish Line Phone Card of the Month

These cards were available through the Finish Line Racing Club. The cards were printed in quantities of 1500 each.

COMPLETE SET (4)	40.00	75.00
1 Jeff Gordon/1500	12.50	25.00
2 Sterling Marlin/1500	6.00	12.00
3 Mark Martin/1500	10.00	20.00
4 Rusty Wallace/1500	10.00	20.00

1995 Finish Line Platinum 5-Unit Phone Cards

There were 500 of each of the cards in this series. The cards could be bought in different unit denomonations, 5, 10, 25, and 60. The cards were sold through the Finish Line Racing Club.

COMPLETE SET (4)	12.50	30.00
COMP. 10 UNIT SET (4)	30.00	50.00
*10 UNIT CARDS: 1X TO 1.5X 5 UNIT CARDS		
COMP. 25 UNIT SET (4)	60.00	80.00
*25 UNIT CARDS: 2X TO 3X 5 UNIT CARDS		
COMP. 60 UNIT SET (4)	160.00	200.00
*60 UNIT CARDS: 5X TO 7X 5 UNIT CARDS		
1 Jeff Gordon	5.00	12.00
2 Mark Martin	4.00	10.00
3 Ricky Rudd	2.50	6.00
4 Rusty Wallace	4.00	10.00

1995 Finish Line SuperTrucks

The inaugural 1995 Finish Line SuperTrucks set features 80-cards that were packaged in 10-card foil packs with 36-packs per box. Sixteen-box case production was limited to 650 cases. Inserts include a Rainbow foil parallel set, along with Calling Cards, Champion's Choice, Super Signatures and Winter Heat Hot Shoes.

COMPLETE SET (80)	4.00	10.00
1 Mike Skinner	.10	.30
2 Butch Gilliland	.05	.15
3 Rick Carelli	.10	.30
4 Walker Evans' Truck	.02	.10
5 Joe Bessey	.05	.15
6 Ken Schrader	.20	.50
7 Scott Lagasse	.10	.30
8 Bob Keselowski's Truck	.02	.10
9 Butch Gilliland's Truck	.02	.10
10 Mike Hulbert	.05	.15
11 Kerry Teague	.05	.15
12 Troy Beebe	.05	.15
13 Walker Evans	.05	.15
14 Joe Ruttman	.05	.15
15 P.J. Jones	.05	.15
16 Jack Sprague's Truck	.02	.10
17 Jeff Gordon	.60	1.50
18 Tobey Butler	.05	.15
19 Jerry Glanville's Truck	.02	.10
20 Roger Mears	.05	.15
21 Bill Sedgwick	.05	.15
22 Gary Collins	.05	.15
23 Walker Evans	.05	.15
24 Sammy Swindell	.10	.30
25 Steve McEachern's Truck	.02	.10
26 Geoff Bodine	.20	.50
27 Terry Labonte	.25	.60
28 Butch Miller	.05	.15
29 Geoff Bodine's Truck	.05	.15
30 Mike Skinner Richard Childress	.10	.30
31 Tommy Archer	.05	.15
32 Steve McEachern	.05	.15
33 Tobey Butler	.05	.15
34 Bob Strait	.05	.15
35 Jerry Glanville	.05	.15
36 Mike Skinner's Truck	.05	.15
37 Joe Bessey	.05	.15
38 P.J. Jones	.05	.15
39 Jack Sprague	.05	.15
40 Tommy Archer's Truck	.02	.10
41 Kerry Teague	.05	.15
42 Roger Mears	.05	.15
43 Ron Hornaday	.10	.30
44 Tommy Archer	.05	.15
45 Scott Lagasse	.10	.30
46 Walker Evans	.05	.15
47 Gary Collins' Truck	.02	.10
48 Jack Sprague	.05	.15
49 Bob Keselowski	.05	.15
50 Geoff Bodine	.20	.50
51 Ken Schrader	.20	.50
52 Tobey Butler's Truck	.02	.10
53 Kerry Teague's Truck	.02	.10
54 Mike Skinner	.10	.30
55 Terry Labonte	.25	.60
56 Troy Beebe	.05	.15
57 Richard Childress	.10	.30
58 Jerry Glanville	.05	.15
59 Butch Miller	.05	.15
60 Terry Labonte's Truck	.05	.15
61 T.J. Clark	.05	.15
62 Butch Gilliland	.05	.15
63 Joe Ruttman	.05	.15
64 Scott Lagasse's Truck	.05	.15
65 Steve McEachern	.05	.15
66 Gary Collins	.05	.15
67 Bob Strait	.05	.15
68 Rick Carelli's Truck	.02	.10
69 Sammy Swindell	.10	.30
70 Ken Schrader's Truck	.02	.10
71 Ron Hornaday	.10	.30
72 T.J. Clark	.05	.15
73 Geoff Bodine	.20	.50
74 Mike Hulbert	.05	.15
75 Ken Schrader	.20	.50
76 P.J. Jones' Truck	.02	.10
77 Roger Mears' Truck	.02	.10
78 Bob Keselowski	.05	.15
79 Rick Carelli	.10	.30
80 Checklist	.02	.10

1995 Finish Line SuperTrucks Rainbow Foil

A parallel set to the regular issue 1995 Finish Line SuperTrucks set, these cards feature a rainbow foil logo on the cardfront. The cards were packaged one per foil pack.

COMPLETE SET (80)	25.00	50.00
*STARS: 2X TO 4X BASIC CARDS		

1995 Finish Line SuperTrucks Calling Cards

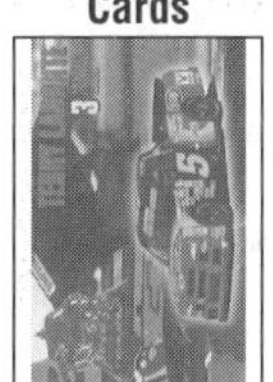

Randomly packed at the rate of approximately 1:18 packs, these Calling Cards carry a phone time value of three minutes with an expiration date of 12/31/1996. Each card features a gold foil Finish Line logo on the cardfront and a serial number of 2100 on the cardback.

COMPLETE SET (10)	5.00	12.00
1 Geoff Bodine	1.00	2.50
2 Rick Carelli	.60	1.50
3 Walker Evans	.30	.75
4 Jerry Glanville	.30	.75
5 Ron Hornaday	.60	1.50
6 P.J. Jones	.30	.75
7 Terry Labonte	1.25	3.00
8 Roger Mears	.30	.75
9 Ken Schrader	1.00	2.50
10 Mike Skinner	.60	1.50

1995 Finish Line SuperTrucks Champion's Choice

Champion's Choice cards were randomly inserted in 1995 Finish Line SuperTrucks packs at the wrapper stated odds of 1:9 packs. The cards feature favorites to win SuperTrucks racing events in 1995.

COMPLETE SET (6)	4.00	10.00
CC1 Roger Mears	.40	1.00
CC2 Terry Labonte	1.50	4.00
CC3 Rick Carelli	.40	1.00
CC4 Ron Hornaday	.60	1.50
CC5 Sammy Swindell	.60	1.50
CC6 Geoff Bodine	1.00	2.50

1995 Finish Line SuperTrucks Super Signature

Super Signature Series cards were randomly inserted in 1995 Finish Line SuperTrucks packs at the wrapper stated odds of 1:9 packs. The 10-cards feature top SuperTrucks drivers printed with a gold foil signature on the cardfront.

COMPLETE SET (10)	10.00	20.00
SS1 Jeff Gordon	4.00	10.00
SS2 Richard Childress	.60	1.50
SS3 Ken Schrader	2.00	4.00
SS4 Jerry Glanville	.60	1.50
SS5 Mike Skinner	1.00	2.50
SS6 Tobey Butler	.60	1.50
SS7 Joe Bessey	.60	1.50
SS8 Scott Lagasse	1.00	2.50
SS9 P.J. Jones	.60	1.50
SS10 Terry Labonte	2.00	5.00

1995 Finish Line SuperTrucks Winter Heat Hot Shoes

Winter Heat Hot Shoes cards are randomly inserted in 1995 Finish Line SuperTrucks packs at the wrapper stated odds of 1:9 packs. The four-cards feature top performers from the SuperTrucks Winter Heat events held in Tucson. The cards are printed with gold foil layering on the cardfront.

COMPLETE SET (4)	2.00	5.00
HS1 Mike Skinner	.60	1.50
HS2 P.J. Jones	.50	1.25
HS3 Rick Carelli	.50	1.25
HS4 Ron Hornaday	.60	1.50

1996 Finish Line

This 100-card set features new looks for '96 of the top Winston Cup drivers and their cars. After teaming up with Classic to produce their '95 line, Finish Line returned to making their own cards in '96. The cards were packaged 10 cards per pack, 36 packs per box and 16 boxes per case. The packs had a suggested retail price of $1.99. There were a total of 1,500 cases produced. The product was distributed through both hobby and retail channels.

COMPLETE SET (100)	4.00	10.00
1 Jeff Gordon	.75	2.00
2 Ted Musgrave	.07	.20
3 Rusty Wallace	.60	1.50
4 Ward Burton's Car	.02	.10
5 Terry Labonte	.25	.60
6 Derrike Cope	.07	.20
7 Steve Grissom	.07	.20
8 Mark Martin	.60	1.50
9 Mark Martin's Car	.25	.60
10 Ricky Rudd	.25	.60
11 Darrell Waltrip	.15	.40
12 Jeff Burton	.25	.60
13 Ernie Irvan	.15	.40
14 Jeremy Mayfield	.15	.40
15 Michael Waltrip's Car	.07	.20
16 Hut Stricklin	.07	.20
17 Brett Bodine	.07	.20
18 Gary DeHart	.07	.20
19 Bobby Hamilton	.07	.20
20 Kyle Petty	.15	.40
21 Derrike Cope's Car	.02	.10
22 Dick Trickle	.07	.20
23 Sterling Marlin	.25	.60
24 Joe Gibbs	.15	.40
25 Bobby Allison	.07	.20
26 Bobby Labonte	.50	1.25
27 Rusty Wallace	.60	1.50
28 Rusty Wallace's Car	.25	.60
29 Morgan Shepherd	.07	.20
30 Geoff Bodine	.07	.20
31 Ricky Craven	.07	.20
32 Jimmy Spencer	.07	.20
33 Ernie Irvan's Car	.07	.20
34 Michael Waltrip	.15	.40
35 Joe Nemechek	.07	.20
36 Ward Burton	.15	.40
37 John Andretti	.07	.20
38 Ken Schrader	.07	.20
39 Mike Wallace	.07	.20
40 Bill Elliott's Car	.15	.40
41 Sterling Marlin	.25	.60
42 Bill Elliott	.30	.75
43 Dale Jarrett	.50	1.25
44 Morgan Shepherd	.07	.20
45 Jimmy Spencer's Car	.02	.10
46 Mike Wallace	.07	.20
47 Chad Little	.07	.20
48 Todd Bodine	.07	.20
49 Bobby Hamilton	.07	.20
50 Larry McReynolds	.02	.10
51 Kenny Wallace	.07	.20
52 Ricky Rudd	.25	.60
53 Steve Grissom	.07	.20
54 Derrike Cope	.07	.20
55 Brett Bodine	.07	.20
56 Darrell Waltrip	.15	.40
57 Ted Musgrave	.07	.20
58 Johnny Benson	.07	.20
59 Geoff Bodine	.07	.20
60 Mark Martin	.60	1.50
61 Michael Waltrip	.15	.40
62 Sterling Marlin's Car	.07	.20
63 Larry McClure	.02	.10
64 Jeff Burton	.25	.60
65 Ward Burton	.15	.40
66 Rick Mast	.07	.20
67 Darrell Waltrip's Car	.07	.20
68 Darrell Waltrip	.15	.40
69 Bobby Labonte	.50	1.25
70 Johnny Benson	.07	.20
71 Todd Bodine	.07	.20
72 Jimmy Makar	.02	.10
73 Hut Stricklin	.07	.20
74 Terry Labonte's Car	.15	.40
75 Joe Nemechek	.07	.20
76 Ricky Craven	.07	.20
77 Bill Elliott	.30	.75
78 Terry Labonte	.25	.60
79 Robert Yates	.02	.10
80 Ricky Rudd's Car	.07	.20
81 Robin Pemberton	.02	.10
82 Ray Evernham	.02	.10
83 Tony Glover	.02	.10
84 David Green	.07	.20
85 Bobby Labonte's Car	.15	.40
86 Kyle Petty	.15	.40
87 Jeff Gordon	.75	2.00
88 Rick Hendrick	.02	.10
89 Ken Schrader	.07	.20
90 Dale Jarrett's Car	.15	.40
91 Felix Sabates	.02	.10
92 Ernie Irvan Jordan Irvan	.15	.40
93 Bill Ingle	.02	.10
94 Jimmy Spencer	.07	.20
95 Jeff Gordon's Car	.30	.75
96 Jack Roush	.02	.10
97 Steve Hmiel	.02	.10
98 Johnny Benson's Car	.02	.10
99 John Andretti	.07	.20
100 Dale Jarrett	.50	1.25

1996 Finish Line Printer's Proof

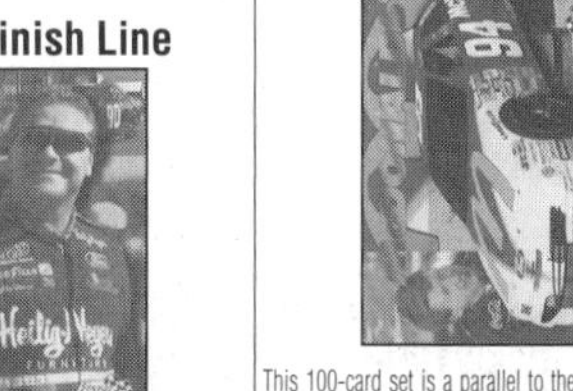

This 100-card set is a parallel to the base set. Each card features a Printer's Proof logo on the front to differentiate it from the base card. Each card is also stamped "one of 500" on the front. The cards were inserted at a rate of one per 18 packs.

COMPLETE SET (100)	150.00	300.00
*PRINT.PROOFS: 5X TO 12X BASE CARDS		

1996 Finish Line Silver

This 100-card set is a parallel to the base set. The cards feature a "Silver 96 Series" logo on the front to differentiate them from the regular cards. The Silver cards were inserted one per pack.

COMPLETE SET (100)	12.00	30.00
*SILVERS: 1X TO 2.5X BASE CARDS		

1996 Finish Line Comin' Back Ernie Irvan

This five-card insert set features Ernie Irvan's come back from his near fatal accident at Michigan in 1994 to his return to the Winston Cup circuit. The cards

use micro-foil technology and are inserted at a rate of one per 18 packs.

COMPLETE SET (5)	5.00	12.00
COMMON CARD (EI1-EI5)	1.25	3.00

1996 Finish Line Gold Signature

This 18-card insert set features the top names in Winston Cup racing. Each card has a facsimile gold signature of that specific driver across the front. The back of the card is sequentially numbered of 1996. The cards are randomly inserted in packs at a rate of one per 36.

COMPLETE SET (18)	40.00	100.00
GS1 Jeff Gordon	12.50	30.00
GS2 Sterling Marlin	4.00	10.00
GS3 Mark Martin	10.00	25.00
GS4 Rusty Wallace	10.00	25.00
GS5 Terry Labonte	4.00	10.00
GS6 Bill Elliott	5.00	12.00
GS7 Bobby Labonte	8.00	20.00
GS8 Ted Musgrave	1.25	3.00
GS9 Geoff Bodine	1.25	3.00
GS10 Bobby Hamilton	1.25	3.00
GS11 Darrell Waltrip	2.50	6.00
GS12 Michael Waltrip	2.50	6.00
GS13 Ernie Irvan	2.50	6.00
GS14 Dale Jarrett	8.00	20.00
GS15 Ken Schrader	1.25	3.00
GS16 Ricky Craven	1.25	3.00
GS17 Ricky Rudd	4.00	10.00
GS18 Kyle Petty	2.50	6.00

1996 Finish Line Man and Machine

Each of the 10 cards from the Man and Machine insert set is printed on 16pt. stock and are fully embossed. Each card features the driver, the owner and the car for the respective 10 teams in the set. The cards were inserted at a rate of one per nine packs.

COMPLETE SET (10)	6.00	15.00
MM1 Jeff Gordon	1.25	3.00
MM2 Mark Martin	1.00	2.50
MM3 Rusty Wallace	1.00	2.50
MM4 Sterling Marlin	.30	.75
MM5 Terry Labonte	.60	1.50
MM6 Ernie Irvan	.30	.75
MM7 Bobby Labonte	.60	1.50
MM8 Bill Elliott	.60	1.50
MM9 Derrike Cope	.15	.40
MM10 Johnny Benson	.15	.40

1996 Finish Line Mega-Phone XL Phone Cards

This four-card insert set offered four $25 dollar oversized phone cards. Each card is die-cut and measures 4" by 7" and shows a horizontal picture of the driver and his car. The cards were made available through redemption cards randomly inserted in packs at a rate of one per 36 packs. There were 8000 of each card made. Also, you only needed one redemption card and $60 to send in to Finish Line to obtain the complete four card set.

COMPLETE SET (4)	20.00	50.00
1 Bill Elliott	4.00	10.00
2 Jeff Gordon	10.00	25.00
3 Mark Martin	8.00	20.00
4 Rusty Wallace	8.00	20.00

1996 Finish Line Rise To The Top Jeff Gordon

This 10-card insert set features Jeff Gordon's "Rise to the Top" to win the 1995 Winston Cup Championship. Each card features micro-foil technology and was randomly inserted at a rate of one per 18 packs.

COMPLETE SET (10)	30.00	80.00
COMMON GORDON (JG1-JG10)	4.00	10.00

1996 Finish Line Black Gold

The 1996 Finish Line Black Gold Limited set was issued in one series totalling 30 cards. The one-card packs carried a suggested retail of $6.00 each. There were 16 boxes per case, 12 packs per box and one card per pack. The cards feature a driver or his car micro photo-etched onto a metal card front. The back is comprised of a 24pt. stock paper. The two pieces, metal front and paper back, were attached to make one card. There was an interactive game that involved one of the cards in the set. The DE - Designated Entry card allowed collectors a chance to win a 1997 Chevy Monte Carlo. By sending in that card or a scratch off BGL card (1:3 packs) that had Bobby Labonte's name on it, they were automatically entered in the drawing. Bobby Labonte was the winner of the NAPA 500 November 8th which was the qualifier for the BGL cards to be winners. There were also two special gold inserts: Jeff Gordon and Bill Elliott. These cards were randomly seeded 1:192 packs. A $25 Black Gold Megaphone XL Jumbo Die-Cut Phone card was randomly seeded 1:12 boxes. The four jumbo die-cut phone cards were printed in quantities of 2,750. Each of the jumbo phone cards carries an expiration date for the phone time of 1/1/2000.

COMPLETE SET (30)	30.00	60.00
C1 Jeff Gordon's Car	2.00	5.00
C2 Rusty Wallace's Car	1.50	4.00
C3 Sterling Marlin's Car	.50	1.25
C4 Terry Labonte's Car	.75	2.00
C5 Mark Martin's Car	1.50	4.00
C6 Ernie Irvan's Car	.40	1.00
C7 Bobby Labonte's Car	1.25	3.00
C8 Kyle Petty's Car	.40	1.00
C9 Ricky Rudd's Car	.60	1.50
C10 Bill Elliott's Car	.75	2.00
C11 Dale Jarrett's Car	1.25	3.00
C12 Darrell Waltrip's Car	.40	1.00
C13 Johnny Benson's Car	.25	.60
C14 Michael Waltrip's Car	.40	1.00
D1 Jeff Gordon	4.00	10.00
D2 Rusty Wallace	3.00	8.00
D3 DE- Designated Entry	.50	1.25
D4 Sterling Marlin	1.25	3.00
D5 Terry Labonte	1.50	4.00
D6 Mark Martin	3.00	8.00
D7 Ernie Irvan	.75	2.00
D8 Bobby Labonte	2.50	6.00
D9 Kyle Petty	.75	2.00
D10 Ricky Rudd	1.25	3.00
D11 Bill Elliott	1.50	4.00
D12 Ted Musgrave	.50	1.25
D13 Darrell Waltrip	.75	2.00
D14 Dale Jarrett	2.50	6.00
D15 Johnny Benson	.50	1.25
D16 Michael Waltrip	.50	1.25
SG1 Jeff Gordon Special Gold	25.00	60.00
SG2 Bill Elliott Special Gold	20.00	50.00
JPC1 Bill Elliott	.60	1.50
JPC2 Jeff Gordon	1.50	4.00
JPC3 Ernie Irvan	.40	1.00
JPC4 Terry Labonte	.60	1.50

1996 Finish Line Diamond Collection $5 Phone Cards

This series of cards was sold through mass retailers. The cards were issued in a black fold out case with each card front featuring a replica diamond and $5 worth of phone time.

COMPLETE SET (8)	15.00	40.00
1 Jeff Gordon	4.00	10.00
2 Bill Elliott	2.00	5.00
3 Dale Jarrett	2.50	6.00
4 Ernie Irvan	1.25	3.00
5 Mark Martin	3.00	8.00
6 Ricky Rudd	2.00	5.00
7 Terry Labonte	2.00	5.00
8 Rusty Wallace	3.00	8.00

1996 Finish Line Phone Pak

This was the first set of phone cards released in pack form. Each card carried a $2 phone value and there were 9500 of each $2 card produced. The cards were packaged three cards per pack, 15-packs per box and 16-boxes per case. A total of 800-cases were produced. Every case, box and phone card was individually numbered.There was also a parallel set of $2 signature cards. They were inserted one per pack and 5000 of each card was produced.

COMPLETE SET (40)	8.00	20.00
WAX BOX	7.50	20.00
1 John Andretti	.08	.25
2 Brett Bodine	.08	.25
3 Geoff Bodine	.08	.25
4 Todd Bodine	.08	.25
5 Jeff Burton	.30	.75
6 Ward Burton	.20	.50
7 Derrike Cope	.08	.25
8 Ricky Craven	.08	.25
9 Bill Elliott	.50	1.25
10 Bill Elliott's Car	.20	.50
11 Jeff Gordon	1.00	2.50
12 Jeff Gordon's Car	.40	1.00
13 Steve Grissom	.08	.25
14 Bobby Hamilton	.08	.25
15 Ernie Irvan	.20	.50
16 Ernie Irvan's Car	.08	.25
17 Dale Jarrett	.60	1.50
18 Bobby Labonte	.60	1.50
19 Bobby Labonte's Car	.20	.50
20 Terry Labonte	.30	.75
21 Terry Labonte's Car	.20	.50
22 Sterling Marlin	.30	.75
23 Sterling Marlin's Car	.20	.50
24 Mark Martin	.75	2.00
25 Mark Martin's Car	.30	.75
26 Ted Musgrave	.08	.25
27 Joe Nemechek	.08	.25
28 Kyle Petty	.20	.50
29 Ricky Rudd	.30	.75
30 Ricky Rudd's Car	.08	.25
31 Ken Schrader	.08	.25
32 Morgan Shepherd	.08	.25
33 Hut Stricklin	.08	.25
34 Dick Trickle	.08	.25
35 Mike Wallace	.08	.25
36 Rusty Wallace	.75	2.00
37 Rusty Wallace's Car	.30	.75
38 Michael Waltrip	.20	.50
39 Darrell Waltrip	.20	.50
40 Darrell Waltrip's Car	.08	.25
P1 Mark Martin Promo	1.25	3.00

1996 Finish Line Phone Pak $2 Signature

This set is essentially a parallel to the basic issue $2 Finish Line Phone Pak cards. Each card includes $2 worth of phone time as well as a facsimile autograph on the cardfront.

COMPLETE SET (40)	7.50	20.00

*$2 SIGNATURE: .6X TO 1.5X BASIC INSERTS

1996 Finish Line Phone Pak $5

This insert series of 24 cards features $5 in phone time value. There were 570 of each of the cards produced and the odd of pulling one from a pack was 1:15. Due to the bankruptcy of Finish Line, the phone time on these cards is not valid.

COMPLETE SET (24)	10.00	25.00
1 John Andretti	.20	.50
2 Brett Bodine	.20	.50
3 Geoff Bodine	.20	.50
4 Jeff Burton	.60	1.50
5 Ward Burton	.40	1.00
6 Ricky Craven	.20	.50
7 Derrike Cope	.20	.50
8 Bill Elliott	1.00	2.50
9 Jeff Gordon	2.00	5.00
10 Bobby Hamilton	.20	.50
11 Ernie Irvan	.40	1.00
12 Dale Jarrett	1.25	3.00
13 Bobby Labonte	1.25	3.00
14 Terry Labonte	.60	1.50
15 Sterling Marlin	.60	1.50
17 Ted Musgrave	.20	.50
18 Kyle Petty	.40	1.00
19 Ricky Rudd	.60	1.50
20 Ken Schrader	.20	.50
21 Morgan Shepherd	.20	.50
22 Rusty Wallace	1.50	4.00
23 Michael Waltrip	.40	1.00
24 Darrell Waltrip	.40	1.00

1996 Finish Line Phone Pak $10

There were 570 of each of the $10 cards. The cards were inserted at a rate of one in 30 packs. Due to the bankruptcy of Finish Line, the phone time on these cards is not valid.

COMPLETE SET (12)	12.00	30.00
1 Geoff Bodine	.40	1.00
2 Bill Elliott	2.00	5.00
3 Jeff Gordon	4.00	10.00
4 Ernie Irvan	.75	2.00
5 Bobby Labonte	2.50	6.00
6 Terry Labonte	1.25	3.00
7 Sterling Marlin	1.25	3.00
8 Mark Martin	3.00	8.00
9 Ricky Rudd	1.25	3.00
10 Ken Schrader	.40	1.00
11 Rusty Wallace	3.00	8.00
12 Darrell Waltrip	.75	2.00

1996 Finish Line Phone Pak $50

This series of insert phone cards features $50 in phone time value. The cards were inserted at a rate of one in 60 packs. Due to the bankruptcy of Finish Line, the phone time on these cards is not valid.

COMPLETE SET (8)	20.00	50.00
1 Bill Elliott	3.00	8.00
2 Jeff Gordon	6.00	15.00
3 Ernie Irvan	1.25	3.00
4 Bobby Labonte	4.00	10.00
5 Terry Labonte	2.00	5.00
6 Mark Martin	5.00	12.00
7 Ricky Rudd	2.00	5.00
8 Rusty Wallace	5.00	12.00

1996 Finish Line Phone Pak $100

There were 280 of each of the $100 phone cards. The cards were inserted one in 120 packs. Due to the bankruptcy of Finish Line, the phone time on these cards is not valid.

COMPLETE SET (6)	30.00	80.00
1 Bill Elliott	5.00	12.00
2 Jeff Gordon	10.00	25.00
3 Ernie Irvan	2.00	5.00
4 Terry Labonte	3.00	8.00
5 Mark Martin	8.00	20.00
6 Rusty Wallace	8.00	20.00

1996 Finish Line Save Mart Phone Cards

This set of three phone cards was distributed at the Save Mart Supermarkets in the Sonoma, California area in conjunction with the Save Mart Supermarkets 300 race. They were used as a promotion to get people to come in to the stores. The phone time on these cards has expired.

COMPLETE SET (3)	2.00	5.00
1 Geoff Bodine/2650	.75	2.00
2 Ernie Irvan/2650	1.00	2.50
3 Save-Mart Car/2650	.40	1.00

1997 Finish Line Phone Pak II

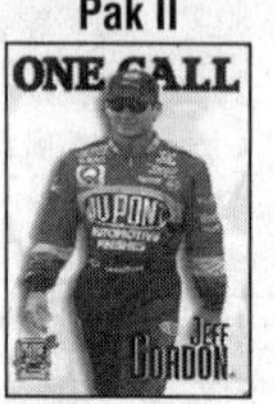

This was the second consecutive year for Finish Line Phone Paks. The set was divided into tiers with each carrying a different phone time value: one call 5-minute cards (#1-37), $5 cards (#39-66), $10 cards (#67-86), $50 cards (#87-94), and $100 cards (#95-100). Each card is individually serial numbered. There was also a special Wild Card insert card that could be used for a random amount of phone time. When calling to collect your prize you would find out what denomination between 5 and 60 minutes you received. The Wild Card was inserted one in 15-packs. Each one call card was numbered of 7950 and each Wild Card was numbered of 4180. The cares were packaged three cards per pack, 15-packs per box and 16-boxes per case.

COMPLETE SET (100)	150.00	300.00
COMP.SET w/o SP's (38)	4.00	10.00
39-66 $5 CARD STATED ODDS 1:7.5		
$5 CARD PRINT RUN 500 SER.#'d SETS		
$10 CARD STATED ODDS 1:15		
$10 CARDS SERIAL NUMBERED OF 360		
$50 CARD STATED ODDS 1:60		
$100 CARD STATED ODDS 1:240		
1 Jeff Gordon	.75	2.00
2 Bill Elliott	.30	.75
3 Mark Martin	.60	1.50
4 Rusty Wallace	.60	1.50
5 Terry Labonte	.30	.75
6 Ernie Irvan	.15	.40
7 Ricky Rudd	.30	.75
8 Bobby Labonte	.50	1.25
9 Sterling Marlin	.30	.75
10 Darrell Waltrip	.15	.40
11 Ted Musgrave	.08	.25
12 Dale Jarrett	.50	1.25
13 Ricky Craven	.08	.25
14 Jeremy Mayfield	.15	.40
15 Eli Gold	.05	.15
16 Michael Waltrip	.15	.40
17 Jimmy Spencer	.08	.25
18 Brett Bodine	.08	.25
19 Geoff Bodine	.08	.25
20 John Andretti	.08	.25
21 Ken Schrader	.08	.25
22 Bobby Hamilton	.08	.25
23 Derrike Cope	.08	.25
24 Ward Burton	.15	.40
25 Joe Nemechek	.08	.25
26 Kenny Wallace	.08	.25
27 Mike Wallace	.08	.25
28 Morgan Shepherd	.08	.25
29 Rick Hendrick	.05	.15
30 Jack Roush	.05	.15
31 Larry McClure	.05	.15
32 Felix Sabates	.05	.15
33 Joe Gibbs	.15	.40
34 Robert Yates	.05	.15
35 Chuck Rider	.05	.15
36 Len Wood	.15	.40
Eddie Wood		
Michael Waltrip		
37 Bill Elliott	.30	.75
38 Wild Card	.05	.15
39 Jeff Gordon $5	2.50	6.00
40 Bill Elliott $5	1.00	2.50
41 Mark Martin $5	2.00	5.00
42 Rusty Wallace $5	2.00	5.00
43 Terry Labonte $5	1.00	2.50
44 Ernie Irvan $5	.50	1.25
45 Ricky Rudd $5	1.00	2.50
46 Bobby Labonte $5	1.50	4.00
47 Sterling Marlin $5	1.00	2.50
48 Darrell Waltrip $5	.50	1.25
49 Ted Musgrave $5	.30	.75
50 Dale Jarrett $5	1.50	4.00
51 Ricky Craven $5	.30	.75
52 Jeremy Mayfield $5	.50	1.25
53 Eli Gold $5	.20	.50
54 Michael Waltrip $5	.50	1.25
55 Jimmy Spencer $5	.30	.75
56 Brett Bodine $5	.30	.75
57 Geoff Bodine $5	.30	.75
58 John Andretti $5	.30	.75
59 Ken Schrader $5	.30	.75
60 Bobby Hamilton $5	.30	.75
61 Derrike Cope $5	.30	.75
62 Ward Burton $5	.50	1.25
63 Joe Nemechek $5	.30	.75
64 Kenny Wallace $5	.30	.75
65 Michael Waltrip $5	.50	1.25
66 Morgan Shepherd $5	.30	.75
67 Rusty Wallace's Car $10	3.00	8.00
68 Sterling Marlin's Car $10	1.25	3.00
69 Terry Labonte's Car $10	1.50	4.00
70 Mark Martin's Car $10	3.00	8.00
71 Geoff Bodine's Car $10	.50	1.25
72 Ricky Rudd's Car $10	1.50	4.00
73 Brett Bodine's Car $10	.50	1.25
74 Ted Musgrave's Car $10	.50	1.25
75 Darrell Waltrip's Car $10	.75	2.00
76 Bobby Labonte's Car $10	2.50	6.00
77 Michael Waltrip's Car $10	.50	1.25
78 Ward Burton's Car $10	.75	2.00
79 Jimmy Spencer's Car $10	.50	1.25
80 Jeff Gordon's Car $10	4.00	10.00
81 Ricky Craven's Car $10	.50	1.25
82 Ernie Irvan's Car $10	.75	2.00
83 Johnny Benson's Car $10	.75	2.00
84 Kyle Petty's Car $10	.75	2.00
85 Dale Jarrett's Car $10	2.50	6.00
86 Bill Elliott's Car $10	1.50	4.00
87 Jeff Gordon $50	12.50	30.00
88 Bill Elliott $50	5.00	12.00
89 Mark Martin $50	10.00	25.00
90 Rusty Wallace $50	10.00	25.00
91 Terry Labonte $50	5.00	12.00
92 Ernie Irvan $50	2.50	6.00
93 Ricky Rudd $50	5.00	12.00
94 Bobby Labonte $50	7.50	20.00
95 Jeff Gordon $100	20.00	50.00
96 Bill Elliott $100	7.50	20.00
97 Mark Martin $100	15.00	40.00
98 Rusty Wallace $100	15.00	40.00
99 Terry Labonte $100	7.50	20.00
100 Ernie Irvan $100	4.00	10.00
P1 Jeff Gordon Promo	2.00	5.00

2000 Firestone Checkered Flag

COMPLETE SET (3)	2.00	5.00
1 Mario Andretti	1.25	3.00
2 Michael Andretti	.30	.75
NNO Mario Andretti	1.25	3.00
/Michael Andretti		

1996 Flair

This 100-card set is the inaugural issue of the Flair brand by Fleer/SkyBox. The cards printed on double thick board feature top drivers from both the Winston Cup and Busch circuits. Cards also featured 100 percent etched-foil and three photos on every basic card. The cards were available through both hobby and retail outlets. The product was distributed via six box cases, with 24 packs per box and five cards per pack. Each pack carried a suggested retail of $4.99.

COMPLETE SET (100)	12.00	30.00
WAX BOX	25.00	60.00
1 John Andretti	.10	.30
2 Johnny Benson	.10	.30
3 Brett Bodine	.10	.30
4 Geoff Bodine	.10	.30
5 Jeff Burton	.40	1.00
6 Ward Burton	.25	.60
7 Derrike Cope	.10	.30
8 Ricky Craven	.10	.30
9 Wally Dallenbach	.10	.30
10 Dale Earnhardt	2.00	5.00
11 Bill Elliott	.50	1.25
12 Jeff Gordon	1.25	3.00
13 Steve Grissom	.10	.30
14 Bobby Hamilton	.10	.30
15 Ernie Irvan	.25	.60
16 Dale Jarrett	.75	2.00
17 Bobby Labonte	.75	2.00
18 Terry Labonte	.40	1.00
19 Dave Marcis	.25	.60
20 Sterling Marlin	.40	1.00
21 Mark Martin	1.00	2.50
22 Rick Mast	.10	.30
23 Jeremy Mayfield	.25	.60
24 Ted Musgrave	.10	.30
25 Joe Nemechek	.10	.30
26 Kyle Petty	.25	.60
27 Robert Pressley	.10	.30
28 Ricky Rudd	.40	1.00
29 Ken Schrader	.10	.30
30 Lake Speed	.10	.30
31 Jimmy Spencer	.10	.30
32 Hut Stricklin	.10	.30
33 Kenny Wallace	.10	.30
34 Mike Wallace	.10	.30
35 Rusty Wallace	1.00	2.50
36 Michael Waltrip	.25	.60
37 Glenn Allen Jr.	.10	.30
38 Rodney Combs	.10	.30
39 David Green	.10	.30
40 Randy LaJoie	.10	.30
41 Chad Little	.10	.30
42 Curtis Markham	.10	.30
43 Mike McLaughlin	.10	.30
44 Patty Moise	.10	.30
45 Phil Parsons	.10	.30
46 Jeff Purvis	.10	.30
47 Bobby Allison	.05	.15
48 Richard Childress	.25	.60
49 Joe Gibbs	.25	.60
50 Rick Hendrick	.05	.15
51 Richard Petty	.40	1.00
52 Jack Roush	.05	.15
53 Ray Evernham	.25	.60
54 Todd Parrott	.05	.15
55 Robin Pemberton	.05	.15
56 David Smith	.05	.15
57 John Andretti's Car	.05	.15
58 Johnny Benson's Car	.05	.15
59 Brett Bodine's Car	.05	.15
60 Geoff Bodine's Car	.05	.15
61 Jeff Burton's Car	.10	.30
62 Ward Burton's Car	.05	.15
63 Derrike Cope's Car	.05	.15
64 Ricky Craven's Car	.05	.15
65 Wally Dallenbach's Car	.05	.15
66 Dale Earnhardt's Car	.75	2.00
67 Bill Elliott's Car	.25	.60
68 Jeff Gordon's Car	.50	1.25
69 Steve Grissom's Car	.05	.15
70 Bobby Hamilton's Car	.05	.15
71 Ernie Irvan's Car	.10	.30
72 Dale Jarrett's Car	.25	.60
73 Bobby Labonte's Car	.25	.60
74 Terry Labonte's Car	.25	.60
75 Dave Marcis' Car	.10	.30
76 Sterling Marlin's Car	.10	.30
77 Mark Martin's Car	.40	1.00
78 Rick Mast's Car	.05	.15
79 Jeremy Mayfield's Car	.10	.30
80 Ted Musgrave's Car	.05	.15
81 Joe Nemechek's Car	.05	.15
82 Kyle Petty's Car	.10	.30
83 Robert Pressley's Car	.05	.15
84 Ricky Rudd's Car	.10	.30
85 Ken Schrader's Car	.05	.15
86 Lake Speed's Car	.05	.15
87 Jimmy Spencer's Car	.05	.15
88 Hut Stricklin's Car	.05	.15
89 Kenny Wallace's Car	.05	.15
90 Mike Wallace's Car	.05	.15
91 Rusty Wallace's Car	.40	1.00
92 Michael Waltrip's Car	.10	.30
93 Dale Jarrett	.60	1.50
Ernie Irvin		
94 Dale Jarrett	.75	2.00
95 Bobby Labonte	.75	2.00
96 Terry Labonte	.40	1.00
97 Mark Martin	1.00	2.50
98 Mike Wallace	.10	.30
99 Jeff Gordon CL (1-67)	.60	1.50
100 Rusty Wallace CL	.40	1.00
(68-100/inserts)		
P1 Jeff Gordon Promo	5.00	10.00

1996 Flair Autographs

This 12-card insert set consist of the top names in NASCAR. Autograph redemption cards were randomly inserted in packs at a rate of one in 100. The redemption card featured one of the 12 drivers on the front and instructions on how and where to redeem it.

COMPLETE SET (12)	500.00	1000.00
1 Ricky Craven	10.00	20.00
2 Dale Earnhardt	150.00	300.00
3 Bill Elliott	20.00	50.00
4 Jeff Gordon	60.00	120.00
5 Ernie Irvan	12.50	30.00
6 Dale Jarrett	12.50	30.00
7 Bobby Labonte	12.50	30.00
8 Terry Labonte	12.50	30.00
9 Sterling Marlin	15.00	40.00
10 Mark Martin	15.00	40.00
11 Ted Musgrave	10.00	20.00
12 Rusty Wallace	20.00	50.00

1996 Flair Center Spotlight

A card from this 10-card insert set was randomly inserted one in five packs. The cards show the cars of leading drivers with 100 percent foil designs and a glittering UV coating. Each card front shows a car with two spotlight type effects in the backgound.

COMPLETE SET (10)	25.00	60.00
1 Johnny Benson	.50	1.25
2 Dale Earnhardt	8.00	20.00
3 Bill Elliott	2.00	5.00
4 Jeff Gordon	5.00	12.00
5 Bobby Hamilton	.50	1.25
6 Bobby Labonte	3.00	8.00
7 Terry Labonte	1.50	4.00
8 Mark Martin	4.00	10.00
9 Ricky Rudd	1.50	4.00
10 Rusty Wallace	4.00	10.00

1996 Flair Hot Numbers

This 10-card insert set featues holofoil stamping and embossed printing to showcase NASCAR's top drivers. The card fronts feature a driver's photo, the driver's car number in holofoil and a facsimile of the driver's signature. Hot Number cards were inserted one in 24 packs.

COMPLETE SET (10)	75.00	150.00
1 Dale Earnhardt	20.00	50.00
2 Bill Elliott	5.00	12.00
3 Jeff Gordon	12.50	30.00
4 Ernie Irvan	2.50	6.00
5 Dale Jarrett	8.00	20.00
6 Bobby Labonte	8.00	20.00
7 Terry Labonte	4.00	10.00
8 Mark Martin	10.00	25.00
9 Ricky Rudd	4.00	10.00
10 Rusty Wallace	10.00	25.00

1996 Flair Power Performance

Cards from this die-cut 10-card set were seeded one in 12 packs. The card fronts feature a driver's photo imposed over a tachometer. The words Power Performance and the driver's name also appear on the front in holofoil stamping.

COMPLETE SET (10)	40.00	100.00
1 Ricky Craven	.75	2.00
2 Dale Earnhardt	12.50	30.00
3 Bill Elliott	3.00	8.00
4 Jeff Gordon	8.00	20.00
5 Dale Jarrett	5.00	12.00
6 Terry Labonte	2.50	6.00
7 Sterling Marlin	2.50	6.00
8 Mark Martin	6.00	15.00
9 Ricky Rudd	2.50	6.00
10 Rusty Wallace	6.00	15.00

1992 Food Lion Richard Petty

This set was issued to employees of the Food Lion supermarket chain. 2,300 of these factory sets were produced and packaged in white boxes with the Food Lion logo on each box. In the summer of 1993, the remaining 400 sets were offered to the public at the cost of $34.

COMPLETE SET (116)	6.00	15.00
1 Daytona, FL February	.05	.10
2 Richard Petty 1964	.30	.75
3 Richard Petty w/Car	.30	.75
4 Richard Petty 1981	.30	.75
5 Rockingham, NC March	.05	.10
6 Richard Petty 1971	.30	.75
7 Richard Petty 1974	.30	.75
8 Richard Petty's Car	.12	.30
9 Richmond, VA March	.05	.10
10 Richard Petty's Car	.12	.30
11 Richard Petty	.30	.75
12 Richard Petty	.30	.75
13 Atlanta, GA March	.05	.10
14 Richard Petty's Car	.12	.30
15 Richard Petty	.30	.75
16 Richard Petty's Car	.12	.30
17 Darlington, SC March	.05	.10
18 Richard Petty	.30	.75
19 Richard Petty's Car	.12	.30
20 Richard Petty's Car	.12	.30
21 Bristol, TN April	.05	.10
22 Richard Petty	.30	.75
23 Richard Petty in Car	.30	.75
24 Richard Petty w/Car	.30	.75
25 N. Wilkesboro, NC April	.05	.10
26 Richard Petty w/Dad	.30	.75
27 Richard Petty's Car	.12	.30
28 Richard Petty's Car	.12	.30
29 Martinsville, VA April	.05	.10
30 Richard Petty	.30	.75
31 Richard Petty	.30	.75
32 Richard Petty	.30	.75
33 Talladega, AL May	.05	.10
34 Richard Petty w/Car	.30	.75
35 Richard Petty's Trailer	.12	.30
36 Richard Petty 1983	.30	.75
37 Charlotte, NC May	.05	.10
38 Richard Petty w/Car	.30	.75
39 Richard Petty on Car	.30	.75
40 Richard Petty 1977	.30	.75
41 Dover, DE May	.05	.10

Richard Petty in Car	.30	.75
Richard Petty	.30	.75
Richard Petty 1984	.30	.75
Sonoma, CA June	.05	.10
Richard Petty w/Car	.30	.75
Richard Petty w/Car	.30	.75
Richard Petty w/Car	.30	.75
Pocono, PA June	.05	.10
Richard Petty	.30	.75
Richard Petty	.30	.75
Richard Petty w/Brother	.30	.75
Brooklyn, MI June	.05	.10
Richard Petty	.30	.75
Richard Petty 1981	.30	.75
Richard Petty w/Car	.30	.75
Daytona, FL July	.05	.10
Richard Petty's Car	.12	.30
Richard Petty 1975	.30	.75
Richard Petty 1984	.30	.75
Pocono, PA July	.05	.10
Richard Petty's Car	.12	.30
Richard Petty	.30	.75
Richard Petty's Car	.12	.30
Talladega, AL July	.05	.10
Richard Petty on Bike	.30	.75
Richard Petty 1984	.30	.75
Richard Petty's Car	.12	.30
Watkins Glen, NY Aug.	.05	.10
Richard Petty w/Car	.30	.75
Richard Petty	.30	.75
Richard Petty	.30	.75
Brooklyn, MI August	.05	.10
Richard Petty w/Brother	.30	.75
Richard Petty 1974	.30	.75
Richard Petty	.30	.75
Bristol, TN August	.05	.10
Richard Petty's Car	.12	.30
Richard Petty	.30	.75
Richard Petty in Car	.30	.75
Darlington, SC Sept.	.05	.10
Richard Petty's Car	.12	.30
Richard Petty	.30	.75
Richard Petty	.30	.75
Richmond, VA September	.05	.10
Richard Petty 1970	.30	.75
Richard Petty's Car	.12	.30
Richard Petty w/Dodge	.30	.75
Dover, DE September	.05	.10
Richard Petty	.30	.75
Richard Petty	.30	.75
Richard Petty	.30	.75
Martinsville, VA Sept.	.05	.10
Richard Petty 1970	.30	.75
Richard Petty 1969	.30	.75
Richard Petty	.30	.75
N. Wilkesboro, NC Oct.	.05	.10
Richard Petty w/Brother	.30	.75
Richard Petty	.30	.75
) Richard Petty	.30	.75
Charlotte, NC October	.05	.10
Richard Petty	.30	.75
Richard Petty w/Car	.30	.75
Richard Petty	.30	.75
Rockingham, NC October	.05	.10
Richard Petty's Car	.12	.30
Richard Petty's Car	.12	.30
Richard Petty Pit Stop	.30	.75
Phoenix, AZ November	.05	.10
Richard Petty	.30	.75
Richard Petty	.30	.75
Richard Petty	.30	.75
Atlanta, GA November	.05	.10
Richard Petty's Car	.12	.30
Richard Petty's Transporter	.12	.30
Richard Petty's Car	.12	.30
0 Richard Petty HOLO	75.00	200.00

1991 Galfield Press Pioneers of Racing

ortedly 3,077 sets were produced. This set was ued in a Pioneers of Racing binder and produced noted NASCAR historian Greg Fielden. Greg sonally signed each of the binders the set came

MPLETE SET (107)	40.00	100.00
ireball Roberts	.60	1.50
Tim Flock		
erb Thomas	.50	1.25
Tim Flock		
loyd Seay	.30	.75
our Abreast Start	.30	.75
im Flock	.50	1.25
Barney Smith		
arol Tillman	.30	.75
arshall Teague	.50	1.25
Herb Thomas		
hil Orr	.30	.75
urtis Turner		
Fireball Roberts		
100,000 at 105 MPH	.30	.75
Bill Holland	.30	.75
Jack Smith	.30	.75
Fonty Flock	.50	1.25
Bob Flock	.30	.75
Curtis Turner	.50	1.25
Fireball Roberts		
Fonty Flock	.50	1.25
Daytona Beach	.30	.75
Jim Reed	.40	1.00
Lee Petty		
John Fish	.30	.75
Curtis Turner	.50	1.25
Sara Christian		
Tim Flock	.50	1.25
Junior Johnson	.60	1.50
Rex White	.60	1.50
Fireball Roberts		
Joe Weatherly	.50	1.25
Marvin Panch		
Eduardo Dibos		
Eddie Skinner	.30	.75
Iggy Katona	.30	.75
Johnny Mantz		
Bill Widenhouse	.30	.75
Buck Baker	.50	1.25
Jimmie Lewallen		
Bobby Johns	.30	.75
Joe Weatherly		
Banjo Matthews	.30	.75
32 Fonty Flock	.50	1.25
Jimmie Lewallen		
33 Joe Guide, Jr.	.30	.75
34 Larry Flynn	.30	.75
35 Lakewood Speedway	.30	.75
36 North Wilkesboro Speedway	.30	.75
37 Fonty Flock	.50	1.25
Marvin Panch		
38 Herb Thomas	.50	1.25
Frank Mundy		
39 Bill O'Dell	.30	.75
40 Jimmy Florian	.30	.75
41 1959 Daytona	.30	.75
42 Paul Goldsmith	.50	1.25
43 Louise Smith	.50	1.25
44 Frank Mundy	.30	.75
45 Doug Cooper	.30	.75
46 Red Vogt	.30	.75
47 Raleigh Speedway	.30	.75
48 Gober Sosebee	.30	.75
Tommy Moon		
Swayne Pritchett		
49 Curtis Turner	.50	1.25
50 Dick Bailey	.30	.75
51 Don Kimberling	.50	1.25
Joe Weatherly		
Eddie Pagan		
Fireball Roberts		
Joe Eubanks		
52 Pee Wee Jones	.30	.75
Jim Reed		
53 Checklist Card	.30	.75
54 Marion Cox	.30	.75
55 Benny Georgeson	.30	.75
57 Cotton Owens	.30	.75
58 Harold Nash	.50	1.25
Bucky Sager		
Ted Rambo		
Mike Brown		
Joe Guide Jr.		
Fireball Roberts		
Dick Rathmann		
59 Danny Letner	.30	.75
60 Bob Flock	.30	.75
61 Tim Flock	.50	1.25
62 Tim Flock	.50	1.25
Herb Thomas		
63 Red Byron	.30	.75
Mickey Rhodes		
64 Tim Flock	.50	1.25
Jim Paschal		
Fonty Flock		
65 Larry Frank	.50	1.25
66 Herb Thomas	.50	1.25
67 Hershel McGriff	.30	.75
68 Fireball Roberts		
69 Curtis Turner	.50	1.25
70 Marshall Teague	.30	.75
71 Hershel McGriff	.30	.75
Frankie Schneider		
72 Bobby Myers	.30	.75
73 Paul Goldsmith	.50	1.25
74 Herschel Buchanan	.30	.75
Joe Guide Jr.		
75 Buddy Shuman	.30	.75
Mickey Fenn		
76 Bob Welborn	.30	.75
77 Axel Anderson	.30	.75
78 Marvin Panch	.50	1.25
Tiny Lund		
Bob Pronger		
Bob Welborn		
79 June Cleveland	.30	.75
80 Tim Flock	.50	1.25
81 Dick Rathmann	.30	.75
82 Glenn Dunnaway	.30	.75
83 Herb Thomas	.50	1.25
84 Cotton Owens	.30	.75
85 Red Byron	.30	.75
86 Fireball Roberts		
87 Joe Weatherly	.50	1.25
88 Tim Flock	.50	1.25
89 Herb Thomas	.50	1.25
90 Gwyn Staley	.30	.75
Charlie Scott		
91 Curtis Turner	.40	1.00
Bobby Isaac		
92 Paul Goldsmith	.50	1.25
Jimmy Thompson		
93 Fireball Roberts		
Roy Jones		
94 Junior Johnson	.60	1.50
95 Lloyd Seay	.30	.75
96 Jimmy Thompson	.30	.75
97 Eduardo Dibos	.30	.75
98 Raymond Parks	.30	.75
99 Daytona Speedweek	.30	.75
100 Tim Flock	.50	1.25
101 Tim Flock	.50	1.25
Joe Lee Johnson		
Spud Murphy		
102 Tim Flock	.50	1.25
Ted Chester		
103 Joe Weatherly	.50	1.25
104 Red Byron	.30	.75
105 Ed Livingston	.30	.75
Friday Hassler		
106 Doug Yates	.30	.75
107 Checklist Card	.30	.75

1992 Hilton G. Hill Gold True Legend

The 16-card set features drivers who raced from 1949-1971. The set includes such greats as Curtis Turner, Tiny Lund and Tim Flock. There was also approximately 20 uncut sheets produced.

COMPLETE SET (16)	4.00	10.00
1 Checklist	.25	.60
2 Bowman Gray Stadium	.25	.60
3 Bob Welborn	.30	.75
4 Tim Flock	.40	1.00
5 Curtis Turner	.40	1.00
6 Bob McGinnis	.30	.75
7 Tiny Lund	.40	1.00
8 Bobby Myers	.30	.75
9 E.H. Weddle	.30	.75
10 PeeWee Jones	.30	.75
11 Johnny Dodson	.30	.75
12 Whitey Norman	.30	.75
13 Jimmie Lewallen	.30	.75
14 Jack Holloway	.30	.75
15 Billy Myers	.30	.75
16 Phillip Smith	.30	.75

1991 Hickory Motor Speedway

This set was produced to honor the 40th Anniversary of Hickory Motor Speedway. Color and black and white photos of the short track's most famous events are featured. The cards were released in complete set form and sold at the track.

COMPLETE SET (12)	2.00	5.00
1 Opening Day Traffic	.10	.30
2 Joe Littlejohn	.10	.30
Ribbon Cutting		
3 The First Race	.10	.30
4 Hickory Today	.10	.30
5 Jack Ingram's Car	.10	.30
Jack's Last Race		
6 Dale Earnhardt	.10	.30
Harry Gant		
Tommy Houston		
Morgan Shepherd		
Dale Jarrett		
Homecoming at Hickory		
7 Max Prestwood Jr.	.10	.30
8 A Packed House	.10	.30
9 Dale Fischlein's Car	.10	.30
Action on the Track		
10 Dale Earnhardt's Car	1.00	2.50
Joe Nemechek's Car		
Busch Action		
11 Robert Huffman w/Car	.20	.50
NNO Cover Card	.10	.30

1994 High Gear Promos

Wheels released this three-card set as a promotional tool for its 1994 High Gear set. All three cards may be found with either silver or gold foil layering.

COMPLETE SILVER SET (3)	6.00	15.00
*GOLD CARDS: .8X TO 2X SILVERS		
P1 Jeff Gordon Silver	3.00	8.00
P2 Rusty Wallace Silver	3.00	5.00
P3 Kyle Petty Silver	2.00	4.00

1995 High Gear Promos

This three-card set was issued to promote the 1995 High Gear release by Wheels. The cards are numbered and often sold in complete set form.

COMPLETE SET (3)	4.00	10.00
P1 Rusty Wallace	1.50	3.00
P2 Jeff Gordon	2.00	5.00
P3 Mark Martin	1.50	4.00

1994-95 Highland Mint/VIP

The 1994-95 Highland Mint cards are replicas of the 1994 VIP series cards. The silver and bronze cards contain 4.25 ounces of metal. Each card is individually numbered, packaged in a lucite display holder and accompanied by a certificate of authenticity. The production mintage according to Highland Mint is listed below. The actual card numbering follows that of the original cards, but we have listed and numbered them below alphabetically for convenience. A 24-karat gold-plated on silver version of the Dale Earnhardt card (numbered of 500) was also produced.

1B Dale Earnhardt/5000	50.00	100.00
1G Dale Earnhardt/500	250.00	500.00
1S Dale Earnhardt/1000	125.00	250.00
2B Bill Elliott/2500	10.00	20.00
2S Bill Elliott/500	50.00	100.00
3B Jeff Gordon/5000	25.00	50.00
3S Jeff Gordon/1000	100.00	175.00
4B Ernie Irvan/5000	10.00	20.00
4S Ernie Irvan/1000	12.50	25.00
5B Mark Martin/5000	20.00	40.00
5S Mark Martin/1000	75.00	150.00
6B Rusty Wallace/5000	20.00	40.00
6S Rusty Wallace/1000	75.00	150.00

1993 Hi-Tech Tire Test

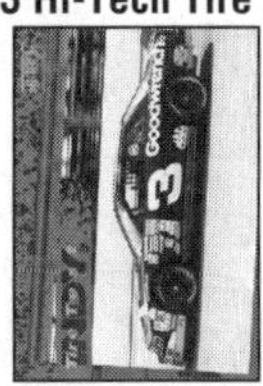

Hi-Tech produced this set commemorating the 1992 NASCAR tire tests at the Indianapolis Motor Speedway. The ten-card set was distributed in two 5-card packs each packed 36 per box. Reportedly, production was limited to 1000 cases.

COMPLETE SET (10)	2.00	5.00
1 Dale Earnhardt's Car	1.00	2.50
2 Darrell Waltrip's Car	.20	.50
3 Davey Allison's car	.30	.75
4 Rusty Wallace's Car	.50	1.25
5 Ernie Irvan's Car	.20	.50
6 Mark Martin's Car	.50	1.25
7 Kyle Petty's Car	.20	.50
8 Land Speed Record at IMS	.10	.30
9 Bill Elliott's Car	.30	.75
10 Brickyard 400 Logo	.10	.30
P1 Rusty Wallace's Car Promo	1.00	2.50
numbered of 15,000		
P2 Davey Allison's Car Promo	1.00	2.50
numbered of 15,000		

1994 Hi-Tech Brickyard 400 Prototypes

Three cards comprise this set released by Hi-Tech to preview its 1994 Brickyard 400 set. Each card is numbered of 20,000.

COMPLETE SET (3)	3.00	8.00
1 Richard Petty w/Car	1.00	2.50
2 Jeff Gordon's Car	2.00	5.00
3 Kyle Petty's Car	.75	2.00

1994 Hi-Tech Brickyard 400

For the second year, Hi-Tech produced a set commemorating the Brickyard 400. The 1994 set was expanded to 70-cards featuring action from the 1993 tire tests at IMS. The cards were packaged 8-cards per pack with 24-packs per box. Reportedly, production was limited to 2,500 12-box cases. Inserts included a Richard Petty set as well as Metamorphosis cards. The Metamorphosis card shows an IndyCar transforming into a stock car racer. It was packed approximately one per box. There was also a 70-card Artist Proof parallel version of the base set. The cards feature a 1 of 200 logo on the front to differentiate them from the base cards. The Artist Proof cards were inserted at a rate of one per box.

COMPLETE SET (70)	10.00	25.00
1 Track Action	.01	.05
2 Rusty Wallace's Car	.20	.50
3 Bobby Hillin's Car	.01	.05
4 Morgan Shepherd's Car	.05	.15
5 Dave Marcis' Car	.01	.05
6 Brett Bodine in Pits	.01	.05
7 Morgan Shepherd's Car	.01	.05
8 Geoff Bodine's Car	.01	.05
9 Dale Earnhardt's Car	.50	1.25
10 Bill Elliott's Car	.10	.30
11 Kenny Wallace's Car	.01	.05
12 Bobby Labonte's Car	.10	.30
13 Geoff Bodine's Car	.01	.05
14 Mark Martin's Car	.20	.50
15 Bill Elliott's Car	.10	.30
16 P.J. Jones' Car	.01	.05
17 John Andretti's Car	.01	.05
18 Darrell Waltrip's Car	.05	.15
19 Mark Martin's Car	.20	.50
20 Jeff Gordon's Car	.30	.75
21 Greg Sacks' Car	.01	.05
22 Terry Labonte's Car	.10	.30
23 Lake Speed's Car	.01	.05
24 Greg Sacks' Car	.01	.05
25 Geoff Bodine's Car	.01	.05
26 Kenny Wallace's Car	.01	.05
27 Mark Martin's Car	.20	.50
Jimmy Spencer's Car		
28 Rusty Wallace's Car	.20	.50
29 Mark Martin's Car	.20	.50
30 Lake Speed in Car	.01	.05
31 Mark Martin's Car	.20	.50
32 Geoff Bodine's Car	.01	.05
Brett Bodine's Car		
33 Race Action	.01	.05
34 Pit Action	.01	.05
35 Action	.01	.05
36 Rick Mast	.05	.15
37 Rusty Wallace	.40	1.00
38 Dale Earnhardt	1.00	2.50
39 Terry Labonte	.20	.50
40 Mark Martin	.40	1.00
41 Geoff Bodine	.01	.05
Todd Bodine		
Brett Bodine		
42 Sterling Marlin	.20	.50
43 D.K. Ulrich	.01	.05
44 Bill Elliott's Car	.10	.30
45 Jimmy Spencer	.05	.15
46 John Andretti	.05	.15
47 Geoff Bodine	.05	.15
48 Darrell Waltrip	.10	.30
49 Dale Jarrett	.25	.60
50 Morgan Shepherd	.05	.15
51 Bobby Labonte	.25	.60
52 Jeff Gordon	.60	1.50
53 Ken Schrader	.05	.15
54 Brett Bodine	.05	.15
55 Lake Speed	.05	.15
56 Michael Waltrip	.10	.30
57 Jimmy Horton	.05	.15
58 Harry Gant	.10	.30
59 Kenny Wallace	.05	.15
60 Kyle Petty	.10	.30
61 Rick Wilson	.05	.15
62 Ted Musgrave	.05	.15
63 Greg Sacks	.05	.15
64 Dave Marcis	.10	.30
65 Todd Bodine	.05	.15
66 Bobby Hillin	.05	.15
67 Derrike Cope	.05	.15
68 Performance History	.01	.05
69 Jeff Gordon	.60	1.50
70 Checklist Card	.01	.05
BYSE1 Metamorphosis Card	.75	2.00

1994 Hi-Tech Brickyard 400 Artist Proofs

This 70-card set is a parallel version of the base set. The cards feature a 1 of 200 logo on the front to differentiate them from the base cards. The Artist Proof cards were inserted at a rate of one per box.

COMPLETE SET (70)	60.00	150.00
*ARTIST PROOFS: 6X TO 15X BASE CARDS		

1994 Hi-Tech Brickyard 400 Richard Petty

Richard Petty is the focus of this Hi-Tech issue. The cards were randomly inserted in 1994 Hi-Tech Brickyard 400 packs and highlight Petty's involvement with the historic race at IMS. The cards were randomly inserted at a rate of one per 20 Hi-Tech Brickyard 400 packs.

COMPLETE SET (6)	2.50	6.00
1 Richard Petty w/Car	1.25	2.50
Becomes King Richard		
2 Richard Petty's Car	.40	1.00
Ceremonial Laps at IMS		
3 Richard Petty's Car	.40	1.00
Thoughts on IMS		
4 Richard Petty w/Car	.40	1.00
5 Richard Petty w/Car	.40	1.00
6 Richard Petty's Car	.40	1.00

1995 HI-Tech Brickyard 400 Prototypes

Three cards comprise this set released by Hi-Tech to preview its 1995 Brickyard 400 set. Each card is numbered of 20,000. Although the cards carry a 1994 date on the copyright line, the cards preview the 1995 set.

COMPLETE SET (3)	4.00	10.00
P1 Mark Martin's Car	1.25	3.00
P2 Ernie Irvan	.75	2.00
P3 Dale Earnhardt	2.50	6.00

1995 Hi-Tech Brickyard 400

In 1995, Hi-Tech again produced a card set commemorating the 1994 Brickyard 400. The cards were released in two separate complete factory sets. The tin box version contained 90 regular cards, 10 Top Ten cards and one Jeff Gordon 23K Gold card. The 90 regular cards were printed on 18 point card stock with gold foil layering. Production was limited to 10,000 factory sets. Hi-Tech also produced the set for distribution in a wooden factory set box with a special Jeff Gordon Gold and Silver card (numbered of 1000). The wooden box version was limited to 1000 sets. Although the cards carry the year 1994 on the copyright line, it's considered a 1995 release.

COMPLETE SET (90)	10.00	25.00
COMP.FACT.SET (101)	25.00	50.00
COMP.WOOD BOX (101)	40.00	100.00
1 Rick Mast's Car	.02	.10
2 Dale Earnhardt's Car	.40	1.00
3 Jeff Gordon's Car UER	.30	.75
card numbered 00		
4 Geoff Bodine's Car	.02	.10
5 Bobby Labonte's Car	.08	.25
6 Bill Elliott's Car	.08	.25
7 Brett Bodine's Car	.02	.10
8 Sterling Marlin's Car	.05	.15
9 Mark Martin's Car	.20	.50
10 Morgan Shepherd's Car	.02	.10
11 Rusty Wallace's Car	.20	.50
12 Greg Sacks' Car	.02	.10
13 Dale Jarrett's Car	.08	.25
14 Michael Waltrip's Car	.05	.15
15 Dave Marcis' Car	.02	.10
16 Ernie Irvan's Car	.05	.15
17 Rich Bickle's Car	.02	.10
18 Hut Stricklin's Car	.02	.10
19 Terry Labonte's Car	.08	.25
20 Wally Dallenbach Jr.'s Car	.02	.10
21 Ken Schrader's Car	.02	.10
22 Jimmy Hensley's Car	.02	.10
23 Todd Bodine's Car	.02	.10
24 Danny Sullivan's Car	.02	.10
25 Darrell Waltrip's Car	.05	.15
26 John Andretti's Car	.02	.10
27 Jeff Purvis' Car	.02	.10
28 Joe Nemechek's Car	.02	.10
29 Jeremy Mayfield's Car	.05	.15
30 Bobby Hamilton's Car	.02	.10
31 Ward Burton's Car	.05	.15
32 Jimmy Spencer's Car	.02	.10
33 Bobby Hillin's Car	.02	.10
34 Kyle Petty's Car	.05	.15
35 Ted Musgrave's Car	.02	.10
36 Jeff Burton's Car	.05	.15
37 Derrike Cope's Car	.02	.10
38 Lake Speed's Car	.02	.10
39 Harry Gant's Car	.05	.15
40 Jeff Gordon Race Action	.30	.75
41 Dale Earnhardt	1.00	2.50
42 Hut Stricklin's Car	.02	.10
43 Wally Dallenbach Jr.'s Car	.02	.10
44 Joe Nemechek	.05	.15
45 Rick Mast	.05	.15
46 Richard Jackson Team	.02	.10
Rick Mast's Crew		
47 Terry Labonte	.20	.50
48 Jeremy Mayfield	.08	.25
49 Bobby Hamilton	.05	.15
50 Bobby Hillin	.05	.15
51 Jeff Burton	.20	.50
52 Kyle Petty	.08	.25
53 Jeff Gordon's Car	.20	.50
Geoff Bodine's Car		
Ken Schrader's Car		
54 Checklist	.02	.10
55 John Andretti	.05	.15
56 Dale Earnhardt	1.00	2.50
57 Danny Sullivan	.05	.15
58 Jimmy Spencer	.05	.15
59 Michael Waltrip	.08	.25
60 Ken Schrader	.05	.15
61 Bobby Labonte	.40	1.00
62 Early-Race	.02	.10
Race Action		
63 Bill Elliott's Car	.08	.25
64 Todd Bodine	.05	.15
65 Ted Musgrave	.05	.15
66 Lake Speed	.05	.15
67 Harry Gant	.08	.25
68 Greg Sacks	.05	.15
69 Jeff Purvis	.05	.15
70 Mark Martin	.50	1.25
71 Rich Bickle	.05	.15
72 Dave Marcis	.05	.15
73 Brett Bodine	.05	.15
74 Geoff Bodine	.05	.15
75 Dale Jarrett	.40	1.00
76 Ward Burton	.08	.25
77 Dale Earnhardt's Car	.40	1.00
78 Darrell Waltrip	.08	.25
79 Ernie Irvan	.08	.25
80 Morgan Shepherd	.05	.15
81 Jimmy Hensley	.05	.15
82 Derrike Cope	.05	.15
83 Rusty Wallace	.50	1.25
84 Sterling Marlin	.20	.50
85 Hut Stricklin	.05	.15
86 Ernie Irvan's Car	.05	.15
87 Dale Earnhardt	1.00	2.50
88 Jeff Gordon	.60	1.50
89 Jeff Gordon's Car	.30	.75
90 Indianapolis Motor Speedway	.02	.10
NNO Jeff Gordon Gold/Silver	25.00	60.00
numbered of 1000		
wooden box insert		
NNO Jeff Gordon Gold/10000	2.00	5.00
tin box insert		

1995 Hi-Tech Brickyard 400 Top Ten

The Top Ten set was issued as an insert into factory sets of 1994 Hi-Tech Brickyard 400. The 10-cards were distributed in both the tin and wooden box versions of the set and were printed on holographic foil stock. Each card was produced with three different background designs: stars, doughnut shaped, and raindrop shaped. The star background version seems to be the toughest to find with cards carrying a 25 percent premium.

COMPLETE SET (10)	7.50	20.00
BY1 Jeff Gordon	1.00	2.50
BY2 Brett Bodine	.10	.25
BY3 Bill Elliott's Car	.15	.40
BY4 Rusty Wallace	.75	2.00
BY5 Dale Earnhardt	1.50	4.00
BY6 Darrell Waltrip	.15	.40
BY7 Ken Schrader	.10	.25
BY8 Michael Waltrip	.15	.40
BY9 Todd Bodine	.10	.25
BY10 Morgan Shepherd	.10	.25

1992 Hooters Alan Kulwicki

This 15-card set is a promotional issue by the restaurant chain Hooters. The cards were sold in complete set form at many of the restaurants as well as given away at some racing events. The cards feature Alan Kulwicki and his Hooters sponsored #7 Ford Thunderbird.

COMPLETE SET (15)	4.00	10.00
COMMON CARD (1-14)	.30	.75

1993 Hoyle Playing Cards

Hoyle produced these three decks of playing cards in early 1993. Each deck features racing stats or race action photos from the era highlighted. All three sets are packaged in similar boxes that differ according to box color: 1947-59 (green), 1960-79 (orange) and 1980-91 (yellow). Although drivers in some photos can be specifically identified, the cards are seldom sold as singles. Therefore, we list only complete set prices for the three card decks.

COMPLETE SET 1947-1959 (54)	1.25	3.00
COMPLETE SET 1960-1979 (54)	1.25	3.00
COMPLETE SET 1980-1991 (54)	1.25	3.00

1995 Images

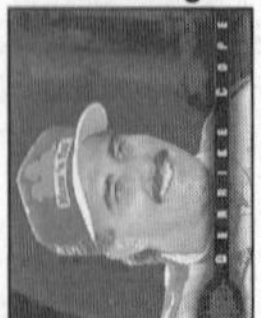

This 100-card set is the inaugural issue for this brand. The product was a joint effort between manufacturers Classic and Finish Line. The set features the top drivers from NASCAR, NHRA, Indy Car and World of Outlaws. The cards have action photography and are printed on 18-point micro-lined foil board. The product came six-cards per pack, 24-packs per box and 16 boxes per case. Each case consisted of 8 red boxes and 8 black boxes. Certain inserts were only available in one color box and not the other. There was also Hot Boxes in which half of each pack would consist of insert cards. A Hot Box could be found 1 in every 4 cases. Two known uncorrected errors exsist in this set. card number 36 Ray Evernham doesn't have a card number on the back of the card and card number 78 Jeff Burton is misnumbered as number 4.

COMPLETE SET (100)	8.00	20.00
1 Al Unser Jr.	.15	.40
2 Rusty Wallace	.60	1.50
3 Dale Earnhardt	1.25	3.00
4 Sterling Marlin	.25	.60
5 Terry Labonte	.25	.60
6 Mark Martin	.40	1.00
7 Geoff Bodine	.07	.20
8 Jeff Burton	.25	.60
9 Lake Speed	.07	.20
10 Ricky Rudd	.25	.60
11 Brett Bodine	.07	.20
12 Derrike Cope	.07	.20
13 John Force	.25	.60
14 Robby Gordon	.07	.20
15 Dick Trickle	.07	.20
16 Ted Musgrave	.07	.20
17 Darrell Waltrip	.15	.40
18 Bobby Labonte	.50	1.25
19 Loy Allen Jr.	.07	.20
20 Walker Evans	.02	.10
21 Morgan Shepherd	.07	.20
22 Joe Amato	.07	.20
23 Jimmy Spencer	.07	.20
24 Jeff Gordon	.75	2.00
25 Ken Schrader	.07	.20
26 Hut Stricklin	.07	.20
27 Steve Kinser	.25	.60
28 Dale Jarrett	.50	1.25
29 Steve Grissom	.07	.20
30 Michael Waltrip	.15	.40
31 Ward Burton	.15	.40
32 Roger Mears	.07	.20
33 Robert Pressley	.07	.20
34 Bill Seebold	.02	.10
35 Mike Skinner RC	.07	.20
36 Ray Evernham UER	.02	.10
Unnumbered		
37 John Andretti	.07	.20
38 Sammy Swindell	.07	.20
39 Larry McReynolds	.02	.10
40 Tony Glover	.02	.10
41 Ricky Craven	.15	.40
42 Kyle Petty	.15	.40
43 Bobby Hamilton	.07	.20
44 David Green	.07	.20
45 Steve Hmiel	.02	.10
46 Bobby Labonte	.50	1.25
47 Darrell Waltrip	.15	.40
48 Jeff Gordon	.75	2.00
49 Al Unser Jr.	.15	.40
50 Dale Earnhardt	1.25	3.00
51 P.J. Jones	.07	.20
52 Ken Schrader	.07	.20
53 Geoff Bodine	.07	.20
54 Sterling Marlin	.25	.60
55 Terry Labonte	.25	.60
56 Morgan Shepherd	.07	.20
57 Robert Pressley	.07	.20
58 Ricky Rudd	.25	.60
59 Ward Burton	.15	.40
60 Rick Carelli	.07	.20
61 Ted Musgrave	.07	.20
62 Kenny Bernstein	.07	.20
63 Jimmy Spencer	.07	.20
64 Brett Bodine	.07	.20
65 Mark Martin	.60	1.50
66 Rusty Wallace	.60	1.50
67 Lake Speed	.07	.20
68 Rick Mast	.07	.20
69 Dick Trickle	.07	.20
70 Michael Waltrip	.15	.40
71 Dave Marcis	.07	.20
72 Jeff Gordon	.75	2.00
73 John Andretti	.07	.20
74 Derrike Cope	.07	.20
75 Todd Bodine	.07	.20
76 Kyle Petty	.15	.40
77 Dale Jarrett	.50	1.25
78 Jeff Burton UER	.25	.60
Numbered 4		
79 Steve Grissom	.07	.20
80 Ernie Irvan	.15	.40
81 Bobby Labonte	.50	1.25
82 Ernie Irvan	.15	.40
83 Bobby Hamilton	.07	.20
84 Sterling Marlin	.25	.60
85 Robby Gordon	.07	.20
86 Todd Bodine	.07	.20
87 Joe Nemechek	.07	.20
88 Mark Martin	.60	1.50
89 Ricky Rudd	.25	.60
90 Mike Wallace	.07	.20
91 Terry Labonte	.25	.60
92 Geoff Bodine	.07	.20
93 Ernie Irvan	.15	.40
94 Rusty Wallace	.50	1.25
95 Ricky Craven	.15	.40
96 John Force	.25	.60
97 Dale Earnhardt	1.25	3.00
98 Jeremy Mayfield	.15	.40
99 Dale Earnhardt CL	.60	1.50
100 Jeff Gordon CL	.40	1.00
P1 Jeff Gordon Promo	7.50	15.00

1995 Images Gold

This 100-card set is a parallel of the base Images set. The cards are printed on Gold foil board and could be found one per pack.

COMPLETE SET (100)	15.00	40.00
*GOLDS: .8X TO 2X BASIC CARDS		

1995 Images Circuit Champions

This 10-card insert set features eight Champions from a variety of racing circuits along with two all-time greats. The acetate cards are sequentially numbered to 675 and inserted at a rate of one per 192 packs. The cards were inserted in both the Red and Black boxes.

COMPLETE SET (10)	60.00	150.00
1 Al Unser Jr.	4.00	10.00
2 Roger Mears	2.00	5.00
3 Bill Seebold	1.00	2.50
4 John Force	6.00	15.00
5 Steve Kinser	6.00	15.00
6 Mike Skinner	2.00	5.00
7 David Green	2.00	5.00
8 Dale Earnhardt	30.00	80.00
9 Glen Wood	1.00	2.50
Leonard Wood		
10 Joe Amato	2.00	5.00

1995 Images Driven

This 15-card insert set features some of the top drivers in NASCAR, NHRA, and IndyCar racing. The cards use holographic foil technology and are sequentially numbered to 1,800. The cards can be found one per 24 packs in the Red Images boxes only.

COMPLETE SET (15)	25.00	60.00
D1 Dale Earnhardt	8.00	20.00
D2 Jeff Gordon	5.00	12.00
D3 Bobby Labonte	3.00	8.00
D4 Sterling Marlin	1.50	4.00
D5 Mark Martin	2.50	6.00
D6 Kyle Petty	1.00	2.50
D7 Ricky Rudd	1.50	4.00
D8 Rusty Wallace	4.00	10.00
D9 Ken Schrader	.50	1.25
D10 John Force	1.50	4.00
D11 Michael Waltrip	1.00	2.50
D12 Robby Gordon	.50	1.25
D13 Terry Labonte	1.50	4.00
D14 Al Unser Jr.	1.00	2.50
D15 Darrell Waltrip	1.00	2.50

1995 Images Hard Chargers

This 10-card insert set uses holographic foil technology to bring the top NASCAR drivers to life. The cards come sequentially numbered to 2,500 and are inserted one per 24 packs in the Black Images boxes only.

COMPLETE SET (10)	20.00	50.00
HC1 Bobby Labonte	3.00	8.00
HC2 Sterling Marlin	1.50	4.00
HC3 Mark Martin	2.50	6.00
HC4 Ricky Rudd	1.50	4.00
HC5 Ken Schrader	.50	1.25
HC6 Rusty Wallace	4.00	10.00
HC7 Michael Waltrip	1.00	2.50
HC8 Jeff Gordon	5.00	12.00
HC9 Dale Earnhardt	8.00	20.00
HC10 Terry Labonte	1.50	4.00

1995 Images Owner's Pride

Owners of some of the top teams in racing are featured in this 15-card insert set. The fronts of the micro-lined, foil-board cards feature a photo of the car. The backs contain a large photo of the owner. Each card is numbered 1 of 5,000 and could be found one per 18 packs. The Owner's Pride cards could be found in both the Red and Black boxes.

COMPLETE SET (15)	12.00	30.00
OP1 Travis Carter	.20	.50
OP2 Richard Childress	.40	1.00
OP3 A.G. Dillard	.20	.50
OP4 Joe Gibbs	.40	1.00
OP5 Jeff Gordon	4.00	10.00
OP6 Junior Johnson	.40	1.00
OP7 Larry McClure	.20	.50
OP8 Jack Roush	.40	1.00
OP9 Ricky Rudd	1.25	3.00
OP10 Felix Sabates	.20	.50
Chaney Sabates		
OP11 Robert Yates	.40	1.00
OP12 Kenny Bernstein	.40	1.00
OP13 Dale Earnhardt	6.00	15.00
OP14 Rick Hendrick	.40	1.00
OP15 Roger Penske	.40	1.00
Don Miller		

1995 Images Race Reflections Dale Earnhardt

The 10-card insert set is a tribute to racing great Dale Earnhardt. The innovative double foil-board cards are randomly inserted in Black boxes only at a rate of one every 32 packs.

COMPLETE SET (10)	40.00	100.00
COMMON CARD (DE1-DE10)	5.00	12.00
*FACSIMILE SIGNATURE: 1X TO 2X BASIC CARDS		

1995 Images Race Reflections Jeff Gordon

This 10-card insert set highlights much of the success Jeff Gordon enjoyed in his career through the middle of 1995. The innovative double foil-board cards are randomly inserted in Red boxes only at a rate of one every 32 packs. There is also a parallel version of each of the ten cards. The parallel features a facsimile signature on the fronts of the cards. The signature cards were randomly inserted at a rate of one every 96 packs.

COMPLETE SET (10)	40.00	100.00
COMMON CARD (JG1-JG10)	5.00	12.00
*FACSIMILE SIGNATURE: 1X TO 2X BASIC CARDS		

1994 IMS Indianapolis 500 Champions Collection

COMPLETE SET (12)	4.00	10.00
NNO Mario Andretti	1.00	2.50
NNO Emerson Fittipaldi	.50	1.25
NNO A.J. Foyt	.60	1.50
NNO Gordon Johncock	.25	.60
NNO Arie Luyendyk	.60	1.50
NNO Tom Sneva	.25	.60
NNO Danny Sullivan	.25	.60
NNO Al Unser Sr.	.75	2.00
NNO Al Unser Jr.	.75	2.00
NNO Rick Mears	.50	1.25
NNO Bobby Rahal	.40	1.00
NNO Johnny Rutherford	.25	.60

1991 IROC

The 1991 IROC set was produced by Dodge and included a short sales brochure covering the Daytona IROC automobile and the 1991 IROC race schedule. Each cardback contains an action photo along with the set title 1991 IROC. Cardfronts contain the driver's photo and career highlights surrounded by a checkered flag border. Distribution was by complete set only sealed in a cello wrapper. The cards later were illegally reprinted. The counterfeits can be distinguished by an incomplete checkered flag design along the card border. One side of the border will be missing approximately 1/4 of the checkered flag.

COMPLETE SET (12)	200.00	400.00
1 Al Unser	15.00	40.00
2 Tom Kendall	6.00	15.00
3 Bob Wollek	6.00	15.00
4 Mark Martin	30.00	80.00
5 Bill Elliott	20.00	50.00
6 Al Unser Jr.	15.00	40.00
7 Scott Pruett	6.00	15.00
8 Geoff Bodine	6.00	15.00
9 Geoff Brabham	6.00	15.00
10 Rusty Wallace	25.00	60.00
11 Dorsey Schroeder	6.00	15.00
12 Dale Earnhardt	60.00	150.00

1997 Jurassic Park

This 61-card set is another uniquely themed set from Wheels. The cards feature the top names in racing and are printed on 24 point stock. Each card has a jungle-like background and is stamped in silver foil. The cards were packed 6 cards per pack and 24 packs per box.

COMPLETE SET (61)	8.00	20.00
1 Jeff Gordon	1.00	2.50
2 Dale Jarrett	.60	1.50
3 Terry Labonte	.30	.75
4 Mark Martin	.75	2.00
5 Rusty Wallace	.75	2.00
6 Bobby Labonte	.60	1.50
7 Sterling Marlin	.30	.75
8 Jeff Burton	.30	.75
9 Ted Musgrave	.08	.25
10 Michael Waltrip	.20	.50
11 David Green	.08	.25
12 Ricky Craven	.08	.25
13 Johnny Benson	.20	.50
14 Jeremy Mayfield	.20	.50
15 Bobby Hamilton	.08	.25
16 Kyle Petty	.20	.50
17 Darrell Waltrip	.20	.50
18 Wally Dallenbach	.08	.25
19 Bill Elliott	.40	1.00
20 Jeff Green	.08	.25
21 Joe Nemechek	.08	.25
22 Derrike Cope	.08	.25
23 Ward Burton	.20	.50
24 Chad Little	.20	.50
25 Mike Skinner	.08	.25
26 Todd Bodine	.08	.25
27 Hut Stricklin	.08	.25
28 Ken Schrader	.08	.25
29 Steve Grissom	.08	.25
30 Robby Gordon RC	.30	.75
31 Kenny Wallace	.08	.25
32 Bobby Hillin	.08	.25
33 Jimmy Spencer	.08	.25
34 John Andretti	.08	.25
35 Steve Park RC	.75	2.00
36 Michael Waltrip	.20	.50
37 Dale Jarrett	.60	1.50
38 Mike McLaughlin	.08	.25
39 Todd Bodine	.08	.25
40 Terry Labonte	.30	.75
41 Jeff Fuller	.08	.25
42 Phil Parsons	.08	.25
43 Jason Keller	.08	.25
44 Mark Martin	.75	2.00
45 Randy LaJoie	.08	.25
46 Joe Nemechek	.08	.25
47 Loy Allen	.08	.25
48 Jeff Gordon	1.00	2.50
49 Mark Martin	.75	2.00
50 Mark Martin	.75	2.00
51 Jeff Gordon	1.00	2.50
52 John Andretti	.08	.25
53 Jimmy Makar	.05	.15
54 Robert Pressley	.08	.25
55 Donnie Wingo	.05	.15
56 Richard Childress	.20	.50
57 Andy Petree	.05	.15
58 Travis Carter	.05	.15
59 Joe Gibbs	.20	.50
60 Checklist	.05	.15
61 Checklist	.05	.15
P1 Mark Martin Promo	2.00	5.00

1997 Jurassic Park Triceratops

This 61-card set is a parallel to the base set. These cards are diecut and feature the image of a triceratops in the background. The cards were randomly inserted in packs at a ratio of 1:2.

COMPLETE SET (61)	15.00	40.00
*TRICERATOPS: .8X TO 2X BASE CARDS		

1997 Jurassic Park Carnivore

This 12-card insert set features the top drivers from the NASCAR circuit. The cards are horizontal and feature the drivers' numbers in the background. The cards were randomly inserted in packs at a ratio of 1:15.

COMPLETE SET (12)	30.00	60.00
C1 Dale Earnhardt	12.50	30.00
C2 Jeff Gordon	4.00	10.00
C3 Dale Jarrett	2.50	6.00
C4 Bobby Labonte	2.50	6.00
C5 Jimmy Spencer	.40	1.00
C6 Bill Elliott	1.50	4.00
C7 Terry Labonte	1.25	3.00
C8 Rusty Wallace	3.00	8.00
C9 Ward Burton	.75	2.00
C10 Mark Martin	3.00	8.00
C11 Todd Bodine	.40	1.00
C12 Sterling Marlin	1.25	3.00

1997 Jurassic Park Pteranodon

This 10-card insert set is printed on clear plastic and contains portrait shots of the top drivers on the NASCAR circuit. The cards were randomly inserted in packs at a ratio of 1:30.

COMPLETE SET (10)	50.00	100.00
P1 Dale Earnhardt	25.00	60.00
P2 Jeff Gordon	6.00	15.00
P3 Bobby Labonte	4.00	10.00
P4 Terry Labonte	2.00	5.00
P5 Rusty Wallace	5.00	12.00
P6 Ward Burton	1.25	3.00
P7 Sterling Marlin	2.00	5.00
P8 Mark Martin	5.00	12.00
P9 Dale Jarrett	4.00	10.00
P10 Kyle Petty	1.25	3.00

1997 Jurassic Park Raptors

This 16-card insert set features drivers on micro-etched cards. The cards were randomly inserted in packs at a ratio of 1:6.

COMPLETE SET (16)	15.00	40.00
R1 Terry Labonte	1.25	3.00
R2 Jeff Gordon	4.00	10.00
R3 Johnny Benson	.75	2.00
R4 Ward Burton	.75	2.00
R5 Bobby Hamilton	.40	1.00
R6 Ricky Craven	.40	1.00
R7 Michael Waltrip	.75	2.00
R8 Bobby Labonte	2.50	6.00
R9 Dale Jarrett	2.50	6.00
R10 Bill Elliott	1.50	4.00
R11 Rusty Wallace	3.00	8.00
R12 Jimmy Spencer	.40	1.00
R13 Sterling Marlin	1.25	3.00
R14 Kyle Petty	.75	2.00
R15 Ken Schrader	.40	1.00
R16 Robby Gordon	1.25	3.00

1997 Jurassic Park Thunder Lizard

This 10-card set features cards that are encased actual lizard skin. The cards were randomly inse in packs at a ratio of 1:90 with each card se numbered of 350.

COMPLETE SET (10)	50.00	120
TL1 Jeff Gordon	20.00	50.
TL2 Dale Jarrett	12.50	30.
TL3 Bobby Labonte	12.50	30.
TL4 Rusty Wallace	15.00	40
TL5 Bill Elliott	8.00	20.
TL6 Jeff Burton	4.00	10.
TL7 Mark Martin	15.00	40.
TL8 Dale Earnhardt	20.00	50
TL9 Mike Skinner	2.00	5
TL10 Robby Gordon	6.00	15.

1997 Jurassic Park T-Rex

This 10-card insert set features cards that are die embossed and micro-etched. The cards w randomly inserted in packs at a ratio of 1:60.

COMPLETE SET (10)	75.00	200.
TR1 Terry Labonte	5.00	12.
TR2 Jeff Gordon	15.00	40.
TR3 Dale Jarrett	10.00	25.
TR4 Bobby Labonte	10.00	25.
TR5 Dale Earnhardt	25.00	60.
TR6 Rusty Wallace	12.50	30.
TR7 Mike Skinner	1.50	4.
TR8 Joe Nemechek	1.50	4.
TR9 Jeremy Mayfield	3.00	8.
TR10 Bill Elliott	6.00	15.

1997 Jurassic Park Th Ride Jeff Gordon

This diecast/card set was available throug redemption program by Wheels and thro RCCA(Racing Collectibles Club of America). The consists of five Jeff Gordon cards, one cover c and a 1:64 Action/RCCA #24 Jeff Gordon Jura Park Hood Opened car.

COMPLETE SET (5)	10.00	25.
COMMON CARD (1-5)	2.00	5.
NNO Cover Card	.40	1.

1992 Just Racing Larr Caudill

This 30-card set features NASCAR driver L Caudill. The sets were sold in complete set f Each set was boxed and sealed and came wi numbered certificate of authenticity. There were 100 signed and numbered cards randomly inse in the sets.

COMPLETE SET (30)	2.00	5.
COMMON CARD (1-30)	.08	
AUTOGRAPHED CARDS	5.00	10.

2006 Kellogg's Racing

This 2-card set was found on boxes of Kellog brand snacks.

COMPLETE SET (2)	2.00	5.
1 Kyle Busch	1.50	4.
2 Terry Labonte	.75	2.

1996 KnightQuest

This 45-card theme set features a theme based King Arthur's time. The drivers are the Knights the track is their battle field. Each card is printed 24-pt paper stock with UV coating and foil stam in silver holographic foil. The set is made up of t subsets: Armor Knights (1-20), Conquerors (21- and Wizards (34-45). The cards are packaged cards per pack, 24 cards per box and 20 boxes case. There were 999 Hobby cases and 699 R cases produced. Wheels also continued its E-Rac Win redemption game for KnightQuest. expiration of both game cards was 5/31/96.

COMPLETE SET (45)	6.00	15.
1 Dale Earnhardt K	1.25	3.
2 Jeff Gordon K	.75	2.
3 Sterling Marlin K	.25	
4 Ted Musgrave K	.07	

5 Mark Martin K	.60	1.50
6 Terry Labonte K	.25	.60
7 Rusty Wallace K	.60	1.50
8 Morgan Shepherd K	.07	.20
9 Bobby Labonte K	.50	1.25
10 Ricky Rudd K	.25	.60
11 Bill Elliott K	.30	.75
12 Ernie Irvan K	.15	.40
13 Ken Schrader K	.07	.20
14 Derrike Cope K	.07	.20
15 Dale Jarrett K	.50	1.25
16 Geoff Bodine K	.07	.20
17 Darrell Waltrip K	.15	.40
18 Kyle Petty K	.15	.40
19 Michael Waltrip K	.15	.40
20 Brett Bodine K	.07	.20
21 Jeff Gordon C	.75	2.00
22 Dale Earnhardt C	1.25	3.00
23 Rusty Wallace C	.60	1.50
24 Mark Martin C	.60	1.50
25 Dale Earnhardt C	1.25	3.00
26 Bobby Labonte C	.50	1.25
27 Kyle Petty C	.15	.40
28 Terry Labonte C	.25	.60
29 Bobby Labonte C	.50	1.25
30 Jeff Gordon C	.75	2.00
31 Jeff Gordon C	.75	2.00
32 Dale Jarrett C	.50	1.25
33 Sterling Marlin C	.25	.60
34 Junior Johnson W	.07	.20
35 Travis Carter W	.02	.10
36 Bob Brannan W	.02	.10
37 Tony Glover W	.02	.10
38 Don Miller W	.02	.10
39 Larry McReynolds W	.02	.10
40 Ray Evernham W	.02	.10
41 Steve Hmiel W	.02	.10
42 Cecil Gordon W	.02	.10
43 Andy Petree W	.02	.10
44 Richard Childress W	.15	.40
45 Don Hawk W	.02	.10

1996 KnightQuest Black Knights

This 45-card set is a parallel to the base set. The cards have a silver and holographic laser gold foil stamping and are printed on 24-pt UV coated paper stock. The cards come sequentially numbered of 899. The odds of pulling a Black Knight card are one per 13 packs. The Black Knight cards were inserted only in hobby packs.

COMPLETE SET (45)	150.00	250.00
*BLACK KNIGHTS: 4X TO 10X BASE CARDS		

1996 KnightQuest Red Knight Preview

This 45-card set is a parallel to the base KnightQuest set. The set was originially distributed at the Winston Cup preview show in Winston-Salem, North Carolina January 20, 1996. It was later made available through a mail order offer. The set comes in a black padded watch style box. The inside is lined in red felt and a logo reading "Preview Edition January 20, 1996 1 of 1996" can be found on the inside lid of the box. Each card is identical to the base KnightQuest cards except for the special red foil preview edition logo that appears on each of the Red Knight cards.

COMPLETE SET (45)	12.00	30.00
*RED KNIGHTS: .8X TO 2X BASE CARDS		

1996 KnightQuest Royalty

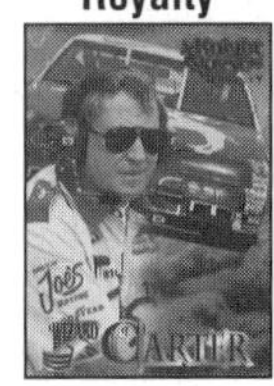

This 45-card set parallel set features 24-pt UV coated paper stock and rich purple foil stamping. The cards are sequentially numbered of 2299. The Royalty cards were seeded one per seven packs. The cards were available in both hobby and retail packs.

COMPLETE SET (45)	50.00	100.00
*ROYALTY: 2.5X TO 6X BASIC CARDS		

1996 KnightQuest White Knights

This 45-card set is parallel to the base set. The cards have a silver and holographic, laser gold foil stamping and are printed on 24-pt UV coated paper stock. The cards come sequentially numbered of 499. White Knight cards were available only in retail packs and inserted at a rate of one per 13 packs.

COMPLETE SET (45)	150.00	300.00
*WHITE KNIGHTS: 5X TO 12X BASIC CARDS		

1996 KnightQuest First Knights

This 10-card insert set features some of the drivers who won Poles in 1995. The cards are printed on foil board and are die-cut. Each card is sequentially numbered of 1,499 and can be found one per 36

packs. The First Knight cards were available in hobby packs.

COMPLETE SET (10)	30.00	80.00
FK1 Dale Earnhardt	8.00	20.00
FK2 Dale Jarrett	3.00	8.00
FK3 Jeff Gordon	5.00	12.00
FK4 Mark Martin	4.00	10.00
FK5 Bobby Labonte	3.00	8.00
FK6 Terry Labonte	1.50	4.00
FK7 Ricky Rudd	1.50	4.00
FK8 Ken Schrader	.50	1.25
FK9 Bill Elliott	2.00	5.00
FK10 Sterling Marlin	1.50	4.00

1996 KnightQuest Knights of the Round Table

The 10-card insert set features the top 10 drivers in Winston Cup. The cards use a gold embossed printing process on 1/4 of the card to show a silhouette of the driver. The other 3/4 of the card show the driver in the car, belted up and ready to go. There are 1,199 of each card and they can be found in both hobby and retail packs at a rate of one per 72 packs.

COMPLETE SET (10)	60.00	150.00
KT1 Jeff Gordon	10.00	25.00
KT2 Dale Earnhardt	15.00	40.00
KT3 Darrell Waltrip	2.00	5.00
KT4 Mark Martin	8.00	20.00
KT5 Terry Labonte	3.00	8.00
KT6 Sterling Marlin	3.00	8.00
KT7 Bill Elliott	4.00	10.00
KT8 Rusty Wallace	8.00	20.00
KT9 Michael Waltrip	2.00	5.00
KT10 Ernie Irvan	2.00	5.00

1996 KnightQuest Kenji Momota

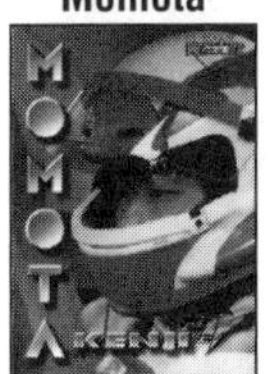

This four-card set features the first Japanese driver to ever race in the SuperTruck series. The cards are printed on 24-pt, UV coated paper stock. They can be found one per 48 packs. There were two different signature versions of card #KMS1. There were 1,500 signature cards produced with an English signature and 1,000 with a Japanese signature. The odds of finding a signature card was one in 480 packs. The Kenji Momota cards were available in both hobby and retail packs.

COMPLETE SET (4)	4.00	10.00
COMMON CARD (KM1-KM4)	1.25	3.00
KMS1A Kenji Momota AUTO American 1500 signed	6.00	15.00
KMS1J Kenji Momota AUTO Japanese 1000 signed	8.00	20.00

1996 KnightQuest Protectors of the Crown

This six-card set features the active Winston Cup Champions. The cards are printed on foil board using embossed technology. Each card is numbered sequentially of 899 and can be found one per hobby 98 packs. There was also an uncut sheet available through the E-Race to Win redemption game. By being unnumbered, the cards on the uncut sheet are different than the regular Protectors of the Crown inserts.

COMPLETE SET (6)	60.00	150.00
UNCUT SHEET	25.00	50.00
PC1 Darrell Waltrip	1.50	4.00
PC2 Dale Earnhardt	12.50	30.00
PC3 Terry Labonte	2.50	6.00
PC4 Rusty Wallace	6.00	15.00
PC5 Bill Elliott	3.00	8.00
PC6 Jeff Gordon	8.00	20.00

1996 KnightQuest Santa Claus

This 5-card set features four of the top names in Winston Cup and Santa Claus. Each card has "Merry Christmas" on the front and "wishing you a Merry Christmas" on the back. Each card is numbered 1 of 1499. There is also parallel green version of each card available in retail packs.

COMPLETE RED SET (5)	25.00	60.00
*GREEN CARDS: .4X TO 1X REDS		
SC1 Dale Earnhardt	10.00	25.00
SC2 Bobby Labonte	4.00	10.00
SC3 Rusty Wallace	5.00	12.00
SC4 Mark Martin	5.00	12.00
SC5 Santa Claus	.30	.75

1991 Langenberg ARCA/Hot Stuff

M.B. Langenberg (H.S.Promotions) produced this set under the name Hot Stuff in 1991. The cards feature drivers of the ARCA PermaTex Supercar Series and were printed on thin white stock. They were originally sold in complete set form.

COMPLETE SET (68)	5.00	10.00
1 Bob Brevak	.07	.20
2 Lee Raymond	.07	.20
3 Carl Miskotten III	.07	.20
4 Mike Fry	.07	.20
5 Scott Stovall	.07	.20
6 Bobby Bowsher	.15	.40
7 Brian Jaeger	.07	.20
8 Bob Dotter Sr.	.15	.40
9 Eric Smith	.07	.20
10 Glenn Brewer	.07	.20
11 Mike Wallace	.60	1.50
12 Roger Blackstock	.07	.20
13 Glenn Sullivan	.07	.20
14 Roger Otto	.07	.20
15 Craig Rubright	.07	.20
16 Roy Payne	.15	.40
17 Billy Simmons	.07	.20
18 Graham Taylor	.07	.20
19 Chris Gehrke	.07	.20
20 Keith Waid	.07	.20
21 Bobby Bowsher	.15	.40
22 Billy Thomas	.07	.20
23 Chet Blanton	.07	.20
24 Dave Jensen	.07	.20
25 Bill Venturini	.15	.40
26 Mike Davis	.07	.20
27 Ken Rowley	.07	.20
28 Charlie Glotzbach	.07	.20
29 Bob Keselowski	.15	.40
30 Wayne Dellinger	.07	.20
31 Cecil Eunice	.07	.20
32 Mark Gibson	.07	.20
33 Dale McDowell	.07	.20
34 Bob Brevak	.07	.20
35 Bobby Gerhart	.07	.20
36 Frank Kimmel	.07	.20
37 Jerry Cook	.07	.20
38 Jerry Hufflin	.07	.20
39 Brad Holman	.07	.20
40 Ben Hess	.15	.40
41 Jimmy Horton	.15	.40
42 Richard Hinds	.07	.20
43 Bill Flowers	.07	.20
44 Ferrel Harris	.07	.20
45 Mark Gibson	.07	.20
46 Joe Booher	.07	.20
47 Ken Ragan	.07	.20
48 Donnie Moran	.07	.20
49 Bobby Massey	.07	.20
50 Checklist	.07	.20
51 Dave Simko	.07	.20
52 David Boggs	.07	.20
53 Larry Couch	.07	.20
54 Dorsey Schroeder	.15	.40
55 Mark Thompson	.07	.20
56 Jerry Hill	.07	.20
57 Gary Weinbroer	.07	.20
58 Scott Hansen	.07	.20
59 Gary Haws	.07	.20
60 Tom Bigelow	.07	.20
61 David Elliott	.07	.20
62 '91 Daytona Action	.07	.20
63 '91 Daytona Action	.07	.20
64 '91 Atlanta Action	.07	.20
65 '88 Dayton Pit Stop	.07	.20
66 Goodyear Tire	.07	.20
67 Hoosier Tire	.07	.20
68 '91 ARCA Schedule	.07	.20

1991 Langenberg ARTGO

This 36-card set was produced by Hot Stuff Promotions of Rockford, Illinois. The cards were

sold at the ARTGO All-Star 100 race, at Rockford Speedway on July 23, 1991.

COMPLETE SET (36)	25.00	50.00
1 Matt Kenseth XRC	20.00	40.00
2 Robbie Reiser	.08	.25
3 Larry Schuler	.08	.25
4 Ed Holmes	.08	.25
5 Al Schill	.08	.25
6 Jerry Wood	.08	.25
7 Todd Coon	.08	.25
8 Bryan Refner	.08	.25
9 Joe Shear	.08	.25
10 John Zeigler	.08	.25
11 Scott Hansen	.08	.25
12 Kregg Hurlbert	.08	.25
13 John Knaus	.08	.25
14 Bill Venturini	.15	.40
15 Johnny Spaw	.08	.25
16 Nolan McBride	.08	.25
17 Monte Gress	.08	.25
18 Tom Carlson	.08	.25
19 David Anspaugh	.08	.25
20 John Loehman	.08	.25
21 Keith Nelson	.08	.25
22 Dennis Berry	.08	.25
23 Dick Harrington	.08	.25
24 Dave Weltmeyer	.08	.25
25 Kevin Cywinski	.08	.25
26 Tony Strupp	.08	.25
27 Jim Weber	.08	.25
28 Steve Carlson	.25	1.00
29 Tracy Schuler	.08	.25
30 Al Schill, Jr.	.08	.25
31 M.G. Gajewski	.08	.25
32 Bob Brownell	.08	.25
33 Joe Shear	.08	.25
34 Dennis Lampman	.08	.25
35 Conrad Morgan	.08	.25
36 Checklist Card	.08	.25

1991 Langenberg Stock Car Champions

This 30-card set features track champions from around the country. Each card in the set carries a "Say NO! To Drugs" logo on the front with each drivers name.

COMPLETE SET (30)	3.00	8.00
1 John Knaus	.10	.30
2 Steve Fraise	.10	.30
3 Keith Berner	.10	.30
4 Brian Ater	.10	.30
5 Tom Rients	.10	.30
6 Kevin Nuttleman	.10	.30
7 Mel Walen	.10	.30
8 Al Humphrey	.10	.30
9 Chris Harat	.10	.30
10 Brad Denney	.10	.30
11 Richie Jensen	.10	.30
12 Jay Stuart	.10	.30
13 Jeff Martin	.10	.30
14 Howard Willis	.10	.30
15 Ronnie Thomas	.10	.30
16 Babe Branscombe	.10	.30
17 Tom Guithues	.10	.30
18 Randy Olson	.10	.30
19 Dennis Setzer	.30	.75
20 Charlie Williamson	.10	.30
21 Bryan Refner	.10	.30
22 Fred Joehnck	.10	.30
23 Roger Otto	.10	.30
24 Terry Cook	.10	.30
25 Roger Avants	.10	.30
26 Larry Mosher	.10	.30
27 Nick Kuipers	.10	.30
28 Terry Lackey	.10	.30
29 Vinny Annarummo	.10	.30
30 Checklist Card	.10	.30

1992 Langenberg ARCA/Flash

M.B. Langenberg produced this set under the name '92 Flash. The cards feature drivers of the ARCA Supercar Series and were printed on slightly thicker card stock than the 1991 release. They were originally sold in complete set form and included an unnumbered Clifford Allison card. Reportedly there were 5,000 sets produced.

COMPLETE SET (111)	8.00	20.00
1 Bill Venturini	.30	.75
2 Bobby Bowsher	.30	.75
3 Bob Keselowski	.08	.25
4 Bob Dotter Sr.	.08	.25
5 Bobby Gerhart	.08	.25
6 Bob Brevak	.08	.25
7 Ben Hess	.08	.25
8 Glenn Brewer	.08	.25
9 Mark Gibson	.08	.25
10 Roy Payne	.08	.25
11 Checklist	.02	.10
12 Jim Clarke	.08	.25
13 Bill Venturini's Car	.08	.25
14 Bobby Bowsher's Car	.08	.25
15 Bob Keselowski	.08	.25
16 Bob Dotter Sr.	.08	.25
17 Bobby Gerhart	.08	.25
18 Bob Brevak	.08	.25
19 Ben Hess	.08	.25
20 Glenn Brewer	.08	.25
21 Mark Gibson	.08	.25
22 Roy Payne	.08	.25
23 Bob Strait	.08	.25
24 Billy Thomas	.08	.25
25 Jerry Huffman	.08	.25
26 Gary Hawes	.08	.25
27 Keith Waid	.08	.25
28 Clay Young's Car Craig Rubright's Car Bob Keselowski's Car '91 Atlanta	.02	.10
29 Jerry Hill	.08	.25
30 Randy Huffman's Car	.02	.10
31 Dale McDowell	.08	.25
32 Roger Blackstock's Car	.02	.10
33 Red Farmer	.30	.75
34 Dave Weltmeyer	.08	.25
35 H.B. Bailey	.08	.25
36 Loy Allen Jr.	.30	.75
37 Bill Venturini Champion	.30	.75
38 Jeff McClure	.08	.25
39 Lee Raymond	.08	.25
40 Dave Mader	.08	.25
41 Andy Genzman	.08	.25
42 Rich Bickle	.30	.75
43 Alan Pruitt	.08	.25
44 Bob Schacht's Car Bill Venturini's Car Bob Keselowski's Car '91 Michigan	.08	.25
45 David Hall	.08	.25
46 Jerry Hufflin	.08	.25
47 Thad Coleman	.08	.25
48 Mike Wren	.08	.25
49 Eddie Bierschwale	.08	.25
50 Tom Sherrill	.08	.25
51 Scotty Sands	.08	.25
52 '92 Daytona Race Action	.02	.10
53 Stan Fox	.30	.75
54 Jimmy Horton	.30	.75
55 Gary Weinbroer's Car	.08	.25
56 Craig Rubright	.08	.25
57 Jerry Churchill	.08	.25
58 Clifford Allison	.30	.75
59 Rich Bickle's Car Roulo Brothers	.08	.25
60 Mike Fry's Car	.08	.25
61 Jeff Purvis	.30	.75
62 Ron Burchette	.08	.25
63 T.W. Taylor	.08	.25
64 Bob Denny	.08	.25
65 Billy Bigley Jr.	.08	.25
66 Charlie Baker	.08	.25
67 Bobby Massey	.08	.25
68 Mike Davis	.08	.25
69 Graham Taylor's Car	.02	.10
70 Tim Fedewa	1.25	3.00
71 Andy Hillenburg	.30	.75
72 Mark Gibson Pit Stop	.02	.10
73 Frank Kimmel	.08	.25
74 Frank Kimmel Pit Stop	.02	.10
75 David Elliott	.08	.25
76 Clay Young	.08	.25
77 Scott Bloomquist's Car	.08	.25
78 Dennis Setzer	.30	.75
79 Dave Jensen	.08	.25
80 Brad Smith's Car	.02	.10
81 Bob Keselowski w/Car Tech Inspection	.02	.10
82 Wayne Dellinger	.08	.25
83 Bobby Woods	.08	.25
84 Paul Holt Jr.	.08	.25
85 Mark Thompson	.08	.25
86 Tim Porter	.08	.25
87 Ken Rowley's Car	.02	.10
88 Jody Gara's Car	.02	.10
89 Mark Harding	.08	.25
90 Tim Priebe's Car	.02	.10
91 James Elliott	.08	.25
92 Wally Finney	.08	.25
93 Richard Hampton's Car	.02	.10
94 T.W. Taylor Pit Stop	.02	.10
95 James Hylton's Car	.02	.10
96 Rich Hayes	.08	.25
97 Joe Booher	.08	.25
98 Eric Smith's Car	.02	.10
99 Ron Otto's Car	.02	.10
100 Bob Williams	.08	.25
101 Tony Schwengel's Car	.02	.10
102 Dave Simko	.08	.25
103 Ben Hess Pit Stop	.02	.10
104 Ken Ragan	.08	.25
105 Maurice Randall's Car	.02	.10
106 Bob Schacht	.08	.25
107 Robbie Cowart	.08	.25
108 Checklist	.02	.10
109 Arca Officials & Sched	.02	.10
110 Hoosier Tire Midwest	.02	.10
NNO Clifford Allison	.75	2.00

1993 Langenberg ARCA/Flash Prototype

M.B. Langenberg produced this prototype card under the name '93 Flash. The Loy Allen card was made as a preview to the 1993 ARCA set that was never produced.

PR1 Loy Allen Jr.	.80	2.00

1994 Langenberg ARCA/Flash

M.B. Langenberg produced this set under the name '94 M.B.L. Flash. The cards feature drivers of the ARCA Supercar Series and were printed on thin card stock with a blue-green cardback. They were originally sold in complete set form. Two promo cards were produced and distributed to advertise the series, but are not considered part of the complete regular set.

COMPLETE SET (100)	10.00	20.00
1 ARCA Cover Card	.08	.25
2 Tim Steele	.20	.50
3 Bob Keselowski	.20	.50
4 Bobby Bowsher	.20	.50
5 Frank Kimmel	.08	.25
6 Bob Brevak	.08	.25
7 Bob Strait	.08	.25
8 Robert Ham	.08	.25
9 Glenn Brewer	.08	.25
10 Ken Allen	.08	.25
11 Bob Dotter Sr.	.08	.25
12 L.W. Miller	.08	.25
13 Rick Sheppard	.08	.25
14 Eric Smith	.08	.25
15 Dave Weltmeyer	.08	.25
16 Craig Rubright	.08	.25
17 Roger Blackstock	.08	.25
18 Jeff Purvis	.20	.50
19 Randy Churchill	.08	.25
20 Mark Thompson	.08	.25
21 Jeep Pflum	.08	.25
22 Curt Dickie	.08	.25
23 Gary Hawes	.08	.25
24 Loy Allen Jr.	.20	.50
25 Brigette Anne Shirley	.08	.25
26 ARCA Officials	.08	.25
27 Jerry Huffman	.08	.25
28 Jimmy Horton	.20	.50
29 Jerry Foyt	.08	.25
30 Todd Coon	.08	.25
31 Ken Rowley	.08	.25
32 Dave Jensen	.08	.25
33 Joe Niemiroski	.08	.25
34 Tony Schwengel	.08	.25
35 Rick Heuser	.08	.25
36 Laura Lane	.08	.25
37 Gary Bradberry	.20	.50
38 Alan Pruitt	.08	.25
39 Danny Kelley	.08	.25
40 Wally Finney	.08	.25
41 Billy Bigley Jr.	.20	.50
42 Bob Schacht	.08	.25
43 Ken Schrader	.20	.50
44 John Wilkinson	.08	.25
45 Billy Thomas	.08	.25
46 Donny Paul	.08	.25
47 David Hall	.08	.25
48 Andy Stone	.08	.25
49 Bob Hill	.08	.25
50 Ron Burchette	.08	.25
51 Red Farmer	.20	.50
52 James Hylton	.20	.50
53 Mike Wallace	.20	.50
54 Tom Bigelow	.08	.25
55 Wayne Larson	.08	.25
56 Peter Gibbons	.08	.25
57 Jeff McClure	.20	.50
58 Andy Farr	.08	.25
59 Kerry Teague	.20	.50
60 Bob Williams	.08	.25
61 Bobby Gerhart	.08	.25
62 Jerry Glanville	.20	.50
63 Marvin Smith	.08	.25
64 Dale Fischlein	.08	.25
65 Rich Bickle	.20	.50
66 Greg Caver	.08	.25
67 Randy Huffman	.08	.25
68 Bill Venturini	.20	.50
69 Dave Simko	.08	.25
70 Tim Porter	.08	.25
71 Jody Gara	.08	.25
72 Perry Tripp	.08	.25
73 Bill Venturini	.20	.50
74 John Stradtman	.08	.25
75 Scotty Sands	.08	.25
76 Rich Hayes	.08	.25
77 Tim Fedewa	1.25	3.00
78 Joey Sonntag	.08	.25
79 Tom Sherrill	.08	.25
80 Delma Cowart	.20	.50
81 Jerry Hill	.08	.25
82 David Boggs	.08	.25
83 Greg Roe	.08	.25
84 Bobby Coyle	.08	.25
85 Mark Gibson	.08	.25
86 Gary Weinbroer	.08	.25
87 1994 ARCA Schedule	.08	.25
88 ARCA Pace Car CL	.08	.25
89 Checklist 21-60	.08	.25
90 Checklist 61-100	.08	.25
91 Tim Steele's Car	.08	.25
92 Bob Keselowski's Car	.08	.25
93 Bobby Bowsher's Car	.08	.25
94 Frank Kimmel's Car	.08	.25
95 Bob Brevak's Car	.08	.25
96 Bob Strait's Car	.08	.25
97 Robert Ham's Car	.08	.25
98 Glenn Brewer's Car	.08	.25
99 Ken Allen's Car	.08	.25
100 Jeff McClure's Car	.08	.25

1992 Limited Editions Promos

Limited Editions released this four-card set to preview its 1992 driver sets. The cards are numbered and feature a card from each of the Gant, Gordon and Glanville sets, marked promo, and a card showing the other four drivers together.

Card	Low	High
COMPLETE SET (4)	2.50	6.00
1 Harry Gant	.60	1.50
2 Kenny Wallace	.25	.60
Jimmy Hensley		
Tommy Houston		
Chuck Bown		
3 Jerry Glanville	.60	1.50
4 Jeff Gordon	4.00	10.00

1992 Limited Editions Chuck Bown

This is one of six Busch series driver sets produced by Limited Editions and distributed in complete set form. Each of the black bordered issues looks similar, but features a different driver. Chuck Bown is the focus of this set. Promo complete sets were also produced with the word "PROMO" on the card fronts. There is no price differnce for the promo version.

Card	Low	High
COMP. FACT SET (15)	1.60	4.00
COMMON CARD (1-15)	.10	.30

1992 Limited Editions Harry Gant

This set is the first in a continuing series of driver sets produced by Limited Editions. The Harry Gant issue differs from the others in that it contains a green border as opposed to black. The cards were distributed in a white box picturing Gant and were individually numbered of 25,000. Uncut sheets of the sets were also made available to members of the Limited Editions Collector Club -- 500 numbered and signed by Gant and 2000 unsigned.

Card	Low	High
COMP. FACT SET (15)	2.00	5.00
HARRY GANT'S CAR (1-15)	.10	.30
HARRY GANT (1-15)	.15	.40

1992 Limited Editions Jerry Glanville

This set is issue number five in a line of Busch series driver sets produced by Limited Editions. Each of the black bordered issues looks similar, but features a different driver. Jerry Glanville is the focus of this set.

Card	Low	High
COMPLETE SET (12)	1.50	4.00
JERRY GLANVILLE'S CAR (1-12)	.10	.30
JERRY GLANVILLE (1-12)	.15	.40

1992 Limited Editions Jeff Gordon

This set is issue number six in a line of Busch series driver sets produced by Limited Editions. Each of the issues looks similar, but features a different driver. Jeff Gordon and the Baby Ruth Race Team are the focus of this set. There were 300 Jeff Gordon autographed cards randomly inserted in the sets. There was also a factory binder. Inside each binder was a promo card of Jeff Gordon, each stamped 1 of 1,000. There were also unstamped versions of the promo card. The 1,000 indicated how many binders there were.

Card	Low	High
COMPLETE SET (12)	3.00	8.00
COMMON CARD (1-12)	.25	.60
AU2 Jeff Gordon AU/300	50.00	120.00

1992 Limited Editions Jimmy Hensley

This is one of six Busch series driver sets produced by Limited Editions and distributed in complete set form. Each of the black bordered issues looks similar, but focuses on a different driver. Jimmy Hensley is the focus of this set.

Card	Low	High
COMP. FACT SET (15)	1.50	4.00
JIMMY HENSLEY'S CAR (1-15)	.10	.30
JIMMY HENSLEY (1-15)	.15	.40

1992 Limited Editions Tommy Houston

This is one of six Busch series driver sets produced by Limited Editions and distributed in complete set form. Each of the black bordered issues looks similar, but features a different driver. Tommy Houston is the focus of this set.

Card	Low	High
COMP. FACT SET (15)	1.50	4.00
TOMMY HOUSTON'S CAR (1-15)	.10	.30
TOMMY HOUSTON (1-15)	.15	.40

1992 Limited Editions Kenny Wallace

This is one of six Busch series driver sets produced by Limited Editions and distributed in complete set form. Each of the black bordered issues looks similar, but features a different driver. Kenny Wallace is the focus of this set.

Card	Low	High
COMPLETE SET (15)	1.50	4.00
KENNY WALLACE'S CAR (1-15)	.10	.30
KENNY WALLACE (1-15)	.15	.40

1995 Lipton Tea Johnny Benson Jr.

Packages of Lipton Tea included one of three Johnny Benson Jr. cards produced in 1995. Each of the three cards features an artist's rendering of a Lipton Tea Racing Team action scene. The cards are unnumbered.

Card	Low	High
COMPLETE SET (3)	2.50	6.00
COMMON CARD	.75	2.00

2006 Little Debbie

This 7-card set was found on boxes of Little Debbie snacks.

Card	Low	High
COMPLETE SET (7)	6.00	12.00

1992 Mac Tools Winner's Cup

Mac Tools produced this set honoring top performers of the NASCAR, Indycar and NHRA racing circuits. The set is titled Winners' Cup Series and mentions it as a series one issue. There was no series two set produced. The cards were packaged in two different packs. Each pack contained 10 cards and a cover card. The cards are unnumbered and have been arranged below alphabetically.

Card	Low	High
COMPLETE SET (21)	6.00	15.00
1 Bobby Allison	.60	1.50
Hut Stricklin		
2 Davey Allison	1.25	3.00
3 Dale Armstrong	.30	.75
4 Ron Ayers	.30	.75
5 Kenny Bernstein	.50	1.25
6 Michael Brotherton	.30	.75
7 Jim Crawford	.30	.75
8 Mike Dunn	.30	.75
9 Harry Gant	.75	2.00
10 Darrell Gwynn	.30	.75
11 Jerry Gwynn	.30	.75
12 Ernie Irvan	.75	2.00
13 Lori Johns	.30	.75
14 Bobby Labonte	1.25	3.00
15 Mark Martin	1.50	4.00
16 Tom McEwen	.30	.75
17 Richard Petty	1.50	4.00
18 Don Prudhomme	.75	2.00
19 Kenny Wallace	.50	1.25
20 Rusty Wallace	1.25	3.00
21 Cover/Checklist Card UER	.20	.50
Hut Stricklin misspelled Strickland		

1993 Maxwell House

The 1993 Maxwell House set was produced by Kraft General Foods for distribution in Maxwell House coffee products. The cards were released in two series of 15-driver cards and one cover card each. Series one features a solid blue border, while the border on series two is a mix of light and dark blue. The cards are often sold in separate series in their original cello wrappers. Note that the copyright date for series one cards is 1992, but the cards were released in early 1993.

Card	Low	High
COMPLETE SET (32)	20.00	50.00
COMPLETE SERIES 1 (16)	8.00	25.00
COMPLETE SERIES 2 (16)	8.00	25.00
1 Bobby Labonte	3.00	8.00
2 Alan Kulwicki	1.50	4.00
3 Davey Allison	1.50	4.00
4 Harry Gant	.25	.60
5 Kyle Petty	.25	.60
6 Mark Martin	4.00	10.00
7 Ricky Rudd	.40	1.00
8 Darrell Waltrip	.25	.60
9 Ernie Irvan	1.50	4.00
10 Rusty Wallace	4.00	10.00
11 Morgan Shepherd	.15	.40
12 Brett Bodine	.15	.40
13 Ken Schrader	.15	.40
14 Dale Jarrett	3.00	8.00
15 Richard Petty	1.50	4.00
16 Bobby Labonte	3.00	8.00
Terry Labonte		
17 Davey Allison	1.50	4.00
Bobby Allison		
18 Richard Petty	1.50	4.00
Kyle Petty		
19 Rusty Wallace	4.00	10.00
Kenny Wallace		
20 Geoff Bodine	.15	.40
Brett Bodine		
21 Darrell Waltrip	.25	.60
Michael Waltrip		
22 Dale Jarrett	3.00	8.00
Ned Jarrett		
23 Sterling Marlin	.25	.60
Coo Coo Marlin		
24 Jeff Gordon	5.00	12.00
Kenny Wallace		
Bobby Labonte		
25 Jeff Gordon	5.00	12.00
26 Kenny Wallace	.15	.40
27 Hut Stricklin	.15	.40
28 Geoff Bodine	.15	.40
29 Terry Labonte	2.00	5.00
30 Bobby Hillin	.15	.40
NNO Cover Card 1	.15	.40
NNO Cover Card 2	.15	.40

1988 Maxx Charlotte

This set contains cards from the second and third printings of 1988 Maxx. The Charlotte name refers to what was believed to be the location of the second and third printings, although all three printings took place at the same location. The set is often called the "First Annual Edition" by collectors. It contains numerous variations from the Myrtle Beach set. The cover cards were printed with two different starburst descriptions (pack versus factory set) in both the Charlotte and Myrtle Beach versions. During the second printing, 10 cards including the two variations of the cover card were changed. The Myrtle Beach notation was removed from the four checklist cards. The special offer price ($19.95) was changed prior to the second printing to $21.45 on the Cover Cards.The Talladega Streaks #10 card was eliminated to make room for Darrell Waltrip. Checklist #19 was changed to reflect this move. On card #26 Phil Parsons, his wife's name was included in the family section on the back of the card. It was excluded in the first printing Myrtle Beach. During the third printing of this set six cards were changed. The #59 1988 Begins card was eliminated to make room for the #59 Brett Bodine card. Checklist #69 was changed to reflect this move. The #43 Daytona International Speedway card was changed to card #47. The #47 Single File card was eliminated. Richard Petty was included in the set on, of course, card #43. Checklist #36 was updated to reflect the changes on cards #43 and #47. On the #88 Ken Bouchard card, the family section was changed to reflect the fact that he and his fiancee, Heidi, were married during the season. There was also a card #99 of Dale Earnhardt that originally wasn't released due to Maxx not getting approval from Dale. The card was later issued with a sticker on it via an insert redemption in the 1994 Maxx Medallion set. (See that set for more on the stickered version.) Then in 1996, as Maxx was going out of business, a signed version of this card was

Card	Low	High
COMPLETE SET (100)	40.00	80.00
COMP.FACT.SET (100)	75.00	150.00
WAX BOX	150.00	250.00
1A Cover Card	.40	1.00
mentions 10 cards		
1B Cover Card	15.00	40.00
mentions 100 cards		
2 Richard Petty's Car	2.00	5.00
3 J.D. McDuffie RC	1.00	2.50
4 Cale Yarborough's Car	1.00	2.50
5 Davey Allison RC	4.00	10.00
6 Rodney Combs RC	1.00	2.50
7 Bobby Allison's Car	.75	2.00
Neil Bonnett's Car		
Geoff Bodine's Car		
Buddy Baker's Car		
8 Mickey Gibbs RC	.60	1.50
9 Atlanta International	3.00	8.00
(with Dale Earnhardt's Car		
10 Darrell Waltrip RC	3.00	8.00
11 Sterling Marlin's Car	1.50	4.00
12 Brad Teague	.40	1.00
13 Alabama Thunder	3.00	8.00
with Dale Earnhardt's Car		
14 Rusty Wallace RC	3.00	8.00
15 Pit Row Action	2.00	5.00
16 Larry Pollard RC	.40	1.00
17 The Winston	3.00	8.00
with Dale Earnhardt's Car		
18 Benny Parsons' Car	1.00	2.50
19 Checklist 1	.40	1.00
no Myrtle Beach line		
20 Neil Bonnett RC	2.00	5.00
21 Martinsville Speedway	.75	2.00
22 Bill Elliott's Car	1.50	4.00
23 Michael Waltrip's Car	1.25	3.00
24 Trevor Boys	.40	1.00
25 Morgan Shepherd RC	1.50	4.00
26 Phil Parsons	.40	1.00
mentions wife Marcia		
27 Darrell Waltrip In Pits	1.25	3.00
28 Hut Stricklin RC	1.00	2.50
29 Richard Childress	1.50	4.00
30 Bobby Allison RC	1.25	3.00
31 Richard Petty's Car	2.00	5.00
Ricky Rudd's Car		
32 Richmond Fairgrounds	.75	2.00
33 Derrike Cope RC	1.25	3.00
34 Neil Bonnett's Car	.75	2.00
35 Geoff Bodine's Car	1.00	2.50
Benny Parsons' Car		
36A Checklist 2	4.00	10.00
no Myrtle Beach line		
card #43 Daytona Int.		
36B Checklist 2	.40	1.00
no Myrtle Beach line		
card #43 Richard Petty		
37 Larry Pearson RC	1.00	2.50
38 Dale Earnhardt in Pits	3.00	8.00
Wrangler		
39 Dave Pletcher RC	.40	1.00
40 Davey Allison ROY	4.00	10.00
41 Alan Kulwicki's Car	1.00	2.50
42 Jimmy Means	.40	1.00
43 Richard Petty RC	5.00	12.00
44 Dave Marcis RC	1.50	4.00
45 Tire Wars	3.00	8.00
Dale Earnhardt's Trailer		
46 Lake Speed RC	1.00	2.50
47 Daytona Int. Speedway	.75	2.00
48 Mark Martin RC	5.00	12.00
49 Dale Earnhardt's Car	3.00	8.00
Davey Allison's Car		
50 Bill Elliott RC	4.00	10.00
51 Ken Ragan	.40	1.00
52 Bobby Hillin RC	1.00	2.50
53 Alabama Int. Speedway	.75	2.00
54 Dale Earnhardt's Car	3.00	8.00
Goodwrench		
55 Buddy Baker RC	1.50	4.00
56 Charlotte Motor Speedway	.75	2.00
57 Rick Wilson Crash	.40	1.00
58 Alan Kulwicki RC	2.50	6.00
59 Brett Bodine RC	1.50	4.00
60 Richard Petty's Car	2.00	5.00
61 Dale Jarrett RC	3.00	8.00
62 Rusty Wallace's Car	1.25	3.00
Geoff Bodine's Car		
63 Terry Labonte RC	3.00	8.00
64 Dave Marcis' Car	.60	1.50
65 Greg Sacks RC	1.00	2.50
66 Jimmy Horton RC	.40	1.00
67 Geoff Bodine RC	1.00	2.50
68 Rick Wilson RC	1.00	2.50
69A Checklist 3	4.00	10.00
no Myrtle Beach line		
card 59 1988 Begins		
69B Checklist 3	.40	1.00
no Myrtle Beach line		
card 59 Brett Bodine		
70 Bill Elliott	1.50	4.00
Fan's Favorite Driver		
71 Mark Stahl	.40	1.00
72 Harry Ranier/Lundy Shop	.40	1.00
73 Phoenix Int. Raceway	.75	2.00
74 Ken Schrader RC	3.00	8.00
75 Darrell Waltrip's Car	1.25	3.00
76 Benny Parsons RC	2.50	6.00
77 Watkins Glen Int.	.75	2.00
78 Phil Barkdoll RC	.40	1.00
79 Speedway Club	.75	2.00
Charlotte Motor Speedway		
80 Sterling Marlin RC	4.00	10.00
81 Ken Schrader's Car	1.25	3.00
82 Riverside International	2.00	5.00
with Richard Petty's Car		
83 Buddy Arrington		
84 Dale Earnhardt's Car	3.00	8.00
Richard Petty's Car		
Bill Elliott's Car		
Double Pleasure		
85 Connie Saylor	.40	1.00
86 North Wilkesboro Speedway	.75	2.00
87 Dale Earnhardt w/Crew	8.00	20.00
Winston Cup Champion		
88 Ken Bouchard RC	.40	1.00
mentions Ken being married		
89 Davey Allison's Car	1.50	4.00
90 Cale Yarborough RC	2.50	6.00
91 Michigan Int. Speedway	.75	2.00
92 Eddie Bierschwale RC	.40	1.00
93 Jim Sauter RC	1.00	2.50
94 Bobby Allison's Car	1.00	2.50
Benny Parsons' Car		
95 Ernie Irvan RC	2.50	6.00
96 Buddy Baker's Car	.60	1.50
97 Filling the Stands	.75	2.00
Charlotte Motor Speedway		
98 Michael Waltrip RC	3.00	8.00
99A Great Body	.60	1.50
Pit Row Scene		
99P Dale Earnhardt Promo	40.00	100.00
100 Checklist 4	.40	1.00
no Myrtle Beach line		

1988 Maxx Myrtle Beach

This was Maxx's first attempt at producing a mass-market racing product. The Myrtle Beach (First Edition) set contains 100 cards including a Cover Card and four checklists. The set was initially introduced at the 1988 Coca Cola 600 in Charlotte. The Myrtle Beach name was attached to this set due to the printer's notation on the four checklists. The 100 standard sized cards comprising this set were issued in complete factory sets which were made available to collectors for the price of $19.95 through an offer on the cover cards. Ten-card shrink-wrapped packs were packaged in 44-count boxes and in 1989 Maxx Combo packs which contained three 10-card '88 packs. It is important to note the combo packs contain cards from all three printings of this set. The Cover Card from this set was produced with two different descriptions located in the yellow starburst on the front of the card. The cover card in the factory sets reads "100 Collector cards...", while the cover card in the shrink-wrapped packs shows "10 Collector cards...". The scarce nature of this set is attributable to the ten variations which it contains. Reportedly 10,000 of the Myrtle Beach sets were produced. The cards listed below are the ten Myrtle Beach variations.

Card	Low	High
COMPLETE SET (100)	175.00	300.00
COMP.FACT.SET (100)	200.00	300.00
1A Cover Card	5.00	10.00
mentions 10 cards		
1B Cover Card	20.00	50.00
mentions 100 cards		
10 Talladega Streaks	15.00	40.00
19 Checklist 1	4.00	10.00
with Myrtle Beach line		
26 Phil Parsons	15.00	40.00
does not mention wife Marcia		
36 Checklist 2	4.00	10.00
with Myrtle Beach line		
43 Daytona Int. Speedway	5.00	12.00
47 Single File	5.00	12.00
with Davey Allison's Car		
59 1988 Begins	4.00	10.00
Daytona Int. Speedway		
69 Checklist 3	4.00	10.00
with Myrtle Beach line		
88 Ken Bouchard	4.00	10.00
mentions Ken being engaged		
100 Checklist 4	4.00	10.00
with Myrtle Beach line		

1989 Maxx Previews

This ten-card set was produced by Maxx to give collectors a preview of the '89 Maxx release. It consists of two Cover cards and eight unnumbered driver cards. These cards were available in '89 Maxx Combo packs. Each combo pack contained three ten-card packs of '88 Maxx and five '89 Preview cards, one of which was a cover card. These cards were collated so one pack contained one half of the Preview set and the other pack contained the other half of the set. The first Cover card features a starburst design and is considered the toughest of the two. The second Cover card features Bill Elliott's car and can be found with either a checklist back or coupon back good for 100 laps toward the 500 needed for a subscription to Grand National Scene.

Card	Low	High
COMPLETE SET (10)	6.00	15.00
1 Geoff Bodine	.50	1.25
2 Bill Elliott	1.50	4.00
3 Bobby Hillin	.60	1.50
4 Sterling Marlin	1.25	3.00
5 Mark Martin	3.00	8.00
6 Richard Petty	2.50	6.00
7 Rusty Wallace	2.00	5.00
8 Michael Waltrip	1.25	3.00
9 Cover Card A	3.00	6.00
Explosion Art Logo		
10 Cover Card B1	.30	.75
Bill Elliott's Car		
Checklist Back		
11 Cover Card B2	.30	.75
Bill Elliott's Car		
100 Laps Back		

1989 Maxx

This set consists of 220 cards featuring drivers, their cars, team owners, crew chiefs, All-Pro crew members, and all-time greats from the NASCAR circuit. It was made available as a mail order set, commonly referred to as the Toolbox set, as a hobby set, and through wax boxes with 48 12-card wax packs, containing ten regular cards, one cover card, and two sticker cards. The set price includes the corrected version of card number 5, Geoff Bodine. A Winston Cup set containing the first one hundred cards of this set was also produced. It was packaged in a yellow box with red checkerboard squares. This set is commonly known as the "Peak" set since it features a picture of Kyle Petty's Peak Antifreeze sponsored car on the box.

Card	Low	High
COMPLETE SET (220)	50.00	100.00
COMP.FACT.SET (220)	60.00	120.00
COMP.TOOLBOX SET (220)	60.00	120.00
COMP.PEAK SET (100)	50.00	100.00
WAX BOX	250.00	350.00
1 Ken Bouchard	.30	.75
Rookie of the Year		
2 Ernie Irvan	1.25	3.00
3 Dale Earnhardt RC	30.00	60.00
4 Rick Wilson	.60	1.50
5A Geoff Bodine ERR	5.00	10.00
last line of text incomplete		
5B Geoff Bodine COR	4.00	8.00
text complete on last line		
6 Mark Martin	3.00	8.00
7 Alan Kulwicki	1.50	4.00
8 Bobby Hillin	.60	1.50
9 Bill Elliott	1.50	4.00
10 Ken Bouchard	.30	.75
11 Terry Labonte	1.50	4.00
12 Bobby Allison	1.00	2.50
13 Robert Gee	.75	2.00
14 Harry Hyde RC	.75	2.00
15 Brett Bodine	.75	2.00
16 Larry Pearson	.30	.75
17 Darrell Waltrip	1.25	3.00
18 Barry Dodson RC	.75	2.00
19 Bill Stavola RC	.75	2.00
Mickey Stavola RC		
20 James Lewter RC	.75	2.00
21 Neil Bonnett	1.25	3.00
22 Tim Brewer RC	.75	2.00
23 Eddie Bierschwale	.30	.75
24 Travis Carter RC	.75	2.00
25 Ken Schrader	1.25	3.00
26 Ricky Rudd RC	4.00	10.00
27 Rusty Wallace	2.00	5.00
28 Davey Allison	2.50	6.00
29 Dale Jarrett	2.50	6.00
30 Michael Waltrip	1.25	3.00
31 Jim Sauter	.75	2.00
32 Todd Parrott RC	.75	2.00
33 Harry Gant RC	1.50	4.00
34 Rodney Combs	.75	2.00
35 Tony Glover RC	.75	2.00
36 Will Lind RC	.75	2.00
37 Cale Yarborough	1.25	3.00
38 Kirk Shelmerdine RC	.75	2.00
39 Ted Conder	.75	2.00
Felix Sabates RC		
40 Raymond Beadle RC	.75	2.00
41 Jim Bown RC	.75	2.00
42 Kyle Petty RC	3.00	8.00
43 Richard Petty	3.00	8.00
44 Jeff Hammond RC	.75	2.00
45 Harry Melling RC	.75	2.00
46 Butch Mock RC	.75	2.00
Bob Rahilly RC		
47 Doug Williams RC	.75	2.00
48 Mickey Gibbs	.30	.75
49 Darrell Bryant RC	.75	2.00
50 Bill Elliott	2.00	5.00
Winston Cup Champion		
51 Walter Bud Moore	.30	.75
52 Jimmy Means	.30	.75
53 Billy Woodruff RC	.75	2.00
54 Rusty Wallace	2.00	5.00
55 Phil Parsons	.30	.75
56 Leonard Wood	.40	1.00
57 Hut Stricklin	.60	1.50
58 Ken Thompson RC	.75	2.00
59 Gary Nelson RC	.75	2.00
60 Dale Earnhardt w/Crew	6.00	15.00
Pit Crew Champs		
61 Rick Hendrick RC	1.25	3.00
62 Barry Dodson	1.00	2.50
63 Roland Wlodyka RC	.75	2.00
64 Danny Schiff	1.00	2.50
Buddy Baker		
65 Gale Wilson RC	.75	2.00
66 Rick Mast RC	.75	2.00
67 Brad Teague	.40	1.00
68 Derrike Cope	.75	2.00
69 Checklist 1-100	.30	.75
70 J.D. McDuffie	.75	2.00
71 Dave Marcis	1.00	2.50
72 David Evans RC	.75	2.00
73 Phil Barkdoll	.40	1.00
74 Ernie Elliott RC	.75	2.00
75 Morgan Shepherd	.75	2.00
76 Dale Inman RC	.75	2.00
77 Junior Johnson	1.00	2.50
78 David Smith RC	.75	2.00
79 Jimmy Fennig RC	.75	2.00
80 Jimmy Horton	.40	1.00
81 Mike Beam RC	.75	2.00
82 Jimmy Makar RC	.75	2.00
83 Lake Speed	.40	1.00
84 Mike Alexander RC	.75	2.00
85 Dennis Connor RC	.75	2.00
86 Mike Hill RC	.75	2.00

87 Richard Childress	.75	2.00
88 Greg Sacks	.75	2.00
89 Waddell Wilson RC	.75	2.00
0 Chad Little RC	1.50	4.00
1 Norman Koshimizu RC	.75	2.00
2 Harold Elliott RC	.75	2.00
3 Cliff Champion RC	.75	2.00
4 Sterling Marlin	1.25	3.00
5 Trevor Boys	.40	1.00
6 Howard Poston (Slick) RC	.75	2.00
7 Jake Elder RC	.75	2.00
8 Chuck Rider RC	.75	2.00
9 Connie Saylor	.40	1.00
00 Bill Elliott	1.50	4.00
Fan's Favorite Driver		
01 Richard Petty's Car	1.00	2.50
Year in Review		
02 Dale Earnhardt's Car	2.50	6.00
Neil Bonnett's Car		
Year in Review		
03 Neil Bonnett's Car	.60	1.50
Alan Kulwicki's Car		
Year in Review		
04 Motorcraft Quality Parts 500	.30	.75
Year in Review		
05 Lake Speed in Pits	.12	.30
Year in Review		
06 Bill Elliott in Pits	.60	1.50
Year in Review		
07 First Union 400	.40	1.00
Year in Review		
08 Dale Earnhardt's Car	2.50	6.00
Year in Review		
09 Winston 500	.40	1.00
Year in Review		
10 Coca Cola 400	.30	.75
Year in Review		
11 Harry Gant in Pits	2.00	5.00
Year in Review		
12 Budweiser 400	.30	.75
Year in Review		
13 Davey Allison's Car	.75	2.00
Year in Review		
14 Alan Kulwicki's Car	.75	2.00
Rusty Wallace's Car		
Year in Review		
15 Bill Elliott's Car	.60	1.50
Rick Wilson's Car		
Year in Review		
16 Sterling Marlin's Car	.50	1.25
Year in Review		
17 Talladega Diehard 500	.40	1.00
Year in Review		
18 Neil Bonnett's Car	.50	1.25
Year in Review		
19 Davey Allison's Car	.75	2.00
Year in Review		
20 Busch 500	.30	.75
Year in Review		
21 Dale Earnhardt's Car	2.50	6.00
Year in Review		
22 Geoff Bodine's Car	.20	.50
Year in Review		
23 Bill Elliott in Pits	.60	1.50
Year in Review		
24 Davey Allison's Car	.75	2.00
Phil Parson's Car		
Dale Jarrett's Car		
Year in Review		
25 Darrell Waltrip's Car	.75	2.00
Sterling Marlin's Car		
Bill Elliott's Car		
Rusty Wallace's Car		
Year in Review		
26 Holly Farms 400	.30	.75
Year in Review		
27 Alan Kulwicki's Car	1.25	3.00
Bill Elliott's Car		
Rusty Wallace's Car		
Davey Allison's Car		
Mark Martin's Car		
Year in Review		
28 Checker 500	.30	.75
Year in Review		
29 Bill Elliott in Pits	.60	1.50
Year in Review		
30 The Winston	.30	.75
Year in Review		
31 Benny Parsons	1.25	3.00
Phil Parsons		
32 Tommy Houston RC	.75	2.00
33 Kenny Bernstein RC	1.25	3.00
34 Jack Roush RC	1.25	3.00
35 Rob Moroso RC	.75	2.00
36 Les Richter RC	.75	2.00
37 Dick Beaty RC	.75	2.00
38 Harold Kinder RC	.75	2.00
39 Checklist 101-160	.40	1.00
40 Darrell Waltrip	1.25	3.00
Michael Waltrip		
41 Bobby Allison	1.00	2.50
Victory Lane		
42 Neil Bonnett	1.25	3.00
Victory Lane		
43 Neil Bonnett	1.25	3.00
Victory Lane		
44 Dale Earnhardt w/Crew	6.00	15.00
Victory Lane		
45 Lake Speed	.40	1.00
Victory Lane		
46 Bill Elliott	1.50	4.00
Victory Lane		
47 Terry Labonte	1.50	4.00
Victory Lane		
48 Dale Earnhardt	6.00	15.00
Teresa Earnhardt		
Victory Lane		
49 Phil Parsons	.30	.75
Victory Lane		
50 Darrell Waltrip	1.25	3.00
Victory Lane		
51 Bill Elliott	1.50	4.00
Victory Lane		
52 Rusty Wallace	2.00	5.00
Victory Lane		
53 Geoff Bodine	.50	1.25
Victory Lane		
54 Rusty Wallace	2.00	5.00
Victory Lane		
55 Bill Elliott	1.50	4.00
Victory Lane		
156 Bill Elliott	1.50	4.00
Victory Lane		
157 Ken Schrader	1.25	3.00
Victory Lane		
158 Ricky Rudd	4.00	10.00
Victory Lane		
159 Davey Allison	2.00	5.00
Victory Lane		
160 Dale Earnhardt	6.00	15.00
Victory Lane		
161 Bill Elliott w/Crew	1.50	4.00
Victory Lane		
162 Davey Allison	2.00	5.00
Victory Lane		
163 Bill Elliott	1.50	4.00
Victory Lane		
164 Darrell Waltrip	1.25	3.00
Victory Lane		
165 Rusty Wallace	2.00	5.00
Victory Lane		
166 Rusty Wallace	2.00	5.00
Victory Lane		
167 Rusty Wallace	2.00	5.00
Victory Lane		
168 Alan Kulwicki	1.50	4.00
Victory Lane		
169 Rusty Wallace	2.00	5.00
Victory Lane		
170 Terry Labonte	1.50	4.00
Junior Johnson		
Victory Lane		
171 Sterling Marlin	1.25	3.00
Victory Lane		
172 Tommy Ellis RC	.75	2.00
173 Billy Hagan RC	.75	2.00
174 Rod Osterlund RC	.75	2.00
175 Elton Sawyer RC	.75	2.00
176 Robert Yates RC	.75	2.00
177 Ed Berrier RC	.75	2.00
178 Kenny Wallace RC	1.50	4.00
179 Joe Thurman RC	.75	2.00
180 Davey Allison	2.00	5.00
Bobby Allison		
181 Richard Petty's Car	1.00	2.50
Classic		
182 Smokey Yunick	.30	.75
Classic		
183 Ralph Moody's Car	.30	.75
Classic		
184 Donnie Allison	.75	2.00
Classic		
185 Marvin Panch's Car	.75	2.00
Johnny Allen's Car		
Classic		
186 Fred Lorenzen	.75	2.00
Classic RC		
187 Wendell Scott's Car	.12	.30
Classic		
188 Curtis Turner	.75	2.00
Classic		
189 Asheville-Weaverville track	.30	.75
Classic		
190 Junior Johnson	.75	2.00
Chris Economaki		
Classic		
191 Darel Dieringer's Car	.12	.30
Classic		
192 Marvin Panch	.75	2.00
Classic		
193 Richard Petty's Car	1.00	2.50
Jack Smith's Car		
Classic		
194 David Pearson	2.50	6.00
Classic		
195 Talladega 1970	.30	.75
Classic		
196 Tim Flock In Car	.75	2.00
Classic		
197 Glenn Fireball Roberts' Car	.50	1.25
Classic		
198 Bobby Isaac	.30	.75
Classic		
199 Wood Brothers 1967	.12	.30
Classic		
200 Ned Jarrett	.75	2.00
Classic		
201 Jack Ingram	.75	2.00
202 Brett Bodine	.60	1.50
Geoff Bodine		
203 Elmo Langley RC	.75	2.00
204 Steve Grissom RC	.75	2.00
205 Ronald Cooper RC	.75	2.00
206 Tim Morgan	.30	.75
Larry McClure Team		
207 Ronnie Silver RC	.75	2.00
208 Jimmy Spencer RC	2.00	5.00
209 Ben Hess RC	.75	2.00
210 Rusty Wallace	2.00	5.00
Kenny Wallace		
211 Bob Whitcomb RC	.75	2.00
212 Billy Standridge RC	.75	2.00
213 Glen Wood	.30	.75
214 L.D. Ottinger RC	.75	2.00
215 David Pearson RC	2.50	6.00
216 Patty Moise RC	1.25	3.00
217 Checklist 162-220	.30	.75
218 Chuck Bown RC	.75	2.00
219 Jimmy Hensley RC	.75	2.00
220 Richard Petty	3.00	8.00
Kyle Petty		

1989 Maxx Stickers

Inserted two per pack in 1989 Maxx, each sticker card features two removable sticker flags. Each flag contains a colored number representing a race car number. The sticker cards are not numbered individually, but have been assigned card numbers below in the order of the left flag number.

COMPLETE SET (20)	25.00	50.00
1 2/33	1.25	3.00
2 3/52	1.25	3.00
3 4/42	1.25	3.00
4 5/43	1.25	3.00
5 6/84	1.25	3.00
6 7/55	1.25	3.00
7 8/57	1.25	3.00
8 9/71	1.25	3.00
9 11/88	1.25	3.00
10 12/68	1.25	3.00
11 15/3	1.25	3.00
12 16/75	1.25	3.00
13 17/83	1.25	3.00
14 21/17	1.25	3.00
15 25/33	1.25	3.00
16 26/43	1.25	3.00
17 27/94	1.25	3.00
18 28/5	1.25	3.00
19 29/27	1.25	3.00
20 30/9	1.25	3.00

1989 Maxx Crisco

This 25-card set contains one Cover card, and 24 driver cards. It was produced by Maxx and distributed by Proctor and Gamble as a complete set. They were given away with a purchase of their product in selected stores throughout the country. They were kept in a floor standup display, featuring Greg Sacks, that held 96 sets. It is reported that one million sets were produced. Two weeks after these sets were shipped to Proctor and Gamble, Greg Sacks parted company with his car owner Buddy Baker and a large portion of these sets were destroyed. However, many of these sets found their way into the hobby through closeout sales.

COMPLETE SET (25)	6.00	15.00
1 Greg Sacks	.30	.75
2 Darrell Waltrip	.60	1.50
3 Ken Schrader	.60	1.50
4 Bill Elliott	.75	2.00
5 Rusty Wallace	1.00	2.50
6 Dale Earnhardt	3.00	8.00
7 Terry Labonte	.75	2.00
8 Geoff Bodine	.25	.60
9 Brett Bodine	.30	.75
10 Davey Allison	1.00	2.50
11 Ricky Rudd	2.00	5.00
12 Kyle Petty	1.50	4.00
13 Alan Kulwicki	.75	2.00
14 Neil Bonnett	.60	1.50
15 Rick Wilson	.30	.75
16 Harry Gant	.75	2.00
17 Richard Petty	1.25	3.00
18 Phil Parsons	.15	.40
19 Sterling Marlin	.60	1.50
20 Bobby Hillin	.30	.75
21 Michael Waltrip	.60	1.50
22 Dale Jarrett	1.00	2.50
23 Morgan Shepherd	.40	1.00
24 Greg Sacks w/Car	.30	.75
NNO Header Card	.15	.40

1990 Maxx

This 200-card set was produced in three different print runs. It was distributed in four different factory sets. The "tin box" set was sold by Maxx through a mail order offer for $29.95, and contains cards from the first printing. The cards from these sets have a glossy finish. The second of the sets was the white box Hobby set distributed to authorized Maxx dealers containing cards from the first printing. The third of the sets was the red/white box Hobby set which contains cards from the second printing. In the second printing four error cards were corrected: number 8 Bobby Hillin, number 28 Davey Allison, number 39 Kirk Shelmerdine, and number 97 Chuck Bown. The fourth of these sets was the red/yellow Hobby set which contains cards from the third printing. In the third printing three error cards were corrected:number 13 Mickey Gibbs, number 69 Checklist, and number 85 Larry McClure. Cards from all three printings of this set were also distributed in wax packs. The packs are distinguishable by the lettering on the bottom of them. Packs from the first printing have white lettering, packs from the second printing have black lettering, and packs form the third printing also have black lettering and have the roman numeral three under the lettering. It is important to note that because of the black borders on these cards they are susceptible to chipping.

COMPLETE SET (200)	10.00	25.00
COMP.FACT.SET WHITE (200)	12.50	30.00
COMP.FACT.SET RED/WHITE (200)	12.50	30.00
COMP.FACT.SET RED/YELLOW (200)	12.50	30.00
1 Terry Labonte	2.00	5.00
2 Ernie Irvan	1.50	4.00
3 Dale Earnhardt	6.00	15.00
4 Phil Parsons	.40	1.00
5 Ricky Rudd	1.50	4.00
6 Mark Martin	4.00	10.00
7 Alan Kulwicki	2.00	5.00
8A Bobby Hillin ERR	.75	2.00
career totals wrong, 332 races		
8B Bobby Hillin COR	.75	2.00
career totals correct, 177 races		
9 Bill Elliott	2.00	5.00
10 Derrike Cope	1.00	2.50
11 Geoff Bodine	.60	1.50
12 Bobby Allison	1.25	3.00
13A Mickey Gibbs ERR	2.50	6.00
only one child listed		
13B Mickey Gibbs COR	.75	2.00
both children listed		
14 A.J. Foyt	1.50	4.00
15 Morgan Shepherd	1.00	2.50
16 Larry Pearson	.40	1.00
17 Darrell Waltrip	1.50	4.00
18 Cale Yarborough	1.50	4.00
19 Barry Dodson	1.00	2.50
20 Bob Whitcomb	.40	1.00
21 Neil Bonnett	1.50	4.00
22 Rob Moroso	.40	1.00
23 Eddie Bierschwale	.40	1.00
24 Cliff Champion		
25 Ken Schrader	1.50	4.00
26 Brett Bodine	.60	1.50
27 Rusty Wallace	2.50	6.00
28A Davey Allison ERR	4.00	10.00
1988 top tens 13		
28B Davey Allison COR	4.00	10.00
1988 top tens 16		
29 Dale Jarrett	2.50	6.00
30 Michael Waltrip	1.25	3.00
31 Jim Sauter	.75	2.00
32 Tony Glover	.40	1.00
33 Harry Gant	1.50	4.00
34 Rodney Combs	.75	2.00
35 Jimmy Fennig	.40	1.00
36 Raymond Beadle	.40	1.00
37 Buddy Parrott RC	1.00	2.50
38 Brandon Baker RC	.75	2.00
39A Kirk Shelmerdine ERR	2.50	6.00
copyright line included		
39B Kirk Shelmerdine COR	1.25	3.00
no copyright		
40 Jim Phillips RC	1.00	2.50
41 Jim Bown	.40	1.00
42 Kyle Petty	2.00	5.00
43 Richard Petty	3.00	8.00
44 Bob Tullius RC	1.00	2.50
45 Richard Childress	1.00	2.50
46 Steve Hmiel RC	1.00	2.50
47 Ronnie Silver	.40	1.00
48 Greg Sacks	.75	2.00
49 Tony Spanos RC	1.00	2.50
50 Darrell Waltrip w/Crew	1.50	4.00
Pit Crew Champions		
51 Junie Donlavey RC	1.00	2.50
52 Jimmy Means	.40	1.00
53 Mike Beam	.40	1.00
54 Jack Roush	1.00	2.50
55 Felix Sabates	1.00	2.50
56 Ted Conder RC	1.00	2.50
57 Hut Stricklin	.75	2.00
58 Ken Ragan	.40	1.00
59 Ronald Cooper	.40	1.00
60 Jeff Hammond	1.00	2.50
61 Elton Sawyer	.40	1.00
62 Leo Jackson RC	1.00	2.50
63 Rick Hendrick	1.00	2.50
64 Dale Inman	.40	1.00
65 Travis Carter		
66 Dick Trickle RC	1.50	4.00
67 Brad Teague	.40	1.00
68 Richard Broome RC	1.00	2.50
69A Checklist A ERR	1.40	4.00
card 85 Tim McClure		
69B Checklist A COR	.40	1.00
card 85 Larry McClure		
70 J.D. McDuffie	.75	2.00
71 Dave Marcis	1.00	2.50
72 Harry Melling	.40	1.00
73 Phil Barkdoll	.40	1.00
74 Leonard Wood	.40	1.00
75 Rick Wilson	.40	1.00
76 Gary Nelson	.40	1.00
77A Ben Hess ERR	2.50	6.00
mentions Hess as single		
77B Ben Hess COR	.40	1.00
mentions Hess as engaged		
78 Larry McReynolds RC	1.00	2.50
79 Darrell Bryant	.40	1.00
80 Jimmy Horton	.40	1.00
81 Kenny Bernstein	1.00	2.50
82 Doug Richert RC	1.00	2.50
83 Lake Speed	.40	1.00
84 Mike Alexander	.40	1.00
85A Larry McClure ERR	1.25	3.00
Tim Morgan on front and back		
85B Larry McClure COR	1.25	3.00
correct name on front and back		
86 Robin Pemberton RC	1.00	2.50
87 Waddell Wilson	.40	1.00
88 Jimmy Spencer	1.00	2.50
89 Rod Osterlund	.40	1.00
90 Stan Barrett RC	1.00	2.50
91 Tommy Ellis	.40	1.00
92 Danny Schiff RC	1.00	2.50
93 Buddy Baker	1.00	2.50
94 Sterling Marlin	1.50	4.00
95 Kenny Wallace	1.00	2.50
96 Tim Brewer	.40	1.00
97A Chuck Bown ERR	2.50	6.00
name Brown on front		
97B Chuck Bown COR	.60	1.50
Bown on front		
98 Butch Miller RC	1.00	2.50
99 Connie Saylor	.40	1.00
100 Darrell Waltrip	1.50	4.00
Fan's Favorite Driver		
101 Dan Ford RC	1.00	2.50
102 Howard Poston Slick	.40	1.00
103 David Evans	.40	1.00
104 Harold Elliott	.40	1.00
105 Ken Thompson	.40	1.00
106 Robert Gee	1.00	2.50
107 James Lewter	.40	1.00
108 Will Lind	.40	1.00
109 Jerry Schweitz RC	1.00	2.50
110 Eddie Wood RC	1.00	2.50
111 Norman Koshimizu	.40	1.00
112 Barry Dodson	1.00	2.50
113 Mike Hill	.40	1.00
114 Jimmy Makar	.40	1.00
115 Barry Dodson	1.00	2.50
116 Dale Earnhardt	6.00	15.00
All Pro		
117 Junior Johnson	1.00	2.50
118 Shawna Robinson RC	2.00	5.00
119 Richard Jackson RC	1.00	2.50
120 Chad Little	1.00	2.50
121 Chuck Rider	.40	1.00
122 L.D. Ottinger	.40	1.00
123 Dennis Connor	.40	1.00
124 Ken Bouchard	.40	1.00
125 Jimmy Hensley	.40	1.00
126 Robert Yates	1.00	2.50
127 Doug Williams	.40	1.00
128 Mark Stahl	.40	1.00
129 Rick Mast	.40	1.00
130 Walter Bud Moore	.40	1.00
131 David Pearson	2.00	5.00
132 Paul Andrews RC	1.00	2.50
133 Tommy Houston	.40	1.00
134 Jack Pennington RC	1.00	2.50
135 Billy Hagan	.40	1.00
136 Joe Thurman	.40	1.00
137A Bill Ingle ERR	2.50	6.00
Billy on front and back		
137B Bill Ingle COR	.60	1.50
Bill on front and back		
138 Patty Moise	1.00	2.50
139 Glen Wood	.40	1.00
140 Billy Standridge	.40	1.00
141 Harry Hyde	.40	1.00
142 Steve Grissom	.40	1.00
143 Bob Rahilly	.40	1.00
144 Butch Mock	.40	1.00
145 Ernie Elliott	.40	1.00
146 Les Richter	.40	1.00
147 Dick Beaty	.40	1.00
148 Harold Kinder	.40	1.00
149 Elmo Langley	.40	1.00
150 Dick Trickle	1.50	4.00
Rookie of the Year		
151 Bobby Hamilton RC	1.50	4.00
152 Jack Ingram	1.00	2.50
153 Bill Stavola	.40	1.00
154 Bob Jenkins RC	1.00	2.50
155 Ned Jarrett	1.00	2.50
156 Benny Parsons	1.50	4.00
157 Jerry Punch RC	1.00	2.50
158 Ken Squier RC	1.00	2.50
159 Chris Economaki RC	1.00	2.50
160 Jack Arute RC	1.00	2.50
161 Dick Berggren RC	1.00	2.50
162 Mike Joy RC	1.00	2.50
163 Barney Hall RC	1.00	2.50
164 Eli Gold RC	1.00	2.50
165 Dick Brooks RC	1.00	2.50
166 Winston Kelley RC	1.00	2.50
167 Darrell Waltrip	1.50	4.00
Year in Review		
168 Rusty Wallace's Car	2.50	6.00
Darrell Waltrip's Car		
Year in Review		
169 Sterling Marlin's Car	1.50	4.00
Year in Review		
170 Pontiac 400	.40	1.00
Year in Review		
171 Harry Gant	1.50	4.00
Year in Review		
172 Bill Elliott's Car	2.00	5.00
Bobby Hillin's Car		
Year in Review		
173 First Union 400	.40	1.00
Year in Review		
174 Darrell Waltrip	1.50	4.00
Year in Review		
175 Davey Allison	2.50	6.00
Year in Review		
176 Sterling Marlin	1.50	4.00
Year in Review		
177 Darrell Waltrip's Car	1.50	4.00
Year in Review		
178 Darrell Waltrip w/Crew	1.50	4.00
Year in Review		
179 Dale Earnhardt w/Crew	6.00	15.00
Teresa Earnhardt		
Year in Review		
180 Banquet Foods 300	.40	1.00
Year in Review		
181 Terry Labonte	2.00	5.00
Year in Review		
182 Bill Elliott	2.00	5.00
Year in Review		
183 Dale Earnhardt's Car	6.00	15.00
Rick Wilson's Car		
Morgan Shepherd's Car		
Ken Schrader's Car		
Year in Review		
184 Bill Elliott	2.00	5.00
Year in Review		
185 Darrell Waltrip's Car	4.00	10.00
Terry Labonte's Car		
Mark Martin's Car		
Dale Jarrett's Car		
Year in Review		
186 Bud At The Glen	.40	1.00
Year in Review		
187 Rusty Wallace's Car	2.50	6.00
Year in Review		
188 Busch 500	.40	1.00
Year in Review		
189 Heinz Southern 500	.40	1.00
Year in Review		
190 Rusty Wallace	2.50	6.00
Year in Review		
191 Dale Earnhardt's Car	6.00	15.00
Year in Review		
192 Richard Petty's Car	3.00	8.00
Kyle Petty's Car		
Year in Review		
193 Richard Childress	1.00	2.50
Year in Review		
194 Michael Waltrip's Car	1.25	3.00
Phil Parsons' Car		
Year in Review		
195 Dale Earnhardt's Car	6.00	15.00
Mark Martin's Car		
Year in Review		
196 Rusty Wallace's Car	2.50	6.00
Year in Review		
197 Rusty Wallace in Pits	2.50	6.00
Year in Review		
198 Rusty Wallace	2.50	6.00
Year in Review		
199 Checklist B	.40	1.00
200 Checklist C	.40	1.00
Club Maxx offer		

1990 Maxx Glossy

This parallel set was issued in factory set form in a colorful tin metal box. Each of the 200-cards was produced during the first printing of 1990 Maxx so all the original error cards were included. Each card is identical to its base issue card except for the addition of an extra glossy surface on the cardfront.

COMP.GLOSSY TIN (200)	30.00	60.00
*GLOSSY: 1X TO 2.5X BASIC CARDS		

1990 Maxx Bill Elliott Vortex Comics

This set was actually issued as a 4-card panel inside Vortex Comics' Legends of NASCAR Bill Elliott comic book. The cards are most often found attached as a panel of four and utilize the same card design found in the regular issue 1990 Maxx set.

COMPLETE SET (4)	1.50	4.00
COMMON CARD (E1-E4)	.40	1.00

1990 Maxx Holly Farms

This is a 30-card set produced by Maxx and distributed by Holly Farms. It consists of 30 driver cards and one prize card, which was for a contest to win a trip to the 1991 Daytona 500. It was distributed as a 30-card set packaged in cello-wrap and given only to Holly Farms employees. As part of a Holly Farms promotion, three-card packs were produced and made available to the public in exchange for proof of purchase seals from Holly Farm products. These cards are distinguishable from regular 1990 Maxx cards by a red, yellow, and black Holly Farms logo located in the upper right hand corner of the card.

COMPLETE SET (30)	6.00	15.00
HF1 Dale Earnhardt	2.00	5.00
HF2 Bill Elliott	.60	1.50
HF3 Darrell Waltrip	.50	1.25
HF4 Rusty Wallace	.75	2.00
HF5 Ken Schrader	.50	1.25
HF6 Richard Petty	1.00	2.50
HF7 Harry Gant	.50	1.25
HF8 Mark Martin	1.25	3.00
HF9 Davey Allison	.75	2.00
HF10 Neil Bonnett	.50	1.25
HF11 Alan Kulwicki	.60	1.50
HF12 Terry Labonte	.60	1.50
HF13 Ricky Rudd	.50	1.25
HF14 Geoff Bodine	.20	.50
HF15 Sterling Marlin	.50	1.25
HF16 Morgan Shepherd	.30	.75
HF17 Kyle Petty	.60	1.50
HF18 Michael Waltrip	.40	1.00
HF19 Phil Parsons	.12	.30
HF20 Dale Jarrett	.75	2.00
HF21 Brett Bodine	.20	.50
HF22 Lake Speed	.12	.30
HF23 Ernie Irvan	.50	1.25
HF24 Junior Johnson	.30	.75
HF25 Cale Yarborough	.50	1.25
HF26 Bobby Allison	.40	1.00
HF27 Derrike Cope	.30	.75
HF28 Bobby Hillin	.25	.60
HF29 Benny Parsons	.50	1.25
HF30 Ned Jarrett	.30	.75

1991 Maxx

This 240-card set was distributed in two different factory sets and in 15-card wax packs. The front of these cards have a black outer border, two shades of blue for the inner border and the drivers' name boxed in yellow at the bottom of the card. The "Deluxe" mail order set contains 240 cards from the regular set , the 20-card Winston Acrylic set, and the 48-card Maxx Update set. The standard hobby factory set is packaged in a blue, shrink-wrapped box with Richard Petty and Bill Elliott cards visible. A special version of this set containing a Bill Elliott autograph card was available through the J.C.Penney catalog.

COMPLETE SET (240)	10.00	25.00
COMP.FACT.SET (240)	12.50	30.00
COMP.MAIL ORDER (308)	20.00	40.00
COMP.JC PENNEY SET (241)	20.00	40.00
WAX BOX	12.50	30.00
1 Rick Mast	.12	.30
2 Rusty Wallace	.50	1.25
3 Dale Earnhardt	1.25	3.00
4 Ernie Irvan	.30	.75
5 Ricky Rudd	.30	.75
6 Mark Martin	.60	1.50
7 Alan Kulwicki	.40	1.00
8 Rick Wilson	.12	.30

9 Bill Elliott .40 1.00
10 Derrike Cope .20 .50
11 Geoff Bodine .12 .30
12 Hut Stricklin .12 .30
13 Ken Bouchard .12 .30
14 A.J. Foyt .20 .50
15 Morgan Shepherd .20 .50
16 Joey Knuckles RC .20 .50
17 Darrell Waltrip .30 .75
18 Greg Sacks .12 .30
19 Chad Little .20 .50
20 Jimmy Hensley .12 .30
21 Dale Jarrett .50 1.25
22 Sterling Marlin .30 .75
23 Eddie Bierschwale .12 .30
24 Mickey Gibbs .12 .30
25 Ken Schrader .20 .50
26 Brett Bodine .12 .30
27 Bobby Allison .25 .60
28 Davey Allison .50 1.25
29 Jeff Hammond .20 .50
30 Michael Waltrip .25 .60
31 Jim Sauter .12 .30
32 Cale Yarborough .30 .75
33 Harry Gant .30 .75
34 Jimmy Makar .12 .30
35 Robert Yates .20 .50
36 Neil Bonnett .30 .75
37 Rick Hendrick .20 .50
38 Harry Hyde .12 .30
39 Kenny Wallace .20 .50
40 Tom Kendall .12 .30
41 Larry Pearson .12 .30
42 Kyle Petty .40 1.00
43 Richard Petty .60 1.50
44 Jimmy Horton .12 .30
45 Mike Beam .12 .30
46 Walter Bud Moore .12 .30
47 Jack Pennington .12 .30
48 James Hylton .12 .30
49 Rodney Combs .12 .30
50 Bill Elliott w/Crew .40 1.00
Pit Crew Champs
51 Jeff Purvis RC .20 .50
52 Jimmy Means .12 .30
53 Bobby Labonte RC 2.50 6.00
54 Richard Childress .20 .50
55 Billy Hagan .12 .30
56 Bill Ingle RC .20 .50
57 Jim Bown .12 .30
58 Ken Ragan .12 .30
59 Larry McReynolds .20 .50
60 Jack Roush .20 .50
61 Phil Parsons .12 .30
62 Harry Melling .12 .30
63 Barry Dodson .12 .30
64 Tony Glover .12 .30
65 Tommy Houston .12 .30
66 Dick Trickle .12 .30
67 Cliff Champion .12 .30
68 Bobby Hamilton .20 .50
69 Gary Nelson .12 .30
70 J.D. McDuffie .12 .30
71 Dave Marcis .20 .50
72 Ernie Elliott .12 .30
73 Phil Barkdoll .12 .30
74 Junie Donlavey .12 .30
75 Chuck Rider .12 .30
76 Ben Hess .12 .30
77 Steve Hmiel .12 .30
78 Felix Sabates .20 .50
79 Tim Brewer .12 .30
80 Tim Morgan .12 .30
81 Larry McClure .12 .30
82 Mark Stahl .12 .30
83 Lake Speed .12 .30
84 Waddell Wilson .12 .30
85 Mike Alexander .12 .30
86 Robin Pemberton .12 .30
87 Junior Johnson .20 .50
88 Leonard Wood .12 .30
89 Kenny Bernstein .20 .50
90 Buddy Baker .20 .50
91 Patty Moise .20 .50
92 Elton Sawyer .12 .30
93 Bob Whitcomb .12 .30
94 Terry Labonte .30 .75
95 Raymond Beadle .12 .30
96 Kirk Shelmerdine .12 .30
97 Chuck Bown .12 .30
98 Jimmy Spencer .20 .50
99 Bobby Hillin .12 .30
100 Rob Moroso .12 .30
Rookie of the Year
101 Rod Osterlund .12 .30
102 Les Richter .12 .30
103 Jimmy Fennig .12 .30
104 Doyle Ford RC .20 .50
105 Elmo Langley .12 .30
106 Richard Jackson .12 .30
107 Jimmy Cox RC .20 .50
108 Dick Beaty .12 .30
109 Kyle Petty's Car .40 1.00
Memorable Moments
110 Bob Tullius .12 .30
111 Buddy Parrott .12 .30
112 H.B. Bailey RC .20 .50
113 Mark Martin's Car .60 1.50
Geoff Bodine's Car
Sterling Marlin's Car
Ernie Irvan's Car
Memorable Moments
114 Billy Standridge .12 .30
115 Doug Williams .12 .30
116 Tracy Leslie RC .20 .50
117 Donnie Allison .20 .50
118 Michael Waltrip Crash .25 .60
Memorable Moments
119 Ed Berrier .12 .30
120 Travis Carter .12 .30
121 Dennis Connor .12 .30
122 Richard Petty's Car .60 1.50
Rob Moroso's Car
Memorable Moments
123 Ward Burton RC 1.25 3.00
124 Bob Rahilly .12 .30
125 Butch Mock
126 Robin Pemberton .12 .30
127 Michael Waltrip's Car .25 .60
Derrike Cope's Car
Memorable Moments
128 Donnie Wingo RC .20 .50
129 Darrell Bryant .12 .30
130 Mike McLaughlin RC .20 .50
131 Robbie Loomis RC .30 .75
132 Charlie Glotzbach RC .20 .50
133 Dave Rezendes RC .20 .50
134 Davey Johnson RC .20 .50
135 Paul Andrews .12 .30
136 Daytona MM .07 .20
137 The Racestoppers .07 .20
138 Jack Ingram .20 .50
139 Joe Nemechek RC .50 1.25
140 Geoff Bodine's Car .40 1.00
Kyle Petty's Car
Ernie Irvan's Car
Memorable Moments
141 Jeffrey Ellis .20 .50
142 Butch Miller .12 .30
143 Bill Venturini RC .20 .50
144 Richard Broome .12 .30
145 Alan Kulwicki in Pits .40 1.00
Memorable Moments
146 Dave Mader RC .20 .50
147 Robert Pressley RC .20 .50
148 Steve Loyd RC .20 .50
149 Ricky Pearson .20 .50
150 Darrell Waltrip .30 .75
Fan's Favorite Driver
151 Don Bierschwale RC .20 .50
152 Leo Jackson .12 .30
153 Tommy Ellis .20 .50
154 Randy Baker RC .20 .50
155 Bill Stavola .12 .30
156 D.K. Ulrich RC .20 .50
157 L.D. Ottinger .12 .30
158 Phoenix MM .07 .20
159 Glen Wood .12 .30
Eddie Wood
Len Wood
160 Andy Petree RC .20 .50
161 Steve Grissom .12 .30
162 Dale Inman .12 .30
163 Charlotte Motor Speedway .07 .20
Memorable Moments
164 Dick Moroso RC .20 .50
165 Doug Richert .12 .30
166 Peter Sospenzo RC .20 .50
167 Chuck Bown .12 .30
Memorable Moments
168 Sandi Fix .12 .30
Miss Winston
169 David Pearson .40 1.00
170 Derrike Cope .20 .50
Year in Review
171 Mark Martin .60 1.50
Year in Review
172 Kyle Petty .40 1.00
Year in Review
173 Dale Earnhardt 1.25 3.00
Year in Review
174 Dale Earnhardt 1.25 3.00
Year in Review
175 Davey Allison .50 1.25
Bobby Allison
Year in Review
176 Brett Bodine .12 .30
Year in Review
177 Geoff Bodine .12 .30
Year in Review
178 Dale Earnhardt 1.25 3.00
Year in Review
179 Dale Earnhardt 1.25 3.00
Year in Review
180 Rusty Wallace .50 1.25
Year in Review
181 Derrike Cope .20 .50
Year in Review
182 Rusty Wallace .50 1.25
Year in Review
183 Harry Gant .30 .75
Year in Review
184 Dale Earnhardt 1.25 3.00
Year in Review
185 Dale Earnhardt 1.25 3.00
Year in Review
186 Geoff Bodine .12 .30
Year in Review
187 Dale Earnhardt 1.25 3.00
Year in Review
188 Ricky Rudd .30 .75
Year in Review
189 Mark Martin .60 1.50
Year in Review
190 Ernie Irvan w/Crew .30 .75
Year in Review
191 Dale Earnhardt .40 1.00
Teresa Earnhardt
Year in Review
192 Dale Earnhardt .40 1.00
Teresa Earnhardt
Year in Review
193 Bill Elliott .40 1.00
Year in Review
194 Geoff Bodine .12 .30
Year in Review
195 Mark Martin .60 1.50
Year in Review
196 Davey Allison w/Crew .50 1.25
(Year in Review
197 Alan Kulwicki .40 1.00
Year in Review
198 Dale Earnhardt 1.25 3.00
Year in Review
199 Morgan Shepherd .20 .50
Year in Review
200 Dale Earnhardt .40 1.00
Teresa Earnhardt
Year in Review
201 Jeff Burton RC 2.00 5.00
202 Larry Hedrick RC .20 .50
203 Todd Bodine RC .20 .50
204 Tom Peck RC .20 .50
205 Kirk Shelmerdine .12 .30
206 David Smith .12 .30
207 Darrell Andrews RC .20 .50
208 Danny Lawrence RC .20 .50
209 Mike Hill .12 .30
210 Norman Koshimizu .12 .30
211 James Lewter .12 .30
212 Will Lind .12 .30
213 Cecil Gordon RC .20 .50
214 Howard Poston .12 .30
215 Eddie Lanier RC .20 .50
216 Troy Martin RC .20 .50
217 Bobby Moody RC .20 .50
218 Henry Benfield RC .20 .50
219 Kirk Shelmerdine .12 .30
220 Dale Earnhardt 1.25 3.00
All Pro
221 Jack Arute .12 .30
222 Dick Berggren .12 .30
223 Dick Brooks .12 .30
224 Chris Economaki .12 .30
225 Eli Gold .12 .30
226 Barney Hall .12 .30
227 Ned Jarrett .20 .50
228 Bob Jenkins .12 .30
229 Mike Joy .12 .30
230 Winston Kelley .12 .30
231 Benny Parsons .30 .75
232 Jim Phillips .12 .30
233 Jerry Punch .12 .30
234 Ken Squier .12 .30
235 Bobby Dotter RC .20 .50
236 Jake Elder .12 .30
237 Checklist 1-60 .07 .20
238 Checklist 61-120 .07 .20
239 Checklist 121-180 .07 .20
240 Checklist 181-240 .07 .20
P1 Bill Elliott Promo 15.00 40.00

1991 Maxx The Winston Acrylics

This 20-card set was distributed as a complete set in the '91 Maxx mail order set and was randomly inserted into '91 Maxx wax packs. They were produced on laser-etched acrylic and are relatively thin when compared to a standard card. Widespread reports show that many of the mail order sets did not contain all of the cards in this set. The cards are unnumbered and have been listed below in alphabetical order.

COMPLETE SET (20) 6.00 15.00
1 Davey Allison 1.00 2.50
2 Brett Bodine .25 .60
3 Geoff Bodine .25 .60
4 Derrike Cope .40 1.00
5 Dale Earnhardt 2.50 6.00
6 Bill Elliott .75 2.00
7 Harry Gant .60 1.50
8 Bobby Hillin .25 .60
9 Alan Kulwicki .75 2.00
10 Terry Labonte .60 1.50
11 Mark Martin 1.25 3.00
12 Phil Parsons .25 .60
13 Kyle Petty .75 2.00
14 Ricky Rudd .60 1.50
15 Ken Schrader .40 1.00
16 Morgan Shepherd .40 1.00
17 Lake Speed .25 .60
18 Dick Trickle .25 .60
19 Rusty Wallace 1.00 2.50
20 Darrell Waltrip .60 1.50

1991 Maxx Update

This 48-card set was distributed in 1991 Maxx "Deluxe" mail order sets and foil packs from the second printing. It was also It contains 33 corrected cards from the 1991 Maxx set and 15 updated cards of drivers such as Dale Earnhardt, Ernie Irvan, Mark Martin, Alan Kulwicki, Richard Petty, and Bobby Labonte.

COMPLETE SET (48) 4.00 10.00
1 Rick Mast .12 .30
3 Dale Earnhardt 1.25 3.00
4 Ernie Irvan .30 .75
5 Ricky Rudd .30 .75
6 Mark Martin .60 1.50
7 Alan Kulwicki .40 1.00
8 Rick Wilson .12 .30
9 Bill Elliott .40 1.00
11 Geoff Bodine .12 .30
12 Hut Stricklin .12 .30
13 Ken Bouchard .12 .30
15 Morgan Shepherd .20 .50
17 Darrell Waltrip .30 .75
22 Sterling Marlin .30 .75
25 Ken Schrader .20 .50
30 Michael Waltrip .25 .60
33 Harry Gant .30 .75
39 Kenny Wallace .20 .50
40 Tom Kendall .12 .30
42 Kyle Petty .40 1.00
43 Richard Petty .60 1.50
49 Rodney Combs .12 .30
50 Bill Elliott .40 1.00
Pit Crew Champions
53 Bobby Labonte RC 2.50 6.00
54 Richard Childress .20 .50
57 Jim Bown .12 .30
58 Ken Ragan .12 .30
66 Dick Trickle .12 .30
68 Bobby Hamilton .20 .50
73 Phil Barkdoll .12 .30
83 Lake Speed .12 .30
85 Mike Alexander .12 .30
94 Terry Labonte .30 .75
97 Chuck Bown .12 .30
98 Jimmy Spencer .20 .50
100 Rob Moroso .12 .30
Rookie of the Year
117 Donnie Allison .20 .50
126 Robin Pemberton .12 .30
132 Charlie Glotzbach RC .20 .50
139 Joe Nemechek RC .50 1.25
141 Jeffrey Ellis RC .20 .50
147 Robert Pressley .20 .50
150 Darrell Waltrip .30 .75
Fan's Favorite Driver
164 Dick Moroso RC .20 .50
165 Doug Richert .12 .30
200 Dale Earnhardt .40 1.00
Teresa Earnhardt
Year in Review
220 Dale Earnhardt 1.25 3.00
All Pro
235 Bobby Dotter RC .20 .50

1991 Maxx Bill Elliott Team Coors/Melling

This 30-card set features Bill Elliott and members of the Coors-Melling Racing Team. Both versions of the set are virtually identical except for the set name on the cardback and that the Elliott set does not include team owner Harry Melling. His card replaced that of Teresa Alligood. Both sets were offered through Bill Elliott's souvenir program and through Maxx's mail order program. All the cards are unnumbered, but have been assigned numbers according to the listing found on the checklist card.

COMPLETE ELLIOTT SET (40) 4.00 10.00
COORS/MELLING VERSION: SAME PRICE
1 Jim Waldrop .12 .30
2 Melvin Turner .12 .30
3 Casey Elliott .12 .30
4 Dan Elliott .12 .30
5 Bill Elliott .40 1.00
6 Diana Pugh .12 .30
7 Bill Elliott's Car .40 1.00
8 Matt Thompson .12 .30
9 Mike Thomas .12 .30
10 Wayne McCord .12 .30
11 Bill Elliott's Pit Crew .40 1.00
Pit Crew Champs
12 Charles Palmer .12 .30
13 Jerry Seabolt .12 .30
14 Denver Harris .12 .30
15 Terron Carver .12 .30
16 Mike Dalrymple .12 .30
17 Alan Palmer .12 .30
18 Michael Rinker .12 .30
19 Doug Shaak .12 .30
20 Bill Elliott .40 1.00
21 Dave Kriska .12 .30
22 Alexis Leras .12 .30
23 Mike Colt .12 .30
24 Chuck Hill
25 Glen Blakely .12 .30
26 Tommy Cole .12 .30
27 Clinton Chumbley .12 .30
28 Mike Brandt .12 .30
29 Phil Seabolt .12 .30
30 Ron Brooks .12 .30
31 Johnny Trammell .12 .30
32 Mike Rich .12 .30
33 Mark Gaddis .12 .30
34 Gregory Trammell .12 .30
35 Wayne Hamby .12 .30
36 Dan Palmer .12 .30
37A Teresa Alligood .12 .30
Elliott Team only
37B Harry Melling .12 .30
Coors/Melling Team only
38 Ernie Elliott .12 .30
39 Team Shops .40 1.00
40 Cover/Checklist Card .07 .20

1991 Maxx McDonald's

This 31-card set was produced by Maxx and distributed in over 250 McDonald's locations in North Carolina and South Carolina between August 30 and October 24, 1991. Any customer purchasing a Bacon, Egg and Cheese Value Meal or a Big Mac Extra Value Meal was given a five-card cellophane pack. Each pack contained one cover card and four driver cards. It features the top 28 finishers in the 1990 NASCAR Winston Cup points race, one McDonald's All-Star Team card, and one cover card. This set contains eight error cards that were corrected in the middle of the press run. The blue portion of the McDonald's All-Star Racing Team logo is missing from the upper right hand corner of all the error cards. It is important to note that due to the nature of the distribution of these cards that a large portion became available to the hobby.

COMPLETE SET (31) 4.00 10.00
1A Dale Earnhardt ERR 2.50 6.00
without blue part of logo
1B Dale Earnhardt COR 1.50 4.00
with blue part of logo
2A Mark Martin ERR 1.25 3.00
without blue part of logo
2B Mark Martin COR .75 2.00
with blue part of logo
3A Geoff Bodine ERR .25 .60
without blue part of logo
3B Geoff Bodine COR .15 .40
with blue part of logo
4A Bill Elliott ERR .75 2.00
without blue part of logo
4B Bill Elliott COR .50 1.25
with blue part of logo
5 Morgan Shepherd .25 .60
6 Rusty Wallace .60 1.50
7 Ricky Rudd .40 1.00
8 Alan Kulwicki .50 1.25
9 Ernie Irvan .40 1.00
10 Ken Schrader .25 .60
11 Kyle Petty .50 1.25
12 Brett Bodine .15 .40
13 Davey Allison .60 1.50
14 Sterling Marlin .40 1.00
15 Terry Labonte .40 1.00
16 Michael Waltrip .30 .75
17 Harry Gant .40 1.00
18 Derrike Cope .25 .60
19 Bobby Hillin .15 .40
20 Darrell Waltrip .40 1.00
21A Dave Marcis ERR .40 1.00
without blue part of logo
21B Dave Marcis COR .25 .60
with blue part of logo
22A Dick Trickle ERR .25 .60
without blue part of logo
22B Dick Trickle COR .15 .40
with blue part of logo
23A Rick Wilson ERR .25 .60
without blue part of logo
23B Rick Wilson COR .15 .40
with blue part of logo
24A Jimmy Spencer ERR .40 1.00
without blue part of logo
24B Jimmy Spencer COR .25 .60
with blue part of logo
25 Dale Jarrett .60 1.50
26 Richard Petty .75 2.00
27 Rick Mast .15 .40
28 Hut Stricklin .15 .40
29 Jimmy Means .15 .40
30 Dale Earnhardt 1.50 4.00
Mark Martin
Bill Elliott
NNO Cover Card .10 .25

1991 Maxx Motorsport

This 40-card set was produced by Maxx for Prospective Marketing International/Ford Motorsport Sportswear. It features the top-ten 1991 Ford race teams and the 1991 Winston Legends champion. It was made available as a sequentially numbered set in orange boxes through the Fall 1992 Ford Motorsport Sportswear and Accessories Catalog. 75,000 of these sets were produced.

COMPLETE SET (40) 6.00 6.00
1 Bill Elliott .50 1.25
2 Davey Allison .60 1.50
3 Wally Dallenbach Jr. .25 .60
4 Sterling Marlin .40 1.00
5 Mark Martin .75 2.00
6 Morgan Shepherd .25 .60
7 Alan Kulwicki .50 1.25
8 Dale Jarrett .60 1.50
9 Geoff Bodine .15 .40
10 Chad Little .25 .60
11 Robert Yates .25 .60
12 Jack Roush .25 .60
13 Walter Bud Moore .15 .40
14 Harry Melling .15 .40
15 Wood Brothers .15 .40
16 Junior Johnson .25 .60
17 Chuck Little .15 .40
18 Junie Donlavey .15 .40
19 Larry McReynolds .25 .60
20 Robin Pemberton .15 .40
21 Donnie Wingo .25 .60
22 Mike Beam .15 .40
23 Ernie Elliott .15 .40
24 Paul Andrews .15 .40
25 Leonard Wood .15 .40
26 Harry Hyde .15 .40
27 Tim Brewer .15 .40
28 Davey Allison's Car .25 .60
29 Bill Elliott's Car .20 .50
30 Davey Allison's Car .25 .60
31 Wally Dallenbach Jr.'s Car .10 .25
32 Sterling Marlin's Car .15 .40
33 Mark Martin's Car .30 .75
34 Morgan Shepherd's Car .10 .25
35 Alan Kulwicki's Car .20 .50
36 Dale Jarrett's Car .25 .60
37 Geoff Bodine's Car .05 .15
38 Chad Little's Car .10 .25
39 Elmo Langley's Car .15 .40
Cale Yarborough's Car
40 Wally Dallenbach Jr. w/Crew .10 .25

1991 Maxx Racing for Kids

These three sheets feature six cards on each that are from the 1990 Maxx set. The cards came on uncut sheets and each card has a "Special Edition Racing for Kids" logo in the upper left hand corner. The cards are a parallel to the regular version. The sheets were issued as a promotional insert in Racing F Kids magazine over three months, January, Februa and March 1991. We've included prices for unc sheets below with the corresponding individual ca numbers after the drivers' name.

COMPLETE SET (3) 30.00 75.0
1 Sheet 1 14.00 35.0
Bill Elliott Pit Champs 50
Michael Waltrip 39
Neil Bonnett 21
Mark Martin 6
Dale Earnhardt 3
Junior Johnson 117
2 Sheet 2 8.00 20.0
Bill Elliott 9
Kyle Petty 42
Derrike Cope 10
Ken Schrader 25
Ricky Rudd 5
Richard Childress 45
3 Sheet 3 10.00 25.0
Richard Petty 43
Rusty Wallace 27
Davey Allison 28
A.J. Foyt 14
Darrell Waltrip 17
Alan Kulwicki 7

1991 Maxx Winston 20th Anniversary Foils

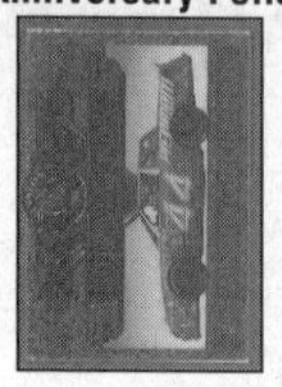

This 21-card set was produced to commemorate 2 years of involvement in the NASCAR circuit by th R.J. Reynolds Tobacco Company. It portrays the pa Winston Cup Champions on foil-etched cards. Th set was made available through multi-pack premiu offers on Winston cigarettes and later through th Club Maxx mail order club. The cards a unnumbered and listed in order by year of Winsto Cup win.

COMPLETE SET (21) 5.00 8.0
1 Richard Petty 1971 Car .30 .7
2 Richard Petty 1972 Car .30 .7
3 Benny Parsons 1973 Car .15 .4
4 Richard Petty 1974 Car .30 .7
5 Richard Petty 1975 Car .30 .7
6 Cale Yarborough 1976 Car .15 .4
7 Cale Yarborough 1977 Car .15 .4
8 Cale Yarborough 1978 Car .15 .4
9 Richard Petty 1979 Car .30 .7
10 Dale Earnhardt 1980 Car .60 1.5
12 Darrell Waltrip 1981 Car .15 .4
12 Darrell Waltrip 1982 Car .15 .4
13 Bobby Allison 1983 Car .12 .3
14 Terry Labonte 1984 Car .15 .4
15 Darrell Waltrip 1985 Car .15 .4
16 Dale Earnhardt 1986 Car .60 1.5
17 Dale Earnhardt 1987 Car .60 1.5
18 Bill Elliott 1988 Car .20 .5
19 Rusty Wallace 1989 Car .25 .6
20 Dale Earnhardt 1990 Car .60 1.5
NNO Checklist .05 .1

1992 Maxx All-Pro Team

This 50-card set was produced by Maxx for Gargoy Performance Eyewear. It features every member the 1991 All-Pro team. The set was made availab through speedway vendors and through Maxx's ma order program.

COMPLETE SET (50) 2.00 4.0
1 Dale Earnhardt .75 2.0
2 Harry Gant .15 .4
3 Mark Martin .30 .7
4 Larry McReynolds .10 .2
5 Kirk Shelmerdine .05 .1
6 Tony Glover .05 .1
7 Larry Wallace .10 .2
8 Leo Jackson .05 .1
9 Eddie Lanier .05 .1
10 Harold Stott .10 .2
11 Andy Petree .05 .1
12 Will Lind .05 .1
13 Kirk Shelmerdine .05 .1
14 Doug Richert .05 .1
15 Tim Brewer .05 .1
16 Scott Robinette .05 .1
17 Darrell Andrews .05 .1
18 Todd Parrott .05 .1
19 David Smith .05 .1
20 Charley Pressley .05 .1
21 Gary Brooks .05 .1
22 Norman Koshimizu .05 .1
23 Danny Myers .05 .1
24 Henry Benfield .05 .1
25 Dan Ford .05 .1
26 Paul Andrews .05 .1
27 Mike Hill .05 .1
28 Will Lind .05 .1
29 Mike Thomas .05 .1
30 Shorty Edwards .10 .2
31 Danny Lawrence .05 .1
32 Devin Barbee .10 .2
33 Ronnie Reavis .05 .1

Ioward Poston (Slick)	.05	.15
Dan Ford	.05	.15
Darrell Dunn	.10	.25
Gale Wilson	.05	.15
Norman Koshimizu	.05	.15
Jerry Schweitz	.05	.15
James Lewter	.05	.15
Abbie Garwood	.10	.25
Mark Osborn	.10	.25
David Little	.10	.25
Wayne Dalton	.05	.15
Troy Martin	.05	.15
Glen Bobo	.10	.25
Bobby Moody	.05	.15
David Munari	.05	.15
) Dale Inman	.05	.15
) Checklist	.05	.10

1992 Maxx Bobby Hamilton

16-card set was produced to honor Bobby ilton as the Winston Cup 1992 Rookie of the . It was distributed as a complete set in one foil .

MPLETE SET (16)	1.25	3.00
BY HAMILTON (1-16)	.10	.30

1992 Maxx Craftsman

eight-card set was produced by Maxx and ributed by Sears. It features drivers with sman sponsorship. It was only made available ose who ordered a red hobby set from the 1992 s Christmas Wish catalog. The unnumbered s have been listed below alphabetically.

MPLETE SET (8)	2.00	5.00
eoff Bodine	.25	.60
ll Elliott	.75	2.00
arry Gant	.60	1.50
obby Hamilton	.40	1.00
erling Marlin	.60	1.50
eg Sacks	.25	.60
arrell Waltrip	.60	1.50
ck Wilson	.25	.60

1992 Maxx IMHOF

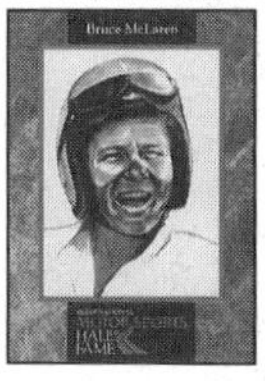

40-card set was produced by Maxx to honor and previous inductees into the International or Sports Hall of Fame. The cards include ches by renowned motorsports artist Jeanne es. These Cards have no number orientation.

MPLETE SET (40)	3.00	8.00
HOF Aerial View	.07	.20
HOF Rotunda	.07	.20
erald Dial Chairman	.07	.20
n Naman Exec. Dir.	.07	.20
HOF Commission	.07	.20
oundbreaking	.07	.20
bon Cutting	.07	.20
nny Gilliand Miss IMHOF	.07	.20
ficial Car Chevy	.07	.20
uck Baker Art	.10	.30
ony Bettenhausen Art	.10	.30
ack Brabham Art	.10	.30
Malcolm Campbell Art	.10	.30
im Clark Art	.10	.30
uan Manuel Fangio Art	.10	.30
im Flock Art	.10	.30
an Gurney Art	.10	.30
nton Hulman(Tony) Art	.10	.30
ed Jarrett Art	.10	.30
unior Johnson Art	.10	.30
arnelli Jones Art	.10	.30
red Lorenzen Art	.10	.30
ruce McLaren Art	.10	.30
tirling Moss Art	.10	.30
arney Oldfield Art	.10	.30
lenn Fireball Roberts Art	.10	.30
Vilbur Shaw Art	.10	.30
arroll Shelby Art	.10	.30
obby Unser Art	.10	.30
ill Vukovich Art	.10	.30
mokey Yunick Art	.10	.30
eanne Barnes Artist	.07	.20
Vinston Cutaway Car	.07	.20
919 Indy Racer	.07	.20
ichard Petty's Car	.10	.30
arrell Waltrip's Car	.07	.20
on Garlits' Car	.07	.20
lenn Fireball Roberts' Car	.07	.20

39 T.G. Shepherd	.07	.20
40 Checklist	.07	.20

1992 Maxx McDonald's

This 37-card set was produced by Maxx and distributed by McDonald's. It was made available exclusively at over 1,300 McDonald's locations throughout 15 states in August 1992. Customers could obtain four-card packs for $.99 each or by purchasing an Extra Value Meal. It features members of the 1992 McDonald's All-Star Race Team and 29 other top NASCAR Winston Cup drivers, plus the respective car owners and crew chiefs of the McDonald's All-Star Racing Team. Like its predecessor, a large amount of these cards found their way into the hobby. Each pack came with a cover card.

COMPLETE SET (37)	4.00	10.00
1 Dale Earnhardt	.75	2.00
Davey Allison		
Bill Elliott		
2 Dale Earnhardt	.75	2.00
3 Davey Allison	.25	.60
4 Bill Elliott	.20	.50
5 Richard Childress	.10	.25
6 Robert Yates	.10	.25
7 Junior Johnson	.10	.25
8 Kirk Shelmerdine	.05	.15
9 Larry McReynolds	.10	.25
10 Tim Brewer	.05	.15
11 Ricky Rudd	.15	.40
12 Harry Gant	.15	.40
13 Ernie Irvan	.15	.40
14 Mark Martin	.30	.75
15 Sterling Marlin	.15	.40
16 Darrell Waltrip	.15	.40
17 Ken Schrader	.10	.25
18 Rusty Wallace	.25	.60
19 Morgan Shepherd	.10	.25
20 Alan Kulwicki	.20	.50
21 Geoff Bodine	.05	.15
22 Michael Waltrip	.12	.30
23 Hut Stricklin	.05	.15
24 Dale Jarrett	.25	.60
25 Terry Labonte	.15	.40
26 Brett Bodine	.05	.15
27 Rick Mast	.05	.15
28 Bobby Hamilton	.10	.25
29 Ted Musgrave	.10	.25
30 Richard Petty	.30	.75
31 Jimmy Spencer	.10	.25
32 Chad Little	.10	.25
33 Derrike Cope	.10	.25
34 Dave Marcis	.10	.25
35 Kyle Petty	.20	.50
36 Dick Trickle	.05	.15
NNO Cover Card	.05	.10

1992 Maxx Motorsport

This 50-card set was produced by Maxx for Prospective Marketing International/Ford Motorsport Sportswear. It features drivers, owners, and crew chiefs from the 13 Ford race teams. This set was only made available through the 1993 Ford Motorsport Sportswear and Accessories Catalog. 50,000 of these sets were made.

COMPLETE SET (50)	2.50	6.00
1 Bill Elliott	.30	.75
2 Davey Allison	.40	1.00
3 Alan Kulwicki	.30	.75
4 Sterling Marlin	.25	.60
5 Mark Martin	.50	1.25
6 Geoff Bodine	.10	.25
7 Brett Bodine	.10	.25
8 Morgan Shepherd	.15	.40
9 Dick Trickle	.10	.25
10 Wally Dallenbach Jr.	.10	.25
11 Jimmy Hensley	.10	.25
12 Charlie Glotzbach	.10	.25
13 Chad Little	.15	.40
14 Junior Johnson	.15	.40
15 Robert Yates	.15	.40
16 Jack Roush	.15	.40
17 Walter Bud Moore	.10	.25
18 Kenny Bernstein	.15	.40
19 Eddie Wood	.10	.25
20 Bill Stavola	.10	.25
21 Cale Yarborough	.25	.60
22 Junie Donlavey	.10	.25
23 Harry Melling	.10	.25
24 Tim Brewer	.10	.25
25 Larry McReynolds	.15	.40
26 Paul Andrews	.10	.25
27 Mike Beam	.10	.25
28 Steve Hmiel	.10	.25
29 Donnie Wingo	.10	.25
30 Donnie Richeson	.15	.40
31 Leonard Wood	.10	.25
32 Ken Wilson	.10	.25
33 Steve Loyd	.10	.25
34 Bob Johnson	.10	.25
35 Gene Roberts	.15	.40
36 Bill Elliott w/Crew	.30	.75
37 Davey Allison w/Crew	.40	1.00
38 Alan Kulwicki w/Crew	.30	.75
39 Sterling Marlin w/Crew	.25	.60
40 Mark Martin w/Crew	.50	1.25
41 Geoff Bodine w/Crew	.10	.25
42 Brett Bodine w/Crew	.10	.25
43 Morgan Shepherd w/Crew	.15	.40
44 Dick Trickle w/Crew	.10	.25
45 Wally Dallenbach Jr. w/Crew	.10	.25
46 Jimmy Hensley w/Crew	.10	.25
47 Charlie Glotzbach w/Crew	.10	.25
48 Chad Little w/Crew	.15	.40
49 Mark Martin's Car	.50	1.25
Alan Kulwicki's Car		
Davey Allison's Car		
Bill Elliott's Car		
Formation Flying		
50 Mark Martin	.50	1.25
Alan Kulwicki		
Davey Allison		
Bill Elliott		

1992 Maxx Red

This 300-card set was made available through hobby sets and 14-card wax packs. Special versions of the hobby sets were distributed through different retail outlets. QVC sold these sets with an autographed Bill Elliott card and Sears sold a set through its catalog that contained the 16-card Bobby Hamilton 1992 Rookie of the Year set and the 8-card Craftsman set.

COMPLETE SET (300)	12.50	30.00
COMP.FACT.SET (304)	15.00	40.00
WAX BOX	12.50	30.00
1 Rick Mast	.10	.25
2 Rusty Wallace	.40	1.00
3 Dale Earnhardt	1.25	3.00
4 Ernie Irvan	.25	.60
5 Ricky Rudd	.25	.60
6 Mark Martin	.50	1.25
7 Alan Kulwicki	.30	.75
8 Rick Wilson	.10	.25
9 Phil Parsons	.10	.25
10 Derrike Cope	.15	.40
11 Bill Elliott	.30	.75
12 Hut Stricklin	.10	.25
13 Bobby Dotter	.10	.25
14 Mike Chase RC	.15	.40
15 Geoff Bodine	.10	.25
16 Wally Dallenbach Jr.	.10	.25
17 Darrell Waltrip	.25	.60
18 Dale Jarrett	.40	1.00
19 Randy LaJoie RC	.15	.40
20 Buddy Baker	.15	.40
21 Morgan Shepherd	.15	.40
22 Sterling Marlin	.25	.60
23 Mike Wallace	.10	.25
24 Kenny Wallace	.15	.40
25 Ken Schrader	.15	.40
26 Brett Bodine	.10	.25
27 Jimmy Hensley	.10	.25
28 Davey Allison	.40	1.00
29 Jeff Gordon	1.50	4.00
30 Michael Waltrip	.20	.50
31 Clifford Allison RC	.20	.50
32 Cecil Eunice RC	.15	.40
33 Harry Gant	.25	.60
34 Chuck Bown	.10	.25
35 Todd Bodine	.10	.25
36 H.B. Bailey	.10	.25
37 Joe Nemechek	.15	.40
38 Dave Rezendes	.10	.25
39 Tommy Houston	.10	.25
40 Tom Kendall	.10	.25
41 Larry Pearson	.10	.25
42 Kyle Petty	.30	.75
43 Richard Petty	.50	1.25
44 Bobby Labonte	.40	1.00
45 Irv Hoerr RC	.15	.40
46 Dick Trickle	.10	.25
47 Greg Sacks	.10	.25
48 James Hylton	.10	.25
49 Stanley Smith	.10	.25
50 Jeff Gordon	1.50	4.00
Rookie of the Year		
51 Jeff Purvis	.10	.25
52 Jimmy Means	.10	.25
53 Bobby Hillin	.10	.25
54 Jack Ingram	.15	.40
55 Ted Musgrave	.15	.40
56 Bill Sedgwick RC	.15	.40
57 Jeff Burton	.20	.50
58 Steve Grissom	.10	.25
59 Patty Moise	.15	.40
60 Elton Sawyer	.10	.25
61 Bill Venturini	.10	.25
62 Mike McLaughlin	.10	.25
63 Ed Berrier	.10	.25
64 Tracy Leslie	.10	.25
65 Shawna Robinson	.25	.60
66 Chad Little	.15	.40
67 Ed Ferree RC	.15	.40
68 Bobby Hamilton	.15	.40
69 Peter Sospenzo	.10	.25
70 John Paul Jr. RC	.15	.40
71 Dave Marcis	.15	.40
72 Jim Bown	.10	.25
73 Phil Barkdoll	.10	.25
74 Tom Peck	.10	.25
75 Joe Ruttman	.10	.25
76 Charlie Glotzbach	.10	.25
77 Rich Bickle RC	.15	.40
78 Larry Phillips RC	.15	.40
79 David Green RC	.30	.75
80 Jack Sprague RC	.15	.40
81 Robert Pressley	.10	.25
82 Mark Stahl	.10	.25
83 Lake Speed	.10	.25
84 Butch Miller	.10	.25
85 Jeff Green RC	.30	.75
86 Ward Burton	.15	.40
87 Dorsey Schroeder RC	.15	.40
88 Ricky Craven RC	.60	1.50
89 Jim Sauter	.10	.25
90 Troy Beebe	.10	.25
91 Bobby Labonte	.40	1.00
BGN Champ		
92 Dave Mader	.10	.25
93 Mickey Gibbs	.10	.25
94 Terry Labonte	.25	.60
95 Eddie Bierschwale	.10	.25
96 Randy Baker	.10	.25
97 Tommy Ellis	.10	.25
98 Jimmy Spencer	.15	.40
99 Bobby Hamilton	.15	.40
Rookie of the Year		
100 Bill Elliott	.30	.75
Most Popular Driver		
101 Ed McClure RC	.15	.40
Teddy McClure RC		
Jerry McClure RC		
102 Richard Childress	.15	.40
103 Rick Hendrick	.15	.40
104 Robert Yates	.15	.40
105 Leo Jackson	.10	.25
106 Larry McClure	.10	.25
107 Tim Morgan	.10	.25
108 Jack Roush	.15	.40
109 Junior Johnson	.15	.40
110 Roger Penske	.15	.40
111 Don Miller	.10	.25
112 Walter Bud Moore	.10	.25
113 Chuck Rider	.10	.25
114 Bobby Allison	.20	.50
115 Bob Bilby	.10	.25
116 Eddie Wood	.10	.25
117 Len Wood	.15	.40
118 Glen Wood	.10	.25
119 Billy Hagan	.10	.25
120 Kenny Bernstein	.15	.40
121 Butch Mock	.10	.25
122 Bob Rahilly	.10	.25
123 Richard Jackson	.10	.25
124 George Bradshaw	.10	.25
125 David Fuge RC	.15	.40
126 Mark Smith RC	.15	.40
127 D.K. Ulrich	.10	.25
128 Ray DeWitt RC	.15	.40
Diane DeWitt RC		
129 Travis Carter	.10	.25
130 Bill Stavola	.10	.25
131 Larry Hedrick	.10	.25
132 Chuck Little	.10	.25
133 Bob Whitcomb	.10	.25
134 Felix Sabates	.15	.40
135 Cale Yarborough	.25	.60
136 Dick Moroso	.10	.25
137 Harry Melling	.10	.25
138 Junie Donlavey	.10	.25
139 Don Bierschwale	.10	.25
140 Sam McMahon III RC	.15	.40
141 A.J. Foyt	.15	.40
142 Jeffrey Ellis	.10	.25
143 Tony Glover	.10	.25
144 Ken Wilson	.10	.25
145 Dale Inman	.10	.25
146 Steve Hmiel	.10	.25
147 Morgan Shepherd w/Crew	.15	.40
Pit Crew Champs		
148 Kirk Shelmerdine	.10	.25
149 Waddell Wilson	.10	.25
150 Larry McReynolds	.15	.40
151 Andy Petree	.10	.25
152 Tony Glover	.10	.25
153 Robin Pemberton	.10	.25
154 Mike Beam	.10	.25
155 Jeff Hammond	.15	.40
156 Richard Broome	.10	.25
157 Eddie Dickerson RC	.15	.40
158 Ernie Elliott	.10	.25
159 Donnie Wingo	.10	.25
160 Paul Andrews	.10	.25
161 Tim Brewer	.10	.25
162 Bill Ingle	.10	.25
163 Jimmy Fennig	.10	.25
164 Dewey Livengood RC	.15	.40
165 Bob Johnson	.10	.25
166 Clyde McLeod	.10	.25
167 Buddy Parrott	.10	.25
168 Doug Williams	.10	.25
169 Steve Loyd	.10	.25
170 Leonard Wood	.10	.25
171 Gene Roberts RC	.15	.40
172 Jimmy Makar	.10	.25
173 Robbie Loomis	.15	.40
174 David Ifft	.10	.25
175 Steve Barkdoll RC	.15	.40
176 Donnie Allison	.15	.40
177 Dennis Connor	.10	.25
178 Barry Dodson	.10	.25
179 Harry Hyde	.10	.25
180 Bob Labonte RC	.15	.40
181 Steve Bird	.10	.25
182 Jeff Hensley	.10	.25
183 Ricky Pearson	.10	.25
184 Scott Houston	.10	.25
185 Eddie Pearson RC	.15	.40
186 Tony Eury RC	.30	.75
187 Donnie Richeson RC	.15	.40
188 Military Cars	.06	.15
Memorable Moments		
189 Sterling Marlin's Car	.10	.25
Memorable Moments		
190 Davey Allison's Car	.15	.40
Darrell Waltrip's Car		
Memorable Moments		
191 Geoff Bodine's Car	.05	.10
Brett Bodine's Car		
Memorable Moments		
192 Kyle Petty's Car	.12	.30
Memorable Moments		
193 Rick Mast's Car	.05	.10
Memorable Moments		
194 Ken Schrader's Car	.05	.15
Memorable Moments		
195 Darrell Waltrip's Car	.10	.25
Memorable Moments		
196 Talladega Speedway	.05	.15
Memorable Moments		
197 Bobby Hamilton's Car	.05	.15
Ted Musgrave's Car		
Memorable Moments		
198 Davey Allison	.15	.40
Dale Jarrett Cars MM		
199 Richmond International	.05	.15
Memorable Moments		
200 Mark Martin's Car	.20	.50
Memorable Moments		
201 Harry Gant's Car	.10	.25
Memorable Moments		
202 Rusty Wallace	.40	1.00
Memorable Moments		
203 Dale Earnhardt's Car	.50	1.25
Memorable Moments		
204 Robert Black	.10	.25
205 Les Richter	.10	.25
206 Dick Beaty	.10	.25
207 Doyle Ford	.10	.25
208 Buster Auton RC	.15	.40
209 Bruce Roney	.10	.25
210 Mike Chaplin RC	.15	.40
211 Chuck Romeo	.15	.40
212 Jimmy Cox	.10	.25
213 Buddy Morrow	.15	.40
214 Tim Earp RC	.15	.40
215 Elmo Langley	.10	.25
216 Jack Whittemore RC	.15	.40
217 Carl Hill	.10	.25
218 Art Krebs RC	.15	.40
219 Gary Nelson	.10	.25
220 Chris Economaki	.10	.25
221 Ned Jarrett	.15	.40
222 Neil Bonnett	.25	.60
223 Mike Joy	.10	.25
224 Dick Berggren	.10	.25
225 Winston Kelley	.10	.25
226 Jack Arute	.10	.25
227 Jim Phillips	.10	.25
228 Ken Squier	.10	.25
229 Beth Bruce	.15	.40
Miss Winston		
230 Renee White	.15	.40
Miss Winston RC		
231 Dale Earnhardt	1.25	3.00
All Pro		
232 Harry Gant	.25	.60
All Pro		
233 Mark Martin	.50	1.25
All Pro		
234 Larry McReynolds	.15	.40
All Pro		
235 Kirk Shelmerdine	.10	.25
Tony Glover		
All Pro		
236 Larry Wallace	.15	.40
All Pro		
237 Leo Jackson	.10	.25
Eddie Lanier		
All Pro		
238 Harold Stott	.15	.40
All Pro		
239 Andy Petree	.10	.25
Will Lind		
All Pro		
240 Kirk Shelmerdine	.10	.25
All Pro		
241 Doug Richert	.10	.25
Tim Brewer		
All Pro		
242 Scott Robinette	.15	.40
All Pro RC		
243 Darrell Andrews	.10	.25
Todd Parrott		
All Pro		
244 David Smith	.10	.25
All Pro		
245 Charley Pressley	.10	.25
Gary Brooks		
All Pro		
246 Norman Koshimizu	.10	.25
All Pro		
247 Danny Myers	.10	.25
Henry Benfield		
All Pro		
248 Dan Ford	.10	.25
All Pro		
249 Paul Andrews	.10	.25
Mike Hill		
All Pro		
250 Will Lind	.10	.25
All Pro		
251 Mike Thomas	.15	.40
Shorty Edwards		
All Pro		
252 Danny Lawrence	.10	.25
All Pro		
253 Devin Barbee RC	.15	.40
Ronnie Reavis		
All Pro RC		
254 Howard Poston (Slick)	.10	.25
All Pro		
255 Dan Ford	.15	.40
Darrell Dunn		
All Pro RC		
256 Gale Wilson	.10	.25
All Pro		
257 Norman Koshimizu	.10	.25
Jerry Schweitz		
All Pro		
258 James Lewter	.10	.25
All Pro		
259 Abbie Garwood RC	.15	.40
Mark Osborn		
All Pro RC		
260 David Little	.15	.40
All Pro		
261 Wayne Dalton	.10	.25
Troy Martin		
All Pro		
262 Glen Bobo	.15	.40
All Pro RC		
263 Bobby Moody	.10	.25
David Munari		
All Pro		
264 Ernie Irvan	.25	.60
Year in Review		
265 Dale Earnhardt	1.25	3.00
Teresa Earnhardt		
Year in Review		
266 Kyle Petty	.30	.75
Year in Review		
267 Ken Schrader	.15	.40
Year in Review		
268 Ricky Rudd	.25	.60
Year in Review		
269 Rusty Wallace	.40	1.00
Year in Review		
270 Darrell Waltrip	.25	.60
Year in Review		
271 Dale Earnhardt	1.25	3.00
Teresa Earnhardt		
Year in Review		
272 Harry Gant	.25	.60
Year in Review		
273 Davey Allison	.40	1.00
Year in Review		
274 Davey Allison	.40	1.00
Deborah Allison		
Year in Review RC		
275 Ken Schrader	.15	.40
Year in Review		
276 Davey Allison w/Crew	.40	1.00
Year in Review		
277 Darrell Waltrip	.25	.60
Year in Review		
278 Davey Allison	.40	1.00
Robert Yates		
Year in Review		
279 Bill Elliott	.30	.75
Year in Review		
280 Rusty Wallace	.40	1.00
Year in Review		
281 Dale Earnhardt	1.25	3.00
Teresa Earnhardt		
Year in Review		
282 Ernie Irvan	.25	.60
Year in Review		
283 Dale Jarrett	.40	1.00
Year in Review		
284 Alan Kulwicki	.30	.75
Year in Review		
285 Harry Gant	.25	.60
Year in Review		
286 Harry Gant	.25	.60
Year in Review		
287 Harry Gant	.25	.60
Year in Review		
288 Harry Gant	.25	.60
Year in Review		
289 Dale Earnhardt	1.25	3.00
Richard Childress		
Year in Review		
290 Geoff Bodine	.10	.25
Year in Review		
291 Davey Allison	.40	1.00
Year in Review		
292 Davey Allison	.40	1.00
Robert Yates		
Year in Review		
293 Mark Martin	.50	1.25
Year in Review		
294 Dale Earnhardt	1.25	3.00
Year in Review		
295 Checklist No. 1	.07	.20
296 Checklist No. 2	.07	.20
297 Checklist No. 3	.07	.20
298 Checklist No. 4	.07	.20
299 Checklist No. 5	.07	.20
300 Checklist No. 6	.07	.20
P1 Bill Elliott Promo	8.00	20.00
Red Border		

1992 Maxx Black

This 300-card set was distributed through hobby sets and 14-card wax packs. The set is a parallel to the Red set with the cards featuring black borders instead of red. It is considered to be the first "premium" racing card. It was produced to be a "hobby" only product. These cards had a 5th Anniversary Edition theme and new logo. Celebrating its anniversary, Maxx inserted cards from their previous sets into factory sets, four per set, and into their wax packs, one per pack.

COMPLETE SET (300)	12.50	30.00
COMP.FACT.SET (304)	15.00	40.00
*STARS: .5X TO 1.2X RED CARDS		
WAX BOX	12.50	30.00
P1 Bill Elliott Promo	8.00	20.00
Black Border		

1992 Maxx Red Update

This 30-card set was produced with the intent of being distributed on the "retail" market. It contains 30 numbered cards and two unnumbered cards, shows updated photos of drivers who changed uniforms along with a few noted personalities. It features the first Maxx cards of Joe Gibbs and Jerry Glanville.

COMPLETE SET (32)	2.50	6.00
U1 Greg Sacks	.12	.30
U2 Geoff Bodine	.12	.30
U3 Jeff Burton	.25	.60
U4 Derrike Cope	.20	.50

U5 Jerry Glanville RC .30 .75
U6 Jeff Gordon 2.00 5.00
U7 Jimmy Hensley .12 .30
U8 Ben Hess .12 .30
U9 Dale Jarrett .50 1.25
U10 Chad Little .20 .50
U11 Mark Martin .60 1.50
U12 Joe Nemechek .20 .50
U13 Bob Schacht RC .20 .50
U14 Stanley Smith .12 .30
U15 Lake Speed .12 .30
U16 Dick Trickle .12 .30
U17 Kenny Wallace .20 .50
U18 Ron McCreary RC .20 .50
U19 Joe Gibbs RC .30 .75
U20 Dick Brooks .12 .30
U21 Bill Connell RC .20 .50
U22 Eli Gold .12 .30
U23 Barney Hall .12 .30
U24 Glenn Jarrett RC .20 .50
U25 Bob Jenkins .12 .30
U26 John Kernan .12 .30
U27 Benny Parsons .30 .75
U28 Pat Patterson RC .20 .50
U29 Randy Pemberton RC .20 .50
U30 Dr. Jerry Punch .12 .30
NNO Eddie Pearson RC .20 .50
NNO Geoff Bodine .12 .30
Make a Wish Foundation

1992 Maxx Black Update

This 32-card set was produced as a "hobby" only product. It contains 30 numbered cards and two unnumbered cards, and shows updated photos of drivers who changed uniforms along with a few noted personalities. It features the first Maxx cards of Joe Gibbs and Jerry Glanville.

COMPLETE SET (32) 2.50 6.00
*STARS: .4X TO 1X RED UPDATES

1992 Maxx Sam Bass

This 11-card set was designed by noted motorsports artist Sam Bass. The set contains paintings of drivers such as Bobby Allison, Richard Petty, and Neil Bonnett. It is important to note this set also contains the only Tim Richmond card made by Maxx. This set was sent free to the buyers of the black mail order set.

COMPLETE SET (11) 3.00 8.00
1 Richard Petty .60 1.50
2 J.D. McDuffie .12 .30
3 Ned Jarrett .20 .50
4 Tim Richmond .20 .50
5 Harold Kinder .12 .30
6 Rob Moroso .12 .30
7 Bobby Allison .25 .60
8 Bill Elliott .40 1.00
9 Junior Johnson .20 .50
10 Neil Bonnett .30 .75
NNO Sam Bass .20 .50

1992 Maxx Texaco Davey Allison

This 20-card set was produced by Maxx and made available at over 1,200 Texaco gas stations in the eastern and southeastern region of the country in February 1992. This set features 1992 Daytona 500 winner Davey Allison and the Robert Yates Texaco Havoline Racing Team. They were available in four-card packs and could be purchased for $.99. Full sets were made available through Club Maxx in July of 1992. 2,000 of the cover cards in this set were autographed and randomly inserted into packs. A large number of these cards found their way into the hobby through factory closeouts.

COMPLETE SET (20) 2.00 5.00
1 Davey Allison .25 .60
2 Davey Allison's Car .25 .60
3 Robert Yates .10 .25
4 Larry McReynolds .10 .25
5 Davey Allison's Car w/Crew .10 .25
6 Davey Allison's Car w/Crew .10 .25
7 Davey Allison's Transporter .10 .25
8 Davey Allison's Car .10 .25
9 Robert Yates .10 .25
Larry McReynolds
10 Davey Allison .25 .60
11 Davey Allison w/Car .25 .60
12 Davey Allison's Car .30 .75
Dale Earnhardt's Car
Leading The Pack
13 Davey Allison in Pits .25 .60
14 Davey Allison .25 .60
Deborah Allison
Robert Yates
Larry McReynolds
15 Davey Allison .25 .60
Larry McReynolds
16 Davey Allison .25 .60
17 Davey Allison .25 .60
Robert Yates
18 Davey Allison .25 .60
Robert Yates
Larry McReynolds
19 Davey Allison .25 .60
Bobby Allison
Robert Yates
Larry McReynolds
20 Davey Allison w/Crew .25 .60
Checklist Card
NNO Davey Allison AU 75.00 150.00

1992 Maxx The Winston

This 50-card set was produced by Maxx and documents the first ever night running of The Winston. 50,000 sets were made and it was made available through Maxx's mail order program.

COMPLETE SET (50) 3.00 8.00
1 Davey Allison .40 1.00
2 Kyle Petty .30 .75
3 Ken Schrader .15 .40
4 Ricky Rudd .25 .60
5 Bill Elliott .30 .75
6 Rusty Wallace .40 1.00
7 Alan Kulwicki .30 .75
8 Ernie Irvan .25 .60
9 Richard Petty .50 1.25
10 Terry Labonte .25 .60
11 Darrell Waltrip .25 .60
12 Harry Gant .25 .60
13 Geoff Bodine .10 .25
14 Dale Earnhardt 1.25 3.00
15 Michael Waltrip .20 .50
16 Dave Mader .10 .25
17 Mark Martin .50 1.25
18 Dale Jarrett .40 1.00
19 Morgan Shepherd .15 .40
20 Hut Stricklin .10 .25
21 Davey Allison's Car .15 .40
22 Kyle Petty's Car .12 .30
23 Ken Schrader's Car .05 .15
24 Ricky Rudd's Car .10 .25
25 Bill Elliott's Car .12 .30
26 Rusty Wallace's Car .15 .40
27 Alan Kulwicki's Car .12 .30
28 Ernie Irvan's Car .10 .25
29 Richard Petty's Car .20 .50
30 Terry Labonte's Car .10 .25
31 Darrell Waltrip's Car .10 .25
32 Harry Gant's Car .10 .25
33 Geoff Bodine's Car .05 .10
34 Dale Earnhardt 's Car .50 1.25
35 Michael Waltrip's Car .07 .20
36 Dave Mader's Car .05 .10
37 Mark Martin's Car .20 .50
38 Dale Jarrett's Car .15 .40
39 Morgan Shepherd's Car .05 .15
40 Hut Stricklin's Car .05 .10
41 Davey Allison's Car .15 .40
42 Davey Allison's Pole Win .40 1.00
43 Michael Waltrip Win .20 .50
44 Final Pace Lap .05 .15
45 First Segment .05 .15
46 Second Segment .05 .15
47 Third Segment .05 .15
48 Davey Allison's Car .15 .40
Kyle Petty's Car
49 Victory Lane .05 .15
50 Davey Allison Win .40 1.00

1993 Maxx

This 300-card set was distributed in complete factory set form and through 12-card wax packs. It is commonly known as the green set for the bright green border. A blue bordered parallel set was released later in the year through Club Maxx. The blue bordered set is known as the Maxx Premier Series and is priced under that title.

COMPLETE SET (300) 8.00 20.00
COMPLETE FACT.SET (300) 10.00 25.00
WAX BOX 15.00 40.00
1 Rick Mast .07 .20
2 Rusty Wallace .60 1.50
3 Dale Earnhardt 1.25 3.00
4 Ernie Irvan .15 .40
5 Ricky Rudd .25 .60
6 Mark Martin .60 1.50
7 Alan Kulwicki .25 .60
8 Sterling Marlin .30 .75
9 Chad Little .07 .20
10 Derrike Cope .07 .20
11 Bill Elliott .30 .75
12 Jimmy Spencer .07 .20
13 Alan Kulwicki's Car .07 .20
Bill Elliott's Car
Memorable Moment
14 Terry Labonte .30 .75
15 Geoff Bodine .07 .20
16 Wally Dallenbach Jr. .07 .20
17 Darrell Waltrip .15 .40
18 Dale Jarrett .50 1.25
19 Tom Peck .07 .20
20 Alan Kulwicki's Car .07 .20
21 Morgan Shepherd .07 .20
22 Bobby Labonte .50 1.25
23 Eddie Bierschwale .02 .10
24 Jeff Gordon CRC 1.25 3.00
25 Ken Schrader .07 .20
26 Brett Bodine .07 .20
27 Hut Stricklin .07 .20
28 Davey Allison .40 1.00
29 Jimmy Horton .07 .20
30 Michael Waltrip .15 .40
31 Steve Grissom .07 .20
32 Charlie Glotzbach .07 .20
33 Harry Gant .15 .40
34 Todd Bodine .07 .20
35 Jeff Purvis .07 .20
36 Ward Burton .15 .40
37 Bill Elliott's Car .07 .20
38 Jerry O'Neill .02 .10
39 Buddy Baker .07 .20
40 Kenny Wallace .07 .20
41 Phil Parsons .07 .20
42 Kyle Petty .15 .40
43 Richard Petty .30 .75
44 Rick Wilson .07 .20
45 Jeff Burton .25 .60
46 Al Unser Jr. .15 .40
47 Bill Venturini .07 .20
48 James Hylton .02 .10
49 Stanley Smith .07 .20
50 Tommy Houston .07 .20
51 Richard Lasater .02 .10
52 Jimmy Means .07 .20
53 Mike Wallace .07 .20
54 Jack Sprague .02 .10
55 Ted Musgrave .07 .20
56 Dale Earnhardt's Car .50 1.25
57 Troy Beebe .02 .10
58 Bill Sedgwick .02 .10
59 Robert Pressley .07 .20
60 Jeff Green .07 .20
61 Kyle Petty's Car .07 .20
62 H.B. Bailey .02 .10
63 Chuck Bown .07 .20
64 Dorsey Schroeder .07 .20
65 Dave Mader .02 .10
66 Jimmy Hensley .07 .20
67 Ed Berrier .02 .10
68 Bobby Hamilton .07 .20
69 Greg Sacks .07 .20
70 Tommy Ellis .02 .10
71 Dave Marcis .07 .20
72 Tracy Leslie .02 .10
73 Phil Barkdoll .07 .20
74 Kyle Petty's Car .07 .20
Memorable Moment
75 Dick Trickle .07 .20
76 Butch Miller .07 .20
77 Mike Potter .02 .10
78 Shawna Robinson .40 1.00
79 Dave Rezendes .07 .20
80 Bobby Dotter .07 .20
81 Lonnie Rush Jr. .02 .10
82 Andy Belmont .07 .20
83 Lake Speed .07 .20
84 Rich Bickle .07 .20
85 Mark Martin's Car .30 .75
86 Mickey Gibbs .02 .10
87 Joe Nemechek .07 .20
88 Sterling Marlin's Car .07 .20
89 Jerry Hill .02 .10
90 Bobby Hillin .07 .20
91 Bob Schacht .02 .10
92 Kerry Teague .02 .10
93 Larry Pearson .07 .20
94 Davey Allison's Car .07 .20
Bill Elliott's Car
Memorable Moment
95 Jim Sauter .02 .10
96 Ed Ferree .02 .10
97 Bobby Hamilton's Car .02 .10
98 Jim Bown .02 .10
99 Ricky Craven .15 .40
100 Junior Johnson .02 .10
101 Robert Yates .02 .10
102 Leo Jackson .02 .10
103 Felix Sabates .02 .10
104 Jack Roush .02 .10
105 Rick Hendrick .02 .10
106 Billy Hagen .02 .10
107 Tim Morgan .02 .10
108 Larry McClure .02 .10
109 Teddy McClure .02 .10
Jerry McClure
Ed McClure
110 Richard Childress .15 .40
111 Roger Penske .02 .10
112 Don Miller .02 .10
113 Bobby Labonte's Car .07 .20
114 Glen Wood .02 .10
115 Len Wood .02 .10
116 Eddie Wood .02 .10
117 Kenny Bernstein .07 .20
118 Walter Bud Moore .02 .10
119 Ray DeWitt .02 .10
120 D.K. Ulrich .02 .10
121 Davey Allison's Car .07 .20
122 Joe Gibbs .15 .40
123 Bill Stavola .02 .10
124 Mickey Stavola .02 .10
125 Richard Jackson .02 .10
126 Chuck Rider .02 .10
127 George Bradshaw .02 .10
128 Mark Smith .02 .10
129 Bobby Allison .07 .20
130 Bob Bilby .02 .10
131 Davey Allison Crash .07 .20
Memorable Moments
132 Larry Hedrick .02 .10
133 Harry Melling .02 .10
134 Junie Donlavey .02 .10
135 Bill Davis .02 .10
136 Cale Yarborough .07 .20
137 Frank Cicci .02 .10
Scott Welliver
138 Dick Moroso .02 .10
139 Butch Mock .02 .10
140 Bob Rahilly .02 .10
141 Don Bierschwale .02 .10
142 Paul Andrews .02 .10
143 Mike Beam .02 .10
144 Larry McReynolds .02 .10
145 Steve Barkdoll .02 .10
146 Robin Pemberton .02 .10
147 Steve Hmiel .02 .10
148 Gary DeHart .02 .10
149 Pete Wright .02 .10
150 Ricky Rudd's Car .07 .20
151 Jake Elder .02 .10
152 Mike Hill .02 .10
153 Tony Glover .02 .10
154 Andy Petree .02 .10
155 Buddy Parrott .02 .10
156 Richard Petty .25 .60
Memorable Moment
157 Leonard Wood .02 .10
158 Donnie Richeson .02 .10
159 Donnie Wingo .02 .10
160 Ken Howes .02 .10
161 Sandy Jones .02 .10
162 Jimmy Makar .02 .10
163 Ken Wilson .02 .10
164 Barry Dodson .02 .10
165 Doug Hewitt .02 .10
166 Howard Comstock .02 .10
167 David Fuge .02 .10
168 Jeff Gordon's Car .50 1.25
169 Robbie Loomis .02 .10
170 Jimmy Fennig .02 .10
171 Bob Johnson .02 .10
172 Doug Richert .02 .10
173 Ernie Elliott .02 .10
174 Doug Williams .02 .10
175 Tim Brewer .02 .10
176 Gil Martin .02 .10
177 Kenny Wallace's Car .02 .10
178 Ray Evernham .02 .10
179 Troy Selberg .02 .10
180 Dennis Connor .02 .10
181 Jeff Hammond .02 .10
182 Dale Inman .02 .10
183 Harry Hyde .02 .10
184 Vic Kangas .02 .10
185 Bob Labonte .02 .10
186 Ken Schrader's Car .02 .10
187 Clyde McLeod .02 .10
188 Ricky Pearson .02 .10
189 Tony Eury .25 .60
190 Alan Kulwicki .15 .40
Winston Cup Champion
191 Jimmy Hensley .07 .20
WC Rookie of the Year
192 Larry McReynolds .02 .10
Crew Chief of the Year
193 Bill Elliott .15 .40
Fan's Favorite Driver
194 Ken Schrader w/Crew .07 .20
Pit Crew Champs
195 Joe Nemechek .07 .20
BGN Champion
196 Ricky Craven .15 .40
BGN Rookie of the Year
197 Ricky Rudd .25 .60
IROC Champion
198 Dick Beaty .02 .10
199 Davey Allison's Car .15 .40
Richard Petty's Car
Bobby Labonte's Car
Mark Martin's Car
Memorable Moment
200 Barney Hall .02 .10
201 Eli Gold .02 .10
202 Ned Jarrett .07 .20
203 Glenn Jarrett .02 .10
204 Dick Berggren .02 .10
205 Jack Arute .02 .10
206 Bob Jenkins .02 .10
207 Benny Parsons .07 .20
208 Jerry Punch .02 .10
209 Joe Moore .02 .10
210 Jim Phillips .02 .10
211 Chris Economaki .02 .10
212 Winston Kelley .02 .10
213 Dick Brooks .02 .10
214 John Kernan .02 .10
215 Mike Joy .02 .10
216 Randy Pemberton .02 .10
217 Allen Bestwick .02 .10
218 Ken Squier .02 .10
219 Neil Bonnett .15 .40
220 Davey Allison Crash .07 .20
Memorable Moment
221 Larry Phillips .02 .10
Brooke Gordon
222 Mike Love .02 .10
Charlie Cragen
223 Steve Murgic .02 .10
Ricky Icenhower
224 Michael Ritch .02 .10
Joe Kosiski
225 Steve Hendren .02 .10
Larry Phillips
226 Darrell Waltrip .07 .20
Memorable Moment
227 Buster Auton .02 .10
228 Jimmy Cox .02 .10
229 Les Richter .02 .10
230 Ray Hill .02 .10
231 Doyle Ford .02 .10
232 Chuck Romeo .02 .10
233 Elmo Langley .02 .10
234 Jack Whittemore .02 .10
235 Walt Green .02 .10
236 Mike Chaplin .02 .10
237 Tim Earp .02 .10
238 Bruce Roney .02 .10
239 Carl Hill .02 .10
240 Mark Connolly .02 .10
241 Gary Miller .02 .10
242 Marlin Wright .02 .10
243 Gary Nelson .02 .10
244 Ernie Irvan's Car .15 .40
245 Richard Petty w/Car .25 .60
Memorable Moment
246 Harry Gant .07 .20
All Pro
247 Tony Glover .02 .10
All Pro
248 David Little .02 .10
All Pro
249 Gary Brooks .02 .10
All Pro
250 Bill Wilburn .02 .10
All Pro
251 Jeff Clark .02 .10
All Pro
252 Shelton Pittman .02 .10
All Pro
253 Scott Robinson .02 .10
All Pro
254 Glen Bobo .02 .10
All Pro
255 James Lewter .02 .10
All Pro
256 Jerry Schweitz .02 .10
All Pro
257 Harold Stott .02 .10
All Pro
258 Ryan Pemberton .02 .10
All Pro
259 Gale Wilson .02 .10
All Pro
260 Danny Glad .02 .10
All Pro
261 Howard Poston (Slick) .02 .10
All Pro
262 Brooke Sealy 1.00 2.50
Miss Winston
263 Geoff Bodine .07 .20
Year in Review
264 Davey Allison .15 .40
Robert Yates
Larry McReynolds
Year in Review
265 Bill Elliott w/Crew .15 .40
Year in Review
266 Bill Elliott .15 .40
Year in Review
267 Bill Elliott .15 .40
Junior Johnson
Year in Review
268 Bill Elliott .15 .40
Year in Review
269 Alan Kulwicki w/Crew .15 .40
Year in Review
270 Davey Allison .15 .40
Robert Yates
Larry McReynolds
Year in Review
271 Mark Martin .30 .75
Jack Roush
Steve Hmiel
Year in Review
272 Davey Allison w/Crew .15 .40
Year in Review
273 Robert Yates .25 .60
Year in Review
274 Dale Earnhardt 3.00 8.00
Kerry Earnhardt
Dale Earnhardt Jr.
Year in Review
275 Harry Gant .07 .20
Year in Review
276 Ernie Irvan .07 .20
Year in Review
277 Alan Kulwicki w/Crew .15 .40
(Year in Review
278 Davey Allison .15 .40
Year in Review
279 Ernie Irvan .07 .20
Year in Review
280 Darrell Waltrip .07 .20
Year in Review
281 Ernie Irvan .07 .20
Year in Review
282 Kyle Petty .15 .40
Felix Sabates
Year in Review
283 Harry Gant .07 .20
Year in Review
284 Darrell Waltrip .07 .20
Year in Review
285 Darrell Waltrip .07 .20
Year in Review
286 Rusty Wallace w/Crew .30 .75
Year in Review
287 Ricky Rudd w/Crew .25 .60
Year in Review
288 Geoff Bodine .07 .20
Year in Review
289 Geoff Bodine w/Crew .07 .20
Year in Review
290 Mark Martin .30 .75
Year in Review
291 Kyle Petty .15 .40
Year in Review
292 Davey Allison .15 .40
Robert Yates
Year in Review
293 Bill Elliott .15 .40
Year in Review
294 Alan Kulwicki .15 .40
Memorable Moment
295 Checklist #1 .02 .10
296 Checklist #2 .02 .10
297 Checklist #3 .02 .10
298 Checklist #4 .02 .10
299 Checklist #5 .02 .10
300 Checklist #6 .02 .10
P1 Bill Elliott Promo 2.00 5.00

1993 Maxx Premier Series

This 300-card set was distributed primarily through the Maxx Club mail order program. It is commonly known as the blue set. Collectors who bought this set were also sent an 8" by 10" chromium card commemorating Dale Earnhardt's six NASCAR Winston Cup titles. The jumbo chromium card of Dale is numbered of 80,000. This card is priced under the 1993 Maxx Premier Plus Jumbo listing.

COMPLETE SET (300) 20.00
1 Rick Mast .15
2 Rusty Wallace 1.25
3 Dale Earnhardt 2.50
4 Ernie Irvan .30
5 Ricky Rudd .50
6 Mark Martin 1.25
7 Alan Kulwicki .50
8 Sterling Marlin .60
9 Chad Little .15
10 Derrike Cope .15
11 Bill Elliott .60
12 Jimmy Spencer .15
13 Alan Kulwicki's Car .15
Bill Elliott's Car
Memorable Moment
14 Terry Labonte .60
15 Geoff Bodine .15
16 Wally Dallenbach Jr. .15
17 Darrell Waltrip .30
18 Dale Jarrett 1.00
19 Tom Peck .15
20 Alan Kulwicki's Car .15
21 Morgan Shepherd .15
22 Bobby Labonte 1.00
23 Eddie Bierschwale .10
24 Jeff Gordon CRC 2.50
25 Ken Schrader .15
26 Brett Bodine .15
27 Hut Stricklin .15
28 Davey Allison .75
29 Jimmy Horton .15
30 Michael Waltrip .30
31 Steve Grissom .15
32 Charlie Glotzbach .15
33 Harry Gant .30
34 Todd Bodine .15
35 Jeff Purvis .15
36 Ward Burton .30
37 Bill Elliott's Car .15
38 Jerry O'Neill .10
39 Buddy Baker .15
40 Kenny Wallace .15
41 Phil Parsons .15
42 Kyle Petty .30
43 Richard Petty .60
44 Rick Wilson .15
45 Jeff Burton .50
46 Al Unser Jr. .30
47 Bill Venturini .15
48 James Hylton .10
49 Stanley Smith .10
50 Tommy Houston .15
51 Richard Lasater .10
52 Jimmy Means .15
53 Mike Wallace .15
54 Jack Sprague .10
55 Ted Musgrave .15
56 Dale Earnhardt's Car 1.00
57 Troy Beebe .10
58 Bill Sedgwick .10
59 Robert Pressley .15
60 Jeff Green .15
61 Kyle Petty's Car .15
62 H.B. Bailey .10
63 Chuck Bown .15
64 Dorsey Schroeder .15
65 Dave Mader .10
66 Jimmy Hensley .15
67 Ed Berrier .10
68 Bobby Hamilton .15
69 Greg Sacks .15
70 Tommy Ellis .10
71 Dave Marcis .15
72 Tracy Leslie .10
73 Phil Barkdoll .15
74 Kyle Petty's Car .15
Memorable Moment
75 Dick Trickle .15
76 Butch Miller .15
77 Mike Potter .10
78 Shawna Robinson .75
79 Dave Rezendes .15
80 Bobby Dotter .15
81 Lonnie Rush Jr. .10
82 Andy Belmont .15
83 Lake Speed .15
84 Rich Bickle .15
85 Mark Martin's Car .60
86 Mickey Gibbs .10
87 Joe Nemechek .15
88 Sterling Marlin's Car .15
89 Jerry Hill .10
90 Bobby Hillin .15
91 Bob Schacht .10
92 Kerry Teague .10
93 Larry Pearson .15
94 Davey Allison's Car .15
Bill Elliott's Car
Memorable Moment
95 Jim Sauter .10
96 Ed Ferree .10
97 Bobby Hamilton's Car .10
98 Jim Bown .10
99 Ricky Craven .30
100 Junior Johnson .15
101 Robert Yates .10
102 Leo Jackson .10
103 Felix Sabates .10
104 Jack Roush .10
105 Rick Hendrick .10
106 Billy Hagen .10
107 Tim Morgan .10
108 Larry McClure .10
109 Teddy McClure .10
Jerry McClure
Ed McClure
110 Richard Childress .30
111 Roger Penske .10
112 Don Miller .10
113 Bobby Labonte's Car .10
114 Glen Wood .10
115 Len Wood .10
116 Eddie Wood .10
117 Kenny Bernstein .15
118 Walter Bud Moore .10
119 Ray DeWitt .10
120 D.K. Ulrich .10
121 Davey Allison's Car .15
122 Joe Gibbs .30
123 Bill Stavola .10

124 Mickey Stavola .10 .20
125 Richard Jackson .10 .20
126 Chuck Rider .10 .20
127 George Bradshaw .10 .20
128 Mark Smith .10 .20
129 Bobby Allison .15 .40
130 Bob Bilby .10 .20
131 Davey Allison Crash .15 .40
Memorable Moments
132 Larry Hedrick .10 .20
133 Harry Melling .10 .20
134 W.C. Donlavey (Junie) .10 .20
135 Bill Davis .10 .20
136 Cale Yarborough .15 .40
137 Frank Cicci .10 .20
Scott Welliver
138 Dick Moroso .10 .20
139 Butch Mock .10 .20
140 Bob Rahilly .10 .20
141 Don Bierschwale .10 .20
142 Paul Andrews .10 .20
143 Mike Beam .10 .20
144 Larry McReynolds .10 .20
145 Steve Barkdoll .10 .20
146 Robin Pemberton .10 .20
147 Steve Hmiel .10 .20
148 Gary DeHart .10 .20
149 Pete Wright .10 .20
150 Ricky Rudd's Car .15 .40
151 Jake Elder .10 .20
152 Mike Hill .10 .20
153 Tony Glover .10 .20
154 Andy Petree .10 .20
155 Buddy Parrott .10 .20
156 Richard Petty .50 1.25
Memorable Moment
157 Leonard Wood .10 .20
158 Donnie Richeson .10 .20
159 Donnie Wingo .10 .20
160 Ken Howes .10 .20
161 Sandy Jones .10 .20
162 Jimmy Makar .10 .20
163 Ken Wilson .10 .20
164 Barry Dodson .10 .20
165 Doug Hewitt .10 .20
166 Howard Comstock .10 .20
167 David Fuge .10 .20
168 Jeff Gordon's Car 1.00 2.50
169 Robbie Loomis .10 .20
170 Jimmy Fennig .10 .20
171 Bob Johnson .10 .20
172 Doug Richert .10 .20
173 Ernie Elliott .10 .20
174 Doug Williams .10 .20
175 Tim Brewer .10 .20
176 Gil Martin .10 .20
177 Kenny Wallace's Car .10 .20
178 Ray Evernham .10 .20
179 Troy Selberg .10 .20
180 Dennis Connor .10 .20
181 Jeff Hammond .10 .20
182 Dale Inman .10 .20
183 Harry Hyde .10 .20
184 Vic Kangas .10 .20
185 Bob Labonte .10 .20
186 Ken Schrader's Car .10 .20
187 Clyde McLeod .10 .20
188 Ricky Pearson .10 .20
189 Tony Eury .50 1.25
190 Alan Kulwicki .30 .75
Winston Cup Champion
191 Jimmy Hensley .15 .40
WC Rookie of the Year
192 Larry McReynolds .10 .20
Crew Chief of the Year
193 Bill Elliott .30 .75
Fan's Favorite Driver
194 Ken Schrader w/Crew .15 .40
Pit Crew Champs
195 Joe Nemechek .15 .40
BGN Champion
196 Ricky Craven .30 .75
BGN Rookie of the Year
197 Ricky Rudd .50 1.25
IROC Champion
198 Dick Beaty .10 .20
199 Davey Allison's Car .30 .75
Richard Petty's Car
Bobby Labonte's Car
Mark Martin's Car
Memorable Moment
200 Barney Hall .10 .20
201 Eli Gold .10 .20
202 Ned Jarrett .15 .40
203 Glenn Jarrett .10 .20
204 Dick Berggren .10 .20
205 Jack Arute .10 .20
206 Bob Jenkins .10 .20
207 Benny Parsons .15 .40
208 Jerry Punch .10 .20
209 Joe Moore .10 .20
210 Jim Phillips .10 .20
211 Chris Economaki .10 .20
212 Winston Kelley .10 .20
213 Dick Brooks .10 .20
214 John Kernan .10 .20
215 Mike Joy .10 .20
216 Randy Pemberton .10 .20
217 Allen Bestwick .10 .20
218 Ken Squier .10 .20
219 Neil Bonnett .30 .75
220 Davey Allison Crash .15 .40
Memorable Moment
221 Larry Phillips .10 .20
Brooke Gordon
222 Mike Love .10 .20
Charlie Cragen
223 Steve Murgic .10 .20
Ricky Icenhower
224 Michael Ritch .10 .20
Joe Kosiski
225 Steve Hendren .10 .20
Larry Phillips
226 Darrell Waltrip .15 .40
Memorable Moment
227 Buster Auton .10 .20
228 Jimmy Cox .10 .20
229 Les Richter .10 .20
230 Ray Hill .10 .20
231 Doyle Ford .10 .20
232 Chuck Romeo .10 .20
233 Elmo Langley .10 .20
234 Jack Whittemore .10 .20
235 Walt Green .10 .20
236 Mike Chaplin .10 .20
237 Tim Earp .10 .20
238 Bruce Roney .10 .20
239 Carl Hill .10 .20
240 Mark Connolly .10 .20
241 Gary Miller .10 .20
242 Marlin Wright .10 .20
243 Gary Nelson .10 .20
244 Ernie Irvan's Car .30 .75
245 Richard Petty w/Car .50 1.25
Memorable Moment
246 Harry Gant .15 .40
All Pro
247 Tony Glover .10 .20
All Pro
248 David Little .10 .20
All Pro
249 Gary Brooks .10 .20
All Pro
250 Bill Wilburn .10 .20
All Pro
251 Jeff Clark .10 .20
All Pro
252 Shelton Pittman .10 .20
All Pro
253 Scott Robinson .10 .20
All Pro
254 Glen Bobo .10 .20
All Pro
255 James Lewter .10 .20
All Pro
256 Jerry Schweitz .10 .20
All Pro
257 Harold Stott .10 .20
All Pro
258 Ryan Pemberton .10 .20
All Pro
259 Gale Wilson .10 .20
All Pro
260 Danny Glad .10 .20
All Pro
261 Howard Poston (Slick) .10 .20
All Pro
262 Brooke Sealy 2.00 5.00
Miss Winston
263 Geoff Bodine .15 .40
Year in Review
264 Davey Allison .30 .75
Robert Yates
Larry McReynolds
Year in Review
265 Bill Elliott w/Crew .30 .75
Year in Review
266 Bill Elliott .30 .75
Year in Review
267 Bill Elliott .30 .75
Junior Johnson
Year in Review
268 Bill Elliott .30 .75
Year in Review
269 Alan Kulwicki w/Crew .30 .75
Year in Review
270 Davey Allison .30 .75
Robert Yates
Larry McReynolds
Year in Review
271 Mark Martin .60 1.50
Jack Roush
Steve Hmiel
Year in Review
272 Davey Allison w/Crew .30 .75
Year in Review
273 Robert Yates .50 1.25
Year in Review
274 Dale Earnhardt 6.00 15.00
Kerry Earnhardt
Dale Earnhardt Jr.
Year in Review
275 Harry Gant .15 .40
Year in Review
276 Ernie Irvan .15 .40
Year in Review
277 Alan Kulwicki w/Crew .30 .75
(Year in Review
278 Davey Allison .30 .75
Year in Review
279 Ernie Irvan .15 .40
Year in Review
280 Darrell Waltrip .15 .40
Year in Review
281 Ernie Irvan .15 .40
Year in Review
282 Kyle Petty .30 .75
Felix Sabates
Year in Review
283 Harry Gant .15 .40
Year in Review
284 Darrell Waltrip .15 .40
Year in Review
285 Darrell Waltrip .15 .40
Year in Review
286 Rusty Wallace w/Crew .60 1.50
Year in Review
287 Ricky Rudd w/Crew .50 1.25
Year in Review
288 Geoff Bodine .15 .40
Year in Review
289 Geoff Bodine w/Crew .15 .40
Year in Review
290 Mark Martin .60 1.50
Year in Review
291 Kyle Petty .30 .75
Year in Review
292 Davey Allison .30 .75
Robert Yates
Year in Review
293 Bill Elliott .30 .75
Year in Review
294 Alan Kulwicki .30 .75
Memorable Moment
295 Checklist #1 .10 .20
296 Checklist #2 .10 .20
297 Checklist #3 .10 .20
298 Checklist #4 .10 .20
299 Checklist #5 .10 .20
300 Checklist #6 .10 .20
P1 Bill Elliott Promo 3.00 8.00

1993 Maxx Baby Ruth Jeff Burton

This four-card set was produced by Maxx and distributed by the Baby Ruth Race Team. It features photos of Baby Ruth driver Jeff Burton.

COMPLETE SET (4) 5.00 10.00
1 Jeff Burton 1.00 2.50
2 Jeff Burton's Car 1.00 2.50
3 Jeff Burton in Pits 1.00 2.50
4 Jeff Burton 1.00 2.50
Gil Martin

1993 Maxx Club Sam Bass Chromium

This 11-card set features the art work of racing artist Sam Bass. The gold bordered cards were printed using Maxx's Chromium technology. According to reports at time of issue, 6,000 sets were produced.

COMPLETE SET (11) 15.00 40.00
1 Bobby Allison 2.00 5.00
2 Bobby Allison 2.00 5.00
3 Rusty Wallace 3.00 8.00
4 Davey Allison 2.50 6.00
Bobby Allison
5 Dale Jarrett's Car 1.00 2.50
6 Rusty Wallace 3.00 8.00
7 Jeff Gordon 4.00 10.00
8 Alan Kulwicki 2.00 5.00
9 Davey Allison 2.50 6.00
10 Jeff Gordon 4.00 10.00
11 Cover Card .75 2.00

1993 Maxx Jeff Gordon

This 20-card set was produced by Maxx and was distributed only in set form through Club Maxx for $4.95 per set. It highlights his career from his early childhood to debut on the Winston Cup circuit. 1,000 Jeff Gordon autographed cards were randomly inserted into the sets at a 1:100 ratio.

COMPLETE SET (20) 7.50 20.00
COMMON CARD (1-20) .60 1.50
JEFF GORDON AUTO 40.00 100.00

1993 Maxx Lowes Foods Stickers

Maxx produced this sticker set for distribution through Lowes Foods Stores. The stickers were distributed over a 5-week period (one per week) and include three drivers per sticker strip. Sticker fronts feature a top Winston Cup driver along with the Maxx and Lowes logos. Backs include Lowes Food Stores coupons. The strips actually are three individual stickers attached together. We've listed and priced the stickers in complete three-sticker strips.

COMPLETE SET (5) 6.00 15.00
1 Jimmy Spencer .75 2.00
Ricky Rudd
Kenny Wallace
2 Bill Elliott 3.00 8.00
Darrell Waltrip
Jeff Gordon
3 Davey Allison 1.25 3.00
Kyle Petty
Bobby Hamilton
4 Terry Labonte 2.00 5.00
Sterling Marlin
Bobby Labonte
5 Morgan Shepherd .75 2.00
Brett Bodine
Ken Schrader

1993 Maxx Motorsport

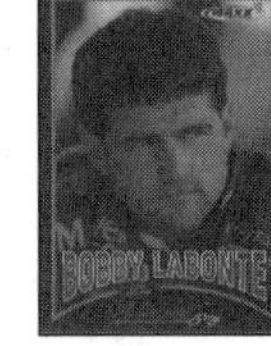

This 50-card set was produced by Maxx and distributed by Ford Motorsports. It consists of Ford's twenty drivers and their cars, plus the cards of the late Davey Allison and Alan Kulwicki.

COMPLETE SET (50) 2.50 6.00
1 Brett Bodine .07 .20
2 Geoff Bodine .07 .20
3 Todd Bodine .07 .20
4 Derrike Cope .07 .20
5 Wally Dallenbach Jr. .07 .20
6 Bill Elliott .30 .75
7 Bobby Hamilton .07 .20
8 Jimmy Hensley .07 .20
9 Bobby Hillin .07 .20
10 P.J. Jones .07 .20
11 Bobby Labonte .40 1.00
12 Sterling Marlin .15 .40
13 Mark Martin .50 1.25
14 Rick Mast .07 .20
15 Ted Musgrave .07 .20
16 Greg Sacks .07 .20
17 Morgan Shepherd .07 .20
18 Lake Speed .07 .20
19 Jimmy Spencer .07 .20
20 Hut Stricklin .07 .20
21 Brett Bodine's Car .02 .10
22 Geoff Bodine's Car .02 .10
23 Todd Bodine's Car .02 .10
24 Derrike Cope's Car .02 .10
25 Wally Dallenbach Jr.'s Car .02 .10
26 Bill Elliott's Car .20 .50
27 Bill Hamilton's Car .02 .10
28 Jimmy Hensley's Car .02 .10
29 Bobby Hillin's Car .02 .10
30 P.J. Jones' Car .02 .10
31 Bobby Labonte's Car .20 .50
32 Sterling Marlin's Car .07 .20
33 Mark Martin's Car .25 .60
34 Rick Mast's Car .02 .10
35 Ted Musgrave's Car .02 .10
36 Greg Sacks' Car .02 .10
37 Morgan Shepherd's Car .02 .10
38 Lake Speed's Car .02 .10
39 Jimmy Spencer's Car .02 .10
40 Hut Stricklin's Car .02 .10
41 Davey Allison .40 1.00
42 Davey Allison's Car .20 .50
43 Alan Kulwicki .20 .50
44 Alan Kulwicki's Car .15 .40
45 Lee Morse .02 .10
46 Michael Kranefuss .02 .10
47 Alan Kulwicki .20 .50
Bill Elliott
48 Manufacturers' Champs .02 .10
49 Davey Allison's Car .20 .50
Takes Richmond
50 Mark Martin's Car .25 .60
Streak Begins

1993 Maxx Premier Plus

This 212-card set was the first "super premium" racing set produced. Factory sets were available through Maxx dealers and Maxx's mail order program. It was also available in eight-card foil packs. Insert cards of the Maxx Mascot and the Maxx Rookie Contenders (1 of 20,000) were included in hobby sets and randomly inserted in foil packs. There is also a version of the Maxx Rookie Contenders card that doesn't have the 1 of 20,000 printed on it.

COMPLETE SET (212) 12.00 30.00
COMP.FACT.SET (212) 12.00 30.00
WAX BOX 15.00 40.00
1 Rick Mast .10 .30
2 Rusty Wallace 1.00 2.50
3 Dale Earnhardt 2.00 5.00
4 Ernie Irvan .25 .60
5 Ricky Rudd .40 1.00
6 Mark Martin 1.00 2.50
7 Alan Kulwicki .40 1.00
8 Sterling Marlin .50 1.25
9 Chad Little .10 .30
10 Derrike Cope .10 .30
11 Bill Elliott .50 1.25
12 Jimmy Spencer .10 .30
13 Alan Kulwicki's Car .25 .60
Bill Elliott's Car
Memorable Moment
14 Terry Labonte .50 1.25
15 Geoff Bodine .10 .30
16 Wally Dallenbach, Jr. .10 .30
17 Darrell Waltrip .25 .60
18 Dale Jarrett .75 2.00
19 Tom Peck .10 .30
20 Alan Kulwicki's Car .25 .60
21 Morgan Shepherd .10 .30
22 Bobby Labonte .75 2.00
23 Kyle Petty's Car .10 .30
Memorable Moment
24 Jeff Gordon CRC 1.50 4.00
25 Ken Schrader .10 .30
26 Brett Bodine .10 .30
27 Hut Stricklin .10 .30
28 Davey Allison .60 1.50
29 Davey Allison's Car .10 .30
Bill Elliott's Car
Memorable Moment
30 Michael Waltrip .25 .60
31 Steve Grissom .10 .30
32 Ken Schrader's Car .05 .15
33 Harry Gant .25 .60
34 Todd Bodine .10 .30
35 Bobby Hamilton's Car .05 .15
36 Ward Burton .25 .60
37 Bill Elliott's Car .10 .30
38 Jerry O'Neill .05 .15
39 Jeff Gordon's Car .75 2.00
40 Kenny Wallace .10 .30
41 Phil Parsons .10 .30
42 Kyle Petty .25 .60
43 Richard Petty .50 1.25
44 Rick Wilson .10 .30
45 Jeff Burton .40 1.00
46 Al Unser Jr. .25 .60
47 Bill Venturini .05 .15
48 Richard Petty .40 1.00
Memorable Moment
49 Stanley Smith .05 .15
50 Tommy Houston .10 .30
51 Bobby Labonte's Car .10 .30
52 Jimmy Means .10 .30
53 Mike Wallace .10 .30
54 Jack Sprague .05 .15
55 Ted Musgrave .10 .30
56 Dale Earnhardt's Car .75 2.00
57 Davey Allison's Car .40 1.00
Richard Petty's Car
Bobby Labonte's Car
Mark Martin's Car
Memorable Moment
58 Jim Sauter .05 .15
59 Robert Pressley .10 .30
60 Davey Allison's Car .10 .30
Kyle Petty's Car
Memorable Moment
61 Kyle Petty's Car .10 .30
62 Davey Allison Crash .10 .30
Memorable Moment
63 Chuck Bown .10 .30
64 Sterling Marlin's Car .10 .30
65 Darrell Waltrip .10 .30
Memorable Moment
66 Jimmy Hensley .10 .30
67 Ernie Irvan's Car .25 .60
68 Bobby Hamilton .10 .30
69 Greg Sacks .10 .30
70 Tommy Ellis .05 .15
71 Dave Marcis .10 .30
72 Tracy Leslie .05 .15
73 Ricky Craven .25 .60
74 Richard Petty w/Car .40 1.00
Memorable Moment
75 Dick Trickle .10 .30
76 Butch Miller .10 .30
77 Jim Bown .05 .15
78 Shawna Robinson .60 1.50
79 Davey Allison's Car .10 .30
80 Bobby Dotter .05 .15
81 Alan Kulwicki .25 .60
Memorable Moment
82 Kenny Wallace's Car .05 .15
83 Lake Speed .10 .30
84 Bobby Hillin .10 .30
85 Mark Martin's Car .25 .60
86 Bob Schacht .05 .15
87 Joe Nemechek .10 .30
88 Ricky Rudd's Car .10 .30
89 Junior Johnson .10 .30
90 Robert Yates .05 .15
91 Leo Jackson .05 .15
92 Felix Sabates .05 .15
93 Jack Roush .05 .15
94 Rick Hendrick .05 .15
95 Billy Hagan .05 .15
96 Tim Morgan .05 .15
97 Larry McClure .05 .15
98 Teddy McClure .05 .15
Jerry McClure
Ed McClure
99 Richard Childress .25 .60
100 Roger Penske .05 .15
101 Don Miller .05 .15
102 Glen Wood .05 .15
103 Len Wood .05 .15
104 Eddie Wood .05 .15
105 Kenny Bernstein .10 .30
106 Walter Bud Moore .05 .15
107 Ray DeWitt .05 .15
108 D.K. Ulrich .05 .15
109 Joe Gibbs .25 .60
110 Bill Stavola .05 .15
111 Mickey Stavola .05 .15
112 Richard Jackson .05 .15
113 Chuck Rider .05 .15
114 George Bradshaw .05 .15
115 Mark Smith .05 .15
116 Bobby Allison .10 .30
117 Bob Bilby .05 .15
118 Larry Hedrick .05 .15
119 Harry Melling .05 .15
120 Junie Donlavey .05 .15
121 Bill Davis .05 .15
122 Cale Yarborough .10 .30
123 Frank Cicci .05 .15
Scott Welliver
124 Dick Moroso .05 .15
125 Butch Mock .05 .15
126 Bob Rahilly .05 .15
127 Paul Andrews .05 .15
128 Mike Beam .05 .15
129 Larry McReynolds .05 .15
130 Tim Brewer .05 .15
131 Robin Pemberton .05 .15
132 Steve Hmiel .05 .15
133 Gary DeHart .05 .15
134 Pete Wright .05 .15
135 Jake Elder .05 .15
136 Mike Hill .05 .15
137 Tony Glover .05 .15
138 Andy Petree .05 .15
139 Buddy Parrott .05 .15
140 Leonard Wood .05 .15
141 Donnie Richeson .05 .15
142 Donnie Wingo .05 .15
143 Ken Howes .05 .15
144 Sandy Jones .05 .15
145 Jimmy Makar .05 .15
146 Ken Wilson .05 .15
147 Barry Dodson .05 .15
148 Doug Hewitt .05 .15
149 Howard Comstock .05 .15
150 David Fuge .05 .15
151 Robbie Loomis .05 .15
152 Jimmy Fennig .05 .15
153 Bob Johnson .05 .15
154 Doug Richert .05 .15
155 Ernie Elliott .05 .15
156 Doug Williams .05 .15
157 Tim Brewer .05 .15
158 Ray Evernham .05 .15
159 Troy Seberg .05 .15
160 Dennis Connor .05 .15
161 Jeff Hammond .05 .15
162 Dale Inman .05 .15
163 Harry Hyde .05 .15
164 Vic Kangas .05 .15
165 Bob Labonte .05 .15
166 Clyde McLeod .05 .15
167 Ricky Pearson .05 .15
168 Tony Eury .40 1.00
169 Ricky Rudd .40 1.00
IROC Champion
170 Dick Beaty .05 .15
171 Ken Schrader w/Crew .10 .30
Pit Crew Champs
172 Alan Kulwicki .25 .60
WC Champion
173 Jimmy Hensley .10 .30
WC Rookie of the Year
174 Larry McReynolds .05 .15
Crew Chief of the Year
175 Bill Elliott .25 .60
Fan's Favorite Driver
176 Joe Nemechek .10 .30
BGN Champion
177 Ricky Craven .25 .60
BGN Rookie of the Year
178 Geoff Bodine .10 .30
Year in Review
179 Davey Allison .25 .60
Year in Review
180 Bill Elliott .25 .60
Year in Review
181 Bill Elliott .25 .60
Year in Review
182 Bill Elliott .25 .60
Year in Review
183 Bill Elliott .25 .60
Junior Johnson
Year in Review
184 Alan Kulwicki .25 .60
Year in Review
185 Davey Allison .25 .60
Year in Review
186 Mark Martin .50 1.25
Year in Review
187 Davey Allison .25 .60
Year in Review
188 Bobby Allison .10 .30
Year in Review
189 Dale Earnhardt 4.00 10.00
Kerry Earnhardt
Dale Earnhardt Jr.
Year in Review
190 Harry Gant .10 .30
Year in Review
191 Ernie Irvan .10 .30
Year in Review
192 Alan Kulwicki .25 .60
Year in Review
193 Davey Allison .10 .30
Robert Yates
Larry McReynolds
Year in Review
194 Ernie Irvan .10 .30
Year in Review
195 Darrell Waltrip .10 .30
Year in Review
196 Ernie Irvan w/Crew .10 .30
Year in Review
197 Kyle Petty .25 .60
Year in Review
198 Harry Gant .10 .30
Year in Review
199 Darrell Waltrip .10 .30
Year in Review
200 Darrell Waltrip .10 .30
Year in Review
201 Rusty Wallace .50 1.25
Year in Review
202 Ricky Rudd .40 1.00
Year in Review
203 Geoff Bodine .10 .30
Year in Review
204 Geoff Bodine .10 .30
Year in Review
205 Mark Martin .50 1.25
Year in Review
206 Kyle Petty .25 .60
Year in Review
207 Davey Allison w/Crew .25 .60
Year in Review
208 Bill Elliott .25 .60
Year in Review
209 Checklist #1 .05 .15
210 Checklist #2 .05 .15
211 Checklist #3 .05 .15
212 Checklist #4 .05 .15
P1 Bill Elliott Promo 5.00 12.00
NNO Mascot Card 1.00 3.00
NNO Jeff Gordon 10.00 25.00
Bobby Labonte
Kenny Wallace

1993 Maxx Premier Plus Jumbos

These three cards commemorate special happenings in the 1992 Winston Cup season. The Alan Kulwicki and Davey Allison cards pay tribute to the two great drivers. The Dale Earnhardt card celebrates his sixth Winston Cup championship. The cards use Maxx's Chromium technology and measure 8" X 10". The Dale Earnhardt card was sold with the 1993 Maxx Premier Series set via the Maxx Club. There were 80,000 of Earnhardt card. The other two cards were sold through the club and retail outlets.

COMPLETE SET (3) 15.00 30.00
1 Davey Allison 3.00 8.00
2 Dale Earnhardt 7.50 15.00
3 Alan Kulwicki 3.00 8.00

1993 Maxx Retail Jumbos

This nine-card set was inserted in special blister retail packs that were distributed in retail outlets

such as K-Mart and Wal-Mart. The jumbo cards measure 3" by 5".

COMPLETE SET (9)	5.00	12.00
1 Darrell Waltrip	.50	1.25
2 Ken Schrader	.25	.60
3 Phil Parsons	.25	.60
4 Sterling Marlin	1.00	2.50
5 Mark Martin	2.00	5.00
6 Dale Jarrett	1.50	4.00
7 Bill Elliott	1.00	2.50
8 Derrike Cope	.25	.60
9 Brett Bodine	.25	.60

1993 Maxx Texaco Davey Allison

This 20-card set was produced by Maxx and made available through Texaco gas stations in the southeastern region of the country. They were distributed in four-card packs and could be purchased for $.99. 5,000 of these cards were autographed by Davey Allison and randomly inserted into packs. The signed cards are different from their base card counterparts by the placement of Davey's printed name on the cardfronts. It is printed in a different location than on the unsigned version -- typically much lower on the cardfront. Like their predecessor, a large number of sets made thier way into the hobby.

COMPLETE SET (20)	4.00	10.00
1 Davey Allison	.40	1.00
2 Davey Allison	.40	1.00
Clifford Allison		
Bobby Allison		
3 Robert Yates	.15	.40
4 Larry McReynolds	.15	.40
5 Davey Allison w/Crew	.15	.40
6 Davey Allison	.15	.40
Robert Yates		
Larry McReynolds		
7 Davey Allison	.40	1.00
8 Davey Allison's Car	.15	.40
Rusty Wallace's Car		
The Winston Pole		
9 Davey Allison Crash	.15	.40
10 Davey Allison	.15	.40
Robert Yates		
Larry McReynolds		
11 Davey Allison	.15	.40
Bobby Allison		
Robert Yates		
12 Davey Allison	.15	.40
Bobby Allison		
13 Davey Allison	.40	1.00
14 Davey Allison	.15	.40
Larry McReynolds		
Robert Yates		
15 Davey Allison in Pits	.15	.40
16 Davey Allison	.15	.40
The Wonder Years		
17 Davey Allison's Car	.15	.40
18 Davey Allison	.15	.40
Bobby Hillin		
19 Davey Allison	.40	1.00
20 Davey Allison w/Crew	.15	.40
Checklist on back		
AU1 Davey Allison AUTO	75.00	150.00

1993 Maxx Winnebago Motorsports

This 11-card set was produced by Maxx and distributed by Winnebago Motorsports. The cards feature drivers in non-racing photos using Winnebago vehicles.

COMPLETE SET (11)	10.00	20.00
1 Sterling Marlin	1.00	2.50
2 Jeff Gordon	4.00	8.00
Bobby Labonte		
Rich Bickle		
Kenny Wallace		
3 Bobby Allison	1.00	2.50
4 Winnebago Motor. Van	.40	1.00
5 Bobby Allison	.75	2.00
Judy Allison		
6 Bobby Allison	.75	2.00
Richard Childress		
Jimmy Spencer		
Ken Schrader		
Sterling Marlin		
Bob Keselowski		
Vectra & Celebrities		
7 Ken Schrader	.75	2.00
8 Tony Bettenhausen	.75	2.00
Stefan Johansson		
9 David Rampy's Funny Car	.40	1.00
10 Bob Keselowski's Car	.40	1.00
NNO Cover Card	.40	1.00

1993 Maxx The Winston

This 51-card set was produced by Maxx and features drivers who raced in the 1993 Winston Select. Each set contains a special chromium Dale Earnhardt card and were originally available through Club Maxx at a price of $10 per set.

COMP.FACT SET (51)	3.00	8.00
1 Dale Earnhardt	.60	1.50
2 Mark Martin	.25	.60
3 Ernie Irvan	.10	.25
4 Ken Schrader	.02	.10
5 Geoff Bodine	.02	.10
6 Darrell Waltrip	.07	.20
7 Sterling Marlin	.07	.20
8 Rusty Wallace	.25	.60
9 Davey Allison	.20	.50
10 Brett Bodine	.02	.10
11 Rick Mast	.02	.10
12 Morgan Shepherd	.02	.10
13 Harry Gant	.07	.20
14 Bill Elliott	.15	.40
15 Terry Labonte	.15	.40
16 Ricky Rudd	.15	.40
17 Jimmy Hensley	.02	.10
18 Michael Waltrip	.07	.20
19 Dale Jarrett	.20	.50
20 Kyle Petty	.07	.20
21 Dale Earnhardt's Car	.40	1.00
22 Mark Martin's Car	.15	.40
23 Ernie Irvan's Car	.07	.20
24 Ken Schrader's Car	.02	.10
25 Geoff Bodine's Car	.02	.10
26 Darrell Waltrip's Car	.02	.10
27 Sterling Marlin's Car	.02	.10
28 Rusty Wallace's Car	.15	.40
29 Davey Allison's Car	.10	.25
30 Brett Bodine's Car	.02	.10
31 Rick Mast's Car	.02	.10
32 Morgan Shepherd's Car	.02	.10
33 Harry Gant's Car	.02	.10
34 Bill Elliott's Car	.07	.20
35 Terry Labonte's Car	.07	.20
36 Ricky Rudd's Car	.02	.10
37 Jimmy Hensley's Car	.02	.10
38 Michael Waltrip's Car	.07	.20
39 Dale Jarrett's Car	.10	.25
40 Kyle Petty's Car	.02	.10
41 Ernie Irvan Pole Win	.10	.25
42 Sterling Marlin Win	.07	.20
43 Charlotte Motor Speedway	.02	.10
44 Winston Starting Lineup	.02	.10
45 First Segment	.02	.10
46 Second Segment	.02	.10
47 Third Segment	.02	.10
48 Third Segment	.02	.10
49 Dale Earnhardt's Car Win	.40	1.00
50 Dale Earnhardt VL	.50	1.25
Brooke Sealy		
51 Dale Earnhardt Chromium	1.00	2.50

1994 Maxx

The 1994 Maxx set was released in two separate series with the first series also being issued as a factory set packaged with four Rookies of the Year inserts. The sets feature the now standard Maxx subsets: Memorable Moments, Year in Review and highlight cards featuring the various NASCAR award winners from 1993. Each series also included randomly packed rookies insert cards with series two also containing an assortment of autographed insert cards. Packaging for each series was similar: 10 cards per pack with 36 packs per box. Jumbo packs were produced for series one with 20-cards per pack.

COMPLETE SET (340)	10.00	25.00
COMP.FACT.SET (244)	12.00	30.00
COMP.SERIES 1 (240)	6.00	15.00
COMP.SERIES 2 (100)	4.00	10.00
WAX BOX SERIES 1	15.00	40.00
WAX BOX SERIES 2	15.00	40.00
1 Rick Mast	.07	.20
2 Rusty Wallace	.60	1.50
3 Dale Earnhardt	1.25	3.00
4 Jimmy Hensley	.07	.20
5 Ricky Rudd	.25	.60
6 Mark Martin	.60	1.50
7 Alan Kulwicki	.25	.60
8 Sterling Marlin	.25	.60
9 P.J. Jones	.07	.20
10 Geoff Bodine	.07	.20
11 Bill Elliott	.30	.75
12 Jimmy Spencer	.07	.20
13 Jeff Gordon	.40	1.00
Memorable Moment		
14 Terry Labonte	.25	.60
15 Lake Speed	.07	.20
16 Wally Dallenbach Jr.	.07	.20
17 Darrell Waltrip	.15	.40
18 Dale Jarrett	.50	1.25
19 Chad Little	.15	.40
20 Bobby Hamilton	.07	.20
21 Morgan Shepherd	.07	.20
22 Bobby Labonte	.50	1.25
23 Dale Earnhardt's Car	.50	1.25
24 Jeff Gordon	1.00	2.50
25 Ken Schrader	.07	.20
26 Brett Bodine	.07	.20
27 Hut Stricklin	.07	.20
28 Davey Allison	.30	.75
29 Ernie Irvan	.15	.40
30 Michael Waltrip	.15	.40
31 Neil Bonnett	.25	.60
32 Jimmy Horton	.07	.20
33 Harry Gant	.07	.20
34 Rusty Wallace's Car	.15	.40
35 Mark Martin's Car	.15	.40
36 Dale Jarrett's Car	.15	.40
37 Loy Allen Jr.	.07	.20
38 Dale Jarrett's Car	.15	.40
Memorable Moment		
39 Kyle Petty's Car	.07	.20
40 Kenny Wallace	.07	.20
41 Dick Trickle	.07	.20
42 Kyle Petty	.15	.40
43 Richard Petty	.25	.60
44 Rick Wilson	.07	.20
45 T.W. Taylor	.02	.10
46 James Hylton	.07	.20
47 Phil Parsons	.07	.20
48 Ernie Irvan's Car	.07	.20
49 Stanley Smith	.02	.10
50 Morgan Shepherd's Car	.02	.10
51 Joe Ruttman	.07	.20
52 Jimmy Means	.07	.20
53 Davey Allison's Car	.15	.40
Memorable Moment		
54 Bill Elliott's Car	.15	.40
55 Ted Musgrave	.07	.20
56 Ken Schrader's Car	.02	.10
57 Bob Schacht	.02	.10
58 Jim Sauter	.02	.10
59 Ricky Rudd w/Car	.15	.40
60 Harry Gant's Car	.07	.20
61 Ken Bouchard	.07	.20
62 Dave Marcis' Car	.07	.20
63 Rich Bickle	.07	.20
64 Darrell Waltrip's Car	.07	.20
65 Jeff Gordon's Car	.30	.75
66 Jeff Burton's Car	.07	.20
67 Geoff Bodine's Car	.02	.10
68 Greg Sacks	.07	.20
69 Tom Kendall	.07	.20
70 Michael Waltrip's Car	.07	.20
71 Dave Marcis	.07	.20
72 John Andretti RC	.07	.20
73 Todd Bodine's Car	.02	.10
74 Bobby Labonte's Car	.15	.40
75 Todd Bodine	.07	.20
76 Brett Bodine's Car	.02	.10
77 Jeff Purvis	.07	.20
78 Rick Mast's Car	.02	.10
79 Rick Carelli RC	.07	.20
80 Wally Dallenbach Jr.'s Car	.02	.10
81 Jimmy Spencer's Car	.02	.10
82 Bobby Hillin's Car	.02	.10
83 Lake Speed's Car	.02	.10
84 Richard Childress	.15	.40
85 Roger Penske	.02	.10
86 Don Miller	.02	.10
87 Jack Roush	.02	.10
88 Joe Gibbs	.15	.40
89 Felix Sabates	.02	.10
90 Bobby Hillin	.07	.20
91 Tim Morgan	.02	.10
92 Larry McClure	.02	.10
93 Teddy McClure	.02	.10
Jerry McClure		
Ed McClure		
94 Glen Wood	.02	.10
95 Len Wood	.02	.10
96 Eddie Wood	.02	.10
97 Junior Johnson	.07	.20
98 Derrike Cope	.07	.20
99 Andy Hillenburg	.07	.20
100 Rick Hendrick	.02	.10
101 Leo Jackson	.02	.10
102 Bobby Allison	.07	.20
103 Bob Bilby	.02	.10
104 Bill Stavola	.02	.10
105 Mickey Stavola	.02	.10
106 Paul Moore (Bud)	.02	.10
107 Chuck Rider	.02	.10
108 Billy Hagan	.02	.10
109 Bill Davis	.02	.10
110 Kenny Bernstein	.07	.20
111 Richard Jackson	.02	.10
112 Ray DeWitt	.02	.10
Diane DeWitt		
113 D.K. Ulrich	.02	.10
114 Cale Yarborough	.07	.20
115 Junie Donlavey	.02	.10
116 Larry Hedrick	.02	.10
117 Robert Yates	.02	.10
118 George Bradshaw	.02	.10
119 Mark Smith	.02	.10
120 David Fuge	.02	.10
121 Harry Melling	.02	.10
122 Atlanta MM	.02	.10
123 Dick Moroso	.02	.10
124 Butch Mock	.02	.10
125 Alan Kulwicki's Transporter	.15	.40
Memorable Moment		
126 Andy Petree	.02	.10
127 Buddy Parrott	.02	.10
128 Steve Hmiel	.02	.10
129 Howard Comstock	.02	.10
130 Jimmy Makar	.02	.10
131 Robin Pemberton	.02	.10
132 Jeff Hammond	.02	.10
133 Tony Glover	.02	.10
134 Leonard Wood	.02	.10
135 Mike Beam	.02	.10
136 Mike Hill	.02	.10
137 Gary DeHart	.02	.10
138 Ray Evernham	.15	.40
139 Ken Howes	.02	.10
140 Jimmy Fennig	.02	.10
141 Barry Dodson	.02	.10
142 Ken Wilson	.02	.10
143 Donnie Wingo	.02	.10
144 Doug Hewitt	.02	.10
145 Pete Wright	.02	.10
146 Tim Brewer	.02	.10
147 Donnie Richeson	.02	.10
148 Sandy Jones	.02	.10
149 Bob Johnson	.02	.10
150 Geoff Bodine's Car	.02	.10
Brett Bodine's Car		
Memorable Moment		
151 Doug Williams	.02	.10
152 Waddell Wilson	.02	.10
153 Doug Richert	.02	.10
154 Larry McReynolds	.02	.10
155 Dennis Connor	.02	.10
156 Harry Hyde	.02	.10
157 Paul Andrews	.02	.10
158 Robbie Loomis	.07	.20
159 Troy Selberg	.02	.10
160 Dale Inman	.02	.10
161 Tony Eury	.25	.60
162 Dale Fischlein	.02	.10
163 Steve Grissom	.07	.20
164 Ricky Craven	.07	.20
165 David Green	.07	.20
166 Chuck Bown	.07	.20
167 Joe Nemechek	.07	.20
168 Ward Burton	.15	.40
169 Bobby Dotter	.07	.20
170 Robert Pressley	.07	.20
171 Hermie Sadler	.07	.20
172 Mike Wallace	.07	.20
173 Tracy Leslie	.07	.20
174 Tom Peck	.07	.20
175 Jeff Burton	.25	.60
176 Rodney Combs	.07	.20
177 Talladega Speedway	.02	.10
Memorable Moments		
178 Tommy Houston	.07	.20
179 Joe Bessey	.07	.20
180 Tim Fedewa	.07	.20
181 Jack Sprague	.07	.20
182 Richard Lasater	.02	.10
183 Roy Payne	.07	.20
184 Shawna Robinson	.30	.75
185 Larry Pearson	.07	.20
186 Jim Bown	.07	.20
187 Nathan Buttke	.02	.10
188 Butch Miller	.07	.20
189 Jason Keller RC	.25	.60
190 Randy LaJoie	.07	.20
191 Dave Rezendes	.07	.20
192 Jeff Green	.07	.20
193 Ed Berrier	.02	.10
194 Troy Beebe	.02	.10
195 Dennis Setzer	.07	.20
196 David Bonnett	.07	.20
197 Steve Grissom	.02	.10
BGN Champion		
198 Hermie Sadler	.02	.10
BGN Rookie of the Year		
199 Rusty Wallace w/Crew	.25	.60
200 Steve Hmiel	.02	.10
Crew Chief of the Year		
201 Jeff Gordon	.60	1.50
WC Rookie of the Year		
202 Bill Elliott	.25	.60
Fan's Favorite Driver		
203 Davey Allison	.15	.40
IROC Champion		
204 Jimmy Horton Crash	.02	.10
Memorable Moment		
205 Dale Jarrett's Car	.15	.40
Kyle Petty's Car		
Memorable Moment		
206 Rusty Wallace's Car	.15	.40
Memorable Moments		
207 Dale Jarrett	.30	.75
Joe Gibbs		
Year in Review		
208 Rusty Wallace	.25	.60
Year in Review		
209 Davey Allison	.15	.40
Year in Review		
210 Morgan Shepherd w/Crew	.02	.10
Year in Review		
211 Dale Earnhardt	.60	1.50
Year in Review		
212 Rusty Wallace	.25	.60
Year in Review		
213 Rusty Wallace w/Crew	.25	.60
Year in Review		
214 Rusty Wallace	.25	.60
Year in Review		
215 Ernie Irvan	.07	.20
Year in Review		
216 Geoff Bodine w/Crew	.02	.10
Year in Review		
217 Sterling Marlin	.15	.40
Year in Review		
218 Dale Earnhardt	.60	1.50
Year in Review		
219 Dale Earnhardt	.60	1.50
Year in Review		
220 Kyle Petty	.07	.20
Year in Review		
221 Ricky Rudd	.15	.40
Year in Review		
222 Dale Earnhardt	.60	1.50
Year in Review		
223 Rusty Wallace	.25	.60
Year in Review		
224 Dale Earnhardt	.60	1.50
Year in Review		
225 Dale Earnhardt	.60	1.50
Year in Review		
226 Mark Martin	.25	.60
Year in Review		
227 Mark Martin	.25	.60
Year in Review		
228 Mark Martin	.25	.60
Year in Review		
229 Mark Martin	.25	.60
Year in Review		
230 Rusty Wallace w/Crew	.25	.60
Year in Review		
231 Rusty Wallace w/Crew	.25	.60
Year in Review		
232 Ernie Irvan	.15	.40
Robert Yates		
Larry McReyonlds		
Year in Review		
233 Rusty Wallace	.25	.60
Year in Review		
234 Ernie Irvan	.07	.20
Year in Review		
235 Rusty Wallace	.25	.60
Year in Review		
236 Mark Martin	.25	.60
Year in Review		
237 Rusty Wallace	.25	.60
Year in Review		
238 Dale Earnhardt	.60	1.50
WC Champion		
Year in Review		
239 Checklist #1	.02	.10
240 Checklist #2	.02	.10
241 Bill Elliott	.30	.75
242 Harry Gant	.15	.40
243 Harry Gant's Car	.07	.20
244 Sterling Marlin	.25	.60
245 Sterling Marlin's Car	.07	.20
246 Terry Labonte	.25	.60
247 Terry Labonte's Car	.15	.40
248 Morgan Shepherd	.07	.20
249 Morgan Shepherd's Car	.02	.10
250 Ernie Irvan	.15	.40
251 Ernie Irvan's Car	.07	.20
252 Dale Jarrett	.50	1.25
253 Dale Jarrett's Car	.15	.40
254 Bobby Labonte	.50	1.25
255 Bobby Labonte's Car	.15	.40
256 Ken Schrader	.07	.20
257 Ken Schrader's Car	.02	.10
258 Mark Martin	.60	1.50
259 Mark Martin's Car	.15	.40
260 Michael Waltrip	.15	.40
261 Michael Waltrip's Car	.07	.20
262 Derrike Cope	.07	.20
263 Hut Stricklin	.07	.20
264 Sterling Marlin	.25	.60
265 Chuck Bown	.07	.20
266 Ted Musgrave	.07	.20
267 Jimmy Spencer	.07	.20
268 Wally Dallenbach Jr.	.07	.20
269 Jeff Purvis	.07	.20
270 Greg Sacks	.07	.20
271 Rich Bickle	.07	.20
272 Bobby Hamilton	.07	.20
273 Dick Trickle's Car	.02	.10
274 Hut Stricklin's Car	.02	.10
275 Terry Labonte's Car	.15	.40
276 Ted Musgrave's Car	.02	.10
277 Greg Sacks' Car	.02	.10
278 Jimmy Hensley's Car	.02	.10
279 Derrike Cope's Car	.02	.10
280 Bobby Hamilton's Car	.02	.10
281 Ricky Rudd's Car	.07	.20
282 Geoff Bodine's Car	.02	.10
283 Kevin Hamlin RC	.02	.10
284 Charley Pressley	.02	.10
285 Jim Long	.02	.10
286 Bill Ingle	.02	.10
287 Peter Sospenzo	.02	.10
288 Freddy Fryar	.02	.10
289 Chris Hussey	.02	.10
290 Mike Hillman	.02	.10
291 Gordon Gibbs	.02	.10
292 Ken Glen	.02	.10
293 Tony Furr	.02	.10
294 Pete Wright	.02	.10
295 Travis Carter	.02	.10
296 Gary Bechtel	.02	.10
Carolyn Bechtel		
297 A.G. Dillard	.07	.20
298 Kenny Wallace	.07	.20
299 Elton Sawyer	.07	.20
300 Rodney Combs	.07	.20
301 Phil Parsons	.07	.20
302 Kevin Lepage RC	.15	.40
303 Johnny Benson RC	.25	.60
304 Mike McLaughlin	.07	.20
305 Patty Moise	.07	.20
306 Larry Pearson	.07	.20
307 Robert Pressley	.07	.20
308 Clyde McLeod	.02	.10
309 Ricky Pearson	.02	.10
310 Gil Martin	.02	.10
311 Fil Martocci	.02	.10
312 Frank Cicci	.02	.10
Scott Welliver		
John Gittler		
313 John Andretti's Car	.02	.10
Memorable Moment		
314 Shawna Robinson's Car	.15	.40
Memorable Moment		
315 Mike Skinner's Car MM	.02	.10
316 Loy Allen Jr.	.02	.10
Memorable Moment		
317 Bob Jenkins	.02	.10
318 Buddy Baker	.02	.10
319 Checklist Card 1	.02	.10
320 Checklist Card 2	.02	.10
321 Joe Nemechek	.02	.10
Winston Select		
322 Rusty Wallace	.25	.60
Winston Select Pole		
323 Winston Select Action	.02	.10
324 Winston Select Action	.02	.10
325 Winston Select Action	.02	.10
326 Ken Schrader's Car	.02	.10
Winston Select		
327 Jeff Gordon's Car	.30	.75
Winston Select		
328 Jeff Gordon	.75	2.00
Winston Select		
329 Winston Select Action	.02	.10
330 Winston Select Action	.02	.10
331 Winston Select Action	.02	.10
332 Geoff Bodine Crash	.02	.10
Winston Select		
333 Winston Select Action	.02	.10
334 Ernie Irvan's Car	.15	.40
Dale Earnhardt's Car		
Ward Burton's Car		
Winston Select		
335 Jeff Gordon's Car	.40	1.00
Rusty Wallace's Car		
Dale Earnhardt's Car		
Winston Select		
336 Geoff Bodine's Car	.02	.10
Ernie Irvan's Car		
Winston Select		
337 Winston Select Action	.02	.10
338 Geoff Bodine's Car	.02	.10
Winston Select		
339 Geoff Bodine	.02	.10
Winston Select		
340 Geoff Bodine	.02	.10
Winston Select		
P11 Bill Elliott Promo	2.00	5.00
numbered 11		
S24 Jeff Gordon Sample	3.00	8.00
numbered 24		
PC Bill Elliott Club Promo	4.00	10.00
unnumbered card		
PS2 Ted Musgrave Promo	.75	2.00
series two promo		
unnumbered card		

1994 Maxx Autographs

Maxx packaged Autographed cards throughout the print run of 1994 series two and Medallion products. Although a few older Maxx issues were included most of the cards signed were from series one 1994 Maxx and the Rookie Class of '94 insert sets. Wrapper stated odds for pulling an autographed card from series two was 1:200 packs. To pull a signed card from Maxx Medallion collectors faced wrapper stated odds of 1:18 packs. Each signed card was crimped with Maxx's corporate seal which reads "J.R. Maxx Inc. Corporate Seal 1988 North Carolina."

COMPLETE SET (37)	600.00	1000.00
1 Rick Mast	6.00	15.00
2 Steve Grissom Rookie Class	6.00	15.00
3 Joe Nemechek Rookie Class	6.00	15.00
4 John Andretti Rookie Class	6.00	15.00
5 Ricky Rudd	15.00	40.00
6 Mark Martin	15.00	40.00
7 Loy Allen Jr. Rookie Class	6.00	15.00
8 Jeremy Mayfield Rookie Class	10.00	25.00
9 Bill Elliott '91 Maxx	40.00	80.00
9 Loy Allen Jr. Rookie Class	6.00	15.00
11 Bill Elliott '92 Maxx Red	30.00	60.00
14 Terry Labonte	12.50	30.00
18 Dale Jarrett	12.50	30.00
20 Buddy Baker '92 Maxx Red	6.00	15.00
20 Buddy Baker '92 Maxx Black	6.00	15.00
22 Bobby Labonte	12.50	30.00
24 Jeff Gordon	75.00	150.00
25 Ken Schrader	6.00	15.00
33 Harry Gant	10.00	25.00
37 Loy Allen Jr.	6.00	15.00
42 Kyle Petty	20.00	40.00
47 Phil Parsons	6.00	15.00
63 Rich Bickle	6.00	15.00
94 Glen Wood	6.00	15.00
95 Len Wood	6.00	15.00
96 Eddie Wood	6.00	15.00
154 Larry McReynolds	6.00	15.00
163 Steve Grissom	6.00	15.00
167 Joe Nemechek	6.00	15.00
168 Ward Burton	10.00	25.00
172 Mike Wallace	6.00	15.00
175 Jeff Burton	8.00	20.00
184 Shawna Robinson	12.50	25.00
227 Mark Martin	15.00	40.00
298 Kenny Wallace	6.00	15.00
307 Robert Pressley	6.00	15.00
318 Buddy Baker	6.00	15.00

1994 Maxx Rookie Class of '94

Maxx produced this set featuring the nine candidates for the 1994 Winston Cup Rookie of the Year award. The cards were distributed in 1994 Maxx series two packs at the stated odds of 1:12.

COMPLETE SET (10)	10.00	20.00
1 Jeff Burton	1.50	4.00
2 Steve Grissom	1.50	4.00
3 Joe Nemechek	1.50	4.00
4 John Andretti	1.50	4.00
5 Ward Burton	1.50	4.00
6 Mike Wallace	.75	2.00
7 Loy Allen Jr.	.75	2.00
8 Jeremy Mayfield	3.00	8.00
9 Billy Standridge	.75	2.00
10 Checklist	.75	2.00

1994 Maxx Rookies of the Year

Maxx produced this set featuring various Winston Cup Rookies of the Year awarded between 1966 and 1993. The cards were distributed in 1994 Maxx series one packs at the wrapper stated odds of 1:1 packs.

COMPLETE SET (16)	10.00	25.00
1 James Hylton	.30	.75
2 Ricky Rudd	1.00	2.50
3 Dale Earnhardt	5.00	12.00

Geoff Bodine .30 .75
Sterling Marlin 1.00 2.50
Rusty Wallace 2.50 6.00
Ken Schrader .30 .75
Alan Kulwicki 1.00 2.50
Davey Allison 1.25 3.00
) Ken Bouchard .30 .75
1 Dick Trickle .30 .75
2 Bobby Hamilton .30 .75
3 Jimmy Hensley .30 .75
4 Kenny Wallace .30 .75
5 Bobby Labonte 2.00 5.00
5 Jeff Gordon 4.00 10.00

1994 Maxx Medallion

axx released the Medallion set in late 1994. The st 55 cards in the set were printed on typical ardboard stock while the last 20 cards were roduced on a clear plastic stock. Packs contained ght total cards; seven regular issue cards and one ear card. Boxes contained 18 packs. Maxx also cluded randomly packed (approximately 1:360) rtificates for 1988 Dale Earnhardt cards (#99) that ad been previously unreleased. Each card carried a old sticker on the front showing the serial number 999 and to help differentiate it from the other card 99 that was released after the bankruptcy of Maxx. so randomly inserted in packs of Medallion were utographed cards. Pricing for those cards can be und under the 1994 Maxx Autograph listing.

OMPLETE SET (75) 12.50 25.00
OMP.SET w/o SP's (55) 3.00 8.00
AX BOX 25.00 50.00
Jeff Gordon's Car .50 1.25
Brett Bodine's Car .05 .15
Bill Elliott .40 1.00
Rusty Wallace .75 2.00
Darrell Waltrip .20 .50
Ken Schrader .08 .25
Michael Waltrip's Car .08 .25
Todd Bodine's Car .05 .15
Morgan Shepherd .08 .25
) Ricky Rudd .30 .75
1 Terry Labonte .30 .75
2 Ted Musgrave's Car .05 .15
3 Sterling Marlin's Car .08 .25
4 Lake Speed .08 .25
5 Bobby Labonte .60 1.50
5 Ernie Irvan's Car .08 .25
7 Greg Sacks' Car .05 .15
3 Jeff Burton .30 .75
3 Joe Nemechek's Car .05 .15
) Bobby Hillin's Car .05 .15
1 Rick Mast's Car .05 .15
2 Wally Dallenbach Jr.'s Car .05 .15
3 Bobby Hamilton .08 .25
4 Kyle Petty .20 .50
5 Jeremy Mayfield's Car .20 .50
5 Derrike Cope's Car .05 .15
7 John Andretti's Car .05 .15
3 Rich Bickle's Car .05 .15
3 A.J. Foyt's Car .05 .15
) Ward Burton .20 .50
1 Jimmy Hensley's Car .05 .15
2 Jeff Purvis .08 .25
3 Mark Martin .75 2.00
4 Hut Stricklin's Car .05 .15
5 Harry Gant .20 .50
5 Geoff Bodine's Car .05 .15
7 Dale Jarrett .60 1.50
3 Dave Marcis' Car .05 .15
) Mike Chase .08 .25
) Jimmy Spencer's Car .05 .15
NASCAR Arrives In .05 .15
2 A Warm Welcome .05 .15
3 Birthday Wishes .05 .15
4 Gentlemen Start Your Engines .05 .15
5 In Formation .05 .15
5 Jeff Gordon's Car .60 1.50
Dale Earnhardt's Car
A Page In History
7 The Youngest Leader .40 1.00
with Jeff Gordon's Car
3 Coming Off Turn One .20 .50
with Jeff Gordon's Car
) Jeff Gordon's Car .40 1.00
Geoff Bodine's Car
Swapping the Lead
0 Jeff Gordon's Car .40 1.00
Just Racin'
1 Dave Marcis' Car .05 .15
Mike Chase's Car
Hitting The Wall
2 Jeff Gordon's Car .40 1.00
Ernie Irvan's Car
Going For The Win
3 Jeff Gordon 1.00 2.50
New Kid in Town
4 NASCAR World .05 .15
5 Checklist Card .05 .15
5 Jeff Gordon 3.00 8.00
7 Bobby Labonte 2.00 5.00
3 Jeff Burton's Car .50 1.25
3 Wally Dallenbach Jr.'s Car .30 .75

60 Brett Bodine .50 1.25
61 Ernie Irvan 1.00 2.50
62 Morgan Shepherd .50 1.25
63 Jimmy Spencer's Car .30 .75
64 Bill Elliott 1.25 3.00
65 Mike Wallace .50 1.25
66 Ricky Rudd 1.25 3.00
67 Ernie Irvan's Car .50 1.25
68 A.J. Foyt 1.00 2.50
69 Rusty Wallace 2.50 6.00
70 Mark Martin 2.50 6.00
71 Ted Musgrave .50 1.25
72 Ricky Rudd's Car .50 1.25
73 Kyle Petty 1.00 2.50
74 Harry Gant .50 1.25
75 Geoff Bodine's Car .30 .75
99SP Dale Earnhardt 1988 Maxx 250.00 400.00

1994 Maxx Motorsport

This 25-card set was produced by Maxx and distributed by Ford Motorsport and Club Maxx. This year's set features top Ford drivers on oversized (approximately 3-1/2" by 5") cards utilizing the metallic printing process commonly found with Maxx Premier Plus. Reportedly, 10,000 sets were produced.

COMPLETE SET (25) 4.00 8.00
1 Ernie Irvan .10 .30
2 Rusty Wallace .75 2.00
3 Mark Martin .75 2.00
4 Bill Elliott .40 1.00
5 Jimmy Spencer .07 .20
6 Ted Musgrave .07 .20
7 Geoff Bodine .07 .20
8 Brett Bodine .07 .20
9 Todd Bodine .07 .20
10 Jeff Burton .30 .75
11 Rick Mast .07 .20
12 Lake Speed .07 .20
13 Morgan Shepherd .07 .20
14 Ricky Rudd .30 .75
15 Derrike Cope .07 .20
16 Hut Stricklin .07 .20
17 Loy Allen Jr. .07 .20
18 Mike Wallace .07 .20
19 Greg Sacks .07 .20
20 Jimmy Hensley .07 .20
21 Rich Bickle .07 .20
22 Bobby Hillin .07 .20
23 Jeremy Mayfield .07 .20
24 Randy LaJoie .07 .20
25 Checklist .04 .10

1994 Maxx Premier Plus

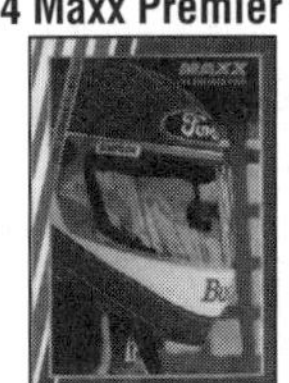

Maxx produced the Premier Plus set for the second year in 1994. The cards were produced using a metallic chromium printing process now standard with Premier Plus. The cards closely resemble those found in series one 1994 Maxx, except for the special printing features and card numbering. An Alan Kulwicki set was produced and randomly inserted in packs. Cards could be found in eight-card packs, 36-pack boxes and complete factory sets which also included six Alan Kulwicki insert cards per set.

COMPLETE SET (200) 10.00 25.00
COMP.FACT.SET (206) 12.00 30.00
WAX BOX 15.00 40.00
1 Rick Mast .10 .30
2 Rusty Wallace 1.00 2.50
3 Dale Earnhardt 2.00 5.00
4 Jimmy Hensley .10 .30
5 Ricky Rudd .40 1.00
6 Mark Martin 1.00 2.50
7 Alan Kulwicki .40 1.00
8 Sterling Marlin .40 1.00
9 Bill Elliott .40 1.00
Fan's Favorite Driver
10 Geoff Bodine .10 .30
11 Bill Elliott .50 1.25
12 Jimmy Spencer .10 .30
13 Jeff Gordon .60 1.50
Memorable Moment
14 Terry Labonte .40 1.00
15 Lake Speed .10 .30
16 Wally Dallenbach Jr. .10 .30
17 Darrell Waltrip .25 .60
18 Dale Jarrett 1.00 2.00
19 Dale Jarrett's Car .25 .60
Memorable Moment
20 Bobby Hamilton .10 .30
21 Morgan Shepherd .10 .30
22 Bobby Labonte .75 2.00
23 Dale Earnhardt's Car .75 2.00
24 Jeff Gordon 1.25 3.00
25 Ken Schrader .10 .30
26 Brett Bodine .10 .30
27 Hut Stricklin .10 .30
28 Davey Allison .60 1.50
29 Ernie Irvan .25 .60
30 Michael Waltrip .25 .60
31 Davey Allison's Car .25 .60
Memorable Moment
32 Jimmy Horton .10 .30
33 Harry Gant .25 .60
34 Rusty Wallace's Car .40 1.00
35 Mark Martin's Car .40 1.00
36 Dale Jarrett's Car .25 .60
37 Travis Carter .05 .15
38 Hut Stricklin's Car .05 .15
39 Kyle Petty's Car .10 .30
40 Kenny Wallace .10 .30
41 Dick Trickle .10 .30
42 Kyle Petty .25 .60
43 Richard Petty .40 1.00
44 Rick Wilson .10 .30
45 Atlanta MM .05 .15
46 Jeff Gordon 1.25 3.00
WC Rookie of the Year
47 Phil Parsons .10 .30
48 Ernie Irvan's Car .10 .30
49 Alan Kulwicki's Transporter .10 .30
Memorable Moment
50 Morgan Shepherd's Car .05 .15
51 Hermie Sadler .10 .30
BGN Rookie of the Year
52 Jimmy Means .10 .30
53 Steve Hmiel .05 .15
54 Bill Elliott's Car .25 .60
55 Ted Musgrave .10 .30
56 Ken Schrader's Car .05 .15
57 Geoff Bodine's Car .05 .15
Brett Bodine's Car
Memorable Moment
58 Davey Allison .60 1.50
IROC Champion
59 Ricky Rudd's Car .10 .30
60 Harry Gant's Car .10 .30
61 Steve Grissom .05 .15
BGN Champion
62 Dave Marcis' Car .10 .30
63 New Hampshire .05 .15
Memorable Moment
64 Darrell Waltrip's Car .10 .30
65 Jeff Gordon's Car .50 1.25
66 Jeff Burton's Car .10 .30
67 Geoff Bodine's Car .05 .15
68 Greg Sacks .10 .30
69 Talladega Speedway .25 .60
Memorable Moment
70 Michael Waltrip's Car .10 .30
71 Dave Marcis .25 .60
72 Jimmy Horton Crash .05 .15
(Memorable Moment
73 Todd Bodine's Car .05 .15
74 Bobby Labonte's Car .25 .60
75 Todd Bodine .10 .30
76 Brett Bodine's Car .05 .15
77 Neil Bonnett .40 1.00
78 Rick Mast's Car .05 .15
79 Dale Jarrett's Car .25 .60
Kyle Petty's Car
Memorable Moment
80 Wally Dallenbach Jr.'s Car .05 .15
81 Jimmy Spencer's Car .05 .15
82 Bobby Hillin's Car .05 .15
83 Lake Speed's Car .05 .15
84 Richard Childress .25 .60
85 Roger Penske .05 .15
86 Don Miller .05 .15
87 Jack Roush .05 .15
88 Joe Gibbs .25 .60
89 Felix Sabates .05 .15
90 Bobby Hillin .10 .30
91 Tim Morgan .05 .15
92 Larry McClure .05 .15
93 Teddy McClure .05 .15
Jerry McClure
Ed McClure
94 Glen Wood .05 .15
95 Len Wood .05 .15
96 Eddie Wood .05 .15
97 Junior Johnson .10 .30
98 Derrike Cope .10 .30
99 Rusty Wallace w/Crew .40 1.00
Pit Crew Champions
100 Rick Hendrick .05 .15
101 Leo Jackson .05 .15
102 Bobby Allison .10 .30
103 Bob Bilby .05 .15
104 Bill Stavola .05 .15
105 Mickey Stavola .05 .15
106 Walter Bud Moore .05 .15
107 Chuck Rider .05 .15
108 Billy Hagan .05 .15
109 Bill Davis .05 .15
110 Kenny Bernstein .10 .30
111 Richard Jackson .05 .15
112 Ray DeWitt .05 .15
Diane DeWitt
113 D.K. Ulrich .05 .15
114 Cale Yarborough .10 .30
115 Junie Donlavey .05 .15
116 Larry Hedrick .05 .15
117 Robert Yates .05 .15
118 Rusty Wallace's Car .40 1.00
Memorable Moment
119 Andy Petree .05 .15
120 Buddy Parrott .05 .15
121 Steve Hmiel .05 .15
122 Howard Comstock .05 .15
123 Jimmy Makar .05 .15
124 Robin Pemberton .05 .15
125 Jeff Hammond .05 .15
126 Tony Glover .05 .15
127 Leonard Wood .05 .15
128 Mike Beam .05 .15
129 Mike Hill .05 .15
130 Gary DeHart .05 .15
131 Ray Evernham .25 .60
132 Ken Howes .05 .15
133 Jimmy Fennig .05 .15
134 Barry Dodson .05 .15
135 Ken Wilson .05 .15
136 Donnie Wingo .05 .15
137 Doug Hewitt .05 .15
138 Pete Wright .05 .15
139 Tim Brewer .05 .15
140 Donnie Richeson .05 .15
141 Sandy Jones .05 .15
142 Bob Johnson .05 .15
143 Doug Williams .05 .15
144 Waddell Wilson .05 .15
145 Doug Richert .05 .15
146 Larry McReynolds .05 .15
147 Paul Andrews .05 .15
148 Robbie Loomis .10 .30
149 Dale Inman .05 .15
150 Steve Grissom .10 .30
151 Ricky Craven .10 .30
152 David Green .10 .30
153 Chuck Bown .10 .30
154 Joe Nemechek .10 .30
155 Ward Burton .25 .60
156 Bobby Dotter .10 .30
157 Robert Pressley .10 .30
158 Hermie Sadler .10 .30
159 Tracy Leslie .10 .30
160 Mike Wallace .10 .30
161 Tom Peck .10 .30
162 Jeff Burton .40 1.00
163 Rodney Combs .10 .30
164 Tommy Houston .10 .30
165 Dale Earnhardt w/Crew 1.00 2.50
WC Champion
166 Dale Jarrett .25 .60
Year in Review
167 Rusty Wallace .40 1.00
Year in Review
168 Davey Allison .40 1.00
Year in Review
169 Morgan Shepherd w/Crew .05 .15
Year in Review
170 Dale Earnhardt 1.00 2.50
Year in Review
171 Rusty Wallace .40 1.00
Year in Review
172 Rusty Wallace w/Crew .40 1.00
Year in Review
173 Rusty Wallace .40 1.00
(Year in Review
174 Ernie Irvan .10 .30
Year in Review
175 Geoff Bodine w/Crew .05 .15
Year in Review
176 Sterling Marlin .25 .60
Year in Review
177 Dale Earnhardt 1.00 2.50
Year in Review
178 Dale Earnhardt w/Crew 1.00 2.50
Year in Review
179 Kyle Petty .10 .30
Year in Review
180 Ricky Rudd .25 .60
Year in Review
181 Dale Earnhardt w/Crew 1.00 2.50
Year in Review
182 Rusty Wallace w/Crew .40 1.00
Year in Review
183 Dale Earnhardt 1.00 2.50
Richard Childress
Year in Review
184 Dale Earnhardt 1.00 2.50
Year in Review
185 Mark Martin .40 1.00
Year in Review
186 Mark Martin .40 1.00
Year in Review
187 Mark Martin .40 1.00
Year in Review
188 Mark Martin w/Crew .40 1.00
Year in Review
189 Rusty Wallace .40 1.00
Year in Review
190 Rusty Wallace w/Crew .40 1.00
Year in Review
191 Ernie Irvan .25 .60
Robert Yates
Larry McReynolds
Year in Review
192 Rusty Wallace .40 1.00
Year in Review
193 Ernie Irvan .25 .60
(Year in Review
194 Rusty Wallace .40 1.00
Year in Review
195 Mark Martin .40 1.00
Jack Roush
Year in Review
196 Rusty Wallace .40 1.00
Year in Review
197 Checklist .05 .15
198 Checklist .05 .15
199 Checklist .05 .15
200 Checklist .05 .15
P1 Bill Elliott Promo 2.50 6.00
unnumbered card

1994 Maxx Premier Plus Alan Kulwicki

Maxx produced these fourteen cards honoring the late Alan Kulwicki to be random inserts in 1994 Premier Plus. Wrapper stated odds for pulling a card was 1:15 packs. Six cards could also be randomly found in each Premier Plus factory set.

COMPLETE SET (14) 8.00 20.00
COMMON CARD (1-14) .75 2.00

1994 Maxx Premier Series

Maxx again offered a special Premier Series set to its Club Maxx members. The 1994 issue included 300 regular cards all featuring new photography and different card design. Eight cards that constitute the first series of the 1994 Maxx Jumbo issue were also included with each complete set.

COMPLETE SET (300) 12.50 30.00
COMP.FACT.SET (308) 15.00 40.00
1 Rick Mast .07 .20

2 Rusty Wallace .60 1.50
3 Dale Earnhardt 1.25 3.00
4 Jimmy Hensley .07 .20
5 Ricky Rudd .25 .60
6 Mark Martin .60 1.50
7 Alan Kulwicki .25 .60
8 Sterling Marlin .25 .60
9 P.J. Jones .07 .20
10 Geoff Bodine .07 .20
11 Bill Elliott .30 .75
12 Jimmy Spencer .07 .20
13 Jeff Gordon .40 1.00
Memorable Moment
14 Terry Labonte .25 .60
15 Lake Speed .07 .20
16 Wally Dallenbach, Jr. .07 .20
17 Darrell Waltrip .15 .40
18 Dale Jarrett .50 1.25
19 Chad Little .07 .20
20 Bobby Hamilton .07 .20
21 Morgan Shepherd .07 .20
22 Bobby Labonte .50 1.25
23 Dale Earnhardt's Car .50 1.25
24 Jeff Gordon .75 2.00
25 Ken Schrader .07 .20
26 Brett Bodine .07 .20
27 Hut Stricklin .07 .20
28 Davey Allison .15 .40
29 Ernie Irvan .15 .40
30 Michael Waltrip .15 .40
31 Neil Bonnett .25 .60
32 Jimmy Horton .07 .20
33 Harry Gant .15 .40
34 Rusty Wallace's Car .25 .60
35 Mark Martin's Car .25 .60
36 Dale Jarrett's Car .15 .40
37 Loy Allen Jr. .07 .20
38 Dale Jarrett's Car .15 .40
Memorable Moment
39 Kyle Petty's Car .07 .20
40 Kenny Wallace .07 .20
41 Dick Trickle .07 .20
42 Kyle Petty .15 .40
43 Richard Petty .25 .60
44 Rick Wilson .07 .20
45 T.W. Taylor .02 .10
46 James Hylton .07 .20
47 Phil Parsons .07 .20
48 Ernie Irvan's Car .15 .40
49 Stanley Smith .02 .10
50 Morgan Shepherd's Car .02 .10
51 Joe Ruttman .07 .20
52 Jimmy Means .07 .20
53 Davey Allison's Car .15 .40
Memorable Moment
54 Bill Elliott's Car .15 .40
55 Ted Musgrave .07 .20
56 Ken Schrader's Car .02 .10
57 Bob Schacht .02 .10
58 Jim Sauter .02 .10
59 Ricky Rudd's Car .07 .20
60 Harry Gant's Car .07 .20
61 Ken Bouchard .07 .20
62 Dave Marcis .07 .20
63 Rich Bickle .07 .20
64 Darrell Waltrip's Car .07 .20
65 Jeff Gordon's Car .30 .75
66 Jeff Burton's Car .07 .20
67 Geoff Bodine's Car .02 .10
68 Greg Sacks .07 .20
69 Tom Kendall .07 .20
70 Michael Waltrip .15 .40
71 Dave Marcis .07 .20
72 John Andretti .07 .20
73 Todd Bodine's Car .02 .10
74 Bobby Labonte's Car .07 .20
75 Todd Bodine .07 .20
76 Brett Bodine's Car .02 .10
77 Jeff Purvis .07 .20
78 Rick Mast's Car .02 .10
79 Rick Carelli .07 .20
80 Wally Dallenbach Jr.'s Car .02 .10
81 Jimmy Spencer's Car .02 .10
82 Bobby Hillin's Car .02 .10
83 Lake Speed's Car .02 .10
84 Richard Childress .15 .40
85 Roger Penske .02 .10
86 Don Miller .02 .10
87 Jack Roush .02 .10
88 Joe Gibbs .15 .40
89 Felix Sabates .02 .10
90 Bobby Hillin .07 .20
91 Tim Morgan .02 .10
92 Larry McClure .02 .10
93 Teddy McClure .02 .10
Jerry McClure
Ed McClure
94 Glen Wood .02 .10
95 Len Wood .02 .10
96 Eddie Wood .02 .10
97 Junior Johnson .07 .20
98 Derrike Cope .07 .20
99 Andy Hillenburg .07 .20
100 Rick Hendrick .02 .10
101 Leo Jackson .02 .10
102 Bobby Allison .07 .20
103 Bob Bilby .02 .10
104 Bill Stavola .02 .10
105 Mickey Stavola .02 .10
106 Walter Bud Moore .02 .10
107 Chuck Rider .02 .10
108 Billy Hagan .02 .10
109 Bill Davis .02 .10
110 Kenny Bernstein .07 .20
111 Richard Jackson .02 .10
112 Ray DeWitt .02 .10
Diane DeWitt
113 D.K. Ulrich .02 .10
114 Cale Yarborough .07 .20
115 Junie Donlavey .02 .10
116 Larry Hedrick .02 .10
117 Robert Yates .02 .10
118 George Bradshaw .02 .10
119 Mark Smith .02 .10
120 David Fuge .02 .10
121 Harry Melling .02 .10
122 Atlanta MM .02 .10
123 Dick Moroso .02 .10
124 Butch Mock .02 .10
125 Alan Kulwicki's Transporter .07 .20
Memorable Moment
126 Andy Petree .02 .10
127 Buddy Parrott .02 .10
128 Steve Hmiel .02 .10
129 Howard Comstock .02 .10
130 Jimmy Makar .02 .10
131 Robin Pemberton .02 .10
132 Jeff Hammond .02 .10
133 Tony Glover .02 .10
134 Leonard Wood .02 .10
135 Mike Beam .02 .10
136 Mike Hill .02 .10
137 Gary DeHart .02 .10
138 Ray Evernham .02 .10
139 Ken Howes .02 .10
140 Jimmy Fennig .02 .10
141 Barry Dodson .02 .10
142 Ken Wilson .02 .10
143 Donnie Wingo .02 .10
144 Doug Hewitt .02 .10
145 Pete Wright .02 .10
146 Tim Brewer .02 .10
147 Donnie Richeson .02 .10
148 Sandy Jones .02 .10
149 Bob Johnson .02 .10
150 Geoff Bodine's Car .02 .10
Brett Bodine's Car
Memorable Moment
151 Doug Williams .02 .10
152 Waddell Wilson .02 .10
153 Doug Richert .02 .10
154 Larry McReynolds .02 .10
155 Dennis Connor .02 .10
156 Harry Hyde .02 .10
157 Paul Andrews .02 .10
158 Robbie Loomis .02 .10
159 Troy Selberg .02 .10
160 Dale Inman .02 .10
161 Tony Eury .25 .60
162 Dave Fischlein .02 .10
163 Steve Grissom .07 .20
164 Ricky Craven .15 .40
165 David Green .07 .20
166 Chuck Bown .07 .20
167 Joe Nemechek .07 .20
168 Ward Burton .07 .20
169 Bobby Dotter .07 .20
170 Robert Pressley .07 .20
171 Hermie Sadler .07 .20
172 Mike Wallace .07 .20
173 Tracy Leslie .07 .20
174 Tom Peck .07 .20
175 Jeff Burton .25 .60
176 Rodney Combs .07 .20
177 New Hampshire .02 .10
Memorable Moment
178 Tommy Houston .07 .20
179 Joe Bessey .07 .20
180 Tim Fedewa .07 .20
181 Jack Sprague .07 .20
182 Richard Lasater .02 .10
183 Roy Payne .07 .20
184 Shawna Robinson .30 .75
185 Larry Pearson .07 .20
186 Jim Bown .07 .20
187 Nathan Buttke .02 .10
188 Butch Miller .07 .20
189 Jason Keller RC .25 .60
190 Randy LaJoie .07 .20
191 Dave Rezendes .07 .20
192 Jeff Green .07 .20
193 Ed Berrier .02 .10
194 Troy Beebe .02 .10
195 Dennis Setzer .07 .20
196 David Bonnett .07 .20
197 Barney Hall .02 .10
198 Eli Gold .02 .10
199 Ned Jarrett .02 .10
200 Benny Parsons .07 .20
201 Jack Arute .02 .10
202 Jerry Punch .02 .10
203 Talladega Speedway .02 .10
Memorable Moment
204 Mike Joy .02 .10
205 Dick Brooks .02 .10
206 Winston Kelley .02 .10
207 Jim Phillips .02 .10
208 John Kernan .02 .10
209 Randy Pemberton .02 .10
210 Ken Squier .02 .10
211 Joe Moore .02 .10
212 Chris Economaki .02 .10
213 Allen Bestwick .02 .10
214 Glenn Jarrett .02 .10
215 Dick Berggren .02 .10
216 Les Richter .02 .10
217 Gary Nelson .02 .10
218 Ray Hill .02 .10
219 Carl Hill .02 .10
220 Chuck Romeo .02 .10
221 Jack Whittemore .02 .10
222 Jimmy Cox .02 .10
223 Bruce Roney .02 .10
224 Marlin Wright .02 .10
225 Mike Chaplin .02 .10
226 Tim Earp .02 .10
227 Doyle Ford .02 .10
228 Buster Auton .02 .10
229 Elmo Langley .02 .10
230 Walt Green .02 .10
231 Gary Miller .02 .10
232 Morris Metcalfe .02 .10
233 Rich Burgdoff .02 .10
234 Jimmy Horton Crash .02 .10
(Memorable Moment
235 Steve Hmiel .02 .10
All Pro
236 Troy Martin .02 .10
All Pro

1994 Maxx Premier Series

237 Gary Brooks	.02	.10
All Pro		
238 Eddie Wood	.02	.10
All Pro		
239 Raymond Fox III	.02	.10
(All Pro		
240 David Smith	.02	.10
All Pro		
241 Robert Yates	.02	.10
All Pro		
242 Todd Parrott	.02	.10
All Pro		
243 David Munari	.02	.10
All Pro		
244 James Lewter	.02	.10
All Pro		
245 Norman Koshimizu	.02	.10
All Pro		
246 Harold Stott	.02	.10
All Pro		
247 Will Lind	.02	.10
(All Pro		
248 Norman Koshimizu	.02	.10
All Pro		
249 Danny Lawrence	.02	.10
All Pro		
250 Dan Ford	.02	.10
All Pro		
251 Barry Beggarly	.02	.10
252 Steve Boley	.02	.10
Jerry Williams		
253 Mel Walen	.02	.10
Larry Phillips		
254 Barry Beggarly	.02	.10
Charlie Cragen		
255 Robert Miller	.02	.10
Tony Ponder		
256 Steve Grissom	.02	.10
BGN Champion		
257 Hermie Sadler	.07	.20
BGN Rookie of the Year		
259 Steve Hmiel	.02	.10
Crew Chief of the Year		
260 Jeff Gordon	.75	2.00
WC Rookie of the Year		
261 Bill Elliott	.25	.60
Fan's Favorite Driver		
262 Davey Allison	.25	.60
IROC Champion		
263 Dale Jarrett's Car	.15	.40
Kyle Petty's Car		
Memorable Moment		
264 Morgan Shepherd's Car	.02	.10
Memorable Moment		
265 Rusty Wallace's Car	.25	.60
Memorable Moment		
266 Dale Jarrett	.25	.60
Year in Review		
267 Rusty Wallace	.25	.60
Year in Review		
268 Davey Allison w/Crew	.15	.40
Year in Review		
269 Morgan Shepherd	.02	.10
Year in Review		
270 Dale Earnhardt	.60	1.50
Year in Review		
271 Rusty Wallace	.25	.60
Year in Review		
272 Rusty Wallace	.25	.60
Year in Review		
273 Rusty Wallace	.25	.60
Year in Review		
274 Ernie Irvan	.07	.20
(Year in Review		
275 Geoff Bodine	.02	.10
Year in Review		
276 Sterling Marlin	.15	.40
Year in Review		
277 Dale Earnhardt	.60	1.50
Year in Review		
278 Dale Earnhardt	.60	1.50
Year in Review		
279 Kyle Petty	.07	.20
(Year in Review		
280 Ricky Rudd	.15	.40
Year in Review		
281 Dale Earnhardt	.60	1.50
Year in Review		
282 Rusty Wallace	.25	.60
Year in Review		
283 Dale Earnhardt	.60	1.50
Year in Review		
284 Dale Earnhardt	.60	1.50
Year in Review		
285 Mark Martin	.25	.60
Year in Review		
286 Mark Martin	.25	.60
Year in Review		
287 Mark Martin	.25	.60
Year in Review		
288 Mark Martin	.25	.60
Year in Review		
289 Rusty Wallace	.25	.60
Year in Review		
290 Rusty Wallace	.25	.60
(Year in Review		
291 Ernie Irvan	.15	.40
Robert Yates		
Larry McReynolds		
Year in Review		
292 Rusty Wallace	.25	.60
Year in Review		
293 Ernie Irvan	.07	.20
Year in Review		
294 Rusty Wallace	.25	.60
Year in Review		
295 Mark Martin	.25	.60
Year in Review		
296 Rusty Wallace	.25	.60
Year in Review		
297 Dale Earnhardt	.60	1.50
Year in Review		
WC Champion		
298 Checklist #1	.02	.10
299 Checklist #2	.02	.10
300 Checklist #3	.02	.10
P11 Bill Elliott Club Promo	2.50	6.00

1994 Maxx Premier Series Jumbos

The Maxx Premier Series Jumbos were distributed in two series; the first eight cards with Maxx Premier Plus factory sets and the second four cards with the Premier Series binder sold through Club Maxx. The twelve cards are actually enlarged (3-1/2" by 5") copies of the corresponding driver's 1994 Premier Plus issue.

COMPLETE SET (12)	10.00	20.00
COMPLETE SERIES 1 (8)	5.00	10.00
COMPLETE SERIES 2 (4)	5.00	10.00
1 Bill Elliott	.60	1.50
2 Ernie Irvan's Car	.40	1.00
3 Dale Jarrett's Car	.60	1.50
4 Mark Martin	1.00	2.50
5 Darrell Waltrip	.60	1.50
6 Richard Petty	.60	1.50
7 Alan Kulwicki	.60	1.50
8 Jeff Gordon	2.00	5.00
9 Rusty Wallace's Car	1.00	2.00
10 Kyle Petty	1.00	2.00
11 Davey Allison	1.25	3.00
12 Harry Gant	1.00	2.00

1994 Maxx The Select 25

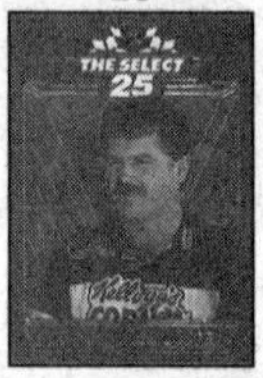

This 25-card chromium set was produced by Maxx and features the top drivers in the 1993 Winston Cup Points standings. These cards were made available in specially marked two packs of Winston Select cigarettes and through a mail-in offer which required 20 Winston Select wrappers and $14.95. This set was closed-out by the manufacturer when the cards set aside for the mail-in offer where not redeemed.

COMPLETE SET (25)	6.00	15.00
1 Dale Earnhardt	1.50	4.00
2 Rusty Wallace	.60	1.50
3 Mark Martin	.60	1.50
4 Dale Jarrett	.50	1.25
5 Kyle Petty	.20	.50
6 Ernie Irvan	.20	.50
7 Morgan Shepherd	.10	.30
8 Bill Elliott	.30	.75
9 Ken Schrader	.10	.30
10 Ricky Rudd	.20	.50
11 Harry Gant	.20	.50
12 Jimmy Spencer	.10	.30
13 Darrell Waltrip	.20	.50
14 Jeff Gordon	.75	2.00
15 Sterling Marlin	.20	.50
16 Geoff Bodine	.10	.30
17 Michael Waltrip	.20	.50
18 Terry Labonte	.30	.75
19 Bobby Labonte	.50	1.25
20 Brett Bodine	.10	.30
21 Rick Mast	.10	.30
22 Wally Dallenbach Jr.	.10	.30
23 Kenny Wallace	.10	.30
24 Hut Stricklin	.10	.30
25 Ted Musgrave	.10	.30

1994 Maxx Texaco Ernie Irvan

Maxx continued the line of Texaco cards in 1994, this year with new team driver Ernie Irvan. For the first time the cards were distributed through foil packs with eight cards per pack. Cards 20-24 were produced with gold foil layering.

COMPLETE SET (50)	2.50	6.00
1 Ernie Irvan	.20	.50
2 Robert Yates	.02	.10
3 Larry McReynolds	.02	.10
4 Ernie Irvan's Car	.02	.10
5 Ernie Irvan's Car	.02	.10
6 Ernie Irvan	.02	.10
Larry McReynolds		
7 Ernie Irvan's Car	.02	.10
In the Driver's Seat		
8 On the Pole	.02	.10
Talladega race action		
9 Ernie Irvan in Pits	.02	.10
10 Ernie Irvan's Car	.02	.10
11 Ernie Irvan's Car	.02	.10
12 Ernie Irvan	.02	.10
A Career in Review		
13 Robert Yates	.02	.10
Follow the Leader		
14 Ernie Irvan's Car w/Crew	.02	.10
15 Ernie Irvan's Transporter	.02	.10
16 Ernie Irvan's Car	.02	.10
Robert Yates Racing Shop		
17 Ernie Irvan's Car	.02	.10
Robert Yates Racing Shop		
18 Ernie Irvan's Shop	.02	.10
Wave of the Future		
19 Ernie Irvan w/Car	.02	.10
20 Ernie Irvan	.02	.10
Robert Yates		
Larry McReynolds		
21 Ernie Irvan	.20	.50
22 Ernie Irvan w/Crew	.02	.10
23 Ernie Irvan	.20	.50
24 Ernie Irvan	.20	.50
25 Jeremy Anderson	.02	.10
26 Gary Beveridge	.02	.10
27 Mike Bumgarner	.02	.10
28 Gene Carrigan	.02	.10
29 Jeff Clark	.02	.10
30 Bret Conway	.02	.10
31 Steve Foster	.02	.10
32 Raymond Fox III	.02	.10
33 Libby Gant	.02	.10
34 Dennis Greene	.02	.10
35 Michael Hanson	.02	.10
36 Eric Horn	.02	.10
37 Vernon Hubbard	.02	.10
38 Gil Kerley	.02	.10
39 Joey Knuckles	.02	.10
40 Norman Koshimizu	.02	.10
41 Dave Kriska	.02	.10
42 Larry Lackey	.02	.10
43 James Lewter	.02	.10
44 Mike Long	.02	.10
45 Nick Ramey	.02	.10
46 Wade Thomas	.02	.10
47 Terry Throneburg	.02	.10
48 Doug Yates	.02	.10
49 Richard Yates	.02	.10
50 Checklist Card	.02	.10

1995 Maxx

Two series were again produced for the 1995 Maxx base brand release. The cards were issued 10 per pack with 36-packs per foil box. Memorable Moments and Victory Lane subsets were included in series one. Several insert sets were distributed over the print run for each series as well. The first card of the Dale Earnhardt Chase the Champion series was included in Maxx one. The popular insert set was distributed by Maxx over the course of the year through five of its different product releases. Series two included a 10-card Bill Elliott Bat Chase insert set packaged approximately 2 cards every 36 packs. A promo card for each series was produced as well.

COMPLETE SET (270)	15.00	40.00
COMP.SERIES 1 (180)	8.00	20.00
COMP.SERIES 2 (90)	4.00	10.00
1 Rick Mast	.07	.20
2 Rusty Wallace	.60	1.50
3 Jeff Gordon's Car	.30	.75
Memorable Moment		
4 Sterling Marlin	.25	.60
5 Terry Labonte	.25	.60
6 Mark Martin	.60	1.50
7 Geoff Bodine	.07	.20
8 Jeff Burton	.25	.60
9 Sterling Marlin	.15	.40
Victory Lane		
10 Ricky Rudd	.25	.60
11 Bill Elliott	.30	.75
12 Derrike Cope	.07	.20
13 Rusty Wallace	.30	.75
Victory Lane		
14 Technical Tidbit	.02	.10
15 Lake Speed	.07	.20
16 Ted Musgrave	.07	.20
17 Darrell Waltrip	.15	.40
18 Dale Jarrett	.50	1.25
19 Loy Allen Jr.	.07	.20
20 Technical Tidbit	.02	.10
Roof Flaps		
21 Morgan Shepherd	.07	.20
22 Bobby Labonte	.50	1.25
23 Hut Stricklin	.07	.20
24 Jeff Gordon	.75	2.00
25 Ken Schrader	.07	.20
26 Brett Bodine	.07	.20
27 Jimmy Spencer	.07	.20
28 Ernie Irvan	.15	.40
29 Steve Grissom	.07	.20
30 Michael Waltrip	.15	.40
31 Ward Burton	.15	.40
32 Dick Trickle	.07	.20
33 Harry Gant	.15	.40
34 Ernie Irvan's Car	.07	.20
Jimmy Spencer's Car		
Memorable Moment		
35 Richard Childress	.15	.40
36 Walter Bud Moore	.02	.10
37 Felix Sabates	.02	.10
38 Ernie Irvan	.07	.20
Victory Lane		
39 Kenny Wallace	.07	.20
40 Bobby Hamilton	.07	.20
41 Joe Nemechek	.07	.20
42 Kyle Petty	.15	.40
43 Richard Petty	.25	.60
44 John Andretti	.07	.20
45 Wally Dallenbach Jr.	.07	.20
46 Ernie Irvan	.07	.20
Victory Lane		
47 Steve Kinser	.07	.20
48 Darlington	.02	.10
Victory Lane		
49 Robert Yates	.02	.10
50 Roger Penske	.02	.10
51 Rusty Wallace's Car	.15	.40
Victory Lane		
52 Glen Wood	.02	.10
53 Len Wood	.02	.10
54 Eddie Wood	.02	.10
55 Jimmy Hensley	.07	.20
56 Don Miller	.02	.10
57 Tim Morgan	.02	.10
58 Terry Labonte	.15	.40
Victory Lane		
59 Larry McClure	.02	.10
60 Rusty Wallace	.30	.75
Victory Lane		
61 Jack Roush	.02	.10
62 Rick Hendrick	.02	.10
63 Talladega Speedway	.02	.10
Victory Lane		
64 Kenny Bernstein	.07	.20
65 Butch Mock	.02	.10
66 Chuck Rider	.02	.10
67 Cale Yarborough	.07	.20
68 Ernie Irvan	.07	.20
Victory Lane		
69 Teddy McClure	.02	.10
70 Joe Gibbs	.15	.40
71 Dave Marcis	.07	.20
72 Jeff Gordon	.40	1.00
Victory Lane		
73 Geoff Bodine	.07	.20
Victory Lane		
74 Richard Jackson	.02	.10
75 Todd Bodine	.07	.20
76 Junior Johnson	.07	.20
77 Greg Sacks	.07	.20
78 Bill Davis	.02	.10
79 D.K. Ulrich	.02	.10
80 Jeff Gordon	.40	1.00
Victory Lane		
81 Travis Carter	.02	.10
82 Bill Stavola	.02	.10
83 Rusty Wallace	.30	.75
Victory Lane		
84 Mickey Stavola	.02	.10
85 Leo Jackson	.02	.10
86 Larry Hedrick	.02	.10
87 Rusty Wallace	.30	.75
Victory Lane		
88 Gary Bechtel	.02	.10
Carolyn Bechtel		
89 Rusty Wallace	.30	.75
Victory Lane		
90 Mike Wallace	.07	.20
91 Bobby Allison	.07	.20
92 Jimmy Spencer	.07	.20
Victory Lane		
93 Junie Donlavey	.02	.10
94 A.G. Dillard	.02	.10
95 Ricky Rudd	.15	.40
Victory Lane		
96 Andy Petree	.02	.10
97 Larry McReynolds	.02	.10
98 Jeremy Mayfield	.15	.40
99 Geoff Bodine	.07	.20
Victory Lane		
100 Buddy Parrott	.02	.10
101 Steve Hmiel	.02	.10
102 Jimmy Spencer	.07	.20
Victory Lane		
103 Ken Howes	.02	.10
104 Leonard Wood	.02	.10
105 Jeff Gordon	.40	1.00
Victory Lane		
106 Bill Ingle	.02	.10
107 Jimmy Fennig	.02	.10
108 Doug Hewitt	.02	.10
109 Mark Martin	.30	.75
Victory Lane		
110 Robin Pemberton	.02	.10
111 Ray Evernham	.02	.10
112 Geoff Bodine	.07	.20
Victory Lane		
113 Donnie Wingo	.02	.10
114 Pete Peterson	.02	.10
115 Rusty Wallace	.30	.75
Victory Lane		
116 Tony Glover	.02	.10
117 Gary DeHart	.02	.10
118 Jimmy Makar	.02	.10
119 Bill Elliott	.15	.40
Victory Lane		
120 Mike Beam	.02	.10
121 Kevin Hamlin	.02	.10
122 Paul Andrews	.02	.10
123 Terry Labonte	.15	.40
Victory Lane		
124 Chris Hussey	.02	.10
125 Mark Martin	.30	.75
IROC Champion		
Memorable Moment		
126 Jim Long	.02	.10
127 Rusty Wallace	.30	.75
Victory Lane		
128 Donnie Richeson	.02	.10
129 Rusty Wallace	.30	.75
Victory Lane		
130 Troy Selberg	.02	.10
131 Tony Furr	.02	.10
132 Mike Hill	.02	.10
133 Geoff Bodine	.07	.20
Victory Lane		
134 Freddy Fryar	.02	.10
135 Philippe Lopez	.02	.10
136 Dale Jarrett	.15	.40
Victory Lane		
137 Jeff Hammond	.02	.10
138 Buddy Barnes	.02	.10
139 Jeff Gordon's Car	.30	.75
Darrell Waltrip's Car		
Terry Labonte's Car		
Ken Schrader's Car		
Victory Lane		
140 Charley Pressley	.02	.10
141 Doug Richert	.02	.10
142 Terry Labonte	.15	.40
Victory Lane		
143 Mike Hillman	.02	.10
144 Derrike Cope's Car	.02	.10
Bobby Hillin's Car		
Billy Standridge's Car		
Memorable Moment		
145 Robbie Loomis	.02	.10
146 Mark Martin	.30	.75
Victory Lane		
147 Harry Gant	.07	.20
Memorable Moment		
148 Bobby Labonte Crash	.15	.40
Memorable Moment		
149 David Green	.07	.20
BGN Champion		
Memorable Moment		
150 David Green	.07	.20
151 Ricky Craven	.07	.20
152 Chad Little	.07	.20
153 Kenny Wallace	.07	.20
154 Robert Pressley	.07	.20
155 Johnny Benson	.15	.40
156 Bobby Dotter	.07	.20
157 Larry Pearson	.02	.10
158 Dennis Setzer	.07	.20
159 Tim Fedewa	.07	.20
160 Jeff Burton	.25	.60
161 Rusty Wallace's Car	.15	.40
162 Mark Martin's Car	.25	.60
163 Ernie Irvan's Car	.07	.20
164 Ken Schrader's Car	.02	.10
165 Morgan Shepherd's Car	.02	.10
166 Ricky Rudd's Car	.07	.20
167 Michael Waltrip's Car	.07	.20
168 Ted Musgrave's Car	.02	.10
169 Jeff Gordon's Car	.30	.75
170 Lake Speed's Car	.02	.10
171 Kyle Petty's Car	.07	.20
172 Sterling Marlin's Car	.07	.20
173 Terry Labonte's Car	.15	.40
174 Darrell Waltrip's Car	.07	.20
175 Dale Jarrett's Car	.15	.40
176 Rick Mast's Car	.02	.10
177 Geoff Bodine's Car	.02	.10
178 Todd Bodine's Car	.02	.10
179 Hut Stricklin's Car	.02	.10
180 Checklist Card	.02	.10
181 Lake Speed	.07	.20
182 Loy Allen Jr.	.07	.20
183 Steve Grissom	.07	.20
184 Dick Trickle	.07	.20
185 Bobby Hamilton	.07	.20
186 John Andretti	.07	.20
187 Charles Hardy	.02	.10
188 Tony Gibson	.02	.10
189 Jeremy Mayfield's Car	.07	.20
190 Jeremy Mayfield	.15	.40
191 Ken Howes	.02	.10
192 Robin Pemberton	.02	.10
193 Chris Hussey	.02	.10
194 Bill Davis	.02	.10
195 Davy Jones	.07	.20
196 Randy LaJoie	.07	.20
197 Donnie Richeson	.02	.10
198 Tony Furr	.02	.10
199 Mike Hill	.02	.10
200 Elton Sawyer	.07	.20
201 Johnny Benson, Jr.	.15	.40
202 Bobby Dotter	.07	.20
203 Andy Petree	.02	.10
204 Ricky Rudd	.25	.60
205 Ricky Rudd's Car	.07	.20
206 Darrell Waltrip	.15	.40
207 Darrell Waltrip's Car	.07	.20
208 Chad Little	.07	.20
209 Hut Stricklin's Car	.02	.10
210 Hut Stricklin	.07	.20
211 Richard Broome	.02	.10
212 Geoff Bodine	.07	.20
213 Geoff Bodine's Car	.02	.10
214 Robert Pressley	.07	.20
215 Mark Martin	.60	1.50
216 Dale Jarrett	.50	1.25
217 Joe Nemechek	.07	.20
218 Joe Nemechek's Car	.02	.10
219 Joe Nemechek	.07	.20
220 Joe Nemechek's Car	.02	.10
221 Bill Elliott	.30	.75
222 Bill Elliott's Car	.15	.40
223 Brett Bodine	.07	.20
224 Brett Bodine's Car	.02	.10
225 Junior Johnson	.07	.20
226 Jimmy Spencer	.07	.20
227 Jimmy Spencer's Car	.02	.10
228 Travis Carter	.02	.10
229 Cecil Gordon	.02	.10
230 Terry Labonte	.25	.60
231 Terry Labonte's Car	.15	.40
232 Terry Labonte	.25	.60
233 Terry Labonte's Car	.15	.40
234 Kyle Petty	.15	.40
235 Kyle Petty's Car	.07	.20
236 Jeff Gordon	.75	2.00
237 Jeff Gordon's Car	.30	.75
238 Scott Lagasse's Truck	.02	.10
239 Scott Lagasse	.07	.20
240 Bobby Labonte	.50	1.25
241 Bobby Labonte's Car	.15	.40
242 David Green's Car	.02	.10
243 Bobby Labonte	.50	1.25
244 Michael Waltrip	.15	.40
245 Michael Waltrip's Car	.07	.20
246 Michael Waltrip	.15	.40
247 Michael Waltrip's Car	.07	.20
248 Ricky Craven	.07	.20
249 Ricky Craven's Car	.02	.10
250 Ricky Craven	.07	.20
251 Ricky Craven's Car	.02	.10
252 Ken Schrader	.07	.20
253 Ken Schrader's Car	.02	.10
254 Ken Schrader	.07	.20
255 Ken Schrader's Car	.02	.10
256 Ken Schrader	.07	.20
257 Ken Schrader's Truck	.02	.10
258 Ray Evernham	.15	.40
259 Joe Gibbs	.15	.40
260 Bob Jenkins	.02	.10
261 Jeff Fuller RC	.07	.20
262 Mike McLaughlin	.07	.20
263 Kenny Wallace	.07	.20
264 Cale Yarborough	.07	.20
265 Chuck Bown	.07	.20
266 Dave Marcis	.15	.40
267 Howard Comstock	.02	.10
268 Jimmy Means	.02	.1
269 Chad Little's Car	.02	.1
270 Checklist Card	.02	.1
P1G Jeff Gordon in Pits Promo	1.00	2.5
Gold Foil		
P1R Jeff Gordon in Pits Promo	1.50	4.0
Red Foil		
P2 Ricky Rudd Promo	.60	1.5
Series Two		
P3 Mark Martin	1.50	4.0
Steve Hmiel		
National Promo Sheet		

1995 Maxx Autographs

This 48-card set features 1995 Maxx series o cards autographed by some of the top personalit in NASCAR. The cards were randomly inserted 1995 Maxx series two packs. To guarantee authenticity, each signed card was crimped w Maxx's corporate seal which reads "J.R. Maxx I Corporate Seal 1988 North Carolina." Most of Johnny Benson cards were signed on the back.

COMPLETE SET (48)	500.00	800.0
5 Terry Labonte	12.50	30.0
7 Geoff Bodine	6.00	15.0
16 Ted Musgrave	6.00	15.0
21 Morgan Shepherd	6.00	15.0
22 Bobby Labonte	12.50	30.0
24 Jeff Gordon	50.00	100.0
25 Ken Schrader	15.00	30.0
30 Michael Waltrip	8.00	20.0
41 Joe Nemechek	6.00	15.0
42 Kyle Petty	12.50	30.0
96 Andy Petree	5.00	10.0
97 Larry McReynolds	6.00	15.0
100 Buddy Parrott	5.00	10.0
101 Steve Hmiel	5.00	10.0
103 Ken Howes	5.00	10.0
104 Leonard Wood	5.00	10.0
106 Bill Ingle	5.00	10.0
108 Doug Hewitt	5.00	10.0
110 Robin Pemberton	5.00	10.0
113 Donnie Wingo	5.00	10.0
114 Pete Peterson	5.00	10.0
116 Tony Glover	5.00	10.0
117 Gary DeHart	5.00	10.0
118 Jimmy Makar	5.00	10.0
120 Mike Beam	5.00	10.0
121 Kevin Hamlin	5.00	10.0
122 Paul Andrews	5.00	10.0
124 Chris Hussey	5.00	10.0
126 Jim Long	5.00	10.0
128 Donnie Richeson	5.00	10.0
130 Troy Selberg	5.00	10.0
131 Tony Furr	5.00	10.0
132 Mike Hill	5.00	10.0
135 Philippe Lopez	5.00	10.0
137 Jeff Hammond	6.00	15.0
138 Buddy Barnes	5.00	10.0
140 Charley Pressley	5.00	10.0
141 Doug Richert	5.00	10.0
143 Mike Hillman	5.00	10.0
145 Robbie Loomis	5.00	10.0
151 Ricky Craven	15.00	30.0
152 Chad Little	15.00	30.0
154 Robert Pressley	6.00	15.0
155 Johnny Benson	15.00	30.0
156 Bobby Dotter	5.00	10.0
157 Larry Pearson	6.00	15.0
158 Dennis Setzer	6.00	15.0
159 Tim Fedewa	6.00	15.0

1995 Maxx Chase the Champion

Dale Earnhardt Chase the Champion cards w distributed over Maxx's five major racing issues 1995: series one and two Maxx (1:36), Premier P (1:24), Premier Series (2 per factory set) a Medallion (1:18). The cards were consecutive numbered and include silver foil layering on t cardfront. Card number 1 was in series one pac cards numbered 2 and 3 were in Premier Series se cards numbered 4 and 5 were inserts in Premier P packs, cards numbered 6 and 7 were inserts series two packs, and numbers 8 through 10 w inserts in Medallion.

COMPLETE SET (10)	40.00	100.0
1 Dale Earnhardt	5.00	12.0
2 Dale Earnhardt	5.00	12.0
3 Dale Earnhardt	5.00	12.0
4 Dale Earnhardt's Car	5.00	12.0
5 Dale Earnhardt	5.00	12.0
6 Dale Earnhardt	5.00	12.0
7 Dale Earnhardt	5.00	12.0
Teresa Earnhardt		
8 Dale Earnhardt	5.00	12.0
9 Dale Earnhardt	5.00	12.0
Richard Childress		
Teresa Earnhardt		
10 Dale Earnhardt	5.00	12.0

1995 Maxx Bill Elliott Bat Chase

lliott's special ThunderBat paint scheme car is ocus of this ten-card set. Series two packs ided two of the Bat Chase insert cards ximately every 36 packs. These sets were also available thru Club Maxx for $5.99 in October. The sets were purchased immediately by both members and dealers. A glow-in-the-dark paint ised on the border of all ten cards. There was a autographed 8" X 10" version of Bill Elliott's derbat card. The card was signed in gold and available through the Maxx Club. Each of the raphed cards were numberd to 500.

PLETE SET (10)	15.00	30.00
MON CARD (1-10)	1.00	3.00
Bill Elliott's Thunderbat	40.00	80.00
utographed 8X10/500		

995 Maxx License to Drive

se to Drive inserts were distributed over three ucts with three different insertion ratios: Maxx s one (1:40), Maxx series two (2:36) and Maxx ier Plus (1:17). The five series two cards were bered with an LTD prefix. Crown Chrome ons of the five Premier Plus cards were also uced and inserted in Maxx Crown Chrome s at the rate of 1:22 packs.

PLETE SET (15)	20.00	50.00
P.MAXX SERIES 1 SET (5)	15.00	30.00
P.MAXX SERIES 2 (5)	10.00	20.00
P.MAXX PREM. PLUS (5)	20.00	40.00
WN CHROME 6-10: SAME PRICE		
ry Labonte's Car	5.00	10.00
rry Gant's Car	3.00	6.00
rling Marlin's Car	4.00	8.00
k Trickle's Car	2.50	5.00
Stricklin's Car	2.50	5.00
d Musgrave's Car	3.00	6.00
rk Martin's Car	6.00	12.00
rd Burton's Car	4.00	8.00
k Mast's Car	3.00	6.00
organ Shepherd's Car	3.00	6.00
ichael Waltrip's Car	2.00	4.00
arrell Waltrip's Car	2.00	4.00
eoff Bodine's Car	1.50	3.00
rett Bodine's Car	1.50	3.00
odd Bodine's Car	1.50	3.00

1995 Maxx Over the Wall

the Wall inserts feature pit scenes of top on Cup race teams. The cards were randomly ted in 1995 Maxx series one packs at the er stated rate of 1:20 packs.

PLETE SET (10)	15.00	40.00
Gordon in Pits	4.00	10.00
tt Bodine in Pits	.40	1.00
Stricklin in Pits	.40	1.00
e Petty in Pits	.75	2.00
rrell Waltrip in Pits	.75	2.00
nny Wallace in Pits	.40	1.00
Schrader in Pits	.40	1.00
Elliott in Pits	1.50	4.00
off Bodine in Pits	.40	1.00
erry Labonte in Pits	1.25	3.00

995 Maxx Stand Ups

six-card set features drivers and cars from on Cup. The cards were produced using a die stand-up" card design and were issued in al retail packs at the rate of one per pack.

PLETE SET (6)	1.25	3.00
1 Geoff Bodine	.15	.40
2 John Andretti's Car	.15	.40
Sterling Marlin's Car		
Geoff Bodine's Car		
3 Jeff Burton	.50	1.25
4 Ernie Irvan's Car	.15	.40
5 Rusty Wallace's Car	.30	.75
6 Richard Petty	.50	1.25

1995 Maxx SuperTrucks

SuperTrucks cards were distributed over three products with three different insertion ratios: Maxx series one (1:40), Maxx Premier Plus (1:17) and Maxx Medallion (1:2). The last 15 cards were numbered with an ST prefix. Unnumbered Crown Chrome versions of the five Premier Plus cards were also produced and inserted in Maxx Crown Chrome packs at the rate of 1:22 packs.

COMPLETE SET (20)	25.00	50.00
COMP.MAXX SET (5)	10.00	20.00
COMP.MAXX PREM. PLUS SET (5)	12.50	25.00
COMP.MAXX MEDALLION (10)	6.00	14.00
*CROWN CHROMES:SAME PRICE AS PREM.PLUS		
1 Mike Skinner's Truck	2.50	5.00
P.J.Jones' Truck		
2 Rick Carelli's Truck	2.00	4.00
3 Tobey Butler's Truck	2.00	4.00
C.Huartson's Truck		
4 Scott Lagasse's Truck	2.50	5.00
T.J.Clark's Truck		
5 Rick Carelli's Truck	2.00	4.00
6 Scott Lagasse's Truck	2.50	5.00
7 Ken Schrader's Truck	5.00	10.00
8 Geoff Bodine's Truck	5.00	10.00
9 Jerry Glanville's Truck	2.50	5.00
10 Rick Carelli's Truck	2.50	5.00
11 John Nemechek's Truck	.75	1.50
12 Sammy Swindell's Truck	.75	2.00
13 Bob Strait's Truck	.75	1.50
14 Mike Chase's Truck	.75	1.50
15 Walker Evans' Truck	.75	1.50
16 Bob Brevak's Truck	.75	1.50
17 Tobey Butler's Truck	.75	1.50
18 Steve Portenga's Truck	.75	1.50
19 Jerry Churchill's Truck	.75	1.50
20 Butch Miller's Truck	.75	1.50

1995 Maxx Top 5 of 2005

Top 5 of 2005 was an exclusive insert to 1995 Maxx series two. The cards were inserted at the wrapper stated rate of 2:36 and featured drivers Maxx felt could be top contenders ten years down the road.

COMPLETE SET (5)	3.00	8.00
TOP1 Ricky Craven	.30	.75
TOP2 Bobby Labonte	2.00	5.00
TOP3 Jason Keller	.60	1.50
TOP4 David Hutio	.30	.75
TOP5 Toby Porter	.30	.75

1995 Maxx Medallion

The second year of the Medallion brand features the "Colors of NASCAR" theme. The 61-card set consists of 30 of the top NASCAR drivers and their cars. Maxx produced 999 cases of this product, which came 18 packs per box with 8 cards per pack. Randomly inserted in packs were On the Road Again, Head-to-Head, Busch Grand National, SuperTrucks, Jeff Gordon Puzzles and the final three Dale Earnhardt Chase the Champion cards. Although the BGN and Head-to-Head cards are numbered differently, as if inserts, most consider the cards part of the regular issue bringing the number of cards in the set to an even 70. Maxx also included a special Checkered Flag Chase box, one per case, that contains parallel cards printed in blue foil.

COMPLETE SET (70)	8.00	20.00
WAX BOX	20.00	50.00
1 Rick Mast	.07	.20
2 Rusty Wallace	.60	1.50
3 Sterling Marlin	.25	.60
4 Terry Labonte	.25	.60
5 Mark Martin	.60	1.50
6 Geoff Bodine	.07	.20
7 Jeff Burton	.25	.60
8 Lake Speed	.07	.20
9 Ricky Rudd	.25	.60
10 Brett Bodine	.07	.20
11 Derrike Cope	.07	.20
12 Ted Musgrave	.07	.20
13 Darrell Waltrip	.15	.40
14 Bobby Labonte	.50	1.25
15 Morgan Shepherd	.07	.20
16 Jimmy Spencer	.07	.20
17 Jeff Gordon	.75	2.00
18 Ken Schrader	.07	.20
19 Hut Stricklin	.07	.20
20 Dale Jarrett	.50	1.25
21 Michael Waltrip	.15	.40
22 Ward Burton	.15	.40
23 John Andretti	.07	.20
24 Kyle Petty	.15	.40
25 Bobby Hamilton	.07	.20
26 Todd Bodine	.07	.20
27 Bobby Hillin	.07	.20
28 Joe Nemechek	.07	.20
29 Mike Wallace	.07	.20
30 Bill Elliott	.30	.75
31 Rick Mast's Car	.02	.10
32 Rusty Wallace's Car	.25	.60
33 Sterling Marlin's Car	.07	.20
34 Terry Labonte's Car	.15	.40
35 Mark Martin's Car	.25	.60
36 Geoff Bodine's Car	.02	.10
37 Jeff Burton's Car	.07	.20
38 Lake Speed's Car	.02	.10
39 Ricky Rudd's Car	.07	.20
40 Brett Bodine's Car	.02	.10
41 Derrike Cope's Car	.02	.10
42 Ted Musgrave's Car	.02	.10
43 Darrell Waltrip's Car	.07	.20
44 Bobby Labonte's Car	.15	.40
45 Morgan Shepherd's Car	.02	.10
46 Jimmy Spencer's Car	.02	.10
47 Jeff Gordon's Car	.40	1.00
48 Ken Schrader's Car	.02	.10
49 Hut Stricklin's Car	.02	.10
50 Dale Jarrett's Car	.15	.40
51 Michael Waltrip's Car	.07	.20
52 Ward Burton's Car	.02	.10
53 John Andretti's Car	.02	.10
54 Kyle Petty's Car	.07	.20
55 Bobby Hamilton's Car	.02	.10
56 Todd Bodine's Car	.02	.10
57 Bobby Hillin's Car	.02	.10
58 Joe Nemechek's Car	.02	.10
59 Mike Wallace's Car	.02	.10
60 Bill Elliott's Car	.15	.40
61 Checklist Card	.02	.10
P1 Ted Musgrave's Car Promo	1.25	3.00
BGN1 Johnny Benson	.15	.40
BGN2 Chad Little	.20	.50
BGN3 Jason Keller	.20	.50
BGN4 Mike McLaughlin	.20	.50
BGN5 Larry Pearson	.20	.50
HTH1 Ricky Craven	.20	.50
HTH2 Ricky Craven's Car	.20	.50
HTH3 Robert Pressley	.20	.50
HTH4 Robert Pressley's Car	.20	.50

1995 Maxx Medallion Blue

Blue foil parallel cards could be found only in Checkered Flag Chase boxes randomly packed in 1995 Maxx Medallion cases (one box per case). All 70 regular issue cards were produced with a special blue foil layering instead of gold.

COMPLETE BLUE SET (70)	100.00	200.00
*BLUE FOILS: 6X TO 12X BASE CARDS		

1995 Maxx Medallion Jeff Gordon Puzzle

Nine Jeff Gordon puzzle cards were produced for and distributed through 1995 Maxx Medallion. Although wrapper stated odds are 1:40, most pack breakers reported much easier ratios on the eight regular cards (numbers 1-3,5-9), about one in four packs, and a much tougher ratio on the short printed card (number 4), about one per case. The number 4 puzzle cards were inserted into the Checkered Flag Chase boxes. Once completed, the puzzle could be returned to Maxx in exchange for a signed 8" by 10" Jeff Gordon card. Maxx reports only 999 of the cards were signed and numbered. Since Maxx has gone out of business numerous extra signed Jeff Gordon photos have surfaced. We have had multiple reports of people having the same numbered photos of 999.

COMPLETE SET (9)	8.00	20.00
1 Jeff Gordon	.75	2.00
2 Jeff Gordon	.75	2.00
3 Jeff Gordon	.75	2.00
4 Jeff Gordon SP	2.50	6.00
5 Jeff Gordon	.75	2.00
6 Jeff Gordon	.75	2.00
7 Jeff Gordon	.75	2.00
8 Jeff Gordon	.75	2.00
9 Jeff Gordon	.75	2.00
NNO Jeff Gordon AUTO/999	60.00	120.00

1995 Maxx Medallion On the Road Again

Unlike many of the 1995 Maxx inserts, On the Road Again was exclusive to one product -- Maxx Medallion. The cards were packaged approximately one every two foil packs and feature top Winston Cup race teams' transporters.

COMPLETE SET (10)	5.00	10.00
OTR1 Ken Schrader's Trans.	.40	1.00
OTR2 Jeff Gordon's Transporter	.75	2.00
OTR3 Terry Labonte's Trans.	.60	1.50
OTR4 Steve Grissom's Trans.	.40	1.00
OTR5 Bill Elliott's Transporter	.60	1.50
OTR6 Jeff Burton's Transporter	.40	1.00
OTR7 Bobby Labonte's Trans.	.60	1.50
OTR8 Lake Speed's Transporter	.40	1.00
OTR9 Derrike Cope's Transporter	.40	1.00
OTR10 Ricky Rudd's Transporter	.60	1.50

1995 Maxx Premier Plus

Maxx again used its chromium printing technology to produce a Premier Plus issue. The cards were distributed in 7-card packs with 36 packs per foil box. In additon to a few new insert sets, Premier Plus included continuations to three other Maxx insert issues. A Crown Chrome parallel release was also produced and issued in its own packs. Crown Chrome came 6-cards to a pack with 24 packs per box. A special Silver Select Dale Earnhardt card was produced and distributed only through Crown Chrome and each was numbered of 750. Maxx reportedly limited production to 9000 numbered boxes.

COMPLETE SET (183)	10.00	25.00
1 Rick Mast	.10	.30
2 Rusty Wallace	1.00	2.50
3 Scott Lagasse	.10	.30
4 Sterling Marlin	.40	1.00
5 Terry Labonte	.50	1.25
6 Mark Martin	1.00	2.50
7 Geoff Bodine	.10	.30
8 Jeff Burton	.40	1.00
9 Ricky Craven	.25	.60
10 Ricky Rudd	.40	1.00
11 Bill Elliott	.50	1.25
12 Derrike Cope	.10	.30
13 Scott Lagasse's SuperTruck	.05	.15
14 Ken Schrader's SuperTruck	.05	.15
15 Lake Speed	.10	.30
16 Ted Musgrave	.10	.30
17 Darrell Waltrip	.25	.60
18 Dale Jarrett	.75	2.00
19 Loy Allen Jr.	.10	.30
20 Steve Kinser	.10	.30
21 Morgan Shepherd	.10	.30
22 Bobby Labonte	.75	2.00
23 Randy LaJoie	.10	.30
24 Jeff Gordon	1.25	3.00
25 Ken Schrader	.10	.30
26 Brett Bodine	.10	.30
27 Jimmy Spencer	.10	.30
28 Ernie Irvan	.25	.60
29 Steve Grissom	.10	.30
30 Michael Waltrip	.25	.60
31 Ward Burton	.25	.60
32 Dick Trickle	.10	.30
33 Harry Gant	.25	.60
34 Terry Labonte's Car	.25	.60
35 Mark Martin's Car	.40	1.00
36 Bobby Labonte's Car	.40	1.00
37 Rusty Wallace's Car	.40	1.00
38 Sterling Marlin's Car	.10	.30
39 Kyle Petty's Car	.10	.30
40 Bobby Hamilton	.10	.30
41 Joe Nemechek	.10	.30
42 Kyle Petty	.25	.60
43 Richard Petty	.40	1.00
44 Brett Bodine's Car	.05	.15
45 John Andretti	.10	.30
46 Todd Bodine's Car	.05	.15
47 Michael Waltrip's Car	.10	.30
48 Dale Jarrett's Car	.40	1.00
49 Joe Nemechek's Car	.05	.15
50 Morgan Shepherd's Car	.05	.15
51 Bill Elliott's Car	.25	.60
52 Ricky Craven's Car	.05	.15
53 Kenny Wallace	.10	.30
54 Bobby Hamilton's Car	.05	.15
55 Jimmy Hensley	.10	.30
56 Ken Schrader's Car	.05	.15
57 Steve Kinser's Car	.05	.15
58 Dick Trickle's Car	.05	.15
59 Ricky Rudd's Car	.10	.30
60 Robert Pressley's Car	.05	.15
61 Ted Musgrave's Car	.05	.15
62 Rick Mast's Car	.05	.15
63 Darrell Waltrip's Car	.10	.30
64 Jeff Gordon's Car	.60	1.50
65 Jeff Burton's Car	.10	.30
66 Geoff Bodine's Car	.05	.15
67 Jimmy Spencer's Car	.05	.15
68 Roger Penske	.05	.15
69 Don Miller	.05	.15
70 Jack Roush	.05	.15
71 Dave Marcis	.25	.60
72 Joe Gibbs	.25	.60
73 Junior Johnson	.10	.30
74 Rick Hendrick	.05	.15
75 Todd Bodine	.10	.30
76 Felix Sabates	.05	.15
77 Greg Sacks	.10	.30
78 Tim Morgan	.05	.15
79 Larry McClure	.05	.15
80 Glen Wood	.05	.15
81 Len Wood	.05	.15
82 Eddie Wood	.05	.15
83 Leo Jackson	.05	.15
84 Bobby Allison	.10	.30
85 Gary Bechtel	.05	.15
Carolyn Bechtel		
86 Bill Stavola	.05	.15
87 Mickey Stavola	.05	.15
88 Walter Bud Moore	.05	.15
89 Chuck Rider	.05	.15
90 Mike Wallace	.10	.30
91 Bill Davis	.05	.15
92 Kenny Bernstein	.10	.30
93 Richard Jackson	.05	.15
94 D.K. Ulrich	.05	.15
95 Cale Yarborough	.10	.30
96 Junie Donlavey	.05	.15
97 Larry Hedrick	.05	.15
98 Jeremy Mayfield	.25	.60
99 Robert Yates	.05	.15
100 Travis Carter	.05	.15
101 Butch Mock	.05	.15
102 Dick Brooks	.05	.15
103 Andy Petree	.05	.15
104 Buddy Parrott	.05	.15
105 Steve Hmiel	.05	.15
106 Jimmy Makar	.05	.15
107 Robin Pemberton	.05	.15
108 Jeff Hammond	.05	.15
109 Tony Glover	.05	.15
110 Leonard Wood	.05	.15
111 Mike Beam	.05	.15
112 Mike Hill	.05	.15
113 Gary DeHart	.05	.15
114 Ray Evernham	.05	.15
115 Ken Howes	.05	.15
116 Bill Ingle	.05	.15
117 Pete Peterson	.05	.15
118 Cecil Gordon	.05	.15
119 Donnie Wingo	.05	.15
120 Doug Hewitt	.05	.15
121 Donnie Richeson	.05	.15
122 Richard Broome	.05	.15
123 Kevin Hamlin	.05	.15
124 Charley Pressley	.05	.15
125 Larry McReynolds	.05	.15
126 Paul Andrews	.05	.15
127 Robbie Loomis	.05	.15
128 Troy Selberg	.05	.15
129 Jimmy Fennig	.05	.15
130 Barry Dodson	.05	.15
131 David Green	.10	.30
132 Ricky Craven	.10	.30
133 Chad Little	.10	.30
134 Kenny Wallace	.10	.30
135 Bobby Dotter	.10	.30
136 Tracy Leslie	.10	.30
137 Larry Pearson	.10	.30
138 Dennis Setzer	.10	.30
139 Robert Pressley	.10	.30
140 Johnny Benson Jr.	.25	.60
141 Terry Labonte	.40	1.00
142 Terry Labonte's Car	.25	.60
143 Ken Schrader	.10	.30
144 Ken Schrader's Car	.05	.15
145 Joe Nemechek	.10	.30
146 Joe Nemechek's Car	.05	.15
147 Jeff Gordon	.60	1.50
Victory Lane		
148 Sterling Marlin	.40	1.00
Victory Lane		
149 Rusty Wallace	.40	1.00
Victory Lane		
150 Ernie Irvan	.10	.30
Victory Lane		
151 Ernie Irvan	.10	.30
Victory Lane		
152 Darlington	.05	.15
Victory Lane		
153 Rusty Wallace in Pits	.40	1.00
Victory Lane		
154 Terry Labonte	.25	.60
Victory Lane		
155 Rusty Wallace	.40	1.00
Victory Lane		
156 Talladega Speedway	.05	.15
Victory Lane		
157 Ernie Irvan w/Crew	.10	.30
Victory Lane		
158 Jeff Gordon	.60	1.50
Victory Lane		
159 Geoff Bodine	.10	.30
Victory Lane		
160 Jeff Gordon	.60	1.50
Victory Lane		
161 Rusty Wallace	.40	1.00
Victory Lane		
162 Rusty Wallace	.40	1.00
Victory Lane		
163 Rusty Wallace	.40	1.00
Victory Lane		
164 Jimmy Spencer	.10	.30
Victory Lane		
165 Ricky Rudd w/Crew	.40	1.00
Victory Lane		
166 Geoff Bodine	.10	.30
Victory Lane		
167 Jimmy Spencer	.10	.30
Victory Lane		
168 Jeff Gordon	.60	1.50
Victory Lane		
169 Mark Martin	.40	1.00
Victory Lane		
170 Geoff Bodine	.10	.30
Victory Lane		
171 Rusty Wallace	.40	1.00
Victory Lane		
172 Bill Elliott	.25	.60
Junior Johnson		
Victory Lane		
173 Terry Labonte	.25	.60
Victory Lane		
174 Rusty Wallace	.40	1.00
Victory Lane		
175 Rusty Wallace	.40	1.00
Victory Lane		
176 Geoff Bodine	.10	.30
Victory Lane		
177 Dale Jarrett	.40	1.00
(Victory Lane		
178 Rockingham Race Action	.05	.15
Victory Lane		
179 Terry Labonte	.25	.60
Victory Lane		
180 Mark Martin	.40	1.00
Victory Lane		
181 Jeff Burton	.40	1.00
Rookie of the Year		
182 Checklist #1	.05	.15
183 Checklist #2	.05	.15
P1 Darrell Waltrip Promo	.60	1.50
Premier Plus Card		
SS1 Dale Earnhardt	30.00	60.00
Silver Select/750		

1995 Maxx Premier Plus Crown Chrome

Crown Chrome is a parallel issue to Maxx's Premier Plus chromium card series. The art used on both sets is identical, but Crown Chrome was produced on clear plastic stock. All the same inserts were produced and packaged as 1995 Premier Plus. Packaging was done 6-cards per pack with 24 packs per box. None of the cards were numbered. The two checklist cards from Premier Plus were done on four Crown Chrome cards increasing the set to 185 total cards. A special Silver Select Dale Earnhardt card was produced and distributed only through Crown Chrome and was numbered of 750. Maxx reportedly limited production to 9000 numbered boxes.

COMPLETE SET (185)	10.00	25.00
*CROWN CHROMES: .4X TO 1X PREM.PLUS		

1995 Maxx Premier Plus PaceSetters

PaceSetter inserts were exclusive to the Maxx Premier Plus and Crown Chrome parallel issues. The cards were packaged approximately 1:17 packs in Premier Plus packs..

COMPLETE SET (9)	25.00	60.00
*CROWN CHROME: .4X TO 1X BASIC INSERTS		
PS1 Mark Martin	5.00	12.00
PS2 Rusty Wallace	5.00	12.00
PS3 Ken Schrader	.60	1.50
PS4 Ricky Rudd	2.00	5.00
PS5 Morgan Shepherd	.60	1.50
PS6 Terry Labonte	2.50	6.00
PS7 Jeff Gordon	6.00	15.00
PS8 Darrell Waltrip	1.25	3.00
PS9 Bill Elliott	2.50	6.00

1995 Maxx Premier Plus Series Two Previews

Five cards were produced to preview the 1995 Maxx series two set. The cards were randomly inserted in Premier Plus packs at the rate of 1:17 packs.

COMPLETE SET (5)	4.00	10.00
*CROWN CHROME: .4X TO 1X BASIC INSERTS		
PRE1 Lake Speed	.75	2.00
PRE2 Jimmy Spencer	.75	2.00
PRE3 Steve Grissom	.75	2.00
PRE4 Dale Jarrett	1.50	4.00
PRE5 Dick Trickle	.75	2.00

1995 Maxx Premier Plus Top Hats

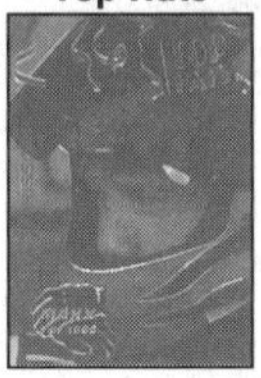

Five cards were produced by Maxx to honor top young Winston Cup drivers. The cards were randomly inserted in Premier Plus packs at the rate of 1:17 packs. A Crown Chrome parallel version was also produced and inserted in packs at the approximate rate of 1:22. Each Top Hat card is numbered 1 of 1995.

COMPLETE SET (5)	5.00	12.00
*CROWN CHROME: .4X TO 1X BASIC INSERTS		
TH1 Ted Musgrave	1.00	2.50

TH2 Ward Burton	1.50	4.00
TH3 Steve Grissom	1.00	2.50
TH4 Jimmy Spencer	1.00	2.50
TH5 Brett Bodine	1.00	2.50

1995 Maxx Premier Plus Retail Jumbos

This six-card set feature jumbo sized cards (3 1/2" X 5") of some of the best Winston Cup drivers. The cards use the Premier Plus chromium printing technology. Originally the cards were only available through Kmart stores but were later distributed via the Maxx Club. In the blister Kmart packs, Jumbo cards came one per along with two 1995 Maxx series one packs and one Texaco Ernie Irvan pack. The cards are unnumbered and checklisted below in alphabetical order.

COMPLETE SET (6)	4.00	10.00
1 Geoff Bodine	.20	.50
2 Jeff Burton	.60	1.50
3 Mark Martin	1.50	4.00
4 Ricky Rudd	.60	1.50
5 Morgan Shepherd	.20	.50
6 Rusty Wallace	1.50	4.00

1995 Maxx Premier Series

Club Maxx members had the chance to purchase the 1995 Maxx Premier Series set directly from Maxx for $64.95 plus shipping charges. Non-members could buy the set for $69.95 plus shipping. Production was limited to 45,000 numbered sets and each factory set included two Dale Earnhardt Chase the Champion cards (#2-3). These Earnhardt cards are priced in the 1995 MAXX Chase the Champion listings. A special gold foil embossed binder to house the set was offered for sale as well.

COMPLETE SET (300)	20.00	40.00
COMPLETE FACT. SET (302)	40.00	80.00
1 Rick Mast	.15	.40
2 Rusty Wallace	1.25	3.00
3 Jeff Gordon's Car	.60	1.50
Memorable Moment		
4 Sterling Marlin	.50	1.25
5 Terry Labonte	.50	1.25
6 Mark Martin	1.25	3.00
7 Geoff Bodine	.15	.40
8 Jeff Burton	.50	1.25
9 Ricky Craven	.15	.40
10 Ricky Rudd	.50	1.25
11 Bill Elliott	.60	1.50
12 Derrike Cope	.15	.40
13 Todd Bodine's Car	.07	.20
Memorable Moment		
14 Tire Wars	.07	.20
Tech Card		
15 Lake Speed	.15	.40
16 Ted Musgrave	.15	.40
17 Darrell Waltrip	.30	.75
18 Dale Jarrett	1.00	2.50
18 Ernie Irvan	.30	.75
19 Loy Allen Jr.	.15	.40
20 Steve Kinser	.15	.40
21 Morgan Shepherd	.15	.40
22 Bobby Labonte	1.00	2.50
23 Randy LaJoie	.15	.40
24 Jeff Gordon	2.00	4.00
25 Ken Schrader	.15	.40
26 Brett Bodine	.15	.40
27 Jimmy Spencer	.15	.40
28 Ernie Irvan	.30	.75
29 Steve Grissom	.15	.40
30 Michael Waltrip	.30	.75
31 Ward Burton	.15	.40
32 Dick Trickle	.15	.40
33 Harry Gant	.30	.75
34 Terry Labonte's Car	.30	.75
35 Mark Martin's Car	.50	1.25
36 Bobby Labonte's Car	.30	.75
37 Rusty Wallace's Car	.50	1.25
38 Sterling Marlin's Car	.15	.40
39 Kyle Petty's Car	.15	.40
40 Bobby Hamilton	.15	.40
41 Joe Nemechek	.15	.40
42 Kyle Petty	.30	.75
43 Richard Petty	.50	1.25
44 Bobby Hillin	.15	.40
45 John Andretti	.15	.40
46 Scott Lagasse	.15	.40
47 Billy Standridge	.15	.40
48 Dale Jarrett's Car	.50	1.25
49 Joe Nemechek's Car	.07	.20
50 Morgan Shepherd's Car	.07	.20
51 Bill Elliott's Car	.30	.75
52 Ricky Craven's Car	.07	.20
53 Kenny Wallace	.15	.40
54 John Andretti's Car	.07	.20
55 Jimmy Hensley	.15	.40
56 Ken Schrader's Car	.07	.20
57 Scott Lagasse's SuperTruck	.07	.20
58 Dick Trickle's Car	.07	.20
59 Ricky Rudd's Car	.15	.40
60 Robert Pressley's Car	.07	.20
61 Ted Musgrave's Car	.07	.20
62 Rick Mast's Car	.07	.20
63 Darrell Waltrip's Car	.15	.40
64 Jeff Gordon's Car	.60	1.50
65 Jeff Burton's Car	.15	.40
66 Geoff Bodine's Car	.07	.20
67 Jimmy Spencer's Car	.07	.20
68 Todd Bodine's Car	.07	.20
69 Michael Waltrip's Car	.15	.40
70 Brett Bodine's Car	.07	.20
71 Dave Marcis	.30	.75
72 Steve Kinser's Car	.07	.20
73 Mike Wallace's Car	.07	.20
74 Maxx Card's Car	.07	.20
75 Todd Bodine	.15	.40
76 Ward Burton's Car	.07	.20
77 Greg Sacks	.15	.40
78 Jeremy Mayfield's Car	.15	.40
79 Loy Allen Jr.'s Car	.07	.20
80 Roger Penske	.07	.20
81 Don Miller	.07	.20
82 Jack Roush	.07	.20
83 Joe Gibbs	.30	.75
84 Felix Sabates	.07	.20
85 Tim Morgan	.07	.20
86 Larry McClure	.07	.20
87 Teddy McClure	.07	.20
Jerry McClure		
Ed McClure		
88 Glen Wood	.07	.20
89 Len Wood	.07	.20
90 Mike Wallace	.15	.40
91 Eddie Wood	.07	.20
92 Junior Johnson	.15	.40
93 Rick Hendrick	.07	.20
94 Leo Jackson	.07	.20
95 Bobby Allison	.15	.40
96 Gary Bechtel	.07	.20
Carolyn Bechtel		
97 Bill Stavola	.07	.20
98 Jeremy Mayfield	.30	.75
99 Mickey Stavola	.07	.20
100 Walter Bud Moore	.07	.20
101 Chuck Rider	.07	.20
102 Ken Schrader's SuperTruck	.07	.20
103 Bill Davis	.07	.20
104 Kenny Bernstein	.15	.40
105 Richard Jackson	.07	.20
106 Ray DeWitt	.07	.20
Diane DeWitt		
107 D.K. Ulrich	.07	.20
108 Cale Yarborough	.15	.40
109 Junie Donlavey	.07	.20
110 Larry Hedrick	.07	.20
111 Robert Yates	.07	.20
112 George Bradshaw	.07	.20
113 Mark Smith	.07	.20
114 David Fuge	.07	.20
115 Travis Carter	.07	.20
116 A.G. Dillard	.07	.20
117 Butch Mock	.07	.20
118 Harry Melling	.07	.20
119 Dick Moroso	.07	.20
120 Dick Brooks	.07	.20
121 Roof Flaps	.07	.20
Tech Card		
122 Andy Petree	.07	.20
123 Buddy Parrott	.07	.20
124 Steve Hmiel	.07	.20
125 Jimmy Makar	.07	.20
126 Robin Pemberton	.07	.20
127 Jeff Hammond	.07	.20
128 Tony Glover	.07	.20
129 Leonard Wood	.07	.20
130 Mike Beam	.07	.20
131 Mike Hill	.07	.20
132 Gary DeHart	.07	.20
133 Ray Evernham	.30	.75
134 Ken Howes	.07	.20
135 Bill Ingle	.07	.20
136 Pete Peterson	.07	.20
137 Cecil Gordon	.07	.20
138 Donnie Wingo	.07	.20
139 Doug Hewitt	.07	.20
140 Phillippe Lopez	.07	.20
141 Chris Hussey	.07	.20
142 Donnie Richeson	.07	.20
143 Richard Broome	.07	.20
144 Kevin Hamlin	.07	.20
145 Ken Glen	.07	.20
146 Charley Pressley	.07	.20
147 Tony Furr	.07	.20
148 Larry McReynolds	.07	.20
149 Dale Fischlein	.07	.20
150 Paul Andrews	.07	.20
151 Robbie Loomis	.07	.20
152 Mike Hillman	.07	.20
153 Troy Selberg	.07	.20
154 Jimmy Fennig	.07	.20
155 Barry Dodson	.07	.20
156 Waddell Wilson	.07	.20
157 Dale Inman	.07	.20
158 Charlie Smith	.07	.20
159 David Green	.15	.40
160 David Green's Car	.07	.20
161 Ricky Craven	.15	.40
162 Ricky Craven's Car	.07	.20
163 Chad Little	.15	.40
164 Chad Little's Car	.07	.20
165 Kenny Wallace	.15	.40
166 Bobby Dotter	.15	.40
167 Tracy Leslie	.15	.40
168 Larry Pearson	.15	.40
169 Dennis Setzer	.15	.40
170 Robert Pressley	.15	.40
171 Johnny Benson Jr.	.15	.40
172 Tim Fedewa	.15	.40
173 Mike McLaughlin	.15	.40
174 Jim Bown	.15	.40
175 Elton Sawyer	.15	.40
176 Jason Keller	.15	.40
177 Rodney Combs	.15	.40
178 Doug Heveron	.15	.40
179 Tommy Houston	.15	.40
180 Kevin Lepage	.15	.40
181 Dirk Stephens	.15	.40
182 Stevie Reeves	.15	.40
183 Phil Parsons	.15	.40
184 Ernie Irvan's Car	.15	.40
Jimmy Spencer's Car		
Memorable Moment		
185 Shawna Robinson	.60	1.50
186 Patty Moise	.15	.40
187 Terry Labonte	.50	1.25
188 Terry Labonte's Car	.30	.75
189 Ken Schrader	.15	.40
190 Ken Schrader's Car	.07	.20
191 Joe Nemechek	.15	.40
192 Joe Nemechek's Car	.07	.20
193 Bobby Hillin's Car	.07	.20
Billy Standridge Cars		
Memorable Moment		
194 Barney Hall	.07	.20
195 Eli Gold	.07	.20
196 Benny Parsons	.15	.40
197 Dr. Jerry Punch	.07	.20
198 Buddy Baker	.15	.40
199 Mike Joy	.07	.20
200 Winston Kelley	.07	.20
201 Jim Phillips	.07	.20
202 John Kernan	.07	.20
203 Randy Pemberton	.07	.20
204 Bill Weber	.07	.20
205 Joe Moore	.07	.20
206 Mark Garrow	.07	.20
207 Allen Bestwick	.07	.20
208 Glenn Jarrett	.07	.20
209 Pat Patterson	.07	.20
210 Dr. Dick Berggren	.07	.20
211 Harry Gant MM	.15	.40
212 Ken Squier	.07	.20
213 Bobby Labonte's Car	.30	.75
Bobby Hamilton's Car		
Rick Mast's Car		
Memorable Moment		
214 Mike Helton	.07	.20
215 Gary Nelson	.07	.20
216 Ray Hill	.07	.20
217 Carl Hill	.07	.20
218 Brian DeHart	.07	.20
219 Jack Whittemore	.07	.20
220 Jimmy Cox	.07	.20
221 Bruce Roney	.07	.20
222 Marlin Wright	.07	.20
223 David Hoots	.07	.20
224 Tim Earp	.07	.20
225 Doyle Ford	.07	.20
226 Buster Auton	.07	.20
227 Elmo Langley	.07	.20
228 Walt Green	.07	.20
229 Gary Miller	.07	.20
230 Morris Metcalfe	.07	.20
231 Rich Burgdoff	.07	.20
232 Jeff Burton	.30	.75
Ward Burton		
Memorable Moment		
233 Larry McReynolds	.07	.20
All Pro		
234 Troy Martin	.07	.20
All Pro		
235 Dan Ford	.07	.20
All Pro		
236 Bill Wilburn	.07	.20
{All Pro		
237 Raymond Fox III	.07	.20
All Pro		
238 David Smith	.07	.20
All Pro		
239 Robert Yates	.07	.20
All Pro		
240 Darrell Andrews	.07	.20
All Pro		
241 Glen Bobo	.07	.20
{All Pro		
242 James Lewter	.07	.20
All Pro		
243 Norman Koshimizu	.07	.20
All Pro		
244 Eric Horn	.07	.20
All Pro		
245 Joe Dan Bailey	.07	.20
All Pro		
246 Joe Lewis	.07	.20
All Pro		
247 Danny Lawrence	.07	.20
All Pro		
248 Slick Poston	.07	.20
All Pro		
249 Derrike Cope's Car	.15	.40
Terry Labonte's Car		
Memorable Moment		
250 David Rogers' Car	.07	.20
WRS National Champion		
251 Mark Burgtorf	.07	.20
David Rogers		
252 Dale Planck	.07	.20
John Knaus		
253 Barry Beggarly	.07	.20
Charlie Cragen		
254 Larry Phillips	.07	.20
Paul Peeples Jr.		
255 David Green	.15	.40
BGN Champion		
256 Johnny Benson Jr.	.15	.40
BGN Rookie of the Year		
257 Jeff Gordon w/Crew	1.00	2.50
Pit Crew Champions		
258 Ray Evernham	.07	.20
Crew Chief of the Year		
259 Jeff Burton	.15	.40
WC Rookie of the Year		
260 Bill Elliott	.30	.75
Fans' Favorite Driver		
261 Mark Martin	.60	1.50
IROC Champion		
262 Jeff Gordon	.75	2.00
Year in Review		
263 Sterling Marlin	.30	.75
Year in Review		
264 Rusty Wallace	.60	1.50
Year in Review		
265 Ernie Irvan	.15	.40
Year in Review		
266 Ernie Irvan	.15	.40
Year in Review		
267 Darlington Speedway	.07	.20
Year in Review		
268 Rusty Wallace in Pits	.50	1.25
Year in Review		
269 Terry Labonte	.30	.75
Year in Review		
270 Rusty Wallace	.60	1.50
Year in Review		
271 Talladega Speedway	.07	.20
Year in Review		
272 Ernie Irvan w/Crew	.15	.40
Year in Review		
273 Jeff Gordon	.75	2.00
Year in Review		
274 Geoff Bodine	.15	.40
Year in Review		
275 Jeff Gordon	.75	2.00
Year in Review		
276 Rusty Wallace	.60	1.50
Year in Review		
277 Rusty Wallace	.60	1.50
Year in Review		
278 Rusty Wallace	.60	1.50
Year in Review		
279 Jimmy Spencer	.15	.40
Year in Review		
280 Ricky Rudd w/ Crew	.30	.75
Year in Review		
281 Geoff Bodine	.15	.40
Year in Review		
282 Jimmy Spencer	.15	.40
Year in Review		
283 Jeff Gordon	.75	2.00
Year in Review		
284 Mark Martin	.60	1.50
Jack Roush		
Year in Review		
285 Geoff Bodine	.15	.40
Year in Review		
286 Rusty Wallace	.60	1.50
Year in Review		
287 Bill Elliott	.30	.75
Junior Johnson		
Year in Review		
288 Terry Labonte	.30	.75
Year in Review		
289 Rusty Wallace w/ Crew	.60	1.50
Year in Review		
290 Rusty Wallace	.60	1.50
Year in Review		
291 Geoff Bodine	.15	.40
Year in Review		
292 Dale Jarrett	.50	1.25
Year in Review		
293 Rockingham Speedway	.07	.20
Year in Review		
294 Terry Labonte	.30	.75
Year in Review		
295 Mark Martin	.60	1.50
{Year in Review		
296 Bobby Labonte Crash	.30	.75
Memorable Moment		
297 Phoenix International	.07	.20
{Memorable Moment		
Tearin' Down The Walls		
298 Checklist #1	.07	.20
299 Checklist #2	.07	.20
300 Checklist #3	.07	.20
P1G Jeff Burton Gold Promo	.40	1.00
P1R Jeff Burton Red Promo	1.25	3.00

1995 Maxx Premier Series Update

This 15-card set is an update to the regular 300 card Premier Series set. The set is packaged in a brown box and was primarily distributed through the Maxx Club.

COMPLETE SET (15)	2.50	5.00
1 Loy Allen	.15	.40
2 Elton Sawyer	.15	.40
3 Hut Stricklin	.15	.40
4 Ward Burton	.30	.75
5 Bobby Hillin	.15	.40
6 Dave Marcis	.30	.75
7 Greg Sacks	.15	.40
8 Jeremy Mayfield	.30	.75
9 Mike Beam	.07	.20
10 Ricky Craven	.15	.40
11 Robert Pressley	.15	.40
12 Ernie Irvan	.30	.75
13 Ernie Irvan in Pits	.15	.40
14 Ernie Irvan's Car	.15	.40
15 Checklist	.07	.20

1995 Maxx Larger than Life Dale Earnhardt

This seven-card set is a 8" X 10" version of card numbers 1-7 of the regular Chase the Champions set. The regular size card #8 from the Maxx Dale Earnhardt Chase the Champion series came along with the seven jumbo cards in a large foil pack. There were a reported 20,000 packs produced. The cards were primarily distributed through the Maxx Club.

COMPLETE SET (7)	15.00	30.00
COMMON CARD (1-7)	2.00	5.00

1996 Maxx

The 1996 Maxx set has a total of 100 cards. The 10-card packs were distributed 36-packs per foil box. The set features the topical subset Memorable Moments (numbers 34, 36, 50, 61, 70, 97 and 98) and closes with checklist cards (numbers 99-100). A wide assortment of insert cards were randomly packed as well. Sterling Marlin was featured on the 1996 Maxx series one wrapper.

COMPLETE SET (100)	6.00	15.00
1 Rick Mast	.07	.20
2 Rusty Wallace	.50	1.25
3 Dale Earnhardt	1.00	2.50
4 Sterling Marlin	.25	.60
5 Terry Labonte	.25	.60
6 Mark Martin	.50	1.25
7 Geoff Bodine	.07	.20
8 Jeff Burton	.25	.60
9 Lake Speed	.07	.20
10 Ricky Rudd	.25	.60
11 Brett Bodine	.07	.20
12 Derrike Cope	.07	.20
13 Joe Nemechek's Car	.02	.10
14 Jimmy Spencer's Car	.02	.10
15 Dick Trickle	.07	.20
16 Ted Musgrave	.07	.20
17 Darrell Waltrip	.15	.40
18 Bobby Labonte	.50	1.25
19 Geoff Bodine's Car	.02	.10
20 Rick Mast's Car	.02	.10
21 Morgan Shepherd	.07	.20
22 Bobby Labonte's Car	.15	.40
23 Jimmy Spencer	.07	.20
24 Jeff Gordon	.60	1.50
25 Ken Schrader	.07	.20
26 Hut Stricklin	.07	.20
27 Darrell Waltrip's Car	.07	.20
28 Dale Jarrett	.50	1.25
29 Steve Grissom	.07	.20
30 Michael Waltrip	.15	.40
31 Kyle Petty's Car	.07	.20
32 Bill Elliott's Car	.15	.40
33 Robert Pressley	.07	.20
34 Jimmy Hensley's Car	.02	.10
Greg Sacks' Car		
Rockingham Rumble		
Memorable Moment		
35 Terry Labonte's Car	.15	.40
36 Ride Across America MM	.02	.10
37 John Andretti	.07	.20
38 Ricky Rudd's Car	.07	.20
39 Michael Waltrip's Car	.07	.20
40 Bobby Hamilton's Car	.02	.10
41 Ricky Craven	.07	.20
42 Kyle Petty	.15	.40
43 Richard Petty	.25	.60
44 Bobby Hamilton	.07	.20
45 Derrike Cope's Car	.02	.10
46 Steve Grissom's Car	.02	.10
47 John Andretti's Car	.02	.10
48 Dale Jarrett's Car	.15	.40
49 Ken Schrader's Car	.02	.10
50 Promising Pole Position MM	.02	.10
51 Morgan Shepherd's Car	.02	.10
52 Robert Yates	.02	.10
53 Rusty Wallace's Car	.25	.60
54 Mark Martin's Car	.25	.60
55 Roger Penske	.02	.10
Don Miller		
56 Ricky Craven's Car	.02	.10
57 Robert Pressley's Car	.02	.10
58 Len Wood	.02	.10
Kim Wood		
Eddie Wood		
Glen Wood		
59 Jeff Burton's Car	.07	.20
60 Richard Jackson	.02	.10
61 Elton Sawyer's Car	.02	.10
Lake Speed's Car		
Bitten By The Monster Mile		
Memorable Moment		
62 Brett Bodine's Car	.02	.10
63 Ted Musgrave's Car	.02	.10
64 Lake Speed's Car	.02	.10
65 Jack Roush	.02	.10
66 Rick Hendrick	.02	.10
67 Chuck Rider	.02	.10
68 Charles Hardy	.02	.10
69 Joe Gibbs	.15	.40
70 Mark Martin's Car	.25	.60
Testing In The Rain MM		
71 Junior Johnson	.07	.20
72 Travis Carter	.02	.10
73 Bobby Allison	.07	.20
74 Johnny Benson Jr.	.15	.40
75 Chad Little	.07	.20
76 Jason Keller	.07	.20
77 Mike McLaughlin	.07	.20
78 Jeff Green	.07	.20
79 Leonard Wood	.02	.10
80 Ray Evernham	.15	.40
81 Bill Ingle	.02	.10
82 Doug Hewitt	.02	.10
83 Robbie Loomis	.02	.10
84 Andy Petree	.02	.10
85 Larry McReynolds	.02	.10
86 Steve Hmiel	.02	.10
87 Joe Nemechek	.07	.20
88 Jeff Gordon's Car	.25	.60
89 Robin Pemberton	.02	.10
90 Mike Beam	.02	.10
91 Ken Howes	.02	.10
92 Howard Comstock	.02	.10
93 Tony Glover	.02	.10
94 Bill Elliott	.30	.75
95 Gary DeHart	.02	.10
96 Jimmy Makar	.02	.10
97 Ted Musgrave's Car	.02	.10
Riding The Wall MM		
98 Dale Jarrett's Car	.15	.40
Ernie Irvan's Car		
On The Comeback Trail MM		
99 Checklist (1-100)	.02	.10
100 Checklist (Chase Cards)	.02	.10
P1 Sterling Marlin Promo	.75	2.00
P2 Terry Labonte	2.00	5.00
Maxx Signed, Sealed,		
Delivered Promo		
P3 Dale Jarrett Promo	1.50	4.00
National 4-Card Sheet		
P4 Steve Grissom Promo	.75	2.00
National 4-Card Sheet		

1996 Maxx Chase the Champion

For the second year, Maxx produced an insert set honoring the previous season's Winston Cup champion. The Chase the Champion cards were distributed over the course of 1996 in various Maxx racing card products. Series one packs contained card #1 at the wrapper stated rate of one in 36. Cards #2 and 3 were inserted in factory sets of '96 Maxx Premier Plus. Cards # 4, 5 and 6 were randomly inserted in packs of '96 Maxx Odyssey at a ra one per 18 packs. Card # 8 was found in Maxx in America packs. Cards #7 and 9-14 were sup to be distributed through packs of Maxx pro scheduled to be released in the second half year. Since Maxx filed for bankruptcy those pro never made it to the market. But the card already been printed and quantities of those did become available in the secondary market.

COMPLETE SET (14)	30.00	8
COMMON CARD	4.00	1

1996 Maxx Family Tie

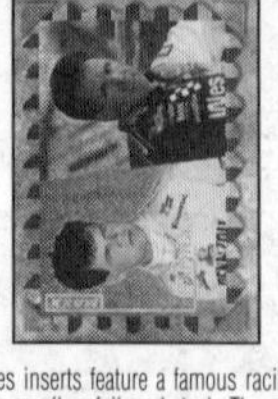

Family Ties inserts feature a famous racing connection on silver foil card stock. The cards randomly inserted in packs at the rate of one in

COMPLETE SET (5)	6.00	1
MINOR STARS	1.50	
FT1 Geoff Bodine	1.00	
Brett Bodine		
Todd Bodine		
FT2 Jeff Burton	1.00	
Ward Burton		
FT3 Terry Labonte	3.00	
Bobby Labonte		
FT4 Rusty Wallace	3.00	
Mike Wallace		
Kenny Wallace		
FT5 Darrell Waltrip	1.50	
Michael Waltrip		

1996 Maxx Sterling Marlin

Randomly inserted in packs at a rate of one in redemption card was issued to be exchanged f 5-card set devoted to Sterling Marlin. The expi date for the exchange card was May 1, 1996.

COMPLETE SET (5)	2.00
COMMON CARD (1-5)	.50

1996 Maxx On The Ro Again

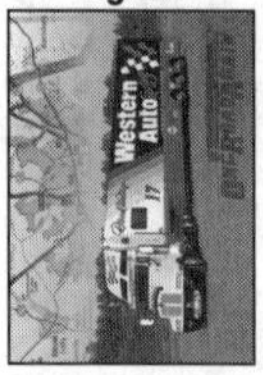

Transporters were again the focus of Maxx's Road inserts. The first five cards of the series randomly inserted in packs at the rate of one packs.

COMPLETE SET (5)	1.50
OTRA1 Kyle Petty's Transporter	.30
OTRA2 Busch Grand National	.30
Transporter	
OTRA3 Rusty Wallace's Trans.	.60
OTRA4 Darrell Waltrip's Trans.	.30
OTRA5 Winston Cup Transporter	.30

1996 Maxx Over the Wall

The 1995 Unocal 76/Rockingham Championship Pit Crew Competition was the of this 10-card Maxx insert set. The cards in the featured pit crew's best time in the comp printed in blue foil. They were randomly inser Maxx packs at the rate of 1:12.

COMPLETE SET (10)	4.00
OTW1 Brett Bodine's Car	.50
OTW2 Kyle Petty's Car	.50
OTW3 Jeff Burton's Car	1.00
OTW4 Derrike Cope's Car	.50
OTW5 Terry Labonte's Car	1.25
OTW6 Geoff Bodine's Car	.50
OTW7 Bobby Labonte's Car	1.50
OTW8 Joe Nemechek's Car	.50
OTW9 Ricky Rudd's Car	1.00
OTW10 Todd Bodine's Car	.50

1996 Maxx Sam Bas

This eight card set consists of Four Driver's an cars, with art work featuring Sam Bass.

COMPLETE SET (8)	3.00
1 Jeff Gordon	2.00
2 Jeff Gordon's Car	.75
3 Jeff Burton	.50
4 Jeff Burton's Car	.25
5 Ricky Craven	.25
6 Ricky Craven's Car	.16
7 Robert Pressley	.25
8 Robert Pressley's Car	.16

1996 Maxx SuperTrucks

Randomly inserted in packs at a rate of one in 12, this 10-card issue features top machines of the NASCAR SuperTrucks Series.

COMPLETE SET (10)	5.00	12.00
ST1 Mike Bliss' Truck	.50	1.25
ST2 Tommy Archer's Truck	.50	1.25
ST3 Rodney Combs' Truck	.50	1.25
ST4 Rodney Combs Jr.'s Truck	.50	1.25
ST5 Chad Little's Truck	.50	1.25
ST6 Derrike Cope's Truck	.50	1.25
ST7 T.J.Clark's Truck	.50	1.25
ST8 Darrell Waltrip's Truck	1.00	2.50
ST9 Kenny Wallace's Truck	.50	1.25
ST10 Kenji Momota's Truck	.50	1.25

1996 Maxx Made in America

This 100-card set was the last Maxx product released before they went out of business. The product was thought to have been distributed by Maxx's printer. The cards feature a car or driver photo on the front with a U.S. flag in the background. There were eight cards per pack and 36 packs per box. The product was originally scheduled to have a special 1988 #99 Dale Earnhardt autograph card inserted one in 6,703 packs. We have received no confirmation that this card ever made it into packs. We have received a few reports of unsigned versions of this card being found in packs.

COMPLETE SET (100)	5.00	12.00
1 Rick Mast	.07	.20
2 Rusty Wallace	.60	1.50
3 Jeff Green	.07	.20
4 Sterling Marlin	.25	.60
5 Terry Labonte	.25	.60
6 Mark Martin	.60	1.50
7 Geoff Bodine	.07	.20
8 Ernie Irvan's Car	.07	.20
9 Lake Speed	.07	.20
10 Ricky Rudd	.25	.60
11 Brett Bodine	.07	.20
12 Derrike Cope	.07	.20
13 Joe Nemechek's Car	.02	.10
14 Jimmy Spencer's Car	.02	.10
15 Jeff Burton's Car	.07	.20
16 Ted Musgrave	.07	.20
17 Darrell Waltrip	.15	.40
18 Bobby Labonte	.50	1.25
19 Lake Speed's Car	.02	.10
20 Rick Mast's Car	.02	.10
21 Michael Waltrip	.15	.40
22 Ward Burton	.15	.40
23 Jimmy Spencer	.02	.10
24 Jeff Gordon	.75	2.00
25 Ken Schrader	.07	.20
26 Jeremy Mayfield's Car	.15	.40
27 Darrell Waltrip's Car	.07	.20
28 Ernie Irvan	.15	.40
29 Bobby Labonte	.50	1.25
30 Johnny Benson's Car	.02	.10
31 Kyle Petty's Car	.07	.20
32 Bill Elliott's Car	.15	.40
33 Robert Pressley	.07	.20
34 Bobby Labonte's Car	.15	.40
35 Terry Labonte's Car	.15	.40
36 Ward Burton's Car	.02	.10
37 John Andretti	.07	.20
38 Ricky Rudd's Car	.07	.20
39 Bobby Hamilton's Car	.02	.10
40 Dale Jarrett's Car	.15	.40
41 Ricky Craven	.07	.20
42 Kyle Petty	.15	.40
43 Richard Petty	.25	.60
44 Bobby Hamilton	.07	.20
45 Derrike Cope's Car	.02	.10
46 Kenny Wallace	.07	.20
47 John Andretti's Car	.02	.10
48 Geoff Bodine's Car	.02	.10
49 Ken Schrader's Car	.02	.10
50 Morgan Shepherd's Car	.02	.10
51 Michael Waltrip's Car	.07	.20
52 Mike McLaughlin's Car	.02	.10
53 Rusty Wallace's Car	.25	.60
54 Mark Martin's Car	.25	.60
55 Tim Fedewa	.07	.20
56 Ricky Craven's Car	.02	.10
57 Robert Pressley's Car	.02	.10
58 Jason Keller's Car	.02	.10
59 Tim Fedewa's Car	.02	.10
60 Larry Pearson's Car	.02	.10
61 Hermie Sadler	.07	.20
62 Jeff Fuller's Car	.02	.10
63 Ted Musgrave's Car	.02	.10
64 David Green	.07	.20
65 Phil Parsons' Car	.02	.10
66 Sterling Marlin's Car	.07	.20
67 Steve Grissom	.07	.20
68 Chad Little's Car	.02	.10
69 Hermie Sadler's Car	.02	.10
70 Jeff Green's Car	.02	.10
71 Phil Parsons	.07	.20
72 Jeff Fuller	.07	.20
73 Jeff Fuller's Car	.02	.10
74 Chad Little	.07	.20
75 Morgan Shepherd	.07	.20
76 Jason Keller	.07	.20
77 Mike McLaughlin	.07	.20
78 Ricky Craven	.07	.20
79 Ricky Craven's Car	.02	.10
80 Michael Waltrip	.15	.40
81 Michael Waltrip's Car	.07	.20
82 Terry Labonte	.25	.60
83 Terry Labonte's Car	.15	.40
84 Joe Nemechek	.07	.20
85 Joe Nemechek's Car	.02	.10
86 Larry Pearson	.07	.20
87 Joe Nemechek	.07	.20
88 Dale Jarrett	.50	1.25
89 Rodney Combs	.07	.20
90 Bobby Labonte's Car	.15	.40
91 Steve Grissom	.07	.20
92 Steve Grissom's Car	.02	.10
93 Kenny Wallace's Car	.02	.10
94 Bill Elliott	.30	.75
95 Kenny Wallace	.07	.20
96 Dale Jarrett	.50	1.25
97 Dale Jarrett's Car	.15	.40
98 Jeremy Mayfield	.15	.40
99 Jeff Burton	.25	.60
100 Checklist	.02	.10

1996 Maxx Made in America Blue Ribbon

Each card in this 15-card insert set features a pop-up design. The car or driver photo on the front of each card can be popped out and formed into the shape of the photo. The cards were inserted one per pack.

COMPLETE SET (15)	2.00	5.00
BR1 Derrike Cope's Car	.03	.15
BR2 Ernie Irvan	.25	.60
BR3 Bill Elliott	.40	1.00
BR4 Ricky Craven	.10	.30
BR5 Michael Waltrip	.25	.60
BR6 Rusty Wallace's Car	.25	.60
BR7 Bobby Labonte's Car	.25	.60
BR8 John Andretti	.10	.30
BR9 Ward Burton	.25	.60
BR10 Ricky Rudd's Car	.10	.30
BR11 Darrell Waltrip's Car	.10	.30
BR12 Johnny Benson's Car	.03	.15
BR13 Sterling Marlin's Car	.10	.30
BR14 Chad Little's Car	.03	.15
BR15 Jeff Green	.10	.30

1996 Maxx Odyssey

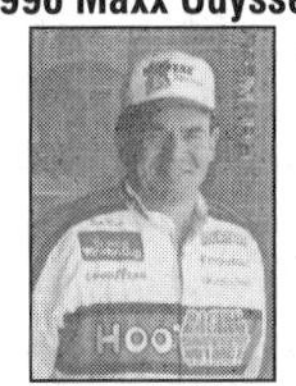

This 100-card set features most of the top names from Winston Cup and Busch racing. The cards were printed on 18 point paper stock as opposed to Maxx's normal 14 point board. Each card front features a driver or car photo, gold foil stamping and the Racing Odyssey logo. Cards were packaged 10 cards per pack and 36 packs per box.

COMPLETE SET (100)	6.00	15.00
1 Rick Mast	.05	.15
2 Rusty Wallace	.50	1.25
3 Jeff Green	.05	.15
4 Sterling Marlin	.20	.50
5 Terry Labonte	.20	.50
6 Mark Martin	.50	1.25
7 Geoff Bodine	.05	.15
8 Geoff Bodine's Car	.02	.10
9 Lake Speed	.05	.15
10 Ricky Rudd	.20	.50
11 Brett Bodine	.05	.15
12 Derrike Cope	.05	.15
13 Joe Nemechek's Car	.02	.10
14 Jimmy Spencer's Car	.02	.10
15 Jeff Burton's Car	.05	.15
16 Ted Musgrave	.05	.15
17 Darrell Waltrip	.10	.30
18 Bobby Labonte	.40	1.00
19 Lake Speed's Car	.02	.10
20 Rick Mast's Car	.02	.10
21 Michael Waltrip	.10	.30
22 Ward Burton	.10	.30
23 Jimmy Spencer	.05	.15
24 Jeff Gordon	.60	1.50
25 Ken Schrader	.05	.15
26 Jeremy Mayfield's Car	.10	.30
27 Darrell Waltrip's Car	.05	.15
28 Ernie Irvan	.10	.30
29 Steve Grissom	.05	.15
30 Johnny Benson's Car	.02	.10
31 Kyle Petty's Car	.05	.15
32 Bill Elliott's Car	.10	.30
33 Robert Pressley	.05	.15
34 Bobby Labonte's Car	.10	.30
35 Terry Labonte's Car	.10	.30
36 Ward Burton's Car	.02	.10
37 John Andretti	.05	.15
38 Ricky Rudd's Car	.05	.15
39 Bobby Hamilton's Car	.02	.10
40 Dale Jarrett's Car	.10	.30
41 Ricky Craven	.05	.15
42 Kyle Petty	.10	.30
43 Richard Petty	.20	.50
44 Bobby Hamilton	.05	.15
45 Derrike Cope's Car	.02	.10
46 Steve Grissom's Car	.02	.10
47 John Andretti's Car	.02	.10
48 Ernie Irvan's Car	.05	.15
49 Ken Schrader's Car	.02	.10
50 Morgan Shepherd's Car	.02	.10
51 Michael Waltrip's Car	.05	.15
52 Mike McLaughlin's Car	.02	.10
53 Rusty Wallace's Car	.10	.30
54 Mark Martin's Car	.20	.50
55 Tim Fedewa	.05	.15
56 Ricky Craven's Car	.02	.10
57 Robert Pressley's Car	.02	.10
58 Jason Keller's Car	.02	.10
59 Tim Fedewa's Car	.02	.10
60 Larry Pearson's Car	.02	.10
61 Hermie Sadler	.05	.15
62 Brett Bodine's Car	.02	.10
63 Ted Musgrave's Car	.02	.10
64 David Green	.05	.15
65 Phil Parsons' Car	.02	.10
66 Steve Grissom's Car	.02	.10
67 Steve Grissom	.05	.15
68 Chad Little's Car	.02	.10
69 Hermie Sadler's Car	.02	.10
70 Jeff Green's Car	.02	.10
71 Phil Parsons	.05	.15
72 Jeff Fuller	.05	.15
73 Jeff Fuller's Car	.02	.10
74 Chad Little	.05	.15
75 Morgan Shepherd	.05	.15
76 Jason Keller	.05	.15
77 Mike McLaughlin	.05	.15
78 Ricky Craven	.05	.15
79 Ricky Craven's Car	.02	.10
80 Michael Waltrip	.10	.30
81 Michael Waltrip's Car	.05	.15
82 Terry Labonte	.20	.50
83 Terry Labonte's Car	.10	.30
84 Joe Nemechek	.05	.15
85 Joe Nemechek's Car	.02	.10
86 Larry Pearson	.05	.15
87 Joe Nemechek	.05	.15
88 Dale Jarrett	.40	1.00
89 Rodney Combs	.05	.15
90 Mike Skinner Will Lind	.05	.15
91 Steve Grissom	.05	.15
92 Steve Grissom's Car	.02	.10
93 Kenny Wallace's Car	.02	.10
94 Bill Elliott	.25	.60
95 Kenny Wallace	.05	.15
96 Dale Jarrett	.40	1.00
97 Dale Jarrett's Car	.10	.30
98 Jeremy Mayfield	.10	.30
99 Jeff Burton	.20	.50
100 Checklist	.02	.10
P1 Bobby Labonte Promo	.75	2.00

1996 Maxx Odyssey Millennium

This 10-card, holographic, die-cut set features Winston Cup drivers and their cars. The cards were randomly inserted in packs at a rate of one per three packs. The series was originally intended to be the first 10 of a larger 30 card set. The rest of the cards were not released due to Maxx's bankruptcy shortly after the release of Odyssey.

COMPLETE SET (10)	5.00	12.00
MM1 Dale Earnhardt's Car	1.00	2.50
MM2 Jimmy Spencer	.30	.75
MM3 Robert Pressley	.30	.75
MM4 Brett Bodine's Car	.20	.50
MM5 Sterling Marlin	.50	1.25
MM6 Jeff Gordon	1.50	4.00
MM7 Bobby Hamilton	.30	.75
MM8 Kyle Petty's Car	.20	.50
MM9 Bill Elliott's Car	.40	1.00
MM10 Terry Labonte's Car	.40	1.00

1996 Maxx Odyssey On The Road Again

This five-card insert features the transporters that bring the race cars and equipment to and from the track. The cards were randomly inserted one in three packs.

COMPLETE SET (5)	.60	1.50
OTRA1 Steve Grissom's Trans.	.12	.30
OTRA2 Michael Waltrip's Trans.	.15	.40
OTRA3 Sterling Marlin's Trans.	.25	.60
OTRA4 Brett Bodine's Trans.	.12	.30
OTRA5 Steve Grissom's Trans.	.12	.30

1996 Maxx Odyssey Radio Active

This 15-card set uses die-cut printing to make pop-up cards. The set features drivers from Winston Cup, Busch and the SuperTruck series. The cards were

randomly inserted in packs at a rate of one per two packs.

COMPLETE SET (15)	3.00	8.00
RA1 Derrike Cope's Car	.07	.20
RA2 Ernie Irvan	.30	.75
RA3 Bill Elliott	.60	1.50
RA4 Ricky Craven	.15	.40
RA5 Michael Waltrip	.30	.75
RA6 Rusty Wallace's Car	.40	1.00
RA7 Bobby Labonte's Car	.30	.75
RA8 John Andretti	.15	.40
RA9 Ward Burton	.30	.75
RA10 Ricky Rudd's Car	.30	.75
RA11 Darrell Waltrip's Car	.07	.20
RA12 Johnny Benson's Car	.07	.20
RA13 Sterling Marlin's Car	.15	.40
RA14 Chad Little's Car	.07	.20
RA15 Jeff Green	.15	.40

1996 Maxx Premier Series

The 1996 Maxx Premier set was issued in one series totalling 300 cards. The cards were sold via mail-order through the Maxx Club. The product was sold in complete set form only. The set features a "Year in Review" yearbook theme and contains NASCAR Winston Cup, Busch Grand National and SuperTruck drivers, owners and crew chiefs. The cards were available with a sheet and binder combination to house the set. Cards #2 and #3 of the Chase the Champion series was available as part of this set. The seven card Superlatives set was also inserted one per factory Premier Series set. Sets originally retailed to Club members for $49.99.

COMPLETE SET (300)	25.00	50.00
1 Rick Mast	.20	.50
2 Rusty Wallace	1.25	3.00
3 Dale Earnhardt	2.50	6.00
4 Sterling Marlin	.60	1.50
5 Terry Labonte	.60	1.50
6 Mark Martin	1.25	3.00
7 Geoff Bodine	.20	.50
8 Jeff Burton	.60	1.50
9 Lake Speed	.20	.50
10 Ricky Rudd	.60	1.50
11 Brett Bodine	.20	.50
12 Derrike Cope	.20	.50
13 Rockingham Rumble MM	.08	.25
14 Rain, Rain, Go Away MM	.08	.25
15 Dick Trickle	.20	.50
16 Ted Musgrave	.20	.50
17 Darrell Waltrip	.40	1.00
18 Bobby Labonte	1.25	3.00
19 Loy Allen	.20	.50
20 Jeremy Mayfield's Car	.20	.50
21 Morgan Shepherd	.20	.50
22 Randy LaJoie	.20	.50
23 Jimmy Spencer	.20	.50
24 Jeff Gordon	1.50	4.00
25 Ken Schrader	.20	.50
26 Hut Stricklin	.20	.50
27 Elton Sawyer	.20	.50
28 Dale Jarrett	1.25	3.00
29 Steve Grissom	.20	.50
30 Michael Waltrip	.40	1.00
31 Ward Burton	.20	.50
32 Chuck Brown	.20	.50
33 Robert Pressley	.20	.50
34 Terry Labonte's Car	.40	1.00
35 Mark Martin's Car	.60	1.50
36 Bobby Labonte's Car	.40	1.00
37 John Andretti	.20	.50
38 Rusty Wallace's Car	.60	1.50
39 Loy Allen's Car	.08	.25
40 Greg Sacks	.20	.50
41 Ricky Craven	.20	.50
42 Kyle Petty	.40	1.00
43 Richard Petty	.60	1.50
44 Bobby Hamilton	.20	.50
45 Jeff Purvis	.20	.50
46 Elton Sawyer's Car	.08	.25
47 Ernie Irvan's Car	.20	.50
48 Joe Nemechek's Car	.08	.25
49 Morgan Shepherd's Car	.08	.25
50 Bill Elliott's Car	.40	1.00
51 Ricky Craven's Car	.08	.25
52 Richard Petty's Car	.40	1.00
53 Ken Schrader's Car	.08	.25
54 Ward Burton's Car	.20	.50
55 Dick Trickle's Car	.08	.25
56 Ricky Rudd's Car	.20	.50
57 Robert Pressley's Car	.08	.25
58 Ted Musgrave's Car	.08	.25
59 Rick Mast's Car	.08	.25
60 Darrell Waltrip's Car	.20	.50
61 Sterling Marlin's Car	.20	.50
62 Geoff Bodine's Car	.08	.25
63 Jimmy Spencer's Car	.08	.25
64 Todd Bodine's Car	.08	.25
65 Michael Waltrip's Car	.20	.50
66 Brett Bodine's Car	.08	.25
67 Derrike Cope's Car	.08	.25
68 John Andretti's Car	.08	.25
69 Steve Grissom's Car	.08	.25
70 Lake Speed's Car	.08	.25
71 Dave Marcis	.40	1.00
72 Kyle Petty's Car	.20	.50
73 Dale Earnhardt's Car	1.00	2.50
74 Ward Burton's Car	.20	.50
75 Todd Bodine	.20	.50
76 Mike Skinner	.20	.50
77 Ron Hornaday Jr.	.20	.50
78 Joe Ruttman	.20	.50
79 Butch Miller	.20	.50
80 Roger Penske	.08	.25
81 Don Miller	.08	.25
82 Larry McClure	.08	.25
83 Jack Roush	.08	.25
84 Joe Gibbs	.40	1.00
85 Felix Sabates	.08	.25
86 Gary Bechtel	.08	.25
87 Joe Nemechek	.20	.50
88 Ernie Irvan	.40	1.00
89 Dale Jarrett's Car	.40	1.00
90 Mike Wallace	.20	.50
91 Len Wood	.08	.25
92 Glen Wood	.08	.25
93 Charles Hardy	.08	.25
94 Bill Elliott	.75	2.00
95 Junior Johnson	.20	.50
96 Rick Hendrick	.08	.25
97 Leo Jackson	.08	.25
98 Jeremy Mayfield	.40	1.00
99 Bobby Allison	.20	.50
100 Carolyn Bechtel	.08	.25
101 Michael Kranefuss	.08	.25
102 Carl Haas	.08	.25
103 Bud Moore	.08	.25
104 Chuck Rider	.08	.25
105 Eddie Wood	.08	.25
106 Richard Jackson	.08	.25
107 Bill Stavola	.08	.25
108 Cale Yarborough	.20	.50
109 Junie Donlavey	.08	.25
110 Larry Hedrick	.08	.25
111 Robert Yates	.08	.25
112 Travis Carter	.08	.25
113 Alan Dillard	.08	.25
114 Butch Mock	.08	.25
115 Harry Melling	.08	.25
116 Bill Davis	.08	.25
117 Kim Wood Hall	.08	.25
118 Mike Wallace's Car	.08	.25
119 Andy Petree	.08	.25
120 Buddy Parrott	.08	.25
121 Steve Hmiel	.08	.25
122 Jimmy Makar	.08	.25
123 Robin Pemberton	.08	.25
124 Tony Glover	.08	.25
125 Leonard Wood	.08	.25
126 Larry McReynolds	.08	.25
127 Gary DeHart	.08	.25
128 Ray Evernham	.40	1.00
129 Ken Howes	.08	.25
130 Bill Ingle	.08	.25
131 Pete Peterson	.08	.25
132 Cecil Gordon	.08	.25
133 Donnie Wingo	.08	.25
134 Doug Hewitt	.08	.25
135 Philippe Lopez	.08	.25
136 Donnie Richeson	.08	.25
137 Richard Broome	.08	.25
138 Kevin Hamlin	.08	.25
139 Charley Pressley	.08	.25
140 Dale Fischlein	.08	.25
141 Paul Andrews	.08	.25
142 Robbie Loomis	.08	.25
143 Troy Selberg	.08	.25
144 Jimmy Fennig	.08	.25
145 Barry Dodson	.08	.25
146 Waddell Wilson	.08	.25
147 Dale Inman	.08	.25
148 Peter Sospenzo	.08	.25
149 Tim Brewer	.08	.25
150 Rick Ren	.08	.25
151 Mike Beam	.08	.25
152 Howard Comstock	.08	.25
153 Jeff Hammond	.08	.25
154 Chris Hussey	.08	.25
155 Todd Parrott	.08	.25
156 Johnny Benson's Car	.08	.25
157 Chad Little's Car	.08	.25
158 Mike McLaughlin's Car	.08	.25
159 Jeff Green's Car	.08	.25
160 Chad Little	.20	.50
161 David Green	.20	.50
162 Jeff Green	.20	.50
163 Curtis Markham	.20	.50
164 Hermie Sadler	.20	.50
165 Jeff Fuller	.20	.50
166 Bobby Dotter	.20	.50
167 Tracy Leslie	.20	.50
168 Larry Pearson	.20	.50
169 Dennis Setzer	.20	.50
170 Ricky Craven	.40	1.00
171 Tim Fedewa	.20	.50
172 Mike McLaughlin	.20	.50
173 Jim Bown	.20	.50
174 Elton Sawyer	.20	.50
175 Jason Keller	.20	.50
176 Rodney Combs	.20	.50
177 Doug Heveron	.20	.50
178 Tommy Houston	.20	.50
179 Kevin Lapage	.20	.50
180 Maxx Car	.08	.25
181 Phil Parsons	.20	.50
182 Ricky Craven's Car	.08	.25
183 Patty Moise	.20	.50
184 Kenny Wallace	.20	.50
185 Terry Labonte BGN	.40	1.00
186 Steve Grissom BGN	.20	.50
187 Steve Grissom's Car	.08	.25
188 Joe Nemechek BGN	.20	.50
189 Joe Nemechek's Car	.08	.25
190 Michael Waltrip BGN	.40	1.00
191 Michael Waltrip's Car	.20	.50
192 Ronnie Silver	.08	.25
193 Barney Hall	.08	.25
194 Eli Gold	.08	.25
195 Benny Parsons	.08	.25
196 Dr. Jerry Punch	.08	.25
197 Buddy Baker	.08	.25
198 Winston Kelley	.08	.25
199 Jim Phillips	.08	.25
200 John Kernan	.08	.25
201 Randy Pemberton	.08	.25
202 Bill Weber	.08	.25
203 Joe Moore	.08	.25
204 Bob Jenkins	.08	.25
205 Allen Bestwick	.08	.25
206 Glenn Jarrett	.08	.25
207 Dr. Dick Berggren	.08	.25
208 Mel Walen	.08	.25
209 Dale Plank	.08	.25
210 Jon Compagnone	.08	.25
211 Paul White	.08	.25
212 Ray Guss	.08	.25
213 Jeff Wildung	.08	.25
214 Phil Warren	.08	.25
215 Mike Helton	.08	.25
216 Gary Nelson	.08	.25
217 Ray Hill	.08	.25
218 Carl Hill	.08	.25
219 Brian DeHart	.08	.25
220 Jack Whittemore	.08	.25
221 Jimmy Cox	.08	.25
222 Bruce Roney	.08	.25
223 Marlin Wright	.08	.25
224 David Hoots	.08	.25
225 Tim Earp	.08	.25
226 Doyle Ford	.08	.25
227 Buster Auton	.08	.25
228 Elmo Langley	.08	.25
229 Walt Green	.08	.25
230 Gary Miller	.08	.25
231 Morris Metcalfe	.08	.25
232 Rich Burgdoff	.08	.25
233 Hoss Berry	.08	.25
234 Steve Peterson	.08	.25
235 Jason Keller's Car	.08	.25
236 Patty Moise's Car	.08	.25
237 Kenny Wallace's Car	.08	.25
238 Kenny Wallace's Car	.08	.25
239 Curtis Markham's Car	.08	.25
240 Tim Fedewa's Car	.08	.25
241 Dennis Setzer's Car	.08	.25
242 Terry Labonte's Car	.40	1.00
243 Jeff Fuller's Car	.08	.25
244 Hermie Sadler's Car	.08	.25
245 Tommy Houston's Car	.08	.25
246 Doug Heveron's Car	.08	.25
247 Kevin Lepage's Car	.08	.25
248 Tracy Leslie's Car	.08	.25
249 Dirk Stephens' Car	.08	.25
250 Testing in the Rain MM	.08	.25
251 Larry Pearson's Car	.08	.25
252 Phil Parson's Car	.08	.25
253 Elton Sawyer's Car	.08	.25
254 Riding the Wall MM	.08	.25
255 On the Comeback Trail MM	.08	.25
256 Larry Phillips WRS National Champion	.08	.25
257 Jeff Fuller BGN Rookie of the Year	.20	.50
258 Johnny Benson BGN Champion	.40	1.00
259 Winston Cup Pit Crew Champs #11 Lowe's Team	.20	.50
260 Ricky Craven Winston Cup Rookie of the Year	.20	.50
261 Bill Elliott Fan Favorite	.40	1.00
262 Dale Earnhardt	1.25	3.00
263 Race 1 - Daytona	.08	.25
264 Race 2 - Rockingham	.08	.25
265 Race 3 - Richmond	.08	.25
266 Race 4 - Atlanta	.08	.25
267 Race 5 - Darlington	.08	.25
268 Race 6 - Bristol	.08	.25
269 Race 7 - North Wilkesboro	.08	.25
270 Race 8 - Martinsville	.08	.25
271 Race 9 - Talladega	.08	.25
272 Race 10 - Sonoma	.08	.25
273 Winston Select Open	.08	.25
274 Winston Select	.08	.25
275 Race 11 - Charlotte	.08	.25
276 Race 12 - Dover	.08	.25
277 Race 13 - Pocono	.08	.25
278 Race 14 - Michigan	.08	.25
279 Race 15 - Daytona	.08	.25
280 Race 16 - New Hampshire	.08	.25
281 Race 17 - Pocono	.08	.25
282 Race 18 - Talladega	.08	.25
283 Race 19 - Indianapolis	.08	.25
284 Race 20 - Watkins Glen	.08	.25
285 Race 21 - Michigan	.08	.25
286 Race 22 - Bristol	.08	.25
287 Race 23 - Darlington	.08	.25
288 Race 24 - Richmond	.08	.25
289 Race 25 - Dover	.08	.25
290 Race 26 - Martinsville	.08	.25
291 Race 27 - North Wilkesboro	.08	.25
292 Race 28 - Charlotte	.08	.25
293 Race 29 - Rockingham	.08	.25
294 Race 30 - Phoenix	.08	.25
295 Race 31 - Atlanta	.08	.25
296 Jeff Gordon Winston Cup Champion	1.00	2.50
297 Mike Skinner SuperTruck Champion	.20	.50
298 Checklist #1	.08	.25
299 Checklist #2	.08	.25
300 Checklist #3	.08	.25
P1G Ricky Craven Gold Promo	.40	1.00
P1R Ricky Craven Red Promo	1.00	2.50

1996 Maxx Premier Series Superlatives

This seven-card insert set was inserted one complete set per factory set of 1996 Maxx Premier Series. The cards take the theme of "the best" and "the most" of the 1995 NASCAR class. For example Ricky Craven is given the title "Most Likely to Succeed." Each card front features a driver and a car photo along with the driver's name and the title Maxx has honored them with.

COMPLETE SET (7)	3.00	8.00
SL1 Bill Elliott	.75	2.00
SL2 Mark Martin	1.25	3.00
SL3 Bobby Labonte	1.25	3.00
SL4 Terry Labonte	.60	1.50
SL5 Bobby Hamilton	.20	.50
SL6 Ricky Craven	.20	.50
SL7 Ken Schrader	.20	.50

1996 Maxx Autographs

These three cards were intended to be inserted into Maxx Signed and Sealed. Due to Maxx's bankruptcy, the Signed and Sealed set was never distributed in a Maxx product. The exact distribution pattern of these cards is unknown.

COMPLETE SET (3)	150.00	250.00
5 Terry Labonte	50.00	100.00

24 Jeff Gordon 60.00 120.00
25 Ken Schrader 25.00 50.00

1996 Maxx Band-Aid Dale Jarrett

This four-card set features Dale Jarrett bearing his NASCAR Busch Grand National sponsor. The cards were issued in boxes of Band-Aid bandages as part of a sales promotion.

COMPLETE SET (4) .75 2.00
1 Dale Jarrett .25 .60
2 Dale Jarrett .25 .60
3 Dale Jarrett's Car .25 .60
4 Dale Jarrett .25 .60
Zachary Jarrett

1996 Maxx Pepsi 500

This five-card set features past winners of the Daytona 500. The cards were originally offered in 12 packs of Pepsi during a regional promotion in the Daytona area in conjunction with the race. They were also offered through the Maxx Club.

COMPLETE SET (5) 1.50 4.00
1 Bobby Allison .40 1.00
2 Geoff Bodine .20 .50
3 Darrell Waltrip .40 1.00
4 Derrike Cope .20 .50
5 Sterling Marlin .60 1.50

1997 Maxx

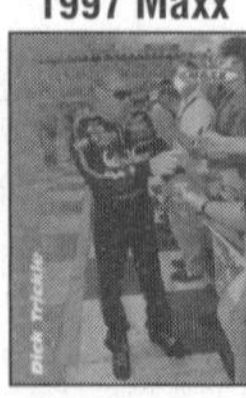

This 120-card set marks Maxx's return to the hobby after a 18 month hiatus. The product was produced and distributed by Upper Deck. Cards were distributed in 10 card packs with 24 packs per box. The packs carried a suggested retail price of $1.99. According to Upper Deck this product contains 50 randomly inserted Dale Earnhardt autographed 1988 Maxx cards.

COMPLETE SET (120) 8.00 20.00
1 Morgan Shepherd .05 .15
2 Rusty Wallace .50 1.25
3 Dale Earnhardt 1.00 2.50
4 Sterling Marlin .20 .50
5 Terry Labonte .20 .50
6 Mark Martin .50 1.25
7 Geoff Bodine .05 .15
8 Hut Stricklin .05 .15
9 Lake Speed .05 .15
10 Ricky Rudd .20 .50
11 Brett Bodine .05 .15
12 Dale Jarrett .40 1.00
13 Bill Elliott .25 .60
14 Dick Trickle .05 .15
15 Wally Dallenbach .05 .15
16 Ted Musgrave .05 .15
17 Darrell Waltrip .10 .30
18 Bobby Labonte .40 1.00
19 Gary Bradberry .05 .15
20 Rick Mast .05 .15
21 Michael Waltrip .10 .30
22 Ward Burton .10 .30
23 Jimmy Spencer .05 .15
24 Jeff Gordon .60 1.50
25 Ricky Craven .05 .15
26 Chad Little .10 .30
27 Kenny Wallace .05 .15
28 Ernie Irvan .10 .30
29 Jeff Green .05 .15
30 Johnny Benson .10 .30
31 Mike Skinner .05 .15
32 Mike Wallace .05 .15
33 Ken Schrader .05 .15
34 Jeff Burton .20 .50
35 David Green .05 .15
36 Derrike Cope .05 .15
37 Jeremy Mayfield .10 .30
38 Dave Marcis .05 .15
39 John Andretti .05 .15
40 Robby Gordon RC .20 .50
41 Steve Grissom .05 .15
42 Joe Nemechek .05 .15
43 Bobby Hamilton .05 .15
44 Kyle Petty .10 .30
45 Elliott Sadler RC 1.50 4.00
46 Morgan Shepherd's Car .02 .10
47 Rusty Wallace's Car .10 .30
48 Dale Earnhardt's Car .40 1.00
49 Sterling Marlin's Car .05 .15
50 Terry Labonte's Car .10 .30
51 Mark Martin's Car .10 .30
52 Geoff Bodine's Car .02 .10
53 Hut Stricklin's Car .02 .10
54 Lake Speed's Car .02 .10
55 Ricky Rudd's Car .05 .15
56 Brett Bodine's Car .02 .10
57 Dale Jarrett's Car .10 .30
58 Bill Elliott's Car .10 .30
59 Dick Trickle's Car .02 .10
60 Wally Dallenbach's Car .02 .10
61 Ted Musgrave's Car .02 .10
62 Darrell Waltrip's Car .02 .10
63 Bobby Labonte's Car .10 .30
64 Gary Bradberry's Car .02 .10
65 Rick Mast's Car .02 .10
66 Michael Waltrip's Car .05 .15
67 Ward Burton's Car .02 .10
68 Jimmy Spencer's Car .02 .10
69 Jeff Gordon's Car .25 .60
70 Ricky Craven's Car .02 .10
71 Chad Little's Car .02 .10
72 Kenny Wallace's Car .02 .10
73 Ernie Irvan's Car .05 .15
74 Jeff Green's Car .02 .10
75 Johnny Benson's Car .02 .10
76 Mike Skinner's Car .02 .10
77 Mike Wallace's Car .02 .10
78 Ken Schrader's Car .02 .10
79 Jeff Burton's Car .02 .10
80 David Green's Car .02 .10
81 Derrike Cope's Car .02 .10
82 Jeremy Mayfield's Car .02 .10
83 Dave Marcis's Car .02 .10
84 John Andretti's Car .02 .10
85 Robby Gordon's Car .10 .30
86 Steve Grissom's Car .02 .10
87 Joe Nemechek's Car .02 .10
88 Bobby Hamilton's Car .02 .10
89 Kyle Petty's Car .05 .15
90 Elliott Sadler's Car .05 .15
91 Terry Labonte PS .10 .30
92 Robbie Gordon PS .10 .30
93 Bobby Labonte PS .20 .50
94 Ward Burton PS .10 .30
95 Bill Elliott PS .10 .30
96 Bill Elliott PS .10 .30
97 Ted Musgrave PS .05 .15
98 Rusty Wallace PS .25 .60
99 Ricky Craven PS .05 .15
100 Bobby Hamilton PS .05 .15
101 Rusty Wallace PS .25 .60
102 Ernie Irvan PS .10 .30
103 Mark Martin PS .25 .60
104 Jeff Burton PS .10 .30
105 Joe Nemechek PS .05 .15
106 Mark Martin MO .25 .60
107 Rusty Wallace MO .25 .60
108 Morgan Shepherd MO .05 .15
109 Derrike Cope MO .05 .15
110 Ricky Rudd MO .10 .30
111 Lake Speed MO .05 .15
112 Sterling Marlin MO .10 .30
113 Michael Waltrip MO .10 .30
114 Terry Labonte MO .10 .30
115 Geoff Bodine MO .05 .15
116 Ken Schrader MO .05 .15
117 Dale Jarrett MO .20 .50
118 Bill Elliott MO .10 .30
119 Darrell Waltrip MO .10 .30
120 Ernie Irvan MO .10 .30
R2 Rusty Wallace Promo 1.00 2.50
NNO Dale Earnhardt/50
1988 Maxx AU

1997 Maxx Chase the Champion

This 10-card set features the top drivers from the NASCAR circuit on micro-etched cards. The cards were randomly inserted in packs at a ratio of 1:5.

COMPLETE SET (10) 10.00 25.00
COMP.GOLD SET (10) 40.00 80.00
*GOLD DCs: 1X TO 2.5X BASIC INSERTS
GOLD DIE CUT STATED ODDS 1:21
C1 Jeff Gordon 4.00 10.00
C2 Mark Martin 3.00 8.00
C3 Terry Labonte 1.25 3.00
C4 Dale Jarrett 2.50 6.00
C5 Jeff Burton 1.25 3.00
C6 Bobby Labonte 2.50 6.00
C7 Ricky Rudd 1.25 3.00
C8 Michael Waltrip .75 2.00
C9 Jeremy Mayfield .75 2.00
C10 Bill Elliott 1.50 4.00

1997 Maxx Flag Firsts

This 25-card set looks back at the first victories of some of today's top NASCAR drivers. The cards were randomly inserted in packs at a ratio of 1:3.

COMPLETE SET (25) 15.00 40.00
FF1 Morgan Shepherd .40 1.00
FF2 Rusty Wallace 3.00 8.00
FF3 Dale Jarrett 2.50 6.00
FF4 Sterling Marlin 1.25 3.00
FF5 Terry Labonte 1.25 3.00
FF6 Mark Martin 3.00 8.00
FF7 Geoff Bodine .40 1.00
FF8 Ken Schrader .40 1.00
FF9 Lake Speed .40 1.00
FF10 Ricky Rudd 1.25 3.00
FF11 Brett Bodine .40 1.00
FF12 Derrike Cope .40 1.00
FF13 Kyle Petty .75 2.00
FF14 Dale Earnhardt 6.00 15.00
FF15 Bobby Hamilton .40 1.00
FF16 John Andretti .40 1.00
FF17 Darrell Waltrip .75 2.00
FF18 Bobby Labonte 2.50 6.00
FF19 Bill Elliott 1.50 4.00
FF20 Ernie Irvan .75 2.00
FF21 Jeff Burton 1.25 3.00
FF22 Ward Burton .75 2.00
FF23 Jimmy Spencer .40 1.00
FF24 Jeff Gordon 4.00 10.00
FF25 Dave Marcis .40 1.00

1997 Maxx Rookies of the Year

This 9-card set features eight of the past winners of the Maxx Winston Cup Rookie of the Year Award. It is important to note that card number MR9 Johnny Benson does not have the Maxx logo with the Rookie of the year logo in the bottom right corner like the other eight cards in the set. The cards were randomly inserted in packs at a ratio of 1:11.

COMPLETE SET (9) 8.00 20.00
MR1 Ken Bouchard .50 1.25
MR2 Dick Trickle .50 1.25
MR3 Rob Moroso .50 1.25
MR4 Bobby Hamilton .50 1.25
MR5 Jimmy Hensley .50 1.25
MR6 Jeff Gordon 5.00 12.00
MR7 Jeff Burton 1.50 4.00
MR8 Ricky Craven .50 1.25
MR9 Johnny Benson 1.00 2.50

1998 Maxx

The 1998 Maxx set was issued in one series totalling 105 cards. This product features a special "Signed, Sealed and Delivered autographed insert card of Richard Petty that earns one lucky collector a free trip to the famous Richard Petty Driving Experience. The set contains the topical subsets: Home Cookin (61-75), License to Drive (76-90), and Front Runners (91-105).

COMPLETE SET (105) 10.00 25.00
1 Jeremy Mayfield .10 .30
2 Rusty Wallace .50 1.25
3 Dale Earnhardt 1.00 2.50
4 Bobby Hamilton .05 .15
5 Terry Labonte .20 .50
6 Mark Martin .50 1.25
7 Geoff Bodine .05 .15
8 Ernie Irvan .10 .30
9 Jeff Burton .20 .50
10 Ricky Rudd .20 .50
11 Johnny Benson .10 .30
12 Dale Jarrett .40 1.00
13 Jerry Nadeau RC .20 .50
14 Steve Park .40 1.00
15 Bill Elliott .25 .60
16 Ted Musgrave .05 .15
17 Darrell Waltrip .10 .30
18 Bobby Labonte .40 1.00
19 Todd Bodine .05 .15
20 Kyle Petty .10 .30
21 Michael Waltrip .10 .30
22 Ken Schrader .05 .15
23 Jimmy Spencer .05 .15
24 Jeff Gordon .60 1.50
25 Ricky Craven .05 .15
26 John Andretti .05 .15
27 Sterling Marlin .20 .50
28 Kenny Irwin .10 .30
29 Mike Skinner .05 .15
30 Derrike Cope .05 .15
31 Jeremy Mayfield's Car .05 .15
32 Rusty Wallace's Car .20 .50
33 Dale Earnhardt's Car .40 1.00
34 Bobby Hamilton's Car .02 .10
35 Terry Labonte's Car .10 .30
36 Mark Martin's Car .20 .50
37 Geoff Bodine's Car .02 .10
38 Ernie Irvan's Car .02 .10
39 Jeff Burton's Car .10 .30
40 Ricky Rudd's Car .05 .15
41 Johnny Benson's Car .02 .10
42 Dale Jarrett's Car .10 .30
43 Jerry Nadeau's Car .10 .30
44 Steve Park's Car .10 .30
45 Bill Elliott's Car .10 .30
46 Ted Musgrave's Car .02 .10
47 Darrell Waltrip's Car .02 .10
48 Bobby Labonte's Car .10 .30
49 Todd Bodine's Car .02 .10
50 Kyle Petty's Car .02 .10
51 Michael Waltrip's Car .05 .15
52 Ken Schrader's Car .02 .10
53 Jimmy Spencer's Car .02 .10
54 Jeff Gordon's Car .25 .60
55 Ricky Craven's Car .02 .10
56 John Andretti's Car .02 .10
57 Sterling Marlin's Car .05 .15
58 Kenny Irwin's Car .05 .15
59 Mike Skinner' s Car .02 .10
60 Derrike Cope's Car .02 .10
61 Jimmy Spencer's Car HC .02 .10
62 Bill Elliott's Car HC .10 .30
63 Darrell Waltrip's Car HC .02 .10
64 Jeff Gordon's Car HC .25 .60
65 John Andretti's Car HC .02 .10
66 Johnny Benson's Car HC .02 .10
67 Jeff Burton's Car HC .10 .30
68 Bobby Hamilton's Car HC .02 .10
69 Ernie Irvan's Car HC .02 .10
70 Dale Jarrett's Car HC .10 .30
71 Bobby Labonte's Car HC .10 .30
72 Terry Labonte's Car HC .10 .30
73 Kyle Petty's Car HC .02 .10
74 Ricky Rudd's Car HC .05 .15
75 Morgan Shepherd HC .02 .10
76 Kenny Irwin's Car HC .10 .30
77 Steve Park's Car LTD .02 .10
78 Jerry Nadeau's Car LTD .10 .30
79 Todd Bodine's Car LTD .02 .10
80 Mike Skinner's Car LTD .02 .10
81 Jeremy Mayfield's Car LTD .02 .10
82 Ricky Craven's Car LTD .02 .10
83 Steve Grissom's Car LTD .02 .10
84 Brett Bodine's Car LTD .02 .10
85 Jeff Burton's Car LTD .05 .15
86 Ward Burton's Car LTD .02 .10
87 Chad Little's Car LTD .02 .10
88 David Green's Car LTD .02 .10
89 John Andretti's Car LTD .02 .10
90 Bobby Labonte's Car LTD .10 .30
91 Jeff Gordon's Car FR .25 .60
92 Dale Jarrett's Car FR .10 .30
93 Mark Martin's Car FR .20 .50
94 Jeff Burton's Car FR .05 .15
95 Dale Earnhardt's Car FR .40 1.00
96 Terry Labonte's Car FR .10 .30
97 Bobby Labonte's Car FR .10 .30
98 Bill Elliott's Car FR .10 .30
99 Rusty Wallace's Car FR .20 .50
100 Ken Schrader's Car FR .02 .10
101 Johnny Benson's Car FR .02 .10
102 Ted Musgrave's Car FR .02 .10
103 Ernie Irvan's Car FR .02 .10
104 Steve Park's Car FR .05 .15
105 Kenny Irwin's Car FR .05 .15

1998 Maxx Focus on a Champion

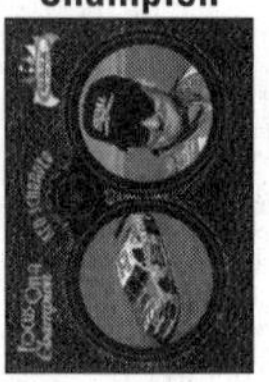

This 15-card set features the top contenders for the Winston Cup Championship. These cards are randomly inserted one per 24 packs.

COMPLETE SET (15) 30.00 80.00
COMP.CEL SET (15) 100.00 200.00
*CEL CARDS: 1X TO 2.5X BASIC INSERTS
FC1 Jeff Gordon 8.00 20.00
FC2 Dale Jarrett 5.00 12.00
FC3 Dale Earnhardt 12.50 30.00
FC4 Mark Martin 6.00 15.00
FC5 Jeff Burton 2.50 6.00
FC6 Kyle Petty 1.50 4.00
FC7 Terry Labonte 2.50 6.00
FC8 Bobby Labonte 5.00 12.00
FC9 Bill Elliott 3.00 8.00
FC10 Rusty Wallace 6.00 15.00
FC11 Ken Schrader .75 2.00
FC12 Johnny Benson 1.50 4.00
FC13 Ted Musgrave .75 2.00
FC14 Ernie Irvan 1.50 4.00
FC15 Kenny Irwin 1.50 4.00

1998 Maxx Swappin' Paint

This 25-card set features the cars of the top contenders for the Winston Cup Championship. These cards are randomly inserted one per three packs.

COMPLETE SET (25) 15.00 30.00
SW1 Steve Park 3.00 8.00
SW2 Terry Labonte's Car 1.00 2.50
SW3 Ernie Irvan's Car .30 .75
SW4 Bobby Hamilton .50 1.25
SW5 Derrike Cope's Car .30 .75
SW6 John Andretti's Car .30 .75
SW7 Geoff Bodine's Car .30 .75
SW8 Hut Stricklin's Car .30 .75
SW9 Jeff Burton's Car 1.00 2.50
SW10 Robert Pressley's Car .30 .75
SW11 Brett Bodine's Car .30 .75
SW12 Rick Mast's Car .30 .75
SW13 Jerry Nadeau's Car 1.00 2.50
SW14 Sterling Marlin's Car .50 1.25
SW15 Johnny Benson's Car .30 .75
SW16 Ted Musgrave's Car .30 .75
SW17 Todd Bodine's Car .30 .75
SW18 Jeremy Mayfield 4.00 10.00
Rusty Wallace
SW19 Mark Martin's Car 1.50 4.00
SW20 Chad Little .50 1.25
SW21 Joe Nemechek's Car .30 .75
SW22 Dick Trickle .50 1.25
SW23 Jimmy Spencer's Car .30 .75
SW24 Kenny Irwin's Car .50 1.25
SW25 Ricky Craven's Car .30 .75

1998 Maxx Teamwork

This 10-card set features the cars and pit crews of the top contenders for the Winston Cup Championship. These cards are randomly inserted one per 11 packs.

COMPLETE SET (10) 10.00 25.00
TW1 Jeff Gordon's Car 2.50 6.00
TW2 Terry Labonte's Car 1.25 3.00
TW3 Ricky Craven's Car .40 1.00
TW4 Mark Martin's Car 2.00 5.00
TW5 Jeff Burton's Car 1.25 3.00
TW6 Ted Musgrave's Car .40 1.00
TW7 Chad Little's Car .40 1.00
TW8 Johnny Benson's Car .40 1.00
TW9 Dale Jarrett's Car 1.25 3.00
TW10 Kenny Irwin's Car .60 1.50

1998 Maxx 1997 Year In Review

The 1997 Maxx Year in Review Boxed Set was issued in one-series factory set totalling 161-base cards, four Award Winners (AW1-AW4) cards and 10 cards (P01-P010) featuring the top finishers.

COMPLETE FACT.SET (175) 12.00 30.00
1 Jeff Gordon .60 1.50
2 Mike Skinner .05 .15
3 Ricky Craven's Car .02 .10
4 Ward Burton's Car .05 .15
5 Hendrick Sweep .10 .30
6 Jeff Gordon's Car .25 .60
7 Mark Martin's Car .20 .50
8 Ernie Irvan's Car .05 .15
9 Dale Earnhardt's Car .50 1.25
10 Ricky Craven's Car .02 .10
11 Rusty Wallace .40 1.00
12 Terry Labonte's Car .10 .30
13 Kyle Petty's Car .05 .15
14 Ricky Rudd's Car .05 .15
15 Ernie Irvan's Car .05 .15
16 Dale Jarrett .40 1.00
17 Robby Gordon .05 .15
18 Johnny Benson's Car .02 .10
19 Geoff Bodine's Car .02 .10
20 Steve Grissom's Car .02 .10
21 Dale Jarrett .40 1.00
22 Dale Jarrett's Car .10 .30
23 Darrell Waltrip .10 .30
24 Michael Waltrip's Car .05 .15
25 Ted Musgrave's Car .02 .10
26 Jeff Burton .20 .50
27 Dale Jarrett's Car .10 .30
28 Steve Grissom's Car .02 .10
29 Jeff Gordon's Car .25 .60
30 Darrell Waltrip's Car .05 .15
31 Jeff Gordon's Car .25 .60
32 Rusty Wallace's Car .20 .50
33 Dale Earnhardt's Car .50 1.25
34 Jeremy Mayfield's Car .05 .15
35 Ted Musgrave's Car .02 .10
36 Jeff Gordon's Car .25 .60
37 Kenny Wallace .05 .15
38 Mark Martin's Car .20 .50
39 Rusty Wallace .50 1.25
40 Ricky Craven's Car .02 .10
41 Mark Martin .50 1.25
42 John Andretti .05 .15
43 Jeff Burton's Car .05 .15
44 Bill Elliott .25 .60
45 Dale Jarrett's Car .10 .30
46 Mark Martin .50 1.25
47 Mark Martin's Car .20 .50
48 Darrell Waltrip's Car .05 .15
49 Ernie Irvan's Car .05 .15
50 Alcatraz Island .02 .10
51 Jeff Gordon's Car .25 .60
52 Jeff Gordon .60 1.50
53 Dale Earnhardt's Car .50 1.25
54 Jeff Burton's Car .05 .15
55 Darrell Waltrip's Car .05 .15
56 Ricky Rudd .20 .50
57 Bobby Labonte .40 1.00
58 Jeff Burton's Car .05 .15
59 Bobby Labonte's Car .10 .30
60 Dave Marcis' Car .02 .10
61 Jeff Gordon .60 1.50
62 Bobby Hamilton's Car .02 .10
63 Derrike Cope's Car .02 .10
64 Morgan Shepherd's Car .02 .10
65 Ward Burton's Car .05 .15
66 Ernie Irvan .10 .30
67 Dale Jarrett .40 1.00
68 Derrike Cope's Car .02 .10
69 Ted Musgrave's Car .02 .10
70 Bill Elliott's Car .10 .30
71 Jeff Gordon .60 1.50
72 Joe Nemechek .05 .15
73 Ricky Rudd .20 .50
74 Jimmy Spencer's Car .02 .10
75 Ted Musgrave's Car .02 .10
76 John Andretti .05 .15
77 Mike Skinner .05 .15
78 Terry Labonte's Car .10 .30
79 Kyle Petty's Car .05 .15
80 Ward Burton's Car .05 .15
81 Jeff Burton .20 .50
82 Ken Schrader .05 .15
83 Hut Stricklin's Car .02 .10
84 Rusty Wallace's Car .20 .50
85 Dale Jarrett .40 1.00
86 Dale Jarrett's Car .10 .30
87 Joe Nemechek .05 .15
88 Johnny Benson's Car .02 .10
89 Ted Musgrave's Car .02 .10
90 Bill Elliott's Car .10 .30
91 Ricky Rudd .20 .50
92 Ernie Irvan's Car .05 .15
93 Kyle Petty's Car .05 .15
94 Michael Waltrip's Car .05 .15
95 Darrell Waltrip's Car .05 .15
96 Jeff Gordon's Car .25 .60
97 Todd Bodine .05 .15
98 Steve Grissom's Car .02 .10
99 Ricky Rudd .20 .50
100 Robby Gordon's Car .02 .10
101 Mark Martin .50 1.25
102 Johnny Benson's Car .02 .10
103 Rusty Wallace's Car .20 .50
104 Bill Elliott's Car .10 .30
105 Jeff Burton's Car .05 .15
106 Dale Jarrett .40 1.00
107 Kenny Wallace .05 .15
108 Steve Grissom's Car .02 .10
109 Geoff Bodine's Car .02 .10
110 David Green's Car .02 .10
111 Jeff Gordon .60 1.50
112 Bobby Labonte .40 1.00
113 Chad Little's Car .02 .10
114 Dick Trickle's Car .02 .10
115 Jeff Burton's Car .05 .15
116 Dale Jarrett .40 1.00
117 Bill Elliott's Car .10 .30
118 Ted Musgrave's Car .02 .10
119 Joe Nemechek .05 .15
120 Kenny Irwin .10 .30
121 Jeff Gordon .60 1.50
122 Ken Schrader .05 .15
123 Ernie Irvan's Car .05 .15
124 John Andretti's Car .02 .10
125 Geoff Bodine's Car .02 .10
126 Mark Martin .50 1.25
127 Mark Martin's Car .20 .50
128 Dale Earnhardt's Car .50 1.25
129 Robby Gordon's Car .02 .10
130 Jeff Gordon's Car .25 .60
131 Jeff Burton .20 .50
132 Ward Burton's Car .05 .15
133 Ricky Craven's Car .02 .10
134 Bobby Hamilton's Car .02 .10
135 Rusty Wallace's Car .20 .50
136 Dale Jarrett .40 1.00
137 Geoff Bodine .05 .15
138 Terry Labonte's Car .10 .30
139 Bobby Labonte's Car .10 .30
140 Darrell Waltrip's Car .05 .15
141 Terry Labonte .20 .50
142 Ernie Irvan .10 .30
143 Kyle Petty's Car .05 .15
144 Mark Martin's Car .20 .50
145 Ken Schrader's Car .02 .10
146 Bobby Hamilton .05 .15
147 Bobby Labonte .40 1.00
148 Sterling Marlin's Car .05 .15
149 Bill Elliott .25 .60
150 Bobby Hamilton .05 .15
151 Dale Jarrett .40 1.00
152 Bobby Hamilton's Car .02 .10
153 Kyle Petty's Car .05 .15
154 Dale Jarrett's Car .10 .30
155 Darrell Waltrip's Car .05 .15
156 Bobby Labonte .40 1.00
157 Geoff Bodine .05 .15
158 Bobby Hamilton's Car .02 .10
159 Mark Martin's Car .20 .50
160 Chad Little's Car .02 .10
161 Checklist .02 .10
AW1 Jeff Gordon 1.25 3.00
AW2 Mike Skinner .20 .50
AW3 Dale Jarrett .75 2.00
AW4 Bill Elliott .50 1.25
PO1 Jeff Gordon 1.25 3.00
PO2 Dale Jarrett .75 2.00
PO3 Mark Martin 1.00 2.50
PO4 Jeff Burton .40 1.00
PO5 Dale Earnhardt 2.00 5.00
PO6 Terry Labonte .50 1.25
PO7 Bobby Labonte .75 2.00
PO8 Bill Elliott .50 1.25
PO9 Rusty Wallace 1.00 2.50
PO10 Ken Schrader .20 .50

1998 Maxx 10th Anniversary

The 1998 Maxx 10th Anniversary set was issued [in] one series totalling 134 cards. The card fron[ts] feature color photos surrounded by a white-borde[r] with the Maxx 10th Anniversary logo in the uppe[r] right corner. The set contains the topical subset[s] Family Ties (91-107), Farewell Tour (108-116) an[d] Racin' Up Wins (117-126).

OMPLETE SET (134) 10.00 25.00
usty Wallace .60 1.50
had Little .20 .50
obby Hamilton .10 .30
erry Labonte .30 .75
Mark Martin .75 2.00
lan Kulwicki .30 .75
eoff Bodine .10 .30
rett Bodine .10 .30
icky Rudd .30 .75
Donnie Allison .10 .30
Jeremy Mayfield .20 .50
Jerry Nadeau RC .30 .75
Jeff Burton .30 .75
Bill Elliott .40 1.00
Elton Sawyer .10 .30
Darrell Waltrip .20 .50
Bobby Labonte .60 1.50
Ward Burton .20 .50
Michael Waltrip .20 .50
David Pearson .20 .50
Bobby Allison .20 .50
Jimmy Spencer .10 .30
Dale Jarrett .60 1.50
Jeff Gordon 1.00 2.50
Johnny Benson .20 .50
Kevin Lepage .10 .30
Davey Allison .40 1.00
Kenny Irwin .20 .50
Ken Schrader .10 .30
Harry Gant .20 .50
Cale Yarborough .20 .50
Ernie Irvan .20 .50
Ned Jarrett .20 .50
Dale Earnhardt Jr. 1.50 4.00
Jeff Green .10 .30
Sterling Marlin .30 .75
Steve Grissom .10 .30
Robert Pressley .10 .30
Richard Petty .30 .75
Kyle Petty .20 .50
John Andretti .10 .30
Benny Parsons .10 .30
Buddy Baker .10 .30
Neil Bonnett .30 .75
Kenny Wallace .10 .30
Rusty Wallace's Car .30 .75
Chad Little's Car .05 .15
Bobby Hamilton's Car .05 .15
Terry Labonte's Car .20 .50
Mark Martin's Car .30 .75
Alan Kulwicki's Car .20 .50
Geoff Bodine's Car .05 .15
Brett Bodine's Car .05 .15
Ricky Rudd's Car .10 .30
Donnie Allison's Car .05 .15
Jeremy Mayfield's Car .10 .30
Jerry Nadeau's Car .20 .50
Jeff Burton's Car .10 .30
Bill Elliott's Car .20 .50
Elton Sawyer .10 .30
Darrell Waltrip's Car .05 .15
Bobby Labonte's Car .20 .50
Ward Burton's Car .10 .30
Michael Waltrip's Car .10 .30
David Pearson's Car .05 .15
Bobby Allison's Car .05 .15
Jimmy Spencer's Car .05 .15
Dale Jarrett's Car .20 .50
Jeff Gordon's Car .40 1.00
Johnny Benson's Car .05 .15
Kevin Lepage's Car .05 .15
Davey Allison's Car .20 .50
Kenny Irwin's Car .10 .30
Ken Schrader's Car .05 .15
Harry Gant's Car .05 .15
Cale Yarborough's Car .10 .30
Ernie Irvan's Car .10 .30
Ned Jarrett's Car .05 .15
Dale Earnhardt Jr.'s Car .75 2.00
Jeff Green's Car .05 .15
Sterling Marlin's Car .10 .30
Steve Grissom's Car .05 .15
Robert Pressley's Car .05 .15
Richard Petty's Car .10 .30
Kyle Petty's Car .10 .30
John Andretti's Car .05 .15
Benny Parsons's Car .05 .15
Buddy Baker's Car .05 .15
Neil Bonnett's Car .05 .15
Kenny Wallace's Car .05 .15
Donnie Allison .10 .30
Bobby Allison .20 .50
Davey Allison .40 1.00
Richard Petty .30 .75
Kyle Petty .20 .50
Dale Earnhardt 1.50 4.00
Dale Earnhardt Jr. 1.50 4.00
Darrell Waltrip .20 .50
Michael Waltrip .20 .50
0 Mike Wallace .10 .30
1 Rusty Wallace .75 2.00
2 Kenny Wallace .10 .30
3 Geoff Bodine .10 .30
4 Brett Bodine .10 .30
5 Todd Bodine .10 .30
6 Terry Labonte .30 .75
7 Bobby Labonte .60 1.50
8 Richard Petty .30 .75
9 Bobby Allison .10 .30
0 Cale Yarborough .10 .30
1 Benny Parsons .10 .30
2 Buddy Baker .10 .30
3 Davey Allison .40 1.00
4 Harry Gant .10 .30
5 Neil Bonnett .30 .75
6 Alan Kulwicki .30 .75
7 B.Elliott/R.Wallace .40 1.00
8 D.Waltrip/R.Wallace .30 .75
9 Dale Earnhardt 1.50 4.00
0 D.Allison/H.Gant .30 .75
1 B.Elliott/D.Allison .30 .75
2 Rusty Wallace .75 2.00
3 Rusty Wallace .75 2.00
4 Jeff Gordon 1.00 2.50
5 Jeff Gordon 1.00 2.50
6 Jeff Gordon 1.00 2.50
7 Checklist .05 .15
8 Checklist .05 .15
9 Checklist .05 .15
0 Checklist .05 .15
131 Checklist .05 .15
132 Checklist .05 .15
133 Checklist .05 .15
134 Checklist .05 .15
P1 Rusty Wallace Promo .75 2.00

1998 Maxx 10th Anniversary Buy Back Autographs

Randomly inserted in packs at a rate of one in 288, this assorted insert set features older MAXX cards that were bought back by Upper Deck and signed by the featured driver. Each card inserted into packs was stamped with Maxx's Seal of Authenticity hologram on the back and hand serial numbered on the front. Some cards later made their into the secondary market without serial numbering but with the hologram on the backs.

1 Bobby Allison '88 #30 10.00 25.00
2 Buddy Baker '88 #55/169 12.50 30.00
3 Brett Bodine '88 #59/149 10.00 25.00
4 Geoff Bodine '88 #67 10.00 25.00
5 Derrick Cope '88 #33/149 7.50 20.00
6 Harry Gant '89 #16
7 Harry Gant '90 #33
8 Harry Gant '91 #17
9 Harry Gant '91 #183
10 Harry Gant '92 NNO
11 Harry Gant '92 #33
12 Harry Gant '92 #272
13 Harry Gant '92 #285
14 Harry Gant '92 #286
15 Harry Gant '92 #287
16 Harry Gant '92 #288
17 Harry Gant '93 #33
18 Harry Gant '93 #246
19 Harry Gant '93 #275
20 Harry Gant '95 #33
21 Jeff Gordon '92 #29
22 Jeff Gordon '92 #50 ROY/10
23 Jeff Gordon '93 #24/10
24 Jeff Gordon '94 #13/10
25 Jeff Gordon '94 #16
26 Ernie Irvan '88 #95/148 15.00 40.00
27 Dale Jarrett '88 #61 25.00 50.00
28 Terry Labonte '88 #63
29 Dave Marcis '88 #44/170 12.50 30.00
30 Benny Parsons '88 #76/153 30.00 60.00
31 Kyle Petty '89 #42
32 Kyle Petty '91 #42
33 Kyle Petty '91 #172
34 Kyle Petty '92 #35
35 Kyle Petty '92 #42
36 Kyle Petty '92 #266
37 Kyle Petty '93 #42
38 Kyle Petty '93 #291
39 Kyle Petty '95 #42
40 K.Petty/R.Petty '89 #220/12
41 Richard Petty '88 #43
42 Richard Petty SSD/250
43 Ken Schrader '88 #74/150 20.00 40.00
44 Morgan Shepherd '88 #25/149 10.00 25.00
45 Lake Speed '88 #46
46 Hut Stricklin '88 #28 7.50 20.00
47 Rusty Wallace '88 #14/297 20.00 50.00
48 Darrell Waltrip '88 #10/179 25.00 60.00
49 Michael Waltrip '88 #98/149 15.00 40.00
50 Cale Yarborough '88 #90/149 10.00 25.00

1998 Maxx 10th Anniversary Card of the Year

Randomly inserted in packs at a rate of one in 23, these insert cards depict highlights from the first 10 years of Maxx.

COMPLETE SET (10) 25.00 60.00
CY1 Davey Allison 3.00 8.00
CY2 Kyle Petty 2.50 6.00
Richard Petty
CY3 Rusty Wallace 5.00 12.00
CY4 Darrell Waltrip 1.50 4.00
CY5 Jeff Gordon 8.00 20.00
CY6 Richard Petty 2.50 6.00
CY7 Rusty Wallace 5.00 12.00
CY8 Dale Jarrett 5.00 12.00
CY9 Mark Martin 6.00 15.00
CY10 Jeff Gordon 8.00 20.00

1998 Maxx 10th Anniversary Champions Past

Randomly inserted in packs at a rate of one in 5, this is the first of a two-tiered insert set that features the past ten Winston Cup Champions.

COMPLETE SET (10) 15.00 40.00
COMP.DIE CUT SET (10) 50.00 120.00
*DIE CUTS : 1X TO 2.5X BASIC INSERTS
CP1 Jeff Gordon 4.00 10.00
CP2 Terry Labonte 1.25 3.00

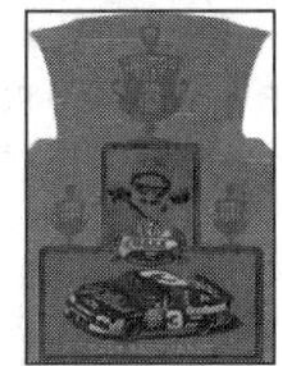

CP3 Dale Earnhardt 6.00 15.00
CP4 Alan Kulwicki 1.25 3.00
CP5 Rusty Wallace 2.50 6.00
CP6 Bill Elliott 1.50 4.00
CP7 Darrell Waltrip .75 2.00
CP8 Bobby Allison .75 2.00
CP9 Richard Petty 1.25 3.00
CP10 Cale Yarborough .75 2.00

1998 Maxx 10th Anniversary Maxximum Preview

Inserted one per pack, this 25-card insert set features the Ionix technology with a unique design of top drivers who are also included in the Maxx Maxximum set.

COMPLETE SET (25) 15.00 30.00
P1 Darrell Waltrip .40 1.00
P2 Rusty Wallace 1.25 3.00
P3 Sterling Marlin .60 1.50
P4 Bobby Hamilton .25 .60
P5 Terry Labonte .60 1.50
P6 Mark Martin 1.50 4.00
P7 Geoff Bodine .25 .60
P8 Ernie Irvan .40 1.00
P9 Jeff Burton .60 1.50
P10 Ricky Rudd .60 1.50
P11 Dale Jarrett 1.25 3.00
P12 Jeremy Mayfield .40 1.00
P13 Jerry Nadeau .60 1.50
P14 Ken Schrader .25 .60
P15 Kyle Petty .40 1.00
P16 Chad Little .40 1.00
P17 Todd Bodine .25 .60
P18 Bobby Labonte 1.25 3.00
P19 Bill Elliott .75 2.00
P20 Mike Skinner .25 .60
P21 Michael Waltrip .40 1.00
P22 John Andretti .25 .60
P23 Jimmy Spencer .25 .60
P24 Jeff Gordon 2.00 5.00
P25 Kenny Irwin .40 1.00

1999 Maxx

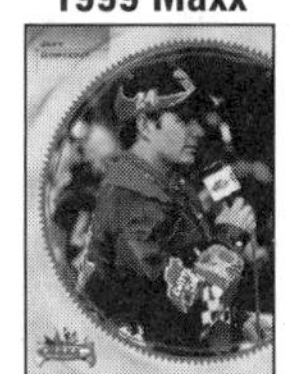

The 1999 Maxx set was issued in one series totalling 90 cards. The set contains cards featuring NASCAR Winston Cup Drivers, NASCAR Winston Cup Cars, and Roots of Racing subset cards.

COMPLETE SET (90) 7.50 20.00
1 Jeff Gordon .75 2.00
2 Jeff Gordon's Car .30 .75
3 Jeff Gordon's Car RR .30 .75
4 Jeff Burton .25 .60
5 Jeff Burton's Car .07 .20
6 Jeff Burton RR .15 .40
7 Dale Jarrett .50 1.25
8 Dale Jarrett's Car .15 .40
9 Dale Jarrett's Car RR .15 .40
10 Ward Burton .15 .40
11 Ward Burton .15 .40
12 Ward Burton .15 .40
13 Bill Elliott .30 .75
14 Bill Elliott's Car .15 .40
15 Bill Elliott's Car RR .15 .40
16 Johnny Benson .15 .40
17 Johnny Benson .15 .40
18 Johnny Benson .15 .40
19 Dale Earnhardt Jr. 1.25 2.50
20 Dale Earnhardt Jr.'s Car .40 1.00
21 Dale Earnhardt Jr.'s Car RR .40 1.00
22 Sterling Marlin .25 .60
23 Sterling Marlin's Car .07 .20
24 Sterling Marlin RR .15 .40
25 Ken Schrader .07 .20
26 Ken Schrader .07 .20
27 Ken Schrader .07 .20
28 Bobby Labonte .50 1.25
29 Bobby Labonte's Car .15 .40
30 Bobby Labonte RR .25 .60
31 Chad Little .15 .40
32 Chad Little .15 .40
33 Chad Little .15 .40
34 Jeremy Mayfield .15 .40
35 Jeremy Mayfield's Car .07 .20
36 Jeremy Mayfield RR .07 .20
37 Ricky Rudd .25 .60
38 Ricky Rudd's Car .07 .20
39 Ricky Rudd's Car RR .07 .20
40 John Andretti .07 .20
41 John Andretti .07 .20
42 John Andretti .07 .20
43 Rusty Wallace .60 1.50
44 Rusty Wallace's Car .25 .60
45 Rusty Wallace RR .30 .75
46 Darrell Waltrip .15 .40
47 Darrell Waltrip's Car .07 .20
48 Darrell Waltrip RR .07 .20
49 Geoffrey Bodine .07 .20
50 Geoffrey Bodine .07 .20
51 Geoffrey Bodine .07 .20
52 Mark Martin .60 1.50
53 Mark Martin's Car .25 .60
54 Mark Martin RR .30 .75
55 Kenny Irwin .15 .40
56 Kenny Irwin's Car .07 .20
57 Kenny Irwin's Car RR .07 .20
58 Mike Skinner .15 .40
59 Mike Skinner .15 .40
60 Mike Skinner .15 .40
61 Kyle Petty .15 .40
62 Kyle Petty's Car .07 .20
63 Kyle Petty's Car RR .07 .20
64 Bobby Hamilton .07 .20
65 Bobby Hamilton .07 .20
66 Bobby Hamilton .07 .20
67 Jerry Nadeau .15 .40
68 Jerry Nadeau .15 .40
69 Jerry Nadeau .15 .40
70 Tony Stewart CRC 1.00 2.50
71 Tony Stewart's Car .30 .75
72 Tony Stewart RR .40 1.00
73 Ernie Irvan .15 .40
74 Ernie Irvan's Car .07 .20
75 Ernie Irvan's Car RR .07 .20
76 Steve Park .40 1.00
77 Steve Park's Car .07 .20
78 Steve Park RR .25 .60
79 Kevin Lepage .07 .20
80 Kevin Lepage .07 .20
81 Kevin Lepage .07 .20
82 Elliott Sadler .15 .40
83 Elliott Sadler .15 .40
84 Elliott Sadler .15 .40
85 Terry Labonte .25 .60
86 Terry Labonte's Car .15 .40
87 Terry Labonte's Car RR .15 .40
88 Dale Earnhardt 1.25 3.00
89 Dale Earnhardt's Car .50 1.25
90 Jeff Gordon CL .40 1.00

1999 Maxx FANtastic Finishes

Randomly inserted in packs at the rate of one in twelve, this 30 card set focuses on the top NASCAR drivers and the closest finishes in their Winston Cup careers.

COMPLETE SET (30) 60.00 120.00
F1 Jeff Gordon's Car 6.00 15.00
F2 Steve Park's Car 3.00 8.00
F3 Elliott Sadler's Car 1.25 3.00
F4 Bobby Hamilton's Car .60 1.50
F5 Rusty Wallace's Car 5.00 12.00
F6 Kyle Petty's Car 1.25 3.00
F7 Kenny Irwin's Car 1.25 3.00
F8 Jerry Nadeau's Car 1.25 3.00
F9 Dale Jarrett's Car 4.00 10.00
F10 Dale Earnhardt's Car 10.00 25.00
F11 Ken Schrader's Car .60 1.50
F12 Jeff Burton's Car 2.00 5.00
F13 Ernie Irvan's Car 1.25 3.00
F14 John Andretti's Car .60 1.50
F15 Dale Earnhardt Jr.'s Car 8.00 20.00
F16 Bill Elliott's Car 2.50 6.00
F17 Mark Martin's Car 5.00 12.00
F18 Mike Skinner's Car 1.25 3.00
F19 Ward Burton's Car 1.25 3.00
F20 Darrell Waltrip's Car 1.25 3.00
F21 Chad Little's Car 1.25 3.00
F22 Ricky Rudd's Car 2.00 5.00
F23 Johnny Benson's Car 1.25 3.00
F24 Terry Labonte's Car 2.00 5.00
F25 Sterling Marlin's Car 2.00 5.00
F26 Kevin Lepage's Car .60 1.50
F27 Jeremy Mayfield's Car 1.25 3.00
F28 Tony Stewart's Car 6.00 15.00
F29 Bobby Labonte's Car 4.00 10.00
F30 Michael Waltrip's Car 1.25 3.00

1999 Maxx Focus on a Champion

Randomly inserted in packs at the rate of one in 1 in 24 this set highlights the top 15 drivers who will be chasing the 1999 NASCAR Winston Cup title.

COMPLETE SET (15) 25.00 60.00
*GOLD CARDS: .8X TO 2X BASIC INSERTS
FC1 Jeff Gordon 3.00 8.00
FC2 Dale Earnhardt 5.00 12.00
FC3 Dale Earnhardt Jr. 4.00 10.00
FC4 Mark Martin 2.50 6.00
FC5 Dale Jarrett 2.00 5.00
FC6 Jeremy Mayfield .60 1.50
FC7 Rusty Wallace 2.50 6.00
FC8 Terry Labonte 1.00 2.50
FC9 Jeff Burton 1.00 2.50
FC10 Ernie Irvan .60 1.50
FC11 Bill Elliott 1.25 3.00
FC12 Bobby Labonte 2.00 5.00
FC13 Jerry Nadeau .60 1.50
FC14 Steve Park 1.50 4.00
FC15 Kenny Irwin .60 1.50

1999 Maxx Race Ticket

Randomly inserted in packs at the rate of one in eight, these scratch off game cards give the collector a chance to instantly win a pair of tickets to a 1999 NASCAR Winston Cup race.

COMPLETE SET (30) 25.00 50.00
RT1 Jerry Nadeau's Car .60 1.50
RT2 Jeff Burton's Car 1.00 2.50
RT3 Jeremy Mayfield's Car .60 1.50
RT4 Dale Earnhardt Jr.'s Car 4.00 10.00
RT5 Steve Park's Car 1.50 4.00
RT6 Kenny Irwin's Car .60 1.50
RT7 Ernie Irvan's Car .60 1.50
RT8 Dale Jarrett's Car 2.00 5.00
RT9 Kevin Lepage's Car .30 .75
RT10 Bill Elliott's Car 1.25 3.00
RT11 Bobby Hamilton's Car .30 .75
RT12 Chad Little's Car .60 1.50
RT13 Brett Bodine's Car .30 .75
RT14 Ken Schrader's Car .30 .75
RT15 Ricky Rudd's Car 1.00 2.50
RT16 Johnny Benson's Car .60 1.50
RT17 John Andretti's Car .30 .75
RT18 Tony Stewart's Car 3.00 8.00
RT19 Mark Martin's Car 2.50 6.00
RT20 Ward Burton's Car .60 1.50
RT21 Elliott Sadler's Car .60 1.50
RT22 Jeff Gordon's Car 3.00 8.00
RT23 Kyle Petty's Car .60 1.50
RT24 Terry Labonte's Car 1.00 2.50
RT25 Sterling Marlin's Car 1.00 2.50
RT26 Darrell Waltrip's Car .60 1.50
RT27 Bobby Labonte's Car 2.00 5.00
RT28 Mike Skinner's Car .60 1.50
RT29 Michael Waltrip's Car .60 1.50
RT30 Rusty Wallace's Car 2.50 6.00

1999 Maxx Racer's Ink

Randomly inserted in packs these cards feature authentic autographs from the top five drivers on the NASCAR Winston Cup circuit and each card was hand numbered to 250.

DE Dale Earnhardt Jr.
JG Jeff Gordon 150.00 250.00
JM Jeremy Mayfield 10.00 25.00
MM Mark Martin 40.00 80.00
RW Rusty Wallace 12.50 30.00

1999 Maxx Racing Images

Randomly inserted in packs at the rate of one in three, this 30 card set features all the new 1999 uniforms and cars with dual photos on the front of each card in Light F/X technology.

COMPLETE SET (30) 12.50 25.00
RI1 Darrell Waltrip .30 .75
RI2 Kevin Lepage .15 .40
RI3 Bobby Labonte 1.00 2.50
RI4 Ricky Rudd .50 1.25
RI5 Jeff Burton .50 1.25
RI6 Brett Bodine .15 .40
RI7 Mike Skinner .30 .75
RI8 John Andretti .15 .40
RI9 Dale Jarrett 1.00 2.50
RI10 Bill Elliott .60 1.50
RI11 Ward Burton .30 .75
RI12 Terry Labonte .50 1.25
RI13 Kenny Irwin .30 .75
RI14 Ken Schrader .15 .40
RI15 Tony Stewart 1.50 4.00
RI16 Sterling Marlin .50 1.25
RI17 Ernie Irvan .30 .75
RI18 Bobby Hamilton .15 .40
RI19 Johnny Benson .30 .75
RI20 Michael Waltrip .30 .75
RI21 Jeremy Mayfield .30 .75
RI22 Chad Little .30 .75
RI23 Rusty Wallace 1.25 3.00
RI24 Jeff Gordon 1.50 4.00
RI25 Steve Park .75 2.00
RI26 Jerry Nadeau .30 .75
RI27 Elliott Sadler .30 .75
RI28 Dale Earnhardt Jr. 2.00 5.00
RI29 Kyle Petty .30 .75
RI30 Mark Martin 1.25 3.00

1999 Maxx Signed, Sealed, and Delivered

Each card in this set was signed by the featured driver and included a postmark style gold foil design on the cardfront. The cardbacks include a congratulatory message from Upper Deck along with hand serial numbering. It is not known exactly how the cards were distributed but they appeared on the market after Upper Deck stopped producing racing cards.

S1 Rusty Wallace/250 40.00 80.00
S3 Jeff Gordon/250 60.00 120.00
S4 Richard Petty/250 50.00 100.00
S5 Jeff Burton/250 10.00 25.00

2000 Maxx

Released as an 85-card set, Maxx is comprised of 39 regular issue driver cards, 20 Race Car cards, 16 Rookie Future cards, nine Front Row Favorites cards and one checklist. Maxx was packaged in 24-pack boxes with packs containing eight cards and carried a suggested retail price of $1.99.

COMPLETE SET (85) 10.00 25.00
1 Dale Jarrett .50 1.25
2 Rusty Wallace .60 1.50
3 Dale Earnhardt 1.25 3.00
4 John Andretti .07 .20
5 Terry Labonte .25 .60
6 Mark Martin .60 1.50
7 Michael Waltrip .15 .40
8 Dale Earnhardt Jr. CRC 1.00 2.50
9 Jerry Nadeau .15 .40
10 Scott Pruett .07 .20
11 Kevin Lepage .07 .20
12 Bobby Hamilton .07 .20
13 Mike Skinner .07 .20
14 Johnny Benson .15 .40
15 Chad Little .15 .40
16 Kenny Wallace .07 .20
17 Matt Kenseth CRC .60 1.50
18 Bobby Labonte .50 1.25
19 Joe Nemechek .07 .20
20 Tony Stewart .75 2.00
21 Elliott Sadler .15 .40
22 Ward Burton .15 .40
23 Ron Hornaday .07 .20
24 Jeff Gordon .75 2.00
25 Robby Gordon .07 .20
26 Randy LaJoie .07 .20
27 Casey Atwood .25 .60
28 Ricky Rudd .25 .60
29 Jeff Burton .25 .60
30 Hank Parker Jr. RC .25 .60
31 Sterling Marlin .25 .60
32 Jeremy Mayfield .07 .20
33 Steve Park .25 .60
34 Kyle Petty .15 .40
35 Darrell Waltrip .15 .40
36 Kevin Grubb .07 .20
37 Adam Petty 3.00 6.00
38 Jason Jarrett .07 .20
39 Lyndon Amick .07 .20
40 Tony Stewart's Car .30 .75
41 Dale Jarrett's Car .15 .40
42 Rusty Wallace's Car .25 .60
43 Dale Earnhardt's Car .50 1.25
44 John Andretti's Car .02 .10
45 Terry Labonte's Car .15 .40
46 Mark Martin's Car .25 .60
47 Matt Kenseth's Car .25 .60
48 Dale Earnhardt Jr.'s Car .40 1.00
49 Jerry Nadeau's Car .15 .40
50 Kyle Petty's Car .07 .20
51 Ward Burton's Car .07 .20
52 Jeremy Mayfield's Car .07 .20
53 Mike Skinner's Car .02 .10
54 Scott Pruett's Car .02 .10
55 Jeff Burton's Car .07 .20
56 Steve Park's Car .07 .20
57 Ricky Rudd's Car .07 .20
58 Bobby Labonte's Car .15 .40
59 Jeff Gordon's Car .30 .75
60 Jimmie Johnson RF RC 4.00 10.00
61 Derrick Gilchrist RF .07 .20
62 Michael Ritch RF .07 .20
63 Kevin Harvick RF .50 1.50
64 Ricky Hendrick RF RC 1.25 3.00
65 Andy Houston RF RC .07 .20
66 Matt Hutter RF .07 .20
67 Jay Sauter RF .07 .20
68 Jamie Skinner RF .07 .20
69 Anthony Lazzaro RF .07 .20
70 Gus Wasson RF .07 .20
71 Greg Biffle RF .25 .60
72 P.J. Jones RF .07 .20
73 Hermie Sadler RF .07 .20

74 Jason Leffler RF	.07	.20
75 Kurt Busch RF	1.50	4.00
76 Bobby Labonte's Car FRF	.15	.40
77 Jeff Gordon's Car FRF	.30	.75
78 Rusty Wallace's Car FRF	.25	.60
79 Ward Burton's Car FRF	.07	.20
80 Tony Stewart's Car FRF	.30	.75
81 Kenny Irwin's Car FRF	.02	.10
82 Mike Skinner's Car FRF	.02	.10
83 Mark Martin's Car FRF	.25	.60
84 Joe Nemechek's Car FRF	.02	.10
85 Rusty Wallace CL	.25	.60

2000 Maxx Collectible Covers

Randomly inserted into packs at one in 72, this 5-card insert set features swatches of authentic car covers. Card backs carry a "CC" prefix followed by the driver's initials.

COMPLETE SET (5)	30.00	80.00
CCBL Bobby Labonte	6.00	15.00
CCDJ Dale Jarrett	6.00	15.00
CCMK Matt Kenseth	8.00	20.00
CCRW Rusty Wallace	6.00	15.00
CCTS Tony Stewart	10.00	25.00

2000 Maxx Drive Time

Randomly inserted into packs at one in three, this 10-card insert highlights some of the top moments from 1999. Card backs carry a "DT" prefix.

COMPLETE SET (10)	6.00	15.00
DT1 Tony Stewart	1.00	2.50
DT2 Jeff Gordon	1.00	2.50
DT3 Ward Burton	.20	.50
DT4 Jeff Burton	.30	.75
DT5 Dale Jarrett	.60	1.50
DT6 Mark Martin	.75	2.00
DT7 Bobby Labonte	.60	1.50
DT8 Rusty Wallace	.75	2.00
DT9 Matt Kenseth	.75	2.00
DT10 Ricky Rudd	.30	.75

2000 Maxx Fantastic Finishes

Randomly inserted into packs at one in 11, this 10-card insert highlights some of the more interesting finishes in 1999. Card backs carry a "FF" prefix.

COMPLETE SET (10)	8.00	20.00
FF1 Dale Earnhardt	2.00	5.00
FF2 Dale Earnhardt Jr.	1.50	4.00
FF3 Terry Labonte	.40	1.00
FF4 Matt Kenseth	1.00	2.50
FF5 Tony Stewart	1.25	3.00
FF6 Jeff Burton	.40	1.00
FF7 Dale Jarrett	.75	2.00
FF8 Bobby Labonte	.75	2.00
FF9 Jeff Gordon	1.25	3.00
FF10 Mark Martin	1.00	2.50

2000 Maxx Focus On A Champion

Randomly inserted into packs at one in 23, this 5-card insert highlights the top drivers chasing the Winston Cup. Card backs carry a "FC" prefix.

COMPLETE SET (5)	12.50	30.00
FC1 Dale Jarrett	2.50	6.00
FC2 Tony Stewart	4.00	10.00
FC3 Bobby Labonte	2.50	6.00
FC4 Jeff Burton	1.25	3.00
FC5 Jeff Gordon	4.00	10.00

2000 Maxx Oval Office

Randomly inserted into packs at one in 72, this 5-card insert highlights the most elite drivers of NASCAR. Card backs carry a "OO" prefix.

COMPLETE SET (5)	30.00	80.00
OO1 Dale Jarrett	5.00	12.00
OO2 Dale Earnhardt	12.50	30.00
OO3 Jeff Gordon	8.00	20.00
OO4 Terry Labonte	2.50	6.00
OO5 Mark Martin	6.00	15.00

2000 Maxx Racer's Ink

Randomly inserted into packs at one in 144, this 16-card insert features authentic autographs from top drivers like Dale Earnhardt and Bobby Labonte as well as a signed card of the late Adam Petty. The cardbacks carry the player's initials as numbering.

COMPLETE SET (16)	600.00	1200.00
AP Adam Petty	75.00	150.00
BL Bobby Labonte	12.50	30.00
CA Casey Atwood	12.50	30.00
DE Dale Earnhardt	250.00	350.00
DJ Dale Jarrett	30.00	60.00
JA John Andretti	10.00	20.00
JB Jeff Burton	10.00	25.00
JM Jeremy Mayfield	15.00	40.00
JR Dale Earnhardt Jr.	100.00	200.00
KS Ken Schrader	10.00	20.00
KW Kenny Wallace	6.00	15.00
RW Rusty Wallace	15.00	40.00
SD Boris Said	12.50	25.00
TL Terry Labonte	15.00	40.00
TS Tony Stewart	75.00	150.00
WB Ward Burton	10.00	25.00

2000 Maxx Speedway Boogie

Randomly inserted into packs at one in 11, this 10-card insert highlights the fastest drivers in NASCAR. Card backs carry a "SB" prefix.

COMPLETE SET (10)	8.00	20.00
SB1 Jeff Gordon	1.25	3.00
SB2 Matt Kenseth	1.00	2.50
SB3 Bobby Labonte	.75	2.00
SB4 Terry Labonte	.40	1.00
SB5 Dale Earnhardt Jr.	1.50	4.00
SB6 Dale Jarrett	.75	2.00
SB7 Mark Martin	1.00	2.50
SB8 Jeff Burton	.40	1.00
SB9 Ricky Rudd	.40	1.00
SB10 Tony Stewart	1.25	3.00

1998 Maxximum

The 1998 Maxximum set was issued in one series totalling 100 cards. The cards feature the new card technology, Ionix, with full-bleed color photography. The set contains the topical subsets: Iron Men (1-25), Steel Chariots (26-50), Armor Clad (51-75), and Heat of Battle (76-100).

COMPLETE SET (100)	20.00	50.00
WAX BOX	30.00	60.00
1 Darrell Waltrip	.30	.75
2 Rusty Wallace	1.25	3.00
3 Dale Earnhardt	2.50	6.00
4 Bobby Hamilton	.15	.40
5 Terry Labonte	.50	1.25
6 Mark Martin	1.25	3.00
7 Geoff Bodine	.15	.40
8 Ernie Irvan	.30	.75
9 Jeff Burton	.50	1.25
10 Ricky Rudd	.50	1.25
11 Dale Jarrett	1.00	2.50
12 Jeremy Mayfield	.30	.75
13 Jerry Nadeau RC	.50	1.25
14 Ken Schrader	.15	.40
15 Kyle Petty	.30	.75
16 Chad Little	.30	.75
17 Todd Bodine	.15	.40
18 Bobby Labonte	1.00	2.50
19 Bill Elliott	.60	1.50
20 Mike Skinner	.15	.40
21 Michael Waltrip	.30	.75
22 John Andretti	.15	.40
23 Jimmy Spencer	.15	.40
24 Jeff Gordon	1.50	4.00
25 Kenny Irwin	.30	.75
26 Darrell Waltrip's Car	.07	.20
27 Rusty Wallace's Car	.50	1.25
28 Dale Earnhardt's Car	1.00	2.50
29 Bobby Hamilton's Car	.07	.20
30 Terry Labonte's Car	.30	.75
31 Mark Martin's Car	.50	1.25
32 Geoff Bodine's Car	.07	.20
33 Ernie Irvan's Car	.07	.20
34 Jeff Burton's Car	.30	.75
35 Ricky Rudd's Car	.15	.40
36 Dale Jarrett's Car	.30	.75
37 Jeremy Mayfield's Car	.07	.20
38 Jerry Nadeau's Car	.30	.75
39 Ken Schrader's Car	.07	.20
40 Kyle Petty's Car	.07	.20
41 Chad Little's Car	.07	.20
42 Todd Bodine's Car	.07	.20
43 Bobby Labonte's Car	.30	.75
44 Bill Elliott's Car	.30	.75
45 Mike Skinner's Car	.07	.20
46 Michael Waltrip's Car	.15	.40
47 John Andretti's Car	.07	.20
48 Jimmy Spencer's Car	.07	.20
49 Jeff Gordon's Car	.60	1.50
50 Kenny Irwin's Car	.07	.20
51 Darrell Waltrip	.30	.75
52 Rusty Wallace	1.25	3.00
53 Dale Earnhardt Jr.	2.00	5.00
54 Bobby Hamilton	.15	.40
55 Terry Labonte	.50	1.25
56 Mark Martin	1.25	3.00
57 Geoff Bodine	.15	.40
58 Ernie Irvan	.30	.75
59 Jeff Burton	.50	1.25
60 Ricky Rudd	.50	1.25
61 Dale Jarrett	1.00	1.50
62 Jeremy Mayfield	.30	.75
63 Jerry Nadeau	.50	1.25
64 Ken Schrader	.15	.40
65 Kyle Petty	.30	.75
66 Chad Little	.30	.75
67 Todd Bodine	.15	.40
68 Bobby Labonte	1.00	2.50
69 Bill Elliott	.60	1.50
70 Mike Skinner	.15	.40
71 Michael Waltrip	.30	.75
72 John Andretti	.15	.40
73 Jimmy Spencer	.15	.40
74 Jeff Gordon	1.50	4.00
75 Kenny Irwin	.30	.75
76 Darrell Waltrip's Car	.07	.20
77 Rusty Wallace	1.25	3.00
78 Dale Earnhardt Jr.	2.00	5.00
79 Bobby Hamilton's Car	.07	.20
80 Terry Labonte's Car	.30	.75
81 Mark Martin's Car	.50	1.25
82 Geoff Bodine's Car	.07	.20
83 Ernie Irvan's Car	.07	.20
84 Jeff Burton's Car	.30	.75
85 Ricky Rudd's Car	.15	.40
86 Dale Jarrett's Car	.30	.75
87 Jeremy Mayfield's Car	.07	.20
88 Jerry Nadeau's Car	.30	.75
89 Ken Schrader's Car	.07	.20
90 Kyle Petty's Car	.07	.20
91 Chad Little's Car	.07	.20
92 Todd Bodine's Car	.07	.20
93 Bobby Labonte's Car	.30	.75
94 Bill Elliott's Car	.30	.75
95 Mike Skinner's Car	.07	.20
96 Michael Waltrip's Car	.15	.40
97 John Andretti's Car	.07	.20
98 Jimmy Spencer's Car	.07	.20
99 Jeff Gordon's Car	.60	1.50
100 Kenny Irwin's Car	.07	.20
S24 Jeff Gordon Sample	1.25	3.00

1998 Maxximum Battle Proven

Randomly inserted in packs at a rate of one in four, this die-cut insert set highlights NASCAR drivers who have each posted more than one career Winston Cup victory.

COMPLETE SET (15)	12.00	30.00
B1 Darrell Waltrip	.60	1.50
B2 Dale Earnhardt	5.00	12.00
B3 Rusty Wallace	2.50	6.00
B4 Bill Elliott	1.25	3.00
B5 Jeff Gordon	3.00	8.00
B6 Mark Martin	2.50	6.00
B7 Terry Labonte	1.00	2.50
B8 Ricky Rudd	1.00	2.50
B9 Geoff Bodine	.30	.75
B10 Ernie Irvan	.60	1.50
B11 Dale Jarrett	2.00	5.00
B12 Kyle Petty	.60	1.50
B13 Sterling Marlin	.60	1.50
B14 Bobby Labonte	2.00	5.00
B15 Jeff Burton	1.00	2.50

1998 Maxximum Field Generals One Star

Sequentially numbered to 2,000, this die-cut insert set is the first of a four-tiered collection showcasing the best Winston Cup drivers.

COMPLETE SET (15)	60.00	120.00
*TWO STAR: .4X TO 1X ONE STARS		
1 Rusty Wallace	8.00	20.00
2 Jeremy Mayfield	2.00	5.00
3 Jeff Gordon	10.00	25.00
4 Terry Labonte	3.00	8.00
5 Dale Jarrett	6.00	15.00
6 Mark Martin	8.00	20.00
7 Jeff Burton	3.00	8.00
8 Kenny Irwin	2.00	5.00
9 Darrell Waltrip	2.00	5.00
10 Dale Earnhardt	15.00	40.00
11 Ernie Irvan	2.00	5.00
12 Bobby Labonte	6.00	15.00
13 Kyle Petty	2.00	5.00
14 Jimmy Spencer	1.00	2.50
15 John Andretti	1.00	2.50

1998 Maxximum Field Generals Three Star Autographs

Sequentially numbered to 100, this double die cut insert set is the third of a four-tiered collection showcasing the best Winston Cup drivers. Each Three Star card was signed by the featured driver. A Four Star parallel was also produced with each signed card being numbered of just 1.

1 Rusty Wallace	40.00	80.00
2 Jeremy Mayfield	25.00	50.00
3 Jeff Gordon	125.00	250.00
4 Terry Labonte	40.00	80.00
5 Dale Jarrett	40.00	80.00
6 Mark Martin	40.00	80.00
7 Jeff Burton	12.50	30.00
8 Kenny Irwin	25.00	50.00
9 Darrell Waltrip	20.00	50.00
10 Dale Earnhardt	250.00	350.00
11 Ernie Irvan	25.00	50.00
12 Bobby Labonte	30.00	60.00
13 Kyle Petty	25.00	50.00
14 Jimmy Spencer	12.50	25.00
15 John Andretti	12.50	25.00

1998 Maxximum First Class

Randomly inserted in packs at a rate of one in three, this insert focuses on 20 drivers who have established themselves to be the most successful drivers on the current Winston Cup circuit.

COMPLETE SET (20)	12.00	30.00
F1 Jeff Gordon	3.00	8.00
F2 Jimmy Spencer	.30	.75
F3 John Andretti	.30	.75
F4 Michael Waltrip	.60	1.50
F5 Bill Elliott	1.25	3.00
F6 Bobby Labonte	2.00	5.00
F7 Kyle Petty	.60	1.50
F8 Ken Schrader	.30	.75
F9 Jeremy Mayfield	.60	1.50
F10 Dale Jarrett	2.00	5.00
F11 Ricky Rudd	1.00	2.50
F12 Jeff Burton	1.00	2.50
F13 Ernie Irvan	.60	1.50
F14 Geoff Bodine	.30	.75
F15 Mark Martin	2.50	6.00
F16 Terry Labonte	1.00	2.50
F17 Bobby Hamilton	.30	.75
F18 Rusty Wallace	2.50	6.00
F19 Darrell Waltrip	.60	1.50
F20 Sterling Marlin	.60	1.50

2000 Maxximum

Released as a 44-card set, Maxximum features top NASCAR drivers in portrait style photographs set on a card with white outlining borders and bronze foil highlights. Maxximum was packaged in 24-pack boxes with each pack containing four cards.

COMPLETE SET (44)	12.50	30.00
1 Dale Jarrett	1.00	2.50
2 Bobby Labonte	1.00	2.50
3 Mark Martin	1.25	3.00
4 Tony Stewart	1.50	4.00
5 Jeff Burton	.50	1.25
6 Jeff Gordon	1.50	4.00
7 Dale Earnhardt	2.50	6.00
8 Rusty Wallace	1.00	3.00
9 Ward Burton	.30	.75
10 Mike Skinner	.15	.40
11 Jeremy Mayfield	.15	.40
12 Terry Labonte	.50	1.25
13 Bobby Hamilton	.15	.40
14 Steve Park	.50	1.25
15 Casey Atwood	.50	1.25
16 Sterling Marlin	.50	1.25
17 John Andretti	.15	.40
18 Wally Dallenbach	.15	.40
19 Kenny Irwin	.30	.75
20 Bill Elliott	.60	1.50
21 Kenny Wallace	.15	.40
22 Chad Little	.30	.75
23 Elliott Sadler	.30	.75
24 Kevin Lepage	.15	.40
25 Kyle Petty	.30	.75
26 Johnny Benson	.30	.75
27 Michael Waltrip	.30	.75
28 Ricky Rudd	.50	1.25
29 Jerry Nadeau	.30	.75
30 Darrell Waltrip	.30	.75
31 Dale Earnhardt Jr. CRC	2.00	5.00
32 Matt Kenseth CRC	1.25	3.00
33 Ron Hornaday	.15	.40
34 Scott Pruett	.15	.40
35 Robby Gordon	.15	.40
36 Stacy Compton RC	.30	.75
37 Randy LaJoie	.15	.40
38 Jimmie Johnson RC	6.00	12.00
39 Kevin Harvick	1.25	3.00
40 Derrick Gilchrist	.15	.40
41 Adam Petty	3.00	6.00
42 Kevin Grubb	.15	.40
43 Hank Parker Jr. RC	.50	1.25
44 Jeff Gordon CL	.60	1.50

2000 Maxximum Die Cuts

Randomly inserted in packs, this 44-card set parallels the base Maxximum set on die-cut cards. Each card is sequentially numbered to 250.

COMPLETE SET (44)	60.00	120.00
*DIE CUTS: 2X TO 5X BASE CARDS		

2000 Maxximum MPH

Randomly inserted in packs, this 44-card set parallels the base set on a die cut card. Each card is sequentially numbered to the driver's car number.

*SINGLES/70-99: 6X TO 15X HI COL.		
*SINGLES/45-69: 8X TO 20X HI COL.		
*SINGLES/30-44: 10X TO 25X HI COL.		
*SINGLES/20-29: 15X TO 30X HI COL.		
38 Jimmie Johnson/92	25.00	60.00

2000 Maxximum Cruise Control

Randomly inserted in packs at the rate of one in four, this 10-card set is die cut along the top and bottom edges of the card. Each card is enhanced with silver foil highlights.

COMPLETE SET (10)	8.00	20.00
CC1 Terry Labonte	.75	2.00
CC2 Bobby Labonte	1.50	4.00
CC3 John Andretti	.25	.60
CC4 Bill Elliott	1.00	2.50
CC5 Dale Earnhardt Jr.	3.00	8.00
CC6 Matt Kenseth	2.00	5.00
CC7 Scott Pruett	.25	.60
CC8 Steve Park	.75	2.00
CC9 Jeff Gordon	2.50	6.00
CC10 Darrell Waltrip	.50	1.25

2000 Maxximum Dialed In

Randomly inserted in packs at the rate of one in 12, this 7-card set features die cut left and right edges and driver portrait photography. Each card contains silver foil highlights.

COMPLETE SET (7)	10.00	25.00
DI1 Dale Jarrett	2.00	5.00
DI2 Tony Stewart	3.00	8.00
DI3 Jeff Gordon	3.00	8.00
DI4 Bobby Labonte	2.00	5.00
DI5 Terry Labonte	1.00	2.50
DI6 Mark Martin	2.50	6.00
DI7 Jeff Burton	1.00	2.50

2000 Maxximum Nifty Fifty

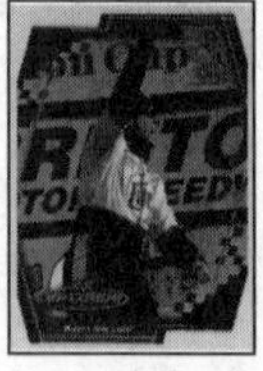

Randomly inserted in packs at the rate of one in this 5-card set pays tribute to Rusty Wallace and victory at the Food City 500 on a card die cut or edges. Each card contains silver foil highlights.

COMPLETE SET (5)	8.00	20.
COMMON R.WALLACE	1.50	4.

2000 Maxximum Pure Adrenaline

Randomly inserted in packs at the rate of one in this 8-card set features die cut cards along the and right edges of the card. Drivers appear on back while their cars appear on the front. Each contains gold foil highlights

COMPLETE SET (8)	8.00	20.
PA1 Tony Stewart	4.00	10.
PA2 Ward Burton	.75	2.
PA3 Bobby Labonte	2.50	6.
PA4 Ricky Rudd	1.25	3.
PA5 Joe Nemechek	.40	1.
PA6 Rusty Wallace	3.00	8.
PA7 Mike Skinner	.40	1.
PA8 Jeff Burton	1.25	3.

2000 Maxximum Roots of Racing

Randomly inserted in packs at the rate of one in this 5-card set spotlights top NASCAR drivers red-bordered die cut card.

COMPLETE SET (5)	8.00	20.
R1 Dale Earnhardt	5.00	12.
R2 Kyle Petty	.60	1.
R3 Tony Stewart	3.00	8.
R4 Dale Jarrett	2.00	5.
R5 Jeff Gordon	3.00	8.

2000 Maxximum Signatures

Randomly inserted in packs at the rate of one in for single autographs, one in 144 for dou autographs, and one in 287 for triple autogra Quadruple autographs are sequentially numbere 100. Several cards were issued as exchange c with an expiration date of 6/14/2001. Bl Alexander did not sign for the set although he have an exchange card inserted into packs.

BE Bill Elliott	20.00	40
CA Casey Atwood	8.00	20
DE Dale Earnhardt	250.00	400
DG Derrick Gilchrist	5.00	12
HP Hank Parker Jr.	6.00	15
JG Joe Gibbs	20.00	40
JJ Jason Jarrett	6.00	15
JL Justin Labonte	6.00	15
JM Jeremy Mayfield	8.00	20
JO Jimmie Johnson	25.00	50
KH Kevin Harvick	12.50	30
KI Kenny Irwin EXCH	2.00	5
LE Jason Leffler	6.00	15
MK Matt Kenseth	20.00	50
NJ Ned Jarrett		
RG Robby Gordon	8.00	20
RR Ricky Rudd	12.50	30
RW Rusty Wallace	12.50	30
SC Stacy Compton	6.00	15
SP Scott Pruett	6.00	15
TS Tony Stewart	40.00	100
WB Ward Burton	12.50	30
DE2 Dale Earnhardt / Dale Earnhardt Jr.	1200.00	1500
DJ2 Dale Jarrett / Jason Jarrett	25.00	50
DN2 Dale Jarrett / Ned Jarrett	40.00	80
DR2 Dale Jarrett / Ricky Rudd	25.00	50
MD2 Matt Waltrip / Darrell Waltrip	30.00	60
MK2 Mark Martin / Matt Kenseth	100.00	200
PE2 Kyle Petty / John Andretti		
RJ2 Rusty Wallace / Jeremy Mayfield	12.50	30
SL2 Tony Stewart / Bobby Labonte		
TB2 Terry Labonte / Bobby Labonte	40.00	100

Ward Burton	25.00	50.00
eff Burton		
Bobby Labonte	60.00	120.00
ony Stewart		
e Gibbs		
Ned Jarrett	50.00	100.00
ale Jarrett		
ason Jarrett		
3 Rusty Wallace	50.00	100.00
enny Wallace		
ike Wallace		
Terry Labonte	40.00	100.00
obby Labonte		
ustin Labonte		
Tony Stewart	100.00	175.00
ason Leffler		
obby Labonte		
e Gibbs		
Mark Martin	100.00	200.00
had Little		
eff Burton		
att Kenseth		

00 Maxximum Young Lions

mly inserted in packs at the rate of one in 24, 0-card set focuses on younger NASCAR s. Each card is die cut in the shape of a lion's and features portrait style photography.

PLETE SET (10)	20.00	50.00
ason Jarrett	.75	2.00
att Kenseth	3.00	8.00
asey Atwood	1.25	3.00
tacy Compton	.75	2.00
dam Petty	5.00	12.00
yndon Amick	.75	2.00
ank Parker Jr.	1.25	3.00
evin Grubb	.75	2.00
immie Johnson	6.00	15.00
Kevin Harvick	5.00	12.00

1995 Metallic mpressions Classic ale Earnhardt 21-Card Tin

lic Impressions produced this 21-card Dale ardt set for Classic Inc. The metal cards were buted in complete set form in a tin box. ction was limited to 9,950 sets with each ing a numbered certificate of authenticity. In of each tin box was a 21st card numbered E1. ured Dale and car owner Richard Childress. lic Impressions also produced a five-card and a rd version of this set. The card fronts are the as the ones in the larger 21 card set. The nce is the numbering on the back. For example ten card set card #5 is the same as card #9 in card set except for the number.

P.FACT SET (21)	12.50	25.00
EARNHARDT'S CAR	.50	1.25
EARNHARDT	.60	1.50
P.FACT 10 CARD SET	10.00	20.00
P.FACT 5 CARD SET	5.00	10.00
le Earnhardt	.60	1.50
ichard Childress		

1995 Metallic npressions Kyle Petty 10-Card Tin

0-card set from Metallic Impressions features Petty on the company's full color embossed cards. The backs have additional photos and entary on Kyle and his many interest. The 10- et was produced in a quantity of 19,950. Each accompanied by an individually numbered cate of Authenticity. There is also a five-card n of this set available in a tin box.

P.10-CARD TIN SET (10)	10.00	20.00
MON CARD	.75	2.00
P.5-CARD TIN SET (5)	4.00	10.00

1995 Metallic mpressions Richard Petty

Richard Petty is the feature of this 5-card set produced by Metallic Impressions in 1995. The metal cards were distributed in complete set form in a tin box. Each card features a picture of King Richard or one of his famous cars.

COMP.FACT SET (5)	4.00	10.00
COMMON PETTY (1-5)	.75	2.00

1995 Metallic Impressions Upper Deck Rusty Wallace

This set was produced in conjunction with Upper Deck. Card fronts show photos of Rusty in every aspect of race-day action. Cards are embossed in sturdy, durable metal with card edges rolled for extra durability and safety. Full-color card backs feature an additional photo, commentary and selected race results. The 20-card set comes in a specifically designed embossed collector's tin with an individually numbered Certificate of Authenticity. There were 12,500 sets produced. There is also a five card version of this set in a tin box.

COMPLETE SET (20)	10.00	25.00
COMMON CARD (1-20)	.75	1.50
COMP.FIVE CARD SET	5.00	10.00

1995 Metallic Impressions Winston Cup Champions 10-Card Tin

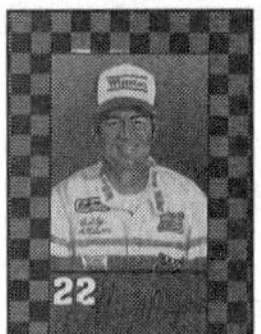

This 10-card set issued by Metallic Impressions features 10 former Winston Cup Champions. The cards are made of embossed metal and come in a tin display box. There were 49,900 sets made.

COMP. FACT SET (10)	12.50	30.00
1 Richard Petty	1.25	3.00
2 Benny Parsons	.75	2.00
3 Cale Yarborough	.75	2.00
4 Dale Earnhardt	5.00	12.00
5 Darrell Waltrip	1.00	2.50
6 Bobby Allison	.75	2.00
7 Terry Labonte	1.25	3.00
8 Bill Elliott	1.25	3.00
9 Rusty Wallace	2.00	5.00
10 Alan Kulwicki	1.25	3.00

1996 Metallic Impressions 25th Anniversary Winston Cup Champions

This 25-card set was produced by Metallic Impressions. The cards were available through packs of Winston cigarettes. There was one card per every two pack of cigarettes. The set was also available by trading in Winston cigarette wrappers.

COMPLETE SET (25)	16.00	40.00
1 Richard Petty	.60	1.50
2 Richard Petty	.60	1.50
3 Benny Parsons	.30	.75
4 Richard Petty	.60	1.50
5 Richard Petty	.60	1.50
6 Cale Yarborough	.30	.75
7 Cale Yarborough	.30	.75
8 Cale Yarborough	.30	.75
9 Richard Petty	.60	1.50
10 Dale Earnhardt	2.50	6.00
11 Darrell Waltrip	.40	1.00
12 Darrell Waltrip	.40	1.00
13 Bobby Allison	.40	1.00
14 Terry Labonte	.60	1.50
15 Darrell Waltrip	.40	1.00
16 Dale Earnhardt	2.50	6.00
17 Dale Earnhardt	2.50	6.00
18 Bill Elliott	.60	1.50
19 Rusty Wallace	1.00	2.50
20 Dale Earnhardt	2.50	6.00
21 Dale Earnhardt	2.50	6.00
22 Alan Kulwicki	.60	1.50
23 Dale Earnhardt	2.50	6.00
24 Dale Earnhardt	2.50	6.00
25 Jeff Gordon	1.50	4.00

1996 Metallic Impressions Avon All-Time Racing Greatest

This five-card sets was produced by Metallic Impressions for Avon. The set was originally sold through the May 1996 Avon catalog. The five NASCAR drivers featured in the set are all former Winston Cup champions. The cards are embossed metal and come in a metal tin.

COMP.FACT SET (5)	10.00	20.00
1 Dale Earnhardt	4.00	10.00
2 Darrell Waltrip	1.00	2.50
3 Bill Elliott	1.25	3.00
4 Terry Labonte	1.25	3.00
5 Rusty Wallace	2.00	5.00

1996 Metallic Impressions Dale Earnhardt Burger King

This 3-card set was prodced by Metallic Impressions and sponsored by Burger King. Each card highlights an eventful year from Dale Earnhardt's career.

COMPLETE SET (3)	6.00	15.00
1 Dale Earnhardt's Car 1987	2.00	5.00
2 Dale Earnhardt 1990	2.00	5.00
3 Dale Earnhardt's Car 1995	2.00	5.00

1996 Metallic Impressions Jeff Gordon Winston Cup Champ 10-Card Tin

Jeff Gordon is the feature of this 10-card set produced by Metallic Impressions. The metal cards were distributed in complete set form in a tin box. Each 10-card set comes with a numbered certificate of authenticity. Metallic Impressions also produced a five-card version of this set.

COMP.10-CARD TIN SET (10)	10.00	25.00
COMMON CARD	1.00	2.50
COMP.5-CARD TIN SET (10)	5.00	12.00

1996 Metallic Impressions Winston Cup Top Five

This five-card set features the Top Five finishers in the 1996 Winston Cup points race. The cards are made of embossed metal and come in a colorful tin. $1.00 from each card set sold went to benefit the continued development of Brenner Children's Hospital.

COMP. FACT SET (5)	5.00	12.00
1 Terry Labonte	.60	1.50
2 Jeff Gordon	1.25	3.00
3 Dale Jarrett	.75	2.00
4 Dale Earnhardt	2.00	5.00
5 Mark Martin	1.00	2.50

1996 M-Force

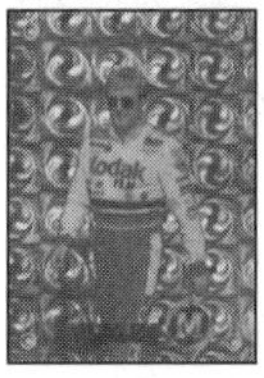

This 45-card set is the first issued by Press Pass under the M-Force brand name. The cards feature 38 point board, two-sided mirror foil, and a damage resistant laminent. The top drivers and cars are included in 1996 race action. The cards were packaged two cards per pack, 24 packs per box and 20 boxes per case. The product was distributed through hobby channels.

COMPLETE SET (45)	12.50	30.00
1 Rusty Wallace	1.25	3.00
2 Rusty Wallace's Car	.50	1.25
3 Dale Earnhardt	2.50	6.00
4 Dale Earnhardt's Car	1.00	2.50
5 Sterling Marlin	.50	1.25
6 Sterling Marlin's Car	.15	.40
7 Terry Labonte	.50	1.25
8 Terry Labonte's Car	.30	.75
9 Mark Martin	1.25	3.00
10 Mark Martin's Car	.50	1.25
11 Ricky Rudd	.50	1.25
12 Ricky Rudd's Car	.15	.40
13 Ted Musgrave	.15	.40
14 Richard Petty	.50	1.25
15 Darrell Waltrip	.30	.75
16 Bobby Allison	.07	.20
17 Bobby Labonte	1.00	3.00
18 Michael Waltrip	.30	.75
19 Jeff Gordon	1.50	4.00
20 Jeff Gordon's Car	.60	1.50
21 Ken Schrader in Car	.15	.40
22 Ernie Irvan	.30	.75
23 Ernie Irvan's Car	.15	.40
24 Steve Grissom	.15	.40
25 Johnny Benson	.15	.40
26 Bobby Hamilton	.15	.40
27 Bobby Hamilton's Car	.07	.20
28 Ricky Craven	.15	.40
29 Ricky Craven's Car	.07	.20
30 Kyle Petty	.30	.75
31 Kyle Petty's Car	.15	.40
32 David Pearson	.07	.20
33 Dale Jarrett	1.00	2.50
34 Dale Jarrett's Car	.30	.75
35 Bill Elliott	.60	1.50
36 Bill Elliott's Car	.30	.75
37 Jeremy Mayfield	.30	.75
38 Jeff Burton	.50	1.25
39 Cale Yarborough	.30	.75
40 Jeff Gordon	1.50	4.00
41 Mark Martin	1.25	3.00
42 Rusty Wallace	1.25	3.00
43 Bill Elliott	.60	1.50
44 Ernie Irvan	.30	.75
45 Dale Earnhardt's Car CL	1.00	2.50
P1 Jeff Gordon Blue Promo	2.00	5.00
P2 Jeff Gordon Green Promo	2.00	5.00
P3 Jeff Gordon Silver Promo	2.00	5.00

1996 M-Force Black

This 12-card insert set features the top drivers from Winston Cup. The fronts of the cards are embossed driver or car portraits on black foil board. The backs feature the same silver mirror foil as the base cards. The Blacks were randomly inserted one in 96 packs.

COMPLETE SET (12)	250.00	500.00
B1 Rusty Wallace	10.00	25.00
B2 Rusty Wallace's Car	4.00	10.00
B3 Dale Earnhardt	20.00	50.00
B4 Dale Earnhardt's Car	8.00	20.00
B5 Terry Labonte	4.00	10.00
B6 Mark Martin	10.00	25.00
B7 Jeff Gordon	12.50	30.00
B8 Jeff Gordon's Car	5.00	12.00
B9 Ernie Irvan	2.50	6.00
B10 Dale Jarrett	8.00	20.00
B11 Bill Elliott	5.00	12.00
B12 Jeff Gordon	12.50	30.00

1996 M-Force Sheet Metal

This 6-card insert set was the first to incorporate actual race used sheet metal into a trading card. The piece of sheet metal along with a photo of the driver is permanently encased in a clear polyurethane card. Cards containing multi-colored pieces of sheet metal carry a 25 percent premium over those that do not. The cards were seeded one in 288 packs and serial numbered of 200.

COMPLETE SET (6)	400.00	800.00
M1 Rusty Wallace	25.00	60.00
M2 Dale Earnhardt	75.00	150.00
M3 Terry Labonte	25.00	60.00
M4 Mark Martin	30.00	80.00
M5 Jeff Gordon	60.00	120.00
M6 Bill Elliott	25.00	60.00

1996 M-Force Silvers

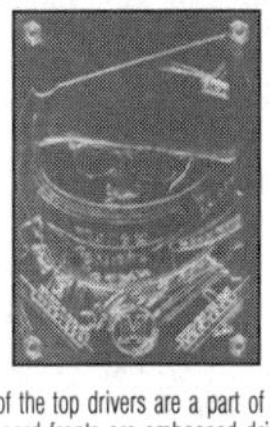

Eighteen of the top drivers are a part of this insert set. The card fronts are embossed driver or car portraits on silver foil board. The backs of the cards feature the same silver mirror foil as the base cards. The Silvers were inserted one in eight packs.

COMPLETE SET (18)	25.00	60.00
S1 Rusty Wallace's Car	1.50	4.00
S2 Dale Earnhardt	8.00	20.00
S3 Dale Earnhardt's Car	3.00	8.00
S4 Sterling Marlin	1.50	4.00
S5 Terry Labonte	1.50	4.00
S6 Terry Labonte's Car	1.00	2.50
S7 Ricky Rudd	1.50	4.00
S8 Richard Petty	1.50	4.00
S9 Bobby Labonte	4.00	10.00
S10 Jeff Gordon's Car	2.00	5.00
S11 Bobby Hamilton's Car	.25	.60
S12 Ricky Craven	.50	1.25
S13 Kyle Petty	1.00	2.50
S14 Jeff Gordon	5.00	12.00
S15 Mark Martin	4.00	10.00
S16 Rusty Wallace	4.00	10.00
S17 Bill Elliott	2.00	5.00
S18 Ernie Irvan	1.00	2.50

1992 Miller Genuine Draft Rusty Wallace

This six-card set was released by the Miller Brewing company. The cards were inserted into twelve packs of Miller Genuine Draft. There were three cards in a white envelope glued inside the twelve packs. Each three cards with envelope is considered a "set." Each card features art work by Sam Bass and measures 3 5/8" X 5 3/8". The front also carries "Miller Brewing Company Reminds You to Please THINK WHEN YOU DRINK." Think when you drink is in a yellow triangle. The cards are blank backed.

COMPLETE SET (6)	6.00	15.00
COMMON CARD	1.25	3.00

1993 Miller Genuine Draft Rusty Wallace Post Cards

This five-card set was available as a send-away offer from Miller Brewing Company. The cards measure 3 1/2" X 5 1/4" and came in a white envelope. There was one cover card in each envelope.

COMPLETE SET (5)	5.00	12.00
COMMON CARD	1.25	3.00
NNO Cover Card	.20	.50

2002 Miller Electric Post Cards

This 4-card set was produced for Miller Electric in 2002. The cards are approximately 4x6. Each card featured one team with each car pictured.

COMPLETE SET (4)	8.00	20.00
1 Dale Earnhardt Jr	5.00	12.00
Steve Park		
Michael Waltrip		
2 Bill Elliott	2.50	6.00
Jeremy Mayfield		
3 Kevin Harvick	2.50	6.00
Jeff Green		
Robby Gordon		
4 Mark Martin	3.00	8.00
Matt Kenseth		
Kurt Busch		
Jeff Burton		

1991 Motorcraft Racing

This 1991 release features members and machines of the Motorcraft Racing teams. The cards were primarily distributed through participating Ford dealerships and are unnumbered. We have listed and numbered the cards below in alphabetical order.

COMPLETE SET (7)	4.00	10.00
1 Bob Glidden's Car	.30	.75
Morgan Shepherd's Car		
2 Bob Glidden w/Car	.30	.75
3 Bob Glidden's Car	.30	.75
4 Bob Glidden Family Racing	.75	2.00
5 Walter Bud Moore	.50	1.25
6 Morgan Shepherd	.75	2.00
7 Morgan Shepherd's Car	.30	.75

1992 Motorcraft Racing

This 1992 release features members and machines of the Motorcraft Racing teams. The cards were primarily distributed in complete set form through participating Ford dealerships and are unnumbered. We have listed and numbered the cards below in alphabetical order.

COMPLETE SET (10)	2.50	6.00
1 Geoff Bodine	.25	.60
2 Geoff Bodine's Car	.10	.25
3 Geoff Bodine's Pit Crew	.25	.60
4 Geoff Bodine	.25	.60
Bob Glidden Cars		
5 Bob Glidden	.25	.60
6 Bob Glidden's Car	.10	.25
7 Bob Glidden	.25	.60
Etta Glidden		
8 Walter Bud Moore	.25	.60
9 Cover Card	.15	.40
10 Motorcraft Special Events	.15	.40

1993 Motorcraft Decade of Champions

This 1993 release honors Motorcraft Quality Part's ten years of motorsports sponsorship. The cards were primarily distributed in complete set form through participating Ford dealerships and are unnumbered. We have listed and numbered the cards below in alphabetical order.

COMPLETE SET (10)	2.50	6.00
1 Geoff Bodine's Car	.40	1.00
2 Manny Esquerra's Truck	.30	.75
3 Bob Glidden's Car	.30	.75
4 Bob Glidden's Car	.30	.75
5 John Jones' Car	.30	.75
6 Mark Oswald's Car	.30	.75
7 Ricky Rudd's Car	.50	1.25
8 Morgan Shepherd's Car	.40	1.00
9 Rickie Smith's Car	.30	.75
NNO Cover Card	.20	.50

1993 Motorcraft Manufacturers Championship

Ford produced this set to honor its 1992 NASCAR Manufacturers' Championship. Eight car and drivers are included along with a trophy card and a cover card. As is common with Motorcraft sets, the cards are unnumbered and listed below alphabetically.

COMPLETE SET (10)	4.00	6.00
1 Davey Allison	.60	1.50
2 Geoff Bodine	.20	.50
3 Bill Elliott	.60	1.25
4 Jimmy Hensley	.20	.50
5 Alan Kulwicki	.40	1.00
6 Sterling Marlin	.30	.75
7 Mark Martin	1.00	2.50
8 Morgan Shepherd	.20	.50
9 Cover Card	.20	.50
10 Trophy Card	.20	.50

1994 MW Windows

This five-card set was produced for distribution at the 1994 National Association of Homebuilders Show held in Las Vegas and was sponsored by MW Windows. The cards are called the Aces Collection and feature four drivers and one checklist card picturing the four. Reportedly, production was held to 7500 complete sets. The cards are unnumbered, but have been assigned numbers below alphabetically with the checklist card last.

COMPLETE SET (5)	5.00	12.00
1 Jeff Gordon	1.50	4.00
2 Bobby Labonte	1.00	2.50
3 Terry Labonte	.75	2.00
4 Ken Schrader	.40	1.00
5 Jeff Gordon	1.25	3.00
Bobby Labonte		
Terry Labonte		
Ken Schrader		
Checklist		

1995 MW Windows

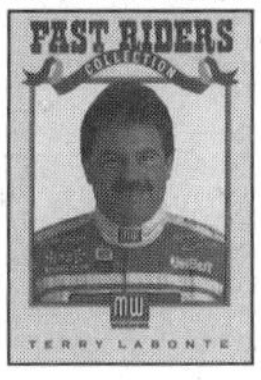

This five-card set was produced for distribution at the 1995 National Association of Homebuilders Show held in Houston and was sponsored by MW Windows. The cards are titled Fast Riders and feature four drivers and one checklist card picturing the four. Reportedly, production was held to 7500 complete sets.The cards are unnumbered, but have been assigned numbers below alphabetically with the checklist card last.

COMPLETE SET (5)	4.00	10.00
1 David Green	.75	2.00
2 Dale Jarrett	1.25	3.00
3 Terry Labonte	1.00	2.50
4 Michael Waltrip	.75	2.00
5 Terry Labonte	1.00	2.50
Michael Waltrip		
Dale Jarrett		
David Green		
Checklist		

2005 NAPA

COMP.UNCUT SET (2)	4.00	10.00
COMPLETE SET (2)	3.00	8.00
NNO Michael Waltrip	.75	2.00
NNO Dale Earnhardt Jr.	3.00	8.00

2004 National Trading Card Day *

PP1 Cover Card	.40	1.00
PP2 Jeff Gordon	1.50	4.00
PP3 Jimmie Johnson	1.25	3.00

PP4 Dale Earnhardt Jr.	1.50	4.00
PP5 Tony Stewart	1.00	2.50

2003 Nilla Wafers Team Nabisco

This set of 4-oversized (roughly 3 1/4" by 4") cards was produced by KF Holdings and issued one per Nabisco product during the 2003 season. Each card was produced with lenticular printing technology on the front and has rounded corners. The cardbacks feature a color photo of the driver, the Team Nabisco logo at the bottom and a copyright date of 2002, although the cards were released in 2003.

COMPLETE SET (4)	12.50	25.00
1 Dale Earnhardt Jr. Oreo	4.00	8.00
2 Dale Earnhardt Jr. Nilla Wafers	4.00	8.00
3 Michael Waltrip	3.00	6.00
4 Dale Earnhardt Jr. Jeff Green Kevin Harvick Michael Waltrip	4.00	8.00

1992 Pace American Canadian Tour

This 50-card set features drivers who raced in the American Canadian Tour. The cards were sold in complete set form and reportedly 30,000 sets were produced. Each set was individually numbered. The cards were produced by Pace Cards, Inc. of Stowe, Vermont.

COMPLETE SET (50)	4.80	12.00
1 Junior Hanley	.05	.15
2 Robbie Crouch	.05	.15
3 Beaver Dragon	.05	.15
4 Kevin Lepage	.05	.15
5 Derek Lynch	.05	.15
6 Brad Leighton	.05	.15
7 Randy MacDonald	.05	.15
8 Dan Beede	.05	.15
9 Roger Laperle	.05	.15
10 Ralph Nason	.05	.15
11 Jean-Paul Cabana	.05	.15
12 Bill Zardo, Sr.	.05	.15
13 Claude Leclerc	.05	.15
14 Robbie Thompson	.05	.15
15 Danny Knoll, Jr.	.05	.15
16 Bill Zardo, Jr.	.05	.15
17 John Greedy	.05	.15
18 Blair Bessett	.05	.15
19 Buzzie Bezanson	.05	.15
20 Phil Pinkham	.05	.15
21 Sylvain Metivier	.05	.15
22 Andre Beaudoin	.05	.15
23 Gord Bennett	.05	.15
24 Donald Forte	.05	.15
25 Jeff Stevens	.05	.15
26 Yvon Bedard	.05	.15
27 Dave Dion	.05	.15
28 Rollie MacDonald	.05	.15
29 Ricky Craven	.40	1.00
30 Chuck Bown	.05	.15
31 Bob Randall	.05	.15
32 Dave Moody	.05	.15
33 Stan Meserve	.05	.15
34 Tom Curley	.05	.15
35 Robbie Crouch	.05	.15
36 Dan Beede	.05	.15
37 Derek Lynch	.05	.15
38 Dan Beede Roger Laperle	.05	.15
39 Randy MacDonald Brad Leighton	.05	.15
40 Randy MacDonald	.05	.15
41 Robbie Thompson	.05	.15
42 Bill Zardo, Sr.	.05	.15
43 Claude Leclerc Brad Leighton	.05	.15
44 John Greedy	.05	.15
45 Roger Laperle Yvon Bedard	.05	.15
46 Gord Bennett	.05	.15
47 Beaver Dragon Ralph Nason	.05	.15
48 Yvon Bedard	.05	.15
49 Jean-Paul Cabana Buzzie Bezanson Sylvain Metivier	.05	.15
50 Randy MacDonald John Greedy	.05	.15

1992 Pepsi Richard Petty

This five-card set features the King of stock car racing, Richard Petty. The cards highlight Richard Petty's career. The cards were a promotional giveaway by Pepsi Co.

COMPLETE SET (5)	2.00	5.00
COMMON CARD	.40	1.00

1993 Pepsi 400 Victory Lane

Produced and distributed by Pepsi, this five-card set honors past winners of the Pepsi 400. The cards are unnumbered and listed below alphabetically. Although no year is present on the cards, they can be distinguished from the 1994 Pepsi 400 release by the orange colored Victory Lane title on the cardfronts.

COMPLETE SET (5)	4.00	10.00
1 Bobby Allison	1.25	3.00
2 Davey Allison	2.00	5.00
3 Buddy Baker	.50	1.25
4 Ernie Irvan	1.25	3.00
5 David Pearson	.50	1.25

1994 Pepsi 400 Victory Lane

Pepsi again produced and distributed a Pepsi 400 commemorative set in 1994. The cards are very similar to the 1993 issue, except they include the year 1994 on the cardfronts, as well as a yellow colored Victory Lane title. The cards are unnumbered and listed below alphabetically.

COMPLETE SET (6)	4.00	8.00
1 Donnie Allison	.50	1.25
2 A.J.Foyt	.50	1.25
3 Richard Petty	1.25	3.00
4 Greg Sacks	.50	1.25
5 Cale Yarborough	.50	1.25
6 Cover/Checklist Card	.10	.30

1996 Pinnacle

The 1996 Pinnacle set was issued in one series totalling 96 cards. This is the first issue under the Pinnacle name brand. The cards features NASCAR's top drivers and their rides printed on 20 point board. Each card has gold foil stamping and UV coating. The set includes these sub-sets; Jeff Gordon Persistence (66-73), Sterling Marlin Sterling (74-77), Hall of Fame (78-81), and Winners (85-89). The cards come 10-cards per pack, 24 packs per box and 16 boxes per case. The packs carried a suggested retail price for $2.49 each.

COMPLETE SET (96)	6.00	15.00
1 Rick Mast	.07	.20
2 Rusty Wallace	.60	1.50
3 Dale Earnhardt	1.25	3.00
4 Sterling Marlin	.25	.60
5 Terry Labonte	.25	.60
6 Mark Martin	.60	1.50
7 Geoff Bodine	.07	.20
8 Hut Stricklin	.07	.20
9 Lake Speed	.07	.20
10 Ricky Rudd	.25	.60
11 Brett Bodine	.07	.20
12 Derrike Cope	.07	.20
13 Dale Jarrett	.50	1.25
14 Joe Nemechek	.07	.20
15 Wally Dallenbach	.07	.20
16 Ted Musgrave	.07	.20
17 Darrell Waltrip	.15	.40
18 Bobby Labonte	.50	1.25
19 Kenny Wallace	.07	.20
20 Bobby Hillin Jr.	.07	.20
21 Michael Waltrip	.15	.40
22 Ward Burton	.15	.40
23 Jimmy Spencer	.07	.20
24 Jeff Gordon	.75	2.00
25 Ken Schrader	.07	.20
26 Morgan Shepherd	.07	.20
27 Bill Elliott	.30	.75
28 Ernie Irvan	.15	.40
29 Bobby Hamilton	.07	.20
30 Johnny Benson	.15	.40
31 Kyle Petty	.15	.40
32 Ricky Craven	.07	.20
33 Robert Pressley	.07	.20
34 John Andretti	.07	.20
35 Jeremy Mayfield	.15	.40
36 Rick Mast's Car	.02	.10
37 Rusty Wallace's Car	.25	.60
38 Dale Earnhardt's Car	.50	1.25
39 Sterling Marlin's Car	.07	.20
40 Terry Labonte's Car	.15	.40
41 Mark Martin's Car	.25	.60
42 Geoff Bodine's Car	.02	.10
43 Ricky Rudd's Car	.07	.20
44 Derrike Cope's Car	.02	.10
45 Ted Musgrave's Car	.02	.10
46 Darrell Waltrip's Car	.07	.20
47 Bobby Labonte's Car	.15	.40
48 Michael Waltrip's Car	.07	.20
49 Ward Burton's Car	.02	.10
50 Jimmy Spencer's Car	.02	.10
51 Jeff Gordon's Car	.30	.75
52 Ernie Irvan's Car	.07	.20
53 Johnny Benson's Car	.02	.10
54 Robert Pressley's Car	.02	.10
55 John Andretti's Car	.02	.10
56 Ricky Craven's Car	.02	.10
57 Kyle Petty's Car	.07	.20
58 Bobby Hamilton's Car	.02	.10
59 Dave Marcis' Car	.07	.20
60 Morgan Shepherd's Car	.02	.10
61 Bobby Hillin's Car	.02	.10
62 Kenny Wallace's Car	.02	.10
63 Joe Nemechek's Car	.02	.10
64 Dale Jarrett's Car	.15	.40
65 Hut Stricklin's Car	.02	.10
66 Jeff Gordon PER	.75	2.00
67 Jeff Gordon PER	.75	2.00
68 Jeff Gordon PER	.75	2.00
69 Jeff Gordon PER	.75	2.00
70 Jeff Gordon PER	.75	2.00
71 Jeff Gordon PER	.75	2.00
72 Jeff Gordon PER	.75	2.00
73 Jeff Gordon PER	.75	2.00
74 Sterling Marlin STE	.15	.40
75 Sterling Marlin STE	.15	.40
76 Sterling Marlin STE	.15	.40
77 Sterling Marlin STE	.15	.40
78 Joe Gibbs HOF	.15	.40
79 Bobby Labonte HOF	.25	.60
80 Jimmy Makar HOF	.02	.10
81 Bobby Labonte's Car HOF	.15	.40
82 Elmo Langley	.02	.10
83 Doyle Ford	.02	.10
84 Buster Auton	.02	.10
85 Jeff Gordon W	.75	2.00
86 Rusty Wallace W	.30	.75
87 Sterling Marlin W	.15	.40
88 Ernie Irvan W	.07	.20
89 Rusty Wallace W	.30	.75
90 Bobby Labonte's Transporter	.15	.40
91 Dale Earnhardt's Transporter	.50	1.25
92 Jeff Gordon's Transporter	.30	.75
93 Sterling Marlin's Transporter	.07	.20
94 Rusty Wallace's Transporter	.25	.60
95 Jeff Gordon CL	.30	.75
96 Mark Martin CL	.25	.60
DS1 Bill Elliott Driver Suit	8.00	20.00

1996 Pinnacle Artist Proofs

This 96-card parallel set features an Artist's Proof logo and rainbow foil stamping to differentiate each card from the base set. The cards were randomly inserted in both hobby and retail packs at a rate of one in 47 and in magazine packs at a rate of one in 75.

COMPLETE SET (96)	20.00	400.00
*ARTIST PROOF: 8X TO 20X BASE CARDS		

1996 Pinnacle Winston Cup Collection

This 96-card set is a parallel version of the base Pinnacle issue. The cards use all-foil dufex printing technology to differentiate themselves from the base Pinnacle cards. The Winston Cup Collection cards were seeded in retail packs one in nine and in hobby and magazine packs at a rate of one in 14.

COMPLETE SET (96)	40.00	80.00
*WC COLLECTION: 2.5X TO 6X BASE CARDS		

1996 Pinnacle Bill's Back

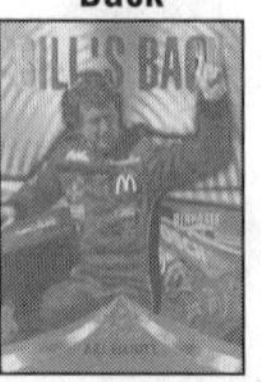

Randomly inserted in hobby and retail packs at a rate of one in 360, this two-card set features NASCAR's perennial fan favorite Bill Elliott. The two card salute captures Bill's return to racing after a potentially career-ending crash. The cards are printed on all-foil dufex card stock.

COMMON CARD (1-2)	8.00	20.00

1996 Pinnacle Checkered Flag

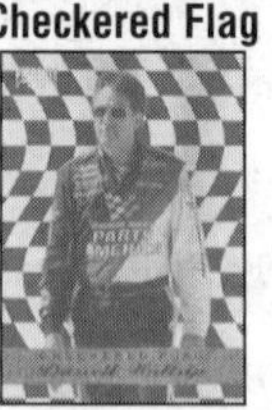

This 15-card insert set features the top names in racing. The cards were available only through magazine packs at a rate of one in 38 packs. The card fronts feature driver photos in front of a checkered flag, rainbow hologram background. The driver's name is in a gold foil stripe across the bottom of each card..

COMPLETE SET (15)	40.00	100.00
1 Jeff Gordon	6.00	15.00
2 Rusty Wallace	5.00	12.00
3 Dale Earnhardt	10.00	25.00
4 Sterling Marlin	2.00	5.00
5 Terry Labonte	2.00	5.00
6 Mark Martin	5.00	12.00
7 Bobby Labonte	4.00	10.00
8 Dale Jarrett	4.00	10.00
9 Bill Elliott	2.50	6.00
10 Ricky Rudd	2.00	5.00
11 Michael Waltrip	1.25	3.00
12 Ricky Craven	.60	1.50
13 Ernie Irvan	1.25	3.00
14 Geoff Bodine	.60	1.50
15 Darrell Waltrip	1.25	3.00

1996 Pinnacle Cut Above

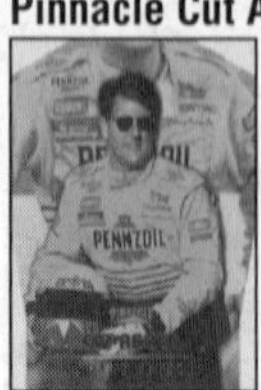

Randomly inserted in retail and hobby packs at a rate of one in 24, this 15-card insert set highlights the top drivers on the circuit. The photo of the driver is impossed over a background of that particular driver's uniform. The card is die-cut and uses gold foil stamping for the driver's name.

COMPLETE SET (15)	30.00	80.00
1 Jeff Gordon	6.00	15.00
2 Bill Elliott	2.50	6.00
3 Terry Labonte	2.00	5.00
4 Ernie Irvan	1.25	3.00
5 Johnny Benson	1.25	3.00
6 Ricky Rudd	2.00	5.00
7 Dale Jarrett	4.00	10.00
8 Rusty Wallace	5.00	12.00
9 Bobby Labonte	4.00	10.00
10 Mark Martin	5.00	12.00
11 Ricky Craven	.60	1.50
12 Robert Pressley	.60	1.50
13 Ted Musgrave	.60	1.50
14 Sterling Marlin	2.00	5.00
15 Geoff Bodine	.60	1.50

1996 Pinnacle Team Pinnacle

Randomly inserted in retail and hobby packs at a rate of one in 90 and magazine packs at a rate of one in 144, each of the 12 cards in this set features a double sided design. The cards display one of NASCAR's top drivers on one side and either their crew chief or owner on the flipside. The driver's side of each card features dufex printing technology.

COMPLETE SET (12)	150.00	350.00
1 Jeff Gordon Ray Evernham	12.50	30.00
2 Rusty Wallace Robin Pemberton	10.00	25.00
3 Dale Earnhardt David Smith	20.00	50.00
4 Dale Jarrett Todd Parrott	8.00	20.00
5 Terry Labonte Gary DeHart	4.00	10.00
6 Mark Martin Steve Hmiel	10.00	25.00
7 Bill Elliott Mike Beam	5.00	12.00
8 Sterling Marlin Tony Glover	4.00	10.00
9 Ricky Rudd Richard Broome	4.00	10.00
10 Jeff Gordon Rick Hendrick	12.50	30.00
11 Dale Earnhardt Richard Childress	20.00	50.00
12 Dale Jarrett Robert Yates	8.00	20.00
P8 Sterling Marlin Promo Tony Glover Promo	2.50	6.00

1996 Pinnacle Pole Position

The 1996 Pinnacle Pole Position set was issued in one series totalling 100 cards. The product was distributed only to K-Mart stores. The set contains the following topical subsets: Drivers (1-25) and The Early Years (72-81). The cards were packaged seven cards per pack, and 24 packs per box. The packs carried a suggested retail price of $1.99.

COMPLETE SET (100)	7.50	20.00
1 John Andretti	.07	.20
2 Rusty Wallace	.60	1.50
3 Dale Earnhardt	1.25	3.00
4 Sterling Marlin	.25	.60
5 Terry Labonte	.25	.60
6 Mark Martin	.60	1.50
7 Geoff Bodine	.07	.20
8 Hut Stricklin	.07	.20
9 Kenny Wallace	.07	.20
10 Ricky Rudd	.25	.60
11 Kyle Petty	.15	.40
12 Ernie Irvan	.15	.40
13 Dale Jarrett	.50	1.25
14 Bill Elliott	.30	.75
15 Jeff Burton	.25	.60
16 Robert Pressley	.07	.20
17 Darrell Waltrip	.15	.40
18 Bobby Labonte	.50	1.25
19 Bobby Hamilton	.07	.20
20 Johnny Benson Jr.	.15	.40
21 Michael Waltrip	.15	.40
22 Ward Burton	.15	.40
23 Jimmy Spencer	.07	.20
24 Jeff Gordon	.75	2.00
25 Ken Schrader	.07	.20
26 Rusty Wallace's Car	.15	.40
27 Dale Earnhardt's Car	.50	1.25
28 Sterling Marlin's Car	.07	.20
29 Terry Labonte's Car	.15	.40
30 Mark Martin's Car	.15	.40
31 Ricky Rudd's Car	.07	.20
32 Brett Bodine's Car	.02	.10
33 Derrike Cope's Car	.02	.10
34 Ted Musgrave's Car	.02	.10
35 Darrell Waltrip's Car	.07	.20
36 Bobby Labonte's Car	.15	.40
37 Michael Waltrip's Car	.07	.20
38 Ward Burton's Car	.02	.10
39 Jimmy Spencer's Car	.02	.10
40 Jeff Gordon's Car	.30	.75
41 Ernie Irvan's Car	.07	.20
42 Kyle Petty's Car	.07	.20
43 Bobby Hamilton's Car	.02	.10
44 Dale Jarrett's Car	.15	.40
45 Johnny Benson's Car	.02	.10
46 Robert Pressley's Car	.02	.10
47 Ricky Craven's Car	.02	.10
48 Bobby Hillin's Car	.02	.10
49 Jeff Burton's Car	.15	.40
50 Joe Nemechek's Car	.02	.10
51 Jeff Gordon 95C	.40	1.00
52 Jeff Gordon 95C	.40	1.00
53 Jeff Gordon 95C	.40	1.00
54 Jeff Gordon 95C	.40	1.00
55 Jeff Gordon 95C	.40	1.00
56 Dale Earnhardt SE	.60	1.50
57 Dale Earnhardt SE	.60	1.50
58 Dale Earnhardt SE	.60	1.50
59 Dale Earnhardt SE	.60	1.50
60 Dale Earnhardt SE	.60	1.50
61 Johnny Benson Jr. RS	.15	.40
62 Johnny Benson Jr. RS	.15	.40
63 Johnny Benson Jr. RS	.15	.40
64 Sterling Marlin WIN	.15	.40
65 Rusty Wallace WIN	.30	.75
66 Michael Waltrip WIN	.15	.40
67 Dale Jarrett WIN	.15	.40
68 Jeff Gordon WIN	.50	1.25
69 Jeff Gordon WIN	.50	1.25
70 Rusty Wallace WIN	.30	.75
71 Sterling Marlin WIN	.15	.40
72 Dale Earnhardt EY	.60	1.50
73 Jeff Gordon EY	.50	1.25
74 Kyle Petty EY	.07	.20
75 Bobby Labonte EY	.15	.40
76 Sterling Marlin EY	.15	.40
77 Mark Martin EY	.30	.75
78 Rusty Wallace EY	.30	.75
79 Terry Labonte EY	.15	.40
80 Ricky Rudd EY	.15	.40
81 Darrell Waltrip EY	.07	.20
82 Ray Evernham	.07	.20
83 Larry McReynolds	.02	.10
84 David Smith	.02	.10
85 Andy Petree	.02	.10
86 Richard Broome	.02	.10
87 Richard Childress	.15	.40
88 Larry McClure	.02	.10
89 Rick Hendrick	.02	.10
90 Filbert Martocci	.02	.10
91 Jack Roush	.02	.10
92 Joe Gibbs	.15	.40
93 Robert Yates	.02	.10
94 John Andretti	.07	.20
95 John Andretti	.07	.20
96 John Andretti	.07	.20
97 John Andretti	.07	.20
98 John Andretti	.07	.20
99 Bill McCarthy CL	.02	.10
100 Gary Miller CL	.02	.10

1996 Pinnacle Pole Position Lightning Fast

This 100-card set is a parallel to the base Pole Position set. The cards feature additional foil treatment on the fronts, but have no text to differentiate themselves from the base cards. The cards were available one in seven packs.

COMPLETE SET (100)	50.00	120.00
*LIGHTNING FAST: 2.5X TO 6X BASE CARDS		

1996 Pinnacle Pole Position Certified Strong

Randomly inserted in packs at a rate of one in 23, this 15-card set features rainbow foil hologram technology. The top drivers in NASCAR make an appearance in this set.

COMPLETE SET (15)	75.00	150.00
1 Jeff Gordon	8.00	20.00
2 Rusty Wallace	6.00	15.00
3 Dale Earnhardt	12.50	30.00
4 Sterling Marlin	2.50	6.00
5 Terry Labonte	2.50	6.00
6 Mark Martin	6.00	15.00
7 Ernie Irvan	1.50	4.00
8 Dale Jarrett	5.00	12.00
9 Jeremy Mayfield	1.50	4.00
10 Ricky Rudd	2.50	6.00
11 Bobby Labonte	5.00	12.00
12 Bobby Hamilton	.75	2.00
13 Bill Elliott	3.00	8.00
14 Kyle Petty	1.50	
15 Ricky Craven	.75	

1996 Pinnacle Pole Position No Limit

This 16-card insert set features the top cars
NASCAR circuit. Each card was printed on
mirror foil board and the front has a shot of t
and the words "speed limit" with the interna
"no" symbol over the top of it. The cards
randomly inserted in packs at a rate of one in 3
Gold Parallel cards feature gold mirror foil
instead of the base silver. The gold cards
seeded one in 240 packs.

COMPLETE SET (16)	100.00
COMP.GOLD SET (16)	400.00
*GOLDS: 1.5X TO 4X BASIC INSERTS	
1 Jeff Gordon	10.00
2 Rusty Wallace	8.00
3 Dale Earnhardt	15.00
4 Sterling Marlin	3.00
5 Terry Labonte	3.00
6 Mark Martin	8.00
7 Ernie Irvan	2.00
8 Robert Pressley	1.00
9 Dale Jarrett	6.00
10 Ricky Rudd	3.00
11 Bill Elliott	4.00
12 Darrell Waltrip	2.00
13 Jeff Burton	3.00
14 Jimmy Spencer	1.00
15 Bobby Labonte	6.00
16 Ken Schrader	1.00

1997 Pinnacle

This 96-card set was produced by Pinnacle B
The set features four topical subsets: Race F
(59-72), Texas Tornado (73-84), New Face (8
and Turn 4 (88-95). Cards were distributed
card packs with 18 packs per box and 24 box
case. The packs carried a suggested retail p
$2.99. A Terry Labonte 24K Gold Collector's
promo card was issued to all members who
the club.

COMPLETE SET (96)	6.00
1 Kyle Petty	.10
2 Rusty Wallace	.40
3 Dale Earnhardt	1.00
4 Sterling Marlin	.20
5 Terry Labonte	.20
6 Mark Martin	.50
7 Geoff Bodine	.05
8 Bill Elliott	.25
9 David Green	.05
10 Ricky Rudd	.20
11 Brett Bodine	.05
12 Derrike Cope	.05
13 Jeremy Mayfield	.10
14 Robby Gordon RC	.20
15 Steve Grissom	.05
16 Ted Musgrave	.05
17 Darrell Waltrip	.10
18 Bobby Labonte	.40
19 Johnny Benson	.10
20 Bobby Hamilton	.05
21 Michael Waltrip	.10
22 Ward Burton	.10
23 Jimmy Spencer	.05
24 Jeff Gordon	.60
25 Ricky Craven	.05
26 Mike Skinner	.05
27 Dale Jarrett	.40
28 Ernie Irvan	.10
29 Jeff Green	.05
30 Kyle Petty's Car	.05
31 Rusty Wallace's Car	.10
32 Dale Earnhardt's Car	.40
33 Sterling Marlin's Car	.05
34 Terry Labonte's Car	.05
35 Mark Martin's Car	.10
36 Geoff Bodine's Car	.02
37 Bill Elliott's Car	.05
38 David Green's Car	.02
39 Ricky Rudd's Car	.05
40 Brett Bodine's Car	.02
41 Derrike Cope's Car	.02
42 Jeremy Mayfield's Car	.10
43 Robby Gordon's Car	.10
44 Steve Grissom's Car	.02
45 Ted Musgrave's Car	.02
46 Darrell Waltrip's Car	.05
47 Bobby Labonte's Car	.10
48 Johnny Benson's Car	.02
49 Bobby Hamilton's Car	.02
50 Michael Waltrip's Car	.05
51 Ward Burton's Car	.02
52 Jimmy Spencer's Car	.02
53 Jeff Gordon's Car	.25
54 Ricky Craven's Car	.02
55 Mike Skinner's Car	.02
56 Dale Jarrett's Car	.10
57 Ernie Irvan's Car	.05
58 Jeff Green's Car	.02

59 Terry Labonte RR .10 .30
60 Dale Jarrett RR .20 .50
61 Mark Martin RR .25 .60
62 Rusty Wallace RR .25 .60
63 Bill Elliott RR .10 .30
64 Bobby Labonte RR .20 .50
65 Ernie Irvan RR .05 .15
66 Dale Earnhardt's Car RR .40 1.00
67 Ricky Rudd RR .10 .30
68 Dale Earnhardt's Car RR .40 1.00
69 Dale Earnhardt RR .50 1.25
70 Dale Earnhardt's Car RR .40 1.00
71 Sterling Marlin RR .10 .30
72 Mike Skinner RR .02 .10
73 Rusty Wallace TT .25 .60
74 Dale Jarrett TT .20 .50
75 Mark Martin TT .25 .60
76 Terry Labonte TT .10 .30
77 Bobby Labonte TT .20 .50
78 Sterling Marlin TT .10 .30
79 Kyle Petty TT .05 .15
80 Ernie Irvan TT .05 .15
81 Bobby Hamilton TT .02 .10
82 Dale Earnhardt TT .50 1.25
83 Michael Waltrip TT .05 .15
84 Dale Earnhardt TT .50 1.25
85 Jeff Green NF .02 .10
86 Mike Skinner NF .02 .10
87 David Green NF .02 .10
88 Johnny Benson's Car T4 .02 .10
89 Dale Jarrett's Car T4 .10 .30
90 Mark Martin's Car T4 .10 .30
91 Dale Earnhardt's Car T4 .40 1.00
92 Rusty Wallace's Car T4 .10 .30
93 Terry Labonte's Car T4 .05 .15
94 Darrell Waltrip's Car T4 .05 .15
95 Dale Earnhardt's Car T4 .40 1.00
96 Rusty Wallace CL .20 .50
C1 Terry Labonte Collector's Club Promo 24K 6.00 15.00

1997 Pinnacle Artist Proofs

This 96-card set is a three-tier parallel of the regular set. The tiers in this set are color coded. The 50 red cards were randomly inserted in packs at a ratio of 1:33. The 36 blue cards were randomly inserted in packs at a ratio of 1:117. Finally, the 100-third tier purple cards were randomly inserted in packs at a ratio of 1:620.

COMPLETE RED SET (50) 25.00 50.00
RED ART.PROOFS: 3X TO 8X BASIC CARDS
BLUE ART.PROOF: 6X TO 15X BASIC CARDS
PURPLE AP: 10X TO 25X BASIC CARDS

1997 Pinnacle Foil

This parallel set was issued in jumbo packs only and distributed primarily through retail magazine accounts. Each card features an all-foil front to differentiate them from the base issue cards.

COMP.FOIL SET (96) 6.00 15.00
FOILS: .4X TO 1X BASE CARDS

1997 Pinnacle Trophy Collection

This 96-card set is a parallel of the regular set. The cards were randomly inserted in packs at a ratio of 1:6.

COMPLETE SET (96) 25.00 60.00
TROPHY COLL: 2X TO 5X BASE CARDS

1997 Pinnacle Chevy Madness

This 3-card insert set is a continuation of the set that was started in 1997 Action Packed. The cards were randomly inserted in packs at a ratio of 1:23.

COMPLETE SET (3) 10.00 25.00
3 Dale Earnhardt's Car 8.00 20.00
4 David Green's Car .50 1.25
5 Jeff Gordon's Car 5.00 12.00

1997 Pinnacle Bobby Labonte Helmets

This 10-card set features ten helmets worn by Bobby Labonte during the 1997 Winston Cup season. Each card has a Dufex surface and features a logo from a

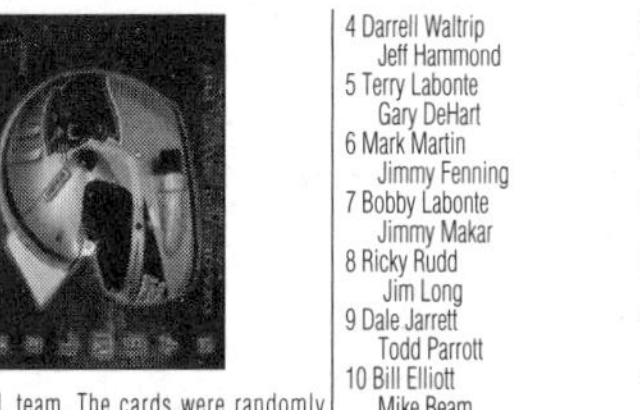

different NFL team. The cards were randomly inserted in hobby packs at a ratio of 1:89.

COMPLETE SET (10) 6.00 15.00
1 Bobby Labonte 1.00 2.50
Carolina Panthers
2 Bobby Labonte 1.00 2.50
Jacksonville Jaguars
3 Bobby Labonte 1.00 2.50
Dallas Cowboys
4 Bobby Labonte 1.00 2.50
Miami Dolphins
5 Bobby Labonte 1.00 2.50
New York Giants
6 Bobby Labonte 1.00 2.50
Detroit Lions
7 Bobby Labonte 1.00 2.50
San Francisco 49ers
8 Bobby Labonte 1.00 2.50
Atlanta Falcons
9 Bobby Labonte 1.00 2.50
Pittsburgh Steelers
10 Bobby Labonte 1.00 2.50
Arizona Cardinals

1997 Pinnacle Spellbound

This 12-card set features 12 drivers, each of whom appears on a letter of the words, "NASCAR RACING". The cards were randomly inserted in packs at a ratio of 1:23.

COMPLETE SET (12) 15.00 40.00
*PROMOS: .2X TO .5X BASIC INSERTS
1N Terry Labonte 1.50 4.00
2A Dale Jarrett 3.00 8.00
3S Dale Earnhardt 8.00 20.00
4C Rusty Wallace 3.00 8.00
5A Mark Martin 4.00 10.00
6R Jeff Gordon 5.00 12.00
7R Bobby Hamilton .50 1.25
8A Kyle Petty 1.00 2.50
9C Ernie Irvan 1.00 2.50
10I Ricky Rudd 1.50 4.00
11N Bill Elliott 2.00 5.00
12G Bobby Labonte 3.00 8.00

1997 Pinnacle Spellbound Autographs

This five-card set features the autographs of five drivers from the regular set. Each of the drivers signed 500 cards. The Jeff Gordon card inserted in packs was actually a redemption that could be redeemed for an autographed card. An insert ratio was not given for these cards.

COMPLETE SET (5) 200.00 400.00
1N Terry Labonte 12.50 30.00
2A Dale Jarrett 12.50 30.00
3S Dale Earnhardt 125.00 250.00
6R Jeff Gordon EXCH 2.00 5.00
6RAU Jeff Gordon AUTO 40.00 80.00
11N Bill Elliott 30.00 75.00

1997 Pinnacle Team Pinnacle

This 10-card insert set features 10 top NASCAR drivers on double-sided cards with their crew chiefs. These cards have red and blue versions. Both colors have the same value. The cards were randomly inserted in packs at a ratio of 1:240.

COMPLETE SET (10) 100.00 200.00
1 Jeff Gordon 10.00 25.00
Ray Evernham
2 Rusty Wallace 6.00 15.00
Robin Pemberton
3 Dale Earnhardt 15.00 40.00
Larry McReynolds
4 Darrell Waltrip 2.00 5.00
Jeff Hammond
5 Terry Labonte 3.00 8.00
Gary DeHart
6 Mark Martin 8.00 20.00
Jimmy Fenning
7 Bobby Labonte 6.00 15.00
Jimmy Makar
8 Ricky Rudd 3.00 8.00
Jim Long
9 Dale Jarrett 6.00 15.00
Todd Parrott
10 Bill Elliott 4.00 10.00
Mike Beam

1997 Pinnacle Certified

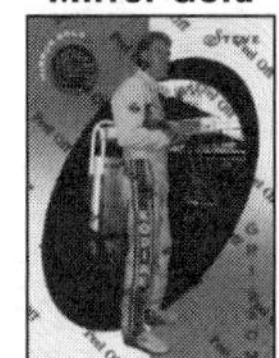

This 100-card set was released by Pinnacle Brands. The set features two topical subsets: War Paint (69-88) and Burning Desire (89-98). Cards were distributed in six card packs with 20 packs per box and 16 boxes per case. The packs carried a suggested retail price of $4.99.

COMPLETE SET (100) 10.00 25.00
1 Kyle Petty .40 1.00
2 Rusty Wallace 1.25 3.00
3 Dale Earnhardt 2.50 6.00
4 Sterling Marlin .60 1.50
5 Terry Labonte .60 1.50
6 Mark Martin 1.25 3.00
7 Bill Elliott .60 1.50
8 Jeremy Mayfield .40 1.00
9 Ted Musgrave .20 .50
10 Ricky Rudd .60 1.50
11 Robby Gordon RC .60 1.50
12 Johnny Benson .40 1.00
13 Bobby Hamilton .20 .50
14 Mike Skinner .20 .50
15 Dale Jarrett 1.00 2.50
16 Steve Grissom .20 .50
17 Darrell Waltrip .40 1.00
18 Bobby Labonte 1.00 2.50
19 Ernie Irvan .40 1.00
20 Jeff Green .20 .50
21 Michael Waltrip .40 1.00
22 Ward Burton .40 1.00
23 Geoff Bodine .20 .50
24 Jeff Gordon 1.50 4.00
25 Ricky Craven .20 .50
26 Jimmy Spencer .20 .50
27 Brett Bodine .20 .50
28 David Green .20 .50
29 John Andretti .20 .50
30 Ken Schrader .20 .50
31 Chad Little .40 1.00
32 Joe Nemecheck .20 .50
33 Hut Stricklin .20 .50
34 Kenny Wallace .20 .50
35 Kyle Petty's Car .07 .20
36 Rusty Wallace's Car .60 1.50
37 Dale Earnhardt's Car 1.00 2.50
38 Sterling Marlin's Car .20 .50
39 Terry Labonte's Car .40 1.00
40 Mark Martin's Car .60 1.50
41 Bill Elliott's Car .40 1.00
42 Jeremy Mayfield's Car .07 .20
43 Jeff Burton's Car .07 .20
44 Ricky Rudd's Car .20 .50
45 Robby Gordon's Car .40 1.00
46 Johnny Benson's Car .07 .20
47 Bobby Hamilton's Car .07 .20
48 Mike Skinner's Car .07 .20
49 Dale Jarrett's Car .20 .50
50 Steve Grissom's Car .07 .20
51 Darrell Waltrip's Car .07 .20
52 Bobby Labonte's Car .40 1.00
53 Ernie Irvan's Car .20 .50
54 Jeff Green's Car .07 .20
55 Michael Waltrip's Car .20 .50
56 Ward Burton's Car .20 .50
57 Geoff Bodine's Car .07 .20
58 Jeff Gordon's Car .60 1.50
59 Terry Labonte's Car .40 1.00
60 Jimmy Spencer's Car .07 .20
61 Brett Bodine's Car .07 .20
62 David Green's Car .07 .20
63 John Andretti's Car .07 .20
64 Ken Schrader's Car .07 .20
65 Chad Little's Car .07 .20
66 Joe Nemecheck's Car .07 .20
67 Hut Stricklin's Car .07 .20
68 Kenny Wallace's Car .07 .20
69 Darrell Waltrip's Car WP .07 .20
70 Darrell Waltrip's Car WP .07 .20
71 Darrell Waltrip's Car WP .07 .20
72 Jeremy Mayfield's Car WP .07 .20
73 Jeremy Mayfield's Car WP .07 .20
74 Jeff Gordon's Car WP .60 1.50
75 Ward Burton's Car WP .07 .20
76 Dale Earnhardt's Car WP 1.00 2.50
77 Bobby Labonte's Car WP .40 1.00
78 Michael Waltrip's Car WP .20 .50
79 Robby Gordon's Car WP .40 1.00
80 Terry Labonte's Car WP .40 1.00
81 Bill Elliott's Car WP .40 1.00
82 Bobby Hamilton's Car WP .07 .20
83 Chad Little's Car WP .07 .20
84 Jeff Green's Car WP .07 .20
85 Jeff Green's Car WP .07 .20
86 Rick Mast's Car WP .07 .20
87 Ernie Irvan's Car WP .20 .50
88 Geoff Bodine's Car WP .07 .20
89 Jeff Gordon BD .75 2.00
90 Terry Labonte BD .40 1.00
91 Mark Martin BD .60 1.50
92 Dale Jarrett BD .60 1.50
93 Dale Earnhardt BD 1.25 3.00
94 Ricky Rudd BD .40 1.00
95 Rusty Wallace BD .60 1.50
96 Bobby Hamilton BD .20 .50
97 Bobby Labonte BD .60 1.50
98 Kyle Petty BD .40 1.00
P6 Mark Martin Promo 2.00 5.00
NNO Checklist 1 .07 .20
NNO Checklist 2 .07 .20

1997 Pinnacle Certified Mirror Blue

This 100-card set is a parallel of the base set. It is important to note that the two checklist cards in this set have a mirror-like finish, but are not labeled as mirror cards. There is only one mirror version, rather than three of each checklist card. The cards were randomly inserted in packs at a ratio of 1:199.

COMPLETE SET (100) 300.00 600.00
*MIRROR BLUES: 4X TO 10X BASIC CARDS

1997 Pinnacle Certified Mirror Gold

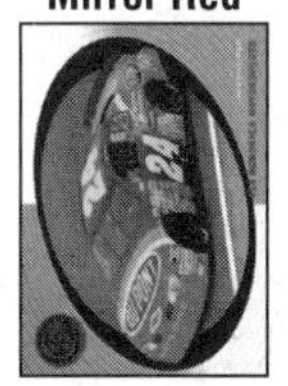

This 100-card set is a parallel of the base set. It is important to note that the two checklist cards in this set have a mirror-like finish, but are not labeled as mirror cards. There is only one mirror version, rather than three of each checklist card. The cards were randomly inserted in packs at a ratio of 1:299.

COMPLETE SET (100) 300.00 750.00
*MIRROR GOLDS: 4X TO 10X BASIC CARDS

1997 Pinnacle Certified Mirror Red

This 100-card set is a parallel of the base set. It is important to note that the two checklist cards in this set have a mirror-like finish, but are not labeled as mirror cards. There is only one mirror version, rather than three of each checklist card. The cards were randomly inserted in packs at a ratio of 1:99.

COMPLETE SET (100) 250.00 500.00
*MIRROR REDS: 3X TO 8X BASIC CARDS

1997 Pinnacle Certified Red

This 100-card set is a parallel of the base set. It is important to note that the two checklist cards in this set do not have a red-bordered front, thus the standard checklist cards are considered to fit this set. The cards were randomly inserted in packs at a ratio of 1:5.

COMPLETE SET (100) 50.00 120.00
*REDS: 1.5X TO 4X BASE CARDS

1997 Pinnacle Certified Certified Team

This 10-card insert set features some of the top stars from the Winston Cup circuit. The cards were randomly inserted in packs at a ratio of 1:19.

COMPLETE SET (10) 15.00 40.00
COMP.GOLD SET (10) 60.00 150.00
*GOLD TEAM: 1.2X TO 3X BASIC INSERTS
GOLD TEAM STATED ODDS: 1:119
1 Dale Earnhardt 6.00 15.00
2 Jeff Gordon 4.00 10.00
3 Ricky Rudd 1.50 4.00
4 Bobby Labonte 2.50 6.00
5 Terry Labonte 1.50 4.00
6 Rusty Wallace 3.00 8.00
7 Mark Martin 3.00 8.00
8 Bill Elliott 1.50 4.00
9 Dale Jarrett 2.50 6.00
10 Jeremy Mayfield 1.00 2.50

1997 Pinnacle Certified Epix

This 10-card insert set features some of the top drivers in NASCAR. The Orange colored base cards were randomly inserted in packs at a ratio of 1:15.

COMPLETE SET (10) 15.00 40.00
COMP.PURPLE SET (10) 25.00 60.00
*PURPLES: .8X TO 2X ORANGE
COMP.EMERALD SET (10) 100.00 200.00
*EMERALDS: 1.5X TO 4X ORANGE
E1 Dale Earnhardt 4.00 10.00
E2 Jeff Gordon 2.50 6.00

E3 Ricky Rudd 1.00 2.50
E4 Bobby Labonte 1.50 4.00
E5 Terry Labonte 1.00 2.50
E6 Rusty Wallace 2.00 5.00
E7 Mark Martin 2.00 5.00
E8 Darrell Waltrip .60 1.50
E9 Dale Jarrett 1.50 4.00
E10 Ernie Irvan .60 1.50

1997 Pinnacle Checkers

This nine-card set was issued through Checkers Drive-In Restaurants. The cards were distributed via single card packs. Each pack has one collector card and t-shirt offer card. You received one pack free with a purchase of a combo meal at all participating Checkers. It took 15 Checkers Racing points to get one free t-shirt. Each t-shirt offer card was worth one point.

COMPLETE SET (9) .80 2.00
1 Ricky Rudd .10 .30
2 Sterling Marlin .10 .30
3 Johnny Benson .08 .25
4 Ricky Rudd .10 .30
5 Sterling Marlin .10 .30
6 Johnny Benson .08 .25
7 Ricky Rudd .10 .30
8 Sterling Marlin .10 .30
9 Johnny Benson .08 .25

1997 Pinnacle Mint

This 30-diecut card set features the top names from the Winston Cup circuit. The cards can be used to hold the coins available in this product. Die-cut cards were distributed two per pack with the regular cards being distributed one per pack. Coins were distributed two per pack. The packs carried a suggested retail price of $2.99.

COMP. DIE CUT SET (30) 5.00 12.00
1 Terry Labonte .25 .60
2 Jeff Gordon .75 2.00
3 Dale Jarrett .40 1.00
4 Darrell Waltrip .15 .40
5 Mark Martin .60 1.50
6 Ricky Rudd .25 .60
7 Rusty Wallace .60 1.50
8 Sterling Marlin .25 .60
9 Bobby Hamilton .07 .20
10 Ernie Irvan .15 .40
11 Bobby Labonte .40 1.00
12 Johnny Benson .15 .40
13 Michael Waltrip .15 .40
14 Jimmy Spencer .07 .20
15 Ted Musgrave .07 .20
16 Geoff Bodine .07 .20
17 Bill Elliott .30 .75
18 John Andretti .07 .20
19 Ward Burton .15 .40
20 Randy LaJoie .07 .20
21 Dale Earnhardt's Car .60 1.50
22 Ricky Rudd's Car .07 .20
23 Dale Jarrett's Car .15 .40
24 Jeff Gordon's Car .40 1.00
25 Terry Labonte's Car .15 .40
26 Mark Martin's Car .25 .60
27 Bobby Labonte's Car .15 .40
28 Ernie Irvan's Car .02 .10
29 Bill Elliott's Car .15 .40
30 Johnny Benson's Car .02 .10
P1 Dale Jarrett Promo 1.25 3.00

1997 Pinnacle Mint Bronze

This 30-card set parallels the die cut card set and has a bronze logo containing the drivers' numbers in place of the die cut area. One foil card was inserted in every pack.

COMPLETE SET (30) 10.00 25.00
*BRONZE: .8X TO 2X DIE CUTS

1997 Pinnacle Mint Gold

This 30-card set parallels the diecut card set and has a gold logo containing the drivers' numbers in place of the diecut area. The cards were randomly inserted in hobby packs at a ratio of 1:48 and in retail packs at a ratio of 1:72.

COMPLETE SET (30) 100.00 200.00
*GOLDS: 6X TO 15X DIE CUTS

1997 Pinnacle Mint Silver

This 30-card set parallels the diecut card set and has a silver logo containing the drivers' numbers in place of the diecut area. The cards were randomly inserted in hobby packs at a ratio of 1:20 and in retail packs at a ratio of 1:30.

COMPLETE SET (30) 40.00 100.00
*SILVERS: 3X TO 8X DIE CUTS

1997 Pinnacle Mint Coins

This 30-coin set parallels the die cut card set. The drivers' portraits and cars are featured on the front of the coins while the Pinnacle Mint logo is featured on the back. The coins are randomly inserted in hobby packs at a ratio of 2:1 and in retail packs at a ratio of 1:1.

COMPLETE SET (30) 12.50 30.00
COMP.NICKEL SET (30) 60.00 150.00
*NICKEL-SILVER: 2X TO 5X BRONZE
NICKEL-SILVER STATED ODDS 1:20
COMP.24K GOLD (30) 250.00 500.00
*24K GOLD PLATED: 6X TO 15X BRONZE
24K GOLD STATED ODDS 1:48
1 Terry Labonte 1.00 2.50
2 Jeff Gordon 2.50 6.00
3 Dale Jarrett 1.25 3.00
4 Darrell Waltrip .50 1.25
5 Mark Martin 1.50 4.00
6 Ricky Rudd .75 2.00
7 Rusty Wallace 1.50 4.00
8 Sterling Marlin .60 1.50
9 Bobby Hamilton .25 .60
10 Ernie Irvan .50 1.25
11 Bobby Labonte 1.25 3.00
12 Johnny Benson .50 1.25
13 Michael Waltrip .50 1.25
14 Jimmy Spencer .25 .60
15 Ted Musgrave .25 .60
16 Geoff Bodine .25 .60
17 Bill Elliott 1.00 2.50
18 John Andretti .25 .60
19 Ward Burton .50 1.25
20 Randy LaJoie .25 .60
21 Dale Earnhardt's Car 2.50 6.00
22 Ricky Rudd's Car .25 .60
23 Dale Jarrett's Car .50 1.25
24 Jeff Gordon's Car 1.00 2.50
25 Terry Labonte's Car .50 1.25
26 Mark Martin's Car .60 1.50
27 Bobby Labonte's Car .50 1.25
28 Ernie Irvan's Car .10 .30
29 Bill Elliott's Car .25 .60
30 Johnny Benson's Car .10 .30

1997 Pinnacle Pepsi Jeff Gordon

This set of 3-promo cards was produced by Pinnacle and distributed through Pepsi. The cards include a color photo of either Jeff Gordon or his car on the front. The backs include a brief bio on the driver's recent career along with the Pinnacle and Pepsi logos at the bottom.

COMPLETE SET (3) 2.00 5.00
1 Jeff Gordon .75 2.00
2 Jeff Gordon's Car .60 1.50
3 Jeff Gordon .75 2.00

1998 Pinnacle Mint

The 1998 Pinnacle Mint set was issued in one series totalling 30 cards. The set offers two coins and three cards per pack. Die-cut cards were also included to provide the perfect fit to make a card-and-coin collectible. The set features 30 drivers with coins that come in brass, nickel-silver, solid silver and solid gold as well as bronze-plated proof coins, silver-plated proof coins, and gold-plated proof coins.

COMPLETE SET (30) 6.00 15.00
1 Jeff Gordon .75 2.00
2 Mark Martin .60 1.50
3 Dale Earnhardt 1.25 3.00
4 Terry Labonte .25 .60
5 Dale Jarrett .50 1.25
6 Bobby Labonte .50 1.25
7 Bill Elliott .30 .75
8 Ted Musgrave .07 .20
9 Ricky Rudd .25 .60
10 Rusty Wallace .60 1.50
12 Michael Waltrip .15 .40
13 Jeff Gordon's Car .30 .75

14 Mark Martin's Car .25 .60
15 Dale Jarrett's Car .15 .40
16 Terry Labonte's Car .15 .40
17 Dale Earnhardt's Car .50 1.25
18 Bobby Labonte's Car .15 .40
19 Bill Elliott's Car .15 .40
20 Ted Musgrave's Car .05 .15
21 Ricky Rudd's Car .07 .20
22 Rusty Wallace's Car .25 .60
23 Jeremy Mayfield's Car .07 .20
24 Michael Waltrip's Car .07 .20
25 Mark Martin MM .30 .75
26 Rusty Wallace MM .30 .75
27 Jeff Gordon MM .40 1.00
28 Dale Jarrett MM .25 .60
29 Ricky Rudd MM .15 .40
30 Ernie Irvan MM .15 .40
P1 Mark Martin Promo 1.00 2.50

1998 Pinnacle Mint Die Cuts

This 30-card set parallels the base (bronze) card set and has a die cut area in place of the bronze area containing the drivers' numbers. The cards were inserted one per hobby pack and two per retail pack.

COMPLETE SET (30) 5.00 12.00
*DIE CUTS: .3X TO .8X BASE CARDS

1998 Pinnacle Mint Championship Mint

This two-card set depicts Jeff Gordon and his car during his 1997 Winston Cup Championship season. These cards were randomly inserted into hobby packs at a ratio of one per 41 packs and into retail packs at a ratio of one per 71 packs.

1 Jeff Gordon 7.50 20.00
2 Jeff Gordon's Car 5.00 12.00

1998 Pinnacle Mint Gold Team

This 30-card set parallels the base set and was randomly inserted in both hobby and retail packs at a rate of one in 47. Each card features a "Gold Team" logo on the front.

COMPLETE SET (30) 125.00 250.00
*GOLD TEAM: 5X TO 12X BASE CARDS

1998 Pinnacle Mint Silver Team

This 30-card set parallels the base set and was randomly inserted in both hobby and retail packs at a rate of 1:15 and 1:23 respectively. Each card features a "Silver Team" logo on the front.

COMPLETE SET (30) 60.00 150.00
*SILVER TEAM: 4X TO 10X BASE CARDS

1998 Pinnacle Mint Coins

This 30-coin set parallels the base card set. These coins were inserted into hobby packs at a ratio of 2:1 and into retail packs at a ratio of 1:1.

COMPLETE SET (30) 10.00 25.00
*GOLD-PLATED: 5X TO 12X BASE COINS
GOLD-PLATED STATED ODDS 1:199
*NICKEL-SILVER: 1.5X TO 4X BASE COINS
NICKEL-SILVER STATED ODDS 1:41
*BRONZE PROOFS: 4X TO 10X BASE COINS
BRONZE PR.PRINT RUN 500 SER.#'d SETS
*GOLD PROOFS: 10X TO 25X BASE COINS
GOLD PROOF PRINT RUN 100 SER.#'d SETS
*SILVER PROOFS: 6X TO 15X BASE COINS
SILV.PROOF PRINT RUN 250 SER.#'d SETS
*SOLID SILVERS: 6X TO 15X BASE COINS
SOLID SILVER ODDS: 1:288 HOB, 1:960 RET
UNPRICED SOLID GOLDS SER.#'d OF 1
1 Jeff Gordon 1.25 3.00
2 Mark Martin 1.00 2.50
3 Dale Earnhardt 2.00 5.00
4 Terry Labonte .40 1.00
5 Dale Jarrett .75 2.00
6 Bobby Labonte .75 2.00
7 Bill Elliott .50 1.25
8 Ted Musgrave .10 .30
9 Ricky Rudd .40 1.00
10 Rusty Wallace 1.00 2.50
11 Jeremy Mayfield .25 .60
12 Michael Waltrip .25 .60
13 Jeff Gordon's Car .50 1.25
14 Mark Martin's Car .40 1.00
15 Dale Jarrett's Car .25 .60
16 Terry Labonte's Car .25 .60
17 Dale Earnhardt's Car .75 2.00
18 Bobby Labonte's Car .25 .60
19 Bill Elliott's Car .25 .60
20 Ted Musgrave's Car .10 .25
21 Ricky Rudd's Car .10 .30
22 Rusty Wallace's Car .40 1.00
23 Jeremy Mayfield's Car .10 .30
24 Michael Waltrip's Car .10 .30
01 Mark Martin MM .50 1.25
02 Rusty Wallace MM .50 1.25
03 Jeff Gordon MM .60 1.50
04 Dale Jarrett MM .40 1.00
05 Ricky Rudd MM .25 .60
06 Ernie Irvan MM .25 .60

1998 Pinnacle Mint Coins Bronze Proof

This 30-card set parallels the base coin set. The set was serially numbered to 500.

COMPLETE SET (30) 100.00 250.00
*BRONZE PROOFS: 4X TO 10X BASE COINS

1998 Pinnacle Mint Championship Mint Coins

Randomly inserted in hobby packs and retail packs at a rate of 1:89 and 1:129 respectively, this set is a metal alloy insert made from the melted hood of Jeff Gordon's 1997 Talladega race car. The retail version contains traditional sized coins, one of Gordon and one of the car. Hobby packs contain a double-sized version of the coins.

COMPLETE SET (4) 60.00 150.00
1A Jeff Gordon's Car 10.00 25.00
1B Jeff Gordon's Car Jumbo 10.00 25.00
2A Jeff Gordon 20.00 50.00
2B Jeff Gordon Jumbo 20.00 50.00

1998 Pinnacle Mint Coins Gold Plated

This 30-card set parallels the coin base set and was randomly inserted in both hobby and retail packs at a rate of one in 199.

COMPLETE SET (30) 175.00 300.00
*GOLD-PLATED: 5X TO 12X BASE COINS

1998 Pinnacle Mint Coins Gold Plated Proofs

This 30-card set parallels the base coin set and was serially numbered to 100.

*GOLD PROOFS: 10X TO 25X BASE COINS

1998 Pinnacle Mint Coins Nickel-Silver

This 30-card set parallels the base coin set and was randomly inserted in both hobby and retail packs at a rate of one in 41.

COMPLETE SET (30) 40.00 100.00
*NICKEL-SILVER: 1.5X TO 4X BASE COINS

1998 Pinnacle Mint Coins Silver Plated Proofs

This 30-card set parallels the base coin set and was serially numbered to 250.

COMPLETE SET (30) 200.00 400.00
*SILVER PROOFS: 6X TO 15X BASE COINS

1998 Pinnacle Mint Coins Solid Silver

This 30-card set parallels the base coin set and was randomly inserted in both hobby and retail packs at a rate of 1:288 and 1:960 respectively.

COMPLETE SET (30) 200.00 400.00
*SOLID SILVERS: 6X TO 15X BASE COINS

1997 Pinnacle Portraits

This set was issued in packs with one oversized card along with a package of standard sized cards. Each features a color photo of the featured driver or his ride.

COMPLETE SET (50) 7.50 20.00
1 Jeff Gordon 1.25 3.00
2 Mark Martin 1.00 2.50
3 Dale Earnhardt 2.00 5.00
4 Terry Labonte .40 1.00
5 Bobby Labonte .75 2.00
6 Bill Elliott .60 1.50
7 Ricky Rudd .40 1.00
8 Dale Jarrett .75 2.00
9 Ted Musgrave .10 .30
10 Jeremy Mayfield .25 .60
11 Johnny Benson .25 .60
12 Ricky Craven .10 .30
13 Michael Waltrip .25 .60
14 Kyle Petty .25 .60
15 Ernie Irvan .25 .60
16 Bobby Hamilton .10 .30
17 Mike Skinner .10 .30
18 Rusty Wallace 1.00 2.50
19 Ken Schrader .10 .30
20 Jimmy Spencer .10 .30
21 Jeff Gordon's Car .50 1.25
22 Mark Martin's Car .40 1.00
23 Dale Earnhardt's Car .75 2.00
24 Terry Labonte's Car .25 .60
25 Bobby Labonte's Car .25 .60
26 Bill Elliott's Car .25 .60
27 Ricky Rudd's Car .10 .30
28 Dale Jarrett's Car .25 .60
29 Ted Musgrave's Car .05 .15
30 Jeremy Mayfield's Car .10 .30
31 Johnny Benson's Car .05 .15
32 Ricky Craven's Car .05 .15
33 Michael Waltrip's Car .10 .30
34 Kyle Petty's Car .10 .30
35 Ernie Irvan's Car .10 .30
36 Bobby Hamilton's Car .05 .15
37 Mike Skinner's Car .05 .15
38 Rusty Wallace's Car .40 1.00
39 Ken Schrader's Car .05 .15
40 Jimmy Spencer's Car .05 .15
41 Mark Martin SS .50 1.25
42 Terry Labonte SS .25 .60
43 Chad Little SS .10 .30
44 Dale Jarrett SS .40 1.00
45 Bill Elliott SS .25 .60
46 David Green SS .10 .30
47 Ernie Irvan SS .10 .30
48 Michael Waltrip SS .25 .60
49 Ted Musgrave SS .05 .15
50 Steve Grissom SS .05 .15

1997 Pinnacle Portraits 8x10

These oversized (roughly 8" x 10") cards were issued one per pack of the Pinnacle Portraits product. Each card was numbered with the driver's initials and the card number. A Dufex parallel version was also created and inserted at the rate of 1:9 packs.

*SINGLES: .6X TO 1.5X BASE CARDS
*DUFEX: 1X TO 2.5X BASIC INSERTS
BE1 Bill Elliott 1.00 2.50
BE2 Bill Elliott 1.00 2.50
BE3 Bill Elliott 1.00 2.50
BE4 Bill Elliott 1.00 2.50
DE1 Dale Earnhardt 3.00 8.00
DE2 Dale Earnhardt 3.00 8.00
DE3 Dale Earnhardt 3.00 8.00
DE4 Dale Earnhardt 3.00 8.00
DJ1 Dale Jarrett 1.25 3.00
DJ2 Dale Jarrett 1.25 3.00
DJ3 Dale Jarrett 1.25 3.00
DJ4 Dale Jarrett 1.25 3.00
JG1 Jeff Gordon 2.00 5.00
JG2 Jeff Gordon 2.00 5.00
JG3 Jeff Gordon 2.00 5.00
JG4 Jeff Gordon 2.00 5.00
MM1 Mark Martin 1.50 4.00
MM2 Mark Martin 1.50 4.00
MM3 Mark Martin 1.50 4.00
MM4 Mark Martin 1.50 4.00
TL1 Terry Labonte .60 1.50
TL2 Terry Labonte .60 1.50
TL3 Terry Labonte .60 1.50
TL4 Terry Labonte .60 1.50

1997 Pinnacle Precision

This 77-card set was distributed in collectible oil cans. The cards themselves are made of steel and carry a 1996 copyright date on the backs. Each can included two 2-card packs of steel cards, one koozie and one static cling decal. The cans carried a suggested retail price of $9.99.

COMPLETE SET (77) 40.00 80.00
1 Bob Brannan .08 .25
2 Rick Hendrick .08 .25
3 Jeff Gordon 1.50 4.00
4 Jeff Gordon Pit Action .75 2.00
5 Jeff Gordon's Car .75 2.00
6 Jeff Gordon 1.50 4.00
7 Ray Evernham .20 .50
8 Jeff Gordon's Car .75 2.00
9 Jeff Gordon 1.50 4.00
10 Don Hawk .08 .25
11 Richard Childress .30 .75
12 Dale Earnhardt's Transporter 1.25 3.00
13 Dale Earnhardt Pit Action 1.25 3.00
14 Dale Earnhardt's Car 1.50 4.00
15 Dale Earnhardt 2.50 6.00
16 David Smith .08 .25
17 Dale Earnhardt's Car 1.50 4.00
18 Dale Earnhardt 2.50 6.00
19 Sterling Marlin's Transporter .08 .25
20 Larry McClure .08 .25
21 Sterling Marlin .50 1.25
22 Sterling Marlin Pit Action .20 .50
23 Sterling Marlin's Car .20 .50
24 Sterling Marlin .50 1.25
25 Shelton Pittman .08 .25
26 Sterling Marlin's Car .20 .50
27 Sterling Marlin .50 1.25
28 Dale Jarrett's Transporter .30 .75
29 Robert Yates .08 .25
30 Dale Jarrett 1.00 2.50
31 Dale Jarrett Pit Action .30 .75
32 Dale Jarrett's Car .30 .75
33 Dale Jarrett 1.00 2.50
34 Todd Parrott .08 .25
35 Dale Jarrett's Car .30 .75
36 Dale Jarrett 1.00 2.50
37 Rusty Wallace's Transporter .30 .75
38 Roger Penske .08 .25
39 Rusty Wallace 1.25 3.00
40 Rusty Wallace Pit Action .30 .75
41 Rusty Wallace's Car .30 .75
42 Rusty Wallace 1.25 3.00
43 Robin Pemberton .08 .25
44 Rusty Wallace's Car .30 .75
45 Rusty Wallace 1.25 3.00
46 Steve Jones .08 .25
47 Bill Elliott .75 2.00
48 Bill Elliott .75 2.00
49 Bill Elliott Pit Action .30 .75
50 Bill Elliott's Car .30 .75
51 Bill Elliott .75 2.00
52 Mike Beam .08 .25
53 Bill Elliott's Car .30 .75
54 Bill Elliott .75 2.00
55 Terry Labonte's Transporter .30 .75
56 Rick Hendrick .08 .25
57 Terry Labonte .50 1.25
58 Terry Labonte Pit Action .30 .75
59 Terry Labonte's Car .30 .75
60 Terry Labonte .50 1.25
61 Gary DeHart .08 .25
62 Terry Labonte's Car .30 .75
63 Terry Labonte .50 1.25
64 Ricky Rudd's Transporter .20 .50
65 Ricky Rudd .50 1.25
66 Ricky Rudd .50 1.25
67 Ricky Rudd Pit Action .20 .50
68 Ricky Rudd's Car .20 .50
69 Ricky Rudd .50 1.25
70 Ricky Rudd .50 1.25
71 Ricky Rudd's Car .20 .50
72 Ricky Rudd .50 1.25
73 Bobby Labonte 1.00 2.50
74 Ricky Craven .20 .50
75 Johnny Benson .30 .75
76 Jeremy Mayfield .30 .75
77 Checklist .08 .25
P0 Bill Elliott Promo 2.00 5.00

1997 Pinnacle Precision Bronze

This 77-card set parallels the base set and was produced with a bronze finish. The cards were randomly inserted into cans at a ratio of 1:4.

COMPLETE SET (77) 100.00 250.00
*BRONZES: 1X TO 2.5X BASIC CARDS

1997 Pinnacle Precision Gold

This 77-card set parallels the base set and was produced with a gold finish. The cards were randomly inserted into cans at a ratio of 1:68.

COMPLETE SET (77) 1000.00 1800.00
*GOLDS: 6X TO 15X BASIC CARDS

1997 Pinnacle Precision Silver

This 77-card set parallels the base set and was produced with a silver finish. The cards were randomly inserted into cans at a ratio of 1:10.

COMPLETE SET (77) 250.00 600.00
*SILVERS: 2.5X TO 6X BASIC CARDS

1997 Pinnacle Precision Terry Labonte Autographs

This is a 7-card Terry Labonte set that features his autograph on each card. Reportedly, only 50 of each card was signed. The cards were randomly inserted in cans at a ratio of 1:1120.

COMMON CARD 60.00 120.00

1997 Pinnacle Totally Certified Platinum Red

Randomly inserted two in every pack, this 100-card set is the base set of this product and is sequentially numbered to 2999. The difference is found in the red design element.

COMPLETE SET (100) 25.00 60.00
1 Kyle Petty .50 1.25
2 Rusty Wallace 2.00 5.00
3 Dale Earnhardt 4.00 10.00
4 Sterling Marlin .75 2.00
5 Terry Labonte .75 2.00
6 Mark Martin 2.00 5.00
7 Bill Elliott 1.00 2.50
8 Jeremy Mayfield .50 1.25
9 Ted Musgrave .30 .75
10 Ricky Rudd .75 2.00
11 Robby Gordon .75 2.00
12 Johnny Benson .50 1.25
13 Bobby Hamilton .30 .75
14 Mike Skinner .30 .75
15 Dale Jarrett 1.50 4.00
16 Steve Grissom .30 .75
17 Darrell Waltrip .30 .75
18 Bobby Labonte 1.50 4.00
19 Ernie Irvan .50 1.25
20 Jeff Green .30 .75
21 Michael Waltrip .50 1.25
22 Ward Burton .50 1.25
23 Geoff Bodine .30 .75
24 Jeff Gordon 2.50 6.00
25 Ricky Craven .30 .75
26 Jimmy Spencer .30 .75
27 Brett Bodine .30 .75
28 David Green .30 .75
29 John Andretti .30 .75
30 Ken Schrader .30 .75
31 Chad Little .30 .75
32 Joe Nemechek .30 .75
33 Hut Stricklin .30 .75
34 Kenny Wallace .30 .75
35 Kyle Petty's Car .30 .75
36 Rusty Wallace's Car .75 2.00
37 Dale Earnhardt's Car 1.50 4.00
38 Sterling Marlin's Car .30 .75
39 Terry Labonte's Car .30 .75
40 Mark Martin's Car .75 2.00
41 Bill Elliott's Car .30 .75
42 Jeremy Mayfield's Car .15 .40
43 Ted Musgrave's Car .15 .40
44 Ricky Rudd's Car .30 .75
45 Robby Gordon's Car .50 1.25
46 Johnny Benson's Car .15 .40
47 Bobby Hamilton's Car .15 .40
48 Mike Skinner's Car .15 .40
49 Dale Jarrett's Car .75 2.00
50 Steve Grissom's Car .15 .40
51 Darrell Waltrip's Car .30 .75
52 Bobby Labonte's Car .75 2.00
53 Ernie Irvan's Car .30 .75
54 Jeff Green's Car .15 .40
55 Michael Waltrip's Car .30 .75
56 Ward Burton's Car .15 .40
57 Geoff Bodine's Car .15 .40
58 Jeff Gordon's Car 1.25 3.00
59 Ricky Craven's Car .15 .40
60 Jimmy Spencer's Car .15 .40
61 Brett Bodine's Car .15 .40
62 David Green's Car .15 .40
63 John Andretti's Car .15 .40
64 Ken Schrader's Car .15 .40
65 Chad Little's Car .15 .40
66 Joe Nemechek's Car .15 .40
67 Hut Stricklin's Car .15 .40
68 Kenny Wallace's Car .15 .40
69 Darrell Waltrip WP .30 .75
70 Darrell Waltrip WP .30 .75
71 Darrell Waltrip WP .30 .75
72 Jeremy Mayfield WP .30 .75
73 Jeremy Mayfield WP .30 .75
74 Jeff Gordon WP 1.25 3.00
75 Ward Burton WP .15 .40
76 Dale Earnhardt WP 2.00 5.00
77 Bobby Labonte WP .75 2.00
78 Michael Waltrip WP .30 .75
79 Robby Gordon WP .50 1.25
80 Terry Labonte WP .50 1.25
81 Bill Elliott WP .50 1.25
82 Bobby Hamilton WP .15 .40
83 Chad Little WP .15 .40
84 Jeff Green WP .15 .40
85 Jeff Green WP .15 .40
86 Rick Mast WP .15 .40
87 Ernie Irvan WP .30 .75
88 Geoff Bodine WP .15 .40
89 Jeff Gordon BD 1.25 3.00
90 Terry Labonte BD .50 1.25
91 Mark Martin BD .75 2.00
92 Dale Jarrett BD .75 2.00
93 Dale Earnhardt BD 2.00 5.00
94 Ricky Rudd BD .50 1.25
95 Rusty Wallace BD .75 2.00
96 Bobby Hamilton BD .15 .40
97 Bobby Labonte BD .75 2.00
98 Kyle Petty BD .30 .75
99 Checklist 1 .15 .40
100 Checklist 2 .15 .40
P10 Ricky Rudd Promo 1.00 2.50

1997 Pinnacle Totally Certified Platinum Blue

Randomly inserted one in every pack, this 100-card set is parallel to the base set and is sequentially numbered to 1,999. The difference is found in the blue design element.

COMPLETE SET (100) 60.00 120.00
*BLUES: .6X TO 1.5X REDS

1997 Pinnacle Totally Certified Platinum Gold

Randomly inserted in packs at the rate of one in 37 packs, this 100-card set is parallel to the base set and is sequentially numbered to 49. The difference is found in the gold design element.

*GOLDS: 5X TO 12X REDS

1991-92 Pioneers of Stock Car Racing

This set was issued in two series of six-cards each. Series one was released in 1991 with series two being issued in 1992.

COMPLETE SET (12) 2.00 5.00
COMPLETE SERIES 1 (6) 1.00 2.50
COMPLETE SERIES 2 (6) 1.00 2.50
1 Rod Long .20 .50
2 Junior Johnson .20 .50
3 Bobby Myers .20 .50
4 Darrell Waltrip .30 .75
Walter Wallace
Freddy Fryar
P.B.Correll
5 Curtis Crider .20 .50
6 Rod Long .20 .50
7 Billy Myers .20 .50
8 Bill Morton .20 .50
9 Gene Glover .20 .50
10 Tim Flock .20 .50
NNO Cover Card Series 1 .07 .20
NNO Cover Card Series 2 .07 .20

2004 Post Cereal

These cards were produced by KF Holdings ar issued in various boxes of Post Cereals in ear 2004. Note that the copyright line on the cardbac lists the year as 2003, but the cards were released 2004. Each was produced with lenticular technolo with alternating photos of the driver and his car the front. There was also a blue decoder lens built to the card that could be used on the postopia.co website as part of an online game. The cardbac feature another color photo of the driver along wi basic statistics.

COMPLETE SET (7) 7.50 15.00
1 Greg Biffle .75 2.00
2 Jeff Burton .75 2.00
3 Kurt Busch .75 2.00
4 Dale Earnhardt Jr. 2.00 5.00
5 Matt Kenseth 1.25 3.00
6 Mark Martin 1.25 3.00
7 Michael Waltrip .75 2.00

1994 Power

In 1994, Pro Set produced only a Power racing se The 150-cards include eight different subset Daytona Beach, Power Teams, Power Winner Power Prospects, Stat Leaders, Power Rigs, Pow Owners and MRN Radio announcers. The cards we packaged 12-cards per foil pack. A Gold parallel s was also produced and inserted one per pack alor with a randomly inserted Dale Earnhardt Hologra card (numbered of 3500). Each of the last 20 car in the set (cars subset) was also produced in a go prism foil version inserted one per special 25-ca retail blister pack.

COMPLETE SET (150) 6.00 15.00
*PRISM CARS: .6X TO 1.5X BASE CARD HI
1 Loy Allen Jr. DB .02 .10
2 Dale Earnhardt DB .50 1.25
3 Ernie Irvan DB .05 .15
4 Sterling Marlin DB .08 .25
5 Jeff Gordon DB .30 .75
6 Richard Childress PT .05 .15
7 Roger Penske PT .01 .05
8 Jack Roush PT .01 .05
9 Robert Yates PT .01 .05
10 Glen Wood PT .01 .05
11 Joe Gibbs PT .05 .15
12 Felix Sabates PT .01 .05
13 Ricky Rudd PT .08 .25
14 Junior Johnson PT .02 .10
15 Joe Hendrick (Papa) PT .01 .05
16 Dale Earnhardt PW .50 1.25
17 Rusty Wallace PW .25 .60
18 Ernie Irvan PW .05 .15
19 Dale Jarrett PW .20 .50
20 Mark Martin PW .25 .60
21 Morgan Shepherd PW .02 .10
22 Kyle Petty PW .05 .15
23 Ricky Rudd PW .08 .25
24 Geoff Bodine PW .02 .10
25 Davey Allison PW .15 .40
26 Loy Allen Jr. PP .02 .10
27 John Andretti PP RC .02 .10
28 Steve Grissom PP .02 .10
29 Ward Burton PP .05 .15
30 Mike Wallace PP .02 .10
31 Joe Nemechek PP .02 .10
32 Todd Bodine PP .02 .10
33 Chuck Bown PP .02 .10
34 Robert Pressley PP .02 .10
35 Jeff Burton PP .08 .25
36 Randy LaJoie PP .02 .10
37 Billy Standridge PP .01 .05
38 Dale Earnhardt SL .50 1.25
39 Rusty Wallace SL .25 .60
40 Terry Labonte SL .08 .25
41 Ricky Rudd SL .08 .25
42 Geoff Bodine SL .02 .10
43 Harry Gant SL .05 .15
44 Mark Martin SL .25 .60
45 Buddy Baker SL .02 .10
46 Darrell Waltrip SL .05 .15
47 Leonard Wood SL .01 .05
48 Dale Inman SL .01 .05
49 Tim Brewer SL .01 .05
50 Harry Hyde SL .01 .05
51 Jeff Hammond SL .01 .05
52 Travis Carter SL .01 .05
53 Buddy Parrott SL .01 .05
54 Rusty Wallace in Pits SL .08 .25
55 Brett Bodine In Pits SL .01 .05
56 Mark Martin in Pits SL .08 .25
57 Bill Elliott in Pits SL .05 .15

Michael Waltrip in Pits SL	.02	.10
Dale Earnhardt's Trans. PR	.20	.50
Darrell Waltrip's Trans. PR	.01	.05
Ernie Irvan's Trans. PR	.02	.10
Mark Martin's Trans. PR	.08	.25
Rusty Wallace's Trans. PR	.08	.25
Richard Petty PO	.08	.25
Junior Johnson PO	.02	.10
Richard Childress PO	.05	.15
Walter Bud Moore PO	.01	.05
Harry Melling PO	.01	.05
Darrell Waltrip PO	.05	.15
Eli Gold MR	.01	.05
Barney Hall MR	.01	.05
Dick Brooks MR	.01	.05
Winston Kelley MR		
Jim Phillips MR		
Joe Moore MR	.01	.05
Allen Bestwick MR		
Fred Armstrong MR		
Bobby Allison	.05	.15
Kenny Bernstein	.02	.10
Rich Bickle	.02	.10
Brett Bodine	.02	.10
Geoff Bodine	.02	.10
George Bradshaw	.01	.05
Travis Carter	.01	.05
Richard Childress	.05	.15
Derrike Cope	.02	.10
Wally Dallenbach Jr.	.02	.10
Bill Davis	.01	.05
Junie Donlavey	.01	.05
Harry Gant	.05	.15
Harry Gant	.05	.15
Joe Gibbs	.05	.15
Jeff Gordon	.30	.75
Jeff Gordon	.30	.75
Bobby Hamilton	.02	.10
Rick Hendrick	.01	.05
Jimmy Hensley	.02	.10
Jimmy Hensley	.02	.10
Ernie Irvan	.05	.15
Richard Jackson	.01	.05
Junior Johnson	.02	.10
Bobby Labonte	.20	.50
Chad Little	.02	.10
Dave Marcis	.05	.15
Sterling Marlin	.08	.25
Sterling Marlin	.08	.25
Rick Mast	.02	.10
Larry McClure	.01	.05
Walter Bud Moore	.01	.05
Ted Musgrave	.02	.10
Roger Penske	.01	.05
Kyle Petty	.05	.15
Kyle Petty	.05	.15
Richard Petty	.08	.25
Chuck Rider	.01	.05
Jack Roush	.01	.05
Felix Sabates	.01	.05
Greg Sacks	.02	.10
Ken Schrader	.02	.10
Lake Speed	.02	.10
Jimmy Spencer	.02	.10
Jimmy Spencer	.02	.10
Hut Stricklin	.02	.10
Dick Trickle	.02	.10
Mike Wallace	.02	.10
Rusty Wallace	.25	.60
Rusty Wallace	.25	.60
Roger Penske	.01	.05
Darrell Waltrip	.05	.15
Michael Waltrip	.05	.15
Pete Wright	.01	.05
Cale Yarborough	.02	.10
Robert Yates	.01	.05
Jeff Burton	.08	.25
Hut Stricklin's Car	.01	.05
Jeff Gordon's Car	.15	.40
Geoff Bodine's Car	.01	.05
Todd Bodine's Car	.01	.05
Randy LaJoie's Car	.01	.05
Derrike Cope's Car	.01	.05
Lake Speed's Car	.01	.05
Ward Burton's Car	.01	.05
Mike Wallace's Car	.01	.05
Terry Labonte's Car	.05	.15
Sterling Marlin's Car	.02	.10
Jimmy Spencer's Car	.01	.05
Michael Waltrip's Car	.02	.10
Brett Bodine's Car	.01	.05
Rick Mast's Car	.01	.05
Harry Gant's Car	.02	.10
Wally Dallenbach Jr.'s Car	.01	.05
Ernie Irvan's Car	.02	.10
Greg Sacks' Car	.01	.05
Darrell Waltrip's Car	.02	.10
Jeff Gordon Promo	2.50	6.00
1 Dale Earnhardt Promo	4.00	10.00
1 Ernie Irvan Promo	1.00	2.50
0 Dale Earnhardt Hologram	15.00	40.00
numbered of 3500		

1994 Power Gold

arallel to the regular 1994 Power set, these insert ds feature a "Gold Cup '94" foil logo on the dfront. The cards are identical to the regular e, except for the logo, and were inserted one per pack.

MPLETE SET (150)	7.50	20.00
OLD CARDS: .8X TO 2X BASIC CARDS		

1994 Power Preview

s 31-card set was issued as a preview to the ver racing set released later in the year. The cards e distributed to hobby outlets in factory set form and included 18 silver foil stamped driver

cards, 12 prism foil car cards and one gold foil Dale Earnhardt tribute card (number 31).

COMPLETE SET (31)	3.00	8.00
1 Geoff Bodine	.02	.10
2 Derrike Cope	.02	.10
3 Wally Dallenbach Jr.	.02	.10
4 Ted Musgrave	.02	.10
5 Jimmy Spencer	.02	.10
6 Michael Waltrip	.07	.20
7 Hut Stricklin	.02	.10
8 Rusty Wallace	.30	.75
9 Darrell Waltrip	.07	.20
10 Dale Jarrett	.25	.60
11 Ken Schrader	.02	.10
12 Jeff Gordon	.50	1.25
13 Ricky Rudd	.15	.40
14 Kyle Petty	.07	.20
15 Mark Martin	.30	.75
16 Harry Gant	.07	.20
17 Harry Gant	.07	.20
Leo Jackson		
18 Bobby Hillin	.02	.10
Junie Donlavey		
19 Mark Martin's Car FOIL	.15	.40
20 Ted Musgrave's Car FOIL	.07	.20
21 Wally Dallenbach's Car FOIL	.07	.20
22 Jeff Gordon's Car FOIL	.30	.75
23 Bobby Hillin's Car FOIL	.07	.20
24 Geoff Bodine's Car FOIL	.07	.20
25 Harry Gant's Car FOIL	.07	.20
26 Kyle Petty's Car FOIL	.07	.20
27 Michael Waltrip's Car FOIL		
28 Hut Stricklin's Car FOIL	.07	.20
29 Dale Jarrett's Car FOIL	.15	.40
30 Derrike Cope's Car FOIL	.07	.20
31 Dale Earnhardt WC Champ	.75	2.00
P16 Harry Gant Promo	.40	1.00
Kit Young Show promo		

1997 Predator Promos

These 6-cards were issued to promote and preview the 1997 Wheels Predator product. Each card is numbered on the back and features the corresponding foil color and design for one of the many parallel sets in the product.

P1 Jeff Gordon Predator	3.00	8.00
P1 Jeff Gordon	3.00	8.00
Predator 1st Slash		
P2 Jeff Gordon Red Wolf	3.00	8.00
P2 Jeff Gordon	3.00	8.00
Red Wolf 1st Slash		
P3 Jeff Gordon Black Wolf	3.00	8.00
P3 Jeff Gordon	3.00	8.00
Black Wolf 1st Slash		

1997 Predator

This 66-card set is another uniquely themed set from Wheels. The cards feature the top names in racing. There are two Double Eagle cards in this product that commemorates Terry Labonte's 1984 and 1996 Winston Cup Championship winning seasons. The Gold Double Eagle card was made available only in First Slash boxes while the Silver Double Eagle card was made available only in the Hobby boxes. The cards were packaged 5 cards per pack, 20 packs per box and 16 boxes per case. The first 375 cases off the press had the First Slash logo stamped on all of the cards in those cases.

COMPLETE SET (66)	6.00	15.00
WAX BOX	40.00	75.00
FIRST SLASH WAX BOX	50.00	90.00
RETAIL WAX BOX	35.00	70.00
1 Jeff Gordon	.75	2.00
2 Terry Labonte	.25	.60
3 Dale Earnhardt	1.25	3.00
4 Dale Jarrett	.50	1.25
5 Mark Martin	.60	1.50
6 Rusty Wallace	.60	1.50
7 Sterling Marlin	.25	.60
8 David Green	.07	.20
9 Jeff Burton	.25	.60
10 Bobby Hamilton	.07	.20
11 Michael Waltrip	.15	.40
12 Bobby Labonte	.50	1.25
13 Ricky Craven	.07	.20
14 Johnny Benson	.15	.40
15 Jeremy Mayfield	.15	.40
16 Hut Stricklin	.07	.20
17 Kyle Petty	.15	.40
18 Darrell Waltrip	.15	.40
19 John Andretti	.07	.20
20 Bill Elliott	.30	.75
21 Robert Pressley	.07	.20
22 Joe Nemechek	.07	.20
23 Derrike Cope	.07	.20
24 Ward Burton	.15	.40
25 Chad Little	.15	.40
26 Mike Skinner	.07	.20
27 Jimmy Spencer	.07	.20
28 Dave Marcis	.07	.20
29 Wally Dallenbach	.07	.20
30 Kenny Wallace	.07	.20
31 Brett Bodine	.07	.20
32 Ted Musgrave	.07	.20
33 Robby Gordon RC	.25	.60
34 Randy LaJoie	.07	.20
35 Jeff Fuller	.07	.20
36 Jason Keller	.07	.20
37 Mike McLaughlin	.07	.20
38 Bobby Labonte	.50	1.25
39 Dale Jarrett	.50	1.25
40 Michael Waltrip	.15	.40
41 Mark Martin	.60	1.50
42 Steve Park RC	1.50	4.00
43 Glenn Allen	.07	.20
44 Jeff Gordon	.75	2.00
45 Terry Labonte	.25	.60
46 Bobby Hamilton	.07	.20
47 Bobby Labonte	.50	1.25
48 Ray Evernham	.07	.20
49 Gary DeHart	.02	.10
50 Todd Parrott	.02	.10
51 Steve Hmiel	.02	.10
52 Robin Pemberton	.02	.10
53 Jimmy Makar	.02	.10
54 Jeff Hammond	.02	.10
55 Larry McReynolds	.02	.10
56 Kevin Hamlin	.02	.10
57 David Smith	.02	.10
58 Richard Childress	.15	.40
59 Joe Gibbs	.15	.40
60 Rick Hendrick	.02	.10
61 Robert Yates	.02	.10
62 Johnny Benson	.15	.40
63 Randy LaJoie	.07	.20
64 Bill Elliott	.30	.75
65 Ron Hornaday	.07	.20
66 Checklist	.02	.10
GD1 Terry Labonte	8.00	20.00
SD1 Terry Labonte	5.00	12.00

1997 Predator Black Wolf First Strike

This set was made available by Wheels through a Collect-N-Purchase offer in which collectors had to collect 8 cards and send them to buy this set directly from Wheels. This 66-card set was packaged in a simulated gatorskin case and was reportedly limited in production to 3,750 sets.

COMPLETE SET (66)	25.00	60.00
*BLACK WOLF FS: 3X TO 6X BASIC CARDS		

1997 Predator First Slash

This parallel set was released in the first 325-cases of the base Predator print run. Each card includes the "First Slash" foil logo on the cardfronts.

COMP.FIRST SLASH (66)	8.00	20.00
*FIRST SLASH: .6X TO 1.5X BASE CARDS		

1997 Predator Grizzly

This 66-card set is a parallel to the base set. These cards are copper foil stamped and are set against a color enhanced background. The cards were randomly inserted into packs at a ratio of 1:5.

COMPLETE SET (66)	40.00	80.00
*GRIZZLY: 2X TO 5X BASE CARDS		

1997 Predator Grizzly First Slash

This parallel set was released in the first 325-cases of the base Predator print run. Each card includes the "First Slash" foil logo on the cardfronts. They were randomly seeded at the rate of 1:5 First Slash packs.

COMP.FS GRIZZLY (66)	60.00	120.00
*FS GRIZZLY: .6X TO 1.5X BASIC GRIZZLY		

1997 Predator Red Wolf

This 66-card set is a parallel to the base set. These cards are red foil stamped and are set against a micro-etched background. The cards were randomly inserted into packs at a ratio of 1:10.

COMPLETE SET (66)	75.00	150.00
*RED WOLF: 3X TO 8X BASIC CARDS		

1997 Predator Red Wolf First Slash

This parallel set was released in the first 325-cases of the base Predator print run. Each card includes the "First Slash" foil logo on the cardfronts. They were randomly seeded at the rate of 1:10 First Slash packs.

COMP.FS RED WOLF (66)	125.00	250.00
*FS RED WOLF: .6X TO 1.5X BASE RED WOLF		

1997 Predator American Eagle

This 10-card insert set features the top drivers from NASCAR. The cards are set against a background of

an eagle. The cards were randomly inserted in packs at a ratio of 1:30.

COMPLETE SET (10)	40.00	80.00
COMP.FIRST SLASH (10)	50.00	100.00
*FIRST SLASH: .5X TO 1.2X BASIC INSERTS		
AE1 Dale Earnhardt	15.00	40.00
AE2 Jeff Gordon	10.00	25.00
AE3 Rusty Wallace	8.00	20.00
AE4 Terry Labonte	3.00	8.00
AE5 Dale Jarrett	6.00	15.00
AE6 Sterling Marlin	3.00	8.00
AE7 Mark Martin	8.00	20.00
AE8 Bobby Labonte	6.00	15.00
AE9 Bill Elliott	4.00	10.00
AE10 Darrell Waltrip	2.00	5.00

1997 Predator Eye of the Tiger

This 8-card insert set features NASCAR top stars on horizontal cards that are foil enhanced and micro-etched. The cards were randomly inserted in packs at a ratio of 1:10.

COMPLETE SET (8)	10.00	25.00
COMP.FIRST SLASH (8)	15.00	40.00
*FIRST SLASH: .5X TO 1.2X BASIC INSERTS		
ET1 Dale Earnhardt	5.00	12.00
ET2 Jeff Gordon	3.00	8.00
ET3 Rusty Wallace	2.50	6.00
ET4 Terry Labonte	1.00	2.50
ET5 Dale Jarrett	2.00	5.00
ET6 Mark Martin	2.50	6.00
ET7 Bobby Labonte	2.00	5.00
ET8 Sterling Marlin	1.00	2.50

1997 Predator Gatorback

This 10-card set is a sublevel parallel of the Gatorback Authentic insert set. The cards feature a simulated crocodile hide distinguishing it from the Gatorback Authentic cards. The cards were randomly inserted in packs at a ratio of 1:40.

COMPLETE SET (10)	40.00	80.00
COMP.FIRST SLASH (10)	50.00	100.00
*FIRST SLASH: .5X TO 1.2X BASIC INSERTS		
GB1 Dale Earnhardt	15.00	40.00
GB2 Jeff Gordon	10.00	25.00
GB3 Mike Skinner	1.00	2.50
GB4 Dale Jarrett	6.00	15.00
GB5 Rusty Wallace	8.00	20.00
GB6 Bobby Labonte	6.00	15.00
GB7 Mark Martin	8.00	20.00
GB8 Sterling Marlin	3.00	8.00
GB9 Darrell Waltrip	2.00	5.00
GB10 Bill Elliott	4.00	10.00

1997 Predator Gatorback Authentic

This 10-card set is the rarest of all Predator insert sets. The cards are highlighted by actual crocodile hide imported from Australia. There are two versions of each card; the white crocodile skin cards are found only in First Slash boxes and the brown crocodile skin cards are found only in Hobby boxes. The cards were randomly inserted in packs at a ratio of 1:120.

COMPLETE SET (10)	125.00	250.00
COMP.FIRST SLASH (10)	200.00	400.00
*FIRST SLASH: .5X TO 1.2X BASIC INSERTS		
GBA1 Dale Earnhardt	30.00	80.00
GBA2 Jeff Gordon	25.00	60.00
GBA3 Mike Skinner	5.00	12.00
GBA4 Dale Jarrett	15.00	40.00
GBA5 Rusty Wallace	15.00	40.00
GBA6 Bobby Labonte	15.00	40.00
GBA7 Mark Martin	20.00	50.00
GBA8 Sterling Marlin	8.00	20.00
GBA9 Darrell Waltrip	6.00	15.00
GBA10 Bill Elliott	10.00	25.00

1997 Predator Golden Eagle

This 10-card insert set features the top drivers from NASCAR. The cards are set against a background of an eagle highlighted by gold foil. The cards were randomly inserted in packs at a ratio of 1:40.

COMPLETE SET (10)	50.00	100.00
COMP.FIRST SLASH (10)	60.00	120.00
*FIRST SLASH: .5X TO 1.2X BASIC INSERTS		
GE1 Dale Earnhardt	12.50	30.00
GE2 Jeff Gordon	8.00	20.00
GE3 Rusty Wallace	6.00	15.00
GE4 Terry Labonte	2.50	6.00
GE5 Dale Jarrett	5.00	12.00
GE6 Sterling Marlin	2.50	6.00
GE7 Mark Martin	6.00	15.00
GE8 Bobby Labonte	5.00	12.00
GE9 Bill Elliott	3.00	8.00
GE10 Darrell Waltrip	1.50	4.00

1993 Press Pass Davey Allison

This five-card set uses prism printing technology to highlight Davey Allison's career. There were 25,000 sets produced and were distributed through a mail in offer in the '93 Press Pass Preview set. The sets could be had for $7.95 + $3.00 shipping and handling. In 1994, Press Pass also made the sets available to members of the Press Pass Club and the Press Pass Dealer Network.

COMPLETE SET (5)	2.00	5.00
1 Davey Allison	.50	1.25
2 Davey Allison	.50	1.25
3 Davey Allison	.50	1.25
4 Davey Allison	.50	1.25
Bobby Allison		
5 Davey Allison	.50	1.25

1993 Press Pass Previews

This 34-card set was the debut set from manufacturer Press Pass. The set was released in the late summer of '93 and features some of the top names in racing. The set originally retailed for $12.95.

COMPLETE SET (34)	8.00	20.00
1 Davey Allison Foil	2.00	4.00
2 Brett Bodine	.15	.40
3 Geoff Bodine	.15	.40
4 Derrike Cope	.15	.40
5 Harry Gant	.30	.75
6 Jimmy Hensley	.15	.40
7 Dale Jarrett	1.00	2.50
8 Alan Kulwicki	.50	1.25
9 Sterling Marlin	.60	1.50
10 Mark Martin	1.50	3.00
11 Kyle Petty	.30	.75
12 Ken Schrader	.15	.40
13 Morgan Shepherd	.15	.40
14 Jimmy Spencer	.15	.40
15 Rusty Wallace	1.25	3.00
16 Joe Gibbs	.30	.75
17 Jeff Gordon	4.00	10.00
Kenny Wallace		
Bobby Labonte		
18A Jeff Gordon	2.50	5.00
Redemption card expired		
18B Jeff Gordon Foil	5.00	12.00
19 Bobby Labonte	1.00	2.50
20 Kenny Wallace	.15	.40
21 Alan Kulwicki	.50	1.25
22 Rusty Wallace	1.25	3.00
23 Bobby Allison	.15	.40
24 Morgan Shepherd's Car	.07	.20
25 Kenny Wallace's Car	.07	.20
26 Jeff Gordon's Car	.75	2.00
27 Dale Jarrett's Car	.30	.75
28 Bobby Labonte's Car	.30	.75
29 Jimmy Spencer's Car	.07	.20
30 Kyle Petty's Car	.15	.40
31 Rusty Wallace's Car	.50	1.25
32 Sterling Marlin's Car	.15	.40
33 Harry Gant's Car	.15	.40
34 Mark Martin's Car	.50	1.25

1994 Press Pass

This 150-card base brand set features top drivers from both the Winston Cup and Busch circuits. The cards came 10-cards to a pack. There were two different 36-count boxes which the packs came in. There was a regular box and a Race Day box. The only difference in the two boxes was the Race Day packs gave the collector the opportunity to pull a Race Day insert card. The Race Day packs were easily identifiable due to the bright yellow star burst on the front of the pack.

COMPLETE SET (150)	8.00	20.00

WAX BOX	20.00	50.00
1 Brett Bodine	.07	.20
2 Geoff Bodine	.07	.20
3 Derrike Cope	.07	.20
4 Wally Dallenbach Jr.	.07	.20
5 Dale Earnhardt	1.25	3.00
6 Harry Gant	.15	.40
7 Jeff Gordon	.75	2.00
8 Bobby Hamilton	.07	.20
9 Jimmy Hensley	.07	.20
10 Bobby Hillin	.07	.20
11 Ernie Irvan	.15	.40
12 Dale Jarrett	.50	1.25
13 Bobby Labonte	.50	1.25
14 Terry Labonte	.25	.60
15 Dave Marcis	.07	.20
16 Sterling Marlin	.25	.60
17 Mark Martin	.60	1.50
18 Rick Mast	.07	.20
19 Jimmy Means	.07	.20
20 Ted Musgrave	.07	.20
21 Kyle Petty	.15	.40
22 Ken Schrader	.07	.20
23 Morgan Shepherd	.07	.20
24 Lake Speed	.07	.20
25 Jimmy Spencer	.07	.20
26 Hut Stricklin	.07	.20
27 Kenny Wallace	.07	.20
28 Rusty Wallace	.75	2.00
29 Darrell Waltrip	.15	.40
30 Michael Waltrip	.15	.40
31 Rusty Wallace	.30	.75
Kenny Wallace		
32 Mark Martin	.30	.75
Jack Roush		
33 Darrell Waltrip	.15	.40
Michael Waltrip		
34 Dale Jarrett	.15	.40
Joe Gibbs		
35 Geoff Bodine	.02	.10
Bobby Hillin		
36 Brett Bodine	.02	.10
Kenny Bernstein		
37 Derrike Cope's Car	.02	.10
38 Morgan Shepherd's Car	.02	.10
39 Bobby Hamilton's Car	.02	.10
40 Jeff Gordon's Car	.30	.75
41 Bobby Hillin's Car	.02	.10
42 Dale Jarrett's Car	.15	.40
43 Ken Schrader's Car	.02	.10
44 Bobby Labonte's Car	.07	.20
45 Jimmy Spencer's Car	.02	.10
46 Kyle Petty's Car	.07	.20
47 Rusty Wallace's Car	.25	.60
48 Geoff Bodine's Car	.02	.10
49 Michael Waltrip's Car	.07	.20
50 Dick Trickle's Car	.02	.10
51 Sterling Marlin's Car	.07	.20
52 Harry Gant's Car	.07	.20
53 Ernie Irvan's Car	.07	.20
54 Mark Martin's Car	.25	.60
55 Todd Bodine	.07	.20
56 Chuck Bown	.07	.20
57 Ward Burton	.15	.40
58 Ricky Craven	.07	.20
59 Bobby Dotter	.07	.20
60 David Green	.07	.20
61 Steve Grissom	.07	.20
62 Joe Nemechek	.07	.20
63 Shawna Robinson	.30	.75
64 Steve Grissom's Car	.02	.10
65 Joe Nemechek's Car	.02	.10
66 Bobby Dotter's Car	.02	.10
67 Ricky Craven's Car	.02	.10
68 Todd Bodine's Car	.02	.10
69 Chuck Bown's Car	.02	.10
70 Shawna Robinson's Car	.07	.20
71 David Green's Car	.02	.10
72 Hermie Sadler's Car	.02	.10
73 Bobby Allison	.07	.20
74 Kenny Bernstein	.07	.20
75 Geoff Bodine	.07	.20
76 Bill Davis	.02	.10
77 Junie Donlavey	.02	.10
78 Joe Gibbs	.15	.40
79 Rick Hendrick	.02	.10
80 Leo Jackson	.02	.10
81 Walter Bud Moore	.02	.10
82 Roger Penske	.02	.10
Don Miller		
83 Chuck Rider	.02	.10
84 Jack Roush	.02	.10
85 Felix Sabates	.02	.10
86 Bill Stavola	.02	.10
Mickey Stavola		
87 Darrell Waltrip	.15	.40
88 Glen Wood	.02	.10
Eddie Wood		
Len Wood		
89 Cale Yarborough	.07	.20
90 Robert Yates	.02	.10
91 Paul Andrews	.02	.10
92 Barry Dodson	.02	.10
93 Ray Evernham	.02	.10
94 Jimmy Fennig	.02	.10
95 Jeff Hammond	.02	.10
96 Doug Hewitt	.02	.10
97 Steve Hmiel	.02	.10
98 Ken Howes	.02	.10
99 Sandy Jones	.02	.10
100 Jimmy Makar	.02	.10
101 Larry McReynolds	.02	.10
102 Buddy Parrott	.02	.10
103 Robin Pemberton	.02	.10
104 Donnie Richeson	.02	.10
105 Doug Williams	.02	.10
106 Ken Wilson	.02	.10
107 Donnie Wingo	.02	.10

108 Leonard Wood	.02	.10
109 Allen Bestwick	.02	.10
110 Dick Brooks	.02	.10
111 Eli Gold	.02	.10
112 Barney Hall	.02	.10
113 Ned Jarrett	.02	.10
114 Winston Kelley	.02	.10
115 Joe Moore	.02	.10
116 Benny Parsons	.07	.20
117 Jim Phillips	.02	.10
118 Rusty Wallace DOY	.30	.75
119 Ken Schrader Pole Win	.02	.10
120 Steve Hmiel	.02	.10
121 Mark Martin TT	.30	.75
122 Dale Jarrett TT	.15	.40
123 Rusty Wallace TT	.30	.75
124 Jeff Gordon ROY	.40	1.00
125 Steve Grissom BGN Champ	.02	.10
126 Joe Nemechek Pop. Driver	.02	.10
127 Davey Allison HR	.25	.60
128 Donnie Allison HR	.07	.20
129 Tim Flock HR	.02	.10
130 Alan Kulwicki HR	.15	.40
131 Fred Lorenzen HR	.02	.10
132 Tiny Lund HR	.02	.10
133 David Pearson HR	.02	.10
134 Glenn Roberts(Fireball) HR	.02	.10
135 Curtis Turner HR	.02	.10
136 Geoff Bodine Art	.02	.10
137 Geoff Bodine Art	.02	.10
138 Derrike Cope Art	.02	.10
139 Speed Racer Art	.02	.10
140 Dale Jarrett Art	.15	.40
141 Mark Martin Art	.30	.75
142 Ken Schrader Art	.02	.10
143 Morgan Shepherd Art	.02	.10
144 Rusty Wallace Art	.40	1.00
145 Harry Gant Farewell	.07	.20
146 Harry Gant Farewell	.07	.20
147 Checklist #1	.02	.10
148 Checklist #2	.02	.10
149 Checklist #3	.02	.10
150 Checklist #4	.02	.10

1994 Press Pass Checkered Flags

This four-card insert set features 1993 multiple race winners. The cards use gold foil stamping and could be found one in every 12 packs.

COMPLETE SET (4)	4.00	10.00
CF1 Dale Earnhardt	2.50	6.00
CF2 Ernie Irvan	.30	.75
CF3 Mark Martin	1.25	3.00
CF4 Rusty Wallace	1.50	4.00

1994 Press Pass Cup Chase

This 30-card set was the first interactive racing game set produced. The specially stamped "Cup Chase" cards were a parallel to the first 30 cards in the set. The collector that owned the Dale Earnhardt Cup Chase card, the 1994 Winston Cup Champion, was able to redeem that card for a special Dale Earnhardt card and an uncut sheet of the 30 Cup Chase cards. An interesting note about the uncut sheet is that in the bottom right hand corner there is a black card and the sheet doesn't have the Dale Earnhardt card on it. The Cup Chase cards were inserted in packs of Press Pass at a rate of one every 18. The cards could be redeemed until March 31, 1995.

COMPLETE SET (30)	75.00	150.00
UNCUT SHEET PRIZE	40.00	100.00
CC1 Brett Bodine	.75	2.00
CC2 Geoff Bodine	.75	2.00
CC3 Derrike Cope	.75	2.00
CC4 Wally Dallenbach Jr.	.75	2.00
CC5 Dale Earnhardt W1	15.00	40.00
CC6 Harry Gant	1.50	4.00
CC7 Jeff Gordon	8.00	20.00
CC8 Bobby Hamilton	.75	2.00
CC9 Jimmy Hensley	.75	2.00
CC10 Bobby Hillin	.75	2.00
CC11 Ernie Irvan	1.50	4.00
CC12 Dale Jarrett	4.00	10.00
CC13 Bobby Labonte	4.00	10.00
CC14 Terry Labonte	2.50	6.00
CC15 Dave Marcis	.75	2.00
CC16 Sterling Marlin	2.50	6.00
CC17 Mark Martin W2	6.00	15.00
CC18 Rick Mast	.75	2.00
CC19 Jimmy Means	.75	2.00
CC20 Ted Musgrave	.75	2.00
CC21 Kyle Petty	1.50	4.00
CC22 Ken Schrader	.75	2.00
CC23 Morgan Shepherd	.75	2.00
CC24 Lake Speed	.75	2.00
CC25 Jimmy Spencer	.75	2.00
CC26 Hut Stricklin	.75	2.00
CC27 Kenny Wallace	.75	2.00
CC28 Rusty Wallace W3	6.00	15.00
CC29 Darrell Waltrip	1.50	4.00
CC30 Michael Waltrip	1.50	4.00
SPCL1 Dale Earnhardt Prize	30.00	60.00

1994 Press Pass Prospects

This five-card insert set uses Thermofoil printing technology to bring five of the top Busch Grand National drivers to collectors. The five drivers were in their rookie years on the Winston Cup circuit in 1994. The cards were randomly seeded at a rate of one per eight packs. The uncut sheet was the prize for returning the second place finisher in the Press Pass Cup Chase

COMPLETE SET (5)	2.50	6.00
UNCUT SHEET PRIZE	7.50	15.00
PP1 Chuck Bown	.40	1.00
PP2 Ward Burton	.75	2.00
PP3 Ricky Craven	.40	1.00
PP4 Steve Grissom	.75	2.00
PP5 Joe Nemechek	.75	2.00

1994 Press Pass Race Day

This 12-card insert set was issued across two Press Pass brands. The first 10 cards in the set were made available through specially marked "Race Day" boxes of Press Pass. The last two cards were randomly inserted in boxes of 1994 VIP. The cards feature drivers who took the checkered flag during 1993 and the 1994 Daytona 500 winner. The cards are printed using the holofoil technology and were randomly inserted in packs at a rate of one per 72.

COMPLETE SET (12)	25.00	60.00
RD1 Davey Allison	2.00	5.00
RD2 Geoff Bodine	.60	1.50
RD3 Ernie Irvan	1.25	3.00
RD4 Dale Jarrett	4.00	10.00
RD5 Mark Martin	5.00	12.00
RD6 Kyle Petty	1.25	3.00
RD7 Jeff Gordon	6.00	15.00
RD8 Morgan Shepherd	.60	1.50
RD9 Rusty Wallace	6.00	15.00
RD10 Dale Earnhardt	10.00	25.00
RD11 Sterling Marlin	2.00	5.00
NNO Cover Card	.30	.75

1994 Press Pass Authentics

These 8" X 10" cards are blown up versions of the five drivers' regular 1994 Press Pass cards. The cards are actually 5" X 7" and framed in a black border. The cards came in two versions: signed and unsigned. There were 1500 cards unsigned and 1000 cards signed. The signed cards were each autographed in gold pen by the driver. All cards are numbered of 2500 no matter if they were signed or unsigned. The cards were made available through the Press Pass Club and to the Press Pass dealer network. The original retail price for each piece was $25 for unsigned and $35 for signed cards.

COMPLETE SET (5)	30.00	80.00
*SIGNED CARDS: 1X TO 2.5X BASE CARDS		
1 Jeff Gordon	12.00	30.00
2 Ernie Irvan	4.00	10.00
3 Mark Martin	7.50	20.00
4 Kyle Petty	4.00	10.00
5 Rusty Wallace	7.50	20.00

1994 Press Pass Holofoils

Press Pass produced this Holofoil set featuring six popular Winston Cup drivers. The cards were sold directly to collectors in complete set form along with a certificate numbering the set one of 15,000 made. The cards contain a photo of the driver printed on holofoil card stock with driver stats on the backs.

COMPLETE SET (6)	4.00	10.00
H1 Dale Earnhardt	2.00	5.00
H2 Jeff Gordon	1.00	2.50
H3 Ernie Irvan	.40	1.00
H4 Mark Martin	.75	2.00
H5 Kyle Petty	.40	1.00
H6 Rusty Wallace	.75	2.00

1995 Press Pass Prototypes

Three cards comprise this release intended to preview the 1995 Press Pass regular set. The cards are numbered and carry the word "Prototype."

COMPLETE SET (3)	3.00	8.00
1 Kyle Petty	.76	2.00
2 Terry Labonte's Car	.75	2.00
3 Jeff Gordon	2.00	5.00

1995 Press Pass

This 145-card base brand set features top drivers from the Winston Cup and Busch Grand National circuits. The cards came 10 cards per pack, 36 packs per box and 20 boxes per case. The set is broken into 10 topical subsets: Winston Cup Drivers (1-36), Winston Cup Cars (37-54), Busch Series Drivers (55-72), Busch Series Cars (73-81), Winston Cup Owners (82-90), Winston Cup Crew Chiefs (91-99), Small Town Saturday Night (100-108), Award Winners (109-117), Heroes of Racing (118-123) SportsKings (124-126), Personal Rides (127-135), Breaking Through (136-143). Also randomly inserted at a rate of one per box in special retail boxes were autograph cards. The only two drivers cards that were autographed are the Sterling Marlin and David Green cards.

COMPLETE SET (145)	10.00	25.00
HOBBY WAX BOX	30.00	55.00
1 Loy Allen Jr.	.07	.20
2 John Andretti	.07	.20
3 Brett Bodine	.07	.20
4 Geoff Bodine	.07	.20
5 Todd Bodine	.07	.20
6 Jeff Burton	.25	.60
7 Ward Burton	.15	.40
8 Derrike Cope	.07	.20
9 Dale Earnhardt	1.25	3.00
10 Jeff Gordon	.75	2.00
11 Steve Grissom	.07	.20
12 Bobby Hamilton	.07	.20
13 Ernie Irvan	.15	.40
14 Dale Jarrett	.50	1.25
15 Bobby Labonte	.50	1.25
16 Terry Labonte	.25	.60
17 Dave Marcis	.15	.40
18 Sterling Marlin	.25	.60
19 Mark Martin	.60	1.50
20 Rick Mast	.07	.20
21 Ted Musgrave	.07	.20
22 Joe Nemechek	.07	.20
23 Kyle Petty	.15	.40
24 Ricky Rudd	.25	.60
25 Greg Sacks	.07	.20
26 Ken Schrader	.07	.20
27 Morgan Shepherd	.07	.20
28 Lake Speed	.07	.20
29 Jimmy Spencer	.07	.20
30 Hut Stricklin	.07	.20
31 Dick Trickle	.07	.20
32 Kenny Wallace	.07	.20
33 Mike Wallace	.07	.20
34 Rusty Wallace	.60	1.50
35 Darrell Waltrip	.15	.40
36 Michael Waltrip Elizabeth Waltrip	.15	.40
37 Morgan Shepherd's Car	.02	.10
38 Jeff Gordon's Car	.30	.75
39 Geoff Bodine's Car	.02	.10
40 Ted Musgrave's Car	.02	.10
41 Dale Earnhardt's Car	.50	1.25
42 Dale Jarrett's Car	.15	.40
43 Terry Labonte's Car	.15	.40
44 Sterling Marlin's Car	.07	.20
45 Ken Schrader's Car	.02	.10
46 Kyle Petty's Car	.07	.20
47 Rusty Wallace's Car	.25	.60
48 Michael Waltrip's Car	.07	.20
49 Brett Bodine's Car	.02	.10
50 John Andretti's Car	.02	.10
51 Ernie Irvan's Car	.07	.20
52 Ricky Rudd's Car	.07	.20
53 Mark Martin's Car	.25	.60
54 Darrell Waltrip's Car	.07	.20
55 Johnny Benson Jr.	.15	.40
56 Jim Bown	.07	.20
57 Ricky Craven	.15	.40
58 Bobby Dotter	.07	.20
59 Tim Fedewa	.07	.20
60 David Green	.07	.20
61 Tommy Houston	.07	.20
62 Jason Keller	.07	.20
63 Randy LaJoie	.07	.20
64 Tracy Leslie	.07	.20
65 Chad Little	.07	.20
66 Mark Martin	.60	1.50
67 Mike McLaughlin	.07	.20
68 Larry Pearson	.07	.20
69 Robert Pressley	.07	.20
70 Elton Sawyer	.07	.20
71 Dennis Setzer	.07	.20
72 Kenny Wallace	.07	.20
73 Dennis Setzer's Car	.02	.10
74 Chad Little's Car	.02	.10
75 Bobby Dotter's Car	.02	.10
76 Ricky Craven's Car	.02	.10
77 Mike McLaughlin's Car	.02	.10
78 Randy LaJoie's Car	.02	.10
79 David Green's Car	.02	.10
80 Larry Pearson's Car	.02	.10
81 Kenny Wallace's Car	.02	.10
82 Richard Childress	.15	.40
83 Rick Hendrick	.02	.10
84 Walter Bud Moore	.02	.10
85 Roger Penske Don Miller	.02	.10
86 Richard Petty	.25	.60
87 Chuck Rider	.02	.10
88 Felix Sabates	.02	.10
89 Cale Yarborough	.07	.20
90 Robert Yates	.02	.10
91 Mike Beam	.02	.10
92 Ray Evernham	.15	.40
93 Steve Hmiel	.02	.10
94 Ken Howes	.02	.10
95 Bill Ingle	.02	.10
96 Larry McReynolds	.02	.10
97 Buddy Parrott	.02	.10
98 Andy Petree	.02	.10
99 Leonard Wood	.02	.10
100 John Andretti ST	.07	.20
101 Geoff Bodine ST	.07	.20
102 Jeff Gordon ST	.40	1.00
103 Steve Kinser ST	.07	.20
104 Mark Martin ST	.30	.75
105 Joe Nemechek ST	.07	.20
106 Ken Schrader ST	.07	.20
107 Jimmy Spencer ST	.07	.20
108 Darrell Waltrip ST	.15	.40
109 Jeff Burton AW	.15	.40
110 Geoff Bodine AW	.07	.20
111 Ray Evernham AW	.07	.20
112 David Green AW	.07	.20
113 Johnny Benson AW	.15	.40
114 David Green AW	.07	.20
115 Dale Earnhardt's Car AW	.50	1.25
116 Mark Martin's Car AW	.25	.60
117 Michael Waltrip's Car AW	.07	.20
118 Buck Baker HR	.07	.20
119 Buddy Baker HR	.07	.20
120 Harry Gant HR	.15	.40
121 J.D. McDuffie HR	.02	.10
122 Marvin Panch HR	.02	.10
123 Lennie Pond HR	.02	.10
124 Bobby Allison S	.07	.20
125 David Pearson S	.07	.20
126 Richard Petty S	.25	.60
127 Geoff Bodine PR	.07	.20
128 Harry Gant PR	.15	.40
129 Jeff Gordon PR	.40	1.00
130 Bobby Hamilton PR	.07	.20
131 Kyle Petty PR	.15	.40
132 Richard Petty PR	.25	.60
133 Ken Schrader PR	.07	.20
134 Morgan Shepherd PR	.07	.20
135 Rusty Wallace PR	.30	.75
136 Jeff Gordon BT	.40	1.00
137 Sterling Marlin BT	.15	.40
138 Jimmy Spencer BT	.07	.20
139 Johnny Benson BT	.15	.40
140 Ricky Craven BT	.15	.40
141 Elton Sawyer BT	.07	.20
142 Dennis Setzer BT	.07	.20
143 Mike Wallace BT	.07	.20
144 Checklist	.02	.10
145 Checklist	.02	.10
A18 Sterling Marlin AUTO	10.00	25.00
A60 David Green AUTO	6.00	12.00

1995 Press Pass Red Hot

This 145-card set is a parallel of the base set. The cards feature a red foil stamping to differentiate them. The Red Hot cards were randomly seeded at a rate of one every two packs.

COMPLETE SET (145)	25.00	60.00
*RED HOTS: 1X TO 2.5X BASE CARDS		

1995 Press Pass Checkered Flags

This eight-card set features Winston Cup drivers who won multiple races in the 1994 season. The cards are gold foil stamped and were inserted in packs at a rate of one per nine.

COMPLETE SET (8)	10.00	25.00
CF1 Geoff Bodine	.30	.75
CF2 Dale Earnhardt	5.00	12.00
CF3 Jeff Gordon	3.00	8.00
CF4 Ernie Irvan	.60	1.50
CF5 Terry Labonte	1.00	2.50
CF6 Mark Martin	2.50	6.00
CF7 Jimmy Spencer	.30	.75
CF8 Rusty Wallace	2.50	6.00

1995 Press Pass Cup Chase

This 36-card insert set is a parallel of the first 36 cards in the base Press Pass set. The cards feature a gold foil stamp "Cup Chase" to differentiate the cards. This is the second year of the interactive game from Press Pass. The rules changed in 1995 so the collector could redeem a Cup Chase card of not only the Winston Cup Champion but the winners of five specific races throughout the year: Daytona 500, Winston Select 500, Coca-Cola 600, Brickyard 400 and the MBNA 500. If you held a Cup Chase card for the winner of any of those five races, you could redeem it for a special holo-prism card of the 1994 winning driver of that specific race. If you had the Winston Cup Champion card (Jeff Gordon), you could redeem that card for the entire set of five special holoprism cards. Odds of finding a Cup Chase card was one per 24 packs. The winning cards could be redeemed until January 31, 1996.

COMPLETE SET (36)	75.00	150.00
1 Loy Allen Jr.	1.25	3.00
2 John Andretti	1.25	3.00
3 Brett Bodine	1.25	3.00
4 Geoff Bodine	1.25	3.00
5 Todd Bodine	1.25	3.00
6 Jeff Burton	2.50	6.00
7 Ward Burton	2.50	6.00
8 Derrike Cope	1.25	3.00
9 Dale Earnhardt Winner Card Expired	12.50	30.00
10 Jeff Gordon Winner Card Expired	10.00	25.00
11 Steve Grissom	1.25	3.00
12 Bobby Hamilton	1.25	3.00
13 Ernie Irvan	2.50	6.00
14 Dale Jarrett	4.00	10.00
15 Bobby Labonte Winner Card Expired	6.00	15.00
16 Terry Labonte	2.50	6.00
17 Dave Marcis	2.50	6.00
18 Sterling Marlin Winner Card Expired	4.00	10.00
19 Mark Martin Winner Card Expired	8.00	20.00
20 Rick Mast	1.25	3.00
21 Ted Musgrave	1.25	3.00
22 Joe Nemechek	1.25	3.00
23 Kyle Petty	2.50	6.00
24 Ricky Rudd	3.00	8.00
25 Greg Sacks	1.25	3.00
26 Ken Schrader	1.25	3.00
27 Morgan Shepherd	1.25	3.00
28 Lake Speed	1.25	3.00
29 Jimmy Spencer	1.25	3.00
30 Hut Stricklin	1.25	3.00
31 Dick Trickle	1.25	3.00
32 Kenny Wallace	1.25	3.00
33 Mike Wallace	1.25	3.00
34 Rusty Wallace	4.00	10.00
35 Darrell Waltrip	2.50	6.00
36 Michael Waltrip	2.50	6.00

1995 Press Pass Cup Chase Prizes

This five-card insert set features the winning drivers of these 1994 races: the Daytona 500, Winston Select 500, Coca-Cola 600, Brickyard 400 and the MBNA 500. The cards were printed using holoprism technology and were made available two different ways. First, the cards were inserted as chiptoppers at a rate of one per hobby case. The cards were also the redemption prizes for the Cup Chase game winners.

COMPLETE SET (5)	30.00	80.00
CCR1 Sterling Marlin	3.00	8.00
CCR2 Dale Earnhardt	15.00	40.00
CCR3 Jeff Gordon	10.00	25.00
CCR4 Jeff Gordon	10.00	25.00
CCR5 Rusty Wallace	8.00	20.00

1995 Press Pass Race Day

This 12-card insert set features winning drivers from the 1994 Winston Cup season. The cards use holofoil technology and were inserted at a rate of one per 24 packs.

COMPLETE SET (12)	30.00	80.00
RD1 Cover Card	.30	.75
RD2 Geoff Bodine	.60	1.50
RD3 Dale Earnhardt	10.00	25.00
RD4 Jeff Gordon	6.00	15.00
RD5 Ernie Irvan	1.25	3
RD6 Dale Jarrett	4.00	10
RD7 Terry Labonte	2.00	5
RD8 Sterling Marlin	2.00	5
RD9 Mark Martin	5.00	12
RD10 Ricky Rudd	2.00	5
RD11 Jimmy Spencer	.60	1
RD12 Rusty Wallace	5.00	12

1996 Press Pass

This 120-card set is the base brand from Press P
It features the best drivers in stock car racing. Th
the first set to ever include each of NASCA
Winston Cup Regional Series champions. The s
also the first to show many of the driver and spo
changes for the 1996 season. The set features
following topical subsets: Winston Cup Drivers
36), Winston Cup Cars (37-54), Busch Gr
National Drivers (55-63), SuperTrucks Drivers
72), Teamwork (73-81), Daytona Winner (82-
Shattered (91-99), Champions (100-108), Winr
Circle (109-112) and '96 Preview (113-119). Ho
product was packaged eight cards per pack
packs per box and 20 boxes per case. Also, inclu
in Hobby only packs was a special Jeff Gor
Championship card. It pays tribute to the 1
Winston Cup Champion. These cards are found
per 480 packs. Retail product was packed eight c
per pack, 36 packs per box and 20 boxes per cas

COMPLETE SET (120)	8.00	20
1 John Andretti	.07	
2 Brett Bodine	.07	
3 Geoff Bodine	.07	
4 Todd Bodine	.07	
5 Jeff Burton	.25	
6 Ward Burton	.15	
7 Derrike Cope	.07	
8 Ricky Craven	.07	
9 Dale Earnhardt	1.25	3
10 Bill Elliott	.30	
11 Jeff Gordon	.75	2
12 Steve Grissom	.07	
13 Bobby Hamilton	.07	
14 Ernie Irvan	.15	
15 Dale Jarrett	.50	1
16 Bobby Labonte	.50	1
17 Terry Labonte	.25	
18 Dave Marcis	.15	
19 Sterling Marlin	.25	
20 Mark Martin	.60	1
21 Rick Mast	.07	
22 Jeremy Mayfield	.15	
23 Ted Musgrave	.07	
24 Joe Nemechek	.07	
25 Kyle Petty	.15	
26 Robert Pressley	.07	
27 Ricky Rudd	.25	
28 Ken Schrader	.07	
29 Morgan Shepherd	.07	
30 Lake Speed	.07	
31 Hut Stricklin	.07	
32 Dick Trickle	.07	
33 Mike Wallace	.07	
34 Rusty Wallace	.60	1
35 Darrell Waltrip	.15	
36 Michael Waltrip	.15	
37 Kyle Petty's Car	.07	
38 Jeff Gordon's Car	.30	
39 Ted Musgrave's Car	.02	
40 Dale Earnhardt's Car	.50	1
41 Bobby Labonte's Car	.15	
42 Terry Labonte's Car	.15	
43 Sterling Marlin's Car	.07	
44 Ricky Craven's Car	.02	
45 Derrike Cope's Car	.02	
46 Bill Elliott's Car	.15	
47 Rusty Wallace's Car	.25	
48 Michael Waltrip's Car	.07	
49 Bobby Hamilton's Car	.07	
50 Dale Jarrett's Car	.15	
51 Ernie Irvan's Car	.07	
52 Ricky Rudd's Car	.07	
53 Mark Martin's Car	.25	
54 Darrell Waltrip's Car	.07	
55 Johnny Benson Jr.	.15	
56 Tim Fedewa	.07	
57 Jeff Fuller	.07	
58 Jeff Green	.07	
59 Jason Keller	.07	
60 Chad Little	.07	
61 Mike McLaughlin	.07	
62 Larry Pearson	.07	
63 Elton Sawyer	.07	
64 Mike Bliss RC	.07	
65 Rick Carelli	.07	
66 Ron Hornaday Jr.	.07	
67 Ernie Irvan	.15	
68 Butch Miller	.07	
69 Joe Ruttman	.07	
70 Bill Sedgwick	.07	
71 Mike Skinner	.07	
72 Bob Strait	.07	
73 Roger Penske TW Don Miller	.07	

obin Pemberton		
Rusty Wallace TW		
arry McClure TW	.07	.20
ony Glover		
Sterling Marlin		
ick Hendrick TW	.07	.20
Gary DeHart		
erry Labonte		
ack Roush TW	.30	.75
Steve Hmiel		
Mark Martin		
oe Gibbs TW	.15	.40
immy Makar		
Bobby Labonte		
eff Gordon TW	.40	1.00
Rick Hendrick		
Ray Evernham		
obert Yates TW	.07	.20
Larry McReynolds		
Dale Jarrett		
ichard Petty TW	.25	.60
Robbie Loomis		
Bobby Hamilton		
harles Hardy TW	.07	.20
Mike Beam		
Bill Elliott		
obby Allison DW	.07	.20
eoff Bodine DW	.07	.20
errike Cope DW	.07	.20
ill Elliott DW	.15	.40
nie Irvan DW	.07	.20
ale Jarrett DW	.15	.40
terling Marlin DW	.15	.40
ichard Petty DW	.25	.60
arrell Waltrip DW	.07	.20
icky Craven S	.07	.20
ll Elliott S	.15	.40
eff Gordon S	.40	1.00
obby Labonte S	.15	.40
erling Marlin S	.15	.40
lark Martin S	.30	.75
yle Petty S	.07	.20
icky Rudd S	.15	.40
usty Wallace S	.30	.75
Jeff Gordon WCC	.40	1.00
rooke Gordon		
Andy Hillenburg	.07	.20
ACA Champion		
Ron Compagnone Jr.	.02	.10
astern Seaboard Champ		
Phil Warren	.02	.10
Mid-Atlantic Champion		
Jeff Wildung	.02	.10
Northwest Champion		
Mel Walen	.02	.10
reat Northern Champion		
Paul White	.02	.10
unbelt Champion		
Dale Planck	.02	.10
Mid-America Champion		
Ray Guss Jr.	.02	.10
entral Champion		
Unocal Race Stoppers WC	.02	.10
Bill Brodrick WC	.02	.10
Jeff Gordon WC	.40	1.00
ohnny Benson Jr.		
Bill Venturini WC	.02	.10
Johnny Benson PRE	.15	.40
David Green PRE	.07	.20
Dale Jarrett PRE	.15	.40
Mike McLaughlin PRE	.07	.20
Morgan Shepherd PRE	.07	.20
Michael Waltrip PRE	.15	.40
Rusty Wallace's Car PRE	.25	.60
Checklist Card	.02	.10
erry Labonte Promo	.75	2.00
Bobby Labonte Gold	2.00	5.00
ational Convention Promo		
Bobby Labonte Red	4.00	10.00
ational Convention Promo		
Gordon Championship	12.50	30.00

1996 Press Pass Scorchers

corchers set is a 120-card parallel version of se set. Each card features red foil stamping to ntiate them from the base cards. The cards are ed in hobby packs at a rate of one per pack.

PLETE SET (120)	30.00	60.00
RCHERS: 1.2X TO 3X BASE CARDS		

1996 Press Pass Torquers

20-card set is a parallel of the base set. Each eatures blue foil stamping to differentiate them the base cards. The cards are in retail packs t a rate of one per pack.

PLETE SET (120)	30.00	60.00
QUERS: 1.2X TO 3X BASE CARDS		

96 Press Pass Burning Rubber

even-card set is the first to incorporate race equipment into trading cards. Press Pass took om winning race cars in the 1995 season and hem cut into pieces. These pieces were then ed to the cards that appear in this set. Each s individually numbered to 500 and the backs n a certificate of authenticity. The cards were ed at a rate of one per 480 packs.

PLETE SET (7)	150.00	300.00
Kyle Petty's Car	12.50	30.00
eff Gordon's Car	30.00	60.00
BR3 Dale Earnhardt's Car	25.00	60.00
BR4 Terry Labonte's Car	12.50	30.00
BR5 Sterling Marlin's Car	12.50	30.00
BR6 Bill Elliott's Car	15.00	40.00
BR7 Mark Martin's Car	15.00	40.00

1996 Press Pass Burning Rubber Die Cast Inserts

These three cards were issued individually in 1996 Press Pass Die Cast Sets. Each set features a group of die cast racing pieces along with one of these Burning Rubber cards. Each card is numbered "1 of 1" on the cardbacks but the announced print runs were printed on the outside of the boxes that housed each set.

1 Bobby Labonte's Car/1008 Burning Rubber II card	30.00	60.00
2 Terry Labonte's Car/1996 Burning Rubber II card	30.00	60.00
3 Rusty Wallace/1996 Race Used Rubber card	30.00	60.00

1996 Press Pass Checkered Flags

This six-card set continues the insert theme started in 1994. The cards feature some of the tops names in NASCAR and were distributed in Wal-Mart only packs at a ratio of 1:9 packs.

COMPLETE SET (6)	8.00	20.00
CF1 Jeff Gordon	3.00	8.00
CF2 Bobby Labonte	2.00	5.00
CF3 Terry Labonte	1.00	2.50
CF4 Sterling Marlin	1.00	2.50
CF5 Mark Martin	2.50	6.00
CF6 Rusty Wallace	2.50	6.00

1996 Press Pass Cup Chase

This 37-card set is the third year in a row for Press Pass' interactive game. This is the first year that you could redeem a Cup Chase driver's card for a prize if they finish in the top 3 in any one of the five selected races. The interactive races are the February 18th Daytona 500, March 10th Purolator 500, April 14th First Union 400, May 5th Save Mart Supermarkets 300, and the June 16th UAW-GM Teamwork 500. The prize for having one of the top three finishers is a limited holographic foil card of that driver. There is also a Grand Prize awarded to those who redeem the 1996 Winston Cup Champion's Cup Chase card at the end of the season. The Grand Prize is an entire 37-card holographic foil cup chase set. Prizes could be redeemed through January 31, 1997. The Cup Chase cards are seeded one per 24 packs.

COMPLETE SET (37)	60.00	120.00
COMP.FOIL SET (37)	25.00	50.00
*FOIL NO-WIN: .4X TO 1X BASIC INSERTS		
*FOIL WIN: .12X TO .3X BASIC INSERTS		
1 John Andretti	.75	2.00
2 Brett Bodine	.75	2.00
3 Geoff Bodine WIN	.75	2.00
4 Todd Bodine	.75	2.00
5 Jeff Burton	2.50	6.00
6 Ward Burton	1.50	4.00
7 Derrike Cope	.75	2.00
8 Ricky Craven	.75	2.00
9 Dale Earnhardt WIN	12.50	30.00
10 Bill Elliott	3.00	8.00
11 Jeff Gordon WIN	8.00	20.00
12 Steve Grissom	.75	2.00
13 Bobby Hamilton	.75	2.00
14 Ernie Irvan	1.50	4.00
15 Dale Jarrett WIN	5.00	12.00
16 Bobby Labonte	5.00	12.00
17 Terry Labonte WIN	2.50	6.00
18 Dave Marcis	1.50	4.00
19 Sterling Marlin	2.50	6.00
20 Mark Martin WIN	6.00	15.00
21 Rick Mast	.75	2.00
22 Jeremy Mayfield	1.50	4.00
23 Ted Musgrave	.75	2.00
24 Joe Nemechek	.75	2.00
25 Kyle Petty	1.50	4.00
26 Robert Pressley	.75	2.00
27 Ricky Rudd WIN	2.50	6.00
28 Ken Schrader WIN	.75	2.00
29 Morgan Shepherd	.75	2.00
30 Lake Speed	.75	2.00
31 Hut Stricklin	.75	2.00
32 Dick Trickle	.75	2.00
33 Mike Wallace	.75	2.00
34 Rusty Wallace WIN	6.00	15.00
35 Darrell Waltrip	1.50	4.00
36 Michael Waltrip	1.50	4.00
37 Johnny Benson, Jr.	1.50	4.00

1996 Press Pass F.Q.S.

This 18-card set uses Nitrokrome technology to bring you nine of the fastest Winston Cup drivers and their cars. F.Q.S is an acronym for Fastest Qualifing Speed. Every driver's card number ends with the letter A, while each driver's car card number ends with the letter B. The cards were randomly inserted at a rate of one per 12 packs.

COMPLETE SET (18)	60.00	125.00
FQS1A Dale Earnhardt	8.00	20.00
FQS1B Dale Earnhardt's Car	3.00	8.00
FQS2A Bill Elliott	2.00	5.00
FQS2B Bill Elliott's Car	1.00	2.50
FQS3A Jeff Gordon	5.00	12.00
FQS3B Jeff Gordon's Car	2.00	5.00
FQS4A Dale Jarrett	3.00	8.00
FQS4B Dale Jarrett's Car	1.00	2.50
FQS5A Bobby Labonte	3.00	8.00
FQS5B Bobby Labonte's Car	1.00	2.50
FQS6A Terry Labonte	1.50	4.00
FQS6B Terry Labonte's Car	1.00	2.50
FQS7A Sterling Marlin	1.50	4.00
FQS7B Sterling Marlin's Car	.50	1.25
FQS8A Mark Martin	4.00	10.00
FQS8B Mark Martin's Car	1.50	4.00
FQS9A Ricky Rudd	1.50	4.00
FQS9B Ricky Rudd's Car	.50	1.25

1996 Press Pass Focused

This set is made up of ten of the top drivers in Winston Cup. Each card is produced on clear acetate stock. The cards were randomly seeded at a rate of one per 72 packs.

COMPLETE SET (10)	60.00	150.00
F1 Dale Earnhardt	15.00	40.00
F2 Bill Elliott	4.00	10.00
F3 Jeff Gordon	10.00	25.00
F4 Ernie Irvan	2.00	5.00
F5 Terry Labonte	3.00	8.00
F6 Sterling Marlin	3.00	8.00
F7 Mark Martin	8.00	20.00
F8 Kyle Petty	2.00	5.00
F9 Ricky Rudd	3.00	8.00
F10 Rusty Wallace	8.00	20.00
P1 Jeff Gordon Promo	2.00	5.00

1996 Press Pass R and N China

This 26-card set was produced by R and N China. Each card is made out of porcelain and is a replica of a 1996 Press Pass card.

COMPLETE SET (26)	125.00	250.00
1 John Andretti	3.00	8.00
5 Jeff Burton	5.00	12.00
8 Ricky Craven	3.00	8.00
9 Dale Earnhardt	30.00	60.00
11 Jeff Gordon	12.50	35.00
13 Bobby Hamilton	3.00	8.00
14 Ernie Irvan	4.00	10.00
15 Dale Jarrett	7.50	20.00
16 Bobby Labonte	7.50	20.00
17 Terry Labonte	6.00	15.00
19 Sterling Marlin	4.00	10.00
20 Mark Martin	10.00	25.00
22 Jeremy Mayfield	3.00	8.00
23 Ted Musgrave	3.00	8.00
24 Joe Nemechek	3.00	8.00
25 Kyle Petty	3.00	8.00
28 Ken Schrader	3.00	8.00
34 Rusty Wallace	10.00	25.00
35 Darrell Waltrip	4.00	10.00
36 Michael Waltrip	4.00	10.00
38 Jeff Gordon's Car	6.00	15.00
42 Terry Labonte's Car	3.00	8.00
47 Rusty Wallace's Car	4.00	10.00
50 Dale Jarrett's Car	4.00	10.00
53 Mark Martin's Car	3.00	8.00
55 Johnny Benson	3.00	8.00

1997 Press Pass

The 1997 Press Pass set was issued in one series totalling 140 cards. The set contains the topical subsets: Winston Cup Drivers (1-30), Winston Cup Cars (31-45), SuperTruck Drivers (46-54), Japan Race (55-63), BGN Drivers (64-78), Back-to-Back (79-90), Highlights (91-109), Champions (110-120), '97 Preview (121-133), and 10 Wins (1334-138). The cards were distributed to both hobby and retail. The hobby product consisted of eight card packs, 24 packs per box and 20 boxes per case. The retail boxes consisted of eight card packs, 32 packs per box and 20 boxes per case. There are two insert cards priced at the bottom of the base set listing. One is the Jeff Gordon Sam Bass Top Flight card. The card was intended to be in the 1996 VIP Top Flight set but was inserted in '97 Press Pass packs at a rate of one in 480 packs. Also a special holofoil Terry Labonte Winston Cup Champion card could be found in packs at a rate of one in 480.

COMPLETE SET (140)	10.00	25.00
1 Terry Labonte	.25	.60
2 Jeff Gordon	.75	2.00
3 Dale Jarrett	.50	1.25
4 Dale Earnhardt	1.25	3.00
5 Mark Martin	.60	1.50
6 Ricky Rudd	.25	.60
7 Rusty Wallace	.60	1.50
8 Sterling Marlin	.25	.60
9 Bobby Hamilton	.07	.20
10 Ernie Irvan	.15	.40
11 Bobby Labonte	.50	1.25
12 Ken Schrader	.07	.20
13 Jeff Burton	.25	.60
14 Michael Waltrip	.15	.40
15 Ted Musgrave	.07	.20
16 Geoff Bodine	.07	.20
17 Rick Mast	.07	.20
18 Morgan Shepherd	.07	.20
19 Ricky Craven	.07	.20
20 Johnny Benson	.15	.40
21 Hut Stricklin	.07	.20
22 Jeremy Mayfield	.15	.40
23 Kyle Petty	.15	.40
24 Kenny Wallace	.07	.20
25 Darrell Waltrip	.15	.40
26 Bill Elliott	.30	.75
27 Robert Pressley	.07	.20
28 Ward Burton	.15	.40
29 Joe Nemechek	.07	.20
30 Mike Skinner	.07	.20
31 Rusty Wallace's Car	.25	.60
32 Dale Earnhardt's Car	.50	1.25
33 Sterling Marlin's Car	.07	.20
34 Terry Labonte's Car	.07	.20
35 Mark Martin's Car	.25	.60
36 Ricky Rudd's Car	.07	.20
37 Bobby Labonte's Car	.15	.40
38 Michael Waltrip's Car	.07	.20
39 Jeff Gordon's Car	.30	.75
40 Ernie Irvan's Car	.02	.10
41 Ricky Craven's Car	.02	.10
42 Kyle Petty's Car	.02	.10
43 Bobby Hamilton's Car	.02	.10
44 Dale Jarrett's Car	.15	.40
45 Bill Elliott's Car	.07	.20
46 Mike Bliss	.07	.20
47 Rick Carelli	.07	.20
48 Ron Hornaday	.07	.20
49 Butch Miller	.07	.20
50 Joe Ruttman	.07	.20
51 Bill Sedgwick	.07	.20
52 Mike Skinner	.07	.20
53 Rusty Wallace	.60	1.50
54 Darrell Waltrip	.15	.40
55 Johnny Benson's Car	.02	.10
56 Dale Earnhardt's Car	.50	1.25
57 Jeff Gordon's Car	.30	.75
58 Ernie Irvan's Car	.02	.10
59 Dale Jarrett's Car	.15	.40
60 Terry Labonte's Car	.07	.20
61 Sterling Marlin's Car	.07	.20
62 Rusty Wallace's Car	.25	.60
63 Michael Waltrip's Car	.07	.20
64 Todd Bodine	.07	.20
65 Rodney Combs	.07	.20
66 Ricky Craven	.07	.20
67 Jeff Fuller	.07	.20
68 David Green	.07	.20
69 Jeff Green	.07	.20
70 Dale Jarrett	.50	1.25
71 Jason Keller	.07	.20
72 Terry Labonte	.25	.60
73 Randy LaJoie	.07	.20
74 Chad Little	.15	.40
75 Mark Martin	.60	1.50
76 Mike McLaughlin	.07	.20
77 Larry Pearson	.15	.40
78 Michael Waltrip	.15	.40
79 Michael Waltrip	.15	.40
80 Dale Jarrett	.50	1.25
81 Bobby Labonte	.50	1.25
82 Terry Labonte	.25	.60
83 Ricky Craven	.07	.20
84 Rusty Wallace	.60	1.50
85 Ken Schrader	.07	.20
86 Mike Wallace	.07	.20
87 Jeremy Mayfield	.15	.40
88 Chad Little	.15	.40
89 Mark Martin	.60	1.50
90 Kenny Wallace	.07	.20
91 Robby Gordon RC	.25	.60
92 Jimmy Johnson	.07	.20
93 Michael Waltrip David Pearson	.15	.40
94 Dale Jarrett	.50	1.25
95 Dale Earnhardt's Car	.50	1.25
96 Jeff Gordon Dale Jarrett's Cars	.30	.75
97 Terry Labonte Richard Petty	.25	.60
98 Sterling Marlin	.25	.60
99 Rusty Wallace's Car	.25	.60
100 Michael Waltrip	.15	.40
101 Ernie Irvan	.15	.40
102 Dale Jarrett	.50	1.25
103 Geoff Bodine	.07	.20
104 Jeff Gordon's Car	.30	.75
105 Jeff Gordon's Car	.30	.75
106 Terry Labonte's Car	.07	.20
107 Ricky Rudd	.25	.60
108 Bobby Hamilton Richard Petty	.25	.60
109 Bobby Labonte	.50	1.25
110 Terry Labonte	.25	.60
111 Randy LaJoie	.07	.20
112 Mark Martin	.60	1.50
113 Ron Hornaday	.07	.20
114 Kelly Tanner	.07	.20
115 Joe Kosiski	.07	.20
116 Lyndon Amick RC	.15	.40
117 Dave Dion	.07	.20
118 Tony Hirschman	.02	.10
119 Chris Raudman	.02	.10
120 Mike Cope	.07	.20
121 Kyle Petty	.15	.40
122 Rusty Wallace's Car	.25	.60
123 Michael Waltrip	.15	.40
124 Dale Jarrett	.50	1.25
125 Chad Little	.15	.40
126 Joe Nemechek	.07	.20
127 Steve Grissom	.07	.20
128 Robby Gordon	.15	.40
129 Mike Wallace	.07	.20
130 Bill Elliott's Car	.07	.20
131 Ken Schrader	.07	.20
132 Wally Dallenbach	.07	.20
133 Derrike Cope	.07	.20
134 Jeff Gordon W	.40	1.00
135 Jeff Gordon W	.40	1.00
136 Jeff Gordon W	.40	1.00
137 Jeff Gordon W	.40	1.00
138 Jeff Gordon W	.40	1.00
139 Checklist	.02	.10
140 Checklist	.02	.10
P1 Dale Jarrett Promo	.75	2.00
P2 Bobby Labonte National Promo	1.25	3.00
P3 Bobby Labonte's Car National Promo	.75	2.00
SB1 Jeff Gordon Sam Bass	20.00	50.00
0 Terry Labonte WC Champ	15.00	40.00

1997 Press Pass Lasers

This 140-card set is a parallel version of the base Press Pass set. The cards feature silver foil and were available only in hobby product. The cards were inserted one per pack.

COMPLETE SET (140)	20.00	50.00
*LASERS: 1.2X TO 3X BASIC CARDS		

1997 Press Pass Oil Slicks

This 140-card set is the top end parallel version in the Press Pass product. The cards feature holographic foil and 100 of each card was produced. The Oil Slicks were only available in the hobby product at a rate of one in 36 packs.

COMPLETE SET (140)	250.00	500.00
*OIL SLICK: 8X TO 20X BASIC CARDS		

1997 Press Pass Torquers

This 140-card set is the retail only parallel version of the Press Pass base set. The cards feature blue foil stamping and were inserted in retail packs at a rate of one per pack.

COMPLETE SET (140)	20.00	50.00
*TORQUERS: 1.2X TO 3X BASIC CARDS		

1997 Press Pass Autographs

This set features autographed cards from the top stars from the Winston Cup and Busch Circuits. These cards were inserted into three Press Pass products: ActionVision, Press Pass Premium, and VIP. The cards were randomly inserted in ActionVision packs at a ratio of 1:160, Press Pass Premuim packs at a ratio of 1:72 packs, and VIP packs at a ratio of 1:60 packs. Each card is numbered on the back "#/35" but a total of 41-different cards were released over the three products. Note that card #27 was produced in two different versions.

COMPLETE SET (41)	800.00	1400.00
1 Terry Labonte ActionVision Press Pass Premuim VIP	12.50	30.00
2 Jeff Gordon Actionvision Press Pass Premium VIP	100.00	175.00
3 Dale Jarrett ActionVision VIP	10.00	25.00
4 Dale Earnhardt ActionVision Press Pass Premium VIP	175.00	300.00
5 Steve Hmiel Press Pass Premium VIP	5.00	10.00
6 Ricky Rudd ActionVision VIP	12.50	30.00
7 Rusty Wallace ActionVision VIP	15.00	40.00
8 Sterling Marlin ActionVision VIP	10.00	25.00
9 Bobby Hamilton Press Pass Premium VIP	10.00	25.00
10 Bobby Labonte Press Pass Premium VIP	12.50	30.00
11 Ken Schrader Press Pass Premium VIP	6.00	15.00
12 Jeff Burton ActionVision VIP	8.00	20.00
13 Michael Waltrip Press Pass Premium VIP	8.00	20.00
14 Ted Musgrave Press Pass Premium VIP	6.00	15.00
15 Geoff Bodine Press Pass Premium VIP	6.00	15.00
16 Ricky Craven VIP	10.00	25.00
17 Johnny Benson Press Pass Premium VIP	12.50	30.00
18 Jeremy Mayfield VIP	10.00	25.00
19 Kyle Petty ActionVision Press Pass Premium VIP	12.50	30.00
20 Bill Elliott ActionVision VIP	25.00	60.00
21 Wood Brothers VIP	5.00	10.00
22 Joe Nemechek Press Pass Premium VIP	6.00	15.00
23 Wally Dallenbach Press Pass Premium VIP	6.00	15.00
24 Robby Gordon Press Pass Premium VIP	10.00	25.00
25 David Green VIP	6.00	15.00
26 Jason Keller Press Pass Premium VIP	6.00	15.00
27 Jeff Green Press Pass Premium VIP	6.00	15.00
27A Robby Gordon Jeff Green Mike Skinner VIP	10.00	25.00
28 Mike McLaughlin Press Pass Premium VIP	6.00	15.00
29 Chad Little VIP	12.50	30.00
30 Jeff Fuller Press Pass Premium VIP	6.00	15.00
31 Todd Bodine Press Pass Premium VIP	6.00	15.00
32 Rodney Combs Press Pass Premium VIP	6.00	15.00
33 Randy LaJoie Press Pass Premium VIP	6.00	15.00
34 Ray Evernham VIP	12.50	30.00
35 Larry McReynolds Press Pass Premium VIP	6.00	15.00
36 Gary DeHart VIP	5.00	10.00
37 Mike Beam VIP	5.00	10.00
38 Darrell Waltrip VIP	15.00	40.00
39 Ward Burton VIP	10.00	25.00
40 Mike Skinner VIP	6.00	15.00

1997 Press Pass Banquet Bound

This 10-card insert set features the top drivers from 1996. The cards are printed on rainbow holofoil board and were inserted one in 12 packs.

COMPLETE SET (10)	12.50	30.00
BB1 Terry Labonte	1.25	3.00
BB2 Jeff Gordon	4.00	10.00
BB3 Dale Jarrett	2.50	6.00
BB4 Dale Earnhardt	6.00	15.00
BB5 Mark Martin	3.00	8.00
BB6 Ricky Rudd	1.25	3.00
BB7 Rusty Wallace	3.00	8.00
BB8 Sterling Marlin	1.25	3.00
BB9 Bobby Hamilton	.40	1.00
BB10 Ernie Irvan	.75	2.00

1997 Press Pass Burning Rubber

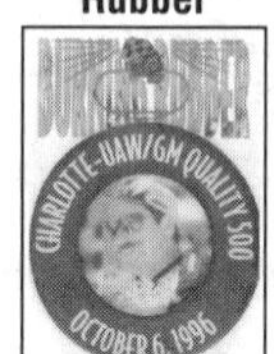

Authentic race-used tires from the top drivers are incorporated in this seven-card insert set. The cards feature an acetate, die-cut design with a photo of the driver in the center with a tire shaped piece of race used rubber surrounding it. Each was serial numbered of 400-cards made. The cards were seeded in packs at a rate of one in 480.

COMPLETE SET (7)	150.00	300.00
BR1 Rusty Wallace	12.50	30.00
BR2 Dale Earnhardt	40.00	80.00
BR3 Terry Labonte	12.50	30.00
BR4 Michael Waltrip	10.00	25.00

BR5 Jeff Gordon	30.00	60.00
BR6 Ernie Irvan	10.00	25.00
BR7 Dale Jarrett	12.50	30.00

1997 Press Pass Clear Cut

Randomly inserted in packs at a rate of one in 18, this 10-card set features drivers who won races in 1996. The cards feature a clear die-cut acetate design.

COMPLETE SET (10)	12.50	30.00
C1 Dale Earnhardt	6.00	15.00
C2 Jeff Gordon	4.00	10.00
C3 Ernie Irvan	.75	2.00
C4 Dale Jarrett	2.50	6.00
C5 Bobby Labonte	2.50	6.00
C6 Terry Labonte	1.25	3.00
C7 Mark Martin	3.00	8.00
C8 Ricky Rudd	1.25	3.00
C9 Rusty Wallace	3.00	8.00
C10 Michael Waltrip	.75	2.00

1997 Press Pass Cup Chase

This was the fourth consecutive year of the popular Press Pass' interactive game. This year if the collector owned a Cup Chase card of one of the three top finishers from any one of the 10 selected Winston Cup race events, the card could be redeemed for a limited gold NitroKrome die cut card of that driver. Card number CC20 was a Field Card to be used in the event that a Winston Cup driver not featured in the set finishes 1st, 2nd, or 3rd at one of the 10 selected races. The prize for the Field Card was one of the 19 featured drivers gold NitroKrome die cut cards drawn at random. At the end of the '97 season, the Winston Cup Champion's Cup Chase card could be redeemed for the entire 20-card gold NitroKrome die cut Cup Chase set. This set included a special card of the 1996 Winston Cup Champion Terry Labonte that was available only through the redemption. Each Cup Chase card could be redeemed for two usages throughout the entire 1997 season. Each time the card was redeemed Press Pass embossed one of the corners. After the card had been embossed twice it is no longer redeemable. The Cup Chase card of the '97 WC Champion could only be redeemed once. The deadline to claim prizes was January 30, 1998. The 10 eligible races were: Feb.16 - Daytona, March 9 - Atlanta, April 6 - Texas, May 4 - Sears Point, May 25 - Charlotte, June 22- California, August 2 - Indianapolis, August 23 - Bristol, September 28 - Martinsville, November 2 - Phoenix. There was also a die cut parallel version of the 20-card set which could not be redeemed for prizes. The die cuts were inserted as chip toppers one per case.

COMPLETE SET (20)	50.00	100.00
COMP.DIE CUT GOLD (20)	75.00	150.00
*DIE CUT GOLD WIN: .6X TO 1.5X BASIC INS.		
*DC GOLD NO-WIN: .8X TO 2X BASIC INS.		
COMP.DIE CUT BLUE (20)	25.00	60.00
*DIE CUT BLUE WIN: .2X TO .5X BASIC INS.		
*DC BLUE NO-WIN: .4X TO 1X BASIC INS.		
CC1 Johnny Benson	1.25	3.00
CC2 Jeff Burton WIN	4.00	10.00
CC3 Ward Burton	1.25	3.00
CC4 Ricky Craven WIN	3.00	6.00
CC5 Dale Earnhardt	10.00	25.00
CC6 Bill Elliott	2.00	5.00
CC7 Jeff Gordon WIN	6.00	15.00
CC8 Bobby Hamilton WIN	2.50	5.00
CC9 Ernie Irvan WIN	3.00	6.00
CC10 Dale Jarrett WIN	4.00	10.00
CC11 Bobby Labonte WIN	4.00	10.00
CC12 Terry Labonte WIN	4.00	10.00
CC13 Sterling Marlin	2.00	5.00
CC14 Mark Martin WIN	5.00	12.00
CC15 Kyle Petty	1.25	3.00
CC16 Ricky Rudd	4.00	10.00
CC17 Ken Schrader	.60	1.50
CC18 Rusty Wallace	5.00	12.00
CC19 Michael Waltrip	1.25	3.00
CC20 Field Card WIN	.60	1.50

1997 Press Pass Victory Lane

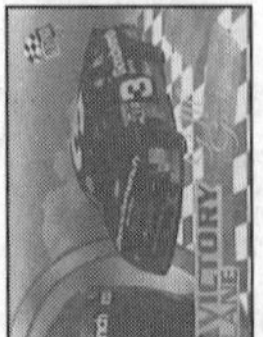

Randomly inserted in packs at a rate of one in 18, this 18-card set was divided with nine cards being drivers and nine cards being driver's cars. The cards are number 1-9 with an A or B extension after the number. All the A cards were shots of the driver while all the B cards were shots of their cars. The A cards were available in hobby packs and the B cards were available in retail packs.

COMPLETE SET (18)	60.00	100.00
COMP.DRIVER SET (9)	45.00	75.00
COMP.CAR SET (9)	15.00	30.00
VL1A Dale Earnhardt	10.00	25.00
VL1B Dale Earnhardt's Car	4.00	10.00
VL2A Jeff Gordon	6.00	15.00
VL2B Jeff Gordon's Car	2.50	6.00
VL3A Ernie Irvan	1.25	3.00
VL3B Ernie Irvan's Car	.30	.75
VL4A Dale Jarrett	4.00	10.00
VL4B Dale Jarrett's Car	1.25	3.00
VL5A Terry Labonte	2.00	5.00
VL5B Terry Labonte's Car	.60	1.50
VL6A Sterling Marlin	2.00	5.00
VL6B Sterling Marlin's Car	.60	1.50
VL7A Ricky Rudd	2.00	5.00
VL7B Ricky Rudd's Car	.60	1.50
VL8A Rusty Wallace	5.00	12.00
VL8B Rusty Wallace's Car	2.00	5.00
VL9A Michael Waltrip	1.25	3.00
VL9B Michael Waltrip's Car	.60	1.50

1998 Press Pass

The 1998 Press Pass set was issued in one series totalling 150 cards and was distributed in eight-card packs. The fronts feature color photos with silver-etched foil highlights. The set contains the topical subsets: NASCAR Winston Cup Drivers (1-27), NASCAR Winston Cup Cars (28-36), NASCAR Busch Series Drivers (37-49), NASCAR Craftsman Truck Series (50-54), 1998 NASCAR Winston Cup Previews (55-63), Teammates (64-81), Champions (82-93), NASCAR Winston Cup Crew Chiefs (94-100), and NASCAR's 50 Greatest Drivers of All-Time (101-150). A special all foil Jeff Gordon Winston Cup Champion card can be found in hobby packs at the rate of one in 480.

COMPLETE SET (150)	12.00	30.00
COMP.REGULAR SET (100)	6.00	15.00
1 Jeff Gordon	.75	2.00
2 Mark Martin	.60	1.50
3 Dale Jarrett	.50	1.25
4 Dale Earnhardt	1.25	3.00
5 Terry Labonte	.25	.60
6 Ricky Rudd	.25	.60
7 Rusty Wallace	.60	1.50
8 Sterling Marlin	.25	.60
9 Bobby Hamilton	.07	.20
10 Ernie Irvan	.15	.40
11 Bobby Labonte	.50	1.25
12 Ken Schrader	.07	.20
13 Jeff Burton	.25	.60
14 Michael Waltrip	.15	.40
15 Ted Musgrave	.07	.20
16 Geoff Bodine	.07	.20
17 Ward Burton	.15	.40
18 Ricky Craven	.15	.40
19 Johnny Benson	.15	.40
20 Jeremy Mayfield	.15	.40
21 Kyle Petty	.15	.40
22 Darrell Waltrip	.15	.40
23 Bill Elliott	.30	.75
24 Mike Skinner	.07	.20
25 David Green	.07	.20
26 Joe Nemechek	.07	.20
27 Wally Dallenbach	.07	.20
28 Rusty Wallace's Car	.25	.60
29 Dale Earnhardt's Car	.50	1.25
30 Terry Labonte's Car	.15	.40
31 Mark Martin's Car	.25	.60
32 Ricky Rudd's Car	.07	.20
33 Bobby Labonte's Car	.02	.10
34 Jeff Gordon's Car	.30	.75
35 Dale Jarrett's Car	.15	.40
36 Bill Elliott's Car	.15	.40
37 Randy LaJoie	.07	.20
38 Todd Bodine	.07	.20
39 Tim Fedewa	.07	.20
40 Kevin Lepage	.07	.20
41 Mark Martin	.60	1.50
42 Mike McLaughlin	.07	.20
43 Jason Keller	.07	.20
44 Steve Park	.50	1.25
45 Dale Jarrett	.50	1.25
46 Dale Earnhardt Jr.	2.00	4.00
47 Kevin Lepage	.15	.40
48 Elliott Sadler	.15	.40
49 Hermie Sadler	.07	.20
50 Rich Bickle	.07	.20
51 Jack Sprague	.07	.20
52 Joe Ruttman	.07	.20
53 Mike Bliss	.07	.20
54 Ron Hornaday	.07	.20
55 Ernie Irvan	.15	.40
56 Kenny Irwin	.15	.40
57 Sterling Marlin	.25	.60
58 Steve Park	.50	1.25
59 Johnny Benson	.15	.40
60 Todd Bodine	.07	.20
61 Bobby Hamilton	.07	.20
62 Ted Musgrave	.07	.20
63 Jimmy Spencer	.07	.20
64 Darren Jolly	.02	.10
65 Jeff Knight	.02	.10
66 Barry Muse	.02	.10
67 Mike Belden	.02	.10
68 Mike Trower	.02	.10
69 Chris Anderson	.02	.10
70 Patrick Donahue	.02	.10
71 Brian Whitesell	.02	.10
72 Ray Evernham	.02	.10
73 J.J. Clodfelter	.02	.10
74 Ben Leslie	.02	.10
75 Dennis Ritchie	.02	.10
76 Mitch Williams	.02	.10
77 Lonnie Dubay	.02	.10
78 Luke Shimp	.02	.10
79 Butch Hylton	.02	.10
80 Steve Spahr	.02	.10
81 Jimmy Fennig	.02	.10
82 Randy LaJoie	.07	.20
83 Jack Sprague	.07	.20
84 Mike Stefanik RC	.07	.20
85 Butch Gilliland	.07	.20
86 Mike Swaim Jr.	.07	.20
87 Hal Goodson	.07	.20
88 Bryan Germone	.07	.20
89 Joe Kosiski	.07	.20
90 Kelly Tanner	.07	.20
91 Gary Scelzi	.07	.20
92 Mark Martin IROC	.60	1.50
93 Andy Green	.02	.10
94 Jimmy Makar	.02	.10
95 Ray Evernham	.02	.10
96 Jimmy Fennig	.02	.10
97 Larry McReynolds	.02	.10
98 Todd Parrott	.02	.10
99 Robin Pemberton	.02	.10
100 WC Schedule CL	.02	.10
101 Jeff Gordon RET	1.25	3.00
102 Mark Martin RET	1.00	2.50
103 Dale Jarrett RET	.75	2.00
104 Dale Earnhardt RET	2.00	5.00
105 Rusty Wallace RET	1.00	2.50
106 Ricky Rudd RET	.40	1.00
107 Bill Elliott RET	.50	1.25
108 Terry Labonte RET	.40	1.00
109 Ralph Earnhardt RET	.25	.60
110 Richie Evans RET	.10	.30
111 Red Farmer RET	.10	.30
112 Ray Hendrick RET	.10	.30
113 Darrell Waltrip RET	.25	.60
114 Tiny Lund RET	.10	.30
115 Jerry Cook RET	.10	.30
116 Geoff Bodine RET	.10	.30
117 Bob Welborn RET	.10	.30
118 Fred Lorenzen RET	.25	.60
119 Herb Thomas RET	.10	.30
120 Tim Flock RET	.25	.60
121 Lee Petty RET	.25	.60
122 Buck Baker RET	.10	.30
123 Rex White RET	.10	.30
124 Ned Jarrett RET	.25	.60
125 Benny Parsons RET	.25	.60
126 Joe Weatherly RET	.10	.30
127 David Pearson RET	.25	.60
128 Bobby Isaac RET	.10	.30
129 Tim Richmond RET	.25	.60
130 Curtis Turner RET	.25	.60
131 Alan Kulwicki RET	.25	.60
132 Bobby Allison RET	.25	.60
133 Cale Yarborough RET	.25	.60
134 Richard Petty RET	.40	1.00
135 Davey Allison RET	.40	1.00
136 Glen Wood RET	.10	.30
137 Harry Gant RET	.25	.60
138 Junior Johnson RET	.25	.60
139 Fireball Roberts RET	.25	.60
140 Neil Bonnett RET	.25	.60
141 Lee Roy Yarborough RET	.10	.30
142 Buddy Baker RET	.25	.60
143 A.J. Foyt RET	.25	.60
144 Red Byron RET	.10	.30
145 Cotton Owens RET	.10	.30
146 Hershel McGriff RET	.10	.30
147 Marvin Panch RET	.10	.30
148 Jack Ingram RET	.10	.30
149 Marshall Teague RET	.10	.30
150 Ernie Irvan CL	.15	.40
P1 Jeff Gordon Promo	2.00	5.00
P2 Mark Martin Club Promo	1.50	4.00
0 Jeff Gordon 1997 Champion	12.50	30.00

1998 Press Pass Oil Slicks

Randomly inserted in hobby packs only at the rate of one in 48, this 100-card set is a partial parallel version of the base set with an all new custom made foil and typography design. Only 100 of each card were produced and are individually numbered.

COMPLETE SET (100)	300.00	600.00
*OIL SLICK: 12X TO 30X BASE CARDS		

1998 Press Pass Autographs

Randomly inserted in hobby packs at the rate of one in 240, this 14-card set features autographed color photos of top NASCAR drivers. Each card was individually numbered.

COMPLETE SET (14)	600.00	1000.00
1 Dale Earnhardt	250.00	350.00
2 Jeff Gordon/60	125.00	250.00
3 Dale Jarrett	25.00	60.00
4 Terry Labonte	20.00	50.00
5 Mark Martin/101	30.00	60.00
6 Bobby Labonte	12.50	30.00
7 Jeff Burton	8.00	20.00
8 Rusty Wallace	20.00	50.00
9 Michael Waltrip/285	10.00	25.00
10 Ricky Craven	7.50	15.00
11 Ricky Rudd	20.00	40.00
12 Mike Skinner	7.50	15.00
13 Darrell Waltrip	20.00	40.00
14 Johnny Benson	15.00	30.00

1998 Press Pass Cup Chase

This was the fifth consecutive year of the popular Press Pass interactive game. This year if the collector owned a Cup Chase card of one of the three top finishers from any one of the 11 selected Winston Cup race events, the card could be redeemed for an all-foil embossed die-cut card of that driver. Card number CC20 is a Field Card. In the event that a Winston Cup driver not featured in the Cup Chase set finishes 1st, 2nd, or 3rd at one of the 11 selected races, the Field Card can be redeemed. The prize for the Field Card is one of the 19 featured drivers die-cut cards drawn at random. At the end of the '98 season, the '98 Winston Cup Champion's Cup Chase card can be redeemed for a special 20-card Cup Chase set. Each Cup Chase card can be redeemed for two uses throughout the entire '98 season. Each time the card is redeemed Press Pass embossed one of the corners. After the card has been embossed twice it is no longer redeemable. The Cup Chase card of the '97 WC Champion can only be redeemed once. Deadline to claim prizes is January 31, 1999. The 11 eligible races are February 15 - Daytona, March 8- Atlanta, April 5 - Texas, May 3 - California, June 6 - Richmond, June 28 - Sears Point, July 26 - Pocono, August 16 - Michigan, September 6 - Darlington, September 27 - Martinsville, October 25 - Phoenix.

COMPLETE SET (20)	75.00	150.00
COMP.DIE CUT SET (19)	25.00	60.00
*DIE CUT WIN: .2X TO .5X BASE INSERTS		
*DIE CUT NO-WIN: .3X TO .8X BASE INS.		
CC1 Johnny Benson	2.00	5.00
CC2 Jeff Burton Win 2	4.00	10.00
CC3 Ward Burton	2.00	5.00
CC4 Ricky Craven	2.00	5.00
CC5 Dale Earnhardt's Car Win 2	10.00	25.00
CC6 Bill Elliott	3.00	8.00
CC7 Jeff Gordon Win 2 Champ	10.00	25.00
CC8 Bobby Hamilton Win	2.00	5.00
CC9 Ernie Irvan	2.00	5.00
CC10 Dale Jarrett Win 2	6.00	15.00
CC11 Bobby Labonte Win 2	6.00	15.00
CC12 Terry Labonte Win 2	5.00	12.00
CC13 Sterling Marlin	2.50	6.00
CC14 Mark Martin Win 2	6.00	15.00
CC15 Kyle Petty	2.00	5.00
CC16 Ricky Rudd Win	4.00	10.00
CC17 Ken Schrader	1.25	3.00
CC18 Rusty Wallace Win 2	6.00	15.00
CC19 Michael Waltrip	2.00	5.00
CC20 Field Card Win 2	2.00	5.00

1998 Press Pass Oil Cans

Randomly inserted in packs at the rate of one in 18, this nine-card set features color photos of top NASCAR Winston Cup drivers on all foil embossed cards.

COMPLETE SET (9)	12.50	30.00
OC1 Jeff Burton	1.25	3.00
OC2 Dale Earnhardt's Car	3.00	8.00
OC3 Jeff Gordon	4.00	10.00
OC4 Dale Jarrett	1.50	4.00
OC5 Bobby Labonte	2.50	6.00
OC6 Terry Labonte	1.50	4.00
OC7 Mark Martin	3.00	8.00
OC8 Ricky Rudd	1.25	3.00
OC9 Rusty Wallace	3.00	8.00

1998 Press Pass Pit Stop

Randomly inserted in packs at the rate of one in 12, this 18-card set features color photos of the hottest teams as they make their record pit stops printed on die-cut cards with intricate foil stamping.

COMPLETE SET (18)	12.50	30.00
PS1 Rusty Wallace's Car	2.50	6.00
PS2 Dale Earnhardt's Car	5.00	12.00
PS3 Sterling Marlin's Car	.75	2.00
PS4 Terry Labonte's Car	1.25	3.00
PS5 Mark Martin's Car	2.00	6.00
PS6 Ricky Rudd's Car	.75	2.00
PS7 Ted Musgrave's Car	.30	.75
PS8 Darrell Waltrip's Car	.60	1.50
PS9 Bobby Labonte's Car	2.00	5.00
PS10 Michael Waltrip's Car	.60	1.50
PS11 Ward Burton's Car	.60	1.50
PS12 Jeff Gordon's Car	3.00	8.00
PS13 Kenny Irwin's Car	.30	.75
PS14 John Andretti's Car	.30	.75
PS15 Kyle Petty's Car	.60	1.50
PS16 Dale Jarrett's Car	1.50	4.00
PS17 Bill Elliott's Car	1.50	4.00
PS18 Jeff Burton's Car	.75	2.00

1998 Press Pass Shockers

Randomly inserted in hobby packs at the rate of one in 12, this 15-card set features color photos of the best NASCAR Winston Cup drivers printed on extra thick die-cut cards.

COMPLETE SET (15)	15.00	40.00
ST1A Terry Labonte	1.50	4.00
ST2A Jeff Gordon	3.00	8.00
ST3A Dale Earnhardt	5.00	12.00
ST4A Dale Jarrett	1.50	4.00
ST5A Mark Martin	2.50	6.00
ST6A Ricky Rudd	1.25	3.00
ST7A Rusty Wallace	2.50	6.00
ST8A Bill Elliott	1.50	4.00
ST9A Bobby Labonte	1.50	4.00
ST10A Kyle Petty	.60	1.50
ST11A Jeff Burton	1.25	3.00
ST12A Michael Waltrip	.60	1.50
ST13A Ted Musgrave	.40	1.00
ST14A Mike Skinner	.40	1.00
ST15A Ward Burton	.60	1.50
P2 Dale Jarrett Promo	2.50	6.00

1998 Press Pass Torpedoes

Randomly inserted in packs at the rate of one in 12, this 15-card set features color photos of the hot cars of the best NASCAR Winston Cup drivers printed on extra thick die-cut cards.

COMPLETE SET (15)	25.00	50.00
ST1B Terry Labonte's Car	1.50	4.00
ST2B Jeff Gordon's Car	3.00	8.00
ST3B Dale Earnhardt's Car	5.00	12.00
ST4B Dale Jarrett's Car	1.50	4.00
ST5B Mark Martin's Car	2.50	6.00
ST6B Ricky Rudd's Car	1.25	3.00
ST7B Rusty Wallace's Car	2.50	6.00
ST8B Bill Elliott's Car	1.50	4.00
ST9B Bobby Labonte's Car	2.00	5.00
ST10B Kyle Petty's Car	.40	1.00
ST11B Jeff Burton's Car	1.25	3.00
ST12B Michael Waltrip's Car	.40	1.00
ST13B Ted Musgrave's Car	.40	1.00
ST14B Mike Skinner's Car	.40	1.00
ST15B Ward Burton's Car	.75	2.00

1998 Press Pass Triple Gear 3 in 1

This nine-card set features actual pieces of race-used tires, firesuits and sheet metal from the pictured driver's car. 33-redemption cards for each driver were produced with eleven cards for each driver inserted in the following products: 1998 Press Pass, 1998 Press Pass Premium, and 1998 VIP.

STG1 Rusty Wallace	100.00	200.00
STG2 Dale Earnhardt	400.00	800.00
STG3 Terry Labonte	75.00	150.00
STG4 Mark Martin	100.00	200.00
STG5 Bobby Labonte	75.00	150.00
STG6 Jeff Gordon	350.00	600.00
STG7 Mike Skinner	50.00	100.00
STG8 Dale Jarrett	75.00	150.00
STG9 Jeff Burton	75.00	150.00

1998 Press Pass Triple Gear Burning Rubber

Randomly inserted in packs at the rate of one in 480, this nine-card set features actual pieces of race-used tires from NASCAR Winston Cup's top drivers. Each card is individually numbered to 250.

TG1 Rusty Wallace	15.00	40.00
TG2 Dale Earnhardt	40.00	80.00
TG3 Terry Labonte	15.00	40.00
TG4 Mark Martin	20.00	50.00
TG5 Bobby Labonte	15.00	40.00
TG6 Jeff Gordon	30.00	60.00
TG7 Mike Skinner	10.00	25.00
TG8 Dale Jarrett	15.00	4
TG9 Jeff Burton	12.50	3

1999 Press Pass

The 1999 Press Pass set was issued in one s
totaling 136 cards. The set contains these su
NASCAR Winston Cup Drivers (1-27), NAS
Winston Cup Machine (28-36), Busch Drivers
51), Super Truck (52-57) Young Guns (58-63),
Chiefs (64-72), NASCAR Series Champions (7
On the Pole (82-94), Winston Cup Preview (9
The final 36-cards of the base issue set fea
"Retro" theme and were inserted one per pack.
cards measure slightly more narrow than a sta
sized card.

COMPLETE SET (136)	12.50	3
WAX BOX	45.00	7
1 Jeff Gordon	.75	
2 Mark Martin	.60	
3 Dale Jarrett	.50	
4 Rusty Wallace	.60	
5 Bobby Labonte	.50	
6 Jeremy Mayfield	.15	
7 Jeff Burton	.25	
8 Dale Earnhardt	1.25	
9 Terry Labonte	.25	
10 Ken Schrader	.07	
11 John Andretti	.07	
12 Ernie Irvan	.15	
13 Jimmy Spencer	.07	
14 Sterling Marlin	.25	
15 Michael Waltrip	.15	
16 Bill Elliott	.30	
17 Bobby Labonte	.50	
18 Johnny Benson	.15	
19 Kenny Irwin	.15	
20 Ward Burton	.15	
21 Darrell Waltrip	.15	
22 Joe Nemechek	.07	
23 Ricky Rudd	.25	
24 Mike Skinner	.07	
25 Robert Pressley	.07	
26 Steve Park	.40	
27 Geoff Bodine	.07	
28 Jeff Gordon's Car	.30	
29 Mark Martin's Car	.25	
30 Dale Jarrett's Car	.15	
31 Rusty Wallace's Car	.25	
32 Bobby Labonte's Car	.15	
33 Jeremy Mayfield's Car	.07	
34 Jeff Burton's Car	.07	
35 Dale Earnhardt's Car	.50	
36 Terry Labonte's Car	.15	
37 Dale Earnhardt Jr.	1.00	
38 Matt Kenseth RC	2.50	
39 Mike McLaughlin	.07	
40 Randy LaJoie	.07	
41 Elton Sawyer	.07	
42 Jason Jarrett	.07	
43 Elliott Sadler	.15	
44 Tim Fedewa	.07	
45 Mike Dillon	.07	
46 Hermie Sadler	.07	
47 Glenn Allen	.07	
48 Dale Jarrett	.50	
49 Mark Martin	.60	
50 Jeff Burton	.25	
51 Michael Waltrip	.15	
52 Ron Barfield ST	.07	
53 Ron Hornaday ST	.07	
54 Jack Sprague ST	.07	
55 Joe Ruttman ST	.07	
56 Jay Sauter ST RC	.07	
57 Rich Bickle ST	.07	
58 Dale Earnhardt Jr. YG	.60	
59 Elliott Sadler YG	.15	
60 Jason Jarrett YG	.07	
61 Tony Stewart YG	.75	
62 Matt Kenseth YG	2.00	
63 Adam Petty YG RC	4.00	
64 Larry McReynolds	.02	
65 Jimmy Makar	.02	
66 Robin Pemberton	.02	
67 Todd Parrott	.02	
68 Ray Evernham	.07	
69 Andy Graves	.02	
70 Jimmy Fennig	.02	
71 Paul Andrews	.02	
72 Jeff Buice	.02	
73 Dale Earnhardt Jr. Champ	.60	
74 Ron Hornaday Champ	.07	
75 Mike Stefanik Champ	.07	
76 Kevin Harvick Champ RC	4.00	
77 Steve Kosiski Champ	.07	
78 Steve Portenga Champ	.07	
79 Jeff Gordon OTP	.40	
80 Rusty Wallace OTP	.30	
81 Ward Burton OTP	.15	
82 Ernie Irvan OTP	.15	
83 Bobby Labonte OTP	.25	
84 Ken Schrader OTP	.07	
85 Kenny Irwin OTP	.07	
86 Bobby Hamilton OTP	.07	
87 Dale Jarrett OTP	.25	
88 Mark Martin OTP	.30	
89 Rick Mast OTP	.07	
90 Jeremy Mayfield OTP	.07	
91 Derrike Cope OTP	.07	
92 Elliott Sadler PRE	.15	
93 Jerry Nadeau PRE	.15	
94 Tony Stewart PRE	.75	
95 Kevin Lepage PRE	.07	
96 Ernie Irvan PRE	.07	
97 Kenny Wallace PRE	.07	
98 Jason Jarrett PRE	.07	
99 Jeff Gordon PRE	.40	
100 Checklist	.02	

Jeff Gordon RET	1.25	3.00
Mark Martin RET	1.00	2.50
Dale Jarrett RET	.75	2.00
Rusty Wallace RET	1.00	2.50
Bobby Labonte RET	.75	2.00
Jeremy Mayfield RET	.25	.60
Jeff Burton RET	.40	1.00
Chad Little RET	.25	.60
Terry Labonte RET	.40	1.00
Ken Schrader RET	.10	.30
John Andretti RET	.10	.30
Ernie Irvan RET	.25	.60
Jimmy Spencer RET	.10	.30
Sterling Marlin RET	.40	1.00
Michael Waltrip RET	.25	.60
Bill Elliott RET	.50	1.25
Bobby Hamilton RET	.10	.30
Johnny Benson RET	.10	.30
Kenny Irwin RET	.25	.60
Ward Burton RET	.25	.60
Darrell Waltrip RET	.25	.60
Joe Nemechek RET	.10	.30
Ricky Rudd RET	.40	1.00
Mike Skinner RET	.10	.30
Robert Pressley RET	.10	.30
Steve Park RET	.60	1.50
Geoff Bodine RET	.10	.30
Bobby Allison RET	.25	.60
Buddy Baker RET	.10	.30
Ned Jarrett RET	.10	.30
David Pearson RET	.25	.60
Richard Petty RET	.40	1.00
Cale Yarborough RET	.25	.60
Junior Johnson RET	.10	.30
Benny Parsons RET	.10	.30
Harry Gant RET	.10	.30
eff Gordon Promo	1.50	4.00
lark Martin Promo	.75	2.00
erry Labonte Promo	.60	1.50
f Gordon 1998 Champ/800	20.00	50.00

1999 Press Pass Autographs

omly inserted in packs at the rate of one in 240, card was individually serial numbered and es an authentic autograph of a leading driver. nnumbered cardbacks contain a congratulatory sage from Press Pass along with the hand n serial number.

PLETE SET (21)	900.00	1500.00
h Bickle/500	5.00	12.00
f Burton/250	10.00	25.00
le Earnhardt/75	350.00	600.00
le Earnhardt Jr./250	75.00	150.00
Elliott/250	30.00	60.00
Evernham/500	10.00	25.00
f Gordon/75	125.00	250.00
dy Graves/250	8.00	20.00
n Hornaday/500	8.00	20.00
nie Irvan/240	20.00	40.00
enny Irwin/249	20.00	40.00
ale Jarrett/250	20.00	50.00
erry Labonte/250	20.00	50.00
andy LaJoie/500	5.00	12.00
ark Martin/235	30.00	60.00
eremy Mayfield/250	20.00	40.00
icky Rudd/245	20.00	40.00
ack Sprague/500	5.00	12.00
ony Stewart/500	40.00	100.00
usty Wallace/70	90.00	150.00
ichael Waltrip/250	10.00	25.00

99 Press Pass Burning Rubber

omly inserted in packs at the rate of one in 480, ine card set features a piece of race-used tire. card was serial numbered of 250.

PLETE SET (9)	200.00	400.00
Terry Labonte's Car	12.50	30.00
Mark Martin's Car	15.00	40.00
Bobby Labonte's Car	12.50	30.00
Jeff Burton's Car	10.00	25.00
Dale Jarrett's Car	12.50	30.00
Ricky Rudd's Car	10.00	25.00
Jeff Gordon's Car	25.00	60.00
Rusty Wallace's Car	12.50	30.00
Dale Earnhardt's Car	25.00	60.00

999 Press Pass Chase Cars

omly inserted in packs at the rate of one in , this 18-card retail only set features laser gold amping.

PLETE SET (18)	30.00	60.00
ale Jarrett's Car	4.00	10.00
obby Labonte's Car	4.00	10.00
ark Martin's Car	5.00	12.00
eremy Mayfield's Car	.60	1.50
en Schrader's Car	.60	1.50
ike Skinner's Car	.60	1.50
ale Earnhardt's Car	10.00	25.00
8B Jeff Burton's Car	2.00	5.00
9B Ricky Rudd's Car	2.00	5.00
10B Michael Waltrip's Car	1.25	3.00
11B Jeff Gordon's Car	6.00	15.00
12B Bill Elliott's Car	2.50	6.00
13B Terry Labonte's Car	2.50	6.00
14B Ernie Irvan's Car	1.25	3.00
15B Johnny Benson's Car	1.25	3.00
16B Sterling Marlin's Car	2.00	5.00
17B Joe Nemechek's Car	.60	1.50
18B Rusty Wallace's Car	5.00	12.00

1999 Press Pass Cup Chase

Randomly inserted in packs at the rate of one in 24, this 20 card set returns sporting an all new design coupled with a combination etch/emboss enhancement on foil board. Collectors could redeem their winning Cup Chase cards for a multi-level embossed die cut version of the cards printed on 24pt. stock.

COMPLETE SET (20)	125.00	250.00
COMP.DIE CUT SET (20)	30.00	80.00
*DIE CUT WIN: .12X TO .3X BASE INSERTS		
*DIE CUT NO-WIN: .25X TO .6X BASE INS.		
1 John Andretti	1.50	4.00
2 Johnny Benson	3.00	8.00
3 Jeff Burton WIN 2	4.00	10.00
4 Dale Earnhardt WIN 2	15.00	40.00
5 Bill Elliott	6.00	15.00
6 Jeff Gordon WIN 2	15.00	40.00
7 Bobby Hamilton	1.50	4.00
8 Ernie Irvan	3.00	8.00
9 Kenny Irwin WIN	4.00	10.00
10 Dale Jarrett WIN 2	8.00	20.00
11 Bobby Labonte WIN 2	8.00	20.00
12 Terry Labonte WIN	6.00	15.00
13 Sterling Marlin	5.00	12.00
14 Mark Martin WIN 2	8.00	20.00
15 Jeremy Mayfield WIN	5.00	12.00
16 Ricky Rudd WIN	8.00	20.00
17 Ken Schrader	1.50	4.00
18 Mike Skinner	1.50	4.00
19 Rusty Wallace WIN	12.00	30.00
20 Field Card WIN	4.00	10.00

1999 Press Pass Oil Cans

Randomly inserted in packs at the rate of one in 18, this nine card sculptured embossed set is printed on shimmering foil board.

COMPLETE SET (9)	20.00	50.00
1 Mark Martin	5.00	12.00
2 Jeff Burton	2.00	5.00
3 Bill Elliott	2.50	6.00
4 Dale Jarrett	4.00	10.00
5 Terry Labonte	2.00	5.00
6 Jeff Gordon	6.00	15.00
7 Bobby Labonte	4.00	10.00
8 Jeremy Mayfield	1.25	3.00
9 Rusty Wallace	5.00	12.00

1999 Press Pass Pit Stop

Randomly inserted in packs at the rate of one in eight, this 18 card set features some of the best cars on the Winston Cup circuit.

COMPLETE SET (18)	12.50	30.00
1 Steve Park's Car	2.00	5.00
2 Rusty Wallace's Car	3.00	8.00
3 Dale Earnhardt's Car	6.00	15.00
4 Bobby Hamilton's Car	.40	1.00
5 Terry Labonte's Car	1.25	3.00
6 Mark Martin's Car	3.00	8.00
7 Ricky Rudd's Car	1.25	3.00
8 Jeremy Mayfield's Car	.75	2.00
9 Johnny Benson's Car	.75	2.00
10 Bobby Labonte's Car	2.50	6.00
11 Michael Waltrip's Car	.75	2.00
12 Jeff Gordon's Car	4.00	10.00
13 Kenny Irwin's Car	.75	2.00
14 Mike Skinner's Car	.40	1.00
15 Ernie Irvan's Car	.75	2.00
16 Dale Jarrett's Car	2.50	6.00
17 Bill Elliott's Car	1.50	4.00
18 Jeff Burton's Car	1.25	3.00

1999 Press Pass Showman

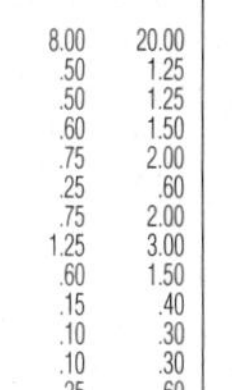

Randomly inserted in packs at the rate of one in eight, this 36-card hobby only set showcases the NASCAR Winston cup drivers on a die-cut laser gold foil card.

COMPLETE SET (18)	25.00	60.00
1A Dale Jarrett	5.00	12.00
2A Bobby Labonte	5.00	12.00
3A Mark Martin	6.00	15.00
4A Jeremy Mayfield	1.50	4.00
5A Ken Schrader	.75	2.00

6A Mike Skinner	.75	2.00
7A Dale Earnhardt Jr.	10.00	25.00
8A Jeff Burton	2.50	6.00
9A Ricky Rudd	2.50	6.00
10A Michael Waltrip	1.50	4.00
11A Jeff Gordon	8.00	20.00
12A Bill Elliott	3.00	8.00
13A Terry Labonte	2.50	6.00
14A Ernie Irvan	1.50	4.00
15A Johnny Benson	1.50	4.00
16A Sterling Marlin	2.50	6.00
17A Joe Nemechek	.75	2.00
18A Rusty Wallace	6.00	15.00
P1 Dale Earnhardt Jr. Promo	2.00	5.00

1999 Press Pass Skidmarks

Randomly inserted in packs at the rate of one in 24, 250 of each base card are specially produced wih real pieces of tire burned into the card.

COMPLETE SET (100)	200.00	400.00
*SKIDMARKS: 5X TO 12X BASE CARDS		
*SKIDMARK RCs: 2X TO 6X BASE CARDS		

1999 Press Pass Triple Gear 3 in 1

Randomly inserted in packs, this nine card set features three pieces of authentic race-used memorabilia (tire, firesuit, and sheetmetal) on a single card. Only 33 cards of each driver produced with each being hand serial numbered on the back in red ink. Eleven of each driver's cards were inserted into 1999 Press Pass, 11 into Press Pass Premium, and 11 into Press Pass VIP.

TG1 Terry Labonte	100.00	250.00
TG2 Mark Martin	150.00	300.00
TG3 Jeff Gordon	250.00	500.00
TG4 Bobby Labonte	125.00	250.00
TG5 Rusty Wallace	125.00	250.00
TG6 Dale Jarrett	125.00	250.00
TG7 Jeff Burton	100.00	200.00
TG8 Mike Skinner	75.00	150.00
TG9 Dale Earnhardt	300.00	600.00

2000 Press Pass

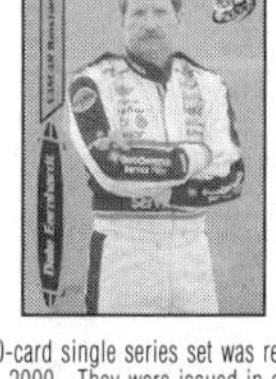

This 100-card single series set was released in January, 2000. They were issued in eight card hobby and retail packs with a SRP of $2.99. The basic cards feature a driver or car portrait with their name on the left of the front. The set has the following subsets: NASCAR Crew Chiefs (28-36), 1999 Replay (37-45), Double Duty (46-54), NASCAR Busch Series (55-63), NASCAR Touring Series Champions (64-72), Shootout (73-81), Generation Now (82-90) and NASCAR 2000 Preview (91-99). There was also a commemorative Dale Jarrett card randomly inserted into packs. This card, which honored his 1999 Winston Cup Championship, is serial numbered to 800. In addition, a Dale Jarrett promotional card was distributed to dealers and hobby media several weeks prior to the product's release. The card is easy to identify by the "PROMO I of I" numbering on the back.

COMPLETE SET (100)	8.00	20.00
1 Dale Jarrett	.50	1.25
2 Bobby Labonte	.50	1.25
3 Mark Martin	.60	1.50
4 Tony Stewart	.75	2.00
5 Jeff Burton	.25	.60
6 Jeff Gordon	.75	2.00
7 Dale Earnhardt	1.25	3.00
8 Rusty Wallace	.60	1.50
9 Ward Burton	.15	.40
10 Mike Skinner	.10	.30
11 Jeremy Mayfield	.10	.30
12 Terry Labonte	.25	.60
13 Bobby Hamilton	.10	.30
14 Steve Park	.25	.60
15 Ken Schrader	.10	.30
16 Sterling Marlin	.25	.60
17 John Andretti	.10	.30
18 Wally Dallenbach Jr.	.10	.30
19 Kenny Irwin	.15	.40
20 Jimmy Spencer	.10	.30
21 Kenny Wallace	.10	.30
22 Chad Little	.15	.40
23 Elliott Sadler	.15	.40
24 Johnny Benson	.15	.40
25 Michael Waltrip	.15	.40
26 Ricky Rudd	.25	.60
27 Darrell Waltrip	.15	.40
28 Robin Pemberton	.05	.15
29 Kevin Hamlin	.05	.15
30 Jimmy Fenning	.05	.15
31 Jimmy Makar	.05	.15
32 Greg Zipadelli	.05	.15
33 Brian Whitesell	.05	.15
34 Larry McReynolds	.05	.15
35 Todd Parrott	.05	.15
36 Frank Stoddard	.05	.15
37 Jeff Gordon	.30	.75
38 Jeff Burton REP	.15	.40
39 Dale Earnhardt Jr. REP CRC	.50	1.25
40 Bobby Labonte REP	.25	.60
41 Dale Jarrett REP	.25	.60
42 Tony Stewart REP	.40	1.00
43 Ernie Irvan REP	.15	.40
44 Tony Stewart REP	.40	1.00
45 Mark Martin REP	.30	.75
46 Dale Earnhardt Jr.'s Car DD	.40	1.00
47 Matt Kenseth's Car DD	.25	.60
48 Mike Skinner's Car DD	.05	.15
49 Mark Martin's Car DD	.25	.60
50 Ken Schrader's Car DD	.05	.15
51 Michael Waltrip's Car DD	.10	.30
52 Bobby Labonte DD	.25	.60
53 Jeff Gordon DD	.30	.75
54 Rusty Wallace DD	.30	.75
55 Tony Stewart	.75	2.00
56 Ward Burton	.15	.40
57 Joe Nemechek	.10	.30
58 Kenny Irwin	.15	.40
59 Mike Skinner	.10	.30
60 Mark Martin	.60	1.50
61 Casey Atwood	.25	.60
62 Dale Earnhardt Jr.	1.00	2.50
63 Jeff Gordon	.75	2.00
64 Matt Kenseth	.60	1.50
65 Steve Park	.25	.60
66 Elliott Sadler	.15	.40
67 Tony Stewart	.75	2.00
68 Kenny Irwin	.15	.40
69 Jeff Burton	.25	.60
70 Dale Earnhardt Jr.	1.00	2.50
71 Jeff Green	.10	.30
72 Matt Kenseth SO	.30	.75
73 Todd Bodine SO	.10	.30
74 Elton Sawyer SO	.10	.30
75 Dave Blaney SO	.10	.30
76 Jason Keller SO	.10	.30
77 Mike McLauglin SO	.10	.30
78 Randy LaJoie SO	.10	.30
79 Casey Atwood SO	.15	.40
80 Dick Trickle SO	.10	.30
81 Joe Nemechek SO	.10	.30
82 Tim Fedewa GN	.10	.30
83 Kevin Grubb GN	.10	.30
84 Jack Sprague GN	.10	.30
85 Dale Earnhardt Jr. GN	.50	1.25
86 Wayne Anderson GN	.05	.15
87 Robert Huffman GN	.05	.15
88 Tony Hirschman GN	.05	.15
89 Sean Woodside GN	.05	.15
90 Bradley Leighton GN	.05	.15
91 Raymond Guss Jr. 00P	.05	.15
92 Dave Blaney 00P	.10	.30
93 Dale Earnhardt Jr. 00P	.50	1.25
94 Matt Kenseth 00P	.30	.75
95 Jerry Nadeau 00P	.15	.40
96 Ricky Rudd 00P	.15	.40
97 Ken Schrader 00P	.10	.30
98 Michael Waltrip 00P	.15	.40
99 Mike Bliss 00P	.10	.30
100 Checklist Card	.05	.15
0 Dale Jarrett 1999 Championship/800	12.50	30.00
P1 Dale Jarrett Promo	1.00	2.50

2000 Press Pass Millennium

Randomly inserted in packs at a rate of one in four. These cards are different from the regular cards in that they have gold foil and the UV coating says "Millennium".

COMPLETE SET (100)	40.00	100.00
*MILLENNIUM: 2X TO 5X BASIC CARDS		

2000 Press Pass Burning Rubber

Inserted one every 480 packs, these cards feature cutting edge technology showcasing swatches of race-used tires. Each card was serial numbered of 200 on the back. According to Press Pass no autographed Burning Rubber cards were inserted into this product, although previously planned.

COMPLETE SET (9)	250.00	500.00
BR1 Dale Jarrett	15.00	40.00
BR2 Mark Martin	20.00	50.00
BR3 Bobby Labonte	15.00	40.00
BR4 Tony Stewart	20.00	50.00
BR5 Jeff Gordon	40.00	80.00
BR6 Dale Earnhardt's Car	40.00	80.00
BR7 Rusty Wallace	15.00	40.00
BR8 Terry Labonte	15.00	40.00
BR9 Dale Earnhardt Jr.	40.00	80.00

2000 Press Pass Cup Chase

Randomly inserted in packs at a rate of one in 48 packs. Press Passâ ™ famous interactive game features a new twist in 2000. The 17-card set gives collectors the chance to redeem winning driverâ ™s cards for a full set of 17 plastic die-cut Cup Chase cards, the 16 drivers and a Dale Jarrett Champion card. Plus an opportunity to win a race-used memorabilia card of the 2000 Winston Cup champion.

COMPLETE SET (17)	125.00	250.00
CC1 John Andretti	2.50	6.00
CC2 Ward Burton WIN	6.00	15.00
CC3 Jeff Burton WIN	6.00	15.00
CC4 Dale Earnhardt	15.00	40.00
CC5 Dale Earnhardt Jr. WIN	20.00	50.00
CC6 Jeff Gordon WIN	12.50	30.00
CC7 Dale Jarrett WIN	7.50	20.00
CC8 Matt Kenseth	6.00	15.00
CC9 Bobby Labonte WIN	7.50	20.00
CC10 Terry Labonte	4.00	10.00
CC11 Mark Martin	7.50	20.00
CC12 Jeremy Mayfield	2.50	6.00
CC13 Ricky Rudd	4.00	10.00
CC14 Mike Skinner	2.50	6.00
CC15 Tony Stewart WIN	10.00	25.00
CC16 Rusty Wallace WIN	10.00	25.00
CC17 Field Card	2.00	5.00

2000 Press Pass Cup Chase Die Cut Prizes

The winning cards from Cup Chase were redeemed for this set of acetate or plastic cards. Each Cup Chase insert card was crimped and returned to the collector. After the end of the 2000 season a Bobby Labonte race used tire card was issued to all collectors that had sent in their Bobby Labonte Cup Chase card in 2000. This car was serial numbered to 650.

COMPLETE SET (17)	15.00	30.00
CC1 John Andretti	.50	1.25
CC2 Ward Burton	.60	1.50
CC3 Jeff Burton	1.00	2.50
CC4 Dale Earnhardt	5.00	12.00
CC5 Dale Earnhardt Jr.	4.00	10.00
CC6 Jeff Gordon	3.00	8.00
CC7 Dale Jarrett	2.00	5.00
CC8 Matt Kenseth	2.50	6.00
CC9 Bobby Labonte	2.00	5.00
CC10 Terry Labonte	1.00	2.50
CC11 Mark Martin	2.50	6.00
CC12 Jeremy Mayfield	.50	1.25
CC13 Ricky Rudd	1.00	2.50
CC14 Mike Skinner	.50	1.25
CC15 Tony Stewart	3.00	8.00
CC16 Rusty Wallace	2.50	6.00
CC17 Dale Jarrett 2000 Champ	2.00	5.00
CCC1 Bobby Labonte Tire/650	15.00	30.00

2000 Press Pass Oil Cans

Randomly inserted in packs at a rate of one in six this all-foil multi-level embossed insert features die-cut images of nine top drivers bursting out of a can.

COMPLETE SET (9)	10.00	25.00
OC1 Tony Stewart	3.00	8.00
OC2 Terry Labonte	1.00	2.50
OC3 Rusty Wallace	2.50	6.00
OC4 Mark Martin	2.50	6.00
OC5 Jeff Burton	1.00	2.50
OC6 Jeff Gordon	3.00	8.00
OC7 Dale Earnhardt's Car	5.00	12.00
OC8 Dale Jarrett	2.00	5.00
OC9 Bobby Labonte	2.00	5.00

2000 Press Pass Pitstop

Randomly inserted in packs at a rate of one in eight. An 18-card micro-embossed die-cut insert puts collectors in the pits with the greatest teams in NASCAR.

COMPLETE SET (18)	10.00	25.00
PS1 Dale Jarrett's Car	.75	2.00
PS2 Rusty Wallace's Car	1.25	3.00
PS3 Dale Earnhardt's Car	2.50	6.00
PS4 Bobby Hamilton's Car	.15	.40
PS5 Terry Labonte's Car	.60	1.50
PS6 Mark Martin's Car	1.25	3.00
PS7 Ricky Rudd's Car	.50	1.25
PS8 Jeremy Mayfield's Car	.15	.40
PS9 Bobby Labonte's Car	1.00	2.50
PS10 Elliott Sadler's Car	.15	.40
PS11 Ward Burton's Car	.30	.75
PS12 Jeff Gordon's Car	1.50	4.00
PS13 Tony Stewart's Car	1.50	4.00
PS14 Kenny Irwin's Car	.30	.75
PS15 Mike Skinner's Car	.15	.40
PS16 Matt Kenseth's Car	1.25	3.00
PS17 Dale Earnhardt Jr.'s Car	2.00	5.00
PS18 Jeff Burton's Car	.50	1.25

2000 Press Pass Showcar Die Cuts

Inserted at a rate of one every twelve retail packs, these cards feature the cars of some of NASCAR's leading drivers on a card die-cut to resemble film cels. Card backs carry an "SC" prefix.

COMPLETE SET (18)	20.00	40.00
SC1 Darrell Waltrip's Car	.50	1.25
SC2 Bobby Labonte's Car	1.50	4.00
SC3 Dale Jarrett's Car	1.50	4.00
SC4 Dale Earnhardt Jr.'s Car	3.00	8.00
SC5 Dale Earnhardt's Car	4.00	10.00
SC6 Jeff Burton's Car	.75	2.00
SC7 Jeff Gordon's Car	2.50	6.00
SC8 Jeremy Mayfield's Car	.30	.75
SC9 John Andretti's Car	.25	.60
SC10 Ken Schrader's Car	.25	.60
SC11 Mark Martin's Car	2.00	5.00
SC12 Mike Skinner's Car	.25	.60
SC13 Ricky Rudd's Car	.75	2.00
SC14 Rusty Wallace's Car	2.00	5.00
SC15 Sterling Marlin's Car	.75	2.00
SC16 Terry Labonte's Car	.75	2.00
SC17 Tony Stewart's Car	2.50	6.00
SC18 Ward Burton's Car	.50	1.25

2000 Press Pass Showman Die Cuts

Randomly inserted in packs at a rate of one in eight, frame by frame action captures eighteen of the most recognizable athletes in NASCAR.

COMPLETE SET (18)	25.00	50.00
*NON-DIE CUT: 1.5X TO 4X BASIC INSERTS		
NON-DIE CUT STATED ODDS 1:100		
SM1 Darrell Waltrip	.60	1.50
SM2 Bobby Labonte	2.00	5.00
SM3 Dale Jarrett	2.00	5.00
SM4 Dale Earnhardt Jr.	4.00	10.00
SM5 Dale Earnhardt Jr.	4.00	10.00
SM6 Jeff Burton	1.00	2.50
SM7 Jeff Gordon	3.00	8.00
SM8 Jeremy Mayfield	.50	1.25
SM9 John Andretti	.50	1.25
SM10 Ken Schrader	.50	1.25
SM11 Mark Martin	2.50	6.00
SM12 Mike Skinner	.50	1.25
SM13 Ricky Rudd	1.00	2.50
SM14 Rusty Wallace	2.50	6.00
SM15 Sterling Marlin	1.00	2.50
SM16 Terry Labonte	1.00	2.50
SM17 Tony Stewart	3.00	8.00
SM18 Ward Burton	.60	1.50

2000 Press Pass Skidmarks

Randomly inserted in packs at a rate of one in 48. Revolutionary technology creates an image on a

trading card using ground-up, race-used tire rubber.

COMPLETE SET (9)	50.00	120.00
SK1 Dale Jarrett	6.00	15.00
SK2 Mark Martin	6.00	15.00
SK3 Bobby Labonte	6.00	15.00
SK4 Tony Stewart	8.00	20.00
SK5 Jeff Gordon	8.00	20.00
SK6 Dale Earnhardt	12.50	30.00
SK7 Rusty Wallace	6.00	15.00
SK8 Terry Labonte	5.00	12.00
SK9 Dale Earnhardt Jr.	8.00	20.00

2000 Press Pass Techno-Retro

Cards from this set are slightly smaller than standard sized. Each measures roughly 2" by 2 1/4" and were inserted one per Press Pass pack.

COMPLETE SET (36)	7.50	20.00
TR1 John Andretti	.10	.30
TR2 Johnny Benson	.15	.40
TR3 Jeff Burton	.25	.60
TR4 Ward Burton	.15	.40
TR5 Wally Dallenbach	.10	.30
TR6 Dale Earnhardt's Car	1.25	3.00
TR7 Dale Earnhardt Jr.	1.00	2.50
TR8 Jeff Gordon	.75	2.00
TR9 Bobby Hamilton	.10	.30
TR10 Kenny Irwin	.15	.40
TR11 Dale Jarrett	.50	1.25
TR12 Bobby Labonte	.50	1.25
TR13 Terry Labonte	.25	.60
TR14 Chad Little	.15	.40
TR15 Sterling Marlin	.25	.60
TR16 Mark Martin	.60	1.50
TR17 Jeremy Mayfield	.10	.30
TR18 Joe Nemechek	.10	.30
TR19 Steve Park	.25	.60
TR20 Ricky Rudd	.25	.60
TR21 Elliott Sadler	.15	.40
TR22 Ken Schrader	.10	.30
TR23 Mike Skinner	.10	.30
TR24 Tony Stewart	.75	2.00
TR25 Rusty Wallace	.60	1.50
TR26 Darrell Waltrip	.15	.40
TR27 Michael Waltrip	.15	.40
TR28 Bobby Allison	.10	.30
TR29 Buddy Baker	.10	.30
TR30 A.J. Foyt	.15	.40
TR31 Ned Jarrett	.10	.30
TR32 Junior Johnson	.10	.30
TR33 Benny Parsons	.10	.30
TR34 Richard Petty	.25	.60
TR35 David Pearson	.15	.40
TR36 Cale Yarborough	.10	.30

2001 Press Pass

Released in late January 2001, this 100-card set features 47 driver cards, 13 racing team cards, 11 replay cards from the 2000 season, 10 touring series cards, 12 shoot out cards, 6 season preview cards, and a checklist/schedule card. Base card stock features full color photos, both action and portrait, with a border along the left side of the card stating the racer's name and a border along the bottom. On the driver cards, a small black and white car photo is placed in the lower left hand corner. A special zero card featuring Bobby Labonte was inserted in Hobby packs only. Press Pass was packaged in 36 pack boxes for Retail and 28 pack boxes for Hobby. Each pack contained eight cards.

COMPLETE SET (100)	10.00	25.00
1 Bobby Labonte	.60	1.50
2 Dale Earnhardt	1.50	4.00
3 Jeff Burton	.25	.60
4 Dale Jarrett	.60	1.50
5 Ricky Rudd	.40	1.00
6 Tony Stewart	1.00	2.50
7 Rusty Wallace	.75	2.00
8 Mark Martin	.75	2.00
9 Jeff Gordon	1.00	2.50
10 Ward Burton	.25	.60
11 Steve Park	.25	.60
12 Mike Skinner	.10	.30
13 Matt Kenseth	1.00	2.50
14 Joe Nemechek	.10	.30
15 Dale Earnhardt Jr.	1.25	3.00
16 Terry Labonte	.40	1.00
17 Ken Schrader	.10	.30
18 Sterling Marlin	.40	1.00
19 Jerry Nadeau	.25	.60
20 Jimmy Spencer	.10	.30
21 John Andretti	.10	.30
22 Jeremy Mayfield	.10	.30
23 Robert Pressley	.10	.30
24 Kenny Wallace	.10	.30
25 Kevin Lepage	.10	.30
26 Elliott Sadler	.25	.60
27 Bobby Hamilton Jr.	.10	.30
28 Dave Blaney	.10	.30
29 Wally Dallenbach Jr.	.10	.30
30 Brett Bodine	.10	.30
31 Darrell Waltrip	.25	.60
32 Stacy Compton	.10	.30
33 Kyle Petty	.25	.60
34 Scott Pruett	.10	.30
35 Jeff Gordon	1.00	2.50
36 Jason Keller	.10	.30
37 Kevin Harvick	.75	2.00
38 Todd Bodine	.10	.30
39 Elton Sawyer	.10	.30
40 Randy LaJoie	.10	.30
41 Casey Atwood	.10	.30
42 David Green	.10	.30
43 Kevin Grubb	.10	.30
44 Hank Parker Jr.	.25	.60
45 Matt Kenseth	1.00	2.50
46 Mark Martin	.75	2.00
47 Tim Fedewa	.10	.30
48 Bobby Labonte's Car	.25	.60
49 Dale Earnhardt's Car	.60	1.50
50 Jeff Burton's Car	.25	.60
51 Dale Jarrett's Car	.25	.60
52 Ricky Rudd's Car	.10	.30
53 Tony Stewart's Car	.40	1.00
54 Rusty Wallace's Car	.40	1.00
55 Mark Martin's Car	.40	1.00
56 Jeff Gordon's Car	.40	1.00
57 Ward Burton's Car	.10	.30
58 Mike Skinner's Car	.07	.20
59 Matt Kenseth's Car	.40	1.00
60 Jeremy Mayfield's Car	.07	.20
61 Jeff Burton REP	.25	.60
62 Matt Kenseth REP	1.00	2.50
63 Bobby Labonte REP	.60	1.50
64 Dale Earnhardt Jr. REP	1.25	3.00
65 Rusty Wallace REP	.60	2.00
66 Dale Jarrett REP	.60	1.50
67 Dale Earnhardt REP	1.50	4.00
68 Tony Stewart REP	1.00	2.50
69 Steve Park REP	.25	.60
70 Jerry Nadeau REP	.25	.60
71 Bobby Labonte REP	.60	1.50
72 Jeff Green	.10	.30
73 Greg Biffle	.25	.60
74 Billy Bigley Jr. RC	.10	.30
75 Garrett Evans RC	.10	.30
76 Brad Leighton	.10	.30
77 Jerry Marquis	.10	.30
78 Robert Huffman	.10	.30
79 Steve Boley	.10	.30
80 Matt Crafton RC	.25	.60
81 Steve Carlson RC	.10	.30
82 Dale Jarrett SO	.60	1.50
83 Mike Skinner SO	.10	.30
84 Rusty Wallace SO	.75	2.00
85 Terry Labonte SO	.40	1.00
86 Ricky Rudd SO	.40	1.00
87 Jeremy Mayfield SO	.10	.30
88 Jeff Gordon SO	1.00	2.50
89 Dale Earnhardt Jr. SO	1.25	3.00
90 Steve Park SO	.25	.60
91 Bobby Labonte SO	.60	1.50
92 Tony Stewart SO	1.00	2.50
93 Jeff Burton SO	.25	.60
94 Elliott Sadler PV	.25	.60
95 Bobby Hamilton Jr. PV	.10	.30
96 Ryan Newman PV RC	3.00	8.00
97 Jeff Burton PV	.25	.60
98 Mark Martin PV	.75	2.00
99 Dale Jarrett PV	.60	1.50
100 Checklist/Schedule	.10	.30
P1 Bobby Labonte Promo	1.00	2.50
0 Bobby Labonte WC Champ	15.00	40.00

2001 Press Pass Millennium

Randomly inserted into packs at one in four, this 100-card set is a complete parallel of the 2001 Press Pass base set.

COMP.MILLENNIUM (100)	50.00	125.00
*MILLENNIUM: 2X TO 5X BASIC CARDS		

2001 Press Pass Autographs

Randomly inserted in packs, this set features a portrait style color photo of the driver on the right side of the card front with a ghosted image of his car to the left. The bottom of the card has a black and silver section with the driver's name. Since the cards were not numbered, we have arranged them in alphabetical order in our checklist. This set also includes one of the last insert cards signed by Dale Earnhardt.

1 John Andretti	7.50	20.00
2 Greg Biffle	12.50	30.00
3 Billy Bigley Jr.	5.00	12.00
4 Dave Blaney	5.00	12.00
5 Brett Bodine	5.00	12.00
6 Todd Bodine	5.00	12.00
7 Steve Boley	5.00	12.00
8 Jeff Burton	12.50	30.00
9 Ward Burton	12.50	30.00
10 Stacy Compton	5.00	12.00
11 Dale Earnhardt	750.00	1000.00
12 Dale Earnhardt Jr.	60.00	120.00
13 Tim Fedewa	5.00	12.00
14 Jeff Gordon	100.00	175.00
15 David Green	5.00	12.00
16 Jeff Green	7.50	20.00
17 Mark Green	5.00	12.00
18 Kevin Grubb	5.00	12.00
19 Bobby Hamilton	10.00	25.00
20 Kevin Harvick	15.00	40.00
21 Robert Huffman	5.00	12.00
22 Dale Jarrett	25.00	60.00
23 Jason Keller	5.00	12.00
24 Matt Kenseth	30.00	60.00
25 Bobby Labonte	15.00	40.00
26 Terry Labonte	15.00	40.00
27 Randy LaJoie	5.00	12.00
28 Brad Leighton	5.00	12.00
29 Chad Little	5.00	12.00
30 Jerry Marquis	5.00	12.00
31 Mark Martin	30.00	60.00
32 Jeremy Mayfield	7.50	20.00
33 Joe Nemechek	7.50	20.00
34 Steve Park	15.00	40.00
35 Hank Parker Jr.	5.00	12.00
36 Robert Pressley	5.00	12.00
37 Ricky Rudd	15.00	40.00
38 Elton Sawyer	5.00	12.00
39 Ken Schrader	10.00	25.00
40 Mike Skinner	5.00	12.00
41 Jimmy Spencer	7.50	20.00
42 Tony Stewart	40.00	100.00
43 Dick Trickle	5.00	12.00
44 Rusty Wallace	15.00	40.00

2001 Press Pass Burning Rubber Drivers

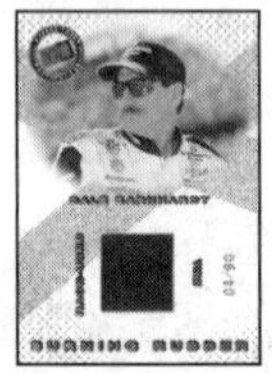

Randomly inserted in Hobby packs at the rate of one in 480, this nine card set features a profile photo of a driver and a square swatch of a race used tire. Card backgrounds are white, and feature a "tire mark" effect through the middle.

COMPLETE SET (9)	400.00	750.00
COMP.CAR SET (9)	300.00	600.00
*CARS: .3X TO .8X DRIVERS		
CAR STATED ODDS 1:720 RETAIL		
BRD1 Jeff Gordon/90	40.00	100.00
BRD2 Rusty Wallace/90	15.00	40.00
BRD3 Dale Earnhardt/90	75.00	150.00
BRD4 Dale Jarrett/90	15.00	40.00
BRD5 Terry Labonte/85	15.00	40.00
BRD6 Mark Martin/90	20.00	50.00
BRD7 Bobby Labonte/90	15.00	40.00
BRD8 Dale Earnhardt Jr./90	50.00	100.00
BRD9 Tony Stewart/90	20.00	50.00

2001 Press Pass Cup Chase

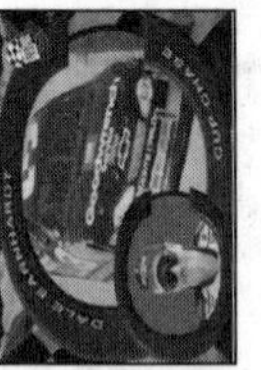

Randomly inserted in packs at the rate of one in 24, this 17-card set features redemption cards with an interactive game. If the pictured driver wins any of the selected races on the back of the card, it could be redeemed (before 1/31/2002) for a complete 17-card set of holofoil die cut cards featuring both drivers and cars. The original Cup Chase insert card was also returned to the collector with a special stamp from Press Pass. These stamped cards are typically worth less than original unstamped copies.

COMPLETE SET (17)	75.00	150.00
CC1 Steve Park	4.00	10.00
CC2 Rusty Wallace	6.00	15.00
CC3 Dale Earnhardt	10.00	25.00
CC4 Jeff Gordon WIN	10.00	25.00
CC5 Terry Labonte	4.00	10.00
CC6 Ken Schrader	1.50	4.00
CC7 Dale Earnhardt Jr.	10.00	25.00
CC8 Jeff Burton WIN	4.00	10.00
CC9 Tony Stewart	6.00	15.00
CC10 Ward Burton	2.50	6.00
CC11 Jeremy Mayfield	1.50	4.00
CC12 Mike Skinner	1.50	4.00
CC13 Ricky Rudd WIN	5.00	12.00
CC14 Dale Jarrett	6.00	15.00
CC15 Matt Kenseth	6.00	15.00
CC16 Bobby Labonte	6.00	15.00
CC17 Field Card WIN	.40	1.00

2001 Press Pass Cup Chase Die Cut Prizes

This set was mailed to the winners of the Cup Chase program, this set includes the 16 driver cards and a Bobby Labonte WC Champ card replacing the Field card from the redemption set. In addition to the full Die Cut set, the winners with the Jeff Gordon redemption card also received a Gordon WC Champ race used rubber card after the season ended. This card has a 2002 date on the cardfront but is considered part of this 2001 prize set listing.

COMPLETE SET (17)	12.50	30.00
*DIE CUT WIN: .06X TO .15X BASE INSERTS		
*DIE CUT NO-WIN: .12X TO .3X BASE INS.		
CC17 Bobby Labonte WC Champ	2.00	5.00
CCC1 Jeff Gordon Tire/400	20.00	50.00

2001 Press Pass Double Burner

Randomly seeded in Hobby packs, this nine card set features a driver portrait photo framed by a gold oval and on the left side has a swatch of a race worn firesuit and on the right, a race worn glove. Each card is sequentially numbered to 100.

DB1 Jeff Gordon	100.00	200.00
DB2 Rusty Wallace	50.00	100.00
DB3 Dale Earnhardt	175.00	350.00
DB4 Dale Jarrett	50.00	100.00
DB5 Tony Stewart	60.00	120.00
DB6 Mark Martin	50.00	100.00
DB7 Matt Kenseth	50.00	100.00
DB8 Dale Earnhardt Jr.	200.00	300.00
DB9 Bobby Labonte	50.00	100.00

2001 Press Pass Ground Zero

Randomly inserted in packs at the rate of one in 18, this nine card set features portrait style photography set against an all foil laser etched background with colors to match each driver's racing team.

COMPLETE SET (9)	40.00	100.00
GZ1 Matt Kenseth	5.00	12.00
GZ2 Rusty Wallace	4.00	10.00
GZ3 Dale Earnhardt	8.00	20.00
GZ4 Jeff Gordon	5.00	12.00
GZ5 Tony Stewart	5.00	12.00
GZ6 Mark Martin	4.00	10.00
GZ7 Dale Jarrett	3.00	8.00
GZ8 Dale Earnhardt Jr.	6.00	15.00
GZ9 Ward Burton	1.25	3.00

2001 Press Pass Showman/Showcar

Randomly inserted in packs at the rate of one in eight, this 24-card set features numbered cards from S1A to S12B. Each driver has two card versions (A and B) where the A version features two profile photos of the driver and the B version features a photo of the car. All cards are printed on rainbow holofoil and are die cut on both the left and right side of this horizontal design.

COMPLETE SET (24)	30.00	80.00
*CARS: .8X TO 2X BASE CARD HI		
S1A Steve Park	1.00	2.50
S1B Steve Park's Car	.50	1.25
S2A Rusty Wallace	3.00	8.00
S2B Rusty Wallace's Car	1.50	4.00
S3A Matt Kenseth	4.00	10.00
S3B Matt Kenseth's Car	2.00	5.00
S4A Jeff Gordon	4.00	10.00
S4B Jeff Gordon's Car	2.00	5.00
S5A Terry Labonte	1.50	4.00
S5B Terry Labonte's Car	.75	2.00
S6A Mark Martin	3.00	8.00
S6B Mark Martin's Car	1.50	4.00
S7A Dale Earnhardt	6.00	15.00
S7B Dale Earnhardt's Car	3.00	8.00
S8A Dale Earnhardt Jr.	5.00	12.00
S8B Dale Earnhardt Jr.'s Car	2.50	6.00
S9A Bobby Labonte	2.50	6.00
S9B Bobby Labonte's Car	1.25	3.00
S10A Tony Stewart	4.00	10.00
S10B Tony Stewart's Car	2.00	5.00
S11A Dale Jarrett	2.50	6.00
S11B Dale Jarrett's Car	1.25	3.00
S12A Mike Skinner	.50	1.25
S12B Mike Skinner's Car	.25	.60

2001 Press Pass Total Memorabilia

Randomly inserted in Hobby packs at the rate of one in 200, this nine card set gives collectors the opportunity to win all race used memorabilia cards of the specific driver who's number is pictured on the card. The cards expired on 1/31/2002.

TM1 Jeff Gordon	.60	1.50
TM2 Rusty Wallace	.40	1.00
TM3 Dale Earnhardt	1.00	2.50
TM4 Dale Jarrett	.40	1.00
TM5 Tony Stewart	.60	1.50
TM6 Mark Martin	.40	1.00
TM7 Matt Kenseth	.40	1.00
TM8 Dale Earnhardt Jr.	.60	1.50
TM9 Bobby Labonte	.40	1.00

2001 Press Pass Triple Burner

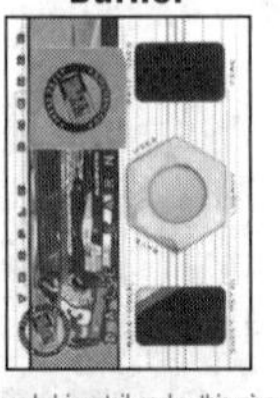

Randomly seeded in retail packs, this nine card set features three swatches of race used memorabilia. On the left side of the card, a swatch of race used sheet metal appears, a race used lugnut is in the middle, and on the right, a swatch of a race used tire appears. Each card is sequentially numbered to 100.

TB1 Jeff Gordon	125.00	250.00
TB2 Rusty Wallace	50.00	100.00
TB3A Dale Earnhardt lug nut	250.00	500.00
TB3B Dale Earnhardt pit board	250.00	500.00
TB4 Dale Jarrett	50.00	100.00
TB5 Tony Stewart	60.00	120.00
TB6 Mark Martin	60.00	120.00
TB7 Matt Kenseth	60.00	120.00
TB8 Dale Earnhardt Jr.	100.00	200.00
TB9 Bobby Labonte	50.00	100.00

2001 Press Pass Velocity

Randomly inserted in packs at the rate of one in eight, this nine card set features driver portrait photos centered on the top of the card in holofoil and a photo of the respective driver's car on the bottom. Names on the bottom are printed in holofoil.

COMPLETE SET (9)	15.00	40.00
VL1 Jeff Gordon	4.00	10.00
VL2 Rusty Wallace	3.00	8.00
VL3 Dale Jarrett	2.50	6.00
VL4 Matt Kenseth	4.00	10.00
VL5 Tony Stewart	4.00	10.00
VL6 Mark Martin	3.00	8.00
VL7 Jeff Burton	1.00	2.50
VL8 Dale Earnhardt Jr.	5.00	12.00
VL9 Dale Earnhardt	6.00	15.00

2001 Press Pass Vintage

Inserted in packs at the rate of one in one, this 27-card set features top NASCAR drivers on a vintage style card. Driver portrait photography is framed by a red line and cards are white bordered. Names appear along the bottom, and racing team names appear along the top.

COMPLETE SET (27)	10.00	2
VN1 Bobby Labonte	1.00	
VN2 Dale Earnhardt	2.50	
VN3 Jeff Burton	.40	
VN4 Dale Jarrett	1.00	
VN5 Ricky Rudd	.60	
VN6 Tony Stewart	1.50	
VN7 Rusty Wallace	1.25	
VN8 Mark Martin	1.25	
VN9 Jeff Gordon	1.50	
VN11 Steve Park	.40	
VN13 Matt Kenseth	1.50	
VN14 Joe Nemechek	.20	
VN15 Dale Earnhardt Jr.	2.00	
VN16 Terry Labonte	.60	
VN17 Ken Schrader	.20	
VN18 Sterling Marlin	.60	
VN19 Jerry Nadeau	.40	
VN20 Jimmy Spencer	.20	
VN21 John Andretti	.20	
VN22 Jeremy Mayfield	.20	
VN23 Robert Pressley	.20	
VN24 Kenny Wallace	.20	
VN25 Kevin Lepage	.20	
VN26 Elliott Sadler	.40	
VN27 Bobby Hamilton	.20	

2002 Press Pass

Issued in early 2002, this 100-card set features of leading NASCAR drivers and the cars they The cards were packaged in 8-card hobby and packs. The following subsets were included base set: NASCAR Busch Series drivers, Craft Truck Series drivers, Replays, and NASCAR To Series drivers. A special insert card (#0) feat Jeff Gordon's 2001 Winston Cup Championshi randomly inserted in packs.

COMPLETE SET (100)	12.50	3
1 John Andretti	.10	
2 Dave Blaney	.10	
3 Brett Bodine	.10	
4 Todd Bodine	.10	
5 Ward Burton	.25	
6 Jeff Burton	.25	
7 Kurt Busch	.40	
8 Stacy Compton	.10	
9 Ricky Craven	.10	
10 Dale Earnhardt Jr.	1.25	
11 Jeff Gordon	1.00	
12 Bobby Hamilton	.10	
13 Kevin Harvick	.75	
14 Ron Hornaday	.10	
15 Dale Jarrett	.60	
16 Buckshot Jones	.10	
17 Matt Kenseth	.75	
18 Bobby Labonte	.60	
19 Terry Labonte	.40	
20 Jason Leffler	.10	
21 Sterling Marlin	.40	
22 Mark Martin	.75	
23 Jeremy Mayfield	.10	
24 Jerry Nadeau	.25	
25 Joe Nemechek	.10	
26 Ryan Newman CRC	.75	
27 Steve Park	.25	
28 Kyle Petty	.25	
29 Ricky Rudd	.40	
30 Elliott Sadler	.25	
31 Ken Schrader	.10	
32 Mike Skinner	.10	
33 Jimmy Spencer	.10	
34 Tony Stewart	.75	
35 Rusty Wallace	.60	
36 Michael Waltrip	.25	
37 Greg Biffle NBS	.25	
38 Larry Foyt NBS RC	.25	
39 David Green NBS	.10	
40 Jeff Green NBS	.10	
41 Kevin Grubb NBS	.10	
42 Tim Fedewa NBS	.10	
43 Kevin Harvick NBS	.75	
44 Jimmie Johnson NBS	.75	
45 Jason Keller NBS	.10	
46 Randy LaJoie NBS	.10	
47 Chad Little NBS	.10	
48 Mike McLaughlin NBS	.10	
49 Jamie McMurray NBS RC	3.00	
50 Ryan Newman NBS	.75	
51 Hank Parker Jr. NBS	.10	
52 Tony Raines NBS	.10	
53 Elton Sawyer NBS	.10	
54 Scott Wimmer NBS RC	.25	
55 Scott Riggs CTS RC	.75	
56 Ricky Hendrick CTS	.50	
57 Jon Wood CTS RC	.25	
58 Jack Sprague CTS	.10	
59 Travis Kvapil CTS RC	.75	
60 Coy Gibbs CTS RC	.25	
61 Matt Crafton CTS	.10	
62 Billy Bigley CTS	.10	
63 Ted Musgrave CTS	.10	
64 Michael Waltrip REP	.25	
65 Kevin Harvick REP	.75	
66 Jeff Gordon REP	1.00	
67 Jeff Burton REP	.25	
68 Elliott Sadler REP	.25	
69 Steve Park REP	.25	
70 Tony Stewart REP	.75	
71 Ryan Newman REP	.75	
72 Sterling Marlin REP	.40	
73 Kerry Earnhardt REP	.25	
74 Shawna Robinson REP	.25	
75 Dale Earnhardt Jr. REP	1.25	
76 Rusty Wallace's Car	.25	
77 Mark Martin's Car	.25	
78 Michael Waltrip's Car	.10	
79 Matt Kenseth's Car	.40	

Bobby Labonte's Car .25 .60
Tony Stewart's Car .40 1.00
Ward Burton's Car .07 .20
Jeff Gordon's Car .40 1.00
Ricky Rudd 's Car .10 .30
Kevin Harvick's Car .40 1.00
Sterling Marlin's Car .07 .20
Dale Jarrett's Car .25 .60
Jeff Burton's Car .07 .20
Steve Carlson NTS .10 .30
Mike Olsen NTS .10 .30
Kyle Berck NTS RC .10 .30
Mike Stefanik NTS .10 .30
Craig Raudman NTS RC .10 .30
Cam Strader NTS RC .10 .30
Brendan Gaughan NTS RC .40 1.00
Kevin Hamlin NTS .10 .30
Jack Sprague CTS Champ .10 .30
Kevin Harvick BGN Champ .75 2.00
Jeff Gordon WC Champ 1.00 2.50
) Dale Earnhardt Jr. CL .50 1.50
eff Gordon 2001 WC Champ 12.50 30.00

2002 Press Pass Platinum

ıed one per pack, this is a parallel to the 2002 ıss Pass set. Each card features a Platinum ɔred foil printing technology on the fronts.

MPLETE SET (100) 20.00 40.00
LATINUM: .6X TO 1.5X BASIC CARDS

2002 Press Pass Autographs

ɜrted in packs at stated odds of one in 72 hobby :ks and one in 240 retail packs, these cards ure autographs from leading NASCAR figures. e Earnhardt Jr. and Tony Stewart did not return r cards in time for pack inclusion and those cards ld be redeemed until December 31, 2002.

obby Allison 8.00 20.00
ohn Andretti 6.00 15.00
Casey Atwood 8.00 20.00
uddy Baker 8.00 20.00
reg Biffle 10.00 25.00
illy Bigley 6.00 15.00
ave Blaney 6.00 15.00
rett Bodine 6.00 15.00
odd Bodine 6.00 15.00
Jeff Burton 8.00 20.00
Ward Burton 15.00 40.00
Kurt Busch 12.50 30.00
Richard Childress 8.00 20.00
Stacy Compton 6.00 15.00
Matt Crafton 6.00 15.00
Ricky Craven 10.00 25.00
Dale Earnhardt Jr. 60.00 120.00
Kerry Earnhardt 12.50 30.00
Tim Fedewa 6.00 15.00
Larry Foyt 6.00 15.00
Coy Gibbs 8.00 20.00
Jeff Gordon 100.00 200.00
David Green 6.00 15.00
Jeff Green 6.00 15.00
Kevin Grubb 6.00 15.00
Kevin Harvick 12.50 30.00
Ricky Hendrick 25.00 50.00
Ron Hornaday 6.00 15.00
Dale Jarrett 25.00 50.00
Ned Jarrett 10.00 25.00
Jimmie Johnson 40.00 80.00
Buckshot Jones 6.00 15.00
Jason Keller 6.00 15.00
Matt Kenseth 15.00 40.00
Travis Kvapil 10.00 25.00
Bobby Labonte 15.00 40.00
Terry Labonte 15.00 40.00
Randy LaJoie 6.00 15.00
Jason Leffler 6.00 15.00
Chad Little 6.00 15.00
Sterling Marlin 25.00 60.00
Mark Martin 30.00 60.00
Mike McLaughlin 6.00 15.00
Jamie McMurray 15.00 40.00
Ted Musgrave 6.00 15.00
Jerry Nadeau 20.00 50.00
Joe Nemechek 6.00 15.00
Ryan Newman 15.00 30.00
Steve Park 8.00 20.00
Hank Parker Jr. 6.00 15.00
Benny Parsons 30.00 60.00
David Pearson 10.00 25.00
Kyle Petty 10.00 25.00
Richard Petty 40.00 80.00
Robert Pressley 6.00 15.00
Tony Raines 6.00 15.00
Scott Riggs 8.00 20.00
Shawna Robinson 15.00 40.00
Ricky Rudd 10.00 25.00
Joe Ruttman 6.00 15.00
Elliott Sadler 10.00 25.00
Elton Sawyer 6.00 15.00
Ken Schrader 8.00 20.00
Mike Skinner 6.00 15.00
Jack Sprague 6.00 15.00
Tony Stewart 40.00 100.00
Rusty Wallace 12.50 30.00
Darrell Waltrip 20.00 50.00
Michael Waltrip 10.00 25.00
Scott Wimmer 8.00 20.00
Glen Wood 6.00 15.00
Jon Wood 8.00 20.00
Cale Yarborough 8.00 20.00

2002 Press Pass Burning Rubber Drivers

Inserted in hobby packs at stated odds of one in 480, these 12 cards feature swatches of race-used tires. Each card was issued to a stated print run of 90 serial numbered sets.

BRD1 Jeff Gordon 40.00 80.00
BRD2 Rusty Wallace 15.00 40.00
BRD3 Dale Earnhardt 50.00 100.00
BRD4 Kevin Harvick 20.00 40.00
BRD5 Dale Jarrett 15.00 40.00
BRD6 Terry Labonte 15.00 40.00
BRD7 Mark Martin 20.00 40.00
BRD8 Bobby Labonte 15.00 40.00
BRD9 Dale Earnhardt Jr. 40.00 80.00
BRD10 Tony Stewart 20.00 40.00
BRD11 Matt Kenseth 20.00 40.00
BRD12 Michael Waltrip 15.00 40.00

2002 Press Pass Burning Rubber Cars

Issued in retail packs at stated odds of one in 720 retail, these 12 cards feature race-worn tire pieces from the noted cars. Each card was serial numbered of 120.

BRC1 Jeff Gordon's Car 40.00 80.00
BRC2 Rusty Wallace's Car 20.00 40.00
BRC3 Dale Earnhardt's Car 50.00 100.00
BRC4 Kevin Harvick's Car 20.00 40.00
BRC5 Dale Jarrett's Car 20.00 40.00
BRC6 Terry Labonte's Car 20.00 40.00
BRC7 Mark Martin's Car 20.00 40.00
BRC8 Bobby Labonte's Car 20.00 40.00
BRC9 Dale Earnhardt Jr.'s Car 40.00 80.00
BRC10 Tony Stewart's Car 20.00 40.00
BRC11 Matt Kenseth's Car 20.00 40.00
BRC12 Michael Waltrip's Car 20.00 40.00

2002 Press Pass Cup Chase

Issued in packs at stated odds of one in 24, these cards feature leading candidates to win races in the eight key NASCAR races. These cards could be redeemed until January 31, 2003 for a complete set of Press Pass Cup Chase Prizes.

CC1 Jeff Burton 7.50 20.00
CC2 Ward Burton WIN 12.50 30.00
CC3 Dale Earnhardt Jr. WIN 12.50 30.00
CC4 Jeff Gordon WIN 12.50 30.00
CC5 Kevin Harvick WIN 12.50 30.00
CC6 Dale Jarrett 7.50 20.00
CC7 Matt Kenseth WIN 12.50 30.00
CC8 Bobby Labonte 7.50 20.00
CC9 Terry Labonte 7.50 20.00
CC10 Mark Martin WIN 12.50 30.00
CC11 Sterling Marlin WIN 12.50 30.00
CC12 Ricky Rudd 6.00 15.00
CC13 Ken Schrader 6.00 15.00
CC14 Steve Park 5.00 12.00
CC15 Tony Stewart 25.00 50.00
CC16 Rusty Wallace 12.50 30.00
CC17 Michael Waltrip 6.00 15.00
CC18 Field Card WIN 10.00 25.00

2002 Press Pass Cup Chase Prizes

This 18-card set was issued as the prize for any basic issue Cup Chase insert card in which the featured driver won at least one race listed on the card's back. Card #CC18 features Jeff Gordon and highlights his 2001 Winston Cup championship in place of the "field" card from the basic insert set. All 18-cards were printed on a clear plastic card stock. A Tony Stewart race used tire card was issued in early 2003 for any collector who submitted their Tony Stewart Cup Chase card (before April 1, 2003) in honor of his 2002 Winston Cup Championship.

COMPLETE SET (18) 12.50 30.00
CC1 Jeff Burton 1.50 4.00
CC2 Ward Burton 1.00 2.50
CC3 Dale Earnhardt Jr. 6.00 15.00
CC4 Jeff Gordon 5.00 12.00
CC5 Kevin Harvick 4.00 10.00
CC6 Dale Jarrett 3.00 8.00
CC7 Matt Kenseth 5.00 12.00
CC8 Bobby Labonte 3.00 8.00
CC9 Terry Labonte 2.00 5.00
CC10 Mark Martin 4.00 10.00
CC11 Mike Skinner 1.50 4.00
CC12 Ricky Rudd 1.50 4.00
CC13 Ken Schrader .50 1.25
CC14 Sterling Marlin 1.50 4.00
CC15 Tony Stewart 5.00 12.00
CC16 Rusty Wallace 4.00 10.00
CC17 Michael Waltrip .50 1.25
CC18 Jeff Gordon WC Champ 5.00 12.00

2002 Press Pass Season's Greetings

Randomly inserted into packs, these three cards wish the collectors good tidings for the holiday season. Each features a picture of Santa Claus.

SG1 Merry Christmas 4.00 10.00
SG2 Happy Holidays 4.00 10.00
SG3 Season's Greetings 4.00 10.00

2002 Press Pass Showman

Issued at hobby packs at stated odds of one in eight for drivers and retail packs at stated odds of one in eight for the car cards. These cards feature drivers who fans come out to root for on the circuit.

COMPLETE SET (12) 20.00 50.00
COMP.CAR SET (8) 10.00 25.00
*CARS: .2X TO .5X DRIVERS
CAR STATED ODDS 1:8 RETAIL
S1A Ward Burton 1.25 3.00
S2A Dale Earnhardt Jr. 6.00 15.00
S3A Jeff Gordon 5.00 12.00
S4A Kevin Harvick 4.00 10.00
S5A Dale Jarrett 3.00 8.00
S6A Steve Park 1.25 3.00
S7A Bobby Labonte 3.00 8.00
S8A Terry Labonte 2.00 5.00
S9A Michael Waltrip 1.25 3.00
S10A Ricky Rudd 1.50 4.00
S11A Tony Stewart 4.00 10.00
S12A Rusty Wallace 3.00 8.00

2002 Press Pass Top Shelf

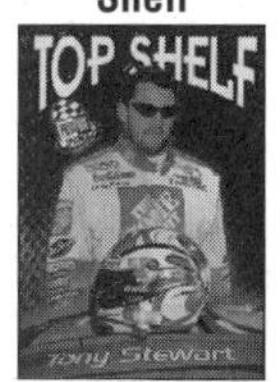

Issued in packs at stated odds of one in 18, these nine cards feature the top group of NASCAR drivers and their helmet on a foil etched card.

COMPLETE SET (9) 25.00 60.00
TS1 Dale Earnhardt Jr. 6.00 15.00
TS2 Jeff Gordon 5.00 12.00
TS3 Kevin Harvick 4.00 10.00
TS4 Dale Jarrett 3.00 8.00
TS5 Bobby Labonte 3.00 8.00
TS6 Terry Labonte 2.00 5.00
TS7 Ricky Rudd 2.00 5.00
TS8 Tony Stewart 4.00 10.00
TS9 Rusty Wallace 3.00 8.00

2002 Press Pass Velocity

Inserted into packs at stated odds of one in eight, these nine cards feature laser etched holofoil with razed type.

COMPLETE SET (9) 10.00 25.00
VL1 Jeff Burton .60 1.50
VL2 Dale Earnhardt Jr. 3.00 8.00
VL3 Jeff Gordon 2.50 6.00
VL4 Kevin Harvick 2.00 5.00
VL5 Dale Jarrett 1.50 4.00
VL6 Bobby Labonte 1.50 4.00
VL7 Sterling Marlin 1.00 2.50
VL8 Mark Martin 2.00 5.00
VL9 Rusty Wallace 1.50 4.00

2002 Press Pass Vintage

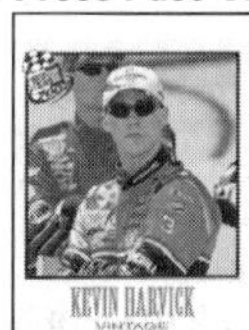

Issued one per pack, these 36 cards feature a mix of today's leading drivers along with some NASCAR legends on a old style card with a black and white picture.

COMPLETE SET (36) 7.50 20.00
VN1 Dave Blaney .20 .50
VN2 Brett Bodine .20 .50
VN3 Jeff Burton .40 1.00
VN4 Ward Burton .40 1.00
VN5 Ricky Craven .20 .50
VN6 Dale Earnhardt Jr. 2.00 5.00
VN7 Jeff Gordon 1.50 4.00
VN8 Bobby Hamilton .20 .50
VN9 Kevin Harvick 1.25 3.00
VN10 Dale Jarrett 1.00 2.50
VN11 Matt Kenseth 1.25 3.00
VN12 Bobby Labonte 1.00 2.50
VN13 Terry Labonte .60 1.50
VN14 Sterling Marlin .60 1.50
VN15 Mark Martin 1.25 3.00
VN16 Jerry Nadeau .40 1.00
VN17 Joe Nemechek .20 .50
VN18 Steve Park .40 1.00
VN19 Ricky Rudd .60 1.50
VN20 Elliott Sadler .40 1.00
VN21 Ken Schrader .20 .50
VN22 Mike Skinner .20 .50
VN23 Jimmy Spencer .20 .50
VN24 Tony Stewart 1.25 3.00
VN25 Rusty Wallace 1.00 2.50
VN26 Michael Waltrip .40 1.00
VN27 Richard Petty .60 1.50
VN28 Bobby Allison .40 1.00
VN29 Buddy Baker .20 .50
VN30 Ned Jarrett .20 .50
VN31 Junior Johnson .20 .50
VN32 Benny Parsons .20 .50
VN33 David Pearson .20 .50
VN34 Darrell Waltrip .40 1.00
VN35 Glen Wood .20 .50
VN36 Cale Yarborough .20 .50

2003 Press Pass

This 100 card set was released in December, 2002. This set was issued in eight card packs which came either 28 packs to a hobby box or 36 packs to a retail box. Both hobby and retail boxes were packed 20 boxes to a case. There was a special card honoring Jamie McMurray's first career win randomly inserted into these packs. In addition, a "King for a Day" entry card was inserted at a stated rate of one in 28 packs.

COMPLETE SET (100) 10.00 25.00
WAX BOX HOBBY (28) 40.00 80.00
1 John Andretti .10 .30
2 Casey Atwood .10 .30
3 Dave Blaney .10 .30
4 Brett Bodine .10 .30
5 Jeff Burton .25 .60
6 Ward Burton .25 .60
7 Kurt Busch .40 1.00
8 Ricky Craven .10 .30
9 Dale Earnhardt Jr. 1.25 3.00
10 Jeff Gordon 1.00 2.50
11 Robby Gordon .10 .30
12 Jeff Green .10 .30
13 Bobby Hamilton .10 .30
14 Kevin Harvick .60 1.50
15 Dale Jarrett .60 1.50
16 Jimmie Johnson 1.00 2.50
17 Matt Kenseth .75 2.00
18 Bobby Labonte .60 1.50
19 Terry Labonte .40 1.00
20 Sterling Marlin .40 1.00
21 Mark Martin .75 2.00
22 Jeremy Mayfield .10 .30
23 Ryan Newman .75 2.00
24 Steve Park .25 .60
25 Kyle Petty .25 .60
26 Ricky Rudd .40 1.00
27 Elliott Sadler .25 .60
28 Ken Schrader .10 .30
29 Mike Skinner .10 .30
30 Jimmy Spencer .10 .30
31 Tony Stewart .75 2.00
32 Rusty Wallace .60 1.50
33 Michael Waltrip .25 .60
34 Greg Biffle NBS .25 .60
35 Kerry Earnhardt NBS .25 .60
36 Scott Wimmer NBS .25 .60
37 Johnny Sauter NBS .25 .60
38 Ricky Hendrick NBS .50 1.25
39 Hank Parker Jr. NBS .10 .30
40 Brian Vickers NBS .50 1.25
41 Scott Riggs NBS .25 .60
42 Chad Little NBS .10 .30
43 Jack Sprague NBS .10 .30
44 Jamie McMurray NBS .60 1.50
45 Casey Mears NBS .25 .60
46 Matt Crafton CTS .10 .30
47 Coy Gibbs CTS .25 .60
48 Travis Kvapil CTS .25 .60
49 Jason Leffler CTS .10 .30
50 Ted Musgrave CTS .10 .30
51 Robert Pressley CTS .10 .30
52 Joe Ruttman CTS .10 .30
53 Dennis Setzer CTS .10 .30
54 Jon Wood CTS .25 .60
55 Dale Earnhardt Jr. DS 1.25 3.00
56 Kevin Harvick DS .60 1.50
57 Elliott Sadler DS .10 .30
58 Kurt Busch DS .40 1.00
59 Jimmie Johnson DS .75 2.00
60 Jeff Gordon DS 1.00 2.50
61 Tony Stewart DS .75 2.00
62 Ryan Newman DS .75 2.00
63 Dale Earnhardt Jr. DS 1.00 2.50
Jimmie Johnson
Ryan Newman
Elliott Sadler
Matt Kenseth
Kurt Busch
64 Jimmie Johnson RR .60 1.50
February 17
65 Jimmie Johnson RR .60 1.50
April 28
66 J.Johnson Dover June RR .60 1.50
67 J.Johnson Dover Sept RR .60 1.50
68 R.Newman Winston RR .60 1.50
69 R.Newman Loudon RR .60 1.50
70 Bouncing Back WCS .25 .60
Jeff Burton
Bobby Labonte
71 A Man of His Word WCS .25 .60
Richard Childress
72 Double Take WCS .40 1.00
Tony Stewart
73 Survivor WCS .10 .30
Ward Burton
74 Rock Steady WCS .40 1.00
Matt Kenseth
75 Kurt-ain Call WCS .25 .60
Kurt Busch
76 Texas Tornado WCS .25 .60
Matt Kenseth
77 Screeching Halt WCS .25 .60
Bobby Labonte
78 The California Kid WCS .40 1.00
Jimmie Johnson
Jeff Gordon
79 Two of a Kind WCS .40 1.00
Jimmie Johnson
80 Ups and Downs WCS .25 .60
Dale Jarrett
81 Pit Bulls WCS .40 1.00
Matt Kenseth
82 Reversal of Fortune WCS .10 .30
Ricky Rudd
83 Defending his Turf WCS .25 .60
Kevin Harvick
84 Rags to Riches WCS .40 1.00
Tony Stewart
85 Jake Hobgood RC .10 .30
86 Kevin Hamlin .10 .30
87 Steve Carlson .10 .30
88 Jeff Fultz RC .10 .30
89 Eric Norris RC .10 .30
90 Andy Santerre RC .40 1.00
91 Rusty Wallace's Car OTW .25 .60
92 Mark Martin's Car OTW .40 1.00
93 Kevin Harvick's Car OTW .25 .60
94 Ryan Newman's Car OTW .40 1.00
95 Matt Kenseth's Car OTW .40 1.00
96 Tony Stewart's Car OTW .40 1.00
97 Ward Burton's Car OTW .10 .30
98 Jeff Gordon's Car OTW .40 1.00
99 Dale Earnhardt Jr.'s Car OTW .50 1.25
100 Jeff Gordon Header .50 1.25
0 Jamie McMurray First Win 8.00 20.00
NNO King for a Day Entry Card .75 2.00

2003 Press Pass Gold Holofoil

Issued at a stated rate of one per pack, this is a parallel to the basic Press Pass set. These cards can be differentiated from the regular cards based on the gold holofoil highlights on the cardfronts instead of silver foil.

COMPLETE SET (100) 25.00 50.00
*PLATINUM: .6X TO 1.5X BASE CARDS

2003 Press Pass Samples

These cards were issued to preview what the 2003 Press Pass set would look like. These cards were stamped "Sample" on the backs and were issued one per Beckett Racing Collector magazine. They were available in the February 2003 issue number 102.

*SAMPLES: 2.5X TO 6X BASIC CARDS

2003 Press Pass Autographs

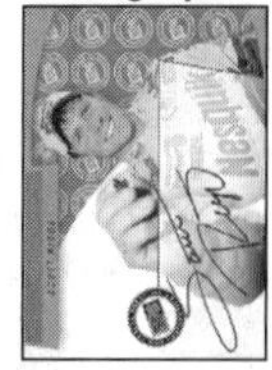

Inserted at a stated rate of one in 72, these 63 signed cards feature a mix of today's NASCAR drivers as well as some legendary drivers from the past. Each card's image was photographed in such a way as to make the driver appear he was signing the card from inside it. Some of these cards were available in packs of 2003 Press Pass, 2003 Press Pass Eclipse or both, and are tagged as such.

1 John Andretti E/P 8.00 20.00
2 Casey Atwood E/P 6.00 15.00
3 Buddy Baker E/P 8.00 20.00
4 Greg Biffle E/P 10.00 25.00
5 Dave Blaney E/P 6.00 15.00
6 Brett Bodine E/P 6.00 15.00
7 Jeff Burton Citgo E 8.00 20.00
8 Jeff Burton Gain E 8.00 20.00
9 Kurt Busch E/P 12.50 30.00
10 Richard Childress E/P 8.00 20.00
11 Matt Crafton E/P 6.00 15.00
12 Ricky Craven E/P 10.00 25.00
13 Bill Davis E/P 6.00 15.00
14 Kerry Earnhardt E 12.50 30.00
15 Coy Gibbs E/P 10.00 25.00
16 Jeff Gordon E/P 100.00 175.00
17 Robby Gordon E/P 10.00 25.00
18 David Green E/P 8.00 20.00
19 Jeff Green E/P 6.00 15.00
20 Mark Green E/P 6.00 15.00
21 Bobby Hamilton E/P 10.00 25.00
22 Kevin Harvick E/P 12.50 30.00
23 Ricky Hendrick E/P 25.00 50.00
24 Shane Hmiel E/P 15.00 30.00
25 Dale Jarrett E/P 20.00 50.00
26 Ned Jarrett E/P 8.00 20.00
27 Jimmie Johnson E/P 40.00 80.00
28 Junior Johnson E/P 8.00 20.00
29 Jason Keller E/P 6.00 15.00
30 Matt Kenseth E/P 15.00 40.00
31 Travis Kvapil E/P 10.00 25.00
32 Bobby Labonte E/P 15.00 40.00
33 Terry Labonte E/P 15.00 40.00
34 Randy LaJoie E/P 6.00 15.00
35 Jason Leffler E/P 6.00 15.00
36 Chad Little E/P 6.00 15.00
37 Mark Martin E/P 30.00 60.00
38 Jeremy Mayfield E/P 10.00 25.00
39 Jamie McMurray E/P 10.00 25.00
40 Casey Mears E/P 10.00 25.00
41 Ted Musgrave E 8.00 20.00
42 Ryan Newman E/P 15.00 30.00
43 Hank Parker Jr. E/P 10.00 25.00
44 Benny Parsons E/P 30.00 60.00
45 David Pearson E/P 20.00 40.00
46 Kyle Petty E/P 12.50 30.00
47 Richard Petty E/P 40.00 80.00
48 Tony Raines E/P 6.00 15.00
49 Scott Riggs E/P 10.00 25.00
50 Ricky Rudd E/P 25.00 50.00
51 Joe Ruttman E/P 6.00 15.00
52 Elliott Sadler E/P 10.00 25.00
53 Johnny Sauter E 8.00 20.00
54 Ken Schrader E/P 10.00 25.00
55 Dennis Setzer E/P 6.00 15.00
56 Mike Skinner E/P 8.00 20.00
57 Jimmy Spencer E/P 8.00 20.00
58 Brian Vickers E/P 10.00 25.00
59 Rusty Wallace E/P 20.00 50.00
60 Michael Waltrip E/P 10.00 25.00
61 Scott Wimmer E/P 10.00 25.00
62 Jon Wood E/P 8.00 20.00
63 Cale Yarborough E/P 10.00 25.00

2003 Press Pass Burning Rubber Cars

Inserted at a stated rate of one in 480 retail packs, these 18 cards feature pieces of race-used tires set against a card featuring the driver's car. These cards were issued to a stated print run of 60 serial numbered sets.

*CARS: .3X TO .8X DRIVERS

2003 Press Pass Burning Rubber Cars Autographs

Randomly inserted into packs, these six-cards form a partial parallel to the Burning Rubber Car insert set. Each card was signed by the featured driver and

serial numbered to his car number.
SOME CARDS NOT PRICED DUE TO SCARCITY
BRT-JG Jeff Gordon's Car/24
BRT-JJ Jimmie Johnson's Car/48 75.00 150.00
BRT-KH Kevin Harvick's Car/29 100.00 200.00
BRT-MK Matt Kenseth's Car/17
BRT-MM Mark Martin's Car/6
BRT-RN Ryan Newman's Car/12
BRT-RW Rusty Wallace's Car/2

2003 Press Pass Burning Rubber Drivers

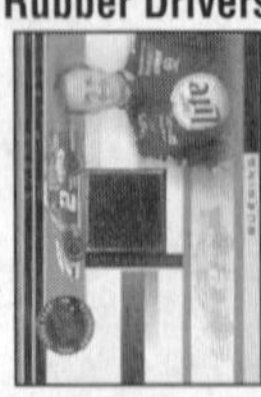

Inserted at a stated rate of one in 480 hobby packs, these 18 cards feature pieces of race-used tires set against a card featuring a picture of the driver. These cards were issued to a stated print run of 50 serial numbered sets.

BRD1 Jeff Gordon 40.00 80.00
BRD2 Ryan Newman 30.00 60.00
BRD3 Kevin Harvick 25.00 50.00
BRD4 Jimmie Johnson 30.00 60.00
BRD5 Rusty Wallace 25.00 50.00
BRD6 Mark Martin 25.00 50.00
BRD7 Matt Kenseth 25.00 50.00
BRD8 Bobby Labonte 20.00 40.00
BRD9 Tony Stewart 30.00 60.00
BRD10 Dale Earnhardt Jr. 40.00 80.00
BRD11 Steve Park 20.00 40.00
BRD12 Sterling Marlin 20.00 40.00
BRD13 John Andretti 15.00 30.00
BRD14 Kyle Petty 15.00 30.00
BRD15 Jimmy Spencer 15.00 30.00
BRD16 Dale Earnhardt 100.00 200.00
BRD17 Dale Jarrett 25.00 50.00
BRD18 Terry Labonte 25.00 50.00

2003 Press Pass Burning Rubber Drivers Autographs

Randomly inserted into packs, these seven cards form a partial parallel to the Burning Rubber Car insert set. These cards were signed by the driver and serial numbered to the driver's car number.

SOME CARDS NOT PRICED DUE TO SCARCITY
BRD-JG Jeff Gordon/24
BRD-JJ Jimmie Johnson/48 75.00 150.00
BRD-KH Kevin Harvick/29 100.00 200.00
BRD-MK Matt Kenseth/17
BRD-MM Mark Martin/6
BRD-RN Ryan Newman/12
BRD-RW Rusty Wallace/2
BRD-TS Tony Stewart/20

2003 Press Pass Cup Chase

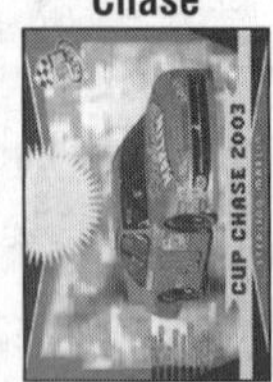

Inserted in Press Pass packs at a rate of one in 28, these cards are part of a year-long contest which allows fans to win a special limited edition plastic Cup Chase card set. The expiration date to send in these cards was January 31, 2004.

CCR1 Jeff Burton 5.00 12.00
CCR2 Ward Burton 5.00 12.00
CCR3 Dale Earnhardt Jr. 12.50 30.00
CCR4 Jeff Gordon 12.50 30.00
CCR5 Kevin Harvick WIN 12.50 30.00
CCR6 Dale Jarrett 8.00 20.00
CCR7 Jimmie Johnson WIN 12.50 30.00
CCR8 Matt Kenseth 15.00 40.00
CCR9 Bobby Labonte 8.00 20.00
CCR10 Terry Labonte 5.00 12.00
CCR11 Mark Martin 8.00 20.00
CCR12 Ryan Newman WIN 12.50 30.00
CCR13 Jeremy Mayfield 3.00 8.00
CCR14 Sterling Marlin 5.00 12.00
CCR15 Tony Stewart 10.00 25.00
CCR16 Rusty Wallace 8.00 20.00
CCR17 Ricky Craven WIN 12.50 30.00
CCR18 Field Card WIN 12.50 30.00

2003 Press Pass Santa Claus

Inserted in packs at stated odds of one in 144 for S1, one in 180 for S2 and one in 720 for S3, these cards feature that sleigh-riding gentleman from the North Pole and were released in time for the 2002 Christmas season.

COMPLETE SET (3) 20.00 40.00
S1 Santa Claus 6.00 15.00
S2 Santa Claus 6.00 15.00
S3 Santa Claus 12.50 30.00

2003 Press Pass Showman

Inserted at a stated rate of one in six hobby packs, these 12 die-cut cards feature two photos, one of which is the driver and the other is that driver's race car.

COMPLETE SET (12) 10.00 25.00
*CARS: .4X TO 1X DRIVERS
CAR STATED ODDS 1:6 RETAIL
S1A Jeff Burton .75 2.00
S2A Ryan Newman 2.50 6.00
S3A Jeff Gordon 3.00 8.00
S4A Kevin Harvick 2.00 5.00
S5A Dale Jarrett 2.00 5.00
S6A Jimmie Johnson 2.50 6.00
S7A Bobby Labonte 2.00 5.00
S8A Sterling Marlin 1.25 3.00
S9A Mark Martin 2.50 6.00
S10A Ricky Rudd 1.25 3.00
S11A Tony Stewart 2.50 6.00
S12A Rusty Wallace 2.00 5.00

2003 Press Pass Snapshots

Issued at a stated rate of one per pack, this 36-card set (measuring approximately 2 3/8" by 2 3/4") features drivers and their most memorable moments of the 2002 NASCAR season.

COMPLETE SET (36) 10.00 25.00
SN1 John Andretti .20 .50
SN2 Casey Atwood .20 .50
SN3 Jeff Burton .40 1.00
SN4 Ward Burton .40 1.00
SN5 Ricky Craven .20 .50
SN6 Dale Earnhardt Jr. 2.00 5.00
SN7 Jeff Gordon 1.50 4.00
SN8 Bobby Hamilton .20 .50
SN9 Kevin Harvick 1.00 2.50
SN10 Dale Jarrett 1.00 2.50
SN11 Jimmie Johnson 1.50 4.00
SN12 Matt Kenseth 1.25 3.00
SN13 Bobby Labonte 1.00 2.50
SN14 Terry Labonte .60 1.50
SN15 Sterling Marlin .60 1.50
SN16 Mark Martin 1.25 3.00
SN17 Ryan Newman 1.25 3.00
SN18 Kurt Busch .60 1.50
SN19 Ricky Rudd .60 1.50
SN20 Elliott Sadler .40 1.00
SN21 Ken Schrader .20 .50
SN22 Mike Skinner .20 .50
SN23 Jimmy Spencer .20 .50
SN24 Tony Stewart 1.25 3.00
SN25 Rusty Wallace 1.00 2.50
SN26 Robby Gordon .20 .50
SN27 Richard Petty .60 1.50
SN28 Bobby Allison .20 .50
SN29 Buddy Baker .20 .50
SN30 Ned Jarrett .40 1.00
SN31 Junior Johnson .20 .50
SN32 Benny Parsons .40 1.00
SN33 David Pearson .40 1.00
SN34 Harry Gant .20 .50
SN35 Glen Wood .20 .50
SN36 Cale Yarborough .40 1.00

2003 Press Pass Top Shelf

Inserted at a state rate of one in eight, these 10 cards feature drivers who are highlighted on silver foil board with an embossed finish.

COMPLETE SET (10) 10.00 25.00
TS1 Dale Earnhardt Jr. 3.00 8.00
TS2 Jeff Gordon 2.50 6.00
TS3 Dale Jarrett 1.50 4.00
TS4 Jimmie Johnson 2.50 6.00
TS5 Bobby Labonte 1.50 4.00
TS6 Mark Martin 2.00 5.00
TS7 Ryan Newman 2.00 5.00
TS8 Tony Stewart 2.00 5.00
TS9 Rusty Wallace 1.50 4.00
TS10 Kevin Harvick 1.50 4.00

2003 Press Pass Velocity

Issued at a stated rate of one in 18, these nine cards feature the driver along with a background photo of his car. These cards were printed on holofoil stock.

COMPLETE SET (9) 15.00 40.00
VC1 Dale Earnhardt Jr. 8.00 20.00
VC2 Jeff Gordon 6.00 15.00
VC3 Dale Jarrett 4.00 10.00
VC4 Jimmie Johnson 6.00 15.00
VC5 Sterling Marlin 2.50 6.00
VC6 Mark Martin 5.00 12.00
VC7 Ricky Rudd 2.50 6.00
VC8 Tony Stewart 5.00 12.00
VC9 Rusty Wallace 4.00 10.00

2004 Press Pass

This 100 card set was released December 9, 2003. This set was issued in eight card packs which came 28 packs to a hobby or retail box. Both hobby and retail boxes were packed 20 boxes to a case. The SRP for both hobby and retail packs was $2.99. There was a special card honoring Ryan Newman's most wins in 2003 randomly inserted into these packs.

COMPLETE SET (100) 10.00 25.00
WAX BOX HOBBY (28) 50.00 75.00
WAX BOX RETAIL (28) 40.00 70.00
1 Greg Biffle .25 .60
2 Dave Blaney .15 .40
3 Brett Bodine .15 .40
4 Todd Bodine .15 .40
5 Jeff Burton .25 .60
6 Ward Burton .25 .60
7 Kurt Busch .40 1.00
8 Ricky Craven .15 .40
9 Dale Earnhardt Jr. 1.00 2.50
(Track in background)
9B Dale Earnhardt Jr. 3.00 8.00
(grandstand visible)
9C Matt Kenseth 3.00 8.00
(Blue sky background)
10 Jeff Gordon 1.00 2.50
(Grandstands in background)
10B Jeff Gordon 3.00 8.00
(infield visible)
11 Robby Gordon .15 .40
12 Kevin Harvick .60 1.50
13 Dale Jarrett .50 1.25
14 Jimmie Johnson .75 2.00
15 Matt Kenseth .75 2.00
(Grandstand in Background)
16 Bobby Labonte .50 1.25
17 Terry Labonte .40 1.00
18 Sterling Marlin .40 1.00
19 Mark Martin .60 1.50
20 Jeremy Mayfield .15 .40
21 Jamie McMurray .40 1.00
(Grandstand in background)
21B Jamie McMurray 2.00 5.00
(infield visible)
22 Casey Mears .25 .60
23 Joe Nemechek .15 .40
24 Ryan Newman .75 2.00
25 Kyle Petty .25 .60
26 Tony Raines .15 .40
27 Ricky Rudd .40 1.00
28 Elliott Sadler .25 .60
29 Ken Schrader .15 .40
30 Jimmy Spencer .15 .40
31 Tony Stewart .60 1.50
(Garage area)
31B Tony Stewart 3.00 8.00
(skyline visible)
32 Rusty Wallace .50 1.25
33 Michael Waltrip .25 .60
34 Kenny Wallace .15 .40
35 Jerry Nadeau .15 .40
36 Christian Fittipaldi RC .15 .40
37 Stacy Compton .15 .40
38 Kyle Busch RC 3.00 8.00
(Grandstand visible)
38B Kyle Busch 6.00 15.00
(infield visible)
39 Coy Gibbs .25 .60
40 David Green .15 .40
41 Kevin Grubb .15 .40
42 Kasey Kahne 1.00 2.50
43 Scott Wimmer .25 .60
44 Chase Montgomery .15 .40
45 Regan Smith RC .15 .40
46 Jimmy Vasser .15 .40
47 Brian Vickers .50 1.25
(track infield visible)
47B Brian Vickers 3.00 8.00
(grandstand visible)
48 Jason Keller .15 .40
49 Matt Crafton .15 .40
50 Rick Crawford .15 .40
51 Carl Edwards .75 2.00
52 Tina Gordon RC .75 2.00
53 Andy Houston .15 .40
54 Travis Kvapil .25 .60
55 Dennis Setzer .15 .40
56 Jon Wood .25 .60
57 Robert Pressley .15 .40
58 Charlie Bradberry RC .25 .60
59 Jeff Jefferson RC .25 .60
60 Steve Carlson .15 .40
61 Andy Santerre .15 .40
62 Todd Szegedy RC .25 .60
63 Robert Huffman .15 .40
64 Rusty Wallace's Car OTW .25 .60
65 Mark Martin's Car OTW .25 .60
66 Dale Earnhardt Jr.'s Car OTW .40 1.00
67 Ryan Newman's Car OTW .25 .60
68 Bobby Labonte's Car OTW .25 .60
(NASCAR Official visible)
68B B.Labonte's Car OTW 1.50 4.00
(no NASCAR Official visible)
69 Tony Stewart's Car OTW .25 .60
70 Kevin Harvick's Car OTW .25 .60
71 Elliott Sadler's Car OTW .15 .40
72 Casey Mears' Car OTW .15 .40
73 Jamie McMurray's Car OTW .15 .40
74 Dale Jarrett's Car OTW .25 .60
75 Kurt Busch's Car OTW .15 .40
75B Kurt Busch's Car OTW SP 1.25 3.00
(NASCAR Official visible)
76 Penske Power WCS .75 2.00
Ryan Newman
Rusty Wallace
77 Figuring It Out WCS .50 1.25
Bobby Labonte
78 One For The Ages WCS .25 .60
Ricky Craven's Car
Kurt Busch's Car
79 Duke-ing It Out WCS .25 .60
Bobby Labonte's Car
80 The Drive for Five WCS#Kurt Busch .75 2.00
Greg Biffle
Matt Kenseth
Jeff Burton
Jack Roush
Mark Martin
81 No Ordinary Joe WCS .25 .60
Joe Nemechek
82 Growing Up Fast WCS .40 1.00
Kurt Busch
83 Spring Reign WCS .75 2.00
Jimmie Johnson
84 Million-dollar Magic WCS .75 2.00
Jimmie Johnson
85 Quiet Confidence WCS .75 2.00
Matt Kenseth
86 In the Groove WCS .40 1.00
Jimmie Johnson's Car
87 Two for the Road WCS .25 .60
Robby Gordon
88 Jamie McMurray RR .40 1.00
89 Casey Mears RR .25 .60
90 Greg Biffle RR .25 .60
91 Dale Earnhardt Jr. DS 1.00 2.50
92 Jamie McMurray DS .40 1.00
93 Jeff Gordon DS 1.00 2.50
94 Kurt Busch DS .40 1.00
95 Jimmie Johnson DS .75 2.00
(Blue bar on card border)
95B Jimmie Johnson DS 2.50 6.00
(Red bar on card border)
96 Casey Mears DS .25 .60
97 Matt Kenseth DS .75 2.00
98 Ryan Newman DS .75 2.00
99 Kevin Harvick DS .60 1.50
100 Matt Kenseth Schedule .75 2.00
0 Ryan Newman/600 15.00 40.00

2004 Press Pass Platinum

Issued at a stated rate of one per pack, this 100-card set is a parallel to the basic Press Pass set. These cards can be differentiated from the regular cards based on the platinum holofoil logos on the cardfronts. They also had a "P" suffix on the card numbers.

COMPLETE SET (100) 15.00 40.00
*PLATINUM: .6X TO 1.5X BASE CARDS

2004 Press Pass Previews

This 48-card set was issued though a joint venture on eBay.com as a special preview of the base set. The cards were identical with the exception of the serial number. Each card was serial numbered to 5.

STATED PRINT RUN 5 SERIAL #'d SETS

2004 Press Pass Samples

This 100 card set is a parallel to the base 2004 Press Pass set without the variations. It was issued 1 per Beckett Racing Collector issue #114, which was the February 2004 Press Pass Eclipse Under Cover date. Each card had the word "SAMPLE" printed across the back.

*SAMPLES: 2X TO 5X BASE CARDS

2004 Press Pass Autographs

Inserted at a stated rate of one in 84 hobby and one in 196 retail, these 55 signed cards feature a mix of today's NASCAR drivers as well as some legendary drivers from the past. Each card's image was placed on the upper left-hand side of the card's horizontal view. Some of these cards were available in packs of 2004 Press Pass, 2004 Press Pass Eclipse or both, and are tagged as such.

1 Bobby Allison P 8.00 20.00
2 Buddy Baker P 8.00 20.00
3 Greg Biffle P 10.00 25.00
4 Dave Blaney P 6.00 15.00
5 Mike Bliss P 6.00 15.00
6 Brett Bodine P 6.00 15.00
7 Todd Bodine P 6.00 15.00
8 Jeff Burton P 8.00 20.00
9 Kurt Busch P 12.50 30.00
10 Kyle Busch P 25.00 60.00
11 Richard Childress P 8.00 20.00
12 Stacy Compton P 6.00 15.00
13 Matt Crafton P 6.00 15.00
14 Ricky Craven P 10.00 25.00
15 Rick Crawford P 6.00 15.00
16 Dale Earnhardt Jr. E 75.00 150.00
17 Kerry Earnhardt E 10.00 25.00
18 Carl Edwards P 20.00 50.00
19 Christian Fittipaldi P 10.00 25.00
20 Coy Gibbs P 6.00 15.00
21 Jeff Gordon P 100.00 175.00
22 Robby Gordon E 8.00 20.00
23 Tina Gordon P 10.00 25.00
24 David Green P 6.00 15.00
25 Kevin Harvick P 12.50 30.00
26 Andy Houston P 6.00 15.00
27 Dale Jarrett P 15.00 40.00
28 Ned Jarrett P 8.00 20.00
29 Jimmie Johnson P 40.00 80.00
30 Kasey Kahne BGN P 25.00 60.00
32 Jason Keller P 6.00 15.00
33 Matt Kenseth P 15.00 40.00
34 Travis Kvapil P 10.00 25.00
35 Bobby Labonte P 15.00 40.00
36 Terry Labonte P 15.00 40.00
37 Damon Lusk P 6.00 15.00
38 Sterling Marlin P 10.00 25.00
39 Mark Martin P 30.00 60.00
40 Jeremy Mayfield 10.00 25.00
41 Mike McLaughlin P 6.00 15.00
42 Jamie McMurray E 10.00 25.00
43 Casey Mears E 10.00 25.00
44 Joe Nemechek P 8.00 20.00
45 Ryan Newman P 15.00 30.00
46 Benny Parsons P 30.00 60.00
47 David Pearson P 10.00 25.00
48 Kyle Petty E 10.00 25.00
49 Richard Petty P 40.00 80.00
50 Tony Raines P 6.00 15.00
51 Scott Riggs P 8.00 20.00
52 Ricky Rudd P 10.00 25.00
53 Johnny Sauter P 8.00 20.00
54 Ken Schrader P 8.00 20.00
55 Dennis Setzer P 6.00 15.00
56 Regan Smith P 6.00 15.00
57 Brian Vickers P 8.00 20.00
58 Kenny Wallace P 10.00 25.00
59 Rusty Wallace P 12.50 30.00
60 Scott Wimmer P 8.00 20.00
61 Glen Wood P 6.00 15.00
62 Jon Wood P 8.00 20.00
63 Robert Yates P 10.00 25.00
64 Cale Yarborough E 8.00 20.00

2004 Press Pass Burning Rubber Autographs

Randomly inserted in packs of 2004 Press Pass, this 8-card set featured NASCAR's hottest drivers along with a swatch of race-used tire along with an autograph. Each card was serial numbered to the driver's car number. The design looked like that of the 2004 Press Pass Burning Rubber Drivers. These were available in both hobby and retail packs of 2004 Press Pass. Some cards are not priced due to scarcity.

BRJG Jeff Gordon/24 250.00 500.00
BRJJ Jimmie Johnson/48 75.00 150.00
BRKB Kurt Busch/97
BRKH Kevin Harvick/29 100.00 200.00
BRMK Matt Kenseth/17
BRMM Mark Martin/6
BRRN Ryan Newman/12
BRRW Rusty Wallace/2

2004 Press Pass Burning Rubber Cars

Inserted at a stated rate of one in 240 retail packs, these 18 cards feature swatches of race-used tires set against a card featuring the driver's car. These cards were issued to a stated print run of 140 serial numbered sets.

BRT1 Jimmie Johnson's Car 15.00 40.
BRT2 Matt Kenseth's Car 12.50 30.
BRT3 Kevin Harvick's Car 12.50 30.
BRT4 Jeff Gordon's Car 20.00 50.
BRT5 Kurt Busch's Car 8.00 20.
BRT6 Mark Martin's Car 15.00 40.
BRT7 Ryan Newman's Car 15.00 40.
BRT8 Bobby Labonte's Car 12.50 30.
BRT9 Rusty Wallace's Car 12.50 30.
BRT10 Dale Earnhardt Jr.'s Car 25.00 60.
BRT11 Michael Waltrip's Car 8.00 20.
BRT12 Jamie McMurray's Car 10.00 25.
BRT13 Tony Stewart's Car 12.50 30.
BRT14 Casey Mears's Car 8.00 20.
BRT15 Terry Labonte's Car 12.50 30.
BRT16 Dale Jarrett's Car 12.50 30.
BRT17 Dale Earnhardt's Car 30.00 80.
BRT18 Robby Gordon's Car 10.00 25.

2004 Press Pass Burnin Rubber Drivers

Inserted at a stated rate of one in 180 retail pa these 18 cards feature pieces of race-used tires against a card featuring the driver. These cards w issued to a stated print run of 70 serial numbe sets.

BRD1 Jimmie Johnson 20.00 50.
BRD2 Matt Kenseth 15.00 40.
BRD3 Kevin Harvick 15.00 40.
BRD4 Jeff Gordon 30.00 60.
BRD5 Kurt Busch 12.50 25.
BRD6 Mark Martin 20.00 50.
BRD7 Ryan Newman 20.00 50.
BRD8 Bobby Labonte 15.00 40.
BRD9 Rusty Wallace 15.00 40.
BRD10 Dale Earnhardt Jr. 40.00 80.
BRD11 Michael Waltrip 12.50 25.
BRD12 Jamie McMurray 12.50 30.
BRD13 Tony Stewart 20.00 40.
BRD14 Casey Mears 12.50 25.
BRD15 Terry Labonte 20.00 40.
BRD16 Dale Jarrett 20.00 40.
BRD17 Dale Earnhardt 50.00 100.
BRD18 Robby Gordon 12.50 30

2004 Press Pass Cup Chase

These 18 cards were issued in packs of 2004 P Pass at a rate of 1:28 hobby and retail packs. T were 17 drivers and 1 field card. If the driver any of the 8 races listed on the back of the car the Nextel Cup Championship that card redeemable, along with $3.95 for s&h, f complete set of 17 of the prize cards. If you hac champion, you were also sent a special memora card of his. The exchange deadline for these January 31, 2005. Cards that were redeemable noted below.

EXCHANGE DEADLINE 01/31/2005
CCR1 Matt Kenseth 12.50 25
CCR2 Jeff Gordon WIN 20.00 40
CCR3 Dale Earnhardt Jr. WIN 20.00 40
CCR4 Bobby Labonte 8.00 20
CCR5 Michael Waltrip 6.00 15
CCR6 Kurt Busch 8.00 20
CCR7 Jimmie Johnson WIN 15.00 30
CCR8 Rusty Wallace 6.00 15
CCR9 Kevin Harvick 8.00 20
CCR10 Sterling Marlin 6.00 15
CCR11 Tony Stewart 8.00 20
CCR12 Mark Martin 6.00 15
CCR13 Terry Labonte 6.00 15
CCR14 Jeff Burton 5.00 12
CCR15 Ryan Newman 10.00 25
CCR16 Elliott Sadler 6.00 15
CCR17 Greg Biffle 6.00 15
CCR18 Field Card 10.00 25

2004 Press Pass Cup Chase Prizes

This 18-card set was issued as the prize for basic issue Cup Chase insert card in which featured driver won at least one race listed or card's back. Card #CC18 features Matt Kenseth highlights his 2003 Winston Cup championsh place of the "field" card from the basic insert se 18-cards were printed on a clear plastic card sto

COMPLETE SET (18) 15.00 40

R1 Matt Kenseth 3.00 8.00
R2 Jeff Gordon 4.00 10.00
R3 Dale Earnhardt Jr. 4.00 10.00
R4 Bobby Labonte 2.00 5.00
R5 Michael Waltrip 1.00 2.50
R6 Kurt Busch 1.50 4.00
R7 Jimmie Johnson 3.00 8.00
R8 Rusty Wallace 2.00 5.00
R9 Kevin Harvick 2.50 6.00
R10 Sterling Marlin 1.50 4.00
R11 Tony Stewart 2.50 6.00
R12 Mark Martin 2.50 6.00
R13 Terry Labonte 1.50 4.00
R14 Jeff Burton 1.00 2.50
R15 Ryan Newman 3.00 8.00
R16 Elliott Sadler 1.00 2.50
R17 Greg Biffle 1.00 2.50
R18 Matt Kenseth Champion 3.00 8.00

2004 Press Pass Schedule

s 4-card set features one of NASCAR's hottest ers with a 2004 Nextel Cup schedule on the k. These cards were packaged inside of blaster es, which were available at most retail stores, as x topper. They were the standard 2 1/2" x 3 1/2".

MPLETE SET (4) 30.00 60.00
ff Gordon 7.50 20.00
mmie Johnson 6.00 15.00
ale Earnhardt Jr. 8.00 20.00
ony Stewart 6.00 15.00

2004 Press Pass Season's Greetings

rted in packs at stated odds of one in 72, these s feature that sleigh-riding gentleman from the h Pole and were released in time for the 2003 stmas season.

MPLETE SET (3) 12.50 30.00
Santa 5.00 12.00
Santa with Sleigh 5.00 12.00
Santa with Tree 5.00 12.00

2004 Press Pass Showcar

ted at a stated rate of one in six retail packs, 12 die-cut cards feature a photo of the featured r's race car.

MPLETE SET (12) 10.00 25.00
Jeff Burton's Car .50 1.25
Kurt Busch's Car 1.00 2.50
Matt Kenseth's Car 2.00 5.00
Dale Earnhardt Jr.'s Car 2.50 6.00
Jeff Gordon's Car 2.50 6.00
Dale Jarrett's Car 1.25 3.00
Jimmie Johnson's Car 2.00 5.00
Bobby Labonte's Car 1.25 3.00
Terry Labonte's Car 1.00 2.50
B Mark Martin's Car 1.50 4.00
B Tony Stewart's Car 1.50 4.00
B Michael Waltrip's Car .50 1.25

2004 Press Pass Showman

ted at a stated rate of one in six retail packs, 12 die-cut cards feature a photo of the featured r.

PLETE SET (12) 12.50 30.00
Jeff Burton .50 1.25
Kurt Busch 1.00 2.50
Matt Kenseth 2.00 5.00
Dale Earnhardt Jr. 2.50 6.00
Jeff Gordon 2.50 6.00
Dale Jarrett 1.25 3.00
Jimmie Johnson 2.00 5.00
Bobby Labonte 1.25 3.00
Terry Labonte 1.00 2.50
Mark Martin 1.50 4.00
Tony Stewart 1.50 4.00
Michael Waltrip .50 1.25

2004 Press Pass Snapshots

d at a stated rate of one per pack, this 36-card measuring approximately 2 3/8" by 2 3/4") features drivers and their most memorable moments of the 2003 NASCAR season along with some retired drivers with highlights from their days of racing.

COMPLETE SET (36) 8.00 20.00
SN1 Greg Biffle .40 1.00
SN2 Jeff Burton .40 1.00
SN3 Ward Burton .40 1.00
SN4 Kurt Busch .60 1.50
SN5 Ricky Craven .20 .50
SN6 Dale Earnhardt Jr. 1.50 4.00
SN7 Jeff Gordon 1.50 4.00
SN8 Robby Gordon .20 .50
SN9 Kevin Harvick 1.25 3.00
SN10 Dale Jarrett 1.00 2.50
SN11 Jimmie Johnson 1.50 4.00
SN12 Matt Kenseth 1.50 4.00
SN13 Bobby Labonte 1.00 2.50
SN14 Terry Labonte .60 1.50
SN15 Sterling Marlin .60 1.50
SN16 Mark Martin 1.25 3.00
SN17 Jamie McMurray .60 1.50
SN18 Casey Mears .40 1.00
SN19 Joe Nemechek .20 .50
SN20 Ryan Newman 1.50 4.00
SN21 Ricky Rudd .60 1.50
SN22 Elliott Sadler .40 1.00
SN23 Michael Waltrip .40 1.00
SN24 Jimmy Spencer .20 .50
SN25 Tony Stewart 1.25 3.00
SN26 Rusty Wallace 1.00 2.50
SN27 Richard Petty .60 1.50
SN28 Buddy Baker .20 .50
SN29 Harry Gant .20 .50
SN30 Ned Jarrett .40 1.00
SN31 Junior Johnson .20 .50
SN32 Benny Parsons .20 .50
SN33 David Pearson .20 .50
SN34 Bobby Allison .20 .50
SN35 Glen Wood .20 .50
SN36 Cale Yarborough .20 .50

2004 Press Pass Top Shelf

Inserted at a state rate of 1:8 in both hobby and retail packs. These 10 cards feature drivers with silver foil names plates and a holofoil embossed finish.

COMPLETE SET (10) 10.00 25.00
TS1 Matt Kenseth 2.00 5.00
TS2 Kevin Harvick 1.50 4.00
TS3 Dale Earnhardt Jr. 2.50 6.00
TS4 Ryan Newman 2.00 5.00
TS5 Jimmie Johnson 2.00 5.00
TS6 Jeff Gordon 2.50 6.00
TS7 Tony Stewart 1.50 4.00
TS8 Bobby Labonte 1.25 3.00
TS9 Terry Labonte .75 2.00
TS10 Kurt Busch .75 2.00

2004 Press Pass Velocity

Issued at a stated rate of one in 18, these nine cards feature the driver along with a background photo of his car. These cards were printed on holofoil stock.

COMPLETE SET (9) 15.00 40.00
VC1 Michael Waltrip .75 2.00
VC2 Rusty Wallace 1.50 4.00
VC3 Kevin Harvick 2.00 5.00
VC4 Mark Martin 2.00 5.00
VC5 Matt Kenseth 2.50 6.00
VC6 Jimmie Johnson 2.50 6.00
VC7 Jeff Gordon 3.00 8.00
VC8 Dale Earnhardt Jr. 3.00 8.00
VC9 Kurt Busch 1.25 3.00

2005 Press Pass

COMPLETE SET (120) 15.00 40.00
COMMON CARD .10 .20
WAX BOX HOBBY (28) 50.00 80.00
WAX BOX RETAIL (24) 35.00 60.00
1 Ward Burton .30 .75
2 Joe Nemechek .20 .50
3 Rusty Wallace .60 1.50
4 Terry Labonte .50 1.25
5 Mark Martin .75 2.00
6 Dale Earnhardt Jr. 1.25 3.00
7 Kasey Kahne 1.25 3.00
8 Scott Riggs .30 .75
9 Ryan Newman 1.00 2.50
10 Michael Waltrip .30 .75
11 Greg Biffle .20 .50
12 Matt Kenseth 1.00 2.50
13 Bobby Labonte .60 1.50
14 Jeremy Mayfield .20 .50
15 Tony Stewart .75 2.00
16 Ricky Rudd .50 1.25
17 Scott Wimmer .30 .75
18 Dave Blaney .20 .50
19 Jeff Gordon 1.25 3.00
20 Brian Vickers .60 1.50
21 Kevin Harvick .75 2.00
22 Jeff Burton .30 .75
23 Robby Gordon .20 .50
24 Ricky Craven .20 .50
25 Boris Said .20 .50
26 Elliott Sadler .30 .75
27 Sterling Marlin .50 1.25
28 Casey Mears .30 .75
29 Jamie McMurray .50 1.25
30 Jeff Green .20 .50
31 Kyle Petty .30 .75
32 Jimmie Johnson 1.00 2.50
33 Ken Schrader .20 .50
34 Brendan Gaughan .30 .75
35 Dale Jarrett .60 1.50
36 Kurt Busch .50 1.25
37 Jason Leffler .20 .50
38 Ron Hornaday .20 .50
39 Kyle Busch .75 2.00
40 Mark McFarland RC .50 1.25
41 Martin Truex Jr. 1.00 2.50
42 Tim Fedewa .20 .50
43 Jason Keller .20 .50
44 Kenny Wallace .20 .50
45 David Green .20 .50
46 Kasey Kahne 1.25 3.00
47 Justin Labonte .50 1.25
48 Greg Biffle .30 .75
49 Andy Houston .20 .50
50 Matt Crafton .20 .50
51 Terry Cook .20 .50
52 Tina Gordon .30 .75
53 Rick Crawford .20 .50
54 Jack Sprague .20 .50
55 Dennis Setzer .20 .50
56 Jon Wood .20 .50
57 Carl Edwards 1.00 2.50
58 Jeff Fultz .20 .50
59 Andy Santerre .20 .50
60 Justin Diercks RC .50 1.25
61 Jeff Jefferson .20 .50
62 Tony Hirschman .20 .50
63 Mike Duncan RC .50 1.25
64 Ryan Newman's Car OTW .50 1.25
65 Dale Earnhardt Jr.'s Car OTW .50 1.25
66 Elliott Sadler's Car OTW .10 .20
67 Bobby Labonte's Car OTW .20 .50
68 Rusty Wallace's Car OTW .20 .50
69 Kurt Busch's Car OTW .10 .20
70 Kevin Harvick's Car OTW .30 .75
71 Dale Jarrett's Car OTW .30 .75
72 Mark Martin's Car OTW .30 .75
73 Dale Earnhardt Jr. NS 1.25 3.00
74 Matt Kenseth NS 1.00 2.50
75 Dale Earnhardt Jr. NS 1.25 3.00
76 Jimmie Johnson NS 1.00 2.50
77 Kurt Busch NS .50 1.25
78 Dale Earnhardt Jr. NS 1.25 3.00
79 Rusty Wallace NS .60 1.50
80 Jeff Gordon NS 1.25 3.00
81 Richard Petty NS .75 2.00
82 Jimmie Johnson NS 1.00 2.50
83 Mark Martin/T.Stewart NS .75 2.00
84 Jeff Gordon NS 1.25 3.00
85 Kasey Kahne RR 1.25 3.00
86 Brian Vickers RR .60 1.50
87 Scott Wimmer RR .30 .75
88 Brendan Gaughan RR .30 .75
89 Scott Riggs RR .30 .75
90 Martin Truex Jr. RR 1.00 2.50
91 Richard Petty Y .75 2.00
92 Joe Hendrick 1.25 3.00
Jeff Gordon
Jimmie Johnson
Terry Labonte
Brian Vickers Y
93 Kevin Harvick Y .75 2.00
94 Dale Earnhardt Jr. Y 1.25 3.00
95 Jeff Gordon Y 1.25 3.00
96 Terry Labonte .50 1.25
Justin Labonte Y
97 Kyle Busch .75 2.00
Kurt Busch Y
98 Rusty Wallace Y .60 1.50
99 Michael Waltrip Y .30 .75
100 Rusty Wallace P .60 1.50
101 Mark Martin P .75 2.00
102 Dale Earnhardt Jr. P 1.25 3.00
103 Michael Waltrip P .30 .75
104 Bobby Labonte P .60 1.50
105 Jeff Gordon P 1.25 3.00
106 Jimmie Johnson P 1.00 2.50
107 Ken Schrader P .20 .50
108 Dale Jarrett P .60 1.50
109 Dale Earnhardt Jr.'s Car .50 1.25
110 Elliott Sadler's Car .30 .75
111 Rusty Wallace's Car .60 1.50
112 Jeff Gordon's Car .50 1.25
113 Dale Earnhardt Jr's Car .50 1.25
114 Jimmie Johnson's Car .50 1.25
115 Mark Martin's Car .75 2.00
116 Ryan Newman's Car 1.00 2.50
117 Kurt Busch's Car .50 1.25
118 Jimmie Johnson's Car .50 1.25
119 WC/BGN Schedule .10 .20
120 Dale Earnhardt Jr 1.25 3.00
Jimmie Johnson
Jeff Gordon CL
NNO Santa Cards

2005 Press Pass Platinum

*PLATINUM: 2.5X TO 6X BASE

2005 Press Pass Previews Silver

COMPLETE SET (9)

2005 Press Pass Samples

These cards were issued to preview the 120-card 2005 Press Pass set. The cards were stamped "Sample" on the backs and were issued one per Beckett Racing magazine Issue #126 February, 2005.

*SAMPLES: 1.5X TO 4X BASE

2005 Press Pass Autographs

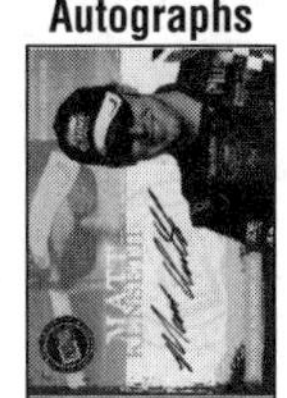

1 Bobby Allison E/P 8.00 20.00
2 Greg Biffle BGN E/P 10.00 25.00
3 Greg Biffle NCS E/P 10.00 25.00
4 Mike Bliss E/P 6.00 15.00
5 Clint Bowyer E/P 12.50 30.00
6 Jeff Burton E 8.00 20.00
7 Kurt Busch E/P 12.50 30.00
8 Kyle Busch BGN E/P 20.00 50.00
9 Kyle Busch NCS E/P 20.00 50.00
10 Richard Childress E 8.00 20.00
11 Terry Cook E/P 8.00 20.00
12 Matt Crafton E/P 8.00 20.00
13 Ricky Craven E/P 10.00 25.00
14 Dale Earnhardt Jr. E 75.00 150.00
15 Kerry Earnhardt E 12.50 30.00
16 Carl Edwards E/P 20.00 50.00
17 Tim Fedewa E 6.00 15.00
18 Brendan Gaughan E/P 12.50 30.00
19 Jeff Gordon E/P 100.00 175.00
20 Tina Gordon E/P 10.00 25.00
21 David Green E/P 6.00 15.00
22 Jeff Green E/P 8.00 20.00
23 Kevin Harvick E/P 12.50 30.00
24 Ron Hornaday E/P 8.00 20.00
25 Andy Houston E/P 6.00 15.00
26 Dale Jarrett E/P 15.00 40.00
27 Jimmie Johnson E/P 40.00 80.00
28 Kasey Kahne BGN E/P 25.00 60.00
29 Kasey Kahne NCS E/P 25.00 60.00
30 Jason Keller E/P 6.00 15.00
31 Matt Kenseth BGN E/P 15.00 40.00
32 Matt Kenseth NCS E/P 15.00 40.00
33 Bobby Labonte E/P 15.00 40.00
34 Justin Labonte E/P 15.00 30.00
35 Terry Labonte E 15.00 40.00
36 Bill Lester E 10.00 25.00
37 Mark Martin E/P 30.00 60.00
38 Jeremy Mayfield E 10.00 25.00
39 Mark McFarland E 10.00 25.00
40 Jamie McMurray 10.00 25.00
41 Casey Mears 10.00 25.00
42 Joe Nemechek E/P 10.00 25.00
43 Ryan Newman E/P 15.00 30.00
44 Steve Park E/P 12.50 30.00
45 Benny Parsons E/P 30.00 60.00
46 David Pearson E/P 10.00 25.00
47 Kyle Petty E 12.50 30.00
48 Richard Petty E/P 40.00 80.00
49 Scott Riggs E/P 8.00 20.00
50 Ricky Rudd E/P 12.50 30.00
51 Boris Said E/P 6.00 15.00
52 Johnny Sauter E 8.00 20.00
53 Ken Schrader E 8.00 20.00
54 Dennis Setzer E/P 6.00 15.00
55 Jack Sprague E/P 6.00 15.00
56 Tony Stewart E/P 40.00 100.00
57 Martin Truex Jr. 15.00 40.00
58 Brian Vickers E/P 10.00 25.00
59 Kenny Wallace E/P 10.00 25.00
60 Rusty Wallace E/P 12.50 30.00
61 Michael Waltrip 10.00 25.00
62 Scott Wimmer E 8.00 20.00
63 Paul Wolfe E 10.00 25.00
64 Glen Wood E/P 6.00 15.00
65 Jon Wood E/P 8.00 20.00
66 Robert Yates E/P 8.00 20.00
67 J.J. Yeley E/P 12.50 30.00

2005 Press Pass Burning Rubber Autographs

This 8-card set was released in packs of 2005 Press Pass. Each card had a swatch of race-used tire along with a signature from the corresponding driver. Each card was serial numbered to the driver's door number. There was a late addition to the set. The Dale Earnhardt Jr. was only available in packs of 2006 Press Pass Legends.

SOME CARDS NOT PRICED DUE TO SCARCITY
BR-DE Dale Earnhardt Jr./8
BR-JJ Jimmie Johnson/48 75.00 150.00
BR-KH Kevin Harvick/29 100.00 200.00
BR-MK Matt Kenseth/17
BR-MM Mark Martin/6
BR-RN Ryan Newman/12
BR-RW Rusty Wallace/2
BR-TS Tony Stewart/20

2005 Press Pass Burning Rubber Cars

*CARS: .3X TO .8X DRIVERS
STATED PRINT RUN 130 SERIAL #'d SETS

2005 Press Pass Burning Rubber Drivers

BRD1 Jimmie Johnson 15.00 40.00
BRD2 Matt Kenseth 15.00 40.00
BRD3 Kevin Harvick 12.50 30.00
BRD4 Jeff Gordon 25.00 60.00
BRD5 Bobby Labonte 12.50 30.00
BRD6 Rusty Wallace 12.50 30.00
BRD7 Dale Earnhardt Jr. 25.00 60.00
BRD8 Michael Waltrip 10.00 25.00
BRD9 Jamie McMurray 10.00 25.00
BRD10 Tony Stewart 20.00 50.00
BRD11 Casey Mears 8.00 20.00
BRD12 Terry Labonte 12.50 30.00
BRD13 Dale Jarrett 12.50 30.00
BRD14 Scott Riggs 8.00 20.00
BRD15 Joe Nemechek 8.00 20.00
BRD16 Ricky Rudd 12.50 30.00
BRD17 Kurt Busch 12.50 30.00
BRD18 Mark Martin 15.00 40.00

2005 Press Pass Burning Rubber Drivers Gold

STATED PRINT RUN 1 SERIAL #'d SET
NOT PRICED DUE TO SCARCITY

2005 Press Pass Cup Chase

CCR1 Kurt Busch Winner 15.00 30.00
CCR2 Dale Jarrett 6.00 15.00
CCR3 Jimmie Johnson Winner 15.00 30.00
CCR4 Jamie McMurray 6.00 15.00
CCR5 Elliott Sadler 6.00 15.00
CCR6 Kevin Harvick Winner 15.00 30.00
CCR7 Jeff Gordon Winner 20.00 40.00
CCR8 Tony Stewart Winner 15.00 30.00
CCR9 Bobby Labonte 6.00 15.00
CCR10 Matt Kenseth 8.00 20.00
CCR11 Greg Biffle Winner 15.00 30.00
CCR12 Michael Waltrip 6.00 15.00
CCR13 Ryan Newman 8.00 20.00
CCR14 Kasey Kahne 10.00 25.00
CCR15 Dale Earnhardt Jr. 10.00 25.00
CCR16 Mark Martin 8.00 20.00
CCR17 Rusty Wallace 6.00 15.00
CCR18 Field Card Winner 15.00 30.00

2005 Press Pass Cup Chase Prizes

COMPLETE SET (18) 15.00 30.00
CCP1 Kurt Busch 1.50 4.00
CCP2 Dale Jarrett 2.00 5.00
CCP3 Jimmie Johnson 3.00 8.00
CCP4 Jamie McMurray 1.50 4.00
CCP5 Elliott Sadler 1.25 3.00
CCP6 Kevin Harvick 2.50 6.00
CCP7 Jeff Gordon 4.00 10.00
CCP8 Tony Stewart 2.50 6.00
CCP9 Bobby Labonte 2.00 5.00
CCP10 Matt Kenseth 3.00 8.00
CCP11 Greg Biffle 1.25 3.00
CCP12 Michael Waltrip 1.25 3.00
CCP13 Ryan Newman 3.00 8.00
CCP14 Kasey Kahne 4.00 10.00
CCP15 Dale Earnhardt Jr. 4.00 10.00
CCP16 Mark Martin 2.50 6.00
CCP17 Rusty Wallace 2.00 5.00
CCP18 Kurt Busch '04 Champ 1.50 4.00
NNO Tony Stewart Firesuit 15.00 30.00

2005 Press Pass Game Face

COMPLETE SET (9) 10.00 25.00
GF1 Dale Jarrett 1.25 3.00
GF2 Jimmie Johnson 2.00 5.00
GF3 Dale Earnhardt Jr. 2.50 6.00
GF4 Kevin Harvick 1.50 4.00
GF5 Bobby Labonte 1.25 3.00
GF6 Jeff Gordon 2.50 6.00
GF7 Tony Stewart 1.50 4.00
GF8 Michael Waltrip .60 1.50
GF9 Mark Martin 1.50 4.00

2005 Press Pass Season's Greetings

1 Santa Claus Snowmobile 10.00 20.00
2 Santa Claus Daytona or Bust 6.00 12.00

2005 Press Pass Showcar

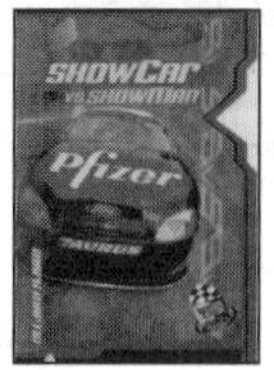

COMPLETE SET (12) 15.00 40.00
*SHOWCARS: .3X TO.8X SHOWMAN
STATED ODDS 1:12

2005 Press Pass Showman

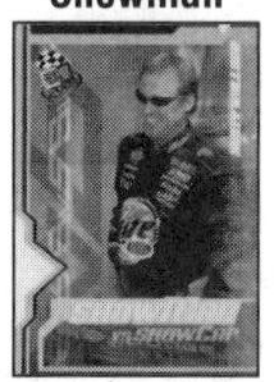

COMPLETE SET (12) 20.00 50.00
COMMON DRIVERS .60 1.50
SEMISTARS 1.00 2.50
UNLISTED STARS 1.50 4.00
STATED ODDS 1:18
SM1 Mark Martin 2.50 6.00
SM2 Kurt Busch 1.50 4.00
SM3 Jimmie Johnson 3.00 8.00
SM4 Dale Earnhardt Jr. 4.00 10.00
SM5 Jeff Gordon 4.00 10.00
SM6 Dale Jarrett 2.00 5.00
SM7 Rusty Wallace 2.00 5.00
SM8 Kevin Harvick 2.50 6.00
SM9 Michael Waltrip 1.00 2.50
SM10 Tony Stewart 2.50 6.00
SM11 Bobby Labonte 2.00 5.00
SM12 Terry Labonte 1.50 4.00

2005 Press Pass Snapshots

COMPLETE SET (36) 10.00 25.00
STATED ODDS 1:2
SN1 Greg Biffle .30 .75
SN2 Dave Blaney .15 .40
SN3 Jeff Burton .30 .75
SN4 Kurt Busch .50 1.25
SN5 Dale Earnhardt Jr. 1.25 3.00
SN6 Carl Edwards 1.00 2.50
SN7 Brendan Gaughan .30 .75
SN8 Jeff Gordon 1.25 3.00
SN9 Jeff Green .15 .40
SN10 Kevin Harvick .75 2.00
SN11 Dale Jarrett .60 1.50
SN12 Jimmie Johnson 1.00 2.50
SN13 Kasey Kahne 1.25 3.00
SN14 Matt Kenseth 1.00 2.50
SN15 Bobby Labonte .60 1.50
SN16 Terry Labonte .50 1.25
SN17 Mark Martin .75 2.00
SN18 Jeremy Mayfield .15 .40
SN19 Joe Nemechek .15 .40
SN20 Scott Riggs .30 .75
SN21 Ricky Rudd .50 1.25
SN22 Elliott Sadler .30 .75
SN23 Ken Schrader .15 .40
SN24 Tony Stewart .75 2.00
SN25 Rusty Wallace .60 1.50
SN26 Michael Waltrip .30 .75
SN27 Bobby Allison .15 .40
SN28 Davey Allison .30 .75
SN29 Geoff Bodine .15 .40
SN30 Harry Gant .30 .75
SN31 Alan Kulwicki .30 .75
SN32 Benny Parsons .15 .40
SN33 David Pearson .15 .40
SN34 Richard Petty .75 2.00
SN35 Glen Wood .15 .40
SN36 Cale Yarborough .15 .40

2005 Press Pass Snapshots Extra

COMPLETE SET (18)
*EXTRA: 1X TO 2.5X BASE

2005 Press Pass Top Ten

COMPLETE SET (10)
TT1 Jeff Gordon 6.00 15.00
TT2 Jimmie Johnson 5.00 12.00
TT3 Dale Earnhardt Jr. 6.00 15.00
TT4 Tony Stewart 4.00 10.00
TT5 Matt Kenseth 5.00 12.00
TT6 Elliott Sadler 1.50 4.00
TT7 Kurt Busch 2.50 6.00
TT8 Mark Martin 4.00 10.00
TT9 Jeremy Mayfield 1.00 2.50
TT10 Ryan Newman 5.00 12.00

2005 Press Pass Velocity

COMPLETE SET (9) 15.00 40.00
V1 Dale Jarrett 1.50 4.00
V2 Jimmie Johnson 2.50 6.00
V3 Jeff Gordon 3.00 8.00
V4 Ricky Rudd 1.25 3.00
V5 Matt Kenseth 2.50 6.00
V6 Michael Waltrip .75 2.00
V7 Dale Earnhardt Jr. 3.00 8.00
V8 Mark Martin 2.50 6.00
V9 Rusty Wallace 2.00 4.00

2006 Press Pass

COMPLETE SET (120) 15.00 40.00
WAX BOX HOBBY (28) 60.00 90.00
WAX BOX RETAIL 50.00 80.00
0 CARD STATED ODDS 1:144
SANTA STATED ODDS 1:72
1 Mike Bliss .20 .50
2 Joe Nemechek .20 .50
3 Martin Truex Jr.
4 Rusty Wallace .60 1.50
5 Kyle Busch
6 Mark Martin .75 2.00
7 Dave Blaney .20 .50
8 Robby Gordon .20 .50
9 Dale Earnhardt Jr. 1.25 3.00
10 Kasey Kahne 1.25 3.00
11 Ryan Newman .75 2.00
12 Greg Biffle .40 1.00
13 Matt Kenseth 1.00 2.50
14 Bobby Labonte .60 1.50
15 Jeremy Mayfield .20 .50
16 Tony Stewart .75 2.00
17 Ricky Rudd .50 1.25
18 Jeff Gordon 1.25 3.00
19 Brian Vickers .60 1.50
20 Kevin Harvick .75 2.00
21 Jeff Burton .30 .75
22 Kevin Lepage .20 .50
23 Sterling Marlin .50 1.25
24 Jamie McMurray .50 1.25
25 Terry Labonte .50 1.25
26 Kyle Petty .30 .75
27 Jimmie Johnson 1.00 2.50
28 Dale Jarrett .60 1.50
29 Kurt Busch .50 1.25
30 Carl Edwards 1.00 2.50
31 Johnny Sauter NBS .30 .75
32 Clint Bowyer NBS 1.25 3.00
33 Martin Truex Jr. NBS .75 2.00
34 J.J. Yeley NBS .50 1.25
35 Denny Hamlin NBS 1.25 3.00
36 Kenny Wallace NBS .20 .50
37 David Green NBS .20 .50
38 Tony Raines NBS .20 .50
39 Jason Keller NBS .20 .50
40 Kasey Kahne NBS 1.25 3.00
41 Reed Sorenson NBS .75 2.00
42 Carl Edwards NBS 1.00 2.50
43 Mike Skinner CTS .20 .50
44 Ron Hornaday CTS .20 .50
45 Terry Cook CTS .20 .50
46 Rick Crawford CTS .20 .50
47 Jack Sprague CTS .20 .50
48 Bill Lester CTS .30 .75
49 Dennis Setzer CTS .20 .50
50 Todd Kluever CTS 1.00 2.50
51 Ricky Craven CTS .20 .50
52 Andy Santerre .20 .50
53 Tony Hirschman .20 .50
54 Justin Diercks .50 1.25
55 Mike Duncan .20 .50
56 Jeff Fultz .20 .50
57 Jeff Jefferson .20 .50
58 Buddy Baker .30 .75
59 Jack Ingram .20 .50
60 Fred Lorenzen .30 .75
61 Lee Petty .50 1.25
62 Rex White .20 .50
63 Donnie Allison .20 .50
64 Neil Bonnett .30 .75
65 Curtis Turner .20 .50
66 Fireball Roberts .30 .75
67 Kyle Busch RR .60 1.50
68 Travis Kvapil RR .30 .75
69 Carl Edwards RR 1.00 2.50
70 Denny Hamlin RR 1.25 3.00
71 Reed Sorenson RR .75 2.00
72 Todd Kluever RR 1.00 2.50
73 Jimmie Johnson's Car OTW 1.00 2.50
74 Dale Jarrett's Car OTW .60 1.50
75 Ricky Rudd's Car OTW .50 1.25
76 Dale Earnhardt Jr's Car OTW 1.25 3.00
77 Jeff Gordon's Car OTW 1.25 3.00
78 Greg Biffle's Car OTW .40 1.00
79 Kevin Harvick's Car OTW .75 2.00
80 Jeff Burton's Car OTW .30 .75
81 Mark Martin's Car OTW .75 2.00
82 Kurt Busch's Car OTW .50 1.25
83 Carl Edwards' Car OTW 1.00 2.50
84 Rusty Wallace's Car OTW .60 1.50
85 Jeff Gordon NS 1.25 3.00
86 Greg Biffle NS .40 1.00
87 Carl Edwards NS 1.00 2.50
88 Kevin Harvick NS .75 2.00
89 Kasey Kahne NS 1.25 3.00
90 Mark Martin NS .75 2.00
91 Jimmie Johnson NS 1.00 2.50
92 Greg Biffle NS .40 1.00
93 Tony Stewart NS .75 2.00
94 Tony Stewart NS .75 2.00
95 Matt Kenseth NS 1.00 2.50
96 Kyle Busch NS .60 1.50
97 Dale Earnhardt Jr. U 1.25 3.00
98 Kasey Kahne U 1.25 3.00
99 Ryan Newman U .75 2.00
100 Tony Stewart U .75 2.00
101 Carl Edwards U 1.00 2.50
102 Martin Truex Jr. U .75 2.00
103 Jimmie Johnson U 1.00 2.50
104 Jeff Gordon U 1.25 3.00
105 Matt Kenseth U 1.00 2.50
106 Dale Jarrett U .60 1.50
107 Kevin Harvick U .75 2.00
108 Kurt Busch U .50 1.25
109 Tony Stewart TT .75 2.00
110 Greg Biffle TT .40 1.00
111 Jimmie Johnson TT 1.00 2.50
112 Rusty Wallace TT .60 1.50
113 Mark Martin TT .75 2.00
114 Kurt Busch TT .50 1.25
115 Jeremy Mayfield TT .20 .50
116 Carl Edwards TT 1.00 2.50
117 Matt Kenseth TT 1.00 2.50
118 Ryan Newman TT .75 2.00
119 Checklist CL .10 .30
120 Tony Stewart Schedule .75 2.00
0 Cup Chase 10 6.00 15.00
Greg Biffle
Jimmie Johnson
Rusty Wallace
Carl Edwards
Jeremy Mayfield
Tony Stewart
Matt Kenseth
Mark martin
Kurt Busch
Ryan Newman
NNO Santa Claus 4.00 10.00

2006 Press Pass Blue

COMPLETE SET (120)
*BLUE: 1.2X TO 3X BASE
STATED ODDS 1 PER HOBBY PACK

2006 Press Pass Previews

COMPLETE SET (54)
(1-42) PRINT RUN 5 SERIAL #'d SETS
(97-108) PRINT RUN 1 SERIAL #'d SET

2006 Press Pass Gold

COMPLETE SET (120)
*GOLD: 1.2X TO 3X BASE
STATED ODDS 1 PER RETAIL PACK

2006 Press Pass Platinum

COMPLETE SET (120)
*PLATINUM: 2.5X TO 6X BASE
STATED PRINT RUN 100 SERIAL #'d SETS

2006 Press Pass Autographs

COMPLETE SET (40)
STATED ODDS 1:84
1 Bobby Allison 8.00 20.00
2 Buddy Baker 7.50 15.00
3 Dave Blaney NC 6.00 15.00
4 Mike Bliss NC 7.50 15.00
5 Clint Bowyer NBS 15.00 40.00
6 Jeff Burton NCS 8.00 20.00
7 Kurt Busch NC 12.50 30.00
8 Kyle Busch NC 20.00 50.00
9 Terry Cook CTS 6.00 15.00
10 Ricky Craven CTS 10.00 25.00
11 Rick Crawford CTS 5.00 12.00
12 Kerry Earnhardt NBS 8.00 20.00
13 Carl Edwards NBS 20.00 50.00
14 Carl Edwards NCS 20.00 50.00
15 Harry Gant 8.00 20.00
16 Jeff Gordon NC 125.00 250.00
17 Robby Gordon NC 10.00 25.00
18 David Green NBS 5.00 12.00
19 Jeff Green NCS 7.50 15.00
20 Denny Hamlin NBS 30.00 60.00
21 Kevin Harvick NC 12.50 30.00
22 Ron Hornaday CTS 6.00 15.00
23 Dale Jarrett NC 15.00 40.00
24 Jimmie Johnson NC 40.00 80.00
25 Kasey Kahne NBS 25.00 60.00
26 Kasey Kahne NC 25.00 60.00
27 Jason Keller NBS 7.50 15.00
28 Matt Kenseth NC 15.00 40.00
29 Todd Kluever CTS 10.00 25.00
30 Travis Kvapil NC 10.00 25.00
31 Bobby Labonte NC 15.00 40.00
32 Justin Labonte NBS 10.00 25.00
33 Bill Lester CTS 10.00 25.00
34 Fred Lorenzen 7.50 15.00
35 Sterling Marlin NC 15.00 30.00
36 Mark Martin NC 30.00 60.00
37 Jeremy Mayfield NC 10.00 25.00
38 Jamie McMurray NC 10.00 25.00
39 Casey Mears NC 10.00 25.00
40 Joe Nemechek NC 8.00 20.00
41 Ryan Newman NC 15.00 30.00
42 Marvin Panch 5.00 12.00
43 Benny Parsons 30.00 60.00
44 David Pearson 10.00 25.00
45 Richard Petty 40.00 80.00
46 Tony Raines NBS 5.00 12.00
47 Ricky Rudd NCS 12.50 30.00
48 Boris Said NC 8.00 20.00
49 Johnny Sauter NBS 8.00 20.00
50 Ken Schrader NCS 8.00 20.00
51 Dennis Setzer CTS 7.50 15.00
52 Jack Sprague CTS 7.50 15.00
53 Tony Stewart NC 40.00 80.00
54 Martin Truex Jr. NBS 15.00 40.00
55 Brian Vickers NC 10.00 25.00
56 Rex White 5.00 12.00
57 Glen Wood 6.00 15.00
58 Jon Wood NBS 6.00 15.00
59 Cale Yarborough 10.00 25.00
60 J.J. Yeley NBS 10.00 25.00

2006 Press Pass Blaster Kmart

COMPLETE SET (6) 8.00 20.00
CEC Carl Edwards 1.50 4.00
DEC Dale Earnhardt Jr. 2.00 5.00
JGC Jeff Gordon 2.00 5.00
KHC Kevin Harvick 1.25 3.00
KKC Kasey Kahne 2.00 5.00
TSC Tony Stewart 1.25 3.00

2006 Press Pass Blaster Target

COMPLETE SET (6) 8.00 20.00
CEB Carl Edwards 1.50 4.00
DEB Dale Earnhardt Jr. 2.00 5.00
JGB Jeff Gordon 2.00 5.00
KHB Kevin Harvick 1.25 3.00
KKB Kasey Kahne 2.00 5.00
TSB Tony Stewart 1.25 3.00

2006 Press Pass Blaster Wal-Mart

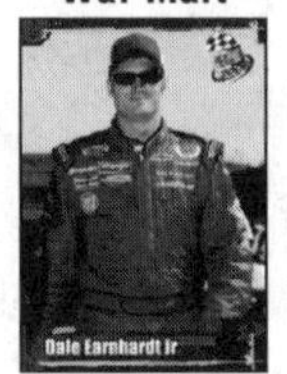

COMPLETE SET (6) 8.00 20.00
CEA Carl Edwards 1.50 4.00
DEA Dale Earnhardt Jr. 2.00 5.00
JGA Jeff Gordon 2.00 5.00
KHA Kevin Harvick 1.25 3.00
KKA Kasey Kahne 2.00 5.00
TSA Tony Stewart 1.25 3.00

2006 Press Pass Burning Rubber Autographs

This 11-card set was available in packs of 2006 Press Pass. Each card had a swatch of race-used tire along with a signature from the corresponding driver. Each card was serial numbered to the driver's door number. The Tony Stewart was a late addition added to the set in October, 2006, and was only available in packs of 2006 Press Pass Legends.

SERIAL #'d TO DRIVER'S DOOR NUMBER
SOME CARDS NOT PRICED DUE TO SCARCITY
BR-CE Carl Edwards/99 60.00 120.00
BR-JG Jeff Gordon/24 250.00 500.00
BR-JJ Jimmie Johnson/48 75.00 150.00
BR-KB Kyle Busch/5
BR-KH Kevin Harvick/29 100.00 200.00
BR-KK Kasey Kahne/9
BR-MK Matt Kenseth/17
BR-MM Mark Martin/6
BR-RN Ryan Newman/12
BR-RW Rusty Wallace/2
BR-TS Tony Stewart/20

2006 Press Pass Burning Rubber Cars

COMPLETE SET (18)
*CARS: .25X TO .6X DRIVERS
STATED PRINT RUN 370 SERIAL #'d SETS

2006 Press Pass Burning Rubber Drivers

STATED ODDS 1:112
STATED PRINT RUN 100 SERIAL #'d SETS
BRD1 Kurt Busch 12.50 30.00
BRD2 Kyle Busch 12.50 30.00
BRD3 Dale Earnhardt Jr. 25.00 60.00
BRD4 Carl Edwards 20.00 50.00
BRD5 Jeff Gordon 25.00 60.00
BRD6 Kevin Harvick 12.50 30.00
BRD7 Dale Jarrett 12.50 30.00
BRD8 Jimmie Johnson 20.00 50.00
BRD9 Kasey Kahne 25.00 60.00
BRD10 Matt Kenseth 20.00 50.00
BRD11 Bobby Labonte 15.00 40.00
BRD12 Terry Labonte 15.00 40.00
BRD13 Mark Martin 20.00 50.00
BRD14 Jamie McMurray 12.50 30.00
BRD15 Ricky Rudd 12.50 30.00
BRD16 Tony Stewart 20.00 50.00
BRD17 Martin Truex Jr. 20.00 50.00
BRD18 Rusty Wallace 15.00 40.00

2006 Press Pass Burning Rubber Drivers Gold

STATED PRINT RUN 1 SERIAL #'d SET
CARDS NOT PRICED DUE TO SCARCITY

2006 Press Pass Cup Chase

STATED ODDS 1:28
EXCH DEADLINE 12/31/06
CCR1 Tony Stewart 8.00 20.00
CCR2 Greg Biffle 6.00 15.00
CCR3 Jimmie Johnson Winner 12.50 25.00
CCR4 Kurt Busch 6.00 12.00
CCR5 Kyle Busch Winner 8.00 20.00
CCR6 Carl Edwards 6.00 15.00
CCR7 Matt Kenseth Winner 8.00 20.00
CCR8 Jamie McMurray 6.00 12.00
CCR9 Ryan Newman 7.50 15.00
CCR10 Jeff Gordon Winner 15.00 30.00
CCR11 Ricky Rudd 4.00 8.00
CCR12 Dale Earnhardt Jr. Winner 15.00 30.00
CCR13 Dale Jarrett 6.00 12.00
CCR14 Kevin Harvick Winner 10.00 25.00
CCR15 Bobby Labonte 5.00 10.00
CCR16 Elliott Sadler 6.00 12.00
CCR17 Jeff Burton Winner 10.00 25.00
CCR18 Field Card Winner 12.50 25.00

2006 Press Pass Cup Chase Prizes

COMPLETE SET (10) 12.50 30.00
CC1 Jimmie Johnson 2.50 6.00
CC2 Matt Kenseth 2.50 6.00
CC3 Denny Hamlin 3.00 8.00
CC4 Kevin Harvick 2.00 5.00
CC5 Dale Earnhardt Jr. 3.00 8.00
CC6 Jeff Gordon 3.00 8.00
CC7 Jeff Burton .75 2.00
CC8 Kasey Kahne 3.00 8.00
CC9 Mark Martin 2.00 5.00
CC10 Kyle Busch 1.50 4.00
CCP1 Jimmie Johnson Firesuit/475 15.00 40.00

2006 Press Pass Game Face

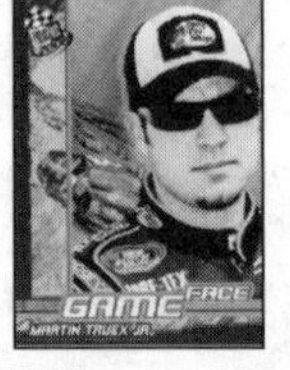

COMPLETE SET (9) 10.00 25.00
COMMON DRIVER .40 1.00
SEMISTARS .60 1.50
UNLISTED STARS 1.00 2.50
STATED ODDS 1:6
GF1 Jeff Gordon 2.50 6.00
GF2 Mark Martin 1.50 4.00
GF3 Ricky Rudd 1.00 2.50
GF4 Dale Earnhardt Jr. 2.50 6.00
GF5 Dale Jarrett 1.25 3.00
GF6 Jimmie Johnson 2.00 5.00
GF7 Bobby Labonte 1.25 3.00
GF8 Martin Truex Jr. 1.50 4.00
GF9 Jeff Burton .60 1.50

2006 Press Pass Snapshots

COMPLETE SET (36) 12.50 30.00
COMMON DRIVERS .20 .50
SEMISTARS .30 .75
UNLISTED STARS .50 1.25
STATED ODDS 1:2
SN1 John Andretti
SN2 Tony Raines .20
SN3 Jeff Burton .30
SN4 Bobby Labonte .60
SN5 Kasey Kahne 1.25
SN6 Terry Cook .20
SN7 Jimmie Johnson 1.00
SN8 Ricky Craven .20
SN9 Rick Crawford .20
SN10 Dave Blaney .20
SN11 Dale Earnhardt Jr. 1.25
SN12 Dennis Setzer .20
SN13 Kyle Petty .30
SN14 John Andretti
SN15 Dale Jarrett .60
SN16 Kenny Wallace
SN17 Jimmie Johnson 1.00
SN18 Kerry Earnhardt
SN19 Martin Truex Jr. .75
SN20 Jason Keller .20
SN21 Todd Kluever 1.00
SN22 Boris Said
SN23 Bobby Labonte .60
SN24 Johnny Sauter .30
SN25 Mark Martin .75
SN26 Ron Hornaday .20
SN27 Ricky Rudd .50
SN28 Ricky Craven .20
SN29 Jeff Burton .30
SN30 Jeff Gordon 1.25
SN31 Dale Jarrett .60
SN32 Mike Skinner .20
SN33 Dave Blaney .20
SN34 Mark Martin .75
SN35 Martin Truex Jr. .75
SN36 Ricky Rudd CL .50

2006 Press Pass Velocity

COMPLETE SET (9) 15.00
COMMON DRIVER .60
SEMISTARS .75
UNLISTED STARS 1.25
STATED ODDS 1:12
VE1 Dale Earnhardt Jr. 3.00
VE2 Mark Martin 2.00
VE3 Carl Edwards 2.50
VE4 Jeff Gordon 3.00
VE5 Ricky Rudd 1.25
VE6 Tony Stewart 2.00
VE7 Martin Truex Jr. 2.00
VE8 Jimmie Johnson 2.50
VE9 Dale Jarrett 1.50

2007 Press Pass

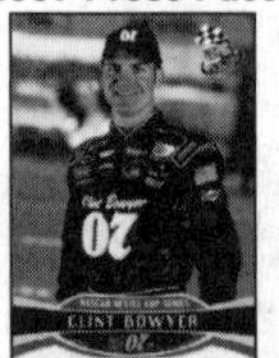

This 120-card set was released December This set was issued in six card packs which car packs to a hobby and 24 packs per retail box. hobby and retail boxes were packed 20 boxes case. The SRP for both hobby and retail packs $2.99. There was a special 00 card honorin 2006 Cup Chase drivers which was inserted packs at a rate of one in 72. There was also a numbered Happy Holidays Santa card which inserted into packs at a rate of one in 72.

COMPLETE SET (120) 15.00
WAX BOX HOBBY (28) 60.00
WAX BOX RETAIL (28) 50.00
1 Matt Kenseth 1.00
2 Jimmie Johnson 1.00
3 Kevin Harvick .75
4 Kyle Busch .50
5 Denny Hamlin 1.00
6 Dale Earnhardt Jr. 1.25
7 Mark Martin .75
8 Jeff Burton .25
9 Jeff Gordon 1.25
10 Kasey Kahne 1.25
11 Tony Stewart .75
12 Greg Biffle .40
13 Carl Edwards .75
14 Kurt Busch .25
15 Casey Mears .30
16 Clint Bowyer .60
17 Ryan Newman .60
18 Scott Riggs .30
19 Jamie McMurray .50
20 Brian Vickers .50
21 Reed Sorenson .50
22 Martin Truex Jr. .75
23 Dale Jarrett .60
24 Bobby Labonte .60
25 Robby Gordon .20
26 J.J. Yeley .30
27 Dave Blaney .20
28 Ken Schrader .20
29 Joe Nemechek .20
30 Sterling Marlin .50
31 Kyle Petty .30
32 David Stremme .50
33 Tony Raines .20
34 Kevin Harvick NBS .75

Carl Edwards NBS	.75	2.00
Denny Hamlin NBS	1.00	2.50
Clint Bowyer NBS	1.00	2.50
J.J. Yeley NBS	.30	.75
Paul Menard NBS	.40	1.00
Jon Wood NBS	.20	.50
David Green NBS	.20	.50
Todd Kluever NBS	.50	1.25
Regan Smith NBS	.20	.50
Danny O'Quinn NBS	.50	1.25
Steve Wallace NBS	.60	1.50
Ron Hornaday CTS	.20	.50
Erik Darnell CTS	.50	1.25
Mike Skinner CTS	.20	.50
Bill Lester CTS	.30	.75
Erin Crocker CTS	.75	2.00
David Regan CTS	.60	1.50
Mike Olsen RC	.50	1.25
Gary Lewis RC	.50	1.25
J.R. Norris RC	.50	1.25
Davey Allison	.40	1.00
Buddy Baker	.25	.60
Neil Bonnett	.25	.60
Fred Lorenzen	.25	.60
Marvin Panch	.15	.40
Fireball Roberts	.25	.60
Rusty Wallace	.50	1.25
Rex White	.15	.40
Glen Wood	.15	.40
Clint Bowyer RR	.75	2.00
Denny Hamlin RR	.75	2.00
Reed Sorenson RR	.50	1.25
David Stremme RR	.50	1.25
Martin Truex Jr. RR	.60	1.50
J.J. Yeley RR	.30	.75
Todd Kluever RR	.50	1.25
Erin Crocker RR	.75	2.00
Erik Darnell RR	.40	1.00
Jeff Gordon's Car OT	.40	1.00
Mark Martin's Car OT	.25	.60
Matt Kenseth's Car OT	.30	.75
Kevin Harvick's car OT	.25	.60
Jimmie Johnson's Car OT	.30	.75
Dale Jarrett's Car OT	.20	.50
Tony Stewart's Car OT	.25	.60
Denny Hamlin's Car OT	.30	.75
Kurt Busch's Car OT	.10	.25
Carl Edwards' Car OT	.25	.60
Terry Labonte's Car OT	.15	.40
Kasey Kahne's Car OT	.40	1.00
Greg Biffle NS	.30	.75
Dale Earnhardt Jr. NS	1.00	2.50
Kurt Busch NS	.25	.60
Carl Edwards NS	.60	1.50
Kasey Kahne NS	1.00	2.50
Denny Hamlin NS	.75	2.00
Tony Stewart NS	.60	1.50
Kyle Busch NS	.50	1.25
Kevin Harvick NS	.60	1.50
Delana Harvick		
Jimmie Johnson NS	.75	2.00
Matt Kenseth NS	.75	2.00
Jimmie Johnson U	.75	2.00
Kevin Harvick U	.60	1.50
Denny Hamlin U	.75	2.00
Kurt Busch U	.25	.60
Jeff Gordon U	1.00	2.50
Kasey Kahne U	1.00	2.50
Greg Biffle U	.30	.75
Tony Stewart U	.60	1.50
Kyle Busch U	.50	1.25
Matt Kenseth U	.75	2.00
Dale Earnhardt Jr. U	1.00	2.50
Jeff Burton U	.25	.60
Matt Kenseth TT	.75	2.00
Jimmie Johnson TT	.75	2.00
Kevin Harvick TT	.60	1.50
Kyle Busch TT	.50	1.25
Denny Hamlin TT	.75	2.00
Dale Earnhardt Jr. TT	1.00	2.50
Mark Martin TT	.60	1.50
Jeff Burton TT	.25	.60
Jeff Gordon TT	1.00	2.50
Kasey Kahne TT	1.00	2.50
Schedule	.10	.25
Juan Pablo Montoya RC	2.00	5.00
Jimmie Johnson CL	.75	2.00
Cup Chase Top 10	4.00	10.00
Santa Happy Holidays	2.50	6.00

2007 Press Pass Blue

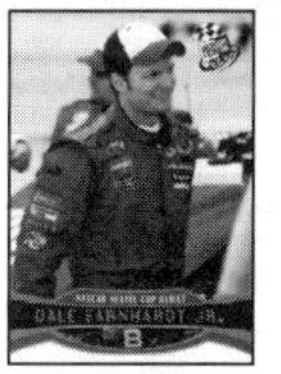

120-card set parallel the base set. It has blue highlights and the card numbers contain a "B" . These were found one per pack in 2007 Press Hobby packs.

PLETE SET (120)	25.00	60.00
JE: .6X TO 1.5X BASE		
TED ODDS 1 PER HOBBY PACK		

2007 Press Pass Gold

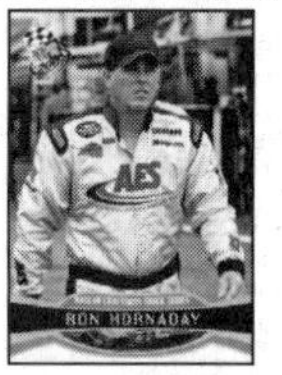

120-card set parallel the base set. It has gold highlights and the card numbers contain a "G" . These were found one per pack in 2007 Press Retail packs.

COMPLETE SET (120)	40.00	80.00
*GOLD: 1.2X TO 3X BASE		

2007 Press Pass Platinum

This 120-card set parallels the base set. They have platinum holofoil highlights and the card numbers contain a "P" prefix. These were found in Hobby packs of 2007 Press Pass. Each card was serial numbered to 100.

*PLATINUM: 4X TO 10X BASE

2007 Press Pass Previews

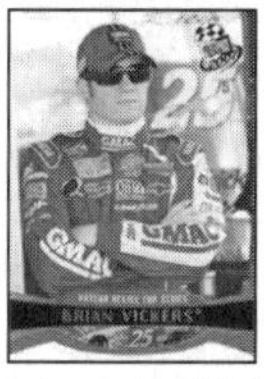

This 56-card set was a partial parallel to the base set. The cards were sold on eBay as a preview to the 2007 Press Pass sets' release. These cards had green foil highlight and were serial numbered to 5 or 1. Cards EB1-EB45 and EB119 were numbered to 5, while cards EB108-EB118 were 1 of 1's.

STATED PRINT RUN (EB1-EB45,EB119) 5 SERIAL #'d SETS
STATED PRINT RUN (EB1-EB108,EB117) 1 SERIAL #'d SET
NOT PRICED DUE TO SCARCITY

2007 Press Pass Autographs

Inserted at a stated rate of one in 84 hobby and one in 96 retail, these 40 signed cards feature a mix of today's NASCAR Nextel Cup drivers as well as Busch Series and Craftsman Truck Series drivers. Some of these cards were available in packs of 2007 Press Pass and 2007 Press Pass Eclipse or both, and are tagged as such.

1 Greg Biffle NC P	10.00	25.00
2 Dave Blaney NC P	6.00	15.00
3 Clint Bowyer NC P	12.50	30.00
4 Kurt Busch NC P	12.50	30.00
5 Kyle Busch	20.00	50.00
6 Jeff Burton NC P	8.00	20.00
7 Terry Cook CTS P	6.00	15.00
8 Rick Crawford CTS P	6.00	15.00
9 Erin Crocker CTS P	15.00	40.00
10 Erik Darnell CTS P	5.00	12.00
12 Carl Edwards NC P	15.00	40.00
13 Jeff Gordon	75.00	150.00
14 David Green NBS P	6.00	15.00
16 Denny Hamlin NC P	30.00	60.00
17 Kevin Harvick NC P	12.50	30.00
18 Ron Hornaday CTS P	6.00	15.00
22 Matt Kenseth NC P	15.00	40.00
23 Todd Kluever NBS P	10.00	25.00
24 Bobby Labonte NC P	15.00	40.00
25 Terry Labonte NC P	15.00	40.00
26 Burney Lamar NBS P	6.00	15.00
27 Bill Lester CTS P	8.00	20.00
28 Sterling Marlin NC P	10.00	25.00
29 Mark Martin NC P	30.00	60.00
30 Jamie McMurray NC P	10.00	25.00
31 Casey Mears NC P	10.00	25.00
33 Joe Nemechek NC P	8.00	20.00
34 Ryan Newman NC P	15.00	30.00
35 Danny O'Quinn NBS P	6.00	15.00
36 David Ragan CTS P	8.00	20.00
37 Tony Raines NC P	6.00	15.00
38 Scott Riggs NC P	5.00	12.00
39 Johnny Sauter NBS P	8.00	20.00
40 Mike Skinner CTS P	6.00	15.00
41 Regan Smith NBS P	6.00	15.00
42 Reed Sorenson NC P	12.50	30.00
43 Tony Stewart NC P	30.00	80.00
44 David Stremme NC P	8.00	20.00
45 Martin Truex Jr. NC P	15.00	40.00
46 Brian Vickers NC P	10.00	25.00
47 Steve Wallace NBS P	12.50	30.00
48 Jon Wood NBS P	5.00	12.00

2007 Press Pass Autographs Press Plates Black

This 26-card set featured the press plates used to make the cards. Each plate was signed by the driver pictured on the card front. The backs had a sticker with the description and the plate color. Each of these plates were 1 of 1's.

1 Clint Bowyer NC
2 Erin Crocker CTS
3 David Green NBS
4 Denny Hamlin NC
5 Kevin Harvick NC
6 Ron Hornaday CTS
7 Matt Kenseth NC
8 Todd Kluever NBS
9 Bobby Labonte NC
10 Terry Labonte NC
11 Burney Lamar NBS
12 Bill Lester CTS
13 Sterling Marlin NC
14 Mark Martin NC
15 Casey Mears NC
16 Joe Nemechek NC
17 Danny O'Quinn NBS
18 Tony Raines NC
19 Johnny Sauter NBS
20 Mike Skinner CTS
21 Regan Smith NBS
22 Reed Sorenson NC
23 Tony Stewart NC
24 Martin Truex Jr. NC
25 Brian Vickers NC
26 Jon Wood NBS

2007 Press Pass Autographs Press Plates Cyan

This 26-card set featured the press plates used to make the cards. Each plate was signed by the driver pictured on the card front. The backs had a sticker with the description and the plate color. Each of these plates were 1 of 1's.

1 Clint Bowyer NC
2 Erin Crocker CTS
3 David Green NBS
4 Denny Hamlin NC
5 Kevin Harvick NC
6 Ron Hornaday CTS
7 Matt Kenseth NC
8 Todd Kluever NBS
9 Bobby Labonte NC
10 Terry Labonte NC
11 Burney Lamar NBS
12 Bill Lester CTS
13 Sterling Marlin NC
14 Mark Martin NC
15 Casey Mears NC
16 Paul Menard NC
17 Joe Nemechek NC
18 Danny O'Quinn NBS
19 Tony Raines NC
20 Johnny Sauter NBS
21 Mike Skinner CTS
22 Regan Smith NBS
23 Reed Sorenson NC
24 Tony Stewart NC
25 Martin Truex Jr. NC
26 Brian Vickers NC
27 Jon Wood NBS

2007 Press Pass Autographs Press Plates Magenta

This 26-card set featured the press plates used to make the cards. Each plate was signed by the driver pictured on the card front. The backs had a sticker with the description and the plate color. Each of these plates were 1 of 1's.

1 Clint Bowyer NC
2 Erin Crocker CTS
3 Carl Edwards NC
4 David Green NBS
5 Denny Hamlin NC
6 Kevin Harvick NC
7 Ron Hornaday CTS
8 Kasey Kahne
9 Matt Kenseth NC
10 Todd Kluever NBS
11 Bobby Labonte NC
12 Terry Labonte NC
13 Burney Lamar NBS
14 Bill Lester CTS
15 Sterling Marlin NC
16 Mark Martin NC
17 Casey Mears NC
18 Joe Nemechek NC
19 Danny O'Quinn NBS
20 Tony Raines NC
21 Johnny Sauter NBS
22 Mike Skinner CTS
23 Regan Smith NBS
24 Reed Sorenson NC
25 Tony Stewart NC
26 Martin Truex Jr. NC
27 Brian Vickers NC
28 Jon Wood NBS

2007 Press Pass Autographs Press Plates Yellow

This 26-card set featured the press plates used to make the cards. Each plate was signed by the driver pictured on the card front. The backs had a sticker with the description and the plate color. Each of these plates were 1 of 1's.

40 Carl Edwards
1 Greg Biffle NC
2 Clint Bowyer NC
3 Erin Crocker CTS

4 David Green NBS
5 Denny Hamlin NC
6 Kevin Harvick NC
7 Ron Hornaday CTS
8 Matt Kenseth NC
9 Todd Kluever NBS
10 Bobby Labonte NC
11 Terry Labonte NC
12 Burney Lamar NBS
13 Bill Lester CTS
14 Sterling Marlin NC
15 Mark Martin NC
16 Casey Mears NC
17 Joe Nemechek NC
18 Danny O'Quinn NBS
19 Tony Raines NC
20 Johnny Sauter NBS
21 Mike Skinner CTS
22 Regan Smith NBS
23 Reed Sorenson NC
24 Tony Stewart NC
25 Martin Truex Jr. NC
26 Brian Vickers NC
27 Jon Wood NBS

2007 Press Pass Burning Rubber Autographs

This 3-card set was a partial parallel to the base Burning Rubber set, with the addition of signatures. Each card was serial numbered to the driver's door number. These rare cards were only found in Hobby packs of 2007 Press Pass.

SOME CARDS NOT PRICED DUE TO SCARCITY		
BRS-JJ Jimmie Johnson/48	75.00	150.00
BRS-KB Kurt Busch/2		
BRS-KH Kevin Harvick/29	100.00	200.00
BRS-MK Matt Kenseth/17		
BRS-TS Tony Stewart/20		

2007 Press Pass Burning Rubber Drivers

This 18-card set featured swatches of race-used, race-win, tires. Each card was noted as to which race the tires were used. They were inserted in packs of 2007 Press Pass Hobby packs at a rate of one in 112, and they were serial numbered to 75 copies. Each card carried a "BRD" prefix to its card number.

BRD1 Jimmie Johnson Daytona 2-19	20.00	50.00
BRD2 Matt Kenseth California 2-19	20.00	50.00
BRD3 Tony Stewart Martinsville 4-2	20.00	50.00
BRD4 Kasey Kahne Texas 4-9	25.00	60.00
BRD5 Kevin Harvick Phoenix 4-22	25.00	60.00
BRD6 Jimmie Johnson Talladega 5-1	20.00	50.00
BRD7 Dale Earnhardt Jr. Richmond 5-6	30.00	80.00
BRD8 Greg Biffle Darlington 5-13	15.00	40.00
BRD9 Kasey Kahne Charlotte 5-28	25.00	60.00
BRD10 Denny Hamlin Pocono 6-11	20.00	50.00
BRD11 Jeff Gordon Sonoma 6-26	30.00	80.00
BRD12 Tony Stewart Daytona 7-1	20.00	50.00
BRD13 Jeff Gordon Chicago 7-9	30.00	80.00
BRD14 Kyle Busch New Hampshire 7-16	15.00	40.00
BRD15 Denny Hamlin Pocono 7-23	20.00	50.00
BRD16 Jimmie Johnson Indianapolis 8-6	25.00	60.00
BRD17 Kevin Harvick Watkins Glen 8-13	25.00	60.00
BRD18 Jeff Burton Dover 9-24	15.00	40.00

2007 Press Pass Burning Rubber Drivers Gold

This 18-card set featured swatches of race-used, race-win, tires and was a parallel to the base Burning Rubber Drivers set. Each card was noted as to which race the tires were used. They were inserted in packs of 2007 Press Pass Hobby packs and were serial numbered 1 of 1. Each card carried a "BRD" prefix to its card number.

NOT PRICED DUE TO SCARCITY

2007 Press Pass Burning Rubber Team

This 18-card set featured swatches of race-used, race-win, tires and was a parallel to the base Burning Rubber Drivers set. Each card was noted as to which race the tires were used. They were inserted in packs of 2007 Press Pass Retail packs at a rate of one in 112, and were serial numbered to 325. Each card carried a "BRT" prefix to its card number. This Team version was printed with a horizontal view.

*TEAM: .3X TO .8X DRIVERS
STATED PRINT RUN 325 SERIAL #'d SETS

2007 Press Pass Cup Chase

These 18 cards were issued in packs of 2007 Press Pass at a rate of one in 20 hobby, and one in 36 retail packs. There were 17 drivers and 1 field card. If the driver pictured on the front qualified for the Chase, that card was redeemable, along with $3.95 for s&h, for a complete set of 12 of the prize cards. The set included only those drivers that qualified for the Chase. If you had the champion, you were also sent a special memorabilia card of his. The exchange deadline for these was December 31, 2007. Cards that were redeemable are noted below. Redeemed cards were stamped by Press Pass and returned. The cards featured the driver's car on the card front.

EXCHANGE DEADLINE 12/31/2007		
CCR1 Jeff Gordon Winner	15.00	40.00
CCR2 Bobby Labonte	5.00	10.00
CCR3 Kasey Kahne	5.00	10.00
CCR4 Matt Kenseth Winner	12.50	25.00
CCR5 Tony Stewart Winner	12.50	25.00
CCR6 Ryan Newman	5.00	10.00
CCR7 Jamie McMurray	5.00	10.00
CCR8 J.Johnson Winner Champ	40.00	80.00
CCR9 Greg Biffle	5.00	10.00
CCR10 Jeff Burton Winner	7.50	15.00
CCR11 Martin Truex Jr. Winner	12.50	25.00
CCR12 Denny Hamlin Winner	12.50	25.00
CCR13 Kurt Busch Winner	12.50	25.00
CCR14 Dale Earnhardt Jr.	6.00	12.00
CCR15 Kyle Busch Winner	12.50	25.00
CCR16 Kevin Harvick Winner	12.50	25.00
CCR17 Carl Edwards Winner	12.50	25.00
CCR18 Field Card Winner	12.50	25.00

2007 Press Pass Race Day

This 12-card set was inserted into packs of 2007 Press Pass at a rate of one in six in both Hobby and Retail packs. The cards carried a "RD" prefix for their card numbers.

COMPLETE SET (12)	15.00	40.00
STATED ODDS 1:6		
RD1 Jeff Gordon	2.50	6.00
RD2 Dale Jarrett	1.25	3.00
RD3 Tony Stewart	1.50	4.00
RD4 Kevin Harvick	1.50	4.00
RD5 Jimmie Johnson	2.00	5.00
RD6 Dale Earnhardt Jr.	2.50	6.00
RD7 Denny Hamlin	2.00	5.00
RD8 Jeff Burton	.60	1.50
RD9 Mark Martin	1.50	4.00
RD10 Kasey Kahne	2.50	6.00
RD11 Martin Truex Jr.	1.50	4.00
RD12 Bobby Labonte	1.25	3.00

2007 Press Pass Snapshots

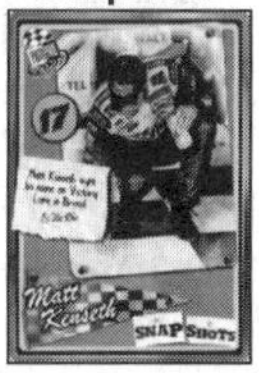

This 36-card insert set was found in packs of 2007 Press Pass. The cards were inserted at a rate of one in two packs.

COMPLETE SET (36)	12.50	25.00
STATED ODDS 1:2		
SN1 Greg Biffle	.50	1.25
SN2 Dave Blaney	.25	.60
SN3 Jeff Burton	.40	1.00
SN4 Kurt Busch	.40	1.00
SN5 Dale Earnhardt Jr.	1.50	4.00
SN6 Carl Edwards	1.00	2.50
SN7 Jeff Gordon	1.50	4.00
SN8 Robby Gordon	.25	.60
SN9 Jeff Green	.25	.60
SN10 Denny Hamlin	1.25	3.00
SN11 Kevin Harvick	1.00	2.50
SN12 Dale Jarrett	.75	2.00
SN13 Jimmie Johnson	1.25	3.00
SN14 Kasey Kahne	1.50	4.00
SN15 Matt Kenseth	1.25	3.00
SN16 Bobby Labonte	.75	2.00
SN17 Terry Labonte	.60	1.50
SN18 Sterling Marlin	.60	1.50
SN19 Mark Martin	1.00	2.50
SN20 Jamie McMurray	.60	1.50
SN21 Joe Nemechek	.25	.60
SN22 Tony Raines	.25	.60
SN23 Scott Riggs	.40	1.00
SN24 Ken Schrader	.25	.60
SN25 Reed Sorenson	.75	2.00
SN26 Tony Stewart	1.00	2.50
SN27 Martin Truex Jr.	1.00	2.50
SN28 David Green	.25	.60
SN29 Paul Menard	.50	1.25
SN30 Danny O'Quinn	.60	1.50
SN31 Regan Smith	.25	.60
SN32 Steve Wallace	.75	2.00
SN33 Jon Wood	.25	.60
SN34 Rick Crawford	.25	.60
SN35 Erik Darnell	.60	1.50
SN36 Ron Hornaday CL	.25	.60

2007 Press Pass Velocity

This 9-card set was inserted into packs of 2007 Press Pass at a rate of one in 12 packs. Each card carried a "V" prefix for its card number.

COMPLETE SET (9)	15.00	40.00
STATED ODDS 1:12		
V1 Kasey Kahne	2.50	6.00
V2 Jimmie Johnson	2.00	5.00
V3 Matt Kenseth	2.00	5.00
V4 Dale Earnhardt Jr.	2.50	6.00
V5 Jeff Gordon	2.50	6.00
V6 Dale Jarrett	1.25	3.00
V7 Jamie McMurray	1.00	2.50
V8 Tony Stewart	1.50	4.00
V9 Denny Hamlin	2.00	5.00

2007 Press Pass K-Mart

This 6-card insert set was available in 2-card bonus packs in the 2007 Press Pass blaster boxes found at K-Mart. Each card carried a "C" suffix for its card number.

COMPLETE SET (6)	15.00	40.00
DE-C Dale Earnhardt Jr.	4.00	10.00
JG-C Jeff Gordon	4.00	10.00
JJ-C Jimmie Johnson	3.00	8.00
KH-C Kevin Harvick	2.50	6.00
KK-C Kasey Kahne	4.00	10.00
TS-C Tony Stewart	2.50	6.00

2007 Press Pass Target

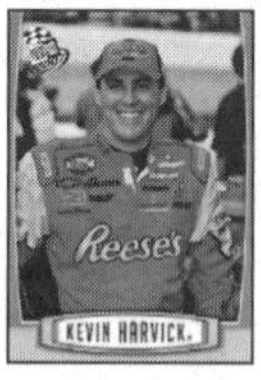

This 6-card insert set was available in 2-card bonus packs in the 2007 Press Pass blaster boxes found at Target. Each card carried a "B" suffix for its card number.

COMPLETE SET (6)	12.50	30.00
DE-B Dale Earnhardt Jr.	4.00	10.00
JG-B Jeff Gordon	4.00	10.00
JJ-B Jimmie Johnson	3.00	8.00
KH-B Kevin Harvick	2.50	6.00
KK-B Kasey Kahne	4.00	10.00
TS-B Tony Stewart	2.50	6.00

2007 Press Pass Target Race Win Tires

This 9-card set featured swatches of race-used, race-win tires. Each card noted the date and location of the victory. These carried a "RW" prefix for the card number. These were only available inside the 2007 Press Pass box blaster packs from Target. Each card was serial numbered to 50.

RW1 Jimmie Johnson Daytona 2-19	40.00	80.00
RW2 Kevin Harvick Phoenix 4-22	30.00	60.00
RW3 Dale Earnhardt Jr. Richmond 5-6	50.00	100.00
RW4 Denny Hamlin Pocono 6-11	25.00	60.00
RW5 Kasey Kahne Michigan 6-18	50.00	100.00
RW6 Jeff Gordon Sonoma 6-26	50.00	100.00
RW7 Tony Stewart Daytona 7-1	25.00	60.00
RW8 Jeff Gordon Chicago 7-9	50.00	100.00
RW9 Matt Kenseth Bristol 8-26	40.00	80.00

2007 Press Pass Wal-Mart

This 6-card insert set was available in 2-card bonus packs in the 2007 Press Pass blaster boxes found at Wal-Mart. Each card carried an "A" suffix for its card number.

COMPLETE SET (6)	12.50	30.00
DE-A Dale Earnhardt Jr.	3.00	8.00
JG-A Jeff Gordon	3.00	8.00
JJ-A Jimmie Johnson	2.50	6.00
KH-A Kevin Harvick	2.00	5.00
KK-A Kasey Kahne	3.00	8.00
TS-A Tony Stewart	2.00	5.00

2007 Press Pass Wal-Mart Autographs

This 6-card autograph set was randomly inserted in blaster box packs found only at Wal-Mart. The cards were serial numbered to 50.

STATED PRINT RUN 50 SERIAL #'d SETS

CE Carl Edwards	75.00	125.00
KH Kevin Harvick	40.00	80.00
MK Matt Kenseth		
MM Mark Martin	75.00	125.00
MT Martin Truex Jr.	40.00	80.00
TS Tony Stewart	60.00	120.00

2008 Press Pass

COMPLETE SET (120)	12.50	30.00
STATED ODDS 0 CARD 1:72		
STATED ODDS 00 CARD 1:72		
WAX BOX HOBBY (28)	60.00	100.00
WAX BOX RETAIL (24)	50.00	75.00
1 Jeff Gordon	1.25	3.00
2 Tony Stewart	1.00	2.50
3 Denny Hamlin	.75	2.00
4 Matt Kenseth	.75	2.00
5 Carl Edwards	.75	2.00
6 Jimmie Johnson	1.00	2.50
7 Jeff Burton	.30	.75
8 Kyle Busch	.60	1.50
9 Clint Bowyer	.60	1.50
10 Kevin Harvick	.60	1.50
11 Martin Truex Jr.	.60	1.50
12 Kurt Busch	.50	1.25
13 Dale Earnhardt Jr.	1.50	4.00
14 Ryan Newman	.50	1.25
15 Greg Biffle	.40	1.00
16 Casey Mears	.30	.75
17 Bobby Labonte	.50	1.25
18 Juan Pablo Montoya	1.25	3.00
19 Jamie McMurray	.40	1.00
20 J.J. Yeley	.40	1.00
21 Mark Martin	.75	2.00
22 Kasey Kahne	1.00	2.50
23 David Ragan	.40	1.00
24 Elliott Sadler	.40	1.00
25 Jeff Green	.20	.50
26 Ricky Rudd	.50	1.25
27 Tony Raines	.20	.50
28 Johnny Sauter	.30	.75
29 Dave Blaney	.20	.50
30 Paul Menard	.40	1.00
31 Scott Riggs	.30	.75
32 Kyle Petty	.30	.75
33 Brian Vickers	.40	1.00
34 Dale Jarrett	.75	2.00
35 Ken Schrader	.20	.50
36 Michael Waltrip	.40	1.00
37 Carl Edwards NBS	.75	2.00
38 Stephen Leicht NBS	.30	.75
39 Marcos Ambrose NBS	1.25	3.00
40 Scott Wimmer NBS	.25	.60
41 Steve Wallace NBS	.60	1.50
42 Todd Kluever NBS	.60	1.50
43 Kelly Bires NBS	.40	1.00
44 Sam Hornish Jr. NBS	.75	2.00
45 Cale Gale NBS	.20	.50
46 Mike Skinner CTS	.20	.50
47 Ron Hornaday CTS	.30	.75
48 Todd Bodine CTS	.20	.50
49 Rick Crawford CTS	.20	.50
50 Jack Sprague CTS	.20	.50
51 Erik Darnell CTS	.30	.75
52 T.J. Bell CTS	.30	.75
53 Travis Kvapil CTS	.30	.75
54 Joey Clanton CTS RC	.60	1.50
55 Buddy Baker	.30	.75
56 Rusty Wallace	.60	1.50
57 Tim Flock	.20	.50
58 Lee Petty	.30	.75
59 Jack Ingram	.20	.50
60 Tim Richmond	.30	.75
61 Dale Earnhardt	2.00	5.00
62 Glen Wood	.20	.50
63 Rex White	.20	.50
64 Jeff Gordon's Car BFS	.50	1.25
65 Martin Truex Jr.'s Car BFS	.25	.60
66 Dale Jarrett's Car BFS	.30	.75
67 Jeff Burton's Car BFS	.12	.30
68 Jimmie Johnson's Car BFS	.40	1.00
69 Jamie McMurray's Car BFS	.15	.40
70 Mark Martin's Car BFS	.30	.75
71 Ricky Rudd's Car BFS	.20	.50
72 Ryan Newman's Car BFS	.20	.50
73 Juan Pablo Montoya NS	1.25	3.00
74 David Gilliland Ricky Rudd NS	.50	1.25
75 Kevin Harvick's Car Mark Martin's Car NS	.30	.75
76 Kevin Harvick NS	.60	1.50
77 Casey Mears NS	.30	.75
78 Juan Pablo Montoya NS	1.25	3.00
79 Martin Truex Jr. NS	.60	1.50
80 Juan Pablo Montoya Kevin Harvick NS	.60	1.50
81 Jimmie Johnson NS	1.00	2.50
82 Juan Pablo Montoya RR	1.25	3.00
83 David Ragan RR	.40	1.00
84 Paul Menard RR	.40	1.00
85 David Reutimann RR	.50	1.25
86 David Ragan NBS RR	.40	1.00
87 Marcos Ambrose RR	1.25	3.00
88 Kevin Harvick's Car U	.25	.60
89 Juan Pablo Montoya's Car U	.50	1.25
90 Martin Truex Jr.'s Car U	.25	.60
91 Jamie McMurray's Car U	.15	.40
92 Jeff Gordon's Car U	.50	1.25
93 Jeff Burton's Car U	.12	.30
94 Kyle Busch's Car U	.25	.60
95 Tony Stewart's Car U	.40	1.00
96 Dale Earnhardt Jr. First Cup Start	1.50	4.00
97 Dale Earnhardt Jr. Rookie All-Star	1.50	4.00
98 Dale Earnhardt Jr. First Cup Win	1.50	4.00
99 Dale Earnhardt Jr. Best Finish	1.50	4.00
100 Dale Earnhardt Jr. Most Wins	1.50	4.00
101 Dale Earnhardt Jr. Daytona Win	1.50	4.00
102 Dale Earnhardt Jr. Talladega	1.50	4.00
103 Dale Earnhardt Jr. Daytona	1.50	4.00
104 Dale Earnhardt Jr. AMP	1.50	4.00
105 Dale Earnhardt Jr. National Guard	1.50	4.00
106 Dale Earnhardt Jr. HMS	1.50	4.00
107 Jimmie Johnson Top 12	1.00	2.50
108 Jeff Gordon Top 12	1.25	3.00
109 Tony Stewart Top 12	1.00	2.50
110 Carl Edwards Top 12	.75	2.00
111 Kurt Busch Top 12	.50	1.25
112 Denny Hamlin Top 12	.75	2.00
113 Martin Truex Jr. Top 12	.60	1.50
114 Matt Kenseth Top 12	.75	2.00
115 Kyle Busch Top 12	.60	1.50
116 Jeff Burton Top 12	.30	.75
117 Kevin Harvick Top 12	.60	1.50
118 Clint Bowyer Top 12	.60	1.50
119 Schedule	.12	.30
120 Michael Waltrip CL	.40	1.00
00 Cup Chase Matt Kenseth Tony Stewart Jeff Gordon Jimmie Johnson Denny Hamlin Kurt Busch Kevin Harvick Carl Edwards Kyle Busch Martin Truex Jr. Jeff Burton Clint Bowyer	4.00	10.00
0 Santa Claus	2.50	6.00

2008 Press Pass Blue

COMPLETE SET (120)	25.00	60.00
*BLUE: 1.2X TO 3X BASE		
STATED ODDS 1 PER RETAIL PACK		

2008 Press Pass Gold

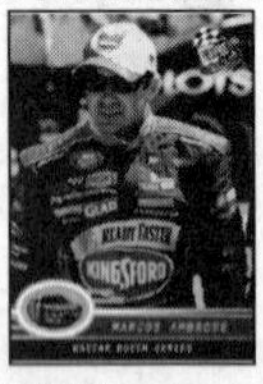

COMPLETE SET (120)
*GOLD: .8X TO 2X BASE
STATED ODDS 1 PER HOBBY PACK

2008 Press Pass Platinum

*PLATINUM: 4X TO 10X BASE
STATED PRINT RUN 100 SERIAL #'d SETS

2008 Press Pass Previews

EB1-EB36,EB96-EB103 STATED PRINT RUN 5 SERIAL #'d SETS
EB107-EB118 STATED PRINT RUN 1 SERIAL #'d SET
NOT PRICED DUE TO SCARCITY

2008 Press Pass Autographs

Gordon was EXCH

STATED ODDS 1:84 H, 1:96 R PP '08		
STATED ODDS 1:20 H, 1:96 R ECLIPSE		
1 A.J. Allmendinger NC P/E	8.00	20.00
2 Aric Almirola NBS P/E	6.00	15.00
3 Marcos Ambrose NBS P/E	15.00	40.00
4 T.J. Bell CTS E	5.00	12.00
5 Greg Biffle NC P/E	12.50	30.00
6 Kelly Bires NBS P/E	8.00	20.00
7 Dave Blaney NC P	8.00	20.00
8 Clint Bowyer NC P/E	15.00	40.00
9 Kurt Busch NC E	15.00	40.00
10 Kyle Busch NC P/E	20.00	50.00
11 Joey Clanton CTS P/E	6.00	15.00
12 Rick Crawford CTS E	6.00	15.00
13 Erik Darnell CTS E	8.00	20.00
14 Dale Earnhardt Jr. NC P/E	75.00	150.00
15 Jeff Gordon NC P/E	125.00	200.00
16 Denny Hamlin NC P/E	20.00	50.00
17 Kevin Harvick NC P/E	15.00	40.00
18 Ron Hornaday CTS P/E	6.00	15.00
19 Dale Jarrett NC P/E	20.00	40.00
20 Jimmie Johnson NC EXCH P	40.00	80.00
21 Kasey Kahne NC P/E	40.00	80.00
22 Matt Kenseth NC P/E	25.00	50.00
23 Todd Kluever NBS P/E	8.00	20.00
24 Travis Kvapil CTS E	6.00	15.00
25 Bobby Labonte NC P/E	15.00	30.00
26 Mark Martin NC P/E	20.00	50.00
27 Casey Mears NC P/E	10.00	25.00
28 Paul Menard NC P/E	10.00	25.00
29 Ryan Newman NC P/E	15.00	30.00
30 David Ragan NC P/E	8.00	20.00
31 Tony Raines NC P/E	6.00	15.00
32 Scott Riggs NC P/E	6.00	15.00
33 Elliott Sadler NC P/E	10.00	25.00
34 Johnny Sauter NBS E	6.00	15.00
35 Ken Schrader NC P/E	6.00	15.00
36 Mike Skinner CTS E	6.00	15.00
37 Regan Smith NC P/E	6.00	15.00
38 Reed Sorenson NC E	10.00	25.00
39 Jack Sprague CTS P/E	5.00	12.00
40 Tony Stewart NC EXCH P	60.00	120.00
41 Martin Truex Jr. NC P/E	15.00	30.00
42 Brian Vickers NC P/E	8.00	20.00
43 Michael Waltrip NC P/E	10.00	25.00
44 Scott Wimmer NBS P/E	8.00	20.00
45 Jon Wood NBS P/E	6.00	15.00
46 J.J. Yeley NC P/E	8.00	20.00

2008 Press Pass Autographs Press Plates Black

CARDS MARKED P AVAIL. IN '08 PP
CARDS MARKED E AVAIL. IN ECLIPSE
STATED PRINT RUN 1 SERIAL #'d SET
NOT PRICED DUE TO SCARCITY

2008 Press Pass Autographs Press Plates Cyan

CARDS MARKED P AVAIL. IN '08 PP
CARDS MARKED E AVAIL. IN ECLIPSE
STATED PRINT RUN 1 SERIAL #'d SET
NOT PRICED DUE TO SCARCITY

2008 Press Pass Autographs Press Plates Magenta

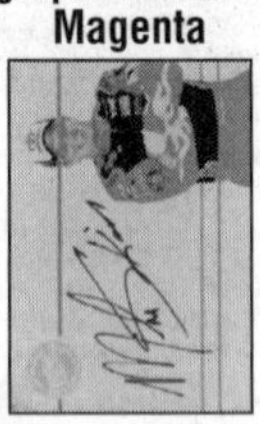

CARDS MARKED P AVAIL. IN '08 PP
CARDS MARKED E AVAIL. IN ECLIPSE
STATED PRINT RUN 1 SERIAL #'d SET
NOT PRICED DUE TO SCARCITY

2008 Press Pass Autographs Press Plates Yellow

CARDS MARKED P AVAIL. IN '08 PP
CARDS MARKED E AVAIL. IN ECLIPSE
STATED PRINT RUN 1 SERIAL #'d SET
NOT PRICED DUE TO SCARCITY

2008 Press Pass Burning Rubber Autographs

SERIAL #'d TO DRIVER'S DOOR #		
SOME NOT PRICED DUE TO SCARCITY		
BR-CM Casey Mears/25	60.00	120.00
BR-DE Dale Earnhardt Jr./8		
BR-DH Denny Hamlin/11		
BR-KB Kyle Busch/5		
BR-KH Kevin Harvick/29	100.00	175.00

2008 Press Pass Burning Rubber Drivers

STATED ODDS 1:112		
STATED PRINT RUN 60 SERIAL #'d SETS		
BRD1 Kevin Harvick Daytona	20.00	40.00
BRD2 Matt Kenseth California	20.00	40.00
BRD3 Jimmie Johnson Las Vegas	15.00	40.00
BRD4 Jimmie Johnson Atlanta	15.00	40.00
BRD5 Kyle Busch Bristol	20.00	40.00
BRD6 Jimmie Johnson Martinsville	15.00	40.00
BRD7 Jeff Burton Texas	15.00	30.00
BRD8 Jeff Gordon Phoenix	30.00	60.00
BRD9 Jeff Gordon Talladega	30.00	60.00
BRD10 Jimmie Johnson Richmond May	15.00	40.00
BRD11 Casey Mears Charlotte	12.50	25.00
BRD12 Martin Truex Jr. Dover	15.00	30.00
BRD13 Jeff Gordon Pocono	30.00	60.00
BRD14 Carl Edwards Michigan	20.00	40.00
BRD15 J.Montoya Infineon	20.00	40.00
BRD16 Denny Hamlin New Hampshire	20.00	40.00
BRD17 Jamie McMurray Daytona	12.50	25.00
BRD18 Tony Stewart Chicago	20.00	40.00
BRD19 Tony Stewart Indianapolis	20.00	40.00
BRD20 Kurt Busch Pocono	12.50	25.00
BRD21 Tony Stewart Watkins	20.00	40.00
BRD22 Kurt Busch Mich.	12.50	25.00
BRD23 Carl Edwards Bristol	20.00	40.00
BRD24 Jimmie Johnson Cal.	15.00	40.00
BRD25 Jimmie Johnson Richmond September	15.00	40.00

2008 Press Pass Burning Rubber Drivers Gold

STATED PRINT RUN 1 SERIAL #'d SET
NOT PRICED DUE TO SCARCITY

2008 Press Pass Burning Rubber Drivers Prime Cuts

*PRIME CUTS: 1.2 X TO 3X DRIVERS
STATED PRINT RUN 25 SERIAL #'d SETS

2008 Press Pass Burning Rubber Teams

*TEAMS: .3X TO .8X DRIVERS
STATED ODDS 1:
STATED PRINT RUN 175 SERIAL #'d SETS

2008 Press Pass Cup Chase

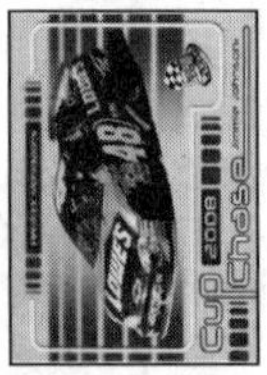

COMPLETE SET (18)	75.00	150.00
STATED ODDS 1:28 H, 1:36 R		
EXCHANGE DEADLINE 12/31/2008		
CC1 Ryan Newman	5.00	10.00
CC2 Matt Kenseth	7.50	15.00
CC3 Jeff Gordon	20.00	40.00
CC4 Dale Earnhardt Jr.	25.00	50.00
CC5 Denny Hamlin	12.50	25.00
CC6 Kevin Harvick	7.50	15.00
CC7 Clint Bowyer	10.00	20.00
CC8 Martin Truex Jr.	10.00	20.00
CC9 Juan Pablo Montoya	7.50	15.00
CC10 Jamie McMurray	5.00	10.00
CC11 Tony Stewart	12.50	25.00
CC12 Jeff Burton	6.00	120.00
CC13 Kasey Kahne	7.50	15.00
CC14 Jimmie Johnson	15.00	30.00
CC15 Carl Edwards	7.50	15.00
CC16 Kurt Busch	6.00	12.00
CC17 Greg Biffle	6.00	12.00
CC18 Field Card	10.00	20.00

2008 Press Pass Race Day

COMPLETE SET (12)	15.00	30.00
COMMON DRIVERS	.25	.60
SEMISTARS	.40	1.00
UNLISTED STARS	.60	1.50
STATED ODDS 1:6		
RD1 Tony Stewart	1.25	3.00
RD2 Ryan Newman	.60	1.50
RD3 Martin Truex Jr.	.75	2.00
RD4 Jeff Gordon	1.50	4.00
RD5 Dale Jarrett	1.00	2.50
RD6 Jeff Burton	.40	1.00
RD7 Brian Vickers	.50	1.25
RD8 Dale Earnhardt Jr.	2.00	5.00
RD9 Matt Kenseth	1.00	2.50
RD10 Juan Pablo Montoya	1.50	4.00
RD11 Carl Edwards	1.00	2.50
RD12 Michael Waltrip	.50	1.25

2008 Press Pass Slideshow

COMPLETE SET (36)	15.00	30.00
COMMON DRIVERS	.20	.50
SEMISTARS	.30	.75
UNLISTED STARS	.50	1.25
STATED ODDS 1:2		
SS1 Casey Mears	.30	.75
SS2 Johnny Sauter	.30	.75
SS3 Jeff Burton	.30	.75
SS4 Kyle Petty	.30	.75
SS5 Sam Hornish Jr.	.75	2.00
SS6 Jimmie Johnson	1.00	2.50
SS7 Todd Bodine	.20	.50
SS8 Jeff Green	.20	.50
SS9 T.J. Bell	.30	.75
SS10 Michael Waltrip	.40	1.00
SS11 Tony Raines	.20	.50
SS12 Dale Earnhardt Jr.	1.50	4.00
SS13 Cale Gale	.20	.50
SS14 Mark Martin	.75	2.00
SS15 Jack Sprague	.20	.50
SS16 Ricky Rudd	.50	1.25
SS17 Tony Stewart	1.00	2.50
SS18 Ron Hornaday	.30	.75
SS19 Mike Skinner	.20	.50
SS20 Jamie McMurray	.40	1.00
SS21 Todd Bodine	.20	.50
SS22 Martin Truex Jr.	.60	1.50
SS23 Kelly Bires	.40	1.00
SS24 Scott Riggs	.30	.75
SS25 Ryan Newman	.50	1.25
SS26 Todd Kluever	.60	1.50
SS27 Travis Kvapil	.30	.75
SS28 Elliott Sadler	.40	1.00
SS29 Jack Sprague	.20	.50
SS30 T.J. Bell	.30	.75
SS31 Joey Clanton	.30	.75
SS32 Stephen Leicht	.30	.75
SS33 Ron Hornaday	.30	.75
SS34 Michael Waltrip	.40	1.00
SS35 Scott Wimmer	.25	.60
SS36 Dale Earnhardt Jr.	1.50	4.00

2008 Press Pass Weekend Warriors

COMPLETE SET (9)	15.00	40.00
COMMON DRIVERS	.30	.75
SEMISTARS	.50	1.25
UNLISTED STARS	.80	2.00
STATED ODDS 1:12		
WW1 Jeff Gordon	2.00	5.00
WW2 Tony Stewart	1.50	4.00
WW3 Jamie McMurray	.60	1.50
WW4 Kevin Harvick	1.00	2.50
WW5 Dale Earnhardt Jr.	2.50	6.00
WW6 Jeff Burton	.50	1.25
WW7 Martin Truex Jr.	1.00	2.50
WW8 Jimmie Johnson	1.50	4.00
WW9 Mark Martin	1.25	3.00

2008 Press Pass Target

COMPLETE SET (6)	8.00	20.00
COMMON DRIVERS	.40	1.00
SEMISTARS	.60	1.50
UNLISTED STARS	1.00	2.50
STATED ODDS 2 PER TARGET BLASTER BOX		
DE-B Dale Earnhardt Jr.	3.00	8.00
JG-B Jeff Gordon	2.50	6.00
JJ-B Jimmie Johnson	2.00	5.00
JM-B Juan Pablo Montoya	2.50	6.00
KK-B Kasey Kahne	2.00	5.00
TS-B Tony Stewart	2.00	5.00

2008 Press Pass Target Victory Tires

RANDOMLY INSERTED IN TARGET BLASTER BOX		
STATED PRINT RUN 50 SERIAL #'d SETS		
TT-CE Carl Edwards Bristol	30.00	60.00
TT-DH Denny Hamlin New Hampshire	25.00	50.00
TT-JG Jeff Gordon Talladega	40.00	80.00
TT-JJ Jimmie Johnson Las Vegas	30.00	60.00
TT-JM J.Montoya Infineon	25.00	50.00
TT-KH Kevin Harvick Daytona	25.00	50.00
TT-MK Matt Kenseth California	25.00	50.00
TT-MT Martin Truex Jr. Dover	20.00	40.00
TT-TS Tony Stewart Indianapolis	30.00	60.00

2008 Press Pass Wal-Mart

COMPLETE SET (6)	8.00	20.00
COMMON DRIVERS	.40	1.00
SEMISTARS	.60	1
UNLISTED STARS	1.00	2
STATED ODDS 2 PER WAL-MART BLASTER BO		
DE-A Dale Earnhardt Jr.	3.00	8
JG-A Jeff Gordon	2.50	6
JJ-A Jimmie Johnson	2.00	5
JM-A Juan Pablo Montoya	2.50	6
KK-A Kasey Kahne	2.00	5
TS-A Tony Stewart	2.00	5

2008 Press Pass Wal Mart Autographs

RANDOMLY INSERTED IN WAL-MART BLASTE BOX		
STATED PRINT RUN 50 SERIAL #'d SETS		
1 Dale Earnhardt Jr.		
2 Carl Edwards EXCH	40.00	80
3 Jeff Gordon	125.00	200
4 Denny Hamlin		
5 Kevin Harvick		
6 Jimmie Johnson	60.00	120
7 Matt Kenseth	40.00	80
8 Mark Martin		
9 Tony Stewart EXCH		
10 Martin Truex Jr.	25.00	50

2002 Press Pass Bosc

Primarily available thru Auto Zone Stores, this card set was produced by Press Pass honoring 100-year anniversary of Bosch Spark Pl Although the cards carry a 2001 copyright year set was released in 2002.

COMPLETE SET (4)	3.00	8
1 Ward Burton	.75	2
2 Jeff Burton	.75	2
3 Sterling Marlin	1.25	3
4 Ken Schrader	.75	2

2002 Press Pass Bria Vickers Fan Club

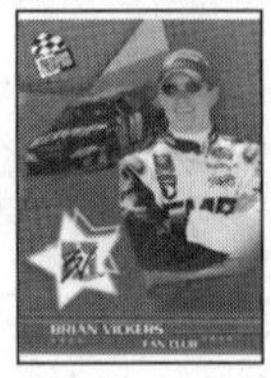

This jumbo sized card was issued to members o Brian Vickers Fan Club in 2002. Press produced the card featuring a Vickers photo o front and a bio on the back. The card is numbered "Series 1" on the back.

SER1 Brian Vickers	7.50	15

1999 Press Pass Brya

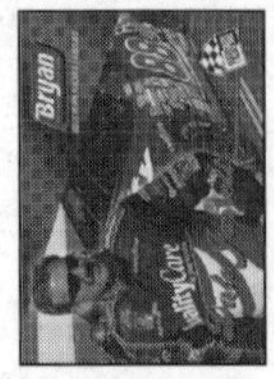

This set was sponsored by Bryan Meat Product produced by Press Pass. Each card include Bryan logo. Complete sets were issued as par sales promotion.

COMPLETE SET (11)	3.00
1 Derrike Cope	.20
2 Geoffery Bodine	.20
3 Todd Bodine	.20
4 David Green	.20
5 Jeff Green	.20
6 Dale Jarrett	.60
7 Jason Jarrett	.20
8 Rusty Wallace	.75
9 Kenny Wallace	.20
10 Darrell Waltrip	.30
11 Michael Waltrip	.30

2006 Press Pass Burnouts

HT1 Kyle Busch	8.00	2
HT2 Jeff Gordon	12.50	3
HT3 Martin Truex Jr	8.00	2
HT4 Kevin Harvick	8.00	2
HT5 Denny Hamlin	8.00	2
HT6 Reed Sorenson	8.00	2
HT7 Carl Edwards	8.00	2
HT8 Clint Bowyer	10.00	2
HT9 J.J. Yeley	6.00	1
HT10 Jimmie Johnson	10.00	2
HT11 Dale Earnhardt Jr.	12.50	3
HT12 Kasey Kahne	8.00	2
HT13 Elliott Sadler	8.00	2
HT14 Mark Martin	8.00	2
HT15 Jeremy Mayfield	6.00	1
HT16 Terry Labonte	6.00	1
HT17 Matt Kenseth	8.00	2
HT18 Ryan Newman	8.00	2

2006 Press Pass Burnouts Holofoil

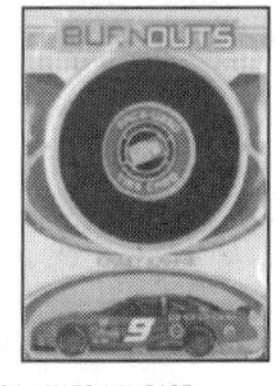

ɪOLOFOIL: .5X TO 1.2X BASE
ʀINT RUN (HT1-HT9) 100 SERIAL #'d SETS
T1-HT9 AVAILABLE IN '06 ECLIPSE
ʀINT RUN (HT10-HT18) 125 SERIAL #'d SETS
T10-HT18 AVAILABLE IN '06 PREMIUM

2007 Press Pass Burnouts

is 6-card set was randomly inserted into retail ster boxes only at Target. Cards 1-3 could only be und in Press Pass Eclipse and cards 4-6 could ly be found in Press Pass Stealth. The cards had a atch of race-used tire and carried a "BO" prefix for card number. The cards were inserted one per x.

)1 Jimmie Johnson 5.00 12.00
)2 Dale Earnhardt Jr. 6.00 15.00
)3 Kevin Harvick 4.00 10.00
)4 Kasey Kahne 6.00 15.00
)5 Tony Stewart 4.00 10.00
)6 Jeff Gordon 6.00 15.00

2007 Press Pass Burnouts Blue

LUE: .8X TO 2X BASE
ATED PRINT RUN 99 SERIAL #'d SETS

2007 Press Pass Burnouts Gold

OLD: .6X TO 1.5X BASE
ATED PRINT RUN 299 SERIAL #'d SETS

2008 Press Pass Burnouts

)MPLETE SET (8)
)1-BO4 ODDS 1 PER TARGET ECLIPSE BLASTER
)X
)5-BO8 ODDS 1 PER TARGET VIP BLASTER BOX
)1 Jeff Gordon 8.00 20.00
)2 Carl Edwards 5.00 12.00
)3 Kevin Harvick 5.00 12.00
)4 Denny Hamlin 5.00 12.00

2008 Press Pass Burnouts Blue

)MPLETE SET (8)
LUE: 1X TO 2.5X BASE
ATED PRINT RUN 99 SERIAL #'d SETS

2008 Press Pass Burnouts Gold

)MPLETE SET (8)
OLD: .6X TO 1.5X BASE
ATED PRINT RUN 299 SERIAL #'d SETS

2000 Press Pass Chef Boyardee

s six-card set was made available one card at a e through insertion in specially marked Chef yardee products. A contest was also conducted t allowed collectors to win signed copies of cards m the set. Those autographs are not cataloged ce they were not certified in any way.

MPLETE SET (6) 8.00 20.00
Bobby Labonte 1.25 3.00
ony Stewart 1.50 4.00
Bobby Labonte 1.25 3.00
ony Stewart 1.50 4.00
oe Gibbs 1.25 3.00
Bobby Labonte 1.50 4.00
Tony Stewart

2001 Press Pass Coca-Cola Racing Family

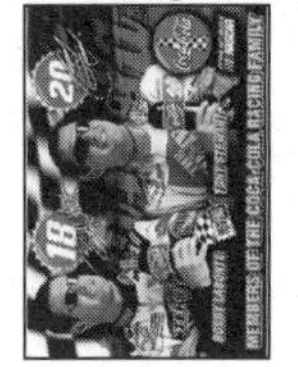

This 3-card set was issued by Press Pass to promote the drivers in the 2001 Coca-Cola Racing Family. Each card features two drivers on the front with a black and white cardback featuring a comprehensive bio of each driver.

COMPLETE SET (3) 3.00 8.00
1 Dale Jarrett 1.00 2.50
Ricky Rudd
2 Bobby Labonte 1.50 4.00
Tony Stewart
3 John Andretti .75 2.00
Kyle Petty

2003 Press Pass Coca-Cola Racing Family

This 12-card set was released in 2003 through Coca-Cola products. Each card was sponsored by Coke, produced by Press Pass, and measures slightly smaller than standard size at 2 1/2" by 3". One card was given away with the purchase of 2 20-ounce bottles of Coca-Cola products at participating stores.

COMPLETE SET (12) 8.00 20.00
COMMON DRIVER .30 .75
SEMISTARS .50 1.25
UNLISTED STARS .60 1.50
1 John Andretti .30 .75
2 Jeff Burton .60 1.50
3 Kurt Busch .60 1.50
4 Bill Elliott .60 1.50
5 Kevin Harvick 1.25 3.00
6 Dale Jarrett 1.25 3.00
7 Bobby Labonte 1.25 3.00
8 Steve Park .50 1.25
9 Kyle Petty .50 1.25
10 Ricky Rudd .75 2.00
11 Tony Stewart 1.50 4.00
12 Michael Waltrip .50 1.25

2003 Press Pass Coca-Cola Racing Family Regional

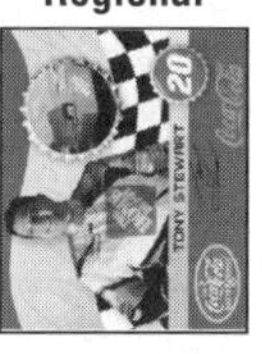

This set was released in 2003 through Coca-Cola products. Each card was sponsored by Coke, produced by Press Pass, and measures slightly smaller than standard size at 2 1/2" by 3". One card was seeded into specially marked cases of Coca-Cola product pimarily in the regional Texas area.

COMPLETE SET (4) 5.00 12.00
1 Bobby Labonte 1.50 4.00
2 Dale Jarrett 1.50 4.00
3 Tony Stewart SP 2.50 6.00
4 Kevin Harvick 1.50 4.00

2003 Press Pass Coca-Cola Racing Family Scratch-off

This 6-card set was released in the Summer of 2003 as the third promotional Press Pass Coca-Cola Family Racing set of the year. The unnumbered cards feature a scratch-off area on the back which gave the collector a chance to win one of several prizes. The contest expired on September 30, 2003.

COMPLETE SET (6) 4.00 10.00
1 John Andretti .50 1.25
2 Kurt Busch 1.00 2.50
3 Kyle Petty .75 2.00
4 Ricky Rudd 1.00 2.50
5 Elliott Sadler .50 1.25
6 Michael Waltrip .75 2.00

2006 Press Pass Collectors Series Making the Show

COMPLETE SET (25)
COM.FACT.SET (26)
MS1 Mark Martin
MS2 Jeff Gordon
MS3 Matt Kenseth
MS4 Ryan Newman
MS5 Denny Hamlin
MS6 Sterling Marlin
MS7 Jimmie Johnson
MS8 J.J. Yeley
MS9 Jamie McMurray
MS10 Terry Labonte
MS11 Carl Edwards
MS12 Dale Jarrett
MS13 Kasey Kahne
MS14 Martin Truex Jr.
MS15 Greg Biffle
MS16 Kevin Harvick
MS17 Tony Stewart
MS18 Jeff Burton
MS19 Kyle Busch
MS20 Scott Riggs
MS21 Ken Schrader
MS22 Bobby Labonte
MS23 Dale Earnhardt Jr.
MS24 Kurt Busch
MS25 Casey Mears CL

2007 Press Pass Collector's Series Box Set

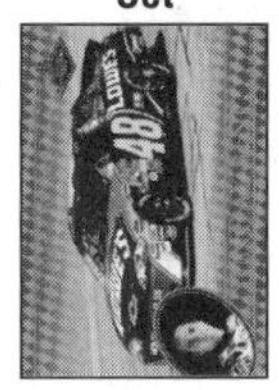

COMPLETE SET (25) 8.00 20.00
COMP.FACT.SET (26) 10.00 25.00
EACH FACT.SET CONTAINS 1 MEM.OR AUTO
SB1 Clint Bowyer .60 1.50
SB2 Jeff Burton .20 .50
SB3 Kurt Busch .20 .50
SB4 Kyle Busch .40 1.00
SB5 Dale Earnhardt Jr. .75 2.00
SB6 Carl Edwards .50 1.25
SB7 Jeff Gordon .75 2.00
SB8 Denny Hamlin .60 1.50
SB9 Kevin Harvick .50 1.25
SB10 Dale Jarrett .40 1.00
SB11 Jimmie Johnson .60 1.50
SB12 Kasey Kahne .75 2.00
SB13 Matt Kenseth .60 1.50
SB14 Bobby Labonte .40 1.00
SB15 Sterling Marlin .30 .75
SB16 Mark Martin .50 1.25
SB17 Jamie McMurray .30 .75
SB18 Juan Pablo Montoya .75 2.00
SB19 Ryan Newman .40 1.00
SB20 Ricky Rudd .30 .75
SB21 Tony Stewart .50 1.25
SB22 David Stremme .40 1.00
SB23 Martin Truex Jr. .50 1.25
SB24 Brian Vickers .30 .75
SB25 Michael Waltrip .20 .50

2003 Press Pass Craftsman

This 30-card set featured Craftsman Truck Series drivers and were available through Craftsman Tools retailers. They were available in packs of 5 cards with the purchase of $35 in Craftsman products. Cards 20-30 are autographed and inserted in packs at a rate of one in 300.

COMP.SET w/o AUTOS (19) 5.00 12.00
1 Ricky Craven .40 1.00
2 Larry Foyt .30 .75
3 Bobby Hamilton .30 .75
4 Rick Crawford .30 .75
5 David Starr .30 .75
6 Dennis Setzer .30 .75
7 Terry Cook .30 .75
8 Bill Lester .30 .75
9 Chad Chaffin .30 .75
10 A.J. Foyt .60 1.50
11 Andy Petree .30 .75
12 Rick Crawford's Truck .20 .50
13 Dennis Setzer's Truck .20 .50
14 Terry Cook's Truck .20 .50
15 2002 Victory Lane .30 .75
Terry Cook
Dennis Setzer
David Starr
16 Winston Cup Series .40 1.00
Ricky Craven
Larry Foyt
17 A.J.Foyt .60 1.50
Larry Foyt
18 Bobby Hamilton Racing .30 .75
Bobby Hamilton
Chad Chaffin
Bill Lester
19 Checklist .20 .50
20 Ricky Craven AU 20.00 40.00
21 Larry Foyt AU 15.00 30.00
22 Bobby Hamilton AU
23 Rick Crawford AU
24 David Starr AU
25 Dennis Setzer AU
26 Terry Cook AU
27 Bill Lester AU
28 Chad Chaffin AU
29 A.J. Foyt AU
30 Andy Petree AU

2001-03 Press Pass Dale Earnhardt

Starting mid-year 2001, this set celebrated the life of Dale Earnhardt with each card featuring an event from the racing life of Earnhardt. Most Press Pass products in 2001 and 2002 included 8 or 9 cards featuring a specific theme with the following insertion ratios for 2001: DE1-DE8 1:48 VIP, DE9-DE16 1:48 Stealth, DE17-DE25 1:48 Optima. The 2002 products included: DE26-DE34 1:72 Press Pass, DE35-DE43 1:72 High Gear, DE35(B)-DE43(B) 1:72 Eclipse, DE44-DE52 1:72 Press Pass Premium, DE53-DE62 1:72 Trackside, DE63-DE70 1:72 VIP, DE71-DE79 1:72 Stealth, DE80-DE88 1:72 Optima, and DE89-DE100 1:72 2003 Press Pass.

COMMON DALE (DE1-DE79) 7.50 15.00
COMMON DALE (DE80-DE100) 10.00 25.00
*CELEBRATION FOILS: 1X TO 2.5X BASIC INS.
CELEB.FOIL PRINT RUN 250 SER.#'d SETS

2003-04 Press Pass 10th Anniversary Earnhardt

This cross brand set was produced by Press Pass in conjunction with their online poll allowing collector's to select their favorite Press Pass Dale Earnhardt cards. They were inserted in packs at a rate of 1:72 in various 2003 and 2004 products: TA1-TA12 inserted in 2003 Press Pass Eclipse, TA13-TA24 2003 Press Pass Premium, TA25-TA37 2003 Press Pass Trackside, TA38-TA50 2003 VIP, TA51-TA63 2003 Press Pass Stealth, TA64-TA76 2003 Press Pass Optima, TA77-TA88 were found in 2004 Press Pass, and TA89-TA100 in 2004 Press Pass Eclipse. The cards are reprints of the originals with a silver foil border and the backs have a description of the card and when it was issued. There is also a gold parallel version of this set.

COMMON EARNHARDT (TA1-TA24) 8.00 20.00
*GOLDS: .8X TO 2X BASIC INSERTS
GOLD PRINT RUN 250 SERIAL #'d SETS

2004 Press Pass Dale Earnhardt Gallery

This cross brand set was produced by Press Pass as a tribute to Dale Earnhardt. They were inserted in packs at a rate of 1:72 in various 2004 and 2005 products: DEG1-DEG9 inserted in 2004 Press Pass Premium, DEG10-DEG18 2004 Press Pass Stealth, DEG19-DEG27 2004 Press Pass Trackside, DEG28-DEG37 2004 VIP, DEG38-DEG45 2004 Press Pass Optima, DEG46-DEG54 2005 Press Pass. The cards are paintings of the Dale with a white border and the backs have a description of the painting. There is also a gold parallel version of this set.

COMMON EARNHARDT 6.00 15.00

2004 Press Pass Dale Earnhardt Gallery Gold

This cross brand set was produced by Press Pass as a tribute to Dale Earnhardt. This is the Gold parallel version which is serial numbered to 200 and randomly inserted into packs of 2004 and 2005 Press Pass products: DEG1-DEG9 inserted in 2004 Press Pass Premium, DEG10-DEG18 2004 Press Pass Stealth, DEG19-DEG27 2004 Press Pass Trackside, DEG28-DEG37 2004 VIP, DEG38-DEG45 2004 Press Pass Optima, DEG46-DEG54 2005 Press Pass. The cards are paintings of the Dale with a white border and the backs have a description of the painting.

*GOLDS: .8X TO 2X
GOLDS STATED PRINT RUN 200 SERIAL #'d SETS

2004 Press Pass Dale Earnhardt The Legacy Victories

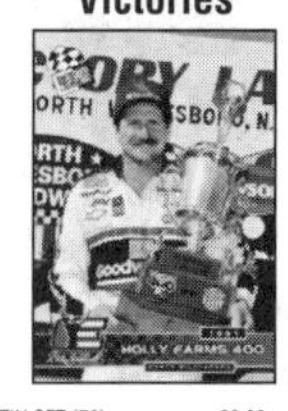

COMP.TIN SET (76) 20.00 40.00
COMPLETE SET (76) 15.00 30.00
COMMON EARNHARDT .50 1.25

2005 Press Pass Dale Earnhardt Victories

COMMON EARNHARDT 4.00 10.00

2007 Press Pass Dale The Movie

COMPLETE SET (50) 15.00 40.00
COMP.FACT.SET (50) 20.00 50.00
1 Dale Earnhardt .60 1.50
Racer's Perspective
2 Dale Earnhardt .60 1.50
Daytona Dominance
3 Dale Earnhardt .60 1.50
Legendary Racer
4 Dale Earnhardt .60 1.50
Son of a Legend
5 Ralph Earnhardt .60 1.50
6 Dale Earnhardt .60 1.50
Picks Up Where His Father Left Off
7 Dale Earnhardt .60 1.50
Darrell Waltrip
8 Dale Earnhardt .60 1.50
Early Cup Racing
9 Dale Earnhardt .60 1.50
First Cup Win
10 Dale Earnhardt .60 1.50
First Championship
11 Dale Earnhardt .60 1.50
Wrangler Sponsorship
12 Dale Earnhardt .60 1.50
Great American Cowboy
13 Dale Earnhardt .60 1.50
One Tough Customer
14 Dale Earnhardt .60 1.50
Richard Childress
15 Dale Earnhardt .60 1.50
16 Wins in 2 Years
16 Dale Earnhardt .60 1.50
Wild Side
17 Danny Chocolate Myers .60 1.50
18 Kelley Earnhardt .60 1.50
Dale Earnhardt Jr.
19 Kerry Earnhardt .60 1.50
20 Dale Earnhardt .60 1.50
Steve Byrnes
21 Dale Earnhardt's Car .60 1.50
Pass in the Grass
22 Dale Earnhardt .60 1.50
Darrell Waltrip Rivalry
23 Dale Earnhardt's Car .60 1.50
Goodwrench Era Begins
24 Dale Earnhardt .60 1.50
Intimidator
25 Dale Earnhardt .60 1.50
Teresa Earnhardt
Four Championships
26 Dale Earnhardt's Car .60 1.50
Brian Williams
27 Dale Earnhardt .60 1.50
Working on the Farm
28 Dale Earnhardt's Car .60 1.50
Final Victory Talladega
29 Dale Earnhardt .60 1.50
Darrell Waltrip DEI
30 Dale Earnhardt .60 1.50
Taylor Nicole Earnhardt
31 Dale Earnhardt .60 1.50
Dale Earnhardt Jr.
32 Dale Earnhardt .60 1.50
Hands On Racer
33 Dale Earnhardt's Car .60 1.50
1986 Daytona 500
34 Dale Earnhardt's Car .60 1.50
1990 Daytona 500
35 Dale Earnhardt's Car .60 1.50
Jeff Gordon's Car
1997 Daytona 500
36 Dale Earnhardt .60 1.50
Girl with Penny
37 Dale Earnhardt's Car .60 1.50
1998 Daytona 500 Final Pit Stop
38 Dale Earnhardt's Car .60 1.50
1998 Daytona 500 Congratulations
39 Dale Earnhardt's Car .60 1.50
1998 Daytona 500 Burnout
40 Dale Earnhardt's Car .60 1.50
1998 Daytona 500 Victory Lane
41 Dale Earnhardt .60 1.50
1998 Daytona 500 Celebration
42 Dale Earnhardt .60 1.50
Reflections
43 Mourning A Legend .60 1.50
44 Steve Park's Car .60 1.50
45 Dale Earnhardt's Car .60 1.50
Bobby Labonte's Car
Kevin Harvick's Car
Jeff Gordon's Car
46 Dale Earnhardt Jr.'s Car .60 1.50
Kevin Harvick's Car
Michael Waltrip's Car
Jimmie Johnson's Car
47 Dale Earnhardt .60 1.50
American Dream
48 Dale Earnhardt .60 1.50
Honored Hero
49 Dale Earnhardt .60 1.50
Career Milestones
50 Dale Earnhardt Statue CL .60 1.50

2004 Press Pass Dale Earnhardt Jr.

COMPLETE TIN SET (74) 10.00 25.00
COMP.SET w/o TIN (72) 6.00 15.00
COMMON DALE JR. .20 .50

2004 Press Pass Dale Earnhardt Jr. Gallery

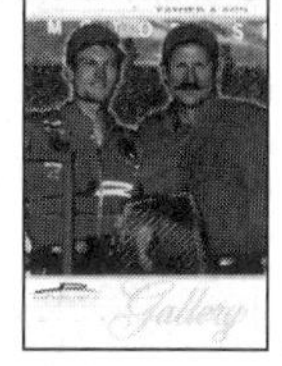

This 8-card set was inserted into the Press Pass Dale Earnhardt Jr. tin sets. There were two cards per sealed set. The cards featured silver foil highlights. Each card carried a "G" prefix for its card numbering.

COMPLETE SET (8) 10.00 25.00
COMMON DALE JR. 2.00 5.00

2004 Press Pass Dale Earnhardt Jr. Tins

COMPLETE SET (4) 12.50 30.00

2002 Press Pass Dale Earnhardt Jr. Firesuit

This card was sent out to collectors who were waiting on a Dale Earnhardt Jr. autograph exchange card that has yet to be redeemed. It shows Dale Jr. in his 1999 Busch Championship celebration and the swatch of firesuit is from the AC Delco uniform from that same season. Some of these were also available in 2003 Press Pass packs.

NNO Dale Earnhardt Jr. 40.00 80.00

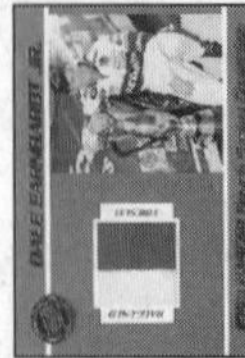

2003 Press Pass Dale Jarrett Fan Club

DJ Dale Jarrett 10.00 25.00

2008 Press Pass Daytona 500 50th Anniversary

COMP.FACT.SET (50) 12.50 25.00
COMPLETE SET (50) 12.50 25.00
COMMON DRIVERS .10 .30
SEMISTARS .20 .50
UNLISTED STARS .30 .75
1 Lee Petty '59 .20 .50
2 Marvin Panch '61 .12 .30
3 Fireball Roberts '62 .12 .30
4 Tiny Lund '63 .12 .30
5 Richard Petty '64 .60 1.50
6 Fred Lorenzen '65 .12 .30
7 Richard Petty '66 .60 1.50
8 Cale Yarborough '68 .25 .60
9 Lee Roy Yarbrough '69 .12 .30
10 Pete Hamilton '70 .12 .30
11 Richard Petty '71 .60 1.50
12 Richard Petty '73 .60 1.50
13 Richard Petty '74 .60 1.50
14 Benny Parsons '75 .20 .50
15 David Pearson '76 .30 .75
16 Cale Yarborough '77 .25 .60
17 Bobby Allison '78 .20 .50
18 Richard Petty '79 .60 1.50
19 Buddy Baker '80 .20 .50
20 Richard Petty '81 .60 1.50
21 Bobby Allison '82 .20 .50
22 Cale Yarborough '83 .25 .60
23 Cale Yarborough '84 .25 .60
24 Geoff Bodine '86 .12 .30
25 Bobby Allison '88 .20 .50
26 Darrell Waltrip '89 .30 .75
27 Derrike Cope '90 .20 .50
28 Ernie Irvan '91 .20 .50
29 Davey Allison '92 .30 .75
30 Dale Jarrett '93 .50 1.25
31 Sterling Marlin '94 .30 .75
32 Sterling Marlin '95 .30 .75
33 Dale Jarrett '96 .50 1.25
34 Jeff Gordon '97 .75 2.00
35 Dale Earnhardt '98 1.25 3.00
36 Jeff Gordon '99 .75 2.00
37 Dale Jarrett '00 .50 1.25
38 Michael Waltrip '01 .25 .60
39 Ward Burton '02 .20 .50
40 Michael Waltrip '03 .25 .60
41 Dale Earnhardt Jr. '04 1.00 2.50
42 Jeff Gordon '05 .75 2.00
43 Jimmie Johnson '06 .60 1.50
44 Kevin Harvick '07 .40 1.00
45 Lee Petty FF .20 .50
46 David Pearson Richard Petty FF .60 1.50
47 Bobby Allison Donnie Allison Cale Yarborough FF .25 .60
48 Dale Earnhardt FF 1.25 3.00
49 Kevin Harvick FF .40 1.00
50 Checklist .20 .50
NNO '08 Winner Tire Redemption 30.00 60.00

2002 Press Pass Delphi

This 7-card promotional set was sponsored by Delphi and produced by Press Pass. Each card features a color image, of drivers Delphi sponsors, on the front and his car on the back.

COMPLETE SET (7) 8.00 20.00
D1 Joe Nemechek .60 1.25
D2 Jeff Gordon 3.00 8.00
D3 Terry Labonte 1.25 3.00
D4 Jimmie Johnson 2.50 6.00
D5 Ricky Hendrick .60 1.25
D6 Jack Sprague .60 1.25
NNO Joe Nemechek's Car (Cover Card) .40 1.00

1999 Press Pass Dew Crew

This 4-card set was sponsored by Mountain Dew and issued as part of a sales promotion in packages of soft drinks.

COMPLETE SET (4) 4.00 10.00
1 Casey Atwood 2.00 5.00
2 Ward Burton .75 2.00
3 Terry Labonte 1.25 3.00
4 Chad Little .40 1.00

2006 Press Pass Dominator Dale Earnhardt

This 33-card set was released in November, 2006 in factory sealed tins. Each tin contained one of 3 oversized jumbo cards. The 33 cards highlighted Dale Earnhardt's career.

COMP.FACT.SET (34) 12.50 30.00
COMPLETE SET (33) 10.00 25.00
1 Dale Earnhardt '76 The Earnly Years .60 1.50
2 Dale Earnhardt '79 ROY .60 1.50
3 Dale Earnhardt '79 Bristol Win .60 1.50
4 Dale Earnhardt '80 Atlanta Win .60 1.50
5 Dale Earnhardt '80 Champion .60 1.50
6 Dale Earnhardt '81 Year in Review .60 1.50
7 Richard Petty '82 Year in Review .60 1.50
8 Dale Earnhardt's Car '83 Year in Review .60 1.50
9 Dale Earnhardt '84 Year in Review .60 1.50
10 Dale Earnhardt '85 Year in Review .60 1.50
11 Dale Earnhardt '86 Champion .60 1.50
12 Dale Earnhardt '86 Atlanta Win .60 1.50
13 Dale Earnhardt '87 Champion .60 1.50
14 Dale Earnhardt's Car '87 Charlotte Win .60 1.50
15 Dale Earnhardt's Car '88 Year in Review .60 1.50
16 Dale Earnhardt '89 Year in Review .60 1.50
17 Dale Earnhardt '90 Champion .60 1.50
18 Dale Earnhardt '91 Champion .60 1.50
19 Dale Earnhardt '92 Year in Review .60 1.50
20 Dale Earnhardt '93 Champion .60 1.50
21 Dale Earnhardt '93 Charlotte Win .60 1.50
22 Dale Earnhardt '94 Champion .60 1.50
23 Dale Earnhardt '94 Talladega Win .60 1.50
24 Dale Earnhardt '96 Year in Review UER .60 1.50
25 Dale Earnhardt '95 Year in Review UER .60 1.50
26 Dale Earnhardt '97 Year in Review .60 1.50
27 Dale Earnhardt '98 Year in Review .60 1.50
28 Dale Earnhardt '98 Daytona 500 Win .60 1.50
29 Dale Earnhardt '99 Year in Review .60 1.50
30 Dale Earnhardt's Car '99 Bristol Win .60 1.50
31 Dale Earnhardt '00 Year in Review .60 1.50
32 Dale Earnhardt's Car '00 Atlanta Win .60 1.50
33 Dale Earnhardt '00 Talladega Win .60 1.50

2006 Press Pass Dominator Dale Earnhardt Jumbo

This 3-card insert set was issued at a rate of one per tin set. Each card was oversized and featured Dale Earnhardt.

COMPLETE SET (3) 8.00 20.00
STATED ODDS 1 PER TIN
SR1 Dale Earnhardt Appeal 3.00 8.00
SR2 Dale Earnhardt 3.00 8.00
SR3 Dale Earnhardt 3.00 8.00

2006 Press Pass Dominator Dale Earnhardt Jr.

This 33-card set was released in November, 2006 in factory sealed tins. Each tin contained one of 3 oversized jumbo cards. The 33 cards highlighted Dale Earnhardt Jr.'s career.

COMP.FACT.SET (34) 12.50 30.00
COMPLETE SET (33) 10.00 25.00
1 Dale Earnhardt Jr. '98 BGN Champ .50 1.25
2 Dale Earnhardt Jr. '99 BGN Champ .50 1.25
3 Dale Earnhardt Jr. '00 Directv 500 Win .50 1.25
4 Dale Earnhardt Jr. '00 Pontiac 400 Win .50 1.25
5 Dale Earnhardt Jr. '00 The Winston Win .50 1.25
6 Dale Earnhardt Jr. '00 Rookie Recap .50 1.25
7 Dale Earnhardt Jr. '01 MBNA 400 Win .50 1.25
8 Dale Earnhardt Jr. '01 EA Sports 500 Win .50 1.25
9 Dale Earnhardt Jr. '01 Pepsi 400 Win .50 1.25
10 Dale Earnhardt Jr. '02 Aaron's 499 Win .50 1.25
11 Dale Earnhardt Jr. '02 EA Sports 500 Win .50 1.25
12 Dale Earnhardt Jr. '03 Aaron's 499 Win .50 1.25
13 Dale Earnhardt Jr.'s Car '03 Checker 500 Win .50 1.25
14 Dale Earnhardt Jr. '03 Breakout Season .50 1.25
15 Dale Earnhardt Jr. '03 Most Popular Driver .50 1.25
16 Dale Earnhardt Jr. '04 Daytona 500 Win .50 1.25
17 Dale Earnhardt Jr.'s Car '04 Golden Corral 500 Win .50 1.25
18 Dale Earnhardt Jr. '04 Chevy 400 Win .50 1.25
19 Dale Earnhardt Jr.'s Car '04 Sharpie 500 Win .50 1.25
20 Dale Earnhardt Jr. '04 EA Sports 500 Win .50 1.25
21 Dale Earnhardt Jr. '04 Checker 500 Win .50 1.25
22 Dale Earnhardt Jr. '04 Inaugural Chase .50 1.25
23 Dale Earnhardt Jr. '04 Most Popular Driver .50 1.25
24 Dale Earnhardt Jr. Martin Truex Jr. '04 Owner BGN Champion .50 1.25
25 Dale Earnhardt Jr.'s Car '05 USG 400 Win .50 1.25
26 Dale Earnhardt Jr. '05 Most Popular Driver .50 1.25
27 Dale Earnhardt Jr. Truex Jr. '05 Owner BGN Champion .50 1.25
28 Dale Earnhardt Jr. '06 Winn-Dixie 250 Win .50 1.25
29 Dale Earnhardt Jr. '06 Ties Dale Sr. BGN Wins .50 1.25
30 Dale Earnhardt Jr. '06 Pontiac 400 Win .50 1.25
31 Dale Earnhardt Jr. '06 Chase .50 1.25
32 Dale Earnhardt Jr. '06 Cars Movie Premiere .50 1.25
33 Dale Earnhardt Jr. '06 Fan Favorite .50 1.25

2006 Press Pass Dominator Dale Earnhardt Jr. Jumbo

This 3-card insert set was issued at a rate of one per tin set. Each card was oversized and featured Dale Earnhardt Jr.

COMPLETE SET (3) 5.00 12.00
STSTED ODDS 1 PER TIN
JR1 Dale Earnhardt Jr. 2.00 5.00
JR2 Dale Earnhardt Jr. 2.00 5.00
JR3 Dale Earnhardt Jr. Competitor 2.00 5.00

2006 Press Pass Dominator Jeff Gordon

This 33-card set was released in November, 2006 in factory sealed tins. Each tin contained one of 3 oversized jumbo cards. The 33 cards highlighted Jeff Gordon's career.

COMP.FACT.SET (34) 12.50 30.00
COMPLETE SET (33) 10.00 25.00
1 Jeff Gordon '92 BGN Pole Record .50 1.25
2 Jeff Gordon '93 125 Qualifying Win .50 1.25
3 Jeff Gordon '93 ROY .50 1.25
4 Jeff Gordon '93 Year in Review .50 1.25
5 Jeff Gordon '94 Brickyard 400 Win .50 1.25
6 Jeff Gordon '94 Year in Review .50 1.25
7 Jeff Gordon '95 Champion .50 1.25
8 Jeff Gordon '95 Year in Review .50 1.25
9 Jeff Gordon '96 Year in Review .50 1.25
10 Jeff Gordon '97 Daytona 500 Win .50 1.25
11 Jeff Gordon '97 Winston Win .50 1.25
12 Jeff Gordon '97 Champion .50 1.25
13 Jeff Gordon '97 Year in Review .50 1.25
14 Jeff Gordon '98 Brickyard 400 Win .50 1.25
15 Jeff Gordon '98 Champion .50 1.25
16 Jeff Gordon '98 Year in Review .50 1.25
17 Jeff Gordon '99 Daytona 500 Win .50 1.25
18 Jeff Gordon '99 Year in Review .50 1.25
19 Jeff Gordon '00 50 Career Wins .50 1.25
20 Jeff Gordon's Car '00 King of the Road .50 1.25
21 Jeff Gordon '00 Year in Review .50 1.25
22 Jeff Gordon '01 Champion .50 1.25
23 Jeff Gordon '01 Year in Review .50 1.25
24 Jeff Gordon '02 Year in Review .50 1.25
25 Jeff Gordon '03 Year in Review .50 1.25
26 Jeff Gordon '04 Year in Review .50 1.25
27 Jeff Gordon '05 Daytona 500 Win .50 1.25
28 Jeff Gordon '05 Year in Review .50 1.25
29 Jeff Gordon '06 Eye on the Prize .50 1.25
30 Jeff Gordon '06 75 Career Wins .50 1.25
31 Jeff Gordon '06 Fan Favorite .50 1.25
32 Jeff Gordon '06 Jeff Gordon Foundation .50 1.25
33 Jeff Gordon '06 Chase .50 1.25

2006 Press Pass Dominator Jeff Gordon Jumbo

This 3-card insert set was issued at a rate of one per tin set. Each card was oversized and featured Jeff Gordon.

COMPLETE SET (3) 5.00 12.00
STATED ODDS 1 PER TIN
JG1 Jeff Gordon 2.00 5.00
JG2 Jeff Gordon Performance 2.00 5.00
JG3 Jeff Gordon 2.00 5.00

2006 Press Pass Dominator Tins

This 3-tin set featured a 33-card set inside for the corresponding driver.

DE Dale Earnhardt 3.00 8.00
JG Jeff Gordon 2.00 5.00
JR Dale Earnhardt Jr. 2.00 5.00

2002 Press Pass Double Burner

Randomly inserted into hobby packs across most 2002 Press Pass products, this set features nine leading drivers. All cards in this set are serial numbered to 100 and include a swatch of a race used glove and firesuit. Some cards were issued via mail redemption cards which carried an expiration date of 1/31/2003.

DB1 Dale Earnhardt Jr. 75.00 200.00
DB2 Jeff Gordon 75.00 200.00
DB3 Kevin Harvick 40.00 80.00
DB4 Dale Jarrett 40.00 80.00
DB5 Bobby Labonte 40.00 80.00
DB6 Terry Labonte 30.00 60.00
DB7 Mark Martin 40.00 80.00
DB8 Tony Stewart 40.00 80.00
DB9 Rusty Wallace 40.00 80.00

2003 Press Pass Double Burner

Issued as part of a year long Press Pass insert program, these 10 cards feature race-used pieces of both firesuits and gloves embedded in a trading card. The cards were issued to a stated print run of 100 serial numbered sets but spread out over a number of their card brands in 2003. Each card was initially released as a redemption card featuring a Press Pass Authentics hologram sticker.

DB1 Jeff Gordon 75.00 150.00
DB2 Ryan Newman 40.00 80.00
DB3 Kevin Harvick 40.00 80.00
DB4 Jimmie Johnson 50.00 100.00
DB5 Rusty Wallace 40.00 80.00
DB6 Mark Martin 50.00 100.00
DB7 Matt Kenseth 40.00 80.00
DB8 Bobby Labonte 30.00 60.00
DB9 Tony Stewart 50.00 100.00
DB10 Dale Earnhardt Jr. 100.00 200.00

2004 Press Pass Double Burner

This 10-card set was randomly inserted in packs across all brands of Press Pass retail products in 2004. These were not available in any hobby packs. Each card was issued as an exchange redeemable for the specified driver's card with a swatch of his race-used glove and a swatch of his race-used firesuit. The cards were serial numbered to 100. These cards were the redemptions. The exchange deadline was January 31, 2005.

COMPLETE SET (10)
*DB EXCHANGE CARDS: .4X TO 1X DB
RANDOM INSERTS IN RETAIL PACKS
DB1 Jeff Gordon 60.00 150.00
DB2 Ryan Newman 50.00 120.00
DB3 Kevin Harvick
DB4 Jimmie Johnson 50.00 120.00
DB5 Rusty Wallace 30.00 80.00
DB6 Mark Martin 50.00 120.00
DB7 Matt Kenseth
DB8 Bobby Labonte 30.00 80.00
DB9 Tony Stewart 40.00 100.00
DB10 Dale Earnhardt Jr. 60.00 150.00

2005 Press Pass Double Burner

DB1 Jeff Gordon 60.00 120.00
DB2 Ryan Newman 50.00 100.00
DB3 Kevin Harvick 40.00 80.00
DB4 Jimmie Johnson 50.00 100.00
DB5 Rusty Wallace 50.00 100.00
DB6 Mark Martin 50.00 100.00
DB7 Matt Kenseth 50.00 100.00
DB8 Bobby Labonte 40.00 80.00
DB9 Tony Stewart 50.00 100.00
DB10 Dale Earnhardt Jr. 75.00 150.00
DB11 Kurt Busch 40.00 80.00
DB12 Brian Vickers 40.00 80.00

2006 Press Pass Double Burner Firesuit-Glove

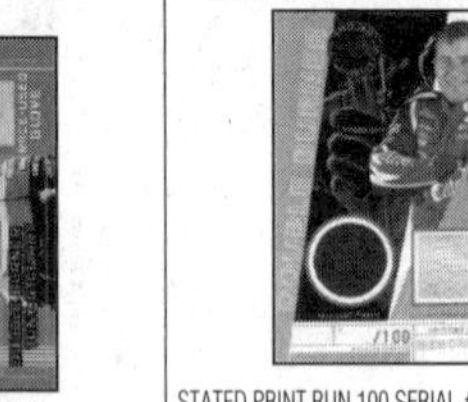

STATED PRINT RUN 100 SERIAL #'d SETS
AVAILABLE IN PACKS OF '06 PREMIUM
DB1 Jeff Gordon 60.00 120.00
DB2 Dale Jarrett 30.00 60.00
DB3 Matt Kenseth 30.00 60.00
DB4 Jimmie Johnson 40.00 80.00
DB5 Kevin Harvick 40.00 80.00
DB6 Dale Earnhardt Jr. 50.00 100.00
DB7 Carl Edwards 40.00 80.00
DB8 Ryan Newman 25.00 50.00
DB9 Tony Stewart 40.00 80.00

2006 Press Pass Double Burner Metal-Tire

AVAILABLE IN PACKS OF '06 PRESS PASS
DB1 Carl Edwards 40.00 80.00
DB2 Dale Earnhardt Jr. 75.00 150.00
DB3 Jeff Gordon 50.00 120.00
DB4 Dale Jarrett 30.00 60.00
DB5 Jimmie Johnson 40.00 80.00
DB6 Mark Martin 40.00 80.00
DB7 Bobby Labonte
DB8 Tony Stewart 40.00 80.00
DB9 Martin Truex Jr. 30.00 60.00

2007 Press Pass Double Burner Firesuit-Glove

DB1 Matt Kenseth 25.00 50.00
DB2 Dale Earnhardt Jr. 50.00 100.00
DB3 Denny Hamlin 30.00 60.00
DB4 Jimmie Johnson 30.00 60.00
DB5 Martin Truex Jr. 25.00 50.00
DB6 Jeff Gordon 40.00 80.00
DB7 Kasey Kahne 30.00 60.00
DB8 Kurt Busch 25.00 50.00
DB9 Carl Edwards 25.00 50.00

2007 Press Pass Double Burner Firesuit-Glove Exchange

STATED PRINT RUN 100 SERIAL #'d SETS
EXCH DEADLINE 01/31/2008

2007 Press Pass Double Burner Metal-Tire

This 9-card set featured swatches of race-used sh metal and race-used tires. These were available packs of 2007 Press Pass as exchange cards, wh were redeemable until December 31, 2007. Ea card is serial numbered to 100 and carried a "D prefix for its card number.

STATED PRINT RUN 100 SERIAL #'d SETS
DB-CE Carl Edwards 40.00 80.0
DB-DE Dale Earnhardt Jr. 75.00 150.0
DB-DH Denny Hamlin 40.00 80.0
DB-JG Jeff Gordon 60.00 120.0
DB-JJ Jimmie Johnson 60.00 120.0
DB-KH Kevin Harvick 50.00 100.0
DB-KK Kasey Kahne 60.00 120.0
DB-MK Matt Kenseth 40.00 80.0
DB-RS Reed Sorenson 30.00 60.0
DB-TS Tony Stewart 50.00 100.0

2007 Press Pass Double Burner Metal-Tire Exchange

This 9-card exchange set pictured swatches of ra used sheet metal and race-used tires. These w available in packs of 2007 Press Pass a redeemable for the actual dual race-used car These were redeemable until December 31, 20 Each card is serial numbered to 100 and carrie "DB" prefix for its card number. Each of these ha Press Pass Authentic hologram sticker. Cards w not returned after they were redeemed.

STATED PRINT RUN 100 SERIAL #'d SETS
EXCH DEADLINE 12/31/2007
DB-CE Carl Edwards 40.00 80.0
DB-DE Dale Earnhardt Jr. 75.00 150.0
DB-DH Denny Hamlin 40.00 80.0
DB-JG Jeff Gordon 60.00 120.0
DB-JJ Jimmie Johnson 60.00 120.0
DB-KH Kevin Harvick 50.00 100.0
DB-KK Kasey Kahne 60.00 120.0
DB-MK Matt Kenseth 40.00 80.0
DB-TS Tony Stewart 50.00 100.0

2008 Press Pass Double Burner Firesuit-Glove

STATED PRINT RUN 100 SERIAL #'d SETS
DBCE Carl Edwards 20.00 50.
DBDJ Dale Jarrett 25.00 50.
DBJG Jeff Gordon 40.00 80.
DBJJ Jimmie Johnson 30.00 60.
DBJM Juan Pablo Montoya 25.00 50.
DBMK Matt Kenseth 20.00 50.
DBMM Mark Martin 30.00 60.
DBMT Martin Truex Jr. 25.00 50.
DBTS Tony Stewart 30.00 60.

2008 Press Pass Double Burner Metal-Tire

STATED PRINT RUN 100 SERIAL #'d SETS
DB-CE Carl Edwards 20.00 50.
DB-DE Dale Earnhardt Jr.
DB-DH Denny Hamlin 15.00 40.
DB-JG Jeff Gordon 60.00 120.
DB-JJ Jimmie Johnson 25.00 60.
DB-JM Juan Pablo Montoya 15.00 40.
DB-KK Kasey Kahne
DB-MM Mark Martin 25.00 60.
DB-MT Martin Truex Jr. 20.00 50.

2002 Press Pass Eclipse

This 50 card set was issued in four card hobby retail packs. In addition, a special promot included two packs and CD-Rom to keep up with values of these cards for $9.99.

COMPLETE SET (50) 12.00 30.
WAX BOX 40.00 100.
1 Jeff Gordon 1.50 4.
2 Tony Stewart 1.25 3.
3 Ricky Rudd .60 1.
4 Sterling Marlin .60 1.
5 Dale Jarrett 1.00 2.
6 Bobby Labonte 1.00 2.
7 Rusty Wallace 1.00 2.
8 Dale Earnhardt Jr. 2.00 5.
9 Kevin Harvick 1.25 3.
10 Jeff Burton .40 1.
11 Ricky Craven .20
12 Matt Kenseth 1.25 3.
13 Ward Burton .40 1.
14 Jerry Nadeau .40 1.
15 Bobby Hamilton .20
16 Ken Schrader .20

Elliott Sadler .40 1.00
Terry Labonte .60 1.50
Dave Blaney .20 .50
Michael Waltrip .40 1.00
Kurt Busch .60 1.50
Joe Nemechek .20 .50
John Andretti .20 .50
Todd Bodine .20 .50
Brett Bodine .20 .50
Steve Park .40 1.00
Kyle Petty .40 1.00
Ryan Newman CRC 1.25 3.00
Jeff Gordon ACC 1.25 3.00
Jeff Gordon ACC 1.25 3.00
Jeff Gordon ACC 1.25 3.00
Jeff Gordon ACC 1.25 3.00
Jeff Gordon ACC 1.25 3.00
Bobby Labonte ACC 1.00 2.50
Jeff Gordon ACC 1.25 3.00
Jeff Gordon ACC 1.25 3.00
Matt Kenseth ACC 1.25 3.00
Jeff Gordon SO 1.25 3.00
Dale Jarrett SO 1.00 2.50
Dale Earnhardt Jr. SO 1.50 4.00
Stacy Compton SO .20 .50
Bobby Labonte SO 1.00 2.50
Ryan Newman SO 1.25 3.00
Ricky Rudd SO .60 1.50
Sterling Marlin SO .60 1.50
Todd Bodine SO .20 .50
Jimmy Spencer SO .20 .50
Ricky Craven SO .20 .50
Kurt Busch SO .60 1.50
Checklist .10 .25
Jeff Gordon Promo 2.50 5.00

002 Press Pass Eclipse Samples

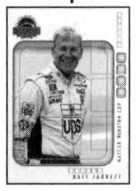

set was issued before the basic Eclipse release romote what the set would look like. The cards e inserted one per Beckett Racing Collector azine.

MPLETE SET (50)
MPLES: 1.5X TO 4X BASIC CARDS

002 Press Pass Eclipse Solar Eclipse

erted one per hobby or retail pack, this is a llel of the 2002 Eclipse basic set.

MPLETE SET (50) 20.00 50.00
LAR ECLIPSE: .8X TO 2X BASE CARD HI

002 Press Pass Eclipse Father and Son Autographs

domly inserted into packs, these five cards re dual signed cards of both fathers and sons have been involved with Nascar. Each card was ed to a stated print run of 100 serial numbered

A.J.Foyt 40.00 100.00
Larry Foyt
Joe Gibbs 30.00 60.00
Coy Gibbs
Ned Jarrett 40.00 100.00
Dale Jarrett
Hank Parker 25.00 50.00
Hank Parker Jr.
Richard Petty 75.00 150.00
Kyle Petty

002 Press Pass Eclipse Racing Champions

ed at stated odds of one per hobby pack and one wo retail packs, this die-cut 36-card set was ted on plastic. The set was foil stamped and ured 2002 Winston Cup winners..

MPLETE SET (36) 12.50 30.00
Michael Waltrip .30 .75
RC2 Steve Park .30 .75
RC3 Jeff Gordon 1.25 3.00
RC4 Kevin Harvick 1.00 2.50
RC5 Dale Jarrett .75 2.00
RC6 Elliott Sadler .30 .75
RC7 Dale Jarrett .75 2.00
RC8 Dale Jarrett .75 2.00
RC9 Bobby Hamilton .15 .40
RC10 Rusty Wallace .75 2.00
RC11 Tony Stewart 1.00 2.50
RC12 Jeff Burton .30 .75
RC13 Jeff Gordon 1.25 3.00
RC14 Jeff Gordon 1.25 3.00
RC15 Ricky Rudd .50 1.25
RC16 Tony Stewart 1.00 2.50
RC17 Dale Earnhardt Jr. 1.50 4.00
RC18 Kevin Harvick 1.00 2.50
RC19 Dale Jarrett .75 2.00
RC20 Bobby Labonte .75 2.00
RC21 Jeff Gordon 1.25 3.00
RC22 Jeff Gordon 1.25 3.00
RC23 Sterling Marlin .50 1.25
RC24 Tony Stewart 1.00 2.50
RC25 Ward Burton .30 .75
RC26 Ricky Rudd .50 1.25
RC27 Dale Earnhardt Jr. 1.50 4.00
RC28 Jeff Gordon 1.25 3.00
RC29 Sterling Marlin .50 1.25
RC30 Ricky Craven .15 .40
RC31 Dale Earnhardt Jr. 1.50 4.00
RC32 Jeff Burton .30 .75
RC33 Joe Nemechek .15 .40
RC34 Bobby Labonte .75 2.00
RC35 Robby Gordon .15 .40
RC36 Richard Petty .30 .75

2002 Press Pass Eclipse Skidmarks

Issued at a stated rate of one in 20, this nine card set features pieces of race-used tires specially treated to enhance the card design.

COMPLETE SET (9) 30.00 80.00
SK1 Terry Labonte 4.00 10.00
SK2 Dale Earnhardt Jr. 8.00 20.00
SK3 Kevin Harvick 6.00 15.00
SK4 Jeff Gordon 8.00 20.00
SK5 Bobby Labonte 6.00 15.00
SK6 Ricky Rudd 3.00 8.00
SK7 Dale Jarrett 6.00 15.00
SK8 Tony Stewart 6.00 15.00
SK9 Rusty Wallace 6.00 15.00

2002 Press Pass Eclipse Supernova

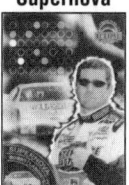

Inserted at a rate of one in eight, this 12 card set featured some of the leading drivers in Nascar.

COMPLETE SET (12) 15.00 40.00
*NUMBERED: 1.2X TO 3X HI COL.
SN1 Jeff Burton 1.00 2.50
SN2 Dale Earnhardt Jr. 8.00 12.00
SN3 Kevin Harvick 3.00 8.00
SN4 Ward Burton 1.25 2.50
SN5 Jeff Gordon 4.00 10.00
SN6 Dale Jarrett 2.50 6.00
SN7 Matt Kenseth 3.00 8.00
SN8 Bobby Labonte 2.50 6.00
SN9 Tony Stewart 3.00 8.00
SN10 Terry Labonte 1.50 4.00
SN11 Ricky Rudd 1.25 3.00
SN12 Rusty Wallace 2.50 6.00

2002 Press Pass Eclipse Under Cover Drivers

Issued at a stated rate of one in 24 hobby packs, these 12 cards feature pieces of car covers included as part of the card. These cards are the 1st time pieces of car covers were used in a set.

*GOLD: .4X TO 1X SILVERS
GOLD PRINT RUN 400 SER.#'d SETS
*GOLD CARS: .6X TO 1.5X SILVERS
GOLD CAR STATED ODDS 1:240 RETAIL
GOLD CAR PRINT RUN 300 SER. #'d SETS
*HOLOFOILS: .8X TO 2X SILVERS
HOLOFOIL PRINT RUN 100 SER.#'d SETS
MULTI-COLORED SWATCH: .6X TO 1.5X HI
CD1 Jimmie Johnson 12.50 30.00
CD2 Jerry Nadeau 8.00 20.00
CD3 Jeff Gordon 15.00 40.00
CD4 Terry Labonte 8.00 20.00
CD5 Bobby Labonte 8.00 20.00
CD6 Tony Stewart 12.50 30.00
CD7 Ken Schrader 6.00 15.00
CD8 Elliott Sadler 6.00 15.00
CD9 Ryan Newman 12.50 30.00
CD10 Ricky Craven 6.00 15.00
CD11 Michael Waltrip 8.00 20.00
CD12 Dale Earnhardt Jr. 20.00 50.00

2002 Press Pass Eclipse Under Cover Double Cover

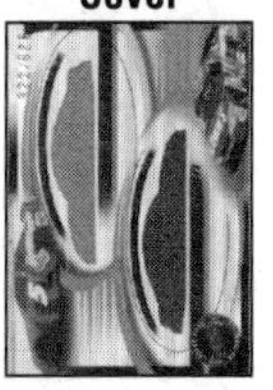

Issued at a stated rate of one in 240 hobby or retail packs, these eight cards feature two pieces of car covers on them. Each of these cards were issued to a stated print run of 625 serial numbered sets.

COMPLETE SET (8) 150.00 300.00
DC1 Jerry Nadeau 15.00 40.00
Jeff Gordon
DC2 Jimmie Johnson 25.00 60.00
Jeff Gordon
DC3 Jeff Gordon 15.00 40.00
Terry Labonte
DC4 Jerry Nadeau 12.50 30.00
Jimmie Johnson
DC5 Terry Labonte 12.50 30.00
Jimmie Johnson
DC6 Terry Labonte 12.50 30.00
Jerry Nadeau
DC7 Bobby Labonte 15.00 40.00
Tony Stewart
DC8 Dale Earnhardt Jr. 25.00 60.00
Michael Waltrip

2002 Press Pass Eclipse Warp Speed

Inserted in packs at a stated rate of one in 12, these eight cards feature some of the fastest drivers on the Nascar circuit. These cards were issued in holo-foil board and plastic for an interesting feel.

COMPLETE SET (8) 10.00 25.00
WS1 Jeff Gordon 3.00 8.00
WS2 Dale Earnhardt Jr. 4.00 10.00
WS3 Rusty Wallace 2.00 5.00
WS4 Dale Jarrett 2.00 5.00
WS5 Tony Stewart 2.50 6.00
WS6 Kevin Harvick 2.50 6.00
WS7 Jeff Burton .75 2.00
WS8 Ricky Rudd 1.25 3.00

2003 Press Pass Eclipse

This 50-card set was issued in five card hobby and four card retail packs with a suggested retail price of $3.99. These went live in March of 2003. The cards featured a white border with silver foil highlights and a full color photo of the drive or his car.

COMPLETE SET (50) 15.00 40.00
WAX BOX HOBBY (24) 60.00 100.00
WAX BOX RETAIL (28) 30.00 80.00
1 Tony Stewart 1.25 3.00
2 Mark Martin 1.25 3.00
3 Kurt Busch .60 1.50
4 Jeff Gordon 1.50 4.00
5 Jimmie Johnson 1.25 3.00
6 Ryan Newman 1.25 3.00
7 Rusty Wallace 1.00 2.50
8 Matt Kenseth 1.25 3.00
9 Dale Jarrett 1.00 2.50
10 Ricky Rudd .60 1.50
11 Dale Earnhardt Jr. 2.00 5.00
12 Jeff Burton .50 1.25
13 Michael Waltrip .50 1.25
14 Ricky Craven .25 .60
15 Bobby Labonte 1.25 3.00
16 Jeff Green .25 .60
17 Sterling Marlin .60 1.50
18 Dave Blaney .25 .60
19 Robby Gordon .25 .60
20 Kevin Harvick 1.00 2.50
21 Kyle Petty .50 1.25
22 Elliott Sadler .50 1.25
23 Terry Labonte .60 1.50
24 Ward Burton .50 1.25
25 Jeremy Mayfield .25 .60
26 Steve Park .50 1.25
27 Jamie McMurray 1.00 2.50
28 Ryan Newman ACC 1.25 3.00
29 Matt Kenseth ACC 1.25 3.00
30 Dale Earnhardt Jr. ACC 2.00 5.00
31 Mark Martin ACC 1.25 3.00
32 Tony Stewart ACC 1.25 3.00
33 Mark Martin ACC 1.25 3.00
34 Ryan Newman ACC 1.25 3.00
35 Jeff Gordon ACC 1.50 4.00
36 Chip Ganassi ACC .25 .60
37 All-American Kid WCS .50 1.25
38 Kansas City Chiefs WCS .50 1.25
39 Holy Cow WCS .25 .60
40 Any Given Sunday WCS .50 1.25
41 Speed Demons WCS .25 .60
42 The Spin Doctor WCS .50 1.25
43 Born to Run WCS .50 1.25
44 High Five WCS .25 .60
45 CHAMP-agne Celebration WCS .50 1.25
46 Jeff Gordon HS 1.50 4.00
47 Ryan Newman HS 1.25 3.00
48 Jimmie Johnson HS 1.25 3.00
49 Dale Earnhardt Jr. HS 2.00 5.00
50 Tony Stewart HS 1.25 3.00

2003 Press Pass Eclipse Solar Eclipse

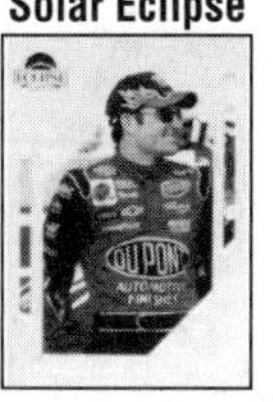

Inserted one per hobby or retail pack, this is a parallel of the 2003 Eclipse base set.

COMPLETE SET (50) 25.00 60.00
*SOLAR ECLIPSE: .6X TO 1.5X

2003 Press Pass Eclipse Double Hot Treads

This 11 card set featured a swatch of race-used tires from 2 drivers per card. The drivers were paired up with a teammate on the opposite sides of the cards. Each card was inserted one per specially marked retail box and each was serial numbered to 999.

DT1 Bobby Labonte 15.00 40.00
Tony Stewart
DT2 Robby Gordon 10.00 25.00
Kevin Harvick
DT3 John Andretti 8.00 20.00
Kyle Petty
DT4 Ward Burton 8.00 20.00
Kenny Wallace
DT5 Sterling Marlin 8.00 20.00
Jamie McMurray
DT6 Matt Kenseth 15.00 40.00
Mark Martin
DT7 Jeff Burton 10.00 25.00
Kurt Busch
DT8 Jeff Gordon 20.00 50.00
Jimmie Johnson
DT9 Ryan Newman 20.00 50.00
Rusty Wallace
DT10 Dale Earnhardt Jr.
Michael Waltrip
DT11 Steve Park
Michael Waltrip

2003 Press Pass Eclipse Racing Champions

Issued at stated odds of one per hobby pack and one in two retail packs, this die-cut 36-card set was printed on plastic. The set was foil stamped and featured 2003 Winston Cup winners..

COMPLETE SET (36) 15.00 40.00
COMMON DRIVER (RC1-RC36) .20 .50
SEMISTARS .40 1.00
UNLISTED STARS .60 1.50
STATED ODDS 1 PER PACK HOBBY
STATED ODDS 1:2 RETAIL
RC1 Tony Stewart 1.25 3.00
RC2 Jimmie Johnson 1.25 3.00
RC3 Ward Burton .50 1.25
RC4 Matt Kenseth 1.25 3.00
RC5 Sterling Marlin .60 1.50
RC6 Tony Stewart 1.25 3.00
RC7 Sterling Marlin .60 1.50
RC8 Kurt Busch .60 1.50
RC9 Matt Kenseth 1.25 3.00
RC10 Bobby Labonte 1.25 3.00
RC11 Dale Earnhardt Jr. 2.00 5.00
RC12 Jimmie Johnson 1.25 3.00
RC13 Tony Stewart 1.25 3.00
RC14 Ryan Newman 1.25 3.00
RC15 Mark Martin 1.25 3.00
RC16 Jimmie Johnson 1.25 3.00
RC17 Dale Jarrett 1.00 2.50
RC18 Matt Kenseth 1.25 3.00
RC19 Ricky Rudd .60 1.50
RC20 Michael Waltrip .50 1.25
RC21 Kevin Harvick 1.00 2.50
RC22 Ward Burton .50 1.25
RC23 Tony Stewart 1.25 3.00
RC24 Dale Jarrett 1.00 2.50
RC25 Jeff Gordon 1.50 4.00
RC26 Jeff Gordon 1.50 4.00
RC27 Matt Kenseth 1.25 3.00
RC28 Ryan Newman 1.25 3.00
RC29 Jimmie Johnson 1.25 3.00
RC30 Jeff Gordon 1.50 4.00
RC31 Dale Earnhardt Jr. 2.00 5.00
RC32 Jamie McMurray 1.00 2.50
RC33 Kurt Busch .60 1.50
RC34 Kurt Busch .60 1.50
RC35 Matt Kenseth 1.25 3.00
RC36 Kurt Busch .60 1.50

2003 Press Pass Eclipse Skidmarks

Issued at a stated rate of one in 18 for both hobby and retail packs. This 18-card set features pieces of race-used tires ground up and specially treated work as into the card design.

COMPLETE SET (18) 125.00 250.00
SM1 John Andretti 4.00 10.00
SM2 Jeff Gordon 8.00 20.00
SM3 Tony Stewart 6.00 15.00
SM4 Rusty Wallace 5.00 12.00
SM5 Ryan Newman 6.00 15.00
SM6 Kurt Busch 5.00 12.00
SM7 Mark Martin 6.00 15.00
SM8 Jimmie Johnson 6.00 15.00
SM9 Matt Kenseth 6.00 15.00
SM10 Jamie McMurray 4.00 10.00
SM11 Terry Labonte 4.00 10.00
SM12 Dale Jarrett 5.00 12.00
SM13 Kevin Harvick 5.00 12.00
SM14 Bobby Labonte 5.00 12.00
SM15 Ward Burton 4.00 10.00
SM16 Robby Gordon 5.00 12.00
SM17 Jeff Green 3.00 8.00
SM18 Jeff Burton 5.00 12.00

2003 Press Pass Eclipse Supernova

Inserted at a rate of one in eight, this 12-card set featured some of the leading drivers in Nascar.

COMPLETE SET (12) 20.00 50.00
SN1 Steve Park 1.25 3.00
SN2 Dale Earnhardt Jr. 5.00 12.00
SN3 Jeff Gordon 4.00 10.00
SN4 Kevin Harvick 2.50 6.00
SN5 Dale Jarrett 2.50 6.00
SN6 Matt Kenseth 3.00 8.00
SN7 Bobby Labonte 3.00 8.00
SN8 Jimmie Johnson 3.00 8.00
SN9 Mark Martin 3.00 8.00
SN10 Michael Waltrip 1.25 3.00
SN11 Tony Stewart 3.00 8.00
SN12 Rusty Wallace 2.50 6.00

2003 Press Pass Eclipse Teammates Autographs

Randomly inserted into packs, these seven cards feature dual signed cards of NASCAR teammates. Each card was issued to a stated print run of 25 serial numbered sets.

SOME NOT PRICED DUE TO SCARCITY
JAKP John Andretti
Kyle Petty
JBKB Jeff Burton
Kurt Busch
JGJJ Jeff Gordon
Jimmie Johnson
KHRG Kevin Harvick
Robby Gordon
MMMK Mark Martin 125.00 200.00
Matt Kenseth
RNRW Ryan Newman
Rusty Wallace
SMJM Sterling Marlin 60.00 100.00
Jamie McMurray

2003 Press Pass Eclipse Under Cover Cars

Issued at a stated rate of one in 240 retail packs, these 17 cards feature pieces of car covers included as part of the card. Each card was also serial numbered to 215 and feature photos of the driver's car.

COMPLETE SET (17)
*CARS: .5X TO 1.2X DRIVERS SILVER
UCT1 Jeff Gordon 20.00 50.00
UCT2 Ryan Newman 15.00 40.00
UCT3 Kevin Harvick 12.50 30.00
UCT4 Jimmie Johnson 12.50 30.00
UCT5 Tony Stewart 15.00 40.00
UCT6 Bobby Labonte 12.50 30.00
UCT7 Dale Earnhardt Jr. 20.00 50.00
UCT8 Jeff Burton 10.00 25.00
UCT9 Ricky Craven 10.00 25.00
UCT10 Terry Labonte 10.00 25.00
UCT11 Michael Waltrip 10.00 25.00
UCT12 Robby Gordon 10.00 25.00
UCT13 Joe Nemechek 10.00 25.00
UCT14 Elliott Sadler 10.00 25.00
UCT15 Jeff Green 10.00 25.00
UCT16 Matt Kenseth 15.00 40.00
UCT17 Mark Martin 15.00 40.00

2003 Press Pass Eclipse Under Cover Cars Autographs

Randomly inserted in retail packs, these 5 cards feature pieces of car covers included as part of the card and a signature of the driver. Each card was also hand numbered to the driver's door number and feature photos of the driver's car.

SOME CARDS NOT PRICED DUE TO SCARCITY
UCTBL Bobby Labonte's Car/18 75.00 150.00
UCTJG Jeff Gordon's Car/24 250.00 500.00
UCTJJ Jimmie Johnson's Car/48 75.00 150.00
UCTRN Ryan Newman's Car/12
UCTTL Terry Labonte's Car/5

2003 Press Pass Eclipse Under Cover Double Cover

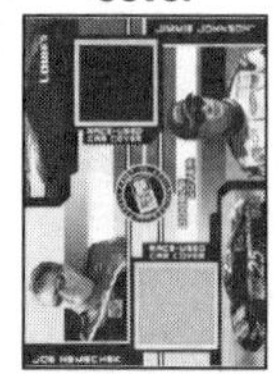

Issued at a stated rate of one in 240 packs, these 9 cards feature pieces of car covers included as part of the card and feature a pair of teammates and a swatch for each driver. Each card was also serial numbered to 530 and feature photos of the drivers.

DC1 Joe Nemechek 12.50 30.00
Jeff Gordon
DC2 Jimmie Johnson 25.00 60.00
Jeff Gordon
DC3 Terry Labonte 15.00 40.00
Jeff Gordon
DC4 Joe Nemechek 12.50 30.00
Jimmie Johnson
DC5 Terry Labonte 12.50 30.00
Jimmie Johnson
DC6 Terry Labonte 10.00 25.00
Joe Nemechek
DC7 Bobby Labonte 20.00 50.00
Tony Stewart
DC8 Kevin Harvick 12.50 30.00
Robby Gordon
DC9 Kevin Harvick 12.50 30.00
Jeff Green

2003 Press Pass Eclipse Under Cover Driver Autographs

Randomly inserted in hobby packs, these 5 cards feature pieces of car covers included as part of the card along with the driver's signature. Each card was also hand numbered to the driver's door number and feature photos of the driver.

SOME CARDS NOT PRICED DUE TO SCARCITY		
UCD-BL Bobby Labonte/18	75.00	150.00
UCD-JG Jeff Gordon/24	250.00	500.00
UCD-JJ Jimmie Johnson/48	75.00	150.00
UCD-RN Ryan Newman/12		
UCD-TL Terry Labonte/5		

2003 Press Pass Eclipse Under Cover Driver Gold

Randomly inserted in hobby packs, these 17 cards feature pieces of car covers included as part of the card. Each card was also serial numbered to 260 and feature photos of the driver and have gold foil highlights.

*GOLDS: .6X TO 1.5X DRIVERS SILVER

2003 Press Pass Eclipse Under Cover Driver Red

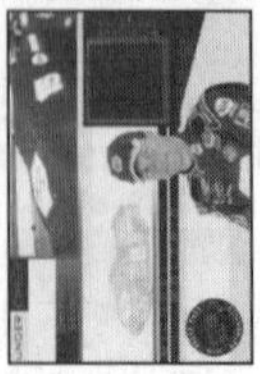

Randomly inserted in hobby packs, these 17 cards feature pieces of car covers included as part of the card. Each card was also serial numbered to 100 and feature photos of the driver and have red foil highlights.

*REDS: .8X TO 2X DRIVERS SILVER

2003 Press Pass Eclipse Under Cover Driver Silver

Randomly inserted in hobby packs, these 17 cards feature pieces of car covers included as part of the card. Each card was also serial numbered to 450 and feature photos of the driver and have silver foil highlights.

*CARS: .5X TO 1.2X
CARS PRINT RUN 215 SERIAL #'d SETS
*GOLDS: .6X TO 1.5X
GOLD PRINT RUN 260 SERIAL #'d SETS
*REDS: .8X TO 2X
RED PRINT RUN 100 SERIAL #'d SETS

UCD1 Jeff Gordon	20.00	40.00
UCD2 Ryan Newman	15.00	30.00
UCD3 Kevin Harvick	12.50	25.00
UCD4 Jimmie Johnson	12.50	25.00
UCD5 Tony Stewart	15.00	30.00
UCD6 Bobby Labonte	12.50	25.00
UCD7 Dale Earnhardt Jr.	20.00	40.00
UCD8 Jeff Burton	8.00	20.00
UCD9 Ricky Craven	8.00	20.00
UCD10 Terry Labonte	10.00	20.00
UCD11 Michael Waltrip	8.00	20.00
UCD12 Robby Gordon	8.00	20.00
UCD13 Joe Nemechek	8.00	20.00
UCD14 Elliott Sadler	8.00	20.00
UCD15 Jeff Green	8.00	20.00
UCD16 Matt Kenseth	15.00	30.00
UCD17 Mark Martin	15.00	30.00

2003 Press Pass Eclipse Warp Speed

Inserted in packs at a stated rate of one in 12, these eight cards feature some of the fastest drivers on the Nascar circuit. These cards were issued in holo-foil board and platinum for an interesting feel. Each card had a "WS" suffix along with its card number.

COMPLETE SET (8)	12.50	30.00
WS1 Jeff Gordon	4.00	10.00
WS2 Dale Earnhardt Jr.	5.00	12.00
WS3 Rusty Wallace	2.50	6.00
WS4 Steve Park	1.25	3.00
WS5 Tony Stewart	3.00	8.00
WS6 Jimmie Johnson	3.00	8.00
WS7 Mark Martin	3.00	8.00
WS8 Michael Waltrip	1.25	3.00

2004 Press Pass Eclipse

This 50-card set was issued in five card hobby and four card retail packs with a suggested retail price of $3.99. These went live in March of 2004. The cards featured a white border with silver foli highlights and a full color photo of the drive or his car.

COMPLETE SET (90)	15.00	40.00
WAX BOX HOBBY (20)	60.00	120.00
1 Matt Kenseth	1.25	3.00
2 Jimmie Johnson	1.25	3.00
2B Jimmie Johnson missing NASCAR official in background	5.00	12.00
3 Dale Earnhardt Jr.	1.50	4.00
4 Jeff Gordon	1.50	4.00
5 Kevin Harvick	1.00	2.50
6 Ryan Newman	1.25	3.00
7 Tony Stewart	1.00	2.50
7B Tony Stewart blue sky grandstand	4.00	10.00
8 Bobby Labonte	.75	2.00
9 Terry Labonte	.60	1.50
10 Kurt Busch	.60	1.50
11 Jeff Burton	.40	1.00
12 Jamie McMurray	.60	1.50
13 Rusty Wallace	.75	2.00
14 Michael Waltrip	.40	1.00
15 Robby Gordon	.25	.60
16 Mark Martin	1.00	2.50
17 Sterling Marlin	.60	1.50
18 Jeremy Mayfield	.25	.60
19 Greg Biffle	.40	1.00
20 Elliott Sadler	.40	1.00
21 Ricky Rudd	.60	1.50
22 Dale Jarrett	1.00	2.50
23 Ricky Craven	.25	.60
24 Kenny Wallace	.25	.60
25 Casey Mears	.40	1.00
26 Ken Schrader	.25	.60
27 Kyle Petty	.40	1.00
28 Rusty Wallace's Car	.40	1.00
29 Mark Martin's Car	.40	1.00
30 Dale Earnhardt Jr.'s Car	.60	1.50
31 Michael Waltrip's Car	.25	.60
32 Matt Kenseth's Car	.60	1.50
33 Bobby Labonte's Car	.40	1.00
34 Tony Stewart's Car	.40	1.00
35 Kevin Harvick's Car	.40	1.00
36 Kurt Busch's Car	.25	.60
37 Brian Vickers	.75	2.00
38 David Green	.25	.60
39 Scott Riggs	.40	1.00
39B Scott Riggs blue sky visible	1.50	4.00
40 Kasey Kahne	1.50	4.00
41 Johnny Sauter	.40	1.00
42 Scott Wimmer	.40	1.00
43 Mike Bliss	.25	.60
44 Stacy Compton	.25	.60
45 Coy Gibbs	.40	1.00
46 Ryan Newman Z	1.25	3.00
47 Dale Earnhardt Jr. Z	1.50	4.00
47B Dale Earnhardt Jr. Z small 8 above large 8	6.00	15.00
48 Jimmie Johnson Z	1.25	3.00
49 Matt Kenseth Z	1.25	3.00
50 Ryan Newman Z	1.25	3.00
51 Matt Kenseth Z	1.25	3.00
52 Dale Earnhardt Jr. Z	1.50	4.00
53 Jeff Gordon Z	1.50	4.00
54 Ryan Newman Z	1.25	3.00
55 Bobby Labonte P	.75	2.00
55B Bobby Labonte P logos not on every white check	3.00	8.00
56 Dale Earnhardt Jr. P	1.50	4.00
57 Jeff Gordon P	1.50	4.00
58 Jimmie Johnson P	1.25	3.00
59 Kevin Harvick P	1.00	2.50
60 Matt Kenseth P	1.25	3.00
61 Michael Waltrip P	.40	1.00
62 Rusty Wallace P	.75	2.00
63 Tony Stewart P	1.00	2.50
64 Tony Stewart WCS	1.00	2.50
65 Ryan Newman's Car WCS	1.25	3.00
66 Bobby Labonte WCS	.75	2.00
67 Kurt Busch WCS	.60	1.50
68 Greg Biffle WCS	.40	1.00
69 Ryan Newman WCS	1.25	3.00
70 Ryan Newman WCS	1.25	3.00
71 Kevin Harvick WCS	1.00	2.50
72 Terry Labonte WCS	.60	1.50
73 Dale Earnhardt Jr. LL	1.50	4.00
74 Kevin Harvick LL	1.00	2.50
75 Jeff Gordon LL	1.50	4.00
76 Mark Martin Rusty Wallace LL	1.00	2.50
77 Matt Kenseth LL	1.25	3.00
78 Dale Earnhardt Jr. Jimmie Johnson LL	1.50	4.00
79 Mark Martin LL	1.00	2.50
80 Michael Waltrip LL	.40	1.00
80B Michael Waltrip LL bright blue sky	1.50	4.00
81 Terry Labonte LL	.60	1.50
82 Robby Gordon Kevin Harvick LL	1.00	2.50
83 Ryan Newman LL	1.25	3.00
84 Tony Stewart LL	1.00	2.50
85 Jimmie Johnson LL	1.25	3.00
86 Jamie McMurray LL	.60	1.50
87 Bobby Labonte LL	.75	2.00
88 Matt Kenseth SM	1.25	3.00
89 Brian Vickers SM	.75	2.00
90 Travis Kvapil SM	.25	.60

2004 Press Pass Eclipse Samples

This 90-card set is a parallel to the base 2004 Press Pass Eclipse set without the variations. It was issued 1 per Beckett Racing Collector issue #117, which was the May 2004 cover date. Each card had the word "SAMPLE" printed across the back.

*SAMPLES: 2X TO 5X BASE

2004 Press Pass Eclipse Destination WIN

This 27-card set featured 2003 race winners celebrating at the track in which they won. The cards are die-cut and produced on a plastic card stock. They were inserted at a rate of 1 in 2 packs.

COMPLETE SET (27)	12.50	30.00
1 Dale Earnhardt Jr.	1.50	4.00
2 Dale Earnhardt Jr.	1.50	4.00
3 Michael Waltrip	.40	1.00
4 Dale Jarrett	.75	2.00
5 Matt Kenseth	1.25	3.00
6 Bobby Labonte	.75	2.00
7 Ricky Craven	.25	.60
8 Kurt Busch	.60	1.50
9 Ryan Newman	1.25	3.00
10 Dale Earnhardt Jr.	1.50	4.00
11 Jeff Gordon	1.50	4.00
12 Kurt Busch	.60	1.50
13 Joe Nemechek	.25	.60
14 Jimmie Johnson	1.25	3.00
15 Ryan Newman	1.25	3.00
16 Tony Stewart	1.00	2.50
17 Robby Gordon	.25	.60
18 Greg Biffle	.40	1.00
19 Jimmie Johnson	1.25	3.00
20 Ryan Newman	1.25	3.00
21 Kevin Harvick	1.00	2.50
22 Terry Labonte	.60	1.50
23 Ryan Newman	1.25	3.00
24 Michael Waltrip	.40	1.00
25 Tony Stewart	1.00	2.50
26 Jeff Gordon	1.50	4.00
27 Dale Earnhardt Jr.	1.50	4.00

2004 Press Pass Eclipse Hyperdrive

This 9-card set featured some of NASCAR's fastest drivers. The cards were designed to be seen on the horizontal angle with a picture of the driver and a smaller image of his car. The cards were produced on a plastic card stock. They were randomly inserted at a rate of 1 in 10 packs.

COMPLETE SET (9)	20.00	50.00
HP1 Michael Waltrip	1.00	2.50
HP2 Rusty Wallace	1.50	4.00
HP3 Tony Stewart	2.00	5.00
HP4 Ryan Newman	2.50	6.00
HP5 Dale Earnhardt Jr.	3.00	8.00
HP6 Mark Martin	2.00	5.00
HP7 Jeff Gordon	3.00	8.00
HP8 Jimmie Johnson	2.50	6.00
HP9 Matt Kenseth	2.50	6.00

2004 Press Pass Eclipse Maxim

This 12-card set featured some of NASCAR's most popular drivers. The cards were designed with a picture of the driver and some foil highlights and were produced on a plastic card stock. They were randomly inserted at a rate of 1 in 6 packs.

COMPLETE SET (12)	15.00	40.00
MX1 Matt Kenseth	2.00	5.00
MX2 Jimmie Johnson	2.00	5.00
MX3 Dale Earnhardt Jr.	2.50	6.00
MX4 Jeff Gordon	2.50	6.00
MX5 Kevin Harvick	1.50	4.00
MX6 Tony Stewart	1.50	4.00
MX7 Bobby Labonte	1.25	3.00
MX8 Kurt Busch	1.00	2.50
MX9 Michael Waltrip	.60	1.50
MX10 Mark Martin	1.50	4.00
MX11 Greg Biffle	.60	1.50
MX12 Dale Jarrett	1.25	3.00

2004 Press Pass Eclipse Skidmarks

Issued at a stated rate of one in 18 for both hobby and retail packs. This 18-card set features pieces of race-used tires ground up and specially treated work as into the card design. There was also a holofoil parallel.

*HOLOFOILS: .6X TO 1.5X BASIC INSERTS
HOLOFOIL PRINT RUN 500 SER.#'d SETS

SM1 Jeff Gordon	10.00	25.00
SM2 Kurt Busch	4.00	10.00
SM3 Jimmie Johnson	8.00	20.00
SM4 Matt Kenseth	8.00	20.00
SM5 Mark Martin	6.00	15.00
SM6 Robby Gordon	2.00	5.00
SM7 Dale Earnhardt Jr.	8.00	20.00
SM8 Terry Labonte	5.00	12.00
SM9 Kevin Harvick	6.00	15.00
SM10 Dale Jarrett	5.00	12.00
SM11 Ryan Newman	8.00	20.00
SM12 Greg Biffle	4.00	10.00
SM13 Tony Stewart	6.00	15.00
SM14 Bobby Labonte	6.00	15.00
SM15 Rusty Wallace	5.00	12.00
SM16 Sterling Marlin	4.00	10.00
SM17 Michael Waltrip	4.00	10.00
SM18 Jamie McMurray	4.00	10.00

2004 Press Pass Eclipse Skidmarks Holofoil

This 18-card set is the parallel of the base set which features pieces of race-used tires ground up and specially treated work as into the card design. These cards had holofoil highlights and were serial numbered to 500.

*HOLOFOILS: .6X TO 1.5X BASIC INSERTS

2004 Press Pass Eclipse Teammates Autographs

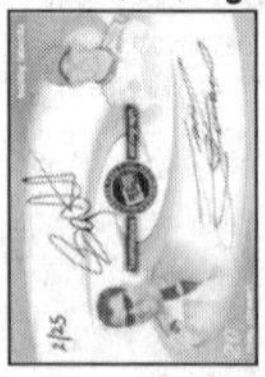

Randomly inserted into packs, these seven cards feature dual signed cards of NASCAR teammates. Each card was issued to a stated print run of 25 serial numbered sets.

1 Robby Gordon Kevin Harvick	125.00	250.00
2 Jimmie Johnson Jeff Gordon	400.00	700.00
3 Greg Biffle Mark Martin	175.00	300.00
4 Bobby Labonte Tony Stewart	200.00	350.00
5 Dale Jarrett Elliott Sadler	100.00	200.00
6 Casey Mears Jamie McMurray	100.00	200.00
7 Ryan Newman Rusty Wallace	150.00	300.00

2004 Press Pass Eclipse Under Cover Autographs

Randomly inserted in retail packs, these 8 cards feature pieces of car covers included as part of the card and a signature of the driver. Each card was also hand numbered to the driver's door number and featured an image of the driver.

SOME CARDS NOT PRICED DUE TO SCARCITY		
UCBL Bobby Labonte/18	75.00	150.00
UCDE Dale Earnhardt Jr./8		
UCJG Jeff Gordon/24	250.00	500.00
UCJJ Jimmie Johnson/48	75.00	150.00
UCKH Kevin Harvick/29	100.00	200.00
UCMM Mark Martin/6		
UCRN Ryan Newman/12		
UCRW Rusty Wallace/2		

2004 Press Pass Eclipse Under Cover Cars

This 15-card set featured a piece of car covers included as part of the card. Each card was also serial numbered to 170 and feature photos of the driver's car.

*CARS: .8X TO 2X DRIVERS SILVER

2004 Press Pass Eclipse Under Cover Double Cover

This 9-card set featured pieces of car covers included as part of the card and feature a pair of teammates and a swatch for each driver. Each card was also serial numbered to 100 and feature photos of the drivers.

DC1 Dale Earnhardt Jr. Michael Waltrip	40.00	100.00
DC2 Rusty Wallace Ryan Newman	30.00	80.00
DC3 Jimmie Johnson Jeff Gordon	40.00	100.00
DC4 Terry Labonte Jeff Gordon	25.00	60.00
DC5 Terry Labonte Jimmie Johnson	15.00	40.00
DC6 Joe Nemechek Terry Labonte	12.50	30.00
DC7 Joe Nemechek Jeff Gordon	20.00	50.00
DC8 Jimmie Johnson Joe Nemechek	15.00	40.00
DC9 Matt Kenseth Jeff Burton	25.00	60.00
DC10 Bobby Labonte Tony Stewart	25.00	60.00
DC11 Kevin Harvick Robby Gordon	25.00	60.00
DC12 Kurt Busch Matt Kenseth	25.00	60.00
DC13 Matt Kenseth Mark Martin	40.00	100.00
DC14 Mark Martin Jeff Burton	20.00	50.00
DC15 Jeff Burton Kurt Busch	15.00	40.00

2004 Press Pass Eclipse Under Cover Driver Gold

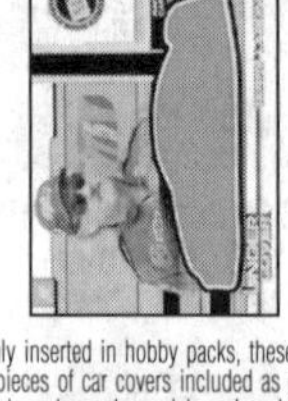

Randomly inserted in hobby packs, these 15 cards feature pieces of car covers included as part of the card. Each card was also serial numbered to 325 and feature photos of the driver and have gold foil highlights.

*GOLD: .6X TO 1.5X DRIVERS SILVER

2004 Press Pass Eclipse Under Cover Driver Red

Randomly inserted in hobby packs, these 15 cards feature pieces of car covers included as part of the card. Each card was also serial numbered to 100 and feature photos of the driver and have red foil highlights.

*RED: 1X TO 2.5X DRIVERS SILVER

2004 Press Pass Eclipse Under Cover Driver Silver

Randomly inserted in hobby packs, these 15 cards feature pieces of car covers included as part of the card. Each card was also serial numbered to 690 and feature photos of the driver and have silver foil highlights.

OVERALL UNDER COVER STATED ODDS 1:10
STATED PRINT RUN 690 SERIAL #'d SETS
*CARS: .8X TO 2X DRIVERS SILVER
CARS INSERTED IN RETAIL PACKS
CAR PRINT RUN 170 SER.#'d SETS
*GOLDS: .6X TO 1.5X SILVERS
GOLD PRINT RUN 325 SER.#'d SETS
*REDS: 1X TO 2.5X SILVERS
RED PRINT RUN 100 SER.#'d SETS

UCD1 Jimmie Johnson	10.00	25
UCD2 Matt Kenseth	10.00	25
UCD3 Kevin Harvick	8.00	20
UCD4 Jeff Gordon	12.50	30
UCD5 Kurt Busch	6.00	15
UCD6 Mark Martin	8.00	20
UCD7 Ryan Newman	10.00	25
UCD8 Bobby Labonte	8.00	20
UCD9 Rusty Wallace	8.00	20
UCD10 Michael Waltrip	5.00	12
UCD11 Robby Gordon	4.00	10
UCD12 Dale Earnhardt Jr.	15.00	40
UCD13 Terry Labonte	6.00	15
UCD14 Tony Stewart	10.00	25
UCD15 Jeff Burton	5.00	12

2005 Press Pass Eclips

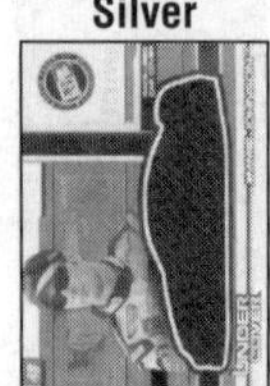

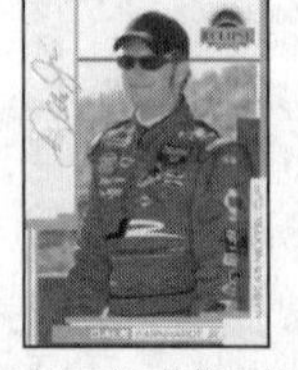

This 90-card set was issued in five card hobby four card retail packs with a suggested retail pri $5.99 for hobby and $2.99 for retail. These wen in March of 2005. The cards featured a white bo with silver foli highlights and a full color photo o drive or his car. The zero card featured Kurt Busc the 2004 Nextel Cup Champion, with two versi gold, numbered to 200, and holofoil numbered t These were found only in hobby packs.

COMPLETE SET (90)	15.00	40
COMMON DRIVER	.25	
SEMISTARS	.40	1
UNLISTED STARS	.60	1
WAX BOX HOBBY (20)	50.00	100
WAX BOX RETAIL (24)	35.00	60
1 Kurt Busch	.60	
2 Jimmie Johnson	1.25	
3 Jeff Gordon	1.50	
4 Mark Martin	1.00	
5 Dale Earnhardt Jr.	1.50	
6 Tony Stewart	1.00	
7 Ryan Newman	1.25	
8 Matt Kenseth	1.25	
9 Elliott Sadler	.40	
10 Jeremy Mayfield	.25	
11 Jamie McMurray	.60	
12 Bobby Labonte	.75	
13 Kasey Kahne	1.50	
14 Kevin Harvick	1.00	
15 Dale Jarrett	.75	
16 Rusty Wallace	.75	
17 Greg Biffle	.40	
18 Joe Nemechek	.25	
19 Michael Waltrip	.40	
20 Sterling Marlin	.60	
21 Casey Mears	.40	
22 Ricky Rudd	.60	
23 Brian Vickers	.75	
24 Terry Labonte	.60	
25 Jeff Green	.25	
26 Ken Schrader	.25	
27 Kyle Petty	.40	
28 Joe Nemechek's Car S	.25	
29 Mark Martin's Car S	.40	
30 Dale Earnhardt Jr's Car S	.60	
31 Scott Riggs' Car S	.25	
32 Ryan Newman's Car S	.40	
33 Michael Waltrip's Car S	.25	
34 Matt Kenseth's Car S	.40	
35 Scott Wimmer's Car S	.25	
36 Jamie McMurray's Car S	.25	
37 Martin Truex Jr.	1.25	
38 Kyle Busch	1.00	
39 Ron Hornaday	.25	
40 Jason Leffler	.25	
41 Jason Keller	.25	
42 Kenny Wallace	.25	
43 Tim Fedewa	.25	
44 David Green	.25	
45 Justin Labonte	.60	
46 Jimmie Johnson Z	1.25	
47 Ryan Newman Z	1.25	
48 Jeff Gordon Z	1.50	
49 Jimmie Johnson Z	1.25	
50 Jimmie Johnson Z	1.25	
51 Kasey Kahne Z	1.50	
52 Kurt Busch Z	.60	
53 Dale Earnhardt Jr. Z	1.50	
54 Kurt Busch Z	.60	
55 Bobby Labonte P	.75	
56 Dale Earnhardt Jr. P	1.50	
57 Jeff Gordon P	1.50	
58 Jimmie Johnson P	1.25	
59 Kevin Harvick P	1.00	
60 Matt Kenseth P	1.25	
61 Michael Waltrip P	.40	
62 Rusty Wallace P	.75	
63 Tony Stewart P	1.00	
64 Ryan Newman's Car NS	.40	
65 J.Gordon/J.Johnson NS	1.50	
66 Tony Stewart NS	1.00	
67 Kurt Busch NS	.60	
68 Jimmie Johnson's Car NS	.40	
69 Tony Stewart NS	1.00	
70 Jeff Gordon NS	1.50	
71 Dale Earnhardt Jr. NS	1.50	
72 J.Gordon/J.Johnson NS	1.50	
73 Dale Earnhardt Jr. LL	1.50	
74 Greg Biffle LL	.40	
75 Jeff Gordon LL	1.50	
76 Brian Vickers LL	.75	
77 Ricky Rudd LL	.60	
78 Kasey Kahne LL	1.50	
79 Mark Martin LL	1.00	
80 Michael Waltrip LL	.40	
81 Terry Labonte LL	.60	
82 Rusty Wallace LL	.75	
83 Dale Jarrett LL	.75	

Tony Stewart LL	1.00	2.50
Jimmie Johnson LL	1.25	3.00
Jamie McMurray LL	.60	1.50
Bobby Labonte LL	.75	2.00
Kurt Busch SM	.60	1.50
Martin Truex Jr. SM	1.25	3.00
Jimmie Johnson SM CL	1.25	3.00
urt Busch Gold/200	6.00	15.00
urt Busch Holofoil/50	12.50	30.00

005 Press Pass Eclipse Samples

se cards were issued to preview the 90-card 5 Eclipse set. The cards were stamped "Sample" the backs and were issued one per Beckett Racing gazine Issue #129 May, 2005.

AMPLES: 1.5X TO 4X

005 Press Pass Eclipse Destination WIN

MPLETE SET (27)	10.00	25.00
ale Earnhardt Jr.	1.25	3.00
Matt Kenseth	1.00	2.50
ale Earnhardt Jr.	1.25	3.00
immie Johnson	1.00	2.50
urt Busch	.50	1.25
lliott Sadler	.30	.75
usty Wallace	.60	1.50
eff Gordon	1.25	3.00
eff Gordon	1.25	3.00
Dale Earnhardt Jr.	1.25	3.00
Jimmie Johnson	1.00	2.50
Mark Martin	.75	2.00
Jimmie Johnson	1.00	2.50
Ryan Newman	1.00	2.50
Jeff Gordon	1.25	3.00
Tony Stewart	.75	2.00
Kurt Busch	.50	1.25
Jeff Gordon	1.25	3.00
Tony Stewart	.75	2.00
Greg Biffle	.30	.75
Dale Earnhardt Jr.	1.25	3.00
Jeremy Mayfield	.15	.40
Dale Earnhardt Jr.	1.25	3.00
Joe Nemechek	.15	.40
Jimmie Johnson	1.00	2.50
Dale Earnhardt Jr.	1.25	3.00
Greg Biffle	.30	.75

005 Press Pass Eclipse Hyperdrive

MPLETE SET (9)	12.50	30.00
1 Michael Waltrip	.75	2.00
2 Bobby Labonte	1.50	4.00
3 Dale Jarrett	1.50	4.00
4 Kevin Harvick	2.00	5.00
5 Dale Earnhardt Jr.	3.00	8.00
6 Mark Martin	2.00	5.00
7 Jeff Gordon	3.00	8.00
8 Jimmie Johnson	2.50	6.00
9 Kurt Busch	1.25	3.00

005 Press Pass Eclipse Maxim

MPLETE SET (12)	15.00	40.00
1 Ryan Newman	2.50	6.00
2 Jimmie Johnson	2.50	6.00
3 Dale Earnhardt Jr.	3.00	8.00
4 Jeff Gordon	3.00	8.00
5 Jamie McMurray	1.25	3.00
6 Tony Stewart	2.00	5.00
7 Terry Labonte	1.25	3.00
8 Dale Jarrett	1.50	4.00
9 Michael Waltrip	.75	2.00
10 Mark Martin	2.00	5.00
11 Kasey Kahne	3.00	8.00
12 Rusty Wallace	1.50	4.00

005 Press Pass Eclipse Skidmarks

1 Jeff Gordon	8.00	20.00
2 Kurt Busch	3.00	8.00
3 Jimmie Johnson	6.00	15.00
4 Matt Kenseth	6.00	15.00
5 Mark Martin	5.00	12.00
6 Elliott Sadler	2.00	5.00
7 Dale Earnhardt Jr.	8.00	20.00

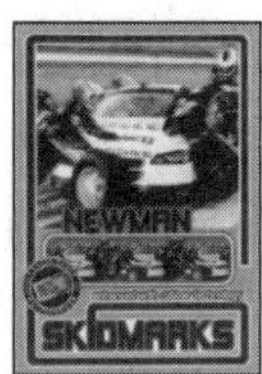

SM8 Ricky Rudd	3.00	8.00
SM9 Kevin Harvick	5.00	12.00
SM10 Dale Jarrett	4.00	10.00
SM11 Ryan Newman	6.00	15.00
SM12 Kasey Kahne	8.00	20.00
SM13 Tony Stewart	5.00	12.00
SM14 Bobby Labonte	4.00	10.00
SM15 Rusty Wallace	4.00	10.00
SM16 Casey Mears	2.00	5.00
SM17 Michael Waltrip	2.00	5.00
SM18 Jamie McMurray	3.00	8.00

2005 Press Pass Eclipse Skidmarks Holofoil

*HOLOFOIL: .6X TO 1.5X SKIDMARKS

2005 Press Pass Eclipse Teammates Autographs

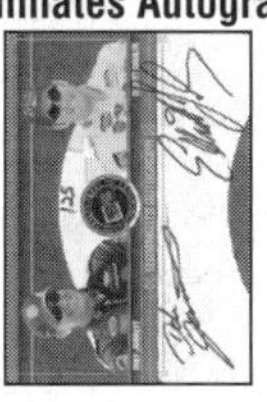

1 Tony Stewart Jason Leffler Bobby Labonte	125.00	200.00
2 Kyle Busch Mark Martin Matt Kenseth	275.00	400.00
3 Ryan Newman Rusty Wallace	75.00	150.00
4 Kasey Kahne Jeremy Mayfield		
5 Dale Jarrett Elliott Sadler	100.00	200.00
6 Jeff Gordon Jimmie Johnson	350.00	600.00
7 Brian Vickers Terry Labonte	60.00	120.00
8 Kyle Busch Carl Edwards	200.00	300.00
9 Matt Kenseth Mark Martin	250.00	350.00

2005 Press Pass Eclipse Under Cover Autographs

SOME CARDS NOT PRICED DUE TO SCARCITY

UCBL Bobby Labonte/18	75.00	150.00
UCDE Dale Earnhardt Jr./8		
UCJG Jeff Gordon/24	250.00	500.00
UCJJ Jimmie Johnson/48	75.00	150.00
UCKH Kevin Harvick/29	100.00	200.00
UCMK Matt Kenseth/17		
UCRN Ryan Newman/12		
UCRW Rusty Wallace/2		
UCTS Tony Stewart/20		

2005 Press Pass Eclipse Under Cover Cars

*CARS: .5X TO 1.2X DRIVERS SILVER

2005 Press Pass Eclipse Under Cover Drivers Holofoil

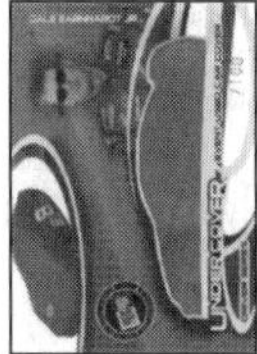

*HOLOFOIL: .6X TO 1.5X SILVER

2005 Press Pass Eclipse Under Cover Driver Red

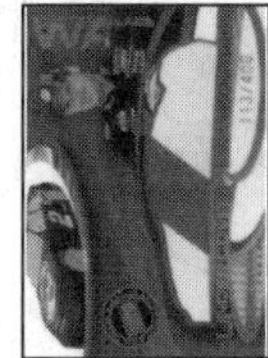

*RED: .5X TO 1.2X SILVER

2005 Press Pass Eclipse Under Cover Drivers Silver

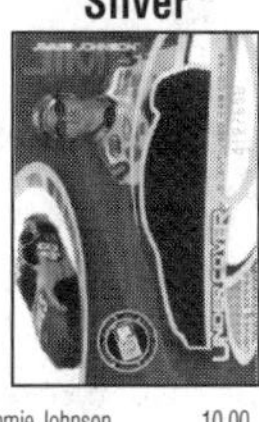

UCD1 Jimmie Johnson	10.00	25.00
UCD2 Matt Kenseth	10.00	25.00
UCD3 Kevin Harvick	8.00	20.00
UCD4 Jeff Gordon	12.50	30.00
UCD5 Kurt Busch	8.00	20.00
UCD6 Mark Martin	8.00	20.00
UCD7 Ryan Newman	10.00	25.00
UCD8 Bobby Labonte	8.00	20.00
UCD9 Rusty Wallace	8.00	20.00
UCD10 Michael Waltrip	6.00	15.00
UCD11 Dale Earnhardt Jr.	15.00	40.00
UCD12 Terry Labonte	8.00	20.00
UCD13 Tony Stewart	10.00	25.00

2005 Press Pass Eclipse Under Cover Double Cover

DC1 Dale Earnhardt Jr. Michael Waltrip	15.00	40.00
DC2 Rusty Wallace Ryan Newman	15.00	40.00
DC3 Jimmie Johnson Jeff Gordon	20.00	50.00
DC4 Kyle Busch Mark Martin	15.00	40.00
DC5 Bobby Labonte Tony Stewart	15.00	40.00
DC6 Kyle Busch Matt Kenseth	15.00	40.00
DC7 Matt Kenseth Mark Martin	15.00	40.00
DC8 Jimmie Johnson Terry Labonte	15.00	40.00
DC9 Jeff Gordon Terry Labonte	15.00	40.00

2006 Press Pass Eclipse

COMPLETE SET (90)	15.00	40.00
WAX BOX HOBBY (20)	90.00	135.00
1 Tony Stewart	1.00	2.50
2 Greg Biffle	.50	1.25
3 Carl Edwards	1.25	3.00
4 Mark Martin	1.00	2.50
5 Jimmie Johnson	1.25	3.00
6 Ryan Newman	1.00	2.50
7 Matt Kenseth	1.25	3.00
8 Rusty Wallace	.75	2.00
9 Jeremy Mayfield	.25	.60
10 Jeff Gordon	1.50	4.00
11 Jamie McMurray	.60	1.50
12 Elliott Sadler	.40	1.00
13 Kevin Harvick	1.00	2.50
14 Dale Jarrett	.75	2.00
15 Joe Nemechek	.25	.60
16 Brian Vickers	.75	2.00
17 Jeff Burton	.40	1.00
18 Dale Earnhardt Jr.	1.50	4.00
19 Kyle Busch	.75	2.00
20 Ricky Rudd	.60	1.50
21 Casey Mears	.40	1.00
22 Kasey Kahne	1.50	4.00
23 Bobby Labonte	.75	2.00
24 Dave Blaney	.25	.60
25 Kyle Petty	.40	1.00
26 Sterling Marlin	.60	1.50
27 Terry Labonte	.60	1.50
28 Martin Truex Jr. NBS	1.00	2.50
29 Clint Bowyer NBS	1.50	4.00
30 Carl Edwards NBS	1.25	3.00
31 Reed Sorenson NBS	1.00	2.50
32 Denny Hamlin NBS	1.50	4.00
33 J.J. Yeley NBS	.60	1.50
34 Johnny Sauter NBS	.40	1.00
35 Jon Wood NBS	.40	1.00
36 Kasey Kahne NBS	1.50	4.00
37 Dale Jarrett WS	.75	2.00
38 Kyle Busch WS	.75	2.00
39 Ryan Newman WS	1.00	2.50
40 Jimmie Johnson WS	1.25	3.00
41 Martin Truex Jr. WS	1.00	2.50
42 Jeff Gordon WS	1.50	4.00
43 Kevin Harvick WS	1.00	2.50
44 Kasey Kahne WS	1.50	4.00
45 Tony Stewart WS	1.00	2.50
46 Greg Biffle P	.50	1.25
47 Rusty Wallace P	.75	2.00
47B Rusty Wallace P Black Jacket	1.50	4.00
48 Brian Vickers P	.75	2.00
49 Kyle Petty P	.40	1.00
50 Tony Stewart P	1.00	2.50
51 Joe Nemechek P	.25	.60
52 Ryan Newman NS	1.00	2.50
53 Dale Jarrett NS	.75	2.00
54 Mark Martin NS	1.00	2.50
55 Jimmie Johnson NS	1.25	3.00
56 Jeff Gordon NS	1.50	4.00
57 Carl Edwards NS	1.25	3.00
57B Carl Edwards NS missing cameraman	2.50	6.00
58 Bobby Labonte TN	.75	2.00
59 Martin Truex Jr. TN	1.00	2.50
60 Kasey Kahne TN	1.50	4.00
60B Kasey Kahne TN missing license	3.00	8.00
61 Greg Biffle TN	.50	1.25
62 Tony Stewart TN	1.00	2.50
63 Dale Earnhardt Jr. TN	1.50	4.00
64 Carl Edwards BA	1.25	3.00
65 Jeremy Mayfield Ryan Newman Rusty Wallace Kurt Busch Matt Kenseth Mark Martin Jimmie Johnson Tony Stewart Greg Biffle Carl Edwards BA	.50	1.25
66 Rusty Wallace BA	.75	2.00
67 Ryan Newman BA	1.00	2.50
68 Mark Martin BA	1.00	2.50
69 Tony Stewart BA	.50	1.25
70 Tony Stewart BA	1.00	2.50
70 Tony Stewart BA	1.00	2.50
71 Tony Stewart BA	1.00	2.50
72 Tony Stewart BA	1.00	2.50
73 Dale Earnhardt Jr. LL	1.50	4.00
74 Jeff Gordon LL	1.50	4.00
75 Dale Jarrett LL	.75	2.00
75B Dale Jarrett LL missing pic in book	1.50	4.00
76 Carl Edwards LL	1.25	3.00
77 Terry Labonte LL	.60	1.50
78 Tony Stewart LL	1.00	2.50
79 Martin Truex Jr. LL	1.00	2.50
80 Rusty Wallace LL	.75	2.00
81 Jimmie Johnson LL	1.25	3.00
82 Mark Martin LL	1.00	2.50
83 Kyle Busch LL	.75	2.00
84 Kevin Harvick LL	1.00	2.50
85 Tony Stewart SM	1.00	2.50
86 Martin Truex Jr. SM	1.00	2.50
87 Kyle Busch SM	.75	2.00
87B Kyle Busch SM d	1.50	4.00
88 Carl Edwards SM	1.25	3.00
89 Ricky Rudd SM	.60	1.50
90 Dale Earnhardt Jr. CL	1.50	4.00
0 Tony Stewart Champ	4.00	10.00

2006 Press Pass Eclipse Hyperdrive

COMPLETE SET (9)	12.50	30.00
STATED ODDS 1:10		
HP1 Carl Edwards	2.50	6.00
HP2 Tony Stewart	2.00	5.00
HP3 Dale Earnhardt Jr.	3.00	8.00
HP4 Jimmie Johnson	2.50	6.00
HP5 Mark Martin	2.00	5.00
HP6 Kasey Kahne	3.00	8.00
HP7 Jeff Gordon	3.00	8.00
HP8 Martin Truex Jr.	2.00	5.00
HP9 Rusty Wallace	1.50	4.00

2006 Press Pass Eclipse Racing Champions

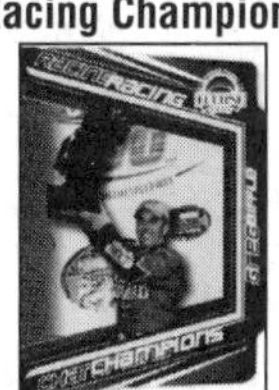

COMPLETE SET (27)	10.00	25.00
STATED ODDS 1:2		
RC1 Jeff Gordon	2.00	5.00
RC2 Greg Biffle	.60	1.50
RC3 Jimmie Johnson	1.50	4.00
RC4 Carl Edwards	1.50	4.00
RC5 Kevin Harvick	1.25	3.00
RC6 Kasey Kahne	2.00	5.00
RC7 Tony Stewart	1.25	3.00
RC8 Dale Earnhardt Jr.	2.00	5.00
RC9 Jeremy Mayfield	.30	.75
RC10 Matt Kenseth	1.50	4.00
RC11 Kyle Busch	1.00	2.50
RC12 Ryan Newman	1.25	3.00
RC13 Dale Jarrett	1.00	2.50
RC14 Mark Martin	1.25	3.00
RC15 Tony Stewart NBS	1.25	3.00
RC16 Mark Martin NBS	1.25	3.00
RC17 Martin Truex Jr. NBS	1.25	3.00
RC18 Carl Edwards NBS	1.50	4.00
RC19 Kevin Harvick NBS	1.25	3.00
RC20 Reed Sorenson NBS	1.25	3.00
RC21 Kasey Kahne NBS	2.00	5.00
RC22 Matt Kenseth NBS	1.50	4.00
RC23 Clint Bowyer NBS	1.50	4.00
RC24 Johnny Sauter NBS	.50	1.25
RC25 David Green NBS	.30	.75
RC26 Ryan Newman NBS	1.25	3.00
RC27 Kyle Busch NBS	1.00	2.50

2006 Press Pass Eclipse Skidmarks

SM1 Kyle Busch	3.00	8.00
SM2 Dale Earnhardt Jr.	6.00	15.00
SM3 Bobby Labonte	3.00	8.00
SM4 Matt Kenseth	5.00	12.00
SM5 Bobby Labonte	3.00	8.00
SM6 Ryan Newman	4.00	10.00
SM7 Jimmie Johnson	5.00	12.00
SM8 Mark Martin	4.00	10.00
SM9 Dale Jarrett	3.00	8.00
SM10 Rusty Wallace	3.00	8.00
SM11 Martin Truex Jr.	4.00	10.00
SM12 Kasey Kahne	6.00	15.00
SM13 Greg Biffle	2.00	5.00
SM14 Jeff Gordon	6.00	15.00
SM15 Carl Edwards	5.00	12.00
SM16 Tony Stewart	4.00	10.00
SM17 Kevin Harvick	4.00	10.00
SM18 Jeff Burton	1.50	4.00

2006 Press Pass Eclipse Skidmarks Holofoil

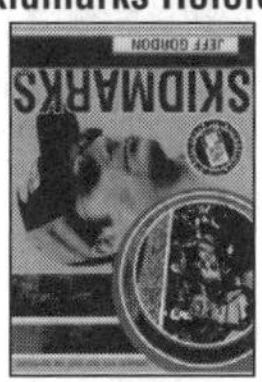

*HOLOFOILS: .8X TO 2X BASE

2006 Press Pass Eclipse Supernova

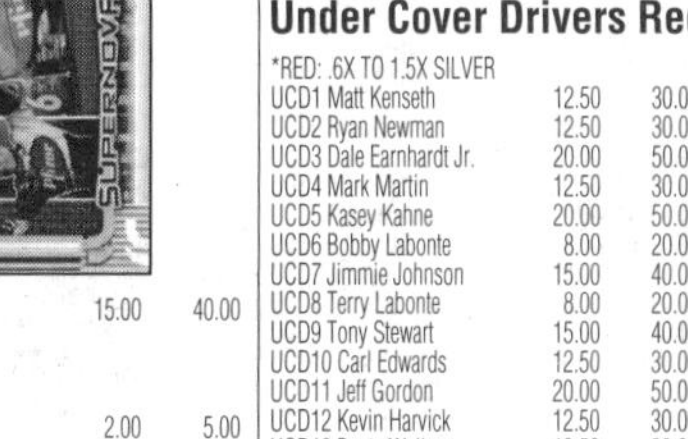

COMPLETE SET (12)	15.00	40.00
SEMISTARS		
UNLISTED STARS		
STATED ODDS 1:5		
SU1 Ryan Newman	2.00	5.00
SU2 Jeff Gordon	3.00	8.00
SU3 Dale Jarrett	1.50	4.00
SU4 Martin Truex Jr.	2.00	5.00
SU5 Tony Stewart	2.00	5.00
SU6 Rusty Wallace	1.50	4.00
SU7 Carl Edwards	2.50	6.00
SU8 Matt Kenseth	2.50	6.00
SU9 Jeff Burton	.75	2.00
SU10 Dale Earnhardt Jr.	3.00	8.00
SU11 Mark Martin	2.00	5.00
SU12 Jimmie Johnson	2.50	6.00

2006 Press Pass Eclipse Teammates Autographs

1 Greg Biffle Matt Kenseth	150.00	250.00
2 Kyle Busch Brian Vickers	60.00	120.00
3 Carl Edwards Mark Martin	125.00	250.00
4 Dale Jarrett Elliott Sadler	75.00	150.00
5 Jimmie Johnson Jeff Gordon	450.00	650.00
6 Kasey Kahne Jeremy Mayfield	150.00	300.00
7 Rusty Wallace Ryan Newman	75.00	150.00

2006 Press Pass Eclipse Under Cover Autographs

SOME NOT PRICED DUE TO SCARCITY

GB Greg Biffle/16		
JG Jeff Gordon/24	300.00	500.00
JJ Jimmie Johnson/48	75.00	150.00
KH Kevin Harvick/29	100.00	200.00
MK Matt Kenseth/17		
MM Mark Martin/6		
RN Ryan Newman/12		
RW Rusty Wallace/2		
TS Tony Stewart/20		

2006 Press Pass Eclipse Under Cover Cars

UCT1 Matt Kenseth	8.00	20.00
UCT2 Ryan Newman	8.00	20.00
UCT3 Dale Earnhardt Jr.	12.50	30.00
UCT4 Mark Martin	8.00	20.00
UCT5 Kasey Kahne	12.50	30.00
UCT6 Bobby Labonte	6.00	15.00
UCT7 Jimmie Johnson	10.00	25.00
UCT8 Terry Labonte	6.00	15.00
UCT9 Tony Stewart	10.00	25.00
UCT10 Carl Edwards	8.00	20.00
UCT11 Jeff Gordon	12.50	30.00
UCT12 Kevin Harvick	8.00	20.00
UCT13 Rusty Wallace	8.00	20.00
UCT14 Greg Biffle	8.00	20.00

2006 Press Pass Eclipse Under Cover Double Cover

DC1 Jimmie Johnson Jeff Gordon	25.00	60.00
DC2 Mark Martin Matt Kenseth	20.00	50.00
DC3 Mark Martin Greg Biffle	15.00	40.00
DC4 Ryan Newman Rusty Wallace	15.00	40.00
DC5 Jeff Gordon Terry Labonte	25.00	60.00
DC6 Matt Kensth Carl Edwards	20.00	50.00
DC7 Carl Edwards Mark Martin	20.00	50.00
DC8 Terry Labonte Jimmie Johnson	15.00	40.00
DC9 Greg Biffle Carl Edwards	20.00	50.00

2006 Press Pass Eclipse Under Cover Drivers Gold

STATED PRINT RUN 1 SERIAL #'d SET
NOT PRICED DUE TO SCARCITY

2006 Press Pass Eclipse Under Cover Drivers Holofoil

*HOLOFOIL: .8X TO 2X SILVER

2006 Press Pass Eclipse Under Cover Drivers Red

*RED: .6X TO 1.5X SILVER

UCD1 Matt Kenseth	12.50	30.00
UCD2 Ryan Newman	12.50	30.00
UCD3 Dale Earnhardt Jr.	20.00	50.00
UCD4 Mark Martin	12.50	30.00
UCD5 Kasey Kahne	20.00	50.00
UCD6 Bobby Labonte	8.00	20.00
UCD7 Jimmie Johnson	15.00	40.00
UCD8 Terry Labonte	8.00	20.00
UCD9 Tony Stewart	15.00	40.00
UCD10 Carl Edwards	12.50	30.00
UCD11 Jeff Gordon	20.00	50.00
UCD12 Kevin Harvick	12.50	30.00
UCD13 Rusty Wallace	12.50	30.00
UCD14 Greg Biffle	12.50	30.00

2006 Press Pass Eclipse Under Cover Drivers Silver

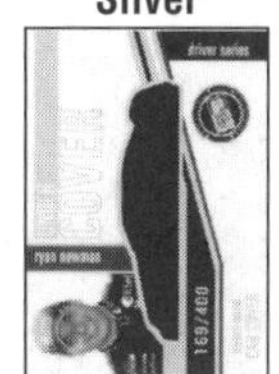

UCD1 Matt Kenseth	8.00	20.00
UCD2 Ryan Newman	8.00	20.00
UCD3 Dale Earnhardt Jr.	12.50	30.00
UCD4 Mark Martin	8.00	20.00
UCD5 Kasey Kahne	12.50	30.00
UCD6 Bobby Labonte	6.00	15.00
UCD7 Jimmie Johnson	10.00	25.00
UCD8 Terry Labonte	6.00	15.00
UCD9 Tony Stewart	10.00	25.00
UCD10 Carl Edwards	8.00	20.00
UCD11 Jeff Gordon	12.50	30.00
UCD12 Kevin Harvick	8.00	20.00
UCD13 Rusty Wallace	8.00	20.00
UCD14 Greg Biffle	8.00	20.00

2007 Press Pass Eclipse

This 90-card set was issued in five card hobby and four card retail packs with a suggested retail price of $5.99 for hobby and $2.99 for retail. These went live in March of 2007. The cards featured a white border with silver foil highlights and a full color photo of the drive or his car. The zero card featured all 10 Cup Chase participants, these were found only in hobby packs and inserted at a rate of one in 72. Hobby boxes contained 24 - five card packs and Retail boxes contained 24 - four card packs and both were packed in 20 box cases.

COMPLETE SET (90)	15.00	40.00
WAX BOX HOBBY (24)	90.00	135.00
WAX BOX RETAIL (24)	50.00	75.00
1 Jimmie Johnson	1.25	3.00
2 Matt Kenseth	1.25	3.00
3 Denny Hamlin	1.25	3.00
4 Kevin Harvick	1.00	2.50
5 Dale Earnhardt Jr.	1.50	4.00
6 Jeff Gordon	1.50	4.00
7 Jeff Burton	.40	1.00
8 Kasey Kahne	1.50	4.00
9 Mark Martin	1.00	2.50
10 Kyle Busch	.75	2.00
11 Tony Stewart	1.00	2.50
12 Carl Edwards	1.00	2.50
13 Greg Biffle	.50	1.25
14 Casey Mears	.40	1.00
15 Kurt Busch	.40	1.00
16 Clint Bowyer	1.25	3.00
17 Ryan Newman	.75	2.00
18 Martin Truex Jr.	1.00	2.50
19 Scott Riggs	.40	1.00
20 Bobby Labonte	.75	2.00
21 Elliott Sadler	.40	1.00
22 Reed Sorenson	.75	2.00
23 Jamie McMurray	.60	1.50
24 Dave Blaney	.25	.60
25 Joe Nemechek	.25	.60
26 Jeff Green	.25	.60
27 J.J. Yeley	.50	1.25
28 Ken Schrader	.25	.60
29 Kyle Petty	.40	1.00
30 David Stremme	.75	2.00
31 Sterling Marlin	.60	1.50
32 Tony Raines	.25	.60
33 Jeff Gordon TO	1.50	4.00
34 Kurt Busch TO	.40	1.00
35 Jimmie Johnson TO	1.25	3.00
36 Ryan Newman TO	.75	2.00
37 Kasey Kahne TO	1.50	4.00
38 Denny Hamlin TO	1.25	3.00
39 Kevin Harvick TO	1.00	2.50
40 Kasey Kahne P	1.50	4.00
41 Dale Earnhardt Jr. P	1.50	4.00
42 Scott Riggs P	.40	1.00
43 Jeff Burton P	.40	1.00
44 Kevin Harvick P	1.00	2.50
45 Kyle Busch P	.75	2.00
46 Casey Mears P	.40	1.00
47 Jeff Gordon P	1.50	4.00
48 Matt Kenseth P	1.25	3.00
49 Matt Kenseth FP	1.25	3.00
50 Jimmie Johnson FP	1.25	3.00
51 Kevin Harvick FP	1.00	2.50
52 Dave Blaney FP	.25	.60
53 Mark Martin FP	1.00	2.50
54 Joe Nemechek FP	.25	.60
55 Jeff Gordon FP	1.50	4.00
56 Sterling Marlin NT	.60	1.50
57 Denny Hamlin NT	1.25	3.00
58 Dale Jarrett NT	.75	2.00
59 Tony Stewart NT	1.00	2.50
60 Joe Nemechek NT	.25	.60
61 J.J. Yeley NT	.50	1.25
62 Rusty Wallace NT	.75	2.00
63 Reed Sorenson NT	.75	2.00
64 Mark Martin	.40	1.00
Kasey Kahne		
Jeff Burton NS		
65 Kevin Harvick NS	1.00	2.50
66 Jeff Burton NS	.40	1.00
67 Tony Stewart NS	1.00	2.50
68 Kasey Kahne NS	1.50	4.00
69 Jimmie Johnson NS	1.25	3.00
70 Tony Stewart NS	1.00	2.50
71 Jimmie Johnson NS	1.25	3.00
72 Jimmie Johnson NS	1.25	3.00
73 Jimmie Johnson NYC	1.25	3.00
74 Matt Kenseth NYC	1.25	3.00
75 Denny Hamlin NYC	1.25	3.00
76 Kevin Harvick NYC	1.00	2.50
77 Dale Earnhardt Jr. NYC	1.50	4.00
78 Tony Stewart NYC	1.00	2.50
79 Jimmie Johnson SM	1.25	3.00
80 Denny Hamlin SM	1.25	3.00
81 Kevin Harvick SM	1.00	2.50
82 Danny O'Quinn SM	.60	1.50
83 Mark Martin SM	1.00	2.50
84 Juan Pablo Montoya RC	3.00	8.00
85 David Gilliland RC	2.00	5.00
86 Paul Menard CRC	2.00	5.00
87 Regan Smith CRC	1.50	4.00
88 Mark Martin	1.00	2.50
89 Dale Jarrett	.75	2.00
0 Cup Chase 10	4.00	10.00
Jimmie Johnson		
Jeff Gordon		
Dale Earnhardt Jr.		
Denny Hamlin		
Matt Kenseth		
Kevin Harvick		
Kasey Kahne		
Kyle Busch		
Jeff Burton		
Mark Martin		
CL Dale Earnhardt Jr. CL	1.50	4.00

2007 Press Pass Eclipse Gold

This 90-card set parallels the basic 2007 Press Pqass Eclipse set. The cards featured gold foil highlights and were serial numbered to 25 copies. The cards carried a "G" prefix for their card numbers.

*GOLD: 8X TO 20X BASE

2007 Press Pass Eclipse Ecliptic

This 12-card set was inserted into packs of 2007 Press Pass Eclipse at a rate of one in six for both Hobby and Retail. The cards were highlighted on a combination of holofoil board and plastic to create a unique finish. The cards carried an "EC" prefix for thier card numbers.

COMPLETE SET (12)	15.00	40.00

EC1 Jimmie Johnson	2.00	5.00
EC2 Mark Martin	1.50	4.00
EC3 Kasey Kahne	2.50	6.00
EC4 Matt Kenseth	2.00	5.00
EC5 Jeff Gordon	2.50	6.00
EC6 Ryan Newman	1.25	3.00
EC7 Tony Stewart	1.50	4.00
EC8 Dale Earnhardt Jr.	2.50	6.00
EC9 Denny Hamlin	2.00	5.00
EC10 Jamie McMurray	1.00	2.50
EC11 Kevin Harvick	1.50	4.00
EC12 Carl Edwards	1.50	4.00

2007 Press Pass Eclipse Hyperdrive

This 9-card set was inserted into packs of 2007 Press Pass Eclipse at a rate of one in 12 for both Hobby and Retail. The cards were highlighted on a combination of holofoil board and plastic to create a unique finish. The cards carried an "HP" prefix for thier card numbers.

COMPLETE SET (9)	12.50	30.00
HD1 Tony Stewart	2.50	6.00
HD2 Matt Kenseth	3.00	8.00
HD4 Kevin Harvick	2.50	6.00
HD5 Jimmie Johnson	3.00	8.00
HD6 Kasey Kahne	4.00	10.00
HD7 Jeff Gordon	4.00	10.00
HD8 Jeff Burton	1.00	2.50
HD9 Dale Earnhardt Jr.	4.00	10.00

2007 Press Pass Eclipse Racing Champions

This 27-card set was inserted into packs of 2007 Press Pass Eclipse at a rate of one in two packs for both Hobby and Retail. Each card carried a "RC" prefix for its card number.

COMPLETE SET (27)	12.50	30.00
RC1 Kasey Kahne	1.25	3.00
RC2 Kevin Harvick	.75	2.00
RC3 Jimmie Johnson	1.00	2.50
RC4 Tony Stewart	.75	2.00
RC5 Matt Kenseth	1.00	2.50
RC6 Greg Biffle	.40	1.00
RC7 Jeff Gordon	1.25	3.00
RC8 Denny Hamlin	1.00	2.50
RC9 Jeff Burton	.30	.75
RC10 Kurt Busch	.30	.75
RC11 Kyle Busch	.60	1.50
RC12 Dale Earnhardt Jr.	1.25	3.00
RC13 Kevin Harvick	.75	2.00
RC14 Carl Edwards	.75	2.00
RC15 Matt Kenseth	1.00	2.50
RC16 Jeff Burton	.30	.75
RC17 Kurt Busch	.30	.75
RC18 Dale Earnhardt Jr.	1.25	3.00
RC19 Denny Hamlin	1.00	2.50
RC20 Kasey Kahne	1.25	3.00
RC21 Clint Bowyer	1.00	2.50
RC22 Greg Biffle	.40	1.00
RC23 Kyle Busch	.60	1.50
RC24 David Gilliland	2.50	6.00
RC25 Paul Menard	.40	1.00
RC26 Tony Stewart	.75	2.00
RC27 Martin Truex Jr.	.75	2.00

2007 Press Pass Eclipse Skidmarks

This 18-card set was inserted into packs of 2007 Press Pass Eclipse at a rate of one in 18 Hobby and Retail packs. The set utilized actual race-used tires to enhance the design elements on the card. Each card carried a "SM" prefix for its card number. There was also a Holofoil parallel which was serial numbered to 250 copies and only available in Hobby packs.

SM1 Dale Earnhardt Jr.	6.00	15.00

2007 Press Pass Eclipse Skidmarks

SM2 Reed Sorenson	3.00	8.00
SM3 Kevin Harvick	3.00	8.00
SM4 Matt Kenseth	4.00	10.00
SM5 Denny Hamlin	3.00	8.00
SM6 Jimmie Johnson	4.00	10.00
SM7 Kyle Busch	2.50	6.00
SM8 Kasey Kahne	3.00	8.00
SM9 Jeff Burton	2.50	6.00
SM10 Tony Stewart	4.00	10.00
SM11 Mark Martin	3.00	8.00
SM12 Scott Riggs	2.00	5.00
SM13 Carl Edwards	3.00	8.00
SM14 Clint Bowyer	3.00	8.00
SM15 Greg Biffle	2.00	5.00
SM16 Jeff Gordon	6.00	15.00
SM17 Ryan Newman	3.00	8.00
SM18 Martin Truex Jr.	2.50	6.00

2007 Press Pass Eclipse Skidmarks Holofoil

This 18-card set was a parallel to the basic Skidmarks set. It was randomly inserted into packs of 2007 Press Pass Eclipse. The set utilized actual race-used tires to enhance the design elements on the card. Each card carried a "SM" prefix for its card number. They were serial numbered to 250 copies and only available in Hobby packs.

*HOLOFOIL: .8X TO 2X BASE

2007 Press Pass Eclipse Teammates Autographs

This 6-card set featured double and triple signed certified autograph cards. The drivers were paired with teammates on the cards and each was serial numbered to just 25 copies. The Gordon/Johnson/Ky.Busch and the Harvick/Bowyer/Burton cards were not released in packs. They were additions that were only available in the Collector's Series Box Set that was released in October 2007.

1 Dale Earnhardt Jr.	250.00	400.00
Martin Truex Jr.		
Paul Menard		
2 Kasey Kahne	200.00	300.00
Scott Riggs		
Elliott Sadler		
3 Juan Pablo Montoya	200.00	300.00
Reed Sorenson		
David Stremme		
4 Denny Hamlin	150.00	250.00
Tony Stewart		
J.J. Yeley		
5 Kurt Busch	100.00	200.00
Ryan Newman		
6 Greg Biffle	275.00	450.00
Carl Edwards		
Matt Kenseth		
7 Jeff Gordon	500.00	650.00
Jimmie Johnson		
Kyle Busch		
8 Kevin Harvick	175.00	350.00
Clint Bowyer		
Jeff Burton		

2007 Press Pass Eclipse Under Cover Autographs

This 7-card set was inserted randomly into Hobby packs of 2007 Press Pass Eclipse. Each card featured a swatch of race-used car cover and a signature of the corresponding driver. The cards were serial numbered to the driver's door number.

SOME CARDS NOT PRICED DUE TO SCARCITY		
UC-DE Dale Earnhardt Jr./8		
UC-GB Greg Biffle/16		
UC-JG Jeff Gordon/24	250.00	400.00
UC-JJ Jimmie Johnson/48	75.00	150.00
UC-KK Kasey Kahne/9		
UC-MK Matt Kenseth/17		
UC-RN Ryan Newman/12		
UC-TS Tony Stewart/20		

2007 Press Pass Eclipse Under Cover Double Cover Name

This 6-card set was inserted randomly into Hobby packs of 2007 Press Pass Eclipse. This set parallels the Under Cover Double Cover NASCAR set. Each card featured a swatch of race-used car cover under the die-cut design of the drivers' names. The cards were serial numbered to 25.

*NAME: 1.2X TO 3X NASCAR

2007 Press Pass Eclipse Under Cover Double Cover NASCAR

This 6-card set was inserted randomly into Hobby packs of 2007 Press Pass Eclipse. This set had a parallel, Under Cover Double Cover Name. Each card featured a swatch of race-used car cover under the die-cut design of the word NASCAR. The cards were serial numbered to 99.

DC1 Carl Edwards	12.50	30.00
Greg Biffle		
DC2 Reed Sorenson	12.50	30.00
David Stremme		
DC3 Jeff Gordon	30.00	60.00
Jimmie Johnson		
DC4 Ryan Newman	15.00	40.00
Kurt Busch		
DC5 Matt Kenseth	15.00	40.00
Carl Edwards		
DC6 Dale Earnhardt Jr.	30.00	60.00
Martin Truex Jr.		

2007 Press Pass Eclipse Under Cover Drivers

This 14-card set was inserted randomly into Hobby packs of 2007 Press Pass Eclipse. Each card featured a swatch of race-used car cover under the die-cut design of a car. The cards were serial numbered to 450.

UCD1 Dale Earnhardt Jr.	15.00	40.00
UCD2 David Stremme	6.00	15.00
UCD3 Reed Sorenson	6.00	15.00
UCD4 Matt Kenseth	8.00	20.00
UCD5 Kevin Harvick	8.00	20.00
UCD6 Greg Biffle	6.00	15.00
UCD7 Jimmie Johnson	10.00	25.00
UCD8 Ryan Newman	8.00	20.00
UCD9 Tony Stewart	10.00	25.00
UCD10 Martin Truex Jr.	8.00	20.00
UCD11 Carl Edwards	6.00	15.00
UCD12 Kasey Kahne	10.00	25.00
UCD13 Jeff Gordon	15.00	40.00
UCD14 Kurt Busch	6.00	15.00

2007 Press Pass Eclipse Under Cover Drivers Name

This 14-card set was inserted randomly into Hobby packs of 2007 Press Pass Eclipse. Each card featured a swatch of race-used car cover under the die-cut design of the driver's name. The cards were serial numbered to 99.

*NAME: .8X TO 2X BASE DRIVERS

2007 Press Pass Eclipse Under Cover Drivers NASCAR

This 14-card set was inserted randomly into Hobby packs of 2007 Press Pass Eclipse. Each card featured a swatch of race-used car cover under the die-cut design of the word "NASCAR". The cards were serial numbered to 270.

*NASCAR: .6X TO 1.5X BASE DRIVERS

2007 Press Pass Eclipse Under Cover Teams

This 14-card set was inserted randomly into Retail packs of 2007 Press Pass Eclipse. Each card featured a swatch of race-used car cover under the die-cut design of a car. The cards were serial numbered to 135.

*TEAMS: .4X TO 1X DRIVERS

2007 Press Pass Eclipse Under Cover Teams NASCAR

This 14-card set was inserted randomly into Retail packs of 2007 Press Pass Eclipse. Each card featured a swatch of race-used car cover under the die-cut design of the word "NASCAR". The cards were serial numbered to 25.

*TEAMS NASCAR: X TO X DRIVERS

2008 Press Pass Eclipse

COMPLETE SET (90)	15.00	40.00
COMMON DRIVERS	.25	.60
SEMISTARS	.40	1.00
UNLISTED STARS	.60	1.50
*SUBSET CARDS: .4X TO 1X BASE		
*CAR CARDS: .15X TO .4X BASE		
*VARIATIONS: 1.5X TO 4X BASE		
WAX BOX HOBBY (24)	100.00	150.00
WAX BOX RETAIL (28)	60.00	100.00
1 Jimmie Johnson	1.25	3.00
2 Jeff Gordon	1.50	4.00
3 Clint Bowyer	.75	2.00
4 Matt Kenseth	1.00	2.50
5 Tony Stewart	1.25	3.00
5B Tony Stewart no background	5.00	12.00
6 Kurt Busch	.60	1.50
7 Jeff Burton	.40	1.00
8 Carl Edwards	1.00	2.50
9 Kevin Harvick	.75	2.00
10 Martin Truex Jr.	.75	2.00
11 Denny Hamlin	1.00	2.50
12 Ryan Newman	.60	1.50
13 Greg Biffle	.50	1.25
14 Jamie McMurray	.50	1.25
15 Bobby Labonte	.60	1.50
16 Kasey Kahne	1.25	3.00
17 Juan Pablo Montoya	1.50	4.00
18 Reed Sorenson	.40	1.00
19 David Ragan	.50	1.25
20 Elliott Sadler	.50	1.25
21 Mark Martin	1.00	2.50
21B Mark Martin Army hat	4.00	10.00
22 Dave Blaney	.25	.60
23 Paul Menard	.50	1.25
24 Kyle Petty	.40	1.00
25 Brian Vickers	.50	1.25
26 Dale Jarrett	1.00	2.50
27 Michael Waltrip	.50	1.25
28 Jeff Gordon RM	1.50	4.00
28B Jeff Gordon RM blank red background	6.00	15.00
29 Ryan Newman RM	.60	1.50
30 Jimmie Johnson RM	1.25	3.00
31 Clint Bowyer RM	.75	2.00
32 Kasey Kahne RM	1.25	3.00
33 Kurt Busch RM	.60	1.50
34 Denny Hamlin RM	1.00	2.50
35 Dave Blaney RM	.25	.60
36 Michael Waltrip RM	.50	1.25
37B Jimmie Johnson TO	5.00	12.00
37 Jimmie Johnson Track background	1.25	3.00
38 Jeff Gordon TO	1.50	4.00
39 Denny Hamlin TO	1.00	2.50
40 Kurt Busch TO	.60	1.50
41 Ryan Newman TO	.60	1.50
42 Kasey Kahne TO	1.25	3.00
43 Martin Truex Jr. TO	.75	2.00
44 Clint Bowyer TO	.75	2.00
45 Jeff Burton TO	.40	1.00
46 Clint Bowyer NS	.75	2.00
47 Carl Edwards NS	1.00	2.50
48 Greg Biffle NS	.50	1.25
49 Jeff Gordon NS	1.50	4.00
50 Jeff Gordon NS	1.50	4.00
51 Jimmie Johnson NS	1.25	3.00
52 Jimmie Johnson NS	1.25	3.00
53 Jimmie Johnson NS	1.25	3.00
54 Rick Hendrick NS	.40	1.00
55 Jeff Gordon's Car LP	.60	1.50
56 Jamie McMurray's Car LP	.20	.50
57 Ryan Newman's Car LP	.25	.60
58 Carl Edwards' Car LP	.40	1.00
59 Martin Truex Jr.'s Car LP	.30	.75
60 David Ragan's Car LP	.20	.50
61 Matt Kenseth's Car LP	.40	1.00
62 Jeff Burton's Car LP	.15	.40
63 Mark Martin's Car LP	.40	1.00
64 Jimmie Johnson's Car LP	.50	1.25
65 Kurt Busch BTF	.60	1.50
66 Ryan Newman BTF	.60	1.50
67 Dale Earnhardt Jr. BTF	2.00	5.00
67B Dale Earnhardt Jr. BTF go-kart	8.00	20.00
68 Brian Vickers BTF	.50	1.25
69 Dario Franchitti BTF	.75	2.00
70 Reed Sorenson BTF	.40	1.00
71 Michael Waltrip BTF	.50	1.25
72 Juan Pablo Montoya BTF	1.50	4.00
73 Jimmie Johnson SO	1.25	3.00
74 Tony Stewart	1.50	4.00
Juan Pablo Montoya SO		
75 Top 10 Drivers SO	1.50	4.00
Jimmie Johnson		
Jeff Gordon		
Kevin Harvick		
Clint Bowyer		
Tony Stewart		
Carl Edwards		
Matt Kenseth		
Kurt Busch		
Kyle Busch		
76 Carl Edwards SO	1.00	2.50
77 Kevin Harvick SO	.75	2.00
78 Tony Stewart SO	1.25	3.00
79 Jeff Gordon SO	1.50	4.00
80 Jeff Burton SO	.40	1.00
81 Jimmie Johnson SO	1.25	3.00
82 Dario Franchitti PREV RC	2.00	5.00
83 J.J. Yeley PREV	.50	1.25
84 Sam Hornish Jr. PREV CRC	2.50	6.00
85 Casey Mears PREV	.40	1.00
85B Casey Mears P Carquest	1.50	4.00
86 Dale Earnhardt Jr. PREV	2.00	5.00
87 Kasey Kahne PREV	1.25	3.00
88 Kyle Busch PREV	.75	2.00
89 Patrick Carpentier PREV RC	2.00	5.00
90 Dale Earnhardt Jr. CL	2.00	5.00

2008 Press Pass Eclips Gold

*GOLD: 5X TO 12X BASE

STATED PRINT RUN 25 SERIAL #'d SETS

2008 Press Pass Eclips Previews

EB1-EB36 SERIAL #'d TO 5 SETS

EB73-EB81 SERIAL #'d TO 1 SET

NOT PRICED DUE TO SCARCITY

2008 Press Pass Eclips Red

STATED PRINT RUN 1 SERIAL #'d SET

NOT PRICED DUE TO SCARCITY

2008 Press Pass Eclips Escape Velocity

COMPLETE SET (12)	15.00	40
STATED ODDS 1:6		
EV1 Jeff Gordon	2.50	6
EV2 Michael Waltrip	.75	2
EV3 Juan Pablo Montoya	2.50	6
EV4 Tony Stewart	2.00	5
EV5 Jamie McMurray	.75	2
EV6 Martin Truex Jr.	1.25	3
EV7 Jimmie Johnson	2.00	5
EV8 Ryan Newman	1.00	2
EV9 Kevin Harvick	1.25	3
EV10 Jeff Burton	.60	1
EV11 Bobby Labonte	1.00	2
EV12 Dale Jarrett	1.50	4

2008 Press Pass Eclips Hyperdrive

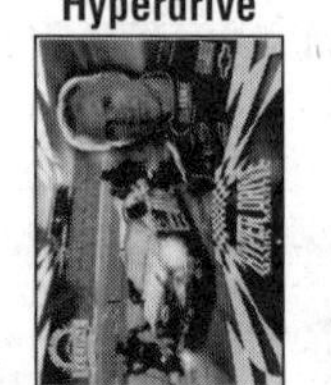

COMPLETE SET (9)	15.00	40
STATED ODDS 1:12		
HP1 Tony Stewart	2.50	6
HP2 Mark Martin	2.00	5
HP3 Jeff Gordon	3.00	8
HP4 Martin Truex Jr.	1.50	4
HP5 Kevin Harvick	1.50	4
HP6 Kasey Kahne	2.50	6
HP7 Matt Kenseth	2.00	5
HP8 Jimmie Johnson	2.50	6
HP9 Jeff Burton	.75	2

2008 Press Pass Eclips Star Tracks

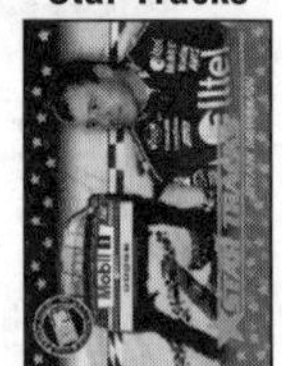

COMPLETE SET (18)	60.00	100
STATED ODDS 1:18		
ST1 Dale Jarrett	4.00	10
ST2 Tony Stewart	5.00	12
ST3 Brian Vickers	2.00	5
ST4 Jeff Gordon	6.00	15
ST5 Mark Martin	4.00	10
ST6 Ryan Newman	2.50	6
ST7 Kevin Harvick	3.00	8
ST8 Kasey Kahne	5.00	12
ST9 Kurt Busch	2.50	6
ST10 Jimmie Johnson	5.00	12
ST11 Jeff Burton	1.50	4
ST12 Martin Truex Jr.	3.00	8
ST13 Matt Kenseth	4.00	10
ST14 Carl Edwards	4.00	10
ST15 Dale Earnhardt Jr.	8.00	20
ST16 Jamie McMurray	2.00	5
ST17 Juan Pablo Montoya	6.00	15
ST18 Michael Waltrip	2.00	5

2008 Press Pass Eclipse Star Tracks Holofoil

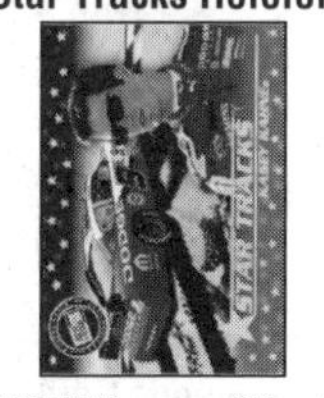

OMPLETE SET (18)	60.00	120.00
HOLO: .6X TO 1.5X BASE		
TATED PRINT RUN 250 SERIAL #'d SETS		

2008 Press Pass Eclipse Stellar

OMPLETE SET (25)	15.00	30.00
TATED ODDS 1:2		
T1 Jimmie Johnson	1.50	4.00
T2 Jeff Gordon	2.00	5.00
T3 Carl Edwards	1.25	3.00
T4 Tony Stewart	1.50	4.00
T5 Kurt Busch	.75	2.00
T6 Matt Kenseth	1.25	3.00
T7 Clint Bowyer	1.00	2.50
T8 Jeff Burton	.50	1.25
T9 Kevin Harvick	1.00	2.50
T10 Denny Hamlin	1.25	3.00
T11 Martin Truex Jr.	1.00	2.50
T12 Greg Biffle	.60	1.50
T13 Jamie McMurray	.60	1.50
T14 Juan Pablo Montoya	2.00	5.00
T15 Kevin Harvick	1.00	2.50
T16 Jeff Burton	.50	1.25
T17 Carl Edwards	1.25	3.00
T18 Denny Hamlin	1.25	3.00
T19 Clint Bowyer	1.00	2.50
T20 Kasey Kahne	1.50	4.00
T21 Matt Kenseth	1.25	3.00
T22 Bobby Labonte	.75	2.00
T23 Juan Pablo Montoya	2.00	5.00
T24 Mike Skinner	.30	.75
T25 Ron Hornaday	.50	1.25

2008 Press Pass Eclipse Teammates Autographs

TATED PRINT RUN 25 SERIAL #'d SETS		
NLESS NOTED BELOW		
V A.J. Allmendinger	75.00	150.00
Brian Vickers/35		
N Kurt Busch	75.00	150.00
Ryan Newman/35		
G Dale Earnhardt Jr.	400.00	650.00
Jeff Gordon		
J Dale Earnhardt Jr.	250.00	400.00
Jimmie Johnson		
M Dale Earnhardt Jr.	175.00	300.00
Casey Mears		
S Kasey Kahne	100.00	200.00
Elliott Sadler/35		
BH Clint Bowyer	125.00	250.00
Jeff Burton		
Kevin Harvick		
HS Kyle Busch	250.00	400.00
Denny Hamlin		
Tony Stewart/35		
MS Dario Franchitti	125.00	250.00
Juan Pablo Montoya		
Reed Sorenson		
GJM Dale Earnhardt Jr.	500.00	800.00
Jeff Gordon		
Jimmie Johnson		
Casey /Mears		

2008 Press Pass Eclipse Under Cover Autographs

ERIAL #'d TO DRIVER'S DOOR #		
OME NOT PRICED DUE TO SCARCITY		
C-DE Dale Earnhardt Jr./8		
C-JG Jeff Gordon/24	200.00	400.00
C-JJ Jimmie Johnson/48		
C-KB Kurt Busch/2		
C-KK Kasey Kahne/9		
C-MK Matt Kenseth/17		
C-MT Martin Truex Jr./1		
C-RN Ryan Newman/12		

2008 Press Pass Eclipse Under Cover Double Cover Name

NAME: .8X TO 2X NASCAR
VERALL R-U STATED ODDS 1:10
TATED PRINT RUN 25 SERIAL #'d SETS

2008 Press Pass Eclipse Under Cover Double Cover NASCAR

VERALL R-U STATED ODDS 1:10		
TATED PRINT RUN 99 SERIAL #'d SETS		
C1 Mark Martin	15.00	40.00
Martin Truex Jr.		
C2 Kevin Harvick	15.00	40.00
Jeff Burton		
C3 Carl Edwards	15.00	40.00
Matt Kenseth		

DC4 Matt Kenseth	12.50	30.00
David Ragan		
DC5 Kurt Busch	12.50	30.00
Ryan Newman		
DC6 Jeff Gordon	25.00	60.00
Jimmie Johnson		
DC7 Carl Edwards	12.50	30.00
David Ragan		

2008 Press Pass Eclipse Under Cover Drivers

OVERALL R-U STATED ODDS 1:10		
STATED PRINT RUN 250 SERIAL #'d SETS		
UCD1 Martin Truex Jr.	8.00	20.00
UCD2 Tony Stewart	10.00	25.00
UCD3 Kevin Harvick	10.00	25.00
UCD4 Kurt Busch	6.00	15.00
UCD5 Carl Edwards	8.00	20.00
UCD6 Mark Martin	8.00	20.00
UCD7 Ryan Newman	8.00	20.00
UCD8 Reed Sorenson	6.00	15.00
UCD9 Matt Kenseth	10.00	25.00
UCD10 David Ragan	6.00	15.00
UCD11 Jeff Burton	8.00	20.00
UCD12 Dale Jarrett	10.00	25.00
UCD13 Michael Waltrip	8.00	20.00
UCD14 Jimmie Johnson	10.00	25.00
UCD15 Jeff Gordon	12.50	30.00

2008 Press Pass Eclipse Under Cover Drivers Eclipse

OVERALL R-U STATED ODDS 1:10
STATED PRINT RUN 1 SERIAL #'d SET
NOT PRICED DUE TO SCARCITY

2008 Press Pass Eclipse Under Cover Drivers Name

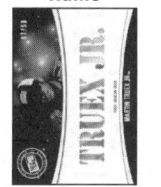

*NAME: .6X TO 1.5X DRIVERS
OVERALL R-U STATED ODDS 1:10
STATED PRINT RUN 50 SERIAL #'d SETS

2008 Press Pass Eclipse Under Cover Drivers NASCAR

*NASCAR: .5X TO 1.2X DRIVERS
OVERALL R-U STATED ODDS 1:10
STATED PRINT RUN 150 SERIAL #'d SETS

2008 Press Pass Eclipse Under Cover Teams

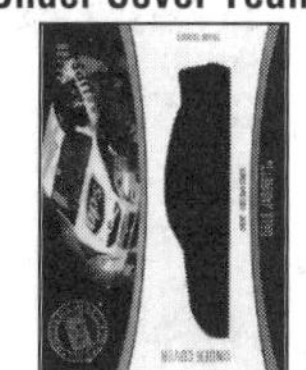

*TEAMS: .6X TO 1.5X DRIVERS
OVERALL R-U STATED ODDS 1:10
STATED PRINT RUN 99 SERIAL #'d SETS

2006 Press Pass Four Wide

FW-BL Bobby Labonte	75.00	150.00
FW-DE Dale Earnhardt Jr.	200.00	400.00
FW-JG Jeff Gordon	250.00	500.00
FW-JJ Jimmie Johnson	125.00	250.00
FW-KH Kevin Harvick	75.00	150.00
FW-MK Matt Kenseth	125.00	250.00
FW-MM Mark Martin	100.00	200.00
FW-RN Ryan Newman	60.00	120.00
FW-RW Rusty Wallace	100.00	200.00
FW-TS Tony Stewart	150.00	300.00

2006 Press Pass Four Wide Checkered Flag

COMPLETE SET (10)
STATED PRINT RUN 1 SERIAL #'d SET
CARDS NOT PRICED DUE TO SCARCITY
FW-BL Bobby Labonte
FW-DE Dale Earnhardt Jr.
FW-JG Jeff Gordon
FW-JJ Jimmie Johnson
FW-KH Kevin Harvick
FW-MK Matt Kenseth
FW-MM Mark Martin
FW-RN Ryan Newman
FW-RW Rusty Wallace
FW-TS Tony Stewart

2007 Press Pass Four Wide

This 9-card set was issued as redemption cards in packs of 2007 Press Pass products. Each card featured swatches of race-used sheet metal, race-used tires, race-used car covers and a large piece of race used firesuit. Each card was serial numbered to 50 and carried a "FW" prefix to its card number. The exchange cards were redeemable until December 31, 2007.

STATED PRINT RUN 50 SERIAL #'d SETS		
FW-DE Dale Earnhardt Jr.	150.00	250.00
FW-DH Denny Hamlin	75.00	150.00
FW-JG Jeff Gordon	200.00	350.00
FW-JJ Jimmie Johnson	75.00	150.00
FW-KH Kevin Harvick	60.00	120.00
FW-KK Kasey Kahne	75.00	150.00
FW-MT Martin Truex Jr.	75.00	150.00
FW-RN Ryan Newman	60.00	120.00
FW-TS Tony Stewart	100.00	200.00

2007 Press Pass Four Wide Exchange

This 9-card exchange set pictured swatches of race-used sheet metal and race-used tires, race-used car covers and a large swatch of race-used firesuit. These were available in packs of 2007 Press Pass and redeemable for the actual four-piece race-used memorabilia cards. These were redeemable until December 31, 2007. Each card is serial numbered to 50 and carried a "FW" prefix for its card number. Each of these had a Press Pass Authentic hologram sticker. Cards were not returned after they were redeemed.

*EXCH: .4X TO 1X FOUR WIDE
EXCH DEADLINE 12/31/2007

2007 Press Pass Four Wide Checkered

This 9-card set was issued as redemption cards in packs of 2007 Press Pass products. Each card featured swatches of race-used sheet metal, race-used tires, race-used car covers and a large piece of race-used checkered flag. Each card was serial numbered to 1 and carried a "FW" prefix to its card number. The exchange cards were redeemable until December 31, 2007.

NOT PRICED DUE TO SCARCITY
FW-DE Dale Earnhardt Jr.
FW-DH Denny Hamlin
FW-JG Jeff Gordon
FW-JJ Jimmie Johnson
FW-KH Kevin Harvick
FW-KK Kasey Kahne
FW-MT Martin Truex Jr.
FW-RN Ryan Newman
FW-TS Tony Stewart

2007 Press Pass Four Wide Checkered Exchange

This 9-card exchange set was issued in packs of 2007 Press Pass products. Each card pictured swatches of race-used sheet metal, race-used tires, race-used car covers and a large piece of race-used checkered flag. Each card was serial numbered to 1 and carried a "FW" prefix to its card number. These exchange cards were redeemable until December 31, 2007 for the actual memorabilia cards.

NOT PRICED DUE TO SCARCITY
EXCH DEADLINE 12/31/2007

2008 Press Pass Four Wide

STATED PRINT RUN 50 SERIAL #'d SETS		
FW-KB Kurt Busch	75.00	150.00
FW-DE1 Dale Earnhardt Jr.	150.00	300.00
FW-DE2 Dale Earnhardt Jr. AMP	200.00	350.00
FW-DE3 Dale Earnhardt Jr. NG	200.00	350.00
FW-CE Carl Edwards	75.00	150.00
FW-JG Jeff Gordon	200.00	350.00
FW-DH Denny Hamlin	100.00	200.00
FW-KH Kevin Harvick	100.00	200.00
FW-JJ Jimmie Johnson	100.00	200.00
FW-KK Kasey Kahne		
FW-MK Matt Kenseth	125.00	250.00
FW-JM Juan Pablo Montoya	60.00	120.00
FW-TS Tony Stewart	150.00	300.00
FW-MT Martin Truex Jr.	60.00	120.00

2008 Press Pass Four Wide Checkered

STATED PRINT RUN 1 SERIAL #'d SET
NOT PRICED DUE TO SCARCITY

2001 Press Pass Excedrin Racing

This three card set was available in specially marked packages of Excedrin. The cards are black and white and feature a picture of the driver front and back.

COMPLETE SET (3)	2.50	6.00
1 David Pearson	.75	2.00
2 Cale Yarborough	.75	2.00
3 Darrell Waltrip	.75	2.00

2000 Press Pass Gatorade Front Runner Award

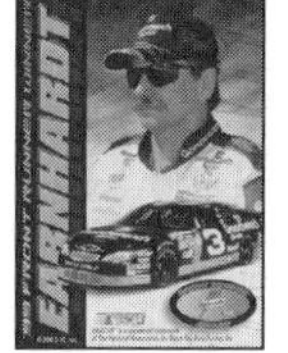

This 12-card set was released by Press Pass in conjunction with Gatorade to honor the 1999 Front Runner Award winners. Three cards were issued at a time over the span of four months (June through September) to collectors that purchased two 32-ounce bottles of Gatorade at participating convenience stores.

COMPLETE SET (12)	10.00	25.00
1 Jeff Burton	.40	1.00
2 Mark Martin	1.25	3.00
3 Steve Park	.60	1.50
4 Tony Stewart	1.50	4.00
5 Dale Jarrett	1.00	2.50
6 Mike Skinner	.20	.50
7 John Andretti	.20	.50
8 Jeff Gordon	1.50	4.00
9 Terry Labonte	.60	1.50
10 Bobby Labonte	1.00	2.50
11 Ward Burton	.30	.75
12 Dale Earnhardt	3.00	8.00

2001 Press Pass Gatorade Front Runner Award

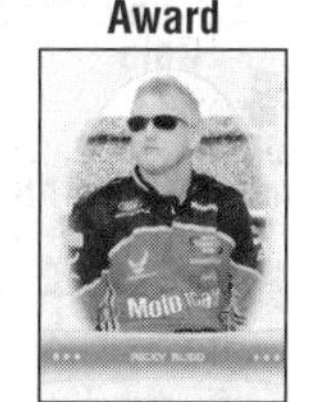

This set was produced by Press Pass and distributed by Gatorade. Each card honors one of the Gatorade Front Runner Award winners from the 2000 Winston Cup season.

COMPLETE SET (10)	6.00	12.00
1 Mark Martin	1.25	3.00
2 Matt Kenseth	1.25	3.00
3 Jeff Gordon	1.50	4.00
4 Jeff Burton	.40	1.00
5 Ward Burton	.40	1.00
6 Jeremy Mayfield	.20	.50
7 Rusty Wallace	1.25	3.00
8 Mike Skinner	.20	.50
9 Jerry Nadeau	.40	1.00
NNO Cover Card	.10	.30

2003 Press Pass Gatorade Jumbos

These cards were produced by Press Pass and sponsored and distributed by Gatorade. Each driver card includes a perforated redemption card at the bottom which could be removed and sent in for a chance to win signed merchandise. The cards with the tab measure roughly 4" by 7 1/4" and 4" by 4 3/4" with the tab removed. Prices below reflect that of cards with the contest tab intact.

COMPLETE SET (4)	5.00	12.00
1 Jimmie Johnson	1.50	4.00
2 Matt Kenseth	1.50	4.00
3 Mark Martin	1.50	4.00
4 Ryan Newman	1.50	4.00

2006 Press Pass Goody's

This 7-card set was produced by Press Pass for Goody's Headache Powders to celebrate the first family of racing, the Pettys. These cards were distributed at Wal-Mart and other retailers in the South. These cards were distributed the summer of 2006 in 4-card packs. Each pack contained a cover card checklist.

COMPLETE SET (7)	5.00	12.00
GCC1 Richard Petty	1.25	3.00
GCC2 Richard Petty	1.25	3.00
GCC3 Kyle Petty	.40	1.00
GCC4 Richard Petty	1.25	3.00
GCC5 Kyle Petty	.40	1.00
GCC6 Kyle Petty	.40	1.00
CL Checklist CL	.15	.40

2001 Press Pass Hot Treads

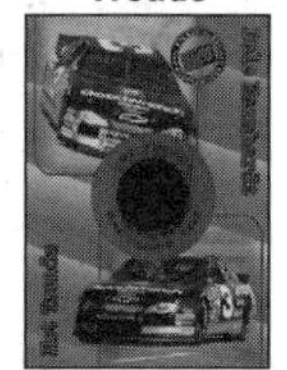

Issued one per High Gear, Press Pass Premier, Stealth and Trackside Special Retail box, these 20 cards feature some of the leading NASCAR drivers. As these cards are printed to different quantities, we have listed the stated print runs in our checklist.

HT1 Bobby Labonte/2405	10.00	25.00
HT2 Tony Stewart/2405	10.00	25.00
HT3 Rusty Wallace/2405	10.00	25.00
HT4 Mike Skinner/2500	6.00	15.00
HT5 Ken Schrader/2500	6.00	15.00
HT6 Dale Earnhardt/1000	25.00	60.00
HT7 Terry Labonte/1000	10.00	25.00
HT8 Joe Nemechek/1000	8.00	20.00
HT9 Dale Jarrett/1000	10.00	25.00
HT10 Ward Burton/1000	8.00	20.00
HT11 Jeff Gordon/1665	15.00	40.00
HT12 Jeremy Mayfield/1660	6.00	15.00
HT13 Mark Martin/1665	10.00	25.00
HT14 Jeff Burton/1660	8.00	20.00
HT15 Dave Blaney/1660	6.00	15.00
HT16 Dale Earnhardt Jr./2405	15.00	40.00
HT17 Steve Park/2400	8.00	20.00
HT18 Matt Kenseth/2405	10.00	25.00
HT19 Ricky Rudd/2400	8.00	20.00
HT20 Bobby Hamilton/2400	6.00	15.00

2001 Press Pass Hot Treads Rookie Rubber

Issued one per special Optima retail box, these six cards feature not only rookies on the NASCAR circuit but a piece of a race-worn tire.

COMPLETE SET (6)	60.00	125.00
RR1 Casey Atwood	5.00	12.00
RR2 Kurt Busch	10.00	25.00
RR3 Ron Hornaday	5.00	12.00
RR4 Andy Houston	5.00	12.00
RR5 Kevin Harvick	12.50	30.00
RR6 Jason Leffler	5.00	12.00

2002 Press Pass Hot Treads

Issued one per special retail box, these cards feature leading drivers and special pieces of memorabilia relating to them. They were issued 8-10 cards at a time in various 2002 Press Pass releases. The final 10-cards feature the popular Coca-Cola family of drivers.

HT1-HT8 ONE PER PRESS PASS SPEC.RETAIL		
HT9-HT16 ONE PER HIGH GEAR SPEC.RETAIL		
HT17-HT24 ONE PER ECLIPSE SPEC.RETAIL		
HT25-HT32 ONE PER PP PREMIUM SPEC.RET.		
HT33-HT42 ONE PER VIP SPEC.RETAIL		
HT1 Steve Park's Car/2300	6.00	15.00
HT2 Ward Burton's Car/2300	6.00	15.00
HT3 Elliott Sadler's Car/2300	5.00	12.00
HT4 Mike Skinner's Car/2300	5.00	12.00
HT5 Tony Stewart's Car/2300	10.00	25.00
HT6 Mark Martin's Car/2300	10.00	25.00
HT7 Michael Waltrip's Car/2300	6.00	15.00
HT8 Dave Blaney's Car/2300	5.00	12.00
HT9 Kevin Harvick's Car/1555	10.00	25.00
HT10 Terry Labonte's Car/1555	6.00	15.00
HT11 Jerry Nadeau's Car/1555	6.00	15.00
HT12 Ken Schrader's Car/1555	6.00	15.00
HT13 Larry Foyt's Car/1555	6.00	15.00
HT14 Jimmie Johnson's Car/1555	10.00	25.00
(Busch Excedrin Car)		
HT15 Jeff Burton's Car/1555	8.00	20.00
HT16 Kurt Busch's Car/1555	10.00	25.00
HT17 Jeff Gordon's Car/2425	10.00	25.00
HT18 Jamie McMurray's Car/2425	10.00	20.00
HT19 Hank Parker Jr's Car/2425	5.00	12.00
HT20 Rusty Wallace's Car/2425	8.00	20.00
HT21 Matt Kenseth's Car/2425	10.00	25.00
HT22 Dale Jarrett's Car/2425	8.00	20.00
HT23 Bobby Labonte's Car/2425	8.00	20.00
HT24 Bobby Hamilton's Car/2425	5.00	12.00
HT25 Dale Earnhardt Jr.'s Car/2375	12.50	30.00
HT26 Sterling Marlin's Car/2375	6.00	15.00
HT27 John Andretti's Car/2375	6.00	15.00
HT28 Jimmy Spencer's Car/2375	6.00	15.00
HT29 Hut Stricklin's Car/2375	5.00	12.00
HT30 Jimmie Johnson/2375	20.00	40.00
(WC Lowe's Car)		
HT31 Ryan Newman's Car/2375	10.00	25.00
HT32 Kyle Petty's Car/2375	6.00	15.00
HT33 Steve Park's Car/900	10.00	25.00
HT34 Michael Waltrip's Car/900	10.00	25.00
HT35 Bobby Labonte's Car/900	8.00	20.00
HT36 Tony Stewart's Car/900	12.50	30.00
HT37 Ricky Rudd's Car/900	10.00	25.00
HT38 Kevin Harvick's Car/900	10.00	25.00
HT39 John Andretti's Car/900	8.00	20.00
HT40 Kyle Petty's Car/900	8.00	20.00
HT41 Dale Jarrett's Car/900	10.00	25.00
HT42 Jeff Burton's Car/900	8.00	20.00

2004 Press Pass Hot Treads

This 18-card set was issued randomly into retail blaster boxes of 2004 Press Pass Eclipse and 2004 Press Pass Premium. The cards featured a swatch of race-used tire. Cards HTR1-HTR9 were available in '04 Press Pass Eclipse blaster boxes and serial numbered to 1100, cards HTR10-HTR18 were available in '04 Press Pass Premium blaster boxes and were serial numbered to 1250. The set also had a silver holofoil parallel.

*HOLOFOILS: .6X TO 1.5X BASIC		
SILVER PRINT RUN 200 SER.#'d SETS		
HTR1 Ricky Rudd	6.00	15.00
HTR2 Dale Earnhardt Jr.	15.00	30.00
HTR3 Jimmie Johnson	10.00	25.00
HTR4 Matt Kenseth	10.00	25.00
HTR5 Ryan Newman	10.00	25.00
HTR6 Kevin Harvick	10.00	25.00
HTR7 Bobby Labonte	8.00	20.00
HTR8 Greg Biffle	8.00	20.00
HTR9 Terry Labonte	10.00	25.00
HTR10 Brian Vickers	8.00	20.00
HTR11 Jeff Gordon	15.00	30.00
HTR12 Tony Stewart	10.00	25.00
HTR13 Rusty Wallace	10.00	25.00
HTR14 Kurt Busch	10.00	25.00
HTR15 Mark Martin	10.00	25.00
HTR16 Michael Waltrip	8.00	20.00
HTR17 Jamie McMurray	8.00	20.00
HTR18 Dale Jarrett	10.00	25.00

2005 Press Pass Hot Treads

HTR1 Dale Earnhardt Jr.	12.50	25.00
HTR2 Mark Martin	10.00	20.00
HTR3 Ryan Newman	10.00	20.00
HTR4 Matt Kenseth	10.00	20.00
HTR5 Kurt Busch	10.00	20.00
HTR6 Kasey Kahne	12.50	25.00
HTR7 Dale Jarrett	10.00	20.00
HTR8 Kevin Harvick	10.00	20.00
HTR9 Rusty Wallace	10.00	20.00
HTR10 Jeff Gordon	12.50	25.00
HTR11 Tony Stewart	10.00	20.00
HTR12 Elliott Sadler	7.50	15.00
HTR13 Jeremy Mayfield	7.50	15.00
HTR14 Martin Truex Jr.	12.50	25.00
HTR15 Michael Waltrip	7.50	15.00
HTR16 Bobby Labonte	7.50	15.00
HTR17 Jamie McMurray	7.50	15.00
HTR18 Jimmie Johnson	10.00	20.00

2005 Press Pass Hot Treads Holofoil

*HOLOFOIL: .6X TO 1.5X HOT TREADS

2007 Press Pass Hot Treads

This 6-card set was randomly inserted into retail blaster boxes only at Wal-Mart. Cards 1-3 could only be found in Press Pass Eclipse and cards 4-6 could only be found in Press Pass Stealth. The cards had a swatch of race-used tire and carried a "HT" prefix for its card number. The cards were inserted one per box.

HT1 Kasey Kahne	6.00	15.00
HT2 Tony Stewart	6.00	15.00
HT3 Jeff Gordon	8.00	20.00
HT4 Jimmie Johnson	6.00	15.00
HT5 Dale Earnhardt Jr.	6.00	15.00
HT6 Kevin Harvick	5.00	12.00

2007 Press Pass Hot Treads Blue

*BLUE: .8X TO 2X BASE
STATED PRINT RUN 99 SERIAL #'d SETS

2007 Press Pass Hot Treads Gold

*GOLD: .6X TO 1.5X BASE
STATED PRINT RUN 99 SERIAL #'d SETS

2008 Press Pass Hot Treads

COMPLETE SET (8)
HO1-HO4 ODDS 1 PER WALMART ECLIPSE BLASTER BOX
HO5-HO8 ODDS 1 PER WALMART VIP BLASTER BOX

HT1 Tony Stewart	6.00	15.00
HT2 Juan Pablo Montoya	5.00	12.00
HT3 Jimmie Johnson	6.00	15.00
HT4 Martin Truex Jr.	5.00	12.00

2008 Press Pass Hot Treads Blue

* BLUE: 1X TO 2.5X BASE
STATED PRINT RUN 99 SERIAL #'d SETS

2008 Press Pass Hot Treads Gold

*GOLD: .6X TO 1.5X BASE
STATED PRINT RUN 299 SERIAL #'d SETS

1999 Press Pass Jeff Gordon Fan Club

JG Jeff Gordon	15.00	40.00

2005 Press Pass Legends

This 50-card set features some of NASCAR's greatest drivers along with some current superstars. They were released in September, 2005 in hobby only 5-card packs. Boxes consisted of 3 mini boxes which each factory sealed, containing 6 packs in each. An entry card for a chance to win a signed lithograph of NASCAR's 50 geartest drivers was inserted into packs at a rate of one in 18.

COMPLETE SET (50)	15.00	40.00
WAX BOX (18)	100.00	150.00
MINI BOX (6)	35.00	60.00
1 Lee Petty	.40	1.00
2 Curtis Turner	.40	1.00
3 Fireball Roberts	.40	1.00
4 Marvin Panch	.25	.60
5 Glen Wood	.25	.60
6 Tiny Lund	.25	.60
7 Fred Lorenzen	.40	1.00
8 Rex White	.25	.60
9 Cale Yarborough	.40	1.00
10 Richard Petty	1.25	3.00
11 Buddy Baker	.40	1.00
12 David Pearson	.40	1.00
13 Bobby Allison	.40	1.00
14 Jack Ingram	.25	.60
15 Benny Parsons	.25	.60
16 Donnie Allison	.40	1.00
17 Harry Gant	.40	1.00
18 Neil Bonnett	.25	.60
19 Dale Earnhardt	2.00	5.00
20 Ricky Rudd	.60	1.50
21 Terry Labonte	.60	1.50
22 Rusty Wallace	.75	2.00
23 Tim Richmond	.40	1.00
24 Mark Martin	1.00	2.50
25 Dale Jarrett	.75	2.00
26 Alan Kulwicki	.60	1.50
27 Davey Allison	.60	1.50
28 Jeff Gordon	1.50	4.00
29 Tony Stewart	1.00	2.50
30 Dale Earnhardt Jr.	1.50	4.00
31 Jimmie Johnson	1.25	3.00
32 Kasey Kahne	1.50	4.00
33 Kyle Busch CRC	1.00	2.50
34 Richard Petty C	1.25	3.00
35 Benny Parsons C	.25	.60
36 Cale Yarborough C	.40	1.00
37 Bobby Allison C	.40	1.00
38 Rusty Wallace C	.75	2.00
39 Alan Kulwicki C	.60	1.50
40 Dale Earnhardt C	2.00	5.00
41 Terry Labonte C	.60	1.50
42 Bobby Labonte C	.75	2.00
43 Jeff Gordon C	1.50	4.00
44 Tony Stewart C	1.00	2.50
45 Matt Kenseth C	1.25	3.00
46 Kurt Busch C	.60	1.50
47 Lee Petty Richard Petty Kyle Petty FT	1.25	3.00
48 Donnie Allison Bobby Allison Davey Allison FT	.60	1.50
49 Terry Labonte Bobby Labonte Justin Labonte FT	.60	1.50
50 Davey Allison Jeff Gordon Richard Petty CL	1.50	4.00
NNO Lithograph Entry Card	3.00	6.00

2005 Press Pass Legends Blue

*BLUE: 1X TO 2.5X BASE

2005 Press Pass Legends Gold

GOLD: 1.2X TO 3X BASE

2005 Press Pass Legends Holofoil

*HOLOFOIL: 2.5X TO 6X BASE

2005 Press Pass Legends Solo

STATED PRINT RUN 1 SERIAL #'d SET
NOT PRICED DUE TO SCARCITY

2005 Press Pass Legends Press Plates Black

STATED PRINT RUN 1 SERIAL #'d SET
NOT PRICED DUE TO SCARCITY

2005 Press Pass Legends Press Plates Cyan

STATED PRINT RUN 1 SERIAL #'d SET
NOT PRICED DUE TO SCARCITY

2005 Press Pass Legends Press Plates Magenta

STATED PRINT RUN 1 SERIAL #'d SET
NOT PRICED DUE TO SCARCITY

2005 Press Pass Legends Press Plates Yellow

STATED PRINT RUN 1 SERAIL #'d SET
NOT PRICED DUE TO SCARCITY

2005 Press Pass Legends Previews

STATED PRINT RUN 5 SERIAL #'d SETS
NOT PRICED DUE TO SCARCITY

2005 Press Pass Legends Autographs Blue

1 Bobby Allison/700	6.00	15.00
2 Buddy Baker/720	8.00	20.00
3 Harry Gant/700	8.00	20.00
4 Fred Lorenzen/700	6.00	15.00
5 Jack Ingram/650	6.00	15.00
6 Marvin Panch/675	6.00	15.00
7 Benny Parsons/700	30.00	60.00
8 David Pearson/650	8.00	20.00
9 Richard Petty/100	40.00	80.00
10 Rex White/700	6.00	15.00
11 Glen Wood/700	6.00	15.00
12 Cale Yarborough/700	6.00	15.00

2005 Press Pass Legends Autographs Black

STATED PRINT RUN 50 UNLESS NOTED BELOW

1 Bobby Allison	15.00	40.00
2 Buddy Baker	15.00	40.00
3 Harry Gant	20.00	50.00
4 Fred Lorenzen	20.00	50.00
5 Jack Ingram/100	15.00	40.00
6 Marvin Panch/100	15.00	40.00
7 Benny Parsons	50.00	100.00
8 David Pearson/100	20.00	50.00
9 Richard Petty	50.00	100.00
10 Rex White	15.00	40.00
11 Glen Wood	12.50	30.00
12 Cale Yarborough	15.00	40.00
13 Kurt Busch	25.00	60.00
14 Dale Earnhardt Jr.	125.00	250.00
15 Jeff Gordon	150.00	300.00
16 Kevin Harvick	40.00	80.00
17 Dale Jarrett	40.00	100.00
18 Jimmie Johnson	60.00	120.00
19 Kasey Kahne	100.00	175.00
20 Matt Kenseth	50.00	100.00
21 Bobby Labonte	30.00	60.00
22 Terry Labonte	60.00	120.00
23 Mark Martin	75.00	150.00
24 Ryan Newman	40.00	80.00
25 Ricky Rudd	30.00	60.00
26 Tony Stewart	100.00	175.00

2005 Press Pass Legends Double Threads Bronze

DT-BK K.Busch/M.Kenseth	12.50	30.00
DT-EW Dale Earnhardt Jr. Michael Waltrip	25.00	60.00
DT-GJ Jeff Gordon Jimmie Johnson	40.00	80.00
DT-KV Kasey Kahne Brian Vickers	20.00	50.00
DT-LG Terry Labonte Jeff Gordon	15.00	40.00
DT-LL Bobby Labonte Terry Labonte	12.50	30.00
DT-MB Mark Martin Kurt Busch	12.50	30.00
DT-MK Mark Martin Matt Kenseth	15.00	40.00
DT-NW Ryan Newman Rusty Wallace	15.00	40.00
DT-SL Tony Stewart Terry Labonte	15.00	40.00

2005 Press Pass Legends Double Threads Gold

*GOLD: .6X TO 1.5X BRONZE

2005 Press Pass Legends Double Threads Silver

*SILVER: .4X TO 1X BRONZE

2005 Press Pass Legends Greatest Moments

COMPLETE SET (18)	40.00	100.00
GM1 Benny Parsons	.75	2.00
GM2 David Pearson Firecracker 400	1.25	3.00
GM3 David Pearson Daytona 500	1.25	3.00
GM4 Richard Petty Daytona 500	4.00	10.00
GM5 Cale Yarborough	1.25	3.00
GM6 Richard Petty Firecracker 400	4.00	10.00
GM7 Dale Earnhardt Winston '87	6.00	15.00
GM8 Bobby Allison Davey Allison	2.00	5.00
GM9 Harry Gant	1.25	3.00
GM10 Davey Allison	2.00	5.00
GM11 Alan Kulwicki	2.00	5.00
GM12 Jeff Gordon	5.00	12.00
GM13 Terry Labonte	2.00	5.00
GM14 Dale Earnhardt Daytona	6.00	15.00
GM15 Dale Earnhardt Winston '00	6.00	15.00
GM16 Kevin Harvick	3.00	8.00
GM17 Dale Earnhardt Jr.	5.00	12.00
GM18 Ricky Craven Kurt Busch	2.00	5.00

2005 Press Pass Legends Heritage

COMPLETE SET (12)	30.00	80.00
HE1 Davey Allison	3.00	8.00
HE2 Jeff Gordon	8.00	20.00
HE3 Dale Jarrett	4.00	10.00
HE4 Alan Kulwicki	3.00	8.00
HE5 Terry Labonte	3.00	8.00
HE6 Mark Martin	5.00	12.00
HE7 David Pearson	2.00	5.00
HE8 Richard Petty	6.00	15.00
HE9 Fireball Roberts	2.00	5.00
HE10 Rusty Wallace	4.00	10.00
HE11 Michael Waltrip	2.00	5.00
HE12 Glen Wood	1.25	3.00

2005 Press Pass Legends Historic Cuts

NOT PRICED DUE TO SCARCITY
1 Davey Allison/5
2 Tim Richmond/2

2005 Press Pass Legends Threads & Treads Bronze

TTDE Dale Earnhardt	25.00	60.00
TTDJ Dale Jarrett	10.00	25.00
TTJG Jeff Gordon	20.00	50.00
TTJJ Jimmie Johnson	15.00	40.00
TTJR Dale Earnhardt Jr.	20.00	50.00
TTKK Kasey Kahne	20.00	50.00
TTMM Mark Martin	12.50	30.00
TTRN Ryan Newman	10.00	25.00
TTRW Rusty Wallace	12.50	30.00
TTTL Terry Labonte	10.00	25.00
TTTS Tony Stewart	12.50	30.00

2005 Press Pass Legends Threads & Treads Gold

*GOLD: .6X TO 1.5X BRONZE

2005 Press Pass Legends Threads & Treads Silver

*SILVER: .5X TO 1.2X BRONZE

2005 Press Pass Legends Tim Richmond Racing Artifacts

COMPLETE SET (3)		
TRF T.Richmond Firesuit B/375	12.50	30.00
TRF T.Richmond Firesuit S/225	15.00	40.00
TRF T.Richmond Firesuit G/99	20.00	50.00
TRG T.Richmond Glove/99	20.00	50.00
TRFG T.Richmond Firesuit Glove/50	30.00	80.00

2006 Press Pass Legends

This 50-card set features some of NASCAR's greatest drivers along with some current superstars. They were released in September, 2006 in hobby only 5-card packs. Boxes consisted of 3 mini boxes which each factory sealed, containing 6 packs in each. An entry card for a chance to win a signed lithograph of NASCAR's 50 geartest drivers was inserted into packs at a rate of one in 18.

COMPLETE SET (50)	12.50	30.00
WAX BOX (18)	75.00	125.00
MINI BOX (6)	35.00	50.00
1 Tim Flock	.25	.60
2 Lee Petty	.60	1.50
3 Marshall Teague	.25	.60
4 Curtis Turner	.25	.60
5 Fireball Roberts	.40	1.00
6 Marvin Panch	.25	.60
7 Ned Jarrett	.40	1.00
8 Glen Wood	.25	.60
9 Tiny Lund	.25	.60
10 Ralph Earnhardt	.60	1.50
11 Fred Lorenzen	.40	1.00
12 Rex White	.25	.60
13 Cale Yarborough	.50	1.25
14 Richard Petty	1.25	3.00
15 Buddy Baker	.40	1.00
16 David Pearson	.60	1.50
17 Bobby Allison	.50	1.25
18 Jack Ingram	.25	.60
19 Benny Parsons	.40	1.00
20 Donnie Allison	.25	.60
21 Darrell Waltrip	.75	2.00
22 Harry Gant	.40	1.00
23 Neil Bonnett	.40	1.00
24 Dale Earnhardt	2.50	6.00
25 Janet Guthrie	.25	.60
26 Terry Labonte	.60	1.50
27 Kyle Petty	.40	1.00
28 Rusty Wallace	.75	2.00
29 Tim Richmond	.40	1.00
30 Mark Martin	1.00	2.50
31 Dale Jarrett	.75	2.00
32 Alan Kulwicki	.60	1.50
33 Davey Allison	.75	2.00
34 Bobby Labonte	.75	2.00
35 Jeff Gordon	1.50	4.00
36 Tony Stewart	1.00	2.50
37 Dale Earnhardt Jr.	1.50	4.00
38 Matt Kenseth	1.25	3.00
39 Kurt Busch	.60	1.50
40 Kevin Harvick	1.00	2.50
41 Jimmie Johnson	1.25	3.00
42 Ryan Newman	1.00	2.50
43 Kasey Kahne	1.50	4.00
44 Carl Edwards	1.25	3.00
45 Denny Hamlin CRC	2.50	6.00
46 Richard Petty Jeff Gordon REC Poles	1.50	4.00
47 Dale Earnhardt Dale Earnhardt Jr. REC	2.50	6.00
48 Richard Petty Jeff Gordon REC Champs	1.50	4.00
49 Richard Petty Jeff Gordon REC Top 10s	1.50	4.00
CL Fred Lorenzen CL	.40	1.00
NNO Lithograph Contest Card	1.50	4.00

2006 Press Pass Legends Blue

This 50-card set was a parallel to the base set. It featured blue foil highlights and carried a "B" prefix on its card number. They were serial numbered to 1999 on the card fronts.

COMPLETE SET (50)	20.00	50.00

*BLUE: .8X TO 2X BASE

2006 Press Pass Legends Bronze

This 50-card set was a parallel to the base set. It featured bronze foil highlights and carried a "Z" prefix on its card number. They were serial numbered to 999 on the card fronts.

COMPLETE SET (50)	40.00	100.00

*BRONZE: 1.2X TO 3X

2006 Press Pass Legends Gold

This 50-card set was a parallel to the base set. It featured bronze foil highlights and carried a " prefix on its card number. They were ser numbered to 299 on the card fronts.

*GOLD: 2.5X TO 6X BASE

2006 Press Pass Legends Holofoil

This 50-card set was a parallel to the base set. It featured holofoil highlights and carried a "H" pre on its card number. They were serial numbered to 99 on the card fronts.

*HOLO: 4X TO 10X BASE

2006 Press Pass Legends Solo

This 50-card set was a parallel to the base set. It featured green foil highlights and carried a "S" pre on its card number. They were serial numbered tc on the card fronts.

NOT PRICED DUE TO SCARCTY

2006 Press Pass Legends Previews

This 49-card set was released in late August, 20 and sold exclusively on eBay. Cards 1-45 were se numbered to 5 and cards 46-49 were each number one of one. These cards are not priced due scarcity. Each card carried an "EB" prefix for its ca number.

NOT PRICED DUE TO SCARCITY

2006 Press Pass Legends Press Plates Black

This 50-card press plate set was a parallel to base set. It featured black press plates used in production of the base cards. They carried a "PF prefix on their card numbering. They were ser numbered to 1.

NOT PRICED DUE TO SCARCITY

2006 Press Pass Legends Press Plates Black Backs

This 50-card press plate set was a parallel to base set. It featured black press plates used in production of the base cards' cardbacks. Th carried a "PPB" prefix on their card numbering an "B" suffix. They were serial numbered to 1.

NOT PRICED DUE TO SCARCITY

2006 Press Pass Legends Press Plates Cyan

This 50-card press plate set was a parallel to base set. It featured cyan press plates used in production of the base cards. They carried a "PP prefix on their card numbering. They were ser numbered to 1.

NOT PRICED DUE TO SCARCITY

2006 Press Pass Legends Press Plates Cyan Backs

This 50-card press plate set was a parallel to base set. It featured cyan press plates used in production of the base cards' cardbacks. Th carried a "PPC" prefix on their card numbering an "B" suffix. They were serial numbered to 1.

NOT PRICED DUE TO SCARCITY

2006 Press Pass Legends Press Plates Magenta

s 50-card press plate set was a parallel to the e set. It featured magenta press plates used in the duction of the base cards. They carried a "PPM" fix on their card numbering. They were serial nbered to 1.

T PRICED DUE TO SCARCITY

2006 Press Pass Legends Press Plates Magenta Backs

s 50-card press plate set was a parallel to the e set. It featured magenta press plates used in the duction of the base cards' cardbacks. They ried a "PPM" prefix on their card numbering and a suffix. They were serial numbered to 1.

T PRICED DUE TO SCARCITY

2006 Press Pass Legends Press Plates Yellow

s 50-card press plate set was a parallel to the e set. It featured yellow press plates used in the duction of the base cards. They carried a "PPY" fix on their card numbering. They were serial nbered to 1.

T PRICED DUE TO SCARCITY

2006 Press Pass Legends Press Plates Yellow Backs

s 50-card press plate set was a parallel to the e set. It featured yellow press plates used in the duction of the base cards' cardbacks. They ried a "PPY" prefix on their card numbering and a suffix. They were serial numbered to 1.

T PRICED DUE TO SCARCITY

2006 Press Pass Legends Autographs Black

s 30-card set featured certified autographs signed black ink. Most of these were serial numbered to see the checklist below for the exceptions. The ds were certified by the manufacturer on their dbacks. The combined rate for all autographs and e-used cards was one in six packs.

Bobby Allison	15.00	40.00
Donnie Allison	15.00	40.00
Buddy Baker		
Harry Gant	20.00	50.00
Janet Guthrie	15.00	40.00
Jack Ingram	15.00	40.00
Ned Jarrett/75	15.00	40.00
Fred Lorenzen/220	12.50	30.00
Marvin Panch/250	12.50	30.00
Benny Parsons	50.00	100.00
David Pearson	25.00	60.00
Richard Petty	50.00	100.00
Rusty Wallace/200	20.00	50.00
Darrell Waltrip/25	75.00	125.00
Rex White	15.00	40.00
Glen Wood	12.50	30.00
Cale Yarborough	15.00	40.00
Jeff Burton	25.00	60.00
Kurt Busch	40.00	80.00
Dale Earnhardt Jr.	125.00	250.00
Carl Edwards	75.00	150.00
Jeff Gordon	125.00	250.00
Jimmie Johnson	60.00	120.00
Kasey Kahne	75.00	150.00
Matt Kenseth	50.00	100.00
Bobby Labonte	30.00	60.00
Terry Labonte	60.00	120.00
Mark Martin	75.00	150.00
Ryan Newman	40.00	80.00
Tony Stewart	100.00	175.00

2006 Press Pass Legends Autographs Blue

s 19-card set featured certified autographs signed blue ink. Most of these were serial numbered to , see the checklist below for the exceptions. The ds were certified by the manufacturer on their dbacks. The combined rate for all autographs and e-used cards was one in six packs.

Bobby Allison	6.00	15.00
Donnie Allison	12.50	30.00
Buddy Baker	8.00	20.00
Greg Biffle/50	25.00	60.00
Harry Gant/600	8.00	20.00
Janet Guthrie/545	12.50	30.00
Kevin Harvick/50	40.00	80.00
Jack Ingram/645	6.00	15.00
Ned Jarrett/205	8.00	20.00
Fred Lorenzen/480	6.00	15.00
Marvin Panch/400	6.00	15.00
Benny Parsons	30.00	60.00
David Pearson	8.00	20.00
Richard Petty/100	40.00	80.00
Rusty Wallace/270	15.00	40.00
Darrell Waltrip/45	75.00	125.00
17 Rex White	6.00	15.00
18 Glen Wood	6.00	15.00
19 Cale Yarborough/645	6.00	15.00

2006 Press Pass Legends Champion Threads & Treads Bronze

This 7-card set features swatches of past champions' firesuit and tire. The cards had bronze foil highlights and each was serial numbered to 399. The cards carried a "CTT" prefix for thier card numbers. The overall odds were combined with other race-used cards and autographs at a rate of one in six packs.

CTT-BL Bobby Labonte	12.50	30.00
CTT-DJ Dale Jarrett	12.50	30.00
CTT-JG Jeff Gordon	20.00	50.00
CTT-KB Kurt Busch	10.00	25.00
CTT-MK Matt Kenseth	15.00	40.00
CTT-TL Terry Labonte	10.00	25.00
CTT-TS Tony Stewart	15.00	40.00

2006 Press Pass Legends Champion Threads & Treads Gold

This 7-card set features swatches of past champions' firesuit and tire. The cards had gold foil highlights and each was serial numbered to 99. The cards carried a "CTT" prefix for thier card numbers. The overall odds were combined with other race-used cards and autographs at a rate of one in six packs.

*GOLD: .8X TO 2X BRONZE

2006 Press Pass Legends Champion Threads & Treads Silver

This 7-card set features swatches of past champions' firesuit and tire. The cards had silver foil highlights and each was serial numbered to 299. The cards carried a "CTT" prefix for thier card numbers. The overall odds were combined with other race-used cards and autographs at a rate of one in six packs.

*SILVER: .6X TO 1.5X BRONZE

2006 Press Pass Legends Champion Threads Bronze

This 7-card set features swatches of past champions' firesuits. The cards had bronze foil highlights and each was serial numbered to 399.The cards carried a "CT" prefix for thier card numbers. The overall odds were combined with other race-used cards and autographs at a rate of one in six packs.

CT-BL Bobby Labonte	10.00	25.00
CT-DJ Dale Jarrett	10.00	25.00
CT-JG Jeff Gordon	15.00	40.00
CT-KB Kurt Busch	8.00	20.00
CT-MK Matt Kenseth	12.50	30.00
CT-TL Terry Labonte	10.00	25.00
CT-TS Tony Stewart	12.50	30.00

2006 Press Pass Legends Champion Threads Gold

This 7-card set features swatches of past champions' firesuits. The cards had gold foil highlights and each was serial numbered to 50. The cards carried a "CT" prefix for thier card numbers. The overall odds were combined with other race-used cards and autographs at a rate of one in six packs.

*GOLD: .6X TO 1.5X BRONZE

2006 Press Pass Legends Champion Threads Patch

This 7-card set features premium patch swatches from past champions' firesuits. The cards had gold foil highlights and each was serial numbered to 25. The cards carried a "CT" prefix for thier card numbers. The overall odds were combined with other race-used cards and autographs at a rate of one in six packs.

CT-BL Bobby Labonte	50.00	100.00
CT-DJ Dale Jarrett	50.00	100.00
CT-JG Jeff Gordon	100.00	200.00
CT-KB Kurt Busch	40.00	80.00
CT-MK Matt Kenseth	60.00	120.00
CT-TL Terry Labonte	50.00	100.00
CT-TS Tony Stewart	75.00	150.00

2006 Press Pass Legends Champion Threads Silver

This 7-card set features swatches of past champions' firesuits. The cards had silver foil highlights and each was serial numbered to 199.The cards carried a "CT" prefix for thier card numbers. The overall odds were combined with other race-used cards and autograhs at a rate of one in six packs.

*SILVER: .5X TO 1.2X BRONZE

2006 Press Pass Legends Heritage Gold

This 15-card set was a parallel to the Heritage Silver set. These were serial numbered to 99 on their card fronts. Each carried an "HE" prefix for its card number.

*GOLD: .6X TO 1.5X SILVER

2006 Press Pass Legends Heritage Silver

This 15-card set was randomly inserted in packs at a rate of one in 18. These were serial numbered to 549 on their card fronts. Each carried an "HE" prefix for its card number.

COMPLETE SET (18)	50.00	120.00
HE1 Richard Petty	5.00	12.00
HE2 David Pearson	2.50	6.00
HE3 Bobby Allison	2.00	5.00
HE4 Darrell Waltrip	3.00	8.00
HE5 Cale Yarborough	2.00	5.00
HE6 Dale Earnhardt	10.00	25.00
HE7 Jeff Gordon	6.00	15.00
HE8 Rusty Wallace	3.00	8.00
HE9 Lee Petty	2.50	6.00
HE10 Tony Stewart	4.00	10.00
HE11 Jimmie Johnson	5.00	12.00
HE12 Dale Earnhardt Jr.	6.00	15.00
HE13 Lee Petty Richard Petty	2.50	6.00
HE14 Bobby Allison Davey Allison	2.00	5.00
HE15 Dale Earnhardt Dale Earnhardt Jr.	10.00	25.00

2006 Press Pass Legends Memorable Moments Gold

This 16-card set was a parallel to the Memorable Moments Silver set. These were serial numbered to 99 on their card fronts. Each carried an "MM" prefix for its card number.

*GOLD: .8X TO 2X SILVER

2006 Press Pass Legends Memorable Moments Silver

This 15-card set was randomly inserted in packs at a rate of one in 12. These were serial numbered to 699 on their card fronts. Each carried an "MM" prefix for its card number.

COMPLETE SET (16)	40.00	100.00
MM1 Bobby Allison	1.50	4.00
MM2 David Pearson Charlotte	2.00	5.00
MM3 Jeff Gordon Charlotte	5.00	12.00
MM4 Jimmie Johnson	4.00	10.00
MM5 David Pearson Darlington	2.00	5.00
MM6 Jeff Gordon Darlington	5.00	12.00
MM7 Dale Earnhardt	8.00	20.00
MM8 Jeff Gordon Darlington '97	5.00	12.00
MM9 Richard Petty North Wilkesboro	4.00	10.00
MM10 Richard Petty Northy Wilkesboro '72	4.00	10.00
MM11 Jeff Gordon North Wilkesboro	5.00	12.00
MM12 Cale Yarborough	1.50	4.00
MM13 Curtis Turner	.75	2.00
MM14 Matt Kenseth	4.00	10.00
MM15 Richard Petty Rockingham	4.00	10.00
MM16 Rusty Wallace	2.50	6.00

2006 Press Pass Legends Racing Artifacts Firesuit Bronze

This 9-card set featured swatches of race-used firesuits. Each card was highlighted with bronze foil and serial numbered to 399. The cards carried an "F" suffix for their card numbering. The odds were combined overall with other race-used memorabilia and autographs cards, and were inserted at a rate of one in six.

AK-F Alan Kulwicki	12.50	30.00
BB-F Buddy Baker	8.00	20.00
CY-F Cale Yarborough	12.50	30.00
DA-F Davey Allison	20.00	50.00
DE-F Dale Earnhardt	20.00	50.00
DP-F David Pearson	12.50	30.00
RW-F Rusty Wallace	8.00	20.00
TL-F Tiny Lund	12.50	30.00
TR-F Tim Richmond	20.00	50.00

2006 Press Pass Legends Racing Artifacts Firesuit Gold

This 9-card set featured swatches of race-used firesuits. Each card was highlighted with gold foil and serial numbered to 99. The cards carried an "F" suffix for their card numbering. The odds were combined overall with other race-used memorabilia and autographs cards, and were inserted at a rate of one in six. This set was a parallel to the Racing Artifacts Firesuit Bronze set.

*GOLD: .6X TO 1.5X BRONZE

2006 Press Pass Legends Racing Artifacts Firesuit Patch

This 9-card set featured premium patch swatches from race-used firesuits. Each card was highlighted with gold foil and serial numbered to 25. The cards carried an "F" suffix for their card numbering. The odds were combined overall with other race-used memorabilia and autographs cards, and were inserted at a rate of one in six. This set was a parallel to the Racing Artifacts Firesuit Bronze set.

*PATCH: 2.5X TO 6X BRONZE

2006 Press Pass Legends Racing Artifacts Firesuit Silver

This 9-card set featured swatches of race-used firesuits. Each card was highlighted with silver foil and serial numbered to 199. The cards carried an "F" suffix for their card numbering. The odds were combined overall with other race-used memorabilia and autographs cards, and were inserted at a rate of one in six. This set was a parallel to the Racing Artifacts Firesuit Bronze set.

*SILVER: .5X TO 1.2X BRONZE

2006 Press Pass Legends Racing Artifacts Glove

This 1-card set featured a swatch of a race-used glove. It was highlighted with gold foil and serial numbered to 10. The cards carried a "G" suffix for its card numbering. The odds were combined overall with other race-used memorabilia and autograph cards, and were inserted at a rate of one in six.

NOT PRICED DUE TO SCARCITY

TR-G Tim Richmond

2006 Press Pass Legends Racing Artifacts Hat

This 1-card set featured a swatch of a Richard Petty's trademark cowboy hat. It was highlighted with gold foil and serial numbered to 99. The cards carried an "H" suffix for its card numbering. The odds were combined overall with other race-used memorabilia and autograph cards, and were inserted at a rate of one in six.

RP-H Richard Petty	60.00	120.00

2006 Press Pass Legends Racing Artifacts Sheet Metal Bronze

This 2-card set featured swatches of race-used sheet metal. Each card was highlighted with bronze foil and serial numbered to 199. The cards carried an "SM" suffix for their card numbering. The odds were combined overall with other race-used memorabilia and autographs cards, and were inserted at a rate of one in six.

BA-SM Bobby Allison	15.00	40.00
BP-SM Benny Parsons	15.00	40.00

2006 Press Pass Legends Racing Artifacts Sheet Metal Gold

This 2-card set featured swatches of race-used sheet metal. Each card was highlighted with gold foil and serial numbered to 50. The cards carried an "SM" suffix for their card numbering. The odds were combined overall with other race-used memorabilia and autographs cards, and were inserted at a rate of one in six. This set was a parallel to the Racing Artifacts Sheet Metal Bronze set.

*GOLD: .6X TO 1.5X BRONZE

2006 Press Pass Legends Racing Artifacts Sheet Metal Silver

This 2-card set featured swatches of race-used sheet metal. Each card was highlighted with silver foil and serial numbered to 99. The cards carried an "SM" suffix for their card numbering. The odds were combined overall with other race-used memorabilia and autographs cards, and were inserted at a rate of one in six. This set was a parallel to the Racing Artifacts Sheet Metal Bronze set.

*SILVER: .5X TO 1.2X BRONZE

2006 Press Pass Legends Racing Artifacts Tire Bronze

This 2-card set featured swatches of race-used tires. Each card was highlighted with bronze foil and serial numbered to 399. The cards carried a "T" suffix for their card numbering. The odds were combined overall with other race-used memorabilia and autographs cards, and were inserted at a rate of one in six.

DE-T Dale Earnhardt	15.00	40.00
RW-T Rusty Wallace	10.00	25.00

2006 Press Pass Legends Racing Artifacts Tire Gold

This 2-card set featured swatches of race-used tires. Each card was highlighted with gold foil and serial numbered to 50. The cards carried a "T" suffix for their card numbering. The odds were combined overall with other race-used memorabilia and autographs cards, and were inserted at a rate of one in six. This set was a parallel to the Racing Artifacts Tires Bronze set.

*GOLD: .6X TO 1.5X BRONZE

2006 Press Pass Legends Racing Artifacts Tire Silver

This 2-card set featured swatches of race-used tires. Each card was highlighted with silver foil and serial numbered to 199. The cards carried a "T" suffix for their card numbering. The odds were combined overall with other race-used memorabilia and autographs cards, and were inserted at a rate of one in six. This set was a parallel to the Racing Artifacts Tires Bronze set.

*SILVER: .5X TO 1.2X BRONZE

2006 Press Pass Legends Racing Cuts

This 7-card set featured cut signatures from past drivers. Most are 1 of 1's, see checklist below for other print runs. These were randomly inserted in packs of Press Pass Legends. They are not priced due to scarcity.

AK Alan Kulwicki/1
DA Davey Allison/1
DE Dale Earnhardt Sr./3
LP Lee Petty/1
TF Tim Flock/2
TL Tiny Lund/12
TR Tim Richmond/1

2006 Press Pass Legends Triple Threads

This 9-card set featured three memorabillia swatches per card. Each card contained a swatch of race-used firesuit, glove and shoe. These were serial numbered to 50.

TT-CE Carl Edwards	60.00	120.00
TT-DE Dale Earnhardt Jr.	75.00	150.00
TT-JG Jeff Gordon	100.00	175.00
TT-JJ Jimmie Johnson		
TT-KH Kevin Harvick	60.00	120.00
TT-MK Matt Kenseth	60.00	120.00
TT-MT Martin Truex Jr.	50.00	100.00
TT-RN Ryan Newman	40.00	80.00
TT-TS Tony Stewart	60.00	120.00

2007 Press Pass Legends

COMPLETE SET (70)	15.00	40.00
COMMON DRIVERS	.20	.50
SEMISTARS	.30	.75
UNLISTED STARS	.50	1.25
WAX BOX	100.00	150.00
MINI BOX	30.00	60.00
1 Lee Petty	.30	.75
2 Louise Smith	.20	.50
3 Marshall Teague	.20	.50
4 Curtis Turner	.30	.75
5 Tim Flock	.20	.50
6 Cotton Owens	.20	.50
7 Glen Wood	.20	.50
8 Marty Robbins	.20	.50
9 Marvin Panch	.20	.50
10 Ralph Earnhardt	.50	1.25
11 Fireball Roberts	.30	.75
12 Rex White	.20	.50
13 Tiny Lund	.20	.50
14 Ned Jarrett	.30	.75
15 David Pearson	.30	.75
16 Fred Lorenzen	.30	.75
17 Jack Ingram	.20	.50
18 Richard Petty	1.00	2.50
19 Bobby Allison	.30	.75
20 Janet Guthrie	.20	.50
21 Cale Yarborough	.30	.75
22 Benny Parsons	.30	.75
23 Donnie Allison	.30	.75
24 Harry Gant	.30	.75
25 Buddy Baker	.30	.75
26 Bud Moore	.20	.50
27 Neil Bonnett	.30	.75
28 Darrell Waltrip	.50	1.25
29 Dale Earnhardt	2.00	5.00
30 Alan Kulwicki	.50	1.25
31 Tim Richmond	.30	.75
32 Rusty Wallace	.60	1.50
33 Ricky Rudd	.50	1.25
34 Dale Jarrett	.60	1.50
35 Mark Martin	.75	2.00
36 Davey Allison	.50	1.25
37 Bobby Labonte	.60	1.50
38 Jeff Burton	.30	.75
39 Tony Stewart	.75	2.00
40 Jeff Gordon	1.25	3.00
41 Matt Kenseth	1.00	2.50
42 Dale Earnhardt Jr.	1.25	3.00
43 Jimmie Johnson	1.00	2.50
44 Juan Pablo Montoya RC	3.00	8.00
45 Kevin Harvick	.75	2.00
46 Ryan Newman	.60	1.50
47 Kurt Busch	.30	.75
48 Carl Edwards	.75	2.00
49 Kasey Kahne	1.25	3.00
50 Denny Hamlin	1.00	2.50
51 Dale Earnhardt N	2.00	5.00
52 Harry Gant N	.30	.75
53 Ricky Rudd N	.50	1.25
54 Fred Lorenzen N	.30	.75
55 Richard Petty N	1.00	2.50
56 Darrell Waltrip N	.50	1.25
57 Fireball Roberts N	.30	.75
58 Cale Yarborough N	.30	.75
59 Kevin Harvick N	.75	2.00
60 David Pearson N	.30	.75
61 Ned Jarrett N	.30	.75
62 Tiny Lund N	.20	.50
63 Bobby Allison Donnie Allison Neil Bonnett N	.30	.75
64 Bobby Allison Donnie Allison Cale Yarborough R	.30	.75
65 Darrell Waltrip Dale Earnhardt R	2.00	5.00
66 Bobby Allison Richard Petty R	1.00	2.50
67 Cale Yarborough Darrell Waltrip R	.50	1.25
68 Dale Earnhardt Jeff Gordon R	2.00	5.00
69 David Pearson Richard Petty R	1.00	2.50
70 Buddy Baker CL	.30	.75

2007 Press Pass Legends Blue

COMPLETE SET (70)	25.00	60.00

*BLUE: 1X TO 2.5X BASE
STATED PRINT RUN 999 SERIAL #'d SETS

2007 Press Pass Legends Bronze

COMPLETE SET (70)	75.00	125.00

*BRONZE: 1.5X TO 4X BASE
STATED PRINT RUN 599 SERIAL #'d SETS

2007 Press Pass Legends Gold

*GOLD: 2.5X TO 6X BASE
STATED PRINT RUN 249 SERIAL #'d SETS

2007 Press Pass Legends Holofoil

*HOLOFOIL: 4X TO 10X BASE
STATED PRINT RUN 99 SERIAL #'d SETS

2007 Press Pass Legends Press Plates Black

STATED PRINT RUN 1 SERIAL #'d SET
NOT PRICED DUE TO SCARCITY

2007 Press Pass Legends Press Plates Black Backs

STATED PRINT RUN 1 SERIAL #'d SET
NOT PRICED DUE TO SCARCITY

2007 Press Pass Legends Press Plates Cyan

STATED PRINT RUN 1 SERIAL #'d SET
NOT PRICED DUE TO SCARCITY

2007 Press Pass Legends Press Plates Cyan Backs

STATED PRINT RUN 1 SERIAL #'d SET
NOT PRICED DUE TO SCARCITY

2007 Press Pass Legends Press Plates Magenta

STATED PRINT RUN 1 SERIAL #'d SET
NOT PRICED DUE TO SCARCITY

2007 Press Pass Legends Press Plates Magenta Backs

STATED PRINT RUN 1 SERIAL #'d SET
NOT PRICED DUE TO SCARCITY

2007 Press Pass Legends Press Plates Yellow

STATED PRINT RUN 1 SERIAL #'d SET
NOT PRICED DUE TO SCARCITY

2007 Press Pass Legends Press Plates Yellow Backs

STATED PRINT RUN 1 SERIAL #'d SET
NOT PRICED DUE TO SCARCITY

2007 Press Pass Legends Previews

STATED PRINT RUN (EB1-EB50) 5 SERIAL #'d SETS
STATED PRINT RUN (EB64-EB69) 1 SERIAL #'d SET
NOT PRICED DUE TO SCARCITY

2007 Press Pass Legends Solo

STATED PRINT RUN 1 SERIAL #'d SET
NOT PRICED DUE TO SCARCITY

2007 Press Pass Legends Autographs Black

OVERALL STATED AU/MEM ODDS 4:18
1 Bobby Allison/49 12.50 30.00
2 Donnie Allison/48 8.00 20.00
3 Buddy Baker/46 10.00 25.00
4 Harry Gant/50 10.00 25.00
5 Janet Guthrie/50 12.50 30.00
6 Jack Ingram/50 8.00 20.00
7 Ned Jarrett/50 10.00 25.00
8 Bud Moore/93 10.00 25.00
9 Cotton Owens/145 8.00 20.00
10 Marvin Panch/50 8.00 20.00
11 David Pearson/48 15.00 40.00
12 Richard Petty/48 60.00 100.00
13 Darrell Waltrip/48 60.00 100.00
14 Rex White/95 12.50 30.00
15 Glen Wood/24 8.00 20.00
16 Cale Yarborough/24 15.00 40.00

2007 Press Pass Legends Autographs Blue

OVERALL STATED AU/MEM ODDS 4:18
1 Bobby Allison/562 10.00 25.00
2 Donnie Allison/644 6.00 15.00
3 Buddy Baker/567 8.00 20.00
4 Kurt Busch/70 15.00 40.00
5 Dale Earnhardt Jr./59 100.00 175.00
6 Carl Edwards/71 40.00 80.00
7 Harry Gant/637 8.00 20.00
8 Jeff Gordon/48 125.00 200.00
9 Janet Guthrie/385 10.00 25.00
10 Denny Hamlin/59 25.00 60.00
11 Kevin Harvick/71 25.00 50.00
12 Jack Ingram/655 6.00 15.00
13 Dale Jarrett/61 15.00 40.00
14 Ned Jarrett/230 8.00 20.00
15 Jimmie Johnson/71 40.00 80.00
16 Matt Kenseth/60 30.00 60.00
17 Mark Martin/62 30.00 60.00
18 Juan Pablo Montoya/73 40.00 80.00
19 Bud Moore/383 10.00 25.00
20 Cotton Owens/361 8.00 20.00
21 Marvin Panch/502 6.00 15.00
22 David Pearson/306 10.00 25.00
23 Richard Petty/570 40.00 75.00
24 Darrell Waltrip/182 40.00 75.00
25 Rex White/594 8.00 20.00
26 Glen Wood/670 6.00 15.00
27 Cale Yarborough/269 10.00 25.00

2007 Press Pass Legends Autographs Inscriptions Black

OVERALL STATED AU/MEM ODDS 4:18
NOT PRICED DUE TO SCARCITY
1 Buddy Baker Gentle Giant/9
2 Buddy Baker Lead Foot/13
3 Buddy Baker Lead Foot w/smiley face/2
4 Jeff Gordon 24/9
5 Bud Moore #15/23
6 Rex White 1960 Champ #4/23
7 Glen Wood Woodchopper only/22

2007 Press Pass Legends Autographs Inscriptions Blue

OVERALL STATED AU/MEM ODDS 4:18
NOT PRICED DUE TO SCARCITY
1 Bobby Allison 3 Daytona 500 wins/23
2 Donnie Allison Alabama Gang/23
3 Dale Jr. 8/7
4 Dale Jr. 07/1
5 Harry Gant Mr. September/23
6 Janet Guthrie 1977 Daytona 500 Top Rookie/23
7 Denny Hamlin 11/9
8 Dale Jarrett #44/9
9 Ned Jarrett #11 Dale's Dad/25
10 Matt Kenseth 03 Cup Champion/9
11 Mark Martin The Kid/9
12 Marvin Panch Pancho/75 10.00 25.00
13 David Pearson Silver Fox 105 Cup Wins only/21
14 Richard Petty 43/19
15 Darrell Waltrip 11 Jaws/15
16 Cale Yarbrough 3 Time Champ/20

2007 Press Pass Legends Cut Signatures

OVERALL STATED AU/MEM ODDS 4:18
NOT PRICED DUE TO SCARCITY
AK Alan Kulwicki/1
BP Benny Parsons/4
DA Davey Allison/3
DE Dale Earnhardt/2
LP Lee Petty/1
LS Louise Smith/2
NB Neil Bonnett/1
TF Tim Flock/1
TL Tiny Lund/4

2007 Press Pass Legends Dale Earnhardt Gold

COMMON DALE 6.00 15.00
STATED PRINT RUN 99 SERIAL #'d SETS

2007 Press Pass Legends Dale Earnhardt Silver

COMPLETE SET (9) 40.00 75.00
COMMON DALE 4.00 10.00
STATED PRINT RUN 499 SERIAL #'d SETS
DE1 Dale Earnhardt 4.00 10.00
DE2 Dale Earnhardt 4.00 10.00
DE3 Dale Earnhardt 4.00 10.00
DE4 Dale Earnhardt 4.00 10.00
DE5 Dale Earnhardt 4.00 10.00

DE6 Dale Earnhardt 4.00 10.00
DE7 Dale Earnhardt 4.00 10.00
DE8 Dale Earnhardt 4.00 10.00
DE9 Dale Earnhardt 4.00 10.00

2007 Press Pass Legends Father & Son Firesuits Bronze

OVERALL STATED AU/MEM ODDS 4:18
STATED PRINT RUN 99 SERIAL #'d SETS
BADA-F B.Allison/Do.Allison 20.00 40.00
RWSW-F R.Wallace/S.Wallace 25.00 50.00

2007 Press Pass Legends Father & Son Firesuits Gold

*GOLD: .6X TO 1.5X BRONZE
OVERALL STATED AU/MEM ODDS 4:18
STATED PRINT RUN 25 SERIAL #'d SETS

2007 Press Pass Legends Father & Son Firesuits Silver

*SILVER: .5X TO 1.2X BRONZE
OVERALL STATED AU/MEM ODDS 4:18
STATED PRINT RUN 50 SERIAL #'d SETS

2007 Press Pass Legends Legends Gallery Gold

COMPLETE SET (12) 15.00 40.00
*GOLD: .8X TO 2X SILVER
STATED PRINT RUN 99 SERIAL #'d SETS

2007 Press Pass Legends Legends Gallery Silver

COMPLETE SET (12) 10.00 25.00
COMMON DRIVERS .40 1.00
SEMISTARS .60 1.50
UNLISTED STARS 1.00 2.50
STATED PRINT RUN 499 SERIAL #'d SETS
LG1 Lee Petty .60 1.50
LG2 Fireball Roberts .60 1.50
LG3 Rusty Wallace 1.25 3.00
LG4 Rex White .40 1.00
LG5 Dale Earnhardt 4.00 10.00
LG6 Curtis Turner .60 1.50
LG7 Fred Lorenzen .60 1.50
LG8 Janet Guthrie .40 1.00
LG9 Glen Wood .40 1.00
LG10 Marshall Teague .40 1.00
LG11 Jack Ingram .40 1.00
LG12 Tim Flock .40 1.00

2007 Press Pass Legends Memorable Moments Gold

*GOLD: .6X TO 1.5X SILVER
STATED PRINT RUN 169 SERIAL#'d SETS

2007 Press Pass Legends Memorable Moments Silver

COMPLETE SET (15) 15.00 40.00
COMMON DRIVERS .50 1.25
SEMISTARS .75 2.00
UNLISTED STARS 1.25 3.00
STATED PRINT RUN 499 SERIAL #'d SETS
MM1 Darrell Waltrip B 1.25 3.00
MM2 Cale Yarborough B .75 2.00
MM3 Jeff Gordon B 3.00 8.00
MM4 Dale Earnhardt B 5.00 12.00
MM5 Rusty Wallace B 1.50 4.00
MM6 Richard Petty D 2.50 6.00
MM7 Bobby Allison Donnie Allison Cale Yarborough D .75 2.00
MM8 Dale Earnhardt D 5.00 12.00
MM9 Darrell Waltrip D 1.25 3.00
MM10 David Pearson D .75 2.00
MM11 Richard Petty D 2.50 6.00
MM12 Bobby Allison Donnie Allison T .75 2.00
MM13 Dale Earnhardt T 5.00 12.00
MM14 Davey Allison T 1.25 3.00
MM15 Dale Earnhardt Jr. T 5.00 12.00

2007 Press Pass Legends Racing Artifacts Firesuit Bronze

OVERALL STATED AU/MEM ODDS 4:18
STATED PRINT RUN 199 SERIAL #'d SETS
UNLESS NOTED BELOW
AG-F Bobby Allison Donnie Allison Neil Bonnett/99 30.00 60.00
AK-F Alan Kulwicki 20.00 40.00
BA-F Bobby Allison 15.00 30.00
BB-F Buddy Baker 12.50 25.00
CY-F Cale Yarborough 12.50 25.00
DE-F Dale Earnhardt 60.00 120.00
DP-F David Pearson 15.00 30.00
DW-F Darrell Waltrip 20.00 40.00
HG-F Harry Gant 12.50 25.00
MR-F Marty Robbins 15.00 30.00
NB-F Neil Bonnett 15.00 30.00
RW-F Rusty Wallace 15.00 30.00
TL-F Tiny Lund 12.50 25.00
TR-F Tim Richmond 12.50 25.00
DAA-F Davey Allison 20.00 40.00
DOA-F Donnie Allison 12.50 25.00

2007 Press Pass Legends Racing Artifacts Firesuit Gold

GOLD: .6X TO 1.5X BRONZE
OVERALL STATED AU/MEM ODDS 4:18
STATED PRINT RUN 50 SERIAL #'d SETS
UNLESS NOTED BELOW
AG-F Bobby Allison Donnie Allison Neil Bonnett/25 40.00 100.00
DE-F Dale Earnhardt 100.00 200.00

2007 Press Pass Legends Racing Artifacts Firesuit Patch

OVERALL STATED AU/MEM ODDS 4:18
STATED PRINT RUN 25 SERIAL #'d SETS
AK-F Alan Kulwicki 125.00 250.00
BA-F Bobby Allison 75.00 125.00
BB-F Buddy Baker
CY-F Cale Yarborough
DE-F Dale Earnhardt 350.00 500.00
DP-F David Pearson
DW-F Darrell Waltrip 100.00 150.00
HG-F Harry Gant
MR-F Marty Robbins 100.00 200.00
NB-F Neil Bonnett 75.00 125.00
RW-F Rusty Wallace
TL-F Tiny Lund
TR-F Tim Richmond 60.00 100.00
DAA-F Davey Allison 150.00 250.00
DOA-F Donnie Allison

2007 Press Pass Legends Racing Artifacts Firesuit Silver

*SILVER: .5X TO 1.2X BRONZE
OVERALL STATED AU/MEM ODDS 4:18
STATED PRINT RUN 99 SERIAL #'d SETS
UNLESS NOTED BELOW
AG-F Bobby Allison Donnie Allison Neil Bonnett 40.00 80.00
DE-F Dale Earnhardt 75.00 150.00

2007 Press Pass Legends Racing Artifacts Hat

OVERALL STATED AU/MEM ODDS 4:18
STATED PRINT RUN 99 SERIAL #'d SETS
RP-H Richard Petty 40.00 80.00

2007 Press Pass Legends Racing Artifacts Sheet Metal Bronze

OVERALL STATED AU/MEM ODDS 4:18
STATED PRINT RUN 199 SERIAL #'d SETS
BA-S Bobby Allison 12.50 30.00
BP-S Benny Parsons 10.00 25.00

2007 Press Pass Legends Racing Artifacts Sheet Metal Gold

*GOLD: .6X TO 1.5X BRONZE
OVERALL STATED AU/MEM ODDS 4:18
STATED PRINT RUN 50 SERIAL #'d SETS

2007 Press Pass Legends Racing Artifacts Sheet Metal Silver

*SILVER: .5X TO 1.2X BRONZE
OVERALL STATED AU/MEM ODDS 4:18
STATED PRINT RUN 99 SERIAL #'d SETS

2007 Press Pass Legends Racing Artifacts Shirt Bronze

OVERALL STATED AU/MEM ODDS 4:18
STATED PRINT RUN 199 SERIAL #'d SETS
BM-SH Bud Moore 8.00 20.00
CO-SH Cotton Owens 6.00 15.00

2007 Press Pass Legends Racing Artifacts Shirt Gold

*GOLD: .6X TO 1.5X BRONZE
OVERALL STATED AU/MEM ODDS 4:18
STATED PRINT RUN 50 SERIAL #'d SETS

2007 Press Pass Legends Racing Artifacts Shirt Silver

*SILVER: .5X TO 1.2X BRONZE
OVERALL STATED AU/MEM ODDS 4:18
STATED PRINT RUN 99 SERIAL #'d SETS

2007 Press Pass Legends Racing Artifacts Tire Bronze

OVERALL STATED AU/MEM ODDS 4:18
STATED PRINT RUN 299 SERIAL #'d SETS
DE-T Dale Earnhardt 20.00 40.00
RW-T Rusty Wallace 15.00 30.00

2007 Press Pass Legends Racing Artifacts Tire Gold

*GOLD: .8X TO 2X BRONZE
OVERALL STATED AU/MEM ODDS 4:18
STATED PRINT RUN 50 SERIAL #'d SETS

2007 Press Pass Legends Racing Artifacts Tire Silver

*SILVER: .6X TO 1.5X BRONZE
OVERALL STATED AU/MEM ODDS 4:18
STATED PRINT RUN 199 SERIAL #'d SETS

2007 Press Pass Legends Signature Series

OVERALL STATED AU/MEM ODDS 1:
STATED PRINT RUN 25 SERIAL #'d SETS
BL Bobby Labonte 125.00 200.00
CE Carl Edwards 200.00 300.00
DH Denny Hamlin 100.00 175.00
DJ Dale Jarrett 75.00 150.00
JG Jeff Gordon 250.00 400.00
JJ Jimmie Johnson 175.00 300.00
JM Juan Pablo Montoya 100.00 175.00
KB Kurt Busch 75.00 150.00
KH Kevin Harvick
MK Matt Kenseth 150.00 250.00
MM Mark Martin 100.00 175.00
MT Martin Truex Jr. 125.00 200.00
PM Paul Menard 60.00 120.00
RN Ryan Newman 100.00 175.00
TS Tony Stewart 150.00 250.00

2007 Press Pass Legends Sunday Swatches Bronze

OVERALL STATED AU/MEM ODDS 4:18
STATED PRINT RUN 199 SERIAL #'d SETS
UNLESS NOTED BELOW
BV-SS Brian Vickers 10.00 20.00
DE-SS Dale Earnhardt Jr. 25.00 50.00
DH-SS Denny Hamlin 20.00 40.00
DJ-SS Dale Jarrett 15.00 30.00
JG-SS Jeff Gordon 25.00 50.00
JJ-SS Jimmie Johnson 20.00 40.00
JM-SS Juan Pablo Montoya/13
JY-SS J.J. Yeley 10.00 20.00
KH-SS Kevin Harvick 20.00 40.00
KK-SS Kasey Kahne 20.00
MT-SS Martin Truex Jr. 15.00 30.00
MW-SS Michael Waltrip 10.00 20.00
PM-SS Paul Menard 15.00 30.00
RS-SS Reed Sorenson 15.00 30.00
TS-SS Tony Stewart 20.00 40.00

2007 Press Pass Legends Sunday Swatches Gold

*GOLD: .8X TO 2X BRONZE
OVERALL STATED AU/MEM ODDS 4:18
STATED PRINT RUN 50 SERIAL #'d SETS

2007 Press Pass Legends Sunday Swatches Silver

*SILVER: .6X TO 1.5X BRONZE
OVERALL STATED AU/MEM ODDS 4:18
STATED PRINT RUN 99 SERIAL #'d SETS

2007 Press Pass Legends Victory Lane Bronze

OVERALL STATED AU/MEM ODDS 4:18
STATED PRINT RUN 199 SERIAL #'d SETS
VL1 Dale Earnhardt Jr. 25.00 50.
VL2 Jeff Gordon 25.00 50.
VL3 Jeff Gordon 25.00 50.
VL4 Denny Hamlin 20.00 40.
VL5 Kevin Harvick 20.00 40.
VL6 Jimmie Johnson 20.00 40.
VL7 Juan Pablo Montoya 20.00 40.
VL8 Tony Stewart 20.00 40.
VL9 Martin Truex Jr. 20.00 40.

2007 Press Pass Legends Victory Lane Gold

*GOLD: .8X TO 2X BRONZE
OVERALL STATED AU/MEM ODDS 4:18
STATED PRINT RUN 25 SERIAL #'d SETS

2007 Press Pass Legends Victory Lane Silver

*SILVER: .6X TO 1.5X BRONZE
OVERALL STATED AU/MEM ODDS 4:18
STATED PRINT RUN 99 SERIAL #'d SETS

2004 Press Pass Makin the Show Collector's Series

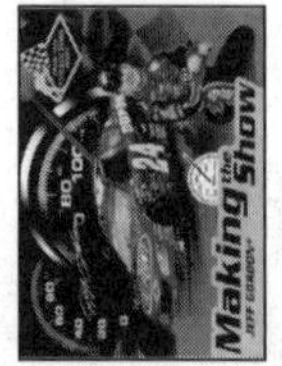

COMPLETE TIN SET (28) 10.00 25.
COMP.SET w/o MEM. (27) 8.00 20.

2002 Press Pass Nabisco Albertsons

Available as a mail-in offer, this four card features the Nabisco team of drivers and sponsored by Albertsons Stores and Nabisco. cardfronts feature one driver while the backs incl photos of the entire team.

COMPLETE SET (4) 4.00 10.
1 Dale Earnhardt Jr. 2.50 6.
2 Kevin Harvick 1.50 4.
3 Steve Park .75 2.
4 Michael Waltrip .75 2.

2003 Press Pass Nabisco Albertsons

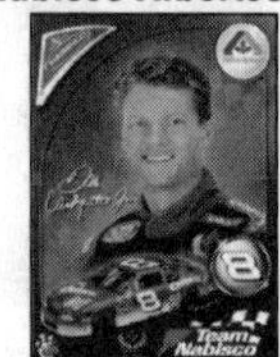

For the second year, a card set was producec Press Pass and sponsored by Team Nabisco Albertsons stores. A complete set of five coulc obtained at participating stores with the purchas Nabisco products.

COMPLETE SET (5) 4.00 10.
1 Dale Earnhardt Jr. 2.50 6.
2 Jeff Green .50 1.
3 Jason Keller .50 1.
4 Steve Park .75 2.
5 Michael Waltrip .75 2.

2004 Press Pass Nilla Wafers

These 4-cards were produced by Press Pass issued on boxes of Nilla Wafers in early 2004. E card was intended to be cut from the outside of box and are priced below as neatly cut cards. E includes a color photo on the front with a very

ple black and white cardback.

Card	Low	High
MPLETE SET (4)	5.00	12.00
Dale Earnhardt Jr.	1.50	4.00
Dale Earnhardt Jr. w/car	1.50	4.00
Dale Earnhardt Jr.'s Oreo Car	1.25	3.00
Michael Waltrip	1.00	2.50

994 Press Pass Optima XL Prototypes

ss Pass released this set to preview its 1994 tima XL line. Two different Rusty Wallace cards re released with the version entitled iver/Owner" the tougher of the two to find. A mplete set is considered three cards with the ier Rusty Wallace version.

Card	Low	High
MPLETE SET (3)	4.00	10.00
Kyle Petty	.75	2.00
Rusty Wallace DD name at bottom of card	1.25	3.00
Rusty Wallace DD Driver/Owner name at top of card	4.00	10.00
Jeff Gordon	2.50	6.00

994 Press Pass Optima XL

s 64-card set was the first time Press Pass issued ds under the Optima XL brand name. The cards larger than the standard card, measuring 2 1/2" x 1/16". There are seven topical subsets that nbine to make up the entire set. Those subsets Spotlight (1-30), Double Duty (31-36), Trophy se (37-42), Dale Earnhardt Racing Family (43-46), R Racing Family (47-49), Winston Cup Scene -58), News Makers (59-64). There is one known iation. The number 43 Teresa Earnhardt card was ginally printed with a picture of both Teresa and e. Early in the production the card was changed be a picture of Teresa. The set price only includes common version. The cards were issued in six d packs which came 24 packs per box and 20 ses per case. There was also a two-card insert set own as Chrome featuring Jeff Gordon and Ernie an. The cards were printed embossed on silver foil l inserted one per 240 packs.

Card	Low	High
MPLETE SET (64)	15.00	40.00
Brett Bodine	.08	.25
Geoff Bodine	.08	.25
Jeff Burton	.30	.75
Dale Earnhardt	2.50	6.00
Harry Gant	.20	.50
Jeff Gordon	1.00	2.50
Steve Grissom	.08	.25
Ernie Irvan	.20	.50
Dale Jarrett	.60	1.50
Terry Labonte	.30	.75
Sterling Marlin	.30	.75
Mark Martin	.75	2.00
Joe Nemechek	.08	.25
Kyle Petty	.20	.50
Ricky Rudd	.30	.75
Greg Sacks	.08	.25
Ken Schrader	.08	.25
Morgan Shepherd	.08	.25
Lake Speed	.08	.25
Jimmy Spencer	.08	.25
Hut Stricklin	.08	.25
Rusty Wallace	.75	2.00
Darrell Waltrip	.20	.50
Michael Waltrip	.20	.50
Ernie Irvan	.20	.50
Jeff Gordon	1.00	2.50
Mark Martin	.75	2.00
Kyle Petty	.20	.50
Ken Schrader	.08	.25
Rusty Wallace	.75	2.00
Geoff Bodine DD	.05	.15
Ernie Irvan DD	.08	.25
Ricky Rudd DD	.20	.50
Ken Schrader DD	.05	.15
Rusty Wallace DD	.40	1.00
Darrell Waltrip DD	.08	.25
Sterling Marlin's Car TC	.08	.25
Jeff Gordon TC	.50	1.25
Terry Labonte's Car TC	.20	.50
Rusty Wallace's Car TC	.30	.75
Dale Earnhardt's Car TC	.75	2.00
Ernie Irvan's Car TC	.08	.25
A Teresa Earnhardt	1.25	3.00
43B Teresa Earnhardt Dale Earnhardt	20.00	50.00
44 Kerry Earnhardt RC	1.50	4.00
45 Kelley Earnhardt RC	1.50	4.00
46 Dale Earnhardt Jr. RC	8.00	20.00
47 Richard Childress	.20	.50
48 Hank Jones	.05	.15
49 Andy Petree	.05	.15
50 Race Day Frenzy WCS	.05	.15
51 Rusty Wallace in Pits WCS	.30	.75
52 Rusty Wallace Mark Martin Ernie Irvan WCS	.20	.50
53 Ricky Rudd's Car WCS	.08	.25
54 Charlotte Motor Speed. WCS	.05	.15
55 Steve Grissom Jeff Burton WCS	.05	.15
56 Jeff Gordon WCS	.50	1.25
57 Joe Nemechek in Plts WCS	.05	.15
58 The Duel in the Sun WCS Charlotte Motor Speed.	.05	.15
59 John Andretti NM RC	.05	.15
60 Shawna Robinson NM	.50	1.25
61 Loy Allen Jr. NM	.05	.15
62 Jeff Gordon NM	.50	1.25
63 Tommy Houston NM	.05	.15
64 Geoff Bodine NM	.05	.15
CC1 Jeff Gordon Chrome	15.00	40.00
CC2 Ernie Irvan Chrome	4.00	10.00

1994 Press Pass Optima XL Red Hot

This 64-card set is a parallel of the base set. It features red foil stamping on the front to set it apart from the base brand. As with the base set, the number 43 Teresa Earnhardt card has a variation. The first ones printed pictured both Teresa and Dale. The more common version features Teresa by herself. The Red Hot cards were inserted at a rate of one per three packs.

Card	Low	High
COMPLETE SET (64)	30.00	80.00
*RED CARDS: 1X TO 2.5X BASIC CARDS		
43B Teresa Earnhardt Dale Earnhardt	60.00	100.00
46 Dale Earnhardt Jr.	8.00	20.00

1994 Press Pass Optima XL Double Clutch

This six-card insert set features drivers who were active on both the Winston Cup and Busch circuits. The cards were inserted at a rate of one per 48 packs. All six cards could also be found in a super pack. These super packs were inserted at a rate of one per 2400 packs.

Card	Low	High
COMPLETE SET (6)	15.00	40.00
DC1 Dale Earnhardt	12.50	30.00
DC2 Ernie Irvan	1.00	2.50
DC3 Terry Labonte	1.50	4.00
DC4 Sterling Marlin	1.50	4.00
DC5 Mark Martin	4.00	10.00
DC6 Morgan Shepherd	.50	1.25

1995 Press Pass Optima XL Prototypes

Press Pass released this set to preview its 1995 Optima XL set. The cards are consecutively numbered and often sold as a 3-card set.

Card	Low	High
COMPLETE SET (3)	3.00	8.00
XL1 Jeff Burton	1.00	2.50
XL2 Darrell Waltrip	.75	2.00
XL3 Mark Martin	2.00	5.00

1995 Press Pass Optima XL

This 60-card set is the second edition of the oversized brand of racing cards produced by Press Pass. The cards measure 2 1/2" X 4 11/16" and use photography from the 1995 season. The set consists of seven subsets: Winston Cup Drivers (1-24), Busch Drivers (25-30), Trophy Case (31-36), Team 24 (37-42), Thunderous Thunderbirds (43-48), Monte Carlo Assault (49-54), and Optima Results (55-59). The product was distributed to both hobby and retail outlets and came six cards per pack, 36 packs per box and 12 boxes per case.

Card	Low	High
COMPLETE SET (60)	10.00	25.00
1 Brett Bodine	.10	.30
2 Geoff Bodine	.10	.30
3 Todd Bodine	.10	.30
4 Derrike Cope	.10	.30
5 Ricky Craven	.10	.30
6 Dale Earnhardt	2.00	5.00
7 Bill Elliott	.50	1.25
8 Jeff Gordon	1.50	3.00
9 Steve Grissom	.10	.30
10 Dale Jarrett	.75	2.00
11 Bobby Labonte	.75	2.00
12 Terry Labonte	.40	1.00
13 Sterling Marlin	.40	1.00
14 Mark Martin	1.00	2.50
15 Ted Musgrave	.10	.30
16 Kyle Petty	.25	.60
17 Robert Pressley	.10	.30
18 Ricky Rudd	.40	1.00
19 Ken Schrader	.10	.30
20 Morgan Shepherd	.10	.30
21 Hut Stricklin	.10	.30
22 Rusty Wallace	1.00	2.50
23 Darrell Waltrip	.25	.60
24 Michael Waltrip	.25	.60
25 Johnny Benson Jr.	.25	.60
26 David Green	.10	.30
27 Jeff Green	.10	.30
28 Jason Keller	.10	.30
29 Chad Little	.10	.30
30 Larry Pearson	.10	.30
31 Jeff Gordon TC	.60	1.50
32 Bobby Labonte TC	.40	1.00
33 Terry Labonte TC	.25	.60
34 Sterling Marlin TC	.25	.60
35 Mark Martin TC	.50	1.25
36 Kyle Petty TC	.10	.30
37 Chad Knaus	.03	.15
38 Ray Evernham	.25	.60
39 Mike Belden	.03	.15
40 Mike Trower	.03	.15
41 Andy Papathanassiou	.03	.15
42 Barry Muse	.03	.15
43 Ted Musgrave's Car	.03	.15
44 Bill Elliott's Car	.25	.60
45 Rusty Wallace's Car	.40	1.00
46 Dale Jarrett's Car	.25	.60
47 Ricky Rudd's Car	.10	.30
48 Mark Martin's Car	.40	1.00
49 Ken Schrader's Car	.03	.15
50 Jeff Gordon's Car	.60	1.50
51 Dale Earnhardt's Car	.75	2.00
52 Bobby Labonte's Car	.25	.60
53 Terry Labonte's Car	.25	.60
54 Sterling Marlin's Car	.10	.30
55 Bill Elliott OR	.40	1.00
56 Jeff Gordon OR	.60	1.50
57 Sterling Marlin OR	.25	.60
58 Mark Martin OR	.50	1.25
59 Ricky Rudd OR	.25	.60
60 Checklist	.03	.15

1995 Press Pass Optima XL Cool Blue

The 60-card Cool Blue set is a parallel of the base Optima XL set. The cards feature blue foil stamping on the fronts and could be found only in retail packs. The Cool Blue cards were inserted at a rate of one per pack.

Card	Low	High
COMPLETE BLUE SET (60)	30.00	60.00
*COOL BLUE: .8X TO 2X BASE CARDS		

1995 Press Pass Optima XL Die Cut

The 60-card Die Cut set is a parallel of the base Optima XL set. Every card is individually die cut to conform to each card's unique design. The Die Cut cards could be found one per 30 packs.

Card	Low	High
COMPLETE SET (60)	200.00	400.00
*DIE CUTS: 5X TO 12X BASE CARDS		

1995 Press Pass Optima XL Red Hot

The 60-card Red Hot set is a parallel of the base Optima XL set. The cards feature red foil stamping on the fronts and were found only in hobby packs. The Red Hot cards were seeded one per pack.

Card	Low	High
COMPLETE RED SET (60)	30.00	60.00
*RED HOTS: .8X TO 2X BASE CARDS		

1995 Press Pass Optima XL JG/XL

This four-card insert set featuring the 1995 Winston Cup champion, Jeff Gordon, created an interesting twist as far as odds of finding the individual cards. The higher the card number the tougher the card was to pull out of a pack. Card number 1 came 1 per 36 packs, card number 2 came 1 per 72 packs, card number 3 came 1:216 packs and card number 4 came 1:864 packs.

Card	Low	High
COMPLETE SET (4)	60.00	150.00
1 Jeff Gordon	2.50	6.00
2 Jeff Gordon	4.00	10.00
3 Jeff Gordon	12.50	30.00
4 Jeff Gordon	40.00	100.00

1995 Press Pass Optima XL Stealth

This 18-card insert set features the top drivers in Winston Cup racing. Each of the 2 1/2" X 4 11/16" insert cards was printed using the embossed foil technology. There have been reports that some of the cards have been found without embossed printing but have shown no premium over the regular issues. The Stealth cards could be found 1 per 18 packs.

Card	Low	High
COMPLETE SET (18)	75.00	150.00
XLS1 Ricky Craven	1.25	3.00
XLS2 Dale Earnhardt	20.00	50.00
XLS3 Bill Elliott	5.00	12.00
XLS4 Jeff Gordon	12.50	30.00
XLS5 Ernie Irvan	2.50	6.00
XLS6 Bobby Labonte	8.00	20.00
XLS7 Terry Labonte	4.00	10.00
XLS8 Sterling Marlin	4.00	10.00
XLS9 Mark Martin	10.00	25.00
XLS10 Ted Musgrave	1.25	3.00
XLS11 Kyle Petty	2.50	6.00
XLS12 Robert Pressley	1.25	3.00
XLS13 Ricky Rudd	4.00	10.00
XLS14 Ken Schrader	1.25	3.00
XLS15 Morgan Shepherd	1.25	3.00
XLS16 Rusty Wallace	10.00	25.00
XLS17 Darrell Waltrip	2.50	6.00
XLS18 Michael Waltrip	2.50	6.00

2000 Press Pass Optima

The 2000 Press Pass Optima product was released in November 2000, and offered a 50-card base set featuring some of the best drivers in the world. Each pack contained 5 cards and carried a suggested retail price of $2.99.

Card	Low	High
COMPLETE SET (50)	8.00	20.00
1 John Andretti	.07	.20
2 Johnny Benson	.15	.40
3 Jeff Burton	.25	.60
4 Ward Burton	.15	.40
5 Dale Earnhardt	1.25	3.00
6 Dale Earnhardt Jr. CRC	1.25	3.00
7 Jeff Gordon	.75	2.00
8 Bobby Hamilton	.07	.20
9 Dale Jarrett	.50	1.25
10 Matt Kenseth CRC	.60	1.50
11 Bobby Labonte	.50	1.25
12 Terry Labonte	.25	.60
13 Kevin Lepage	.07	.20
14 Chad Little	.15	.40
15 Sterling Marlin	.25	.60
16 Mark Martin	.60	1.50
17 Jeremy Mayfield	.07	.20
18 Jerry Nadeau	.15	.40
19 Joe Nemechek	.07	.20
20 Steve Park	.25	.60
21 Ricky Rudd	.25	.60
22 Mike Skinner	.07	.20
23 Elliott Sadler	.15	.40
24 Tony Stewart	.75	2.00
25 Rusty Wallace	.50	1.50
26 Darrell Waltrip	.15	.40
27 Michael Waltrip	.15	.40
28 Casey Atwood BGN	.25	.60
29 Todd Bodine BGN	.07	.20
30 David Green BGN	.07	.20
31 Mark Green BGN	.07	.20
32 Kevin Harvick BGN	.60	1.50
33 Jason Keller BGN	.07	.20
34 Jeff Green BGN	.07	.20
35 Hermie Sadler BGN	.07	.20
36 Matt Kenseth BGN	.30	.75
37 Hank Parker Jr. BGN RC	.25	.60
38 Randy LaJoie BGN	.07	.20
39 Elton Sawyer BGN	.07	.20
40 Jeff Burton WCL	.15	.40
41 Ward Burton WCL	.07	.20
42 Ricky Rudd WCL	.15	.40
43 Dale Earnhardt Jr. WCL	.60	1.50
44 Mark Martin WCL	.30	.75
45 Dale Jarrett WCL	.25	.60
46 Matt Kenseth WCL	.30	.75
47 Bobby Labonte WCL	.25	.60
48 Tony Stewart WCL	.60	1.50
49 Rusty Wallace WCL	.30	.75
50 Steve Park WCL CL	.15	.40
P1 Matt Kenseth Promo	1.25	3.00

2000 Press Pass Optima Platinum

Inserted at one per pack, this 50-card set is a complete parallel of the 2000 Press Pass Optima base set. Each card was produced using a special Platinum holofoil stamping.

Card	Low	High
COMP.PLATINUM SET (50)	12.00	30.00
*PLATINUM: .6X TO 1.5X BASE CARDS		

2000 Press Pass Optima Cool Persistence

Randomly inserted into packs at one in 18, this 6-card insert set features drivers that have what it takes to get to the front. Card backs carry a "CP" prefix.

Card	Low	High
COMPLETE SET (6)	8.00	20.00
CP1 Dale Earnhardt Jr.	6.00	15.00
CP2 Jeff Gordon	4.00	10.00
CP3 Dale Jarrett	2.50	6.00
CP4 Bobby Labonte	2.50	6.00
CP5 Terry Labonte	1.25	3.00
CP6 Rusty Wallace	3.00	8.00

2000 Press Pass Optima Encore

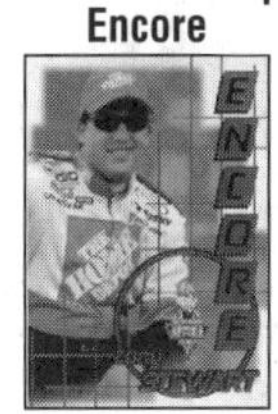

Randomly inserted into packs at one in 8, this 9-card insert set features drivers on a gold-foil stamped card. Card backs carry an "EN" prefix.

Card	Low	High
COMPLETE SET (9)	6.00	15.00
EN1 Dale Jarrett	1.25	3.00
EN2 Bobby Labonte	1.25	3.00
EN3 Mark Martin	1.50	4.00
EN4 Dale Earnhardt Jr.	3.00	8.00
EN5 Jeff Gordon	2.00	5.00
EN6 Dale Earnhardt's Car	3.00	8.00
EN7 Tony Stewart	2.00	5.00
EN8 Jeremy Mayfield	.20	.50
EN9 Rusty Wallace	1.50	4.00

2000 Press Pass Optima G Force

Inserted at one per pack, this 27-card "set within a set" features rainbow-foil and a unique glossy coat. Card backs carry a "GF" prefix.

Card	Low	High
COMPLETE SET (27)	8.00	20.00
GF1 Johnny Benson	.30	.75
GF2 Jeff Burton	.50	1.25
GF3 Ward Burton	.30	.75
GF4 Wally Dallenbach	.15	.40
GF5 Dale Earnhardt's Car	2.50	6.00
GF6 Dale Earnhardt Jr.	2.50	6.00
GF7 Jeff Gordon	1.50	4.00
GF8 Bobby Hamilton	.15	.40
GF9 Dale Jarrett	1.00	2.50
GF10 Matt Kenseth	1.25	3.00
GF11 Bobby Labonte	1.00	2.50
GF12 Terry Labonte	.50	1.25
GF13 Kevin Lepage	.15	.40
GF14 Chad Little	.30	.75
GF15 Sterling Marlin	.50	1.25
GF16 Mark Martin	1.25	3.00
GF17 Jeremy Mayfield	.15	.40
GF18 Joe Nemechek	.15	.40
GF19 Steve Park	.50	1.25
GF20 Ricky Rudd	.50	1.25
GF21 Elliott Sadler	.30	.75
GF22 Mike Skinner	.15	.40
GF23 Tony Stewart	1.50	4.00
GF24 Kenny Wallace	.15	.40
GF25 Rusty Wallace	1.25	3.00
GF26 Darrell Waltrip	.30	.75
GF27 David Green CL	.15	.40

2000 Press Pass Optima Race Used Lugnuts Drivers

Randomly inserted into hobby packs at one in 120, this 20-card set features actual pitstop-used lugnuts. Card backs carry a "LD" prefix. Please note that the hobby version pictures the driver while the retail cards feature the car. Cards LD1-LD14 have a stated print run of 100 sets while cards LD15-LD20 have a stated print run of 55 sets.

Card	Low	High
COMPLETE SET (20)	600.00	1200.00
*CAR CARDS: .3X TO .8X DRIVERS		
LD1 Dave Blaney	10.00	25.00
LD2 Jeff Burton	12.50	30.00
LD3 Ward Burton	12.50	30.00
LD4 Dale Jarrett	20.00	50.00
LD5 Terry Labonte	20.00	50.00
LD6 Kevin Lepage	10.00	25.00
LD7 Chad Little	10.00	25.00
LD8 Sterling Marlin	15.00	40.00
LD9 Mark Martin	30.00	80.00
LD10 Jeremy Mayfield	12.50	30.00
LD11 Jerry Nadeau	10.00	25.00
LD12 Ricky Rudd	12.50	30.00
LD13 Elliott Sadler	10.00	25.00
LD14 Rusty Wallace	25.00	60.00
LD15 Dale Earnhardt/55	100.00	200.00
LD16 Dale Earnhardt Jr./55	100.00	200.00
LD17 Jeff Gordon/55	100.00	200.00
LD18 Matt Kenseth/55	40.00	100.00
LD19 Bobby Labonte/55	40.00	100.00
LD20 Tony Stewart/55	40.00	100.00

2000 Press Pass Optima On the Edge

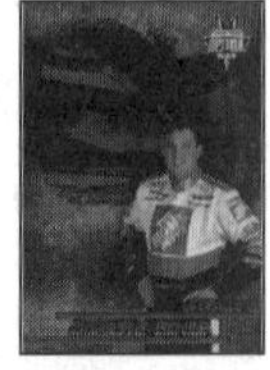

Randomly inserted into packs at one in 24, this 6-card insert set features drivers that take it to the edge. Card backs carry an "OE" prefix.

Card	Low	High
COMPLETE SET (6)	15.00	40.00
OE1 Dale Earnhardt's Car	6.00	15.00
OE2 Dale Earnhardt Jr.	6.00	15.00
OE3 Jeff Gordon	4.00	10.00
OE4 Bobby Labonte	2.50	6.00
OE5 Matt Kenseth	3.00	8.00
OE6 Tony Stewart	4.00	10.00

2000 Press Pass Optima Overdrive

Randomly inserted into packs at one in 8, this 12-card insert set features some of the fastest drivers on a die cut gold foil based card. Card backs carry an "OD" prefix.

Card	Low	High
COMPLETE SET (12)	6.00	15.00
*SQUARE CUT: 1.5X TO 4X BASIC INSERTS		
SQUARE CUT STATED ODDS 1:48		
SQUARE CUT PRINT RUN 350 SER.#'D SETS		
OD1 Jeff Burton	.60	1.50
OD2 Casey Atwood	.60	1.50
OD3 Mike Skinner	.20	.50
OD4 Jeff Gordon	2.00	5.00
OD5 Dale Jarrett	1.25	3.00
OD6 Bobby Labonte	1.25	3.00
OD7 Mark Martin	1.50	4.00
OD8 Tony Stewart	2.00	5.00
OD9 Rusty Wallace	1.50	4.00
OD10 Matt Kenseth	1.50	4.00
OD11 Ward Burton	.40	1.00
OD12 Ricky Rudd	.60	1.50

2001 Press Pass Optima

This 50 card set, featuring the leading drivers in NASCAR was issued during 2001 and released in 5-card packs. The set includes the following subsets: Busch Grand National drivers (#28-39), and Winston Cup Leaders (#40-50). A Kevin Harvick Double Duty insert (numbered "0" and serial numbered of 550) was also inserted in packs at the rate of 1:480.

Card	Low	High
COMPLETE SET (50)	8.00	20.00
WAX BOX HOBBY	40.00	80.00
1 Dave Blaney	.08	.25
2 Jeff Burton	.20	.50
3 Ward Burton	.20	.50
4 Kurt Busch CRC	.30	.75
5 Dale Earnhardt Jr.	1.00	2.50
6 Jeff Gordon	.75	2.00
7 Bobby Hamilton	.08	.25
8 Kevin Harvick CRC	.60	1.50
9 Dale Jarrett	.50	1.25
10 Matt Kenseth	.60	1.50
11 Bobby Labonte	.50	1.25
12 Terry Labonte	.30	.75
13 Sterling Marlin	.30	.75
14 Mark Martin	.60	1.50
15 Jerry Nadeau	.20	.50
16 Joe Nemechek	.08	.25
17 Steve Park	.20	.50
18 Kyle Petty	.20	.50
19 Robert Pressley	.08	.25
20 Ricky Rudd	.30	.75
21 Elliott Sadler	.20	.50
22 Ken Schrader	.08	.25
23 Mike Skinner	.08	.25
24 Jimmy Spencer	.08	.25
25 Tony Stewart	.75	2.00
26 Rusty Wallace	.60	1.50
27 Michael Waltrip	.20	.50
28 Jeff Green BGN	.08	.25
29 David Green BGN	.08	.25
30 Kevin Grubb BGN	.08	.25
31 Kevin Harvick BGN	.60	1.50
32 Jimmie Johnson BGN	.60	1.50

33 Jason Keller BGN .08 .25
34 Randy LaJoie BGN .08 .25
35 Chad Little BGN .08 .25
36 Mike McLaughlin BGN .08 .25
37 Ryan Newman BGN RC 2.50 6.00
38 Hank Parker Jr. BGN .20 .50
39 Elton Sawyer BGN .08 .25
40 Jeff Burton WCL .20 .50
41 Dale Earnhardt Jr. WCL 1.00 2.50
42 Jeff Gordon WCL .75 2.00
43 Kevin Harvick WCL .60 1.50
44 Dale Jarrett WCL .50 1.25
45 Mark Martin WCL .60 1.50
46 Steve Park WCL .20 .50
47 Ricky Rudd WCL .30 .75
48 Tony Stewart WCL .75 2.00
49 Rusty Wallace WCL .60 1.50
50 Bobby Labonte WCL CL .50 1.25
0 Kevin Harvick Double Duty/500 15.00 40.00

2001 Press Pass Optima Gold

Issued one per pack, this is a complete parallel of the Optima set. Each card was enhanced with gold foil layering.

COMP.GOLD SET (50) 12.00 30.00
*GOLDS: .6X TO 1.5X BASE CARDS

2001 Press Pass Optima Cool Persistence

Issued at stated odds of one in six, these 12 cards feature drivers who stay cool under extreme race pressure.

COMPLETE SET (12) 8.00 20.00
CP1 Jeff Burton .50 1.25
CP2 Ward Burton .50 1.25
CP3 Dale Earnhardt Jr. 2.50 6.00
CP4 Jeff Gordon 2.00 5.00
CP5 Kevin Harvick 1.50 4.00
CP6 Dale Jarrett 1.25 3.00
CP7 Bobby Labonte 1.25 3.00
CP8 Terry Labonte .75 2.00
CP9 Steve Park .50 1.25
CP10 Ricky Rudd .75 2.00
CP11 Mike Skinner .25 .60
CP12 Rusty Wallace 1.50 4.00

2001 Press Pass Optima G Force

Inserted one per pack, cards from this set feature the top drivers from the base set. This is a continuation of Press Pass's concept of the "set within a set."

COMPLETE SET (27) 10.00 25.00
GF1 Jeff Burton .40 1.00
GF2 Ward Burton .40 1.00
GF3 Kurt Busch .60 1.50
GF4 Dale Earnhardt Jr. 2.00 5.00
GF5 Jeff Gordon 1.50 4.00
GF6 Bobby Hamilton .20 .50
GF7 Kevin Harvick 1.25 3.00
GF8 Dale Jarrett 1.00 2.50
GF9 Matt Kenseth 1.25 3.00
GF10 Bobby Labonte 1.00 2.50
GF11 Terry Labonte .60 1.50
GF12 Sterling Marlin .60 1.50
GF13 Mark Martin 1.25 3.00
GF14 Jeremy Mayfield .20 .50
GF15 Jerry Nadeau .40 1.00
GF16 Joe Nemechek .20 .50
GF17 Steve Park .40 1.00
GF18 Kyle Petty .40 1.00
GF19 Robert Pressley .20 .50
GF20 Ricky Rudd .60 1.50
GF21 Elliott Sadler .40 1.00
GF22 Ken Schrader .20 .50
GF23 Mike Skinner .20 .50
GF24 Jimmy Spencer .20 .50
GF25 Tony Stewart 1.50 4.00
GF26 Rusty Wallace 1.25 3.00
GF27 Michael Waltrip .40 1.00

2001 Press Pass Optima Race Used Lugnuts Cars

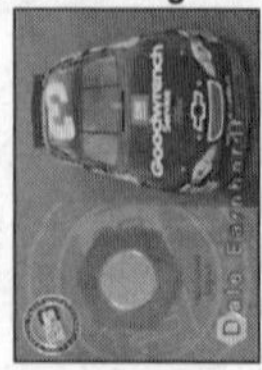

Inserted in retail packs at stated odds of one in 250, these 16 cards featuring driver's cars. Each card also included a piece of race used lugnut that was viewable from both the front and back sides of the card.

LNC1 Jeff Burton's Car 12.50 30.00
LNC2 Ward Burton's Car 12.50 30.00
LNC3 Dale Earnhardt's Car 100.00 250.00
LNC4 Dale Earnhardt Jr.'s Car 40.00 100.00
LNC5 Jeff Gordon's Car 50.00 120.00
LNC6 Kevin Harvick's Car 20.00 50.00
LNC7 Dale Jarrett's Car 15.00 40.00
LNC8 Matt Kenseth's Car 25.00 60.00
LNC9 Terry Labonte's Car 20.00 50.00
LNC10 Bobby Labonte's Car 15.00 40.00
LNC11 Sterling Marlin's Car 12.50 30.00
LNC12 Mark Martin's Car 15.00 40.00
LNC13 Steve Park's Car 12.50 30.00
LNC14 Ricky Rudd's Car 12.50 30.00
LNC15 Tony Stewart's Car 25.00 60.00
LNC16 Rusty Wallace's Car 15.00 40.00

2001 Press Pass Optima Race Used Lugnuts Drivers

Inserted in hobby packs at stated odds of one in 150, these 16 cards feature leading drivers in NASCAR. Each card also included a piece of race used lugnut that was viewable from both the front and back sides of the card. The hobby version (numbered of 100 unless noted) features a picture of the driver while the retail version (numbered of 115 unless noted) features their car.

LND0 Dale Earnhardt/45 125.00 250.00
LND1 Jeff Burton 12.50 30.00
LND2 Ward Burton 12.50 30.00
LND3 Dale Earnhardt Jr. 40.00 100.00
LND4 Jeff Gordon 50.00 120.00
LND5 Kevin Harvick 20.00 50.00
LND6 Dale Jarrett 15.00 40.00
LND7 Matt Kenseth 25.00 60.00
LND8 Terry Labonte 20.00 50.00
LND9 Bobby Labonte 15.00 40.00
LND10 Sterling Marlin 12.50 30.00
LND11 Mark Martin 20.00 40.00
LND12 Steve Park 12.50 30.00
LND13 Ricky Rudd 12.50 30.00
LND14 Tony Stewart 25.00 60.00
LND15 Rusty Wallace 15.00 40.00

2001 Press Pass Optima On the Edge

Inserted at stated odds of one in nine, these nine cards feature drivers who have a chance of winning the Winston Cup.

COMPLETE SET (9) 10.00 25.00
OE1 Dale Earnhardt Jr. 3.00 8.00
OE2 Jeff Gordon 2.50 6.00
OE3 Kevin Harvick 2.00 5.00
OE4 Dale Jarrett 1.50 4.00
OE5 Mark Martin 2.00 5.00
OE6 Steve Park .60 1.50
OE7 Ricky Rudd 1.00 2.50
OE8 Tony Stewart 2.50 6.00
OE9 Rusty Wallace 2.00 5.00

2001 Press Pass Optima Up Close

Inserted at stated odds of one in 12, these six cards feature drivers who deserve to have a closer look taken at their careers.

COMPLETE SET (6) 8.00 20.00
UC1 Dale Earnhardt Jr. 2.50 6.00
UC2 Jeff Gordon 2.00 5.00
UC3 Kevin Harvick 1.50 4.00
UC4 Dale Jarrett 1.25 3.00
UC5 Mark Martin 1.50 4.00
UC6 Rusty Wallace 1.50 4.00

2002 Press Pass Optima

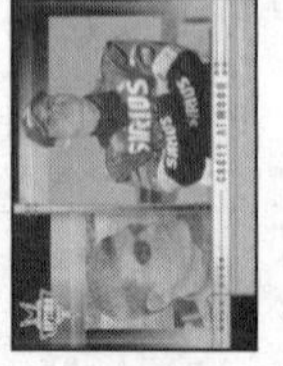

This fifty card set was released in October, 2002. It was issued in five card hobby or retail packs which were packed 24 packs per box and 20 boxes per case with an SRP of $2.99 per pack. The card featuring both Jeff Gordon and Jimmie Johnson was issued in hobby packs at a stated rate of one in 480.

COMPLETE SET (50) 10.00 25.00
WAX BOX HOBBY 30.00 60.00
WAX BOX RETAIL (24) 30.00 60.00
1 Casey Atwood .10 .30
2 Dave Blaney .10 .30
3 Jeff Burton .25 .60
4 Ward Burton .25 .60
5 Kurt Busch .40 1.00
6 Ricky Craven .10 .30
7 Dale Earnhardt Jr. 1.25 3.00
8 Jeff Gordon 1.00 2.50
9 Robby Gordon .10 .30
10 Jeff Green .10 .30
11 Bobby Hamilton .10 .30
12 Kevin Harvick .75 2.00
13 Dale Jarrett .60 1.50
14 Jimmie Johnson CRC .75 2.00
15 Matt Kenseth .75 2.00
16 Bobby Labonte .60 1.50
17 Terry Labonte .40 1.00
18 Sterling Marlin .40 1.00
19 Mark Martin .75 2.00
20 Jeremy Mayfield .10 .30
21 Ryan Newman CRC .75 2.00
22 Steve Park .10 .30
23 Kyle Petty .25 .60
24 Ricky Rudd .40 1.00
25 Elliott Sadler .25 .60
26 Ken Schrader .10 .30
27 Jimmy Spencer .10 .30
28 Tony Stewart .75 2.00
29 Rusty Wallace .60 1.50
30 Michael Waltrip .25 .60
31 Greg Biffle .25 .60
32 Tony Raines .10 .30
33 Ricky Hendrick .50 1.25
34 Jason Keller .10 .30
35 Randy LaJoie .10 .30
36 Mike McLaughlin .10 .30
37 Jamie McMurray RC 3.00 8.00
38 Casey Mears RC 1.00 2.50
39 Hank Parker Jr. .10 .30
40 Scott Riggs RC .75 2.00
41 Johnny Sauter RC .25 .60
42 Jack Sprague .10 .30
43 Brian Vickers 1.50 4.00
44 Scott Wimmer RC .25 .60
45 Dale Earnhardt Jr. YG 1.25 3.00
46 Ryan Newman YG .75 2.00
47 Jimmie Johnson YG .75 2.00
48 Kevin Harvick YG .75 2.00
49 Kurt Busch YG .40 1.00
50 Matt Kenseth YG .75 2.00
0 Jeff Gordon 20.00 50.00
Jimmie Johnson

2002 Press Pass Optima Gold

Issued at a stated rate of one pack, this is a parallel to the Optima basic set. Each card features gold foil highlights on the front.

*GOLDS: .6X TO 1.5X BASE CARDS

2002 Press Pass Optima Samples

These cards were issued before the release of the Optima product to highlight what the cards would look like. The cards were inserted one per Beckett Racing Collector magazine.

*SAMPLES: 3X TO 8X BASE CARDS

2002 Press Pass Optima Cool Persistence

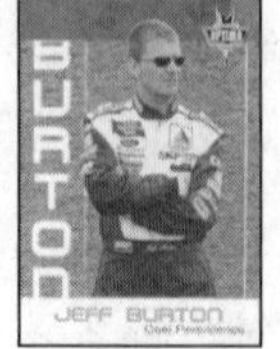

Inserted at a stated rate of one in six, these 12 cards features how persistence pays off for these drivers which stay cool under pressure.

COMPLETE SET (12) 10.00 25.00
CP1 Jeff Burton .60 1.50
CP2 Dale Earnhardt Jr. 3.00 8.00
CP3 Jeff Gordon 2.50 6.00
CP4 Kevin Harvick 2.00 5.00
CP5 Dale Jarrett 1.50 4.00
CP6 Jimmie Johnson 2.00 5.00
CP7 Matt Kenseth 2.00 5.00
CP8 Terry Labonte 1.00 2.50
CP9 Sterling Marlin 1.00 2.50
CP10 Mark Martin 2.00 5.00
CP11 Tony Stewart 2.00 5.00
CP12 Rusty Wallace 1.50 4.00

2002 Press Pass Optima Fan Favorite

Issued at a stated rate of one per pack, these 27 die-cut card set gives all the information needed to join these driver's fan clubs.

COMPLETE SET (27) 8.00 20.00
FF1 Casey Atwood .20 .50
FF2 Jeff Burton .40 1.00
FF3 Ward Burton .40 1.00
FF4 Kurt Busch .60 1.50
FF5 Ricky Craven .20 .50
FF6 Dale Earnhardt Jr. 2.00 5.00
FF7 Jeff Gordon 1.50 4.00
FF8 Robby Gordon .20 .50
FF9 Kevin Harvick 1.25 3.00
FF10 Dale Jarrett 1.00 2.50
FF11 Jimmie Johnson 1.25 3.00
FF12 Matt Kenseth 1.25 3.00
FF13 Bobby Labonte 1.00 2.50
FF14 Terry Labonte .60 1.50
FF15 Sterling Marlin .60 1.50
FF16 Mark Martin 1.25 3.00
FF17 Jeremy Mayfield .20 .50
FF18 Ryan Newman 1.25 3.00
FF19 Steve Park .20 .50
FF20 Kyle Petty .40 1.00
FF21 Ricky Rudd .60 1.50
FF22 Jeff Green .20 .50
FF23 Ken Schrader .20 .50
FF24 Jimmy Spencer .20 .50
FF25 Tony Stewart 1.25 3.00
FF26 Rusty Wallace 1.00 2.50
FF27 Dave Blaney .20 .50

2002 Press Pass Optima Q and A

Issued at a stated rate of one in nine, these nine cards feature racers answering frequently asked fan questions on these holo-foil etched cards.

COMPLETE SET (9) 10.00 25.00
QA1 Kurt Busch 1.00 2.50
QA2 Dale Earnhardt Jr. 3.00 8.00
QA3 Jimmie Johnson 2.00 5.00
QA4 Matt Kenseth 2.00 5.00
QA5 Bobby Labonte 1.50 4.00
QA6 Mark Martin 2.00 5.00
QA7 Ricky Rudd 1.00 2.50
QA8 Sterling Marlin 1.00 2.50
QA9 Tony Stewart 2.00 5.00

2002 Press Pass Optima Race Used Lugnuts Autographs

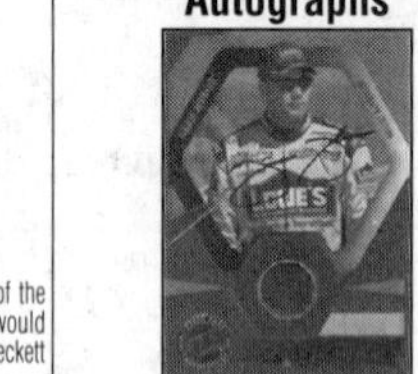

Randomly inserted into packs, these cards feature not only pieces of race-used lugnuts but also the drivers signature on the card. Each of these cards were signed to the driver's car number. Due to market scarcity pricing is not provided for every card.

LNDA6 Jeff Gordon/24 250.00 500.00
LNDA7 Kevin Harvick/29 100.00 200.00
LNDA9 Jimmie Johnson/48 100.00 175.00
LNDA10 Matt Kenseth/17
LNDA11 Bobby Labonte/18 75.00 150.00
LNDA13 Mark Martin/6
LNDA14 Ryan Newman/12
LNDA17 Tony Stewart/20
LNDA18 Rusty Wallace/2

2002 Press Pass Optima Race Used Lugnuts Cars

Randomly inserted into retail packs, these 18 card feature slices of race-used lugnuts on a photo of the driver's car. Each of these cards were issued to a stated print run of 100 sets.

LNC1 Jeff Burton's Car 12.50 30.00
LNC2 Ward Burton's Car 12.50 30.00
LNC3 Kurt Busch's Car 15.00 40.00

LNC4 Dale Earnhardt's Car/10
LNC5 Dale Earnhardt Jr.'s Car 40.00 100.00
LNC6 Jeff Gordon's Car 40.00 100.00
LNC7 Kevin Harvick's Car 25.00 60.00
LNC8 Dale Jarrett's Car 15.00 40.00
LNC9 Jimmie Johnson's Car 25.00 60.00
LNC10 Matt Kenseth's Car 20.00 50.00
LNC11 Bobby Labonte's Car 15.00 40.00
LNC12 Terry Labonte's Car 15.00 40.00
LNC13 Mark Martin's Car 20.00 50.00
LNC14 Ryan Newman's Car 20.00 50.00
LNC15 Ricky Rudd's Car 12.50 30.00
LNC16 Elliott Sadler's Car 10.00 25.00
LNC17 Tony Stewart's Car 30.00 80.00
LNC18 Rusty Wallace's Car 20.00 50.00

2002 Press Pass Optima Race Used Lugnuts Drivers

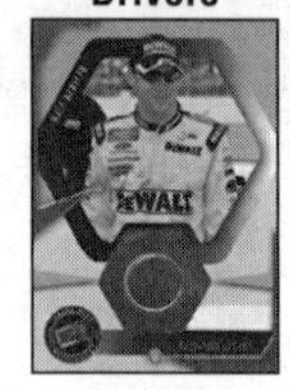

Issued in hobby packs at a stated rate of one in 160, these 18 cards feature pieces of race-used lugnuts placed on a car featuring a driver. With the exception of Dale Earnhardt Sr, these cards were issued to a stated press run of 100 sets. The Earnhardt card was issued to a stated run of 10 sets and due to market scarcity, no pricing is provided.

LND1 Jeff Burton 12.50 30.00
LND2 Ward Burton 12.50 30.00
LND3 Kurt Busch 15.00 40.00
LND4 Dale Earnhardt/10
LND5 Dale Earnhardt Jr. 50.00 100.00
LND6 Jeff Gordon 50.00 100.00
LND7 Kevin Harvick 25.00 60.00
LND8 Dale Jarrett 15.00 40.00
LND9 Jimmie Johnson 25.00 60.00
LND10 Matt Kenseth 20.00 50.00
LND11 Bobby Labonte 15.00 40.00
LND12 Terry Labonte 15.00 40.00
LND13 Mark Martin 20.00 50.00
LND14 Ryan Newman 20.00 50.00
LND15 Ricky Rudd 12.50 30.00
LND16 Elliott Sadler 10.00 25.00
LND17 Tony Stewart 30.00 80.00
LND18 Rusty Wallace 20.00 50.00

2002 Press Pass Optima Up Close

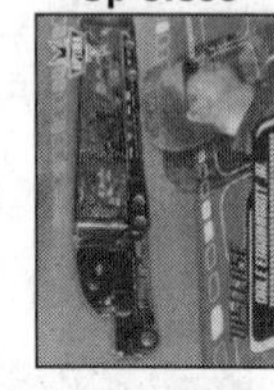

Issued at a stated rate on one in 12, these six cards feature information about the "home away from homes" for these six NASCAR drivers.

COMPLETE SET (6) 8.00 20.00
UC1 Dale Jarrett 1.50 4.00
UC2 Jeff Gordon 2.50 6.00
UC3 Ryan Newman 2.00 5.00
UC4 Jimmie Johnson 2.00 5.00
UC5 Rusty Wallace 1.50 4.00
UC6 Dale Earnhardt Jr. 3.00 8.00

2003 Press Pass Optima

This fifty card set was released in October, 2003. It was issued in five card hobby or retail packs which were packed 28 packs per box with an SRP of $2.99 per pack. The base cards featured a color photo of the driver along with a smaller black and white photo of the driver.

COMPLETE SET (50) 10.00 25.00
WAX BOX HOBBY (28) 40.00 75.00
1 Greg Biffle CRC .20 .50
2 Dave Blaney .10 .25
3 Jeff Burton .20 .50
4 Ward Burton .20 .50
5 Kurt Busch .30 .75
6 Dale Earnhardt Jr. 1.00 2.50
7 Jeff Gordon .75 2.00
8 Robby Gordon .10 .25
9 Kevin Harvick .50 1.
10 Dale Jarrett .50 1.
11 Jimmie Johnson .60 1.
12 Matt Kenseth .60 1.
13 Bobby Labonte .50 1.
14 Terry Labonte .30 .
15 Sterling Marlin .30 .
16 Mark Martin .60 1.
17 Jamie McMurray CRC .50 1.
18 Joe Nemechek .10 .
19 Ryan Newman .60 1.
20 Kyle Petty .20 .
21 Ricky Rudd .30 .
22 Elliott Sadler .20 .
23 Jimmy Spencer .10 .
24 Tony Stewart .60 1.
25 Kenny Wallace .10 .
26 Rusty Wallace .50 1.
27 Michael Waltrip .20 .
28 Jason Keller .10 .
29 Stacy Compton .10 .
30 David Green .10 .
31 Kasey Kahne RC 5.00 12.
32 Johnny Sauter .20 .
33 Mike McLaughlin .10 .
34 Chase Montgomery RC .30 .
35 Jimmy Vasser RC .10 .
36 Brian Vickers .40 1.
37 Damon Lusk RC .30 .
38 Mike Bliss .10 .
39 Scott Wimmer .20 .
40 Dale Earnhardt Jr. UC 1.00 2.
41 Bobby Labonte UC .50 1.
42 Elliott Sadler UC .20 .
43 Kevin Harvick UC .50 1.
44 Tony Stewart UC .60 1.
45 Kurt Busch UC .30 .
46 Dale Earnhardt Jr. TV .75 2.
47 Dale Earnhardt Jr. Music .75 2.
48 Dale Earnhardt Jr. Magazines .75 2.
49 Dale Earnhardt Jr. Talk Shows .75 2.
50 Ryan Newman CL .30 .
NNO Signings Contest Card 2.00 5.

2003 Press Pass Optim Gold

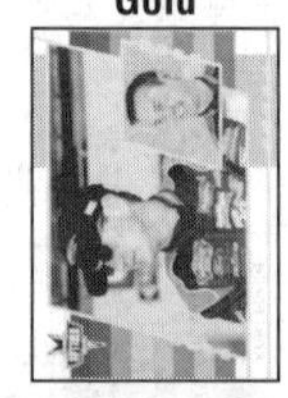

ssued at a stated rate of one pack, this is a paralle the Optima basic set. Each card features gold highlights on the front.

COMPLETE SET (50) 15.00 40.
*GOLDS: .6X TO 1.5X BASE

2003 Press Pass Optim Samples

This 50-card set was a parallel of the base set w the exception of the word "SAMPLE" printed on back of each card. These cards were found Beckett Racing Collector December 2003, Is #112. There was one card per magazine.

*SAMPLES: 2.5X TO 6X BASE

2003 Press Pass Optim Cool Persistence

COMPLETE SET (12) 10.00 25.
CP1 Dale Earnhardt Jr. 2.50 6.
CP2 Jimmie Johnson 1.50 4.
CP3 Mark Martin 1.50 4.
CP4 Ricky Rudd .75 2.
CP5 Terry Labonte .75 2.
CP6 Dale Jarrett 1.25 3.
CP7 Bobby Labonte 1.25 3.
CP8 Jeff Gordon 2.00 5.
CP9 Tony Stewart 1.50 4.
CP10 Rusty Wallace 1.25 3.
CP11 Matt Kenseth 1.50 4.
CP12 Kevin Harvick 1.25 3.

2003 Press Pass Optim Fan Favorite

COMPLETE SET (27) 8.00 20.
FF1 Jimmie Johnson 1.00 2.
FF2 Jeff Burton .30 .
FF3 Matt Kenseth 1.00 2.
FF4 Joe Nemechek .15 .
FF5 Jamie McMurray .75 2.
FF6 Dale Earnhardt Jr. 1.50 4.
FF7 Jeff Gordon 1.25 3.

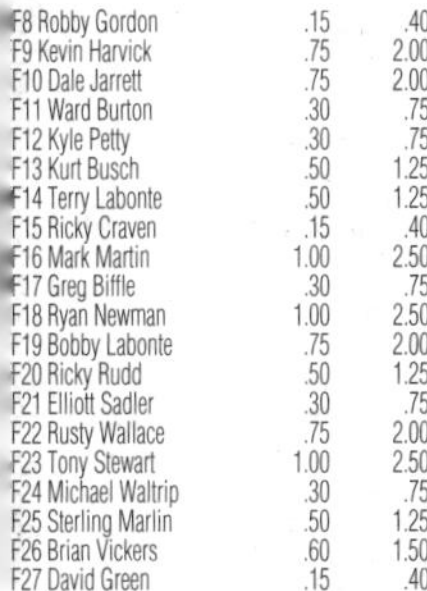

F8 Robby Gordon .15 .40
F9 Kevin Harvick .75 2.00
F10 Dale Jarrett .75 2.00
F11 Ward Burton .30 .75
F12 Kyle Petty .30 .75
F13 Kurt Busch .50 1.25
F14 Terry Labonte .50 1.25
F15 Ricky Craven .15 .40
F16 Mark Martin 1.00 2.50
F17 Greg Biffle .30 .75
F18 Ryan Newman 1.00 2.50
F19 Bobby Labonte .75 2.00
F20 Ricky Rudd .50 1.25
F21 Elliott Sadler .30 .75
F22 Rusty Wallace .75 2.00
F23 Tony Stewart 1.00 2.50
F24 Michael Waltrip .30 .75
F25 Sterling Marlin .50 1.25
F26 Brian Vickers .60 1.50
F27 David Green .15 .40

2003 Press Pass Optima Q and A

sued at a stated rate of one in eight, these nine ards feature racers answering frequently asked fan uestions on these holo-foil etched cards.

COMPLETE SET (9) 10.00 25.00
A1 Tony Stewart 1.50 4.00
A2 Ward Burton .50 1.25
A3 Jeff Gordon 2.00 5.00
A4 Dale Jarrett 1.25 3.00
A5 Greg Biffle .50 1.25
A6 Ryan Newman 1.50 4.00
A7 Joe Nemechek .25 .60
A8 Kurt Busch .75 2.00
A9 Bobby Labonte 1.25 3.00

2003 Press Pass Optima Thunder Bolts Cars

andomly inserted into retail packs, these 18 cards ature slices of race-used lugnuts on a photo of the river's car. Each of these cards were issued to a ated print run of 95 sets with the exception of the ale Earnhardt which had 3 and Kevin Harvick which ad 20 copies produced. These were avalible only in tail packs.

TATED PRINT RUN 95 SERIAL #'d SETS
BT1 Jeff Gordon's Car 25.00 60.00
BT2 Ryan Newman's Car 20.00 50.00
BT3 Kevin Harvick's Car/20
BT4 Jimmie Johnson's Car 15.00 40.00
BT5 Rusty Wallace's Car 12.50 30.00
BT6 Mark Martin's Car 15.00 40.00
BT7 Matt Kenseth's Car 15.00 40.00
BT8 Bobby Labonte's Car 10.00 25.00
BT9 Terry Labonte's Car 12.50 30.00
BT10 Dale Earnhardt Jr.'s Car 30.00 80.00
BT11 Dale Earnhardt's Car/3
BT12 Jeff Burton's Car 10.00 25.00
BT13 Ward Burton's Car 10.00 25.00
BT14 Kurt Busch's Car 10.00 25.00
BT15 Dale Jarrett's Car 15.00 40.00
BT16 Tony Stewart's Car 20.00 50.00
BT17 Sterling Marlin's Car 10.00 25.00
BT18 Michael Waltrip's Car 10.00 25.00

2003 Press Pass Optima Thunder Bolts Cars Autographs

andomly inserted into retail packs, these 9 cards ature slices of race-used lugnuts on a photo of the river's car along with a signature from the orresponding driver. These cards were limited and and numbered to the driver's door number. Some of ese cards are not priced due to scarcity. These ere avalible only in hobby packs.

OME CARDS NOT PRICED DUE TO SCARCITY
BT-BL Bobby Labonte's Car/18 75.00 150.00
BT-JG Jeff Gordon's Car/24 250.00 500.00
BT-JJ Jimmie Johnson's Car/48 75.00 150.00
BT-KH Kevin Harvick's Car/29 100.00 200.00
BT-MK Matt Kenseth's Car/17
BT-MM Mark Martin's Car/6
BT-RN Ryan Newman's Car/12
BT-RW Rusty Wallace's Car/2
BT-TL Terry Labonte's Car/5

2003 Press Pass Optima Thunder Bolts Drivers

andomly inserted into retail packs, these 18 cards ature slices of race-used lugnuts on a photo of the river's car. Each of these cards were issued to a ated print runs of 65, 60, 15 or 3 and noted below the checklist. These were avalible only in hobby acks.

BD1 Jeff Gordon/60 50.00 100.00
BD2 Ryan Newman/60 40.00 80.00
BD3 Kevin Harvick/15
BD4 Jimmie Johnson/60 30.00 60.00

TBD5 Rusty Wallace/60 20.00 50.00
TBD6 Mark Martin/60 30.00 60.00
TBD7 Matt Kenseth/60 30.00 60.00
TBD8 Bobby Labonte/60 15.00 40.00
TBD9 Terry Labonte/60 20.00 50.00
TBD10 Dale Earnhardt Jr./65 60.00 120.00
TBD11 Dale Earnhardt/3
TBD12 Jeff Burton/65 15.00 40.00
TBD13 Ward Burton/65 15.00 40.00
TBD14 Kurt Busch/65 15.00 40.00
TBD15 Dale Jarrett/65 25.00 60.00
TBD16 Tony Stewart/65 40.00 80.00
TBD17 Sterling Marlin/65 15.00 40.00
TBD18 Michael Waltrip/65 15.00 40.00

2003 Press Pass Optima Thunder Bolts Drivers Autographs

Randomly inserted into retail packs, these 9 cards feature slices of race-used lugnuts on a photo of the driver's car along with a signature from the corresponding driver. These cards were limited and hand numbered to the driver's door number. Some of these cards are not priced due to scarcity. These were avalible only in hobby packs.

TBD-BL Bobby Labonte/18 75.00 150.00
TBD-JG Jeff Gordon/24 250.00 500.00
TBD-JJ Jimmie Johnson/48 75.00 150.00
TBD-KH Kevin Harvick/29 100.00 200.00
TBD-MK Matt Kenseth/17
TBD-MM Mark Martin/6
TBD-RN Ryan Newman/12
TBD-RW Rusty Wallace/2
TBD-TL Terry Labonte/5

2003 Press Pass Optima Young Guns

Randomly inserted in packs at a rate of 1:12, this 6-card set featured some of NASCAR's young superstars. Each card number carried a prefix of "YG".

COMPLETE SET (6) 8.00 20.00
YG1 Dale Earnhardt Jr. 3.00 8.00
YG2 Elliott Sadler .60 1.50
YG3 Jamie McMurray 1.50 4.00
YG4 Kevin Harvick 1.50 4.00
YG5 Jimmie Johnson 2.00 5.00
YG6 Kurt Busch 1.00 2.50

2004 Press Pass Optima

This 100-card set was released in October, 2004. It was issued in five card hobby or retail packs which were packed 28 packs per hobby box and 24 per retail box with an SRP of $2.99 per pack. The base cards featured a color photo of the driver along with a smaller photo of the driver's face.

COMPLETE SET (100) 15.00 40.00
COMMON CARD (1-100)
COMMON DRIVER .10 .30
SEMISTARS .25 .60
UNLISTED STARS .40 1.00
WAX BOX HOBBY (28) 50.00 80.00
WAX BOX RETAIL (24) 35.00 70.00
1 Greg Biffle .25 .60
2 Ward Burton .25 .60
3 Kurt Busch .40 1.00
4 Dale Earnhardt Jr. 1.00 2.50
5 Brendan Gaughan CRC .25 .60
6 Jeff Gordon 1.00 2.50
7 Robby Gordon .10 .30
8 Kevin Harvick .60 1.50
9 Dale Jarrett .50 1.25
10 Jimmie Johnson .75 2.00
11 Kasey Kahne CRC 1.25 3.00
12 Matt Kenseth .75 2.00
13 Bobby Labonte .50 1.25
14 Terry Labonte .40 1.00
15 Mark Martin .60 1.50
16 Jeremy Mayfield .10 .30
17 Jamie McMurray .40 1.00
18 Casey Mears .25 .60
19 Ryan Newman .75 2.00
20 Kyle Petty .25 .60
21 Scott Riggs CRC .25 .60
22 Elliott Sadler .25 .60
23 Boris Said .10 .30
24 Tony Stewart .60 1.50
25 Brian Vickers CRC .50 1.25
26 Rusty Wallace .50 1.25
27 Michael Waltrip .25 .60
28 Casey Atwood .10 .30
29 Mike Bliss .10 .30
30 Clint Bowyer RC 2.50 6.00
31 Stacy Compton .10 .30
32 Ron Hornaday .10 .30
33 J.J. Yeley RC 1.50 4.00
34 Johnny Sauter .25 .60
35 Kenny Wallace .10 .30
36 Joe Nemechek .10 .30
37 Martin Truex Jr. RC 2.50 6.00
38 Justin Labonte .40 1.00
39 Matt Kenseth .75 2.00
40 Terry Cook RC .50 1.25
41 Matt Crafton .10 .30
42 Carl Edwards .75 2.00
43 Tina Gordon RC .75 2.00
44 Bill Lester RC .50 1.25
45 Steve Park .25 .60
46 Dennis Setzer .10 .30
47 Jack Sprague .10 .30
48 Jon Wood .25 .60
49 Kasey Kahne YG 1.00 2.50
50 Scott Wimmer YG CRC .25 .60
51 Brian Vickers YG .50 1.25
52 Scott Riggs YG .25 .60
53 Brendan Gaughan YG .25 .60
54 Kyle Busch YG RC 3.00 8.00
55 Dale Earnhardt Jr.'s Car RV .40 1.00
56 Matt Kenseth's Car RV .40 1.00
57 Ryan Newman's Car RV .40 1.00
58 Jimmie Johnson's Car RV .40 1.00
59 Elliott Sadler's Car RV .10 .30
60 Rusty Wallace's Car RV .10 .30
61 Mark Martin's Car RV .25 .60
62 Jeff Gordon's Car RV .40 1.00
63 Kurt Busch's Car RV .10 .30
64 Kyle Petty CS .25 .60
65 Elliott Sadler CS .25 .60
66 Ward Burton CS .25 .60
67 Jeff Green CS .10 .30
68 Jeff Gordon CS 1.00 2.50
69 Dale Jarrett CS .50 1.25
70 Ricky Craven CS .10 .30
71 Terry Labonte CS .40 1.00
72 Kyle Petty CS .25 .60
73 Dale Earnhardt Jr. CP 1.00 2.50
74 Casey Mears CP .25 .60
75 Brian Vickers CP .50 1.25
76 Jeff Gordon CP 1.00 2.50
77 Jimmie Johnson CP .75 2.00
78 Kasey Kahne CP 1.00 2.50
79 Tony Stewart CP .60 1.50
80 Matt Kenseth CP w/ President George W. Bush 1.50 4.00
81 Rusty Wallace CP .50 1.25
82 Brendan Gaughan RR .25 .60
83 Dale Earnhardt Jr. RR 1.00 2.50
84 Brian Vickers RR .50 1.25
85 Kevin Harvick RR .60 1.50
86 Tony Stewart RR .60 1.50
87 Kasey Kahne RR 1.00 2.50
88 Dale Earnhardt Jr. SS 1.00 2.50
89 Kevin Harvick SS .60 1.50
90 Jimmie Johnson SS .75 2.00
91 Casey Mears SS .25 .60
92 Michael Waltrip SS .25 .60
93 Elliott Sadler SS .25 .60
94 Jeff Gordon SS 1.00 2.50
95 Matt Kenseth NP .75 2.00
96 Kurt Busch NP .40 1.00
97 Casey Mears NP .25 .60
98 Greg Biffle NP .25 .60
99 Jon Wood NP .25 .60
100 Jeff Gordon CL 1.00 2.50
NNO Signings Entry Card Dale Jr. 2.50 6.00

2004 Press Pass Optima Gold

Randomly inserted in packs of 2004 Press Pass Optima, this 100-card set is a parallel to the basic set. Each card features gold foil highlights on the front and is serial numbered to 100.

COMPLETE SET (100)
*GOLD: 2.5X TO 6X BASE

2004 Press Pass Optima Samples

This 90-card set is a parallel to the base 2004 Press Pass Optima set without the variations. It was issued 1 per Beckett Racing Collector issue #124, which was the December 2004 cover date. Each card had the word "SAMPLE" printed across the back.

*SAMPLES: 1.5X TO 4X BASE
STATED ODDS 1 PER BRC 124

2004 Press Pass Optima Cool Persistence

This 12-card set featured NASCAR's hottest stars. Cards were produced with a holographic image of

the driver. They were randomly inserted at a rate of 1 in 6 packs.

COMPLETE SET (12) 12.50 30.00
COMMON CARD (CP1-CP12)
COMMON DRIVER .40 1.00
SEMISTARS .60 1.50
UNLISTED STARS 1.00 2.50
STATED ODDS 1:6
CP1 Jeff Gordon 2.50 6.00
CP2 Terry Labonte 1.00 2.50
CP3 Dale Earnhardt Jr. 2.50 6.00
CP4 Mark Martin 1.50 4.00
CP5 Ricky Rudd 1.00 2.50
CP6 Jimmie Johnson 2.00 5.00
CP7 Ryan Newman 2.00 5.00
CP8 Tony Stewart 1.50 4.00
CP9 Matt Kenseth 2.00 5.00
CP10 Bobby Labonte 1.25 3.00
CP11 Dale Jarrett 1.25 3.00
CP12 Kasey Kahne 2.50 6.00

2004 Press Pass Optima Fan Favorite

This 27-card set featured NASCAR's hottest stars interacting with fans. Cards had a die-cut design and pictured fan interaction with the drivers. They were randomly inserted at a rate of 1 in 2 packs.

COMPLETE SET (27) 10.00 25.00
FF1 Greg Biffle .25 .60
FF2 Ward Burton .25 .60
FF3 Kurt Busch .40 1.00
FF4 Dale Earnhardt Jr. 1.00 2.50
FF5 Brendan Gaughan .25 .60
FF6 Jeff Gordon 1.00 2.50
FF7 Robby Gordon .15 .40
FF8 Kevin Harvick .60 1.50
FF9 Dale Jarrett .50 1.25
FF10 Jimmie Johnson .75 2.00
FF11 Kasey Kahne 1.00 2.50
FF12 Matt Kenseth .75 2.00
FF13 Bobby Labonte .50 1.25
FF14 Terry Labonte .40 1.00
FF15 Mark Martin .60 1.50
FF16 Casey Mears .25 .60
FF17 Joe Nemechek .15 .40
FF18 Ryan Newman .75 2.00
FF19 Kyle Petty .25 .60
FF20 Ricky Rudd .40 1.00
FF21 Elliott Sadler .25 .60
FF22 Tony Stewart .60 1.50
FF23 Brian Vickers .50 1.25
FF24 Rusty Wallace .50 1.25
FF25 Michael Waltrip .25 .60
FF26 Davey Allison .25 .60
FF27 Alan Kulwicki CL .25 .60

2004 Press Pass Optima G Force

This 6-card set featured NASCAR's hottest stars and their cars. The cards had silver foil highlights. They were randomly inserted at a rate of 1 in 12 packs.

COMPLETE SET (6) 12.50 30.00
GF1 Dale Earnhardt Jr. 3.00 8.00
GF2 Jeff Gordon 3.00 8.00
GF3 Tony Stewart 2.00 5.00
GF4 Michael Waltrip .75 2.00
GF5 Jimmie Johnson 2.50 6.00
GF6 Rusty Wallace 1.50 4.00

2004 Press Pass Optima Q&A

This 9-card set featured NASCAR's hottest stars. Cards had silver foild and etched highlights. They were randomly inserted at a rate of 1 in 8 packs.

COMPLETE SET (9) 12.50 30.00
QA1 Jeff Gordon 2.50 6.00
QA2 Mark Martin 1.50 4.00
QA3 Matt Kenseth 2.00 5.00
QA4 Tony Stewart 1.50 4.00
QA5 Elliott Sadler .60 1.50
QA6 Jimmie Johnson 2.00 5.00
QA7 Kurt Busch 1.00 2.50
QA8 Michael Waltrip .60 1.50
QA9 Dale Earnhardt Jr. 2.50 6.00

2004 Press Pass Optima Thunder Bolts Autographs

Randomly inserted into hobby and retail packs, these 7 cards feature slices of race-used lugnuts on a photo of the driver along with a signature from the corresponding driver. These cards were limited and hand numbered to the driver's door number. Some of these cards are not priced due to scarcity. The Dale Earnhardt Jr. was only available in packs of 2005 Press Pass Legends which was released in July of 2005.

SOME CARDS NOT PRICED DUE TO SCARCITY
TBBG Brendan Gaughan/77 50.00 100.00
TBBL Bobby Labonte/18 75.00 150.00
TBDE Dale Earnhardt Jr./8
TBJG Jeff Gordon/24 250.00 500.00
TBKK Kasey Kahne/9
TBMK Matt Kenseth/17
TBRN Ryan Newman/12
TBRW Rusty Wallace/2

2004 Press Pass Optima Thunder Bolts Cars

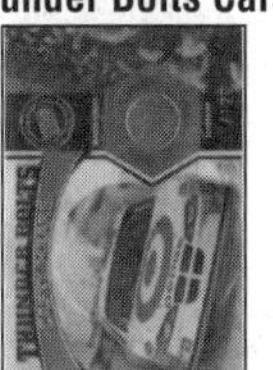

Randomly inserted into retail packs, these 18 cards feature slices of race-used lugnuts on a photo of the driver's car. Each of these cards were issued to a stated print run of 120 sets with the exception of the Dale Earnhardt which had only 3 copies produced. These were available only in retail packs. The stated odds were 1 in 240 retail packs.

*CARS: .4X TO 1X DRIVERS
TBT18 Dale Earnhardt's Car/3

2004 Press Pass Optima Thunder Bolts Drivers

Randomly inserted into hobby packs at a rate of 1 in 68 packs, these 18 cards feature slices of race-used lugnuts on a photo of the driver's car. Each of these cards were serial numbered to 70 with the exception of Dale Earnhardt which only had 3 copies produced.

TBD1 Dale Earnhardt Jr. 40.00 80.00
TBD2 Kasey Kahne 30.00 60.00
TBD3 Tony Stewart 25.00 50.00
TBD4 Michael Waltrip 12.50 25.00
TBD5 Ryan Newman 30.00 60.00
TBD6 Kevin Harvick 25.00 50.00
TBD7 Rusty Wallace 25.00 50.00
TBD8 Matt Kenseth 25.00 50.00
TBD9 Jimmie Johnson 30.00 60.00
TBD10 Brendan Gaughan 15.00 30.00
TBD11 Bobby Labonte 20.00 40.00
TBD12 Dale Jarrett 20.00 40.00
TBD13 Jeff Gordon 50.00 100.00
TBD14 Mark Martin 25.00 50.00
TBD15 Jamie McMurray 20.00 40.00
TBD16 Kurt Busch 15.00 30.00
TBD17 Casey Mears 15.00 30.00
TBD18 Dale Earnhardt/3

2005 Press Pass Optima

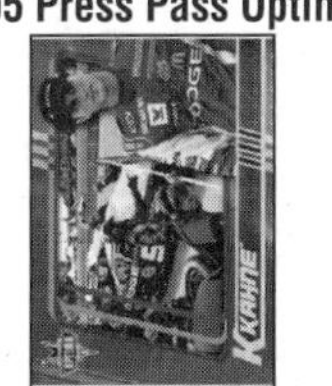

COMPLETE SET (100) 15.00 40.00
WAX BOX HOBBY (28) 50.00 80.00
COMP.CUP CHASE SET (10) 12.50 30.00
*CUP CHASE: 2X TO 5X BASE
CUP CHASE STATED ODDS 1:14
SIGNINGS ENTRY STATED ODDS 1:28
1 John Andretti .10 .30
2 Greg Biffle .25 .60
2B Greg Biffle Cup Chase 1.25 3.00
3 Dave Blaney .10 .30
4 Mike Bliss .10 .30
5 Jeff Burton .25 .60
6 Kurt Busch .40 1.00
6B Kurt Busch Cup Chase 2.00 5.00
7 Kyle Busch CRC .60 1.50
8 Dale Earnhardt Jr. 1.00 2.50
9 Carl Edwards CRC .75 2.00
9B Carl Edwards Cup Chase 4.00 10.00
10 Jeff Gordon 1.00 2.50
11 Kevin Harvick .60 1.50
12 Dale Jarrett .50 1.25
13 Jimmie Johnson .75 2.00
13B Jimmie Johnson Cup Chase 4.00 10.00
14 Kasey Kahne 1.00 2.50
15 Matt Kenseth .75 2.00
15B Matt Kenseth Cup Chase 4.00 10.00
16 Bobby Labonte .50 1.25
17 Sterling Marlin .40 1.00
18 Mark Martin .60 1.50
18B Mark Martin Cup Chase 3.00 8.00
19 Jeremy Mayfield .10 .30
19B Jeremy Mayfield Cup Chase .60 1.50
20 Jamie McMurray .40 1.00
21 Casey Mears .25 .60
22 Joe Nemechek .10 .30
23 Ryan Newman .75 2.00
23B Ryan Newman Cup Chase 4.00 10.00
24 Ricky Rudd .40 1.00
25 Elliott Sadler .25 .60
26 Ken Schrader .10 .30
27 Tony Stewart .60 1.50
27B Tony Stewart Cup Chase 3.00 8.00
28 Brian Vickers .50 1.25
29 Rusty Wallace .50 1.25
29B Rusty Wallace Cup Chase 2.50 6.00
30 Scott Wimmer .25 .60
31 Clint Bowyer BGN 1.00 2.50
32 Carl Edwards BGN .75 2.00
33 David Green .10 .30
34 Denny Hamlin BGN RC 3.00 8.00
35 Kasey Kahne BGN 1.00 2.50
36 Jason Keller BGN .10 .30
37 Reed Sorenson BGN RC 2.50 6.00
38 Martin Truex Jr. BGN .75 2.00
39 J.J. Yeley BGN .40 1.00
40 Terry Cook CTS .25 .60
41 Rick Crawford CTS .10 .30
42 Ron Hornaday CTS .10 .30
43 Todd Kluever CTS RC 1.25 3.00
44 Bill Lester CTS .40 1.00
45 Ken Schrader CTS .10 .30
46 Dennis Setzer CTS .10 .30
47 Mike Skinner CTS .10 .30
48 Jack Sprague CTS .10 .30
49 Martin Truex Jr. YG .75 2.00
50 Carl Edwards YG .75 2.00
51 Kasey Kahne YG 1.00 2.50
52 Reed Sorenson YG 2.00 5.00
53 Clint Bowyer YG 1.00 2.50
54 Kyle Busch YG .60 1.50
55 Dale Jarrett RR .50 1.25
56 Dale Earnhardt Jr. RR 1.00 2.50
57 Mark Martin RR .60 1.50
58 Jeff Gordon RR 1.00 2.50
59 Bobby Labonte RR .50 1.25
60 Martin Truex Jr. RR .75 2.00
61 Carl Edwards RR .75 2.00
62 Jimmie Johnson RR .75 2.00
63 Kurt Busch RR .40 1.00
64 Elliott Sadler DP .25 .60
65 Jeff Green DP .10 .30
66 Tony Stewart DP .60 1.50
67 Jimmie Johnson DP .75 2.00
68 Greg Biffle DP .25 .60
69 Ryan Newman DP .75 2.00
70 Scott Wimmer DP .25 .60
71 Casey Mears DP .25 .60
72 Mark Martin CP .60 1.50
73 Rusty Wallace CP .50 1.25
74 Dale Earnhardt Jr. CP 1.00 2.50
75 Mark Martin CP .60 1.50
76 Elliott Sadler CP .25 .60
77 Sterling Marlin CP .40 1.00
78 Jamie McMurray CP .40 1.00
79 Dale Jarrett CP .50 1.25
80 Mark Martin CP .60 1.50
81 Kurt Busch CP .40 1.00
82 Mark Martin DT .60 1.50
83 Kyle Petty DT .25 .60
84 Carl Edwards DT .75 2.00
85 Jimmie Johnson DT .75 2.00
86 Jeff Burton DT .25 .60
87 Dale Jarrett DT .50 1.25
88 Jeff Gordon's Car RTV .40 1.00
89 Tony Stewart's Car RTV .25 .60
90 Jeremy Mayfield's Car RTV
91 Kevin Harvick's Car RTV .60 1.50
92 Jimmie Johnson's Car RTV .25 .60
93 Dale Earnhardt Jr's Car RTV .40 1.00
94 Greg Biffle's Car RTV .10 .30
95 Jimmie Johnson R&R .75 2.00
96 Bobby Labonte R&R .50 1.25
97 Rusty Wallace R&R .50 1.25
98 Dale Jarrett R&R .50 1.25
99 Mark Martin R&R .60 1.50
100 Tony Stewart CL .60 1.50
NNO Carl Edwards Signings Entry 2.50 6.00

2005 Press Pass Optima Gold

*GOLD: 3X TO 8X BASE

2005 Press Pass Optima Samples

*SAMPLES: X TO X BASE

2005 Press Pass Optima Cool Persistence

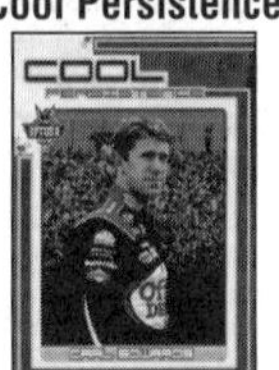

COMPLETE SET (12) 12.50 30.00
STATED ODDS 1:6
CP1 Jeff Gordon 2.50 6.00

CP2 Ricky Rudd 1.00 2.50
CP3 Mark Martin 1.50 4.00
CP4 Jimmie Johnson 2.00 5.00
CP5 Rusty Wallace 1.25 3.00
CP6 Carl Edwards 2.00 5.00
CP7 Dale Jarrett 1.25 3.00
CP8 Sterling Marlin 1.00 2.50
CP9 Kevin Harvick 1.50 4.00
CP10 Jeff Burton .60 1.50
CP11 Bobby Labonte 1.25 3.00
CP12 Tony Stewart 1.50 4.00

2005 Press Pass Optima Corporate Cuts Drivers

STATED ODDS 1:168
STATED PRINT RUN 120 SERIAL #'d SETS
CCD1 Tony Stewart 20.00 50.00
CCD2 Bobby Labonte 15.00 40.00
CCD3 Kasey Kahne 25.00 60.00
CCD4 Jeremy Mayfield 10.00 25.00
CCD5 Greg Biffle 12.50 30.00
CCD6 Dale Jarrett 15.00 40.00
CCD7 Kurt Busch 12.50 30.00
CCD8 Mark Martin 20.00 50.00
CCD9 Matt Kenseth 20.00 50.00

2005 Press Pass Optima Corporate Cuts Cars

*CARS: .4X TO 1X DRIVERS

2005 Press Pass Optima Fan Favorite

COMPLETE SET (27) 10.00 25.00
STATED ODDS 1:2
FF1 John Andretti .15 .40
FF2 Greg Biffle .25 .60
FF3 Dave Blaney .15 .40
FF4 Jeff Burton .25 .60
FF5 Kurt Busch .40 1.00
FF6 Kyle Busch .60 1.50
FF7 Carl Edwards .75 2.00
FF8 Jeff Gordon 1.00 2.50
FF9 Robby Gordon .15 .40
FF10 Kevin Harvick .60 1.50
FF11 Dale Jarrett .50 1.25
FF12 Jimmie Johnson .75 2.00
FF13 Kasey Kahne 1.00 2.50
FF14 Matt Kenseth .75 2.00
FF15 Bobby Labonte .50 1.25
FF16 Terry Labonte .40 1.00
FF17 Mark Martin .60 1.50
FF18 Jamie McMurray .40 1.00
FF19 Casey Mears .25 .60
FF20 Joe Nemechek .15 .40
FF21 Kyle Petty .25 .60
FF22 Ricky Rudd .40 1.00
FF23 Elliott Sadler .25 .60
FF24 Tony Stewart .60 1.50
FF25 Martin Truex Jr. .75 2.00
FF26 Rusty Wallace .50 1.25
FF27 Scott Wimmer .25 .60

2005 Press Pass Optima G Force

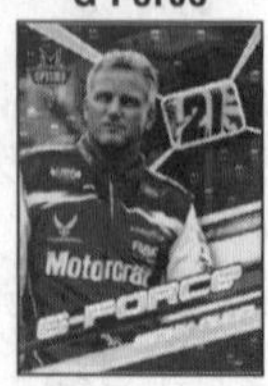

COMPLETE SET (6) 12.50 30.00
STATED ODDS 1:12
GF1 Martin Truex Jr. 2.50 6.00
GF2 Jimmie Johnson 2.50 6.00
GF3 Ricky Rudd 1.25 3.00
GF4 Mark Martin 2.00 5.00
GF5 Jeff Gordon 3.00 8.00
GF6 Dale Jarrett 1.50 4.00

2005 Press Pass Optima Q & A

COMPLETE SET (9) 12.50 30.00
STATED ODDS 1:8
QA1 Mark Martin 1.50 4.00
QA2 Kyle Busch 1.50 4.00
QA3 Elliott Sadler .60 1.50
QA4 Carl Edwards 2.00 5.00
QA5 Jeff Gordon 2.50 6.00
QA6 Dale Earnhardt Jr. 2.50 6.00
QA7 Tony Stewart 1.50 4.00
QA8 Kasey Kahne 2.50 6.00
QA9 Sterling Marlin 1.00 2.50

2005 Press Pass Optima Thunder Bolts Autographs

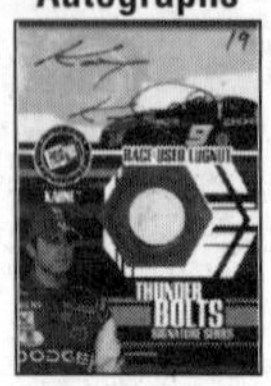

This 8-card set was available in packs of 2005 Press Pass Optima. Each card had a slice of a race-used lugnut and a signature from the corresponding driver. The cards were serial numbered to the driver's door number. There was a late addition to the set. Dale Earnhardt Jr. was only available in packs of 2006 Press Pass Legends.

SOME NOT PRICED DUE TO SCARCITY
TB-JG Jeff Gordon/24 250.00 500.00
TB-JJ Jimmie Johnson/48 75.00 150.00
TB-KB Kurt Busch/97 50.00 100.00
TB-KK Kasey Kahne/9
TB-MM Mark Martin/6
TB-RN Ryan Newman/12
TB-TS Tony Stewart/20
TB-DE Dale Earnhardt Jr./8

2006 Press Pass Optima

This 100-card set featured top drivers from all levels of NASCAR, Nextel Cup, Busch Series and Craftman Trucks. They were released in October of 2006. Hobby packs consisted of five cards and 24 packs per box. Retail packs consisted of four cards and 28 packs per box.

COMPLETE SET (100) 15.00 40.00
WAX BOX HOBBY (28) 50.00 80.00
WAX BOX RETAIL (24) 40.00 70.00
1 Joe Nemechek .20 .50
2 Clint Bowyer CRC 2.50 6.00
3 Martin Truex Jr. CRC 1.50 4.00
4 Kurt Busch .50 1.25
4B Kyle Busch Chase 3.00 8.00
5 Kyle Busch .60 1.50
6 Mark Martin .75 2.00
6B Mark Martin Chase 4.00 10.00
7 Robby Gordon .20 .50
8 Dale Earnhardt Jr. 1.25 3.00
8B Dale Earnhardt Jr. Chase 6.00 15.00
9 Kasey Kahne 1.25 3.00
9B Kasey Kahne Chase 6.00 15.00
10 Scott Riggs .30 .75
11 Denny Hamlin CRC 4.00 10.00
11B Denny Hamlin Chase 6.00 15.00
12 Ryan Newman .75 2.00
13 Sterling Marlin .50 1.25
14 Greg Biffle .40 1.00
15 Matt Kenseth 1.00 2.50
15B Matt Kenseth Chase 5.00 12.00
16 J.J. Yeley CRC 1.00 2.50
17 Tony Stewart .75 2.00
18 Ken Schrader .20 .50
19 Jeff Gordon 1.25 3.00
19B Jeff Gordon Chase 6.00 15.00
20 Brian Vickers .60 1.50
21 Jamie McMurray .50 1.25
22 Kevin Harvick .75 2.00
22B Kevin Harvick Chase 4.00 10.00
23 Jeff Burton .30 .75
23B Jeff Burton Chase 1.50 4.00
24 David Stremme CRC 2.00 5.00
25 Reed Sorenson CRC 2.00 5.00
26 Casey Mears .30 .75
27 Bobby Labonte .60 1.50
28 Terry Labonte .50 1.25
29 Kyle Petty .30 .75
30 Jimmie Johnson 1.00 2.50
30B Jimmie Johnson Chase 5.00 12.00
31 Dale Jarrett .60 1.50
32 Tony Raines .20 .50
33 Carl Edwards 1.00 2.50
34 Todd Kluever NBS 1.00 2.50
35 Clint Bowyer NBS 1.25 3.00
36 Paul Menard NBS .40 1.00
37 Denny Hamlin NBS 1.25 3.00
38 Kevin Harvick NBS .75 2.00
39 David Green NBS .20 .50
40 Regan Smith NBS .20 .50
41 Jon Wood NBS .30 .75
42 Danny O'Quinn Jr. NBS RC .60 1.50
43 Carl Edwards NBS 1.00 2.50
44 Steve Wallace NBS RC 1.25 3.00
45 Burney Lamar NBS RC .75 2.00
46 Mike Skinner CTS .20 .50
47 David Ragan CTS RC 1.00 2.50
48 Rick Crawford CTS .20 .50
49 Bill Lester CTS .30 .75
50 Ron Hornaday CTS .20 .50
51 Erik Darnell CTS RC .60 1.50
52 Dale Jarrett's Car HS .25 .60
53 Jeff Gordon's Car HS .50 1.25
54 Jamie McMurray's Car HS .20 .50
55 Tony Stewart's Car HS .30 .75
56 Kurt Busch's Car HS .20 .50
57 Mark Martin's Car HS .30 .75
58 Jeff Burton's Car HS .12 .30
59 Terry Labonte's Car HS .20 .50
60 Dale Earnhardt Jr.'s Car HS .50 1.25
61 Jimmie Johnson's Car HS .40 1.00
62 Bobby Labonte's Car HS .25 .60
63 Matt Kenseth's Car HS .40 1.00
64 Jeff Gordon CP 1.25 3.00
65 Richard Petty CP 1.00 2.50
66 Jimmie Johnson CP 1.00 2.50
67 Mark Martin CP .75 2.00
68 Dale Earnhardt Jr. CP 1.25 3.00
69 Kyle Petty CP .30 .75
70 Tony Stewart CP .75 2.00
71 Kasey Kahne CP 1.25 3.00
72 Bill Lester CP .30 .75
73 Clint Bowyer YG 1.25 3.00
74 Denny Hamlin YG 1.25 3.00
75 Reed Sorenson YG .75 2.00
76 David Stremme YG .75 2.00
77 Martin Truex Jr. YG .75 2.00
78 J.J. Yeley YG .50 1.25
79 Matt Kenseth RTV Dover 1.00 2.50
80 Denny Hamlin RTV Pocono 1.25 3.00
81 Kasey Kahne RTV Michigan 1.25 3.00
82 Jeff Gordon RTV Sonoma 1.25 3.00
83 Tony Stewart RTV Daytona .75 2.00
84 Jeff Gordon RTV Chicago 1.25 3.00
85 Kyle Busch RTV New Hamp. .60 1.50
86 Denny Hamlin RTV Pocono 1.25 3.00
87 Jimmie Johnson RTV Indy 1.00 2.50
88 Kevin Harvick RTV Wat. Glen .75 2.00
89 Matt Kenseth RTV Michigan 1.00 2.50
90 Matt Kenseth RTV Bristol 1.00 2.50
91 Rusty Wallace 84 ROTY .60 1.50
92 Rusty Wallace 1st Win '86 .60 1.50
93 Rusty Wallace 89 Champ .60 1.50
94 Rusty Wallace 50th Win .60 1.50
95 Rusty Wallace Last Win .60 1.50
96 Rusty Wallace Short Track .60 1.50
97 Mark Martin VOTC .75 2.00
98 Jimmie Johnson VOTC 1.00 2.50
99 Matt Kenseth VOTC 1.00 2.50
CL Dale Jarrett CL .60 1.50
NNO Elvis Presley Promo 2.00 5.00

2006 Press Pass Optima Gold

This 100-card set was a parallel to the base Optima set. Each card featured gold foil highlights and was serial numbered to 100.

*GOLD: 4X TO 10X BASE
*GOLD: 2X TO 5X BASE CRCs

2006 Press Pass Optima Fan Favorite

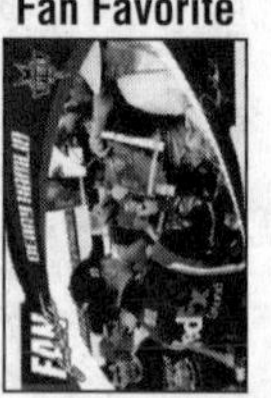

This 27-card set featured top drivers interacting with fans These cards carried an "FF" prefix for their card numbering. They were inserted into packs at a rate of one in two packs.

COMPLETE SET (27) 12.50 30.00
STATED ODDS 1:2
FF1 Clint Bowyer 2.00 5.00
FF2 Jeff Burton .50 1.25
FF3 Kurt Busch .75 2.00
FF4 Dale Earnhardt Jr. 2.00 5.00
FF5 Carl Edwards 1.50 4.00
FF6 Jeff Gordon 2.00 5.00
FF7 Denny Hamlin 2.00 5.00
FF8 Kevin Harvick 1.25 3.00
FF9 Dale Jarrett 1.00 2.50
FF10 Jimmie Johnson 1.50 4.00
FF11 Kasey Kahne 2.00 5.00
FF12 Terry Labonte .75 2.00
FF13 Sterling Marlin .75 2.00
FF14 Mark Martin 1.25 3.00
FF15 Jamie McMurray .75 2.00
FF16 Joe Nemechek .30 .75
FF17 Ryan Newman 1.25 3.00
FF18 Kyle Petty .50 1.25
FF19 Scott Riggs .50 1.25
FF20 Ken Schrader .30 .75
FF21 Tony Stewart 1.25 3.00
FF22 Paul Menard .60 1.50
FF23 David Green .30 .75
FF24 Rick Crawford .30 .75
FF25 Ron Hornaday .30 .75
FF26 Bill Lester .50 1.25
FF27 David Regan 1.50 4.00

2006 Press Pass Optima Pole Position

This 9-card set featured drivers who sat on the pole during the past season. They were inserted in packs at a rate of one in eight. Each card carried a "PP" prefix for its card number.

COMPLETE SET (9) 12.50 30.00
STATED ODDS 1:8
PP1 Jeff Burton .60 1.50
PP2 Kurt Busch 1.00 2.50
PP3 Greg Biffle .75 2.00
PP4 Kasey Kahne 2.50 6.00
PP5 Jimmie Johnson 2.00 5.00
PP6 Kyle Busch 1.25 3.00
PP7 Ryan Newman 1.50 4.00
PP8 Denny Hamlin 2.50 6.00
PP9 Scott Riggs .60 1.50

2006 Press Pass Optima Q & A

This 12-card set featured NASCAR's hottest stars. These cards were inserted into packs at a rate of one in six. Each card carried a "QA" prefix for its card numbering.

COMPLETE SET (12) 10.00 25.00
QA1 Jimmie Johnson 1.50 4.00
QA2 Martin Truex Jr. 1.25 3.00
QA3 Kasey Kahne 2.00 5.00
QA4 Jeff Burton .50 1.25
QA5 Kevin Harvick 1.25 3.00
QA6 Kurt Busch .75 2.00
QA7 Dale Earnhardt Jr. 2.00 5.00
QA8 Reed Sorenson 1.25 3.00
QA9 Jamie McMurray .75 2.00
QA10 Dale Jarrett 1.00 2.50
QA11 Jeff Gordon 2.00 5.00
QA12 Tony Stewart 1.25 3.00

2006 Press Pass Optima Rookie Relics Cars

This 15-card set featured swatches of sheet metal and tire from the corresponding drivers' roookie season. This is a retail parallel version of the Driver hobby version. These were serial numbered to 50. Each card carried an "RRT" prefix for its card number.

*CARS: .4X TO 1X DRIVERS

2006 Press Pass Optima Rookie Relics Drivers

This 15-card set featured swatches of sheet metal and tire from the corresponding drivers' roookie season. This set had a retail parallel Cars version. These were serial numbered to 50. Each card carried an "RRD" prefix for its card number.

RRD1 Clint Bowyer 25.00 60.00
RRD2 Denny Hamlin/40 60.00 120.00
RRD3 Reed Sorenson 25.00 60.00
RRD4 David Stremme 20.00 50.00
RRD5 Martin Truex Jr. 25.00 60.00
RRD6 J.J. Yeley 20.00 50.00
RRD7 Kyle Busch 25.00 60.00
RRD8 Kasey Kahne 60.00 120.00
RRD9 Jamie McMurray 25.00 60.00
RRD10 Ryan Newman 25.00 60.00
RRD11 Kevin Harvick 50.00 100.00
RRD12 Matt Kenseth 50.00 100.00
RRD13 Tony Stewart 50.00 100.00
RRD14 Jeff Burton 40.00 80.00
RRD15 Jeff Gordon 60.00 120.00

2005 Press Pass Panorama

This 81-card set was released in retail blaster boxes of 2005 Press Pass Optima, Press Pass Stealth,

Press pass Trackside and VIP. Cards PPP1-PPP18 were available in Press Pass Stealth. Cards PPP19-PPP36 were available in Press Pass Trackside. Cards PPP37-PPP54 were available in VIP. Cards PPP55-PPP81 were available in Press Pass Optima. When arranged properly, nine consecutive card backs made up trackside scenes.

COMPLETE SET (81) 25.00 60.00
PPP1 John Andretti .20 .50
PPP2 Jeff Burton .30 .75
PPP3 Jeff Gordon 1.25 3.00
PPP4 Denny Hamlin 2.00 5.00
PPP5 Dale Jarrett .60 1.50
PPP6 Matt Kenseth 1.00 2.50
PPP7 Bobby Labonte .60 1.50
PPP8 Terry Labonte .50 1.25
PPP9 Ricky Rudd .50 1.25
PPP10 Jack Sprague .20 .50
PPP11 Kevin Harvick .75 2.00
PPP12 Jimmie Johnson 1.00 2.50
PPP13 Mark Martin .75 2.00
PPP14 Tony Stewart .75 2.00
PPP15 Martin Truex Jr. .75 2.00
PPP16 Rusty Wallace .60 1.50
PPP17 Michael Waltrip .30 .75
PPP18 J.J. Yeley .50 1.25
PPP19 Jeff Burton .30 .75
PPP20 Jeff Gordon 1.25 3.00
PPP21 Jimmie Johnson 1.00 2.50
PPP22 Bill Lester .60 1.50
PPP23 J.J. Yeley .50 1.25
PPP24 Michael Waltrip .30 .75
PPP25 Jimmie Johnson 1.00 2.50
PPP26 Dale Jarrett .60 1.50
PPP27 Jeff Gordon 1.25 3.00
PPP28 Kevin Harvick .75 2.00
PPP29 Bobby Labonte .60 1.50
PPP30 Jeff Gordon 1.25 3.00
PPP31 Ricky Rudd .50 1.25
PPP32 Tony Stewart .75 2.00
PPP33 Dale Earnhardt Jr. 1.25 3.00
PPP34 Rusty Wallace .60 1.50
PPP35 Terry Labonte .50 1.25
PPP36 Jimmie Johnson 1.00 2.50
PPP37 Jeff Gordon 1.25 3.00
PPP38 Jeff Gordon 1.25 3.00
PPP39 Jeff Gordon 1.25 3.00
PPP40 Dale Jarrett .60 1.50
PPP41 Dale Jarrett .60 1.50
PPP42 Dale Jarrett .60 1.50
PPP43 Jimmie Johnson 1.00 2.50
PPP44 Jimmie Johnson 1.00 2.50
PPP45 Rusty Wallace .60 1.50
PPP46 Tony Stewart .75 2.00
PPP47 Tony Stewart .75 2.00
PPP48 Bobby Labonte .60 1.50
PPP49 Bobby Labonte .60 1.50
PPP50 Johnny Sauter .30 .75
PPP51 Paul Wolfe .40 1.00
PPP52 Todd Kluever 1.25 3.00
PPP53 Jack Sprague .20 .50
PPP54 Bill Lester .60 1.50
PPP55 Martin Truex Jr. .75 2.00
PPP56 Lee Petty .50 1.25
PPP57 Tony Raines .20 .50
PPP58 Dale Jarrett .60 1.50
PPP59 Jimmie Johnson 1.00 2.50
PPP60 Kasey Kahne 1.25 3.00
PPP61 Rusty Wallace .60 1.50
PPP62 Tony Stewart .75 2.00
PPP63 Bobby Labonte .60 1.50
PPP64 Rusty Wallace .60 1.50
PPP65 Martin Truex Jr. .75 2.00
PPP66 Ricky Craven .20 .50
PPP67 Ron Hornaday .20 .50
PPP68 Clint Bowyer 1.25 3.00
PPP69 Jack Sprague .20 .50
PPP70 Jason Keller .20 .50
PPP71 Johnny Sauter .30 .75
PPP72 Ricky Rudd .50 1.25
PPP73 J.J. Yeley .50 1.25
PPP74 Terry Cook .20 .50
PPP75 Kerry Earnhardt .30 .75
PPP76 Denny Hamlin 2.00 5.00
PPP77 Dennis Setzer .20 .50
PPP78 Rex White .20 .50
PPP79 Buddy Baker .30 .75
PPP80 Martin Truex Jr. .75 2.00
PPP81 Dave Blaney .20 .50

1995 Press Pass Premium

This 36-card set features the top 36 Winston Cup drivers. The first issue of the Premium brand by Press Pass was printed in a quantity of 18,000 boxes. The cards use gold foil stamping and are printed on 24-point stock. The cards came 3 per pack, 36 packs per box and 8 boxes per case.

COMP.GOLD SET (36) 10.00 25.00
1 Dale Earnhardt 2.00 5.00
2 Mark Martin 1.00 2.50
3 Rusty Wallace 1.00 2.50
4 Ken Schrader .10 .30
5 Ricky Rudd .40 1.0
6 Morgan Shepherd .10 .3
7 Terry Labonte .40 1.0
8 Jeff Gordon 1.25 3.0
9 Darrell Waltrip .25 .6
10 Michael Waltrip .25 .6
11 Ted Musgrave .10 .3
12 Sterling Marlin .40 1.0
13 Kyle Petty .25 .6
14 Dale Jarrett .75 2.0
15 Geoff Bodine .10 .3
16 Brett Bodine .10 .3
17 Todd Bodine .10 .3
18 Bobby Labonte .75 2.0
19 Ernie Irvan .25 .6
20 Richard Petty .40 1.0
21 Greg Sacks .10 .3
22 Joe Nemechek .10 .3
23 Steve Grissom .10 .3
24 John Andretti .10 .3
25 Ricky Craven .10 .3
26 Steve Kinser .10 .3
27 Robert Pressley .10 .3
28 Randy LaJoie .10 .3
29 Davy Jones .10 .3
30 Mark Martin 1.00 2.5
31 Rusty Wallace 1.00 2.5
32 Ricky Rudd .40 1.0
33 Jeff Gordon 1.25 3.0
34 Kyle Petty .25 .6
35 Ken Schrader .10 .3
36 Sterling Marlin .40 1.0
P1 Kyle Petty Prototype Holofoil Card 1.00 2.5

1995 Press Pass Premium Holofoil

This 36-card set is a parallel to the base set. Th cards feature holofoil printing technology and we inserted at a rate of one per pack.

COMPLETE SET (36) 20.00 50.00
*HOLOFOIL STARS: 1X TO 2.5X BASIC CARDS

1995 Press Pass Premium Red Hot

This 36-card set is a parallel of the base set. Th cards are red foil stamped and inserted at a rate one per nine packs.

COMPLETE SET (36) 100.00 250.0
*RED HOTS: 4X TO 10X BASIC CARDS

1995 Press Pass Premium Hot Pursuit

This nine-card insert set features nine of the be drivers in Winston Cup. The cards use NitroKron printing technology and were inserted at a rate of o per 18 packs.

COMPLETE SET (9) 25.00 60.0
HP1 Geoff Bodine .60 1.5
HP2 Dale Earnhardt 10.00 25.0
HP3 Jeff Gordon 6.00 15.0
HP4 Dale Jarrett 4.00 10.0
HP5 Mark Martin 5.00 12.0
HP6 Kyle Petty 1.25 3.0
HP7 Ricky Rudd 2.00 5.0
HP8 Ken Schrader .60 1.5
HP9 Rusty Wallace 5.00 12.0

1995 Press Pass Premium Phone Cards $5

This 9-card set is the first phone card insert issu by Press Pass. The cards featured $5 worth of pho time and were inserted at the rate of one per packs. There was also a parallel 9-card set of $ phone cards. The odds of finding one of the $ cards was one in 864 packs. Ken Schrader, Sterli Marlin and Geoff Bodine also had autographe versions of both $5 and $50 phone cards. The od of finding a signed phone card was one every 2 packs. Finally there were 18 $1995 Jeff Gord phone cards produced. All 18 of the cards we signed in a special white ink pen. Odds of findi one of the $1995 phone cards was one in 36,0 packs. The phone time expired 1/31/1996.

COMPLETE $5 SET (9) 15.00 40.0
*AUTOGRAPHED $5 CARDS: 4X TO 10X
*AUTOGRAPHED $50 CARDS: 8X TO 20X
COMP. $50 SET (9) 100.00 200.0
*$50 CARDS: 1.25X TO 3X BASIC $5 CARDS
1 Geoff Bodine .40 1.0
2 Jeff Gordon 4.00 10.0
3 Dale Jarrett 2.50 6.0
4 Terry Labonte 1.25 3.0
5 Sterling Marlin 1.25 3.0
6 Mark Martin 3.00 8.0
7 Kyle Petty .75 2.0
8 Ken Schrader .40 1.0

Michael Waltrip .75 2.00
Jeff Gordon $1995 AUTO

1996 Press Pass Premium

e 1996 Press Pass Premium set issued in one ies totalling 45 cards. The cards came in three d packs with a holofoil card in every pack. The set ntains the topical subsets: Premium Drivers (1-32) d Premium Cars (33-45).

Card	Low	High
OMPLETE SET (45)	8.00	20.00
Jeff Gordon	1.25	3.00
Dale Earnhardt	2.00	5.00
Sterling Marlin	.40	1.00
Mark Martin	.75	2.50
Rusty Wallace	1.00	2.50
Terry Labonte	.40	1.00
Ted Musgrave	.10	.30
Bill Elliott	.50	1.25
Ricky Rudd	.40	1.00
Bobby Labonte	.75	2.00
Morgan Shepherd	.10	.30
Michael Waltrip	.25	.60
Dale Jarrett	.75	2.00
Bobby Hamilton	.10	.30
Derrike Cope	.10	.30
Geoff Bodine	.10	.30
Ken Schrader	.10	.30
John Andretti	.10	.30
Darrell Waltrip	.25	.60
Brett Bodine	.10	.30
Ward Burton	.25	.60
Ricky Craven	.10	.30
Steve Grissom	.10	.30
Joe Nemechek	.10	.30
Robert Pressley	.10	.30
Kyle Petty	.25	.60
Jeremy Mayfield	.25	.60
Jeff Burton	.40	1.00
Ernie Irvan	.25	.60
Wally Dallenbach	.10	.30
Johnny Benson	.25	.60
Chad Little	.10	.30
Michael Waltrip's Car	.10	.30
Jeff Gordon's Car	.60	1.50
Dale Earnhardt's Car	.75	2.00
Bobby Labonte's Car	.25	.60
Terry Labonte's Car	.25	.60
Ricky Craven's Car	.03	.15
Bill Elliott's Car	.25	.60
Rusty Wallace's Car	.40	1.00
Dale Jarrett's Car	.25	.60
Bobby Hamilton's Car	.03	.15
Ernie Irvan's Car	.10	.30
Ricky Rudd's Car	.10	.30
Mark Martin's Car Checklist	.40	1.00
Bobby Labonte Promo Holofoil	1.25	3.00

1996 Press Pass Premium Emerald Proofs

is 45-card set is a parallel to the base Press Pass emium set. The card features emerald foil mping and are individually numbered of 380. The ds were randomly inserted in packs at a rate of 6 packs.

OMPLETE SET (45) 200.00 400.00
MER.PROOFS: 5X TO 12X BASIC CARDS

1996 Press Pass Premium Holofoil

is 45-card set is a parallel of the base Press Pass emium set. The cards feature a holofoil printing ocess that differentiate them from the base set. The lofoil cards were inserted one per pack.

OMPLETE SET (45) 12.50 30.00
OLOFOILS: .8X TO 2X BASIC CARDS

1996 Press Pass Premium $5 Phone Cards

ndomly inserted in packs at a rate of one in 36, s nine-card insert set features some of the best vers in Winston Cup. Each card is worth $5 in one time and carries an expiration of 4/30/97. ere are two parallel versions of the $5 set, a $10 and a $20 set. The cards are indentical except ey carry $10 and $20 worth of phone time spectively. The $10 cards were randomly inserted packs at 1:216. The $20 cards were randomly erted 1:864. There is also a $1,996 Mark Martin one Card. Any of the phone cards that have had pin numbered scratched usually are worth .25X .50X a mint phone card.

Card	Low	High
OMPLETE SET (9)	10.00	25.00
.00 DOLLAR SET (9)	15.00	40.00
10 CARDS: .6X TO 1.5X $5 CARDS		
20.00 DOLLAR SET (9)	30.00	75.00
*$20 CARDS: 1.2X TO 3X $5 CARDS		
1 Mark Martin		
1 Johnny Benson	.50	1.25
2 Ricky Craven	.25	.60
3 Bill Elliott	1.00	2.50
4 Dale Jarrett	1.50	4.00
5 Bobby Labonte	1.50	4.00
6 Sterling Marlin	.75	2.00
7 Mark Martin	2.00	5.00
8 Kyle Petty	.50	1.25
9 Michael Waltrip	.50	1.25

1996 Press Pass Premium Burning Rubber II

This seven-card set is the second edition of the race-used tire cards. The cards feature an actual tire look. There is an all-foil hub surrounded by the race-tire rubber. Tires from the 1996 Daytona race were acquired to use on the cards. The cards were inserted in both hobby and retail products. Cards BR1-BR4 could be found in hobby packs, while BR5-BR7 could be found in retail packs. The odds of finding a Burning Rubber card were 1:288 packs and each card was serial numbered of 500.

Card	Low	High
COMPLETE SET (7)	300.00	600.00
BR1 Jeff Gordon's Car	40.00	100.00
BR2 Mark Martin's Car	20.00	50.00
BR3 Dale Jarrett's Car	15.00	40.00
BR4 Ken Schrader's Car	15.00	40.00
BR5 Dale Earnhardt's Car	50.00	100.00
BR6 Rusty Wallace's Car	15.00	40.00
BR7 Ernie Irvan's Car	15.00	40.00

1996 Press Pass Premium Crystal Ball

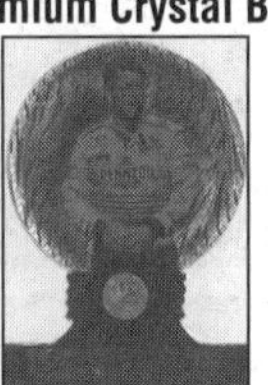

Randomly inserted in packs at a rate of one in 18, this 12-card insert set uses die-cut printing to bring some of the top drivers into view. The cards use a crystal ball design and feature the driver in the crystal ball with his name in script across the base.

Card	Low	High
COMPLETE SET (12)	30.00	80.00
CB1 Johnny Benson	1.25	3.00
CB2 Ricky Craven	.60	1.50
CB3 Dale Earnhardt	10.00	25.00
CB4 Bill Elliott	2.50	6.00
CB5 Jeff Gordon	6.00	15.00
CB6 Ernie Irvan	1.25	3.00
CB7 Dale Jarrett	4.00	10.00
CB8 Bobby Labonte	4.00	10.00
CB9 Terry Labonte	2.00	5.00
CB10 Sterling Marlin	2.00	5.00
CB11 Mark Martin	5.00	12.00
CB12 Rusty Wallace	5.00	12.00

1996 Press Pass Premium Hot Pursuit

Randomly inserted in packs at a rate of one in 18, this nine-card insert set features Press Pass' NitroKrome printing technology. The cards feature the top names in Winston Cup racing.

Card	Low	High
COMPLETE SET (9)	25.00	60.00
HP1 Dale Earnhardt UER Misspelled Earnheardt on the back	8.00	20.00
HP2 Bill Elliott	2.00	5.00
HP3 Jeff Gordon	5.00	12.00
HP4 Ernie Irvan	1.00	2.50
HP5 Bobby Labonte	3.00	8.00
HP6 Mark Martin	4.00	10.00
HP7 Ricky Rudd	1.50	4.00
HP8 Rusty Wallace	4.00	10.00
HP9 Michael Waltrip	1.00	2.50

1997 Press Pass Premium

The 1997 Press Pass Premium set was issued in one series totalling 45 cards. Cards were distributed in 3 card packs with 36 packs per box. The packs carried a suggested retail price of $3.29.

Card	Low	High
COMPLETE SET (45)	8.00	20.00
1 Terry Labonte	.40	1.00
2 Jeff Gordon	1.25	3.00
3 Dale Jarrett	.75	2.00
4 Dale Earnhardt	2.00	5.00
5 Mark Martin	1.00	2.50
6 Ricky Rudd	.40	1.00
7 Rusty Wallace	1.00	2.50
8 Sterling Marlin	.40	1.00
9 Bobby Hamilton	.10	.30
10 Ernie Irvan	.25	.60
11 Bobby Labonte	.75	2.00
12 Ken Schrader	.10	.30
13 Jeff Burton	.40	1.00
14 Michael Waltrip	.25	.60
15 Ted Musgrave	.10	.30
16 Ricky Craven	.10	.30
17 Johnny Benson	.25	.60
18 Wally Dallenbach	.10	.30
19 Jeremy Mayfield	.25	.60
20 Kyle Petty	.25	.60
21 Bill Elliott	.50	1.25
22 Ward Burton	.25	.60
23 Joe Nemechek	.10	.30
24 Chad Little	.25	.60
25 Darrell Waltrip	.25	.60
26 Robby Gordon RC	.40	1.00
27 Mike Skinner Robby Gordon David Green	.25	.60
28 Rusty Wallace's Car	.40	1.00
29 Dale Earnhardt's Car	.75	2.00
30 Terry Labonte's Car	.25	.60
31 Mark Martin's Car	.40	1.00
32 Ricky Rudd's Car	.10	.30
33 Jeff Gordon's Car	.50	1.25
34 Bobby Hamilton's Car	.05	.15
35 Dale Jarrett's Car	.25	.60
36 Bill Elliott's Car	.25	.60
37 Bill Elliott	.50	1.25
38 Jeff Gordon	1.25	3.00
39 Ernie Irvan	.25	.60
40 Dale Jarrett	.75	2.00
41 Bobby Labonte	.75	2.00
42 Sterling Marlin	.40	1.00
43 Mark Martin	1.00	2.50
44 Rusty Wallace	1.00	2.50
45 Checklist	.05	.15
P1 Jeff Gordon Promo	2.00	5.00
P2 Dale Jarrett MO Promo	4.00	10.00
P3 Ernie Irvan MO Promo	2.50	6.00

1997 Press Pass Premium Emerald Proofs

The 45-card set is a parallel to the base Press Pass Premium set. The cards feature emerald foil stamping and are individually numbered of 380. The cards were randomly inserted in packs at a ratio of 1:45.

COMPLETE SET (45) 200.00 400.00
*EMER.PROOFS: 5X TO 12X BASE CARDS

1997 Press Pass Premium Mirrors

This 45-card set, which were issued one per pack, is a parallel to the base Press Pass Premium set. The cards feature a foil background.

COMPLETE SET (45) 15.00 40.00
*MIRRORS: .8X TO 2X BASE CARDS

1997 Press Pass Premium Oil Slicks

This 45-card set is a parallel to the base Press Pass Premium set. The cards feature a rainbow foil Press Pass Premium logo and are individually numbered of 100. The cards were randomly inserted in packs at a ratio of 1:96.

*OIL SLICKS: 8X TO 20X BASIC CARDS

1997 Press Pass Premium Crystal Ball

This 12-card insert set features some of the top names from NASCAR. The cards use a crystal ball design and feature the driver in the crystal ball with his name across the base. The cards were randomly inserted in packs at a ratio of 1:18.

Card	Low	High
COMPLETE SET (12)	25.00	50.00
COMP.DIE CUT SET (12)	50.00	100.00
*DIE CUTS: .6X TO 1.5X BASIC INSERTS		
DIE CUT STATED ODDS 1:36		
CB1 Ricky Craven	.60	1.50
CB2 Dale Earnhardt's Car	4.00	10.00
CB3 Bill Elliott	2.50	6.00
CB4 Jeff Gordon	6.00	15.00
CB5 Ernie Irvan	1.25	3.00
CB6 Dale Jarrett	4.00	10.00
CB7 Bobby Labonte	4.00	10.00
CB8 Terry Labonte	2.00	5.00
CB9 Sterling Marlin	2.00	5.00
CB10 Mark Martin	5.00	12.00
CB11 Ricky Rudd	2.00	5.00
CB12 Rusty Wallace	5.00	12.00

1997 Press Pass Premium Double Burners

This five-card insert set features pieces of race-used tire rubber and race-used driver uniforms on the same card. The piece of the driver's uniform appears on the front of the card while the piece of the driver's tire appears on the back. Cards that contain multi-colored pieces of cloth carry a 25 percent premium over those that do not. The cards were randomly inserted in packs at a ratio of 1:432 and are individually numnered of 350.

Card	Low	High
COMPLETE SET (5)	200.00	400.00
DB1 Dale Earnhardt	75.00	150.00
DB2 Jeff Gordon	50.00	100.00
DB3 Terry Labonte	20.00	50.00
DB4 Rusty Wallace	25.00	60.00
DB5 Michael Waltrip	15.00	40.00

1997 Press Pass Premium Lap Leaders

This 12-card insert set features cel cards that are printed on acetate. The cards are randomly inserted in packs at a ratio of 1:12.

Card	Low	High
COMPLETE SET (12)	15.00	40.00
LL1 Dale Earnhardt	10.00	25.00
LL2 Bill Elliott	2.50	6.00
LL3 Jeff Gordon	6.00	15.00
LL4 Ernie Irvan	1.25	3.00
LL5 Dale Jarrett	4.00	10.00
LL6 Bobby Labonte	4.00	10.00
LL7 Terry Labonte	2.00	5.00
LL8 Mark Martin	5.00	12.00
LL9 Kyle Petty	1.25	3.00
LL10 Ricky Rudd	2.00	5.00
LL11 Rusty Wallace	5.00	12.00
LL12 Michael Waltrip	1.25	3.00

1998 Press Pass Premium

The 1998 Press Pass Premium set was issued in one series totalling 54 cards. The 3-card packs retail for $3.49 each. The set contains the topical subsets: NASCAR Busch Series (1-13), NASCAR Winston Cup Cars (14-27), and NASCAR Winston Cup Drivers (28-53).

Card	Low	High
COMPLETE SET (54)	12.00	30.00
1 Randy LaJoie	.15	.40
2 Tim Fedewa	.15	.40
3 Mike McLaughlin	.15	.40
4 Elliott Sadler	.30	.75
5 Tony Stewart RC	6.00	15.00
6 Jeff Burton	.40	1.00
7 Michael Waltrip	.40	1.00
8 Dale Jarrett	1.00	2.50
9 Mark Martin	1.25	3.00
10 Jason Keller	.15	.40
11 Hermie Sadler	.15	.40
12 Dale Earnhardt Jr.	2.00	5.00
13 Joe Nemechek	.15	.40
14 Rusty Wallace's Car	.50	1.25
15 Dale Earnhardt's Car	1.00	2.50
16 Bobby Hamilton's Car	.10	.25
17 Terry Labonte's Car	.30	.75
18 Mark Martin's Car	.50	1.25
19 Ricky Rudd's Car	.15	.40
20 Bobby Labonte's Car	.30	.75
21 Jeff Gordon's Car	.60	1.50
22 Johnny Benson's Car	.15	.40
23 Kenny Irwin's Car	.25	.60
24 John Andretti's Car	.05	.15
25 Dale Jarrett's Car	.30	.75
26 Bill Elliott's Car	.30	.75
27 Jeff Burton's Car	.15	.40
28 Jeff Gordon	1.50	4.00
29 Dale Jarrett	1.00	2.50
30 Mark Martin	1.25	3.00
31 Jeff Burton	.40	1.00
32 Dale Earnhardt	2.50	6.00
33 Terry Labonte	.50	1.25
34 Bobby Labonte	.75	2.00
35 Bill Elliott	.60	1.50
36 Rusty Wallace	1.25	3.00
37 Ken Schrader	.15	.40
38 Johnny Benson	.40	1.00
39 Ted Musgrave	.15	.40
40 Jeremy Mayfield	.30	.75
41 Ernie Irvan	.30	.75
42 John Andretti	.15	.40
43 Bobby Hamilton	.25	.60
44 Ricky Rudd	.50	1.25
45 Michael Waltrip	.30	.75
46 Ricky Craven	.15	.40
47 Jimmy Spencer	.30	.75
48 Geoff Bodine	.15	.40
49 Ward Burton	.30	.75
50 Sterling Marlin	.50	1.25
51 Todd Bodine	.15	.40
52 Joe Nemechek	.15	.40
53 Mike Skinner	.15	.40
54 Kenny Irwin CL	.60	1.50
P1 Jeff Gordon Promo	2.00	5.00
0 Dale Earnhardt Daytona	30.00	60.00

1998 Press Pass Premium Reflectors

This 54-card set is a parallel of the regular base set. These cards were randomly inserted at a ratio of one in 8 packs.

COMPLETE SET (54) 75.00 150.00
*REFLECTOR VETS: 2X TO 5X BASE CARDS
*REFLECTOR RCs: .6X TO 1.5X BASE CARDS

1998 Press Pass Premium Flag Chasers

Randomly inserted in packs at a rate of one in 2, this 27-card insert set features multi-dimensional all-foil, die-cut cards with intricate micro-etching of the top NASCAR Winston Cup drivers and cars.

Card	Low	High
COMPLETE SET (27)	15.00	40.00
COMP.REF. SET (27)	150.00	300.00
*REFLECTORS: 3X TO 8X BASIC INSERTS		
FC1 Jeff Gordon	3.00	8.00
FC2 Steve Park	1.00	2.50
FC3 Dale Jarrett	2.00	5.00
FC4 Mark Martin	2.50	6.00
FC5 Jeff Burton	1.00	2.50
FC6 Rusty Wallace	2.50	6.00
FC7 Ricky Rudd	1.00	2.50
FC8 Terry Labonte	1.00	2.50
FC9 Bobby Labonte	1.50	4.00
FC10 Ernie Irvan	.60	1.50
FC11 Johnny Benson	.60	1.50
FC12 Michael Waltrip	.60	1.50
FC13 Bill Elliott	1.25	3.00
FC14 Ken Schrader	.30	.75
FC15 Wally Dallenbach	.30	.75
FC16 Kenny Irwin	.60	1.50
FC17 Ricky Craven	.30	.75
FC18 Mike Skinner	.30	.75
FC19 Rusty Wallace's Car	1.00	2.50
FC20 Dale Earnhardt's Car	2.00	5.00
FC21 Terry Labonte's Car	.60	1.50
FC22 Ricky Rudd's Car	.30	.75
FC23 Bobby Labonte's Car	.60	1.50
FC24 Jeff Gordon's Car	1.25	3.00
FC25 Dale Jarrett's Car	.60	1.50
FC26 Bill Elliott's Car	.60	1.50
FC27 Jeff Burton's Car	.30	.75

1998 Press Pass Premium Rivalries

Randomly inserted in packs at a rate of one in 6, this 12-card insert set celebrates NASCAR's 50th anniversary with inter-locking die-cut cards that depict the top six driver duels from NASCAR's premier division.

Card	Low	High
COMPLETE SET (12)	20.00	50.00
1A Jeff Burton	1.25	3.00
1B Jeff Gordon	4.00	10.00
2A David Pearson	.40	1.00
2B Richard Petty	.75	2.00
3A Dale Earnhardt	6.00	15.00
3B Rusty Wallace	3.00	8.00
4A Cale Yarborough	.40	1.00
4B Bobby Allison	.40	1.00
5A Mark Martin	3.00	8.00
5B Dale Jarrett	2.50	6.00
6A Jeff Gordon's Car	1.50	4.00
6B Dale Earnhardt's Car	2.50	6.00

1998 Press Pass Premium Steel Horses

Randomly inserted in packs at a rate of one in 12, this 12-card insert set highlights the top NASCAR Winston Cup cars in an all-foil, die-cut, embossed and etched set.

Card	Low	High
COMPLETE SET (12)	20.00	50.00
SH1 Rusty Wallace's Car	4.00	10.00
SH2 Dale Earnhardt's Car	8.00	20.00
SH3 Terry Labonte's Car	2.50	6.00
SH4 Mark Martin's Car	4.00	10.00
SH5 Ricky Rudd's Car	1.25	3.00
SH6 Bobby Labonte's Car	2.50	6.00
SH7 Jeff Gordon's Car	5.00	12.00
SH8 Kenny Irwin's Car	1.25	3.00
SH9 Sterling Marlin's Car	1.25	3.00
SH10 Dale Jarrett's Car	2.50	6.00
SH11 Bill Elliott's Car	2.50	6.00
SH12 Jeff Burton's Car	1.25	3.00

1998 Press Pass Premium Triple Gear Firesuit

Randomly inserted in packs at a rate of one in 432, this 9-card insert set features authentic pieces of the drivers' firesuits. These cards are numbered to 150.

Card	Low	High
TGF1 Rusty Wallace	30.00	80.00
TGF2 Dale Earnhardt	125.00	250.00
TGF3 Terry Labonte	25.00	60.00
TGF4 Mark Martin	30.00	80.00
TGF5 Bobby Labonte	25.00	60.00
TGF6 Jeff Gordon	100.00	200.00
TGF7 Mike Skinner	15.00	40.00
TGF8 Dale Jarrett	25.00	60.00
TGF9 Jeff Burton	20.00	50.00

1999 Press Pass Premium

This 54-card set was issued by Press Pass as a premium hobby product with three cards per pack. The set features cards of most of the leading NASCAR drivers and a few of their cars. A parallel reflector set was issued at the rate of one every eight packs and is valued at a multiple of the regular cards. A special Jeff Gordon Daytona card was randomly inserted in packs and is listed at the end of these listings.

Card	Low	High
COMPLETE SET (72)	12.50	30.00
1 John Andretti	.15	.40
2 Johnny Benson	.30	.75
3 Geoff Bodine	.15	.40
4 Jeff Burton	.50	1.25
5 Ward Burton	.30	.75
6 Dale Earnhardt	2.50	6.00
7 Bill Elliott	.60	1.50
8 Jeff Gordon	1.50	4.00
9 Bobby Hamilton	.15	.40
10 Ernie Irvan	.30	.75
11 Kenny Irwin	.30	.75
12 Dale Jarrett	1.00	2.50
13 Bobby Labonte	1.00	3.00
14 Terry Labonte	.50	1.25
15 Chad Little	.30	.75
16 Sterling Marlin	.50	1.25
17 Mark Martin	1.25	3.00
18 Jeremy Mayfield	.30	.75
19 Joe Nemechek	.15	.40
20 Steve Park	.75	2.00

21 Ricky Rudd	.50	1.25
22 Elliott Sadler	.30	.75
23 Tony Stewart CRC	2.00	5.00
24 Mike Skinner	.15	.40
25 Jimmy Spencer	.15	.40
26 Rusty Wallace	1.25	3.00
27 Michael Waltrip	.30	.75
28 Jeff Gordon's Car	.60	1.50
29 Mark Martin's Car	.50	1.25
30 Dale Jarrett's Car	.30	.75
31 Rusty Wallace's Car	.50	1.25
32 Jeff Burton's Car	.30	.75
33 Bobby Labonte's Car	.30	.75
34 Jeremy Mayfield's Car	.07	.20
35 Dale Earnhardt's Car	1.00	2.50
36 Terry Labonte's Car	.30	.75
37 Mike Skinner's Car	.07	.20
38 John Andretti's Car	.07	.20
39 Kenny Irwin's Car	.15	.40
40 Joe Nemechek	.15	.40
41 Dale Earnhardt Jr.	2.00	5.00
42 Tim Fedewa	.15	.40
43 Jeff Gordon	1.50	4.00
44 Ken Schrader	.15	.40
45 Terry Labonte	.50	1.25
46 Matt Kenseth RC	3.00	8.00
47 Randy LaJoie	.15	.40
48 Mark Martin	1.25	3.00
49 Mike McLaughlin	.15	.40
50 Michael Waltrip	.30	.75
51 Hermie Sadler	.15	.40
52 Jason Keller	.15	.40
53 Todd Bodine	.15	.40
54 Jason Jarrett CL	.30	.75
P1 Dale Earnhardt Jr. Promo	2.00	5.00
0 Jeff Gordon Daytona	15.00	40.00

1999 Press Pass Premium Reflectors

Issued at stated odds of one in eight, these cards parallel the Press Pass Premium set. Each card was coated with a peel-off clear "reflector shield" designed to protect the cardfronts from scrathes. The stated print run was 1975 serial numbered sets.

COMPLETE SET (54)	100.00	200.00
*REFLECTORS: 2X TO 5X BASE CARDS		
*REFLECTOR RCs: 1X TO 2.5X BASE CARDS		

1999 Press Pass Premium Badge of Honor

These cards were inserted one every two packs. The card back resembles a shield with the drivers car number on it. There is also a non-die-cut reflector set issued to these cards which are issued one every 24 packs.

COMPLETE SET (28)	15.00	40.00
COMP.REFLECT.SET (28)	200.00	400.00
*REFLECTORS: 3X TO 8X BASIC INSERTS		
BH1 Rusty Wallace	2.50	6.00
BH2 Dale Earnhardt Jr.	4.00	10.00
BH3A Michael Waltrip	.60	1.50
BH3B Jimmy Spencer	.30	.75
BH4 Terry Labonte	1.00	2.50
BH5 Mark Martin	2.50	6.00
BH6 Ricky Rudd	1.00	2.50
BH7 Jeremy Mayfield	.60	1.50
BH8 Johnny Benson	.60	1.50
BH9 Bobby Labonte	2.50	6.00
BH10 Jeff Gordon	3.00	8.00
BH11 Kenny Irwin	.60	1.50
BH12 Mike Skinner	.30	.75
BH13 Ernie Irvan	.60	1.50
BH14 Dale Jarrett	2.00	5.00
BH15 Bill Elliott	1.25	3.00
BH16 Jeff Burton	1.00	2.50
BH17 Chad Little	.60	1.50
BH18 Kevin Lepage	.30	.75
BH19 Dale Earnhardt's Car	2.50	6.00
BH20 Terry Labonte's Car	.50	1.25
BH21 Mark Martin's Car	1.25	3.00
BH22 Jeremy Mayfield's Car	.30	.75
BH23 Bobby Labonte's Car	1.25	3.00
BH24 Jeff Gordon's Car	1.50	4.00
BH25 Dale Jarrett's Car	1.00	2.50
BH26 Dale Earnhardt Jr.'s Car	2.00	5.00
BH27 Jeff Burton's Car	.50	1.25

1999 Press Pass Premium Burning Desire

This six card insert set was issued with progressing insert ratios, the odds are noted next to each driver. This set also featured race used rubber on the card.

COMPLETE SET (6)	50.00	120.00
FD1B Jeff Gordon 1:240	12.50	30.00
FD2B Dale Earnhardt Jr. 1:192	12.50	30.00
FD3B Jeremy Mayfield 1:144	3.00	8.00
FD4B Jeff Burton 1:72	4.00	10.00
FD5B Dale Jarrett 1:36	5.00	12.00
FD6B Tony Stewart 1:18	6.00	15.00

1999 Press Pass Premium Extreme Fire

This six card insert set was issued with progressing insert ratios, the odds are noted next to each driver. This set also featured race used rubber on the card.

COMPLETE SET (6)	40.00	100.00
FD1A Jeff Gordon 1:240	10.00	25.00
FD2A Dale Earnhardt 1:192	12.50	30.00
FD3A Rusty Wallace 1:144	7.50	15.00
FD4A Mark Martin 1:72	6.00	15.00
FD5A Terry Labonte 1:36	3.00	8.00
FD6A Bobby Labonte 1:18	3.00	8.00

1999 Press Pass Premium Race Used Firesuit

Inserted at the rate of one every 432 packs these nine cards feature pieces of the racing firesuits worn by various drivers. The Jeff Gordon Firesuit was not available at time of issue but was only available via a mail redemption card. The stated print run was 250 serial numbered sets.

COMPLETE SET (9)	400.00	800.00
F1 Jeff Gordon	60.00	150.00
F2 Rusty Wallace	30.00	80.00
F3 Dale Earnhardt	100.00	200.00
F4 Bobby Labonte	20.00	50.00
F5 Terry Labonte	20.00	50.00
F6 Mark Martin	30.00	80.00
F7 Mike Skinner	15.00	40.00
F8 Dale Jarrett	25.00	60.00
F9 Jeff Burton	20.00	50.00

1999 Press Pass Premium Steel Horses

Inserted one every 12 packs, these 12 cards feature pictures of some of the leading cars on the NASCAR circuit. Each card was produced in a die-cut shape of a galloping horse.

COMPLETE SET (12)	20.00	50.00
SH1 Rusty Wallace's Car	5.00	12.00
SH4 Terry Labonte's Car	2.00	5.00
SH5 Mark Martin's Car	5.00	12.00
SH6 Dale Earnhardt Jr.'s Car	8.00	20.00
SH7 Jeremy Mayfield's Car	1.25	3.00
SH8 Bobby Labonte's Car	5.00	12.00
SH9 Jeff Gordon's Car	6.00	15.00
SH10 Dale Jarrett's Car	4.00	10.00
SH11 Bill Elliott's Car	2.50	6.00
SH12 Jeff Burton's Car	2.00	5.00
SH22 Dale Earnhardt's Car	10.00	25.00
SH32 Mike Skinner's Car	.60	1.50

2000 Press Pass Premium

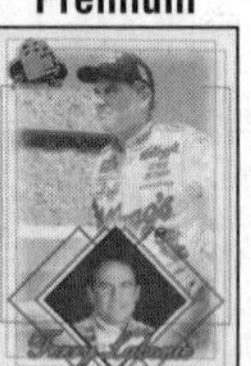

2000 Press Pass Premium was released as a 72-card three tier base set. Contenders (numbers 1-45) were inserted at three in one, Champs and Challengers (numbers 46-63) were inserted at one in three, and Premium Choice (numbers 64-72) were inserted at one in 12. This set also features a "ZERO" card which pays tribute to the 2000 Daytona 500 winner. Press Pass Premium was packaged at 24-packs per box, 4-cards per pack, and packs carried a suggested retail price of $3.99.

COMPLETE SET (72)	40.00	100.00
COMP.SET w/o SP'S (45)	6.00	15.00
1 Steve Park	.60	1.50
2 Rusty Wallace	1.50	4.00
3 Bobby Hamilton	.20	.50
4 Terry Labonte	.60	1.50
5 Mark Martin	1.50	4.00
6 Michael Waltrip	.40	1.00
7 Jeremy Mayfield	.20	.50
8 Kevin Lepage	.20	.50
9 Bobby Labonte	1.25	3.00
10 Tony Stewart	2.00	5.00
11 Elliott Sadler	.40	1.00
12 Ward Burton	.40	1.00
13 Jeff Gordon	2.00	5.00
14 Jerry Nadeau	.40	1.00
15 Jimmy Spencer	.20	.50
16 Ricky Rudd	.60	1.50
17 Mike Skinner	.20	.50
18 Joe Nemechek	.20	.50
19 Sterling Marlin	.60	1.50
20 Kenny Irwin	.40	1.00
21 John Andretti	.20	.50
22 Kenny Wallace	.20	.50
23 Geoffrey Bodine	.20	.50
24 Darrell Waltrip	.40	1.00
25 Dale Jarrett	1.25	3.00
26 Chad Little	.40	1.00
27 Jeff Burton	.60	1.50
28 Rusty Wallace's Car	.60	1.50
29 Jeremy Mayfield's Car	.08	.25
30 Terry Labonte's Car	.40	1.00
31 Mark Martin's Car	.60	1.50
32 Joe Nemechek's Car	.08	.25
33 Matt Kenseth CRC	.60	1.50
34 Bobby Labonte's Car	.40	1.00
35 Tony Stewart's Car	.75	2.00
36 Jeff Gordon's Car	.75	2.00
37 Sterling Marlin's Car	.20	.50
38 Ricky Rudd's Car	.20	.50
39 Jeff Burton's Car	.20	.50
40 Dave Blaney	.20	.50
41 Mike Bliss	.20	.50
42 Scott Pruett RC	.20	.50
43 Dale Earnhardt Jr. CRC	2.50	6.00
44 Matt Kenseth	1.50	4.00
45 Stacy Compton CL	.20	.50
46 Dale Jarrett	1.50	4.00
47 Jeff Gordon	2.50	6.00
48 Terry Labonte	.75	2.00
49 Dale Earnhardt	4.00	10.00
50 Rusty Wallace	2.00	5.00
51 Darrell Waltrip	.50	1.25
52 Mark Martin	2.00	5.00
53 Dale Earnhardt Jr.	3.00	8.00
54 Jeremy Mayfield	.25	.60
55 Matt Kenseth	2.00	5.00
56 Bobby Labonte	1.50	4.00
57 Tony Stewart	2.50	6.00
58 Ward Burton	.50	1.25
59 Ricky Rudd	.75	2.00
60 Mike Skinner	.25	.60
61 John Andretti	.25	.60
62 Scott Pruett	.25	.60
63 Jeff Burton	.75	2.00
64 Dale Earnhardt	5.00	12.00
65 Jeff Gordon	3.00	8.00
66 Dale Earnhardt Jr.	4.00	10.00
67 Tony Stewart	3.00	8.00
68 Dale Jarrett	2.00	5.00
69 Mark Martin	2.50	6.00
70 Bobby Labonte	2.00	5.00
71 Jeff Burton	1.25	3.00
72 Ward Burton	.60	1.50
0 Dale Jarrett Daytona 500 Win	20.00	50.00
P1 Bobby Labonte Promo	1.00	2.50

2000 Press Pass Premium Reflectors

This 72-card set parallels the base Press Pass Premium set. Each card was enhanced with a rainbow holographic all-foil cardfront. Cards numbered 1-45 were inserted one per pack, while numbers 46-63 were seeded at the rate of 1:12 and numbers 64-72 were seeded at 1:48 packs.

COMP.SET w/o SP's (45)	12.50	30.00
*REFLECTORS 1-45: .8X TO 2X BASE CARDS		
*REFLECTORS 46-63: 1.5X TO 4X BASE CARDS		
*REFLECTORS 64-72: 2X TO 5X BASE CARDS		

2000 Press Pass Premium In The Zone

Randomly inserted in packs at one in 12, this 12-card set showcases NASCAR's most intense drivers on all-foil cards enhanced with micro-etching. Card backs carry an "IZ" prefix.

COMPLETE SET (12)	15.00	40.00
IZ1 Tony Stewart	3.00	8.00
IZ2 Bobby Labonte	2.00	5.00
IZ3 Sterling Marlin	1.00	2.50
IZ4 Jeff Gordon	3.00	8.00
IZ5 Matt Kenseth	2.50	6.00
IZ6 Jeff Burton	1.00	2.50
IZ7 Mark Martin	2.50	6.00
IZ8 Dale Jarrett	2.00	5.00
IZ9 Dale Earnhardt Jr.	4.00	10.00
IZ10 Ward Burton	.60	1.50
IZ11 Rusty Wallace	2.50	6.00
IZ12 Terry Labonte	1.00	2.50

2000 Press Pass Premium Performance Driven

Randomly seeded in packs at one in 24, this 6-card set features some of NASCAR's highest performance drivers. Card fronts contain a color portrait shot of the driver set against a black and white action shot of the respective car. Each card is all-foil and is enhanced with micro-etching. Card backs carry a "PD" prefix.

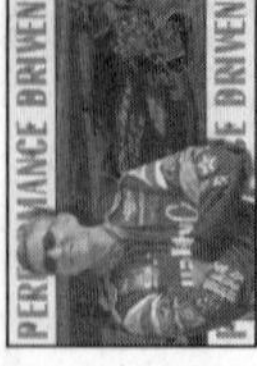

COMPLETE SET (6)	15.00	40.00
PD1 Dale Jarrett	3.00	8.00
PD2 Jeff Gordon	5.00	12.00
PD3 Tony Stewart	5.00	12.00
PD4 Dale Earnhardt Jr.	6.00	15.00
PD5 Mark Martin	4.00	10.00
PD6 Dale Earnhardt	10.00	25.00

2000 Press Pass Premium Race Used Firesuit

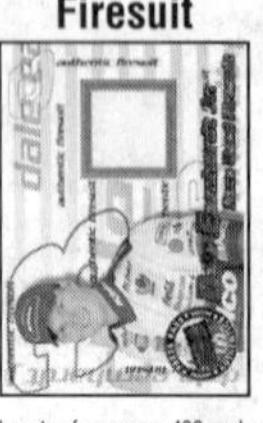

Inserted at the rate of one every 480 packs these nine cards feature pieces of the racing firesuits worn by various drivers.

COMPLETE SET (9)	400.00	800.00
F1 Dale Earnhardt Jr./130	75.00	150.00
F2 Rusty Wallace	25.00	60.00
F3 Dale Earnhardt	100.00	200.00
F4 Jeff Gordon	75.00	150.00
F5 Terry Labonte	25.00	60.00
F6 Bobby Labonte	25.00	60.00
F7 Tony Stewart	30.00	80.00
F8 Dale Jarrett	25.00	60.00
F9 Jeff Burton	20.00	50.00

2001 Press Pass Premium

This product was released in April 2001, and featured an 81-card base set that was broken into tiers as follows: 50 Base Veterans (3:1), 19 Champs and Challengers (1:3), and 12 Premium Choice cards (1:12). Each pack contained 4-cards and carried a suggested retail price of $2.99.

COMPLETE SET (81)	60.00	120.00
CARD 0 AND 00 STATED ODDS 1:240		
WAX BOX HOBBY	75.00	125.00
1 John Andretti	.25	.60
2 Jeff Burton	.50	1.25
3 Dale Earnhardt	4.00	10.00
4 Ward Burton	.50	1.25
5 Dale Earnhardt Jr.	3.00	8.00
6 Jeff Gordon	2.50	6.00
7 Bobby Hamilton	.25	.60
8 Dale Jarrett	1.00	2.50
9 Buckshot Jones	.25	.60
10 Matt Kenseth	1.50	4.00
11 Bobby Labonte	1.50	4.00
12 Jerry Nadeau	.50	1.25
13 Sterling Marlin	.75	2.00
14 Mark Martin	1.50	4.00
15 Jeremy Mayfield	.25	.60
16 Robert Pressley	.25	.60
17 Joe Nemechek	.25	.60
18 Steve Park	.50	1.25
19 Kyle Petty	.50	1.25
20 Ricky Rudd	.75	2.00
21 Elliott Sadler	.50	1.25
22 Ken Schrader	.25	.60
23 Mike Skinner	.25	.60
24 Dave Blaney	.25	.60
25 Tony Stewart	2.00	5.00
26 Rusty Wallace	1.50	4.00
27 Michael Waltrip	.50	1.25
28 Steve Park	.50	1.25
29 Rusty Wallace	1.50	4.00
30 Dale Earnhardt	4.00	10.00
31 Terry Labonte	.75	2.00
32 Dale Earnhardt Jr.	2.50	6.00
33 Michael Waltrip	.50	1.25
34 Bobby Labonte	1.50	4.00
35 Tony Stewart	2.00	5.00
36 Jeff Gordon	2.50	6.00
37 Ricky Rudd	.75	2.00
38 Mike Skinner	.25	.60
39 Joe Nemechek	.25	.60
40 Ken Schrader	.25	.60
41 Sterling Marlin	.75	2.00
42 Kyle Petty	.50	1.25
43 Kevin Harvick CRC	1.50	4.00
44 Dale Jarrett	1.00	2.50
45 Casey Atwood	.25	.60
46 Kurt Busch CRC	.75	2.00
47 Ron Hornaday	.25	.60
48 Andy Houston	.25	.60
49 Kevin Harvick	1.50	4.00
50 Jason Leffler CL	.25	.60
51 Dale Earnhardt CC	4.00	10.00
52 Jeff Gordon CC	2.50	6.00
53 Dale Jarrett CC	1.50	4.00
54 Bobby Labonte CC	1.50	4.00
55 Terry Labonte CC	1.00	2.50
56 Rusty Wallace CC	2.00	5.00
57 Jeff Burton CC	.60	1.50
58 Ward Burton CC	.60	1.50
59 Dale Earnhardt Jr. CC	3.00	8.00
60 Bobby Hamilton CC	.30	.75
61 Matt Kenseth CC	2.00	5.00
62 Sterling Marlin CC	1.00	2.50
63 Mark Martin CC	2.00	5.00
64 Jeremy Mayfield CC	.30	.75
65 Steve Park CC	.60	1.50
66 Ricky Rudd CC	1.00	2.50
67 Mike Skinner CC	.30	.75
68 Tony Stewart CC	2.50	6.00
69 Michael Waltrip CC	.60	1.50
70 Terry Labonte PC	1.50	4.00
71 Mike Skinner PC	.75	2.00
72 Dale Earnhardt Jr. PC	6.00	15.00
73 Jeff Gordon PC	5.00	12.00
74 Dale Jarrett PC	3.00	8.00
75 Sterling Marlin PC	2.00	5.00
76 Bobby Labonte PC	3.00	8.00
77 Dale Earnhardt PC	8.00	20.00
78 Mark Martin PC	5.00	10.00
79 Ricky Rudd PC	1.25	3.00
80 Tony Stewart PC	5.00	12.00
81 Rusty Wallace PC	4.00	10.00
0 Michael Waltrip Daytona Win	8.00	20.00
00 Jeff Gordon No Bull 5 Win	10.00	25.00

2001 Press Pass Premium Gold

Randomly inserted into packs, this 83-card set is a complete gold foil parallel of the 2001 Press Pass Premium base set. Cards 1-50 were issued at one per pack, cards 51-69 at 1:12 packs, and cards 70-83 at 1:48 packs.

COMP.SET w/o SP's (50)	20.00	50.00
*GOLD 1-50: .8X TO 2X BASE CARDS		
*GOLD 51-69: 1.2X TO 3X BASE CARDS		
*GOLD 70-81: 2X TO 5X BASE CARDS		

2001 Press Pass Premium In The Zone

Randomly inserted into packs at the rate of one in 12, this twelve card insert set features drivers that are determined to "go the distance". Card backs carry an "IZ" prefix.

COMPLETE SET (12)	20.00	50.00
IZ1 Jeff Burton	.75	2.00
IZ2 Dale Earnhardt Jr.	5.00	12.00
IZ3 Dale Earnhardt	6.00	15.00
IZ4 Sterling Marlin	1.25	3.00
IZ5 Jeff Gordon	4.00	10.00
IZ6 Dale Jarrett	1.50	4.00
IZ7 Matt Kenseth	2.50	6.00
IZ8 Bobby Labonte	2.50	6.00
IZ9 Mike Skinner	.40	1.00
IZ10 Mark Martin	2.50	6.00
IZ11 Ricky Rudd	1.25	3.00
IZ12 Rusty Wallace	2.50	6.00

2001 Press Pass Premium Performance Driven

Randomly inserted into packs at the rate of one in 24, this nine card insert set features drivers that are performance driven. Card backs carry a "PD" prefix.

COMPLETE SET (9)	40.00	100.00
PD1 Sterling Marlin	2.00	5.00
PD2 Dale Earnhardt Jr.	8.00	20.00
PD3 Dale Earnhardt	10.00	25.00
PD4 Jeff Gordon	6.00	15.00
PD5 Bobby Labonte	4.00	10.00
PD6 Mark Martin	4.00	10.00
PD7 Ricky Rudd	2.00	5.00
PD8 Tony Stewart	5.00	12.00
PD9 Rusty Wallace	4.00	10.00

2001 Press Pass Premium Race Used Firesuit Drivers

Randomly inserted into hobby packs at the rate of one in 480, this nine card insert set features swatches of actual race-used firesuits. Card ba carry a "FD" prefix. The hobby version pictures driver and each was serial numbered of 100. T retail version features their cars and each was se numbered of 120.

*CARS: .4X TO .8X DRIVERS		
FD0 Dale Earnhardt Jr.	75.00	150.
FD1 Jeff Gordon	75.00	150.
FD2 Mark Martin	30.00	80.
FD3 Dale Earnhardt	100.00	200.
FD4 Matt Kenseth	30.00	80.
FD5 Bobby Labonte	25.00	60.
FD6 Mike Skinner	15.00	40.
FD7 Tony Stewart	25.00	60.
FD8 Rusty Wallace	25.00	60.

2002 Press Pass Premium

This 81-card set was released in May, 2002. This was issued in four card hobby or retail packs wh came 24 packs to a box and 20 boxes to a case w an SRP of $3.99 per pack. In addition, a special c honoring Ward Burton's Daytona 500 win w inserted at approximately a one per case rate.

COMPLETE SET (81)	30.00	80.
COMP.SET w/o SP's (50)	10.00	25.
WAX BOX HOBBY (24)	50.00	90.
WAX BOX RETAIL (24)	40.00	80.
1 John Andretti	.15	.4
2 Brett Bodine	.15	.4
3 Jeff Burton	.30	.7
4 Ward Burton	.30	.7
5 Kurt Busch	.50	1.2
6 Ricky Craven	.15	.4
7 Dale Earnhardt Jr.	1.50	4.
8 Jeff Gordon	1.25	3.
9 Jeff Green	.15	.4
10 Bobby Hamilton	.15	.4
11 Kevin Harvick	1.00	2.5
12 Dale Jarrett	.75	2.
13 Jimmie Johnson CRC	1.00	2.5
14 Buckshot Jones	.15	.4
15 Matt Kenseth	1.00	2.5
16 Bobby Labonte	.75	2.
17 Terry Labonte	.50	1.2
18 Sterling Marlin	.50	1.2
19 Mark Martin	1.00	2.5
20 Jeremy Mayfield	.15	.4
21 Jerry Nadeau	.30	.7
22 Joe Nemechek	.15	.4
23 Ryan Newman CRC	1.00	2.5
24 Kyle Petty	.30	.7
25 Ricky Rudd	.50	1.2
26 Elliott Sadler	.30	.7
27 Ken Schrader	.15	.4
28 Mike Skinner	.15	.4
29 Jimmy Spencer	.15	.4
30 Tony Stewart	1.00	2.5
31 Hut Stricklin	.15	.4
32 Rusty Wallace	.75	2.
33 Michael Waltrip	.30	.7
34 Jimmie Johnson's Car	.50	1.2
35 Ryan Newman's Car	.50	1.2
36 Dale Earnhardt Jr.'s Car	.60	1.5
37 Jeff Burton's Car	.15	.4
38 Jeff Gordon's Car	.50	1.2
39 Kevin Harvick's Car	.50	1.2
40 Dale Jarrett's Car	.30	.
41 Matt Kenseth's Car	.50	1.2
42 Sterling Marlin's Car	.15	.4
43 Mark Martin's Car	.50	1.2
44 Tony Stewart's Car	.50	1.2
45 Ricky Rudd's Car	.15	.4
46 Jeff Gordon SW	1.25	3.
47 Michael Waltrip SW	.30	.
48 Tony Stewart SW	1.00	2.5
49 Jimmie Johnson SW	1.00	2.5
50 Tony Stewart CL	.50	1.2
51 Jeff Gordon CH	2.50	6.
52 Dale Jarrett CH	1.50	4.
53 Bobby Labonte CH	1.50	4.
54 Terry Labonte CH	1.00	2.5
55 Rusty Wallace CH	1.50	4.
56 Jeff Burton CH	.60	1.5
57 Ward Burton CH	.30	.
58 Kurt Busch CH	1.00	2.5
59 Ricky Craven CH	.30	.
60 Dale Earnhardt Jr. CH	3.00	8.
61 Kevin Harvick CH	2.00	5.
62 Jimmie Johnson CH	2.00	5.
63 Matt Kenseth CH	2.00	5.
64 Sterling Marlin CH	1.00	2.5
65 Mark Martin CH	2.00	5.
66 Ryan Newman CH	2.00	5.
67 Ricky Rudd CH	1.00	2.5
68 Tony Stewart CH	2.00	5.
69 Michael Waltrip CH	.60	1.5
70 Jeff Burton PC	1.25	3.
71 Dale Earnhardt Jr. PC	5.00	12.
72 Jeff Gordon PC	4.00	10.
73 Kevin Harvick PC	3.00	8.
74 Dale Jarrett PC	2.50	6.
75 Jimmie Johnson PC	3.00	8.
76 Bobby Labonte PC	2.50	6.
77 Terry Labonte PC	1.50	4.
78 Sterling Marlin PC	1.50	4.
79 Mark Martin PC	3.00	8.
80 Tony Stewart PC	3.00	8.
81 Rusty Wallace PC	2.50	6.
0 Ward Burton Daytona Win	10.00	25.

2002 Press Pass Premium Red Reflectors

nserted at an overall stated rate of one per pack, this s a parallel to the Premium basic set. Cards umbered 51 through 69 were issued at a stated rate f one in 12 and cards numbered 70 through 81 ere issued at a stated rate of one in 48.

COMPLETE SET (81) 100.00 200.00
COMP.SET w/o SP's (50) 15.00 40.00
1-50 RED REF: .8X TO 2X BASIC CARDS
51-69 RED REF: 1X TO 2.5X BASIC CARDS
70-81 RED REF: 1X TO 2.5X BASIC CARDS

2002 Press Pass Premium Samples

hese cards were issued before the release of the remium product to promote what the set would look ke. The cards were inserted one per Beckett Racing ollector magazine.

SAMPLES: 2X TO 5X BASIC CARDS

2002 Press Pass Premium In The Zone

ssued in packs at a stated rate of one in 12, these olofoil gold double-etched 12 cards feature nformation on how leading NASCAR drivers make it the finish line.

COMPLETE SET (12) 15.00 40.00
Z1 Jeff Burton .75 2.00
Z2 Ward Burton .75 2.00
Z3 Dale Earnhardt Jr. 4.00 10.00
Z4 Jeff Gordon 3.00 8.00
Z5 Kevin Harvick 2.50 6.00
Z6 Dale Jarrett 2.00 5.00
Z7 Matt Kenseth 2.50 6.00
Z8 Bobby Labonte 2.00 5.00
Z9 Sterling Marlin 1.25 3.00
Z10 Mark Martin 2.50 6.00
Z11 Tony Stewart 2.50 6.00
Z12 Rusty Wallace 2.00 5.00

2002 Press Pass Premium Performance Driven

ssued at a stated rate of one in 24, these nine silver oil double-etched cards feature information on how ASCAR drivers are motivated to succeed.

COMPLETE SET (9) 20.00 50.00
PD1 Dale Earnhardt Jr. 6.00 15.00
PD2 Jeff Gordon 5.00 12.00
PD3 Kevin Harvick 4.00 10.00
PD4 Dale Jarrett 3.00 8.00
PD5 Bobby Labonte 3.00 8.00
PD6 Mark Martin 4.00 10.00
PD7 Ricky Rudd 2.00 5.00
PD8 Tony Stewart 4.00 10.00
PD9 Rusty Wallace 3.00 8.00

2002 Press Pass Premium Race Used Firesuit Cars

nserted at a stated rate of one in 480 retail packs, hese 12 cards feature race-used swatches of driver's resuits. Each of these cards were issued to a stated rint run of 90 serial numbered sets.

MULTI-COLORED SWATCH: .6X TO 1.5X HI
FC1 Jeff Gordon 50.00 120.00
FC2 Mark Martin 25.00 60.00
FC3 Matt Kenseth 25.00 60.00
FC4 Bobby Labonte 20.00 50.00
FC5 Dale Jarrett 20.00 50.00

FC6 Tony Stewart 25.00 60.00
FC7 Rusty Wallace 20.00 50.00
FC8 Terry Labonte 15.00 40.00
FC9 Sterling Marlin 15.00 40.00
FC10 Ken Schrader 12.50 30.00
FC11 Dale Earnhardt 50.00 120.00
FC12 Dale Earnhardt Jr. 40.00 100.00

2002 Press Pass Premium Race Used Firesuit Drivers

Inserted at a stated rate of one in 480 hobby packs, these 12 cards feature swatches of race-used firesuits. Each of these cards were issued to a stated print run of 80 serial numbered sets.

MULTI-COLORED SWATCH: .6X TO 1.5X HI
FD1 Jeff Gordon 60.00 150.00
FD2 Mark Martin 30.00 80.00
FD3 Matt Kenseth 30.00 80.00
FD4 Bobby Labonte 25.00 60.00
FD5 Dale Jarrett 25.00 60.00
FD6 Tony Stewart 30.00 80.00
FD7 Rusty Wallace 25.00 60.00
FD8 Terry Labonte 20.00 50.00
FD9 Sterling Marlin 20.00 50.00
FD10 Ken Schrader 15.00 40.00
FD11 Dale Earnhardt 75.00 150.00
FD12 Dale Earnhardt Jr. 50.00 120.00

2003 Press Pass Premium

This 81-card set was released in April, 2003. This set was issued in five card hobby or four card retail packs which came 24 packs to a hobby box and 28 packs to a retail box with an SRP of $3.99 per pack. Cards 51-68 were short printed and came in packs at a rate of one in three and cards 69-81 were also short printed and they were inserted at a rate of one in 12. In addition, a special card honoring Michael Waltrip's Daytona 500 win was inserted at approximately a one per case rate.

COMPLETE SET (81) 75.00 125.00
COMP.SET w/o SPs (50) 10.00 25.00
WAX BOX HOBBY (24) 60.00 100.00
WAX BOX RETAIL (28) 40.00 75.00
1 John Andretti .15 .40
2 Todd Bodine .15 .40
3 Jeff Burton .30 .75
4 Ward Burton .30 .75
5 Kurt Busch .50 1.25
6 Ricky Craven .15 .40
7 Dale Earnhardt Jr. 1.50 4.00
8 Jeff Gordon 1.25 3.00
9 Robby Gordon .15 .40
10 Jeff Green .15 .40
11 Kevin Harvick .75 2.00
12 Dale Jarrett .75 2.00
13 Jimmie Johnson 1.00 2.50
14 Matt Kenseth 1.00 2.50
15 Bobby Labonte .75 2.00
16 Terry Labonte .50 1.25
17 Sterling Marlin .50 1.25
18 Mark Martin 1.00 2.50
19 Jerry Nadeau .30 .75
20 Joe Nemechek .15 .40
21 Ryan Newman 1.00 2.50
22 Steve Park .30 .75
23 Kyle Petty .30 .75
24 Ricky Rudd .50 1.25
25 Elliott Sadler .30 .75
26 Mike Skinner .15 .40
27 Tony Stewart 1.00 2.50
28 Kenny Wallace .15 .40
29 Rusty Wallace .75 2.00
30 Michael Waltrip .30 .75
31 Greg Biffle CRC .30 .75
32 Jamie McMurray CRC .75 2.00
33 Casey Mears CRC .30 .75
34 Jeff Burton's Car .15 .40
35 Kurt Busch's Car .30 .75
36 Dale Earnhardt Jr.'s Car .60 1.50
37 Jeff Gordon's Car .50 1.25
38 Kevin Harvick's Car .30 .75
39 Dale Jarrett's Car .30 .75
40 Jimmie Johnson's Car .50 1.25
41 Elliott Sadler's Car .15 .40
42 Matt Kenseth's Car .50 1.25
43 Mark Martin's Car .50 1.25
44 Michael Waltrip's Car .15 .40
45 Greg Biffle's Car .10 .30
46 Dale Earnhardt Jr. 1.50 4.00
47 Robby Gordon .15 .40
48 Dale Earnhardt Jr. 1.50 4.00
49 Jeff Green .15 .40
50 Dale Earnhardt Jr. 1.50 4.00
Steve Park
Michael Waltrip CL
51 Terry Labonte CC 1.00 2.50
52 Rusty Wallace CC 1.50 4.00
53 Jeff Gordon CC 2.50 6.00
54 Dale Jarrett CC 1.50 4.00
55 Bobby Labonte CC 1.50 4.00
56 Tony Stewart CC 2.00 5.00
57 Jeff Burton CC .50 1.25
58 Kurt Busch CC 1.00 2.50
59 Dale Earnhardt Jr. CC 3.00 8.00
60 Kevin Harvick CC 1.50 4.00
61 Jimmie Johnson CC 2.00 5.00
62 Matt Kenseth CC 2.00 5.00
63 Sterling Marlin CC 1.00 2.50
64 Mark Martin CC 2.00 5.00
65 Ryan Newman CC 3.00 8.00
66 Steve Park CC .50 1.25
67 Ward Burton CC .50 1.25
68 Michael Waltrip CC .50 1.25
69 Kurt Busch PC 1.50 4.00
70 Dale Earnhardt Jr.PC 5.00 12.00
71 Jeff Gordon PC 4.00 10.00
72 Dale Jarrett PC 2.50 6.00
73 Jimmie Johnson PC 3.00 8.00
74 Bobby Labonte PC 2.50 6.00
75 Mark Martin PC 3.00 8.00
76 Ryan Newman PC 3.00 8.00
77 Steve Park PC 1.00 2.50
78 Tony Stewart PC 3.00 8.00
79 Rusty Wallace PC 2.50 6.00
80 Michael Waltrip PC 1.00 2.50
81 Jeff Burton PC 1.00 2.50
0 Michael Waltrip 15.00 30.00

2003 Press Pass Premium Red Reflectors

Inserted at an overall stated rate of one per pack, this is a parallel to the Premium basic set. Cards numbered 51 through 69 were issued at a stated rate of one in 12 and cards numbered 70 through 81 were issued at a stated rate of one in 48.

COMP.SET w/o SPs (50) 20.00 50.00
*RED REFLECT.1-50: .8X TO 2X BASE CARD HI
*RED REFLECT.51-68: 1X TO 2.5X BASE CARD
*RED REFLECT.69-81: 1X TO 2.5X BASE CARD

2003 Press Pass Premium Samples

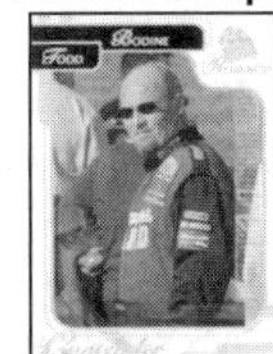

This 50-card set was a parallel of the base set with the exception of the word "SAMPLE" printed on the back of each card. These cards were found in Beckett Racing Collector June 2003, Issue #106. There was one card per magazine.

*SINGLES: 2X TO 5X BASE CARD HI

2003 Press Pass Premium Hot Threads Cars Autographs

Randomly inserted in retail packs, these 9 cards feature race-used swatches of driver's firesuits along with a signature of the corresponding driver. These cards were limited and hand numbered to the driver's door number. Some cards are not priced due to scarcity.

SOME CARDS NOT PRICED DUE TO SCARCITY
HTD-BL Bobby Labonte's Car/18 75.00 150.00
HTD-JG Jeff Gordon's Car/24 250.00 500.00
HTD-JJ Jimmie Johnson's Car/48 100.00 175.00
HTD-KH Kevin Harvick's Car/29 100.00 200.00
HTD-MK Matt Kenseth's Car/17
HTD-MM Mark Martin's Car/6
HTD-RN Ryan Newman's Car/12
HTD-RW Rusty Wallace's Car/2
HTD-TL Terry Labonte's Car/5

2003 Press Pass Premium Hot Threads Drivers Autographs

Randomly inserted in hobby packs, these 9 cards feature race-used swatches of driver's firesuits along with a signature of the corresponding driver. These cards were limited and hand numbered to the driver's door number. Some cards are not priced due to scarcity.

SOME CARDS NOT PRICED DUE TO SCARCITY
HTT-BL Bobby Labonte/18 75.00 150.00
HTT-JG Jeff Gordon/24 250.00 500.00
HTT-JJ Jimmie Johnson/48 100.00 175.00
HTT-KH Kevin Harvick/29 100.00 200.00
HTT-MK Matt Kenseth/17
HTT-MM Mark Martin/6
HTT-RN Ryan Newman/12
HTT-RW Rusty Wallace/2
HTTT-TL Terry Labonte/5

2003 Press Pass Premium Hot Threads Cars

Inserted at a stated rate of one in 72 retail packs, these 14 cards feature race-used swatches of driver's firesuits. Each of these cards were issued to a stated print run of 160 serial numbered sets.

*CARS: .3X TO .8X DRIVERS
CAR STATED ODDS 1:72
STATED PRINT RUN 160 SERIAL #'d SETS
HTT13 Ward Burton/475 12.50 30.00
HTT14 Terry Labonte/475 12.50 30.00

2003 Press Pass Premium Hot Threads Drivers

Inserted at a stated rate of one in 72 hobby packs, these 15 cards feature race-used swatches of driver's firesuits. Each of these cards were issued to a stated print run of 285 serial numbered sets with the exception of Ward Burton and Terry Labonte which only had 100 copies produced. Please note the premiums on the multi-color swatches.

*MULTI-COLOR SWATCHES: 1.5X TO 3X
HTD0 Dale Earnhardt 50.00 100.00
HTD1 Jeff Gordon 40.00 100.00
HTD2 Ryan Newman 20.00 50.00
HTD3 Kevin Harvick 20.00 50.00
HTD4 Jimmie Johnson 20.00 50.00
HTD5 Rusty Wallace 15.00 40.00
HTD6 Mark Martin 20.00 50.00
HTD7 Matt Kenseth 20.00 50.00
HTD8 Bobby Labonte 15.00 40.00
HTD9 Tony Stewart 20.00 50.00
HTD10 Dale Earnhardt Jr. 50.00 100.00
HTD11 Dale Jarrett 15.00 40.00
HTD12 Sterling Marlin 12.50 30.00
HTD13 Ward Burton/100 20.00 40.00
HTD14 Terry Labonte/100 20.00 50.00

2003 Press Pass Premium In the Zone

Issued in packs at a stated rate of one in 12, these holofoil gold double-etched 12 cards feature information on how leading NASCAR drivers make it to the finish line.

COMPLETE SET (12) 20.00 40.00
IZ1 Dale Earnhardt Jr. 3.00 8.00
IZ2 Jeff Gordon 2.50 6.00
IZ3 Dale Jarrett 1.50 4.00
IZ4 Jimmie Johnson 2.00 5.00
IZ5 Matt Kenseth 2.00 5.00
IZ6 Mark Martin 2.00 5.00
IZ7 Ryan Newman 2.00 5.00
IZ8 Steve Park .60 1.50
IZ9 Ricky Rudd 1.00 2.50
IZ10 Tony Stewart 2.00 5.00
IZ11 Rusty Wallace 1.50 4.00
IZ12 Michael Waltrip .60 1.50

2003 Press Pass Premium Performance Driven

Issued at a stated rate of one in 24, these nine silver foil double-etched cards feature information on how NASCAR drivers are motivated to succeed.

COMPLETE SET (9) 20.00 50.00
PD1 Dale Earnhardt Jr. 5.00 12.00
PD2 Jeff Gordon 4.00 10.00
PD3 Jimmie Johnson 3.00 8.00
PD4 Mark Martin 3.00 8.00
PD5 Kurt Busch 1.50 4.00
PD6 Steve Park 1.00 2.50
PD7 Tony Stewart 3.00 8.00
PD8 Rusty Wallace 2.50 6.00
PD9 Michael Waltrip 1.00 2.50

2004 Press Pass Premium

This 81-card set was released in May, 2004. This set was issued in five card hobby or four card retail packs which came 20 packs to a hobby box and 24 packs to a retail box with an SRP of $3.99 per pack. Cards 51-69 were short printed and came in packs at a rate of one in three and cards 70-81 were also short printed and they were inserted at a rate of one in 10. In addition, a special card honoring Dale Earnhardt Jr.'s Daytona 500 win was inserted at approximately a one per case rate.

COMP.SET w/o SP's (50) 10.00 25.00
COMPLETE SET (81) 40.00 80.00
COMMON CARD
CC COMMON DRIVERS (51-69) .40 1.00
CC SEMISTARS .60 1.50
CC UNLISTED STARS 1.00 2.50
CC 51-69 STATED ODDS 1:3
PC COMMON DRIVERS (51-69) .75 2.00
PC SEMISTARS 1.25 3.00
PC UNLISTED STARS 1.50 4.00
PC 70-81 STATED ODDS 1:10
0 CARD STATED ODDS 1:480
WAX BOX HOBBY (20) 60.00 120.00
WAX BOX RETAIL (24) 40.00 75.00
1 Dale Earnhardt Jr. 1.25 3.00
2 Tony Stewart .75 2.00
3 Kevin Harvick .75 2.00
4 Jimmie Johnson 1.00 2.50
5 Joe Nemechek .20 .50
6 Elliott Sadler .40 .75
7 Jeff Gordon 1.25 3.00
8 Matt Kenseth 1.00 2.50
9 Dale Jarrett .60 1.50
10 Bobby Labonte .60 1.50
11 Greg Biffle .40 .75
12 Casey Mears .40 .75
13 Kurt Busch .50 1.25
14 Ward Burton .40 .75
15 Ricky Rudd .50 1.25
16 Terry Labonte .50 1.25
17 Kyle Petty .40 .75
18 Ricky Craven .20 .50
19 Jeremy Mayfield .20 .50
20 Rusty Wallace .60 1.50
21 Ryan Newman 1.00 2.50
22 Jeff Green .20 .50
23 Robby Gordon .20 .50
24 Jamie McMurray .50 1.25
25 Sterling Marlin .50 1.25
26 Michael Waltrip .40 .75
27 Ken Schrader .20 .50
28 Jeff Burton .40 .75
29 Mark Martin .75 2.00
30 Kevin Lepage .20 .50
31 Brendan Gaughan CRC .40 .75
32 Kasey Kahne CRC 1.50 4.00
33 Scott Riggs CRC .40 .75
34 Johnny Sauter .40 .75
35 Brian Vickers CRC .60 1.50
36 Scott Wimmer CRC .40 .75
37 Rusty Wallace's Car .40 .75
38 Mark Martin's Car .40 .75
39 Dale Earnhardt Jr's Car .50 1.25
40 Michael Waltrip's Car .20 .50
41 Matt Kenseth's Car .50 1.25
42 Jeff Gordon's Car .50 1.25
43 Kevin Harvick's Car .40 .75
44 Jimmie Johnson's Car .50 1.25
45 Kurt Busch's Car .20 .50
46 Dale Earnhardt Jr. NS 1.25 3.00
47 Elliott Sadler NS .40 .75
48 Dale Jarrett NS .60 1.50
49 Greg Biffle NS .40 .75
50 Tony Stewart CL .75 2.00
51 Terry Labonte CC 1.00 2.50
52 Rusty Wallace CC 1.25 3.00
53 Jeff Gordon CC 2.50 6.00
54 Dale Jarrett CC 1.25 3.00
55 Bobby Labonte CC 1.25 3.00
56 Tony Stewart CC 1.50 4.00
57 Matt Kenseth CC 2.00 5.00
58 Jimmie Johnson CC 2.00 5.00
59 Dale Earnhardt Jr. CC 2.50 6.00
60 Kevin Harvick CC 1.50 4.00
61 Ryan Newman CC 2.00 5.00
62 Jeff Burton CC .60 1.50
63 Jamie McMurray CC 1.00 2.50
64 Michael Waltrip CC .60 1.50
65 Robby Gordon CC .40 1.00
66 Elliott Sadler CC .60 1.50
67 Sterling Marlin CC 1.00 2.50
68 Greg Biffle CC .60 1.50
69 Ward Burton CC .60 1.50
70 Michael Waltrip PC 1.25 3.00
71 Rusty Wallace PC 2.00 5.00
72 Tony Stewart PC 2.50 6.00
73 Bobby Labonte PC 2.00 5.00
74 Matt Kenseth PC 3.00 8.00
75 Jimmie Johnson PC 3.00 8.00
76 Dale Jarrett PC 2.00 5.00
77 Kevin Harvick PC 2.50 6.00
78 Robby Gordon PC .75 2.00
79 Jeff Gordon PC 4.00 10.00
80 Dale Earnhardt Jr. PC 4.00 10.00
81 Kurt Busch PC 1.50 4.00
0 Dale Earnhardt Jr. Daytona 10.00 25.00

2004 Press Pass Premium Previews

This 36-card set was a partial parallel of the base set, but each card was serial numbered to 5. The cards were offered via eBay auctions before the base set was released.

COMPLETE SET (36)
STATED PRINT RUN 5 SERIAL #'d SETS

2004 Press Pass Premium Samples

This 50-card set is a parallel to the base 2004 Press Pass Premium set without the variations. It was issued 1 per Beckett Racing Collector issue #118, which was the June 2004 cover date. Each card had the word "SAMPLE" printed across the back.

*SAMPLES: 2X TO 5X BASIC

2004 Press Pass Premium Asphalt Jungle

This 6-card set featured some of racing's hottest drivers. The cards were designed to be viewed at a horizontal angle and they pictured the driver with his car in the background. They were inserted at a rate of 1 in 10 packs.

COMPLETE SET (6) 12.50 30.00
A1 Tony Stewart 2.00 5.00
A2 Jeff Gordon 3.00 8.00
A3 Ryan Newman 3.00 8.00
A4 Jimmie Johnson 3.00 8.00
A5 Dale Earnhardt Jr. 3.00 8.00
A6 Kevin Harvick 2.00 5.00

2004 Press Pass Premium Hot Threads Autographs

This 9-card set was available in packs of 2004 Press Pass Premium. Each card had a swatch of a race-used firesuit and a signature from the corresponding driver. The cards were serial numbered to the driver's door number. There was a late addition to the set. Dale Earnhardt Jr. was only available in packs of 2006 Press Pass Legends.

HT-DE Dale Earnhardt Jr./8
HT-JG Jeff Gordon/24 250.00 500.00
HT-JJ Jimmie Johnson/48 100.00 175.00
HT-KH Kevin Harvick/29 100.00 200.00
HT-MK Matt Kenseth/17
HT-MM Mark Martin/6
HT-RN Ryan Newman/12
HT-RW Rusty Wallace/2
HT-TS Tony Stewart/20

2004 Press Pass Premium Hot Threads Drivers Bronze

Randomly inserted into hobby packs, these 16 cards feature race-used swatches of driver's firesuits. Each of these cards were issued to a stated print run of 125 serial numbered sets. These cards also had the word "Bronze" on the front to distinguish the level. Please note there was also a retail version of the Bronze level. The difference between them was the driver's car number ghosted in the background behind the swatch on the retail version.

HTD1 Jimmie Johnson 20.00 50.00
HTD2 Matt Kenseth 20.00 50.00
HTD3 Kevin Harvick 15.00 40.00
HTD4 Jeff Gordon 25.00 60.00
HTD5 Kurt Busch 10.00 25.00
HTD6 Mark Martin 15.00 40.00
HTD7 Ryan Newman 15.00 40.00
HTD8 Bobby Labonte 15.00 40.00
HTD9 Rusty Wallace 15.00 40.00
HTD10 Tony Stewart 15.00 40.00
HTD11 Dale Earnhardt Jr. 25.00 60.00
HTD12 Dale Jarrett 12.50 30.00
HTD13 Sterling Marlin 12.50 30.00
HTD14 Terry Labonte 15.00 40.00
HTD15 Michael Waltrip 10.00 25.00
HTD16 Dale Earnhardt 30.00 80.00

2004 Press Pass Premium Hot Threads Drivers Bronze Retail

Randomly inserted into retail packs, these 16 cards feature race-used swatches of driver's firesuits. Each of these cards were issued to a stated print run of 125 serial numbered sets. These cards also had the word "Bronze" on the front to distinguish the level. Please note there was also a hobby version of the Bronze level. The difference between them was the driver's car number ghosted in the. The difference was the driver's car number was ghosted on the background behind the swatch on the retail version.

*RETAIL: .4X TO 1X BRONZE
HTT1 Jimmie Johnson 20.00 50.00
HTT2 Matt Kenseth 20.00 50.00
HTT3 Kevin Harvick 15.00 40.00
HTT4 Jeff Gordon 25.00 60.00
HTT5 Kurt Busch 10.00 25.00
HTT6 Mark Martin 15.00 40.00
HTT7 Ryan Newman 15.00 40.00
HTT8 Bobby Labonte 15.00 40.00
HTT9 Rusty Wallace 15.00 40.00
HTT10 Tony Stewart 15.00 40.00
HTT11 Dale Earnhardt Jr. 25.00 60.00
HTT12 Dale Jarrett 12.50 30.00
HTT13 Sterling Marlin 12.50 30.00
HTT14 Terry Labonte 15.00 40.00
HTT15 Michael Waltrip 10.00 25.00
HTT16 Dale Earnhardt 30.00 80.00

2004 Press Pass Premium Hot Threads Drivers Gold

Randomly inserted into hobby packs, these 16 cards feature race-used swatches of driver's firesuits. Each of these cards were issued to a stated print run of 50 serial numbered sets. These cards also had the word "Gold" on the front to distinguish the level. Please note these were premium patch swatches.

*GOLD: 1.2X TO 2.5X BRONZE
STATED PRINT RUN 50 SERIAL #'d SETS

2004 Press Pass Premium Hot Threads Drivers Silver

Randomly inserted into hobby packs, these 16 cards feature race-used swatches of driver's firesuits. Each of these cards were issued to a stated print run of 75 serial numbered sets. These cards also had the word "Silver" on the front to distinguish the level. Please note these were multi-color swatches.

*SILVER: .6X TO 1.5X BRONZE

2004 Press Pass Premium In the Zone

This 6-card set featured some of racing's hottest drivers. The card fronts featured an image of the driver and had gold holofoil highlights. They were inserted at a rate of 1 in 6 packs. There was also a serial numbered parallel set.

COMPLETE SET (12) 12.50 30.00
IZ1 Bobby Labonte 1.50 4.00
IZ2 Dale Earnhardt Jr. 3.00 8.00
IZ3 Dale Jarrett 1.50 4.00
IZ4 Jeff Gordon 3.00 8.00
IZ5 Jimmie Johnson 2.50 6.00
IZ6 Terry Labonte 1.25 3.00
IZ7 Matt Kenseth 2.50 6.00
IZ8 Michael Waltrip 1.00 2.50
IZ9 Ricky Rudd 1.25 3.00
IZ10 Rusty Wallace 1.50 4.00
IZ11 Ryan Newman 2.50 6.00
IZ12 Tony Stewart 2.00 5.00

2004 Press Pass Premium Performance Driven

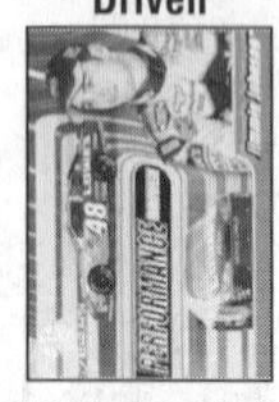

This 9-card set featured some of racing's hottest drivers. The card fronts featured an image of the driver and his car with silver holofoil highlights. They were inserted at a rate of 1 in 20 packs.

COMPLETE SET (9) 15.00 40.00
PD1 Tony Stewart 4.00 10.00
PD2 Ryan Newman 5.00 12.00
PD3 Rusty Wallace 3.00 8.00
PD4 Ricky Rudd 2.50 6.00
PD5 Kurt Busch 2.50 6.00
PD6 Jimmie Johnson 5.00 12.00
PD7 Jeff Gordon 6.00 15.00
PD8 Dale Jarrett 3.00 8.00
PD9 Dale Earnhardt Jr. 6.00 15.00

2005 Press Pass Premium

This 81-card set was released in May, 2005. This set was issued in five card hobby or four card retail packs which came 20 packs to a hobby box and 24 packs to a retail box with an SRP of $3.99 per pack. Cards 51-69 were short printed and came in packs at a rate of one in three and cards 70-81 were also short printed and they were inserted at a rate of one in 10. In addition, a special card honoring Jeff Gordon's Daytona 500 win was inserted at a rate of approximately one per case.

COMP.SET w/o SPs (1-50) 15.00 40.00
0 CARD STATED ODDS 1:72
WAX BOX HOBBY (20) 50.00 80.00
WAX BOX RETAIL (24) 35.00 60.00
1 John Andretti .25 .60
2 Greg Biffle .40 1.00
3 Jeff Burton .40 1.00
4 Kurt Busch .60 1.50
5 Dale Earnhardt Jr. 1.50 4.00
6 Carl Edwards CRC 1.25 3.00
7 Jeff Gordon 1.50 4.00
8 Jeff Green .25 .60
9 Kevin Harvick 1.00 2.50
10 Dale Jarrett .75 2.00
11 Jimmie Johnson 1.25 3.00
12 Kasey Kahne 1.50 4.00
13 Matt Kenseth 1.25 3.00
14 Bobby Labonte .75 2.00
15 Terry Labonte .60 1.50
16 Jason Leffler .25 .60
17 Kevin Lepage .25 .60
18 Sterling Marlin .60 1.50
19 Mark Martin 1.00 2.50
20 Jeremy Mayfield .25 .60
21 Jamie McMurray .60 1.50
22 Casey Mears .40 1.00
23 Joe Nemechek .25 .60
24 Ryan Newman 1.25 3.00
25 Kyle Petty .40 1.00
26 Scott Riggs .40 1.00
27 Ricky Rudd .60 1.50
28 Elliott Sadler .40 1.00
29 Ken Schrader .25 .60
30 Tony Stewart 1.00 2.50
31 Brian Vickers .75 2.00
32 Rusty Wallace .75 2.00
33 Michael Waltrip .40 1.00
34 Scott Wimmer .40 1.00
35 Kyle Busch CRC 1.00 2.50
36 Travis Kvapil CRC .25 .60
37 Kurt Busch's Car M .25 .60
38 Jimmie Johnson's Car M .40 1.00
39 Rusty Wallace's Car M .25 .60
40 Jeff Gordon's Car M .60 1.50
41 Tony Stewart's Car M .25 .60
42 Michael Waltrip's Car M .25 .60
43 Kevin Harvick's Car M .25 .60
44 Dale Jarrett's Car M .75 2.00
45 Robby Gordon's Car M .25 .60
46 Tony Stewart S 1.00 2.50
47 Michael Waltrip S .40 1.00
48 Jimmie Johnson S 1.25 3.00
49 Dale Jarrett S .75 2.00
50 Tony Stewart CL 1.00 2.50
51 Terry Labonte CC 2.00 5.00
52 Rusty Wallace CC 2.50 6.00
53 Jeff Gordon CC 5.00 12.00
54 Dale Jarrett CC 2.50 6.00
55 Bobby Labonte CC 2.50 6.00
56 Tony Stewart CC 3.00 8.00
57 Matt Kenseth CC 4.00 10.00
58 Kurt Busch CC 2.00 5.00
59 Jimmie Johnson CC 4.00 10.00
60 Mark Martin CC 3.00 8.00
61 Dale Earnhardt Jr. CC 5.00 12.00
62 Ryan Newman CC 4.00 10.00
63 Jeremy Mayfield CC .75 2.00
64 Jamie McMurray CC 2.00 5.00
65 Kasey Kahne CC 5.00 12.00
66 Kevin Harvick CC 3.00 8.00
67 Joe Nemechek CC .75 2.00
68 Ricky Rudd CC 2.00 5.00
69 Jeff Burton CC 1.25 3.00
70 Jeff Burton PC 1.50 4.00
71 Dale Earnhardt Jr. PC 6.00 15.00
72 Jeff Gordon PC 6.00 15.00
73 Ryan Newman PC 5.00 12.00
74 Jimmie Johnson PC 5.00 12.00
75 Ricky Rudd PC 2.50 6.00
76 Bobby Labonte PC 3.00 8.00
77 Mark Martin PC 4.00 10.00
78 Kevin Harvick PC 4.00 10.00
79 Tony Stewart PC 4.00 10.00
80 Rusty Wallace PC 3.00 8.00
81 Kurt Busch PC 2.50 6.00
0 Jeff Gordon Daytona 10.00 25.00
LEG1 Davey Allison Promo 3.00 8.00

2005 Press Pass Premium Samples

COMPLETE SET (50)
*SAMPLES: 1.5X TO 4X BASE

2005 Press Pass Premium Asphalt Jungle

COMPLETE SET (6) 15.00 30.00
AJ1 Jimmie Johnson 2.50 6.00
AJ2 Mark Martin 2.00 5.00
AJ3 Jeff Gordon 3.00 8.00
AJ4 Bobby Labonte 1.50 4.00
AJ5 Tony Stewart 2.00 5.00
AJ6 Rusty Wallace 1.50 4.00

2005 Press Pass Premium Hot Threads Autographs

SOME CARDS NOT PRICED DUE TO SCARCITY
HT-BL Bobby Labonte/18 75.00 150.00
HT-BV Brian Vickers/25 100.00 200.00
HT-DE Dale Earnhardt Jr./8
HT-JG Jeff Gordon/24 350.00 600.00
HT-JJ Jimmie Johnson/48 100.00 175.00
HT-KK Kasey Kahne/9
HT-MK Matt Kenseth/17
HT-RW Rusty Wallace/2
HT-TL Terry Labonte/5
HT-TS Tony Stewart/20

2005 Press Pass Premium Hot Threads Cars

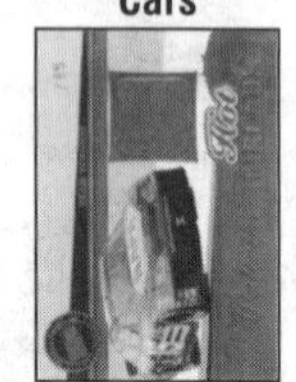

*CARS: .4X TO 1X DRIVERS
HTT1 Kurt Busch 10.00 25.00
HTT2 Jimmie Johnson 15.00 40.00
HTT3 Jeff Gordon 20.00 50.00
HTT4 Dale Earnhardt Jr. 20.00 50.00
HTT5 Tony Stewart 15.00 40.00
HTT6 Ryan Newman 15.00 40.00
HTT7 Matt Kenseth 12.50 30.00
HTT8 Kevin Harvick 12.50 30.00
HTT9 Bobby Labonte 10.00 25.00
HTT10 Rusty Wallace 10.00 25.00
HTT11 Dale Jarrett 10.00 25.00
HTT12 Terry Labonte 10.00 25.00
HTT13 Michael Waltrip 8.00 20.00
HTT14 Sterling Marlin 10.00 25.00

2005 Press Pass Premium Hot Threads Drivers

HTD1 Kurt Busch 10.00 25.00
HTD2 Jimmie Johnson 15.00 40.00
HTD3 Jeff Gordon 20.00 50.00
HTD4 Dale Earnhardt Jr. 20.00 50.00
HTD5 Tony Stewart 15.00 40.00
HTD6 Ryan Newman 15.00 40.00
HTD7 Matt Kenseth 12.50 30.00
HTD8 Kevin Harvick 12.50 30.00
HTD9 Bobby Labonte 10.00 25.00
HTD10 Rusty Wallace 10.00 25.00
HTD11 Dale Jarrett 10.00 25.00
HTD12 Terry Labonte 10.00 25.00
HTD13 Michael Waltrip 8.00 20.00
HTD14 Sterling Marlin 10.00 25.00

2005 Press Pass Premium Hot Threads Drivers Gold

CARDS NOT PRICED DUE TO SCARCITY

2005 Press Pass Premium In the Zone

COMPLETE SET (12) 15.00 30.00
IZ1 Michael Waltrip .75 2.00
IZ2 Rusty Wallace 1.50 4.00
IZ3 Tony Stewart 2.00 5.00
IZ4 Ryan Newman 2.50 6.00
IZ5 Jeff Burton .75 2.00
IZ6 Kevin Harvick 2.00 5.00
IZ7 Jimmie Johnson 2.50 6.00
IZ8 Dale Jarrett 1.50 4.00
IZ9 Jeff Gordon 3.00 8.00
IZ10 Dale Earnhardt Jr. 3.00 8.00
IZ11 Matt Kenseth 2.50 6.00
IZ12 Bobby Labonte 1.50 4.00

2005 Press Pass Premium In the Zone Elite Edition

*ELITE EDITION: 1X TO 2.5X IN THE ZONE

2005 Press Pass Premium Performance Driven

COMPLETE SET (9) 25.00 50.00
PD1 Dale Earnhardt Jr. 5.00 12.00
PD2 Dale Jarrett 2.50 6.00
PD3 Kevin Harvick 3.00 8.00
PD4 Jeff Gordon 5.00 12.00
PD5 Jimmie Johnson 4.00 10.00
PD6 Bobby Labonte 2.50 6.00
PD7 Jeff Burton 1.25 3.00
PD8 Rusty Wallace 2.50 6.00
PD9 Tony Stewart 3.00 8.00

2006 Press Pass Premium

This 81-card set was released in May, 2005. This set was issued in five card hobby or four card retail packs which came 20 packs to a hobby box and 24 packs to a retail box with an SRP of $3.99 per pack. Cards 53-71 were short printed and came in packs at a rate of one in three and cards 72-83 were also short printed and they were inserted at a rate of one in 10. In addition, a special card honoring Jimmie Johnson's Daytona 500 win was inserted at a rate of approximately one per case.

COMPLETE SET (83) 90.00 150.00
COMP.SET w/o SPs (45) 10.00 25.00
ZERO CARD STATED ODDS 1:72
WAX BOX HOBBY (20) 60.00 90.00
WAX BOX RETAIL (24) 50.00 80.00
CC STATED ODDS 1:3
PC STATED ODDS 1:10
1 Greg Biffle .60 1.50
2 Dave Blaney .30 .75
3 Jeff Burton .50 1.25
4 Kurt Busch .75 2.00
5 Kyle Busch 1.00 2.50
6 Dale Earnhardt Jr. 2.00 5.00
7 Carl Edwards 1.50 4.00
8 Jeff Gordon 2.00 5.00
9 Jeff Green .30 .75
10 Kevin Harvick 1.25 3.00
11 Dale Jarrett 1.00 2.50
12 Jimmie Johnson 1.50 4.00
13 Kasey Kahne 2.00 5.00
14 Matt Kenseth 1.50 4.00
15 Bobby Labonte 1.00 2.50
16 Terry Labonte .75 2.00
17 Sterling Marlin .75 2.00
18 Mark Martin 1.25 3.00
19 Jeremy Mayfield .30 .75
20 Casey Mears .50 1.25
21 Joe Nemechek .30 .75

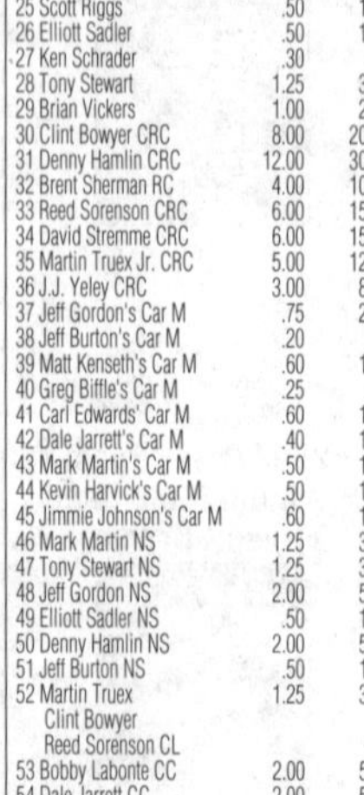

22 Ryan Newman 1.25 3.00
23 Kyle Petty .50 1.25
24 Tony Raines .30 .75
25 Scott Riggs .50 1.25
26 Elliott Sadler .50 1.25
27 Ken Schrader .30 .75
28 Tony Stewart 1.25 3.00
29 Brian Vickers 1.00 2.50
30 Clint Bowyer CRC 8.00 20.00
31 Denny Hamlin CRC 12.00 30.00
32 Brent Sherman RC 4.00 10.00
33 Reed Sorenson CRC 6.00 15.00
34 David Stremme CRC 6.00 15.00
35 Martin Truex Jr. CRC 5.00 12.00
36 J.J. Yeley CRC 3.00 8.00
37 Jeff Gordon's Car M .75 2.00
38 Jeff Burton's Car M .20 .50
39 Matt Kenseth's Car M .60 1.50
40 Greg Biffle's Car M .25 .60
41 Carl Edwards' Car M .60 1.50
42 Dale Jarrett's Car M .40 1.00
43 Mark Martin's Car M .50 1.25
44 Kevin Harvick's Car M .50 1.25
45 Jimmie Johnson's Car M .60 1.50
46 Mark Martin NS 1.25 3.00
47 Tony Stewart NS 1.25 3.00
48 Jeff Gordon NS 2.00 5.00
49 Elliott Sadler NS .50 1.25
50 Denny Hamlin NS 2.00 5.00
51 Jeff Burton NS .50 1.25
52 Martin Truex 1.25 3.00
Clint Bowyer
Reed Sorenson CL
53 Bobby Labonte CC 2.00 5.00
54 Dale Jarrett CC 2.00 5.00
55 Tony Stewart CC 2.50 6.00
56 Kurt Busch CC 1.50 4.00
57 Jeff Gordon CC 4.00 10.00
58 Matt Kenseth CC 3.00 8.00
59 Terry Labonte CC 1.50 4.00
60 Carl Edwards C 3.00 8.00
61 Jimmie Johnson C 3.00 8.00
62 Kasey Kahne C 4.00 10.00
63 Dale Earnhardt Jr. C 4.00 10.00
64 Greg Biffle C 1.25 3.00
65 Mark Martin C 2.50 6.00
66 Jeff Burton C 1.00 2.50
67 Kyle Busch C 2.00 5.00
68 Kevin Harvick C 2.50 6.00
69 Casey Mears C 1.00 2.50
70 Sterling Marlin C 1.50 4.00
71 Elliott Sadler C 1.00 2.50
72 Mark Martin PC 4.00 10.00
73 Jimmie Johnson PC 5.00 12.00
74 Martin Truex Jr. PC 4.00 10.00
75 Tony Stewart PC 4.00 10.00
76 Jeff Gordon PC 6.00 15.00
77 Dale Jarrett PC 3.00 8.00
78 Ryan Newman PC 4.00 10.00
79 Carl Edwards PC 5.00 12.00
80 Dale Earnhardt Jr. PC 6.00 15.00
81 Matt Kenseth PC 5.00 12.00
82 Kasey Kahne PC 6.00 15.00
83 Jeff Burton PC 1.50 4.00
0 Jimmie Johnson Daytona 6.00 15.00

2006 Press Pass Premium Asphalt Jungle

COMPLETE SET (6) 10.00 25.00
COMMON DRIVERS .40 1.00
SEMISTARS .60 1.50
UNLISTED STARS 1.00 2.50
AJ1 Dale Earnhardt Jr. 2.50 6.00
AJ2 Mark Martin 1.50 4.00
AJ3 Jeff Gordon 2.50 6.00
AJ4 Tony Stewart 1.50 4.00
AJ5 Jimmie Johnson 2.00 5.00
AJ6 Dale Jarrett 1.25 3.00

2006 Press Pass Premium Hot Threads Autographs

STATED PRINT RUN SERIAL #'d TO DRIVER'S DOOR NUMBER
SOME NOT PRICED DUE TO SCARCITY
HT-JJ Jimmie Johnson 100.00 175.00
HT-KH Kevin Harvick 100.00 175.00
HT-KK Kasey Kahne
HT-RW Rusty Wallace
HT-TS Tony Stewart

2006 Press Pass Premium Hot Threads Drivers

HTD1 Tony Stewart 20.00 50.00
HTD2 Matt Kenseth 15.00 40.00
HTD3 Dale Earnhardt Jr. 25.00 60.00
HTD4 Carl Edwards 20.00 50.00
HTD5 Jimmie Johnson 20.00 50.00
HTD6 Kevin Harvick 15.00 40.00
HTD7 Dale Jarrett 15.00 40.00
HTD8 Kasey Kahne 20.00 50.0
HTD9 Terry Labonte 12.50 30.0
HTD10 Ryan Newman 15.00 40.0
HTD11 Jeff Gordon 40.00 80.0
HTD12 Denny Hamlin 25.00 60.0
HTD13 Brian Vickers 12.50 30.0
HTD14 Kyle Busch 15.00 40.0
HTD15 Reed Sorenson 12.50 30.0

2006 Press Pass Premium Hot Threads Drivers Gold

STATED PRINT RUN 1 SERIAL #'d SET
NOT PRICED DUE TO SCARCITY

2006 Press Pass Premium In the Zone

COMPLETE SET (12) 15.00 40.0
IZ1 Dale Earnhardt Jr. 4.00 10.0
IZ2 Carl Edwards 3.00 8.0
IZ3 Dale Jarrett 2.00 5.0
IZ4 Tony Stewart 2.50 6.0
IZ5 Matt Kenseth 3.00 8.0
IZ6 Kurt Busch 1.50 4.0
IZ7 Jimmie Johnson 3.00 8.0
IZ8 Kevin Harvick 2.50 6.0
IZ9 Martin Truex Jr. 2.50 6.0
IZ10 Jeff Gordon 4.00 10.0
IZ11 Mark Martin 2.50 6.0
IZ12 Bobby Labonte 2.00 5.0

2006 Press Pass Premium In the Zone Red

*RED: .8X TO 2X BASIC

2007 Press Pass Premium

This 81-card set was released in April, 2007. Th set was issued in five card hobby or four card reta packs which came 20 packs to a hobby box with a SRP of $4.99 per pack and 24 packs to a retail bo with an SRP of $2.99 per pack. Cards 71-7 Daytona Dominators, were short-printed and inserte at a rate of one in three packs. Cards 77-82, Fa Favorites, were short-printed and inserted in packs a rate of one in 10 packs. The RCs and CRCs, 83-9 were also short-printed and inserted into packs at rate of one in 20 packs. In addition, a special ca honoring Kevin Harvick's Daytona 500 win wa inserted at a rate of one in 60 packs. A 2007 Pre Pass Stealth Chrome preview card of Juan Pab Montoya was also inserted as a box topper in eve hobby box.

COMPLETE SET (90) 40.00 100.0
COMP.SET W/O SPs (70) 15.00 40.0
STEALTH PREVIEW STATED ODDS 1:20H
WAX BOX HOBBY (20) 60.00 100.0
WAX BOX RETAIL (24) 50.00 75.0
1 Jimmie Johnson CL .75 2.0
2 Mark Martin .60 1.5
3 Clint Bowyer .75 2.0
4 Martin Truex Jr. .60 1.5
5 Kurt Busch .25 .6
6 Kyle Busch .50 1.2
7 Dale Earnhardt Jr. 1.00 2.5
8 Kasey Kahne 1.00 2.5
9 Scott Riggs .25 .6
10 Denny Hamlin .75 2.0
11 Ryan Newman .50 1.2
12 Joe Nemechek .15 .4
13 Sterling Marlin .40 1.0
14 Greg Biffle .30 .7
15 Matt Kenseth .75 2.0
16 J.J. Yeley .30 .7
17 Elliott Sadler .25 .6
18 Tony Stewart .60 1.5
19 Ken Schrader .15 .4
20 Dave Blaney .15 .4
21 Jeff Gordon 1.00 2.5
22 Casey Mears .25 .6
23 Kevin Harvick .60 1.5
24 Jeff Burton .25 .6
25 David Stremme .50 1.2
26 Reed Sorenson .50 1.2
27 Bobby Labonte .50 1.2
28 Dale Jarrett .50 1.2

9 Kyle Petty .25 .60
0 Jimmie Johnson .75 2.00
1 Jeff Green .15 .40
2 Brian Vickers .40 1.00
3 Carl Edwards .60 1.50
4 Kasey Kahne's Car M 1.00 2.50
5 Jeff Gordon's Car M 1.00 2.50
6 Kevin Harvick's Car M .60 1.50
7 Tony Stewart's Car M .60 1.50
8 Kurt Busch's Car M .25 .60
9 Denny Hamlin's Car M .75 2.00
0 Reed Sorenson's Car M .50 1.25
1 Dale Jarrett's Car M .50 1.25
2 Matt Kenseth's Car M .75 2.00
3 Martin Truex Jr.'s Car M .60 1.50
4 Carl Edwards' Car M .60 1.50
5 Jimmie Johnson's Car M .75 2.00
6 Tony Stewart SW .60 1.50
7 David Gilliland 1.50 4.00
Ricky Rudd SW
8 Tony Stewart SW .60 1.50
9 Jeff Gordon SW 1.00 2.50
0 Jack Sprague SW .15 .40
1 Kevin Harvick SW .60 1.50
2 Dale Earnhardt Jr. RTTC 1.00 2.50
3 Denny Hamlin RTTC .75 2.00
4 Tony Stewart RTTC .60 1.50
5 Carl Edwards RTTC .60 1.50
6 Matt Kenseth RTTC .75 2.00
7 Jeff Gordon RTTC 1.00 2.50
8 Kasey Kahne RTTC 1.00 2.50
9 Jimmie Johnson RTTC .75 2.00
0 Greg Biffle RTTC .30 .75
1 Elliott Sadler RTTC .25 .60
2 Jimmie Johnson MD .75 2.00
3 Joe Nemechek MD .15 .40
4 Kyle Petty MD .25 .60
5 Dale Earnhardt Jr. MD 1.00 2.50
6 David Stremme .30 .75
J.J. Yeley MD
7 Tony Stewart MD .60 1.50
8 Mark Martin MD .60 1.50
9 Jeff Gordon MD 1.00 2.50
0 J.J. Yeley MD .30 .75
1 Jimmie Johnson DD 1.25 3.00
2 Jeff Gordon DD 1.50 4.00
3 Dale Earnhardt Jr. DD 1.50 4.00
4 Dale Jarrett DD .75 2.00
5 Michael Waltrip DD .40 1.00
6 Tony Stewart DD 1.00 2.50
7 Dale Earnhardt Jr. FF 2.00 5.00
8 Jeff Gordon FF 2.00 5.00
9 Kasey Kahne FF 2.00 5.00
0 Tony Stewart FF 1.25 3.00
1 Mark Martin FF 1.25 3.00
2 Jimmie Johnson FF 1.50 4.00
3 A.J. Allmendinger RD RC 6.00 15.00
4 David Gilliland RD RC 5.00 12.00
5 Paul Menard RD CRC 4.00 10.00
6 Juan Pablo Montoya RD RC 8.00 20.00
7 David Ragan RD CRC 5.00 12.00
8 David Reutimann RD RC 5.00 12.00
9 Regan Smith RD CRC 4.00 10.00
0 Jon Wood RD CRC 5.00 12.00
) Kevin Harvick Daytona 4.00 10.00

2007 Press Pass Premium Red

STATED PRINT RUN 15 SERIAL #'d SETS
R71-R90) PRINT RUN 5 SERIAL #'d SETS

2007 Press Pass Premium Concrete Chaos

his 6-card set was inserted into packs of 2007 ress Pass Premium at a rate of one in nine. The ard numbers had a "CC" prefix.

OMPLETE SET (6) 10.00 25.00
C1 Jeff Gordon 2.50 6.00
C2 Dale Earnhardt Jr. 2.50 6.00
C3 Jimmie Johnson 2.00 5.00
C4 Tony Stewart 1.50 4.00
C5 Dale Jarrett 1.25 3.00
C6 Mark Martin 1.50 4.00

2007 Press Pass Premium Hot Threads Autographs

his 8-card set was randomly inserted into packs of 007 Press Pass Premium. The cards were hand umbered to the driver's car door number. Some of e cards are not priced due to scarcity. Each card as a swatch of the coresponding driver's race-worn resuit along with the driver's signature.

ERIAL #'d TO DRIVER'S DOOR NUMBER
OME CARDS NOT PRICED DUE TO SCARCITY
T-BL Bobby Labonte 60.00 120.00
T-DE Dale Earnhardt Jr.
T-JG Jeff Gordon 250.00 400.00
T-JJ Jimmie Johnson 100.00 175.00
T-KB Kyle Busch
T-KB Kurt Busch
T-MK Matt Kenseth
T-TS Tony Stewart

2007 Press Pass Premium Hot Threads Drivers

his 16-card set was randomly inserted into packs of 007 Press Pass Premium. Each card has a swatch the coresponding driver's race-worn firesuit.The cards were serial numbered to 145 and they were highlighted with silver foil.

HTD1 Kasey Kahne 15.00 40.00
HTD2 Martin Truex Jr. 12.50 30.00
HTD3 Ryan Newman 10.00 25.00
HTD4 Reed Sorenson 10.00 25.00
HTD5 Tony Stewart 15.00 40.00
HTD6 Denny Hamlin 15.00 40.00
HTD7 Kurt Busch 15.00 40.00
HTD8 Jeff Gordon 25.00 60.00
HTD9 Bobby Labonte 12.50 30.00
HTD10 J.J. Yeley 12.50 30.00
HTD11 Dale Earnhardt Jr. 20.00 50.00
HTD12 Matt Kenseth 12.50 30.00
HTD13 Kyle Busch 10.00 25.00
HTD14 Carl Edwards 12.50 30.00
HTD15 Jimmie Johnson 15.00 40.00
HTD16 Juan Pablo Montoya 15.00 40.00

2007 Press Pass Premium Hot Threads Patch

This 27-card set was randomly inserted into packs of 2007 Press Pass Premium. Each card has a patch-swatch of the coresponding driver's race-worn firesuit.The cards were individually serial numbered to quantities of 20 or less. The cards are not priced due to scarcity.

NOT PRICED DUE TO SCARCITY
HTP1 Dale Earnhardt Coke/10
HTP2 Jeff Gordon Pepsi/15
HTP3 Jeff Gordon DuPont/8
HTP4 Martin Truex Jr. Bass Pro/15
HTP5 Denny Hamlin Fed Ex/15
HTP6 Denny Hamlin Flag/8
HTP7 Kyle Busch Tucan Sam/20
HTP8 Kasey Kahne Stanley/10
HTP9 Kasey Kahne Valvoline/15
HTP10 J.J. Yeley Interstate Batteries/10
HTP11 Jimmie Johnson Lowe's/15
HTP12 Jimmie Johnson Nextel Cup/10
HTP13 Dale Earnhardt Jr. DEI/10
HTP14 Dale Earnhardt Jr. Wrangler/8
HTP15 Kurt Busch Penske Racing/10
HTP16 Tony Stewart Joe Gibbs Racing/8
HTP17 Tony Stewart Home Depot/15
HTP18 Bobby Labonte Pop Secret/10
HTP19 Bobby Labonte Victory Junction Gang/10
HTP20 Carl Edwards Coke/8
HTP21 Carl Edwards Gillette Young Guns/8
HTP22 Matt Kenseth Carhartt/10
HTP23 Matt Kenseth RL Carriers/6
HTP24 Juan Pablo Montoya Havoline/5
HTP25 Juan Pablo Montoya Raybestos/15
HTP26 Reed Sorenson Target/10
HTP27 Ryan Newman Alltel/10

2007 Press Pass Premium Hot Threads Team

This 16-card set was randomly inserted into packs of 2007 Press Pass Premium. Each card has a swatch of the coresponding driver's race-worn firesuit.The cards were serial numbered to 160 and they were highlighted with silver foil.

*TEAM: .3X TO .8X DRIVERS
STATED PRINT RUN 160 SERIAL #'d SETS
HTT1 Kasey Kahne 12.50 30.00
HTT2 Martin Truex Jr. 10.00 25.00
HTT3 Ryan Newman 10.00 20.00
HTT4 Reed Sorenson 10.00 10.00
HTT5 Tony Stewart 12.50 30.00
HTT6 Denny Hamlin 12.50 30.00
HTT7 Kurt Busch 10.00 25.00
HTT8 Jeff Gordon 20.00 50.00
HTT9 Bobby Labonte 10.00 25.00
HTT10 J.J. Yeley 10.00 25.00
HTT11 Dale Earnhardt Jr. 15.00 40.00
HTT12 Matt Kenseth 10.00 25.00
HTT13 Kyle Busch 10.00 20.00
HTT14 Carl Edwards 10.00 25.00
HTT15 Jimmie Johnson 12.50 30.00
HTT16 Juan Pablo Montoya 12.50 30.00

2007 Press Pass Premium Performance Driven

This 12-card set was inserted into packs of 2007 Press Pass Premium at a rate of one in five packs. The cards carried a "PD" prefix for their card numbering. This set had a hobby only parallel whichg was serial numbered to 250.

COMPLETE SET (12) 15.00 40.00
PD1 Bobby Labonte 1.50 4.00
PD2 Kasey Kahne 3.00 8.00
PD3 Dale Earnhardt Jr. 3.00 8.00
PD4 Denny Hamlin 2.50 6.00
PD5 Michael Waltrip .75 2.00
PD6 Jimmie Johnson 2.50 6.00
PD7 Kurt Busch .75 2.00
PD8 Tony Stewart 2.00 5.00
PD9 Dale Jarrett 1.50 4.00
PD10 Jeff Gordon 3.00 8.00
PD11 Mark Martin 2.00 5.00
PD12 Juan Pablo Montoya 3.00 8.00

2007 Press Pass Premium Performance Driven Red

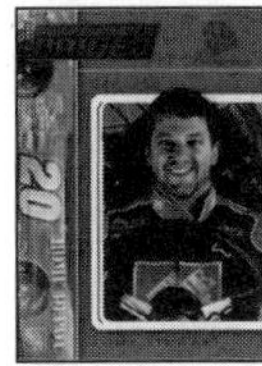

This 12-card set was inserted into packs of 2007 Press Pass PremiumThe cards carried a "PD" prefix for their card numbering. This set was a hobby only parallel which was serial numbered to 250.

*RED: 1X TO 2.5X BASE

2008 Press Pass Premium

COMPLETE SET (90) 40.00 80.00
COMP.SET w/o SP's (72) 10.00 25.00
COMMON DRIVERS .25 .60
SEMISTARS .40 1.00
UNLISTED STARS .60 1.50
COMMON FLASHBACK .40 1.00
SEMISTARS FB .60 1.50
UNLISTED STARS FB 1.00 2.50
FLASHBACK STATED ODDS 1:3
COMMON OPENING DAY .60 1.50
SEMISTARS OD 1.00 2.50
UNLISTED STARS OD 1.50 4.00
OPENING DAY STATED ODDS 1:10
COMMON ROOKIE DEBUT .50 1.25
SEMISTARS RD .75 2.00
UNLISTED STARS RD 1.25 3.00
ROOKIE DEBUT STATED ODDS 1:20
ZERO CARD STATED ODDS 1:60
WAX BOX HOBBY (20) 75.00 100.00
WAX BOX RETAIL (24) 50.00 75.00
1 Dale Earnhardt Jr. CL 2.00 5.00
2 Regan Smith .25 .60
3 Clint Bowyer .75 2.00
4 Martin Truex Jr. .75 2.00
5 Kurt Busch .60 1.50
6 Casey Mears .40 1.00
7 David Ragan .50 1.25
8 Mark Martin 1.00 2.50
9 Kasey Kahne 1.25 3.00
10 Denny Hamlin 1.00 2.50
11 Ryan Newman .60 1.50
12 Paul Menard .50 1.25
13 Greg Biffle .50 1.25
14 Matt Kenseth 1.00 2.50
15 Kyle Busch .75 2.00
16 Elliott Sadler .50 1.25
17 Tony Stewart 1.25 3.00
18 Dave Blaney .25 .60
19 Jeff Gordon 1.50 4.00
20 Jamie McMurray .40 1.00
21 Travis Kvapil .40 1.00
22 Kevin Harvick .75 2.00
23 Jeff Burton .40 1.00
24 David Gilliland .60 1.50
25 Reed Sorenson .40 1.00
26 Juan Pablo Montoya 1.50 4.00
27 Bobby Labonte .60 1.50
28 Dale Jarrett 1.00 2.50
29 Jimmie Johnson 1.25 3.00
30 Michael Waltrip .50 1.25
31 Scott Riggs .40 1.00
32 Brian Vickers .50 1.25
33 A.J. Allmendinger .40 1.00
34 Dale Earnhardt Jr. 2.00 5.00
35 J.J. Yeley .50 1.25
36 Carl Edwards 1.00 2.50
37 Dale Earnhardt Jr.'s Car M .75 2.00
38 Kevin Harvick's Car M .30 .75
39 Michael Waltrip's Car M .20 .50
40 Martin Truex Jr.'s Car M .30 .75
41 Jimmie Johnson's Car M .50 1.25
42 Denny Hamlin's Car M .40 1.00
43 Jeff Gordon's Car M .60 1.50
44 Kyle Busch's Car M .30 .75
45 Juan Pablo Montoya's Car M .60 1.50
46 Mark Martin's Car M .40 1.00
47 Tony Stewart's Car M .50 1.25
48 Dale Jarrett's Car M .30 .75
49 Dale Earnhardt Jr. 2.00 5.00
SW Shootout
50 Jimmie Johnson 1.25 3.00
SW Daytona Pole
51 Dale Earnhardt Jr. 2.00 5.00
SW Gatorade Duel
52 Denny Hamlin 1.00 2.50
SW Gatorade Duel
53 Tony Stewart 1.25 3.00
SW Camping World 300
54 Kurt Busch EOP .60 1.50
55 Jimmie Johnson EOP 1.25 3.00
56 Carl Edwards EOP 1.00 2.50
57 Dale Earnhardt Jr. EOP 2.00 5.00
58 Matt Kenseth EOP 1.00 2.50
59 Jeff Gordon EOP 1.50 4.00
60 Kasey Kahne EOP 1.25 3.00
61 Tony Stewart EOP 1.25 3.00
62 Martin Truex Jr. EOP .75 2.00
63 Kyle Busch EOP .75 2.00
64 Juan Pablo Montoya EOP 1.50 4.00
65 Denny Hamlin EOP 1.00 2.50
66 Kevin Harvick EOP .75 2.00
67 J.J. Yeley MD .50 1.25
68 Tony Stewart MD 1.25 3.00
69 Jimmie Johnson MD 1.25 3.00
70 Carl Edwards MD 1.00 2.50
71 Dale Earnhardt Jr. MD 2.00 5.00
72 Juan Pablo Montoya MD 1.50 4.00
73 Mark Martin F 1.50 4.00
74 Jimmie Johnson F 2.00 5.00
75 Dale Earnhardt Jr. F 3.00 8.00
76 Clint Bowyer F 1.25 3.00
77 Reed Sorenson F .60 1.50
78 Carl Edwards F 1.50 4.00
79 Jeff Gordon F 2.50 6.00
80 Kyle Busch F 1.25 3.00
81 Greg Biffle F .75 2.00
82 Jeff Gordon OD 4.00 10.00
83 Jimmie Johnson OD 3.00 8.00
84 Dale Earnhardt Jr. OD 5.00 12.00
85 Tony Stewart OD 3.00 8.00
86 Carl Edwards OD 2.50 6.00
87 Patrick Carpentier RD RC 5.00 12.00
88 Dario Franchitti RD RC 5.00 12.00
89 Sam Hornish Jr. RD CRC 6.00 15.00
90 Michael McDowell RD RC 8.00 20.00
0 Ryan Newman Daytona 6.00 15.00

2008 Press Pass Premium Red

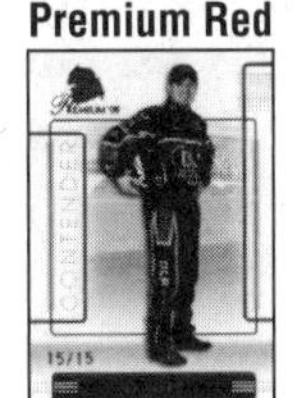

(1-72) STATED PRINT RUN 15 SERIAL #'d SETS
(73-90) STATED PRINT RUN 5 SERIAL #'d SETS
NOT PRICED DUE TO SCARCITY

2008 Press Pass Premium Clean Air

COMPLETE SET (12) 12.50 30.00
COMMON DRIVERS .30 .75
SEMISTARS .50 1.25
UNLISTED STARS .75 2.00
STATED ODDS 1:5
CA1 Jeff Gordon 2.00 5.00
CA2 Martin Truex Jr. 1.00 2.50
CA3 Michael Waltrip .50 1.25
CA4 Dale Earnhardt Jr. 2.50 6.00
CA5 Mark Martin 1.25 3.00
CA6 Kevin Harvick 1.25 3.00
CA7 Matt Kenseth 1.25 3.00
CA8 Kasey Kahne 2.00 5.00
CA9 Jeff Burton .50 1.25
CA10 Jimmie Johnson 1.50 4.00
CA11 Bobby Labonte 1.00 2.50
CA12 Tony Stewart 1.50 4.00

2008 Press Pass Premium Going Global

COMPLETE SET (6) 15.00 40.00
COMMON DRIVERS .40 1.00
SEMISTARS .60 1.50
UNLISTED STARS 1.00 2.50
STATED ODDS 1:9
GG1 Dale Earnhardt Jr. 3.00 8.00
GG2 Patrick Carpentier 1.25 3.00
GG3 Tony Stewart 2.00 5.00
GG4 Juan Pablo Montoya 2.50 6.00
GG5 Jeff Gordon 2.50 6.00
GG6 Dario Franchitti 1.25 3.00

2008 Press Pass Premium Going Global Red

COMPLETE SET (6) 25.00 60.00
*RED: .8X TO 2X BASIC
STATED PRINT RUN 250 SERIAL #'d SETS

2008 Press Pass Premium Hot Threads Autographs

SERIAL #'d TO DRIVER'S DOOR NUMBER
SOME NOT PRICED DUE TO SCARCITY
HTDH Denny Hamlin/11
HTJG Jeff Gordon/24 250.00 400.00
HTKH Kevin Harvick/29 100.00 200.00
HTMK Matt Kenseth/17
HTMM Mark Martin/8
HTMT Martin Truex Jr./1
HTMW Michael Waltrip/55 60.00 120.00

2008 Press Pass Premium Hot Threads Drivers

STATED ODDS 1:40
STATED PRINT RUN 120 SERIAL #'d SETS
HTD1 Kevin Harvick 15.00 40.00
HTD2 Martin Truex Jr. 12.50 30.00
HTD3 Brian Vickers 10.00 25.00
HTD4 Jimmie Johnson 20.00 50.00
HTD5 Denny Hamlin 15.00 40.00
HTD6 Juan Pablo Montoya 12.50 30.00
HTD7 Dale Jarrett 15.00 40.00
HTD8 Carl Edwards 15.00 40.00
HTD9 Jeff Gordon 25.00 60.00
HTD10 Ryan Newman 12.50 30.00
HTD11 Dario Franchitti 10.00 25.00
HTD12 Kurt Busch 10.00 25.00
HTD13 Mark Martin 20.00 50.00
HTD14 Paul Menard 10.00 25.00
HTD15 Reed Sorenson 10.00 25.00
HTD16 Matt Kenseth 20.00 50.00
HTD17 Tony Stewart 20.00 50.00
HTD18 Dale Earnhardt Jr. AMP 50.00 100.00
HTD19 Dale Earnhardt Jr. NG 50.00 100.00

2008 Press Pass Premium Hot Threads Drivers Gold

STATED PRINT RUN 1 SERIAL #'d SET
NOT PRICED DUE TIO SCARCITY

2008 Press Pass Premium Hot Threads Patches

SERIAL #'d TO 27 OR LESS SEE CHECKLISTS BELOW
NOT PRICED DUE TO SCARCITY
HTP1 Kurt Busch
U.S. Flag
HTP2 Carl Edwards
CE Signature
HTP3 Carl Edwards
Ford Racing/6
HTP4 Carl Edwards
NASCAR bar
HTP5 Jeff Gordon
Bosch Spark Plugs/8
HTP6 Jeff Gordon
Goodyear
HTP7 Jeff Gordon
NASCAR bar
HTP8 Denny Hamlin
Fed Ex/4
HTP9 Kevin Harvick
Pennzoil
HTP10 Kevin Harvick
Saftey Kleen/6
HTP11 Kevin Harvick
U.S. Flag/6
HTP12 Dale Jarrett
Coca Cola/8
HTP13 Dale Jarrett
UPS/12
HTP14 Dale Jarrett
NASCAR bar
HTP15 Jimmie Johnson
Delphi/8
HTP16 Jimmie Johnson
Hendrick Motorsports/6
HTP17 Jimmie Johnson
NASCAR bar/6
HTP18 Matt Kenseth #17/4
HTP19 Matt Kenseth
Kraft Singles
HTP20 Bobby Labonte
Hamburger Helper/8
HTP21 Bobby Labonte
Pillsbury/6
HTP22 Bobby Labonte
U.S. Flag/6
HTP23 Mark Martin
U.S. Army/27
HTP24 Mark Martin
Mighty/6
HTP25 Mark Martin
NASCAR bar/5
HTP26 Mark Martin
U.S. Flag
HTP27 Paul Menard
Menards
HTP28 Paul Menard
Turtle Wax/22
HTP29 Paul Menard
NASCAR bar/5
HTP30 Juan Pablo Montoya
Big Red
HTP31 Juan Pablo Montoya
Havoline
HTP32 Juan Pablo Montoya
NASCAR bar/5
HTP33 Juan Pablo Montoya
Columbian Flag
HTP34 Ryan Newman
Gatorade/5
HTP35 Ryan Newman
Gillette Young Guns/7
HTP36 Ryan Newman
NASCAR bar
HTP37 Ryan Newman
U.S. Flag
HTP38 Reed Sorenson
Ganassi Racing/8
HTP39 Reed Sorenson
NASCAR bar/6
HTP40 Tony Stewart #20
HTP41 Tony Stewart
Smoke
HTP42 Tony Stewart
NASCAR bar
HTP43 Tony Stewart
U.S. Flag/8
HTP44 Martin Truex Jr.
Bass Pro/3
HTP45 Martin Truex Jr.
DEI logo
HTP46 Brian Vickers #83/9
HTP47 Brian Vickers
Red Bull/15
HTP48 Brian Vickers
NASCAR bar/6
HTP49 Brian Vickers
U.S. Flag
HTP50 Michael Waltrip
Best Western/14
HTP51 Michael Waltrip
NAPA/14
HTP52 Michael Waltrip
NASCAR bar/6

2008 Press Pass Premium Hot Threads Team

*TEAMS: .4X TO 1X DRIVERS
STATED PRINT RUN 120 SERIAL #'d SETS

2008 Press Pass Premium Previews

EB1-EB36 STATED PRINT RUN 5 SERIAL #'d SETS
EB54-EB66 STATED PRINT RUN 1 SERIAL #'d SET
NOT PRICED DUE TO SCARCITY

2008 Press Pass Premium Target

COMPLETE SET (6) 12.50 30.00
STATED ODDS 2 PER TARGET BLASTER BOX
TA1 Matt Kenseth 2.00 5.00
TA2 Denny Hamlin 2.00 5.00
TA3 Kevin Harvick 2.00 5.00
TA4 Tony Stewart 2.50 6.00
TA5 Dale Earnhardt Jr. 4.00 10.00
TA6 Juan Pablo Montoya 3.00 8.00

2008 Press Pass Premium Team Signed Baseballs

GAN Dario Franchitti
Juan Pablo Montoya
Reed Sorenson
GIB Kyle Busch
Denny Hamlin
Tony Stewart
HMS Dale Earnhardt Jr.
Jeff Gordon
Jimmie Johnson
Casey Mears
ROU Carl Edwards 125.00 200.00
Matt Kenseth
Jamie McMurray#David Ragan

2008 Press Pass Premium Wal-Mart

COMPLETE SET (6) 12.50 30.00
STATED ODDS 2 PER WALMART BLASTER BOX
WM1 Dale Earnhardt Jr. 4.00 10.00
WM2 Jimmie Johnson 2.50 6.00
WM3 Kasey Kahne 3.00 8.00
WM4 Carl Edwards 2.00 5.00
WM5 Jeff Gordon 3.00 8.00
WM6 Martin Truex Jr. 1.50 4.00

2003 Press Pass Race Exclusives

These cards were issued one at a time for select race winners in 2003. Each card follows the format or even parallels a regular issue 2003 card with the addition of a race winning date and mention printed on the front. All cards were sealed in a Beckett Graded Services card holder, but not graded. We've listed the cards alphabetically below.

1 Dale Earnhardt Jr. 15.00 25.00
Daytona Shootout 2/8/03
2 Michael Waltrip 12.00 20.00
Daytona 500 2/16/03

2004 Press Pass Rookie Class

This 6-card set was available in retail packs of 2004 VIP. They were inserted into the '04 VIP retail blaster boxes at a rate of 1 per box. The cards featured 6 of the top upcoming drivers making their Nextel Cup debuts in 2004.

COMPLETE SET (6) 8.00 20.00
RC1 Kasey Kahne 4.00 10.00

RC2 Johnny Sauter	1.00	2.50
RC3 Brian Vickers	1.50	4.00
RC4 Brendan Gaughan	1.50	4.00
RC5 Scott Riggs	1.00	2.50
RC6 Scott Wimmer	1.00	2.50

1998 Press Pass Signings

This 39-card set contains the autographs of the top drivers and crew chiefs on the Winston Cup and Busch circuits. These cards were inserted into 1998 Press Pass Premium at a ratio of one per 48 packs, 1998 Press Pass Stealth at a ratio of one per 72 packs and 1998 VIP at a ratio of one per 60 packs.

COMPLETE SET (39)	700.00	1200.00
1 Jeff Gordon	100.00	175.00
Press Pass Premium		
Press Pass Stealth		
VIP		
2 Dale Jarrett	12.50	30.00
Press Pass Premium		
Press Pass Stealth		
VIP		
3 Dale Earnhardt	175.00	300.00
Press Pass Premium		
Press Pass Stealth		
VIP		
4 Terry Labonte	12.50	30.00
Press Pass Premium		
Press Pass Stealth		
VIP		
5 Ricky Rudd	10.00	25.00
Press Pass Premium		
Press Pass Stealth		
VIP		
6 John Andretti	6.00	15.00
Press Pass Stealth		
VIP		
7 Sterling Marlin	12.50	30.00
Press Pass Stealth		
VIP		
8 Bobby Hamilton	10.00	25.00
Press Pass Stealth		
VIP		
9 Ernie Irvan	8.00	20.00
Press Pass Stealth		
VIP		
10 Bobby Labonte	12.50	30.00
Press Pass Stealth		
VIP		
11 Ken Schrader	6.00	15.00
Press Pass Premium		
12 Jeff Burton	8.00	20.00
Press Pass Premium		
VIP		
13 Michael Waltrip	10.00	25.00
Press Pass Premium		
Press Pass Stealth		
14 Ted Musgrave	6.00	15.00
Press Pass Stealth		
VIP		
15 Geoff Bodine	6.00	15.00
Press Pass Stealth		
VIP		
16 Ward Burton	8.00	20.00
Press Pass Stealth		
VIP		
17 Ricky Craven	10.00	25.00
Press Pass Premium		
18 Johnny Benson	8.00	20.00
Press Pass Premium		
VIP		
20 Wally Dallenbach	6.00	15.00
VIP		
21 Tony Stewart	40.00	100.00
Press Pass Stealth		
22 Bill Elliott	12.50	30.00
Press Pass Premium		
Press Pass Stealth		
VIP		
23 Mike Skinner	6.00	15.00
Press Pass Premium		
Press Pass Stealth		
VIP		
24 David Green	6.00	15.00
Press Pass Premium		
25 Joe Nemechek	6.00	15.00
Press Pass Premium		
VIP		
26 Kenny Irwin	15.00	40.00
Press Pass Stealth		
27 Steve Park	10.00	25.00
Press Pass Premium		
Press Pass Stealth		
VIP		
28 Robin Pemberton	4.00	10.00
Press Pass Premium		
VIP		
29 Larry McReynolds	6.00	15.00
Press Pass Premium		
Press Pass Stealth		
VIP		
30 Jimmy Makar	4.00	10.00
Press Pass Premium		
VIP		
31 Ray Evernham	10.00	25.00
Press Pass Premium		
Press Pass Stealth		
VIP		
32 Todd Parrott	4.00	10.00
Press Pass Premium		
Press Pass Stealth		
VIP		
33 Randy LaJoie	6.00	15.00
Press Pass Premium		
VIP		
34 Robert Pressley	6.00	15.00
Press Pass Stealth		
VIP		
35 Tim Fedewa	6.00	15.00
Press Pass Premium		
VIP		
36 Kevin Lepage	6.00	15.00
Press Pass Premium		
VIP		
37 Mike McLaughlin	6.00	15.00
Press Pass Stealth		
VIP		
38 Jason Keller	6.00	15.00
Press Pass Premium		
VIP		
39 Dale Earnhardt Jr.	250.00	350.00
Press Pass Premium		
Press Pass Stealth		
VIP		
40 Jimmy Spencer	6.00	15.00
Press Pass Stealth		
VIP		

1998 Press Pass Signings Gold

This 9-card set is a partial parallel of the Press Pass signings set. Each driver signed 100 cards for this set. These cards were inserted into 1998 Press Pass Premium and into 1998 VIP packs.

1 Jeff Gordon	125.00	250.00
Press Pass Premium		
VIP		
2 Dale Jarrett	30.00	60.00
Press Pass Premium		
VIP		
3 Dale Earnhardt	250.00	450.00
Press Pass Premium		
VIP		
4 Terry Labonte	40.00	80.00
Press Pass Premium		
VIP		
10 Bobby Labonte	30.00	60.00
VIP		
12 Jeff Burton	25.00	50.00
Press Pass Premium		
VIP		
13 Michael Waltrip	20.00	50.00
Press Pass Premium		
VIP		
22 Bill Elliott	75.00	125.00
Press Pass Premium		
VIP		
40 Jimmy Spencer	15.00	30.00
VIP		

1999 Press Pass Signings

Inserted in Press Pass Premium packs at stated odds of one in 48, these cards feature authentic autographs of past and present NASCAR personalities. Most cards were hand serial numbered on the back and each features silver foil highlights on the front. They are often confused with the 2000 Press Pass Signings since that year's cards also featured a 1999 copyright line year. The real 1999 Signings inserts feature the words "Press Pass Signings" vertically in the background of the driver photo. Also note that additional Signings cards, including Dale Earnhardt Jr. and Matt Kenseth, were released with the 2003 VIP Tin factory set. Those Signings cards feature different serial numbering and most were signed in black ink or a very dark blue ink instead of the basic bright blue ink.

1 Glenn Allen/1500	6.00	15.00
2 Bobby Allison/500	15.00	30.00
3 John Andretti/370	6.00	15.00
4 Buddy Baker/1500	6.00	15.00
5A Johnny Benson/750	6.00	15.00
5B Johnny Benson/620	6.00	15.00
6A Dave Blaney Blue/750	6.00	15.00
6B Dave Blaney Black/500	6.00	15.00
7 Brett Bodine/750	6.00	15.00
8 Todd Bodine/500	6.00	15.00
9A Jeff Burton/250	10.00	25.00
9B Jeff Burton/500	8.00	20.00
10 Ward Burton/500	10.00	25.00
11 Derrike Cope/500	8.00	20.00
12 Wally Dallenbach/500	6.00	15.00
13 Mike Dillon/500	6.00	15.00
14 Dale Earnhardt/400	175.00	350.00
15A Dale Earnhardt Jr./875	75.00	150.00
16 Tim Fedewa/690	6.00	15.00
17 Jeff Fuller/500	4.00	10.00
18 Harry Gant/1450	6.00	15.00
19 Jeff Gordon/400	75.00	150.00
20 David Green/770	6.00	15.00
21 Jeff Green	6.00	15.00
22 Bobby Hamilton/480	10.00	25.00
23 Ernie Irvan/225	20.00	50.00
24 Kenny Irwin/380	20.00	50.00
25A Dale Jarrett Blue/600	12.50	30.00
25B Dale Jarrett Black/60	20.00	50.00
26 Jason Jarrett/1500	6.00	15.00
27A Ned Jarrett/400	8.00	20.00
27B Ned Jarrett Blue/355	8.00	20.00
28 Jason Keller/500	6.00	15.00
29A Matt Kenseth Blue/500	30.00	60.00
29B Matt Kenseth Black/155	30.00	60.00
30 Bobby Labonte/500	12.50	30.00
31 Terry Labonte/400	12.50	30.00
32 Randy LaJoie/750	6.00	15.00
33 Kevin Lepage/500	6.00	15.00
34 Chad Little/500	8.00	20.00
35A Jimmy Makar Blue/700	8.00	20.00
35B Jimmy Makar Black/500	8.00	20.00
36 Sterling Marlin/750	12.50	30.00
37 Mark Martin/430	30.00	60.00
38A Jeremy Mayfield Blue/490	8.00	20.00
38B Jeremy Mayfield Black/500	8.00	20.00
39A Mike McLaughlin Blue/750	6.00	15.00
39B Mike McLaughlin Black/475	6.00	15.00
40A Larry McReynolds Blue/750	8.00	20.00
40B Larry McReynolds Black/500	8.00	20.00
41 Joe Nemechek	6.00	15.00
42 Steve Park/900	8.00	20.00
43A Todd Parrott Blue/975	4.00	10.00
43B Todd Parrott Black/500	4.00	10.00
44 Robin Pemberton/750	4.00	10.00
45 Andy Petree	6.00	15.00
46 Robert Pressley/1000	6.00	15.00
47 Ricky Rudd/550	15.00	30.00
48A Elliott Sadler Blue/650		
48B Elliott Sadler Black/250		
49 Hermie Sadler/500	6.00	15.00
50 Elton Sawyer	6.00	15.00
51 Ken Schrader/1575	6.00	15.00
52A Mike Skinner Blue/350	6.00	15.00
52B Mike Skinner Black/395	6.00	15.00
53 Jimmy Spencer/650	8.00	20.00
54 Jack Sprague/750	6.00	15.00
55 Tony Stewart/500	40.00	100.00
56 Rusty Wallace	12.50	30.00
57 Darrell Waltrip/175	20.00	50.00
58 Michael Waltrip/500		

1999 Press Pass Signings Gold

Inserted in packs at stated odds of one in 480, these cards feature authentic autographs of leading drivers. Each card features gold foil highlights on the front, was hand serial numbered on the back, and signed in gold ink unless noted below. They are often confused with the 2000 Press Pass Signings since that year's cards also featured a 1999 copyright line year. The real 1999 Signings inserts feature the words "Press Pass Signings" vertically in the background of the driver photo. Some cards were also issued in 2003 as part of the Press Pass VIP holiday tin factory set.

1 Ward Burton/70	40.00	80.00
2 Derrike Cope/100	15.00	40.00
3 Dale Earnhardt/100	300.00	500.00
4A Dale Earnhardt Jr. Gold/85	100.00	200.00
4B Dale Earnhardt Jr. Blue/125	100.00	200.00
5 Jeff Gordon/100	100.00	200.00
6 Bobby Hamilton/100	25.00	60.00
7 Jeff Hammond/100	25.00	60.00
8 Ernie Irvan/105	25.00	50.00
9 Dale Jarrett/100	30.00	60.00
10 Jason Keller/95	15.00	40.00
11 Matt Kenseth/100	40.00	80.00
12 Bobby Labonte/100	20.00	50.00
13 Terry Labonte/100	40.00	80.00
14 Jimmy Makar/700	15.00	40.00
(signed in blue ink)		
15 Mark Martin/100	75.00	150.00
16 Jeremy Mayfield/110	15.00	40.00
17 Mike McLaughlin/100	15.00	40.00
18 Larry McReynolds/100	15.00	40.00
19 Joe Nemechek/100	15.00	40.00
20 Todd Parrott/100	15.00	40.00
21 Robin Pemberton/100	15.00	40.00
22 Ricky Rudd/100	25.00	60.00
23 Elliott Sadler/65	30.00	60.00
24 Mike Skinner/100	15.00	40.00
25 Jimmy Spencer/100	15.00	40.00
26 Tony Stewart/100	60.00	120.00
27 Frank Stoddard/100	15.00	40.00
28 Rusty Wallace Blue/100	40.00	80.00
29 Darrell Waltrip/100	30.00	60.00

2000 Press Pass Signings

Randomly inserted in packs at a rate of one in 240. This autograph program featured over 60-current and past drivers. Each card features the autograph in a large area below the photo with the set name and driver's name vertically on the left. The cardbacks feature a 1999 copyright date line but were issued as a 2000 year set so they are often sold or mistaken to be the 1999 release. The cards were spread throughout all of the 2000 Press Pass products. Unlike previous years these cards were not serial numbered.

1 Bobby Allison	7.50	20.00
2 John Andretti	7.50	20.00
3 Casey Atwood	10.00	25.00
4 Buddy Baker	7.50	20.00
5 Dave Blaney	5.00	12.00
6 Brett Bodine	5.00	12.00
7 Todd Bodine	5.00	12.00
8 Jeff Burton	8.00	20.00
9 Ward Burton	10.00	25.00
10 Richard Childress	7.50	20.00
11 Stacy Compton	5.00	12.00
12 Wally Dallenbach	5.00	12.00
13 Bill Davis	4.00	8.00
14 Dale Earnhardt	175.00	350.00
15 Dale Earnhardt Jr.	60.00	120.00
16 Jimmy Elledge	4.00	8.00
17 Tim Fedewa	5.00	12.00
18 Jimmy Fennig	4.00	8.00
19 A.J. Foyt	30.00	60.00
20 Jeff Gordon	100.00	175.00
21 David Green	5.00	12.00
22 Jeff Green	5.00	12.00
23 Mark Green	5.00	12.00
24 Kevin Grubb	5.00	12.00
25 Bobby Hamilton	10.00	25.00
26 Jeff Hammond	5.00	12.00
27 Dale Jarrett	12.50	30.00
28 Ned Jarrett	7.50	20.00
29 Jason Keller	5.00	12.00
30 Matt Kenseth	15.00	40.00
31 Terry Labonte	12.50	30.00
32 Randy LaJoie	5.00	12.00
33 Kevin Lepage	5.00	12.00
34 Chad Little	7.50	20.00
35 Jimmy Makar	4.00	8.00
36 Sterling Marlin	12.50	30.00
37 Mark Martin	30.00	60.00
38 Jeremy Mayfield	10.00	25.00
39 Larry McReynolds	5.00	12.00
40 Joe Nemechek	5.00	12.00
41 Steve Park	10.00	25.00
42 Hank Parker Jr.	5.00	12.00
43 Todd Parrott	4.00	8.00
44 Benny Parsons	30.00	60.00
45 David Pearson	20.00	40.00
46 Robin Pemberton	4.00	8.00
47 Robert Pressley	5.00	12.00
48 Scott Pruett	5.00	12.00
49 Tony Raines	5.00	12.00
50 Ricky Rudd	12.50	30.00
51 Elliott Sadler	5.00	12.00
52 Hermie Sadler	5.00	12.00
53 Elton Sawyer	7.50	20.00
54 Ken Schrader	7.50	20.00
55 Mike Skinner	5.00	12.00
56 Peter Sospenzo	4.00	8.00
57 Tony Stewart	40.00	100.00
58 Frank Stoddard	4.00	8.00
59 Dick Trickle	5.00	12.00
60 Kenny Wallace	10.00	25.00
61 Darrell Waltrip	20.00	50.00
62 Michael Waltrip	10.00	25.00
63 Greg Zippadeli	4.00	8.00

2000 Press Pass Signings Gold

Randomly inserted in packs at a rate of one in 475, Press Pass Signings Gold was a parallel to the base insert set with each autograph signed in gold ink. The cards were inserted across all 2000 Press Pass hobby pack products with each serial numbered of 100 made. The cardbacks feature a 1999 copyright date line but were issued as a 2000 year set so they are often sold or mistaken to be the 1999 release.

1 Bobby Allison	12.50	30.00
2 John Andretti	12.50	30.00
3 Buddy Baker	12.50	30.00
4 Dave Blaney	6.00	15.00
5 Brett Bodine	8.00	20.00
6 Jeff Burton	15.00	40.00
7 Ward Burton	15.00	40.00
8 Stacy Compton	8.00	20.00
9 Dale Earnhardt	300.00	500.00
10 Dale Earnhardt Jr.	100.00	200.00
11 A.J. Foyt	30.00	80.00
12 Jeff Gordon	125.00	250.00
13 Bobby Hamilton	25.00	60.00
14 Dale Jarrett	30.00	60.00
15 Ned Jarrett	12.50	30.00
16 Matt Kenseth	50.00	100.00
17 Bobby Labonte		
18 Terry Labonte	40.00	80.00
19 Chad Little	12.50	30.00
20 Mark Martin	75.00	150.00
21 Jeremy Mayfield	15.00	40.00
22 Joe Nemechek	8.00	20.00
23 Steve Park	15.00	40.00
24 Benny Parsons	50.00	100.00
25 David Pearson	25.00	60.00
26 Robert Pressley	8.00	20.00
27 Ricky Rudd	20.00	50.00
28 Elliott Sadler	15.00	40.00
29 Mike Skinner	8.00	20.00
30 Tony Stewart	60.00	120.00
31 Kenny Wallace	15.00	40.00
32 Darrell Waltrip	30.00	80.00
33 Michael Waltrip	20.00	50.00

2001 Press Pass Signings

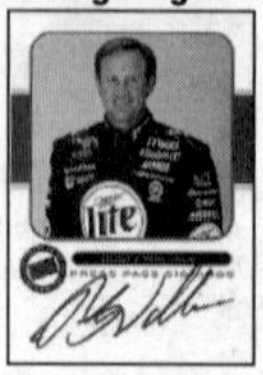

Issued in various 2001 Press Pass products at different odds, these cards feature authentic autographs along with silver foil layering on the fronts. A few cards were issued as exchange cards in packs that carried one of three different expiration dates: July 31, 2002, September 11, 2002 or October 30, 2002.

STATED ODDS 1:48 PREMIUM HOB/RET
STATED ODDS 1:96 OPTIMA HOB,1:120 RET
ODDS 1:96 STEALTH HOB, 1:120 STL RET
ODDS 1:120 TRACKSIDE HOB, 1:240 RET
STATED ODDS 1:72 VIP HOB, 1:120 RET

1 John Andretti	8.00	20.00
PPP/TS/VIP/Stealth		
2 Casey Atwood	8.00	20.00
PPP/VIP/Stealth		
3 Greg Biffle	10.00	25.00
VIP/Stealth		
4 Dave Blaney	5.00	12.00
PPP/TS/VIP/Stealth		
5 Brett Bodine	5.00	12.00
PPP/TS/VIP/Stealth		
6 Todd Bodine	5.00	12.00
TS/Stealth		
7 Jeff Burton	8.00	20.00
PPP/TS/VIP		
8 Ward Burton	10.00	25.00
PPP/TS/VIP/Stealth		
9 Kurt Busch	15.00	40.00
PPP/TS/VIP/Stealth		
10 Stacy Compton	5.00	12.00
TS/VIP/Stealth		
11 Ricky Craven	8.00	20.00
PPP/TS/VIP/Stealth		
12 Dale Earnhardt Jr.	75.00	150.00
(PPP/Stealth/Trackside/VIP		
13 Tim Fedewa	5.00	12.00
PPP/VIP/Stealth		
14 A.J.Foyt	15.00	40.00
VIP/Stealth		
15 Jeff Gordon	100.00	175.00
TS/VIP/Stealth		
16 David Green	5.00	12.00
Stealth		
17 Jeff Green	5.00	12.00
PPP/VIP		
18 Mark Green	5.00	12.00
VIP		
19 Kevin Grubb	5.00	12.00
PPP/VIP/Stealth		
20 Bobby Hamilton	10.00	25.00
PPP		
21 Kevin Harvick Busch	12.50	30.00
PPP/VIP/Stealth		
22 Kevin Harvick	12.50	30.00
WC /VIP/Stealth		
23 Ron Hornaday	5.00	12.00
TS/VIP/Stealth		
24 Dale Jarrett	15.00	40.00
PPP/TS/VIP/Stealth		
25 Buckshot Jones	8.00	20.00
VIP/Stealth		
26 Jason Keller	5.00	12.00
VIP/Stealth		
27 Matt Kenseth	15.00	40.00
PPP/TS/VIP/Stealth		
28 Bobby Labonte	15.00	40.00
PPP/TS/VIP/Stealth		
29 Terry Labonte	12.50	30.00
TS/VIP/Stealth		
30 Randy LaJoie	5.00	12.00
VIP/Stealth		
31 Jason Leffler	5.00	12.00
Stealth		
32 Chad Little	5.00	12.00
VIP/Stealth		
33 Sterling Marlin	12.50	30.00
PPP/VIP/Stealth		
34 Mark Martin	30.00	60.00
PPP/TS/VIP/Stealth		
35 Jeremy Mayfield	10.00	25.00
PPP/Stealth		
36 Mike McLaughlin	5.00	12.00
PPP/VIP/Stealth		
37 Jerry Nadeau	8.00	20.00
VIP/Stealth		
38 Joe Nemechek	5.00	12.00
PPP/TS/VIP/Stealth		
39 Ryan Newman	20.00	40.00
PPP/VIP/Stealth		
40 Steve Park EXCH	25.00	60.00
PPP/TS/VIP		
41 Hank Parker Jr.	5.00	12.00
VIP/Stealth		
42 Kyle Petty	10.00	25.00
PPP/TS/VIP/Stealth		
43 Richard Petty	40.00	80.00
VIP/Stealth		
44 Robert Pressley	5.00	12.00
PPP/TS/VIP/Stealth		
45 Tony Raines	5.00	12.00
PPP/VIP/Stealth		
46 Ricky Rudd	10.00	25.00
PPP/TS/VIP/Stealth		
47 Elliott Sadler	10.00	25.00
PPP/VIP/Stealth		
48 Elton Sawyer	5.00	12.00
VIP/Stealth		
49 Ken Schrader	8.00	20.00
PPP/TS/VIP/Stealth		
50 Jimmy Spencer	8.00	20.00
PPP/TS/VIP/Stealth		
51 Tony Stewart	40.00	100.0
PPP/TS/VIP		
52 Rusty Wallace	12.50	30.0
PPP/TS/VIP/Stealth		
53 Darrell Waltrip	20.00	50.0
PPP/TS/VIP/Stealth		
54 Michael Waltrip	10.00	25.0
VIP/Stealth		
55 Robert Yates	8.00	20.0
TS		
56 Greg Zipadelli	5.00	12.0

2001 Press Pass Signings Gold

Randomly inserted in various 2001 Press Pa products, these cards parallel the Press Pa Signings insert set. Each card was serial number to 50 and featured gold foil layering on the front. few cards were issued as redemption cards in pack Those cards could be redeemed until July 31, 200 The Dale Earnhardt Jr. card was issued via ma redemption in 2003.

1 John Andretti	25.00	60.0
PPP/TS/VIP/Stealth		
2 Casey Atwood	25.00	60.0
PPP/TS/VIP/Stealth		
3 Dave Blaney	15.00	40.0
PPP/TS/Stealth		
4 Brett Bodine	15.00	40.0
PPP/TS/VIP/Stealth		
5 Todd Bodine	15.00	40.0
VIP/Stealth		
6 Jeff Burton	30.00	80.0
TS/VIP/Stealth		
7 Ward Burton	30.00	80.0
PPP/TS/VIP/Stealth		
8 Kurt Busch	50.00	120.0
PPP/TS/VIP/Stealth		
9 Stacy Compton	15.00	40.0
TS/VIP/Stealth		
10 Ricky Craven	30.00	80.0
PPP/TS/VIP/Stealth		
11 Dale Earnhardt Jr.	150.00	300.0
12 A.J. Foyt	40.00	100.0
VIP/Stealth		
13 Jeff Gordon	150.00	300.0
Stealth		
14 Kevin Harvick	75.00	150.0
WC /VIP/Stealth		
15 Ron Hornaday	15.00	40.0
TS/VIP/Stealth		
16 Dale Jarrett	40.00	100.0
PPP/TS/VIP/Stealth		
17 Buckshot Jones	25.00	60.0
VIP/Stealth		
18 Matt Kenseth	40.00	100.0
PPP/TS/VIP/Stealth		
19 Bobby Labonte	30.00	60.0
Stealth		
20 Terry Labonte	50.00	120.0
TS/VIP/Stealth		
21 Jason Leffler	15.00	40.0
Stealth		
22 Sterling Marlin	40.00	100.0
TS/VIP/Stealth		
23 Mark Martin	75.00	150.0
PPP/TS/VIP/Stealth		
24 Jeremy Mayfield	30.00	80.0
Stealth		
25 Jerry Nadeau	25.00	60.0
VIP/Stealth		
26 Joe Nemechek	15.00	40.0
PPP/TS/VIP/Stealth		
27 Kyle Petty	30.00	80.0
PPP/TS/VIP/Stealth		
28 Robert Pressley	15.00	40.0
PPP/TS/VIP/Stealth		
29 Ricky Rudd	30.00	80.0
PPP/TS/VIP/Stealth		
30 Elliott Sadler	30.00	80.0
TS/VIP/Stealth		
31 Ken Schrader	25.00	60.0
PPP/TS/VIP/Stealth		
32 Jimmy Spencer	25.00	60.0
PPP/TS/VIP/Stealth		
33 Tony Stewart	100.00	175.0
PPP/TS/VIP/Stealth		
34 Rusty Wallace	40.00	80.0
PPP/TS/VIP/Stealth		
35 Darrell Waltrip	60.00	150.0
PPP/TS/VIP/Stealth		
36 Michael Waltrip	25.00	60.0
VIP/Stealth		

2001 Press Pass Signings Transparent

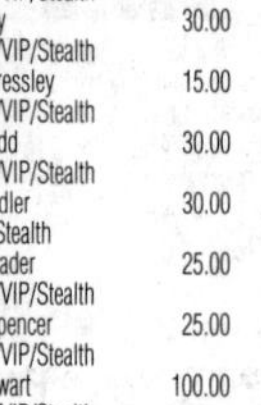

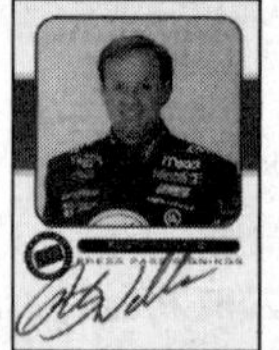

Randomly inserted in packs, these 12-cards featu authentic autographs of leading NASCAR drive printed and signed on plastic stock. The cards we serial numbered to 100 and a few were issued packs as exchange cards. Those exchange card

ld be redeemed until July 31, 2002.
leff Burton 15.00 40.00
VIP/Stealth
Vard Burton 15.00 40.00
PPP/TS/VIP/Stealth
Dale Earnhardt Jr. 100.00 200.00
Dale Jarrett 30.00 60.00
PPP/TS/VIP/Stealth
Matt Kenseth 50.00 100.00
PPP/TS/VIP/Stealth
Bobby Labonte 20.00 50.00
Stealth
Mark Martin 50.00 100.00
PPP/TS/VIP/Stealth
eremy Mayfield 15.00 40.00
Stealth
Kyle Petty 15.00 40.00
PPP/TS/VIP/Stealth
Ricky Rudd 15.00 40.00
PPP/TS/VIP/Stealth
Tony Stewart 60.00 120.00
VIP/Stealth
Rusty Wallace 40.00 80.00
PPP/TS/VIP/Stealth
Darrell Waltrip 30.00 80.00
PPP/TS/VIP/Stealth

2002 Press Pass Signings

ued at different rates depending on the product se cards were inserted in, these 74-cards include authentic autograph of the featured driver. We e notated next to the driver's name which duct(s) their autographs appeared in. Please note some of the cards were not ready for inclusion in ks and those cards could be redeemed until June 2003. The Dale Earnhardt Jr. was the most able of the redemptions.

ATED ODDS 1:48H, 1:72R PP PREMIUM
ATED ODDS 1:120H, 1:240R TRACKSIDE
ATED ODDS 1:72 HOBBY VIP
ATED ODDS 1:96 H, 1:240R STEALTH

ohn Andretti O/P/S/T/V 6.00 15.00
uddy Baker O/P/S/T/V 8.00 20.00
yle Berck O/P/S/T/V 6.00 15.00
reg Biffle O/S/V 10.00 25.00
ave Blaney O/P/S/T/V 8.00 20.00
rett Bodine O/P/S/V 6.00 15.00
odd Bodine O/P/S/T/V 6.00 15.00
eff Burton O/S/T/V 8.00 20.00
Vard Burton O/P/S/T/V 8.00 20.00
Kurt Busch O/P/S/T/V 12.50 30.00
Steve Carlson O/P/S/T/V 6.00 15.00
Matt Crafton O/P/S/T/V 6.00 15.00
Ricky Craven O/P/S/V 10.00 25.00
Dale Earnhardt Jr. P/T 60.00 120.00
Kerry Earnhardt O/P/S/T/V 10.00 25.00
Larry Foyt O/P/S/T/V 8.00 20.00
Coy Gibbs O/P/S/T/V 6.00 15.00
Jeff Gordon O/P/S/T/V 100.00 175.00
Robby Gordon O/P/S/T/V 8.00 20.00
David Green O/P/S/T/V 6.00 15.00
Jeff Green O/P/S/T/V 6.00 15.00
Mark Green O/P/S/V 6.00 15.00
Bobby Hamilton O/P/S/T/V 10.00 25.00
Kevin Hamlin O/P/S/T/V 6.00 15.00
Jeff Hammond 10.00 25.00
Kevin Harvick O/P/S/T/V 12.50 30.00
Dale Jarrett O/P/S/T/V 15.00 40.00
Ned Jarrett O/P/S/T/V 8.00 20.00
Jimmie Johnson O/P/S/T/V 40.00 80.00
Junior Johnson O/P/S/T/V 10.00 25.00
Buckshot Jones O/P/S/T/V 8.00 20.00
Jason Keller O/P/S/V 8.00 20.00
Matt Kenseth O/P/S/T/V 15.00 40.00
Travis Kvapil O/P/S/T/V 8.00 20.00
Bobby Labonte O/P/S/T/V 15.00 40.00
Terry Labonte O/S/T/V 15.00 40.00
Randy Lajoie O/P/S/T/V 6.00 15.00
Jason Leffler O/P/S/T/V 6.00 15.00
Chad Little O/P/S/V 6.00 15.00
Sterling Marlin O/P/S/T/V 12.50 30.00
Mark Martin O/P/S/T/V 30.00 60.00
Jeremy Mayfield O/P/S/T/V 10.00 25.00
Mike McLaughlin O/S/V 6.00 15.00
Jamie McMurray O/P/S/T/V 10.00 25.00
Casey Mears O/S/V 12.50 30.00
Ted Musgrave O/P/S/T/V 6.00 15.00
Jerry Nadeau O/P/S/T/V 6.00 15.00
Ryan Newman O/P/S/T/V 15.00 30.00
Hank Parker Jr. O/P/S/T/V 6.00 15.00
Benny Parsons O/P/S/T/V 30.00 60.00
David Pearson O/P/S/T/V 15.00 40.00
Kyle Petty O/P/S/T/V 10.00 25.00
Richard Petty O/P/S/T/V 40.00 80.00
Craig Raudman O/P/S/T/V 6.00 15.00
Ricky Rudd O/P/S/T/V 8.00 20.00
Joe Ruttman O/P/S/T/V 8.00 20.00
Elliott Sadler O/S/V 8.00 20.00
Johnny Sauter O/P/S/T/V 8.00 20.00
Ken Schrader O/P/S/T/V 6.00 15.00
Dennis Setzer O/P/S/V 6.00 15.00
Mike Skinner O/S/V 6.00 15.00
Jimmy Spencer O/P/S/T/V 8.00 20.00
Jack Sprague O/P/S/T/V 8.00 20.00
Mike Stefanik O/P/S/T/V 6.00 15.00
Tony Stewart O 40.00 100.00
Cam Strader O/P/S/T/V 6.00 15.00
Hut Stricklin O/P/S/T/V 6.00 15.00
Rusty Wallace O/P/S/V 12.50 30.00
Michael Waltrip O/P/S/T/V 10.00 25.00
Scott Wimmer O/P/S/T/V 8.00 20.00
Glen Wood O/P/S/T/V 6.00 15.00
Jon Wood O/P/S/T/V 8.00 20.00
Cale Yarborough O/P/S/T/V 10.00 25.00

2002 Press Pass Signings Gold

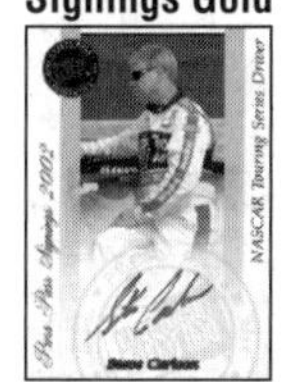

This set, which is a partial parallel of the Signings insert set features driver's signatures in Gold Ink. Each of these cards were issued to a stated print run of 50 serial numbered sets.

1 Bobby Allison O/P/S/T/V 40.00 80.00
2 John Andretti O/P/S/T/V 20.00 50.00
3 Buddy Baker O/P/S/T/V 25.00 60.00
4 Kyle Berck O/P/S/T/V 20.00 50.00
5 Greg Biffle O/S/V 40.00 100.00
6 Dave Blaney O/P/S/T/V 25.00 60.00
7 Brett Bodine O/P/S/T/V 20.00 50.00
8 Todd Bodine O/P/S/T/V 20.00 50.00
9 Jeff Burton O/S/T/V 30.00 80.00
10 Ward Burton O/P/S/T/V 25.00 60.00
11 Kurt Busch O/P/S/T/V 40.00 80.00
12 Steve Carlson O/P/S/T/V 20.00 50.00
13 Matt Crafton O/P/S/T/V 20.00 50.00
14 Dale Earnhardt Jr. 125.00 250.00
15 Kerry Earnhardt O/P/S/T/V 30.00 80.00
16 Larry Foyt O/P/S/T/V 25.00 60.00
17 Coy Gibbs P/S/T/V 20.00 50.00
18 Jeff Gordon O/P/S/T/V 150.00 300.00
19 David Green O/P/S/T/V 20.00 50.00
20 Jeff Green O/P/S/T/V 20.00 50.00
21 Mark Green O/P/S/V 20.00 50.00
22 Bobby Hamilton O/P/S/T/V 30.00 80.00
23 Kevin Hamlin O/P/S/T/V 20.00 50.00
24 Kevin Harvick O/P/S/T/V 40.00 80.00
25 Dale Jarrett O/P/S/T/V 40.00 100.00
26 Ned Jarrett O/P/S/T/V 25.00 60.00
27 Jimmie Johnson O/P/S/T/V 60.00 120.00
28 Junior Johnson O/P/S/T/V 30.00 80.00
29 Buckshot Jones O/P/S/T/V 25.00 60.00
30 Jason Keller O/P/S/V 25.00 60.00
31 Matt Kenseth O/P/S/T/V 50.00 120.00
32 Travis Kvapil O/P/S/T/V 30.00 80.00
33 Bobby Labonte O/P/S/T/V 30.00 60.00
34 Terry Labonte O/S/T/V 50.00 120.00
35 Randy Lajoie O/P/S/T/V 20.00 50.00
36 Jason Leffler O/P/S/T/V 20.00 50.00
37 Chad Little P/S/T/V 20.00 50.00
38 Sterling Marlin O/P/S/T/V 40.00 100.00
39 Mark Martin O/P/S/T/V 75.00 150.00
40 Jeremy Mayfield O/P/S/T/V 30.00 80.00
41 Jamie McMurray O/P/S/T/V 30.00 60.00
42 Casey Mears O/S/V 30.00 80.00
43 Ted Musgrave O/P/S/T/V 20.00 50.00
44 Jerry Nadeau O/P/S/T/V 20.00 50.00
45 Ryan Newman O/P/S/T/V 30.00 60.00
46 Hank Parker Jr. O/S/T/V 20.00 50.00
47 Benny Parsons O/P/S/T/V 50.00 100.00
48 David Pearson O/P/S/T/V 50.00 120.00
49 Kyle Petty O/P/S/T/V 30.00 80.00
50 Richard Petty O/P/S/T/V 50.00 100.00
51 Craig Raudman O/P/S/T/V 20.00 50.00
52 Ricky Rudd O/P/S/T/V 25.00 60.00
53 Joe Ruttman P/S/T/V 25.00 60.00
54 Elliott Sadler O/S/V 25.00 60.00
55 Johnny Sauter P/S/T/V 25.00 60.00
56 Ken Schrader O/P/S/T/V 20.00 50.00
57 Dennis Setzer O/P/S/T/V 20.00 50.00
58 Mike Skinner O/S/V 20.00 50.00
59 Jimmy Spencer O/P/S/T/V 25.00 60.00
60 Jack Sprague P/S/T/V 25.00 60.00
61 Mike Stefanik O/P/S/T/V 20.00 50.00
62 Cam Strader O/P/S/T/V 20.00 50.00
63 Hut Stricklin O/P/S/T/V 20.00 50.00
64 Rusty Wallace O/P/S/T/V 50.00 100.00
65 Darrell Waltrip O/P/S/T/V 40.00 100.00
66 Michael Waltrip O/P/S/T/V 25.00 60.00
67 Scott Wimmer P/S/T/V 25.00 60.00
68 Glen Wood O/P/S/T/V 20.00 50.00
69 Jon Wood O/P/S/T/V 20.00 50.00
70 Cale Yarborough O/P/S/T/V 30.00 80.00

2002 Press Pass Signings Transparent

Randomly inserted into packs, these nine cards feature clear plastic cards signed in blue ink by the featured driver. Note that Tony Stewart only signed cards for this version of the Signings inserts. Each card in this set was issued to a stated print run of 100 serial numbered cards. The Dale Earnhardt Jr. cards were issued via mail redemptions fulfilled in 2003.

1 Dale Earnhardt Jr. 100.00 200.00
2 Jeff Gordon O/P/S/T/V 125.00 250.00
3 Kevin Harvick O/P/S/T/V 25.00 60.00
4 Dale Jarrett O/P/S/T/V 30.00 60.00
5 Matt Kenseth O
6 Bobby Labonte O/P/S/T/V 20.00 50.00
7 Ryan Newman O/P/S/T/V 15.00 40.00
8 Ricky Rudd O/P/S/T/V 15.00 40.00
9 Tony Stewart O/P/S/T/V 60.00 120.00
10 Rusty Wallace O/P/S/T/V 40.00 80.00

2003 Press Pass Signings

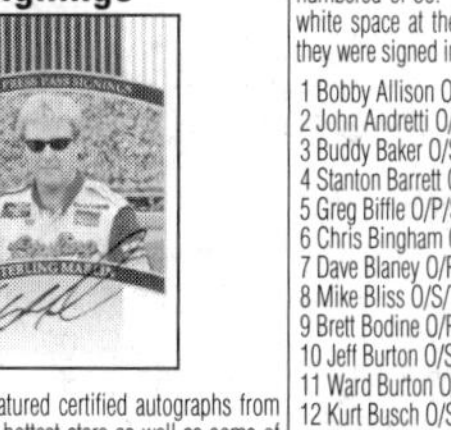

This 75-card set featured certified autographs from some of NASCAR's hottest stars as well as some of the retired greats. Some of these cards were found in packs of 2003 Press Pass, 2003 Press Pass Stealth, 2003 Press Pass Trackside, 2003 VIP or a combination of these and are tagged as such. The stated odd were 1 in 48 packs in Press Pass Premium, and 1 in 84 packs in Press Pass Stealth,Press Pass Trackside and VIP. The card fronts have a designated white space at the bottom for the autographs.

STATED ODDS 1:84 2003 TRACKSIDE
STATED ODDS 1:84 2003 VIP

1 Bobby Allison O/S/T/V 15.00 40.00
2 John Andretti O/P/S/T/V 8.00 20.00
3 Buddy Baker O/S/T/V 8.00 20.00
4 Stanton Barrett O/S/T/V 8.00 20.00
5 Greg Biffle O/P/S/T/V 10.00 25.00
6 Chris Bingham O/S 10.00 25.00
7 Dave Blaney O/P/S/T/V 6.00 15.00
8 Mike Bliss O/S/T/V 6.00 15.00
9 Brett Bodine O/P/S/T/V 6.00 15.00
10 Jeff Burton O/S/V 8.00 20.00
11 Ward Burton O/P/S/T/V 8.00 20.00
12 Kurt Busch O/S/T/V 12.50 30.00
13 Steve Carlson O/P/S/T/V 6.00 15.00
14 Matt Crafton O/S/V 8.00 20.00
15 Ricky Craven O/P/S/T/V 10.00 25.00
16 Rick Crawford O/S/T/V 6.00 15.00
17 Dale Earnhardt Jr. O/S/V/04PP 60.00 120.00
18 Kerry Earnhardt O/S 12.50 30.00
19 Carl Edwards O/S/V 25.00 60.00
20 Christian Fittipaldi O/S/T/V 8.00 20.00
21 Jeff Fultz O/P/S/T/V 6.00 15.00
22 Coy Gibbs O/S/T/V 6.00 15.00
23 Jeff Gordon O/P/S/T/V 100.00 175.00
24 Robby Gordon O/P/S/T/V 10.00 25.00
25 Tina Gordon O/S/V 10.00 25.00
26 David Green O/S/T/V 6.00 15.00
27 Jeff Green P/T 6.00 15.00
28 Kevin Hamlin O/P/S/T/V 6.00 15.00
29 Kevin Harvick O/P/S/T/V 12.50 30.00
30 Shane Hmiel O/S/T/V 15.00 40.00
31 Jake Hobgood O/P/S/T/V 6.00 15.00
32 Andy Houston O/S/T/V 6.00 15.00
33 Dale Jarrett O/P/S/T/V 15.00 40.00
34 Ned Jarrett O/S/T/V 10.00 25.00
35 Jimmie Johnson O/P/S/T/V 40.00 80.00
36 Kasey Kahne O 40.00 80.00
37 Jason Keller O/P/S/T/V 8.00 20.00
38 Matt Kenseth O/P/S/T/V 15.00 40.00
39 Travis Kvapil O/P/S/T/V 10.00 25.00
40 Bobby Labonte O/P/S/T/V 15.00 40.00
41 Terry Labonte O/P/S/T/V 15.00 40.00
42 Randy LaJoie O/P/S/T/V 6.00 15.00
43 Damon Lusk O/S/T/V 6.00 15.00
44 Steadman Marlin O/S/T/V 8.00 20.00
45 Sterling Marlin O/P/S/T/V 12.50 30.00
46 Mark Martin O/P/S/T/V 30.00 60.00
47 Jeremy Mayfield O/P/S/T/V 10.00 25.00
48 Jamie McMurray O/S/T/V 10.00 25.00
49 Casey Mears O/S/T/V 10.00 25.00
50 Chase Montgomery O/S/V 8.00 20.00
51 Jerry Nadeau O/S/T/V 10.00 25.00
52 Joe Nemechek O/S/T/V 8.00 20.00
53 Ryan Newman O/P/S/T/V 15.00 30.00
54 Eric Norris O/S/T/V 10.00 25.00
55 Steve Park P/T 15.00 40.00
56 Benny Parsons O/S/T/V 30.00 60.00
57 David Pearson O/S/T/V 15.00 40.00
58 Kyle Petty O/P/S/T/V 10.00 25.00
59 Richard Petty O/S/T/V 40.00 80.00
60 Tony Raines O/S/T/V 6.00 15.00
61 Scott Riggs O/P/S/T/V 10.00 25.00
62 Ricky Rudd O/P/S/T/V 12.50 30.00
63 Andy Santerre O/P/S/T/V 8.00 20.00
64 Johnny Sauter O/P/S/T/V 8.00 20.00
65 Ken Schrader O/S/T/V 8.00 20.00
66 Mike Skinner O/P/S/T/V 8.00 20.00
67 Regan Smith O/S/V 6.00 15.00
68 Jimmy Spencer O/S/T/V 8.00 20.00
69 Jack Sprague O/S/V 6.00 15.00
70 Tony Stewart O/S/V 40.00 100.00
71 Jimmy Vasser O/S/V 8.00 20.00
72 Brian Vickers O/S/T/V 10.00 25.00
73 Rusty Wallace O/P/S/T/V 12.50 30.00
74 Michael Waltrip O/P/S/T/V 10.00 25.00
75 Scott Wimmer O/S/T/V 10.00 25.00
76 Glen Wood O/S/T/V 6.00 15.00
77 Jon Wood O/S/V 8.00 20.00
78 Cale Yarborough O/S/T/V 10.00 25.00
79 Robert Yates O/S/T/V 20.00 40.00

2003 Press Pass Signings Gold

This 75-card set featured certified autographs from some of NASCAR's hottest stars as well as some of the retired greats. Some of these cards were found in packs of 2003 Press Pass, 2003 Press Pass Stealth, 2003 Press Pass Trackside, 2003 VIP or a combination of these and are tagged as such. The cards were randomly inserted in packs and hand numbered of 50. The card fronts have a designated white space at the bottom for the autographs, and they were signed in gold.

1 Bobby Allison O/S/T/V 30.00 80.00
2 John Andretti O/P/S/T 15.00 40.00
3 Buddy Baker O/S/T/V 15.00 40.00
4 Stanton Barrett O/S/T/V 15.00 40.00
5 Greg Biffle O/P/S/T/V 25.00 60.00
6 Chris Bingham O/S 20.00 50.00
7 Dave Blaney O/P/S/T/V 15.00 40.00
8 Mike Bliss O/S/T/V 12.50 30.00
9 Brett Bodine O/P/S/T/V 12.50 30.00
10 Jeff Burton O/S/V 20.00 50.00
11 Ward Burton O/P/S/T/V 20.00 50.00
12 Kurt Busch O/S/T/V 40.00 80.00
13 Steve Carlson O/P/S/T/V 12.50 30.00
14 Matt Crafton O/S/V 15.00 40.00
15 Ricky Craven O/P/S/T/V 20.00 50.00
16 Rick Crawford O/S/V 12.50 30.00
17 Dale Earnhardt Jr. O/S/V/04PP 125.00 250.00
18 Kerry Earnhardt O/S 25.00 60.00
19 Carl Edwards O/S/V 60.00 120.00
20 Christian Fittipaldi O/S/T/V 15.00 40.00
21 Jeff Fultz O/P/S/T/V 12.50 30.00
22 Coy Gibbs O/S/T/V 12.50 30.00
23 Jeff Gordon O/P/S/T/V 150.00 300.00
24 Robby Gordon O/P/S/T/V 20.00 50.00
25 Tina Gordon O/S/V 25.00 50.00
26 David Green O/S/T/V 12.50 30.00
27 Jeff Green O/P/S/T 12.50 30.00
28 Kevin Hamlin O/P/S/T/V 12.50 30.00
29 Kevin Harvick O/P/S/T/V 40.00 80.00
30 Shane Hmiel O/S/V 30.00 80.00
31 Jake Hobgood O/P/S/T/V 12.50 30.00
32 Andy Houston O/S/T/V 12.50 30.00
33 Dale Jarrett O/P/S/T/V 40.00 100.00
34 Ned Jarrett O/S/T/V 15.00 40.00
35 Jimmie Johnson O/P/S/T/V 60.00 120.00
36 Kasey Kahne O 125.00 250.00
37 Jason Keller O/P/S/T/V 15.00 40.00
38 Matt Kenseth O/P/S/T/V 60.00 120.00
39 Travis Kvapil O/P/S/T/V 20.00 50.00
40 Bobby Labonte O/P/S/T/V 30.00 60.00
41 Terry Labonte O/P/S/T/V 60.00 120.00
42 Randy LaJoie O/P/S/T/V 12.50 30.00
43 Damon Lusk O/S/T/V 12.50 30.00
44 Steadman Marlin O/S/T/V 15.00 40.00
45 Sterling Marlin O/P/S/T/V 40.00 100.00
46 Mark Martin O/P/S/T/V 75.00 150.00
47 Jeremy Mayfield O/P/S/T/V 20.00 50.00
48 Jamie McMurray O/S/T/V 30.00 60.00
49 Casey Mears O/S/T/V 25.00 60.00
50 Chase Montgomery O/S/V 15.00 40.00
51 Jerry Nadeau O/S/T/V 20.00 50.00
52 Joe Nemechek O/S/T/V 15.00 40.00
53 Ryan Newman O/P/S/T/V 30.00 60.00
54 Eric Norris O/S/T/V 20.00 50.00
55 Steve Park O/P/S/T 60.00 120.00
56 Benny Parsons O/S/T/V 50.00 100.00
57 David Pearson O/S/T/V 30.00 80.00
58 Kyle Petty O/P/S/T/V 20.00 50.00
59 Richard Petty O/S/T/V 50.00 100.00
60 Tony Raines O/S/T/V 12.50 30.00
61 Scott Riggs O/P/S/T/V 15.00 40.00
62 Ricky Rudd O/P/S/T/V 25.00 60.00
63 Elliott Sadler O
64 Andy Santerre O/P/S/T/V 15.00 40.00
65 Johnny Sauter O/P/S/T/V 15.00 40.00
66 Ken Schrader O/S/T/V 15.00 40.00
67 Mike Skinner O/P/S/T/V 15.00 40.00
68 Regan Smith O/S/V 12.50 30.00
69 Jimmy Spencer O/S/T/V 15.00 40.00
70 Jack Sprague O/S/ V 12.50 30.00
71 Tony Stewart O/S/V 100.00 175.00
72 Brian Vickers O/S/T/V 50.00 100.00
73 Kenny Wallace 20.00 50.00
74 Rusty Wallace O/S 50.00 100.00
75 Michael Waltrip O/P/S/T/V 25.00 60.00
76 Scott Wimmer O/S/T/V 20.00 50.00
77 Glen Wood O/S/T/V 12.50 30.00
78 Jon Wood O/S/V 15.00 40.00
79 Cale Yarborough O/S/T/V 20.00 50.00
80 Robert Yates O/S/T/V 30.00 80.00

2003 Press Pass Signings Transparent

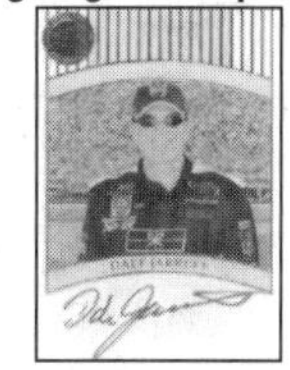

This 8-card set featured certified autographs from some of NASCAR's hottest stars. Some of these cards were found in packs of 2003 Press Pass, 2003 Press Pass Stealth, 2003 Press Pass Trackside, 2003 VIP or a combination of these and are tagged as such. The cards were randomly inserted and hand numbered to 100. The cards were of the same design as the basic version with the exception that these were done on a clear plastic card stock.

1 Kurt Busch O/S/T/V 30.00 60.00
2 Jeff Gordon O/P/S/T/V 125.00 250.00
3 Kevin Harvick O/P/S/T/V 30.00 60.00
4 Dale Jarrett O/P/S/T/V 30.00 60.00
5 Jimmie Johnson O/P/S/T/V 50.00 100.00
6 Bobby Labonte O/P/S/T/V 20.00 50.00
7 Ryan Newman O/P/S/T/V 15.00 40.00
8 Tony Stewart O/S/V 60.00 120.00

2004 Press Pass Signings

This 70-card set featured certified autographs from some of NASCAR's hottest stars as well as some of the retired greats. Some of these cards were found in packs of 2004 Press Pass Optima, 2004 Press Pass Premium, 2004 Press Pass Stealth, 2004 Press Pass Trackside, 2004 VIP or a combination of these and are tagged as such. The stated odd were 1 in 48

packs in Press Pass Premium, and 1 in 84 packs in Press Pass Stealth,Press Pass Trackside and VIP.

1 Bobby Allison O/P/S/T/V 8.00 20.00
2 Greg Biffle BGN T/V 10.00 25.00
3 Greg Biffle NC O/S/T/V 10.00 25.00
4 Dave Blaney O/V 6.00 15.00
5 Mike Bliss T/V 6.00 15.00
6 Clint Bowyer S/T/V 12.50 30.00
7 Charlie Bradberry T/V 6.00 15.00
8 Jeff Burton O/T/V 8.00 20.00
9 Kurt Busch S/T/V 12.50 30.00
10 Kyle Busch O/P/S/T/V 25.00 60.00
11 Steve Carlson P/S/T/V 6.00 15.00
12 Stacy Compton T/V 6.00 15.00
13 Terry Cook O 8.00 20.00
14 Matt Crafton T/V 8.00 20.00
15 Ricky Craven O/P/S/T/V 10.00 25.00
16 Rick Crawford O 8.00 20.00
17 Dale Earnhardt Jr. O/T/V 60.00 120.00
18 Carl Edwards O/P/S/T/V 25.00 50.00
19 Tim Fedewa O/T/V 8.00 20.00
20 Brendan Gaughan O/P/S/T/V 12.50 30.00
21 Jeff Gordon O/P/S/T/V 100.00 175.00
22 Robby Gordon O/T/V 10.00 25.00
23 Tina Gordon O 10.00 25.00
24 David Green O/P/S/T/V 6.00 15.00
25 Jeff Green O/V 8.00 20.00
26 Kevin Harvick O/P/S/T/V 12.50 30.00
27 Ron Hornaday T/V 10.00 25.00
28 Robert Huffman P/S/T/V 6.00 15.00
29 Dale Jarrett O/P/S/T/V 15.00 40.00
30 Ned Jarrett 8.00 20.00
31 Jeff Jefferson S/T/V 6.00 15.00
32 Jimmie Johnson O/P/S/T/V 40.00 80.00
33 Kasey Kahne BGN O/S/T/V 25.00 60.00
34 Kasey Kahne NCS O/S/T/V 25.00 60.00
35 Jason Keller O/S/T/V 6.00 15.00
36 Matt Kenseth BGN O/V 15.00 40.00
37 Matt Kenseth NCS O/P/S/T/V 15.00 40.00
38 Bobby Labonte O/P/S/T/V 15.00 40.00
39 Terry Labonte O/S/T/V 15.00 40.00
40 Sterling Marlin O/P/S/T/V 12.50 30.00
41 Mark Martin O/T/V 30.00 60.00
42 Jeremy Mayfield O/S/T/V 10.00 25.00
43 Jamie McMurray O 10.00 25.00
44 Casey Mears O/P/S/T 10.00 25.00
45 Paul Menard V 10.00 25.00
46 Joe Nemechek O 10.00 25.00
47 Ryan Newman O/P/S/T/V 15.00 30.00
48 Steve Park O 15.00 40.00
49 Benny Parsons P/S/T/V 30.00 60.00
50 David Pearson P/S/T/V 10.00 25.00
51 Kyle Petty O/P/S/T/V 10.00 25.00
52 Richard Petty O/P/S/T/V 40.00 80.00
53 Scott Riggs O/S/T/V 8.00 20.00
54 Ricky Rudd O/P/S/T/V 10.00 25.00
55 Andy Santerre P/S/T/V 6.00 15.00
56 Johnny Sauter NCS T/V 8.00 20.00
57 Dennis Setzer P/S/T/V 6.00 15.00
59 Tony Stewart O/P/S/T 40.00 80.00
59 Jack Sprague O 6.00 15.00
60 Todd Szegedy S/T/V 6.00 15.00
61 Martin Truex Jr. O 15.00 40.00
62 Kenny Wallace T/V 10.00 25.00
63 Rusty Wallace O/S/T/V 12.50 30.00
64 Michael Waltrip O/P/S/T/V 10.00 25.00
65 Scott Wimmer O/P/S/T/V 8.00 20.00
66 Glen Wood O/P/S/T/V 6.00 15.00
67 Jon Wood O/P/S/T/V 8.00 20.00
68 Cale Yarborough O/P/S/T/V 10.00 25.00
69 Robert Yates P/S/T/V 8.00 20.00
70 J.J. Yeley T/V 12.50 30.00

2004 Press Pass Signings Gold

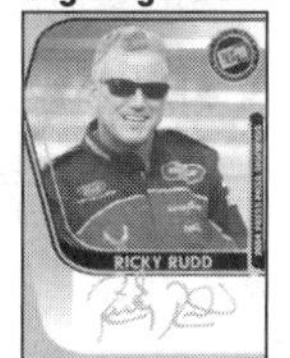

This 66-card set featured certified autographs from some of NASCAR's hottest stars as well as some of the retired greats. Some of these cards were found in packs of 2004 Press Pass Optima, 2004 Press Pass Premium, 2004 Press Pass Stealth, 2004 Press Pass Trackside, 2004 VIP or a combination of these and are tagged as such. The cards were randomly inserted in packs and hand numbered of 50. The card fronts have a designated white space at the bottom for the autographs, and they were signed in gold.

*UNLISTED GOLDS: 1X TO 2.5X BASIC SIGNINGS

1 Bobby Allison O/P/S/T/V 20.00 50.00
2 Greg Biffle BGN S/T/V 25.00 60.00
3 Greg Biffle NC O/S/T/V 25.00 60.00
4 Dave Blaney O/V 25.00 60.00
5 Mike Bliss T/V 15.00 40.00
6 Clint Bowyer S/T/V 20.00 50.00
7 Charlie Bradberry T/V 15.00 40.00
8 Jeff Burton O/T/V 25.00 60.00
9 Kurt Busch O/S/T/V 40.00 80.00
10 Kyle Busch O/P/S/T/V 125.00 250.00
11 Steve Carlson P/S/T/V 15.00 40.00
12 Stacy Compton T/V 15.00 40.00
13 Matt Crafton T/V 20.00 50.00
14 Ricky Craven O/P/S/T/V 25.00 60.00
15 Rick Crawford O 20.00 50.00
16 Dale Earnhardt Jr. O/P/S/T/V 125.00 250.00
17 Carl Edwards O/P/S/T/V 50.00 100.00
18 Tim Fedewa O 20.00 50.00
19 Brendan Gaughan O/P/S/T/V 30.00 80.00
20 Jeff Gordon O/P/S/T/V 150.00 300.00
21 Robby Gordon O/T/V 25.00 60.00
22 David Green O/P/S/T/V 15.00 40.00
23 Jeff Green O/V 20.00 50.00
24 Kevin Harvick O/P/S/T/V 40.00 80.00
25 Ron Hornaday T/V 25.00 60.00
26 Robert Huffman P/S/T/V 15.00 40.00
27 Dale Jarrett O/P/S/T/V 40.00 100.00
28 Jeff Jefferson S/T/V 15.00 40.00
29 Jimmie Johnson O/P/S/T/V 60.00 120.00
30 Kasey Kahne BGN O/S/T/V 60.00 120.00
31 Kasey Kahne NC O/S/T/V 75.00 150.00
32 Jason Keller O/S/T/V 15.00 40.00
33 Matt Kenseth BGN O/V 40.00 80.00
34 Matt Kenseth NCS O/P/S/T/V 50.00 100.00
35 Bobby Labonte O/P/S/T/V 30.00 60.00
36 Terry Labonte O/S/T/V 60.00 120.00
37 Sterling Marlin O/P/S/T/V 40.00 100.00
38 Mark Martin O/T/V 75.00 150.00
39 Jeremy Mayfield O/S/T/V 25.00 60.00
40 Jamie McMurray O/T/V 30.00 80.00
41 Casey Mears O/P/S/T/V 25.00 60.00
42 Paul Menard V 30.00 80.00
43 Ryan Newman/20 O/P/S/T/V 50.00 100.00
44 Steve Park O 25.00 60.00
45 Benny Parsons P/S/T/V 50.00 100.00
46 David Pearson P/S/T/V 25.00 60.00
47 Kyle Petty O/P/S/T/V 25.00 60.00
48 Richard Petty O/P/S/T/V 50.00 100.00
49 Scott Riggs O/S/T/V 20.00 50.00
50 Ricky Rudd O/P/S/T/V 25.00 60.00
51 Andy Santerre P/S/T/V 15.00 40.00
52 Johnny Sauter BGN T/V 20.00 50.00
53 Johnny Sauter NCS T/V 20.00 50.00
54 Dennis Setzer P/S/T/V 15.00 40.00
55 Tony Stewart O/S/T/V 100.00 175.00
56 Todd Szegedy S/T/V 15.00 40.00
57 Martin Truex Jr. O 100.00 200.00
58 Kenny Wallace T/V 25.00 60.00
59 Rusty Wallace O/P/S/T/V 50.00 100.00
60 Michael Waltrip O/P/S/T/V 25.00 60.00
61 Scott Wimmer O/S/T/V 20.00 50.00
62 Glen Wood O/P/S/T/V 15.00 40.00
63 Jon Wood O/P/S/T/V 20.00 50.00
64 Cale Yarborough O/P/S/T/V 25.00 60.00
65 Robert Yates O/P/S/T/V 20.00 50.00
66 J.J. Yeley T/V 30.00 80.00

2004 Press Pass Signings Transparent

This 11-card set featured certified autographs from some of NASCAR's hottest stars. Some of these cards were found in packs of 2004 Press Pass Optima, 2004 Press Pass Premium, 2004 Press Pass Stealth, 2004 Press Pass Trackside or a combination of these and are tagged as such. The cards were randomly inserted in packs and hand numbered of 100. The cards were produced on a transparent plactic stock.

1 Jeff Gordon O/P/S/T 125.00 250.00
2 Kevin Harvick O/P/S/T 30.00 60.00
3 Jimmie Johnson O/P/S/T 50.00 100.00
4 Matt Kenseth O/P/S/T 40.00 80.00
5 Bobby Labonte O/P/S/T 20.00 50.00
6 Ryan Newman O/S/T 15.00 40.00
7 Richard Petty O/P/T 50.00 100.00
8 Ricky Rudd O/P/T 40.00 80.00
9 Tony Stewart O/S/T 60.00 120.00
10 Rusty Wallace O/P/S/T 40.00 80.00
11 Michael Waltrip O/P/S/T 20.00 50.00

2005 Press Pass Signings

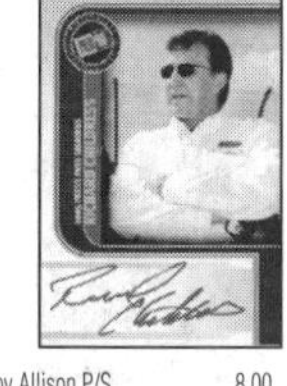

1 Bobby Allison P/S 8.00 20.00
2 John Andretti S 7.50 15.00
3 Dave Blaney 6.00 15.00
4 Clint Bowyer 12.50 30.00
5 Kurt Busch P/S 12.50 30.00
6 Kyle Busch 20.00 50.00
7 Richard Childress P/S 8.00 20.00
8 Terry Cook P/S 7.50 15.00
9 Ricky Craven 10.00 25.00
10 Rick Crawford 7.50 15.00
11 Justin Diercks P/S 8.00 20.00
12 Mike Duncan P/S 7.50 15.00
13 Dale Earnhardt Jr. 60.00 120.00
14 Carl Edwards BGN 25.00 50.00
15 Carl Edwards NC 25.00 50.00
16 Jeff Fultz P/S 7.50 15.00
17 Harry Gant P/S 8.00 20.00
18 Jeff Gordon P/S 100.00 175.00
19 David Green 6.00 15.00
20 Jeff Green P/S 7.50 15.00
21 Denny Hamlin 40.00 80.00
22 Kevin Harvick P/S 12.50 30.00
23 Tony Hirschman P/S 7.50 15.00
24 Dale Jarrett P/S 15.00 40.00
25 Jeff Jefferson P/S 7.50 15.00
26 Jimmie Johnson P/S 40.00 80.00
27 Kasey Kahne BGN S 25.00 60.00
28 Kasey Kahne NC P/S 25.00 60.00
29 Matt Kenseth BGN
30 Matt Kenseth NC P/S 15.00 40.00
31 Travis Kvapil 10.00 25.00
32 Bobby Labonte 15.00 40.00
33 Justin Labonte P/S 8.00 20.00
34 Terry Labonte 15.00 40.00
35 Bill Lester S 10.00 25.00

36 Fred Lorenzen P/S 8.00 20.00
37 Sterling Marlin 12.50 30.00
38 Mark Martin P/S 30.00 60.00
39 Jeremy Mayfield S 10.00 25.00
40 Jamie McMurray 10.00 25.00
41 Casey Mears 10.00 25.00
42 Joe Nemechek P/S 8.00 20.00
43 Ryan Newman P/S 15.00 30.00
44 Benny Parsons P/S 30.00 60.00
45 David Pearson P/S 10.00 25.00
46 Richard Petty P/S 40.00 80.00
47 Scott Riggs P/S 7.50 15.00
48 Ricky Rudd P/S 12.50 30.00
49 Boris Said S 8.00 20.00
50 Andy Santerre P/S 7.50 15.00
51 Dennis Setzer P/S 7.50 15.00
52 Reed Sorenson 15.00 40.00
53 Jack Sprague P/S 7.50 15.00
54 David Stremme 25.00 50.00
55 Tony Stewart P/S 40.00 80.00
56 Brian Vickers S 10.00 25.00
57 Kenny Wallace 10.00 25.00
58 Rusty Wallace 12.50 30.00
59 Michael Waltrip P/S 10.00 25.00
60 Rex White P/S 7.50 15.00
61 Scott Wimmer P/S 7.50 15.00
62 Glen Wood P/S 6.00 15.00
63 Jon Wood S 7.50 15.00
64 Cale Yarborough P/S 8.00 20.00
65 J.J. Yeley 10.00 25.00

2005 Press Pass Signings Gold

3 Clint Bowyer 20.00 50.00
4 Kurt Busch P/S 40.00 80.00
5 Kyle Busch NC 125.00 200.00
8 Ricky Craven 15.00 40.00
9 Rick Crawford 12.50 30.00
10 Justin Diercks P/S 20.00 40.00
11 Mike Duncan P/S 15.00 30.00
13 Carl Edwards BGN 60.00 120.00
14 Carl Edwards NC 75.00 150.00
17 Jeff Gordon P/S 150.00 300.00
20 Denny Hamlin 100.00 175.00
21 Kevin Harvick P/S 40.00 80.00
23 Dale Jarrett P/S 40.00 100.00
25 Jimmie Johnson P/S 60.00 120.00
26 Kasey Kahne BGN S 60.00 120.00
27 Kasey Kahne NC P/S 60.00 120.00
28 Matt Kenseth P/S 50.00 100.00
30 Bobby Labonte 30.00 60.00
31 Justin Labonte P/S 30.00 60.00
32 Terry Labonte 40.00 80.00
35 Sterling Marlin 40.00 100.00
36 Mark Martin P/S 75.00 150.00
38 Jamie McMurray 30.00 60.00
41 Ryan Newman P/S 30.00 60.00
42 Benny Parsons P/S 50.00 100.00
44 Richard Petty P/S 50.00 100.00
50 Reed Sorenson 40.00 80.00
52 Tony Stewart P/S 100.00 175.00
53 David Stremme 40.00 80.00
54 Martin Truex Jr. 40.00 80.00
55 Brian Vickers S 20.00 50.00
57 Rusty Wallace 50.00 100.00
58 Michael Waltrip P/S 25.00 60.00
64 J.J. Yeley 20.00 50.00

2005 Press Pass Signings Platinum

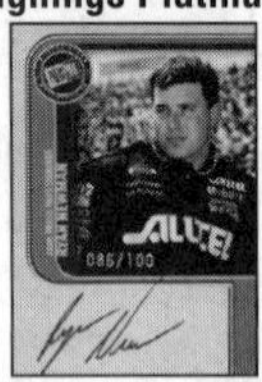

STSTED PRINT RUN 100 SERIAL #'d SETS
SOME CARDS WERE RELEASED w/o SERIAL #'s
3 Dave Blaney 12.50 30.00
4 Kurt Busch P/S 30.00 60.00
5 Kyle Busch 40.00 80.00
11 Dale Earnhardt Jr. 100.00 200.00
13 Carl Edwards BGN 50.00 100.00
14 Carl Edwards NC 60.00 120.00
17 Jeff Gordon P/S 100.00 200.00
18 David Green 10.00 25.00
20 Denny Hamlin 60.00 120.00
21 Kevin Harvick P/S 25.00 60.00
23 Dale Jarrett P/S 30.00 60.00
25 Jimmie Johnson P/S 50.00 100.00
27 Kasey Kahne NC P/S 40.00 80.00
28 Matt Kenseth NC P/S 40.00 80.00
29 Bobby Labonte 20.00 50.00
30 Justin Labonte P/S 15.00 30.00
31 Terry Labonte 20.00 40.00
34 Sterling Marlin 25.00 60.00
35 Mark Martin P/S 50.00 100.00
37 Jamie McMurray 20.00 50.00
39 Ryan Newman P/S 15.00 40.00
40 Benny Parsons P/S 40.00 80.00
42 Richard Petty P/S 50.00 100.00
48 Reed Sorenson 15.00 40.00
50 Tony Stewart P/S 60.00 120.00
51 David Stremme 30.00 60.00
52 Brian Vickers S 15.00 40.00
53 Michael Waltrip P/S 20.00 50.00

2006 Press Pass Signings

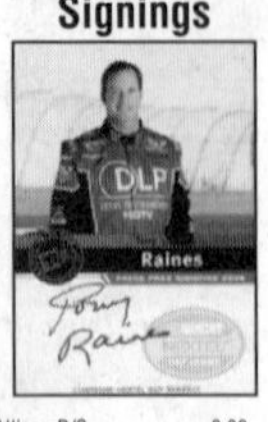

1 Bobby Allison P/S 8.00 20.00
2 Donnie Allison S 8.00 20.00
3 Buddy Baker P/S 7.50 15.00
4 Greg Biffle NC S 10.00 25.00
5 Dave Blaney NC S 6.00 15.00
6 Clint Bowyer NC S 15.00 40.00
7 Jeff Burton NC S 8.00 20.00
8 Kurt Busch NC S 12.50 30.00
9 Kyle Busch NC S 20.00 50.00
10 Terry Cook CTS P/S 6.00 15.00
11 Rick Crawford CTS S 5.00 12.00
12 Erin Crocker CTS P/S 20.00 50.00
13 Erik Darnell CTS S 8.00 20.00
14 Dale Earnhardt Jr. NC S 60.00 120.00
15 Carl Edwards 20.00 50.00
16 Harry Gant P/S 8.00 20.00
17 Jeff Gordon NC P/S 100.00 175.00
18 Robby Gordon NC S 10.00 25.00
19 David Green NBS P/S 5.00 12.00
20 Denny Hamlin V 30.00 60.00
21 Kevin Harvick NC P/S 12.50 30.00
22 Ron Hornaday CTS P/S 6.00 15.00
23 Jack Ingram P/S 6.00 15.00
24 Dale Jarrett NC P/S 15.00 40.00
25 Jimmie Johnson NC P/S 40.00 80.00
26 Kasey Kahne NC P/S 25.00 60.00
27 Matt Kenseth NC P/S 15.00 40.00
28 Todd Kluever NBS S 10.00 25.00
29 Bobby Labonte NC S 15.00 40.00
30 Terry Labonte NC S 15.00 40.00
31 Bill Lester CTS S 10.00 25.00
32 Fred Lorenzen P/S 7.50 15.00
33 Sterling Marlin NC S 15.00 30.00
34 Mark Martin NC S 30.00 60.00
35 Jeremy Mayfield NC S 8.00 20.00
36 Mark McFarland NBS S 8.00 20.00
37 Jamie McMurray 10.00 25.00
38 Casey Mears NC P/S 10.00 25.00
39 Paul Menard 12.50 30.00
40 Joe Nemechek NC P/S 6.00 15.00
41 Ryan Newman NC S 15.00 30.00
42 Danny O'Quinn CTS S 15.00 30.00
43 Marvin Panch P/S 5.00 12.00
44 Benny Parsons P/S 30.00 60.00
45 David Pearson S 10.00 25.00
46 Richard Petty P/S 40.00 80.00
47 Tony Raines NC P/S 5.00 12.00
48 Scott Riggs NC P/S 6.00 15.00
49 Elliott Sadler NC S 20.00 50.00
50 Johnny Sauter V 8.00 20.00
51 Ken Schrader NC S 8.00 20.00
52 Brent Sherman NC S 12.50 30.00
53 Mike Skinner CTS P/S 8.00 20.00
54 Regan Smith NBS S 6.00 15.00
55 Reed Sorenson V 12.50 30.00
56 David Stremme NC P/S 12.50 30.00
57 Tony Stewart NC P/S 40.00 100.00
58 Martin Truex Jr. NC P/S 15.00 40.00
59 Brian Vickers NC S 10.00 25.00
60 Rex White P/S 5.00 12.00
61 Glen Wood P/S 6.00 15.00
62 Jon Wood NBS P/S 6.00 15.00
63 Cale Yarborough P/S 10.00 25.00
64 J.J. Yeley 12.50 30.00
NNO Entry Card Dale Jr. 1.50 4.00

2006 Press Pass Signings Gold

1 Bobby Allison P/S 15.00 40.00
2 Donnie Allison S 15.00 40.00
3 Buddy Baker P/S 12.50 30.00
4 Greg Biffle NC S 25.00 60.00
5 Clint Bowyer NC S 30.00 80.00
6 Jeff Burton NC S 20.00 50.00
7 Kurt Busch NC S 40.00 80.00
8 Kyle Busch NC S 60.00 120.00
9 Terry Cook CTS P/S 12.50 30.00
10 Rick Crawford CTS S 10.00 25.00
11 Erik Darnell CTS S 15.00 40.00
12 Dale Earnhardt Jr. NC S 125.00 250.00
13 Harry Gant P/S 20.00 50.00
14 Jeff Gordon NC P/S 150.00 300.00
15 Robby Gordon NC S 20.00 50.00
16 David Green NBS P/S 10.00 25.00
18 Kevin Harvick NC P/S 40.00 80.00
17 Denny Hamlin V 50.00 100.00
19 Ron Hornaday CTS P/S 12.50 30.00
20 Jack Ingram P/S 10.00 25.00
21 Dale Jarrett NC P/S 30.00 80.00
22 Jimmie Johnson NC P/S 60.00 120.00
23 Kasey Kahne NC P/S 60.00 120.00
24 Matt Kenseth NC P/S 50.00 100.00
25 Todd Kluever NBS S 30.00 60.00
26 Bobby Labonte NC S 30.00 80.00
27 Terry Labonte NC S 30.00 80.00
28 Bill Lester CTS S 25.00 60.00
29 Fred Lorenzen P/S 12.50 30.00
30 Sterling Marlin NC S 30.00 60.00
31 Mark Martin NC S 60.00 120.00
32 Jeremy Mayfield NC S 15.00 40.00
33 Mark McFarland NBS S 15.00 40.00
34 Casey Mears NC P/S 25.00 60.00
35 Joe Nemechek NC P/S 12.50 30.00
36 Ryan Newman NC S 30.00 60.00
37 Danny O'Quinn CTS S 30.00 60.00
38 Marvin Panch P/S 10.00 25.00
39 Benny Parsons P/S 50.00 100.00
40 David Pearson S 20.00 50.00
41 Richard Petty P/S 60.00 120.00
42 Tony Raines NC P/S 10.00 25.00
43 Scott Riggs NC P/S 12.50 30.00
44 Elliott Sadler NC S 40.00 100.00
45 Ken Schrader NC S 15.00 40.00
46 Brent Sherman NC S 20.00 50.00
47 Mike Skinner CTS P/S 12.50 30.00
48 Regan Smith NBS S 12.50 30.00
50 Tony Stewart NC P/S 100.00 175.00
51 David Stremme NC P/S 30.00 80.00
49 Reed Sorenson V 40.00 80.00
52 Martin Truex Jr. NC P/S 40.00 80.00
53 Brian Vickers NC S 20.00 50.00
54 Rex White P/S 12.50 30.00
55 Glen Wood P/S 12.50 30.00
56 Jon Wood NBS P/S 12.50 30.00
57 Cale Yarborough P/S 20.00 50.00

2006 Press Pass Signings Silver

1 Bobby Allison P/S 12.50 30.00
2 Donnie Allison S 15.00 40.00
3 Buddy Baker P/S 10.00 25.00
4 Greg Biffle NC S
5 Clint Bowyer NC S 20.00 50.00
6 Jeff Burton NC S 15.00 40.00
7 Kurt Busch NC S 30.00 60.00
8 Kyle Busch NC S 40.00 80.00
9 Terry Cook CTS P/S 8.00 20.00
10 Rick Crawford CTS S 6.00 15.00
11 Erin Crocker CTS P/S 30.00 60.00
12 Erik Darnell CTS S 10.00 25.00
13 Dale Earnhardt Jr. NC S 100.00 200.00
14 Carl Edwards 40.00 80.00
15 Harry Gant P/S 12.50 30.00
16 Jeff Gordon/50 P/S 125.00 250.00
17 Robby Gordon NC S 15.00 30.00
18 David Green NBS P/S 6.00 15.00
19 Jeff Green V 15.00 40.00
20 Denny Hamlin V 40.00 80.00
21 Kevin Harvick NC P/S 25.00 60.00
22 Ron Hornaday CTS P/S 10.00 25.00
23 Jack Ingram P/S 8.00 20.00
24 Dale Jarrett NC P/S 20.00 50.00
25 Jimmie Johnson NC P/S 50.00 100.00
26 Kasey Kahne NC P/S 40.00 80.00
27 Matt Kenseth NC P/S 40.00 80.00
28 Todd Kluever NBS S 25.00 60.00
29 Terry Labonte NC S 20.00 50.00
30 Bill Lester CTS S 15.00 40.00
31 Fred Lorenzen P/S 10.00 25.00
32 Sterling Marlin NC S 20.00 40.00
33 Mark Martin NC S 40.00 80.00
34 Jeremy Mayfield NC S 10.00 25.00
35 Mark McFarland NBS S 10.00 25.00
36 Jamie McMurray 20.00 50.00
37 Casey Mears NC P/S 12.50 30.00
38 Joe Nemechek NC P/S 8.00 20.00
39 Ryan Newman NC S 15.00 40.00
40 Danny O'Quinn CTS S 20.00 40.00
41 Marvin Panch P/S 8.00 20.00
42 Benny Parsons P/S 40.00 80.00
43 David Pearson S 12.50 30.00
44 Richard Petty P/S 50.00 100.00
45 Tony Raines NC P/S 6.00 15.00
46 Scott Riggs NC P/S 8.00 20.00
47 Elliott Sadler NC S 25.00 60.00
48 Ken Schrader NC S 10.00 25.00
49 Brent Sherman NC S 15.00 40.00
50 Mike Skinner CTS P/S 6.00 15.00
51 Regan Smith NBS S 8.00 20.00
52 Reed Sorenson V 15.00 40.00
53 Tony Stewart NC P/S 60.00 120.00
54 David Stremme NC P/S 20.00 50.00
55 Martin Truex Jr. NC P/S 20.00 50.00
56 Brian Vickers NC S 15.00 40.00
57 Rex White P/S 6.00 15.00
58 Glen Wood P/S 8.00 20.00
59 Jon Wood NBS P/S 8.00 20.00
60 Cale Yarborough P/S 12.50 30.00

2007 Press Pass Signings

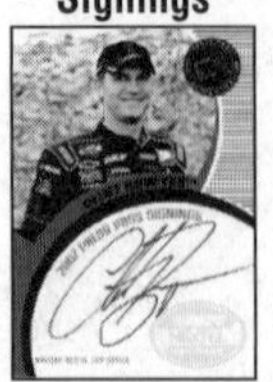

This 39-card set was available in packs of 2007 Press Pass Premium, Press Pass Stealth, 2007 Traks and 2007 VIP products. The cards were certified by the manufacturer. There were three parallel sets, some of which were just partial parallels. In Premium the cards were inserted at a rate of one in 20 hobby packs. The Juan Pablo Montoya without sunglasses was only released in the Collector's Series Box Set.

STATED ODDS 1:20 PREMIUM H
STATED ODDS 1:96 PREMIUM R
STATED ODDS 1:20 STEALTH CHROME
STATED ODDS 1:96 STEALTH R
STATED ODDS 1:84 TRAKS H
STATED ODDS 1:96 TRAKS R
1 Bobby Allison P/S 8.00 20.00
2 Donnie Allison P/S 8.00 20.00
3 A.J. Allmendinger NC S/T 8.00 20.00
4 Aric Almirola NBS T 8.00 20.00
5 Marcos Ambrose NBS S/T 20.00 40.00
6 Buddy Baker P/S 6.00 15.00
7 Greg Biffle NC T 8.00 20.00
8 Dave Blaney NC P/S/T 5.00 12.00
9 Todd Bodine CTS S/T 6.00 15.00
10 Clint Bowyer NC P/S/T 12.50 30.00
11 Jeff Burton NC P/S/T 8.00 20.00
12 Kurt Busch NC S/T 12.50 30.00
13 Kyle Busch NC P/S/T 20.00 50.00
14 Rick Crawford CTS P/S/T 5.00 12.00
15 Erik Darnell CTS P/S/T 6.00 15.00
16 Kertus Davis NBS S/T 5.00 12.00
17 Dale Earnhardt Jr. NC P/S/T 60.00 120.00
18 Carl Edwards NC S/T 15.00 40.00
19 Cale Gale NBS S/T 6.00 15.00
20 Harry Gant P/S 6.00 15.00
21 David Gilliland NC P/S/T 8.00 20.00
22 Jeff Gordon NC P/S/T 100.00 175.00
23 Jeff Green NC P/S/T 5.00 12.00
24 Janet Guthrie P/S 8.00 20.00
25 Denny Hamlin NC S/T 30.00 60.00
26 Kevin Harvick NC P/S/T 12.50 30.00
27 Eric Holmes T
28 Ron Hornaday CTS P/S/T 5.00 12.00
29 Sam Hornish Jr. NBS T 12.50 25.00
30 Jack Ingram P/S 5.00 12.00
31 Dale Jarrett NC S/T 15.00 40.00
32 Jimmie Johnson NC P/S/T 30.00 60.00
33 Kasey Kahne NC P/S/T 20.00 50.00
34 Matt Kenseth NC P/S/T 15.00 40.00
35 Kraig Kinser CTS S/T 8.00 20.00
36 Todd Kluever NBS S/T 10.00 25.00
37 Travis Kvapil CTS S/T 5.00 12.00
38 Bobby Labonte NC P/S/T 12.50 30.00
39 Stephen Leicht 8.00 20.00
40 Greg Lewis T 6.00 15.00
41 Fred Lorenzen P/S 6.00 15.00
42 Sterling Marlin NC P/S/T 10.00 25.00
43 Mark Martin NC P/S/T 30.00 60.00
44 Jamie McMurray NC S/T 8.00 20.00
45 Casey Mears NC T 10.00 25.00
46 Paul Menard NC P/S/T 8.00 20.00
47 Junior Miller T
48 Juan Pablo Montoya NC P/S/T 40.00 80.00
49 Juan Pablo Montoya w/o glasses NC 50.00 100.00
50 Joe Nemechek NC S/T 5.00 12.00
51 Ryan Newman NC S/T 15.00 30.00
52 J.R. Norris T
53 Mike Olsen T 6.00 15.00
54 Marvin Panch P/S 6.00 15.00
55 David Pearson P/S 8.00 20.00
56 Timothy Peters NBS S/T 6.00 15.00
57 Richard Petty P/S 30.00 60.00
58 David Ragan NC S/T 10.00 25.00
59 Tony Raines NC 6.00 15.00
60 David Reutimann NC S/T 15.00 40.00
61 Scott Riggs NC P/S/T 6.00 15.00
62 Elliott Sadler NC P/S/T 10.00 25.00
63 Johnny Sauter NC P/S/T 6.00 15.00
64 Tim Schendel T 6.00 15.00
65 Ken Schrader NC S/T 6.00 15.00
66 Regan Smith NC S/T 6.00 15.00
67 Reed Sorenson NC T 10.00 25.00
68 Mike Stefanik T
69 Tony Stewart NC P/S/T 30.00 60.00
70 David Stremme NC T 10.00 25.00
71 Martin Truex Jr. NC P/S/T 15.00 40.00
72 Brian Vickers NC S/T 8.00 20.00
73 Rusty Wallace P/S 12.50 30.00
74 Steve Wallace 8.00 20.00
75 Michael Waltrip NC S/T 10.00 25.00
76 Rex White P/S 6.00 15.00
77 Scott Wimmer NBS S/T 6.00 15.00
78 Glen Wood P/S 5.00 12.00
79 Jon Wood NBS S/T 5.00 12.00
80 Jon Wood NC S/T 6.00 15.00
81 Cale Yarborough P/S 8.00 20.00
82 J.J. Yeley NC P/S/T 10.00 25.00

2007 Press Pass Signings Press Plates Black

STATED PRINT RUN 1 SERIAL #'d SET
NOT PRICED DUE TO SCARCITY

2007 Press Pass Signings Press Plates Cyan

NOT PRICED DUE TO SCARCITY
STATED PRINT RUN 1 SERIAL #'d SET

2007 Press Pass Signings Press Plates Magenta

STATED PRINT RUN 1 SERIAL #'d SET
NOT PRICED DUE TO SCARCITY

2007 Press Pass Signings Press Plates Yellow

NOT PRICED DUE TO SCARCITY
STATED PRINT RUN 1 SERIAL #'d SET

2007 Press Pass Signings Blue

STATED PRINT RUN 25 SERIAL #'d SETS
1 A.J. Allmendinger NC 40.00 80.00
2 Clint Bowyer NC 40.00 80.00
3 Jeff Burton NC 30.00 60.00
4 Kurt Busch NC 40.00 80.00
5 Kyle Busch NC 100.00 175.00
6 Dale Earnhardt Jr. NC 175.00 300.00
7 David Gilliland NC 50.00 100.00
8 Jeff Gordon NC 125.00 200.00
9 Jeff Green NC
10 Denny Hamlin NC 100.00 175.00
11 Kevin Harvick NC 75.00 150.00
12 Dale Jarrett NC
13 Jimmie Johnson NC 75.00 150.00
14 Kasey Kahne NC
15 Matt Kenseth NC 75.00 150.00
16 Bobby Labonte NC 50.00 100.00
17 Sterling Marlin NC
18 Mark Martin NC 60.00 120.00
19 Jamie McMurray NC
20 Paul Menard NC 30.00 60.00
21 Juan Pablo Montoya NC 75.00 150.00
22 Joe Nemechek NC
23 Ryan Newman NC 50.00 100.00
24 David Ragan NC 40.00 80.00
25 David Reutimann NC 30.00 60.00
26 Scott Riggs NC 30.00 60.00
27 Elliott Sadler NC 25.00 50.00
28 Johnny Sauter NC
29 Ken Schrader NC
30 Regan Smith NC 25.00 50.00
31 Tony Stewart NC 125.00 250.00
32 Martin Truex Jr. NC 75.00 150.00
33 Brian Vickers NC
34 Michael Waltrip NC
35 J.J. Yeley NC

2007 Press Pass Signings Blue Daytona

This 8-card set was available in packs of 2007 Press Pass Premium, Press Pass Stealth, 2007 Traks and 2007 VIP products. The cards were certified by the manufacturer. This was one of three parallel sets to the basic Signings set. The cards were serial numbered to 150 copies and included only past Daytona winners.

STATED PRINT RUN 150 SERIAL #'d SETS
1 Bobby Allison P 10.00 25.00
2 Buddy Baker P 8.00 20.00
3 Fred Lorenzen 8.00 20.00
4 Marvin Panch 8.00 20.00
5 David Pearson 10.00 25.00
6 Richard Petty 40.00 80.00
7 Rusty Wallace
8 Cale Yarborough 10.00 25.00

2007 Press Pass Signings Gold

This 25-card set was available in packs of 2007 Press Pass Premium, Press Pass Stealth, 2007 Traks and 2007 VIP products. The cards were certified by the manufacturer. This was one of three parallel sets to the basic Signings set. The cards were serial numbered to 50 copies. The Juan Pablo Montoya without sunglasses was only released in the Collector's Series Box Set.

STATED PRINT RUN 50 SERIAL #'d SETS
1 A.J. Allmendinger NC S/T 15.00 40.00
2 Aric Almirola NBS T 15.00 40.00
3 Marcos Ambrose NBS S/T 40.00 80.00
4 Greg Biffle NC T 15.00 40.00
5 Dave Blaney NC P/S/T 12.50 30.00
6 Todd Bodine CTS S/T 12.50 30.00
7 Clint Bowyer NC P/S/T 25.00 60.00
8 Jeff Burton NC P/S/T 20.00 50.00
9 Kurt Busch NC S/T 30.00 60.00
10 Kyle Busch NC P/S/T 60.00 120.00
11 Rick Crawford CTS P/S/T 12.50 30.00
12 Erik Darnell CTS P/S/T 15.00 40.00
13 Kertus Davis NBS S/T 10.00 25.00
14 Dale Earnhardt Jr. NC P/S/T 125.00 250.00
15 Carl Edwards NC S/T 40.00 80.00
16 Cale Gale NBS S/T 15.00 40.00
17 David Gilliland NC P/S/T 25.00 60.00
18 Jeff Gordon NC P/S/T 150.00 300.00
19 Jeff Green NC P/S/T 12.50 30.00
20 Denny Hamlin NC P/S/T 50.00 100.00
21 Kevin Harvick NC P/S/T 40.00 80.00
22 Ron Hornaday CTS P/S/T 12.50 30.00
23 Sam Hornish Jr. NBS T 25.00 50.00
24 Dale Jarrett NC S/T 25.00 60.00
25 Jimmie Johnson NC P/S/T 50.00 120.00
26 Kasey Kahne NC/20 P/S/T 75.00 150.00
27 Matt Kenseth NC P/S/T 30.00 80.00
28 Kraig Kinser CTS S/T 30.00 60.00
29 Todd Kluever NBS S/T
30 Travis Kvapil CTS S/T 20.00 50.00
31 Bobby Labonte NC P/S/T 30.00 80.00
32 Stephen Leicht 15.00 30.00
33 Sterling Marlin NC P/S/T 20.00 50.00
34 Mark Martin NC P/S/T 50.00 100.00
35 Jamie McMurray NC S/T 30.00 60.00
36 Casey Mears NC T 20.00 40.00
37 Paul Menard NC P/S/T 20.00 50.00
38 Juan Pablo Montoya NC P/S/T 75.00 150.00
39 Juan Pablo Montoya w/o glasses NC 60.00 120.00
40 Joe Nemechek NC S/T 12.50 30.00
41 Ryan Newman NC S/T 20.00 50.00
42 Timothy Peters NBS S/T 12.50 30.00
43 Tony Raines 15.00 30.00
44 David Ragan NC S/T 20.00 50.00
45 David Reutimann NC S/T
46 Scott Riggs NC P/S/T 12.50 30.00
47 Elliott Sadler NC S/T 25.00 50.00
48 Johnny Sauter NC S/T 25.00 50.00
49 Ken Schrader NC S/T 12.50 30.00
50 Regan Smith NC S/T 25.00 50.00
51 Reed Sorenson NC T
52 Tony Stewart NC P/S/T 75.00 150.00
53 David Stremme NC T 30.00 60.00
54 Martin Truex Jr. NC P/S/T 30.00 60.00
55 Brian Vickers NC S/T 20.00 50.00
56 Michael Waltrip NC S/T 30.00 60.00
57 Scott Wimmer NBS S/T 15.00 40.00
58 Jon Wood NC S/T 15.00 40.00
59 J.J. Yeley NC P/S/T 20.00 50.00

2007 Press Pass Signings Silver

This 24-card set was available in packs of 2007 Press Pass Premium, Press Pass Stealth, 2007 Traks and 2007 VIP products. The cards were certified by the manufacturer. This was one of three parallel sets to the basic Signings set. The cards were serial numbered to 100 copies. The Juan Pablo Montoya without sunglasses was only released in the Collector's Series Box Set.

STATED PRINT RUN 100 SERIAL #'d SETS

1 Aric Almirola NBS T 12.50 30.
2 Marcos Ambrose NBS S/T 30.00 60.
3 Greg Biffle NC T 20.00 40.
4 Dave Blaney NC P/S/T 8.00 20
5 Todd Bodine CTS S/T 10.00 25.
6 Clint Bowyer NC P/S/T 15.00 40.
7 Jeff Burton NC P/S/T 15.00 40.
8 Kurt Busch NC S/T 25.00 50.
9 Kyle Busch NC P/S/T 40.00 80.
10 Rick Crawford CTS 8.00 20.
11 Erik Darnell CTS P/S/T 10.00 25.
12 Kertus Davis NBS S/T 10.00 25.
13 Dale Earnhardt Jr. NC P/S/T 100.00 175.
14 Carl Edwards NC S/T
15 Cale Gale NBS S/T 8.00 20.
16 David Gilliland NC P/S/T 15.00 40.
17 Jeff Gordon NC P/S/T 100.00 200.
18 Jeff Green NC P/S/T 8.00 20.
19 Denny Hamlin NC S/T 40.00 80.
20 Kevin Harvick NC P/S/T 25.00 60.
21 Ron Hornaday CTS P/S/T 8.00 20.
22 Sam Hornish Jr. NBS T 15.00 40.
23 Dale Jarrett NC S/T 20.00 50.
24 Jimmie Johnson NC P/T 40.00 80.
25 Kasey Kahne NC/45 P/S/T 50.00 100
26 Matt Kenseth NC P/S/T 20.00 50.
27 Kraig Kinser CTS S/T 15.00 40.
28 Todd Kluever NBS S/T 15.00 40.
29 Travis Kvapil CTS S/T
30 Bobby Labonte NC P/S/T 25.00 60
31 Stephen Leicht 10.00 25
32 Sterling Marlin NC P/S/T 12.50 30.
33 Mark Martin NC P/S/T 40.00 80.
34 Jamie McMurray NC S/T 20.00 50.
35 Casey Mears NC T 12.50 30
36 Paul Menard NC P/S/T 12.50 30
37 Juan Pablo Montoya NC P/S/T 50.00 100
38 Juan Pablo Montoya w/o glasses NC 60.00 120
39 Joe Nemechek NC S/T 8.00 20
40 Ryan Newman NC S/T 15.00 40
41 Timothy Peters NBS S/T 10.00 25
42 David Ragan NC S/T 15.00 40
43 Tony Raines NC 8.00 20
44 David Reutimann NC S/T 12.50 30
45 Scott Riggs NC P/S/T 10.00 25
46 Elliott Sadler NC S/T 15.00 40
47 Johnny Sauter NC S/T 15.00 40
48 Ken Schrader NC S/T 8.00 20
49 Regan Smith NC S/T 8.00 20
50 Reed Sorenson NC T 15.00 40
51 Tony Stewart NC P/S/T 50.00 100
52 David Stremme NC T 12.50 30
53 Martin Truex Jr. NC P/S/T 20.00 50
54 Michael Waltrip NC S/T 15.00 40
55 Scott Wimmer NBS S/T 10.00 25
56 Jon Wood NC S/T 10.00 25
57 J.J. Yeley NC P/S/T 12.50 30

2008 Press Pass Signings

STATED ODDS PREMIUM 1:20
STATED ODDS STEATH CHROME 1:20
STATED ODDS SPEEDWAY 1:84
1 Bobby Allison 8.00 20
2 Donnie Allison 8.00 20
3 A.J. Allmendinger 8.00 20
4 Aric Almirola 10.00 25
5 Buddy Baker 8.00 20
6 Dave Blaney 5.00 12
7 Clint Bowyer 15.00 40
8 Colin Braun 12.00 30
9 Kurt Busch 12.00 30
11 Landon Cassill 12.00 30
12 Bryan Clauson 8.00 20
13 Rick Crawford 5.00 12
14 Erik Darnell 8.00 20
15 Dale Earnhardt Jr. AMP 100.00 175
16 Dale Earnhardt Jr. NG 100.00 175
17 Carl Edwards
18 Cale Gale 5.00 12
19 Harry Gant 8.00 20
20 David Gilliland 12.00 30
21 Jeff Gordon 60.00 120
22 Janet Guthrie 8.00 20
23 Denny Hamlin 20.00 50
24 Kevin Harvick 15.00 40
25 Ron Hornaday 8.00 20
26 Sam Hornish Jr. 12.50 30
27 Jack Ingram 5.00 12
28 Dale Jarrett 20.00 50
29 Jimmie Johnson 25.00 60
30 Kasey Kahne 25.00 60
31 Matt Kenseth 20.00 50
32 Travis Kvapil 8.00 20
33 Bobby Labonte 12.00 30
34 Joey Logano 75.00 150
35 Fred Lorenzen 5.00 12
36 Mark Martin 20.00 50
37 Michael McDowell 12.00 30
38 Jamie McMurray 10.00 25
39 Casey Mears 8.00 20
40 Paul Menard 10.00 25
41 Joe Nemechek 5.00 12
42 Ryan Newman 12.00 30

2005 Press Pass Signings Gold

Marvin Panch 5.00 12.00
David Pearson 12.00 30.00
Richard Petty 25.00 60.00
David Ragan 10.00 25.00
David Reutimann 12.00 30.00
Elliott Sadler 10.00 25.00
Mike Skinner 5.00 12.00
Regan Smith 5.00 12.00
Reed Sorenson 8.00 20.00
Jack Sprague 5.00 12.00
Tony Stewart 25.00 60.00
Martin Truex Jr. 15.00 40.00
Brian Vickers 10.00 25.00
Michael Waltrip 10.00 25.00
Rex White 5.00 12.00
Scott Wimmer 6.00 15.00
Glen Wood 5.00 12.00
Cale Yarborough 10.00 25.00
J.J. Yeley 10.00 25.00

2008 Press Pass Signings Press Plates Black

TATED PRINT RUN 1 SERIAL #'d SET
OT PRICED DUE TO SCARCITY

2008 Press Pass Signings Press Plates Cyan

TATED PRINT RUN 1 SERIAL #'d SET
OT PRICED DUE TO SCARCITY

2008 Press Pass Signings Press Plates Magenta

TATED PRINT RUN 1 SERIAL #'d SET
OT PRICED DUE TO SCARCITY

2008 Press Pass Signings Press Plates Yellow

TATED PRINT RUN 1 SERIAL #'d SET
OT PRICED DUE TO SCARCITY

2008 Press Pass Signings Blue

TATED PRINT RUN 25 SERIAL #'d SETS
NLESS NOTED IN CHECKLIST BELOW
Bobby Allison/100 10.00 25.00
A.J. Allmendinger 20.00 50.00
Dave Blaney 12.00 30.00
Clint Bowyer 40.00 100.00
Kurt Busch 30.00 80.00
Kyle Busch 175.00 300.00
Dale Earnhardt Jr./8
Jeff Gordon 175.00 300.00
Denny Hamlin 50.00 120.00
Kevin Harvick 50.00 100.00
Sam Hornish Jr. 30.00 60.00
Dale Jarrett 40.00 100.00
Jimmie Johnson 60.00 120.00
Kasey Kahne 75.00 150.00
Matt Kenseth 60.00 120.00
Bobby Labonte 40.00 80.00
Mark Martin 50.00 100.00
Michael McDowell 20.00 50.00
Jamie McMurray 25.00 60.00
Paul Menard 25.00 60.00
Joe Nemechek 12.00 30.00
Ryan Newman 30.00 80.00
David Pearson/100 15.00 40.00
Richard Petty/100 30.00 80.00
David Ragan 25.00 60.00
David Reutimann 30.00 80.00
Elliott Sadler 25.00 60.00
Regan Smith 12.00 30.00
Reed Sorenson 20.00 50.00
Tony Stewart 75.00 150.00
Brian Vickers 25.00 60.00
Michael Waltrip 25.00 60.00
Rex White/100 6.00 15.00
Cale Yarborough/100 12.00 30.00
J.J. Yeley 25.00 60.00

2008 Press Pass Signings Gold

TATED PRINT RUN 50 SERIAL #'d SETS
A.J. Allmendinger 12.00 30.00
Aric Almirola 15.00 40.00
Kelly Bires 15.00 40.00
Dave Blaney 8.00 20.00
Clint Bowyer 30.00 60.00
Kurt Busch 20.00 50.00
Kyle Busch 75.00 150.00
Landon Cassill 20.00 50.00
Rick Crawford 8.00 20.00
Erik Darnell 12.00 30.00
Dale Earnhardt Jr. AMP/25 125.00 250.00
Dale Earnhardt Jr. NG/25 125.00 250.00
Carl Edwards 40.00 80.00
Dario Franchitti 25.00 60.00
Cale Gale 8.00 20.00
David Gilliland 20.00 50.00
Jeff Gordon 125.00 250.00
Denny Hamlin 30.00 80.00
Kevin Harvick 30.00 60.00
Ron Hornaday 12.00 30.00
Sam Hornish Jr. 30.00 80.00
Dale Jarrett 60.00 120.00
Jimmie Johnson 60.00 120.00
Kasey Kahne 50.00 100.00
Matt Kenseth 40.00 80.00
Brad Keselowski 40.00 80.00
Travis Kvapil 12.00 30.00
Bobby Labonte 20.00 50.00
Joey Logano 200.00 350.00
Mark Martin 40.00 80.00
Michael McDowell 20.00 50.00
Jamie McMurray 15.00 40.00
Paul Menard 15.00 40.00
Chase Miller 20.00 50.00

35 Joe Nemechek 8.00 20.00
36 Ryan Newman 20.00 50.00
37 David Ragan 15.00 40.00
38 Scott Riggs 12.00 30.00
39 Elliott Sadler 15.00 40.00
40 Mike Skinner 8.00 20.00
41 Regan Smith 8.00 20.00
42 Reed Sorenson 12.00 30.00
43 Tony Stewart 50.00 100.00
44 Martin Truex Jr. 25.00 60.00
45 Brian Vickers 15.00 40.00
46 Scott Wimmer 10.00 25.00
47 J.J. Yeley 15.00 40.00

2008 Press Pass Signings Silver

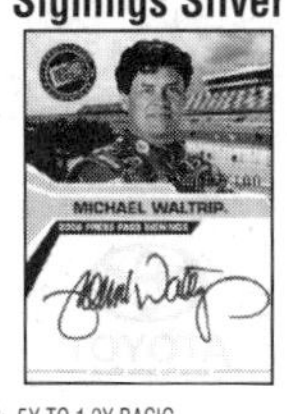

*SILVER: .5X TO 1.2X BASIC
STATED PRINT RUN 100 SERIAL #'d SETS
1 A.J. Allmendinger 10.00 25.00
2 Aric Almirola 12.00 30.00
3 Dave Blaney 6.00 15.00
4 Clint Bowyer 20.00 50.00
5 Colin Braun 15.00 40.00
6 Kurt Busch 15.00 40.00
7 Kyle Busch 60.00 120.00
8 Landon Cassill 15.00 40.00
9 Bryan Clauson 10.00 25.00
10 Rick Crawford 6.00 15.00
11 Erik Darnell 10.00 25.00
12 Dale Earnhardt Jr. AMP/50 125.00 200.00
13 Dale Earnhardt Jr. NG/50 125.00 200.00
14 Carl Edwards 30.00 60.00
15 Cale Gale 6.00 15.00
16 Denny Hamlin 40.00 80.00
17 Kevin Harvick 20.00 50.00
18 Ron Hornaday 10.00 25.00
19 Sam Hornish Jr. 15.00 40.00
20 Dale Jarrett 30.00 60.00
21 Kasey Kahne 40.00 80.00
22 Matt Kenseth 25.00 50.00
23 Travis Kvapil 10.00 25.00
24 Bobby Labonte 15.00 40.00
25 Joey Logano 100.00 175.00
26 Mark Martin 30.00 60.00
27 Michael McDowell 15.00 40.00
28 Jamie McMurray 12.00 30.00
29 Casey Mears 10.00 25.00
30 Paul Menard 12.00 30.00
31 Joe Nemechek 6.00 15.00
32 Ryan Newman 15.00 40.00
33 David Ragan 12.00 30.00
34 David Reutimann 15.00 40.00
35 Elliott Sadler 12.00 30.00
36 Mike Skinner 6.00 15.00
37 Regan Smith 6.00 15.00
38 Reed Sorenson 10.00 25.00
39 Jack Sprague 6.00 15.00
40 Tony Stewart 40.00 80.00
41 Martin Truex Jr. 20.00 50.00
42 Brian Vickers 12.00 30.00
43 Michael Waltrip 12.00 30.00
44 Scott Wimmer 8.00 20.00
45 J.J. Yeley 12.00 30.00

2008 Press Pass Speedway

COMPLETE SET (100) 15.00 40.00
WAX BOX HOBBY (36) 60.00 100.00
WAX BOX RETAIL (24) 50.00 75.00
1 Aric Almirola CRC .40 1.00
2 Clint Bowyer .60 1.50
3 Jeff Burton .30 .75
4 Dale Earnhardt Jr. 1.50 4.00
5 Jeff Gordon 1.25 3.00
6 Kevin Harvick .60 1.50
7 Jimmie Johnson 1.00 2.50
8 Casey Mears .30 .75
9 Paul Menard .40 1.00
10 Scott Riggs .30 .75
11 Martin Truex Jr. .60 1.50
12 Kurt Busch .50 1.25
13 Patrick Carpentier RC .60 1.50
14 Dario Franchitti RC .60 1.50
15 Sam Hornish Jr. CRC .75 2.00
16 Kasey Kahne 1.00 2.50
17 Bobby Labonte .50 1.25
18 Juan Pablo Montoya 1.25 3.00
19 Ryan Newman .50 1.25
20 Elliott Sadler .40 1.00
21 Greg Biffle .40 1.00
22 Carl Edwards .75 2.00
23 David Gilliland .50 1.25
24 Matt Kenseth .75 2.00
25 Travis Kvapil .30 .75
26 Jamie McMurray .40 1.00
27 David Ragan .40 1.00
28 Dave Blaney .20 .50
29 Kyle Busch .60 1.50
30 Denny Hamlin .75 2.00
31 Dale Jarrett .75 2.00
32 David Reutimann .50 1.25
33 Tony Stewart 1.00 2.50
34 Brian Vickers .40 1.00
35 Michael Waltrip .40 1.00
36 J.J. Yeley .40 1.00
37 Clint Bowyer NNS .60 1.50
38 Cale Gale NNS .20 .50
39 Brad Keselowski NNS RC 1.25 3.00
40 Scott Wimmer NNS .25 .60
41 Bryan Clauson NNS RC .30 .75
42 Dario Franchitti NNS .60 1.50
43 Chase Miller NNS RC .50 1.25
44 Marcos Ambrose NNS 1.25 3.00
45 Carl Edwards NNS .75 2.00
46 David Ragan NNS .40 1.00
47 Kyle Busch NNS .60 1.50
48 David Reutimann NNS .50 1.25
49 Ron Hornaday CTS .30 .75
50 Jack Sprague CTS .20 .50
51 Colin Braun CTS RC .50 1.25
52 Rick Crawford CTS .20 .50
53 Erik Darnell CTS .30 .75
54 Mike Skinner CTS .20 .50
55 Tony Eury Jr. RC .75 2.00
56 Chad Knaus .60 1.50
57 Steve Letarte RC .75 2.00
58 Greg Zipadelli .60 1.50
59 Kevin Harvick SH .60 1.50
60 Ryan Newman SH .50 1.25
61 Jeff Gordon SH 1.25 3.00
62 Dale Earnhardt Jr. SH 1.50 4.00
63 Aric Almirola SH .40 1.00
64 Mark Martin SH .75 2.00
65 Elliott Sadler SH .40 1.00
66 Martin Truex Jr. SH .60 1.50
67 Kevin Harvick UTH .60 1.50
68 Dale Earnhardt Jr. UTH 1.50 4.00
69 Bobby Labonte UTH .50 1.25
70 Jeff Burton UTH .30 .75
71 Jimmie Johnson UTH 1.00 2.50
72 Ryan Newman UTH .50 1.25
73 Jeff Gordon UTH 1.25 3.00
74 Martin Truex Jr. UTH .60 1.50
75 Tony Stewart UTH 1.00 2.50
76 Denny Hamlin's Car RSG .30 .75
77 Dale Earnhardt Jr.'s Car RSG .60 1.50
78 Jeff Gordon's Car RSG .50 1.25
79 Carl Edwards's Car RSG .30 .75
80 Martin Truex Jr.'s Car RSG .25 .60
81 Tony Stewart's Car RSG .40 1.00
82 Martin Truex Jr.'s Car WS .25 .60
83 Kyle Busch's Car WS .25 .60
84 Tony Stewart's Car WS .40 1.00
85 Jeff Gordon's Car WS .50 1.25
86 Jamie McMurray's Car WS .15 .40
87 Jeff Burton's Car WS .12 .30
88 Jimmie Johnson's Car WS .40 1.00
89 Brian Vickers' Car WS .15 .40
90 Carl Edwards' Car WS .30 .75
91 Dale Earnhardt Jr.'s Car H .60 1.50
92 Dario Franchitti
Juan Pablo Montoya H .60 1.50
93 Ryan Newman's Car
Kurt Busch's Car H .20 .50
94 Kyle Busch H .60 1.50
95 Carl Edwards H .75 2.00
96 Jeff Burton's Car
Kevin Harvick's Car
Clint Bowyer's Car H .12 .30
97 Dale Jarrett Fans H .75 2.00
98 Ryan Newman H .50 1.25
99 Kyle Busch H .60 1.50
100 Jeff Burton CL .30 .75

2008 Press Pass Speedway Gold

COMPLETE SET (100) 25.00 60.00
*GOLDS: 1X TO 2.5X BASE
STATED ODDS 1 PER PACK

2008 Press Pass Speedway Holofoil

*HOLOFOIL: 6X TO 15X BASE
STATED PRINT RUN 50 SERIAL #'d SETS

2008 Press Pass Speedway Previews

(EB1-EB48) STATED PRINT RUN 5 SERIAL #'d SETS
(EB91-EB99) STATED PRINT RUN 1 SERIAL #'d SET
NOT PRICED DUE TO SCARCITY

2008 Press Pass Speedway Red

STATED PRINT RUN 10 SERIAL #'d SETS
NOT PRICED DUE TO SCARCITY

2008 Press Pass Speedway Blur

COMPLETE SET (9) 15.00 40.00
STATED ODDS 1:12
B1 Jimmie Johnson 2.50 6.00
B2 Matt Kenseth 2.00 5.00
B3 Dale Earnhardt Jr. 4.00 10.00

B4 Ryan Newman 1.25 3.00
B5 Jeff Gordon 3.00 8.00
B6 Martin Truex Jr. 1.50 4.00
B7 Clint Bowyer 1.50 4.00
B8 Tony Stewart 2.50 6.00
B9 Kevin Harvick 1.50 4.00

2008 Press Pass Speedway Cockpit

COMPLETE SET (27) 12.00 30.00
STATED ODDS 1:2
CP1 Dave Blaney .20 .50
CP2 Clint Bowyer .60 1.50
CP3 Jeff Burton .30 .75
CP4 Kurt Busch .50 1.25
CP5 Kyle Busch .60 1.50
CP6 Dario Franchitti .60 1.50
CP7 Jeff Gordon 1.25 3.00
CP8 Kevin Harvick .60 1.50
CP9 Dale Jarrett .75 2.00
CP10 Jimmie Johnson 1.00 2.50
CP11 Matt Kenseth .75 2.00
CP12 Bobby Labonte .50 1.25
CP13 Mark Martin .75 2.00
CP14 Jamie McMurray .40 1.00
CP15 Casey Mears .30 .75
CP16 Paul Menard .40 1.00
CP17 Ryan Newman .50 1.25
CP18 Kyle Petty .30 .75
CP19 David Reutimann .50 1.25
CP20 Elliott Sadler .40 1.00
CP21 Regan Smith .20 .50
CP22 Reed Sorenson .30 .75
CP23 Tony Stewart 1.00 2.50
CP24 Martin Truex Jr. .60 1.50
CP25 Brian Vickers .40 1.00
CP26 Michael Waltrip .40 1.00
CP27 J.J. Yeley .40 1.00

2008 Press Pass Speedway Corporate Cuts Drivers

STATED PRINT RUN 80 SERIAL #'d SETS
CD-AA Aric Almirola 6.00 15.00
CD-CE Carl Edwards 10.00 25.00
CD-DF Dario Franchitti 6.00 15.00
CD-DJ Dale Jarrett 15.00 40.00
CD-DR David Ragan 12.00 30.00
CD-JM Jamie McMurray 10.00 25.00
CD-KH Kevin Harvick 15.00 40.00
CD-MK Matt Kenseth 12.00 30.00
CD-MM Mark Martin 12.00 30.00
CD-MT Martin Truex Jr. 10.00 25.00
CD-MW Michael Waltrip 8.00 20.00
CD-RN Ryan Newman 8.00 20.00
CD-TS Tony Stewart 15.00 40.00
CD -DH Denny Hamlin 10.00 25.00
CD-JPM Juan Pablo Montoya 10.00 25.00
CD-KuB Kurt Busch 8.00 20.00
CD-KyB Kyle Busch 15.00 40.00

2008 Press Pass Speedway Corporate Cuts Drivers Patches

NOT PRICED DUE TO SCARCITY
CD-AA Aric Almirola/26
CD-CE Carl Edwards/13
CD-DF Dario Franchitti
CD-DJ Dale Jarrett
CD-DR David Ragan
CD-JM Jamie McMurray
CD-KH Kevin Harvick
CD-MK Matt Kenseth/12
CD-MM Mark Martin/29
CD-MT Martin Truex Jr./17
CD-MW Michael Waltrip/13
CD-RN Ryan Newman/15
CD-TS Tony Stewart
CD -DH Denny Hamlin
CD-JPM Juan Pablo Montoya/7
CD-KuB Kurt Busch
CD-KyB Kyle Busch

2008 Press Pass Speedway Corporate Cuts Team

*TEAM: .3X TO .8X DRIVERS
STATED PRINT RUN 165 SERIAL #'d SETS

2008 Press Pass Speedway Garage Graphs

CK Chad Knaus 15.00 40.00
GZ Greg Zipadelli 12.00 30.00
SL Steve Letarte 12.00 30.00
TE Tony Eury Jr. 15.00 40.00

2008 Press Pass Speedway Garage Graphs Duals

EE Dale Earnhardt Jr.
Tony Eury Jr. 200.00 350.00
GL Jeff Gordon
Steve Letarte 175.00 300.00
JK Jimmie Johnson
Chad Knaus 75.00 150.00
SZ Tony Stewart
Greg Zipadelli 100.00 200.00

2008 Press Pass Speedway Test Drive

COMPLETE SET (12) 12.00 30.00
STATED ODDS 1:6
TD1 Jeff Gordon 2.00 5.00
TD2 Kurt Busch .75 2.00
TD3 Mark Martin 1.25 3.00
TD4 Tony Stewart 1.50 4.00
TD5 Martin Truex Jr. 1.00 2.50
TD6 Ryan Newman .75 2.00
TD7 Dale Earnhardt Jr. 2.50 6.00
TD8 Jeff Burton .50 1.25
TD9 Michael Waltrip .60 1.50
TD10 Carl Edwards 1.25 3.00
TD11 Jimmie Johnson 1.50 4.00
TD12 Kasey Kahne 1.50 4.00

1998 Press Pass Stealth

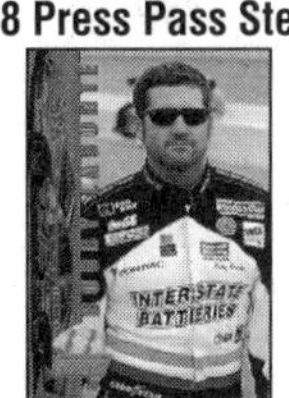

The 1998 Press Pass Stealth set was issued in one series totalling 60 cards. The set features silver foil stamping and UV coating and highlighted with a shimmering metal effect specially produced on the NASCAR Winston Cup Series. The set contains the topical subset: Teammates (45-59).

COMPLETE SET (60) 12.50 30.00
1 Dale Earnhardt's Car .75 2.00
2 Dale Earnhardt's Car .75 2.00
3 Richard Childress .30 .75
4 Jeff Burton .30 .75
5 Jeff Burton's Car .12 .30
6 Jack Roush .25 .60
7 Bill Elliott .60 1.50
8 Bill Elliott's Car .25 .60
9 Joe Garone .12 .30
10 Jeff Gordon 1.25 3.00
11 Jeff Gordon's Car .50 1.25
12 Ray Evernham .25 .60
13 Kenny Irwin .50 1.25
14 Kenny Irwin's Car .20 .50
15 Robert Yates .25 .60
16 Dale Jarrett .75 2.00
17 Dale Jarrett's Car .30 .75
18 Todd Parrott .20 .50
19 Bobby Labonte .75 2.00
20 Bobby Labonte's Car .30 .75
21 Jimmy Makar .20 .50
22 Terry Labonte .50 1.25
23 Terry Labonte's Car .20 .50
24 Andy Graves .12 .30
25 Mark Martin 1.00 2.50
26 Mark Martin's Car .40 1.00
27 Jimmy Fennig .12 .30
28 Ricky Rudd .40 1.00
29 Ricky Rudd's Car .15 .40
30 Bill Ingle .12 .30
31 Rusty Wallace 1.00 2.50
32 Rusty Wallace's Car .40 1.00
33 Robin Pemberton .12 .30
34 Michael Waltrip .30 .75
35 Michael Waltrip's Car .12 .30
36 Glen Wood .12 .30
37 Dale Earnhardt Jr. 2.00 5.00
38 Jason Keller .12 .30
39 Randy LaJoie .12 .30
40 Mark Martin 1.00 2.50
41 Mike McLaughlin .12 .30
42 Elliott Sadler .25 .60
43 Hermie Sadler .12 .30
44 Tony Stewart RC 4.00 10.00
45 Dale Jarrett TM .75 2.00
46 Kenny Irwin TM .50 1.25
47 Jeff Gordon TM 1.25 3.00
48 Terry Labonte TM .50 1.25
49 Jeremy Mayfield TM .25 .60
50 Rusty Wallace TM 1.00 2.50
51 Jeff Burton TM .30 .75
52 Ted Musgrave TM .20 .50
53 Chad Little TM .20 .50
54 Johnny Benson TM .30 .75
55 Mark Martin TM 1.00 2.50
56 Sterling Marlin TM .50 1.25
57 Joe Nemechek TM .12 .30
58 Mike Skinner TM .12 .30
59 Dale Earnhardt's Car TM .75 2.00
60 Dale Earnhardt Jr. CL 2.00 5.00
P1 Jeff Gordon Promo 2.00 5.00
0 Jeff Gordon Champ Bronze 1:110 5.00 12.00
0 Jeff Gordon Champ Silver 1:220 10.00 25.00
0 Jeff Gordon Champ Gold 1:440 20.00 50.00

1998 Press Pass Stealth Fusion

This parallel set features red foil on the cardfronts. There was one Fusion red foil card per Stealth pack.

COMPLETE SET (60) 15.00 40.00
*FUSION VETS: 1.2X TO 3X BASE CARDS
*FUSION RCs: .6X TO 1.5X BASE CARDS

1998 Press Pass Stealth Awards

Randomly inserted in progressive odds at a rate of 1:22 through 1:420, this insert set honors those drivers who have proven their excellence and risen to the top in 6 key categories: Most Laps Completed (1:22), All Charged Up (1:68), Top Rookie (1:90), Most Money Won (1:120), Most Poles (1:200), and Most Wins (1:420).

COMPLETE SET (7) 100.00 200.00
1 Jeremy Mayfield 1:22 1.25 3.00
2 Jeff Burton 1:68 2.50 6.00
3 Kenny Irwin 1:90 2.00 5.00
4 Mark Martin 1:120 6.00 15.00
5 Jeff Gordon 1:200 8.00 20.00
6 Mark Martin 1:420 15.00 40.00
7 Jeff Gordon 1:420 25.00 60.00

1998 Press Pass Stealth Fan Talk

Randomly inserted in packs at a rate of one in 10, this all-foil, micro-etched insert set gives fans their chance to say why their favorite driver is the best in the business.

COMPLETE SET (9) 10.00 25.00
COMP.DIE CUT SET (9) 40.00 80.00
*DIE CUTS: .6X TO 1.5X BASIC INSERTS
1 Dale Earnhardt 6.00 15.00
2 Bill Elliott 1.25 3.00
3 Jeff Gordon 3.00 8.00
4 Dale Jarrett 2.00 5.00
5 Bobby Labonte 2.00 5.00
6 Terry Labonte 1.00 2.50
7 Mark Martin 2.50 6.00
8 Ricky Rudd 1.00 2.50
9 Rusty Wallace 2.50 6.00

1998 Press Pass Stealth Octane

Randomly inserted in packs at a rate of one in 2, this insert offers a "set within a set" that features the top 18 NASCAR Winston Cup drivers and their rides on all-foil, micro-etched cards.

COMPLETE SET (36) 15.00 30.00
COMP.DIE CUT SET (36) 50.00 120.00
*DIE CUTS: 1.2X TO 3X BASIC INSERTS
1 John Andretti .25 .60
2 John Andretti's Car .10 .30

3 Johnny Benson .50 1.25
4 Johnny Benson's Car .10 .30
5 Jeff Burton .75 2.00
6 Jeff Burton's Car .25 .60
7 Ward Burton .50 1.25
8 Ward Burton's Car .25 .60
9 Dale Earnhardt's Car 1.50 4.00
10 Dale Earnhardt's Car 1.50 4.00
11 Bill Elliott 1.00 2.50
12 Bill Elliott's Car .50 1.25
13 Jeff Gordon 2.50 6.00
14 Jeff Gordon's Car 1.00 2.50
15 Ernie Irvan .50 1.25
16 Ernie Irvan's Car .25 .60
17 Dale Jarrett 1.50 4.00
18 Dale Jarrett's Car .50 1.25
19 Bobby Labonte 1.50 4.00
20 Bobby Labonte's Car .50 1.25
21 Terry Labonte .75 2.00
22 Terry Labonte's Car .50 1.25
23 Sterling Marlin .75 2.00
24 Sterling Marlin's Car .50 1.25
25 Mark Martin 2.00 5.00
26 Mark Martin's Car .75 2.00
27 Jeremy Mayfield .25 .60
28 Jeremy Mayfield's Car .10 .30
29 Ricky Rudd .75 2.00
30 Ricky Rudd's Car .25 .60
31 Mike Skinner .25 .60
32 Mike Skinner's Car .10 .30
33 Jimmy Spencer .25 .60
34 Jimmy Spencer's Car .10 .30
35 Rusty Wallace 2.00 5.00
36 Rusty Wallace's Car .75 2.00

1998 Press Pass Stealth Race Used Gloves

Randomly inserted in packs at a rate of one in 400, this eight-card insert set features a piece of race-used gloves from top NASCAR Winston Cup drivers like Jeff Gordon and Mark Martin. These cards are numbered to 205. Cards with multi-colored cloth carry a 25 percent premium.

G1 Rusty Wallace 15.00 40.00
G2 Jeff Burton 10.00 25.00
G3 Terry Labonte 15.00 40.00
G4 Mark Martin 15.00 40.00
G5 Bobby Labonte 15.00 40.00
G6 Jeff Gordon 40.00 80.00
G7 Dale Jarrett 15.00 40.00
G8 Dale Earnhardt 50.00 100.00

1998 Press Pass Stealth Stars

Randomly inserted in packs at a rate of one in 6, this 18-card insert set features NASCAR Winston Cup superstars on all-foil.

COMPLETE SET (18) 15.00 40.00
COMP.DIE CUT SET (18) 100.00 200.00
*DIE CUTS: 1.2X TO 3X BASIC INSERTS
1 Johnny Benson .40 1.00
2 Jeff Burton 1.25 3.00
3 Dale Earnhardt Jr. 5.00 12.00
4 Bill Elliott 1.50 4.00
5 Jeff Gordon 4.00 10.00
6 Bobby Hamilton .40 1.00
7 Kenny Irwin .75 2.00
8 Dale Jarrett 2.50 6.00
9 Bobby Labonte 2.50 6.00
10 Terry Labonte 1.25 3.00
11 Sterling Marlin 1.25 3.00
12 Mark Martin 3.00 8.00
13 Jeremy Mayfield .40 1.00
14 Ted Musgrave .40 1.00
15 Ricky Rudd 1.25 3.00
16 Jimmy Spencer .40 1.00
17 Rusty Wallace 3.00 8.00
18 Michael Waltrip .75 2.00

1999 Press Pass Stealth

This sixty card set features a mix of drivers, crew chiefs, cars and equipment needed to run on the NASCAR circuit. With three cards in each group the card backs formed a panoramic picture of the team hauler.

COMPLETE SET (60) 10.00 25.00
*FUSION RC's: .6X TO 1.5X HI COLUMN
1 Jeff Burton .40 1.00
2 Jeff Burton's Car .10 .30
3 Frank Stoddard .05 .15
4 Ward Burton .25 .60
5 Ward Burton's Car .10 .30
6 Tommy Baldwin .05 .15
7 Dale Earnhardt 2.00 5.00
8 Dale Earnhardt's Car .75 2.00
9 Kevin Hamlin .05 .15
10 Jeff Gordon 1.25 3.00
11 Jeff Gordon's Car .50 1.25
12 Rick Hendrick .05 .15
13 Dale Jarrett .75 2.00
14 Dale Jarrett's Car .25 .60
15 Todd Parrott .05 .15
16 Bobby Labonte .75 2.00
17 Bobby Labonte's Car .25 .60
18 Jimmy Makar .05 .15
19 Terry Labonte .40 1.00
20 Terry Labonte's Car .25 .60
21 John Hendrick .05 .15
22 Mark Martin 1.00 2.50
23 Mark Martin's Car .40 1.00
24 Jack Roush .05 .15
25 Jeremy Mayfield .25 .60
26 Jeremy Mayfield's Car .10 .30
27 Michael Kranefuss .05 .15
28 Mike Skinner .10 .30
29 Mike Skinner's Car .05 .15
30 Larry McReynolds .05 .15
31 Tony Stewart CRC 1.50 4.00
32 Tony Stewart's Car .50 1.25
33 Joe Gibbs .25 .60
34 Rusty Wallace 1.00 2.50
35 Rusty Wallace's Car .40 1.00
36 Robin Pemberton .05 .15
37 Casey Atwood RC 1.00 2.50
38 Dave Blaney RC .10 .30
39 Dale Earnhardt Jr. 1.50 4.00
40 Jeff Gordon 1.25 3.00
41 Jeff Green .10 .30
42 Jason Keller .10 .30
43 Matt Kenseth RC 3.00 8.00
44 Randy LaJoie .10 .30
45 Mark Martin 1.00 2.50
46 Mike McLaughlin .10 .30
47 Elton Sawyer .10 .30
48 Michael Waltrip .25 .60
49 Caterpillar Stop Watch TT .05 .15
50 Dupont Air Gun TT .05 .15
51 Exide Car Jack TT .05 .15
52 Quality Care Gas Can TT .05 .15
53 Goodwrench Tool Cart TT .05 .15
54 Home Depot Ratchet TT .05 .15
55 Interstate Generator TT .05 .15
56 Kelloggs Tires TT .05 .15
57 Miller Lite Headphones TT .05 .15
58 Jeremy Mayfield's Car .05 .15
59 Lowes Lugnuts TT .05 .15
60 Valvoline Springs TT CL .05 .15
P1 Tony Stewart Promo Big Numbers 1.00 2.50

1999 Press Pass Stealth Fusion

Inserted one per pack, this parallel of the base set was printed on metalized foil stock and over stamped in laser gold foil.

COMPLETE SET (60) 15.00 40.00
*FUSION: 1X TO 2.5X BASIC CARDS
*FUSION RC's: .6X TO 1.5X BASIC CARDS

1999 Press Pass Stealth Big Numbers

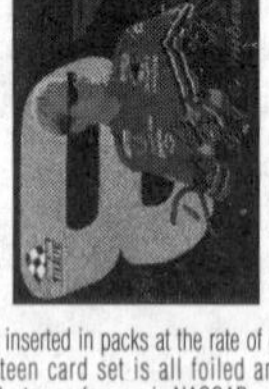

Randomly inserted in packs at the rate of one in six, this eighteen card set is all foiled and etched featuring the top performers in NASCAR.

COMPLETE SET (18) 20.00 50.00
*DIE CUTS: 1X TO 2.5X BASIC INSERTS
DIE CUT STATED ODDS 1:18
BN1 Ward Burton .50 1.25
BN2 Jeff Burton .75 2.00
BN3 Dale Earnhardt 4.00 10.00
BN4 Dale Earnhardt Jr. 3.00 8.00
BN5 Dale Earnhardt Jr. 3.00 8.00
BN6 Mike Skinner .25 .60
BN7 Jeff Gordon 2.50 6.00
BN8 Jeff Gordon 2.50 6.00
BN9 Bobby Hamilton .25 .60
BN10 Dale Jarrett 1.50 4.00
BN11 Bobby Labonte 1.50 4.00
BN12 Terry Labonte .75 2.00
BN13 Sterling Marlin .75 2.00
BN14 Mark Martin 2.00 5.00
BN15 Jeremy Mayfield .50 1.25
BN16 Tony Stewart 2.50 6.00
BN17 Rusty Wallace 2.00 5.00
BN18 Michael Waltrip .50 1.25

1999 Press Pass Stealth Headlines

Randomly inserted in packs at increasing ratios this set features a interactive heat transfer technology.

Collectors would touch the black screen to reveal the "Stealth Headline."

COMPLETE SET (9) 40.00 100.00
SH1 Jeff Gordon 10.00 25.00
SH2 Dale Earnhardt 12.50 30.00
SH3 Dale Earnhardt Jr. 8.00 20.00
SH4 Mark Martin 5.00 12.00
SH5 Rusty Wallace 5.00 12.00
SH6 Tony Stewart 3.00 8.00
SH7 Dale Earnhardt Jr. 4.00 10.00
SH8 Dale Jarrett 2.50 6.00
SH9 Terry Labonte 2.00 5.00

1999 Press Pass Stealth Octane SLX

Randomly inserted in packs at the rate of one in two these cards feature a mix of leading NASCAR drivers and the cars they drive.

COMPLETE SET (36) 12.50 30.00
*DIE CUTS: .8X TO 2X BASIC INSERTS
DIE CUT STATED ODDS 1:11
01 John Andretti .15 .40
02 Ward Burton .30 .75
03 Jeff Burton .50 1.25
04 Dale Earnhardt Jr. 2.00 5.00
05 Dale Earnhardt Jr. 2.00 5.00
06 Jeff Gordon 1.50 4.00
07 Jeff Gordon 1.50 4.00
08 Bobby Hamilton .15 .40
09 Ernie Irvan .30 .75
010 Dale Jarrett 1.00 2.50
011 Terry Labonte .50 1.25
012 Bobby Labonte 1.00 2.50
013 Sterling Marlin .50 1.25
014 Mark Martin 1.25 3.00
015 Jeremy Mayfield .30 .75
016 Joe Nemechek .15 .40
017 Ricky Rudd .50 1.25
018 Ken Schrader .30 .75
019 Mike Skinner .15 .40
020 Jimmy Spencer .15 .40
021 Tony Stewart 1.50 4.00
022 Elliott Sadler .15 .40
023 Michael Waltrip .30 .75
024 Dale Earnhardt Jr.'s Car .75 2.00
025 Dale Earnhardt Jr.'s Car .75 2.00
026 Jeff Gordon's Car .60 1.50
027 Jeff Burton's Car .15 .40
028 Dale Earnhardt's Car 1.00 2.50
029 Tony Stewart's Car .60 1.50
030 Bobby Labonte's Car .30 .75
031 Terry Labonte's Car .30 .75
032 Ward Burton's Car .10 .30
033 Elliott Sadler's Car .10 .20
034 Jeff Gordon's Car .60 1.50
035 Dale Jarrett's Car .30 .75
036 Mark Martin's Car .50 1.25

1999 Press Pass Stealth Race Used Gloves

Randomly inserted in packs at the rate of one in 480, these cards feature a swatch of race used glove.

G1 Jeff Burton/150 20.00 50.00
G2 Jeff Gordon/24 150.00 300.00
G3 Dale Earnhardt's Car/30 200.00 400.00
G4 Dale Jarrett/25 125.00 250.00
G5 Bobby Labonte/150 25.00 60.00
G6 Terry Labonte/150 25.00 60.00
G7 Mark Martin/150 40.00 80.00
G8 Tony Stewart/150 50.00 120.00
G9 Rusty Wallace/150 30.00 80.00

1999 Press Pass Stealth SST Cars

Randomly inserted in packs at the rate of one in 23, these cards come partially covered with a black peel off, remove the peel off to find a smaller picture of the driver's ride.

COMPLETE SET (9) 15.00 40.00
SS1 Dale Earnhardt Jr.'s Car 1.50 4.00
SS2 Dale Earnhardt's Car 2.00 5.00
SS3 Jeff Gordon's Car 1.25 3.00
SS4 Dale Jarrett's Car .75 2.00
SS5 Bobby Labonte's Car .75 2.00
SS6 Terry Labonte's Car .40 1.00
SS7 Mark Martin's Car 1.00 2.50
SS8 Tony Stewart's Car 1.25 3.00
SS9 Rusty Wallace's Car 1.00 2.50

1999 Press Pass Stealth SST Drivers

Randomly inserted in packs at the rate of one in 95, these cards come partially covered with a black peel off, remove the peel to find a smaller picture of the driver.

COMPLETE SET (9) 30.00 80.00
SS1 Dale Earnhardt Jr. 3.00 8.00
SS2 Dale Earnhardt's Car 2.50 6.00
SS3 Jeff Gordon 2.50 6.00
SS4 Dale Jarrett 1.50 4.00
SS5 Bobby Labonte 1.50 4.00
SS6 Terry Labonte .75 2.00
SS7 Mark Martin 2.00 5.00
SS8 Tony Stewart 2.50 6.00
SS9 Rusty Wallace 2.00 5.00

2000 Press Pass Stealth

Released in October 2000, Stealth features a 72-card base set divided up into three subsets. Card numbers 1-54 are from the Winston Cup, numbers 55-63 are BGN, and numbers 64-72 are Fan Favorites. Three cards were released for each racing team, and when the backs are laid together, they form the image of a race pit scene. Stealth was packaged in 24-pack boxes with packs containing six cards and carried a suggested retail price of 2.99.

COMPLETE SET (72) 6.00 15.00
1 Steve Park .20 .50
2 Steve Park's Car .07 .20
3 Paul Andrews .07 .20
4 Rusty Wallace .50 1.25
5 Rusty Wallace's Car .20 .50
6 Robin Pemberton .07 .20
7 Dale Earnhardt 1.25 3.00
8 Dale Earnhardt's Car .50 1.25
9 Kevin Hamlin .07 .20
10 Terry Labonte .30 .75
11 Terry Labonte's Car .12 .30
12 Gary DeHart .07 .20
13 Mark Martin .60 1.50
14 Mark Martin's Car .25 .60
15 Jimmy Fennig .07 .20
16 Dale Earnhardt Jr. CRC 1.00 2.50
17 Dale Earnhardt Jr.'s Car .40 1.00
18 Tony Eury .15 .40
19 Jeremy Mayfield .07 .20
20 Jeremy Mayfield's Car .05 .10
21 Peter Sospenzo .07 .20
22 Matt Kenseth CRC .60 1.50
23 Matt Kenseth's Car .25 .60
24 Robbie Reiser .15 .40
25 Bobby Labonte .50 1.25
26 Bobby Labonte's Car .20 .50
27 Jimmy Makar .12 .30
28 Tony Stewart .75 2.00
29 Tony Stewart's Car .30 .75
30 Greg Zipadelli .15 .40
31 Ward Burton .15 .40
32 Ward Burton's Car .05 .15
33 Tommy Baldwin .15 .40
34 Jeff Gordon .75 2.00
35 Jeff Gordon's Car .30 .75
36 Robbie Loomis .15 .40
37 Jerry Nadeau .15 .40
38 Jerry Nadeau's Car .05 .15
39 Tony Furr .07 .20
40 Ricky Rudd .25 .60
41 Ricky Rudd's Car .05 .15
42 Mike McSwain .05 .10
43 Mike Skinner .07 .20
44 Mike Skinner's Car .05 .10
45 Larry McReynolds .15 .40
46 Dale Jarrett .50 1.25
47 Dale Jarrett's Car .20 .50
48 Todd Parrott .12 .30
49 Chad Little .12 .30
50 Chad Little's Car .05 .10
51 Jeff Hammond .15 .40
52 Jeff Burton .20 .50
53 Jeff Burton's Car .07 .20
54 Frank Stoddard .07 .20
55 Casey Atwood BGN .25 .60
56 Jeff Green BGN .07 .20
57 Matt Kenseth BGN .60 1.50
58 Todd Bodine BGN .07 .20
59 Randy LaJoie BGN .07 .20
60 Jason Keller BGN .07 .20
61 David Green BGN .07 .20
62 Kevin Harvick BGN .60 1.50
63 Elton Sawyer BGN .07 .20
64 Bobby Labonte FF .50 1.25
65 Jeff Gordon FF .75 2.00
66 Tony Stewart FF .75 2.00
67 Terry Labonte FF .30 .75
68 Dale Jarrett FF .50 1.25
69 Ricky Rudd FF .25 .60
70 Dale Earnhardt Jr. FF 1.00 2.50
71 Rusty Wallace FF .50 1.25
72 Casey Atwood CL .25 .60

2000 Press Pass Stealth Behind the Numbers

Randomly inserted in packs at the rate of one in 12, this 9-card set features heat transfer technology that upon touch of a finger, reveals information about the driver.

COMPLETE SET (9) 15.00 40.00
BN1 Matt Kenseth 3.00 8.00
BN2 Dale Earnhardt Jr. 5.00 12.00
BN3 Mark Martin 3.00 8.00
BN4 Rusty Wallace 2.50 6.00
BN5 Dale Jarrett 2.50 6.00
BN6 Tony Stewart 4.00 10.00
BN7 Jeff Gordon 4.00 10.00
BN8 Terry Labonte 1.50 4.00
BN9 Bobby Labonte 2.50 6.00

2000 Press Pass Stealth Fusion

Randomly inserted in packs at the rate of one in one, this 36-card set is billed as the set within a set. Each card is die cut and features full color photography of drivers and their cars.

COMPLETE SET (36) 10.00 25.00
*FUSION RED: .6X TO 1.5X BASIC INSERTS
RED STATED ODDS 1:8
*FUSION GREEN: 1.2X TO 3X BASIC INSERTS
GREEN STATED ODDS 1:18
GREEN PRINT RUN 1000 SER.#'d SETS
FS1 Dale Jarrett 1.00 2.50
FS2 Dale Jarrett's Car .40 1.00
FS3 Dale Jarrett 1.00 2.50
FS4 Bobby Labonte 1.00 2.50
FS5 Bobby Labonte's Car .40 1.00
FS6 Bobby Labonte 1.00 2.50
FS7 Rusty Wallace 1.00 2.50
FS8 Rusty Wallace's Car .40 1.00
FS9 Rusty Wallace 1.00 2.50
FS10 Mark Martin 1.25 3.00
FS11 Mark Martin's Car .50 1.25
FS12 Mark Martin 1.25 3.00
FS13 Jeff Gordon 1.50 4.00
FS14 Jeff Gordon's Car .60 1.50
FS15 Jeff Gordon 1.50 4.00
FS16 Dale Earnhardt Jr. 2.00 5.00
FS17 Dale Earnhardt Jr.'s Car .75 2.00
FS18 Dale Earnhardt Jr. 2.00 5.00
FS19 Matt Kenseth 1.25 3.00
FS20 Matt Kenseth's Car .50 1.25
FS21 Matt Kenseth 1.25 3.00
FS22 Tony Stewart 1.50 4.00
FS23 Tony Stewart .60 1.50
FS24 Tony Stewart 1.50 4.00
FS25 Jeff Burton .40 1.00
FS26 Jeff Burton's Car .15 .40
FS27 Jeff Burton .40 1.00
FS28 Jeremy Mayfield .15 .40
FS29 Jeremy Mayfield .05 .15
FS30 Jeremy Mayfield .15 .40
FS31 Ward Burton .30 .75
FS32 Ward Burton .12 .30
FS33 Ward Burton .30 .75
FS34 Tony Stewart 1.50 4.00
FS35 Tony Stewart's Car .60 1.50
FS36 Tony Stewart 1.50 4.00

2000 Press Pass Stealth Intensity

Randomly inserted in packs at the rate of one in 18, this 9-card set features multiple driver photos on an all foil micro-etched card stock.

COMPLETE SET (9) 20.00 50.00
IN1 Dale Jarrett 2.50 6.00
IN2 Mark Martin 3.00 8.00
IN3 Bobby Labonte 2.50 6.00
IN4 Tony Stewart 4.00 10.00
IN5 Jeff Gordon 4.00 10.00
IN6 Dale Earnhardt's Car 2.50 6.00
IN7 Rusty Wallace 2.50 6.00
IN8 Mike Skinner .40 1.00
IN9 Dale Earnhardt Jr. 5.00 12.00

2000 Press Pass Stealth Profile

Randomly inserted in packs progressively from one in 10 to one in 419, this 10-card set features an all-

foil micro-etched card stock and portrait photos drivers.

COMPLETE SET (10) 75.00 150.0
PR1 Dale Jarrett 2.00 5.0
PR2 Ward Burton 1.25 3.0
PR3 Tony Stewart 6.00 15.0
PR4 Bobby Labonte 3.00 8.0
PR5 Rusty Wallace 2.00 6.0
PR6 Mark Martin 2.00 6.0
PR7 Matt Kenseth 6.00 15.0
PR8 Dale Earnhardt Jr. 8.00 20.0
PR9 Jeff Gordon 30.00 80.0
PR10 Dale Earnhardt 30.00 80.0

2000 Press Pass Stealt Race Used Gloves

Randomly inserted in packs at the rate of one in 4 this 12-card set features authentic swatches of ra worn gloves. Stated print runs are placed next to driver's name.

COMPLETE SET (12)
G1 Bobby Labonte/100 25.00 50.0
G2 Rusty Wallace/100 30.00 60.0
G3 Dale Earnhardt/100 100.00 200.0
G4 Jeff Burton/100 25.00 50.0
G5 Terry Labonte/100 30.00 60.0
G6 Mark Martin/50 40.00 80.0
G7 Jeff Gordon/100 60.00 120.0
G8 Dale Earnhardt Jr./50 100.00 200.0
G9 Matt Kenseth/100 30.00 60.0
G10 Mike Skinner/100 15.00 30.0
G11 Dale Jarrett/50 50.00 100.0
G12 Tony Stewart/100 50.00 100.0

2000 Press Pass Stealt SST

Randomly inserted in packs at the rate of one eight, this 12-card set features embossed photos an all foil card stock.

COMPLETE SET (12) 15.00 40.0
SST1 Dale Jarrett 1.50 4.0
SST2 Bobby Labonte 1.50 4.0
SST3 Mark Martin 2.00 5.0
SST4 Jeff Gordon 2.50 6.0
SST5 Tony Stewart 2.50 6.0
SST6 Jeff Burton .60 1.5
SST7 Matt Kenseth 2.00 5.0
SST8 Rusty Wallace 1.50 4.0
SST9 Ward Burton .50 1.2
SST10 Terry Labonte 1.00 2.5
SST11 Ricky Rudd .75 2.0
SST12 Dale Earnhardt Jr. 3.00 8.0

2001 Press Pass Stealt

Issued in 2001, this 72 card set features a r between the leading NASCAR drivers and cards the cars they drive. The cards were issued in 6-c packs.

COMPLETE SET (72) 12.50 30.0
WAX BOX HOBBY 40.00 75.0
1 Steve Park .30
2 Steve Park's Car .30
3 Steve Park .30
4 Rusty Wallace .75 2.5
5 Rusty Wallace's Car .30
6 Rusty Wallace .75 2.5
7 Terry Labonte .50 1.2
8 Terry Labonte's Car .30
9 Terry Labonte .50 1.2
10 Mark Martin 1.00 2.5
11 Mark Martin's Car .30
12 Mark Martin 1.00 2.5
13 Dale Earnhardt Jr. 1.50 4.0
14 Dale Earnhardt Jr.'s Car .60 1.5
15 Dale Earnhardt Jr. 1.50 4.0
16 Michael Waltrip .30
17 Michael Waltrip's Car .15
18 Michael Waltrip .30
19 Bobby Labonte .75 2.0
20 Bobby Labonte's Car .30
21 Bobby Labonte .75 2.0
22 Tony Stewart 1.25 3.0
23 Tony Stewart's Car .50 1.2
24 Tony Stewart 1.25 3.0
25 Ward Burton .30
26 Ward Burton's Car .15
27 Ward Burton .30
28 Jeff Gordon 1.25 3.0

9 Jeff Gordon's Car	.50	1.25
0 Jeff Gordon	1.25	3.00
1 Ricky Rudd	.50	1.25
2 Ricky Rudd's Car	.30	.75
3 Ricky Rudd	.50	1.25
4 Kevin Harvick CRC	1.25	3.00
5 Kevin Harvick's Car	.50	1.25
6 Kevin Harvick	1.25	3.00
7 Mike Skinner	.15	.40
8 Mike Skinner's Car	.05	.15
9 Mike Skinner	.15	.40
0 Dale Jarrett	.75	2.00
1 Dale Jarrett's Car	.30	.75
2 Dale Jarrett	.75	2.00
3 Jeff Burton	.30	.75
4 Jeff Burton's Car	.15	.40
5 Jeff Burton	.30	.75
6 Greg Biffle BGN	.30	.75
7 David Green BGN	.15	.40
8 Jeff Green BGN	.15	.40
9 Kevin Grubb BGN	.15	.40
0 Kevin Harvick BGN	1.25	3.00
1 Randy LaJoie BGN	.15	.40
2 Chad Little BGN	.15	.40
3 Hank Parker Jr. BGN	.30	.75
4 Elton Sawyer BGN	.15	.40
5 Jeff Gordon WIN	1.00	2.50
6 Jeff Gordon WIN	1.00	2.50
7 Jeff Gordon WIN	1.00	2.50
8 Jeff Gordon WIN	1.00	2.50
9 Jeff Gordon WIN	1.00	2.50
0 Jeff Gordon WIN	1.00	2.50
1 Jeff Gordon WIN	1.00	2.50
2 Jeff Gordon WIN	1.00	2.50
3 Jeff Gordon WIN	1.00	2.50
4 Steve Park SST	.30	.75
5 Jeff Gordon SST	1.25	3.00
6 Dale Earnhardt Jr. SST	1.50	4.00
7 Mark Martin SST	1.00	2.50
8 Kevin Harvick SST	1.25	3.00
9 Dale Jarrett SST	.75	2.00
0 Tony Stewart SST	1.25	3.00
1 Rusty Wallace SST	1.00	2.50
2 Michael Waltrip SST CL	.15	.40

2001 Press Pass Stealth Holofoils

sued one per pack, these cards parallel the Stealth sic set. Each card was enhanced with holofoil inting.

OMPLETE SET (72)	50.00	100.00
HOLOFOILS: .8X TO 2X BASE CARDS		

2001 Press Pass Stealth Behind The Numbers

ndomly inserted into packs, these six cards feature ading drivers printed on a hexagon shaped card at can folded to form one of three different images. e stated odds were 1:48 packs.

OMPLETE SET (6)	30.00	80.00
N1 Kevin Harvick	8.00	20.00
N2 Mark Martin	6.00	15.00
N3 Dale Jarrett	5.00	12.00
N4 Terry Labonte	3.00	8.00
N5 Tony Stewart	8.00	20.00
N6 Rusty Wallace	6.00	15.00

2001 Press Pass Stealth Fusion

ndomly inserted into packs, these nine cards ature top drivers printed with on holofoil card ock. The stated odds were 1:12 packs.

OMPLETE SET (9)	20.00	50.00
Dale Earnhardt Jr.	6.00	15.00
2 Jeff Gordon	5.00	12.00
3 Dale Jarrett	3.00	8.00
4 Bobby Labonte	3.00	8.00
5 Terry Labonte	2.00	5.00
6 Mark Martin	4.00	10.00
7 Steve Park	1.25	3.00
8 Tony Stewart	5.00	12.00
9 Rusty Wallace	4.00	10.00

2001 Press Pass Stealth Lap Leaders

sued one per pack, these 36-die cut cards feature -drivers who led NASCAR races along with 18- rds featuring their rides. Each card was created th a clear plastic parallel with the 18-drivers sued at the rate of 1:8 hobby packs and the cars retail packs.

OMPLETE SET (36)	8.00	20.00
OMP.CLEAR CARS (18)	8.00	20.00
LEAR CARS: 1X TO 2.5X BASIC INSERTS		
LEAR CAR STATED ODDS 1:8 RETAIL		
OMP.CLEAR DRIVER (18)	12.50	30.00
LEAR DRIVER: 1X TO 2.5X BASIC INSERTS		
EAR DRIVER STATED ODDS 1:8 HOBBY		
1 Steve Park	.30	.75
LL2 Rusty Wallace	1.00	2.50
LL3 Terry Labonte	.50	1.25
LL4 Dale Earnhardt Jr.	1.50	4.00
LL5 Michael Waltrip	.30	.75
LL6 Matt Kenseth	1.00	2.50
LL7 Bobby Labonte	.75	2.00
LL8 Tony Stewart	1.25	3.00
LL9 Ward Burton	.30	.75
LL10 Jeff Gordon	1.25	3.00
LL11 Ricky Rudd	.50	1.25
LL12 Kevin Harvick	1.25	3.00
LL13 Mike Skinner	.15	.40
LL14 Joe Nemechek	.15	.40
LL15 Sterling Marlin	.50	1.25
LL16 Bobby Hamilton	.15	.40
LL17 Dale Jarrett	.75	2.00
LL18 Jeff Burton	.30	.75
LL19 Steve Park's Car	.30	.75
LL20 Rusty Wallace's Car	.30	.75
LL21 Terry Labonte's Car	.30	.75
LL22 Dale Earnhardt Jr.'s Car	.60	1.50
LL23 Michael Waltrip's Car	.15	.40
LL24 Matt Kenseth's Car	.50	1.25
LL25 Bobby Labonte's Car	.30	.75
LL26 Tony Stewart's Car	.50	1.25
LL27 Ward Burton's Car	.15	.40
LL28 Jeff Gordon's Car	.50	1.25
LL29 Ricky Rudd's Car	.30	.75
LL30 Kevin Harvick's Car	.50	1.25
LL31 Mike Skinner's Car	.05	.15
LL32 Joe Nemechek's Car	.05	.15
LL33 Sterling Marlin's Car	.05	.15
LL34 Bobby Hamilton's Car	.05	.15
LL35 Dale Jarrett's Car	.30	.75
LL36 Jeff Burton's Car	.15	.40

2001 Press Pass Stealth Profile

Randomly inserted into packs, these six cards feature leading NASCAR drivers laser etched on holofoil cardstock. The cards were randomly inserted in packs regressively with odds of 1:10 (#SP6) to 1:120 (#SP1).

SP1 Mark Martin	4.00	10.00
SP2 Kevin Harvick	5.00	12.00
SP3 Tony Stewart	5.00	12.00
SP4 Rusty Wallace	3.00	8.00
SP5 Jeff Gordon	6.00	15.00
SP6 Dale Earnhardt Jr.	6.00	15.00

2001 Press Pass Stealth Race Used Glove Cars

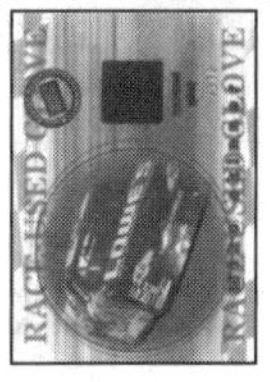

Inserted into retail packs at stated odds of one in 480, these 12 cards feature race-worn pieces of racing gloves. The print runs are notated next to each driver in our checklist.

RGC1 Jeff Gordon/50	60.00	150.00
RGC2 Rusty Wallace/120	20.00	50.00
RGC3 Michael Waltrip/170	15.00	40.00
RGC4 Tony Stewart/120	20.00	50.00
RGC5 Terry Labonte/120	15.00	40.00
RGC6 Mark Martin/50	40.00	100.00
RGC7 Matt Kenseth/120	20.00	50.00
RGC8 Dale Earnhardt Jr./50	75.00	200.00
RGC9 Jeff Burton/170	10.00	25.00
RGC10 Bobby Labonte/120	15.00	40.00
RGC11 Kevin Harvick/120	25.00	60.00
RGC12 Mike Skinner/170	10.00	25.00

2001 Press Pass Stealth Race Used Glove Drivers

Inserted into hobby packs at stated odds of one in 230, these 12 cards feature race-worn pieces of racing gloves. The print runs are notated next to each driver in our checklist.

RGD1 Jeff Gordon/50	100.00	200.00
RGD2 Rusty Wallace/120	25.00	60.00
RGD3 Michael Waltrip/170	20.00	50.00
RGD4 Tony Stewart/120	25.00	60.00
RGD5 Terry Labonte/120	20.00	50.00
RGD6 Mark Martin/50	60.00	120.00
RGD7 Matt Kenseth/120	25.00	60.00
RGD8 Dale Earnhardt Jr./50	125.00	250.00
RGD9 Jeff Burton/170	12.50	30.00
RGD10 Bobby Labonte/120	20.00	50.00
RGD11 Kevin Harvick/120	30.00	80.00
RGD12 Mike Skinner/170	12.50	30.00

2002 Press Pass Stealth

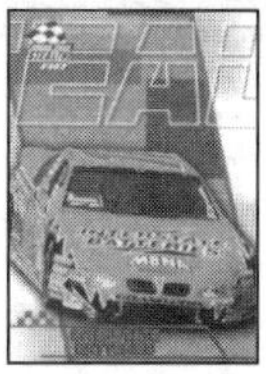

This 72 card set was released in September, 2002. These cards were issued in six card hobby or retail packs which came 24 packs per box with 20 boxes per case. When the three cards featuring either the driver or the team are placed together, a picture of the team's transporter is visible as if a puzzle was joined together.

COMPLETE SET (72)	10.00	25.00
WAX BOX HOBBY	40.00	75.00
WAX BOX RETAIL (24)	30.00	60.00
1 Rusty Wallace	.60	1.50
2 Rusty Wallace's Car	.25	.60
3 Rusty Wallace	.60	1.50
4 Terry Labonte	.40	1.00
5 Terry Labonte's Car	.10	.30
6 Terry Labonte	.40	1.00
7 Mark Martin	.75	2.00
8 Mark Martin's Car	.30	.75
9 Mark Martin	.75	2.00
10 Dale Earnhardt Jr.	1.25	3.00
11 Dale Earnhardt Jr.'s Car	.50	1.25
12 Dale Earnhardt Jr.	1.25	3.00
13 Ryan Newman CRC	.75	2.00
14 Ryan Newman's Car	.30	.75
15 Ryan Newman	.75	2.00
16 Matt Kenseth	.75	2.00
17 Matt Kenseth's Car	.30	.75
18 Matt Kenseth	.75	2.00
19 Bobby Labonte	.60	1.50
20 Bobby Labonte's Car	.25	.60
21 Bobby Labonte	.60	1.50
22 Tony Stewart	.75	2.00
23 Tony Stewart's Car	.30	.75
24 Tony Stewart	.75	2.00
25 Ward Burton	.25	.60
26 Ward Burton's Car	.10	.30
27 Ward Burton	.25	.60
28 Jeff Gordon	1.00	2.50
29 Jeff Gordon's Car	.40	1.00
30 Jeff Gordon	1.00	2.50
31 Kevin Harvick	.75	2.00
32 Kevin Harvick's Car	.30	.75
33 Kevin Harvick	.75	2.00
34 Sterling Marlin	.40	1.00
35 Sterling Marlin's Car	.10	.30
36 Sterling Marlin	.40	1.00
37 Jimmie Johnson CRC	.75	2.00
38 Jimmie Johnson's Car	.30	.75
39 Jimmie Johnson	.75	2.00
40 Dale Jarrett	.60	1.50
41 Dale Jarrett's Car	.25	.60
42 Dale Jarrett	.60	1.50
43 Jeff Burton	.25	.60
44 Jeff Burton's Car	.10	.30
45 Jeff Burton	.25	.60
46 Greg Biffle	.25	.60
47 Mike McLaughlin	.10	.30
48 Randy LaJoie	.10	.30
49 Chad Little	.10	.30
50 Hank Parker Jr.	.10	.30
51 Jamie McMurray RC	2.50	6.00
52 Jimmie Johnson's Car SST	.30	.75
53 Kevin Harvick's Car SST	.30	.75
54 Dale Jarrett's Car SST	.25	.60
55 Dale Earnhardt Jr.'s Car SST	.50	1.25
56 Matt Kenseth's Car SST	.30	.75
57 Jeff Burton's Car SST	.10	.30
58 Mark Martin's Car SST	.30	.75
59 Rusty Wallace's Car SST	.25	.60
60 Jeff Gordon's Car SST	.40	1.00
61 Tony Stewart's Car SST	.30	.75
62 Bobby Labonte's Car SST	.25	.60
63 Robby Gordon's Car SST	.05	.15
64 Dale Earnhardt Jr. WW	1.25	3.00
65 Kevin Harvick WW	.75	2.00
66 Bobby Labonte WW	.60	1.50
67 Terry Labonte WW	.40	1.00
68 Mark Martin WW	.75	2.00
69 Jimmie Johnson WW	.75	2.00
70 Tony Stewart WW	.75	2.00
71 Jeff Gordon WW	1.00	2.50
72 Rusty Wallace checklist	.30	.75
Ryan Newman checklist		

2002 Press Pass Stealth Gold

Issued at a stated rate of one per pack, this is a parallel of the Stealth set. These cards can be differentiated a by the gold foil stamping instead of the basic issue silver.

COMPLETE SET (72)	15.00	40.00
*GOLDS: .8X TO 2X BASIC CARDS		

2002 Press Pass Stealth Samples

These cards were issued before the release of the Stealth product to both herald the set and to show what these cards would look like. The cards were inserted one per Beckett Racing Collector magazine.

*SAMPLES: 2.5X TO 6X BASE CARDS

2002 Press Pass Stealth Behind the Numbers

Issued at stated odds ranging from one in 48 (card #BN9) to one in 240 (#BN1), these nine cards feature cards which celebrate the accomplishments and milestones of the featured drivers.

BN1 Kevin Harvick	10.00	25.00
BN2 Mark Martin	10.00	25.00
BN3 Dale Jarrett	10.00	25.00
BN4 Terry Labonte	6.00	15.00
BN5 Tony Stewart	4.00	10.00
BN6 Rusty Wallace	4.00	10.00
BN7 Jimmie Johnson	4.00	10.00
BN8 Bobby Labonte	3.00	8.00
BN9 Jeff Gordon	4.00	10.00

2002 Press Pass Stealth EFX

Issued at stated odds of one in eight, these 12 cards feature information on how NASCAR drivers stay cool while racing during summertime. Each card was printed with an all-foil design.

COMPLETE SET (12)	10.00	25.00
FX1 Ricky Rudd	.60	1.50
FX2 Sterling Marlin	.75	2.00
FX3 Rusty Wallace	1.25	3.00
FX4 Dale Earnhardt Jr.	2.50	6.00
FX5 Jeff Gordon	2.00	5.00
FX6 Kevin Harvick	1.50	4.00
FX7 Tony Stewart	1.50	4.00
FX8 Dale Jarrett	1.25	3.00
FX9 Jeff Burton	.50	1.25
FX10 Ryan Newman	1.50	4.00
FX11 Jimmie Johnson	1.50	4.00
FX12 Terry Labonte	.75	2.00

2002 Press Pass Stealth Fusion

Cards from this set were issued at a stated rate of one in 12 packs. They feature information on how a driver learns to become an elite NASCAR driver in this all holo, gold-foil stamped insert set.

COMPLETE SET (12)	15.00	40.00
F1 Jeff Burton	.60	1.50
F2 Dale Earnhardt Jr.	3.00	8.00
F3 Jeff Gordon	2.50	6.00
F4 Kevin Harvick	2.00	5.00
F5 Dale Jarrett	1.50	4.00
F6 Jimmie Johnson	2.00	5.00
F7 Bobby Labonte	1.50	4.00
F8 Sterling Marlin	1.00	2.50
F9 Mark Martin	2.00	5.00
F10 Ryan Newman	2.00	5.00
F11 Tony Stewart	2.00	5.00
F12 Rusty Wallace	1.50	4.00

2002 Press Pass Stealth Lap Leaders

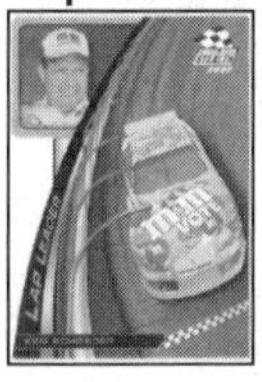

Inserted at a stated rate of one per pack, this 27-car die-cut set features NASCAR drivers who have led races for at least one lap.

COMPLETE SET (27)	8.00	20.00
LL1 John Andretti	.15	.40
LL2 Casey Atwood	.15	.40
LL3 Jeff Burton	.30	.75
LL4 Ward Burton	.30	.75
LL5 Kurt Busch	.40	1.00
LL6 Dale Earnhardt Jr.	1.50	4.00
LL7 Jeff Gordon	1.25	3.00
LL8 Robby Gordon	.15	.40
LL9 Jeff Green	.15	.40
LL10 Bobby Hamilton	.15	.40
LL11 Kevin Harvick	1.00	2.50
LL12 Dale Jarrett	.75	2.00
LL13 Jimmie Johnson	1.00	2.50
LL14 Matt Kenseth	1.00	2.50
LL15 Bobby Labonte	.75	2.00
LL16 Terry Labonte	.50	1.25
LL17 Sterling Marlin	.50	1.25
LL18 Mark Martin	1.00	2.50
LL19 Jeremy Mayfield	.15	.40
LL20 Ryan Newman	1.00	2.50
LL21 Kyle Petty	.30	.75
LL22 Ricky Rudd	.40	1.00
LL23 Ken Schrader	.15	.40
LL24 Mike Skinner	.15	.40
LL25 Jimmy Spencer	.15	.40
LL26 Tony Stewart	1.00	2.50
LL27 Rusty Wallace	.75	2.00

2002 Press Pass Stealth Profile

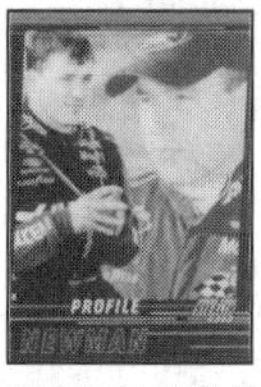

Issued at a stated rate of one in 24, this nine-card plastic set features personal information about leading NASCAR drivers.

COMPLETE SET (9)	20.00	50.00
P1 Jeff Gordon	5.00	12.00
P2 Mark Martin	4.00	10.00
P3 Tony Stewart	4.00	10.00
P4 Kevin Harvick	4.00	10.00
P5 Matt Kenseth	4.00	10.00
P6 Jimmie Johnson	4.00	10.00
P7 Ryan Newman	4.00	10.00
P8 Dale Jarrett	3.00	8.00
P9 Bobby Labonte	3.00	8.00

2002 Press Pass Stealth Race Used Glove Cars

Issued at a stated rate of one in 480 retail packs, these 16 cards feature pieces of race-used gloves set upon cards featuring the cars of leading NASCAR drivers. These cards were issued to a state print run of 85 serial numbered sets. The Dale Jarrett and Dale Earnhardt cards were issued to a stated print run of 10 sets and those cards are not priced due to market scarcity.

GLC1 Jeff Gordon's Car	30.00	80.00
GLC2 Rusty Wallace's Car	12.50	30.00
GLC3 Tony Stewart's Car	20.00	50.00
GLC4 Terry Labonte's Car	15.00	40.00
GLC5 Mark Martin's Car	15.00	40.00
GLC6 Matt Kenseth's Car	15.00	40.00
GLC7 Dale Earnhardt Jr.'s Car	30.00	80.00
GLC8 Jeff Burton's Car	10.00	25.00
GLC9 Bobby Labonte's Car	12.50	30.00
GLC10 Kevin Harvick's Car	12.50	30.00
GLC11 Mike Skinner's Car	8.00	20.00
GLC12 Ryan Newman's Car	15.00	40.00
GLC13 Jimmie Johnson's Car	15.00	40.00
GLC14 Dale Jarrett's Car/10		
GLC15 Ken Schrader's Car	8.00	20.00
GLC16 Dale Earnhardt's Car/10		

2002 Press Pass Stealth Race Used Glove Drivers

Inserted into hobby packs at a stated rate of one in 480, these 16 cards feature race-used glove swatches set against a photo of the driver. These cards were issued to a stated print run of 50 serial numbered sets.

GLD1 Jeff Gordon	60.00	120.00
GLD2 Rusty Wallace	20.00	50.00
GLD3 Tony Stewart	40.00	80.00
GLD4 Terry Labonte	25.00	60.00
GLD5 Mark Martin	25.00	60.00
GLD6 Matt Kenseth	25.00	60.00
GLD7 Dale Earnhardt Jr.	60.00	120.00
GLD8 Jeff Burton	15.00	40.00
GLD9 Bobby Labonte	20.00	50.00
GLD10 Kevin Harvick	20.00	50.00
GLD11 Mike Skinner	12.50	30.00
GLD12 Ryan Newman	25.00	60.00
GLD13 Jimmie Johnson	25.00	60.00
GLD14 Dale Jarrett/10		
GLD15 Ken Schrader	12.50	30.00
GLD16 Dale Earnhardt/10		

2003 Press Pass Stealth

This 72 card set was released in September, 2003. These cards were issued in six card hobby or retail packs which came 28 packs per box with an SRP of $2.99. When the three cards featuring either the

driver or the team are placed together, the card backs feature a picture of the team's car as if a puzzle was joined together. As a bonus there was a Dale Earnhardt Sunday Money card numbered 0/0 inserted at a rate of 1 in 480 packs.

COMPLETE SET (72)	10.00	25.00
ZERO CARD STATED ODDS 1:480		
WAX BOX HOBBY (28)	45.00	80.00
1 Rusty Wallace	.60	1.50
2 Rusty Wallace's Car	.25	.60
3 Rusty Wallace	.60	1.50
4 Terry Labonte	.40	1.00
5 Terry Labonte's Car	.10	.30
6 Terry Labonte	.40	1.00
7 Mark Martin	.75	2.00
8 Mark Martin's Car	.25	.60
9 Mark Martin	.75	2.00
10 Dale Earnhardt Jr.	1.25	3.00
11 Dale Earnhardt Jr.'s Car	.50	1.25
12 Dale Earnhardt Jr.	1.25	3.00
13 Michael Waltrip	.25	.60
14 Michael Waltrip's Car	.05	.15
15 Michael Waltrip	.25	.60
16 Matt Kenseth	.75	2.00
17 Matt Kenseth's Car	.25	.60
18 Matt Kenseth	.75	2.00
19 Bobby Labonte	.60	1.50
20 Bobby Labonte's Car	.25	.60
21 Bobby Labonte	.60	1.50
22 Tony Stewart	.75	2.00
23 Tony Stewart's Car	.25	.60
24 Tony Stewart	.75	2.00
25 Ricky Rudd	.40	1.00
26 Ricky Rudd's Car	.10	.30
27 Ricky Rudd	.40	1.00
28 Ward Burton	.25	.60
29 Ward Burton's Car	.05	.15
30 Ward Burton	.25	.60
31 Jeff Gordon	1.00	2.50
32 Jeff Gordon's Car	.40	1.00
33 Jeff Gordon	1.00	2.50
34 Jimmie Johnson	.75	2.00
35 Jimmie Johnson's Car	.25	.60
36 Jimmie Johnson	.75	2.00
37 Dale Jarrett	.60	1.50
38 Dale Jarrett's Car	.25	.60
39 Dale Jarrett	.60	1.50
40 Kurt Busch	.40	1.00
41 Kurt Busch's Car	.10	.30
42 Kurt Busch	.40	1.00
43 Jeff Burton	.25	.60
44 Jeff Burton's Car	.05	.15
45 Jeff Burton	.25	.60
46 Scott Wimmer BGN	.25	.60
47 David Green BGN	.10	.30
48 Kerry Earnhardt BGN	.25	.60
49 Kevin Grubb BGN	.10	.30
50 Jason Keller BGN	.10	.30
51 Mike McLaughlin BGN	.10	.30
52 Johnny Sauter BGN	.25	.60
53 Jimmy Vasser BGN RC	.10	.30
54 Brian Vickers BGN	.50	1.25
55 Rusty Wallace SST	.60	1.50
56 Terry Labonte SST	.40	1.00
57 Dale Earnhardt Jr. SST	1.25	3.00
58 Kerry Earnhardt SST	.25	.60
59 Michael Waltrip SST	.25	.60
60 Bobby Labonte SST	.60	1.50
61 Ward Burton SST	.25	.60
62 Jeff Gordon SST	1.00	2.50
63 Jimmie Johnson SST	.75	2.00
64 Jeff Gordon SF	1.00	2.50
65 Ricky Rudd SF	.40	1.00
66 Dale Jarrett SF	.60	1.50
67 Jimmie Johnson SF	.75	2.00
68 Terry Labonte SF	.40	1.00
69 Mark Martin SF	.75	2.00
70 Tony Stewart SF	.75	2.00
71 Rusty Wallace SF	.60	1.50
72 Dale Earnhardt Jr.	.75	2.00
Matt Kenseth CL		
0 Dale Earnhardt Sunday Money	12.50	30.00

2003 Press Pass Stealth Red

Issued at a stated rate of one per pack, this is a parallel of the Stealth set. These cards can be differentiated by the red foil stamping instead of the basic issue silver.

*REDS: .8X TO 2X BASIC

2003 Press Pass Stealth Samples

This 50-card set was a parallel of the base set with the exception of the word "SAMPLE" printed on the back of each card. These cards were found in Beckett Racing Collector November 2003, Issue #111. There was one card per magazine.

*SAMPLES: 2.5X TO 6X BASE CARDS

2003 Press Pass Stealth EFX

Issued at stated odds of one in eight, these 12 cards feature information on how NASCAR drivers stay cool while racing during summertime. Each card was printed with an all-foil design.

FX1 Jeff Burton	.50	1.25
FX2 Greg Biffle	.50	1.25
FX3 Dale Earnhardt Jr.	2.50	6.00
FX4 Jeff Gordon	2.00	5.00
FX5 Ryan Newman	1.50	4.00
FX6 Jimmie Johnson	1.50	4.00
FX7 Bobby Labonte	1.25	3.00
FX8 Terry Labonte	.75	2.00
FX9 Ricky Rudd	.75	2.00
FX10 Tony Stewart	1.50	4.00
FX11 Rusty Wallace	1.25	3.00
FX12 Michael Waltrip	.50	1.25

2003 Press Pass Stealth Fusion

Cards from this set were issued at a stated rate of one in 12 packs. They feature information on how a driver learns to become an elite NASCAR driver in this all holo, gold-foil stamped insert set.

FU1 Jeff Burton	.60	1.50
FU2 Casey Mears	.60	1.50
FU3 Dale Earnhardt Jr.	3.00	8.00
FU4 Jeff Gordon	2.50	6.00
FU5 Kevin Harvick	2.00	5.00
FU6 Jamie McMurray	1.00	2.50
FU7 Jimmie Johnson	2.00	5.00
FU8 Bobby Labonte	1.50	4.00
FU9 Mark Martin	2.00	5.00
FU10 Ricky Rudd	1.00	2.50
FU11 Rusty Wallace	1.50	4.00
FU12 Michael Waltrip	.60	1.50

2003 Press Pass Stealth Gear Grippers Cars

Issued at a stated rate of one in 240 retail packs, these 18 cards feature pieces of race-used gloves set upon cards featuring the cars of leading NASCAR drivers. These cards were issued to a state print run of 150 serial numbered sets. The Dale Earnhardt card was issued to a stated print run of 3 sets and the Michael Waltrip was numbered to 30. The Earnhardt cards are not priced due to scarcity.

*CARS: .25X TO .6X DRIVERS

GGT1 Jeff Gordon	25.00	60.00
GGT2 Ryan Newman	20.00	50.00
GGT3 Kevin Harvick	15.00	40.00
GGT4 Jimmie Johnson	20.00	50.00
GGT5 Rusty Wallace	12.50	30.00
GGT6 Mark Martin	20.00	50.00
GGT7 Ken Schrader	10.00	25.00
GGT8 Tony Stewart	20.00	50.00
GGT9 Terry Labonte	12.50	30.00
GGT10 Dale Earnhardt Jr.	25.00	60.00
GGT11 Dale Earnhardt/3		
GGT12 Michael Waltrip/30	20.00	40.00
GGT13 Jeff Burton	10.00	25.00
GGT14 Dale Jarrett	12.50	30.00
GGT15 Joe Nemechek	10.00	25.00
GGT16 Ward Burton	10.00	25.00
GGT17 Ricky Craven	8.00	20.00
GGT18 Bobby Labonte	15.00	40.00

2003 Press Pass Stealth Gear Grippers Cars Autographs

This 8-card set was randomly inserted retail packs. These cards feature pieces of race-used gloves set

upon cards featuring the cars of leading NASCAR drivers along with the driver's signature. These cards were limited and hand numbered to the corresponding driver's door number. Some of these cards are not priced due to scarcity.

SERIAL #'s TO CAR NUMBER
SOME CARDS NOT PRICED DUE TO SCARCITY

JG Jeff Gordon's Car/24	250.00	500.00
JJ Jimmie Johnson's Car/48	100.00	175.00
KH Kevin Harvick's Car/29	100.00	200.00
MK Matt Kenseth's Car/17		
MM Mark Martin's Car/6		
RN Ryan Newman's Car/12		
RW Rusty Wallace's Car/2		
TL Terry Labonte's Car/5		

2003 Press Pass Stealth Gear Grippers Drivers

Issued at a stated rate of one in 180 retail packs, these 18 cards feature pieces of race-used gloves set upon cards featuring the drivers of leading NASCAR teams. These cards were issued to a state print run of 75 serial numbered sets. The Dale Earnhardt card was issued to a stated print run of 3 sets and the Michael Waltrip was numbered to 30. The Earnhardt cards are not priced due to scarcity.

STATED PRINT RUN 75 SERIAL #'d SETS

GGD1 Jeff Gordon	50.00	100.00
GGD2 Ryan Newman	40.00	80.00
GGD3 Kevin Harvick	30.00	60.00
GGD4 Jimmie Johnson	30.00	80.00
GGD5 Rusty Wallace	25.00	50.00
GGD6 Mark Martin	40.00	80.00
GGD7 Ken Schrader	20.00	40.00
GGD8 Tony Stewart	40.00	80.00
GGD9 Terry Labonte	25.00	50.00
GGD10 Dale Earnhardt Jr.	50.00	100.00
GGD11 Dale Earnhardt/3		
GGD12 Michael Waltrip/30	25.00	50.00
GGD13 Jeff Burton	15.00	40.00
GGD14 Dale Jarrett	20.00	50.00
GGD15 Joe Nemechek	20.00	40.00
GGD16 Ward Burton	15.00	40.00
GGD17 Ricky Craven	15.00	30.00
GGD18 Bobby Labonte	30.00	60.00

2003 Press Pass Stealth Gear Grippers Drivers Autographs

This 8-card set was randomly inserted hobby packs. These cards feature pieces of race-used gloves set upon cards featuring the drivers along with the their signature. These cards were limited and hand numbered to the corresponding driver's door number. Some of these cards are not priced due to scarcity.

JG Jeff Gordon/24	250.00	500.00
JJ Jimmie Johnson/48	100.00	175.00
KH Kevin Harvick/29	100.00	200.00
MK Matt Kenseth/17		
MM Mark Martin/6		
RN Ryan Newman/12		
RW Rusty Wallace/2		
TL Terry Labonte/5		

2003 Press Pass Stealth No Boundaries

Issued at a stated rate of one per pack, this 25-card set features the interaction fans have with their favorite leading NASCAR drivers.

NB1 Kevin Grubb	.20	.50
NB2 Kerry Earnhardt	.40	1.00
NB3 Jason Keller	.20	.50
NB4 Mike McLaughlin	.20	.50
NB5 Johnny Sauter	.40	1.00
NB6 Regan Smith	.20	.50
NB7 Jimmy Vasser	.20	.50
NB8 Scott Wimmer	.40	1.00
NB9 Greg Biffle	.40	1.00
NB10 Jeff Burton	.40	1.00
NB11 Dale Earnhardt Jr.	2.00	5.00
NB12 Jeff Gordon	1.50	4.00
NB13 Kevin Harvick	1.25	3.00
NB14 Dale Jarrett	1.00	2.50
NB15 Matt Kenseth	1.25	3.00
NB16 Jimmie Johnson	1.25	3.00
NB17 Bobby Labonte	1.00	2.50
NB18 Terry Labonte	.60	1.50
NB19 Mark Martin	1.25	3.00
NB20 Jamie McMurray	.60	1.50
NB21 Casey Mears	.40	1.00
NB22 Ricky Rudd	.60	1.50
NB23 Jimmy Spencer	.20	.50
NB24 Rusty Wallace	1.00	2.50
NB25 Michael Waltrip	.40	1.00

2003 Press Pass Stealth Profile

Issued at a stated rate of one in 24, this nine-card plastic set features personal information about leading NASCAR drivers.

PR1 Dale Earnhardt Jr.	5.00	12.00
PR2 Jeff Gordon	4.00	10.00
PR3 Dale Jarrett	2.50	6.00
PR4 Jimmie Johnson	3.00	8.00
PR5 Bobby Labonte	2.50	6.00
PR6 Mark Martin	3.00	8.00
PR7 Ryan Newman	3.00	8.00
PR8 Rusty Wallace	2.50	6.00

2003 Press Pass Stealth Supercharged

Issued at stated odds ranging from one in 48 (card #SC9) to one in 168 (#BN1), these nine cards feature cards which celebrate the accomplishments and milestones of the featured drivers.

SC1 Jeff Gordon	20.00	50.00
SC2 Jimmie Johnson	12.50	25.00
SC3 Dale Earnhardt Jr.	12.50	30.00
SC4 Rusty Wallace	7.50	15.00
SC5 Michael Waltrip	4.00	10.00
SC6 Mark Martin	5.00	10.00
SC7 Ward Burton	4.00	8.00
SC8 Kerry Earnhardt	4.00	8.00
SC9 Terry Labonte	5.00	10.00

2004 Press Pass Stealth

Press Pass Stealth was released in May of 2004. This 100-card set featured NASCAR's hottest drivers. Photography from this set was taken during Speedweeks at Daytona in February and this was the first time drivers were pictured with their new teams for 2004. Cards were packaged 4 to a pack in both hobby and retail. Hobby boxes contained 28 packs while retail had only 24 packs, but both were packed 20 boxes to a case. The SRP for both hobby and retail was $2.99 per pack.

COMPLETE SET (100)	12.50	30.00
WAX BOX HOBBY (28)	40.00	70.00
WAX BOX RETAIL (24)	40.00	70.00
1 Kurt Busch	.40	1.00
2 Kurt Busch's Car	.15	.40
3 Kurt Busch	.40	1.00
4 Dale Jarrett	.50	1.25
5 Dale Jarrett's Car	.25	.60
6 Dale Jarrett	.50	1.25
7 Jimmie Johnson	.75	2.00
8 Jimmie Johnson's Car	.25	.60
9 Jimmie Johnson	.75	2.00
10 Jamie McMurray	.40	1.00
11 Jamie McMurray's Car	.15	.40
12 Jamie McMurray	.40	1.00
13 Sterling Marlin	.40	1.00
14 Sterling Marlin's Car	.15	.40
15 Sterling Marlin	.40	1.00
16 Robby Gordon	.15	.40
17 Robby Gordon's Car	.15	.40
18 Robby Gordon	.15	.40
19 Kevin Harvick	.60	1.50
20 Kevin Harvick's Car	.25	.60
21 Kevin Harvick	.60	1.50
22 Brian Vickers CRC	.50	1.25
23 Brian Vickers' Car	.25	.60
24 Brian Vickers	.50	1.25
25 Jeff Gordon	1.00	2.50
26 Jeff Gordon's Car	.40	1.00
27 Jeff Gordon	1.00	2.50
28 Ricky Rudd	.40	1.00
29 Ricky Rudd's Car	.15	.40
30 Ricky Rudd	.40	1.00
31 Tony Stewart	.60	1.50
32 Tony Stewart's Car	.25	.60
33 Tony Stewart	.60	1.50
34 Michael Waltrip	.25	.60
35 Michael Waltrip's Car	.15	.40
36 Michael Waltrip	.25	.60
37 Matt Kenseth	.75	2.00
38 Matt Kenseth's Car	.25	.60
39 Matt Kenseth	.75	2.00
40 Bobby Labonte	.50	1.25
41 Bobby Labonte's Car	.25	.60
42 Bobby Labonte	.50	1.25
43 Greg Biffle	.25	.60
44 Greg Biffle's Car	.15	.40
45 Greg Biffle	.25	.60
46 Ryan Newman	.75	2.00
47 Ryan Newman's Car	.25	.60
48 Ryan Newman	.75	2.00
49 Scott Riggs CRC	.25	.60
50 Scott Riggs' Car	.15	.40
51 Scott Riggs	.25	.60
52 Dale Earnhardt Jr.	1.00	2.50
53 Dale Earnhardt Jr.'s Car	.40	1.00
54 Dale Earnhardt Jr.	1.00	2.50
55 Mark Martin	.60	1.50
56 Mark Martin's Car	.25	.60
57 Mark Martin	.60	1.50
58 Terry Labonte	.40	1.00
59 Terry Labonte's Car	.15	.40
60 Terry Labonte	.40	1.00
61 Rusty Wallace	.50	1.25
62 Rusty Wallace's Car	.25	.60
63 Rusty Wallace	.50	1.25
64 Mike Bliss	.15	.40
65 Kyle Busch RC	3.00	8.00
66 Paul Wolfe RC	.75	2.00
67 Jason Keller	.15	.40
68 Paul Menard RC	.75	2.00
69 Billy Parker Jr. RC	1.00	2.50
70 David Green	.15	.40
71 Martin Truex Jr. RC	2.50	6.00
72 J.J. Yeley RC	1.50	4.00
73 Jeff Burton WW	.25	.60
74 Mark Martin WW	.60	1.50
75 Matt Kenseth WW	.75	2.00
76 Kevin Harvick WW	.60	1.50
77 Johnny Sauter WW	.15	.40
78 Kasey Kahne WW CRC	1.25	3.00
79 Greg Biffle WW	.25	.60
80 Joe Nemechek WW	.15	.40
81 Robby Gordon WW	.15	.40
82 Robby Gordon SST	.15	.40
83 Dale Earnhardt Jr. SST	1.00	2.50
84 Michael Waltrip SST	.25	.60
85 Matt Kenseth SST	.75	2.00
86 Jeff Gordon SST	1.00	2.50
87 Kevin Harvick SST	.60	1.50
88 Jimmie Johnson SST	.75	2.00
89 Dale Jarrett SST	.50	1.25
90 Kurt Busch SST	.40	1.00
91 Rusty Wallace SF	.50	1.25
92 Jamie McMurray SF	.40	1.00
93 Kevin Harvick SF	.60	1.50
94 Jimmie Johnson SF	.75	2.00
95 Kurt Busch SF	.40	1.00
96 Tony Stewart SF	.60	1.50
97 Matt Kenseth SF	.75	2.00
98 Michael Waltrip SF	.25	.60
99 Dale Earnhardt Jr. SF	1.00	2.50
100 Kevin Harvick CL	.60	1.50

2004 Press Pass Stealth Samples

This 100-card set is a parallel to the base 2004 Press Pass Stealth set without the variations. It was issued 1 per Beckett Racing Collector issue #119, which was the July 2004 cover date. Each card had the word "SAMPLE" printed across the back.

*SAMPLES: 2X TO 5X BASE
STATED ODDS 1 PER BRC119

2004 Press Pass Stealth X-Ray

This 100-card set was a parallel to the base set and was serial numbered to 100. This set was sometimes referred to as a 'Gold Parallel' due to its gold foil highlights and the serial numbering and there was no notation of 'X-Ray' on the cards, just on the wrappers. The cards had an "EB" prefix for their numbering on the cardbacks. These were only available in hobby packs.

COMPLETE SET (100)
*RCs: 3X TO 8X BASE CARDS
STATED PRINT RUN 100 SERIAL #'d SETS

2004 Press Pass Stealth EFX

Randomly inserted in packs at a rate of 1:10, this 12-card set featured some of NASCAR's hottest drivers. The cards had holofoil designs with gold foil stamping. The cards had an "EF" prefix for their numbering on the cardbacks.

EF1 Dale Earnhardt Jr.	2.50	6.00
EF2 Jeff Gordon	2.50	6.00
EF3 Jimmie Johnson	2.00	5.00
EF4 Tony Stewart	1.50	4.00
EF5 Ryan Newman	2.00	5.00
EF6 Kurt Busch	1.00	2.50
EF7 Mark Martin	1.50	4.00
EF8 Rusty Wallace	1.25	3.00
EF9 Michael Waltrip	.75	2.00
EF10 Brian Vickers	1.25	3.00
EF11 Ricky Rudd	1.00	2.50
EF12 Matt Kenseth	2.00	5.00

2004 Press Pass Stealth Fusion

Randomly inserted in packs at a rate of 1:24. These cards had a lenticular design and had a prefix of "FU" for their card numbering on the cardbacks.

COMPLETE SET (9)	20.00	50.00
FU1 Jeff Gordon	6.00	15.00
FU2 Terry Labonte	2.50	6.00
FU3 Dale Earnhardt Jr.	6.00	15.00
FU4 Michael Waltrip	2.00	5.00
FU5 Ryan Newman	5.00	12.00
FU6 Rusty Wallace	3.00	8.00
FU7 Kurt Busch	2.50	6.00
FU8 Mark Martin	4.00	10.00
FU9 Bobby Labonte	3.00	8.00

2004 Press Pass Stealth Gear Grippers Autographs

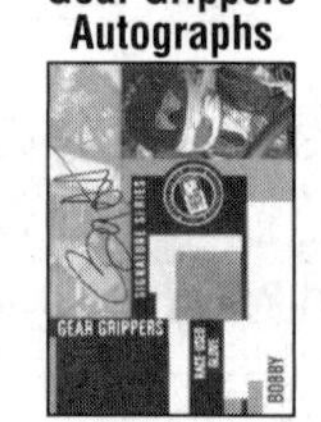

Randomly inserted in hobby packs only, this 7-card set featured a swatch of race-used glove from the corresponding driver and his signature. The cards were serial numbered to the respective driver's door number. These cards had a "HT" prefix for the card numbering on their cardbacks. The Dale Earnhardt Jr. was not released until July 2005 in packs of Press Pass Legends. The Bobby Labonte was also released late and was randomly inserted into the 2005 Box Blaster sets.

HT-DE Dale Earnhardt Jr./8		
HT-JG Jeff Gordon/24	250.00	500.00
HT-JJ Jimmie Johnson/48	100.00	175.00
HT-KH Kevin Harvick/29	100.00	200.00
HT-MK Matt Kenseth/17		
HT-MM Mark Martin/6		
HT-RN Ryan Newman/12		
HT-RW Rusty Wallace/2		
HT-BL Bobby Labonte/18	75.00	150.00

2004 Press Pass Stealth Gear Grippers Drivers

Randomly inserted into hobby packs only at a rate of 1:168. This 18-card set featured a swatch of the corresponding driver's race-used glove and a photo of him. The cards carried a "GGD" prefix for their card numbering on the cardbacks.

GGD1 Jimmie Johnson	25.00	60.00
GGD2 Matt Kenseth	25.00	60.00
GGD3 Kevin Harvick	20.00	50.00
GGD4 Jeff Gordon	30.00	80.00
GGD5 Kurt Busch	15.00	40.00
GGD6 Ryan Newman	25.00	60.00
GGD7 Bobby Labonte	15.00	40.00
GGD8 Rusty Wallace	20.00	50.00
GGD9 Dale Earnhardt Jr.	40.00	100.00
GGD10 Michael Waltrip	12.50	30.00
GGD11 Jeff Burton	12.50	30.00
GGD12 Dale Jarrett	20.00	50.00
GGD13 Terry Labonte	20.00	50.00
GGD14 Robby Gordon	12.50	30.00
GGD15 Ward Burton	10.00	25.00
GGD16 Tony Stewart	20.00	50.00
GGD17 Mark Martin	20.00	50.00
GGD18 Greg Biffle	12.50	30.00

2004 Press Pass Stealt Gear Grippers Drivers Retail

Randomly inserted into retail packs only at a rate 1:240. This 18-card set featured a swatch of t corresponding driver's race-used glove and a ph of his car. The cards carried a "GGT" prefix for th card numbering on the cardbacks.

*CARS: .3X TO .8X DRIVERS

GGT1 Jimmie Johnson	20.00	50.0
GGT2 Matt Kenseth	20.00	50.0
GGT3 Kevin Harvick	15.00	40.0
GGT4 Jeff Gordon	25.00	60.0
GGT5 Kurt Busch	12.50	30.0
GGT6 Ryan Newman	20.00	50.0
GGT7 Bobby Labonte	12.50	30.0
GGT8 Rusty Wallace	15.00	40.0
GGT9 Dale Earnhardt Jr.	30.00	80.0
GGT10 Michael Waltrip	10.00	25.0
GGT11 Jeff Burton	10.00	25.0
GGT12 Dale Jarrett	15.00	40.0
GGT13 Terry Labonte	15.00	40.0
GGT14 Robby Gordon	10.00	25.0
GGT15 Ward Burton	8.00	20.0
GGT16 Tony Stewart	15.00	40.0
GGT17 Mark Martin	15.00	40.0
GGT18 Greg Biffle	10.00	25.0

2004 Press Pass Stealt No Boundaries

Randomly inserted into packs only at a rate of 1 This 27-card set featured an embossed die-c design printed on foil cards. The set featured sor of NASCAR's hottest drivers and some you prospects. The cards carried an "NB" prefix for th card numbering on the cardbacks.

NB1 Clint Bowyer	1.50	4.0
NB2 Kyle Busch	1.50	4.0
NB3 David Green	.30	.7
NB4 Mike Bliss	.30	.7
NB5 Damon Lusk	.30	.7
NB6 Paul Menard	1.25	3.0
NB7 Billy Parker Jr.	1.25	3.0
NB8 Martin Truex Jr.	2.50	6.0
NB9 J.J. Yeley	1.50	4.0
NB10 Ward Burton	.50	1.2
NB11 Dale Earnhardt Jr.	2.00	5.0
NB12 Jeff Gordon	2.00	5.0
NB13 Kevin Harvick	1.25	3.0
NB14 Dale Jarrett	1.00	2.5
NB15 Jimmie Johnson	1.50	4.0
NB16 Matt Kenseth	1.50	4.0
NB17 Bobby Labonte	1.00	2.5
NB18 Terry Labonte	.75	2.0
NB19 Mark Martin	1.25	3.0
NB20 Scott Riggs	.50	1.2
NB21 Joe Nemechek	.30	.7
NB22 Ryan Newman	1.50	4.0
NB23 Ricky Rudd	.75	2.0
NB24 Elliott Sadler	.50	1.2
NB25 Rusty Wallace	1.00	2.5
NB26 Michael Waltrip	.50	1.2
NB27 Scott Wimmer	.50	1.2

2004 Press Pass Stealt Profile

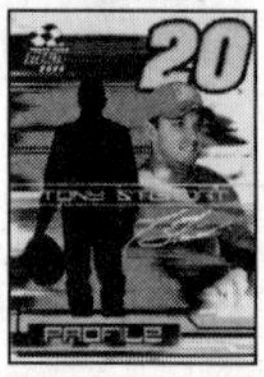

Randomly inserted into packs only at a progress rate of 1:14 to 1:112. The individual card od released by Press Pass are listed net to the drive name in the checklist provided. This 12-card featured foild cards with gold foil highlights. T cards carried a "P" prefix for their card numbering the cardbacks.

P1 Jeff Gordon 1:112	12.50	30.0
P2 Jimmie Johnson 1:112	10.00	25.0
P3 Dale Earnhardt Jr. 1:112	10.00	25.0
P4 Kurt Busch 1:112	8.00	20.0
P5 Matt Kenseth 1:48	5.00	12.0
P6 Jamie McMurray 1:48	4.00	10.0
P7 Tony Stewart 1:48	5.00	12.0
P8 Scott Riggs 1:48	4.00	10.0
P9 Greg Biffle 1:14	3.00	8.0
P10 Bobby Labonte 1:14	3.00	8.0
P11 Michael Waltrip 1:14	3.00	8.0
P12 Dale Jarrett 1:14	3.00	8.0

2005 Press Pass Stealt

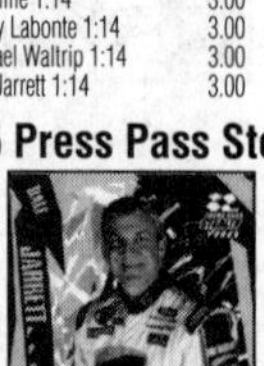

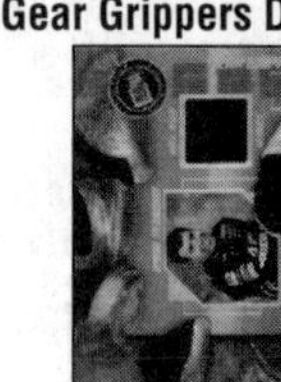

MPLETE SET (100)	12.50	30.00
X BOX HOBBY (28)	50.00	80.00
X BOX RETAIL (24)	35.00	60.00
erling Marlin	.40	1.00
asey Kahne	1.00	2.50
mie McMurray	.40	1.00
erling Marlin's Car	.15	.40
asey Kahne's Car	.40	1.00
mie McMurray's Car	.10	.25
erling Marlin	.40	1.00
asey Kahne	1.00	2.50
mie McMurray	.40	1.00
Ryan Newman	.75	2.00
Rusty Wallace	.50	1.25
Scott Wimmer	.25	.60
Ryan Newman's Car	.25	.60
Rusty Wallace's Car	.15	.40
Scott Wimmer's Car	.10	.25
Ryan Newman	.75	2.00
Rusty Wallace	.50	1.25
Scott Wimmer	.25	.60
Dale Jarrett	.50	1.25
Ricky Rudd	.40	1.00
Matt Kenseth	.75	2.00
Dale Jarrett's Car	.15	.40
Ricky Rudd's Car	.15	.40
Matt Kenseth's Car	.25	.60
Dale Jarrett	.50	1.25
Ricky Rudd	.40	1.00
Matt Kenseth	.75	2.00
Greg Biffle	.25	.60
Kurt Busch	.40	1.00
Terry Labonte	.40	1.00
Greg Biffle's Car	.10	.25
Kurt Busch's Car	.15	.40
Terry Labonte's Car	.15	.40
Greg Biffle	.25	.60
Kurt Busch	.40	1.00
Terry Labonte	.40	1.00
Jeff Burton	.25	.60
Dale Earnhardt Jr.	1.00	2.50
Jimmie Johnson	.75	2.00
Jeff Burton's Car	.10	.25
Dale Earnhardt Jr.'s Car	.40	1.00
Jimmie Johnson's Car	.25	.60
Jeff Burton	.25	.60
Dale Earnhardt Jr.	1.00	2.50
Jimmie Johnson	.75	2.00
Jason Leffler	.15	.40
Kevin Harvick	.60	1.50
Jeff Gordon	1.00	2.50
Jason Leffler's Car	.10	.25
Kevin Harvick's Car	.25	.60
Jeff Gordon's Car	.40	1.00
Jason Leffler	.15	.40
Kevin Harvick	.60	1.50
Jeff Gordon	1.00	2.50
Tony Stewart	.60	1.50
Michael Waltrip	.25	.60
Bobby Labonte	.50	1.25
Tony Stewart's Car	.25	.60
Michael Waltrip's Car	.10	.25
Bobby Labonte's Car	.15	.40
Tony Stewart	.60	1.50
Michael Waltrip	.25	.60
Bobby Labonte	.50	1.25
Tim Fedewa	.15	.40
Clint Bowyer	1.00	2.50
David Stremme	1.00	2.50
Kasey Kahne	1.00	2.50
J.J. Yeley	.40	1.00
Justin Labonte	.40	1.00
Tony Raines	.15	.40
David Green	.15	.40
Kenny Wallace	.15	.40
Terry Cook	.25	.60
Mike Skinner	.15	.40
Rick Crawford	.15	.40
Kerry Earnhardt	.25	.60
Ken Schrader	.15	.40
Ron Hornaday	.15	.40
Todd Kluever RC	1.25	3.00
Bill Lester	.15	.40
Dennis Setzer	.15	.40
Rusty Wallace H	.50	1.25
Dale Earnhardt Jr. H	1.00	2.50
Michael Waltrip H	.25	.60
Bobby Labonte H	.50	1.25
Tony Stewart H	.60	1.50
Jeff Gordon H	1.00	2.50
Kevin Harvick H	.60	1.50
Jimmie Johnson H	.75	2.00
Kurt Busch H	.40	1.00
Tony Stewart SF	.60	1.50
Bobby Labonte SF	.50	1.25
Rusty Wallace SF	.50	1.25
Matt Kenseth SF	.75	2.00
Ricky Rudd SF	.40	1.00
Jimmie Johnson SF	.75	2.00
Jeff Gordon SF	1.00	2.50
Michael Waltrip SF	.25	.60
Kevin Harvick SF	.60	1.50
Jeff Gordon CL	1.00	2.50

005 Press Pass Stealth Previews

TED PRINT RUN 5 SERIAL #'d SETS
DS NOT PRICED DUE TO SCARCITY

005 Press Pass Stealth Samples

MPLES: 2X TO 5X BASE

2005 Press Pass Stealth X-Ray

*X-RAY: 3X TO 8X BASE

2005 Press Pass Stealth EFX

COMPLETE SET (12)	15.00	40.00
EFX1 Jeff Gordon	2.50	6.00
EFX2 Jimmie Johnson	2.00	5.00
EFX3 Dale Jarrett	1.25	3.00
EFX4 Michael Waltrip	.60	1.50
EFX5 Tony Stewart	1.50	4.00
EFX6 Martin Truex Jr.	2.00	5.00
EFX7 Terry Labonte	1.00	2.50
EFX8 Bobby Labonte	1.25	3.00
EFX9 Kevin Harvick	1.50	4.00
EFX10 Jeff Burton	.60	1.50
EFX11 Rusty Wallace	1.25	3.00
EFX12 Matt Kenseth	2.00	5.00

2005 Press Pass Stealth Fusion

COMPLETE SET (12)	50.00	100.00
FU1 Jeff Gordon 1:112	15.00	40.00
FU2 Jimmie Johnson 1:112	10.00	25.00
FU3 Ryan Newman 1:112	8.00	20.00
FU4 Michael Waltrip 1:112	6.00	15.00
FU5 Terry Labonte 1:48	4.00	10.00
FU6 Rusty Wallace 1:48	4.00	10.00
FU7 Tony Stewart 1:48	4.00	10.00
FU8 Matt Kenseth 1:48	4.00	10.00
FU9 Dale Jarrett 1:14	2.50	6.00
FU10 Kevin Harvick 1:14	2.50	6.00
FU11 Jeff Burton 1:14	2.00	5.00
FU12 Bobby Labonte 1:14	2.50	6.00

2005 Press Pass Stealth Gear Grippers Autographs

This 8-card set was available in packs of 2005 Press Pass Stealth. Each card had a swatch of a race-used glove and a signature from the corresponding driver. The cards were serial numbered to the driver's door number. There was a late addition to the set. Tony Stewart was only available in packs of 2006 Press Pass Legends.

SERIAL #'d TO CAR NUMBER
SOME CARDS NOT PRICED DUE TO SCARCITY

GG-BV Brian Vickers/25	100.00	200.00
GG-DE Dale Earnhardt Jr./8		
GG-JG Jeff Gordon/24	250.00	500.00
GG-KH Kevin Harvick/29	100.00	175.00
GG-MM Mark Martin/6		
GG-MW Michael Waltrip/15		
GG-TL Terry Labonte/5		
GG-TS Tony Stewart/20		

2005 Press Pass Stealth Gear Grippers Cars

*CARS: .3X TO .8X DRIVERS

2005 Press Pass Stealth Gear Grippers Drivers

GGD1 Jamie McMurray	20.00	50.00
GGD2 Matt Kenseth	20.00	50.00
GGD3 Kevin Harvick	15.00	40.00
GGD4 Jeff Gordon	30.00	80.00
GGD5 Kurt Busch	15.00	40.00
GGD6 Ryan Newman	25.00	60.00
GGD7 Bobby Labonte	15.00	40.00
GGD8 Rusty Wallace	15.00	40.00
GGD9 Michael Waltrip	12.50	25.00

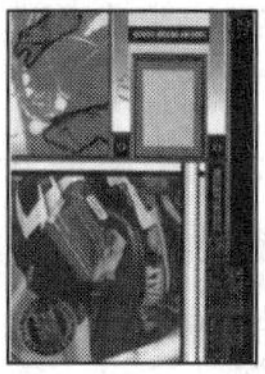

GGD10 Jeff Burton	12.50	25.00
GGD11 Dale Jarrett	15.00	40.00
GGD12 Terry Labonte	15.00	40.00
GGD13 Tony Stewart	20.00	50.00
GGD14 Scott Riggs	12.50	30.00
GGD15 Brian Vickers	12.50	30.00
GGD16 Joe Nemechek	10.00	25.00
GGD17 Greg Biffle	12.50	30.00
GGD18 Dale Earnhardt Jr.	30.00	80.00

2005 Press Pass Stealth No Boundaries

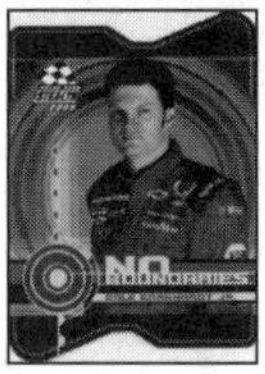

COMPLETE SET (27)	15.00	40.00
NB1 Michael Waltrip	.60	1.50
NB2 Rusty Wallace	1.25	3.00
NB3 Tony Stewart	1.50	4.00
NB4 Ken Schrader	.40	1.00
NB5 Ricky Rudd	1.00	2.50
NB6 Kyle Petty	.60	1.50
NB7 Ryan Newman	2.00	5.00
NB8 Joe Nemechek	.40	1.00
NB9 Bobby Labonte	1.25	3.00
NB10 Matt Kenseth	2.00	5.00
NB11 Jimmie Johnson	2.00	5.00
NB12 Dale Jarrett	1.25	3.00
NB13 Kevin Harvick	1.25	3.00
NB14 Jeff Gordon	2.50	6.00
NB15 Dale Earnhardt Jr.	2.50	6.00
NB16 Kurt Busch	1.00	2.50
NB17 Jeff Burton	.60	1.50
NB18 John Andretti	.40	1.00
NB19 J.J. Yeley	1.00	2.50
NB20 Jon Wood	.60	1.50
NB21 Kenny Wallace	.40	1.00
NB22 Martin Truex Jr.	2.00	5.00
NB23 Justin Labonte	1.00	2.50
NB24 Denny Hamlin	2.50	6.00
NB25 David Green	.40	1.00
NB26 Tim Fedewa	.40	1.00
NB27 Clint Bowyer	2.50	6.00

2005 Press Pass Stealth Profile

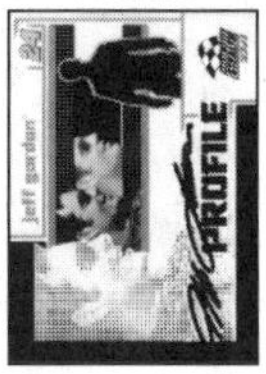

COMPLETE SET (9)	20.00	50.00
PR1 Jeff Gordon	8.00	20.00
PR2 Jimmie Johnson	6.00	15.00
PR3 Dale Earnhardt Jr.	8.00	20.00
PR4 Jeff Burton	2.00	5.00
PR5 Mark Martin	5.00	12.00
PR6 Rusty Wallace	4.00	10.00
PR7 Kevin Harvick	4.00	10.00
PR8 Bobby Labonte	4.00	10.00
PR9 Tony Stewart	5.00	12.00

2006 Press Pass Stealth

This 97-card set was released in late June 2006. Cards 91-97 featured the drivers competing in the Nextel Cup for the first time. Each of these Cup Rookie Cards were short-printed and inserted into hobby packs at a rate of one in 20. Each of these cards featured the RC logo. The basic card design featured thick cardstock with gold foil Stealth logos and colorfoil design highlights. Hobby boxes contained 20-five card packs. The SRP for packs were $4.99.

COMPLETE SET (97)	50.00	100.00
COMP.SET w/o SPs (90)	15.00	40.00
WAX BOX HOBBY (20)	60.00	90.00
SPs (91-97) STATED ODDS 1:20		
1 Greg Biffle	.40	1.00
2 Dave Blaney	.20	.50
3 Jeff Burton	.30	.75
4 Kurt Busch	.50	1.25
5 Kyle Busch	.60	1.50
6 Dale Earnhardt Jr.	1.25	3.00
7 Carl Edwards	1.00	2.50
8 Jeff Gordon	1.25	3.00
9 Robby Gordon	.20	.50
10 Jeff Green	.20	.50
11 Kevin Harvick	.75	2.00
12 Dale Jarrett	.60	1.50
13 Jimmie Johnson	1.00	2.50
14 Kasey Kahne	1.25	3.00
15 Matt Kenseth	1.00	2.50
16 Terry Labonte	.50	1.25
17 Bobby Labonte	.60	1.50
18 Sterling Marlin	.50	1.25
19 Mark Martin	.75	2.00
20 Jamie McMurray	.50	1.25
21 Casey Mears	.30	.75
22 Joe Nemechek	.20	.50
23 Ryan Newman	.75	2.00
24 Kyle Petty	.30	.75
25 Tony Raines	.20	.50
26 Scott Riggs	.30	.75
27 Elliott Sadler	.30	.75
28 Tony Stewart	.75	2.00
29 Brian Vickers	.60	1.50
30 A.J. Foyt IV NBS RC	1.00	2.50
31 David Green NBS	.20	.50
32 Todd Kluever NBS	1.00	2.50
33 Mark McFarland NBS	.20	.50
34 Paul Menard NBS	.40	1.00
35 Danny O'Quinn NBS RC	.60	1.50
36 Clint Bowyer NBS	1.25	3.00
37 Greg Biffle NBS	.40	1.00
38 Jon Wood NBS	.30	.75
39 Kevin Harvick's Rig	.75	2.00
40 Jimmie Johnson's Rig	.40	1.00
41 Matt Kenseth's Rig	.40	1.00
42 Jeff Burton's Rig	.12	.30
43 Martin Truex Jr.'s Rig	.25	.60
44 Dale Jarrett's Rig	.25	.60
45 Jeff Gordon's Rig	.50	1.25
46 Carl Edwards' Rig	.40	1.00
47 Dale Earnhardt Jr.'s Rig	.50	1.25
48 Roush Racing TM	.40	1.00
Matt Kenseth		
Mark Martin		
Greg Biffle		
Jamie McMurray		
Ca		
49 Joe Gibbs Racing TM	1.25	3.00
Tony Stewart		
Denny Hamlin		
J.J. Yeley		
50 Richard Childress Racing TM	1.25	3.00
Kevin Harvick		
Jeff Burton		
Clint Bowyer		
51 Evernham Motorsports TM	1.25	3.00
Kasey Kahne		
Jeremy Mayfield		
Scott Riggs		
52 Dale Earnhardt Inc. TM	.75	2.00
Martin Truex Jr.		
Dale Earnhardt Jr.		
53 Chip Ganassi Racing TM	.75	2.00
Casey Mears		
David Stremme		
Reed Sorenson		
54 Hendrick Motorsports TM	1.25	3.00
Jeff Gordon		
Terry Labonte		
Jimmie Johnson		
Brian		
55 Penske Racing TM	.75	2.00
Kurt Busch		
Ryan Newman		
56 Robert Yates Racing TM	.60	1.50
Dale Jarrett		
Elliott Sadler		
57 Dale Earnhardt Jr. F	1.25	3.00
58 Jeff Gordon F	1.25	3.00
59 Dale Jarrett F	.60	1.50
60 Tony Stewart F	.75	2.00
61 Martin Truex Jr. F	.75	2.00
62 Carl Edwards F	1.00	2.50
63 Terry Labonte F	.50	1.25
64 Kasey Kahne F	1.25	3.00
65 Jimmie Johnson F	1.00	2.50
66 Kevin Harvick F	.75	2.00
67 Bobby Labonte F	.60	1.50
68 Mark Martin F	.75	2.00
69 Kevin Harvick DD	.75	2.00
70 Kasey Kahne DD	1.25	3.00
71 Dale Earnhardt Jr. DD	1.25	3.00
72 Carl Edwards DD	1.00	2.50
73 Denny Hamlin DD	1.25	3.00
74 Matt Kenseth DD	1.00	2.50
75 J.J. Yeley DD	.50	1.25
76 Clint Bowyer DD	1.25	3.00
77 Reed Sorenson DD	.75	2.00
78 Brian Vickers DD	.60	1.50
79 Tony Stewart DD	.75	2.00
80 Kyle Busch DD	.60	1.50
81 Greg Biffle DD	.40	1.00
82 Dale Earnhardt '79 RS	2.00	5.00
83 Dale Earnhardt '79 RS	2.00	5.00
84 Dale Earnhardt '79 RS	2.00	5.00
85 Dale Earnhardt '79 RS	2.00	5.00
86 Dale Earnhardt '79 RS	2.00	5.00
87 Dale Earnhardt '79 RS	2.00	5.00
88 Dale Earnhardt '79 RS	2.00	5.00
89 Dale Earnhardt '79 RS	2.00	5.00
90 Jimmie Johnson	1.25	3.00
Jeff Gordon CL		
91 Clint Bowyer CRC	5.00	12.00
92 Denny Hamlin CRC	8.00	20.00
93 Brent Sherman CRC	2.50	6.00
94 Reed Sorenson CRC	4.00	10.00
95 David Stremme CRC	4.00	10.00
96 Martin Truex Jr. CRC	3.00	8.00
97 J.J. Yeley CRC	2.00	5.00

2006 Press Pass Stealth X-Ray

This 97-card set is a parallel to the base set. Each card is serial numbered to 100 and carries an 'X' prefix for its card number.

*X-RAY: 2.5X TO 6X BASE

2006 Press Pass Stealth Autographed Hat Entry

These cards are redemption cards for a Press Pass Hat signed by the corresponding driver on the card. Press Pass had these hats signed at Daytona's Speedweeks in early 2006. The deadline to redeem these cards was January 31, 2007.

STATED PRINT RUN 1 SERIAL #'d SET
EXCH DEADLINE 06/30/2007

PPH1 Greg Biffle
PPH2 Clint Bowyer
PPH3 Jeff Burton
PPH4 Kurt Busch
PPH5 Dale Earnhardt Jr.
PPH6 Carl Edwards
PPH7 Jeff Gordon
PPH8 Kevin Harvick
PPH9 Denny Hamlin
PPH10 Dale Jarrett
PPH11 Jimmie Johnson
PPH12 Kasey Kahne
PPH13 Matt Kenseth
PPH14 Bobby Labonte
PPH15 Mark Martin
PPH16 Jeremy Mayfield
PPH17 Jamie McMurray
PPH18 Casey Mears
PPH19 Ryan Newman
PPH20 Elliott Sadler
PPH21 Reed Sorenson
PPH22 Tony Stewart
PPH23 David Stremme
PPH24 Martin Truex Jr.
PPH25 Brian Vickers
PPH26 J.J. Yeley
PPH27 Mark McFarland

2006 Press Pass Stealth Corporate Cuts

This 14-card set featured a swatch of a sponsor shirt worn by the driver pictured on the front during the 2005 Nextel Cup season. Each card is serial numbered to 250 copies. The card number carried a 'CCD' prefix.These were available in 2006 Press Pass Stealth Hobby and Retail packs. They were inserted along with Gear Grippers at a combined rate of one in 40 hobby packs and a combined rate of one in 112 retail packs.

CCD1 Greg Biffle	8.00	20.00
CCD2 Jeremy Mayfield	8.00	20.00
CCD3 Dale Earnhardt Jr.	15.00	40.00
CCD4 Carl Edwards	12.50	30.00
CCD5 Reed Sorenson	10.00	25.00
CCD6 Dale Jarrett	10.00	25.00
CCD7 David Stremme	8.00	20.00
CCD8 Kasey Kahne	15.00	40.00
CCD9 Matt Kenseth	12.50	30.00
CCD10 Tony Stewart	12.50	30.00
CCD11 Kurt Busch	8.00	20.00
CCD12 Clint Bowyer	8.00	20.00
CCD13 Ryan Newman	8.00	20.00
CCD14 Jeff Burton	8.00	20.00

2006 Press Pass Stealth EFX

This 12-card set was inserted into packs of Press Pass Stealth at a rate of one in 14 to one in 112 packs progressively. The individual odds are listed below next to each card. The cards featured the top drivers on the Nextel Cup circuit and used holofoil technology to highlight the cards. Each card carried an 'EFX' prefix on the card numbers.

COMPLETE SET (12)	20.00	50.00
STATED ODDS 1:14 TO 1:112 PROGRESSIVE		
EFX1 Tony Stewart 1:112	5.00	12.00
EFX2 Dale Earnhardt Jr. 1:112	8.00	20.00
EFX3 Jeff Gordon 1:112	8.00	20.00
EFX4 Jimmie Johnson 1:112	6.00	16.00
EFX5 Martin Truex Jr. 1:48	3.00	8.00
EFX6 Mark Martin 1:48	3.00	8.00
EFX7 Dale Jarrett 1:48	2.50	6.00
EFX8 Carl Edwards 1:48	4.00	10.00
EFX9 Terry Labonte 1:14	1.50	4.00
EFX10 Greg Biffle 1:14	1.25	3.00
EFX11 Matt Kenseth 1:14	3.00	8.00
EFX12 Kyle Busch 1:14	2.00	5.00

2006 Press Pass Stealth Gear Grippers Autographs

This 9-card set featured a swatch of a race-used glove along with the corresponding driver's signature. Each card was hand numbered to the driver's door number. These were inserted into hobby packs only. Some of these cards are not priced due to scarcity.

CB Clint Bowyer/7		
CM Casey Mears/42	100.00	175.00
DE Dale Earnhardt Jr./8		
DH Denny Hamlin/11		
JG Jeff Gordon/24	250.00	500.00
KH Kevin Harvick/29	100.00	200.00
MK Matt Kenseth/17		
MM Mark Martin/6		
RN Ryan Newman/12		
TS Tony Stewart/20		

2006 Press Pass Stealth Gear Grippers Drivers

This 18-card set featured a swatch of a driver's glove that had been worn during a race by the corresponding driver on the card. Each card was serial numbered to . These cards were only found in hobby packs of Press Pass Stealth and inserted at a combined rate of one in 40 along with the Corporate Cuts insert. Each card carried a 'GGD' prefix for its card number.

GGD1 Jeff Gordon	40.00	100.00
GGD2 Ryan Newman	15.00	40.00
GGD3 Dale Jarrett	15.00	40.00
GGD4 J.J. Yeley	15.00	40.00
GGD5 Tony Stewart	25.00	60.00
GGD6 Dale Earnhardt Jr.	40.00	100.00
GGD7 Matt Kenseth	25.00	60.00
GGD8 Kevin Harvick	20.00	50.00
GGD9 Denny Hamlin	25.00	60.00
GGD10 Kasey Kahne	40.00	80.00
GGD11 Reed Sorenson	15.00	40.00
GGD12 Casey Mears	12.50	30.00
GGD13 Jimmie Johnson	25.00	60.00
GGD14 Clint Bowyer	12.50	30.00
GGD15 Mark Martin	25.00	60.00
GGD16 Martin Truex Jr.	20.00	50.00
GGD17 Carl Edwards	25.00	60.00
GGD18 Jeff Burton	12.50	30.00

2006 Press Pass Stealth Hot Pass

This 27-card set featured the top drivers in NASCAR. Each card was designed to look like a "Hot Pass" ticket from the track. The cards carried an 'HP' prefix for the card number. These were inserted in packs at a rate of one in two.

COMPLETE SET (27)	15.00	40.00
HP1 Greg Biffle	.75	2.00
HP2 Dave Blaney	.40	1.00
HP3 Clint Bowyer	2.50	6.00
HP4 Jeff Burton	.60	1.50
HP5 Kurt Busch	1.00	2.50
HP6 Kyle Busch	1.25	3.00
HP7 Dale Earnhardt Jr.	2.50	6.00
HP8 Carl Edwards	2.00	5.00
HP9 Jeff Gordon	2.50	6.00
HP10 Robby Gordon	.40	1.00
HP11 Denny Hamlin	2.50	6.00
HP12 Kevin Harvick	1.50	4.00
HP13 Dale Jarrett	1.25	3.00
HP14 Jimmie Johnson	2.00	5.00
HP15 Kasey Kahne	2.50	6.00
HP16 Matt Kenseth	2.00	5.00
HP17 Bobby Labonte	1.25	3.00
HP18 Mark Martin	1.50	4.00
HP19 Jeremy Mayfield	.40	1.00
HP20 Joe Nemechek	.40	1.00
HP21 Ryan Newman	1.50	4.00
HP22 Tony Raines	.40	1.00
HP23 Ken Schrader	.40	1.00
HP24 David Stremme	1.50	4.00
HP25 Tony Stewart	1.50	4.00
HP26 Martin Truex Jr.	1.50	4.00
HP27 J.J. Yeley	1.00	2.50

2006 Press Pass Stealth Profile

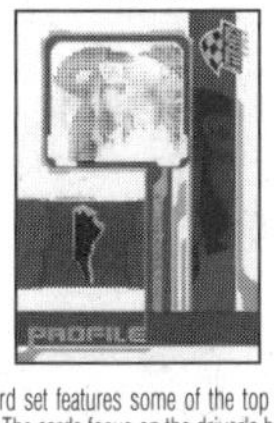

This 9-card set features some of the top drivers in NASCAR. The cards focus on the driver's home state. The cards have the state cut into the card along with their profile. These cards were inserted into packs at a rate of one in 10. Each card carried a 'P' prefix for its card number.

COMPLETE SET (9)	20.00	50.00
P1 Dale Earnhardt Jr.	4.00	10.00
P2 Mark Martin	2.50	6.00
P3 Jeff Gordon	4.00	10.00
P4 Kasey Kahne	4.00	10.00
P5 Dale Jarrett	2.00	5.00
P6 Jimmie Johnson	3.00	8.00
P7 Tony Stewart	2.50	6.00
P8 Martin Truex Jr.	2.50	6.00
P9 Kevin Harvick	2.50	6.00

2006 Press Pass Stealth Retail

This 97-card set was released in late June 2006. Cards 91-97 featured the drivers competing in the Nextel Cup for the first time. Each of these Cup Rookie Cards were short-printed and inserted into retail packs at a rate of one in 6. Each of these cards featured the RC logo. The basic card design featured thick cardstock with silver foil Stealth logos. Retail boxes contained 24-four card packs. The SRP for packs were $2.99.

COMPLETE SET (97)	40.00	80.00
COMP.SET w/o SPs (90)	15.00	40.00
WAX BOX RETAIL (24)	40.00	70.00
1 Greg Biffle	.30	.75
2 Dave Blaney	.15	.40
3 Jeff Burton	.25	.60
4 Kurt Busch	.40	1.00
5 Kyle Busch	.50	1.25
6 Dale Earnhardt Jr.	1.00	2.50
7 Carl Edwards	.75	2.00
8 Jeff Gordon	1.00	2.50
9 Robby Gordon	.15	.40
10 Jeff Green	.15	.40
11 Kevin Harvick	.60	1.50
12 Dale Jarrett	.50	1.25
13 Jimmie Johnson	.75	2.00
14 Kasey Kahne	1.00	2.50
15 Matt Kenseth	.75	2.00
16 Terry Labonte	.40	1.00
17 Bobby Labonte	.50	1.25
18 Sterling Marlin	.40	1.00
19 Mark Martin	.60	1.50
20 Jamie McMurray	.40	1.00
21 Casey Mears	.25	.60
22 Joe Nemechek	.15	.40
23 Ryan Newman	.75	2.00
24 Kyle Petty	.25	.60
25 Tony Raines	.15	.40
26 Scott Riggs	.25	.60
27 Elliott Sadler	.25	.60
28 Tony Stewart	.60	1.50
29 Brian Vickers	.60	1.50
30 A.J. Foyt IV NBS RC	.75	2.00
31 David Green NBS	.15	.40
32 Todd Kluever NBS	.75	2.00
33 Mark McFarland NBS	.15	.40
34 Paul Menard NBS	.30	.75
35 Danny O'Quinn NBS RC	.50	1.25
36 Clint Bowyer NBS	1.00	2.50
37 Greg Biffle NBS	.30	.75
38 Jon Wood NBS	.25	.60
39 Kevin Harvick's Rig	.60	1.50
40 Jimmie Johnson's Rig	.75	2.00
41 Matt Kenseth's Rig	.75	2.00
42 Jeff Burton's Rig	.25	.60
43 Martin Truex Jr.'s Rig	.75	2.00
44 Dale Jarrett's Rig	.50	1.25
45 Jeff Gordon's Rig	1.00	2.50
46 Carl Edwards' Rig	.75	2.00
47 Dale Earnhardt Jr.'s Rig	1.00	2.50
48 Roush Racing TM	.30	.75
Matt Kenseth		
Mark Martin		
Greg Biffle		
Jamie McMurray		
Ca		
49 Joe Gibbs Racing TM	1.00	2.50
Tony Stewart		
Denny Hamlin		
J.J. Yeley		
50 Richard Childress Racing TM	1.00	2.50
Kevin Harvick		
Jeff Burton		
Clint Bowyer		
51 Evernham Motorsports TM	1.00	2.50
Kasey Kahne		
Jeremy Mayfield		
Scott Riggs		
52 Dale Earnhardt Inc. TM	.75	2.00
Martin Truex Jr.		
Dale Earnhardt Jr.		
53 Chip Ganassi Racing TM	.60	1.50
Casey Mears		
David Stremme		
Reed Sorenson		
54 Hendrick Motorsports TM	1.00	2.50
Jeff Gordon		
Terry Labonte		
Jimmie Johnson		
Brian		
55 Penske Racing TM	.75	2.00
Kurt Busch		
Ryan Newman		
56 Robert Yates Racing TM	.50	1.25
Dale Jarrett		
Elliott Sadler		
57 Dale Earnhardt Jr. F	1.00	2.50
58 Jeff Gordon F	1.00	2.50
59 Dale Jarrett F	.50	1.25
60 Tony Stewart F	.60	1.50
61 Martin Truex Jr. F	.75	2.00
62 Carl Edwards F	.75	2.00
63 Terry Labonte F	.40	1.00
64 Kasey Kahne F	1.00	2.50
65 Jimmie Johnson F	.75	2.00
66 Kevin Harvick F	.60	1.50
67 Bobby Labonte F	.50	1.25
68 Mark Martin F	.60	1.50
69 Kevin Harvick DD	.60	1.50
70 Kasey Kahne DD	1.00	2.50
71 Dale Earnhardt Jr. DD	1.00	2.50
72 Carl Edwards DD	.75	2.00
73 Denny Hamlin DD	1.00	2.50
74 Matt Kenseth DD	.75	2.00
75 J.J. Yeley DD	.40	1.00
76 Clint Bowyer DD	1.00	2.50
77 Reed Sorenson DD	.60	1.50
78 Brian Vickers DD	.60	1.50
79 Tony Stewart DD	.60	1.50
80 Kyle Busch DD	.50	1.25
81 Greg Biffle DD	.30	.75
82 Dale Earnhardt '79 RS	1.50	4.00
83 Dale Earnhardt '79 RS	1.50	4.00
84 Dale Earnhardt '79 RS	1.50	4.00
85 Dale Earnhardt '79 RS	1.50	4.00
86 Dale Earnhardt '79 RS	1.50	4.00
87 Dale Earnhardt '79 RS	1.50	4.00
88 Dale Earnhardt '79 RS	1.50	4.00
89 Dale Earnhardt '79 RS	1.50	4.00
90 Jimmie Johnson	1.00	2.50
Jeff Gordon CL		
91 Clint Bowyer CRC	5.00	12.00
92 Denny Hamlin CRC	5.00	12.00
93 Brent Sherman CRC	2.50	6.00
94 Reed Sorenson CRC	4.00	10.00
95 David Stremme CRC	4.00	10.00
96 Martin Truex Jr. CRC	3.00	8.00
97 J.J. Yeley CRC	2.00	5.00

2006 Press Pass Stealth Retail Gear Grippers Cars

This 18-card set featured a swatch of a driver's glove that had been worn during a race by the corresponding driver on the card. Each card was serial numbered to . These cards were only found in retail packs of Press Pass Stealth and inserted at a combined rate of one in 112 along with the Corporate Cuts insert. Each card carried a 'GGT' prefix for its card number.

*CARS: .3X TO .8X DRIVERS

2007 Press Pass Stealth Chrome

COMPLETE SET (90)	20.00	50.00
STATED ODDS L1 VARIATION 1:60		
STATED ODDS L2 VARIATION 1:120		
WAX BOX HOBBY (24)	80.00	110.00
1 Greg Biffle	.50	1.25
2 Clint Bowyer	1.25	3.00
3 Jeff Burton	.40	1.00
4 Kurt Busch	.40	1.00
5 Kyle Busch	.75	2.00
6 Dale Earnhardt Jr.	1.50	4.00
6A Dale Earnhardt Jr. L1	3.00	8.00
2-white dots		
6B Dale Earnhardt Jr. L2	6.00	15.00
2-white dots w/line		
7 Carl Edwards	1.00	2.50
8 Jeff Gordon	1.50	4.00
8A Jeff Gordon L1	3.00	8.00
-white dot in corners		
8B Jeff Gordon L2	6.00	15.00
-white dot -background text		
9 Denny Hamlin	1.25	3.00
10 Kevin Harvick	1.00	2.50
11 Dale Jarrett	.75	2.00
12 Jimmie Johnson	1.25	3.00
13 Kasey Kahne	1.50	4.00
14 Matt Kenseth	1.25	3.00
15 Bobby Labonte	.75	2.00
16 Mark Martin	1.00	2.50
17 Jamie McMurray	.60	1.50
18 Casey Mears	.40	1.00
19 Ryan Newman	.75	2.00
20 Scott Riggs	.40	1.00
21 Ricky Rudd	.60	1.50
22 Elliott Sadler	.40	1.00
23 Reed Sorenson	.75	2.00
24 Tony Stewart	1.00	2.50
25 Martin Truex Jr.	1.00	2.50
26 Brian Vickers	.60	1.50
27 J.J. Yeley	.50	1.25
28 Michael Waltrip	.40	1.00
29 A.J. Allmendinger RC	2.50	6.00
30 David Gilliland RC	2.50	6.00
31 Paul Menard CRC	1.50	4.00
32 Juan Pablo Montoya RC	4.00	10.00
32A Juan Pablo Montoya L1	3.00	8.00
2 yellow corners		
32B Juan Pablo Montoya L2	6.00	15.00
2 yellow corners -NNCS line		
33 David Ragan CRC	2.00	5.00
34 David Reutimann RC	2.00	5.00
35 Regan Smith CRC	1.50	4.00
36 Jon Wood CRC	2.00	5.00
37 Marcos Ambrose NBS RC	1.25	3.00
38 Clint Bowyer NBS	1.25	3.00
39 Carl Edwards NBS	1.00	2.50
40 Kevin Harvick NBS	1.00	2.50
41 Stephen Leicht NBS RC	1.00	2.50
42 David Ragan NBS	1.00	2.50
43 David Reutimann NBS	2.00	5.00
44 Reed Sorenson NBS	.75	2.00
45 Steve Wallace NBS	.75	2.00
46 Mark Martin's Rig	.40	1.00
47 Dale Earnhardt Jr.'s Rig	1.50	4.00
48 Kasey Kahne's Rig	.60	1.50
49 Denny Hamlin's Rig	.50	1.25
50 Matt Kenseth's Rig	.50	1.25
51 Tony Stewart's Rig	.40	1.00
52 Jeff Gordon's Rig	.60	1.50
53 Dale Jarrett's Rig	.30	.75
54 Jimmie Johnson's Rig	.50	1.25
55 Martin Truex Jr.'s Crew PC	.40	1.00
56 Kurt Busch's Crew GC	.15	.40
57 Dale Jr.'s Crew PC	.60	1.50
58 Greg Biffle's Crew GC	.20	.50
59 Tony Stewart's Crew GC	.40	1.00
60 Jeff Gordon's Crew GC	.60	1.50
61 Jeff Burton's Crew GC	.15	.40
62 Bobby Labonte's Crew GC	.30	.75
63 Jimmie Johnson's Crew GC	.50	1.25
63A Jimmie Johnson's Car		
GC L1 yellow hose	2.50	6.00
64 Clint Bowyer	.40	1.00
Kevin Harvick		
Jeff Burton		
65 Denny Hamlin	.50	1.25
Tony Stewart		
J.J. Yeley		
66 David Gilliland	1.25	3.00
Ricky Rudd		
67 Ryan Newman	.40	1.00
Kurt Busch		
68 Joe Nemechek	1.50	4.00
Mark Martin		
Sterling Marlin		
Regan Smith		
69 Carl Edwards	1.25	3.00
Greg Biffle		
Matt Kenseth		
Jamie McMurray		
David Ragan		
70 Reed Sorenson	.75	2.00
Juan Pablo Montoya		
David Stremme		
71 Martin Truex Jr.	1.50	4.00
Dale Earnhardt Jr.		
Paul Menard		
72 Casey Mears	1.50	4.00
Kyle Busch		
Jimmie Johnson		
Jeff Gordon		
73 J.J. Yeley DD	.50	1.25
74 David Ragan DD	1.00	2.50
75 Denny Hamlin DD	1.25	3.00
76 David Reutimann DD	2.00	5.00
77 Kevin Harvick DD w/w/sil stripes	1.00	2.50
77A Kevin Harvick DD L1		
w/sil/w stripes	2.00	5.00
78 David Gilliland DD	1.25	3.00
79 Carl Edwards DD	1.00	2.50
80 Greg Biffle DD	.50	1.25
81 Reed Sorenson DD	.75	2.00
82 Dale Earnhardt Jr. PO	1.50	4.00
83 Jimmie Johnson PO	1.25	3.00
84 Kasey Kahne PO	1.25	3.00
84A Kasey Kahne PO L1 -logo-squares	3.00	8.00
85 Matt Kenseth PO	1.25	3.00
86 Kevin Harvick PO	1.00	2.50
87 Tony Stewart PO	1.00	2.50
88 Jeff Burton PO	.40	1.00
89 Jeff Gordon PO	1.50	4.00
90 Dale Earnhardt Jr. CL	1.50	4.00

2007 Press Pass Stealth Chrome Exclusives

*EXCLUSIVES: 4X TO 10X BASE
STATED PRINT RUN 99 SERIAL #'d SETS

2007 Press Pass Stealth Chrome Platinum

*PLATINUM: 8X TO 20X BASE
STATED PRINT RUN 25 SERIAL #'d SETS

2007 Press Pass Stealth

COMPLETE SET (90)	12.50	30.00
WAX BOX RETAIL (28)	50.00	75.00
1 Greg Biffle	.30	.75
2 Clint Bowyer	.75	2.00
3 Jeff Burton	.25	.60
4 Kurt Busch	.25	.60
5 Kyle Busch	.50	1.25
6 Dale Earnhardt Jr.	1.00	2.50
7 Carl Edwards	.60	1.50
8 Jeff Gordon	1.00	2.50
9 Denny Hamlin	.75	2.00
10 Kevin Harvick	.60	1.50
11 Dale Jarrett	.50	1.25
12 Jimmie Johnson	.75	2.00
13 Kasey Kahne	1.00	2.50
14 Matt Kenseth	.75	2.00
15 Bobby Labonte	.50	1.25
16 Mark Martin	.60	1.50
17 Jamie McMurray	.40	1.00
18 Casey Mears	.25	.60
19 Ryan Newman	.50	1.25
20 Scott Riggs	.25	.60
21 Ricky Rudd	.40	1.00
22 Elliott Sadler	.25	.60
23 Reed Sorenson	.50	1.25
24 Tony Stewart	.60	1.50
25 Martin Truex Jr.	.60	1.50
26 Brian Vickers	.40	1.00
27 J.J. Yeley	.30	.75
28 Michael Waltrip	.25	.60
29 A.J. Allmendinger RC	1.50	4.00
30 David Gilliland RC	1.25	3.00
31 Paul Menard CRC	1.25	3.00
32 Juan Pablo Montoya RC	2.00	5.00
33 David Ragan CRC	1.25	3.00
34 David Reutimann RC	1.25	3.00
35 Regan Smith CRC	1.00	2.50
36 Jon Wood CRC	1.25	3.00
37 Marcos Ambrose NBS RC	.75	2.00
38 Clint Bowyer NBS	.75	2.00
39 Carl Edwards NBS	.60	1.50
40 Kevin Harvick NBS	.60	1.50
41 Stephen Leicht NBS RC	.60	1.50
42 David Ragan NBS	.60	1.50
43 David Reutimann NBS	1.25	3.00
44 Reed Sorenson NBS	.50	1.25
45 Steve Wallace NBS	.50	1.25
46 Mark Martin's Rig	.40	1.00
47 Dale Earnhardt Jr.'s Rig	.60	1.50
48 Kasey Kahne's Rig	.60	1.50
49 Denny Hamlin's Rig	.50	1.25
50 Matt Kenseth's Rig	.50	1.25
51 Tony Stewart's Rig	.40	1.00
52 Jeff Gordon's Rig	.60	1.50
53 Dale Jarrett's Rig	.30	.75
54 Jimmie Johnson's Rig	.50	1.25
55 Martin Truex Jr.'s Crew PC	.40	1.00
56 Kurt Busch's Crew GC	.15	.40
57 Dale Jr.'s Crew PC	.60	1.50
58 Greg Biffle's Crew GC	.20	.50
59 Tony Stewart's Crew GC	.40	1.00
60 Jeff Gordon's Crew GC	.60	1.50
61 Jeff Burton's Crew GC	.15	.40
62 Bobby Labonte's Crew GC	.30	.75
63 Jimmie Johnson's Crew GC	.50	1.25
64 Clint Bowyer	.25	.60
Kevin Harvick		
Jeff Burton		
65 Denny Hamlin	.30	.75
Tony Stewart		
J.J. Yeley		
66 David Gilliland	1.50	4.00
Ricky Rudd		
67 Ryan Newman	.25	.60
Kurt Busch		
68 Joe Nemechek	1.00	2.50
Mark Martin		
Sterling Marlin		
Regan Smith		
69 Carl Edwards	.75	2.00
Greg Biffle		
Matt Kenseth		
Jamie McMurray		
David Ragan		
70 Reed Sorenson	.50	1.25
Juan Pablo Montoya		
David Stremme		
71 Martin Truex Jr.	1.00	2.50
Dale Earnhardt Jr.		
Paul Menard		
72 Casey Mears	1.00	2.50
Kyle Busch		
Jimmie Johnson		
Jeff Gordon		
73 J.J. Yeley DD	.30	.75
74 David Ragan DD	.60	1.50
75 Denny Hamlin DD	.75	2.00
76 David Reutimann DD	1.25	3.00
77 Kevin Harvick DD	.60	1.50
78 David Gilliland DD	1.50	4.00
79 Carl Edwards DD	.60	1.50
80 Greg Biffle DD	.30	.75
81 Reed Sorenson DD	.50	1.25
82 Dale Earnhardt Jr. PO	1.00	2.50
83 Jimmie Johnson PO	.75	2.00
84 Kasey Kahne PO	1.00	2.50
85 Matt Kenseth PO	.75	2.00
86 Kevin Harvick PO	.60	1.50
87 Tony Stewart PO	.60	1.50
88 Jeff Burton PO	.25	.60
89 Jeff Gordon PO	1.00	2.50
90 Dale Earnhardt Jr. CL	1.00	2.50

2007 Press Pass Stealth Previews

(EB1-EB45) STATED PRINT RUN 5 SERIAL #'d SETS
(EB82-EB90) STATED PRINT RUN 1 SERIAL #'d SET
NOT PRICED DUE TO SCARCITY
EB1 Greg Biffle
EB2 Clint Bowyer
EB3 Jeff Burton
EB4 Kurt Busch
EB5 Kyle Busch
EB6 Dale Earnhardt Jr.
EB7 Carl Edwards
EB8 Jeff Gordon
EB9 Denny Hamlin
EB10 Kevin Harvick
EB11 Dale Jarrett
EB12 Jimmie Johnson
EB13 Kasey Kahne
EB14 Matt Kenseth
EB15 Bobby Labonte
EB16 Mark Martin
EB17 Jamie McMurray
EB18 Casey Mears
EB19 Ryan Newman
EB20 Scott Riggs
EB21 Ricky Rudd
EB22 Elliott Sadler
EB23 Reed Sorenson
EB24 Tony Stewart
EB25 Martin Truex Jr.
EB26 Brian Vickers
EB27 J.J. Yeley
EB28 Michael Waltrip
EB29 A.J. Allmendinger
EB30 David Gilliland
EB31 Paul Menard
EB32 Juan Pablo Montoya
EB33 David Ragan
EB34 David Reutimann
EB35 Regan Smith
EB36 Jon Wood
EB37 Marcos Ambrose NBS
EB38 Clint Bowyer NBS
EB39 Carl Edwards NBS
EB40 Kevin Harvick NBS
EB41 Stephen Leicht NBS
EB42 David Ragan NBS
EB43 David Reutimann NBS
EB44 Reed Sorenson NBS
EB45 Steve Wallace NBS
EB82 Dale Earnhardt Jr. PO
EB83 Jimmie Johnson PO
EB84 Kasey Kahne PO
EB85 Matt Kenseth PO
EB86 Kevin Harvick PO
EB87 Tony Stewart PO
EB88 Jeff Burton PO
EB89 Jeff Gordon PO
EB90 Dale Earnhardt Jr. CL

2007 Press Pass Stealth Battle Armor Autographs

SERIAL #'d TO DRIVER'S DOOR NUMBER		
SOME CARDS NOT PRICED DUE TO SCARCITY		
BAS-DE Dale Earnhardt Jr./8		
BAS-JG Jeff Gordon/24		
BAS-JJ Jimmie Johnson/48	100.00	175.00
BAS-MK Matt Kenseth/17		
BAS-RN Ryan Newman/12		

2007 Press Pass Stealth Battle Armor Drivers

STATED ODDS 1:40 HOBBY		
STATED PRINT RUN 150 SERIAL #'d SETS		
BAD1 Jeff Gordon	40.00	80.00
BAD2 Greg Biffle	15.00	40.00
BAD3 Denny Hamlin	20.00	50.00
BAD4 David Ragan	20.00	50.00
BAD5 Ryan Newman	20.00	50.00
BAD6 Dale Earnhardt Jr.	40.00	80.00
BAD7 Carl Edwards	25.00	60.00
BAD8 Jimmie Johnson	25.00	60.00
BAD9 Jeff Burton	20.00	50.00
BAD10 Tony Stewart	25.00	60.00
BAD11 Kurt Busch	20.00	50.00
BAD12 Casey Mears	20.00	50.00
BAD13 Matt Kenseth	25.00	60.00
BAD14 Kyle Busch	20.00	50.00
BAD15 Kasey Kahne SP/8		
BAD16 Dale Jarrett	20.00	50.00
BAD17 Martin Truex Jr.	15.00	40.00
BAD18 Juan Pablo Montoya	25.00	60.00
BAD19 Mark Martin	25.00	60.00
BAD20 Reed Sorenson	20.00	50.00
BAD21 J.J. Yeley	20.00	50.00
BAD22 David Reutimann	20.00	50.00
BAD23 Bobby Labonte	20.00	50.00
BAD24 David Stremme	15.00	40.00

2007 Press Pass Stealth Battle Armor Teams

*TEAMS: .4X TO 1X DRIVERS
STATED ODDS 1:112 RETAIL
STATED PRINT RUN 85 SERIAL #'d SETS

2007 Press Pass Stealth Fusion

COMPLETE SET (9)	12.50	30.00
STATED ODDS 1:10		
F1 Dale Jarrett	1.50	4.00
F2 Jeff Gordon	3.00	8.00
F3 Tony Stewart	2.00	5.00
F4 Michael Waltrip	.75	2.00
F5 Jimmie Johnson	2.50	6.00
F6 Denny Hamlin	2.50	6.00
F7 Dale Earnhardt Jr.	3.00	8.00
F8 Juan Pablo Montoya	3.00	8.00
F9 Kevin Harvick	2.00	5.00

2007 Press Pass Stealth Mach 07

COMPLETE SET (12)	40.00	100.00
STATED ODDS 1:14-1:112 PROGRESSIVE		
M7-1 Dale Earnhardt Jr.	10.00	25.00
M7-2 Jeff Gordon	12.50	30
M7-3 Tony Stewart	5.00	12
M7-4 Juan Pablo Montoya	5.00	12
M7-5 Kasey Kahne	5.00	12
M7-6 Jimmie Johnson	6.00	15
M7-7 Kevin Harvick	5.00	12
M7-8 Denny Hamlin	4.00	10
M7-9 Mark Martin	4.00	10
M7-10 Jeff Burton	3.00	8
M7-11 Bobby Labonte	3.00	8
M7-12 Dale Jarrett	3.00	8

2007 Press Pass Steal Maximum Access

COMPLETE SET (27)	15.00	40
STATED ODDS 1:2		
MA1 A.J. Allmendinger	4.00	10
MA2 Greg Biffle	.75	
MA3 Clint Bowyer	2.00	
MA4 Jeff Burton	.60	
MA5 Kyle Busch	1.25	
MA6 Dale Earnhardt Jr.	2.50	
MA7 Carl Edwards	1.50	
MA8 Jeff Gordon	2.50	
MA9 David Gilliland	4.00	10
MA10 Denny Hamlin	2.00	
MA11 Kevin Harvick	1.50	
MA12 Dale Jarrett	1.25	
MA13 Jimmie Johnson	2.00	
MA14 Kasey Kahne	2.50	
MA15 Matt Kenseth	2.00	
MA16 Bobby Labonte	1.25	
MA17 Mark Martin	1.50	
MA18 Casey Mears	.60	
MA19 Paul Menard	.75	
MA20 Juan Pablo Montoya	2.50	
MA21 Ryan Newman	1.25	
MA22 David Ragan	1.50	
MA23 Ricky Rudd	1.00	
MA24 Reed Sorenson	1.25	
MA25 Tony Stewart	1.50	
MA26 Martin Truex Jr.	1.50	
MA27 Brian Vickers	1.00	

2007 Press Pass Steal Maximum Access Autographs

STATED PRINT RUN 25 SERIAL #'d SETS		
NOT PRICED DUE TO SCARCITY		
MA1 A.J. Allmendinger	30.00	60
MA2 Greg Biffle EXCH		
MA3 Clint Bowyer	60.00	120
MA4 Jeff Burton EXCH		
MA5 Kyle Busch		
MA6 Dale Earnhardt Jr.	125.00	200
MA7 Carl Edwards EXCH	50.00	100
MA8 Jeff Gordon EXCH	125.00	200
MA9 David Gilliland EXCH	60.00	120
MA10 Denny Hamlin EXCH	75.00	150
MA11 Kevin Harvick	40.00	80
MA12 Dale Jarrett	40.00	80
MA13 Jimmie Johnson	60.00	120
MA14 Kasey Kahne EXCH		
MA15 Matt Kenseth		
MA16 Bobby Labonte EXCH	40.00	80
MA17 Mark Martin	60.00	120
MA18 Casey Mears		
MA19 Paul Menard EXCH	60.00	120
MA20 Juan Pablo Montoya EXCH	75.00	150
MA21 Ryan Newman EXCH	50.00	100
MA22 David Ragan	30.00	60
MA23 Ricky Rudd EXCH	60.00	120
MA24 Reed Sorenson EXCH		
MA25 Tony Stewart EXCH	60.00	120
MA26 Martin Truex Jr. EXCH	50.00	100
MA27 Brian Vickers	35.00	60

2008 Press Pass Steal Chrome

COMPLETE SET (90)	15.00	4
WAX BOX HOBBY	75.00	12
1 Greg Biffle	.50	
2 Dave Blaney	.25	
3 Clint Bowyer	.75	
4 Jeff Burton	.40	
5 Kurt Busch	.60	
6 Scott Riggs	.40	
7 Patrick Carpentier RC	3.00	

Dale Earnhardt Jr.	2.00	5.00
Carl Edwards	1.00	2.50
Dario Franchitti RC	3.00	8.00
Jeff Gordon	1.50	4.00
B Jeff Gordon blue background VAR	6.00	15.00
Denny Hamlin	1.00	2.50
Kevin Harvick	.75	2.00
Sam Hornish Jr.	1.00	2.50
Dale Jarrett	1.00	2.50
Jimmie Johnson	1.25	3.00
Kasey Kahne	1.25	3.00
B Kasey Kahne missing KK logo VAR	5.00	12.00
Matt Kenseth	1.00	2.50
Travis Kvapil	.40	1.00
Bobby Labonte	.60	1.50
Mark Martin	1.00	2.50
Jeremy Mayfield	.25	.60
Jamie McMurray	.50	1.25
Casey Mears	.40	1.00
Paul Menard	.50	1.25
Juan Pablo Montoya	1.50	4.00
Ryan Newman	.60	1.50
Kyle Petty	.40	1.00
David Ragan	.50	1.25
Elliott Sadler	.50	1.25
Reed Sorenson	.40	1.00
Tony Stewart	1.25	3.00
Martin Truex Jr.	.75	2.00
Brian Vickers	.50	1.25
Michael Waltrip	.50	1.25
J.J. Yeley	.50	1.25
Clint Bowyer NNS	.75	2.00
Bryan Clauson NNS RC	1.50	4.00
Carl Edwards NNS	1.00	2.50
Dario Franchitti NNS	.75	2.00
Cale Gale NNS	.25	.60
Kevin Harvick NNS	.75	2.00
Brad Keselowski NNS RC	6.00	15.00
Tony Stewart NNS	1.25	3.00
Scott Wimmer NNS	.30	.75
Martin Truex Jr.'s Rig C	.30	.75
Mark Martin's Rig C	.40	1.00
Ryan Newman's Rig C	.25	.60
Matt Kenseth's Rig C	.40	1.00
Tony Stewart's Rig C	.50	1.25
Kevin Harvick's Rig C	.30	.75
Jeff Burton's Rig C	.15	.40
Dale Earnhardt Jr.'s Rig C	.75	2.00
Carl Edwards' Rig C	.40	1.00
Mark Martin's Car GC	.40	1.00
Casey Mears's Car GC	.15	.40
Denny Hamlin's Car GC	.40	1.00
Greg Biffle's Car GC	.20	.50
Tony Stewart's Car GC	.50	1.25
Jeff Gordon's Car GC	.60	1.50
Jeff Burton's Car GC	.15	.40
Juan Pablo Montoya's Car GC	.60	1.50
Jimmie Johnson's Car GC	.50	1.25
B Jimmie Johnson's Car GC without right front tire changer VAR	5.00	12.00
Juan Pablo Montoya / Dario Franchitti / Reed Sorenson	1.50	4.00
Aric Almirola / Mark Martin / Martin Truex Jr. / Paul Menard / Regan Smith	.75	2.00
Kasey Kahne / Elliott Sadler / Patrick Carpentier	1.25	3.00
Jimmie Johnson / Jeff Gordon / Dale Earnhardt Jr. / Casey Mears	2.00	5.00
Denny Hamlin / Tony Stewart / Kyle Busch	1.25	3.00
Jeff Burton / Clint Bowyer / Kevin Harvick	.75	2.00
B Jeff Burton / Kevin Harvick / Clint Bowyer VAR	3.00	8.00
Greg Biffle / Jamie McMurray / Carl Edwards / Matt Kenseth / David Ragan	1.00	2.50
Brian Vickers / A.J. Allmendinger	.40	1.00
Travis Kvapil / David Gilliland	.60	1.50
Greg Biffle DO	.50	1.25
Clint Bowyer DO	.75	2.00
Kyle Busch DO	.75	2.00
Carl Edwards DO	1.00	2.50
Dario Franchitti DO	.75	2.00
Kevin Harvick DO	.75	2.00
Matt Kenseth DO	1.00	2.50
David Ragan DO	.50	1.25
Tony Stewart DO	1.25	3.00
B Stewart DO 20s in background design VAR	5.00	12.00
Clint Bowyer PM	.75	2.00
Dale Earnhardt Jr. PM	2.00	5.00
B Dale Jr. PM Only 1 trophy in background VAR	8.00	20.00
Jeff Gordon PM	1.50	4.00
Denny Hamlin PM	1.00	2.50
Kevin Harvick PM	.75	2.00
Ryan Newman PM	.60	1.50
Tony Stewart PM	1.25	3.00
Martin Truex Jr. PM	.75	2.00
Jimmie Johnson PM	1.25	3.00

008 Press Pass Stealth Chrome Exclusives

XCLUSIVES: 4X TO 10X BASE
ATED PRINT RUN 25 SERIAL #'d SETS

008 Press Pass Stealth Chrome Exclusives Gold

XCLUSIVES GOLD: 2.5X TO 6X BASE
ATED PRINT RUN 99 SERIAL #'d SETS

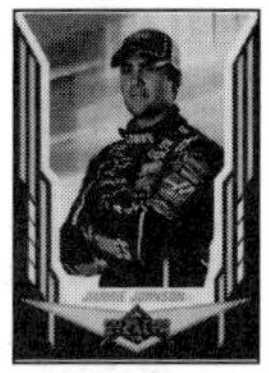

2008 Press Pass Stealth

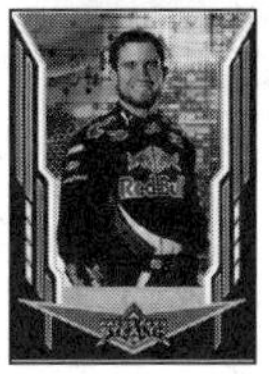

COMPLETE SET (90)	15.00	40.00
WAX BOX	50.00	75.00
1 Greg Biffle	.40	1.00
2 Dave Blaney	.20	.50
3 Clint Bowyer	.60	1.50
4 Jeff Burton	.30	.75
5 Kurt Busch	.50	1.25
6 Scott Riggs	.30	.75
7 Patrick Carpentier RC	2.00	5.00
8 Dale Earnhardt Jr.	1.50	4.00
9 Carl Edwards	.75	2.00
10 Dario Franchitti RC	2.00	5.00
11 Jeff Gordon	1.25	3.00
12 Denny Hamlin	.75	2.00
13 Kevin Harvick	.60	1.50
14 Sam Hornish Jr.	.30	.75
15 Dale Jarrett	.75	2.00
16 Jimmie Johnson	1.00	2.50
17 Kasey Kahne	1.00	2.50
18 Matt Kenseth	.75	2.00
19 Travis Kvapil	.30	.75
20 Bobby Labonte	.50	1.25
21 Mark Martin	.75	2.00
22 Jeremy Mayfield	.20	.50
23 Jamie McMurray	.40	1.00
24 Casey Mears	.30	.75
25 Paul Menard	.40	1.00
26 Juan Pablo Montoya	1.25	3.00
27 Ryan Newman	.50	1.25
28 Kyle Petty	.30	.75
29 David Ragan	.40	1.00
30 Elliott Sadler	.40	1.00
31 Reed Sorenson	.30	.75
32 Tony Stewart	1.00	2.50
33 Martin Truex Jr.	.60	1.50
34 Brian Vickers	.40	1.00
35 Michael Waltrip	.40	1.00
36 J.J. Yeley	.40	1.00
37 Clint Bowyer NNS	.60	1.50
38 Bryan Clauson NNS RC	1.00	2.50
39 Carl Edwards NNS	.75	2.00
40 Dario Franchitti NNS	.60	1.50
41 Cale Gale NNS	.20	.50
42 Kevin Harvick NNS	.60	1.50
43 Brad Keselowski NNS RC	4.00	10.00
44 Tony Stewart NNS	1.00	2.50
45 Scott Wimmer NNS	.25	.60
46 Martin Truex Jr.'s Rig C	.25	.60
47 Mark Martin's Rig C	.30	.75
48 Ryan Newman's Rig C	.20	.50
49 Matt Kenseth's Rig C	.30	.75
50 Tony Stewart's Rig C	.40	1.00
51 Kevin Harvick's Rig C	.25	.60
52 Jeff Burton's Rig C	.12	.30
53 Dale Earnhardt Jr.'s Rig C	.60	1.50
54 Carl Edwards' Rig C	.30	.75
55 Mark Martin's Car GC	.30	.75
56 Casey Mears's Car GC	.12	.30
57 Denny Hamlin's Car GC	.30	.75
58 Greg Biffle's Car GC	.15	.40
59 Tony Stewart's Car GC	.40	1.00
60 Jeff Gordon's Car GC	.50	1.25
61 Jeff Burton's Car GC	.12	.30
62 Juan Pablo Montoya's Car GC	.50	1.25
63 Jimmie Johnson's Car GC	.40	1.00
64 Juan Pablo Montoya / Dario Franchitti / Reed Sorenson	.60	1.50
65 Aric Almirola / Mark Martin / Martin Truex Jr. / Paul Menard / Regan Smith	.60	1.50
66 Kasey Kahne / Elliott Sadler / Patrick Carpentier	.40	1.00
67 Jimmie Johnson / Jeff Gordon / Dale Earnhardt Jr. / Casey Mears	1.50	4.00
68 Denny Hamlin / Tony Stewart / Kyle Busch	1.00	2.50
69 Jeff Burton / Clint Bowyer / Kevin Harvick	.60	1.50
70 Greg Biffle / Jamie McMurray / Carl Edwards / Matt Kenseth / David Ragan	.75	2.00
71 Brian Vickers / A.J. Allmendinger	.30	.75
72 Travis Kvapil / David Gilliland	.30	.75
73 Greg Biffle DO	.40	1.00
74 Clint Bowyer DO	.60	1.50
75 Kyle Busch DO	.60	1.50
76 Carl Edwards DO	.75	2.00
77 Dario Franchitti DO	.60	1.50
78 Kevin Harvick DO	.60	1.50
79 Matt Kenseth DO	.75	2.00
80 David Ragan DO	.40	1.00
81 Tony Stewart DO	1.00	2.50
82 Clint Bowyer PM	.60	1.50
83 Dale Earnhardt Jr. PM	1.50	4.00
84 Jeff Gordon PM	1.25	3.00
85 Denny Hamlin PM	.75	2.00
86 Kevin Harvick PM	.60	1.50
87 Ryan Newman PM	.50	1.25
88 Tony Stewart PM	1.00	2.50
89 Martin Truex Jr. PM	.60	1.50
90 Jimmie Johnson PM	1.00	2.50

2008 Press Pass Stealth Battle Armor Autographs

SERIAL #'d TO DRIVERS DOOR NUMBER
SOME NOT PRICED DUE TO SCARCITY

BASDH Denny Hamlin/11		
BASKH Kevin Harvick/29	200.00	300.00
BASKK Kasey Kahne/9		
BASMK Matt Kenseth/17		
BASMM Mark Martin/8		
BASTS Tony Stewart/20		

2008 Press Pass Stealth Battle Armor Drivers

STATED ODDS 1:40
STATED PRINT RUN 120 SERIAL #'d SETS

BAD1 Jimmie Johnson	20.00	50.00
BAD2 Michael Waltrip	10.00	25.00
BAD3 Jeff Gordon	40.00	80.00
BAD4 Patrick Carpentier	12.00	30.00
BAD5 Carl Edwards	15.00	40.00
BAD6 Kasey Kahne	40.00	80.00
BAD7 Juan Pablo Montoya	10.00	25.00
BAD8 Ryan Newman	12.00	30.00
BAD9 Reed Sorenson	8.00	20.00
BAD10 Mark Martin	15.00	40.00
BAD11 Dario Franchitti	15.00	40.00
BAD12 Kurt Busch	12.00	30.00
BAD13 Martin Truex Jr.	12.00	30.00
BAD14 Matt Kenseth	15.00	40.00
BAD15 Elliott Sadler	10.00	25.00
BAD16 Kyle Busch	15.00	40.00
BAD17 Kevin Harvick	15.00	40.00
BAD18 Denny Hamlin	15.00	40.00
BAD19 Dale Jarrett	15.00	40.00
BAD20 Tony Stewart	15.00	40.00
BAD21 Jeff Burton	8.00	20.00
BAD22 Casey Mears	8.00	20.00
BAD23 Dale Earnhardt Jr.	40.00	80.00

2008 Press Pass Stealth Battle Armor Teams

*TEAMS: .4X TO 1X DRIVERS
STATED PRINT RUN 115 SERIAL #'d SETS

2008 Press Pass Stealth Mach 08

PROGRESSIVE ODDS 1:14-1:112

M8-1 Jeff Gordon	20.00	50.00
M8-2 Dale Earnhardt Jr.	15.00	40.00
M8-3 Tony Stewart	10.00	25.00
M8-4 Jimmie Johnson	10.00	25.00
M8-5 Mark Martin	4.00	10.00
M8-6 Martin Truex Jr.	2.50	6.00
M8-7 Kevin Harvick	5.00	12.00
M8-8 Juan Pablo Montoya	2.50	6.00
M8-9 Ryan Newman	2.50	6.00
M8-10 Jeff Burton	3.00	8.00
M8-11 Dario Franchitti	3.00	8.00
M8-12 Dale Jarrett	4.00	10.00

2008 Press Pass Stealth Maximum Access

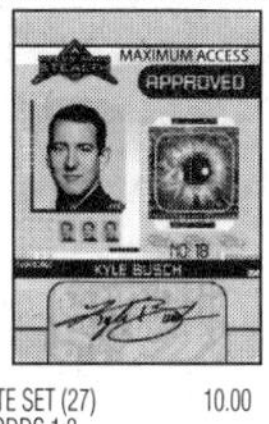

COMPLETE SET (27)	10.00	25.00
STATED ODDS 1:2		
MA1 A.J. Allmendinger	.60	1.50
MA2 Greg Biffle	.75	2.00
MA3 Dave Blaney	.40	1.00
MA4 Clint Bowyer	1.25	3.00
MA5 Jeff Burton	.60	1.50
MA6 Kurt Busch	1.00	2.50
MA7 Kyle Busch	1.25	3.00
MA8 Dale Earnhardt Jr.	3.00	8.00
MA9 Carl Edwards	1.50	4.00
MA10 Jeff Gordon	2.50	6.00
MA11 Denny Hamlin	1.50	4.00
MA12 Kevin Harvick	1.25	3.00
MA13 Dale Jarrett	1.50	4.00
MA14 Jimmie Johnson	2.00	5.00
MA15 Matt Kenseth	1.50	4.00
MA16 Bobby Labonte	1.00	2.50
MA17 Mark Martin	1.50	4.00
MA18 Jamie McMurray	.75	2.00
MA19 Casey Mears	.60	1.50
MA20 Juan Pablo Montoya	2.50	6.00
MA21 Ryan Newman	1.00	2.50
MA22 David Ragan	.75	2.00
MA23 Reed Sorenson	.60	1.50
MA24 Tony Stewart	2.00	5.00
MA25 Martin Truex Jr.	1.25	3.00
MA26 Brian Vickers	.75	2.00
MA27 Michael Waltrip	.75	2.00

2008 Press Pass Stealth Maximum Access Autographs

STATED PRINT RUN 25 SERIAL #'d SETS

MA1 A.J. Allmendinger	20.00	50.00
MA2 Greg Biffle	40.00	80.00
MA3 Dave Blaney	30.00	60.00
MA4 Clint Bowyer	60.00	120.00
MA5 Jeff Burton	40.00	80.00
MA6 Kurt Busch	20.00	50.00
MA7 Kyle Busch	150.00	250.00
MA8 Dale Earnhardt Jr.	250.00	400.00
MA9 Carl Edwards	125.00	250.00
MA10 Jeff Gordon	250.00	400.00
MA11 Denny Hamlin	60.00	120.00
MA12 Kevin Harvick	50.00	100.00
MA13 Dale Jarrett	60.00	120.00
MA14 Jimmie Johnson	75.00	150.00
MA15 Matt Kenseth	60.00	120.00
MA16 Bobby Labonte	60.00	120.00
MA17 Mark Martin	50.00	100.00
MA18 Jamie McMurray	30.00	60.00
MA19 Casey Mears	30.00	60.00
MA20 Juan Pablo Montoya	50.00	100.00
MA21 Ryan Newman	50.00	100.00
MA22 David Ragan	40.00	80.00
MA23 Reed Sorenson		
MA24 Tony Stewart	60.00	120.00
MA25 Martin Truex Jr.	50.00	100.00
MA26 Brian Vickers	40.00	80.00
MA27 Michael Waltrip	40.00	80.00

2008 Press Pass Stealth Previews

EB1-EB45 PRINT RUN SERIAL #'d TO 5 SETS
EB82-EB90 PRINT RUN SERIAL #'d TO 1 SET
NOT PRICED DUE TO SCARCITY

2008 Press Pass Stealth Synthesis

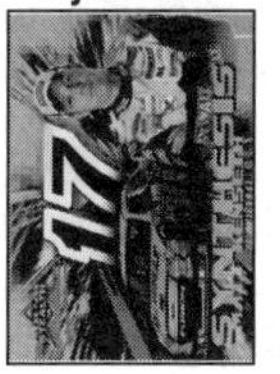

COMPLETE SET (9)	10.00	25.00
STATED ODDS 1:10		
S1 Jimmie Johnson	1.50	4.00
S2 Clint Bowyer	1.00	2.50
S3 Jeff Burton	.50	1.25
S4 Tony Stewart	1.50	4.00
S5 Matt Kenseth	1.25	3.00
S6 Bobby Labonte	.75	2.00
S7 Dale Earnhardt Jr.	2.50	6.00
S8 Michael Waltrip	.60	1.50
S9 Jeff Gordon	2.00	5.00

1999 Press Pass Tony Stewart Fan Club

NNO Tony Stewart	10.00	25.00

2002 Press Pass Tony Stewart Fan Club

NNO Tony Stewart	10.00	25.00

2003 Press Pass Top Prospects Memorabilia

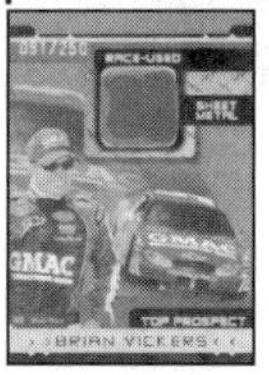

This 24-card set featured 6 of NASCAR's young prospects. Each driver had 4 versions: a swatch of glove numbered to 100, a swatch of shoe numbered to 200, a swatch of sheet metal numbered to 250 and a swatch of tire numbered to 400. These cards were available in: 2003 Press Pass Optima at a rate of 1 in 130, 2003 Press Pass Stealth at a rate of 1 in 124 packs and 2003 Press Pass Trackside at a rate of 1 in 168.

BVG Brian Vickers Glove/100	20.00	50.00
BVM Brian Vickers Sheet Metal/250	20.00	50.00
BVS Brian Vickers Shoe/200	20.00	50.00
BVT Brian Vickers Tire/400	10.00	25.00
CBG Chad Blount Glove/100	6.00	15.00
CBM Chad Blount Sheet Metal/250	6.00	15.00
CBS Chad Blount Shoe/200	6.00	15.00
CBT Chad Blount Tire/400	5.00	12.00
SHG Shane Hmiel Glove/100	12.50	30.00
SHM Shane Hmiel Sheet Metal/250	12.50	30.00
SHS Shane Hmiel Shoe/200	12.50	30.00
SHT Shane Hmiel Tire/400	10.00	25.00
SMG Steadman Marlin Glove/100	8.00	20.00
SMM Steadman Marlin Sheet Metal/250	8.00	20.00
SMS Steadman Marlin Shoe/200	8.00	20.00
SMT Steadman Marlin Tire/400	6.00	15.00
SRG Scott Riggs Glove/100	8.00	20.00
SRM Scott Riggs Sheet Metal/250	8.00	20.00
SRS Scott Riggs Shoe/200	8.00	20.00
SRT Scott Riggs Tire/400	6.00	15.00
SWG Scott Wimmer Glove/100	8.00	20.00
SWM Scott Wimmer Sheet Metal/250	8.00	20.00
SWS Scott Wimmer Shoe/200	8.00	20.00
SWT Scott Wimmer Tire/400	6.00	15.00

2004 Press Pass Top Prospects Memorabilia

This 22-card set featured race-used swatches of the top young drivers in NASCAR. There were sheet metal and tire cards available in 2004 Press Pass Trackside at a rate of 1 in 84 packs, and they were serial numbered to 200 (sheet metal) and 350 (tire). There were glove and shoe swatches available in 2004 Press Pass Optima at a rate of 1 in 84 packs, and they were serial numbered to 100 (glove) and 150 (shoe).

COMPLETE SET (22)
GLOVE/SHOE STATED ODDS 1:98 '04 OPTIMA
GLOVE PRINT RUN 100 SERIAL #'d SETS
SHEET METAL PRINT RUN 200 SERIAL #'d SETS
SHOE PRINT RUN 150 SERIAL #'d SETS
TIRE PRINT RUN 350 SERIAL #'d SETS

CBT Clint Bowyer Tire	10.00	25.00
CBSM Clint Bowyer Metal	15.00	40.00
KBG Kyle Busch Glove	25.00	60.00
KBT Kyle Busch Tire	20.00	50.00
KBSM Kyle Busch Metal	40.00	80.00
THG Tracy Hines Glove	10.00	25.00
THS Tracy Hines Shoe	8.00	20.00
KKG Kasey Kahne Glove	40.00	80.00
KKS Kasey Kahne Shoe	25.00	50.00
KKT Kasey Kahne Tire	20.00	40.00
KKSM Kasey Kahne Metal	30.00	60.00
PMG Paul Menard Glove	10.00	25.00
PMS Paul Menard Shoe	10.00	25.00
PMT Paul Menard Tire	8.00	20.00
PMSM Paul Menard Metal	12.50	30.00
BPSM Billy Parker Metal	12.50	30.00
MTT Martin Truex Jr. Tire	15.00	40.00
MTSM Martin Truex Jr. Metal		
PWT Paul Wolfe Tire	6.00	15.00
PWSM Paul Wolfe Metal	8.00	20.00
JYT J.J. Yeley Tire	10.00	25.00
JYSM J.J. Yeley Metal	12.50	30.00

2005 Press Pass Top Prospects Memorabilia

CE-G Carl Edwards Glove	40.00	80.00
CE-S Carl Edwards Shoe	30.00	60.00
CE-SM Carl Edwards Metal	40.00	80.00
CE-T Carl Edwards Tire	12.50	30.00
DH-S Denny Hamlin Shoe	25.00	50.00
DH-SM Denny Hamlin Metal	25.00	50.00
DH-T Denny Hamlin Tire	15.00	40.00
DS-G David Stremme Glove	15.00	40.00
DS-T David Stremme Tire	12.50	30.00
JL-G Justin Labonte Glove	10.00	25.00
JL-SM Justin Labonte Metal	10.00	25.00
JL-T Justin Labonte Tire	8.00	20.00
JW-G Jon Wood Glove	8.00	20.00
JW-S Jon Wood Shoe	8.00	20.00
JW-SM Jon Wood Metal	8.00	20.00
MT-G Martin Truex Jr. Glove	15.00	40.00
MT-S Martin Truex Jr. Shoe	15.00	40.00
MT-SM Martin Truex Jr. Metal	20.00	50.00
MT-T Martin Truex Jr. Tire	8.00	20.00
RS-G Reed Sorenson Glove	15.00	40.00
RS-SM Reed Sorenson Metal	15.00	40.00
RS-T Reed Sorenson Tire	8.00	20.00

2006 Press Pass Top Prospects Gloves

This 6-card set featured swatches of race-used gloves from some of NASCAR's hottest prospects. Each card was serial numbered to 199 and carried a "G" suffix for its card number.

BL-G Burney Lamar	8.00	20.00
DO-G Danny O'Quinn	10.00	25.00
EC-G Erin Crocker	12.50	30.00
RS-G Regan Smith	8.00	20.00
SW-G Steve Wallace	10.00	25.00
TK-G Todd Kluever	12.50	30.00

2006 Press Pass Top Prospects Sheet Metal

This 6-card set featured swatches of race-used sheet metal from some of NASCAR's hottest prospects. Each card was serial numbered to 199 and carried an "M" suffix for its card number.

BL-M Burney Lamar	10.00	25.00
DO-M Danny O'Quinn	10.00	25.00
EC-M Erin Crocker	15.00	40.00
RS-M Regan Smith	10.00	25.00
SW-M Steve Wallace	15.00	40.00
TK-M Todd Kluever	15.00	40.00

2006 Press Pass Top Prospects Shoes

This 6-card set featured swatches of race-used shoes from some of NASCAR's hottest prospects. Each card was serial numbered to 199 and carried an "S" suffix for its card number.

BL-S Burney Lamar	8.00	20.00
DO-S Danny O'Quinn	10.00	25.00
EC-S Erin Crocker	12.50	30.00
RS-S Regan Smith	8.00	20.00
SW-S Steve Wallace	8.00	20.00
TK-S Todd Kluever	15.00	40.00

2006 Press Pass Top Prospects Tires Autographs

This 4-card set featured swatches of race-used tires from some of NASCAR's hottest prospects along with signatures. Each card was serial numbered to 25 and carried a "T" suffix for its card number.

EC-T Erin Crocker	40.00	80.00
MM-T Mark McFarland	30.00	60.00
RS-T Regan Smith		
SW-T Steve Wallace		
TK-T Todd Kluever	50.00	100.00

2006 Press Pass Top Prospects Tires Gold

This 7-card set featured swatches of race-used tires from some of NASCAR's hottest prospects. Most cards were serial numbered to 100 and carried a "T" suffix for its card number. See below for exceptions to serial numbering. This set was a parallel to the Silver version.

*GOLD: .5X TO 1.2X SILVER

BL-T Burney Lamar	10.00	25.00
DO-T Danny O'Quinn	8.00	20.00
EC-T Erin Crocker	12.50	30.00
MM-T Mark McFarland	8.00	20.00
RS-T Regan Smith/199		
SW-T Steve Wallace/199	12.50	30.00
TK-T Todd Kluever	15.00	40.00

2006 Press Pass Top Prospects Tires Silver

This 5-card set featured swatches of race-used tires from some of NASCAR's hottest prospects. Most cards were serial numbered to 500 and carried a "T" suffix for its card number.

BL-T Burney Lamar	8.00	20.00
DO-T Danny O'Quinn	6.00	15.00
EC-T Erin Crocker	12.50	30.00
MM-T Mark McFarland	6.00	15.00
TK-T Todd Kluever	10.00	25.00

2007 Press Pass Top Prospects Gloves

STATED PRINT RUN 200 SERIAL #'d SETS

AA-G Aric Almirola	8.00	20.00
MA-G Marcos Ambrose	12.50	30.00
SH-G Shane Huffman	10.00	25.00
DRE-G David Reutimann	10.00	25.00

2007 Press Pass Top Prospects Sheet Metal

STATED PRINT RUN 350 SERIAL #'d SETS

AA-SM Aric Almirola	6.00	15.00
MA-SM Marcos Ambrose	25.00	50.00
SH-SM Shane Huffman	8.00	20.00
DRA-SM David Ragan	8.00	20.00
DRE-SM David Reutimann	12.50	30.00

2007 Press Pass Top Prospects Sheet Metal-Tire

STATED PRINT RUN 75 SERIAL #'d SETS

AA-ST Aric Almirola	20.00	40.00
MA-ST Marcos Ambrose		
SH-ST Shane Huffman	20.00	40.00
DRA-ST David Ragan	25.00	50.00
DRE-ST David Reutimann	25.00	50.00

2007 Press Pass Top Prospects Shoes

STATED PRINT RUN 200 SERIAL #'d SETS

AA-S Aric Almirola	8.00	20.00
MA-S Marcos Ambrose	12.50	30.00
SH-S Shane Huffman	10.00	25.00
DRA-S David Ragan	8.00	20.00
DRE-S David Reutimann	15.00	40.00

2007 Press Pass Top Prospects Tire Autographs

STATED PRINT RUN 25 SERIAL #'d SETS

AA-A Aric Almirola	40.00	80.00
MA-A Marcos Ambrose	50.00	100.00
SH-A Shane Huffman	40.00	80.00
SL-A Stephen Leicht	40.00	80.00
DRA-A David Ragan	60.00	120.00
DRE-A David Reutimann	60.00	120.00
SHO-A Sam Hornish Jr.		

2007 Press Pass Top Prospects Tires Gold

*GOLD: .5X TO 1.2X SILVER
STATED PRINT RUN 99 SERIAL #'d SETS

2007 Press Pass Top Prospects Tires Silver

STATED PRINT RUN 250 SERIAL #'d SETS

AA-T Aric Almirola	10.00	25.00
DG-T David Gilliland	10.00	25.00
MA-T Marcos Ambrose	15.00	40.00
SH-T Shane Huffman	10.00	25.00
SL-T Stephen Leicht	8.00	20.00
DRa-T David Ragan	8.00	20.00
DRe-T David Reutimann	8.00	20.00
SHo-T Sam Hornish Jr.	8.00	20.00

2008 Press Pass Top Prospects Gloves

STATED PRINT RUN 175 SERIAL #'d SETS

BC-G Bryan Clauson	10.00	25.00
BK-G Brad Keselowski	15.00	40.00
CB-G Colin Braun	10.00	25.00
CM-G Chase Miller	8.00	20.00
LC-G Landon Cassill	12.00	30.00

2008 Press Pass Top Prospects Metal-Tire

STATED PRINT RUN 75 SERIAL #'d SETS

BC-ST Bryan Clauson	12.00	30.00
BK-ST Brad Keselowski	20.00	50.00
CB-ST Colin Braun	12.00	30.00
CM-ST Chase Miller	10.00	25.00
LC-ST Landon Cassill	15.00	40.00

2008 Press Pass Top Prospects Sheet Metal

STATED PRINT RUN 175 SERIAL #'d SETS

BC-SM Bryan Clauson	10.00	25.00
BK-SM Brad Keselowski	15.00	40.00
CB-SM Colin Braun	10.00	25.00
CM-SM Chase Miller	8.00	20.00
LC-SM Landon Cassill	12.00	30.00

2008 Press Pass Top Prospects Shoes

STATED PRINT RUN 175 SERIAL #'d SETS

BK-S Brad Keselowski	10.00	25.00
CB-S Colin Braun	8.00	20.00
CM-S Chase Miller	6.00	15.00
LC-S Landon Cassill	10.00	25.00

2008 Press Pass Top Prospects Tires

STATED PRINT RUN 330 SERIAL #'d SETS

BCT Bryan Clauson	5.00	12.00
BKT Brad Keselowski	8.00	20.00
CBT Colin Braun	6.00	15.00
CMT Chase Miller	4.00	10.00
KBT Kelly Bires	5.00	12.00
LCT Landon Cassill	8.00	20.00

2008 Press Pass Top Prospects Tires Autographs

STATED PRINT RUN 25 SERIAL #'d SETS

BC-AT Bryan Clauson	30.00	60.00
BK-AT Brad Keselowski		
CB-AT Colin Braun	40.00	80.00
CM-AT Chase Miller	30.00	60.00
KB-AT Kelly Bires		
LC-AT Landon Cassill	40.00	80.00

2008 Press Pass Top Prospects Tires Gold

*GOLD: .5X TO 1.2X BASIC

2006 Press Pass Top 25 Drivers & Rides

This 50-card set was released at retail locations and carried an SRP of $9.99. It featured the top 25 Nextel Cup drivers. Each driver had a car card produced along with a driver card. This set was packaged in black & yellow blister packs with Top 25 Drivers & Rides printed on it. This set contained a first year card of Brent Sherman.

COMPLETE SET (50)	10.00	20.00
COMP.FACT SET (50)	10.00	20.00
COMP.DRIVERS SET (25)	6.00	12.00
COMP.CARS SET (25)	4.00	8.00
SEMISTARS	.25	.60
UNLISTED STARS	.40	1.00
C1 Martin Truex Jr.'s Car	.25	.60
C2 Kurt Busch's Car	.15	.40
C3 Kyle Busch's Car	.20	.50
C4 Mark Martin's Car	.25	.60
C5 Clint Bowyer's Car	.40	1.00
C6 Dale Earnhardt Jr.'s Car	.40	1.00
C7 Kasey Kahne's Car	.40	1.00
C8 Denny Hamlin's Car	.40	1.00
C9 Ryan Newman's Car	.25	.60
C10 Greg Biffle's Car	.12	.30
C11 Matt Kenseth's Car	.30	.75
C12 J.J. Yeley's Car	.15	.40
C13 Tony Stewart's Car	.25	.60
C14 Jeff Gordon's Car	.40	1.00
C15 Kevin Harvick's Car	.25	.60
C16 Jeff Burton's Car	.10	.25
C17 Elliott Sadler's Car	.10	.25
C18 David Stremme's Car	.25	.60
C19 Reed Sorenson's Car	.25	.60
C20 Casey Mears' Car	.15	.40
C21 Bobby Labonte's Car	.20	.50
C22 Jimmie Johnson's Car	.30	.75
C23 Brent Sherman's Car	.20	.50
C24 Dale Jarrett's Car	.20	.50
C25 Carl Edwards' Car	.30	.75
D1 Martin Truex Jr.	.75	2.00
D2 Kurt Busch	.40	1.00
D3 Kyle Busch	.50	1.25
D4 Mark Martin	.60	1.50
D5 Clint Bowyer	1.00	2.50
D6 Dale Earnhardt Jr.	1.00	2.50
D7 Kasey Kahne	1.00	2.50
D8 Denny Hamlin	1.00	2.50
D9 Ryan Newman	.75	2.00
D10 Greg Biffle	.30	.75
D11 Matt Kenseth	.75	2.00
D12 J.J. Yeley	.40	1.00
D13 Tony Stewart	.60	1.50
D14 Jeff Gordon	1.00	2.50
D15 Kevin Harvick	.60	1.50
D16 Jeff Burton	.25	.60
D17 Elliott Sadler	.25	.60
D18 David Stremme	.60	1.50
D19 Reed Sorenson	.60	1.50
D20 Casey Mears	.25	.60
D21 Bobby Labonte	.50	1.25
D22 Jimmie Johnson	.75	2.00
D23 Brent Sherman	.50	1.25
D24 Dale Jarrett	.50	1.25
D25 Carl Edwards	.75	2.00

2002 Press Pass Total Memorabilia Power Pick

Issued in packs at stated odds of 1:200 across all 2002 Press Pass brands, these nine cards were redemptions that were to be used for a chance to win complete runs of all 2002 Press Pass memorabilia cards for the featured driver. The collector would have to mail this card to Press Pass for a chance to be a winner. Five winners per driver were awarded. The expiration date for the contest was January 31, 2003.

TM0 Dale Earnhardt	5.00	12.00
TM1 Dale Earnhardt Jr.	4.00	10.00
TM2 Jeff Gordon	3.00	8.00
TM3 Kevin Harvick	3.00	6.00
TM4 Dale Jarrett	2.00	5.00
TM5 Bobby Labonte	2.00	5.00
TM6 Terry Labonte	1.50	4.00
TM7 Mark Martin	2.50	6.00
TM8 Tony Stewart	2.50	6.00
TM9 Rusty Wallace	2.00	5.00

2003 Press Pass Total Memorabilia Power Pick

Inserted at a stated rate of one in 200, these 10 cards are contest cards which allowed collectors to enter a drawing to win all the memorabilia cards of a driver which were issued in 2002. Out of all the entries, only five winners will be selected for each driver.

TM1 Jeff Gordon	8.00	20.00
TM2 Ryan Newman	6.00	15.00
TM3 Kevin Harvick	5.00	12.00
TM4 Jimmie Johnson	6.00	15.00
TM5 Rusty Wallace	6.00	15.00
TM6 Mark Martin	6.00	15.00
TM7 Matt Kenseth	6.00	15.00
TM8 Bobby Labonte	5.00	12.00
TM9 Tony Stewart	6.00	15.00
TM10 Dale Earnhardt Jr.	8.00	20.00

2004 Press Pass Total Memorabilia Power Pick

This 10-card set was randomly inserted in packs across all brands of Press Pass hobby and retail products in 2004. Each card was issued as an entry card for a chance to win an entire run of each of the specified driver's memorabilia cards issued in 2004 by Press Pass. There were 5 winners drawn for each of the 10 drivers. The entry deadline was January 31, 2005.

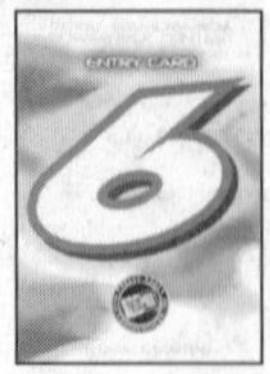

TM1 Jeff Gordon	12.50	25.00
TM2 Ryan Newman	4.00	10.00
TM3 Kevin Harvick	4.00	10.00
TM4 Jimmie Johnson	5.00	12.00
TM5 Rusty Wallace	3.00	8.00
TM6 Mark Martin	4.00	10.00
TM7 Matt Kenseth	4.00	10.00
TM8 Bobby Labonte	4.00	10.00
TM9 Tony Stewart	4.00	10.00
TM10 Dale Earnhardt Jr.	10.00	20.00

2005 Press Pass Total Memorabilia Power Pick

TM1 Jeff Gordon	6.00	15.00
TM2 Ryan Newman	5.00	12.00
TM3 Kevin Harvick	5.00	12.00
TM4 Jimmie Johnson	5.00	12.00
TM5 Rusty Wallace	5.00	12.00
TM6 Mark Martin	5.00	12.00
TM7 Matt Kenseth	5.00	12.00
TM8 Bobby Labonte	5.00	12.00
TM9 Tony Stewart	5.00	12.00
TM10 Dale Earnhardt Jr.	6.00	15.00
TM11 Brian Vickers	5.00	12.00
TM12 Kurt Busch	5.00	12.00

2000 Press Pass Trackside

Released as a 72-card set, Trackside Racing featured top Winston Cup drivers on cards 1-27, top race winners on cards 28-36, Busch Series drivers on cards 37-45, crew chiefs on cards 46-54, Wood Brother's milestones on cards 55-63, and track scenes on cards 64-72. Boxes contained 24 packs with six cards per pack and carried a suggested retail price of 2.99.

COMPLETE SET (72)	10.00	25.00
1 Steve Park	.25	.60
2 Dale Earnhardt	1.25	3.00
3 Bobby Hamilton	.12	.30
4 Terry Labonte	.25	.60
5 Michael Waltrip	.15	.40
6 Dale Earnhardt Jr. CRC	1.00	2.50
7 Jeff Gordon	.75	2.00
8 Jerry Nadeau	.15	.40
9 Mike Skinner	.12	.30
10 Joe Nemechek	.12	.30
11 Sterling Marlin	.25	.60
12 Kenny Irwin	.15	.40
13 Bobby Labonte	.50	1.25
14 Tony Stewart	.75	2.00
15 Ward Burton	.15	.40
16 Johnny Benson Jr.	.15	.40
17 John Andretti	.12	.30
18 Dave Blaney	.12	.30
19 Rusty Wallace	.60	1.50
20 Mark Martin	.60	1.50
21 Jeremy Mayfield	.12	.30
22 Matt Kenseth CRC	.60	1.50
23 Chad Little	.15	.40
24 Ricky Rudd	.25	.60
25 Darrell Waltrip	.15	.40
26 Dale Jarrett	.50	1.25
27 Jeff Burton	.25	.60
28 Jeff Burton's Car	.12	.30
29 Dale Earnhardt Jr.'s Car	.40	1.00
30 Jeff Gordon's Car	.30	.75
31 Rusty Wallace's Car	.25	.60
32 Mark Martin's Car	.25	.60
33 Bobby Labonte's Car	.15	.40
34 Dale Jarrett's Car	.15	.40
35 Tony Stewart's Car	.30	.75
36 Dale Earnhardt's Car	.50	1.25
37 Jeff Green BGN	.12	.30
38 Elton Sawyer BGN	.12	.30
39 Casey Atwood BGN	.25	.60
40 Todd Bodine BGN	.12	.30
41 Ricky Hendrick BGN RC	1.25	3.00
42 Justin Labonte BGN	.12	.30
43 Hank Parker Jr. BGN RC	.25	.60
44 Kenny Irwin BGN	.15	.40
45 Mark Green BGN	.12	.30
46 Robin Pemberton	.07	.20
47 Peter Sospenso	.07	.20
48 Jimmy Makar	.07	.20
49 Greg Zippadelli	.07	.20
50 Tommy Baldwin	.07	.20
51 Larry McReynolds	.07	.20
52 Jimmy Elledge	.07	.20
53 Ryan Pemberton	.07	.20
54 Todd Parrott	.07	.20
55 Glen Wood WBM	.07	.20
56 Cale Yarborough WBM	.12	.30
57 A.J. Foyt WBM	.15	.40
58 David Pearson WBM	.15	.40
59 David Pearson WBM	.15	.40
60 Buddy Baker WBM	.12	.30
61 Dale Jarrett WBM	.25	.60
62 Elliott Sadler WBM	.15	.40
63 Wood Brothers WBM	.07	.20
64 Grand Stands	.07	.20
65 Infield	.07	.20
66 Rigs	.07	.20
67 Garage	.07	.20
68 Pit Row	.07	.20
69 Around the Track	.07	.20
70 Pre-Race Activities	.07	.20
71 Flags	.07	.20
72 Checklist	.07	.20
P1 Mark Martin Promo	.75	2.00
NNO Jeff Burton Power Pick	2.50	6.00
NNO Chad Little Power Pick	2.00	5.00
NNO Mark Martin Power Pick	3.00	8.00
NNO Scott Pruett Power Pick	2.00	5.00

2000 Press Pass Trackside Die Cuts

Inserted in packs at the rate of one in one, this 45-card set parallels the first 45 cards from the Press Pass Trackside base set in die-cut form.

COMPLETE SET (45)	20.00	50.00

*DIE CUTS: .8X TO 2X BASE CARDS

2000 Press Pass Trackside Golden

Randomly inserted in packs at the rate of one in 110, this 45-card set parallels the first 45 cards of the Press Pass Trackside base set. Cards contain gold borders and each card is sequentially numbered to 50.

COMPLETE SET (72)	500.00	1000.00

*GOLDEN: 15X TO 30X BASE CARDS

2000 Press Pass Trackside Dialed In

Randomly inserted in packs at the rate of one in eight, this 12-card set features top NASCAR drivers on a holofoil die-cut card in the shape of the gauges in a NASCAR race car.

COMPLETE SET (12)	20.00	50.00
DI1 Dale Jarrett	1.50	4.00
DI2 Bobby Labonte	1.50	4.00
DI3 Mark Martin	2.00	5.00
DI4 Jeff Gordon	2.50	6.00
DI5 Tony Stewart	2.50	6.00
DI6 Jeff Burton	.60	1.50
DI7 Matt Kenseth	2.00	5.00
DI8 Rusty Wallace	1.50	4.00
DI9 Dale Earnhardt	4.00	10.00
DI10 Terry Labonte	1.00	2.50
DI11 Ricky Rudd	.75	2.00
DI12 Dale Earnhardt Jr.	3.00	8.00

2000 Press Pass Trackside Generation.now

Randomly inserted in packs at the rate of one in 18, this six card set features top young NASCAR drivers on an all holofoil card. Card backs carry a "GN" prefix.

COMPLETE SET (6)	12.50	30.00
GN1 Matt Kenseth	2.50	6.00
GN2 Dale Earnhardt Jr.	4.00	10.00
GN3 Casey Atwood	1.00	2.50
GN4 Elliott Sadler	.60	1.50
GN5 Tony Stewart	3.00	8.00
GN6 Jeff Gordon	3.00	8.00

2000 Press Pass Trackside Panorama

Randomly inserted in packs, the last 9 cards of this set are short-printed. Cards P1-P27 are inserted at the rate of one in one, and cards P28-P36 are inserted at the rate of one in 12. These cards are

smaller than the base set, measuring 2" X 3 1/2", and contain wide angle action photography.

COMPLETE SET (36)	25.00	50.00
P1 Steve Park	.60	1.50
P2 John Andretti	.25	.60
P3 Bobby Hamilton	.40	1.00
P4 Terry Labonte	1.00	2.50
P5 Michael Waltrip	.60	1.50
P6 Brett Bodine		
P7 Jeremy Mayfield	.25	.60
P8 Johnny Benson Jr.	.60	1.50
P9 Kevin Lepage		
P10 Elliott Sadler	.50	1.25
P11 Ward Burton	.50	1.25
P12 Jerry Nadeau	.50	1.25
P13 Jimmy Spencer	.50	1.25
P14 Ricky Rudd	.75	2.00
P15 Mike Skinner	.25	.60
P16 Scott Pruett		
P17 Joe Nemechek	.25	.60
P18 Robert Pressley		
P19 Sterling Marlin	1.00	2.50
P20 Kenny Irwin	1.00	2.50
P21 Casey Atwood	.75	2.00
P22 Kenny Wallace		
P23 Geoffrey Bodine	.25	.60
P24 Darrell Waltrip	.50	1.25
P25 Wally Dallenbach		
P26 Dave Blaney		
P27 Chad Little CL	.40	1.00
P28 Dale Earnhardt	4.00	10.00
P29 Jeff Burton	.60	1.50
P30 Rusty Wallace	1.50	4.00
P31 Jeff Gordon	2.50	6.00
P32 Dale Jarrett	1.50	4.00
P33 Matt Kenseth	2.00	5.00
P34 Bobby Labonte	1.50	4.00
P35 Mark Martin	2.00	5.00
P36 Tony Stewart	2.50	6.00

2000 Press Pass Trackside Pit Stoppers

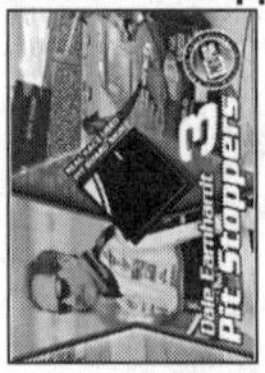

Randomly inserted in packs at the rate of one in 240, this 13-card set features swatches of race-used pit-stop signs. Each card was serial numbered of 200-sets produced.

COMPLETE SET (13)	500.00	800.00
PS1 Ward Burton	12.50	30.00
PS2 Rusty Wallace	15.00	40.00
PS3 Dale Earnhardt	40.00	100.00
PS4 Bobby Labonte	12.50	30.00
PS5 Terry Labonte	12.50	30.00
PS6 Mark Martin	20.00	50.00
PS7 Tony Stewart	25.00	60.00
PS8 Elliott Sadler	12.50	30.00
PS9 Dave Blaney	12.50	30.00
PS10 Jeremy Mayfield	10.00	25.00
PS11 Matt Kenseth	20.00	50.00
PS12 Jeff Burton	10.00	25.00
PS13 Dale Earnhardt Jr.	30.00	80.00

2000 Press Pass Trackside Runnin N' Gunnin

Randomly inserted in packs at the rate of one in six, this 9-card set features top NASCAR racers on a holofoil card. Each card features the driver on one half and his car on the other.

COMPLETE SET (9)	10.00	25.00
RG1 Tony Stewart	2.00	5.00
RG2 Dale Earnhardt Jr.	2.50	6.00
RG3 Rusty Wallace	1.25	3.00
RG4 Mark Martin	1.50	4.00
RG5 Terry Labonte	.75	2.00
RG6 Jeff Gordon	2.00	5.00
RG7 Jeff Burton	.50	1.25
RG8 Dale Jarrett	1.25	3.00
RG9 Bobby Labonte	1.25	3.00

2000 Press Pass Trackside Too Tough To Tame

Randomly inserted in packs at the rate of one in 24, this 9-card set showcases nine top NASCAR drivers. Cards are all holofoil and picture both the driver and his car.

COMPLETE SET (9)	25.00	60.
TT1 Dale Jarrett	3.00	8.
TT2 Mark Martin	4.00	10.
TT3 Bobby Labonte	3.00	8.
TT4 Tony Stewart	5.00	12.
TT5 Jeff Gordon	5.00	12.
TT6 Dale Earnhardt	8.00	20.
TT7 Rusty Wallace	3.00	8.
TT8 Terry Labonte	2.00	5.
TT9 Dale Earnhardt Jr.	6.00	15.

2001 Press Pass Trackside

This is the second year that Press Pass has issue set using the Trackside brand name. The base consists of 63 cards and there are also t subsets:Teammates (cards numbered 64-81) a Charity Spotlight (cards numbered 82-89).

COMPLETE SET (90)	12.50	30.
WAX BOX HOBBY	30.00	60.
WAX BOX RETAIL	30.00	60.
1 Dale Earnhardt Jr.	1.00	2.
2 Jeff Gordon	.75	2.
3 Dale Earnhardt	1.25	3.
4 Bobby Hamilton	.08	
5 Kevin Harvick CRC	.60	1.
6 Terry Labonte	.30	
7 Jerry Nadeau	.20	
8 Joe Nemechek	.08	
9 Steve Park	.20	
10 Mike Skinner	.08	
11 Michael Waltrip	.20	
12 Ron Hornaday	.08	
13 Bobby Labonte	.50	1.
14 Ken Schrader	.08	
15 Tony Stewart	.75	2.
16 Todd Bodine	.08	
17 Jeff Burton	.20	
18 Kurt Busch CRC	.30	
19 Ricky Craven	.08	
20 Andy Houston	.08	
21 Dale Jarrett	.50	1.
22 Matt Kenseth	.60	1.
23 Mark Martin	.60	1.
24 Jeremy Mayfield	.08	
25 Robert Pressley	.08	
26 Ricky Rudd	.30	
27 Elliott Sadler	.20	
28 Jimmy Spencer	.08	
29 Rusty Wallace	.60	1.
30 John Andretti	.08	
31 Casey Atwood	.08	
32 Dave Blaney	.08	
33 Ward Burton	.20	
34 Stacy Compton	.08	
35 Buckshot Jones	.08	
36 Jason Leffler	.08	
37 Sterling Marlin	.30	
38 Kyle Petty	.20	
39 Steve Park's Car	.20	
40 Rusty Wallace's Car	.20	
41 Terry Labonte's Car	.20	
42 Mark Martin's Car	.20	
43 Dale Earnhardt Jr.'s Car	.60	1.
44 Michael Waltrip's Car	.08	
45 Matt Kenseth's Car	.20	
46 Bobby Labonte's Car	.20	
47 Tony Stewart's Car	.30	
48 Jeff Gordon's Car	.30	
49 Dale Jarrett's Car	.20	
50 Jeff Burton's Car	.08	
51 Jeff Green	.08	
52 Elton Sawyer	.08	
53 Kevin Harvick	.60	1.
54 Hank Parker Jr.	.20	
55 Mark Green	.08	
56 Chad Little	.08	
57 Greg Biffle	.20	
58 David Green	.08	
59 Jason Keller	.08	
60 Randy LaJoie	.08	
61 Mike McLaughlin	.08	
62 Jeff Purvis	.08	
63 Tim Fedewa	.08	
64 Kevin Harvick TM	.60	1.
65 Mike Skinner TM	.08	
66 Bobby Labonte TM	.50	1.
67 Tony Stewart TM	.75	2.
68 Ricky Rudd TM	.30	
69 Dale Jarrett TM	.50	1.
70 Rusty Wallace TM	.60	1.
71 Jeremy Mayfield TM	.08	
72 Joe Nemechek TM	.08	
73 Bobby Hamilton TM	.08	
74 Sterling Marlin TM	.30	
75 Jason Leffler TM	.08	
76 Kyle Petty TM	.20	
77 Buckshot Jones TM	.08	
78 Andy Houston TM	.08	
79 Ricky Craven TM	.08	
80 Terry Labonte TM	.30	
81 Jerry Nadeau TM	.20	
82 Kyle Petty CS	.20	
83 Ricky Craven CS	.08	

Ward Burton CS .20 .50
Jeff Gordon CS .75 2.00
Dale Jarrett CS .50 1.25
Joe Nemechek CS .08 .25
Tony Stewart CS .75 2.00
Rusty Wallace CS .60 1.50
Checklist .02 .10

2001 Press Pass Trackside Die Cuts

erted at one per pack, this 90-card set is a nplete die-cut parallel of the 2001 Press Pass ackside base set.

MPLETE SET (90) 30.00 80.00
IE CUTS: .8X TO 2X BASE CARDS

2001 Press Pass Trackside Golden

erted at one in 120 packs, this 90-card set is a nplete gold-foil die-cut parallel of the 2001 Press ss Trackside base set.

MPLETE SET (90) 750.00 1500.00
OLDEN: 10X TO 25X BASE CARDS

2001 Press Pass Trackside Dialed In

ndomly inserted into packs at one in 8, this 12-d insert features illuminating dial settings anced by a special UV coating. Card backs carry)" prefix.

MPLETE SET (12) 12.50 30.00
Steve Park .75 2.00
Rusty Wallace 2.50 6.00
Dale Earnhardt 5.00 12.00
Jeff Gordon 3.00 8.00
Terry Labonte 1.25 3.00
Mark Martin 2.50 6.00
Bobby Labonte 2.00 5.00
Dale Earnhardt Jr. 4.00 10.00
Sterling Marlin 1.25 3.00
0 Jeff Burton .75 2.00
1 Dale Jarrett 2.00 5.00
2 Michael Waltrip .75 2.00

2001 Press Pass rackside Mirror Image

ndomly inserted into packs at one in 18, this 9-d insert features driver photos with special cked-ice etching. Card backs carry a "MI" prefix.

MPLETE SET (9) 15.00 40.00
1 Dale Jarrett 2.00 5.00
2 Rusty Wallace 2.50 6.00
3 Dale Earnhardt 5.00 12.00
4 Tony Stewart 3.00 8.00
5 Jeff Gordon 3.00 8.00
6 Mark Martin 2.50 6.00
7 Ricky Rudd 1.25 3.00
8 Dale Earnhardt Jr. 4.00 10.00
9 Terry Labonte 1.25 3.00

2001 Press Pass rackside Pit Stoppers Cars

ndomly inserted into retail packs at a rate of one in), this 12-card insert features pieces of actual pit p signs. Card backs carry a "PSC" prefix. This sion pictures the driver's car.

C1 Dale Earnhardt Jr.'s Car/250 30.00 80.00
C2 Tony Stewart's Car/250 15.00 40.00
C3 Dale Earnhardt's Car
C4 Ward Burton's Car/305 8.00 20.00
C5 Rusty Wallace's Car 30.00 80.00
PSC6 Terry Labonte's Car 15.00 40.00
PSC7 Bobby Labonte's Car 15.00 40.00
PSC8 Dave Blaney's Car 8.00 20.00
PSC9 Matt Kenseth's Car/250 20.00 50.00
PSC10 Steve Park's Car/100 8.00 20.00
PSC11 Michael Waltrip's Car/200 10.00 25.00
PSC12 Joe Nemechek's Car 8.00 20.00

2001 Press Pass Trackside Pit Stoppers Drivers

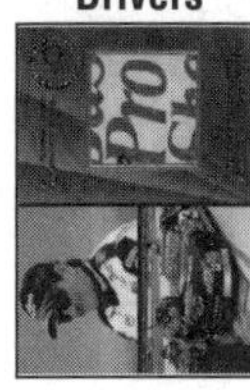

Randomly inserted into hobby packs at a rate of one in 480, this 12-card insert features pieces of actual pit stop signs. Card backs carry a "PSD" prefix. This version pictures the driver.

PSD1 Dale Earnhardt Jr./100 50.00 120.00
PSD2 Tony Stewart/100 25.00 60.00
PSD3 Dale Earnhardt/10
PSD4 Ward Burton 12.50 30.00
PSD5 Rusty Wallace/30 60.00 120.00
PSD6 Terry Labonte 25.00 60.00
PSD7 Bobby Labonte 25.00 60.00
PSD8 Dave Blaney 12.50 30.00
PSD9 Matt Kenseth/100 30.00 80.00
PSD10 Steve Park/100 12.50 30.00
PSD11 Michael Waltrip/75 20.00 40.00
PSD12 Joe Nemechek 12.50 30.00

2001 Press Pass Trackside Runnin N' Gunnin

Randomly inserted into packs at one in 6, this 9-card insert features drivers that do plenty of "running and gunning" on the track. Card backs carry a "RG" prefix.

COMPLETE SET (9) 12.50 30.00
RG1 Ricky Rudd .75 2.00
RG2 Dale Earnhardt Jr. 2.50 6.00
RG3 Rusty Wallace 1.50 4.00
RG4 Mark Martin 1.50 4.00
RG5 Terry Labonte .75 2.00
RG6 Jeff Gordon 2.00 5.00
RG7 Tony Stewart 2.00 5.00
RG8 Kevin Harvick 1.50 4.00
RG9 Bobby Labonte 1.25 3.00

2002 Press Pass Trackside

This 90-card set was released in June, 2002. This set was issued in six card packs which came 24 packs to a box and 20 boxes to a case. The pack SRP was $2.99.

COMPLETE SET (90) 12.50 30.00
WAX BOX HOBBY 30.00 60.00
1 Dale Earnhardt Jr. 1.25 3.00
2 Jeff Gordon 1.00 2.50
3 Robby Gordon .10 .30
4 Jeff Green .10 .30
5 Bobby Hamilton .10 .30
6 Kevin Harvick .75 2.00
7 Jimmie Johnson CRC .75 2.00
8 Terry Labonte .40 1.00
9 Jerry Nadeau .25 .60
10 Steve Park .25 .60
11 Mike Skinner .10 .30
12 Michael Waltrip .25 .60
13 Bobby Labonte .60 1.50
14 Ken Schrader .10 .30
15 Tony Stewart .75 2.00
16 Dave Blaney .10 .30
17 Brett Bodine .10 .30
18 Jeff Burton .25 .60
19 Kurt Busch .40 1.00
20 Ricky Craven .10 .30
21 Dale Jarrett .60 1.50
22 Matt Kenseth .75 2.00
23 Mark Martin .75 2.00
24 Ryan Newman CRC .75 2.00
25 Ricky Rudd .40 1.00
26 Elliott Sadler .25 .60
27 Rusty Wallace .60 1.50
28 John Andretti .10 .30
29 Shawna Robinson .25 .60
30 Ward Burton .25 .60
31 Buckshot Jones .10 .30
32 Sterling Marlin .40 1.00
33 Jeremy Mayfield .10 .30
34 Kyle Petty .25 .60
35 Jimmy Spencer .10 .30
36 Hut Stricklin .10 .30
37 Ricky Hendrick NBS .50 1.25
38 Randy LaJoie NBS .10 .30
39 Mike McLaughlin NBS .10 .30
40 Johnny Sauter NBS RC .25 .60
41 Hank Parker Jr. NBS .10 .30
42 Scott Riggs NBS RC .75 2.00
43 Kerry Earnhardt NBS .25 .60
44 Jack Sprague NBS .10 .30
45 Scott Wimmer NBS RC .25 .60
46 Matt Crafton CTS .10 .30
47 Coy Gibbs CTS RC .25 .60
48 Travis Kvapil CTS RC .75 2.00
49 Ted Musgrave CTS .10 .30
50 Robert Pressley CTS .10 .30
51 Jon Wood CTS RC .25 .60
52 Dale Earnhardt Jr. RD 1.25 3.00
53 Jeff Gordon RD 1.00 2.50
54 Kevin Harvick RD .75 2.00
55 Dale Jarrett RD .60 1.50
56 Jimmie Johnson RD .75 2.00
57 Ryan Newman RD .75 2.00
58 Tony Stewart RD .75 2.00
59 Rusty Wallace RD .60 1.50
60 Ricky Rudd RD .40 1.00
61 Mark Martin RD .75 2.00
62 Bobby Labonte RD .60 1.50
63 Terry Labonte RD .40 1.00
64 Rusty Wallace's Car .25 .60
65 Terry Labonte's Car .10 .30
66 Mark Martin's Car .40 1.00
67 Dale Earnhardt Jr.'s Car .50 1.25
68 Michael Waltrip's Car .10 .30
69 Matt Kenseth's Car .40 1.00
70 Bobby Labonte's Car .25 .60
71 Tony Stewart's Car .40 1.00
72 Jeff Gordon's Car .40 1.00
73 Dale Earnhardt Jr. TM 1.25 3.00
74 Michael Waltrip TM .25 .60
75 Steve Park TM .25 .60
76 Kurt Busch TM .40 1.00
77 Matt Kenseth TM .75 2.00
78 Mark Martin TM .75 2.00
79 Jeff Burton TM .25 .60
80 Tony Stewart TM .75 2.00
81 Bobby Labonte TM .60 1.50
82 Jeff Gordon TM 1.00 2.50
83 Jimmie Johnson TM .75 2.00
84 Terry Labonte TM .40 1.00
85 Jerry Nadeau TM .25 .60
86 Dale Jarrett TM .60 1.50
87 Ricky Rudd TM .40 1.00
88 Rusty Wallace TM .60 1.50
89 Ryan Newman TM .75 2.00
90 Dale Earnhardt Jr. CL .75 2.00
Kerry Earnhardt

2002 Press Pass Trackside Golden

Randomly inserted into hobby packs, this is a partial parallel to the Trackside set. These cards were issued to a stated print run of 50 serial numbered sets. Only the first 45 cards from the set are included in this parallel version.

*GOLDEN: 12X TO 30X BASIC CARDS

2002 Press Pass Trackside Samples

These cards were issued to preview what the Press Pass Trackside set would look like. The cards were inserted one per Beckett Racing Collector magazine.

*SAMPLES: 2.5X TO 6X BASE CARDS

2002 Press Pass Trackside Dialed In

Issued at a stated rate of one in eight, these 12 cards feature some on NASCAR's best drivers on cards which are illuminated by mirror-foil and enhanced etching.

COMPLETE SET (12) 12.50 30.00
DI1 Jeff Burton .60 1.50
DI2 Dale Earnhardt, Jr. 3.00 8.00
DI3 Jeff Gordon 2.50 6.00
DI4 Kevin Harvick 2.00 5.00
DI5 Dale Jarrett 1.50 4.00
DI6 Jimmie Johnson 2.00 5.00
DI7 Bobby Labonte 1.50 4.00
DI8 Terry Labonte 1.00 2.50
DI9 Sterling Marlin 1.00 2.50
DI10 Mark Martin 2.00 5.00
DI11 Tony Stewart 2.00 5.00
DI12 Rusty Wallace 1.50 4.00

2002 Press Pass Trackside Generation Now

Inserted at a stated rate of one in 36, this eight card set features leading drivers on cards which have been etched, printed on foil and also gold foil stamped.

COMPLETE SET (8) 25.00 50.00
GN1 Kevin Harvick 4.00 10.00
GN2 Tony Stewart 4.00 10.00
GN3 Dale Earnhardt Jr. 6.00 15.00
GN4 Jimmie Johnson 4.00 10.00
GN5 Ryan Newman 4.00 10.00
GN6 Matt Kenseth 4.00 10.00
GN7 Kurt Busch 2.00 5.00
GN8 Elliott Sadler 1.25 3.00

2002 Press Pass Trackside License to Drive

Inserted at a stated rate of one per pack, these 36 cards feature the development of leading NASCAR drivers.

COMPLETE SET (36) 10.00 25.00
*DIE CUTS: .6X TO 1.5X BASIC INSERTS
1 John Andretti .20 .50
2 Dave Blaney .20 .50
3 Brett Bodine .20 .50
4 Jeff Burton .40 1.00
5 Ward Burton .40 1.00
6 Kurt Busch .60 1.50
7 Ricky Craven .20 .50
8 Dale Earnhardt Jr. 2.00 5.00
9 Jeff Gordon 1.50 4.00
10 Robby Gordon .20 .50
11 Jeff Green .20 .50
12 Bobby Hamilton .20 .50
13 Kevin Harvick 1.25 3.00
14 Dale Jarrett 1.00 2.50
15 Jimmie Johnson 1.25 3.00
16 Buckshot Jones .20 .50
17 Matt Kenseth 1.25 3.00
18 Bobby Labonte 1.00 2.50
19 Terry Labonte .60 1.50
20 Sterling Marlin .60 1.50
21 Mark Martin 1.25 3.00
22 Jeremy Mayfield .20 .50
23 Jerry Nadeau .40 1.00
24 Ryan Newman 1.25 3.00
25 Steve Park .40 1.00
26 Kyle Petty .40 1.00
27 Ricky Rudd .60 1.50
28 Elliott Sadler .40 1.00
29 Ken Schrader .20 .50
30 Mike Skinner .20 .50
31 Jimmy Spencer .20 .50
32 Tony Stewart 1.25 3.00
33 Hut Stricklin .20 .50
34 Rusty Wallace 1.00 2.50
35 Michael Waltrip .40 1.00
36 Checklist .08 .25

2002 Press Pass Trackside Mirror Image

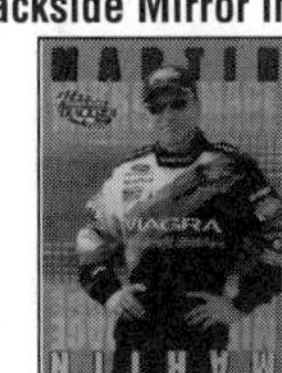

Inserted at a stated rate of one in 18, these nine cards feature questions about who might mirror the success of each driver.

COMPLETE SET (9) 20.00 50.00
MI1 Dale Earnhardt Jr. 4.00 10.00
MI2 Jeff Gordon 3.00 8.00
MI3 Kevin Harvick 2.50 6.00
MI4 Dale Jarrett 2.00 5.00
MI5 Bobby Labonte 2.00 5.00
MI6 Terry Labonte 1.25 3.00
MI7 Mark Martin 2.50 6.00
MI8 Tony Stewart 2.50 6.00
MI9 Rusty Wallace 2.00 5.00

2002 Press Pass Trackside Pit Stoppers Cars

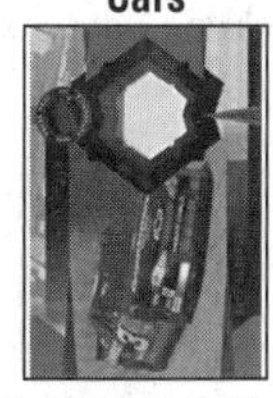

Inserted at a stated rate of one in 240 retail packs, these 15 cards feature swatches of race-used pit signs set against a photo of the featured driver's car. Each card was issued to a different print run total as noted below.

PSC1 Bobby Labonte's Car/350 10.00 25.00
PSC2 Tony Stewart's Car/350 15.00 40.00
PSC3 Steve Park's Car/300 8.00 20.00
PSC4 Dale Earnhardt Jr.'s Car/50 100.00 200.00
PSC5 Kevin Harvick's Car/200 15.00 40.00
PSC6 Ryan Newman's Car/350 15.00 40.00
PSC7 Terry Labonte's Car/350 10.00 25.00
PSC8 Rusty Wallace's Car/350 12.50 30.00
PSC9 Ricky Craven's Car/200 8.00 20.00
PSC10 Ken Schrader's Car/200 8.00 20.00
PSC11 Sterling Marlin's Car/250 8.00 20.00
PSC12 Jimmy Spencer's Car/350 8.00 20.00
PSC13 Matt Kenseth's Car/60 50.00 100.00
PSC14 Ward Burton's Car/125 8.00 20.00
PSC15 Dale Earnhardt's Car/20

2002 Press Pass Trackside Pit Stoppers Drivers

Inserted at a stated rate of one in 480 hobby packs, these 15 cards feature swatches of race-used pit signs set against a photo of the featured driver. Each card was issued to a different print run as noted below.

PSD1 Bobby Labonte/150 15.00 40.00
PSD2 Tony Stewart/150 25.00 60.00
PSD3 Steve Park/150 12.50 30.00
PSD4 Dale Earnhardt Jr./50 100.00 200.00
PSD5 Kevin Harvick/100 30.00 60.00
PSD6 Ryan Newman/175 25.00 60.00
PSD7 Terry Labonte/175 15.00 40.00
PSD8 Rusty Wallace/175 20.00 50.00
PSD9 Ricky Craven/100 12.50 30.00
PSD10 Ken Schrader/150 12.50 30.00
PSD11 Sterling Marlin/150 12.50 30.00
PSD12 Jimmy Spencer/175 12.50 30.00
PSD13 Matt Kenseth/60 40.00 100.00
PSD14 Ward Burton/100 12.50 30.00
PSD15 Dale Earnhardt/20

2002 Press Pass Trackside Runnin N' Gunnin

Issued at a stated rate of one in six, these nine cards feature drivers who never let you see them sweat.

COMPLETE SET (9) 10.00 25.00
RG1 Dale Earnhardt Jr. 2.50 6.00
RG2 Jeff Gordon 2.00 5.00
RG3 Kevin Harvick 1.50 4.00
RG4 Bobby Labonte 1.25 3.00
RG5 Matt Kenseth 1.50 4.00
RG6 Dale Jarrett 1.25 3.00
RG7 Ricky Rudd .75 2.00
RG8 Tony Stewart 1.50 4.00
RG9 Rusty Wallace 1.25 3.00

2003 Press Pass Trackside

This 90-card set was released in June, 2003. This set was issued in six card packs which came 24 packs to a box. The pack SRP was $2.99. There was a King for a Day entry card, inserted in packs at a rate of 1 per box, which was for a chance to spend a day at a Richard Petty Driving School.

COMPLETE SET (81) 10.00 25.00
WAX BOX HOBBY (28) 40.00 75.00
1 Greg Biffle CRC .25 .60
2 Jeff Burton .25 .60
3 Kurt Busch .40 1.00
4 Dale Jarrett .60 1.50
5 Matt Kenseth .75 2.00
6 Mark Martin .75 2.00
7 Ricky Rudd .40 1.00
8 Elliott Sadler .25 .60
9 Dave Blaney .10 .30
10 John Andretti .10 .30
11 Ward Burton .25 .60
12 Sterling Marlin .40 1.00
13 Jeremy Mayfield .10 .30
14 Jamie McMurray CRC .60 1.50
15 Casey Mears CRC .25 .60
16 Ryan Newman .75 2.00
17 Kenny Wallace .10 .30
18 Rusty Wallace .60 1.50
19 Dale Earnhardt Jr. 1.25 3.00
20 Jeff Gordon 1.00 2.50
21 Robby Gordon .10 .30
22 Jeff Green .10 .30
23 Kevin Harvick .75 2.00
24 Jimmie Johnson .75 2.00
25 Bobby Labonte .60 1.50
26 Terry Labonte .40 1.00
27 Joe Nemechek .10 .30
28 Steve Park .25 .60
29 Tony Stewart .75 2.00
30 Michael Waltrip .25 .60
31 Ricky Craven .10 .30
32 Jerry Nadeau .25 .60
33 Mike Skinner .10 .30
34 Stanton Barrett BGN RC .10 .30
35 Mike Bliss BGN .10 .30
36 Stacy Compton BGN .10 .30
37 Kerry Earnhardt BGN .25 .60
38 Coy Gibbs BGN .25 .60
39 Damon Lusk BGN RC .10 .30
40 Chad Blount BGN RC .40 1.00
41 Shane Hmiel BGN RC 1.25 3.00
42 Jason Keller BGN .10 .30
43 Randy LaJoie BGN .10 .30
44 Scott Riggs BGN .25 .60
45 Brian Vickers BGN .50 1.25
46 Matt Crafton CTS .10 .30
47 Rick Crawford CTS RC .10 .30
48 Carl Edwards CTS RC 2.50 6.00
49 Andy Houston CTS .10 .30
50 Travis Kvapil CTS .25 .60
51 Jason Leffler CTS .10 .30
52 Robert Pressley CTS .10 .30
53 Dennis Setzer CTS .10 .30
54 Jon Wood CTS .25 .60
55 Rusty Wallace FA .60 1.50
Kenny Wallace FA
56 Brett Bodine FA .10 .30
Todd Bodine FA
57 Jeff Burton FA .25 .60
Ward Burton FA
58 Sterling Marlin FA .40 1.00
Steadman Marlin FA
59 Dale Jarrett FA .60 1.50
Ned Jarrett FA
60 Kyle Petty FA .75 2.00
Richard Petty FA
61 Rusty Wallace in Pits .25 .60
62 Dale Earnhardt Jr. in Pits .50 1.25
63 Ryan Newman in Pits .30 .75
64 Kerry Earnhardt in Pits .10 .30
65 Michael Waltrip in Pits .10 .30
66 Greg Biffle in Pits .10 .30
67 Bobby Labonte in Pits .25 .60
68 Kevin Harvick in Pits .30 .75
69 Robby Gordon in Pits .10 .30
70 Elliott Sadler in Pits .10 .30
71 Dale Jarrett in Pits .25 .60
72 Jeff Burton in Pits .10 .30
73 Kenny Wallace TM .25 .60
Ward Burton TM
74 Tony Stewart TM .75 2.00
Bobby Labonte TM
75 Elliott Sadler TM .60 1.50
Dale Jarrett TM
76 Rusty Wallace TM .75 2.00
Ryan Newman TM
77 John Andretti TM .25 .60
Kyle Petty TM
78 Mark Martin TM .75 2.00
Jeff Burton TM
Greg Biffle TM
Matt Kenseth TM
Kurt Busch TM
79 Jimmie Johnson TM 1.00 2.50
Jeff Gordon TM
80 Casey Mears TM .60 1.50
Jamie McMurray TM
Sterling Marlin TM
81 Rusty Wallace CL .60 1.50
NNO King for a Day Yellow 1.00 2.50

2003 Press Pass Trackside Golden

This partial parallel featurd gold highlights on the cards and each was serial numbered to 50.

*GOLDEN: 10X TO 25X BASE

2003 Press Pass Trackside Gold Holofoil

This parallel set of 81 cards featured gold foil highlights and was inserted in packs at a rate of one per pack.

COMPLETE SET (81)	15.00	40.00

*SINGLES: .6X TO 1.5X BASE CARD HI

2003 Press Pass Trackside Samples

This 81-card set was a parallel of the base set with the exception of the word "SAMPLE" printed on the back of each card. These cards were found in Beckett Racing Collector August 2003, Issue #108. There was one card per magazine.

*SAMPLES: 2.5X TO 6X BASIC

2003 Press Pass Trackside Dialed In

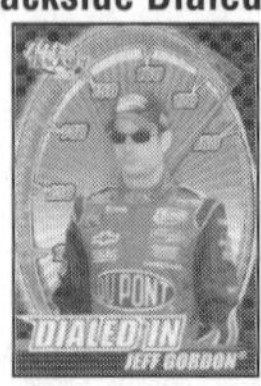

Issued at a stated rate of one in eight, these 12 cards feature some on NASCAR's best drivers on cards which are illuminated by mirror-foil and enhanced etching. These cards also featured a "DI" prefix on the card numbers.

COMPLETE SET (12)	12.50	30.00
DI1 Kerry Earnhardt	.50	1.25
DI2 Dale Earnhardt Jr.	2.50	6.00
DI3 Jeff Gordon	2.00	5.00
DI4 Dale Jarrett	1.25	3.00
DI5 Jimmie Johnson	1.50	4.00
DI6 Bobby Labonte	1.25	3.00
DI7 Terry Labonte	.75	2.00
DI8 Ricky Rudd	.75	2.00
DI9 Ryan Newman	1.50	4.00
DI10 Tony Stewart	1.50	4.00
DI11 Rusty Wallace	1.25	3.00
DI12 Michael Waltrip	.50	1.25

2003 Press Pass Trackside Hat Giveaway

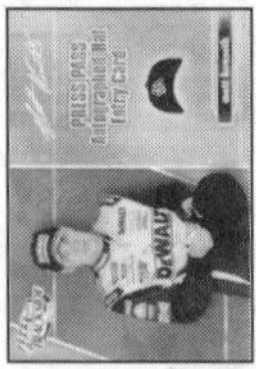

Randomly inserted in packs at a rate of one per box. This 30-card set of entry cards were good for a chance to win an autographed hat of the corresponding driver. The sweepstakes ended on January 31, 2004.

PPH1 John Andretti	.75	2.00
PPH2 Greg Biffle	1.50	4.00
PPH3 Brett Bodine	.75	2.00
PPH4 Jeff Burton	1.50	4.00
PPH5 Kurt Busch	2.50	6.00
PPH6 Ricky Craven	.75	2.00
PPH7 Jeff Gordon	6.00	15.00
PPH8 Robby Gordon	.75	2.00
PPH9 Jeff Green	.75	2.00
PPH10 Kevin Harvick	5.00	12.00
PPH11 Dale Jarrett	4.00	10.00
PPH12 Jimmie Johnson	5.00	12.00
PPH13 Matt Kenseth	5.00	12.00
PPH14 Bobby Labonte	4.00	10.00
PPH15 Sterling Marlin	2.50	6.00
PPH16 Mark Martin	5.00	12.00
PPH17 Jeremy Mayfield	.75	2.00
PPH18 Jamie McMurray	4.00	10.00
PPH19 Casey Mears	1.50	4.00
PPH20 Jerry Nadeau	1.50	4.00
PPH21 Ryan Newman	5.00	12.00
PPH22 Steve Park	1.50	4.00
PPH23 Kyle Petty	1.50	4.00
PPH24 Ricky Rudd	2.50	6.00
PPH25 Elliott Sadler	1.50	4.00
PPH26 Mike Skinner	.75	2.00
PPH27 Tony Stewart	5.00	12.00
PPH28 Kenny Wallace	.75	2.00
PPH29 Rusty Wallace	4.00	10.00
PPH30 Michael Waltrip	1.50	4.00

2003 Press Pass Trackside Hot Pursuit

Inserted at a stated rate of one in 28 packs, these 8 cards feature the some of NASCAR's leading drivers. Each card carried a prefix of "HP" as part of the card number.

COMPLETE SET (8)	15.00	30.00
STATED ODDS 1:28		
HP1 Kerry Earnhardt	.75	2.00
HP2 Dale Earnhardt Jr.	4.00	10.00
HP3 Jimmie Johnson	2.50	6.00
HP4 Kevin Harvick	2.50	6.00
HP5 Ryan Newman	2.50	6.00
HP6 Tony Stewart	2.50	6.00
HP7 Michael Waltrip	.75	2.00
HP8 Elliott Sadler	.75	2.00

2003 Press Pass Trackside License to Drive

Inserted at a stated rate of one per pack, these 27 cards feature the development of leading NASCAR drivers.

COMPLETE SET (27)	10.00	20.00
STATED ODDS 1 PER PACK		
LD1 Greg Biffle	.30	.75
LD2 Todd Bodine	.15	.40
LD3 Ward Burton	.30	.75
LD4 Dale Earnhardt Jr.	1.50	4.00
LD5 Jeff Gordon	1.25	3.00
LD6 Brett Bodine	.15	.40
LD7 Ricky Craven	.15	.40
LD8 Bobby Labonte	.75	2.00
LD9 Robby Gordon	.15	.40
LD10 Jeff Burton	.30	.75
LD11 Elliott Sadler	.30	.75
LD12 Jerry Nadeau	.30	.75
LD13 Ryan Newman	1.00	2.50
LD14 Steve Park	.30	.75
LD15 Ricky Rudd	.50	1.25
LD16 Ken Schrader	.15	.40
LD17 Jimmy Spencer	.15	.40
LD18 Tony Stewart	1.00	2.50
LD19 Rusty Wallace	.75	2.00
LD20 Michael Waltrip	.30	.75
LD21 Mike Skinner	.15	.40
LD22 Kyle Petty	.30	.75
LD23 Kevin Grubb	.15	.40
LD24 Steadman Marlin	.15	.40
LD25 Damon Lusk	.15	.40
LD26 Scott Wimmer	.30	.75
LD27 Jimmy Vasser Checklist	.15	.40

2003 Press Pass Trackside Mirror Image

Inserted at a stated rate of one in 18, these nine cards feature questions about who might mirror the success of each driver.

COMPLETE SET (9)	12.50	30.00
MI1 Kerry Earnhardt	.60	1.50
MI2 Dale Earnhardt Jr.	3.00	8.00
MI3 Jeff Gordon	2.50	6.00
MI4 Mark Martin	2.00	5.00
MI5 Bobby Labonte	1.50	4.00
MI6 Terry Labonte	1.00	2.50
MI7 Tony Stewart	2.00	5.00
MI8 Rusty Wallace	1.50	4.00
MI9 Michael Waltrip	.60	1.50

2003 Press Pass Trackside Pit Stoppers Cars

Randomly inserted in retail packs, these 18 cards feature swatches of race-used pit signs set against a photo of the featured driver's car. Each card was issued to a a stated print run of 175 with the exceptions of Dale Earnhardt of 3 and Matt Kenseth of 17. The Earnhardt and Kenseth are not priced due to scarcity.

PST1 Jeff Gordon	25.00	60.00
PST2 Terry Labonte	12.50	30.00
PST3 Kevin Harvick	12.50	30.00
PST4 Jimmie Johnson	15.00	40.00
PST5 Rusty Wallace	12.50	30.00
PST6 Bobby Labonte	15.00	40.00
PST7 Tony Stewart	15.00	40.00
PST8 Ryan Newman	15.00	40.00
PST9 Dale Earnhardt/3		
PST10 Sterling Marlin	10.00	25.00
PST11 Ward Burton	10.00	25.00
PST12 Michael Waltrip	10.00	25.00
PST13 Robby Gordon	10.00	25.00
PST14 Jeff Green	8.00	20.00
PST15 Jamie McMurray	10.00	25.00
PST16 Matt Kenseth/10		
PST17 Steve Park	8.00	20.00
PST18 Dale Earnhardt Jr.	25.00	60.00

2003 Press Pass Trackside Pit Stoppers Cars Autographs

Randomly inserted in retail packs, these 8 cards feature swatches of race-used pit signs set against a photo of the featured driver's car along with a signature of the corresponding driver. The cards were limited and hand numbered to the driver's door number. Some of the cards are not priced due to scarcity.

SOME CARDS NOT PRICED DUE TO SCARCITY		
BL Bobby Labonte's Car/18	75.00	150.00
JJ Jimmie Johnson's Car/48	75.00	150.00
KH Kevin Harvick's Car/29	100.00	200.00
MK Matt Kenseth's Car/17		
MM Mark Martin's Car/6		
RN Ryan Newman's Car/12		
RW Rusty Wallace's Car/2		
TL Terry Labonte's Car/5		

2003 Press Pass Trackside Pit Stoppers Drivers

Randomly inserted in hobby packs at a rate of one in 180, these 18 cards feature swatches of race-used pit signs set against a photo of the featured driver. Each card was issued to a a stated print run of 100 with the exceptions of Dale Earnhardt of 3 and Matt Kenseth of 17. The Earnhardt and Kenseth are not priced due to scarcity.

PSD1 Jeff Gordon	40.00	80.00
PSD2 Terry Labonte	15.00	40.00
PSD3 Kevin Harvick	15.00	40.00
PSD4 Jimmie Johnson	20.00	50.00
PSD5 Rusty Wallace	15.00	40.00
PSD6 Bobby Labonte	20.00	50.00
PSD7 Tony Stewart	20.00	50.00
PSD8 Ryan Newman	20.00	50.00
PSD9 Dale Earnhardt/3		
PSD10 Sterling Marlin	12.50	30.00
PSD11 Ward Burton	12.50	30.00
PSD12 Michael Waltrip	12.50	30.00
PSD13 Robby Gordon	12.50	30.00
PSD14 Jeff Green	10.00	25.00
PSD15 Jamie McMurray	12.50	30.00
PSD16 Matt Kenseth/10		
PSD17 Steve Park	12.50	25.00
PSD18 Dale Earnhardt Jr.	40.00	80.00

2003 Press Pass Trackside Pit Stoppers Drivers Autographs

Randomly inserted in hobby packs, these 8 cards feature swatches of race-used pit signs set against a photo of the featured driver along with a his signature. The cards were limited and hand numbered to the driver's door number. Some of the cards are not priced due to scarcity.

SOME CARDS NOT PRICED DUE TO SCARCITY		
PSD-BL Bobby Labonte/18	75.00	150.00
PSD-JJ Jimmie Johnson/48	75.00	150.00
PSD-KH Kevin Harvick/29	100.00	200.00
PSD-MK Matt Kenseth/17		
PSD-MM Mark Martin/6		
PSD-RN Ryan Newman/12		
PSD-RW Rusty Wallace/2		
PSD-TL Terry Labonte/5		

2003 Press Pass Trackside Runnin n' Gunnin

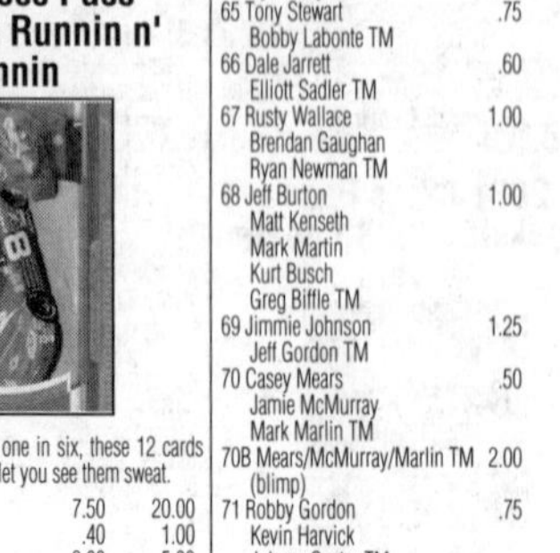

Issued at a stated rate of one in six, these 12 cards feature drivers who never let you see them sweat.

COMPLETE SET (12)	7.50	20.00
RG1 Kerry Earnhardt	.40	1.00
RG2 Dale Earnhardt, Jr.	2.00	5.00
RG3 Jeff Gordon	1.50	4.00
RG4 Dale Jarrett	1.00	2.50
RG5 Bobby Labonte	1.00	2.50
RG6 Jimmie Johnson	1.25	3.00
RG7 Ricky Rudd	.60	1.50
RG8 Rusty Wallace	1.00	2.50
RG9 Michael Waltrip	.40	1.00
RG10 Ryan Newman	1.25	3.00
RG11 Kevin Harvick	1.25	3.00
RG12 Matt Kenseth	1.25	3.00

2004 Press Pass Trackside

This 120-card set was released in June, 2004. This set was issued in six card packs which came 28 packs to a box. The pack SRP was $2.99. The set had 6 short-printed background variations as noted in the checklist below.

COMPLETE SET (120)	15.00	40.00
WAX BOX HOBBY (28)	40.00	70.00
WAX BOX RETAIL (24)	40.00	70.00
1 Brendan Gaughan CRC	.30	.75
1B Brendan Gaughan (no print on wall)	1.25	3.00
2 Kasey Kahne CRC	1.50	4.00
3 Sterling Marlin	.50	1.25
4 Jamie McMurray	.50	1.25
5 Casey Mears	.30	.75
6 Ryan Newman	1.00	2.50
7 Rusty Wallace	.60	1.50
8 Scott Wimmer CRC	.30	.75
9 Kyle Petty	.30	.75
10 Jeremy Mayfield	.15	.40
11 Jeff Green	.15	.40
12 Greg Biffle	.30	.75
13 Kurt Busch	.50	1.25
14 Jeff Burton	.30	.75
15 Dale Jarrett	.60	1.50
16 Matt Kenseth	1.00	2.50
17 Mark Martin	.75	2.00
18 Elliott Sadler	.30	.75
19 Dale Earnhardt Jr.	1.25	3.00
20 Jeff Gordon	1.25	3.00
20B Jeff Gordon (dark background)	5.00	12.00
21 Robby Gordon	.15	.40
22 Kevin Harvick	.75	2.00
23 Jimmie Johnson	1.00	2.50
24 Bobby Labonte	.60	1.50
25 Terry Labonte	.50	1.25
26 Joe Nemechek	.15	.40
27 Scott Riggs CRC	.30	.75
28 Tony Stewart	.75	2.00
29 Brian Vickers CRC	.60	1.50
30 Michael Waltrip	.30	.75
31 Kyle Busch RC	4.00	10.00
32 Stacy Compton	.15	.40
33 Kenny Wallace	.15	.40
34 Paul Menard RC	1.00	2.50
35 Jason Keller	.15	.40
36 J.J. Yeley RC	2.00	5.00
37 Ron Hornaday	.15	.40
38 Billy Parker Jr. RC	1.25	3.00
39 Martin Truex Jr. RC	3.00	8.00
39B Martin Truex Jr. (missing official)	5.00	12.00
40 Casey Atwood	.15	.40
41 Tim Fedewa	.15	.40
42 Clint Bowyer RC	3.00	8.00
43 Matt Crafton	.15	.40
44 Rick Crawford	.15	.40
45 Tina Gordon RC	1.00	2.50
46 Andy Houston	.15	.40
47 Steve Park	.15	.40
48 Jon Wood	.30	.75
49 Terry Cook RC	.60	1.50
50 Jack Sprague	.15	.40
51 Dennis Setzer	.15	.40
52 Rusty Wallace's Car HS	.30	.75
52B Rusty Wallace's Car HS (no official)	1.25	3.00
53 Dale Earnhardt Jr.'s Car HS	.50	1.25
54 Kasey Kahne's Car HS	.50	1.25
55 Ryan Newman's Car HS	.50	1.25
56 Michael Waltrip's Car HS	.15	.40
57 Greg Biffle's Car HS	.15	.40
58 Bobby Labonte's Car HS	.30	.75
59 Kevin Harvick's Car HS	.30	.75
60 Robby Gordon's Car HS	.15	.40
61 Elliott Sadler's Car HS	.15	.40
62 Dale Jarrett's Car HS	.30	.75
63 Jimmie Johnson's Car HS	.40	1.00
64 Jeff Green Kyle Petty TM	.30	.75
65 Tony Stewart Bobby Labonte TM	.75	2.00
66 Dale Jarrett Elliott Sadler TM	.60	1.50
67 Rusty Wallace Brendan Gaughan Ryan Newman TM	1.00	2.50
68 Jeff Burton Matt Kenseth Mark Martin Kurt Busch Greg Biffle TM	1.00	2.50
69 Jimmie Johnson Jeff Gordon TM	1.25	3.00
70 Casey Mears Jamie McMurray Mark Marlin TM	.50	1.25
70B Mears/McMurray/Marlin TM (blimp)	2.00	5.00
71 Robby Gordon Kevin Harvick Johnny Sauter TM	.75	2.00
72 Dale Earnhardt Jr. Michael Waltrip TM	1.25	3.00
73 Joe Nemechek Scott Riggs TM	.30	.75
74 Scott Wimmer Dave Blaney TM	.30	.75
75 Jeremy Mayfield Kasey Kahne TM	1.25	3.00
76 Rick Hendrick H	.15	.40
77 Geoff Bodine H	.15	.40
78 Tim Richmond H	.15	.40
79 Benny Parsons Darrell Waltrip H	.30	.75
80 Ken Schrader H	.15	.40
81 Jack Sprague H	.15	.40
82 Ricky Craven H	.15	.40
83 Jerry Nadeau H	.30	.75
84 Ricky Hendrick Kyle Busch H	.75	2.00
85 Jimmie Johnson H	1.00	2.50
86 Joe Nemechek H	.15	.40
87 Brian Vickers H	.60	1.50
88 Ricky Rudd H	.50	1.25
89 Jeff Gordon H	1.25	3.00
90 Terry Labonte H	.50	1.25
91 Brian Vickers LD	.60	1.50
92 Kyle Busch LD	.75	2.00
93 Kasey Kahne LD	1.25	3.00
94 Casey Atwood LD	.15	.40
95 Jon Wood LD	.30	.75
96 Kurt Busch LD	.50	1.25
97 Billy Parker Jr. LD	.60	1.50
98 Casey Mears LD	.30	.75
99 Martin Truex Jr. LD	1.50	4.00
100 Dale Earnhardt Jr. TT	1.25	3.00
101 Greg Biffle TT	.30	.75
102 Kevin Harvick TT	.75	2.00
103 Ryan Newman TT	1.00	2.50
104 Casey Mears TT	.30	.75
105 Tony Stewart TT	.75	2.00
106 Bobby Labonte TT	.60	1.50
107 Sterling Marlin TT	.50	1.25
108 Jeff Gordon Jimmie Johnson Brian Vickers TT	1.25	3.00
109 Dale Earnhardt Jr. F	1.25	3.00
110 Michael Waltrip F	.30	.75
111 Jeff Gordon F	1.25	3.00
112 Jimmie Johnson F	1.00	2.50
113 Mark Martin F	.75	2.00
114 Rusty Wallace F	.60	1.50
115 Kevin Harvick F	.75	2.00
115B Kevin Harvick F (blue sky)	3.00	8.00
116 Tony Stewart F	.75	2.00
117 Matt Kenseth F	1.00	2.50
118 Ryan Newman F	1.00	2.50
119 Bobby Labonte F	.60	1.50
120 Jeff Gordon Jimmie Johnson CL	1.25	3.00

2004 Press Pass Trackside Golden

This 120-card parallel set featurd gold highlights on the cards and each was serial numbered to 100.

*GOLDEN: 2.5X TO 6X BASE

2004 Press Pass Trackside Previews

This 42-card set was a partial parallel of the base set, but each card was serial numbered to 5. The cards were offered via eBay auctions before the base set was released.

COMPLETE SET (42)
STATED PRINT RUN 5 SERIAL #'d SETS

2004 Press Pass Trackside Samples

This 120-card set is a parallel to the base 2 Press Pass Trackside set without the variations. was issued 1 per Beckett Racing Collector is #120, which was the August 2004 cover date. E card had the word "SAMPLE" printed across back.

*SAMPLES: 1.5X TO 4X BASIC

2004 Press Pass Trackside Dialed In

Issued at a stated rate of one in eight, these 12 ca feature some on NASCAR's best drivers on ca which are illuminated by mirror-foil and enhan etching. These cards also featured a "DI" prefix the card numbers.

COMPLETE SET (12)	12.50	30.
DI1 Jimmie Johnson	3.00	8.
DI2 Dale Earnhardt Jr.	4.00	10.
DI3 Jeff Gordon	4.00	10.
DI4 Michael Waltrip	1.25	3.
DI5 Jamie McMurray	1.50	4.
DI6 Tony Stewart	2.50	6.
DI7 Sterling Marlin	1.50	4.
DI8 Bobby Labonte	2.00	5.
DI9 Kurt Busch	1.50	4.
DI10 Brian Vickers	2.00	5.
DI11 Casey Mears	1.25	3.
DI12 Rusty Wallace	2.00	5.

2004 Press Pass Trackside Hat Giveawa

Randomly inserted in packs at a rate of 1 in packs. This 39-card set of entry cards were good a chance to win an autographed hat of corresponding driver. The sweepstakes ended January 31, 2005.

COMPLETE SET (39)		
PPH1 Greg Biffle	1.50	4.
PPH2 Dave Blaney	1.00	2.
PPH3 Jeff Burton	1.50	4.
PPH4 Ward Burton	1.50	4.
PPH5 Kurt Busch	2.50	6.
PPH6 Dale Earnhardt Jr.	6.00	15.
PPH7 Brendan Gaughan	1.50	4.
PPH8 Jeff Gordon	8.00	20.
PPH9 Jeff Green	1.00	2.
PPH10 Kevin Harvick	4.00	10.
PPH11 Ron Hornaday	1.00	2.
PPH12 Dale Jarrett	3.00	8.
PPH13 Jimmie Johnson	5.00	12.
PPH14 Kasey Kahne	6.00	15.
PPH15 Bobby Labonte	3.00	8.
PPH16 Terry Labonte	2.50	6.
PPH17 Kevin Lepage	1.00	2.
PPH18 Sterling Marlin	2.50	6.
PPH19 Mark Martin	4.00	10.
PPH20 Jeremy Mayfield	1.00	2.
PPH21 Jamie McMurray	2.50	6.
PPH22 Casey Mears	1.50	4.
PPH23 Joe Nemechek	1.00	2.
PPH24 Ryan Newman	5.00	12.
PPH25 Scott Riggs	1.50	4.
PPH26 Ricky Rudd	2.50	6.
PPH27 Elliott Sadler	1.50	4.
PPH28 Johnny Sauter	1.50	4.
PPH29 Ken Schrader	1.00	2.
PPH30 Tony Stewart	4.00	10.
PPH31 Brian Vickers	3.00	8
PPH32 Rusty Wallace	3.00	8.
PPH33 Michael Waltrip	1.50	4.
PPH34 Scott Wimmer	1.50	4
PPH35 Martin Truex Jr.	6.00	15.
PPH36 Ricky Craven	1.00	2.
PPH37 Robby Gordon	1.00	2
PPH38 Matt Kenseth	5.00	12.
PPH39 Kyle Petty	1.50	4.

2004 Press Pass Trackside Hot Pass

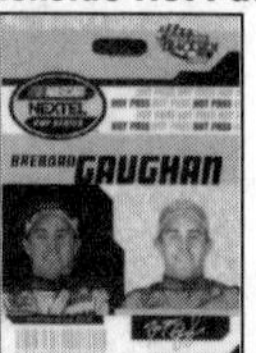

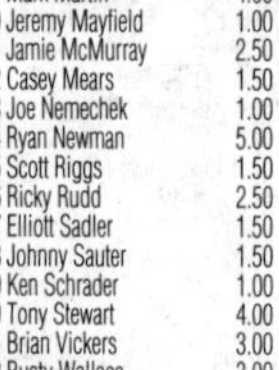

Inserted at a stated rate of 1 in 2 packs, these cards feature the some of NASCAR's leading driv Each card carried a prefix of "HP" as part of the number. The cards were also designed to look li pit pass for the track. A few drivers have a Ne Cup and Busch Series version and are noted in checklist below.

COMPLETE SET (27)	12.50	30.
HP1 Greg Biffle	.50	1

Jeff Burton .50 1.25
Ward Burton .50 1.25
Ricky Craven .30 .75
Dale Earnhardt Jr. 2.00 5.00
Brendan Gaughan .50 1.25
Jeff Gordon 2.00 5.00
Robby Gordon .30 .75
Jimmie Johnson 1.50 4.00
0 Bobby Labonte 1.00 2.50
1 Terry Labonte .75 2.00
2 Ryan Newman 1.50 4.00
3 Kyle Petty .50 1.25
4 Ricky Rudd .75 2.00
5 Elliott Sadler .50 1.25
6 Tony Stewart 1.25 3.00
7 Rusty Wallace 1.00 2.50
8 Michael Waltrip .50 1.25
9 Scott Wimmer BGN .50 1.25
0 Greg Biffle BGN .50 1.25
1 Kevin Harvick BGN 1.25 3.00
2 Kasey Kahne BGN 2.50 6.00
3 Kenny Wallace BGN .30 .75
4 Tim Fedewa BGN .30 .75
5 Johnny Sauter BGN .50 1.25
6 Robby Gordon BGN .30 .75
7 J.J. Yeley BGN 2.00 5.00

2004 Press Pass Trackside Hot Pass National

IPLETE SET (27) 15.00 40.00
IONAL: 1X TO 2.5X BASE

2004 Press Pass Trackside Hot Pursuit

ted at a stated rate of one in 28 packs, these 9 feature the some of NASCAR's leading drivers. card carried a prefix of "HP" as part of the card ber.

IPLETE SET (9) 12.50 30.00
Dale Earnhardt Jr. 4.00 10.00
Jimmie Johnson 4.00 10.00
Michael Waltrip 1.25 3.00
Jeff Gordon 5.00 12.00
Rusty Wallace 2.50 6.00
Matt Kenseth 4.00 10.00
Casey Mears 1.25 3.00
Dale Jarrett 2.50 6.00
Kevin Harvick 3.00 8.00

2004 Press Pass Trackside Pit Stoppers Cars

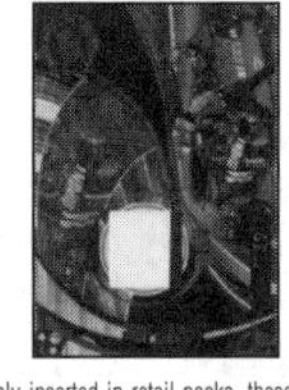

omly inserted in retail packs, these 17 cards re swatches of race-used pit signs set against a o of the featured driver's car. Each card was ed to a a stated print run of 150 with the ption of Matt Kenseth which had 17 copies uced. The Kenseth is not priced due to scarcity.

RS: .4X TO 1X DRIVERS
1 Jeff Gordon 25.00 60.00
2 Terry Labonte 12.50 30.00
3 Kevin Harvick 25.00 60.00
4 Jimmie Johnson 20.00 50.00
5 Rusty Wallace 15.00 40.00
6 Bobby Labonte 15.00 40.00
7 Tony Stewart 20.00 50.00
8 Ryan Newman 15.00 40.00
9 Dale Earnhardt
10 Sterling Marlin 10.00 25.00
11 Jeff Burton 10.00 25.00
12 Michael Waltrip 10.00 25.00
13 Jamie McMurray 15.00 40.00
14 Matt Kenseth/20
15 Dale Earnhardt Jr. 25.00 60.00
16 Scott Riggs 10.00 25.00
17 Joe Nemechek 8.00 20.00

2004 Press Pass Trackside Pit Stoppers Drivers

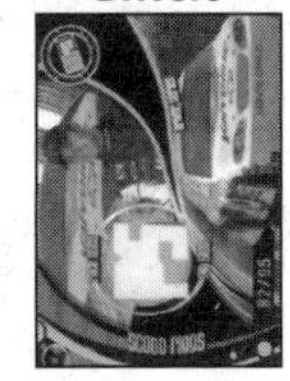

omly inserted in hobby packs at a rate of one in these 17 cards feature swatches of race-used pit set against a photo of the featured driver. Each was issued to a a stated print run of 95 with the ptions of Kevin Harvick of 40 and Matt Kenseth of 20. The Kenseth is not priced due to scarcity.

COMPLETE SET (17)
STATED ODDS 1:168
STATED PRINT RUN 95 SERIAL #'d SETS
PSD1 Jeff Gordon 30.00 60.00
PSD2 Terry Labonte 15.00 30.00
PSD3 Kevin Harvick/40 30.00 60.00
PSD4 Jimmie Johnson 25.00 50.00
PSD5 Rusty Wallace 20.00 40.00
PSD6 Bobby Labonte 20.00 40.00
PSD7 Tony Stewart 25.00 50.00
PSD8 Ryan Newman 20.00 40.00
PSD9 Dale Earnhardt
PSD10 Sterling Marlin 12.50 25.00
PSD11 Jeff Burton 12.50 25.00
PSD12 Michael Waltrip 12.50 25.00
PSD13 Jamie McMurray 20.00 40.00
PSD14 Matt Kenseth/20
PSD15 Dale Earnhardt Jr. 30.00 60.00
PSD16 Scott Riggs 12.50 25.00
PSD17 Joe Nemechek 10.00 20.00

2004 Press Pass Trackside Pit Stoppers Autographs

Randomly inserted in hobby packs, these 8 cards feature swatches of race-used pit signs set against a photo of the featured driver along with a his signature. The cards were limited and hand numbered to the driver's door number. Some of the cards are not priced due to scarcity.

COMPLETE SET (8)
SERIAL #'d TO DRIVER'S DOOR NUMBER
SOME CARDS NOT PRICED DUE TO SCARCITY
PS-BL Bobby Labonte/18 75.00 150.00
PS-DE Dale Earnhardt Jr./8
PS-KH Kevin Harvick/29 100.00 200.00
PS-MK Matt Kenseth/17
PS-RN Ryan Newman/12
PS-RW Rusty Wallace/2
PS-SR Scott Riggs/10
PS-TS Tony Stewart/20

2004 Press Pass Trackside Runnin n' Gunnin

Issued at a stated rate of one in six, these 12 cards feature drivers who never let you see them sweat.

COMPLETE SET (12) 10.00 25.00
RG1 Dale Earnhardt Jr. 1.50 4.00
RG2 Jeff Gordon 1.50 4.00
RG3 Jimmie Johnson 1.25 3.00
RG4 Michael Waltrip .40 1.00
RG5 Bobby Labonte .75 2.00
RG6 Tony Stewart 1.00 2.50
RG7 Scott Riggs .40 1.00
RG8 Greg Biffle .40 1.00
RG9 Terry Labonte .60 1.50
RG10 Rusty Wallace .75 2.00
RG11 Jamie McMurray .60 1.50
RG12 Matt Kenseth 1.25 3.00

2005 Press Pass Trackside

COMPLETE SET (100) 15.00 30.00
WAX BOX HOBBY (28) 50.00 80.00
WAX BOX RETAIL (24) 35.00 60.00
1 Jeff Burton .30 .75
2 Dale Earnhardt Jr. 1.25 3.00
2B Dale Earnhardt Jr. no car 2.50 6.00
3 Jeff Gordon 1.25 3.00
4 Kevin Harvick .75 2.00
5 Jimmie Johnson 1.00 2.50
6 Bobby Labonte .60 1.50
7 Terry Labonte .50 1.25
8 Joe Nemechek .20 .50
9 Scott Riggs .30 .75
10 Tony Stewart .75 2.00
11 Brian Vickers .60 1.50
12 Kyle Busch CRC .75 2.00
13 Jeff Green .20 .50
14 Kasey Kahne 1.25 3.00
14B Kasey Kahne no white t-shirt 2.50 6.00
15 Travis Kvapil CRC .30 .75
16 Sterling Marlin .50 1.25
17 Jeremy Mayfield .20 .50
18 Jamie McMurray .50 1.25
19 Casey Mears .30 .75
20 Ryan Newman 1.00 2.50
21 Kyle Petty .30 .75
22 Ken Schrader .20 .50
23 Rusty Wallace .60 1.50
24 Scott Wimmer .30 .75
25 John Andretti .20 .50
26 Greg Biffle .30 .75
27 Kurt Busch .50 1.25
28 Carl Edwards CRC 1.00 2.50
28B Carl Edwards no wire 2.00 5.00
29 Dale Jarrett .60 1.50
30 Matt Kenseth 1.00 2.50
31 Mark Martin .75 2.00
32 Ricky Rudd .50 1.25
33 Elliott Sadler .30 .75
34 Clint Bowyer 1.25 3.00
35 Justin Labonte .50 1.25
36 David Green .20 .50
37 Denny Hamlin RC 3.00 8.00
38 Jon Wood .30 .75
39 Paul Wolfe .30 .75
40 Johnny Sauter .30 .75
41 Reed Sorenson RC 4.00 10.00
41B Reed Sorenson no reflection 6.00 15.00
42 Jason Keller .20 .50
43 Martin Truex Jr. 1.00 2.50
44 Kenny Wallace .20 .50
45 J.J. Yeley .50 1.25
46 Terry Cook .20 .50
47 Ricky Craven .20 .50
48 Rick Crawford .20 .50
49 Kerry Earnhardt .30 .75
50 Todd Kluever RC 1.50 4.00
51 Ken Schrader .20 .50
52 Ron Hornaday .20 .50
53 Dennis Setzer .20 .50
54 Jack Sprague .20 .50
55 Rusty Wallace's Car HS .20 .50
56 Kasey Kahne's Car HS .50 1.25
57 Ryan Newman's Car HS .30 .75
58 Michael Waltrip's Car HS .10 .25
59 Bobby Labonte's Car HS .20 .50
60 Tony Stewart's Car HS .30 .75
61 Jeff Gordon's Car HS .50 1.25
61B Jeff Gordon's Car HS no orange spots 1.00 2.50
62 Kevin Harvick's Car HS .30 .75
63 Jeff Burton's Car HS .10 .25
64 Elliott Sadler's Car HS .10 .25
65 Jimmie Johnson's Car HS .30 .75
66 Dale Jarrett's Car HS .20 .50
67 J.Green/K.Petty TM .30 .75
68 Stewart/Leffler/B.Labonte TM .75 2.00
69 D.Jarrett/E.Sadler/ TM .60 1.50
70 J.Gordon/J.Johnson TM 1.25 3.00
71 Mears/Marlin/McMurray TM .50 1.25
72 Blaney/J.Burton/Harvick TM .75 2.00
73 Riggs/Said/Nemechek TM .30 .75
74 K.Kahne/J.Mayfield TM 1.25 3.00
75 T.Labonte/Vickers/Ky.Busch TM .75 2.00
76 Kurt Busch Kyle Busch FA .75 2.00
77 Rusty Wallace Kenny Wallace FA .60 1.50
78 Terry Labonte Justin Labonte FA .50 1.25
79 Richard Petty Kyle Petty FA .75 2.00
80 Bobby Labonte Terry Labonte FA .60 1.50
81 Jon Wood Glen Wood FA .30 .75
82 Dale Earnhardt Jr. GP 1.25 3.00
83 Jeff Gordon GP 1.25 3.00
84 Jeff Burton GP .30 .75
85 Kevin Harvick GP .75 2.00
86 Jimmie Johnson GP 1.00 2.50
86B Jimmie Johnson GP no Chevy logo 2.00 5.00
87 Bobby Labonte GP .60 1.50
88 Tony Stewart GP .75 2.00
89 Michael Waltrip GP .30 .75
90 Dale Jarrett GP .60 1.50
91 Ricky Rudd GP .50 1.25
92 Rusty Wallace GP .60 1.50
93 Matt Kenseth GP 1.00 2.50
94 Dale Earnhardt Jr. F 1.25 3.00
95 Jeff Gordon F 1.25 3.00
96 Jimmie Johnson F 1.00 2.50
97 Tony Stewart F .75 2.00
98 Rusty Wallace F .60 1.50
99 Dale Jarrett F .60 1.50
100 Dale Earnhardt Jr. CL 1.25 3.00

2005 Press Pass Trackside Golden

*GOLDEN: 2.5X TO 6X BASE

2005 Press Pass Trackside Previews

NOT PRICED DUE TO SCARCITY

2005 Press Pass Trackside Dialed In

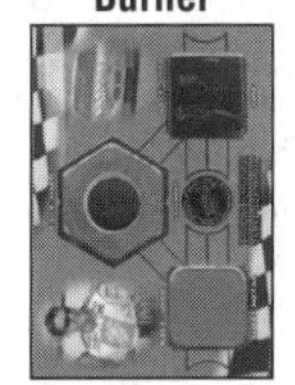

COMPLETE SET (9) 10.00 25.00
DI1 Jimmie Johnson 2.50 6.00
DI2 Kevin Harvick 2.00 5.00
DI3 Jeff Gordon 3.00 8.00
DI4 Michael Waltrip .75 2.00
DI5 Tony Stewart 2.00 5.00
DI6 Bobby Labonte 1.50 4.00
DI7 Matt Kenseth 2.50 6.00
DI8 Dale Jarrett 1.50 4.00
DI9 Rusty Wallace 1.50 4.00

2005 Press Pass Trackside Hat Giveaway

COMPLETE SET (46)
PPH1 John Andretti .75 2.00
PPH2 Dave Blaney .75 2.00
PPH3 Jeff Burton 1.50 4.00
PPH4 Kurt Busch 2.50 6.00
PPH5 Kyle Busch 4.00 10.00
PPH6 Dale Earnhardt Jr. 6.00 15.00
PPH7 Carl Edwards 4.00 10.00
PPH8 Jeff Gordon 6.00 15.00
PPH9 Jeff Green .75 2.00
PPH10 Kevin Harvick 4.00 10.00
PPH11 Dale Jarrett 3.00 8.00
PPH12 Jimmie Johnson 5.00 12.00
PPH13 Kasey Kahne 6.00 15.00
PPH14 Matt Kenseth 5.00 12.00
PPH15 Travis Kvapil 1.50 4.00
PPH16 Terry Labonte 2.50 6.00
PPH17 Bobby Labonte 3.00 8.00
PPH18 Jason Leffler .75 2.00
PPH19 Kevin Lepage .75 2.00
PPH20 Jeremy Mayfield .75 2.00
PPH21 Jamie McMurray 2.50 6.00
PPH22 Casey Mears 1.50 4.00
PPH23 Joe Nemechek .75 2.00
PPH24 Ryan Newman 5.00 12.00
PPH25 Kyle Petty 1.50 4.00
PPH26 Scott Riggs 1.50 4.00
PPH27 Ricky Rudd 2.50 6.00
PPH28 Elliott Sadler 1.50 4.00
PPH29 Boris Said .75 2.00
PPH30 Ken Schrader .75 2.00
PPH31 Tony Stewart 4.00 10.00
PPH32 Brian Vickers 3.00 8.00
PPH33 Rusty Wallace 3.00 8.00
PPH34 Michael Waltrip 1.50 4.00
PPH35 Scott Wimmer 1.50 4.00
PPH36 Martin Truex Jr. 5.00 12.00
PPH37 Boston Reid 5.00 12.00
PPH38 Reed Sorenson 6.00 15.00
PPH39 David Green .75 2.00
PPH40 Kenny Wallace .75 2.00
PPH41 Rick Crawford .75 2.00
PPH42 Blake Feese 5.00 12.00
PPH43 Sterling Marlin 2.50 6.00
PPH44 Greg Biffle 1.50 4.00
PPH45 Mark Martin 4.00 10.00
PPH46 Mike Bliss .75 2.00

2005 Press Pass Trackside Hot Pass

COMPLETE SET (27) 12.50 30.00
1 John Andretti .30 .75
2 Jeff Burton .50 1.25
3 Dale Earnhardt Jr. 2.00 5.00
4 Jeff Gordon 2.00 5.00
5 Jeff Green .30 .75
6 Kevin Harvick 1.25 3.00
7 Dale Jarrett 1.00 2.50
8 Jimmie Johnson 1.50 4.00
9 Matt Kenseth 1.50 4.00
10 Bobby Labonte 1.00 2.50
11 Terry Labonte .75 2.00
12 Ryan Newman 1.50 4.00
13 Mark Martin 1.25 3.00
14 Ricky Rudd .75 2.00
15 Ken Schrader .30 .75
16 Tony Stewart 1.25 3.00
17 Rusty Wallace 1.00 2.50
18 Michael Waltrip .50 1.25
19 Denny Hamlin 2.00 5.00
20 Kasey Kahne 2.00 5.00
21 Kenny Wallace .30 .75
22 Tim Fedewa .30 .75
23 Jason Keller .30 .75
24 Martin Truex Jr. 1.50 4.00
25 David Green .30 .75
26 David Stremme 2.00 5.00
27 J.J. Yeley .75 2.00

2005 Press Pass Trackside Hot Pass National

Available at the 2005 National Convention held in July 2005 in Chicago, Il.

COMPLETE SET (27) 12.50 30.00
*NATIONAL: .4X TO 1X BASE

2005 Press Pass Trackside Hot Pursuit

COMPLETE SET (9) 20.00 50.00
HP1 Kevin Harvick 3.00 8.00
HP2 Jimmie Johnson 4.00 10.00
HP3 Matt Kenseth 4.00 10.00
HP4 Jeff Gordon 4.00 10.00
HP5 Rusty Wallace 2.50 6.00
HP6 Ryan Newman 4.00 10.00
HP7 Ricky Rudd 2.00 5.00

HP8 Tony Stewart 3.00 8.00
HP9 Bobby Labonte 2.50 6.00

2005 Press Pass Trackside Pit Stoppers Autographs

SOME CARDS NOT PRICED DUE TO SCARCITY
PSDE Dale Earnhardt Jr./8
PSJG Jeff Gordon/24 250.00 500.00
PSJJ Jimmie Johnson/48 75.00 150.00
PSRN Ryan Newman/12
PSRW Rusty Wallace/2
PSSR Scott Riggs/10
PSTS Tony Stewart/20

2005 Press Pass Trackside Pit Stoppers Cars

*CARS: .4X TO 1X DRIVERS

2005 Press Pass Trackside Pit Stoppers Drivers

PSD1 Jeff Gordon 25.00 60.00
PSD2 Terry Labonte 12.50 30.00
PSD3 Jimmie Johnson 20.00 50.00
PSD4 Rusty Wallace 15.00 40.00
PSD5 Tony Stewart 20.00 50.00
PSD6 Ryan Newman 20.00 50.00
PSD7 Sterling Marlin 12.50 30.00
PSD8 Michael Waltrip 12.50 30.00
PSD9 Jamie McMurray 12.50 30.00
PSD10 Matt Kenseth 20.00 50.00
PSD11 Scott Riggs 12.50 30.00
PSD12 Joe Nemechek 12.50 30.00
PSD13 Bobby Labonte 15.00 40.00
PSD14 Dale Earnhardt Jr. 25.00 60.00

2005 Press Pass Trackside Runnin n' Gunnin

COMPLETE SET (12) 10.00 25.00
RG1 Dale Earnhardt Jr. 2.00 5.00
RG2 Jeff Gordon 2.00 5.00
RG3 Jimmie Johnson 1.50 4.00
RG4 Ryan Newman 1.50 4.00
RG5 Bobby Labonte 1.00 2.50
RG6 Tony Stewart 1.25 3.00
RG7 Matt Kenseth 1.50 4.00
RG8 Dale Jarrett 1.00 2.50
RG9 Terry Labonte .75 2.00
RG10 Rusty Wallace 1.00 2.50
RG11 Kevin Harvick 1.25 3.00
RG12 Jeff Burton .50 1.25

2002 Press Pass Triple Burner

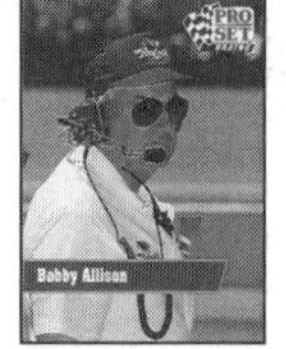

Randomly inserted into retail packs across several Press Pass products, this set features nine leading drivers' cars. All cards in this set are serial numbered to 100 and include three different swatches: race used lugnut, sheet metal and tire.

TB1 Dale Earnhardt Jr. 200.00 350.00
TB2 Jeff Gordon 200.00 350.00
TB3 Kevin Harvick 60.00 120.00
TB4 Dale Jarrett 50.00 100.00
TB5 Bobby Labonte 50.00 100.00
TB6 Terry Labonte 50.00 100.00
TB7 Mark Martin 60.00 120.00
TB8 Tony Stewart 60.00 120.00
TB9 Rusty Wallace 50.00 100.00

2003 Press Pass Triple Burner

These 10-cards are also part of a continuing Press Pass year long insert program. It kicked off with the 2003 Press Pass set in which 14-copies of each card were released. Each card contains race-used pieces of tires, sheet metal and lugnuts. They were intially issued as redemption cards and included a Press Pass Authentics hologram seal of authenticity.

TB1 Jeff Gordon 100.00 200.00

TB2 Ryan Newman 60.00 120.00
TB3 Kevin Harvick 60.00 120.00
TB4 Jimmie Johnson 60.00 120.00
TB5 Rusty Wallace 60.00 120.00
TB6 Mark Martin 75.00 150.00
TB7 Matt Kenseth 60.00 120.00
TB8 Bobby Labonte 60.00 120.00
TB9 Tony Stewart 75.00 150.00
TB10 Dale Earnhardt Jr. 75.00 150.00

2004 Press Pass Triple Burner Exchange

This 10-card set was randomly inserted in packs across all brands of Press Pass hobby products in 2004. These were not available in any retail packs. Each card was issued as an exchange redeemable for the specified driver's card with a swatch of his race-used tire, a swatch of his race-used sheet metal and a slice of his race-used lugnut. The cards were serial numbered to 100. These cards were the redemptions. The exchange deadline was January 31, 2005.

*TB EXCHANGE CARDS: .4X TO 1X TB
RANDOM INSERTS IN HOBBY PACKS
TB1 Jeff Gordon 125.00 250.00
TB2 Ryan Newman 75.00 150.00
TB3 Kevin Harvick 60.00 120.00
TB4 Jimmie Johnson 75.00 150.00
TB5 Rusty Wallace 60.00 120.00
TB6 Mark Martin 60.00 120.00
TB7 Matt Kenseth 75.00 150.00
TB8 Bobby Labonte 50.00 100.00
TB9 Tony Stewart 60.00 120.00
TB10 Dale Earnhardt Jr. 100.00 200.00

2005 Press Pass Triple Burner Exchange

*EXCHANGE: .5X TO 1X BASE
TB1 Jeff Gordon 125.00 250.00
TB2 Ryan Newman 75.00 150.00
TB3 Kevin Harvick 60.00 120.00
TB4 Jimmie Johnson 75.00 150.00
TB5 Rusty Wallace 60.00 120.00
TB6 Mark Martin 100.00 200.00
TB7 Matt Kenseth 100.00 200.00
TB8 Bobby Labonte 50.00 100.00
TB9 Tony Stewart 75.00 150.00
TB10 Dale Earnhardt Jr. 125.00 250.00
TB11 Kurt Busch 60.00 120.00
TB12 Brian Vickers 50.00 100.00

2005 Press Pass UMI Cup Chase

This 11-card set features the 10 drivers from the 2005 Cup Chase along with a checklist card featuring all 10 drivers from the Cup Chase photo shoot. This set was available with purchase of the 2005 UMI Nextel Cup Series Yearbook and the 2006 UMI Preview and Press Guide.

COMP.FACT.SET (11) 15.00 30.00
1 Cup Chase Drivers 2.00 5.00
Greg Biffle
Jimmie Johnson
Rusty Wallace
Carl Edwards
Jeremy Mayfield
Tony Stewart
Matt Kenseth
Mark Martin
Kurt Busch
Ryan Newman CL
2 Tony Stewart 1.50 4.00
3 Greg Biffle .60 1.50
4 Rusty Wallace 1.25 3.00
5 Jimmie Johnson 2.00 5.00
6 Kurt Busch 1.00 2.50
7 Mark Martin 1.50 4.00
8 Jeremy Mayfield .40 1.00
9 Matt Kenseth 2.00 5.00
10 Carl Edwards 2.00 5.00
11 Ryan Newman 2.00 5.00

1991 Pro Set Prototypes

This Prototype set was released by Pro Set in its own cello wrapper and features the Bobby Allison Racing Team. Although the cards are unnumbered, they have been assigned numbers below according to alphabetical order. They are often sold as a complete set.

COMPLETE SET (4) 1.25 3.00
P1 Bobby Allison .75 2.00
P2 Hut Stricklin .40 1.00
P3 Hut Stricklin's Car .40 1.00
P4 Cover Card .25 .60

1991 Pro Set

This was Pro Set's first NASCAR release in a run of sets produced by the company from 1991-1994. The set features star drivers, cars and crew members of the top Winston Cup teams. Three cards containing errors were corrected in a later printing and a 37-

card Legends insert was also included with the release. The cards were packaged 12 per foil pack with 36 packs per box. One thousand signed cards of Bobby Allison (card number 38) were also randomly inserted as was a special hologram card featuring the Winston Cup Trophy (numbered of 5000). The Allison cards were signed using a black fine line Sharpie pen.

COMPLETE SET (143) 10.00 25.00
WAX BOX 15.00 30.00
1 Rick Mast .12 .30
2 Richard Jackson .12 .30
3 Bob Johnson RC .20 .50
4 Rick Mast w/Car .07 .20
5 Rusty Wallace .50 1.25
6 Rusty Wallace .50 1.25
7 Jimmy Makar .12 .30
8 Rusty Wallace's Car .30 .75
9 Ernie Irvan's Car .20 .50
10 Don Miller RC .20 .50
11 Bill Venturini RC .20 .50
12 Roger Penske RC .30 .75
13 Ernie Irvan .30 .75
14 Ernie Irvan .30 .75
15 Larry McClure .12 .30
16 Tony Glover .12 .30
17 Ricky Rudd .30 .75
18A Rick Hendrick ERR .30 .75
pictured in dark sweater and white shirt
18B Rick Hendrick COR .20 .50
updated photo
19 Waddell Wilson .12 .30
20 Ricky Rudd's Car .20 .50
21 Mark Martin .60 1.50
22 Jack Roush .20 .50
23 Robin Pemberton .12 .30
24 Steve Hmiel .12 .30
25 Mark Martin's Car .40 1.00
26 Rick Wilson .12 .30
27 Beth Bruce .12 .30
Ms. Winston
28 Harry Hyde .12 .30
29 Rick Wilson's Car .07 .20
30 Bob Whitcomb .12 .30
31 Buddy Parrott .12 .30
32 Derrike Cope's Car .12 .30
33 Geoff Bodine .12 .30
34 Junior Johnson .20 .50
35 Tim Brewer .12 .30
36 Geoff Bodine's Car .07 .20
37 Hut Stricklin .12 .30
38A Bobby Allison ERR .40 1.00
text mentions son-in-law
38B Bobby Allison COR .25 .60
no son-in-law mentioned
39 Hut Stricklin's Car .07 .20
40 Morgan Shepherd .20 .50
41 Walter Bud Moore .12 .30
42 Morgan Shepherd's Car .12 .30
43 Dale Jarrett .50 1.25
44 Dale Jarrett's Car .30 .75
45 Junior Johnson .20 .50
46 Mike Beam .12 .30
47 Sterling Marlin's Car .20 .50
48 Mickey Gibbs .12 .30
49 Barry Dodson .12 .30
50 Ken Schrader .20 .50
51 Rick Hendrick .20 .50
52 Richard Broome .12 .30
53 Doug Williams .12 .30
54 Kyle Petty .40 1.00
55 Ned Jarrett .50 1.25
Dale Jarrett
56 Cale Yarborough .30 .75
57 Terry Labonte .30 .75
58 Chuck Rider .12 .30
59 Bill Ingle .20 .50
60 Michael Waltrip's Car .15 .40
61 Ken Schrader's Car .12 .30
62 Jimmy Fennig .12 .30
63 Harry Gant .30 .75
64 Andy Petree RC .20 .50
65 Richard Petty .60 1.50
66 Dale Inman .12 .30
67 Robbie Loomis RC .30 .75
68 Richard Petty's Car .40 1.00
69 Jimmy Means .12 .30
70 Jimmy Means' Car .07 .20
71 Dave Marcis .20 .50
72 Dave Marcis' Car .12 .30
73 Lake Speed .12 .30
74 Geoff Bodine .12 .30
75 George Bradshaw RC .20 .50
76 Joe Ruttman RC .20 .50
77 Butch Mock .12 .30
78 Bob Rahilly .12 .30
79 Joe Ruttman's Car .12 .30
80 Terry Labonte .30 .75
81 Steve Loyd RC .20 .50
82 Terry Labonte's Car .20 .50
83 Jimmy Spencer .20 .50
84 Travis Carter .12 .30
85 Jimmy Spencer's Car .12 .30
86 Bobby Hillin .12 .30
87 Kyle Petty .40 1.00
88 Felix Sabates .20 .50
89 Gary Nelson .12 .30
90 Wally Dallenbach Jr. RC .20 .50
91 Danny Glad RC .20 .50
92 Paul Andrews .12 .30
93 Alan Kulwicki .40 1.00
94 Alan Kulwicki's Car .25 .60
95 Ted Little .20 .50
96 Jeff Hammond .20 .50
97 Kenny Bernstein .20 .50
98 Brett Bodine's Car .07 .20
99 Mark Martin .60 1.50
100 Lake Speed's Car .07 .20
101 Wayne Bumgarner RC .20 .50
102 Brett Bodine .12 .30
103 Ted Musgrave RC .30 .75
104 Ted Musgrave's Car .20 .50
105 Larry Pearson .12 .30
106 Larry Hedrick RC .20 .50
107 Robert Harrington RC .20 .50
108 Len Wood .12 .30
109 Eddie Wood .12 .30
110 Leonard Wood .12 .30
111 Buddy Baker .20 .50
112 Dick Moroso RC .20 .50
113 Dick Moroso .20 .50
David Ifft
114 J.D. McDuffie .12 .30
115 Stanley Smith RC .20 .50
116 Eddie Bierschwale .12 .30
117 Darrell Waltrip .30 .75
118 Darrell Waltrip w/Car .20 .50
119 Darrell Waltrip's Car .20 .50
120 Chuck Little .20 .50
Alfred Allen RC
121 Greg Sacks .12 .30
122 Junie Donlavey .12 .30
123 Leo Jackson .12 .30
124 Bill Stavola .12 .30
125 Renee White Ms. Winston .12 .30
126 Geoff Bodine .12 .30
127 Ken Schrader .20 .50
128 Ricky Rudd .30 .75
129 Harry Gant .30 .75
130 Richard Petty .60 1.50
131 Bobby Hamilton's Car .12 .30
132 Felix Sabates .20 .50
Gary Nelson
133 Alan Kulwicki .40 1.00
134 Alan Kulwicki Army Car .25 .60
135 Winston Showcar .07 .20
136 Greg Sacks Navy Car .07 .20
137 Mickey Gibbs Air Force Car .07 .20
138 Buddy Baker Marines Car .12 .30
139 D.Marcis Coast Guard Car .12 .30
140 T. Wayne Robertson RC .20 .50
141 Ricky Rudd .30 .75
142 Brett Bodine .12 .30
143A Phil Parsons ERR .20 .50
text reads Due to Health Problems...
143B Phil Parsons COR .12 .30
text omits Due to Health Problems...
AU38 Bobby Allison AUTO 40.00 80.00
NNO Winston Cup HOLO/5000 8.00 20.00

1991 Pro Set Legends

Pro Set produced this 37-card set as an insert into its 1991 Winston Cup Racing packs. The cards seemed to have been produced in the same quantities as the regular issue and are often sold together as a set. Donnie Allison's card (number L11) contains an error that was later corrected.

COMPLETE SET (37) 2.00 5.00
L1 Dick Brooks .12 .30
L2 Buck Baker .20 .50
L3 Fred Lorenzen .20 .50
L4 Ned Jarrett .20 .50
L5 Dick Hutcherson .12 .30
L6 Marilyn Green .12 .30
L7 Harold Kinder .12 .30
L8 Coo Coo Marlin .20 .50
L9 Ralph Seagraves .12 .30
L10 Paul Bud Moore .12 .30
L11A Donnie Allison ERR .20 .50
text reads BGN crew chief
L11B Donnie Allison COR .20 .50
text reads WC crew chief
L12 Glen Wood .12 .30
L13 Marvin Panch .20 .50
L14 Cale Yarborough .30 .75
L15 Neil Castles (Soapy) .12 .30
L16 Maurice Petty .30 .75
L17 Junior Johnson .20 .50
L18 Tim Flock .20 .50
L19 Smokey Yunick .12 .30
L20 Larry Frank .12 .30
L21 Cotton Owens .12 .30
L22 Ralph Moody Jr. .20 .50
L23 Bob Welborn .12 .30
L24 Neil Bonnett .30 .75
L25 Edwin Matthews (Banjo) .12 .30
L26 Sam McQuagg .12 .30
L27 Jim Paschal .12 .30
L28 David Pearson .40 1.00
L29 Tom Pistone .12 .30
L30 Jack Smith .12 .30
L31 Bobby Allison .25 .60
L32 Charles Ellington .12 .30
L33 Paul Goldsmith .12 .30
L34 Pete Hamilton .12 .30
L35 Rex White .20 .50
L36 Elmo Langley .12 .30
L37 Benny Parsons .30 .75

1991 Pro Set Petty Family Prototypes

Pro Set issued four cards to preview the release of the 1991 Pro Set Petty Family set. The unnumbered cards came in their own cello wrapper and are often sold as a complete set.

COMPLETE SET (4) 1.50 4.00
P1 Lee Petty's Car .30 .75
P2 Maurice Petty .75 2.00
P3 Richard Petty's Car .60 1.50
P4 Cover Card .20 .50

1991 Pro Set Petty Family

Pro Set produced this 50-card set in factory set form. It highlights the careers of Richard and the rest of the Petty racing family. The set was released again in 1992 as part of a special Petty Gift Pack containing a custom card album.

COMP. FACT SET (50) 1.50 4.00
1 Maurice Petty Art .30 .75
Richard Petty ART
Lee Petty ART
2 1949 Reaper Shed .30 .75
3 Lee Petty's Car 1949 .05 .15
4 Lee Petty's Car 1949 .05 .15
5 Lee Petty w/Car 1950 .15 .40
6 Lee Petty's Car 1951 .05 .15
7 Lee Petty's Car 1952 .05 .15
8 Lee Petty's Car 1953 .05 .15
9 Lee Petty .30 .75
Richard Petty
Maurice Petty 1954
10 Lee Petty's Car 1955 .05 .15
11 Lee Petty's Car 1956 .05 .15
12 Lee Petty's Car 1957 .05 .15
13 Richard Petty 1958 .30 .75
14 Lee Petty's Car .05 .15
Johnny Beauchamp's Car
15 Lee Petty .30 .75
Richard Petty
Maurice Petty 1960
16 Richard Petty's Car 1961 .12 .30
17 Richard Petty 1962 .30 .75
18 Richard Petty's Car .12 .30
Lee Petty's Car 1963
19 Richard Petty's Car 1964 .12 .30
20 Richard Petty's Car 1965 .12 .30
21 Richard Petty's Car 1966 .12 .30
22 Richard Petty 1967 .30 .75
23 Richard Petty's Car 1968 .12 .30
24 Richard Petty's Car 1969 .12 .30
25 Maurice Petty Art .15 .40
26 Maurice Petty .15 .40
Buddy Baker
27 Richard Petty's Car 1972 .12 .30
28 Petty Family .30 .75
29 Maurice Petty 1974 .15 .40
30 Petty Family .30 .75
31 Richard Petty's Transporter .12 .30
32 Richard Petty's Car 1977 .12 .30
33 Richard Petty's Car 1978 .12 .30
34 Richard Petty ART .30 .75
Kyle Petty
35 Richard Petty's Car .12 .30
Kyle Petty's Car
36 Richard Petty's Car .12 .30
Kyle Petty's Car
37 Petty Family .30 .75
38 Richard Petty's Car 1983 .12 .30
39 Kyle Petty's Car 1984 .07 .20
40 Dick Brooks' Car .01 .05
41 Richard Petty's Car 1986 .12 .30
42 Richard Petty's Car 1987 .12 .30
43 Richard Petty's Car 1989 .12 .30
44 Petty Enterprises .30 .75
45 Lee Petty .15 .40
46 Maurice Petty .15 .40
47 Richard Petty .30 .75
48 Kyle Petty .20 .50
49 Richard Petty .30 .75
Maurice Petty
50 Richard Petty Museum .30 .75

1992 Pro Set Prototypes

This Prototype set was released by Pro Set in its own cello wrapper. Although the cards are unnumbered, they have been assigned numbers below according to alphabetical order.

COMPLETE SET (4) 2.00 5.00
P1 Dale Earnhardt 1.50 4.00
P2 Sterling Marlin .50 1.25
P3 Morgan Shepherd .30 .75
P4 Cover Card .10 .30

1992 Pro Set

This was Pro Set's second NASCAR release. The set features star drivers, cars and crew members of the top Winston Cup teams from the previous season. Six cards containing errors were corrected in a later printing and a 32-card Legends insert was also included with the release. The Club only factory set, of which 6,000 were made, contained the corrected cards. Cards were packaged 12 per foil pack with 36

packs per box. A special hologram card featuring a Dale Earnhardt Winston Cup Champion logo (numbered of 5000) was produced and randomly distributed through packs. The card originally had a white border, but was later changed to black creating the variation.

COMPLETE SET (248) 10.00 25.00
COMP.FACT.SET (280) 15.00 40.00
1 Dale Earnhardt 1.25 3.00
2 Alan Kulwicki .30 .75
3 Steve Grissom .10 .25
4 Jimmy Hensley .10 .25
5 Tommy Houston .10 .25
6 Bobby Labonte .40 1.00
7 Joe Nemechek .15 .40
8 Robert Pressley .10 .25
9 Kenny Wallace .15 .40
10 Mike Wallace .10 .25
11 Rick Mast's Transporter .05 .10
12 Rusty Wallace's Transporter .15 .40
13 Geoff Bodine .10 .25
14 Ricky Rudd's Transporter .10 .25
15 Alan Kulwicki's Transporter .12 .30
16 Derrike Cope's Transporter .05 .15
17 Harry Gant's Transporter .10 .25
18 Kyle Petty's Transporter .12 .30
19 Dave Marcis' Transporter .05 .15
20 Ernie Irvan w/Pit Crew .25 .60
21 Terry Labonte's Transporter .10 .25
22 Jimmy Spencer's Transporter .05 .15
23 Michael Waltrip .20 .50
24 Dale Jarrett .40 1.00
25 Derrike Cope's Car .05 .15
26 Kirk Shelmerdine .10 .25
27 Mike Wallace's Car .05 .10
28 Terry Labonte .25 .60
29 Joe Ruttman .10 .25
30 Kyle Petty .30 .75
31 Ricky Craven RC .60 1.50
32 Clifford Allison RC .20 .50
33 Shawna Robinson .25 .60
34 Dorsey Schroeder RC .15 .40
35 Terry Labonte .25 .60
36 Phil Parsons' Car .05 .10
37 Jimmy Means' Car .05 .10
38 Dave Marcis' Car .05 .10
39 Richard Childress .15 .40
40 Hut Stricklin's Transporter .05 .10
41 Davey Allison's Transporter .15 .40
42 Rick Mast .10 .25
43 Richard Petty .50 1.25
44 Kyle Petty .30 .75
45 Richard Petty .50 1.25
46 Chad Little's Transporter .05 .15
47 Jimmy Means .10 .25
48 Dave Marcis .15 .40
49 Harry Gant .25 .60
50 Lake Speed .10 .25
51 Jimmy Spencer .15 .40
52 Bobby Hillin .10 .25
53 Chad Little .15 .40
54 Eddie Bierschwale .10 .25
55 Jack Sprague RC .15 .40
56 Dick Trickle w/Car .10 .25
57 Charlie Glotzbach .10 .25
58 Phil Barkdoll .10 .25
59 Dale Earnhardt 's Car .50 1.25
60 Ernie Irvan .25 .60
61 Mark Martin's Car .20 .50
62 Geoff Bodine's Car .05 .10
63 Bobby Hamilton's Car .05 .15
64A Dorsey Schroeder's Car ERR .05 .15
crew chief Junior Dunlavey
64B Dorsey Schroeder's Car COR .05 .15
crew chief Junie Dunlavey
65 Jimmy Spencer's Car .05 .15
66 Geoff Bodine .10 .25
67A Hut Stricklin .10 .25
pictured in Chevy hat
67B Hut Stricklin .10 .25
pictured without Chevy hat
68 Mickey Gibbs .10 .25
69 Wally Dallenbach Jr. .10 .25
70 Ted Musgrave .15 .40
71 Mark Martin .50 1.25
72 Larry Pearson .10 .25
73 Greg Sacks .10 .25
74 Phil Parsons .10 .25
75 Rick Wilson .10 .25
76 Dick Trickle's Car .05 .10
77 Greg Sacks' Car .05 .10
78 Ted Musgrave's Car .05 .15
79 Junior Johnson .15 .40
80 Tony Glover .10 .25
81 Tim Brewer .10 .25
82 Sterling Marlin .25 .60
83 Jeff Hammond .15 .40
84 Leonard Wood .10 .25
85 Andy Petree .10 .25
86 Robin Pemberton .10 .25
87 Robbie Loomis .15 .40
88 Buddy Baker .15 .40
89 J.D.McDuffie w/Car .10 .25
90 Steve Hmiel .10 .25
91 Jimmy Makar .10 .25
92 Michael Waltrip's Transporter .07 .20
93 Darrell Waltrip .25 .60
94 Ricky Rudd .25 .60
95 Ernie Irvan .25 .60
96 Mark Martin .50 1.25
97 Darrell Waltrip .25 .60
98 Ken Schrader .15 .40
99 Rusty Wallace .40 1.00
100 Alan Kulwicki .30 .75
101 Geoff Bodine .10 .25
102 Michael Waltrip .20 .50
103 Hut Stricklin .10 .25
104 Ken Schrader .15 .40
105 Dale Jarrett .40 1.00
106 Jim Sauter .10 .25
107 Rusty Wallace's Car .15 .40
108 Ernie Irvan's Car .10 .25
109 Ricky Rudd's Car .10 .25
110 Hut Stricklin's Car .05 .10
111 Michael Waltrip's Car .07 .20
112 Harry Gant's Car .10 .25
113 Kyle Petty's Car .12 .30
114 Richard Petty's Car .20 .50
115 Rusty Wallace .40 1.00
116 Terry Labonte's Car .10 .25
117 Stanley Smith .10 .25
118 Eddie Dickerson RC .15 .40
119 Doug Williams .10 .25
120 Donnie Wingo .10 .25
121 Steve Loyd .10 .25
122 David Ifft .10 .25
123 Dick Trickle's Transporter .05 .10
124 Richard Petty's Transporter .20 .50
125 Ward Burton .15 .40
126 Morgan Shepherd .15 .40
127 Todd Bodine .10 .25
128 Jeff Gordon 1.50 4.00
129 Bill Ingle .10 .25
130A Waddell Wilson ERR .10 .25
reads joined WC in 1979
130B Waddell Wilson COR .10 .25
reads joined WC in 1963
131 Doug Richert .10 .25
132 Dale Inman .10 .25
133 Ricky Rudd .25 .60
134 Morgan Shepherd .15 .40
135 Jeff Burton .20 .50
136 Tommy Ellis .10 .25
137 Allen Bestwick .15 .40
138 Barry Dodson .10 .25
139 Bobby Hamilton's Trans. .05 .15
140 Beth Bruce .15 .40
Ms.Winston RC
141 Bill Venturini .10 .25
142 Bob Johnson .10 .25
143 Bob Rahilly .10 .25
144 Bobby Allison .20 .50
145 Bobby Dotter .10 .25
146 Brett Bodine .10 .25
147 Buddy Parrott .10 .25
148 Butch Miller .10 .25
149 Cale Yarborough .25 .60
150 Rick Mast's Car .05 .10
151 Cecil Gordon
152 Alan Kulwicki's Car .12 .30
153 Chad Little .15 .40
154 Dick Trickle's Car .05 .10
155 Ted Musgrave's Car .05 .15
156 Brett Bodine's Car .05 .10
157 Chuck Bown .10 .25
158 Chad Little's Car .05 .15
159 Chuck Rider .10 .25
160 Morgan Shepherd's Car .05 .15
161 Dale Earnhardt 1.25 3.00
162 Sterling Marlin's Car .10 .25
163 Danny Myers .10 .25
164A David Fuge ERR .15 .40
wrong photo, wearing mustache
164B David Fuge COR .15 .40
correct photo, wearing beard RC
165 Ken Schrader's Car .05 .15
166 Dave Rezendes .10 .25
167 David Evans .10 .25
168 Dick Brooks .10 .25
169A Felix Sabates ERR .15 .40
back reads car #43
169B Felix Sabates COR .15 .40
back reads car #42
170 Gene Roberts RC .15 .40
171 Jack Pennington .10 .25
172 Dale Earnhardt's Transporter .50 1.25
173 Ken Wilson .10 .25
174 Sterling Marlin's Transporter .10 .25
175 Renee White .15 .40
Ms.Winston RC
176 Rodney Combs .10 .25
177 Sterling Marlin .25 .60
178 Michael Waltrip's Car .07 .20
179 Winston Kelley .10 .25
180 Brett Bodine .10 .25
181 Wally Dallenbach Jr.'s Car .05 .10
182 Dale Earnhardt 1.25 3.00
183 Davey Allison .40 1.00
184 Mark Martin's Transporter .20 .50
185 Donnie Richeson RC .15 .40
186 Eddie Wood .15 .40
Len Wood
187 Eli Gold .10 .25
188 Red Farmer .10 .25
Tommy Allison Jr
189 Gary Nelson .10 .25
190 Harry Gant .25 .60
191 Jack Ingram .15 .40
192 Jay Smith RC .15 .40
193 Phil Parsons' Transporter .05 .10
194 Joey Knuckles .10 .25
Ryan Pemberton
195 L.D. Ottinger .10 .25
196 Mark Cronquist RC
197 Elton Sawyer .15 .40
Patty Moise
198 Mike Beam .10 .25
199 Neil Bonnett .25 .60
200 Butch Mock .10 .25
Bob Rahilly
Dick Trickle's Car
201 Paul Andrews .10 .25
202 Ernie Irvan's Transporter .10 .25
203 Robert Yates .15 .40
204 Richard Broome .10 .25
205 Wally Dallenbach Jr.'s Trans. .05 .10
206 Tracy Leslie .10 .25
207 Will Lind .10 .25
208 Barney Hall .10 .25
209 Darrell Waltrip's Car .10 .25
210 Danny Lawrence .10 .25
211 Davey Allison .40 1.00
212 Dennis Connor .10 .25
213 Dick Rahilly RC .15 .40
214 Gary DeHart RC .15 .40
215 Neil Bonnett .25 .60
Buddy Baker
Mike Joy
Announcers
216 James Hylton .10
217 Jimmy Fennig .10
218 Jimmy Horton .10
219 Keith Almond .10
220 Marc Reno RC .15
221 Shelton Pittman .10
222 Brett Bodine's Transporter .05
223 Davey Allison w/Crew .40
224 Dale Earnhardt w/Crew 1.25
225 Geoff Bodine's Transporter .05
226 Walter Smith RC .15
227 NASCAR Softball Team .05
228 Troy Beebe .10
229 Davey Allison 's Car .15
230 David Green RC .30
231 Dewey Livengood RC .15
232 Ed Berrier .10
233 Eddie Lanier .10
234 Irv Hoerr RC .15
235 Jim Phillips .10
236 Larry McReynolds .15
237 Joe Moore .10
238 Jimmy Means' Transporter .05
239 David Smith .10
240 Morgan Shepherd's Pit Crew .15
241 Harry Gant DOY .25
242 Mark Martin Busch Pole .50
243 Larry McReynolds .15
244 Tom Peck .10
245 Darrell Waltrip's Transporter .10
246 Travis Carter .10
247 Morgan Shepherd's Trans. .05
248A Walter Bud Moore ERR .10
Paul on front
248B Walter Bud Moore COR .10
Walter on front
NNO Dale Earnhardt HOLO 25.00 6
5000 White
NNO Dale Earnhardt HOLO 25.00 6
5000 Black

1992 Pro Set Legend

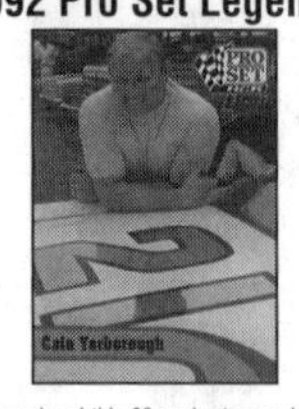

Pro Set produced this 32-card set as an inser its 1992 Winston Cup Racing packs. The c seemed to have been produced in the s quantities as the regular issue and are often together as a set. Dick Hutcherson's card (nu L4) contains a wrong photo that was later correc

COMPLETE SET (32) 2.00
L1 Buck Baker .10
L2 Fred Lorenzen .10
L3 Ned Jarrett .10
L4A Dick Hutcherson ERR .15
photo of Johnny Rutherford
L4B Dick Hutcherson COR .15
correct photo
L5 Coo Coo Marlin .07
L6 Paul Bud Moore .07
L7 Donnie Allison .10
L8 Marvin Panch .07
L9 Neil Castles (Soapy) .07
L10 Maurice Petty .10
L11 Tim Flock .07
L12 Smokey Yunick .07
L13 Larry Frank .07
L14 Cotton Owens .07
L15 Ralph Moody Jr. .07
L16 Bob Welborn .07
L17 Marilyn Green .07
L18 Edwin Matthews (Banjo) .07
L19 Sam McQuagg .07
L20 Jim Paschal .07
L21 David Pearson .10
L22 Tom Pistone .07
L23 Jack Smith .07
L24 Charles Ellington .07
L25 Pete Hamilton .07
L26 Rex White .07
L27 Elmo Langley .07
L28 Benny Parsons .10
L29 Harold Kinder .07
L30 Cale Yarborough .10
L31 Junior Johnson .10
L32 Bobby Allison .20

1992 Pro Set Maxwe House

Pro Set produced this 30-card set for Ma House. The cards were distributed in six-card through Maxwell House filter packs. There we different title cards available in those packs. Ar to obtain a complete set at $5.00 with 2 pro purchase or $15.00 without the POPs was included in the promotion. The set features d from the top NASCAR teams with a special emp on Sterling Marlin and the Maxwell House R Team. The first 100 people who responded mail-in offer received a special set of autographed by Sterling Marlin or Junior Johns

COMPLETE SET (30) 3.00
1 Title Card .08
2 Sterling Marlin .15

terling Marlin .15 .40
unior Johnson .08 .25
terling Marlin's Car .08 .25
terling Marlin's Transporter .08 .25
ike Beam .08 .25
terling Marlin's Car .08 .25
icky Rudd .15 .40
Davey Allison .40 1.00
Harry Gant .15 .40
Ernie Irvan .15 .40
Mark Martin .60 1.50
Darrell Waltrip .15 .40
Ken Schrader .08 .25
Rusty Wallace .60 1.50
Morgan Shepherd .08 .25
Alan Kulwicki .25 .60
Geoff Bodine .08 .25
Michael Waltrip .15 .40
Hut Stricklin .08 .25
Dale Jarrett .50 1.25
Terry Labonte .30 .75
Brett Bodine .08 .25
Richard Petty .25 .60
Kyle Petty .15 .40
Jimmy Spencer .08 .25
Rick Mast .08 .25
Wally Dallenbach Jr. .08 .25
Sterling Marlin w/Car .15 .40

1992 Pro Set Racing Club

rds from this set were issued over the course of 1992 and 1993 race seasons and distributed to mbers of the Pro Set Racing Club. The cards lude an RCC prefix on the numbers and feature vers and events from both NASCAR Winston Cup NHRA racing. Finish Line's Racing Club also ributed the cards in complete set form.

MPLETE SET (8) 6.00 15.00
Kenny Bernstein's Car 301.70 MPH .75 2.00
Charlotte Motor Speedway One Hot Night .50 1.25
Clifford Allison 1.25 3.00
Clifford Allison In Memorium 1.25 3.00
oe Amato Cruz Pedregon Warren Johnson 1992 Champions .75 2.00
Richard Petty's Car The King's Last Race .75 2.00
Fastest NHRA Drivers Pat Austin Kenny Bernstein Doug Herbert Don Prudhomme Joe Amato Scott Kalitta Rance McDaniel .50 1.25
he Winston 1993 .50 1.25

1992 Pro Set Rudy Farms

Set produced this 20-card set for Rudy Farms es. The cards were distributed in Rudy Farms ndwiches via a 3-card cello packs. The set ures cards from the regular issue Pro Set release have been re-numbered. The five card Legends es is considered part of the 20-card regular set. Legends cards are numbered 1-5. We have ed the L prefix to make it easier to read. An um was also produced for distribution with nplete sets. The 5 card Legends set was also ilable through a proofs-of-purchase mail-in offer n R.B Rice sausage.

MPLETE SET (20) 18.00 30.00
. RICE SET (5) 3.00 8.00
icky Rudd .75 2.00
avey Allison 1.00 2.50
arry Gant .75 2.00
rnie Irvan .75 2.00
lark Martin 1.50 4.00
terling Marlin .75 2.00
arrell Waltrip .75 2.00
en Schrader .40 1.00
usty Wallace 1.50 4.00
Morgan Shepherd .40 1.00
Alan Kulwicki .75 2.00
Geoff Bodine .40 1.00
Michael Waltrip .40 1.00
Kyle Petty .75 2.00
Richard Petty 1.00 2.50
Ned Jarrett .40 1.00
David Pearson .40 1.00
Cale Yarborough .75 2.00
Junior Johnson .40 1.00
Bobby Allison .75 2.00

1992 Pro Set Tic Tac Hut Stricklin

Pro Set produced this 6-card set for Tic Tac. The cards were distributed in 2-card cello packs through Tic Tac four packs. The set focuses on Hut Stricklin and the associate sponsored Tic Tac Racing Team.

COMPLETE SET (6) 2.00 4.00
1 Hut Stricklin .40 1.00
2 Bobby Allison .40 1.00
3 Jimmy Fennig .20 .50
4 Keith Almond .20 .50
5 Hut Stricklin's Car .20 .50
6 Hut Stricklin .40 1.00

1994 Quality Care Glidden/Speed

Ford produced this set as a continuation of their Motorcraft Racing issues released previously. Unlike the red colored Motorcraft cards, this set is designed primarily in blue to follow the paint scheme of the Quality Care Racing Teams. Lake Speed and Bob Glidden are the two featured drivers. The cards are unnumbered and listed alphabetically below.

COMPLETE SET (10) 2.50 6.00
1 Bob Glidden .40 1.00
2 Bob Glidden's Car .25 .50
3 Bob Glidden's Car .25 .50
4 Walter Bud Moore .25 .50
5 Lake Speed's Pit Crew .25 .50
6 Lake Speed .40 1.00
7 Lake Speed's Car .25 .50
8 Lake Speed's Car .25 .50
9 Lake Speed's Car Bob Glidden's Car .25 .50
10 Cover Card .25 .50

1996 Racer's Choice

This 110-card set was the first time Pinnacle issued a set under the Racer's Choice brand name. The black bordered cards feature top Winston Cup stars and their cars. The cards were packaged eight cards per pack; 36 packs per box and 20 boxes per case. Suggested retail price on a pack was 99 cents. Also randomly inserted in the bottom of hobby boxes was a 5" X 7" Jeff Gordon 1995 Championship card. The card features the dufex printing technology and could be found one in every three boxes. It is priced at the end of the base set listing.

COMPLETE SET (110) 6.00 15.00
WAX BOX HOBBY 20.00 40.00
WAX BOX RETAIL 15.00 30.00
1 Rick Mast .05 .15
2 Rusty Wallace .50 1.25
3 Dale Earnhardt 1.00 2.50
4 Sterling Marlin .20 .50
5 Terry Labonte .20 .50
6 Mark Martin .50 1.25
7 Ward Burton .10 .30
8 Joe Nemechek .05 .15
9 Jeff Gordon .60 1.50
10 Ted Musgrave .05 .15
11 Michael Waltrip .10 .30
12 Johnny Benson, Jr. .10 .30
13 Bill Elliott .25 .60
14 Bobby Labonte .40 1.00
15 Ricky Rudd .20 .50
16 Dale Jarrett .40 1.00
17 Bobby Hamilton .05 .15
18 Ken Schrader .05 .15
19 Derrike Cope .05 .15
20 Brett Bodine .05 .15
21 Darrell Waltrip .10 .30
22 John Andretti .05 .15
23 Jeremy Mayfield .10 .30
24 Ernie Irvan .10 .30
25 Lake Speed .05 .15
26 Rusty Wallace's Car .10 .30
27 Dale Earnhardt's Car .40 1.00
28 Sterling Marlin's Car .05 .15
29 Terry Labonte's Car .10 .30
30 Mark Martin's Car .10 .30
31 Jimmy Spencer's Car .02 .10
32 Dale Jarrett's Car .10 .30
33 Ricky Rudd's Car .05 .15
34 Derrike Cope's Car .02 .10
35 Ward Burton's Car .02 .10
36 Ted Musgrave's Car .02 .10
37 Darrell Waltrip's Car .05 .15
38 Bobby Labonte's Car .10 .30
39 Michael Waltrip w/Car .05 .15
40 Jeff Gordon's Car .25 .60
41 Ernie Irvan's Car .05 .15
42 Johnny Benson, Jr.'s Car .02 .10
43 Brett Bodine's Car .02 .10
44 Ricky Craven's Car .02 .10
45 Bobby Hamilton's Car .02 .10
46 Morgan Shepherd's Car .02 .10
47 Joe Nemechek's Car .02 .10
48 Bill Elliott's Car .10 .30
49 Jeremy Mayfield's Car .10 .30
50 John Andretti's Car .02 .10
51 Jeff Gordon WCC .30 .75
52 Jeff Gordon WCC .30 .75
53 Jeff Gordon WCC .30 .75
54 Jeff Gordon WCC .30 .75
55 Jeff Gordon WCC Danielle Randall Jim Brochhausen .30 .75
56 Dale Earnhardt I Don Hawk .50 1.25
57 Dale Earnhardt I .50 1.25
58 Dale Earnhardt I .50 1.25
59 Dale Earnhardt I .50 1.25
60 Dale Earnhardt I .50 1.25
61 Ted Musgrave HC .02 .10
62 Ted Musgrave HC Howard Comstock .02 .10
63 Ted Musgrave HC Brittany Musgrave .02 .10
64 Ted Musgrave HC .02 .10
65 Ted Musgrave HC .02 .10
66 Bobby Labonte OF .10 .30
67 Bobby Labonte OF .10 .30
68 Bobby Labonte OF Donna Labonte .10 .30
69 Bobby Labonte OF .10 .30
70 Bobby Labonte OF .10 .30
71 Sterling Marlin PH .10 .30
72 Sterling Marlin PH Clifton Marlin Paula Marlin Sutherlin Marlin Steadman Marlin .10 .30
73 Sterling Marlin PH .10 .30
74 Sterling Marlin PH Tony Glover .10 .30
75 Sterling Marlin PH .10 .30
76 John Andretti's Car .02 .10
77 Joe Nemechek's Car .02 .10
78 Michael Waltrip's Car .05 .15
79 Doyle Ford .02 .10
80 Jimmy Cox .02 .10
81 Elmo Langley .02 .10
82 Rusty Wallace RW .25 .60
83 Jeff Gordon RW .30 .75
84 Dale Earnhardt RW .50 1.25
85 Mark Martin RW .25 .60
86 Mark Martin RW .25 .60
87 Ward Burton RW Tabitha Burton Sarah Burton Jeb Burton .02 .10
88 Ricky Rudd RW Linda Rudd .10 .30
89 Dale Earnhardt RW .50 1.25
90 Jeff Gordon BC .30 .75
91 Dale Jarrett BC .10 .30
92 Dale Earnhardt BC .50 1.25
93 Mark Martin BC .25 .60
94 Bobby Labonte BC .10 .30
95 Terry Labonte BC .10 .30
96 Ricky Rudd BC .10 .30
97 Ken Schrader BC .02 .10
98 Bill Elliott BC .10 .30
99 Sterling Marlin BC .10 .30
100 John Andretti BC .02 .10
101 Rick Mast BC .02 .10
102 Ted Musgrave BC .02 .10
103 David Green BC .02 .10
104 Hut Stricklin BC .02 .10
105 Darrell Waltrip BC .05 .15
106 Johnny Benson Jr. R .10 .30
107 Johnny Benson Jr. R .10 .30
108 Johnny Benson Jr. R .10 .30
109 Mark Martin CL .25 .60
110 Jeff Gordon CL .30 .75
J52 Jeff Gordon 5x7 2.50 6.00
P9 Jeff Gordon Promo 2.00 5.00
P99 Sterling Marlin Promo .75 2.00

1996 Racer's Choice Artist's Proofs

The 110-card Artist's Proof set is a parallel to the base set. Each card features copper foil and an Artist's Proof logo to differentiate them from the base cards. The cards were seeded one per 35 regular packs and one per 17 jumbo packs.

COMPLETE SET (110) 125.00 250.00
*ARTIST PROOFS: 10X TO 25X BASE CARDS

1996 Racer's Choice Speedway Collection

The 110-card Speedway Collection set is a parallel to the base set. The cards feature silver foil and a Speedway Collection logo to differentiate them from the base cards. The cards were inserted one per six regular packs and one per three jumbo packs.

COMPLETE SET (110) 15.00 40.00
*SPEEDWAY COLL: 1.5X TO 4X BASE CARDS

1996 Racer's Choice Top Ten

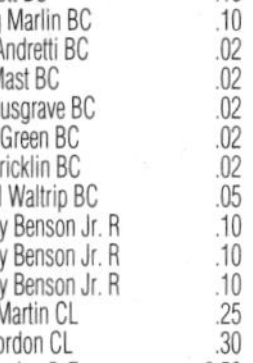

This 10-card insert set features the drivers who finished in the Top Ten in the 1995 Winston Cup points standings. The cards were printed on foil board and use micro-etched highlights. Top Ten cards were randomly inserted in packs at a rate of one in 69 regular packs and of one in 35 jumbo packs.

COMPLETE SET (10) 60.00 125.00
1 Jeff Gordon 12.50 30.00
2 Dale Earnhardt 20.00 50.00
3 Sterling Marlin 4.00 10.00
4 Mark Martin 10.00 25.00
5 Rusty Wallace 10.00 25.00
6 Terry Labonte 4.00 10.00
7 Ted Musgrave 1.25 3.00
8 Bill Elliott 5.00 12.00
9 Ricky Rudd 4.00 10.00
10 Bobby Labonte 8.00 20.00
P2 Dale Earnhardt Promo 4.00 10.00

1996 Racer's Choice Up Close with Dale Earnhardt

This 7-card insert set could be found in hobby only packs. The cards feature Winston Cup great Dale Earnhardt. The cards were randomly inserted in hobby packs at a rate of one in 31.

COMPLETE SET (7) 15.00 40.00
DALE EARNHARDT CARD (1-7) 2.50 6.00

1996 Racer's Choice Up Close with Jeff Gordon

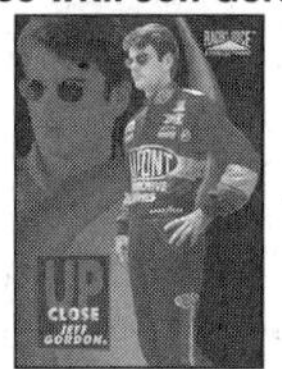

This 7-card insert set features 1995 Winston Cup Champion Jeff Gordon. The cards were seeded in retail packs at a rate of one in 31.

COMPLETE SET (7) 12.00 30.00
JEFF GORDON CARD (1-7) 2.00 5.00

1996 Racer's Choice Sundrop

One card was inserted in each specially marked 12-packs of Sundrop citrus soda. The cards come in an opaque wrapper attached to the cardboard packaging of the 12-packs. There were signed copies of each of the three cards also randomly inserted in the soft drink packages. The autographed cards were not certified in any way and are otherwise indistinguishable from the unsigned regular cards. Many dealers have left the signed cards in the opaque wrappers to distinguish the origin of the card.

COMPLETE SET (3) 6.00 15.00
COMMON CARD (SD1-SD3) 2.00 5.00

1997 Racer's Choice

This 106-card set was produced by Pinnacle Brands. The white bordered cards feature the top Winston Cup stars and their cars. Cards were distributed in eight card packs with 36 pack in a box. The packs carried a suggested retail price of $.99.

COMPLETE SET (106) 6.00 15.00
1 Morgan Shepherd .05 .15
2 Rusty Wallace .50 1.25
3 Dale Earnhardt 1.00 2.50
4 Sterling Marlin .20 .50
5 Terry Labonte .20 .50
6 Mark Martin .50 1.25
7 Geoff Bodine .05 .15
8 Hut Stricklin .05 .15
9 Chad Little .10 .30
10 Ricky Rudd .20 .50
11 Brett Bodine .05 .15
12 Derrike Cope .05 .15
13 Jeremy Mayfield .10 .30
14 Robby Gordon RC .20 .50
15 Steve Grissom .05 .15
16 Ted Musgrave .05 .15
17 Darrell Waltrip .10 .30
18 Bobby Labonte .40 1.00
19 John Andretti .05 .15
20 Bobby Hamilton .05 .15
21 Michael Waltrip .10 .30
22 Ward Burton .10 .30
23 Jimmy Spencer .05 .15
24 Jeff Gordon .60 1.50
25 Ricky Craven .05 .15
26 Kyle Petty .10 .30
27 Dale Earnhardt 1.00 2.50
28 Ernie Irvan .10 .30
29 Joe Nemechek .05 .15
30 Johnny Benson .10 .30
31 Mike Skinner .05 .15
32 Dale Jarrett .40 1.00
33 Ken Schrader .05 .15
34 Bill Elliott .25 .60
35 David Green .05 .15
36 Morgan Shepherd's Car .02 .10
37 Rusty Wallace's Car .10 .30
38 Dale Earnhardt's Car .40 1.00
39 Sterling Marlin's Car .05 .15
40 Terry Labonte's Car .10 .30
41 Mark Martin's Car .10 .30
42 Geoff Bodine's Car .02 .10
43 Hut Stricklin's Car .02 .10
44 Chad Little's Car .02 .10
45 Ricky Rudd's Car .05 .15
46 Brett Bodine's Car .02 .10
47 Derrike Cope's Car .02 .10
48 Jeremy Mayfield's Car .02 .10
49 Robby Gordon's Car .10 .30
50 Steve Grissom's Car .02 .10
51 Ted Musgrave's Car .02 .10
52 Darrell Waltrip's Car .02 .10
53 Bobby Labonte's Car .10 .30
54 John Andretti's Car .02 .10
55 Bobby Hamilton's Car .02 .10
56 Michael Waltrip's Car .05 .15
57 Ward Burton's Car .02 .10
58 Jimmy Spencer's Car .02 .10
59 Geoff Bodine's Car .02 .10
60 Ricky Craven's Car .02 .10
61 Kyle Petty's Car .02 .10
62 Dale Earnhardt's Car .40 1.00
63 Ernie Irvan's Car .02 .10
64 Joe Nemechek's Car .02 .10
65 Johnny Benson's Car .02 .10
66 Mike Skinner's Car .02 .10
67 Dale Jarrett's Car .10 .30
68 Ken Schrader's Car .02 .10
69 Bill Elliott's Car .10 .30
70 David Green's Car .02 .10
71 Gary Nelson SS .02 .10
72 Robert Yates SS .02 .10
73 Robin Pemberton SS .02 .10
74 Kyle Petty SS .10 .30
75 Geoff Bodine SS .05 .15
76 Earl Barban SS .02 .10
77 Jeremy Mayfield SS .10 .30
78 Steve Grissom SS .05 .15
79 Mike Skinner SS .05 .15
80 Richard Childress SS .10 .30
81 Chocolate Meyers SS .02 .10
82 Ward Burton SS .10 .30
83 Chad Little SS .10 .30
84 Buddy Parrott SS .02 .10
85 Jimmy Cox SS .02 .10
86 Richard Petty SS .05 .15
87 Mike Skinner R .05 .15
88 David Green R .05 .15
89 Robby Gordon R .10 .30
90 Dale Earnhardt TR .50 1.25
91 Rusty Wallace TR .25 .60
92 Sterling Marlin TR .05 .15
93 Terry Labonte TR .10 .30
94 Mark Martin TR .25 .60
95 Ricky Rudd TR .10 .30
96 Ted Musgrave TR .05 .15
97 Johnny Benson TR .10 .30
98 Bobby Labonte TR .20 .50
99 Bobby Hamilton TR .05 .15
100 Michael Waltrip TR .10 .30
101 Ward Burton TR .10 .30
102 Ricky Craven TR .05 .15
103 Ernie Irvan TR .10 .30
104 Dale Earnhardt TR .50 1.25
105 Dale Jarrett TR .20 .50
106 Dale Earnhardt CL .50 1.25
P5 Terry Labonte Promo 1.00 2.50

1997 Racer's Choice Showcase Series

The 106-card Showcase Series is a parallel to the base set. The cards feature silver foil to differentiate them from the base cards. The cards were randomly inserted in packs at a ratio of 1:7.

COMPLETE SET (106) 40.00 80.00
*SHOWCASE SERIES: 2.5X TO 6X BASE CARDS

1997 Racer's Choice Busch Clash

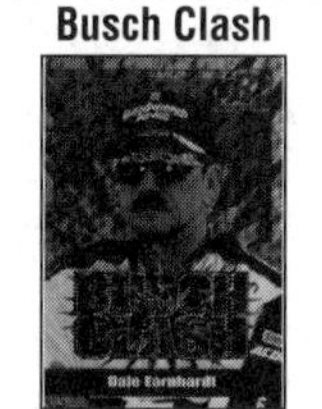

This 14-card insert highlights those NASCAR drivers who have appeared in the Busch Clash. The cards were randomly inserted in hobby packs at a ratio of 1:47 and in magazine packs at a ratio of 1:23.

COMPLETE SET (14) 50.00 120.00
1 Dale Earnhardt 12.50 30.00
2 Terry Labonte 2.50 6.00
3 Johnny Benson 1.50 4.00
4 Ward Burton 1.50 4.00
5 Mark Martin 6.00 15.00
6 Ricky Craven .75 2.00
7 Ernie Irvan 1.50 4.00
8 Jeff Gordon 8.00 20.00
9 Ted Musgrave .75 2.00
10 Jeremy Mayfield 1.50 4.00
11 Dale Earnhardt 12.50 30.00
12 Dale Jarrett 5.00 12.00
13 Bobby Labonte 5.00 12.00
14 Rusty Wallace 6.00 15.00

1997 Racer's Choice Chevy Madness

This 6-card set is the continuation of the set that started in 1997 Action Packed and ended in 1997 Pinnacle. The cards were randomly inserted in hobby packs at a ratio of 1:17 and in magazine packs at a ratio of 1:8.

COMPLETE SET (6) 12.50 30.00
7 Jeff Gordon 4.00 10.00
8 Dale Earnhardt 6.00 15.00
9 Ricky Craven .40 1.00
10 Robby Gordon 1.25 3.00
11 Jeff Green .40 1.00
12 Terry Labonte 1.25 3.00

1997 Racer's Choice High Octane

This 15-card set features the top 15 drivers from the Winston Cup circuit. The cards were randomly inserted in hobby packs at a ratio of 1:23 and in magazine packs at a ratio of 1:12.

COMPLETE SET (15) 50.00 100.00
COMP.GLOW SET (15) 100.00 200.00
*GLOW: .6X TO 1.5X BASIC INSERTS
1 Terry Labonte 2.50 6.00
2 Dale Earnhardt 10.00 25.00
3 Jeff Gordon 6.00 15.00
4 Dale Jarrett 4.00 10.00
5 Mark Martin 5.00 12.00
6 Rusty Wallace 5.00 12.00
7 Bill Elliott 3.00 8.00
8 Bobby Labonte 4.00 10.00
9 Ernie Irvan 1.50 4.00
10 Kyle Petty 1.50 4.00
11 Ricky Rudd 2.00 5.00
12 Johnny Benson 1.50 4.00
13 Ward Burton 1.25 3.00
14 Ted Musgrave 1.00 2.50
15 Dale Earnhardt 10.00 25.00

1997 Race Sharks

This 45-card set is another uniquely themed set from Wheels. The cards feature the top names in racing. The cards are printed on 36 point paper. Each card has a wave like background and is stamped in silver foil. The cards were packaged three cards per pack, 24 packs per box and 16 boxes per case. There were a total of 1250 numbered cases. The first 375 cases off the press had the First Bite logo stamped on all the cards in those cases.

COMPLETE SET (45) 5.00 12.00
1 Dale Earnhardt 1.25 3.00
2 Jeff Gordon .75 2.00
3 Dale Jarrett .50 1.25
4 Terry Labonte .25 .60
5 Rusty Wallace .60 1.50
6 Mark Martin .60 1.50
7 Sterling Marlin .25 .60
8 Bill Elliott .30 .75
9 Bobby Labonte .50 1.25
10 Bobby Hamilton .07 .20
11 Darrell Waltrip .15 .40
12 Michael Waltrip .15 .40
13 Mike Wallace .07 .20
14 Kyle Petty .15 .40
15 Ken Schrader .07 .20
16 Ricky Craven .07 .20
17 Derrike Cope .07 .20
18 Jeff Burton .25 .60
19 Ward Burton .15 .40
20 Robert Pressley .07 .20
21 Joe Nemechek .07 .20
22 Brett Bodine .07 .20
23 Jimmy Spencer .07 .20
24 Chad Little .07 .20
25 Bobby Labonte .50 1.25
26 Terry Labonte .25 .60
27 Mark Martin .60 1.50
28 Jeff Green .07 .20
29 David Green .07 .20
30 Dale Jarrett .50 1.25
31 Joe Gibbs .15 .40
32 Richard Childress .15 .40
33 Bobby Allison .07 .20
34 Dale Jarrett .50 1.25
35 Jeff Gordon .75 2.00
36 Jeff Gordon .75 2.00
37 Rusty Wallace .60 1.50

38 Sterling Marlin	.25	.60
39 Rusty Wallace	.60	1.50
40 Jeff Gordon	.75	2.00
41 Dale Jarrett	.50	1.25
42 Rusty Wallace	.60	1.50
43 Jeff Gordon	.75	2.00
44 Checklist	.02	.10
45 Checklist	.02	.10
P1 Jeff Gordon Promo	2.50	6.00

1997 Race Sharks First Bite

The First Bite parallels were issued in the first 375-cases of the basic issue Race Sharks product. Each card was stamped with a special "First Bite" logo on the fronts.

COMP.FIRST BITE SET (45)	6.00	15.00
*FIRST BITE: .6X TO 1.5X BASE CARDS		

1997 Race Sharks Great White

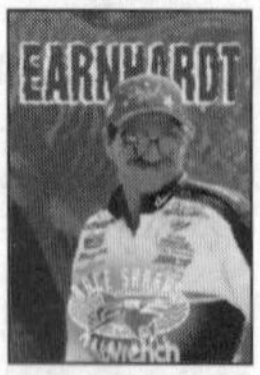

This 45-card set was made available through a redemption program using letter cards inserted in Race Sharks packs. Each card is a parallel of the base cards along with a "Great White" logo.

COMPLETE SET (45)	15.00	40.00
*GREAT WHITE: 1.2X TO 3X BASE CARDS		

1997 Race Sharks Hammerhead

This 45-card set is a parallel to the base Race Sharks set. The cards are die-cut in a hammerhead shape to keep with the theme. There were 1350 of each card produced and odds of pulling one out of a pack were one in eight packs. There is also a First Bite version of the Hammerhead parallel. These cards were inserted one in eight First Bite packs.

COMPLETE SET (45)	40.00	80.00
*HAMMERHEAD: 2.5X TO 6X BASIC CARDS		

1997 Race Sharks Hammerhead First Bite

The First Bite parallels were issued in the first 375-cases of the basic issue Race Sharks product. Each card was stamped with a special "First Bite" logo on the fronts. Stated odds were 1:8 packs.

COMP.FIRST BITE (45)	50.00	100.00
*FIRST BITE: .5X TO 1.2X HAMMERHEAD		

1997 Race Sharks Tiger Shark

This 45-card set is the toughest level parallel in the Race Sharks brand. The Tiger Shark cards were double foil stamped and micro-etched. There is 675 of each card available. The odds of pulling a Tiger Shark card were one in 16 packs.

COMPLETE SET (45)	60.00	150.00
*TIGER SHARKS: 3X TO 8X BASIC CARDS		

1997 Race Sharks Great White Shark's Teeth

This 10-card insert set features the dominant drivers on the NASCAR circuit. Each card also features a real Shark's tooth embedded in the card. The odds of pulling one of these cards is one in 96 packs. The First Bite versions of the Great White cards featured white sharks teeth as opposed to gray colored sharks teeth on the regular Great Whites.

COMPLETE SET (10)	150.00	300.00
COMP.FIRST BITE (10)	200.00	400.00
*FIRST BITE: .5X TO 1.2X BASIC INSERTS		
GW1 Dale Earnhardt	40.00	100.00
GW2 Jeff Gordon	25.00	60.00
GW3 Terry Labonte	8.00	20.00
GW4 Dale Jarrett	15.00	40.00
GW5 Rusty Wallace	20.00	50.00
GW6 Mark Martin	20.00	50.00
GW7 Bobby Labonte	15.00	40.00
GW8 Bill Elliott	10.00	25.00
GW9 Sterling Marlin	8.00	20.00
GW10 Ricky Craven	2.50	6.00

1997 Race Sharks Shark Attack

Just when you thought it was safe to go back into your favorite hobby store. That was the slogan Wheels used to promote their Race Sharks product. The 10-card Shark Attack set featured micro-etched cards and a simulated embossed shark's tooth. The cards were randomly seeded one in 48 packs.

COMPLETE SET (10)	60.00	120.00
COMP.FIRST BITE (10)	75.00	150.00
*FIRST BITE: .5X TO 1.2X SHARK ATTACK		
COMP.FB PREVIEW (10)	10.00	25.00
*FB PREVIEWS: .1X TO .2X SHARK ATTACK		
SA1 Dale Earnhardt	15.00	40.00
SA2 Jeff Gordon	10.00	25.00
SA3 Dale Jarrett	6.00	15.00
SA4 Rusty Wallace	8.00	20.00
SA5 Terry Labonte	3.00	8.00
SA6 Sterling Marlin	3.00	8.00
SA7 Michael Waltrip	2.00	5.00
SA8 Kyle Petty	2.00	5.00
SA9 Ward Burton	2.00	5.00
SA10 Jeff Burton	3.00	8.00

1997 Race Sharks Shark Tooth Signatures

This 25-card set features autographs of Winston Cup and Busch Grand National drivers, crew chiefs, owners and other racing personalities. The cards were inserted one per 24 packs.

COMPLETE SET (25)	300.00	600.00
COMP.FIRST BITE (25)	500.00	1000.00
*FIRST BITE: .5X TO 1.2X BASIC AUTOS		
FIRST BITE PRINT RUN 400 SER.#'d SETS		
ST1 Dale Earnhardt/300	200.00	300.00
ST2 Jeff Gordon/400	50.00	100.00
ST3 Dale Jarrett	12.50	30.00
ST4 Terry Labonte	12.50	30.00
ST5 Sterling Marlin/600	12.50	30.00
ST6 Bill Elliott/600	15.00	40.00
ST7 Ricky Craven	6.00	15.00
ST8 Robert Pressley	6.00	15.00
ST9 Jeff Burton	8.00	20.00
ST10 Ward Burton	8.00	20.00
ST11 Bobby Labonte/800	12.50	30.00
ST12 Joe Nemechek/800	6.00	15.00
ST13 Chad Little	6.00	15.00
ST14 David Green	6.00	15.00
ST15 Jeff Green	6.00	15.00
ST16 Joe Gibbs	20.00	50.00
ST17 Todd Parrott	6.00	15.00
ST18 Jeff Hammond	6.00	15.00
ST19 Charlie Pressley	3.00	6.00
ST20 Joey Knuckles	3.00	6.00
ST21 David Smith	3.00	6.00
ST22 Brad Parrott	6.00	15.00
ST23 Eddie Dickerson	3.00	6.00
ST24 Randy Dorton/1200	6.00	15.00
ST25 Jimmy Johnson	3.00	6.00

1997 Race Sharks Tiger Shark First Bite

The First Bite parallels were issued in the first 375-cases of the basic issue Race Sharks product. Each card was stamped with a special "First Bite" logo on the fronts. Stated odds were 1:16 packs.

COMP.FIRST BITE (45)	100.00	200.00
*FIRST BITE: .5X TO 1.2X TIGER SHARK		

1991 Racing Concepts Shawna Robinson

This nine-card set features one of the most popular female drivers ever to race NASCAR, Shawna Robinson. The set was distributed through Sparky's and were originally sold with cards 1-6 and a Sparky's coupon that could be redeemed for one of the cards, 7-9, with purchase.

COMPLETE SET (9)	5.00	12.00
1 Cover Card	.15	.40
2 Shawna Robinson	.60	1.50
3 Shawna Robinson	.60	1.50
4 Shawna Robinson	.60	1.50
5 Shawna Robinson	.60	1.50
6 Shawna Robinson	.60	1.50
Dwight Huffman		
Dennis Combs		
7 Shawna Robinson	.60	1.50
8 Shawna Robinson	.75	2.00
David Pearson		
9 Shawna Robinson	.60	1.50

1992 Redline Graphics Short Track

Redline Graphics produced this set featuring race action scenes from various short track races. The cards primarily picture exciting crashes caught by the photographer.

COMPLETE SET (30)	4.00	8.00
1 Cover Card	.10	.30
Mark Lamoreaux's Car		
Conrad Morgan's Car		
2 Late Model Sandwich	.25	.60
Tom Carlson's Car		
Conrad Morgan's Car		
Jason Keller's Car		
3 Elko Speedway	.10	.30
Brian Johnson's Car		
Bret Berg's Car		
4 Window Shot #1	.10	.30
M.G.Gajewski's Car		
Al Schill's Car		
5 Window Shot #2	.10	.30
M.G.Gajewski's Car		
Al Schill's Car		
6 Veteran and Rookie	.10	.30
Mel Walen's Car		
Tim Johnson's Car		
7 Lift Off	.10	.30
Mark Lamoreaux's Car		
Conrad Morgan's Car		
8 Orbit	.10	.30
Mark Lamoreaux's Car		
Conrad Morgan's Car		
9 Landing	.10	.30
Mark Lamoreaux's Car		
Conrad Morgan's Car		
10 Aftermath	.10	.30
Mark Lamoreaux's Car		
11 Inside Move	.10	.30
Dennis Barta's Car		
Tom Gille's Car		
12 Three Deep	.10	.30
Tom Karnish's Car		
Gary Petrash's Car		
Loren Petrash's Car		
13 Roof Dance	.10	.30
Tom Karnish's Car		
Gary Petrash's Car		
Loren Petrash's Car		
14 The Ride Continues	.10	.30
Tom Karnish's Car		
Gary Petrash's Car		
Loren Petrash's Car		
15 Finally Over	.10	.30
Tom Karnish's Car		
Gary Petrash's Car		
Loren Petrash's Car		
Steve Murgic's Car		
16 Miraculous	.10	.30
Tom Karnish's Car		
Gary Petrash's Car		
Loren Petrash's Car		
17 High Speed Wipeout	.10	.30
Loren Petrash's Car		
18 Front Stretch Mishap	.10	.30
Bruce Lee's Car		
Mike Mohn's Car		
19 Prelude to Defeat	.10	.30
Don Jenkins' Car		
Pete Moore's Car		
20 Oh No!	.20	.50
Rich Bickle's Car		
Don Jenkins' Car		
Pete Moore's Car		
21 Fabulous Race	.20	.50
Rich Bickle's Car		
Mike Garvey's Car		
22 Raceway Park	.10	.30
Doug Balombini's Car		
Christian Elder's Car		
23 Champion	.10	.30
Mike Tuma's Car		
Steve Fredrickson's Car		
24 Hobby Crash	.10	.30
Danny Hron's Car		
25 Show Car	.20	.50
Mike Mohn w/Car		
26 Parking Lot	.10	.30
multi-car crash		
27 Ouch!	.10	.30
Ken Reiser's Car		
28 Father and Son	.20	.50
Steve Murgic's Car		
Mike Murgic's Car		
29 Infamous Turn Four	.10	.30
Robbie Reiser's Car		
30 Checklist Card	.10	.30

1992 Redline Racing Harry Gant

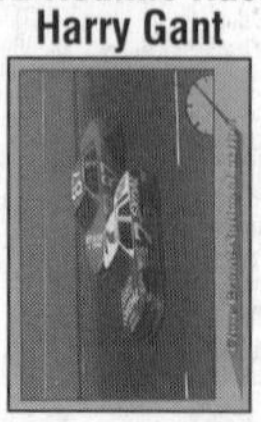

This set is one of four issues produced in 1992 by Redline Racing entitled My Life in Racing. The set focuses on the life of Harry Gant with text written in story form on the cardbacks. The four driver sets were packaged together in factory set form 24-sets per display box. Each set includes a colorful factory box and was limited to a production run of 25,000.

COMP. FACT SET (30)	3.00	8.00
COMMON CARD (1-30)	.10	.30
P1 Harry Gant Prototype	.60	1.50

1992 Redline Racing Rob Moroso

This set is one of four issues produced in 1992 by Redline Racing entitled My Life in Racing. The set focuses on the life and tragic death of Rob Moroso with text written in story form on the cardbacks. The four driver sets were packaged together in factory set form 24-sets per display box. Each set includes a colorful factory set box and was limited to a production run of 25,000.

COMP. FACT SET (30)	2.50	6.00
COMMON CARD (1-30)	.10	.30
P1 Rob Moroso Prototype	.40	1.00

1992 Redline Racing Ken Schrader

This set is one of four issues produced in 1992 by Redline Racing entitled My Life in Racing. The set focuses on the life of Ken Schrader with text written in story form on the cardbacks. The four driver sets were packaged together in factory set form 24-sets per display box. Each set includes a colorful factory box and was limited to a production run of 25,000.

COMP. FACT SET (30)	2.50	6.00
COMMON CARD (1-30)	.08	.25
P1 Ken Schrader Prototype	.60	1.50

1992 Redline Racing Cale Yarborough

This set is one of four issues produced in 1992 by Redline Racing entitled My Life in Racing. The set focuses on the life of Cale Yarborough with text written in story form on the cardbacks. The four sets were packaged together in factory set form 24-sets per display box. Each set includes a colorful factory box and was limited to a production run of 25,000.

COMP. FACT SET (30)	2.50	6.00
COMMON CARD (1-30)	.08	.25
P1 Cale Yarborough Prototype	.60	1.50

1992 Redline Standups

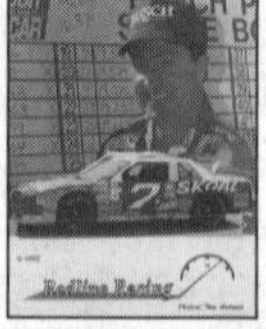

Redline Racing and Photo File of New York produced this unique set in 1992. Each card could be folded in such a way as to stand-up independently. The cards were packed one per foil pack (48-packs per box) and contain a full bleed color photo on the front. Another photo and brief driver stats are on the cardback with the set name and die cut photo of the driver's car on the stand-up support piece. Uncut sheets of the 36-card set have also been made available.

COMPLETE SET (36)	5.00	12.00
1 Rick Mast	.07	.20
2 Dave Marcis	.07	.20
3 Richard Petty	.25	.60
4 Bobby Labonte	.60	1.50
5 Jimmy Means	.07	.20
6 Mark Martin	.75	2.00
7 Alan Kulwicki	.25	.60
8 Rick Wilson	.07	.20
9 Bill Elliott	.40	1.00
10 Derrike Cope	.07	.20
11 Geoff Bodine	.07	.20
12 Jack Ingram	.07	.20
13 Dick Trickle	.07	.20
14 Jeff Burton	.15	.40
15 Morgan Shepherd	.07	.20
16 Tom Peck	.07	.20
17 Darrell Waltrip	.15	.40
18 Jimmy Spencer	.07	.20
19 Chad Little	.07	.20
20 Bobby Hillin	.07	.20
21 Dale Jarrett	.60	1.50
22 Sterling Marlin	.15	.40
23 Bobby Hamilton	.07	.20
24 Kyle Petty	.15	.40
25 Ken Schrader	.07	.20
26 Brett Bodine	.07	.20
27 Chuck Bown	.07	.20
28 Kenny Wallace	.07	.20
29 Joe Nemechek	.07	.20
30 Terry Labonte	.40	1.00
31 Steve Grissom	.07	.20
32 Jimmy Hensley	.07	.20
33 Harry Gant	.15	.40
34 Harry Gant	.15	.40
35 Bobby Labonte	.60	1.50
36 Doyle Ford	.07	.20

1992 RSS Motorsports Haulers

RSS Motorsports released these cards in complete set form. They feature transporter drivers for top NASCAR race teams. Jerry Schweitz is included in the set twice with the second card bearing a "promotional card" logo on the cardback. The checklist card contains two misnumbered cards.

COMPLETE SET (30)	1.25	3.00
1 Richard Bostick Jr.	.05	.15
2 Jerry Seabolt	.05	.15
3 Ken J. Hartley	.05	.15
4 George R. Colwell	.05	.15
5 Carroll Hoss Berry	.05	.15
6 Terry Hall	.05	.15
7 Robin Metdepenningen	.05	.15
8 Buster Auton	.05	.15
9 Henry Benfield	.05	.15
10 Gale W. Wilson	.05	.15
11 Peter Jellen	.05	.15
12 Tommy Rigsbee	.05	.15
13 Harold Hughes	.05	.15
14 Gene Starnes	.05	.15
15 Bill McCarthy	.05	.15
16 Bryan Dorsey	.05	.15
17 Dennis Ritchie	.05	.15
18 Joe Lewis	.05	.15
19 Mike Powell	.05	.15
20 Steve Foster	.05	.15
21 Jerry Schweitz	.05	.15
22 Ted Harrison	.05	.15
23 Norman Koshimizu	.05	.15
24 Charlie Hyde	.05	.15
25 Mike Culbertson	.05	.15
26 Jim Baldwin	.05	.15
27 Bart Creasman	.05	.15
28 Jerry Schweitz Promo	.05	.15
29 Checklist Card UER	.05	.15
cards 26 and 28 misnumbered		
30 Cover Card	.05	.15

1997 SB Motorsports

This 100-card set captures the top names in Winston Cup racing, including drivers, owners, crew chiefs, crew members and announcers. Each card carries complete updated stats through the 1996 racing season. The cards were packaged six per pack with 36 packs per box and 16 boxes per case. SB stands for manufacturer Score Board.

COMPLETE SET (100)	6.00	15.00
1 Dale Earnhardt	1.00	2.50
2 Jeff Gordon	.60	1.50
3 Terry Labonte	.25	.60
4 Dale Jarrett	.40	1.00
5 Robby Gordon RC	.25	.60
6 Mark Martin	.50	1.25
7 Ricky Rudd	.25	.60
8 Richard Petty	.25	.60
9 Ken Schrader	.07	.20
10 Ernie Irvan	.15	.40
11 Sterling Marlin	.25	.60
12 Bobby Labonte	.40	1.00
13 Ted Musgrave	.07	.20
14 Bobby Hamilton	.07	.20
15 Jimmy Spencer	.07	.20
16 Michael Waltrip	.15	.40
17 Jeff Burton	.25	.60
18 Rick Mast	.07	.20
19 Geoff Bodine	.07	.20
20 Ricky Craven	.07	.20
21 Morgan Shepherd	.07	.20
22 Johnny Benson	.15	.40
23 Jeremy Mayfield	.15	.40
24 Wally Dallenbach	.07	.20
25 Brett Bodine	.07	.20
26 Larry Hedrick	.02	.10
27 Ned Jarrett	.02	.10
28 Darrell Waltrip	.15	
29 Hut Stricklin	.07	
30 Richard Petty	.25	
31 Kyle Petty	.15	
32 Robert Yates	.02	
33 Mike Skinner	.07	
34 Robin Pemberton	.02	
35 Ray Evernham	.07	
36 Larry McReynolds	.02	
37 Mike Wallace	.07	
38 Steve Park RC	1.00	2
39 Steve Grissom	.07	
40 Dale Jarrett	.40	1
41 Dale Earnhardt	1.00	2
42 Mark Martin	.50	1
43 Ricky Rudd	.25	
44 Wood Brothers	.02	
45 Robby Gordon's Car	.15	
46 Rusty Wallace's Car	.25	
47 Dale Earnhardt's Car	.40	1
48 Sterling Marlin's Car	.07	
49 Mark Martin's Car	.25	
50 Dale Earnhardt's Car CL	.40	1
51 Bobby Labonte's Car	.15	
52 Michael Waltrip's Car	.07	
53 Ernie Irvan's Car	.02	
54 Darrell Waltrip's Car	.02	
55 Dale Jarrett's Car	.15	
56 Dave Rezendes	.07	
57 Sterling Marlin	.25	
58 Ken Schrader	.07	
59 Richard Childress	.15	
60 Wood Brothers	.02	
61 Tony Glover	.02	
62 Steve Hmiel	.02	
63 The Rainbow Warriors	.02	
64 Steve Grissom	.07	
65 Larry McClure	.02	
66 Ernie Irvan	.15	
67 Jerry Punch	.07	
68 Shelton Pittman	.02	
69 Jack Roush	.02	
UER Roush Racing		
70 Geoff Bodine	.07	
71 Robert Pressley	.07	
72 John Andretti	.07	
73 Ward Burton	.15	
74 Dick Trickle	.07	
75 Dave Marcis	.07	
76 Kenny Wallace	.07	
77 Todd Bodine	.07	
78 Gary DeHart	.02	
79 Ron Hornaday	.07	
80 David Green	.07	
81 Randy Dorton	.02	
82 Kellogg's Crew	.02	
83 Johnny Benson	.15	
84 Jeremy Mayfield	.15	
85 Mike Skinner	.07	
86 #25 Hendrick Team	.02	
87 Bobby Labonte	.40	1
88 Jimmy Johnson	.07	
89 Jimmy Spencer	.07	
90 Michael Waltrip	.15	
91 Morgan Shepherd	.07	
92 Dale Earnhardt	1.00	2
93 Dale Jarrett	.40	1
94 Rick Hendrick	.02	
95 Mark Martin	.50	1
96 Ricky Rudd	.25	
97 Ernie Irvan	.15	
98 Sterling Marlin	.25	
99 Kyle Petty	.15	
100 Sterling Marlin's Car CL	.02	

1997 SB Motorsports Autographs

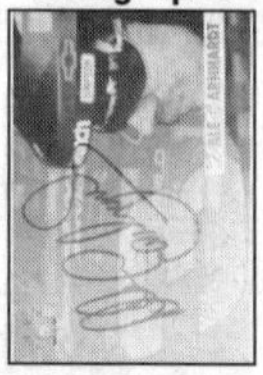

Five drivers from the Winston Cup circuit ha signed insert cards for the 1997 SB Motorsp prodcut. The cards were inserted at the rate of 1: Packs. Each card was sequentially hand-numb on the front and did not contain a card number.

COMPLETE SET (5)	450.00	800.
1 Dale Earnhardt/500	200.00	400.
2 Jeff Gordon/250	50.00	100.
3 Robby Gordon/500	10.00	25.
4 Dale Jarrett	20.00	50.
5 Terry Labonte	12.50	30.

1997 SB Motorsports Race Chat

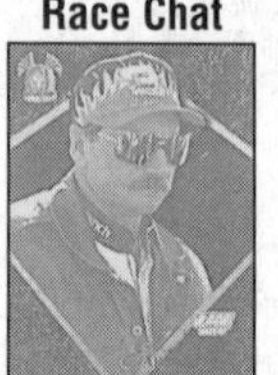

This 10-card insert set features quotes on the ba of each card from drivers, owners, and crew ch about the driver featured on the card. The qu give insight as to how they feel about racing their competitors. The cards were seeded one ir packs.

COMPLETE SET (10)	20.00	50
RC1 Dale Earnhardt	10.00	25
RC2 Ricky Craven	.75	2
RC3 Ernie Irvan	1.50	4
RC4 Dale Jarrett	4.00	10

5 Sterling Marlin 2.50 6.00
6 Mark Martin 5.00 12.00
7 Johnny Benson 1.50 4.00
8 Ricky Rudd 2.50 6.00
9 Bobby Labonte 4.00 10.00
10 Kyle Petty 1.50 4.00

1997 SB Motorsports Winston Cup Rewind

31-card insert set commemorates highlights n each Winston Cup events of 1996. The cards e randomly inserted in packs at a rate of one in 8 ks.

MPLETE SET (31) 25.00 60.00
1 Dale Jarrett 2.00 5.00
2 Dale Earnhardt's Car 2.00 5.00
3 Ted Musgrave .40 1.00
4 Johnny Benson .75 2.00
5 Ward Burton .75 2.00
6 Mark Martin 2.50 6.00
7 Robert Pressley .40 1.00
8 Ricky Craven .40 1.00
9 Sterling Marlin 1.25 3.00
10 Wally Dallenbach .40 1.00
11 Dale Jarrett 2.00 5.00
12 Bobby Labonte 2.00 5.00
13 Geoff Bodine .40 1.00
14 Bobby Hamilton .40 1.00
15 Dave Marcis .40 1.00
16 Ernie Irvan .75 2.00
17 Ricky Rudd 1.25 3.00
18 Jeremy Mayfield .75 2.00
19 Dale Jarrett 2.00 5.00
20 Dale Earnhardt's Car 2.00 5.00
21 Jeff Burton 1.25 3.00
22 Mark Martin 2.50 6.00
23 Hut Stricklin .40 1.00
24 Ernie Irvan .75 2.00
25 Bobby Labonte 2.00 5.00
26 Bobby Hamilton .40 1.00
27 Ted Musgrave .40 1.00
28 Ricky Craven .40 1.00
29 Ricky Rudd 1.25 3.00
30 Bobby Hamilton .40 1.00
31 Terry Labonte's Car/1996 1.25 3.00

996 Score Board Dale Earnhardt

MPLETE SET (10) 8.00 20.00
MMON DALE EARNHARDT 1.00 2.50

1997 Score Board IQ

s set contains 50 cards and was distributed in 2-d packs, with 30 packs in each box. The IQ ation is used by Score Board stands for "Insert ality".

MPLETE SET (50) 10.00 25.00
ale Earnhardt 2.00 5.00
eff Gordon 1.25 3.00
erry Labonte .40 1.00
ale Jarrett .75 2.00
ichael Waltrip .25 .60
ark Martin 1.00 2.50
ale Jarrett .75 2.00
obby Labonte .75 2.00
obby Gordon RC .40 1.00
Rick Mast .10 .30
Geoff Bodine .10 .30
Sterling Marlin .40 1.00
Jeff Burton .40 1.00
Ward Burton .25 .60
Darrell Waltrip .25 .60
Ken Schrader .10 .30
Kyle Petty .25 .60
Bobby Hamilton .10 .30
Ernie Irvan .25 .60
Steve Grissom .10 .30
Ted Musgrave .10 .30
Jeremy Mayfield .25 .60
Ricky Rudd .40 1.00
Ricky Craven .10 .30
Hut Stricklin .10 .30
Jeff Gordon 1.25 3.00
Dale Earnhardt 2.00 5.00
Dale Jarrett .75 2.00
Terry Labonte .40 1.00
Richard Childress .25 .60
Rick Hendrick .10 .30
Richard Petty .40 1.00
Robert Yates .05 .15
Joe Gibbs .25 .60
Ray Evernham .25 .60
Larry McReynolds .05 .15
Jeff Gordon 1.25 3.00
Dale Earnhardt 2.00 5.00
Rusty Wallace's Car .40 1.00
Dale Earnhardt's Car .75 2.00
Sterling Marlin's Car .10 .30
Mark Martin's Car .40 1.00
Bobby Labonte's Car .25 .60
Michael Waltrip's Car .10 .30
Jeff Gordon's Car .50 1.25
46 Ernie Irvan's Car .10 .30
47 Robby Gordon's Car .25 .60
48 Bobby Hamilton's Car .05 .15
49 Dale Jarrett's Car .25 .60
50 Terry Labonte / Jeff Gordon / Ricky Craven .60 1.50
P1 Dale Jarrett Promo .60 1.50

1997 Score Board IQ $10 Phone Cards

These cards feature a foil-stamped design and each card carries $10 of phone time. They are inserted one per ten packs.

COMPLETE SET (10) 10.00 25.00
PC1 Dale Earnhardt 3.00 8.00
PC2 Rusty Wallace's Car .60 1.50
PC3 Bobby Labonte 1.25 3.00
PC4 Dale Earnhardt's Car 1.25 3.00
PC5 Sterling Marlin .60 1.50
PC6 Mark Martin 1.50 4.00
PC7 Michael Waltrip .40 1.00
PC8 Dale Jarrett 1.25 3.00
PC9 Ricky Rudd .60 1.50
PC10 Ernie Irvan .40 1.00

1997 Score Board IQ Remarques

These cards feature the original artwork of renowned artist Sam Bass. Ten of his more famous artworks were reprinted on canvas stock in order to create these cards. These cards are serial numbered from 101 to 570 and are autographed by Bass. These cards are inserted one per 65 packs.

COMPLETE SET (10) 150.00 300.00
COMP.BASS FINISHED (10) 250.00 500.00
*BASS FINISHED: .6X TO 1.5X BASIC INSERTS
SB1 Dale Earnhardt 30.00 80.00
SB2 Jeff Gordon 20.00 50.00
SB3 Richard Childress 4.00 10.00
SB4 Ernie Irvan 4.00 10.00
SB5 Rusty Wallace's Car 6.00 15.00
SB6 Darrell Waltrip 4.00 10.00
SB7 Richard Petty 6.00 15.00
SB8 Bobby Labonte 12.50 30.00
SB9 Alan Kulwicki 4.00 10.00
SB10 Terry Labonte 6.00 15.00

1997 Score Board Seven-Eleven Phone Cards

This 4-card set was sponsored and distributed by 7-11 Stores, licensed through Score Board, and features phone time by Frontier Communications. Each card features the driver's image on the front along with his ride and the phone card instructions on the back.

COMPLETE SET (4) 5.00 12.00
1 Dale Earnhardt 3.00 8.00
2 Sterling Marlin 1.00 2.50
3 Dale Jarrett 1.25 3.00
4 Michael Waltrip .75 2.00

1995 Select Promos

Pinnacle Brands distributed these cards as a cello wrapped set to preview its 1995 Select release. Four of the cards are promo versions of regular issue cards, along with a promo Jeff Gordon Dream Machines card. A sixth (cover) card was included as well.

COMPLETE SET (6) 8.00 20.00
12 Jeff Gordon 2.00 5.00
24 Kyle Petty .60 1.50
128 Loy Allen Jr. .40 1.00
136 Geoff Bodine .40 1.00
DM8 Jeff Gordon's Car Dream Machine 6.00 15.00
NNO Cover Card .10 .30

1995 Select

This 150-card set is the first racing set produced from manufacturer Pinnacle. The cards came eight cards per pack, 24 packs per box and 24 boxes per case. There were 2,950 numbered cases produced. The set features six topical subsets: Owners (73-90), Crew Chief (91-108), In the Blood (109-117), Young Stars (118-128), Idols (129-134), Pole Sitters (135-136). In the original set the only card with ties to Dale Earnhardt was card number 41, a picture of his car. In the middle of 1995 Dale signed a spokesperson agreement with Pinnacle. Pinnacle then issued a special Select number 151 card Dale to complete the set. This card was distributed to dealers that ordered the Select product. The card is not part of the regular set price. Also randomly inserted in the bottom of the boxes were a Jeff Gordon Jumbo and a Jumbo Geoff Bodine Magic Motion card. These two cards are priced at the bottom of the listing.

COMPLETE SET (150) 10.00 25.00
1 Loy Allen Jr. .08 .25
2 John Andretti .08 .25
3 Brett Bodine .08 .25
4 Geoff Bodine .08 .25
5 Todd Bodine .08 .25
6 Jeff Burton .30 .75
7 Ward Burton .20 .50
8 Derrike Cope .08 .25
9 Wally Dallenbach Jr. .08 .25
10 Dave Marcis .20 .50
11 Harry Gant .20 .50
12 Jeff Gordon 1.00 2.50
13 Steve Grissom .08 .25
14 Bobby Hamilton .08 .25
15 Ernie Irvan .20 .50
16 Dale Jarrett .60 1.50
17 Bobby Labonte .60 1.50
18 Terry Labonte .30 .75
19 Sterling Marlin .30 .75
20 Mark Martin .75 2.00
21 Rick Mast .08 .25
22 Ted Musgrave .08 .25
23 Joe Nemechek .08 .25
24 Kyle Petty .20 .50
25 Ricky Rudd .30 .75
26 Greg Sacks .08 .25
27 Ken Schrader .08 .25
28 Morgan Shepherd .08 .25
29 Lake Speed .08 .25
30 Jimmy Spencer .08 .25
31 Hut Stricklin .08 .25
32 Kenny Wallace .08 .25
33 Mike Wallace .08 .25
34 Rusty Wallace .75 2.00
35 Darrell Waltrip .20 .50
36 Michael Waltrip .20 .50
37 Morgan Shepherd's Car .05 .15
38 Jeff Gordon's Car .50 1.25
39 Geoff Bodine's Car .05 .15
40 Ted Musgrave's Car .05 .15
41 Dale Earnhardt's Car .50 1.25
42 Dale Jarrett's Car .20 .50
43 Terry Labonte's Car .20 .50
44 Sterling Marlin's Car .08 .25
45 Ken Schrader's Car .05 .15
46 Kyle Petty's Car .08 .25
47 Rusty Wallace's Car .30 .75
48 Michael Waltrip's Car .08 .25
49 Brett Bodine's Car .05 .15
50 Lake Speed's Car .05 .15
51 Ernie Irvan's Car .08 .25
52 Ricky Rudd's Car .08 .25
53 Mark Martin's Car .08 .25
54 Darrell Waltrip's Car .08 .25
55 Johnny Benson Jr. .20 .50
56 Jim Bown .08 .25
57 Ricky Craven .08 .25
58 Bobby Dotter .08 .25
59 Tim Fedewa .08 .25
60 David Green .08 .25
61 Tommy Houston .08 .25
62 Jason Keller .08 .25
63 Randy LaJoie .08 .25
64 Tracy Leslie .08 .25
65 Chad Little .08 .25
66 Mark Martin .75 2.00
67 Mike McLaughlin .08 .25
68 Larry Pearson .08 .25
69 Robert Pressley .08 .25
70 Elton Sawyer .08 .25
71 Dennis Setzer .08 .25
72 Kenny Wallace .08 .25
73 Richard Petty OWN .30 .75
74 Leo Jackson OWN .05 .15
75 Bobby Allison OWN .08 .25
76 Richard Childress OWN .20 .50
77 Geoff Bodine OWN .08 .25
78 Joe Gibbs OWN .20 .50
79 Kenny Bernstein OWN .08 .25
80 Bill Davis OWN .05 .15
81 Cale Yarborough OWN .08 .25
82 Rick Hendrick OWN .05 .15
83 Roger Penske OWN / Don Miller OWN .05 .15
84 Chuck Rider OWN .05 .15
85 Ricky Rudd OWN .20 .50
86 Jack Roush OWN .05 .15
87 Felix Sabates OWN .05 .15
88 Darrell Waltrip OWN .20 .50
89 Glen Wood OWN / Eddie Wood OWN / Len Wood OWN .05 .15
90 Robert Yates OWN .05 .15
91 Paul Andrews .05 .15
92 Ray Evernham .05 .15
93 Jeff Hammond .05 .15
94 Steve Hmiel .05 .15
95 Ken Howes .05 .15
96 Jimmy Makar .05 .15
97 Larry McReynolds .05 .15
98 Buddy Parrott .05 .15
99 Leonard Wood .05 .15
100 Andy Petree .05 .15
101 Jimmy Fennig .05 .15
102 Mike Beam .05 .15
103 Tony Glover .05 .15
104 Doug Hewitt .05 .15
105 Donnie Richeson .05 .15
106 Bill Ingle .05 .15
107 Donnie Wingo .05 .15
108 Robin Pemberton .05 .15
109 Richard Petty IB / Kyle Petty IB .30 .75
110 Geoff Bodine IB / Todd Bodine IB / Brett Bodine IB .08 .25
111 Rusty Wallace IB / Kenny Wallace IB / Mike Wallace IB .40 1.00
112 Davey Allison IB / Bobby Allison IB .30 .75
113 Darrell Waltrip IB / Michael Waltrip IB .20 .50
114 Bobby Labonte IB / Terry Labonte IB .30 .75
115 Dale Jarrett IB / Ned Jarrett IB .30 .75
116 David Pearson IB / Larry Pearson IB .08 .25
117 Jeff Burton IB / Ward Burton IB .20 .50
118 Jeff Gordon YS .50 1.25
119 Jeff Burton YS .20 .50
120 Loy Allen Jr. YS .08 .25
121 Todd Bodine YS .08 .25
122 John Andretti YS .08 .25
123 Joe Nemechek YS .08 .25
124 Kenny Wallace YS .08 .25
125 Bobby Labonte YS .30 .75
126 Ricky Craven YS .08 .25
127 Johnny Benson YS .20 .50
128 Chad Little YS .08 .25
129 Richard Petty I / Mark Martin I .40 1.00
130 David Pearson I / Ken Schrader I .08 .25
131 Bobby Allison I / Kyle Petty I .20 .50
132 Cale Yarborough I / Ricky Rudd I .20 .50
133 Junior Johnson I / Darrell Waltrip I .20 .50
134 Alan Kulwicki I / Geoff Bodine I .20 .50
135 Ernie Irvan PS .20 .50
136 Geoff Bodine PS .08 .25
137 Ted Musgrave PS .08 .25
138 Ricky Rudd PS .20 .50
139 Chuck Bown PS .08 .25
140 Rusty Wallace PS .40 1.00
141 Jeff Gordon PS .50 1.25
142 Rick Mast PS .08 .25
143 Mark Martin PS .40 1.00
144 Loy Allen Jr. PS .08 .25
145 Harry Gant PS .20 .50
146 Jimmy Spencer PS .08 .25
147 Checklist .05 .15
148 Checklist .05 .15
149 Checklist .05 .15
150 Checklist .05 .15
151S Dale Earnhardt Dealer Mail Out 4.00 10.00
NNO Jeff Gordon YS Jumbo 6.00 15.00
NNO G.Bodine Magic Motion 2.50 6.00

1995 Select Flat Out

This 150-card set is a parallel to the base set. The cards feature all foil Gold Rush printing and have a Flat Out logo on the back to differentiate them from the base cards. Flat Out cards were randomly inserted at a rate of one per three packs. Pinnacle also released a Flat Out version of the Dale Earnhardt card mentioned in the base set blurb (card number 151). This card is not included in the complete set price.

COMPLETE SET (150) 50.00 120.00
*FLAT OUT: 2.5X TO 6X BASE CARDS
151FO Dale Earnhardt Dealer Mail Out 6.00 15.00

1995 Select Dream Machines

This 12-card insert set features of the top Winston Cup Driver's cars. The cards are printed on an all-foil board and use Dufex technology. Dream Machine cards were randomly inserted one per 48 packs.

COMPLETE SET (12) 40.00 100.00
DM1 Geoff Bodine's Car 1.00 2.50
DM2 Rusty Wallace's Car 8.00 20.00
DM3 Mark Martin's Car 8.00 20.00
DM4 Ken Schrader's Car 1.00 2.50
DM5 Ricky Rudd's Car 3.00 8.00
DM6 Morgan Shepherd's Car 1.00 2.50
DM7 Ernie Irvan's Car 2.00 5.00
DM8 Jeff Gordon's Car 10.00 25.00
DM9 Michael Waltrip's Car 2.00 5.00
DM10 Darrell Waltrip's Car 2.00 5.00
DM11 Kyle Petty's Car 2.00 5.00
DM12 Terry Labonte's Car 3.00 8.00

1995 Select Skills

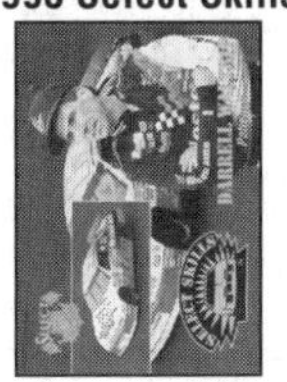

Some of Winston Cup racing's top drivers are featured in this 18-card insert set. The cards feature all-foil, Gold Rush printing technology and were randomly seeded one per 12 packs.

COMPLETE SET (18) 30.00 60.00
SS1 Rusty Wallace 5.00 12.00
SS2 Mark Martin 5.00 12.00
SS3 Jeff Gordon 6.00 15.00
SS4 Ernie Irvan 1.25 3.00
SS5 Terry Labonte 2.00 5.00
SS6 Ricky Rudd 2.00 5.00
SS7 Kyle Petty 1.25 3.00
SS8 Ken Schrader .60 1.50
SS9 Morgan Shepherd .60 1.50
SS10 Geoff Bodine .60 1.50
SS11 Ted Musgrave .60 1.50
SS12 Michael Waltrip 1.25 3.00
SS13 John Andretti .60 1.50
SS14 Todd Bodine .60 1.50
SS15 Sterling Marlin 2.00 5.00
SS16 Darrell Waltrip 1.25 3.00
SS17 Jimmy Spencer .60 1.50
SS18 Harry Gant 1.25 3.00

1994 SkyBox

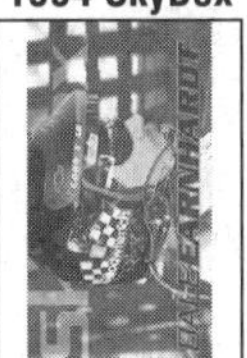

This 27-card set is the first NASCAR issue by manufacturer SkyBox. The cards are oversized 4 1/2" X 2 1/2" and feature some of the top names in Winston Cup racing. The set includes a Anatomy of a Pit Stop subset (14-17). Card number 27, the SkyBox Winston Cup car that Dick Trickle drove in a few races, was redeemable for a card of the 1994 Brickyard 400 Winner. You could send that card in with $1.50 and receive a card of Jeff Gordon holding the Brickyard 400 trophy (expiration date 12/31/1995). This card is not included in the set price.

COMPLETE FACT.SET (27) 6.00 15.00
1 Dale Earnhardt 2.00 5.00
2 Darrell Waltrip's Car .15 .40
3 Ernie Irvan's Car .15 .40
4 Jeff Gordon's Car 1.00 3.00
5 Terry Labonte's Car .30 .75
6 Wally Dallenbach Jr.'s Car .07 .20
7 Kyle Petty's Car .15 .40
8 Lake Speed's Car .07 .20
9 Mark Martin's Car .60 1.50
10 Morgan Shepherd's Car .07 .20
11 Ricky Rudd's Car .15 .40
12 Rusty Wallace's Car .50 1.25
13 Sterling Marlin's Car .15 .40
14 Anatomy of a Pit Stop .07 .20
15 Anatomy of a Pit Stop .07 .20
16 Anatomy of a Pit Stop .07 .20
17 Anatomy of a Pit Stop .07 .20
18 Bare Frame .07 .20
19 Chevy Engine .07 .20
20 Jacked up Body .07 .20
21 Finished Body .07 .20
22 Sanding Body .07 .20
23 Finished Race Car .07 .20
24 Geoff Bodine's Car / Todd Bodine's Car .07 .20
25 Darrell Waltrip's Car / Michael Waltrip's Car .15 .40
26 John Andretti's Cars .07 .20
NNO Dick Trickle's Car / Exchange Card Expired .15 .40
NNO Jeff Gordon / Exchanged Card Redemption 2.50 5.00

1997 SkyBox Profile

This 80-card set was Fleer/Skybox's first NASCAR release under the SkyBox brand name. The product was highlighted by a autographed card redemption program. Cards were distributed in five card packs with 24 packs per box and 6 or 12 boxes per case. The packs carried a suggested retail price of $4.99.

COMPLETE SET (80) 8.00 20.00
1 John Andretti .10 .30
2 Johnny Benson .25 .60
3 Derrike Cope .10 .30
4 Ricky Craven .10 .30
5 Dale Earnhardt 2.00 5.00
6 Bill Elliott .50 1.25
7 Jeff Gordon 1.25 3.00
8 Robby Gordon RC .40 1.00
9 Steve Grissom .10 .30
10 David Green .10 .30
11 Bobby Hamilton .10 .30
12 Bobby Hillin .10 .30
13 Ernie Irvan .25 .60
14 Dale Jarrett .75 2.00
15 Bobby Labonte .75 2.00
16 Terry Labonte .40 1.00
17 Dave Marcis .10 .30
18 Sterling Marlin .40 1.00
19 Mark Martin 1.00 2.50
20 Rick Mast .10 .30
21 Jeremy Mayfield .25 .60
22 Ted Musgrave .10 .30
23 Joe Nemechek .10 .30
24 Ricky Rudd .40 1.00
25 Ken Schrader .10 .30
26 Morgan Shepherd .10 .30
27 Hut Stricklin .10 .30
28 Dick Trickle .10 .30
29 Kenny Wallace .10 .30
30 Rusty Wallace 1.00 2.50
31 Michael Waltrip .25 .60
32 Richard Childress OWN .25 .60
33 Richard Petty OWN .10 .30
34 Rick Hendrick OWN .03 .15
35 Robert Yates OWN .03 .15
36 Joe Gibbs OWN .25 .60
37 Cale Yarborough OWN .03 .15
38 Jack Roush OWN .03 .15
39 Ray Evernham CC .10 .30
40 Larry McReynolds CC .03 .15
41 Gary DeHart CC .03 .15
42 Todd Parrott CC .03 .15
43 Marc Reno CC .03 .15
44 Steve Hmiel MG CC .03 .15
45 Robin Pemberton CC .03 .15
46 Todd Bodine .10 .30
47 Jason Keller .10 .30
48 Randy LaJoie .10 .30
49 Phil Parsons .10 .30
50 Steve Park RC 3.00 6.00
51 Buckshot Jones RC .10 .30
52 Jeff Fuller .10 .30
53 Tracy Leslie .10 .30
54 Elton Sawyer .10 .30
55 Jeff Green .10 .30
56 Mike McLaughlin .10 .30
57 Ron Barfield .10 .30
58 Glen Allen Jr. .10 .30
59 Kevin Lepage .10 .30
60 Rodney Combs .10 .30
61 Tim Fedewa .10 .30
62 Rusty Wallace's Car .40 1.00
63 Dale Earnhardt's Car .75 2.00
64 Sterling Marlin's Car .10 .30
65 Terry Labonte's Car .25 .60
66 Mark Martin's Car .40 1.00
67 Ricky Rudd's Car .10 .30
68 Bobby Labonte's Car .40 1.00
69 Michael Waltrip's Car .10 .30
70 Jeff Gordon's Car .50 1.25
71 Ernie Irvan's Car .03 .15
72 Ken Schrader's Car .03 .15
73 Derrike Cope's Car .03 .15
74 Jeremy Mayfield's Car .03 .15
75 Robby Gordon's Car .25 .60
76 Bobby Hamilton's Car .03 .15
77 Dale Jarrett's Car .40 1.00
78 Bill Elliott's Car .25 .60
79 David Green's Car .03 .15
80 Checklist .03 .15
D1 Jeff Gordon Daytona 15.00 40.00
P1 Jeff Gordon Promo .75 2.00

1997 SkyBox Profile Autographs

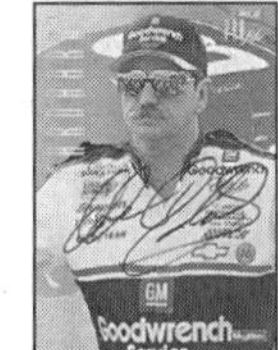

This 47-card insert set contains autograph redemption cards from each driver in this set. 11,100 cards total were set aside to be redeemed in this program. Each Winston Cup and Busch driver signed 200 cards, with the exception of Randy LaJoie who signed 500. The cards were randomly inserted in packs at a ratio of 1:24.

COMPLETE SET (47) 750.00 1500.00
1 John Andretti 10.00 20.00
2 Johnny Benson 10.00 20.00
3 Derrike Cope 7.50 15.00
4 Ricky Craven 7.50 15.00
5 Dale Earnhardt 150.00 300.00
6 Bill Elliott 30.00 80.00
7 Jeff Gordon 75.00 150.00
8 Robby Gordon 10.00 20.00
9 Steve Grissom 7.50 15.00
10 David Green 7.50 15.00
11 Bobby Hamilton 10.00 25.00
12 Bobby Hillin 7.50 15.00
13 Ernie Irvan 12.50 30.00
14 Dale Jarrett 25.00 60.00
15 Bobby Labonte 12.50 30.00
16 Terry Labonte 15.00 40.00
17 Dave Marcis 10.00 20.00
18 Sterling Marlin 12.50 30.00

19 Mark Martin	40.00	80.00
20 Rick Mast	7.50	15.00
21 Jeremy Mayfield	10.00	20.00
22 Ted Musgrave	7.50	15.00
23 Joe Nemechek	7.50	15.00
24 Ricky Rudd	12.50	30.00
25 Ken Schrader	10.00	20.00
26 Morgan Shepherd	7.50	15.00
27 Hut Stricklin	7.50	15.00
28 Dick Trickle	7.50	15.00
29 Kenny Wallace	7.50	15.00
30 Rusty Wallace	25.00	60.00
31 Michael Waltrip	8.00	20.00
46 Todd Bodine	7.50	15.00
47 Jason Keller	7.50	15.00
48 Randy LaJoie	7.50	15.00
49 Phil Parsons	7.50	15.00
50 Steve Park	10.00	20.00
51 Buckshot Jones	10.00	20.00
52 Jeff Fuller	7.50	15.00
53 Tracy Leslie	7.50	15.00
54 Elton Sawyer	7.50	15.00
55 Jeff Green	7.50	15.00
56 Mike McLaughlin	7.50	15.00
57 Ron Barfield	7.50	15.00
58 Glen Allen	7.50	15.00
59 Kevin Lepage	7.50	15.00
60 Rodney Combs	7.50	15.00
61 Tim Fedewa	7.50	15.00

1997 SkyBox Profile Break Out

This 9-card insert set features young drivers who could become stars in NASCAR. The cards were randomly inserted in packs at a ratio of 1:4.

COMPLETE SET (9)	6.00	15.00
B1 Jeff Gordon	4.00	10.00
B2 Robby Gordon	1.25	3.00
B3 Ron Barfield	.40	1.00
B4 Johnny Benson	.75	2.00
B5 Steve Park	8.00	20.00
B6 Ricky Craven	.40	1.00
B7 Bobby Labonte	2.50	6.00
B8 Jeremy Mayfield	.75	2.00
B9 David Green	.40	1.00

1997 SkyBox Profile Pace Setters

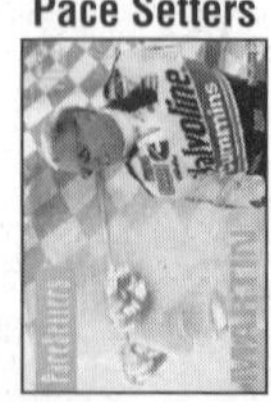

This 9-card insert set covers those drivers whose performances have secured their spots in the record books. The cards were randomly inserted in packs at a ratio of 1:10.

COMPLETE SET (9)	25.00	60.00
E1 Dale Earnhardt	12.50	30.00
E2 Terry Labonte	2.50	6.00
E3 Bill Elliott	3.00	8.00
E4 Ricky Rudd	2.50	6.00
E5 Jeff Gordon	8.00	20.00
E6 Dale Jarrett	5.00	12.00
E7 Michael Waltrip	1.50	4.00
E8 Rusty Wallace	6.00	15.00
E9 Mark Martin	6.00	15.00

1997 SkyBox Profile Team

This 9-card set features the strongest teams in NASCAR. Each card front pictures the driver, crew chief and car owner. The cards were randomly inserted in packs at a ratio of 1:100.

COMPLETE SET (9)	200.00	400.00
T1 Terry Labonte	8.00	20.00
T2 Jeff Gordon	25.00	60.00
T3 Dale Jarrett	15.00	40.00
T4 Dale Earnhardt	40.00	100.00
T5 Mark Martin	20.00	50.00
T6 Ricky Rudd	8.00	20.00
T7 Ernie Irvan	5.00	12.00
T8 Bill Elliott	10.00	25.00
T9 Rusty Wallace	20.00	50.00

1992 Slim Jim Bobby Labonte

Produced for and distributed by Slim Jim, the Bobby Labonte set includes 27 car and driver cards with one cover/checklist card and one bi-fold autograph card. The autograph card (number 13) is not signed but is a bi-fold card intended to be large enough unfolded for the driver to sign. The back of the checklist card included an offer to purchase additional sets at $5 each with 5 proofs of purchases from Slim Jim products. Regardless, the Slim Jim Bobby Labonte set is thought to be one of the toughest individual driver card sets to find.

COMPLETE SET (29)	7.50	20.00
1 Cover/Checklist Card	.40	1.00
2 Bobby Labonte's Car	.40	1.00
3 Bobby Labonte	.75	2.00
4 Bobby Labonte's Car	.40	1.00
5 Bob Labonte Sr.	.40	1.00
6 Bobby Labonte's Car	.40	1.00
7 Bobby Labonte Terry Labonte	.75	2.00
8 Bobby Labonte	.75	2.00
9 Bobby Labonte in Pits	.40	1.00
10 Bobby Labonte's Car	.40	1.00
11 Bobby Labonte	.75	2.00
12 Bobby Labonte's Car	.40	1.00
13 Bobby Labonte Auto.Card Unsigned Bi-Fold Card	.40	1.00
14 Bobby Labonte in Pits	.40	1.00
15 Bobby Labonte	.75	2.00
16 Bobby Labonte's Car Steve Grissom's Car Dale Earnhardt's Car	.40	1.00
17 Bobby Labonte	.75	2.00
18 Bobby Labonte in Pits	.40	1.00
19 Bobby Labonte's Car	.40	1.00
20 Bobby Labonte's Car Chad Little's Car	.40	1.00
21 Bobby Labonte	.75	2.00
22 Bobby Labonte's Car	.40	1.00
23 Bobby Labonte Donna Labonte	.40	1.00
24 Bobby Labonte Bob Labonte Sr.	.40	1.00
25 Bobby Labonte	.75	2.00
26 Bobby Labonte's Car	.40	1.00
27 Bobby Labonte's Car	.40	1.00
28 Bobby Labonte w/Car	.40	1.00
29 Bobby Labonte w/Car	.40	1.00

1994 Slim Jim David Green

Similar to the 1992 set, the 1994 release was produced for and distributed by Slim Jim. New driver David Green is the set's focus that includes 16 driver and car cards with one checklist card and one bi-fold autograph card. The autograph card (number 48) is not signed but is a bi-fold card intended to be large enough unfolded for the driver to sign. Cards from the Slim Jim David Green set are numbered consecutively after the 1992 Bobby Labonte set.

COMPLETE SET (18)	6.00	12.00
31 Checklist Card	.20	.50
32 David Green	.40	1.00
33 David Green in Pits	.20	.50
34 David Green	.40	1.00
35 David Green	.40	1.00
36 David Green Action	.20	.50
37 David Green's Car	.20	.50
38 David Green	.40	1.00
39 Eddie Lowery	.20	.50
40 Curt Clouttier	.20	.50
41 Charlie Smith	.20	.50
42 David Green	.40	1.00
43 David Green Steve Grissom	.20	.50
44 David Green's Car	.20	.50
45 David Green	.40	1.00
46 David Green	.20	.50
47 David Green's Car Hermie Sadler's Car	.20	.50
48 David Green Bi-Fold	.40	1.00

1995 SP

This 150-card set is the inaugural SP brand issue from Upper Deck. The set is made up of seven subsets: Cup Contenders (1-30), Drivers (31-74), Cars (75-116), Premier Prospects (117-120), Owners (121-135) and Crew Chiefs (136-150). The product came seven cards per pack, 32 packs per box and six boxes per case. The original suggested retail price per pack was $3.99 and the product was available only through hobby outlets. At the time it was announced that SP Racing was the lowest produced SP product across the 5 major sports that have that brand. Also, SP was delayed a month from its original release date so that it could include a special Comebacks Hologram insert card of Ernie Irvan and Michael Jordan. The Comebacks card could be found one per 192 packs.

COMPLETE SET (150)	10.00	25.00
1 Rick Mast CC	.10	.30
2 Rusty Wallace CC	1.00	2.50
3 Sterling Marlin CC	.40	1.00
4 Terry Labonte CC	.40	1.00
5 Mark Martin CC	1.00	2.50
6 Geoff Bodine CC	.10	.30
7 Jeff Burton CC	.40	1.00
8 Lake Speed CC	.10	.30
9 Ricky Rudd CC	.40	1.00
10 Brett Bodine CC	.10	.30
11 Derrike Cope CC	.10	.30
12 Bobby Hamilton CC	.10	.30
13 Ted Musgrave CC	.10	.30
14 Darrell Waltrip CC	.25	.60
15 Bobby Labonte CC	.75	2.00
16 Morgan Shepherd CC	.10	.30
17 Joe Nemechek CC	.10	.30
18 Jeff Gordon CC	1.25	3.00
19 Ken Schrader CC	.10	.30
20 Hut Stricklin CC	.10	.30
21 Dale Jarrett CC	.75	2.00
22 Steve Grissom CC	.10	.30
23 Michael Waltrip CC	.25	.60
24 Ward Burton CC	.10	.30
25 Todd Bodine CC	.10	.30
26 Robert Pressley CC	.10	.30
27 Bill Elliott CC	.50	1.25
28 John Andretti CC	.10	.30
29 Ricky Craven CC	.10	.30
30 Kyle Petty CC	.25	.60
31 Rick Mast	.10	.30
32 Rusty Wallace	1.00	2.50
33 Rusty Wallace	1.00	2.50
34 Sterling Marlin	.40	1.00
35 Sterling Marlin	.40	1.00
36 Terry Labonte	.40	1.00
37 Mark Martin	1.00	2.50
38 Mark Martin	1.00	2.50
39 Geoff Bodine	.10	.30
40 Jeff Burton	.40	1.00
41 Lake Speed	.10	.30
42 Ricky Rudd	.40	1.00
43 Brett Bodine	.10	.30
44 Derrike Cope	.10	.30
45 Bobby Hamilton	.10	.30
46 Dick Trickle	.10	.30
47 Ted Musgrave	.10	.30
48 Darrell Waltrip	.25	.60
49 Bobby Labonte	.75	2.00
50 Morgan Shepherd	.10	.30
51 Chuck Bown	.10	.30
52 Jeff Purvis	.10	.30
53 Jimmy Hensley	.10	.30
54 Jimmy Spencer	.10	.30
55 Jeff Gordon	1.25	3.00
56 Jeff Gordon	1.25	3.00
57 Ken Schrader	.10	.30
58 Hut Stricklin	.10	.30
59 Randy LaJoie	.10	.30
60 Dale Jarrett	.75	2.00
61 Steve Grissom	.10	.30
62 Michael Waltrip	.25	.60
63 Ward Burton	.25	.60
64 Todd Bodine	.10	.30
65 Robert Pressley	.10	.30
66 Jeremy Mayfield	.25	.60
67 Mike Wallace	.10	.30
68 Bill Elliott	.50	1.25
69 John Andretti	.10	.30
70 Chad Little	.10	.30
71 Joe Nemechek	.10	.30
72 Dave Marcis	.25	.60
73 Ricky Craven	.10	.30
74 Kyle Petty	.25	.60
75 Rick Mast's Car	.05	.15
76 Rusty Wallace's Car	.40	1.00
77 Rusty Wallace's Car	.40	1.00
78 Sterling Marlin's Car	.10	.30
79 Terry Labonte's Car	.25	.60
80 Mark Martin's Car	.40	1.00
81 Geoff Bodine's Car	.05	.15
82 Jeff Burton's Car	.10	.30
83 Lake Speed's Car	.05	.15
84 Ricky Rudd's Car	.10	.30
85 Brett Bodine's Car	.05	.15
86 Derrike Cope's Car	.05	.15
87 Bobby Hamilton's Car	.05	.15
88 Dick Trickle's Car	.05	.15
89 Ted Musgrave's Car	.05	.15
90 Darrell Waltrip's Car	.10	.30
91 Bobby Labonte's Car	.40	1.00
92 Morgan Shepherd's Car	.05	.15
93 Chad Little's Car	.05	.15
94 Jeff Purvis' Car	.05	.15
95 Jimmy Hensley's Car	.05	.15
96 Jimmy Spencer's Car	.05	.15
97 Jeff Gordon's Car	.60	1.50
98 Ken Schrader's Car	.05	.15
99 Hut Stricklin's Car	.05	.15
100 Jeff Gordon's Car	.60	1.50
101 Dale Jarrett's Car	.40	1.00
102 Steve Grissom's Car	.05	.15
103 Michael Waltrip's Car	.10	.30
104 Ward Burton's Car	.10	.30
105 Todd Bodine's Car	.05	.15
106 Robert Pressley's Car	.05	.15
107 Jeremy Mayfield's Car	.10	.30
108 Mike Wallace's Car	.05	.15
109 Bill Elliott's Car	.25	.60
110 Bill Elliott's Car	.25	.60
111 John Andretti's Car	.05	.15
112 Kenny Wallace's Car	.05	.15
113 Joe Nemechek's Car	.05	.15
114 Dave Marcis's Car	.10	.30
115 Ricky Craven's Car	.05	.15
116 Kyle Petty's Car	.10	.30
117 Ricky Craven PP	.10	.30
118 Robert Pressley PP	.10	.30
119 Randy LaJoie PP	.10	.30
120 Davy Jones PP	.10	.30
121 Rick Hendrick OWN	.05	.15
122 Jack Roush OWN	.05	.15
123 Roger Penske OWN Rusty Wallace	.40	1.00
124 Joe Gibbs OWN	.25	.60
125 Felix Sabates OWN	.05	.15
126 Bobby Allison OWN	.10	.30
127 Richard Petty OWN	.40	1.00
128 Cale Yarborough OWN	.10	.30
129 Robert Yates OWN	.05	.15
130 Darrell Waltrip OWN	.25	.60
131 Bill Elliott OWN	.50	1.25
132 Geoff Bodine OWN	.10	.30
133 Junior Johnson OWN	.10	.30
134 Ricky Rudd OWN	.40	1.00
135 Glen Wood OWN	.05	.15
136 Robin Pemberton	.05	.15
137 Steve Hmiel	.05	.15
138 Larry McReynolds	.05	.15
139 Robbie Loomis	.05	.15
140 Ray Evernham	.25	.60
141 Howard Comstock	.05	.15
142 Gary DeHart	.05	.15
143 Paul Andrews	.05	.15
144 Bill Ingle	.05	.15
145 Jimmy Makar	.05	.15
146 Barry Dodson	.05	.15
147 Jimmy Fennig	.05	.15
148 Leonard Wood	.05	.15
149 Pete Peterson	.05	.15
150 Ken Howes	.05	.15
JG1 Jeff Gordon Promo	2.00	5.00
CB1 Ernie Irvan HOLO Michael Jordan	8.00	20.00

1995 SP Die Cuts

This 150-card set is a parallel to the regular SP set. Each card is a die cut replica of the base cards. There was one die cut card per pack.

COMPLETE SET (150)	30.00	75.00
*DIE CUT STARS: 1.25X TO 3X BASIC CARDS		

1995 SP Back-To-Back

This three-card insert set features the only three drivers to win back-to-back Daytona 500's. The cards feature a forward and reverse image on holographic board. Richard Petty won the event seven times including '73 and '74. Cale Yarborough was a four time winner including '83 and '84. Sterling Marlin's made the set for his '94 and '95 trips to the winner's circle. The cards were randomly inserted at a ratio of 1:81 packs.

COMPLETE SET (3)	10.00	25.00
BB1 Richard Petty	5.00	12.00
BB2 Cale Yarborough	4.00	10.00
BB3 Sterling Marlin	5.00	12.00

1995 SP Speed Merchants

The 30-card set uses HoloView technology to feature the top drivers and up and coming stars in Winston Cup racing. The cards were seeded one per five packs. There was also a die cut parallel version of the Speed Merchant cards. The die cut cards were randomly inserted one per 74 packs.

COMPLETE SET (30)	25.00	60.00
*DIE CUTS: 2X TO 5X BASIC INSERTS		
SM1 Kyle Petty	1.25	3.00
SM2 Rusty Wallace	5.00	12.00
SM3 Bill Elliott	2.50	6.00
SM4 Sterling Marlin	2.00	5.00
SM5 Terry Labonte	2.00	5.00
SM6 Mark Martin	5.00	12.00
SM7 Geoff Bodine	.60	1.50
SM8 Jeff Burton	2.00	5.00
SM9 Steve Grissom	.60	1.50
SM10 Ricky Rudd	2.00	5.00
SM11 Brett Bodine	.60	1.50
SM12 Derrike Cope	.60	1.50
SM13 Ward Burton	1.25	3.00
SM14 Mike Wallace	.60	1.50
SM15 Robert Pressley	.60	1.50
SM16 Ted Musgrave	.60	1.50
SM17 Darrell Waltrip	1.25	3.00
SM18 Bobby Labonte	4.00	10.00
SM19 Ricky Craven	.60	1.50
SM20 Davy Jones	.60	1.50
SM21 Morgan Shepherd	.60	1.50
SM22 Randy LaJoie	.60	1.50
SM23 Jeremy Mayfield	1.25	3.00
SM24 Jeff Gordon	6.00	15.00
SM25 Ken Schrader	.60	1.50
SM26 Todd Bodine	.60	1.50
SM27 John Andretti	.60	1.50
SM28 Dale Jarrett	4.00	10.00
SM29 Greg Sacks	.60	1.50
SM30 Michael Waltrip	1.25	3.00

1996 SP

The 1996 SP hobby set was issued in one series totalling 84 cards. The set contains the topical subsets: Driver Cards (1-42), Cup Contenders (43-74) and RPM (75-84). The 7-card packs retailed for $4.39 each. There were 20 packs per box and 12 boxes per case. The product was distributed through hobby channels only. Also, included as an insert in packs was a card titled Driving Aces. The card is a double sided card with Dale Earnhardt on one side and Jeff Gordon on the other. This card was inserted in packs at a rate of one in 257 and is priced at the bottom of this set.

COMPLETE SET (84)	12.00	30.00
WAX BOX	30.00	60.00
1 Rick Mast	.10	.30
2 Rusty Wallace	1.00	2.50
3 Dale Earnhardt	1.50	4.00
4 Sterling Marlin	.40	1.00
5 Terry Labonte	.40	1.00
6 Mark Martin	1.00	2.50
7 Geoff Bodine	.10	.30
8 Hut Stricklin	.10	.30
9 Lake Speed	.10	.30
10 Ricky Rudd	.40	1.00
11 Brett Bodine	.10	.30
12 Derrike Cope	.10	.30
13 Bill Elliott	.50	1.25
14 Bobby Hamilton	.10	.30
15 Wally Dallenbach	.10	.30
16 Ted Musgrave	.10	.30
17 Darrell Waltrip	.25	.60
18 Bobby Labonte	.75	2.00
19 Loy Allen	.10	.30
20 Morgan Shepherd	.10	.30
21 Michael Waltrip	.25	.60
22 Ward Burton	.25	.60
23 Jimmy Spencer	.10	.30
24 Jeff Gordon	1.25	3.00
25 Ken Schrader	.10	.30
26 Kyle Petty	.25	.60
27 Bobby Hillin	.10	.30
28 Ernie Irvan	.25	.60
29 Steve Grissom	.10	.30
30 Johnny Benson	.25	.60
31 Dave Marcis	.10	.30
32 Jeremy Mayfield	.25	.60
33 Robert Pressley	.10	.30
34 Jeff Burton	.40	1.00
35 Joe Nemechek	.10	.30
36 Dale Jarrett	.75	2.00
37 John Andretti	.10	.30
38 Kenny Wallace	.10	.30
39 Mike Wallace	.10	.30
40 Dick Trickle	.10	.30
41 Ricky Craven	.10	.30
42 Chad Little	.10	.30
43 Jeff Gordon CC	.75	2.00
44 Sterling Marlin CC	.10	.30
45 Mark Martin CC	.60	1.50
46 Rusty Wallace CC	.60	1.50
47 Terry Labonte CC	.25	.60
48 Ted Musgrave CC	.05	.15
49 Bill Elliott CC	.25	.60
50 Ricky Rudd CC	.25	.60
51 Bobby Labonte CC	.50	1.25
52 Morgan Shepherd CC	.05	.15
53 Michael Waltrip CC	.25	.60
54 Dale Jarrett CC	.50	1.25
55 Bobby Hamilton CC	.05	.15
56 Derrike Cope CC	.05	.15
57 Geoff Bodine CC	.05	.15
58 Ken Schrader CC	.05	.15
59 John Andretti CC	.05	.15
60 Darrell Waltrip CC	.10	.30
61 Brett Bodine CC	.05	.15
62 Kenny Wallace CC	.05	.15
63 Ward Burton CC	.10	.30
64 Lake Speed CC	.05	.15
65 Ricky Craven CC	.05	.15
66 Jimmy Spencer CC	.05	.15
67 Steve Grissom CC	.05	.15
68 Joe Nemechek CC	.05	.15
69 Ernie Irvan CC	.10	.30
70 Kyle Petty CC	.10	.30
71 Johnny Benson CC	.10	.30
72 Jeff Burton CC	.25	.60
73 Dave Marcis CC	.05	.15
74 Jeremy Mayfield CC	.10	.30
75 Michael Waltrip RPM	.25	.60
76 Dale Jarrett RPM	.50	1.25
77 Johnny Benson RPM	.10	.30
78 Ricky Craven RPM	.05	.15
79 Rusty Wallace RPM	.60	1.50
80 Jeff Gordon RPM	.75	2.00
81 Terry Labonte RPM	.25	.60
82 Sterling Marlin RPM	.10	.30
83 Mark Martin RPM	.60	1.50
84 Ernie Irvan RPM	.10	.30
S1 Rusty Wallace Promo	1.50	4.00
KR1 Dale Earnhardt Jeff Gordon Aces	40.00	100.00

1996 SP Driving Force

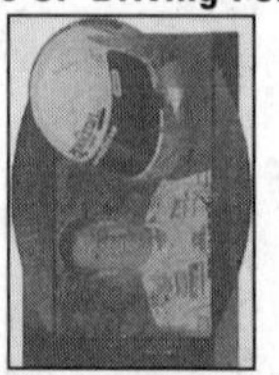

Randomly inserted in packs at a rate of one in 30, this 10-card set featues the top up and coming drivers on the NASCAR circuit. The die-cut cards incorporate a driver's photo and a picture of the driver's helmet on the front.

COMPLETE SET (10)	20.00	50.00
DF1 Johnny Benson	2.50	6.00
DF2 Jeremy Mayfield	2.50	6.00
DF3 Brett Bodine	1.25	3.00
DF4 Robert Pressley	1.25	3.00
DF5 Jeff Burton	4.00	10.00
DF6 Ricky Craven	1.25	3.00
DF7 Wally Dallenbach	1.25	3.00
DF8 Bobby Labonte	8.00	20.00
DF9 Kenny Wallace	1.25	3.00
DF10 Bobby Hamilton	1.25	3.00

1996 SP Holoview Maximum Effects

This 25-card insert set features holoview prin[t] technology to bring your favorite driver to life. [The] cards put the driver's photo in motion and [were] randomly inserted one in six packs. There is al[so a] parallel die-cut version of this set inserted one i[n ...] packs.

COMPLETE SET (25)	50.00	120
COMP. DIE-CUT SET (25)	200.00	500
*DIE CUTS: 1.5X TO 4X BASIC INSERTS		
ME1 Jeff Gordon	10.00	25
ME2 Rusty Wallace	8.00	20
ME3 Dale Earnhardt	12.50	30
ME4 Sterling Marlin	3.00	8
ME5 Terry Labonte	3.00	8
ME6 Mark Martin	8.00	20
ME7 Geoff Bodine	1.00	2
ME8 Johnny Benson	2.00	5
ME9 Derrike Cope	1.00	2
ME10 Ricky Rudd	3.00	8
ME11 Ricky Craven	1.00	2
ME12 John Andretti	1.00	2
ME13 Ken Schrader	1.00	2
ME14 Ernie Irvan	2.00	5
ME15 Steve Grissom	1.00	2
ME16 Ted Musgrave	1.00	2
ME17 Darrell Waltrip	2.00	5
ME18 Bobby Labonte	6.00	15
ME19 Kyle Petty	2.00	5
ME20 Bobby Hamilton	1.00	2
ME21 Kenny Wallace	1.00	2
ME22 Dale Jarrett	6.00	15
ME23 Bill Elliott	4.00	10
ME24 Jeremy Mayfield	2.00	5
ME25 Jeff Burton	3.00	8

1996 SP Racing Legen[ds]

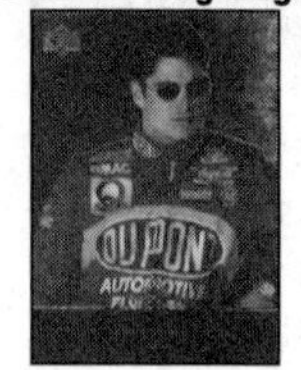

This cross brand insert set features the final cards from the 25 card series. The cards w[ere] randomly inserted in packs at a rate of one in 15.

COMPLETE SET (5)	15.00	40
RL21 Rusty Wallace	6.00	15
RL22 Bill Elliott	3.00	8
RL23 Mark Martin	6.00	15
RL24 Jeff Gordon	8.00	20
RL25 Header	.40	1

1996 SP Richard Petty/STP 25th Anniversary

Randomly inserted in packs at a rate of one in [...] this nine-card set provides a historical perspe[ctive] on the 25 year relationship between two of [the] biggest names in racing. The cards use an intri[cate] die cut process to make them unique.

COMPLETE SET (9)	40.00	100
COMMON CARD (RP1-RP9)	5.00	12

1997 SP

This 126-card set was produced by Upper Dec[k and] was distributed in packs in three tiers. The cards [are] designated by flags on their borders. The single [flag] cards are randomly inserted in packs at a ratio of [...] The double flag cards are randomly inserted in p[acks] at a ratio of 1:3. The triple flag cards are rand[omly] inserted in packs at a ratio of 1:7. The double and triple flag tiers contain 21 cards each. C[ards] were distributed in seven card packs with 20 p[acks] per box and 12 boxes per cases. 1000 cases of [the] product were produced.

COMPLETE SET (126)	100.00	200
COMP.SINGLE FLAG (84)	6.00	15
1 Morgan Shepherd	.10	
2 Rusty Wallace	1.00	2
3 Dale Earnhardt 3F	15.00	40
4 Sterling Marlin	.40	1
5 Terry Labonte	.40	1
6 Mark Martin 2F	5.00	12
7 Geoff Bodine	.10	
8 Hut Stricklin	.10	
9 Lake Speed	.10	
10 Ricky Rudd	.40	1
11 Brett Bodine	.10	
12 Dale Jarrett	.75	2
13 Bill Elliott	.50	1
14 Bobby Hamilton	.10	

illy Dallenbach	.10	.30
i Musgrave	.10	.30
rrell Waltrip 3F	2.50	6.00
bby Labonte	.75	2.00
y Allen	.10	.30
k Mast	.10	.30
chael Waltrip 2F	1.25	3.00
rd Burton 2F	1.25	3.00
nmy Spencer	.10	.30
f Gordon 3F	12.00	30.00
ky Craven 3F	1.25	3.00
e Petty	.25	.60
bby Hillin	.10	.30
ie Irvan	.25	.60
bert Pressley	.10	.30
nny Benson 2F	1.25	3.00
ve Marcis	.25	.60
emy Mayfield	.25	.60
n Schrader 2F	.60	1.50
f Burton	.40	1.00
ad Little	.25	.60
rrike Cope	.10	.30
nn Andretti	.10	.30
nny Wallace	.10	.30
k Trickle	.10	.30
vid Green 3F	1.25	3.00
ke Wallace	.10	.30
e Nemechek	.10	.30
rgan Shepherd's Car	.05	.15
sty Wallace's Car	.40	1.00
le Earnhardt's Car 3F	6.00	15.00
rling Marlin's Car	.10	.30
ry Labonte's Car 2F	1.25	3.00
rk Martin's Car	.40	1.00
off Bodine's Car	.05	.15
t Stricklin's Car	.05	.15
ke Speed's Car	.05	.15
ky Rudd's Car 2F	.60	1.50
ett Bodine's Car	.05	.15
le Jarrett's Car	.25	.60
l Elliott's Car 3F	2.50	6.00
bby Hamilton's Car 2F	.30	.75
lly Dallenbach's Car	.05	.15
i Musgrave's Car	.05	.15
rrell Waltrip's Car	.10	.30
bby Labonte's Car	.25	.60
y Allen's Car	.05	.15
k Mast's Car	.05	.15
chael Waltrip's Car	.10	.30
rd Burton's Car	.10	.30
nmy Spencer's Car 2F	.30	.75
f Gordon's Car	.60	1.50
ky Craven's Car	.05	.15
e Petty's Car 3F	.60	1.50
bby Hillin's Car	.05	.15
ie Irvan's Car	.10	.30
bert Pressley's Car 3F	.60	1.50
nny Benson's Car	.10	.30
ve Marcis's Car	.10	.30
emy Mayfield's Car	.10	.30
n Schrader's Car	.05	.15
f Burton's Car	.25	.60
ad Little's Car	.05	.15
rrike Cope's Car 2F	.30	.75
nn Andretti's Car	.05	.15
nny Wallace's Car	.05	.15
k Trickle's Car	.05	.15
vid Green's Car 3F	.60	1.50
ke Wallace	.10	.30
e Nemechek	.10	.30
sty Wallace 3F	8.00	20.00
rling Marlin 2F	2.00	5.00
ry Labonte 3F	5.00	12.00
rk Martin 2F	5.00	12.00
off Bodine	.10	.30
ke Speed	.10	.30
ky Rudd 3F	4.00	10.00
e Jarrett 2F	4.00	10.00
Elliott 2F	2.50	6.00
bby Hamilton	.10	.30
lly Dallenbach	.10	.30
i Musgrave	.10	.30
rrell Waltrip	.25	.60
bby Labonte 2F	4.00	10.00
chael Waltrip	.25	.60
ard Burton	.25	.60
mmy Spencer	.10	.30
ff Gordon 2F	6.00	15.00
cky Craven	.10	.30
yle Petty 3F	2.50	6.00
nie Irvan 2F	1.25	3.00
hnny Benson	.25	.60
eremy Mayfield	.25	.60
en Schrader 3F	1.25	3.00
ff Burton	.40	1.00
errike Cope	.10	.30
ohn Andretti	.10	.30
enny Wallace	.10	.30
usty Wallace 3F	8.00	20.00
erling Marlin	.40	1.00
erry Labonte 3F	5.00	12.00
ark Martin 3F	8.00	20.00
cky Rudd 2F	2.00	5.00
ale Jarrett 3F	6.00	15.00
ll Elliott	.50	1.25
obby Labonte 2F	4.00	10.00
mmy Spencer 2F	.60	1.50
eff Gordon 3F	12.00	30.00
yle Petty	.25	.60
nie Irvan 3F	2.50	6.00
icky Craven 2F	.60	1.50
en Schrader	.10	.30
eff Gordon Sample	1.50	4.00

997 SP Super Series

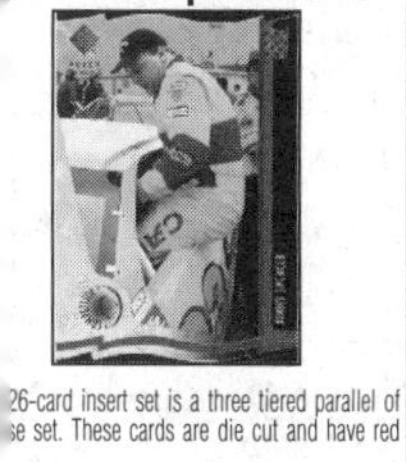

26-card insert set is a three tiered parallel of se set. These cards are die cut and have red borders to differentiate them from the base set. The single flag cards are randomly inserted in packs at a ratio of 1:5. The double flag cards are randomly inserted in packs at a ratio of 1:40. The triple flag cards are randomly inserted in packs at a ratio of 1:240. The double flag and triple flag tiers include 21-cards each.

COMP.SINGLE FLAG (84)	90.00	150.00

*SINGLE FLAGS: 4X TO 10X BASE CARDS
*DOUBLE FLAGS 2X TO 5X BASE CARDS
*TRIPLE FLAGS 2.5X TO 6X BASE CARDS

1997 SP Race Film

This 10-card insert set features film technology to capture race moments. Each card is numbered of 400. The cards were randomly inserted in packs at a ratio of 1:63.

COMPLETE SET (10)	60.00	120.00
RD1 Jeff Gordon	12.50	30.00
RD2 Rusty Wallace	10.00	25.00
RD3 Dale Earnhardt	15.00	40.00
RD4 Sterling Marlin	4.00	10.00
RD5 Terry Labonte	4.00	10.00
RD6 Mark Martin	10.00	25.00
RD7 Dale Jarrett	8.00	20.00
RD8 Ernie Irvan	2.50	6.00
RD9 Bill Elliott	5.00	12.00
RD10 Ricky Rudd	4.00	10.00

1997 SP SPx Force Autographs

This 4-card set features Upper Deck's holoview technology. Each of the four drivers signed 100 cards each. The cards were randomly inserted in packs at a ratio of 1:480.

COMPLETE SET (4)	300.00	500.00
SF1 Jeff Gordon	125.00	250.00
SF2 Rusty Wallace	75.00	150.00
SF3 Ricky Craven	40.00	80.00
SF4 Terry Labonte	50.00	100.00

1998 SP Authentic

The 1998 SP Authentic set was issued in one series totalling 84 cards. The 5-card packs retail for a suggested price of $4.99 each. The set contains the topical subset: Victory Lap (69-84).

COMPLETE SET (84)	15.00	40.00
1 Jeremy Mayfield	.30	.75
2 Rusty Wallace	1.25	3.00
3 Dale Earnhardt	2.50	6.00
4 Bobby Hamilton	.15	.40
5 Terry Labonte	.50	1.25
6 Mark Martin	1.25	3.00
7 Geoff Bodine	.15	.40
8 Hut Stricklin	.15	.40
9 Jeff Burton	.50	1.25
10 Ricky Rudd	.50	1.25
11 Johnny Benson	.30	.75
12 Dale Jarrett	1.00	2.50
13 Jerry Nadeau RC	.50	1.25
14 Steve Park	1.00	2.50
15 Bill Elliott	.60	1.50
16 Ted Musgrave	.15	.40
17 Darrell Waltrip	.30	.75
18 Bobby Labonte	1.00	2.50
19 Todd Bodine	.15	.40
20 Kyle Petty	.30	.75
21 Michael Waltrip	.30	.75
22 Ken Schrader	.15	.40
23 Jimmy Spencer	.15	.40
24 Jeff Gordon	1.50	4.00
25 Ricky Craven	.15	.40
26 John Andretti	.15	.40
27 Sterling Marlin	.50	1.25
28 Kenny Irwin	.30	.75
29 Mike Skinner	.15	.40
30 Derrike Cope	.15	.40
31 Ernie Irvan	.30	.75
32 Joe Nemechek	.15	.40
33 Kenny Wallace	.15	.40
34 Ward Burton	.30	.75
35 Jeremy Mayfield's Car	.15	.40
36 Rusty Wallace's Car	.50	1.25
37 Dale Earnhardt's Car	1.00	2.50
38 Bobby Hamilton's Car	.07	.20
39 Terry Labonte's Car	.30	.75
40 Mark Martin's Car	.50	1.25
41 Geoff Bodine's Car	.07	.20
42 Hut Stricklin's Car	.07	.20
43 Jeff Burton's Car	.15	.40
44 Ricky Rudd's Car	.15	.40
45 Johnny Benson's Car	.07	.20
46 Dale Jarrett's Car	.30	.75
47 Jerry Nadeau's Car	.30	.75
48 Steve Park's Car	.30	.75
49 Bill Elliott's Car	.30	.75
50 Ted Musgrave's Car	.07	.20
51 Darrell Waltrip's Car	.15	.40
52 Bobby Labonte's Car	.30	.75
53 Todd Bodine's Car	.07	.20
54 Kyle Petty's Car	.15	.40
55 Michael Waltrip's Car	.15	.40
56 Ken Schrader's Car	.07	.20
57 Jimmy Spencer's Car	.07	.20
58 Jeff Gordon's Car	.60	1.50
59 Ricky Craven's Car	.07	.20
60 John Andretti's Car	.07	.20
61 Sterling Marlin's Car	.15	.40
62 Kenny Irwin's Car	.15	.40
63 Mike Skinner's Car	.07	.20
64 Derrike Cope's Car	.07	.20
65 Ernie Irvan's Car	.15	.40
66 Joe Nemechek's Car	.07	.20
67 Kenny Wallace's Car	.07	.20
68 Ward Burton's Car	.15	.40
69 Darrell Waltrip VL	.30	.75
70 Rusty Wallace VL	1.25	3.00
71 Bill Elliott VL	.60	1.50
72 Jeff Gordon VL	1.50	4.00
73 Geoff Bodine VL	.15	.40
74 Terry Labonte VL	.50	1.25
75 Mark Martin VL	1.25	3.00
76 Ricky Rudd VL	.50	1.25
77 Ernie Irvan VL	.30	.75
78 Dale Jarrett VL	1.00	2.50
79 Kyle Petty VL	.30	.75
80 Sterling Marlin VL	.50	1.25
81 Dave Marcis VL	.30	.75
82 Bobby Labonte VL	1.00	2.50
83 Ken Schrader VL	.15	.40
84 Jimmy Spencer VL	.15	.40
SPA2 Rusty Wallace Sample	1.50	4.00

1998 SP Authentic Behind the Wheel

Randomly inserted in packs at a rate of one in 4, this is the first of a three-tiered insert set that features 20 of the top NASCAR Winston Cup drivers, with each level boasting its own special insert ratio and foil treatment. Level 1 features a silver foil.

COMPLETE SET (20)	20.00	50.00
COMP.GOLD SET (20)	50.00	100.00

*GOLDS: .8X TO 2X BASIC INSERTS
GOLD STATED ODDS 1:12
*DIE CUTS: 5X TO 12X BASIC INSERTS
DIE CUTS PRINT RUN 100 SER.#'D SETS

BW1 Jeff Gordon	4.00	10.00
BW2 Dale Jarrett	2.50	6.00
BW3 Mark Martin	3.00	8.00
BW4 Jeff Burton	1.25	3.00
BW5 Terry Labonte	1.25	3.00
BW6 Bobby Labonte	2.50	6.00
BW7 Bill Elliott	1.50	4.00
BW8 Rusty Wallace	3.00	8.00
BW9 Ken Schrader	.40	1.00
BW10 Johnny Benson	.75	2.00
BW11 Ted Musgrave	.40	1.00
BW12 Jeremy Mayfield	.75	2.00
BW13 Ernie Irvan	.75	2.00
BW14 Kyle Petty	.75	2.00
BW15 Bobby Hamilton	.40	1.00
BW16 Ricky Rudd	1.25	3.00
BW17 Michael Waltrip	.75	2.00
BW18 Ricky Craven	.40	1.00
BW19 Kenny Irwin	.75	2.00
BW20 Steve Park	2.50	6.00

1998 SP Authentic Mark of a Legend

Randomly inserted in packs at a rate of one in 168, this five card insert set features autographs from all-time NASCAR greats.

COMPLETE SET (5)	150.00	250.00
M1 Richard Petty/220	40.00	80.00
M2 David Pearson	20.00	50.00
M3 Benny Parsons	30.00	60.00
M4 Ned Jarrett	15.00	40.00
M5 Cale Yarborough/220	15.00	40.00

1998 SP Authentic Sign of the Times

Randomly inserted in packs at a rate of one in 24, this is the first of a two-tiered insert set that contains autographs from today's top NASCAR stars including Jeff Gordon, Mark Martin and Rusty Wallace. Each card features the driver's car along with a large box in the lower right that features the signature. The basic inserts feature blue foil. Some cards were initially issued as redemptions in packs that carried an expiration date of 6/30/1999.

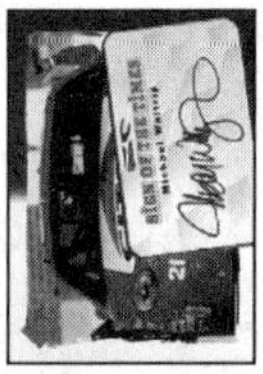

COMPLETE SET (10)	100.00	200.00
S1 Rusty Wallace's Car	12.50	30.00
S2 Ted Musgrave's Car	5.00	12.00
S3 Ricky Craven's Car	5.00	12.00
S4 Sterling Marlin's Car	10.00	25.00
S5 John Andretti's Car	5.00	12.00
S6 Michael Waltrip's Car	10.00	25.00
S7 Darrell Waltrip's Car	8.00	20.00
S8 Jeremy Mayfield's Car	6.00	15.00
S9 Kenny Irwin's Car	12.50	30.00
S10 Bobby Hamilton's Car	10.00	25.00

1998 SP Authentic Sign of the Times Red

Randomly inserted in packs at a rate of one in 96, this is the second of a two-tiered insert set that contains autographs from today's top NASCAR stars including Jeff Gordon, Mark Martin and Rusty Wallace. Each card features the driver's car along with a large box in the lower right that features the signature. The red foil version also included hand numbering on the backs. Some cards were initially issued as redemptions in packs that carried an expiration date of 6/30/1999.

COMPLETE SET (10)	400.00	800.00
ST1 Jeff Gordon's Car/45	150.00	300.00
ST2 Ernie Irvan's Car	15.00	40.00
ST3 Dale Earnhardt's Car	250.00	350.00
ST4 Kyle Petty's Car	15.00	40.00
ST5 Terry Labonte's Car	50.00	100.00
ST6 Mark Martin's Car	30.00	60.00
ST7 Dale Jarrett's Car/239	30.00	60.00
ST8 Jeff Burton's Car	10.00	25.00
ST9 Bobby Labonte's Car	12.50	30.00
ST10 Ricky Rudd's Car	15.00	40.00

1998 SP Authentic Traditions

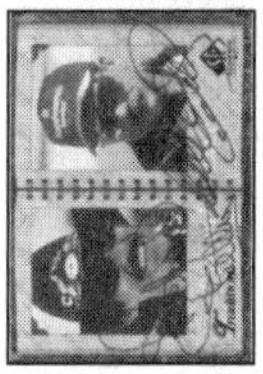

Randomly inserted in packs at a rate of one in 288, this five card insert set features two authentic autographs: one from a NASCAR legend, and one from a current NASCAR superstar. Some cards were initially issued as redemptions in packs that carried an expiration date of 7/15/1999.

COMPLETE SET (5)	800.00	1200.00
T1 Richard Petty Dale Earnhardt	350.00	500.00
T2 David Pearson Jeff Gordon	200.00	350.00
T3 Benny Parsons Terry Labonte	100.00	200.00
T4 Ned Jarrett Dale Jarrett	100.00	175.00
T5 Cale Yarborough Rusty Wallace	60.00	120.00

1999 SP Authentic

This 83 card set produced by Upper Deck was issued in four card packs. Cards numbered from 73 through 83 were produced in shorter supply than the other cards with 73 through 82 having a print run of 1000 cards and 83 having a print run of 500 signed cards. Card number 83 was also an exchange card that expired on May 25, 2000.

COMPLETE SET (83)	150.00	300.00
COMP.SET w/o SP's (72)	12.50	30.00
1 Jeff Gordon	1.50	4.00
2 Dale Earnhardt	2.50	6.00
3 Tony Stewart CRC	2.00	5.00
4 Dale Jarrett	1.00	2.50
5 Bobby Labonte	1.00	2.50
6 Ken Schrader	.15	.40
7 Jerry Nadeau	.30	.75
8 Mike Skinner	.15	.40
9 Kyle Petty	.30	.75
10 Johnny Benson	.30	.75
11 Kenny Irwin	.30	.75
12 Ward Burton	.30	.75
13 Kevin Lepage	.15	.40
14 Ernie Irvan	.30	.75
15 Jeff Burton	.50	1.25
16 Rusty Wallace	1.25	3.00
17 Jeremy Mayfield	.30	.75
18 Elliott Sadler	.30	.75
19 Bill Elliott	.60	1.50
20 Mark Martin	1.25	3.00
21 Michael Waltrip	.30	.75
22 Robert Pressley	.15	.40
23 Ricky Rudd	.50	1.25
24 Geoffrey Bodine	.15	.40
25 John Andretti	.15	.40
26 Darrell Waltrip	.30	.75
27 Steve Park	.75	2.00
28 Chad Little	.30	.75
29 Bobby Hamilton	.15	.40
30 Dale Earnhardt Jr.	2.00	5.00
31 Jason Keller	.15	.40
32 Kenny Irwin's Car	.08	.20
33 Geoffrey Bodine's Car	.08	.20
34 Robert Pressley's Car	.08	.20
35 Kevin Lepage's Car	.08	.20
36 Tony Stewart's Car	.60	1.50
37 Dale Earnhardt Jr's Car	.75	2.00
38 Ernie Irvan's Car	.15	.40
39 Jeff Burton's Car	.15	.40
40 Chad Little's Car	.08	.20
41 Rusty Wallace's Car	.50	1.25
42 Steve Park's Car	.30	.75
43 Mike Skinner's Car	.08	.20
44 Jeremy Mayfield's Car	.15	.40
45 Elliott Sadler's Car	.08	.20
46 Bill Elliott's Car	.30	.75
47 Darrell Waltrip's Car	.15	.40
48 John Andretti's Car	.08	.20
49 Kyle Petty's Car	.08	.20
50 Johnny Benson's Car	.15	.40
51 Jeff Gordon's Car	.60	1.50
52 Dale Jarrett's Car	.30	.75
53 Dale Earnhardt's Car	1.00	2.50
54 Terry Labonte's Car	.30	.75
55 Bobby Labonte's Car	.30	.75
56 Jerry Nadeau's Car	.15	.40
57 Ricky Rudd's Car	.15	.40
58 Bobby Hamilton's Car	.08	.20
59 Michael Waltrip's Car	.15	.40
60 Ken Schrader's Car	.08	.20
61 Mark Martin's Car	.50	1.25
62 Mark Martin CLASS	.60	1.50
63 Darrell Waltrip CLASS	.15	.40
64 Rusty Wallace CLASS	.60	1.50
65 Jeff Gordon CLASS	.75	2.00
66 Dale Earnhardt Jr. CLASS	1.00	2.50
67 Bobby Labonte CLASS	.50	1.25
68 Jeremy Mayfield CLASS	.15	.40
69 Terry Labonte CLASS	.50	1.25
70 Jeff Burton CLASS	.30	.75
71 Dale Jarrett CLASS	.50	1.25
72 Dale Earnhardt Jr. CL	1.00	2.50
73 Bobby Labonte SP	5.00	12.00
74 Ward Burton SP	2.50	6.00
75 Jeremy Mayfield SP	2.50	6.00
76 Mark Martin SP	6.00	15.00
77 Rusty Wallace SP	6.00	15.00
78 Jeff Burton SP	3.00	8.00
79 Dale Earnhardt SP	12.50	30.00
80 Dale Jarrett SP	5.00	12.00
81 Tony Stewart SP	7.50	20.00
82 Jeff Gordon SP	7.50	20.00
83 Dale Earnhardt Jr. SP AUTO/500	60.00	120.00

1999 SP Authentic Overdrive

This is a parallel set to the regular SP Authentic set. These cards are randomly inserted in packs and cards numbered 1 to 72 were printed in quantity of 200 cards each while cards numbered 73 through 83 were printed to the car number of the driver. Similar to the regular set, the Dale Earnhardt Jr.card was also autographed.

*SINGLES 1-72: 3X TO 8X BASIC CARDS
1-72 STATED PRINT RUN 200 SER.#'d SETS

73 Bobby Labonte SP/18		
74 Ward Burton SP/22	25.00	60.00
75 Jeremy Mayfield SP/12		
76 Mark Martin SP/6		
77 Rusty Wallace SP/2		
78 Jeff Burton SP/99	25.00	60.00
79 Dale Earnhardt SP/3		
80 Dale Jarrett SP/88	40.00	100.00
81 Tony Stewart SP/20	100.00	250.00
82 Jeff Gordon SP/24	125.00	300.00
83 D.Earnhardt Jr. SP AU/3		

1999 SP Authentic Cup Challengers

Inserted one every 23 packs, these cards feature 10 of the leading contenders for the Winston Cup title.

COMPLETE SET (10)	30.00	60.00
CC1 Jeff Gordon	6.00	15.00
CC2 Dale Jarrett	4.00	10.00
CC3 Jeff Burton	2.00	5.00
CC4 Rusty Wallace	5.00	12.00
CC5 Mark Martin	5.00	12.00
CC6 Jeremy Mayfield	1.25	3.00
CC7 Ward Burton	1.25	3.00
CC8 Bobby Labonte	4.00	10.00
CC9 Tony Stewart	6.00	15.00
CC10 Elliott Sadler	1.25	3.00

1999 SP Authentic Driving Force

Inserted one every 11 packs, these cards feature 11 drivers who are considered among the keys to bringing more fans to the NASCAR races.

COMPLETE SET (11)	20.00	40.00
DF1 Bobby Labonte	2.00	5.00
DF2 Terry Labonte	1.00	2.50
DF3 Jeremy Mayfield	.60	1.50
DF4 Mark Martin	2.50	6.00
DF5 Rusty Wallace	2.50	6.00
DF6 Jeff Burton	1.00	2.50
DF7 Dale Earnhardt	5.00	12.00
DF8 Jeff Gordon	3.00	8.00
DF9 Dale Earnhardt Jr.	4.00	10.00
DF10 Elliott Sadler	.60	1.50
DF11 Tony Stewart	3.00	8.00

1999 SP Authentic In the Driver's Seat

Inserted one every four packs, these nine cards feature racers who are considered the shapers of NASCAR. Card number DS6 was not produced.

COMPLETE SET (9)	12.50	30.00
DS1 Dale Earnhardt	3.00	8.00
DS2 Jeremy Mayfield	.40	1.00
DS3 Rusty Wallace	1.50	4.00
DS4 Tony Stewart	2.00	5.00
DS5 Bobby Labonte	1.25	3.00
DS7 Dale Earnhardt Jr.	2.50	6.00
DS8 Mark Martin	1.50	4.00
DS9 Jeff Burton	.60	1.50
DS10 Jeff Gordon	2.00	5.00

1999 SP Authentic Sign of the Times

Inserted one every 11 packs, these 26 cards feature signatures of NASCAR drivers. Several cards were issued via mail exchange cards.

COMPLETE SET (26)	500.00	1000.00
BE Bill Elliott	12.50	30.00
BH Bobby Hamilton	10.00	25.00
BL Bobby Labonte	12.50	30.00
CL Chad Little	6.00	15.00
DE Dale Earnhardt	200.00	400.00
DJ Dale Jarrett	12.50	30.00
EI Ernie Irvan	8.00	20.00
GB Geoffrey Bodine	6.00	15.00
JA John Andretti	6.00	15.00
JB Jeff Burton	8.00	20.00
JG Jeff Gordon	75.00	150.00
JM Jeremy Mayfield	6.00	15.00
JN Jerry Nadeau	8.00	20.00
KL Kevin Lepage	4.00	10.00
KP Kyle Petty	10.00	25.00
KS Ken Schrader	6.00	15.00
MM Mark Martin	40.00	80.00
MS Mike Skinner	6.00	15.00
RW Rusty Wallace	12.50	30.00
SM Sterling Marlin	8.00	20.00
SP Steve Park	8.00	20.00
TL Terry Labonte	12.50	30.00
TS Tony Stewart	40.00	80.00
WB Ward Burton	8.00	20.00
DEJ Dale Earnhardt Jr.	60.00	120.00
JBN Johnny Benson	6.00	15.00

2000 SP Authentic

Released as a 90-card set, SP Authentic features 45 regular cards, 30 SP Performance cards, and 15 SP Supremacy cards. SP Authentic was packaged in 24-pack boxes with four cards per pack and carried a suggested retail price of $3.99. Cards numbered from 46 through 75 had a stated print run of 2500 sets while cards numbered from 76 through 90 had a stated print run on 1000 sets.

COMPLETE SET (90)	60.00	120.00
COMP.SET w/o SP's (45)	10.00	25.00
WAX BOX	175.00	300.00
1 Bobby Labonte	1.00	2.50
2 Mark Martin	1.25	3.00
3 Ward Burton	.30	.75
4 Jeff Burton	.50	1.25
5 Dale Earnhardt	2.50	6.00
6 Rusty Wallace	1.00	3.00
7 Dale Jarrett	1.00	2.50
8 Ricky Rudd	.50	1.25
9 Jeremy Mayfield	.15	.40
10 Tony Stewart	2.00	5.00
11 Terry Labonte	.50	1.25
12 Jeff Gordon	1.50	4.00
13 Bill Elliott	.60	1.50
14 Justin Labonte	.15	.40
15 Chad Little	.30	.75
16 Mike Skinner	.15	.40
17 Sterling Marlin	.50	1.25
18 Johnny Benson	.30	.75
19 Dale Earnhardt Jr. CRC	2.00	5.00
20 Steve Park	.50	1.25
21 Matt Kenseth CRC	1.25	3.00
22 John Andretti	.15	.40
23 Bobby Hamilton	.15	.40
24 Kevin Lepage	.15	.40
25 P.J. Jones	.15	.40
26 Michael Waltrip	.30	.75
27 Joe Nemechek	.15	.40
28 Kenny Irwin	.30	.75
29 Elliott Sadler	.30	.75
30 Jerry Nadeau	.30	.75
31 Kyle Petty	.30	.75
32 Stacy Compton RC	.30	.75
33 Robby Gordon	.15	.40
34 Darrell Waltrip	.30	.75
35 Scott Pruett	.15	.40
36 Todd Bodine	.15	.40
37 Randy LaJoie	.15	.40
38 Jason Leffler	.15	.40
39 Jimmie Johnson RC	7.50	15.00
40 Kurt Busch	3.00	8.00
41 Kevin Grubb	.15	.40
42 Hank Parker Jr. RC	.50	1.25
43 Jason Keller	.15	.40
44 Kevin Harvick	1.25	3.00
45 Casey Atwood	.50	1.25
46 Chad Little PER	1.25	3.00
47 Mike Skinner PER	.75	2.00
48 Johnny Benson PER	1.25	3.00
49 Kenny Wallace PER	.75	2.00
50 John Andretti PER	.75	2.00
51 Bobby Hamilton PER	.75	2.00
52 Kevin Lepage PER	.75	2.00
53 Michael Waltrip PER	1.25	3.00
54 Joe Nemechek PER	.75	2.00
55 Kenny Irwin PER	1.25	3.00
56 Elliott Sadler PER	1.25	3.00
57 Robert Pressley PER	.75	2.00
58 Dick Trickle PER	.75	2.00
59 Stacy Compton PER	1.25	3.00
60 Robby Gordon PER	.75	2.00
61 Jason Leffler PER	.75	2.00
62 Justin Labonte PER	.75	2.00
63 Jason Jarrett PER	.75	2.00
64 Jerry Nadeau PER	1.25	3.00
65 Jay Sauter PER	.75	2.00
66 Lyndon Amick PER	.75	2.00
67 Jimmie Johnson PER	7.50	15.00
68 Michael Ritch PER	.75	2.00
69 Tony Raines PER RC	1.25	3.00
70 Darrell Waltrip PER	1.25	3.00
71 Kevin Grubb PER	.75	2.00
72 Hank Parker Jr. PER	2.00	5.00
73 Jason Keller PER	.75	2.00
74 Kevin Harvick PER	6.00	15.00
75 Casey Atwood PER	2.00	5.00
76 Bobby Labonte SUP	5.00	12.00
77 Mark Martin SUP	6.00	15.00
78 Ward Burton SUP	1.50	4.00
79 Jeff Burton SUP	3.00	8.00
80 Dale Earnhardt SUP	10.00	25.00
81 Rusty Wallace SUP	6.00	15.00
82 Dale Jarrett SUP	5.00	12.00
83 Ricky Rudd SUP	3.00	8.00
84 Jeremy Mayfield SUP	1.50	4.00
85 Tony Stewart SUP	10.00	25.00
86 Terry Labonte SUP	3.00	8.00
87 Jeff Gordon SUP	7.50	20.00
88 Bill Elliott SUP	3.00	8.00
89 Dale Earnhardt Jr. SUP	10.00	25.00
90 Matt Kenseth SUP	8.00	20.00
P88 Dale Jarrett Promo	1.00	2.50

2000 SP Authentic Overdrive Gold

Randomly inserted in packs, this 90-card set parallels the base SP Authentic set with each card sequentially numbered to the driver's car number.

*1-45 SINGLES/70-99: 8X TO 20X HI COL.
*1-45 SINGLES/45-69: 12.5X TO 25X HI COL.
*1-45 SINGLES/30-44: 15X TO 30X HI COL.
*1-45 SINGLES/20-29: 20X TO 40X HI COL.
*46-75 SINGLES/70-99: 2X TO 5X HI COL.
*46-75 SINGLES/45-69: 2.5X TO 6X HI COL.
*46-75 SINGLES/30-44: 5X TO 10X HI COL.
*46-75 SINGLES/20-29: 7.5X TO 15X HI COL.
*76-90 SINGLES/70-99: 1X TO 2.5X HI COL.
*76-90 SINGLES/20-29: 4X TO 8X HI COL.

39 Jimmie Johnson/92	25.00	60.00
40 Kurt Busch/99	20.00	50.00

2000 SP Authentic Overdrive Silver

Randomly inserted in packs, this 90-card set parallels the base SP Authentic with each card sequentially numbered to 250.

*SILVERS 1-45: 4X TO 10X BASE CARDS
*SILVERS 46-75: .8X TO 2X BASE CARDS
*SILVERS 76-90: .4X TO 1X BASE CARDS

39 Jimmie Johnson	10.00	25.00
40 Kurt Busch	6.00	15.00

2000 SP Authentic Dominance

Randomly inserted in packs at the rate of one in 24, this 6-card set spotlights the most dominating NASCAR drivers. The cards contain foil highlights.

COMPLETE SET (6)	20.00	50.00
D1 Tony Stewart	8.00	20.00
D2 Dale Earnhardt Jr.	8.00	20.00
D3 Matt Kenseth	5.00	12.00
D4 Rusty Wallace	5.00	12.00
D5 Jeremy Mayfield	.60	1.50
D6 Jeff Burton	2.00	5.00

2000 SP Authentic Driver's Seat

Randomly inserted in packs at the rate of one in four, this 10-card set features close up shots of the racer in his car. Each card contains silver foil highlights.

COMPLETE SET (10)	8.00	20.00
DS1 Dale Jarrett	1.25	3.00
DS2 Bobby Labonte	1.25	3.00
DS3 Mark Martin	1.50	4.00
DS4 Tony Stewart	2.50	6.00
DS5 Jeff Burton	.60	1.50
DS6 Jeff Gordon	2.00	5.00
DS7 Matt Kenseth	1.50	4.00
DS8 Rusty Wallace	1.50	4.00
DS9 Ward Burton	.40	1.00
DS10 Mike Skinner	.20	.50

2000 SP Authentic High Velocity

Randomly inserted in packs at the rate of one in 12, this 7-card set features portrait photos of drivers and action photos of their cars. Each card contains silver foil highlights.

COMPLETE SET (8)	4.00	10.00
HV1 Ricky Rudd	.60	1.50
HV2 Bill Elliott	.75	2.00
HV3 Darrell Waltrip	.40	1.00
HV4 Terry Labonte	.60	1.50
HV5 Kyle Petty	.40	1.00
HV6 Jeremy Mayfield	.20	.50
HV7 Sterling Marlin	.60	1.50
HV8 Casey Atwood	.60	1.50

2000 SP Authentic Power Surge

Randomly inserted in packs at the rate of one in 24, this 7-card set highlights NASCAR drivers who take their cars to the limit week after week.

COMPLETE SET (7)	25.00	60.00
PS1 Dale Earnhardt	10.00	25.00
PS2 Jeff Gordon	6.00	15.00
PS3 Tony Stewart	8.00	20.00
PS4 Dale Earnhardt Jr.	8.00	20.00
PS5 Matt Kenseth	5.00	12.00
PS6 Mark Martin	5.00	12.00
PS7 Dale Jarrett	4.00	10.00

2000 SP Authentic Race for the Cup

Randomly inserted in packs at the rate of one in 12, this 10-card set features top NASCAR contenders.

COMPLETE SET (10)	8.00	20.00
R1 Jeff Gordon	2.00	5.00
R2 Dale Jarrett	1.25	3.00
R3 Ward Burton	.40	1.00
R4 Jeff Burton	.60	1.50
R5 Mark Martin	1.50	4.00
R6 Bobby Labonte	1.25	3.00
R7 Tony Stewart	2.50	6.00
R8 Rusty Wallace	1.50	4.00
R9 Ricky Rudd	.60	1.50
R10 Jeremy Mayfield	.20	.50

2000 SP Authentic Sign of the Times

Randomly inserted in packs at the rate of one in 11, this set features authentic autographs from some of NASCAR's finest. Some cards were released through exchange cards inserted into packs. Most drivers signed the cards with a blue felt tip pen while a few can be found with either blue or black ink. The basic inserts were printed with bronze colored ink wording on the fronts and feature a silver hologram Upper Deck logo on the back. A Gold parallel set was also produced with each card hand serial numbered of 25. The Gold version was printed with gold ink on the front and a gold hologram on back. Any additions to this list are appreciated.

BB Brett Bodine	5.00	12.00
BE Bill Elliott	15.00	40.00
BH Bobby Hamilton	10.00	25.00
BI Greg Biffle	12.50	30.00
BL Bobby Labonte EXCH		
CL Chad Little	5.00	12.00
CR Rick Crawford	6.00	15.00
DE Dale Earnhardt	300.00	450.00
DG Derrick Gilchrist	5.00	12.00
DJ Dale Jarrett	12.50	30.00
DM Dave Marcis	6.00	15.00
DT Dick Trickle	5.00	12.00
EI Ernie Irvan	8.00	20.00
ES Elliott Sadler	15.00	40.00
GB Geoff Bodine	5.00	12.00
GW Gus Wasson	5.00	12.00
HE Hermie Sadler	5.00	12.00
HI Bobby Hillin	5.00	12.00
HS Hut Stricklin	5.00	12.00
JA John Andretti	6.00	15.00
JB Jeff Burton	8.00	20.00
JG Jeff Gordon	75.00	150.00
JI Jimmie Johnson	40.00	80.00
JK Jason Keller	5.00	12.00
JM Jeremy Mayfield	6.00	15.00
JN Jerry Nadeau	6.00	15.00
JO Joe Nemechek	5.00	12.00
JR Dale Earnhardt Jr.	60.00	120.00
JS Jamie Skinner SP	60.00	120.00
JY Jay Sauter	5.00	12.00
KB Kurt Busch	15.00	40.00
KH Kevin Harvick	15.00	40.00
KL Kevin Lepage	5.00	12.00
LA Lyndon Amick	8.00	20.00
MH Matt Hutter	5.00	12.00
MK Matt Kenseth	15.00	40.00
MM Mark Martin	50.00	100.00
MS Mike Skinner	5.00	12.00
PJ P.J. Jones	5.00	12.00
PR Scott Pruett	5.00	12.00
RB Rich Bickle	5.00	12.00
RG Robby Gordon	6.00	15.00
RH Ron Hornaday	5.00	12.00
RL Randy LaJoie	5.00	12.00
RM Rick Mast	5.00	12.00
RP Robert Pressley	5.00	12.00
RW Rusty Wallace	15.00	40.00
SA Elton Sawyer	5.00	12.00
SC Stacy Compton	5.00	12.00
SM Sterling Marlin	8.00	20.00
SP Steve Park	6.00	15.00
TB Todd Bodine	5.00	12.00
TF Tim Fedewa	5.00	12.00
TL Terry Labonte	15.00	40.00
TR Tony Raines	5.00	12.00
WA Mike Wallace	6.00	15.00
WD Wally Dallenbach	5.00	12.00

2000 SP Authentic Sign of the Times Gold

Randomly inserted in packs, this set parallels the base Sign of the Times set on cards that feature a Gold colored background. Each card was sequentially hand numbered to 25 and includes a gold hologram Upper Deck logo on the back

*GOLD #'d: 1.5X TO 4X BASIC AUTOS

BH Bobby Hamilton	40.00	100.00
DE Dale Earnhardt	500.00	1000.00
JG Jeff Gordon	250.00	400.00

JI Jimmie Johnson	125.00	250.00
JR Dale Earnhardt Jr.	250.00	450.00
KH Kevin Harvick	75.00	150.00
MK Matt Kenseth	75.00	150.00

1996 SPx

This is the inaugural racing issue of Upper Deck's popular SPx brand. The 25-card set features holoview technology and has a die cut design. The one-card packs retailed for $3.49 each. There were 28 packs per box and 12 boxes per case. Randomly inserted in packs were special cards of Terry Labonte and Jeff Gordon. The Terry Labonte card commemorated his record breaking 514 consecutive starts. These cards were seeded one in 47 packs. The Jeff Gordon card was a tribute to the hottest young star in racing. His card was seeded one in 71 packs. There were also autograph cards of both drivers. The Terry Labonte seeded in packs was actually an autograph redemption card. This card was available one in 395 packs. The Jeff Gordon card was an autographed version of the tribute card and was also seeded one in 395 packs. There was also a Jeff Gordon Sample card that was issued as a promo.

COMPLETE SET (25)	15.00	40.00
1 Jeff Gordon	3.00	8.00
2 Rusty Wallace	2.50	6.00
3 Dale Earnhardt	5.00	12.00
4 Sterling Marlin	1.00	2.50
5 Terry Labonte	1.00	2.50
6 Mark Martin	2.50	6.00
7 Jeff Burton	1.00	2.50
8 Bobby Hamilton	.40	1.00
9 Lake Speed	.40	1.00
10 Ricky Rudd	1.00	2.50
11 Brett Bodine	.40	1.00
12 Derrike Cope	.40	1.00
13 Jeremy Mayfield	.60	1.50
14 Ricky Craven	.40	1.00
15 Johnny Benson	.60	1.50
16 Ted Musgrave	.40	1.00
17 Darrell Waltrip	.60	1.50
18 Bobby Labonte	2.00	5.00
19 Steve Grissom	.40	1.00
20 Kyle Petty	.60	1.50
21 Michael Waltrip	.60	1.50
22 Ernie Irvan	.60	1.50
23 Dale Jarrett	2.00	5.00
24 Bill Elliott	1.25	3.00
25 Ken Schrader	.40	1.00
C1 Terry Labonte COMM	6.00	15.00
C1A Terry Labonte Commemorative AU	12.50	30.00
T1 Jeff Gordon Tribute	10.00	25.00
T1A Jeff Gordon Tribute AU	50.00	120.00
S1 Jeff Gordon Sample	3.00	8.00

1996 SPx Gold

This 25-card set is a parallel to the base SPx set. The cards feautre a gold foil stamping and could be pulled one in seven packs.

COMPLETE SET (25)	60.00	150.00

*GOLDS: 1X TO 2.5X BASE CARDS

1996 SPx Elite

Randomly inserted in packs at a rate of one in 23, this five-card set features some of the top names in racing. The cards use the same holoview technology as the base SPx cards.

COMPLETE SET (5)	25.00	60.00
E1 Jeff Gordon	10.00	25.00
E2 Dale Jarrett	6.00	15.00
E3 Terry Labonte	3.00	8.00
E4 Rusty Wallace	8.00	20.00
E5 Ernie Irvan	2.00	5.00

1997 SPx

This 25-card set features the top names from the Winston Cup circuit. It is important to note that a significant percentage of base cards that were pulled from packs contain minor surface foil damage on the left side on each card. This has made the supply of Mint cards very small. Cards were distributed in three cards packs with 18 packs per box and 12 boxes per case. The packs carried a suggested retail price of $4.99.

COMPLETE SET (25)	15.00	40.00
1 Robby Gordon RC	.60	1.50
2 Rusty Wallace	1.50	4.00
3 Dale Earnhardt	3.00	8.00
4 Sterling Marlin	.60	1.50
5 Terry Labonte	.60	1.50
6 Mark Martin	1.50	4.00
7 Geoff Bodine	.20	.50
8 Dale Jarrett	1.25	3.00
9 Ernie Irvan	.40	1.00
10 Ricky Rudd	.60	1.50
11 Mike Skinner	.20	.50
12 Johnny Benson	.40	1.00
13 Kyle Petty	.40	1.00
14 John Andretti	.20	.50
15 Jeff Burton	.60	1.50
16 Ted Musgrave	.20	.50
17 Darrell Waltrip	.40	1.00
18 Bobby Labonte	1.25	3.00
19 Bobby Hamilton	.20	.50
20 Bill Elliott	.75	2.00
21 Michael Waltrip	.40	1.00
22 Ken Schrader	.20	.50
23 Jimmy Spencer	.20	.50
24 Jeff Gordon	2.00	5.00
25 Ricky Craven	.20	.50
S2 Rusty Wallace Promo	1.25	3.00

1997 SPx Blue

This 25-card insert set is a parallel of the base set and were inserted one per pack. These cards differ from the base cards in that the car number in the bottom right corner of the card is in blue foil rather than grey foil.

COMPLETE SET (25)	20.00	50.00

*BLUES: .6X TO 1.5X BASIC CARDS

1997 SPx Gold

This 25-card insert set is a parallel of the base set. These cards differ from the base cards in that the car number in the bottom right corner of the card is in gold foil rather than grey foil. The cards were randomly inserted in packs at a ratio of 1:75.

COMPLETE SET (25)	250.00	500.00

*GOLDS: 5X TO 12X BASIC CARDS

1997 SPx Silver

This 25-card insert set is a parallel of the base set. These cards differ from the base cards in that the car number in the bottom right corner of the card is in silver foil rather than grey foil. The cards were randomly inserted in packs at a ratio of 1:5.

COMPLETE SET (25)	40.00	100.00

*SILVERS: 1.2X TO 3X BASIC CARDS

1997 SPx SpeedView Autographs

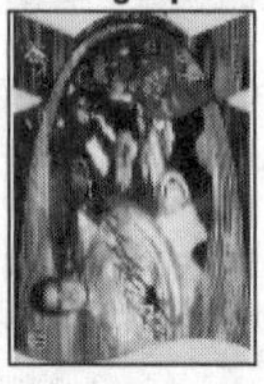

This 10-card insert set features the top driver on the Winston Cup Circuit. Each card is autographed and has three photos of the driver on the front of the card. The cards were randomly inserted in packs at a ratio of 1:175.

COMPLETE SET (10)	175.00	350.00
SV1 Jeff Gordon	75.00	150.00
SV2 Rusty Wallace	15.00	30.00
SV3 Bill Elliott	15.00	40.00
SV4 Sterling Marlin	8.00	20.00
SV5 Terry Labonte	12.50	30.00
SV6 Mark Martin	15.00	40.00
SV7 Dale Jarrett	12.50	30.00
SV8 Ernie Irvan	8.00	20.00
SV9 Bobby Labonte	12.50	30.00
SV10 Ricky Rudd	8.00	20.00

1997 SPx Tag Team

This five- card insert set features the top pairs of teammates in NASCAR. The cards were randomly inserted in packs at a ratio of 1:55.

COMPLETE SET (5)	50.00	120.00
TT1 Terry Labonte Jeff Gordon	15.00	40.00
TT2 Dale Jarrett Ernie Irvan	7.50	20.00
TT3 Mark Martin Jeff Burton	10.00	25.00
TT4 Jeff Gordon Ricky Craven	15.00	40.00
TT5 Richard Petty Kyle Petty	6.00	

1997 SPx Tag Tea[m] Autographs

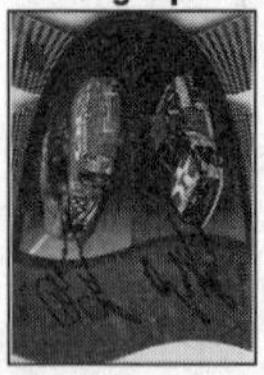

This five-card insert set is a parallel of the ba[se] team set. Each card from this set is signed b[y] drivers featured on the card. The card[s] randomly inserted in packs at a ratio of 1:2,50[0]

COMPLETE SET (5)	350.00	6
TA1 Terry Labonte Jeff Gordon	100.00	2
TA2 Dale Jarrett Ernie Irvan	40.00	
TA3 Mark Martin Jeff Burton	40.00	1
TA4 Jeff Gordon Ricky Craven	75.00	1
TA5 Richard Petty Kyle Petty	50.00	1

1996 Speedflix

The 1996 Speedflix Racing set was issued [in] series totalling 87 cards. The set includ[es] following subsets: Black Lighting (5[...]) Champion In Motion (55-62), Back on Trac[k] 66), Relentless Opponent (67-70), Champi[...] Form (71-74), Million Dollar Bill (75-78[)] Winning Style (79-82). The cards use len[ticular] animation to bring movement to every car[d]. cards were packaged 5 cards per pack in both[h] and retail packs. Jumbo packs had eight ca[rds] pack.

COMPLETE SET (87)	10.00
WAX BOX	30.00
1 Rusty Wallace	.50
2 Sterling Marlin	.20
3 Terry Labonte	.20
4 Bill Elliott	.25
5 John Andretti	.05
6 Bobby Hamilton	.05
7 Darrell Waltrip	.10
8 Michael Waltrip	.10
9 Jeff Gordon	.60
10 Dale Jarrett	.40
11 Johnny Benson Jr.	.10
12 Rick Mast	.05
13 Geoff Bodine	.05
14 Ward Burton	.10
15 Kenny Wallace	.05
16 Jeff Gordon	.60
17 Dale Earnhardt	1.00
18 Rusty Wallace	.50
19 Sterling Marlin	.20
20 Mark Martin	.50
21 Ricky Rudd	.20
22 Darrell Waltrip	.10
23 Bobby Labonte	.40
24 Dale Jarrett	.40
25 Ricky Craven	.05
26 Johnny Benson Jr.	.10
27 Joe Nemechek	.05
28 Ernie Irvan	.10
29 Jeff Burton	.20
30 Terry Labonte	.20
31 Bobby Hillin Jr.	.05
32 John Andretti	.05
33 Mike Wallace	.05
34 Kyle Petty	.10
35 Lake Speed	.05
36 Rusty Wallace's Car in pits	.10
37 Dale Earnhardt's Car in pits	.40
38 Sterling Marlin's Car in pits	.05
39 Terry Labonte's Car in pits	.10
40 Mark Martin's Car in pits	.10
41 Ricky Rudd's Car in pits	.05
42 Bill Elliott's Car in pits	.10
43 Ernie Irvan's Car in pits	.05
44 Jeff Gordon's Car in pits	.25
45 Bobby Labonte's Car in pits	.10
46 Terry Labonte DT	.10
47 Dale Jarrett DT	.10
48 Michael Waltrip DT	.10
49 Kenny Wallace DT	.02
50 Mark Martin DT	.10
51 Dale Earnhardt BL	.50
52 Dale Earnhardt BL	.50
53 Dale Earnhardt BL	.50
54 Dale Earnhardt BL	.50
55 Jeff Gordon CM	.25
56 Jeff Gordon CM	.25
57 Jeff Gordon CM	.25
58 Jeff Gordon CM	.25
59 Jeff Gordon CM	.25
60 Jeff Gordon CM	.25
61 Jeff Gordon CM	.25
62 Jeff Gordon CM	.25
63 Ernie Irvan BT	.05
64 Ernie Irvan BT	.05
65 Ernie Irvan BT	.05
66 Ernie Irvan BT	.05
67 Mark Martin RO	.10
68 Mark Martin RO	.10

rk Martin RO	.10	.30
rk Martin RO	.10	.30
sty Wallace CF	.10	.30
sty Wallace CF	.10	.30
sty Wallace CF	.10	.30
sty Wallace CF	.10	.30
Elliott MDB	.10	.30
Elliott MDB	.10	.30
Elliott MDB	.10	.30
Elliott MDB	.10	.30
ky Rudd WS	.10	.30
ky Rudd WS	.10	.30
ky Rudd WS	.10	.30
ky Rudd WS	.10	.30
e Earnhardt W	.50	1.25
f Gordon W	.30	.75
e Earnhardt W	.50	1.25
Gordon CL	.30	.75
rk Martin CL	.10	.30
le Jarrett Promo	1.50	4.00

996 Speedflix Artist Proof's

7-card set is a parallel to the base Speedflix e cards feature a gold foil Artist Proof stamp front of each card to differentiate them from se set. Odds of pulling an Artist Proof card is 24 packs.

LETE SET (87)	125.00	250.00
ST PROOFS: 5X TO 12X BASE CARDS		

996 Speedflix Clear Shots

2-card insert set features almost clear lar technology. It mixes an acetate card with lar technology. The cards were inserted in packs at a rate of one in 31.

LETE SET (12)	80.00	175.00
Earnhardt	20.00	50.00
Gordon	12.50	30.00
ing Marlin	4.00	10.00
y Wallace	10.00	25.00
by Labonte	8.00	20.00
Labonte	4.00	10.00
Jarrett	8.00	20.00
Martin	10.00	25.00
Elliott	5.00	12.00
ie Irvan	2.50	6.00
Musgrave	1.25	3.00
nny Benson Jr.	2.50	6.00

1996 Speedflix In Motion

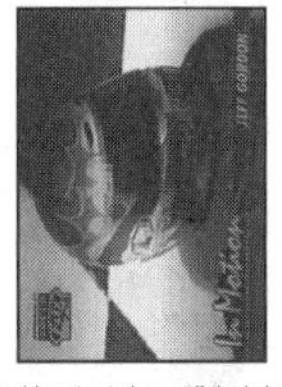

-card insert set shows off the helmets of the vers on the Winston Cup circuit. The helmets tured in multi-phase lenticular animation. In cards were seeded one in 48 packs.

LETE SET (10)	40.00	100.00
Earnhardt's Helmet	12.50	30.00
Gordon's Helmet	8.00	20.00
ing Marlin's Helmet	2.50	6.00
Wallace's Helmet	6.00	15.00
Bodine's Helmet	.75	2.00
Labonte's Helmet	2.50	6.00
ell Waltrip's Helmet	1.50	4.00
Martin's Helmet	6.00	15.00
Musgrave's Helmet	.75	2.00
Elliott's Helmet	3.00	8.00

1996 Speedflix ProMotion

-card insert set allows collectors to see their s on the move. The cards use multi-phase ar animation to show drivers getting in and their cards. ProMotion cards were randomly one per nine packs.

LETE SET (12)	25.00	60.00
Earnhardt	8.00	20.00
Gordon	5.00	12.00
ing Marlin	1.50	4.00
Wallace	4.00	10.00
ael Waltrip	1.00	2.50
Labonte	1.50	4.00
Jarrett	3.00	8.00
Martin	4.00	10.00
Elliott	2.00	5.00
ell Waltrip	1.00	2.50

11 Bobby Hamilton	.50	1.25
12 Johnny Benson Jr.	1.00	2.50

1997 SportsCom FanScan

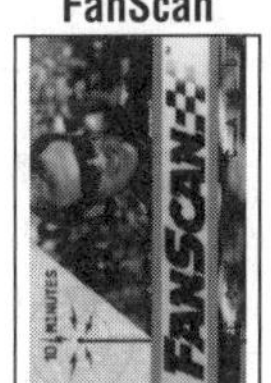

This series of cards was produced by SportsCom, Inc. Each was to be used similar to a phone card except that the phone call would be connected to the featured driver's team radios during a Winston Cup race, just like a scanner. Each card featured 10-minutes worth of time that expired on 12/31/1997. However, the holder could also purchase additional time at the rate of $1.49 per minute thereafter.

COMPLETE SET (12)	7.50	20.00
1 Jeff Burton	.60	1.50
2 Dale Earnhardt	2.50	6.00
3 Jeff Gordon	1.50	4.00
4 Bobby Hamilton	.30	.75
5 Ernie Irvan	.60	1.50
6 Dale Jarrett	1.00	2.50
7 Sterling Marlin	.60	1.50
8 Mark Martin	1.25	3.00
9 Ted Musgrave	.30	.75
10 Richard Petty	.75	2.00
11 Ken Schrader	.40	1.00
12 Rusty Wallace	1.25	3.00

1998 SportsCom FanScan

Each card in this set was to be used similar to a phone card except that the phone call would be connected to the featured driver's team radios during a Winston Cup race, just like a scanner. Each card featured 20-Units (3-minutes = 1-unit) worth of time that expired on 3/31/1998. However, the holder could also purchase additional time at the rate of $1.49 per minute thereafter.

COMPLETE SET (9)	6.00	15.00
1 Dale Earnhardt	2.50	6.00
2 Jeff Gordon	1.50	4.00
3 Ernie Irvan	.60	1.50
4 Dale Jarrett	1.00	2.50
5 Sterling Marlin	.60	1.50
6 Mark Martin	1.25	3.00
7 Ken Schrader	.40	1.00
8 Rusty Wallace	1.25	3.00
9 Darrell Waltrip	.40	1.00

1999 SportsCom FanScan

This series marks the second year of cards produced by SportsCom, Inc. Each was to be used similar to a phone card except that the phone call would be connected to the featured driver's team radios during a Winston Cup race, just like a scanner. Each card featured 7-minutes worth of time that expired on 3/31/1999. However, the holder could also purchase additional time at the rate of $1.49 per minute thereafter.

COMPLETE SET (9)	6.00	15.00
1 Dale Earnhardt	2.50	6.00
2 Jeff Gordon	1.50	4.00
3 Ernie Irvan	.60	1.50
4 Dale Jarrett	1.00	2.50
5 Sterling Marlin	.60	1.50
6 Mark Martin	1.25	3.00
7 Ken Schrader	.40	1.00
8 Rusty Wallace	1.25	3.00
9 Darrell Waltrip	.40	1.00

1991 Sports Legends Bobby Allison

K and M Cards produced this set honoring Bobby Allison as part of a continuing Sports Legends card series. The set was issued in factory set form in an oversized box numbered as series three. The cards in each series look very similar with just the driver's name on the cardfronts.

COMP. FACT SET (30)	2.00	5.00
COMMON CARD (BA1-BA30)	.12	.30
P1 Bobby Allison Prototype	.40	1.00
Donnie Allison		
Neil Bonnett		
Red Border		
P2 Bobby Allison Prototype	.40	1.00
Donnie Allison		
Neil Bonnett		
Yellow Border		

1991 Sports Legends Donnie Allison

K and M Cards produced this set honoring Donnie Allison as part of a continuing Sports Legends card series. The set was issued in factory set form in an oversized box numbered as series four. The cards in each series look very similar with just the driver's name on the cardfronts. The Donnie Allison cards were printed with a red border.

COMPLETE SET (30)	2.00	5.00
DA1 Donnie Allison w/Car	.05	.10
Busch Buick		
DA2 Donnie Allison	.10	.25
Donnie Allison and Family		
DA3 Kenny Allison	.05	.15
in the Winner's Circle		
DA4 Ronald Allison w/Car	.01	.05
in Victory Lane		
DA5 Donald Allison	.05	.15
in Pits		
DA6 Hut Stricklin	.05	.15
Pam, Hut and Taylor		
DA7 Donnie Allison	.10	.25
Donnie's First Race Car		
DA8 Donnie Allison	.10	.25
Rockingham, NC, 1968		
DA9 Donnie Allison	.10	.25
1968 World 600 Pole		
DA10 Donnie Allison	.10	.25
Donnie and Pat		
DA11 Donnie Allison	.10	.25
Donnie's First Sportsman's Race		
DA12 Donnie Allison	.12	.30
Bobby Allison		
DA13 Donnie Allison w/Car	.05	.10
1969 Banjo Matthews Ford		
DA14 Donnie Allison	.10	.25
1969		
DA15 Donnie Allison w/Car	.10	.25
1972 Bud Moore Ford		
DA16 Donnie Allison's Car	.05	.15
Bobby Allison's Car		
Neil Bonnett's Car		
Practice Run		
DA17 Donnie Allison	.15	.40
Bobby Allison		
Neil Bonnett		
DA18 Donnie Allison	.10	.25
1971 - Talladega		
DA19 Donnie Allison w/Car	.10	.25
DiGard Racing Team		
DA20 Donnie Allison	.12	.30
Bobby Allison		
The Allison Brothers and Wives		
DA21 Donnie Allison	.15	.40
Bobby Allison		
Neil Bonnett		
The Alabama Gang		
DA22 Donnie Allison	.12	.30
Bobby Allison		
in Birmingham		
DA23 Donnie Allison	.10	.25
Donnie Takes Checkered Flag		
In Macon, Georgia		
DA24 Donnie Allison	.12	.30
Bobby Allison		
Winston Cup Wives Auxiliary Dance		
DA25 Donnie Allison	.10	.25
Visiting Jimmy & Rosalynn Carter		
DA26 Donnie Allison w/Car	.10	.25
Kenny Childers' Coal Mining Cars		
DA27 Donnie Allison	.12	.30
Bobby Allison		
The Allison Brothers		
DA28 Donnie Allison's Car	.05	.10
Driving All-Pro Circuit		
DA29 Donnie Allison	.10	.25
Statistics		
DA30 Donnie Allison	.10	.25
Statistics cont'd.		

1991 Sports Legends Neil Bonnett

K and M Cards produced this set honoring Neil Bonnett as part of a continuing Sports Legends card series. The set was issued in factory set form in an oversized box numbered as series five. The cards in each series look very similar with just the driver's name on the cardfronts. The Neil Bonnett cards were printed with a red border.

COMP. FACT SET (30)	2.00	5.00
NB1 Neil Bonnett w/Car	.15	.40
Ford Mustang		
NB2 Neil Bonnett	.15	.40
Neil Bonnett and Family		
NB3 Neil Bonnett	.15	.40
Neil, Lawrence and Josephine Bonnett		
NB4 Neil Bonnett w/Car	.15	.40
Daytona International Speedway		
NB5 Neil Bonnett	.15	.40
A Young Neil Bonnett		
NB6 Neil Bonnett w/Car	.15	.40
1974 Birmingham, Alabama		
NB7 Neil Bonnett's Car	.05	.15
Cale Yarborough's Car		
1974 Talladega, Alabama		
NB8 Neil Bonnett	.15	.40
Victory Lane at Atlanta Raceway		
NB9 Neil Bonnett	.15	.40
1980 Talladega, Alabama		
NB10 Neil Bonnett		
Neil Before A Winston Cup Race		
NB11 Neil Bonnett	.15	.40
Donnie Allison		
Bobby Allison		
The Alabama Gang		
NB12 Neil Bonnett w/Car	.15	.40
1981		
NB13 Neil Bonnett w/Crew	.15	.40
Home Away From Home		
NB14 Neil Bonnett	.15	.40
Neil in Victory Lane		
NB15 Neil Bonnett	.15	.40
1981		
NB16 Neil Bonnett w/Cars	.15	.40
Bessemer, Alabama		
NB17 Neil Bonnett	.15	.40
Neil at Indianapolis		
NB18 Neil Bonnett's Car	.05	.15
Leader of the Pack		
NB19 Neil Bonnett	.15	.40
1982 The World 600		
NB20 Neil Bonnett	.15	.40
1983 The Busch Clash		
NB21 Neil Bonnett's Car	.05	.15
Atlanta International Speedway		
NB22 Neil Bonnett	.15	.40
1983 "Journal 500"		
NB23 Neil Bonnett	.15	.40
IROC		
NB24 Neil Bonnett	.15	.40
1984 Daytona Beach, Florida		
NB25 Neil Bonnett	.15	.40
1985 Winston Cup Awards		
NB26 Neil Bonnett w/Car	.15	.40
Neil's Toy		
NB27 Neil Bonnett	.15	.40
Neil's Pastime		
NB28 Neil Bonnett	.15	.40
David Bonnett		
NB29 Neil Bonnett w/Car	.15	.40
#11 Coca-Cola Car		
NB30 Neil Bonnett	.15	.40
Statistics		

1991 Sports Legends Harry Hyde

K and M Cards produced this set honoring Harry Hyde as part of a continuing Sports Legends card series. The set was issued in factory set form in an oversized box numbered as series eight. The cards in each series look very similar with just the driver's name on the cardfronts. The Harry Hyde cards were printed with a red border.

COMP. FACT SET (30)	2.00	5.00
HH1 Harry Hyde	.10	.25
Tim Richmond		
1986		
HH2 Tim Richmond	.10	.25
July 4, 1986		
HH3 Harry Hyde	.05	.15
1990		
HH4 Tim Richmond's Car	.05	.10
1986		
HH5 Harry Hyde	.10	.25
Rick Hendrick		
HH6 Harry Hyde	.05	.15
Tim Richmond		
HH7 Ken Schrader's Car	.05	.10
1988		
HH8 Harry Hyde	.05	.15
1990		
HH9 Harry Hyde	.05	.15
Tim Richmond		
1986		
HH10 Harry Hyde	.10	.25
Tim Richmond		
1986		
HH11 Harry Hyde	.10	.25
Buddy Baker		
Harry and Buddy Baker		
HH12 Harry Hyde	.05	.15
Harry and "Tiger"		
HH13 Bobby Unser w/Car	.15	.40
Pikes Peak Climb		
HH14 Harry Hyde	.05	.15
Harry Helping Out		
HH15 Bobby Isaac's Car	.01	.05
Hill Climb		
HH16 Harry Hyde	.10	.25
Buddy Baker		
1973		
HH17 Bobby Isaac's Car	.01	.05
1971		
HH18 Harry Hyde w/Car	.01	.05
#4 Big Auto Wreckers T-Model		
HH19 Harry Hyde	.05	.15
1986		
HH20 Harry Hyde	.05	.15
Buddy Baker		
1973		
HH21 Harry Hyde	.05	.15
1968		
HH22 Harry Hyde w/Car	.05	.15
Little 8		
HH23 Harry Hyde w/Car	.05	.15
#8 Thundermug		
HH24 Bobby Isaac's Car	.01	.05
1971		
HH25 Harry Hyde	.05	.15
Jesse Baird		
1954		
HH26 Harry Hyde w/Car	.05	.15
Crashed Car		
HH27 Harry Hyde	.05	.15
1970		
HH28 Harry Hyde w/Car	.05	.15
1947		
HH29 Harry Hyde w/Car	.05	.15
Career Highlights		
HH30 Harry Hyde	.05	.15
Career Highlights cont'd.		
P1 Harry Hyde Prototype	.15	.40

1991 Sports Legends Dale Jarrett

K and M Cards produced this set honoring Dale Jarrett as part of a continuing Sports Legends card series. The set was issued in factory set form in an oversized box numbered as series ten. The cards in each series look very similar with just the driver's name on the cardfronts. The Dale Jarrett cards were printed with a dark blue border.

COMP. FACT SET (30)	2.50	6.00
DJ1 Dale Jarrett	.12	.30
1991		
DJ2 Dale Jarrett	.12	.30
Ned Jarrett		
1989		
DJ3 Dale Jarrett's Car	.05	.10
1989		
DJ4 Dale Jarrett w/Car	.12	.30
1991		
DJ5 Dale Jarrett	.12	.30
Ned Jarrett		
1991		
DJ6 Dale Jarrett w/Crew	.12	.30
1991		
DJ7 Dale Jarrett w/Car	.12	.30
1990		
DJ8 Dale Jarrett's Car	.05	.10
Davey Allison's Car		
1991		
DJ9 Dale Jarrett w/Crew	.12	.30
1991		
DJ10 Dale Jarrett	.12	.30
Ned Jarrett		
Dale and Ned		
DJ11 Dale Jarrett	.12	.30
1991		
DJ12 Dale Jarrett w/Car	.12	.30
Contract for Life		
DJ13 Dale Jarrett	.12	.30
1991		
DJ14 Dale Jarrett	.12	.30
1990		
DJ15 Dale Jarrett	.12	.30
1987		
DJ16 Dale Jarrett's Car	.05	.10
1987		
DJ17 Dale Jarrett	.12	.30
Cale Yarborough		
1988 Dale and Cale		
DJ18 Dale Jarrett w/Car	.12	.30
1989		
DJ19 Dale Jarrett's Car	.05	.10
1985		
DJ20 Dale Jarrett's Car	.05	.10
1987		
DJ21 Dale Jarrett	.12	.30
1987		
DJ22 Dale Jarrett	.12	.30
1986		
DJ23 Dale Jarrett	.12	.30
Statistics		
DJ24 Dale Jarrett w/Car	.12	.30
1982		
DJ25 Dale Jarrett Crash	.12	.30
1979 Rockingham		
DJ26 Dale Jarrett	.12	.30
Andy Petree		
Jimmy and Andy		
DJ27 Dale Jarrett's Car	.05	.10
1980		
DJ28 Dale Jarrett	.12	.30
1959		
DJ29 Dale Jarrett w/Car	.12	.30
second year		
DJ30 Dale Jarrett	.12	.30
Statistics		
P1 Dale Jarrett Prototype	.60	1.50

1991 Sports Legends Ned Jarrett

K and M Cards produced this set honoring Ned Jarrett as the first in a continuing Sports Legends card series. The set was issued in factory set form in an oversized box numbered as series one. The cards in each series look very similar with just the driver's name on the cardfronts. The Ned Jarrett cards were printed with a yellow border.

COMP. FACT SET (30)	2.00	5.00
NJ1 Ned Jarrett	.10	.25
Ned's Racing Years		
NJ2 Ned Jarrett	.10	.25
Meet Mr. & Mrs. Ned Jarrett		
NJ3 Ned Jarrett	.25	.60
Glenn Jarrett		
Dale Jarrett		
Daytona Family Portrait		
NJ4 Ned Jarrett	.25	.60
Dale Jarrett		
Another Jarrett Victory		
NJ5 Ned Jarrett	.10	.25
with Ronald Reagan		
Presidential Interview		
NJ6 Ned Jarrett	.10	.25
1988 Gentleman Ned		
Businessman Ned		
NJ7 Ned Jarrett	.10	.25
A Family Gathering		
NJ8 Ned Jarrett	.10	.25
Ned and Donald 1942		
NJ9 Ned Jarrett	.10	.25
1937 Ford Coupe		
NJ10 Ned Jarrett	.10	.25
1955 Southern 500		
NJ11 Ned Jarrett	.10	.25
The Look of 1957		
NJ12 Ned Jarrett	.10	.25
1957-Hickory Speedway		
NJ13 Ned Jarrett	.10	.25
1965 - A Consistent Driver		
NJ14 Ned Jarrett w/Car	.10	.25
1960 - Hickory Speedway		
NJ15 Ned Jarrett's Car	.05	.10
1961 Season		
NJ16 Ned Jarrett w/Car	.10	.25
1962 Season		
NJ17 Ned Jarrett	.10	.25
Bud Allman		
Ned and Bud		
NJ18 Ned Jarrett w/Car	.10	.25
1964 Season		
NJ19 Ned Jarrett w/Car	.10	.25
1965 Season		
NJ20 Ned Jarrett's Car	.10	.25
Curtis Turner's Car		
Running Tough		
NJ21 Ned Jarrett	.10	.25
1965 Darlington 500		
NJ22 Ned Jarrett	.10	.25
A Family Grows Up		
NJ23 Ned Jarrett	.10	.25
Sweet Victory		
1965 Darlington 500		
NJ24 Ned Jarrett	.10	.25
The Bondy Long Racing Team		
NJ25 Ned Jarrett	.10	.25
Eye Protection		
NJ26 Ned Jarrett	.10	.25
Retirement Speech - 1966		
NJ27 Ned Jarrett	.10	.25
Dale Jarrett		
NJ28 Ned Jarrett	.10	.25
Barney Hall		
1986 Ned and Barney		
NJ29 Ned Jarrett	.10	.25
After Retirement		
NJ30 Ned Jarrett	.10	.25
Statistics		

1991 Sports Legends Rob Moroso

K and M Cards produced this set honoring Rob Moroso as part of a continuing Sports Legends card series. The set was issued in factory set form in an oversized box numbered as series six. The Rob Moroso cards were printed with a different design than most other Sports Legends sets. The cards feature Moroso's name in a black and gold strip running across the bottom of the cardfront. A special art print card portraying Moroso was inserted into 3,000 of the sets.

COMPLETE SET (30)	2.00	5.00
COMMON CARD (RM1-RM30)	.07	.20
P1 Rob Moroso Prototype	.40	1.00

1991 Sports Legends Phil Parsons

K and M Cards produced this set honoring Phil Parsons as part of a continuing Sports Legends card series. The set was issued in factory set form in an oversized box numbered as series nine. The cards in each series look very similar with just the driver's name on the cardfronts. The Phil Parsons cards were printed with a red border.

COMP. FACT SET (30)	2.00	5.00
PP1 Phil Parsons w/Car	.05	.15
1990		

PP2 Phil Parsons .05 .15
Going To Work
PP3 Phil Parsons .05 .15
1983 Talladega
PP4 Phil Parsons' Car .01 .05
October 1980 Charlotte
PP5 Phil Parsons .05 .15
Phil and Marcia
PP6 Phil Parsons .05 .15
Keeping in Shape
PP7 Phil Parsons .05 .15
Phil in Indy Car
PP8 Phil Parsons .05 .15
Phil's Lifelong Dream
PP9 Phil Parsons' Car .01 .05
1980 North Wilkesboro, NC
PP10 Phil Parsons w/Car .05 .15
1980 North Wilkesboro
PP11 Phil Parsons' Car .01 .05
1980 Charlotte, NC
PP12 Phil Parsons' Car .01 .05
1981
PP13 Phil Parsons' Car .01 .05
1981 Daytona Beach, FL
PP14 Phil Parsons' Car .01 .05
May 1981
PP15 Phil Parsons' Car .01 .05
1982 Richmond, VA
PP16 Phil Parsons .05 .15
1982 Bristol
PP17 Phil Parsons .05 .15
Charlotte, NC
PP18 Phil Parsons .25 .60
with Dale Earnhardt's Car
1983 Daytona Beach, FL
PP19 Phil Parsons' Car .01 .05
1984 Bristol, TN
PP20 Phil Parsons .05 .15
1984 Wedding
PP21 Phil Parsons' Car .01 .05
1986 Twenty-Four Hours at Daytona
PP22 Phil Parsons' Car .05 .15
1982 Charlotte, NC
PP23 Phil Parsons .05 .15
1988 Victory Lane
PP24 Phil Parsons .05 .15
Million Dollar Man
PP25 Phil Parsons .15 .40
Benny Parsons
Phil & Benny
PP26 Phil Parsons .05 .15
Kinsley's First Birthday
PP27 Phil Parsons .05 .15
1990 Bowling Tournament
PP28 Phil Parsons .05 .15
1991
PP29 Phil Parsons' Car .01 .05
April, 1991
PP30 Phil Parsons .05 .15
Statistics
P1 Phil Parsons Prototype .60 1.50

1991 Sports Legends Wendell Scott

K and M Cards produced this set honoring Wendell Scott as part of a continuing Sports Legends card series. The set was issued in factory set form in an oversized box numbered as series thirteen. The cards in each series look very similar with just the driver's name on the cardfronts. The Wendell Scott cards were printed with a yellow border.

COMP. FACT SET (30) 2.00 5.00
WS1 Wendell Scott w/Car .05 .15
Fayeteville, NC
WS2 Wendell Scott's Car .01 .05
May 1968 Charlotte Motor Speedway
WS3 Wendell Scott .05 .15
1986
WS4 Wendell Scott .05 .15
Fayetteville, NC
WS5 Wendell Scott .05 .15
October 7, 1973
WS6 Wendell Scott w/Car .05 .15
Fayetteville Motor Speedway
WS7 Wendell Scott .05 .15
1955 Daytona Beach, Fl
WS8 Wendell Scott .05 .15
Wendell and Michael
WS9 Wendell Scott .05 .15
July, 1968 Bristol, TN
WS10 Wendell Scott .05 .15
Danville, VA
WS11 Wendell Scott .05 .15
Wendell, Wendell Jr., and Franklin
WS12 Wendell Scott's Car .01 .05
September, 1966 Darlington, SC
WS13 Wendell Scott .05 .15
WS14 Wendell Scott .15 .40
Cale Yarborough
1983
WS15 Wendell Scott .05 .15
1977
WS16 Wendell Scott .05 .15
WS17 Wendell Scott .05 .15
1973
WS18 Wendell Scott .05 .15
March 4, 1961
WS19 Wendell Scott .05 .15
1963
WS20 Wendell Scott .05 .15
1988
WS21 Wendell Scott .05 .15
with Richard Pryor
Career Achievements
WS22 Wendell Scott w/Car .05 .15
July 20, 1962
WS23 Wendell Scott .05 .15
December 1, 1963
WS24 Wendell Scott .05 .15
1977
WS25 Wendell Scott w/Car .05 .15
1969
WS26 Wendell Scott w/Car .05 .15
Danville, VA
WS27 Wendell Scott .05 .15
1988 Championships
WS28 Wendell Scott .05 .15
1989
WS29 Wendell Scott .05 .15
1987
WS30 Wendell Scott .05 .15
Statistics

1991 Sports Legends Hut Stricklin

K and M Cards produced this set honoring Hut Stricklin as part of a continuing Sports Legends card series. The set was issued in factory set form in an oversized box numbered as series twelve. The Hut Stricklin cards were printed with a different design than most other Sports Legends sets. The cards feature Stricklin's name in a white and blue strip running across the bottom of the cardfront.

COMP. FACT SET (30) 2.00 5.00
HS1 Hut Stricklin w/Car .05 .15
Raybestos Buick
HS2 Hut Stricklin .05 .15
Winston Cup
HS3 Hut Stricklin .05 .15
December 6, 1989
HS4 Hut Stricklin .05 .15
December 6, 1989 Hut Stricklin Day
HS5 Hut Stricklin .05 .15
1989
HS6 Hut Stricklin .05 .15
1987 North Wilkesboro, NC
HS7 Hut Stricklin's Car .10 .25
Davey Allison's Car
1989
HS8 Hut Stricklin .05 .15
1987 Charlotte, NC
HS9 Hut Stricklin .05 .15
November 22, 1987 Atlanta, GA
HS10 Hut Stricklin .05 .15
1986
HS11 Hut Stricklin w/Car .05 .15
1986 Charlotte
Daytona Dash Champion
HS12 Hut Stricklin w/Car .05 .15
1986 Birmingham, AL
HS13 Hut Stricklin w/Car .05 .15
1987 Rougemont, NC
HS14 Hut Stricklin w/Car .05 .15
1986 Montgomery, AL
HS15 Hut Stricklin's Car .07 .20
1985 Montgomery, AL
HS16 Hut Stricklin w/Car .05 .15
1985 Birmingham, AL
HS17 Hut Stricklin .05 .15
1972 Calera, AL
HS18 Hut Stricklin w/Car .05 .15
1984 Birmingham, AL
HS19 Hut Stricklin w/Crew .05 .15
1984
HS20 Hut Stricklin .05 .15
1977
HS21 Hut Stricklin w/Car .05 .15
1981
HS22 Hut Stricklin's Car .01 .05
1980 Birmingham, AL
HS23 Hut Stricklin .05 .15
November 1987 Atlanta, GA
HS24 Hut Stricklin .05 .15
1987 Charlotte/Daytona Dash
HS25 Hut Stricklin .05 .15
1991 Talladega, AL
HS26 Hut Stricklin .05 .15
1986 Charlotte
Daytona Dash Champion
HS27 Hut Stricklin .05 .15
1978
HS28 Hut Stricklin .05 .15
Kenny Allison
Donald Allison
1982 Montgomery, AL All-Pro Race
HS29 Hut Stricklin .05 .15
Career Highlights
HS30 Hut Stricklin's Car .01 .05
Statistics
P1 Hut Stricklin Prototype .60 1.50

1991 Sports Legends Herb Thomas

K and M Cards produced this set honoring Herb Thomas as the second in a continuing Sports Legends card series. The set was issued in factory set form in an oversized box numbered as series two. The cards in each series look very similar with just the driver's name on the cardfronts. The Herb Thomas cards were printed with a light blue border.

COMP. FACT SET (30) 2.00 5.00
HT1 Herb Thomas w/Car .05 .15
Darlington, SC 1952
HT2 Herb Thomas' Car .01 .05
Herb Thomas
HT3 Herb Thomas .05 .15
1st NASCAR Grand National
HT4 Herb Thomas w/Car .05 .15
Hudson Hornet
HT5 Herb Thomas' Car .05 .15
Slick Smith's Car
Iggy Katona's Car
1951 - Southern 500
HT6 Herb Thomas' Car .01 .05
Hillsboro, NC 1951
HT7 Herb Thomas .05 .15
1951 - Grand National Champion
HT8 Herb Thomas' Car .05 .15
Marshall Teague's Car
Herb and brother, Donald
HT9 Herb Thomas .05 .15
Racing's First Real "Superstar"
HT10 Herb Thomas' Car .05 .15
Buck Baker's Car
Lee Petty's Car
Jimmy Lewallan's Car
Ralph Liguori's Car
Richmond, VA, 1953
HT11 Herb Thomas' Car .01 .05
High Point, NC, 1953
HT12 Herb Thomas' Car .01 .05
Gene Comstock's Car
Darlington, SC, 1953
HT13 Herb Thomas' Car .01 .05
Matt Gowen's Car
Fonty Flock's Car
Herb Battles For Lead
HT14 Herb Thomas w/Car .05 .15
Wilson, NC, 1953
HT15 Herb Thomas' Car .01 .05
1954 Daytona Beach Modified
Sportsman Race
HT16 Herb Thomas' Car .01 .05
Daytona Beach, FL, 1954
HT17 Herb Thomas' Car .01 .05
Daytona Beach, 1954
HT18 Herb Thomas' Car .01 .05
Atlanta, GA, 1954
HT19 Herb Thomas' Car .01 .05
Savannah, GA, 1954
HT20 Herb Thomas' Car .01 .05
Darlington, SC, 1954
HT21 Herb Thomas w/Crew .05 .15
Darlington, SC, 1954
HT22 Herb Thomas in Pits .05 .15
Pit Stop - 1954 Style
HT23 Herb Thomas' Car .01 .05
Darlington, SC, 1954
HT24 Herb Thomas' Car .05 .10
Buck Baker's Car
Charlotte, NC, 1955
HT25 Herb Thomas' Car .01 .05
Ralph Liguori's Car
Darlington, SC, 1955
HT26 Herb Thomas .05 .15
Darlington, SC, 1955
HT27 Herb Thomas' Car .05 .10
Tiny Lund's Car
Darlington, SC, 1956
HT28 Herb Thomas' Car .01 .05
Daytona Beach, 1952
HT29 Herb Thomas w/Car .05 .15
1956 Chevrolet
HT30 Herb Thomas .05 .15
Grand National Record
P1 Herb Thomas Prototype .15 .40

1991 Sports Legends Cale Yarborough

K and M Cards produced this set honoring Cale Yarborough as part of a continuing Sports Legends card series. The set was issued in factory set form in an oversized box numbered as series eleven. The cards in each series look very similar with just the driver's name on the cardfronts. The Cale Yarborough cards were printed with an orange border.

COMP. FACT SET (30) 2.00 5.00
COMMON CARD (CY1-CY30) .07 .20
P1 Cale Yarborough Prototype .75 2.00

1992 Sports Legends Buck Baker

K and M Cards produced this set honoring Buck Baker as part of a continuing Sports Legends card series. The set was issued in factory set form in an oversized box numbered as series fifteen. The Buck Baker cards were printed with a design featuring his name in a red strip running across the bottom of the card front.

COMP. FACT SET (30) 2.00 5.00
COMMON CARD (BB1-BB30) .07 .20
P1 Buck Baker Prototype .40 1.00

1992 Sports Legends Alan Kulwicki

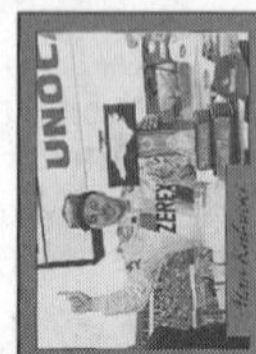

K and M Cards produced this set honoring Alan Kulwicki as part of a continuing Sports Legends card series. The set was issued in factory set form in an oversized box numbered as series seven. The cards in each series look very similar with just the driver's name on the cardfronts. The Alan Kulwicki cards were printed with an orange border.

COMP. FACT SET (30) 3.00 8.00
COMMON CARD (AK1-AK30) .15 .40
P1 Alan Kulwicki Prototype .75 2.00

1992 Sports Legends Fred Lorenzen

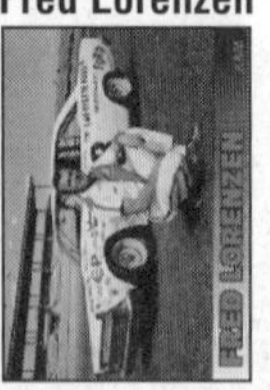

Produced in 1992 by K and M Cards, this Fred Lorenzen commemorative set was issued in factory set form. The cardfronts feature a photo of Lorenzen with backs containing text relating to the photo. The cards are numbered on back inside an outline of a trophy and checkered flag.

COMPLETE SET (16) 2.00 4.00
COMMON CARD (1-16) .08 .25

1992 Sports Legends Rusty Wallace

K and M Cards produced this set honoring Rusty Wallace as part of a continuing Sports Legends card series. The set was issued in factory set form in an oversized box numbered as series fourteen. The cards in each series look very similar with just the driver's name on the cardfronts.

COMPLETE SET (30) 2.50 6.00
COMMON CARD (1-30) .10 .30
P1 Rusty Wallace Prototype 1.00 2.50

1985 SportStars Photo-Graphics Stickers

SportStars Photo-Graphics Inc. produced this set on sticker card stock. The backs are blank and the fronts feature both a driver and car photo. They look very similar to the 1986 SportStars release, but are much smaller, measuring approximately 2" by 3."

COMPLETE SET (8) 40.00 75.00
NNO Mario Andretti 4.00 10.00
NNO A.J.Foyt 4.00 10.00
NNO David Pearson ERR 4.00 10.00
Daivd on Front
NNO David Pearson COR 4.00 10.00
David on Front
NNO Richard Petty 5.00 12.00
NNO Al Unser Sr. 3.00 8.00
NNO Darrell Waltrip 4.00 10.00
NNO Cale Yarborough 3.00 8.00

1986 SportStars Photo-Graphics

This 13-card set was produced by SportStars, Inc. The cards are a little larger than standard size, measuring 2 3/4" X 3 1/2". The cards have a white border and picture both the driver and his car. The backs contain only driver name, birth date and place, hometown and current car. The also have a "SportStars Photo-GRAPHICS" copyright on the back. Four of the cards appear to be in shorter supply than the others: Bodine, Earnhardt, Gant, and Richmond. All the cards are unnumbered and appear below numbered in alphabetical order. The list represents the 13 known regular versions. Some variations of these cards exist.

COMPLETE SET (13) 400.00 800.00
1 Bobby Allison 6.00 15.00
2 Geoff Bodine SP 50.00 100.00
3 Neil Bonnett 20.00 50.00
4 Dale Earnhardt SP 125.00 250.00
5 Bill Elliott 10.00 25.00
6 A.J. Foyt 10.00 25.00
Stock Car
7 A.J. Foyt 15.00 40.00
Indy Car
8 Harry Gant SP 40.00 80.00
9 Terry Labonte 25.00 60.00
10 Richard Petty 15.00 40.00
11 Tim Richmond SP 60.00 120.00
12 Darrell Waltrip 6.00 15.00
13 Cale Yarborough 6.00 15.00

1992 SportStars Racing Collectibles

This 16-card set features four top drivers from the mid to late '70's. Card number 1 was inserted loosely in Racing Collectibles magazines and given to dealers who sold the magazine. The other cards came as a stitched in insert in the magazines.

COMPLETE SET (16) 4.00 10.00
1 Joe Weatherly .30 .75
2 Joe Weatherly .30 .75
3 Joe Weatherly .30 .75
4 Joe Weatherly .30 .75
5 Dave Marcis .30 .75
6 Dave Marcis .30 .75
7 Dave Marcis .30 .75
8 Dave Marcis .30 .75
9 Mark Donohue .30 .75
10 Mark Donohue .30 .75
11 Mark Donohue .30 .75
12 Mark Donohue .30 .75
13 Janet Guthrie .30 .75
14 Janet Guthrie .30 .75
15 Janet Guthrie .30 .75
16 Janet Guthrie .30 .75

2006 Stanley Tools Promo

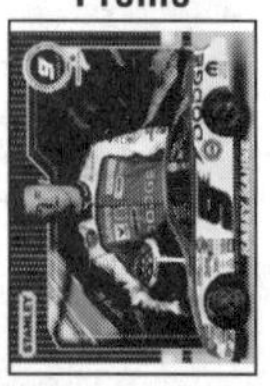

COMPLETE SET (6) 4.00 10.00
COMP.SHEET 5.00 12.00
1 Erin Crocker 2.50 6.00
2 Kasey Kahne 1.50 4.00
3 Jeremy Mayfield .25 .60
4 Scott Riggs .40 1.00
5 Kasey Kahne First Win 1.50 4.00
6 Stanley Header Card .20 .50
6 Stanley Tools Cover Card .20 .50

1993 Stove Top

Issued in two different three-card packs in Stove Top Stuffing packages, the cards feature an artist's rendering of a NASCAR driver on the cardfronts. Cardbacks include a driver career summary and stats. The cards are unnumbered and listed below alphabetically.

COMPLETE SET (6) 2.40 6.00
1 Jeff Gordon 1.00 2.50
2 Bobby Hamilton .20 .50
3 Bobby Labonte .60 1.50
4 Kenny Wallace .20 .50
5 Rusty Wallace .75 2.00
6 Michael Waltrip .30 .75

1972 STP

STP Corporation produced and distributed these cards as a promotion in 1972. These are some of the earliest known NASCAR cards and, thus, are highly sought after by collectors. Cards were printed on white stock with blue lettering on the cardbacks which contain the STP name and address. Photos are full-bleed and the cards are unnumbered.

COMPLETE SET (11) 400.00 800.00
1 Bobby Allison 40.00 100.00
2 Buddy Baker 30.00 80.00
3 Richard Brooks 25.00 60.00
4 Charlie Glotzbach 25.00 60.00
5 James Hylton 25.00 60.00
6 Elmo Langley 25.00 60.00
7 Fred Lorenzen 30.00 80.00
8 Fred Lorenzen w/Car 30.00 80.00
9 Dave Marcis 30.00
10 Benny Parsons 30.00
11 Richard Petty 50.00

1991 STP Richard Pe

Using nine cards from the Richard Pett anniversary set, Traks produced this 10-car for First Brands Corp. and STP. A cover/c card was added as the tenth card in the set.

COMPLETE SET (10) 4.00
1 Richard Petty .60
A Winning Combination
2 Richard Petty's Car .25
The Racer's Edge
3 Richard Petty .60
Richard Lee + STP = 43
4 Richard Petty's Car .60
Kyle Petty in Pits
Son of a Gun!
5 Richard Petty's Car .25
Pre-flight Checklist
6 Richard Petty .60
The Fan's Choice
7 Richard Petty's Car .25
Greased Lightning
8 Richard Petty w/Car .60
Happy Anniversary
9 Richard Petty .60
The King
10 Checklist .07

1992 STP Daytona 5

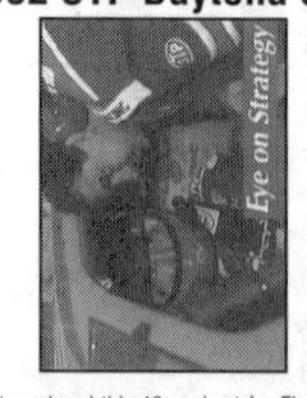

Pro Set produced this 10-card set for First (STP). The set commemorates Richard Pett entry in the Daytona 500. It was made av through redeeming the proof-of-purchase fr STP product.

COMPLETE SET (10) 4.00
1 Richard Petty .50
2 Richard Petty in Car .50
3 Green Flag .40
race action
4 Richard Petty's Car .50
5 Richard Petty in Pits .50
6 Daytona 500 Fans .40
7 Richard Petty in Pits .40
8 Davey Allison .60
9 Richard Petty .50
10 Checklist .20

1996 STP 25th Anniversary

Cards were distributed through a mail in c cases of STP. The six-card set features a cov and five cards with the different paint schen Bobby Hamilton, driver of the Richard Petty pontiac, ran under during the 1996 Winst season.

COMPLETE SET (6) 2.00
COMMON CARD .40
NNO Cover Card .08

1991 Sunbelt Racin Legends

COMPLETE SET (11) 2.00
1 Richard Petty .50
2 Rusty Wallace .40
3 Dale Earnhardt 1.00
4 Davey Allison .40
5 Ricky Rudd .25
6 Mark Martin .50
7 Darrell Waltrip .25
8 Harry Gant .25
9 Bill Elliott .30
10 Checklist Card .05
NNO Cover Card .05

1991 Superior Raci Metals

This 12-card set features some of the best n Winston Cup racing. The cards were sold mail and through Superior Performance's network. The cards feature the were the firs cards ever produced to feature a Winston Cup The cards are unnumbered and listed be alphabetical order.

COMPLETE SET (12) 60.00

errike Cope 4.00 10.00
ll Elliott 8.00 20.00
arry Gant 6.00 15.00
obby Hamilton 4.00 10.00
nie Irvan 6.00 15.00
erling Marlin 6.00 15.00
ark Martin 12.00 30.00
il Parsons 2.50 6.00
yle Petty 8.00 20.00
Richard Petty 12.00 30.00
Ken Schrader 4.00 10.00
Darrell Waltrip 6.00 15.00

2001 Super Shots Hendrick Motorsports

set was issued by Super Shots to commemorate 100th win of Hendrick Motorsports. Each card res a current or past Hendrick Racing driver who ributed to the feat with the final two being ted to the Hendrick family and a list of all 100-. The final card is a double sized jumbo card ring the entire Hendrick Racing Team. Each ry boxed set could also have been upgraded to de one of 8 different banner memorabilia cards Jeff Gordon Raced-Used Tire card.

MP.FACT.SET (22) 10.00 25.00
Geoff Bodine .30 .75
Tim Richmond .30 .75
Darrell Waltrip .50 1.25
with Michael Waltrip
Ken Schrader .50 1.25
Darrell Waltrip .50 1.25
Ricky Rudd .50 1.25
Terry Labonte .60 1.50
Jeff Gordon 1.00 2.50
Jeff Gordon 1.00 2.50
Jeff Gordon 1.00 2.50
Jeff Gordon 1.00 2.50
Terry Labonte .60 1.50
Terry Labonte .60 1.50
Terry Labonte .75 2.00
Jeff Gordon
Ricky Craven
Jeff Gordon 1.00 2.50
Terry Labonte .60 1.50
Jeff Gordon 1.00 2.50
Jerry Nadeau .30 .75
Jeff Gordon 1.00 2.50
Papa Joe Hendrick .30 .75
John Hendrick
Rick Hendrick
100-Win list .20 .50
2 Race Team Jumbo .50 1.25
Jeff Gordon Tire 15.00 40.00

2001 Super Shots Hendrick Motorsports Silver

parallel set to the basic issue Super Shots drick set features silver foil highlights on the ronts. They were distributed in complete factory orm along with 2-silver Banner cards and one om autographed card. Reportedly, 500-Silver ry sets were produced.

MP.FACT.SET (24) 150.00 250.00
VERS: 2X TO 5X BASIC CARDS

2001 Super Shots Hendrick Motorsports Victory Banners

e 8-cards were issued one per factory boxed set 001 Super Shots Hendrick Motorsports. Each was serial numbered of 775 and includes a ch taken from the 100th Victory Banner layed in victory lane at Michigan on June 10, . Silver factory sets included both of the final silver foil Banner cards.

MPLETE SET (8) 60.00 150.00
1 Jerry Nadeau 5.00 12.00
2 Jeff Gordon 12.50 30.00
3 Terry Labonte 6.00 15.00
4 Ricky Rudd 6.00 15.00
5 Darrell Waltrip 6.00 15.00
6 Ken Schrader 5.00 12.00
7 Tim Richmond 5.00 12.00
8 Geoff Bodine 5.00 12.00
1 Jeff Gordon/500 30.00 60.00
Terry Labonte/500
2 Hendrick Race Team/500 15.00 40.00

2001 Super Shots Hendrick Motorsports Autographs

1 Jeff Gordon/71 75.00 150.00
2 Jerry Nadeau/72 10.00 20.00
3 Terry Labonte/71 20.00 40.00
4 Darrell Waltrip/71 25.00 50.00

HSA5 Ken Schrader/72 10.00 20.00
HSA6 Ricky Rudd/71 10.00 20.00

2001 Super Shots Race-Used Tire Jumbos

These cards were issued by Super Shots, Inc. in 2001. Each is an oversized jumbo card featuring a swatch of race used tire from the featured driver.

RW1 Rusty Wallace/1000 10.00 20.00
JGG1 Jeff Gordon Gold/2001 8.00 20.00
JGS1 Jeff Gordon's Car Silver/2001 6.00 15.00

2001 Super Shots Sears Point CHP

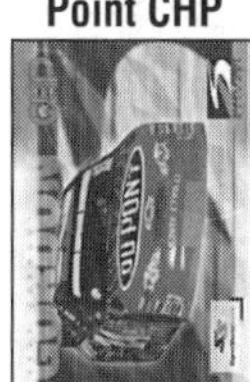

These cards were produced by Super Shots for the California Highway Patrol and were given away at Sears Point Raceway to commemorate the NASCAR race that season.

COMPLETE SET (6) 3.00 8.00
SP1 Sears Point Raceway .20 .50
SP2 Bobby Labonte's Car .50 1.25
SP3 Tony Stewart's Car .75 2.00
SP4 Jeff Gordon's Car .75 2.00
SP5 Kevin Harvick's Car .60 1.50
SP6 Dale Jarrett's Car .50 1.25

2002 Super Shots California Speedway

For the second year in a row a set of 6-cards was produced by Super Shots for the California Speedway. The cards were also sponsored by the California Highway Patrol and each features a driver's car from the race with the final card showing the track itself.

COMPLETE SET (6) 3.00 7.00
CS1 Kevin Harvick's Car .60 1.50
CS2 Bobby Labonte's Car .50 1.25
CS3 Ward Burton's Car .30 .75
CS4 Tony Stewart's Car .75 2.00
CS5 Rusty Wallace's Car .50 1.25
CS6 California Speedway .20 .50

2004 Super Shots CHP Sonoma

COMPLETE SET (5) 6.00 15.00
1 Jeff Gordon 2.50 6.00
2 Jimmie Johnson 2.00 5.00
3 Kasey Kahne 2.50 6.00
4 Terry Labonte 1.00 2.50
5 Jamie McMurray 1.00 2.50

1991 Texas World Speedway

This 10-card set was released by Texas World Speedway in conjunction with the reopening of the track in 1991. The cards feature a turquoise-blue border and some of the top names in racing. The Tim Richmond card was one of the first produced after his death in 1988 and was the best selling card in the set. There were a reported 50,000 sets were produced.

COMPLETE SET (10) 1.25 3.00
1 Benny Parsons .15 .40
2 Buddy Baker .10 .25
3 Bobby Isaac .05 .15
4 Cale Yarborough .15 .40
5 Richard Petty .30 .75
6 Tim Richmond .10 .25
7 Richard Petty .30 .75
Bill France
8 Cale Yarborough .15 .40
9 Darrell Waltrip .15 .40
NNO Cover Card .05 .10

1989-90 TG Racing Masters of Racing

The 1989-90 Masters of Racing set was produced and distributed by TG Racing which used its extensive photo files to produce a history of stock car racing on cards. The 1989 issue (numbers 1-152) was broken down into four series of 38-cards each, with each series featuring a different colored border. The set was sold by series (originally $7.95 each) directly to the card hobby. Part two (numbers 153-262) of the Masters of Racing was released in the summer of 1990 under the title White Gold. The 1990 set was sold in complete factory set form only, not by series. A special Masters of Racing album was produced as well to house the cards.

COMPLETE SET (262) 60.00 135.00
COMP.SERIES 1 (152) 60.00 120.00
COMP.SERIES 2 (110) 7.50 20.00
1 Cover Card .20 .50
Gun Gray 1-38
2 Red Byron .30 .75
3 Red Byron's Car .20 .50
First Champion
4 Starting Lineup .20 .50
1963 Atlanta 500
5 Speedy Thompson .30 .75
6 Speedy Thompson .20 .50
Darlington 1956
7 Buck Baker .60 1.50
8 Buck Baker w/Car .60 1.50
9 Buck Baker .60 1.50
Speedy Thompson
Carl Kiekhaefer
300 and 300B
10 Henley Gray .30 .75
11 Henley Gray's Car .20 .50
12 Ralph Earnhardt 1.00 2.50
13 The Wreck .20 .50
1960 Modified-Sportsman 250
14 Paul Goldsmith .60 1.50
15 Paul Goldsmith w/Car .60 1.50
16 Bill Seifert .30 .75
17 Bill Seifert w/Car .30 .75
18 Edwin Matthews w/Car .30 .75
19 Edwin Matthews w/Car .30 .75
20 Johnny Thompson w/Car .30 .75
21 Johnny Thompson w/Car .30 .75
Jacksonville 1950
22 Glenn Roberts(Fireball) 1.25 3.00
23 Glenn Roberts(Fireball) w/Car 1.25 3.00
24 Glenn Roberts(Fireball) 1.25 3.00
In Action
25 Lennie Pond .30 .75
26 Lennie Pond w/Car .30 .75
27 David Pearson's Car .30 .75
Junior Johnson's Car
Ned Jarrett's Car
Marvin Panch's Car
Fireball Roberts' Car
256 Wins
28 Sam McQuagg .30 .75
29 Sam McQuagg w/Car .30 .75
30 Gober Sosebee .30 .75
31 Gober Sosebee's Car .20 .50
On The Beach
32 Larry Frank .60 1.50
33 Larry Frank w/Car .60 1.50
34 Eddie Pagan .30 .75
35 Curtis Crider .30 .75
36 Curtis Crider w/Car .30 .75
37 Tiny Lund's Car .30 .75
Fireball Roberts' Cars
Bristol 1963
38 Checklist .20 .50
Cards 1-38
39 Cover Card .20 .50
Red Fox 39-76
David Pearson's Car
Earl Brooks' Car
40 Lloyd Dane .30 .75
41 David Pearson w/Car .60 1.50
42 David Pearson w/Car .60 1.50
Champion 1968-69
43 David Pearson .60 1.50
Pearson 1976
44 Roy Tyner's Car .20 .50
45 David Ezell .30 .75
46 Lee Roy Yarborough .60 1.50
47 Lee Roy Yarborough w/Car .60 1.50
Big Track Champ
48 Marshall Teague .30 .75
49 Night Time .20 .50
1964 Columbia 200
50 Jabe Thomas .30 .75
51 Dirt Track .20 .50
1963 Orange Speedway
52 Billy Carden .30 .75
53 Billy Carden's Car .20 .50
Birmingham Fairgrounds
54 Ed Samples .30 .75
55 Ed Samples' Car .20 .50
Greensboro 1947
56 Jack Smith w/Car .30 .75
57 Jack Smith w/Car .30 .75
Red Fox
58 Ralph Moody Jr. w/Car .30 .75
59 David Pearson's Car 1.00 2.50
Richard Petty's Car
Junior Johnson's Car
Hillsboro 1964
60 David Pearson .60 1.50
Goat Power
61 Tiny Lund .60 1.50
62 Tiny Lund w/Car .60 1.50
55 lb. Fish Story
63 Tiny Lund w/Car .60 1.50
Tiny Wins the Big One
64 Marvin Panch .60 1.50
65 The 5 Heroes .20 .50
1963 Daytona
66 Wilkesboro 1962 .20 .50
67 Marvin Panch w/Car .60 1.50
Ford in '64
68 Cotton Owens .30 .75
69 Cotton Owens w/Car .30 .75
70 Tommy Gale w/Car .30 .75
71 Tiny Lund 1.50 4.00
Marty Robbins
The Hat
72 Jack Smith's Car .20 .50
Cotton Owens' Car
Red Fox Edges Cotton
73 Johnny Allen .60 1.50
74 Johnny Allen w/Car .60 1.50
75 Lee Roy Yarborough 1.00 2.50
Junior Johnson
Herb Nab
Victory Lane
76 Checklist .20 .50
Cards 39-76 with Cotton Owens
77 Cover Card .20 .50
Sky Blue 77-114 with Junior Johnson
78 Walter Ballard .30 .75
79 Walter Ballard's Car .20 .50
80 Darel Dieringer .30 .75
81 Darel Dieringer's Car .20 .50
82 Ray Erickson .30 .75
83 Ray Erickson w/Car .30 .75
Pioneer
84 Dick Hutcherson w/Car .30 .75
85 Dick Hutcherson's Car .20 .50
86 Ramo Stott .30 .75
87 Ramo Stott w/Car .30 .75
88 Don White .30 .75
89 Don White's Car .20 .50
90 Dick Hutcherson .30 .75
Ramo Stott
Don White
Keokuk, Iowa
91 Glen Wood .30 .75
92 Rex White w/Car .30 .75
93 Rex White's Car .20 .50
94 Jimmie Lewallen .30 .75
95 Jimmie Lewallen w/Car .20 .50
96 Darel Dieringer 1.00 2.50
Junior Johnson
97 Banks Simpson .30 .75
98 Paul Lewis w/Car .30 .75
99 Glen Wood's Car .30 .75
Rex White's Car
Winston-Salem 1961
100 Junior Johnson 1.25 3.00
101 Junior Johnson's Car .60 1.50
Darlington 1965
102 Junior Johnson w/Car 1.25 3.00
103 Joe Millikan .30 .75
104 Junior Johnson .60 1.50
Ray Fox
Cheat 'N Eat
105 Bobby Myers .30 .75
Billy Myers
106 Reino Tulonen w/Car .30 .75
107 World 600 1963 .20 .50
108 Coo Coo Marlin .60 1.50
109 Coo Coo Marlin w/Car .60 1.50
110 Bobby Myers .30 .75
111 Billy Myers .30 .75
112 Billy Myers .30 .75
Bowman Gray Stadium
113 Bobby Myers .30 .75
114 Checklist .20 .50
Cards 77-114
115 Cover Card .20 .50
Burnt Orange 115-152
Bobby Isaac's Car
Tiny Lund's car
116 Buddy Arrington .30 .75
117 Buddy Arrington's Car .20 .50
118 Bill Blair w/Car .30 .75
119 Bill Blair w/Car .30 .75
120 Earl Brooks w/Car .30 .75
121 Earl Brooks w/Car .30 .75
122 Charlie Glotzbach .30 .75
123 Charlie Glotzbach w/Car .30 .75
Famous Chevy
124 Charlie Glotzbach w/Car .30 .75
125 Gene Cline w/Car .30 .75
126 Nelson Stacy .30 .75
127 Nelson Stacy w/Car .30 .75
128 Jim Reed .30 .75
129 Jim Reed w/Car .30 .75
130 Charlie Glotzbach w/Car .30 .75
131 Bobby Isaac's Car .30 .75
132 Neil Castles' Car .20 .50
133 Buddy Arrington's Car .20 .50
134 Fireball Roberts in Pits .60 1.50
Quick Stop
135 Neil Castles .30 .75
136 Neil Castles' Car .20 .50
137 Red Farmer .30 .75
138 Red Farmer's Car .20 .50
139 Big Winner .30 .75
Fred Lorenzen's Car
1964 Martinsville
140 Pete Hamilton .30 .75
141 Pete Hamilton w/Car .20 .50
142 Gwyn Staley .30 .75
143 Fred Lorenzen .60 1.50
Fred and Donna
144 Gwyn Staley .30 .75
Enoch Staley
Charlie Combs
North Wilkesboro
145 Bobby Isaac w/Car .60 1.50
146 G.C. Spencer .30 .75
147 Bob Derrington .30 .75
148 Earl Brooks' Car .20 .50
Lorenzen's Car
Nelson Stacy's Car
The Pack
149 Fred Lorenzen .60 1.50
150 Fred Lorenzen w/Car .60 1.50
151 Fred Lorenzen w/Car .60 1.50
152 Checklist .20 .50
Cards 115-152
153 Cover Card .07 .20
White Gold 153-262
Red Byron's Car
154 Bob Flock .10 .30
155 Bob Flock's Car .07 .20
Red Byron's Car
Whitewalls
156 Fonty Flock .20 .50
157 Fonty Flock's Car .10 .30
1947 Champion
158 Tim Flock .20 .50
159 Tim Flock w/Car .20 .50
Automatic
160 Fonty Flock .20 .50
Tim Flock
Bob Flock
Carl Flock
161 James Hylton .10 .30
162 James Hylton's Car .07 .20
163 James Hylton w/Car .10 .30
Rookie Sensation
164 Perk Brown .10 .30
165 Perk Brown's Car .07 .20
166 Joe Frasson .10 .30
167 Joe Frasson's Car .07 .20
168 Jack Handle w/Car .10 .30
169 Louise Smith .20 .50
170 Louise Smith .20 .50
First Lady
171 Lee Petty .40 1.00
Louise Smith
Janet Guthrie
Lella Lombardi
Christine Beckers
Racers All
172 Marshall Teague .20 .50
Interior
173 Marshall Teague w/Car .20 .50
Exterior
174 George Follmer .10 .30
175 George Follmer's Car .07 .20
Special Breed
176 George Follmer w/Car .10 .30
Hawk Ford
177 Bob Wellborn's Car .07 .20
Rex White's Car
Jim Reed's Car
Champions
178 Bob Burcham w/Car .10 .30
179 Tommy Moon .10 .30
180 Wendell Scott .40 1.00
181 Wendell Scott's Car .20 .50
Independent
182 Wendell Scott's Car .20 .50
David Pearson's Car
Late Win
183 Dick Linder .10 .30
184 Larry Shurter .10 .30
185 Johnny Halford .10 .30
186 Johnny Halford's Car .07 .20
High Pockets
187 Jim Paschal's Car .07 .20
Fonty Flock's Car
Joe Eubanks' Car
Rough Day
188 Butch Lindley .10 .30
189 Butch Lindley's Car .07 .20
LMS Whiz
190 Checklist .07 .20
Cards 153-190
191 Donnie Allison .40 1.00
192 Donnie Allison's Car .20 .50
Banner Year
193 Donnie Allison's Car .20 .50
Heartbreaker
194 Bob Welborn .10 .30
195 Hershel McGriff .10 .30
196 Hershel McGriff .10 .30
197 Hershel McGriff's Car .07 .20
The Comeback
198 Roscoe Pappy Hough .10 .30
199 Roscoe Pappy Hough's Car .07 .20
Double Dip
200 Ned Jarrett .20 .50
201 Ned Jarrett w/Car .20 .50
14-Lap Winner
202 Ned Jarrett w/Car .20 .50
No Cigar
203 Ned Jarrett w/Car .20 .50
Barely Lived
204 Joe Eubanks .10 .30
205 Joe Eubanks' Car .07 .20
That North Turn
206 Richard Brickhouse .10 .30
207 Richard Brickhouse's Car .07 .20
'70 Superbird
208 Tom Pistone .20 .50
209 Tom Pistone's Car .10 .30
Go-Go-Go
210 Buddy Shuman .10 .30
211 Marshall Teague .10 .30
Bob Flock
Ed Samples
Buddy Shuman
The Inlaw
212 Jody Ridley .10 .30
213 Jody Ridley's Car .07 .20
Unbelievable
214 Lee Petty .40 1.00
215 Lee Petty's Car .20 .50
Deflated
216 Maurice Petty .20 .50
217 Maurice Petty .20 .50
Mickey Who?
218 Al Holbert .10 .30
219 Al Holbert's Car .07 .20
Top Rookie
220 Dick Brooks .10 .30
221 Dick Brooks' Car .07 .20
Pete Hamilton's Car
Last Race
222 Dick Brooks' Car .07 .20
High Hopes
223 Dick Rathmann w/Car .10 .30
224 Dick Rathmann's Car .07 .20
Last to First
225 Jim Vandiver .10 .30
226 Jim Vandiver's Car .07 .20
Man On Move
227 Gene White .10 .30
228 Checklist .07 .20
Cards 191-228
Skyboxes 1953
229 Dick May .10 .30
230 Dick May's Car .07 .20
D.D. Dandy
231 Herb Thomas .20 .50
232 Herb Thomas .20 .50
Marshall Teague
The Secret?
233 Donald Thomas .10 .30
234 Fans' Race .07 .20
1950 North Wilkesboro
235 Jim Paschal .10 .30
236 Jim Paschal w/Car .10 .30
Pontiac Sweep
237 Jim Paschal w/Car .10 .30
Richard Petty Power
238 Jim Paschal's Car .07 .20
69 Javelin
239 Frank Mundy .10 .30
240 Frank Mundy .10 .30
The Rebel
241 Frankie Schneider .10 .30
242 Joe Lee Johnson .10 .30
243 Joe Lee Johnson w/Car .10 .30
Tradersville
244 Dink Widenhouse .10 .30
245 Dink Widenhouse's Car .07 .20
Dink's Dilemma
246 Dave Marcis .20 .50
247 Dave Marcis' Car .10 .30
Flying High
248 Bill Rexford .10 .30
249 Bill Rexford w/Car .10 .30
1950 Champ
250 Cale Yarborough .20 .50
251 Cale Yarborough .20 .50
252 Cale Yarborough w/Car .20 .50
Ford In 1962
253 Cale Yarborough w/Car .20 .50
New Shoes
254 Cale Yarborough w/Car .20 .50
Old Yeller
255 Cale Yarborough's Car .10 .30
1981 Buick
256 Elmo Langley .20 .50
257 Elmo Langley's Car .10 .30
Green Machine
258 Ray Hendrick .10 .30
259 Ray Hendrick .10 .30
Perk Brown
Rivals
260 Ron Bouchard .10 .30
261 Ron Bouchard w/Car .10 .30
Lucky 13
262 Checklist .07 .20
Cards 229-262
Dave Marcis
Red, White, Blue

1991 TG Racing Tiny Lund

T.G.Racing released this 55-card set highlighting the career of Tiny Lund. The cards were sold in complete set form. Reportedly 20,000 sets were produced.

COMP. FACT SET (55) 4.00 10.00
1 Tiny Lund .10 .25
Art Cover
2 Tiny Lund .10 .25
Statistics
3 Tiny Lund .10 .25
A Boy and His Dog
4 Tiny Lund .10 .25
Stylish in '50s
5 Tiny Lund .10 .25
Biker First
6 Tiny Lund's Car .05 .10
Hometown Hero
7 Tiny Lund's Car .05 .10
Blurry Win
8 Tiny Lund .10 .25
Trackside Wedding
9 Tiny Lund's Car .05 .10
Brushy Mountain
10 Tiny Lund w/Car .10 .25
For A Friend
11 Tiny Lund .10 .25
Tom Pistone
Laurel and Hardy
12 Tiny Lund w/Car .10 .25
Fish Camp Chevy
13 Tiny Lund .10 .25
The Fish Camp
14 Tiny Lund .10 .25
Louis Vogt
Legend Signs On
15 Tiny Lund .10 .25
Record Catch
16 Tiny Lund's Car .10 .25
Fred Lorenzen's Car
Tiny and Fred
17 Tiny Lund w/Car .10 .25
Cinderfella
18 Tiny Lund .10 .25
Fireball Roberts
Ned Jarrett
Fred Lorenzen
The Big Four
19 Carnegie Medal .05 .10
20 Tiny Lund .10 .25
They Knew Him
21 Tiny Lund .10 .25
Tiny Lund Day
22 Tiny Lund .10 .25
Atlanta Victory
23 Tiny Lund .10 .25
Miss Firebird
24 Tiny Lund's Car .05 .10
Tom Pistone's Car
Serious Racing
25 Tiny Lund .15 .40
Dick Hutcherson
Cale Yarborough
Ned Jarrett
Buddy Baker
Buck Baker
Playboy Bunny
26 Tiny Lund .10 .25
Buddy Baker
Brooks Robinson
Favorite Player
27 Tiny Lund's Car .05 .10
Fred Lorenzen's Car
Slippin', Slidin'
28 Tiny Lund's Car .05 .10
Hard Charger
29 Tiny Lund .10 .25
Movie Premiere
30 Tiny Lund .10 .25
Ride of Her Life
31 Tiny Lund .10 .25
Baby Alligator
32 Tiny Lund .10 .25

Buddy Baker
Paul Bud Moore
The Quartet
33 Tiny Lund .10 .25
Wanda's Wedding
34 Tiny Lund .10 .25
His Pets
35 Tiny Lund .10 .25
Buck Baker
Pretty Ladies
36 Tiny Lund's Car .05 .10
Talladega 1969
37 Tiny Lund .10 .25
Tom Pistone
Bill France Sr.
France Serves
38 Tiny Lund .10 .25
Seiichi Suzuki
Big In Japan
39 Tiny Lund .10 .25
Sushi and Saki
40 Tiny Lund .10 .25
Joan Crawford
41 Tiny Lund .10 .25
Wrecking Crew
42 Tiny Lund .10 .25
Bob Baskowitz
Mountain Dew
43 Tiny Lund .10 .25
A New Seat
44 Tiny Lund .10 .25
Santa Claus
45 Tiny Lund .10 .25
Kids Loved Him
46 Tiny Lund .10 .25
Andy Granatelli
STP's Andy
47 Tiny Lund .10 .25
Another Trophy
48 Tiny Lund .10 .25
President Richard Nixon
49 Tiny Lund w/Car .10 .25
Two Loves
50 Tiny Lund .10 .25
Proud Man
51 Tiny Lund .10 .25
Marty Robbins
52 Tiny Lund .10 .25
Canadian Tribute
53 1976 Marquee .05 .10
54 The Batter's Box .10 .25
June 1, 1991
55 Tiny Lund's Car .10 .25
Checklist back
P1 Tiny Lund Prototype .50 1.25
borderless, numbered 55

1991 TG Racing David Pearson

T.G.Racing released this six-card set highlighting the career of David Pearson. The cards were sold in complete set form.

COMP. FACT SET (6) 10.00 25.00
COMMON CARD (1-6) 2.00 5.00

1991 TG Racing Wendell Scott

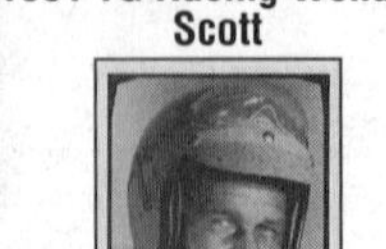

T.G.Racing released this six-card set highlighting the career of Wendell Scott. The cards were sold in complete set form.

COMP. FACT SET (6) 3.00 8.00
COMMON CARD (1-6) .60 1.50

1991-92 TG Racing Masters of Racing Update

TG Racing reprinted the original Masters of Racing set in this "Update" form. This set was released in complete factory set form in a colorful box. Three cards were added to the original set and all cards contain a blue border as opposed to the various border colors of the original cards. Although the cards are marked 1991 on the copyright line, they are considered a 1992 release. Four promo cards were produced to promote the set. They are not considered part of the complete set price.

COMP.FACT SET (265) 10.00 25.00
1 Cover Card .05 .10
Gun Gray 1-38
2 Red Byron .20 .50
3 Red Byron's Car .07 .20
First Champion
4 Starting Lineup .07 .20
1963 Atlanta 500
5 Speedy Thompson .20 .50
6 Speedy Thompson .20 .50
Darlington 1956
7 Buck Baker .20 .50
8 Buck Baker w/Car .20 .50
9 Buck Baker .07 .20
Speedy Thompson
Carl Kiekhaefer
300 and 300B
10 Henley Gray .20 .50
11 Henley Gray's Car .07 .20
12 Ralph Earnhardt .40 1.00
13 The Wreck .07 .20
1960 Modified-Sportsman 250
14 Paul Goldsmith .12 .30
15 Paul Goldsmith w/Car .12 .30
16 Bill Seifert .20 .50
17 Bill Seifert w/Car .20 .50
18 Edwin Matthews w/Car .12 .30
19 Edwin Matthews w/Car .12 .30
20 Johnny Thompson w/Car .20 .50
21 Johnny Thompson w/Car .20 .50
Jacksonville 1950
22 Glenn Roberts(Fireball) .30 .75
23 Glenn Roberts(Fireball) w/Car .30 .75
24 Glenn Roberts(Fireball) .30 .75
In Action
25 Lennie Pond .20 .50
26 Lennie Pond w/Car .20 .50
27 David Pearson's Car .40 1.00
Junior Johnson's Car
Ned Jarrett's Car
Marvin Panch's Car
Fireball Roberts' Car
256 Wins
28 Sam McQuagg .12 .30
29 Sam McQuagg w/Car .12 .30
30 Gober Sosebee .20 .50
31 Gober Sosebee's Car .07 .20
On The Beach
32 Larry Frank .12 .30
33 Larry Frank w/Car .12 .30
34 Eddie Pagan .20 .50
35 Curtis Crider .20 .50
36 Curtis Crider w/Car .20 .50
37 Tiny Lund's Car .12 .30
Fireball Roberts' Cars
Bristol 1963
38 Checklist .07 .20
Cards 1-38
39 Cover Card .15 .40
Red Fox 39-76
David Pearson's Car
Earl Brooks' Car
40 Lloyd Dane .12 .30
41 David Pearson w/Car .40 1.00
42 David Pearson w/Car .40 1.00
Champion 1968-69
43 David Pearson .40 1.00
Pearson 1976
44 Roy Tyner's Car .07 .20
45 David Ezell .20 .50
46 Lee Roy Yarborough .20 .50
47 Lee Roy Yarborough w/Car .20 .50
Big Track Champ
48 Marshall Teague .20 .50
49 Night Time .07 .20
1964 Columbia 200
50 Jabe Thomas .20 .50
51 Dirt Track .07 .20
1963 Orange Speedway
52 Billy Carden .20 .50
53 Billy Carden's Car .07 .20
Birmingham Fairgrounds
54 Ed Samples .20 .50
55 Ed Samples' Car .07 .20
Greensboro 1947
56 Jack Smith w/Car .12 .30
57 Jack Smith w/Car .12 .30
Red Fox
58 Ralph Moody Jr. w/Car .20 .50
59 David Pearson's Car .15 .40
Richard Petty's Car
Junior Johnson's Car
Hillsboro 1964
60 David Pearson .40 1.00
Goat Power
61 Tiny Lund .20 .50
62 Tiny Lund w/Car .20 .50
55 lb. Fish Story
63 Tiny Lund w/Car .20 .50
Tiny Wins the Big One
64 Marvin Panch .20 .50
65 The 5 Heroes .07 .20
1963 Daytona
66 Wilkesboro 1962 .07 .20
67 Marvin Panch w/Car .20 .50
Ford in '64
68 Cotton Owens .12 .30
69 Cotton Owens w/Car .12 .30
70 Tommy Gale w/Car .20 .50
71 Tiny Lund .20 .50
Marty Robbins
The Hat
72 Jack Smith's Car .05 .10
Cotton Owens' Car
Red Fox Edges Cotton
73 Johnny Allen .20 .50
74 Johnny Allen w/Car .20 .50
75 Lee Roy Yarborough .20 .50
Junior Johnson
Herb Nab
Victory Lane
76 Checklist .12 .30
Cards 39-76 with Cotton Owens
77 Cover Card .07 .20
Sky Blue 77-114 with Junior Johnson
78 Walter Ballard .20 .50
79 Walter Ballard's Car .07 .20
80 Darel Dieringer .12 .30
81 Darel Dieringer's Car .05 .10
82 Ray Erickson .20 .50
83 Ray Erickson w/Car .20 .50
Pioneer
84 Dick Hutcherson w/Car .12 .30
85 Dick Hutcherson's Car .05 .10
86 Ramo Stott .20 .50
87 Ramo Stott w/Car .20 .50
88 Don White .20 .50
89 Don White's Car .07 .20
90 Dick Hutcherson .20 .50
Ramo Stott
Don White
Keokuk, Iowa
91 Glen Wood .12 .30
92 Rex White w/Car .20 .50
93 Rex White's Car .07 .20
94 Jimmie Lewallen .12 .30
95 Jimmie Lewallen w/Car .12 .30
96 Darel Dieringer .20 .50
Junior Johnson
97 Banks Simpson .20 .50
98 Paul Lewis w/Car .20 .50
99 Glen Wood's Car .07 .20
Rex White's Car
Winston-Salem 1961
100 Junior Johnson .20 .50
101 Junior Johnson's Car .07 .20
Darlington 1965
102 Junior Johnson w/Car .20 .50
103 Joe Millikan .20 .50
104 Junior Johnson .20 .50
Ray Fox
Cheat 'N Eat
105 Bobby Myers .20 .50
Billy Myers
106 Reino Tulonen w/Car .20 .50
107 World 600 1963 .07 .20
108 Coo Coo Marlin .12 .30
109 Coo Coo Marlin w/Car .12 .30
110 Ray Fox .20 .50
111 Billy Myers .20 .50
112 Billy Myers .20 .50
Bowman Gray Stadium
113 Ray Fox .20 .50
114 Checklist .07 .20
Cards 77-114
115 Cover Card .07 .20
Burnt Orange 115-152
Bobby Isaac's Car
Tiny Lund's car
116 Buddy Arrington .12 .30
117 Buddy Arrington's Car .05 .10
118 Bill Blair w/Car .12 .30
119 Bill Blair w/Car .12 .30
120 Earl Brooks w/Car .20 .50
121 Earl Brooks w/Car .20 .50
122 Charlie Glotzbach .20 .50
123 Charlie Glotzbach w/Car .20 .50
Famous Chevy
124 Charlie Glotzbach w/Car .20 .50
125 Gene Cline w/Car .20 .50
126 Nelson Stacy .20 .50
127 Nelson Stacy w/Car .20 .50
128 Jim Reed .12 .30
129 Jim Reed w/Car .12 .30
130 Charlie Glotzbach w/Car .20 .50
131 Bobby Isaac's Car .05 .10
132 Neil Castles' Car .05 .10
133 Buddy Arrington's Car .05 .10
134 Fireball Roberts in Pits .30 .75
Quick Stop
135 Neil Castles .12 .30
136 Neil Castles' Car .05 .10
137 Red Farmer .20 .50
138 Red Farmer's Car .07 .20
139 Big Winner .20 .50
Fred Lorenzen's Car
1964 Martinsville
140 Pete Hamilton .12 .30
141 Pete Hamilton w/Car .12 .30
142 Gwyn Staley .20 .50
143 Fred Lorenzen .20 .50
Fred and Donna
144 Gwyn Staley .20 .50
Enoch Staley
Charlie Combs
North Wilkesboro
145 Bobby Isaac w/Car .12 .30
146 G.C. Spencer .12 .30
147 Bob Derrington .20 .50
148 Earl Brooks' Car .07 .20
Lorenzen's Car
Nelson Stacy's Car
The Pack
149 Fred Lorenzen .20 .50
150 Fred Lorenzen w/Car .20 .50
151 Fred Lorenzen w/Car .20 .50
152 Checklist .07 .20
Cards 115-152
153 Cover Card .07 .20
White Gold 153-262
Red Byron's Car
154 Bob Flock .20 .50
155 Bob Flock's Car .07 .20
Red Byron's Car
Whitewalls
156 Fonty Flock .20 .50
157 Fonty Flock's Car .07 .20
1947 Champion
158 Tim Flock .20 .50
159 Tim Flock w/Car .20 .50
Automatic
160 Fonty Flock .07 .20
Tim Flock
Bob Flock
Carl Flock
161 James Hylton .12 .30
162 James Hylton's Car .05 .10
163 James Hylton w/Car .12 .30
Rookie Sensation
164 Perk Brown .20 .50
165 Perk Brown's Car .07 .20
166 Joe Frasson .20 .50
167 Joe Frasson's Car .07 .20
168 Jack Handle w/Car .20 .50
169 Louise Smith .12 .30
170 Louise Smith .12 .30
First Lady
171 Lee Petty .30 .75
Louise Smith
Janet Guthrie
Lella Lombardi
Christine Beckers
Racers All
172 Frank Warren .20 .50
173 Frank Warren's Car .07 .20
174 George Follmer .20 .50
175 George Follmer's Car .07 .20
Special Breed
176 George Follmer w/Car .20 .50
Hawk Ford
177 Bob Wellborn's Car .07 .20
Rex White's Car
Jim Reed's Car
Champions
178 Bob Burcham w/Car .20 .50
179 Tommy Moon .20 .50
180 Wendell Scott .12 .30
181 Wendell Scott's Car .05 .10
Independent
182 Wendell Scott's Car .15 .40
David Pearson's Car
Late Win
183 Dick Linder .20 .50
184 Larry Shurter .20 .50
185 Johnny Halford .20 .50
186 Johnny Halford's Car .07 .20
High Pockets
187 Jim Paschal's Car .07 .20
Fonty Flock's Car
Joe Eubanks' Car
Rough Day
188 Butch Lindley .20 .50
189 Butch Lindley's Car .07 .20
LMS Whiz
190 Checklist .07 .20
Cards 153-190
191 Donnie Allison .20 .50
192 Donnie Allison's Car .07 .20
Banner Year
193 Donnie Allison's Car .07 .20
Heartbreaker
194 Bob Welborn .12 .30
195 Hershel McGriff .20 .50
196 Hershel McGriff .20 .50
197 Hershel McGriff's Car .07 .20
The Comeback
198 Roscoe Pappy Hough .20 .50
199 Roscoe Pappy Hough's Car .07 .20
Double Dip
200 Ned Jarrett .20 .50
201 Ned Jarrett w/Car .20 .50
14-Lap Winner
202 Ned Jarrett w/Car .20 .50
No Cigar
203 Ned Jarrett w/Car .20 .50
Barely Lived
204 Joe Eubanks .20 .50
205 Joe Eubanks' Car .07 .20
That North Turn
206 Richard Brickhouse .20 .50
207 Richard Brickhouse's Car .07 .20
'70 Superbird
208 Tom Pistone .12 .30
209 Tom Pistone's Car .05 .10
Go-Go-Go
210 Buddy Shuman .20 .50
211 Marshall Teague .20 .50
Bob Flock
Ed Samples
Buddy Shuman
The Inlaw
212 Jody Ridley .20 .50
213 Jody Ridley's Car .07 .20
Unbelievable
214 Lee Petty .30 .75
215 Lee Petty's Car .12 .30
Deflated
216 Maurice Petty .30 .75
217 Maurice Petty .30 .75
Mickey Who?
218 Al Holbert .20 .50
219 Al Holbert's Car .07 .20
Top Rookie
220 Dick Brooks .12 .30
221 Dick Brooks' Car .05 .10
Pete Hamilton's Car
Last Race
222 Dick Brooks' Car .05 .10
High Hopes
223 Dick Rathmann w/Car .12 .30
224 Dick Rathmann's Car .05 .10
Last to First
225 Jim Vandiver .20 .50
226 Jim Vandiver's Car .07 .20
Man On Move
227 Gene White .20 .50
228 Checklist .07 .20
Cards 191-228
Skyboxes 1953
229 Dick May .20 .50
230 Dick May's Car .07 .20
D.D. Dandy
231 Herb Thomas .12 .30
232 Herb Thomas .20 .50
Marshall Teague
The Secret?
233 Donald Thomas .20 .50
234 Fans' Race .07 .20
1950 North Wilkesboro
235 Jim Paschal .12 .30
236 Jim Paschal w/Car .12 .30
Pontiac Sweep
237 Jim Paschal w/Car .12 .30
Richard Petty Power
238 Jim Paschal's Car .05 .10
69 Javelin
239 Frank Mundy .12 .30
240 Frank Mundy .12 .30
The Rebel
241 Frankie Schneider .20 .50
242 Joe Lee Johnson .20 .50
243 Joe Lee Johnson w/Car .12 .30
Tradersville
244 Dink Widenhouse .20 .50
245 Dink Widenhouse's Car .07 .20
Dink's Dilemma
246 Dave Marcis .20 .50
247 Dave Marcis' Car
Flying High
248 Bill Rexford .12 .30
249 Bill Rexford w/Car .12 .30
1950 Champ
250 Cale Yarborough .30 .75
251 Cale Yarborough .30 .75
252 Cale Yarborough w/Car .30 .75
Ford In 1962
253 Cale Yarborough w/Car .30 .75
New Shoes
254 Cale Yarborough w/Car .30 .75
Old Yeller
255 Cale Yarborough's Car .12 .30
1981 Buick
256 Elmo Langley .12 .30
257 Elmo Langley's Car .05 .10
Green Machine
258 Ray Hendrick .20 .50
259 Ray Hendrick .20 .50
Perk Brown
Rivals
260 Ron Bouchard .20 .50
261 Ron Bouchard w/Car .20 .50
Lucky 13
262 Bobby Myers .20 .50
263 Bobby Myers .20 .50
Darlington
264 Checklist .20 .50
Cards 229-262
Dave Marcis
Red, White, Blue
265 Tommy Moon w/Car .20 .50
P1 Larry Frank Promo .60 1.50
P2 Charlie Glotzbach Promo 1.00 2.50
P3 Charlie Owens Promo .60 1.50
Cotton's Ride
P4 Donald Thomas Promo 1.00 2.50
numbered 233

1994 Tide Ricky Rudd

Proctor and Gamble produced and released this set featuring Ricky Rudd and the Tide Racing Team. The ten-card set was given away wherever the Tide showcar was on display during the 1995 Winston Cup season and was released in complete set form.

COMPLETE SET (10) 3.20 8.00
1 Ricky Rudd w/Car .30 .75
2 Ricky Rudd's Car .30 .75
3 Ricky Rudd .50 1.25
4 Ricky Rudd .30 .75
Bill Ingle
5 Ricky Rudd in Pits .30 .75
6 Ricky Rudd .50 1.25
7 Ricky Rudd's Transporter .30 .75
8 Ricky Rudd .30 .75
Linda Rudd
9 Ricky Rudd .30 .75
Linda Rudd
10 Ricky Rudd .30 .75
Linda Rudd

1991 Tiger Tom Pistone

This is a 15 card set consisting of 3 color and 12 black and white cards produced by "If Its Racing". The set covers Tom's career from 1954 to his victory in a legends race at Hickory Speedway in 1987.

COMPLETE SET (15) 1.50 4.00
1 Tom Pistone .10 .25
2 Tom Pistone .10 .25
3 Tom Pistone .10 .25
4 Tom Pistone .10 .25
5 Tom Pistone .10 .25
6 Tom Pistone .10 .25
7 Tom Pistone .10 .25
Andy Granatelli
8 Tom Pistone .10 .25
9 Tom Pistone .10 .25
10 Tom Pistone .10 .25
11 Tom Pistone .10 .25
12 Tom Pistone .10 .25
13 Tom Pistone .50 1.25
Richard Petty
14 Tom Pistone .15 .40
Tiny Lund
15 Tom Pistone .10 .25
P1 Tom Pistone Promo .60 1.50

1991 Track Pack Yesterday's Heroes

This 48-card set features some of the greatest names to ever run the NASCAR circuit. The set includes David Pearson, Ned Jarrett and Benny Parsons to name a few. The cards are listed in alphabetical order.

COMPLETE SET (48) 6.00 15.00
1 Cover Card .12 .30
2 Bill Blair .20 .50
3 Neil Bonnett .50 1.25
4 Dick Brooks .20 .50
5 Neil Castles .20 .50
6 Neil Castles .20 .50
7 Richard Childress .30 .75
8 Lloyd Dane .20 .50
9 Tim Flock .30 .75
10 Larry Frank .20 .50
11 Dick Hutcherson .20 .50
12 Ned Jarrett .30 .75
13 JoeLee Johnson .20 .50
14 Elmo Langley .20 .50
15 Jimmie Lewallen .20 .50
16 Fred Lorenzen .30 .75
17 CooCoo Marlin .30 .75
18 Banjo Matthews .20 .50
19 Banjo Matthews .20 .50
20 Sam McQuagg .20 .50
21 Ralph Moody .30 .75
22 Ralph Moody .30 .75
23 Bud Moore .20 .50
24 Frank Mundy .20 .50
25 Benny Parsons .50 1.25
26 Jim Paschal .20 .50
27 David Pearson .60 1.50
28 David Pearson .60 1.50
29 Tom Pistone .20 .50
30 Dick Rathmann .20 .50
31 Jim Reed .20 .50
32 Bill Rexford .20 .50
33 Jim Roper .20 .50
34 Jack Smith .20 .50
35 Jack Smith .20 .50
36 Louise Smith .20 .50
37 G.C. Spencer .20 .50
38 G.C. Spencer .20 .50
39 Herb Thomas .20 .50
40 Bob Welborn .20 .50
41 Bob Welborn .20 .50
42 Rex White .30 .75
43 Glen Wood .20 .50
44 Glen Wood .20 .50
45 Cale Yarborough .50 1.25
46 Cale Yarborough .50 1.25
47 Smokey Yunick .20 .50
48 Checklist Card .12 .30

1991 Traks Promos

This 6-card set was issued to promote the 1 Traks set. Each card is essentially identical to base issue card except for the card numbering back.

COMPLETE SET (6) 20.00 35
P1 Ernie Irvan 2.00 5
P2 Mark Martin 4.00 10
P3 Kyle Petty 2.50 6
P4 Richard Petty The King 4.00 10
P5 Richard/Lee Petty 4.00 10
P6 Richard Petty 4.00 10

1991 Traks

In addition to a 200-card factory set, the pre edition Traks set was distributed in 15-card p with 30 packs per box in late 1991. The set feat the top Busch and Winston Cup drivers along owners and other racing team members. Traks included the first regular issue NASCAR card of Gordon (number 1). The set was available factory wooden box version. These were distrib through some of the television shopping chan 1,000 sets were produced.

COMPLETE SET (200) 15.00 40
COMP.FACT.SET (200) 15.00 40
WAX BOX 40.00 70
1 Jeff Gordon RC 12.00 30
2 Rusty Wallace .60 1
3A Dale Earnhardt 1.50 4
Trademark reads
...than Sports Image, Inc is â ¦
3B Dale Earnhardt 1.50 4
Trademark reads
...than Sports Image, Inc. at
racing venuesâ ¦
4 Ernie Irvan .40 1
5 Ricky Rudd .40 1
6 Mark Martin .75 2
7 Alan Kulwicki .50 1
8 Rick Wilson .15
9 Troy Beebe RC .25
10 Ernie Irvan w/Car .40 1
11 Larry McClure .15
Ed McClure
Teddy McClure
Jerry McClure
12 Hut Stricklin .15
13 High Speed Chaos .10
14 Bobby Hillin .15
15 Morgan Shepherd .25
16 Eddie Lanier RC .25
17 Jeff Hammond .25
18 Mike Wallace RC .40
19 Chad Little .25
20 Bobby Hillin .15
21 Dale Jarrett .60
22 Sterling Marlin .40
23 Danny Myers RC .25
24 Barry Dodson .15
25 Ken Schrader .25
26 Neil Bonnett .40
27A Mike Colyer RC .25
Traks car logo on back
27B Mike Colyer RC .25
Traks car logo on back is removed
28 Davey Allison .60
29 Phil Parsons .15
30 Michael Waltrip .30
31 Steve Grissom .15
32 Dale Jarrett .60
33 Harry Gant .40
34 Todd Bodine RC .25
35 Chuck Rider .15
36 Kenny Wallace .25
37 Roger Penske RC .40
38 Jimmy Makar .15
39 Don Miller RC .25
40 Felix Sabates .25
41 Kyle Petty's Transporter .20
42 Kyle Petty .50
43 Richard Petty .75
44 Dale Inman .15
45 Bob Bilby RC .25
46 Robert Yates .25
47 Kyle Petty .50
48 Sprague Turner RC .25
49 Doug Richert .15
50 Mark Martin .75
51 Mike McLaughlin RC .25
52 Butch Miller .15
53 Harold Elliott .15
54 Richard Childress .25
55 Ted Musgrave w/Car .40
56 Tommy Ellis .15
57 Kirk Shelmerdine .15
58 Larry McClure .15
59 Robert Pressley RC .25
60 Tim Morgan .15
61 Dick Trickle .15
62 Leonard Wood .15
63 Chuck Bown .15
64 Glen Wood .15
65 Steve Loyd RC .25
66 Cale Yarborough .40
67 Jimmy Johnson .25
Rick Hendrick
68 Ricky Rudd's Car .15
69 Travis Carter .15
70 Tony Glover .15
71 Dave Marcis .25
72 Waddell Wilson .15
73 Alan Kulwicki's Car .20
74 Jimmy Fennig .15
75 Michael Waltrip .30
76 Ken Wilson RC .25

avid Smith .15 .40
unior Johnson .25 .60
ave Rezendes RC .25 .60
ony Furr RC .25 .60
ed Conder .15 .40
like Beam .15 .40
/alter Bud Moore .15 .40
erry Labonte .40 1.00
chard Petty w/Car .75 2.00
onnie Wingo RC .25 .60
oe Nemechek RC .60 1.50
ton Sawyer .25 .60
atty Moise
oug Williams .15 .40
mmy Martin RC .25 .60
ichard Broome .15 .40
reg Moore RC .25 .60
ank Jones RC
erry Labonte .40 1.00
ill Lind .15 .40
om Peck RC .25 .60
organ Shepherd .25 .60
mmy Spencer .25 .60
eo Jackson .15 .40
Max Helton RC .25 .60
Bruce Roney RC .25 .60
Keith Almond RC .25 .60
Dale Earnhardt 1.50 4.00
rademark reads
.than Sports Image, Inc is â¦
Dale Earnhardt 1.50 4.00
rademark reads
.than Sports Image, Inc. at
acing venuesâ¦
Bob Tomlinson RC .25 .60
Benny Ertel RC .25 .60
Tommy Houston .15 .40
Cecil Gordon RC .25 .60
David Green RC .40 1.00
Robin Pemberton .15 .40
David Green's Car .15 .40
John Mulloy RC .25 .60
Harry Gant .40 1.00
Ed Whitaker RC .25 .60
Bobby Moody RC .25 .60
Steve Hmiel .15 .40
Red Farmer RC .25 .60
Eddie Jones RC .25 .60
Bill Stavola .15 .40
Mickey Stavola
David Ifft RC .25 .60
Dick Moroso RC .25 .60
Eddie Wood .15 .40
Len Wood .15 .40
Lou LaRosa RC .25 .60
Rusty Wallace .60 1.50
Rob Moroso .15 .40
Ned Jarrett .25 .60
Tom Higgins RC .25 .60
Frank Edwards RC .25 .60
Steve Waid RC .25 .60
Steve Waid RC .25 .60
Jim Phillips .15 .40
ame in black type on front
Jim Phillips .15 .40
ame in white type on front
John Ervin RC .25 .60
Winston Kelley .15 .40
rst name "Kelly" on back of card
ame in black type on front
Winston Kelley .15 .40
rst name spelled correct on back
ame in white type on front
Allen Bestwick RC .40 1.00
ame in black type on front
Allen Bestwick RC .40 1.00
ame in white type on front
Dick Brooks .15 .40
ame in black type on front
Dick Brooks .15 .40
ame in white type on front
Ricky Rudd Winner .40 1.00
Eli Gold .15 .40
ame in black type on front
Eli Gold .15 .40
ame in white type on front
Joe Hendrick (Papa) RC .40 1.00
Barney Hall .15 .40
Tim Brewer .15 .40
George Bradshaw RC .25 .60
John Wilson RC .25 .60
Robbie Loomis RC .40 1.00
Benny Parsons .40 1.00
Jack Steele RC .25 .60
Gary Nelson .15 .40
Ed Brasefield RC .25 .60
Jake Speed .15 .40
Bill Brodrick RC .25 .60
Robert Black RC .25 .60
Carl Hill RC .25 .60
Jimmy Means .15 .40
Mark Garrow RC .25 .60
Lynda Petty RC .25 .60
D.K. Ulrich RC .25 .60
Davey Allison .60 1.50
Jimmy Cox RC .25 .60
Clyde Booth RC .25 .60
John Kernan RC .25 .60
Marlin Wright RC .25 .60
Scott Houston RC .25 .60
Wayne Bumgarner RC .25 .60
Jeff Hensley RC .25 .60
Bill Davis RC .25 .60
Bob Jenkins .15 .40
Scott Cluka RC .25 .60
Sterling Marlin .40 1.00
Tommy Allison RC .25 .60
Hubert Hensley RC .25 .60
Steve Bird RC .25 .60
John Hall RC .25 .60
L.D. Ottinger ERR .15 .40
L.D. Ottinger COR .15 .40
Kyle Petty .50 1.25
Felix Sabates
Gary Nelson
Andy Petree RC .25 .60
Joe Moore RC .25 .60
Shelton Pittman RC .25 .60
Ricky Pearson RC .25 .60

178 Ed Berrier .15 .40
179 Rusty Wallace .60 1.50
180 Richard Yates RC .25 .60
181 Frank Cicci RC .25 .60
Scott Welliver RC
182 Clyde McLeod RC .25 .60
183 A.G. Dillard RC .25 .60
184 Larry McReynolds .25 .60
185 Joey Knuckles RC .25 .60
186A Teresa Earnhardt RC .50 1.25
Trademark reads
...than Sports Image, Inc is â¦
186B Teresa Earnhardt RC .50 1.25
Trademark reads
...than Sports Image, Inc. at
racing venuesâ¦
187 Rick Hendrick .25 .60
188 Jerry Punch .15 .40
189A Tim Petty RC .25 .60
Team colors are blue and red
189B Tim Petty RC .25 .60
Team colors are orange and yellow
190A Dale Earnhardt 1.50 4.00
Trademark reads
...than Sports Image, Inc is â¦
190B Dale Earnhardt 1.50 4.00
Trademark reads
...than Sports Image, Inc. at
racing venues..."
191 Checklist #1 .10 .25
192 Checklist #2 .10 .25
193 Checklist #3 .10 .25
194 Checklist #4 .10 .25
195 Checklist #5 .10 .25
196 Checklist #6 .10 .25
197 Checklist #7 .10 .25
198 Checklist #8 .10 .25
199 Patriotic Statement .10 .25
200 Richard Petty .75 2.00
The King

1991 Traks Mello Yello Kyle Petty

Traks issued a special set to commemorate Kyle Petty and the Mello Yello race team in 1991. A cover/checklist card (number 13) was also included.

COMPLETE SET (13) 4.00 10.00
COMMON CARD (1-13) .40 1.00

1991 Traks Mom-n-Pop's Biscuits Dale Earnhardt

In conjunction with Traks, Mom-n-Pop's produced this set for distribution in its microwavable sandwich products in 1991. The cards were cello packed with one card and one cover card per pack. Dale Earnhardt is the featured driver due to Mom-n-Pop's associate sponsorship of the RCR racing team. The "Biscuits" cards look very similar to the "Ham" cards produced the same year. A numbered (of 20,000) uncut sheet version of the 6-cards was also produced and offered through packs of 1993 Wheels Mom-n-Pop's cards at $20.00 for the pair of Biscuit and Ham sheets.

COMPLETE SET (6) 5.00 12.00
COMMON CARD (1-6) 1.00 2.50

1991 Traks Mom-n-Pop's Ham Dale Earnhardt

In conjunction with Traks, Mom-n-Pop's produced this set for distribution in its country ham products in 1991. The cards were cello packed with one card and one cover card per pack. Dale Earnhardt is the featured driver due to Mom-n-Pop's associate sponsorship of the RCR racing team. The "Ham" cards look very similar to the "Biscuit" cards produced the same year. A numbered (of 20,000) uncut sheet version of the 6-cards was also produced and offered through packs of 1993 Wheels Mom-n-Pop's cards at $20.00 for the pair of Biscuit and Ham sheets.

COMPLETE SET (6) 5.00 12.00
COMMON CARD (1-6) 1.00 2.50

1991 Traks Richard Petty

The Richard Petty 20th anniversary set was Traks' first racing card release. The issue chronicles Petty's life in racing and was distributed in 12-card packs. It was also distributed as a factory set. Cards 1-25 were packaged in a replica model of Petty's 1972 Plymouth and cards 26-50 were packaged in a replica model of his 1991 Pontiac.

COMPLETE SET (50) 4.00 8.00
COMPLETE FACT.SET (50) 5.00 10.00
WAX BOX 5.00 12.00
1 Richard Petty .25 .60
2 Richard Petty's Car .10 .25
3 Richard Petty's Car .10 .25
4 Richard Petty w/Car .25 .60
5 Richard Petty's Car .10 .25
6 Richard Petty w/Car .25 .60
Gang's all Here
7 Richard Petty's Car .10 .25
Under Cover
8 Richard Petty w/Car .25 .60
Race Day
9 Richard Petty .25 .60
All Smiles
10 Richard Petty in Pits .25 .60
The Treatment
11 Richard Petty w/Car .25 .60
On Top of the World
12 Richard Petty's Car .10 .25
Leading the Way
13 Richard Petty's Car .10 .25
Winner's Circle
14 Richard Petty .25 .60
The Beard
15 Richard Petty's Car .10 .25
What a Following
16 Richard Petty's Car .10 .25
True Colors
17 Richard Petty's Car .10 .25
And Petty's Away
18 Richard Petty .25 .60
Through the Years
19 Richard Petty .25 .60
The King
20 Richard Petty's Car .10 .25
STP Pontiacs
21 Richard Petty w/Car .25 .60
Southern Pride
22 Richard Petty's Car .50 1.25
Dale Earnhardt's Car
Darrell Waltrip's Car
Lead Draft
23 Richard Petty in Pits .25 .60
Under the Gun
24 Richard Petty's Car .10 .25
The High Line
25 Richard Petty's Car .10 .25
Memories
26 Richard Petty's Car .10 .25
Round the Bend
27 Richard Petty .25 .60
Famous Smile
28 Richard Petty's Car .10 .25
Battle Scarred
29 Richard Petty .25 .60
Man of Miles
30 Richard Petty in Pits .25 .60
Team Work
31 Richard Petty's Car .10 .25
Sunday Drive
32 Richard Petty w/Car .25 .60
It's Getting Heavy
33 Richard Petty in Pits .25 .60
Wilkesboro Bash
34 Richard Petty's Car .10 .25
Line Drive
35 Richard Petty's Car .10 .25
Waiting for The King
36 Richard Petty .25 .60
Thanks for the Memories
37 Richard Petty w/Car .25 .60
Suited Up
38 Richard Petty in Pits .25 .60
Every Second Counts
39 Richard Petty .25 .60
The King's Office
40 Richard Petty's Car .10 .25
Famous 43
41 Richard Petty w/Car .25 .60
The High Bank
42 Richard Petty in Pits .25 .60
Pit Action
43 Richard Petty .25 .60
Happy Anniversary
44 Richard Petty .25 .60
Long Rider
45 Richard Petty's Car .10 .25
Tools of the Trade
46 Richard Petty .25 .60
In Appreciation
47 Richard Petty .25 .60
Most Photographed
48 Richard Petty .25 .60
Fan's Choice
49 Richard Petty w/Car .25 .60
Traditions
50 Richard Petty w/Car .25 .60
Profile of the King

1992 Traks

In addition to a 200-card factory set, the 1992 Traks set was distributed in 12-card packs with 30 packs per box. The set features the top Busch and Winston Cup drivers along with owners and other racing team members. Variations on several cards exist with the versions differing according to either pack or factory set distribution. Traks also included randomly packed autographed insert cards.

COMPLETE SET (200) 8.00 20.00
COMP.FACT.SET (200) 10.00 25.00
1 Rick Mast .05 .15
2 Rusty Wallace .50 1.25
3 Dale Earnhardt 1.25 3.00
4 Ernie Irvan .10 .30
5 Ricky Rudd .20 .50
6 Mark Martin .50 1.25
7 Alan Kulwicki .20 .50
8 Rick Wilson .05 .15
9 Phil Parsons .05 .15
10 Ricky Craven RC .02 .10
11 Bobby Labonte .40 1.00
12 Hut Stricklin .05 .15
13 Sam Bass .02 .10
14 Bobby Allison .10 .30
15 Rusty Wallace .25 .60
Mike Wallace
Kenny Wallace
16 Race Stoppers .02 .10
17 Darrell Waltrip .10 .30
18 Dale Jarrett .40 1.00
19 Cale Yarborough .10 .30
20 Doyle Ford .02 .10
21 Morgan Shepherd .05 .15
22 Sterling Marlin .25 .60
23 Kenny Wallace .02 .10
Barry Dodson
24 Kenny Wallace .05 .15
25 Ken Schrader .05 .15
26 Brett Bodine .05 .15
27 Ward Burton .10 .30
28 Davey Allison .30 .75
29A Andy Hillenburg .05 .15
red stripe under name on back
29B Andy Hillenburg .05 .15
green stripe under name on back
30 Michael Waltrip .10 .30
31 Steve Grissom .05 .15
32 Dale Jarrett .40 1.00
33 Harry Gant .10 .30
34 Todd Bodine .05 .15
35 Robert Yates .02 .10
36 Kenny Wallace .05 .15
37 Roger Penske .02 .10
38 Mark Martin .50 1.25
39 Don Miller .02 .10
40 Chany Sabates .02 .10
Felix Sabates
41 Troy Beebe .02 .10
42 Kyle Petty .10 .30
43 Richard Petty .30 .75
44 Bobby Labonte .40 1.00
45 Butch Miller .05 .15
46 Chuck Rider .02 .10
47 Dale Inman .02 .10
48 Jack Sprague RC .05 .15
49 Doug Richert .02 .10
50 Jimmy Makar .02 .10
51 Mike McLaughlin .05 .15
52 Jimmy Means .05 .15
53 Waddell Wilson .02 .10
54 Richard Childress .10 .30
55 Ted Musgrave .05 .15
56 Darrell Waltrip .10 .30
57 Kirk Shelmerdine .02 .10
58 Larry McClure .02 .10
59 Robert Pressley .05 .15
60 Dale Earnhardt in Pits .30 .75
61 Dick Trickle .05 .15
62 Leonard Wood .05 .15
63 Chuck Bown .05 .15
64 Elmo Langley .02 .10
65 Barry Dodson .02 .10
66 Chad Little .10 .30
67 Elton Sawyer .05 .15
68 Ed McClure .02 .10
69A Kyle Petty .10 .30
no green stripe under name on back
69B Kyle Petty .10 .30
green stripe under name on back
70 Tony Glover .02 .10
71 Dave Marcis .10 .30
72A Rusty Wallace .25 .60
Eddie Dickerson
title on back in white letters
72B Rusty Wallace .25 .60
Eddie Dickerson
title on back in black letters
73 Alan Kulwicki .20 .50
74 Jimmy Fennig .02 .10
75 Michael Waltrip .10 .30
76 Ken Wilson .05 .15
77 David Smith .05 .15
78 Junior Johnson .05 .15
79 Dave Rezendes .05 .15
80 Bruce Roney .02 .10
81 Eddie Lanier .02 .10
82 Mike Beam .02 .10
83 Walter Bud Moore .02 .10
84 Terry Labonte .25 .60
85 Richard Petty .30 .75
86 Donnie Wingo .02 .10
87 Joe Nemechek .05 .15
88 Greg Moore .02 .10
89 Doug Williams .02 .10
90 Jimmy Martin .02 .10
91 Richard Broome .02 .10
92 Hut Stricklin .05 .15
Bobby Allison
93 Hank Jones .02 .10
94 Terry Labonte .25 .60
95 Will Lind .02 .10
96 Tom Peck .05 .15
97 Morgan Shepherd .05 .15
98 Jimmy Spencer .05 .15
99 Jeff Burton .20 .50
100 Max Helton .02 .10
101 Jeff Gordon 2.00 5.00
102 Keith Almond .02 .10
103 Dale Earnhardt 1.25 3.00
104 Ernie Irvan .10 .30
105 Greg Wilson .02 .10
106 Tommy Houston .05 .15
107 Ed Whitaker .02 .10
108 David Green .05 .15
109 Robin Pemberton .02 .10
110 Mike Colyer .02 .10
111 Jerry McClure .02 .10
112 Cecil Gordon .02 .10
113A Jimmy Johnson .02 .10
name on back in white letters
113B Jimmy Johnson .02 .10
name on back in black letters
114 Neil Bonnett .10 .30
115 Steve Hmiel .02 .10
116 Charles Farmer .02 .10
117 Eddie Jones .02 .10
118 Mickey Stavola .02 .10
Bill Stavola
119 Leo Jackson .02 .10
120 Dick Moroso .02 .10
121 Eddie Wood .02 .10
122 Len Wood .02 .10
123 Lou LaRosa .02 .10
124A Rusty Wallace .50 1.25
name on back in white letters
124B Rusty Wallace .50 1.25
name on back in black letters
125 Bobby Hillin .05 .15
126 Ned Jarrett .05 .15
127 Ken Schrader .05 .15
128 Travis Carter .02 .10
129 Frank Edwards .02 .10
130 Tom Higgins .02 .10
Steve Waid
131 Jim Phillips .02 .10
Winston Kelley
Dick Brooks
132 John Ervin .02 .10
133A Harry Gant .10 .30
no line on back
133B Harry Gant .10 .30
red line on back
133C Harry Gant .10 .30
black line on back
134 Allen Bestwick .02 .10
135 Barney Hall .02 .10
136 Ricky Rudd .10 .30
Rick Hendrick
137 Eli Gold .02 .10
138 Joe Hendrick (Papa) .02 .10
139 John Wilson .02 .10
140 Tim Brewer .02 .10
141 George Bradshaw .02 .10
142 Kyle Petty .10 .30
143 Robbie Loomis .05 .15
144 Benny Parsons .05 .15
145 Danny Myers .02 .10
146 Harry Gant .10 .30
Ed Whitaker
147 Jeff Hammond .02 .10
148 Donnie Richeson .02 .10
149 Bill Brodrick .02 .10
150 Robert Black .02 .10
151 Carl Hill .02 .10
152 Mike Wallace .05 .15
153 Mark Garrow .02 .10
154 Lynda Petty .02 .10
155A Ted Musgrave ERR .02 .10
D.K.Ulrich
Mugrave on front
155B Ted Musgrave COR .02 .10
D.K.Ulrich
Musgrave on front
156 Davey Allison .50 1.25
157 Jimmy Cox .02 .10
158 Clyde Booth .02 .10
159 Bob Bilby .02 .10
160 Marlin Wright .02 .10
161 Gary Nelson .02 .10
162 Jake Elder .02 .10
163 Jeff Hensley .02 .10
164 Bill Davis .02 .10
165 Tracy Leslie .05 .15
166 Tommy Ellis .05 .15
167 Sterling Marlin .25 .60
168 Tony Eury .40 1.00
169 Teddy McClure .02 .10
170 Steve Bird .02 .10
171A Paul Andrews .02 .10
name on back in white letters
171B Paul Andrews .02 .10
name on back in black letters
172 Brad Parrott .02 .10
173A Eddie Dickerson .02 .10
name on back in white letters
173B Eddie Dickerson .02 .10
name on back in black letters
174 Andy Petree .02 .10
175 Dale Earnhardt w/Crew .40 1.00
176A Shelton Pittman .02 .10
name on back in white letters
176B Shelton Pittman .02 .10
name on back in black letters
177 Ricky Pearson .02 .10
Robert Pressley
178 Ed Berrier .02 .10
179A Rusty Wallace .50 1.25
name on back in white letters
179B Rusty Wallace .50 1.25
name on back in black letters
180 Richard Yates .02 .10
181 Scott Welliver .02 .10
Frank Cicci
182 Clyde McLeod .02 .10
183 A.G. Dillard .05 .15
184 Larry McReynolds .02 .10
185 Joey Knuckles .02 .10
186 Rodney Combs .05 .15
187 Rick Hendrick .02 .10
188 Jerry Punch .02 .10
189 Tim Morgan .02 .10
190 Dale Earnhardt 1.25 3.00
191 Sterling Marlin .05 .15
Darrell Waltrip Crash
192 Safe and Sure .02 .10
checklist back
193 Dale Earnhardt's Car .10 .30
checklist back
194 Rick Mast's Car .02 .10
checklist back
195 Follow the Signs .02 .10
checklist back
196 Kyle Petty's Car .05 .15
checklist back
197 Thread the Needle .02 .10
checklist back
198 Darrell Waltrip's Car .05 .15
checklist back
199 Rick Wilson's Car .02 .10
checklist back
200 Richard Petty .25 .60
Lynda Petty
P1 Benny Parsons Prototype 1.50 4.00
P2 Kyle Petty Prototype 2.00 5.00
P3 Richard Petty Prototype 8.00 20.00
P4 Rusty Wallace Prototype 4.00 10.00

1992 Traks Autographs

This set was distributed randomly throughout 1992 Traks packs. A maximum of 5000 cards were signed by each driver and many cards can be found, as well, without signatures. The Ricky Rudd card is considered a short print signed due to the seemingly large number of available copies unsigned. Unsigned cards typically sell for a fraction of autographed issues. The set is highlighted by a dual signed Dale Earnhardt and Richard Petty card (number A1).

COMPLETE SET (10) 250.00 400.00
A1 Dale Earnhardt 175.00 300.00
Richard Petty
A2 Rusty Wallace 30.00 60.00
A3 Harry Gant 6.00 15.00
A4 Ernie Irvan 8.00 20.00
A5 Ricky Rudd SP 12.50 30.00
A6 Kyle Petty 10.00 25.00
A7 Jeff Gordon 50.00 100.00
A8 Bobby Labonte 15.00 40.00
A9 Benny Parsons 30.00 60.00
NNO Cover Card 4.00 10.00

1992 Traks Alliance Robert Pressley

The 1992 Traks Alliance Racing Team Robert Pressley set is very similar to the 1993-94 Alliance Robert Pressley and Dennis Setzer issues. The Traks version includes the Traks logo on the cardfronts along with a black border.

COMPLETE SET (12) 4.00 8.00
1 Cover/Checklist Card .25 .60
2 Robert Pressley .25 .60
Victory Circle
3 Robert Pressley's Transporter .25 .60
4 Robert Pressley's Transporter .25 .60
5 Robert Pressley's Cars .25 .60
6 Robert Pressley .60 1.50
7 Robert Pressley's Car .25 .60
8 Robert Pressley's Car .25 .60
9 Robert Pressley's Pit Crew .25 .60
10 Robert Pressley .60 1.50
11 Ricky Pearson .25 .60
12 Robert Pressley's Transporter .25 .60

1992 Traks ASA

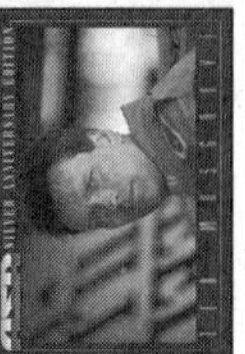

To commemorate the 25th anniversary of the American Speed Association, Traks released a special 50-card boxed set featuring many past greats of the ASA circuit as well as then current drivers.

COMPLETE SET (51) 2.00 5.00
1 Josh DuVall .07 .20
2 Glenn Allen Jr. .07 .20
3 Mike Eddy Crew .07 .20
4 Mike Eddy .07 .20
5 Pat Schauer .07 .20
6 Tim Fedewa .10 .30
7 Tom Jones .07 .20
8 Tony Raines .07 .20
9 Jay Sauter .07 .20
10 Jeff Neal .07 .20
11 Terry Baldry .07 .20
12 Dennis Lampman .07 .20

Card	Low	High
13 Rusty Wallace w/Car	.40	1.00
14 Johnny Benson Jr.	.20	.50
15 Bob Senneker Crew	.07	.20
16 Bob Senneker	.07	.20
17 Dean South	.07	.20
18 John Wilson	.07	.20
19 Bruce VanderLaan	.07	.20
20 Dave Jackson	.07	.20
21 Chris Weiss	.07	.20
22 Tim Fedewa	.10	.30
23 Butch Fedewa	.07	.20
24 Gary St.Amant	.07	.20
25 Bud St. Amant	.07	.20
26 Dave Jackson	.07	.20
27 Glenn Allen Sr.	.07	.20
28 Tom Harrington Car	.07	.20
29 Dennis Vogel Car	.07	.20
30 Field of Dreams	.07	.20
31 Mario Caputo (Chip)	.07	.20
32 Kenny Wallace	.10	.30
33 Dick Trickle	.10	.30
34 Butch Miller	.07	.20
35 Scott Hansen	.07	.20
36 Alan Kulwicki w/Car	.30	.75
37 Jim Sauter Car	.07	.20
38 Bobby Allison w/Car	.15	.40
39 Davey Allison w/Car	.40	1.00
40 Jimmy Fennig	.07	.20
41 Mark Martin	.40	1.25
42 Darrell Waltrip w/Car	.07	.20
43 Harold Fair Sr.	.07	.20
44 Kenny Adams	.07	.20
45 Kent Stauffer	.07	.20
46 Dave Taylor	.07	.20
47 Terry Baker	.07	.20
48 Howie Lettow	.07	.20
49 Harold Alan Fair Jr.	.07	.20
50 Ted Musgrave	.10	.30
NNO Souvenir Order Form Card	.07	.20

1992 Traks Baby Ruth Jeff Gordon

For the first of two years, Traks released a special set featuring the Baby Ruth sponsored Busch Series race team in 1992 with Jeff Gordon as the focus. Gordon is featured on two cards with the others devoted to his car and crew.

Card	Low	High
COMPLETE SET (4)	4.00	10.00
1 Jeff Gordon	2.00	4.00
2 Jeff Gordon	2.00	4.00
3 Jeff Gordon's Car	.50	1.00
4 Jeff Gordon's Crew	.50	1.00

1992 Traks Country Star Racing

This 13-card set features Dick Trickle and the number 2 Country Star sponsored car he drove on the Busch Grand National circuit. The set was released both as a subset to the Country Star Collection set and as an individual set.

Card	Low	High
COMPLETE SET (13)	2.40	6.00
1 Dick Trickle	.30	.75
2 Dick Trickle	.30	.75
3 Ted Conder	.20	.50
4 Dick Trickle	.30	.75
Ken Schrader		
5 Mark Connolly	.20	.50
6 Dick Trickle	.30	.75
7 Danny Dias	.20	.50
8 Dick Trickle	.30	.75
9 Bill Tucker	.20	.50
Bob Benton		
Joe Kloiber		
Mike Timmerman		
Wendy Connolly		
Robin Richert		
10 Dick Trickle	.30	.75
11 Brian Grinstead	.20	.50
12 Ad Card	.20	.50
NNO Checklist Card	.20	.50

1992 Traks Goody's

Drivers of the 1992 Goody's 300 are featured on this 25-card Traks release. The set was distributed in its own box through hobby outlets and includes most of the top drivers of 1992.

Card	Low	High
COMPLETE SET (25)	5.00	10.00
1 Bobby Labonte	.50	1.25
2 Kenny Wallace	.08	.25

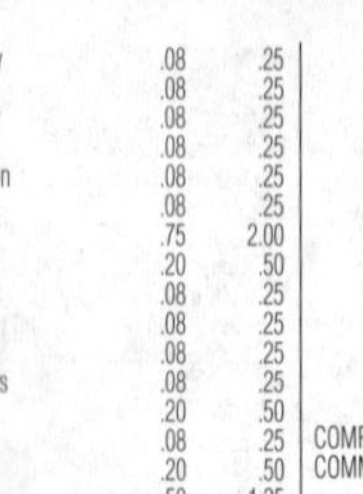

Card	Low	High
3 Robert Pressley	.08	.25
4 Chuck Bown	.08	.25
5 Jimmy Hensley	.08	.25
6 Todd Bodine	.08	.25
7 Tommy Houston	.08	.25
8 Steve Grissom	.08	.25
9 Jeff Gordon	.75	2.00
10 Jeff Burton	.20	.50
11 David Green	.08	.25
12 Tracy Leslie	.08	.25
13 Butch Miller	.08	.25
14 Dave Rezendes	.08	.25
15 Ward Burton	.20	.50
16 Ed Berrier	.08	.25
17 Harry Gant	.20	.50
18 Dale Jarrett	.50	1.25
19 Dale Earnhardt	1.25	3.00
20 Ernie Irvan	.20	.50
21 Davey Allison	.40	1.00
22 Morgan Shepherd	.08	.25
23 Michael Waltrip	.20	.50
24 Ken Schrader	.08	.25
25 Richard Petty	.30	.75

1992 Traks Kodak Ernie Irvan

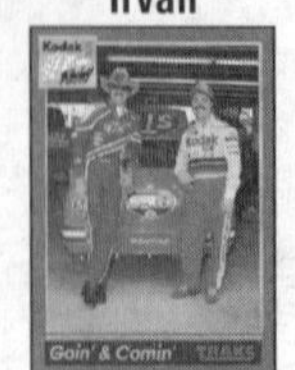

The Kodak Film Racing team and Ernie Irvan were the focus of this 25-card Traks release. The cards were distributed in specially marked 2-packs of Kodak Gold Plus film, as well as in complete factory sets. Five cards (numbers 1,6,11,16,21,25) were also produced with gold foil embossing on the card fronts for distribution in the factory sets. An offer for uncut press sheets featuring the five gold cards was also included. Many of the cards are very similar to ones included in the Ernie Irvan team set also issued in 1992.

Card	Low	High
COMPLETE SET (25)	15.00	25.00
1A Ernie Irvan	1.25	2.50
Richard Petty		
1B Ernie Irvan Gold	2.00	4.00
Richard Petty		
2 Teddy McClure	.50	1.00
3 Tim Morgan	.50	1.00
4 Robert Larkins	.50	1.00
5 Shelton Pittman	.50	1.00
6A Ernie Irvan	1.25	2.50
6B Ernie Irvan Gold	2.00	4.00
7 Larry McClure	.50	1.00
8 Jerry McClure	.50	1.00
9 Tony Glover	.50	1.00
10 Clint Ballard	.50	1.00
11A Ernie Irvan's Car	.50	1.00
11B Ernie Irvan's Car Gold	1.00	2.00
12 Jerry Puckett	.50	1.00
13 Ernie Irvan's Car	.50	1.00
14 Zeke Lester	.50	1.00
15 Randall Helbert	.50	1.00
16A Ernie Irvan	1.25	2.50
16B Ernie Irvan Gold	2.00	4.00
17 Bill Marsh	.50	1.00
18 Johnny Townsend	.50	1.00
19 Teddy McClure	.50	1.00
Larry McClure		
Tim Morgan		
Jerry McClure		
Ed McClure		
20 Ernie Irvan w/Crew	.50	1.00
Win at the Glen		
21A Ernie Irvan in Pits	1.25	2.50
21B Ernie Irvan in Pits Gold	2.00	4.00
22 George Gardner	.50	1.00
23 Power Builders	.50	1.00
24 Ed McClure	.50	1.00
25 Ernie Irvan w/Car	.50	1.00
Checklist		

1992 Traks Mom-n-Pop's Ham Dale Earnhardt

Produced by Traks, Mom-n-Pop's distributed this set in its country ham products in 1992. The cards were cello packed with one card and one cover card per pack. Dale Earnhardt is the featured driver due to Mom-n-Pop's associate sponsorship of the RCR racing team. A special "Pig" card (5000 made) was produced as well and randomly inserted in packs. The card was printed with a gold foil border and features a ghosted holographic image of Earnhardt's signature to prevent counterfeiting. Mom-n-Pop's Ham Christmas packaging distributed in North and South Carolina included the special card. A numbered (of 20,000) uncut sheet version of the 6-cards was also produced and offered through packs of 1993 Wheels Mom-n-Pop's cards.

Card	Low	High
COMPLETE SET (6)	10.00	20.00
1 Dale Earnhardt w/Crew	2.00	4.00
2 Dale Earnhardt's Car	2.00	4.00
3 Dale Earnhardt	2.00	4.00
Richard Childress		
4 Dale Earnhardt in Pits	2.00	4.00
5 Dale Earnhardt	2.00	4.00
6 Dale Earnhardt	2.00	4.00
NNO Dale Earnhardt	12.00	30.00
with Thunder the pig		

1992 Traks Benny Parsons

Benny Parsons and his career in racing is the focus of this 50-card release distributed to the hobby in 1992. 25,000 sets were printed and individually serial numbered with a certificate included with each boxed set.

Card	Low	High
COMP. FACT SET (50)	2.00	5.00
COMMON CARD (1-50)	.07	.20

1992 Traks Racing Machines

Traks produced the Racing Machines series to highlight the cars, rigs and race action of NASCAR racing. The 100-card set was distributed in 12-card packs. Cases were numbered up to a maximum of 2500 10-box cases with 36 packs per box. A special 20-card bonus set was also inserted two cards per pack as well as one set per Racing Machines factory set. Four prototype cards were issued for the release, but are not considered part of the complete set.

Card	Low	High
COMPLETE SET (100)	8.00	20.00
COMP.FACT.SET (120)	10.00	25.00
WAX BOX	10.00	25.00
1 Dale Earnhardt's Transp.	.50	1.25
2 Rusty Wallace's Car	.30	.75
3 Dale Earnhardt's Car	.60	1.50
4 Ernie Irvan's Car	.07	.20
5 Ricky Rudd's Car	.07	.20
Ken Schrader's Car		
6 Mark Martin's Car	.30	.75
7 Alan Kulwicki in Pits	.07	.20
8 Dick Trickle's Car	.02	.10
9 Dale Earnhardt's Car	.60	1.50
Ricky Rudd's Car		
Harry Gant's Car		
10 Ernie Irvan's Transp.	.07	.20
11 Rick Mast's Car	.02	.10
12 Hut Stricklin's Car	.02	.10
13 Kyle Petty's Car	.07	.20
Pre-Race Check Off		
14 Sterling Marlin's Car	.07	.20
15 Geoff Bodine's Transp.	.02	.10
16 Wally Dallenbach Jr.'s Car	.02	.10
17 Darrell Waltrip in Pits	.07	.20
18 Richard Petty's Transp.	.07	.20
19 Richard Petty in Pits	.07	.20
20 Ken Schrader's Transp.	.02	.10
21 Morgan Shepherd in Pits	.02	.10
22 Sterling Marlin's Car	.07	.20
23 Darrell Waltrip's Transp.	.07	.20
24 Rusty Wallace w/Truck	.40	1.00
25 Ken Schrader's Car	.02	.10
26 Bobby Hamilton's Transp.	.02	.10
27 Round and Round	.02	.10
Martinsville Speedway		
28 Davey Allison's Car	.15	.40
29 Harry Gant's Transp.	.02	.10
30 Michael Waltrip's Car		
31 Steve Grissom	.02	.10
Roddenberry Car		
32 Steve Grissom	.02	.10
Channellock Car		
33 Harry Gant in Pits	.02	.10
34 Dale Earnhardt's Car	.75	2.00
Davey Allison's Car		
35 Davey Allison's Transp.	.15	.40
36 Michael Waltrip's Car		
Under Cover		
37 Darrell Waltrip's Car	.07	.20
Pre Race Preparation		
38 Hut Stricklin In Pits UER	.02	.10
40 Jeff Gordon's Car	.75	2.00
Davey Allison's Car		
41 Sterling Marlin in Pits	.07	.20
42 Kyle Petty's Car	.07	.20
43 Richard Petty's Car	.07	.20
44 Dale Earnhardt's Car	.60	1.50
Ricky Rudd's Car		
45 Sterling Marlin in Pits	.07	.20
46 Kyle Petty's Transp.	.07	.20
47 Rick Mast's Car	.02	.10
48 Ken Schrader in Pits	.02	.10
49 Morgan Shepherd's Trans.	.02	.10
50 Brett Bodine w/Car	.07	.20
51 Alan Kulwicki 's Car	.07	.20
52 Wally Dallenbach Jr. in Pits	.02	.10
53 Mark Martin's Transp.	.20	.50
54 Dale Earnhardt in Pits	.60	1.50
55 Richard Petty's Transporter	.07	.20
Line Forms Here		
56 Pre-Race Pageantry	.02	.10
Multi-Car Starting Grid		
57 Bobby Labonte in Pits	.20	.50
58 Ricky Rudd's Car	.20	.50
Rusty Wallace's Car		
59 Robert Pressley's Car	.02	.10
60 Bobby Labonte's Car	.20	.50
Harry Gant's Car		
61 Rick Mast's Transp.	.02	.10
62 Lightning Fast	.02	.10
Race Action		
63 Chuck Bown's Car	.02	.10
64 Rusty Wallace's Motorhome	.20	.50
65 Davey Allison's Car	.15	.40
Michael Waltrip's Car		
66 Ted Musgrave's Transp.	.02	.10
67 Bobby Hamilton in Pits	.02	.10
68 Bobby Hamilton's Car	.02	.10
69 Ernie Irvan in Pits	.07	.20
70 Lake Speed Crash	.02	.10
71 Dave Marcis' Car	.07	.20
72 Michael Waltrip's Transp.		
73 Mark Martin in Pits	.30	.75
74 Sterling Marlin's Transp.	.07	.20
75 Harry Gant's Car	.02	.10
Brett Bodine's Car		
76 Mark Martin in Pits	.30	.75
77 Alan Kulwicki's Transp.	.07	.20
78 Rusty Wallace in Pits	.30	.75
79 Dick Trickle's Transp.	.02	.10
80 Richard Petty Action	.07	.20
81 Rusty Wallace's Transp.	.20	.50
82 Terry Labonte w/Car	.30	.75
83 Michael Waltrip's Car		
84 Dale Earnhardt	.60	1.50
Morgan Shepherd		
Hut Stricklin Cars		
85 Jimmy Hensley's Transp.	.02	.10
86 Terry Labonte's Transp.	.20	.50
87 Kyle Petty's Car	.07	.20
88 Wally Dallenbach Jr.'s Trans.	.02	.10
89 Dale Earnhardt in Pits	.60	1.50
90 Jimmy Hensley's Car	.02	.10
91 Dale Earnhardt's Car	.50	1.25
Tommy Houston's Car		
92 Sterling Marlin's Car	.07	.20
Ricky Rudd's Car		
93 Davey Allison's Car	.15	.40
Morgan Shepherd's Car		
94 Terry Labonte Crash	.20	.50
95 Ernie Irvan in Pits	.07	.20
96 Derrike Cope's Transp.	.02	.10
97 Richard Petty in Pits	.07	.20
checklist back		
98 Bobby Labonte's Car	.20	.50
Terry Labonte's Car		
Rusty Wallace's Car		
Ernie Irvan's Car		
Freight Train		
checklist back		
99 Davey Allison's Car	.15	.40
checklist back		
100 Dale Earnhardt's Car	.50	1.25
Richard Petty's Car		
checklist back		
P1 Dale Earnhardt's	4.00	10.00
Transporter Promo		
P26 Bobby Hamilton's	1.00	2.50
Transporter Promo		
P51 Alan Kulwicki's Car	2.00	5.00
Promo		
P76 Mark Martin in Pits	2.50	6.00
Promo		

1992 Traks Racing Machines Bonus

Inserted two per pack in 1992 Traks Racing Machines packs and one complete set per regular factory set, the cards feature top drivers and cars in the style of regular issue 1992 Traks cards.

Card	Low	High
COMPLETE SET (20)	2.50	5.00
1B Charlotte Under Lights	.01	.05
2B Barry Dodson	.01	.05
3B Dale Earnhardt's Car	.60	1.50
4B Jimmy Spencer	.02	.10
5B Gary DeHart	.01	.05
6B Steve Loyd	.01	.05
7B Harry Gant MAC Team	.07	.20
8B Dick Trickle	.02	.10
9B Bobby Dotter's Car	.01	.05
10B Ricky Craven	.20	.50
11B Junior Johnson	.02	.10
12B Joe Nemechek w/Car	.02	.10
13B Terry Labonte w/Car	.30	.75
14B Kenny Wallace	.02	.10
15B Jimmy Hensley	.02	.10
16B Mark Martin's Car	.30	.75
Wally Dallenbach Jr.'s Car		
17B Mike Wallace	.02	.10
18B Jeff Burton	.20	.50
Ward Burton		
19B Tom Peck w/Car	.02	.10
20B Jeff Gordon Baby Boomer	2.00	4.00

1992 Traks Team Sets

This 200-card release was actually distributed as eight separate 25-card team sets. Cards from the eight sets were consecutively numbered though to form a complete set of 200. Each team set was sold in a cardboard rack-style pack shaped like that team's race car.

Card	Low	High
COMPLETE SET (200)	20.00	40.00
COMPLETE EARNHARDT (25)	5.00	10.00
COMPLETE D.ALLISON (25)	3.00	6.00
COMPLETE K.PETTY (25)	2.50	5.00
COMPLETE M.WALTRIP (25)	2.50	5.00
COMPLETE IRVAN (25)	2.50	5.00
COMPLETE D.WALTRIP (25)	2.50	5.00
COMPLETE STRICKLIN (25)	2.00	5.00
COMPLETE R.PETTY (25)	2.50	5.00
1 Dale Earnhardt's Car	.20	.50
Driving Force		
2 Dale Earnhardt	.75	2.00
3 Dale Earnhardt's Car	.20	.50
Davey Allison's Car		
Familiar Position		
4 Dale Earnhardt's Car	.20	.50
Flying Aces		
5 Kirk Shelmerdine	.10	.30
6 David Smith	.10	.30
7 Will Lind	.10	.30
8 Danny Myers	.10	.30
9 Hank Jones	.10	.30
10 Eddie Lanier	.10	.30
11 Danny Lawrence	.10	.30
12 Cecil Gordon	.10	.30
13 Dale Earnhardt	.20	.50
Richard Childress		
Winning Combo		
14 Richard Childress	.10	.30
15 Dale Earnhardt w/crew	.20	.50
Party Time		
16 Dale Earnhardt's Cars	.75	2.00
Childress Promotions		
17 Dale Earnhardt	.75	2.00
Family Tradition		
18 Dale Earnhardt	.75	2.00
Cool Customer		
19 Dale Earnhardt's Car	.20	.50
New Names		
20 Dale Earnhardt's Car	.20	.50
Inspection Time		
21 Dale Earnhardt	.75	2.00
Friends of the Forest		
22 Dale Earnhardt's Planes	.20	.50
Air Goodwrench		
23 Dale Earnhardt	.75	2.00
1991 Busch Clash		
24 Dale Earnhardt's Cars	.20	.50
Arsenal		
25 Dale Earnhardt's Car	.20	.50
Checklist		
26 Davey Allison	.40	1.00
27 Robert Yates	.10	.30
28 Davey Allison's Car	.20	.50
Star Power		
29 Davey Allison in Pits	.20	.50
Controlled Frenzy		
30 Ryan Pemberton	.10	.30
31 Richard Yates	.10	.30
32 Larry McReynolds	.10	.30
33 Gary Beveridge	.10	.30
34 Joey Knuckles	.10	.30
35 Tommy Allison	.10	.30
36 Mike Bumgarner	.10	.30
37 Terry Throneburg	.10	.30
38 Eric Horn	.10	.30
39 Gil Kerley	.10	.30
40 Raymond Fox III	.10	.30
41 Norman Koshimizu	.10	.30
42 Davey Allison	.40	1.00
Five-Time Winner		
43 Motor Minds	.10	.30
Engine Builders		
44 Davey Allison	.40	1.00
Fantastic Phoenix		
45 James Lewter	.10	.30
46 Vernon Hubbard	.10	.30
47 Devin Barbee	.10	.30
48 Doug Yates	.10	.30
49 Davey Allison	.40	1.00
Larry McReynolds		
Robert Yates		
Triple Threats		
50 Davey Allison w/crew	.40	1.00
Checklist		
51 Kyle Petty	.20	.50
Confident Smile		
52 Felix Sabates	.10	.30
53 Felix Sabates	.10	.30
Success Story		
54 Gary Nelson	.10	.30
55 Kyle Petty	.20	.50
Rocky Top		
56 John Wilson	.10	.30
57 Larry Barnes Jr.	.10	.30
58 Jerry Windell	.10	.30
59 Barry Cook	.10	.30
60 Scott Palmer	.10	.30
61 Charles Lane	.10	.30
62 Richard Bostick	.10	.30
63 Earl Ramey	.10	.30
Doug Hess		
Machine Shop		
64 Scott Grant	.10	.30
Jerry Brady		
Cylinder Specialists		
65 Jim Sutton	.10	.30
66 Steve Knipe	.10	.30
67 Dick Seidenspinner	.10	.30
68 Donnie Richeson	.10	.30
69 Jim Long	.10	.30
70 Mike Ford	.10	.30
71 Len Sherrill	.10	.30
72 Glenn Funderburke	.10	.30
73 Rick Brakefield	.10	.30
74 Kyle Petty	.20	.50
Lean on Me		
75 Kyle Petty's Car	.10	.30
Checklist		
76 Michael Waltrip	.20	.50
77 Michael Waltrip	.10	.30
Chuck Rider		
Strategy Session		
78 Chuck Rider	.10	.30
79 Michael Waltrip's Car	.10	.30
Bahari Racing		
80 Lowrance Harry	.10	.30
81 Richmond Gage	.10	.30
82 Michael Waltrip in Pits	.10	.30
Seconds Count		
83 Bill Ingle	.10	.30
84 Engine Room	.10	.30
Michael Waltrip's Engine Builders		
85 Mark Cronquist	.10	.30
86 Mike Windsor	.10	.30
Jeff Rumple		
Body By Bahari		
87 Jon Leibensperger	.10	.30
88 Jeff Dixon	.10	.30
Paul Chencutt		
Bryan Smith		
Custom Made		
89 Jeff Dixon	.10	.30

Card	Price
90 Assembly Room	.10
Michael Waltrip's Crew	
91 Barry Swift	.10
92 Ray Hall	.10
93 Tim Lancaster	.10
94 Tommy Rigsbee	.10
95 Michael Waltrip	.20
Game Face	
96 Ronnie Silver	.10
97 Jeff Chandler	.10
98 BGN Team	.10
with Ronnie Silver	
99 Michael Waltrip's Transporter	.10
100 Michael Waltrip's Car	.10
Checklist	
101 Dale Earnhardt's Car	.20
Davey Allison's Car	
Ernie Irvan's Car	
Bobby Labonte's Car	
Kyle Petty's Car	
5 Laps From Victory	
102 Ernie Irvan's Car	.10
Kodak Film Chevrolet	
103 Tim Morgan	.10
104 Larry McClure	.10
105 Teddy McClure	.10
106 Ed McClure	.10
107 Shelton Pittman	.10
108 Ernie Irvan	.30
109 Ernie Irvan's Car	.10
Beat the Clock	
110 Johnny Townsend	.10
111 Tony Glover	.10
112 Jerry McClure	.10
113 Zeke Lester	.10
114 Bill Marsh	.10
115 Randall Helbert	.10
116 Clint Ballard	.10
117 Randall Latonis	.10
118 George Gardner	.10
119 Ernie Irvan	.30
'91 Daytona 500	
120 Teddy McClure	.10
Larry McClure	
Tim Morgan	
Jerry McClure	
Ed McClure	
121 Ernie Irvan's Car	.10
Morgan/McClure Racing Shop	
122 Power Builders	.10
with Runt Pittman	
123 Jerry Puckett	.10
124 Ernie Irvan w/crew	.30
Win at The Glen	
125 Ernie Irvan w/Car	.30
Checklist	
126 Western Auto Store	.10
127 Darrell Waltrip	.20
Winning Smile	
128 Joe Carver Sr.	.10
129 Jeff Hammond	.10
130 Darrell Waltrip's Car	.10
Strong Finisher	
131 Bobby Waltrip	.10
132 Clifford Smith	.10
133 Keith Sawyer	.10
134 Doug Richert	.10
135 Jake Elder	.10
136 Carolyn Waltrip	.10
137 Ronnie Hoover	.10
138 Darrell Waltrip in Pits	.10
Jacked Up	
139 Billy Hodges	.10
140 Scott Mercer	.10
David Menear	
Support Staff	
141 Lisa Sigmon	.10
142 Darrell Waltrip	.20
143 Jeff Hammond	.10
Standing Tall	
144 Bob Sutton	.10
145 Gregg Buchanan	.10
146 Tom McCrimmon	.10
147 Robbie Hancock	.10
Greg Carpenter	
Body Men	
148 Glen Skillman	.10
Joe Parlato	
Built to Last	
149 Ron McLeod	.10
Danny Shull	
Tide Connections	
150 Darrell Waltrip's Transporter	.10
Checklist	
151 Hut Stricklin	.10
Race Ready	
152 Hut Stricklin	.20
153 Hut Stricklin's Car	.10
154 Hut Stricklin in Pits	.10
Full Service	
155 Hut Stricklin's Transporter	.10
Mike Culbertson	
Big Rig	
156 Keith Armond	.10
157 Jimmy Fennig	.10
158 Carolyn Freeman	.10
159 Brad Parrott	.10
160 Mike Basinger	.10
161 Glen Bobo	.10
162 Chris Meade	.10
163 Mike Boling	.10
164 Mike Culbertson	.10
165 Tom Bagen	.10
166 Tracie Honeycutt	.10
Lou Ann Kropp	
Front Office	
167 Kenny Freeman	.10
Glen Bobo	
Paint and Body Shop	
168 Horsepower	.10
Engine Builders	
169 C.B.Lee	.10
Mike Basinger	
Square One	
170 Bobby Allison's Car	.10
171 Bob Bilby	.10
172 Nathan Sams	.10
173 Frank Plessinger	.10
174 Tom Kincaid	.10
175 Bobby Allison	.20
Checklist	

ichard Petty	.30	.75
Mike Cheek	.10	.30
Roger Pierce	.10	.30
Johnny Cline	.10	.30
eff Chamberlain		
he Royal Colors		
Wade Thornburg	.10	.30
uddy Pugh		
tafford Wood		
mmy Walker		
aking Shape		
Dale Inman	.10	.30
Ken Perkins	.10	.30
Petty Power	.10	.30
ngine Builders		
Richard Petty w/Crew	.30	.75
ome Team		
Richard Petty w/Crew	.30	.75
way Team		
Robbie Loomis	.20	.50
Martha Bonkemeyer	.10	.30
Kerry Lawrence	.10	.30
From the Ground Up	.10	.30
abricators		
Wade Thornburg	.10	.30
Stafford Wood	.10	.30
ynda Petty	.10	.30
Bob Riffle	.10	.30
David Walker	.10	.30
ouise Loftin	.30	.75
with Richard Petty		
Randy Cox	.10	.30
ance Hill	.10	.30
immy Martin	.10	.30
Richie Barsz	.10	.30
Richard Petty	.30	.75
he King		
hecklist		

1993 Traks

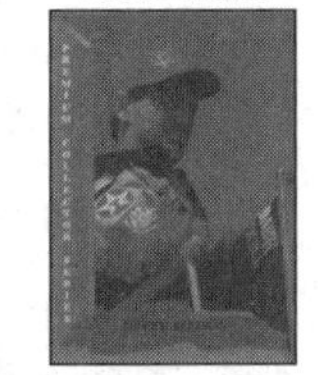

993 Traks set was released in 12-card packs 30 packs per box. The set is divided into two , although released together in packs. The two Silver cards (last 50-cards) were much difficult to pull from packs than series one, he difference in value. 1993 marked the first of the now traditional Traks First Run parallel set. The 1-150 First Runs were packaged two per pack.

PLETE SET (200)	12.50	30.00
P.SET w/o SP's (150)	5.00	12.00
P.SILVER SET (50)	12.50	25.00
BOX SERIES 1	15.00	30.00
JT SILVER SHEET	15.00	30.00
k Mast's Car	.02	.10
ty Wallace Win	.30	.75
y Labonte's Car	.15	.40
e Irvan's Car	.07	.20
Bonnett	.25	.60
k Martin	.50	1.50
Kulwicki	.25	.60
ling Marlin's Car	.07	.20
e Wallace	.07	.20
mmy Allison	.02	.10
ke Beam	.02	.10
nmy Spencer	.07	.20
ck Trickle	.07	.20
rry Labonte	.30	.75
ur Wide	.02	.10
alladega Speedway		
ally Dallenbach, Jr.	.07	.20
nny Parsons	.07	.20
le Jarrett's Car	.15	.40
m Peck	.07	.20
bby Hamilton's Car	.02	.10
organ Shepherd	.07	.20
bby Labonte	.50	1.25
oy Selburg	.02	.10
f Gordon's Car	.50	1.25
sty Wallace's Car	.15	.40
ecklist		
ett Bodine	.07	.20
an Kulwicki Early Ride	.15	.40
vey Allison	.40	1.00
ddy Parrott	.02	.10
chael Waltrip	.15	.40
eve Grissom's Car	.02	.10
rk Martin's Car	.15	.40
en Schrader's Car		
rry Gant	.15	.40
dd Bodine's Car	.02	.10
awna Robinson	.40	1.00
nny Bernstein	.07	.20
f Burton	.25	.60
Wood	.02	.10
f Gordon CRC	1.00	2.50
bby Hillin	.07	.20
l Parsons' Car	.02	.10
rd Burton	.15	.40
odwrench 500	.02	.10
ockingham		
k Wilson	.07	.20
e Nemechek	.07	.20
Unser Jr.'s Car	.15	.40
Schrader	.07	.20
e Wright	.02	.10
bert Yates	.02	.10
le Inman	.02	.10
ecklist		
ve Hmiel	.02	.10
my Means's Car	.02	.10
ce Roney	.02	.10
n Fedewa RC	.07	.20
d Musgrave	.07	.20
rk Martin's Car	.15	.40
on Keller's Car	.02	.10
sty Wallace	.60	1.50

59 Bill Stavola	.02	.10
Mickey Stavola		
60 Mark Martin's Busch Car	.15	.40
61 Tom Brewer	.02	.10
62 Donnie Richeson	.02	.10
63 Chuck Bown	.07	.20
64 Larry Hedrick	.02	.10
65 Joe Nemechek	.15	.40
Ricky Craven		
Todd Bodine		
66 Gary DeHart	.02	.10
67 Mark Martin	.60	1.50
68 Greg Sacks' Car	.02	.10
69 Davey Allison	.40	1.00
Robert Yates		
70 Harry Gant's Car	.02	.10
71 Walter Bud Moore	.02	.10
72 Andy Hillenburg	.07	.20
73 Ray Evernham	.07	.20
74 Sterling Marlin	.30	.75
75 Checklist #3	.02	.10
76 Ned Jarrett	.07	.20
77 Miller 400	.02	.10
Michigan International		
78 Mark Martin's Car	.15	.40
79 Glen Wood	.02	.10
Leonard Wood		
80 Hermie Sadler RC	.07	.20
81 Jerry Glanville	.07	.20
82 Alan Kulwicki First Win	.15	.40
83 Lake Speed's Car	.02	.10
84 Al Unser Jr.	.15	.40
85 Ward Burton	.07	.20
Todd Bodine		
86 Larry McReynolds	.02	.10
87 Greg Sacks	.07	.20
88 Ken Schrader's Car	.02	.10
89 Ken Howes	.02	.10
90 Bobby Hillin's Car	.02	.10
91 Don Miller	.02	.10
92 Joe Ruttman	.07	.20
93 Bill Brodrick	.02	.10
94 David Green	.07	.20
95 Joey Knuckles	.02	.10
96 Derrike Cope	.07	.20
97 Bill Davis	.02	.10
98 Derrike Cope's Car	.02	.10
99 Ricky Craven	.15	.40
100 Davey Allison	.40	1.00
101 Junior Johnson	.07	.20
102 Carl Hill	.02	.10
103 Dick Trickle's Car	.02	.10
104 Dave Marcis	.07	.20
105 Larry Pearson's Car	.02	.10
106 Rick Mast	.07	.20
107 Eli Gold	.02	.10
108 D.K. Ulrich	.02	.10
109 Mark Martin's Car	.15	.40
110 Hanes 500	.02	.10
Martinsville		
111 Jimmy Johnson	.02	.10
112 Buster Auton	.02	.10
113 Waddell Wilson	.02	.10
114 Eddie Wood	.02	.10
115 Clyde McLeod	.02	.10
116 Rick Hendrick	.02	.10
117 Bobby Dotter's Car	.02	.10
118 Jimmy Hensley	.07	.20
119 Jerry McClure	.02	.10
Tim Morgan		
Larry McClure		
Ed McClure		
Teddy McClure		
120 Dave Rezendes	.02	.10
121 Jack Sprague's Car	.02	.10
122 Tony Glover	.02	.10
123 Cale Yarborough	.07	.20
124 Jimmy Means	.07	.20
125 Michael Waltrip's Trans.	.02	.10
checklist		
126 Roy Payne	.02	.10
127 Davey Allison	.40	1.00
128 Davey Allison's Car	.15	.40
129 Doug Richert	.02	.10
130 Robert Pressley	.07	.20
131 Ken Wilson	.02	.10
132 Motorcraft 500	.02	.10
Atlanta Motorspeedway		
133 Jay Luckwaldt	.02	.10
134 Donnie Wingo	.02	.10
135 Billy Hagan	.02	.10
136 Ricky Rudd's Car	.07	.20
The Winston		
137 Jack Roush	.02	.10
138 Joe Gibbs	.15	.40
139 Robbie Loomis	.02	.10
140 Jimmy Fennig	.02	.10
141 Chuck Rider	.02	.10
142 Alan Kulwicki On Pole	.15	.40
143 Red Farmer	.02	.10
144 Jim Bown	.02	.10
145 Rusty Wallace in Pits	.15	.40
146 Ricky Pearson	.02	.10
147 Coca Cola 600	.02	.10
Charlotte Motorspeedway		
148 Pam Rimer	.02	.10
Valli Elliott		
Lisa Shrowder		
149 Bobby Allison	.07	.20
150 Checklist #6	.02	.10
151 Jeff Gordon	4.00	10.00
152 Sterling Marlin	.75	2.00
153 Jeff Burton	.60	1.50
154 Jimmy Spencer	.25	.60
155 Ted Musgrave	.25	.60
156 Ricky Craven	.50	1.25
157 Harry Gant	.50	1.25
158 Tracy Leslie	.12	.30
159 Wally Dallenbach, Jr.	.25	.60
160 Jack Sprague	.12	.30
161 Mark Martin	2.00	5.00
162 Shawna Robinson	1.00	2.50
163 Tommy Houston	.25	.60
164 Rusty Wallace	2.00	5.00
165 Chuck Bown	.25	.60
166 Joe Nemechek	.25	.60
167 Ken Schrader	.25	.60
168 Rick Hendrick	.12	.30
169 Larry Pearson	.25	.60
170 Rick Mast	.25	.60
171 Robert Yates	.12	.30
172 Hermie Sadler RC	.25	.60
173 Morgan Shepherd	.25	.60
174 Mike Wallace	.25	.60
175 Tom Peck	.12	.30
checklist		
176 Bobby Labonte	1.25	3.00
177 Lake Speed	.25	.60
178 Davey Allison	1.25	3.00
Bobby Allison		
179 Derrike Cope	.25	.60
180 Walter Bud Moore	.12	.30
181 Rusty Wallace	2.00	5.00
182 Ward Burton	.50	1.25
183 Bobby Dotter	.12	.30
184 Terry Labonte	.75	2.00
185 Todd Bodine	.25	.60
186 Michael Waltrip	.50	1.25
187 Roy Payne	.12	.30
188 Junior Johnson	.25	.60
189 Jack Roush	.12	.30
190 Davey Allison	1.50	4.00
191 David Green	.25	.60
192 Greg Sacks	.25	.60
193 Steve Grissom	.25	.60
194 Robert Pressley	.25	.60
195 Dick Trickle	.25	.60
196 Alan Kulwicki MEM	1.00	2.50
The Champ		
197 Al Unser Jr.	.50	1.25
198 Brett Bodine	.25	.60
199 Chuck Rider	.12	.30
200 Davey Allison	1.50	4.00
P1 Jeff Gordon Promo	4.00	10.00
P2 Rusty Wallace Promo	2.00	5.00

1993 Traks First Run

First Run cards were issued for the first time in 1993 and inserted two per pack in regular issue Traks. The series two Silver cards were much tougher to pull than series one. The cards can be distinguished from regular Traks cards by the inclusion of a "First Run" logo on the card fronts, otherwise they're identical to the regular issue release. Many of the First Run single cards are priced below using a multiplier of the regular issue cards.

COMPLETE SET (200)	60.00	125.00
COMP.SET w/o SP's (150)	10.00	25.00
COMP.SILVER SET (50)	50.00	100.00

*STARS 1-150: 1.5X TO 4X BASIC CARDS
*STARS 151-200: 2X TO 5X BASIC CARDS

1993 Traks Kodak Ernie Irvan

Once again, in 1993, Traks released a commemorate set featuring the Kodak Film Racing Team and driver Ernie Irvan. The cards are oversized (3-3/4" by 5-1/4") with a design very similar to the 1992 set. All six cards were issued with gold foil borders in a cardboard factory set type package. Reportedly 4,000 of these sets were produced and most of them were given away at Kodak's hospitality tent at Daytona.

COMPLETE FACTORY SET (6)	6.00	15.00
1 Ernie Irvan w/Car	2.00	4.00
Man and Machine		
2 Inside Out	1.00	2.00
3 Ernie Irvan w/Crew	2.00	4.00
Beat the Heat		
4 Ernie Irvan in Pits	1.00	2.00
Bird's Eye View		
5 Ernie Irvan	2.00	4.00
Worst to First		
6 Ernie Irvan's Car	1.00	2.00
200 mph in NYC		

1993 Traks Preferred Collector

This 20-card set was made available through the Traks Club. The cards feature some of the top drivers in NASCAR Winston Cup racing. The backs list stats for the driver's career and the 1992 season. President George Bush is featured on card number 15 with Richard Petty.

COMPLETE SET (20)	6.00	15.00
1 Michael Waltrip	.25	.60
2 Brett Bodine	.20	.50
3 Terry Labonte	.40	1.00
4 Kyle Petty	.25	.60
5 Alan Kulwicki	.40	1.00
6 Mark Martin	.75	2.00
7 Morgan Shepherd	.20	.50
9 Darrell Waltrip	.25	.60
10 Hut Stricklin	.20	.50
11 Rusty Wallace	.50	1.25
12 Ken Schrader	.20	.50
13 Dale Jarrett	.50	1.25
14 Ernie Irvan	.40	1.00
15 Richard Petty	.40	1.00
George Bush		
16 Richard Petty	.40	1.00
17 Harry Gant	.25	.60
18 Jimmy Hensley	.20	.50
19 Dick Trickle	.20	.50
20 Davey Allison	.40	1.00

1993 Traks Trivia

The 1993 Traks Trivia set was released to retail outlets in a blister type packaging in complete set form. The 50-cards contain photos of NASCAR drivers on front with small photos on back along with six racing trivia questions.

COMP. FACT SET (50)	5.00	10.00
1 Mark Martin	.20	.50
2 Jeff Gordon	.60	1.50
3 Rusty Wallace	.20	.50
4 Davey Allison	.20	.50
5 Jeff Purvis	.05	.15
6 Mark Martin	.20	.50
7 Jimmy Hensley	.05	.15
8 Sterling Marlin	.10	.30
9 Alan Kulwicki	.20	.50
10 Davey Allison's Helmet	.10	.30
11 Rusty Wallace	.20	.50
12 Jimmy Spencer	.05	.15
13 Joe Nemechek	.05	.15
14 Terry Labonte	.10	.30
15 Harry Gant	.05	.15
16 Wally Dallenbach Jr.	.05	.15
17 Al Unser Jr.	.10	.30
18 Davey Allison	.20	.50
Bobby Allison		
19 Mark Martin	.20	.50
20 Lake Speed	.05	.15
21 Morgan Shepherd	.05	.15
22 Bobby Labonte	.05	.15
23 Mark Martin	.20	.50
24 Jeff Gordon	.60	1.50
25 Ken Schrader	.05	.15
26 Brett Bodine	.05	.15
27 Morgan Shepherd's Car	.05	.15
28 Davey Allison	.20	.50
29 Rusty Wallace	.20	.50
30 Michael Waltrip	.10	.30
31 Bobby Labonte	.05	.15
32 Mark Martin	.20	.50
33 Harry Gant	.05	.15
34 Davey Allison w/Crew	.20	.50
35 Alan Kulwicki	.20	.50
36 Jeff Gordon	.60	1.50
37 Mark Martin	.20	.50
38 Jeff Gordon's Car	.25	.60
39 Rusty Wallace	.20	.50
40 Davey Allison	.20	.50
Jerry Glanville		
41 Mark Martin	.20	.50
42 Dave Marcis	.05	.15
43 Ken Schrader	.05	.15
44 Greg Sacks	.05	.15
45 Jeff Gordon	.60	1.50
46 Bobby Hillin	.05	.15
47 Ted Musgrave	.05	.15
48 Bobby Allison	.05	.15
49 Derrike Cope	.05	.15
50 Rick Mast	.05	.15

1994 Traks

1994 Traks was released in two series of 100-cards each through 12-card packs. Boxes contained 30-packs. Series one cards were produced with gold foil layering while series two included silver foil. There were a couple of uncorrected error cards in the second series. The Ned Jarrett card was supposed to be number 134 but all of them were issued with the number 123 on the back. Also, the Tracy Leslie card was supposed to be number 148 but all of them were issued with the number 127 on the back. That means there are two different number 123's and two different number 127's. Club only factory sets were also produced with a 5-card Cartoons insert set per factory issue. A First Run factory set (400 sets made) was produced for sale to Club members at $35.00 as well that included a Cartoons set autographed by the card's artist.

COMPLETE SET (200)	10.00	25.00
COMP.SERIES 1 (100)	4.00	10.00
COMP.SERIES 2 (100)	4.00	10.00
WAX BOX SERIES 1	20.00	40.00
WAX BOX SERIES 2	20.00	40.00
1 Rick Mast	.07	.20
2 Rusty Wallace	.60	1.50
3 Sterling Marlin	.25	.60
4 Ward Burton's Car	.02	.10
5 Terry Labonte	.25	.60
6 Mark Martin	.60	1.50
7 Alan Kulwicki	.25	.60
8 Jeff Burton	.25	.60
9 Mike Wallace	.07	.20
10 Jeff Gordon's Car	.40	1.00
11 Junior Johnson	.07	.20
12 Bobby Allison	.07	.20
13 Dale Jarrett	.50	1.25
14 Sterling Marlin's Car	.07	.20
15 Lake Speed	.07	.20
16 Ted Musgrave	.07	.20
17 Ricky Rudd	.25	.60
18 Joe Gibbs	.15	.40
19 Davey Allison	.40	1.00
20 Buddy Parrott	.02	.10
21 Morgan Shepherd	.07	.20
22 Bobby Labonte	.50	1.25
23 Ken Schrader	.07	.20
24 Jeff Gordon	.75	2.00
25 Neil Bonnett	.07	.20
Checklist #1		
26 Brett Bodine	.07	.20
27 Larry McReynolds	.02	.10
28 Ernie Irvan	.15	.40
29 Neil Bonnett	.25	.60
30 Michael Waltrip	.15	.40
31 Steve Grissom	.07	.20
32 Bruce Roney	.02	.10
33 Harry Gant	.15	.40
34 Derrike Cope	.07	.20
35 Shawna Robinson	.30	.75
36 Jeff Gordon	.75	2.00
37 Mark Martin's Car	.25	.60
38 Jimmy Hensley	.07	.20
39 Ricky Craven	.07	.20
40 Robert Yates	.02	.10
41 Dennis Setzer	.07	.20
42 Kenny Bernstein	.07	.20
43 Wally Dallenbach, Jr.	.07	.20
44 David Green	.07	.20
45 Ernie Irvan	.15	.40
46 Sterling Marlin	.25	.60
47 Joe Bessey	.07	.20
48 Bobby Labonte	.50	1.25
49 Michael Waltrip's Car	.07	.20
50 Neil Bonnett	.07	.20
Checklist #2		
51 Morgan Shepherd's Car	.02	.10
52 Jimmy Means	.07	.20
53 Loy Allen Jr.'s Car	.02	.10
54 Steve Hmiel	.02	.10
55 Ricky Rudd	.25	.60
56 Jimmy Spencer	.07	.20
57 Roger Penske	.02	.10
58 Ken Schrader	.07	.20
59 Bobby Labonte's Car	.25	.60
60 Mark Martin	.60	1.50
61 Derrike Cope's Car	.02	.10
62 Rusty Wallace	.60	1.50
63 Chuck Bown	.07	.20
64 Cale Yarborough	.07	.20
65 Dale Jarrett	.50	1.25
66 Ernie Irvan	.15	.40
67 Todd Bodine	.07	.20
68 Loy Allen Jr.	.07	.20
69 Morgan Shepherd	.07	.20
70 Terry Labonte's Car	.15	.40
71 Dave Marcis	.15	.40
72 Rusty Wallace's Car	.25	.60
73 Harry Gant	.15	.40
74 Bobby Dotter	.07	.20
75 Ken Schrader's Car	.02	.10
Brett Bodine's Car		
Checklist #3		
76 Robert Pressley	.07	.20
77 Leo Jackson	.02	.10
78 Brett Bodine	.07	.20
79 Ward Burton	.15	.40
80 Rusty Wallace	.60	1.50
81 Andy Hillenburg	.07	.20
82 Mark Martin	.60	1.50
83 Ray Evernham	.15	.40
84 Ricky Rudd's Car	.07	.20
85 Joe Nemechek	.07	.20
86 Jeff Gordon	.75	2.00
87 Ken Wilson	.02	.10
88 Carl Hill	.02	.10
89 Hermie Sadler	.07	.20
BGN Rookie of the Year		
90 Bobby Hillin	.07	.20
91 Ernie Irvan	.15	.40
92 Larry Pearson	.07	.20
93 Kenny Wallace	.07	.20
94 Ernie Irvan's Car	.07	.20
95 Jack Roush	.02	.10
96 Terry Labonte	.25	.60
97 Greg Sacks	.07	.20
98 Jimmy Makar	.02	.10
99 Harry Gant	.15	.40
100 Mark Martin's Car	.25	.60
Checklist #4		
101 Ernie Irvan	.15	.40
102 Rusty Wallace	.60	1.50
103 Dale Jarrett	.50	1.25
104 Mike McLaughlin	.07	.20
105 Billy Hagan	.02	.10
106 Jeff Gordon	.75	2.00
107 Jeremy Mayfield RC	.75	2.00
108 Dale Jarrett's Car	.25	.60
109 Sterling Marlin's Car	.07	.20
110 John Andretti RC	.07	.20
111 Kyle Petty	.15	.40
112 Sterling Marlin's Car	.07	.20
113 Mark Martin	.60	1.50
114 Bobby Allison	.07	.20
115 Jimmy Hensley	.07	.20
116 Harry Gant	.15	.40
117 Mike Beam	.02	.10
118 Terry Labonte	.25	.60
119 Eddie Wood	.02	.10
120 Rodney Combs	.07	.20
121 Morgan Shepherd	.07	.20
122 Mike Wallace's Car	.02	.10
123 Bobby Labonte	.50	1.25
124 Gary DeHart	.02	.10
125 Ricky Rudd's Car	.07	.20
Checklist #5		
126 Sterling Marlin	.25	.60
127 Ward Burton	.15	.40
128 Chuck Bown	.07	.20
129 Elton Sawyer	.07	.20
130 Ricky Rudd	.25	.60
131 Ken Schrader	.07	.20
132 Jimmy Fennig	.02	.10
133 Brett Bodine	.07	.20
134 Ned Jarrett	.02	.10
UER Numbered 123		
135 Ernie Irvan	.15	.40
136 Larry Hedrick	.02	.10
137 Kyle Petty	.15	.40
138 Todd Bodine's Car	.02	.10
139 Todd Bodine	.07	.20
140 Harry Gant's BGN Car	.07	.20
141 Bobby Allison	.07	.20
142 Charley Pressley	.02	.10
143 Loy Allen Jr.	.07	.20
144 Mark Martin	.60	1.50
145 Lake Speed's Car	.02	.10
146 Dale Jarrett	.50	1.25
147 Dave Marcis	.15	.40
148 Tracy Leslie	.07	.20
UER Numbered 127		
149 Lake Speed	.07	.20
150 Ernie Irvan's Car	.07	.20
Checklist #6		
151 Ted Musgrave	.07	.20
152 Terry Labonte	.25	.60
153 Len Wood	.02	.10
154 Michael Waltrip	.15	.40
155 Tim Fedewa	.07	.20
156 Glen Wood	.02	.10
Leonard Wood		
157 Rusty Wallace	.60	1.50
158 Tony Glover	.02	.10
159 Steve Grissom	.07	.20
160 Ernie Irvan's Car	.07	.20
161 Jeff Burton	.25	.60
162 Buster Auton	.02	.10
163 Ernie Irvan	.15	.40
164 Jim Bown	.07	.20
165 Derrike Cope	.07	.20
166 Harry Gant	.15	.40
167 Ken Howes	.02	.10
168 Ken Schrader's BGN Car	.02	.10
169 Robbie Loomis	.07	.20
170 Mike Wallace	.07	.20
171 Jeff Gordon	.75	2.00
172 Richard Jackson	.02	.10
173 Rick Mast	.07	.20
174 Jason Keller RC	.25	.60
175 Race Action	.02	.10
Checklist #7		
176 Mark Martin	.60	1.50
177 Greg Sacks	.07	.20
178 Elmo Langley	.02	.10
179 Doug Richert	.02	.10
180 Dick Trickle	.07	.20
181 Donnie Richeson	.02	.10
182 Sterling Marlin	.25	.60
183 Joe Nemechek	.07	.20
184 Kenny Wallace	.07	.20
185 Kyle Petty	.15	.40
186 Wally Dallenbach Jr.	.07	.20
187 Rusty Wallace's Car	.25	.60
188 Morgan Shepherd	.07	.20
189 Waddell Wilson	.02	.10
190 Ricky Craven's BGN Car	.07	.20
191 Ricky Rudd	.25	.60
192 Donnie Wingo	.02	.10
193 Rusty Wallace	.60	1.50
194 Chuck Bown's Car	.02	.10
195 Robert Pressley	.07	.20
196 Troy Selberg	.02	.10
197 Ted Musgrave's Car	.02	.10
198 Ernie Irvan	.15	.40
199 Benny Parsons	.07	.20
200 Jeff Gordon in Pits	.40	1.00
Checklist #8		
P1 Ernie Irvan's Car Prototype	.40	1.00
P2 Mark Martin T10 Prototype	2.00	5.00

1994 Traks First Run

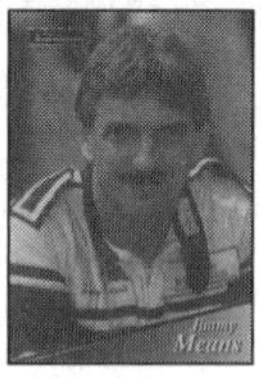

Packaged one per 1994 Traks foil pack, First Run is a parallel set to the regular Traks issue. The cards can be distinguished only by the presence of the "First Run" Traks logo. 400 factory First Run sets were also produced and offered to Traks Club members. Each factory set included a Cartoons insert set signed by artist Bill Stanford.

COMPLETE SET (200)	15.00	40.00
COMP.SERIES 1 (100)	10.00	20.00
COMP.SERIES 2 (100)	10.00	20.00

*FIRST RUN CARDS: 1.25X TO 2.5X BASIC CARDS

1994 Traks Autographs

Randomly inserted in both series one and two packs, these inserts are a specially designed card with each signed by the featured driver. A 13th card (cover/checklist card) was also inserted. A maximum of 3500 of each card was signed.

COMPLETE SET (13)	75.00	150.00
A1 Todd Bodine	5.00	12.00
A2 Jeff Burton	10.00	25.00
Ward Burton		
A3 Harry Gant	6.00	15.00
A4 Jeff Gordon	50.00	100.00
A5 Steve Grissom	5.00	12.00
A6 Ernie Irvan	8.00	20.00
A7 Sterling Marlin	10.00	25.00
A8 Mark Martin	15.00	40.00
A9 Joe Nemechek	6.00	15.00
A10 Robert Pressley	5.00	12.00
A11 Ken Schrader	6.00	15.00
A12 Rusty Wallace	12.50	30.00

NNO Cover Card Checklist back	3.00	8.00

1994 Traks Winners

The Traks Winners cards are a Holofoil stamped issue randomly inserted in series two packs of 1994 Traks racing. The cards feature early 1994 race winners that also had cards in Traks series one.

COMPLETE SET (25)	10.00	25.00
W1 Sterling Marlin	.50	1.25
W2 Rusty Wallace	1.25	3.00
W3 Ernie Irvan	.30	.75
W4 Ernie Irvan	.30	.75
W5 Terry Labonte	.50	1.25
W6 Rusty Wallace	1.25	3.00
W7 Ernie Irvan	.30	.75
W8 Jeff Gordon	1.50	4.00
W9 Rusty Wallace	1.25	3.00
W10 Terry Labonte	.50	1.25
W11 Joe Nemechek	.15	.40
W12 Harry Gant	.30	.75
W13 Terry Labonte	.50	1.25
W14 Mark Martin	1.25	3.00
W15 Ricky Craven	.15	.40
W16 David Green	.15	.40
W17 Hermie Sadler	.15	.40
W18 Derrike Cope	.15	.40
W19 Ricky Craven	.15	.40
W20 Mike Wallace	.15	.40
W21 Jeff Gordon	1.50	4.00
W22 Jeff Gordon	1.50	4.00
W23 Ken Schrader	.15	.40
W24 Rusty Wallace	1.25	3.00
W25 Elton Sawyer	.15	.40

1994 Traks Auto Value

In conjunction with Auto Value stores, Traks issued a set featuring 50 NASCAR drivers and racing personalities and one cover/checklist card. The cards were released in packs and were free with the purchase of a specific dollar purchase or purchase of certain items. The packs could also be purchased outright. Reportedly, 84,456 of these sets were produced.

COMPLETE SET (51)	5.00	12.00
1 Sterling Marlin	.20	.50
2 Brett Bodine	.08	.25
3 Robert Pressley	.08	.25
4 Ted Musgrave	.08	.25
5 Harry Gant	.15	.40
6 Ward Burton	.08	.25
7 Michael Waltrip	.15	.40
8 Jimmy Spencer	.08	.25
9 Dale Jarrett	.60	1.50
10 Jack Roush	.08	.25
11 Steve Grissom	.08	.25
12 Morgan Shepherd	.08	.25
13 Ricky Rudd	.15	.40
14 Chuck Bown	.08	.25
15 Neil Bonnett	.20	.50
16 Rick Hendrick	.08	.25
17 Lake Speed	.08	.25
18 Todd Bodine	.08	.25
19 Jeff Burton	.08	.25
20 Greg Sacks	.08	.25
21 Rusty Wallace	.75	2.00
22 Rick Mast	.08	.25
23 Loy Allen Jr.	.08	.25
24 Chuck Rider	.08	.25
25 Jeff Gordon	1.25	2.50
26 Bobby Hillin	.08	.25
27 Bobby Labonte	.60	1.50
28 Dick Trickle	.08	.25
29 Terry Labonte	.40	1.00
30 Joe Nemechek	.08	.25
31 Wally Dallenbach Jr.	.08	.25
32 Bobby Allison	.08	.25
33 Mark Martin	.75	2.00
34 Alan Kulwicki	.25	.60
35 Jimmy Hensley	.08	.25
36 Walter Bud Moore	.08	.25
37 Davey Allison	.40	1.00
38 Dave Marcis	.08	.25
39 Derrike Cope	.08	.25
40 Ned Jarrett	.08	.25
41 Ken Schrader	.08	.25
42 Junior Johnson	.08	.25
43 Ernie Irvan	.25	.60
44 Jimmy Means	.08	.25
45 Robert Yates	.08	.25
46 Roger Penske	.08	.25
47 Joe Gibbs	.08	.25
48 Derrike Cope's Car Ted Musgrave's Car	.08	.25
49 Rusty Wallace's Car Ken Schrader's Car	.20	.50
50 Ricky Rudd's Car Nose to Tail	.08	.25
NNO Checklist Card	.15	.40

1994 Traks Cartoons

The Traks Cartoons set was produced for and distributed with 1994 Traks factory sets and First Run factory sets offered to Traks Club members. The cards are oversized and measure approximately 8" X 10". First Run factory sets included a numbered Cartoons set signed the card's artist, Bill Stanford.

COMPLETE SET (5)	4.00	15.00
C1 Mark Martin	2.50	6.00
C2 Rusty Wallace	2.50	6.00
C3 Sterling Marlin	1.00	2.50
C4 Kyle Petty	.60	1.50
C5 Jeff Gordon	3.00	8.00

1994 Traks Preferred Collector

This is the second 20-card set made available only to Traks club members. The cards continue in numbering where the 1993 series left off. The cards feature some of the top drivers in NASCAR Winston Cup racing. The backs include stats for the driver's career and the 1993 season. The last two cards in the set are tributes to Davey Allison and Alan Kulwicki.

COMPLETE SET (20)	6.00	15.00
21 Rusty Wallace	.75	2.00
22 Harry Gant	.20	.50
23 Sterling Marlin	.40	1.00
24 Mark Martin	.75	2.00
25 Ted Musgrave	.10	.30
26 Greg Sacks	.10	.30
27 Ken Schrader	.10	.30
28 Morgan Shepherd	.10	.30
29 Lake Speed	.10	.30
30 Jimmy Spencer	.10	.30
31 Dick Trickle	.10	.30
32 Terry Labonte	.40	1.00
33 Jeff Gordon	1.00	2.50
34 Ernie Irvan	.20	.50
35 Bobby Labonte	.60	1.50
36 Brett Bodine	.10	.30
37 Neil Bonnett	.20	.50
38 Derrike Cope	.10	.30
39 Alan Kulwicki	.40	1.00
40 Davey Allison	.50	1.25

1994 Traks Hermie Sadler

Traks produced this individual set to commemorate the new Virginia is for Lovers Racing Team. The cards were distributed primarily through souvenir trailers and feature driver Hermie Sadler.

COMPLETE SET (10)	1.50	3.00
1 Hermie Sadler	.25	.60
2 Don Beverley	.10	.30
3 Hermie Sadler's Car	.10	.30
4 Hermie Sadler	.25	.60
5 Bobby King	.10	.30
6 Hermie Sadler's Car	.10	.30
7 Hermie Sadler	.25	.60
8 Hermie Sadler w/Crew	.10	.30
9 Hermie Sadler BGN ROY	.10	.30
10 Hermie Sadler's Transporter	.10	.30

1995 Traks

1995 Traks was released in one single series set of 75-cards through 12-card packs. Boxes contained 36-packs and production was limited to 2500 20-box cases. Dale Earnhardt was included in the set for the first time since 1992. The cards were released with an autographed Richard Petty promo card inserted along with other inserts: First Run parallel, Behind the Scenes, On the Rise, Race Scapes, Racing Machines, Series Stars and Challengers. Each insert set was also produced with a First Run parallel version. The Racing Machines and Series Stars First Run parallels were only available as part of the prizes for winners of the Challengers interactive game. A random insert in packs was a autographed Richard Petty card. The cards were inserted at a rate of one in 600 packs.

COMPLETE SET (75)	6.00	15.00
1 Geoff Bodine	.05	.15
2 John Andretti	.05	.15
3 Harry Gant	.05	.15
4 Jeff Gordon	.60	1.50
5 Bobby Labonte	.40	1.00
6 Sterling Marlin	.20	.50
7 Johnny Benson Jr.	.08	.25
8 Ward Burton	.08	.25
9 Ernie Irvan	.08	.25
10 Steve Grissom	.05	.15
11 Dennis Setzer	.05	.15
12 Greg Sacks	.05	.15
13 Rusty Wallace	.50	1.25
14 Brett Bodine	.05	.15
15 Loy Allen Jr.	.05	.15
16 Ted Musgrave	.05	.15
17 Jeremy Mayfield	.08	.25
18 Dale Jarrett	.40	1.00
19 Steve Kinser	.05	.15
20 Chad Little	.05	.15
21 Dave Marcis	.05	.15
22 Kyle Petty	.08	.25
23 Ricky Rudd	.20	.50
24 Hermie Sadler	.05	.15
25 Mike Wallace	.05	.15
26 Jeff Gordon	.60	1.50
27 Dale Earnhardt	1.00	2.50
28 Ricky Craven	.05	.15
29 David Green	.05	.15
30 Mark Martin	.50	1.25
31 Rick Mast	.05	.15
32 Joe Nemechek	.05	.15
33 Todd Bodine	.05	.15
34 Kyle Petty	.08	.25
35 Tommy Houston	.05	.15
36 Robert Pressley	.05	.15
37 Morgan Shepherd	.05	.15
38 Dick Trickle	.05	.15
39 Jeff Burton	.20	.50
40 Geoff Bodine	.05	.15
41 Terry Labonte	.20	.50
42 Ken Schrader	.05	.15
43 Dale Jarrett	.40	1.00
44 Kenny Wallace	.05	.15
45 Bobby Hamilton	.05	.15
46 Rusty Wallace	.50	1.25
47 Brett Bodine	.05	.15
48 Mark Martin	.50	1.25
49 Michael Waltrip	.08	.25
50 Ward Burton	.08	.25
51 Kyle Petty	.08	.25
52 Jeff Gordon	.60	1.50
53 Mark Martin	.50	1.25
54 Geoff Bodine	.05	.15
55 Ken Schrader	.05	.15
56 Jeff Burton	.20	.50
57 Randy LaJoie	.05	.15
58 Jeff Gordon	.60	1.50
59 Ernie Irvan	.08	.25
60 Dale Jarrett	.40	1.00
61 Terry Labonte	.20	.50
62 Mark Martin	.50	1.25
63 Ricky Rudd	.20	.50
64 Ken Schrader	.05	.15
65 Morgan Shepherd	.05	.15
66 Rusty Wallace	.50	1.25
67 Derrike Cope	.05	.15
68 Jeff Gordon	.60	1.50
69 Michael Waltrip	.08	.25
70 Todd Bodine	.05	.15
71 Sterling Marlin	.20	.50
72 Sterling Marlin	.20	.50
73 Ricky Rudd	.20	.50
74 Ernie Irvan	.08	.25
75 Rusty Wallace	.50	1.25
P26 Jeff Gordon Prototype First Run Card	1.50	4.00
NNO Richard Petty Auto	40.00	80.00

1995 Traks First Run

Packaged one per 1995 Traks foil pack, First Run is a parallel set to the regular Traks issue. The cards can be distinguished only by the presence of the "First Run" Traks logo on the cardfront. Each card in the regular set, as well as all insert sets were produced with a First Run parallel. First Run versions of Racing Machines and Series Stars inserts were only available as prizes in the Challengers interactive contest.

COMPLETE SET (75)	10.00	25.00
*FIRST RUN: .8X TO 2X BASIC CARDS		

1995 Traks Behind The Scenes

Behind the Scenes was produced by Traks as an insert in its 1995 Traks packs. The cards focus on non-drivers that make the sport of racing run. A parallel First Run version of each card was also produced. Wrapper stated odds of pulling a Behind the Scenes card is approximately two per pack.

COMPLETE SET (25)	2.00	4.00
*FIRST RUNS: 1.25X TO 3X BASIC INSERT		
BTS1 Steve Hmiel	.08	.25
BTS2 Rick Hendrick	.08	.25
BTS3 Joe Gibbs	.08	.25
BTS4 Chuck Rider	.08	.25
BTS5 Buddy Parrott	.08	.25
BTS6 Jack Roush	.08	.25
BTS7 Larry McReynolds	.08	.25
BTS8 Roger Penske	.08	.25
BTS9 Robbie Loomis	.08	.25
BTS10 Glen Wood Leonard Wood	.08	.25
BTS11 Paul Andrews	.08	.25
BTS12 Robert Yates	.08	.25
BTS13 Cale Yarborough	.08	.25
BTS14 Jimmy Johnson	.08	.25
BTS15 Tony Glover	.08	.25
BTS16 Ray Evernham	.08	.25
BTS17 Eddie Wood	.08	.25
BTS18 Andy Petree	.08	.25
BTS19 Carl Hill	.08	.25
BTS20 Richard Jackson	.08	.25
BTS21 Bruce Roney	.08	.25
BTS22 Junior Johnson	.08	.25
BTS23 Leo Jackson	.08	.25
BTS24 Len Wood	.08	.25
BTS25 Kenny Bernstein	.08	.25
P1 Steve Hmiel Prototype	.40	1.00

1995 Traks Challengers

Challengers is a 15-card interactive game randomly packed in 1995 Traks packs. Production was limited to less than 2000 of each card and the top prize was a complete First Run set of all 1995 Traks cards. Contest winners were required to redeem the cards of both the top Challenger and Rookie Challenger points drivers according to Traks' point rating system. Jeff Gordon was the Challengers winner and the Rookie Challengers winner was Ricky Craven. The original expiration date of November 1995 was extended to April 15, 1996.

COMPLETE SET (15)	40.00	80.00
COMP. FIRST RUN SET	40.00	100.00
*FIRST RUN: .5X TO 1.2X BASIC INSERTS		
C1 Jeff Gordon Winner Card	8.00	20.00
C2 Kyle Petty	1.25	3.00
C3 Ken Schrader	.75	2.00
C4 Terry Labonte	2.50	6.00
C5 Ricky Rudd	2.50	6.00
C6 Rusty Wallace	6.00	15.00
C7 Dale Jarrett	5.00	12.00
C8 Mark Martin	6.00	15.00
C9 Geoff Bodine	.75	2.00
C10 Sterling Marlin	2.50	6.00
C11 Morgan Shepherd	.75	2.00
C12 Steve Kinser	.75	2.00
C13 Ricky Craven Winner Card	.75	2.00
C14 Robert Pressley	.75	2.00
C15 Randy LaJoie	.75	2.00

1995 Traks On The Rise

On the Rise inserts focus on the top future stars of the Winston Cup and Busch racing circuits. The cards were packed approximately one per pack in 1995 Traks. A First Run parallel of each card was also randomly issued through packs. Jeff Burton's card was also released as a prototype.

COMPLETE SET (20)	2.50	5.00
*FIRST RUNS: 1X TO 2.5X BASIC INSERTS		
OTR1 Johnny Benson Jr.	.15	.40
OTR2 Steve Kinser	.10	.25
OTR3 Mike Wallace	.10	.25
OTR4 Larry Pearson	.10	.25
OTR5 Bobby Dotter	.10	.25
OTR6 Dennis Setzer	.10	.25
OTR7 David Green	.10	.25
OTR8 Steve Grissom	.10	.25
OTR9 Hermie Sadler	.10	.25
OTR10 Mike McLaughlin	.10	.25
OTR11 Joe Nemechek	.10	.25
OTR12 John Andretti	.10	.25
OTR13 Ted Musgrave	.10	.25
OTR14 Jeff Burton	.30	.75
OTR15 Ward Burton	.15	.40
OTR16 Kenny Wallace	.10	.25
OTR17 Ricky Craven	.10	.25
OTR18 Robert Pressley	.10	.25
OTR19 Chad Little	.10	.25
OTR20 Bobby Labonte	.60	1.50
P1 Jeff Burton Prototype numbered OTR14	.50	1.25

1995 Traks Race Scapes

Traks Race Scapes inserts were produced with art renderings of race scenes on the cardfront and checklists on the cardbacks. The cards were packed approximately one in every three packs of 1995 Traks.

COMPLETE SET (10)	.50	1.25
RS1 Checklist 1	.05	.15
RS2 Checklist 2	.05	.15
RS3 Checklist 3	.05	.15
RS4 Checklist 4	.05	.15
RS5 Checklist 5	.05	.15
RS6 Checklist 6	.05	.15
RS7 Checklist 7	.05	.15
RS8 Checklist 8	.05	.15
RS9 Contest Rules	.05	.15
RS10 1995 Winston Cup Sked.	.05	.15

1995 Traks Racing Machines

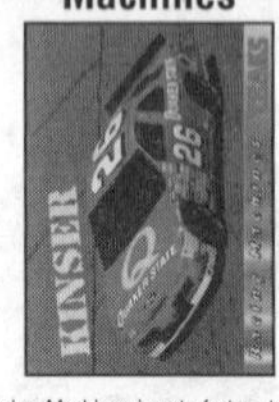

Traks Racing Machines inserts feature top Winston Cup cars printed on prism foil card stock. The cards were inserted at the wrapper stated rate of approximately 1:30 packs. A First Run parallel of each card was also produced as a prize to winners of the Challengers interactive contest.

COMPLETE SET (20)	30.00	60.00
*FIRST RUNS: .3X TO .8X BASIC INSERTS		
RM1 Todd Bodine	.60	1.50
RM2 Sterling Marlin	2.00	5.00
RM3 Geoff Bodine	.60	1.50
RM4 Bobby Hamilton	.60	1.50
RM5 Ricky Rudd	2.00	5.00
RM6 Terry Labonte	2.00	5.00
RM7 Jeff Gordon	6.00	15.00
RM8 Morgan Shepherd	.60	1.50
RM9 Mark Martin	5.00	12.00
RM10 Rusty Wallace	5.00	12.00
RM11 Rick Mast	.60	1.50
RM12 Dale Jarrett	4.00	10.00
RM13 Dick Trickle	.60	1.50
RM14 Ken Schrader	.60	1.50
RM15 Michael Waltrip	1.00	2.50
RM16 Steve Kinser	.60	1.50
RM17 Ted Musgrave	.60	1.50
RM18 Kyle Petty	1.00	2.50
RM19 Jeff Burton	2.00	5.00
RM20 Bobby Labonte	4.00	10.00

1995 Traks Series Stars

Traks Series Stars inserts feature top Winston Cup drivers printed on foil card stock. Each card was covered with a removable static cling "fan" sticker to protect the cardfront. The cards were inserted at the wrapper stated rate of approximately 1:30 packs. A First Run parallel of each card was also produced and available only as a prize to winners of the Challengers interactive contest.

COMPLETE SET (20)	25.00	60.00
*FIRST RUN: .3X TO .8X BASIC INSERTS		
SS1 Ken Schrader	.60	1.50
SS2 Terry Labonte	2.00	5.00
SS3 Morgan Shepherd	.60	1.50
SS4 Rusty Wallace	5.00	12.00
SS5 Mark Martin	5.00	12.00
SS6 Derrike Cope	.60	1.50
SS7 Sterling Marlin	2.00	5.00
SS8 Jeff Gordon	6.00	15.00
SS9 Harry Gant	.60	1.50
SS10 Geoff Bodine	.60	1.50
SS11 Ernie Irvan	1.00	2.50
SS12 Brett Bodine	.60	1.50
SS13 Michael Waltrip	1.00	2.50
SS14 Dick Trickle	.60	1.50
SS15 Ted Musgrave	.60	1.50
SS16 Ricky Rudd	2.00	5.00
SS17 Kyle Petty	1.00	2.50
SS18 Rick Mast	.60	1.50
SS19 Dale Earnhardt	10.00	25.00
SS20 Dale Jarrett	4.00	10.00

1995 Traks Auto Value

In conjunction with Auto Value stores, Traks issued a set featuring 50 NASCAR drivers and racing personalities for the second straight year. The cards were distributed through Auto Value stores in cello packs.

COMPLETE SET (51)	6.00	15.00
1 Jeff Gordon	2.00	5.00
2 Steve Grissom	.10	.30
3 Randy LaJoie	.10	.30
4 Junior Johnson	.10	.30
5 Jeff Burton	.30	.75
6 Geoff Bodine		.10
7 Kyle Petty		.20
8 Robert Pressley		.10
9 Greg Sacks		.10
10 Morgan Shepherd		.10
11 John Andretti		.10
12 Paul Andrews		.10
13 Brett Bodine		.10
14 Steve Hmiel		.10
15 Ernie Irvan		.20
16 Joe Gibbs		.20
17 Ray Evernham		.10
18 Ricky Craven		.10
19 Derrike Cope		.10
20 Ward Burton		.20
21 Todd Bodine		.10
22 Bobby Hamilton		.10
23 Rick Hendrick		.10
24 Dale Jarrett		.40
25 Bobby Labonte		.40
26 Steve Kinser		.10
27 Dave Marcis		.20
28 Sterling Marlin		.30
29 Mark Martin		.50
30 Rick Mast		.10
31 Jeremy Mayfield		.20
32 Michael Waltrip		.20
33 Ted Musgrave		.10
34 Robert Yates		.10
35 Cale Yarborough		.10
36 Buddy Parrott		.10
37 Mike Wallace		.10
38 Joe Nemechek		.10
39 Larry McReynolds		.10
40 Roger Penske		.10
41 Dick Trickle		.10
42 Kenny Wallace		.10
43 Jack Roush		.10
44 Ken Schrader		.10
45 Rusty Wallace		.50
46 Kenny Bernstein		.10
47 Terry Labonte		.30
48 Race Action		.10
49 Race Action		.10
50 Race Aciton		.10
NNO Checklist		.10

1995 Traks 5th Anniversary

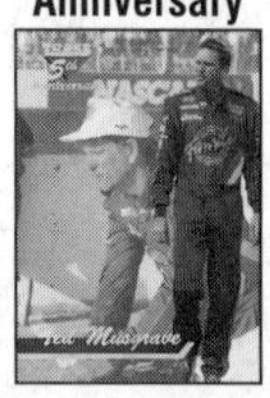

Traks introduced a new premium brand unc name of 5th Anniversary in 1995. The releas distributed in 8-card packs with 24-packs pe Each case contained eight boxes of Tra Anniversary and four boxes of Gold. Repo production was limited to 1000 cases. Inse include Clear Contenders and Retrospective.

COMPLETE SET (80)	8.00
1 Mark Martin	.60
2 Steve Grissom	.07
3 Dale Earnhardt	1.25
4 Jeff Gordon	.75
5 Ricky Rudd	.25
6 Geoff Bodine	.07
7 Sterling Marlin	.25
8 Johnny Benson Jr.	.15
9 Rusty Wallace	.60
10 John Andretti	.07
11 Derrike Cope	.07
12 Ernie Irvan	.15
13 Ted Musgrave	.07
14 Chad Little	.07
15 Kyle Petty	.15
16 Brett Bodine	.07
17 Ricky Craven	.15
18 David Green	.07
19 Terry Labonte	.25
20 Dale Jarrett	.50
21 Ward Burton	.15
22 Mike Wallace	.07
23 Morgan Shepherd	.07
24 Robert Pressley	.07
25 Todd Bodine	.07
26 Joe Nemechek	.07
27 Rick Mast	.07
28 Ken Schrader	.07
29 Kenny Wallace	.07
30 Jeff Burton	.25
31 Michael Waltrip	.15
32 Dick Trickle	.07
33 Bobby Labonte	.50
34 Bobby Hamilton	.07
35 Hut Stricklin	.07
36 Sterling Marlin	.25
37 Ricky Rudd	.25
38 Jeff Gordon	.75
39 Terry Labonte	.25
40 Mark Martin	.60
41 Dale Jarrett	.50
42 Rusty Wallace	.60
43 Todd Bodine's Car	.02
44 Sterling Marlin's Car	.07
45 Geoff Bodine's Car	.02
46 Bobby Hamilton's Car	.02
47 Ricky Rudd's Car	.07
48 Terry Labonte's Car	.15
49 Jeff Gordon's Car	.40
50 Morgan Shepherd's Car	.02
51 Mark Martin's Car	.25
52 Rusty Wallace's Car	.25
53 Michael Waltrip's Car	.07
54 Dale Jarrett's Car	.15
55 Dick Trickle's Car	.02
56 Rick Mast's Car	.02
57 Ricky Craven's Car	.02
58 Joe Nemechek's Car	.02
59 Ted Musgrave's Car	.02

Kyle Petty's Car .07 .20
Jeff Burton's Car .07 .20
Bobby Hamilton's Car .02 .10
Steve Grissom's Car .02 .10
Robert Pressley's Car .02 .10
Jack Roush .02 .10
Steve Hmiel .02 .10
Robert Yates .02 .10
Gary DeHart .02 .10
Cale Yarborough .07 .20
Larry McClure .02 .10
Robin Pemberton .02 .10
Ed McClure .02 .10
Larry McReynolds .02 .10
Andy Petree .02 .10
Joe Gibbs .15 .40
Tony Glover .02 .10
Rick Hendrick .02 .10
Jimmy Makar .02 .10
Paul Andrews .02 .10
Ray Evernham .02 .10
Ray Evernham Promo .40 1.00
Sterling Marlin's Car Promo .50 1.25
Mark Martin Promo 1.25 3.00
Mark Martin Promo/4000 2.00 5.00
St.Louis Show Promo

1995 Traks 5th Anniversary Gold

s 80-card set is a parallel to the base Traks 5th niversary set. The cards feature a gold foil mping and came in the blue Anniversary packs. h 12 box case of Traks 5th Anniversary came with r boxes of Anniversary Gold and eight boxes of base Anniversary product.

MPLETE SET (80) 15.00 40.00
OLDS: .6X TO 1.5X BASIC CARDS

1995 Traks 5th Anniversary Clear Contenders

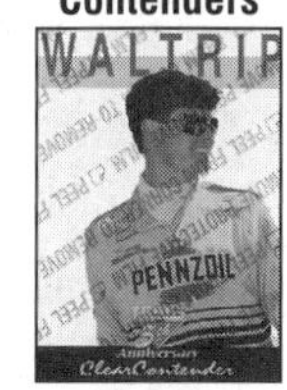

ar Contenders were randomly inserted in packs of ks 5th Anniversary Gold. Wrapper stated insertion o is 1:3 packs. The cards feature 10 of the top SCAR drivers on clear plastic card stock.

MPLETE SET (10) 12.00 30.00
Dale Earnhardt 5.00 12.00
Mark Martin 2.50 6.00
Jeff Gordon 3.00 8.00
Sterling Marlin 1.00 2.50
Ted Musgrave .30 .75
Rusty Wallace 2.50 6.00
Bobby Labonte 2.00 5.00
Michael Waltrip .60 1.50
Terry Labonte 1.00 2.50
) Morgan Shepherd .30 .75

1995 Traks 5th Anniversary Jumbos

s 10-card set features the top drivers in Winston . The cards are a jumbo sized card (3"X5") and e inserted in the bottom of Anniversary boxes at a of one per three boxes. There was also a Gold allel version of the jumbo cards. The cards were erted at a rate of one per case. There were 100 of h gold card made.

MPLETE SET (10) 10.00 25.00
OLDS: 1.2X TO 3X BASIC INSERTS
Jeff Gordon 2.50 6.00
Terry Labonte .75 2.00
Rusty Wallace 2.00 5.00
Morgan Shepherd .25 .60
Ted Musgrave .25 .60
Dale Earnhardt 4.00 10.00
Sterling Marlin .75 2.00
Michael Waltrip .50 1.25
Bobby Labonte 1.50 4.00
) Mark Martin 2.00 5.00

1995 Traks 5th Anniversary Retrospective

ospective cards were randomly inserted in 1995 ks 5th Anniversary Gold packs only. Wrapper d insertion ratio is 1:3 packs. The 15-cards were ted on holofoil prism card stock and feature a o of the driver's first Traks card on the back.

MPLETE SET (15) 8.00 20.00
Mark Martin 1.25 3.00
Dale Earnhardt 2.50 6.00
Jeff Gordon 1.50 4.00
Ricky Rudd .50 1.25
Sterling Marlin .50 1.25
Rusty Wallace 1.25 3.00
Dale Jarrett 1.00 2.50
Terry Labonte .50 1.25
Kyle Petty .30 .75
Ken Schrader .15 .40

R11 Ernie Irvan .30 .75
R12 Geoff Bodine .15 .40
R13 Morgan Shepherd .15 .40
R14 Cale Yarborough .15 .40
R15 Richard Petty .40 1.00

1995 Traks Valvoline

Traks produced this set for Valvoline in celebration of 100-years of auto racing. The cards were available in factory set form directly from Valvoline with the purchase of a case of oil or any Valvoline oil change. Each set was packaged in a tin replica Mark Martin race car and offered for sale at $12.95. The black-bordered cards feature an art rendering of a great race car from racing's past with one representative car from each year.

COMP.FACT SET (101) 7.50 20.00
1 J.Frank Duryea's Car .05 .15
Duryea Motor Wagon
2 A.L.Riker's Car .05 .15
3 Bollee Jamin .05 .15
4 George Heath's Car .05 .15
5 Camille Jenatzy's Car .05 .15
6 Fernand Charron's Car .05 .15
7 Henri Fournier's Car .05 .15
8 Barney Oldfield's Car .05 .15
9 H.T.Thomas' Car .05 .15
10 George Heath's Car .05 .15
11 B.F.Dingley's Car .05 .15
12 Joseph Tracy's Car .05 .15
13 Scipion Borghese's Car .05 .15
14 Louis Wagner's Car .05 .15
15 Carl Fisher's Car .05 .15
16 Bob Burman's Car .05 .15
17 Ray Harroun's Car .05 .15
18 Joe Dawson's Car .05 .15
19 Jules Goux's Car .05 .15
20 Rene Thomas' Car .05 .15
21 Ralph dePalma's Car .05 .15
22 Dario Resta's Car .05 .15
23 WWI Ambulance .05 .15
The War Years
24 Dodge 4 Staff Car .05 .15
The War Years
25 Albert Guyot's Car .05 .15
26 Gaston Chevrolet's Car .05 .15
27 Tommy Milton's Car .05 .15
28 Jimmy Murphy's Car .05 .15
29 Albert Guyot's Car .05 .15
30 Jean Chassagne's Car .05 .15
31 Dave Lewis' Car .05 .15
32 Jules Goux's Car .05 .15
33 Robert Benoist's Car .05 .15
34 Louis Meyer's Car .05 .15
35 Ray Keech's Car .05 .15
36 Billy Arnold's Car .05 .15
37 Lou Schneider's Car .05 .15
38 Fred Frame's Car .05 .15
39 Henry Birkin's Car .05 .15
40 Bill Cummings' Car .05 .15
41 Malcolm Campbell's Car .05 .15
42 Louis Meyer's Car .05 .15
43 Bernd Rosemeyer's Car .05 .15
44 Louis Meyer's Car .05 .15
45 Wilbur Shaw's Car .05 .15
46 Ted Horn's Car .05 .15
47 Floyd Davis' Car .05 .15
Mauri Rose's Car
48 Daimler Dingo .05 .15
The War Years
49 Willys Jeep .05 .15
The War Years
50 Red Ball Express .05 .15
The War Years
51 M-4 Sherman Tank .05 .15
The War Years
52 George Robson's Car .05 .15
53 Mauri Rose's Car .05 .15
54 Johnny Mauro's Car .05 .15
55 Red Byron's Car .05 .15
56 Johnnie Parsons' Car .05 .15
57 Lee Walerd's Car .05 .15
58 Alberto Ascari's Car .05 .15
59 Bill Vukovich's Car .05 .15
60 Lee Petty's Car .08 .25
61 Bob Sweikert's Car .05 .15
62 Fireball Roberts' Car .08 .25
63 Juan Manuel Fangio's Car .05 .15
64 Jimmy Bryan's Car .05 .15
65 Lee Petty's Car .08 .25
66 Jim Rathmann's Car .05 .15
67 A.J.Foyt's Car .20 .50
68 Joe Weatherly's Car .05 .15
69 Parnelli Jones' Car .08 .25
70 Ken Miles' Car .05 .15
71 Jim Clark's Car .05 .15
72 Don Garlits' Car .08 .25
73 Richard Petty's Car .30 .75
74 David Pearson's Car .08 .25
75 Mario Andretti's Car .20 .50
76 Ferrari 512S Roadster .05 .15
77 Don Garlits' Car .08 .25
78 Ronnie Sox's Car .05 .15
79 Gordon Johncock's Car .08 .25
80 Don Prudhomme's Car .08 .25
81 Bobby Allison's Car
82 Buddy Baker's Car .08 .25
83 A.J.Foyt's Car .20 .50
84 Tom Sneva's Car .08 .25
85 Richard Petty's Car .30 .75
86 Benny Parsons' Car .08 .25
87 Bobby Unser's Car
88 Gordon Johncock's Car .08 .25
89 Cale Yarborough's Car .08 .25
90 Joe Amato's Car .05 .15
91 Ron Bouchard's Car .05 .15
92 Shirley Muldowney's Car .20 .50
93 Al Unser's Car .20 .50
94 Neil Bonnett's Car .20 .50
95 Ken Schrader's Car .08 .25
96 Bobby Rahal's Car .08 .25
97 Rusty Wallace's Car .60 1.50
98 Al Unser Jr.'s Car .20 .50
99 Mark Martin's Car .60 1.50
100 Jeff Gordon's Car .75 2.00
NNO Cover Card .05 .15
Checklist

1996 Traks Review and Preview

This 50-card set features top drivers from the Winston Cup circuit. The cards use gold foil stamping and UV coating. The product was packaged 12 boxes per case, 24 packs per box and eight cards per pack.

COMPLETE SET (50) 6.00 15.00
1 Sterling Marlin .25 .60
2 Bobby Hamilton .07 .20
3 Ted Musgrave .07 .20
4 Robert Pressley .07 .20
5 Mark Martin .50 1.25
6 Dale Jarrett .40 1.00
7 Joe Nemechek .07 .20
8 Kyle Petty .15 .40
9 Ward Burton .15 .40
10 Ernie Irvan .15 .40
11 Mark Martin .50 1.25
12 Kyle Petty .15 .40
13 Johnny Benson .15 .40
14 Ward Burton .15 .40
15 Jeff Gordon .60 1.50
16 John Andretti .07 .20
17 Sterling Marlin .25 .60
18 Ted Musgrave .07 .20
19 Ernie Irvan .15 .40
20 Jeff Burton .25 .60
21 Ricky Craven .07 .20
22 Dale Jarrett .40 1.00
23 Morgan Shepherd .07 .20
24 Ken Schrader .07 .20
25 Robert Pressley .07 .20
26 Bobby Hamilton .07 .20
27 Geoff Bodine .07 .20
28 Michael Waltrip .15 .40
29 Joe Nemechek .07 .20
30 Steve Grissom .07 .20
31 Morgan Shepherd .07 .20
32 Sterling Marlin .25 .60
33 Hut Stricklin .07 .20
34 Rick Mast .07 .20
35 Kyle Petty .15 .40
36 Mark Martin .60 1.50
37 Dale Earnhardt 1.00 2.50
38 Derrike Cope .07 .20
39 Dale Jarrett .40 1.00
40 Brett Bodine .07 .20
41 Ernie Irvan .15 .40
42 Ken Schrader .07 .20
43 Ted Musgrave .07 .20
44 Ernie Irvan .15 .40
45 Geoff Bodine .07 .20
46 Mike Wallace .07 .20
47 Checklist I .15 .40
Dale Jarrett's Car on front -
48 Checklist II .07 .20
Ernie Irvan's Car on front
49 Checklist III .07 .20
Mike Wallace
Jeff Burton's Cars on front
50 Checklist IV .07 .20
Geoff Bodine's Car on front
P1 Sterling Marlin Promo .40 1.00
P2 Mark Martin's Car Promo .50 1.25

1996 Traks Review and Preview First Run

This 50-card set is a parallel to the base set. The cards feature a "First Run" logo on the front of each card in the bottom right hand corner. The first run cards were inserted one per pack.

COMPLETE SET (50) 10.00 25.00
*FIRST RUN: .8X TO 2X BASIC CARDS

1996 Traks Review and Preview Magnets

This 50-card parallel set features the top Winston Cup circuit drivers. The cards are a parallel to the base cards and are printed on magnet stock. Two magnet cards were inserted in every box. They were not found in packs.

COMPLETE SET (50) 25.00 60.00
*MAGNETS: 3X TO 8X BASIC CARDS

1996 Traks Review and Preview Liquid Gold

Inserted at a rate of one per 24 packs, the Liquid Gold cards feature top names in Winston Cup racing. The cards have vibrant colors and gold accents.

COMPLETE SET (20) 15.00 40.00
LG1 Dale Jarrett 3.00 8.00
LG2 Ernie Irvan 1.25 3.00
LG3 Mark Martin 4.00 10.00
LG4 Jeff Burton 2.00 5.00
LG5 Bobby Hamilton .60 1.50
LG6 Morgan Shepherd .60 1.50
LG7 John Andretti .60 1.50
LG8 Steve Grissom .60 1.50
LG9 Rick Mast .60 1.50
LG10 Mike Wallace .60 1.50
LG11 Derrike Cope .60 1.50
LG12 Robert Pressley .60 1.50
LG13 Ward Burton 1.25 3.00
LG14 Kyle Petty 1.25 3.00
LG15 Ricky Craven .60 1.50
LG16 Sterling Marlin 2.00 5.00
LG17 Geoff Bodine .60 1.50
LG18 Jeff Gordon 5.00 12.00
LG19 Brett Bodine .60 1.50
LG20 Ted Musgrave .60 1.50

1996 Traks Review and Preview Triple-Chase

This 20-card insert set is the base set that features the top drivers in Winston Cup. The cards were inserted one per pack. There are two parallel versions: Gold and Holofoil. The Gold cards feature gold foil stamping and are inserted at a rate of one per three packs. The Holofoil cards feature holofoil highlights and were inserted one per 48 packs.

COMPLETE SET (20) 2.00 5.00
COMP.HOLO.SET (20) 40.00 80.00
*HOLOFOILS: 6X TO 15X BASIC INSERTS
COMP.GOLD SET (20) 3.00 8.00
*GOLDS: .6X TO 1.5X BASIC INSERTS
TC1 Sterling Marlin .25 .60
TC2 Ted Musgrave .07 .20
TC3 Mark Martin .40 1.00
TC4 Morgan Shepherd .07 .20
TC5 Michael Waltrip .15 .40
TC6 Dale Jarrett .40 1.00
TC7 Bobby Hamilton .07 .20
TC8 Todd Bodine .07 .20
TC9 Geoff Bodine .07 .20
TC10 Kyle Petty .15 .40
TC11 Ernie Irvan .15 .40
TC12 Steve Grissom .07 .20
TC13 Robert Pressley .07 .20
TC14 Ricky Craven .07 .20
TC15 Sterling Marlin's Car .07 .20
TC16 Mark Martin's Car .15 .40
TC17 Ernie Irvan's Car .02 .10
TC18 Kyle Petty's Car .02 .10
TC19 Ted Musgrave's Car .02 .10
TC20 Dale Jarett's Car .07 .20

2006 TRAKS

COMPLETE SET (110) 20.00 50.00
WAX BOX HOBBY (28) 40.00 70.00
WAX BOX RETAIL (24) 40.00 70.00
1 Greg Biffle .50 1.25
2 Dave Blaney .25 .60
3 Clint Bowyer CRC 3.00 8.00
4 Jeff Burton .40 1.00
5 Kurt Busch .60 1.50
6 Kyle Busch .75 2.00
7 Dale Earnhardt Jr. 1.50 4.00
8 Carl Edwards 1.25 3.00
9 Jeff Gordon 1.50 4.00
10 Robby Gordon .25 .60
11 Jeff Green .25 .60
12 Denny Hamlin CRC 3.00 8.00
13 Kevin Harvick 1.00 2.50
14 Dale Jarrett .75 2.00
15 Jimmie Johnson 1.25 3.00
16 Kasey Kahne 1.50 4.00
17 Matt Kenseth 1.25 3.00
18 Bobby Labonte .75 2.00
19 Terry Labonte .60 1.50
20 Sterling Marlin .60 1.50
21 Mark Martin 1.00 2.50
22 Jeremy Mayfield .25 .60
23 Casey Mears .40 1.00
24 Joe Nemechek .25 .60
25 Ryan Newman 1.00 2.50
26 Kyle Petty .40 1.00
27 Scott Riggs .40 1.00
28 Elliott Sadler .40 1.00
29 Ken Schrader .25 .60
30 Brent Sherman RC 1.50 4.00
31 Reed Sorenson CRC 2.50 6.00
32 Tony Stewart 1.00 2.50
33 David Stremme CRC 2.50 6.00
34 Martin Truex Jr. CRC 2.00 5.00
35 Brian Vickers .75 2.00
36 J.J. Yeley CRC 1.25 3.00
37 Martin Truex Jr.'s Car .50 1.25
38 Kurt Busch's Car .25 .60
39 Mark Martin's Car .40 1.00
40 Dale Earnhardt Jr.'s Car .60 1.50
41 Kasey Kahne's Car .60 1.50
42 Denny Hamlin's Car .60 1.50
43 Ryan Newman's Car .50 1.25
44 Greg Biffle's Car .20 .50
45 Matt Kenseth's Car .50 1.25
46 Tony Stewart's Car .40 1.00
47 Jeff Gordon's Car .60 1.50
48 Kevin Harvick's Car .40 1.00
49 Jeff Burton's Car .15 .40
50 Elliott Sadler's Car .15 .40
51 Bobby Labonte's Car .30 .75
52 Jimmie Johnson's Car .50 1.25
53 Dale Jarrett's Car .30 .75
54 Carl Edwards' Car .50 1.25
55 A.J. Foyt IV NBS RC 1.25 3.00
56 David Green NBS .25 .60
57 Todd Kluever NBS 1.25 3.00
58 Mark McFarland NBS .25 .60
59 Paul Menard NBS .50 1.25
60 Danny O'Quinn NBS RC .75 2.00
61 Johnny Sauter NBS .40 1.00
62 Regan Smith NBS .25 .60
63 Jon Wood NBS .40 1.00
64 Rick Crawford CTS .25 .60
65 Erin Crocker CTS RC 3.00 8.00
66 Erik Darnell CTS RC .75 2.00
67 Ron Hornaday CTS .25 .60
68 Mark Martin CTS 1.00 2.50
69 Mike Skinner CTS .25 .60
70 Bobby Allison .50 1.25
71 Davey Allison .75 2.00
72 Donnie Allison .25 .60
73 Buddy Baker .40 1.00
74 Dale Earnhardt 2.50 6.00
75 Harry Gant .40 1.00
76 Jack Ingram .25 .60
77 Alan Kulwicki .60 1.50
78 Tiny Lund .25 .60
79 Marvin Panch .25 .60
80 Benny Parsons .40 1.00
81 David Pearson .60 1.50
82 Lee Petty .60 1.50
83 Richard Petty 1.25 3.00
84 Tim Richmond .40 1.00
85 Fireball Roberts .40 1.00
86 Curtis Turner .25 .60
87 Rusty Wallace .75 2.00
88 Rex White .25 .60
89 Glen Wood .25 .60
90 Cale Yarborough .50 1.25
91 Chip Ganassi Racing Hdqtrs .40 1.00
92 Dale Earnhardt Inc. Hdqtrs 1.00 2.50
93 Evernham Motorsports Hdqtrs .40 1.00
94 Hendrick Motorsports Hdqtrs .40 1.00
95 Joe Gibbs Racing Hdqtrs .40 1.00
96 Penske Racing Hdqtrs .40 1.00
97 Richard Childress Racing Hdqtrs .40 1.00
98 Robert Yates Racing Hdqtrs .40 1.00
99 Roush Racing Hdqtrs .40 1.00
100 Martin Truex Jr.'s Car PS .50 1.25
101 Mark Martin's Car PS .40 1.00
102 Sterling Marlin's Car PS .25 .60
103 Greg Biffle's Car PS .20 .50
104 Matt Kenseth's Car PS .50 1.25
105 Kevin Harvick's Car PS .40 1.00
106 Jeff Burton's Car PS .15 .40
107 Elliott Sadler's Car PS .15 .40
108 Dale Jarrett's Car PS .30 .75
109 Carl Edwards' Car PS .50 1.25
110 Checklist CL .15 .40

2006 TRAKS Autographs

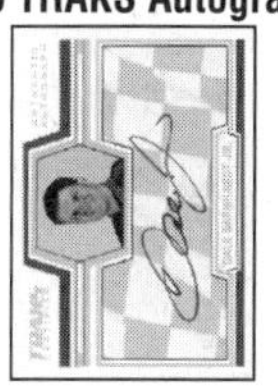

STATED ODDS 1:56
1 Greg Biffle NC 10.00 25.00
2 Dave Blaney NC 6.00 15.00
3 Clint Bowyer NC 12.50 30.00
4 Jeff Burton NC 8.00 20.00
5 Kurt Busch NC 12.50 30.00
6 Kyle Busch NC SP 20.00 50.00
7 Erin Crocker CTS 20.00 50.00
8 Dale Earnhardt Jr. NC SP
9 Carl Edwards 20.00 50.00
10 Jeff Gordon NC SP
11 Robby Gordon NC 8.00 20.00
12 David Green NBS 7.50 15.00
13 Denny Hamlin 30.00 60.00
14 Kevin Harvick NC SP 20.00 50.00
15 Ron Hornaday CTS 7.50 15.00
16 Dale Jarrett NC SP 20.00 50.00
17 Jimmie Johnson NC SP 40.00 80.00
18 Kasey Kahne NC SP 25.00 60.00
19 Matt Kenseth NC SP 15.00 40.00
20 Todd Kluever NBS 10.00 25.00
21 Bobby Labonte NC 15.00 40.00
22 Terry Labonte NC 15.00 40.00
23 Sterling Marlin NC 12.50 30.00
24 Mark Martin NC SP 60.00 120.00
25 Jeremy Mayfield NC SP 12.50 30.00
26 Casey Mears NC SP
27 Joe Nemechek NC 8.00 20.00
28 Ryan Newman NC SP 15.00 30.00
29 Tony Raines NC 7.50 15.00
30 Scott Riggs NC SP 10.00 25.00
31 Elliott Sadler NC 20.00 50.00
32 Johnny Sauter NBS 7.50 15.00
33 Mike Skinner CTS 7.50 15.00
34 Reed Sorenson NC 12.50 30.00
35 David Stremme NC 12.50 30.00
36 Tony Stewart NC 40.00 100.00
37 Martin Truex Jr. NC 15.00 40.00
38 Brian Vickers NC 10.00 25.00
39 Jon Wood NBS 7.50 15.00
40 J.J. Yeley NC 12.50 30.00

2006 TRAKS Autographs 100

STATED PRINT RUN 100 SERIAL #'d SETS
1 Greg Biffle NC 15.00 40.00
2 Dave Blaney NC 10.00 25.00
3 Clint Bowyer NC 15.00 40.00
4 Kurt Busch NC 12.50 30.00
5 Erin Crocker CTS 50.00 100.00
6 Robby Gordon NC 10.00 25.00
7 David Green NBS 8.00 20.00
8 Kevin Harvick NC 25.00 60.00
9 Ron Hornaday CTS 8.00 20.00
10 Dale Jarrett NC 25.00 60.00
11 Todd Kluever NBS 25.00 60.00
12 Bobby Labonte NC 20.00 50.00
13 Terry Labonte NC 20.00 50.00
14 Casey Mears NC 12.50 30.00
15 Tony Raines NC 8.00 20.00
16 Scott Riggs NC 12.50 30.00
17 Johnny Sauter NBS 8.00 20.00
18 David Stremme NC 20.00 50.00
19 Martin Truex, Jr. NC 20.00 50.00
20 Jon Wood NBS 8.00 20.00

2006 TRAKS Autographs 25

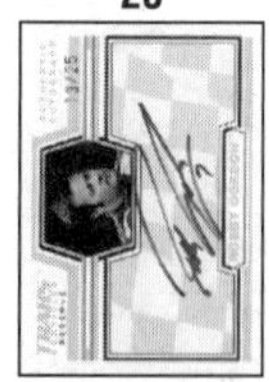

STATED PRINT RUN 25 SERIAL #'d SETS

2006 TRAKS Stickers

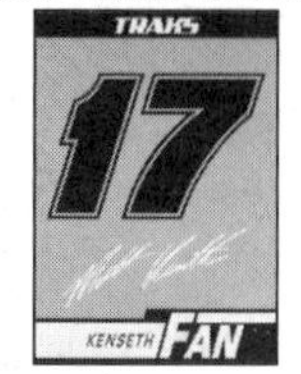

COMPLETE SET (36) 10.00 20.00
STATED ODDS 1 PER PACK
1 Martin Truex Jr. .75 2.00
01 Joe Nemechek .15 .40
2 Kurt Busch .40 1.00
5 Kyle Busch .50 1.25
6 Mark Martin .60 1.50
7 Robby Gordon .15 .40
07 Clint Bowyer 1.00 2.50
8 Dale Earnhardt Jr. 1.00 2.50
9 Kasey Kahne 1.00 2.50
10 Scott Riggs .25 .60
11 Denny Hamlin 1.00 2.50
12 Ryan Newman .75 2.00
14 Sterling Marlin .40 1.00
16 Greg Biffle .30 .75
17 Matt Kenseth .75 2.00
18 J.J. Yeley .40 1.00
19 Jeremy Mayfield .15 .40
20 Tony Stewart .60 1.50
21 Ken Schrader .15 .40
22 Dave Blaney .15 .40
24 Jeff Gordon 1.00 2.50
25 Brian Vickers .60 1.50
26 Jamie McMurray .40 1.00
29 Kevin Harvick .60 1.50
31 Jeff Burton .25 .60
38 Elliott Sadler .25 .60
40 David Stremme .60 1.50
41 Reed Sorenson .60 1.50
42 Casey Mears .25 .60
43 Bobby Labonte .50 1.25
44 Terry Labonte .40 1.00
45 Kyle Petty .25 .60
48 Jimmie Johnson .75 2.00
66 Jeff Green .15 .40
88 Dale Jarrett .50 1.25
99 Carl Edwards .75 2.00

2007 Traks

COMPLETE SET (100) 12.50 30.00
COMMON DRIVERS .15 .40
SEMISTARS .25 .60
UNLISTED STARS .40 1.00
WAX BOX HOBBY (24) 50.00 80.00
WAX BOX RETAIL (24) 40.00 75.00
1 Greg Biffle .30 .75
2 Jeff Burton .25 .60
3 Kyle Busch .50 1.25
4 Kurt Busch .25 .60
5 Dale Earnhardt Jr. 1.00 2.50
6 Carl Edwards .60 1.50
7 Robby Gordon .15 .40
8 Jeff Gordon 1.00 2.50
9 Denny Hamlin .75 2.00
10 Kevin Harvick .60 1.50
11 Dale Jarrett .50 1.25
12 Jimmie Johnson .75 2.00
13 Kasey Kahne 1.00 2.50
14 Matt Kenseth .75 2.00
15 Bobby Labonte .50 1.25
16 Sterling Marlin .40 1.00
17 Jamie McMurray .40 1.00

18 Casey Mears .25 .60
19 Joe Nemechek .15 .40
20 Ryan Newman .50 1.25
21 Kyle Petty .25 .60
22 Tony Raines .15 .40
23 Scott Riggs .25 .60
24 Ricky Rudd .40 1.00
25 Johnny Sauter .25 .60
26 Ken Schrader .15 .40
27 Reed Sorenson .50 1.25
28 Tony Stewart .60 1.50
29 Martin Truex Jr. .60 1.50
30 Brian Vickers .40 1.00
31 Michael Waltrip .25 .60
32 A.J. Allmendinger RC 1.50 4.00
33 Paul Menard CRC 1.25 3.00
34 Juan Pablo Montoya RC 2.00 5.00
35 David Ragan CRC 1.25 3.00
36 Regan Smith CRC 1.00 2.50
37 Aric Almirola NBS RC .60 1.50
38 Marcos Ambrose NBS RC .75 2.00
39 Kertus Davis NBS RC .50 1.25
40 Cale Gale NBS RC .40 1.00
41 Sam Hornish Jr. NBS RC .60 1.50
42 Shane Huffman NBS RC .60 1.50
43 Todd Kluever NBS .50 1.25
44 Stephen Leicht NBS RC .60 1.50
45 Timothy Peters NBS RC .40 1.00
46 Steve Wallace NBS .50 1.25
47 Scott Wimmer NBS .25 .60
48 Jon Wood NBS .15 .40
49 Todd Bodine CTS .15 .40
50 Rick Crawford CTS .15 .40
51 Erik Darnell CTS .40 1.00
52 Ron Hornaday CTS .15 .40
53 Travis Kvapil CTS .25 .60
54 Mike Skinner CTS .20 .50
55 T.J. Bell CTS RC .15 .40
56 Carl Edwards' Car CTG .25 .60
57 Dale Jarrett's Car CTG .20 .50
58 Jeff Gordon's Car CTG .50 1.25
59 Kasey Kahne's Car CTG .40 1.00
60 Ryan Newman CTG .50 1.25
61 Tony Stewart's Car CTG .40 1.00
62 Jimmie Johnson CTG .30 .75
63 Darrell Waltrip CTG .40 1.00
64 David Stremme MG .50 1.25
65 Mark Martin 1.00 2.50
Regan Smith MG
66 Kasey Kahne MG 1.00 2.50
67 Kurt Busch MG .25 .60
68 David Reutimann MG 1.25 3.00
69 Juan Pablo Montoya MG 1.00 2.50
70 Elliott Sadler MG .25 .60
71 Jimmie Johnson MG .75 2.00
72 Kyle Busch MG .50 1.25
73 Dale Earnhardt Jr. MG 1.00 2.50
74 Jeff Gordon MG 1.00 2.50
75 Tony Stewart GP .60 1.50
76 Dale Jarrett GP .50 1.25
77 Martin Truex Jr. GP .60 1.50
78 Kevin Harvick GP .60 1.50
79 Dale Earnhardt Jr. GP 1.00 2.50
80 Bobby Labonte GP .50 1.25
81 Jimmie Johnson GP .75 2.00
82 Martin Truex Jr.'s Car NFS .60 1.50
83 Dale Earnhardt Jr.'s Car NFS 1.00 2.50
84 Kasey Kahne's Car NFS 1.00 2.50
85 Matt Kenseth's Car NFS .75 2.00
86 Tony Stewart's Car NFS .60 1.50
87 Jeff Gordon's Car NFS 1.00 2.50
88 Kevin Harvick's Car NFS .60 1.50
89 Jimmie Johnson's Car NFS .75 2.00
90 Ricky Rudd's Car NFS .40 1.00
91 Jeff Burton FT .25 .60
92 Kurt Busch FT .25 .60
93 Dale Earnhardt Jr. FT 1.00 2.50
94 Jeff Gordon FT 1.00 2.50
95 Denny Hamlin FT .75 2.00
96 Jimmie Johnson FT .75 2.00
97 Kasey Kahne FT 1.00 2.50
98 Matt Kenseth FT .75 2.00
99 Tony Stewart FT .60 1.50
100 Dale Jarrett CL .50 1.25

2007 Traks Gold

COMPLETE SET (100) 25.00 50.00
*GOLD: X TO X BASE
STATED ODDS 1 PER HOBBY PACK

2007 Traks Holofoil

*HOLOFOIL: 4X TO 10X BASE
STATED PRINT RUN 50 SERIAL #'d SETS

2007 Traks Previews

(EB1-EB48) STATED PRINT RUN 5 SERIAL #'d SETS
(EB75-EB81) STATED PRINT RUN 1 SERIAL #'d SET
NOT PRICED DUE TO SCARCITY

2007 Traks Red

STATED PRINT RUN 10 SERIAL #'d SETS
NOT PRICED DUE TO SCARCITY

2007 Traks Corporate Cuts Driver

STATED ODDS 1:112
STATED PRINT RUN 99 SERIAL #'d SETS
CCD1 Reed Sorenson 10.00 25.00
CCD2 Kasey Kahne 15.00 40.00
CCD3 David Ragan 12.50 30.00
CCD4 Dale Jarrett 15.00 40.00
CCD5 Matt Kenseth 15.00 40.00
CCD6 Denny Hamlin 15.00 40.00
CCD7 David Stremme 10.00 25.00
CCD8 Kurt Busch 15.00 40.00
CCD9 Ryan Newman 10.00 25.00
CCD10 Carl Edwards 15.00 40.00
CCD11 Greg Biffle 12.50 30.00
CCD12 Dale Earnhardt Jr. 20.00 50.00
CCD13 Tony Stewart 15.00 40.00
CCD14 Michael Waltrip 12.50 30.00
CCD15 Mark Martin 15.00 40.00
CCD16 J.J. Yeley 10.00 25.00
CCD17 Juan Pablo Montoya 15.00 40.00
CCD18 David Reutimann 12.50 30.00

2007 Traks Corporate Cuts Patch

NOT PRICED DUE TO SCARCITY
STATED PRINT RUNS VARY SEE CHECKLIST BELOW
CCD1 Reed Sorenson/6
CCD2 Kasey Kahne/12
CCD3 David Ragan/15
CCD4 Dale Jarrett/10
CCD5 Matt Kenseth/12
CCD6 Denny Hamlin/10
CCD7 David Stremme/6
CCD8 Kurt Busch/6
CCD9 Ryan Newman/15
CCD10 Carl Edwards/12
CCD11 Greg Biffle/15
CCD12 Dale Earnhardt Jr./8
CCD13 Tony Stewart/4
CCD14 Michael Waltrip/12
CCD15 Mark Martin/15
CCD16 J.J. Yeley/15
CCD17 Juan Pablo Montoya/5
CCD18 David Reutimann/15

2007 Traks Corporate Cuts Team

*TEAM: .4X TO 1X DRIVER
STATED ODDS 1:112
STATED PRINT RUN 180 SERIAL #'d SETS

2007 Traks Driver's Seat

COMPLETE SET (27) 12.50 30.00
COMMON DRIVERS .40 1.00
SEMISTARS .60 1.50
UNLISTED STARS 1.00 2.50
STATED ODDS 1:2
*VARIATIONS: 1.5X TO 4X BASIC
VARIATION STATED ODDS 1:210
VARIATION HAS DOOR # IN PLACE OF LAP #
DS1 David Stremme 1.25 3.00
DS2 Jeff Gordon 2.50 6.00
DS3 Martin Truex Jr. 1.50 4.00
DS4 Tony Stewart 1.50 4.00
DS5 Ryan Newman 1.25 3.00
DS6 Mark Martin 1.50 4.00
DS7 Bobby Labonte 1.25 3.00
DS8 Jimmie Johnson 2.00 5.00
DS9 Kasey Kahne 2.50 6.00
DS10 Brian Vickers 1.00 2.50
DS11 Matt Kenseth 1.50 4.00
DS12 Kevin Harvick 1.50 4.00
DS13 Sterling Marlin 1.00 2.50
DS14 Dale Earnhardt Jr. 2.50 6.00
DS15 David Gilliland 2.00 5.00
DS16 Greg Biffle .75 2.00
DS17 Casey Mears .60 1.50
DS18 Kurt Busch .60 1.50
DS19 Michael Waltrip .60 1.50
DS20 Jeff Burton .60 1.50
DS21 Juan Pablo Montoya 2.50 6.00
DS22 Dale Jarrett 1.25 3.00
DS23 Johnny Sauter .60 1.50
DS24 Carl Edwards 1.50 4.00
DS25 J.J. Yeley .75 2.00
DS26 Ricky Rudd 1.00 2.50
DS27 Ken Schrader .40 1.00

2007 Traks Hot Pursuit

COMPLETE SET (12) 10.00 25.00
COMMON DRIVERS .50 1.25
SEMISTARS .75 2.00
UNLISTED STARS 1.25 3.00
STATED ODDS 1:6
HP1 Jeff Gordon 3.00 8.00
HP2 Kyle Busch 1.50 4.00
HP3 Tony Stewart 2.00 5.00
HP4 Martin Truex Jr. 2.00 5.00
HP5 Mark Martin 2.00 5.00
HP6 Carl Edwards 2.00 5.00
HP7 Jimmie Johnson 2.50 6.00
HP8 Kasey Kahne 3.00 8.00
HP9 Juan Pablo Montoya 3.00 8.00
HP10 Dale Earnhardt Jr. 3.00 8.00
HP11 Matt Kenseth 2.50 6.00
HP12 Kevin Harvick 2.00 5.00

2007 Traks Track Time

COMPLETE SET (9) 12.50 30.00
COMMON DRIVER .50 1.25
SEMISTARS .75 2.00
UNLISTED STARS 1.25 3.00
STATED ODDS 1:12
TT1 Dale Earnhardt Jr. 3.00 8.00
TT2 Juan Pablo Montoya 3.00 8.00
TT3 Kevin Harvick 2.00 5.00
TT4 Jimmie Johnson 2.50 6.00
TT5 Dale Jarrett 1.50 4.00
TT6 Jeff Gordon 3.00 8.00
TT7 David Gilliland 5.00 12.00
TT8 Tony Stewart 2.00 5.00
TT9 Martin Truex Jr. 2.00 5.00

2007 Traks Target Exclusives

COMPLETE SET (6) 5.00 12.00
COMMON DRIVER .20 .50
SEMISTARS .30 .75
UNLISTED STARS .50 1.25
STATED ODDS 2 PER TARGET BLASTER BOX
DE-A Dale Earnhardt Jr. 1.25 3.00
JG-A Jeff Gordon 1.25 3.00
JJ-A Jimmie Johnson 1.00 2.50
KH-A Kevin Harvick .75 2.00
KK-A Kasey Kahne 1.25 3.00
TS-A Tony Stewart .75 2.00

2007 Traks Wal-Mart Exclusives

COMPLETE SET (6) 5.00 12.00
COMMON DRIVER .20 .50
SEMISTARS .30 .75
UNLISTED STARS .50 1.25
STATED ODDS 2 PER WAL-MART BLASTER BOX
DE-B Dale Earnhardt Jr. 1.25 3.00
JG-B Jeff Gordon 1.25 3.00
JJ-B Jimmie Johnson 1.00 2.50
KH-B Kevin Harvick .75 2.00
KK-B Kasey Kahne 1.25 3.00
TS-B Tony Stewart .75 2.00

2007 Traks Driver's Seat National

COMPLETE SET (27) 10.00 25.00
DS1 David Stremme 1.00 2.50
DS2 Jeff Gordon 2.00 5.00
DS3 Martin Truex Jr. 1.25 3.00
DS4 Tony Stewart 1.25 3.00
DS5 Ryan Newman 1.00 2.50
DS6 Mark Martin 1.25 3.00
DS7 Bobby Labonte 1.00 2.50
DS8 Jimmie Johnson 1.50 4.00
DS9 Kasey Kahne 2.00 5.00
DS10 Brian Vickers .75 2.00
DS11 Matt Kenseth 1.50 4.00
DS12 Kevin Harvick 1.25 3.00
DS13 Sterling Marlin .75 2.00
DS14 Dale Earnhardt Jr. 2.00 5.00
DS15 David Gilliland 3.00 8.00
DS16 Greg Biffle .60 1.50
DS17 Casey Mears .50 1.25
DS18 Kurt Busch .50 1.25
DS19 Michael Waltrip .50 1.25
DS20 Jeff Burton .50 1.25
DS21 Juan Pablo Montoya 2.00 5.00
DS22 Dale Jarrett 1.00 2.50
DS23 Johnny Sauter .50 1.25
DS24 Carl Edwards 1.25 3.00
DS25 J.J. Yeley .60 1.50
DS26 Ricky Rudd .75 2.00
DS27 Ken Schrader .30 .75

1996 Ultra

This 200-card set is the first NASCAR set produced by Fleer. The set was distributed in 10-card packs with a suggested retail of $2.49 each. The set contains the following topical subsets: Busch Drivers (120-139), Car Owners (140-148), Award Winners (149-156), Road Warriors (157-166) and Race Action (167-200).

COMPLETE SET (200) 10.00 25.00
WAX BOX 40.00 80.00
1 Jeff Gordon .75 2.00
2 Jeff Gordon .75 2.00
3 Jeff Gordon's Car .30 .75
4 Ray Evernham .02 .10
5 Dale Earnhardt 1.25 3.00
6 Dale Earnhardt 1.25 3.00
7 Dale Earnhardt's Car .50 1.25
8 Andy Petree .02 .10
9 Mark Martin .60 1.50
10 Mark Martin .60 1.50
11 Mark Martin's Car .15 .40
12 Steve Hmiel .02 .10
13 Sterling Marlin .25 .60
14 Sterling Marlin .25 .60
15 Sterling Marlin's Car .07 .20
16 Tony Glover .02 .10
17 Rusty Wallace .60 1.50
18 Rusty Wallace .60 1.50
19 Rusty Wallace's Car .15 .40
20 Robin Pemberton .02 .10
21 Terry Labonte .25 .60
22 Terry Labonte .25 .60
23 Terry Labonte's Car .07 .20
24 Gary DeHart .02 .10
25 Ted Musgrave .07 .20
26 Ted Musgrave .07 .20
27 Ted Musgrave's Car .02 .10
28 Howard Comstock .02 .10
29 Bobby Labonte .50 1.25
30 Bobby Labonte .50 1.25
31 Bobby Labonte's Car .15 .40
32 Jimmy Makar .02 .10
33 Bill Elliott .30 .75
34 Bill Elliott .30 .75
35 Bill Elliott's Car .15 .40
36 Mike Beam .02 .10
37 Ricky Rudd .25 .60
38 Ricky Rudd .25 .60
39 Ricky Rudd's Car .07 .20
40 Bill Ingle .02 .10
41 Bobby Hamilton .07 .20
42 Bobby Hamilton .07 .20
43 Bobby Hamilton's Car .02 .10
44 Michael Waltrip .15 .40
45 Michael Waltrip .15 .40
46 Michael Waltrip's Car .07 .20
47 Dale Jarrett .50 1.25
48 Dale Jarrett .50 1.25
49 Dale Jarrett's Car .15 .40
50 Morgan Shepherd .07 .20
51 Morgan Shepherd .07 .20
52 Morgan Shepherd's Car .02 .10
53 Derrike Cope .07 .20
54 Derrike Cope .07 .20
55 Derrike Cope's Car .02 .10
56 Geoff Bodine .07 .20
57 Geoff Bodine .07 .20
58 Geoff Bodine's Car .02 .10
59 Ken Schrader .07 .20
60 Ken Schrader .07 .20
61 Ken Schrader's Car .02 .10
62 John Andretti .07 .20
63 John Andretti .07 .20
64 John Andretti's Car .02 .10
65 Tim Brewer .02 .10
66 Brett Bodine .07 .20
67 Brett Bodine .07 .20
68 Brett Bodine's Car .02 .10
69 Rick Mast .07 .20
70 Rick Mast .07 .20
71 Rick Mast's Car .02 .10
72 Ward Burton .15 .40
73 Ward Burton .15 .40
74 Ward Burton's Car .02 .10
75 Lake Speed .07 .20
76 Lake Speed .07 .20
77 Lake Speed's Car .02 .10
78 Ricky Craven .07 .20
79 Ricky Craven .07 .20
80 Ricky Craven's Car .02 .10
81 Dick Trickle .07 .20
82 Dick Trickle .07 .20
83 Dick Trickle's Car .02 .10
84 Steve Grissom .07 .20
85 Steve Grissom .07 .20
86 Steve Grissom's Car .02 .10
87 Jimmy Spencer .07 .20
88 Jimmy Spencer .07 .20
89 Jimmy Spencer's Car .02 .10
90 Kyle Petty .15 .40
91 Kyle Petty .15 .40
92 Kyle Petty's Car .07 .20
93 Robert Pressley .07 .20
94 Robert Pressley .07 .20
95 Robert Pressley's Car .02 .10
96 Joe Nemechek .07 .20
97 Joe Nemechek .07 .20
98 Joe Nemechek's Car .02 .10
99 Jeremy Mayfield .15 .40
100 Jeremy Mayfield .15 .40
101 Jeremy Mayfield's Car .07 .20
102 Jeff Burton .25 .60
103 Jeff Burton .25 .60
104 Jeff Burton's Car .07 .20
105 Todd Bodine .07 .20
106 Todd Bodine .07 .20
107 Todd Bodine's Car .02 .10
108 Mike Wallace .07 .20
109 Mike Wallace .07 .20
110 Mike Wallace's Car .02 .10
111 Dave Marcis .15 .40
112 Dave Marcis .15 .40
113 Dave Marcis' Car .07 .20
114 Hut Stricklin .07 .20
115 Hut Stricklin .07 .20
116 Hut Stricklin's Car .02 .10
117 Ernie Irvan .15 .40
118 Ernie Irvan .15 .40
119 Ernie Irvan's Car .07 .20
120 Johnny Benson, Jr. .15 .40
121 Johnny Benson, Jr.'s Car .02 .10
122 Chad Little .07 .20
123 Chad Little's Car .02 .10
124 Mike McLaughlin .07 .20
125 Mike McLaughlin's Car .02 .10
126 Jeff Green .07 .20
127 Jeff Green's Car .02 .10
128 Jason Keller .07 .20
129 Jason Keller's Car .02 .10
130 Larry Pearson .07 .20
131 Larry Pearson's Car .02 .10
132 Phil Parsons .07 .20
133 Phil Parsons' Car .02 .10
134 Tim Fedewa .07 .20
135 Tim Fedewa's Car .02 .10
136 Elton Sawyer .07 .20
137 Elton Sawyer's Car .02 .10
138 Patty Moise .07 .20
139 Patty Moise's Car .02 .10
140 Rick Hendrick .02 .10
141 Richard Childress .15 .40
142 Jack Roush .02 .10
143 Larry McClure .02 .10
144 Roger Penske .02 .10
145 Joe Gibbs .15 .40
146 Richard Petty .25 .60
147 Bobby Allison .07 .20
148 Glen Wood .02 .10
149 Ricky Craven A .07 .20
150 Andy Petree A .02 .10
151 Ray Evernham A .02 .10
152 Jeff Gordon A .40 1.00
153 Johnny Benson, Jr. A .15 .40
154 Chad Little A .07 .20
155 Bill Elliott A .15 .40
156 Ernie Irvan A .15 .40
157 Jeff Gordon's Helmet .60 1.50
158 Geoff Bodine's Helmet .02 .10
159 Ted Musgrave's Helmet .02 .10
160 Derrike Cope's Helmet .02 .10
161 Rusty Wallace's Helmet .15 .40
162 Kyle Petty's Helmet .07 .20
163 Morgan Shepherd's Helmet .02 .10
164 Ricky Rudd's Helmet .15 .40
165 Mark Martin's Helmet .15 .40
166 Bobby Labonte's Helmet .15 .40
167 Daytona 500 Race Action .02 .10
168 Jeff Gordon's Car RW .30 .75
169 Terry Labonte RW .15 .40
170 Jeff Gordon RW .40 1.00
Bobby Labonte
Terry Labonte
171 Bobby Labonte's Car RW .15 .40
172 Jeff Gordon RW .60 1.50
Brooke Gordon
173 Dale Earnhardt RW .60 1.50
174 Rusty Wallace's Car RW .15 .40
175 Dale Earnhardt's Car RW .50 1.25
176 Dale Earnhardt .15 .40
Mark Martin's Car
177 Bobby Labonte's Car RW .15 .40
178 Kyle Petty RW .07 .20
179 UAW GM Teamwork 500 .02 .10
Race Action
180 Bobby Labonte RW .25 .60
181 Jeff Gordon's Car .15 .40
Race Action
182 Jeff Gordon's Car .15 .40
Race Action
183 Dale Jarrett RW .15 .40
184 Ken Schrader's Car RW .02 .10
185 Dale Earnhardt .60 1.50
Teresa Earnhardt
186 Mark Martin's Car RW .15 .40
187 Dale Earnhart's Car RW .50 1.25
188 Terry Labonte's Car RW .07 .20
189 Mountain Dew Southern 500 .02 .10
Darlington Race Action
190 Rusty Wallace's Car RW .15 .40
191 Jeff Gordon in Pits RW .30 .75
192 Dale Earnhardt RW .60 1.50
193 Mark Martin RW .30 .75
194 Joe Nemechek's Car .02 .10
Race Action
195 Ward Burton RW .07 .20
196 Ricky Rudd RW .15 .40
197 Dale Earnhardt in Pits RW .50 1.25
198 David Green w/Car .07 .20
199 Sterling Marlin .15 .40
Paula Marlin
Steadman Marlin
Sutherlin Marlin RW
200 Dale Earnhardt's Car .15 .40
Jeff Gordon's Car
Rusty Wallace's Car
Jimmy Spencer's Car
Ken Schrader's Car
Winston Select Race Action
P1 Jeff Gordon Promo Sheet 1.50 3.00
five cards featured
NNO Checklist #1 .02 .10
NNO Checklist #2 .02 .10

1996 Ultra Autographs

This 37-card insert set features the top drivers or Winston Cup circuit. The autographed cards ha front and back design that looks like a card in regular set but the front of the card has a silver seal stating "Mark of Authenticity" in a ci surrounding the Ultra logo. The Ultra logo is different than the one used on the regular card fro The back has the words " Certified Autograph C and carries no number. An autograph redemp card was inserted one per 24 packs. This redemp card would have to be sent in to Fleer to obtain actual autograph card. The autograph redempti expired on 12/31/96.

COMPLETE SET (37) 500.00 1000
1 John Andretti 7.50 20
2 Johnny Benson 7.50 20
3 Brett Bodine 6.00 12
4 Geoff Bodine 6.00 12
5 Todd Bodine 6.00 15
6 Ward Burton 8.00 20
7 Derrike Cope 6.00 12
8 Ricky Craven 6.00 12
9 Dale Earnhardt 175.00 350
10 Bill Elliott 30.00 60
11 Jeff Gordon 60.00 120
12 Ernie Irvan 10.00 25
13 Dale Jarrett 20.00 50
14 Jason Keller 6.00 12
15 Bobby Labonte 12.50 30
16 Terry Labonte 12.50 30
17 Chad Little 7.50 20
18 Dave Marcis 7.50 20
19 Sterling Marlin 10.00 25
20 Mark Martin 12.50 30
21 Rick Mast 6.00 12
22 Jeremy Mayfield 7.50 20
23 Mike McLaughlin 6.00 12
24 Patty Moise 7.50 20
25 Ted Musgrave 6.00 12
26 Joe Nemechek 6.00 12
27 Kyle Petty 10.00 25
28 Richard Petty 40.00 80
29 Ricky Rudd 10.00 25
30 Elton Sawyer 6.00 12
31 Ken Schrader 7.50 20
32 Morgan Shepherd 6.00 12
33 Lake Speed 6.00 12
34 Jimmy Spencer 6.00 12
35 Dick Trickle 6.00 12
36 Rusty Wallace 12.50 30
37 Michael Waltrip 8.00 20

1996 Ultra Champions Club

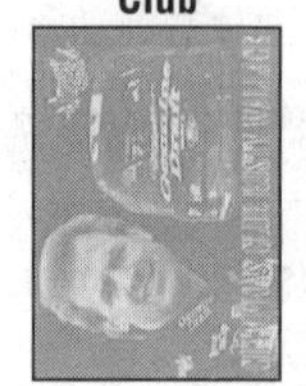

Randomly inserted in packs at a rate of one in this five-card set features former NASCAR Win Cup Champions. The cards are printed on silver board and show both a picture of the driver and current car they were driving.

COMPLETE SET (5) 5.00 12
1 Rusty Wallace 1.25 3
2 Dale Earnhardt 2.50 6
3 Bill Elliott .60 1
4 Terry Labonte .50 1
5 Jeff Gordon 1.50 4

1996 Ultra Flair Previe

This 10-card insert set pinpoints NASCAR's drivers of '95 in a preview of Fleer's super-prem Flair product line. Randomly inserted in packs rate of one in 12 packs, each of these cards feat 100 percent etched foil processing.

COMPLETE SET (10) 35.00 75
1 Jeff Gordon 5.00 12
2 Dale Earnhardt 8.00 20
3 Sterling Marlin 1.50 4
4 Mark Martin 4.00 10
5 Rusty Wallace 4.00 10
6 Terry Labonte 1.50 4
7 Ted Musgrave .50 1
8 Bill Elliott 2.00 5
9 Ricky Rudd 1.50 4
10 Bobby Labonte 3.00 8

1996 Ultra Golden Memories

This nine-card insert set highlights the '95 seas most memorable moments. The silver foil board cards are printed on uses a checkered flag ground behind every front photo. The cards randomly inserted in packs at a rate of one in

MPLETE SET (9)	6.00	15.00
nie Irvan	.50	1.25
ard Burton	.50	1.25
erling Marlin	.75	2.00
le Earnhardt	4.00	10.00
n Schrader	.25	.60
rry Labonte	.75	2.00
bby Labonte	1.50	4.00
rry Labonte	.75	2.00
hn Andretti	.25	.60

1996 Ultra Season Crowns

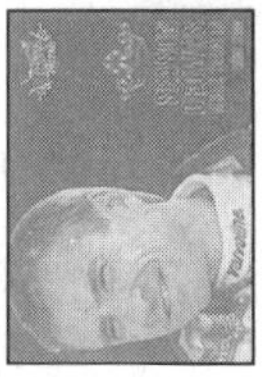

domly inserted in packs at a rate of one in four, 15-card insert set features statistical leaders in s such as wins, poles, most laps led and top 5 ners from '95.

MPLETE SET (15)	15.00	40.00
rry Labonte	.60	1.50
ff Gordon	2.00	5.00
le Earnhardt	3.00	8.00
ff Gordon	2.00	5.00
le Earnhardt	3.00	8.00
ark Martin	1.50	4.00
ff Gordon	2.00	5.00
ark Martin	1.50	4.00
le Earnhardt	3.00	8.00
eff Gordon	2.00	5.00
eff Gordon	2.00	5.00
Dale Earnhardt's Car	1.25	3.00
Jeff Gordon's Car		
Chad Little	.20	.50
David Green	.20	.50
Dale Earnhardt	3.00	8.00

996 Ultra Thunder and Lightning

10-card insert set features teams generating der on the tracks and lightning in the pits. The s use multi-colored foil backgrounds to bring he colors of NASCAR Winston Cup cars. The s could be found at a rate of one per four packs.

MPLETE SET (10)	5.00	12.00
ett Bodine's Car	.10	.30
ett Bodine's Car	.10	.30
ff Gordon's Car	1.00	2.50
ff Gordon's Car	1.00	2.50
le Earnhardt's Car	1.50	4.00
le Earnhardt's Car	1.50	4.00
erling Marlin's Car	.25	.60
erling Marlin's Car	.25	.60
bby Labonte's Car	.50	1.25
Bobby Labonte's Car	.50	1.25

1996 Ultra Update

1996 Ultra Update set was issued in one series ling 100 cards. The 10-card packs retail for 9 each. The set contains the topical subsets: CAR Winston Cup Drivers (1-33), NASCAR h Grand National Drivers (34-43), Hot Start (44- NASCAR Winston Cup Cars (47-79), Precious ls (80-83) and Fresh Start (84-98). The cards ure a large Ultra logo in gold foil as the drop. The set updates the first Ultra issue of 5 by providing shots of driver changes and sor changes. There were 24 packs per box and oxes per case.

PLETE SET (100)	8.00	20.00
hn Andretti	.07	.20
hnny Benson Jr.	.15	.40
ett Bodine	.07	.20
off Bodine	.07	.20
f Burton	.25	.60
ard Burton	.15	.40
rrike Cope	.07	.20
cky Craven	.07	.20
ally Dallenbach Jr.	.07	.20
ale Earnhardt	1.25	3.00
ill Elliott	.30	.75
eff Gordon	.75	2.00
teve Grissom	.07	.20
obby Hamilton	.07	.20
rnie Irvan	.15	.40
ale Jarrett	.40	1.00
obby Labonte	.40	1.00
18 Terry Labonte	.25	.60
19 Dave Marcis	.15	.40
20 Sterling Marlin	.25	.60
21 Mark Martin	.40	1.00
22 Rick Mast	.07	.20
23 Jeremy Mayfield	.15	.40
24 Ted Musgrave	.07	.20
25 Joe Nemechek	.07	.20
26 Kyle Petty	.15	.40
27 Robert Pressley	.07	.20
28 Ricky Rudd	.25	.60
29 Ken Schrader	.07	.20
30 Hut Stricklin	.07	.20
31 Kenny Wallace	.07	.20
32 Rusty Wallace	.50	1.25
33 Michael Waltrip	.15	.40
34 Glenn Allen Jr.	.07	.20
35 Rodney Combs	.07	.20
36 David Green	.07	.20
37 Randy LaJoie	.07	.20
38 Chad Little	.07	.20
39 Curtis Markham	.07	.20
40 Mike McLaughlin	.07	.20
41 Patty Moise	.07	.20
42 Phil Parsons	.07	.20
43 Jeff Purvis	.07	.20
44 Dale Jarrett HS	.15	.40
45 Dale Earnhardt HS	.60	1.50
46 Jeff Gordon HS	.40	1.00
47 John Andretti's Car	.02	.10
48 Johnny Benson's Car	.02	.10
49 Brett Bodine's Car	.02	.10
50 Geoff Bodine's Car	.02	.10
51 Jeff Burton's Car	.07	.20
52 Ward Burton's Car	.02	.10
53 Derrike Cope's Car	.02	.10
54 Ricky Craven's Car	.02	.10
55 Wally Dallenbach's Car	.02	.10
56 Dale Earnhardt's Car	.50	1.25
57 Bill Elliott's Car	.15	.40
58 Jeff Gordon's Car	.30	.75
59 Steve Grissom's Car	.02	.10
60 Bobby Hamilton's Car	.02	.10
61 Ernie Irvan's Car	.07	.20
62 Dale Jarrett's Car	.15	.40
63 Bobby Labonte's Car	.15	.40
64 Terry Labonte's Car	.15	.40
65 Dave Marcis' Car	.07	.20
66 Sterling Marlin's Car	.07	.20
67 Mark Martin's Car	.25	.60
68 Rick Mast's Car	.02	.10
69 Jeremy Mayfield's Car	.15	.40
70 Ted Musgrave's Car	.02	.10
71 Joe Nemechek's Car	.02	.10
72 Kyle Petty's Car	.07	.20
73 Robert Pressley's Car	.02	.10
74 Ricky Rudd's Car	.07	.20
75 Ken Schrader's Car	.02	.10
76 Hut Stricklin's Car	.02	.10
77 Kenny Wallace's Car	.02	.10
78 Rusty Wallace's Car	.15	.40
79 Michael Waltrip's Car	.07	.20
80 Dale Earnhardt Olympic Car	.15	.40
81 Terry Labonte Ironman Car	.15	.40
82 Bobby Hamilton 25th Anniversary	.02	.10
83 Brett Bodine Gold Car	.02	.10
84 Wally Dallenbach Jimmy Means	.02	.10
85 Jeff Burton Buddy Parrott	.07	.20
86 Dale Jarrett Todd Parrott	.15	.40
87 Hut Stricklin Philippe Lopez	.02	.10
88 Michael Waltrip Eddie Wood Leonard Wood	.15	.40
89 M.Shepherd 75 Team Remington Arms	.02	.10
90 Kenny Wallace	.07	.20
91 Ernie Irvan	.15	.40
92 Rick Mast	.07	.20
93 Geoff Bodine	.07	.20
94 Ricky Rudd Richard Broome	.15	.40
95 Brett Bodine Donnie Richeson	.02	.10
96 Dale Earnhardt David Smith	.60	1.50
97 Steve Grissom Bill Ingle	.02	.10
98 Johnny Benson	.15	.40
99 Checklist (1-100)	.02	.10
100 Checklist (inserts)	.02	.10
P1 Ernie Irvan Promo	.40	1.00

1996 Ultra Update Autographs

This 12-card insert set features the top names in NASCAR. The cards found in packs were redemption cards. These cards could be sent in to receive an autographed card of the driver who appeared on the front of the card. The redemption cards were seeded one in 100 packs.

COMPLETE SET (12)	400.00	800.00
1 Ricky Craven	6.00	12.00
2 Dale Earnhardt	175.00	350.00
3 Bill Elliott	30.00	60.00
4 Jeff Gordon	75.00	150.00
5 Ernie Irvan	10.00	25.00
6 Dale Jarrett	20.00	50.00
7 Bobby Labonte	12.50	30.00
8 Terry Labonte	12.50	30.00
9 Sterling Marlin	10.00	25.00
10 Mark Martin	15.00	40.00
11 Ted Musgrave	6.00	12.00
12 Rusty Wallace	20.00	50.00

1996 Ultra Update Proven Power

Randomly inserted in packs at a rate of one in 72, this 15-card set uses a reflective graphic design and

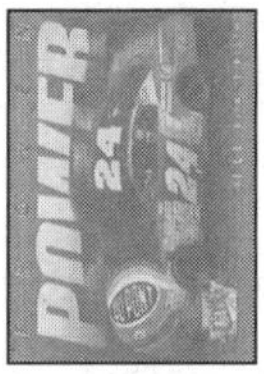

100 percent foil treatments to showcase the point leaders from the 1995 and 1996 seasons.

COMPLETE SET (15)	125.00	225.00
1 Ricky Craven	2.00	5.00
2 Dale Earnhardt	30.00	80.00
3 Bill Elliott	8.00	20.00
4 Jeff Gordon	20.00	50.00
5 Bobby Hamilton	2.00	5.00
6 Dale Jarrett	10.00	25.00
7 Bobby Labonte	10.00	25.00
8 Terry Labonte	6.00	15.00
9 Sterling Marlin	6.00	15.00
10 Mark Martin	10.00	25.00
11 Jeremy Mayfield	4.00	10.00
12 Ted Musgrave	2.00	5.00
13 Ricky Rudd	6.00	15.00
14 Ken Schrader	2.00	5.00
15 Rusty Wallace	12.50	30.00

1996 Ultra Update Rising Star

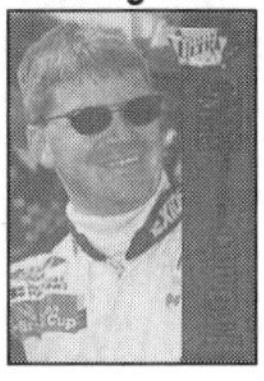

Randomly inserted in packs at a rate of one in four, this five-card set focuses on the newest drivers on the Winston Cup circuit. The cards use gold foil and thermo-embossed black ink to make the card have a tire like texture.

COMPLETE SET (5)	2.00	5.00
1 John Andretti	.40	1.00
2 Johnny Benson Jr.	.75	2.00
3 Jeff Burton	.75	2.00
4 Ricky Craven	.40	1.00
5 Jeremy Mayfield	.75	2.00

1996 Ultra Update Winner

Randomly inserted in packs at a rate of one in three, this 18-card set honors at least one winner from every track in the 1995 season. The cards feature a portrait of the winning driver on the front with track info and dates on the back.

COMPLETE SET (18)	12.00	30.00
1 Jeff Gordon	1.50	4.00
2 Terry Labonte	.50	1.25
3 Bobby Labonte	.75	2.00
4 Jeff Gordon	1.50	4.00
5 Sterling Marlin	.50	1.25
6 Kyle Petty	.30	.75
7 Dale Earnhardt	2.50	6.00
8 Rusty Wallace	1.00	2.50
9 Bobby Labonte	.75	2.00
10 Jeff Gordon	1.50	4.00
11 Mark Martin	.75	2.00
12 Ricky Rudd	.50	1.25
13 Dale Jarrett	.75	2.00
14 Terry Labonte	.50	1.25
15 Ward Burton	.30	.75
16 Dale Earnhardt	2.50	6.00
17 Sterling Marlin	.50	1.25
18 Mark Martin	.75	2.00

1996 Ultra Boxed Set

This 15-card set was issued by Fleer. The set was issued in a gray and black checkered box and features the top names in Winston Cup racing. The sets were primarily sold through retail mail order catalogs.

COMP. FACT SET (15)	7.50	15.00
1 Jeff Gordon	1.00	2.50
2 Dale Earnhardt	2.00	4.00
3 Sterling Marlin	.40	1.00
4 Mark Martin	.75	2.00
5 Rusty Wallace	.75	2.00
6 Terry Labonte	.50	1.25
7 Ted Musgrave	.15	.40
8 Bill Elliott	.50	1.25
9 Ricky Rudd	.40	1.00
10 Bobby Labonte	.60	1.50
11 Morgan Shepherd	.15	.40
12 Michael Waltrip	.25	.60
13 Dale Jarrett	.60	1.50
14 Bobby Hamilton	.15	.40
15 Derrike Cope	.15	.40

1997 Ultra

This 100-card set features the same popular design Fleer used for the Baseball and Football Ultra lines. The cards use full-bleed photography with UV

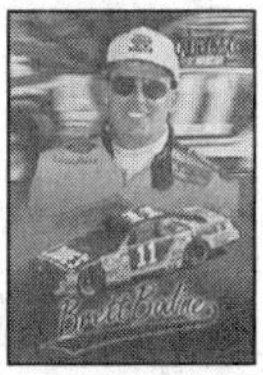

coating and foil stamping along with the driver's name written in script across the front of each card. The card contains an image of each driver and a still shot of his car superimposed over an action photo of the vehicle. There were 3,000 cases produced. The cards were packaged nine cards per pack, 24 packs per box and six boxes per case. There were three specially themed insert cards. Card number C1 is Terry Labonte, NASCAR Winston Cup Champion. The card was inserted at a rate of one in 180 packs. 500 of these cards were inserted into packs that carried an autograph redemption. Card number P1 is Bill Elliott, 1996 Most Popular Driver. This card was seeded one in 12 packs. Also, Johnny Benson, NASCAR Rookie of the Year, appears on card number R1. The Benson cards were randomly inserted one in 72 packs.

COMPLETE SET (100)	6.00	15.00
1 John Andretti	.07	.20
2 Johnny Benson	.15	.40
3 Brett Bodine	.07	.20
4 Geoff Bodine	.07	.20
5 Jeff Burton	.25	.60
6 Ward Burton	.15	.40
7 Derrike Cope	.07	.20
8 Ricky Craven	.07	.20
9 Wally Dallenbach	.07	.20
10 Dale Earnhardt	1.25	3.00
11 Bill Elliott	.30	.75
12 Jeff Gordon	.75	2.00
13 Bobby Hamilton	.07	.20
14 Bobby Hillin	.07	.20
15 Ernie Irvan	.15	.40
16 Dale Jarrett	.50	1.25
17 Bobby Labonte	.50	1.25
18 Terry Labonte	.25	.60
19 Dave Marcis	.15	.40
20 Sterling Marlin	.25	.60
21 Mark Martin	.60	1.50
22 Rick Mast	.07	.20
23 Jeremy Mayfield	.15	.40
24 Ted Musgrave	.07	.20
25 Joe Nemechek	.07	.20
26 Kyle Petty	.15	.40
27 Robert Pressley	.07	.20
28 Ricky Rudd	.25	.60
29 Ken Schrader	.07	.20
30 Morgan Shepherd	.07	.20
31 Lake Speed	.07	.20
32 Jimmy Spencer	.07	.20
33 Hut Stricklin	.07	.20
34 Dick Trickle	.07	.20
35 Kenny Wallace	.07	.20
36 Rusty Wallace	.60	1.50
37 Michael Waltrip	.15	.40
38 Robby Gordon's Car	.15	.40
39 Terry Labonte's Car	.15	.40
40 Dale Jarrett's Car	.15	.40
41 Jeff Gordon's Car	.30	.75
42 Mark Martin's Car	.25	.60
43 Dale Earnhardt's Car	.50	1.25
44 Ricky Rudd's Car	.07	.20
45 Sterling Marlin's Car	.07	.20
46 Rusty Wallace's Car	.25	.60
47 Bobby Hamilton's Car	.02	.10
48 Bill Elliott's Car	.15	.40
49 Bobby Labonte's Car	.15	.40
50 Jeremy Mayfield's Car	.15	.40
51 Johnny Benson's Car	.02	.10
52 Ted Musgrave's Car	.02	.10
53 Ricky Craven's Car	.02	.10
54 Ernie Irvan's Car	.07	.20
55 Michael Waltrip's Car	.07	.20
56 Jeff Burton's Car	.07	.20
57 Jimmy Spencer's Car	.02	.10
58 Bobby Allison	.07	.20
59 Richard Childress	.15	.40
60 Joe Gibbs	.15	.40
61 Rick Hendrick	.02	.10
62 Richard Petty	.25	.60
63 Jack Roush	.02	.10
64 Robert Yates	.02	.10
65 Cale Yarborough	.07	.20
66 Steve Hmiel	.02	.10
67 Mike Beam	.02	.10
68 David Smith	.02	.10
69 Eddie Wood Len Wood	.02	.10
70 Ray Evernham	.15	.40
71 Todd Parrott	.02	.10
72 Larry McReynolds	.02	.10
73 Tech Talk - Tires	.02	.10
74 Tech Talk - Fuel Cell	.02	.10
75 Tech Talk - Roof Flaps	.02	.10
76 Tech Talk - Motor	.02	.10
77 Tech Talk - Seat	.02	.10
78 Tech Talk - Rear Spoiler	.02	.10
79 Tech Talk - Generator	.02	.10
80 Tech Talk - Jack Stob	.02	.10
81 Tech Talk - Track Bar Hole	.02	.10
82 Todd Bodine	.07	.20
83 David Green	.07	.20
84 Jeff Green	.07	.20
85 Jason Keller	.07	.20
86 Randy LaJoie	.07	.20
87 Chad Little	.07	.20
88 Curtis Markham	.07	.20
89 Phil Parsons	.07	.20
90 Larry Pearson	.07	.20
91 Jeff Purvis	.07	.20
92 Mike McLaughlin	.07	.20
93 Patty Moise	.07	.20
94 Glenn Allen	.07	.20
95 Kevin Lepage	.07	.20
96 Rodney Combs	.07	.20
97 Tim Fedewa	.07	.20
98 Dennis Setzer	.07	.20
99 Checklist	.02	.10
100 Checklist	.02	.10
C1 Terry Labonte	8.00	20.00
C1A Terry Labonte Auto	60.00	120.00
P1 Bill Elliott	1.00	2.50
R1 Johnny Benson	2.50	6.00
S1 Mark Martin Sample	1.25	3.00

1997 Ultra AKA

This 10-card insert set captures the personalities of racing's very best drivers. The cards were randomly seeded one in 24 packs.

COMPLETE SET (10)	40.00	80.00
A1 Dale Earnhardt	12.50	30.00
A2 Jeff Gordon	8.00	20.00
A3 Terry Labonte	2.50	6.00
A4 Dale Jarrett	5.00	12.00
A5 Bill Elliott	3.00	8.00
A6 Mark Martin	6.00	15.00
A7 Bobby Labonte	5.00	12.00
A8 Ernie Irvan	1.50	4.00
A9 Rusty Wallace	6.00	15.00
A10 Ricky Craven	.75	2.00

1997 Ultra Inside Out

This 15-card set uses laser-cut technology to bring the action inside the car to life. The cards feature top names in NASCAR and were inserted one in six packs.

COMPLETE SET (15)	25.00	60.00
DC1 Dale Earnhardt	8.00	20.00
DC2 Jeff Gordon	5.00	12.00
DC3 Terry Labonte	1.50	4.00
DC4 Dale Jarrett	3.00	8.00
DC5 Bill Elliott	2.00	5.00
DC6 Sterling Marlin	1.50	4.00
DC7 Mark Martin	4.00	10.00
DC8 Ernie Irvan	1.00	2.50
DC9 Rusty Wallace	4.00	10.00
DC10 Johnny Benson	1.00	2.50
DC11 Ricky Rudd	1.50	4.00
DC12 Bobby Labonte	3.00	8.00
DC13 Ricky Craven	.50	1.25
DC14 Bobby Hamilton	.50	1.25
DC15 Michael Waltrip	1.00	2.50

1997 Ultra Shoney's

This 16-card set was offered through a special promotion at Shoney's restaurants. These cards maintain the same design of the 1997 Ultra cards with the exception of the Shoney's logo on the top part of the card back.

COMPLETE SET (16)	8.00	20.00
1 Johnny Benson	.30	.75
2 Ward Burton	.30	.75
3 Dale Earnhardt	3.00	8.00
4 Jeff Gordon	1.50	4.00
5 Bobby Hamilton	.30	.75
6 Dale Jarrett	1.00	2.50
7 Bobby Labonte	1.00	2.50
8 Terry Labonte	.60	1.50
9 Sterling Marlin	.50	1.25
10 Mark Martin	1.25	3.00
11 Ted Musgrave	.30	.75
12 Ricky Rudd	.50	1.25
13 Michael Waltrip	.50	1.25
14 Hut Stricklin	.30	.75
15 Richard Petty	.60	1.50
16 Randy LaJoie	.30	.75

1997 Ultra Update

This 97-card set was the second Ultra NASCAR set issued in 1997. The cards were distributed in nine card packs with 24 packs per box and 6 and 12 boxes per case. The packs carried a suggested retail price of $2.49.

COMPLETE SET (97)	8.00	20.00
1 Jeff Gordon	.75	2.00
2 Dale Earnhardt	1.25	3.00
3 Dale Jarrett	.50	1.25
4 Mark Martin	.60	1.50
5 Terry Labonte	.25	.60
6 Bill Elliott	.30	.75
7 Rusty Wallace	.60	1.50
8 Ernie Irvan	.15	.40
9 Sterling Marlin	.25	.60
10 Bobby Hamilton	.08	.20
11 Bobby Labonte	.50	1.25
12 John Andretti	.08	.20
13 Robby Gordon RC	.25	.60
14 Ken Schrader	.08	.20
15 Michael Waltrip	.15	.40
16 Ted Musgrave	.08	.20
17 Ricky Rudd	.25	.60
18 Johnny Benson	.15	.40
19 Jeremy Mayfield	.15	.40
20 Derrike Cope	.08	.20
21 Ricky Craven	.08	.20
22 Steve Grissom	.08	.20
23 Rick Mast	.08	.20
24 Dick Trickle	.08	.20
25 Kenny Wallace	.08	.20
26 Hut Stricklin	.08	.20
27 Joe Nemechek	.08	.20
28 David Green	.08	.20
29 Morgan Shepherd	.08	.20
30 Bobby Hillin	.08	.20
31 Glenn Jarrett	.04	.10
32 Ned Jarrett	.08	.20
33 Benny Parsons	.04	.10
34 Dr. Jerry Punch	.04	.10
35 Dave Despain	.04	.10
36 Bill Weber	.04	.10
37 Ken Squire	.04	.10
38 Jack Arute	.04	.10
39 Larry McReynolds	.04	.10
40 Ray Evernham	.15	.40
41 Mike Beam	.04	.10
42 Gary DeHart	.04	.10
43 Jimmy Fennig	.04	.10
44 Marc Reno	.04	.10
45 Joe Gibbs	.15	.40
46 Cale Yarborough	.04	.10
47 Richard Petty	.25	.60
48 Andy Petree	.04	.10
49 Rick Hendrick	.04	.10
50 Richard Childress	.15	.40
51 Robert Yates	.04	.10
52 Jack Roush	.04	.10
53 Ron Barfield	.04	.10
54 Todd Bodine	.08	.20
55 Tim Fedewa	.08	.20
56 Jeff Fuller	.08	.20
57 Jeff Green	.08	.20
58 Jason Keller	.08	.20
59 Randy LaJoie	.08	.20
60 Tracy Leslie	.08	.20
61 Kevin Lepage	.08	.20
62 Mike McLaughlin	.08	.20
63 Steve Park RC	3.00	6.00
64 Phil Parsons	.08	.20
65 Elton Sawyer	.08	.20
66 Glenn Allen	.08	.20
67 Tech Talk Helmet	.04	.10
68 Tech Talk Front Grille	.04	.10
69 Tech Talk Ground Clearance	.04	.10
70 Tech Talk Air Filters	.04	.10
71 Tech Talk Springs	.04	.10
72 Tech Talk Dashboard	.04	.10
73 Tech Talk Fuel Fillers	.04	.10
74 Tech Talk Gloves	.04	.10
75 Tech Talk War Wagon	.04	.10
76 Rusty Wallace's Car	.25	.60
77 Dale Earnhardt's Car	.50	1.25
78 Sterling Marlin's Car	.08	.20
79 Terry Labonte's Car	.15	.40
80 Mark Martin's Car	.25	.60
81 Hut Stricklin's Car	.04	.10
82 Ricky Rudd's Car	.08	.20
83 Ted Musgrave's Car	.04	.10
84 Bobby Labonte's Car	.15	.40
85 Michael Waltrip's Car	.08	.20
86 Jeff Gordon's Car	.30	.75
87 Ricky Craven's Car	.04	.10
88 Ernie Irvan's Car	.15	.40
89 Johnny Benson's Car	.04	.10
90 Ken Schrader's Car	.04	.10
91 Jeremy Mayfield's Car	.15	.40
92 Steve Grissom's Car	.04	.10
93 Bobby Hamilton's Car	.04	.10
94 Dale Jarrett's Car	.15	.40
95 Bill Elliott's Car	.15	.40
96 Checklist	.04	.10
97 Checklist	.04	.10

1997 Ultra Update Autographs

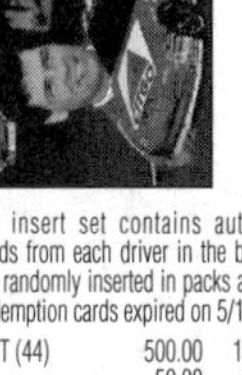

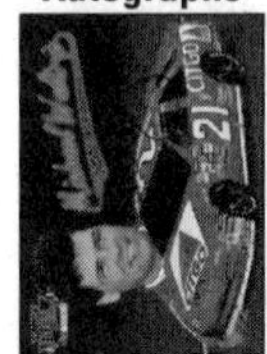

This 44-card insert set contains autograph redemption cards from each driver in the base set. The cards were randomly inserted in packs at a ratio of 1:25. The redemption cards expired on 5/1/98.

COMPLETE SET (44)	500.00	1000.00
1 Jeff Gordon	50.00	120.00
2 Dale Earnhardt	150.00	300.00
3 Dale Jarrett	25.00	50.00
4 Mark Martin	30.00	60.00
5 Terry Labonte	12.50	30.00
6 Bill Elliott	30.00	60.00
7 Rusty Wallace	15.00	30.00
8 Ernie Irvan	12.50	30.00
9 Sterling Marlin	15.00	40.00
10 Bobby Hamilton	10.00	25.00

11 Bobby Labonte	12.50	30.00
12 John Andretti	10.00	25.00
13 Robby Gordon	10.00	25.00
14 Ken Schrader	10.00	25.00
15 Michael Waltrip	8.00	20.00
16 Ted Musgrave	10.00	25.00
17 Ricky Rudd	12.50	30.00
18 Johnny Benson	10.00	25.00
19 Jeremy Mayfield	10.00	25.00
20 Derrike Cope	7.50	15.00
21 Ricky Craven	7.50	15.00
22 Steve Grissom	7.50	15.00
23 Rick Mast	7.50	15.00
24 Dick Trickle	7.50	15.00
25 Kenny Wallace	7.50	15.00
26 Hut Stricklin	7.50	15.00
27 Joe Nemechek	7.50	15.00
28 David Green	7.50	15.00
29 Morgan Shepherd	7.50	15.00
30 Bobby Hillin	7.50	15.00
53 Ron Barfield	7.50	15.00
54 Todd Bodine	7.50	15.00
55 Tim Fedewa	7.50	15.00
56 Jeff Fuller	7.50	15.00
57 Jeff Green	7.50	15.00
58 Jason Keller	7.50	15.00
59 Randy LaJoie	7.50	15.00
60 Tracy Leslie	7.50	15.00
61 Kevin Lepage	7.50	15.00
62 Mike McLaughlin	7.50	15.00
63 Steve Park	12.50	30.00
64 Phil Parsons	7.50	15.00
65 Elton Sawyer	7.50	15.00
66 Glenn Allen	7.50	15.00

1997 Ultra Update Double Trouble

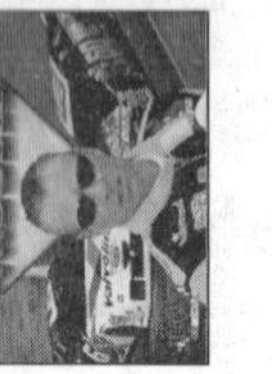

This eight-card insert set features top drivers on both the Winston Cup and Busch circuits. The cards were randomly inserted in packs at a stated ratio of 1:4.

COMPLETE SET (8)	4.00	10.00
DT1 Mark Martin	2.50	6.00
DT2 Dick Trickle	.30	.75
DT3 Bobby Labonte	2.00	5.00
DT4 Ricky Craven	.30	.75
DT5 Michael Waltrip	.60	1.50
DT6 Dale Jarrett	2.00	5.00
DT7 Terry Labonte	1.00	2.50
DT8 Joe Nemechek	.30	.75

1997 Ultra Update Driver View

This 10-card insert set offers an up-close view, with laser cut cards, into the window net of some of the top Winston Cup stars. The cards were randomly inserted in packs at a ratio of 1:8.

COMPLETE SET (10)	15.00	40.00
D1 Jeff Gordon	5.00	12.00
D2 Dale Jarrett	3.00	8.00
D3 Bill Elliott	2.00	5.00
D4 Bobby Labonte	3.00	8.00
D5 Sterling Marlin	1.50	4.00
D6 Dale Earnhardt	8.00	20.00
D7 Mark Martin	4.00	10.00
D8 Terry Labonte	1.50	4.00
D9 Ricky Rudd	1.50	4.00
D10 Bobby Hamilton	.50	1.25

1997 Ultra Update Elite Seats

This 10-card set features ten of the top drivers on the Winston Cup circuit on special 40-point stock cards. The cards were randomly inserted in packs at a ratio of 1:12.

COMPLETE SET (10)	25.00	60.00
E1 Jeff Gordon	5.00	12.00
E2 Dale Earnhardt	8.00	20.00
E3 Bill Elliott	2.00	5.00
E4 Ernie Irvan	1.00	2.50
E5 Ricky Rudd	1.50	4.00
E6 Dale Jarrett	3.00	8.00
E7 Terry Labonte	1.50	4.00
E8 Mark Martin	4.00	10.00
E9 Rusty Wallace	4.00	10.00
E10 Ricky Craven	.50	1.25

1983 UNO Racing

This 30-card promotional set features UNO sponsored cars from 1980-83 and the drivers who drove them. The cards usually have a photo of the driver standing next to the UNO car on the front of the card. The back of the card has the UNO logo and looks like a card from an UNO card game. The sets were originally distributed via give aways.

COMPLETE SET (30)	125.00	250.00
1 Tim Richmond	2.50	6.00
2 Neil Bonnett	5.00	12.00
3 Tim Richmond	2.50	6.00
4 Lake Speed	1.50	4.00
5 D.K. Ulrich	1.50	4.00
6 Tim Richmond	2.50	6.00
7 Buddy Baker Ron Bouchard	1.50	4.00
8 Tim Richmond	2.50	6.00
9 Tim Richmond	2.50	6.00
10 Tim Richmond	2.50	6.00
11 Buddy Baker	1.50	4.00
12 Tim Richmond	2.50	6.00
13 Kyle Petty	2.50	6.00
14 Lake Speed	1.50	4.00
15 Tim Richmond	2.50	6.00
16 Kyle Petty	2.50	6.00
17 Tim Richmond	2.50	6.00
18 Tim Richmond	2.50	6.00
19 Kyle Petty	2.50	6.00
20 Buddy Baker	1.50	4.00
21 Buddy Baker	1.50	4.00
22 Tim Richmond	2.50	6.00
23 Richard Petty	15.00	30.00
24 Tim Richmond	2.50	6.00
25 Buddy Baker	1.50	4.00
26 Tim Richmond	2.50	6.00
27 Dale Earnhardt	50.00	80.00
28 Darrell Waltrip	2.50	6.00
29 Bobby Allison	2.50	6.00
30 Buddy Baker	1.50	4.00

1995 Upper Deck

Issued in two series over the first half of 1995, Upper Deck released both products through 10-card packs with 36-packs per box. Both series included several insert sets including the popular Predictor redemption cards and one Silver or Gold parallel card in every pack. Series one hobby packs featured a Jeff Gordon Salute card randomly inserted (1:108 packs) and the retail version a Sterling Marlin Salute (1:108 packs). A special Sterling Marlin Back-to-Back Salute card was randomly seeded in series two retail packs (1:108). As with most Upper Deck issues, subsets abound. Series one included Championship Pit Crew, Star Rookies, Images of '95 and Next in Line. Series two featured New for '95, Did You Know, Speedway Legends and more Star Rookies.

COMPLETE SET (300)	12.50	30.00
COMP.SERIES 1 SET (150)	8.00	20.00
COMP.SERIES 2 SET (150)	6.00	15.00
WAX BOX HOBBY SER.1	20.00	50.00
WAX BOX HOBBY SER.2	20.00	50.00
1 Rusty Wallace	.60	1.50
2 Jeff Gordon	.75	2.00
3 Bill Elliott	.30	.75
4 Kyle Petty	.15	.40
5 Darrell Waltrip	.15	.40
6 Ernie Irvan	.15	.40
7 Dale Jarrett	.50	1.25
8 Mark Martin	.60	1.50
9 Michael Waltrip	.15	.40
10 Rick Mast	.07	.20
11 Sterling Marlin	.25	.60
12 Chad Little	.07	.20
13 Geoff Bodine	.07	.20
14 Ricky Rudd	.25	.60
15 Lake Speed	.07	.20
16 Ted Musgrave	.07	.20
17 Morgan Shepherd	.07	.20
18 Bobby Labonte	.50	1.25
19 Ken Schrader	.07	.20
20 Brett Bodine	.07	.20
21 Jimmy Spencer	.07	.20
22 Harry Gant	.15	.40
23 Dick Trickle	.07	.20
24 Derrike Cope	.07	.20
25 Kenny Wallace	.07	.20
26 Jeff Burton	.25	.60
27 Chuck Bown	.07	.20
28 John Andretti	.07	.20
29 Loy Allen Jr.	.07	.20
30 Hut Stricklin	.07	.20
31 Steve Grissom	.07	.20
32 Ward Burton	.15	.40
33 Robert Pressley	.07	.20
34 Joe Nemechek	.07	.20
35 Wally Dallenbach Jr.	.07	.20
36 Jeff Purvis	.07	.20
37 Terry Labonte	.25	.60
38 Jimmy Hensley	.07	.20
39 Dave Marcis	.07	.20
40 Todd Bodine	.07	.20
41 Greg Sacks	.07	.20
42 Mike Wallace	.07	.20
43 Jeremy Mayfield	.15	.40
44 Rusty Wallace with Car	.30	.75
45 Jeff Gordon with Car	.40	1.00
46 Bill Elliott with Car	.15	.40
47 Kyle Petty with Car	.15	.40
48 Darrell Waltrip with Car	.15	.40
49 Ernie Irvan with Car	.15	.40
50 Dale Jarrett with Car	.25	.60
51 Mark Martin with Car	.30	.75
52 Michael Waltrip with Car	.15	.40
53 Rick Mast with Car	.07	.20
54 Sterling Marlin with Car	.15	.40
55 Chad Little with Car	.07	.20
56 Geoff Bodine with Car	.07	.20
57 Ricky Rudd with Car	.15	.40
58 Lake Speed with Car	.07	.20
59 Ted Musgrave with Car	.07	.20
60 Morgan Shepherd with Car	.07	.20
61 Bobby Labonte with Car	.25	.60
62 Ken Schrader with Car	.07	.20
63 Brett Bodine with Car	.07	.20
64 Jimmy Spencer with Car	.07	.20
65 Harry Gant with Car	.15	.40
66 Dick Trickle with Car	.07	.20
67 Jeremy Mayfield with Car	.07	.20
68 Kenny Wallace with Car	.07	.20
69 Rusty Wallace's Car	.25	.60
70 Jeff Gordon's Car	.30	.75
71 Bill Elliott's Car	.15	.40
72 Kyle Petty's Car	.07	.20
73 Darrell Waltrip's Car	.07	.20
74 Ernie Irvan's Car	.07	.20
75 Dale Jarrett's Car	.15	.40
76 Mark Martin's Car	.25	.60
77 Michael Waltrip's Car	.07	.20
78 Rick Mast's Car	.02	.10
79 Sterling Marlin's Car	.07	.20
80 Chad Little's Car	.02	.10
81 Geoff Bodine's Car	.02	.10
82 Ricky Rudd's Car	.07	.20
83 Lake Speed's Car	.02	.10
84 Ted Musgrave's Car	.02	.10
85 Morgan Shepherd's Car	.02	.10
86 Bobby Labonte's Car	.25	.60
87 Ken Schrader's Car	.02	.10
88 Brett Bodine's Car	.02	.10
89 Jimmy Spencer's Car	.02	.10
90 Harry Gant's Car	.07	.20
91 Dick Trickle's Car	.02	.10
92 Derrike Cope's Car	.02	.10
93 Kenny Wallace's Car	.02	.10
94 Jeff Burton's Car	.07	.20
95 Chuck Bown's Car	.02	.10
96 John Andretti's Car	.02	.10
97 Loy Allen Jr.'s Car	.02	.10
98 Hut Stricklin's Car	.02	.10
99 Steve Grissom's Car	.02	.10
100 Ward Burton's Car	.07	.20
101 Robert Pressley's Car	.02	.10
102 Joe Nemechek's Car	.02	.10
103 Wally Dallenbach Jr.'s Car	.02	.10
104 Jeff Purvis' Car	.02	.10
105 Terry Labonte's Car	.15	.40
106 Jimmy Hensley's Car	.02	.10
107 Dave Marcis' Car	.07	.20
108 Todd Bodine's Car	.02	.10
109 Greg Sacks' Car	.02	.10
110 Mike Wallace's Car	.02	.10
111 Jeremy Mayfield's Car	.07	.20
112 Rick Mast's Car NIL	.02	.10
113 Sterling Marlin's Car NIL	.07	.20
114 Bobby Labonte's Car NIL	.25	.60
115 Geoff Bodine NIL	.07	.20
116 Ricky Rudd's Car NIL	.07	.20
117 Lake Speed's Car NIL	.02	.10
118 Ted Musgrave's Car NIL	.02	.10
119 Morgan Shepherd's Car NIL	.02	.10
120 Ward Burton's Car NIL	.07	.20
121 Ken Schrader's Car NIL	.02	.10
122 Brett Bodine's Car NIL	.02	.10
123 Jimmy Spencer's Car NIL	.02	.10
124 Dick Trickle's Car NIL	.02	.10
125 Derrike Cope's Car NIL	.02	.10
126 Kenny Wallace NIL	.07	.20
127 John Andretti	.07	.20
128 Ward Burton	.15	.40
129 Steve Grissom	.07	.20
130 Jeremy Mayfield	.15	.40
131 Jeff Burton	.25	.60
132 Joe Nemechek	.07	.20
133 Michael Jordan CPC	2.50	6.00
134 Reggie Jackson CPC	.15	.40
135 Joe Montana CPC	2.00	5.00
136 Ken Griffey Jr. CPC	2.00	5.00
137 Rusty Wallace's Car	.25	.60
138 Jeff Gordon's Car	.30	.75
139 Bill Elliott's Car	.15	.40
140 Kyle Petty's Car	.07	.20
141 Darrell Waltrip's Car	.07	.20
142 Ernie Irvan's Car	.07	.20
143 Dale Jarrett's Car	.15	.40
144 Mark Martin's Car	.25	.60
145 Michael Waltrip's Car	.07	.20
146 Ford Engine	.02	.10
147 Chevy Engine	.02	.10
148 Pontiac Engine	.02	.10
149 Rusty Wallace CL	.15	.40
150 Rusty Wallace CL	.15	.40
151 Richard Petty SL	.25	.60
152 Cale Yarborough SL	.07	.20
153 Junior Johnson SL	.07	.20
154 Harry Gant SL	.07	.20
155 Bobby Allison SL	.07	.20
156 David Pearson SL	.07	.20
157 Ned Jarrett SL	.07	.20
158 Glen Wood SL	.02	.10
159 Benny Parsons SL	.07	.20
160 Smokey Yunick SL	.02	.10
161 Rusty Wallace DYK	.30	.75
162 Terry Labonte DYK	.15	.40
163 Jeff Gordon DYK	.40	1.00
164 Mark Martin DYK	.30	.75
165 Dale Jarrett DYK	.25	.60
166 Geoff Bodine DYK	.07	.20
167 Ricky Rudd DYK	.15	.40
168 Jeff Burton DYK	.07	.20
169 Sterling Marlin DYK	.15	.40
170 Darrell Waltrip DYK	.15	.40
171 Bobby Labonte DYK	.25	.60
172 Ken Schrader DYK	.07	.20
173 Kyle Petty DYK	.15	.40
174 John Andretti DYK	.07	.20
175 Ted Musgrave DYK	.07	.20
176 Randy LaJoie SR	.07	.20
177 Steve Kinser SR	.07	.20
178 Robert Pressley SR	.07	.20
179 Ricky Craven SR	.07	.20
180 Davy Jones SR	.07	.20
181 Rick Mast	.07	.20
182 Rusty Wallace	.60	1.50
183 Rusty Wallace	.60	1.50
184 Sterling Marlin	.25	.60
185 Terry Labonte	.25	.60
186 Terry Labonte	.25	.60
187 Mark Martin	.60	1.50
188 Mark Martin	.60	1.50
189 Geoff Bodine	.07	.20
190 Jeff Burton	.25	.60
191 Lake Speed	.07	.20
192 Ricky Rudd	.25	.60
193 Brett Bodine	.07	.20
194 Derrike Cope	.07	.20
195 Dick Trickle	.07	.20
196 Ted Musgrave	.07	.20
197 Darrell Waltrip	.15	.40
198 Bobby Labonte	.50	1.25
199 Morgan Shepherd	.07	.20
200 Randy LaJoie	.07	.20
201 Jimmy Spencer	.07	.20
202 Jeff Gordon	.75	2.00
203 Ken Schrader	.07	.20
204 Steve Kinser	.07	.20
205 Loy Allen Jr.	.07	.20
206 Dale Jarrett	.50	1.25
207 Ernie Irvan	.15	.40
208 Steve Grissom	.07	.20
209 Michael Waltrip	.15	.40
210 Ward Burton	.15	.40
211 Jimmy Hensley	.07	.20
212 Robert Pressley	.07	.20
213 John Andretti	.07	.20
214 Greg Sacks	.07	.20
215 Ricky Craven	.07	.20
216 Kyle Petty	.15	.40
217 Jeff Purvis	.07	.20
218 Gary Bradberry	.07	.20
219 Dave Marcis	.07	.20
220 Todd Bodine	.07	.20
221 Davy Jones	.07	.20
222 Kenny Wallace	.07	.20
223 Joe Nemechek	.07	.20
224 Mike Wallace	.07	.20
225 Bill Elliott	.30	.75
226 Chad Little	.07	.20
227 Jeremy Mayfield	.15	.40
228 Rick Mast SD	.07	.20
229 Rusty Wallace SD	.30	.75
230 Sterling Marlin SD	.15	.40
231 Terry Labonte SD	.15	.40
232 Mark Martin SD	.30	.75
233 Geoff Bodine SD	.07	.20
234 Jeff Burton SD	.15	.40
235 Lake Speed SD	.07	.20
236 Ricky Rudd SD	.15	.40
237 Brett Bodine SD	.07	.20
238 Derrike Cope SD	.07	.20
239 Dick Trickle SD	.07	.20
240 Ted Musgrave SD	.07	.20
241 Darrell Waltrip SD	.15	.40
242 Bobby Labonte SD	.25	.60
243 Morgan Shepherd SD	.07	.20
244 Randy LaJoie SD	.07	.20
245 Jimmy Spencer SD	.07	.20
246 Jeff Gordon SD	.40	1.00
247 Ken Schrader SD	.07	.20
248 Steve Kinser SD	.07	.20
249 Loy Allen Jr. SD	.07	.20
250 Dale Jarrett SD	.25	.60
251 Steve Grissom SD	.07	.20
252 Michael Waltrip SD	.15	.40
253 Ward Burton SD	.15	.40
254 Jimmy Hensley SD	.07	.20
255 Robert Pressley SD	.07	.20
256 John Andretti SD	.07	.20
257 Greg Sacks SD	.07	.20
258 Ricky Craven SD	.07	.20
259 Kyle Petty SD	.15	.40
260 Gary Bradberry SD	.07	.20
261 Dave Marcis SD	.07	.20
262 Todd Bodine SD	.07	.20
263 Davy Jones SD	.07	.20
264 Kenny Wallace SD	.07	.20
265 Joe Nemechek SD	.07	.20
266 Mike Wallace SD	.07	.20
267 Bill Elliott SD	.15	.40
268 Chad Little SD	.07	.20
269 Jeremy Mayfield SD	.07	.20
270 Rusty Wallace's Car	.25	.60
271 Sterling Marlin's Car	.07	.20
272 Terry Labonte's Car	.15	.40
273 Geoff Bodine's Car	.02	.10
274 Jeff Burton's Car	.07	.20
275 Brett Bodine's Car	.02	.10
276 Dick Trickle's Car	.02	.10
277 Ted Musgrave's Car	.02	.10
278 Darrell Waltrip's Car	.07	.20
279 Bobby Labonte's Car	.07	.20
280 Randy LaJoie's Car	.02	.10
281 Jeff Gordon's Car	.30	.75
282 Ken Schrader's Car	.02	.10
283 Steve Kinser's Car	.02	.10
284 Loy Allen Jr.'s Car	.02	.10
285 Dale Jarrett's Car	.15	.40
286 Steve Grissom's Car	.02	.10
287 Jimmy Hensley's Car	.02	.10
288 Robert Pressley's Car	.02	.10
289 John Andretti's Car	.02	.10
290 Greg Sacks' Car	.02	.10
291 Ricky Craven's Car	.07	.20
292 Kyle Petty's Car	.07	.20
293 Jeff Purvis' Car	.02	.10
294 Gary Bradberry's Car	.02	.10
295 Dave Marcis' Car	.07	.20
296 Davy Jones' Car	.02	.10
297 Kenny Wallace's Car	.02	.10
298 Joe Nemechek's Car	.02	.10
299 Bill Elliott's Car	.15	.40
300 Checklist (151-300)	.02	.10
UD1 Sterling Marlin Salute	8.00	20.00
UD2 Jeff Gordon Salute	12.50	30.00
UD3 Sterling Marlin BB Salute	6.00	15.00
RW1 Rusty Wallace Promo Series One Silver Foil	.75	2.00
PR1 Rusty Wallace Promo Series One Gold Foil	.75	2.00
PR2 Rusty Wallace Promo Series Two Silver Foil	.75	2.00

1995 Upper Deck Gold Signature/Electric Gold

Gold parallel cards were produced for both series of 1995 Upper Deck -- Gold Signature for series one and Electric Gold for series two. The parallel versions look very similar to the regular issue Upper Deck cards with the addition of either a gold foil facsimile signature or the word "Electric" in gold foil on the card fronts. The Gold cards were randomly inserted at the wrapper stated rate of 1:35 packs for either series.

COMPLETE GOLD SET (300)	350.00	700.00
COMP.GOLD SIG.SET (150)	200.00	400.00
COMP. ELE.GOLD SET (150)	150.00	300.00
*GOLD STARS: 8X TO 20X BASE CARDS		

1995 Upper Deck Silver Signature/Electric Silver

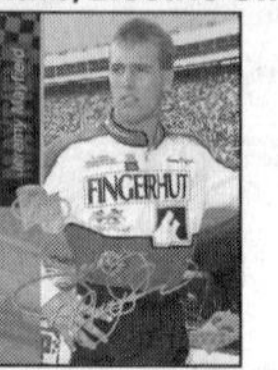

Silver parallel cards were produced for both series of 1995 Upper Deck -- Silver Signature for series one and Electric Silver for series two. The parallel versions look very similar to the regular issue Upper Deck cards with the addition of either a silver foil facsimile signature or the word "Electric" in refractive silver foil on the card fronts. The Silver cards were inserted at the wrapper stated rate of one per hobby or retail pack for either series and two per magazine distributor pack.

COMPLETE SILVER SET (300)	25.00	60.00
*SILVERS: .8X TO 2X BASE CARDS		

1995 Upper Deck Autographs

Randomly inserted in series two 1995 Upper Deck, the Autograph inserts were seeded approximately 1:300 packs. Reportedly, over 5000 total cards were signed for inclusion in packs.

COMPLETE SET (30)	700.00	1200.00
181 Rick Mast	8.00	20.00
182 Rusty Wallace	12.50	30.00
186 Terry Labonte	15.00	40.00
187 Mark Martin	30.00	60.00
189 Geoff Bodine	8.00	20.00
190 Jeff Burton	12.50	30.00
191 Lake Speed	8.00	20.00
195 Dick Trickle	8.00	20.00
196 Ted Musgrave	8.00	20.00
197 Darrell Waltrip	20.00	50.00
199 Morgan Shepherd	8.00	20.00
201 Jimmy Spencer	12.50	30.00
202 Jeff Gordon	125.00	250.00
205 Loy Allen Jr.	8.00	20.00
206 Dale Jarrett	25.00	60.00
207 Ernie Irvan	20.00	40.00
208 Steve Grissom	8.00	20.00
209 Michael Waltrip	8.00	20.00
210 Ward Burton	20.00	40.00
212 Robert Pressley	8.00	20.00
213 John Andretti	8.00	20.00
214 Greg Sacks	8.00	20.00
215 Ricky Craven	12.50	30.00
216 Kyle Petty	25.00	50.00
219 Dave Marcis	12.50	30.00
220 Todd Bodine	8.00	20.00
222 Kenny Wallace	8.00	20.00
223 Joe Nemechek	8.00	20.00
224 Mike Wallace	8.00	20.00
225 Bill Elliott	30.00	60.00

1995 Upper Deck Illustrations

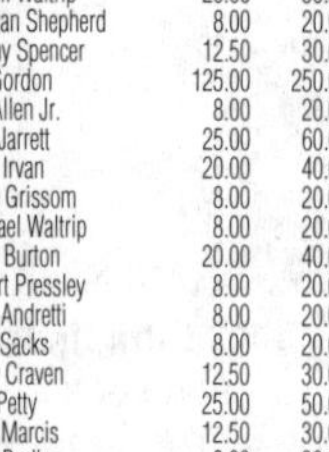

Illustrations cards were randomly inserted in Upper Deck series two hobby packs at the rate of 1:15 packs. The cards feature portraits of ten legendary drivers painted by noted artists Jeanne Barne Jim Aukland.

COMPLETE SET (10)	12.00	3
I1 Smokey Yunick	.25	
I2 Bobby Allison	.50	
I3 Junior Johnson	.50	
I4 Cale Yarborough	.50	
I5 David Pearson	.50	
I6 Benny Parsons	.50	
I7 Ned Jarrett	.50	
I8 Bill Elliott	2.00	
I9 Jeff Gordon	5.00	1
I10 Rusty Wallace	4.00	1

1995 Upper Deck Jumbos

Upper Deck issued the Oversized box inserts i 5-card series. The cards could be found pack one per at the bottom of each foil box of either s one or two 1995 Upper Deck. The cards essentially an enlarged (5" X 7") version of a re issue Upper Deck card. Complete series of 5- were offered on some Upper Deck packs in exch for 15 wrappers and $3 per series.

COMPLETE SET (10)	15.00	4
OS1 Rusty Wallace	5.00	1
OS2 Kyle Petty	1.25	
OS3 Jeff Gordon	6.00	1
OS4 Mark Martin	5.00	1.
OS5 Ernie Irvan	1.25	
OS6 Ken Schrader	.60	
OS7 Bill Elliott	2.50	
OS8 Geoff Bodine	.60	
OS9 Ricky Rudd	2.00	
OS10 Terry Labonte	2.00	

1995 Upper Deck Predictor Race Winne

Upper Deck included its popular Pred redemption cards in both series racing prod Series one packs included randomly inserted packs) Predictor Race Winners cards. If the fea driver won any of the 31 Winston Cup races of the card (along with $3) could be exchanged special parallel set. A longshot card was includ cover races that none of the nine other driver won. The winning cards are designated below often carry a slight premium since they exchangeable. The parallel prize cards differ on the cardbacks. Each prize card has a short biography as opposed to contest rules redemption game expired 2/1/96. Upper produced a special Predictor Race Winner s both the 1995 Daytona 500 and Coca-Cola 6 Charlotte. The cards feature a gold foil stamp the race date and use the same rules as the re issue Predictor cards, except that the featured would have to win that specific race. The lon wound up being the winning card for both races

COMPLETE SET (10)	25.00	6
COMP. WIN PRIZE SET (10)	7.50	1
*PRIZE CARDS: .15X TO .4X BASIC INSERTS		
COMP.DAYTONA 500 (10)	25.00	6
*DAYTONA 500: .4X TO 1X BASIC INSERTS		
COMP.COCA-COLA 600 (10)	25.00	6
*COCA-COLA 600: .4X TO 1X BASIC INSERTS		
P1 Rusty Wallace WIN	4.00	1
P2 Mark Martin WIN	4.00	1
P3 Ricky Rudd	1.50	
P4 Jeff Gordon WIN	5.00	1
P5 Bill Elliott	2.00	
P6 Geoff Bodine	.50	
P7 Dale Jarrett WIN	3.00	
P8 Terry Labonte WIN	1.50	
P9 Jimmy Spencer	.50	
P10 Long Shot WIN	.25	

1995 Upper Deck Predictor Series Poin

Upper Deck included its popular Pred redemption cards in both series one and two r products. Series two packs included rand inserted (1:17 packs) Predictor Series Points c If the featured driver won the 1995 Winston Points Championship, the card (along with $3) be exchanged for a special parallel set. A lon card was included to cover drivers not feature individual cards. The winning card, Jeff Gordo

...nated below and often carries a slight premium ...e it was the only exchangeable card for the ...est. The parallel prize cards differ only on the ...backs. Each prize card has a short driver ...raphy as opposed to contest rules. The ...nption game expired 2/1/96.

...PLETE SET (10)	12.00	30.00
...P. WIN PRIZE SET (10)	7.50	15.00
...ZE CARDS: .2X TO .5X BASIC INSERTS		
Rusty Wallace	3.00	8.00
Sterling Marlin	1.25	3.00
Terry Labonte	1.25	3.00
Mark Martin	3.00	8.00
Bobby Labonte	2.50	6.00
Jeff Gordon Win	4.00	10.00
Dale Jarrett	2.50	6.00
Kyle Petty	.75	2.00
Bill Elliott	1.50	4.00
) Long Shot	.20	.50

1995 Upper Deck Jeff Gordon Phone Cards

...set was sold to both hobby and retail outlets. ...cards were sold in complete set form with each ...in the set carrying five minutes of phone time.

...PLETE SET (5)	5.00	12.00
...MON CARD (1-5)	1.25	3.00

995 Upper Deck Rusty Wallace Phone Cards

...set was sold to both hobby and retail outlets. ...cards were sold in complete set form with each ...in the set carrying five minutes of phone time.

...PLETE SET (5)	4.00	10.00
...MON CARD (1-5)	.75	2.00

1996 Upper Deck

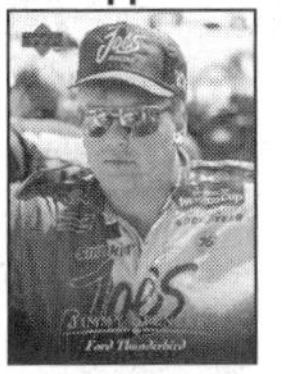

...1996 Upper Deck set totals 150 cards. This is ...econd year of Upper Deck Motorsports. The set ...res the following topical subsets: Drivers (1-... Scrapbook (41-80), Precision Performers (81-... and The History Book (121-150). The product ...available through both hobby and retail ...nels. There were 12 boxes per case with each ...containing 28 packs. 10 cards came per pack ...had a suggested retail of $1.99. In addition to ...erous insert sets, Upper Deck produced two ...al Jeff Gordon single card inserts highlighting ...hampionship 1995 season. Each of the cards ...res a die-cut design and light F/X printing. The ...s were randomly inserted at the rate of 1:108 ...s.

...PLETE SET (150)	7.50	20.00
...k Mast	.07	.20
...sty Wallace	.60	1.50
...erling Marlin	.25	.60
...rry Labonte	.25	.60
...rk Martin	.60	1.50
...off Bodine	.07	.20
...f Burton	.25	.60
...ke Speed	.07	.20
...cky Rudd	.25	.60
...rett Bodine	.07	.20
...errike Cope	.07	.20
...obby Hamilton	.07	.20
...ick Trickle	.07	.20
...ed Musgrave	.07	.20
...arrell Waltrip	.15	.40
...obby Labonte	.50	1.25
...Morgan Shepherd	.07	.20
...had Little	.07	.20
...eff Purvis	.07	.20
...oy Allen Jr.	.07	.20
...mmy Spencer	.07	.20
...eff Gordon	.75	2.00
...en Schrader	.07	.20
...ut Stricklin	.07	.20
...rnie Irvan	.15	.40
...ale Jarrett	.50	1.25
...teve Grissom	.07	.20
...Michael Waltrip	.15	.40
...Ward Burton	.15	.40
...odd Bodine	.07	.20
...obert Pressley	.07	.20
...eremy Mayfield	.15	.40
...Mike Wallace	.07	.20
...ill Elliott	.30	.75
...ohn Andretti	.07	.20
...enny Wallace	.07	.20
...oe Nemechek	.07	.20
...ave Marcis	.15	.40
...icky Craven	.07	.20
...yle Petty SB	.07	.20
...ick Mast SB	.02	.10
...usty Wallace SB	.30	.75
...terling Marlin SB	.15	.40
...erry Labonte SB	.15	.40
...Mark Martin SB	.30	.75
...eoff Bodine SB	.02	.10
...ff Burton SB	.07	.20
...ake Speed SB	.02	.10
...icky Rudd SB	.15	.40
...rett Bodine SB	.02	.10
...errike Cope SB	.02	.10
...obby Hamilton SB	.02	.10
...ick Trickle SB	.02	.10
...ed Musgrave SB	.02	.10
...arrell Waltrip SB	.07	.20
...obby Labonte SB	.25	.60
...organ Shepherd SB	.02	.10
...nie Irvan SB	.07	.20
...nie Irvan SB	.07	.20
...nie Irvan SB	.07	.20
61 Jimmy Spencer SB	.02	.10
62 Jeremy Mayfield SB	.15	.40
63 Mike Wallace SB	.02	.10
64 Ken Schrader SB	.02	.10
65 Hut Stricklin SB	.02	.10
66 Dale Jarrett SB	.25	.60
67 Steve Grissom SB	.02	.10
68 Michael Waltrip SB	.15	.40
69 Ward Burton SB	.07	.20
70 Todd Bodine SB	.02	.10
71 Robert Pressley SB	.02	.10
72 Jeff Gordon SB	.40	1.00
73 Jeff Gordon SB	.40	1.00
74 Bill Elliott SB	.15	.40
75 John Andretti SB	.02	.10
76 Kenny Wallace SB	.02	.10
77 Joe Nemechek SB	.02	.10
78 Dave Marcis SB	.07	.20
79 Ricky Craven SB	.02	.10
80 Kyle Petty PP	.07	.20
81 Rick Mast PP	.02	.10
82 Rusty Wallace PP	.30	.75
83 Sterling Marlin PP	.15	.40
84 Terry Labonte PP	.15	.40
85 Mark Martin PP	.30	.75
86 Geoff Bodine PP	.02	.10
87 Jeff Burton PP	.07	.20
88 Lake Speed PP	.02	.10
89 Ricky Rudd PP	.15	.40
90 Brett Bodine PP	.02	.10
91 Derrike Cope PP	.02	.10
92 Bobby Hamilton PP	.02	.10
93 Dick Trickle PP	.02	.10
94 Ted Musgrave PP	.02	.10
95 Darrell Waltrip PP	.07	.20
96 Bobby Labonte PP	.25	.60
97 Morgan Shepherd PP	.02	.10
98 Jeff Gordon PP	.40	1.00
99 Mark Martin PP	.30	.75
100 Michael Waltrip PP	.15	.40
101 Jimmy Spencer PP	.02	.10
102 Jeff Gordon PP	.40	1.00
103 Ken Schrader PP	.02	.10
104 Hut Stricklin PP	.02	.10
105 Ernie Irvan PP	.07	.20
106 Dale Jarrett PP	.25	.60
107 Steve Grissom PP	.02	.10
108 Michael Waltrip PP	.15	.40
109 Ward Burton PP	.07	.20
110 Todd Bodine PP	.02	.10
111 Robert Pressley PP	.02	.10
112 Jeremy Mayfield PP	.15	.40
113 Mike Wallace PP	.02	.10
114 Bill Elliott PP	.15	.40
115 John Andretti PP	.02	.10
116 Kenny Wallace PP	.02	.10
117 Joe Nemechek PP	.02	.10
118 Dave Marcis PP	.07	.20
119 Ricky Craven PP	.02	.10
120 Kyle Petty HB	.07	.20
121 Rick Hendrick HB	.02	.10
122 Jack Roush HB	.02	.10
123 Roger Penske HB	.02	.10
124 Joe Gibbs HB	.15	.40
125 Felix Sabates HB	.02	.10
126 Bobby Allison HB	.07	.20
127 Richard Petty HB	.25	.60
128 Cale Yarborough HB	.07	.20
129 Robert Yates HB	.02	.10
130 Darrell Waltrip HB	.07	.20
131 Bill Elliott HB	.15	.40
132 Geoff Bodine HB	.02	.10
133 Sterling Marlin HB	.15	.40
134 Ricky Rudd HB	.15	.40
135 Dave Marcis HB	.07	.20
136 Rusty Wallace HB	.30	.75
137 Ernie Irvan HB	.07	.20
138 Jeff Gordon HB	.40	1.00
139 Richard Petty HB	.25	.60
140 Ned Jarrett HB	.07	.20
141 Benny Parsons HB	.07	.20
142 Rusty Wallace HB	.30	.75
143 Jeff Burton HB	.07	.20
144 Smokey Yunick HB	.02	.10
145 Junior Johnson HB	.07	.20
146 Ken Schrader HB	.07	.20
147 Harry Gant HB	.07	.20
148 Rusty Wallace HB	.30	.75
149 Kyle Petty HB	.07	.20
150 Jeff Gordon HB	.40	1.00
C1 Jeff Gordon Tribute	10.00	25.00
C2 Jeff Gordon Tribute	10.00	25.00
JG1 Jeff Gordon Promo	2.00	5.00

1996 Upper Deck All-Pro

This 10-card set features the members of the Upper Deck All-Pro team. The cards could be found on average one per every 36 packs of 1996 Upper Deck series one.

COMPLETE SET (10)	25.00	60.00
AP1 Jeff Gordon	10.00	25.00
AP2 Terry Labonte	3.00	8.00
AP3 Ray Evernham	1.00	2.50
AP4 Rick Hendrick	.50	1.25
AP5 Rusty Wallace	8.00	20.00
AP6 Robin Pemberton	.50	1.25
AP7 Mark Martin	8.00	20.00
AP8 Ted Musgrave	1.00	2.50
AP9 Steve Hmiel	.50	1.25
AP10 Jack Roush	.50	1.25

1996 Upper Deck Predictor Poles

This 10-card interactive game set features nine drivers plus one Longshot card. The object to the game was to find a card for a driver who won any of

the 31 pole positions for a 1996 race. If you had a winning card it was redeemable for a special version of all 10 Retail Predictors. The cards came only in retail packs at a rate of one per 12 packs. The expiration date to redeem winning cards was 2/1/1997. The Prize set was a 10-card set featuring the same fronts as the game cards. The difference is on the back. The cards are numbered RP1-RP10 just like the game cards but instead of having "How to play Predictor" game rules each card has a brief bio on that particular driver.

COMPLETE SET (10)	10.00	25.00
REDEMPTION SET (10)	5.00	12.00
*PRIZE CARDS: .2X TO .5X BASIC INSERTS		
RP1 Jeff Gordon WIN	4.00	10.00
RP2 Mark Martin WIN	3.00	8.00
RP3 Rusty Wallace	3.00	8.00
RP4 Ernie Irvan	.75	2.00
RP5 Bobby Labonte	2.50	6.00
RP6 Bill Elliott	1.50	4.00
RP7 Sterling Marlin	1.25	3.00
RP8 Ricky Rudd	1.25	3.00
RP9 Rick Mast	.40	1.00
RP10 Longshot WIN	.20	.50

1996 Upper Deck Predictor Wins

This 10-card interactive game set features nine drivers plus one Longshot card. The object to the game was to have a card for a driver who won any of the 31 races in 1996. If you had a winning card it was redeemable for a special version of all 10 Hobby Predictors. The cards came only in hobby packs at a rate of one per 12 packs. The winning cards expired for redemption on 2/1/1997. The Prize set was a 10-card set featuring the same fronts as the game cards. The difference is on the back. The cards are numbered HP1-HP10 just like the game cards but instead of having "How to play Predictor" game rules each card has a brief bio on that particular driver.

COMPLETE SET (10)	12.00	30.00
COMP.PRIZE SET (10)	6.00	15.00
*PRIZE CARDS: .2X TO .5X BASIC INSERTS		
HP1 Jeff Gordon WIN	4.00	10.00
HP2 Rusty Wallace WIN	3.00	8.00
HP3 Sterling Marlin WIN	1.25	3.00
HP4 Bobby Labonte	2.50	6.00
HP5 Mark Martin	3.00	8.00
HP6 Ricky Rudd	1.25	3.00
HP7 Terry Labonte WIN	1.25	3.00
HP8 Kyle Petty	.40	1.00
HP9 Dale Jarrett WIN	2.50	6.00
HP10 Longshot WIN	.20	.50

1996 Upper Deck Racing Legends

This 10-card set salutes the legends of racing as well as potential future legends. The set was available across brand lines in 1996. The cards are randomly inserted one per 24 packs.

COMPLETE SET (10)	10.00	25.00
RLC1 Richard Petty	2.50	6.00
RLC2 Cale Yarborough	2.00	5.00
RLC3 Bobby Allison	1.00	2.50
RLC4 Ned Jarrett	1.00	2.50
RLC5 Dave Marcis	1.00	2.50
RLC6 Junior Johnson	1.00	2.50
RLC7 David Pearson	2.00	5.00
RLC8 Harry Gant	2.00	5.00
RLC9 Darrell Waltrip	2.00	5.00
RLC10 Cover Card	1.00	2.50

1996 Upper Deck Virtual Velocity

This 15-card die-cut set features some of the top drivers in Winston Cup racing. The cards are die cut and feature light F/X processing. The cards were inserted at a rate of one per six packs. A parallel gold version was done of each card and was inserted at a rate of one per 72 packs.

COMPLETE SILVER SET (15)	12.00	30.00
COMP.GOLD SET (15)	75.00	150.00
*GOLDS: 1.5X TO 4X BASIC INSERTS		
VV1 Jeff Gordon	3.00	8.00
VV2 Rusty Wallace	2.50	6.00
VV3 Geoff Bodine	.30	.75
VV4 Sterling Marlin	1.00	2.50
VV5 Terry Labonte	1.00	2.50
VV6 Mark Martin	2.50	6.00
VV7 Bill Elliott	1.25	3.00
VV8 Darrell Waltrip	.60	1.50
VV9 Ted Musgrave	.30	.75
VV10 Ricky Rudd	1.00	2.50
VV11 Morgan Shepherd	.30	.75
VV12 John Andretti	.30	.75
VV13 Bobby Labonte	2.00	5.00
VV14 Michael Waltrip	.60	1.50
VV15 Kyle Petty	.30	.75

1996 Upper Deck Jeff Gordon Profiles

This 20-card set features highlights from Jeff Gordon's racing career. The cards are 5" X 7" and were available through special retail outlets as well as hobby shops.

COMPLETE SET (20)	6.00	15.00
COMMON CARD (1-20)	.40	1.00

1996 Upper Deck Road To The Cup

The 1996 Upper Deck Road To The Cup set was issued in one series totalling 150 cards. The 12-card packs had a suggested retail of $1.99 each. The set contains the topical subsets: Drivers (RC1-RC50), Screamin' Steel (RC51-RC90), Changin' Gears (RC91-RC120), Award Winner (RC121-RC135), Truckin' 96 (RC136-RC145) and Role Models (RC146-RC150). It is the first Upper Deck set to include Dale Earnhardt. In honor getting Dale inked Upper Deck went back and made a number 301 card for its 1995 Upper Deck set. The card was seeded one in 95 packs. Also, they produced a Dale Earnhardt Tribute Card. This card was randomly inserted one in 190 packs. There is also a single insert of a Jeff Gordon Commemorative card. This card was inserted one in 72 packs and features 2-D technology.

COMPLETE SET (150)	10.00	25.00
RC1 Jeff Gordon	.75	2.00
RC2 Sterling Marlin	.25	.60
RC3 Mark Martin	.60	1.50
RC4 Rusty Wallace	.60	1.50
RC5 Terry Labonte	.25	.60
RC6 Ted Musgrave	.07	.20
RC7 Bill Elliott	.30	.75
RC8 Ricky Rudd	.25	.60
RC9 Bobby Labonte	.50	1.25
RC10 Morgan Shepherd	.07	.20
RC11 Michael Waltrip	.15	.40
RC12 Dale Jarrett	.50	1.25
RC13 Bobby Hamilton	.07	.20
RC14 Derrike Cope	.07	.20
RC15 Geoff Bodine	.07	.20
RC16 Ken Schrader	.07	.20
RC17 John Andretti	.07	.20
RC18 Darrell Waltrip	.15	.40
RC19 Brett Bodine	.07	.20
RC20 Kenny Wallace	.07	.20
RC21 Ward Burton	.15	.40
RC22 Lake Speed	.07	.20
RC23 Ricky Craven	.07	.20
RC24 Jimmy Spencer	.07	.20
RC25 Steve Grissom	.07	.20
RC26 Joe Nemechek	.07	.20
RC27 Ernie Irvan	.15	.40
RC28 Kyle Petty	.15	.40
RC29 Johnny Benson	.15	.40
RC30 Jeff Burton	.25	.60
RC31 Mike Wallace	.07	.20
RC32 Dave Marcis	.15	.40
RC33 Hut Stricklin	.07	.20
RC34 Bobby Hillin	.07	.20
RC35 Elton Sawyer	.07	.20
RC36 Loy Allen	.07	.20
RC37 Rick Mast	.07	.20
RC38 Jeff Purvis	.07	.20
RC39 Robert Pressley	.07	.20
RC40 Wally Dallenbach	.07	.20
RC41 Jeremy Mayfield	.15	.40
RC42 Dale Earnhardt	1.25	3.00
RC43 Chad Little	.07	.20
RC44 Mike McLaughlin	.07	.20
RC45 Jason Keller	.07	.20
RC46 Randy LaJoie	.07	.20
RC47 Tim Fedewa	.07	.20
RC48 Jeff Fuller	.07	.20
RC49 David Green	.07	.20
RC50 Patty Moise	.07	.20
RC51 Jeff Gordon's Car	.30	.75
RC52 Mark Martin's Car	.25	.60
RC53 Rusty Wallace's Car	.25	.60
RC54 Terry Labonte's Car	.15	.40
RC55 Ted Musgrave's Car	.02	.10
RC56 Bill Elliott's Car	.15	.40
RC57 Ricky Rudd's Car	.07	.20
RC58 Bobby Labonte's Car	.15	.40
RC59 Morgan Shepherd's Car	.02	.10
RC60 Michael Waltrip's Car	.07	.20
RC61 Dale Jarrett's Car	.15	.40
RC62 Bobby Hamilton's Car	.02	.10
RC63 Derrike Cope's Car	.02	.10
RC64 Geoff Bodine's Car	.02	.10
RC65 Ken Schrader's Car	.02	.10
RC66 John Andretti's Car	.02	.10
RC67 Darrell Waltrip's Car	.07	.20
RC68 Brett Bodine's Car	.02	.10
RC69 Rick Mast's Car	.02	.10
RC70 Ward Burton's Car	.02	.10
RC71 Lake Speed's Car	.02	.10
RC72 Ricky Craven's Car	.02	.10
RC73 Jimmy Spencer's Car	.02	.10
RC74 Chad Little's Car	.02	.10
RC75 Joe Nemechek's Car	.02	.10
RC76 Robert Pressley's Car	.02	.10
RC77 Kyle Petty's Car	.07	.20
RC78 Jeremy Mayfield's Car	.07	.20
RC79 Jeff Burton's Car	.07	.20
RC80 Mike Wallace's Car	.02	.10
RC81 Dave Marcis's Car	.07	.20
RC82 Hut Stricklin's Car	.02	.10
RC83 Bobby Hillin's Car	.02	.10
RC84 Elton Sawyer's Car	.02	.10
RC85 Loy Allen's Car	.02	.10
RC86 Kenny Wallace's Car	.02	.10
RC87 Jeff Purvis's Car	.02	.10
RC88 Ernie Irvan's Car	.07	.20
RC89 Wally Dallenbach's Car	.02	.10
RC90 Johnny Benson's Car	.02	.10
RC91 Mark Martin	.60	1.50
RC92 Rusty Wallace	.60	1.50
RC93 Ricky Rudd	.25	.60
RC94 Bobby Labonte	.50	1.25
RC95 Morgan Shepherd	.07	.20
RC96 Michael Waltrip	.15	.40
RC97 Dale Jarrett	.50	1.25
RC98 Bobby Hamilton	.07	.20
RC99 Geoff Bodine	.07	.20
RC100 Ken Schrader	.07	.20
RC101 Darrell Waltrip	.15	.40
RC102 Brett Bodine	.07	.20
RC103 Rick Mast	.07	.20
RC104 Ward Burton	.15	.40
RC105 Lake Speed	.07	.20
RC106 Jimmy Spencer	.07	.20
RC107 Steve Grissom	.07	.20
RC108 Joe Nemechek	.07	.20
RC109 Robert Pressley	.07	.20
RC110 Kyle Petty	.15	.40
RC111 Jeremy Mayfield	.15	.40
RC112 Jeff Burton	.25	.60
RC113 Mike Wallace	.07	.20
RC114 Dave Marcis	.15	.40
RC115 Hut Stricklin	.07	.20
RC116 Dick Trickle	.07	.20
RC117 Loy Allen	.07	.20
RC118 Kenny Wallace	.07	.20
RC119 Wally Dallenbach	.07	.20
RC120 Johnny Benson	.15	.40
RC121 Jeff Gordon	.75	2.00
RC122 Rick Hendrick	.02	.10
RC123 Ray Evernham	.02	.10
RC124 Jeff Gordon	.75	2.00
RC125 Sterling Marlin	.25	.60
RC126 Mark Martin	.60	1.50
RC127 Rusty Wallace	.60	1.50
RC128 Terry Labonte	.25	.60
RC129 Ted Musgrave	.07	.20
RC130 Bill Elliott	.30	.75
RC131 Ricky Rudd	.25	.60
RC132 Bobby Labonte	.50	1.25
RC133 Ricky Craven	.07	.20
RC134 Bobby Hamilton	.07	.20
RC135 Johnny Benson	.15	.40
RC136 Ernie Irvan	.15	.40
RC137 Geoff Bodine	.07	.20
RC138 Geoff Bodine	.07	.20
RC139 Todd Bodine	.07	.20
RC140 Jimmy Hensley	.07	.20
RC141 Darrell Waltrip	.15	.40
RC142 Kenny Wallace	.07	.20
RC143 Derrike Cope	.07	.20
RC144 Ted Musgrave	.07	.20
RC145 Mike Wallace	.07	.20
RC146 Ricky Craven	.07	.20
RC147 Jeff Burton	.25	.60
RC148 Jeff Gordon	.75	2.00
RC149 Jimmy Hensley	.07	.20
RC150 Bobby Hamilton	.07	.20
301 Dale Earnhardt	12.50	30.00
DE1 Dale Earnhardt	10.00	25.00
JG1 Jeff Gordon	8.00	20.00

1996 Upper Deck Road To The Cup Autographs

Randomly inserted in hobby packs only at a rate of one in 16, this insert set features authentic signatures from top NASCAR drivers. Card number H7 was supposed to be Bill Elliott. Due to a crash at Talladega on April 28, 1996, Bill was unable to sign his cards and was dropped from the set.

COMPLETE SET (29)	400.00	700.00
H1 Jeff Gordon	75.00	150.00
H2 Sterling Marlin	15.00	40.00
H3 Mark Martin	15.00	40.00
H4 Rusty Wallace	12.50	30.00
H5 Terry Labonte	12.50	30.00
H6 Ted Musgrave	7.50	15.00
H8 Ricky Rudd	10.00	25.00
H9 Bobby Labonte	12.50	30.00
H10 Morgan Shepherd	7.50	15.00
H11 Michael Waltrip	8.00	20.00
H12 Dale Jarrett	12.50	30.00
H13 Bobby Hamilton	10.00	25.00
H14 Derrike Cope	7.50	15.00
H15 Geoff Bodine	7.50	15.00
H16 Ken Schrader	7.50	15.00
H17 John Andretti	7.50	15.00
H18 Darrell Waltrip	15.00	30.00
H19 Brett Bodine	7.50	15.00
H20 Kenny Wallace	7.50	15.00
H21 Ward Burton	8.00	20.00
H22 Lake Speed	7.50	15.00
H23 Ricky Craven	7.50	15.00
H24 Jimmy Spencer	7.50	15.00
H25 Steve Grissom	7.50	15.00
H26 Joe Nemechek	7.50	15.00
H27 Ernie Irvan	10.00	25.00
H28 Kyle Petty	10.00	25.00
H29 Johnny Benson	10.00	25.00
H30 Jeff Burton	8.00	20.00

1996 Upper Deck Road To The Cup Diary of a Champion

Randomly inserted in packs at a rate of one in six, this 10-card insert set captures moments of "a day in the life of Jeff Gordon" both on and off the track.

COMPLETE SET (10)	6.00	15.00
COMMON GORDON (DC1-DC10)	1.00	2.50

1996 Upper Deck Road To The Cup Game Face

This 10-card insert set was available only in special retail packs. Each card includes the Game Face logo and was inserted one per pack.

COMPLETE SET (10)	4.00	10.00
GF1 Jeff Gordon	1.50	4.00
GF2 Rusty Wallace	1.25	3.00
GF3 Ernie Irvan	.30	.75
GF4 Dale Jarrett	1.00	2.50
GF5 Terry Labonte	.50	1.25
GF6 Mark Martin	1.25	3.00
GF7 Kyle Petty	.30	.75
GF8 Bobby Labonte	1.00	2.50
GF9 Bill Elliott	.60	1.50
GF10 Ricky Rudd	.50	1.25

1996 Upper Deck Road To The Cup Jumbos

This five-card set was available through a wrapper redemption offer. The cards measure 5" X 7" and feature some of the top names in Winston Cup.

COMPLETE SET (5)	3.00	8.00
WC1 Jeff Gordon	1.25	3.00
WC2 Rusty Wallace	1.00	2.50
WC3 Ernie Irvan	.25	.60
WC4 Dale Jarrett	.75	2.00
WC5 Bill Elliott	.50	1.25

1996 Upper Deck Road To The Cup Leaders of the Pack

Randomly inserted in packs at a rate of one in 35, this five-card insert set features the top motorsports drivers according to miles and/or laps led.

COMPLETE SET (5)	10.00	25.00
LP1 Jeff Gordon	5.00	12.00
LP2 Rusty Wallace	4.00	10.00
LP3 Ernie Irvan	1.00	2.50
LP4 Dale Jarrett	3.00	8.00
LP5 Terry Labonte	1.50	4.00

1996 Upper Deck Road To The Cup Predictor Points

Randomly inserted in packs at a rate of one in 22. In this 10-card insert set, the Terry Labonte card was the winning card and was redeemable for a special Championship Journal Redemption set.

COMPLETE SET (10)	12.00	30.00
PP1 Jeff Gordon	4.00	10.00
PP2 Sterling Marlin	1.25	3.00
PP3 Mark Martin	3.00	8.00
PP4 Rusty Wallace	3.00	8.00
PP5 Terry Labonte WIN	1.25	3.00
PP6 Ted Musgrave	.40	1.00
PP7 Bill Elliott	1.50	4.00
PP8 Dale Jarrett	2.50	6.00
PP9 Bobby Labonte	2.50	6.00
PP10 Longshot	.20	.50

1996 Upper Deck Road To The Cup Predictor Points Prizes

This 10-card set is the redemption for the winning Terry Labonte card from the Predictor Points game. The cards feature gold micro-etched foil boarders coupled with silver micro-etched backgrounds. The driver's photo is impossed on top of this silver background. Dale Earnhardt takes the place of the longshot card from the Predictor game.

COMPLETE SET (10)	10.00	25.00
PR1 Jeff Gordon	2.50	6.00
PR2 Sterling Marlin	.75	2.00
PR3 Mark Martin	2.00	5.00
PR4 Rusty Wallace	2.00	5.00
PR5 Terry Labonte	.75	2.00
PR6 Ted Musgrave	.25	.60
PR7 Bill Elliott	1.00	2.50
PR8 Dale Jarrett	1.50	4.00
PR9 Bobby Labonte	1.50	4.00
PR10 Dale Earnhardt	3.00	8.00

1996 Upper Deck Road To The Cup Predictor Top 3

Randomly inserted in packs at a rate of one in 22. In this 10-card insert set, if the drivers whose helmets are pictured on the card finish in first, second and third in any order of any race in the 1996 season, that card was redeemable for a special 15-card set. The expiration date to return these cards was February 10,1997.

COMPLETE SET (10)	15.00	40.00
T1 Jeff Gordon Rusty Wallace Terry Labonte	1.50	4.00
T2 Terry Labonte Dale Jarrett Sterling Marlin	1.25	3.00
T3 Jeff Gordon Ernie Irvan Longshot WIN	1.50	4.00
T4 Rusty Wallace Darrell Waltrip Longshot	1.25	3.00
T5 Mark Martin Rusty Wallace Bobby Labonte	1.25	3.00
T6 Sterling Marlin Jeff Gordon Longshot WIN	7.50	15.00
T7 Jeff Gordon Mark Martin Johnny Benson	1.50	4.00
T8 Ricky Rudd Mark Martin Bill Elliott	1.25	3.00
T9 Mark Martin Ted Musgrave Longshot	1.25	3.00
T10 Rusty Wallace Terry Labonte Kyle Petty	1.25	3.00

1996 Upper Deck Road To The Cup Predictor Top 3 Prizes

This 15-card set is the redemption prize for any of the winning Top 3 Predictor game cards. The cards feature individual drivers unlike the game which featured three driver's helmets per card. The cards are done in gold foil and have a portrait shot of the driver impossed over the top of the foil.

COMPLETE SET (15)	10.00	25.00
R1 Jeff Gordon	2.50	6.00
R2 Rusty Wallace	2.00	5.00
R3 Ernie Irvan	.50	1.25
R4 Sterling Marlin	.75	2.00
R5 Terry Labonte	.75	2.00
R6 Mark Martin	2.00	5.00
R7 Darrell Waltrip	.50	1.25
R8 Bobby Labonte	1.50	4.00
R9 Dale Jarrett	1.50	4.00
R10 Ricky Rudd	.75	2.00
R11 Bill Elliott	1.00	2.50
R12 Ted Musgrave	.25	.60
R13 Kyle Petty	.50	1.25
R14 Johnny Benson	.50	1.25
R15 Longshot	.10	.30

1996 Upper Deck Road To The Cup Racing Legends

Randomly inserted in packs at a rate of one in 23, this 10-card insert set is a cross-brand chase set featuring active and retired motorsport drivers. The first ten cards from the Racing Legends series were inserted in 1996 Upper Deck.

COMPLETE SET (10)	20.00	50.00
RL11 Terry Labonte	3.00	8.00
RL12 Bobby Labonte	6.00	15.00
RL13 Sterling Marlin	3.00	8.00
RL14 Ernie Irvan	2.00	5.00
RL15 Dale Jarrett	6.00	15.00
RL16 Kyle Petty	2.00	5.00
RL17 Geoff Bodine	1.00	2.50
RL18 Ricky Rudd	3.00	8.00
RL19 Ken Schrader	1.00	2.50
RL20 Header	.50	1.25

1997 Upper Deck Hot Wheels Kyle Petty

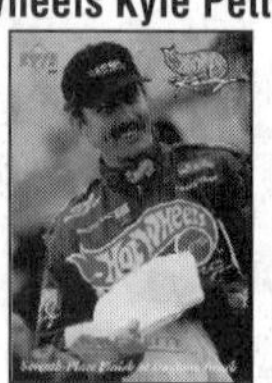

This 5-card set was produced by Upper Deck and made available by Toys 'R Us through a special point-of-purchase offer that would enable a collector to get the set of cards after buying $5.00 worth of Hot Wheels products.

COMPLETE SET (5)	2.00	5.00
HW1 Kyle Petty	.40	1.00
HW2 Kyle Petty's Car	.40	1.00
HW3 Kyle Petty's Car	.40	1.00
HW4 Kyle Petty	.40	1.00
HW5 Kyle Petty's Car	.40	1.00

1997 Upper Deck Road To The Cup

This 150-card set features six topical subsets: Heroes of the Hardtop (1-45), Power Plants (46-89), Inside Track (90-104), Haulin' (105-120), Alternators (121-142), and Thunder Struck(143-150). Cards were distributed in ten card packs with 28 packs per box and 12 boxes per case. The packs carried a suggested retail price of $2.49.

COMPLETE SET (150)	8.00	20.00
1 Terry Labonte	.25	.60
2 Jeff Gordon	.75	2.00
3 Dale Jarrett	.50	1.25
4 Dale Earnhardt	1.25	3.00
5 Mark Martin	.60	1.50
6 Ricky Rudd	.25	.60
7 Rusty Wallace	.60	1.50
8 Sterling Marlin	.25	.60
9 Bobby Hamilton	.07	.20
10 Ernie Irvan	.15	.40
11 Bobby Labonte	.50	1.25
12 Bill Elliott	.30	.75
13 Kyle Petty	.15	.40
14 Ken Schrader	.07	.20
15 Jeff Burton	.25	.60
16 Michael Waltrip	.15	.40
17 Jimmy Spencer	.07	.20
18 Ted Musgrave	.07	.20
19 Geoff Bodine	.07	.20
20 Rick Mast	.07	.20
21 Morgan Shepherd	.07	.20
22 Ricky Craven	.07	.20
23 Johnny Benson	.15	.40
24 Hut Stricklin	.07	.20
25 Lake Speed	.07	.20
26 Brett Bodine	.07	.20
27 Wally Dallenbach	.07	.20
28 Jeremy Mayfield	.15	.40
29 Kenny Wallace	.07	.20
30 Darrell Waltrip	.15	.40
31 John Andretti	.07	.20
32 Robert Pressley	.07	.20
33 Ward Burton	.15	.40
34 Joe Nemechek	.07	.20
35 Derrike Cope	.07	.20
36 Dick Trickle	.07	.20
37 Dave Marcis	.15	.40
38 Steve Grissom	.07	.20
39 Mike Wallace	.07	.20
40 Chad Little	.07	.20
41 Gary Bradberry	.07	.20
42 David Green	.07	.20
43 Bobby Hillin	.07	.20
44 Terry Labonte's Car	.15	.40
45 Jeff Gordon's Car	.30	.75
46 Dale Jarrett's Car	.15	.40
47 Mark Martin's Car	.25	.60
48 Ricky Rudd's Car	.07	.20
49 Rusty Wallace's Car	.25	.60
50 Sterling Marlin's Car	.07	.20
51 Bobby Hamilton's Car	.02	.10
52 Ernie Irvan's Car	.07	.20
53 Bobby Labonte's Car	.15	.40
54 Bill Elliott's Car	.15	.40
55 Kyle Petty's Car	.07	.20
56 Ken Schrader's Car	.02	.10
57 Jeff Burton's Car	.07	.20
58 Michael Waltrip's Car	.07	.20
59 Jimmy Spencer's Car	.02	.10
60 Ted Musgrave's Car	.02	.10
61 Geoff Bodine's Car	.02	.10
62 Rick Mast's Car	.02	.10
63 Morgan Shepherd's Car	.02	.10
64 Ricky Craven's Car	.02	.10
65 Johnny Benson's Car	.02	.10
66 Hut Stricklin's Car	.02	.10
67 Lake Speed's Car	.02	.10
68 Brett Bodine's Car	.02	.10
69 Wally Dallenbach's Car	.02	.10
70 Jeremy Mayfield's Car	.15	.40
71 Kenny Wallace's Car	.02	.10
72 Darrell Waltrip's Car	.07	.20
73 John Andretti's Car	.02	.10
74 Robert Pressley's Car	.02	.10
75 Ward Burton's Car	.02	.10
76 Joe Nemechek's Car	.02	.10
77 Derrike Cope's Car	.02	.10
78 Dick Trickle's Car	.02	.10
79 Dave Marcis's Car	.07	.20
80 Steve Grissom's Car	.02	.10
81 Mike Wallace's Car	.02	.10
82 Chad Little's Car	.02	.10
83 Gary Bradberry's Car	.02	.10
84 David Green's Car	.02	.10
85 Bobby Hillin's Car	.02	.10
86 Terry Labonte	.25	.60
87 Jeff Gordon	.75	2.00
88 Dale Jarrett	.50	1.25
89 Mark Martin	.60	1.50
90 Ricky Rudd	.25	.60
91 Rusty Wallace	.60	1.50
92 Sterling Marlin	.25	.60
93 Bobby Hamilton	.07	.20
94 Ernie Irvan	.15	.40
95 Bobby Labonte	.50	1.25
96 Bill Elliott	.30	.75
97 Kyle Petty	.15	.40
98 Ken Schrader	.07	.20
99 Jeff Burton	.25	.60
100 Ted Musgrave	.07	.20
101 Ricky Craven	.07	.20
102 Johnny Benson	.15	.40
103 Darrell Waltrip	.15	.40
104 John Andretti	.07	.20
105 Derrike Cope	.07	.20
106 Terry Labonte's Trans.	.15	.40
107 Jeff Gordon's Trans.	.25	.60
108 Dale Jarrett's Trans.	.15	.40
109 Jeff Burton's Trans.	.07	.20
110 Ricky Rudd's Trans.	.07	.20
111 Sterling Marlin's Trans.	.07	.20
112 Rick Mast's Trans.	.02	.10
113 Michael Waltrip's Trans.	.07	.20
114 Ken Schrader's Trans.	.02	.10
115 Steve Grissom's Trans.	.02	.10
116 Kyle Petty's Trans.	.07	.20
117 Darrell Waltrip's Trans.	.07	.20
118 Bobby Labonte's Trans.	.15	.40
119 Bill Elliott's Trans.	.15	.40
120 Chad Little's Trans.	.02	.10
121 Dale Earnhardt's Trans.	.50	1.25
122 Brett Bodine's Trans.	.02	.10
123 Geoff Bodine's Trans.	.02	.10
124 Rusty Wallace	.60	1.50
125 Sterling Marlin	.25	.60
126 Bobby Hamilton	.07	.20
127 Ernie Irvan	.15	.40
128 Bobby Labonte	.50	1.25
129 Kyle Petty	.15	.40
130 Ken Schrader	.07	.20
131 Ted Musgrave	.07	.20
132 Rick Mast	.07	.20
133 Morgan Shepherd	.07	.20
134 Ricky Craven	.07	.20
135 Hut Stricklin	.07	.20
136 Lake Speed	.07	.20
137 Brett Bodine	.07	.20
138 Wally Dallenbach	.07	.20
139 Darrell Waltrip	.15	.40
140 Robert Pressley	.07	.20
141 Joe Nemechek	.07	.20
142 Derrike Cope	.07	.20
143 Steve Grissom	.07	.20
144 Mike Wallace	.07	.20
145 Chad Little	.07	.20
146 David Green	.07	.20
147 Mark Martin	.60	1.50
148 Ricky Rudd	.25	.60
149 Gary Bradberry	.07	.20
150 John Andretti	.07	.20

1997 Upper Deck Road To The Cup Cup Quest

This 10-card insert set features the top stars from the Winston Cup circuit. Each card in the basic insert set was printed with a green background and serial numbered of 5000.

COMPLETE SET (10)	25.00	60.00
COMP.WHITE CUP QUEST (10)	60.00	120.00
*WHITE CUP QUEST: .8X TO 2X GREEN		
WHITE PRINT RUN 1000 SER.#'d SETS		
COMP.CHECKERED (10)	750.00	1500.00
*CHECKERED: 6X TO 15X GREEN		
CHECKERED PRINT RUN 100 SER.#'d SETS		
CQ1 Terry Labonte	1.50	4.00
CQ2 Jeff Gordon	5.00	12.00
CQ3 Dale Earnhardt	8.00	20.00
CQ4 Dale Jarrett	3.00	8.00
CQ5 Rusty Wallace	4.00	10.00
CQ6 Ernie Irvan	1.00	2.50
CQ7 Mark Martin	4.00	10.00
CQ8 Sterling Marlin	1.50	4.00
CQ9 Bobby Hamilton	.50	1.25
CQ10 Ricky Rudd	1.50	4.00

1997 Upper Deck Road To The Cup Million Dollar Memoirs

This 20-card set features five of top driver on the Winston Cup circuit. Each driver has four cards in the set. The cards were randomly inserted in packs at a ratio of 1:23.

COMPLETE SET (20)	60.00	150.00
MM1 Terry Labonte	2.50	6.00
MM2 Terry Labonte	2.50	6.00
MM3 Terry Labonte	2.50	6.00
MM4 Terry Labonte	2.50	6.00
MM5 Jeff Gordon	8.00	20.00
MM6 Jeff Gordon	8.00	20.00
MM7 Jeff Gordon	8.00	20.00
MM8 Jeff Gordon	8.00	20.00
MM9 Rusty Wallace	6.00	15.00
MM10 Rusty Wallace	6.00	15.00
MM11 Rusty Wallace	6.00	15.00
MM12 Rusty Wallace	6.00	15.00
MM13 Dale Jarrett	5.00	12.00
MM14 Dale Jarrett	5.00	12.00
MM15 Dale Jarrett	5.00	12.00
MM16 Dale Jarrett	5.00	12.00
MM17 Bill Elliott	3.00	8.00
MM18 Bill Elliott	3.00	8.00
MM19 Bill Elliott	3.00	8.00
MM20 Bill Elliott	3.00	8.00

1997 Upper Deck Road To The Cup Million Dollar Memoirs Autographs

This 20-card set is a parallel to the base Million Dollar Memoirs set. Each card in this set is autographed. The cards were randomly inserted in packs at a ratio of 1:109.

COMPLETE SET (20)	500.00	1000.00
MM1 Terry Labonte	12.50	30.00
MM2 Terry Labonte	12.50	30.00
MM3 Terry Labonte	12.50	30.00
MM4 Terry Labonte	12.50	30.00
MM5 Jeff Gordon	60.00	120.00
MM6 Jeff Gordon	60.00	120.00
MM7 Jeff Gordon	60.00	120.00
MM8 Jeff Gordon	60.00	120.00
MM9 Rusty Wallace	12.50	30.00
MM10 Rusty Wallace	12.50	30.00
MM11 Rusty Wallace	12.50	30.00
MM12 Rusty Wallace	12.50	30.00
MM13 Dale Jarrett	12.50	30.00
MM14 Dale Jarrett	12.50	30.00
MM15 Dale Jarrett	12.50	30.00
MM16 Dale Jarrett	12.50	30.00
MM17 Bill Elliott	20.00	50.00
MM18 Bill Elliott	20.00	50.00
MM19 Bill Elliott	20.00	50.00
MM20 Bill Elliott	20.00	50.00

1997 Upper Deck Road To The Cup Piece of the Action

This 9-card set features pieces of a driver's seat, safety harness and window net incorporated into a trading card. The cards were seeded one in 1117 packs.

COMPLETE SET (9)	250.00	500.00
1 Jeff Gordon Seat Cover	20.00	50.00
2 Jeff Gordon Shoulder Harness	20.00	50.00
3 Jeff Gordon Window Net	20.00	50.00
4 Dale Jarrett Seat Cover	12.50	25.00
5 Dale Jarrett Shoulder Harness	12.50	25.00
6 Dale Jarrett Window Net	12.50	25.00
7 Rusty Wallace Seat Cover	12.50	25.00
8 Rusty Wallace Shoulder Harness	12.50	25.00
9 Rusty Wallace Window Net	12.50	25.00

1997 Upper Deck Road To The Cup Predictor Plus

This 30-card set features a scratch-off redemption game that gave collectors three chances to win. Each card has three scratch off areas that correspond to Starting Position, Laps Led, and Finish Position. There were three levels of prizes available for the winning cards. The cards featuring drivers that were winners in one of the three categories could be redeemed for a cel card of that driver. The cards that were winners in two categories could be redeemed for a complete set of die cut cel cards. Finally, the cards that were winners in all three areas could be redeemed for a complete set of cel cards and a complete base set of 1997 Upper Deck Road to the Cup. The prices below are for unscratched cards. These cards expired on 1/30/98. The cards were randomly inserted in packs at a ratio of 1:11.

COMPLETE SET (30)	40.00	80.00
*CEL PRIZES: 1X TO 2.5X BASIC INSERTS		
*DIE CUT PRIZES: 1.2X TO 3X BASIC INSERTS		
1 Terry Labonte	.60	1.50
2 Jeff Gordon	2.00	5.00
3 Dale Jarrett	1.25	3.00
4 Sterling Marlin WIN	.60	1.50
5 Ricky Craven	.20	.50
6 Ernie Irvan WIN	.40	1.00
7 Rusty Wallace	1.50	4.00
8 Mark Martin	1.50	4.00
9 Terry Labonte	.60	1.50
10 Bill Elliott	.75	2.00
11 Jeff Gordon WIN	2.00	5.00
12 Geoff Bodine WIN 3	.20	.50
13 Dale Jarrett WIN	1.25	3.00
14 Rusty Wallace	1.50	4.00
15 Jeremy Mayfield	.40	1.00
16 Mark Martin	1.50	4.00
17 Ken Schrader WIN	.20	.50
18 Jimmy Spencer WIN	.20	.50
19 Ted Musgrave	.20	.50
20 Darrell Waltrip	.40	1.00
21 Jeff Burton	.60	1.50
22 Ward Burton WIN	.40	1.00
23 Ricky Rudd WIN	.60	1.50
24 Johnny Benson WIN	.40	1.00
25 Kyle Petty WIN	.40	1.00
26 Bobby Hamilton WIN 3	.20	.50
27 Terry Labonte	.60	1.50
28 Jeff Gordon	2.00	5.00
29 Bobby Labonte WIN 2	1.25	3.00
30 Bill Elliott WIN	.75	2.00

1997 Upper Deck Road To The Cup Premiere Position

This 48-card insert set showcases drivers who won the pole in one of 24 races in the 1996 season and early 1997 season. Each card features a die cut. The cards were randomly inserted in packs at a ratio of 1:5.

COMPLETE SET (48)	75.00	150.00
PP1 Terry Labonte	1.25	3.00
PP2 Jeff Gordon	4.00	10.00
PP3 Johnny Benson	.75	2.00
PP4 Dale Earnhardt	6.00	15.00
PP5 Terry Labonte	1.25	3.00
PP6 Terry Labonte	1.25	
PP7 Ricky Craven	.40	
PP8 Rusty Wallace	3.00	
PP9 Ernie Irvan	.75	
PP10 Sterling Marlin	1.25	
PP11 Jeff Gordon	4.00	1
PP12 Jeff Gordon	4.00	1
PP13 Bobby Hamilton	.40	
PP14 Rusty Wallace	3.00	
PP15 Ricky Craven	.40	
PP16 Ernie Irvan	.75	
PP17 Mark Martin	3.00	
PP18 Rusty Wallace	3.00	
PP19 Jeremy Mayfield	.75	
PP20 Jeff Gordon	4.00	1
PP21 Jeff Gordon	4.00	1
PP22 Dale Jarrett	2.50	
PP23 Jeff Burton	1.25	
PP24 Dale Jarrett	2.50	
PP25 Mark Martin	3.00	
PP26 Rusty Wallace	3.00	
PP27 Dale Jarrett	2.50	
PP28 Jeff Gordon	4.00	1
PP29 Mark Martin	3.00	
PP30 Ernie Irvan	.75	
PP31 Bobby Hamilton	.40	
PP32 Jeff Gordon	4.00	1
PP33 Bobby Labonte	2.50	
PP34 Terry Labonte	1.25	
PP35 Dale Jarrett	2.50	
PP36 Ricky Rudd	1.25	
PP37 Bobby Labonte	2.50	
PP38 Bobby Hamilton	.40	
PP39 Bobby Labonte	2.50	
PP40 Bobby Labonte	2.50	
PP41 Mark Martin	3.00	
PP42 Jeff Gordon	4.00	1
PP43 Terry Labonte	1.25	
PP44 Rusty Wallace	3.00	
PP45 Dale Jarrett	2.50	
PP46 Dale Jarrett	2.50	
PP47 Dale Jarrett	2.50	
PP48 Jeff Burton	1.25	

1998 Upper Deck Diamond Vision

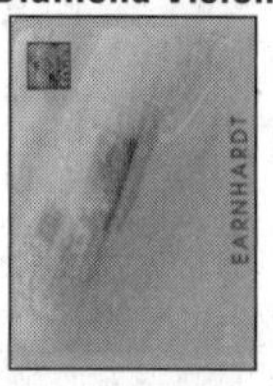

This 15-card set focuses on 15 of the top driv NASCAR utilizing motion technology. Th Gordon Reeltime card was randomly insert packs at a ratio of 1:500. Cards were distribu one card packs with 16 packs per box and 12 per case. The packs carried a suggested retail of $7.99.

COMPLETE SET (15)	25.00	6
1 Jeff Gordon	3.00	
2 Rusty Wallace	2.50	
3 Dale Earnhardt	5.00	1
4 Sterling Marlin	1.00	
5 Terry Labonte	1.00	
6 Mark Martin	2.50	
7 Dale Jarrett	2.00	
8 Bill Elliott	1.25	
9 Ernie Irvin	.60	
10 Ricky Rudd	1.00	
11 Jeff Burton	.60	
12 Ricky Craven	.60	
13 Bobby Labonte	2.00	
14 Kyle Petty	.60	
15 Robby Gordon	.40	
RT1 Jeff Gordon RT	50.00	10

1998 Upper Deck Diamond Vision Signature Moves

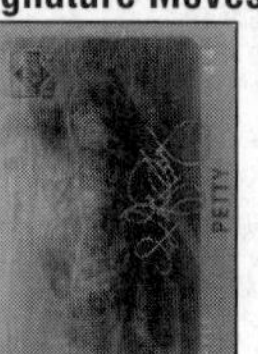

This 15-card insert set is a parallel to the bas This set features facsimile signatures on each The cards were randomly inserted in packs at a of 1:3.

COMPLETE SET (15)	100.00	20
1 Jeff Gordon	10.00	2
2 Rusty Wallace	8.00	2
3 Dale Earnhardt	15.00	4
4 Sterling Marlin	3.00	
5 Terry Labonte	3.00	
6 Mark Martin	8.00	2
7 Dale Jarrett	6.00	1
8 Bill Elliott	4.00	1
9 Ernie Irvin	2.00	
10 Ricky Rudd	3.00	
11 Jeff Burton	2.00	
12 Ricky Craven	2.00	
13 Bobby Labonte	6.00	1
14 Kyle Petty	2.00	
15 Robby Gordon	1.25	

1998 Upper Deck Diamond Vision Visic of a Champion

This 4-card insert set features four past Winsto champions. The cards were randomly inser

...ks at a ratio of 1:40.

...MPLETE SET (4) 60.00 150.00
...1 Rusty Wallace 10.00 25.00
...2 Dale Earnhardt 20.00 50.00
...3 Jeff Gordon 12.50 30.00
...4 Terry Labonte 4.00 10.00

1998 Upper Deck Road To The Cup

...e 1998 Upper Deck Road to the Cup set consists ... 120 standard size cards. The fronts feature full ...ed photos of the driver or the driver's car. A silver ...nd lines the left side of the card where the driver's ...me and Upper Deck logo are found. The set ...ntains the subsets: Taurus Time (46-60), Days of ...ytona (61-75), Young Guns (76-85), Viva Las ...gas (86-100), Double Barrel (101-115), and ...ecklists (116-120).

...MPLETE SET (120) 15.00 35.00
...AX BOX 25.00 60.00
Kevin Lepage .10 .30
Rusty Wallace 1.00 2.50
Dale Earnhardt 2.00 5.00
Bobby Hamilton's Car .05 .15
Terry Labonte .40 1.00
Mark Martin's Car .40 1.00
Geoff Bodine's Car .05 .15
Hut Stricklin .10 .30
Jeff Burton's Car .10 .30
Ricky Rudd .40 1.00
Brett Bodine's Car .05 .15
Jeremy Mayfield .25 .60
Jerry Nadeau RC .40 1.00
Loy Allen's Car .05 .15
Bill Elliott's Car .25 .60
Jeff Green .10 .30
Darrell Waltrip .25 .60
Bobby Labonte's Car .25 .60
David Green .10 .30
Dale Jarrett .75 2.00
Michael Waltrip .25 .60
Ward Burton .25 .60
Jimmy Spencer .10 .30
Jeff Gordon 1.25 3.00
Randy LaJoie's Car .05 .15
Johnny Benson .25 .60
Gary Bradberry .10 .30
Kenny Irwin .25 .60
Dave Marcis .25 .60
Derrike Cope .10 .30
Mike Skinner .10 .30
Ron Hornaday .10 .30
Ken Schrader .10 .30
Rick Mast .10 .30
Todd Bodine .10 .30
Ernie Irvan .25 .60
Dick Trickle's Car .05 .15
Robert Pressley .10 .30
Wally Dallenbach .10 .30
Sterling Marlin's Car .10 .30
Steve Grissom .10 .30
Joe Nemechek's Car .05 .15
John Andretti .10 .30
Kyle Petty's Car .10 .30
Kenny Wallace .10 .30
Rusty Wallace's Car .40 1.00
Mark Martin's Car .40 1.00
Geoff Bodine's Car .05 .15
Ricky Rudd's Car .10 .30
Jeremy Mayfield's Car .10 .30
Jerry Nadeau's Car .25 .60
Chad Little's Car .05 .15
Michael Waltrip's Car .10 .30
Jimmy Spencer's Car .05 .15
Johnny Benson's Car .10 .30
Kenny Irwin's Car .10 .30
Kenny Wallace's Car .05 .15
Dale Jarrett's Car .25 .60
Bill Elliott's Car .25 .60
Jeff Burton's Car .10 .30
NASCAR Gold Car .05 .15
Jimmy Spencer's Car .05 .15
Rusty Wallace's Car .40 1.00
Jeremy Mayfield .25 .60
Geoff Bodine's Car .05 .15
Jeff Gordon 1.25 3.00
John Andretti .10 .30
Bobby/Terry Labonte .75 2.00
Terry Labonte's Car .25 .60
Bobby Labonte's Car .25 .60
Chad Little's Car .05 .15
Sterling Marlin's Car .10 .30
Dave Marci's Car .10 .30
Jerry Nadeau's Car .25 .60
Dale Earnhardt 2.00 5.00
Kenny Irwin .25 .60
Jerry Nadeau's Car .25 .60
Todd Bodine .10 .30
Johnny Benson's Car .10 .30
John Andretti .10 .30
Jeremy Mayfield .25 .60
Kevin Lepage .10 .30
Dale Earnhardt Jr.'s Car .50 1.25
Randy LaJoie .10 .30
Mike Skinner's Car .05 .15
Rusty Wallace's Car .40 1.00
Ernie Irvan's Car .10 .30
Jeff Gordon's Car .50 1.25
Jeff Burton .40 1.00
Dale Jarrett's Car .25 .60
Bill Elliott's Car .25 .60
Jeremy Mayfield's Car .10 .30
Johnny Benson's Car .10 .30
Dale Earnhardt Jr.'s Car VL .50 1.25
Kyle Petty's Car .10 .30
Rick Mast's Car .05 .15
97 Terry Labonte's Car .25 .60
98 Ricky Rudd .40 1.00
99 Chad Little's Car .05 .15
100 Mark Martin's Car .40 1.00
101 Mark Martin 1.00 2.50
102 Dale Jarrett .75 2.00
103 Joe Nemechek .10 .30
104 Dave Marcis .25 .60
105 Hermie Sadler .10 .30
106 Michael Waltrip .25 .60
107 Dick Trickle .10 .30
108 Jeff Burton .40 1.00
109 Derrike Cope .10 .30
110 John Andretti .10 .30
111 Mike Wallace .10 .30
112 Robert Pressley .10 .30
113 Elliott Sadler .25 .60
114 Randy LaJoie .10 .30
115 Tony Stewart RC 6.00 15.00
116 Checklist (1-50) .05 .15
117 Checklist (51-100) .05 .15
118 Checklist (101-AN25) .05 .15
119 Checklist (AN26-CS18) .05 .15
120 Checklist (CQ1-W5) .05 .15

1998 Upper Deck Road To The Cup 50th Anniversary

Randomly inserted in packs at a rate of one in four, this 50-card insert set, highlights the top names in NASCAR from the past 50 years. The card fronts feature color photography surrounded by a blue border.

COMPLETE SET (50) 15.00 40.00
AN1 Bill France Sr. .10 .30
AN2 Daytona Beach .10 .30
AN3 Jim Roper's Car .10 .30
AN4 Tim Flock .25 .60
AN5 Hudson Hornet .10 .30
AN6 Fireball Roberts .25 .60
AN7 Smokey Yunick .25 .60
AN8 Buck Baker .25 .60
AN9 Ned Jarrett .25 .60
AN10 Richard Petty .50 1.25
AN11 Junior Johnson .25 .60
AN12 David Pearson .25 .60
AN13 Ned Jarrett .25 .60
AN14 Richard Petty .50 1.25
AN15 Ford Turino .10 .30
AN16 Buddy Baker's Car .10 .30
AN17 Richard Petty's Car .25 .60
AN18 David Pearson .25 .60
AN19 Winston Show Car .10 .30
AN20 Bobby Allison .25 .60
AN21 Richard Petty .50 1.25
AN22 Benny Parsons .25 .60
AN23 NASCAR Silver Anniversary .10 .30
AN24 Junior Johnson .25 .60
AN25 Cale Yarborough .25 .60
AN26 David Pearson .25 .60
AN27 Richard Petty .50 1.25
AN28 Bobby Allison's Car .10 .30
AN29 Rusty Wallace's Car .75 2.00
AN30 Darrell Waltrip's Car .25 .60
AN31 Bobby Hillin's Car .10 .30
AN32 Cale Yarborough's Car .10 .30
AN33 Benny Parsons's Car .10 .30
AN34 Ernie Irvan's Car .25 .60
AN35 Darrell Waltrip .50 1.25
AN36 Richard Petty's Car .25 .60
AN37 Bill Elliott's Car .50 1.25
AN38 Davey Allison .50 1.25
AN39 Davey Allison/Bobby Allison .50 1.25
AN40 Rusty Wallace 2.00 5.00
AN41 Richard Petty .50 1.25
AN42 Alan Kulwicki .50 1.25
AN43 Jeff Gordon 2.50 6.00
AN44 Terry Labonte .75 2.00
AN45 Terry Labonte .75 2.00
AN46 Suzuka Speedway .10 .30
AN47 Jeff Gordon 2.50 6.00
AN48 Jeremy Mayfield's Car .25 .60
AN49 Dale Earnhardt 4.00 10.00
AN50 Las Vegas Speedway .10 .30

1998 Upper Deck Road To The Cup 50th Anniversary Autographs

Randomly inserted in hobby packs only, this 10-card insert set is limited and hand-numbered to 50. Each card offers an autograph from a top name in NASCAR's 50-year history. The card fronts feature color photography surrounded by a blue border.

COMPLETE SET (10) 600.00 1000.00
AN13 Ned Jarrett 30.00 50.00
AN14 Richard Petty 40.00 80.00
AN18 David Pearson 30.00 50.00
AN25 Cale Yarborough 30.00 50.00
AN35 Darrell Waltrip 35.00 60.00
AN39 Bobby Allison 30.00 50.00
AN40 Rusty Wallace 60.00 120.00
AN44 Terry Labonte 60.00 120.00
AN47 Jeff Gordon 100.00 200.00
AN49 Dale Earnhardt 250.00 450.00

1998 Upper Deck Road To The Cup Cover Story

Randomly inserted in packs at a rate of one in 11, this 16-card insert set features hand-picked photos and in-depth prose from the editors of Tuff Stuff magazine and Winston Cup Scene.

COMPLETE SET (16) 15.00 40.00

CS1 Ernie Irvan .50 1.25
CS2 Terry Labonte .75 2.00
CS3 Darrell Waltrip .50 1.25
CS4 Kyle Petty .50 1.25
CS5 Rusty Wallace 2.00 5.00
CS6 Alan Kulwicki .50 1.25
CS7 Bill Elliott .50 1.25
CS8 Jeff Gordon 2.50 6.00
CS9 WC Grand National Scene .10 .30
CS10 Dale Earnhardt 4.00 10.00
CS11 Ernie Irvan .50 1.25
CS12 Rusty Wallace 2.00 5.00
CS13 Jeff Gordon 2.50 6.00
CS14 Indianapolis Motor Speedway .10 .30
CS15 Jeff Gordon Terry Labonte Ricky Craven 2.50 6.00
CS16 Jeff Gordon Darrell Waltrip 2.50 6.00

1998 Upper Deck Road To The Cup Cup Quest Turn 1

Sequentially numbered to 4,000, this is the first tier of a five-tiered insert set focused on the top ten drivers contending for this year's Winston Cup title.

COMPLETE SET (10) 20.00 50.00
COMP.TURN 2 SET (10) 30.00 80.00
*TURN 2: .6X TO 1.5X BASIC INSERTS
TURN 2 PRINT RUN 2000 SER.#'D SETS
COMP.TURN 3 SET (10) 60.00 150.00
*TURN 3 CARDS: 1.2X TO 3X BASIC INSERTS
TURN 3 PRINT RUN 1000 SER.#'D SETS
*TURN 4: 4X TO 10X BASIC INSERTS
TURN 4 PRINT RUN 100 SER.#'D SETS
CQ1 Jeff Gordon's Car 6.00 15.00
CQ2 Rusty Wallace's Car 5.00 12.00
CQ3 Kenny Irwin's Car 1.50 4.00
CQ4 Jeremy Mayfield's Car 1.50 4.00
CQ5 Terry Labonte's Car 3.00 8.00
CQ6 Mark Martin's Car 5.00 12.00
CQ7 Bobby Labonte's Car 3.00 8.00
CQ8 Dale Jarrett's Car 3.00 8.00
CQ9 Jeff Burton's Car 1.50 4.00
CQ10 Ernie Irvan's Car 1.50 4.00

1998 Upper Deck Road To The Cup Winning Materials

Randomly inserted in packs at a rate of one in 999, this 5-card insert set sports special cards with authentic race-used pieces of the engine, along with an actual piece of a driver's race-worn fire suit.

COMPLETE SET (5) 200.00 400.00
W1 Rusty Wallace 20.00 50.00
W2 Jeremy Mayfield 12.50 30.00
W3 Dale Jarrett 15.00 40.00
W4 Bobby Labonte 20.00 50.00
W5 Jeff Burton 15.00 40.00

1998 Upper Deck UD Authentics

RW Rusty Wallace 15.00 30.00

1997 Upper Deck Victory Circle

The 1997 Upper Deck set was issued in one series totalling 120 cards. The set contains the topical subsets: Driver (1-50), Momentum (51-100) Local Legends (101-115) and Track Facts (116-120). The cards were packaged 10 cards per pack, 28 packs per box and 12 boxes per case. Each pack carried a suggested retail price of $2.49.

COMPLETE SET (120) 8.00 20.00
1 Rick Mast .07 .20
2 Rusty Wallace .60 1.50
3 Dale Earnhardt 1.25 3.00
4 Sterling Marlin .25 .60
5 Terry Labonte .25 .60
6 Mark Martin .60 1.50
7 Geoff Bodine .07 .20
8 Hut Stricklin .07 .20
9 Lake Speed .07 .20
10 Ricky Rudd .25 .60
11 Brett Bodine .07 .20
12 Derrike Cope .07 .20
13 Bill Elliott .30 .75
14 Bobby Hamilton .07 .20
15 Wally Dallenbach .07 .20
16 Ted Musgrave .07 .20
17 Darrell Waltrip .15 .40
18 Bobby Labonte .50 1.25
19 Loy Allen .07 .20
20 Morgan Shepherd .07 .20
21 Michael Waltrip .15 .40
22 Ward Burton .15 .40
23 Jimmy Spencer .07 .20
24 Jeff Gordon .75 2.00
25 Ken Schrader .07 .20
26 Kyle Petty .15 .40
27 Bobby Hillin .07 .20
28 Ernie Irvan .15 .40
29 Jeff Purvis .07 .20
30 Johnny Benson .15 .40
31 Dave Marcis .15 .40
32 Jeremy Mayfield .15 .40
33 Robert Pressley .07 .20
34 Jeff Burton .25 .60
35 Joe Nemechek .07 .20
36 Dale Jarrett .50 1.25
37 John Andretti .07 .20
38 Kenny Wallace .07 .20
39 Elton Sawyer .07 .20
40 Dick Trickle .07 .20
41 Ricky Craven .07 .20
42 Chad Little .07 .20
43 Todd Bodine .07 .20
44 David Green .07 .20
45 Randy LaJoie .07 .20
46 Larry Pearson .07 .20
47 Jason Keller .07 .20
48 Hermie Sadler .07 .20
49 Mike McLaughlin .07 .20
50 Tim Fedewa .07 .20
51 Rick Mast's Car .02 .10
52 Rusty Wallace's Car .25 .60
53 Ricky Craven's Car .02 .10
54 Sterling Marlin's Car .07 .20
55 Terry Labonte's Car .15 .40
56 Mark Martin's Car .25 .60
57 Geoff Bodine's Car .02 .10
58 Hut Stricklin's Car .02 .10
59 Lake Speed's Car .02 .10
60 Ricky Rudd's Car .07 .20
61 Brett Bodine's Car .02 .10
62 Derrike Cope's Car .02 .10
63 Bill Elliott's Car .15 .40
64 Bobby Hamilton's Car .02 .10
65 Wally Dallenbach's Car .02 .10
66 Ted Musgrave's Car .02 .10
67 Darrell Waltrip's Car .07 .20
68 Bobby Labonte's Car .15 .40
69 Loy Allen's Car .02 .10
70 Morgan Shepherd's Car .02 .10
71 Michael Waltrip's Car .07 .20
72 Ward Burton's Car .02 .10
73 Jimmy Spencer's Car .02 .10
74 Jeff Gordon's Car .30 .75
75 Ken Schrader's Car .02 .10
76 Kyle Petty's Car .07 .20
77 Bobby Hillin's Car .02 .10
78 Ernie Irvan's Car .07 .20
79 Jeff Purvis's Car .02 .10
80 Johnny Benson's Car .02 .10
81 Dave Marcis's Car .07 .20
82 Jeremy Mayfield's Car .15 .40
83 Robert Pressley's Car .02 .10
84 Jeff Burton's Car .07 .20
85 Joe Nemechek's Car .02 .10
86 Dale Jarrett's Car .15 .40
87 John Andretti's Car .02 .10
88 Kenny Wallace's Car .02 .10
89 Elton Sawyer's Car .15 .40
90 Dick Trickle's Car .02 .10
91 Chad Little's Car .02 .10
92 Todd Bodine's Car .02 .10
93 David Green's Car .02 .10
94 Randy LaJoie's Car .02 .10
95 Larry Pearson's Car .02 .10
96 Jason Keller's Car .02 .10
97 Hermie Sadler's Car .02 .10
98 Mike McLaughlin's Car .02 .10
99 Tim Fedewa's Car .02 .10
100 Patty Moise's Car .02 .10
101 Dale Jarrett .50 1.25
102 Ricky Rudd .25 .60
103 Rusty Wallace .60 1.50
104 Sterling Marlin .25 .60
105 Geoff Bodine .07 .20
106 John Andretti .07 .20
107 Jeremy Mayfield .15 .40
108 Terry Labonte .25 .60
109 Mark Martin .60 1.50
110 Derrike Cope .07 .20
111 Jeff Gordon .75 2.00
112 Ricky Craven .07 .20
113 Ted Musgrave .07 .20
114 Joe Nemechek .07 .20
115 Bill Elliott .30 .75
116 Kenny Wallace .07 .20
117 Darrell Waltrip .15 .40
118 Bobby Labonte .50 1.25
119 North Wilkesboro Speedway .02 .10
120 North Wilkesboro Speedway .02 .10

1997 Upper Deck Victory Circle Championship Reflections

Randomly inserted in packs at a rate of one in 4, this 10-card set highlights the top ten finishers in the point standings for the 1996 Winston Cup season.

COMPLETE SET (10) 10.00 25.00
CR1 Terry Labonte .75 2.00
CR2 Jeff Gordon 2.50 6.00
CR3 Dale Jarrett 1.50 4.00
CR4 Dale Earnhardt 4.00 10.00
CR5 Mark Martin 2.00 5.00
CR6 Ricky Rudd .75 2.00
CR7 Rusty Wallace 2.00 5.00
CR8 Sterling Marlin .75 2.00
CR9 Bobby Hamilton .25 .60
CR10 Ernie Irvan .50 1.25

1997 Upper Deck Victory Circle Crowning Achievement

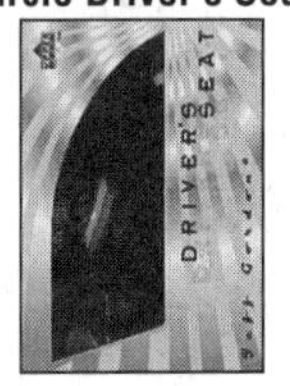

Randomly inserted in packs at a rate of one in 35, this five-card set takes a look back at Terry Labonte's record breaking season. The cards used a double die-cut design.

COMPLETE SET (5) 15.00 40.00
TERRY LABONTE CARD (CA1-CA5) 3.00 8.00

1997 Upper Deck Victory Circle Driver's Seat

Randomly inserted in packs at a rate of one in 69, this 10-card set takes cel technology and applies it to racing cards. The cards are best viewed when held up to light.

COMPLETE SET (10) 50.00 120.00
DS1 Dale Earnhardt 20.00 50.00
DS2 Jeff Gordon 12.50 30.00
DS3 Terry Labonte 4.00 10.00
DS4 Ken Schrader 1.25 3.00
DS5 Sterling Marlin 4.00 10.00
DS6 Mark Martin 10.00 25.00
DS7 Rusty Wallace 10.00 25.00
DS8 Bobby Labonte 8.00 20.00
DS9 Ernie Irvan 2.50 6.00
DS10 Dale Jarrett 8.00 20.00

1997 Upper Deck Victory Circle Generation Excitement

This five-card set highlights some of the up and coming stars of NASCAR's Winston Cup circuit. The cards were inserted one in 11 packs.

COMPLETE SET (5) 6.00 15.00
GE1 Jeff Gordon 4.00 10.00
GE2 Bobby Hamilton .40 1.00
GE3 Johnny Benson .75 2.00
GE4 Ricky Craven .40 1.00
GE5 Bobby Labonte 2.50 6.00

1997 Upper Deck Victory Circle Piece of the Action

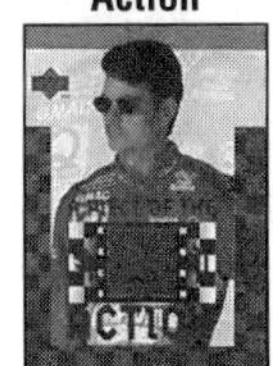

This 9-card set features pieces of a driver's gloves, shoes, and firesuit incorporated into a trading card. The cards were seeded one in 699 packs.

COMPLETE SET (9) 200.00 400.00
FS1 Jeff Gordon Firesuit 20.00 50.00
FS2 Jeff Gordon Glove 20.00 50.00
FS3 Jeff Gordon Shoe 20.00 50.00
FS4 Rusty Wallace Firesuit 8.00 20.00
FS5 Rusty Wallace Glove 8.00 20.00
FS6 Rusty Wallace Shoe 8.00 20.00
FS7 Dale Jarrett Firesuit 8.00 20.00
FS8 Dale Jarrett Glove 8.00 20.00
FS9 Dale Jarrett Shoe 8.00 20.00

1997 Upper Deck Victory Circle Predictor

This 10-card is an interactive predictor game. Each card has a specific goal stamped on the front. If that driver accomplishes that goal anytime during the 1997 Winston Cup season that card may be redeemed for a 10 card prize set. These cards expired on 2/1/1998. The predictor cards were inserted one per 21 packs.

COMPLETE SET (10) 20.00 50.00
COMP.PRIZE CEL SET (10) 40.00 100.00
*PRIZE CARDS: .8X TO 2X BASIC INSERTS
PE1 Jeff Gordon WIN 6.00 15.00
PE2 Rusty Wallace WIN 5.00 12.00
PE3 Dale Jarrett WIN 4.00 10.00
PE4 Sterling Marlin 2.00 5.00
PE5 Terry Labonte 2.00 5.00
PE6 Mark Martin WIN 5.00 12.00
PE7 Bobby Labonte WIN 4.00 10.00
PE8 Ernie Irvan WIN 1.25 3.00
PE9 Bill Elliott 2.50 6.00
PE10 Ricky Rudd 2.00 5.00

1997 Upper Deck Victory Circle Victory Lap

Randomly inserted in packs at a rate of one in 109, this 10-card set is a hobby only insert. The cards feature die-cut technology and a checkered flag design. Each of the drivers in this set visited victory lane in 1996. The cards were inserted one per 109 packs.

COMPLETE SET (10) 150.00 300.00
VL1 Dale Earnhardt 40.00 100.00
VL2 Jeff Gordon 25.00 60.00
VL3 Bobby Labonte 15.00 40.00
VL4 Dale Jarrett 15.00 40.00
VL5 Ernie Irvan 5.00 12.00
VL6 Sterling Marlin 8.00 20.00
VL7 Ricky Rudd 8.00 20.00
VL8 Geoff Bodine 2.50 6.00
VL9 Bobby Hamilton 2.50 6.00
VL10 Rusty Wallace 20.00 50.00

1998 Upper Deck Victory Circle

The 1998 Upper Deck Victory Circle set was issued in one series totalling 135 cards. The set contains the topical subsets: Season Highlights (91-105), Freeze Frame (106-120), and Hard Chargers (121-135).

COMPLETE SET (150) 15.00 40.00
1 Morgan Shepherd .08 .25
2 Rusty Wallace .75 2.00
3 Dale Earnhardt 1.50 4.00
4 Sterling Marlin .30 .75
5 Terry Labonte .30 .75
6 Mark Martin .75 2.00
7 Geoff Bodine .08 .25
8 Hut Stricklin .08 .25
9 Lake Speed .08 .25
10 Ricky Rudd .30 .75
11 Brett Bodine .08 .25
12 Dale Jarrett .60 1.50
13 Bill Elliott .40 1.00
14 Dick Trickle .08 .25
15 Wally Dallenbach .08 .25
16 Ted Musgrave .08 .25
17 Darrell Waltrip .20 .50
18 Bobby Labonte .60 1.50
19 Gary Bradberry .08 .25
20 Rick Mast .08 .25
21 Michael Waltrip .20 .50
22 Ward Burton .20 .50
23 Jimmy Spencer .08 .25
24 Jeff Gordon 1.00 2.50
25 Ricky Craven .08 .25
26 Chad Little .08 .25
27 Kenny Wallace .08 .25
28 Ernie Irvan .20 .50
29 Steve Park .60 1.50
30 Johnny Benson .20 .50
31 Mike Skinner .08 .25

1998 Upper Deck Victory Circle

32 Mike Wallace .08 .25
33 Ken Schrader .08 .25
34 Jeff Burton .30 .75
35 David Green .08 .25
36 Derrike Cope .08 .25
37 Jeremy Mayfield .20 .50
38 Dave Marcis .20 .50
39 John Andretti .08 .25
40 Robby Gordon .08 .25
41 Steve Grissom .08 .25
42 Joe Nemechek .08 .25
43 Bobby Hamilton .08 .25
44 Kyle Petty .20 .50
45 Kenny Irwin .20 .50
46 Morgan Shepherd's Car .05 .15
47 Rusty Wallace's Car .30 .75
48 Dale Earnhardt's Car .60 1.50
49 Sterling Marlin's Car .08 .25
50 Terry Labonte's Car .20 .50
51 Mark Martin's Car .30 .75
52 Geoff Bodine's Car .05 .15
53 Hut Stricklin's Car .05 .15
54 Lake Speed's Car .05 .15
55 Ricky Rudd's Car .08 .25
56 Brett Bodine's Car .05 .15
57 Dale Jarrett's Car .20 .50
58 Bill Elliott's Car .20 .50
59 Dick Trickle's Car .05 .15
60 Wally Dallenbach's Car .05 .15
61 Ted Musgrave's Car .05 .15
62 Darrell Waltrip's Car .20 .50
63 Bobby Labonte's Car .20 .50
64 Gary Bradberry's Car .05 .15
65 Rick Mast's Car .05 .15
66 Michael Waltrip's Car .08 .25
67 Ward Burton's Car .08 .25
68 Jimmy Spencer's Car .05 .15
69 Jeff Gordon's Car .40 1.00
70 Ricky Craven's Car .05 .15
71 Chad Little's Car .08 .25
72 Kenny Wallace's Car .05 .15
73 Ernie Irvan's Car .08 .25
74 Steve Park's Car .20 .50
75 Johnny Benson's Car .05 .15
76 Mike Skinner's Car .05 .15
77 Mike Wallace's Car .05 .15
78 Ken Schrader's Car .05 .15
79 Jeff Burton's Car .08 .25
80 David Green's Car .05 .15
81 Derrike Cope's Car .05 .15
82 Jeremy Mayfield's Car .08 .25
83 Dave Marcis's Car .08 .25
84 John Andretti's Car .05 .15
85 Robby Gordon's Car .05 .15
86 Steve Grissom's Car .05 .15
87 Joe Nemechek's Car .05 .15
88 Bobby Hamilton's Car .05 .15
89 Kyle Petty's Car .08 .25
90 Kenny Irwin's Car .08 .25
91 Mike Skinner .08 .25
92 Jeff Gordon .60 1.50
Terry Labonte
Ricky Craven
93 Jeff Gordon 1.00 2.50
94 Robby Gordon .08 .25
95 Dale Jarrett .60 1.50
96 Jeff Burton .30 .75
97 Mark Martin .75 2.00
98 Mark Martin .75 2.00
99 Joe Nemechek .08 .25
100 Jeff Gordon 1.00 2.50
101 Mike Skinner .08 .25
102 John Andretti .08 .25
103 Ricky Rudd .30 .75
104 Todd Bodine .08 .25
105 Jeff Gordon 1.00 2.50
106 Mark Martin .75 2.00
107 Geoff Bodine .08 .25
108 Kenny Irwin .20 .50
109 Dave Marcis .20 .50
110 Rusty Wallace .75 2.00
111 Ricky Rudd .30 .75
112 Bobby Labonte .60 1.50
113 Ernie Irvan .20 .50
114 Kenny Wallace .08 .25
115 Mike Skinner .08 .25
116 Dale Jarrett .60 1.50
117 Mark Martin .75 2.00
118 Terry Labonte .30 .75
119 Jeff Gordon 1.00 2.50
120 Jeff Gordon 1.00 2.50
121 Derrike Cope .08 .25
122 Jeremy Mayfield .20 .50
123 Robby Gordon .08 .25
124 Ricky Craven .08 .25
125 Ernie Irvan .20 .50
126 Terry Labonte .30 .75
127 Johnny Benson .20 .50
128 Mike Skinner .08 .25
129 Kyle Petty .20 .50
130 Wally Dallenbach .08 .25
131 Rick Mast .08 .25
132 Morgan Shepherd .08 .25
133 Michael Waltrip .20 .50
134 Ted Musgrave .08 .25
135 Ricky Rudd .30 .75
136 Ricky Craven .08 .25
137 Geoff Bodine .08 .25
138 Morgan Shepherd .08 .25
139 Ted Musgrave .08 .25
140 Mark Martin .75 2.00
141 Darrell Waltrip .20 .50
142 Rusty Wallace .75 2.00
143 Jeff Burton .30 .75
144 Bill Elliott .40 1.00
145 Ricky Rudd .30 .75
146 Terry Labonte .30 .75
147 Bobby Labonte .60 1.50
148 Steve Grissom .08 .25
149 Dale Jarrett .60 1.50
150 Ernie Irvan .20 .50

1998 Upper Deck Victory Circle 32 Days of Speed

Randomly inserted in packs at the rate of one in four, this 32-card set features color photos of one of the drivers from each of the 32 NASCAR Winston Cup races.

COMPLETE SET (32) 20.00 40.00

*GOLD CARDS: 8X TO 20X BASIC INSERTS
GOLD PRINT RUN 97 SER.#'D SETS
D1 Mike Skinner .15 .40
D2 Jeff Gordon 1.50 4.00
D3 Rusty Wallace 1.25 3.00
D4 Robby Gordon .15 .40
D5 Dale Jarrett 1.00 2.50
D6 Jeff Burton .50 1.25
D7 Rusty Wallace 1.25 3.00
D8 Kenny Wallace .15 .40
D9 Mark Martin 1.25 3.00
D10 Mark Martin 1.25 3.00
D11 Jeff Gordon 1.50 4.00
D12 Ricky Rudd .50 1.25
D13 Bobby Hamilton .15 .40
D14 Ernie Irvan .30 .75
D15 Joe Nemechek .15 .40
D16 John Andretti .15 .40
D17 Ken Schrader .15 .40
D18 Dale Jarrett 1.00 2.50
D19 Ricky Rudd .50 1.25
D20 Todd Bodine .15 .40
D21 Johnny Benson .30 .75
D22 Kenny Wallace .15 .40
D23 Bobby Labonte 1.00 2.50
D24 Bill Elliott .60 1.50
D25 Ken Schrader .15 .40
D26 Mark Martin 1.25 3.00
D27 Ward Burton .30 .75
D28 Bobby Labonte 1.00 2.50
D29 Terry Labonte .50 1.25
D30 Bobby Hamilton .15 .40
D31 Bobby Hamilton .15 .40
D32 Jeff Gordon 1.50 4.00

1998 Upper Deck Victory Circle Autographs

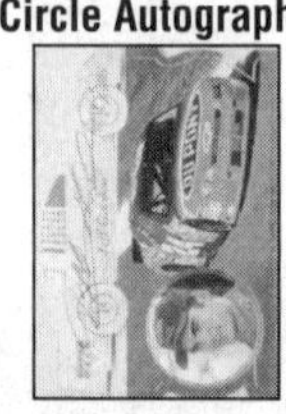

Randomly inserted in packs, this five-card set features autographed color photos of favorite NASCAR Winston Cup drivers printed on unique die-cut cards. Each card was individually hand-serial numbered to 250.

COMPLETE SET (5) 250.00 500.00
AG1 Jeff Gordon 50.00 100.00
AG2 Jeff Burton 10.00 25.00
AG3 Dale Jarrett 25.00 60.00
AG4 Mark Martin 40.00 80.00
AG5 Terry Labonte 20.00 50.00

1998 Upper Deck Victory Circle Piece of the Engine

Randomly inserted in packs at the rate of one in 999, this five-card set features color photos of drivers with an actual race-used piece of the engine from the top cars in NASCAR contained in the card. There were two cards of each driver produced. Cards PE6-PE10 feature a race date the engine piece was used.

COMPLETE SET (10) 300.00 700.00
PE1 Darrell Waltrip 15.00 40.00
PE2 Rusty Wallace 20.00 50.00
PE3 Dale Jarrett 20.00 50.00
PE4 Ernie Irvan 15.00 40.00
PE5 Bobby Labonte 15.00 40.00
PE6 Darrell Waltrip 15.00 40.00
PE7 Rusty Wallace 20.00 50.00
PE8 Dale Jarrett 20.00 50.00
PE9 Ernie Irvan 15.00 40.00
PE10 Bobby Labonte 15.00 40.00

1998 Upper Deck Victory Circle Point Leaders

Randomly inserted in packs at the rate of one in 13, this 20-card set features color photos of drivers who finished in the top 20 in the final point standings for the season.

COMPLETE SET (20) 50.00 100.00
PL1 Jeff Gordon 5.00 12.00
PL2 Dale Jarrett 3.00 8.00
PL3 Mark Martin 4.00 10.00
PL4 Jeff Burton 1.50 4.00
PL5 Dale Earnhardt 8.00 20.00
PL6 Terry Labonte 1.50 4.00
PL7 Bobby Labonte 3.00 8.00
PL8 Bill Elliott 2.00 5.00
PL9 Rusty Wallace 4.00 10.00
PL10 Ken Schrader .50 1.25
PL11 Johnny Benson 1.00 2.50
PL12 Ted Musgrave .50 1.25
PL13 Jeremy Mayfield 1.00 2.50
PL14 Ernie Irvan 1.00 2.50
PL15 Kyle Petty 1.00 2.50
PL16 Bobby Hamilton .50 1.25
PL17 Ricky Rudd 1.50 4.00
PL18 Michael Waltrip 1.00 2.50
PL19 Ricky Craven .50 1.25
PL20 Jimmy Spencer .50 1.25

1998 Upper Deck Victory Circle Predictor Plus

Randomly inserted in packs at the rate of one in 23, this 20-card set features scratch-off game cards which enabled the collector to win prizes if the driver pictured on the card achieved the goals displayed after scratching off the special cars on the card.

COMPLETE SET (20) 30.00 60.00
*CEL REDEMPT: .5X TO 1.25X BASIC INS.
1 Ernie Irvan 1.25 3.00
2 Rusty Wallace 5.00 12.00
3 Dale Jarrett 4.00 10.00
4 Sterling Marlin 2.00 5.00
5 Terry Labonte 2.00 5.00
6 Mark Martin 5.00 12.00
7 Geoff Bodine .60 1.50
8 Hut Stricklin .60 1.50
9 Lake Speed .60 1.50
10 Ricky Rudd 2.00 5.00
11 Brett Bodine .60 1.50
12 Bill Elliott 2.50 6.00
13 Kyle Petty 1.25 3.00
14 Jeff Burton 2.00 5.00
15 Jeremy Mayfield 1.25 3.00
16 Ricky Craven .60 1.50
17 Ted Musgrave .60 1.50
18 Bobby Labonte 4.00 10.00
19 Mike Skinner .60 1.50
20 Johnny Benson 1.25 3.00

1998 Upper Deck Victory Circle Sparks of Brilliance

Randomly inserted in packs at the rate of one in 84, this ten-card set features color photos of top drivers with their accomplishments on the track during the 1997 season.

COMPLETE SET (10) 200.00 400.00
SB1 Jeff Gordon 15.00 40.00
SB2 Rusty Wallace 10.00 25.00
SB3 Dale Earnhardt 25.00 60.00
SB4 Ernie Irvan 4.00 10.00
SB5 Terry Labonte 6.00 15.00
SB6 Mark Martin 12.00 30.00
SB7 Bobby Labonte 10.00 25.00
SB8 Ricky Rudd 5.00 12.00
SB9 Dale Jarrett 10.00 25.00
SB10 Jeff Burton 4.00 10.00

1999 Upper Deck Holiday Santa Suit

Cards from this set were mailed out during the 1999 year end holiday season to Upper Deck dealers and other customers. Each card features a driver dressed as Santa along with a swatch cut from the Santa suit that the driver wore for the photo shoot.

NNO Rusty Wallace 15.00 40.00

1999 Upper Deck MVP ProSign

These Autographs were signed for the cancelled 1999 Upper Deck MVP product but placed in packs of 2000 SP Authentic at the rate of 1:40

BB Brett Bodine 6.00 15.00

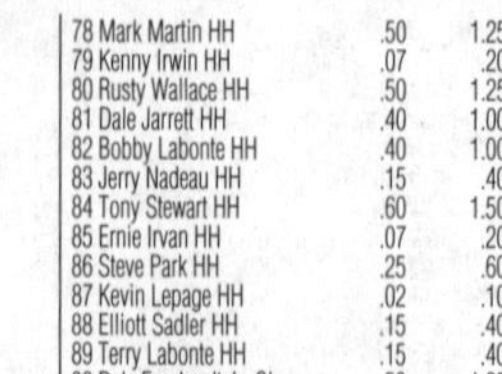

DJR Dale Jarrett Silver 30.00 60.00
DWH Darrell Waltrip Gold 20.00 40.00
DWR Darrell Waltrip Silver 20.00 40.00
JB Johnny Benson 6.00 15.00
JGH Jeff Gordon Gold 300.00 500.00
JGR Jeff Gordon Silver 300.00 500.00
JJH Jason Jarrett Gold 10.00 25.00
JJR Jason Jarrett Silver 10.00 25.00
JR Dale Earnhardt Jr. 60.00 120.00
KP Kyle Petty 15.00 30.00
KSH Ken Schrader Gold 8.00 20.00
KSR Ken Schrader Silver 8.00 20.00
MKH Matt Kenseth Gold 30.00 80.00
MKR Matt Kenseth Silver 20.00 50.00
MW Mike Wallace 7.50 20.00
TSH Tony Stewart Gold 40.00 100.00
TSR Tony Stewart Silver 40.00 100.00

1999 Upper Deck Road to the Cup

The 1999 Upper Deck Road to the Cup product was released in late 1999, and featured a 90-card base set that was broken into tiers as follows: 30 Veteran Drivers, 30 Car cards, and 15 Fan Favorites, and 15 Happy Hour cards.

COMPLETE SET (90) 10.00 25.00
WAX BOX 30.00 60.00
1 Kenny Irwin .15 .40
2 Dale Jarrett .50 1.25
3 Terry Labonte .25 .60
4 Geoff Bodine .07 .20
5 John Andretti .07 .20
6 Tony Stewart CRC 1.00 2.50
7 Ricky Rudd .25 .60
8 Jeremy Mayfield .15 .40
9 Chad Little .15 .40
10 Darrell Waltrip .15 .40
11 Bobby Labonte .50 1.25
12 Ken Schrader .07 .20
13 Sterling Marlin .25 .60
14 Mike Skinner .07 .20
15 Kevin Lepage .07 .20
16 Jeff Burton .25 .60
17 Elliott Sadler .15 .40
18 Mark Martin .60 1.50
19 Bill Elliott .30 .75
20 Steve Park .40 1.00
21 Jerry Nadeau .15 .40
22 Rusty Wallace .60 1.50
23 Bobby Hamilton .07 .20
24 Jeff Gordon .75 2.00
25 Randy LaJoie .07 .20
26 Dale Earnhardt 1.25 3.00
27 Ernie Irvan .15 .40
28 Johnny Benson .15 .40
29 Kyle Petty .15 .40
30 Dale Earnhardt Jr. 1.00 2.50
31 Jeremy Mayfield's Car .07 .20
32 Terry Labonte's Car .15 .40
33 John Andretti's Car .02 .10
34 Kyle Petty's Car .07 .20
35 Darrell Waltrip's Car .02 .10
36 Geoff Bodine's Car .02 .10
37 Dale Earnhardt Jr.'s Car .40 1.00
38 Bobby Labonte's Car .15 .40
39 Ken Schrader's Car .02 .10
40 Johnny Benson's Car .02 .10
41 Sterling Marlin's Car .07 .20
42 Ernie Irvan's Car .07 .20
43 Jeff Gordon's Car .30 .75
44 Mike Skinner's Car .07 .20
45 Kevin Lepage's Car .02 .10
46 Jeff Burton's Car .07 .20
47 Ricky Rudd's Car .07 .20
48 Dale Jarrett's Car .15 .40
49 Kenny Irwin's Car .07 .20
50 Randy LaJoie's Car .02 .10
51 Elliott Sadler's Car .02 .10
52 Steve Park's Car .15 .40
53 Chad Little's Car .02 .10
54 Jerry Nadeau's Car .07 .20
55 Bobby Hamilton's Car .02 .10
56 Bill Elliott's Car .15 .40
57 Mark Martin's Car .25 .60
58 Tony Stewart's Car .30 .75
59 Rusty Wallace's Car .25 .60
60 Dale Earnhardt's Car .50 1.25
61 Jeff Gordon FF .40 1.00
62 Terry Labonte FF .15 .40
63 Dale Jarrett FF .40 1.00
64 Darrell Waltrip FF .07 .20
65 Bill Elliott FF .07 .20
66 Tony Stewart FF .60 1.50
67 Dale Earnhardt Jr. FF .75 2.00
68 Ernie Irvan FF .07 .20
69 Kyle Petty FF .07 .20
70 Bobby Labonte FF .40 1.00
71 Kenny Irwin FF .07 .20
72 Jeremy Mayfield FF .07 .20
73 Ricky Rudd FF .15 .40
74 Mark Martin FF .50 1.25
75 Rusty Wallace FF .50 1.25
76 Jeremy Mayfield HH .07 .20
77 Jeff Gordon HH .40 1.00
78 Mark Martin HH .50 1.25
79 Kenny Irwin HH .07 .20
80 Rusty Wallace HH .50 1.25
81 Dale Jarrett HH .40 1.00
82 Bobby Labonte HH .40 1.00
83 Jerry Nadeau HH .15 .40
84 Tony Stewart HH .60 1.50
85 Ernie Irvan HH .07 .20
86 Steve Park HH .25 .60
87 Kevin Lepage HH .02 .10
88 Elliott Sadler HH .15 .40
89 Terry Labonte HH .15 .40
90 Dale Earnhardt Jr. CL .50 1.25

1999 Upper Deck Road to the Cup A Day in the Life

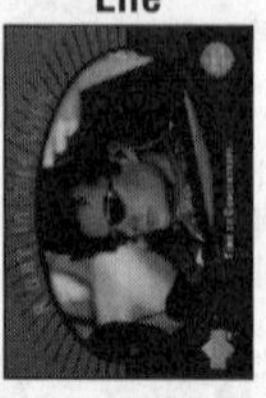

Randomly inserted in packs at the rate of one in six, this 10-card insert set details a day in the life of Jeff Gordon. Card backs carry a "JG" prefix.

COMPLETE SET (10) 5.00 12.00
COMMON GORDON (JG1-JG10) .50 1.25

1999 Upper Deck Road to the Cup NASCAR Chronicles

Randomly inserted in packs at the rate of one in two, This twenty card set features the journeys the top drivers have taken to make it to the NASCAR Winston Cup Circuit. Card backs carry a "NC" prefix.

COMPLETE SET (20) 15.00 40.00
NC1 Bobby Labonte 1.50 4.00
NC2 Jeff Gordon 2.50 6.00
NC3 Rusty Wallace 2.00 5.00
NC4 Terry Labonte .75 2.00
NC5 Kyle Petty .50 1.25
NC6 Kevin Lepage .25 .60
NC7 Jeff Burton .75 2.00
NC8 Jeremy Mayfield .50 1.25
NC9 Elliott Sadler .50 1.25
NC10 Mark Martin 2.00 5.00
NC11 Dale Earnhardt 4.00 10.00
NC12 Kenny Irwin .50 1.25
NC13 Bill Elliott 1.00 2.50
NC14 Dale Earnhardt Jr. 3.00 8.00
NC15 John Andretti .25 .60
NC16 Ricky Rudd .75 2.00
NC17 Dale Jarrett 1.50 4.00
NC18 Jerry Nadeau .50 1.25
NC19 Tony Stewart 2.50 6.00
NC20 Steve Park 1.25 3.00

1999 Upper Deck Road to the Cup Road to the Cup Bronze Level 1

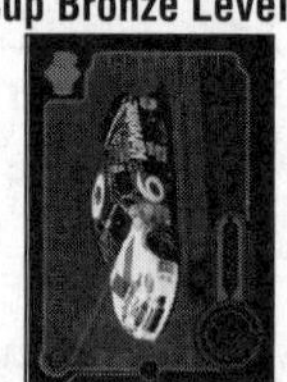

Randomly inserted in packs at the rate of one in twelve. This set features ten drivers who competed for the NASCAR Winston Cup Championship. The cardbacks carry a "RTTC" prefix and the Level 1 cards featured bronze foil printing on the cardfronts and were not die cut. There were two die cut parallel sets produced as well: Level 2 Silver (1:23 packs) and Level 3 Gold (1:48 packs).

COMP.LEVEL 1 SET (10) 20.00 40.00
COMP.LEVEL 2 SILVER (10) 30.00 60.00
*LEVEL 2 SILVERS: .6X TO 1.5X LEVEL 1
COMP.LEVEL 3 GOLD (10) 50.00 100.00
*LEVEL 3 GOLDS: 1X TO 2.5X LEVEL 1
RTTC1 Jeff Gordon 5.00 12.00
RTTC2 Mark Martin's Car 1.50 4.00
RTTC3 Rusty Wallace 4.00 10.00
RTTC4 Terry Labonte 1.50 4.00
RTTC5 Bobby Labonte 3.00 8.00
RTTC6 Jeremy Mayfield 1.00 2.50
RTTC7 Jeff Burton 1.50 4.00
RTTC8 Dale Jarrett 3.00 8.00
RTTC9 Ricky Rudd 1.50 4.00
RTTC10 Dale Earnhardt Jr. 6.00 15.00

1999 Upper Deck Road to the Cup Signature Collection

Randomly inserted in packs at the rate of one in 999, this set features actual autographs of top NASCAR drivers. The cards look similar to the Victory Circle

Signature Collection but can be differentiated by circular shaped player image and the inclusion o Road to the Cup logo on the cardfronts. T cardbacks carry the driver's initials as numberi Cards of some drivers were released later without "Road to the Cup" logo on the fronts.

DE Dale Earnhardt
DJ Dale Jarrett
JB Jeff Burton 8.00 20.
JG Jeff Gordon 100.00 200.
KP Kyle Petty
MM Mark Martin 40.00 80.
RW Rusty Wallace 12.50 30.
SP Steve Park 12.50 30.
TS Tony Stewart 40.00 100.
DEJR Dale Earnhardt Jr. 60.00 120.

1999 Upper Deck Roac to the Cup Signature Collection Checkered Flag

These Autographs were signed for the cancel 1999 Upper Deck Road to the Cup Checkered F product but placed in packs of 2000 SP Authenti the rate of 1:40. Each card looks nearly identica the basic 1999 Upper Deck Road to the C Signature Collection cards except for the inclusio both the Victory Circle and Checkered Flag (logos on the cardfronts.

BL Bobby Labonte 12.50 30.
DE Dale Earnhardt 250.00 500.
JB Jeff Burton 12.50 25.
JG Jeff Gordon 100.00 175.
MS Mike Skinner 10.00 20.
RW Rusty Wallace 20.00 50.
TS Tony Stewart 40.00 100.
DEJR Dale Earnhardt Jr. 60.00 120.

1999 Upper Deck Roac to the Cup Tires of Daytona

Randomly inserted in packs at the rate of one in 5 This set features a piece of a race-used tire fro Winston Cup car raced at Daytona. Card backs c a "T" prefix.

COMPLETE SET (5) 175.00 350.
T1 Jeff Gordon 40.00 80.
T2 Rusty Wallace 25.00 50.
T3 Jeremy Mayfield 20.00 40.
T4 Mark Martin 30.00 60.
T5 Jeff Burton 12.50 30.

1999 Upper Deck Roac to the Cup Tires of Daytona Autographed

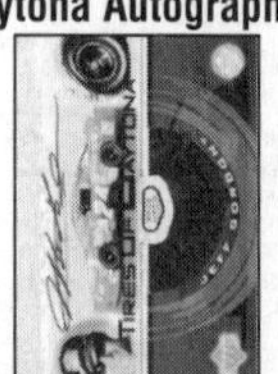

Randomly inserted in packs, this set features a pi of a race-used tire from a Winston Cup car race Daytona, and is autographed to the driver's number. Card backs carry a "TS" prefix. Most ca were issued mail redemption cards that carried expiration date of 7/1/2000.

TS1 Jeff Gordon/24 300.00 500.
TS2 Mark Martin/6
TS3 Rusty Wallace/2
TS4 Jeremy Mayfield/12

1999 Upper Deck Roac to the Cup Upper Deck Profiles

Randomly inserted in packs at the rate of one eleven, this fifteen card set gets up close a onal with 15 of NASCAR's Winston Cup drivers. backs carry a "P" prefix.

MPLETE SET (15)	40.00	80.00
Jeremy Mayfield	1.25	3.00
Terry Labonte	2.00	5.00
Dale Earnhardt	10.00	25.00
Jerry Nadeau	1.25	3.00
Dale Jarrett	4.00	10.00
Steve Park	3.00	8.00
Mark Martin	5.00	12.00
Bobby Labonte	4.00	10.00
Kenny Irwin	1.25	3.00
Dale Earnhardt Jr.	8.00	20.00
Tony Stewart	6.00	15.00
Elliott Sadler	1.25	3.00
Rusty Wallace	5.00	12.00
Jeff Burton	2.00	5.00
Jeff Gordon	6.00	15.00

999 Upper Deck Victory Circle

1999 Upper Deck Victory Circle set was issued ne series totalling 89 cards. The set contains the subsets: 55 Veterans and 34 Car cards.

MPLETE SET (89)	10.00	25.00
K BOX	30.00	60.00
ale Jarrett	.50	1.25
errike Cope	.07	.20
ff Gordon	.75	2.00
cky Rudd	.25	.60
obby Labonte	.50	1.25
ark Martin	.60	1.50
remy Mayfield	.15	.40
erry Labonte	.25	.60
usty Wallace	.60	1.50
Geoff Bodine	.07	.20
Ward Burton	.15	.40
Brett Bodine	.07	.20
Jeff Green	.07	.20
Dale Earnhardt Jr.	1.00	2.50
Jerry Nadeau	.15	.40
Kenny Irwin	.15	.40
Bill Elliott	.30	.75
Ernie Irvan	.15	.40
Darrell Waltrip	.15	.40
John Andretti	.07	.20
Kyle Petty	.15	.40
Steve Park	.40	1.00
Jeff Burton	.25	.60
Ken Schrader	.07	.20
Johnny Benson	.15	.40
Dave Marcis	.07	.20
Wally Dallenbach	.07	.20
Michael Waltrip	.15	.40
Bobby Hamilton	.07	.20
Sterling Marlin	.25	.60
Chad Little	.15	.40
Dick Trickle	.07	.20
Joe Nemechek	.07	.20
Mike Skinner	.07	.20
Kenny Wallace	.07	.20
Robert Pressley	.07	.20
Steve Grissom	.07	.20
Kevin Lepage	.07	.20
Mike Wallace	.07	.20
Rick Mast	.07	.20
Jeff Gordon's Car	.30	.75
Rusty Wallace's Car	.25	.60
Bill Elliott's Car	.15	.40
Johnny Benson's Car	.02	.10
Mark Martin's Car	.25	.60
Sterling Marlin's Car	.07	.20
Darrell Waltrip's Car	.02	.10
Jerry Nadeau's Car	.15	.40
Terry Labonte's Car	.15	.40
Dale Earnhardt Jr.'s Car	.40	1.00
Ernie Irvan's Car	.02	.10
Dale Jarrett's Car	.15	.40
Jeff Green's Car	.02	.10
Jeff Burton's Car	.07	.20
Geoff Bodine's Car	.02	.10
Chad Little's Car	.07	.20
Brett Bodine's Car	.02	.10
Jeremy Mayfield's Car	.07	.20
Steve Park's Car	.07	.20
Kenny Irwin's Car	.07	.20
Derrike Cope's Car	.02	.10
Kevin Lepage's Car	.02	.10
Bobby Hamilton's Car	.02	.10
Ken Schrader's Car	.02	.10
Kyle Petty's Car	.07	.20
John Andretti's Car	.02	.10
Ricky Rudd's Car	.07	.20
Bobby Labonte's Car	.15	.40
Michael Waltrip's Car	.07	.20
Joe Nemechek's Car	.02	.10
Kenny Wallace's Car	.02	.10
Mike Skinner's Car	.02	.10
Robert Pressley's Car	.02	.10
Ward Burton's Car	.07	.20
Mark Martin	.60	1.50
Jeff Gordon	.75	2.00
Jeremy Mayfield	.07	.20
Rusty Wallace	.60	1.50
Mark Martin's Car	.25	.60
Jeff Gordon	.75	2.00
Rusty Wallace	.60	1.50
Steve Park	.40	1.00
Dale Earnhardt	1.25	3.00
Jeff Gordon	.75	2.00
Dale Earnhardt Jr.	1.00	2.50
Elliott Sadler	.15	.40
Mike McLaughlin	.07	.20
Tony Stewart	.75	2.00
Rusty Wallace CL	.30	.75

1999 Upper Deck Victory Circle UD Exclusives

Randomly inserted into packs, this hobby-only insert is a complete parallel of the 1999 Upper Deck Victory Circle base set. Each card is individually serial numbered to 99.

COMPLETE SET (89)	400.00	800.00
*EXCLUSIVES: 10X TO 25X BASIC CARDS		

1999 Upper Deck Victory Circle Income Statement

Randomly inserted into packs at one in 2, this 15-card insert set features some of the top money-makers from 1999. Card backs carry an "IS" prefix

COMPLETE SET (15)	10.00	25.00
IS1 Jeff Gordon	2.00	5.00
IS2 Bobby Labonte	1.25	3.00
IS3 Bill Elliott	.75	2.00
IS4 Rusty Wallace	1.50	4.00
IS5 Jeff Burton	.60	1.50
IS6 Kenny Irwin	.40	1.00
IS7 Jeremy Mayfield	.40	1.00
IS8 Dale Jarrett	1.25	3.00
IS9 Ken Schrader	.20	.50
IS10 Mark Martin	1.50	4.00
IS11 Ricky Rudd	.60	1.50
IS12 John Andretti	.20	.50
IS13 Ernie Irvan	.40	1.00
IS14 Terry Labonte	.60	1.50
IS15 Dale Earnhardt Jr.	2.50	6.00

1999 Upper Deck Victory Circle Magic Numbers

Randomly inserted into packs at the rate of one in 999, this set features actual race-used numbers peeled off from the side of the top cars in NASCAR. Card backs carry a "M" prefix.

COMPLETE SET (4)	250.00	400.00
M1 Mark Martin	20.00	50.00
M2 Bobby Labonte	20.00	50.00
M3 Dale Jarrett	20.00	50.00
M4 Rusty Wallace	20.00	50.00

1999 Upper Deck Victory Circle Magic Numbers Autographs

Randomly inserted into packs, this set features authentic autographs as well as actual race-used numbers peeled off from the side of the top cars in NASCAR. Card backs carry a "M" prefix. Print runs are listed in our checklist.

M1 Mark Martin/6		
M2 Bobby Labonte/18	300.00	400.00
M3 Dale Jarrett/88	125.00	200.00
M4 Rusty Wallace/2		

1999 Upper Deck Victory Circle Signature Collection

Randomly inserted into packs at one in 100, this 20-card insert set features authentic signatures from NASCAR's top drivers. The cards look similar to the Road to the Cup Signature Collection but can be differentiated by the rectangular shaped player image and the lack of a Victory Circle logo on the cardfronts. The cardbacks carry the player's initials as numbering.

BL Bobby Labonte	12.50	30.00
DE Dale Earnhardt		
DJ Dale Jarrett	20.00	50.00
DW Darrell Waltrip	15.00	40.00
EI Ernie Irvan	12.50	30.00
ES Elliott Sadler	10.00	25.00
JA John Andretti	10.00	25.00
JB Jeff Burton	8.00	20.00
JG Jeff Gordon	75.00	150.00
JM Jeremy Mayfield	10.00	25.00
JN Jerry Nadeau	12.50	30.00
KI Kenny Irwin	15.00	40.00
KP Kyle Petty	12.50	30.00
MM Mark Martin	25.00	50.00
MW Michael Waltrip	10.00	25.00
RR Ricky Rudd	20.00	40.00
RW Rusty Wallace	12.50	30.00
SP Steve Park	12.50	30.00
TL Terry Labonte	12.50	30.00
DEJ Dale Earnhardt Jr.	60.00	120.00

1999 Upper Deck Victory Circle Speed Zone

Randomly inserted into packs at one in 2, this 15-card insert set features drivers that feel the need for speed. Card backs carry a "SZ" prefix.

COMPLETE SET (15)	15.00	30.00
SZ1 Bobby Labonte	1.25	3.00
SZ2 Mark Martin	1.50	4.00
SZ3 Jeff Gordon	2.00	5.00
SZ4 Ernie Irvan	.40	1.00
SZ5 Bill Elliott	.75	2.00
SZ6 Rusty Wallace	1.50	4.00
SZ7 Jeff Burton	.60	1.50
SZ8 Dale Jarrett	1.25	3.00
SZ9 Terry Labonte	.60	1.50
SZ10 Dale Earnhardt Jr.	2.50	6.00
SZ11 Steve Park	1.00	2.50
SZ12 Jeremy Mayfield	.40	1.00
SZ13 John Andretti	.20	.50
SZ14 Bobby Hamilton	.20	.50
SZ15 Ken Schrader	.20	.50

1999 Upper Deck Victory Circle Track Masters

Randomly inserted into packs at one in 11, this 15-card insert set features drivers that have "mastered" almost every track in the Northern Hemisphere. Card backs carry a "TM" prefix.

COMPLETE SET (15)	40.00	80.00
TM1 Jeff Gordon	6.00	15.00
TM2 Dale Jarrett	4.00	10.00
TM3 Ernie Irvan	1.25	3.00
TM4 Sterling Marlin	2.00	5.00
TM5 Rusty Wallace	5.00	12.00
TM6 Mark Martin	5.00	12.00
TM7 Jeff Burton	2.00	5.00
TM8 Bobby Hamilton	.60	1.50
TM9 Terry Labonte	2.00	5.00
TM10 Jeremy Mayfield	1.25	3.00
TM11 Bobby Labonte	4.00	10.00
TM12 Bill Elliott	2.50	6.00
TM13 Darrell Waltrip	1.25	3.00
TM14 John Andretti	.60	1.50
TM15 Dale Earnhardt Jr.	8.00	20.00

1999 Upper Deck Victory Circle Victory Circle

Randomly inserted into packs at one in 23, this 9-card insert set features top drivers on die cut card stock. Card backs carry a "V" prefix.

COMPLETE SET (9)	40.00	80.00
V1 Dale Earnhardt	12.50	30.00
V2 Bobby Labonte	5.00	12.00
V3 Terry Labonte	2.50	6.00
V4 Jeff Burton	2.50	6.00
V5 Mark Martin	6.00	15.00
V6 Dale Jarrett	5.00	12.00
V7 Jeremy Mayfield	1.50	4.00
V8 Jeff Gordon	8.00	20.00
V9 Rusty Wallace	6.00	15.00

2000 Upper Deck MVP

Released early in 2000, this 102 card set was issued in 10-card packs which came 28 packs per box with an SRP of $1.59 per pack. This set is evenly mixed between NASCAR drivers and the cars they drive.

COMPLETE SET (102)	8.00	20.00
1 Dale Jarrett	.40	1.00
2 Rusty Wallace	.50	1.25
3 Dale Earnhardt	1.00	2.50
4 John Andretti	.05	.15
5 Terry Labonte	.20	.50
6 Mark Martin	.50	1.25
7 Ken Schrader	.05	.15
8 Mike McLaughlin	.05	.15
9 Boris Said RC	.05	.15
10 Kyle Petty	.10	.30
11 Kevin Lepage	.05	.15
12 Bobby Hamilton	.05	.15
13 Mike Skinner	.05	.15
14 Johnny Benson	.10	.30
15 Chad Little	.05	.15
16 Kenny Wallace	.05	.15
17 John Nemechek Tribute	.05	.15
Joe Nemechek		
18 Bobby Labonte	.40	1.00
19 Jerry Nadeau	.10	.30
20 Tony Stewart	.60	1.50
21 Elliott Sadler	.10	.30
22 Ward Burton	.10	.30
23 Ernie Irvan	.10	.30
24 Jeff Gordon	.60	1.50
25 Bill Elliott	.25	.60
26 Ricky Craven	.05	.15
27 Michael Waltrip	.10	.30
28 Geoffrey Bodine	.05	.15
29 Jeff Burton	.20	.50
30 Robert Pressley	.05	.15
31 Sterling Marlin	.20	.50
32 Jeremy Mayfield	.05	.15
33 Steve Park	.20	.50
34 Matt Kenseth CRC	.50	1.25
35 Darrell Waltrip	.10	.30
36 Dave Marcis	.05	.15
37 Michael Waltrip	.10	.30
38 Jason Jarrett	.05	.15
39 Ricky Rudd	.20	.50
40 Casey Atwood	.20	.50
41 Jason Keller	.05	.15
42 Rick Mast	.05	.15
43 Bobby Hamilton Jr. RC	.10	.30
44 Randy LaJoie	.05	.15
45 Dick Trickle	.05	.15
46 Adam Petty	1.50	4.00
47 Hank Parker Jr. RC	.20	.50
48 Tony Stewart's Car	.25	.60
49 Robert Pressley's Car	.02	.10
50 Dick Trickle's Car	.02	.10
51 Elliott Sadler's Car	.02	.10
52 Dave Marcis's Car	.02	.10
53 Kenny Wallace's Car	.02	.10
54 Johnny Benson's Car	.02	.10
55 Geoffrey Bodine's Car	.02	.10
56 Ward Burton's Car	.05	.15
57 Bobby Hamilton Jr.'s Car	.02	.10
58 Mark Martin's Car	.20	.50
59 Hank Parker Jr.'s Car	.05	.15
60 Jason Jarrett's Car	.02	.10
61 Jason Keller's Car	.02	.10
62 Dale Jarrett's Car	.10	.30
63 Rusty Wallace's Car	.20	.50
64 Jeff Burton's Car	.10	.30
65 Jeff Gordon's Car	.25	.60
66 Jeremy Mayfield's Car	.02	.10
67 Kevin Lepage's Car	.02	.10
68 Bill Elliott's Car	.10	.30
69 Darrell Waltrip's Car	.05	.15
70 Steve Park's Car	.10	.30
71 Chad Little's Car	.05	.15
72 Terry Labonte's Car	.10	.30
73 Adam Petty's Car	.60	1.50
74 Kyle Petty's Car	.05	.15
75 Bobby Labonte's Car	.10	.30
76 Matt Kenseth's Car	.20	.50
77 Ernie Irvan's Car	.05	.15
78 Tony Stewart's Car	.25	.60
79 Casey Atwood's Car	.10	.30
80 Michael Waltrip's Car	.05	.15
81 Ricky Rudd's Car	.05	.15
82 Mike Skinner's Car	.02	.10
83 Ken Schrader's Car	.02	.10
84 Bobby Hamilton's Car	.02	.10
85 Dale Jarrett	.40	1.00
Ned Jarrett		
86 John Andretti's Car	.02	.10
87 Dale Earnhardt's Car	.40	1.00
88 Mike McLaughlin's Car	.02	.10
89 Jerry Nadeau's Car	.10	.30
90 Randy LaJoie's Car	.02	.10
91 Sterling Marlin's Car	.05	.15
92 Dale Jarrett	.40	1.00
93 Dale Earnhardt Jr.	.75	2.00
94 Boris Said RC	.05	.15
95 Terry Labonte	.20	.50
96 Darrell Waltrip	.10	.30
97 Ricky Rudd	.20	.50
98 Dale Earnhardt Jr.'s Car	.30	.75
99 Matt Kenseth	.50	1.25
100 Wally Dallenbach	.05	.15
101 Tony Stewart CL	.30	.75
102 Jeff Gordon CL	.30	.75

2000 Upper Deck MVP Gold Script

Randomly inserted in hobby packs, this is a parallel set to the MVP base set with a gold facsimile autograph on the card fronts. These cards are serial numbered to 125.

COMPLETE SET (102)	250.00	500.00
*GOLD SCRIPT: 8X TO 20X BASE CARDS		

2000 Upper Deck MVP Silver Script

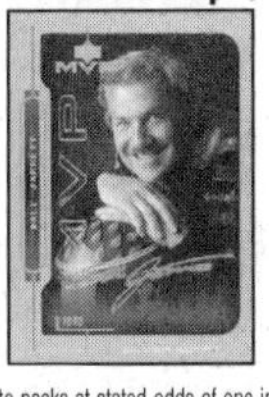

Inserted into packs at stated odds of one in two, this is a parallel to the Upper Deck MVP set with a silver facsimile autograph on the card fronts.

COMPLETE SET (102)	15.00	40.00
*SILVER SCRIPTS: .8X TO 2X BASE CARDS		

2000 Upper Deck MVP Super Script

Randomly inserted in hobby packs, this is a parallel to the basic set. These cards are all serial numbered to the driver's car number. Please note that cards with a print run of less than 20 are not priced.

*SINGLES/70-99: 15X TO 40X BASE CARDS

*SINGLES/45-69: 20X TO 50X BASE CARDS
*SINGLES/30-44: 40X TO 80X BASE CARDS
*SINGLES/20-29: 40X TO 80X BASE CARDS

2000 Upper Deck MVP Cup Quest 2000

Issued at stated odds of one in seven, these 10 cards honor the drivers with the best chance of finishing the year as Winston Cup champion.

COMPLETE SET (10)	10.00	25.00
CQ1 Dale Earnhardt	2.50	6.00
CQ2 Dale Earnhardt Jr.	2.00	5.00
CQ3 Terry Labonte	.50	1.25
CQ4 Ward Burton	.30	.75
CQ5 Tony Stewart	1.50	4.00
CQ6 Jeff Burton	.50	1.25
CQ7 Dale Jarrett	1.00	2.50
CQ8 Bobby Labonte	1.00	2.50
CQ9 Jeff Gordon	1.50	4.00
CQ10 Mark Martin	1.25	3.00

2000 Upper Deck MVP Legends in the Making

Inserted at stated odds of one in 13, these 10 cards feature drivers who have the best chance to become legendary figures in NASCAR history.

LM1 Jeff Gordon	2.00	5.00
LM2 Matt Kenseth	1.50	4.00
LM3 Bobby Labonte	1.25	3.00
LM4 Terry Labonte	.60	1.50
LM5 Dale Earnhardt Jr.	2.50	6.00
LM6 Dale Jarrett	1.25	3.00
LM7 Mark Martin	1.50	4.00
LM8 Jeff Burton	.60	1.50
LM9 Casey Atwood	.60	1.50
LM10 Tony Stewart	2.00	5.00

2000 Upper Deck MVP Magic Numbers

Inserted at stated odds of one in 391, these five cards feature not only the drivers pictured but a real piece of a race-driven NASCAR car on them.

MBL Bobby Labonte's Car	20.00	50.00
MDJ Dale Jarrett's Car	20.00	50.00
MMK Matt Kenseth's Car	20.00	50.00
MRW Rusty Wallace's Car	20.00	50.00
MTS Tony Stewart's Car	20.00	50.00

2000 Upper Deck MVP Magic Numbers Autographs

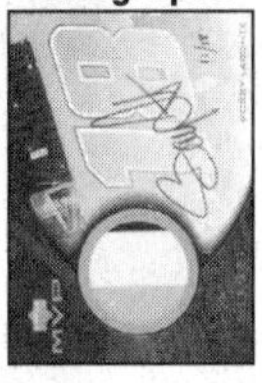

Randomly inserted to packs, these cards parallel the Magic Number insert set. These cards are serial numbered to the car number and have been autographed by the honored driver.

MABL Bobby Labonte's Car/18	200.00	350.00
MADJ Dale Jarrett's Car/88	75.00	150.00
MAMK Matt Kenseth's Car/17	250.00	400.00
MARW Rusty Wallace's Car/2		
MATS Tony Stewart's Car/20	200.00	400.00

2000 Upper Deck MVP NASCAR Gallery

Inserted in packs at stated odds of one in 27, these nine cards focus on the most collectible drivers in NASCAR.

NG1 Terry Labonte	1.00	2.50
NG2 Tony Stewart	3.00	8.00
NG3 Mark Martin	2.50	6.00
NG4 Jeff Burton	1.00	2.50
NG5 Dale Earnhardt Jr.	4.00	10.00
NG6 Matt Kenseth	2.50	6.00
NG7 Dale Jarrett	2.00	5.00
NG8 Casey Atwood	1.00	2.50
NG9 Jeff Gordon	3.00	8.00
NG10 Bobby Labonte	2.00	5.00

2000 Upper Deck MVP NASCAR Stars

Inserted at stated odds of one in five, these 11 cards highlight the sport's top drivers.

COMPLETE SET (11)	10.00	25.00
NS1 Tony Stewart	1.25	3.00
NS2 Jeff Gordon	1.25	3.00
NS3 Dale Earnhardt	2.00	5.00
NS4 Jeff Burton	.40	1.00
NS5 Dale Jarrett	.75	2.00
NS6 Mark Martin	1.00	2.50
NS7 Bobby Labonte	.75	2.00
NS8 Terry Labonte	.40	1.00
NS9 Matt Kenseth	1.00	2.50
NS10 Casey Atwood	.40	1.00
NS11 Dale Earnhardt Jr.	1.50	4.00

2000 Upper Deck MVP ProSign

Inserted at stated odds of one in 144, these 15 cards feature autographs of leading drivers. All these cards were released at redemptions and had a redemption deadline of October 7, 2000. Bobby Labonte did not return his cards so none of his cards were signed.

PSBL Bobby Labonte EXCH	4.00	10.00
PSCA Casey Atwood	15.00	40.00
PSDJ Dale Jarrett	12.50	30.00
PSDW Darrell Waltrip	20.00	50.00
PSJA John Andretti	7.50	20.00
PSJB Jeff Burton	10.00	25.00
PSJG Jeff Gordon	200.00	350.00
PSJM Jeremy Mayfield	15.00	30.00
PSJR Dale Earnhardt Jr.	60.00	120.00
PSKS Ken Schrader	6.00	15.00
PSMK Matt Kenseth	15.00	40.00
PSMM Mark Martin	20.00	50.00
PSRW Rusty Wallace	15.00	40.00
PSTS Tony Stewart	30.00	80.00
PSWB Ward Burton	10.00	25.00

2000 Upper Deck Racing

Released as a 45-card base set, 2000 Upper Deck features all rainbow holofoil cards with gold foil highlights and featured close up portrait style photography. Upper Deck was packaged in 24-pack boxes with packs containing four cards and carried a suggested retail price of $2.99.

COMPLETE SET (45)	10.00	25.00
1 Dale Jarrett	.75	2.00
2 Bobby Labonte	.75	2.00
3 Mark Martin	1.00	2.50
4 Tony Stewart	1.25	3.00
5 Jeff Burton	.40	1.00
6 Jeff Gordon	1.25	3.00
7 Dale Earnhardt	2.00	5.00
8 Rusty Wallace	1.00	2.50
9 Ward Burton	.25	.60
10 Mike Skinner	.10	.30
11 Jeremy Mayfield	.10	.30
12 Terry Labonte	.40	1.00
13 Bobby Hamilton	.10	.30
14 Steve Park	.40	1.00
15 Race Day	.05	.15
16 Sterling Marlin	.40	1.00
17 John Andretti	.10	.30
18 Wally Dallenbach	.10	.30
19 Kenny Irwin	.25	.60
20 Bill Elliott	.50	1.25
21 Kenny Wallace	.10	.30
22 Chad Little	.25	.60
23 Elliott Sadler	.25	.60

2000 Upper Deck Racing

24 Kevin Lepage	.10	.30
25 Kyle Petty	.25	.60
26 Johnny Benson	.25	.60
27 Michael Waltrip	.25	.60
28 Ricky Rudd	.40	1.00
29 Jerry Nadeau	.25	.60
30 Darrell Waltrip	.25	.60
31 Dale Earnhardt Jr. CRC	1.50	4.00
32 Matt Kenseth CRC	1.00	2.50
33 Jason Keller	.10	.30
34 Scott Pruett RC	.10	.30
35 Robby Gordon	.10	.30
36 Stacy Compton RC	.25	.60
37 Randy LaJoie	.10	.30
38 Jimmie Johnson RC	5.00	12.00
39 Kevin Harvick	1.00	2.50
40 Power Pit	.05	.15
41 Garage Work	.05	.15
42 Short Tracks	.05	.15
43 Hank Parker Jr. RC	.40	1.00
44 Casey Atwood	.40	1.00
45 Tony Stewart CL	.60	1.50

2000 Upper Deck Racing Brickyard's Best

Randomly inserted in packs at the rate of one in 95, this eight card set features swatches of a tire that was used in the inaugural Brickyard 400 race in 1994.

COMPLETE SET (8)	125.00	250.00
BB1 Rusty Wallace	12.50	30.00
BB2 Mark Martin	12.50	30.00
BB3 Bill Elliott	10.00	25.00
BB4 Darrell Waltrip	10.00	25.00
BB5 Dale Jarrett	12.50	30.00
BB6 Jeff Gordon	20.00	50.00
BB7 Ernie Irvan	10.00	25.00
BB8 Kyle Petty	10.00	25.00

2000 Upper Deck Racing High Groove

Randomly inserted in packs at the rate of one in 12, this six card set features top NASCAR drivers in a holographic foil card. Each card pictures the driver in the upper left hand corner and a large action shot of the car.

COMPLETE SET (6)	15.00	40.00
HG1 Jeff Burton	1.00	2.50
HG2 Dale Earnhardt Jr.	4.00	10.00
HG3 Matt Kenseth	2.50	6.00
HG4 Tony Stewart	3.00	8.00
HG5 Dale Earnhardt	5.00	12.00
HG6 Jeff Gordon	3.00	8.00

2000 Upper Deck Racing Record Pace

Randomly inserted in packs at the rate of one in three, this 9-card set features the driver with action shots of his car on an all rainbow holofoil card.

COMPLETE SET (9)	12.50	30.00
RP1 Jeff Burton	.60	1.50
RP2 Bobby Labonte	1.25	3.00
RP3 Dale Earnhardt	3.00	8.00
RP4 Mark Martin	1.50	4.00
RP5 Jeff Gordon	2.00	5.00
RP6 Dale Earnhardt Jr.	2.50	6.00
RP7 Dale Jarrett	1.25	3.00
RP8 Matt Kenseth	1.50	4.00
RP9 Tony Stewart	2.00	5.00

2000 Upper Deck Racing Road Signs

Randomly seeded in packs at the rate of one in 72, this 26-card set features authentic autographs of NASCAR drivers. Due to the tragic death of Adam Petty, his exchange cards were redeemable for autographs of other drivers from all 2000 Upper Deck Racing products.

RSAP Adam Petty EXCH	25.00	50.00
RSBL Bobby Labonte	12.50	30.00
RSCA Casey Atwood	6.00	15.00
RSDE Dale Earnhardt	300.00	450.00
RSDJ Dale Jarrett	12.50	30.00
RSES Elliott Sadler	10.00	25.00
RSJA John Andretti		
RSJB Jeff Burton		
RSJG Jeff Gordon	125.00	250.00
RSJM Jeremy Mayfield EXCH	8.00	20.00
RSJN Jerry Nadeau		
RSJR Dale Earnhardt Jr.	60.00	120.00
RSKG Kevin Grubb		
RSKH Kevin Harvick	15.00	40.00
RSKP Kyle Petty EXCH	20.00	40.00
RSKS Ken Schrader	8.00	20.00
RSLA Lyndon Amick	6.00	15.00
RSMK Matt Kenseth	30.00	60.00
RSMM Mark Martin	20.00	50.00
RSPA Steve Park		
RSRH Ron Hornaday	6.00	15.00
RSRR Ricky Rudd	15.00	40.00
RSRW Rusty Wallace	20.00	50.00
RSTL Terry Labonte		
RSTS Tony Stewart SP	175.00	300.00
RSWB Ward Burton	8.00	20.00

2000 Upper Deck Racing Speeding Ticket

Randomly inserted in packs at the rate of one in 12, this six card set features top drivers on an all rainbow holofoil insert card with gold foil highlights.

COMPLETE SET (6)	15.00	40.00
ST1 Jeff Gordon	3.00	8.00
ST2 Bobby Labonte	2.00	5.00
ST3 Dale Earnhardt Jr.	4.00	10.00
ST4 Tony Stewart	3.00	8.00
ST5 Dale Earnhardt	5.00	12.00
ST6 Dale Jarrett	2.00	5.00

2000 Upper Deck Racing Tear Aways

Randomly inserted in packs at the rate of one in 750, this 14-card set features swatches of race used windshield tear-aways.

COMPLETE SET (4)	75.00	150.00
TACA Casey Atwood	8.00	20.00
TADJ Dale Jarrett	10.00	25.00
TAMK Matt Kenseth	12.50	30.00
TARW Rusty Wallace	12.50	30.00

2000 Upper Deck Racing Thunder Road

Randomly inserted in packs at the rate of one in 12, this six card set features portrait shots of drivers with their cars in the background. Cards are all holographic foil with bronze foil highlights.

COMPLETE SET (6)	12.50	30.00
TR1 Kyle Petty	.60	1.50
TR2 Rusty Wallace	2.50	6.00
TR3 Mark Martin	2.50	6.00
TR4 Ricky Rudd	1.00	2.50
TR5 Jeff Gordon	3.00	8.00
TR6 Tony Stewart	3.00	8.00

2000 Upper Deck Racing Trophy Dash

Randomly inserted in packs at the rate of one in 72, this nine card set features both veterans and young stars on an all holofoil card stock.

COMPLETE SET (9)	50.00	120.00
TD1 Terry Labonte	2.50	6.00
TD2 Dale Earnhardt Jr.	10.00	25.00
TD3 Bobby Labonte	5.00	12.00
TD4 Matt Kenseth	6.00	15.00
TD5 Jeff Burton	2.50	6.00
TD6 Dale Earnhardt	12.50	30.00
TD7 Jeff Gordon	8.00	20.00
TD8 Dale Jarrett	5.00	12.00
TD9 Tony Stewart	8.00	20.00

2000 Upper Deck Racing Winning Formula

Randomly inserted in packs at the rate of one in 23, this six card set focuses on the top young drivers of the 2000 Winston Cup Series. Cards are issued in split format with a driver portrait on the right side and his car on the left.

COMPLETE SET (6)	25.00	60.00
WF1 Bobby Labonte	4.00	10.00
WF2 Mark Martin	5.00	12.00
WF3 Dale Earnhardt	10.00	25.00
WF4 Dale Jarrett	4.00	10.00
WF5 Tony Stewart	6.00	15.00
WF6 Jeff Gordon	6.00	15.00

2000 Upper Deck Racing CHP

This was a four card set produced for the California Highway Patrol and was given out at the California Speedway for the 2000 season.

COMPLETE SET (4)	2.00	4.00
1 Rusty Wallace	.75	2.00
2 Jeremy Mayfield	.25	.60
3 Mark Martin	.75	2.00
4 California Speedway	.12	.30

2000 Upper Deck Victory Circle

This 85 card set was issued in 10 card packs, with 24 packs per box and a SRP of $2.99 per pack. This set features a mix of leading drivers and their cars.

COMPLETE SET (85)	10.00	25.00
1 Hank Parker Jr. RC	.30	.75
2 Todd Bodine	.08	.25
3 Rick Mast	.08	.25
4 Rusty Wallace	.75	2.00
5 Jason Jarrett	.08	.25
6 Michael Waltrip	.20	.50
7 Ken Schrader	.08	.25
8 Steve Park	.30	.75
9 Dale Earnhardt	1.50	4.00
10 Jeremy Mayfield	.08	.25
11 Mike Skinner	.08	.25
12 Jason Keller	.08	.25
13 Lyndon Amick	.08	.25
14 Johnny Benson	.20	.50
15 Jeff Burton	.30	.75
16 Jeff Gordon	1.00	2.50
17 Kenny Wallace	.08	.25
18 Bobby Labonte	.60	1.50
19 Kevin Lepage	.08	.25
20 Geoffrey Bodine	.08	.25
21 Bill Elliott	.40	1.00
22 Tony Stewart	1.00	2.50
23 Kyle Petty	.20	.50
24 Darrell Waltrip	.20	.50
25 Mark Martin	.75	2.00
26 John Andretti	.08	.25
27 Brett Bodine	.08	.25
28 Ward Burton	.20	.50
29 Casey Atwood	.30	.75
30 Ernie Irvan	.20	.50
31 Matt Kenseth CRC	.75	2.00
32 Bobby Hamilton	.08	.25
33 Mike McLaughlin	.08	.25
34 Dale Jarrett	.60	1.50
35 Sterling Marlin	.30	.75
36 Elliott Sadler	.20	.50
37 Dale Earnhardt Jr. CRC	1.25	3.00
38 Terry Labonte	.30	.75
39 Chad Little	.08	.25
40 Kenny Irwin	.20	.50
41 Ricky Rudd	.30	.75
42 Derrike Cope	.08	.25
43 Ned Jarrett	.08	.25
44 Dick Trickle	.08	.25
45 Wally Dallenbach	.08	.25
46 Adam Petty	2.00	5.00
47 David Green	.08	.25
48 Robert Pressley	.08	.25
49 Ricky Craven	.08	.25
50 Bobby Hamilton Jr. RC	.20	.50
51 Randy LaJoie	.08	.25
52 Ward Burton's Car	.08	.25
53 Bobby Labonte's Car	.20	.50
54 Casey Atwood's Car	.20	.50
55 Dale Earnhardt's Car	.60	1.50
56 Dale Earnhardt Jr.'s Car	.50	1.25
57 Dale Jarrett's Car	.20	.50
58 Jeff Burton's Car	.20	.50
59 Jeff Gordon's Car	.40	1.00
60 Mark Martin's Car	.30	.75
61 Matt Kenseth's Car	.30	.75
62 Rusty Wallace's Car	.30	.75
63 Terry Labonte's Car	.20	.50
64 Tony Stewart's Car	.40	1.00
65 Jeff Gordon's Car	.40	1.00
66 Jeff Gordon's Car	.40	1.00
67 Tony Stewart's Car	.40	1.00
68 Casey Atwood's Car	.20	.50
69 Dale Jarrett's Car	.20	.50
70 Dale Earnhardt's Car	.60	1.50
71 Rusty Wallace's Car	.30	.75
72 Bobby Labonte's Car	.20	.50
73 Jeff Gordon's Car	.40	1.00
74 Jeff Burton's Car	.20	.50
75 Mark Martin's Car	.30	.75
76 Ernie Irvan's Car	.08	.25
77 Adam Petty's Car	.75	2.00
78 Dale Earnhardt Jr.'s Car	.50	1.25
79 Darrell Waltrip's Car	.08	.25
80 Tony Stewart's Car	.40	1.00
81 Johnny Benson	.20	.50
82 John Andretti	.08	.25
83 Matt Kenseth	.75	2.00
84 Terry Labonte's Car	.20	.50
85 Tony Stewart CL	.50	1.25

2000 Upper Deck Victory Circle Exclusives Level 1 Silver

Randomly inserted in hobby packs, these cards parallel the base set and are serial numbered to 250 in a silver bar at the bottom of the card front.

COMPLETE SET (85)	60.00	150.00

*EXCLUSIVES L1: 4X TO 10X BASE CARDS

2000 Upper Deck Victory Circle Exclusives Level 2 Gold

Randomly inserted into packs, this parallel set is numbered to the driver's car number in a gold bar at the bottom of the card front.

*SINGLES/70-99: 10X TO 25X HI COL.
*SINGLES/45-69: 12X TO 30X HI COL.
*SINGLES/30-44: 25X TO 50X HI COL.
*SINGLES/20-29: 40X TO 80X HI COL.

2000 Upper Deck Victory Circle A Day in the Life

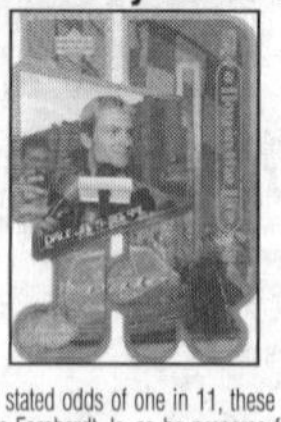

Inserted at stated odds of one in 11, these six cards follow Dale Earnhardt Jr. as he prepares for a race day.

COMPLETE SET (6)	10.00	25.00
COMMON DALE JR. (JR1-JR6)	2.00	5.00
COMP.LTD SET (6)	75.00	150.00

*LTD CARDS: 3X TO 6X BASIC INSERTS
LTD STATED ODDS 1:287

2000 Upper Deck Victory Circle Income Statement

Inserted in packs at stated odds of one in nine, these 10 die-cut cards feature NASCAR's top drivers and their top payouts during the 1999 season.

COMPLETE SET (10)	8.00	20.00
COMP.LTD SET (10)	15.00	40.00

*LTD CARDS: .8X TO 2X BASIC INSERTS
LTD STATED ODDS 1:23

IS1 Jeff Gordon	1.25	3.00
IS2 Jeff Burton	.40	1.00
IS3 Bobby Labonte	.75	2.00
IS4 Dale Jarrett	.75	2.00
IS5 Tony Stewart	1.25	3.00
IS6 Mark Martin	1.00	2.50
IS7 Ward Burton	.25	.60
IS8 Rusty Wallace	1.00	2.50
IS9 Matt Kenseth	1.00	2.50
IS10 Casey Atwood	.40	1.00

2000 Upper Deck Victory Circle Signature Collection

Inserted in packs at stated odds of one in 143, these 10-cards feature autographs from top drivers. A Gold foil parallel set for some cards was also produced. The cards were all released as redemptions and needed to be sent in by October 1, 2000.

CA Casey Atwood	8.00	20.00
DJ Dale Jarrett	12.50	30.00
DW Darrell Waltrip		
JB Jeff Burton	8.00	20.00
JG Jeff Gordon	60.00	120.00
JM Jeremy Mayfield	8.00	20.00
MK Matt Kenseth	20.00	50.00
RW Rusty Wallace	12.50	30.00
TS Tony Stewart	30.00	80.00
WB Ward Burton	8.00	20.00

2000 Upper Deck Victory Circle Signature Collection Gold

These cards are a gold foil parallel to the basic Signature Collection inserts. Each card was hand serial numbered to the driver's car number on the front and features a large gold foil area at the bottom of the cardfronts that includes the signature.

1 Casey Atwood/27		
2 Ward Burton/22		
3 Jeff Gordon/24		
4 Dale Jarrett/88	60.00	150.00
5 Tony Stewart/20		
6 Darrell Waltrip/66	40.00	80.00

2000 Upper Deck Victory Circle PowerDeck

Issued in packs at different odds, these six cards capture NASCAR action on digital trading cards. Stated odds for card one thru four are 1:23, and cards five and six are 1:287.

PD1 Dale Earnhardt	12.00	30.00
PD2 Dale Earnhardt Jr.	10.00	25.00
PD3 Rusty Wallace	5.00	12.00
PD4 Tony Stewart	8.00	20.00
PD5 Jeff Gordon	15.00	40.00
PD6 Dale Earnhardt Jr.	20.00	50.00

2000 Upper Deck Victory Circle Victory Circle

Inserted at stated odds of one in seven, these nine die-cut cards showcase drivers who won races in 1999.

COMP.LTD SET (9)	50.00	120.00

*LTD CARDS: 3X TO 6X BASIC INSERTS
LTD STATED ODDS 1:71

V1 Bobby Labonte	.75	
V2 Matt Kenseth	1.00	
V3 Rusty Wallace	1.00	
V4 Jeff Burton	.40	
V5 Casey Atwood	.40	
V6 Dale Jarrett	.75	
V7 Mark Martin	1.00	
V8 Terry Labonte	.40	
V9 Dale Earnhardt Jr.	1.50	

2000 Upper Deck Victo Circle Winning Materi Autographed Victory H

Randomly inserted into packs, this insert set fea pieces of caps worn by Drivers in victory circle a with an autograph. Cards are numberd to 30.

HBL Bobby Labonte	150.00	30
HJB Jeff Burton	100.00	20
HMM Mark Martin	150.00	30
HRW Rusty Wallace	125.00	25

2000 Upper Deck Victo Circle Winning Materi Combination

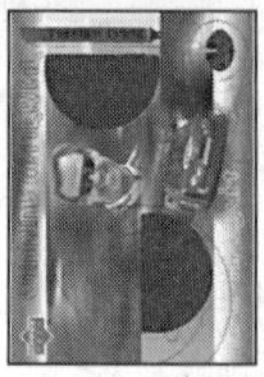

Randomly inserted into packs, these four c feature pieces of race-worn firesuits along with used tires. These cards are serial numbered to 5

CDJ Dale Jarrett	40.00	10
CMK Matt Kenseth	60.00	12
CMM Mark Martin	50.00	12
CRW Rusty Wallace	40.00	10

2000 Upper Deck Victo Circle Winning Materi Firesuit

Inserted into packs at stated odds of one in these five cards feature pieces of race-worn fires

FSDJ Dale Jarrett	15.00	4
FSMK Matt Kenseth	25.00	5
FSMM Mark Martin	15.00	4
FSRW Rusty Wallace	15.00	4
FSWB Ward Burton	12.50	3

2000 Upper Deck Victo Circle Winning Materi Tire

Inserted into packs at stated odds of one in these 10 cards feature pieces of race-used tires.

TBL Bobby Labonte	25.00	6
TCA Casey Atwood	20.00	5
TDE Dale Earnhardt		
TDJ Dale Jarrett	25.00	6
TJG Jeff Gordon	75.00	15
TJR Dale Earnhardt Jr.	75.00	15
TMK Matt Kenseth	25.00	6
TMM Mark Martin	25.00	6
TRW Rusty Wallace	25.00	6
TTS Tony Stewart	25.00	6

1995 US Air Greg Sac

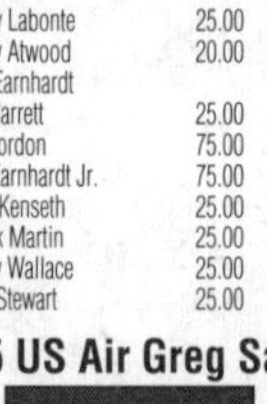

US Air produced and distributed this set feat Greg Sacks and the US Air Racing Team. The black bordered cards are not numbered and l below alphabetically.

COMPLETE SET (5)	2.00	
1 Tony Furr	.40	
2 Greg Sacks' Car	.40	
3 Greg Sacks in Pits	.40	

eg Sacks UER	.60	1.50
birthdate incorrect		
K. Ulrich	.40	1.00

992 U.S. Playing Card

set is actually a deck of playing cards featuring Junior Johnson Race Team and driver Bill Elliott. e the majority of the cards from the set show a playing card design, a few include photos of ıson and Elliott. The cardbacks feature Bill tt's car.

IP. FACT SET (56)	1.25	3.00
MON CARD (1-56)	.01	.05
ELLIOTT CARDS	.20	.50

007 Valvoline Racing

IP.FACT SET (25)	7.50	15.00
IPLETE SET (25)	6.00	12.00
) Shelly Payne	.30	.75
Scott Riggs		
Antron Brown		
) Jay Payne	.30	.75
) Ron Kisher	.30	.75
) Shelly Payne	.30	.75
) Ron Capps	.50	1.25
) Angelle Sampey	1.00	2.50
) Richie Stevens Jr.	.30	.75
) Antron Brown	.50	1.25
) Gary Scelzi	.50	1.25
) Scott Riggs	.30	.75
) Scott Riggs' Car	.30	.75
) Kasey Kahne	1.25	3.00
) Elliott Sadler	.30	.75
) Tony Schumacher	.50	1.25
) Jack Beckman		
) Bob Newberry	.30	.75
) Steve Francis	.30	.75
) Conventional Valvoline	.12	.30
) Durablend Valvoline	.12	.30
) Maxlife Valvoline	.12	.30
) Maxlife Synthetic Valvoline	.12	.30
) Synpower Valvoline	.12	.30
) VR1 Racing Valvoline	.12	.30
) FAQs 1	.12	.30
) FAQs 2	.12	.30

2002 Velveeta Jeff Burton

e 3-card set was sponsored by Kraft and issued art of boxes of Velveeta Shells and Cheese. Each was to be cut from the box of product. The s measure roughly 2 1/2" by 3 1/2" when cleanly

IPLETE SET (3)	5.00	10.00
MON CARD (1-3)	1.50	4.00

1994 VIP

100-card set was the first issued by card maker s Pass under the VIP brand name. The cards are ed on 24-point stock and are foil stamped on sides. There are four topical subsets: Portraits 81), Alabama Gang (82-84), Heroes of Racing 90), Master Mechanics (91-99). The Portraits et features nine water color paintings for racing t Jeanne Barnes. There were reportedly 3,500 s made. Each case contained 20 boxes, with 36 s per box and 6 cards per pack.

IPLETE SET (100)	10.00	25.00
(BOX	30.00	60.00
y Allen Jr.	.10	.30
ett Bodine	.10	.30
eoff Bodine	.10	.30
dd Bodine	.10	.30
uck Bown	.10	.30
ff Burton	.40	1.00
ard Burton	.25	.60
errike Cope	.10	.30
ally Dallenbach Jr.	.10	.30
Dale Earnhardt	2.00	5.00
Harry Gant	.25	.60
Jeff Gordon	1.25	3.00
Steve Grissom	.10	.30
Bobby Hamilton	.10	.30
Jimmy Hensley	.10	.30
Ernie Irvan	.25	.60
Dale Jarrett	.75	2.00
Bobby Labonte	.75	2.00
Terry Labonte	.40	1.00
Sterling Marlin	.40	1.00
Mark Martin	1.00	2.50
Rick Mast	.10	.30
Ted Musgrave	.10	.30
Joe Nemechek	.10	.30
Kyle Petty	.25	.60
Ricky Rudd	.40	1.00
Greg Sacks	.10	.30
Ken Schrader	.10	.30
Morgan Shepherd	.10	.30
Lake Speed	.10	.30
Jimmy Spencer	.10	.30
Hut Stricklin	.10	.30
33 Mike Wallace	.10	.30
34 Rusty Wallace	1.00	2.50
35 Darrell Waltrip	.25	.60
36 Michael Waltrip	.25	.60
37 Morgan Shepherd w/Car	.05	.15
38 Jeff Gordon w/Car	1.25	3.00
39 Geoff Bodine w/Car	.05	.15
40 Ted Musgrave w/Car	.05	.15
41 Derrike Cope w/Car	.05	.15
42 Dale Earnhardt w/Car	2.00	5.00
43 Dale Jarrett w/Car	.75	2.00
44 Terry Labonte w/Car	.40	1.00
45 Ken Schrader w/Car	.05	.15
46 Bobby Labonte w/Car	.75	2.00
47 Kyle Petty w/Car	.10	.30
48 Rusty Wallace 's Car	.25	.60
49 Michael Waltrip w/Car	.10	.30
50 Brett Bodine w/Car	.05	.15
51 Ernie Irvan w/Car	.10	.30
52 Ricky Rudd w/Car	.25	.60
53 Mark Martin w/Car	1.00	2.50
54 Darrell Waltrip w/Car	.10	.30
55 Johnny Benson RC	.40	1.00
56 Ricky Craven	.10	.30
57 Bobby Dotter	.10	.30
58 David Green	.10	.30
59 Tracy Leslie	.10	.30
60 Chad Little	.10	.30
61 Mike McLaughlin	.10	.30
62 Larry Pearson	.10	.30
63 Tom Peck	.10	.30
64 Robert Pressley	.10	.30
65 Dennis Setzer	.10	.30
66 Kenny Wallace	.10	.30
67 Tom Peck's Car	.05	.15
68 Bobby Dotter w/Car	.05	.15
69 Ricky Craven w/Car	.05	.15
70 Mike McLaughlin w/Car	.05	.15
71 David Green w/Car	.05	.15
72 Hermie Sadler's Car	.05	.15
73 Harry Gant ART	.10	.30
74 Jeff Gordon ART	.60	1.50
75 Ernie Irvan ART	.10	.30
76 Dale Jarrett ART	.40	1.00
77 Sterling Marlin ART	.25	.60
78 Mark Martin ART	.40	1.00
79 Kyle Petty ART	.10	.30
80 Morgan Shepherd ART	.05	.15
81 Rusty Wallace ART	.40	1.00
82 Bobby Allison RF	.10	.30
83 Donnie Allison RF	.10	.30
84 Red Farmer RF	.05	.15
85 Ned Jarrett HR	.05	.15
86 Junior Johnson HR	.10	.30
87 Ralph Moody HR	.05	.15
88 Benny Parsons HR	.10	.30
89 Wendell Scott HR	.10	.30
90 Cale Yarborough HR	.10	.30
91 Paul Andrews MM	.05	.15
92 Barry Dodson MM	.05	.15
93 Jeff Hammond MM	.05	.15
94 Steve Hmiel MM	.05	.15
95 Jimmy Makar MM	.05	.15
96 Larry McReynolds MM	.05	.15
97 Buddy Parrott MM	.05	.15
98 Robin Pemberton MM	.05	.15
99 Andy Petree MM	.05	.15
100 Checklist	.05	.15
P1 Jeff Gordon's Car Prototype	2.00	5.00
P2 Ernie Irvan Prototype	1.25	3.00
P3 Harry Gant Prototype	.75	2.00
P4 Rusty Wallace Prototype	2.00	5.00

1994 VIP Driver's Choice

The nine-card insert set features the drivers, as chosen by their peers, as the most likely to win the 1994 Winston Cup Championship. The cards were seeded one per eight packs.

COMPLETE SET (9)	10.00	25.00
DC1 Dale Earnhardt	5.00	12.00
DC2 Ernie Irvan	.60	1.50
DC3 Dale Jarrett	2.00	5.00
DC4 Sterling Marlin	1.00	2.50
DC5 Mark Martin	2.50	6.00
DC6 Kyle Petty	.60	1.50
DC7 Ken Schrader	.30	.75
DC8 Morgan Shepherd	.30	.75
DC9 Rusty Wallace	2.50	6.00

1994 VIP Gold Signature

This seven-card set was originally inserted in packs of VIP via redemption cards. Inserted at a rate of one per 240 packs was a redemption card that had a driver's facsimile signature in a gold foil stamping across the front. There were only 1,500 of each of the seven redemption cards. This redemption card was then used to receive a 24K Gold Signature card. The prices below are for the 24K Gold Signature cards and not the redemption card.

COMPLETE SET (7)	125.00	250.00
EC1 Dale Earnhardt	25.00	60.00
EC2 Harry Gant	3.00	8.00
EC3 Jeff Gordon	15.00	40.00
EC4 Ernie Irvan	3.00	8.00
EC5 Mark Martin	12.50	30.00
EC6 Kyle Petty	3.00	8.00
EC7 Rusty Wallace	12.50	30.00
SEC1 Super Exchange Card Exp.	.75	2.00

1994 VIP Member's Only

Although these two cards do not carry the VIP logo, they utilize the same design as the 1994 VIP set. They were distributed directly to participants of Press Pass' Member's Only collecting club. The cards are unnumbered and carry a blue foil "Member's Only" logo.

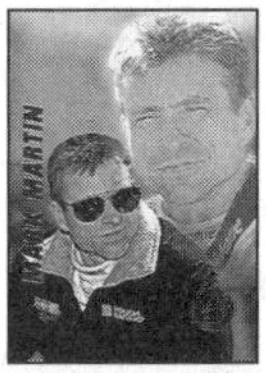

COMPLETE SET (2)	6.00	15.00
1 Geoff Bodine	2.00	5.00
2 Mark Martin	4.00	10.00

1995 VIP Promos

Press Pass produced this set to preview its 1995 VIP set. Each of the four cards can be found with either Red or Gold foil layering on the cardfront. While the Gold cards are not numbered, the Red foil versions are individually numbered of 6000 produced.

COMPLETE SET (4)	1.00	2.50
*RED CARDS: 1.2X TO 3X GOLDS		
1G Dale Jarrett Gold	.40	1.00
2G Bobby Labonte Gold	.40	1.00
3G Michael Waltrip Gold	.20	.50
4G Derrike Cope Gold	.20	.50

1995 VIP

This 64-card set represents the second year for the VIP brand. The cards feature top personalities from NASCAR racing. Each card is gold-foil stamped and is printed on 24-point stock.There are four topical subsets: Heroes of Racing (46-50), Track Dominators (51-54), Master Mechanics (55-59), SuperTruck (60-63). The cards came packed six cards per pack. There were 24 packs per box and 16 boxes per case.

COMPLETE SET (64)	10.00	25.00
WAX BOX	45.00	80.00
1 John Andretti	.10	.30
2 Brett Bodine	.10	.30
3 Geoff Bodine	.10	.30
4 Todd Bodine	.10	.30
5 Jeff Burton	.40	1.00
6 Ward Burton	.25	.60
7 Derrike Cope	.10	.30
8 Ricky Craven	.10	.30
9 Dale Earnhardt	2.00	5.00
10 Bill Elliott	.50	1.25
11 Jeff Gordon	1.25	3.00
12 Steve Grissom	.10	.30
13 Bobby Hamilton	.10	.30
14 Dale Jarrett	.75	2.00
15 Bobby Labonte	.75	2.00
16 Terry Labonte	.40	1.00
17 Randy LaJoie	.10	.30
18 Sterling Marlin	.40	1.00
19 Mark Martin	1.00	2.50
20 Ted Musgrave	.10	.30
21 Joe Nemechek	.10	.30
22 Kyle Petty	.25	.60
23 Robert Pressley	.10	.30
24 Ricky Rudd	.40	1.00
25 Ken Schrader	.10	.30
26 Morgan Shepherd	.10	.30
27 Dick Trickle	.10	.30
28 Rusty Wallace	1.00	2.50
29 Darrell Waltrip	.25	.60
30 Michael Waltrip	.25	.60
31 Jeff Gordon	1.25	3.00
32 Sterling Marlin	.40	1.00
33 Mark Martin	1.00	2.50
34 Kyle Petty	.25	.60
35 Ricky Rudd	.40	1.00
36 Ken Schrader	.10	.30
37 Johnny Benson Jr.	.25	.60
38 Rodney Combs	.10	.30
39 Bobby Dotter	.10	.30
40 David Green	.10	.30
41 Chad Little	.10	.30
42 Mike McLaughlin	.10	.30
43 Larry Pearson	.10	.30
44 Dennis Setzer	.10	.30
45 Kenny Wallace	.10	.30
46 Bobby Allison HR	.10	.30
47 Ernie Irvan HR	.25	.60
48 Elmo Langley HR	.05	.15
49 Richard Petty HR	.40	1.00
50 Tim Richmond HR	.10	.30
51 Bill Elliott TD	.40	1.00
52 Sterling Marlin TD	.40	1.00
53 Mark Martin TD	.50	1.25
54 Darrell Waltrip TD	.25	.60
55 Jeff Andrews MM	.05	.15
56 Danny Glad MM	.05	.15
57 Charlie Siegars MM	.05	.15
58 Rick Wetzel MM	.05	.15
59 Gregg Wilson MM	.05	.15
60 Geoff Bodine's Truck	.05	.15
61 Jeff Gordon's Truck	.40	1.00
62 Ken Schrader's Truck	.05	.15
63 Mike Skinner's Truck	.05	.15
64 Checklist	.05	.15

1995 VIP Cool Blue

This 64-card set is a parallel of the base set. These hobby only cards feature a blue foil stamping, while the retail cards feature a red foil stamping. Cool Blue cards were available one per pack in Hobby packs.

COMPLETE SET (64)	15.00	40.00
*COOL BLUE: .8X TO 2X BASE CARDS		

1995 VIP Emerald Proofs

This 64-card set is a parallel of the base set. The cards feature a emerald color foil stamping and are numbered of 380. The cards were randomly inserted at a rate of one per 32 packs.

COMPLETE SET (64)	250.00	500.00
*EMER.PROOFS: 5X TO 12X BASIC CARDS		

1995 VIP Red Hot

This 64-card set is a parallel of the base set. These hobby only cards feature a red foil stamping and were available one per Retail pack.

COMPLETE SET (64)	15.00	40.00
*RED HOTS: .8X TO 2X BASIC CARDS		

1995 VIP Autographs

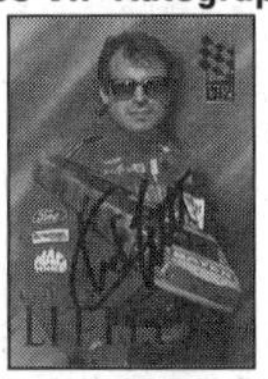

This 24-card insert set consists of autographed regular VIP cards. The only way to tell the difference in one of these cards and one signed at a show or a track, is that the ones from packs don't have the UV coating. Press Pass does this intentionally to make them easier for the drivers to sign and to differentiate the insert cards. There were more than 30,000 signed cards inserted in the VIP packs at a rate of one per 24 packs. Each card was not signed in equal quantities.

COMPLETE SET (24)	175.00	350.00
7 Derrike Cope	6.00	15.00
8 Ricky Craven	6.00	15.00
11 Jeff Gordon	50.00	100.00
13 Bobby Hamilton	10.00	25.00
18 Sterling Marlin	8.00	20.00
19 Mark Martin	15.00	40.00
20 Ted Musgrave	6.00	15.00
22 Kyle Petty	15.00	40.00
25 Ken Schrader	10.00	25.00
37 Johnny Benson	10.00	25.00
38 Rodney Combs	6.00	15.00
39 Bobby Dotter	6.00	15.00
40 David Green	6.00	15.00
41 Chad Little	8.00	20.00
42 Mike McLaughlin	6.00	15.00
43 Larry Pearson	6.00	15.00
44 Dennis Setzer	6.00	15.00
45 Kenny Wallace	6.00	15.00
47 Ernie Irvan HR	10.00	25.00
55 Jeff Andrews MM	5.00	10.00
56 Danny Glad MM	5.00	10.00
57 Charlie Siegars MM	5.00	10.00
58 Rick Wetzel MM	5.00	10.00
59 Gregg Wilson MM	5.00	10.00

1995 VIP Fan's Choice

This nine-card insert set features the top nine Winston Cup drivers as voted by the Press Pass VIP Club members. The cards are printed on either gold or silver foil board. Fan's Choice Silver cards could be found at a rate of one per six packs. Gold cards were packaged at the rate of 1:30 packs.

COMPLETE SILVER SET (9)	10.00	25.00
*GOLDS: 1X TO 2.5X BASIC INSERTS		
FC1 Dale Earnhardt	6.00	15.00
FC2 Bill Elliott	1.50	4.00
FC3 Jeff Gordon	4.00	10.00
FC4 Terry Labonte	1.25	3.00
FC5 Sterling Marlin	1.25	3.00
FC6 Mark Martin	3.00	8.00
FC7 Ricky Rudd	1.25	3.00
FC8 Ken Schrader	.40	1.00
FC9 Rusty Wallace	3.00	8.00

1995 VIP Helmets

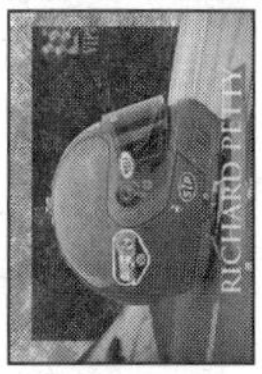

This nine-card insert set uses Nitrokrome technology along with etched foil printed on silver or gold foil to bring out the color in some of the best Winston Cup drivers' helmets. The Silver cards were randomly inserted in packs at a rate of one per 18 with Gold cards packed at 1:90.

COMPLETE SILVER SET (9)	20.00	50.00
*GOLDS: .6X TO 1.5X BASIC INSERTS		
H1 Geoff Bodine	1.25	3.00
H2 Jeff Burton	4.00	10.00
H3 Derrike Cope	1.25	3.00
H4 Jeff Gordon	12.50	30.00
H5 Kyle Petty	2.50	6.00
H6 Ricky Rudd	4.00	10.00
H7 Richard Petty 1960's	4.00	10.00
H8 Richard Petty 1980's	4.00	10.00
H9 Richard Petty 1990's	4.00	10.00

1995 VIP Reflections

This five-card insert set features the artwork of Jeanne Barnes. The card fronts show a portrait of the driver as if you were looking at him from head on. The card backs show a portrait of the driver as if you were standing behind him. The cards are printed on both silver and gold foil board with Silver cards inserted at a rate of one per 72 packs. Gold cards were packaged 1:360 packs.

COMPLETE SILVER SET (5)	25.00	60.00
*GOLDS: 1.2X TO 3X BASIC INSERTS		
R1 Ricky Craven	1.00	2.50
R2 Jeff Gordon	10.00	25.00
R3 Sterling Marlin	3.00	8.00
R4 Mark Martin	8.00	20.00
R5 Rusty Wallace	8.00	20.00

1996 VIP

The 1996 VIP set was issued in one series totalling 54 cards. The cards are packaged six cards per pack, 24 packs per box and 16 boxes per case. Each card is printed on 24 point board and has foil stamping and UV coating.

COMPLETE SET (54)	8.00	20.00
1 John Andretti	.10	.30
2 Johnny Benson	.25	.60
3 Geoff Bodine	.10	.30
4 Jeff Burton	.40	1.00
5 Ward Burton	.25	.60
6 Ricky Craven	.10	.30
7 Wally Dallenbach	.10	.30
8 Dale Earnhardt	2.00	5.00
9 Bill Elliott	.50	1.25
10 Jeff Gordon	1.25	3.00
11 Bobby Hamilton	.10	.30
12 Ernie Irvan	.25	.60
13 Dale Jarrett	.75	2.00
14 Bobby Labonte	.75	2.00
15 Terry Labonte	.40	1.00
16 Sterling Marlin	.40	1.00
17 Mark Martin	1.00	2.50
18 Jeremy Mayfield	.25	.60
19 Ted Musgrave	.10	.30
20 Joe Nemechek	.10	.30
21 Kyle Petty	.25	.60
22 Robert Pressley	.10	.30
23 Ricky Rudd	.40	1.00
24 Ken Schrader	.10	.30
25 Morgan Shepherd	.10	.30
26 Mike Skinner	.10	.30
27 Rusty Wallace	1.00	2.50
28 Darrell Waltrip	.25	.60
29 Michael Waltrip	.25	.60
30 Jeff Gordon	1.25	3.00
31 Mark Martin	.75	2.00
32 David Green	.10	.30
33 Jeff Green	.10	.30
34 Jason Keller	.10	.30
35 Chad Little	.25	.60
36 Mike McLaughlin	.10	.30
37 Jeff Gordon's Car	.50	1.25
38 Dale Earnhardt's Car	.75	2.00
39 Bill Elliott's Car	.25	.60
40 Rusty Wallace's Car	.40	1.00
41 Dale Jarrett's Car	.25	.60
42 Bobby Hamilton's Car	.05	.15
43 Ernie Irvan's Car	.10	.30
44 Ricky Rudd's Car	.10	.30
45 Mark Martin's Car	.40	1.00
46 Ray Evernham	.25	.60
47 Steve Hmiel	.05	.15
48 Larry McReynolds	.05	.15
49 David Smith	.05	.15
50 Jeff Andrews	.05	.15
51 Danny Glad	.05	.15
52 Charlie Siegars	.05	.15
53 Rick Wetzel	.05	.15
54 Checklist	.05	.15
P1 Mark Martin Promo	2.00	5.00
P2 Kyle Petty Club Promo	2.00	5.00

1996 VIP Emerald Proofs

This 54-card set is a parallel to the base VIP set. The cards feature a metallic green foil stamping to differentiate them. There are 380 of each of the 54 cards and they were inserted at a rate of one per 40 packs.

COMPLETE SET (54)	200.00	400.00
*EMER.PROOFS: 4X TO 10X BASE CARDS		

1996 VIP Torquers

This 54-card set is a parallel to the base VIP set. The cards feature blue foil stamping and could be pulled at a rate of one per pack.

COMPLETE SET (54)	10.00	25.00
*TORQUERS: .6X TO 1.5X BASE CARDS		

1996 VIP Autographs

This 26-card set features desirable autographs from NASCAR's biggest stars. More than 25,000 autographs were inserted in packs of VIP at a rate of one per 24 packs.

COMPLETE SET (26)	400.00	800.00
1 Jeff Andrews	4.00	8.00
2 Johnny Benson	10.00	25.00
3 Geoff Bodine	7.50	15.00
4 Jeff Burton	8.00	20.00
5 Ricky Craven	7.50	15.00
6 Dale Earnhardt	175.00	300.00
7 Danny Glad	4.00	8.00
8 Jeff Gordon	60.00	120.00
9 David Green	7.50	15.00
10 Jeff Green	7.50	15.00
11 Steve Hmiel	4.00	8.00
12 Ernie Irvan	10.00	25.00
13 Jason Keller	7.50	15.00
14 Bobby Labonte	12.50	30.00
15 Chad Little	10.00	25.00
16 Jeremy Mayfield	10.00	25.00
17 Mike McLaughlin	7.50	15.00
18 Ted Musgrave	7.50	15.00
19 Joe Nemechek	7.50	15.00
20 Robert Pressley	7.50	15.00
21 Charlie Siegars	4.00	8.00
22 Mike Skinner	7.50	15.00
23 David Smith	4.00	8.00
24 Rusty Wallace	12.50	30.00
25 Michael Waltrip	8.00	20.00
26 Rick Wetzel	4.00	8.00

1996 VIP Dale Earnhardt Firesuit

Randomly inserted in packs at a rate of one in 384, this two-card set incorporates a piece of Dale Earnhardt's uniform in each card. There were four different color variations Gold foil 1:512, Silver foil 1:384 in Wal-mart only packs, Blue foil 1:2048, and Green 1:6144.

DE1B Dale Earnhardt B	50.00	100.00
DE1S Dale Earnhardt S	50.00	100.00
DE1GL Dale Earnhardt GLD	50.00	100.00
DE1GR Dale Earnhardt GRN	75.00	150.00
DE2B Dale Earnhardt B	50.00	100.00
DE2S Dale Earnhardt S	50.00	100.00
DE2GL Dale Earnhardt GLD	50.00	100.00
DE2GR Dale Earnhardt GRN	75.00	150.00

1996 VIP Head Gear

Randomly inserted in packs at a rate of one in 16, this nine-card set features today's top Winston Cup talent with their helmets in an all-foil design. There was also a die cut version of each Head Gear card and they were inserted at a rate of one in 96 packs.

COMPLETE SET (9)	20.00	50.00
COMPLETE DIE CUT SET (9)	60.00	120.00
*DIE CUTS: .8X TO 2X BASIC INSERTS		
HG1 Ricky Craven	.60	1.50
HG2 Dale Earnhardt	10.00	25.00

HG3 Jeff Gordon	6.00	15.00
HG4 Ernie Irvan	1.25	3.00
HG5 Mark Martin	5.00	12.00
HG6 Ricky Rudd	2.00	5.00
HG7 Rusty Wallace	5.00	12.00
HG8 Darrell Waltrip	1.25	3.00
HG9 Michael Waltrip	1.25	3.00

1996 VIP Sam Bass Top Flight

Randomly inserted in packs at a rate of one in 48, this five-card set features art work from renowned racing artist Sam Bass. The cards come with a silver foil border. There is also a gold foil version inserted at a rate of one in 144 packs.

COMPLETE SET (5)	40.00	100.00
COMPLETE GOLD SET (5)	60.00	150.00
*GOLDS: .6X TO 1.5X BASIC INSERTS		
SB1 Dale Earnhardt	12.50	30.00
SB2 Bill Elliott	3.00	8.00
SB3 Terry Labonte	2.50	6.00
SB4 Mark Martin	6.00	15.00
SB5 Rusty Wallace	6.00	15.00

1996 VIP War Paint

Randomly inserted in packs at a rate of one in 12, this 18-card set features the Winston Cup cars with wildest paint jobs mixed with all-foil NitroKrome technology.

COMPLETE SET (18)	25.00	60.00
COMP.GOLD SET (18)	50.00	120.00
*GOLDS: .8X TO 2X BASIC INSERTS		
WP1 Rusty Wallace's Car	3.00	8.00
WP2 Dale Earnhardt's Car	6.00	15.00
WP3 Sterling Marlin's Car	1.00	2.50
WP4 Terry Labonte's Car	2.00	5.00
WP5 Mark Martin's Car	3.00	8.00
WP6 Ricky Rudd's Car	1.00	2.50
WP7 Ted Musgrave's Car	.50	1.25
WP8 Darrell Waltrip's Car	1.00	2.50
WP9 Bobby Labonte's Car	2.00	5.00
WP10 Michael Waltrip's Car	.50	1.25
WP11 Ward Burton's Car	1.00	2.50
WP12 Jeff Gordon's Car	4.00	10.00
WP13 Ernie Irvan's Car	1.00	2.50
WP14 Ricky Craven's Car	.50	1.25
WP15 Kyle Petty's Car	1.00	2.50
WP16 Bobby Hamilton's Car	.50	1.25
WP17 Dale Jarrett's Car	2.00	5.00
WP18 Bill Elliott's Car	2.00	5.00

1997 VIP

This 50-card set features stars from the top three NASCAR divisions (Winston Cup, Busch Grand National and Truck racing) and was distributed in seven-card packs with a suggested retail price of $3.99. The set was printed on extra thick 24 pt. card stock with two different foil stampings on the front.

COMPLETE SET (50)	8.00	20.00
1 Johnny Benson	.25	.60
2 Geoff Bodine	.10	.30
3 Jeff Burton	.40	1.00
4 Ward Burton	.25	.60
5 Ricky Craven	.10	.30
6 Dale Earnhardt	2.00	5.00
7 Bill Elliott	.60	1.50
8 Jeff Gordon	1.25	3.00
9 Robby Gordon RC	.40	1.00
10 Bobby Hamilton	.10	.30
11 Ernie Irvan	.25	.60
12 Dale Jarrett	.75	2.00
13 Bobby Labonte	.75	2.00
14 Terry Labonte	.40	1.00
15 Sterling Marlin	.40	1.00
16 Mark Martin	1.00	2.50
17 Ted Musgrave	.10	.30
18 Joe Nemechek	.10	.30
19 Kyle Petty	.25	.60
20 Ricky Rudd	.40	1.00
21 Ken Schrader	.10	.30
22 Mike Skinner	.10	.30
23 Rusty Wallace	1.00	2.50
24 Darrell Waltrip	.25	.60
25 Michael Waltrip	.25	.60
26 David Green	.10	.30
27 Chad Little	.10	.30
28 Todd Bodine	.10	.30
29 Tim Fedewa	.10	.30
30 Jeff Fuller	.10	.30
31 Jeff Green	.10	.30
32 Jason Keller	.10	.30
33 Randy LaJoie	.10	.30
34 Kevin Lepage	.10	.30
35 Mark Martin	1.00	2.50
36 Mike McLaughlin	.10	.30
37 Rich Bickle	.10	.30
38 Mike Bliss	.10	.30
39 Rick Carelli	.10	.30
40 Ron Hornaday	.10	.30
41 Kenny Irwin RC	2.00	4.00
42 Tammy Jo Kirk	.05	.15
43 Butch Miller	.10	.30
44 Joe Ruttman	.10	.30
45 Jack Sprague	.10	.30
46 Jeff Burton	.25	.60
47 Dale Jarrett	.75	2.00
48 Mark Martin	1.00	2.50
49 Bruton Smith Eddie Gossage	.05	.15
50 Checklist	.05	.15
P1 Dale Jarrett Promo	1.50	4.00

1997 VIP Explosives

This 50-card set is parallel to the regular base set and is similar in design. The difference is found in the technology used in etching and in the foil board it is printed on. These cards were inserted one per pack.

COMP.EXPLOSIVE SET (50)	15.00	40.00
*EXPLOSIVE: .8X TO 2X BASIC CARDS		
P1 Dale Jarrett Promo	2.00	5.00

1997 VIP Oil Slicks

Randomly inserted in hobby only packs at the rate of one in 64, this 50-card set is a custom made foil parallel version of the regular base VIP set. Only 100 of each card was produced and are individually numbered.

COMPLETE SET (50)	300.00	600.00
*OIL SLICKS: 8X TO 20X BASIC CARDS		

1997 VIP Head Gear

Randomly inserted in packs at the rate of one in 16, this nine-card set features the hottest drivers and driver helmets on the Winston Cup circuit and are printed on cards with an all foil NitroKrome embossed design.

COMPLETE SET (9)	15.00	40.00
COMP.DIE CUT SET (9)	40.00	75.00
*DIE CUT: .6X TO 1.5X BASIC INSERTS		
HG1 Dale Earnhardt	6.00	15.00
HG2 Bill Elliott	2.00	5.00
HG3 Jeff Gordon	4.00	10.00
HG4 Ernie Irvan	.75	2.00
HG5 Mark Martin	3.00	8.00
HG6 Kyle Petty	.75	2.00
HG7 Ricky Rudd	1.25	3.00
HG8 Rusty Wallace	3.00	8.00
HG9 Michael Waltrip	.75	2.00

1997 VIP Knights of Thunder

Randomly inserted in packs at the rate of one in 30, this six-card set features reproductions of original artworks of leading drivers by Race Artist, Sam Bass.

COMPLETE SET (6)	20.00	50.00
COMP. GOLD SET (6)	60.00	150.00
*GOLDS: 1X TO 2.5X BASIC INSERTS		
KT1 Dale Earnhardt	10.00	25.00
KT2 Jeff Gordon	6.00	15.00
KT3 Dale Jarrett	4.00	10.00
KT4 Bobby Labonte	4.00	10.00
KT5 Terry Labonte	2.00	5.00
KT6 Rusty Wallace	5.00	12.00

1997 VIP Precious Metal

Randomly inserted in packs at the rate of one in 384, this set features color photos on authentic race-used sheet metal from top drivers and incorporated into a thick laminated card. Each card is individually numbered to 500 and comes with a certificate of authenticity.

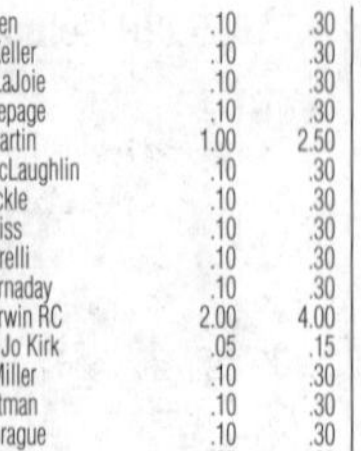

COMPLETE SET (5)	125.00	250.00
*MULTI-COLOR METAL: .75X TO 1.25X		
SM1 Jeff Gordon	40.00	100.00
SM2 Bobby Labonte	15.00	40.00
SM3 Bill Elliott	20.00	50.00
SM4 Terry Labonte	15.00	40.00
SM5 Rusty Wallace	15.00	40.00

1997 VIP Ring of Honor

Randomly inserted in packs at the rate of one in 10, this 12-card set features color photos of top NASCAR tracks and drivers who have tamed them. The set is printed on thick card stock and clear acetate.

COMPLETE SET (12)	15.00	40.00
COMP.DIE-CUT SET (12)	30.00	60.00
*DIE CUTS: .6X TO 1.5X BASIC INSERTS		
RH1 Rusty Wallace's Car	4.00	10.00
RH2 Dale Earnhardt's Car	8.00	20.00
RH3 Sterling Marlin's Car	1.50	4.00
RH4 Terry Labonte's Car	1.50	4.00
RH5 Mark Martin's Car	4.00	10.00
RH6 Ricky Rudd's Car	1.50	4.00
RH7 Bobby Labonte's Car	3.00	8.00
RH8 Jeff Gordon's Car	5.00	12.00
RH9 Ernie Irvan's Car	1.00	2.50
RH10 Bobby Hamilton's Car	.50	1.25
RH11 Dale Jarrett's Car	3.00	8.00
RH12 Bill Elliott's Car	2.50	6.00

1998 VIP

The 1998 VIP set was issued in one series totalling 50 cards. The card fronts feature full bleed color photography with two channels of etched foil stamping. The set contains the topical subsets: Winston Drivers (1-27), Busch Drivers (28-36), Winston Cars (37-46), and Las Vegas Motor Speedway (47-50).

COMPLETE SET (50)	12.00	30.00
WAX BOX	40.00	80.00
1 John Andretti	.12	.30
2 Johnny Benson	.40	1.00
3 Geoff Bodine	.15	.40
4 Jeff Burton	.40	1.00
5 Ward Burton	.30	.75
6 Dale Earnhardt	2.50	6.00
7 Bill Elliott	.75	2.00
8 Jeff Gordon	1.50	4.00
9 Bobby Hamilton	.25	.60
10 Ernie Irvan	.40	1.00
11 Kenny Irwin	.60	1.50
12 Dale Jarrett	1.00	2.50
13 Bobby Labonte	1.00	2.50
14 Terry Labonte	.60	1.50
15 Sterling Marlin	.60	1.50
16 Mark Martin	1.25	3.00
17 Jeremy Mayfield	.30	.75
18 Ted Musgrave	.25	.60
19 Joe Nemechek	.15	.40
20 Steve Park		
21 Robert Pressley		
22 Ricky Rudd	.50	1.25
23 Ken Schrader	.15	.40
24 Mike Skinner	.15	.40
25 Jimmy Spencer	.30	.75
26 Rusty Wallace	1.00	2.50
27 Michael Waltrip	.40	1.00
28 Dale Earnhardt Jr.	2.50	6.00
29 Tim Fedewa	.15	.40
30 Jason Keller	.15	.40
31 Randy LaJoie	.15	.40
32 Mark Martin	1.25	3.00
33 Mike McLaughlin	.15	.40
34 Elliott Sadler	.30	.75
35 Hermie Sadler	.15	.40
36 Tony Stewart RC	6.00	15.00
37 Jeff Burton's Car	.15	.40
38 Dale Earnhardt's Car	1.00	2.50
39 Bill Elliott's Car	.30	.75
40 Jeff Gordon's Car	.60	1.50
41 Dale Jarrett's Car	.40	1.00
42 Bobby Labonte's Car	.40	1.00
43 Terry Labonte's Car	.25	.60
44 Chad Little's Car	.10	.25
45 Mark Martin's Car	.50	1.25
46 Rusty Wallace's Car	.40	1.00
47 Mark Martin	1.25	3.00
48 Dale Jarrett	1.00	2.50
49 Roush Racing	1.25	3.00
50 Mark Martin CL		
P1 Jeremy Mayfield Promo	1.00	2.50

1998 VIP Explosives

Randomly inserted one in every pack, this parallel to the base set is etched using a special custom die and printed on a unifoil board.

COMPLETE SET (50)	20.00	50.00
*EXPLOSIVE VETS: 1X TO 2.5X BASE CARDS		
*EXPLOSIVE RCs: .6X TO 1.5X BASE CARDS		

1998 VIP Driving Force

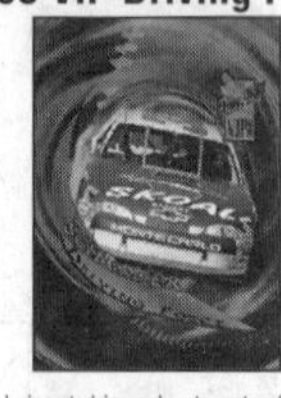

Randomly inserted in packs at a rate of one in 10, this 18-card insert set features NASCAR's stock cars printed on all-foil cards.

COMPLETE SET (18)	20.00	50.00
COMP.DIE CUT SET (18)	40.00	100.00
*DIE CUTS: .6X TO 1.5X BASIC INSERTS		
DF1 John Andretti's Car	.40	1.00
DF2 Johnny Benson's Car	1.00	2.50
DF3 Jeff Burton's Car	1.00	2.50
DF4 Ward Burton's Car	.75	2.00
DF5 Dale Earnhardt's Car	6.00	15.00
DF6 Bill Elliott's Car	2.00	5.00
DF7 Jeff Gordon's Car	4.00	10.00
DF8 Bobby Hamilton's Car	.60	1.50
DF9 Kenny Irwin's Car	1.50	4.00
DF10 Dale Jarrett's Car	2.50	6.00
DF11 Bobby Labonte's Car	2.50	6.00
DF12 Terry Labonte's Car	1.50	4.00
DF13 Sterling Marlin's Car	1.50	4.00
DF14 Mark Martin's Car	3.00	8.00
DF15 Jeremy Mayfield's Car	.75	2.00
DF16 Ricky Rudd's Car	1.25	3.00
DF17 Ken Schrader's Car	.40	1.00
DF18 Rusty Wallace's Car	2.50	6.00

1998 VIP Head Gear

Randomly inserted in packs at a rate of one in 16, this 9-card insert set was printed on all-foil and customed sculptured to resemble a driver's helmet.

COMPLETE SET (9)	15.00	40.00
COMP.DIE CUT SET (9)	25.00	60.00
*DIE CUTS: .6X TO 1.5X BASIC INSERTS		
HG1 Jeff Burton	1.00	2.50
HG2 Dale Earnhardt	6.00	15.00
HG3 Bill Elliott	2.00	5.00
HG4 Jeff Gordon	4.00	10.00
HG5 Dale Jarrett	2.50	6.00
HG6 Bobby Labonte	2.50	6.00
HG7 Terry Labonte	1.50	4.00
HG8 Mark Martin	3.00	8.00
HG9 Rusty Wallace	2.50	6.00

1998 VIP Lap Leaders

Randomly inserted in packs at a rate of one in 20, this 9-card insert features the top NASCAR rides on micro-embossed, super thick all-foil board.

COMPLETE SET (9)	15.00	40.00
COMP.ACETATE SET (9)	30.00	80.00
*ACETATES: .8X TO 2X BASIC INSERTS		
LL1 Jeff Burton's Car	1.00	2.50
LL2 Dale Earnhardt's Car	6.00	15.00
LL3 Jeff Gordon's Car	4.00	10.00
LL4 Dale Jarrett's Car	2.00	5.00
LL5 Bobby Labonte's Car	2.00	5.00
LL6 Terry Labonte's Car	2.00	5.00
LL7 Mark Martin's Car	3.00	8.00
LL8 Jeremy Mayfield's Car	1.00	2.50
LL9 Rusty Wallace's Car	3.00	8.00

1998 VIP NASCAR Country

Randomly inserted in packs at a rate of one in 10, this 9-card insert helps celebrate NASCAR's 50th Anniversary. The cards feature the top NASCAR Winston Cup drivers teamed up with today's top country music.

COMPLETE SET (9)	12.50	30.00
COMP.DIE CUT SET (9)	30.00	80.00
*DIE CUTS: .8X TO 2X BASIC INSERTS		
NC1 Dale Earnhardt	6.00	15.00
NC2 Bill Elliott	1.50	4.00
NC3 Jeff Gordon	4.00	10.00
NC4 Dale Jarrett	2.50	6.00
NC5 Bobby Labonte	2.50	6.00
NC6 Terry Labonte	1.25	3.00
NC7 Mark Martin	3.00	8.00
NC8 Ricky Rudd	1.25	3.00
NC9 Rusty Wallace	3.00	8.00

1998 VIP Triple Gear Sheet Metal

Randomly inserted in packs at a rate of one in 384, this 9-card insert set offers race-used sheet metal from the top NASCAR Winston Cup teams. Cards with multi-color pieces of sheet metal carry a 25% premium over those that do not. These cards are numbered to 225.

TGS1 Rusty Wallace	30.00	80.00
TGS2 Dale Earnhardt	100.00	200.00
TGS3 Terry Labonte	20.00	50.00
TGS4 Mark Martin	30.00	80.00
TGS5 Bobby Labonte	20.00	50.00
TGS6 Jeff Gordon	75.00	150.00
TGS7 Mike Skinner	15.00	40.00
TGS8 Dale Jarrett	20.00	50.00
TGS9 Jeff Burton	15.00	40.00

1999 VIP

This 50 card set was issued in six card hobby packs. The set features a mix of cards of drivers and the cars they drive.

COMPLETE SET (50)	12.50	30.00
1 John Andretti	.10	.30
2 Johnny Benson	.25	.60
3 Chad Little	.25	.60
4 Jeff Burton	.40	1.00
5 Ward Burton	.25	.60
6 Derrike Cope	.10	.30
7 Dale Earnhardt	2.00	5.00
8 Jeff Gordon	1.25	3.00
9 David Green	.10	.30
10 Bobby Hamilton	.10	.30
11 Kenny Irwin	.25	.60
12 Dale Jarrett	.75	2.00
13 Bobby Labonte	.75	2.00
14 Terry Labonte	.40	1.00
15 Sterling Marlin	.40	1.00
16 Mark Martin	1.00	2.50
17 Jeremy Mayfield	.25	.60
18 Joe Nemechek	.10	.30
19 Steve Park	.60	1.50
20 Ricky Rudd	.40	1.00
21 Elliott Sadler	.25	.60
22 Ken Schrader	.10	.30
23 Mike Skinner	.10	.30
24 Jimmy Spencer	.10	.30
25 Tony Stewart CRC	1.50	4.00
26 Rusty Wallace	1.00	2.50
27 Michael Waltrip	.25	.60
28 Casey Atwood RC	1.00	2.50
29 Dave Blaney RC	.10	.30
30 Dale Earnhardt Jr.	1.50	4.00
31 Jeff Gordon BGN	1.25	3.00
32 Jason Keller	.10	.30
33 Matt Kenseth RC	3.00	8.00
34 Randy LaJoie	.10	.30
35 Mark Martin BGN	1.00	2.50
36 Mike McLaughlin	.10	.30
37 Elton Sawyer	.10	.30
38 Jimmy Spencer BGN	.10	.30
39 Dick Trickle	.10	.30
40 Jeff Burton's Car	.05	.15
41 Dale Earnhardt's Car	.75	2.00
42 Jeff Gordon's Car	.50	1.25
43 Dale Jarrett' Car	.25	.60
44 Bobby Labonte's Car	.25	.60
45 Terry Labonte's Car	.25	.60
46 Mark Martin's Car	.40	1.00
47 Jeremy Mayfield's Car	.10	.30
48 Tony Stewart's Car	.50	1.25
49 Rusty Wallace's Car	.40	1.00
50 Jeff Burton CL Mark Martin CL	.50	1.25
P1 Mark Martin Promo	.75	2.00

1999 VIP Explosives

This parallel set, issued one per pack, features that are meticulously etched on foil board.

COMPLETE SET (50)	30.00	
*EXPLOSIVES: 1X TO 2.5X BASE CARD HI		
*EXPLOSIVE RCs: .6X TO 1.5X BASE CARD HI		

1999 VIP Explosives Lasers

This parallel set, issued exclusively in hobby at a rate of one in 19, features the explosive taken to a more intense level.

COMPLETE SET (50)	150.00	
*EXP.LASERS: 5X TO 12X BASE CARD HI		
*EXP.LASER RCs: 3X TO 8X BASE CARD HI		

1999 VIP Double Tak

Inserted one every 29 packs, these six cards "transformation" of leading drivers in their moments.

COMPLETE SET (6)	25.00	
DT1 Jeff Gordon	8.00	
DT2 Rusty Wallace	6.00	
DT3 Tony Stewart	8.00	
DT4 Dale Earnhardt Jr.	10.00	
DT5 Terry Labonte	2.50	
DT6 Mark Martin	6.00	

1999 VIP Head Gear

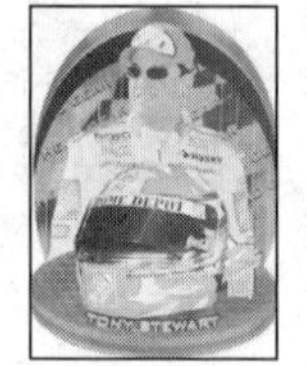

This nine card set inserted one every 10 features up close shots of nine helmets drivers who wear them.

COMPLETE SET (9)	12.50	
HG1 Jeff Gordon	3.00	
HG2 Rusty Wallace	2.50	
HG3 Tony Stewart	3.00	
HG4 Dale Earnhardt Jr.	4.00	
HG5 Terry Labonte	1.00	
HG6 Mark Martin	2.50	
HG7 Bobby Labonte	2.00	
HG8 Dale Jarrett	2.00	
HG9 Jeff Burton	1.00	

1999 VIP Head Gear Plastic

This is a parallel to the basic Head Gear Each card was made of plastic and issued one 39 packs. A tenth card featuring Dale Earnhardt a Winston Cup driver was added to this parallel set.

COMPLETE SET (10)	25.00	
*PLASTIC: .6X TO 1.5X BASIC INSERTS		
HG10 Dale Earnhardt Jr.	7.50	

1999 VIP Lap Leader

These nine cards, inserted one every 20 feature all plastic foil stamped cards on nine leading NASCAR drivers.

COMPLETE SET (9)	30.00	
LL1 Jeff Gordon	6.00	
LL2 Rusty Wallace	5.00	
LL3 Dale Earnhardt	10.00	

.4 Dale Earnhardt Jr. 8.00 20.00
.5 Terry Labonte 2.00 5.00
.6 Mark Martin 5.00 12.00
.7 Bobby Labonte 4.00 10.00
.8 Dale Jarrett 4.00 10.00
.9 Jeff Burton 2.00 5.00

1999 VIP Out of the Box

sued one every nine packs, these 12 cards feature -foil gold stamped highlights of 12 driver's reers.

OMPLETE SET (12) 12.50 30.00
B1 Jeff Gordon 3.00 8.00
B2 Ricky Rudd 1.00 2.50
B3 Dale Earnhardt's Car 2.00 5.00
B4 Dale Earnhardt Jr. 4.00 10.00
B5 Terry Labonte 1.00 2.50
B6 Mark Martin 2.50 6.00
B7 Bobby Labonte 2.00 5.00
B8 Dale Jarrett 2.00 5.00
B9 Jeff Burton 1.00 2.50
B10 Rusty Wallace 2.50 6.00
B11 Tony Stewart 3.00 8.00
B12 Ward Burton .60 1.50

1999 VIP Rear View Mirror

sued at a stated rate of one in six packs, these nine rds feature a drivers rear view mirror perspective.

OMPLETE SET (9) 10.00 25.00
M1 Jeff Gordon 2.50 6.00
M2 Dale Jarrett 1.50 4.00
M3 Dale Earnhardt 4.00 10.00
M4 Dale Earnhardt Jr. 3.00 8.00
M5 Jeff Burton .75 2.00
M6 Mark Martin 2.00 5.00
M7 Terry Labonte .75 2.00
M8 Rusty Wallace 2.00 5.00
M9 Tony Stewart 2.50 6.00

1999 VIP Sheet Metal

sued one every 384 packs, these nine cards atures pieces of race used sheet metal from six fferent drivers.

OMPLETE SET (8) 500.00 1000.00
MULTI-COLOR METAL: .75X TO 1.25X
M1 Rusty Wallace 30.00 60.00
M2 Dale Earnhardt's Car 100.00 250.00
M3 Jeff Gordon 60.00 120.00
M4 Terry Labonte 20.00 50.00
M5 Mark Martin 30.00 80.00
M6 Tony Stewart 30.00 80.00
M7 Dale Jarrett 20.00 50.00
M8 Bobby Labonte 20.00 50.00

1999 VIP Vintage Performance

ese cards were inserted in Retail boxes as a box opper at a rate of one per retail box. They were aled in a cellophane rapper.

OMPLETE SET (9) 8.00 20.00
Dale Jarrett 1.25 3.00
Rusty Wallace 1.50 4.00
Mark Martin 1.50 4.00
Jeff Gordon 2.00 5.00
Jeff Burton .60 1.50
Bobby Labonte 1.25 3.00
Jeremy Mayfield .40 1.00
Dale Earnhardt's Car 1.25 3.00
Terry Labonte .60 1.50

2000 VIP

leased as a 50-card set, Press Pass VIP features Driver cards, eight Winston Cup 2000 Victory rds, three Big Payoff cards, six A Decade of Firsts cards, nine 50 Win Club cards, four Back to Back Championship cards and one checklist. VIP was packaged in 28-pack boxes with packs containing six cards and carried a suggested retail price of $2.99.

COMPLETE SET (50) 12.50 30.00
1 Bobby Labonte .75 2.00
2 Mark Martin 1.00 2.50
3 Ward Burton .25 .60
4 Dale Earnhardt 2.00 5.00
5 Rusty Wallace .75 2.00
6 Jeff Burton .30 .75
7 Ricky Rudd .40 1.00
8 Dale Jarrett .75 2.00
9 Terry Labonte .50 1.25
10 Jeremy Mayfield .12 .30
11 Tony Stewart 1.25 3.00
12 Jeff Gordon 1.25 3.00
13 Chad Little .20 .50
14 Johnny Benson .30 .75
15 Mike Skinner .12 .30
16 Sterling Marlin .50 1.25
17 Dale Earnhardt Jr. CRC 1.50 4.00
18 Matt Kenseth CRC 1.00 2.50
19 Dale Jarrett V .75 2.00
20 Bobby Labonte V .75 2.00
21 Jeff Burton V .30 .75
22 Ward Burton V .25 .60
23 Rusty Wallace V .75 2.00
24 Dale Earnhardt Jr. V 1.50 4.00
25 Mark Martin V 1.00 2.50
26 Jeff Gordon V 1.25 3.00
27 Tony Stewart V 1.25 3.00
28 Dale Jarrett NB .75 2.00
29 Jeff Gordon NB 1.25 3.00
30 Jeff Burton NB .30 .75
31 Rusty Wallace DF .75 2.00
32 Jeff Gordon DF 1.25 3.00
33 Jeff Burton DF .30 .75
34 Jeff Gordon DF 1.25 3.00
35 Mark Martin DF 1.00 2.50
36 Tony Stewart DF 1.25 3.00
37 David Pearson 50 W .50 1.25
38 Darrell Waltrip 50 W .25 .60
39 Bobby Allison 50 W .40 1.00
40 Cale Yarborough 50 W .40 1.00
41 Dale Earnhardt's Car 50 W 2.00 5.00
42 Junior Johnson 50 W .30 .75
43 Ned Jarrett 50 W .30 .75
44 Rusty Wallace 50 W .75 2.00
45 Jeff Gordon 50 W 1.25 3.00
46 Cale Yarborough DT .40 1.00
47 Darrell Waltrip DT .25 .60
48 Dale Earnhardt's Car DT 2.00 5.00
49 Jeff Gordon DT 1.25 3.00
50 Winston Cup/CL .12 .30
P1 Dale Earnhardt Jr. Promo 4.00 10.00

2000 VIP Explosives

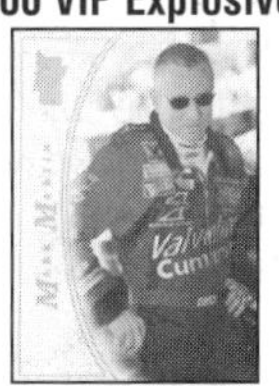

Randomly inserted in packs at the rate of one in one, this 50-card set parallels the base Press Pass VIP set on cards with enhanced canvas card stock.

COMPLETE SET (50) 40.00 80.00
*EXPLOSIVES 1X TO 2.5X BASE CARDS

2000 VIP Explosives Lasers

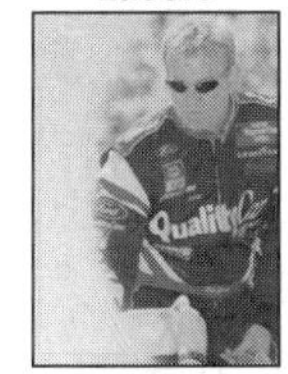

Randomly inserted in packs at the rate of one in 20, this 50-card set parallels the base Press Pass VIP set on cards enhanced with all gold laser holofoil. Each card is sequentially numbered to 200 and Hobby Only.

COMPLETE SET (50) 200.00 400.00
*EXP.LASERS 4X TO 10X BASE CARDS

2000 VIP Head Gear

Randomly inserted in packs at the rate of one in 10, this 6-card set showcases the custom markings of some of NASCAR's driver's helmets.

COMPLETE SET (6) 12.50 30.00
COMP.EXPLOSIVES (6) 25.00 60.00
*EXPLOSIVES .8X TO 2X BASIC INSERTS
EXPLOSIVES STATED ODDS 1:30
COMP.EXP.LAS DIE CUT (6) 40.00 100.00
*EXP.LAS.DIE CUT 1.2X TO 3X HI
EXP.LASER DIE CUT ODDS 1:60
HG1 Jeff Gordon 2.50 6.00
HG2 Rusty Wallace 1.50 4.00
HG3 Tony Stewart 2.50 6.00
HG4 Dale Earnhardt Jr. 3.00 8.00
HG5 Terry Labonte 1.00 2.50
HG6 Dale Jarrett 1.50 4.00

2000 VIP Head Gear Explosives Laser Die Cuts

Randomly inserted in packs at the rate of one in 60, this 6-card set parallels the base Head Gear insert set on cards enhanced with a laser gold foil die cut card stock.

COMPLETE SET (6) 40.00 100.00
*EXP.LAS.DIE CUT: 1.2X TO 3X BASIC INS.

2000 VIP Lap Leaders

Randomly inserted in packs at the rate of one in five, this 12-card set features top NASCAR drivers for whom it is common to come around the last turn leading the pack.

COMPLETE SET (12) 10.00 25.00
COMP.EXPLOSIVES (12) 20.00 50.00
*EXPLOSIVES .8X TO 2X BASIC INSERTS
EXPLOSIVES STATED ODDS 1:15
COMP.EXP.LASER (12) 25.00 60.00
*EXP.LASERS 1X TO 2.5X BASIC INSERTS
EXP.LASERS STATED ODDS 1:20 HOB
LL1 Jeff Gordon 2.00 5.00
LL2 Tony Stewart 2.00 5.00
LL3 Bobby Labonte 1.25 3.00
LL4 Jeff Burton .60 1.50
LL5 Dale Jarrett 1.25 3.00
LL6 Rusty Wallace 1.50 4.00
LL7 Mark Martin 1.50 4.00
LL8 Mike Skinner .20 .50
LL9 Terry Labonte .60 1.50
LL10 Ward Burton .40 1.00
LL11 Ricky Rudd .60 1.50
LL12 Jeremy Mayfield .20 .50

2000 VIP Making the Show

Randomly inserted in packs at the rate of one in one, this 24-card set features drivers that qualify week after week on an all foil die cut card.

COMPLETE SET (24) 6.00 15.00
MS1 Bobby Labonte 1.00 2.50
MS2 Chad Little .30 .75
MS3 Elliott Sadler .15 .40
MS4 Dale Earnhardt Jr. 2.00 5.00
MS5 Dale Jarrett 1.00 2.50
MS6 Jeff Burton .50 1.25
MS7 Jeff Gordon 1.50 4.00
MS8 Jeremy Mayfield .15 .40
MS9 Joe Nemechek .15 .40
MS10 Johnny Benson .30 .75
MS11 Kenny Irwin .15 .40
MS12 Mark Martin 1.25 3.00
MS13 Matt Kenseth 1.25 3.00
MS14 Mike Skinner .15 .40
MS15 Ricky Rudd .50 1.25
MS16 Kenny Wallace .15 .40
MS17 Rusty Wallace 1.25 3.00
MS18 Sterling Marlin .50 1.25
MS19 Steve Park .15 .40
MS20 Terry Labonte .50 1.25
MS21 Tony Stewart 1.50 4.00
MS22 Michael Waltrip .30 .75
MS23 Ward Burton .30 .75
MS24 Wally Dallenbach/CL .25 .60

2000 VIP Rear View Mirror

Randomly inserted in packs at the rate of one in 20, this 6-card set focuses on on top drivers. Each card is printed on all foil card stock with enhanced foil stamping.

COMPLETE SET (6) 30.00 80.00
COMP.EXPLOSIVE (6) 60.00 150.00
*EXPLOSIVE: .8X TO 2X BASIC INSERTS
EXPLOSIVE STATED ODDS 1:60
COMP.EXP.LASER DIE CUT (6) 100.00 250.00
*EXP.LASER DCs: 1X TO 2.5X BASIC INSERTS
EXP.LASER DIE CUT STATED ODDS 1:130
RM1 Bobby Labonte 4.00 10.00
RM2 Rusty Wallace 5.00 12.00
RM3 Dale Earnhardt 10.00 25.00
RM4 Dale Earnhardt Jr. 8.00 20.00
RM5 Mark Martin 5.00 12.00
RM6 Tony Stewart 6.00 15.00

2000 VIP Sheet Metal

Randomly inserted in packs at the rate of one in 384, this 9-card set contains a swatch of race used sheet metal from nine of NASCAR's top drivers.

COMPLETE SET (10) 500.00 1000.00
*MULTI-COLOR METAL: 1X TO 1.5X
SM1 Ward Burton 12.50 30.00
SM2 Jeff Burton 12.50 30.00
SM3 Dale Earnhardt 100.00 200.00
SM4 Terry Labonte 15.00 40.00
SM5 Mark Martin 30.00 80.00
SM6 Tony Stewart 30.00 80.00
SM7 Dale Earnhardt Jr. 60.00 120.00
SM8 Bobby Labonte 15.00 40.00
SM9 Jeff Gordon 60.00 120.00
SM10 Dale Earnhardt Jr. 50.00 100.00

2000 VIP Under the Lights

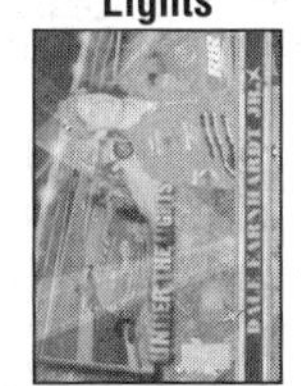

Randomly inserted in packs at the rate of one in 15, this 8-card set features NASCAR night vision on this all foil insert card.

COMPLETE SET (8) 12.50 30.00
COMP.EXPLOSIVES (8) 25.00 60.00
*EXPLOSIVES: .8X TO 2X BASIC INSERTS
EXPLOSIVES STATED ODDS 1:45
COMP.EXP.LASER (8) 50.00 120.00
*EXP.LASERS: 1.5X TO 4X BASIC INSERTS
EXPLOSIVE LASER ODDS 1:90 HOBBY
EXP.LASER PRINT RUN 250 SER.#'d SETS
UL1 Jeff Gordon 3.00 8.00
UL2 Dale Jarrett 2.00 5.00
UL3 Bobby Labonte 2.00 5.00
UL4 Dale Earnhardt Jr. 4.00 10.00
UL5 Tony Stewart 3.00 8.00
UL6 Rusty Wallace 2.50 6.00
UL7 Mark Martin 2.50 6.00
UL8 Mike Skinner .30 .75

2001 VIP

This 50 card set features four sub sets, 18 NASCAR Winston Cup Drivers 1-18, nine Sunday Money 2001 cards 19-27, 11 Rookie Thunder cards 28-38, and 11 All Stars cards 39-49, with one checklist card 50. VIP was available in hobby and retail stores in 24 pack boxes or retail only in a specially packed box containing one Hot Treads card.

COMPLETE SET (50) 12.50 30.00
WAX BOX HOBBY 50.00 90.00
WAX BOX RETAIL 35.00 75.00
1 Bobby Labonte 1.00 2.50
2 Mark Martin 1.25 3.00
3 Ward Burton .40 1.00
4 Steve Park .40 1.00
5 Rusty Wallace 1.25 3.00
6 Jeff Burton .40 1.00
7 Ricky Rudd .75 2.00
8 Dale Jarrett 1.00 2.50
9 Terry Labonte .75 2.00
10 Kevin Harvick CRC 1.25 3.00
11 Tony Stewart 1.50 4.00
12 Jeff Gordon 1.50 4.00
13 Michael Waltrip .40 1.00
14 Ken Schrader .20 .50
15 Mike Skinner .20 .50
16 Sterling Marlin .75 2.00
17 Dale Earnhardt Jr. 2.00 5.00
18 Jeremy Mayfield .20 .50
19 Michael Waltrip SM .40 1.00
20 Steve Park SM .40 1.00
21 Jeff Gordon SM 1.50 4.00
22 Kevin Harvick SM 1.25 3.00
23 Dale Jarrett SM 1.00 2.50
24 Elliott Sadler SM .40 1.00
25 Bobby Hamilton SM .20 .50
26 Rusty Wallace SM 1.25 3.00
27 Tony Stewart SM 1.50 4.00
28 Ricky Rudd RT .75 2.00
29 Sterling Marlin RT .75 2.00
30 Rusty Wallace RT 1.25 3.00
31 Ken Schrader RT .20 .50
32 Bobby Hamilton RT .20 .50
33 Jeff Gordon RT 1.50 4.00
34 Jeff Burton RT .40 1.00
35 Ricky Craven RT .20 .50
36 Mike Skinner RT .20 .50
37 Tony Stewart RT 1.50 4.00
38 Matt Kenseth RT 1.50 4.00
39 Terry Labonte AS .75 2.00
40 Sterling Marlin AS .75 2.00
41 Rusty Wallace AS 1.25 3.00
42 Michael Waltrip AS .40 1.00
43 Jeff Gordon AS 1.50 4.00
44 Jimmy Spencer AS .20 .50
45 Dale Earnhardt Jr. AS 2.00 5.00
46 Mark Martin AS 1.25 3.00
47 Jeremy Mayfield AS .20 .50
48 Tony Stewart AS 1.50 4.00
49 Ricky Craven AS .20 .50
50 Jeff Gordon CL .75 2.00

2001 VIP Explosives

Inserted at one per pack, this 50-card set is an all-foil parallel of the 2001 VIP base set.

COMPLETE SET (50) 25.00 60.00
*EXPLOSIVES: .8X TO 2X BASE CARDS

2001 VIP Explosives Lasers

Inserted at one in 20 hobby packs, this 50-card set parallels the 2001 VIP base set, and are serial numbered to 420.

COMPLETE SET (50) 150.00 400.00
*LASERS 3X TO 8X BASE CARDS

2001 VIP Driver's Choice

Randomly inserted into packs at one in 18, this 8-card insert highlights each driver's car of choice. Card backs carry a "DC" prefix.

COMPLETE SET (8) 15.00 40.00
COMP.TRANS SET (8) 75.00 150.00
*TRANS: .6X TO 1.5X BASIC INSERTS
TRANS STATED ODDS 1:48
COMP.PREC.METAL (8) 150.00 300.00
*PREC.METAL: 2.5X TO 6X BASIC INSERTS
PREC.METAL STATED ODDS 1:480 HOBBY
PREC.METAL PRINT RUN 100 SER.#'D SETS
DC1 Jeff Gordon 5.00 12.00
DC2 Dale Jarrett 3.00 8.00
DC3 Bobby Labonte 3.00 8.00
DC4 Dale Earnhardt Jr. 6.00 15.00
DC5 Tony Stewart 5.00 12.00
DC6 Rusty Wallace 4.00 10.00
DC7 Kevin Harvick 4.00 10.00
DC8 Michael Waltrip 1.25 3.00

2001 VIP Head Gear

Randomly inserted into packs at one in 16, this 6-card insert features driver profile images as well as head shots. Card backs carry a "HG" prefix.

COMPLETE SET (6) 12.50 30.00
COMP.DIE CUT SET (6) 50.00 120.00
*DIE CUTS: 1.5X TO 4X BASIC INSERTS
DIE CUT STATED ODDS 1:60
HG1 Jeff Gordon 5.00 12.00
HG2 Rusty Wallace 4.00 10.00
HG3 Kevin Harvick 4.00 10.00
HG4 Dale Earnhardt Jr. 6.00 15.00
HG5 Sterling Marlin 1.50 4.00
HG6 Dale Jarrett 3.00 8.00

2001 VIP Making the Show

This 24-card "set within a set" features some of the best drivers in NASCAR. These cards were issued at one per pack.

COMPLETE SET (24) 8.00 20.00
1 Steve Park .40 1.00
2 Rusty Wallace 1.25 3.00
3 Terry Labonte .75 2.00
4 Mark Martin 1.25 3.00
5 Dale Earnhardt Jr. 2.00 5.00
6 Jeremy Mayfield .20 .50
7 Michael Waltrip .40 1.00
8 Matt Kenseth 1.50 4.00
9 Bobby Labonte 1.00 2.50
10 Tony Stewart 1.50 4.00
11 Ward Burton .40 1.00
12 Jeff Gordon 1.50 4.00
13 Jimmy Spencer .20 .50
14 Ricky Rudd .75 2.00
15 Kevin Harvick 1.25 3.00
16 Mike Skinner .20 .50
17 Joe Nemechek .20 .50
18 Ken Schrader .20 .50
19 Sterling Marlin .75 2.00
20 Kyle Petty .40 1.00
21 Bobby Hamilton .20 .50
22 Todd Bodine .20 .50
23 Dale Jarrett 1.00 2.50
24 Jeff Burton CL .40 1.00

2001 VIP Mile Masters

Randomly inserted into packs at one in 6, this 12-card insert highlights drivers that have logged thousands of miles throughout their career. Card backs carry a "MM" prefix.

COMPLETE SET (12) 15.00 40.00
COMP.PREC.METAL (12) 125.00 300.00
*PREC.METAL: 2.5X TO 6X BASIC INSERTS
PREC.METAL STATED ODDS 1:100 HOBBY
PREC.METAL PRINT RUN 325 SER.#'d SETS
COMP.TRANS SET (12) 25.00 60.00
*TRANS: 1X TO 2.5X BASIC INSERTS
TRANS STATED ODDS 1:18
MM1 Jeff Gordon 3.00 8.00
MM2 Tony Stewart 3.00 8.00
MM3 Michael Waltrip .75 2.00
MM4 Dale Earnhardt Jr. 4.00 10.00
MM5 Dale Jarrett 2.00 5.00
MM6 Rusty Wallace 2.00 5.00
MM7 Ward Burton .75 2.00
MM8 Mike Skinner .30 .75
MM9 Terry Labonte 1.25 3.00
MM10 Jeff Burton .75 2.00
MM11 Ricky Rudd 1.00 2.50
MM12 Kevin Harvick 2.50 6.00

2001 VIP Rear View Mirror

Randomly inserted into packs at one in 24, this 6-card insert features a special in-car driver shot on an embossed foil-based card. Card backs carry a "RV" prefix.

COMPLETE SET (6) 15.00 40.00
COMP.DIE CUT SET (6) 80.00 200.00
*DIE CUTS: 2X TO 5X BASIC INSERTS
DIE CUT STATED ODDS 1:120
RV1 Bobby Labonte 3.00 8.00
RV2 Rusty Wallace 4.00 10.00
RV3 Kevin Harvick 4.00 10.00
RV4 Dale Earnhardt Jr. 6.00 15.00
RV5 Ricky Rudd 2.00 5.00
RV6 Tony Stewart 5.00 12.00

2001 VIP Sheet Metal Drivers

Randomly inserted into hobby packs at one in 420, this 12-card insert features an actual swatch of race-used sheet metal. Card backs carry a "SD" prefix. Please note that each card was individually serial numbered to 75.

*CARS: .3X TO .8X DRIVERS
CARS STATED ODDS 1:544 RETAIL
CARS PRINT RUN 120 SER.#'d SETS
SD1 Steve Park 15.00 40.00
SD2 Ward Burton 15.00 40.00
SD3 Dale Earnhardt 150.00 300.00

SD4 Tony Stewart	30.00	80.00
SD5 Terry Labonte	25.00	60.00
SD6 Dale Jarrett	25.00	60.00
SD7 Bobby Labonte	25.00	60.00
SD8 Dale Earnhardt Jr.	50.00	120.00
SD9 Jeff Gordon	50.00	120.00
SD10 Michael Waltrip	25.00	60.00
SD11 Kevin Harvick	30.00	38.00
SD12 Matt Kenseth	30.00	38.00

2002 VIP

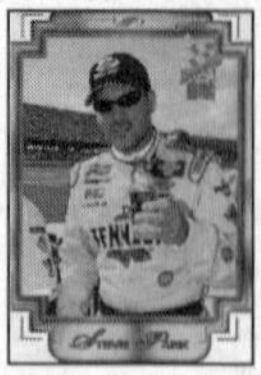

This 50-card set was issued in either four-card hobby or retail packs. Each card was printed with gold foil layering.

COMPLETE SET (50)	10.00	25.00
WAX BOX HOBBY	40.00	80.00
WAX BOX RETAIL	30.00	60.00
1 Steve Park	.25	.60
2 Rusty Wallace	.60	1.50
3 Terry Labonte	.40	1.00
4 Mark Martin	.75	2.00
5 Dale Earnhardt Jr.	1.50	3.00
6 Ryan Newman CRC	.75	2.00
7 Matt Kenseth	.75	2.00
8 Bobby Labonte	.60	1.50
9 Tony Stewart	.75	2.00
10 Ward Burton	.25	.60
11 Jeff Gordon	1.25	2.50
12 Ricky Rudd	.40	1.00
13 Kevin Harvick	.75	2.00
14 Sterling Marlin	.40	1.00
15 John Andretti	.10	.30
16 Jimmie Johnson CRC	.75	2.00
17 Dale Jarrett	.60	1.50
18 Jeff Burton	.25	.60
19 Ward Burton SG	.25	.60
20 Matt Kenseth SG	.75	2.00
21 Tony Stewart SG	.75	2.00
22 Sterling Marlin SG	.40	1.00
23 Jimmie Johnson SG	.75	2.00
24 Matt Kenseth SG	.75	2.00
25 Bobby Labonte SG	.60	1.50
26 Dale Earnhardt Jr. SG	1.50	3.00
27 Tony Stewart SG	.75	2.00
28 Jeff Gordon SG	1.25	2.50
29 Kevin Harvick AS	.75	2.00
30 Ryan Newman AS	.75	2.00
31 Rusty Wallace AS	.60	1.50
32 Tony Stewart AS	.75	2.00
33 Dale Earnhardt Jr. AS	1.50	3.00
34 Jimmie Johnson AS	.75	2.00
35 Jeff Burton AS	.25	.60
36 Mark Martin AS	.75	2.00
37 Terry Labonte SA	.40	1.00
38 Sterling Marlin SA	.40	1.00
39 Ricky Rudd SA	.40	1.00
40 Mark Martin PP	.75	2.00
41 Cale Yarborough PP	.10	.30
42 Ward Burton PP	.25	.60
43 Bobby Allison PP	.10	.30
44 Rusty Wallace PP	.60	1.50
45 Junior Johnson PP	.10	.30
46 Dale Jarrett PP	.60	1.50
47 David Pearson PP	.10	.30
48 Jeff Gordon PP	1.25	2.50
49 Richard Petty PP	.40	1.00
50 Jeff Gordon CL	.60	1.50
Jimmie Johnson CL		

2002 VIP Explosives

Issued at a stated rate of one per pack, this is a parallel version of the VIP set. Each card was printed on silver foil card stock with gold foil accents.

COMPLETE SET (50)	20.00	50.00
*EXPLOSIVES: 1X TO 2.5X BASE CARD HI		

2002 VIP Explosives Lasers

Issued at a stated rate of one in 20, this is a parallel to the VIP Explosives set. These cards can be differentiated from the basic Explosives set by the inclusion of a prismatic foil background on the cardfronts. The stated pirnt run was 420 serial numbered sets.

*EXPLOSIVES LASERS: 4X TO 10X BASE CARD HI

2002 VIP Samples

This set was issued to preview and promote the VIP set before it was released to the general public. Each card features the word" SAMPLE" on the back. They were issued one per Beckett Racing Collector magazine.

*SAMPLES: 2.5X TO 6X BASIC CARDS

2002 VIP Driver's Choice

Issued at a stated rate of one in 18, these nine cards feature information on where the leading drivers prefer to race.

COMPLETE SET (9)	15.00	40.00
*TRANSPARENT: .8X TO 2X BASIC INSERTS		
TRANSPARENT STATED ODDS 1:48		
*TRANSPARENT LTD: 1.2X TO 3X BASIC INSERTS		
TRANS.LTD PRINT RUN 100 SER.#'d SETS		
DC1 Jeff Gordon	5.00	12.00
DC2 Dale Jarrett	3.00	8.00
DC3 Bobby Labonte	3.00	8.00
DC4 Dale Earnhardt Jr.	6.00	15.00
DC5 Tony Stewart	4.00	10.00
DC6 Rusty Wallace	3.00	8.00
DC7 Kevin Harvick	4.00	10.00
DC8 Mark Martin	4.00	10.00
DC9 Jimmie Johnson	4.00	10.00

2002 VIP Head Gear

Inserted at stated odds of one in 12, these nine cards feature information on how drivers gear up for race day. Each card features a driver photo set against a background of his race day helmet.

COMPLETE SET (9)	12.50	30.00
*DIE CUTS: 1X TO 2.5X BASIC INSERTS		
HG1 Jeff Gordon	4.00	10.00
HG2 Rusty Wallace	2.50	6.00
HG3 Kevin Harvick	3.00	8.00
HG4 Dale Earnhardt Jr.	5.00	12.00
HG5 Ward Burton	1.00	2.50
HG6 Dale Jarrett	2.50	6.00
HG7 Tony Stewart	3.00	8.00
HG8 Terry Labonte	1.50	4.00
HG9 Mark Martin	3.00	8.00

2002 VIP Making the Show

Inserted at a stated rate of one per pack, this 24 card set features information on how these drivers made it onto the NASCAR circuit. Each card was produced in a die-cut design.

COMPLETE SET (24)	8.00	20.00
MS1 Steve Park	.40	1.00
MS2 Rusty Wallace	1.00	2.50
MS3 Mike Skinner	.20	.50
MS4 Terry Labonte	.60	1.50
MS5 Mark Martin	1.25	3.00
MS6 Dale Earnhardt Jr.	2.00	5.00
MS7 Ryan Newman	1.25	3.00
MS8 Matt Kenseth	1.25	3.00
MS9 Bobby Labonte	1.00	2.50
MS10 Jeremy Mayfield	.20	.50
MS11 Tony Stewart	1.25	3.00
MS12 Ward Burton	.40	1.00
MS13 Jeff Gordon	1.50	4.00
MS14 Ricky Rudd	.60	1.50
MS15 Kevin Harvick	1.25	3.00
MS16 Robby Gordon	.20	.50
MS17 Ken Schrader	.20	.50
MS18 Sterling Marlin	.60	1.50
MS19 John Andretti	.20	.50
MS20 Kyle Petty	.40	1.00
MS21 Jimmie Johnson	1.25	3.00
MS22 Dale Jarrett	1.00	2.50
MS23 Jeff Burton	.40	1.00
MS24 Ricky Rudd CL	.60	1.50

2002 VIP Mile Masters

Inserted at a stated rate of one in six, these 12 cards feature drivers who are masters on the race track. Each card was produced on holofoil card stock.

COMPLETE SET (12)	12.50	30.00
*TRANSPARENT: .8X TO 2X BASIC INSERTS		
*TRANSPARENT LTD: 1.2X TO 3X BASIC INSERTS		
MM1 Jeff Gordon	3.00	8.00
MM2 Tony Stewart	2.50	6.00
MM3 Jimmie Johnson	2.50	6.00
MM4 Dale Earnhardt Jr.	4.00	10.00
MM5 Dale Jarrett	2.00	5.00
MM6 Rusty Wallace	2.00	5.00
MM7 Ryan Newman	2.50	6.00
MM8 Mark Martin	2.50	6.00
MM9 Terry Labonte	1.25	3.00
MM10 Jeff Burton	.75	2.00
MM11 Ricky Rudd	1.00	2.50
MM12 Kevin Harvick	2.50	6.00

2002 VIP Race Used Sheet Metal Cars

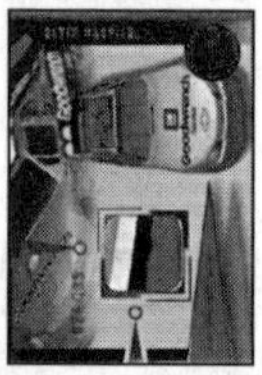

Issued at a stated rate of one in 460 retail packs, these 16 cards feature a genuine piece of race-used sheet metal set upon a card showing the car of the featured driver. These cards were issued to a stated print run of 135 sets.

SC1 Jeff Gordon's Car	40.00	100.00
SC2 Kevin Harvick's Car	15.00	40.00
SC3 Bobby Labonte's Car	15.00	40.00
SC4 Terry Labonte's Car	15.00	40.00
SC5 Ryan Newman's Car	25.00	60.00
SC6 Steve Park's Car	12.50	30.00
SC7 Ken Schrader's Car	12.50	30.00
SC8 Tony Stewart's Car	20.00	50.00
SC9 Mark Martin's Car	20.00	50.00
SC10 Matt Kenseth's Car	15.00	40.00
SC11 Rusty Wallace's Car	15.00	40.00
SC12 Jimmie Johnson's Car	25.00	60.00
SC13 Ward Burton's Car	12.50	30.00
SC14 Dale Jarrett's Car	15.00	40.00
SC15 Dale Earnhardt Jr.'s Car	60.00	120.00
SC16 Dale Earnhardt's Car		

2002 VIP Race Used Sheet Metal Drivers

Issued at a stated rate of one in 220 packs, these 16 cards feature a genuine piece of race-used sheet metal set upon a card with the picture of the featured driver. These cards were issued to a stated print run of 130 sets. The Dale Earnhardt Sr. card was issued to a stated print run of 50 sets.

SD1 Jeff Gordon	40.00	100.00
SD2 Kevin Harvick	15.00	40.00
SD3 Bobby Labonte	15.00	40.00
SD4 Terry Labonte	15.00	40.00
SD5 Ryan Newman	20.00	50.00
SD6 Steve Park	12.50	30.00
SD7 Ken Schrader	12.50	30.00
SD8 Tony Stewart	20.00	50.00
SD9 Mark Martin	20.00	50.00
SD10 Matt Kenseth	15.00	40.00
SD11 Rusty Wallace	15.00	40.00
SD12 Jimmie Johnson	25.00	60.00
SD13 Ward Burton	12.50	30.00
SD14 Dale Jarrett	15.00	40.00
SD15 Dale Earnhardt Jr.	60.00	120.00
SD16 Dale Earnhardt/50	200.00	400.00

2002 VIP Rear View Mirror

Inserted at a stated rate of one in 24, these six cards feature gold foil embossing and honor the very best drivers on the NASCAR circuit.

COMPLETE SET (6)	15.00	40.00
*DIE CUTS: .8X TO 2X BASIC INSERTS		
RM1 Bobby Labonte	3.00	8.00
RM2 Rusty Wallace	3.00	8.00
RM3 Kevin Harvick	4.00	10.00
RM4 Mark Martin	4.00	10.00
RM5 Jeff Gordon	5.00	12.00
RM6 Tony Stewart	4.00	10.00

2003 VIP

This 50-card set was issued in either five-card hobby or retail packs and packed in 28 pack boxes. This set was released in July of 2003. The SRP for packs was $2.99. Each card was printed with gold foil layering.

COMPLETE SET (50)	10.00	25.00
WAX BOX HOBBY (28)	40.00	80.00
WAX BOX RETAIL (24)	40.00	70.00
1 Jeff Burton	.25	.60
2 Ward Burton	.25	.60
3 Kurt Busch	.40	1.00
4 Dale Earnhardt Jr.	1.25	3.00
5 Jeff Gordon	1.00	2.50
6 Kevin Harvick	.60	1.50
7 Dale Jarrett	.60	1.50
8 Jimmie Johnson	.75	2.00
9 Matt Kenseth	.75	2.00
10 Bobby Labonte	.60	1.50
11 Terry Labonte	.40	1.00
12 Mark Martin	.75	2.00
13 Joe Nemechek	.10	.30
14 Ryan Newman	.75	2.00
15 Ricky Rudd	.40	1.00
16 Tony Stewart	.75	2.00
17 Rusty Wallace	.60	1.50
18 Michael Waltrip	.25	.60
19 Michael Waltrip SG	.25	.60
20 Dale Jarrett SG	.60	1.50
21 Matt Kenseth SG	.75	2.00
22 Bobby Labonte SG	.60	1.50
23 Ricky Craven SG	.10	.30
24 Kurt Busch SG	.40	1.00
25 Ryan Newman SG	.75	2.00
26 Dale Earnhardt Jr. SG	1.25	3.00
27 Jeff Gordon SG	1.00	2.50
28 Jimmie Johnson AS	.75	2.00
29 Ryan Newman AS	.75	2.00
30 Jeff Gordon AS 2001	1.00	2.50
31 Dale Earnhardt Jr. AS	1.25	3.00
32 Terry Labonte AS	.40	1.00
33 Mark Martin AS	.75	2.00
34 Jeff Gordon AS 1997	1.00	2.50
35 Michael Waltrip AS	.25	.60
36 Jeff Gordon AS 1995	1.00	2.50
37 Cale Yarborough LEG	.25	.60
38 David Pearson LEG	.25	.60
39 Benny Parsons LEG	.25	.60
40 Bobby Allison LEG	.25	.60
41 Ned Jarrett LEG	.25	.60
42 Richard Petty LEG	.40	1.00
43 Buddy Baker LEG	.25	.60
44 Harry Gant LEG	.25	.60
45 Glen Wood LEG	.10	.30
46 Ryan Newman HR	.75	2.00
47 Bobby Labonte HR	.60	1.50
48 Jimmie Johnson HR	.75	2.00
49 Rusty Wallace HR	.60	1.50
50 Dale Jarrett HR	.60	1.50

2003 VIP Explosives

Issued at a stated rate of one per pack, this is a parallel version of the VIP set. Each card was printed on silver foil card stock with gold foil accents.

COMPLETE SET (50)	15.00	40.00
*EXPLOSIVES: 1X TO 2.5X BASE CARDS		

2003 VIP Laser Explosive

Issued at a stated rate of one in 20, this is a parallel to the VIP Explosives set. These cards can be differentiated from the basic Explosives set by the inclusion of a prismatic foil background on the cardfronts. The stated pirnt run was 240 serial numbered sets.

LASERS: 4X TO 10X BASE CARDS
STATED ODDS 1:20

2003 VIP Samples

This 50-card set was a parallel of the base set with the exception of the word "SAMPLE" printed on the back of each card. These cards were found in Beckett Racing Collector September 2003, Issue #109. There was one card per magazine.

*SAMPLES: 2.5X TO 6X BASE

2003 VIP Tin

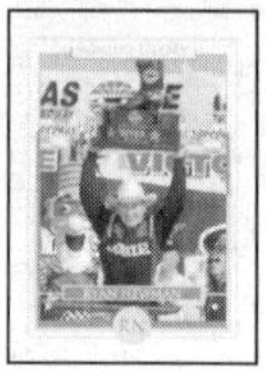

This 50-card set is a parallel to the basic VIP set. This set was sold exclusively at retail outlets and was packaged in a commemorative tin featuring Dale Earnhardt Jr. Each factory set also included a random autograph or memorabilia card that was from a set that was previously released with a few cards making their first appearance. Each card had a "CT" prefix. The factory tins had an SRP of $29.99.

COMP.FACT.TIN SET (51)	25.00	40.00
COMPLETE SET (50)	10.00	25.00
*SINGLES: .4X TO 1X BASIC CARDS		

2003 VIP Driver's Choice

Issued at a stated rate of one in 12, these nine cards feature information on where the leading drivers prefer to race.

*DIE CUTS: 1.2X TO 3X BASIC INSERTS		
DIE CUTS STATED ODDS 1:60		
DC1 Jimmie Johnson	2.00	5.00
DC2 Dale Earnhardt Jr.	3.00	8.00
DC3 Jeff Gordon	2.50	6.00
DC4 Dale Jarrett	1.50	4.00
DC5 Ward Burton	.60	1.25
DC6 Terry Labonte	1.00	2.50
DC7 Mark Martin	2.00	5.00
DC8 Rusty Wallace	1.50	4.00
DC9 Michael Waltrip	.60	1.25

2003 VIP Driver's Choice National

COMPLETE SET (9)	15.00	40.00
*NATIONAL: 1X TO 2.5X BASE		

2003 VIP Head Gear

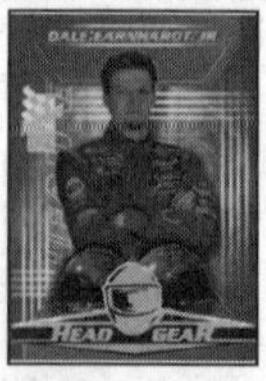

Inserted at stated odds of one in 24, these six cards feature information on how drivers gear up for race day. Each card features a driver photo set against a background of his race day helmet.

*DIE CUTS: .8X TO 2X BASIC INSERTS		
DIE CUTS STATED ODDS 1:72		
HG1 Jimmie Johnson	3.00	8.00
HG2 Dale Earnhardt Jr.	5.00	12.00
HG3 Jeff Gordon	4.00	10.00
HG4 Dale Jarrett	2.50	6.00
HG5 Rusty Wallace	2.50	6.00
HG6 Mark Martin	3.00	8.00

2003 VIP Head Gear National

COMPLETE SET (6)	20.00	50.00
*NATIONAL: 1X TO 2.5X BASE		

2003 VIP Lap Leaders

This 9-card set was randomly inserted in packs a rate of one in 18 packs. These cards featu holofoil etched technology.

*TRANS: .8X TO 2X BASIC INSERTS		
*TRANS LTD: 2X TO 5X BASIC INSERTS		
LL1 Jeff Gordon	4.00	10.0
LL2 Dale Earnhardt Jr.	5.00	12.0
LL3 Bobby Labonte	2.50	6.0
LL4 Rusty Wallace	2.50	6.0
LL5 Jimmie Johnson	3.00	8.0
LL6 Mark Martin	3.00	8.0
LL7 Michael Waltrip	1.00	2.5
LL8 Dale Jarrett	2.50	6.0
LL9 Kerry Earnhardt	1.00	2.5

2003 VIP Lap Leaders National

COMPLETE SET (9)	20.00	50.0
*NATIONAL: 1X TO 2.5X BASE		

2003 VIP Making the Show

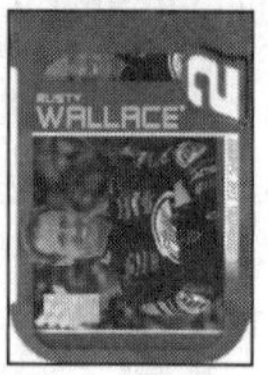

Inserted at a stated rate of one per pack, this 24 c set features information on how these drivers mad onto the NASCAR circuit. Each card was produced a die-cut design.

MS1 Rusty Wallace	1.00	2.5
MS2 Terry Labonte	.60	1.5
MS3 Mark Martin	1.25	3.0
MS4 Dale Earnhardt Jr.	2.00	5.0
MS5 Kerry Earnhardt	.40	1.0
MS6 Michael Waltrip	.40	1.0
MS7 Greg Biffle	.40	1.0
MS8 Bobby Labonte	1.00	2.5
MS9 Jeremy Mayfield	.20	.5
MS10 Tony Stewart	1.25	3.0
MS11 Ricky Rudd	.60	1.5
MS12 Ward Burton	.40	1.0
MS13 Kenny Wallace	.20	.5
MS14 Jeff Gordon	1.50	4.0
MS15 Kevin Harvick	1.00	2.5
MS16 Elliott Sadler	.40	1.0
MS17 Casey Mears	.40	1.0
MS18 Jamie McMurray	.60	1.5
MS19 Kyle Petty	.40	1.0
MS20 Jimmie Johnson	1.25	3.0
MS21 Ken Schrader	.20	.5
MS22 Todd Bodine	.20	.5
MS23 Dale Jarrett	1.00	2.5
MS24 Jeff Burton CL	.40	1.0

2003 VIP Mile Masters

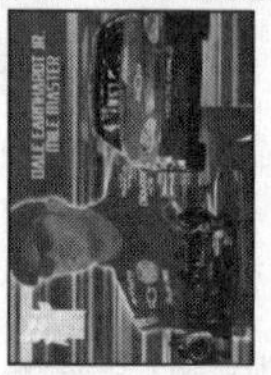

Inserted at a stated rate of one in six, these 12 ca feature drivers who are masters on the race tra Each card was produced on holofoil card stock.

COMPLETE SET (12)	10.00	25.0
*TRANS: .8X TO 2X BASIC INSERTS		
TRANS STATED ODDS 1:18		
*TRANS LTD: 3X TO 8X BASIC INSERTS		
TRANS LTD STATED ODDS 1:72		
TRANS LTD PRINT RUN 325 SERIAL #'d SETS		
MM1 Kerry Earnhardt	.60	1.5
MM2 Dale Earnhardt Jr.	2.50	6.0
MM3 Jeff Gordon	2.00	5.0
MM4 Dale Jarrett	1.25	3.0
MM5 Jimmie Johnson	1.50	4.0
MM6 Bobby Labonte	1.25	3.0
MM7 Terry Labonte	.75	2.0
MM8 Mark Martin	1.50	4.0
MM9 Ricky Rudd	.75	2.0
MM10 Tony Stewart	1.50	4.0
MM11 Rusty Wallace	1.25	3.0
MM12 Michael Waltrip	.60	1.5

2003 VIP Mile Masters National

COMPLETE SET (12)	15.00	40.0
*NATIONAL: 1X TO 2.5X BASE		

2003 VIP Tradin' Paint Cars

Randomly inserted in retail packs, these 18 ca feature a genuine piece of race-used sheet metal upon a card showing the car of the featured driver.

se cards were issued to a stated print run of 160 with the exception of Dale Earnhardt who was ed to just 3 copies and is not priced due to the 's scarcity.

1 Jeff Gordon's Car	25.00	60.00
2 Ryan Newman's Car	20.00	50.00
3 Kevin Harvick's Car	15.00	40.00
4 Jimmie Johnson's Car	25.00	60.00
5 Dale Jarrett's Car	15.00	40.00
6 Mark Martin's Car	25.00	60.00
7 Matt Kenseth's Car	20.00	50.00
8 Bobby Labonte's Car	12.50	30.00
9 Tony Stewart's Car	20.00	50.00
10 Dale Earnhardt Jr.'s Car	25.00	60.00
11 Jeff Burton's Car	10.00	25.00
12 Kurt Busch's Car	12.50	30.00
13 Dale Earnhardt's Car/3		
14 Robby Gordon's Car	10.00	25.00
15 Michael Waltrip's Car	12.50	30.00
16 Ward Burton's Car	10.00	25.00
17 Rusty Wallace's Car	15.00	40.00
18 Terry Labonte's Car	15.00	40.00

2003 VIP Tradin' Paint Car Autographs

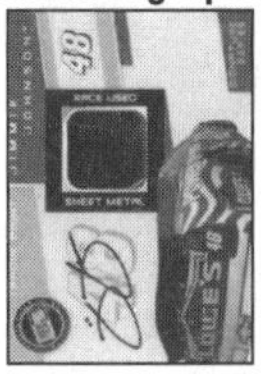

domly inserted in retail packs, these 8 cards re a genuine piece of race-used sheet metal set a card showing the car of the featured driver g with his signature. These cards were limited hand numbered to the corresponding driver's number. Some of these cards are not priced to scarcity.

ME CARDS NOT PRICED DUE TO SCARCITY		
Bobby Labonte's Car/18	75.00	150.00
immie Johnson's Car/48	100.00	175.00
Kevin Harvick's Car/29	100.00	200.00
Matt Kenseth's Car/17		
Mark Martin's Car/6		
Ryan Newman's Car/12		
Rusty Wallace's Car/2		
Terry Labonte's Car/5		

2003 VIP Tradin' Paint Drivers

domly inserted in retail packs at a rate of one in these 18 cards feature a genuine piece of race- sheet metal set upon a card showing the driver. se cards were issued to a stated print run of 110 with the exception of Mark Martin who was ed to just 65 copies.

1 Jeff Gordon	40.00	80.00
2 Ryan Newman	30.00	60.00
3 Kevin Harvick	25.00	50.00
4 Jimmie Johnson	40.00	80.00
5 Dale Jarrett	25.00	50.00
6 Mark Martin/65	40.00	80.00
7 Matt Kenseth	30.00	60.00
8 Bobby Labonte	20.00	40.00
9 Tony Stewart	30.00	60.00
10 Dale Earnhardt Jr.	40.00	80.00
11 Jeff Burton	15.00	30.00
12 Kurt Busch	20.00	40.00
13 Dale Earnhardt		
14 Robby Gordon	15.00	30.00
15 Michael Waltrip	20.00	40.00
16 Ward Burton	15.00	30.00
17 Rusty Wallace	25.00	50.00
18 Terry Labonte	25.00	50.00

2003 VIP Tradin' Paint Driver Autographs

domly inserted in retail packs, these 8 cards re a genuine piece of race-used sheet metal set a card showing the featured driver along with signature. These cards were limited and hand numbered to the corresponding driver's door number. Some of these cards are not priced due to scarcity.

SOME CARDS NOT PRICED DUE TO SCARCITY		
BL Bobby Labonte/18	75.00	150.00
JJ Jimmie Johnson/48	100.00	175.00
KH Kevin Harvick/29	100.00	200.00
MK Matt Kenseth/17		
MM Mark Martin/6		
RN Ryan Newman/12		
RW Rusty Wallace/2		
TL Terry Labonte/5		

2004 VIP

This 90-card set was issued in either five-card hobby or retail packs in 28 pack boxes. This set was released in August of 2004. The SRP for packs was $2.99. Each card was printed with gold foil layering.

COMPLETE SET (90)	15.00	40.00
COMMON CARD	.08	.20
COMMON DRIVER	.20	.50
SEMISTARS	.30	.75
UNLISTED STARS	.60	1.25
WAX BOX HOBBY (20)	40.00	80.00
WAX BOX RETAIL (24)	35.00	70.00
0 CARD STATED ODDS 1:160		
1 Jeff Burton	.30	.75
2 Ward Burton	.30	.75
3 Kurt Busch	.60	1.25
4 Dale Earnhardt Jr.	1.25	3.00
5 Jeff Gordon	1.25	3.00
6 Kevin Harvick	.75	2.00
7 Dale Jarrett	.60	1.50
8 Jimmie Johnson	1.00	2.50
9 Matt Kenseth	1.00	2.50
10 Bobby Labonte	.60	1.50
11 Terry Labonte	.60	1.25
12 Mark Martin	.75	2.00
13 Joe Nemechek	.20	.50
14 Ryan Newman	1.00	2.50
15 Ricky Rudd	.60	1.25
16 Tony Stewart	.75	2.00
17 Rusty Wallace	.60	1.50
18 Michael Waltrip	.30	.75
19 Greg Biffle	.30	.75
20 Kasey Kahne CRC	1.50	4.00
21 Robby Gordon	.20	.50
22 Kyle Petty	.30	.75
23 Scott Wimmer CRC	.30	.75
24 Jeremy Mayfield	.20	.50
25 Casey Mears	.20	.50
26 Jamie McMurray	.60	1.25
27 Brian Vickers CRC	.60	1.50
28 Dale Earnhardt Jr.'s Car R	.50	1.25
29 Michael Waltrip's Car R	.20	.50
30 Kevin Harvick's Car R	.30	.75
31 Rusty Wallace's Car R	.30	.75
32 Casey Mears' Car R	.20	.50
33 Jamie McMurray's Car R	.20	.50
34 Ryan Newman's Car R	.60	1.25
35 Scott Wimmer's Car R	.20	.50
36 Tony Stewart's Car R	.30	.75
37 Bobby Labonte's Car R	.30	.75
38 Jeff Gordon's Car R	.60	1.25
39 Jimmie Johnson's Car R	.60	1.25
40 Ricky Rudd's Car R	.20	.50
41 Kasey Kahne's Car R	.60	1.25
42 Jeff Burton's Car R	.20	.50
43 Dale Earnhardt Jr. SG	1.25	3.00
44 Matt Kenseth SG	1.00	2.50
45 Matt Kenseth SG	1.00	2.50
46 Dale Earnhardt Jr. SG	1.25	3.00
47 Jimmie Johnson SG	1.00	2.50
48 Kurt Busch SG	.60	1.25
49 Elliott Sadler SG	.30	.75
50 Rusty Wallace SG	.60	1.50
51 Jeff Gordon SG	1.25	3.00
52 Jeff Gordon SG	1.25	3.00
53 Dale Earnhardt Jr. SG	1.25	3.00
54 Mark Martin SG	.75	2.00
55 Dale Earnhardt Jr. HR	1.25	3.00
56 Jeff Gordon HR	1.25	3.00
57 Jimmie Johnson HR	1.00	2.50
58 Terry Labonte HR	.60	1.25
59 Sterling Marlin HR	.60	1.25
60 Tony Stewart HR	.75	2.00
61 Rusty Wallace HR	.60	1.50
62 Dale Jarrett HR	.60	1.50
63 Ryan Newman HR	1.00	2.50
64 Bobby Allison L	.30	.75
65 Davey Allison L	.60	1.25
66 Benny Parsons L	.30	.75
67 Buddy Baker L	.30	.75
68 Alan Kulwicki L	.60	1.25
69 Neil Bonnett L	.20	.50
70 Glen Wood L	.30	.75
71 Harry Gant L	.30	.75
72 Richard Petty L	.60	1.25
73 Elliott Sadler BTN	.30	.75
74 Jeff Gordon BTN	1.25	3.00
75 Tony Stewart BTN	.75	2.00
76 Scott Wimmer BTN	.30	.75
77 Dale Earnhardt Jr. BTN	1.25	3.00
78 Johnny Sauter BTN	.30	.75
79 Ryan Newman BTN	1.00	2.50
80 Jimmie Johnson BTN	1.00	2.50
81 Bobby Labonte BTN	.60	1.50
82 Richard Petty ATW	.60	1.25
83 David Pearson ATW	.30	.75
84 Bobby Allison ATW	.30	.75
85 Darrell Waltrip ATW	.60	1.25
86 Cale Yarborough ATW	.30	.75
87 Dale Earnhardt ATW	2.00	5.00
88 Jeff Gordon ATW	1.25	3.00
89 Rusty Wallace ATW	.60	1.50
90 Dale Earnhardt Jr. CL	1.25	3.00
0 Dale Earnhardt Sunday Money	10.00	25.00

2004 VIP Driver's Choice

Issued at a stated rate of one in 10, these six cards feature information on where the leading drivers prefer to race.

COMPLETE SET (6)	10.00	25.00
DC1 Jimmie Johnson	2.00	5.00
DC2 Dale Earnhardt Jr.	2.50	6.00
DC3 Jeff Gordon	2.50	6.00
DC4 Rusty Wallace	1.25	3.00
DC5 Sterling Marlin	1.00	2.50
DC6 Michael Waltrip	.60	1.50

2004 VIP Driver's Choice Die Cuts

This 6-card set is a die cut parallel to the basic Driver's Choice set. These cards were inserted at a rate of one in 40 packs.

COMPLETE SET (6)	15.00	40.00
*DIE CUTS: .8X TO 2X BASIC		

2004 VIP Head Gear

Inserted at stated odds of 1 in 5, these 12 cards feature information on how drivers gear up for race day. Each card features a driver photo set against a background of his race day helmet.

COMPLETE SET (12)	10.00	25.00
STATED ODDS 1:5		
HG1 Dale Earnhardt Jr.	2.50	6.00
HG2 Jeff Gordon	2.50	6.00
HG3 Kevin Harvick	1.50	4.00
HG4 Jimmie Johnson	2.00	5.00
HG5 Kasey Kahne	2.50	6.00
HG6 Matt Kenseth	2.00	5.00
HG7 Joe Nemechek	.40	1.00
HG8 Ricky Rudd	1.00	2.50
HG9 Elliott Sadler	.60	1.50
HG10 Tony Stewart	1.50	4.00
HG11 Rusty Wallace	1.25	3.00
HG12 Michael Waltrip	.60	1.50

2004 VIP Head Gear Transparent

Inserted at stated odds of 1 in 18, this 12-card parallel set features information on how drivers gear up for race day and is printed on a plastic card stock. Each card features a driver photo set against a background of his race day helmet.

COMPLETE SET (12)	15.00	40.00
*TRANS: .8X TO 2X BASIC		

2004 VIP Lap Leaders

This 9-card set was randomly inserted in packs at a rate of 1 in 8 packs. These cards featured holofoil etched technology.

COMPLETE SET (9)	12.50	30.00
STATED ODDS 1:8		
LL1 Mark Martin	2.00	5.00
LL2 Dale Earnhardt Jr.	3.00	8.00
LL3 Kasey Kahne	3.00	8.00
LL4 Ryan Newman	2.50	6.00
LL5 Michael Waltrip	.75	2.00
LL6 Tony Stewart	2.00	5.00
LL7 Jeff Gordon	3.00	8.00
LL8 Bobby Labonte	1.50	4.00
LL9 Rusty Wallace	1.50	4.00

2004 VIP Lap Leaders Transparent

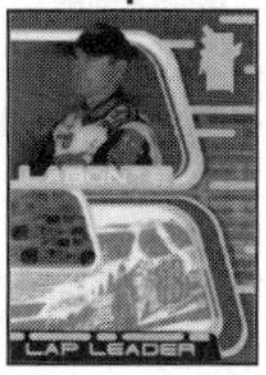

This 9-card set was randomly inserted in packs at a rate of 1 in 20 packs. These cards featured holofoil etched technology and are printed on a plastic card stock.

COMPLETE SET (9)	20.00	50.00
*TRANS: .8X TO 2X BASIC		

2004 VIP Making the Show

Inserted at a stated rate of 1 in 2 packs, this 27-card set features information on how these drivers made it onto the NASCAR circuit. Each card was produced in a die-cut design.

COMPLETE SET (27)	10.00	25.00
MS1 Joe Nemechek	.25	.60
MS2 Rusty Wallace	.75	2.00
MS3 Scott Wimmer	.40	1.00
MS4 Ward Burton	.40	1.00
MS5 Dale Earnhardt Jr.	1.50	4.00
MS6 Kasey Kahne	1.50	4.00
MS7 Scott Riggs	.40	1.00
MS8 Ryan Newman	1.25	3.00
MS9 Michael Waltrip	.40	1.00
MS10 Greg Biffle	.40	1.00
MS11 Matt Kenseth	1.25	3.00
MS12 Bobby Labonte	.75	2.00
MS13 Jeremy Mayfield	.25	.60
MS14 Tony Stewart	1.00	2.50
MS15 Ricky Rudd	.60	1.50
MS16 Jeff Gordon	1.50	4.00
MS17 Brian Vickers	.75	2.00
MS18 Kevin Harvick	1.00	2.50
MS19 Sterling Marlin	.60	1.50
MS20 Casey Mears	.40	1.00
MS21 Jamie McMurray	.60	1.50
MS22 Jeff Green	.25	.60
MS23 Jimmie Johnson	1.25	3.00
MS24 Brendan Gaughan	.40	1.00
MS25 Robby Gordon	.25	.60
MS26 Mark Martin	1.00	2.50
MS27 Jeff Burton CL	.40	1.00

2004 VIP Samples

This 90-card set is a parallel to the base 2004 VIP set without the variations. It was issued 1 per Beckett Racing Collector issue #121, which was the September 2004 cover date. Each card had the word "SAMPLE" printed across the back.

COMPLETE SET (90)
COMMON CARD (1-90)
*SAMPLES: 2X TO 5X BASE

2004 VIP Tradin' Paint Autographs

Randomly inserted in retail packs, these 4 cards feature a genuine piece of race-used sheet metal set upon a card showing the featured driver along with his signature. These cards were limited and hand numbered to the corresponding driver's door number. Some of these cards are not priced due to scarcity. The Jimmie Johnson and Jeff Gordon were not released until July 2005 in packs of Press Pass Legends. The Scott Wimmer was not released until October 2004 in the boxed sets of 2004 Press Pass Making the Show Collector's Series. The card went into products un-numbered, but it was confirmed by Press Pass that 22 copies exist.

SOME CARDS NOT PRICED DUE TO SCARCITY		
TP-BV Brian Vickers/25	100.00	200.00
TP-DE Dale Earnhardt Jr./8		
TP-JG Jeff Gordon/24	250.00	500.00
TP-JJ Jimmie Johnson/48	100.00	175.00
TP-KH Kevin Harvick/29	100.00	200.00
TP-MM Mark Martin/6		
TP-TS Tony Stewart/20		
TP-SW Scott Wimmer/22	50.00	100.00

2004 VIP Tradin' Paint Bronze

Randomly inserted in retail packs, these 18 cards feature a genuine piece of race-used sheet metal set upon a card showing the driver. These cards were issued to a stated print run of 130 sets with the exception of Joe Nemechek who was limited to just 50 copies. Each card has the word "Bronze" printed on the front near the serial number to note the level. Please note there are 2 other levels of the this insert.

*BRONZE: .4X TO 1X SILVER
TPT13 Joe Nemechek/50

2004 VIP Tradin' Paint Gold

Randomly inserted in hobby and retail packs, these 18 cards feature a genuine piece of race-used sheet metal set upon a card showing the driver. These cards were issued to a stated print run of 50 sets. Each card has the word "Gold" printed on the front near the serial number to note the level. Please note there are 2 other levels of the this insert.

*GOLD: .6X TO 1.5X SILVER

2004 VIP Tradin' Paint Silver

Randomly inserted in retail packs, these 18 cards feature a genuine piece of race-used sheet metal set upon a card showing the driver. These cards were issued to a stated print run of 70 sets with the exception of Joe Nemechek who was limited to just 50 copies. Each card has the word "Silver" printed on the front near the serial number to note the level. Please note there are 2 other levels of the this insert.

TPD1 Dale Earnhardt Jr.	50.00	100.00
TPD2 Jeff Gordon	50.00	100.00
TPD3 Jimmie Johnson	25.00	60.00
TPD4 Tony Stewart	26.00	60.00
TPD5 Ryan Newman	20.00	50.00
TPD6 Kevin Harvick	15.00	40.00
TPD7 Matt Kenseth	15.00	40.00
TPD8 Bobby Labonte	15.00	40.00
TPD9 Rusty Wallace	15.00	40.00
TPD10 Kurt Busch	12.50	30.00
TPD11 Robby Gordon	12.50	30.00
TPD12 Dale Jarrett	20.00	50.00
TPD13 Joe Nemechek/50	15.00	40.00
TPD14 Jeff Burton	12.50	30.00
TPD15 Scott Wimmer	12.50	30.00
TPD16 Brian Vickers	15.00	40.00
TPD17 Mark Martin	25.00	60.00
TPD18 Michael Waltrip	15.00	40.00

2005 VIP

5cards per pack hobby - 4 cards per pack retail

COMPLETE SET (90)	15.00	40.00
COMMON CARD	.10	.30
COMMON DRIVERS	.20	.50
SEMISTARS	.30	.75
UNLISTED STARS	.50	1.25
WAX BOX HOBBY (20)	40.00	70.00
WAX BOX RETAIL (24)	35.00	60.00
1 Greg Biffle	.30	.75
2 Jeff Burton	.30	.75
3 Kurt Busch	.50	1.25
4 Kyle Busch CRC	.75	2.00
5 Dale Earnhardt Jr.	1.25	3.00
6 Carl Edwards CRC	1.00	2.50
7 Jeff Gordon	1.25	3.00
8 Robby Gordon	.20	.50
9 Kevin Harvick	.75	2.00
10 Dale Jarrett	.60	1.50
11 Jimmie Johnson	1.00	2.50
12 Kasey Kahne	1.25	3.00
13 Matt Kenseth	1.00	2.50
14 Travis Kvapil CRC	.30	.75
15 Bobby Labonte	.60	1.50
16 Terry Labonte	.50	1.25
17 Mark Martin	.75	2.00
18 Sterling Marlin	.50	1.25
19 Jeremy Mayfield	.20	.50
20 Jamie McMurray	.50	1.25
21 Casey Mears	.30	.75
22 Joe Nemechek	.20	.50
23 Ryan Newman	1.00	2.50
24 Kyle Petty	.30	.75
25 Ricky Rudd	.50	1.25
26 Elliott Sadler	.30	.75
27 Tony Stewart	.75	2.00
28 Brian Vickers	.60	1.50
29 Rusty Wallace	.60	1.50
30 Scott Wimmer	.30	.75
31 Rusty Wallace's Car R	.30	.75
32 Jamie McMurray's Car R	.20	.50
33 Dale Earnhardt Jr's Car R	.50	1.25
34 Matt Kenseth's Car R	.50	1.25
35 Bobby Labonte's Car R	.30	.75
36 Kurt Busch's Car R	.20	.50
37 Ricky Rudd's Car R	.20	.50
38 Scott Wimmer's Car R	.10	.30
39 Tony Stewart's Car R	.30	.75
40 Elliott Sadler's Car R	.10	.30
41 Jeff Burton's Car R	.10	.30
42 Jimmie Johnson's Car R	.50	1.25
43 Jeff Gordon SG	1.25	3.00
44 Greg Biffle SG	.30	.75
45 Jimmie Johnson SG	1.00	2.50
46 Carl Edwards SG	1.00	2.50
47 Kevin Harvick SG	.75	2.00
48 Jeff Gordon SG	1.25	3.00
49 Greg Biffle SG	.30	.75
50 Kurt Busch SG	.50	1.25
51 Jeff Gordon SG	1.25	3.00
52 Greg Biffle SG	.30	.75
53 Kasey Kahne SG	1.25	3.00
54 Jimmie Johnson SG	1.00	2.50
55 Kasey Kahne HR	1.25	3.00
56 Ryan Newman HR	1.00	2.50
57 Martin Truex Jr. HR	1.00	2.50
58 Mark Martin HR	.75	2.00
59 Ryan Newman HR	1.00	2.50
60 Mark Martin HR	.75	2.00
61 Elliott Sadler HR	.30	.75
62 Brian Vickers HR	.60	1.50
63 Jeff Gordon HR	1.25	3.00
64 Terry Labonte F	.50	1.25
65 Terry Labonte F	.50	1.25
66 Terry Labonte F	.50	1.25
67 Mark Martin F	.75	2.00
68 Mark Martin F	.75	2.00
69 Mark Martin F	.75	2.00
70 Rusty Wallace F	.60	1.50
71 Rusty Wallace F	.60	1.50
72 Rusty Wallace F	.60	1.50
73 Dale Earnhardt Jr. BN	1.25	3.00
74 Jeff Gordon BN	1.25	3.00
75 Terry Labonte BN	.50	1.25
76 Jimmie Johnson BN	1.00	2.50
77 Mark Martin BN	.75	2.00
78 Tony Stewart BN	.75	2.00
79 Rusty Wallace BN	.60	1.50
80 Bobby Labonte BN	.60	1.50
81 Dale Jarrett BN	.60	1.50
82 Jeff Burton BN	.30	.75
83 Bobby Labonte ATML	.60	1.50
84 Rusty Wallace ATML	.60	1.50
85 Jeff Gordon ATML	1.25	3.00
86 Tony Stewart ATML	.75	2.00
87 Mark Martin ATML	.75	2.00
88 Jeff Burton ATML	.30	.75
89 Dale Jarrett ATML	.60	1.50
90 Wallace/Martin/T.Labonte CL	.75	2.00

2005 VIP Previews

CARDS NOT PRICED DUE TO SCARCITY

2005 VIP Samples

*SAMPLES: 1.5X TO 4X BASE

2005 VIP Driver's Choice

COMPLETE SET (6)	12.50	30.00
DC1 Jimmie Johnson	2.00	5.00
DC2 Dale Earnhardt Jr.	2.50	6.00
DC3 Jeff Gordon	2.50	6.00
DC4 Rusty Wallace	1.25	3.00
DC5 Sterling Marlin	1.00	2.50
DC6 Tony Stewart	1.50	4.00

2005 VIP Driver's Choice Die Cuts

COMPLETE SET (6)	20.00	50.00
*DIE CUTS: 1X TO 2.5X BASE		

2005 VIP Head Gear

COMPLETE SET (12)	12.50	30.00
1 Jeff Burton	.60	1.50

2 Jeff Gordon 2.50 6.00
3 Kevin Harvick 1.50 4.00
4 Jimmie Johnson 2.00 5.00
5 Kasey Kahne 2.50 6.00
6 Matt Kenseth 2.00 5.00
7 Joe Nemechek .40 1.00
8 Carl Edwards 2.00 5.00
9 Elliott Sadler .60 1.50
10 Tony Stewart 1.50 4.00
11 Rusty Wallace 1.25 3.00
12 Dale Jarrett 1.25 3.00

2005 VIP Head Gear Transparent

COMPLETE SET (12) 20.00 50.00
*TRANSPARENT: 1X TO 2.5X BASE

2005 VIP Lap Leaders

COMPLETE SET (9) 15.00 40.00
1 Mark Martin 2.00 5.00
2 Dale Earnhardt Jr. 3.00 8.00
3 Kasey Kahne 3.00 8.00
4 Elliott Sadler .75 2.00
5 Matt Kenseth 2.50 6.00
6 Tony Stewart 2.00 5.00
7 Jeff Gordon 3.00 8.00
8 Bobby Labonte 1.50 4.00
9 Rusty Wallace 1.50 4.00

2005 VIP Making The Show

COMPLETE SET (27) 10.00 25.00
1 Joe Nemechek .30 .75
2 Rusty Wallace 1.00 2.50
3 Scott Wimmer .50 1.25
4 Martin Truex Jr. 1.50 4.00
5 Dale Earnhardt Jr. 2.00 5.00
6 Kasey Kahne 2.00 5.00
7 Scott Riggs .50 1.25
8 Ryan Newman 1.50 4.00
9 Matt Kenseth 1.50 4.00
10 Greg Biffle .50 1.25
11 John Andretti .30 .75
12 Bobby Labonte 1.00 2.50
13 Jeremy Mayfield .30 .75
14 Tony Stewart 1.25 3.00
15 Boris Said .30 .75
16 Jeff Gordon 2.00 5.00
17 Brian Vickers 1.00 2.50
18 Kevin Harvick 1.25 3.00
19 Sterling Marlin .75 2.00
20 Casey Mears .50 1.25
21 Jamie McMurray .75 2.00
22 Jeff Green .30 .75
23 Jimmie Johnson 1.50 4.00
24 Jason Leffler .30 .75
25 Mike Bliss .30 .75
26 Mark Martin 1.25 3.00
27 Jeff Burton .50 1.25

2005 VIP Tradin' Paint Autographs

COMPLETE SET (7)
SOME CARDS NOT PRICED DUE TO SCARCITY
DE Dale Earnhardt Jr./8
JJ Jimmie Johnson/48 100.00 175.00
KH Kevin Harvick/29 100.00 200.00
KK Kasey Kahne/9
MK Matt Kenseth/17
MM Mark Martin/6
TS Tony Stewart/20

2005 VIP Tradin' Paint Cars

*CARS: .3X TO .8X DRIVERS

2005 VIP Tradin' Paint Drivers

TPD1 Dale Earnhardt Jr. 50.00 100.00
TPD2 Jeff Gordon 50.00 100.00
TPD3 Jimmie Johnson 30.00 60.00
TPD4 Tony Stewart 30.00 60.00
TPD5 Terry Labonte 30.00 60.00
TPD6 Kevin Harvick 30.00 60.00
TPD7 Matt Kenseth 30.00 60.00
TPD8 Bobby Labonte 25.00 50.00
TPD9 Rusty Wallace 25.00 50.00
TPD10 Kurt Busch 25.00 50.00
TPD11 Kasey Kahne 40.00 80.00
TPD12 Dale Jarrett 30.00 60.00
TPD13 Joe Nemechek 12.50 25.00
TPD14 Scott Riggs 12.50 25.00
TPD15 Scott Wimmer 12.50 25.00
TPD16 Brian Vickers 15.00 30.00
TPD17 Mark Martin 30.00 60.00

2006 VIP

COMPLETE SET (96) 15.00 40.00
COMP.SET w/o SPs (90) 10.00 25.00
COMMON DRIVERS .20 .50
SEMISTARS .30 .75
UNLISTED STARS .50 1.25
WAX BOX HOBBY (20) 50.00 80.00
WAX BOX RETAIL (24) 40.00 70.00
CRC STATED ODDS 1:6
1 Greg Biffle .40 1.00
2 Jeff Burton .30 .75
3 Kurt Busch .50 1.25
4 Kyle Busch .60 1.50
5 Dale Earnhardt Jr. 1.25 3.00
6 Carl Edwards 1.00 2.50
7 Jeff Gordon 1.25 3.00
8 Robby Gordon .20 .50
9 Kevin Harvick .75 2.00
10 Dale Jarrett .60 1.50
11 Jimmie Johnson 1.00 2.50
12 Kasey Kahne 1.25 3.00
13 Matt Kenseth 1.00 2.50
14 Bobby Labonte .60 1.50
15 Terry Labonte .60 1.50
16 Mark Martin .75 2.00
17 Sterling Marlin .50 1.25
18 Jamie McMurray .50 1.25
19 Casey Mears .30 .75
20 Joe Nemechek .20 .50
21 Ryan Newman .75 2.00
22 Kyle Petty .30 .75
23 Scott Riggs .30 .75
24 Elliott Sadler .30 .75
25 Ken Schrader .20 .50
26 Tony Stewart .75 2.00
27 Brian Vickers .60 1.50
28 Jeff Gordon's Car R .50 1.25
29 Kurt Busch's Car R .20 .50
30 Dale Jarrett's Car R .25 .60
31 Kevin Harvick's Car R .30 .75
32 Mark Martin's Car R .30 .75
33 Martin Truex Jr.'s Car R .25 .60
34 Matt Kenseth's Car R .40 1.00
35 Jimmie Johnson's Car R .40 1.00
36 Carl Edwards' Car R .40 1.00
37 Kasey Kahne's Car R .50 1.25
38 Jeff Burton's Car R .10 .30
39 Tony Stewart's Car R .30 .75
40 Jimmie Johnson SG 1.00 2.50
41 Matt Kenseth SG 1.00 2.50
42 Jimmie Johnson SG 1.00 2.50
43 Kasey Kahne SG 1.25 3.00
44 Kurt Busch SG .50 1.25
45 Tony Stewart SG .75 2.00
46 Kasey Kahne SG 1.25 3.00
47 Kevin Harvick SG .75 2.00
48 Jimmie Johnson SG 1.00 2.50
49 Dale Earnhardt Jr. SG 1.25 3.00
50 Greg Biffle SG .40 1.00
51 Kasey Kahne SG 1.25 3.00
52 Jimmie Johnson BTN 1.00 2.50
53 Dale Jarrett BTN .60 1.50
54 Dale Earnhardt Jr. BTN 1.25 3.00
55 Tony Stewart BTN .75 2.00
56 Carl Edwards BTN 1.00 2.50
57 Jeff Burton BTN .30 .75
58 Terry Labonte BTN .50 1.25
59 Mark Martin BTN .75 2.00
60 Jeff Gordon BTN 1.25 3.00
61 Jamie McMurray BTN .50 1.25
62 Kasey Kahne BTN 1.25 3.00
63 Greg Biffle BTN .40 1.00
64 Kurt Busch BTN .50 1.25
65 Ryan Newman RF .75 2.00
66 Kasey Kahne RF 1.25 3.00
67 Jeff Gordon RF 1.25 3.00
68 Greg Biffle RF .40 1.00
69 Kurt Busch RF .50 1.25
70 Dale Jarrett RF .60 1.50
71 Jimmie Johnson RF 1.00 2.50
72 Tony Stewart RF .75 2.00
73 Martin Truex Jr. AS .75 2.00
74 Kasey Kahne AS 1.25 3.00
75 Scott Riggs AS .30 .75
76 Kyle Petty AS .30 .75
77 Kyle Busch AS .60 1.50
78 Kevin Harvick AS .75 2.00
79 Jimmie Johnson AS 1.00 2.50
80 Dale Jarrett IF .60 1.50
81 Bobby Labonte IF .60 1.50
82 Mark Martin IF .75 2.00
83 Dale Earnhardt Jr. IF 1.25 3.00
84 Jimmie Johnson IF 1.00 2.50
85 Carl Edwards IF 1.00 2.50
86 Casey Mears IF .30 .75
87 Kevin Harvick IF .75 2.00
88 Jeff Gordon IF 1.25 3.00
89 Kurt Busch IF .50 1.25
90 Clint Bowyer CRC 3.00 8.00
91 Denny Hamlin CRC 3.00 8.00
92 Reed Sorenson CRC 2.50 6.00
93 David Stremme CRC 2.50 6.00
94 Martin Truex Jr. CRC 2.00 5.00
95 J.J. Yeley CRC 1.25 3.00
CL Jeff Gordon CL 1.25 3.00

2006 VIP Head Gear

COMPLETE SET (12) 12.50 30.00
HG1 Terry Labonte .75 2.00
HG2 Jimmie Johnson 1.50 4.00
HG3 Kasey Kahne 2.00 5.00
HG4 Dale Jarrett 1.00 2.50
HG5 Denny Hamlin 2.00 5.00
HG6 Mark Martin 1.25 3.00
HG7 Jeff Gordon 2.00 5.00
HG8 Tony Stewart 1.25 3.00
HG9 Kurt Busch .75 2.00
HG10 Kevin Harvick 1.25 3.00
HG11 Bobby Labonte 1.00 2.50
HG12 Jeff Burton .50 1.25

2006 VIP Head Gear Transparent

COMPLETE SET (12) 20.00 50.00
*TRANS: .8X TO 2X BASE

2006 VIP Lap Leader

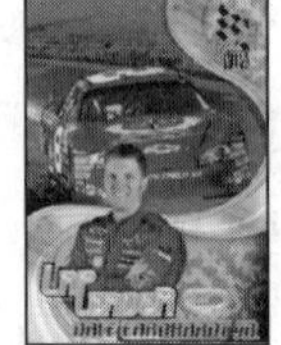

COMPLETE SET (9) 10.00 25.00
LL1 Tony Stewart 1.00 2.50
LL2 Mark Martin 1.00 2.50
LL3 Dale Earnhardt Jr. 1.50 4.00
LL4 Kasey Kahne 1.50 4.00
LL5 Jimmie Johnson 1.25 3.00
LL6 Dale Jarrett .75 2.00
LL7 Jeff Gordon 1.50 4.00
LL8 Kurt Busch .60 1.50
LL9 Jeff Burton .40 1.00

2006 VIP Lap Leader Transparent

COMPLETE SET (9) 15.00 40.00
*TRANS: .8X TO 2X BASE

2006 VIP Making the Show

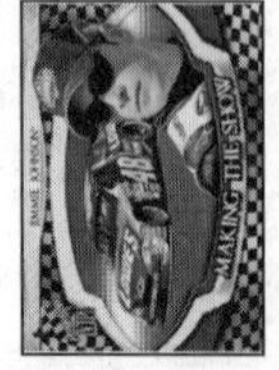

COMPLETE SET (25) 15.00 40.00
MS1 Mark Martin .75 2.00
MS2 Jeff Gordon 1.25 3.00
MS3 Matt Kenseth 1.00 2.50
MS4 Ryan Newman .75 2.00
MS5 Denny Hamlin 1.25 3.00
MS6 Sterling Marlin .50 1.25
MS7 Jimmie Johnson 1.00 2.50
MS8 J.J. Yeley .50 1.25
MS9 Jamie McMurray .50 1.25
MS10 Terry Labonte .50 1.25
MS11 Carl Edwards 1.00 2.50
MS12 Dale Jarrett .60 1.50
MS13 Kasey Kahne 1.25 3.00
MS14 Martin Truex Jr. .75 2.00
MS15 Greg Biffle .40 1.00
MS16 Kevin Harvick .75 2.00
MS17 Tony Stewart .75 2.00
MS18 Jeff Burton .30 .75
MS19 Kyle Busch .60 1.50
MS20 Scott Riggs .30 .75
MS21 Ken Schrader .20 .50
MS22 Bobby Labonte .60 1.50
MS23 Dale Earnhardt Jr. 1.25 3.00
MS24 Kurt Busch .50 1.25
MS25 Casey Mears .30 .75

2006 VIP Rookie Stripes

RS1 Clint Bowyer 20.00 50.00
RS2 Denny Hamlin 50.00 100.00
RS3 Reed Sorenson 20.00 50.00
RS4 David Stremme 15.00 40.00
RS5 Martin Truex Jr. 25.00 60.00
RS6 J.J. Yeley 20.00 50.00

2006 VIP Rookie Stripes Autographs

RS-CB Clint Bowyer 100.00 175.00
RS-DH Denny Hamlin 300.00 400.00
RS-DS David Stremme 60.00 150.00

2006 VIP Tradin' Paint Autographs

SERIAL #'D TO CAR NUMBER
SOME NOT PRICED DUE TO SCARCITY
TP-DE Dale Earnhardt Jr./8
TP-JG Jeff Gordon/24 250.00 500.00
TP-JJ Jimmie Johnson/48 100.00 175.00
TP-KK Kasey Kahne/9
TP-TS Tony Stewart/20

2006 VIP Tradin' Paint Cars Bronze

*CARS: .3X TO .8X DRIVERS SILVER

2006 VIP Tradin' Paint Drivers Gold

*GOLD: .5X TO 1.2X SILVER

2006 VIP Tradin' Paint Drivers Silver

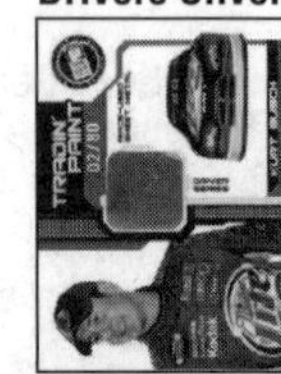

TPD1 Clint Bowyer 15.00 40.00
TPD2 Kurt Busch 20.00 50.00
TPD3 Kyle Busch 25.00 60.00
TPD4 Dale Earnhardt Jr. 50.00 120.00
TPD5 Carl Edwards 30.00 80.00
TPD6 Jeff Gordon 60.00 120.00
TPD7 Kevin Harvick 25.00 60.00
TPD8 Denny Hamlin 30.00 80.00
TPD9 Dale Jarrett 25.00 60.00
TPD10 Jimmie Johnson 40.00 100.00
TPD11 Kasey Kahne 40.00 100.00
TPD12 Brian Vickers 15.00 40.00
TPD13 Bobby Labonte 25.00 60.00
TPD14 Jeff Burton 20.00 50.00
TPD15 Ryan Newman 25.00 60.00
TPD16 Reed Sorenson 25.00 60.00
TPD17 Tony Stewart 40.00 100.00
TPD18 Terry Labonte 25.00 60.00

2007 VIP

COMPLETE SET 20.00 50.00
COMP.SET w/o SPs (83) 12.50 30.00
COMMON DRIVERS .20 .50
SEMISTARS .30 .75
UNLISTED STARS .50 1.25
SP STATED ODDS 1:8
WAX BOX HOBBY (20) 50.00 80.00
WAX BOX RETAIL (24) 45.00 75.00
1 Martin Truex Jr. CL .75 2.00
2 Greg Biffle .40 1.00
3 Clint Bowyer 1.00 2.50
4 Jeff Burton .30 .75
5 Kurt Busch .30 .75
6 Kyle Busch .60 1.50
7 Dale Earnhardt Jr. 1.25 3.00
8 Carl Edwards .75 2.00
9 Jeff Gordon 1.25 3.00
10 Jeff Green .20 .50
11 Denny Hamlin 1.00 2.50
12 Kevin Harvick .75 2.00
13 Dale Jarrett .60 1.50
14 Jimmie Johnson 1.00 2.50
15 Kasey Kahne 1.25 3.00
16 Matt Kenseth 1.00 2.50
17 Bobby Labonte .60 1.50
18 Sterling Marlin .50 1.25
19 Mark Martin .75 2.00
20 Jamie McMurray .50 1.25
21 Casey Mears .30 .75
22 Joe Nemechek .20 .50
23 Kyle Petty .30 .75
24 Tony Raines .20 .50
25 Ricky Rudd .50 1.25
26 Reed Sorenson .60 1.50
27 Tony Stewart .75 2.00
28 David Stremme .60 1.50
29 Martin Truex Jr. .75 2.00
30 Brian Vickers .50 1.25
31 Michael Waltrip .30 .75
32 J.J. Yeley .40 1.00
33 Richard Childress PB .30 .75
34 Ray Evernham PB .25 .60
35 Joe Gibbs PB
36 Rick Hendrick PB
37 Jack Roush PB .25 .60
38 Robert Yates PB .25 .60
39 Chip Ganassi PB
40 Ken Schrader's Car R .07 .20
41 Tony Stewart's Car R .30 .75
42 Kurt Busch's Car R .12 .30
43 Jeff Gordon's Car R .50 1.25
44 Michael Waltrip Racing AN .12 .30
45 Joe Gibbs Racing AN
46 Roush Racing AN .10 .25
47 Bill Davis Racing AN
48 Evernham Motorsports AN .10 .25
49 Martin Truex Jr.'s Car SV .30 .75
50 Dale Earnhardt Jr.'s Car SV .50 1.25
51 Sterling Marlin's Car SV .20 .50
52 Tony Stewart's Car SV .30 .75
53 Jeff Gordon's Car SV .50 1.25
54 Jamie McMurray's Car SV .20 .50
55 Jimmie Johnson's Car SV .40 1.00
56 Ricky Rudd's Car SV .20 .50
57 Brian Vickers' Car SV .20 .50
58 Dale Jarrett's Car SV .25 .60
59 Kevin Harvick Red C .75 2.00
60 Jimmie Johnson Red C 1.00 2.50
61 Mark Martin Red C .75 2.00
62 Jeff Burton Red C .30 .75
63 Tony Stewart Red C .75 2.00
64 Johnny Sauter Red C .30 .75
65 Matt Kenseth Red C 1.00 2.50
66 Ryan Newman Red C .60 1.50
67 Dale Earnhardt Jr. Red C 1.25 3.00
68 Martin Truex Jr. Red C .75 2.00
69 Kevin Harvick Daytona AP .75 2.00
70 Matt Kenseth California AP 1.00 2.50
71 Jimmie Johnson Las Vegas AP 1.00 2.50
72 Jimmie Johnson Atlanta AP 1.00 2.50
73 Kyle Busch Bristol AP .60 1.50
74 Jimmie Johnson Martinsville AP 1.00 2.50
75 Jeff Burton Texas AP .30 .75
76 Jeff Gordon Phoenix AP 1.25 3.00
77 Jeff Gordon Talladega AP 1.25 3.00
78 Jimmie Johnson Richmond AP 1.00 2.50
79 Jeff Gordon Darlington AP 1.25 3.00
80 Casey Mears Charlotte AP .30 .75
81 Martin Truex Jr. Dover AP .75 2.00
82 Jeff Gordon Pocono AP 1.25 3.00
83 Carl Edwards Michigan AP .75 2.00
84 A.J. Allmendinger SP RC 2.50 6.00
85 David Gilliland SP RC 2.00 5.00
86 Paul Menard SP CRC 1.50 4.00
87 Juan Pablo Montoya SP RC 3.00 8.00
88 David Ragan SP CRC 2.00 5.00
89 David Reutimann SP RC 2.00 5.00
90 Regan Smith SP CRC 1.25 3.00

2007 VIP Previews

STATED PRINT RUN (EB1-EB32) 5 SERIAL #'d SETS
STATED PRINT RUN (EB84-EB90) 1 SERIAL #'d SET
NOT PRICED DUE TO SCARCITY

2007 VIP Gear Gallery

COMPLETE SET (12) 15.00 40.00
COMMON DRIVERS .50 1.25
SEMISTARS .75 2.00
UNLISTED STARS 1.25 3.00
STATED ODDS 1:4
GG1 Ryan Newman 1.50 4.00
GG2 Kevin Harvick 2.00 5.00
GG3 Dale Jarrett 1.50 4.00
GG4 Jeff Gordon 3.00 8.00
GG5 Juan Pablo Montoya 3.00 8.00
GG6 Ricky Rudd 1.25 3.00
GG7 Mark Martin 2.00 5.00
GG8 Michael Waltrip .75 2.00
GG9 Tony Stewart 2.00 5.00
GG10 Jimmie Johnson 2.50 6.00
GG11 David Gilliland 2.50 6.00
GG12 Kyle Busch 1.50 4.00

2007 VIP Gear Gallery Transparent

COMPLETE SET (12) 25.00 60.00
*TRANS: .6X TO 1.5X BASIC
STATED ODDS 1:15

2007 VIP Get A Grip Autographs

SERIAL #'d TO DRIVERS' DOOR NUMBER
SOME NOT PRICED DUE TO SCARCITY
GG-DE Dale Earnhardt Jr./8
GG-JM Juan Pablo Montoya/42 60.00 120.00
GG-JY J.J. Yeley/18
GG-KH Kevin Harvick/29 100.00 200.00
GG-KK Kasey Kahne/9
GG-MK Matt Kenseth/17

2007 VIP Get A Grip Drivers

OVERALL R-U STATED ODDS 1:40
STATED PRINT RUN 70 SERIAL #'d SETS
GGD1 Mark Martin 20.00
GGD2 Carl Edwards 20.00
GGD3 Michael Waltrip 12.50
GGD4 Jamie McMurray 12.50
GGD5 Regan Smith 8.00
GGD6 Ryan Newman 12.50
GGD7 Juan Pablo Montoya 25.00
GGD8 Kasey Kahne 25.00
GGD9 Elliott Sadler 15.00
GGD10 Matt Kenseth 20.00
GGD11 Dale Jarrett 20.00
GGD12 Tony Stewart 25.00
GGD13 Jeff Gordon 40.00
GGD14 Joe Nemechek 8.00
GGD15 Scott Riggs 8.00
GGD16 Reed Sorenson 12.50
GGD17 Denny Hamlin 20.00
GGD18 Kevin Harvick 15.00
GGD19 Dave Blaney 8.00
GGD20 David Stremme 12.50
GGD21 Clint Bowyer 20.00
GGD22 Brian Vickers 15.00
GGD23 Kyle Busch 15.00
GGD24 David Ragan 15.00
GGD25 Jeff Burton 15.00
GGD26 A.J. Allmendinger 15.00
GGD27 Dale Earnhardt Jr. 40.00
GGD28 Martin Truex Jr. 15.00
GGD29 Jimmie Johnson 25.00

2007 VIP Get A Grip Teams

*TEAMS: .5X TO 1X DRIVERS
OVERALL R-U ODDS 1:112 RETAIL
STATED PRINT RUN 70 SERIAL #'d SETS

2007 VIP Pedal To Th Metal

OVERALL R-U ODDS 1:40 HOBBY
OVERALL R-U ODDS 1:112 RETAIL
STATED PRINT RUN 50 SERIAL #'d SETS
PM1 Tony Stewart 40.00
PM2 Elliott Sadler 25.00
PM3 Dale Earnhardt Jr. 50.00
PM4 Michael Waltrip 20.00
PM5 Kasey Kahne 40.00
PM6 Carl Edwards 30.00
PM7 Jamie McMurray 20.00
PM8 Jeff Gordon 50.00
PM9 Kevin Harvick 40.00

2007 VIP Rookie Strip

OVERALL R-U ODDS 1:40 HOBBY
OVERALL R-U ODDS 1:112 RETAIL
STATED PRINT RUN 100 SERIAL #'d SETS
RS1 A.J. Allmendinger 15.00
RS2 Paul Menard 20.00
RS3 Juan Pablo Montoya 30.00
RS4 David Ragan 25.00
RS5 David Reutimann 15.00
RS6 Regan Smith 15.00

2007 VIP Rookie Strip Autographs

STATED PRINT RUN 25 SERIAL #'d SETS
RS-AJ A.J. Allmendinger 40.00
RS-JM Juan Pablo Montoya 100.00
RS-PM Paul Menard 40.00
RS-RS Regan Smith 50.00
RS-DRA David Ragan 50.00
RS-DRE David Reutimann 40.00

2007 VIP Sunday Bes

COMPLETE SET (25) 15.00
COMMON DRIVERS .25
SEMISTARS .40
UNLISTED STARS .60
STATED ODDS 1:2
SB1 Clint Bowyer 1.25
SB2 Jeff Burton .40
SB3 Kurt Busch .40
SB4 Kyle Busch .75
SB5 Dale Earnhardt Jr. 1.50
SB6 Carl Edwards 1.00
SB7 Jeff Gordon 1.50
SB8 Denny Hamlin 1.25
SB9 Kevin Harvick 1.00
SB10 Dale Jarrett .75
SB11 Jimmie Johnson 1.25
SB12 Kasey Kahne 1.50
SB13 Matt Kenseth 1.25
SB14 Bobby Labonte .75
SB15 Sterling Marlin .60
SB16 Mark Martin 1.00
SB17 Jamie McMurray .60
SB18 Juan Pablo Montoya 1.50
SB19 Ryan Newman .75
SB20 Ricky Rudd .60
SB21 Tony Stewart 1.00
SB22 David Stremme .75
SB23 Martin Truex Jr. 1.00
SB24 Brian Vickers .60
SB25 Michael Waltrip .40

2007 VIP Trophy Clu

TC1 Tony Stewart 2.50
TC2 Dale Jarrett 2.00

C3 Jimmie Johnson	3.00	8.00
C4 Dale Earnhardt Jr.	4.00	10.00
C5 Jeff Burton	1.00	2.50
C6 Kurt Busch	1.00	2.50
C7 Denny Hamlin	3.00	8.00
C8 Ryan Newman	2.00	5.00
C9 Jeff Gordon	4.00	10.00

1996 Viper Promos

heels produced this 3-card promo set to advertise new Viper card line. The cards were distributed ounted in a simulated snake skin binder.

OMPLETE SET (3)	10.00	25.00
1 Bobby Labonte	2.00	5.00
2 Rusty Wallace	3.00	8.00
3 Jeff Gordon	5.00	12.00

1996 Viper

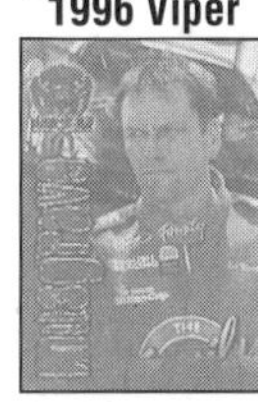

is 78-card set features many of the top names in inston Cup. The cards use the theme of the snake th the Viper logo appearing in the top left hand rner of each card. Cards are printed on 24-point ock. There are both hobby and retail boxes of per. Each box contains 24-packs with five cards r pack. Each card in the first 325 cases printed rried a special First Strike logo. These First Strike rds parallel the base set and inserts and were ckaged separately in specially marked boxes and cks.

OMPLETE SET (78)	10.00	25.00
Dale Earnhardt	1.50	4.00
Jeff Gordon	1.00	2.50
Sterling Marlin	.30	.75
Mark Martin	.75	2.00
Terry Labonte	.30	.75
Rusty Wallace	.75	2.00
Bill Elliott	.40	1.00
Bobby Labonte	.60	1.50
Ward Burton	.20	.50
0 Bobby Hamilton	.10	.25
1 Dale Jarrett	.60	1.50
2 Ted Musgrave	.10	.25
3 Darrell Waltrip	.20	.50
4 Kyle Petty	.20	.50
5 Ken Schrader	.10	.25
6 Michael Waltrip	.20	.50
7 Derrike Cope	.10	.25
8 Jeff Burton	.30	.75
9 Ricky Craven	.10	.25
0 Steve Grissom	.10	.25
1 Robert Pressley	.10	.25
2 Joe Nemechek	.10	.25
3 Jeremy Mayfield	.20	.50
4 Mike Wallace	.10	.25
5 Johnny Benson	.20	.50
6 Jimmy Spencer	.10	.25
7 Tony Glover	.05	.15
8 Steve Hmiel	.05	.15
9 Mike Beam	.05	.15
0 Larry McReynolds	.05	.15
1 Robin Pemberton	.05	.15
2 Jimmy Makar	.05	.15
3 Richard Childress	.20	.50
4 Joe Gibbs	.20	.50
5 Jack Roush	.05	.15
6 Roger Penske	.05	.15
7 Mark Martin	.75	2.00
8 Bobby Labonte	.60	1.50
9 Terry Labonte	.30	.75
0 Jeff Gordon	1.00	2.50
1 Rusty Wallace	.75	2.00
2 Jeff Gordon	1.00	2.50
3 Dale Earnhardt	1.50	4.00
4 Mark Martin	.75	2.00
5 Mark Martin	.75	2.00
6 Ward Burton	.20	.50
7 Chad Little	.20	.50
8 Mike McLaughlin	.10	.25
9 Jason Keller	.10	.25
0 David Green	.10	.25
1 Larry Pearson	.20	.50
2 Jeff Fuller	.10	.25
3 David Green	.10	.25
4 Hermie Sadler	.10	.25
5 Bobby Dotter	.10	.25
6 Terry Labonte	.30	.75
7 Mark Martin	.75	2.00
8 Dale Jarrett	.60	1.50
9 Michael Waltrip	.20	.50
0 Joe Nemechek	.10	.25
1 Ken Schrader	.10	.25
2 Mike Wallace	.10	.25
3 Randy Porter	.10	.25
4 Mike Skinner	.10	.25
5 Joe Ruttman	.10	.25
6 Ron Hornaday	.10	.25
7 Butch Miller	.10	.25
8 Rick Carelli	.10	.25
9 Bill Sedgwick	.10	.25
0 Tobey Butler	.10	.25
1 Steve Portenga	.10	.25
2 Bob Keselowski	.10	.25
3 Ken Schrader	.10	.25
4 Johnny Benson	.20	.50
5 Mike Chase	.10	.25
6 Checklist	.05	.15
7 Checklist	.05	.15
8 Cover Card	.05	.15
3 Dale Earnhardt Promo	2.00	5.00
3FS Dale Earnhardt Promo First Strike card	2.50	6.00

1996 Viper First Strike

ese cards were issued in the first 325-cases of the se 1996 Viper card release. Each is identical to its base Viper card with the addition of the "First Strike" diamond shaped silver logo on the cardfront. All First Strike cards were issued through their own specially marked packs and boxes.

COMPLETE SET (78)	20.00	50.00
*FIRST STRIKE: 1X TO 2.5X BASE CARDS		

1996 Viper Red Cobra

The Red Cobra parallel set was issued in its own factory set box that featured replica snake skin on the outside. Each card is identical to its base Viper counterpart with the difference of red foil on the cardfronts instead of silver.

COMPLETE SET (78)	15.00	40.00
*RED COBRA: 1.25X TO 3X BASE CARDS		

1996 Viper Black Mamba

This 78-card set is a hobby only parallel version of the base Viper set. The Black Mamba cards feature black foil stamping to differentiate them from the base silver foil cards. They were randomly seeded in hobby packs at a rate of one per 13 packs and were sequentially numbered of 499. There was also a special Black Mamba #R3 Dale Earnhardt card randomly inserted in packs.

COMPLETE SET (78)	150.00	300.00
*BLACK MAMBA: 4X TO 10X BASE CARDS		
R3B Dale Earnhardt Black	25.00	60.00

1996 Viper Black Mamba First Strike

This set parallels the Black Mamba insert set. The cards were inserted at a rate of 1:13 First Strike packs. The cards feature the First Strike logo on the fronts.

COMPLETE SET (78)	400.00	600.00
*FIRST STRIKE: .8X TO 2X BLACK MAMBA		

1996 Viper Green Mamba

This 78-card set is retail only parallel to the base Viper set. The cards are randomly inserted in retail only packs at a rate of one per 13 packs. The cards feature green foil stamping and are sequentially numbered of 349.

COMPLETE SET (78)	250.00	450.00
*GREEN MAMBA: .4X TO 1X BLACK MAMBA		

1996 Viper Copperhead Die Cuts

This 78-card set is a parallel of the base Viper set. The cards feature a copper foil stamping and were randomly inserted at a rate of one in seven packs. Each Copperhead card is die cut and sequentially numbered of 1399.

COMPLETE SET (78)	60.00	150.00
*COPPERHEAD: 2.5X TO 6X BASE CARDS		

1996 Viper Busch Clash

This 16-card set features drivers who captured a pole in 1995. The cards have many of the drivers holding the traditional Busch Pole plaque. The cards were inserted at a rate of one in eight packs. There was also a First Strike version available in First Strike boxes at a rate of one in eight packs

COMPLETE SET (16)	30.00	75.00
COMP.FIRST STRIKE (16)	50.00	100.00
*FIRST STRIKE: .6X TO 1.5X BASIC INSERTS		
B1 Terry Labonte	2.00	5.00
B2 John Andretti	.60	1.50
B3 Hut Stricklin	.60	1.50
B4 David Green	.60	1.50
B5 Jeff Gordon	6.00	15.00
B6 Darrell Waltrip	1.25	3.00
B7 Dale Jarrett	4.00	10.00
B8 Sterling Marlin	2.00	5.00
B9 Rick Mast	.60	1.50
B10 Dave Marcis	.60	1.50
B11 Mark Martin	5.00	12.00
B12 Ken Schrader	.60	1.50
B13 Ted Musgrave	.60	1.50
B14 Dale Earnhardt	10.00	25.00
B15 Bobby Labonte	4.00	10.00
B16 Bill Elliott	2.50	6.00

1996 Viper Cobra

This 10-card insert set ten of the top 15 finishers in the 1995 Winston Cup points race. The cards are randomly inserted one per 48 packs. The First Strike version featured the same odds and were inserted only in First Strike boxes.

COMPLETE SET (10)	75.00	125.00
COMP. FIRST STRIKE (10)	80.00	200.00
*FIRST STRIKE: .5X TO 1.2X BASIC INSERTS		
C1 Dale Earnhardt	25.00	60.00

C2 Jeff Gordon	15.00	40.00
C3 Bobby Labonte	10.00	25.00
C4 Mark Martin	12.50	30.00
C5 Sterling Marlin	5.00	12.00
C6 Rusty Wallace	12.50	30.00
C7 Terry Labonte	5.00	12.00
C8 Bill Elliott	6.00	15.00
C9 Bobby Hamilton	1.50	4.00
C10 Dale Jarrett	10.00	25.00

1996 Viper Dale Earnhardt

This set was available through a redemption of a winning viper venom card. The set features seven time Winston Cup Champion Dale Earnhardt and comes in a simulated snake skin case.

COMPLETE SET (3)	15.00	40.00
COMMON CARD	7.50	20.00

1996 Viper Diamondback

This eight-card insert set features a patch of simulated rattlesnake skin next to the picture of the driver on the fronts of the cards. The cards are randomly inserted in packs one per 72 packs. Each card is sequentially numbered of 1,499. The First Strike version were cards inserted into specially marked boxes of Viper First Strike. The cards are a parallel to the base inserts.

COMPLETE SET (8)	60.00	175.00
COMP.FIRST STRIKE (8)	100.00	200.00
*FIRST STRIKE: .6X TO 1.5X BASIC INSERTS		
D1 Jeff Gordon	10.00	25.00
D2 Dale Earnhardt	15.00	40.00
D3 Bobby Labonte	6.00	15.00
D4 Mark Martin	8.00	20.00
D5 Terry Labonte	3.00	8.00
D6 Rusty Wallace	8.00	20.00
D7 Sterling Marlin	3.00	8.00
D8 Bill Elliott	4.00	10.00

1996 Viper Diamondback Authentic

This eight-card insert set features authentic diamondback rattlesnake skin attached to each horizontally-oriented card. The cards are inserted at a rate of one per 120 packs and are sequentially numbered of 749. There was also a parallel First Strike version that was available in specially marked Viper First Strike boxes.

COMPLETE SET (8)	100.00	200.00
COMP.CALIFORNIA SET (8)	250.00	500.00
*CALIFORNIA: 1X TO 2X BASIC INSERTS		
COMP. FIRST STRIKE (8)	150.00	300.00
*FIRST STRIKE: .5X TO 1.2X BASIC INSERTS		
DA1 Jeff Gordon	15.00	40.00
DA2 Dale Earnhardt	25.00	60.00
DA3 Sterling Marlin	5.00	12.00
DA4 Bobby Labonte	10.00	25.00
DA5 Rusty Wallace	12.50	30.00
DA6 Terry Labonte	5.00	12.00
DA7 Mark Martin	12.50	30.00
DA8 Bill Elliott	6.00	15.00

1996 Viper King Cobra

This 10-card set is a jumbo sized parallel to the Viper Cobra insert set. The cards measure 3" X 5" and were inserted into boxes of Viper at a rate of one per three boxes. Each card is sequentially numbered of 699. The First Strike version is a parallel to the base cards and comes in specially marked Viper First Strike boxes.

COMPLETE SET (10)	75.00	125.00
COMP.FIRST STRIKE (10)	80.00	200.00
*FIRST STRIKE: .6X TO 1.5X BASIC INSERTS		
KC1 Dale Earnhardt	25.00	60.00
KC2 Jeff Gordon	15.00	40.00
KC3 Dale Jarrett	10.00	25.00
KC4 Bill Elliott	6.00	15.00
KC5 Terry Labonte	5.00	12.00
KC6 Bobby Hamilton	1.50	4.00
KC7 Rusty Wallace	12.50	30.00
KC8 Mark Martin	12.50	30.00
KC9 Bobby Labonte	10.00	25.00
KC10 Sterling Marlin	5.00	12.00

1996 Viper Dale Earnhardt Cobra Mom-n-Pop's

This three-card set was available directly from Mom-n-Pop's. The cards are similar to the three card Viper Dale Earnhardt redemption set except these cards are Cobra cards. The cards come in a simulated snake skin case with red crushed velvet on the inside.

COMPLETE SET (3)	10.00	25.00
COMMON CARD (1-3)	4.80	12.00

1997 Viper

This 82-card set features many of the top names in Winston Cup. The cards use the theme of the snake with the Viper logo appearing in the top left hand corner of each card. There are both hobby and retail boxes of Viper. Each hobby box contains 24 packs with six cards per pack. Each retail box contains 30 packs with five cards per pack. There were 200 Eastern cases and 1,000 Western cases produced. The difference in these cases is the Diamondback Authentic cards. The Eastern cases contain cards that were not produced from Western Diamondback snake skin, but facsimile skin. Each 16-box hobby case contains 12 regular boxes and four First Strike boxes. Each card in the First Strike boxes carried a special First Strike logo.

COMPLETE SET (82)	8.00	20.00
1 Jeff Gordon	.75	2.00
2 Dale Jarrett	.50	1.25
3 Terry Labonte	.25	.60
4 Mark Martin	.60	1.50
5 Rusty Wallace	.60	1.50
6 Bobby Labonte	.50	1.25
7 Sterling Marlin	.25	.60
8 Jeff Burton	.25	.60
9 Ted Musgrave	.07	.20
10 Michael Waltrip	.15	.40
11 David Green	.07	.20
12 Ricky Craven	.07	.20
13 Johnny Benson	.15	.40
14 Jeremy Mayfield	.15	.40
15 Bobby Hamilton	.07	.20
16 Kyle Petty	.15	.40
17 Darrell Waltrip	.15	.40
18 Wally Dallenbach	.07	.20
19 Bill Elliott	.30	.75
20 Robert Pressley	.07	.20
21 Joe Nemechek	.07	.20
22 Derrike Cope	.07	.20
23 Ward Burton	.15	.40
24 Chad Little	.07	.20
25 Mike Skinner	.07	.20
26 Brett Bodine	.07	.20
27 Hut Stricklin	.07	.20
28 Dave Marcis	.15	.40
29 Ken Schrader	.07	.20
30 Steve Grissom	.07	.20
31 Robby Gordon RC	.25	.60
32 Kenny Wallace	.07	.20
33 Bobby Hillin, Jr.	.07	.20
34 Jimmy Spencer	.07	.20
35 Dick Trickle	.07	.20
36 John Andretti	.07	.20
37 Steve Park RC	2.00	4.00
38 Jeff Burton	.25	.60
39 Michael Waltrip	.15	.40
40 Dale Jarrett	.50	1.25
41 Mike McLaughlin	.07	.20
42 Todd Bodine	.07	.20
43 Bobby Labonte	.50	1.25
44 Jeff Fuller	.07	.20
45 Kyle Petty	.15	.40
46 Jason Keller	.07	.20
47 Mark Martin	.60	1.50
48 Randy LaJoie	.07	.20
49 Joe Nemechek	.07	.20
50 Glenn Allen	.07	.20
51 Jeff Gordon	.75	2.00
52 Rusty Wallace	.60	1.50
53 Dale Jarrett	.50	1.25
54 Jeff Burton	.25	.60
55 Dale Jarrett	.50	1.25
56 Jeff Hammond	.02	.10
57 Andy Petree	.02	.10
58 Robbie Loomis	.02	.10
59 Mike Beam	.02	.10
60 Buddy Parrott	.02	.10
61 Roger Penske	.02	.10
62 Bill Davis	.02	.10
63 Travis Carter	.02	.10
64 Chuck Rider	.02	.10
65 Felix Sabates	.02	.10
66 Larry Hedrick	.02	.10
67 Rusty Wallace's Car	.25	.60
68 Dale Earnhardt's Car	.50	1.25
69 Terry Labonte's Car	.15	.40
70 Mark Martin's Car	.25	.60
71 Brett Bodine's Car	.02	.10
72 Bobby Labonte's Car	.15	.40
73 Jimmy Spencer's Car	.02	.10
74 Jeff Gordon's Car	.30	.75
75 Mike Skinner's Car	.02	.10
76 Robby Gordon's Car	.15	.40
77 Wally Dallenbach's Car	.02	.10
78 Kyle Petty's Car	.07	.20
79 Dale Jarrett's Car	.15	.40
80 Bill Elliott's Car	.15	.40
81 Checklist	.02	.10
82 Checklist	.02	.10
P1 Dale Jarrett Promo	.60	1.50
P2 Jeff Gordon Promo	1.00	2.50

1997 Viper Black Racer

This 82-card insert set is a parallel to the base Viper set. This features cards that are horizontal and have the Black Racer logo. The First Strike version of these cards were inserted into specially marked boxes of Viper First Strike. The cards were randomly inserted hobby packs, First Strike packs and retail packs at a ratio of 1:5

COMPLETE SET (82)	50.00	100.00
*BLACK RACERS: 3X TO 8X BASIC CARDS		

1997 Viper Black Racer First Strike

Cards from the First Strike parallel set were only available from specially marked First Strike boxes. Each card was printed with a "First Strike" logo on the cardfront and were randomly seeded at the rate of 1:5 packs.

COMP.FIRST STRIKE (82)	75.00	150.00
*FIRST STRIKE: .5X TO 1.2X BASIC INSERTS		

1997 Viper First Strike

Cards from the First Strike parallel set were only available from specially marked First Strike boxes. Each Viper case of 16-boxes contained 12-regular and 4-First Strike wax boxes. Each card was printed with a "First Strike" logo on the cardfront.

COMPLETE SET (82)	12.00	30.00
*FIRST STRIKE: .5X TO 1.2X BASE CARDS		

1997 Viper Anaconda Jumbos

This 13-card insert set features oversized cards featuring the top stars of the Winston Cup circuit. The cards were randomly inserted as chiptoppers at a ratio of one per two hobby boxes.

COMPLETE SET (13)	50.00	100.00
A1 Terry Labonte	2.50	6.00
A2 Jeff Gordon	8.00	20.00
A3 Dale Jarrett	5.00	12.00
A4 Bobby Labonte	5.00	12.00
A5 Dale Earnhardt	12.50	30.00
A6 Rusty Wallace	6.00	15.00
A7 Darrell Waltrip	1.50	4.00
A8 Joe Nemechek	.75	2.00
A9 Jeremy Mayfield	1.50	4.00
A10 Bill Elliott	3.00	8.00
A11 Jeff Burton	2.50	6.00
A12 Mark Martin	6.00	15.00
A13 Kyle Petty	1.50	4.00

1997 Viper Cobra

This 10-card insert set is highlighted by micro-etched cards that are die cut. The cards were randomly inserted in hobby packs at a ratio of 1:24.

COMPLETE SET (10)	40.00	80.00
COMP. FIRST STRIKE SET (10)	50.00	100.00
*FIRST STRIKE: .5X TO 1.2X BASIC INSERTS		
C1 Dale Earnhardt	15.00	40.00
C2 Jeff Gordon	8.00	20.00
C3 Bobby Labonte	5.00	12.00
C4 Terry Labonte	2.50	6.00
C5 Rusty Wallace	6.00	15.00
C6 Bill Elliott	3.00	8.00
C7 Sterling Marlin	2.50	6.00
C8 Mark Martin	6.00	15.00
C9 Dale Jarrett	5.00	12.00
C10 Kyle Petty	1.50	4.00

1997 Viper Diamondback

The 10-card insert set features a patch of simulated rattlesnake skin next to the picture of the driver on the fronts of the cards. The First Strike version of these cards were inserted into specially marked boxes of Viper First Strike. The cards were randomly inserted in hobby and First Strike packs at a ratio of 1:48 and inserted in retail packs at a ratio of 1:30.

COMPLETE SET (10)	60.00	120.00
COMP. FIRST STRIKE SET (10)	75.00	150.00
*FIRST STRIKE: .5X TO 1.2X BASIC INSERTS		
DB1 Jeff Gordon	10.00	25.00
DB2 Dale Jarrett	6.00	15.00
DB3 Bobby Labonte	6.00	15.00
DB4 Rusty Wallace	8.00	20.00
DB5 Bill Elliott	4.00	10.00
DB6 Jeff Burton	3.00	8.00
DB7 Mark Martin	8.00	20.00
DB8 Dale Earnhardt	15.00	40.00
DB9 Mike Skinner	1.00	2.50
DB10 Robby Gordon	3.00	8.00

1997 Viper Diamondback Authentic

This 10-card insert set features authentic diamondback rattlesnake skin attached to each card. The First Strike version of these cards were inserted into specially marked boxes of Viper First Strike. There are four different versions of each card: Western, Eastern, Western First Strike and Eastern First Strike. The cards were randomly inserted in hobby and First Strike packs at a ratio of 1:96 and inserted in retail packs at a ratio of 1:90.

COMPLETE SET (10)	100.00	250.00
COMP. FIRST STRIKE SET (10)	200.00	400.00
*FIRST STRIKE: .5X TO 1.2X BASIC INSERTS		
COMP.EASTERN SET (10)	250.00	500.00
*EASTERN DIAM: .5X TO 1.2X BASIC INSERTS		
COMP.EASTERN FS (10)	300.00	600.00
*EAST.FIRST STRIKE: .8X TO 2X BASIC INS.		
DBA1 Jeff Gordon	15.00	40.00
DBA2 Dale Jarrett	8.00	20.00
DBA3 Bobby Labonte	8.00	20.00
DBA4 Rusty Wallace	10.00	25.00
DBA5 Bill Elliott	8.00	20.00
DBA6 Jeff Burton	6.00	15.00
DBA7 Mark Martin	10.00	25.00
DBA8 Dale Earnhardt	25.00	60.00
DBA9 Mike Skinner	5.00	12.00
DBA10 Robby Gordon	6.00	15.00

1997 Viper King Cobra

This 10-card insert set features oversized, die-cut cards portraiting the top stars of the Winston Cup circuit. The cards were randomly inserted as chiptoppers at a ratio of one per two First Strike boxes.

COMPLETE SET (10)	75.00	150.00
KC1 Dale Earnhardt	20.00	50.00
KC2 Jeff Gordon	10.00	25.00
KC3 Bobby Labonte	6.00	15.00
KC4 Terry Labonte	3.00	8.00
KC5 Rusty Wallace	8.00	20.00
KC6 Bill Elliott	4.00	10.00
KC7 Sterling Marlin	3.00	8.00
KC8 Mark Martin	8.00	20.00
KC9 Dale Jarrett	6.00	15.00
KC10 Kyle Petty	2.00	5.00

1997 Viper Sidewinder

This 16-card insert set features stars from Winston Cup series on die-cut cards. The First Strike version of these cards were inserted into specially marked boxes of Viper First Strike. The cards were randomly inserted in hobby, First Strike and retail packs at a ratio of 1:6.

COMPLETE SET (16)	15.00	40.00
COMP.FIRST STRIKE (10)	20.00	50.00
*FIRST STRIKE: .5X TO 1.2X BASIC INSERTS		
S1 Terry Labonte	1.50	4.00
S2 Jeff Gordon	5.00	12.00
S3 Johnny Benson	1.00	2.50
S4 Ward Burton	1.00	2.50
S5 Bobby Hamilton	.50	1.25
S6 Ricky Craven	.50	1.25
S7 Michael Waltrip	1.00	2.50
S8 Bobby Labonte	3.00	8.00
S9 Dale Jarrett	3.00	8.00
S10 Bill Elliott	2.00	5.00
S11 Rusty Wallace	4.00	10.00
S12 Jimmy Spencer	.50	1.25
S13 Sterling Marlin	1.50	4.00
S14 Kyle Petty	1.00	2.50
S15 Ken Schrader	.50	1.25
S16 Robby Gordon	1.50	4.00

1997 Viper Snake Eyes

This 12-card insert set features stars from Winston Cup series on horizontal cards. The First Strike version of these cards were inserted into specially marked boxes of Viper First Strike. The cards were randomly inserted in hobby, First Strike and retail packs at a ratio of 1:12.

COMPLETE SET (12) 25.00 60.00
COMP.FIRST STRIKE (12) 40.00 80.00
*FIRST STRIKE: .5X TO 1.2X BASIC INSERTS
SE1 Dale Earnhardt 10.00 25.00
SE2 Jeff Gordon 6.00 15.00
SE3 Dale Jarrett 4.00 10.00
SE4 Bobby Labonte 4.00 10.00
SE5 Jimmy Spencer .60 1.50
SE6 Bill Elliott 2.50 6.00
SE7 Terry Labonte 2.00 5.00
SE8 Rusty Wallace 5.00 12.00
SE9 Jeff Burton 2.00 5.00
SE10 Mark Martin 5.00 12.00
SE11 Brett Bodine .60 1.50
SE12 Sterling Marlin 2.00 5.00

1992 Wheels Kyle Petty

This 14-card set features Kyle Petty and the Mello Yello team. The cards were packaged in a rack display blister with the Title Card appearing on the front of the package. There were 30,000 silver foil stamped sets made. The original suggested retail was $12. Each of the card backs featured artwork from Sam Bass. There was a gold parallel version of the set that was produced in a quantity of 12,000. The gold version originally retailed for $15.

COMP.SILVER SET (14) 2.50 6.00
*GOLD CARDS: 1X TO 2X SILVERS
1 Title Card .20 .50
2 Kyle Petty .30 .75
3 Felix Sabates .20 .50
4 Robin Pemberton .20 .50
5 Kyle Petty's Car .20 .50
6 Kyle Petty .30 .75
7 Kyle Petty .30 .75
8 Kyle Petty .30 .75
9 Kyle Petty .30 .75
10 Kyle Petty in Pits .20 .50
11 Kyle Petty's Car .20 .50
12 Kyle Petty's Car .20 .50
13 Kyle Petty .30 .75
14 Kyle Petty's Car Art .20 .50

1992 Wheels Dale Earnhardt Tribute Hologram

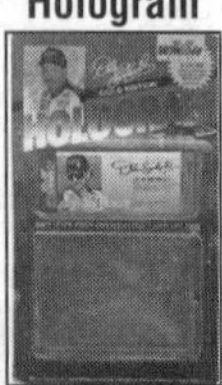

This single Dale Earnhardt holographic card comes in a snap-it deluxe card holder. It is packaged in a blister pack along with a AuthenTicket. There are four different versions; silver, gold, platinum and gold fascimile autographed. In each version the AuthenTicket is serial numbered.

1A Dale Earnhardt 6.00 15.00
Facsimile Signature
1G Dale Earnhardt Gold 2.00 5.00
1P Dale Earnhardt Platinum 2.50 6.00
1S Dale Earnhardt Silver 2.00 5.00

1992 Wheels Bill Elliott Tribute Hologram

This single Bill Elliott holographic card comes in a snap-it deluxe card holder. It is packaged in a blister pack along with a AuthenTicket. There were three different versions: silver, gold, and platinum.

1G Bill Elliott Gold 1.25 3.00
1P Bill Elliott Platinum 1.50 4.00
1S Bill Elliott Silver 1.25 3.00

1992 Wheels Harry Gant Tribute Hologram

This single Harry Gant holographic card comes in a snap-it deluxe card holder. It is packaged in a blister pack along with a AuthenTicket. There are four different versions; silver, gold, platinum and silver facsimile autographed.

1A Harry Gant 4.00 10.00
Facsimile Autograph
1G Harry Gant Gold 1.25 3.00
1P Harry Gant Platinum 1.50 4.00
1S Harry Gant Silver 1.25 3.00

1992 Wheels Rusty Wallace

This 14-card set features Rusty Wallace and the Miller Genuine Draft team. The cards were packaged in a rack display blister with the Title Card appearing on the front of the package. There were 35,000 silver foil stamped sets made. The original suggested retail was $12. Each of the card backs featured artwork from Tim Bruce. There was a gold parallel version of the set that was produced in a quantity of 15,000. The gold set originally retailed for $15.

COMPLETE SILVER SET (14) 3.00 8.00
*GOLD CARDS: 1X TO 2X SILVERS
1 Title Card .30 .75
2 Rusty Wallace .40 1.00
3 Roger Penske .30 .75
4 Buddy Parrott .30 .75
5 Rusty Wallace's Car .30 .75
6 Rusty Wallace .40 1.00
7 Bill Wilburn .30 .75
8 Rusty Wallace w/Crew .30 .75
9 Rusty Wallace .40 1.00
Mike Wallace
Kenny Wallace
10 Rusty Wallace .40 1.00
11 Rusty Wallace .40 1.00
12 Rusty Wallace .40 1.00
13 Rusty Wallace .40 1.00
14 Rusty Wallace Art .30 .75

1993 Wheels Mom-n-Pop's Dale Earnhardt

The 1993 Dale Earnhardt Mom-n-Pop's set was produced by Wheels and features photos of Dale's wins during the first half of 1993. The cards were packed one card and one cover card per cello pack in various ham, biscuit and sandwich products. A coupon was included as well offering complete sets and uncut sheets of previous year's sets.

COMPLETE SET (6) 6.00 12.00
COMMON CARD (1-6) 1.00 2.50

1993 Wheels Rookie Thunder Promos

This Promo set previews the 1993 Wheels Rookie Thunder release. The cards are numbered as a group and are often sold as complete sets.

COMPLETE SET (5) 5.00 12.00
P1 Richard Petty .75 2.00
P2 Jeff Gordon 2.50 6.00
P3 Kenny Wallace .40 1.00
P4 Bobby Labonte 1.25 3.00
P5 Davey Allison 1.25 3.00

1993 Wheels Rookie Thunder

This 100-card set features Rookie of the Year drivers from 1958-1993. The cards were printed on 24-pt stock and feature UV coating. The cards were packaged eight card per pack, 30 packs per box and 20 boxes per case.

COMPLETE SET (100) 6.00 15.00
1 Shorty Rollins .01 .05
2 Richard Petty .10 .30
3 David Pearson .02 .10
4 Woodie Wilson .01 .05
5 Tom Cox .01 .05
6 Billy Wade .01 .05
7 Doug Cooper .01 .05
8 Sam McQuagg .01 .05
9 James Hylton .01 .05
10 Donnie Allison .02 .10
11 Dick Brooks .01 .05
12 Bill Dennis .01 .05
13 Walter Ballard .01 .05
14 Larry Smith .01 .05
15 Lennie Pond .01 .05
16 Earl Ross .01 .05
17 Bruce Hill .01 .05
18 Skip Manning .01 .05
19 Ricky Rudd .10 .30
20 Ronnie Thomas .01 .05
21 Jody Ridley .02 .10
22 Ron Bouchard .01 .05
23 Geoff Bodine .02 .10
24 Sterling Marlin .15 .40
25 Rusty Wallace .25 .60
26 Ken Schrader .02 .10
27 Alan Kulwicki .10 .30
28 Davey Allison .20 .50
29 Ken Bouchard .02 .10
30 Dick Trickle .02 .10
31 Jimmy Hensley .02 .10
32 Jeff Gordon CRC .50 1.25
33 Bobby Labonte .20 .50
34 Kenny Wallace .02 .10
35 Rich Bickle .02 .10
36 Joe Nemechek .02 .10
37 Jeff Gordon .50 1.25
38 Ricky Craven .07 .20
39 Hermie Sadler RC .02 .10
40 Tim Fedewa .02 .10
41 Joe Bessey .02 .10
42 Roy Payne .01 .05
43 Nathan Buttke .01 .05
44 Ricky Rudd .10 .30
45 Geoff Bodine .02 .10
46 Rusty Wallace .25 .60
47 Ken Schrader .02 .10
48 Alan Kulwicki .07 .20
49 Davey Allison .20 .50
50 Jeff Gordon .50 1.25
51 Jeff Gordon .50 1.25
52 Bobby Labonte .20 .50
53 Kenny Wallace .02 .10
54 Kenny Wallace .02 .10
55 Dick Brooks .01 .05
56 Davey Allison .20 .50
57 Alan Kulwicki .10 .30
58 Alan Kulwicki .10 .30
59 Alan Kulwicki .10 .30
60 Rusty Wallace's Car .07 .20
61 Richard Petty .10 .30
62 Jeff Gordon w/Car .50 1.25
63 Kenny Wallace .02 .10
64 Bobby Labonte .20 .50
65 Rusty Wallace .25 .60
66 Rusty Wallace .25 .60
67 Rusty Wallace .25 .60
68 Rusty Wallace .25 .60
69 Hermie Sadler RC .02 .10
70 Jeff Gordon .50 1.25
71 Jeff Gordon .50 1.25
72 Bobby Labonte .20 .50
73 Bobby Labonte .20 .50
74 Kenny Wallace .02 .10
75 Kenny Wallace .02 .10
76 Ricky Craven .07 .20
77 Joe Nemechek .02 .10
78 Bobby Labonte .20 .50
79 Richard Petty .10 .30
80 Richard Petty .10 .30
81 Bobby Labonte .20 .50
82 Jeff Gordon .50 1.25
83 Kenny Wallace .02 .10
84 Davey Allison .20 .50
85 Davey Allison .20 .50
86 Alan Kulwicki .07 .20
87 Rusty Wallace .25 .60
88 Ricky Rudd .10 .30
89 Ricky Rudd .10 .30
90 Rusty Wallace .25 .60
91 Geoff Bodine .02 .10
92 Bobby Labonte .20 .50
93 Jeff Gordon's Car .25 .60
94 Bobby Labonte in Pits .07 .20
95 Richard Petty's Car .07 .20
David Pearson's Car
96 Richard Petty .10 .30
97 Jeff Gordon .50 1.25
98 Jeff Gordon .50 1.25
Ken Schrader
99 Richard Petty .10 .30
100 Davey Allison .20 .50

1993 Wheels Rookie Thunder Platinum

This 100-card set is a parallel to the base set. The cards feature a platinum foil stamping to differentiate them from the base cards. There was one Platinum card per pack.

COMPLETE SET (100) 15.00 40.00
*PLATINUM: 1X TO 2.5X BASIC CARDS

1993 Wheels Rookie Thunder SPs

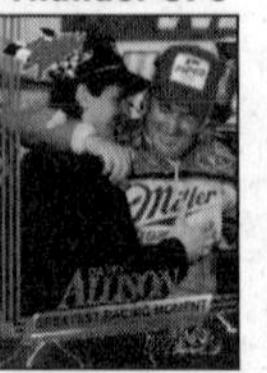

This seven-card insert set features some of the top names in NASCAR history. The cards are similar in design to the base set cards but with the only visable difference being on the bottom front of the cards is a lighting strike background instead of the blue marblized background of the regular cards. The SP cards could be found one per box.

COMPLETE SET (7) 10.00 25.00
SP1 Terry Labonte 1.25 3.00
SP2 Davey Allison 2.00 5.00
Bobby Allison
SP3 Davey Allison 2.00 5.00
SP4 Alan Kulwicki 1.25 3.00
SP5 Alan Kulwicki 1.25 3.00
SP6 Richard Petty 1.25 3.00
SP7 Richard Petty 1.25 3.00

1994 Wheels Harry Gant Promos

This Promo set was produced to advertise the 1994 Wheels Harry Gant set. The cards are individually numbered and often sold as a set of five.

COMPLETE SET (5) 1.50 4.00
P1 Harry Gant .40 1.00
First Daytona Race
P2 Harry Gant .40 1.00
Rookie Contender
P3 Harry Gant .40 1.00
Staying Focused
P4 Harry Gant .40 1.00
All Business
P5 Harry Gant .40 1.00
Harley Harry

1994 Wheels Harry Gant

This 80-card set pays tribute to racing great Harry Gant. The cards are a retrospective of Harry's career, plus the last 15 cards in the set are of other racing personalities holding a sign "I love Harry." The cards were packaged six cards per pack, 24 packs per box and 20 boxes per case. There were 1,500 cases produced. Randomly inserted in boxes were a 4" X 6" Signature card and a 4" X 6" Signature Hologram card. There were 3,300 of the Signature card produced and 1,000 of the Signature Hologram card produced. The odds of finding the Signature card was one in nine boxes. The odds of finding the Signature Hologram card was one in 30 boxes. Five promo cards were produced as well (numbers P1-P5).

COMPLETE SET (80) 5.00 12.00
1 Harry Gant .10 .25
Baby Harry
2 Harry Gant .10 .25
Third Grade
3 Harry Gant .10 .25
High School Years
4 Harry Gant .10 .25
High School Years
5 Harry Gant .10 .25
High School Years
6 Harry Gant .10 .25
High School Years
7 Harry Gant's Bike .07 .20
First Harley '54
8 Harry Gant's Car .07 .20
First Race Car '65
9 Harry Gant .10 .25
First Race in Daytona
10 Harry Gant .10 .25
'64 Chevelle
11 Harry Gant .10 .25
Money Man
12 Harry Gant .10 .25
Dick Trickle
Two Champions
13 Harry Gant .10 .25
Feature Winner
14 Harry Gant .10 .25
Weigh-In
15 Harry Gant .10 .25
First Trophy
16 Harry Gant .10 .25
'73 Track Champion
17 Harry Gant .10 .25
Fillin' Up
18 Harry Gant .10 .25
Harry's Steak Place
19 Harry Gant .10 .25
'79 Rookie On The Pole
20 Harry Gant .10 .25
'81 All Smiles
21 Harry Gant .10 .25
Ned Jarrett
'82 Cool Harry
22 Harry Gant .10 .25
Peggy Gant
23 Harry Gant .10 .25
'83 Ready To Roll
24 Harry Gant .10 .25
Hal Needham
Burt Reynolds
Three Amigos
25 Harry Gant .10 .25
Hal Needham
West Coast Bandits
26 Harry Gant .10 .25
Hal Needham
Clowning Around
27 Harry Gant .10 .25
Rolling In The Dough
28 Harry Gant .10 .25
Buckling In
29 Harry Gant w/Car .10 .25
Bandit On Tour
30 Harry Gant .10 .25
Donna Gant
Debbie Gant
Harry's Girls
31 Harry Gant .10 .25
Peggy Gant
32 Harry Gant .10 .25
Harry's Classics
33 Harry Gant .10 .25
Virginia National Bank
34 Harry Gant .10 .25
National 500
35 Harry Gant .10 .25
TranSouth 500
36 Harry Gant .10 .25
Peggy Gant
Like Cola 500
37 Harry Gant .10 .25
Southern 500
38 Harry Gant .10 .25
Delaware 500
39 Harry Gant .10 .25
Sovran Bank 500
40 Harry Gant .10 .25
Delaware 500
41 Harry Gant .10 .25
Peggy Gant
Holly Farms 400
42 Harry Gant .10 .25
TranSouth 500
43 Harry Gant .10 .25
Miller Genuine Draft
44 Harry Gant .10 .25
Winston 500
45 Harry Gant .10 .25
Heinz Southern 500
46 Harry Gant .10 .25
Miller Genuine Draft
47 Harry Gant .10 .25
Peak 500
48 Harry Gant .10 .25
Peggy Gant
Goody's 500
49 Harry Gant .10 .25
Bud 500
50 Harry Gant .10 .25
Champion 400
51 Harry Gant .10 .25
Life Begins at 51
52 Harry Gant .10 .25
Family Affair
53 Harry Gant .10 .25
New Face On Tour
54 Harry Gant .10 .25
All-American Boy
55 Harry Gant .10 .25
Bandit On The Loose
56 Harry Gant .10 .25
Handsome Harry
57 Harry Gant .10 .25
High Price of Success
58 Harry Gant .10 .25
'85 IROC Champion
59 Harry Gant .10 .25
'91 Myers' Brothers Award
60 Harry Gant .10 .25
'91 NMPA Driver of
61 Harry Gant .10 .25
Remembering
62 Harry Gant .10 .25
Winding Down
63 Harry Gant .10 .25
Leader of the Pack
64 Harry Gant .10 .25
Phoenix Bound
65 Harry Gant .10 .25
A Fond Farewell
66 Jeff Gordon .75 2.00
67 Ernie Irvan .15 .40
68 Sterling Marlin .25 .60
69 Derrike Cope .10 .25
70 Bobby Labonte .50 1.25
71 Larry Hedrick .07 .20
72 Benny Parsons .07 .20
73 Rusty Wallace .60 1.50
74 Mark Martin .60 1.50
75 Kyle Petty .15 .40
76 Ray Cooper .07 .20
77 Andy Petree .07 .20
78 Eddie Masencup .07 .20
79 Brian Buchauer .07 .20
80 Johnny Hayes .07 .20
1994 Jeff Gordon 5.00 10.00
Harry Gant set
HGS1 Harry Gant 4x6 AUTO 6.00 15.00
3300 produced
NNO Harry Gant 4x6 HOLO 6.00 15.00
1000 produced

1994 Wheels Harry Gant Gold

This 80-card set is a parallel to the base Wheels Harry Gant set. The cards feature gold foil stamping and were inserted one per pack.

COMPLETE GOLD SET (80) 15.00 30.00
*GOLDS: 1.5X TO 3X BASIC CARDS

1994 Wheels Harry Gant Down On The Farm

This five-card insert set gives a close look at Harry on his farm in Taylorsville, North Carolina. The cards are randomly inserted at a rate of one per box.

COMPLETE SET (5) 5.00 12.00
COMMON CARD (SP1-SP5) 1.00 3.00

1996 Wheels Dale Earnhardt Mom-n-Pop's

This three-card set features seven-time Winston Cup champion Dale Earnhardt. The cards were produced by Wheels and were inserted into Mom-n-Pop's products.

COMPLETE SET (3) 7.50 15.00
COMMON CARD (MPC1-MPC3) 2.50 5.00

1998 Wheels

The 1998 Wheels set was issued in one series totalling 100 cards. The set contains the topical subsets: NASCAR Winston Cup Drivers (1-30), NASCAR Winston Cup Cars (31-45), NASCAR Busch Series Drivers (46-59), NASCAR Busch Series Cars (60-63), NASCAR Craftsman Tru Series Drivers (64-68), NASCAR Winston Cup Cr Chiefs (69-75), NASCAR Winston Cup Owners (7 81), Daytona 500 Winners (82-90), and Te Members (91-100).

COMPLETE SET (100) 8.00 20.0
1 John Andretti .07
2 Johnny Benson .15
3 Geoff Bodine .07
4 Todd Bodine .07
5 Jeff Burton .25
6 Ward Burton .15
7 Ricky Craven .07
8 Wally Dallenbach .07
9 Dale Earnhardt 1.25
10 Bill Elliott .30
11 Jeff Gordon .75
12 David Green .07
13 Bobby Hamilton .07
14 Ernie Irvan .15
15 Kenny Irwin .15
16 Dale Jarrett .50
17 Bobby Labonte .50
18 Terry Labonte .25
19 Sterling Marlin .25
20 Mark Martin .60
21 Jeremy Mayfield .15
22 Ted Musgrave .07
23 Joe Nemechek .07
24 Steve Park .50
25 Ricky Rudd .25
26 Ken Schrader .07
27 Mike Skinner .07
28 Jimmy Spencer .07
29 Rusty Wallace .60
30 Michael Waltrip .15
31 John Andretti's Car .02
32 Johnny Benson's Car .02
33 Jeff Burton's Car .07
34 Dale Earnhardt's Car .50
35 Bill Elliott's Car .15
36 Jeff Gordon's Car .30
37 Kenny Irwin's Car .07
38 Dale Jarrett's Car .15
39 Bobby Labonte's Car .15
40 Terry Labonte's Car .15
41 Sterling Marlin's Car .07
42 Mark Martin's Car .25
43 Jeremy Mayfield's Car .07
44 Ricky Rudd's Car .07
45 Rusty Wallace's Car .25
46 Jeff Burton .25
47 Dale Earnhardt Jr. 1.25
48 Tim Fedewa .07
49 Dale Jarrett .50
50 Jason Jarrett RC .07
51 Jason Keller .07
52 Randy LaJoie .07
53 Mark Martin .60
54 Mike McLaughlin .07
55 Joe Nemechek .07
56 Elliott Sadler .15
57 Hermie Sadler .07
58 Tony Stewart RC 3.00
59 Michael Waltrip .15
60 Dale Earnhardt Jr.'s Car .50
61 Randy LaJoie's Car .02
62 Elliott Sadler's Car .02
63 Tony Stewart's Car .75
64 Rich Bickle .07
65 Mike Bliss .07
66 Ron Hornaday .07
67 Joe Ruttman .07
68 Jack Sprague .07
69 Ray Evernham .07
70 Jimmy Fenning .02
71 Andy Graves .02
72 Jimmy Makar .02
73 Larry McReynolds .02
74 Todd Parrott .02
75 Robin Pemberton .02
76 Richard Childress .15
77 Bill Elliott .30
78 Joe Gibbs .15
79 John Hendrick .02
80 Jack Roush .07
81 Ricky Rudd .25
82 Geoff Bodine .07
83 Dale Earnhardt 1.25
84 Bill Elliott .30
85 Jeff Gordon .75
86 Ernie Irvan .15
87 Dale Jarrett .50
88 Fred Lorenzen .07
89 Sterling Marlin .25
90 Richard Petty .25
91 Craig Lund .02
92 Chocolate Myers .02
93 Jack Lewis .02
94 Steve Muse .02
95 Jerry Hailey .02
96 Mike Moore .02
97 David Rogers .02
98 Larry McReynolds .02
99 Dale Earnhardt's Car .50
100 Checklist .02
P1 Mark Martin Promo 1.25
0 Mark Martin Las Vegas 15.00

1998 Wheels Golden

This 100-card set is a parallel of the regular base Each card is serial numbered to 50. These ca were randomly inserted into hobby packs at a rati 1 per 68.

COMPLETE SET (100) 600.00 1000.
*GOLDEN: 15X TO 40X BASE CARDS
*GOLDEN RCs: 8X TO 20X

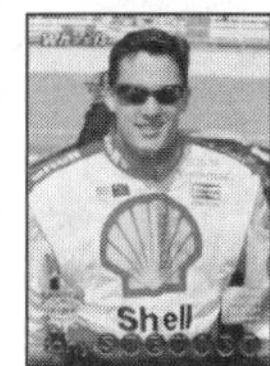

1998 Wheels 50th Anniversary

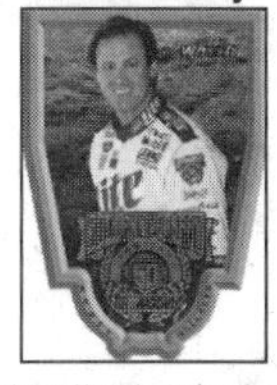

ndomly inserted in packs at a rate of one in 2, this -card insert set celebrates NASCAR's 50th niversary. This "set within a set" shows off the st talented drivers and their cars in NASCAR nston Cup racing. Each card is intricately die-cut d includes a customized micro-etched foil atment.

MPLETE SET (27)	12.00	30.00
Johnny Benson	.50	1.25
Jeff Burton	.75	2.00
Dale Earnhardt	4.00	10.00
Bill Elliott	1.00	2.50
Jeff Gordon	2.50	6.00
Kenny Irwin	.50	1.25
Dale Jarrett	1.50	4.00
Bobby Labonte	1.50	4.00
Terry Labonte	.75	2.00
0 Sterling Marlin	.75	2.00
1 Mark Martin	2.00	5.00
2 Ricky Rudd	.75	2.00
3 Jimmy Spencer	.25	.60
4 Rusty Wallace	2.00	5.00
5 Michael Waltrip	.50	1.25
6 Johnny Benson's Car	.10	.30
7 Jeff Burton's Car	.25	.60
8 Dale Earnhardt's Car	1.50	4.00
9 Bill Elliott's Car	.50	1.25
0 Jeff Gordon's Car	1.00	2.50
1 Kenny Irwin's Car	.25	.60
2 Dale Jarrett's Car	.50	1.25
3 Bobby Labonte's Car	.50	1.25
4 Terry Labonte's Car	.50	1.25
5 Sterling Marlin's Car	.25	.60
6 Mark Martin's Car	.75	2.00
7 Rusty Wallace's Car	.75	2.00

1998 Wheels Autographs

ndomly inserted in packs at a rate of one in 240, s 14-card insert set features autographs from top SCAR drivers and aspiring rookies. No more than) individually numbered and autographed cards re issued per driver.

MPLETE SET (14)	400.00	750.00
Dale Earnhardt	175.00	350.00
Jeff Gordon/200	125.00	250.00
Dale Jarrett/200	25.00	60.00
Terry Labonte/150	20.00	50.00
Bobby Labonte/200	12.50	30.00
Jimmy Spencer	10.00	25.00
Jeff Burton/200	10.00	25.00
Geoff Bodine	6.00	15.00
Michael Waltrip	10.00	25.00
Ricky Craven/200	10.00	25.00
Ricky Rudd	10.00	25.00
Mike Skinner	6.00	15.00
Kenny Irwin/200	20.00	40.00
Johnny Benson/200	10.00	25.00

1998 Wheels Custom Shop

ndomly inserted in packs at the rate of one in 192. emption cards for this set allowed the collector to stomize his own card by selecting one of three nts and three backs for each card. The collector n received his custom-made card by return mail n his chosen front and back selection.

MPLETE SET (3)	40.00	80.00
RIZE CARDS: .4X TO 1X BASIC INSERTS		
DJ Dale Jarrett	10.00	25.00
JG Jeff Gordon	15.00	40.00
RW Rusty Wallace	12.50	30.00

1998 Wheels Double Take

ndomly inserted in packs at a rate of one in 72, s 9-card insert set is a first-time offer that features hnology that allows you to change the exposure of card front. Watch your favorite NASCAR Winston p driver magically transform into his NASCAR e.

MPLETE SET (9)	75.00	150.00
Jeff Burton	2.50	6.00

E2 Dale Earnhardt	12.50	30.00
E3 Bill Elliott	3.00	8.00
E4 Jeff Gordon	8.00	20.00
E5 Dale Jarrett	5.00	12.00
E6 Bobby Labonte	5.00	12.00
E7 Terry Labonte	2.50	6.00
E8 Mark Martin	6.00	15.00
E9 Rusty Wallace	6.00	15.00

1998 Wheels Green Flags

Randomly inserted in packs at a rate of one in 8, this 18-card insert set showcases NASCAR's fiercest cars in an etched, all-foil, emerald green foil set.

COMPLETE SET (18)	25.00	60.00
GF1 John Andretti's Car	.60	1.50
GF2 Johnny Benson's Car	.60	1.50
GF3 Jeff Burton's Car	1.25	3.00
GF4 Dale Earnhardt's Car	8.00	20.00
GF5 Bill Elliott's Car	2.50	6.00
GF6 Jeff Gordon's Car	5.00	12.00
GF7 Bobby Hamilton's Car	.60	1.50
GF8 Kenny Irwin's Car	1.25	3.00
GF9 Dale Jarrett's Car	2.50	6.00
GF10 Bobby Labonte's Car	2.50	6.00
GF11 Terry Labonte's Car	2.50	6.00
GF12 Sterling Marlin's Car	1.25	3.00
GF13 Mark Martin's Car	4.00	10.00
GF14 Ricky Rudd's Car	1.25	3.00
GF15 Mike Skinner's Car	.60	1.50
GF16 Jimmy Spencer's Car	.60	1.50
GF17 Rusty Wallace's Car	4.00	10.00
GF18 Michael Waltrip's Car	.60	1.50

1998 Wheels Jackpot

Randomly inserted in packs at a rate of one in 12, this 9-card insert set recognizes NASCAR's Winston Cup's biggest winners over the past five years on embossed all-foil technology.

COMPLETE SET (9)	15.00	40.00
J1 Dale Earnhardt	8.00	20.00
J2 Bill Elliott	2.00	5.00
J3 Jeff Gordon	5.00	12.00
J4 Dale Jarrett	3.00	8.00
J5 Bobby Labonte	3.00	8.00
J6 Terry Labonte	1.50	4.00
J7 Jeremy Mayfield	1.00	2.50
J8 Ricky Rudd	1.50	4.00
J9 Rusty Wallace	4.00	10.00

1999 Wheels

This 100 card set featuring all foil stamping consists of the following subsets: 37-54 Busch drivers, 55-72 Winston Cup cars, 73-81 Teams, 82-87 Crew Chiefs, 88-93 Truck Series drivers, 94-100 Top Prospects.

COMPLETE SET (100)	10.00	25.00
1 John Andretti	.07	.20
2 Johnny Benson	.15	.40
3 Geoffrey Bodine	.07	.20
4 Jeff Burton	.25	.60
5 Ward Burton	.15	.40
6 Derrike Cope	.07	.20
7 Kenny Wallace	.07	.20
8 Wally Dallenbach	.07	.20
9 Dale Earnhardt	1.25	3.00
10 Bill Elliott	.30	.75
11 David Green	.07	.20
12 Jeff Gordon	.75	2.00
13 Bobby Hamilton	.07	.20
14 Ernie Irvan	.15	.40
15 Kenny Irwin	.15	.40
16 Dale Jarrett	.50	1.25
17 Bobby Labonte	.50	1.25
18 Terry Labonte	.25	.60
19 Kevin Lepage	.07	.20
20 Chad Little	.15	.40
21 Sterling Marlin	.25	.60
22 Mark Martin	.60	1.50
23 Jeremy Mayfield	.15	.40
24 Ted Musgrave	.07	.20
25 Jerry Nadeau	.15	.40
26 Joe Nemechek	.07	.20
27 Steve Park	.40	1.00
28 Ricky Rudd	.25	.60
29 Elliott Sadler	.15	.40
30 Ken Schrader	.07	.20
31 Mike Skinner	.07	.20
32 Jimmy Spencer	.07	.20
33 Tony Stewart CRC	1.00	2.50
34 Rusty Wallace	.60	1.50
35 Darrell Waltrip	.15	.40
36 Michael Waltrip	.15	.40
37 Casey Atwood BGN RC	.40	1.00
38 Todd Bodine BGN	.07	.20
39 Dale Earnhardt Jr. BGN	1.00	2.50
40 Tim Fedewa BGN	.07	.20
41 Jeff Fuller BGN	.07	.20
42 Jeff Gordon BGN	.75	2.00
43 Jeff Green BGN	.07	.20
44 Dave Blaney BGN RC	.07	.20
45 Jason Keller BGN	.07	.20
46 Matt Kenseth BGN RC	2.50	6.00
47 Randy LaJoie BGN	.07	.20
48 Mark Martin BGN	.60	1.50
49 Mike McLaughlin BGN	.07	.20
50 Elton Sawyer BGN	.07	.20
51 Jimmy Spencer BGN	.07	.20
52 Kevin Grubb	.07	.20
53 Mark Green BGN RC	.07	.20
54 Glenn Allen BGN	.07	.20
55 Rusty Wallace's Car	.25	.60
56 Dale Earnhardt's Car	.50	1.25
57 Terry Labonte's Car	.15	.40
58 Mark Martin's Car	.25	.60
59 Bobby Labonte's Car	.15	.40
60 Jeff Gordon's Car	.30	.75
61 Dale Jarrett's Car	.15	.40
62 Bill Elliott's Car	.15	.40
63 Jeff Burton's Car	.07	.20
64 Derrike Cope's Car	.02	.10
65 Dale Earnhardt Jr.'s Car	.40	1.00
66 Mike Skinner's Car	.02	.10
67 Joe Nemechek's Car	.02	.10
68 Tony Stewart's Car	.30	.75
69 Wally Dallenbach's Car	.02	.10
70 Ricky Rudd's Car	.07	.20
71 Chad Little's Car	.07	.20
72 Jeff Gordon's Car	.30	.75
73 Robin Pemberton TC	.02	.10
74 Rusty Wallace TC	.60	1.50
75 Roger Penske TC	.02	.10
76 Jimmy Makar TC	.02	.10
77 Bobby Labonte TC	.50	1.25
78 Joe Gibbs TC	.15	.40
79 Todd Parrott TC	.02	.10
80 Dale Jarrett TC	.50	1.25
81 Robert Yates TC	.02	.10
82 Larry McReynolds TC	.02	.10
83 Tony Furr TC	.02	.10
84 Frank Stoddard TC	.02	.10
85 Greg Zipadelli TC	.02	.10
86 Jeff Hammond TC	.02	.10
87 Sammy Johns TC	.02	.10
88 Kevin Harvick CTS RC	4.00	10.00
89 Jay Sauter CTS RC	.07	.20
90 Jack Sprague CTS	.07	.20
91 Greg Biffle CTS RC	3.00	8.00
92 Mike Bliss CTS	.07	.20
93 Mike Stefanik CTS	.07	.20
94 Dave Blaney TP	.07	.20
95 Tony Stewart	.75	2.00
96 Dale Earnhardt Jr. TP	1.00	2.50
97 Elliott Sadler TP	.15	.40
98 Matt Kenseth TP	2.00	5.00
99 Casey Atwood TP	1.25	3.00
100 Justin Labonte TP CL RC	.07	.20
P1 Bobby Labonte Promo	.75	2.00
P2 Jeff Gordon Promo	1.25	3.00

1999 Wheels Golden

Randomly inserted in packs at the rate of one in 77, this parallel set is limited to only 50 of each card, and is accented with gold foil stamping.

COMPLETE SET (100)	400.00	800.00
*GOLDEN VETERANS: 20X TO 50X		
*GOLDEN RCs: 10X TO 25X		

1999 Wheels Autographs

Randomly inserted in packs at the rate of one in 240 these cards feature authentic autographs of leading NASCAR figures. Each driver signed a different number of cards. We have noted below the print run of all cards that were hand serial numbered on the backs. Additionally, some cards were also issued without serial numbering in the 2003 VIP Tin factory sets.

1 Glenn Allen/300	7.50	20.00
2 John Andretti/100	7.50	20.00
3 Johnny Benson/200	7.50	20.00
4 Jeff Burton/150	8.00	20.00
5 Derrike Cope/295	7.50	20.00
6 Dale Earnhardt Jr./75	125.00	250.00
7 Jeff Fuller/350	7.50	20.00
8 Jeff Gordon/75	125.00	250.00
9 Dale Jarrett/100	25.00	60.00
10 Bobby Labonte/250	12.50	30.00
11 Terry Labonte/250	20.00	50.00
12 Kevin Lepage/250	7.50	20.00
13 Chad Little/350	7.50	20.00
14 Mike McLaughlin/200	7.50	20.00
15 Mark Martin/100	40.00	80.00
16 Todd Parrott/500	7.50	20.00
17 Robin Pemberton	7.50	20.00
18 Robert Pressley/196	7.50	20.00
19 Ricky Rudd/100	12.50	30.00
20 Ken Schrader/199	10.00	25.00
21 Jimmy Spencer	7.50	20.00
22 Tony Stewart/350	40.00	100.00
23 Frank Stoddard	7.50	20.00
24 Michael Waltrip/200	10.00	25.00

1999 Wheels Circuit Breaker

Randomly inserted in packs at the rate of one in 24, this nine-card set of the top record-setters of the sport is printed on plastic and foil stamped.

COMPLETE SET (9)	25.00	60.00
CB1 Terry Labonte	2.00	5.00
CB2 Bobby Labonte	3.00	8.00
CB3 Dale Earnhardt	8.00	20.00
CB4 Mark Martin	4.00	10.00
CB5 Jeff Gordon	5.00	12.00
CB6 Ricky Rudd	1.50	4.00
CB7 Rusty Wallace	3.00	8.00
CB8 Dale Jarrett	3.00	8.00
CB9 Mark Martin	4.00	10.00

1999 Wheels Custom Shop

Randomly inserted in packs at the rate of one in 192, this redemption set was redesigned to let the collector choose the material used (paper, foil, or plastic) in addition to design.

COMPLETE SET (5)	75.00	175.00
*PRIZE CARDS: .4X TO 1X BASIC INSERTS		
CS1 Bobby Labonte	10.00	25.00
CS2 Jeff Gordon	15.00	40.00
CS3 Dale Earnhardt Jr.	15.00	40.00
CS4 Mark Martin	12.50	30.00
CS5 Rusty Wallace	10.00	25.00

1999 Wheels Dialed In

Randomly inserted in packs at the rate of one in twelve, this all-foil, die-cut, micro-etched nine card set featured drivers who are among the best in the Winston Cup circuit.

COMPLETE SET (9)	25.00	60.00
DI1 Jeff Gordon	5.00	12.00
DI2 Rusty Wallace	3.00	8.00
DI3 Dale Earnhardt's Car	8.00	20.00
DI4 Dale Earnhardt Jr.	6.00	15.00
DI5 Terry Labonte	2.00	5.00
DI6 Mark Martin	4.00	10.00
DI7 Bobby Labonte	3.00	8.00
DI8 Dale Jarrett	3.00	8.00
DI9 Jeff Burton	1.25	3.00

1999 Wheels Flag Chasers Daytona Seven

Randomly inserted in packs at the rate of one in 565, this five-card set features progessive ratios for the different color flag swatches.

COMPLETE SET (5)	250.00	600.00
BLACK/WHITE/YELLOW PRICED BELOW		
BLACK/WHITE/YELLOW ODDS 1:3424		
BLACK/WHITE/YELLOW SERIAL #'D TO 69		
GREEN/RED PRICED BELOW		
GREEN/RED STATED ODDS 1:3634		
RED/GREEN CARDS SER.#'D TO 65		
*BLUE-YELLOW: 1X TO 2X BASIC INSERTS		
BLUE-YELLOW STATED ODDS 1:5250		
BLUE-YELLOW CARDS SER.#'D TO 45		
*CHECKERED: .8X TO 2X BASIC INSERTS		
CHECKERED STATED ODDS 1:6562		
CHECKERED CARDS SERIAL #'D TO 36		
DS1 Jeff Gordon	40.00	100.00
DS2 Dale Earnhardt	40.00	100.00
DS3 Rusty Wallace	30.00	80.00
DS4 Mark Martin	30.00	80.00
DS5 Terry Labonte	30.00	80.00

1999 Wheels High Groove

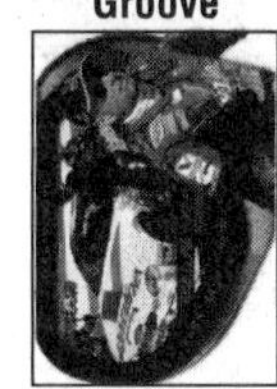

Randomly inserted in packs at the rate of one in eight, this nine card set pairs cards of famed tracks with the drivers who excel on those tracks.

COMPLETE SET (9)	12.50	30.00
HG1 Bobby Labonte	2.50	6.00
HG2 Ernie Irvan	.75	2.00
HG3 Jeff Gordon	4.00	10.00
HG4 Dale Earnhardt's Car	2.50	6.00
HG5 Mark Martin	3.00	8.00
HG6 Rusty Wallace	3.00	8.00
HG7 Jeff Gordon	4.00	10.00
HG8 Dale Jarrett	2.50	6.00
HG9 Mark Martin	3.00	8.00

1999 Wheels Runnin and Gunnin

Inserted in packs at the rate of one per pack for the basic paper version and one in twelve packs for the foil version; this 36-card set features leading personalities from NASCAR.

COMPLETE SET (36)	12.50	30.00
COMP.FOIL SET (36)	100.00	200.00
*FOIL CARDS: 2.5X TO 6X BASIC INSERTS		
RG1 Mark Martin	2.00	5.00
RG2 Rusty Wallace	2.00	5.00
RG3 Dale Earnhardt's Car	1.50	4.00
RG4 Terry Labonte	.75	2.00
RG5 Dale Jarrett	1.50	4.00
RG6 Bill Elliott	1.00	2.50
RG7 Mike Skinner	.25	.60
RG8 Bobby Labonte	1.50	4.00
RG9 Jeff Gordon	2.50	6.00
RG10 Michael Waltrip	.50	1.25
RG11 Jeff Burton	.75	2.00
RG12 Ernie Irvan	.50	1.25
RG13 Dale Earnhardt Jr.	3.00	8.00
RG14 Ward Burton	.50	1.25
RG15 Wally Dallenbach	.25	.60
RG16 Ricky Rudd	.75	2.00
RG17 Jeremy Mayfield	.50	1.25
RG18 Tony Stewart	2.50	6.00
RG19 Johnny Benson	.50	1.25
RG20 Geoffrey Bodine	.25	.60
RG21 Derrike Cope	.25	.60
RG22 Bobby Hamilton	.25	.60
RG23 Matt Kenseth	1.25	3.00
RG24 Chad Little	.50	1.25
RG24B Kevin Lepage	.25	.60
RG25 Sterling Marlin	.75	2.00
RG26 David Green	.25	.60
RG27 Ted Musgrave	.25	.60
RG28 Joe Nemechek	.25	.60
RG29 Jeff Gordon	2.50	6.00
RG30 Ken Schrader	.25	.60
RG31 Darrell Waltrip	.50	1.25
RG32 John Andretti	.25	.60
RG33 Jimmy Spencer	.25	.60
RG34 Elliott Sadler	.50	1.25
RG35 Kenny Irwin	.50	1.25

2003 Wheels American Thunder

This 50-card set was released in May, 2003. These cards were found in 5-card hobby packs with 24 pack boxes with pack SRP of $5.99 and 4-card retail packs with 28 pack boxes with an SRP of $2.99.

COMPLETE SET (50)	12.50	25.00
WAX BOX HOBBY (24)	60.00	100.00
WAX BOX RETAIL (28)	50.00	100.00
1 John Andretti	.15	.40
2 Jeff Burton	.30	.75
3 Ward Burton	.30	.75
4 Kurt Busch	.50	1.25
5 Dale Earnhardt Jr.	1.50	4.00
6 Jeff Gordon	1.25	3.00
7 Jeff Green	.15	.40
8 Kevin Harvick	.75	2.00
9 Dale Jarrett	.75	2.00
10 Jimmie Johnson	1.00	2.50
11 Matt Kenseth	1.00	2.50
12 Bobby Labonte	.75	2.00
13 Terry Labonte	.50	1.25
14 Sterling Marlin	.50	1.25
15 Mark Martin	1.00	2.50
16 Jamie McMurray CRC	.75	2.00
17 Ryan Newman	1.00	2.50
18 Steve Park	.30	.75
19 Tony Stewart	1.00	2.50
20 Rusty Wallace	.75	2.00
21 Michael Waltrip	.30	.75
22 Jeff Gordon SS	1.25	3.00
23 Dale Jarrett SS	.75	2.00
24 Bobby Labonte SS	.75	2.00
25 Terry Labonte SS	.50	1.25
26 Tony Stewart SS	1.00	2.50
27 Rusty Wallace SS	.75	2.00
28 Bobby Labonte DT	.75	2.00
29 Steve Park DT	.30	.75
30 Ryan Newman DT	1.00	2.50
31 Dale Jarrett DT	.75	2.00
32 Tony Stewart DT	1.00	2.50
33 Michael Waltrip DT	.30	.75
34 Jimmie Johnson DT	1.00	2.50
35 Jeff Burton DT	.30	.75
36 Mark Martin DT	1.00	2.50
37 Dale Earnhardt Jr. CC	1.50	4.00
38 Mark Martin CC	1.00	2.50
39 Michael Waltrip CC	.30	.75
40 Matt Kenseth CC	1.00	2.50
41 Bobby Labonte CC	.75	2.00
42 Ryan Newman CC	1.00	2.50
43 Jeff Gordon CC	1.25	3.00
44 Steve Park CC	.30	.75
45 Ward Burton CC	.30	.75
46 Dale Jr.'s Transporter	.60	1.50
47 Michael Waltrip's Transporter	.10	.30
48 Jimmie Johnson's Transporter	.50	1.25
49 Mark Martin's Transporter	.50	1.25
50 Dale Jarrett's Transporter Checklist Card	.30	.75
P1 Jeff Gordon Promo	3.00	6.00

2003 Wheels American Thunder Born On

This 50-card set is a parallel of the basic Wheels American Thunder set. These cards were serial numbered to 100 and carried a "BO" prefix for the card numbers.

*BORN ON: 5X TO 12X BASIC CARDS

2003 Wheels American Thunder Holofoil

This 50-card set is a parallel to the basic Wheels American Thunder set. These cards were inserted at a rate of one per pack. These cards feature a "P" prefix on the card numbers.

COMPLETE SET (50)	15.00	40.00
*HOLOFOIL: .8X TO 2X BASIC CARDS		

2003 Wheels American Thunder Previews

This 36-card set was issued though a joint venture on eBay.com as a special preview of the base set. The cards were identical with the exception of the serial number. Each card was serial numbered to 5.

STATED PRINT RUN 5 SERIAL #'d SETS

2003 Wheels American Thunder Samples

This 50-card set was a parallel of the base set with the exception of the word "SAMPLE" printed on the back of each card. These cards were found in Beckett Racing Collector July 2003, Issue #107. There was one card per magazine. These cards also featured a "P" prefix on the card number.

*SAMPLES: 2X TO 5X BASE CARD HI

2003 Wheels American Thunder American Eagle

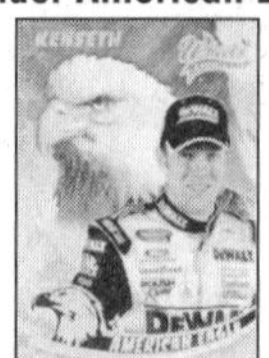

This 9-card set was randomly inserted in packs at a rate of one in 18. The feature foil etched cards of NASCAR's leading drivers. The cards carried an "AE" prefix for their card numbers.

COMPLETE SET (9)	20.00	40.00
*GOLDEN: 2.5X TO 6X AMERICAN EAGLE		
STATED PRINT RUN 100 SERIAL #'d SETS		
AE1 Rusty Wallace	2.50	6.00
AE2 Tony Stewart	3.00	8.00
AE3 Ryan Newman	3.00	8.00
AE4 Matt Kenseth	3.00	8.00
AE5 Jeff Gordon	4.00	10.00
AE6 Jimmie Johnson	3.00	8.00
AE7 Bobby Labonte	2.50	6.00
AE8 Kurt Busch	1.50	4.00
AE9 Ward Burton	1.00	2.50

2003 Wheels American Thunder American Muscle

This 11-card set was randomly inserted in packs at a rate of one in 12. The feature foil etched cards of NASCAR's leading drivers. The cards carried an "AM" prefix for their card numbers.

COMPLETE SET (11) 15.00 40.00
STATED ODDS 1:12
AM1 Dale Earnhardt Jr. 4.00 10.00
AM2 Jeff Gordon 3.00 8.00
AM3 Kevin Harvick 2.00 5.00
AM4 Jimmie Johnson 2.50 6.00
AM5 Bobby Labonte 2.00 5.00
AM6 Mark Martin 2.50 6.00
AM7 Ryan Newman 2.50 6.00
AM8 Steve Park .75 2.00
AM9 Tony Stewart 2.50 6.00
AM10 Rusty Wallace 2.00 5.00
AM11 Michael Waltrip .75 2.00

2003 Wheels American Thunder Cool Threads

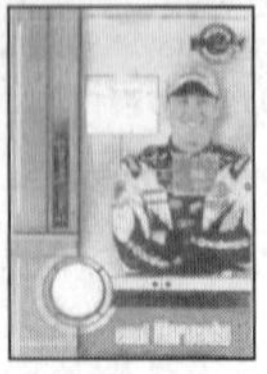

This 8-card set was randomly inserted in packs. They feature swatches of shirtsworn by drivers during races. The cards carried a "CT" prefix for their card numbers and were serial numbered to 285.

STATED PRINT RUN 285 SERIAL #'d SETS
CT1 Jeff Burton 10.00 25.00
CT2 Kevin Harvick 12.50 30.00
CT3 Ryan Newman 12.50 30.00
CT4 Kenny Wallace 10.00 25.00
CT5 Mark Martin 12.50 30.00
CT6 Jeff Gordon 30.00 60.00
CT7 Dale Jarrett 12.50 30.00
CT8 Jamie McMurray 12.50 30.00

2003 Wheels American Thunder Dale Earnhardt Retrospective

This 9-card set featured cards with images of reprinted Dale Earnhardt Wheels cards on them. These cards were randoimly inserted in packs at a rate of one in 72.

COMMON EARNHARDT (AT1-AT9) 10.00 25.00
STATED ODDS 1:72
*FOIL: .8X TO 2X BASIC EARNHARDT
FOIL STATED PRINT RUN 250 SERIAL #'d SETS

2003 Wheels American Thunder Head to Toe

This 10-card set featured swatches of race-used hats and shoes. Each card was serial numbered to 40 and carried an "HT" prefix for its card number.

STATED PRINT RUN 40 SERIAL #'d SETS
HT1 Jeff Burton 25.00 60.00
HT2 Ricky Craven 25.00 60.00
HT3 Matt Kenseth 50.00 100.00
HT4 Sterling Marlin 40.00 80.00
HT5 Mark Martin 40.00 80.00
HT6 Mike Skinner 20.00 50.00
HT7 Tony Stewart 50.00 100.00
HT8 Rusty Wallace 50.00 100.00
HT9 Michael Waltrip 20.00 50.00
HT10 Joe Nemechek 20.00 50.00

2003 Wheels American Thunder Heads Up Goodyear

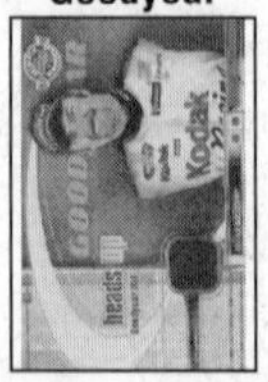

This 17-card set featured a swatch of a Goodyear hat worn during speedweeks at Daytona. Each card is serial numbered to 90 and features an "HUG" prefix on the card number.

STATED PRINT RUN 90 SERIAL #'d SETS
HUG1 Jeff Burton 10.00 25.00
HUG2 Robby Gordon 8.00 20.00
HUG3 Kevin Harvick 15.00 40.00
HUG4 Dale Jarrett 15.00 40.00
HUG5 Matt Kenseth 15.00 40.00
HUG6 Ryan Newman 20.00 50.00
HUG7 Steve Park 10.00 25.00
HUG8 Rusty Wallace 15.00 40.00
HUG9 Jeremy Mayfield 8.00 20.00
HUG10 Ward Burton 10.00 25.00
HUG11 Mark Martin 15.00 40.00
HUG12 Mike Skinner 8.00 20.00
HUG13 Dave Blaney 8.00 20.00
HUG14 Kurt Busch 10.00 25.00
HUG15 Ricky Rudd 10.00 25.00
HUG16 Ricky Craven 8.00 20.00
HUG17 Terry Labonte 12.50 30.00

2003 Wheels American Thunder Heads Up Manufacturer

This 34-card set featured a swatch of a Manufacturers hat worn during speedweeks at Daytona. Each card is serial numbered to 90 and features an "HUM" prefix on the card number.

STATED PRINT RUN 90 SERIAL #'d SETS
HUM1 John Andretti 8.00 20.00
HUM2 Brett Bodine 8.00 20.00
HUM3 Jeff Burton 10.00 25.00
HUM4 Jeff Gordon 25.00 60.00
HUM5 Robby Gordon 8.00 20.00
HUM6 Jeff Green 8.00 20.00
HUM7 Kevin Harvick 15.00 40.00
HUM8 Dale Jarrett 15.00 40.00
HUM9 Jimmie Johnson 20.00 50.00
HUM10 Matt Kenseth 15.00 40.00
HUM11 Bobby Labonte 15.00 40.00
HUM12 Jamie McMurray 10.00 25.00
HUM13 Casey Mears 10.00 25.00
HUM14 Jerry Nadeau 10.00 25.00
HUM15 Ryan Newman 20.00 50.00
HUM16 Steve Park 10.00 25.00
HUM17 Kyle Petty 10.00 25.00
HUM18 Elliott Sadler 10.00 25.00
HUM19 Rusty Wallace 15.00 40.00
HUM20 Jeremy Mayfield 8.00 20.00
HUM21 Tony Stewart 25.00 60.00
HUM22 Ward Burton 10.00 25.00
HUM23 Michael Waltrip 10.00 25.00
HUM24 Greg Biffle 10.00 25.00
HUM25 Mark Martin 20.00 50.00
HUM26 Sterling Marlin 12.50 30.00
HUM27 Kenny Wallace 8.00 20.00
HUM28 Mike Skinner 8.00 20.00
HUM29 Dave Blaney 8.00 20.00
HUM30 Kurt Busch 10.00 25.00
HUM31 Ricky Rudd 10.00 25.00
HUM32 Ricky Craven 8.00 20.00
HUM33 Terry Labonte 12.50 30.00
HUM34 Joe Nemechek 8.00 20.00

2003 Wheels American Thunder Heads Up Team

This 31-card set featured a swatch of a the driver's team hat worn during speedweeks at Daytona. Each card is serial numbered to either 60 or 90 and is noted below in the checklist and features an "HUT" prefix on the card number.

RANDOM INSERTS IN PACKS
HUT1 John Andretti/90 8.00 20.00
HUT2 Jeff Burton/90 10.00 25.00
HUT3 Jeff Gordon/60 30.00 80.00
HUT4 Robby Gordon/60 10.00 25.00
HUT5 Jeff Green/60 10.00 25.00
HUT6 Kevin Harvick/60 20.00 50.00
HUT7 Dale Jarrett/90 15.00 40.00
HUT8 Jimmie Johnson/90 20.00 50.00
HUT9 Matt Kenseth/90 15.00 40.00
HUT10 Bobby Labonte/60 20.00 50.00
HUT11 Jamie McMurray/60 15.00 40.00
HUT12 Casey Mears/60 12.50 30.00
HUT13 Ryan Newman/90 20.00 50.00
HUT14 Steve Park/90 10.00 25.00
HUT15 Kyle Petty/90 10.00 25.00
HUT16 Elliott Sadler/60 12.50 30.00
HUT17 Rusty Wallace/60 20.00 50.00
HUT18 Jeremy Mayfield/60 10.00 25.00
HUT19 Tony Stewart/60 30.00 80.00
HUT20 Ward Burton/90 10.00 25.00
HUT21 Michael Waltrip/60 12.50 30.00
HUT22 Greg Biffle/90 10.00 25.00
HUT23 Mark Martin/90 20.00 50.00
HUT24 Sterling Marlin/90 12.50 30.00
HUT25 Mike Skinner/60 10.00 25.00
HUT26 Dale Earnhardt Jr./60 60.00 120.00
HUT27 Dave Blaney/60 10.00 25.00
HUT28 Kurt Busch/60 12.50 30.00
HUT29 Ricky Rudd/90 10.00 25.00
HUT30 Terry Labonte/90 12.50 30.00
HUT31 Joe Nemechek/60 10.00 25.00

2003 Wheels American Thunder Heads Up Winston

This 34-card set featured a swatch of a Winston hat worn during speedweeks at Daytona. Each card is serial numbered to 90 and features an "HUW" prefix on the card number.

STATED PRINT RUN 90 SERIAL #'d SETS
HUW1 John Andretti 10.00 25.00
HUW2 Brett Bodine 10.00 25.00
HUW3 Jeff Burton 12.50 30.00
HUW4 Jeff Gordon 30.00 80.00
HUW5 Robby Gordon 10.00 25.00
HUW6 Jeff Green 10.00 25.00
HUW7 Kevin Harvick 20.00 50.00
HUW8 Dale Jarrett 20.00 50.00
HUW9 Jimmie Johnson 25.00 60.00
HUW10 Matt Kenseth 20.00 50.00
HUW11 Bobby Labonte 20.00 50.00
HUW12 Jamie McMurray 15.00 40.00
HUW13 Casey Mears 12.50 30.00
HUW14 Jerry Nadeau 12.50 30.00
HUW15 Ryan Newman 25.00 60.00
HUW16 Steve Park 12.50 30.00
HUW17 Kyle Petty 12.50 30.00
HUW18 Elliott Sadler 12.50 30.00
HUW19 Rusty Wallace 20.00 50.00
HUW20 Jeremy Mayfield 10.00 25.00
HUW21 Tony Stewart 30.00 80.00
HUW22 Ward Burton 12.50 30.00
HUW23 Michael Waltrip 12.50 30.00
HUW24 Greg Biffle 12.50 30.00
HUW25 Mark Martin 25.00 60.00
HUW26 Sterling Marlin 15.00 40.00
HUW27 Kenny Wallace 10.00 25.00
HUW28 Mike Skinner 10.00 25.00
HUW29 Dave Blaney 10.00 25.00
HUW30 Kurt Busch 12.50 30.00
HUW31 Ricky Rudd 12.50 30.00
HUW32 Ricky Craven 10.00 25.00
HUW33 Terry Labonte 15.00 40.00
HUW34 Joe Nemechek 10.00 25.00

2003 Wheels American Thunder Post Mark

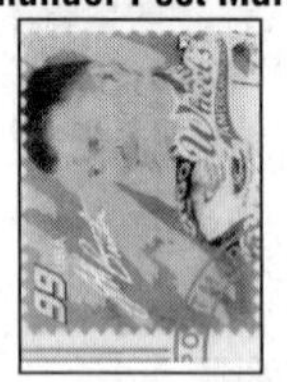

This 18-card set was printed on clear plastic and was about the size of a postage stamp. They were inserted into packs at a rate of one in eight. These cards carried a "PM" prefix for their card numbers.

COMPLETE SET (18) 25.00 50.00
STATED ODDS 1:8
PM1 Jeff Burton .75 2.00
PM2 Ward Burton .75 2.00
PM3 Kurt Busch 1.25 3.00
PM4 Dale Earnhardt Jr. 4.00 10.00
PM5 Jeff Gordon 3.00 8.00
PM6 Jeff Green .40 1.00
PM7 Kevin Harvick 2.00 5.00
PM8 Dale Jarrett 2.00 5.00
PM9 Jimmie Johnson 2.50 6.00
PM10 Matt Kenseth 2.50 6.00
PM11 Bobby Labonte 2.00 5.00
PM12 Jamie McMurray 2.00 5.00
PM13 Mark Martin 2.50 6.00
PM14 Ryan Newman 2.50 6.00
PM15 Steve Park .75 2.00
PM16 Tony Stewart 2.50 6.00
PM17 Rusty Wallace 2.00 5.00
PM18 Michael Waltrip .75 2.00

2003 Wheels American Thunder Pushin Pedal

Randomly inserted in packs, these 14 cards featured swatches of race-used shoes. The cards were serial numbered to 285 with the exceptions of Robby Gordon of 300, Mike Skinner and Ricky Craven of 175.

UNLESS NOTED PRINT RUN 285 SETS
PP1 Jeff Burton 8.00 20.00
PP2 Jeff Gordon 20.00 50.00
PP3 Robby Gordon/300 8.00 20.00
PP4 Matt Kenseth 12.50 30.00
PP5 Mark Martin 12.50 30.00
PP6 Mike Skinner/175 8.00 20.00
PP7 Tony Stewart 15.00 40.00
PP8 Rusty Wallace 10.00 25.00
PP9 Michael Waltrip 8.00 20.00
PP10 Ricky Craven/175 8.00 20.00
PP11 Jimmie Johnson 15.00 40.00
PP12 Sterling Marlin 10.00 25.00
PP13 Terry Labonte 10.00 25.00
PP14 Joe Nemechek 6.00 15.00

2003 Wheels American Thunder Rookie Class

This 11-card set was interactive with the actual performance of the specified drivers. If the card was a winner it could be redeemed for a prize set.

COMPLETE SET (11) 10.00 25.00
RANDOM INSERTS IN PACKS
RC1 Ryan Newman WIN 3.00 8.00
RC2 Greg Biffle WIN 3.00 8.00
RC3 Jamie McMurray WIN 2.50 6.00
RC4 Casey Mears 1.50 4.00
RC5 Jack Sprague .60 1.50
RC6 Scott Riggs 1.50 4.00
RC7 Chad Blount .60 1.50
RC8 Coy Gibbs WIN 3.00 8.00
RC9 Damon Lusk WIN .60 1.50
RC10 Chase Montgomery 1.00 2.50
RC11 Regan Smith .60 1.50

2003 Wheels American Thunder Rookie Class Prizes

This 11-card set was the redemption set for any of the redeemed winner cards. The cards were the same as the basic set with the exception of foil highlights and a uv-coating.

COMPLETE SET (11)
COMP.SET WINSTON CUP (5) 6.00 15.00
COMP.SET BUSCH SERIES (6)
RC1 Ryan Newman 4.00 10.00
RC2 Greg Biffle 1.25 3.00
RC3 Jamie McMurray 2.00 5.00
RC4 Casey Mears 1.25 3.00
RC5 Jack Sprague .75 2.00
RC6 Scott Riggs
RC7 Chad Blount
RC8 Coy Gibbs
RC9 Damon Lusk
RC10 Chase Montgomery
RC11 Regan Smith
NNO Jamie McMurray Tire/600 8.00 20.00

2003 Wheels American Thunder Rookie Thunder

This 36-card set was randomly inserted in packs at a rate of one per pack. Each card carried a prefix of "RT" for the card number.

COMPLETE SET (36) 8.00 20.00
STATED ODDS 1 PER PACK
RT1 John Andretti .25 .60
RT2 Greg Biffle .50 1.25
RT3 Brett Bodine .25 .60
RT4 Jeff Burton .50 1.25
RT5 Ward Burton .50 1.25
RT6 Kurt Busch .75 2.00
RT7 Ricky Craven .25 .60
RT8 Dale Earnhardt Jr. 2.50 6.00
RT9 Jeff Gordon 2.00 5.00
RT10 Robby Gordon .25 .60
RT11 Jeff Green .25 .60
RT12 Kevin Harvick 1.25 3.00
RT13 Dale Jarrett 1.25 3.00
RT14 Jimmie Johnson 1.50 4.00
RT15 Matt Kenseth 1.50 4.00
RT16 Bobby Labonte 1.25 3.00
RT17 Terry Labonte .75 2.00
RT18 Sterling Marlin .75 2.00
RT19 Mark Martin 1.50 4.00
RT20 Casey Mears .50 1.25
RT21 Jamie McMurray 1.25 3.00
RT22 Jerry Nadeau .50 1.25
RT23 Joe Nemechek .25 .60
RT24 Ryan Newman 1.50 4.00
RT25 Steve Park .50 1.25
RT26 Kyle Petty .50 1.25
RT27 Ricky Rudd .75 2.00
RT28 Elliott Sadler .50 1.25
RT29 Ken Schrader .25 .60
RT30 Mike Skinner .25 .60
RT31 Jack Sprague .25 .60
RT32 Tony Stewart 1.50 4.00
RT33 Kenny Wallace .25 .60
RT34 Rusty Wallace 1.25 3.00
RT35 Michael Waltrip .50 1.25
RT36 Checklist .25 .60

2003 Wheels American Thunder Thunder Road

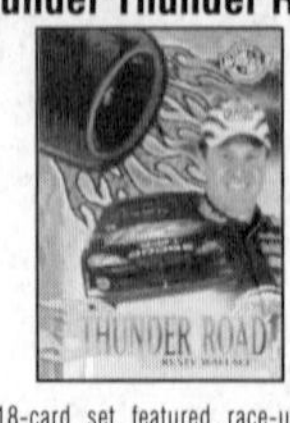

This 18-card set featured race-used tires incorporated into the card design. They were inserted in packs at a rate of one in 18. Each card carried a "TR" prefix in its card numbers.

COMPLETE SET (18) 75.00 150.00
STATED ODDS 1:18
TR1 Dale Earnhardt Jr. 10.00 25.00
TR2 Jeff Gordon 8.00 20.00
TR3 Tony Stewart 6.00 15.00
TR4 Rusty Wallace 5.00 12.00
TR5 Ryan Newman 6.00 15.00
TR6 Kurt Busch 4.00 10.00
TR7 Mark Martin 6.00 15.00
TR8 Jimmie Johnson 6.00 15.00
TR9 Matt Kenseth 6.00 15.00
TR10 Michael Waltrip 2.50 6.00
TR11 Steve Park 2.50 6.00
TR12 Jamie McMurray 5.00 12.00
TR13 Kevin Harvick 5.00 12.00
TR14 Bobby Labonte 5.00 12.00
TR15 Ward Burton 2.50 6.00
TR16 Robby Gordon 1.00 2.50
TR17 Jeff Green 1.00 2.50
TR18 Jeff Burton 2.50 6.00

2003 Wheels American Thunder Triple Hat

This 14-card set features three swatches of hats that were worn during Daytona Speedweeks. The cards are serial numbered to 25 and are not priced due to scarcity.

STATED PRINT RUN 25 SERIAL #'d SETS
NOT PRICED DUE TO SCARCITY
TH1 Steve Park
TH2 Rusty Wallace
TH3 Jeff Burton
TH4 Jamie McMurray
TH5 Michael Waltrip
TH6 Bobby Labonte
TH7 Jeff Gordon 60.00 100.00
TH8 Kevin Harvick
TH9 Jimmie Johnson
TH10 Dale Jarrett
TH11 Sterling Marlin
TH12 Tony Stewart
TH13 Ricky Rudd
TH14 Greg Biffle

2004 Wheels American Thunder

This 90-card set was released in September, 2004. These cards were found in 5-card hobby packs with 20 pack boxes with pack SRP of $5.99 and 4-card retail packs with 28 pack boxes with an SRP of $2.99. There was also a zero card of Air Force One in honor of President George W. Bush's trip to the Daytona 500 in February. The stated odds for this card was 1 in 72 packs.

COMPLETE SET (90) 15.00 40.00
WAX BOX HOBBY (20) 60.00 120.00
1 Jeff Burton .30 .75
2 Kurt Busch .50 1.25
3 Ricky Craven .20 .50
4 Dale Earnhardt Jr. 1.25 3.00
5 Jeff Gordon 1.25 3.00
6 Robby Gordon .20 .50
7 Jeff Green .20 .50
8 Kevin Harvick .75 2.00
9 Dale Jarrett .60 1.50
10 Jimmie Johnson 1.00 2.50
11 Kasey Kahne CRC 1.50 4.00
12 Matt Kenseth 1.00 2.50
13 Bobby Labonte .60 1.50
14 Terry Labonte .50 1.25
15 Sterling Marlin .50 1.25
16 Mark Martin .75 2.00
17 Jeremy Mayfield .20 .50
18 Jamie McMurray .50 1.25
19 Casey Mears .20 .50
20 Joe Nemechek .20 .50
21 Ryan Newman 1.00 2.
22 Ricky Rudd .50 1.
23 Elliott Sadler .30
24 Tony Stewart .75 2.
25 Brian Vickers CRC .60 1.
26 Rusty Wallace .60 1.
27 Michael Waltrip .30
28 Brendan Gaughan CRC .30
29 Scott Riggs CRC .30
30 Scott Wimmer CRC .30
31 Jimmie Johnson's Rig Rt. 66 .50 1.
32 Sterling Marlin's Rig Rt. 66 .20
33 Dale Earnhardt Jr.'s Rig Rt. 66 .50 1.
34 Jeff Gordon's Rig Rt. 66 .50 1.
35 Rusty Wallace's Rig Rt. 66 .30
36 Michael Waltrip's Rig Rt. 66 .20
37 Matt Kenseth AS 1.00 2.
38 Ryan Newman AS 1.00 2.
39 Tony Stewart AS .75 2.
40 Michael Waltrip AS .30
41 Dale Earnhardt Jr. AS 1.25 3.
42 Jeff Gordon AS 1.25 3.
43 Kasey Kahne AS 1.25 3.
44 Elliott Sadler AS .30
45 Rusty Wallace AS .60 1.
46 Rusty Wallace's Car HR .30
47 Dale Earnhardt's Car HR .50 1.
48 Scott Rigg's Car HR .20
49 Michael Waltrip's Car HR .20
50 Bobby Labonte's Car HR .30
51 Scott Wimmer's Car HR .20
52 Jeff Gordon's Car HR .50 1.
53 Mark Martin's Car HR .30
54 Jimmie Johnson's Car HR .50 1.
55 Michael Waltrip DT .30
56 Rusty Wallace DT .60 1.
57 Ricky Rudd DT .50 1.
58 Elliott Sadler DT .30
59 Bobby Labonte DT .60 1.
60 Matt Kenseth DT 1.00 2.
61 Kevin Harvick DT .75 2.
62 Dale Earnhardt Jr. DT 1.25 3.
63 Kurt Busch DT .50 1.
64 Kasey Kahne RR 1.25 3.
65 Jeff Gordon RR 1.25 3.
66 Jamie McMurray RR .50 1.
67 Michael Waltrip RR .30
68 Bobby Labonte RR .60 1.
69 Dale Earnhardt Jr. RR 1.25 3.
70 Mark Martin RR .75 2.
71 Ricky Craven RR .20
72 Jimmie Johnson RR 1.00 2.
73 Elliott Sadler RR .30
74 Brian Vickers RR .60 1.
75 Kevin Harvick RR .75 2.
76 Jeff Gordon CC 1.25 3.
77 Dale Earnhardt Jr. CC 1.25 3.
78 Tony Stewart CC .75 2.
79 Rusty Wallace CC .60 1.
80 Terry Labonte CC .50 1.
81 Michael Waltrip CC .30
82 Jeff Burton CC .30
83 Dale Jarrett CC .60 1.
84 Jimmie Johnson CC 1.00 2.
85 Kasey Kahne RT 1.25 3.
86 Brian Vickers RT .60 1.
87 Scott Wimmer RT .30
88 Brendan Gaughan RT .30
89 Scott Riggs RT .30
90 Kahne/Busch/McMurray CL 1.25 3.
0 Daytona 500 Air Force One 2.00 5.
NNO American Chopper Promo .75 2.

2004 Wheels America[n] Thunder Samples

This 90-card set is a parallel to the base 20[04] Wheels American Thunder set without the variatio[ns]. It was issued 1 per Beckett Racing Collector is[sue] #123, which was the November 2004 cover d[ate]. Each card had the word "SAMPLE" printed acr[oss] the back.

*SAMPLES: 2X TO 5X BASE

2004 Wheels America[n] Thunder American Eag[le]

This 12-card set was randomly inserted in packs [at a] rate of 1 in 6. The feature foil etched card[s of] NASCAR's leading drivers. The cards carried an "[AE]" prefix for their card numbers.

COMPLETE SET (12) 12.50 30.
AE1 Jeff Burton .60 1.
AE2 Jeff Gordon 2.50 6.
AE3 Dale Jarrett 1.25 3.
AE4 Jimmie Johnson 2.00 5.
AE5 Bobby Labonte 1.25 3.
AE6 Terry Labonte 1.00 2.
AE7 Greg Biffle .60 1.
AE8 Jamie McMurray 1.00 2.
AE9 Ricky Rudd 1.00 2.
AE10 Brian Vickers 1.25 3.
AE11 Rusty Wallace 1.25 3.
AE12 Michael Waltrip .60 1.

2004 Wheels America[n] Thunder Golden Eagle

This 12-card set is a parallel to the basic Ameri[can] Eagle set. These cards were serial numbered to [...] and carried an "AE" prefix for their card numbers.

*GOLDEN: 1.5X TO 4X AMERICAN

004 Wheels American Thunder American Muscle

9-card set was randomly inserted in packs at a of 1 in 10. The feature foil etched cards of CAR's leading drivers. The cards carried an prefix for their card numbers.

PLETE SET (9) 12.50 30.00
Dale Earnhardt Jr. 3.00 8.00
Kevin Harvick 2.00 5.00
Jimmie Johnson 2.50 6.00
Jeff Gordon 3.00 8.00
Rusty Wallace 1.50 4.00
Tony Stewart 2.00 5.00
Kasey Kahne 3.00 8.00
Bobby Labonte 1.50 4.00
Kurt Busch 1.25 3.00

004 Wheels American 'hunder Cool Threads

15-card set was randomly inserted in packs. feature swatches of shirts worn by drivers g races. The cards carried a "CT" prefix for their numbers and were serial numbered to 525.

Jeff Burton 8.00 20.00
Dale Earnhardt Jr. 20.00 40.00
Jeff Gordon 15.00 40.00
Kevin Harvick 8.00 20.00
Dale Jarrett 8.00 20.00
Matt Kenseth 12.50 30.00
Sterling Marlin 8.00 20.00
Mark Martin 10.00 25.00
Jamie McMurray 10.00 25.00
) Casey Mears 8.00 20.00
Joe Nemechek 8.00 20.00
2 Ryan Newman 10.00 25.00
3 Scott Riggs 8.00 20.00
4 Kenny Wallace 8.00 20.00
5 Michael Waltrip 8.00 20.00

004 Wheels American Thunder Cup Quest

PLETE SET (12) 30.00 60.00
Jimmie Johnson 6.00 15.00
Dale Earnhardt Jr. 8.00 20.00
Jeff Gordon 10.00 25.00
Tony Stewart 5.00 12.00
Bobby Labonte 4.00 10.00
Ryan Newman 6.00 15.00
Dale Jarrett 4.00 10.00
Mark Martin 5.00 12.00
Michael Waltrip 2.50 6.00
0 Terry Labonte 3.00 8.00
1 Jeff Burton 2.50 6.00
2 Ricky Rudd 3.00 8.00

004 Wheels American Thunder Head to Toe

9-card set featured swatches of race-used hats shoes. Each card was serial numbered to 100, unless noted in the checklist below and carried an "HT" prefix for its card number.

UNLESS OTHERWISE NOTED
HT1 Jeff Burton/50 10.00 25.00
HT2 Ward Burton 10.00 25.00
HT3 Dale Earnhardt Jr. 50.00 100.00
HT4 Jeff Gordon/50 75.00 150.00
HT5 Matt Kenseth 25.00 60.00
HT6 Terry Labonte 15.00 40.00
HT7 Mark Martin/50 25.00 60.00
HT8 Joe Nemechek 10.00 25.00
HT9 Scott Riggs 10.00 25.00

2004 Wheels American Thunder Post Mark

This 27-card set was printed on clear plastic and was about the size of a postage stamp. They were inserted into packs at a rate of 1 in 2. These cards carried a "PM" prefix for their card numbers.

COMPLETE SET (27) 10.00 25.00
STATED ODDS 1:2
PM1 Ward Burton .40 1.00
PM2 Joe Nemechek .25 .60
PM3 Rusty Wallace .75 2.00
PM4 Terry Labonte .60 1.50
PM5 Mark Martin 1.00 2.50
PM6 Dale Earnhardt Jr. 1.50 4.00
PM7 Scott Riggs .40 1.00
PM8 Ryan Newman 1.25 3.00
PM9 Michael Waltrip .40 1.00
PM10 Greg Biffle .40 1.00
PM11 Matt Kenseth 1.25 3.00
PM12 Bobby Labonte .75 2.00
PM13 Tony Stewart 1.00 2.50
PM14 Ricky Rudd .60 1.50
PM15 Scott Wimmer .40 1.00
PM16 Jeff Gordon 1.50 4.00
PM17 Brian Vickers .75 2.00
PM18 Kevin Harvick 1.00 2.50
PM19 Robby Gordon .25 .60
PM20 Casey Mears .25 .60
PM21 Jamie McMurray .60 1.50
PM22 Jeff Green .25 .60
PM23 Kyle Petty .40 1.00
PM24 Jimmie Johnson 1.25 3.00
PM25 Brendan Gaughan .40 1.00
PM26 Jeff Burton .40 1.00
PM27 Kasey Kahne CL 1.50 4.00

2004 Wheels American Thunder Pushin Pedal

Randomly inserted in packs, these 15 cards featured swatches of race-used shoes. The cards were serial numbered to 275 unless noted in the checklist below..

PP1 Greg Biffle 6.00 15.00
PP2 Jeff Burton/200 8.00 20.00
PP3 Ward Burton 8.00 20.00
PP4 Kurt Busch 8.00 20.00
PP5 Dale Earnhardt Jr. 20.00 50.00
PP6 Jeff Gordon/200 25.00 60.00
PP7 Robby Gordon 6.00 15.00
PP8 Kevin Harvick 10.00 25.00
PP9 Jimmie Johnson 12.50 30.00
PP10 Matt Kenseth 12.50 30.00
PP11 Terry Labonte 10.00 25.00
PP12 Mark Martin/200 12.50 30.00
PP13 Joe Nemechek 6.00 15.00
PP14 Scott Riggs 6.00 15.00
PP15 Tony Stewart 10.00 25.00

2004 Wheels American Thunder Thunder Road

This 18-card set featured race-used tires incorporated into the card design. They were inserted in packs at a rate of one in 18. Each card carried a "TR" prefix in its card numbers.

TR1 Rusty Wallace 4.00 10.00
TR2 Terry Labonte 3.00 8.00
TR3 Mark Martin 5.00 12.00
TR4 Dale Earnhardt Jr. 8.00 20.00
TR5 Ryan Newman 6.00 15.00
TR6 Michael Waltrip 2.00 5.00
TR7 Robby Gordon 1.25 3.00
TR8 Matt Kenseth 6.00 15.00
TR9 Bobby Labonte 4.00 10.00
TR10 Tony Stewart 5.00 12.00
TR11 Ricky Rudd 3.00 8.00
TR12 Jeff Gordon 8.00 20.00
TR13 Brian Vickers 4.00 10.00
TR14 Sterling Marlin 3.00 8.00
TR15 Jamie McMurray 4.00 10.00
TR16 Jimmie Johnson 6.00 15.00
TR17 Dale Jarrett 4.00 10.00
TR18 Jeff Burton 2.00 5.00

2004 Wheels American Thunder Triple Hat

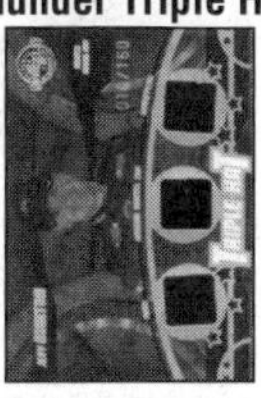

This 35-card set features three swatches of hats that were worn during Daytona Speedweeks. The cards are serial numbered to 160.

TH1 Kurt Busch 12.50 30.00
TH2 Ricky Craven 10.00 25.00
TH3 Jeff Gordon 40.00 100.00
TH4 Jeff Green 8.00 20.00
TH5 Dale Jarrett 15.00 40.00
TH6 Jimmie Johnson 25.00 60.00
TH7 Kasey Kahne 30.00 80.00
TH8 Matt Kenseth 15.00 40.00
TH9 Bobby Labonte 12.50 30.00
TH10 Terry Labonte 25.00 60.00
TH11 Sterling Marlin 15.00 40.00
TH12 Mark Martin 20.00 50.00
TH13 Jamie McMurray 15.00 40.00
TH14 Casey Mears 10.00 25.00
TH15 Joe Nemechek 8.00 20.00
TH16 Kyle Petty 12.50 30.00
TH17 Scott Riggs 10.00 25.00
TH18 Ricky Rudd 10.00 25.00
TH19 Elliott Sadler 12.50 30.00
TH20 Johnny Sauter 8.00 20.00
TH21 Tony Stewart 25.00 60.00
TH22 Brian Vickers 15.00 40.00
TH23 Rusty Wallace 15.00 40.00
TH24 Michael Waltrip 12.50 30.00
TH25 Scott Wimmer 10.00 25.00
TH26 Greg Biffle 10.00 25.00
TH27 Jeff Burton 10.00 25.00
TH28 Ward Burton 10.00 25.00
TH29 Brendan Gaughan 12.50 30.00
TH30 Kevin Lepage 8.00 20.00
TH31 Jeremy Mayfield 10.00 25.00
TH32 Ken Schrader 12.50 30.00
TH33 Dale Earnhardt Jr. 40.00 100.00
TH34 Robby Gordon 10.00 25.00
TH35 Ryan Newman 20.00 50.00

2005 Wheels American Thunder

COMPLETE SET (90) 15.00 40.00
WAX BOX HOBBY (20) 60.00 100.00
WAX BOX RETAIL (24) 50.00 80.00
1 John Andretti .20 .50
2 Greg Biffle .30 .75
3 Jeff Burton .30 .75
4 Kurt Busch .50 1.25
5 Kyle Busch CRC .75 2.00
6 Dale Earnhardt Jr. 1.25 3.00
7 Carl Edwards CRC 1.00 2.50
8 Jeff Gordon 1.25 3.00
9 Robby Gordon .20 .50
10 Kevin Harvick .75 2.00
11 Dale Jarrett .60 1.50
12 Jimmie Johnson 1.00 2.50
13 Kasey Kahne 1.25 3.00
14 Matt Kenseth 1.00 2.50
15 Travis Kvapil CRC .30 .75
16 Bobby Labonte .60 1.50
17 Terry Labonte .50 1.25
18 Jason Leffler .20 .50
19 Sterling Marlin .50 1.25
20 Mark Martin .75 2.00
21 Jeremy Mayfield .20 .50
22 Jamie McMurray .50 1.25
23 Casey Mears .30 .75
24 Joe Nemechek .20 .50
25 Ricky Rudd .50 1.25
26 Elliott Sadler .30 .75
27 Tony Stewart .75 2.00
28 Brian Vickers .60 1.50
29 Rusty Wallace .60 1.50
30 Scott Wimmer .30 .75
31 Jimmie Johnson's Rig Rt. 66 .30 .75
32 Mark Martin's Rig RT. 66 .30 .75
33 Jeff Burton's Rig Rt. 66 .20 .50
34 Jeff Gordon's Rig Rt. 66 .50 1.25
35 Kevin Harvick's Rig Rt. 66 .30 .75
36 Dale Earnhardt Jr's Rig Rt. 66 .50 1.25
37 Mark Martin AS .75 2.00
38 Dale Earnhardt Jr. AS 1.25 3.00
39 Matt Kenseth AS 1.00 2.50
40 Jeff Gordon AS 1.25 3.00
41 Martin Truex Jr. AS 1.00 2.50
42 Dale Jarrett AS .60 1.50
43 Tony Stewart AS .75 2.00
44 Bobby Labonte AS .60 1.50
45 Rusty Wallace AS .60 1.50
46 Kevin Harvick's Car HR .30 .75
47 Rusty Wallace's Car HR .30 .75
48 Elliott Sadler's Car HR .20 .50
49 Mark Martin's Car HR .30 .75
50 Tony Stewart's Car HR .30 .75
51 Dale Jarrett's Car HR .30 .75
52 Jeff Gordon's Car HR .50 1.25
53 Jimmie Johnson's Car HR .30 .75
54 Kasey Kahne DT 1.25 3.00
55 Carl Edwards DT 1.00 2.50
56 Rusty Wallace DT .60 1.50
57 Dale Earnhardt Jr. DT 1.25 3.00
58 Tony Stewart DT .75 2.00
59 Bobby Labonte DT .60 1.50
60 Jimmie Johnson DT 1.00 2.50
61 Kyle Busch DT .75 2.00
62 Ricky Rudd DT .50 1.25
63 Jeff Gordon DT 1.25 3.00
64 Carl Edwards RR 1.00 2.50
65 Jeff Gordon RR 1.25 3.00
66 Jeremy Mayfield RR .20 .50
67 Jimmie Johnson RR 1.00 2.50
68 Bobby Labonte RR .60 1.50
69 Dale Earnhardt Jr. RR 1.25 3.00
70 Mark Martin RR .75 2.00
71 Jeff Burton RR .30 .75
72 Dale Jarrett RR .60 1.50
73 Tony Stewart RR .75 2.00
74 Kyle Busch RR .75 2.00
75 Martin Truex Jr. RR 1.00 2.50
76 Jamie McMurray CC .50 1.25
77 Dale Earnhardt Jr. CC 1.25 3.00
78 Kasey Kahne CC 1.25 3.00
79 John Andretti CC .20 .50
80 Martin Truex Jr. CC 1.00 2.50
81 Scott Wimmer CC .30 .75
82 Travis Kvapil CC .30 .75
83 Ricky Rudd CC .50 1.25
84 Jimmie Johnson CC 1.00 2.50
85 Kyle Busch RT .75 2.00
86 Travis Kvapil RT .30 .75
87 Carl Edwards RT 1.00 2.50
88 Reed Sorenson RT RC 2.50 6.00
89 Denny Hamlin RT RC 3.00 8.00
90 C.Edwards/Ky.Busch CL 1.00 2.50

2005 Wheels American Thunder Previews

STATED PRINT RUN 5 SERIAL #'d SETS
UNLESS OTHERWISE NOTED BELOW

2005 Wheels American Thunder Samples

COMPLETE SET (90)
*SAMPLES: 1.5X TO 4X BASE
STATED ODDS 1 PER BRC 135

2005 Wheels American Thunder American Eagle

COMPLETE SET (12) 12.50 30.00
AE1 Jeff Burton .60 1.50
AE2 Dale Earnhardt Jr. 2.50 6.00
AE3 Dale Jarrett 1.25 3.00
AE4 Rusty Wallace 1.25 3.00
AE5 Bobby Labonte 1.25 3.00
AE6 Martin Truex Jr. 2.00 5.00
AE7 Jeff Gordon 2.50 6.00
AE8 Joe Nemechek .40 1.00
AE9 Ricky Rudd 1.00 2.50
AE10 Mark Martin 1.50 4.00
AE11 Jimmie Johnson 2.00 5.00
AE12 Greg Biffle .60 1.50

2005 Wheels American Thunder Golden Eagle

HOBBY ONLY
COMPLETE SET (12)
*GOLDEN EAGLE: 1.5X TO 4X AMERICAN EAGLE

2005 Wheels American Thunder American Muscle

COMPLETE SET (9) 15.00 40.00
AM1 Mark Martin 2.00 5.00
AM2 Kevin Harvick 2.00 5.00
AM3 Jimmie Johnson 2.50 6.00
AM4 Jeff Gordon 3.00 8.00
AM5 Carl Edwards 2.50 6.00
AM6 Dale Earnhardt Jr. 3.00 8.00
AM7 Greg Biffle .75 2.00

AM8 Elliott Sadler .75 2.00
AM9 Kurt Busch 1.25 3.00

2005 Wheels American Thunder Cool Threads

CT1 Jeff Gordon 15.00 40.00
CT2 Casey Mears 6.00 15.00
CT3 Sterling Marlin 8.00 20.00
CT4 Dale Earnhardt Jr. 15.00 40.00
CT5 Matt Kenseth 10.00 25.00
CT6 Mark Martin 12.50 30.00
CT7 Scott Riggs 6.00 15.00
CT8 Joe Nemechek 6.00 15.00
CT9 Kurt Busch 8.00 20.00
CT10 Jamie Mcmurray 8.00 20.00
CT11 Kevin Harvick 8.00 20.00
CT12 Dale Jarrett 8.00 20.00
CT13 Ryan Newman 12.50 30.00

2005 Wheels American Thunder Double Hat

DH1 John Andretti 6.00 15.00
DH2 Mike Bliss 6.00 15.00
DH3 Carl Edwards 12.50 30.00
DH4 Bobby Labonte 10.00 25.00
DH5 Terry Labonte 10.00 25.00
DH6 Jason Leffler 6.00 15.00
DH7 Kevin Lepage 6.00 15.00
DH8 Ryan Newman 12.50 30.00
DH9 Boris Said 6.00 15.00

2005 Wheels American Thunder Head to Toe

HT1 Carl Edwards 20.00 50.00
HT2 Greg Biffle 15.00 40.00
HT3 Kurt Busch 15.00 40.00
HT4 Dale Earnhardt Jr. 25.00 60.00
HT5 Terry Labonte 15.00 40.00
HT6 Tony Stewart 25.00 60.00
HT7 Bobby Labonte 15.00 40.00
HT8 Joe Nemechek 10.00 25.00
HT9 Scott Riggs 10.00 25.00
HT10 Jeff Gordon 30.00 80.00
HT11 Matt Kenseth 20.00 50.00
HT12 Mark Martin 20.00 50.00
HT13 Jimmie Johnson/60 25.00 60.00

2005 Wheels American Thunder License to Drive

COMPLETE SET (9) 12.50 30.00
1 Carl Edwards 3.00 8.00
2 Travis Kvapil 1.00 2.50
3 Jason Leffler .60 1.50
4 David Stremme 3.00 8.00
5 Martin Truex Jr. 3.00 8.00
6 J.J. Yeley 1.50 4.00
7 Clint Bowyer 4.00 10.00
8 Denny Hamlin 3.00 8.00
9 Jon Wood 1.00 2.50

2005 Wheels American Thunder Medallion

COMPLETE SET (27) 10.00 25.00
MD1 John Andretti .25 .60
MD2 Kyle Busch 1.00 2.50
MD3 Rusty Wallace .75 2.00
MD4 Terry Labonte .60 1.50
MD5 Mark Martin 1.00 2.50
MD6 Joe Nemechek .25 .60
MD7 Casey Mears .40 1.00
MD8 Tony Raines .25 .60
MD9 Dale Jarrett .75 2.00

MD10 Bobby Labonte .75 2.00
MD11 Tony Stewart 1.00 2.50
MD12 Ricky Rudd .60 1.50
MD13 Sterling Marlin .60 1.50
MD14 Jeff Gordon 1.50 4.00
MD15 Kevin Harvick 1.00 2.50
MD16 Robby Gordon .25 .60
MD17 Johnny Sauter .40 1.00
MD18 Jeff Green .25 .60
MD19 Kyle Petty .40 1.00
MD20 Jimmie Johnson 1.25 3.00
MD21 Mike Bliss .25 .60
MD22 Jeff Burton .40 1.00
MD23 Elliott Sadler .40 1.00
MD24 Kenny Wallace .25 .60
MD25 Paul Wolfe .40 1.00
MD26 Kasey Kahne 1.50 4.00
MD27 Scott Wimmer CL .40 1.00

2005 Wheels American Thunder Pushin Pedal

PP1 Greg Biffle 10.00 25.00
PP2 Kurt Busch 10.00 25.00
PP3 Dale Earnhardt Jr. 25.00 60.00
PP4 Terry Labonte 12.50 30.00
PP5 Kevin Harvick 12.50 30.00
PP6 Joe Nemechek 8.00 20.00
PP7 Scott Riggs 8.00 20.00
PP8 Tony Stewart 25.00 60.00
PP9 Carl Edwards 15.00 40.00
PP10 Bobby Labonte 12.50 30.00
PP11 Mark Martin 15.00 40.00
PP12 Jeff Gordon 25.00 60.00
PP13 Jimmie Johnson/60 20.00 50.00
PP14 Matt Kenseth 15.00 40.00

2005 Wheels American Thunder Single Hat

SH1 Jeff Burton 8.00 20.00
SH2 Martin Truex Jr. 12.50 30.00

2005 Wheels American Thunder Thunder Road

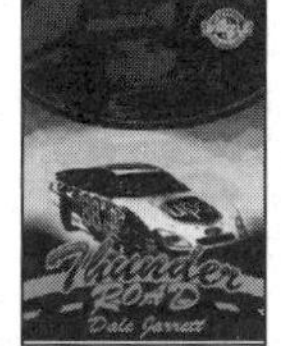

TR1 Rusty Wallace 4.00 10.00
TR2 Terry Labonte 3.00 8.00
TR3 Mark Martin 5.00 12.00
TR4 Dale Earnhardt Jr. 8.00 20.00
TR5 Kurt Busch 3.00 8.00
TR6 Kasey Kahne 8.00 20.00
TR7 Kyle Busch 5.00 12.00
TR8 Travis Kvapil 2.00 5.00
TR9 Bobby Labonte 4.00 10.00
TR10 Tony Stewart 5.00 12.00
TR11 Ricky Rudd 3.00 8.00
TR12 Jeff Gordon 8.00 20.00
TR13 Carl Edwards 6.00 15.00
TR14 Sterling Marlin 3.00 8.00
TR15 Martin Truex Jr. 6.00 15.00
TR16 Jimmie Johnson 6.00 15.00
TR17 Dale Jarrett 4.00 10.00
TR18 Jeff Burton 2.00 5.00

2005 Wheels American Thunder Triple Hat

TH1 Greg Biffle 12.50 30.00
TH2 Kurt Busch 12.50 30.00
TH3 Kyle Busch 15.00 40.00
TH4 Dale Earnhardt Jr. 30.00 80.00
TH5 Jeff Gordon 30.00 80.00
TH6 Jeff Green 6.00 15.00
TH7 Kevin Harvick 20.00 50.00
TH8 Dale Jarrett 15.00 40.00
TH9 Jimmie Johnson 25.00 60.00
TH10 Kasey Kahne 30.00 80.00
TH11 Matt Kenseth 25.00 60.00

TH12 Travis Kvapil	8.00	20.00
TH13 Sterling Marlin	12.50	30.00
TH14 Mark Martin	20.00	50.00
TH15 Jeremy Mayfield	10.00	25.00
TH16 Jamie McMurray	12.50	30.00
TH17 Casey Mears	6.00	15.00
TH18 Joe Nemechek	8.00	20.00
TH19 Kyle Petty	8.00	20.00
TH20 Scott Riggs	6.00	15.00
TH21 Ricky Rudd	12.50	30.00
TH22 Elliott Sadler	12.50	30.00
TH23 Tony Stewart	25.00	60.00
TH24 Brian Vickers	12.50	30.00
TH25 Rusty Wallace	15.00	40.00
TH26 Scott Wimmer	8.00	20.00

2006 Wheels American Thunder

This 96-card set was released in September, 2006. These cards were found in 5-card hobby packs with 20 pack boxes with pack SRP of $5.99 and 4-card retail packs with 24 pack boxes with an SRP of $2.99. The six Cup Rookie Cards were each randomly inserted into packs and serial numbered to 350. Each of the contained an autograph. The David Stremme was issued in packs as a redemption, but the actual cards were ready and shipped from Press Pass by the time the product went live. The checklist card had "CL" for its card number.

COMP.SET w/o SPs (90)	12.50	30.00
CRC STATED PRINT RUN 350 SERIAL #'d SETS		
WAX BOX HOBBY (20)	75.00	125.00
WAX BOX RETAIL (24)	40.00	75.00
1 Greg Biffle	.40	1.00
2 Dave Blaney	.20	.50
3 Jeff Burton	.30	.75
4 Kurt Busch	.50	1.25
5 Kyle Busch	.60	1.50
6 Dale Earnhardt Jr.	1.25	3.00
7 Carl Edwards	1.00	2.50
8 Jeff Gordon	1.25	3.00
9 Robby Gordon	.20	.50
10 Jeff Green	.20	.50
11 Kevin Harvick	.75	2.00
12 Dale Jarrett	.60	1.50
13 Jimmie Johnson	1.00	2.50
14 Kasey Kahne	1.25	3.00
15 Matt Kenseth	1.00	2.50
16 Bobby Labonte	.60	1.50
17 Terry Labonte	.50	1.25
18 Sterling Marlin	.50	1.25
19 Mark Martin	.75	2.00
20 Jeremy Mayfield	.20	.50
21 Jamie McMurray	.50	1.25
22 Casey Mears	.30	.75
23 Joe Nemechek	.20	.50
24 Ryan Newman	.75	2.00
25 Kyle Petty	.30	.75
26 Tony Raines	.20	.50
27 Scott Riggs	.30	.75
28 Elliott Sadler	.30	.75
29 Ken Schrader	.20	.50
30 Tony Stewart	.75	2.00
31 Matt Kenseth DT	1.00	2.50
32 Dale Earnhardt Jr. DT	1.25	3.00
33 Terry Labonte DT	.50	1.25
34 Jimmie Johnson DT	1.00	2.50
35 Tony Stewart DT	.75	2.00
36 Carl Edwards DT	1.00	2.50
37 Jeff Gordon DT	1.25	3.00
38 Kyle Busch DT	.60	1.50
39 Mark Martin DT	.75	2.00
40 Jamie McMurray DT	.50	1.25
41 Jeff Burton DT	.30	.75
42 Bobby Labonte DT	.60	1.50
43 Jeff Gordon's Car HR	1.25	3.00
44 Mark Martin's Car HR	.75	2.00
45 Dale Jarrett's Car HR	.60	1.50
46 Jeff Burton's Car HR	.30	.75
47 Dale Earnhardt Jr.'s Car HR	1.25	3.00
48 Jimmie Johnson's Car HR	1.00	2.50
49 Terry Labonte's Car HR	.50	1.25
50 Tony Stewart's Car HR	.75	2.00
51 Bobby Labonte's Car HR	.60	1.50
52 Kasey Kahne's Car HR	1.25	3.00
53 Martin Truex Jr.'s Car HR	.75	2.00
54 Kevin Harvick's Car HR	.75	2.00
55 Jamie McMurray's Car HR	.50	1.25
56 Sterling Marlin's Car HR	.50	1.25
57 Bobby Labonte's Car HR	.60	1.50
58 Carl Edwards' Car HR	1.00	2.50
59 Dave Blaney GR	.20	.50
60 Kasey Kahne GR	1.25	3.00
61 Tony Stewart GR	.75	2.00
62 Ken Schrader GR	.20	.50
63 Robby Gordon GR	.20	.50
64 Greg Biffle SS	.40	1.00
65 Jeff Burton SS	.30	.75
66 Jimmie Johnson SS	1.00	2.50
67 Joe Nemechek SS	.20	.50
68 Kevin Harvick SS	.75	2.00
69 Ken Schrader SS	.20	.50
70 Jeff Gordon SS	1.25	3.00
71 Tony Stewart SS	.75	2.00
72 Jimmie Johnson MIA	1.00	2.50
73 Jeff Gordon MIA	1.25	3.00
74 Dale Earnhardt Jr. MIA	1.25	3.00
75 Tony Stewart MIA	.75	2.00
76 Mark Martin MIA	.75	2.00
77 Dale Jarrett MIA	.60	1.50
78 Carl Edwards MIA	1.00	2.50
79 Kasey Kahne MIA	1.25	3.00
80 Ryan Newman MIA	.75	2.00
81 Bobby Labonte MIA	.60	1.50
82 Matt Kenseth NN	1.00	2.50
83 Jimmie Johnson NN	1.00	2.50
84 Greg Biffle NN	.40	1.00
85 Dale Earnhardt Jr. NN	1.25	3.00
86 Mark Martin NN	.75	2.00
87 Kasey Kahne NN	1.25	3.00
88 Tony Stewart NN	.75	2.00
89 Kevin Harvick NN	.75	2.00
90 Clint Bowyer RT AU CRC	25.00	60.00
91 Denny Hamlin RT AU CRC	40.00	80.00
92 Reed Sorenson RT AU CRC	15.00	40.00
93 David Stremme RT AU CRC	12.50	30.00
94 Martin Truex Jr. RT AU CRC	15.00	40.00
95 J.J. Yeley RT AU CRC	12.50	30.00
CL Jeff Gordon CL	1.25	3.00

2006 Wheels American Thunder American Muscle

This 9-card set was randomly inserted in packs at a rate of 1 in 10. The feature foil etched cards of NASCAR's leading drivers. The cards carried an "AM" prefix for their card numbers.

COMPLETE SET (9)	12.50	30.00
AM1 Mark Martin	1.50	4.00
AM2 Jeff Gordon	2.50	6.00
AM3 Tony Stewart	1.50	4.00
AM4 Dale Jarrett	1.25	3.00
AM5 Martin Truex Jr.	1.50	4.00
AM6 Jeff Burton	.60	1.50
AM7 Dale Earnhardt Jr.	2.50	6.00
AM8 Terry Labonte	1.00	2.50
AM9 Jimmie Johnson	2.00	5.00

2006 Wheels American Thunder American Racing Idol

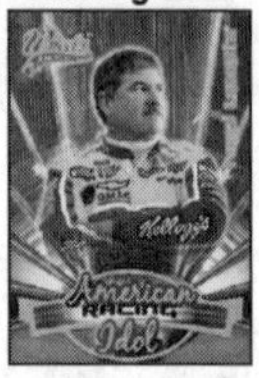

This 12-card set was randomly inserted in packs at a rate of 1 in 6. The feature foil etched cards of NASCAR's leading drivers. The cards carried an "RI" prefix for their card numbers.

COMPLETE SET (12)	15.00	40.00
RI1 Jimmie Johnson	2.50	6.00
RI2 Terry Labonte	1.25	3.00
RI3 Dale Earnhardt Jr.	3.00	8.00
RI4 Jeff Burton	.75	2.00
RI5 Mark Martin	2.00	5.00
RI6 Jeff Gordon	3.00	8.00
RI7 Kasey Kahne	3.00	8.00
RI8 Kevin Harvick	2.00	5.00
RI9 Dale Jarrett	1.50	4.00
RI10 Tony Stewart	2.00	5.00
RI11 Matt Kenseth	2.50	6.00
RI12 Martin Truex Jr.	2.00	5.00

2006 Wheels American Thunder American Racing Idol Golden

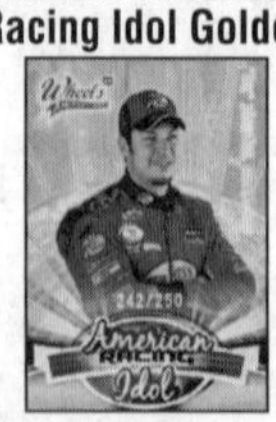

This 12-card set is a parallel to the basic American Racing Idol set. These cards were serial numbered to 250 and carried an "RI" prefix for their card numbers.

*GOLDEN: 1.2X TO 3X BASE

2006 Wheels American Thunder Cool Threads

This 15-card set was randomly inserted in packs. They feature swatches of shirts worn by drivers during races. The cards carried a "CT" prefix for their card numbers and were serial numbered to 329.

CT1 Reed Sorenson	8.00	20.00
CT2 Scott Riggs	6.00	15.00
CT3 Martin Truex Jr.	10.00	25.00
CT4 Dale Earnhardt Jr.	15.00	40.00
CT5 Casey Mears	6.00	15.00
CT6 Kurt Busch	12.50	30.00
CT7 Jeff Gordon	15.00	40.00
CT8 Kasey Kahne	12.50	30.00
CT9 David Stremme	6.00	15.00
CT10 Ryan Newman	8.00	20.00
CT11 Jeremy Mayfield	6.00	15.00
CT12 Kevin Harvick	10.00	25.00
CT13 Mark Martin	10.00	25.00
CT14 Matt Kenseth	10.00	25.00
CT15 Dale Jarrett	10.00	25.00

2006 Wheels American Thunder Double Hat

This 27-card set features two swatches of hats that were worn during Daytona Speedweeks. The cards are serial numbered to 99.

DH1 Greg Biffle	15.00	40.00
DH2 Clint Bowyer	12.50	30.00
DH3 Jeff Burton	12.50	30.00
DH4 Kurt Busch	12.50	30.00
DH5 Dale Earnhardt Jr.	40.00	100.00
DH6 Carl Edwards	20.00	50.00
DH7 Jeff Gordon	40.00	100.00
DH8 Denny Hamlin	20.00	50.00
DH9 Kevin Harvick	15.00	40.00
DH10 Dale Jarrett	15.00	40.00
DH11 Jimmie Johnson	25.00	60.00
DH12 Kasey Kahne	25.00	60.00
DH13 Matt Kenseth	20.00	50.00
DH14 Mark Martin	20.00	50.00
DH15 Jeremy Mayfield	8.00	20.00
DH16 Jamie McMurray	10.00	25.00
DH17 Casey Mears	8.00	20.00
DH18 Ryan Newman	10.00	25.00
DH19 Tony Raines	8.00	25.00
DH20 Scott Riggs	8.00	20.00
DH21 Elliott Sadler	15.00	40.00
DH22 Reed Sorenson	10.00	25.00
DH23 Tony Stewart	25.00	60.00
DH24 David Stremme	8.00	20.00
DH25 Martin Truex Jr.	8.00	20.00
DH26 Brian Vickers	12.50	30.00
DH27 J.J. Yeley	10.00	25.00

2006 Wheels American Thunder Grandstand

This 27-card set was designed to look like a ticket stub and was about 2 1/2" by 3". They were inserted into packs at a rate of 1 in 2. These cards carried a "GS" prefix for their card numbers.

COMPLETE SET (27)	10.00	25.00
GS1 Jeff Burton	.50	1.25
GS2 Kurt Busch	.75	2.00
GS3 Kyle Busch	1.00	2.50
GS4 Dale Earnhardt Jr.	2.00	5.00
GS5 Carl Edwards	1.50	4.00
GS6 Jeff Gordon	2.00	5.00
GS7 Denny Hamlin	2.00	5.00
GS8 Kevin Harvick	1.25	3.00
GS9 Dale Jarrett	1.00	2.50
GS10 Jimmie Johnson	1.50	4.00
GS11 Kasey Kahne	2.00	5.00
GS12 Matt Kenseth	1.50	4.00
GS13 Terry Labonte	.75	2.00
GS14 Bobby Labonte	1.00	2.50
GS15 Sterling Marlin	.75	2.00
GS16 Mark Martin	1.25	3.00
GS17 Casey Mears	.50	1.25
GS18 Jamie McMurray	.75	2.00
GS19 Ryan Newman	1.25	3.00
GS20 Scott Riggs	.50	1.25
GS21 Tony Stewart	1.25	3.00
GS22 Martin Truex Jr.	1.25	3.00
GS23 David Green	.30	.75
GS24 Burney Lamar	1.25	3.00
GS25 Rick Crawford	.30	.75
GS26 Ron Hornaday	.30	.75
GS27 Bill Lester CL	.50	1.25

2006 Wheels American Thunder Head to Toe

This 15-card set featured swatches of race-used hats and shoes. Each card was serial numbered to 99, unless noted in the checklist below and carried an "HT" prefix for its card number.

HT1 Scott Riggs	6.00	15.00
HT2 Ryan Newman	12.50	30.00
HT3 David Stremme	8.00	20.00
HT4 Tony Stewart	20.00	50.00
HT5 Reed Sorenson	10.00	25.00
HT6 Jeremy Mayfield	6.00	15.00
HT7 Martin Truex Jr.	10.00	25.00
HT8 Casey Mears	6.00	15.00
HT9 Dale Earnhardt Jr.	50.00	100.00
HT10 Kevin Harvick	15.00	40.00
HT11 Matt Kenseth	25.00	60.00
HT12 Jimmie Johnson/35	75.00	125.00
HT13 Mark Martin	25.00	60.00
HT14 Jeff Gordon	50.00	100.00
HT15 Carl Edwards	20.00	50.00

2006 Wheels American Thunder Pushin' Pedal

Randomly inserted in packs, these 15 cards featured swatches of race-used shoes. The cards were serial numbered to 199 unless noted in the checklist below..

PP1 Dale Earnhardt Jr.	25.00	60.00
PP2 Scott Riggs	6.00	15.00
PP3 David Stremme	8.00	20.00
PP4 Tony Stewart	15.00	40.00
PP5 Ryan Newman	10.00	25.00
PP6 Casey Mears	8.00	20.00
PP7 Kevin Harvick	15.00	40.00
PP8 Reed Sorenson	10.00	25.00
PP9 Jeremy Mayfield	6.00	15.00
PP10 Martin Truex Jr.	10.00	25.00
PP11 Mark Martin	12.50	30.00
PP12 Carl Edwards	15.00	40.00
PP13 Jeff Gordon	25.00	60.00
PP14 Jimmie Johnson/35	60.00	120.00
PP15 Bobby Labonte	8.00	20.00

2006 Wheels American Thunder Single Hat

This 8-card set features a swatch of hat that was worn during Daytona Speedweeks. The cards are serial numbered to 99.

SH1 Dave Blaney	6.00	15.00
SH2 Jeff Green	6.00	15.00
SH3 Bobby Labonte	10.00	25.00
SH4 Terry Labonte	10.00	25.00
SH5 Sterling Marlin	12.50	30.00
SH6 Joe Nemechek	6.00	15.00
SH7 Kyle Petty	8.00	20.00
SH8 Ken Schrader	10.00	25.00

2006 Wheels American Thunder Thunder Road

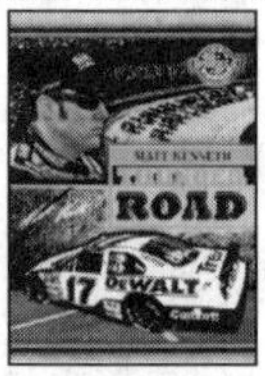

This 18-card set featured race-used tires incorporated into the card design. They were inserted in packs at a rate of one in 18. Each card carried a "TR" prefix in its card numbers.

TR1 Jamie McMurray	3.00	8.00
TR2 Dale Earnhardt Jr.	8.00	20.00
TR3 Bobby Labonte	4.00	10.00
TR4 Jimmie Johnson	6.00	15.00
TR5 Kevin Harvick	5.00	12.00
TR6 Tony Stewart	5.00	12.00
TR7 Martin Truex Jr.	5.00	12.00
TR8 Sterling Marlin	3.00	8.00
TR9 Dale Jarrett	4.00	10.00
TR10 Jeff Gordon	8.00	20.00
TR11 Mark Martin	5.00	12.00
TR12 Terry Labonte	3.00	8.00
TR13 Scott Riggs	2.00	5.00
TR14 Kasey Kahne	8.00	20.00
TR15 Jeff Burton	2.00	5.00
TR16 Kurt Busch	3.00	8.00
TR17 Matt Kenseth	6.00	15.00
TR18 Carl Edwards	6.00	15.00

2006 Wheels American Thunder Thunder Strokes

This 13-card set was inserted into packs of Wheels American Thunder. Each card was serial numbered to 100 copies. These autographed cards were certified authentic by the manufacturer and was stated on the card backs.

1 Clint Bowyer	20.00	50.00
2 Kurt Busch	12.50	30.00
3 Dale Earnhardt Jr.	75.00	150.00
4 Bobby Labonte	20.00	50.00
5 Sterling Marlin	15.00	40.00
6 Mark Martin	30.00	80.00
7 Casey Mears	12.50	30.00
8 Scott Riggs	12.50	30.00
9 Reed Sorenson	15.00	40.00
10 David Stremme	12.50	30.00
11 Martin Truex Jr./400	15.00	40.00
12 Danny O'Quinn	15.00	40.00
13 Erin Crocker	30.00	60.00

2007 Wheels American Thunder

COMPLETE SET (90)		
COMP.SET w/o SPs (83)	12.50	30.00
COMMON DRIVERS	.25	.60
SEMISTARS	.40	1.00
UNLISTED STARS	.60	1.50
RT AU INSCRIPTIONS 50 SERIAL #'d SETS		
UNLESS NOTED BELOW		
WAX BOX HOBBY	60.00	120.00
WAX BOX RETAIL	50.00	100.00
1 Jeff Gordon CL	1.50	4.00
2 Greg Biffle	.50	1.25
3 Jeff Burton	.40	1.00
4 Clint Bowyer	1.25	3.00
5 Kurt Busch	.40	1.00
6 Kyle Busch	.75	2.00
7 Dale Earnhardt Jr.	1.50	4.00
8 Carl Edwards	1.00	2.50
9 Jeff Gordon	1.50	4.00
10 Jeff Green	.25	.60
11 Denny Hamlin	1.25	3.00
12 Kevin Harvick	1.00	2.50
13 Dale Jarrett	.75	2.00
14 Jimmie Johnson	1.25	3.00
15 Kasey Kahne	1.50	4.00
16 Matt Kenseth	1.25	3.00
17 Bobby Labonte	.75	2.00
18 Sterling Marlin	.60	1.50
19 Mark Martin	1.00	2.50
20 Jamie McMurray	.60	1.50
21 Casey Mears	.40	1.00
22 Joe Nemechek	.25	.60
23 Ryan Newman	.75	2.00
24 Kyle Petty	.40	1.00
25 Tony Raines	.25	.60
26 Scott Riggs	.40	1.00
27 Ricky Rudd	.60	1.50
28 Elliott Sadler	.40	1.00
29 Johnny Sauter	.40	1.00
30 Ken Schrader	.25	.60
31 Reed Sorenson	.75	2.00
32 David Stremme	.75	2.00
33 Tony Stewart	1.00	2.50
34 Martin Truex Jr.	1.00	2.50
35 Brian Vickers	.60	1.50
36 Michael Waltrip	.40	1.00
37 Mark Martin's Car DT	.40	1.00
38 Martin Truex Jr.'s Car DT	.40	1.00
39 Dale Earnhardt Jr.'s Car DT	.60	1.50
40 Ryan Newman's Car DT	.30	.75
41 Sterling Marlin's Car DT	.25	.60
42 Greg Biffle's Car DT	.20	.50
43 Matt Kenseth's Car DT	.50	1.25
44 Tony Stewart's Car DT	.40	1.00
45 Jeff Gordon's Car DT	.60	1.50
46 Jamie McMurray's Car DT	.25	.60
47 Jeff Burton's Car DT	.15	.40
48 Jimmie Johnson's Car DT	.50	1.25
49 Carl Edwards' Car HR	.40	1.00
50 Jeff Gordon's Car HR	.60	1.50
51 Martin Truex Jr.'s Car HR	.40	1.00
52 Tony Stewart's Car HR	.40	1.00
53 Kevin Harvick's Car HR	.40	1.00
54 Jimmie Johnson's Car HR	.50	1.25
55 Ricky Rudd's Car HR	.25	.60
56 Denny Hamlin's Car HR	.50	1.25
57 Dale Earnhardt Jr.'s Car HR	.60	1.50
58 Brian Vickers' Car HR	.25	.60
59 Bobby Labonte's Car HR	.30	.75
60 Jeff Gordon RW	1.50	4.00
61 Tony Stewart RW	1.00	2.50
62 Ryan Newman RW	.75	2.00
63 Ricky Rudd RW	.60	1.50
64 Carl Edwards RW	1.00	2.50
65 Elliott Sadler RW	.40	1.00
66 Kevin Harvick RW	1.00	2.50
67 Greg Biffle BP	.50	1.25
68 Tony Stewart BP	1.00	2.50
69 Michael Waltrip BP	.40	1.00
70 Jeff Gordon BP	1.50	4.00
71 Jeff Burton BP	.40	1.00
72 Jamie McMurray BP	.60	1.50
73 Sterling Marlin HC	.60	1.50
74 Tony Stewart HC	1.00	2.50
75 Reed Sorenson HC	.75	2.00
76 Jeff Gordon HC	1.50	4.00
77 Kurt Busch HC	.40	1.00
78 J.J. Yeley HC	.50	1.25
79 Bobby Labonte HC	.75	2.00
80 Dale Earnhardt Jr. HC	1.50	4.00
81 Jeff Burton HC	.40	1.00
82 Ricky Rudd HC	.60	1.50
83 Kyle Busch HC	.75	2.00
84 A.J. Allmendinger RT AU/345 RC	20.00	40.00
84B A.J. Allmendinger RT AU/50 Dinger	25.00	50.00
85 David Gilliland RT AU RC EXCH	25.00	50.00
86 Paul Menard RT AU/365 CRC	15.00	30.00
86B Paul Menard RT AU/1 #01		
87 Juan Pablo Montoya RT AU/300 RC	40.00	80.00
87B Juan Pablo Montoya RT AU/50 JPM	60.00	120.00
88 David Ragan RT AU/305 CRC	15.00	30.00
89 David Reutimann RT AU/310 RC	15.00	30.00
89B David Reutimann RT AU/50 Bea K	20.00	40.00
90 Regan Smith RT AU/310 CRC	12.50	30.00
90B Regan Smith RT AU/50 Army Strong	25.00	50.00

2007 Wheels American Thunder Previews

(EB1-EB36) STATED PRINT RUN 5 SERIAL #'d SETS
(EB49-EB59) STATED PRINT RUN 1 SERIAL #'d SET
NOT PRICED DUE TO SCARCITY

2007 Wheels American Thunder American Dreams

COMPLETE SET (12)	15.00	4
COMMON DRIVERS	.40	
SEMISTARS	.60	
UNLISTED STARS	1.00	
STATED ODDS 1:6		
AD1 Kevin Harvick	1.50	
AD2 Matt Kenseth	2.00	
AD3 Jimmie Johnson	2.00	
AD4 Kyle Busch	1.25	
AD5 Jeff Burton	.60	
AD6 Jeff Gordon	2.50	
AD7 Casey Mears	.60	
AD8 Martin Truex Jr.	1.50	
AD9 Carl Edwards	1.50	
AD10 Dale Earnhardt Jr.	2.50	
AD11 Juan Pablo Montoya	2.50	
AD12 Tony Stewart	1.50	

2007 Wheels America Thunder American Dreams Gold

COMPLETE SET (12)	40.00	10
*GOLD: 1.5X TO 4X BASIC		
STATED PRINT RUN 250 SERIAL #'d SETS		

2007 Wheels America Thunder American Muscle

COMPLETE SET (9)	12.50	3
COMMON DRIVERS	.40	
SEMISTARS	.60	
UNLISTED STARS	1.00	
STATED ODDS 1:10		
AM1 Mark Martin	1.50	
AM2 Tony Stewart	1.50	
AM3 Matt Kenseth	2.00	
AM4 Jimmie Johnson	2.00	
AM5 Kyle Busch	1.25	
AM6 Martin Truex Jr.	1.50	
AM7 Kevin Harvick	1.50	
AM8 Ricky Rudd	1.00	
AM9 Jeff Gordon	2.50	

2007 Wheels America Thunder Cool Thread

OVERALL R-U ODDS 1:10		
STATED PRINT RUN 299 SERIAL #'d SETS		
CT1 A.J. Allmendinger	6.00	1
CT2 Michael Waltrip	6.00	1
CT3 Mark Martin	8.00	2
CT4 Brian Vickers	6.00	1
CT5 Dale Jarrett	12.50	3
CT6 Dale Earnhardt Jr.	15.00	4
CT7 Martin Truex Jr.	6.00	1
CT8 Casey Mears	6.00	1
CT9 Ryan Newman	8.00	2
CT10 Carl Edwards	10.00	2
CT11 Reed Sorenson	6.00	1
CT12 Kurt Busch	6.00	1
CT13 Jeff Gordon	15.00	4
CT14 Juan Pablo Montoya	10.00	2
CT15 Matt Kenseth	10.00	2
CT16 Jimmie Johnson	10.00	2

2007 Wheels America Thunder Double Hat

OVERALL R-U ODDS 1:10		
STATED PRINT RUN 99 SERIAL #'d SETS		
DH1 Tony Raines	6.00	1
DH2 Ricky Rudd	12.50	3
DH3 Regan Smith	8.00	2
DH4 Brian Vickers	6.00	1
DH5 Jamie McMurray	6.00	1
DH6 Jeff Burton	8.00	2
DH7 Tony Stewart	12.50	3

2007 Wheels America Thunder Head to Toe

OVERALL R-U ODDS 1:10		
STATED PRINT RUN 99 SERIAL #'d SETS		
HT1 Michael Waltrip	10.00	2
HT2 Tony Stewart	20.00	5
HT3 Martin Truex Jr.	15.00	4
HT4 Kasey Kahne	20.00	5
HT5 Dale Earnhardt Jr.	25.00	6
HT6 Dale Jarrett	15.00	4

7 David Ragan 10.00 25.00
8 Elliott Sadler 12.50 30.00
9 J.J. Yeley 10.00 25.00
10 Paul Menard 12.50 30.00
11 Scott Riggs 10.00 25.00
12 David Stremme 10.00 25.00
13 Matt Kenseth 15.00 40.00
14 Jeff Gordon 25.00 60.00

2007 Wheels American Thunder Pushin' Pedal

VERALL R-U ODDS 1:10
ATED PRINT RUN 99 SERIAL #'d SETS
1 Dale Earnhardt Jr. 20.00 50.00
2 Tony Stewart 15.00 40.00
3 Dale Jarrett 15.00 40.00
4 Denny Hamlin 12.50 30.00
5 Michael Waltrip 10.00 25.00
6 Jamie McMurray 8.00 20.00
7 J.J. Yeley 8.00 20.00
8 Carl Edwards 12.50 30.00
9 Martin Truex Jr. 10.00 25.00
10 Regan Smith 8.00 20.00
11 David Reutimann 10.00 25.00
12 Bobby Labonte 10.00 25.00
13 Juan Pablo Montoya 12.50 30.00
14 Jimmie Johnson 15.00 40.00
15 Reed Sorenson 10.00 25.00
16 Jeff Gordon 20.00 50.00

2007 Wheels American Thunder Single Hat

VERALL R-U ODDS 1:10
ATED PRINT RUN 99 SERIAL #'d SETS
1 A.J. Allmendinger 10.00 25.00
2 Joe Nemechek 6.00 15.00

2007 Wheels American Thunder Starting Grid

ATED ODDS 1:2
1 Jeff Burton .40 1.00
2 Dale Earnhardt Jr. 1.50 4.00
3 Jeff Gordon 1.50 4.00
4 Dale Jarrett .75 2.00
5 Jimmie Johnson 1.25 3.00
6 Sterling Marlin .60 1.50
7 Jamie McMurray .60 1.50
8 Martin Truex Jr. 1.00 2.50
9 Brian Vickers .60 1.50
10 Michael Waltrip .40 1.00
11 Mark Martin 1.00 2.50
12 Cale Gale .60 1.50
13 Todd Kluever .75 2.00
14 Scott Wimmer .40 1.00
15 T.J. Bell .60 1.50
16 Kelly Bires .60 1.50
17 Todd Bodine .25 .60
18 Joey Clanton .60 1.50
19 Rick Crawford .25 .60
20 Erik Darnell .60 1.50
21 Ron Hornaday .25 .60
22 Kraig Kinser .60 1.50
23 Travis Kvapil .40 1.00
24 Mike Skinner .25 .60
25 Jack Sprague .25 .60

2007 Wheels American Thunder Thunder Road

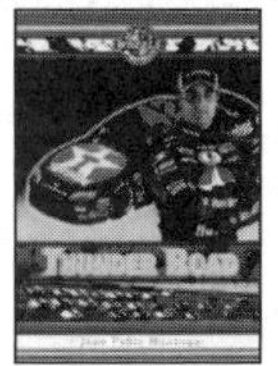

ATED ODDS 1:18
1 Jimmie Johnson 6.00 15.00
2 Michael Waltrip 4.00 10.00
3 Martin Truex Jr. 4.00 10.00
4 Jamie McMurray 4.00 10.00
5 Ryan Newman 4.00 10.00
6 Dale Jarrett 4.00 10.00
7 Jeff Gordon 8.00 20.00
8 Kevin Harvick 5.00 12.00
9 Bobby Labonte 4.00 10.00
10 Dale Earnhardt Jr. 8.00 20.00
11 Denny Hamlin 5.00 12.00
12 Jeff Burton 4.00 10.00
13 Brian Vickers 4.00 10.00
14 Matt Kenseth 6.00 15.00
15 Kasey Kahne 6.00 15.00
16 Sterling Marlin 4.00 10.00
17 Tony Stewart 6.00 15.00
18 Juan Pablo Montoya 8.00 20.00

2007 Wheels American Thunder Thunder Strokes

ATED ODDS 1:20
Aric Almirola 8.00 20.00
Marcos Ambrose 15.00 40.00
Greg Biffle 8.00 20.00
Dave Blaney 8.00 20.00
Todd Bodine 8.00 20.00
Clint Bowyer 25.00 50.00
Kurt Busch 12.50 30.00

8 Kyle Busch 15.00 40.00
9 Rick Crawford 6.00 15.00
10 Erik Darnell 6.00 15.00
11 Kertus Davis 8.00 20.00
12 Dale Earnhardt Jr. 75.00 150.00
13 Carl Edwards 25.00 50.00
14 Jeff Gordon 100.00 200.00
15 Jeff Green 6.00 15.00
16 David Gilliland 12.50 30.00
17 Denny Hamlin 30.00 60.00
18 Kevin Harvick 15.00 40.00
19 Sam Hornish Jr. 15.00 40.00
20 Dale Jarrett 15.00 40.00
21 Jimmie Johnson 30.00 60.00
22 Matt Kenseth 25.00 60.00
23 Todd Kluever 8.00 20.00
24 Travis Kvapil 6.00 15.00
25 Bobby Labonte 15.00 40.00
26 Stephen Leicht 10.00 25.00
27 Sterling Marlin
28 Mark Martin 30.00 60.00
29 Casey Mears 10.00 25.00
30 Joe Nemechek 8.00 20.00
31 Ryan Newman 10.00 25.00
32 Timothy Peters 6.00 15.00
33 Tony Raines 6.00 15.00
34 Johnny Sauter 8.00 20.00
35 Ken Schrader 8.00 20.00
36 Reed Sorenson 10.00 25.00
37 Tony Stewart 30.00 60.00
38 David Stremme 10.00 25.00
39 Martin Truex Jr. 15.00 40.00
40 Brian Vickers 10.00 25.00
41 Steve Wallace 10.00 25.00
42 Michael Waltrip 12.50 30.00
43 Jon Wood 6.00 15.00
44 J.J. Yeley 10.00 25.00

2007 Wheels American Thunder Thunder Strokes Press Plates Black

STATED PRINT RUN 1 SERIAL #'d SET
NOT PRICED DUE TO SCARCITY

2007 Wheels American Thunder Thunder Strokes Press Plates Cyan

STATED PRINT RUN 1 SERIAL #'d SET
NOT PRICED DUE TO SCARCITY

2007 Wheels American Thunder Thunder Strokes Press Plates Magenta

STATED PRINT RUN 1 SERIAL #'d SET
NOT PRICED DUE TO SCARCITY

2007 Wheels American Thunder Thunder Strokes Press Plates Yellow

STATED PRINT RUN 1 SERIAL #'d SET
NOT PRICED DUE TO SCARCITY

2007 Wheels American Thunder Triple Hat

OVERALL R-U ODDS 1:10
STATED PRINT RUN 99 SERIAL #'d SETS
TH1 Greg Biffle 10.00 25.00
TH2 Dave Blaney 8.00 20.00
TH3 Clint Bowyer 20.00 40.00
TH4 Kurt Busch 10.00 25.00
TH5 Kyle Busch 20.00 40.00
TH6 Dale Earnhardt Jr. 40.00 80.00
TH7 Carl Edwards 20.00 40.00
TH8 Jeff Gordon 40.00 80.00
TH9 David Gilliland 30.00 60.00
TH10 Denny Hamlin 20.00 40.00
TH11 Kevin Harvick 30.00 60.00
TH12 Dale Jarrett 15.00 40.00
TH13 Jimmie Johnson 30.00 60.00
TH14 Kasey Kahne 30.00 60.00
TH15 Matt Kenseth 15.00 40.00
TH16 Bobby Labonte 15.00 40.00
TH17 Mark Martin 25.00 50.00
TH18 Casey Mears 10.00 25.00
TH19 Paul Menard 10.00 25.00
TH20 Juan Pablo Montoya 15.00 40.00
TH21 Ryan Newman 10.00 25.00
TH22 Kyle Petty 10.00 25.00
TH23 David Ragan 8.00 20.00
TH24 David Reutimann 15.00 40.00
TH25 Scott Riggs 8.00 20.00
TH26 Elliott Sadler 12.50 30.00
TH27 Ken Schrader 10.00 25.00
TH28 Reed Sorenson 10.00 25.00
TH29 David Stremme 10.00 25.00
TH30 Martin Truex Jr. 12.50 30.00
TH31 Michael Waltrip 12.50 30.00
TH32 J.J. Yeley 10.00 25.00

1994 Wheels High Gear

This 200-card set was issued in two 100-card series. The cards are printed on 24-pt paper stock, and use UV coating and silver foil stamping. The set features top Winston Cup and Busch Grand National drivers along with crew chiefs, owner, and mechanics. There are five topical subsets; Awards (70-74), Winners (75-87), Busch Clash (88-99), Earnhardt Family (179-186), Winners (187-200). There were 3,000 numbered cases of the first series and 1,000 numbered cases of the second series. Cards came packaged six cards per pack; 24 packs per box and 24 boxes per case. In series one High Gear boxes there was a possibility of pulling a Jeff Gordon Busch Clash signature card. There were 1,500 of these cards and each was individually numbered of 1,500 on the back in black pen. They were randomly inserted in packs of series one at a rate of 1:1152 packs. In series two boxes and boxes of High Gear Day One, there was a Mark Martin "Feel the Heat" autographed card. There were 1,000 of these cards, inserted in packs at a rate of one per 1152 packs.

COMPLETE SET (200) 20.00 50.00
COMP.SERIES 1 (100) 6.00 15.00
COMP.SERIES 2 (100) 15.00 40.00
WAX BOX SERIES 2 40.00 80.00
1 Dale Earnhardt 1.25 3.00
2 Rusty Wallace .60 1.50
3 Mark Martin .60 1.50
4 Ken Schrader .07 .20
5 Ernie Irvan .15 .40
6 Geoff Bodine .07 .20
7 Harry Gant .15 .40
8 Ricky Rudd .25 .60
9 Sterling Marlin .25 .60
10 Rick Mast .07 .20
11 Michael Waltrip .15 .40
12 Terry Labonte .25 .60
13 Bobby Labonte .50 1.25
14 Dick Trickle .07 .20
15 Rick Wilson .07 .20
16 Kenny Wallace .07 .20
17 Hut Stricklin .07 .20
18 Wally Dallenbach, Jr. .07 .20
19 Jimmy Hensley .07 .20
20 Ted Musgrave .07 .20
21 Bobby Hillin .07 .20
22 Dave Marcis .15 .40
23 Derrike Cope .07 .20
24 Neil Bonnett .25 .60
25 Lake Speed .07 .20
26 Robert Yates .02 .10
27 Leo Jackson .02 .10
28 Richard Petty .25 .60
29 Junior Johnson .07 .20
30 Rick Hendrick .02 .10
31 Bobby Allison .07 .20
32 Felix Sabates .02 .10
33 Richard Childress .15 .40
34 Bill Davis .07 .20
35 Cale Yarborough .07 .20
36 Jack Roush .02 .10
37 Chuck Rider .02 .10
38 Andy Petree .02 .10
39 Buddy Parrott .02 .10
40 Jimmy Makar .02 .10
41 Mike Hill .02 .10
42 Mike Beam .02 .10
43 Charley Pressley .02 .10
44 Ray Evernham .02 .10
45 Larry McReynolds .02 .10
46 Steve Hmiel .02 .10
47 Ricky Craven .07 .20
48 David Green .07 .20
49 Bobby Dotter .07 .20
50 Robert Pressley .07 .20
51 Joe Bessey .07 .20
52 Tim Fedewa .07 .20
53 Mike McLaughlin .07 .20
54 Roy Payne .07 .20
55 Larry Pearson .07 .20
56 Mike Wallace .07 .20
57 Tracy Leslie .07 .20
58 Tom Peck .07 .20
59 Hermie Sadler .07 .20
60 Chuck Bown .07 .20
61 Todd Bodine .07 .20
62 Shawna Robinson .30 .75
63 Randy LaJoie .07 .20
64 Ward Burton .15 .40
65 Jeff Burton .25 .60
66 Joe Nemechek .07 .20
67 Steve Grissom .07 .20
68 Harry Gant .15 .40
69 Tommy Houston .07 .20
70 Rusty Wallace's Pit Crew .15 .40
71 Rusty Wallace .30 .75
Driver of the Year
72 Steve Grissom .02 .10
BGN Champion
73 Jeff Gordon .75 2.00
Winston Cup Rookie of the Year
74 Hermie Sadler .07 .20
BGN Rookie of the Year
75 Dale Jarrett WIN .15 .40
76 Rusty Wallace WIN .25 .60
77 Davey Allison WIN .15 .40
78 Morgan Shepherd WIN .02 .10
79 Dale Earnhardt WIN .60 1.50
80 Rusty Wallace WIN .25 .60
81 Rusty Wallace WIN .25 .60
82 Rusty Wallace WIN .25 .60
83 Ernie Irvan WIN .07 .20
84 Geoff Bodine WIN .02 .10
85 Dale Earnhardt BB WIN .60 1.50
86 Kyle Petty WIN .07 .20
87 Ricky Rudd WIN .15 .40
88 Kyle Petty BC .07 .20
89 Mark Martin BC .30 .75
90 Ken Schrader BC .02 .10
91 Rusty Wallace BC .30 .75
92 Dale Earnhardt BC .60 1.50
93 Brett Bodine BC .02 .10
94 Geoff Bodine BC .02 .10
95 Ernie Irvan BC .07 .20
96 Bobby Labonte BC .15 .40
97 Jeff Gordon BC .40 1.00
98 Harry Gant BC .07 .20
99 P.J. Jones BC .02 .10
100 Davey Allison's Car .40 1.00
Alan Kulwicki's Car
101 Jeff Gordon .75 2.00
102 Todd Bodine .07 .20
103 Wally Dallenbach Jr. .07 .20
104 Sterling Marlin .25 .60
105 Terry Labonte .25 .60
106 Mark Martin .60 1.50
107 Geoff Bodine .07 .20
108 Jeff Burton .25 .60
109 Ward Burton .15 .40
110 Mike Wallace .07 .20
111 Derrike Cope .07 .20
112 Chuck Bown .07 .20
113 Robert Pressley .07 .20
114 John Andretti RC .07 .20
115 Lake Speed .07 .20
116 Ted Musgrave .07 .20
117 Darrell Waltrip .15 .40
118 Dale Jarrett .50 1.25
119 Loy Allen Jr. .07 .20
120 Bobby Hamilton .07 .20
121 Morgan Shepherd .07 .20
122 Kyle Petty .15 .40
123 Hut Stricklin .07 .20
124 Joe Nemechek .07 .20
125 Jimmy Hensley .07 .20
126 Brett Bodine .07 .20
127 Jimmy Spencer .07 .20
128 Ernie Irvan .15 .40
129 Steve Grissom .07 .20
130 Greg Sacks .07 .20
131 Tony Glover .02 .10
132 Barry Dodson .02 .10
133 Pete Wright .02 .10
134 Chris Hussey .02 .10
135 Gary DeHart .02 .10
136 Doug Hewitt .02 .10
137 Paul Andrews .02 .10
138 Bill Ingle .02 .10
139 Jimmy Fennig .02 .10
140 Jeff Hammond .02 .10
141 Donnie Richeson .02 .10
142 Leonard Wood .02 .10
143 Robbie Loomis .02 .10
144 Larry Hedrick .02 .10
145 Billy Hagan .02 .10
146 Travis Carter .02 .10
147 Roger Penske .02 .10
148 Richard Jackson .02 .10
149 Larry McClure .02 .10
150 Bill Stavola .02 .10
151 Mickey Stavola .02 .10
152 Eddie Wood .02 .10
153 Glen Wood .02 .10
154 Len Wood .02 .10
155 Ricky Rudd .25 .60
156 Butch Mock .02 .10
157 D.K. Ulrich .02 .10
158 Joe Gibbs .15 .40
159 Don Miller .02 .10
160 Eddie Masencup .02 .10
161 Mike Colyer .02 .10
162 Hank Jones .02 .10
163 Harry Gant .15 .40
164 Kenny Wallace .07 .20
165 Terry Labonte .25 .60
166 Morgan Shepherd .07 .20
167 Chad Little .07 .20
168 Ernie Irvan .15 .40
169 Shawna Robinson .30 .75
170 Mike McLaughlin .07 .20
171 Elton Sawyer .07 .20
172 Dirk Stephens .02 .10
173 Ken Schrader .07 .20
174 Dennis Setzer .07 .20
175 Mark Martin .60 1.50
176 Jim Bown .07 .20
177 Bobby Labonte .50 1.25
178 Ed Whitaker .02 .10
179 Tony Eury .25 .60
180 Kelley Earnhardt 5.00 12.00
Kerry Earnhardt
Dale Earnhardt Jr
181 Kelley Earnhardt RC 3.00 8.00
182 Kerry Earnhardt RC 3.00 8.00
183 Dale Earnhardt Jr. RC 15.00 30.00
184 Teresa Earnhardt .60 1.50
185 Don Hawk .02 .10
186 Dale Earnhardt WIN .60 1.50
187 Rusty Wallace WIN .25 .60
188 Dale Earnhardt BB WIN .60 1.50
189 Mark Martin WIN .25 .60
190 Mark Martin WIN .25 .60
191 Mark Martin WIN .25 .60
192 Mark Martin WIN .25 .60
193 Rusty Wallace WIN .25 .60
194 Rusty Wallace WIN .25 .60
195 Ernie Irvan WIN .07 .20
196 Rusty Wallace WIN .25 .60
197 Ernie Irvan WIN .07 .20
198 Rusty Wallace WIN .25 .60
199 Mark Martin WIN .25 .60
200 Rusty Wallace WIN .25 .60
MMS1 Mark Martin AUTO 15.00 40.00
Feel The Heat
NNO Jeff Gordon BC AUTO/1500 25.00 60.00

1994 Wheels High Gear Day One

This 100-card set is a parallel to the 1994 High Gear series two set. The cards were packaged separately in six card packs. There were 24 packs per box and 24 boxes per case. The cards that went into the first 500 cases of High Gear series two off the press were stamped with a silver foil "Day 1" logo to differentiate them from the regular series two cards.

COMPLETE SET (100) 20.00 50.00
*DAY ONES: .6X to 1.5X SER.2 BASIC CARDS

1994 Wheels High Gear Day One Gold

This 100-card set is a parallel to the base Day One set. The cards feature a gold foil stamped "Day 1" logo to differentiate them from the base Day One cards. The gold cards were randomly inserted in packs of Day One at a rate of one card per two packs.

COMPLETE SET (100) 50.00 125.00
*GOLD CARDS: 1.2X TO 3X BASIC DAY ONE

1994 Wheels High Gear Gold

This 200-card set was issued in two series and is a parallel to the base High Gear cards. The cards featured gold foil stamping and the word "GOLD" appears below the High Gear logo on the front. There were 20 cards in the first series that were produced in shorter quantity than the other 80 in that series. Due to a UV coating problem cards 1, 6, 11, 16, 25, 30, 35, 40, 41, 46, 51, 56, 61, 66, 71, 76, 81, 86, 91, 96 were produced in smaller quantities. The majority of these cards were produced in 15-35 percent less quantities. Cards 1, 6, 71, 81, and 91 were the shortest at 40-50 percent less quantites.

COMPLETE SET (200) 60.00 150.00
COMP.SERIES 1 SET (100) 20.00 50.00
COMP.SERIES 2 SET (100) 40.00 100.00
*GOLDS: 1.2X TO 3X BASE CARDS
*GOLD SPs 1/6/71/81/91: 2X TO 5X
183 Dale Earnhardt Jr. 25.00 50.00

1994 Wheels High Gear Dominators

This 7-card insert set features Jumbo size cards (4" by 6") of the top drivers in Winston Cup racing. The cards were distributed as box inserts in High Gear series one and two, along with High Gear Day One. Cards D1-D3 were available in series one boxes at a rate of one in six. Card D4 was available in High Gear Day One boxes at a rate of one in eight. Cards D5-D7 were available in series two boxes at a rate of one in six. There are 3,000 of each of the cards D1-D3, while there are 1,750 of the cards D4-D7.

COMPLETE SET (7) 60.00 120.00
COMP.SERIES 1 (3) 30.00 60.00
COMP.SERIES 2 (3) 30.00 60.00
D1 Mark Martin 6.00 15.00
D2 Rusty Wallace 6.00 15.00
D3 Dale Earnhardt 20.00 40.00
D4 Ernie Irvan 6.00 15.00
D5 Jeff Gordon 12.50 30.00
D6 Mark Martin 8.00 20.00
D7 Harry Gant 6.00 15.00

1994 Wheels High Gear Legends

This six-card insert set features some of the greatest names in racing history. The cards were issued in series one, series two and High Gear Day One boxes. Series one boxes offered cards LS1-LS3 at an average of one Legends card per box. Series two and High Gear Day One boxes offered cards LS4-LS6 at a rate of one per box (24 packs).

COMPLETE SET (6) 12.00 25.00
COMP.SERIES 1 (3) 5.00 10.00
COMP.SERIES 2 (3) 7.00 15.00
LS1 Cale Yarborough 2.00 4.00
LS2 David Pearson 2.00 4.00
LS3 Bobby Allison 2.00 4.00
LS4 Richard Petty 4.00 8.00
LS5 Benny Parsons 2.00 4.00
LS6 Ned Jarrett 2.00 4.00

1994 Wheels High Gear Mega Gold

This 12-card insert set features 12 of the best drivers in Winston Cup. Cards are on all gold board and could be found at a rate of one per 12 packs. There was also a special Dale Earnhardt 7-Time Champion card. This card is the same as the regular card except that the entire card is embossed and comes with a 7-Time Champion seal on the front. The sets were also sold on QVC. There were 3,900 sets offered, including the 7-time Dale Earnhardt card for $99. An uncut sheet of all 13 cards was available. There are two different versions of uncut sheets also. The common version is a blank back sheet. The more difficult versions has complete card backs.

COMPLETE SET (12) 25.00 60.00
MG1 Dale Earnhardt 10.00 25.00
MG1S Dale Earnhardt 15.00 40.00
7-Time Champ
MG2 Ernie Irvan 1.25 3.00
MG3 Rusty Wallace 5.00 12.00
MG4 Mark Martin 5.00 12.00
MG5 Jeff Gordon 6.00 15.00
MG6 Ken Schrader .60 1.50
MG7 Geoff Bodine .60 1.50
MG8 Ricky Rudd 2.00 5.00
MG9 Kyle Petty 1.25 3.00
MG10 Terry Labonte 2.00 5.00
MG11 Darrell Waltrip 1.25 3.00
MG12 Michael Waltrip 1.25 3.00

1994 Wheels High Gear Power Pak Teams

There are three individually boxed driver's team sets that are part of the Power Pak Teams: 21-card Dale Earnhardt, 34-card Harry Gant and 41-card Rusty Wallace sets. Each team set is individually boxed and features that driver and their team. There was also a gold parallel version of each of the sets. There were 800 cases produced. There were 36 sets in each case and the cases were packaged in the following ratios: 15 Dale Earnhardt sets, 10 Rusty Wallace sets, 5 Harry Gant sets, 3 Gold Dale Earnhardt sets, 2 Gold Rusty Wallace sets and 1 Gold Harry Gant set.

COMP.EARNHARDT SET (21) 8.00 20.00
COMP.GANT SET (34) 4.00 10.00
COMP.WALLACE SET (41) 5.00 12.00
COMP.GOLD EARNHARDT (21) 20.00 40.00
COMP.GOLD GANT (34) 10.00 20.00
COMP.GOLD WALLACE (41) 12.50 25.00
*GOLD CARDS: .8X TO 2X BASIC CARDS
E1 Richard Childress .30 .75
E2 Andy Petree .30 .75
E3 Dale Earnhardt 1.50 4.00
E4 Dale Earnhardt 1.50 4.00
Richard Childress
E5 Dale Earnhardt 1.50 4.00
Andy Petree
E6 David Smith .30 .75
E7 Danny Meyers .30 .75
E8 Danny Lawrence .30 .75
E9 Eddie Lanier .30 .75
E10 Jimmy Elledge .30 .75
E11 Joe Dan Bailey .30 .75
E12 Jim Baldwin .30 .75
E13 Craig Donley .30 .75
E14 John Mulloy .30 .75
E15 Gene Dehart .30 .75
E16 Jim Cook .30 .75
Hal Carter
E17 RCR Enterprises Office .30 .75
E18 Dale Earnhardt in Pits .30 .75
E19 Dale Earnhardt w/Crew 1.50 4.00
E20 Dale Earnhardt's Car .30 .75
E21 Dale Earnhardt's Car .30 .75
checklist card numbered CL
G1 Harry Gant .40 1.00
G2 Leo Jackson .25 .60
G3 Charley Pressley .25 .60
G4 Billy Abernathy .25 .60
G5 Ricky Viers .25 .60
G6 David Rogers .25 .60
G7 Jimmy Penland .25 .60
G8 Allen Hester .25 .60
G9 Jay Guy .25 .60
G10 Ellis Frazier .25 .60
G11 Hoss Berry .25 .60
G12 Eddie Masencup .25 .60
G13 Shaun Woods .25 .60

G14 Renee Forrest .25 .60
G15 Phil Banks .25 .60
G16 Joe Schmaling .25 .60
G17 Bruce Morris .25 .60
G18 Dean Johnson .25 .60
G19 DeWayne Felkel .25 .60
G20 Jim Presnell .25 .60
G21 Jan McDougald .25 .60
G22 Marc Parks .25 .60
G23 Jerry Vess .25 .60
G24 Teddy Blackwell .25 .60
G25 Roger Chastain .25 .60
G26 Brad Turner .25 .60
G27 Kent Mashburn .25 .60
G28 Harry Gant in Pits .25 .60
G29 Harry Gant .40 1.00
G30 Harry Gant in Pits .25 .60
G31 Harry Gant's Car .25 .60
G32 Harry Gant's Car .25 .60
G33 Harry Gant's Car .25 .60
G34 Harry Gant's Car .25 .60
checklist card numbered CL
W1 Roger Penske .25 .60
W2 Rusty Wallace .50 1.25
W3 Don Miller .25 .60
W4 Dick Paysor .25 .60
W5 Buddy Parrott .25 .60
W6 Todd Parrott .25 .60
W7 Brad Parrott .25 .60
W8 Bill Wilburn .25 .60
W9 Scott Robinson .25 .60
W10 Paul VanderLaan .25 .60
W11 Gary Brooks .25 .60
W12 Earl Barban Jr. .25 .60
W13 Jeff Thousand .25 .60
W14 Nick Ollila .25 .60
W15 Angela Crawford .25 .60
W16 Stella Paysor .25 .60
W17 Lori Wetzel .25 .60
W18 Dave Hoffert .25 .60
W19 Robert Pressley .25 .60
W20 Dennis Beaver .25 .60
W21 Jerry Branz .25 .60
W22 David Munari .25 .60
W23 Rocky Owenby .25 .60
Barry Poovey
W24 Jamie Freeze .25 .60
Mike Wingate
W25 Steve Triplett .25 .60
James Shoffner
W26 Phil Ditmars .25 .60
Eric Durchman
W27 Ronnie Phillips .25 .60
Billy Woodruff
W28 Matt King .25 .60
Jimmy Zamrzla
W29 Mark Campbell .25 .60
W30 David Evans .25 .60
W31 Tony Lambert .25 .60
David Little
W32 David Kenny .25 .60
Dave Roberts
W33 Bo Schlager .25 .60
Mark Armstrong
W34 Rusty Wallace .50 1.25
Buddy Parrott
W35 Rusty Wallace .50 1.25
W36 Rusty Wallace in Pits .25 .60
W37 Rusty Wallace .50 1.25
W38 Rusty Wallace w/Car .25 .60
W39 Rusty Wallace .50 1.25
W40 Rusty Wallace's Car .25 .60
W41 Rusty Wallace's Car .25 .60
checklist card numbered CL

1994 Wheels High Gear Rookie Shootout Autographs

This seven-card insert set features seven of the drivers that were competing for the '94 Winston Cup Rookie of the Year. Cards RS1-RS3 were available in series one boxes. There were 1,500 of each of the three cards and they were randomly seeded at one card per 384 packs. Cards RS4-RS7 were available in series two High Gear boxes and series two High Gear Day One boxes. There were 1,000 of each of the four cards and they were randomly inserted at a rate of one card per 288 packs.

COMPLETE SET (7) 60.00 120.00
RS1 Steve Grissom AUTO/1500 6.00 15.00
RS2 Ward Burton AUTO/1500 6.00 15.00
RS3 Jeff Burton AUTO/1500 8.00 20.00
RS4 Joe Nemechek AUTO/1000 8.00 20.00
RS5 Mike Wallace AUTO/1000 8.00 20.00
RS6 Loy Allen Jr. AUTO/1000 6.00 15.00
RS7 John Andretti AUTO/1000 8.00 20.00

1994 Wheels High Gear Rookie Thunder Update

This 5-card insert set features four former Rookies of the Year. The cards were an update to the 93 Wheels Rookie Thunder set. The cards were packaged in three card cellophane packs and you got one pack in the top of 1994 High Gear series one boxes. There was one checklist and two cards in each pack. The four driver cards came in two versions, a base version and a platinum parallel version.

COMPLETE SET (5) 8.00 20.00
*PLATINUM: 1X TO 2.5X BASIC CARDS
101 Hermie Sadler 1.00 2.00
102 Jeff Gordon 3.00 6.00
103 Bobby Hamilton 1.00 2.00
104 Dale Earnhardt 4.00 10.00
NNO Checklist Card .25 .50

1995 Wheels High Gear

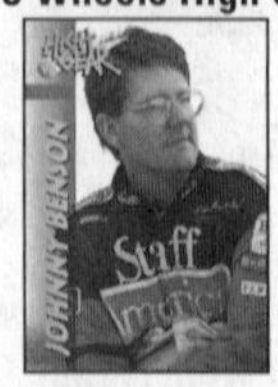

This 100-card set features top drivers from both Winston Cup and Busch Circuits. The cards are printed on 24-point paper and display silver foil stamping and UV coating. There were 1,000 cases produced. Each case contained 20 boxes, with 24 packs per box and six cards per pack. There were also two randomly inserted autograph cards. Terry Labonte was featured on an "IceMan" card and Steve Kinser was featured on "The Outlaw" card. The autograph cards were randomly inserted at a rate of one per 480 packs. The set also included two subsets; Split Shift (61-68), and Race Winner (86-97).

COMPLETE SET (100) 8.00 20.00
COMP.E-RACE TO WIN SET (10) .25 .50
1 Dale Earnhardt 1.25 3.00
2 Rusty Wallace .60 1.50
3 Mark Martin .60 1.50
4 Ricky Rudd .25 .60
5 Morgan Shepherd .07 .20
6 Jeff Gordon .75 2.00
7 Darrell Waltrip .15 .40
8 Terry Labonte .25 .60
9 Michael Waltrip .15 .40
10 Ted Musgrave .07 .20
11 Geoff Bodine .07 .20
12 Ken Schrader .07 .20
13 Bill Elliott .30 .75
14 Lake Speed .07 .20
15 Sterling Marlin .25 .60
16 Rick Mast .07 .20
17 Kyle Petty .15 .40
18 Ernie Irvan .15 .40
19 Dale Jarrett .50 1.25
20 Brett Bodine .07 .20
21 Bobby Labonte .50 1.25
22 Todd Bodine .07 .20
23 Jeff Burton .25 .60
24 Joe Nemechek .07 .20
25 Steve Grissom .07 .20
26 Derrike Cope .07 .20
27 John Andretti .07 .20
28 Mike Wallace .07 .20
29 Ward Burton .15 .40
30 Loy Allen Jr. .07 .20
31 Richard Childress .15 .40
32 Roger Penske .02 .10
33 Jack Roush .02 .10
34 Rick Hendrick .02 .10
35 Ricky Rudd OWN .25 .60
36 Robert Yates .02 .10
37 Junior Johnson .07 .20
38 Bobby Allison .07 .20
39 Felix Sabates .02 .10
40 Cale Yarborough .07 .20
41 Andy Petree .02 .10
42 Charlie Pressley .02 .10
43 Ray Evernham .07 .20
44 Larry McReynolds .02 .10
45 Steve Hmiel .02 .10
46 Robbie Loomis .02 .10
47 Paul Andrews .02 .10
48 Jeff Hammond .02 .10
49 Doug Hewitt .02 .10
50 Gary Dehart .02 .10
51 Kenny Wallace .07 .20
52 Ricky Craven .07 .20
53 Dennis Setzer .07 .20
54 Johnny Benson .15 .40
55 David Green .07 .20
56 Hermie Sadler .07 .20
57 Elton Sawyer .07 .20
58 Chad Little .07 .20
59 Larry Pearson .07 .20
60 Mike McLaughlin .07 .20
61 Terry Labonte SS .15 .40
62 Mike Wallace SS .02 .10
63 Mark Martin SS .30 .75
64 Kenny Wallace SS .02 .10
65 Ken Schrader SS .02 .10
66 Bobby Labonte SS .25 .60
67 Joe Nemechek SS .02 .10
68 Harry Gant SS .07 .20
69 Johnny Benson Jr. BGN ROY .15 .40
70 David Green BGN Champ .02 .10
71 Dale Earnhardt's Car .50 1.25
72 Rusty Wallace's Car .25 .60
73 Mark Martin's Car .25 .60
74 Ken Schrader's Car .02 .10
75 Ricky Rudd's Car .07 .20
76 Morgan Shepherd's Car .02 .10
77 Terry Labonte's Car .15 .40
78 Jeff Gordon's Car .30 .75
79 Darrell Waltrip's Car .07 .20
80 Bill Elliott's Car .15 .40
81 Sterling Marlin's Car .07 .20
82 Lake Speed's Car .02 .10
83 Ted Musgrave's Car .02 .10
84 Michael Waltrip's Car .07 .20
85 Geoff Bodine's Car .02 .10
86 Dale Earnhardt RW .60 1.50
87 Rusty Wallace RW .30 .75
88 Mark Martin RW .30 .75
89 Ricky Rudd RW .15 .40
90 Terry Labonte RW .15 .40
91 Jeff Gordon RW .40 1.00
92 Bill Elliott RW .15 .40
93 Sterling Marlin RW .15 .40
94 Geoff Bodine RW .02 .10
95 Dale Jarrett RW .25 .60
96 Ernie Irvan RW .07 .20
97 Jimmy Spencer RW .02 .10
98 Jeff Gordon in Pits .30 .75
99 Jeff Burton ROY .25 .60
100 Bill Elliott FF .15 .40
SKS1 Steve Kinser AU/1500 10.00 20.00
TLS1 Terry Labonte AU/1500 12.50 30.00
NNO E-Race to Win .02 .10
(Unscratched)
NNO E-Race to Win (Winner) .02 .10

1995 Wheels High Gear Day One

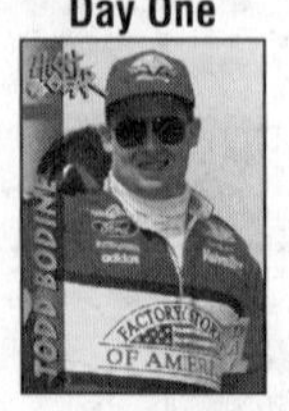

This 100-card set is a separately packaged version of the base '95 High Gear set. The cards feature a silver foil stamped "Day 1" logo to distinguish them from the base cards. The cards in the first 500 cases off the press were stamped with this "Day 1" logo. There were two subsets; Split Shift (61-68), and Race Winner (86-97). They were packaged six cards to a pack, 24 packs to a box and 20 boxes per case.

COMPLETE SET (100) 10.00 25.00
1 Dale Earnhardt 2.00 5.00
2 Rusty Wallace 1.00 2.50
3 Mark Martin 1.00 2.50
4 Ricky Rudd .40 1.00
5 Morgan Shepherd .10 .30
6 Jeff Gordon 1.25 3.00
7 Darrell Waltrip .25 .60
8 Terry Labonte .40 1.00
9 Michael Waltrip .25 .60
10 Ted Musgrave .10 .30
11 Geoff Bodine .10 .30
12 Ken Schrader .10 .30
13 Bill Elliott .50 1.25
14 Lake Speed .10 .30
15 Sterling Marlin .40 1.00
16 Rick Mast .10 .30
17 Kyle Petty .25 .60
18 Ernie Irvan .25 .60
19 Dale Jarrett .75 2.00
20 Brett Bodine .10 .30
21 Bobby Labonte .75 2.00
22 Todd Bodine .10 .30
23 Jeff Burton .40 1.00
24 Joe Nemechek .10 .30
25 Steve Grissom .10 .30
26 Derrike Cope .10 .30
27 John Andretti .10 .30
28 Mike Wallace .10 .30
29 Ward Burton .25 .60
30 Loy Allen Jr. .10 .30
31 Richard Childress .25 .60
32 Roger Penske .05 .15
33 Jack Roush .05 .15
34 Rick Hendrick .05 .15
35 Ricky Rudd OWN .40 1.00
36 Robert Yates .05 .15
37 Junior Johnson .10 .30
38 Bobby Allison .10 .30
39 Felix Sabates .05 .15
40 Cale Yarborough .10 .30
41 Andy Petree .05 .15
42 Charlie Pressley .05 .15
43 Ray Evernham .10 .30
44 Larry McReynolds .05 .15
45 Steve Hmiel .05 .15
46 Robbie Loomis .05 .15
47 Paul Andrews .05 .15
48 Jeff Hammond .05 .15
49 Doug Hewitt .05 .15
50 Gary Dehart .05 .15
51 Kenny Wallace .10 .30
52 Ricky Craven .10 .30
53 Dennis Setzer .10 .30
54 Johnny Benson .25 .60
55 David Green .10 .30
56 Hermie Sadler .10 .30
57 Elton Sawyer .10 .30
58 Chad Little .10 .30
59 Larry Pearson .10 .30
60 Mike McLaughlin .10 .30
61 Terry Labonte SS .25 .60
62 Mike Wallace SS .05 .15
63 Mark Martin SS .50 1.25
64 Kenny Wallace SS .05 .15
65 Ken Schrader SS .05 .15
66 Bobby Labonte SS .40 1.00
67 Joe Nemechek SS .05 .15
68 Harry Gant SS .10 .30
69 Johnny Benson BGN ROY .25 .60
70 David Green BGN Champ .05 .15
71 Dale Earnhardt's Car .75 2.00
72 Rusty Wallace's Car .40 1.00
73 Mark Martin's Car .40 1.00
74 Ken Schrader's Car .05 .15
75 Ricky Rudd's Car .10 .30
76 Morgan Shepherd's Car .05 .15
77 Terry Labonte's Car .25 .60
78 Jeff Gordon's Car .50 1.25
79 Darrell Waltrip's Car .10 .30
80 Bill Elliott's Car .25 .60
81 Sterling Marlin's Car .10 .30
82 Lake Speed's Car .05 .15
83 Ted Musgrave's Car .05 .15
84 Michael Waltrip's Car .10 .30
85 Geoff Bodine's Car .05 .15
86 Dale Earnhardt RW 1.00 2.50
87 Rusty Wallace RW .50 1.25
88 Mark Martin RW .50 1.25
89 Ricky Rudd RW .25 .60
90 Terry Labonte RW .25 .60
91 Jeff Gordon RW .60 1.50
92 Bill Elliott RW .25 .60
93 Sterling Marlin RW .25 .60
94 Geoff Bodine RW .05 .15
95 Dale Jarrett RW .40 1.00
96 Ernie Irvan RW .10 .30
97 Jimmy Spencer RW .05 .15
98 Jeff Gordon in Pits .50 1.25
99 Jeff Burton ROY .40 1.00
100 Bill Elliott FF .25 .60

1995 Wheels High Gear Day One Gold

This 100-card set is a parallel to the base Day One set. The cards feature a gold foil stamping on the Day One logo on the front of the card. The cards were inserted one per High Gear Day One pack.

COMPLETE SET (100) 25.00 60.00
*DAY ONE GOLD: 1X TO 2.5X BASE DAY ONES

1995 Wheels High Gear Gold

This 100-card set is a parallel to the base High Gear set. The cards feature gold foil stamping and the word "gold" appears under the High Gear logo on the fronts of the cards. The cards were found one per pack.

COMPLETE SET (100) 15.00 40.00
*GOLDS: 1X TO 2.5X BASIC CARDS

1995 Wheels High Gear Busch Clash

This 16-card insert set features the drivers who qualified for the 1995 Busch Clash. Each card was printed in silver foil as well as a gold foil parallel. The silver cards use MicroEtch printing technology and were inserted at the ratio of 1:8 packs.

COMPLETE SET (16) 20.00 50.00
*GOLD: .8X TO 2X BASIC INSERT
UNCUT GOLD SHEET 20.00 40.00
BC1 Loy Allen Jr. .50 1.25
BC2 Geoff Bodine .50 1.25
BC3 Ted Musgrave .50 1.25
BC4 Bill Elliott 2.00 5.00
BC5 Ernie Irvan 1.00 2.50
BC6 Rusty Wallace 4.00 10.00
BC7 Jeff Gordon 5.00 12.00
BC8 Dale Earnhardt 8.00 20.00
BC9 Rick Mast .50 1.25
BC10 Mark Martin 4.00 10.00
BC11 Jimmy Spencer .25 .60
BC12 Ward Burton 1.00 2.50
BC13 Ricky Rudd 1.50 4.00
BC14 Sterling Marlin 1.50 4.00
BC15 Greg Sacks .50 1.25
BC16 David Green .50 1.25

1995 Wheels High Gear Dominators

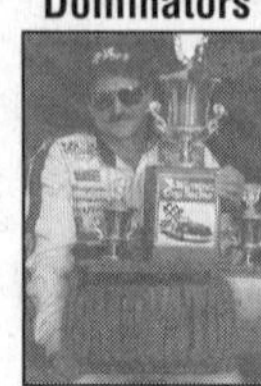

This four-card insert set feaures top Winston Cup drivers on 3 1/2" by 5" cards. The cards are numbered of 1,750 on the backs of the card. They came in a white envelope and were inserted in boxes at a rate of one per seven boxes. The Rusty Wallace (D1) was available in Day One boxes and the other three (D2-D4) were found in regular High Gear boxes. A four card uncut sheet of the Dominators was also produced. There was also a Mini-Dominator version of each of the four cards. These cards were a standard size replica of the jumbo card. The cards were distributed the same as their larger versions and were inserted 1:168 packs.

COMPLETE SET (4) 30.00 80.00
UNCUT 4 CARD SHEET 50.00 100.00
*MINI.DOMI: .4X TO 1X BASIC DOMINATOR
MINI DOMINATOR STATED ODDS 1:168
D1 Rusty Wallace/1750 10.00 25.00
D2 Terry Labonte/1750 4.00 10.00
D3 Dale Earnhardt/1750 20.00 50.00
D4 Geoff Bodine/1750 1.25 3.00

1995 Wheels High Gear Legends

This three-card insert set features three of the all time legends of Stock Car racing. The cards are printed on silver foil board and were inserted one per 24 packs.

COMPLETE SET (3) 4.00 10.00
L1 Junior Johnson 1.50 4.00
L2 Fred Lorenzen 1.50 4.00
L3 Red Farmer 1.50 4.00

1998 Wheels High Gear

The 1998 High Gear set was issued in one series totalling 72 cards. The cards feature color photos printed on 24 pt. board with multi-level foil stamping. The set contains the topical subsets: NASCAR Winston Cup Drivers (1-27), NASCAR Winston Cup Cars (28-36), NASCAR Busch Series Drivers (37-41), NASCAR Craftsman Truck Drivers (42-45), Awards (46-54), '98 Preview (55-63), and Carmeleon (64-71).

COMPLETE SET (72) 8.00 20.00
1 Jeff Gordon .75 2.00
2 Dale Jarrett .50 1.25
3 Mark Martin .60 1.50
4 Jeff Burton .25 .60
5 Dale Earnhardt 1.25 3.00
6 Terry Labonte .25 .60
7 Bobby Labonte .50 1.25
8 Bill Elliott .30 .75
9 Rusty Wallace .60 1.50
10 Ken Schrader .07 .20
11 Johnny Benson .15 .40
12 Ted Musgrave .07 .20
13 Jeremy Mayfield .15 .40
14 Ernie Irvan .15 .40
15 Kyle Petty .15 .40
16 Bobby Hamilton .07 .20
17 Ricky Rudd .25 .60
18 Michael Waltrip .15 .40
19 Ricky Craven .07 .20
20 Jimmy Spencer .07 .20
21 Ward Burton .15 .40
22 Sterling Marlin .25 .60
23 Darrell Waltrip .15 .40
24 Joe Nemechek .07 .20
25 Mike Skinner .07 .20
26 David Green .07 .20
27 Wally Dallenbach Jr. .07 .20
28 Rusty Wallace's Car .25 .60
29 Dale Earnhardt's Car .50 1.25
30 Terry Labonte's Car .15 .40
31 Mark Martin's Car .25 .60
32 Bobby Labonte's Car .25 .60
33 Jeff Gordon's Car .30 .75
34 Dale Jarrett's Car .15 .40
35 Bill Elliott's Car .15 .40
36 Jeff Burton's Car .07 .20
37 Randy LaJoie .07 .20
38 Todd Bodine .07 .20
39 Steve Park .50 1.25
40 Phil Parsons .07 .20
41 Elliott Sadler .15 .40
42 Rich Bickle .07 .20
43 Jack Sprague .07 .20
44 Joe Ruttman .07 .20
45 Ron Hornaday Jr. .07 .20
46 Mark Martin .60 1.50
47 Brian Whitesell .02 .10
48 Dale Earnhardt's Car .50 1.25
49 Mike Skinner .07 .20
50 Jeff Gordon .75 2.00
51 Jeff Burton .25 .60
52 Jimmy Fenning .02 .10
53 Charlie Siegars .02 .10
54 Dale Jarrett .50 1.25
55 Johnny Benson .15 .40
56 Todd Bodine .07 .20
57 Robert Pressley .07 .20
58 Bobby Hamilton .07 .20
59 Ernie Irvan .15 .40
60 Kenny Irwin .15 .40
61 Sterling Marlin .25 .60
62 Steve Park .50 1.25
63 John Andretti .07 .20
64 Dale Earnhardt's Car .50 1.25
65 Terry Labonte's Car .15 .40
66 Ricky Rudd's Car .07 .20
67 Bobby Labonte's Car .25 .60
68 Michael Waltrip's Car .07 .20
69 Jeff Gordon's Car .30 .75
70 Darrell Waltrip's Car .07 .20
71 Bill Elliott's Car .15
72 Checklist .02
P1 Bobby Labonte Promo 1.50 4.

1998 Wheels High Gea First Gear

Inserted one per pack, this 72-card set is an all-micro-etched parallel version of the base set.

COMPLETE SET (72) 12.00 30.
*FIRST GEAR: .6X TO 1.5X BASIC CARDS

1998 Wheels High Gea MPH

Randomly inserted in hobby only packs at the rat one in 40, this 72-card set is parallel to the base with a special MVP foil-stamping. Only 100 of e card was produced and individually numbered.

COMPLETE SET (72) 300.00 600.
*MPH CARDS: 10X TO 25X BASE CARDS

1998 Wheels High Gea Pure Gold

Randomly inserted in packs at the rate of one in this nine-card set commemorates NASCAR's 5 anniversary and features color photos of the best time drivers printed on all-foil cards.

COMPLETE SET (9) 10.00 25.
PG1 Dale Earnhardt 5.00 12.
PG2 Richard Petty .60 1.
PG3 Jeff Gordon 3.00 8.
PG4 Terry Labonte 1.00 2.
PG5 Mark Martin 2.50 6.
PG6 Darrell Waltrip .60 1.
PG7 Ned Jarrett .30 .
PG8 Bill Elliott 1.25 3.
PG9 Rusty Wallace 2.50 6.

1998 Wheels High Gea Autographs

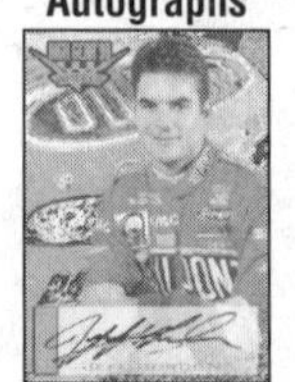

Randomly inserted in packs at the rate of one in 1 this set features autographed cards of top NASC Winston Cup drivers with a certificate of authenti printed on the back. All of the cards except Jim Spencer feature hand written serial numbering on backs as noted below. The Jimmy Spencer card actually released in 2003 through the VIP Tin fac set program. The unnumbered cards are checklis below in alphabetical order.

COMPLETE SET (23) 750.00 1250.
1 Johnny Benson/250 12.50 30.
2 Jeff Burton/250 10.00 25.
3 Ward Burton/250 10.00 20.
4 Ricky Craven/200 7.50 15.
5 Wally Dallenbach/250 7.50 15.
6 Dale Earnhardt/50 250.00 400.
7 Bill Elliott/250 25.00 60.
8 Jeff Gordon/50 150.00 300.
9 Bobby Hamilton/250 10.00 25.
10 Ernie Irvan/225 12.50 30.
11 Dale Jarrett/200 20.00 50.
12 Bobby Labonte/250 12.50 30.
13 Terry Labonte/150 25.00 60.
14 Mark Martin/100 40.00 80.
15 Jeremy Mayfield/250 12.50 30.
16 Ted Musgrave/250 7.50 15.
17 Joe Nemechek/250 7.50 15.
18 Kyle Petty/200 12.50 30.
19 Ken Schrader/250 10.00 20.
20 Mike Skinner/250 7.50 15.
21 Jimmy Spencer 12.50 30.
22 Darrell Waltrip/250 15.00 40.
23 Michael Waltrip/250 10.00 25.

1998 Wheels High Gea Custom Shop

Randomly inserted in packs at the rate of one in 1 redemption cards for this five-card set allowed collector to customize his own card by selecting of three fronts and three backs for each card. collector then received his custom-made card return mail with his chosen front and back selecti

COMPLETE SET (5) 100.00 200.
*PRIZE CARDS: .4X TO 1X BASIC INSERTS
CS1 Dale Earnhardt EXCH 30.00 80.
CS2 Jeff Gordon EXCH 20.00 50.

3 Mark Martin EXCH 15.00 40.00
4 Terry Labonte EXCH 6.00 15.00
5 Dale Jarrett EXCH 12.50 30.00

998 Wheels High Gear Gear Jammers

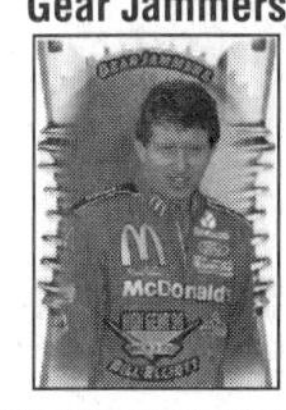

domly inserted in packs at the rate of one in two, 27-card set features color photos printed on die-foil stamped cards.

MPLETE SET (27) 10.00 25.00
Rusty Wallace 2.00 5.00
Dale Earnhardt's Car 1.50 4.00
Sterling Marlin .75 2.00
Terry Labonte .75 2.00
Mark Martin 2.00 5.00
Ricky Rudd .75 2.00
Ted Musgrave .25 .60
Darrell Waltrip .50 1.25
Bobby Labonte 1.50 4.00
0 Michael Waltrip .50 1.25
1 Ward Burton .50 1.25
2 Jeff Gordon 2.50 6.00
3 Bobby Hamilton .25 .60
4 Kyle Petty .50 1.25
5 Dale Jarrett 1.50 4.00
6 Bill Elliott 1.00 2.50
7 Jeff Burton .75 2.00
8 Wally Dallenbach .25 .60
9 Jimmy Spencer .25 .60
0 Ken Schrader .25 .60
1 Johnny Benson .50 1.25
2 David Green .25 .60
3 Mike Skinner .25 .60
4 Joe Nemechek .25 .60
5 Jeremy Mayfield .50 1.25
6 Ricky Craven .25 .60
7 Morgan Shepherd .25 .60

998 Wheels High Gear High Groove

domly inserted in packs at the rate of one in 10, nine-card set features color photos of cars onging to top drivers printed on die-cut, foil nped cards.

MPLETE SET (9) 12.00 30.00
1 Rusty Wallace's Car 2.00 5.00
2 Dale Earnhardt's Car 4.00 10.00
3 Terry Labonte's Car 1.25 3.00
4 Mark Martin's Car 2.00 5.00
5 Jeff Gordon's Car 2.50 6.00
6 Bobby Labonte's Car 2.00 5.00
7 Dale Jarrett's Car 1.25 3.00
8 Bill Elliott's Car 1.25 3.00
9 Jeff Burton's Car .60 1.50

998 Wheels High Gear Man and Machine Drivers

domly inserted in hobby packs only at the rate of in 20, this nine-card set features color portraits op drivers printed on interlocking all-foil cards e to be matched with the retail only version of set containing color photos of their cars.

MPLETE SET (9) 30.00 75.00
MP.CAR SET (9) 15.00 40.00
RS: .25X TO .6X DRIVERS
1 Jeff Gordon 5.00 12.00
2 Mark Martin 4.00 10.00
3 Dale Jarrett 3.00 8.00
4 Jeff Burton 1.50 4.00
5 Terry Labonte 1.50 4.00
6 Bobby Labonte 3.00 8.00
7 Dale Earnhardt 8.00 20.00
8 Bill Elliott 2.00 5.00
9 Rusty Wallace 4.00 10.00

998 Wheels High Gear Top Tier

domly inserted in packs, this eight-card set ures color photos of the top eight 1997 NASCAR ston Cup finishers printed on all-foil cards. The rtion ratios are printed after the driver's name.

MPLETE SET (8) 25.00 60.00
Jeff Gordon 1:384 15.00 40.00
Dale Jarrett 1:192 12.50 30.00
Mark Martin 1:100 6.00 15.00

TT4 Jeff Burton 1:60 2.50 6.00
TT5 Dale Earnhardt 1:40 10.00 25.00
TT6 Terry Labonte 1:40 2.00 5.00
TT7 Bobby Labonte 1:20 2.00 5.00
TT8 Bill Elliott 1:20 1.50 4.00

1999 Wheels High Gear

The 1999 High Gear set was issued in one series totalling 72 cards. They were issued in six card hobby packs or five card retail packs. The set contains the topical subsets: NASCAR Winston Cup Drivers (1-27), NASCAR Winston Cup Cars (28-36), NASCAR Busch Drivers (37-45), Awards (46-54), '99 Preview (55-63), and Carmeleon (64-71).

COMPLETE SET (72) 10.00 25.00
WAX BOX HOBBY 50.00 100.00
WAX BOX RETAIL 20.00 50.00
1 Jeff Gordon .75 2.00
2 Mark Martin .60 1.50
3 Dale Jarrett .50 1.25
4 Rusty Wallace .60 1.50
5 Jeff Burton .25 .60
6 Bobby Labonte .50 1.25
7 Jeremy Mayfield .15 .40
8 Dale Earnhardt 1.25 3.00
9 Terry Labonte .25 .60
10 Bobby Hamilton .07 .20
11 John Andretti .07 .20
12 Ken Schrader .07 .20
13 Sterling Marlin .25 .60
14 Jimmy Spencer .07 .20
15 Chad Little .07 .20
16 Ward Burton .15 .40
17 Michael Waltrip .15 .40
18 Bill Elliott .30 .75
19 Ernie Irvan .15 .40
20 Johnny Benson .07 .20
21 Mike Skinner .07 .20
22 Ricky Rudd .25 .60
23 Robert Pressley .07 .20
24 Kenny Irwin .07 .20
25 Geoff Bodine .07 .20
26 Joe Nemechek .07 .20
27 Steve Park .40 1.00
28 Rusty Wallace's Car .25 .60
29 Dale Earnhardt's Car .50 1.25
30 Terry Labonte's Car .15 .40
31 Mark Martin's Car .25 .60
32 Bobby Labonte's Car .15 .40
33 Jeff Gordon's Car .30 .75
34 Dale Jarrett's Car .15 .40
35 Bill Elliott's Car .15 .40
36 Jeff Burton's Car .07 .20
37 Dale Earnhardt Jr. 1.00 2.50
38 Matt Kenseth RC 2.50 6.00
39 Mike McLaughlin .07 .20
40 Randy LaJoie .07 .20
41 Mark Martin .60 1.50
42 Jason Jarrett .07 .20
43 Michael Waltrip .15 .40
44 Tim Fedewa .07 .20
45 Tony Stewart .75 2.00
46 Jeff Gordon .75 2.00
47 Bill Elliott .30 .75
48 Dale Earnhardt's Car .50 1.25
49 Kenny Irwin .15 .40
50 Mark Martin .60 1.50
51 Jeff Burton .25 .60
52 Ray Evernham .07 .20
53 Bobby Hamilton .07 .20
54 Jeff Gordon .75 2.00
55 Ward Burton .15 .40
56 Geoff Bodine .07 .20
57 Darrell Waltrip .15 .40
58 Jeff Gordon .75 2.00
59 Kenny Wallace .07 .20
60 Ted Musgrave .07 .20
61 Tony Stewart .75 2.00
62 Elliott Sadler .15 .40
63 Jerry Nadeau .15 .40
64 Dale Earnhardt's Car .50 1.25
65 Terry Labonte's Car .15 .40
66 Bobby Labonte's Car .15 .40
67 Kenny Irwin's Car .02 .10
68 Rusty Wallace's Car .25 .60
69 Jeff Gordon's Car .30 .75
70 Dale Jarrett's Car .15 .40
71 Ernie Irvan's Car .02 .10
72 Jeff Gordon CL .40 1.00
P1 Jeff Gordon Promo 1.00 2.50

1999 Wheels High Gear First Gear

Inserted one per pack, this 72-card set is an all-foil micro-etched parallel version of the base set.

COMPLETE SET (72) 25.00 50.00
*FIRST GEAR: 1X TO 2.5X BASIC CARDS

1999 Wheels High Gear MPH

Randomly inserted in hobby packs at the rate of one in 40, this 72-card set is parallel to the base set with special holofoil-stamping. Only 125 of each card were produced and individually numbered.

COMPLETE SET (72) 250.00 500.00
*MPH VETS: 10X TO 25X BASE CARDS
*MPH RCs: 3X TO 8X BASE CARDS

1999 Wheels High Gear Autographs

Randomly inserted in packs at the rate of one in 100, this 25-card set features autographed color photos of top NASCAR Winston Cup drivers with a certificate of authenticity. The cards are checklisted below in alphabetical order.

COMPLETE SET (25) 800.00 1300.00
1 John Andretti/350 8.00 20.00
2 Johnny Benson/350 10.00 25.00
3 Geoffrey Bodine/350 8.00 20.00
4 Ward Burton/350 10.00 25.00
5 Jeff Burton/350 8.00 20.00
6 Dale Earnhardt/55 250.00 400.00
7 Dale Earnhardt Jr./350 75.00 150.00
8 Bill Elliott/350 15.00 40.00
9 Jeff Gordon/100 100.00 200.00
10 Bobby Hamilton/350 10.00 25.00
11 Ernie Irvan/350 10.00 25.00
12 Kenny Irwin 15.00 40.00
13 Dale Jarrett/350 20.00 50.00
14 Bobby Labonte/250 12.50 30.00
15 Terry Labonte/100 50.00 100.00
16 Chad Little/350 8.00 20.00
17 Sterling Marlin/350 12.50 30.00
18 Mark Martin/200 30.00 60.00
19 Jeremy Mayfield/350 10.00 25.00
20 Joe Nemechek/350 8.00 20.00
21 Robert Pressley/350 8.00 20.00
22 Ricky Rudd/350 12.50 30.00
23 Ken Schrader/350 10.00 25.00
24 Mike Skinner/350 8.00 20.00
25 Jimmy Spencer/350 8.00 20.00
26 Michael Waltrip/350 10.00 25.00

1999 Wheels High Gear Custom Shop

Randomly inserted in packs at the rate of one in 200, redemption cards for this five-card set allowed the collector to customize his own card by selecting one of three fronts and three backs for each card. The collector then received his custom-made card by return mail with his chosen front and back selection.

COMPLETE SET (5) 125.00 250.00
*PRIZE CARDS: .4X TO 1X BASIC INSERTS
CSDE Dale Earnhardt EXCH 20.00 50.00
CSJG Jeff Gordon EXCH 15.00 40.00
CSJR Dale Earnhardt Jr. EXCH 15.00 40.00
CSMM Mark Martin EXCH 10.00 25.00
CSTL Terry Labonte EXCH 10.00 25.00

1999 Wheels High Gear Flag Chasers

This five card insert set features pieces of racing flags used in 1998 races. They were issued in different colors with the following insert ratios: Green: 1:2600 (numbered to 65), Yellow 1:2450 (numbered to 69); Blue-Yellow 1:3900 (numbered to 45); Black 1:2450 (numbered to 69); Red 1:2600 (numbered to 65); White 1:2450 (numbered to 69) and Checkered 1:5000 (numbered to 36). Overall ratio for flag insertion was one in 400 packs.

BLACK/WHITE/YELLOW PRICED BELOW
*GREEN/RED: .3X TO .8X BASIC INSERTS
*BLUE-YELLOW: .6X TO 1.5X BASIC INS.
*CHECKERED: 1X TO 2X BASIC INSERTS
FC1 Jeff Gordon 60.00 120.00
FC2 Mark Martin 50.00 100.00
FC3 Terry Labonte 50.00 100.00
FC4 Rusty Wallace 40.00 100.00
FC5 Dale Earnhardt 75.00 150.00

1999 Wheels High Gear Gear Shifters

Randomly inserted in packs at the rate of one in two, this 27-card set features color photos printed on die-cut, foil stamped cards.

COMPLETE SET (27) 15.00 30.00
GS1 Jeff Gordon 2.50 6.00
GS2 Mark Martin 2.00 5.00
GS3 Dale Jarrett 1.50 4.00
GS4 Rusty Wallace 2.00 5.00
GS5 Jeff Burton .75 2.00
GS6 Bobby Labonte 1.50 4.00
GS7 Jeremy Mayfield .50 1.25
GS8 Dale Earnhardt 4.00 10.00
GS9 Terry Labonte .75 2.00
GS10 Bobby Hamilton .25 .60
GS11 John Andretti .25 .60
GS12 Ken Schrader .25 .60
GS13 Sterling Marlin .75 2.00
GS14 Jimmy Spencer .25 .60
GS15 Chad Little .25 .60
GS16 Ward Burton .50 1.25
GS17 Michael Waltrip .50 1.25
GS18 Bill Elliott 1.00 2.50
GS19 Ernie Irvan .50 1.25
GS20 Johnny Benson .25 .60
GS21 Mike Skinner .25 .60
GS22 Ricky Rudd .75 2.00
GS23 Darrell Waltrip .50 1.25
GS24 Kenny Irwin .25 .60
GS25 Geoffrey Bodine .25 .60
GS26 Robert Pressley .25 .60
GS27 Steve Park CL 1.25 3.00

1999 Wheels High Gear Hot Streaks

Randomly inserted in packs at the rate of one in ten, this six-card gold foil set focuses on the legendary streaks of NASCAR drivers.

COMPLETE SET (6) 10.00 25.00
HS1 Jeff Gordon 3.00 8.00
HS2 Terry Labonte 1.00 2.50
HS3 Dale Earnhardt's Car 2.00 5.00
HS4 Ricky Rudd 1.00 2.50
HS5 Mark Martin 2.50 6.00
HS6 Dale Jarrett 2.00 5.00

1999 Wheels High Gear Man and Machine Drivers

Randomly inserted in Hobby packs at the rate of one in ten, this nine-card set features color portraits of top drivers and their machines in an interlocking set. (Hobby: 1A-9A, Retail: 1B-9B)

COMPLETE SET (9) 15.00 40.00
COMP.CAR SET (9) 12.50 30.00
*CARS: .3X TO .8X DRIVERS
MM1A Jeff Gordon 3.00 8.00
MM2A Mark Martin 2.50 6.00
MM3A Dale Jarrett 2.00 5.00
MM4A Jeff Burton 1.00 2.50
MM5A Terry Labonte 1.00 2.50
MM6A Bobby Labonte 2.00 5.00
MM7A Jeremy Mayfield .60 1.50
MM8A Jimmy Spencer .30 .75
MM9A Rusty Wallace 2.50 6.00

1999 Wheels High Gear Top Tier

Randomly inserted in packs, this eight-card set features color photos of the top eight 1998 NASCAR Winston Cup finishers printed on all-foil cards. The insertion ratios are printed after the driver's name.

COMPLETE SET (8) 30.00 80.00
TT1 Jeff Gordon 1:400 15.00 40.00
TT2 Mark Martin 1:200 8.00 20.00
TT3 Dale Jarrett 1:100 4.00 10.00
TT4 Rusty Wallace 1:80 4.00 10.00
TT5 Jeff Burton 1:40 1.25 3.00
TT6 Bobby Labonte 1:40 2.50 6.00
TT7 Jeremy Mayfield 1:20 1.25 3.00
TT8 Dale Earnhardt's Car 1:20 4.00 10.00

2000 Wheels High Gear

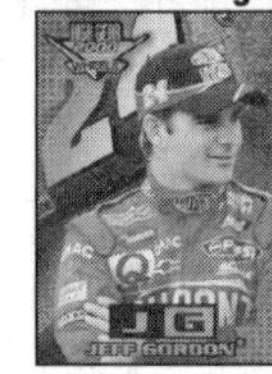

The 2000 High Gear set was released as a 72-card set that featured 72 of NASCAR's top stars on extra thick, 24-point stock. Released in both Hobby and Retail packs, this product carried a suggested retail price of $3.99 for 6-card Hobby packs, and $2.99 for 4-card Retail packs.

COMPLETE SET (72) 12.50 30.00
WAX BOX HOBBY 60.00 100.00
WAX BOX RETAIL 40.00 80.00
1 Dale Jarrett .50 1.25
2 Bobby Labonte .50 1.25
3 Mark Martin .60 1.50
4 Jeff Gordon .75 2.00
5 Tony Stewart .75 2.00
6 Jeff Burton .30 .75
7 Dale Earnhardt 1.25 3.00
8 Rusty Wallace .60 1.50
9 Ward Burton .20 .50
10 Mike Skinner .10 .30
11 Jeremy Mayfield .10 .30
12 Terry Labonte .30 .75
13 Bobby Hamilton .10 .30
14 Ken Schrader .10 .30
15 Sterling Marlin .30 .75
16 Steve Park .30 .75
17 Kenny Irwin .20 .50
18 John Andretti .10 .30
19 Jimmy Spencer .10 .30
20 Ricky Rudd .30 .75
21 Wally Dallenbach .10 .30
22 Kenny Wallace .10 .30
23 Kevin Lepage .10 .30
24 Chad Little .20 .50
25 Elliott Sadler .20 .50
26 Darrell Waltrip .20 .50
27 Michael Waltrip .20 .50
28 Rusty Wallace's Car .30 .75
29 Ward Burton's Car .10 .30
30 Mark Martin's Car .30 .75
31 Bobby Labonte's Car .20 .50
32 Tony Stewart's Car .40 1.00
33 Jeff Gordon's Car .30 .75
34 Mike Skinner's Car .07 .20
35 Dale Jarrett's Car .20 .50
36 Jeff Burton's Car .10 .30
37 Dale Earnhardt Jr. 1.00 2.50
38 Matt Kenseth .60 1.50
39 Jeff Green .10 .30
40 Elton Sawyer .10 .30
41 Jeff Gordon .75 2.00
42 Randy LaJoie .10 .30
43 Dave Blaney .10 .30
44 Mike McLaughlin .10 .30
45 Casey Atwood .30 .75
46 Jeff Gordon .75 2.00
47 Tony Stewart .75 2.00
48 Jeff Gordon .75 2.00
49 Bobby Labonte .50 1.25
50 Jeff Burton .30 .75
51 Bobby Labonte .50 1.25
52 Bobby Labonte .50 1.25
53 Todd Parrott .07 .20
54 Doug Yates .07 .20
55 Rusty Wallace's Car .30 .75
56 Kenny Wallace's Car .07 .20
57 Elliott Sadler's Car .07 .20
58 Mark Martin's Car .30 .75
59 Jeff Gordon's Car .30 .75
60 Bobby Labonte's Car .20 .50
61 Tony Stewart's Car .40 1.00
62 John Andretti's Car .07 .20
63 Dale Jarrett's Car .20 .50
64 Dave Blaney .10 .30
65 Dale Earnhardt Jr. 1.00 2.50
66 Matt Kenseth .60 1.50
67 Jerry Nadeau .20 .50
68 Michael Waltrip .20 .50
69 Kenny Irwin .20 .50
70 Joe Nemechek .10 .30
71 John Andretti .10 .30
72 Jeff Fuller CL .10 .30
2000 T.Stewart High Gear 2.00 5.00

2000 Wheels High Gear First Gear

Inserted one per pack, this 72-card set features NASCAR's top stars on extra thick, 24-point stock with full foil card fronts.

COMPLETE SET (72) 25.00 50.00
*FIRST GEAR: 1X TO 2.5X BASE CARDS

2000 Wheels High Gear MPH

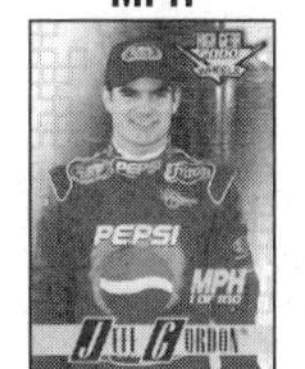

Randomly inserted in packs at 1 in 40, this Hobby only insert parallels the base set and features each base card with a gold holofoil stamp. Each card is sequentially ink-jet numbered to 100.

COMPLETE SET (72) 75.00 150.00
*MPH CARDS: 6X TO 12X BASE CARDS

2000 Wheels High Gear Autographs

Randomly inserted into packs at one in 100, this insert set features authentic autographs from drivers like Dale Earnhardt and Matt Kenseth. The unnumbered cards are listed below in alphabetical

order for convenience. Please note that the copyright year on the backs is 1999, but the cards were issued in 2000. Finally, some cards were only issued in 2003 in the VIP Tin factory sets.

COMPLETE SET (28) 500.00 1000.00
1 John Andretti 10.00 25.00
2 Casey Atwood 10.00 25.00
3 Dave Blaney 6.00 15.00
4 Mike Bliss 5.00 10.00
5 Brett Bodine 5.00 10.00
6 Geoffrey Bodine 6.00 15.00
7 Todd Bodine 5.00 10.00
8 Jeff Burton 10.00 25.00
9 Dale Earnhardt 175.00 350.00
10 Dale Earnhardt Jr. 60.00 120.00
11 Tim Fedewa 5.00 10.00
12 Kevin Grubb 5.00 10.00
13 Bobby Hamilton 10.00 25.00
14 Dale Jarrett 20.00 50.00
15 Jason Keller 6.00 15.00
16 Matt Kenseth 30.00 60.00
17 Bobby Labonte 12.50 30.00
18 Terry Labonte 15.00 40.00
19 Randy LaJoie 5.00 10.00
20 Chad Little 6.00 15.00
21 Jeremy Mayfield 10.00 25.00
22 Mike McLaughlin 5.00 10.00
23 Ricky Rudd 10.00 25.00
24 Elliott Sadler 6.00 15.00
25 Mike Skinner 6.00 15.00
26 Tony Stewart 40.00 100.00
27 Kenny Wallace 5.00 10.00
28 Michael Waltrip 12.50 30.00

2000 Wheels High Gear Custom Shop

Randomly inserted in packs at one in 200, this 5-card insert allowed collectors to "custom-design" their own all-foil etched card from combinations of fronts and backs showcasing five of NASCAR's hottest drivers. Card backs are numbered using the driver's initials, and carry a "CS" prefix. The cards expired on March 31, 2001.

*PRIZE CARDS: .4X TO 1X BASIC INSERTS
CSDE Dale Earnhardt Jr. EXCH 20.00 50.00
CSDJ Dale Jarrett EXCH 15.00 40.00
CSJG Jeff Gordon EXCH 20.00 50.00
CSMK Mark Martin EXCH 15.00 40.00
CSTS Tony Stewart EXCH 15.00 40.00

2000 Wheels High Gear Flag Chasers

Randomly inserted in packs at one in 400, this 5-card insert features some of NASCAR'S top drivers and real pieces of all seven flags that were used during the 1999 NASCAR Winston Cup season. Card backs carry a "FC" prefix.

COMPLETE SET (5) 250.00 500.00
BLCK/WHT/YELL/GRN/RED PRICED BELOW
BLK/WHT/YEL/GRN/REDS #'D TO 75
*BLUE-YELLOW: .6X TO 1.5X BASIC INS.
BLUE-YELLOW CARDS #'D TO 45
*CHECKERED: 1X TO 2X BASIC INSERTS
CHECKERED STATED ODDS 1:5000
CHECKERED CARDS #'D TO 35
*CHECKERED W/BLUE ORNG: 1.5X TO 2.5X
FC1 Dale Jarrett 30.00 80.00
FC2 Jeff Gordon 50.00 120.00
FC3 Dale Earnhardt 75.00 150.00
FC4 Mark Martin 30.00 80.00
FC5 Tony Stewart 25.00 60.00

2000 Wheels High Gear Gear Shifters

Randomly inserted in packs at one in two, this 27-card insert features most of the best drivers in NASCAR. Card backs carry a "GS" prefix.

COMPLETE SET (27) 10.00 25.00
GS1 Dale Jarrett 1.25 3.00
GS2 Mark Martin 1.50 4.00
GS3 Bobby Labonte 1.25 3.00
GS4 Tony Stewart 2.00 5.00
GS5 Jeff Burton .75 2.00
GS6 Jeff Gordon 2.00 5.00
GS7 Dale Earnhardt 3.00 8.00
GS8 Rusty Wallace 1.50 4.00
GS9 Ward Burton .50 1.25

GS10 Terry Labonte .75 2.00
GS11 Mike Skinner .30 .75
GS12 Jeremy Mayfield .30 .75
GS13 Matt Kenseth 1.50 4.00
GS14 Bobby Hamilton .30 .75
GS15 Dave Blaney .30 .75
GS16 Sterling Marlin .75 2.00
GS17 John Andretti .30 .75
GS18 Kenny Irwin .50 1.25
GS19 Kevin Lepage .30 .75
GS20 Steve Park .75 2.00
GS21 Darrell Waltrip .50 1.25
GS22 Kenny Wallace .30 .75
GS23 Dale Earnhardt Jr. 2.50 6.00
GS24 Elliott Sadler .50 1.25
GS25 Michael Waltrip .50 1.25
GS26 Casey Atwood .75 2.00
GS27 Ricky Rudd .75 2.00

2000 Wheels High Gear Man and Machine Cars

Randomly inserted in Retail packs at the rate of one in ten, this nine-card set features color portraits of top drivers and their machines in an interlocking set.

COMPLETE SET (9) 10.00 25.00
MM1B Tony Stewart's Car 3.00 8.00
MM2B Dale Earnhardt Jr.'s Car 4.00 10.00
MM3B Rusty Wallace's Car 2.50 6.00
MM4B Mark Martin's Car 2.50 6.00
MM5B Terry Labonte's Car 1.25 3.00
MM6B Jeff Gordon's Car 3.00 8.00
MM7B Jeff Burton's Car 1.25 3.00
MM8B Dale Jarrett's Car 2.00 5.00
MM9B Bobby Labonte's Car 2.00 5.00

2000 Wheels High Gear Man and Machine Drivers

Randomly inserted in Hobby packs at the rate of one in ten, this nine-card set features color portraits of top drivers and their machines in an interlocking set.

COMPLETE SET (9) 15.00 30.00
MM1A Tony Stewart 4.00 10.00
MM2A Dale Earnhardt Jr. 5.00 12.00
MM3A Rusty Wallace 3.00 8.00
MM4A Mark Martin 3.00 8.00
MM5A Terry Labonte 1.50 4.00
MM6A Jeff Gordon 4.00 10.00
MM7A Jeff Burton 1.50 4.00
MM8A Dale Jarrett 2.50 6.00
MM9A Bobby Labonte 2.50 6.00

2000 Wheels High Gear Sunday Sensation

Randomly inserted in packs at one in 18, this 9-card insert features nine all plastic cards of superstars that make Monday morning's headlines. Card backs carry an "OC" prefix.

COMPLETE SET (9) 20.00 40.00
OC1 Tony Stewart 5.00 12.00
OC2 Terry Labonte 2.00 5.00
OC3 Rusty Wallace 4.00 10.00
OC4 Mark Martin 4.00 10.00
OC5 Jeff Burton 2.00 5.00
OC6 Jeff Gordon 5.00 12.00
OC7 Dale Earnhardt's Car 8.00 20.00
OC8 Dale Jarrett 3.00 8.00
OC9 Bobby Labonte 3.00 8.00

2000 Wheels High Gear Top Tier

Randomly inserted in packs one in 20, this 9-card die-cut insert features the top nine drivers of the 1999 NASCAR Winston Cup season. Card backs carry a "TT" prefix.

COMPLETE SET (9) 25.00 50.00
TT1 Dale Jarrett 4.00 10.00
TT2 Bobby Labonte 4.00 10.00
TT3 Mark Martin 5.00 12.00
TT4 Jeff Gordon 6.00 15.00
TT5 Tony Stewart 6.00 15.00
TT6 Jeff Burton 2.50 6.00
TT7 Dale Earnhardt 10.00 25.00
TT8 Rusty Wallace 5.00 12.00
TT9 Ward Burton 1.50 4.00

2000 Wheels High Gear Vintage

Issued one per special retail box, these three cards feature some of the leading drivers on the NASCAR circuit.

COMPLETE SET (3) 6.00 15.00
V1 Dale Jarrett 2.00 5.00
V2 Mark Martin 2.50 6.00
V3 Tony Stewart 3.00 8.00

2000 Wheels High Gear Winning Edge

Randomly inserted in packs at one in ten, this 9-card insert features foil-etched cards that highlight some of the attention-getting moves of top drivers. Card backs carry a "WE" prefix.

COMPLETE SET (9) 15.00 30.00
WE1 Dale Jarrett 2.50 6.00
WE2 Mark Martin 3.00 8.00
WE3 Bobby Labonte 2.50 6.00
WE4 Tony Stewart 4.00 10.00
WE5 Jeff Gordon 4.00 10.00
WE6 Dale Earnhardt 6.00 15.00
WE7 Rusty Wallace 3.00 8.00
WE8 Terry Labonte 1.50 4.00
WE9 Dale Earnhardt Jr. 5.00 12.00

2001 Wheels High Gear

The 2001 Wheels High Gear product was released in March 2001, and featured a 72-card base set and is broken into subset as follows: 27 Veterans (1-27), 6 NASCAR Winston Cup Machines (28-33), 12 NASCAR Busch Series (34-45), 6 NASCAR Winston Cup Carmeleons (46-51), 6 2000 Highlights (52-57), 6 Contingency Awards (58-63), and 9 NASCAR Winston Cup Previews (64-72). Each pack contained 4-cards and carried a suggested retail price of $2.99.

COMPLETE SET (72) 12.50 30.00
1 Bobby Labonte .75 2.00
2 Dale Earnhardt 2.00 5.00
3 Dale Jarrett .75 2.00
4 Jeff Burton .30 .75
5 Tony Stewart 1.25 3.00
6 Rusty Wallace .75 2.00
7 Ricky Rudd .40 1.00
8 Mark Martin 1.00 2.50
9 Ward Burton .30 .75
10 Mike Skinner .12 .30
11 Matt Kenseth 1.00 2.50
12 Steve Park .30 .75
13 Dale Earnhardt Jr. 1.50 4.00
14 Robert Pressley .12 .30
15 Ken Schrader .12 .30
16 Sterling Marlin .50 1.25
17 Terry Labonte .50 1.25
18 Joe Nemechek .12 .30
19 Kenny Wallace .12 .30
20 Bobby Hamilton .20 .50
21 John Andretti .12 .30
22 Jimmy Spencer .25 .60
23 Jerry Nadeau .25 .60
24 Jeremy Mayfield .12 .30
25 Dave Blaney .12 .30
26 Elliott Sadler .25 .60
27 Tony Stewart WCM 1.25 3.00
28 Ward Burton WCM .30 .75
29 Matt Kenseth WCM 1.00 2.50
30 Ricky Rudd WCM .40 1.00
31 Dale Jarrett WCM .75 2.00
32 Rusty Wallace WCM .75 2.00
33 Kevin Grubb BGN .12 .30
34 Hank Parker Jr. BGN .12 .30
35 Todd Bodine BGN .12 .30
36 Jeff Green BGN .12 .30
37 Jason Keller BGN .12 .30
38 Kevin Harvick BGN 1.00 2.50
39 Randy LaJoie BGN .12 .30
40 Matt Kenseth BGN 1.00 2.50
41 Elton Sawyer BGN .12 .30
42 David Green BGN .12 .30
43 Jason Leffler BGN .12 .30
44 Casey Atwood BGN .40 1.00
45 Ken Schrader's Car .05 .10
46 Ward Burton's Car .12 .30
47 Sterling Marlin's Car .20 .50
48 Bobby Labonte's Car .30 .75
49 Mark Martin's Car .40 1.00
50 Elliott Sadler's Car .12 .30
51 Terry Labonte's Car .20 .50
52 Rusty Wallace HL .75 2.00
53 Jerry Nadeau HL .25 .60
54 Steve Park HL .30 .75
55 Matt Kenseth HL 1.00 2.50
56 Dale Earnhardt Jr. HL 1.50 4.00
57 Bobby Labonte HL .75 2.00
58 Rusty Wallace CA .75 2.00
59 Matt Kenseth CA 1.00 2.50
60 Jeff Burton CA .30 .75
61 Dale Earnhardt CA 2.00 5.00
62 Jimmy Makar CA .20 .50
63 Rusty Wallace CA .75 2.00
64 Elliott Sadler WCP .25 .60
65 Bobby Hamilton WCP .20 .50
66 Ryan Newman WCP RC 5.00 12.00
67 Jeff Burton WCP .30 .75
68 Sterling Marlin WCP .50 1.25
69 Mark Martin WCP 1.00 2.50
70 Dale Jarrett WCP .75 2.00
71 Ricky Craven WCP .12 .30
72 2001 WC Schedule .12 .30

2001 Wheels High Gear First Gear

Inserted one per pack, this set features an all foil card with holofoil printing.

COMPLETE SET (72) 40.00 100.00
*FIRST GEAR: 1X TO 2.5X BASE CARDS

2001 Wheels High Gear MPH

Inserted at a rate of 1:30 hobby, this set features an all foil card with rainbow holofoil printing and is individually numbered to 100.

COMP.MPH SET (72) 300.00 600.00
*MPH CARDS: 4X TO 10X BASE CARDS

2001 Wheels High Gear Autographs

Randomly inserted into packs, this 33-card set features authentic signatures from drivers like Jeff Gordon and Dale Earnhardt. Card backs are unnumbered.

1 John Andretti
2 Dave Blaney 6.00 15.00
3 Brett Bodine 6.00 15.00
4 Todd Bodine 6.00 15.00
5 Jeff Burton 8.00 20.00
6 Ward Burton 10.00 25.00
7 Stacy Compton 6.00 15.00
8 Dale Earnhardt 850.00 1100.00
9 Dale Earnhardt Jr. 100.00 200.00
10 Jeff Gordon 100.00 200.00
11 David Green 6.00 15.00
12 Jeff Green 6.00 15.00
13 Mark Green 6.00 15.00
14 Bobby Hamilton 10.00 25.00
15 Kevin Harvick 12.50 30.00
16 Dale Jarrett 20.00 50.00
17 Jason Keller 6.00 15.00
18 Matt Kenseth 15.00 40.00
19 Terry Labonte 15.00 40.00
20 Chad Little 7.50 20.00
21 Jeremy Mayfield 7.50 20.00
22 Sterling Marlin 12.50 30.00
23 Mark Martin 40.00 80.00
24 Joe Nemechek 6.00 15.00
25 Hank Parker Jr. 6.00 15.00
26 Robert Pressley 6.00 15.00
27 Ricky Rudd 12.50 30.00
28 Elton Sawyer 6.00 15.00
29 Ken Schrader 6.00 15.00
30 Mike Skinner 7.50 20.00
31 Tony Stewart 30.00 80.00
32 Dick Trickle 6.00 15.00
33 Rusty Wallace 20.00 50.00

2001 Wheels High Gear Custom Shop

Randomly inserted into packs at the rate of one in 200, this 5-card insert set features an interactive card that allows the collector to custom-design their own foil-based card. He would select one of 3-different front and back card designs and Press Pass would build the card to his specifications.

COMPLETE SET (5) 80.00 200.00
*PRIZE CARDS: .4X TO 1X BASIC INSERTS
CSBL Bobby Labonte EXCH 10.00 25.00
CSDEJ Dale Earnhardt Jr. EXCH 20.00 50.00
CSJG Jeff Gordon EXCH 15.00 40.00
CSMK Matt Kenseth EXCH 12.50 30.00
CSTS Tony Stewart EXCH 12.50 30.00

2001 Wheels High Gear Flag Chasers

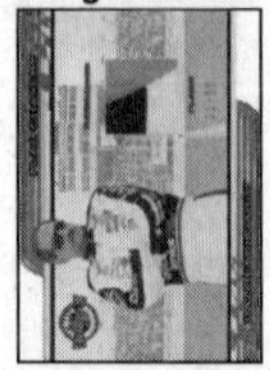

Randomly inserted into packs at the average rate of one in 325, this set features swatches of actual race-used flags. Card backs carry a "FC" prefix.

COMPLETE SET (5) 250.00 500.00
BLACK PRICED BELOW
BLACK CARDS #'D TO 75
*GREEN/RED/WHITE/YELLOW: .4X TO 1X
GREEN/RED/WHITE/YELLOW CARDS #'D TO 75
*BLUE-YELLOW: .4X TO 1X BASIC INSERTS
BLUE-YELLOW CARDS #'D TO 45
*CHECKERED CARDS: .6X TO 1.5X
CHECKERED CARDS #'D TO 35
*CHECKERED W/BLUE ORANGE 2X TO 5X
FC1 Bobby Labonte 25.00 60.00
FC2 Tony Stewart 25.00 60.00
FC3 Dale Earnhardt 100.00 200.00
FC4 Matt Kenseth 30.00 80.00
FC5 Dale Earnhardt Jr. 50.00 120.00

2001 Wheels High Gear Gear Shifters

Randomly inserted into packs at the rate of one in 2, this 27-card "set within a set" features the best drivers in NASCAR. Card backs carry a "GS" prefix.

COMPLETE SET (27) 12.50 30.00
GS1 Bobby Labonte 1.25 3.00
GS2 Dale Earnhardt 3.00 8.00
GS3 Dale Jarrett 1.25 3.00
GS4 Jeff Burton .50 1.25
GS5 Tony Stewart 2.00 5.00
GS6 Rusty Wallace 1.50 4.00
GS7 Ricky Rudd .75 2.00
GS8 Mark Martin 1.50 4.00
GS9 Ward Burton .50 1.25
GS10 Elliott Sadler .50 1.25
GS11 Mike Skinner .25 .60
GS12 Matt Kenseth 1.50 4.00
GS13 Steve Park .50 1.25
GS14 Dale Earnhardt Jr. 2.50 6.00
GS15 Robert Pressley .25 .60
GS16 Ken Schrader .25 .60
GS17 Sterling Marlin .75 2.00
GS18 Terry Labonte .75 2.00
GS19 Joe Nemechek .25 .60
GS20 Kenny Wallace .25 .60
GS21 Bobby Hamilton .25 .60
GS22 John Andretti .25 .60
GS23 Jimmy Spencer .25 .60
GS24 Jerry Nadeau .50 1.25
GS25 Jeremy Mayfield .25 .60
GS26 Dave Blaney .25 .60
GS27 Bobby Labonte 1.25 3.00

2001 Wheels High Gear Hot Streaks

Randomly inserted into packs at the rate of one in 10, this 9-card insert set features drivers that know how to have repeat success. Card backs carry a "HS" prefix.

COMPLETE SET (9) 20.00 50.00
HS1 Tony Stewart 4.00 10.00
HS2 Bobby Labonte 2.50 6.00
HS3 Dale Earnhardt 6.00 15.00
HS4 Mark Martin 3.00 8.00
HS5 Dale Jarrett 2.50 6.00
HS6 Ricky Rudd 1.50 4.00
HS7 Matt Kenseth 3.00 8.00
HS8 Dale Earnhardt Jr. 5.00 12.00
HS9 Jeff Burton 1.00 2.50

2001 Wheels High Gear Man and Machine Drivers

Randomly inserted into packs at the rate of one in 10, this 18-card insert set is broken into two subsets: MM1A-MM9A were issued in hobby packs (drivers), and cards MM1B-MM9B issued into retail packs (machines).

COMP.DRIVERS SET (9) 20.00 50.00
COMP.CAR SET (9) 15.00 40.00
*CARS: .3X TO .8X DRIVERS
MM1A Tony Stewart 4.00 10.00
MM2A Bobby Labonte 2.50 6.00
MM3A Rusty Wallace 3.00 8.00
MM4A Mark Martin 3.00 8.00
MM5A Dale Jarrett 2.50 6.00
MM6A Dale Earnhardt 6.00 15.00
MM7A Dale Earnhardt Jr. 5.00 12.00
MM8A Jeff Burton 1.00 2.50
MM9A Ward Burton 1.00 2.50

2001 Wheels High Gear Sunday Sensation

Randomly inserted into packs at the rate of one in 18, this plastic 9-card insert set features drivers that usually make Monday's headlines. Card backs carry a "SS" prefix.

COMPLETE SET (9) 15.00 40.00
SS1 Dale Jarrett 2.50 6.00
SS2 Rusty Wallace 2.50 6.00
SS3 Matt Kenseth 3.00 8.00
SS4 Steve Park 1.00 2.50
SS5 Tony Stewart 4.00 10.00
SS6 Dale Earnhardt 6.00 15.00
SS7 Bobby Labonte 2.50 6.00
SS8 Ward Burton 1.00 2.50
SS9 Jeff Burton 1.00 2.50

2001 Wheels High Gear Top Tier

Randomly inserted into packs at the rate of one in 20, this insert set features the top six drivers from the 2001 season. Card backs carry a "TT" prefix.

COMPLETE SET (6) 12.50 30.00
COMP.HOLOFOIL SET (6) 60.00 150.00
*HOLOFOILS: 1.5X TO 4X BASIC INSERTS
HOLOFOIL STATED ODDS 1:450
HOLOFOIL PRINT RUN 250 SER.#'D SETS
TT1 Bobby Labonte 3.00 8.00
TT2 Dale Earnhardt 8.00 20.00
TT3 Jeff Burton 1.25 3.00
TT4 Dale Jarrett 3.00 8.00
TT5 Ricky Rudd 1.50 4.00
TT6 Tony Stewart 5.00 12.00

2002 Wheels High Gear

The 2002 Wheels High Gear product was released in February 2002, and featured a 72-card base set broken into subsets as follows: 27 Veterans (1-27), 6 NASCAR Winston Cup Machines (28-33), 12 NASCAR Busch Series (34-45), 6 NASCAR Winston Cup Carmeleons (46-54), 6 2001 Highlights (55-60), 4 Contingency Awards (61-64), 2 Champ (65 and 66), and 4 NASCAR Winston Cup Previews (68-70). Each pack contained 4-cards and carried a suggested retail price of $2.99.

COMPLETE SET (72) 12.00 30.00
COMMON CARD (1-72) .08 .25
COMMON DRIVER (1-72) .15 .40
WAX BOX HOBBY (20) 50.00 90.00
WAX BOX RETAIL (16) 40.00 80.00
1 Dave Blaney .15 .40
2 Jeff Burton .30 .75
3 Ward Burton .30 .75
4 Kurt Busch .50 1.25
5 Ricky Craven .15 .40
6 Dale Earnhardt Jr. 1.50 4.00
7 Jeff Gordon 1.25 3.00
8 Bobby Hamilton .15 .40
9 Kevin Harvick 1.00 2.50
10 Dale Jarrett .75 2.00
11 Matt Kenseth 1.00 2.50
12 Bobby Labonte .75 2.00
13 Terry Labonte .50 1.25
14 Sterling Marlin .50 1.25
15 Mark Martin 1.00 2.50
16 Jerry Nadeau .30 .75
17 Joe Nemechek .15 .40
18 Steve Park .30 .75
19 Kyle Petty .30 .75
20 Robert Pressley .15 .40
21 Ricky Rudd .50 1.25
22 Elliott Sadler .30 .75
23 Ken Schrader .15 .40
24 Jimmy Spencer .15 .40
25 Tony Stewart 1.00 2.50
26 Rusty Wallace .75 2.00
27 Michael Waltrip .30 .75
28 Jeff Gordon's Car .50 1.25
29 Kevin Harvick's Car .50 1.25
30 Dale Jarrett's Car .30 .75
31 Ricky Rudd's Car .15 .40
32 Tony Stewart's Car .50 1.25
33 Rusty Wallace's Car .30 .75
34 Jeff Green BGN .15 .40
35 David Green BGN .15 .40
36 Kevin Grubb BGN .15 .40
37 Kevin Harvick BGN 1.00 2.50
38 Jimmie Johnson BGN 1.00 2.50
39 Jason Keller BGN .15
40 Randy LaJoie BGN .15
41 Chad Little BGN .15
42 Jamie McMurray BGN RC 4.00 10
43 Ryan Newman BGN 1.00 2
44 Hank Parker Jr. BGN .15
45 Elton Sawyer BGN .15
46 Dale Earnhardt Jr.'s Car .75 2
47 Jeff Gordon's Car .50 1
48 Kevin Harvick's Car .50 1
49 Dale Jarrett's Car .30
50 Bobby Labonte's Car .30
51 Ricky Rudd's Car .15
52 Ken Schrader's Car .08
53 Jimmy Spencer's Car .15
54 Tony Stewart's Car .50 1
55 Dale Earnhardt Jr. HL 1.50 4
56 Jeff Gordon HL 1.25 3
57 Kevin Harvick HL 1.00 2
58 Sterling Marlin HL .50 1
59 Steve Park HL .30
60 Michael Waltrip HL .30
61 Jeff Gordon CA 1.25 3
62 Jeff Gordon CA 1.25 3
63 Sterling Marlin CA .50 1
64 Kevin Harvick CA 1.00 2
65 Jeff Gordon WC Champ 1.25 3
66 Kevin Harvick BGN Champ 1.00 2
67 Ryan Newman PRE 1.00 2
68 Robby Gordon PRE .15
69 Jeff Green PRE .15
70 Jimmie Johnson PRE 1.00 2
71 Jeff Gordon WC Sched. .60 1
72 Kevin Harvick CL .50 1
P1 Power Pick Entry Card .08

2002 Wheels High Gea[r] First Gear

Inserted at a rate of one per pack, this paralle[l] features all-foil cardfronts with gold holofoil prin[t]

COMPLETE FIRST GEAR (72) 40.00 100
*FIRST GEAR: 1X TO 2.5X BASIC CARDS

2002 Wheels High Gea[r] MPH

Inserted at a rate of 1:30 hobby packs, this features an all-foil card with holofoil printing. card was individually serial numbered to 100.

COMP.MPH SET (72) 200.00 400
*MPH CARDS: 5X TO 12X BASIC CARDS

2002 Wheels High Gea[r] Autographs

This set features autographs of NASCAR drivers Winston Cup, Busch, and Craftsman Truck se inserted at a rate of 1:60 hobby packs and 1 retail packs. The cards were not numbered and been listed below alphabetically. The Dale Earnh Jr. was not released in the 2002 product, he released in 2004 Wheels High Gear.

1 Bobby Allison 15.00 30
2 Casey Atwood 12.50 25
3 Buddy Baker 6.00 15
4 Greg Biffle 10.00 25
5 Dave Blaney 6.00 15
6 Brett Bodine 6.00 15
7 Todd Bodine 6.00 15
8 Jeff Burton 8.00 20
9 Ward Burton 10.00 25
10 Kurt Busch 12.50 30
11 Richard Childress 8.00 20
12 Stacy Compton 6.00 15
13 Matt Crafton 6.00 15
14 Dale Earnhardt Jr. 200.00 400
15 Larry Foyt 6.00 15
16 Coy Gibbs 8.00 20
17 Jeff Gordon 100.00 200
18 David Green 6.00 15
19 Jeff Green 6.00 15
20 Bobby Hamilton 10.00 25
21 Kevin Harvick 12.50 30
22 Ricky Hendrick 25.00 50
23 Ron Hornaday 6.00 15
24 Dale Jarrett 20.00 50
25 Ned Jarrett 6.00 15
26 Jimmie Johnson 40.00 80
27 Jason Keller 6.00 15
28 Matt Kenseth 15.00 40
29 Travis Kvapil 8.00 20
30 Bobby Labonte 15.00 40
31 Terry Labonte 15.00 40
32 Randy LaJoie 6.00 15
33 Chad Little 6.00 15
34 Sterling Marlin 15.00 40
35 Mark Martin 40.00 80
36 Mike McLaughlin 6.00 15
37 Jamie McMurray 10.00 25
38 Ted Musgrave 6.00 15
39 Jerry Nadeau 8.00 20
40 Joe Nemechek 6.00 15
41 Ryan Newman 15.00 30

nny Parsons	30.00	60.00
vid Pearson	15.00	40.00
le Petty	15.00	30.00
chard Petty	40.00	80.00
bert Pressley	6.00	15.00
ny Raines	6.00	15.00
ott Riggs	10.00	25.00
cky Rudd	20.00	40.00
e Ruttman	6.00	15.00
on Sawyer	6.00	15.00
n Schrader	8.00	20.00
ke Skinner	6.00	15.00
ck Sprague	6.00	15.00
ny Stewart	40.00	100.00
sty Wallace	12.50	30.00
rrell Waltrip	20.00	50.00
chael Waltrip	10.00	25.00
ott Wimmer	12.50	25.00
n Wood	8.00	20.00
le Yarborough	15.00	30.00
bert Yates	6.00	15.00

02 Wheels High Gear Custom Shop

mly inserted into packs at the rate of one in his 5-card insert set features an interactive card llows the collector to custom-design their own sed card. Card backs carry a "CS" prefix along e driver's initials.

Dale Jarrett EXCH	12.50	25.00
Jeff Gordon EXCH	20.00	40.00
Kevin Harvick EXCH	12.50	30.00
Ryan Newman EXCH	12.50	30.00
Tony Stewart EXCH	12.50	30.00

02 Wheels High Gear Flag Chasers

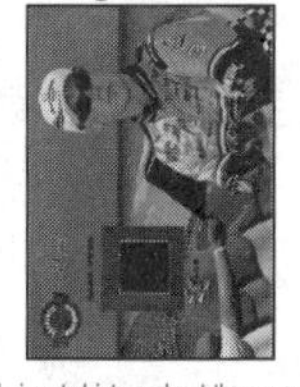

mly inserted into packs at the average rate of 400, this set features swatches of actual race-lags. Several different parallels were produced ach version being serial numbered. Card backs "FC" prefix.

E CARDS #'D TO 130
OW CARDS: .5X TO 1X BASIC INSERTS
W CARDS #'D TO 110
K/GREEN/RED: .5X TO 1X BASIC INSERTS
K/GREEN/RED CARDS #'D TO 90
E-YELLOW: .8X TO 2X BASIC INSERTS
-YELLOW CARDS #'D TO 40
CKERED CARDS: 2X TO 5X
CKERED W/BLUE ORANGE 3X TO 8X
KERED CARDS #'D TO 10

ale Earnhardt Jr.	50.00	120.00
eff Gordon	50.00	100.00
evin Harvick	30.00	60.00
ale Jarrett	25.00	60.00
ony Stewart	30.00	60.00

02 Wheels High Gear High Groove

ie cut card features foil stamping and photos driver and his car. They were inserted at a rate

PLETE SET (27)	12.00	30.00
ave Blaney	.25	.60
eff Burton	.50	1.25
Vard Burton	.50	1.25
urt Busch	.75	2.00
icky Craven	.25	.60
ale Earnhardt Jr.	2.50	6.00
eff Gordon	2.00	5.00
obby Hamilton	.25	.60
evin Harvick	1.50	4.00
Dale Jarrett	1.25	3.00
Matt Kenseth	1.50	4.00
Bobby Labonte	1.25	3.00
Terry Labonte	.75	2.00
Sterling Marlin	.75	2.00
Mark Martin	1.50	4.00
Jerry Nadeau	.50	1.25
Joe Nemechek	.25	.60
Steve Park	.50	1.25
Kyle Petty	.50	1.25
Robert Pressley	.25	.60
Ricky Rudd	.75	2.00
Elliott Sadler	.50	1.25
Ken Schrader	.25	.60
Jimmy Spencer	.25	.60

HG25 Tony Stewart	1.50	4.00
HG26 Rusty Wallace	1.25	3.00
HG27 Michael Waltrip	.50	1.25

2002 Wheels High Gear Hot Streaks

Inserted at a rate of 1:10, this 9-card set features top drivers from 2001. Each card was printed on holofoil card stock.

COMPLETE SET (9)	15.00	40.00
HS1 Jeff Burton	1.00	2.50
HS2 Dale Earnhardt Jr.	5.00	12.00
HS3 Jeff Gordon	4.00	10.00
HS4 Kevin Harvick	3.00	8.00
HS5 Dale Jarrett	2.50	6.00
HS6 Steve Park	1.00	2.50
HS7 Ricky Rudd	1.50	4.00
HS8 Tony Stewart	3.00	8.00
HS9 Rusty Wallace	2.50	6.00

2002 Wheels High Gear Man and Machine Drivers

Randomly inserted into packs at the rate of one in 10, this insert was divided into two different sets: MM1A-MM9A were issued in hobby packs (drivers), and cards MM1B-MM9B issued into retail packs (machines). Each card was die-cut so that both the driver and car version would fit together like a puzzle.

COMPLETE SET (9)	15.00	40.00
*CARS: .4X TO 1X DRIVERS		
MM1A Dale Earnhardt Jr.	5.00	12.00
MM2A Jeff Gordon	4.00	10.00
MM3A Kevin Harvick	3.00	8.00
MM4A Dale Jarrett	2.50	6.00
MM5A Bobby Labonte	2.50	6.00
MM6A Steve Park	1.00	2.50
MM7A Ricky Rudd	1.50	4.00
MM8A Tony Stewart	3.00	8.00
MM9A Rusty Wallace	2.50	6.00

2002 Wheels High Gear Sunday Sensation

Randomly inserted into packs at the rate of one in 18, this foil laser-etched 9-card insert set features drivers that usually make Monday's headlines. The cardbacks carry an "SS" prefix.

COMPLETE SET (9)	15.00	40.00
SS1 Ward Burton	1.25	3.00
SS2 Jeff Burton	1.25	3.00
SS3 Ricky Rudd	2.00	5.00
SS4 Jeff Gordon	5.00	12.00
SS5 Kevin Harvick	4.00	10.00
SS6 Dale Jarrett	3.00	8.00
SS7 Sterling Marlin	2.00	5.00
SS8 Tony Stewart	4.00	10.00
SS9 Rusty Wallace	3.00	8.00

2002 Wheels High Gear Top Tier

Randomly inserted into packs at the rate of one in 20, this insert set features the top six drivers from the 2001 season. Each card was printed on clear plastic card stock. Cardbacks carry a "TT" prefix.

COMPLETE SET (6)	15.00	40.00
*NUMBERED: 1.2X TO 3X BASIC INSERTS		
FOIL CARDS SERIAL #'d OF 250		
TT1 Jeff Gordon	6.00	15.00
TT2 Tony Stewart	5.00	12.00
TT3 Sterling Marlin	2.50	6.00
TT4 Ricky Rudd	2.00	5.00
TT5 Dale Jarrett	4.00	10.00
TT6 Bobby Labonte	4.00	10.00

2003 Wheels Autographs

Issued at a stated rate of one in 60, these 52 cards feature most of the leading drivers on the NASCAR circuit.

1 John Andretti AT/HG	6.00	15.00
2 Casey Atwood AT/HG	10.00	25.00
3 Greg Biffle Blue BGN HG	10.00	25.00
4 Greg Biffle Red WC AT	10.00	25.00
5 Dave Blaney AT/HG	6.00	15.00
6 Brett Bodine AT/HG	6.00	15.00
7 Todd Bodine AT	6.00	15.00
8 Jeff Burton Citgo AT	8.00	20.00
9 Jeff Burton Gain AT	8.00	20.00
10 Ward Burton AT	10.00	25.00
11 Kurt Busch AT/HG	12.50	30.00
12 Matt Crafton AT/HG	6.00	15.00
13 Ricky Craven AT/HG	10.00	25.00
14 Kerry Earnhardt AT	12.50	30.00
15 Coy Gibbs AT/HG	8.00	20.00
16 Jeff Gordon AT/HG	100.00	200.00
17 Robby Gordon AT/HG	8.00	20.00
18 David Green AT/HG	6.00	15.00
19 Jeff Green AT/HG	6.00	15.00
20 Mark Green AT/HG	6.00	15.00
21 Bobby Hamilton AT/HG	10.00	25.00
22 Kevin Harvick AT/HG	12.50	30.00
23 Ricky Hendrick AT/HG	25.00	50.00
24 Shane Hmiel AT/HG	15.00	30.00
25 Dale Jarrett AT/HG	15.00	40.00
26 Jimmie Johnson AT/HG	40.00	80.00
27 Jason Keller AT/HG	6.00	15.00
28 Matt Kenseth AT/HG	15.00	40.00
29 Travis Kvapil AT/HG	10.00	25.00
30 Bobby Labonte AT/HG	15.00	40.00
31 Terry Labonte AT/HG	15.00	40.00
32 Randy LaJoie AT/HG	6.00	15.00
33 Jason Leffler AT/HG	6.00	15.00
34 Chad Little AT/HG	6.00	15.00
35 Sterling Marlin AT	12.50	30.00
36 Mark Martin AT/HG	30.00	60.00
37 Jeremy Mayfield AT/HG	20.00	40.00
38 Jamie McMurray Havoline AT	10.00	25.00
39 Jamie McMurray Williams AT/HG	10.00	25.00
40 Casey Mears Phillips 66 AT/HG	10.00	25.00
41 Casey Mears Target AT	10.00	25.00
42 Ted Musgrave AT/HG	10.00	25.00
43 Jerry Nadeau AT	10.00	25.00
44 Joe Nemechek AT/HG	6.00	15.00
45 Ryan Newman AT/HG	15.00	30.00
46 Hank Parker Jr. AT/HG	6.00	15.00
47 Kyle Petty AT/HG	12.50	30.00
48 Tony Raines AT/HG	6.00	15.00
49 Scott Riggs AT/HG	10.00	25.00
50 Ricky Rudd AT/HG	12.50	30.00
51 Joe Ruttman AT/HG	6.00	15.00
52 Elliott Sadler AT/HG	10.00	25.00
53 Johnny Sauter AT/HG	8.00	20.00
54 Ken Schrader AT/HG	8.00	20.00
55 Dennis Setzer AT/HG	6.00	15.00
56 Mike Skinner AT/HG	10.00	25.00
57 Jimmy Spencer AT/HG	6.00	15.00
58 Brian Vickers AT/HG	10.00	25.00
59 Rusty Wallace AT/HG	12.50	30.00
60 Michael Waltrip	10.00	25.00
61 Scott Wimmer AT/HG	10.00	25.00
62 Jon Wood AT/HG	8.00	20.00

2003 Wheels High Gear

This set was released in January 2003. These cards were issued in 6-card hobby packs with an SRP of $3.99. They came 20-packs to a box and 20-boxes to a case. The retail version was issued four cards per pack with an $2.99 SRP and packaged 28-packs to a box and 20-boxes to a case. There was a special 0 card honoring Tony Stewart as the 2002 NASCAR champion and those cards were inserted at a stated rate of one in 400 packs. In addition, two cards (one hobby and the other retail only) featuring Kerry Earnhardt were issued in packs with a "KE" prefix, those cards were issued at a stated rate of one in 70 packs.

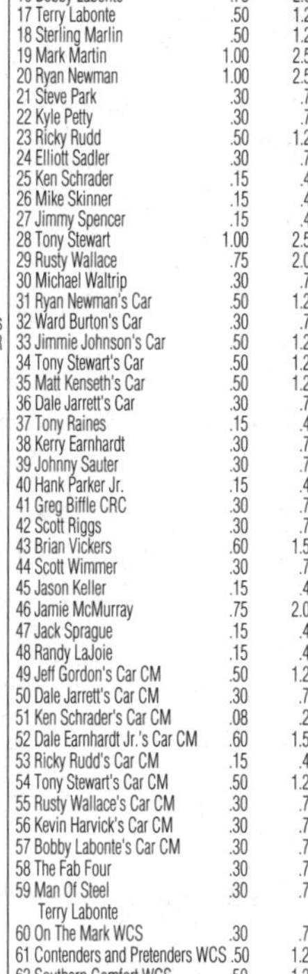

COMPLETE SET (72)	12.50	30.00
WAX BOX HOBBY (20)	50.00	80.00
1 John Andretti	.15	.40
2 Dave Blaney	.15	.40
3 Brett Bodine	.15	.40
4 Jeff Burton	.30	.75
5 Ward Burton	.30	.75
6 Kurt Busch	.50	1.25
7 Ricky Craven	.15	.40
8 Dale Earnhardt Jr.	1.50	4.00
9 Robby Gordon	.15	.40
10 Jeff Gordon	1.25	3.00
11 Jeff Green	.15	.40
12 Kevin Harvick	.75	2.00
13 Dale Jarrett	.75	2.00
14 Jimmie Johnson	1.00	2.50
15 Matt Kenseth	1.00	2.50
16 Bobby Labonte	.75	2.00
17 Terry Labonte	.50	1.25
18 Sterling Marlin	.50	1.25
19 Mark Martin	1.00	2.50
20 Ryan Newman	1.00	2.50
21 Steve Park	.30	.75
22 Kyle Petty	.30	.75
23 Ricky Rudd	.50	1.25
24 Elliott Sadler	.30	.75
25 Ken Schrader	.15	.40
26 Mike Skinner	.15	.40
27 Jimmy Spencer	.15	.40
28 Tony Stewart	1.00	2.50
29 Rusty Wallace	.75	2.00
30 Michael Waltrip	.30	.75
31 Ryan Newman's Car	.50	1.25
32 Ward Burton's Car	.30	.75
33 Jimmie Johnson's Car	.50	1.25
34 Tony Stewart's Car	.50	1.25
35 Matt Kenseth's Car	.50	1.25
36 Dale Jarrett's Car	.30	.75
37 Tony Raines	.15	.40
38 Kerry Earnhardt	.30	.75
39 Johnny Sauter	.30	.75
40 Hank Parker Jr.	.15	.40
41 Greg Biffle CRC	.30	.75
42 Scott Riggs	.30	.75
43 Brian Vickers	.60	1.50
44 Scott Wimmer	.30	.75
45 Jason Keller	.15	.40
46 Jamie McMurray	.75	2.00
47 Jack Sprague	.15	.40
48 Randy LaJoie	.15	.40
49 Jeff Gordon's Car CM	.50	1.25
50 Dale Jarrett's Car CM	.30	.75
51 Ken Schrader's Car CM	.08	.20
52 Dale Earnhardt Jr.'s Car CM	.60	1.50
53 Ricky Rudd's Car CM	.15	.40
54 Tony Stewart's Car CM	.50	1.25
55 Rusty Wallace's Car CM	.30	.75
56 Kevin Harvick's Car CM	.30	.75
57 Bobby Labonte's Car CM	.30	.75
58 The Fab Four	.30	.75
59 Man Of Steel Terry Labonte	.30	.75
60 On The Mark WCS	.30	.75
61 Contenders and Pretenders WCS	.50	1.25
62 Southern Comfort WCS	.50	1.25
63 Feeling Like A New Man WCS	.50	1.25
64 Tony Stewart NA	.75	2.00
65 Ryan Newman NA	.75	2.00
66 Jeff Green NA	.15	.40
67 Scott Riggs NA	.30	.75
68 Ryan Newman NA	.75	2.00
69 Greg Biffle NA	.30	.75
70 Elliott Sadler 2003 Preview	.30	.75
71 Kevin Harvick 2003 Preview	.60	1.50
72 Tony Stewart CL	.60	1.50
KE1 Kerry Earnhardt HOBBY	5.00	12.00
KE2 Kerry Earnhardt RETAIL	6.00	15.00
0 Tony Stewart Champion	10.00	25.00

2003 Wheels High Gear Blue Hawaii SCDA Promos

This 72-card set was a parallel to the basic set of Wheels High Gear. This set had blue foil highlights and each card was slabbed by SCD Authentic. The labels read Racing Champions Press Pass Exclusive Blue Parallel Hawaii Edition, Wheels High Gear. There were reports that between 5 and 10 copies of each card were available.

*BLUE HAWAII: X TO X BASE CARDS

2003 Wheels High Gear First Gear

Issued at a stated rate of one per pack, this is a parallel to the High Gear set. These cards can be differentiated from the regular cards by the silver foil cardstock and gold foil highlights.

COMPLETE SET (72)	25.00	50.00
*FIRST GEAR: .8X TO 2X BASE CARDS		

2003 Wheels High Gear MPH

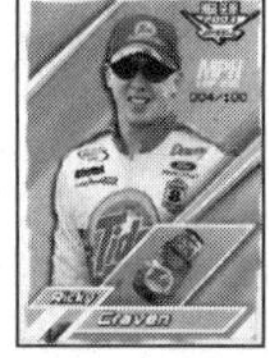

Randomly inserted into packs, this is a parallel to the basic set. These cards can be differentiated as they were treated with special holofoil stamping and were issued to 100 serial numbered sets.

*MPH: 5X TO 12X BASE CARDS

2003 Wheels High Gear Samples

These cards were issued to preview the 72-card 2003 High Gear set. The cards were stamped "Sample" on the backs and were issued one per Beckett Racing Collector magazine.

*SAMPLES: 2X TO 5X BASE CARDS

2003 Wheels High Gear Custom Shop

Issued at a stated rate of one in 200, these five cards feature some of the most popular drivers on the Winston Cup circuit. Collectors were able to use these redemption cards by choosing from a variety of front and back designs to create their own custom card. The expiration date for the exchange cards is 6/30/2004.

COMPLETE SET (5)	60.00	120.00
*PRIZE CARDS: .5X TO 1.2X BASIC INSERTS		
45-DIFFERENT PRIZES ISSUED VIA MAIL		
CSDE Dale Earnhardt Jr. EXCH	20.00	40.00
CSJG Jeff Gordon EXCH	15.00	30.00
CSJJ Jimmie Johnson EXCH	12.50	25.00
CSRN Ryan Newman EXCH	12.50	25.00
CSTS Tony Stewart EXCH	12.50	25.00

2003 Wheels High Gear Custom Shop Autograph Redemption

These cards were initially released as redemption cards in packs of 2003 Wheels High Gear. Each card features the front of the typical Custom Shop insert with a sticker attached to the cardback with an explanation of the redemption program and an expiration date (June 30, 2004). The cardbacks also include a "Press Pass Authentics" hologram sticker.

CSDE Dale Earnhardt Jr. EXCH
CSJG Jeff Gordon EXCH
CSJJ Jimmie Johnson EXCH
CSRN Ryan Newman EXCH
CSTS Tony Stewart EXCH

2003 Wheels High Gear Dale Earnhardt Retrospective

Issued at a stated rate of one in 72, these nine cards feature a look back at some of the most popular High Gear Dale Earnhardt cards ever issued. A Foil parallel set was also issued and serial numbered to 250.

COMMON EARNHARDT	10.00	25.00
*FOILS: .8X TO 2X BASIC INSERTS		

2003 Wheels High Gear Flag Chasers Black

Randomly inserted into packs, these cards feature a race-used black flag piece embedded into a card. These cards were issued to a stated print run of 90 serial numbered sets. Six other flag colors were also produced as parallels of each card in varying quantities as noted below.

*BLUE/YELLOW FLAGS: .8X TO 2X BLACK
BLUE/YELLOW FLAGS SER.#'d TO 45
CHECKERED FLAGS SERIAL #'d TO 25
*CHECKERED FLAGS: NOT PRICED DUE TO SCARCITY
*GREEN FLAGS: .3X TO .8X BLACK FLAGS
GREEN FLAGS SERIAL #'d TO 90
*RED FLAGS: .3X TO .8X BLACK FLAGS
RED FLAGS SERIAL #'d TO 90
*WHITE FLAGS: .3X TO .8X BLACK FLAGS
WHITE FLAGS SERIAL #'d TO 90
*YELLOW FLAGS: .3X TO .8X BLACK FLAGS
YELLOW FLAGS SERIAL #'d TO 90
POWER PICK ENTRY CARD ODDS 1:20

FC1 Dale Earnhardt Jr.	75.00	150.00
FC2 Jeff Gordon	60.00	120.00
FC3 Jimmie Johnson	30.00	80.00
FC4 Ryan Newman	30.00	80.00
FC5 Tony Stewart	40.00	100.00
FC6 Matt Kenseth	30.00	80.00
FC7 Jamie McMurray	30.00	60.00
FC8 Kurt Busch	30.00	60.00
FC9 Mark Martin	40.00	100.00
FC10 Ward Burton	20.00	50.00
NNO Power Pick Entry Card	1.50	4.00

2003 Wheels High Gear Full Throttle

Issued at a stated rate of one in six, these nine cards feature high-speed competitors in this set made of clear plastic stock.

COMPLETE SET (9)	10.00	25.00
FT1 Kevin Harvick	1.25	3.00
FT2 Jeff Gordon	2.00	5.00
FT3 Ryan Newman	1.50	4.00
FT4 Jimmie Johnson	1.50	4.00
FT5 Dale Jarrett	1.25	3.00
FT6 Rusty Wallace	1.25	3.00
FT7 Dale Earnhardt Jr.	2.50	6.00
FT8 Mark Martin	1.50	4.00
FT8 Tony Stewart	1.50	4.00
FT9 Matt Kenseth	1.50	4.00

2003 Wheels High Gear High Groove

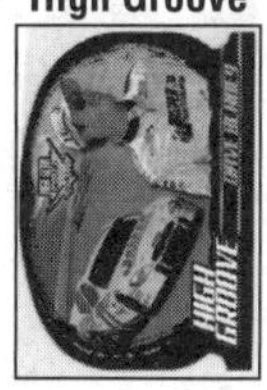

Issued at a stated rate of one in two, these 27 cards feature some of the leading drivers in NASCAR. Each card was die-cut and features a photo of the driver and his car.

COMPLETE SET (27)	10.00	25.00
HG1 Dave Blaney	.25	.60
HG2 Jeff Burton	.50	1.25
HG3 Ward Burton	.50	1.25
HG4 Kurt Busch	.75	2.00
HG5 Ricky Craven	.25	.60
HG6 Dale Earnhardt Jr.	2.50	6.00
HG7 Jeff Gordon	2.00	5.00
HG8 Robby Gordon	.25	.60
HG9 Jeff Green	.25	.60
HG10 Kevin Harvick	1.25	3.00
HG11 Dale Jarrett	1.25	3.00
HG12 Jimmie Johnson	1.50	4.00
HG13 Matt Kenseth	1.50	4.00
HG14 Bobby Labonte	1.25	3.00
HG15 Terry Labonte	.75	2.00
HG16 Sterling Marlin	.75	2.00
HG17 Mark Martin	1.50	4.00
HG18 Ryan Newman	1.50	4.00
HG19 Steve Park	.50	1.25
HG20 Kyle Petty	.50	1.25
HG21 Ricky Rudd	.75	2.00
HG22 Elliott Sadler	.50	1.25
HG23 Ken Schrader	.25	.60
HG24 Jimmy Spencer	.25	.60
HG25 Tony Stewart	1.50	4.00
HG26 Rusty Wallace	1.25	3.00
HG27 Michael Waltrip	.50	1.25

2003 Wheels High Gear Hot Treads

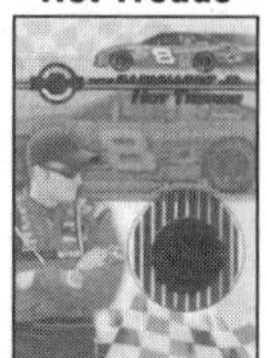

Randomly inserted in retail packs only, these 19 cards feature leading NASCAR drivers. These cards were issued to a stated print run of 425 serial numbered sets.

HT0 Michael Waltrip	10.00	25.00
HT1 John Andretti	6.00	15.00
HT2 Jeff Burton	8.00	20.00
HT3 Ward Burton	8.00	20.00
HT4 Kurt Busch	12.50	30.00
HT5 Jeff Gordon	15.00	40.00
HT6 Kevin Harvick	12.50	30.00
HT7 Jimmie Johnson	12.50	30.00
HT8 Matt Kenseth	12.50	30.00

HT9 Bobby Labonte	10.00	25.00
HT10 Sterling Marlin	8.00	20.00
HT11 Mark Martin	12.50	30.00
HT12 Jamie McMurray	10.00	25.00
HT13 Ryan Newman	12.50	30.00
HT14 Steve Park	10.00	25.00
HT15 Kyle Petty	10.00	25.00
HT16 Tony Stewart	15.00	30.00
HT17 Rusty Wallace	12.50	30.00
HT18 Dale Earnhardt Jr.	15.00	40.00

2003 Wheels High Gear Man

Issued at a stated rate of one in 10 hobby packs, these nine foil-embossed die-cut cards feature photos of leading drivers. A "Machine" version of each card was produced for retail packs. Collectors could interlock both the Man and Machine cards similar to a puzzle.

COMPLETE SET (9)	15.00	40.00
*MACHINE: .4X TO 1X MAN CARDS		
MACHINE STATED ODDS 1:10 RETAIL		
MM1A Jimmie Johnson	2.50	6.00
MM2A Kevin Harvick	2.00	5.00
MM3A Rusty Wallace	2.00	5.00
MM4A Tony Stewart	2.50	6.00
MM5A Ryan Newman	2.50	6.00
MM6A Dale Earnhardt Jr.	4.00	10.00
MM7A Dale Jarrett	2.00	5.00
MM8A Bobby Labonte	2.00	5.00
MM9A Jeff Gordon	3.00	8.00

2003 Wheels High Gear Sunday Sensation

Issued at a stated rate of one in 18, these nine silver foil micro-etched cards feature both NASCAR drivers and the tracks they won races on in 2002.

COMPLETE SET (9)	25.00	60.00
SS1 Matt Kenseth	4.00	10.00
SS2 Sterling Marlin	2.00	5.00
SS3 Mark Martin	4.00	10.00
SS4 Jeff Gordon	5.00	12.00
SS5 Jimmie Johnson	4.00	10.00
SS6 Ryan Newman	4.00	10.00
SS7 Tony Stewart	4.00	10.00
SS8 Ward Burton	1.25	3.00
SS9 Dale Earnhardt Jr.	6.00	15.00

2003 Wheels High Gear Top Tier

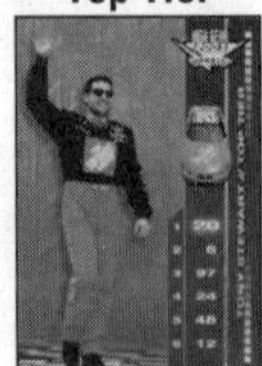

Issued at a stated rate of one in 12, these six cards feature the top drivers from the 2002 NASCAR season. Each was printed on special holofoil card stock.

COMPLETE SET (6)	8.00	20.00
TT1 Tony Stewart	2.00	5.00
TT2 Mark Martin	2.00	5.00
TT3 Kurt Busch	1.00	2.50
TT4 Jeff Gordon	2.50	6.00
TT5 Jimmie Johnson	2.00	5.00
TT6 Ryan Newman	2.00	5.00

2004 Wheels Autographs

These 59 cards were signed by the drivers pictured on them and inserted in packs at a rate of one in 60. They were certified by the manufacturer on the card backs.

1 Bobby Allison HG	8.00	20.00
2 Greg Biffle HG	10.00	25.00
3 Dave Blaney HG	6.00	15.00
4 Mike Bliss HG	8.00	20.00
5 Brett Bodine HG	8.00	20.00
6 Todd Bodine HG	8.00	20.00
7 Clint Bowyer AT	12.50	30.00
8 Jeff Burton HG	8.00	20.00
9 Ward Burton HG	10.00	25.00
10 Kurt Busch HG	12.50	30.00
11 Kyle Busch HG	25.00	60.00
12 Terry Cook AT	8.00	20.00
13 Stacy Compton HG	8.00	20.00
14 Matt Crafton HG	8.00	20.00
15 Ricky Craven HG	10.00	25.00
16 Rick Crawford HG	8.00	20.00
17 Dale Earnhardt Jr. AT	60.00	120.00
18 Kerry Earnhardt HG	15.00	40.00
19 Carl Edwards HG	20.00	50.00
20 Tim Fedewa AT	8.00	20.00
21 Christian Fittipaldi HG	8.00	20.00
22 Brendan Gaughan AT	10.00	25.00
23 Coy Gibbs HG	8.00	20.00
24 Jeff Gordon HG	100.00	200.00
25 Robby Gordon AT	10.00	25.00
26 Tina Gordon HG	10.00	25.00
27 David Green HG	8.00	20.00
28 Jeff Green AT	8.00	20.00
29 Kevin Harvick HG	12.50	30.00
30 Andy Houston HG	8.00	20.00
31 Dale Jarrett HG	15.00	40.00
32 Ned Jarrett HG	8.00	20.00
33 Jimmie Johnson HG	40.00	80.00
34 Kasey Kahne HG	25.00	60.00
35 Jason Keller HG	8.00	20.00
36 Matt Kenseth HG	15.00	40.00
37 Travis Kvapil HG	10.00	25.00
38 Bobby Labonte HG	15.00	40.00
39 Terry Labonte HG	15.00	40.00
40 Damon Lusk HG	8.00	20.00
41 Sterling Marlin HG	12.50	30.00
42 Mark Martin HG	30.00	60.00
43 Jeremy Mayfield HG	10.00	25.00
44 Mike McLaughlin HG	8.00	20.00
45 Jamie McMurray HG	10.00	25.00
46 Casey Mears HG	10.00	25.00
47 Joe Nemechek HG	8.00	20.00
48 Ryan Newman HG	15.00	30.00
49 Billy Parker Jr. AT	10.00	25.00
50 Benny Parsons HG	30.00	60.00
51 David Pearson HG	12.50	30.00
52 Kyle Petty HG	15.00	40.00
53 Richard Petty HG	40.00	80.00
54 Tony Raines HG	8.00	20.00
55 Scott Riggs HG	10.00	25.00
56 Ricky Rudd HG	12.50	30.00
57 Elliott Sadler AT	15.00	40.00
58 Johnny Sauter HG	12.50	30.00
59 Ken Schrader HG	8.00	20.00
60 Dennis Setzer HG	8.00	20.00
61 Regan Smith HG	8.00	20.00
62 Jack Sprague AT	8.00	20.00
63 Tony Stewart AT	40.00	100.00
64 Martin Truex Jr.	15.00	40.00
65 Brian Vickers HG	10.00	25.00
66 Kenny Wallace HG	10.00	25.00
67 Rusty Wallace HG	12.50	30.00
68 Michael Waltrip AT	10.00	25.00
69 Scott Wimmer HG	10.00	25.00
70 Glen Wood HG	8.00	20.00
71 Jon Wood HG	8.00	20.00
72 Cale Yarborough HG	10.00	25.00
73 J.J. Yeley AT	12.50	30.00

2004 Wheels High Gear

This set was released in late January 2004. These cards were issued in 5-card hobby packs with an SRP of $2.99. They came 20-packs to a box and 20-boxes to a case. The retail version was issued four cards per pack with an $2.99 SRP and packaged 28-packs to a box and 20-boxes to a case. There was a special 0 card honoring Matt Kenseth as the 2003 NASCAR champion and those cards were inserted at a stated rate of one in 480 packs.

COMPLETE SET (72)	12.50	30.00
COMMON CARD (1-72)	.10	.25
WAX BOX HOBBY (20)	50.00	90.00
1 Greg Biffle	.30	.75
2 Dave Blaney	.20	.50
3 Jeff Burton	.30	.75
4 Kurt Busch	.50	1.25
5 Ricky Craven	.20	.50
6 Dale Earnhardt Jr.	1.25	3.00
7 Robby Gordon	.20	.50
8 Jeff Gordon	1.25	3.00
9 Kevin Harvick	.75	2.00
10 Dale Jarrett	.60	1.50
11 Jimmie Johnson	1.00	2.50
12 Matt Kenseth	1.00	2.50
13 Bobby Labonte	.60	1.50
14 Terry Labonte	.50	1.25
15 Sterling Marlin	.50	1.25
16 Mark Martin	.75	2.00
17 Jamie McMurray	.50	1.25
18 Casey Mears	.30	.75
19 Joe Nemechek	.20	.50
20 Ryan Newman	1.00	2.50
21 Kyle Petty	.30	.75
22 Ricky Rudd	.50	1.25
23 Elliott Sadler	.30	.75
24 Jimmy Spencer	.20	.50
25 Tony Stewart	.75	2.00
26 Rusty Wallace	.60	1.50
27 Michael Waltrip	.30	.75
28 Terry Labonte C	.30	.75
29 Dale Earnhardt Jr.'s Car C	.50	1.25
30 Kurt Busch's Car C	.10	.25
31 Bobby Labonte's Car C	.30	.75
32 Elliott Sadler's Car C	.10	.25
33 Ricky Rudd's Car C	.20	.50
34 Jeff Gordon's Car C	.50	1.25
35 Robby Gordon's Car C	.10	.25
36 Jimmie Johnson's Car C	.50	1.25
37 David Green	.20	.50
38 Brian Vickers	.60	1.50
39 Scott Riggs CRC	.30	.75
40 Kasey Kahne	1.25	3.00
41 Scott Wimmer	.30	.75
42 Coy Gibbs	.30	.75
43 Mike Bliss	.20	.50
44 Johnny Sauter	.30	.75
45 Kyle Busch RC	4.00	10.00
46 Matt Kenseth NA	1.00	2.50
47 Jamie McMurray NA	.50	1.25
48 Ryan Newman NA	1.00	2.50
49 Matt Kenseth NA	1.00	2.50
50 Dale Earnhardt Jr. NA	1.25	3.00
51 Jimmie Johnson NA	1.00	2.50
52 Jeff Gordon NA	1.25	3.00
53 Brian Vickers NA	.60	1.50
54 David Stremme NA RC	2.00	5.00
55 Rusty Wallace's Car	.30	.75
56 Bobby Labonte's Car	.30	.75
57 Jimmie Johnson's Car	.50	1.25
58 Kevin Harvick's Car	.30	.75
59 Jeff Gordon's Car	.50	1.25
60 Matt Kenseth's Car	.50	1.25
61 Dale Earnhardt Jr. Feb. 2003	1.25	3.00
62 Rusty Wallace May 2003	.60	1.50
63 Ryan Newman June 2003	1.00	2.50
64 Kurt Busch July 2003	.50	1.25
65 Bobby Labonter Sept. 2003	.60	1.50
66 Michael Waltrip Oct. 2003	.30	.75
67 Jamie McMurray's Car PREV	.20	.50
68 Kurt Busch's Car PREV	.50	1.25
69 Joe Nemechek's Car PREV	.10	.25
70 Scott Wimmer's Car PREV	.20	.50
71 Scott Riggs' Car PREV	.20	.50
72 Jimmie Johnson CL	1.00	2.50
0 Matt Kenseth Champ	8.00	20.00

2004 Wheels High Gear MPH

Randomly inserted into packs, this is a parallel to the basic set. These cards can be differentiated as they were treated with special holofoil stamping and were issued to 100 serial numbered sets.

COMPLETE SET (72)
*VETERANS: 5X TO 12X BASE CARD HI
*RCs: 4X TO 10X BASE CARD HI

2004 Wheels High Gear Samples

These cards were issued to preview the 72-card 2004 High Gear set. The cards were stamped "Sample" on the backs and were issued one per Beckett Racing Collector magazine Issue #115 March, 2004.

*SAMPLES: 2X TO 5X BASE
STATED ODDS 1 PER BRC 115

2004 Wheels High Gear Custom Shop

Issued at a stated rate of one in 200, these five cards feature some of the most popular drivers on the Winston Cup circuit. Collectors were able to use these redemption cards by choosing from a variety of front and back designs to create their own custom card.

CSDE Dale Earnhardt Jr.	20.00	40.00
CSJG Jeff Gordon	20.00	40.00
CSJJ Jimmie Johnson	15.00	30.00
CSKH Kevin Harvick	12.50	25.00
CSTS Tony Stewart	12.50	25.00

2004 Wheels High Gear Dale Earnhardt Jr.

This 6-card set featured Dale Earnhardt Jr. in 6 different cards and were available only in specially marked blister boxes.

COMPLETE SET (6)	15.00	40.00
DJR1 Dale Earnhardt Jr.	3.00	6.00
DJR2 Dale Earnhardt Jr.	3.00	6.00
DJR3 Dale Earnhardt Jr.	3.00	6.00
DJR4 Dale Earnhardt Jr.	3.00	6.00
DJR5 Dale Earnhardt Jr.	3.00	6.00
DJR6 Dale Earnhardt Jr.	3.00	6.00

2004 Wheels High Gear Flag Chasers Black

Randomly inserted into packs, these cards feature a race-used black flag piece embedded into a card.

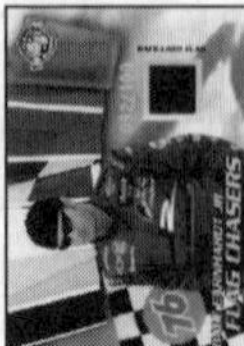

These cards were issued to a stated print run of 90 serial numbered sets. Six other flag colors were also produced as parallels of each card in varying quantities as noted below.

STATED PRINT RUN 100 SER.#'d SETS
ENTRY CARD STATED ODDS 1:20
*BLUE FLAGS: .6X TO 1.5X BLACK
BLUE FLAG PRINT RUN 50 SER.#'d SETS
*CHECKERED FLAGS: 1X TO 2.5X BLACK
CHECKERED FLAG PRINT RUN 35 SER.#'d SETS
*GREEN FLAGS: .5X TO 1X BLACK
*RED FLAGS: .5X TO 1X BLACK
*WHITE FLAGS: .5X TO 1X BLACK
*YELLOW FLAGS: .5X TO 1X BLACK
GRN/RED/WHT/YELL SER.#'d OF 100

FC1 Jimmie Johnson	25.00	50.00
FC2 Kevin Harvick	30.00	60.00
FC3 Bobby Labonte	20.00	40.00
FC4 Michael Waltrip	15.00	30.00
FC5 Tony Stewart	30.00	60.00
FC6 Jeff Gordon	40.00	80.00
FC7 Dale Earnhardt Jr.	40.00	80.00
FC8 Ryan Newman	30.00	60.00
FC9 Matt Kenseth	30.00	60.00
NNO Entry Card	1.25	3.00

2004 Wheels High Gear Full Throttle

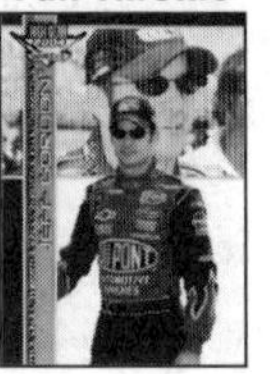

Issued at a stated rate of one in 18, these six cards feature high-speed competitors in this set made of clear plastic stock.

COMPLETE SET (6)	12.50	30.00
FT1 Jimmie Johnson	3.00	8.00
FT2 Jeff Gordon	4.00	10.00
FT3 Ryan Newman	3.00	8.00
FT4 Tony Stewart	2.50	6.00
FT5 Matt Kenseth	3.00	8.00
FT6 Kevin Harvick	2.50	6.00

2004 Wheels High Gear High Groove

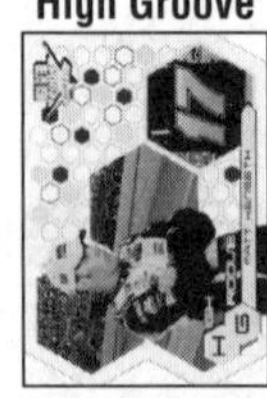

Issued at a stated rate of one per pack, these 27 cards feature some of the leading drivers in NASCAR. Each card was die-cut and features a photo of the driver and his car.

COMPLETE SET (27)	8.00	20.00
HG1 Greg Biffle	.40	1.00
HG2 Jeff Burton	.40	1.00
HG3 Kurt Busch	.60	1.50
HG4 Ricky Craven	.25	.60
HG5 Dale Earnhardt Jr.	1.50	4.00
HG6 Jeff Gordon	1.50	4.00
HG7 Robby Gordon	.25	.60
HG8 Kevin Harvick	1.00	2.50
HG9 Dale Jarrett	.75	2.00
HG10 Jimmie Johnson	1.25	3.00
HG11 Matt Kenseth	1.25	3.00
HG12 Bobby Labonte	.75	2.00
HG13 Terry Labonte	.60	1.50
HG14 Sterling Marlin	.60	1.50
HG15 Mark Martin	1.00	2.50
HG16 Jamie McMurray	.60	1.50
HG17 Casey Mears	.40	1.00
HG18 Joe Nemechek	.25	.60
HG19 Ryan Newman	1.25	3.00
HG20 Kyle Petty	.40	1.00
HG21 Ricky Rudd	.60	1.50
HG22 Elliott Sadler	.40	1.00
HG23 Dave Blaney	.25	.60
HG24 Jimmy Spencer	.25	.60
HG25 Tony Stewart	1.00	2.50
HG26 Rusty Wallace	.75	2.00
HG27 Michael Waltrip	.40	1.00

2004 Wheels High Gear Machine

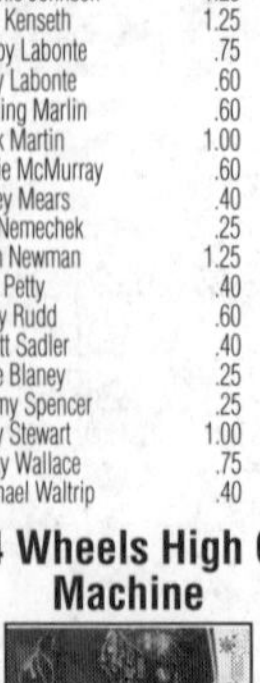

Issued at a stated rate of one in 10 retail sets, these nine foil-embossed diecut cards feature the cars of leading drivers.

COMPLETE SET (9)	15.00	40.00
*MACHINE: .4X TO 1X MAN		
STATED ODDS 1:10 RETAIL		
MM1B Tony Stewart	2.00	5.00
MM2B Kurt Busch	1.00	2.50
MM3B Jeff Gordon	3.00	8.00
MM4B Michael Waltrip	.60	1.50
MM5B Kevin Harvick	2.00	5.00
MM6B Jimmie Johnson	2.50	6.00
MM7B Matt Kenseth	2.50	6.00
MM8B Dale Jarrett	1.25	3.00
MM9B Dale Earnhardt Jr.	3.00	8.00

2004 Wheels High Gear Man

Issued at a stated rate of one in 10 hobby packs, these nine foil-embossed die-cut cards feature photos of leading drivers. A "Machine" version of each card was produced for retail packs. Collectors could interlock both the Man and Machine cards similar to a puzzle.

COMPLETE SET (9)	15.00	40.00
MM1A Tony Stewart	2.00	5.00
MM2A Kurt Busch	1.00	2.50
MM3A Jeff Gordon	3.00	8.00
MM4A Michael Waltrip	.60	1.50
MM5A Kevin Harvick	2.00	5.00
MM6A Jimmie Johnson	2.50	6.00
MM7A Matt Kenseth	2.50	6.00
MM8A Dale Jarrett	1.25	3.00
MM9A Dale Earnhardt Jr.	3.00	8.00

2004 Wheels High Gear Sunday Sensation

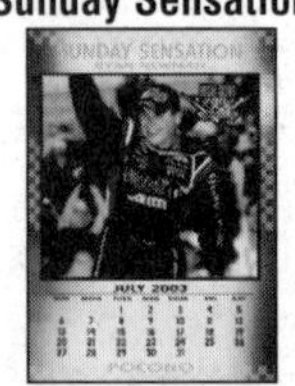

Issued at a stated rate of one in 18, these nine silver foil micro-etched cards feature both NASCAR drivers and the tracks they won races on in 2003.

COMPLETE SET (9)	10.00	25.00
SS1 Michael Waltrip	.50	1.25
SS2 Matt Kenseth	1.50	4.00
SS3 Dale Earnhardt Jr.	2.00	5.00
SS4 Jimmie Johnson	1.50	4.00
SS5 Tony Stewart	1.25	3.00
SS6 Ryan Newman	1.50	4.00
SS7 Kevin Harvick	1.25	3.00
SS8 Ryan Newman	1.50	4.00
SS9 Jeff Gordon	2.00	5.00

2004 Wheels High Gear Top Ten

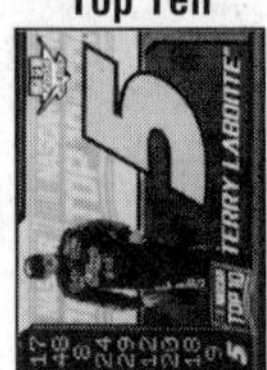

Issued at a stated rate of one in 12, these nine cards feature the top drivers from the 2003 NASCAR season. Each was printed on special holofoil card stock.

COMPLETE SET (9)	12.50	30.00
TT1 Matt Kenseth	3.00	8.00
TT2 Jimmie Johnson	3.00	8.00
TT3 Dale Earnhardt Jr.	4.00	10.00
TT4 Jeff Gordon	4.00	10.00
TT5 Kevin Harvick	2.50	6.00
TT6 Ryan Newman	3.00	8.00
TT7 Tony Stewart	2.50	6.00
TT8 Bobby Labonte	2.00	5.00
TT9 Terry Labonte	1.50	4.00

2004 Wheels High Gear Winston Victory Lap Tribute

This 6-card set was randomly inserted in packs at a rate of one in 48. The card feature some of the most memorable drivers who won Winston Championships.

COMPLETE SET (6)	40.00	1(
*GOLDS: 1X TO 2.5X BASIC INSERTS		
GOLD PRINT RUN 100 SER.#'d SETS		
WVL1 Jeff Gordon	8.00	
WVL2 Terry Labonte	6.00	
WVL3 Richard Petty	8.00	
WVL4 Dale Earnhardt	12.50	
WVL5 Darrell Waltrip	6.00	
WVL6 Cale Yarborough	5.00	

2005 Wheels Autogra

These 67 cards were signed by the drivers p on them and inserted in packs at a rate of one in both Wheels American Thunder and Wheel Gear packs. They were certified by the manuf on the card backs.

1 Bobby Allison	8.00	
2 Greg Biffle BGN	10.00	
3 Greg Biffle NC	10.00	
4 Mike Bliss	8.00	
5 Clint Bowyer	12.50	
6 Kurt Busch	12.50	
7 Kyle Busch BGN	20.00	
8 Kyle Busch NC	20.00	
9 Terry Cook	8.00	
10 Matt Crafton	8.00	
11 Ricky Craven	10.00	
12 Rick Crawford	7.50	
13 Dale Earnhardt Jr.	60.00	1
14 Kerry Earnhardt	12.50	
15 Tim Fedewa	8.00	
16 Brendan Gaughan	10.00	
17 Jeff Gordon	75.00	1
18 Robby Gordon	10.00	
19 Tina Gordon	10.00	
20 David Green	8.00	
21 Jeff Green	8.00	
22 Kevin Harvick	12.50	
23 Ron Hornaday	8.00	
24 Andy Houston	8.00	
25 Dale Jarrett	15.00	
26 Jimmie Johnson	40.00	
27 Kasey Kahne BGN	25.00	
28 Kasey Kahne NC	25.00	
29 Jason Keller	8.00	
30 Matt Kenseth BGN	15.00	
31 Matt Kenseth NC	15.00	
32 Bobby Labonte	15.00	
33 Justin Labonte	15.00	
34 Terry Labonte	15.00	
35 Sterling Marlin	12.50	
36 Mark Martin	30.00	
37 Jeremy Mayfield	10.00	
38 Mark McFarland	8.00	
39 Jamie McMurray	10.00	
40 Casey Mears	10.00	
41 Joe Nemechek	10.00	
42 Ryan Newman	15.00	
43 Steve Park	25.00	
44 Benny Parsons	30.00	
45 David Pearson	10.00	
46 Kyle Petty	8.00	
47 Richard Petty	40.00	
48 Scott Riggs	8.00	
49 Ricky Rudd	12.50	
50 Boris Said	10.00	
51 Johnny Sauter	10.00	
52 Ken Schrader CTS	10.00	
53 Ken Schrader NC	10.00	
54 Dennis Setzer	8.00	
55 Jack Sprague	6.00	
56 Tony Stewart	40.00	1
57 Martin Truex Jr.	15.00	
58 Brian Vickers	10.00	
59 Kenny Wallace	8.00	
60 Rusty Wallace	12.50	
61 Michael Waltrip	10.00	
62 Scott Wimmer	8.0	
63 Paul Wolfe	10.00	
64 Glen Wood	6.00	
65 Jon Wood	8.00	
66 Cale Yarborough	8.00	
67 J.J. Yeley	12.50	

2005 Wheels High Ge

This set was released in late January 2005. cards were issued in 5-card hobby packs w SRP of $2.99. They came 20-packs to a box a boxes to a case. The retail version was issu cards per pack with an $2.99 SRP and packag packs to a box and 20-boxes to a case. There special 0 card honoring Kurt Busch as th NASCAR champion and those cards were ins a stated rate of one in 480 packs.

COMPLETE SET (90)	12.50
COMMON CARD	.08
0 CARD STATED ODDS 1:72	
FLAG CHASERS ENTRY STATED ODDS 1:20	
WAX BOX HOBBY (20)	50.00
WAX BOX RETAIL (24)	35.00
1 Joe Nemechek	.20

usty Wallace .60 1.50
lark Martin .75 2.00
ale Earnhardt Jr. 1.25 3.00
asey Kahne 1.25 3.00
cott Riggs .30 .75
yan Newman 1.00 2.50
lichael Waltrip .30 .75
reg Biffle .30 .75
Matt Kenseth 1.00 2.50
Bobby Labonte .60 1.50
Jeremy Mayfield .20 .50
Tony Stewart .75 2.00
Ricky Rudd .50 1.25
Scott Wimmer .30 .75
Jeff Gordon 1.25 3.00
Brian Vickers .60 1.50
Kevin Harvick .75 2.00
Elliott Sadler .30 .75
Sterling Marlin .50 1.25
Casey Mears .30 .75
Jamie McMurray .50 1.25
Jimmie Johnson 1.00 2.50
Ken Schrader .20 .50
Brendan Gaughan .30 .75
Dale Jarrett .60 1.50
Kurt Busch .50 1.25
Martin Truex Jr. 1.00 2.50
Kyle Busch .75 2.00
Jason Leffler .20 .50
Greg Biffle .30 .75
David Green .20 .50
Ron Hornaday .20 .50
Jason Keller .20 .50
Tim Fedewa .20 .50
Kasey Kahne 1.25 3.00
Tony Stewart's Car C .30 .75
Rusty Wallace's Car C .20 .50
Elliott Sadler's Car C .08 .20
Kasey Kahne's Car C .50 1.25
Kevin Harvick's Car C .30 .75
Dale Jarrett's Car C .20 .50
Bobby Labonte's Car C .20 .50
Ryan Newman's Car C .08 .20
Ricky Rudd's Car C .20 .50
Kurt Busch A .50 1.25
Martin Truex Jr. A 1.00 2.50
Tony Stewart A .75 2.00
Kasey Kahne A 1.25 3.00
Ryan Newman A 1.00 2.50
Matt Kenseth A 1.00 2.50
Dale Earnhardt Jr. A 1.25 3.00
Jeff Gordon A 1.25 3.00
Jimmie Johnson A 1.00 2.50
Jimmie Johnson's Car .30 .75
Matt Kenseth's Car .30 .75
Ryan Newman's Car .30 .75
Tony Stewart's Car .30 .75
Jeff Gordon's Car .50 1.25
Michael Waltrip's Car .08 .20
Dale Earnhardt Jr.'s Car .50 1.25
Jamie McMurray's Car .20 .50
Mark Martin's Car .30 .75
Matt Kenseth NI 1.00 2.50
Dale Earnhardt Jr. NI 1.25 3.00
Jeff Gordon NI 1.25 3.00
Dale Earnhardt Jr. NI 1.25 3.00
Jamie McMurray NI .50 1.25
Tony Stewart NI .75 2.00
Jimmie Johnson NI 1.00 2.50
Rusty Wallace NI .60 1.50
Dale Earnhardt Jr. NI 1.25 3.00
Jimmie Johnson IF 1.00 2.50
Kasey Kahne IF 1.25 3.00
Dale Earnhardt Jr. IF 1.25 3.00
Michael Waltrip IF .30 .75
Jeff Gordon IF 1.25 3.00
Tony Stewart IF .75 2.00
Martin Truex Jr. RS 1.00 2.50
Jeff Gordon RS 1.25 3.00
Elliott Sadler RS .30 .75
Ryan Newman RS 1.00 2.50
Jimmie Johnson RS 1.00 2.50
Dale Earnhardt Jr. RS 1.25 3.00
Rusty Wallace P .60 1.50
Kyle Busch P .50 1.25
Jason Leffler P .20 .50
Dale Jarrett P .60 1.50
Terry Labonte P .50 1.25
Matt Kenseth 1.00 2.50
Kurt Busch
Mark Martin CL
urt Busch '04 Champion 8.00 20.00
) Flag Chasers Entry Card 1.50 4.00

005 Wheels High Gear MPH

domly inserted into packs, this is a parallel to the c set. These cards can be differentiated as they treated with special holofoil stamping and were ed to 100 serial numbered sets. They were lable in hobby only packs and carry an "M" x for the card numbers.

H: 4X TO 10X BASE

005 Wheels High Gear Previews Green

se cards were issued to preview the first 36-cards he base 2005 High Gear set. Each card was ed to a stated print run of five serial numbered Due to secondary market scarcity no pricing is ided.

MPLETE SET (36)

2005 Wheels High Gear Previews Silver

These cards were issued to preview cards 73-78 of the base 2005 High Gear set. Each card was issued to a stated print run of one serial numbered set. Due to secondary market scarcity no pricing is provided.

COMPLETE SET (6)

2005 Wheels High Gear Samples

These cards were issued to preview the 90-card 2005 High Gear set. The cards were stamped "Sample" on the backs and were issued one per Beckett Racing magazine Issue #127 March, 2005.

*SAMPLES: 1.5X TO 4X BASE

2005 Wheels High Gear Flag Chasers Black

Randomly inserted into packs, these cards feature a race-used black flag piece embedded into a card. These cards were issued to a stated print run of 55 serial numbered sets. Six other flag colors were also produced as parallels of each card in varying quantities as noted below. The overall stated odds were 1 in 144 packs.

COMPLETE SET (9)
FC1 Kasey Kahne 40.00 100.00
FC2 Rusty Wallace 20.00 50.00
FC3 Tony Stewart 20.00 50.00
FC4 Jimmie Johnson 25.00 60.00
FC5 Ryan Newman 25.00 60.00
FC6 Kevin Harvick 20.00 50.00
FC7 Dale Earnhardt Jr. 40.00 100.00
FC8 Jeff Gordon 40.00 100.00
FC9 Mark Martin 25.00 60.00

2005 Wheels High Gear Flag Chasers Blue-Yellow

Randomly inserted into packs, these cards feature a race-used blue-yellow flag piece embedded into a card. This set parallels the basic Flag Chasers Black set.These cards were issued to a stated print run of 25 serial numbered sets. The overall stated odds are 1 in 144 packs.

*BLUE-YELLOW: .6X TO 1.5X BLACK

2005 Wheels High Gear Flag Chasers Checkered

Randomly inserted into packs, these cards feature a race-used checkered flag piece embedded into a card. This set parallels the basic Flag Chasers Black set.These cards were issued to a stated print run of 10 serial numbered sets. The overall stated odds are 1 in 144 packs.

NOT PRICED DUE TO SCARCITY

2005 Wheels High Gear Flag Chasers Green

Randomly inserted into packs, these cards feature a race-used green flag piece embedded into a card. This set parallels the basic Flag Chasers Black set.These cards were issued to a stated print run of 55 serial numbered sets. The overall stated odds are 1 in 144 packs.

*GREEN: .4X TO 1X BLACK

2005 Wheels High Gear Flag Chasers Red

Randomly inserted into packs, these cards feature a race-used red flag piece embedded into a card. This set parallels the basic Flag Chasers Black set.These cards were issued to a stated print run of 55 serial numbered sets. The overall stated odds are 1 in 144 packs.

*RED: .4X TO 1X BLACK

2005 Wheels High Gear Flag Chasers White

Randomly inserted into packs, these cards feature a race-used white flag piece embedded into a card. This set parallels the basic Flag Chasers Black set.These cards were issued to a stated print run of 55 serial numbered sets. The overall stated odds are 1 in 144 packs.

*WHITE: .4X TO 1X BLACK

2005 Wheels High Gear Flag Chasers Yellow

Randomly inserted into packs, these cards feature a race-used yellow flag piece embedded into a card. This set parallels the basic Flag Chasers Black set.These cards were issued to a stated print run of 55 serial numbered sets. The overall stated odds are 1 in 144 packs.

*YELLOW: .4X TO 1X BLACK

2005 Wheels High Gear Flag to Flag

Issued at a stated rate of one in two packs, these 27 cards feature some of the leading drivers in NASCAR. Each card was die-cut and features a photo of the driver and his car.

COMPLETE SET (27) 10.00 25.00
FF1 Greg Biffle .40 1.00
FF2 Ward Burton .40 1.00
FF3 Dale Earnhardt Jr. 1.50 4.00
FF4 Brendan Gaughan .40 1.00
FF5 Jeff Gordon 1.50 4.00
FF6 Jeff Green .25 .60
FF7 Kevin Harvick 1.00 2.50
FF8 Dale Jarrett .75 2.00
FF9 Jimmie Johnson 1.25 3.00
FF10 Kasey Kahne 1.50 4.00
FF11 Matt Kenseth 1.25 3.00
FF12 Bobby Labonte .75 2.00
FF13 Terry Labonte .60 1.50
FF14 Mark Martin 1.00 2.50
FF15 Jeremy Mayfield .40 1.00
FF16 Jamie McMurray .60 1.50
FF17 Casey Mears .40 1.00
FF18 Joe Nemechek .25 .60
FF19 Ryan Newman 1.25 3.00
FF20 Kyle Petty .40 1.00
FF21 Ricky Rudd .60 1.50
FF22 Elliott Sadler .40 1.00
FF23 Ken Schrader .25 .60
FF24 Tony Stewart 1.00 2.50
FF25 Brian Vickers .75 2.00
FF26 Rusty Wallace .75 2.00
FF27 Michael Waltrip .40 1.00

2005 Wheels High Gear Full Throttle

Issued at a stated rate of one in 12, these six cards feature high-speed competitors in this set made of clear plastic stock. Each card carried a "FT" prefix for its card number.

COMPLETE SET (6) 10.00 25.00
FT1 Dale Earnhardt Jr. 2.50 6.00
FT2 Tony Stewart 1.50 4.00
FT3 Kevin Harvick 1.50 4.00
FT4 Jeff Gordon 2.50 6.00
FT5 Dale Jarrett 1.25 3.00
FT6 Jimmie Johnson 2.00 5.00

2005 Wheels High Gear Machine

Issued at a stated rate of one in seven retail packs, these nine foil-embossed cards feature the cars of leading drivers. Each card carried an "MMB" prefix for its card number.

COMPLETE SET (9) 8.00 20.00
*MACHINE: 1X TO 2.5X MAN

2005 Wheels High Gear Man

Issued at a stated rate of one in five hobby packs, these nine foil-embossed cards feature photos of leading drivers. A "Machine" version of each card was produced for retail packs. Each card carried an "MMA" prefix for its card number.

COMPLETE SET (9) 10.00 25.00
MMA1 Michael Waltrip .50 1.25
MMA2 Terry Labonte .75 2.00
MMA3 Jamie McMurray .75 2.00
MMA4 Dale Earnhardt Jr. 2.00 5.00
MMA5 Jimmie Johnson 1.50 4.00
MMA6 Mark Martin 1.25 3.00
MMA6 Kasey Kahne 2.00 5.00
MMA7 Jeff Gordon 2.00 5.00
MMA8 Tony Stewart 1.25 3.00
MMA9 Rusty Wallace 1.00 2.50

2005 Wheels High Gear Top Tier

Issued at a stated rate of one in nine, these ten cards feature the top drivers from the 2004 NASCAR season. Each was printed on special holofoil card stock.

COMPLETE SET (10) 12.50 30.00
TT1 Kurt Busch 1.00 2.50
TT2 Jimmie Johnson 2.00 5.00
TT3 Jeff Gordon 2.50 6.00
TT4 Mark Martin 1.50 4.00
TT5 Dale Earnhardt Jr. 2.50 6.00
TT6 Tony Stewart 1.50 4.00
TT7 Ryan Newman 2.00 5.00
TT8 Matt Kenseth 2.00 5.00
TT9 Elliott Sadler .60 1.50
TT10 Jeremy Mayfield .60 1.50

2006 Wheels Autographs

These 53 cards were signed by the drivers pictured on them and inserted in packs at a rate of one in 40 in both Wheels American Thunder and Wheels High Gear packs. They were certified by the manufacturer on the card backs.

1 Bobby Allison 10.00 20.00
2 Donnie Allison 12.50 30.00
3 Buddy Baker 7.50 15.00
4 Greg Biffle 10.00 25.00
5 Dave Blaney 7.50 15.00
6 Clint Bowyer NBS 20.00 40.00
7 Jeff Burton NC 8.00 20.00
8 Kurt Busch NC 12.50 30.00
9 Kyle Busch NC 20.00 50.00
10 Terry Cook CTS 7.50 15.00
11 Ricky Craven CTS 10.00 20.00
12 Rick Crawford 7.50 15.00
13 Kerry Earnhardt 10.00 20.00
14 Carl Edwards NBS 20.00 50.00
15 Carl Edwards NC 20.00 50.00
16 Harry Gant 7.50 15.00
17 Jeff Gordon NC 125.00 250.00
18 Robby Gordon 10.00 20.00
19 David Green NBS 7.50 15.00
20 Jeff Green 7.50 15.00
21 Denny Hamlin NBS 30.00 60.00
22 Kevin Harvick NC 12.50 30.00
23 Ron Hornaday CTS 7.50 15.00
24 Jack Ingram 7.50 15.00
25 Dale Jarrett NC 15.00 40.00
26 Jimmie Johnson NC 30.00 60.00
27 Kasey Kahne NBS 25.00 60.00
28 Kasey Kahne NC 25.00 60.00
29 Jason Keller NBS 7.50 15.00
30 Matt Kenseth NBS 15.00 40.00
31 Matt Kenseth NC 15.00 40.00
32 Todd Kluever CTS 10.00 25.00
33 Travis Kvapil NC 10.00 20.00
34 Bobby Labonte NC 15.00 40.00
35 Justin Labonte NBS 10.00 25.00
36 Bill Lester CTS 10.00 25.00
37 Fred Lorenzen 10.00 20.00
38 Sterling Marlin NC 20.00 40.00
39 Mark Martin NC 40.00 80.00
40 Jeremy Mayfield NC 12.50 25.00
41 Jamie McMurray NC 10.00 25.00
42 Casey Mears NC 10.00 25.00
43 Joe Nemechek NC 7.50 15.00
44 Ryan Newman NC 15.00 30.00
45 Marvin Panch 7.50 15.00
46 Benny Parsons 30.00 60.00
47 David Pearson 10.00 25.00
48 Richard Petty 40.00 80.00
49 Tony Raines NBS 10.00 20.00
50 Ricky Rudd 12.50 30.00
51 Boris Said NC 7.50 15.00
52 Johnny Sauter 7.50 15.00
53 Ken Schrader CTS 10.00 20.00
54 Dennis Setzer 7.50 15.00
55 Mike Skinner 7.50 15.00
56 Reed Sorenson NBS 12.50 30.00
57 Jack Sprague CTS 7.50 15.00
58 Tony Stewart NC 50.00 100.00
59 Brian Vickers NC 10.00 25.00
60 Rusty Wallace 12.50 30.00
61 Rex White 7.50 15.00
62 Scott Wimmer NC 7.50 15.00
63 Glen Wood 7.50 15.00
64 Jon Wood NBS 7.50 15.00
65 Cale Yarborough 10.00 20.00
66 Robert Yates 7.50 15.00
67 J.J. Yeley 10.00 25.00

2006 Wheels High Gear

This set was released in late January 2006. These cards were issued in 5-card hobby packs with an SRP of $3.99. They came 20-packs to a box and 20-boxes to a case. The retail version was issued four cards per pack with an $2.99 SRP and packaged 24-packs to a box and 20-boxes to a case. There was a special 0 card honoring Tony Stewart as the 2005 NASCAR champion and those cards were inserted at a stated rate of one in 72 packs. The Daytona Variation cards were also included in packs at a rate of one in 14. The four cards included are past Daytona 500 winners and they feature a logo on the card. Jeff Gordon's variation is card number 16 and Sterling Marlin's variation is number 26.

COMPLETE SET (90) 15.00 40.00
WAX BOX HOBBY (20) 60.00 120.00
WAX BOX RETAIL (24)
1 Tony Stewart 1.00 2.50
2 Greg Biffle .50 1.25
3 Carl Edwards 1.25 3.00
4 Mark Martin 1.00 2.50
5 Jimmie Johnson 1.25 3.00
6 Ryan Newman 1.00 2.50
7 Matt Kenseth 1.25 3.00
8 Rusty Wallace .75 2.00
9 Jeremy Mayfield .25 .60
10 Jeff Gordon 1.50 4.00
11 Jamie McMurray .60 1.50
12 Elliott Sadler .40 1.00
13 Kevin Harvick 1.00 2.50
14 Dale Jarrett .75 2.00
14B Dale Jarrett Daytona 3.00 8.00
15 Joe Nemechek .25 .60
16 Brian Vickers .75 2.00
16B Jeff Gordon Daytona 6.00 15.00
17 Jeff Burton .40 1.00
18 Dale Earnhardt Jr. 1.50 4.00
18B Dale Earnhardt Jr. Daytona 6.00 15.00
19 Kyle Busch .75 2.00
20 Ricky Rudd .60 1.50
21 Casey Mears .40 1.00
22 Kasey Kahne 1.50 4.00
23 Bobby Labonte .75 2.00
24 Kyle Petty .40 1.00
25 Sterling Marlin .60 1.50
26 Ken Schrader .25 .60
26B Sterling Marlin Daytona 2.50 6.00
27 Robby Gordon .25 .60
28 Martin Truex Jr. NBS 1.00 2.50
29 Clint Bowyer NBS 1.50 4.00
30 Reed Sorenson NBS 1.00 2.50
31 Carl Edwards NBS 1.25 3.00
32 Denny Hamlin NBS 1.50 4.00
33 Johnny Sauter NBS .40 1.00
34 David Green NBS .25 .60
35 Jason Keller NBS .25 .60
36 J.J. Yeley NBS .60 1.50
37 Dennis Setzer CTS .25 .60
38 Ron Hornaday CTS .25 .60
39 Mike Skinner CTS .25 .60
40 Ken Schrader CTS .25 .60
41 Ricky Craven CTS .25 .60
42 Terry Cook CTS .25 .60
43 Todd Kluever CTS 1.25 3.00
44 Rick Crawford CTS .25 .60
45 Bill Lester CTS .40 1.00
46 Rusty Wallace's Car C .30 .75
47 Dale Earnhardt Jr.'s Car C .60 1.50
48 Kasey Kahne's Car C .60 1.50
49 Matt Kenseth's Car C .50 1.25
50 Carl Edwards' Car C .50 1.25
51 Tony Stewart's Car C .40 1.00
52 Kevin Harvick's Car C .40 1.00
53 Dale Jarrett's Car C .30 .75
54 Jeff Burton's Car C .15 .40
55 Tony Stewart NA 1.00 2.50
56 Kyle Busch NA .75 2.00
57 Martin Truex Jr. NA 1.00 2.50
58 Carl Edwards NA 1.25 3.00
59 Ryan Newman NA 1.00 2.50
60 Tony Stewart NA 1.00 2.50
61 Tony Stewart NA 1.00 2.50
62 Tony Stewart NA 1.00 2.50
63 Ryan Newman NA 1.00 2.50
64 Carl Edwards CM 1.25 3.00
65 Tony Stewart CM 1.00 2.50
66 Dale Jarrett CM .75 2.00
67 Jeff Gordon CM 1.50 4.00
68 Jimmie Johnson CM 1.25 3.00
69 Jeff Burton CM .40 1.00
70 Reed Sorenson PREV CRC 1.25 3.00
71 Sterling Marlin PREV .60 1.50
72 Bobby Labonte PREV .75 2.00
73 David Stremme PREV CRC 1.25 3.00
74 Mark Martin PREV 1.00 2.50
75 Mark McFarland PREV .25 .60
76 Mark Martin FF 1.00 2.50
77 Dale Jarrett FF .75 2.00
78 Jimmie Johnson FF 1.25 3.00
79 Dale Earnhardt Jr. FF 1.50 4.00
80 Jeff Gordon FF 1.50 4.00
81 Kasey Kahne FF 1.50 4.00
82 Tony Stewart FF 1.00 2.50
83 Martin Truex Jr. FF 1.00 2.50
84 Rusty Wallace FF .75 2.00
85 Kasey Kahne NI 1.50 4.00
86 Jeff Green NI .25 .60
87 Ryan Newman NI 1.00 2.50
88 Tony Stewart NI 1.00 2.50
89 Rusty Wallace 1.00 2.50
Mark Martin NI
90 Jeff Gordon CL 1.50 4.00
0 Tony Stewart Champ 6.00 15.00
NNO Daytona Power Pick 2.00 5.00

2006 Wheels High Gear MPH

Randomly inserted into packs, this is a parallel to the basic set. These cards can be differentiated as they were treated with special holofoil stamping and were issued to 100 serial numbered sets. They were available in hobby only packs and carry an "M" prefix for the card numbers.

*MPH: 4X TO 10X BASE

2006 Wheels High Gear Previews Green

These cards were issued to preview the first 36-cards of the base 2005 High Gear set. Each card was issued to a stated print run of five serial numbered sets. Due to secondary market scarcity no pricing is provided.

COMPLETE SET (36)

2006 Wheels High Gear Previews Silver

These cards were issued to preview cards 76-84 of the base 2006 High Gear set. Each card was issued to a stated print run of one serial numbered set. Due to secondary market scarcity no pricing is provided.

COMPLETE SET (9)

2006 Wheels High Gear Flag Chasers Black

Randomly inserted into packs, these cards feature a race-used black flag piece embedded into a card. These cards were issued to a stated print run of 110 serial numbered sets. The overall odds for Flag Chasers are 1 in 40 packs. Six other flag colors were also produced as parallels of each card in varying quantities as noted below.

FC1 Carl Edwards 15.00 40.00
FC2 Jeff Gordon 25.00 60.00
FC3 Dale Earnhardt Jr. 25.00 60.00
FC4 Tony Stewart 20.00 50.00
FC5 Kasey Kahne 20.00 50.00
FC6 Ryan Newman 15.00 40.00
FC7 Kevin Harvick 15.00 40.00
FC8 Dale Jarrett 15.00 40.00
FC9 Jimmie Johnson 20.00 50.00

2006 Wheels High Gear Flag Chasers Blue-Yellow

Randomly inserted into packs, these cards feature a race-used blue-yellow flag piece embedded into a card. These cards were issued to a stated print run of 65 serial numbered sets. The overall odds for Flag Chasers are 1 in 40 packs. This set parallels the Flag Chasers Black set.

*BLUE-YELLOW: .8X TO 2X BLACK

2006 Wheels High Gear Flag Chasers Checkered

Randomly inserted into packs, these cards feature a race-used checkered flag piece embedded into a card. These cards were issued to a stated print run of 3 serial numbered sets. The overall odds for Flag Chasers are 1 in 40 packs. This set parallels the Flag Chasers Black set.

CARDS NOT PRICED DUE TO SCARCITY

2006 Wheels High Gear Flag Chasers Green

Randomly inserted into packs, these cards feature a race-used green flag piece embedded into a card. These cards were issued to a stated print run of 110 serial numbered sets. The overall odds for Flag Chasers are 1 in 40 packs. This set parallels the Flag Chasers Black set.

*GREEN: .4X TO 1X BLACK

2006 Wheels High Gear Flag Chasers Red

Randomly inserted into packs, these cards feature a race-used red flag piece embedded into a card. These cards were issued to a stated print run of 110 serial numbered sets. The overall odds for Flag Chasers are 1 in 40 packs. This set parallels the Flag Chasers Black set.

*RED: .4X TO 1X BLACK

2006 Wheels High Gear Flag Chasers White

Randomly inserted into packs, these cards feature a race-used white flag piece embedded into a card. These cards were issued to a stated print run of 110 serial numbered sets. The overall odds for Flag Chasers are 1 in 40 packs. This set parallels the Flag Chasers Black set.

*WHITE: .4X TO 1X BLACK

2006 Wheels High Gear Flag Chasers Yellow

Randomly inserted into packs, these cards feature a race-used yellow flag piece embedded into a card. These cards were issued to a stated print run of 110 serial numbered sets. The overall odds for Flag Chasers are 1 in 40 packs. This set parallels the Flag Chasers Black set.

*YELLOW: .4X TO 1X BLACK

2006 Wheels High Gear Flag to Flag

Issued at a stated rate of one in two packs, these 27 cards feature some of the leading drivers in NASCAR. Each card was die-cut and features a photo of the driver and his car.

COMPLETE SET (27)	12.50	30.00
FF1 Greg Biffle	.60	1.50
FF2 Jeff Burton	.50	1.25
FF3 Casey Mears	.50	1.25
FF4 Kyle Busch	1.00	2.50
FF5 Dale Earnhardt Jr.	2.00	5.00
FF6 Carl Edwards	1.50	4.00
FF7 Jeff Gordon	2.00	5.00
FF8 Robby Gordon	.30	.75
FF9 Kevin Harvick	1.25	3.00
FF10 Dale Jarrett	1.00	2.50
FF11 Jimmie Johnson	1.50	4.00
FF12 Kasey Kahne	2.00	5.00
FF13 Matt Kenseth	1.50	4.00
FF14 Bobby Labonte	1.00	2.50
FF15 Sterling Marlin	.75	2.00
FF16 Mark Martin	1.25	3.00
FF17 Jeremy Mayfield	.30	.75
FF18 Jamie McMurray	.75	2.00
FF19 Ryan Newman	1.25	3.00
FF20 Kyle Petty	.50	1.25
FF21 Scott Riggs	.50	1.25
FF22 Elliott Sadler	.50	1.25
FF23 Ken Schrader	.30	.75
FF24 Tony Stewart	1.25	3.00
FF25 Martin Truex Jr.	1.25	3.00
FF26 Brian Vickers	1.00	2.50
FF27 Rusty Wallace	1.00	2.50

2006 Wheels High Gear Full Throttle

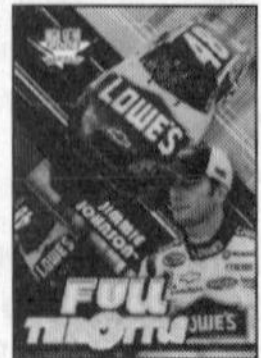

Issued at a stated rate of one in 12, these six cards feature high-speed competitors in this set made of clear plastic stock. Each card carried a "FT" prefix for its card number.

COMPLETE SET (6)	12.50	30.00
FT1 Martin Truex Jr.	2.50	6.00
FT2 Jimmie Johnson	3.00	8.00
FT3 Jeff Gordon	4.00	10.00
FT4 Dale Earnhardt Jr.	4.00	10.00
FT5 Mark Martin	2.50	6.00
FT6 Tony Stewart	2.50	6.00

2006 Wheels High Gear Man & Machine (Machine)

Issued at a stated rate of one in seven retail packs, these nine foil-embossed cards feature the cars of

leading drivers. Each card carried an "MMB" prefix for its card number.

COMPLETE SET (9)
*MACHINE: .8X TO 2X MAN

2006 Wheels High Gear Man & Machine (Man)

Issued at a stated rate of one in five hobby packs, these nine foil-embossed cards feature photos of leading drivers. A "Machine" version of each card was produced for retail packs. Each card carried an "MMA" prefix for its card number.

COMPLETE SET (9)	12.50	25.00
MMA1 Tony Stewart	2.00	5.00
MMA2 Jeff Gordon	3.00	8.00
MMA3 Jimmie Johnson	2.50	6.00
MMA4 Dale Earnhardt Jr.	3.00	8.00
MMA5 Mark Martin	2.00	5.00
MMA6 Dale Jarrett	1.50	4.00
MMA7 Martin Truex Jr.	2.00	5.00
MMA8 Jeff Burton	.75	2.00
MMA9 Ricky Rudd	1.25	3.00

2006 Wheels High Gear Top Tier

Issued at a stated rate of one in nine, these ten cards feature the top drivers from the 2005 NASCAR season. Each was printed on special holofoil card stock.

COMPLETE SET (9)	15.00	40.00
TT1 Tony Stewart	3.00	8.00
TT2 Greg Biffle	1.50	4.00
TT3 Carl Edwards	4.00	10.00
TT4 Mark Martin	3.00	8.00
TT5 Jimmie Johnson	4.00	10.00
TT6 Ryan Newman	3.00	8.00
TT7 Matt Kenseth	4.00	10.00
TT8 Rusty Wallace	2.50	6.00
TT9 Jeremy Mayfield	.75	2.00

2007 Wheels Autographs

These 42 cards were signed by the drivers pictured on them and inserted in packs at a rate of one in 40 in 2007 Wheels High Gear Hobby packs, and one in 96 in Retail packs of 2007 Wheels High Gear. They were certified by the manufacturer on the card backs. They were available in packs of Wheels High Gear and Wheels American Thunder, or both, and are noted below.

1 Greg Biffle NC HG	10.00	25.00
2 Dave Blaney NC HG	8.00	20.00
3 Clint Bowyer NC HG	12.50	30.00
4 Jeff Burton NC HG	8.00	20.00
5 Kurt Busch NC HG	12.50	30.00
6 Kyle Busch NC HG	20.00	50.00
7 Rick Crawford	6.00	15.00
8 Erin Crocker CTS HG	20.00	50.00
9 Erik Darnell CTS HG	6.00	15.00
10 Dale Earnhardt Jr. NC HG	60.00	120.00
11 Carl Edwards NC HG	20.00	50.00
12 David Green NBS HG		
13 Jeff Green NC HG	6.00	15.00
14 Denny Hamlin NC HG	30.00	60.00
15 Kevin Harvick NC HG	12.50	30.00
16 Ron Hornaday CTS HG	6.00	15.00
17 Jimmie Johnson NC HG	30.00	60.00
18 Kasey Kahne NC HG	25.00	60.00
19 Matt Kenseth NC HG	15.00	40.00
20 Todd Kluever NBS HG	10.00	25.00
21 Bobby Labonte NC HG	15.00	40.00
22 Terry Labonte NC HG	15.00	40.00
23 Burney Lamar NBS HG	8.00	20.00
24 Bill Lester CTS HG	8.00	20.00
25 Mark Martin NC HG	30.00	60.00
26 Jamie McMurray NC HG	10.00	25.00
27 Casey Mears NC HG	10.00	25.00
28 Paul Menard NBS HG	8.00	20.00
29 Joe Nemechek NC HG	8.00	20.00
30 Ryan Newman NC HG	15.00	30.00
31 Danny O'Quinn NBS HG	8.00	20.00
32 Tony Raines NC HG	6.00	15.00
33 David Ragan CTS HG	8.00	20.00
34 Mike Skinner CTS HG	6.00	15.00
35 Reed Sorenson NC HG	12.50	30.00
36 Regan Smith NBS HG	8.00	20.00
37 David Stremme NC HG	12.50	30.00
38 Tony Stewart NC HG	40.00	100.00
39 Martin Truex Jr. NC HG	15.00	40.00
40 Brian Vickers NC HG	10.00	25.00
41 Steve Wallace NBS HG	10.00	25.00
42 Jon Wood NBS HG	6.00	15.00
43 J.J. Yeley NC HG	10.00	25.00

2007 Wheels Autographs Press Plates Black

This 42-card set featured the press plates used to make the cards. Each plate was signed by the driver pictured on the card front. The backs had a sticker with the description and the plate color. Each of these plates were 1 of 1's.

NOT PRICED DUE TO SCARCITY

2007 Wheels Autographs Press Plates Cyan

This 42-card set featured the press plates used to make the cards. Each plate was signed by the driver pictured on the card front. The backs had a sticker with the description and the plate color. Each of these plates were 1 of 1's.

NOT PRICED DUE TO SCARCITY

2007 Wheels Autographs Press Plates Magenta

This 42-card set featured the press plates used to make the cards. Each plate was signed by the driver pictured on the card front. The backs had a sticker with the description and the plate color. Each of these plates were 1 of 1's.

NOT PRICED DUE TO SCARCITY

2007 Wheels Autographs Press Plates Yellow

This 42-card set featured the press plates used to make the cards. Each plate was signed by the driver pictured on the card front. The backs had a sticker with the description and the plate color. Each of these plates were 1 of 1's.

NOT PRICED DUE TO SCARCITY

2007 Wheels High Gear

This 90-card base set featured six additional variations and two short-printed cards, none of which were included in the base set price. The variations were inserted in both Hobby and Retail packs at a rate of one in 60. The variations are card #3 Denny Hamlin with a blurred background, #5 Dale Earnhardt Jr. with red in the background in place of blue, #6 Jeff Gordon with the #24 missing from the pit wagon in the background, #71 kevin Harvick CM with the warning signs behind him reversed, the running sign is above the guy getting hit with the projectile and falling sign, #73 Jimmie Johnson with the ink colors reversed on the magazine cover, "Take That" is in yellow, #88 Juan Pablo Montoya with the green infield pictured in the background. The zero card short print is Jimmie Johnson '06 Champion, which was inserted in packs at a rate of one in 60 in both Hobby and Retail. The other short print is the NNO Daytona Entry Card which was inserted at a rate of one in 20 in both Hobby and Retail packs. It was a entry for a chance to win a signed flag and helmet acquired during Daytona's Speedweeks. The promotion ended October 31, 2007 and the winner was notified by November 15, 2007.

COMPLETE SET (90)	15.00	40.00
WAX BOX HOBBY (20)	60.00	80.00
WAX BOX RETAIL (24)	45.00	70.00
1 Jimmie Johnson	1.00	2.50
2 Matt Kenseth	1.00	2.50
3 Denny Hamlin	1.00	2.50
3B Denny Hamlin blurred	5.00	12.00
4 Kevin Harvick	.75	2.00
5 Dale Earnhardt Jr. blue	1.25	3.00
5B Dale Earnhardt Jr. red	6.00	15.00
6 Jeff Gordon	1.25	3.00
6B Jeff Gordon -yellow 24	6.00	15.00
7 Jeff Burton	.30	.75
8 Kasey Kahne	1.25	3.00
9 Mark Martin	.75	2.00
10 Kyle Busch	.60	1.50
11 Tony Stewart	.75	2.00
12 Greg Biffle	.40	1.00
13 Carl Edwards	.75	2.00
14 Casey Mears	.30	.75
15 Kurt Busch	.30	.75
16 Clint Bowyer	1.00	2.50
17 Ryan Newman	.60	1.50
18 Martin Truex Jr.	.75	2.00
19 Scott Riggs	.30	.75
20 Bobby Labonte	.60	1.50
21 Elliott Sadler	.30	.75
22 Reed Sorenson	.60	1.50
23 Jamie McMurray	.50	1.25
24 Joe Nemechek	.20	.50
25 Jeff Green	.20	.50
26 J.J. Yeley	.40	1.00
27 Robby Gordon	.20	.50
28 Ken Schrader	.20	.50
29 David Stremme	.60	1.50
30 Sterling Marlin	.50	1.25
31 Tony Raines	.20	.50
32 Kevin Harvick NBS	.75	2.00
33 Carl Edwards NBS	.75	2.00
34 Denny Hamlin NBS	1.00	2.50
35 Paul Menard NBS	.40	1.00
36 Jon Wood NBS	.20	.50
37 Danny O'Quinn NBS	.50	1.25
38 Regan Smith NBS	.20	.50
39 Steve Wallace NBS	.60	1.50
40 Ron Hornaday CTS	.20	.50
41 Rick Crawford CTS	.20	.50
42 Mike Skinner CTS	.20	.50
43 Erik Darnell CTS	.50	1.25
44 Bill Lester CTS	.30	.75
45 David Ragan CTS	.75	2.00
46 Eric Holmes RC	.60	1.50
47 Mike Olsen	.60	1.50
48 Mike Stefanik	.20	.50
49 Junior Miller RC	.60	1.50
50 Tim Schendel RC	.60	1.50
51 Gary Lewis RC	.60	1.50
52 J.R. Norris RC	.60	1.50
53 Rip Michels RC	.60	1.50
54 Tony Stewart NA	.75	2.00
55 Kasey Kahne NA	1.25	3.00
56 Jimmie Johnson NA	1.00	2.50
57 Kasey Kahne NA	1.25	3.00
58 Matt Kenseth NA	1.00	2.50
59 Kevin Harvick NA	.75	2.00
60 Denny Hamlin NA	1.00	2.50
61 Kasey Kahne NA	1.25	3.00
62 Tony Stewart NA	.75	2.00
63 Tony Stewart NA	.75	2.00
64 Kevin Harvick NA	.75	2.00
65 Denny Hamlin NA	1.00	2.50
66 Denny Hamlin CM	1.00	2.50
67 Kasey Kahne CM	1.25	3.00
68 Ryan Newman CM	.60	1.50
69 Reed Sorenson CM	.60	1.50
70 Matt Kenseth CM	1.00	2.50
71 Kevin Harvick CM	.75	2.00
71B Kevin Harvick CM mixed signs	4.00	10.00
72 Scott Riggs CM	.30	.75
73 Jimmie Johnson NI red take	1.00	2.50
73B Jimmie Johnson NI yellow take	5.00	12.00
74 Carl Edwards NI	.75	2.00
75 Kasey Kahne NI	1.25	3.00
76 Kevin Harvick NI	.75	2.00
77 Jeff Gordon NI	1.25	3.00
78 Clint Bowyer's Car C	.40	1.00
79 Kasey Kahne's Car C	.50	1.25
80 Ryan Newman's Car C	.25	.60
81 Tony Stewart's Car C	.30	.75
82 Jeff Gordon's Car C	.50	1.25
83 Kevin Harvick's Car C	.75	2.00
84 Greg Biffle's Car C	.15	.40
85 Kyle Busch's Car C	.25	.60
86 David Gilliland	1.50	4.00
87 Paul Menard	1.50	4.00
88 Juan Pablo Montoya	2.50	6.00
88B Juan Pablo Montoya infield	6.00	15.00
89 Jon Wood	1.50	4.00
CL Jeff Gordon CL	1.25	3.00
NNO Daytona Entry Card	1.00	2.50
0 Jimmie Johnson Champion	4.00	10.00

2007 Wheels High Gear Final Standings Gold

This 31-card set was a partial parallel to the base set. The cards are serial numbered to the corresponding driver's final position at the conclusion of the 2006 season. Each card carried a "FS" prefix for its card number.

FS1 Jimmie Johnson/1		
FS2 Matt Kenseth/2		
FS3 Denny Hamlin/3		
FS4 Kevin Harvick/4		
FS5 Dale Earnhardt Jr./5		
FS6 Jeff Gordon/6		
FS7 Jeff Burton/7		
FS8 Kasey Kahne/8		
FS9 Mark Martin/9		
FS10 Kyle Busch/10		
FS11 Tony Stewart/11		
FS12 Greg Biffle/13		
FS13 Carl Edwards/12		
FS14 Casey Mears/14		
FS15 Kurt Busch/16		
FS16 Clint Bowyer/17		
FS17 Ryan Newman/18		
FS18 Martin Truex Jr./19		
FS19 Scott Riggs/20		
FS20 Bobby Labonte/21		
FS21 Elliott Sadler/22		
FS22 Reed Sorenson/24		
FS23 Jamie McMurray/25	15.00	40.00
FS24 Joe Nemechek/27	6.00	15.00
FS25 Jeff Green/28	6.00	15.00
FS26 J.J. Yeley/29		
FS27 Robby Gordon/30		
FS28 Ken Schrader/31	6.00	15.00
FS29 David Stremme/33	8.00	20.00
FS30 Sterling Marlin/34	15.00	30.00
FS31 Tony Raines/35	8.00	20.00

2007 Wheels High Gear MPH

This 90-card set was a parallel of the base set. Each card was serial numbered to 100 and carried a "M" prefix for its card number. The cards were highlighted with a holofoil design.

*MPH: 4X TO 10X BASIC

2007 Wheels High Gear Previews

This 55-card set was a partial parallel to the base set. It was available via eBay prior to the release of 2007 Wheels High Gear. Cards EB1-EB39 and EB54-EB65 were serial numbered to 5 copies while cards EB86-EB89 were 1 of 1's.

NOT PRICED DUE TO SCARCITY

2007 Wheels High Gear Driven

This 27-card set was inserted in packs of 2007 Wheels High Gear at a rate of one in two in both Hobby and Retail packs. The cards carried a "DR" prefix for their card numbers.

COMPLETE SET (27)	12.50	30.00
DR1 Mark Martin	1.25	3.00
DR2 Jeff Burton	.50	1.25
DR3 Reed Sorenson	1.00	2.50
DR4 Jimmie Johnson	1.50	4.00
DR5 Robby Gordon	.30	.75
DR6 Martin Truex Jr.	1.25	3.00
DR7 Kevin Harvick	1.25	3.00
DR8 Matt Kenseth	1.50	4.00
DR9 Denny Hamlin	1.50	4.00
DR10 Greg Biffle	.60	1.50
DR11 Ryan Newman	1.00	2.50
DR12 Tony Stewart	1.25	3.00
DR13 Clint Bowyer	1.50	4.00
DR14 Jeff Gordon	2.00	5.00
DR15 Jamie McMurray	.75	2.00
DR16 Bobby Labonte	1.00	2.50
DR17 Kurt Busch	.50	1.25
DR18 Dale Earnhardt Jr.	2.00	5.00
DR19 J.J. Yeley	.60	1.50
DR20 Carl Edwards	1.25	3.00
DR21 Kasey Kahne	2.00	5.00
DR22 Ken Schrader	.30	.75
DR23 David Stremme	1.00	2.50
DR24 Sterling Marlin	.75	2.00
DR25 Jeff Green	.30	.75
DR26 Dave Blaney	.30	.75
DR27 Tony Raines	.30	.75

2007 Wheels High Gear Flag Chasers Black

Randomly inserted into packs, these cards feature a race-used black flag piece embedded into a card. These cards were issued to a stated print run of 89 serial numbered sets. The overall odds for Flag Chasers are one in 40 Hobby and one in 112 Retail packs. Six other flag colors were also produced as parallels of each card in varying quantities.

FC1 Dale Earnhardt Jr.	25.00	60.00
FC2 Carl Edwards	15.00	40.00
FC3 Kevin Harvick	20.00	50.00
FC4 Tony Stewart	20.00	50.00
FC5 Jimmie Johnson	20.00	50.00
FC6 Denny Hamlin	20.00	50.00
FC7 Mark Martin	20.00	50.00
FC8 Jeff Gordon	25.00	60.00
FC9 Kasey Kahne	25.00	60.00
FC10 Matt Kenseth	15.00	40.00

2007 Wheels High Gear Flag Chasers Blue-Yellow

Randomly inserted into packs, these cards feature a race-used blue-yellow flag piece embedded into a card. These cards were issued to a stated print run of 50 serial numbered sets. The overall odds for Flag Chasers are one in 40 Hobby and one in 112 Retail packs. This set parallels the Flag Chasers Black set.

*BLUE-YELLOW: .6X TO 1.5X BLACK

2007 Wheels High Gear Flag Chasers Checkered

Randomly inserted into packs, these cards feature a race-used checkered flag piece embedded into a card. These cards were issued to a stated print run of 10 serial numbered sets. The overall odds for Flag Chasers are one in 40 Hobby and one in 112 Retail packs. This set parallels the Flag Chasers Black set.

NOT PRICED DUE TO SCARCITY

2007 Wheels High Gear Flag Chasers Green

Randomly inserted into packs, these cards feature a race-used green flag piece embedded into a card. These cards were issued to a stated print run of 89 serial numbered sets. The overall odds for Flag Chasers are one in 40 Hobby and one in 112 Retail packs. This set parallels the Flag Chasers Black set.

*GREEN: .4X TO 1X BLACK

2007 Wheels High Gear Flag Chasers Red

Randomly inserted into packs, these cards feature a race-used red flag piece embedded into a card. These cards were issued to a stated print run of 89 serial numbered sets. The overall odds for Flag Chasers are one in 40 Hobby and one in 112 Retail packs. This set parallels the Flag Chasers Black set.

*RED: .4X TO 1X BLACK

2007 Wheels High Gear Flag Chasers White

Randomly inserted into packs, these cards feature a race-used white flag piece embedded into a card. These cards were issued to a stated print run of 89 serial numbered sets. The overall odds for Flag Chasers are one in 40 Hobby and one in 112 Retail packs. This set parallels the Flag Chasers Black set.

*WHITE: .4X TO 1X BLACK

2007 Wheels High Gea Flag Chasers Yellow

Randomly inserted into packs, these cards featu race-used yellow flag piece embedded into a c These cards were issued to a stated print run o serial numbered sets. The overall odds for Chasers are one in 40 Hobby and one in 112 R packs. This set parallels the Flag Chasers Black s

*YELLOW: .4X TO 1X BLACK

2007 Wheels High Gea Full Throttle

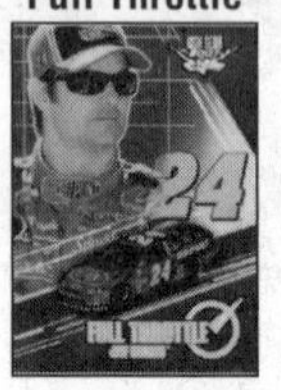

This 9-card set was randomly inserted in pack 2007 Wheels High Gear at a rate of one in six both Hobby and Retail packs. Each card carri "FT" prefix for its card number.

COMPLETE SET (9)	12.50	30
FT1 Jeff Gordon	2.50	6
FT2 Reed Sorenson	1.25	3
FT3 Kevin Harvick	1.50	4
FT4 Dale Earnhardt Jr.	2.50	6
FT5 Kasey Kahne	2.50	6
FT6 Jimmie Johnson	2.00	5
FT7 Mark Martin	1.50	4
FT8 Tony Stewart	1.50	4
FT9 Martin Truex Jr.	1.50	4

2007 Wheels High Gea Last Lap

This 8-card set featured three swatches of race-u flag embedded into the card. The swatches w green, white and checkered. Each card was s numbered to 10 copies. They were available in Hobby and Retail packs of 2007 Wheels High Ge

NOT PRICED DUE TO SCARCITY

LL1 Kasey Kahne
LL2 Matt Kenseth
LL3 Jimmie Johnson
LL4 Kevin Harvick
LL5 Tony Stewart
LL6 Jeff Gordon
LL7 Denny Hamlin
LL8 Dale Earnhardt Jr.

2007 Wheels High Gea Top Tier

This 10-card set was randomly inserted in pack 2007 Wheels High Gear at a rate of one in fou both Hobby and Retail packs. Each card carri "TT" prefix to its card numbering.

COMPLETE SET (10)	15.00	40
TT1 Jimmie Johnson	2.50	6
TT2 Matt Kenseth	2.50	6
TT3 Denny Hamlin	2.50	6
TT4 Kevin Harvick	2.00	5
TT5 Dale Earnhardt Jr.	3.00	8
TT6 Jeff Gordon	3.00	8
TT7 Jeff Burton	.75	2
TT8 Kasey Kahne	3.00	8
TT9 Mark Martin	2.00	5
TT10 Kyle Busch	1.50	4

2008 Wheels Autograp

STATED ODDS 1:40

1 A.J. Allmendinger NC HG	10.00	25
2 Marcos Ambrose NBS HG	20.00	40
3 Greg Biffle NC HG	10.00	25
4 Kelly Bires CTS HG	6.00	15
5 Dave Blaney NC HG	6.00	15
6 Clint Bowyer NC HG	20.00	40
7 Kurt Busch NC HG	15.00	30
8 Joey Clanton CTS HG	6.00	15
9 Rick Crawford CTS HG	6.00	15

ale Earnhardt Jr. NC HG 75.00 150.00
eff Gordon NC HG EXCH 100.00 175.00
enny Hamlin NC HG 25.00 50.00
evin Harvick NC HG 15.00 40.00
on Hornaday CTS HG 6.00 15.00
ale Jarrett NC HG 20.00 40.00
immie Johnson NC HG EXCH 40.00 80.00
asey Kahne NC HG 30.00 60.00
att Kenseth NC HG 25.00 50.00
ravis Kvapil CTS HG 6.00 15.00
obby Labonte NC HG 15.00 30.00
ark Martin NC HG 20.00 50.00
yan Newman NC HG 15.00 30.00
avid Ragan NC HG 8.00 20.00
ony Raines NC HG 6.00 15.00
cott Riggs NC HG 8.00 20.00
lliott Sadler NC HG 10.00 25.00
ohnny Sauter NC HG 6.00 15.00
en Schrader NC HG 6.00 15.00
egan Smith NC HG 6.00 15.00
ack Sprague CTS HG 6.00 15.00
ony Stewart NC HG EXCH 40.00 80.00
avid Stremme NC HG 10.00 25.00
artin Truex Jr. NC HG 15.00 30.00
rian Vickers NC HG 10.00 25.00
ichael Waltrip NC HG 10.00 25.00
cott Wimmer NBS HG 6.00 15.00
on Wood NC HG 6.00 15.00
.J. Yeley NC HG 8.00 20.00

2008 Wheels tographs Press Plates Black

TED PRINT RUN 1 SERIAL #'d SET
PRICED DUE TO SCARCITY

2008 Wheels tographs Press Plates Cyan

TED PRINT RUN 1 SERIAL #'d SET
PRICED DUE TO SCARCITY

2008 Wheels tographs Press Plates Magenta

TED PRINT RUN 1 SERIAL #'d SET
PRICED DUE TO SCARCITY

2008 Wheels tographs Press Plates Yellow

TED PRINT RUN 1 SERIAL #'d SET
PRICED DUE TO SCARCITY

2008 Wheels Autographs Chase Edition

leff Gordon, Jimmie Johnson and Tony Stewart . were issued as exchange cards in packs, but redeemed later in the year for the actual cards.

TED PRINT RUN 25 SERIAL #'d SETS
nt Bowyer NC 50.00 100.00
rt Busch NC 40.00 80.00
f Gordon NC 150.00 300.00
nny Hamlin NC 50.00 100.00
vin Harvick NC 60.00 120.00
nmie Johnson NC EXCH 100.00 200.00
tt Kenseth NC 75.00 150.00
ny Stewart NC EXCH 100.00 200.00
rtin Truex Jr. NC 60.00 120.00

)08 Wheels High Gear

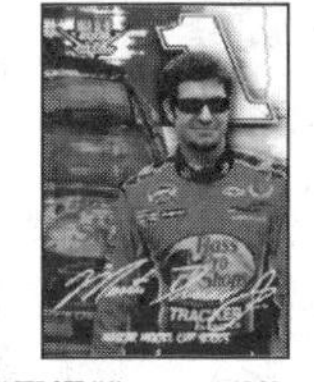

IPLETE SET (90) 15.00 40.00
) CARD STATED ODDS 1:60
ATION STATED ODDS 1:60
: ALONG ENTRY STATED ODDS 1:20
TONA ENTRY STATED ODDS 1:20
BOX HOBBY (20) 60.00 90.00
. BOX RETAIL (24) 50.00 75.00
nmie Johnson .75 2.00
immie Johnson Yellow 48 4.00 10.00
f Gordon 1.00 2.50
nt Bowyer .50 1.25
tt Kenseth .60 1.50
le Busch .50 1.25
ny Stewart .75 2.00
rt Busch .40 1.00
f Burton .25 .60
rl Edwards .60 1.50
evin Harvick .50 1.25
artin Truex Jr. .50 1.25
enny Hamlin .60 1.50
yan Newman .40 1.00
reg Biffle .30 .75
amie McMurray .30 .75
obby Labonte .40 1.00
asey Kahne .75 2.00
uan Pablo Montoya 1.00 2.50
eed Sorenson .25 .60
avid Ragan .30 .75
lliott Sadler .30 .75
ark Martin .60 1.50
aul Menard .30 .75
yle Petty .25 .60
rian Vickers .30 .75
ale Jarrett .60 1.50
ichael Waltrip .30 .75
arcos Ambrose NBS 1.00 2.50
29 Kelly Bires NBS .30 .75
30 Clint Bowyer NBS .50 1.25
31 Jeff Burton NBS .25 .60
32 Carl Edwards NBS .60 1.50
33 Denny Hamlin NBS .60 1.50
34 Kevin Harvick NBS .50 1.25
35 Steve Wallace NBS .50 1.25
36 Scott Wimmer NBS .20 .50
37 Todd Bodine CTS .15 .40
38 Rick Crawford CTS .15 .40
39 Erik Darnell CTS .25 .60
40 Ron Hornaday CTS .25 .60
41 Mike Skinner CTS .15 .40
42 Jack Sprague CTS .15 .40
43 Kevin Harvick DD .50 1.25
44 Kevin Harvick DD .50 1.25
45 Jack Sprague DD .15 .40
46 Matt Kenseth's Car C .25 .60
47 Tony Stewart's Car C .30 .75
47B Tony Stewart's Car C Purple Top 1.50 4.00
48 Clint Bowyer's Car C .20 .50
49 Jeff Burton's Car C .10 .25
50 Kyle Petty's Car C .10 .25
51 Kevin Harvick's Car C .20 .50
52 Jeff Gordon's Car C .40 1.00
53 Dale Jarrett's Car C .25 .60
54 Carl Edwards' Car C .25 .60
55 Jimmie Johnson NA .75 2.00
56 Jeff Gordon NA 1.00 2.50
57 Juan Pablo Montoya NA 1.00 2.50
58 Jeff Gordon NA 1.00 2.50
59 Matt Kenseth NA .60 1.50
60 Jeff Gordon NA 1.00 2.50
60B Jeff Gordon CA with hat 5.00 12.00
61 Jimmie Johnson NA .75 2.00
62 Jeff Gordon NA 1.00 2.50
63 Denny Hamlin NA .60 1.50
64 Martin Truex Jr.'s Car EL .20 .50
65 Kurt Busch's Car EL .15 .40
66 Matt Kenseth's Car EL .25 .60
67 Jeff Gordon's Car EL .40 1.00
68 Kevin Harvick's Car EL .20 .50
69 Jeff Burton's Car EL .10 .25
70 Reed Sorenson's Car EL .10 .25
71 Jimmie Johnson's Car EL .30 .75
72 Carl Edwards' Car EL .25 .60
72B Carl Edwards' Car EL -car on track 1.25 3.00
73 Juan Pablo Montoya NI 1.00 2.50
74 Kasey Kahne NI .75 2.00
75 Tony Stewart NI .75 2.00
76 Casey Mears NI .25 .60
77 Clint Bowyer NI .50 1.25
78 Jimmie Johnson NI .75 2.00
79 Jeff Burton NI .25 .60
80 Dale Earnhardt Jr. P 1.25 3.00
81 Dale Earnhardt Jr. P 1.25 3.00
82 Dale Earnhardt Jr. P 1.25 3.00
82B Dale Earnhardt Jr. P w/o helicopter 6.00 15.00
83 Dale Earnhardt Jr. P 1.25 3.00
84 Dale Earnhardt Jr. P 1.25 3.00
85 Dale Earnhardt Jr. P 1.25 3.00
85B Dale Earnhardt Jr. P w/o can 6.00 15.00
86 Dario Franchitti's Car P .20 .50
87 Sam Hornish Jr.'s Car P .25 .60
88 Patrick Carpentier's Car P .20 .50
89 Kyle Busch's Car P .20 .50
90 Dale Earnhardt Jr. CL 1.25 3.00
0 Jimmie Johnson Champ 4.00 10.00
NNO Daytona Entry Card 1.50 4.00
NNO Ride Along Entry Card 1.25 3.00

2008 Wheels High Gear Final Standings

SOME NOT PRICED DUE TO SCARCITY
F1 Jimmie Johnson/1
F2 Jeff Gordon/2
F3 Clint Bowyer/3
F4 Matt Kenseth/4
F5 Kyle Busch/5
F6 Tony Stewart/6
F7 Kurt Busch/7
F8 Jeff Burton/8
F9 Carl Edwards/9
F10 Kevin Harvick/10
F11 Martin Truex Jr./11
F12 Denny Hamlin/12
F13 Ryan Newman/13
F14 Greg Biffle/14
F15 Jamie McMurray/17
F16 Bobby Labonte/18
F17 Kasey Kahne/19
F18 Juan Pablo Montoya/20
F19 Reed Sorenson/22
F20 David Ragan/23
F21 Elliott Sadler/25 6.00 15.00
F22 Mark Martin/27 12.50 25.00
F23 Paul Menard/34 6.00 15.00
F24 Kyle Petty/35 5.00 12.00
F25 Brian Vickers/38 4.00 10.00
F26 Dale Jarrett/41 20.00 40.00
F27 Michael Waltrip/44 6.00 15.00

2008 Wheels High Gear MPH

*MPH: 3X TO 8X BASE
STATED PRINT RUN 100 SERIAL #'d SETS

2008 Wheels High Gear Previews

(EB1-EB27,EB80-EB85) STATED PRINT RUN 5 SERIAL #'d SETS
(EB86-EB89) STATED PRINT RUN 1 SERIAL #'d SET
NOT PRICED DUE TO SCARCITY

2008 Wheels High Gear Driven

COMPLETE SET (27) 8.00 20.00
STATED ODDS 1:2
DR1 Jimmie Johnson 1.25 3.00
DR2 Tony Stewart 1.25 3.00
DR3 Kurt Busch .60 1.50
DR4 Clint Bowyer .75 2.00
DR5 David Ragan .50 1.25
DR6 Kyle Petty .40 1.00
DR7 Elliott Sadler .50 1.25
DR8 Bobby Labonte .60 1.50
DR9 Kevin Harvick .75 2.00
DR10 Mark Martin 1.00 2.50
DR11 Dale Jarrett 1.00 2.50
DR12 Kasey Kahne 1.25 3.00
DR13 Dave Blaney .25 .60
DR14 Greg Biffle .50 1.25
DR15 Martin Truex Jr. .75 2.00
DR16 Michael Waltrip .50 1.25
DR17 Reed Sorenson .40 1.00
DR18 Denny Hamlin 1.00 2.50
DR19 Matt Kenseth 1.00 2.50
DR20 Jeff Burton .40 1.00
DR21 Ryan Newman .60 1.50
DR22 Jeff Gordon 1.50 4.00
DR23 Brian Vickers .50 1.25
DR24 Jamie McMurray .50 1.25
DR25 Carl Edwards 1.00 2.50
DR26 Juan Pablo Montoya 1.50 4.00
DR27 A.J. Allmendinger .40 1.00

2008 Wheels High Gear Flag Chasers Black

OVERALL FLAG CHASERS STATED ODDS 1:40
STATED PRINT RUN 89 SERIAL #'d SETS
FC1 Mark Martin 8.00 20.00
FC2 Tony Stewart 10.00 25.00
FC3 Jeff Gordon 15.00 40.00
FC4 Kevin Harvick 10.00 25.00
FC5 Juan Pablo Montoya 8.00 20.00
FC6 Jimmie Johnson 12.50 30.00
FC7 Carl Edwards 8.00 20.00
FC8 Kasey Kahne 12.50 30.00
FC9 Matt Kenseth 10.00 25.00

2008 Wheels High Gear Flag Chasers Blue-Yellow

*BLUE-YELLOW: 1X TO 2.5X BLACK
OVERALL FLAG CHASERS STATED ODDS 1:40
STAED PRINT RUN 50 SERIAL #'d SETS

2008 Wheels High Gear Flag Chasers Checkered

OVERALL FLAG CHASERS STATED ODDS 1:40
STATED PRINT RUN 20 SERIAL #'d SETS

2008 Wheels High Gear Flag Chasers Green

*GREEN: .6X TO 1.5X BLACK
OVERALL FLAG CHASERS STATED ODDS 1:40
STATED PRINT RUN 60 SERIAL #'d SETS

2008 Wheels High Gear Flag Chasers Red

*RED: .4X TO 1X BLACK
OVERALL FLAG CHASERS STATED ODDS 1:40
STATED PRINT RUN 89 SERIAL #'d SETS

2008 Wheels High Gear Flag Chasers White

*WHITE: .5X TO 1.2X BLACK
OVERALL FLAG CHASERS STATED ODDS 1:40
STATED PRINT RUN 65 SERIAL #'d SETS

2008 Wheels High Gear Flag Chasers Yellow

*YELLOW: .4X TO 1X BLACK
OVERALL FLAG CHASERS STATED ODDS 1:40
STATED PRINT RUN 89 SERIAL #'d SETS

2008 Wheels High Gear Full Throttle

COMPLETE SET (9) 12.50 30.00
STATED ODDS 1:6
FT1 Jeff Gordon 2.00 5.00
FT2 Mark Martin 1.25 3.00
FT3 Kevin Harvick 1.00 2.50
FT4 Juan Pablo Montoya 2.00 5.00
FT5 Carl Edwards 1.25 3.00
FT6 Jeff Burton .50 1.25
FT7 Jimmie Johnson 1.50 4.00

FT8 Martin Truex Jr. 1.00 2.50
FT9 Tony Stewart 1.50 4.00

2008 Wheels High Gear Last Lap

STATED PRINT RUN 10 SERIAL #'d SETS
NOT PRICED DUE TO SCARCITY

2008 Wheels High Gear Last Lap Holofoil

STATED PRINT RUN 5 SERIAL #'d SETS
NOT PRICED DUE TO SCARCITY

2008 Wheels High Gear The Chase

COMPLETE SET (12) 15.00 40.00
STATED ODDS 1:4
TC1 Jimmie Johnson 2.00 5.00
TC2 Jeff Gordon 2.50 6.00
TC3 Clint Bowyer 1.25 3.00
TC4 Matt Kenseth 1.50 4.00
TC5 Kyle Busch 1.25 3.00
TC6 Tony Stewart 2.00 5.00
TC7 Kurt Busch 1.00 2.50
TC8 Jeff Burton .60 1.50
TC9 Carl Edwards 1.50 4.00
TC10 Kevin Harvick 1.25 3.00
TC11 Martin Truex Jr. 1.25 3.00
TC12 Denny Hamlin 1.50 4.00

1998 Wheels Terry Labonte Fan Club

NNO Terry Labonte 6.00 15.00

1991 Winner's Choice New England Drivers

Winner's Choice, Inc. produced this set in 1991 featuring popular New England area drivers of various race circuits. The black-bordered cards look very similar to 1991 Winner's Choice Modifieds cards and include a color driver or car photo surrounded by a checkered flag frame. The cards were packaged and sold in complete factory set form.

COMPLETE SET (120) 5.00 12.00
1 Cover Card .02 .10
2 Tony Hirschman .07 .20
3 Mike Hirschman's Car .02 .10
4 Mike Rowe .07 .20
5 Mike Rowe's Car .02 .10
6 Steve Knowlton .07 .20
7 Steve Knowlton's Car .02 .10
8 Bobby Dragon .07 .20
9 Bobby Dragon's Car .02 .10
10 Tony Sylvester .07 .20
11 Tony Sylvester's Car .02 .10
12 Dave Dion .07 .20
13 Dave Dion's Car .02 .10
14 Mike Weeden .07 .20
15 Mike Weeden's Car .02 .10
16 Bobby Gahan .07 .20
17 Bobby Gahan's Car .02 .10
18 Dean Ferri .07 .20
19 Dean Ferri's Car .02 .10
20 Lloyd Gillie .07 .20
21 Lloyd Gillie's Car .02 .10
22 Joey Kourafas .07 .20
23 Joey Kourafas' Car .02 .10
24 Jimmy Field .07 .20
25 Jimmy Field's Car .02 .10
26 Mike Johnson .07 .20
27 Mike Johnson's Car .02 .10
28 Dick McCabe .07 .20
29 Dick McCabe's Car .02 .10
30 Rick Miller .07 .20
31 Rick Miller's Car .02 .10
32 Joe Bessey .15 .40
33 Joe Bessey's Car .07 .20
34 Donny Ling Jr. .07 .20
35 Donny Ling Jr.'s Car .02 .10
36 Jamie Aube .07 .20
37 Jamie Aube's Car .02 .10
38 Ron Lamell Jr. .07 .20
39 Ron Lamell Jr.'s Car .02 .10
40 Checklist Card .02 .10
41 Mike Maietta .07 .20
42 Mike Maietta's Car .02 .10
43 Tom Bolles .07 .20
44 Tom Bolles' Car .02 .10
45 Tom Rowe .07 .20
46 Tom Rowe's Car .02 .10
47 Kelly Moore .07 .20
48 Kelly Moore's Car .02 .10
49 Bobby Gada .07 .20
50 Bobby Gada's Car .02 .10
51 Pete Rondeau .07 .20
52 Pete Rondeau's Car .02 .10
53 Dale Shaw .07 .20
54 Dale Shaw's Car .02 .10
55 Mike Olsen .07 .20
56 Mike Olsen's Car .02 .10
57 Bob Randall .07 .20
58 Bob Randall's Car .02 .10
59 Billy Clark .07 .20
60 Billy Clark's Car .02 .10
61 Tracy Gordon .07 .20
62 Tracy Gordon's Car .02 .10
63 Paul Richardson .07 .20
64 Paul Richardson's Car .02 .10
65 Glenn Cusack .07 .20
66 Glenn Cusack's Car .02 .10
67 Barney McRae .07 .20
68 Barney McRae's Car .02 .10
69 Pete Fiandaca .07 .20
70 Pete Fiandaca's Car .02 .10
71 Jeff Spraker .07 .20
72 Jeff Spraker's Car .02 .10
73 Stub Fadden .07 .20
74 Stub Fadden's Car .02 .10
75 Bruce Haley .07 .20
76 Bruce Haley's Car .02 .10
77 Pete Silva .07 .20
78 Pete Silva's Car .02 .10
79 Paul Johnson .07 .20
80 Paul Johnson's Car .02 .10
81 Checklist Card .02 .10
82 Dave Davis .07 .20
83 Dave Davis' Car .02 .10
84 Jimmy Burns .07 .20
85 Jimmy Burns' Car .02 .10
86 Bub Bilodeau .07 .20
87 Bub Bilodeau's Car .02 .10
88 Dave Darveau .07 .20
89 Dave Darveau's Car .02 .10
90 Glenn Sullivan .07 .20
91 Glenn Sullivan's Car .02 .10
92 Ricky Harrison .07 .20
93 Ricky Harrison's Car .02 .10
94 Billy Holbrook .07 .20
95 Billy Holbrook's Car .02 .10
96 John Marsh .07 .20
97 John Marsh's Car .02 .10
98 Ricky Craven .75 2.00
99 Ricky Craven's Car .40 1.00
100 Mike Stefanik .15 .40
101 Mike Stefanik's Car .07 .20
102 Bob Brunell .07 .20
103 Bob Brunell's Car .02 .10
104 Al Hammond .07 .20
105 Al Hammond's Car .02 .10
106 Babe Branscombe .07 .20
107 Babe Branscombe's Car .02 .10
108 Jeff Zuidemen .07 .20
109 Jeff Zuidemen's Car .02 .10
110 Jeff Barry .07 .20
111 Jeff Barry's Car .02 .10
112 Jerry Marquis .07 .20
113 Jerry Marquis' Car .02 .10
114 Art Tappen .07 .20
115 Art Tappen's Car .02 .10
116 Mike Rowe .07 .20
Tom Rowe
Father and Son
117 Mike Maietta .07 .20
Mike Maietta Jr.
Father and Son
118 Bentley Warren .07 .20
119 Bentley Warren's Car .02 .10
120 Checklist Card .02 .10

1991 Winner's Choice Ricky Craven

One of Winner's Choice's first card sets, this issue focuses on the career of up-and-coming driver Ricky Craven. The cards were released in complete factory set form with Craven pictured on the set box. A contest entry card was included with each set exchangeable for a chance to win Ricky Craven's 1990 Rookie of the Year driver's suit.

COMPLETE FACT.SET (31) 10.00 20.00
1 Ricky Craven .30 .75
Boyhood photo
2 Ricky Craven w/Car .30 .75
3 Ricky Craven w/Car .30 .75
4 Ricky Craven w/Car .30 .75
5 Ricky Craven's Car .12 .30
Early Disappointments
6 Ricky Craven .30 .75
7 Ricky Craven w/Car .30 .75
8 Ricky Craven w/Car .30 .75
9 Ricky Craven's Car .12 .30
10 Ricky Craven's Car .12 .30
11 Ricky Craven w/Car .30 .75
12 Ricky Craven's Car .12 .30
13 Ricky Craven .30 .75
14 Ricky Craven w/Car .30 .75
15 Ricky Craven .30 .75
16 Ricky Craven .30 .75
Cathleen Craven
17 Richard Petty .60 1.50
Ricky Craven
18 Ricky Craven .30 .75
19 Ricky Craven's Car .30 .75
Chuck Bown's Car
20 Ricky Craven .30 .75
21 Ricky Craven .30 .75
22 Ricky Craven .30 .75
Cathleen Craven
23 Ricky Craven .30 .75
24 Ricky Craven w/Crew .30 .75
25 Ricky Craven .30 .75
26 Ricky Craven's Car .12 .30
27 Ricky Craven's Car .12 .30
28 Ricky Craven .30 .75
29 Ricky Craven .30 .75
30 Ricky Craven .30 .75
NNO Contest Entry Card .07 .20

1992 Winner's Choice Busch

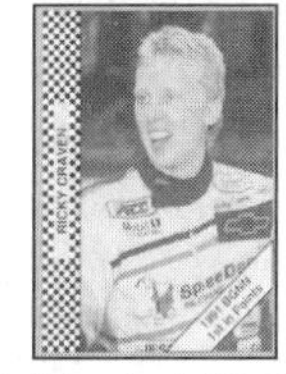

Winner's Choice released a full 150-card set featuring the top drivers of the Winston Cup Busch Series. The cards were distributed in factory set form, as well as through 12-card foil packs. Randomly inserted autographed cards were included in some foil packs.

COMPLETE SET (150) 10.00 25.00
COMP.FACT.SET (150) 10.00 25.00
1 Cover Card .02 .10
2 Ricky Craven .30 .75
3 Ricky Craven .30 .75
4 Ricky Craven's Car .20 .50
5 Dick McCabe .08 .25
6 Dick McCabe's Car .02 .10
7 Billy Clark .08 .25
8 Billy Clark's Car .20 .50
9 Jamie Aube .08 .25
10 Jamie Aube's Car .02 .10
11 Kelly Moore .08 .25
12 Kelly Moore's Car .02 .10
13 Joey Kourafas .08 .25
14 Joey Kourafas' Car .02 .10
15 Tony Hirschman .08 .25
16 Tony Hirschman's Car .02 .10
17 Tony Hirschman .08 .25
18 Stub Fadden .08 .25
19 Stub Fadden's Car .02 .10
20 Mike Rowe .08 .25
21 Mike Rowe's Car .02 .10
22 Dale Shaw .08 .25
23 Dale Shaw's Car .02 .10
24 Dave Dion .08 .25
25 Dave Dion's Car .02 .10
26 Joe Bessey .20 .50
27 Joe Bessey's Car .08 .25
28 Bobby Gada .08 .25
29 Bobby Gada's Car .20 .50
30 Jeff Barry .08 .25
31 Jeff Barry's Car .02 .10
32 Ken Bouchard .20 .50
33 Peter Daniels .08 .25
34 Peter Daniels' Car .02 .10
35 Barney McRae .08 .25
36 Barney McRae's Car .20 .50
37 Mike Olsen .08 .25
38 Mike Olsen's Car .02 .10
39 Bob Brunell .08 .25
40 Bob Brunell's Car .20 .50
41 Donny Ling Jr. .08 .25
42 Donny Ling Jr.'s Car .02 .10
43 Dean Ferri .08 .25
44 Dean Ferri's Car .02 .10
45 Jeff Sprakcr .08 .25
46 Jeff Spraker's Car .02 .10
47 Rick Miller .08 .25
48 Rick Miller's Car .02 .10
49 Lloyd Gillie .08 .25
50 Lloyd Gillie's Car .02 .10
51 Checklist Card .02 .10
52 Curtis Markham .20 .50
53 Curtis Markham's Car .08 .25
54 Ron Lamell .08 .25
55 Ron Lamell's Car .02 .10
56 Bobby Dragon .08 .25
57 Bobby Dragon's Car .20 .50
58 Mike Weeden .08 .25
59 Mike Weeden's Car .02 .10
60 Babe Branscombe .08 .25
61 Babe Branscombe's Car .20 .50
62 Kenny Wallace .30 .75
63 Kenny Wallace's Car .20 .50
64 Robert Pressley .20 .50
65 Robert Pressley's Car .08 .25
66 Chuck Bown .20 .50
67 Chuck Bown's Car .08 .25
68 Joe Nemechek .30 .75
69 Joe Nemechek's Car .20 .50
70 Todd Bodine .30 .75
71 Todd Bodine's Car .20 .50
72 Tom Peck .08 .25
73 Tom Peck's Car .02 .10
74 Steve Grissom .20 .50
75 Steve Grissom's Car .08 .25
76 Jeff Gordon 8.00 20.00
77 Jeff Gordon's Car 3.00 8.00
78 Jeff Burton 1.00 2.50
79 Jeff Burton's Car .50 1.25
80 David Green .30 .75
81 David Green's Car .20 .50
82 Butch Miller .08 .25
83 Butch Miller's Car .20 .50
84 Dave Rezendes .08 .25
85 Dave Rezendes' Car .02 .10
86 Ward Burton .75 2.00
87 Ward Burton's Car .30 .75
88 Ed Berrier .08 .25
89 Ed Berrier's Car .02 .10
90 Troy Beebe .08 .25
91 Troy Beebe's Car .02 .10

92 Ed Ferree .08 .25
93 Ed Ferree's Car .02 .10
94 Jim Bown .08 .25
95 Jim Bown's Car .02 .10
96 Tony Siscone .08 .25
97 Tony Siscone's Car .02 .10
98 Shawna Robinson 3.00 6.00
99 Shawna Robinson's Car .30 .75
100 Checklist Card .02 .10
101 Mike Maietta .08 .25
102 Mike Maietta's Car .02 .10
103 Tracy Gordon .08 .25
104 Tracy Gordon's Car .02 .10
105 Tony Papale .08 .25
106 Tony Papale's Car .02 .10
107 Jerry Marquis .08 .25
108 Jerry Marquis' Car .02 .10
109 Dave St. Clair .08 .25
110 Dave St. Clair's Car .02 .10
111 Steve Nelson .08 .25
112 Steve Nelson's Car .02 .10
113 Glenn Cusack .08 .25
114 Glenn Cusack's Car .02 .10
115 Jeff Zuideman .08 .25
116 Jeff Zuideman's Car .02 .10
117 Ed Carroll .08 .25
118 Ed Carroll's Car .02 .10
119 Tom Rosati .08 .25
120 Tom Rosati's Car .02 .10
121 Jim McCallum .08 .25
122 Jim McCallum's Car .02 .10
123 Eddy Carroll Jr. .08 .25
124 Eddy Carroll Jr.'s Car .02 .10
125 Bob Randall .08 .25
126 Bob Randall's Car .20 .50
127 Pete Fiandaca .08 .25
128 Pete Fiandaca's Car .02 .10
129 Bobby Gahan .08 .25
130 Bobby Gahan's Car .20 .50
131 Scott Bachand .08 .25
132 Scott Bachand's Car .02 .10
133 Tom Bolles .08 .25
134 Tom Bolles' Car .02 .10
135 Pete Silva .08 .25
136 Pete Silva's Car .02 .10
137 Jimmy Field .08 .25
138 Jimmy Field's Car .02 .10
139 Tony Sylvester .08 .25
140 Tony Sylvester's Car .02 .10
141 Mike Johnson .08 .25
142 Mike Johnson's Car .02 .10
143 Mike Maietta Jr. .08 .25
144 Mike Maietta Jr.'s Car .02 .10
145 Jimmy Hensley .08 .25
146 Jimmy Hensley's Car .02 .10
147 Sam Ard .08 .25
148 Sam Ard's Car .02 .10
149 Mike Greenwell .08 .25
150 Checklist Card .02 .10

1992 Winner's Choice Busch Autographs

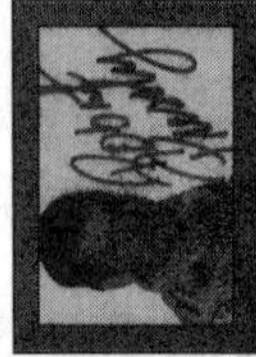

These four-cards were randomly inserted in 1992 Winner's Choice Busch foil packs. Gold borders and Gold paint pen signatures highlight the cardfronts. Reportedly, 500 of each card was autographed. The cards are unnumbered and arranged below alphabetically.

COMPLETE SET (4) 80.00 160.00
1 Chuck Bown/500 25.00 40.00
2 Ricky Craven/500 25.00 40.00
3 Robert Pressley/500 25.00 40.00
4 Kenny Wallace/500 25.00 40.00

1992 Winner's Choice Mainiac

Winner's Choice Race Cards produced this set in 1992 featuring drivers from various tracks in Maine. The cardfronts include a black and white driver photo inside a maroon colored border. The 50-cards were sold in complete set form through Winner's Choice and area tracks.

COMPLETE SET (50) 3.00 6.00
1 Cover Card .05 .15
2 Steve Reny .05 .15
3 Paul Pierce .05 .15
4 Ralph Hanson .05 .15
5 Billy Penfold .05 .15
6 Kim Gray .05 .15
7 Jimmy Burns .05 .15
8 Mary LeBlanc .05 .15
9 Doug Ripley .05 .15
10 Bob Libby .05 .15
11 Steve Chicoine .05 .15
12 Kenny Wright .05 .15
13 Mark Cyr .05 .15
14 Barry Babb .05 .15
15 David Wilcox .05 .15
16 Steve Blood .05 .15
17 Forest Peaslee .05 .15
18 Jamie Peaslee .05 .15
19 Chuck LaChance .05 .15
20 Steve Nelson .05 .15
21 Gary Smith .05 .15
22 Jerry Babb .05 .15
23 Bob Young .05 .15
24 Ray Penfold .05 .15
25 Andy Santerre .60 1.50
26 Dave McLaughlin .05 .15
27 Jon Lizotte .05 .15
28 Mike Kimball .05 .15
29 Benji Rowe .05 .15
30 John Phippen Jr. .05 .15
31 Casey Nash .05 .15
32 Joe Bowser .05 .15
33 Gene Wasson Jr. .05 .15
34 Gary Bellefleur Jr. .05 .15
35 Dick Belisle .05 .15
36 Cary Martin .05 .15
37 Lloyd Poland .05 .15
38 Moe Belanger .05 .15
39 Andy Lude .05 .15
40 Ron Benjamin .05 .15
41 Tania Schafer .05 .15
42 Bobby Babb .05 .15
43 Brad Hammond .05 .15
44 Ken Beasley .05 .15
45 Danny Grover .05 .15
46 Buster Grover .05 .15
47 Mark Billings .05 .15
48 Elaine Grover .05 .15
49 Gabe Gaboury .05 .15
50 Checklist Card .05 .15
blankbacked

1989 Winners Circle

One of the most sought after stock car racing sets, the 1989 Winners Circle set was primarily distributed to kids as part of a drug awareness program in North Carolina. The cards were also given out at many race tracks including the Richmond International Speedway in February, 1989. The 45 black-bordered cards feature star drivers from the early days of NASCAR. The checklist was intended to be card number 13, but is actually numbered "A." Reportedly only 150 of the 1A card of Lee Petty were produced. The set price doesn't include this card. A card album to house the set was also made available. Counterfeits have also been reported.

COMPLETE SET (45) 350.00 700.00
1A Lee Petty 250.00 400.00
without NASCAR on back
1B Lee Petty 20.00 40.00
with NASCAR on back
2 Fred Lorenzen 20.00 40.00
3 Tom Pistone 10.00 20.00
4 Tiny Lund 15.00 30.00
5 Paul Goldsmith 10.00 20.00
6 Dick Hutcherson 7.50 15.00
7 Louise Smith 10.00 20.00
8 Charlie Glotzbach 7.50 15.00
9 Bob Welborn 7.50 15.00
10 Bob Flock 7.50 15.00
11 Fonty Flock 10.00 20.00
12 Tim Flock 10.00 20.00
13 Checklist 3.00 8.00
Card actually numbered A
14 Ethel Mobley 10.00 20.00
15 Cotton Owens 7.50 15.00
16 David Pearson 10.00 20.00
17 Glen Wood 10.00 20.00
18 Bobby Isaac 15.00 30.00
19 Joe Lee Johnson 7.50 15.00
20 G.C. Spencer 7.50 15.00
21 Jack Smith 7.50 15.00
22 Frank Mundy 7.50 15.00
23 Bill Rexford 7.50 15.00
24 Dick Rathmann 7.50 15.00
25 Bill Blair 7.50 15.00
26 Darel Dieringer 7.50 15.00
27 Speedy Thompson 7.50 15.00
28 Donald Thomas 7.50 15.00
29 Marvin Panch 10.00 20.00
30 Buddy Shuman 7.50 15.00
31 Neil Castles 7.50 15.00
32 Buck Baker 10.00 20.00
33 Curtis Turner 10.00 20.00
34 Larry Frank 10.00 20.00
35 Lee Roy Yarborough 10.00 20.00
36 Ralph Liguori 7.50 15.00
37 Wendell Scott 15.00 30.00
38 Jim Paschal 7.50 15.00
39 Johnny Allen 10.00 20.00
40 Jimmie Lewallen 7.50 15.00
41 Maurice Petty 10.00 20.00
42 Nelson Stacy 7.50 15.00
43 Glenn Roberts(Fireball) 15.00 30.00
44 Edwin Matthews (Banjo) 7.50 15.00
45 Pete Hamilton 7.50 15.00

1995 Western Steer Earnhardt Next Generation

This 4-card set features Dale Earnhardt and three of his kids Kerry, Kelly, and Dale Jr. The cards were distributed by Western Steer and were produced using lenticular 3-D technology. There are three regular size cards and one Jumbo card. Reportedly, a total of 2500 sets were produced. There is also a black binder that was available to hold all four of the cards. The cards were available through the WSMP restaurants, Sports Image souvenir trailers and mail order.

COMPLETE SET (4) 15.00 30.00
1 Dale Earnhardt 2.50 5.00
Kerry Earnhardt
2 Dale Earnhardt 2.50 5.00
Kelley Earnhardt
3 Dale Earnhardt 7.50 15.00
Dale Earnhardt Jr.
JUM Dale Earnhardt 4.00 8.00
Kerry Earnhardt
Kelley Earnhardt
Dale Earnhardt Jr.
5"x7" Blank back

1995 Zenith

This is the inaugural set of Pinnacle's Zenith Racing brand. The 83-card set consists of five different subsets: Hot Guns (1-33), Mean Rides (34-58), End of the Day (59-68), Joe Gibbs Racing (69-75), and Championship Quest (78-83). The product came six cards per pack, with 24 packs per box and 16 boxes per case. The suggested retail price of a pack was $3.99.

COMPLETE SET (83) 8.00 20.00
1 Rick Mast HG .10 .30
2 Rusty Wallace HG .75 2.00
3 Dale Earnhardt HG 1.50 4.00
4 Sterling Marlin HG .40 1.00
5 Hut Stricklin HG .10 .30
6 Mark Martin HG .75 2.00
7 Geoff Bodine HG .10 .30
8 Jeff Burton HG .40 1.00
9 Lake Speed HG .10 .30
10 Ricky Rudd HG .40 1.00
11 Brett Bodine HG .10 .30
12 Derrike Cope HG .10 .30
13 Jeremy Mayfield HG .25 .60
14 Joe Nemechek HG .10 .30
15 Dick Trickle HG .10 .30
16 Ted Musgrave HG .10 .30
17 Darrell Waltrip HG .25 .60
18 Bobby Labonte HG .60 1.50
19 Bobby Hillin HG .10 .30
20 Morgan Shepherd HG .10 .30
21 Kenny Wallace HG .10 .30
22 Jimmy Spencer HG .10 .30
23 Jeff Gordon HG 1.00 2.50
24 Ken Schrader HG .10 .30
25 Terry Labonte HG .40 1.00
26 Todd Bodine HG .10 .30
27 Dale Jarrett HG .60 1.50
28 Steve Grissom HG .10 .30
29 Michael Waltrip HG .25 .60
30 Bobby Hamilton HG .10 .30
31 Robert Pressley HG .10 .30
32 Ricky Craven HG .10 .30
33 John Andretti HG .10 .30
34 Rick Mast's Transporter .05 .15
35 Rusty Wallace's Transporter .40 1.00
36 Dale Earnhardt's Transporter .75 2.00
37 Sterling Marlin's Transporter .10 .30
38 Terry Labonte's Transporter .10 .30
39 Mark Martin's Transporter .40 1.00
40 Geoff Bodine's Transporter .05 .15
41 Jeremy Mayfield's Trans. .10 .30
42 Ricky Rudd's Transporter .10 .30
43 Brett Bodine's Transporter .05 .15
44 Jimmy Spencer's Transporter .05 .15
45 Dick Trickle's Transporter .05 .15
46 Ted Musgrave's Transporter .05 .15
47 Darrell Waltrip's Transporter .10 .30
48 Bobby Labonte's Transporter .25 .60
49 Morgan Shepherd's Trans. .05 .15
50 Bill Elliott's Transporter .10 .30
51 Jeff Gordon's Transporter .40 1.00
52 Robert Pressley's Transporter .05 .15
53 Dale Jarrett's Transporter .25 .60
54 Michael Waltrip's Transporter .10 .30
55 Jeff Burton's Transporter .10 .30
56 John Andretti's Transporter .05 .15
57 Kyle Petty's Transporter .10 .30
58 Bobby Hamilton's Transporter .05 .15
59 Kenny Wallace EOD .10 .30
60 John Andretti EOD .10 .30
61 Ted Musgrave EOD .10 .30
62 Jimmy Spencer EOD .10 .30
63 Bobby Labonte EOD .60 1.50
64 Jeff Gordon EOD 1.00 2.50
65 Robert Pressley EOD .10 .30
66 Bobby Hillin EOD .10 .30
67 Bobby Hamilton EOD .10 .30
68 Brett Bodine EOD .10 .30
69 Cruz Pedregon JG .10 .30
70 Cruz Pedregon JG .10 .30
71 Cory McClenathan JG .10 .30
72 Cory McClenathan JG .10 .30
73 Jim Yates JG .05 .15
74 Jim Yates JG .05 .15
75 Bobby Labonte JG .60 1.50
76 Dale Earnhardt .75 2.00
Checklist
77 Jeff Gordon .50 1.25
Checklist
78 Jeff Gordon CQ 1.25 3.00
79 Jeff Gordon CQ 1.25 3.00
80 Jeff Gordon CQ 1.25 3.00
81 Jeff Gordon CQ 1.25 3.00
82 Jeff Gordon CQ 1.25 3.00
83 Jeff Gordon CQ 1.25 3.00
P3 Dale Earnhardt HG Promo 5.00 12.00

1995 Zenith Helmets

The 10 cards in this set were randomly inserted in Zenith Racing at a rate of one per 72 packs. The cards feature the helmets of some of Winston Cup's top drivers captured in all-foil Dufex printing technology.

COMPLETE SET (10) 50.00 120.00
1 Dale Earnhardt 15.00 40.00
2 Rusty Wallace 8.00 20.00
3 Jeff Gordon 10.00 25.00
4 Mark Martin 8.00 20.00
5 Bill Elliott 4.00 10.00
6 Bobby Labonte 6.00 15.00
7 Sterling Marlin 4.00 10.00
8 Ted Musgrave 1.25 3.00
9 Terry Labonte 4.00 10.00
10 Ricky Rudd 4.00 10.00
P8 Ted Musgrave Promo 2.00 5.00

1995 Zenith Tribute

This two-card insert set pays tribute to racing superstars: Dale Earnhardt and Jeff Gordon. The cards were inserted at a rate of one per 120 packs. The cards use all-foil Dufex printing technology to picture these two racing greats.

1 Dale Earnhardt 12.50 30.00
2 Jeff Gordon 12.50 30.00

1995 Zenith Winston Winners

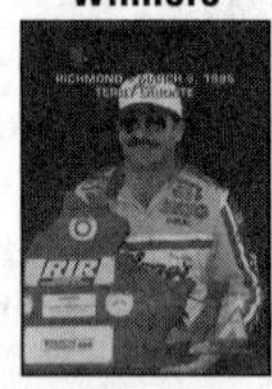

This 25-card set is a retrospective look at the winners of the first 25 Winston Cup races of the 1995 season. The cards feature all-gold foil card stock and could be found at a rate of one in six packs of Zenith Racing.

COMPLETE SET (25) 30.00 80.00
1 Sterling Marlin 1.50 4.00
2 Jeff Gordon 4.00 10.00
3 Terry Labonte 1.50 4.00
4 Jeff Gordon 4.00 10.00
Ray Evernham
5 Sterling Marlin 1.50 4.00
6 Jeff Gordon 4.00 10.00
7 Dale Earnhardt 6.00 15.00
8 Rusty Wallace 3.00 8.00
9 Mark Martin 3.00 8.00
10 Dale Earnhardt 6.00 15.00
Teresa Earnhardt
11 Bobby Labonte 2.50 6.00
12 Kyle Petty 1.00 2.50
13 Terry Labonte 1.50 4.00
14 Bobby Labonte 2.50 6.00
15 Jeff Gordon 4.00 10.00
16 Jeff Gordon 4.00 10.00
17 Dale Jarrett 2.50 6.00
18 Sterling Marlin 1.50 4.00
Paula Marlin
Sutherlin Marlin
19 Dale Earnhardt 6.00 15.00
20 Mark Martin 3.00 8.00
21 Bobby Labonte 2.50 6.00
Donna Labonte
Tyler Labonte
22 Terry Labonte 1.50 4.00
23 Jeff Gordon 4.00 10.00
24 Dale Earnhardt 6.00 15.00
25 Jeff Gordon 4.00 10.00
Brooke Gordon

1995 Zenith Z-Team

This 12 card set features the top Winston Cup drivers. The full body driver's photo is located on a Z-Team pedestal with a prismatic and metallic background that contains various colors. The Z-Team cards were inserted at a rate of one per 48 packs in Zenith Racing.

COMPLETE SET (12) 75.00 150.00
1 Dale Earnhardt 15.00 40.00
2 Jeff Gordon 10.00 25.00
3 Bobby Labonte 6.00 15.00
4 Terry Labonte 4.00 10.00
5 Sterling Marlin 4.00 10.00
6 Ken Schrader 1.25 3.00
7 Michael Waltrip 2.50 6.00
8 Ricky Rudd 4.00 10.00
9 Ted Musgrave 1.25 3.00
10 Morgan Shepherd 1.25 3.00
11 Rusty Wallace 8.00 20.00
12 Mark Martin 8.00 20.00

1996 Zenith

This 100-card set is the second issue of the Zenith brand by Pinnacle. The set is made up of 10 different subsets and includes the top drivers for NASCAR racing. Topical subsets include Road Pilots (1-34), Heavenly View (35-49), Sunrise (50-64), Black by Design (65-68), Tribute (69,70), Rookie of the Year (71,72), Championship Style (73-80), Trilogy (81-85), Robert Yates Racing (86-90), and Winners (91-98). A Dale Earnhardt commemorative card was inserted at the rate of 1:6025 with each being hand serial numbered of 94. The cards were packaged six cards per pack, 24 packs per box and 16 boxes per case. Suggested retail price for a pack was $3.99.

COMPLETE SET (100) 15.00 40.00
1 Dale Earnhardt 2.00 5.00
2 Jeff Gordon 1.25 3.00
3 Sterling Marlin .40 1.00
4 Terry Labonte .40 1.00
5 Ricky Rudd .40 1.00
6 Mark Martin 1.00 2.50
7 Bill Elliott .50 1.25
8 Ernie Irvan .25 .60
9 Rusty Wallace 1.00 2.50
10 Dale Jarrett .75 2.00
11 Geoff Bodine .10 .30
12 Derrike Cope .10 .30
13 Michael Waltrip .25 .60
14 Brett Bodine .10 .30
15 Ted Musgrave .10 .30
16 Hut Stricklin .10 .30
17 Rick Mast .10 .30
18 Darrell Waltrip .25 .60
19 Bobby Labonte .75 2.00
20 Jeff Burton .25 .60
21 Jeremy Mayfield .25 .60
22 Ken Schrader .10 .30
23 Johnny Benson .25 .60
24 Lake Speed .10 .30
25 John Andretti .10 .30
26 Robert Pressley .10 .30
27 Kyle Petty .25 .60
28 Ricky Craven .25 .60
29 Bobby Hamilton .10 .30
30 Joe Nemechek .10 .30
31 Morgan Shepherd .10 .30
32 Bobby Hillin .10 .30
33 Jimmy Spencer .10 .30
34 Ward Burton .25 .60
35 Dale Earnhardt's Car HV .75 2.00
36 Jeff Gordon's Car HV .50 1.25
37 Sterling Marlin's Car HV .10 .30
38 Mark Martin's Car HV .40 1.00
39 Terry Labonte's Car HV .25 .60
40 Bobby Labonte's Car HV .25 .60
41 Darrell Waltrip's Car HV .10 .30
42 Ernie Irvan's Car HV .10 .30
43 Dale Jarrett's Car HV .25 .60
44 Bobby Hamilton's Car HV .05 .15
45 Bill Elliott's Car HV .25 .60
46 Joe Nemechek's Car HV .05 .15
47 Ted Musgrave's Car HV .05 .15
48 Kyle Petty's Car HV .10 .30
49 Michael Waltrip's Car HV .10 .30
50 Dale Earnhardt S 1.00 2.50
51 Jeff Gordon S .60 1.50
52 Mark Martin S .50 1.25
53 Ricky Rudd S .25 .60
54 Terry Labonte S .25 .60
55 Kyle Petty S .10 .30
56 Bobby Hillin S .05 .15
57 Ted Musgrave S .05 .15
58 Ken Schrader S .05 .15
59 John Andretti S .05
60 Dale Jarrett S .40
61 Johnny Benson S .10
62 Michael Waltrip S .25
63 Bobby Labonte S .40
64 Ernie Irvan S .10
65 Dale Earnhardt BD 1.00
66 Dale Earnhardt BD 1.00
67 Dale Earnhardt BD 1.00
68 Dale Earnhardt BD 1.00
69 Dale Earnhardt T 1.00
70 Terry Labonte T .25
71 Ricky Craven ROY .05
72 Ricky Craven ROY .05
73 Jeff Gordon CS .50
74 Jeff Gordon CS .50
75 Jeff Gordon CS .50
76 Jeff Gordon CS .50
77 Jeff Gordon CS .50
78 Jeff Gordon CS .50
79 Jeff Gordon CS .50
80 Jeff Gordon CS .50
81 Kenny Wallace TRI .05
82 Kenny Wallace TRI .05
83 Kenny Wallace TRI .05
84 Kenny Wallace TRI .05
85 Kenny Wallace TRI .05
86 Robert Yates RYR .05
87 Ernie Irvan RYR .10
88 Larry McReynolds RYR .05
89 Dale Jarrett RYR .40
90 Todd Parrott RYR .05
91 Jeff Gordon W .60
92 Jeff Gordon W .60
93 Terry Labonte W .25
94 Rusty Wallace W .50
95 Sterling Marlin W .25
96 Rusty Wallace W .50
97 Dale Jarrett W .40
98 Jeff Gordon .60
Brooke Gordon W
99 Jeff Gordon CL .50
100 Bill Elliott CL .25
WC1 Dale Earnhardt/94 150.00 30
Seven Wonders

1996 Zenith Artist Proc

This 100-card set is a parallel to the base set set features the base cards printed on Gold Rai holofoil. The cards were randomly seeded in pac a rate of 1:24.

COMPLETE SET (100) 300.00 60
*ARTIST PROOFS: 4X TO 10X BASE CARD HI

1996 Zenith Champio Salute

This 26-card insert set pays tribute to the pa years of NASCAR Winston Cup racing. Each features a photo of the drivers championship The rings include a real diamond chip mounte the surface of the card. The cards were rand inserted 1:90.

COMPLETE SET (26) 300.00 60
1 Jeff Gordon 15.00 4
2 Dale Earnhardt 25.00 6
3 Dale Earnhardt 25.00 6
4 Alan Kulwicki 3.00
5 Dale Earnhardt 25.00 6
6 Dale Earnhardt 25.00 6
7 Rusty Wallace 12.50 3
8 Bill Elliott 6.00 1
9 Dale Earnhardt 25.00 6
10 Dale Earnhardt 25.00 6
11 Darrell Waltrip 3.00
12 Terry Labonte 5.00 1
13 Bobby Allison 1.50
14 Darrell Waltrip 3.00
15 Darrell Waltrip 3.00
16 Dale Earnhardt 25.00 6
17 Richard Petty 3.00
18 Cale Yarborough 1.50
19 Cale Yarborough 1.50
20 Cale Yarborough 1.50
21 Richard Petty 3.00
22 Richard Petty 3.00
23 Benny Parsons 1.50
24 Richard Petty 3.00
25 Richard Petty 3.00
26 Richard Childress 1.50
P12 Bobby Allison Promo 2.00

1996 Zenith Highligh

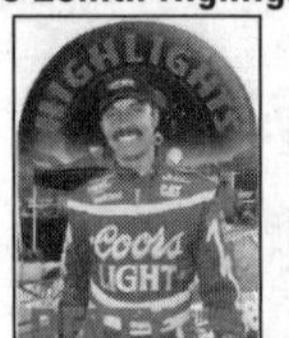

This 15-card insert set features top drive Winston Cup racing. The cards are die-cu stamped and randomly seeded 1:11 packs.

COMPLETE SET (15) 30.00 8
1 Dale Earnhardt 8.00 2
2 Jeff Gordon 5.00 1
3 Sterling Marlin 1.50
4 Mark Martin 4.00 1
5 Ricky Rudd 1.50
6 Darrell Waltrip 1.00
7 Geoff Bodine .50
8 Bobby Labonte 3.00
9 Terry Labonte 1.50
10 Michael Waltrip 1.00
11 Ken Schrader .50
12 Jimmy Spencer .50
13 Kyle Petty 1.00
14 Ernie Irvan 1.00
15 Bill Elliott 2.00

1986 Ace Drag

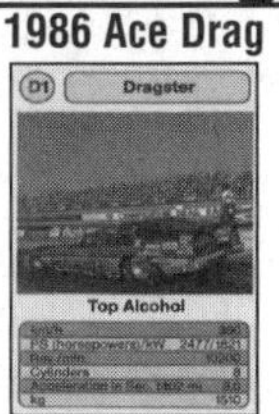

...et was made in West Germany for the British ...ny Ace. The cards are actually part of a Trump ...game featuring drag racing photos on the ...ont with a playing card back and rounded ...s. The playing card deck contains 32-cards ...e cover/rule card. Drivers are not specifically ...fied on the cards, but are included below as

...PLETE SET (33)	4.00	10.00
...nny Car	.10	.30
...nny Car	.10	.30
...nny Car	.10	.30
...nny Car	.20	.50
...m Hoover		
...ck Car	.20	.50
...b Glidden		
...ck Car	.10	.30
...ck Car	.10	.30
... Dragster	.20	.50
...y Johnson		
...ng Shot	.10	.30
...ng Shot	.10	.30
...ng Shot	.10	.30
...ng Shot	.10	.30
...p Alcohol	.10	.30
...p Alcohol	.10	.30
...p Alcohol	.10	.30
...p Alcohol	.20	.50
...m Hoover		
...ortsman Pro	.10	.30
...ortsman Pro	.10	.30
...ortsman Pro	.10	.30
...rtsman Pro	.10	.30
...Fuel Funny Car	.10	.30
...Fuel Funny Car	.20	.50
...ymond Beadle		
...Fuel Funny Car	.10	.30
...Fuel Funny Car	.10	.30
...agster Truck	.10	.30
...agster Truck	.10	.30
...agster Truck	.10	.30
...agster Truck	.10	.30
...agster Truck	.10	.30
...agster Truck	.10	.30
...agster Truck	.10	.30
...agster Truck	.10	.30
...Cover Card	.10	.30
...me rules on back		

1994 Action Packed NHRA

...Packed expanded their auto racing card line ...4 with their first set featuring popular drivers ...RA. The card fronts feature a ghosted white ...ound with gold lettering for the driver's name. ...ing included 6-card packs and 24-pack boxes ...opular driver's photos on the wrapper fronts. ...Gold insert cards were randomly distributed in

...LETE SET (42)	7.50	20.00
...FACT.SET (42)	7.50	20.00
...e Hill	.60	1.50
...t Kalitta	.30	.75
...ny Bernstein	.60	1.50
...Dunn	.20	.50
...e McDaniel	.20	.50
... McClenathan	.30	.75
...Amato	.30	.75
...McCulloch	.20	.50
...g Herbert	.20	.50
...mmy Johnson Jr.	.20	.50
...ie Hill's Car	.30	.75
...tt Kalitta's Car	.10	.30
...ny Bernstein's Car	.30	.75
...e Dunn's Car	.10	.30
...ce McDaniel's Car	.10	.30
...y McClenathan's Car	.10	.30
... Amato's Car	.10	.30
...McCulloch's Car	.10	.30
...g Herbert's Car	.10	.30
...mmy Johnson Jr.'s Car	.10	.30
...n Force	1.50	3.00
...ck Etchells	.20	.50
...z Pedregon	.30	.75
...Hofmann	.20	.50
...n Hoover	.20	.50
...rren Johnson	.20	.50
...t Johnson	.20	.50
...tt Geoffrion	.20	.50
29 Larry Morgan	.20	.50
30 Mark Pawuk	.20	.50
31 Tom McEwen	.20	.50
32 Shirley Muldowney	.60	1.50
33 Darrell Gwynn	.20	.50
34 Don Garlits	.60	1.50
35 Bob Glidden's Car	.10	.30
36 Don Prudhomme	.60	1.50
37 Cory McClenathan's Car	.10	.30
38 Pat Austin's Car	.10	.30
39 John Force's Car	.75	2.00
40 Jim Epler's Car	.10	.30
41 Warren Johnson's Car	.10	.30
42 Warren Johnson's Car	.10	.30
DR1 Eddie Hill Promo	1.50	4.00

1994 Action Packed NHRA 24K Gold

Randomly inserted in 1994 Action Packed Drag racing packs, each card includes the now standard 24Kt. Gold logo on the card front. These Gold cards are essentially parallel versions of the corresponding driver's regular issue. Wrapper stated odds for pulling a 24K Gold card are 1:96.

COMPLETE SET (6)	100.00	200.00
31G Tom McEwen	15.00	30.00
32G Shirley Muldowney	25.00	50.00
33G Darrell Gwynn	15.00	30.00
34G Don Garlits	25.00	50.00
35G Bob Glidden's Car	15.00	30.00
36G Don Prudhomme	20.00	40.00

1994 Action Packed Winston Drag Racing 24K Gold

This three-card set was produced by Action Packed and distributed through the Winston Cup Catalog and by Action Packed dealers. The cards were printed using Action Packed's 24K Gold process and feature NHRA stars John Force, Eddie Hill, and Warren Johnson.

COMPLETE SET (3)	12.00	30.00
1 John Force	6.00	15.00
2 Eddie Hill	4.00	10.00
3 Warren Johnson	3.00	8.00

1995 Action Packed NHRA

The 1995 Action Packed NHRA set was one of the first racing sets to be released after Action Packed became a Pinnacle brand. The set focuses on the top stars of NHRA with subsets on three of the more popular drivers: Joe Amato, Kenny Bernstein, and John Force. The standard packaging of 6-cards per pack and 24-packs per box was used with a four-tier insert card program: Silver Streak parallel, Autographs, Junior Dragster Champs, and 24K Gold.

COMPLETE SET (42)	6.00	15.00
1 Scott Kalitta's Car	.15	.40
2 Larry Dixon's Car	.15	.40
3 Cory McClenathan's Car	.20	.50
4 Connie Kalitta's Car	.20	.50
5 Joe Amato's Car	.15	.40
6 Kenny Bernstein's Car	.30	.75
7 Mike Dunn's Car	.15	.40
8 Pat Austin's Car	.15	.40
9 Tommy Johnson Jr.'s Car	.15	.40
10 Shelly Anderson's Car	.15	.40
11 John Force's Car	.40	1.00
12 Cruz Pedregon's Car	.20	.50
13 Al Hofmann's Car	.15	.40
14 Chuck Etchells's Car	.15	.40
15 K.C. Spurlock's Car	.15	.40
16 Gordie Bonin's Car	.15	.40
17 Jim Epler's Car	.15	.40
18 Dean Skuza's Car	.15	.40
19 Gary Bolger's Car	.15	.40
20 Kenji Okazaki's Car	.15	.40
21 Darrell Alderman's Car	.15	.40
22 Scott Geoffrion's Car	.15	.40
23 Warren Johnson's Car	.15	.40
24 Jim Yates' Car	.15	.40
25 Kurt Johnson's Car	.15	.40
26 Joe Amato	.30	.75
27 Joe Amato's Car	.20	.50
28 Joe Amato's Car	.20	.50
29 Joe Amato	.30	.75
30 Kenny Bernstein	.40	1.00
31 Kenny Bernstein's Car	.30	.75
32 Kenny Bernstein's Car	.30	.75
33 Kenny Bernstein's Car	.30	.75
34 Kenny Bernstein's Car	.30	.75
35 Kenny Bernstein's Car	.30	.75
36 John Force	1.00	2.50
37 John Force's Car	.40	1.00
38 John Force's Car	.40	1.00
39 John Force's Car	.40	1.00
40 John Force's Car	.40	1.00
41 Eddie Hill	.40	1.00
42 Joe Gibbs	.30	.75
P11 John Force's Car Prototype	2.00	5.00

1995 Action Packed NHRA Silver Streak

Action Packed introduced a Pinnacle Brands tradition to its 1995 NHRA set with the addition of a full parallel set -- Silver Streak. The cards were randomly inserted in 1995 Action Packed NHRA packs at the rate of approximately one card every six foil packs. The cards were printed with a silver foil background on the driver photo and the Silver Streak logo on the card back.

COMPLETE SET (42) 40.00 80.00
*SINGLES: 2X TO 5X BASE CARDS

1995 Action Packed NHRA Autographs

This 16-card insert set features the top drivers in the NHRA signatures. Each card is hand numbered of 500. The Kenny Bernstein and John Force cards were numbered of 125. The cards were available one per 24 packs.

COMPLETE SET (16)	300.00	600.00
1 Scott Kalitta	10.00	25.00
2 Larry Dixon	10.00	25.00
3 Cory McClenathan	15.00	40.00
6 K.Bernstein/125	90.00	150.00
7 Mike Dunn	10.00	25.00
9 Tommy Johnson	10.00	25.00
10 Shelly Anderson	10.00	25.00
11 John Force/125	100.00	175.00
12 Cruz Pedregon	15.00	40.00
13 Al Hofmann	10.00	25.00
21 Darrell Alderman	10.00	25.00
22 Scott Geoffrion	10.00	25.00
23 Warren Johnson	10.00	25.00
24 Jim Yates	10.00	25.00
25 Kurt Johnson	10.00	25.00
41 Eddie Hill	15.00	40.00

1995 Action Packed NHRA 24K Gold

Randomly inserted in 1995 Action Packed NHRA packs, each card includes the standard 24Kt. Gold logo on the card front. These Gold cards are essentially parallel versions of the Kenny Bernstein and John Force subset cards. Wrapper stated odds for pulling a 24K Gold card are 1:96.

COMPLETE SET (10)	125.00	250.00
30 Kenny Bernstein	12.50	25.00
31 Kenny Bernstein	12.50	25.00
32 Kenny Bernstein	12.50	25.00
33 Kenny Bernstein	12.50	25.00
34 Kenny Bernstein	12.50	25.00
35 Kenny Bernstein	12.50	25.00
36 John Force	20.00	40.00
37 John Force	20.00	40.00
38 John Force	20.00	40.00
39 John Force	20.00	40.00
40 John Force	20.00	40.00

1995 Action Packed NHRA Jr. Dragster Champs

Randomly inserted in 1995 Action Packed NHRA packs, this set provides a preview of future NHRA hopefuls -- Junior National Championship winners. Cards were packed approximately one per 48 foil packs.

COMPLETE SET (8)	20.00	40.00
1 Richard Thompson	3.00	6.00
2 Chris Bear	3.00	6.00
3 Richard Coury Jr.	3.00	6.00
4 Jamie Lynn Innes	3.00	6.00
5 James Antonnette	3.00	6.00
6 Barrie Wagers	3.00	6.00
7 Michelle Banach	3.00	6.00
8 Mark Lowry	3.00	6.00

1993 Advanced Images Quick Eight Racing

This set was produced by Advanced Images and licensed through the Quick Eight Racing Association. Each card features a driver's car image with a black border on the front. The cardbacks include a checkered flag border with detailed driver information.

COMPLETE SET (25)	5.00	12.00
1 Ken Regenthal's Car	.30	.75
2 Rick Moore's Car	.30	.75
3 James Smith Jr.'s Car	.30	.75
4 Mike Elliott's Car	.30	.75
5 Ken Regenthal's Car	.30	.75
6 Dale Brinsfield's Car	.30	.75
7 Paul Dunlap's Car	.30	.75
8 Steve Sechler's Car	.30	.75
9 Dennis Houck's Car	.30	.75
10 Tom Stewart's Car	.30	.75
11 Barry Blackwell's Car	.30	.75
12 Dallas Cornelius's Car	.30	.75
13 Danny Crouse's Car	.30	.75
14 Charles Harris's Car	.30	.75
15 John McClain's Car	.30	.75
16 Don Plemmons's Car	.30	.75
17 Sonny Tindall's Car	.30	.75
18 Sam Snyder's Car	.30	.75
19 Kenneth Tripp's Car	.30	.75
20 Jerry Williams's Car	.30	.75
21 Herb Atkins's Car	.30	.75
22 Buzz Varner's Car	.30	.75
23 Gary McKee's Car	.30	.75
24 Rex Michael Shelton's Car	.30	.75
25 Kenny Farrell's Car	.30	.75

1990 Big Time Drag

This 21-card set features some of drag racings most popular cars. There is everything from Tom Hoover's Showtime Funny Car to Roger Gustin's Jet Funny Car. There were 1,500 sets produced. The cards are listed below in alphabetical order

COMPLETE SET (21)	12.00	30.00
1 Bob Bealieu	.60	1.50
2 Charles Carpenter's Car	.60	1.50
3 Jim Druer	.60	1.50
4 Artie Farmer	.60	1.50
5 Gordy Foust's Car	.60	1.50
6 Roger Gustin's Car	.60	1.50
7 Al Hanna's Car	.60	1.50
8 Tom Hoover's Car	.80	2.00
9 Tom Jacobson's Car	.60	1.50
10 Donnie Little	.60	1.50
11 Jeff Littleton's Car	.60	1.50
12 Jerry Moreland's Car	.60	1.50
13 Rocky Pirrone	.60	1.50
14 Dick Rosberg	.60	1.50
15 Lou Sattelmaier's Car	.60	1.50
16 Paul Strommen's Car	.60	1.50
17 Ken Thurm's Car	.60	1.50
18 William Townes	.60	1.50
19 Roy Trevino's Car	.60	1.50
20 Bob Vandergriff	.60	1.50
21 Norm Wizner's Car	.60	1.50

1990 Big Time Drag Stickers

This 21-card sticker set is a parallel to the 1990 Big Time Drag set. The same photos were used in each set. There were 500 sticker sets produced.

COMPLETE SET (21)	40.00	75.00
1 Bob Bealieu	1.50	4.00
2 Charles Carpenter's Car	1.50	4.00
3 Jim Druer	1.50	4.00
4 Artie Farmer	1.50	4.00
5 Gordy Foust's Car	1.50	4.00
6 Roger Gustin's Car	1.50	4.00
7 Al Hanna's Car	1.50	4.00
8 Tom Hoover's Car	2.00	5.00
9 Tom Jacobson's Car	1.50	4.00
10 Donnie Little	1.50	4.00
11 Jeff Littleton's Car	1.50	4.00
12 Jerry Moreland's Car	1.50	4.00
13 Rocky Pirrone	1.50	4.00
14 Dick Rosberg	1.50	4.00
15 Lou Sattelmaier's Car	1.50	4.00
16 Paul Strommen's Car	1.50	4.00
17 Ken Thurm's Car	1.50	4.00
18 William Townes	1.50	4.00
19 Roy Trevino's Car	1.50	4.00
20 Bob Vandergriff	1.50	4.00
21 Norm Wizner's Car	1.50	4.00

1991 Big Time Drag

Big Time Drag Cards, Inc. of Roseville, Michigan produced this 96-card set in complete factory set form. The first 24-cards highlight the careers of Don Garlits and Norm Day. The final card is an unnumbered cover card.

COMPLETE SET (96)	12.50	25.00
1 Don Garlits in Car	.50	1.25
2 Don Garlits in Car	.50	1.25
3 Don Garlits' Car	.50	1.25
4 Don Garlits' Car	.50	1.25
5 Don Garlits' Car	.50	1.25
6 Don Garlits' Car	.50	1.25
7 Don Garlits' Car	.50	1.25
8 Don Garlits' Car	.50	1.25
9 Don Garlits' Car	.50	1.25
10 Don Garlits' Car	.50	1.25
11 Don Garlits' Car	.50	1.25
12 Don Garlits' Car	.50	1.25
13 Norm Day Cover Card	.02	.20
14 Norm Day's Car	.10	.30
15 Norm Day's Car	.10	.30
16 Norm Day's Car	.10	.30
17 Norm Day's Car	.10	.30
18 Norm Day	.20	.50
19 Norm Day's Car	.10	.30
20 Norm Day W/Crew	.20	.50
21 Don Garlits' Car	.50	1.25
22 Norm Day's Car	.10	.30
23 Norm Day's Car	.10	.30
24 Norm Day's Car	.10	.30
25 Tom Hoover's Car	.20	.50
26 Jerry Caminito's Car	.10	.30
27 Wyatt Radke's Car	.10	.30
28 Cruz Pedregon's Car	.20	.50
29 Wayne Torkelson's Car	.10	.30
30 Whit Bazemore's Car	.10	.30
31 Bruce Larson's Car	.10	.30
32 Joe Amato's Car	.50	1.25
33 Bunny Burkett	.10	.30
34 Joe Amato's Car	.50	1.25
35 Della Woods w/Car	.10	.30
36 Della Woods' Car	.10	.30
37 Al Dapozzo's Car	.10	.30
38 Richard Hartman's Car	.10	.30
39 Richard Hartman	.10	.30
40 Bruce Larson's Car	.10	.30
41 Bob Vanscriver's Car	.10	.30
42 Jerry Caminito's Car Wyatt Radke's Car	.10	.30
43 Wayne Bailey's Car	.10	.30
44 Tom Hoover's Car Bruce Larson's Car	.20	.50
45 Jim Feurer's Car	.10	.30
46 Jim Feurer's Car	.10	.30
47 Blake Wiggins' Car	.10	.30
48 Randy Moore	.10	.30
49 Randy Moore's Car	.10	.30
50 Carolyn Melendy's Car	.10	.30
51 Sonny Leonard's Motor	.02	.20
52 Wally Bell's Car	.10	.30
53 Gary Grahner's Car	.10	.30
54 Bill Kuhlmann's Car	.10	.30
55 Tom Jacobson's Car	.10	.30
56 Ken Thurm's Car	.10	.30
57 Al Hanna's Car	.10	.30
58 Donnie Little's Car	.10	.30
59 Lou Sattelmaier's Car	.10	.30
60 Gordy Foust's Car	.10	.30
61 Charles Carpenter's Car	.10	.30
62 Tom Hoover's Car	.20	.50
63 Roy Trevino's Car	.10	.30
64 Jim Feurer w/Car	.10	.30
65 Paul Strommen's Car	.10	.30
66 Roger Gustin's Car	.10	.30
67 Jack Joyce's Car	.10	.30
68 Jerry Moreland's Car	.10	.30
69 Jeff Littleton's Car	.10	.30
70 Norm Wizner's Car	.10	.30
71 Kenneth Tripp Jr.'s Car	.10	.30
72 Tim McAmis' Car	.10	.30
73 Tom McEwen's Car	.20	.50
74 Tom McEwen's Car	.20	.50
75 Tom Hoover's Car	.20	.50
76 Ken Karsten Jr.'s Car	.10	.30
77 Johnny West's Car	.10	.30
78 Brian Gahm's Car	.10	.30
79 Wally Bell's Car	.10	.30
80 Roger Gustin's Car	.10	.30
81 Bob Bunker's Car	.10	.30
82 Terry Leggett's Car	.10	.30
83 Mike Ashley's Car	.10	.30
84 Al Hanna's Car	.10	.30
85 Whit Bazemore's Car	.10	.30
86 Wally Bell's Car	.10	.30
87 Aggi Hendriks' Car	.10	.30
88 Bruce Larson's Car	.10	.30
89 Darrell Amberson's Car	.10	.30
90 Bob Vanscriver's Car	.10	.30
91 John H. Rocca's Car	.10	.30
92 Wayne Bailey	.10	.30
93 K.S. Pittman's Car	.10	.30
94 Jack Ostrander's Car	.10	.30
95 Bob Vandergriff's Car	.10	.30
NNO Cover Card	.02	.20

1994 Card Dynamics Joe Amato

This three-card set features the five-time Winston Top Fuel Champion. The cards are made of polished aluminum and come in a display box. There were 10,000 sets made. Each set comes with a certificate of authenticity.

COMPLETE SET (3)	5.00	12.00
COMMON CARD	2.00	5.00

1994 Card Dynamics Kenny Bernstein

This three-card set features the "King of Speed." The cards are made of polished aluminum and come in a display box. There were 10,000 sets made. Each set comes with a certificate of authenticity.

COMPLETE SET (3)	5.00	12.00
COMMON CARD	2.00	5.00

1994 Card Dynamics Eddie Hill

This three-card set features the 1994 Winston Top Fuel Champion. The cards are made of polished aluminum and come in a display box. There were 10,000 sets made. Each set comes with a certificate of authenticity.

COMPLETE SET (3)	5.00	12.00
COMMON CARD	2.00	5.00

1994 Card Dynamics Don Prudhomme

This three-card set features drag racing legend Don "The Snake" Prudhomme. The cards are made of polished aluminum and come in a display box. There were 10,000 sets made. Each set comes with a certificate of authenticity.

COMPLETE SET (3)	5.00	12.00
COMMON CARD	2.00	5.00

1989 Checkered Flag IHRA

Checkered Flag Inc. produced sets in 1989 and 1990 featuring drivers and cars of the International Hot Rod Association. The cards were sold in complete factory set form. The 1989 set features black borders and horizontally oriented car cards with a few individual driver cars. The final card, number 100, is a checklist.

COMPLETE SET (100)	15.00	25.00
1 Richard Holcomb's Car	.10	.30
2 Richard Holcomb's Car	.10	.30
3 Usif Lawson's Car	.10	.30
4 Scott Weis' Car	.10	.30
5 Butch Kernodle's Car	.10	.30
6 Paul Hall's Car	.10	.30
7 Bogie Kell's Car	.10	.30
8 Kurt Neighbor's Car	.10	.30
9 Gary Rettell's Car	.10	.30
10 Steve Litton's Car	.10	.30
11 Melinda Green's Car	.10	.30
12 Don DeFluiter's Car	.10	.30
13 Mark Thomas' Car	.10	.30
14 Gary Rettell's Car	.10	.30
15 Bob Gilbertson's Car	.10	.30
16 Greg Moss	.20	.50
17 Dan Nimmo's Car	.10	.30
18 Phil Sebring's Car	.10	.30
19 Dennis Ramey	.20	.50
20 Dennis Ramey's Car	.10	.30
21 Ted Osborne's Car	.10	.30
22 Mark Osborne's Car	.10	.30
23 Garley Daniels' Car	.10	.30
24 Danny Estep's Car	.10	.30
25 Tim Freeman's Car	.10	.30
26 George Supinski's Car	.10	.30
27 Dave Northrop's Car	.10	.30
28 Jerry Taylor's Car	.10	.30
29 Mike Davis' Car	.10	.30
30 Jim Yates' Car	.10	.30
31 Harold Denton	.20	.50
32 Harold Denton's Car	.10	.30
33 Ed Dixon's Car	.10	.30
34 Ed Dixon	.20	.50
35 Terry Adams	.20	.50
36 Terry Adams' Car	.10	.30
37 Harold Robinson's Car	.10	.30
38 Larry Morgan's Car	.10	.30
39 Tim Nabors' Car	.10	.30
40 Steve Schmidt's Car	.10	.30
41 Neil Moyer's Car	.10	.30
42 Joe Sway's Car	.10	.30
43 John Nobile's Car	.10	.30
44 John Nobile's Car	.10	.30
45 Shirl Greer's Car	.10	.30
46 Shirl Greer's Car	.10	.30
47 Dave Miller's Car	.10	.30
48 Dave Miller's Car	.10	.30
49 Billy Ewing's Car	.10	.30
50 Clay Broadwater's Car	.10	.30
51 Gary Litton's Car	.10	.30
52 Keith Jackson's Car	.10	.30
53 Whit Bazemore	.20	.50
54 Craig Cain's Car	.10	.30
55 Esua Speed's Car	.10	.30
56 Ed Hoover's Car	.10	.30
57 Ed Hoover's Car	.10	.30
58 Kenneth Tripp Jr.'s Car	.10	.30
59 Kenneth Tripp Sr.'s Car	.10	.30
60 Billy DeWitt's Car	.10	.30
61 Billy DeWitt	.20	.50
62 Scotty Cannon's Car	.10	.30
63 Scotty Cannon	.20	.50
64 Michael Martin	.20	.50
65 Michael Martin's Car	.10	.30
66 Gordy Hmiel's Car	.10	.30
67 Gordy Hmiel's Car	.10	.30
68 Sam Snyder's Car	.10	.30
69 Terry Housley's Car	.10	.30
70 Jim Ray's Car	.10	.30
71 John leppert's Car	.10	.30
72 Frankie Foster's Car	.10	.30
73 Buddy McGowan's Car	.10	.30
74 Brian Gahm's Car	.10	.30
75 Bob Dickson's Car	.10	.30
76 Walter Henry's Car	.10	.30
77 Gene Fryer's Car	.10	.30
78 Terry Leggett's Car	.10	.30
79 Blake Wiggins' Car	.10	.30
80 Tim Nabors' Car	.10	.30
81 Ernest Wrenn's Car	.10	.30
82 Donnie Little's Car	.10	.30
83 Mike Ashley's Car	.10	.30
84 Ron Miller's Car	.10	.30
85 Danny Bastianelli's Car	.10	.30
86 Tracy Eddins' Car	.10	.30
87 Kurt Neighbor's Car	.10	.30
88 Greg Moss' Car	.10	.30
89 Greg Moss' Car	.10	.30
90 Bogie Kell's Car	.10	.30
91 Jerry Gulley's Car	.10	.30
92 Ernest Wrenn's Car	.10	.30
93 Don DeFluiter	.20	.50
94 Blake Wiggins	.20	.50
95 Barry Shirley's Car	.10	.30
96 Ken Regenthal's Car UER	.10	.30
97 Donnie Little's Car	.10	.30
98 Rick Hord's Car	.10	.30

99 Ricky Bowie's Car .10 .30
100 Checklist Card .10 .30

1990 Checkered Flag IHRA

Checkered Flag Race Cards Inc. produced sets in 1989 and 1990 featuring drivers and cars of the International Hot Rod Association. The cards were sold in complete factory set form. The 1990 set features white borders and horizontally oriented car cards. The final card, #100, is a checklist. An unnumbered cover card was produced as well featuring an order form to purchase additional sets at $17.50 each.

COMPLETE SET (101) 8.00 16.00
1 Mike Ashley's Car .07 .20
2 Ronnie Sox's Car .20 .50
3 Scotty Cannon's Car .20 .50
4 Jeff Littleton's Car .07 .20
5 Gordy Foust's Car .07 .20
6 Donnie Little's Car .07 .20
7 Bob Vandergriff's Car .07 .20
8 Terry Leggett's Car .07 .20
9 Ken Regenthal's Car .07 .20
10 Ed Hoover's Car .07 .20
11 Stanley Barker's Car .07 .20
12 Tim McAmis' Car .07 .20
13 Sam Snyder's Car .07 .20
14 Brian Gahm's Car .07 .20
15 Blake Wiggins' Car .07 .20
16 Ken Karsten Jr.'s Car .07 .20
17 Eddie Harris' Car .07 .20
18 Carolyn Melendy's Car .07 .20
19 Stuart Norman's Car .07 .20
20 Terry Leggett's Car .07 .20
21 Ron Iannotti's Car .07 .20
22 Michael Martin's Car .07 .20
23 Jeff Ensslin's Car .07 .20
24 Tim McAmis' Car .07 .20
25 Al Billes' Car .07 .20
26 Gordy Hmiel's Car .07 .20
27 Manny DeJesus' Car .07 .20
28 Brian Gahm's Car .07 .20
29 Ray Ervin's Car .07 .20
30 Wally Stroupe's Car .07 .20
31 Chuck VanVallis' Car .07 .20
32 Ken Karsten Jr.'s Car .07 .20
33 Ed Hoover's Car .07 .20
34 Ronnie Sox w/Car .25 .60
35 Scotty Cannon's Car .20 .50
36 Bob Vandergriff's Car .07 .20
37 Mike Ashley's Car .07 .20
38 Gordy Foust's Car .07 .20
39 Blake Wiggins' Car .07 .20
40 Ken Regenthal's Car .07 .20
41 Tracy Eddins' Car .07 .20
42 Steve Litton's Car .07 .20
43 Mark Thomas' Car .07 .20
44 Johnny West's Car .07 .20
45 Jerry Gulley's Car .07 .20
46 Bob Gilbertson's Car .07 .20
47 Dan Nimmo's Car .07 .20
48 Ronnie Midyette's Car .07 .20
49 Phil Sebring's Car .07 .20
50 Art Hendey's Car .07 .20
51 Bogie Kell's Car .07 .20
52 Greg Moss' Car .07 .20
53 Gary Litton's Car .07 .20
54 Ricky Bowie's Car .07 .20
55 Frank Kramberger's Car .07 .20
56 Keith Jackson's Car .07 .20
57 Clay Broadwater's Car .07 .20
58 Tommy Mauney's Car .07 .20
59 Ed Dixon's Car .07 .20
60 David Drongowski's Car .07 .20
61 Carlton Phillips' Car .07 .20
62 Harold Denton's Car .07 .20
63 Charlie Garrett's Car .07 .20
64 Joe Sway's Car .07 .20
65 Tim Nabors' Car .07 .20
66 Tommy Mauney's Car .07 .20
67 Terry Adams' Car .07 .20
68 Harold Denton's Car .07 .20
69 Terry Housley's Car .07 .20
70 Doug Kirk's Car .07 .20
71 Ed Dixon's Car .07 .20
72 Terry Walters' Car .07 .20
73 Neil Moyer's Car .07 .20
74 Harold Robinson's Car .07 .20
75 Jack Revelle's Car .07 .20
76 Don Kohler's Car .07 .20
77 Michael Brotherton's Car .20 .50
78 Richard Holcomb's Car .07 .20
79 Wayne Bailey's Car .07 .20
80 Fred Farndon's Car .07 .20
81 Chris Karamesines' Car .20 .50
82 John Carey's Car .07 .20
83 Melvin Eaves' Car .07 .20
84 Carroll Smoot's Car .07 .20
85 Gene Fryer's Car .07 .20
86 Craig Cain's Car .07 .20
87 Joe Groves' Car .07 .20
88 Ron Miller's Car .07 .20
89 Buddy McGowan's Car .07 .20
90 Frank Daniels' Car .07 .20
91 Mark Osborne's Car .07 .20
92 Tim Freeman's Car .07 .20
93 Ted Osborne's Car .07 .20
94 Danny Estep's Car .07 .20
95 Bruce Abbott's Car .07 .20
96 Aggi Hendriks' Car .07 .20
97 Tim Butler's Car .07 .20
98 Bob Vanscive's Car .07 .20
99 Usif Lawson's Car .07 .20
100 Checklist Card .07 .20
NNO Cover Card .07 .20
complete set order form on back

1965 Donruss Spec Sheet

Donruss produced this 66-card set sponsored by Hot Rod magazine for distribution in gum wax packs. The cards primarily feature top cars from a wide variety of drag racing and show events, but also cover road racing and IndyCar. The most noteworthy card, #49, features Bobby Unser and his Pikes Peak Hill Climb championship.

COMPLETE SET (66) 125.00 250.00
1 Bill Burke's Car 2.50 6.00
Mel Chastain's Car
Bonneville Streamliner
2 Fred Larson's Car 2.00 4.00
Ready to Go
3 Sam Parriott's Car 2.00 4.00
Blown Ford Engine
4 Jack Lufkin's Car 2.50 6.00
Triple Threat 'Vette
5 1925 T-Roadster 2.00 4.00
6 Show Winner 2.00 4.00
7 Agelesss Street Rod 2.00 4.00
8 315 Horsepower 2.00 4.00
9 Bob Summers' Car 2.00 4.00
Bill Summers' Car
700 Horsepower
10 Hot Rod Fever 2.00 4.00
11 East African Safari 2.00 4.00
12 Beauty and Comfort 2.00 4.00
13 Record Runs 2.00 4.00
14 Ted Wingate's Car 2.00 4.00
Pair Duces
15 Six Pots 2.00 4.00
16 Howard Peck's Car 2.50 6.00
'64 Buick Mill
17 What a Machine 2.00 4.00
18 Al Eckstrand's Car 2.50 6.00
Dodge Super Stock
19 Kurtis Roadster 2.00 4.00
20 World's Fastest 2.00 4.00
21 Super Super Stock 2.00 4.00
22 Hot Rod Dictionary 2.00 4.00
23 Well Dressed Mill 2.00 4.00
24 Custom Pick-Up 2.00 4.00
25 Bob-Tailed T 2.00 4.00
26 Jess Van Deventer's Car 2.00 4.00
Fiery Chevy
27 Offy Engine 2.00 4.00
28 334 Cubic Inches 2.00 4.00
29 Jack Williams' Car 2.00 4.00
Points Champion
30 Abandoned 2.00 4.00
31 Salt Flats 2.00 4.00
32 LeRoi Tex Smith's Car 2.00 4.00
Experimental Roadster
33 Modified Sport Car 2.00 4.00
34 Instant Roadster 2.00 4.00
35 1923 Dodge 2.00 4.00
36 L.A. Roadsters 2.00 4.00
37 Howard Brown's Car 2.00 4.00
137 Quarter
38 A Real Winner 2.00 4.00
39 Steve LaBonge's Car 2.00 4.00
Crusing Model A
40 Mark 27 2.00 4.00
41 Owners Pride 2.00 4.00
42 Roman Red 2.00 4.00
43 Tom McMullen's Car 2.00 4.00
Flamed Roadster
44 Hot Rod Dictionary 2.00 4.00
45 Detailed Custom 2.00 4.00
46 306 Streamliner 2.00 4.00
47 The Wedge 2.00 4.00
48 The Oakland Lational 2.00 4.00
49 Bobby Unser's Car 2.50 6.00
Hill Climb Champ
50 Tony Nancy's Car 2.00 4.00
Off the Line
51 Hot Rod Dictionary 2.00 4.00
52 Bob Herda's Car 2.00 4.00
Record Holder
53 Bobby Unser w/Car 2.50 6.00
Pikes Peak Champ
54 National Championship 2.00 4.00
55 Hot Rod Dictionary 2.00 4.00
56 John Mazmanian's Car 2.00 4.00
Boss
57 1964 Indianapolis 500 2.00 4.00
58 Hot Rod Dictionary 2.00 4.00
59 Connie Kalitta's Car 2.50 6.00
Nitro Loaded
60 Off the Line 2.00 4.00
61 Chuck Griffith's Car 2.00 4.00
Starlighter
62 National Drags 2.00 4.00
63 '35 Custom 2.00 4.00
64 Tom Spaulding's Car 2.00 4.00
Going Cart
65 Hot Rod Dictionary 2.00 4.00
66 Hot Rod Dictionary 2.00 4.00

1993 Finish Line NHRA Prototypes

This Prototype set was released by Finish Line in its own cello wrapper. Although the cards are unnumbered, they have been assigned numbers below according to alphabetical order.

COMPLETE SET (4) 2.00 5.00
1 Scott Geoffrion .60 1.50
2 Cory McClenathan's Car .60 1.50
3 Cruz Pedregon .75 2.00
4 Cover Card .10 .30

1993 Finish Line NHRA

For the first time Finish Line produced their own card set with this 1993 NHRA release. The set features star drivers, cars and crew members of the top NHRA teams of the previous season. The cards were packaged 12 per foil pack with 36 packs per box and 25-cards per jumbo pack. Insert sets included a 17-card Speedways issue and a 9-card Autographs set.

COMPLETE SET (133) 4.00 10.00
1 Joe Amato .07 .20
2 Joe Amato .07 .20
3 Joe Amato's Car .02 .10
4 Shelly Anderson .07 .20
5 Dale Armstrong .02 .10
6 Pat Austin .02 .10
7 Pat Austin's Car .01 .05
8 Walt Austin .02 .10
Pat Austin
9 Lee Beard .02 .10
10 Kenny Bernstein .20 .60
11 Kenny Bernstein's Car .07 .20
12 Kenny Bernstein .20 .60
13 Jim Brissette .02 .10
14 Michael Brotherton .02 .10
15 Michael Brotherton's Car .01 .05
16 Fuzzy Carter .02 .10
17 Wes Cerny .02 .10
18 Dannielle DePorter .02 .10
19 Darrell Gwynn .07 .20
20 Jim Head .02 .10
21 Doug Herbert .02 .10
22 Eddie Hill .20 .60
23 Eddie Hill .20 .60
24 Eddie Hill's Car .07 .20
25 Tommy Johnson Jr. .07 .20
26 Tommy Johnson Sr. .07 .20
Tommy Johnson Jr.
Wendy Johnson
27 Kim LaHaie .02 .10
28 Cory McClenathan .20 .60
29 Cory McClenathan .20 .60
30 Cory McClenathan's Car .07 .20
31 Ed McCulloch .02 .10
32 Ed McCulloch's Car .01 .05
33 John Medlen .02 .10
34 Jack Ostrander .02 .10
35 Jim Prock .02 .10
36 Don Prudhomme .20 .60
37 Don Prudhomme's Car .07 .20
38 Tim Richards .02 .10
39 Al Segrini .02 .10
40 Gene Snow .07 .20
41 Ken Veney .02 .10
42 Tom Anderson .02 .10
43 Whit Bazemore .02 .10
44 Gary Bolger .02 .10
45 Jerry Caminito .02 .10
46 Austin Coil .02 .10
47 Gary Densham .02 .10
48 Chuck Etchells .02 .10
49 Chuck Etchells' Car .01 .05
50 Jim Epler .02 .10
51 Gary Evans .02 .10
52 Bernie Fedderly .02 .10
53 John Force .50 1.25
54 John Force .50 1.25
55 John Force's Car .20 .60
56 Richard Hartman .02 .10
57 Al Hofmann .07 .20
58 Al Hofmann .07 .20
59 Al Hofmann's Car .02 .10
60 Tom Hoover .07 .20
61 Tom Hoover's Car .02 .10
62 Gordon Minor .02 .10
63 Mike Green .02 .10
64 Mark Oswald .02 .10
65 Cruz Pedregon .20 .60
66 Cruz Pedregon .20 .60
67 Cruz Pedregon's Car .07 .20
68 Bill Schultz .02 .10
69 Johnny West .02 .10
70 Del Worsham .02 .10
71 Chuck Worsham .02 .10
72 Bruce Allen .02 .10
73 Bruce Allen's Car .01 .05
74 Greg Anderson .02 .10
Kurt Johnson
75 Don Beverley .02 .10
76 Gary Brown .02 .10
77 Kenny Delco .02 .10
78 Jerry Eckman .02 .10
79 Jerry Eckman .02 .10
80 Jerry Eckman's Car .01 .05
81 Alban Gauthier's Car .01 .05
82 Scott Geoffrion .02 .10
83 Scott Geoffrion .02 .10
84 Scott Geoffrion's Car .01 .05
85 Bob Glidden .07 .20
86 Bob Glidden's Car .02 .10
87 Etta Glidden W/Crew .07 .20
88 Jerry Haas .02 .10
89 Dave Hutchens .02 .10
Mike Sullivan
90 Frank Iaconio .02 .10
91 Bill Jenkins .02 .10
92 Warren Johnson .07 .20
93 Warren Johnson .07 .20
94 Warren Johnson's Car .02 .10
95 Joe Lepone Jr. .02 .10
96 Larry Morgan .02 .10
97 Larry Morgan's Car .01 .05
98 Bill Orndorff .02 .10
99 Mark Pawuk .02 .10
100 Paul Rebeschi Jr. .02 .10
101 David Reher .02 .10
Buddy Morrison
102 Gordie Rivera .02 .10
103 Tom Roberts .02 .10
104 Harry Scribner .02 .10
105 Rickie Smith .02 .10
106 Jim Yates .02 .10
107 James Bernard w/Bike .01 .05
108 Bryon Hines .02 .10
109 Steve Johnson w/Bike .01 .05
110 John Mafaro .02 .10
111 John Myers .02 .10
112 David Schultz .02 .10
113 John Smith w/Bike .01 .05
114 Blaine Johnson .02 .10
115 Bob Newberry .02 .10
116 Steve Johns .02 .10
117 Greg Stanfield .02 .10
118 Chad Guilford .02 .10
119 Edmond Richardson .02 .10
120 Jeg Coughlin Jr. .02 .10
121 Pat Austin's Car .01 .05
122 Bill Barney .02 .10
123 Anthony Bartone's Car .01 .05
124 David Nickens .02 .10
125 Buster Couch .02 .10
126 Steve Evans .02 .10
127 Bob Frey .02 .10
128 Dave McClelland .02 .10
129 Larry Minor .02 .10
130 Wally Parks .02 .10
131 Shirley Muldowney .20 .60
132 Del Worsham's Car .01 .05
133 Larry Meyer .02 .10

1993 Finish Line NHRA Autographs

Finish Line produced this nine-card set with each card individually signed by the featured driver. The cards were randomly inserted in 1993 Finish Line foil and jumbo packs.

COMPLETE SET (9) 100.00 180.00
1 Joe Amato 7.50 20.00
2 Cory McClenathan 7.50 20.00
3 Kenny Bernstein 18.00 30.00
4 Cruz Pedregon 7.50 20.00
5 John Force 25.00 50.00
6 Al Hofmann 6.00 15.00
7 Warren Johnson 7.50 20.00
8 Scott Geoffrion 6.00 15.00
9 Jerry Eckman 6.00 15.00

1993 Finish Line NHRA Speedways

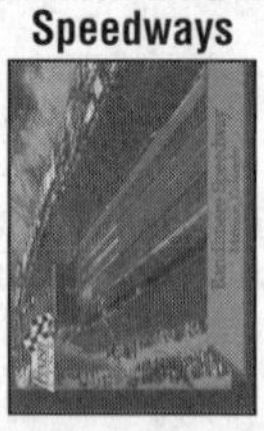

NHRA race tracks are the focus of this 17-card insert set produced by Finish Line. The cards were randomly packed in 1993 Finish Line NHRA foil and jumbo packs.

COMPLETE SET (17) 1.50 3.00
T1 Pomona Raceway .10 .20
T2 Firebird International .10 .20
T3 Houston Raceway Park .10 .20
T4 Gainesville Raceway .10 .20
T5 Rockingham Dragway .10 .20
T6 Atlanta Dragway .10 .20
T7 Memphis International .10 .20
T8 Old Bridge Township .10 .20
T9 National Trail Raceway .10 .20
T10 Sanair Int'l Dragway .10 .20
T11 Bandimere Speedway .10 .20
T12 Sears Point Int'l .10 .20
T13 Seattle International .10 .20
T14 Brainerd Int'l Raceway .10 .20
T15 Indianapolis Raceway .10 .20
T16 Maple Grove Raceway .10 .20
T17 Texas Motorplex .10 .20

1970 Fleer Dragstrips

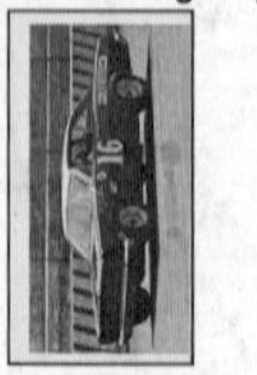

Fleer produced this 10-card set primarily as backers for their Dragstrips stickers. With each 5-cent wax pack, collector's received one of these cards and a group of automotive stickers. The cards are oversized (approximately 2-1/2" by 4-1/2") and blankbacked as are the sticker sheets. The black and white cards feature uncaptioned photos of top racers with an emphasis on Andy Granatelli and the STP IndyCar race team. We've assigned card numbers according to alphabetical order.

COMPLETE SET (10) 175.00 300.00
STICKER INSERTS 5.00 10.00
1 Darel Dierenger's Car 15.00 25.00
2 Don Garlits' Car 60.00 100.00
3 Andy Granatelli 20.00 35.00
4 Dan Gurney's Car 20.00 35.00
5 Graham Hill's Car 20.00 35.00
6 Parnelli Jones' Car 30.00 50.00
Andy Granatelli
7 Joe Leonard's Car 15.00 25.00
8 Joe Leonard's Car 15.00 25.00
Andy Granatelli
9 Ken Miles' Car 15.00 25.00
Lloyd Ruby's Car
MK II Ford
10 Art Pollard's Car 15.00 25.00

1971 Fleer AHRA Drag Champs

This is the first of three consecutive sets Fleer released featuring stars of AHRA drag racing. Wax packs contained five-cards and one stick of gum. There were three different wrappers produced, each featuring a different drag racer. Although virtually all of the 63-cards feature racing cars in action, three cards were devoted to the top champions in each drag racing category. An American and Canadian version was produced with the American cards printed on white card stock and are unnumbered. The Canadian set was numbered (listed below in that order) and printed on a cream colored paper stock.

COMPLETE SET (63) 200.00 350.00
*CANADIAN CARDS: SAME VALUE
1 Arlen Vanke's Car 3.00 6.00
2 John Wiebe's Car 4.00 8.00
3 Terry Hedrick's Car 3.00 6.00
4 Steve Carbone's Car 3.00 6.00
5 Leroy Goldstein's Car 3.00 6.00
6 Pat Foster's Car 3.00 6.00
7 Don Schumacher's Car 3.00 6.00
8 Don Gay's Car 4.00 8.00
Roy Gay's Car
9 Dick Harrell's Car 3.00 6.00
10 Bill Jenkins' Car 3.00 6.00
11 Kenny Safford's Car 3.00 6.00
12 John Elliot's Car 3.00 6.00
13 Pat Minick's Car 3.00 6.00
14 Arnie Behling's Car 3.00 6.00
15 Gene Snow's Car 4.00 8.00
16 Jay Howell's Car 3.00 6.00
17 Norm Tanner's Car 3.00 6.00
18 Don Garlits' Car 4.00 8.00
19 Ray Alley's Car 3.00 6.00
20 K.S. Pittman's Car 3.00 6.00
21 Ed Miller's Car 3.00 6.00
22 Funny Car Champs 4.00 8.00
Jay Howell
Tom McEwen
Danny Ongais
Leroy Goldstein
Gene Snow
Mart Higgenbotham
23 Chris Karamesines' Car 4.00 8.00
24 Super Stock Champs 4.00 8.00
Dick Harrell
Ed Miller
Don Nicholson
Bill Hielscher
Dave Lyall
Herb McCandless
25 Jim Nicoll's Car 4.00 8.00
26 Dick Landy's Car 3.00 6.00
27 Shirley Shahan's Car 3.00 6.00
28 John McFadde's Car 3.00 6.00
29 Leonard Hughes' Car 3.00 6.00
30 Eddie Schartman's Car 3.00 6.00
31 Ed Terry's Car 3.00 6.00
32 Hubert Platt's Car 3.00 6.00
33 Gary Kimball's Car 3.00 6.00
34 Gary Watson's Car 3.00 6.00
35 Rich Siroonian's Car 3.00 6.00
36 Richard Tharp's Car 3.00
37 Jake Johnston's Car 3.00
38 Ronnie Sox's Car 4.00
39 Charles Therwanger's Car 3.00
40 Don Grotheer's Car 3.00
41 Pete Robinson's Car 3.00
42 Ron O'Donnell's Car 3.00
43 Dick Loehr's Car 3.00
44 Tom Hoover's Car 4.00
45 Dale Young's Car 3.00
46 Warren Gunter's Car 3.00
47 Bruce Larson's Car 3.00
48 Paula Murphy's Car 3.00
49 Bob Murray's Car 3.00
50 Jim Liberman's Car 3.00
51 Sam Auxier Jr.'s Car 3.00
52 Duane Ong's Car 3.00
53 Preston Davis' Car 3.00
54 Top Fuel Champs 4.00
Richard Tharp
Jim Nicoll
Bob Murray
Don Garlits
Chris Karamesines
John Wiebe
Don Cook
Jimmy King
55 Jimmy King's Car 3.00
56 Ron Martin's Car 3.00
57 Jerry Mallicoat's Car 3.00
Tom Chamblis' Car
58 Jerry Miller's Car 3.00
59 Tommy Ivo's Car 3.00
60 Bill Hielscher's Car 3.00
61 Tony Nancy's Car 3.00
62 Fritz Callier's Car 3.00
63 Don Nicholson's Car 3.00

1971 Fleer Stick Shi

Similar to the 1970 Dragstrips release, Flee Shift cards were issued primarily as backers f Shift race stickers. With each 10-cent wa collector's received one of these cards and a of race stickers. The cards are ove (approximately 2-1/2" by 4-1/2") and blank as are the sticker sheets. The black and whit feature captioned photos of cars and r Although only nine cards can be confirmed, is thought to consist of ten cards. Any addit this list are appreciated.

COMPLETE SET (9) 400.00 7
STICKER INSERTS 5.00
1 Kelly Brown's Dragster 40.00
The Unsinkable Kelly Brown
2 Dragster at Lion's Drag Strip 40.00
3 Plymouth Superbird 40.00
4 Plymouth GTX 40.00
5 Dan Ongais 50.00 1
Driving the Winningest
Funny Car ever
6 Don Burns 40.00
A real crowd pleaser
The VW Bug
7 Don Prudhomme 75.00 1
8 Chris Karamesines 60.00 1
9 Don Garlits 75.00 1

1972 Fleer AHRA Dr Nationals

For the second consecutive year, Fleer release featuring stars of AHRA drag racing. Wax contained five-cards and one stick of gum set size was increased to 70-cards. There i speculation that based on the odd set size cards may have been printed in shorter supp others. Again, most of the cards feature drag cars in action, but a larger number (versus th set) were devoted to top drivers as well. An A and Canadian version was produced w American cards printed on white card stock the Canadian set was printed on a cream paper stock.

COMPLETE SET (70) 275.00 4
AMERICAN/CANADIAN SAME VALUE
1 Don Garlits' Car 5.00
2 Don Garlits 6.00
3 Don Garlits' Car 5.00
4 Phil Schofield's Car 4.00
5 Charlie Thurwanger's Car 4.00
6 Bill Leavitt's Car 4.00
7 Fritz Callier's Car 4.00
8 Richard Tharp's Car 5.00
9 John Wiebe's Car 4.00
10 Steve Carbone 4.00
11 Kenny Sanford's Car 4.00
12 Jim Hayter's Car 4.00
13 Herb McCandless' Car 4.00
14 Don Grotheer's Car 4.00
15 Mike Fons' Car 4.00
16 Ronnie Sox's Car 5.00
17 Joe Rundle's Car 4.00
18 Bill Jenkins' Car 4.00
19 Dick Landy's Car 4.00
20 Don Carlton's Car 4.00
21 Mart Higginbotham 4.00
22 Gene Snow 5.00
23 Butch Maas' Car 4.00
24 Dale Pulde's Car 5.00

Mickey Thompson's Car		
ary Watson's Car	4.00	8.00
om McEwen	5.00	10.00
on Prudhomme	6.00	12.00
ary Cochran	4.00	8.00
om Hoover	5.00	10.00
ene Snow's Car	5.00	10.00
teve Carbone's Car	4.00	8.00
ohn Paxton's Car	4.00	8.00
ohn Wiebe	4.00	8.00
ennis Baca's Car	4.00	8.00
ripp Shumake's Car	4.00	8.00
Mart Higginbotham's Car	4.00	8.00
hris Karamesines	5.00	10.00
ary Cochran's Car	4.00	8.00
on Cook's Car	4.00	8.00
ic Brown's Car	4.00	8.00
hris Karamesines' Car	5.00	10.00
onnie Sox	5.00	10.00
Buddy Martin		
om Hoover's Car	5.00	10.00
ary Burgin's Car	4.00	8.00
ohn Lombardo's Car	4.00	8.00
on Prudhomme's Car	5.00	10.00
om McEwen's Car	5.00	10.00
eroy Goldstein's Car	4.00	8.00
ussell Long's Car	4.00	8.00
on Moody's Car	4.00	8.00
on Schumacher's Car	4.00	8.00
oug Rose's Car	4.00	8.00
arry Christopherson's Car	4.00	8.00
om Grove's Car	4.00	8.00
im Dunn's Car	4.00	8.00
im King's Car	4.00	8.00
utch Leal's Car	4.00	8.00
ill Jenkins' Car	4.00	8.00
on Moody's Car	4.00	8.00
lare Sanders' Car	4.00	8.00
im Nicoll's Car	4.00	8.00
ecil Lankford's Car	4.00	8.00
im Walther's Car	4.00	8.00
alph Gould's Car	4.00	8.00
ale Pulde's Car	5.00	10.00
Mickey Thompson's Car		
ave Beebe's Car	4.00	8.00
oe Lee's Car	4.00	8.00
oug Rose's Car	4.00	8.00
ale Pulde's Car	5.00	10.00
Mickey Thompson's Car		
ary Watson's Car	4.00	8.00

973 Fleer AHRA Race USA

USA was Fleer's final AHRA release. Wax packs contained five-cards and one stick of gum and different wrappers were produced. The set size was increased to 74-cards. There is some ulation that based on the odd set size, some s may have been printed in shorter supply than s. Many of the cards feature drag racing cars in n, but several focus on the top drivers as well.

MPLETE SET (74)	275.00	450.00
m McEwen	5.00	10.00
m McEwen's Car	5.00	10.00
m McEwen's Car	5.00	10.00
n Prudhomme's Car	6.00	12.00
n Prudhomme's Car	6.00	12.00
n Prudhomme's Car	5.00	10.00
ike Randall's Car	4.00	8.00
ll Leavitt's Car	4.00	8.00
chard Tharp's Car	4.00	8.00
ob Lambeck's Car	4.00	8.00
utch Leal's Car	4.00	8.00
ick Landy	4.00	8.00
ick Landy's Car	4.00	8.00
ary Kimball's Car	4.00	8.00
arry Kimball's Car		
om Hoover's Car	5.00	10.00
om Hoover w/Car	5.00	10.00
on Nicholson's Car	4.00	8.00
en Holthe's Car	4.00	8.00
on Grotheer's Car	4.00	8.00
ddie Shartman's Car	4.00	8.00
Vayne Gapp's Car	4.00	8.00
eyy Brown's Car	4.00	8.00
ogo Eads' Car	4.00	8.00
ene Dunlap's Car	4.00	8.00
Mart Higginbotham's Car	4.00	8.00
teve Carbone's Car	4.00	8.00
on Cook's Car	4.00	8.00
ary Cochran's Car	4.00	8.00
Mike Burkart's Car	4.00	8.00
om Akin's Car	4.00	8.00
on Garlits DOY	5.00	10.00
arry Christopherson w/car	4.00	8.00
arry Christopherson's Car	4.00	8.00
onnie Sox's Car	5.00	10.00
onnie Sox	5.00	10.00
Buddy Martin		
on Schumacher's Car	4.00	8.00
oe Satmary's Car	4.00	8.00
oe Satmary's Car	4.00	8.00
cott Shafiroff's Car	4.00	8.00
at Foster's Car	4.00	8.00
hris Karamesines' Car	5.00	10.00
ave Russell's Car	4.00	8.00
wig Zigler	4.00	8.00
onnie Martin's Car	5.00	10.00

45 Mickey Thompson w/Car	4.00	8.00
46 Dale Pulde's Car	4.00	8.00
47 Henry Harrison's Car	4.00	8.00
48 Ed McCulloch's Car	5.00	10.00
49 Ed McCulloch's Car	5.00	10.00
50 John Wiebe	5.00	10.00
51 Gary Watson's Car	4.00	8.00
52 Arlen Vanke's Car	4.00	8.00
53 Duane Jacobsen's Car	4.00	8.00
54 Ronnie Runyon's Car	4.00	8.00
55 Jerry Baker's Car	4.00	8.00
56 Barrie Poole's Car	4.00	8.00
57 Bobby Yowell's Car	4.00	8.00
58 Don Garlits' Car	6.00	12.00
59 Don Garlits' Car	5.00	10.00
60 Don Garlits' Car	5.00	10.00
61 Jeg Coughlin's Car	4.00	8.00
62 Mike Sullivan's Car	4.00	8.00
63 Jon Petrie's Car	4.00	8.00
64 Bob Riffle's Car	4.00	8.00
65 Dave Hough's Car	4.00	8.00
66 The Mob Dragster	4.00	8.00
67 The Mob Dragster	4.00	8.00
68 Jeb Allen's Car	4.00	8.00
69 Jim Nicoll's Car	5.00	10.00
70 Ed Sigmon's Car	4.00	8.00
71 Gene Snow	5.00	10.00
72 Gene Snow's Car	5.00	10.00
73 Jake Johnston's Car	4.00	8.00
74 Chip Woodall's Car	4.00	8.00

1997 Hi-Tech NHRA

COMPLETE SET (40)	12.50	30.00
COMMON DRIVERS	.25	.60
SEMISTARS	.40	1.00
UNLISTED STARS	.50	1.25
HT-1 NHRA Header Card	.20	.50
HT-2 Joe Amato	.30	.75
HT-3 Shelly Anderson	.30	.75
HT-4 Kenny Bernstein	.50	1.25
HT-5 larry Dixon	.50	1.25
HT-6 Mike Dunn	.20	.50
HT-7 Eddie Hill	.20	.50
HT-8 Connie Kalitta	.20	.50
HT-9 Scott Kalitta	.50	1.25
HT-10 Cory McClenathan	.50	1.25
HT-11 Cristen Powell	.20	.50
HT-12 Gary Scelzi	.50	1.25
HT-13 Randy Anderson	.20	.50
HT-14 Whit Bazemore	.60	1.50
HT-15 Gary Densham	.30	.75
HT-16 John Force	1.25	3.00
HT-17 Al Hofmann	.20	.50
HT-18 Dean Skuza	.30	.75
HT-19 Mark Oswald	.20	.50
HT-20 Cruz Pedregon	.60	1.50
HT-21 Tony Pedregon	.60	1.50
HT-22 Ron Capps	.50	1.25
HT-23 Del Worsham	.60	1.50
HT-24 Darrell Alderman	.20	.50
HT-25 Mike Edwards	.20	.50
HT-26 Scott Geoffrion	.20	.50
HT-27 Bob Glidden	.20	.50
HT-28 Chuck Harris	.20	.50
HT-29 Kurt Johnson	.60	1.50
HT-30 Warren Johnson	.60	1.50
HT-31 Tom Martino	.20	.50
HT-32 Steve Schmidt	.20	.50
HT-33 Jim Yates	.30	.75
HT-34 Hector Arana	.20	.50
HT-35 Matt Hines	.50	1.25
HT-36 Steve Johnson	.20	.50
HT-37 John Myers	.20	.50
HT-38 Dave Schultz	.30	.75
HT-39 Angelle Seeling	1.00	2.50
HT-40 John Smith	.20	.50

1997 Hi-Tech NHRA Christmas Tree

COMPLETE SET (9)	4.00	10.00
XM-1 Joe Amato	.30	.75
XM-2 Kenny Bernstein	.50	1.25
XM-3 John Force	1.25	3.00
XM-4 Eddie Hill	.20	.50
XM-5 Warren Johnson	.60	1.50
XM-6 Scott Kalitta	.50	1.25
XM-7 Tony Pedregon	.60	1.50
XM-8 Dave Schultz	.30	.75
XM-9 Jim Yates	.30	.75

1997 Hi-Tech NHRA Funny Car

COMPLETE SET (11)	5.00	12.00
FC-1 Funny Car Header Card	.20	.50
FC-2 Whit Bazemore	.60	1.50
FC-3 Gary Densham	.30	.75
FC-4 John Force	1.25	3.00
FC-5 Al Hofmann	.20	.50
FC-6 Dean Skuza	.30	.75
FC-7 Mark Oswald	.20	.50
FC-8 Cruz Pedregon	.60	1.50
FC-9 Del Worsham	.60	1.50
FC-10 Tony Pedregon	.60	1.50
FC-11 Ron Capps	.50	1.25

1997 Hi-Tech NHRA John Force

COMPLETE SET (8)	8.00	20.00
COMMON FORCE	1.25	3.00

1997 Hi-Tech NHRA Pro Stock

COMPLETE SET (9)	2.50	6.00
PS-1 Pro Stock Header Card	.20	.50
PS-2 Darrell Alderman	.20	.50
PS-3 Mike Edwards	.20	.50
PS-4 Scott Geoffrion	.20	.50
PS-5 Kurt Johnson	.60	1.50
PS-6 Warren Johnson	.60	1.50
PS-7 Steve Schmidt	.20	.50
PS-8 Jim Yates	.30	.75
PS-9 Tom Martino	.20	.50

1997 Hi-Tech NHRA Pro Stock Bike

COMPLETE SET (7)	2.00	6.00
PB-1 Pro Stock Bike Header Card	.20	.50
PB-2 Matt Hines	.50	1.25
PB-3 John Myers	.20	.50
PB-4 Dave Schultz	.30	.75
PB-5 Angelle Seeling	1.00	2.50
PB-6 John Smith	.20	.50
PB-7 Steve Johnson	.20	.50

1997 Hi-Tech NHRA Top Fuel

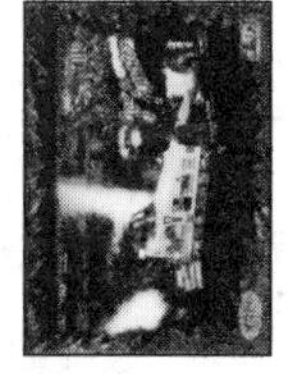

COMPLETE SET (12)	3.00	8.00
TF-1 Top Fuel Header Card	.20	.50
TF-2 Joe Amato	.30	.75
TF-3 Shelly Anderson	.30	.75
TF-4 Kenny Bernstein	.50	1.25
TF-5 Larry Dixon	.50	1.25
TF-6 Mike Dunn	.20	.50
TF-7 Eddie Hill	.20	.50
TF-8 Connie Kalitta	.20	.50
TF-9 Scott Kalitta	.50	1.25
TF-10 Cory McClenathan	.50	1.25
TF-11 Cristen Powell	.20	.50
TF-12 Gary Scelzi	.50	1.25

1993-97 Kustom Kards Bunny Burkett

This nine-card set was produced by Kustom Kards and features Bunny and the cars she has driven through the years. Cards from this set were distributed by her team through trackside souvenir stands and autoshow appearances. Each features a black border and features a card number made up of the year, her initials, and the final overall card number which we've included below.

COMPLETE SET (9)	3.00	8.00
COMMON CARD (1-9)	.40	1.00

1989 Mega Drag

Mega Promotions Inc. of Florida released this set in mid-1989 featuring the top names in drag racing. The cards were sold in factory set form directly from Mega at the original price of $19.95 plus $3 shipping. A series two set was planned but never materialized.

COMPLETE SET (110)	100.00	200.00
1 Darrell Gwynn	1.50	3.00
2 Darrell Gwynn's Car	1.25	2.50
3 Eddie Hill	2.00	4.00
4 Eddie Hill's Car	2.00	4.00
5 Eddie Hill's Car	2.00	4.00
6 Joe Amato	2.00	4.00
7 Joe Amato's Car	1.25	2.50
8 Mike Dunn	1.25	2.50
9 Mike Dunn's Car	1.00	2.25
10 Morris Johnson Jr.	1.25	2.50
11 Morris Johnson Jr.'s Car	1.00	2.25
12 Ed McCulloch	1.25	2.50
13 Ed McCulloch's Car	1.00	2.25
14 Mike Troxel	1.25	2.50
15 Mike Troxel's Car	1.00	2.25
16 Dale Pulde	1.50	3.00
17 Jerry Haas	1.25	2.50
18 Jerry Haas' Car	1.00	2.25
19 Bruce Allen	1.25	2.50
20 Bruce Allen's Car	1.00	2.25
21 Shirley Muldowney	2.00	4.00
22 Shirley Muldowney's Car	2.00	4.00
23 Bill Kuhlman	1.25	2.50
24 Bill Kuhlman's Car	1.00	2.25
25 Rickie Smith	1.25	2.50
26 Rickie Smith's Car	1.00	2.25
27 Jim Feurer's Car	1.00	2.25
28 Denny Lucas	1.25	2.50
29 Denny Lucas' Car	1.00	2.25
30 Bruce Larson	1.25	2.50
31 Bruce Larson's Car	1.00	2.25
32 Tony Christian	1.25	2.50
33 Tony Christian's Car	1.00	2.25
34 John Martin	1.25	2.50
35 John Martin's Car	1.00	2.25
36 Frank Bradley	1.25	2.50
37 Frank Bradley's Car	1.00	2.25
38 Gary Ormsby	1.25	2.50
39 Gary Ormsby's Car	1.00	2.25
40 Kenny Koretsky	1.25	2.50
41 Kenny Koretsky's Car	1.00	2.25
42 Scott Geoffrion	1.25	2.50
43 Scott Geoffrion's Car	1.00	2.25
44 Earl Whiting	1.25	2.50
45 Earl Whiting's Car	1.00	2.25
46 Jerry Caminito	1.25	2.50
47 Jerry Caminito's Car	1.00	2.25
48 Darrell Alderman	1.50	3.00
49 Darrell Alderman's Car	1.25	2.50
50 Roland Leong	1.25	2.50
51 Roland Leong's Car	1.00	2.25
52 Gordie Rivera	1.25	2.50
53 Gordie Rivera's Car	1.00	2.25
54 R.C. Sherman's Car	1.00	2.25
55 Frank Manzo	1.25	2.50
56 Frank Manzo's Car	1.00	2.25
57 Frank Iaconio	1.25	2.50
58 Frank Iaconio's Car	1.00	2.25
59 Don Campanello	1.25	2.50
60 Don Campanello's Car	1.00	2.25
61 Bob Newberry's Car	1.00	2.25
62 Nick Nikolis	1.25	2.50
63 Nick Nikolis' Car	1.00	2.25
64 John Speelman's Car	1.00	2.25
65 Chuck Etchells	1.50	3.00
66 Chuck Etchells' Car	1.25	2.50
67 Paul Smith	1.25	2.50
68 Paul Smith's Car	1.00	2.25
69 Mark Pawuk	1.25	2.50
70 Mark Pawuk's Car	1.00	2.25
71 Arnie Karp	1.25	2.50
72 Arnie Karp's Car	1.00	2.25
73 Frank Sanchez	1.25	2.50
74 Frank Sanchez's Car	1.00	2.25
75 Lori Johns	1.50	3.00
76 Lori Johns' Car	1.25	2.50
77 Bubba Sewell's Car	1.00	2.25
78 Della Woods	1.25	2.50
79 Della Woods' Car	1.00	2.25
80 Brian Raymer's Car	1.00	2.25
81 Tim Grose	1.25	2.50
82 Tim Grose's Car	1.00	2.25
83 Tom Conway's Car	1.00	2.25
84 Darrell Amberson	1.25	2.50
85 Darrell Amberson's Car	1.00	2.25
86 Jim Head	1.25	2.50
87 Jim Head's Car	1.00	2.25
88 Doc Halladay	1.25	2.50
89 Doc Halladay's Car	1.00	2.25
90 Dal Denton's Car	1.00	2.25
91 Dick LaHaie	1.25	2.50
92 Dick LaHaie's Car	1.00	2.25
93 Don Coonce	1.25	2.50
94 Don Coonce's Car	1.00	2.25
95 Jerry Eckman	1.25	2.50
96 Jerry Eckman's Car	1.00	2.25
97 Harold Lewelling's Car	1.00	2.25
98 Domenic Santucci Sr.'s Car	1.00	2.25
99 Al Hanna's Car	1.00	2.25
100 Gene Snow	1.50	3.00
101 Gene Snow's Car	1.25	2.50
102 Joe Lepone Jr.	1.25	2.50
103 Joe Lepone Jr.'s Car	1.00	2.25
104 Hank Enders	1.25	2.50
105 Hank Enders' Car	1.00	2.25
106 Lee Dean's Car	1.00	2.25
107 Dennis Piranio's Car	1.00	2.25
108 Don Garlits	2.00	4.00
109 Don Garlits' Car	2.00	4.00
110 Checklist	1.00	2.25

2007 NHRA Powerade Countdown to the Championship

COMPLETE SET (17)		
1 Brandon Bernstein		
2 Larry Dixon		
3 Rod Fuller		
4 Tony Schumacher		
5 Ron Capps		
6 Robert Hight		
7 Tony Pedregon		
8 Gary Scelzi		
9 Greg Anderson		
10 Dave Connolly		
11 Jeg Coughlin		
12 Allen Johnson		
13 Chip Ellis		
14 Andrew Hines		
15 Peggy Llewellyn		
16 Matt Smith		
NNO Cover Card		

2005 Press Pass NHRA

COMP.FACT.SET (51)	15.00	40.00
COMPLETE SET (50)	12.50	30.00
1 David Baca RC	.50	1.25
2 Brandon Bernstein RC	1.00	2.50
3 Dave Grubnic RC	.50	1.25
4 Doug Herbert	.50	1.25
5 Doug Kalitta RC	.50	1.25
6 Scott Kalitta	.50	1.25
7 Morgan Lucas RC	.40	1.00
8 Cory McLenathan RC	.25	.60
9 Clay Millican RC	.40	1.00
10 Tony Schumacher RC	1.00	2.50
11 Scott Weis	.15	.40
12 Tony Bartone	.50	1.25
13 Whit Bazemore	.50	1.25
14 Phil Burkart Jr. RC	.40	1.00
15 Ron Capps	.50	1.25
16 John Force Green	2.00	5.00
17 John Force Red	2.00	5.00
18 John Force Ashley Force RC	2.00	5.00
19 Bob Gilbertson	.15	.40
20 Robert Hight RC	.40	1.00
21 Eric Medlen RC	1.25	3.00
22 Cruz Pedregon	1.00	2.50
23 Frank Pedregon RC	.40	1.00
24 Tony Pedregon	1.00	2.50
25 Gary Scelzi	.50	1.25
26 Tim Wilkerson RC	.40	1.00
27 Del Worsham	.15	.40
28 Bruce Allen	.15	.40
29 Greg Anderson	.50	1.25
30 Dave Connolly RC	.40	1.00
31 Jeg Coughlin Jr.	.50	1.25
32 Mike Edwards	.15	.40
33 Vieri Gaines RC	.25	.60
34 Allen Johnson RC	.40	1.00
35 Kurt Johnson	.50	1.25
36 Warren Johnson RC	.40	1.00
37 Kenny Koretsky	.25	.60
38 Ron Krisher RC	.40	1.00
39 Larry Morgan	.15	.40
40 Jason Line RC	.40	1.00
41 Richie Stevens RC	.40	1.00
42 Jim Yates	.15	.40
43 Antron Brown RC	.50	1.25
44 Andrew Hines RC	.50	1.25
45 Steve Johnson	.40	1.00
46 Angelle Sampey	1.00	2.50
47 Geno Scali RC	.40	1.00
48 Karen Stoffer RC	.25	.60
49 GT Tonglet RC	.40	1.00
50 Craig Treble RC	.40	1.00

2005 Press Pass NHRA Autographs

1 John Force	125.00	250.00
2 Tony Schumacher	25.00	50.00
3 Doug Kalitta		
4 Scott Kalitta		
5 Scott Weis		
6 Dave Grubnic		
7 Cory McClenathan	15.00	30.00
8 Doug Herbert		
9 Clay Millican		
10 Morgan Lucas		
11 Gary Scelzi	25.00	50.00
12 Whit Bazemore		
13 Tim Wilkerson		
14 Ron Capps	25.00	50.00
15 Frank Pedregon	20.00	40.00
16 Tony Bartone		
17 Greg Anderson		
18 Jason Line	20.00	40.00
19 Jeg Coughlin Jr.		
20 Kenny Koretsky	15.00	30.00
21 Richie Stevens		
22 Vieri Gaines	15.00	30.00
23 Bob Gilbertson	12.50	25.00
24 Angelle Sampey		
25 Antron Brown	10.00	20.00
26 Craig Treble	15.00	30.00
27 Larry Morgan	15.00	30.00
28 Mike Edwards	12.50	25.00
29 Geno Scali		
30 Steve Johnson	20.00	40.00
31 Karen Stoffer	15.00	30.00
32 Eric Medlen	200.00	300.00
33 Robert Hight		
34 Melanie Troxel		

2005 Press Pass NHRA Cool Threads Gold

*GOLD: .6X TO 1.5X RED

2005 Press Pass NHRA Cool Threads Green

*GREEN: .8X TO 2X RED

2005 Press Pass NHRA Cool Threads Red

CT1 Tim Wilkerson	12.50	25.00
CT2 Bob Gilbertson	10.00	20.00
CT3 Tony Bartone	12.50	25.00
CT4 Greg Anderson	12.50	25.00
CT5 Jason Line	12.50	25.00
CT6 Kenny Koretsky	10.00	20.00
CT7 Del Worsham	10.00	20.00
CT8 Phil Burkart	12.50	25.00
CT9 John Force		
CT10 Eric Medlen	12.50	25.00
CT11 Robert Hight	12.50	25.00

1991 Pro Set NHRA

This was Pro Set's first NHRA release in a run of sets produced by the company from 1991-1993. The set features star drivers, cars and crew members of the top NHRA teams. The cards were packaged 10 per foil pack with 36 packs per box. Signed cards of Don Garlits, number 105, that were UV coated and autographed in silver ink were also randomly inserted.

COMPLETE SET (130)	5.00	12.00
1 Joe Amato	.30	1.00
2 Gary Ormsby	.05	.15
3 Dick LaHaie	.05	.15
4 Lori Johns	.08	.25
5 Gene Snow	.08	.25
6 Eddie Hill	.30	1.00
7 Frank Bradley	.05	.15
8 Kenny Bernstein	.30	1.00
9 Frank Hawley	.05	.15
10 Shirley Muldowney	.30	1.00
11 Chris Karamesines	.08	.25
12 Jim Head	.05	.15

13 Don Prudhomme .08 .25
14 Tommy Johnson Jr. .08 .25
15 Michael Brotherton .05 .15
16 Darrell Gwynn .08 .25
17 John Force RC .60 1.50
18 Ed McCulloch .05 .15
19 Bruce Larson .05 .15
20 Mark Oswald .05 .15
21 Jim White .05 .15
22 K.C. Spurlock .05 .15
23 Tom Hoover .08 .25
24 Richard Hartman .05 .15
25 Scott Kalitta .30 1.00
26 Jerry Caminito .05 .15
27 Al Hofmann .05 .15
28 Glenn Mikres .05 .15
29 Chuck Etchells .05 .15
30 John Myers .05 .15
31 Paula Martin .05 .15
32 Mike Dunn .05 .15
33 Connie Kalitta .08 .25
34 Darrell Alderman .05 .15
35 Bob Glidden .08 .25
36 Jerry Eckman .05 .15
37 Larry Morgan .05 .15
38 Warren Johnson .08 .25
39 Rickie Smith .05 .15
40 Mark Pawuk .05 .15
41 Bruce Allen .05 .15
42 Joe Lepone Jr. .05 .15
43 Kenny Delco .05 .15
44 Scott Geoffrion .05 .15
45 Gordie Rivera .05 .15
46 Jerry Haas .05 .15
47 Buddy Ingersoll .05 .15
48 Jim Yates .05 .15
49 Butch Leal .05 .15
50 Joe Amato's Car .05 .15
51 Gary Ormsby's Car .02 .10
52 Dick LaHaie's Car .02 .10
53 Lori Johns' Car .02 .10
54 Gene Snow's Car .02 .10
55 Eddie Hill's Car .08 .25
56 Frank Bradley's Car .02 .10
57 Kenny Bernstein's Car .08 .25
58 Frank Hawley's Car .02 .10
59 Shirley Muldowney's Car .08 .25
60 Chris Karamesines' Car .05 .15
61 Jim Head's Car .02 .10
62 Don Prudhomme's Car .05 .15
63 Tommy Johnson Jr.'s Car .05 .15
64 Michael Brotherton's Car .02 .10
65 Darrell Gwynn's Car .05 .15
66 John Force's Car .30 1.00
67 Ed McCulloch's Car .02 .10
68 Bruce Larson's Car .02 .10
69 Mark Oswald's Car .02 .10
70 Jim White's Car .02 .10
71 K.C. Spurlock's Car .02 .10
72 Tom Hoover's Car .05 .15
73 Richard Hartman's Car .02 .10
74 Scott Kalitta's Car .02 .10
75 Jerry Caminito's Car .02 .10
76 Al Hofmann's Car .02 .10
77 Glenn Mikres' Car .02 .10
78 Chuck Etchells' Car .02 .10
79 Whit Bazemore's Car .02 .10
80 Paula Martin's Car .02 .10
81 David Schultz .02 .10
82 Darrell Alderman's Car .02 .10
83 Bob Glidden's Car .05 .15
84 Jerry Eckman's Car .02 .10
85 Larry Morgan's Car .02 .10
86 Warren Johnson's Car .08 .25
87 Rickie Smith's Car .02 .10
88 Mark Pawuk's Car .02 .10
89 Bruce Allen's Car .02 .10
90 Joe Lepone Jr.'s Car .02 .10
91 Kenny Delco's Car .02 .10
92 Scott Geoffrion's Car .02 .10
93 Gordie Rivera's Car .02 .10
94 Jerry Haas' Car .02 .10
95 Buddy Ingersoll's Car .02 .10
96 Jim Yates' Car .02 .10
97 Butch Leal's Car .02 .10
98 Buster Couch .05 .15
99 Fuzzy Carter .05 .15
100 Austin Coil .05 .15
101 Tim Richards .05 .15
102 Bob Glidden Family .05 .15
103 Kenny Bernstein Funny Car .08 .25
104 Don Prudhomme Funny Car .08 .25
105 Don Garlits .30 1.00
106 Dale Armstrong .05 .15
107 Tom McEwen .08 .25
108 Dave McClelland .05 .15
109 Steve Evans .05 .15
110 Bob Frey .05 .15
111 Deb Brittsan Miss Winston .05 .15
112 Safety Safari .02 .10
113 Gary Densham .05 .15
114 Frank Iaconio .05 .15
115 Don Beverly .05 .15
116 Lee Beard .05 .15
117 Wyatt Radke .05 .15
118 John Medlen .05 .15
119 Gary Brown .05 .15
120 Bernie Fedderly .05 .15
121 Rahn Tobler .05 .15
122 Del Worsham .05 .15
123 Kim LaHaie .05 .15
124 Larry Meyer .05 .15
125 Freddie Neely .05 .15
126 Dan Pastorini .08 .25
127 Bill Jenkins .05 .15
128 Wally Parks .05 .15
129 Connie Kalitta's Car .05 .15
130 Whit Bazemore .05 .15
AU105 Don Garlits AUTO 45.00 75.00

1992 Pro Set NHRA

This was Pro Set's second NHRA release. The set features star drivers, cars and crew members of the top NHRA teams of the previous season. The cards were packaged 12 per foil pack with 36 packs per box. 1,500 factory sets were also produced for distribution to Pro Set Racing Club members. A special hologram card featuring a Pro Set Racing logo (numbered of 5000) was produced and randomly distributed through packs. The card originally had a white border, but was later changed to black creating a variation.

COMPLETE SET (200) 6.00 15.00
COMP.FACT.SET (200) 6.00 14.00
1 Joe Amato .07 .20
2 Kenny Bernstein .20 .60
3 Don Prudhomme
4 Frank Hawley .01 .05
5 Eddie Hill .20 .60
6 Tom McEwen .07 .20
7 Gene Snow .07 .20
8 Dick LaHaie .02 .10
9 Cory McClenathan .07 .20
10 Jim Head .02 .10
11 Tommy Johnson Jr. .07 .20
12 Pat Austin .07 .20
13 Scott Kalitta .20 .60
14 Cruz Pedregon .20 .60
15 Doug Herbert .07 .20
16 Gary Ormsby .07 .20
17 Paula Martin 's Car .01 .05
18 Frank Bradley .02 .10
19 Jack Ostrander .02 .10
20 Jim Dunn .02 .10
21 Connie Kalitta .20 .60
22 Pat Dakin .02 .10
23 Jim Murphy's Car .01 .05
24 Bobby Baldwin .02 .10
25 Kenny Koretsky .01 .05
26 Russ Collins .01 .05
27 Shirley Muldowney .20 .60
28 Kim LaHaie .01 .05
29 Gene Snow .20 .60
30 Eddie Hill .20 .60
31 Don Prudhomme .20 .60
32 Kenny Bernstein .20 .60
33 Joe Amato .20 .60
34 Del Worsham .02 .10
35 John Force .50 1.25
36 Tom Gilbertson .01 .05
37 Gary Ritter .01 .05
38 Johnny West .01 .05
39 Mark Sievers .01 .05
40 Jim Epler .02 .10
41 Ron Sutherland .01 .05
42 Wyatt Radke .02 .10
43 Freddie Neely .02 .10
44 Gordon Mineo .02 .10
45 Paula Martin .02 .10
46 Glenn Mikres .01 .05
47 John Force .50 1.25
48 Jim White .02 .10
49 Ed McCulloch .07 .20
50 Mark Oswald .02 .10
51 Al Hofmann .02 .10
52 Tom Hoover .07 .20
53 Richard Hartman .02 .10
54 Jerry Caminito .02 .10
55 Chuck Etchells .07 .20
56 Gary Densham .02 .10
57 Whit Bazemore .01 .05
58 Gary Bolger .02 .10
59 Jim Murphy .01 .05
60 Al Hofmann .07 .20
61 Del Worsham .02 .10
62 Mark Oswald .02 .10
63 Ed McCulloch .07 .20
64 Mike Dunn .02 .10
65 Warren Johnson .07 .20
66 Larry Morgan .02 .10
67 Scott Geoffrion .02 .10
68 Bob Glidden .20 .60
69 Jerry Eckman .02 .10
70 Bruce Allen .02 .10
71 Jim Yates .07 .20
72 Rickie Smith .02 .10
73 Butch Leal .02 .10
74 Joe Lepone Jr. .02 .10
75 Gary Brown .01 .05
76 Harry Scribner .01 .05
77 Paul Rebeschi Jr. .01 .05
78 Joseph Folgore .01 .05
79 Steve Schmidt .02 .10
80 Brad Klein .01 .05
81 Gordie Rivera .02 .10
82 Don Beverly .02 .10
83 Jerry Haas .01 .05
84 Frank Iaconio .02 .10
85 Vincent Khoury .01 .05
86 Kenny Delco .01 .05
87 Ray Franks .02 .10
88 Daryl Thompson .01 .05
89 Mark Pawuk .02 .10
90 Jerry Eckman .02 .10
91 Bob Glidden .20 .60
92 Scott Geoffrion .02 .10
93 Larry Morgan .02 .10
94 Warren Johnson .07 .20
95 Buddy Ingersoll .01 .05
96 Steve Johnson W/Bike .02 .10
97 Paul Gast's Bike .01 .05
98 James Bernard's Bike .01 .05
99 John Myers' Bike .07 .20
100 David Schultz's Bike .07 .20
101 Joe Amato's Car .07 .20
102 Kenny Bernstein's Car .07 .20
103 Don Prudhomme's Car .07 .20
104 Michael Brotherton's Car .01 .05
105 Eddie Hill's Car .07 .20
106 Tom McEwen's Car .01 .05
107 Gene Snow's Car .01 .05
108 Kim LaHaie's Car .01 .05
109 Cory McClenathan's Car .01 .05
110 Jim Head's Car .01 .05
111 Tommy Johnson Jr.'s Car .01 .05
112 Pat Austin's Car .01 .05
113 Scott Kalitta's Car .07 .20
114 Ed McCulloch's Car .01 .05
115 Doug Herbert's Car .01 .05
116 Frank Bradley's Car .01 .05
117 John Force's Car .50 1.25
118 Cruz Pedregon's Car .07 .20
119 Mark Oswald's Car .01 .05
120 Del Worsham's Car .01 .05
121 Al Hofmann's Car .01 .05
122 Tom Hoover's Car .01 .05
123 Richard Hartman's Car .01 .05
124 Jerry Caminito's Car .01 .05
125 Chuck Etchells' Car .01 .05
126 Gary Densham's Car .01 .05
127 Whit Bazemore's Car .01 .05
128 Gary Bolger's Car .01 .05
129 Gordon Mineo's Car .01 .05
130 Freddie Neely's Car .01 .05
131 Jerry Haas' Car .01 .05
132 Joe Lepone Jr.'s Car .01 .05
133 Gordie Rivera's Car .01 .05
134 Gary Brown's Car .01 .05
135 Harry Scribner's Car .01 .05
136 Warren Johnson's Car .01 .05
137 Larry Morgan's Car .01 .05
138 Scott Geoffrion's Car .01 .05
139 Rickie Smith's Car .01 .05
140 Bob Glidden's Car .07 .20
141 Frank Iaconio's Car .01 .05
142 Jerry Eckman's Car .01 .05
143 Jim Yates' Car .01 .05
144 Bruce Allen's Car .01 .05
145 Mark Pawuk's Car .01 .05
146 Kenny Delco's Car .01 .05
147 Kurt Johnson .01 .05
148 Mike Sullivan .01 .05
Dave Hutchens
149 Tom Anderson .01 .05
150 Bernie Fedderly .01 .05
151 John Davis .01 .05
152 Fuzzy Carter .01 .05
153 Dale Armstrong .01 .05
154 Tim Richards .01 .05
155 Ken Veney .01 .05
156 Jim Prock .01 .05
157 Austin Coil .01 .05
158 Chuck Worsham .01 .05
159 Richard Hartman .01 .05
Ray Strasser
160 Tom Roberts .01 .05
161 George Hoover .01 .05
162 Bill Schultz .01 .05
163 Larry Meyer .01 .05
164 John Medlen .01 .05
165 Walt Austin .01 .05
166 Greg Anderson .01 .05
167 Rusty Glidden .01 .05
Etta Glidden
168 Bill Orndorff .01 .05
169 Dave Butner .01 .05
170 Buddy Morrison .01 .05
David Reher
171 Rich Purdy .01 .05
172 Morris Johnson Jr. .01 .05
173 Lee Beard .01 .05
174 Rahn Tobler .01 .05
175 Dannielle DePorter .01 .05
176 Chris Karamesines .01 .05
177 Michael Brotherton .01 .05
178 Bill Jenkins .01 .05
179 Darrell Gwynn .07 .20
180 Larry Minor .01 .05
181 Buster Couch .01 .05
182 Don Garlits .20 .60
183 Dave McClelland .01 .05
184 Steve Evans .01 .05
185 Bob Frey .01 .05
186 Brock Yates .01 .05
187 Wally Parks .01 .05
188 John Mullin .01 .05
189 NHRA Softball Team .01 .05
190 Safety Safari .01 .05
191 Deb Brittsan Miss Winston .01 .05
192 Gary Evans .01 .05
193 Jim Brissette .01 .05
194 Blaine Johnson's Car .01 .05
195 Pat Austin's Car .01 .05
196 David Nickens' Car .01 .05
197 Jeff Taylor's Car .01 .05
198 John Calvert's Car .01 .05
199 John Asta's Car .01 .05
200 Scott Richardson's Car .01 .05
NNO Trophy HOLO White 30.00 80.00
NNO Trophy HOLO Black 30.00 80.00

1992 Pro Set Kenny Bernstein

Pro Set produced this set to highlight the careers of Kenny Bernstein and his crew. The cards were primarily distributed through Bernstein's souvenir outlets.

COMPLETE SET (7) 1.50 4.00
1 Kenny Bernstein .20 .50
2 Kenny Bernstein w/Crew .20 .50
3 Dale Armstrong .12 .30
4 Wes Cerny .12 .30
5 Kenny Bernstein .20 .50
6 Kenny Bernstein's Car .07 .20
NNO Cover Card .07 .20

1965 Topps Hot Rods

Topps produced this 66-card set for distribution in 5-cent gum wax packs. The cards feature a wide range of cars from hot rods and racers to custom and dream cars. Three different cardback variations exist. All 66-cards were produced on gray card stock, while only 44 different cards exist with white backs. The 22-card yellow back variations seem to be the toughest to find. They were issued in the "Win-A-Card" Milton Bradley board game distributed in 1968. That game also included cards from Topps' 1967 football card and 1968 baseball card sets.

COMPLETE SET (66) 200.00 325.00
1 Super Marauder 3.00 5.00
2 New Breed T.V. Car 3.00 5.00
3 Dragenet 29 3.00 5.00
4 Li'l Deuce 3.00 5.00
5 T Plus 11 3.00 5.00
6 Cabriolet 3.00 5.00
7 Rodster 3.00 5.00
8 The Tangerine 3.00 5.00
9 Les Po Po 3.00 5.00
10 Li'l Beauty 3.00 5.00
11 Twister T 3.00 5.00
12 XPAK 400 3.00 5.00
13 XMSC 210 3.00 5.00
14 El Capitola 3.00 5.00
15 Life of Riley T.V. Car 3.00 5.00
16 The Pumkin 3.00 5.00
17 Mustang 3.00 5.00
18 X-Tura 3.00 5.00
19 R&C Dream Truck 3.00 5.00
20 1957 Thunderbird 3.00 5.00
21 Curled Flame 3.00 5.00
22 Surf Woody 3.00 5.00
23 Surf Woody 3.00 5.00
24 Turbo-Sonic 3.00 5.00
25 Drag T 3.00 5.00
26 Flaky T 3.00 5.00
27 Black Beauty 3.00 5.00
28 Ruby T 3.00 5.00
29 Bimimi Wagon 3.00 5.00
30 Cyclops 3.00 5.00
31 Emperor 3.00 5.00
32 Cosma Ray 3.00 5.00
33 Lemans Cadillac 3.00 5.00
34 Beatnik Bandit 3.00 5.00
35 Rotar 3.00 5.00
36 Silhouette 3.00 5.00
37 Roanoke Valley Special 3.00 5.00
38 Beach Baron 3.00 5.00
39 Show Boat 3.00 5.00
40 The Mysterion 3.00 5.00
41 Chuck Hepler's Car 3.00 5.00
The Fugitive
42 Willy Mack's Car 3.00 5.00
The Snapper
43 Rose Gennuso's Car 3.00 5.00
Flaming Special
44 Weekly Norman's Car 3.50 6.00
The Lightning Rod
45 Kamakai One 3.00 5.00
46 Little Old Bucket 3.00 5.00
47 Golden Rod 3.00 5.00
48 John Albright's Car 3.50 6.00
Bo Weevil
49 Devil Cart 3.00 5.00
50 Funnel Master 3.00 5.00
51 Jim Nelson's Car 3.50 6.00
Dode Martin's Car
Modified Dart
52 Gary Cagle's Car 3.50 6.00
Newhouse Special
53 The Riviera 3.00 5.00
54 The Undertaker 3.00 5.00
55 The Rushin' Roulette 3.00 5.00
56 T-Bird 3.00 5.00
57 Eddie Hill's Car 3.50 6.00
Texas Terror
58 Li'l Coffin 3.00 5.00
59 The Honey 3.00 5.00
60 Dode Martin's Car 3.50 6.00
The Drag Master
61 The Blazer 3.00 5.00
62 The Streamline 3.00 5.00
63 The Strip Star 3.00 5.00
64 Angelo Giampetroni's Car 3.00 5.00
Li'l Billy
65 The Wild Dream 3.00 5.00
66 The Road Blazer 3.00 5.00

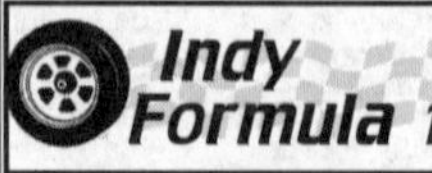

1983 A and S Racing Indy

A and S Racing Collectables produced IndyCar sets from 1983-87. The 1983 set featured 51-cards sold in complete set form and includes the first card of driver Al Unser Jr. There was no card number 13 produced -- the checklist card was unnumbered and blankbacked.

COMPLETE SET (51) 15.00 30.00
1 Rick Mears .75 2.00
2 Dennis Firestone .15 .40
3 Chip Mead .15 .40
4 Chris Kneifel .15 .40
5 Chip Ganassi .15 .40
6 Howdy Holmes .15 .40
7 Steve Krisloff UER .15 .40
8 Pancho Carter .15 .40
9 Chet Fillip .15 .40
10 Phil Caliva .15 .40
11 Geoff Brabham .15 .40
12 Jerry Sneva .15 .40
14 Herm Johnson .15 .40
15 Spike Gehlhausen .15 .40
16 Steve Chassey .15 .40
17 Pete Halsmer .15 .40
18 Kevin Cogan .15 .40
19 Teo Fabi .15 .40
20 Greg Leffler .15 .40
21 Johnny Rutherford .75 2.00
22 Tony Bettenhausen .15 .40
23 Tom Frantz .15 .40
24 George Snider .15 .40
25 Michael Chandler .15 .40
26 Danny Sullivan .30 .75
27 Doug Heveron .15 .40
28 Roger Mears .15 .40
29 Josele Garza .15 .40
30 Mike Mosley .15 .40
31 Scott Brayton .30 .75
32 Jerry Karl .15 .40
33 Mario Andretti 1.25 3.00
34 Bobby Rahal .30 .75
35 Gordon Smiley .15 .40
36 Derek Daly .15 .40
37 Phil Krueger .15 .40
38 John Mahler .15 .40
39 Bill Alsup .15 .40
40 John Paul Jr. .15 .40
41 Jim Buick .15 .40
42 Jim Hickman .15 .40
43 Al Unser Jr. .75 2.00
44 Hector Rebaque .15 .40
45 Bill Tempero .15 .40
46 Dick Ferguson .15 .40
47 Tom Sneva .30 .75
48 Al Unser .75 2.00
49 Gordon Johncock .30 .75
50 Dick Simon .15 .40
51 Gary Bettenhausen .15 .40
NNO Checklist .15 .40

1984 A and S Racing Indy

The 1984 A and S Racing Indy set features 50 of the top drivers on the IndyCar circuit, along with one checklist card (#13). An offer to purchase 1983 complete sets for $8.50 was included on the checklist card. The cards are very similar in appearance to the other A and S Indy sets produced from 1983-87.

COMPLETE SET (51) 15.00 30.00
1 Al Unser .60 1.50
2 Phil Krueger .15 .40
3 Howdy Holmes .15 .40
4 Roger Mears .15 .40
5 Johnny Rutherford .60 1.50
6 Michael Chandler .15 .40
7 Pancho Carter .15 .40
8 Dick Ferguson .15 .40
9 Phil Caliva .15 .40
10 Rick Mears .60 1.50
11 Pete Halsmer .15
12 Derek Daly .15
13 Checklist .15
14 Steve Chassey .15
15 Josele Garza .15
16 Mario Andretti .75 2
17 Chris Kneifel .15
18 Al Loquasto .15
19 Dennis Firestone .15
20 Teo Fabi .15
21 George Snider .15
22 Patrick Bedard .15
23 Gary Bettenhausen .15
24 Dick Simon .15
25 Tom Sneva .30
26 Herm Johnson .15
27 Scott Brayton .30
28 Bill Tempero .15
29 Danny Ongais .15
30 John Paul Jr. .15
31 Tom Bagley .15
32 Gordon Johncock .30
33 Desire Wilson .15
34 Greg Leffler .15
35 Chip Ganassi .15
36 Michael Andretti .60 1
37 Doug Heveron .15
38 Steve Krisloff .15
39 Geoff Brabham .15
40 Bill Alsup .15
41 Kevin Cogan .15
42 Chuck Ciprich .15
43 Mike Mosley .15
44 Chip Mead .15
45 Tony Bettenhausen .15
46 Jerry Karl .15
47 Al Unser Jr. .60 1
48 Chet Fillip .15
49 Bill Vukovich Jr. .15
50 Bobby Rahal .60 1
51 Tom Bigelow .15

1985 A and S Racing Indy

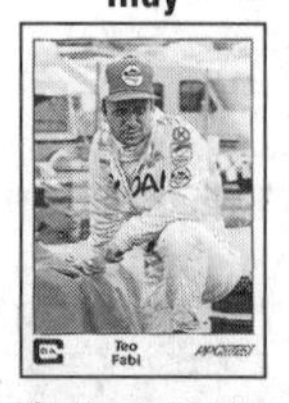

The top IndyCar drivers are featured on cards the 1985 A and S Racing Indy set. The set originally released in complete set form on checklist card, number 13, was produced along an unnumbered card featuring announcer Don The checklist card features an offer to purc 1983-1985 complete sets directly from A and S autographed uncut card sheet was offere collectors as well at a cost of $110. The Jac Villeneuve card in this set is the uncle of the PPG series winner.

COMPLETE SET (52) 15.00 30
1 Mario Andretti 1.25 2
2 Roberto Guerrero .25
3 Derek Daly .15
4 John Paul Jr. .15
5 Chet Fillip .15
6 Al Holbert .15
7 Stan Fox .15
8 Steve Chassey .15
9 Chip Ganassi .15
10 Mike Mosley .15
11 Michael Chandler .15
12 Bobby Rahal .50 1
13 Checklist .15
14 Johnny Parsons Jr. .15
15 Howdy Holmes .15
16 Geoff Brabham .15
17 Pete Halsmer .15
18 Dick Ferguson .15
19 Gary Bettenhausen .15
20 Gordon Johncock .25
21 Roger Mears .15
22 Ed Pimm .15
23 Emerson Fittipaldi .25
24 Al Unser Jr. .50 1
25 Rick Mears .50 1
26 Bill Alsup .15
27 Spike Gehlhausen .15
28 Teo Fabi .15
29 Herm Johnson .15
30 Tom Sneva .25
31 Dick Simon .15
32 Tom Gloy .15
33 Dale Coyne .15
34 Patrick Bedard .15
35 Al Unser .50 1
36 Jerry Karl .15
37 Chris Kneifel .15
38 George Snider .15
39 Tony Bettenhausen .15
40 Johnny Rutherford .50 1
41 Scott Brayton .25
42 Michael Andretti .50 1
43 Randy Lewis .15
44 Phil Krueger .15
45 Pancho Carter .15
46 Dennis Firestone .15
47 Kevin Cogan .15
48 Jacques Villeneuve .15
49 Arie Luyendyk .25
50 Mario Andretti .60 1
Michael Andretti

Unser .50 1.25
Al Unser Jr.
Don Hein .15 .40

1986 A and S Racing Indy

S Racing released this 50-card set in complete orm. The cards feature the top IndyCar nalities and very closely resemble the other sets released by the company between 1983-87. ast card in the set features a checklist and an to purchase 1983-1986 complete sets directly A and S. An autographed uncut card sheet was offered to collectors as well at a cost of $110.

PLETE SET (50) 15.00 30.00
Unser .50 1.25
rio Andretti .75 2.00
ike Gehlhausen .15 .40
sele Garza .15 .40
erson Fittipaldi .25 .60
Pimm .15 .40
le Coyne .15 .40
berto Guerrero .25 .60
ncho Carter .15 .40
l Unser Jr. .50 1.25
ete Halsmer .15 .40
eorge Snider .15 .40
asoline Alley .15 .40
ichael Roe .15 .40
ick Simon .15 .40
ohnny Rutherford .50 1.25
teve Chassey .15 .40
eoff Brabham .15 .40
om Bigelow .15 .40
erm Johnson .15 .40
rie Luyendyk .25 .60
het Fillip .15 .40
ohn Paul Jr. .15 .40
hip Ganassi .15 .40
cott Brayton .25 .60
hil Krueger .15 .40
evin Cogan .15 .40
ohnny Parsons Jr. .15 .40
ennis Firestone .15 .40
obby Rahal .50 1.25
m Crawford .15 .40
om Sneva .25 .60
erek Daly .15 .40
ick Ferguson .15 .40
ordon Johncock .25 .60
cott Brayton .25 .60
ancho Carter
rie Luyendyk ROY .25 .60
anny Sullivan T10 .15 .40
merson Fittipaldi T10 .15 .40
ick Mears T10 .25 .60
acques Villeneuve .15 .40
upert Keegan .15 .40
ichael Andretti .50 1.25
owdy Holmes .15 .40
ick Mears .50 1.25
ony Bettenhausen .15 .40
ary Bettenhausen .15 .40
aul Boesel .15 .40
anny Sullivan .25 .60
hecklist .15 .40

1987 A and S Racing Indy

S Racing released this 50-card set in complete orm. The cards feature the top Indy Car onalities and very closely resemble the other sets released by the company between 1983-87. number 13 features a checklist along with an to purchase 1983-1987 complete sets directly A and S. Fifty uncut card sheets signed by all 's were again offered to collectors at a cost of

PLETE SET (50) 12.50 25.00
obby Rahal .40 1.00
rio Andretti .50 1.25
om Carnegie
eve Chassey .15 .40
m Sneva .25 .60
off Brabham .15 .40
erson Fittipaldi .25 .60
e Coyne .15 .40
ry Bettenhausen .15 .40
Unser .40 1.00
ck Mears' Record .25 .60
oberto Moreno .15 .40
cott Brayton .25 .60
hecklist .15 .40
J. Foyt .40 1.00

15 Phil Krueger .15 .40
16 Jan Lammers .15 .40
17 Ed Pimm .15 .40
18 Michael Andretti w/Car .40 1.00
19 George Snider .15 .40
20 Mario Andretti w/Car .50 1.25
21 Spike Gehlhausen .15 .40
22 Johnny Rutherford .40 1.00
23 Mike Nish .15 .40
24 Kevin Cogan .15 .40
25 Josele Garza .15 .40
26 Tony Bettenhausen .15 .40
27 Rick Miaskiewicz .15 .40
28 Pancho Carter .15 .40
29 Arie Luyendyk .25 .60
30 Al Unser Jr. .40 1.00
31 Dennis Firestone .15 .40
32 Raul Boesel .15 .40
33 Dominic Dobson .15 .40
34 Danny Sullivan .25 .60
35 Derek Daly .15 .40
36 Ian Ashley .15 .40
37 Randy Lewis .15 .40
38 Jim Crawford .15 .40
39 Rick Mears .40 1.00
40 Johnny Parsons Jr. .15 .40
41 Dick Simon .15 .40
42 Jacques Villeneuve .15 .40
43 Roberto Guerrero .25 .60
44 Desire Wilson .15 .40
45 Danny Sullivan .25 .60
Rick Mears
Michael Andretti
46 Dominic Dobson ROY .15 .40
47 Bobby Rahal Winner .25 .60
48 Mario Andretti Winner .50 1.25
49 Johnny Rutherford Winner .25 .60
50 Tony Bettenhausen .15 .40
Gary Bettenhausen

1986 Ace Formula One

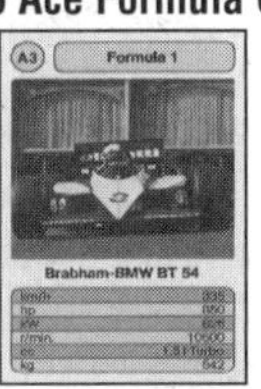

This set was made in West Germany for the British company Ace. The cards actually resemble a deck of playing cards with Formula One driver photos on the cardfront with a red playing card type back. The cards are unnumbered and listed below alphabetically. A German version of the set was also produced entitled Top Ace. There is no price difference between the two versions.

COMPLETE SET (33) 2.50 6.00
A1 Alfa Romeo 185T .08 .25
A2 Arrows BMW A8 .08 .25
A3 Brabham BMW BT54 .08 .25
A4 Ferrari 156/85 .08 .25
B1 Ligier Renault JS25 .08 .25
B2 McLaren TAG/Porsche .08 .25
B3 Osella Alfa Romeo FA1F .08 .25
B4 Renault RE60 .08 .25
C1 Lotus Renault 97T .08 .25
C2 Minardi Motori Moder.M185 .08 .25
C3 RAM Hart 03 .08 .25
C4 Spirit Hart 101B .08 .25
D1 Toleman Hart .08 .25
D2 Tyrrell Cosworth 012 .08 .25
D3 Williams Honda FW10 .08 .25
D4 Zakspeed 841 .08 .25
E1 Alfa Romeo 184T .08 .25
E2 Arrows BMW A7 .08 .25
E3 ATS BMW D7 .08 .25
E4 Brabham BMW BT53 .08 .25
F1 Ferrari 126C4 .08 .25
F2 Ligier Renault JS23 .08 .25
F3 RAM Hart 02 .08 .25
F4 Williams Honda FW09B .08 .25
G1 Lotus Renault 95T .08 .25
G2 McLaren TAG/Porsche .08 .25
G3 Renault RE50 .08 .25
G4 Toleman Hart TG184 .08 .25
H1 Brabham BMW BT52B .08 .25
H2 Lotus Renault 94T .08 .25
H3 Renault RE40 .08 .25
H4 Ferrari 126C3 .08 .25
NNO Cover Card .08 .25

1986 Ace Indy

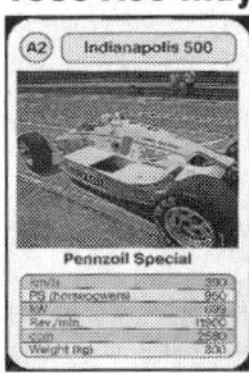

This set was made in West Germany for the British company Ace. The cards are actually part of a Trump card game featuring IndyCar photos on the cardfront with a playing card back and rounded corners. The playing card deck contains 32-cards with one cover/rule card. Drivers are not specifically indentified on the cards, but are included below as noted.

COMPLETE SET (33) 3.00 8.00
A1 Amway Special .25 .60
Scott Brayton
A2 Pennzoil Special .25 .60
Rick Mears
A3 Kraco Special .25 .60
Michael Andretti
A4 Gilmore Special .25 .60
A.J.Foyt
B1 Living Well Special .25 .60
Arie Luyendyk
B2 Intersport March .15 .40
Jim Ward
B3 Budweiser Lola .25 .60
Bobby Rahal
B4 Bryd's Valpack March .15 .40
Rich Vogler
C1 Scheid Tyre Special Buick .15 .40
Derek Daly
C2 STP Special .07 .20
C3 Veedol Special .15 .40
Mike Mosley
C4 Sunoco Special .15 .40
Gary Bettenhausen
D1 Rislone Special .07 .20
D2 STP Eagle Special .15 .40
Wally Dallenbach Sr.
D3 McLaren Special .15 .40
Gordon Johncock
D4 Wynn's Special Offy .15 .40
Sam Sessions
E1 Lightning Special .07 .20
E2 Thermo King Special .07 .20
E3 A.J.Foyt Gilmore Special .25 .60
A.J.Foyt's Car
E4 Eagle Chevrolet .07 .20
F1 Tone Valvoline Special .07 .20
F2 Valvoline Special .07 .20
F3 Advan Special .07 .20
F4 Valvoline Spirit Honda .07 .20
G1 Lacatop Special .07 .20
G2 Vermont March Special .07 .20
G3 Gilmore Karco Special .25 .60
Michael Andretti
G4 Marlboro BRM Special .07 .20
H1 Nova Indy 47 .07 .20
H2 Indy Midget .07 .20
Mel Kenyon
H3 Indy Midget .07 .20
H4 Clubmann Indy Stocker .07 .20
NNO Cover Card .07 .20
Game rules on back

1987 Ace Formula One

This set was made in West Germany for the British company Ace. The cards actually resemble a deck of playing cards with Formula One driver photos on the cardfront with a blue playing card type back. The set contains 32 individual driver cards with one cover card picturing Alain Prost. The cards are unnumbered and listed below alphabetically.

COMPLETE SET (33) 3.00 8.00
1 Michele Alboreto .07 .20
2 Philippe Alliot .07 .20
3 Rene Arnoux .07 .20
4 Allen Berg .07 .20
5 Gerhard Berger .15 .40
6 Thierry Boutsen .07 .20
7 Martin Brundle .07 .20
8 Alex Caffi .07 .20
9 Ivan Capelli .07 .20
10 Eddie Cheever .07 .20
11 Christian Danner .07 .20
12 Andrea deCesaris .07 .20
13 Johnny Dumfries .07 .20
14 Teo Fabi .07 .20
15 Piercarlo Ghinzani .07 .20
16 Stefan Johansson .07 .20
17 Alan Jones .07 .20
18 Jacques Laffite .07 .20
19 Nigel Mansell .25 .60
20 Satoro Nakajma .07 .20
21 Alessandro Nannini .07 .20
22 Jonathan Palmer .07 .20
23 Riccardo Patrese .15 .40
24 Nelson Piquet .15 .40
25 Alain Prost .15 .40
26 Keke Rosberg .15 .40
27 Huub Rothengatter .07 .20
28 Ayrton Senna .50 1.25
29 Philippe Streiff .07 .20
30 Marc Surer .07 .20
31 Patrick Tambay .07 .20
32 Derek Warwick .07 .20
33 Cover Card .07 .20
Alain Prost

1990 Action Packed Indy Prototypes

Action Packed prepared these four prototype cards to demonstrate their printing technology to the racing card industry. Each card features the standard gold foil border along with an embossed driver photo on the cardfront. Backs carry a short driver biography and 1989 race results. The four cards are skip numbered.

COMPLETE SET (4) 150.00 300.00
1 Emerson Fittipaldi 40.00 75.00

6 Mario Andretti 75.00 125.00
22 Rick Mears 40.00 75.00
23 Pancho Carter 30.00 60.00

1991 All World Indy

All World, in cooperation with A and S Racing, produced an Indy Car set in both 1991 and '92. The 1991 issue contained 100-cards featuring individual driver cards, race by race highlight cards of the previous season and All-Time Greats and Past Champion subset cards. Foil packs contained nine cards and factory sets were produced. Signed cards from this set were randomly inserted in 1992 All World packs, although they have no distinguishing characteristics to differentiate them from regular issue cards. An offer to purchase past A and S Racing sets was also included in packs.

COMPLETE SET (100) 1.50 4.00
1 Al Unser Jr. .08 .25
2 Bill Vukovich III .01 .05
3 Tero Palmroth .01 .05
4 John Andretti .02 .10
5 Mario Andretti .20 .50
6 Tony Bettenhausen .01 .05
7 Tom Sneva .02 .10
8 Willy T. Ribbs .01 .05
9 Bobby Rahal .02 .10
10 Danny Sullivan .02 .10
11 Buddy Lazier .01 .05
12 Stan Fox .01 .05
13 Checklist 1 UER .01 .05
14 Dean Hall .01 .05
15 Arie Luyendyk .02 .10
16 Eddie Cheever .01 .05
17 Scott Goodyear .01 .05
18 Jon Beekhuis .01 .05
19 Jeff Wood .01 .05
20 Emerson Fittipaldi .02 .10
21 Pancho Carter W/Family .01 .05
22 Mike Groff .01 .05
23 Rocky Moran .01 .05
24 Roberto Guerrero .08 .25
25 Michael Andretti .08 .25
26 Didier Theys .01 .05
27 Geoff Brabham .01 .05
28 Randy Lewis .01 .05
29 Michael Greenfield .01 .05
30 Rick Mears .08 .25
31 Gary Bettenhausen .01 .05
32 Raul Boesel .01 .05
33 Michael Andretti .08 .25
John Andretti
34 Dominic Dobson .01 .05
35 Al Unser .08 .25
36 Kevin Cogan .01 .05
37 Wally Dallenbach Jr. .01 .05
38 Jim Crawford .01 .05
39 Scott Brayton .02 .10
40 Hiro Matsushita .01 .05
41 Jeff Andretti .01 .05
42 '90 Indy Standings .01 .05
43 Emerson Fittipaldi Win .02 .10
44 Arie Luyendyk Win .02 .10
45 Al Unser Jr. WIN .08 .25
46 Eddie Cheever ROY .01 .05
47 Guido Dacco .01 .05
48 Tony Bettenhausen .01 .05
Gary Bettenhausen
49 Steve Chassey .01 .05
50 Derek Daly .01 .05
51 Scott Pruett .01 .05
52 Phil Krueger .01 .05
53 Bernard Jourdain .01 .05
54 Johnny Rutherford .02 .10
55 Ludwig Heimrath Jr. .01 .05
56 Scott Atchison .01 .05
57 John Jones .01 .05
58 Scott Harrington .01 .05
59 Davy Jones .01 .05
60 Steve Saleen .01 .05
61 Gordon Johncock .01 .05
62 Dale Coyne .01 .05
63 Bill Vukovich III .01 .05
64 Bernard Jourdain .01 .05
Scott Pruett
65 Emerson Fittipaldi WIN .02 .10
66 Michael Andretti WIN .08 .25
67 Danny Sullivan WIN .02 .10
68 Jim Hurtubise .01 .05
69 Sheldon Kinser .01 .05
70 Al Holbert .01 .05
71 Sam Hanks ATG .01 .05
72 Duane Carter Sr. ATG .01 .05
73 Tony Bettenhausen Sr. ATG .01 .05
74 Rick Mears Winner .08 .25
75 Al Unser Jr. .08 .25
Bobby Rahal
76 Checklist 2 UER .01 .05
77 '90 Phoenix Race .01 .05
78 '90 Long Beach Race .01 .05
79 '90 Indy 500 Mile Race .01 .05
80 '90 Milwaukee Race .01 .05
81 '90 Detroit Race .01 .05
82 '90 Portland Race .01 .05
83 '90 Cleveland Race .01 .05
84 '90 Meadowlands Race .01 .05
85 '90 Toronto Race .01 .05
86 '90 Michigan 500 Race .01 .05
87 '90 Denver Race .01 .05
88 '90 Vancouver Race .01 .05
89 '90 Mid Ohio Race .01 .05
90 '90 Elkhart Lake Race .01 .05
91 '90 Nazareth Race .01 .05
92 '90 Laguna Seca Race .01 .05
93 Johnny Rutherford PPGC .02 .10
94 Rick Mears PPGC .08 .25
95 Al Unser PPGC .02 .10
96 Mario Andretti PPGC .20 .50
97 Bobby Rahal PPGC .02 .10
99 Emerson Fittipaldi PPGC .02 .10
100 Al Unser Jr. PPGC .08 .25
P1 Al Unser Jr. Promo 1.50 4.00
P2 Al Unser Jr.'s Car Promo 1.00 2.50

1992 All World Indy

All World, in cooperation with A and S Racing, produced an Indy Car set in both 1991 and '92. The 1992 issue again contained 100-cards featuring individual driver cards and Where are They Now, Careers, and All-Time Greats subset cards. Foil packs contained nine cards and factory sets were produced as well. Autographed cards from the 1991 All World Indy set were randomly seeded throughout the run of 1992 packs. Reportedly, 100 cards were signed by 40 different drivers. The cards cannot otherwise be distinguished from regular issue 1991 cards and, therefore, generally do not carry a significant premium over other signed cards. An offer to purchase uncut sheets of the set for $19.95 was included on the wrapper.

COMPLETE SET (100) 1.50 4.00
1 Michael Andretti .08 .25
2 Mike Groff .01 .05
3 Dean Hall .01 .05
4 Gary Bettenhausen .01 .05
5 Willy T. Ribbs .01 .05
6 Scott Pruett .01 .05
7 Scott Goodyear .01 .05
8 Bobby Rahal .08 .25
9 Eddie Cheever .01 .05
10 Phil Krueger .01 .05
11 Arie Luyendyk .05 .15
12 Michael Greenfield .01 .05
13 Checklist .01 .05
14 Stan Fox .01 .05
15 John Andretti .05 .15
16 Guido Dacco .01 .05
17 Kevin Cogan .01 .05
18 Danny Sullivan .05 .15
19 Mark Dismore .01 .05
20 Emerson Fittipaldi .05 .15
21 Al Unser Jr. .08 .25
22 Didier Theys .01 .05
23 Geoff Brabham .01 .05
24 Buddy Lazier .01 .05
25 Mario Andretti .20 .50
26 Dale Coyne .01 .05
27 Roberto Guerrero .08 .25
28 Dominic Dobson .01 .05
29 Johnny Parsons Jr. .01 .05
30 Al Unser .05 .15
31 Tony Bettenhausen .01 .05
32 Scott Brayton .05 .15
33 Gordon Johncock .05 .15
34 Tero Palmroth .01 .05
35 Dennis Vitolo .01 .05
36 Bernard Jourdain .01 .05
37 Hiro Matsushita .01 .05
38 Ted Prappas .01 .05
39 Jeff Wood .01 .05
40 Jeff Andretti .01 .05
41 Rick Mears .08 .25
42 Pancho Carter .01 .05
43 Jim Crawford .01 .05
44 Randy Lewis .01 .05
45 Buddy Lazier .01 .05
Bob Lazier
46 Michael Andretti .08 .25
47 Jeff Andretti .01 .05
48 John Andretti .05 .15
49 Mario Andretti .08 .25
Michael Andretti
John Andretti
Jeff Andretti
The Andretti Family
50 Mario Andretti .08 .25
Michael Andretti
John Andretti
The Andretti Trifecta
51 Norman Schwartzkopf .05 .15
Pancho Carter
Johnny Rutherford
Al Unser Sr.
52 Rich Vogler .01 .05
53 Al Loquasto .01 .05
54 Checklist .01 .05
55 Rodger Ward ATG .01 .05
56 Louis Meyer ATG .01 .05
57 Wally Dallenbach Sr. ATG .01 .05
58 Johnnie Parsons ATG .01 .05
59 Troy Ruttman ATG .01 .05
60 Parnelli Jones ATG .01 .05
61 Eddie Sachs ATG .01 .05
62 Johnny Boyd ATG .01 .05
63 Lloyd Ruby ATG .01 .05
64 Bill Vukovich Jr. ATG .01 .05
65 George Snider .01 .05
66 Gene Hartley .01 .05
67 Howdy Holmes .01 .05
68 Lee Kunzman .01 .05
69 Larry Rice .01 .05
70 Mario Andretti C .20 .50
71 Arie Luyendyk C .01 .05
72 Gordon Johncock C .05 .15
73 Scott Goodyear C .01 .05
74 Pancho Carter C .01 .05
75 Jim Crawford C .01 .05
76 John Andretti C .05 .15
77 Johnny Rutherford C .05 .15
78 Danny Sullivan C .05 .15
79 Michael Andretti C .08 .25
80 Emerson Fittipaldi C .05 .15
81 Bobby Rahal C .05 .15
82 Steve Chassey C .01 .05
83 Checklist .01 .05
84 Al Unser Jr. .08 .25
85 Roberto Guerrero .08 .25
86 Eddie Cheever .01 .05
87 Tom Sneva .01 .05
88 Scott Pruett .01 .05
89 Phil Krueger .01 .05
90 Rick Mears .05 .15
91 Al Unser .05 .15
92 Tony Bettenhausen .01 .05
93 Dominic Dobson .01 .05
94 Scott Brayton .05 .15
95 Randy Lewis .01 .05
96 Geoff Brabham .01 .05
97 Mike Groff .01 .05
98 Gary Bettenhausen .01 .05
99 Didier Theys .01 .05
100 Kevin Cogan .01 .05

1911 American Tobacco Auto Drivers

This 25-card set was produced for The American Tobacco Company. Each card includes a small ad for either Hassan or Mecca Cigarettes on the cardback. All 25 cards were produced with both ad back variations. The cards measure 2 1/2 x 1 3/4 and came with square corners. The cards are unnumbered and feature top race car drivers of the day from both North America and Europe representing all types of auto racing events. They were packaged one card per 10 cigarette pack and two per 20 cigarette pack. The cards were inserted in cigarette packs starting on March 27th, 1911 and ending on March 31st, 1911. Special thanks to Jon Hardgrove for providing much of this information.

COMPLETE SET (25) 90.00 800.00
1 David Bruce-Brown 15.00 25.00
2 Bob Burman 15.00 25.00
3 Louis Chevrolet 30.00 50.00
4 Walter Christie 15.00 25.00
5 Demoget 15.00 25.00
6 Ralph dePalma 30.00 50.00
7 Bert Dingley 15.00 25.00
8 Arthur Duray 15.00 25.00
9 Henri Fournier 15.00 25.00
10 Harry E. Grant 15.00 25.00
11 Victor Hemery 15.00 25.00
12 Camille Jenatzy UER 15.00 25.00
13 Vincenzo Lancia 15.00 25.00
14 Herbert Lyttle 15.00 25.00
15 Fred Marriott 15.00 25.00
16 Harry Mitchner 15.00 25.00
17 R. Mulford 15.00 25.00
18 Felice Nazarro 15.00 25.00
19 Barney Oldfield 30.00 50.00
20 George H. Robertson 15.00 25.00
21 Joe Seymour 15.00 25.00
22 Lewis P. Strang 15.00 25.00
23 Francois Szisz 15.00 25.00
24 Joseph Tracy UER 15.00 25.00
Misspelled Tracey
25 Louis Wagner 15.00 25.00

1980 Avalon Hill USAC Race Game

This 33-card set was part of a board game. The cards feature the Indy drivers who raced in the 1980 Indianapolis 500. An interesting note is the appearance of NASCAR Winston Cup driver Tim Richmond. He finished 9th in the race. The cards are numbered in order of finish in the race.

COMPLETE SET (33) 75.00 125.00
1 Johnny Rutherford 2.50 6.00
2 Tom Sneva 1.50 4.00
3 Gary Bettenhausen 1.50 4.00
4 Gordon Johncock 1.50 4.00
5 Rick Mears 1.50 4.00
6 Pancho Carter 1.50 4.00
7 Danny Ongais 1.50 4.00
8 Tom Bigelow 1.25 3.00
9 Tim Richmond 3.00 8.00
10 Greg Leffler 1.25 3.00
11 Billy Engelhart 1.25 3.00
12 Billy Vukovich 1.25 3.00
13 Don Whittington 1.25 3.00

14 A.J.Foyt	3.00	8.00
15 George Snider	1.25	3.00
16 Dennis Firestone	1.25	3.00
17 Jerry Sneva	1.25	3.00
18 Hurley Haywood	1.25	3.00
19 Bobby Unser	1.50	4.00
20 Mario Andretti	4.00	10.00
21 Jerry Karl	1.25	3.00
22 Dick Simon	1.25	3.00
23 Roger Rager	1.25	3.00
24 Jim McElreath	1.25	3.00
25 Gordon Smiley	1.25	3.00
26 Johnny Parsons	1.25	3.00
27 Al Unser	2.50	6.00
28 Tom Bagley	1.25	3.00
29 Spike Gehlhausen	1.25	3.00
30 Bill Ehittington	1.25	3.00
31 Dick Ferguson	1.25	3.00
32 Mike Mosley	1.25	3.00
33 Larry Cannon	1.25	3.00

1986 BOSCH Indy

Bosch Spark Plugs produced this set featuring top IndyCar drivers. Each card is unnumbered and features a driver photo and car photo on the cardfront. Cardbacks contain driver career information and stats.

COMPLETE SET (8)	150.00	250.00
1 Mario Andretti	35.00	60.00
2 Emerson Fittipaldi	15.00	30.00
3 Bruno Giacomelli	12.50	25.00
4 Howdy Holmes	12.50	25.00
5 Rick Mears	15.00	30.00
6 Danny Sullivan	15.00	30.00
7 Al Unser, Jr.	25.00	50.00
8 Al Unser, Sr.	20.00	40.00

1991 Carms Formula One

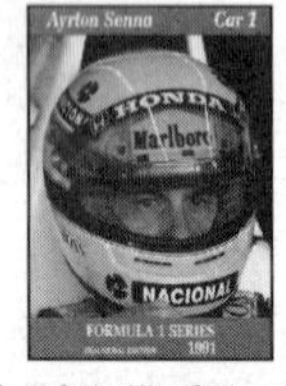

Carms Sports Cards of Nova Scotia produced this set featuring the top drivers of Formula One racing. Most drivers have three cards: a portrait, a car photo, and a driver photo in his car. The last card in the set is a cover card complete with ordering information for additional sets. Cards were sold in factory set form with Ayrton Senna's car featured on the box.

COMPLETE SET (105)	12.50	30.00
1 Ayrton Senna	2.00	4.00
2 Ayrton Senna's Car	.75	2.00
3 Ayrton Senna	2.00	4.00
4 Gerhard Berger	.30	.75
5 Gerhard Berger's Car	.20	.50
6 Gerhard Berger	.30	.75
7 Saturo Nakajima	.20	.50
8 Saturo Nakajima's Car	.08	.25
9 Saturo Nakajima	.20	.50
10 Stefano Modena	.20	.50
11 Stefano Modena's Car	.08	.25
12 Stefano Modena	.20	.50
13 Nigel Mansell	.75	2.00
14 Nigel Mansell's Car	.30	.75
15 Nigel Mansell	.75	2.00
16 Riccardo Patrese	.30	.75
17 Riccardo Patrese's Car	.20	.50
18 Riccardo Patrese	.30	.75
19 Martin Brundle	.20	.50
20 Martin Brundle's Car	.08	.25
21 Martin Brundle	.20	.50
22 Mark Blundell	.20	.50
23 Mark Blundell's Car	.08	.25
24 Mark Blundell	.20	.50
25 Michele Alboreto	.20	.50
26 Michele Alboreto's Car	.08	.25
27 Michele Alboreto	.20	.50
28 Alex Caffi	.20	.50
29 Alex Caffi's Car	.08	.25
30 Alex Caffi	.20	.50
31 Mika Hakkinen	.20	.50
32 Mika Hakkinen's Car	.08	.25
33 Mika Hakkinen	.20	.50
34 Julian Bailey	.20	.50
35 Julian Bailey's Car	.08	.25
36 Julian Bailey	.20	.50
37 Olivier Grouillard	.20	.50
38 Olivier Grouillard's Car	.08	.25
39 Olivier Grouillard	.20	.50
40 Mauricio Gugelmin	.20	.50
41 Mauricio Gugelmin's Car	.08	.25
42 Mauricio Gugelmin	.20	.50
43 Ivan Capelli	.20	.50
44 Ivan Capelli's Car	.08	.25
45 Ivan Capelli	.20	.50
46 Gabriele Tarquini	.20	.50
47 Gabriele Tarquini's Car	.08	.25
48 Gabriele Tarquini	.20	.50
49 Stefan Johansson	.30	.75
50 Stefan Johansson's Car	.20	.50
51 Stefan Johansson	.30	.75
52 Roberto Moreno	.20	.50
53 Roberto Moreno's Car	.08	.25
54 Roberto Moreno	.20	.50
55 Nelson Piquet	.20	.50
56 Nelson Piquet's Car	.08	.50
57 Nelson Piquet	.20	.50
58 Emanuele Pirro	.20	.50
59 Emanuele Pirro's Car	.08	.25
60 Emanuele Pirro	.20	.50
61 J.J. Lehto	.20	.50
62 J.J. Lehto's Car	.08	.25
63 J.J. Lehto	.20	.50
64 Pierluigi Martini	.20	.50
65 Pierluigi Martini's Car	.08	.25
66 Pierluigi Martini	.20	.50
67 Gianni Morbidelli	.20	.50
68 Gianni Morbidelli's Car	.08	.25
69 Gianni Morbidelli	.20	.50
70 Thierry Boutsen	.20	.50
71 Thierry Boutsen's Car	.08	.25
72 Thierry Boutsen	.20	.50
73 Erik Comas	.20	.50
74 Erik Comas' Car	.08	.25
75 Erik Comas	.20	.50
76 Alain Prost	.30	.75
77 Alain Prost's Car	.20	.50
78 Alain Prost	.30	.75
79 Jean Alesi	.20	.50
80 Jean Alesi's Car	.08	.25
81 Jean Alesi	.20	.50
82 Eric Bernard	.20	.50
83 Eric Bernard's Car	.08	.25
84 Eric Bernard	.20	.50
85 Aguri Suzuki	.20	.50
86 Aguri Suzuki's Car	.08	.25
87 Aguri Suzuki	.20	.50
88 Pedro Matos Chaves	.20	.50
89 Pedro Matos Chaves' Car	.08	.25
90 Bertrand Gachot	.20	.50
91 Bertrand Gachot's Car	.08	.25
92 Bertrand Gachot	.20	.50
93 Andrea deCesaris	.20	.50
94 Andrea deCesaris' Car	.08	.25
95 Andrea deCesaris	.20	.50
96 Nicola Larini	.20	.50
97 Nicola Larini's Car	.08	.25
98 Nicola Larini	.20	.50
99 Eric Van de Poele	.20	.50
100 Eric Van de Poele's Car	.08	.25
101 Mario Andretti	.75	2.00
102 Mario Andretti's Car	.30	.75
103 Gilles Villeneuve	.75	2.00
104 Gilles Villeneuve's Car	.30	.75
105 Cover Card	.08	.25

1997 CART Schedule Cards

This set was proedcued for the 1997 CART season with each glossy card featuring a CART 97 logo on the front along with a color image of the driver. The backs of these cards contain the 1997 CART schedule with no manufacturer identification. The cards are unnumbered and appear in alphabetical order.

COMPLETE SET (6)	1.25	3.00
1 Michael Andretti	.50	1.25
2 Mark Blundell	.20	.50
3 Gil De Ferran	.25	.60
4 Christian Fittipaldi	.25	.60
5 Max Papis	.20	.50
6 Jimmy Vasser	.30	.75

1939 Churchman's Kings of Speed

This European tobacco issue is part of a bigger 50 card set. The set was issued by Imperial Tobacco Company and carries the theme speed. There were 13 car cards as part of the set. Other subsets were Aviators, Motorcycle racers, Bicycle racers, Boatsmen, Winter Olympians and Summer Olympians. The cards measure 1 3/8" X 2 5/8" and feature artwork of the drivers for card fronts. The backs give a bio of the driver pictured.

COMPLETE SET (13)	20.00	35.00
11 Captain G.E.T. Eyston	1.25	3.00
12 John Cobb	1.25	3.00
13 Major Goldie Gardner	1.25	3.00
14 Ab Jenkins	1.25	3.00
15 Birabongse Bira Prince of Siam	1.25	3.00
16 Rudolf Caracciola	1.25	3.00
17 Charlie Dodson	1.25	3.00
18 Louis Gerard	1.25	3.00
19 Percy Maclure	1.25	3.00
20 Raymond Mays	1.25	3.00
21 Tazio Nuvolari	1.25	3.00
22 Richard Seaman	1.25	3.00
23 J.P. Wakefield	1.25	3.00

1992 Collect-A-Card Andretti Racing

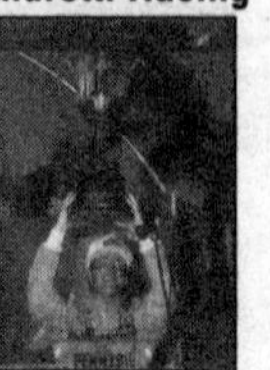

This Collect-A-Card set highlights the racing careers of Andretti family members Mario, Michael, Jeff and John. The cards were issued in 10-card packs as well as complete factory sets. Packs included randomly inserted 24K Gold autograph cards (250 of each made) of each of the four drivers. Factory sets included a special Hologram card featuring the CART/PPG IndyCar World Series Championship trophy.

COMPLETE SET (100)	1.50	4.00
1 Checklist Card	.05	.10
2 Mario Andretti's Car 1961 Lebanon Valley	.05	.15
3 Mario Andretti's Car 1967 Daytona Beach	.05	.15
4 Mario Andretti	.15	.40
5 Mario Andretti's Car 1965 Terre Haute	.05	.15
6 Mario Andretti's Car 1965 Indianapolis	.05	.15
7 Jeff Andretti	.05	.15
8 John Andretti	.05	.15
9 Mario Andretti's Car 1963 Allentown	.05	.15
10 Mario Andretti in Car	.05	.15
11 Mario Andretti's Car 1966 Indiana State FG	.05	.15
12 Mario Andretti in Car 1965 Indianapolis	.05	.15
13 Mario Andretti Aldo Andretti 1956 Langhorne	.15	.40
14 Mario Andretti in Car 1966 Indianapolis	.15	.40
15 Mario Andretti	.15	.40
16 Mario Andretti's Car 1967 Daytona Beach	.05	.15
17 Mario Andretti's Car 1967 Sebring	.05	.15
18 Mario Andretti's Car 1971 South Africa	.05	.15
19 Mario Andretti's Car 1967 St. Jovite	.05	.15
20 Mario Andretti's Car 1967 Riverside	.05	.15
21 Mario Andretti's Car 1972 Watkins Glen	.05	.15
22 Mario Andretti's Car 1967 Trenton	.05	.15
23 Mario Andretti's Car 1964 Allentown	.05	.15
24 Mario Andretti in Car 1964 Trenton	.05	.15
25 Mario Andretti's Car 1967 Indianapolis	.05	.15
26 John Andretti's Car 1990 Indianapolis	.01	.05
27 John Andretti's Car 1988 Indianapolis	.01	.05
28 John Andretti's Car 1987 Elkhart Lake	.01	.05
29 John Andretti's Car 1989 Daytona	.01	.05
30 John Andretti	.05	.15
31 John Andretti	.05	.15
32 John Andretti Car Michael Andretti Car Mario Andretti Car 1988 LeMans	.15	.40
33 John Andretti's Car 1988 Indianapolis	.01	.05
34 John Andretti's Car 1982 Dorney Park	.01	.05
35 John Andretti in Car	.01	.05
36 John Andretti's Car 1987 Mid-Ohio	.01	.05
37 John Andretti's Car 1988 Melbourne	.01	.05
38 John Andretti's Car 1989 Nuremberg	.01	.05
39 John Andretti	.05	.15
40 John Andretti's Car 1991 Milwaukee	.01	.05
41 Mario Andretti's Car A.J. Foyt's Car 1991 Indianapolis	.05	.10
42 Michael Andretti Mario Andretti Al Unser Jr.	.15	.40
43 Michael Andretti Mario Andretti 1991 Portland	.15	.40
44 Michael Andretti	.10	.25
45 Michael Andretti's Car 1991 Laguna Seca	.05	.10
46 Michael Andretti's Car 1990 Portland	.05	.10
47 Michael Andretti	.10	.25
48 Michael Andretti's Car 1989 Cleveland	.05	.10
49 Michael Andretti's Car 1988 Laguna Seca	.05	.10
50 Michael Andretti's Car 1988 Laguna Seca	.05	.10
51 Mario Andretti's Car 1969 Nazareth	.05	.15
52 Mario Andretti's Car 1986 Phoenix	.05	.15
53 Mario Andretti's Car 1986 Cleveland	.05	.15
54 Michael Andretti's Car 1986 Cleveland	.05	.10
55 Mario Andretti	.15	.40
56 Mario Andretti's Car 1988 Nazareth	.05	.15
57 Mario Andretti	.15	.40
58 Michael Andretti's Car 1987 Michigan	.05	.10
59 Mario Andretti's Car 1987 Long Beach	.05	.15
60 Mario Andretti	.15	.40
61 Mario Andretti's Car 1984 Mid-Ohio	.05	.15
62 Mario Andretti's Car 1984 Michigan	.05	.15
63 Michael Andretti's Car 1984 Indianapolis	.05	.10
64 Michael Andretti's Car 1990 Meadowlands	.05	.10
65 Mario Andretti's Car 1969 Sebring	.05	.15
66 Jeff Andretti	.05	.15
67 Michael Andretti's Car 1991 Milwaukee	.05	.10
68 Michael Andretti Carl Haas	.10	.25
69 Mario Andretti Michael Andretti Jeff Andretti 1969 Nazareth	.15	.40
70 Mario Andretti's Car 1978 Long Beach	.05	.15
71 Mario Andretti	.15	.40
72 Mario Andretti's Car Dan Gurney's Car Gordon Johncock's Car 1969 Indianapolis	.15	.40
73 Mario Andretti's Car 1966 LeMans	.05	.15
74 Jeff Andretti's Car 1991 Long Beach	.01	.05
75 Mario Andretti's Car Jeff Andretti's Car John Andretti's Car Michael Andretti's Car	.15	.40
76 Mario Andretti Michael Andretti Jeff Andretti	.15	.40
77 Michael Andretti in Pits 1991 Indianapolis	.10	.25
78 Mario Andretti A.J. Foyt Rick Mears	.10	.25
79 Michael Andretti	.10	.25
80 Mario Andretti's Car 1987 Elkhart Lake	.05	.15
81 Mario Andretti in Car 1988 Cleveland	.05	.15
82 Jeff Andretti's Car 1991 Queensland	.01	.05
83 Mario Andretti's Transporter	.05	.15
84 Jeff Andretti	.05	.15
85 Michael Andretti Paul Newman	.20	.50
86 1990 Indianapolis	.15	.40
87 Jeff Andretti	.05	.15
88 Michael Andretti Car Mario Andretti Car 1984 Daytona	.05	.15
89 Mario Andretti's Car 1977 Sweden	.05	.15
90 Mario Andretti	.15	.40
91 Michael Andretti Car Jeff Andretti Car Mario Andretti Car 1991 Daytona	.15	.40
92 Jeff Andretti's Car 1985 Cleveland	.01	.05
93 Mario Andretti Jeff Andretti in Car 1986 Mid-Ohio	.15	.40
94 Jeff Andretti's Car 1987 Phoenix	.01	.05
95 Jeff Andretti's Car 1988 Phoenix	.01	.05
96 Mario Andretti Collage 35 Years of Racing	.15	.40
97 Mario Andretti Michael Andretti Jeff Andretti 1969 Indianapolis	.15	.40
98 Mario Andretti	.15	.40
99 Michael Andretti	.10	.25
100 Checklist Card	.05	.10
NNO PPG Cup HOLO	.50	1.00

1987 Formula One Italian

This set was produced in Italy in 1987 and features popular drivers of the Formula One circuit. The cards are unnumbered, oversized (2-3/4" by 4") and have rounded corners. A 1987 yearly calendar makes up the cardback, while cardfronts typically show two small driver photos along with an F1 car shot. The cards are listed below alphabetically according to the alphabetized pair of drivers featured.

COMPLETE SET (16)	8.00	20.00
1 Michele Alboreto Stefan Johansson	.60	1.50
2 Rene Arnoux Jacques Laffite	.40	1.00
3 Gerhard Berger Teo Fabi	.60	1.50
4 Thierry Boutsen Marc Surer	.40	1.00
5 Martin Brundle Eddie Cheever	.60	1.50
6 Ivan Capeli Christian Danner	.40	1.00
7 Elio DeAngelis Riccardo Patrese	.60	1.50
8 Andrea DeCesais Alessandro Nannini	.40	1.00
9 Johnny Dumfries Ayrton Senna	1.50	4.00
10 Alan Jones Patrick Tambay	.60	1.50
11 Nigel Mansell Nelson Piguet	.75	2.00
12 Jonathan Palmer	.40	1.00
13 Alain Prost	.60	1.50
14 Alain Prost Keke Rosberg	.60	1.50
15 Checklist Card w/drivers	.40	1.00
16 Cover Card w/cars	.40	1.00

1992 Golden Era Grand Prix The Early Years

This 25-card set was produced by Rainbow Press of Loughton Essex England. The cards feature illustrations by British artist Robert R. Wisdom. The cards depict a colorful selection of the most thrilling and spectacular racing cars to ever grace the Grand Prix circuits of the World, driven by the famous and legendary drivers of the day.

COMPLETE SET (25)	4.00	10.00
1 Jimmy Murphy's Car	.20	.50
2 Antonio Ascari's Car	.20	.50
3 Bugatti Type 35B	.20	.50
4 Robert Benoist's Car	.20	.50
5 Auto Union A-Type	.20	.50
6 Alfa Romeo Tipo B	.20	.50
7 Von Brauchitsch's Car	.20	.50
8 Raymond Mays' Car	.20	.50
9 Mercedes W125	.20	.50
10 Giuseppe Farina's Car	.20	.50
11 Tazio Nuvolari's Car	.20	.50
12 Mercedes W163	.20	.50
13 Peter Whitehead's Car	.20	.50
14 Giuseppe Farina's Car	.20	.50
15 Juan Manuel Fangio's Car	.20	.50
16 Alberto Ascari's Car	.20	.50
17 Juan Manuel Fangio's Car	.20	.50
18 Alberto Ascari's Car	.20	.50
19 Stirling Moss' Car	.40	1.00
20 Stirling Moss' Car	.40	1.00
21 Stirling Moss' Car	.40	1.00
22 Mike Hawthorn's Car	.20	.50
23 Jack Brabham's Car	.20	.50
24 Phil Hill's Car	.20	.50
25 Jim Clark's Car	.20	.50
NNO Cover Card	.08	.25

1978-79 Grand Prix

The 1978-79 Grand Prix set was produced with an album intended to house the 240-card set. The album is written entirely in French. The card fronts feature a color photo of a top Grand Prix driver, while the backs include the card number and, on most, a short card title.

COMPLETE SET (240)	75.00	135.00
1 Mario Andretti	2.00	5.00
2 Bruno Giacomelli	.30	.75
3 Jan Lammers	.30	.75
4 Didier Pironi Jean Pierre Jaussaud	.30	.75
5 Al Unser	1.50	4.00
6 Markku Alen	.30	.75
7 Tony Carello	.30	.75
8 Mario Andretti	2.00	5.00
9 Mario Andretti's Car	1.00	2.00
10 Carlos Reutemann's Car	.20	.50
11 Didier Pironi's Car	.20	.50
12 James Hunt's Car	.20	.50
13 Niki Lauda's Car	.30	.75
14 Mario Andretti's Car	1.00	2.00
15 Gilles Villeneuve's Car	.30	.75
16 Arturo Merzario's Car	.20	.50
17 Jean Pierre Jarier's Car	.20	.50
18 Emerson Fittipaldi	1.25	3.00
19 Carlos Reutemann's Car	.20	.50
20 Emerson Fittipaldi's Car	.60	1.50
21 Niki Lauda's Car	.30	.75
22 Grand Prix Action	.20	.50
23 Gilles Villeneuve's Car	.30	.75
24 Ronnie Peterson's Car	.20	.50
25 Alan Jones' Car	.30	.75
26 Eddie Cheever's Car	.30	.75
27 Jacques Laffite's Car	.20	.50
28 Ronnie Peterson		.30
29 Patrick Depailler's Car		.20
30 Riccardo Patrese's Car		.30
31 Jean Pierre Jabouille's Car		.20
32 John Watson's Car		.20
33 Didier Pironi's Car		.20
34 Eddie Cheever's Car		.30
35 Carlos Reutemann's Car		.20
36 Rolf Stommelen's Car		.20
37 Rene Arnoux's Car		.20
38 Carlos Reutemann		.30
39 Carlos Reutemann's Car		.20
40 Mario Andretti's Car		1.00
41 Alan Jones' Car		.30
42 Patrick Depailler's Car		.20
43 Clay Regazzoni's Car Gilles Villeneuve's Car		.40
44 Jody Scheckter's Car		.20
45 Hans Stuck's Car		.20
46 Lamberto Leoni's Car		.20
47 Jacques Laffite's Car Riccardo Patrese's Car		.20
48 Patrick Depailler		.30
49 Grand Prix Action		.20
50 Niki Lauda's Car		.30
51 Carlos Reutemann's Car		.20
52 Patrick Tambay's Car		.20
53 Didier Pironi Riccardo Patrese		.30
54 John Watson's Car		.20
55 Jean Pierre Jabouille's Car		.20
56 Mario Andretti's Car		1.00
57 Wolf-Ford		.20
58 Mario Andretti		2.00
59 Mario Andretti's Car		1.00
60 Alan Jones' Car		.30
61 Carlos Reutemann's Car		.20
62 Gilles Villeneuve's Car		.30
63 Bruno Giacomelli's Car		.20
64 Didier Pironi's Car Rene Arnoux's Car Rolf Stommelen's Car		.20
65 Rene Arnoux' Car		.20
66 Brett Lunger's Car		.20
67 Jochen Mass' Car		.20
68 Mario Andretti's Car		1.00
69 Jacques Laffite's Car		.20
70 Jody Scheckter's Car		.20
71 James Hunt's Car		.20
72 Jacques Laffite		.30
73 Ronnie Peterson's Car		.20
74 John Watson's Car		.20
75 Hector Rebaque's Car		.20
76 Emilio Villota's Car		.20
77 Rupert Keegan's Car		.20
78 Niki Lauda		.60
79 Niki Lauda's Car		.30
80 Mario Andretti's Car		1.00
81 Riccardo Patrese's Car		.30
82 Patrick Tambay's Car		.20
83 Mario Andretti's Car		1.00
84 Ronnie Peterson's Car		.20
85 Geoff Brabham's Car		.30
86 Clay Regazzoni's Car		.20
87 Grand Prix Action		.20
88 Mario Andretti's Car		1.00
89 Ronnie Peterson's Car		.20
90 James Hunt's Car		.20
91 Riccardo Patrese's Car		.30
92 Niki Lauda's Car		.30
93 James Hunt's Car		.20
94 Jody Scheckter's Car		.20
95 Jacques Laffite's Car		.20
96 Alan Jones' Car		.30
97 Carlos Reutemann's Car		.20
98 Carlos Reutemann		.30
99 Carlos Reutemann's Car		.20
100 Niki Lauda's Car		.30
101 Mario Andretti's Car		1.00
102 Patrick Depailler's Car		.20
103 Alan Jones' Car		.30
104 Grand Prix Action		.20
105 Hans Stuck's Car		.20
106 Patrick Tambay's Car		.20
107 Bruno Giacomelli's Car		.20
108 Mario Andretti's Car		1.00
109 Jody Scheckter's Car		.20
110 Jody Scheckter		.30
111 Jacques Laffite's Car		.20
112 Harald Ertl		.30
113 Emerson Fittipaldi's Car		.60
114 Didier Pironi Emerson Fittipaldi		.60
115 Keke Rosberg's Car		.30
116 John Watson's Car		.20
117 Gilles Villeneuve's Car		.30
118 Ronnie Peterson's Car		.20
119 Patrick Depailler's Car Niki Lauda's Car		.30
120 Vittorio Brambilla's Car		.20
121 Mario Andretti's Car		1.00
122 Niki Lauda's Car		.30
123 Gilles Villeneuve's Car Patrick Depailler's Car Hans Stuck's Car		.40
124 Nelson Piquet's Car		.30
125 Carlos Reutemann's Car		.20
126 Jean Pierre Jabouille's Car		.20
127 Derek Daly's Car		.20
128 Mario Andretti		2.00
129 John Watson's Car		.20
130 Jean Pierre Jabouille's Car		.20
131 Michael Bleekemolen's Car		.20
132 Gilles Villeneuve's Car		.30
133 Emerson Fittipaldi's Car		.60
134 Patrick Tambay's Car		.20
135 James Hunt's Car		.20
136 Jochen Mass' Car		.20
137 Derek Daly's Car		.20
138 John Watson		.30

i Lauda's Car	.30	.75
rio Andretti's Car	1.00	2.00
nnie Peterson's Car	.20	.50
nnie Peterson	.30	.75
n Watson's Car	.20	.50
es Villeneuve's Car	.30	.75
rick Tambay's Car	.20	.50
orio Brambilla's Car	.20	.50
son Piquet's Car	.30	.75
los Reutemann's Car	.20	.50
los Reutemann	.30	.75
n Jones' Car	.30	.75
n Pierre Jabouille's Car	.20	.50
n Pierre Jarier's Car	.20	.50
nes Hunt's Car	.20	.50
ick Tambay's Car	.20	.50
y Regazzoni	.60	1.50
rson Fittipaldi		
ne Arnoux's Car	.20	.50
bby Rahal's Car	.40	1.00
es Villeneuve's Car	.30	.75
es Villeneuve	.40	1.00
dy Scheckter's Car	.20	.50
n Pierre Jarier's Car	.20	.50
ccardo Patrese's Car	.30	.75
nd Prix Action	.20	.50
nd Prix Action	.20	.50
ek Daly's Car	.20	.50
son Piquet's Car	.30	.75
e Rosberg's Car	.30	.75
no Giacomelli's Car	.20	.50
rc Surer's Car	.20	.50
rch-BMW	.20	.50
ek Daly's Car	.20	.50
ro Necchi's Car	.20	.50
x Dias Ribeiro's Car	.20	.50
e Rosberg's Car	.30	.75
Lammers' Car	.20	.50
ders Olofsson's Car	.20	.50
rick Gaillard's Car	.20	.50
son Piquet's Car	.30	.75
ek Warwick's Car	.20	.50
in Prost's Car	.40	1.00
co Serra's Car	.20	.50
berto Grano's Car	.20	.50
nin Hahne's Car	.20	.50
mens Schickentanz's Car	.20	.50
s Heyer's Car		
lo Facetti's Car	.20	.50
tini Finotto's Car		
li Bergmeistr's Car	.20	.50
Siegst's Car		
don Spice's Car	.20	.50
dy Pilette's Car		
mut Bauer's Car	.20	.50
emans' Car	.20	.50
wig's Car		
) Wollek's Car	.20	.50
ri Pescarolo's Car		
lie Cheever's Car	.40	1.00
gio Francia's Car		
naso Pantera's Car	.20	.50
ns Heyer's Car	.20	.50
ald Ertl's Car	.20	.50
Stommelen's Car	.20	.50
ier Pironi's Car	.20	.50
Pierre Jaussaud's Car		
ier Pironi	.30	.75
Wollek's Car	.20	.50
en Barth's Car		
ick Depailler's Car	.20	.50
Pierre Jabouille's Car		
ault Alpine A442A	.20	.50
sche 936	.20	.50
Stommelen's Car	.20	.50
fred Schurti's Car		
man's Car	.20	.50
ques Laffite's Car	.20	.50
Schuppan's Car		
nd Prix 78-79	.20	.50
Berlinetta Boxer	.20	.50
ni Jaussaud's Car	.20	.50
Unser	1.50	4.00
Unser's Car	.75	2.00
nd Prix 78-79	.20	.50
n Sneva's Car	.40	1.00
by Unser's Car	.60	1.50
y Dallenbach Sr.'s Car		
et Guthrie's Car	.60	1.50
io Andretti's Car	1.00	2.00
tin Schanche's Car	.20	.50
reas Bentza's Car	.20	.50
Anderson's Car	.20	.50
nd Prix 78-79	.20	.50
Fassbender's Car	.20	.50
ero Laine's Car	.20	.50
nz Wurz's Car	.20	.50
n Pierre Nicolas' Car	.20	.50
n Ragnotti's Car	.20	.50
kku Alen's Car	.20	.50
nu Nikkola's Car	.20	.50
ers Kullang's Car	.20	.50
n Pierre Nicolas' Car	.20	.50
Preston's Car	.20	.50
sun 160J	.20	.50
ota Celica	.20	.50
tti Airikkala's Car	.20	.50
n Waldegaard's Car	.20	.50
y Pond's Car	.20	.50
y Carello's Car	.20	.50
ert Staepelaere's Car	.20	.50
z Wittmann's Car	.20	.50
er Clark's Car	.20	.50
hel Mouton's Car	.20	.50
nard Darniche's Car	.20	.50
nio Zanini's Car	.20	.50

1992 Grid Formula One

Released in foil packs and complete factory set form, this 200-card issue features top Formula One drivers and machines. The cards were produced with gold foil layering on the cardfronts and heavy UV coating. The set is highlighted by a large number of Ayrton Senna cards.

COMPLETE SET (200)	3.00	7.00
COMPLETE FACT.SET (200)	3.00	7.00
1 Ayrton Senna's Car	.08	.25
2 Gerhard Berger's Car	.02	.10
3 Olivier Grouillard's Car	.01	.05
4 Andrea deCesaris' Car	.01	.05
5 Nigel Mansell's Car	.05	.15
6 Riccardo Patrese's Car	.01	.05
7 Eric van de Poele's Car	.01	.05
8 Damon Hill's Car	.05	.15
9 Giovanna Amati's Car	.01	.05
10 Michele Alboreto's Car	.01	.05
11 Aguri Suzuki's Car	.01	.05
12 Mika Hakkinen's Car	.01	.05
13 Johnny Herbert's Car	.01	.05
14 Andrea Chiesa's Car	.01	.05
15 Gabriele Tarquini's Car	.01	.05
16 Karl Wendlinger's Car	.01	.05
17 Paul Belmondo's Car	.01	.05
18 Michael Schumacher's Car	.05	.15
19 Martin Brundle's Car	.01	.05
20 J.J. Lehto's Car	.01	.05
21 Pierluigi Martini's Car	.01	.05
22 Christian Fittipaldi's Car	.01	.05
23 Gianni Morbidelli's Car	.01	.05
24 Thierry Boutsen's Car	.01	.05
25 Erik Comas' Car	.01	.05
26 Jean Alesi's Car	.02	.10
27 Ivan Capelli's Car	.01	.05
28 Ukyo Katayama's Car	.01	.05
29 Bertrand Gachot's Car	.01	.05
30 Stefano Modena's Car	.01	.05
31 Mauricio Gugelmin's Car	.01	.05
32 Roberto Moreno's Car	.01	.05
33 Perry McCarthy's Car	.01	.05
34 Ayrton Senna	.10	.30
35 Gerhard Berger	.08	.25
36 Olivier Grouillard	.02	.10
37 Andrea deCesaris	.02	.10
38 Nigel Mansell	.08	.25
39 Riccardo Patrese	.05	.15
40 Eric van de Poele	.02	.10
41 Damon Hill	.08	.25
42 Giovanna Amati	.02	.10
43 Michele Alboreto	.02	.10
44 Aguri Suzuki	.02	.10
45 Mika Hakkinen	.02	.10
46 Johnny Herbert	.02	.10
47 Andrea Chiesa	.02	.10
48 Gabriele Tarquini	.02	.10
49 Karl Wendlinger	.02	.10
50 Paul Belmondo	.02	.10
51 Michael Schumacher	.08	.25
52 Martin Brundle	.02	.10
53 J.J. Lehto	.02	.10
54 Pierluigi Martini	.02	.10
55 Christian Fittipaldi	.02	.10
56 Gianni Morbidelli	.02	.10
57 Thierry Boutsen	.02	.10
58 Erik Comas	.02	.10
59 Jean Alesi	.05	.15
60 Ivan Capelli	.02	.10
61 Bertrand Gachot	.02	.10
62 Ukyo Katayama	.02	.10
63 Stefano Modena	.02	.10
64 Mauricio Gugelmin	.02	.10
65 Roberto Moreno	.02	.10
66 Perry McCarthy	.02	.10
67 Ayrton Senna	.10	.30
68 Gerhard Berger	.08	.25
69 Olivier Grouillard	.02	.10
70 Andrea deCesaris	.02	.10
71 Nigel Mansell	.08	.25
72 Riccardo Patrese	.05	.15
73 Eric van de Poele	.02	.10
74 Damon Hill	.08	.25
75 Giovanna Amati	.02	.10
76 Michele Alboreto	.02	.10
77 Aguri Suzuki	.02	.10
78 Mika Hakkinen	.02	.10
79 Johnny Herbert	.02	.10
80 Andrea Chiesa	.02	.10
81 Gabriele Tarquini	.02	.10
82 Karl Wendlinger	.02	.10
83 Paul Belmondo	.02	.10
84 Michael Schumacher	.08	.25
85 Martin Brundle	.02	.10
86 J.J. Lehto	.02	.10
87 Pierluigi Martini	.02	.10
88 Christian Fittipaldi	.02	.10
89 Gianni Morbidelli	.02	.10
90 Thierry Boutsen	.02	.10
91 Erik Comas	.02	.10
92 Jean Alesi	.05	.15
93 Ivan Capelli	.02	.10
94 Bertrand Gachot	.02	.10
95 Ukyo Katayama	.02	.10
96 Stefano Modena	.02	.10
97 Mauricio Gugelmin	.02	.10
98 Roberto Moreno	.02	.10
99 Perry McCarthy	.02	.10
100 Ayrton Senna	.05	.15
Alain Prost		
Nelson Piquet		
101 Ayrton Senna Winner	.08	.25
102 Ayrton Senna	.05	.15
Gerhard Berger		
J.J.Lehto		
103 Jean Alesi	.05	.15
Ayrton Senna		
Nigel Mansell		
104 Nelson Piquet	.02	.10
Stefano Modena		
Riccardo Patrese		
105 Ayrton Senna	.05	.15
Riccardo Patrese		
Nigel Mansell		
106 Nigel Mansell	.05	.15
Alain Prost		
Ayrton Senna		
107 Nigel Mansell	.05	.15
Gerhard Berger		
Alain Prost		
108 Riccardo Patrese	.05	.15
Nigel Mansell		
Jean Alesi		
109 Ayrton Senna	.05	.15
Nigel Mansell		
Riccardo Patrese		
110 Ayrton Senna Win	.08	.25
111 Nigel Mansell	.05	.15
Ayrton Senna		
Alain Prost		
112 Riccardo Patrese Win	.02	.10
113 Nigel Mansell	.05	.15
Alain Prost		
Riccardo Patrese		
114 Gerhard Berger	.05	.15
Ayrton Senna		
Riccardo Patrese		
115 Ayrton Senna Win	.08	.25
116 South Africa Race Track	.01	.05
117 Mexico Race Track	.01	.05
118 Brazil Race Track	.01	.05
119 Spain Race Track	.01	.05
120 San Marino Race Track	.01	.05
121 Monaco Race Track	.01	.05
122 Canada Race Track	.01	.05
123 France Race Track	.01	.05
124 England Race Track	.01	.05
125 Germany Race Track	.01	.05
126 Hungary Race Track	.01	.05
127 Belgium Race Track	.01	.05
128 Italy Race Track	.01	.05
129 Portugal Race Track	.01	.05
130 Japan Race Track	.01	.05
131 Australia Race Track	.01	.05
132 Frank Williams	.01	.05
133 Don Dennis	.01	.05
134 Tom Walkinshaw	.01	.05
135 Luca di Montezemolo	.01	.05
136 Gerard Larrousse	.01	.05
137 Eddie Jordan	.01	.05
138 Giancarlo Minardi	.01	.05
139 Charlie Moody	.01	.05
140 Ken Tyrrell	.01	.05
141 Peter Collins	.01	.05
142 Jackie Oliver	.01	.05
143 Guy Ligier	.01	.05
144 Andrea Sasetti	.01	.05
145 Dennis Nursey	.01	.05
146 Gabriele Rumi	.01	.05
147 Gianpaola Dallara	.01	.05
148 Gilles Villeneuve's Car	.02	.10
149 Gilles Villeneuve's Car	.02	.10
150 Gilles Villeneuve's Car	.02	.10
151 Gilles Villeneuve's Car	.02	.10
152 Gilles Villeneuve's Car	.02	.10
153 Gilles Villeneuve's Car	.02	.10
154 Gilles Villeneuve's Car	.02	.10
155 Gilles Villeneuve's Car	.02	.10
156 Gilles Villeneuve's Car	.02	.10
157 Gilles Villeneuve's Car	.02	.10
158 Checklist Card	.01	.05
159 Gilles Villeneuve	.05	.15
160 Davy Jones	.02	.10
161 Mark Blundell	.02	.10
162 Al Unser Jr.	.08	.25
163 David Coulthard	.05	.15
164 Rubens Barrichello	.05	.15
165 Alan McNish	.02	.10
166 Checklist Card	.01	.05
167 Paul Tracy	.05	.15
168 Emanuelle Naspetti	.02	.10
169 Alessandro Zanardi	.02	.10
170 Eddie Irvine	.02	.10
171 Antonio Tamburini	.02	.10
172 Jacques Villeneuve	.08	.25
173 Jordi Gene	.02	.10
174 Michael Bartels	.02	.10
175 Jimmy Vasser	.02	.10
176 Eric Bachelart	.02	.10
177 Robby Gordon	.50	1.25
178 Alberto Ascari	.02	.10
179 Alberto Ascari's Car	.01	.05
180 Graham Hill	.02	.10
181 Graham Hill's Car	.01	.05
182 Emerson Fittipaldi	.05	.15
183 Emerson Fittipaldi's Car	.01	.05
184 Keke Rosberg	.05	.15
185 1982 Ferrari	.01	.05
186 Ayrton Senna	.10	.30
187 Ayrton Senna's Car	.08	.25
188 Ayrton Senna	.10	.30
189 Ayrton Senna's Car	.08	.25
190 Alain Prost	.05	.15
191 Jordan's First Points	.01	.05
192 Nigel Mansell's Car	.05	.15
193 Bertrand Gachot's Car	.01	.05
194 Michael Schumacher	.08	.25
195 Nelson Piquet's Car	.01	.05
196 J.P.Balestre	.02	.10
197 Alain Prost	.05	.15
198 Nigel Mansell Crash	.02	.10
199 Saturo Nakajima	.02	.10
200 Michael Andretti's Car	.05	.15

1960 Hawes Wax Indy

Although often considered to be one of the first American auto racing card sets, the 50-card Hawes Wax issue was printed by Parkhurst in Canada for distribution in Hawes Wax products. This set features 39 cards portraying Indy 500 race winners from 1911-1959; 11 cards featuring race action scenes, and one card featuring the Purdue University Marching Band. Cardbacks are printed in both English and French. It's interesting to note that card #50 lists the winners of the Parkhurst Zip Gum Hockey Contest originally offered on the backs of 1958-59 Parkhurst hockey cards. Oversized versions (approximately 3" by 4") of six cards exist featuring the fronts of 12 Hawes Wax cards (#9/26/29/31/33/35/37/38/39/40/43/44) placed back-to-back. Reportedly, the six cards were part of a game produced in Canada that also included additional cards of non-racing subjects. These six cards are valued at approximately $20.00 each.

COMPLETE SET (50)	500.00	800.00
1 Ray Harroun	12.00	20.00
2 Joe Dawson	12.00	20.00
3 Jules Goux	12.00	20.00
4 Rene Thomas	12.00	20.00
5 Ralph dePalma	15.00	25.00
6 Dario Resta	12.00	20.00
7 Howard Wilcox	12.00	20.00
8 Gaston Chevrolet	15.00	25.00
9 Tommy Milton	12.00	20.00
10 Jimmy Murphy	12.00	20.00
11 Tommy Milton	12.00	20.00
12 L.L.Corum	12.00	20.00
Joe Boyer		
13 Peter DePaolo	12.00	20.00
14 Frank Lockhart	12.00	20.00
15 George Souders	12.00	20.00
16 Louis Meyer	12.00	20.00
17 Ray Keech	12.00	20.00
18 Billy Arnold	12.00	20.00
19 Louis Schneider	12.00	20.00
20 Fred Frame	12.00	20.00
21 Louis Meyer	12.00	20.00
22 Bill Cummings	12.00	20.00
23 Kelly Petillo	12.00	20.00
24 Louis Meyer	12.00	20.00
25 Wilbur Shaw	12.00	20.00
26 Floyd Roberts	12.00	20.00
27 Wilbur Shaw	12.00	20.00
28 Purdue University Band	12.00	20.00
29 Mauri Rose	12.00	20.00
Floyd Davis		
(Rose pictured)		
30 George Robson	12.00	20.00
31 Mauri Rose	12.00	20.00
32 Rodger Ward VL	15.00	25.00
33 Bill Holland	12.00	20.00
34 Johnnie Parsons	15.00	25.00
35 Lee Wallard	12.00	20.00
36 Troy Ruttman	12.00	20.00
37 Bill Vukovich	15.00	25.00
38 Start of Parade Lap	12.00	20.00
race action		
39 Bob Sweikert	12.00	20.00
40 Pat Flaherty	12.00	20.00
41 Sam Hanks	12.00	20.00
42 Jimmy Bryan	12.00	20.00
43 Rodger Ward	15.00	25.00
44 Tony Bettenhausen in Pits	15.00	25.00
45 Rodger Ward w/wife	15.00	25.00
46 The Borg-Warner Trophy	12.00	20.00
47 Main Gate of IMS	12.00	20.00
48 IMS Museum	12.00	20.00
49 Paul Russo in Pits	12.00	20.00
50 Parade Lap	12.00	20.00
back lists winners of		
Zip Gum Hockey Contest		

1992 Hi-Tech Indy Prototypes

Hi-Tech produced this 6-card set to promote several upcoming releases. The cards represent samples from different sets intended to be released by Hi-Tech. The cover card mentions that 15,000 Prototype sets were produced. The sets were also sold matted under glass and framed. The matting carried the number (of 15,000) for each set.

COMPLETE SET (6)		
1 Mario Andretti	1.50	4.00
2 Al Unser Jr's Car	1.50	4.00
Scott Goodyear's Car		
3 Michael Andretti	1.00	2.50
4 Paul Newman	2.00	5.00
5 Cover Card	.40	1.00
6 Scott Goodyear	1.50	4.00

1992 Hi-Tech Mario Andretti

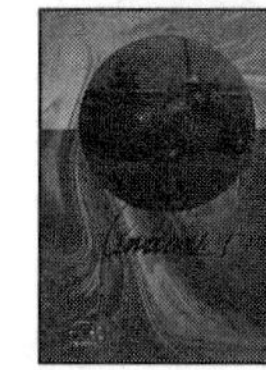

Hi-Tech produced this set in 1992, but actually released it in early 1993. The cards were distributed in factory set form in a tin box package. The set commemorates the long career of Mario Andretti and was limited to 100,000 51-card sets. A #52 card was also produced (5000 made) with 2500 signed copies randomly inserted in some factory sets. It is not considered part of the complete set price.

COMPLETE FACTORY SET (51)	10.00	20.00
1 Mario Andretti	.30	.75
2 Mario Andretti	.30	.75
Aldo Andretti		
3 Mario Andretti's Car	.12	.30
White Hudson		
4 Mario Andretti's Car	.12	.30
Fuel Activator Special		
5 Mario Andretti in Car	.30	.75
6 Mario Andretti	.30	.75
Ed Mataka		
Bill Mataka		
7 Mario Andretti in Car	.30	.75
8 Mario Andretti in Car	.30	.75
9 Mario Andretti in Car	.30	.75
10 Mario Andretti in Car	.30	.75
11 Mario Andretti in Car	.30	.75
12 Mario Andretti	.30	.75
13 Mario Andretti	.30	.75
14 Mario Andretti in Car	.30	.75
15 Mario Andretti's Car	.20	.50
A.J.Foyt's Car		
16 Mario Andretti	.30	.75
Clint Brawner		
17 Mario Andretti	.30	.75
Chuck Rodee		
18 Mario Andretti in Car	.30	.75
19 Mario Andretti	.30	.75
20 Mario Andretti's Car	.12	.30
21 Mario Andretti in Car	.30	.75
22 Mario Andretti	.30	.75
23 Mario Andretti w/Car	.30	.75
24 Mario Andretti in Car	.30	.75
25 Mario Andretti's Car	.12	.30
26 Mario Andretti	.30	.75
27 Mario Andretti in Car	.30	.75
28 Mario Andretti in Car	.30	.75
29 Mario Andretti in Car	.30	.75
30 Mario Andretti	.30	.75
Jackie Ickx		
31 Mario Andretti in Car	.30	.75
32 Mario Andretti in Car	.30	.75
33 Mario Andretti in Car	.30	.75
34 Mario Andretti	.30	.75
35 Mario Andretti in Car	.30	.75
36 Mario Andretti	.30	.75
37 Mario Andretti in Car	.30	.75
38 Mario Andretti's Car	.12	.30
39 Mario Andretti's Car	.12	.30
40 Mario Andretti	.30	.75
41 Mario Andretti in Car	.30	.75
42 Mario Andretti's Car	.12	.30
43 Mario Andretti's Car	.12	.30
44 Mario Andretti	.30	.75
Michael Andretti		
45 Mario Andretti	.30	.75
46 Mario Andretti	.30	.75
Al Unser Jr.		
Tom Sneva		
47 Mario Andretti	.30	.75
48 Mario Andretti	.30	.75
49 Mario Andretti's Car	.20	.50
A.J.Foyt's Car		
Rick Mears' Car		
50 Mario Andretti's Car	.12	.30
51 Checklist Card	.07	.20
52 Mario Andretti Signature Card	.30	.75
Unsigned		
P1 Mario Andretti Prototype	.60	1.50
unnumbered card		

1993 Hi-Tech Indy Prototypes

Hi-Tech produced these six-cards to preview the 1993 IndyCar set. The cards are numbered P1/6, P2/6, etc. and are often sold as a complete set.

COMPLETE SET (6)	8.00	16.00
P1 Danny Sullivan	1.50	3.00
P2 Scott Goodyear	1.50	3.00
P3 Eddie Cheever's Car	.75	2.00
P4 Bobby Rahal's Car FOIL	1.50	3.00
P5 Eddie Cheever's Car FOIL	.75	2.00
P6 Al Unser's Car FOIL	2.00	4.00

1993 Hi-Tech Indy

Hi-Tech produced this set featuring drivers of the 1992 Indianapolis 500. The cards were released in 10-card packs with 36-packs per box. Reportedly, production was limited to 4000 cases. Cards from the Checkered Flag Finishers set were randomly inserted into packs.

COMPLETE SET (81)	4.00	10.00
1 Roberto Guerrero	.08	.25
2 Eddie Cheever	.05	.15
3 Mario Andretti	.30	.75
4 Arie Luyendyk	.08	.25
5 Gary Bettenhausen	.08	.25
6 Michael Andretti	.15	.40
7 Scott Brayton	.05	.15
8 Danny Sullivan	.08	.25
9 Rick Mears	.15	.40
10 Bobby Rahal	.08	.25
11 Emerson Fittipaldi	.15	.40
12 Al Unser Jr.	.15	.40
13 Stan Fox	.05	.15
14 John Andretti	.15	.40
15 Eric Bachelart	.05	.15
16 Philippe Gache	.05	.15
17 Scott Pruett	.05	.15
18 John Paul Jr.	.05	.15
19 Paul Tracy	.08	.25
20 Jeff Andretti	.15	.40
21 Jim Crawford	.05	.15
22 Al Unser	.08	.25
23 A.J. Foyt	.15	.40
24 Buddy Lazier	.05	.15
25 Raul Boesel	.05	.15
26 Brian Bonner	.05	.15
27 Lyn St. James	.08	.25
28 Jimmy Vasser	.05	.15
29 Dominic Dobson	.05	.15
30 Tom Sneva	.08	.25
31 Gordon Johncock	.08	.25
32 Ted Prappas	.05	.15
33 Scott Goodyear	.05	.15
34 Al Unser Jr.	.15	.40
Indy Champ		
35 Roberto Guerrero	.08	.25
Pole Win		
36 Al Unser Jr.	.15	.40
37 Scott Goodyear	.05	.15
38 Al Unser	.08	.25
39 Eddie Cheever	.05	.15
40 Danny Sullivan	.08	.25
41 Bobby Rahal	.08	.25
42 Raul Boesel	.05	.15
43 John Andretti	.15	.40
44 A.J. Foyt	.15	.40
45 John Paul Jr.	.05	.15
46 Lyn St. James	.08	.25
47 Dominic Dobson	.05	.15
48 Michael Andretti	.15	.40
49 Buddy Lazier	.05	.15
50 Arie Luyendyk	.08	.25
51 Ted Prappas	.05	.15
52 Gary Bettenhausen	.08	.25
53 Jeff Andretti	.15	.40
54 Brian Bonner	.05	.15
55 Paul Tracy	.08	.25
56 Jimmy Vasser	.05	.15
57 Scott Brayton	.05	.15
58 Mario Andretti	.30	.75
59 Emerson Fittipaldi	.15	.40
60 Jim Crawford	.05	.15
61 Rick Mears	.15	.40
62 Stan Fox	.05	.15
63 Philippe Gache	.05	.15
64 Gordon Johncock	.08	.25
65 Scott Pruett	.05	.15
66 Tom Sneva	.08	.25
67 Eric Bachelart	.05	.15
68 Roberto Guerrero	.08	.25
69 1992 Pace Car	.05	.15
70 Roberto Guerrero	.20	.50
Eddie Cheever		
Mario Andretti		
71 Mario Andretti's Car	.08	.25
Michael Andretti's Car		
72 Al Unser Jr.'s Car	.08	.25
73 Race Start	.05	.15
74 Pit Crew Practice	.05	.15
75 Tom Sneva's Car	.05	.15
Jimmy Vasser's Car		
76 Nelson Piquet's Car	.05	.15
77 Gordon Johncock's Car	.05	.15
78 Protective Coverings	.05	.15
Pit Row		
79 Eric Bachelart's Car	.05	.15
80 Race Accidents	.05	.15
81 Checklist Card	.05	.15

1993 Hi-Tech Indy Checkered Flag Finishers

Randomly inserted in 1993 Hi-Tech Indy packs, these 12-cards feature top drivers printed on holographic foil card stock.

COMPLETE SET (12)	15.00	30.00
SP2 Scott Goodyear	1.00	2.00

SP4 Eddie Cheever	1.00	2.00
SP5 Danny Sullivan	1.50	3.00
SP6 Bobby Rahal	1.50	3.00
SP7 Raul Boesel	1.00	2.00
SP8 John Andretti	1.50	3.00
SP10 John Paul Jr.	1.00	2.00
SP11 Lyn St. James	1.00	2.00
SP12 Dominic Dobson	1.00	2.00

1994 Hi-Tech Indy Prototypes

Hi-Tech produced these three cards to preview the 1994 IndyCar set. The cards are numbered P1/3, P2/3 and P3/3 and are often sold as a complete set.

COMPLETE SET (3)	4.00	8.00
P1 Nigel Mansell's Car	.75	2.00
P2 Mario Andretti's Car	1.00	2.50
P3 Mario Andretti	1.50	4.00

1994 Hi-Tech Indy

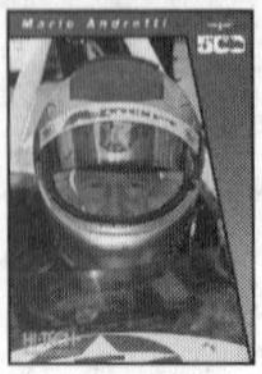

The 1993 Indianapolis 500 is the subject of this Hi-Tech production. The cards were distributed in complete set form with all insert cards. There were a reported 25,000 sets produced.

COMPLETE SET (51)	4.00	8.00
1 Cover Card	.05	.15
Emerson Fittipaldi		
2 Emerson Fittipaldi	.15	.40
3 Arie Luyendyk's Car	.05	.15
4 Nigel Mansell	.15	.40
5 Raul Boesel's Car	.05	.15
6 Mario Andretti	.30	.75
7 Scott Brayton's Car	.05	.15
8 Scott Goodyear	.05	.15
9 Al Unser Jr.	.15	.40
10 Teo Fabi's Car	.05	.15
11 John Andretti	.15	.40
12 Stefan Johansson	.05	.15
13 Al Unser	.15	.40
14 Jimmy Vasser	.05	.15
15 Kevin Cogan	.05	.15
16 Davy Jones	.05	.15
17 Eddie Cheever in Pits	.05	.15
18 Gary Bettenhausen	.08	.25
19 Hiro Matsushita's Car	.05	.15
20 Stephan Gregoire in Pits	.05	.15
21 Tony Bettenhausen's Car	.05	.15
22 Willy T. Ribbs	.05	.15
23 Didier Theys' Car	.05	.15
24 Dominic Dobson	.05	.15
25 Jim Crawford	.05	.15
26 Lyn St. James	.15	.40
27 Geoff Brabham's Car	.05	.15
28 Robby Gordon's Car	.08	.25
29 Roberto Guerrero	.05	.15
30 Jeff Andretti's Car	.05	.15
31 Paul Tracy	.08	.25
32 Stan Fox in Pits	.05	.15
33 Nelson Piquet	.05	.15
34 Danny Sullivan	.08	.25
35 Mark Smith	.05	.15
36 Bobby Rahal	.15	.40
37 Stephan Gregoire	.08	.25
Nelson Piquet		
Robby Gordon		
Stefan Johansson		
Nigel Mansell		
1993 Rookies		
38 A.J. Foyt's Car	.08	.25
Foyt Salute		
39 Arie Luyendyk Pole Win	.05	.15
40 Arie Luyendyk	.15	.40
Mario Andretti		
Raul Boesel		
41 The Staring Grid	.05	.15
42 Arie Luyendyk's Car	.05	.15
Mario Andretti's Car		
Raul Boesel's Car		
Pace Lap		
43 The Start	.05	.15
Indy 500		
44 Pit Action	.05	.15
45 Nigel Mansell in Pits	.05	.15
46 Jeff Andretti's Car	.05	.15
Roberto Guerrero's Car		
Crash		
47 Emerson Fittipaldi's Car	.05	.15
Checkered Flag		
48 Emerson Fittipaldi Winner	.05	.15
49 Rick Mears	.05	.15
Brian Armenoff		
Race Rick Contest		
50 Brian Armenoff	.05	.15
51 Checklist Card	.05	.15

1994 Hi-Tech Indy Championship Drivers

Inserted one set per 1994 Hi-Tech Indy factory set, these cards feature top IndyCar drivers with extensive biographical information on the cardback.

COMPLETE SET (36)	7.50	15.00
CD1 Jeff Andretti	.20	.50
CD2 John Andretti	.30	.75
CD3 Mario Andretti	.50	1.25
CD4 Michael Andretti	.30	.75
CD5 Ross Bentley	.20	.50
CD6 Gary Bettenhausen	.20	.50
CD7 Raul Boesel	.20	.50
CD8 Scott Brayton	.20	.50
CD9 Robbie Buhl	.20	.50
CD10 Eddie Cheever	.20	.50
CD11 Jim Crawford	.20	.50
CD12 Dominic Dobson	.20	.50
CD13 Emerson Fittipaldi	.30	.75
CD14 A.J. Foyt	.40	1.00
CD15 Stan Fox	.20	.50
CD16 Scott Goodyear	.20	.50
CD17 Mike Groff	.20	.50
CD18 Roberto Guerrero	.20	.50
CD19 Stefan Johansson	.20	.50
CD20 Gordon Johncock	.20	.50
CD21 Buddy Lazier	.20	.50
CD22 Arie Luyendyk	.20	.50
CD23 Rick Mears	.30	.75
CD24 Johnny Parsons Jr.	.20	.50
CD25 Ted Prappas	.20	.50
CD26 Scott Pruett	.20	.50
CD27 Bobby Rahal	.30	.75
CD28 Johnny Rutherford	.30	.75
CD29 Lyn St. James	.30	.75
CD30 Mark Smith	.20	.50
CD31 Tom Sneva	.20	.50
CD32 Danny Sullivan	.30	.75
CD33 Didier Theys	.20	.50
CD34 Paul Tracy	.30	.75
CD35 Al Unser Jr.	.20	.50
CD36 Jimmy Vasser	.20	.50

1994 Hi-Tech Indy A.J. Foyt

A.J.Foyt is the focus of this Hi-Tech issue. The cards were inserted one set per 1994 Hi-Tech Indy factory set and highlight Foyt's first and last races, as well as his four wins at IMS.

COMPLETE SET (6)	2.50	5.00
COMMON CARD (AJ1-AJ6)	.50	1.00

1994 Hi-Tech Indy Rick Mears

Rick Mears is the focus of this Hi-Tech issue. The cards were inserted one set per 1994 Hi-Tech Indy factory set and highlight Mears' first and last races, as well as his four wins at IMS.

COMPLETE SET (6)	2.50	5.00
COMMON CARD (RM1-RM6)	.50	1.00

1995 Hi-Tech Indy Championship Drivers

This 11-card set features some of the top drivers on the IndyCar circuit. The sets were sold in complete set form at Indianapolis Motor Speedway. They were also made available to Hi-Tech Club members.

COMPLETE SET (11)	6.00	15.00
CD1 Al Unser Jr.	.75	2.00
CD2 Eddie Cheever	.30	.75
CD3 Emerson Fittipaldi	.75	2.00
CD4 Scott Pruett	.30	.75
CD5 Raul Boesel	.30	.75
CD6 Paul Tracy	.50	1.25
CD7 Jacques Villeneuve	.50	1.25
CD8 Michael Andretti	.75	2.00
CD9 Danny Sullivan	.50	1.25
CD10 Paul Newman	.75	2.00
CD11 Mario Andretti	1.25	3.00

1997 Hi-Tech IRL

This set commemorates the first season of the Indy Racing League. The set comes in a factory box that contains all 94-cards and a Dodge Viper Pace Car die-cast. There are six different sets within the factory set box. The 38-card base set features drivers from the IRL circuit. The 20-card Indy 500 set features the 80th Anniversary of the Indy 500. There was also a 10-card Disney 200 set, a nine card Phoenix set, a eight-card tribute to Scott Brayton and a eight-card set featuring the Dodge Viper.

COMP.FACT.SET (94)	10.00	25.00
COMP. IRL SET (38)	4.00	10.00
1 IRL Cover Card	.07	.20
2 Scott Sharp	.15	.40
3 Buzz Calkins	.15	.40
4 Robbie Buhl	.15	.40
5 Richie Hearn	.15	.40
6 Roberto Guerrero	.15	.40
7 Mike Groff	.15	.40
8 Arie Luyendyk	.30	.75
9 Tony Stewart XRC	2.00	5.00
10 Davey Hamilton	.07	.20
11 Johnny O'Connell	.07	.20
12 Michele Alboreto	.07	.20
13 Lyn St.James	.15	.40
14 Stephan Gregoire	.07	.20
15 Buddy Lazier	.15	.40
16 John Paul Jr.	.07	.20
17 Eddie Cheever	.07	.20
18 Johnny Parsons	.07	.20
19 Scott Brayton	.30	.75
20 David Kudrave	.07	.20
21 Michel Jourdain	.07	.20
22 Jim Guthrie	.07	.20
23 Fermin Velez	.07	.20
24 Eliseo Salazar	.07	.20
25 Johnny Unser	.15	.40
26 Stan Wattles	.07	.20
27 Davy Jones	.15	.40
28 Paul Durant	.07	.20
29 Alessandro Zampedri	.07	.20
30 Danny Ongais	.07	.20
31 Hideshi Matsuda	.07	.20
32 Scott Harrington	.07	.20
33 Racin Gardner	.07	.20
34 Mark Dismore	.07	.20
35 Joe Gosek	.07	.20
36 Brad Murphey	.07	.20
37 Marco Greco	.07	.20
NNO Checklist	.07	.20

1997 Hi-Tech IRL Disney 200

These 10-cards were issued along with the rest of the 1997 Hi-Tech IRL release in factory set form. The set was produced to commemorate the inaugural Disney 200 IRL event.

COMPLETE SET (10)	2.50	6.00
D1 Disney Track	.08	.25
D2 The Field	.08	.25
D3 Tony Stewart	1.50	4.00
Buzz Calkins' Cars		
D4 Mike Groff's Car	.15	.40
D5 Johnny Parson	.40	1.00
Eddie Chever's Cars		
D6 Stephan Gregoire	.40	1.00
Buddy Lazier's Cars		
D7 Michele Alboreto's Car	.15	.40
D8 The Field	.08	.25
D9 Buzz Calkins' Car	.15	.40
D10 Buzz Calkins	.30	.75

1997 Hi-Tech IRL Indy 500

This set features top drivers and cars that participated in the Indy 500. The set was issued one per 1997 Hi-Tech IRL factory set.

COMPLETE SET (20)	2.50	6.00
I1 Indy 500 Cover Card	.07	.20
I2 Scott Brayton	.20	.50
I3 Starting Grid	.07	.20
I4 Alessa Zampedri's Car	.10	.30
Michel Jourdain's Car		
Buzz Calkins' Car		
I5 The Field	.07	.20
I6 Viper Pace Car	.07	.20
I7 A.J. Foyt	.50	1.25
I8 Scott Sharp's Car	.20	.50
I9 Michele Alboreto's Car	.10	.30
I10 Eliseo Salazar's Car	.20	.50
I11 Viper Pace Car	.07	.20
I12 Robbie Buhl's Car	.20	.50
I13 Danny Ongais's Car	.10	.30
I14 Buddy Lazier's Car	.20	.50
I15 Davy Jones's Car	.20	.50
I16 Richie Hearn's Car	.20	.50
I17 Alessandro Zampedri's Car	.10	.30
I18 Roberto Guerrero's Car	.20	.50
I19 Buddy Lazier's Car	.20	.50
I20 Buddy Lazier	.30	.75

1997 Hi-Tech IRL Phoenix

This set features top driver's and participants in the IRL event run in Phoenix. One set was included in each 1997 Hi-Tech IRL factory set.

COMPLETE SET (10)	1.25	3.00
P1 Phoenix Track	.07	.20
P2 Tony George	.15	.40
P3 Scott Brayton's Car	.15	.40
P4 Pace Car	.07	.20
P5 The Field	.07	.20
P6 Pace Car	.07	.20
P7 Roberto Guerrero's Car	.60	1.50
Tony Stewart's Car		
P8 Arie Luyendyk's Car	.15	.40
Scott Brayton's Car		
P9 Arie Luyendyk	.20	.50
P10 Cover Card	.07	.20

1997 Hi-Tech IRL Scott Brayton

This set is a tribute to Scott Brayton. One set was included in each 1997 Hi-Tech IRL factory set.

COMPLETE SET (8)	.75	2.00
COMMON CARD (BR1-BR8)	.10	.30

1997 Hi-Tech IRL Viper Pace Car

This set features the Dodge Viper Pace car for the Indy 500. One 8-card set was included in each 1997 Hi-Tech IRL factory set.

COMPLETE SET (8)	.20	.50
COMMON CARD (V1-V8)	.02	.10

1988 Heraclio Fournier Formula One

This set of 34-cards are pieces of a card game produced in Spain. They contain a typical playing card back, are a small size (2-1/4" by 3-1/2) and feature Grand Prix drivers on the cardfront. All text is in Spanish and the cards are numbered similarly to other playing card decks.

COMPLETE SET (34)	4.00	10.00
1A Rosenberg's Car	.07	.20
1B Riccardo Patrese's Car	.20	.50
1C Rene Arnoux's Car	.07	.20
1D Martin Brundle's Car	.10	.30
2A Michele Alboreto's Car	.10	.30
2B Alan Jones' Car	.07	.20
2C Patrick Tambay's Car	.07	.20
2D Thierry Boutsen's Car	.10	.30
3A Stefan Johansson's Car	.10	.30
3B Pierluigi Martini's Car	.10	.30
3C Piercarlo Ghinzani's Car	.07	.20
3D Gerhard Berger's Car	.20	.50
4A Alain Prost's Car	.20	.50
4B Ayrton Senna's Car	.75	2.00
4C Thackwell's Car	.07	.20
4D Jonathan Palmer's Car	.07	.20
5A Emerson Fittipaldi's Car	.20	.50
5B Rick Mears' Car	.20	.50
5C Al Unser Jr.'s Car	.30	.75
5D Mauricio Gugelmin's Car	.10	.30
6A Kaiser's Car	.07	.20
6B Thackwell's Car	.07	.20
6C Philippe Streiff's Car	.07	.20
6D Raphanel's Car	.07	.20
7A Morin's Car	.07	.20
7B Huysmann's Car	.07	.20
7C Nicola Larini's Car	.07	.20
7D Trolle's Car	.07	.20
8A Stefano Modena's Car	.07	.20
8B Yannick Dalmas' Car	.07	.20
8C Artzlet's Car	.07	.20
8D Birne's Car	.07	.20
NNO Cover Card	.07	.20
Rene Arnoux's Car		

2002 Indianapolis 500

This set of 16-cards was released at the 2002 Indianapolis 500 as a perforated sheet. Each card features a color photo of an IRL driver surrounded by a brown border. The cardbacks are a simple white card stock with black lettering.

COMPLETE SET (16)	7.50	15.00
1 Alex Barron	.30	.75
2 Billy Boat	.30	.75
3 Robbie Buhl	.30	.75
4 Eddie Cheever Jr.	.40	1.00
5 Airton Dare	.30	.75
6 Sarah Fisher	1.00	2.50
7 Felipe Giaffone	.30	.75
8 Sam Hornish Jr.	.60	1.50
9 Buddy Lazier	.40	1.00
10 Arie Luyendyk	.40	1.00
11 George Mack	.30	.75
12 Robby McGehee	.30	.75
13 Greg Ray	.40	1.00
14 Scott Sharp	.60	1.50
15 Al Unser Jr.	.60	1.50
16 Jeff Ward	.30	.75

1991 K-Mart

K-Mart produced and distributed this two card set in 1991 featuring the K-Mart/Texaco Havoline sponsored IndyCar Racing Team.

COMPLETE SET (2)	1.25	3.00
1 Mario Andretti	.75	2.00
2 Michael Andretti	.40	1.00

1992 K-Mart

This two card set was produced and distributed by K-Mart Stores in 1992. It features the K-Mart/Texaco Havoline sponsored IndyCar Racing Team.

COMPLETE SET (2)	1.25	3.00
1 Mario Andretti	.75	2.00
2 Michael Andretti	.50	1.25

1993 K-Mart

K-Mart produced and distributed this two card set in 1992 featuring the K-Mart/Texaco Havoline sponsored IndyCar Racing Team. The cards are distinguishable by the silver border.

COMPLETE SET (2)	1.25	3.00
1 Mario Andretti	.75	2.00
2 Nigel Mansell	.40	1.00

1994 K-Mart

Silver and black borders help distinguish the fourth K-Mart issue from the previous three releases. It again features the K-Mart/Texaco Havoline sponsored IndyCar Racing Team headlined by Mario Andretti.

COMPLETE SET (2)	1.25	3.00
1 Mario Andretti	.75	2.00
2 Nigel Mansell	.40	1.00

1991 Langenberg American IndyCar Series

Langenberg Racing produced this set entitled 1991 Hot Stuff. The set features then present and past drivers of the American IndyCar Series. The set features the only Unser to run at the IRL's 1996 Indy 500, Johnny. The set also includes Rodger Ward, the winner of the 1959 and 1962 Indy 500.

COMPLETE SET (18)	4.00	10.00
1 Cover Card	.10	.30

Bill Tempero's Car		
2 Bill Tempero		.20
3 Robby Unser in Car		.30
4 Johnny Unser		.30
5 Jimmy Santos		.20
6 Rick Sutherland		.20
7 Jim Buick		.20
8 Eddie Miller		.20
9 Bob Tankersley		.20
10 Bill Hansen		.20
11 Rocco Desimone		.20
12 Don Johnson		.20
13 Ken Petrie		.20
14 Kevin Whitesides		.20
15 Ken Petrie's Car		.20
Eddie Miller's Car		
16 Todd Snyder's Car		.30
Robby Unser's Car		
17 Rodger Ward		.30
18 Checklist Card		.10
1991 Schedule on back		

1991 Legends of In

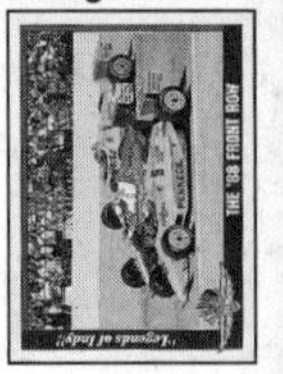

The first of two Legends of Indy sets was p in 1991 by Collegiate Collection of Ken celebrate the 75th Indy 500. The car distributed in complete set form and feature present stars of the IndyCar circuit. An a house the cards was also produced and o sold for $8.95 plus $2.50 shipping. The fina the set could have been redeemed for a spe of the 1991 race winner Rick Mears.

COMPLETE SET (100)	6.00	
1 The Start	.02	
2 Largest Starting Field	.02	
1933 field		
3 Norman Batten	.02	
4 Parnelli Jones' Car	.05	
A Turbine Almost Wins		
5 Paul Russo's Car	.02	
Fageol's Twin Coach Special		
6 Eddie Sachs' Car	.02	
A.J.Foyt's Car		
The Sachs/Foyt Duel		
7 Transporters	.02	
8 Bill Holland's Car	.02	
Mauri Rose's Car		
Holland and the EZY sign		
9 Carl Graham Fisher	.02	
Arthur Newby		
Frank Wheeler		
James Allison		
The Track Founders		
10 New Garage Area	.02	
11 The Brick Surface	.02	
12 Jim Clark's Car	.02	
Rear-Engine Almost Wins		
13 First Rear Engine to Start	.02	
1939 Rear-Engine Car		
14 Ralph dePalma in Pits	.02	
15 Mary Fendrich Hulman	.02	
16 Pete DePaolo	.05	
17 Johnnie Parsons' Car	.02	
18 Lee Wallard	.05	
Cinderella Man		
19 Arie Luyendyk's Car	.10	
Fastest 500		
20 Sam Hanks' Car	.02	
Wins with an Experiment		
21 Pre-500 Garage Area	.02	
22 The 1911 Front Row	.02	
23 First Pace Car	.02	
1911 race		
24 Pit Stop	.02	
3 Bud Car		
25 Jules Goux w/Car	.05	
26 Economical Maxwell	.02	
27 Tony Hulman	.02	
Luke Walton		
28 Freddie Agabashian's Car	.02	
A Diesel On The Pole		
29 Tommy Milton	.05	
Louis Meyer		
Presentation Pace Car		
30 Wilbur Shaw	.05	
31 Rick Mears' Car	.10	
Rick's Records		
32 Eddie Rickenbacker	.05	
Tony Hulman		
33 Lou Moore's Car	.02	
34 Dale Evans' Car	.02	
35 Duke Nalon's Crash	.05	
Duke's Lucky Escape		
36 Tangled Start	.02	
37 Wilbur Shaw's Crash	.05	

aw Clears the Wall		
ly Effort By Ford	.02	.10
k Mears' Car	.10	.30
ardon Johncock's Car		
e Closest Finish		
mpson Special	.02	.10
ester Gardner's Car	.02	.10
el Consumption		
ck Brabham's Car	.02	.10
nelli Jones w/Crew	.10	.30
e First 150		
ly Devore's Car	.02	.10
e Six-Wheeler		
e Leonard's Car	.05	.15
rbine Almost Wins		
bby Unser w/Car	.20	.50
ester Miller w/Car	.05	.15
Hopped-Up Model T		
nny Sullivan's Car	.10	.30
eedway's First Event	.02	.10
otorcycles	.02	.10
bby Rahal's Car	.10	.30
ck Mears' Car		
vin Cogan's Car		
e Closest Finish		
e Stutz Team	.02	.10
et Miller's Car	.02	.10
rage Fire	.02	.10
bby Johns' Car	.02	.10
nokey's Sidecar		
ck to Asphalt	.02	.10
n Clark's Car	.05	.15
ar-Engine Win		
w Tower and Pit Lane	.02	.10
Unser Jr.'s Car	.20	.50
erson Fittipaldi's Car		
mo And Little Al		
ve Lewis' Car	.02	.10
0's First Front Drive		
eamliners	.02	.10
n Sneva w/Crew	.10	.30
debakers	.02	.10
Victory Lane	.02	.10
ny Hulman	.40	1.00
J.Foyt		
p Of Honor		
et Guthrie w/Car	.20	.50
e 1923 Lineup	.02	.10
erson Fittipaldi w/Car	.20	.50
nning A Million		
loons	.02	.10
bby Unser's Car	.10	.30
nning In The Rain		
Unser's Car	.20	.50
nset Winner		
y Ruttman's Car	.02	.10
is Schwitzer's Car	.02	.10
eedway's First Race		
k Mears' Car	.20	.50
nny Sullivan's Car		
Unser's Car		
e '88 Front Row		
ph dePalma w/Car	.05	.15
Palma Pushes Home		
Vukovich's Car	.05	.15
mmy Bryan's Car		
ky Laps the Field		
wers' Meeting	.02	.10
e Pagoda	.02	.10
e Old Front Gate	.02	.10
n Sneva's Car	.10	.30
rage Doors		
ial View, 1922	.02	.10
ial View Today	.02	.10
mmy Murphy's Car	.05	.15
st Winner from the Pole		
l Of Fame Museum	.02	.10
Rathmann's Car	.05	.15
dger Ward's Car		
thmann/Ward Duel		
rio Andretti	.50	1.25
dy Granatelli		
rio Wins For Andy		
Harroun's Car	.02	.10
e Marmon Wasp		
nny Rutherford's Car	.10	.30
ree For JR		
l Russo's Car	.02	.10
e Novi		
ak Days	.02	.10
Vinter's Scene	.02	.10
t Card	.02	.10
t Card	.02	.10
t Card	.02	.10
t Card	.02	.10
t Card	.02	.10
t Card	.02	.10
t Card	.02	.10
t Card	.02	.10
Cover Card	.02	.10
91 Winner card		
er on back		
Rick Mears	10.00	25.00
91 Race Winner		

992 Legends of Indy

t of two Legends of Indy sets was produced in y G.S.S. of Indiana to celebrate the Indy 500. The cards were distributed in 10-card packs and feature past and present stars of the IndyCar circuit. Factory sets numbered of 25,000 were wrapped in a blister type packaging. An album to house the cards was also produced and offered for sale, along with the 1991 card album, for $9.95 plus $2.50 shipping. The coupon for the album offer also contained an offer to purchase complete sets of the 1991 series at $14.95 plus $3.50 shipping.

COMPLETE SET (100)	4.00	10.00
1 Rick Mears	.08	.25
Four Time Winner		
2 Rick Mears' Car	.05	.15
3 Michael Andretti's Car	.08	.25
4 Arie Luyendyk's Car	.05	.15
5 Al Unser Jr.'s Car	.08	.25
6 John Andretti's Car	.05	.15
7 Gordon Johncock's Car	.02	.10
8 Mario Andretti's Car	.08	.25
9 Stan Fox's Car	.02	.10
10 Tony Bettenhausen in Pits	.02	.10
11 Danny Sullivan's Car	.02	.10
12 Emerson Fittipaldi's Car	.05	.15
13 Scott Pruett's Car	.02	.10
14 Dominic Dobson's Car	.02	.10
15 Randy Lewis's Car	.02	.10
16 Jeff Andretti's Car	.02	.10
17 Hiro Matsushita's Car	.02	.10
18 Scott Brayton's Car	.02	.10
19 Bernard Jourdain's Car	.02	.10
20 Bobby Rahal in Pits	.05	.15
21 Geoff Brabham's Car	.02	.10
22 Pancho Carter's Car	.02	.10
23 Gary Bettenhausen's Car	.02	.10
24 Tero Palmroth's Car	.02	.10
25 Mike Groff's Car	.02	.10
26 John Paul Jr.'s Car	.02	.10
27 Jim Crawford's Car	.02	.10
28 Scott Goodyear's Car	.02	.10
29 A.J. Foyt Jr.'s Car	.08	.25
30 Kevin Cogan's Car	.02	.10
31 Roberto Guerrero's Car	.05	.15
32 Eddie Cheever's Car	.02	.10
33 Willy T. Ribbs's Car	.02	.10
34 Buddy Lazier's Car	.02	.10
35 Hiro Matsushita's Car	.02	.10
36 Willy T. Ribbs	.02	.10
37 Arie Luyendyk	.05	.15
with Dan Quayle		
Special Visitor		
38 Danny Sullivan's Car	.02	.10
39 1991 Pace Car	.02	.10
40 John Andretti's Car	.05	.15
Scott Pruett's Car		
Gordon Johncock's Car		
Race Action		
41 The General	.02	.10
Norman Schwartzkopf		
42 Rick Mears' Car	.05	.15
Michael Andretti's Car		
43 Rick Mears' Car	.05	.15
A.J.Foyt's Car		
Mario Andretti's Car		
Illustrious Front Row		
44 Rick Mears' Car	.05	.15
Checker for Mears		
45 1991 Start	.02	.10
46 A.J.Foyt's Car	.05	.15
Ovation for A.J.		
47 1980 Pace Car	.02	.10
48 1981 Pace Car	.02	.10
49 1982 Pace Car	.02	.10
50 1983 Pace Car	.02	.10
51 1984 Pace Car	.02	.10
52 1985 Pace Car	.02	.10
53 1986 Pace Car	.02	.10
54 1987 Pace Car	.02	.10
55 1988 Pace Car	.02	.10
56 1989 Pace Car	.02	.10
57 A.J.Foyt w/Car	.20	.50
Tony George		
A.J.Foyt 's 34TH		
58 Mario Andretti's Car	.08	.25
Dihedral Wings		
59 Hall of Fame Museum	.02	.10
60 Alberto Ascari's Car	.02	.10
Ferrari At Indy		
61 Janet Guthrie	.05	.15
Dick Simon		
Janet Qualifies		
62 Al Unser's Car	.05	.15
Yard of Bricks		
63 1968 Pace Lap	.02	.10
64 A.J.Foyt's Car	.08	.25
Johnny Rutherford's Car		
Two Tough Texans		
65 Yellow Flag	.02	.10
66 How They Line Up	.02	.10
67 Pre-Race Laps	.02	.10
68 1969 Start	.02	.10
69 Mario Andretti's Car	.08	.25
Mario's Backup Wins		
70 Joe Leonard in Pits	.02	.10
with Andy Granatelli		
Leonard Pit Stop		
71 Parnelli Jones' Car	.02	.10
Don Branson's Car		
Jim Hurtubise's Car		
1963 Front Row		
72 Al Unser's Car	.05	.15
Victory Lane is Moved		
73 Tommy Milton	.02	.10
Harry Stutz		
Howdy Wilcox		
with cars		
HCS Specials		
74 Chet Miller's Car	.02	.10
Front Drive Novis		
75 Peter Revson w/Car	.02	.10
Revson's Upset		
76 Danny Sullivan's Car	.05	.15
Mario Andretti's Car		
77 Lloyd Ruby in Pits	.02	.10
78 Tom Sneva's Car	.02	.10
Al Unser's Car		
Al Unser Jr.'s Car		
Sneva's Dilemma		
79 Eddie Sachs	.02	.10
Eddie and His Wheel		
80 Dan Gurney's Car	.02	.10
Dan and Mickey's Debut		
81 Mark Donohue's Car	.02	.10
82 Duane Carter Sr.'s Car	.02	.10
Low-Profile Tires		
83 Balloons	.02	.10
84 Tom Sneva's Car	.02	.10
Danny Ongais' Car		
Rick Mears' Car		
200 MPH Front Row		
85 Pit Stops	.02	.10
86 Pat Flaherty	.02	.10
Winning in a T-Shirt		
87 Victory Circle	.02	.10
88 Mike Mosley's Car	.02	.10
Tom Sneva's Car		
Tom Bigelow's Car		
Scott Brayton's Car		
Turn One Parking		
89 Bobby Rahal	.08	.25
Victory Circle Baby		
90 Gordon Johncock w/Car	.05	.15
'77 Heatbreak		
91 Roger McCluskey's Car	.02	.10
Aerodynamic Experiment		
92 Parnelli Jones in Pits	.05	.15
Andy Granatelli		
Parnelli and the Turbine		
93 1911 Lineup	.02	.10
94 Bill Cheesbourg's Car	.02	.10
Twin Porsche		
95 Bobby Rahal's Car	.05	.15
Kevin Cogan's Car		
Race to the Checker		
96 Tony Bettenhausen	.02	.10
Paul Russo		
Relief Drivers		
97 Parnelli Jones' Car	.02	.10
Famous Smokestack		
98 Old Main Entrance	.02	.10
99 Sam Hanks	.02	.10
Jimmy Bryan Car		
1957/58 Winner		
100 Checklist Card	.02	.10
P1 Michael Andretti's Car	.40	1.00
Prototype Card		

1992 Limited Appeal Formula One

Cars of ten of the top 1991 Formula One drivers are the featured subject of this set produced by Limited Appeal of England. The cardfronts include a color photo in an attractive white ghosted-out border. The backs include driver information from the 1991 season and carry a 1992 year copyright line. The unnumbered cards are listed below alphabetically and were released as a complete set (Nigel Mansell was featured on the set wrapper).

COMPLETE SET (10)	4.00	10.00
1 Mark Blundell	.30	.75
2 Ivan Capelli	.30	.75
3 Erik Comas	.30	.75
4 Andrea deCesaris	.30	.75
5 Mika Hakkinen	.30	.75
6 Nigel Mansell	.60	1.50
7 Stefano Modena	.30	.75
8 Alain Prost	.40	1.00
9 Michael Schumacher	.75	2.00
10 Ayrton Senna	1.25	3.00

1962 Marhoefer Indy

Marhoefer Meats of Muncie Indiana distributed this Indy car set in 1962 through its various meat products. The cards feature top IndyCar drivers in black and white photos. As is common with most issues distributed with meat products, the cards were produced with a wax film covering and are often found with product stains. The unnumbered cards are oversized (approximately 4" by 5-1/4") and contain rounded corners.

COMPLETE SET (16)	250.00	500.00
1 Chuck Arnold	18.00	30.00
2 Don Branson	18.00	30.00
3 Bob Christie	18.00	30.00
4 Don Davis	18.00	30.00
5 A.J.Foyt	50.00	75.00
6 Elmer George	18.00	30.00
7 Cliff Griffith	18.00	30.00
8 Gene Hartley	18.00	30.00
9 Roger McCluskey	18.00	30.00
10 Dick Rathmann	18.00	30.00
11 Lloyd Ruby	18.00	30.00
12 Eddie Sachs	18.00	30.00
13 Len Sutton	18.00	30.00
14 Jack Turner	18.00	30.00
15 Rodger Ward	20.00	35.00
16 Wayne Weiler	18.00	30.00

1993 Maxx Williams Racing

This 100-card set was produced by Maxx and features present and past drivers of the Williams Formula One racing team. It was sold through Club Maxx for $14.95 per set.

COMPLETE SET (100)	7.50	20.00
1 Nigel Mansell	.25	.60
2 Riccardo Patrese	.10	.30
3 Alain Prost	.10	.30
4 Damon Hill	.10	.30
5 Mark Blundell	.07	.20
6 Thierry Boutsen	.07	.20
7 Jean-Louis Schlesser	.07	.20
8 Martin Brundle	.07	.20
9 Jonathan Palmer	.07	.20
10 Jacques Laffite	.07	.20
11 Keke Rosberg	.07	.20
12 Nelson Piquet	.10	.30
13 Derek Daly	.07	.20
14 Carlos Reutemann	.10	.30
15 Mario Andretti	.75	2.00
16 Alan Jones	.10	.30
17 Clay Regazzoni	.07	.20
18 The Helmets	.02	.10
19 Frank Williams	.07	.20
20 Patrick Head	.07	.20
21 Adrian Newey	.07	.20
22 David Brown	.07	.20
23 The Conference Centre	.02	.10
24 The Trophies	.02	.10
25 The Crash Test	.02	.10
26 Clay Regazzoni's Car	.02	.10
27 Alan Jones' Car	.07	.20
28 Alan Jones' Car	.07	.20
29 Alan Jones' Car	.07	.20
30 Alan Jones' Car	.07	.20
31 Alan Jones' Car	.07	.20
32 Alan Jones' Car	.07	.20
33 Alan Jones' Car	.07	.20
34 Alan Jones' Car	.07	.20
35 Alan Jones	.25	.60
Jackie Stewart		
36 Alan Jones' Car	.07	.20
37 Alan Jones	.10	.30
38 Alan Jones' Car	.07	.20
39 Carlos Reutemann's Car	.07	.20
40 Carlos Reutemann's Car	.07	.20
41 Alan Jones' Car	.07	.20
42 Keke Rosberg's Car	.02	.10
43 Keke Rosberg's Car	.02	.10
44 Keke Rosberg's Car	.02	.10
45 Keke Rosberg's Car	.02	.10
46 Keke Rosberg's Car	.02	.10
47 Keke Rosberg's Car	.02	.10
48 Nigel Mansell's Car	.10	.30
49 Nigel Mansell	.25	.60
50 Nigel Mansell	.25	.60
51 Nelson Piquet's Car	.07	.20
52 Nigel Mansell's Car	.10	.30
53 Nigel Mansell's Car	.10	.30
54 Nigel Mansell's Car	.10	.30
55 Nigel Mansell's Car	.10	.30
56 Nigel Mansell's Car	.10	.30
57 Nigel Mansell's Car	.10	.30
58 Nelson Piquet's Car	.07	.20
59 Nigel Mansell's Car	.10	.30
60 Nigel Mansell's Car	.10	.30
61 Nigel Mansell's Car	.10	.30
62 Nigel Mansell	.25	.60
63 Nelson Piquet's Car	.07	.20
64 Nelson Piquet's Car	.07	.20
65 Nigel Mansell's Car	.10	.30
66 Nelson Piquet's Car	.07	.20
67 Nigel Mansell	.25	.60
68 Nigel Mansell's Car	.10	.30
69 Nelson Piquet's Car	.07	.20
70 Nigel Mansell's Car	.10	.30
71 Thierry Boutsen's Car	.02	.10
72 Thierry Boutsen	.10	.30
Riccardo Patrese		
73 Riccardo Patrese's Car	.07	.20
74 Thierry Boutsen's Car	.02	.10
75 Riccardo Patrese's Car	.07	.20
76 Nigel Mansell's Car	.10	.30
77 Nigel Mansell's Car	.10	.30
78 Nigel Mansell's Car	.10	.30
79 Nigel Mansell's Car	.10	.30
80 Riccardo Patrese's Car	.07	.20
81 Nigel Mansell's Car	.10	.30
82 Nigel Mansell's Car	.10	.30
83 Nigel Mansell's Car	.10	.30
84 Nigel Mansell's Car	.10	.30
85 Nigel Mansell's Car	.10	.30
86 Nigel Mansell's Car	.10	.30
87 Riccardo Patrese's Car	.07	.20
88 Nigel Mansell's Car	.10	.30
89 Nigel Mansell's Car	.10	.30
90 Nigel Mansell's Car	.10	.30
91 Nigel Mansell's Car	.10	.30
92 Nigel Mansell's Car	.10	.30
93 Keke Rosberg's Car	.02	.10
94 Alan Jones' Car	.07	.20
95 Alan Jones' Car	.07	.20
96 Nigel Mansell's Car	.10	.30
97 Ford Cosworth DFV	.02	.10
98 Honda V6	.02	.10
99 Judd V8	.02	.10
100 Renault V10	.02	.10

1971 Mobil The Story of Grand Prix Motor Racing

This 36-card set highlights some of the great drivers and their cars from 1906 to 1969. Famous names like Ralph de Palma and Jackie Stewart are depicted on the fronts of the cards via artist renderings. The set was sponsored by Mobil and issued in Europe.

COMPLETE SET (36)	12.50	25.00
1 Szisz Renault's Car	.30	.75
2 Felice Nazzaro's Car	.30	.75
3 C.Lautenschlager's Car	.30	.75
4 Georges Boillot's Car	.30	.75
5 C.Lautenschlager's Car	.30	.75
6 Ralph de Palma's Car	.75	1.50
7 Jimmy Murphy's Car	.30	.75
8 P. Bordino's Car	.30	.75
9 H.Segrave's Car	.30	.75
10 G.Campari's Car	.30	.75
11 M.Costantini's Car	.30	.75
12 R.Benoist's Car	.30	.75
13 Rene Dreyfus' Car	.30	.75
14 Sir Henry Birkin's Car	.30	.75
15 Luigi Fagioli's Car	.30	.75
16 Tazio Nuvolari's Car	.30	.75
17 R.Carraciola's Car	.30	.75
18 Tazio Nuvolari's Car	.30	.75
19 B.Rosemeyer's Car	.30	.75
20 Richard Seaman's Car	.30	.75
21 Louis Chiron's Car	.30	.75
22 Jean Pierre Wimille's Car	.30	.75
23 Baron de Graffenried's Car	.30	.75
24 Giuseppe Farina's Car	.30	.75
25 Alberto Ascari's Car	.30	.75
26 Mike Hawthorn's Car	.30	.75
27 Juan Manuel Fangio's Car	.50	1.00
28 Tony Brooks's Car	.30	.75
29 Peter Collins' Car	.30	.75
30 Juan Manuel Fangio's Car	.50	1.00
31 Stirling Moss' Car	.50	1.00
32 Mike Hawthorn's Car	.30	.75
33 Jack Brabham's Car	.30	.75
34 Graham Hill's Car	.50	1.00
35 Jim Clark's Car	.30	.75
36 Jackie Stewart's Car	.75	1.50

1973 Nabisco Sugar Daddy Speedway Collection

Cards from the Speedway Collection set were inserted into Sugar Daddy and Sugar Mama candies in 1973. A wall poster was also produced that was used by collectors to mount their card sets using the adhesive on the cardbacks.The cards themselves are small (approximately 1" by 2-3/4") and feature art renderings of cars from various auto racing circuits along with a racing sponsor logo on the right side of the cardfront. The sponsor logos were to be cut out and mounted separately to the poster. A few of the cards pertain to a particular driver as noted below. There were also six 5" X 7" premiums also issued with the set. The premium cards were available in the bottom of the Sugar Daddy's boxes. They were printed on text-weight paper.

COMPLETE SET (25)	400.00	700.00
1 Jackie Stewart's Car	20.00	40.00
Formula 1		
2 Peter Revson's Car	15.00	25.00
Can-Am		
3 Mark Donohue's Car	15.00	25.00
AMC Javelin Trans-Am		
4 Mario Andretti's Car	20.00	40.00
Jackie Ickx's Car		
Ferrari 312P IMC		
5 Porsche 917 IMC	15.00	25.00
6 Al Unser's Car	20.00	40.00
Championship		
7 A.J.Foyt's Car	20.00	40.00
Stock Car		
8 Renault Alpine Rally	15.00	25.00
9 Ford Bronco Off-Road	15.00	25.00
10 Datsun 510 2-5 Challenge	15.00	25.00
11 Ferrari Daytona IMC	15.00	25.00
12 Volkswagon Bug Off-Road	15.00	25.00
13 Don Garlits' Car	20.00	40.00
Fuel Dragster		
14 Ed McCulloch's Car	20.00	40.00
Funny Car		
15 Bill Jenkins' Car	15.00	25.00
Pro Stock Eliminator		
16 Fiat Abarth 3000	15.00	25.00
Hill Climb		
17 Corvette A-Production	15.00	25.00
18 John Morton's Car	15.00	25.00
Datsun 240Z C-Production		
19 MK1 Sprite	15.00	25.00
H-Production		
20 Blue Flame	15.00	25.00
Land Speed Record		
21 Goldenrod	15.00	25.00
Land Speed Record		
22 Gary Bettenhausen's Car	20.00	40.00
Sprint Car USAC Sprint		
23 David Hobbs' Car	20.00	40.00
McLaren M10B Formula 5000		
24 Mach 71 Ford Formula B	15.00	25.00
25 Lynx-VW Formula Vee	15.00	25.00

1931 Ogden's Motor Races

This 50-card series features artist renderings of cars and motorcycles at various racing events in 1931. The cards were produced for Imperial Tobacco Company of Great Britain and Ireland's Ogden cigarettes branch. The cards measure 1 3/8" X 2 5/8". The fronts of the cards depict cars or motorcycles in race action. "Ogden's Cigarettes" and the title and date of the event are on the front of every card. The card backs state at the top "Motor Races 1931" and "A series of 50". This dating gives the specific year all the racing events featured were run. The latest event featured is October 17, 1931, which in turn leads us to believe that the cards were probably not produced or issued until 1932. The cards backs also feature a brief story on the event featured on that card. The bottom of the card backs state "Issued by Ogden's." The series is broken into two groups, automobile races and motorcycle races. Cards 1-33 are the automobile races and cards 34-50 feature the motorcycle races.

COMPLETE SET (50)	200.00	400.00
1 Sir Malcom Campbell	3.00	8.00
Blue Bird, Daytona, Feb 5		
2 Swedish Winter Grand Prix	3.00	8.00
Feb. 23		
3 Argentine National Grand Prix	3.00	8.00
March		
4 Tunis Grand Prix, March 29	3.00	8.00
5 Austrailian Grand Prix, March	3.00	8.00
6 The Italian, 1000 Miles Race	3.00	8.00
April 11-12		
7 Monaco Grand Prix, April 20	3.00	8.00
8 The Double Twelve Race	3.00	8.00
Brooklands, May 8-9		
10 Grand Prix, Casablanca	3.00	8.00
May 17		
11 Italian Grand Prix, Monza	3.00	8.00
May 24		
12 The 500 Miles Race	3.00	8.00
Indianapolis, May 30		
13 Ernesto Maserati	3.00	8.00
Royal Prix de Roma, June 7		
14 Grand Prix d'Endurance	3.00	8.00
LeMans, June 12-13		
15 Grand Prix, Automobile	3.00	8.00
Club de France, June 21		
16 Southport 100 Mile Race	3.00	8.00
June 27		
17 Junior Car Club, High-Speed	3.00	8.00
Trial, July 4		
18 Belgian 24-Hours Race	3.00	8.00
July 4-5		
19 Irish Grand Prix, Saorstat Cup	3.00	8.00
July 5		
20 Irish Grand Prix, Eireann Cup	3.00	8.00
July 6		
21 Shelsley Walsh Hill Climb	3.00	8.00
July 11		
22 Belgian Grand Prix, July 12	3.00	8.00
23 Sand Race, Skegness, July 18	3.00	8.00
24 The German Grand Prix	3.00	8.00
July 19		
25 Relay Race, Brooklands	3.00	8.00
July 25		
26 Circuit de Dieppe	3.00	8.00
(1500 cc. class), July 26		
27 Circuit de Dieppe	3.00	8.00
(over 1500 cc. class), July 26		
28 Mile Record, Brooklands	3.00	8.00
August 8		
30 Mont Ventoux Hill Climb	3.00	8.00
August 30		
31 Monza Grand Prix, Sept. 6	3.00	8.00
32 Circuit des Routes pavees	3.00	8.00

Sept 13
33 Sir Henry Birkin 3.00 8.00
at Brooklands, Oct. 17
34 The 100-Miles Sand Race 3.00 8.00
Southport, May 9
35 The Austrian Tourist Trophy 3.00 8.00
May 10
36 Junior Motorcycle Tourist 3.00 8.00
Trophy, June 15
37 Lightweight Motorcycle 3.00 8.00
Tourist Trophy, June 17
38 Senior Motorcycle 3.00 8.00
Tourist Trophy, June 19
40 F.I.C.M. Grand Prix 3.00 8.00
(250cc and 500cc Classes), June 28
41 German Grand Prix 3.00 8.00
(500cc class), July 5
42 Dutch Motorcycle 3.00 8.00
Tourist Trophy, July 11
43 Italian Tourist Trophy, July 12 3.00 8.00
44 Phoenix Park Road Races 3.00 8.00
July 18
45 Belgian Grand Prix, July 19 3.00 8.00
46 The Dieppe Grand Prix, July 3.00 8.00
47 Ulster Grand Prix, Sept. 5 3.00 8.00
48 Swedish Grand Prix, Sept. 6 3.00 8.00
49 Manx Junior Grand Prix 3.00 8.00
Sept. 8
50 Manx Senior Grand Prix 3.00 8.00
Sept. 10

1962 Petpro Limited Grand Prix Racing Cars

This 35-card set was issued by Petpro Limited of Crawley, Sussex England. The cards feature artist paintings of many of the top Grand Prix cards than raced between 1939 and 1961. The cards measure 2 1/2" X 1 1/8".

COMPLETE SET (35) 15.00 30.00
1 Tony Brook's Car .40 1.00
2 Achille Varzi's Car .40 1.00
3 W.F. Moss' Car .40 1.00
4 Tony Rolt's Car .40 1.00
5 B. Bira's Car .40 1.00
6 Reg Parnell's Car .40 1.00
7 Louis Rosier's Car .40 1.00
8 Guiseppe Farina's Car .40 1.00
9 Guiseppe Farina's Car .40 1.00
10 Arthur Dobson's Car .40 1.00
11 Joe Kelly's Car .40 1.00
12 Peter Whitehead's Car .40 1.00
13 Froilan Gonzales' Car .40 1.00
14 International Racing Flags .40 1.00
15 Lance Macklin's Car .40 1.00
16 Mike Hawthorn's Car .40 1.00
17 Juan Manuel Fangio's Car .60 1.50
18 Ken Wharton's Car .40 1.00
19 Tony Rolt's Car .40 1.00
20 Jack Brabham's Car .40 1.00
21 John Surtees' Car .40 1.00
22 Albert Ascari's Car .40 1.00
23 Jean Behra's Car .40 1.00
24 Karl Kling's Car .40 1.00
25 Stirling Moss' Car UER .75 2.00
name mispelled Sterling
26 Jean Behra's Car .40 1.00
27 Archie Scot Brown's Car .40 1.00
28 Froilan Gonzales' Car .40 1.00
29 Chuck Daigh's Car .40 1.00
30 Jack Brabham's Car .40 1.00
31 Jimmy Clark's Car .40 1.00
32 Phil Hill's Car .40 1.00
33 Joachim Bonnier's Car .40 1.00
34 Graham Hill's Car .60 1.50
35 Stirling Moss' Car .75 2.00

1991 Pro Tracs Formula One

Canadian based Pro Tracs produced this 1991 issue focusing on Formula One drivers and top F1 teams. The cards were distributed in 10-card packs with 36-packs per box. The set is sometimes called Vroom, the name contained on foil boxes.

COMPLETE SET (200) 4.00 10.00
1 Ayrton Senna .30 .75
2 Ayrton Senna's Car .10 .30
3 Gerhard Berger .07 .20
4 Gerhard Berger's Car .02 .10
5 Saturo Nakajima .02 .10
6 Saturo Nakajima's Car .01 .05
7 Stefano Modena .02 .10
8 Stefano Modena's Car .01 .05
9 Nigel Mansell .10 .30
10 Nigel Mansell's Car .07 .20
11 Riccardo Patrese .07 .20
12 Riccardo Patrese's Car .02 .10
13 Martin Brundle .02 .10
14 Martin Brundle's Car .01 .05
15 Martin Brundle's Car .01 .05
16 Mark Blundell .02 .10
17 Mark Blundell's Car .01 .05
18 Mark Blundell's Car .01 .05
19 Michele Alboreto .02 .10
20 Michele Alboreto's Car .01 .05
21 Michele Alboreto's Car .01 .05
22 Alex Caffi .02 .10
23 Alex Caffi's Car .01 .05
24 Stefan Johansson .07 .20
25 Stefan Johansson's Car .02 .10
26 Mika Hakkinen .02 .10
27 Mika Hakkinen's Car .01 .05
28 Julian Bailey .02 .10
29 Julian Bailey's Car .01 .05
30 Johnny Herbert .02 .10
31 Johnny Herbert's Car .01 .05
32 Olivier Grouillard .02 .10
33 Olivier Grouillard's Car .01 .05
34 Olivier Grouillard's Car .01 .05
35 Mauricio Gugelmin .02 .10
36 Mauricio Gugelmin's Car .01 .05
37 Ivan Capelli .02 .10
38 Ivan Capelli's Car .01 .05
39 Gabriele Tarquini .02 .10
40 Gabriele Tarquini's Car .01 .05
41 Stefan Johansson .07 .20
42 Stefan Johansson's Car .02 .10
43 Fabrizio Barbazza .02 .10
44 Fabrizio Barbazza's Car .01 .05
45 Roberto Moreno .02 .10
46 Roberto Moreno's Car .01 .05
47 Roberto Moreno's Car .01 .05
48 Nelson Piquet .07 .20
49 Nelson Piquet's Car .02 .10
50 Nelson Piquet's Car .02 .10
51 Emanuele Pirro .02 .10
52 Emanuele Pirro's Car .01 .05
53 J.J. Lehto .02 .10
54 J.J. Lehto's Car .01 .05
55 Pierluigi Martini .02 .10
56 Pierluigi Martini's Car .01 .05
57 Gianni Morbidelli .02 .10
58 Gianni Morbidelli's Car .01 .05
59 Thierry Boutsen .02 .10
60 Thierry Boutsen's Car .01 .05
61 Erik Comas .02 .10
62 Erik Comas' Car .01 .05
63 Alain Prost .07 .20
64 Alain Prost's Car .02 .10
65 Jean Alesi .02 .10
66 Jean Alesi's Car .01 .05
67 Eric Bernard .02 .10
68 Eric Bernard's Car .01 .05
69 Aguri Suzuki .02 .10
70 Aguri Suzuki's Car .01 .05
71 Pedro Matos Chaves .02 .10
72 Pedro Matos Chaves' Car .01 .05
73 Bertrand Gachot .02 .10
74 Bertrand Gachot's Car .01 .05
75 Andrea deCesaris .02 .10
76 Andrea deCesaris' Car .01 .05
77 Nicola Larini .02 .10
78 Nicola Larini's Car .01 .05
79 Eric Van de Poele .02 .10
80 Eric Van de Poele's Car .01 .05
81 USA Race Track .01 .05
82 Brazil Race Track .01 .05
83 San Marino Race Track .01 .05
84 Monaco Race Track .01 .05
85 Canada Race Track .01 .05
86 Mexico Race Track .01 .05
87 France Race Track .01 .05
88 Great Britain Track .01 .05
89 Germany Race Track .01 .05
90 Hungary Race Track .01 .05
91 Belgium Race Track .01 .05
92 Italy Race Track .01 .05
93 Portugal Race Track .01 .05
94 Spain Race Track .01 .05
95 Japan Race Track .01 .05
96 Australia Race Track .01 .05
97 Ayrton Senna's Car .10 .30
98 Ayrton Senna's Car .10 .30
99 Ayrton Senna's Car .10 .30
100 Ayrton Senna's Car .10 .30
101 Ayrton Senna's Car .10 .30
102 Ayrton Senna's Car .10 .30
103 Ayrton Senna's Car .10 .30
104 Ayrton Senna's Car .10 .30
105 Ayrton Senna's Car .10 .30
106 Ayrton Senna .30 .75
107 Ayrton Senna .30 .75
108 Alain Prost .07 .20
109 Alain Prost's Car .02 .10
110 Alain Prost's Car .02 .10
111 Alain Prost's Car .02 .10
112 Alain Prost's Car .02 .10
113 Alain Prost's Car .02 .10
114 Alain Prost's Car .02 .10
115 Alain Prost's Car .02 .10
116 Alain Prost's Car .02 .10
117 Alain Prost's Car .02 .10
118 Alain Prost .07 .20
119 Alain Prost's Car .02 .10
120 Alain Prost .07 .20
121 Nigel Mansell's Car .07 .20
122 Nigel Mansell's Car .07 .20
123 Nigel Mansell's Car .07 .20
124 Nigel Mansell's Car .07 .20
125 Nigel Mansell's Car .07 .20
126 Nigel Mansell's Car .07 .20
127 Nigel Mansell's Car .07 .20
128 Nigel Mansell's Car .07 .20
129 Nigel Mansell's Car .07 .20
130 Nigel Mansell's Car .07 .20
131 Nigel Mansell .10 .30
132 Porsche Engine .01 .05
133 Yamaha Engine .01 .05
134 Lamborghini Engine .01 .05
135 Honda Engine .01 .05
136 Ferrari Engine .01 .05
137 Ford Engine .01 .05
138 Renault Engine .01 .05
139 Ilmor Engine .01 .05
140 Judd Engine .01 .05
141 Judd Engine .01 .05
142 Honda Engine .01 .05
143 Ford Engine .01 .05
144 Ayrton Senna's Car .10 .30
145 Alain Prost .07 .20
146 Nelson Piquet .07 .20
147 Ayrton Senna's Car .10 .30
148 Ayrton Senna .30 .75
149 Riccardo Patrese's Car .02 .10
150 Gerhard Berger's Car .02 .10
151 Ayrton Senna .30 .75
152 Ayrton Senna's Car .10 .30
153 San Marino .01 .05
154 Ayrton Senna's Car .10 .30
155 Monaco .01 .05
156 Monaco .01 .05
157 Nelson Piquet's Car .02 .10
158 Nigel Mansell's Car .07 .20
159 Nelson Piquet's Car .02 .10
160 French Grand Prix .01 .05
161 Aguri Suzuki .02 .10
Eric Bernard
162 Riccardo Patrese .07 .20
Alain Prost
163 Great Britain Grand Prix .01 .05
164 Silverstone GB .01 .05
165 Ayrton Senna's Car .10 .30
Nigell Mansell's Car
166 Ayrton Senna .30 .75
167 Hockenheim GER .01 .05
168 Start GER .01 .05
169 Thierry Boutsen .02 .10
170 Thierry Boutsen's Car .01 .05
171 Martin Donnelly's Car .01 .05
172 Ayrton Senna .10 .30
Gerhard Berger
173 Start HUN .01 .05
174 View BEL .01 .05
175 Ferrari ITA .01 .05
176 Start ITA .01 .05
177 Monza ITA .01 .05
178 Race Grid POR .01 .05
179 Nigel Mansell's Car .07 .20
180 Nigel Mansell .10 .30
181 Alain Prost .07 .20
182 Alain Prost's Car .02 .10
183 SPA .01 .05
184 Nelson Piquet .07 .20
185 Roberto Moreno .07 .20
Nelson Piquet
186 Johnny Herbert's Car .01 .05
187 Nelson Piquet .07 .20
188 Stag Hotel AUS .01 .05
189 Yannick Dalmas' Car .01 .05
190 Jody Scheckter .02 .10
191 Keke Rosberg's Car .01 .05
192 Niki Lauda .07 .20
193 Colin Chapman .07 .20
Nigel Mansell
194 Patrick Tambay's Car .01 .05
195 John Watson .02 .10
196 Gilles Villeneuve's Car .07 .20
197 Gilles Villeneuve's Car .07 .20
198 Alain Prost's Car .02 .10
199 Checklist .01 .05
200 Checklist .01 .05

2007 Rittenhouse IRL

COMPLETE SET (54) 15.00 40.00
COMMON DRIVERS .15 .40
SEMISTARS .25 .60
UNLISTED STARS .40 1.00
WAX BOX HOBBY 70.00 100.00
WAX BOX ARCHIVES 400.00 750.00
1 Danica Patrick RC 2.50 6.00
2 Danica Patrick's Car 1.00 2.50
3 Danica Patrick RC 2.50 6.00
4 Dan Wheldon RC 1.00 2.50
5 Dan Wheldon's Car .40 1.00
6 Dan Wheldon RC 1.00 2.50
7 Tony Kanaan RC 1.00 2.50
8 Tony Kanaan's Car .40 1.00
9 Tony Kanaan RC 1.00 2.50
10 Scott Dixon RC .25 .60
11 Scott Dixon's Car .10 .25
12 Scott Dixon RC .25 .60
13 Vitor Meira RC .25 .60
14 Vitor Meira's Car .10 .25
15 Vitor Meira RC .25 .60
16 Milka Duno RC 1.25 3.00
17 Milka Duno's Car .60 1.50
18 Milka Duno RC 1.25 3.00
19 Marco Andretti RC 1.00 2.50
20 Marco Andretti's Car .40 1.00
21 Marco Andretti RC 1.00 2.50
22 Dario Franchitti RC 1.00 2.50
23 Dario Franchitti's Car .40 1.00
24 Dario Franchitti RC 1.00 2.50
25 Tomas Scheckter RC .40 1.00
26 Tomas Scheckter's Car .15 .40
27 Tomas Scheckter RC .40 1.00
28 Scott Sharp .25 .60
29 Scott Sharp's Car .10 .25
30 Scott Sharp .25 .60
31 Kosuke Matsuura RC .25 .60
32 Kosuke Matsuura's Car .10 .25
33 Kosuke Matsuura RC .25 .60
34 Ed Carpenter RC .25 .60
35 Ed Carpenter's Car .10 .25
36 Ed Carpenter RC .25 .60
37 Buddy Rice RC .25 .60
38 Buddy Rice's Car .10 .25
39 Buddy Rice RC .25 .60
40 Jeff Simmons RC .25 .60
41 Jeff Simmons' Car .10 .25
42 Jeff Simmons RC .25 .60
43 Marty Roth RC .25 .60
44 Marty Roth's Car .10 .25
45 Marty Roth RC .25 .60
46 Sarah Fisher RC 1.50 4.00
47 Sarah Fisher's Car .60 1.50
48 Sarah Fisher RC 1.50 4.00
49 A.J. Foyt IV .40 1.00
50 A.J. Foyt IV Car .15 .40
51 A.J. Foyt IV .40 1.00
52 Darren Manning RC .50 1.25
53 Darren Manning's Car .20 .50
54 Darren Manning RC .50 1.25
P1 Danica Patrick Promo 4.00 10.00
NNO Dario Franchitti Indy 500 Champ. 12.50 25.00

2007 Rittenhouse IRL Autographs

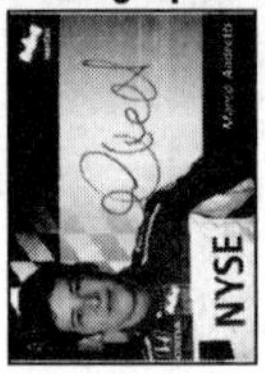

STATED ODDS 1:12
1 Marco Andretti 15.00 30.00
2 Ed Carpenter 10.00 20.00
3 Scott Dixon 10.00 20.00
4 Milka Duno 20.00 40.00
5 Sarah Fisher 20.00 40.00
6 Dario Franchitti 15.00 30.00
7 A.J. Foyt IV 10.00 20.00
8 Tony Kanaan 15.00 30.00
9 Darren Manning 10.00 20.00
10 Kosuke Matsuura 7.50 15.00
11 Vitor Meira 10.00 20.00
12 Danica Patrick 275.00 400.00
13 Buddy Rice 7.50 15.00
14 Tomas Scheckter 7.50 15.00
15 Scott Sharp 10.00 20.00
16 Jeff Simmons 10.00 20.00
17 Dan Wheldon 15.00 30.00

2007 Rittenhouse IRL Foyt 50th Anniversary

COMPLETE SET (9) 30.00 60.00
STATED ODDS 1:24 4.00 8.00
1 A.J. Foyt 1958 4.00 8.00
2 A.J. Foyt '61 Indy 500 Champion 4.00 8.00
3 A.J. Foyt '61 Indy 500 Champion 4.00 8.00
4 A.J. Foyt '64 Indy 500 Champion 4.00 8.00
5 A.J. Foyt 1964 Indy 500 Champion 4.00 8.00
6 A.J. Foyt '67 Indy 500 Champion 4.00 8.00
7 A.J. Foyt '67 Indy 500 Champion 4.00 8.00
8 A.J. Foyt '77 Indy 500 Champion 4.00 8.00
9 A.J. Foyt '07 4.00 8.00

2007 Rittenhouse IRL Foyt 50th Anniversary Autograph

STATED ODDS 1:864
NNO A.J. Foyt 75.00 125.00

2007 Rittenhouse IRL Road to Victory Indy 500

COMPLETE SET (9) 10.00 20.00
STATED ODDS 1:8
V1 Dario Franchitti 1.25 3.00
V2 Dario Franchitti 1.25 3.00
V3 Dario Franchitti 1.25 3.00
V4 Dario Franchitti 1.25 3.00
V5 Dario Franchitti 1.25 3.00
V6 Dario Franchitti 1.25 3.00
V7 Dario Franchitti 1.25 3.00
V8 Dario Franchitti 1.25 3.00
V9 Dario Franchitti 1.25 3.00

2007 Rittenhouse IRL Shades of Victory

COMPLETE SET (9) 12.50 30.00
COMMON DRIVER .25 .60
SEMISTARS .40 1.00
UNLISTED STARS .60 1.50
STATED ODDS 1:12
R1 Danica Patrick 4.00 10.00
R2 Dan Wheldon 1.50 4.00
R3 Dario Franchitti 1.50 4.00
R4 Tony Kanaan 1.50 4.00
R5 Vitor Meira .40 1.00
R6 Scott Dixon .40 1.00
R7 Buddy Rice .40 1.00
R8 Marco Andretti 1.50 4.00
R9 A.J. Foyt IV .60 1.50

1970 Shell Racing Cars of the World

COMPLETE SET (48)
1 1901 Panhard
2 1901 Renault
3 1906 Locomobile
4 1908 Mors
5 1910 Bugatti
6 1913 Peugeot
7 1914 Mercedes
8 1919 Ballot
9 1921 Sunbeam Talbot Darracoq
10 1923 Voisin
11 1924 Duesenberg
12 1927 Delage
13 1927 Fiat Type 806
14 1928 Amilcar
15 1930 Bugatti
16 1931 Alfa Romeo
17 1935 Gilmore Special
18 1938 Auto Union
19 1938 Mercedes Benz
20 1946 Sparks
21 1950 Wynn
22 1950 Alfa Romeo
23 1950 Lago Talbot
24 1951 HWM
25 1952 Connaught
26 1952 Ferrari
27 1954 Lancia
28 1955 Mercedes Benz
29 1956 Maserati 250F
30 1956 Lycoming Special
31 1957 Cooper 500
32 1957 Maserati
33 1957 Lister Jaguar
34 1958 Vanwall
35 1959 Cooper
36 1959 BRM
37 1959 Aston Martin DBR 4/250
38 1960 Ferrari
39 1960 Lotus
40 1960 Lotus Climax
41 1961 Ferguson
42 1961 Ferrari
43 1961 SAAB
44 1961 Peugeot
45 1961 Cooper
46 1961 Elfin
47 1962 BRM
48 1962 Lola

1995 SkyBox Indy 500

This 108-card set was the first Indy set produced by SkyBox. The oversized cards 2 1/2" X 4 1/2" feature the top names in Indy Car racing. There are two topical subsets within the set: Qualifying Position (19-51) and Finishing Position (73-105). The also a special 1994 Indy Champion inser Unser Jr. The card was randomly inserted at a one per 44 packs. A special Jacques Villeneu 500 Winner mail away card was produced a Both cards are priced at the bottom of the set but not included in the set price.

COMPLETE SET (108) 8.00
1 Cover Card .10
Checklist Back
2 IMS Speedway .10
World's Greatest Race Course
3 Borg-Warner Trophy .10
4 IMS Speedway .10
A New Look for the Speedway
5 Paul Tracy's Car .10
Penske PC23 Chassis
6 Robby Gordon's Car .10
Lola T94/00 Chassis
7 Michael Andretti's Car .20
Reynard 941 Chassis
8 Paul Tracy .15
Al Unser
Emerson Fittipaldi's Car
Penske Racing Teams
9 Stefan Johansson .10
State-of-the-Art Helmets
10 Bryan Herta .20
A.J.Foyt
11 Emerson Fittipaldi w/Car .20
12 Mario Andretti w/Car .20
Pole Run
13 Jacques Villeneuve .20
Fastest Rookie Qualifier
14 Al Unser Jr. .20
Roger Penske
With Crew
15 Al Unser Sr. .20
Retires
16 Johnny Rutherford in Car .15
17 Bobby Rahal in Car .15
18 Emerson Fittipaldi .20
Raul Boesel
Al Unser Jr.
19 Al Unser Jr. in Car .20
20 Raul Boesel .10
21 Emerson Fittipaldi .20
22 Jacques Villeneuve in Car .20
23 Michael Andretti in Car .20
24 Lyn St. James .10
25 Nigel Mansell .15
26 Arie Luyendyk .15
27 Mario Andretti in Car .20
28 John Andretti .15
29 Eddie Cheever .10
30 Dominic Dobson .10
31 Stan Fox .10
32 Hideshi Matsuda .10
33 Dennis Vitolo .10
34 Jimmy Vasser .10
35 Scott Sharp .15
36 Hiro Matsushita .10
37 Robby Gordon .15
38 Roberto Guerrero .15
39 Brian Till .10
40 Bryan Herta .10
41 Scott Brayton .10
42 Teo Fabi .15
43 Paul Tracy .15
44 Adrian Fernandez .10
45 Stefan Johansson .10
46 Bobby Rahal .15
47 Mauricio Gugelmin .10
48 John Paul Jr. .10
49 Mike Groff .10
50 Marco Greco .10
51 Scott Goodyear .10
52 Al Unser Jr. .20
MVP for the Month of May
53 Jim Nabors .10
Back Home Again
54 Robby Gordon .15
Roberto Guerrero
Bryan Till
Ready To Roll
55 IMS Speedway .10
The Greatest Spectacle in Racing
56 IMS Speedway .10
Showtime
57 IMS Speedway .10
The 78th Edition
58 Dennis Vitolo's Car .10
59 Mario Andretti in Pits .20
60 Mike Groff's Car .10
Dominic Dobson's Car
61 Adrian Fernandez's Car .10
62 Jacques Villeneuve's Car .20
Takes the Lead
63 Robby Gordon's Car .10
Raul Boesel's Car
Wheel-to-Wheel
64 Hideshi Matsuda's Car .10
Hits the Wall
65 Dennis Vitolo's Car .10
Nigel Mansell's Car
Tangle in Turn Three
66 Emerson Fittipaldi's Car .15
Pull's Away
67 Emerson Fittipaldi's Car .15
Emmo's Day Comes to an End
68 Stan Fox's Car .10
Brings Out Final caution
69 Al Unser Jr.'s Car .20
Salute to the New Champion
70 Al Unser Jr. in Car .20
Heads to Victory Lane
71 Al Unser Jr. WIN .20
Number Two for the Record Books
72 Al Unser Jr. WIN .20

l Unser Jr. .20 .50
acques Villeneuve .20 .50
3obby Rahal .15 .40
immy Vasser .10 .25
Robby Gordon .15 .40
Michael Andretti .20 .50
Teo Fabi .15 .40
Eddie Cheever .10 .25
Bryan Herta .10 .25
John Andretti .15 .40
Mauricio Gugelmin .10 .25
Brian Till .10 .25
Stan Fox .10 .25
Hiro Matsushita .10 .25
Stefan Johansson .10 .25
Scott Sharp .15 .40
Emerson Fittipaldi .20 .50
Arie Luyendyk .15 .40
Lyn St.James .10 .25
Scott Brayton .15 .40
Raul Boesel .10 .25
Nigel Mansell .15 .40
Paul Tracy .15 .40
Hideshi Matsuda .10 .25
John Paul Jr. .10 .25
Dennis Vitolo .10 .25
Marco Greco .10 .25
Adrian Fernandez .10 .25
Dominic Dobson .10 .25
Scott Goodyear .10 .25
Mike Groff .10 .25
Mario Andretti .20 .50
Roberto Guerrero .15 .40
Al Unser Jr. .20 .50
Mario Andretti .20 .50
Al Unser Jr. .20 .50
1994 Indianapolis
Al Unser Jr.'s Car Promo .75 2.00
Jacques Villeneuve Promo .75 2.00
Jacques Villeneuve WIN .75 2.00
Al Unser Jr. Champion .75 2.00

1995 SkyBox Indy 500 Heir to Indy

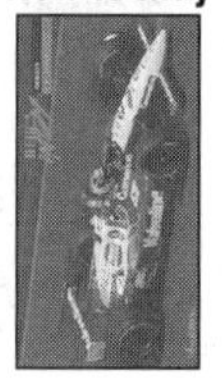

six-card insert set features some of the best of youngest drivers on the Indy circuit. The cards printed on silver foil board and were inserted at e of one per 29 packs.

MPLETE SET (6) 15.00 30.00
ul Boesel 2.00 5.00
mmy Vasser 2.00 5.00
bby Gordon 2.50 6.00
chael Andretti 2.50 6.00
ul Tracy 2.50 6.00
cques Villeneuve 5.00 10.00

1995 SkyBox Indy 500 Past Champs

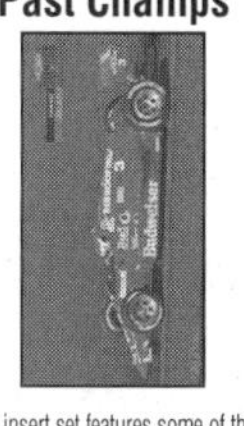

18-card insert set features some of the Indy 500 ers since 1962. The cards were printed on silver board and were inserted randomly at a rate of per 10 packs.

MPLETE SET (18) 15.00 40.00
Unser Jr. 1.50 4.00
merson Fittipaldi 1.50 4.00
ck Mears 1.50 4.00
e Luyendyk .75 2.00
Unser 1.25 3.00
bby Rahal 1.25 3.00
nny Sullivan .75 2.00
m Sneva .75 2.00
rdon Johncock .75 2.00
obby Unser 1.25 3.00
ohnny Rutherford 1.25 3.00
Mark Donohue .75 2.00
Mario Andretti 1.50 4.00
J. Foyt 1.50 4.00
raham Hill .75 2.00
im Clark .75 2.00
arnelli Jones .75 2.00
odger Ward .75 2.00

1996 SkyBox Indy 500

1996 SkyBox Indy set was issued in a single card series. The cards feature the drivers of the Indy 500. The cards were standard size for the time in SkyBox racing cards history. There are topical subsets within the set: Qualifying tion (10-42), Indy 500 Car Owners (50-54), hing Position (55-87), Anatomy of the Modern Car (91-99).

MPLETE SET (100) 6.00 15.00
ristian Fittipaldi .10 .25

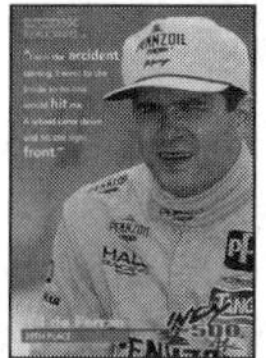

2 Firestone's Return .05 .15
3 Honda's Comeback .05 .15
4 Dick Simon .10 .25
Lyn St.James
5 Scott Brayton .10 .25
6 Qualifying Highlights .05 .15
7 Scott Brayton w/Crew .10 .25
8 Al Unser, Jr. .40 1.00
9 Emerson Fittipaldi .15 .40
10 Scott Brayton's Car .05 .15
11 Arie Luyendyk's Car .05 .15
12 Scott Goodyear's Car .05 .15
13 Michael Andretti's Car .10 .25
14 Jacques Villeneuve's Car .15 .40
15 Mauricio Gugelmin's Car .05 .15
16 Robby Gordon's Car .10 .25
17 Scott Pruett's Car .05 .15
18 Jimmy Vasser's Car .05 .15
19 Hiro Matsushita's Car .05 .15
20 Stan Fox's Car .05 .15
21 Andre Ribeiro's Car .05 .15
22 Roberto Guerrero's Car .05 .15
23 Eddie Cheever's Car .05 .15
24 Teo Fabi's Car .05 .15
25 Paul Tracy's Car .10 .25
26 Alessandro Zampedri's Car .05 .15
27 Danny Sullivan's Car .05 .15
28 Gil de Ferran's Car .05 .15
29 Hideshi Matsuda's Car .05 .15
30 Bobby Rahal's Car .10 .25
31 Raul Boesel's Car .05 .15
32 Buddy Lazier's Car .05 .15
33 Eliseo Salazar's Car .05 .15
34 Adrian Fernandez's Car .05 .15
35 Eric Bachelart's Car .05 .15
36 Christian Fittipaldi's Car .05 .15
37 Lyn St. James's Car .10 .25
38 Carlos Guerrero's Car .05 .15
39 Scott Sharp's Car .05 .15
40 Stefan Johansson's Car .05 .15
41 Davy Jones's Car .05 .15
42 Bryan Herta's Car .05 .15
43 Robby Gordon in Pits .10 .25
44 Green Flag .05 .15
45 Stan Fox's Car .05 .15
46 Scott Goodyear's Car .05 .15
Arie Luyendyk's Car
47 Scott Goodyear's Car .05 .15
48 Checkered Flag .05 .15
49 Jacques Villeneuve .30 .75
50 Joe Montana 1.25 3.00
Chip Ganassi
51 Roger Penske .05 .15
52 Paul Newman .10 .25
Carl Haas
53 A.J. Foyt .15 .40
54 Walter Payton 1.00 2.50
Dale Coyne
55 Jacques Villeneuve .30 .75
56 Christian Fittipaldi .10 .25
57 Bobby Rahal .15 .40
58 Eliseo Salazar .10 .25
59 Robby Gordon .15 .40
60 Mauricio Gugelmin .10 .25
61 Arie Luyendyk .10 .25
62 Teo Fabi .10 .25
63 Danny Sullivan .10 .25
64 Hiro Matsushita .10 .25
65 Alessandro Zampedri .10 .25
66 Roberto Guerrero .10 .25
67 Bryan Herta .10 .25
68 Scott Goodyear .10 .25
69 Hideshi Matsuda .10 .25
70 Stefan Johansson .10 .25
71 Scott Brayton .10 .25
72 Andre Ribeiro .10 .25
73 Scott Pruett .10 .25
74 Raul Boesel .10 .25
75 Adrian Fernandez .10 .25
76 Jimmy Vasser .10 .25
77 Davy Jones .10 .25
78 Paul Tracy .15 .40
79 Michael Andretti .60 1.50
80 Scott Sharp .10 .25
81 Buddy Lazier .10 .25
82 Eric Bachelart .10 .25
83 Gil de Ferran .10 .25
84 Stan Fox .10 .25
85 Eddie Cheever .10 .25
86 Lyn St. James .15 .40
87 Carlos Guerrero .10 .25
88 Jacques Villeneuve w/Crew .30 .75
89 Mauricio Gugelmin .10 .25
90 Scott Goodyear .10 .25
91 Feel the 500 - Tires/Gas .05 .15
92 Feel the 500 - Suspension .05 .15
93 Feel the 500 - Cockpit .05 .15
94 Feel the 500 - Engine .05 .15
95 Feel the 500 - Rear End .05 .15
96 Feel the 500 - Hauler .05 .15
97 Feel the 500 - Ground Effects .05 .15
98 Feel the 500 - Noise Piece .05 .15
99 Feel the 500 - IMS .05 .15
100 Checklist .05 .15

1996 SkyBox Indy 500 Champions Collection

Randomly inserted in packs at a rate of one in five, this six-card insert set features six former Indy 500 Champions. The cards printed on silver foil board offers pictures of the past champions standing next to the Borg-Warner Trophy on the fronts of the cards and sitting in the actual winning car they drove on the backs.

COMPLETE SET (6) 6.00 15.00
1 Al Unser, Jr. 3.00 6.00
2 Emerson Fittipaldi 1.00 2.50
3 Bobby Rahal 1.00 2.50
4 Arie Luyendyk .75 2.00
5 Danny Sullivan .75 2.00
6 Jacques Villeneuve 2.50 5.00

1996 SkyBox Indy 500 Rookies of the Year

This nine-card insert set features the Indy 500 Rookies of the Year from 1987-94. This includes the Co-Rookies of the Year in 1989, Bernard Jourdain and Scott Pruett. The cards feature gold foil stamping and are die cut. Rookie of the Year cards could be found at a rate of one per three packs.

COMPLETE SET (9) 6.00 15.00
1 Fabrizio Barbazza .40 1.00
2 Billy Vukovich III .40 1.00
3 Bernard Jourdain .40 1.00
4 Scott Pruett .40 1.00
5 Eddie Cheever .40 1.00
6 Jeff Andretti .75 2.00
7 Lyn St. James .75 2.00
8 Nigel Mansell 1.50 4.00
9 Jacques Villeneuve 1.50 4.00

1926 Sport Company of America Racing

This eight-card racing set was issued by Spalding Sporting Goods in 1926. The racing cards are just part of a larger mulit-sport set. The cards measure 1 1/2 x 2 1/4. The front features a glossy finished black and white framed photograph of the driver with his name and sport below the picture. The backs carry a detailed biography of the driver's achievements. Also on the back is the copyright date, Nov. 1926, and the Sports Co. of America S.F. title. The cards came in a glassine envelope along with a coupon for Spalding Sporting Goods. The front of the coupon reads "Sport-Scrip" "Value Ten Cents". The back of the coupon detailed how the coupon could be redeemed for ten cents worth of Spalding Sporting Goods.

COMPLETE SET (8) 162.50 325.00
1 Earl Cooper 25.00 40.00
2 Ralph De Palma 35.00 60.00
3 Ralph De Palo 25.00 40.00
4 Harry Hartz 25.00 40.00
5 Benny Hill 25.00 40.00
6 Bob McDonough 25.00 40.00
7 Tommy Milton 25.00 40.00
8 Barney Oldfield 35.00 60.00

1978 Sports I.D. Patches

This set features full color pictures of some of the top drivers in Indy Car on cloth patches. The patches are not numbered, so they appear below alphabetically.

COMPLETE SET (12) 100.00 200.00
1 Mario Andretti 15.00 30.00
2 Gary Bettenhausen 10.00 20.00
3 Wally Dallenbach Sr. 10.00 20.00
4 A.J. Foyt 15.00 30.00
5 Gordon Johncock 10.00 20.00
6 Sheldon Kinser 10.00 20.00
7 Danny Ongais 10.00 20.00
8 Johnny Parsons 10.00 20.00
9 Johnny Rutherford 12.50 25.00
10 Tom Sneva 12.50 25.00
11 Al Unser 15.00 30.00
12 Bobby Unser 12.50 25.00

1954 Stark and Wetzel Indy Winners

Stark and Wetzel Meats produced and distributed these cards in 1954. The issue features past winners of the Indy 500 and their cars. Since the cards were distributed in packages of meat products, they were produced with a wax covering that is often found stained making Near Mint copies especially tough to find. The cards are blankbacked and have lightly perforated edges. The cards are unnumbered and listed below in order of winning year.

COMPLETE SET (37) 600.00 1000.00
1911 Ray Harroun 18.00 30.00
1912 Joe Dawson 18.00 30.00
1913 Jules Goux 18.00 30.00
1914 Rene Thomas 18.00 30.00
1915 Ralph DePalma 25.00 40.00
1916 Dario Resta 18.00 30.00
1919 Howard Wilcox 18.00 30.00
1920 Gaston Chevrolet 25.00 40.00
1921 Tommy Milton 18.00 30.00
1922 Jimmy Murphy 18.00 30.00
1923 Tommy Milton 18.00 30.00
1924 Joe Boyer 18.00 30.00
L.L.Corum
1925 Peter DePaolo 18.00 30.00
1926 Frank Lockhart 18.00 30.00
1927 George Souders 18.00 30.00
1928 Louis Meyer 18.00 30.00
1929 Ray Keech 18.00 30.00
1930 Billy Arnold 18.00 30.00
1931 Louis Schneider 18.00 30.00
1932 Fred Frame 18.00 30.00
1933 Louis Meyer 18.00 30.00
1934 Bill Cummings 18.00 30.00
1935 Kelly Petillo 18.00 30.00
1936 Louis Meyer 18.00 30.00
1937 Wilbur Shaw 25.00 40.00
1938 Floyd Roberts 18.00 30.00
1939 Wilbur Shaw 25.00 40.00
1940 Wilbur Shaw 25.00 40.00
1941 Floyd Davis 25.00 40.00
Mauri Rose
1946 George Robson 18.00 30.00
1947 Mauri Rose 25.00 40.00
1948 Mauri Rose 25.00 40.00
1949 Bill Holland 18.00 30.00
1950 Johnnie Parsons 25.00 40.00
1951 Lee Wallard 18.00 30.00
1952 Troy Ruttman 18.00 30.00
1953 Bill Vukovich 18.00 30.00

1966 Strombecker

These cards were presumably made in Europe by the Strombecker Corporation. There are 12 known unnumbered cards with each featuring a type of race car from various manufacturers. The cardfronts include a gold or yellow border, a color photo of the car and the flag of the manufacturer's home country. The backs are blue and include detailed stats on the featured car.

COMPLETE SET (12) 150.00 300.00
1 BRM Formula One 12.50 25.00
2 Cobra 12.50 25.00
3 Cooper Formula One 12.50 25.00
4 Ferrari Formula One 12.50 25.00
5 Ferrari GTO 12.50 25.00
6 Ford GT 12.50 25.00
7 Jaguar D-Type 12.50 25.00
8 Jaguar XK-E 12.50 25.00
9 Lotus 19 12.50 25.00
10 Lotus 38 12.50 25.00
11 Plymouth Barracuda 12.50 25.00
12 Porsche 904 12.50 25.00

1911 Turkey Red Automobile Series

This 50-card set features most of the race cars from the early 1900's. The cards were made in New York City and released in the Turkish cigarette brand from the American Tobacco Company. The cards measure 2" X 2 5/8" and came one per pack or box. Many of the card backs talk about the 1910 Vanderbilt Cup and therefore it has been determined that the set was issued either in late 1910 or in 1911. There is a possibility that the set was released over a period of years from 1909-1911. The set was reprinted by Bowman in 1953 and called Antique Autos. The reprint cards have 3-D backs that required the wearing of 3-D glasses for reading.

COMPLETE SET (50) 350.00 600.00
1 Acme Racer 7.50 15.00
2 Alco Racer 7.50 15.00
3 Apperson Racer 7.50 15.00
4 Baker Electric Racer 7.50 15.00
5 Benz Racer 7.50 15.00
6 Buick Racer 7.50 15.00
7 Cadillac Racer 7.50 15.00
8 Chadwick Racer 7.50 15.00
9 Chalmers-Detroit Racer 7.50 15.00
10 Corbin Racer 7.50 15.00
11 De Dietrcih Racer 7.50 15.00
12 Fiat Racer 7.50 15.00
13 Ford Racer 7.50 15.00
14 Franklin Racer 7.50 15.00
15 Gaeth Racer 7.50 15.00
16 Haynes Racer 7.50 15.00
17 Hotchkiss Racer 7.50 15.00
18 Hudson Racer 7.50 15.00
19 Isotta Racer 7.50 15.00
20 Knox Racer 7.50 15.00
21 Lancia Racer 7.50 15.00
22 Locomobile Racer 7.50 15.00
23 Lozier Racer 7.50 15.00
24 Matheson Racer 7.50 15.00
25 Maxwell Racer 7.50 15.00
26 Mercedes Racer 7.50 15.00
27 Mitchell Racer 7.50 15.00
28 Moline Racer 7.50 15.00
29 National Racer 7.50 15.00
30 Oldsmobile Racer 7.50 15.00
31 Packard Racer 7.50 15.00
32 Palmer-Singer Racer 7.50 15.00
33 Panhard Racer 7.50 15.00
34 Peerless Racer 7.50 15.00
35 Pierce-Arrow Racer 7.50 15.00
36 Pope-Hartford Racer 7.50 15.00
37 Premier Racer 7.50 15.00
38 Pullman Racer 7.50 15.00
39 Rainier Racer 7.50 15.00
40 Rambler Racer 7.50 15.00
41 Renault Racer 7.50 15.00
42 Reo Racer 7.50 15.00
43 Simplex Racer 7.50 15.00
44 Stearns Racer 7.50 15.00
45 Stevens-Duryea Racer 7.50 15.00
46 Stoddard-Dayton Racer 7.50 15.00
47 Studebaker Racer 7.50 15.00
48 Thomas Racer 7.50 15.00
49 White Racer 7.50 15.00
50 Winton Racer 7.50 15.00

1930 Wills' Cigarettes

This eight-card European tobacco issue is part of a bigger 50 card set. The cards were produced by Imperial Tobacco Company of Great Britain and Ireland. The set features all types of transportation vehicles. The cards measure 1 3/8" X 2 5/8" and feature artwork of the vehicles for card fronts. The backs give a bio of the car pictured.

COMPLETE SET (8) 15.00 30.00
23 Malcom Campbell 2.00 5.00
24 Sir Henry Seagrave 2.00 5.00
25 Captain Henry Birkin 2.00 5.00
26 Mrs. Victor Bruce 2.00 5.00
27 Boris Ivanonski 2.00 5.00
28 Kay Don 2.00 5.00
29 Rudolf Carcciola 2.00 5.00
30 Sv. Holbrook 2.00 5.00

1938 Wills' Cigarettes

This European tobacco issue is part of a bigger 50 card set. The set is titled Speed and features all types of transportation vehicles. The cards measure 1 3/8" X 2 5/8" and feature artwork of the vehicles for card fronts. The backs give a bio of the car pictured.

COMPLETE SET (8) 10.00 20.00
16 Captain G.E.T. Eyston 1.25 3.00
17 Malcom Campbell 1.25 3.00
18 Ab Jenkins 1.25 3.00
19 John Cobb 1.25 3.00
20 Major Goldie Gardner 1.25 3.00
21 Raymond Mays 1.25 3.00
22 Rudolf Caracciola 1.25 3.00
23 Bernt Rosemeyer 1.25 3.00

1991 Bull Ring

Bull Ring Race Cards produced this set in 1991 featuring popular drivers of short track competition. The cards include a color driver photo on the cardfront and a driver career summary on the back. Butch Lindley, Card number 1 is a memorial card.

COMPLETE SET (144) 6.00 12.00
1 Butch Lindley .02 .10
2 Jerry Goodwin .02 .10
3 Todd Massey .02 .10
4 Bobby Gill .02 .10
5 Rich Bickle .07 .20
6 Freddie Query .02 .10
7 Mike Garvey .02 .10
8 Jay Fogelman .02 .10
9 Andy Thurman .02 .10
10 Beano Francis .02 .10
11 David Smith .02 .10
12 Karen Schulz .02 .10
13 Jerry McCart .02 .10
14 Rick Crawford .02 .10
15 Mark Day .02 .10
16 Hal Goodson .02 .10
17 Jerry Allen VanHorn .02 .10
18 Joe Frasson .02 .10
19 Kevin Smith .02 .10
20 Sammy Pegram .02 .10
21 Donnie York .02 .10
22 Doug Noe .02 .10
23 Dickie Linville .02 .10
24 Granny Tatroe's Car .02 .10
25 Mike Cope .02 .10
26 Robby Faggart .02 .10
27 James Trammell .02 .10
28 Billy Bigley, Jr. .02 .10
29 Mitchell Barrett .02 .10
30 Scott Kilby .02 .10
31 Brian Pack .02 .10
32 Randy Porter .02 .10
33 Jimmy McClain .02 .10
34 Larry Beaver .02 .10
35 Robby Johnson .02 .10
36 David Russell .02 .10
37 Larry Raines .02 .10
38 Steve Walker .02 .10
39 Stephen Grimes .02 .10
40 Dale Fischlein .02 .10
41 Max Prestwood, Jr. .02 .10
42 Tres Wilson .02 .10
43 Jerry Williams .02 .10
44 Larry Caudill .07 .20
45 Phil Gann .02 .10
46 Danny Blevins .02 .10
47 Ronnie Payne .07 .20
48 Mike Miller .02 .10
49 Debbie Lunsford .02 .10
50 John Gerstner II .02 .10
51 Chrissy Oliver .02 .10
52 Scotty Lovelady .02 .10
53 Duke Southard .02 .10
54 Bob Pressley .02 .10
55 Debris Brown .02 .10
56 Robert Powell .02 .10
57 Jason Keller .75 2.00
58 John Kelly .02 .10
59 Robert Pressley .20 .50
60 Don Carlton .02 .10
61 Mike Pressley .07 .20
62 Smiley Rich .02 .10
63 Mark Miner .02 .10
64 John Earl Barton .02 .10
65 Rodger Gentry .02 .10
66 Wesley Mills .02 .10
67 Joey Sims .02 .10
68 Lloyd Slagle .02 .10
69 Sidney Minton .02 .10
70 Ronnie Davidson .02 .10
71 Donnie Bishop .02 .10
72 Johnny Cochran .02 .10
73 Scott Sutherland .02 .10
74 Jack Sprague .20 .50
75 Robert Huffman .02 .10
76 Tim Roberts .02 .10
77 Ted Hodgdon .02 .10
78 Gary Bradberry .07 .20
79 Steve Holzhausen .02 .10
80 Danny Shortt .02 .10
81 Lee Faulk .02 .10
82 Barry Beggarly .07 .20
83 Rodney Howard .02 .10
84 Kevin Evans .02 .10
85 Greg Hendrix .02 .10
86 Tim Gordon .02 .10
87 Danny Slack .02 .10
88 Chris Mullinax .02 .10
89 Brian Butler .02 .10
90 Randy Couch .02 .10
91 Dennis Setzer .07 .20
92 Dick Anderson .02 .10
93 Junior Niedecken .02 .10
94 Gary Nix .02 .10
95 Terry Davis .02 .10
96 Charlie Stokes .02 .10
97 Marty Ward .02 .10
98 Jody Ridley .02 .10
99 Chris Diamond .02 .10
100 Tom Usry .02 .10
101 Robin Hayes .02 .10
102 Johnny Reynolds .02 .10
103 Shelton McNair, Jr. .02 .10
104 Grump Wills .02 .10
105 Jeff Agnew .02 .10
106 Ronald Walls .02 .10
107 Eddie Hanks .02 .10
108 Mickey York .02 .10
109 Larry Ogle .02 .10
110 Jacky Workman .02 .10
111 Tuck Trentham .02 .10
112 Richard Landreth, Jr. .02 .10
113 David Rogers .02 .10

114 Mike Harmon .02 .10
115 Toby Porter .02 .10
116 Stacy Compton .40 1.00
117 Ricky Vaughn .02 .10
118 Tommy Grimes .02 .10
119 Mike McSwain .02 .10
120 Roy Chatham .02 .10
121 Johnny Rumley .02 .10
122 Doug Strickland .02 .10
123 Tommy Ruff .02 .10
124 Jeff Williams .02 .10
125 Mike Love .02 .10
126 A.J. Sanders .02 .10
127 Dallas Wilcox .02 .10
128 Dennis Crump .02 .10
129 Kevin Barrett .02 .10
130 Mike Toemmes .02 .10
131 Gene Pack .02 .10
132 Robbie Ferguson .02 .10
133 Buddy Vance .02 .10
134 Ralph Carnes .02 .10
135 Rick Lambert .02 .10
136 Bart Ingram .02 .10
137 Pete Orr .02 .10
138 Shawna Robinson .60 1.50
139 Mike Porter .02 .10
140 Scott Green .02 .10
141 Darrell Holman .02 .10
142 Jeff Finley .02 .10
143 Junior Franks .02 .10
144 Jabe Jones .02 .10

1992 Bull Ring

This 200-card set was the second complete set produced by Bull Ring Race Cards. The 1992 features popular drivers of short track competition. The cards include a color driver photo on the cardfront with a blue border and a driver career summary and biographical information on the back.

COMPLETE SET (200) 15.00 25.00
1 Checklist Card .02 .10
2 Jerry Goodwin .02 .10
3 Beano Francis .02 .10
4 Edward Jordan .02 .10
5 Rickie Bickle .15 .40
6 Stacy Compton .40 1.00
7 Mike Garvey .02 .10
8 Jay Fogelman .02 .10
9 C.J. Johnson .02 .10
10 Chad Chaffin .15 .40
11 David Rogers .02 .10
12 Karen Schulz .02 .10
13 Jerry McCart .02 .10
14 Rick Crawford .02 .10
15 Clay Brown .02 .10
16 Hal Goodson .02 .10
17 Jerry A. Van Horn .02 .10
18 Joe Frasson .02 .10
19 Scotty Lovelady .02 .10
20 Dallas Wilcox .02 .10
21 Sammy Pegram .02 .10
22 Doug Noe .02 .10
23 Brad Sorenson .02 .10
24 Mike Harmon .02 .10
25 Mike Cope .02 .10
26 Tuck Trentham .02 .10
27 Danny Fair .02 .10
28 Billy Bigley, Jr. .02 .10
29 Chris Mullinax .02 .10
30 Mike Love .02 .10
31 Gary Balough .02 .10
32 Randy Porter .02 .10
33 Jimmy McClain .02 .10
34 Scott Green .02 .10
35 Wesley Mills .02 .10
36 David Russell .02 .10
37 Larry Raines .02 .10
38 Pete Orr .02 .10
39 Robert Huffman .02 .10
40 Chrissy Oliver .02 .10
Checklist back
41 Max Prestwood, Jr. .02 .10
42 Tres Wilson .02 .10
43 Mike Borghi .02 .10
44 Larry Caudill .15 .40
45 Duke Southard .02 .10
46 Wade Buttrey .02 .10
47 Phil Warren .02 .10
48 Jack Sprague .15 .40
49 Debbie Lunsford .02 .10
50 Mike Buffkin .02 .10
51 Jeff Purvis .15 .40
52 Tammy Kirk .02 .10
53 Charlie Ragan, Jr. .02 .10
54 Bob Pressley .02 .10
55 Debris Brown .02 .10
56 Robert Powell .02 .10
57 Jason Keller .25 .60
58 Jeff Agnew .02 .10
59 Robert Pressley .15 .40
60 Ralph Carnes .02 .10
61 Tim Steele .15 .40
62 Buckshot Jones .60 1.50
63 Chuck Abell .02 .10
64 John Earl Barton .02 .10
65 Robert Hester .02 .10
66 Freddie Query .02 .10
67 Rodney Howard .02 .10
68 Mark Day .02 .10
69 Sidney Minton .02 .10
70 Granny Tatroe .02 .10
71 Donnie Bishop .02 .10
72 Eddie Mercer .02 .10
73 John Livinston, Jr. .02 .10
74 Wayne Willard .02 .10
75 Bobby Brack .02 .10
76 Dennis Schoenfeld .02 .10
77 Johnny Chapman .02 .10
78 Gary Bradberry .15 .40
79 Robby Faggart .02 .10
80 Randy Porter .02 .10
Checklist back
81 Mike Pressley .02 .10
82 Barry Beggarly .08 .25
83 Bubba Gale .02 .10
84 Sean Graham .02 .10
85 Joe Winchell .02 .10
86 Bubba Adams .02 .10
87 Ron Barfield .15 .40
88 Mike McCrary, Jr. .02 .10
89 Steve Walker .02 .10
90 Stan Eads .02 .10
91 Todd Massey .02 .10
92 Dick Anderson .02 .10
93 Junior Niedecken .02 .10
94 Johnny Reynolds .02 .10
95 Robert Elliott .02 .10
96 Jack Cook .02 .10
97 Marty Ward .02 .10
98 Jody Ridley .15 .40
99 Charlie Stokes .02 .10
100 Chrissy Oliver .02 .10
101 Eddie Perry .02 .10
102 Claude Gwin, Jr. .02 .10
103 Shelton McNair, Jr. .02 .10
104 Charles Powell III .02 .10
105 Jeff Agnew .02 .10
106 P.B. Crowell III .02 .10
107 Eddie Hanks .02 .10
108 Tink Reedy .02 .10
109 Larry Ogle .02 .10
110 David Showers .02 .10
111 David Rogers .02 .10
112 Danny Sikes .02 .10
113 Charlie Brown .02 .10
114 Roy Hendrick .02 .10
115 Randy Bynum .02 .10
116 Mike Howell .02 .10
117 Mark Miner .02 .10
118 Danny Shortt .02 .10
119 Kevin Smith .02 .10
120 Larry Caudill .08 .25
Checklist back
121 Johnny Rumley .08 .25
122 Mickey York .02 .10
123 Dickie Linville .02 .10
124 A.W. Kirby, Jr. .02 .10
125 Mike Love .02 .10
126 Gary Nix .02 .10
127 Jeff Burkett .02 .10
128 Rick Lambert .02 .10
129 Marc Kinley .02 .10
130 Mardy Lindley .02 .10
131 Mitchell Barrett .02 .10
132 Robbie Ferguson .02 .10
133 Rodney Combs, Jr. .15 .40
134 Ned Combs .02 .10
135 Terry Davis .02 .10
136 Bobby Knox .02 .10
137 Richard Hargrove .02 .10
138 Curtis Markham .08 .25
139 Stephen Grimes .02 .10
140 Penn Crim, Jr. .02 .10
141 Brian Butler .02 .10
142 Terry Lee .02 .10
143 David Bonnett .15 .40
144 Lloyd Slagle .02 .10
145 Greg Motes .02 .10
146 Don Carlton .02 .10
147 David Smith .02 .10
148 Darrell Holman .02 .10
149 Orvil Reedy .02 .10
150 Craig Gower .02 .10
151 Bill Posey .02 .10
152 Phil Gann .02 .10
153 Bugs Hairfield .02 .10
154 Ronnie Thomas .02 .10
155 Dennis Southerlin .02 .10
156 Brian King .02 .10
157 Ed Meredith .02 .10
158 Andy Houston .02 .10
159 Ronnie Roach .02 .10
160 Checklist Card .02 .10
161 Elton Sawyer .15 .40
162 Danny Blevins .02 .10
163 Greg Marlowe .02 .10
164 Mike Reynolds .02 .10
165 Tommy Spangler .02 .10
166 Dennis Setzer .15 .40
167 Jabe Jones .02 .10
168 Jacky Workman .02 .10
169 Jimmy Cope .02 .10
170 Mike Dillon .08 .25
171 Bobby Gill .02 .10
172 Chris Diamond .02 .10
173 Scott Kilby .02 .10
174 Pete Hughes .02 .10
175 Donnie York .02 .10
176 Junior Franks .02 .10
177 Ron Young .02 .10
178 Tom Usry .02 .10
179 Greg Hendrix .02 .10
180 Toby Porter .02 .10
181 Mike Hovis .02 .10
182 Richard Landreth, Jr. .02 .10
183 Kevin Barrett .02 .10
184 Marty Houston .02 .10
185 G.C. Campbell .02 .10
186 Tony Ponder .02 .10
187 Danny Slack .02 .10
188 Michael McSwain .02 .10
189 Kevin Evans .02 .10
190 Tim Roberts .02 .10
191 Greg Cecil .02 .10
192 A.J. Sanders .02 .10
193 Richard Starkey .02 .10
194 Hal Perry .02 .10
195 Dennis Crump .02 .10
196 Rob Underwood .02 .10
197 Donn Fenn .02 .10
198 Mark Cox .02 .10
199 Lee Tissot .02 .10
200 Butch Lindley .02 .10

2002 Choice Rising Stars

This set was produced in 2002 by Choice Marketing. Each card was printed on glossy card stock with a full color driver image on the front and a black and white cardback. The set features some of the top short track drivers in the country.

COMPLETE SET (28) 12.00 30.00
1 Chris Wimmer .30 .75
2 Pat Kelly .30 .75
3 Zach Niessner .30 .75
4 Gary St.Amant .40 1.00
5 Joey Clanton .30 .75
6 Jake Hodges .30 .75
7 Rich Gardner .30 .75
8 Scott Null .30 .75
9 Greg Williams .30 .75
10 J.C. Beattie .30 .75
11 Jeff Emery .30 .75
12 Robbie Pyle .40 1.00
13 John Silverthorne .30 .75
14 Ed Brown .30 .75
15 Doug Mahlik .30 .75
16 Brandon Miller .30 .75
17 Wayne Anderson .30 .75
18 Kyle Busch 2.50 6.00
19 Russ Tuttle .30 .75
20 Chad Wood .30 .75
21 Dan Fredrickson .30 .75
22 Reed Sorenson XRC 1.00 2.50
23 Mike Garvey .40 1.00
24 Rick Beebe .40 1.00
25 Todd Kluever XRC .75 2.00
26 Greg Stewart .30 .75
27 Kevin Cywinski .30 .75
28 Mike Cope .40 1.00

1992 Corter Selinsgrove and Clinton County Speedways

Corter Race Cards produced this set commemorating drivers of the Pennsylvania Selinsgrove and Clinton County Speedways. Sets were packaged in a plastic case and each was individually numbered of 1,200.

COMPLETE SET (36) 5.00 12.00
1 David Corter's Car .10 .30
2 Steve Campbell's Car .10 .30
3 Lenny Krautheim's Car .10 .30
4 Dale Schweikart's Car .10 .30
5 Barry Knouse's Car .10 .30
6 Jim Nace .20 .50
7 Dennis Hahn .20 .50
8 Richard Jensen's Car .10 .30
9 Bill Glenn's Car .10 .30
10 George Fultz's Car .10 .30
11 Todd Shaffer .20 .50
12 Craig Lindsey's Car .10 .30
13 Penrose Kester's Car .10 .30
14 Eric Hons' Car .10 .30
15 Luke Hoffner's Car .10 .30
16 Jim Stine w/Car .20 .50
17 Alan Cole's Car .10 .30
18 Fred Rahmer's Car .10 .30
19 Ed Shafer's Car .10 .30
20 Steve Byers' Car .10 .30
21 Donald Schick, Jr.'s Car .10 .30
22 Dustin Hoffman w/Car .20 .50
23 James Gearhart .20 .50
24 Wesley Matthews w/Car .20 .50
25 John Hafer's Car .10 .30
26 Glenn Fitzcharles' Car .10 .30
27 Arthur Probst, Jr. .20 .50
28 Scott Barrett's Car .10 .30
29 Franklin Benfer's Car .10 .30
30 Dwayne Wasson .20 .50
31 Jerry Hollenbach w/Car .20 .50
32 Chuck Reinert, Jr.'s Car .10 .30
33 David Matthews w/Car .20 .50
34 Robby Smith's Car .10 .30
35 C.W. Smith's Car .10 .30
36 Robin Johnson .20 .50

1993 Corter Selinsgrove and Clinton County Speedways

This 36-card set is the second edition from Corter Race Cards. The sets feature drivers and their cars

that raced at the Pennsylvania speedway. There were 1,000 sets produced. Each set comes in a snap it case and has a cover card with the number of 1,000 that each particular set is. An uncut sheet of the set was given to each of the drivers that appeared in the set.

COMPLETE SET (36) 4.00 10.00
1 Richie Jensen .10 .30
2 Steve Campbell .10 .30
3 Lenny Krautheim III .10 .30
4 Dale Schweikart .10 .30
5 Dwayne Wasson .20 .50
6 Jim Nace .20 .50
7 Dustin Hoffman .20 .50
8 Chuck Reinert Jr. .10 .30
9 Boyd Toner Sr. .10 .30
10 George Fultz .10 .30
11 Jim Stine .20 .50
12 Craig Lindsey .10 .30
13 David Brouse Sr. .10 .30
14 Eric Hons .10 .30
15 Luke Hoffner .10 .30
16 Vern Wasson .10 .30
17 Alan Cole .10 .30
18 James Gearhart .20 .50
19 Ed Shafer .20 .50
In Memory
20 Pen Kester's Car .10 .30
21 Don Schick Jr. .10 .30
22 Timothy Bowmaster .10 .30
23 Larry Bair .10 .30
24 Bob Bertasavage .10 .30
25 John Hafer's Car .10 .30
26 Glenn Fitzcharles .20 .50
27 Wayne Peeling .10 .30
28 Dave Lundgren .10 .30
29 Bill Crawford .10 .30
30 Grover Graham .10 .30
31 Loren Armes .10 .30
32 Edward Overdorf .10 .30
33 Ron Kramer .10 .30
34 Robby Smith .10 .30
35 Joey Borich .10 .30
36 Christa Koch .10 .30
Ms.Selinsgrove

1991 Dirt Trax

Volunteer Racing produced this set in two series. Each series was released in its own plastic factory set box. The cards were printed on thin stock and carry blue borders and yellow cardbacks.

COMPLETE SET (72) 6.00 12.00
COMPLETE SERIES 1 (36) 3.00 6.00
COMPLETE SERIES 2 (36) 3.00 6.00
1 Buck Simmons .07 .20
2 Herman Goddard .07 .20
3 H.E. Vinegard .07 .20
4 Billy Moyer Jr.'s Car UER .10 .30
Moyers on front
5 Rodney Combs .20 .50
6 Bob Pierce .07 .20
7 Jack Boggs .20 .50
8 Jack Pennington .07 .20
9 Ronnie Johnson .10 .30
10 Hot Rod LaMance .07 .20
11 Scott Bloomquist .20 .50
12 Donnie Moran .10 .30
13 Eddie Carrier's Car .07 .20
14 Ed Basey .07 .20
15 Dale McDowell .07 .20
16 Ed Gibbons .07 .20
17 Mike Balzano .10 .30
18 John Gill's Car .07 .20
19 Jack Trammell .10 .30
20 Skip Arp .07 .20
21 David Bilbrey .07 .20
22 James Cline .07 .20
23 Wade Knowles .10 .30
24 Joe Meadows' Car .07 .20
25 Gary Hall's Car .07 .20
26 Bob Cowen .07 .20
27 Bob Wearing, Jr. .10 .30
28 Rusty Goddard .07 .20
29 Scott Sexton .07 .20
30 Steve Francis .20 .50
31 Billy Ogle, Jr. .10 .30
32 Barry Hurt .07 .20
33 Mark Vineyard .07 .20
34 Bobby Thomas's Car .07 .20
35 John Mason's Car .07 .20
36 Cover Card .07 .20
Checklist 1-36
37 Buck Simmons .07 .20
38 Jerry Inmon .07 .20
Mississippi Flyer
39 Billy Moyer .20 .50
40 Mike Head .07 .20
41 Stan Massey .07 .20
42 Mike Duvall .10 .30
Flintstone Flyer
43 Jack Pennington .07 .20
44 Jeff Purvis .30 .75
45 Eddie Pace .07 .20
46 Bill Ingram .07 .20
47 Hot Rod LaMance .07 .20
48 Ricky Weeks' Car .07 .20
49 Lynn Geisler .07 .20
50 Kevin Claycomb .07 .20
51 Nathan Durboraw .07 .20
52 Doug McCammon .07 .20
53 Ed Basey .07 .20
54 C.J. Rayburn .07 .20
55 Bobby Thomas .07 .20
56 Gary Stuhler .07 .20
57 Davey Johnson .10 .30
58 Clay Kelley .07 .20
59 Chub Frank .20 .50
60 Tom Rients .07 .20
61 Todd Andrews .07 .20
62 Paul Croft's Car .07 .20
63 Wendall Wallace .07 .20
64 Tom Helfrich w/Car .07 .20
65 John Jones .07 .20
66 Tony Cardin w/Car .07 .20
67 Dion Deason's Car .07 .20
68 Marty Calloway .07 .20
69 Mark Gansmann .07 .20
70 Jeff Treece .07 .20
71 Darrell Lanigan .07 .20
72 Cover Card .07 .20
Checklist 37-72

1992 Dirt Trax

Volunteer Racing Promotions produced this set featuring popular drivers of the Dirt Track Series. The blue bordered cards were sold in complete factory set form as well as through 10-card cello wrappers called wax pax. There were four Gold cards also produced (1000 of each) as a random insert in packs.

COMPLETE SET (100) 5.00 12.00
1 Cover/Checklist Card .05 .15
2 Freddy Smith .15 .40
3 Jerry Inmon .05 .15
4 Delmas Conley .05 .15
5 Herman Goddard .05 .15
6 Tom Nesbitt .05 .15
7 Larry Moore .05 .15
8 Billy Moyer .15 .40
9 Mike Head .05 .15
10 Bob Pierce .05 .15
11 Rodney Combs .15 .40
12 Jack Boggs .08 .25
13 Mike Duvall .08 .25
14 Ronnie Johnson .08 .25
15 Rick Aukland .08 .25
16 Steve Kosiski .05 .15
17 Scott Bloomquist .15 .40
18 Bill Ingram .05 .15
19 Rod LaMance .05 .15
20 Donnie Moran .08 .25
21 Ed Basey .05 .15
22 Pete Parker .05 .15
23 Delbert Smith .05 .15
24 Nathan Durboraw .05 .15
25 Rex Richey .05 .15
26 Bill Ogle Sr. .05 .15
27 Mike Balzano .08 .25
28 Tom Rients .05 .15
29 John Gill .08 .25
30 Skip Arp .05 .15
31 David Bilbrey .05 .15
32 Clay Kelley .05 .15
33 Chub Frank .15 .40
34 Todd Andrews .05 .15
35 Wade Knowles .08 .25
36 Bill Frye .08 .25
37 Kevin Weaver .08 .25
38 Joe Meadows .05 .15
39 John Booper Bare .05 .15
40 Ron Davies .05 .15
41 Gary Hall .05 .15
42 John Jones .05 .15
43 Dick Barton .05 .15
44 Andy Dill .05 .15
45 Steve Francis .15 .40
46 Davey Johnson .08 .25
47 Billy Ogle Jr. .08 .25
48 Troy Green .05 .15
49 Gary Green .05 .15
50 Jake Lowry .05 .15
51 Checklist Card .05 .15
52 Ronnie Johnson .08 .25
Jack Boggs
Scott Bloomquist
53 Roger Bagwell .05 .15
54 Randy Boggs .05 .15
55 Denny Bonebrake .05 .15
56 Marty Calloway .05 .15
57 Tony Cardin .05 .15
58 Perry County Speedway .05 .15
59 Gene Chupp .05 .15
60 Kevin Claycomb .05
61 Phil Coltrane .05
62 Tootle Estes .05
63 Red Farmer .15
64 Mark Gansmann .05
65 Lynn Geisler .05
66 Ed Gibbons .05
67 Matt Gilardi .05
68 Rusty Goddard .05
69 Tom Helfrich .05
70 Doug Ingalls .05
71 Joe Kosiski .05
72 Darrell Lanigan .05
73 Freddie Lee .05
74 Tiny Lund .15
75 John Mason .05
76 Stan Massey .05
77 Larry McDaniels .05
78 Dale McDowell .05
79 Ben Miley .05
80 Buddy Morris .05
81 David Moyer .05
82 Eddie Pace .05
83 Jack Pennington .05
84 C.J. Rayburn .05
85 Scott Sexton .05
86 Steve Shaver .05
87 Buck Simmons .05
88 Jeff Smith .05
89 Steve Smith .08
90 Steve Smith .08
91 Gary Stuhler .05
92 Charlie Swartz .05
93 Bobby Thomas .05
94 Jack Trammell .08
95 Carl Trimmer .05
96 Wendall Wallace .05
97 Bob Wearing Jr. .05
Bob Wearing Sr.
98 Ricky Weeks .05
99 Johnny Williams .05
100 Ivan Russell .05

2003 Dirt Trax

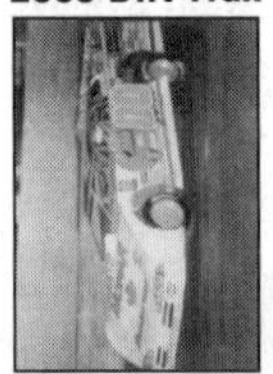

Volunteer Racing Promotions produced thi featuring popular drivers of various Dirt Track S The borderless cards were sold in complete fa set form and printed on very thin glossy stock cards were not numbered but have been assi card numbers below based upon the listings o two checklist cards.

COMPLETE SET (50) 8.00 20
1 Todd Andrews .20
2 Skip Arp's Car .20
3 Rick Aukland's Car .40
4 Shannon Babb's Car .40
5 Mike Balzano .40
6 Brian Birkhofer .20
7 Robbie Blair .40
8 Randle Chupp .20
9 Delmas Conley's Car .20
10 R.J. Conley's Car .20
11 Rod Conley's Car .20
12 Ray Cook's Car .20
13 Mike Duvall's Car .40
14 Rick Eckert .40
15 Terry English's Car .40
16 Dennis Erb Jr.'s Car .40
17 Chris Francis .40
18 Steve Francis .60
19 Chub Frank .60
20 Bill Frye's Car .40
21 John Gill's Car .40
22 Bart Hartman's Car .20
23 Mike Head's Car .20
24 Tim Hitt's Car .20
25 Checklist 1 .20
26 Duayne Hommell's Car .40
27 Davey Johnson .40
28 Johnny Johnson's Car .20
29 Mike Johnson .20
30 Ronnie Johnson's Car .40
31 Randy Korte's Car .20
32 Jimmy Mars .20
33 Dale McDowell .20
34 Matt Miller .40
35 Donnie Moran .40
36 Billy Moyer's Car .60
37 Terrence Nowell's Car .20
38 Don O'Neal's Car .20
39 Earl Pearson Jr. .20
40 Terry Phillips's Car .40
41 Bob Pierce's Car .20
42 Dan Schlieper .20
43 Steve Shaver .20
44 Clint Smith's Car .20
45 Freddy Smith's Car .60
46 Jeff Smith's Car .20
47 Gary Stuhler .20
48 Wendall Wallace's Car .20
49 Chris Francis .60
Steve Francis
50 Checklist 2 .20

1991 DK IMCA Dirt Tra

This 53-card set features Dirt Track drivers fro IMCA series. The cards were issued in comple form.

LETE SET (53)	6.00	12.00
klist Card	.07	.20
Gallaher	.07	.20
Watts	.07	.20
y Breuer	.07	.20
Daughters	.07	.20
Carr	.07	.20
Shryock	.07	.20
Dralle	.07	.20
Strothman	.07	.20
Johnson	.07	.20
ty Patterson	.07	.20
in Cale	.07	.20
Jackson	.07	.20
y Ryan	.07	.20
de Russell	.07	.20
ve Sutliff	.07	.20
in Birkhofer	.07	.20
y Pilcher	.07	.20
n Richard	.07	.20
y Stewart	2.00	5.00
ve Hennies	.07	.20
Johnson	.07	.20
id Birkhofer	.07	.20
e Fitzpatrick	.07	.20
lie Frink	.07	.20
Jennings	.07	.20
e Smith	.07	.20
nk Springsteen	.07	.20
Wood	.07	.20
Stewart	.07	.20
ve Fraise	.07	.20
Martin	.07	.20
Guss, Jr.	.07	.20
y Webb	.07	.20
ny Smyser	.07	.20
Verly	.07	.20
ry Walker	.07	.20
g Kastli	.07	.20
Boyse	.07	.20
Alkey	.07	.20
Wendling	.07	.20
Forsyth	.07	.20
an Wanner	.07	.20
Johnson	.07	.20
g Hopkins	.07	.20
g Jacobs	.07	.20
by Greiner Jr.	.07	.20
nny Johnson	.07	.20
rel DeFrance	.07	.20
ty Gall	.07	.20
dy Krampe	.07	.20
Pallister	.07	.20
LeKander	.07	.20

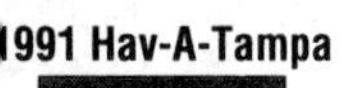

1991 Hav-A-Tampa

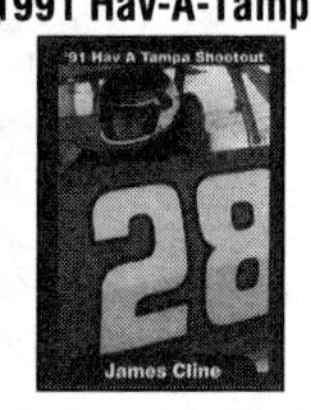

ed by Volunteer Racing, this 28-card set drivers and cars of the Hav-A-Tampa series. ds feature black borders with color photos re distributed in complete set form. The checklist card is not numbered, but was d to be card #1.

LETE SET (28)	3.00	6.00
r Card	.08	.25
ecklist		
numbered		
4 Drivers	.08	.25
m Photo		
ngram	.08	.25
Reaid	.08	.25
my Mosteller		
1 Champion		
Reaid	.08	.25
ichey	.08	.25
ey Combs Sr.	.15	.40
Coltrane	.08	.25
Knowles	.15	.40
e Head	.08	.25
Basey	.08	.25
es Cline	.08	.25
by Thomas	.08	.25
ger Howell's Car UER	.08	.25
e misspelled Grainger		
nie Johnson's Car	.08	.25
ick Rainey	.08	.25
ne Echols' Car	.08	.25
die Lee's Car	.08	.25
ne McCullough	.08	.25
Stansberry	.08	.25
ngram's Car	.08	.25
e Nicholson	.08	.25
n Jones	.08	.25
d Moyer's Car	.08	.25
Massey	.08	.25
Arp	.08	.25
Summerville	.08	.25
dy Morris w/Car	.08	.25

1992 Hav-A-Tampa

er Racing Promotions produced this set g drivers of the Hav-A-Tampa Series. The clude the top 24 drivers of the series along checklist card and were sold in complete set

LETE SET (28)	4.00	8.00
r/Checklist Card	.10	.30

2 Top 24 Group	.10	.30
3 Jimmy Mosteller	.10	.30
4 Red Farmer Capitol Sports Radio	.10	.30
5 Buddy Morris	.10	.30
6 Ronnie Johnson's Car	.10	.30
7 Phil Coltrane's Car	.10	.30
8 Rex Richey's Car	.10	.30
9 Wade Knowles' Car	.20	.50
10 Rodney Combs' Car	.20	.50
11 Bobby Turner's Car	.10	.30
12 Dale McDowell's Car	.10	.30
13 Mike Head's Car	.10	.30
14 Stan Massey w/car	.10	.30
15 Tony Reaid's Car	.10	.30
16 Freddie Lee's Car	.10	.30
17 Ricky Williams' Car	.10	.30
18 Jody Summerville's Car	.10	.30
19 David Chancy's Car	.10	.30
20 Greg Knight's Car	.10	.30
21 Bobby Thomas' Car	.10	.30
22 Rodney Martin's Car	.10	.30
23 Granger Howell's Car	.10	.30
24 Buckshot Miles' Car	.10	.30
25 Wayne Echols' Car	.10	.30
26 Buster Goss' Car	.10	.30
27 John Jones' Car	.10	.30
28 Ed Basey's Car	.10	.30

1995 Hav-A-Tampa

Speed Graphics produced this set featuring drivers of the Hav-A-Tampa Series. The cards include the top personalities of the series along with a checklist card and were sold in complete set form.

COMPLETE SET (42)	6.00	15.00
1 Cover Card	.15	.40
2 Bill Frye	.25	.60
3 Drivers Meeting 1994 Shootout	.15	.40
4 Jeff Smith	.15	.40
5 Ronnie Johnson	.25	.60
6 Jack Boggs	.30	.75
7 Dale McDowell	.15	.40
8 Clint Smith	.15	.40
9 Rodney Martin	.15	.40
10 Dixie Speedway	.15	.40
11 Freddy Smith	.30	.75
12 Jeff Smith	.15	.40
13 Larry Moore	.15	.40
14 David Gibson	.15	.40
15 Danny McClure	.15	.40
16 Kenny Morrow	.15	.40
17 C.S.Fitzgerald	.15	.40
18 DeWayne Johnson	.15	.40
19 Kenny Merchant	.15	.40
20 Bill Ogle Jr.	.25	.60
21 Johnny Virden	.15	.40
22 Bobby Thomas	.15	.40
23 Gar Dickson	.15	.40
24 Mike Carter	.15	.40
25 Wendall Wallace	.15	.40
26 Rex Richey	.15	.40
27 Tony Reaid	.15	.40
28 Earl Pearson Jr.	.15	.40
29 Rick Aukland	.25	.60
30 Donnie Moran UER Donnnie on front	.25	.60
31 Billy Moyer	.30	.75
32 Curtis Gattis	.15	.40
33 Frank Ingram	.15	.40
34 Marshall Green	.15	.40
35 Mark Miner	.15	.40
36 Ray Cook	.15	.40
37 Stan Massey	.15	.40
38 Rod LaMance	.15	.40
39 Mike Duvall	.25	.60
40 Bill Ingram	.15	.40
41 Jimmy Mosteller Founder	.15	.40
42 HAT Officials Nick Masters David Roberts Jim Harrah Checklist back	.15	.40

1991 JAGS

JAGS Race Cards produced this set featuring top drivers of Dirt Late Model competition. This was the first of four sets and featured a light gray card border.

COMPLETE SET (50)	6.00	12.00
1 Scott Bloomquist	.30	.75
2 Jack Boggs' Car	.10	.30
3 Donnie Moran's Car	.20	.50
4 Mike Duvall	.20	.50

5 Gene Chupp's Car	.07	.20
6 Gary Stuhler's Car	.07	.20
7 Ronnie Johnson's Car	.07	.20
8 John Gill	.20	.50
9 James Cline's Car	.07	.20
10 C.J. Rayburn's Car	.07	.20
11 Jim Curry	.10	.30
12 Mike Balzano's Car	.20	.50
13 Rex Richey's Car	.07	.20
14 Kris Patterson	.10	.30
15 Tony Cardin	.10	.30
16 Eddie Carrier	.10	.30
17 Mike Head's Car	.07	.20
18 John Provenzano	.10	.30
19 Bill Frye's Car	.07	.20
20 Steve Francis	.30	.75
21 Randy Boggs' Car	.07	.20
22 Roger Long	.10	.30
23 Daryl Key	.10	.30
24 Bob Pohlman	.10	.30
25 Scott Bloomquist's Car	.20	.50
26 Johnny Stokes' Car	.07	.20
27 Steve Barnett	.10	.30
28 Rex McCroskey	.10	.30
29 Mitch Johnson	.10	.30
30 Wade Knowles	.20	.50
31 Darrell Mooneyham	.10	.30
32 John Mason's Car	.07	.20
33 Ken Essary's Car	.07	.20
34 Wendall Wallace	.10	.30
35 Leslie Essary	.10	.30
36 Rodney Franklin	.10	.30
37 Jerry Inmon	.10	.30
38 Tom Rients	.10	.30
39 Earl Pepper Newby	.10	.30
40 Bob Wearing Jr.	.10	.30
41 Dale McDowell	.10	.30
42 John Booper Bare	.10	.30
43 Buck Simmons' Car	.07	.20
44 Steve Kosiski's Car	.07	.20
45 John Jones' Car	.07	.20
46 Hot Rod LaMance's Car	.07	.20
47 Ricky Weeks' Car	.07	.20
48 Billy Scott	.10	.30
49 Ed Basey's Car	.07	.20
50 Bob Pierce	.10	.30

1992 JAGS

JAGS Race Cards produced this set featuring top drivers of Dirt Late Model competition. This was the second of four sets released by JAGS and featured a light blue card border. The set was distributed in two separate series.

COMPLETE SET (256)	15.00	30.00
COMPLETE SERIES 1 (128)	7.50	15.00
COMPLETE SERIES 2 (128)	7.50	15.00
1 Skip Arp	.05	.15
2 Rick Aukland	.08	.25
3 Doug Ault	.05	.15
4 Mark Banal	.05	.15
5 Dick Barton	.05	.15
6 Shannon Bearden	.05	.15
7 Mike Bechelli	.05	.15
8 Jim Bernheisel	.05	.15
9 Scott Bloomquist	.15	.40
10 Jack Boggs	.15	.40
11 Johnny Bone Jr.	.05	.15
12 Mike Brown	.05	.15
13 Tony Cardin	.05	.15
14 Darrell Carpenter	.05	.15
15 Denny Chamberlain	.05	.15
16 Kevin Claycomb	.05	.15
17 Mike Clonce	.05	.15
18 Phil Coltrane	.05	.15
19 Paul Croft	.05	.15
20 Randy Dunn	.05	.15
21 Hank Edwards	.05	.15
22 Rick Egersdorf	.05	.15
23 Terry English	.08	.25
24 Dennis Erb	.08	.25
25 Ken Essary	.05	.15
26 Rocky Estes	.05	.15
27 Danny Felker	.05	.15
28 Ed Ferree	.05	.15
29 Jeff Floyd	.05	.15
30 Chub Frank	.15	.40
31 Rollie Frink	.05	.15
32 Bill Frye	.08	.25
33 Lynn Geisler	.05	.15
34 Ed Gibbons	.05	.15
35 Herman Goddard	.05	.15
36 Gary Green	.05	.15
37 Marshall Green	.05	.15
38 Kevin Gundaker	.05	.15
39 Phil Hall	.05	.15
40 Paul Harris	.05	.15
41 Mike Head	.05	.15
42 Tom Helfrich	.05	.15
43 Jack Hewitt	.08	.25
44 Brian Hickman	.05	.15
45 Bob Hill	.05	.15
46 Don Hobbs	.05	.15
47 Bruce Hogue	.05	.15
48 J.D. Howard	.05	.15
49 Charlie Hughes	.05	.15
50 Sam Hurd	.05	.15
51 Doug Ingalls	.05	.15
52 Bill Ingram	.05	.15
53 Mike Jewell	.05	.15
54 Johnny Johnson	.05	.15
55 Ronnie Johnson	.08	.25
56 Harvey Jones Jr.	.05	.15
57 Gary Keeling	.05	.15
58 Ed Kosiski	.05	.15
59 Steve Kosiski	.05	.15
60 Willy Kraft	.05	.15
61 Ted Lackey	.05	.15
62 Larry Lambeth	.05	.15
63 Steve Landrum	.05	.15
64 Darrell Lanigan	.05	.15
65 Jerry Lark	.05	.15
66 John Lawhorn	.05	.15
67 Tommy Lawell	.05	.15
68 Rick Lebow	.05	.15
69 Mike Luna	.05	.15
70 Donald Marsh	.05	.15
71 Bill Martin	.05	.15
72 Stan Massey	.05	.15
73 Doug McCammon	.05	.15
74 Gary McPherson	.05	.15
75 Audie McWilliams	.05	.15
76 Joe Meadows	.05	.15
77 Buckshot Miles	.05	.15
78 Brett Miller	.05	.15
79 Larry Moore	.05	.15
80 Donnie Moran	.08	.25
81 David Moyer	.05	.15
82 Tom Nesbitt	.05	.15
83 Bill Ogle	.08	.25
84 Don O'Neal	.05	.15
85 Eddie Pace	.05	.15
86 Pete Parker	.05	.15
87 Bob Pierce	.05	.15
88 Ronnie Poche	.05	.15
89 Al Purkey	.05	.15
90 Jim Rarick	.05	.15
91 Frank Reaber	.05	.15
92 Tony Reaid	.05	.15
93 Joe Rice	.05	.15
94 Rex Richey	.05	.15
95 Eddie Rickman	.05	.15
96 Jerry Robertson	.05	.15
97 Jeff Robinson	.05	.15
98 Steve Russell	.05	.15
99 Doug Sanders	.05	.15
100 Charlie Schaffer	.05	.15
101 Ken Schrader	.05	.15
102 Frank Seder	.05	.15
103 Randy Sellars	.05	.15
104 Scott Sexton	.05	.15
105 Paul Shafer	.05	.15
106 Steve Shaver	.05	.15
107 Clint Smith	.05	.15
108 Delbert Smith	.05	.15
109 Earl Smith	.05	.15
110 Steve Smith	.08	.25
111 Gibby Steinhaus	.05	.15
112 Charlie Swartz	.05	.15
113 Dick Taylor	.05	.15
114 Bobby Thomas	.05	.15
115 Jack Trammell	.08	.25
116 John Utsman	.05	.15
117 Troy VanderVeen	.05	.15
118 H.E. Vineyard	.05	.15
119 Wendall Wallace	.05	.15
120 Bob Wearing Jr.	.05	.15
121 Kevin Weaver	.08	.25
122 Gary Webb	.05	.15
123 Doug Wiggs	.05	.15
124 Rick Williams	.05	.15
125 Randy Woodling	.05	.15
126 Jeff Aikey's Car	.05	.15
127 Tony Albright's Car	.05	.15
128 Chris Anderson's Car	.05	.15
129 Todd Anderson's Car	.05	.15
130 Todd Andrews' Car	.05	.15
131 Brian Ater	.08	.25
132 Steve Baker	.08	.25
133 Mike Balzano's Car	.08	.25
134 Jr. Banks	.08	.25
135 John Booper Bare's Car	.05	.15
136 Joe Barnett	.08	.25
137 Steve Barnett	.08	.25
138 Ed Basey's Car	.05	.15
139 Dave Bilbrey's Car	.05	.15
140 Randy Boggs' Car	.05	.15
141 Don Bohlander's Car	.05	.15
142 Denny Bonebrake's Car	.05	.15
143 Mike Bowers' Car	.05	.15
144 Jay Brinkley	.08	.25
145 Randy Carte	.08	.25
146 David Chancy	.08	.25
147 Gene Chupp	.08	.25
148 Jimmy Clifton's Car	.05	.15
149 Tory Collins' Car	.05	.15
150 Delmas Conley's Car	.05	.15
151 Rick Corbin's Car	.05	.15
152 Jim Curry's Car	.05	.15
153 Jim Donofrio's Car	.05	.15
154 Nelson Dowd's Car	.05	.15
155 Bryan Dunaway	.05	.15
156 Mike Duvall's Car	.08	.25
157 Rick Eckert	.08	.25
158 Leslie Essary	.08	.25
159 Don Eyerly's Car	.05	.15
160 Lee Fleetwood	.08	.25
161 Randy Floyd	.08	.25
162 Steve Francis' Car	.08	.25
163 Rodney Franklin	.08	.25
164 Andy Fries	.08	.25
165 Andy Genzman's Car	.05	.15
166 John Gill's Car	.05	.15
167 Ray Godsey's Car	.05	.15
168 Barry Goodman's Car	.05	.15
169 Gary Gorby	.08	.25
170 Troy Green's Car	.05	.15
171 Phil Gregory's Car	.05	.15
172 Don Gross' Car	.05	.15
173 Johnny Schuler's Car	.05	.15
174 Dave Hoffman's Car	.05	.15
175 Dewayne Hughes' Car	.05	.15
176 Mike Hurlbert's Car	.05	.15
177 Ricky Idom's Car	.05	.15
178 Ricky Ingalls	.08	.25
179 Jerry Inmon	.08	.25
180 Tony Izzo Jr.	.08	.25
181 Mitch Johnson's Car	.05	.15
182 John Jones' Car	.05	.15
183 (Big) Jim Kelly's Car	.05	.15
184 Daryl Key's Car	.05	.15
185 Terry King's Car	.05	.15
186 Wade Knowles's Car	.05	.15
187 Joe Kosiski's Car	.05	.15
188 Hot Rod LaMance's Car	.05	.15
189 Freddie Lee's Car	.05	.15
190 Junior Lemmings	.08	.25
191 Joe Littlejohn's Car	.05	.15
192 Roger Long's Car	.05	.15
193 B.K. Luna	.08	.25
194 Garry Mahoney	.08	.25
195 Donnie Marcoullier Jr.	.08	.25
196 Bill Mason's Car	.05	.15
197 John Mason's Car	.05	.15
198 Lance Matthees' Car	.05	.15
199 Rex McCroskey's Car	.05	.15
200 Dale McDowell's Car	.05	.15
201 Ben Miley	.08	.25
202 Matt Miller	.08	.25
203 Matt Mitchell	.08	.25
204 Darrell Mooneyham	.08	.25
205 Bill Morgan	.08	.25
206 Mike Mullvain	.08	.25
207 Terry Muskrat's Car	.05	.15
208 Earl Pepper Newby	.08	.25
209 Bobby Joe Nicely's Car	.05	.15
210 Mike Norris' Car	.05	.15
211 Keith Nosbisch's Car	.05	.15
212 Jimmy Nowlin	.08	.25
213 Chuck Nutzmann's Car	.05	.15
214 Mike Nutzmann's Car	.05	.15
215 Lee Olibas's Car	.05	.15
216 Jim O'Conner	.08	.25
217 Marty O'Neal	.08	.25
218 Skip Pannell's Car	.05	.15
219 Kris Patterson's Car	.05	.15
220 Terry Phillips	.08	.25
221 Bob Pohlman Jr.'s Car	.05	.15
222 John Provenzano	.08	.25
223 C.J. Rayburn	.05	.15
224 Jerry Rice	.08	.25
225 Tom Rients	.05	.15
226 Kevin Roderick's Car	.05	.15
227 Todd Rust's Car	.05	.15
228 Ed Sans Jr.'s Car	.05	.15
229 Eric Sayre's Car	.05	.15
230 Darwin Scarlett's Car	.05	.15
231 Billy Scott	.08	.25
232 Russ Sell's Car	.05	.15
233 Steve Shute's Car	.05	.15
234 Buck Simmons' Car	.05	.15
235 Lavon Sloan's Car	.05	.15
236 Buddy Smith's Car	.05	.15
237 Sonny Smyser	.08	.25
238 Tommy Snell's Car	.05	.15
239 Mark Stevens	.08	.25
240 Johnny Stokes	.08	.25
241 Jim Tyron's Car	.05	.15
242 Wren Turner	.08	.25
243 Johnny Virdon's Car	.05	.15
244 Mike Walker's Car	.05	.15
245 Bob Wearing Jr.'s Car	.05	.15
246 Ricky Weeks' Car	.05	.15
247 Jimmie White	.08	.25
248 Dill Whittymore	.08	.25
249 Sam Williams' Car	.05	.15
250 Charlie Williamson's Car	.05	.15
NNO Cover Card Checklist 85-125	.05	.15
NNO Cover Card Checklist 43-84	.05	.15
NNO Cover Card Checklist 126-167	.05	.15
NNO Cover Card Checklist 1-42	.05	.15
NNO Cover Card Checklist 210-250	.05	.15
NNO Cover Card Checklist 168-209	.05	.15

1993 JAGS

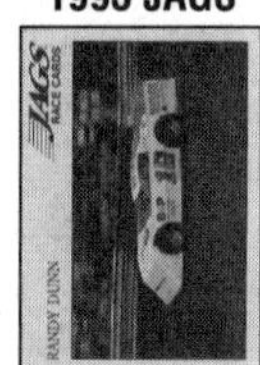

JAGS Race Cards produced this set featuring top drivers of Dirt Late Model competition. This was the third of four sets released by JAGS and featured a light tan border.

COMPLETE SET (52)	4.00	10.00
1 Tony Albright	.07	.20
2 Stan Amacher	.07	.20
3 Scott Bloomquist	.20	.50
4 Mike Boland	.07	.20
5 Jimmy Burwell	.07	.20
6 Marty Calloway	.07	.20
7 Randle Chupp	.07	.20
8 Kevin Coffey	.07	.20
9 Gar Dickson	.07	.20
10 Ed Dixon	.07	.20
11 Patrick Duggan	.07	.20
12 Randy Dunn	.07	.20
13 Jimmy Edwards Jr.	.07	.20
14 Paul Feistritzer	.07	.20
15 Mike Freeman	.07	.20
16 Fred F. Flatt	.07	.20
17 John Gill	.10	.30
18 Ray Guss Jr.	.07	.20
19 Billy Hicks	.07	.20
20 Kent Hicks	.07	.20
21 Casey Huffman	.07	.20
22 Sonny Huskey	.07	.20
23 Bill Ingram	.07	.20
24 Frank Ingram	.07	.20
25 Willy Kraft	.07	.20
26 Darrell Lanigan	.07	.20
27 B.K. Luna	.07	.20
28 Mike Luna	.07	.20
29 Gary Mann	.07	.20
30 Mark DIRT Martin	.07	.20
31 Dale McDowell	.07	.20
32 Monty Miller	.07	.20
33 Tony W. Moody	.07	.20
34 Donnie Moran	.10	.30
35 Billy Moyer	.20	.50
36 Ken Nosbisch	.07	.20
37 Bill Palmer	.07	.20
38 Pete Parker	.07	.20
39 Steve D. Russell	.07	.20
40 Doug Sanders	.07	.20
41 Randy Sellars	.07	.20
42 Terry Shannon	.07	.20
43 Clint Smith	.07	.20
44 Freddy Smith	.20	.50
45 Jeff Smith	.07	.20
46 Josh Tarter	.07	.20
47 John A. Utsman	.07	.20
48 Jeff Walker	.07	.20
49 Kevin Weaver	.10	.30
50 Randy Weaver	.07	.20
51 Cover Card Checklist	.07	.20
NNO Jennifer Dunn Miss JAGS	.07	.20

1994 JAGS

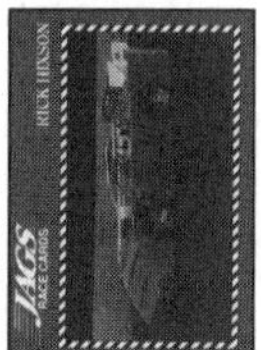

JAGS Race Cards produced this set featuring top drivers of Dirt Late Model competition. This was the last of four sets released by JAGS and featured a purple border.

COMPLETE SET (63)	4.00	10.00
1 Tony Albright	.07	.20
2 Brian Ater	.07	.20
3 Steve Barnett	.07	.20
4 Wade Beaty	.07	.20
5 Eddie Benfield	.07	.20
6 Scott Bloomquist	.20	.50
7 Jackie Boggs Jr.	.07	.20
8 Rudy Boutwell	.07	.20
9 Jay Brinkley	.07	.20
10 Dave Burks	.07	.20
11 Ronnie Caldwell	.07	.20
12 Buster Cardwell	.07	.20
13 Randall Carte	.07	.20
14 Kevin Coffey	.07	.20
15 Ray Cook	.07	.20
16 Billy Drake	.07	.20
17 Patrick Duggan	.07	.20
18 Bryan Dunaway	.07	.20
19 Rick Eckert	.10	.30
20 Terry English	.10	.30
21 Wayne Fielden	.07	.20
22 Steve Francis	.20	.50
23 Billy Hicks	.07	.20
24 Rick Hixson	.07	.20
25 Larry Isley	.07	.20
26 Travis Johnson	.07	.20
27 Gary Keeling	.07	.20
28 Kenny LeCroy	.07	.20
29 Jr. Lemmings	.07	.20
30 Roger Long	.07	.20
31 Keith Longmire	.07	.20
32 Mike Luna	.07	.20
33 Gary Mabe	.07	.20
34 Tom Maddox	.07	.20
35 Robby Mason	.07	.20
36 Gary May	.07	.20
37 Jimmy McCormick	.07	.20
38 Dale McDowell	.07	.20
39 Gary McPherson	.07	.20
40 Byron L. Michael	.07	.20
41 Donnie Moran	.10	.30
42 Mike Mullvain	.07	.20
43 Billy Ogle Jr.	.10	.30
44 Carnell Parker	.07	.20
45 Jamie Perry	.07	.20

46 Bob Pierce	.07	.20
47 Phillip Richardson	.07	.20
48 Bobby Richey Jr.	.07	.20
49 Rick Rogers	.07	.20
50 Joe Ross Jr.	.07	.20
51 Randy Sellars	.07	.20
52 Scott Sexton	.07	.20
53 J.R. Shickel	.07	.20
54 Freddy Smith	.20	.50
55 Jeff Smith	.07	.20
56 Dick Taylor	.07	.20
57 Paul Tims	.07	.20
58 Mike Tinker	.07	.20
59 Leroy Vann	.07	.20
60 Kevin Weaver	.10	.30
61 Neil P. Welch	.07	.20
62 Rick Williams	.07	.20
63 Cover Card Checklist	.07	.20

1995 JSK Iceman

JSK Collectable Promotions produced this 27-card set featuring drivers of the Iceman Super Car Series. The cards are numbered according to the driver's car number and were distributed through souvenir stands at series' tracks. Set production was limited to 4000 sets that had an original cost of $12.50. Uncut sheets (52 made) were distributed for the set as well at a cost of $17.

COMPLETE SET (27)	5.00	12.00
1 Dennis Berry's Car	.30	.75
4 Scott Baker's Car	.20	.50
6 Tom Fedewa's Car	.20	.50
7 Jason Mignogna's Car	.20	.50
9 Matt Hutter's Car	.20	.50
10 Stan Perry's Car	.20	.50
13 Jerry Cook's Car	.20	.50
15 Kenny Phillips' Car	.20	.50
20 Ed Hage's Car	.20	.50
21 Dan Morse's Car	.20	.50
24 Dave Kuhlman's Car	.20	.50
32 Dennis Strickland's Car	.20	.50
48 Kenny Howard's Car	.20	.50
56 Chase Howe w/Car	.20	.50
65 Tim Ice's Car	.40	1.00
69 Ron Allen's Car	.20	.50
70 Fred Campbell's Car	.30	.75
72 Scott Hantz's Car	.20	.50
77 Kenny Sword's Car	.20	.50
81 Gary Camelot's Car	.20	.50
83 Bob Sibila's Car	.20	.50
90 Tim Curry's Car	.20	.50
97 Steve Sauve's Car	.20	.50
99 John Sawatsky's Car	.20	.50
0 Chuck Roumell's Car	.30	.75
NNO Cover Card set order form on back	.20	.50
NNO Schedule Card	.20	.50

1995 JSK Iceman Past Champions

JSK Collectable Promotions produced this 7-card set featuring past champs of the Iceman Super Car Series. Six cards focus on the champion drivers and cars, along with one cover card. The cards are numbered according to the driver's car number. Set production was limited to 4000 sets that had an original cost of $5. Uncut sheets (52 made) were distributed for the set as well at a cost of $7.

COMPLETE SET (7)	2.50	6.00
40 Bruce Vanderlaan's Car	.40	1.00
51/52 Dennis Berry's Car Butch Miller's Car	.40	1.00
61 Dennis Berry w/Car	.40	1.00
65 Tim Ice w/Car	.75	2.00
70 Fred Campbell's Car	.40	1.00
0 Chuck Roumell's Car	.40	1.00
NNO Cover Card set order form on back	.40	1.00

1995 JSK S.O.D. Sprints

JSK Collectable Promotions produced this 24-card set featuring drivers of the S.O.D. Sprints series. The cards are numbered according to the driver's car number and were distributed through souvenir stands at series' tracks. Set production was limited to 4000 sets that had an original cost of $10. Uncut sheets (52 made) were distributed for the set as well at a cost of $15.

COMPLETE SET (24)	4.00	10.00
1 Scott Seaton's Car	.20	.50
2 Mike Katz's Car	.20	.50
3S Brian Tyler's Car	.20	.50
5 Steve VanNote's Car	.20	.50
6 Jeff Bloom's Car	.20	.50
10 Ron Koehler's Car	.20	.50
16 Mike Mouch's Car	.20	.50
20 Bill Tyler's Car	.20	.50
21 Rocky Fisher's Car	.20	.50
22R Jay Sherston's Car	.20	.50
35 Ryan Katz's Car	.20	.50
37 Hank Lower's Car	.20	.50
42 Gary Fedewa's Car	.30	.75
43 Dan Osburn's Car	.20	.50
44J Bill Jacoby's Car	.20	.50
47 Bob Clark's Car	.20	.50
49 Lisa Ward's Car	.20	.50
72 Pat York's Car	.20	.50
77B Steve Burch's Car	.20	.50
77T John Turner's Car	.20	.50
83 Wayne Landon's Car	.20	.50
NNO John Boy Hotchkiss numbered JB	.20	.50
NNO Cover Card set order form on back	.20	.50
NNO Schedule Card	.20	.50

1990 K and W Dirt Track

K and W Race Cards produced a series of sets featuring drivers of DIRT Modifieds sold through local area tracks. A percentage of set sales proceeds went to the DIRT driver's injury fund. This 42-card set was the first edition in the series and was printed with color photos surrounded by a black border on the cardfront. Cardbacks were printed in black and white. Reportedly, 2,500 sets were produced and 500 of each card were made available to the drivers. The remaining 2,000 sets were then distributed. The unnumbered cards are listed below alphabetically.

COMPLETE SET (42)	3.00	8.00
1 Steve Ay	.08	.25
2 Johnny Bennett Jr.	.08	.25
3 Dave Bently	.08	.25
4 Frances Blauvelt	.08	.25
5 Billy Brennen	.08	.25
6 Ed Brown Jr.	.08	.25
7 Hal Browning	.08	.25
8 Barry Buckhart	.08	.25
9 Tom Capie	.08	.25
10 Darryl Carman	.08	.25
11 Richard Cass	.08	.25
12 Chic Cossaboone	.08	.25
13 Brian Donley	.08	.25
14 Joe Edwards	.08	.25
15 Rick Elliott	.08	.25
16 Butch Glisson	.08	.25
17 Garry Gollub	.08	.25
18 Newt Hartman	.08	.25
19 Frank Hayes	.08	.25
20 Jim Horton Sr.	.15	.40
21 Jimmy Horton	.20	.50
22 James Jackson	.08	.25
23 Bucky Kell	.08	.25
24 Robbie Keller	.08	.25
25 Bear Kelly	.08	.25
26 Ron Keys	.08	.25
27 Roger Laureno	.08	.25
28 John Leach	.08	.25
29 Mick MacNeir	.08	.25
30 Jimmy Martin	.08	.25
31 Ernie Miles Jr.	.08	.25
32 Jamie Mills	.08	.25
33 Brad Nash	.08	.25
34 Fred Orchard Jr.	.08	.25
35 Bobby Parks	.08	.25
36 Richie Pratt	.08	.25
37 Scott Pursell	.08	.25
38 Erwin Schlenger	.08	.25
39 Glenn Smith	.08	.25
40 Paul Weaver	.08	.25
41 Wayne Weaver	.08	.25
42 Edward Zehner	.08	.25

1991 K and W Dirt Track

This set of 50-cards featuring top Northeast DIRT Track drivers was produced and distributed by Kand W Race Cards. The black bordered cards include 49-drivers and one cover/checklist card and were released in complete set form. A percentage of set sales proceeds went to the DIRT driver's injury fund. Reportedly, 2,500 sets were produced and 500 of each card were made available to the drivers. The remaining 2,000 sets were then distributed.

COMPLETE SET (50)	4.00	10.00
1 Brett Hearn	.08	.25
2 Billy Pauch	.08	.25
3 Doug Hoffman	.08	.25
4 Scott Irwin	.08	.25
5 Johnny Betts	.08	.25
6 Chip Slocum	.08	.25
7 Fred Brightbill	.08	.25
8 Glenn Smith	.08	.25
9 Rick Elliott	.08	.25
10 John Leach	.08	.25
11 Jamie Mills	.08	.25
12 Wayne Weaver	.08	.25
13 Ron Keys	.08	.25
14 Newt Hartman	.08	.25
15 Garry Gollub	.08	.25
16 Mark Kenyon	.08	.25
17 Jimmy Chester	.08	.25
18 Sam Martz	.08	.25
19 John Pinter	.08	.25
20 Bobby Wilkins	.08	.25
21 Hal Browning	.08	.25
22 Donnie Wetmore	.08	.25
23 Tom Capie	.08	.25
24 Bucky Kell	.08	.25
25 Chic Cossaboone	.08	.25
26 Randy Glenski	.08	.25
27 Roger Laureno	.08	.25
28 Dave Adams	.08	.25
29 Bobby Parks	.08	.25
30 Pete Visconti	.08	.25
31 Ronnie Tobias	.08	.25
32 Richie Pratt	.08	.25
33 Frank Cozze	.08	.25
34 Jack Johnson	.08	.25
35 Jimmy Horton	.20	.50
36 Toby Tobias Jr.	.08	.25
37 Scott Pursell	.08	.25
38 Kenny Tremont	.08	.25
39 Steve Paine	.08	.25
40 Billy Decker	.08	.25
41 Whitey Kidd Jr.	.08	.25
42 Tom Peck	.15	.40
43 Ernie Miles Jr.	.08	.25
44 Bill Tanner	.08	.25
45 Fred Orchard	.08	.25
46 Bob Lineman	.08	.25
47 Deron Rust	.08	.25
48 Gary Bruckler	.08	.25
49 Craig Von Dohren	.08	.25
50 Cover Card Checklist	.08	.25

1991 K and W URC Sprints

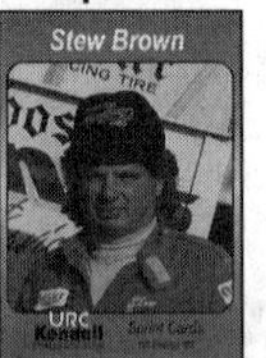

This set of 43-cards featuring top drivers of the United Racing Club Sprint Car series was produced and distributed by Kand W Race Cards. The blue bordered cards include 41-drivers, one cover/checklist card and a card of Miss URC. Reportedly 2,500 sets were produced and 500 of each card were made available to the drivers. The remaining 2,000 sets were then distributed.

COMPLETE SET (43)	5.00	12.00
1 Glenn Fitzcharles	.15	.40
2 Bruce Thompson	.15	.40
3 Jimmy Martin	.15	.40
4 Billy Ellis	.15	.40
5 Lou Cicconi Jr.	.20	.50
6 Stew Brown	.15	.40
7 Sam Gangemi	.15	.40
8 Mike Conway	.15	.40
9 Todd Rittenhouse	.15	.40
10 Mike Wells	.15	.40
11 Wayne Rice	.15	.40
12 Dave McGough	.15	.40
13 Dan Nerl	.15	.40
14 Tom Wanner	.15	.40
15 Bob Kellar	.15	.40
16 Tim Higgins	.15	.40
17 Bruce Bowen	.15	.40
18 Mares Stellfox	.15	.40
19 Kramer Williamson	.15	.40
20 Jerry Dinnen	.15	.40
21 Ray Winiecki Jr.	.15	.40
22 Tony Smolenyak	.15	.40
23 Billy Hughes	.15	.40
24 Bob Swavely	.15	.40
25 Fran Hogue	.15	.40
26 Gary Hieber	.15	.40
27 John Jenkins	.15	.40
28 Jim Baker	.15	.40
29 Jon Holmquist Jr.	.15	.40
30 Lance Dewease	.15	.40
31 Midge Miller	.15	.40
32 Dave McGough	.15	.40
33 Mike Haggenbottom	.15	.40
34 Bob Fisher Jr.	.15	.40
35 Jon Eldreth	.15	.40
36 Rich Bates	.15	.40
37 Don Souders Jr.	.15	.40
38 Larry Winchell	.15	.40
39 Greg Coverdale	.15	.40
40 Ralph Stettenbauer	.15	.40
41 Glenn Fitzcharles	.15	.40
42 Kolleen Reimel Miss URC	.15	.40
43 Cover Card Checklist	.15	.40

1992 K and W Dirt Track

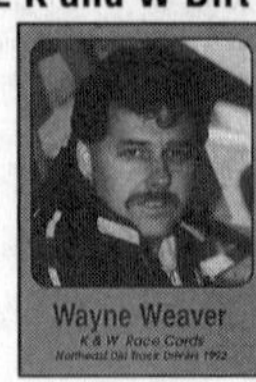

K and W Race Cards produced a series of sets featuring drivers of DIRT Modifieds sold through local area tracks. A percentage of set sales proceeds went to the DIRT driver's injury fund. This 65-card set was printed with color photos surrounded by an orange-red border on the cardfront. Cardbacks were printed in black and white. 2,500 of each card were produced and 500 of those cards were made available to the drivers. The remaining 2,000 sets were then distributed.

COMPLETE SET (65)	3.00	8.00
1 Billy Pauch	.05	.15
2 Doug Hoffman	.05	.15
3 Brett Hearn	.05	.15
4 Bob McCreadie	.05	.15
5 Jimmy Horton	.20	.50
6 Jack Johnson	.05	.15
7 Toby Tobias Jr.	.05	.15
8 Ronnie Tobias	.05	.15
9 Steve Paine	.05	.15
10 Kenny Tremont	.05	.15
11 Billy Decker	.05	.15
12 Rick Elliott	.05	.15
13 Bobby Wilkins	.05	.15
14 Tom Hager	.05	.15
15 Kevin Collins	.05	.15
16 David Lape	.05	.15
17 C.D. Coville	.05	.15
18 Duane Howard	.05	.15
19 Frank Cozze	.05	.15
20 Ron Keys	.05	.15
21 John Leach	.05	.15
22 Roger Laureno	.05	.15
23 Dave Adams	.05	.15
24 Chic Cossaboone	.05	.15
25 Jimmy Chester	.05	.15
26 Garry Gollub	.05	.15
27 Glenn Smith	.05	.15
28 Jamie Mills	.05	.15
29 Wayne Weaver	.05	.15
30 John Pinter	.05	.15
31 Randy Glenski	.05	.15
32 Buck Ward	.05	.15
33 Richie Pratt	.05	.15
34 H.J. Bunting, III	.05	.15
35 Deron Rust	.05	.15
36 Bobby Sapp	.05	.15
37 Greg Humlhanz	.05	.15
38 Ed Brown, Jr.	.05	.15
39 David Hill	.05	.15
40 John Bennett, Jr.	.05	.15
41 Landy Adams	.05	.15
42 Pete Visconti	.05	.15
43 Scott Pursell	.05	.15
44 Chip Slocum	.05	.15
45 Tom Capie	.05	.15
46 Whitey Kidd, Jr.	.05	.15
47 Ernie Miles, Jr.	.05	.15
48 Bill Tanner	.05	.15
49 Bobby Parks	.05	.15
50 Craig Von Dohren	.05	.15
51 Tom Mayberry	.05	.15
52 Dennis Bailey	.05	.15
53 Jeff Strunk	.05	.15
54 Rick Schaffer	.05	.15
55 Jack Follweiler	.05	.15
56 Tom Carberry	.05	.15
57 Fred Dmuchowski	.05	.15
58 Steve Bottcher	.05	.15
59 Joe Plazek	.05	.15
60 Smokey Warren	.05	.15
61 Ray Swinehart	.05	.15
62 Bucky Kell	.05	.15
63 Newt Hartman	.05	.15
64 Sam Martz	.05	.15
65 Checklist Card	.05	.15

1994 K and W Dirt Track

K and W Race Cards produced a series of sets featuring drivers of DIRT Modifieds sold through local area tracks. A percentage of set sales proceeds went to the local driver's injury fund. This 40-card set was printed with color photos surrounded by a blue border on the cardfront. Cardbacks were printed in black and white. Reportedly, 2,500 sets were produced and 500 of each card were made available to the drivers. The remaining 2,000 sets were then distributed.

COMPLETE SET (40)	4.00	10.00
1 Brett Hearn	.10	.30
2 Doug Hoffman	.10	.30
3 Bob McCreadie	.10	.30
4 Bobby Wilkins	.10	.30
5 Billy Pauch	.10	.30
6 Mitch Gibbs	.10	.30
7 Toby Tobias, Jr.	.10	.30
8 Kenny Tremont	.10	.30
9 Rick Elliott	.10	.30
10 Duane Howard	.10	.30
11 Jimmy Horton	.20	.50
12 Kevin Collins	.10	.30
13 Steve Paine	.10	.30
14 Pete Visconti	.10	.30
15 Jack Johnson	.10	.30
16 Craig Von Dohren	.10	.30
17 Billy Decker	.10	.30
18 Randy Glenski	.10	.30
19 Frank Cozze	.10	.30
20 Ray Swinehart	.10	.30
21 Roger Laureno	.10	.30
22 David Lape	.10	.30
23 Tom Mayberry	.10	.30
24 Ron Keys	.10	.30
25 Ronnie Tobias	.10	.30
26 Fred Dmuchowski	.10	.30
27 John Leach	.10	.30
28 Joe Plazek	.10	.30
29 Bucky Kell	.10	.30
30 Jamie Mills	.10	.30
31 Tom Hager	.10	.30
32 Dave Adams	.10	.30
33 Bobby Sapp	.10	.30
34 Jimmy Chester	.10	.30
35 Greg Humlhanz	.10	.30
36 Deron Rust	.10	.30
37 Chip Slocum	.10	.30
38 Rick Schaffer	.10	.30
39 Jeff Strunk	.10	.30
40 Cover/Checklist Card	.10	.30

1995 K and W Dirt Track

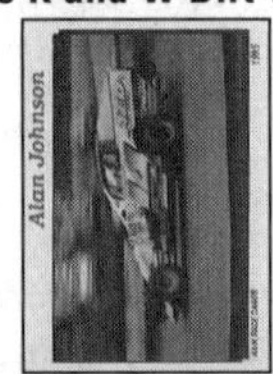

K and W Race Cards produced a series of sets featuring drivers of DIRT Modifieds sold through local area tracks. A percentage of set sales proceeds went to the local driver's injury fund. This 42-card set was printed with color photos surrounded by a white border on the cardfront. Cardbacks were printed in black and white. Reportedly, 2,500 sets were produced and 500 of each card were made available to the drivers. The remaining 2,000 sets were then distributed.

COMPLETE SET (42)	5.00	12.00
1 Bob McCreadie	.10	.30
2 Dale Planck	.10	.30
3 Brett Hearn	.10	.30
4 Doug Hoffman	.10	.30
5 Rick Elliott	.10	.30
6 Mitch Gibbs	.10	.30
7 Alan Johnson	.10	.30
8 Jack Johnson	.10	.30
9 Danny Johnson	.20	.50
10 Bobby Wilkins	.10	.30
11 Joe Plazek	.10	.30
12 Billy Pauch	.10	.30
13 Jimmy Horton	.30	.75
14 Kenny Tremont	.10	.30
15 Craig Von Dohren	.10	.30
16 Frank Cozze	.10	.30
17 Garry Gollub	.10	.30
18 Meme DeSantis	.10	.30
19 Steve Paine	.10	.30
20 Billy Decker	.10	.30
21 Jimmy Chester	.10	.30
22 Wade Hendrickson	.10	.30
23 Billy Pauch	.10	.30
24 H.J. Bunting, III	.10	.30
25 David Lape	.10	.30
26 Dave Adams	.10	.30
27 Pete Visconti	.10	.30
28 Sammy Beavers	.10	.30
29 Ron Keys	.10	.30
30 Norman Short Jr.	.10	.30
31 Fred Dmuchowski	.10	.30
32 Randy Glenski	.10	.30
33 Tom Hager	.10	.30
34 Roger Laureno	.10	.30
35 John Leach	.10	.30
36 Greg Humlhanz	.10	.30
37 Jamie Mills	.10	.30
38 Mike Sena	.10	.30
39 Deron Rust	.10	.30
40 John Wyers	.10	.30
41 Wayne Weaver	.10	.30
42 Cover/Checklist Card	.10	.30

1990 Langenberg Rockford Speedway/Hot Stuff

M.B. Langenberg produced this set in 1990 under the title Hot Stuff. The cards feature drivers of various circuits that raced at the Rockford (Illinois) Speedway. As with most Langenberg sets, the cards feature a checkered flag design and black an cardbacks. The card numbering is unusual i begins with 1001 and ends with 1045. shortened the numbering in the listings as r below.

COMPLETE SET (45)	3.00
1 John Ganley	.07
2 Jim Rieger	.07
3 Mark Higby	.07
4 Gary Anderson	.07
5 Tom Cormack	.07
6 Bob Torkelson	.07
7 Walter Reitz	.07
8 Bobby Wilberg	.07
9 Curt Tillman	.07
10 John Knaus	.07
11 Bobby Davis	.07
12 Steve Erickson	.07
13 Dale Cox	.07
14 Dave Cox	.07
15 Gary Loos	.07
16 Bob Parisot	.07
17 Jim Reynolds	.07
18 Dave Wagner	.07
19 Terry Rahl	.07
20 Dennis Miller	.07
21 Larry Schuler	.07
22 Bart Reinen	.07
23 Jeff Watson	.07
24 Bill McCoy	.07
25 Nolan McBride	.07
26 Dave Nelson	.07
27 Brad Wagner	.07
28 Dave Foltz	.07
29 Mark Hartline	.07
30 B.J.Sparkman	.07
31 Jon Reynolds	.07
32 Tom Gille	.07
33 Bryan Young	.07
34 Bobby LaPier	.07
35 Todd Aldrich	.07
36 Mike Lloyd	.07
37 Don Russell	.07
38 Dana Czach	.07
39 Bruce Tucker	.07
40 Tim Loos	.07
41 Steve Gray	.07
42 Dan Johnson	.07
43 Murt Dunn	.07
44 Jerry Gille	.07
45 Al Sheppard	.07

1991 Langenberg Rockford Speedwa

This 66-card set features various drivers wh at the Rockford (Illinois) Speedway. The produced by M.B. Langenberg. It was the consecutive year a Rockford Speedway s issued.

COMPLETE SET (66)	4.00
1 Curt Tillman	.07
2 Ricky Bilderback	.07
3 Jerry Gille	.07
4 Scott Dolliver	.07
5 Tom Gille	.07
6 Jim Reynolds	.07
7 Kurt Danko	.07
8 Don Russell	.07
9 Bruce Devoy	.07
10 Brian Johnson	.07
11 Robert Parisot	.07
12 Murt Dunn	.07
13 Dennis Miller	.07
14 Tom Graves	.07
15 Daryl Luepkes	.07
16 Ron Smykay	.07
17 Bobby Hacker	.07
18 Roy Crettol	.07
19 Jeff Taber	.07
20 Dave Lapier	.07
21 Ricky Bilderback Dennis Miller John Knaus	.07
22 Allan Merfeld	.07
23 Dale Yardley	.07
24 Mike Lloyd	.07
25 Jeff Watson	.07
26 John Knaus	.07
27 Bill McCoy	.07
28 Scott Lawver Tom Schneider Doug Fermanich	.07
29 George Compo	.07
30 Mike O'Leary	.07
31 Gene Hill	.07
32 Rodney Gilley	.07
33 Brad Wagner	.07
34 Bob Miller	.07
35 Doug Fermanich	.07
36 Darrell Williams	.07
37 Scott Bryden	.07
38 Mike Martindale	.07
39 Mike Loos	.07
40 Alan Sheppard	.07
41 Mark Magee	.07
42 Gary Head	.07
43 Bobby Wilberg	.07
44 B.J. Sparkman	.07
45 Nolan McBride	.07
46 Elmo Deery	.07
47 Thomas Powell	.07
48 Todd Aldrich	.07
49 Jim Sanders	.07
50 Dave Lee	.07
51 Dale Cox	.07
52 Patrick Rossmann	.07
53 Derrick Spack	.07
54 Lon Ritz	.07

rry Ahlquist	.07	.20
ave Wagner	.07	.20
an Burdick	.07	.20
ana Czach	.07	.20
rry O'Brien	.07	.20
bby Wilberg	.10	.30
ary Head		
rad Wagner		
urt Danko		
ockford Speedway	.07	.20
ockford Speedway	.07	.20
ockford Speedway	.07	.20
ave Wagner	.07	.20
ill McCoy		
ruce Devoy		
ichard Sanders		
obert Parisot		
ott Tripp	.07	.20
rian Steward		
om Ragner Sr.		
hecklist Card	.07	.20

1991 Langenberg Seekonk Speedway

Langenberg produced this set of 29 cards. The feature various drivers who have raced at onk Speedway. This set was done in nction with the tracks 45th anniversary.

PLETE SET (29)	3.00	8.00
ny Annarummo	.10	.30
Lee	.10	.30
k Houlihan	.10	.30
k Martin	.10	.30
my Wilkins	.10	.30
y Cerullo	.10	.30
Ellis	.10	.30
my Kuhn	.10	.30
n Tripp	.10	.30
vid Berghman	.10	.30
n Dionne	.10	.30
rl Stevens	.10	.30
ayne Dion	.10	.30
ny Kias, Jr.	.10	.30
ed Astle, Jr.	.10	.30
n McCallum	.10	.30
uce Taylor	.10	.30
ff Mecure	.10	.30
anny Dias	.10	.30
b Stockel	.10	.30
ke Santiano	.10	.30
chard Hanatow	.10	.30
bby Tripp	.10	.30
n Proulx	.10	.30
Anthony Venditti	.10	.30
mmy Kuhn	.10	.30
ekonk Speedway	.10	.30
hecklist 1-29	.10	.30
ver Card	.10	.30

1992 Langenberg Rockford Speedway

as the third consecutive year M.B. Langenberg ced a Rockford Speedway set. The cards various drivers who have run at the track.The d set is listed in alphabetical order.

PLETE SET (61)	5.00	12.00
y Ahlquist	.08	.25
y Bilderback	.08	.25
y Bilderback	.08	.25
rge Bohn	.08	.25
tty Bryden	.08	.25
Burdick	.08	.25
rge Compo	.08	.25
Danko	.08	.25
Darnell	.08	.25
k Deery	.08	.25
eve DeMarb	.08	.25
eve DeMarb	.08	.25
ott Dolliver	.08	.25
ve Ebrecht	.08	.25
ry Eckel	.08	.25
nn Ganley	.08	.25
hn Ganley	.08	.25
ry Gille	.08	.25
m Gille	.08	.25
m Gille	.08	.25
dney Gilley	.08	.25
m Graves	.08	.25
bby Hacker	.08	.25
ry Head	.08	.25
ry Head	.08	.25
an Johnson	.08	.25
n Johnson	.08	.25
hn Knaus	.08	.25
hn Knaus	.08	.25
m Kurth	.08	.25
chie Lane	.08	.25
rty Langenberg	.08	.25
ke Lloyd	.08	.25
ryl Luepkes	.08	.25
rk Magee	.08	.25
ly McCoy	.08	.25
ry Meisman	.08	.25
Miller	.08	.25
nes Nuelle	.08	.25
Papini, III	.08	.25
Parisot	.08	.25
m Powell	.08	.25
Reynolds	.08	.25
n Robinson	.08	.25
ephan Rubeck	.08	.25
di Rushiti	.08	.25
vin Smith	.08	.25
. Sparkman	.08	.25
. Sparkman	.08	.25
orge Sparkman	.08	.25
Taber	.08	.25
52 Brad Wagner	.08	.25
53 Brad Wagner	.08	.25
54 David Wagner	.08	.25
55 Rob Wagner	.08	.25
56 Howie Ware	.08	.25
57 Jeff Watson	.08	.25
58 Jeff Watson	.08	.25
59 Bobby Wilberg	.08	.25
60 Bobby Wilberg	.08	.25
61 Darrell Williams	.08	.25

1992 Racing Legends Sprints

Racing Legends produced this set in 1992 to highlight the stars of Sprint Car racing. The 30-card set was released in factory set form with a certificate numbering it amongst the production run of 10,000 sets.

COMPLETE SET (30)	5.00	12.00
1 Steve Kinser w/Car	.60	1.50
2 Sammy Swindell w/Car	.40	1.00
3 Sammy Swindell	.40	1.00
4 Johnny Herrera's Car	.10	.30
5 Johnny Herrera	.20	.50
6 Steve Beitler's Car	.10	.30
7 Steve Beitler	.10	.30
8 Joe Gaerte's Car	.10	.30
9 Mark Kinser's Car	.10	.30
10 Mark Kinser	.20	.50
11 Dave Blaney's Car	1.00	2.50
12 Bobby Fletcher's Car	.10	.30
13 Stevie Smith's Car	.10	.30
14 Stevie Smith Jr.	.20	.50
15 Steve Stambaugh's Car	.10	.30
16 Kenny Jacobs' Car	.10	.30
17 Fred Rahmer's Car	.10	.30
18 Glenn Fitzcharles' Car	.10	.30
19 Jim Carr's Car	.10	.30
20 Joey Kuhn's Car	.10	.30
21 Bobby Weaver's Car	.10	.30
22 Paul Lotier's Car	.10	.30
23 Cris Eash's Car	.10	.30
24 Johnny Mackison Jr.'s Car	.10	.30
25 Bobby Allen's Car	.10	.30
26 Me Me DeSantis' Car	.10	.30
27 Randy Wolfe's Car	.10	.30
28 Bobby Davis Jr.'s Car	.10	.30
29 Donnie Krietz Jr.'s Car	.10	.30
30 Brent Kaeding's Car	.20	.50

1992 STARS Modifieds

Short Track Auto Racing Stars (STARS) released this 48-card set in 1992. The cards were sold in complete set form and feature photos of top drivers of the STARS modifieds series.

COMPLETE SET (48)	6.00	15.00
1 Blaine Aber	.10	.30
2 Dub Barnhouse	.10	.30
3 Mike Balzano w/Car	.10	.30
4 Bob Adams, Jr.	.10	.30
5 Dick Barton	.10	.30
6 Booper Bare	.10	.30
7 Andy Bond	.10	.30
8 Jack Boggs	.20	.50
9 Larry Bond	.10	.30
10 Todd Andrews	.10	.30
11 Jim Gentry	.10	.30
12 Keith Berner	.10	.30
13 Bob Cowen	.10	.30
14 Jim Curry	.10	.30
15 Darrell Lanigan w/Car	.10	.30
16 Rodney Franklin	.10	.30
17 Nathan Durboraw w/Car	.10	.30
18 Ron Davies	.10	.30
19 Denny Chamberlain	.10	.30
20 Mark Banal	.10	.30
21 Mike Duvall	.20	.50
22 Chub Frank	.10	.30
23 Paul Davis	.10	.30
24 B.A. Malcuit	.10	.30
25 Davey Johnson w/Car	.20	.50
26 Rocky Hodges	.10	.30
27 Tim Hitt	.10	.30
28 Lynn Geisler	.10	.30
29 Don Gross	.10	.30
30 Bob Wearing, Jr. w/Car	.10	.30
31 Gary Stuhler w/Car	.10	.30
32 Freddy Smith	.30	.75
33 Buck Simmons	.10	.30
34 Steve Shaver w/Car	.10	.30
35 Harold Redman	.10	.30
36 Bob Pierce	.10	.30
37 Mark Myers	.10	.30
38 Donnie Moran	.20	.50
39 Billy Moyer w/Car	.30	.75
40 John Mason	.10	.30
41 Chuck Maloney	.10	.30
42 Ed Gibbons	.10	.30
43 Steve Francis	.30	.75
44 Butch McGill w/Car	.10	.30
45 Rodney Combs Hillbilly 100 Winner	.30	.75
46 Larry Moore w/Car	.10	.30
47 Joe Meadows' Car	.10	.30
NNO Cover Card Checklist	.10	.30

1994 STARS Modifieds

Short Track Auto Racing Stars (STARS) licensed this 54-card set released in 1994. The cards were sold in complete set form and feature action photos of top drivers of the STARS modifieds series.

COMPLETE SET (54)	4.80	12.00
1 Davey Johnson	.15	.40
2 Todd Andrews	.08	.25
3 Dan Armbruster	.08	.25
4 Rick Aukland	.08	.25
5 Mike Balzano	.08	.25
6 John Booper Bare	.08	.25
7 Steve Barnett	.08	.25
8 Scott Bloomquist	.15	.40
9 Larry Bond	.08	.25
10 Denny Bonebrake	.08	.25
11 Kevin Claycomb	.08	.25
12 D.J. Cline	.08	.25
13 Delmas Conley	.08	.25
14 R.J. Conley	.08	.25
15 Rod Conley	.08	.25
16 Ron Davies	.08	.25
17 Nathan Durboraw	.08	.25
18 Mike Duvall	.15	.40
19 Terry Eaglin	.08	.25
20 Rick Eckert	.15	.40
21 Vince Fanello	.08	.25
22 Steve Francis	.25	.60
23 Chub Frank	.08	.25
24 Ed Gibbons	.08	.25
25 Ed Griffin	.08	.25
26 Don Gross	.08	.25
27 Doug Hall	.08	.25
28 Mike Harrison	.08	.25
29 Scott Hartley	.08	.25
30 Bart Hartman	.08	.25
31 Billy Hicks	.08	.25
32 Tim Hitt	.08	.25
33 Bruce Hordusky	.08	.25
34 Bubby James	.08	.25
35 Tony Izzo Jr.	.08	.25
36 Darrell Lanigan	.08	.25
37 John Mason	.08	.25
38 Donnie Moran	.15	.40
39 Billy Moyer	.25	.60
40 Don O'Neal	.08	.25
41 Bob Pierce	.08	.25
42 Dick Potts	.08	.25
43 C.J. Rayburn	.08	.25
44 Brian Ruhlman	.08	.25
45 Steve Shaver	.08	.25
46 Eddie Smith	.08	.25
47 Freddy Smith	.25	.60
48 Michael Smith	.08	.25
49 Gary Stuhler	.08	.25
50 Kevin Weaver	.08	.25
51 Greg Williams	.08	.25
52 Rick Workman	.08	.25
53 Ricky Weeks	.08	.25
NNO Checklist/Cover Card	.08	.25

1992 Traks Dirt

The 1992 Traks Dirt set features 15 numbered DIRT modified driver cards and one unnumbered cover/checklist card. The set was distributed by Traks through hobby channels.

COMPLETE SET (16)	1.60	4.00
1 Dave Lape	.10	.30
2 Jack Johnson	.10	.30
3 Alan Johnson	.10	.30
4 Jeff Trombley	.10	.30
5 Brett Hearn	.10	.30
6 Steve Paine	.10	.30
7 Jeff Heotzler	.10	.30
8 Joe Plazek	.10	.30
9 Dick Larkin	.10	.30
10 Billy Decker	.10	.30
11 Frank Cozze	.10	.30
12 Bob McCreadie	.10	.30
13 Kenny Tremont	.10	.30
14 Doug Hoffman	.10	.30
15 Danny Johnson	.10	.30
NNO Checklist Card	.10	.30

1992 Volunteer Racing East Alabama Speedway

This 20-card set feautres some of the top drivers that have run dirt cars at East Alabama Speedway. The set was produced by Volunteer racing and includes drivers like Buck Simmons, Jack Boggs and Scott Bloomquist. Also, included are a couple of cards of Busch Grand National regular Jeff Purvis.

COMPLETE SET (20)	2.50	6.00
1 Checklist Card	.08	.25
2 Bobby Thomas	.08	.25
3 Bud Lunsford	.08	.25
4 Charlie Hughes	.08	.25
5 Buck Simmons	.15	.40
6 Billy Thomas	.08	.25
7 Don Hester	.08	.25
8 Tom Helfrich	.08	.25
9 Larry Moore	.08	.25
10 Jeff Purvis	.30	.75
11 Jeff Purvis	.30	.75
12 Buddy Boutwell	.08	.25
13 Jeff Purvis	.30	.75
14 Jack Boggs	.08	.25
15 Billy Moyer	.30	.75
16 Freddy Smith	.30	.75
17 Bobby Thomas	.08	.25
18 Scott Bloomquist	.15	.40
19 Jimmy Thomas	.15	.40
20 Parade Lap	.08	.25

1992 Volunteer Racing Lernersville Speedway Series One

This 72-card set features some of the top sprint car drivers to have raced at Lernersville Speedway. This is the first of a two set series produced by Volunteer Racing. The set includes such notables as Brad Doty and an unnumbered promo card of Dale and Lou Blaney.

COMPLETE SET (72)	3.20	8.00
1 Checklist Card (1-36)	.05	.15
2 Checklist Card (37-72)	.05	.15
3 Jim Andrews	.05	.15
4 Johnny Axe	.05	.15
5 Bob Axe	.05	.15
6 Johnny Beaber	.05	.15
7 Johnny Beaber	.05	.15
8 Lou Blaney	.05	.15
9 Lou Blaney	.05	.15
10 John Braymer	.05	.15
11 John Britsky	.05	.15
12 Paul Brown	.05	.15
13 Mark Cassella	.05	.15
14 Ron Davies	.05	.15
15 Brad Doty	.08	.25
16 Bill Emig	.05	.15
17 Ernie Gardina	.05	.15
18 Lou Gentile	.05	.15
19 Lou Gentile	.05	.15
20 Dale Hafer	.05	.15
21 Dave Hess	.05	.15
22 Dave Hoffman	.05	.15
23 Dave Hoffman	.05	.15
24 Chuck Kennedy	.05	.15
25 Denny Keppel	.05	.15
26 Bob Kirchner	.05	.15
27 Mark Lezanic	.05	.15
28 Rick Majors	.05	.15
29 Jerry Matus	.05	.15
30 Chuck McDowell	.05	.15
31 Kevin McKinney	.05	.15
32 Ben Miley	.05	.15
33 Ben Miley	.05	.15
34 Jim Minton	.05	.15
35 Brian Muehlman	.05	.15
36 Carl Murdick	.05	.15
37 Bill Nobles	.05	.15
38 Mike Norris	.05	.15
39 Gary Pease	.05	.15
40 Dave Pegher	.05	.15
41 Barry Peters	.05	.15
42 Tom Phillips	.05	.15
43 Frank Raiti	.05	.15
44 Craig Rankin	.05	.15
45 L.B. Roenigk	.05	.15
46 Terry Rosenberger	.05	.15
47 Deek Scott	.05	.15
48 Herb Scott	.05	.15
49 Jack Sodeman	.05	.15
50 Ralph Spithaler, Jr.	.05	.15
51 Al Stivenson	.05	.15
52 Rod Stockdale	.05	.15
53 Rick Strong	.05	.15
54 Tom Sturgis	.05	.15
55 Mike Sutton	.05	.15
56 Dick Swartzlander	.05	.15
57 Mel Swartzlander	.05	.15
58 Dave Thompson	.05	.15
59 Tom Valasek	.05	.15
60 Blackie Watt	.05	.15
61 Blackie Watt	.05	.15
62 Blackie Watt	.05	.15
63 Bob Wearing	.05	.15
64 Bob Wearing	.05	.15
65 Bob Wearing	.05	.15
66 Bob Wearing	.05	.15
67 Don Wigton	.05	.15
68 Ted Wise	.05	.15
69 Russ Woolsey	.05	.15
70 Helen Martin	.05	.15
71 Don Martin	.05	.15
NNO Dale Blaney Lou Blaney Promo card	.08	.25

1992 Volunteer Racing Lernersville Speedway Series Two

This is the second set of the Lernersville Speedway cards produced by Volunteer Racing. The 72-card set features various sprint car drivers to have raced at Lernersville Speedway. The set includes a card of the 1995 World of Outlaw champion, Dave Blaney.

COMPLETE SET (72)	3.20	8.00
1 Checklist Card 1	.05	.15
2 Checklist Card 2	.05	.15
3 Earl Bauman	.05	.15
4 Johnny Beaber	.05	.15
5 Rodney Beltz	.05	.15
6 Rodney Beltz	.05	.15
7 Helene Bergtes	.05	.15
8 Dave Blaney	.50	1.25
9 Lou Blaney	.05	.15
10 Lou Blaney	.05	.15
11 Lou Blaney	.05	.15
12 Tony Burke	.05	.15
13 Ben Bussard	.05	.15
14 Tim Campbell	.05	.15
15 Marty Edwards	.05	.15
16 Bob Felmlee	.05	.15
17 Rick Ferkel	.05	.15
18 Bucky Fleming	.05	.15
19 George Frederick	.05	.15
20 Lynn Geisler	.05	.15
21 Lou Gentile	.05	.15
22 Lou Gentile	.05	.15
23 Rod George	.05	.15
24 Bob Graham	.05	.15
25 Mark Harvanek	.05	.15
26 Mark Hein	.05	.15
27 Gary Henry	.05	.15
28 Dave Hess	.05	.15
29 Dave Hoffman	.05	.15
30 Callen Hull	.05	.15
31 Tom Jarrett	.05	.15
32 Chuck Kennedy	.05	.15
33 Bud Kunkel	.05	.15
34 Ed Lynch, Sr.	.05	.15
35 Jean Lynch	.05	.15
36 Ed Lynch, Jr.	.05	.15
37 Don Luffy	.05	.15
38 Ed Lynch, Jr.	.05	.15
39 Ed Lynch, Sr.	.05	.15
40 Lynn Geisler	.05	.15
41 Bob Wearing	.05	.15
42 Ben Miley	.05	.15
43 Art Malies	.05	.15
44 Angelo Mariani	.05	.15
45 Don Martin	.05	.15
46 Jerry Matus	.05	.15
47 Brian Muehlman	.05	.15
48 Glenn Noland	.05	.15
49 Gary Pease	.05	.15
50 Dave Pegher	.05	.15
51 Barry Peters	.05	.15
52 Andy Phillips	.05	.15
53 Tom Phillips	.05	.15
54 Joe Pitkavish	.05	.15
55 Ralph Quarterson	.05	.15
56 Ralph Quarterson	.05	.15
57 Ralph Quarterson	.05	.15
58 Tommy Quarterson	.05	.15
59 Craig Rankin	.05	.15
60 Donny Roenigk	.05	.15
61 Dave Rupp	.05	.15
62 Barb Smith Ron Smith	.05	.15
63 Jack Sodeman	.05	.15
64 Bill Steinbach	.05	.15
65 William VanGuilder	.05	.15
66 Chuck Ward	.05	.15
67 Blackie Watt	.05	.15
68 Blackie Watt	.05	.15
69 Blackie Watt	.05	.15
70 Bob Wearing	.05	.15
71 Bobby Wearing	.05	.15
NNO Bucky Ogle Promo Card	.08	.25

1991 Winner's Choice Modifieds

Winner's Choice, Inc. produced this set in 1991 featuring popular Modified car drivers with 14-cards devoted to the late Richie Evans. The black-bordered cards look very similar to 1991 Winner's Choice New England cards and include a color driver or car photo surrounded by a checkered flag frame. The cards were packaged and sold in complete factory set form.

COMPLETE SET (104)	6.00	15.00
1 Cover Card	.02	.10
2 Carl Pasteryak	.05	.15
3 Carl Pasteryak's Car	.02	.10
4 Tony Ferrante Jr.	.05	.15
5 Tony Ferrante Jr.'s Car	.02	.10
6 Tim Arre	.05	.15
7 Tim Arre's Car	.02	.10
8 Johnny Bush	.05	.15
9 Johnny Bush's Car	.02	.10
10 Jan Leaty	.05	.15
11 Jan Leaty's Car	.02	.10
12 Bob Park	.05	.15
13 Bob Park's Car	.02	.10
14 Richie Gallup	.05	.15
15 Richie Gallup's Car	.02	.10
16 Doug Heveron	.05	.15
17 Doug Heveron's Car	.02	.10
18 Jeff Fuller	.10	.30
19 Jeff Fuller's Car	.02	.10
20 Charlie Rudolph	.05	.15
21 Charlie Rudolph's Car	.02	.10
22 Satch Worley	.05	.15
23 Satch Worley's Car	.02	.10
24 George Brunnhoelzl	.05	.15
25 George Brunnhoelzl's Car	.02	.10
26 Randy Hedger	.05	.15
27 Randy Hedger's Car	.02	.10
28 S.J. Evonsion	.05	.15
29 S.J. Evonsion's Car	.02	.10
30 Mike Ewanitsko	.05	.15
31 Mike Ewanitsko's Car	.02	.10
32 Wayne Anderson	.05	.15
33 Wayne Anderson's Car	.02	.10
34 Steve Park	1.50	3.00
35 Checklist Card	.02	.10
36 Steve Park's Car	.50	1.25
37 Tom Bolles	.05	.15
38 Tom Bolles' Car	.02	.10
39 Ed Kennedy	.05	.15
40 Ed Kennedy's Car	.02	.10
41 Jerry Marquis	.05	.15
42 Jerry Marquis' Car	.02	.10
43 Rick Fuller	.10	.30
44 Rick Fuller's Car	.02	.10
45 Stan Greger	.05	.15
46 Stan Greger's Car	.02	.10
47 Dan Avery	.05	.15
48 Dan Avery's Car	.02	.10
49 Charlie Pasteryak	.05	.15
50 Charlie Pasteryak's Car	.02	.10
51 Bruce D'Alessandro	.05	.15
52 Bruce D'Alessandro's Car	.02	.10
53 Jamie Tomaino	.05	.15
54 Jamie Tomaino's Car	.02	.10
55 Bruce Haley	.05	.15
56 Bruce Haley's Car	.02	.10
57 Gary Drew	.05	.15
58 Gary Drew's Car	.02	.10
59 Mike Stefanik	.30	.75
60 Mike Stefanik's Car	.02	.10
61 Willie Elliott	.05	.15
62 Willie Elliott's Car	.02	.10
63 Kirby Monteith	.05	.15
64 Kirby Monteith's Car	.02	.10
65 George Kent	.05	.15
66 George Kent's Car	.02	.10
67 John Preston	.05	.15
68 John Preston's Car	.02	.10
69 Reggie Ruggiero	.05	.15
70 Checklist Card	.02	.10
71 Reggie Ruggiero's Car	.02	.10
72 Pete Rondeau	.05	.15
73 Pete Rondeau's Car	.02	.10
74 Tom Baldwin	.10	.30
75 Tom Baldwin's Car	.02	.10
76 Greg Tomaino	.05	.15
77 Greg Tomaino's Car	.02	.10
78 Ted Christopher	.05	.15
79 Ted Christopher's Car	.02	.10
80 Bo Gunning	.05	.15
81 Bo Gunning's Car	.02	.10
82 Bob Potter	.05	.15
83 Bob Potter's Car	.02	.10
84 Tony Hirschman	.05	.15
85 Tony Hirschman's Car	.02	.10
86 Steve Chowansky	.05	.15
87 Steve Chowansky's Car	.02	.10
88 Mike Christopher	.05	.15
89 Mike Christopher's Car	.02	.10
90 Richie Evans	.30	.75
91 Richie Evans' Car One of His First Cars	.10	.30
92 Richie Evans' Car One of Many Early Wins	.10	.30
93 Richie Evans w/Car 1973 at Stafford	.30	.75
94 Richie Evans' Car Modified Madness	.10	.30
95 Richie Evans w/Car Daytona Inter.Speedway	.30	.75
96 Richie Evans w/Car Another of Many Wins	.30	.75
97 Richie Evans' Car Supermodified	.10	.30
98 Richie Evans May 6, 1983	.30	.75
99 Richie Evans' Car 1983 at Martinsville	.10	.30
100 Richie Evans w/Car 1985 Thompson Ice Breaker	.30	.75
101 Richie Evans w/Car 1985 Spring Sizzler	.30	.75
102 Richie Evans 1985 Thompson Speedway	.30	.75
103 Richie Evans 1985	.30	.75
104 Checklist Card	.02	.10
NNO Cover Card	.02	.10

1987 World of Outlaws

This marked the first year of World of Outlaws factory sets produced by James International Art, Inc. The cards are skip numbered and include two different number one Steve Kinser cards. The set is most famous for including the first card of Jeff Gordon. While the card sets from 1987-90 look very similar, the 1987 set can be differentiated by the driver's name appearing in a blue box on the cardfront.

COMPLETE SET (52)	40.00	80.00

1A Steve Kinser XRC	2.00	5.00
1987 Race Highlights		
1B Steve Kinser	2.00	5.00
Summary of 1987 Stats		
2 Brad Doty	.60	1.50
3 Bobby Davis Jr.	.15	.40
4 Jac Haudenschild	.75	2.00
5 Ron Shuman	.15	.40
6 Mark Kinser	1.25	3.00
7 Danny Smith	.15	.40
8 Johnny Herrera	.15	.40
9 Cris Eash	.15	.40
10 Craig Keel	.15	.40
11 Rich Bubak	.15	.40
12 Sammy Swindell	.75	2.00
13 Lee Brewer Jr.	.15	.40
14 Bobby Allen	.15	.40
15 Jimmy Sills	.15	.40
16 Tim Gee	.15	.40
17 Dave Blaney	3.00	8.00
18 Greg Wooley	.15	.40
19 Tommie Estes Jr.	.15	.40
22 Kenny Jacobs	.15	.40
23 Keith Kauffman	.15	.40
24 Rocky Hodges	.15	.40
25 Lealand McSpadden	.15	.40
26 Darrell Hanestad	.15	.40
27 Rick Ungar	.15	.40
28 Rickey Hood	.15	.40
29 Tony Armstrong	.15	.40
30 Shane Carson	.15	.40
31 Steve Siegel	.15	.40
32 Terry Gray	.15	.40
33 Andy Hillenburg	.60	1.50
34 Joey Allen	.15	.40
35 Steve Kent	.15	.40
36 Brent Kaeding	.40	1.00
37 Stevie Smith Jr.	.60	1.50
38 Jack Hewitt	.40	1.00
39 Terry McCarl	.15	.40
41 Steve Butler	.15	.40
42 Jeff Swindell	.60	1.50
43 Chuck Gurney	.15	.40
44 Ted Lee	.15	.40
45 Richard Griffin	.15	.40
47 Joe Gaerte	.15	.40
48 Bobby Fletcher	.15	.40
49 Jason McMillen	.15	.40
50 Randy Smith	.15	.40
51 Tim Green	.15	.40
52 Jeff Gordon XRC	30.00	60.00
NNO Cover Card	.15	.40
Checklist		

1988 World of Outlaws

James International Art again produced a World of Outlaws set in 1988. The cards were released in factory set form only and are skip numbered. The set includes early cards of popular drivers Jeff Gordon and Steve Kinser. Two unnumbered driver cards were part of the set as well as an unnumbered checklist card. While the card sets from 1987-90 look very similar, the 1988 set can be differentiated by the driver's name appearing in a red box on the cardfront.

COMPLETE SET (48)	20.00	50.00
1 Steve Kinser	1.50	4.00
2 Sammy Swindell	.60	1.50
3 Bobby Davis Jr.	.10	.30
6 Andy Hillenburg	.25	.60
7 Cris Eash	.10	.30
8 Jac Haudenschild	.60	1.50
10 Danny Smith	.10	.30
11 Greg Wooley	.10	.30
12 Bobby Allen	.10	.30
13 Jeff Swindell	.25	.60
14 Johnny Herrera	.10	.30
16 Jimmy Sills	.10	.30
17 Joey Allen	.10	.30
18 Lee Brewer Jr.	.10	.30
19 Craig Keel	.10	.30
20 Tony Armstrong	.10	.30
21 Kenny Jacobs	.10	.30
22 Tommie Estes Jr.	.10	.30
23 Jack Hewitt	.25	.60
24 Tim Green	.10	.30
25 Rich Bubak	.10	.30
26 Joe Gaerte	.10	.30
27 Robbie Stanley	.10	.30
28 Terry McCarl	.10	.30
29 Donnie Kreitz Jr.	.10	.30
30 Steve Siegel	.10	.30
31 Steve Kent	.10	.30
32 Keith Kauffman	.10	.30
33 Rick Ungar	.10	.30
34 Rocky Hodges	.10	.30
35 Tim Gee	.10	.30
36 Steve Butler	.10	.30
38 Randy Wolfe	.10	.30
39 Ron Shuman	.10	.30
40 Jim Carr	.10	.30
41 Chuck Miller	.10	.30
43 Danny Burton	.10	.30
45 Gary Dunkle	.10	.30
46 Rickey Hood	.10	.30
48 Lealand McSpadden	.10	.30
50 Chuck Gurney	.10	.30
54 Jeff Gordon	20.00	40.00
NNO Cover Card	.10	.30
Checklist		
NNO Max Dumesny	.10	.30
NNO Brent Kaeding	.25	.60

1989 World of Outlaws

For the third year, James International Art produced a World of Outlaws set in 1989. The cards were released in factory set form only with a 32-card standard sized set and a 13-card postcard sized set together. Although packaged together, the two sets are often considered independent issues and, therefore, listed separately. The 32-card set is again skip-numbered and includes several unnumbered cards as well. The numbered cards are listed according to 1989 final points standings. While the card sets from 1987-90 look very similar, the 1989 set can be differentiated by the driver's name appearing in a yellow box on the cardfront.

COMPLETE SET (32)	10.00	20.00
1 Bobby Davis Jr.	.10	.30
2 Jeff Swindell	.40	1.00
3 Cris Eash	.10	.30
4 Tim Green	.10	.30
5 Joe Gaerte	.10	.30
6 Jac Haudenschild	.75	2.00
7 Andy Hillenburg	.40	1.00
8 Keith Kauffman	.10	.30
9 Doug Wolfgang	.40	1.00
10 Steve Siegel	.10	.30
11 Craig Keel	.10	.30
13 Steve Beitler	.10	.30
14 Jack Hewitt	.25	.60
15 Bobby Allen	.10	.30
16 Johnny Herrera	.10	.30
17 Dave Blaney	3.00	6.00
19 Kenny Jacobs	.10	.30
20 Danny Smith	.10	.30
21 Brent Kaeding	.10	.30
25 Joey Allen	.10	.30
29 Danny Lasoski	.25	.60
31 Rickey Hood	.10	.30
33 Mark Kinser	.60	1.50
34 Steve Kinser	1.50	4.00
35 Frankie Kerr	.25	.60
38 Tommie Estes Jr.	.10	.30
64 Ron Shuman	.10	.30
65 Rich Vogler	.10	.30
NNO Cover Card	.10	.30
Checklist		
NNO Wayne C. Helland	.10	.30
NNO Lealand McSpadden	.10	.30
NNO Jimmy Sills	.10	.30

1989 World of Outlaws Postcards

This 13-card set was included as an insert into 1989 World of Outlaws factory sets. The cards are oversized (3-1/2" by 5") and numbered according to the featured car's number.

COMPLETE SET (13)	4.00	8.00
2 Andy Hillenburg's Car	.60	1.50
2S Steve Siegel's Car	.25	.60
4 Tim Green	.25	.60
Let's Do It		
Car 4		
7TW Joe Gaerte's Car	.25	.60
8D Doug Wolfgang's Car	.60	1.50
10 Bobby Davis Jr.'s Car	.50	1.25
11X Jeff Swindell's Car	.60	1.50
14 Tim Green's Car	.25	.60
17E Cris Eash's Car	.25	.60
48 Keith Kauffman's Car	.25	.60
77 Pit Action	.25	.60
NNO Jim Kingwell	.25	.60
NNO Transporter Hauler	.25	.60

1990 World of Outlaws

For the fourth year, James International Art produced a World of Outlaws set. The cards were released in factory set form only with a 36-card standard sized set and a 10-card postcard sized set together. Although packaged together, the two sets are often considered independent issues and, therefore, listed separately. The 36-card set is again skip-numbered and includes the first card of popular driver Sammy Swindell. Two unnumbered cards were produced as well. The cards are listed according to 1990 final points standings. While the card sets from 1987-90 look very similar, the 1990 set can be differentiated by the driver's name appearing in an orange box on the cardfront.

COMPLETE SET (36)	7.50	20.00
1 Steve Kinser	1.50	4.00
2 Doug Wolfgang	.40	1.00
3 Joe Gaerte	.10	.30
4 Bobby Davis Jr.	.10	.30
5 Stevie Smith Jr.	.40	1.00
6 Cris Eash	.10	.30
7 Dave Blaney	1.50	4.00
8 Keith Kauffman	.10	.30
9 Steve Beitler	.10	.30
10 Sammy Swindell	.75	2.00
11 Johnny Herrera	.10	.30
13 Bobby Allen	.10	.30
14 Jac Haudenschild	.75	2.00
16 Danny Lasoski	.10	.30
17 Kenny Jacobs	.10	.30
18 Jeff Swindell	.25	.60
19 Andy Hillenburg	.25	.60
20 Danny Smith	.10	.30
21 Brent Kaeding	.25	.60
22 Jim Carr	.10	.30
23 Lee Brewer Jr.	.10	.30
28 Jack Hewitt	.25	.60
30 Tim Green	.10	.30
31 Jimmy Sills	.10	.30
34 Rickey Hood	.10	.30
40 Mike Peters	.10	.30
41 Joey Kuhn	.10	.30
42 Steve Smith Sr.	.10	.30
43 Craig Keel	.10	.30
46 Ed Lynch Jr.	.10	.30
49 Rick Ferkel	.10	.30
50 Rick Ungar	.10	.30
NNO J.W. Hunt	.10	.30
NNO Cover Card	.10	.30
Checklist		

1990 World of Outlaws Postcards

This 13-card set was included as an insert into 1990 World of Outlaws factory sets. The cards are oversized (3-1/2" by 5") and are numbered according to the featured car's number.

COMPLETE SET (10)	4.00	8.00
1 Sammy Swindell	1.25	2.50
1A Bobby Allen	.25	.60
7C Dave Blaney's Car	1.00	2.50
8 Doug Wolfgang's Car	.60	1.50
10 Bobby Davis Jr.'s Car	.25	.60
11 Steve Kinser's Car	1.00	2.50
23S Frankie Kerr's Car	.40	1.00
69 Brent Kaeding's Car	.40	1.00
77 Stevie Smith Jr.'s Car	.40	1.00
NNO Only the Best Go Four	.25	.60

1991 World of Outlaws

James International Art produced the largest World of Outlaws set to date in 1991. The cards were released in 10-card foil pack form with a 114-card regular set and four Most Wanted insert cards. The cards were redesigned from previous issues and contain a yellow border. Production and packaging problems resulted in a reportedly shorter print run for the 1991 set. Cards numbered 112-114 are considered in shorter supply. A Steve Kinser Promo card was released as well and is not considered part of the regular set.

COMPLETE SET (114)	20.00	40.00
WAX BOX	15.00	30.00
1 Checklist	.10	.30
2 Steve Kinser	1.50	3.00
3 Mark Kinser	.60	1.50
4 Joe Gaerte	.10	.30
5 Stevie Smith Jr.	.40	1.00
6 Dave Blaney	1.00	2.50
7 Johnny Herrera	.10	.30
8 Steve Beitler	.10	.30
9 Jim Carr	.10	.30
10 Checklist	.10	.30
11 Sammy Swindell	.75	2.00
12 Gary Cameron II	.10	.30
13 Bobby Davis Jr.	.10	.30
14 Bobby Allen	.10	.30
15 Danny Lasoski	.10	.30
16 Doug Wolfgang	.40	1.00
17 Greg Hodnett	.10	.30
18 Keith Kauffman	.10	.30
19 Jac Haudenschild	.75	2.00
20 Jeff Swindell	.40	1.00
21 Craig Keel	.10	.30
22 Gary Wright	.10	.30
23 Dale Laakso	.10	.30
24 Terry Gray	.10	.30
25 Kenny Jacobs	.10	.30
26 Aaron Berryhill	.10	.30
27 Danny Smith	.10	.30
28 Mike Peters	.10	.30
29 Cris Eash	.10	.30
30 Brent Kaeding	.25	.60
31 Ronnie Day	.10	.30
32 Donnie Kreitz Jr.	.10	.30
33 Frankie Kerr	.25	.60
34 Terry McCarl	.10	.30
35 Jimmy Sills	.10	.30
36 Steve Kent	.10	.30
37 Tommie Estes Jr.	.10	.30
38 Dan Hamilton	.10	.30
39 Darrell Hanestad	.10	.30
40 Paul McMahan	.10	.30
41 Jason McMillen	.10	.30
42 Toni Lutar	.10	.30
43 Tim Green	.10	.30
44 Greg DeCaires IV	.10	.30
45 Ricky Stenhouse	.10	.30
46 Bobby Fletcher	.10	.30
47 Paul Lotier	.10	.30
48 Shane Carson	.10	.30
49 Steve Siegel	.10	.30
50 Rich Bubak	.10	.30
51 Bobby McMahan	.10	.30
52 Chuck Miller	.10	.30
53 Lealand McSpadden	.10	.30
54 Dennis Rodriguez	.10	.30
55 Rickie Gaunt	.10	.30
56 Lee Brewer Jr.	.10	.30
57 Rick Hirst	.10	.30
58 Rickey Hood	.10	.30
59 Jason Earls	.10	.30
60 Ron Shuman	.10	.30
61 Checklist	.10	.30
62 Ted Johnson	.10	.30
63 Dion Appleby	.10	.30
64 Tom Basinger	.10	.30
65 Dale Blaney	.10	.30
66 Billy Boat	.10	.30
67 Greg Brown	.10	.30
68 Steve Butler	.10	.30
69 Dan Dietrich	.10	.30
70 Checklist	.10	.30
71 Kevin Doty	.10	.30
72 Kenny French	.10	.30
73 Rick Haas	.10	.30
74 Jack Hewitt	.25	.60
75 Larry Hillerod	.10	.30
76 Rocky Hodges	.10	.30
77 Sparky Howard	.10	.30
78 Chris Ikard	.10	.30
79 Howard Kaeding	.10	.30
80 Todd Kane	.10	.30
81 Dave Kelly	.10	.30
82 Kelly Kinser	.10	.30
83 Joey Kuhn	.10	.30
84 Nick Losasso	.10	.30
85 Ed Lynch Jr.	.10	.30
86 Rick Martin	.10	.30
87 Fred Rahmer	.10	.30
88 Nick Rescino	.10	.30
89 Tommy Scott	.10	.30
90 Todd Shaffer	.10	.30
91 Terry Shepherd	.10	.30
92 Steve Smith Sr.	.10	.30
93 Steve Stambaugh	.10	.30
94 Jason Statler	.10	.30
95 Mitch Sue	.10	.30
96 Bobby Weaver	.10	.30
97 Max Dumesny	.10	.30
98 Melinda Dumesny	.10	.30
99 Skip Jackson	.10	.30
100 Jamie Moyle	.10	.30
101 Steve Kinser's Car	.75	2.00
102 Mark Kinser's Car	.10	.30
103 Joe Gaerte	.10	.30
104 Dave Blaney's Car	.75	2.00
105 Johnny Herrera's Car	.10	.30
106 Steve Beitler's Car	.10	.30
107 Sammy Swindell's Car	.50	1.25
108 Bobby Davis Jr.'s Car	.10	.30
109 Greg Hodnett's Car	.10	.30
110 Gary Wright's Car	.10	.30
111 Terry Gray's Car	.10	.30
112 Aaron Berryhill's Car SP	1.50	3.00
113 Frankie Kerr's Car SP	1.50	3.00
114 Jimmy Sills' Car SP	1.25	2.50
P1 Steve Kinser Promo	2.00	5.00

1991 World of Outlaws Most Wanted

This six-card Most Wanted set was issued in both foil packs of 1991 World of Outlaws and in complete set form. The four driver cards were released through packs first and then re-issued as a complete set with the cover and checklist cards. The card design is very similar to other Most Wanted sets, but can be distinguished by the border color of black.

COMPLETE SET (6)	5.00	10.00
1 Stevie Smith Jr.	.75	2.00
2 Danny Lasoski	1.50	3.00
3 Jimmy Sills	.60	1.50
4 Bobby Davis Jr.	.75	2.00
NNO Checklist Card	.30	.75
NNO Cover Card	.30	.75
World of Outlaws logo		
and complete set offer		

1992 World of Outlaws Most Wanted

James International Art produced only 12-card Most Wanted set in 1992. The card design is very similar to other Most Wanted sets, but can be distinguished by the border color of Maroon. The cover card describes the set as Most Wanted series two.

COMPLETE SET (12)	5.00	10.00
2 Johnny Herrera	.30	.75
3 Steve Beitler	.30	.75
4 Jack Hewitt	.30	.75
5 Sammy Swindell	.75	2.00
6 Jim Carr	.30	.75
7 Danny Smith	.30	.75
8 Keith Kauffman	.30	.75
9 Lee Blaney	.30	.75
10 Andy Hillenburg	.30	.75
NNO Cover Card	.25	.60
World of Outlaws logo		
and complete set offer		
NNO Checklist Card	.25	.60

1993 World of Outlaws Most Wanted

James International Art produced only a 12-card Most Wanted set in 1993. The card design is very similar to other Most Wanted sets, but can be distinguished by the border color of blue. The cover card describes the set as Most Wanted series three.

COMPLETE SET (12)	5.00	10.00
1 Dave Blaney	1.00	2.50
2 Kenny Jacobs	.50	1.25
3 Craig Keel	.30	.75
4 Joe Gaerte	.30	.75
5 Ed Lynch Jr.	.30	.75
6 Tommie Estes Jr.	.30	.75
7 Cris Eash	.30	.75
8 Garry Lee Maier	.30	.75
9 Gary Cameron II	.30	.75
10 Kevin Huntley	.30	.75
NNO Cover Card	.25	.60
World of Outlaws logo		
and complete set offer		
NNO Checklist Card	.25	.60
complete set/sheet		
offer on back		

1994 World of Outlaws

After a two year hiatus, James International once again produced a regular issue World of Outlaws set in 1994, as well as a Most Wanted set. The cards were re-designed and include 50 to the set released in a factory set box.

COMPLETE SET (50)	10.00	20.00
1 Checklist	.10	.30
2 Steve Kinser	1.00	2.50
3 Dave Blaney	.75	2.00
4 Stevie Smith Jr.	.40	
5 Kenny Jacobs	.10	
6 Andy Hillenburg	.25	
7 Jac Haudenschild	.60	
8 Greg Hodnett	.25	
9 Johnny Herrera	.10	
10 Richard Day	.10	
11 Steve Beitler	.10	
12 Craig Keel	.10	
13 Jeff Swindell	.25	
14 Mark Kinser	.40	
15 Aaron Berryhill	.10	
16 Joe Gaerte	.10	
17 Danny Lasoski	.25	
18 Terry McCarl	.10	
19 Bobby Davis Jr.	.10	
20 Ed Lynch Jr.	.10	
21 Bobby Allen	.10	
22 Donnie Kreitz Jr.	.10	
23 Keith Kauffman	.10	
24 Danny Smith	.10	
25 Gary Wright	.10	
26 Johnny Mackison Jr.	.10	
27 Jim Carr	.10	
28 Randy Smith	.10	
29 Garry Lee Maier	.10	
30 Steve Kent	.10	
31 Max Dumesny	.10	
32 Jimmy Sills	.10	
33 Gary Cameron II	.10	
34 Kevin Huntley	.10	
35 Rocky Hodges	.10	
36 Brent Kaeding	.25	
37 Frankie Kerr	.25	
38 Tim Green	.10	
39 Fred Rahmer	.25	
40 Steve Smith Sr.	.25	
41 Brad Noffsinger	.10	
42 Randy Hannagan	.10	
43 Garry Rush	.10	
44 Jason McMillen	.10	
45 Todd Kane	.10	
46 Dale Blaney	.10	
47 Rusty McClure	.10	
48 Kevin Pylant	.10	
49 Rod Henderson	.10	
50 Ron Shuman	.10	

1994 World of Outlaw Most Wanted

James International Art this 12-card Most W set in 1994. The card design is very similar to Most Wanted sets, but can be distinguished border color of brown. The cover card describ set as Most Wanted series four and includes a to purchase complete sets or uncut sheets previous year's sets.

COMPLETE SET (12)	5.00
1 Steve Kinser	1.25
2 Greg Hodnett	.30
3 Mark Kinser	.75
4 Frankie Kerr	.40
5 Aaron Berryhill	.30
6 Terry McCarl	.30
7 Jeff Swindell	.40
8 Brent Kaeding	.40
9 Lance Dewease	.30
10 Steve Kent	.30
NNO Cover Card	.25
offer for complete	
sets/sheets on back	
NNO Checklist Card	.25
offer for complete	
sets/sheets on back	

Multi Sport

1968 American Oil Winners Circle *

This set of 12 perforated game cards mea approximately 2 5/8" by 2 1/8". There are "le and "right side" game cards which had matched to win a car or a cash prize. The "righ game cards have a color drawing of a s personality in a circle on the left, surround laurel leaf twigs, and a short career summary right. There is a color bar on the bottom of th piece carrying a dollar amount and the words side". The "left side" game cards carry a recta drawing of a sports personality or a phot Camaro or a Corvette. A different color bar dollar amount and the words "left side" are un picture. On a dark blue background, the "righ

ks carry the rules of the game, and the "left side" ds show a "Winners Circle". The cards are umbered and checklisted below in alphabetical er.

arnelli Jones 2.00 5.00
left side

1994-95 Assets *

duced by Classic, the 1994 Assets set features s from basketball, hockey, football, baseball, and racing. The set was released in two series of 50 ds each. 1,994 cases were produced of each es. This standard-sized card set features a player to with his name in silver letters on the lower left er and the Assets logo on the upper right. The k has a color photo on the left side along with a graphy on the right side of the card. A Sprint ne card is randomly inserted in each five-card k.

ale Earnhardt .75 2.00
Dale Earnhardt .75 2.00
Jeff Gordon .40 1.00
Jeff Gordon .40 1.00

1994-95 Assets Silver Signature *

s 48-card standard-size set was randomly rted at a rate of four per box. The cards are tical to the first twenty-four cards in the each es, except that these show a silver facsimile ograph on their fronts. The first 24 cards espond to cards 1-24 in the first series while the nd 24 cards correspond to cards 51-74 in the nd series.

.VER SIGS: 1.2X TO 3X BASIC CARDS

994-95 Assets Die Cuts *

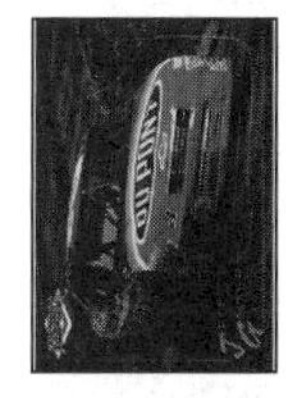

s 25-card standard-size set was randomly rted into packs. DC1-10 were included in series while DC11-25 were included in series two s. These cards feature the player on the card and ability to separate the player's photo. The back ains information about the player on the section e card that is separable.

Dale Earnhardt 7.50 15.00
9 Jeff Gordon's Car 1.50 4.00

994-95 Assets Phone Cards One Minute/$2 *

suring 2" by 3 1/4", these cards have rounded ers and were inserted one per pack. Cards 1-24 in first series packs while 25-48 were included second series packs. The front features the er's photo and on the side is how long the card ood for. The Assets logo is in the bottom left er. The back gives instructions on how to use phone card. The first series cards expired on ember 1, 1995 while the second series cards red on March 31, 1996. The cards with a $2 logo worth a mulitple of the regular cards. Please refer e values below for these cards.

NUMB.REVEALED: .2X to .5X BASIC INS.
O DOLLAR: .5X TO 1.2X BASIC INSERTS
ale Earnhardt 1.25 3.00
eff Gordon .60 1.50

1994-95 Assets Phone Cards $5 *

These cards measure 2" by 3 1/4", have rounded corners and were randomly inserted into packs. Cards 1-5 were inserted into first series packs while 6-15 were in second series packs. The front features the player's photo, with "Five Dollars" written in cursive script along the left edge. In the bottom left corner is the Assets logo. The back gives instructions on how to use the phone card. Series one cards expired on December 1, 1995 while second series cards expired on March 31, 1996.

*PIN NUMBER REVEALED: .2X TO .5X
9 Jeff Gordon 1.00 2.50

1994-95 Assets Phone Cards $25 *

These rounded corner cards measuring 2" by 3 1/4" were randomly inserted into first series packs. The front features the player's photo, with "Twenty-five Dollars" written in cursive script along the left edge. In the bottom left corner is the Classic Assets logo. The back gives instructions on how to use the phone card. These cards are listed in alphabetical order. Two combo cards were available to dealers at the rate of one per every six second-series boxes ordered. The cards expired on December 1, 1995.

*PIN NUMBER REVEALED: .2X TO .5X
1 Dale Earnhardt 3.00 8.00

1994-95 Assets Phone Cards $1000 *

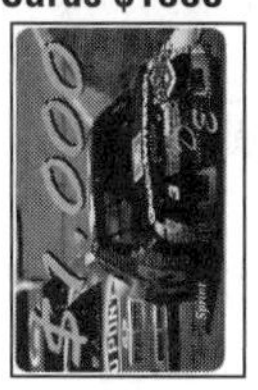

Measuring 2" by 3 1/4", these rounded-corner cards were randomly inserted in first-series packs. The fronts feature color player photos, with "One Thousand Dollars" in cursive script along the left edge. The backs give instructions on how to use the phone cards. The cards expired December 1, 1995.

*PIN NUMBER REVEALED: HALF VALUE
1 Dale Earnhardt 60.00 120.00

1995 Assets Gold *

This 50-card set measures the standard size. The fronts feature borderless player action photos with the player's name printed in gold at the bottom. The backs carry a portrait of the player with his name, career highlights, and statistics. The Dale Earnhardt card was pulled from circulation early in the product's release and is considered a Short Print (SP).

1 Dale Earnhardt SP 6.00 15.00

1995 Assets Gold Printer's Proofs *

These parallel card were randomly seeded at the rate of 1:18 packs. They feature the words "Printer's Proof" on the cardfronts.

1 Dale Earnhardt SP 10.00 25.00

1995 Assets Gold Silver Signatures *

These parallel cards were inserted one per pack. They feature a silver foil facsimile signature on the cardfronts.

1 Dale Earnhardt SP 5.00 12.00

1995 Assets Gold Die Cuts Silver *

This 20-card set was randomly inserted in packs at a rate of one in 18. The fronts feature a borderless player color action photo with a diamond-shaped top and the player's action taking place in front of the card name. The backs carry the card name, player's name and career highlights. The cards are numbered on the backs. Gold versions were inserted at a rate of one in 72 packs.

*GOLDS: 1.2X to 3X SILVERS
SDC10 Dale Earnhardt 2.00 5.00

1995 Assets Gold Phone Cards $2 *

This 47-card set was randomly inserted in packs and measures 2 1/8" by 3 3/8". The fronts feature color action player photos with the player's name below. The $2 calling value is printed vertically down the left. The backs carry the instructions on how to use the cards which expired on 7/31/96. The cards are unnumbered.

*PIN NUMBER REVEALED: HALF VALUE
1 Dale Earnhardt 2.50 5.00

1995 Assets Gold Phone Cards $5 *

This 16-card set measures 2 1/8" by 3 3/8" and was randomly inserted in packs. The fronts feature color action player photos with the player's name below. The $5 calling value is printed vertically down the left. The backs carry the instructions on how to use the cards which expired on 7/31/96. The cards are unnumbered. The Microlined versions are inserted at a rate of one in 18 packs versus one in six packs for the basic $5 card.

*MICROLINED: .6X TO 1.5X BASIC INSERTS
MICROLINED STATED ODDS 1:18
*PIN NUMBER REVEALED: HALF VALUE
12 Dale Earnhardt 2.50 6.00

1995 Assets Gold Phone Cards $1000 *

This five-card set measures 2 1/8" by 3 3/8". The fronts feature color action player photos with the player's name below. The $1000 calling value is printed on the left. The backs carry the instructions on how to use the cards which expired on 7/31/96. The cards are unnumbered and checklisted below in alphabetical order.

*PIN NUMBER REVEALED:HALF VALUE
2 Dale Earnhardt

1996 Assets *

The 1996 Classic Assets was issued in one set totalling 50 cards. This 50-card premium set has a tremendous selection of the top athletes in the world headlines. Each card features action photos, up-to-date statistics and is printed on high-quality, foil-stamped stock. Hot Print cards are parallel cards randomly inserted in Hot Packs and are valued at a multiple of the regular cards below.

3 Todd Bodine .05 .15
9 Dale Earnhardt 1.00 2.50
21 Sterling Marlin .08 .25
22 Mark Martin .30 .75
27 Ted Musgrave .05 .15

1996 Assets Hot Prints *

These parallel cards were randomly seeded in 1996 Assets Hot Packs. Each card is marked Hot Print on the cardfront.

*HOT PRINTS: 1.2X TO 3X BASIC CARDS

1996 Assets A Cut Above *

The even cards were randomly inserted in retail packs at a rate of one in eight, and the odd cards were inserted in clear asset packs at a rate of one in 20, this 20-card die-cut set is composed of 10 phone cards and 10 trading cards. The cards have rounded corners except for one which is cut in a straight corner design. The fronts feature a color action player cut-out superimposed over a gray background with the words "cut above" printed throughout and resembled to be cut so it displays a basketball game behind it. The backs carry a color action player photo with the player's name and a short career summary.

CA6 Mark Martin 1.25 3.00
CA17 Sterling Marlin 1.00 2.50

1996 Assets A Cut Above Phone Cards *

This 10-card set, which were inserted at a rate of one in eight, measures approximately 2 1/8" by 3 3/8" have rounded corners except for one corner which is cut out and made straight. The fronts feature a color action player cut-out superimposed over a gray background with the words "cut above" printed throughout and resembled to be cut so that it displays a game going on behind the background. The backs carry the instructions on how to use the card. The cards expired on 1/31/97.

*PIN NUMBER REVEALED: HALF VALUE
1 Dale Earnhardt 6.00 15.00

1996 Assets Crystal Phone Cards *

Randomly inserted in retail packs at a rate of one in 250, this high-tech, 10-card insert set contains clear holographic phone cards worth five minutes of long distance calling time. The cards measure approximately 2 1/8" by 3 3/8" with rounded corners. The fronts display a color action double-image player cut-out on a clear crystal background with the player's name printed vertically on the side. The backs carry instructions on how to use the card. The cards expired January 31, 1997. Twenty dollar phone cards of these athletes were issued, they are valued as a multiple of the cards below.

*TWENTY DOLLAR CARDS: 1X TO 2.5X
$20 CARDS STATED ODDS 1:250
*PIN NUMBER REVEALED: HALF VALUE
3 Dale Earnhardt 5.00 12.00

1996 Assets Phone Cards $2 *

This 30-card set was inserted in retail packs at a rate of 1 per pack with a minimum value of $2 per phone card. The cards measure approximately 2 1/8" by 3 3/8" with rounded corners. The fronts display color aciton player photos with the player's name in a red bar below. The backs carry the instructions on how to use the cards and the expiration date of 1/31/97. Hot Print parallel cards were randomly inserted in Hot Packs. These cards are valued as a multiple of the cards below.

*PIN NUMBER REVEALED: HALF VALUE
*ONE DOLLAR CARDS: HALF VALUE
*HOT PRINTS: 1.5X TO 4X BASIC INSERTS
6 Dale Earnhardt 1.50 4.00
12 Sterling Marlin .60 1.50
13 Mark Martin .75 2.00

1996 Assets Phone Cards $5 *

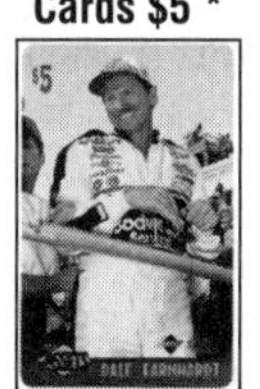

This 20-card set was randomly inserted in retail packs at a rate of 1 in 5. The cards measure approximately 2 1/8" by 3 3/8" with rounded corners. The fronts display color action player photos with the player's name in a red bar below. The backs carry the instructions on how to use the cards and the expiration date of 1/31/97.

*PIN NUMBER REVEALED: HALF VALUE
6 Dale Earnhardt 2.50 6.00
10 Mark Martin 1.25 3.00

1996 Assets Phone Cards $10 *

This 10-card set was randomly inserted in packs at a rate of 1 in 20. The cards measure approximately 2 1/8" by 3 3/8" with rounded corners. The fronts display color action player photos with the player's name in a red bar below. The backs carry the instructions on how to use the cards and the expiration date of 1/31/97.

*PIN NUMBER REVEALED: HALF VALUE
3 Dale Earnhardt 4.00 10.00

1996 Assets Phone Cards $20 *

This five card set measures approximately 2 1/8" by 3 3/8" with rounded corners and were randomly inserted in retail packs. The fronts display color action player photos with the player's name. The backs carry the instructions on how to use the cards and the expiration date of 1/31/97.

*PIN NUMBER REVEALED: HALF VALUE
1 Dale Earnhardt 8.00 20.00

1996 Assets Phone Cards $100 *

This five card set, randomly inserted in packs, measures approximately 2 1/8" by 3 3/8" with rounded corners. The fronts display color action player photos with the player's name. The backs carry the instructions on how to use the cards and the expiration date of 1/31/97.

*PIN NUMBER REVEALED: HALF VALUE
1 Dale Earnhardt 10.00 25.00

1996 Assets Silksations *

Randomly inserted in retail packs at a rate of one in 100, this 10-card standard-size set features duplexed fabric-stock with top athletes. The fronts display a color action player cut-out with a two-tone background. The player's name is printed below. The backs carry a head photo of the player made to appear as if it is coming out of a square hole in gold cloth. The player's name and a short career summary are below. The cards are numbered with a "S" prefix and sequenced in alphabetical order.

3 Dale Earnhardt 10.00 25.00

1995 Classic Five-Sport Previews *

Randomly inserted in 1995 Classic hockey packs, this five-card standard-size set salutes the leaders and the up-and-coming rookies of the five sports. Borderless fronts have a full-color action shot with gold foil stamp of "preview" and the player's name, school and position printed vertically on the right side of the card. The player's sport's ball (or tire) is printed in a montage on the right. Backs have another full-color action shot and also a biography, statistics and profile. The cards are numbered with a "SP" prefix.

SP1 Dale Earnhardt 5.00 5.00

1995 Classic Five-Sport *

The 1995 Classic Five Sport set was issued in one series of 200 standard-size cards. Cards were issued in 10-card regular packs (SRP $1.99). Boxes contained 36 packs. One autographed card was guaranteed in each pack and one certified autographed card (with an embossed logo) appeared in each box. There were also memorabilia redemption cards included in some packs and were guaranteed in at least one pack per box. Borderless fronts feature color player action photos. Balls of the sport run vertically down the right side with the player's name, position, and team name printed on them. Tires are used for racing cards, while pucks are used for hockey cards. The backs carry another color player action photo with the player's name, biographical information, career highlights, and statistics. The cards are numbered and divided into the five sports as follows: Basketball (1-42), Football (43-92), Baseball (93-122), Hockey (123-160), Racing (161-180), Alma Maters (181-190), Picture Perfect (191-200).

*SILVER DCs: .8X TO 2X BASIC CARDS
ONE SILVER PER HOBBY PACK
*RED DCs: 2.5X TO 6X BASIC CARDS
RANDOM INSERTS IN RETAIL JUMBOS
*PRINT.PROOFS: 4X TO 10X BASIC CARDS
PPs RANDOM INSERTS IN HOBBY PACKS
161 Dale Earnhardt .75 2.00
162 John Andretti .02 .10
163 Derrike Cope .02 .10
164 Richard Childress .02 .10
165 Rusty Wallace .25 .60
166 Bobby Labonte .20 .50
167 Brett Bodine .02 .10
168 Michael Waltrip .02 .10
169 Sterling Marlin .15 .40
170 Kyle Petty .07 .20
171 Ricky Rudd .15 .40
172 Jeff Burton .15 .40
173 Dick Trickle .02 .10
174 Ernie Irvan .07 .20
175 Dale Jarrett .25 .60
176 Darrell Waltrip .07 .20
177 Geoff Bodine .02 .10
178 Ted Musgrave .02 .10
179 Morgan Shepherd .02 .10
180 Todd Bodine .02 .10

1995 Classic Five-Sport Autographs *

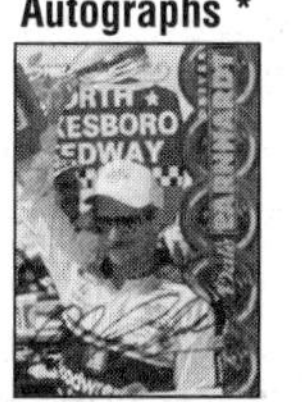

This set was randomly inserted into packs. Borderless fronts feature color player action photos. The backs carry a "Congratulations" message stating that it is an autographed 1995 Five Sport Autograph Edition Card with the sport's ball pictured at the bottom. The cards are unnumbered.

*CLASSIC SIGNINGS: SAME VALUE
*CLASSIC SIGNINGS/225: 1.2X TO 3X
161A Dale Earnhardt/635 200.00 350.00
161B Dale Earnhardt/225 350.00 500.00
163 Derrike Cope/225
Not Confirmed
164 Richard Childress/225 2.00 5.00
166 Bobby Labonte/225 12.50 30.00
167 Brett Bodine/225 2.00 5.00
168 Michael Waltrip/225
Not Confirmed
169 Sterling Marlin/225 6.00 15.00
170 Kyle Petty/225 4.00 10.00
171 Ricky Rudd/225 2.00 5.00
172 Jeff Burton/225
Not Confirmed
173 Dick Trickle/225 2.00 5.00
174 Ernie Irvan/225 4.00 10.00
175 Dale Jarrett/225 6.00 15.00
176 Darrell Waltrip/225 2.00 5.00
177 Geoff Bodine/225 2.00 5.00
178 Ted Musgrave/225 2.00 5.00
179 Morgan Shepherd/225 2.00 5.00
180 Todd Bodine/225 2.00 5.00

1995 Classic Five-Sport Classic Standouts *

Randomly inserted in regular packs at a rate of one in 216, this 10-card standard-size set features both the hot new stars and the established elite of all five sports. Fronts have full-color action player cutouts set against a gold and black foil background. The player's name is printed in gold foil at the top. Backs contain a full-color action shot with the player's name printed in yellow and a career highlights box. The cards are numbered with a "CS" prefix.

CS3 Dale Earnhardt 5.00 12.00

1995 Classic Five-Sport Hot Box Autographs *

This set of six autographed standard-sized cards were randomly inserted in Hobby Hot boxes. The cards are identical to the regular Hot box inserts with the exception of a player's signature on the front.

3 Dale Earnhardt/635 250.00 400.00

1995 Classic Five-Sport On Fire *

Ten of the 20-cards in this set were released in Hobby Hot Packs while the other ten were released in retail Hot packs. Fronts have full-color player cutouts set against a flame background with the On Fire logo printed at the bottom. The player's name is printed vertically in white type on the left side. backs feature biography and players's statistics.

H3 Dale Earnhardt 4.00 10.00

1995 Classic Five-Sport Phone Cards $3 *

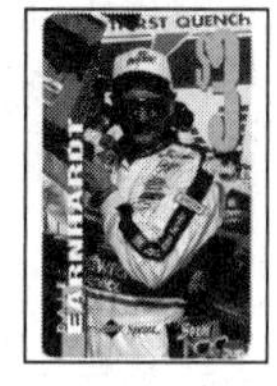

The five-card set of $3 Phone Cards were found one per 72 retail packs. The credit-card size plastic pieces have a borderless front with a full-color action player photo and the $3 emblem printed on the upper right in blue. The player's name is printed in white type vertically on the lower left. The Sprint logo appears on the bottom also. White backs carry information of how to place calls using the card.

1 Dale Earnhardt 2.00 5.00

1995 Classic Five-Sport Phone Cards $4 *

These cards were inserted randomly into packs at a rate of one in 72 and featured the five top prospects or performers of the individual sports. The borderless fronts feature full-color action photos with the athlete's name printed in white across the bottom. The Sprint logo and $4 are printed along the top. White backs contain information about placing calls using the card.

1 Dale Earnhardt 2.50 6.00

1995 Classic Five-Sport Record Setters *

This 10-card standard-size set was inserted in retail packs and feature the stars and rookies of the five sports. The fronts display full-bleed color action photos; the set title "Record Setters" iin prismatic block lettering appears toward the bottom. On a sepia-tone photo, the backs carry a player profile. The cards are numbered on the back with an "RS" prefix and hand-numbered out of 1250.

RS4 Dale Earnhardt 4.00 10.00

1995 Classic Five-Sport Strive For Five *

This interactive game card set consists of 65 cards to be used like playing cards. Collector's gained a full suit of cards to redeem prizes. The odds of finding the card in packs were one in 10. Fronts are bordered in metallic silver foil and picture the player in full-color action. The cards are numbered on both top and bottom in silver foil and the player's name is printed vertically in silver foil. Backs have green backgrounds with the game rules printed in white type.

RC1 John Andretti	.20	.50
RC2 Dick Trickle	.20	.50
RC3 Kyle Petty	.30	.75
RC4 Bobby Labonte	.40	1.00
RC5 Ricky Rudd	.30	.75
RC6 Darrell Waltrip	.30	.75
RC7 Dale Jarrett	.40	1.00
RC8 Brett Bodine	.20	.50
RC9 Geoff Bodine	.20	.50
RC10 Ernie Irvan	.30	.75
RC11 Jeff Burton	.40	1.00
RC12 Sterling Marlin	.40	1.00
RC13 Rusty Wallace	.40	1.00

1995 Classic National *

This 20-card multi-sport set was issued by Classic to commemorate the 16th National Sports Collectors Convention in St. Louis. The fronts display color player photos that have a metallic sheen and are edged on the left by a jagged rust-colored stripe. A stripe of the same color cuts across the bottom and carries the player's name. The backs feature a color closeup photo at top and player profile at the bottom. The set included a certificate of limited edition, with the serial number out of 9,995 sets produced. One thousand Sprint 20-minute phone cards featuring Ki-Jana Carter were also distributed.

NC4 Dale Earnhardt	2.00	5.00

1996 Classic Signings *

The 1996 Classic Signings set consists of 100 standard-size cards. This series is distinguished from the regular issue by a silver foil facsimile autograph and a silver-foil "Autograph Edition" toward the bottom. The die cut cards were inserted one in four packs. The blue and red signature cards were randomly inserted in regular five-sport Hot Boxes and are identical to the regular card with the exception of a red foil signature on the front.

*DIE CUTS: .5X TO 1.2X BASIC CARDS
*RED SIGS: 1X TO 2.5X BASIC CARDS
1995 FIVE-SPORT RED SIG: SAME PRICE
*BLUE SIGS: 3X TO 8X BASIC CARDS

S79 Dale Earnhardt	.60	1.50
S80 John Andretti	.01	.05
S81 Rusty Wallace	.25	.60
S82 Bobby Labonte	.20	.50
S83 Michael Waltrip	.01	.05
S84 Sterling Marlin	.10	.30
S85 Brett Bodine	.01	.05
S86 Kyle Petty	.05	.15
S87 Ricky Rudd	.10	.30
S88 Ernie Irvan	.10	.30
S89 Darrell Waltrip	.05	.15
S90 Geoff Bodine	.01	.05

1996 Classic Signings Etched in Stone *

This 10-card set, printed on 16-point foil board, was randomly inserted in Hot boxes only. Hot boxes were distributed at a rate of 1:5 cases.

9 Mark Martin	2.50	6.00

1996 Classic Signings Freshly Inked *

This 30-card set was randomly inserted one in every ten 1996 Classic Signings packs. The fronts feature borderless player color action photos with the player's name printed in gold foil across the bottom. The backs carry an artist's drawing of the player with the player's name at the top.

FS27 John Andretti	1.00	2.50
FS28 Derrike Cope	.40	1.00
FS29 Todd Bodine	.60	1.50
FS30 Jeff Burton	5.00	8.00

1996 Clear Assets *

The 1996 Clear Assets set was issued in one series totaling 70 cards. The set features 75 upscale acetate cards of the most collectible athletes from baseball, basketball, football, hockey and auto racing. Also included is the debut appearance by many of the top players entering the 1996 football draft. Release date was April 1996.

60 Ricky Rudd	.08	.15
61 Bobby Hamilton	.08	.15
62 Dale Jarrett	.20	.50
63 Brett Bodine	.05	.05
64 Dale Earnhardt	.60	1.50
65 Sterling Marlin	.20	.25
66 Mark Martin	.25	.60
67 Ted Musgrave	.05	.05
68 Bobby Labonte	.20	.50
69 Ricky Craven	.05	.05
70 Kyle Petty	.08	.15

1996 Clear Assets Phone Cards $2 *

Inserted at a rate of one per pack, this 30-card set of acetate phone cards features many of the biggest names in sports. The Sprint phone cards carry expiration dates of 10/1/97.

*PIN NUMBER REVEALED: HALF VALUE
*$1 CARDS: .2X TO .5X $2 CARDS

4 Mark Martin	.40	1.00
19 Dale Earnhardt	1.50	4.00

1996 Clear Assets Phone Cards $5 *

Inserted at a rate of 1:10 packs, this 20-card set of acetate phone cards features many of the biggest names in sports. The Sprint phone cards carry expiration dates of 10/1/97.

*PIN NUMBER REVEALED:HALF VALUE

4 Dale Earnhardt	2.50	6.00

1996 Clear Assets Phone Cards $10 *

Inserted at a rate of 1:30 packs, this 10-card set of acetate phone cards features many of the biggest names in sports. The Sprint phone cards carry expiration dates of 10/1/97.

*PIN NUMBER REVEALED:HALF VALUE

3 Dale Earnhardt	5.00	12.00
8 Mark Martin	2.50	6.00

1996 Clear Assets 3X *

Randomly inserted in packs at a rate of one in 100, this 10-card set is another first from Classic. The cards resemble triplexed cards with acetate in the middle and an opaque covering.

X1 Mark Martin	5.00	12.00

1972-83 Dimanche/Derniere Heure *

The blank-backed photo sheets in this multi-sport set measure approximately 8 1/2" by 11" and feature white-bordered color sports star photos from Dimanche Derniere Heure, a Montreal newspaper. The player's name, position and biographical information appear within the lower white margin. All text is in French. A white vinyl album was available for storing the photo sheets. Printed on the album's spine are the words, "Mes Vedettes du Sport" (My Stars of Sport).The photos are unnumbered and are checklisted below in alphabetical order according to sport or team as follows: Montreal Expos baseball players (1-117; National League baseball players (118-130); Montreal Canadiens hockey players (131-177); wrestlers (178-202); prize fighters (203-204); auto racing drivers (205-208); women's golf (209); Patof the circus clown (210); and CFL (211-278).

205 Emerson Fittipaldi	3.00	6.00
206 Alan Jones	1.50	3.00
207 Jody Scheckter	2.00	4.00
208 Patrick Tambay	1.50	3.00

1937 Kellogg's Pep Stamps *

Kellogg's distributed these multi-sport stamps inside specially marked Pep brand cereal boxes in 1937. They were originally issued in four-stamp blocks along with an instructional type tab at the top. The tab contained the sheet number. We've noted the sheet number after each athlete's name below. Note that six athletes appear on two sheets, thereby making those six double prints. There were 24-different sheets produced. We've catalogued the unnumbered stamps below in single loose form according to sport (AR- auto racing, AV- aviation, BB- baseball, BX- boxing, FB- football, GO- golf, HO- horses, SW- swimming, TN- tennis). Stamps can often be found intact in blocks of four along with the tab. Complete blocks of stamps are valued at roughly 50 percent more than the total value of the four individual stamps as priced below. An album was also produced to house the set.

AR1 Billy Arnold 6	7.50	15.00
AR2 Bill Cummings 2	7.50	15.00
AR3 Ralph DePalma 14	10.00	20.00
AR4 Tommy Milton 8	7.50	15.00
AR5 Mauri Rose 10	12.50	25.00
AR6 Wilbur Shaw 24	12.50	25.00

1976 Nabisco Sugar Daddy 1 *

This set of 25 tiny (approximately 1 1/16" by 2 3/4") cards features action scenes from a variety of popular sports from around the world. One card was included in specially marked Sugar Daddy and Sugar Mama candy bars. The set is referred to as "Sugar Daddy Sports World - Series 1" on the backs of the cards. The cards are in color with a relatively wide white border around the front of the cards.

4 Auto Racing	5.00	10.00

1996 No Fear *

This eight-card jumbo-sized set was issued through No Fear. It is a multi-sport set that features a posed color player shot on the front and a white back featuring a slogan by No Fear. The mode of distribution is unclear. The cards are not numbered and checklisted below in alphabetical order.

4 Robby Gordon	.40	1.00

1991 Pro Set Pro Files *

These cards measure the standard size. The fronts have full-bleed color photos, with facsimile autographs inscribed across the bottom of the pictures. Reportedly only 150 of each were produced and approximately 100 of each were handed out as part of a contest on the Pro Files TV show. Each week viewers were invited to send in their names and addresses to a Pro Set post office box. All subjects in the set made appearances on the TV show. The show was hosted by Craig James and Tim Brant and was aired on Saturday nights in Dallas and sponsored by Pro Set. The cards were subtitled "Signature Series". The cards are unnumbered and are listed in alphabetical order by subject in the checklist below. All of the cards were facsimile autographed except for Anne Smith who signed all of her cards personally.

11 Rusty Wallace	10.00	25.00

1994 Score Board National Promos *

Distributed during the 1994 National Sports Collectors Convention, this 20-card standard-size multi-sport set features four subsets: Salute to 1994 Draft Stars (1-5), Centers of Attention (6-9), Texas Heroes (10-13, 20), and Salute to Racing's Greatest (14-18). The borderless fronts feature color action cutouts on multi-colored metallic backgrounds. The players name, position, and team name appear randomly placed on arcs. The borderless backs feature a color head shot on a ghosted backgound. The players name and biography appear at the top with the player's stats and profile at the bottom. The cards are numbered on the back with an "NC" prefix. The sets were given away to attendees at Classic's National Convention Party. Each set included a certificate of authenticity, giving the set serial number out of a total of 9,900 sets produced. There were five different checklist cards created using the fronts of other cards in the set. The complete set price includes only one of the checklist cards.

14 Dale Earnhardt	1.50	4.00
1979-1981		
15 Dale Earnhardt	1.50	4.00
1982-1984		
16 Dale Earnhardt	1.50	4.00
1985-1987		
17 Dale Earnhardt	1.50	4.00
Teresa Earnhardt		
1988-1990		
18 Dale Earnhardt	1.50	4.00
1991-1993		
20B Dale Earnhardt	1.25	3.00
Checklist Card		

1989-91 Sports Illustrated for Kids *

Since its debut issue in January 1989, SI for Kids has included a perforated sheet of nine standard-size cards bound into each magazine. The cards were consecutively numbered 1-324 through December 1991. The athletes featured represent an extremely wide spectrum of sports. Each card features color photos with variously colored borders. The borders are as follows: aqua (1-108), green (109-207), woodgrain (208-216), red (217-315), marble (316-324). The player's name is printed in a white bar at the top, while his or her sport appears at the bottom. The backs carry biographical information, career highlights, and a trivia question with answer. The cards' magazine issue date appears on the back in very small type. Although originally distributed in sheet form, the cards are frequently traded as singles. Thus, they are priced individually. The value of an intact sheet is equal to the sum of the nine cards plus a premium of up to 20%.

41 Mario Andretti	1.25	3.00
54 Lyn St. James	.40	1.00
187 Danny Sullivan	.40	1.00
196 Lori Johns	.40	1.00
257 Al Unser Jr.	.60	1.50
290 Rick Mears	.60	1.50

1992-00 Sports Illustrated for Kids *

Since its debut issue in January 1989, SI for Kids has included a perforated sheet of nine standard-size cards bound into each magazine. In January 1992, the card numbers started over at card #1. This listing comprises only the racing subject cards contained from that magazine through the last 2000 issue. Each card features color photos with borders of various designs and colors. The athlete's name is printed at the top while his sport appears at the bottom. The backs carry biographical information, career highlights, and a trivia question with answer. The cards' magazine issue date appears on the back in very small type. Although originally distributed in sheet form the cards are frequently traded as singles -- thus they are priced individually below.

48 Darrell Waltrip	.75	2.00
66 Richard Petty	1.50	4.00
114 Nigel Mansell	.30	.75
255 Joe Amato	.08	.25
334 Geoff Bodine	.40	1.00
480 Dale Jarrett	.60	1.00
602 Jeff Gordon	1.50	4.00
728 Eddie Cheever	.08	.25
735 Jeff Gordon	1.25	3.00
801 John Force	.40	1.00
828 Ron Hornaday	.08	.25

2001-02 Sports Illustrated for Kids *

Since its debut issue in January 1989, SI for Kids has included a perforated sheet of nine standard-size cards bound into each magazine. In January 2001, for the second time, the card numbers started over at card #1. The athletes featured represent an extremely wide spectrum of sports, but we've listed only the auto racing subjects below. Although originally distributed in sheet form, the cards are frequently traded as singles. Thus, they are priced individually.

78 Dale Jarrett	.40	1.00
126 Dale Earnhardt Jr.	2.00	5.00
148 Michael Schumacher	.15	.75
160 Jeff Gordon	1.25	3.00
196 Helio Castroneves	.15	.50

2003 Sports Illustrated for Kids *

Since its debut issue in January 1989, SI for Kids has included a perforated sheet of nine standard-size cards bound into each magazine. In January 2001, for the second time, the card numbers started over at 1. Listed below are the racing cards issued in magazines that carry 2003 cover dates. Although originally distributed in sheet form, the cards are frequently traded as singles. Thus, they are priced individually.

243 Jimmie Johnson's Car	.15	.40
306 Gil de Ferran	.15	.40
324 Matt Kenseth	.75	2.00

2005 Sports Illustrated for Kids *

459 Kurt Busch	.75	1.00
495 Jeff Gordon	2.00	4.00
519 Dan Wheldon	2.00	3.00

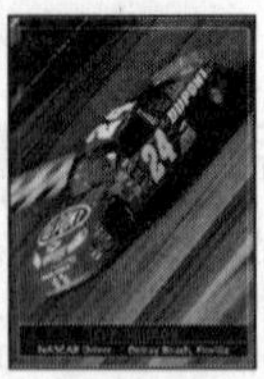

2006 Sports Illustrated for Kids

9 Tony Stewart NASCAR
69 Kasey Kahne's Car NASCAR
85 Sam Hornish's Car Racing

2007 Sports Illustrated for Kids

117 Colin McRae Racing	.10	.30
125 Brad Coleman Auto Racing		
153 Denny Hamlin NASCAR		

1996 Visions *

The 1996 Classic Visions set consists of 150 standard-size cards. The fronts feature full-bleed color action player photos. The player's position and name are presented in blue foil, while the Classic logo and set title "96 Visions" are stamped in gold foil. The back carries a second color photo, college statistics, biography, and a player fact.

108 Dale Earnhardt's Car	.30	.75
109 Dale Jarrett	.20	.50
110 Mark Martin	.25	.60
111 Ernie Irvan	.05	.15
112 Ricky Rudd	.15	.25
113 Bobby Labonte	.20	.50
114 Rusty Wallace's Car	.15	.40
115 Michael Waltrip	.01	.15
116 Sterling Marlin	.15	.40
117 Dick Trickle	.01	.05
118 John Andretti	.01	.05
119 Darrell Waltrip	.01	.15
120 Kyle Petty	.05	.15
124 Dale Earnhardt	.75	2.00
127 Mark Martin	.25	.60

1996 Visions Signings *

The 1996 Visions Signings set consists of 100 standard-size cards. The fronts feature full-bleed color action player photos. The player's position and name are stamped in prismatic foil along with the Classic logo and set title "96 Visions Signings." This set contains standouts from five sports grouped together in this order: basketball, football, hockey, baseball and racing. Cards were distributed in six-card packs. Release date was June 1996. The main allure to this product, in addition to the conventional inserts, were autographed memorabilia redemption cards inserted one per 10 packs.

88 Dale Jarrett	.20	.50
89 Mark Martin	.25	.60
90 Ernie Irvan	.05	.15
91 Ricky Rudd	.15	.40
92 Bobby Labonte	.20	.50
93 Michael Waltrip	.01	.15
94 Sterling Marlin	.15	.40
95 Dick Trickle	.01	.05
96 Darrell Waltrip	.05	.15
97 Kyle Petty	.05	.15
98 John Andretti	.01	.05
99 Rusty Wallace's Car	.15	.40
100 Dale Earnhardt's Car	.30	.75

1996 Visions Signings Autographs Silver *

Certified autographed cards were inserted in Visions Signings packs at a rate of 1:12. Some players signed only silver cards, some signed gold and silver cards. Silver cards were individually numbered; the quantity is listed after the player name.

89A Mark Martin/315	15.00	30.00
90A Ernie Irvan/265	3.00	8.00
91A Ricky Rudd/285	6.00	15.
93A Michael Waltrip/285	3.00	8.
95A Dick Trickle/285	3.00	8.

2004 SportCoins

3 Dale Earnhardt	20.00	35
3 b-RCR 35th Anniversary/1003		
8 Dale Earnhardt Jr	20.00	35.
8 b-DEI/4008		
18 Bobby Labonte	15.00	25.
'00 Champion		
b-Joe Gibbs Racing/518		
20 Tony Stewart	18.00	30.
'02 Champion		
b-Joe Gibbs Racing/520		
24 Jeff Gordon	20.00	35
Flames 24 b-HMS 20th Anniversary/2024		
24 Jeff Gordon	25.00	40.
Flames 24		
b-Brickyard 400 Winner/2024		
29 Kevin Harvick	18.00	30.
Goodwrench 29		
b-RCR 35th Anniversary/529		
30 Johnny Sauter	25.00	40.
AOL 30 b-RCR 35th Anniversary/50		
31 Robby Gordon	18.00	30.
Cingular 31 b-Gas On Flames/531		
31 Robby Gordon	15.00	25
Cingular 31		
b-RCR 35th Anniversary/531		
43 Richard Petty	20.00	35
The King b-Accomplishments/500		
48 Jimmie Johnson	18.00	30.
48 b-HMS 20th Anniversary/548		
NNO Petty Enterprises/500	18.00	30.
NNO Coca Cola 600 20th Anniversary/825	15.00	25

2005 SportCoins

2 Rusty Wallace	15.00	30
Miller Lite Last Call b-Penske/1002		
3 Dale Earnhardt	20.00	35
3 b-DEI/1503		
3 Dale Earnhardt	20.00	35
'98 Daytona b-3/2003		
5 Kyle Busch	15.00	25
Kellogg's b-HMS/505		
6 Mark Martin	18.00	30
6 b-Roush/506		
8 Dale Earnhardt Jr.	20.00	35
8 b-DEI/10,008		
8 Dale Earnhardt	20.00	35
'04 Daytona b-8/2008		
8 Martin Truex Jr.	15.00	30
8 b-Chance 2/508		
9 Kasey Kahne	15.00	30
9 b-Evernham/1009		
12 Ryan Newman	12.50	25
12 b-Penske/512		
15 Michael Waltrip	15.00	25
15 b-DEI/515		
16 Greg Biffle	15.00	25
16 b-Roush/516		
17 Matt Kenseth	18.00	30
DeWalt 17 b-Roush/517		
18 Bobby Labonte	15.00	25
Interstate Batteries 18		
b-Joe Gibbs Racing/1518		
19 J.Mayfield/19 b-Evernham/519	12.50	25
20 Tony Stewart	18.00	30
Home Depot 20 b-JGR/1520		
21 Ricky Rudd	15.00	25
21 b-Wood Brothers/521		
24 Jeff Gordon	20.00	35
DuPont Flames 24 b-HMS/5024		
24 Jeff Gordon	20.00	35
'05 Daytona Winner		
b-24 Flames/5024		
24 Jeff Gordon		
Jeff Gordon Network b-24 Flames		
Fan Club Exclusive		
25 Brian Vickers	15.00	25
GMAC 25 b-HMS/525		
29 Kevin Harvick	18.00	30
Goodwrench b-RCR/1029		
31 Jeff Burton	15.00	25
Cingular 31 b-RCR/531		
43 Richard Petty	20.00	35
The King b-Accomplishments Gold/543		
48 Jimmie Johnson	20.00	35
Lowe's 48 b-HMS/1048		
97 Kurt Busch	15.00	25
Sharpie 97 b-Roush/597		
99 Carl Edwards	25.00	40
99 b-Roush/599		
01 Joe Nemechek	15.00	25
Army b-MB2		
07 Dave Blaney	20.00	35
Jack Daniel's b-RCR/1007		

2000-01 Action Racing ollectables Ceramic 1:12

	EX	NM-MT
Earnhardt oodwrench 97 Monte Carlo Crash/5004 2001	250.00	500.00
Earnhardt oodwrench Taz 2000	175.00	300.00
Gordon Pont	250.00	500.00

003 Action Road Racing 1:12

	EX	NM-MT
Earnhardt ale Earnhardt Jr. ndy Pilgrim elly Collins 001 C5-R Corvette RCCA/100	400.00	650.00

1990-03 Action Racing lectables Pit Wagon Banks 1:16

1:16 scale replicas of Pit Wagons were produced by Racing Collectibles. ARC began producing them in 1994 ch is a coin bank.

	EX	NM-MT
y Wallace rd Motorsports	30.00	60.00
y Wallace iller Genuine Draft/2508 1995	25.00	60.00
y Wallace iller Lite 1997	25.00	60.00
y Wallace iller Lite plastic case/3500 1998	25.00	60.00
Earnhardt oodwrench/3000 1995	50.00	120.00
Earnhardt oodwrench 94 Champ/5000 19955	50.00	100.00
Earnhardt oodwrench RCCA/2500 1996	50.00	120.00
Earnhardt oodwrench 7-Time Champion	60.00	120.00
Earnhardt oodwrench Plus Bass Pro 1998	75.00	175.00
Earnhardt oodwrench 1999	75.00	150.00
Earnhardt oodwrench th Anniversary/2508 1999	50.00	120.00
Earnhardt oodwrench Taz No Bull	80.00	175.00
Earnhardt oodwrench Peter Max paint 2000	100.00	200.00
Earnhardt rangler/2508 1999	50.00	120.00
Earnhardt heaties/3756 1997	75.00	150.00
Earnhardt Jr. C Delco Superman/4308 1999	40.00	80.00
Elliott udweiser/2508 1994	30.00	80.00
Musgrave amily Channel 1994	10.00	20.00
le Jarrett terstate Batteries	15 00	30.00
Gordon uPont 1993 ROY 1994	60.00	150.00
Gordon uPont 1996 Monte Carlo/2500	60.00	120.00
Gordon uPont Superman/3504 1999	35.00	75.00
Gordon urassic Park 3 1997	50.00	120.00
Gordon epsi/2508 1999	25.00	50.00
ey Allison avoline RCCA 1990	30.00	60.00
ey Allison avoline Mac Tools RCCA 1993	30.00	80.00
ie Irvan avoline	20.00	40.00
ie Irvan ac Tools	20.00	40.00
nny Irwin avoline Joker	40.00	60.00
in Harvick nap-On/7494 2002	30.00	60.00
hael Waltrip ennzoil/2508 1994	10.00	25.00
Nemechek eineke/2508 1994	15.00	30.00
le Petty ello Yello	15.00	30.00
l Bonnett ountry Time/5216 1994	20.00	50.00
le Jarrett uality Care Batman	35.00	60.00
Elliott ac Tonight 1997	15.00	40.00
Elliott cDonald's/2508 1995	20.00	35.00
ale Earnhardt egacy/3333 2003	20.00	35.00

1998 Action Racing Collectables 1:18

	EX	NM-MT
Earnhardt oodwrench Plus Bass Pro	125.00	250.00
Earnhardt oodwrench Plus Daytona/4008	75.00	150.00
Earnhardt oodwrench Silver 95 Monte Carlo/7000	200.00	300.00
Earnhardt heaties	100.00	200.00

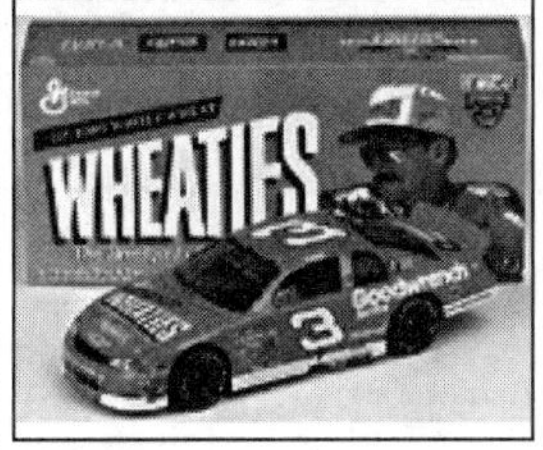

	EX	NM-MT
1997 Monte Carlo/7008		
24 Jeff Gordon DuPont Chromalusion	125.00	225.00
28 Kenny Irwin Joker	50.00	100.00
31 Dale Earnhardt Jr. Sikkens Blue 1997 Monte Carlo/7596	50.00	120.00
31 Dale Earnhardt Jr. Wrangler 1997 Monte Carlo/7596	50.00	120.00
88 Dale Jarrett Batman	60.00	100.00

1999 Action Racing Collectables 1:18

These 1:18 scale cars were distributed by Action through their distributor network.

	EX	NM-MT
1 Dale Earnhardt Jr. Coke	70.00	100.00
1 Steve Park Pennzoil/2508	25.00	60.00
1 Steve Park Pennzoil Shark	30.00	75.00
2 Ron Fellows John Paul Jr. Chris Kneifel Goodwrench C5-R Corvette	30.00	80.00
2 Rusty Wallace Miller Lite/2508	30.00	80.00
2 Rusty Wallace Miller Lite Harley/3504	30.00	80.00
3 Dale Earnhardt Coke	75.00	150.00
3 Dale Earnhardt Goodwrench/4008	75.00	150.00
3 Dale Earnhardt Goodwrench Sign/3000	100.00	200.00
3 Dale Earnhardt Goodwrench Sign Last Lap/2508	175.00	300.00
3 Dale Earnhardt Wrangler	75.00	150.00
3 Dale Earnhardt Jr. AC Delco	75.00	150.00
3 Dale Earnhardt Jr. AC Delco Superman	75.00	150.00
5 Terry Labonte K-Sentials/2508	25.00	60.00
5 Terry Labonte Kellogg's NASCAR Racers/2508	30.00	60.00
8 Dale Earnhardt Jr. Budweiser 2000/2508	60.00	120.00
10 Ricky Rudd Tide Kid's	30.00	60.00
18 Bobby Labonte Interstate Batteries NASCAR Racers/2508	30.00	80.00
20 Tony Stewart Home Depot/5508	60.00	120.00
20 Tony Stewart Home Depot Habitat/10,008	25.00	60.00
24 Jeff Gordon DuPont	60.00	125.00
24 Jeff Gordon DuPont Superman/3000	75.00	150.00
24 Jeff Gordon DuPont NASCAR Racers	75.00	150.00
24 Jeff Gordon Pepsi	50.00	100.00
24 Jeff Gordon Pepsi Star Wars/3000	30.00	80.00
27 Casey Atwood Castrol	25.00	60.00
31 Dale Earnhardt Jr. Mom 'N' Pop's 1996 Monte Carlo/2508	50.00	100.00
31 Dale Earnhardt Jr. Sikkens White 1997 Monte Carlo	70.00	120.00
36 Ernie Irvan M&M's	20.00	50.00
36 Ernie Irvan M&M's Countdown	20.00	50.00
36 Ernie Irvan M&M's Millennium	25.00	60.00
40 Sterling Marlin Coors Lite Brooks & Dunn	40.00	100.00
55 Kenny Wallace Square D NASCAR Racers/2508	25.00	60.00
88 Dale Jarrett Quality Care	30.00	60.00

2000 Action Racing Collectables 1:18

These 1:18 scale cars were distributed by Action through their distributor network.

	EX	NM-MT
3 Dale Earnhardt Goodwrench	150.00	250.00
3 Dale Earnhardt Goodwrench Peter Max/3000	250.00	400.00
3 Dale Earnhardt Goodwrench Taz No Bull	150.00	250.00
3 Ron Fellows Justan Bell Cris Kneifel Goodwrench C5-R Corvette	100.00	150.00
4 Franck Freon Andy Pilgrim Kelly Collins Goodwrench C5-R Corvette	100.00	150.00
8 Dale Earnhardt Jr. Bud/3504	75.00	150.00
8 Dale Earnhardt Jr. Budweiser Olympic	80.00	125.00
18 Bobby Labonte Interstate Batteries All Star Game	30.00	60.00
20 Tony Stewart Home Depot	50.00	100.00
20 Tony Stewart Home Depot ROY/2508	30.00	60.00
24 Jeff Gordon DuPont/3504	50.00	100.00
24 Jeff Gordon DuPont Millennium/3504	60.00	120.00
24 Jeff Gordon DuPont Peanuts	75.00	125.00
24 Jeff Gordon DuPont Winston	75.00	125.00
24 Jeff Gordon Pepsi	50.00	100.00
25 Jerry Nadeau Holigan Coast Guard/2004	25.00	50.00
28 Ricky Rudd Havoline Marines/2000	30.00	60.00
36 Ken Schrader M&M's Keep Back/2004	30.00	60.00
66 Darrell Waltrip Big K Route 66 Flames	30.00	80.00
88 Dale Jarrett Quality Care/2004	30.00	60.00
88 Dale Jarrett Quality Care Air Force	35.00	70.00
94 Bill Elliott McDonald's/2004	30.00	60.00
94 Bill Elliott McDonald's 25th Anniversary	30.00	60.00

2001 Action Racing Collectables 1:18

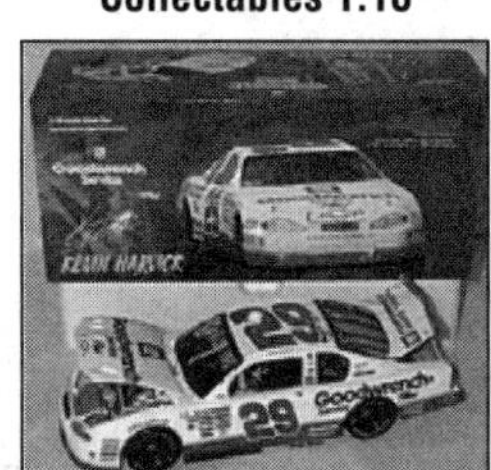

	EX	NM-MT
2 Ron Fellows Johnny O'Connell Franck Freon Chris Kneifel C5-R Corvette/8748	45.00	100.00
2 Ron Fellows Johnny O'Connell Franck Freon Chris Kneifel C5-R Corvette raced version/1008	70.00	150.00
3 Dale Earnhardt Goodwrench w/sonic decal/20,004	50.00	100.00
3 Dale Earnhardt Goodwrench Oreo Daytona/3000	175.00	300.00
3 Dale Earnhardt Dale Earnhardt Jr Andy Pilgrim Kelly Collins C5-R Corvette/16,752	100.00	200.00
3 Dale Earnhardt Dale Earnhardt Jr Andy Pilgrim Kelly Collins C5-R Corvette raced version/1008	125.00	250.00
3 Dale Earnhardt Dale Earnhardt Jr Andy Pilgrim Kelly Collins C5-R Corvette 24Kt.Gold/2000	175.00	300.00
3 Dale Earnhardt Dale Earnhardt Jr Andy Pilgrim Kelly Collins C5-R Corvette Color Chrome/7500	75.00	150.00
3 Dale Earnhardt Dale Earnhardt Jr Andy Pilgrim Kelly Collins C5-R Corvette Color Chrome Raced Version/7500	100.00	200.00
3 Dale Earnhardt Dale Earnhardt Jr Andy Pilgrim Kelly Collins C5-R Corvette Platinum/2508	150.00	250.00
9 Bill Elliott Dodge Spiderman	35.00	75.00
18 Bobby Labonte Interstate Batteries Cal Ripken	40.00	80.00
18 Bobby Labonte Interstate Batteries Coke Bear/2508	30.00	60.00
20 Tony Stewart Home Depot Coke Bear/2504	40.00	80.00
24 Jeff Gordon DuPont Flames/2508	75.00	150.00
29 Kevin Harvick Goodwrench/6000	50.00	120.00
29 Kevin Harvick Goodwrench Taz/3504	60.00	120.00
88 Dale Jarrett UPS Flames/3000	40.00	80.00

2002 Action Racing Collectables 1:18

	EX	NM-MT
3 Dale Earnhardt Goodwrench Oreo/2508	75.00	135.00
3 Dale Earnhardt Jr. Oreo Color Chrome/2508	70.00	120.00
3 Dale Earnhardt Jr. Nilla Wafers/3504	60.00	100.00
3 Dale Earnhardt Jr. Oreo/4008	50.00	100.00
8 Dale Earnhardt Jr. Bud/3504	60.00	100.00
8 Dale Earnhardt Jr. Bud Color Chrome/2508	75.00	135.00
8 Dale Earnhardt Jr. Bud All-Star/4512	45.00	80.00
8 Dale Earnhardt Jr. Looney Tunes/3384	45.00	80.00
24 Jeff Gordon DuPont Flames/4008	45.00	80.00
24 Jeff Gordon DuPont Bugs Bunny/2472	45.00	80.00
24 Jeff Gordon DuPont 200th Ann./3504	45.00	80.00
29 Kevin Harvick Goodwrench/4008	40.00	80.00
29 Kevin Harvick Goodwrench ET/3000	40.00	80.00
29 Kevin Harvick Goodwrench Taz/1008	45.00	80.00
40 Sterling Marlin Coors Light/1800	60.00	100.00
48 Jimmie Johnson Lowe's Sylvester&Tweety/2268	40.00	80.00
NNO Dale Earnhardt Monte Carlo SS/11,952	60.00	100.00

2002 Action/RCCA 1:18

	EX	NM-MT
8 Dale Earnhardt Jr. Bud MLB All-Star/504	60.00	100.00
8 Dale Earnhardt Jr. Looney Tunes/504	60.00	100.00
24 Jeff Gordon DuPont Bugs Bunny/504	45.00	80.00
48 Jimmie Johnson Lowe's Sylvester &Tweety/504	40.00	80.00
NNO Dale Earnhardt Monte Carlo SS/408	125.00	250.00
NNO Dale Earnhardt Monte Carlo SS Color Chrome/1008	125.00	250.00

2003 Action Racing Collectables 1:18

	EX	NM-MT
3 Dale Earnhardt Foundation/3876	50.00	100.00
8 Dale Earnhardt Jr. Bud/3832	60.00	100.00
8 Dale Earnhardt Jr. Bud All-Star Game/3324	60.00	100.00
8 Dale Earnhardt Jr. Bud StainD/2748	50.00	90.00
8 Dale Earnhardt Jr. Dirty Mo Posse/4002	60.00	100.00
8 Dale Earnhardt Jr. E Concert/3024	60.00	100.00
8 Dale Earnhardt Jr. Oreo Ritz/504	50.00	100.00
8 Tony Stewart 3 Doors Down/1836	50.00	80.00
20 Tony Stewart Home Depot/2532	50.00	80.00
24 Jeff Gordon DuPont Flames/2094	50.00	80.00
24 Jeff Gordon Pepsi Billion $/1996	50.00	80.00
24 Jeff Gordon DuPont Wright Brothers/1804	50.00	80.00
48 Jimmie Johnson Lowe's Power of Pride/1866	40.00	80.00
NNO Jeff Gordon Monte Carlo SS/4842	75.00	150.00

2003 Action/RCCA 1:18

	EX	NM-MT
8 Dale Earnhardt Jr. Bud/600	50.00	80.00

2004 Action Road Racing 1:18

	EX	NM-MT
2 Dale Earnhardt Jr. Tony Stewart Andy Wallace/Citgo/7188	50.00	80.00
2 Dale Earnhardt Jr./Tony Stewart Andy Wallace Citgo Brushed Metal/300	60.00	100.00
2 Dale Earnhardt Jr. Tony Stewart Andy Wallace Citgo GM Dealers/516	50.00	80.00
2 Dale Earnhardt Jr. Tony Stewart Andy Wallace Citgo Raced w/tire/6684	60.00	100.00
4 Jimmie Johnson Butch Leitzinger Elliott Forbes-Robinson/Boss/1812	40.00	80.00
8 Dale Earnhardt Jr. Boris Said Corvette C-5R/4014	90.00	135.00
8 Dale Earnhardt Jr./Boris Said/Corvette C-5R GM Dealers/324	90.00	135.00
8 Dale Earnhardt Jr. Boris Said Corvette C-5R RCCA/600	90.00	135.00
20 Tony Stewart Andy Wallace Citgo/936	50.00	80.00
20 Tony Stewart Andy Wallace Citgo Color Chrome/204	60.00	100.00
20 Tony Stewart Andy Wallace Citgo QVC/204	60.00	100.00
20 Tony Stewart Andy Wallace Citgo RCCA/204	60.00	100.00
09 Robby Gordon Doug Goad Stephan Gregorie Milka Duno Citgo/1170	50.00	80.00

2004 Action Racing Collectables 1:18

	EX	NM-MT
2 Rusty Wallace Miller Lite/1248	50.00	80.00
2 Rusty Wallace Miller Lite Last Call/1224	60.00	100.00
8 Dale Earnhardt Jr. Bud/1788	60.00	100.00
8 Dale Earnhardt Jr. Bud Born On Feb. 15	60.00	100.00
NNO Dale Earnhardt Monte Carlo SS/5060	40.00	65.00
NNO Dale Earnhardt Jr. Monte Carlo SS/6840	40.00	65.00

2005 Action Racing Collectables 1:18

	EX	NM-MT
8 Dale Earnhardt Jr. Bud/1194	50.00	80.00
8 Dale Earnhardt Jr. Bud Born On Feb.12/624	50.00	80.00
8 Dale Earnhardt Jr. Bud Born On Feb.17/630	50.00	80.00
8 Dale Earnhardt Jr. Bud Born On Feb.20/1056	50.00	80.00

2005 Action/RCCA 1:18

	EX	NM-MT
8 Dale Earnhardt Jr. Bud Color Chrome/288	60.00	100.00
8 Dale Earnhardt Jr. Bud Born On Feb.12 Color Chrome/140	60.00	100.00
8 Dale Earnhardt Jr. Bud Born On Feb.17 Color Chrome/88	60.00	100.00
8 Dale Earnhardt Jr. Bud Born On Feb.20 Color Chrome/200	60.00	100.00

2006 Action Racing Collectables 1:18

	EX	NM-MT
8 Dale Earnhardt Jr. Bud 3 Days of Dale Tribute/2437	75.00	125.00
8 Dale Earnhardt Jr. Bud Father's Day/612	75.00	125.00
8 Dale Earnhardt Jr. Bud Father's Day GM Dealers/204	75.00	125.00
24 Jeff Gordon DuPont Hot Hues Foose Design	60.00	100.00
NNO Dale Earnhardt Hall of Fame Dale Tribute/2508	60.00	100.00
NNO Dale Earnhardt Hall of Fame Dale Tribute GM Dealers/180	60.00	100.00

2006 Action/RCCA 1:18

	EX	NM-MT
8 Dale Earnhardt Jr. Bud 3 Days of Dale Tribute Color Chrome/333	100.00	150.00
8 Dale Earnhardt Jr. Bud Father's Day Chrome/408	75.00	150.00

1994 Action Racing Collectables 1:24

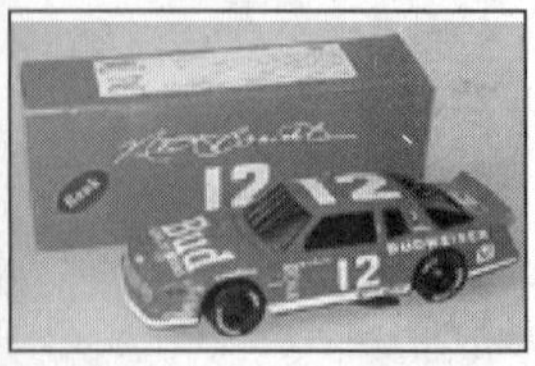

These 1:24 scale replicas were produced by Action Racing Collectibles. Most pieces were packaged in a blue or red box and have the Action Racing Collectibles logo or the Racing Collectibles Inc. logo on the box.

	EX	NM-MT
1 Winston Show Car	20.00	40.00
2 Ricky Craven DuPont	30.00	80.00
2 Mark Martin Miller American 1984 ASA Bank	30.00	60.00
2 Rusty Wallace Ford Motorsports Bank/3504	100.00	175.00
3 Dale Earnhardt Goodwrench 1994 Lumina Bank/5016	200.00	350.00
3 Dale Earnhardt Wrangler 1984 Monte Carlo Bank/5016	250.00	350.00
3 D.Earnhardt Wrangler 1988 Monte Carlo Aerocoupe Bank/5016	250.00	400.00
5 Terry Labonte Kellogg's Bank/2508	150.00	300.00
7 Alan Kulwicki Hooters	75.00	150.00
7 Alan Kulwicki Zerex	60.00	120.00
8 Kenny Wallace Red Dog Bank	40.00	80.00
11 Bill Elliott Budweiser/2508	75.00	150.00
11 Bill Elliott Budweiser Bank	50.00	90.00
11 Darrell Waltrip Budweiser 1984 Monte Carlo Bank	50.00	100.00
11 Darrell Waltrip Budweiser 1984 Thunderbird	50.00	125.00
11 Darrell Waltrip Bud Red 1986 Monte Carlo Bank	40.00	80.00
12 Neil Bonnett Budweiser White 1984 Monte Carlo	40.00	100.00
12 Neil Bonnett Bud White 1984 Monte Carlo Bank	60.00	100.00
12 Neil Bonnett Bud Red 1986 Monte Carlo Bank/5000	40.00	75.00
15 Lake Speed Quality Care/2508	8.00	20.00
16 Ted Musgrave Family Channel Bank	100.00	200.00
16 Ted Musgrave Primestar	8.00	20.00
21 David Pearson Chattanooga Chew Bank/3500	40.00	80.00
28 Ernie Irvan Havoline	30.00	60.00
28 Dale Jarrett Havoline Bank	35.00	60.00
41 Joe Nemechek Meineke/2508	15.00	30.00
42 Kyle Petty Mello Yello/2508	60.00	100.00
51 Neil Bonnett Country Time Bank	70.00	120.00
75 Buddy Baker Valvoline Bank	40.00	80.00
94 Bill Elliott McDonald's	25.00	45.00
98 Derrike Cope Fingerhut/2508	8.00	20.00

1994 Action/RCCA 1:24

These 1:24 scale pieces were distributed through Action's Racing Collectibles Club of America.

	EX	NM-MT
1 Jeff Gordon Baby Ruth Revell/7500	100.00	200.00
2 Rusty Wallace Ford Motorsports	45.00	90.00
2 Rusty Wallace Miller Genuine Draft 1995 Thunderbird	45.00	90.00
3 Richard Childress Black Gold Bank	30.00	50.00
3 Dale Earnhardt Goodwrench In Memory of Neil/5016	250.00	400.00
3 Dale Earnhardt Goodwrench Bank/5016	125.00	250.00
3 Dale Earnhardt Wrangler 1981 Pontiac Bank/5016	200.00	300.00
3 Dale Earnhardt Wrangler 1985 Monte Carlo Bank/5016	200.00	300.00
3 Dale Earnhardt Wrangler 1987 Monte Carlo	400.00	500.00
3 Dale Earnhardt Wrangler 1987 Monte Carlo Bank/5016	250.00	400.00
9 Ted Musgrave Action Racing Collectables	20.00	40.00
16 Ted Musgrave Primestar Bank	30.00	60.00
18 Dale Jarrett Interstate Batteries/2608	125.00	200.00
23 Jimmy Spencer Smokin' Joe's	200.00	350.00
25 Ken Schrader Budweiser Bank	40.00	60.00
28 Ernie Irvan Havoline Bank retail	20.00	40.00
28 Ernie Irvan Havoline Bank gold foil sticker/13,500	25.00	50.00
30 Michael Waltrip Pennzoil	50.00	100.00
51 Neil Bonnett Country Time/5216	125.00	200.00

1995 Action Racing Collectables 1:24

	EX	NM-MT
1 Rick Mast Skoal in acrylic case	40.00	80.00
2 Dale Earnhardt Wrangler 1981 Pontiac/5016	250.00	400.00
2 Rusty Wallace Miller Genuine Draft/7500	75.00	150.00
2 Rusty Wallace Miller Genuine Draft Bank/15,000	60.00	120.00
2/43 Dale Earnhardt Richard Petty 7&7 Champions 2-Bank Set	125.00	250.00
3 Richard Childress Black Gold 1978	25.00	60.00
3 Richard Childress CRC Chemical Bank/5004 1980 Oldsmobile	25.00	50.00
3 Dale Earnhardt Goodwrench/6000	175.00	300.00
3 Dale Earnhardt Goodwrench Black Window Promo	60.00	150.00
3 Dale Earnhardt Goodwrench Bank Sports Image	60.00	120.00
3 Dale Earnhardt Goodwrench Bank 1994 Winston Cup Champion with headlights	75.00	150.00
3 Dale Earnhardt Goodwrench Bank without headlights	60.00	150.00
3 Dale Earnhardt Goodwrench Brickyard/10,000	150.00	300.00
3 Dale Earnhardt Goodwrench Silver Bank GM logo on hood black wheels	300.00	500.00
3 Dale Earnhardt Goodwrench Silver Bank GM logo on hood with red wheels	300.00	500.00
3 Dale Earnhardt Goodwrench Silver Bank GM Parts logo on hood with black wheels	175.00	350.00
3 Dale Earnhardt Goodwrench Silver Bank GM Parts logo on hood with red wheels	250.00	500.00
3 Dale Earnhardt Goodwrench Silver Desk Set	100.00	175.00
3 Dale Earnhardt Wrangler 1981 Pontiac/5016	300.00	450.00
3 Dale Earnhardt Wrangler 1985 Monte Carlo Aerocoupe/6000	275.00	400.00
3 Dale Earnhardt Wrangler 1987 Monte Carlo/6000	250.00	400.00
3 Jeff Green Goodwrench/5004	30.00	75.00
3/24 Dale Earnhardt Jeff Gordon Brickyard 2-car set/5000	125.00	250.00
4 Sterling Marlin Kodak/5004	15.00	40.00
6 Mark Martin Folgers 1991 Bank/5004	75.00	150.00
6 Mark Martin Valvoline/5496	40.00	80.00
6 Mark Martin Valvoline Brickyard/8520	50.00	120.00
6 Mark Martin VValvoline Brickyard Bank/5004	25.00	60.00
7 Geoff Bodine Exide	8.00	20.00
7 Alan Kulwicki Hooters Bank/2508	60.00	125.00
9 Ted Musgrave Action/2508	12.50	30.00
10 Ricky Rudd Tide Bank/5004	15.00	40.00
11 Brett Bodine Lowe's Bank/5004	15.00	35.00
11 Darrell Waltrip Mountain Dew/6000	60.00	120.00
15 Dale Earnhardt Wrangler 1983 Thunderbird/5004	300.00	450.00
21 Buddy Baker Valvoline Bank 1983 Thunderbird/5004	40.00	80.00
21 Neil Bonnett Hodgdon Bank/5004	30.00	60.00
22 Bobby Allison Miller High Life/5004 1983 Buick	60.00	120.00
22 Bobby Allison Miller High Life 1983 Buick Bank/5004	50.00	100.00
23 Jimmy Spencer Camel/5004	125.00	200.00
24 Jeff Gordon DuPont Bank/9504	100.00	200.00
24 Jeff Gordon DuPont 1995 Champion Bank/20,124	50.00	100.00
25 Ken Schrader Bud Bank/6204	20.00	50.00
27 Rusty Wallace Kodiak Bank/6210 1989 Grand Prix in plastic case	125.00	200.00
28 Ernie Irvan Havoline Employee Bank/13,500	100.00	175.00
28 Ernie Irvan Havoline retail Bank/8000	20.00	35.00
28 Dale Jarrett Havoline Bank/7992	30.00	60.00
35 Alan Kulwicki Quincy's Steakhouse Bank/6000	60.00	120.00
42 Kyle Petty Coors Light/5004	35.00	60.00
88 Ernie Irvan Havoline Bank Promo	15.00	40.00
88 Darrell Waltrip Gatorade 1977 Olds Bank/2508	70.00	110.00
94 Bill Elliott McDonald's Bank/5004	25.00	50.00
94 Bill Elliott McDonald's Thunderbat Bank/5000	50.00	120.00
95 David Green Busch Beer Bank/4704	20.00	50.00

1995 Action/RCCA 1:24

	EX	NM-MT
1 Rick Mast Skoal in acrylic case/7500	40.00	70.00
1 Winston Show Car Bank/3504	25.00	50.00
2 Dale Earnhardt Wrangler 1981 Pontiac Bank/5016	150.00	250.00
2/43 Dale Earnhardt Richard Petty 7 and 7 Special 2-car set	150.00	250.00
3 Richard Childress CRC Chemical 1980 Olds/3500	50.00	100.00
3 Dale Earnhardt Goodwrench 1988 Monte Carlo Aerocoupe/5016	300.00	450.00
3 Dale Earnhardt Goodwrench with SkyBox card/5016	125.00	250.00
3 Dale Earnhardt Goodwrench Bank with headlights	50.00	120.00
3 Dale Earnhardt Goodwrench Bank without headlights	50.00	120.00
3 Dale Earnhardt Goodwrench Silver GM Parts with black wheels	300.00	600.00
3 Dale Earnhardt Goodwrench Silver GM Parts red wheels	250.00	500.00
3 Dale Earnhardt Goodwrench Silver GM black wheels	400.00	750.00
3 Dale Earnhardt Goodwrench Silver GM with red wheels	400.00	750.00
3 Dale Earnhardt Wrangler 1984 Monte Carlo blue deck lid/5016	200.00	400.00
3 Dale Earnhardt Wrangler 1984 Monte Carlo yellow deck lid/5016	200.00	400.00
3 Jeff Green Goodwrench Bank/2508	25.00	50.00
4 Sterling Marlin Kodak Bank/2508	20.00	50.00
6 Mark Martin Folgers 1991/2508	150.00	250.00
6 Mark Martin Valvoline Bank/4500	30.00	50.00
6 Mark Martin Valvoline Brickyard Bank	40.00	70.00
7 Geoff Bodine Exide Bank/2508	15.00	40.00
7 Alan Kulwicki Hooters Bank/5004	75.00	150.00
7 Alan Kulwicki Zerex Bank/2508	90.00	150.00
9 Ted Musgrave RCCA/2508	15.00	40.00
10 Ricky Rudd Tide/2508	40.00	70.00
11 Brett Bodine Lowe's/2508	12.00	30.00
11 Darrell Waltrip Mountain Dew Bank 1981 Buick/5000	45.00	80.00
15 Dale Earnhardt Wrangler Bank 1983 T-bird/10,008	125.00	250.00
22 Bobby Allison Miller High Life/5004 1983 Buick	20.00	50.00
24 Jeff Gordon DuPont/5004	150.00	250.00
25 Ken Schrader Bud/5004	35.00	60.00
26 Hut Stricklin Quaker State/2508	15.00	40.00
27 Rusty Wallace Kodiak 1989 Grand Prix/5000	250.00	400.00
28 Dale Jarrett Havoline/5016	40.00	80.00
42 Kyle Petty Coors Light Bank/5004	35.00	60.00
42 Kyle Petty Coors Light Pumpkin/5004 in plastic case	150.00	300.00
88 Ernie Irvan Havoline Bank	15.00	40.00
88 Darrell Waltrip Gatorade Bank 1980 Monte Carlo/2508	50.00	100.00
94 Bill Elliott McDonald's/5004	25.00	50.00
94 Bill Elliott McDonald's Thunderbat	75.00	150.00
95 David Green Busch Beer/2508	20.00	50.00

1995-96 Action Racing Collectables SuperTrucks 1:24

	EX	NM-MT
3 Mike Skinner Goodwrench 1995	25.00	40.00
3 Mike Skinner Goodwrench 1996	20.00	40.00
7 Geoff Bodine Exide/6000 1995	15.00	40.00
16 Ron Hornaday Action 1995	20.00	40.00
16 Ron Hornaday NAPA 1996	20.00	40.00
24 Jack Sprague Quaker State Bank/3500 1996	12.50	30.00
28 Ernie Irvan NAPA/4008	30.00	45.00
71 Kenji Momota Marukatsu/4008 1995	20.00	40.00
84 Joe Ruttman Mac Tools/5004	15.00	40.00
84 Joe Ruttman Mac Tools Bank	30.00	45.00
98 Butch Miller Raybestos Bank/6000 1995	15.00	40.00

1995-96 Action/RCCA SuperTrucks 1:24

The top SuperTruck driver's trucks are featured in these die-cast pieces. Most pieces were distributed either through the Action Dealer Network or Action's Racing Collectibles Club of America. Some were made available through both outlets. There are two versions of most trucks, a bank and a regular version. The banks have a slot in the truck bed for the coin.

	EX	NM-MT
3 Mike Skinner Goodwrench Bank 1995	35.00	50.00
3 Mike Skinner Goodwrench Bank/1000 1996	40.00	6
6 Rick Carelli Total Petroleum	30.00	4
6 Rick Carelli Total Petroleum Bank	30.00	4
7 Geoff Bodine Exide Bank	20.00	4
16 Ron Hornaday Action Bank/6004 1995	15.00	4
16 Ron Hornaday NAPA 1996	20.00	4
16 Ron Hornaday NAPA Bank 1996	20.00	4
16 Ron Hornaday NAPA Gold 1996	35.00	6
16 Ron Hornaday NAPA Gold Bank 1996	35.00	6
16 Ron Hornaday Papa John's 1995	25.00	4
16 Ron Hornaday Papa John's Bank Platinum Series 1995	25.00	4
24 Scott Lagasse DuPont 1995	30.00	4
24 Scott Lagasse DuPont Bank 1995	30.00	4
24 Jack Sprague Quaker State/2500	20.00	4
28 Ernie Irvan NAPA Bank	30.00	5
52 Ken Schrader AC Delco/2508 1995	20.00	4
52 Ken Schrader AC Delco Bank Platinum Series/5004 1995	20.00	4
71 Kenji Momota Marukatsu Bank	30.00	4
80 Joe Ruttman JR's Garage	30.00	6
84 Joe Ruttman Mac Tools	25.00	4

1996 Action Racing Collectables 1:24

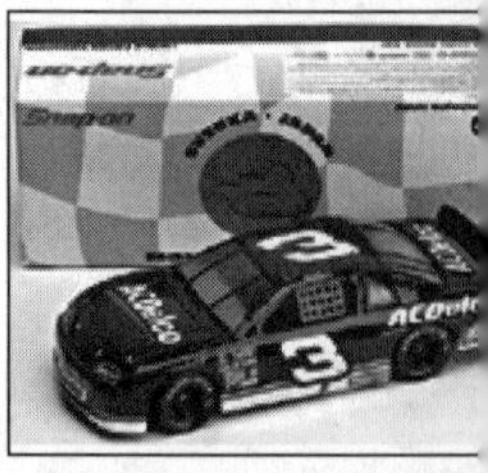

These 1:24 scale replicas were produced by Action Collectibles. Most pieces were packaged in a blue box ar the Action Racing Collectibles logo or the Racing Colle Inc. logo on the box. The banks were issued in the same with a blue "Bank" sticker attached to the sides. All 199 have black windows.

	EX	NM
2 Mark Martin Miller 1985 ASA	30.00	7
2 Mark Martin Miller 1985 ASA Bank/6000	35.00	7
2 Rusty Wallace Miller Splash	70.00	12
2 Rusty Wallace Miller Genuine Draft Silver 25th Anniversary	40.00	10
2 Rusty Wallace Miller Splash Bank	40.00	7
3 Dale Earnhardt AC-Delco	100.00	20
3 Dale Earnhardt AC-Delco Snap-On	75.00	20
3 Dale Earnhardt Goodwrench 1996 Monte Carlo	75.00	15
3 Dale Earnhardt Olympic Bank	100.00	20
3 Dale Earnhardt Olympic Food City Promo box	100.00	25
3 Dale Earnhardt Olympic Goodwrench Box	250.00	35
3 Dale Earnhardt Olympic Green Box	200.00	40
3 Dale Earnhardt Olympic Green Box No Trademark on Hood of Car	75.00	20
3 Dale Earnhardt Olympic Mom-n-Pop's box	100.00	22
3 Dale Earnhardt Olympic Sports Image blue box	75.00	20
5 Terry Labonte Kellogg's Iron Man Silver Bank/10,000	75.00	15
5 Terry Labonte Kellogg's Japan Bank	40.00	8
6 Mark Martin Valvoline Bank	30.00	6
7 Geoff Bodine QVC Bank	20.00	5
10 Ricky Rudd Tide	40.00	8
10 Ricky Rudd Tide Bank	35.00`	6
14 Jeff Green Tide Racing For Kids	20.00	4
15 Dale Earnhardt Wrangler 1982 Thunderbird Bank/2508	125.00	25
18 Bobby Labonte Interstate Batteries	45.00	9
18 Bobby Labonte Interstate Batteries Pro Football Hall of Fame	75.00	15
21 Michael Waltrip Citgo	15.00	4
21 Michael Waltrip Citgo Star Trek Bank	25.00	5
22 Ward Burton	25.00	4

Item	EX	NM-MT
MBNA Bank/5000		
eff Gordon	35.00	75.00
DuPont Bank/12,500		
m Richmond	50.00	100.00
Folgers 1987 Monte Carlo Bank/7500		
en Schrader	20.00	50.00
Bud Bank/6204		
eve Grissom	25.00	50.00
Flintstones Bank		
o Driver Association	20.00	50.00
Scooby-Doo		
eve Grissom	25.00	50.00
WCW Bank/5000		
o Driver Association	25.00	50.00
Scooby-Doo Bank/10,000		
ike Skinner	30.00	80.00
Snap-On/5000		
Mike Skinner	70.00	125.00
Snap-On Promo		
obby Gordon	25.00	50.00
Tonka Bank		
yle Petty	30.00	60.00
Coors Light/7500		
yle Petty	35.00	60.00
Coors Light Black Bank/7500		
obby Hamilton	20.00	50.00
STP '72 Blue		
obby Hamilton	15.00	40.00
STP '72 Blue Bank/2500		
obby Hamilton	20.00	50.00
STP '72 Blue&Red		
obby Hamilton	15.00	40.00
STP '72 Blue&Red Bank/2500		
obby Hamilton	20.00	50.00
STP '79 Blue&Red		
ed sides/blue roof		
obby Hamilton	15.00	40.00
STP '79 Blue&Red Bank/2500		
ed sides/blue roof		
obby Hamilton	20.00	50.00
STP '84 Blue&Red		
blue sides w/red stripes		
obby Hamilton	15.00	40.00
STP '84 Blue&Red Bank/2500		
blue sides w/red stripes		
obby Hamilton	25.00	60.00
STP Silver 25th Anniversary		
obby Hamilton	20.00	50.00
STP Silver		
25th Anniversary Bank/2500		
ason Keller	15.00	40.00
Halloween Havoc/5004		
rnie Irvan	30.00	70.00
Havoline		
nie Irvan	25.00	60.00
Havoline Bank		
ale Jarrett	30.00	60.00
Quality Care		
eremy Mayfield	20.00	50.00
RCA		

1996 Action/RCCA 1:24

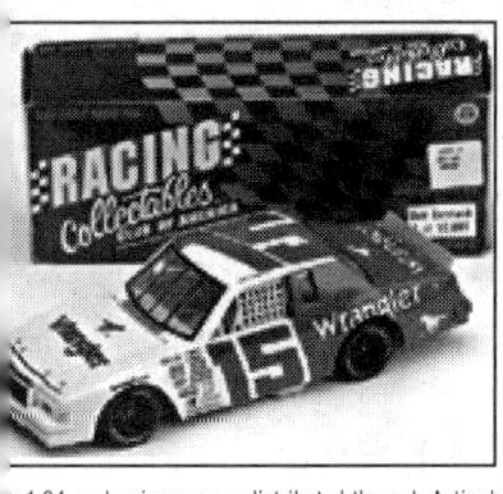

e 1:24 scale pieces were distributed through Action's ng Collectibles Club of America. The pieces are 1:24 cas of the cars that have raced in NASCAR. Each was d in a black RCCA box or colorful box with the team's s. The banks were issued in the same boxes with the on of a "Bank" sticker to the box. All 1996 banks feature windows.

Item	EX	NM-MT
nston Show Car/7000	25.00	50.00
sty Wallace	45.00	70.00
Miller Genuine Draft Bank		
sty Wallace	30.00	80.00
Miller Genuine Draft		
Silver 25th Anniversary Bank		
sty Wallace	45.00	90.00
Miller Genuine Draft		
e Earnhardt	40.00	100.00
AC-Delco Bank		
e Earnhardt	60.00	150.00
Goodwrench Bank		
ry Labonte	100.00	175.00
Kellogg's Iron Man Silver		
ry Labonte	30.00	80.00
Kellogg's Japan/5000		
rk Martin	40.00	80.00
Valvoline Thunderbird		
arrell Waltrip	35.00	75.00
Budweiser 1984 Monte Carlo Bank		
eil Bonnett	40.00	75.00
Budweiser 1984 Monte Carlo Bank		
ff Green	25.00	60.00
Racing For Kids Bank		
ale Earnhardt	150.00	300.00
Wrangler		
1982 Thunderbird/10,000		
ale Earnhardt	100.00	175.00
Wrangler 1982 Thunderbird Bank		
arrell Waltrip	30.00	60.00
Parts America		
arrell Waltrip	25.00	50.00
Parts America Bank/5000		
arrell Waltrip	50.00	100.00
Tide 1988 Monte Carlo		
obby Labonte	20.00	50.00
Interstate Batteries Bank/5000		
obby Labonte	35.00	75.00
Interstate Batteries		
Pro Football HOF Bank/10,000		
eil Bonnett	25.00	60.00
Hodgdon 1981 Buick/5004		
ichael Waltrip	20.00	50.00
Citgo Bank/5000		
21 Michael Waltrip	30.00	60.00
Citgo Star Trek		
22 Bobby Allison	35.00	60.00
Miller American/2500		
1985 Monte Carlo		
22 Ward Burton	20.00	50.00
MBNA/5000		
24 Jeff Gordon	40.00	80.00
DuPont/12,500		
25 Tim Richmond	50.00	100.00
Folgers 1987 Monte		
Carlo Bank/5000		
25 Ken Schrader	20.00	50.00
Bud/3500		
28 Ernie Irvan	25.00	50.00
Havoline Bank		
29 Steve Grissom	25.00	60.00
Flintstones/10,000		
29 Steve Grissom	25.00	60.00
WCW/5000		
30 Johnny Benson	25.00	60.00
Pennzoil Bank/5000		
31 Mike Skinner	40.00	80.00
Lowe's Bank		
31 Mike Skinner	40.00	100.00
Snap-On Bank/3500		
33 Robert Pressley	25.00	60.00
Skoal/5000		
42 Kyle Petty	35.00	65.00
Coors Light Bank/5000		
42 Robby Gordon	30.00	60.00
Tonka/3500		
42 Kyle Petty	40.00	65.00
Coors Light Black/5000		
43 Bobby Hamilton	20.00	50.00
STP '72 Blue/3500		
43 Bobby Hamilton	20.00	50.00
STP '72 Blue&Red/3500		
43 Bobby Hamilton	20.00	50.00
STP '79 Blue&Red/3500		
red sides/blue roof		
43 Bobby Hamilton	20.00	50.00
STP '84 Blue&Red/3500		
blue sides w/red stripes		
43 Bobby Hamilton	25.00	60.00
STP Silver 25th Anniversary		
57 Jason Keller	20.00	50.00
Halloween Havoc Bank/3500		
88 Ernie Irvan	25.00	60.00
Havoline Bank		
88 Dale Jarrett	35.00	60.00
Quality Care Bank		
94 Bill Elliott	25.00	60.00
McDonald's Bank/5000		
99 Jeff Burton	20.00	50.00
Exide Bank/3500		

1997 Action Racing Collectables 1:24

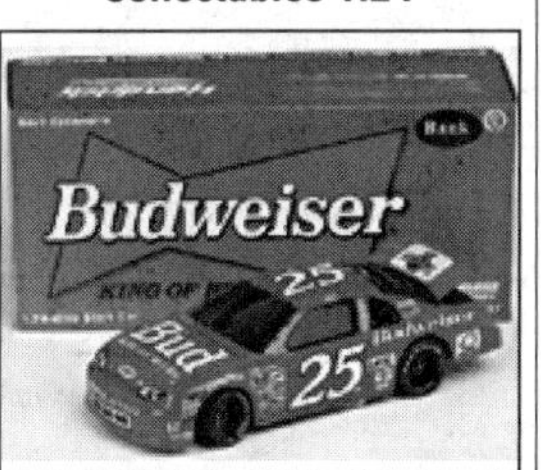

These 1:24 scale replicas were produced by Action Racing Collectibles. Most pieces were packaged in a blue box and have the Action Racing Collectibles logo or the Racing Collectibles Inc. logo on the box. The banks were issued in the same boxes with the addition of a "Bank" sticker on the sides. Note that all banks in this series have black windows.

Item	EX	NM-MT
1 Hermie Sadler	15.00	40.00
DeWalt Bank/3500		
1 Gargoyles 500 Promo	10.00	20.00
2 Rusty Wallace	30.00	60.00
Miller Lite/10,500		
2 Rusty Wallace	25.00	50.00
Miller Japan/7500		
2 Rusty Wallace	25.00	60.00
Miller Lite Texas Bank/7584		
3 Dale Earnhardt	60.00	120.00
AC Delco Bank		
3 Dale Earnhardt	60.00	150.00
Goodwrench Bank		
3 Dale Earnhardt	40.00	80.00
Goodwrench Plus		
3 Dale Earnhardt	40.00	80.00
Goodwrench Plus Bank		
3 Dale Earnhardt	60.00	120.00
Goodwrench Brickyard/7500		
3 Dale Earnhardt	125.00	225.00
Lowes Food Bank/7992		
3 Dale Earnhardt	60.00	120.00
Wheaties Hood Open		
black window netting		
3 Dale Earnhardt	100.00	200.00
Wheaties HO black		
netting Snap-On Tools		
3 Dale Earnhardt	40.00	100.00
Wheaties mail-In		
red window netting		
3 Dale Earnhardt	75.00	150.00
Wheaties Snap-On Bank		
3 Dale Earnhardt	100.00	200.00
Wheaties Sports Image		
3 Dale Earnhardt	100.00	200.00
Wrangler Bank		
1984 Monte Carlo Daytona paint		
3 Steve Park	40.00	100.00
AC Delco Bank/6504		
3 Ricky Rudd	35.00	80.00
Piedmont 1983		
Monte Carlo Bank/3500		
4 Sterling Marlin	15.00	40.00
Kodak Bank/6300		
4 Sterling Marlin	15.00	40.00
Kodak Mac Tools Bank/1500		
6 Mark Martin	30.00	60.00
Valvoline		
6 Mark Martin	40.00	75.00
Valvoline Mac Tools		
8 Hut Stricklin	8.00	20.00
Circuit City		
9 Jeff Burton	20.00	50.00
Track Gear Bank/3500		
10 Phil Parsons	8.00	20.00
Channellock/3500		
10 Ricky Rudd	30.00	50.00
Tide Bank/6000		
11 Brett Bodine	8.00	20.00
Close Call/8004		
12 Kenny Wallace	8.00	20.00
Gray Bar/6504		
14 Steve Park	50.00	125.00
Burger King/6000		
16 Ted Musgrave	8.00	20.00
Primestar/5604		
17 Darrell Waltrip	15.00	40.00
Parts America Bank		
Blue&White		
17 Darrell Waltrip	25.00	60.00
Parts America Bank		
Chrome		
17 Darrell Waltrip	15.00	40.00
Parts America Bank		
Green w/green number		
17 Darrell Waltrip	15.00	40.00
Parts America Bank		
Green w/white no.		
17 Darrell Waltrip	15.00	40.00
Parts America Bank		
Orange		
17 Darrell Waltrip	15.00	40.00
Parts America Bank		
Red&White		
17 Darrell Waltrip	15.00	40.00
Parts America Bank		
Yellow&White		
18 Bobby Labonte	25.00	60.00
Interstate Batteries		
18 Bobby Labonte	75.00	150.00
Interstate Batteries Mac Tools		
22 Bobby Allison	40.00	80.00
Miller American Bank/5304		
1985 Monte Carlo		
22 Ward Burton	20.00	40.00
MBNA/5292		
22 Ward Burton	20.00	40.00
MBNA Gold Bank		
23 Jimmy Spencer	40.00	100.00
Camel		
24 Jeff Gordon	50.00	100.00
DuPont		
24 Jeff Gordon	50.00	100.00
DuPont Mac Tools		
24 Jeff Gordon	50.00	100.00
DuPont Brickyard/7500		
black windows		
24 Jeff Gordon	100.00	200.00
DuPont ChromaPremier Promo		
24 Jeff Gordon	125.00	250.00
DuPont CromaPremier		
Sports Image/7500		
24 Jeff Gordon	75.00	150.00
DuPont ChromaPremier Bank/28,000		
24 Jeff Gordon	40.00	75.00
DuPont Million Dollar Date Bank		
24 Jeff Gordon	40.00	75.00
DuPont Million $ Date		
Mac Tools Bank		
24 Jeff Gordon	75.00	150.00
Jurassic Park 3		
24 Jeff Gordon	50.00	100.00
Jurassic Park 3 Bank		
25 Ricky Craven	20.00	40.00
Bud/3500		
25 Ricky Craven	25.00	60.00
Bud Bank/8400		
26 Rich Bickle	15.00	40.00
KFC Bank/3852		
27 Kenny Irwin	30.00	60.00
Action/3500		
27 Kenny Irwin	20.00	50.00
G.I. Joe Bank/5000		
27 Kenny Irwin	25.00	60.00
Tonka/5700		
27 Kenny Irwin	25.00	60.00
Tonka Mac Tools/1500		
27 Rusty Wallace	75.00	135.00
Miller Genuine Draft		
1990 Grand Prix Bank/6000		
in plastic case		
29 Jeff Green	25.00	60.00
Tom & Jerry		
29 Elliott Sadler	25.00	50.00
Phillips 66 Bank/3500		
30 Johnny Benson	8.00	30.00
Pennzoil		
31 Mike Skinner	15.00	40.00
Lowe's		
31 Mike Skinner	15.00	30.00
Lowe's Japan/5000		
31 Mike Skinner	15.00	30.00
Lowe's Japan Bank/6500		
32 Dale Jarrett	20.00	50.00
White Rain Bank/7956		
33 Ken Schrader	35.00	55.00
Skoal Bank		
36 Todd Bodine	20.00	40.00
Stanley Bank		
36 Derrike Cope	15.00	40.00
Skittles Bank/6708		
37 Mark Green	10.00	25.00
Timber Wolf/3500		
37 Jeremy Mayfield	15.00	40.00
K-Mart RC-Cola Bank/6000		
40 Robby Gordon	20.00	50.00
Coors Light Bank/7500		
41 Steve Grissom	20.00	50.00
Kodiak Bank		
42 Joe Nemechek	10.00	30.00
BellSouth/7716		
46 Wally Dallenbach	8.00	20.00
First Union/6792		
60 Mark Martin	35.00	60.00
Winn Dixie Bank		
71 Dave Marcis	25.00	60.00
Realtree Bank		
71 Dave Marcis	25.00	60.00
Realtree Making of Champions Bank		
75 Rick Mast	8.00	20.00
Remington/6000		
75 Rick Mast	15.00	30.00
Remington Camo		
81 Kenny Wallace	15.00	40.00
Square D Bank		
88 Dale Jarrett	25.00	50.00
Quality Care/5960		
88 Dale Jarrett	25.00	60.00
Quality Care Mac Tools/4000		
88 Dale Jarrett	35.00	60.00
Quality Care Brickyard/7500		
94 Bill Elliott	45.00	80.00
McDonald's Bank		
94 Bill Elliott	25.00	50.00
Mac Tonight/8700		
96 David Green	15.00	40.00
Caterpillar Bank/6504		
99 Jeff Burton	15.00	40.00
Exide		
99 Jeff Burton	15.00	40.00
Exide Mac Tools/4000		
00 Buckshot Jones	15.00	40.00
Aqua Fresh/3500		

1997 Action/RCCA 1:24

These 1:24 scale pieces were distributed through Action's Racing Collectibles Club of America. The pieces are 1:24 replicas of the cars that have raced in NASCAR. All banks in this series have black windows.

Item	EX	NM-MT
2 Rusty Wallace	30.00	60.00
Miller Lite Bank		
2 Rusty Wallace	30.00	60.00
Miller Japan Bank/5000		
2 Rusty Wallace	60.00	100.00
Miller Lite Texas		
3 Dale Earnhardt	60.00	120.00
AC Delco/1200		
3 Dale Earnhardt	125.00	250.00
Goodwrench/3500		
3 Dale Earnhardt	60.00	120.00
Goodwrench Plus		
3 Dale Earnhardt	60.00	120.00
Goodwrench Plus Bank/10,000		
3 Dale Earnhardt	150.00	250.00
Lowes Food/10,000		
3 Dale Earnhardt	100.00	200.00
Wheaties Bank		
3 Dale Earnhardt	150.00	250.00
Wrangler 1984 Monte		
Carlo Daytona/10,000		
3 Steve Park	100.00	175.00
AC Delco		
3 Ricky Rudd	50.00	100.00
Piedmont 1983 Monte Carlo/3500		
4 Sterling Marlin	15.00	40.00
Kodak/2500		
6 Mark Martin	35.00	60.00
Valvoline Bank		
9 Jeff Burton	20.00	50.00
Track Gear/3500		
10 Phil Parsons	20.00	50.00
Channellock Bank/2500		
10 R.Rudd/Tide/2500	25.00	50.00
11 Brett Bodine	15.00	40.00
Close Call Bank/2500		
12 Kenny Wallace	15.00	40.00
Gray Bar Bank/2500		
14 Steve Park	50.00	100.00
Burger King Bank/5000		
16 Ted Musgrave	15.00	40.00
Primestar Bank/2500		
17 Darrell Waltrip	15.00	40.00
Parts America		
Blue&White/6000		
17 Darrell Waltrip	30.00	80.00
Parts America Chrome/6000		
17 Darrell Waltrip	15.00	40.00
Parts America Green		
with green number/6000		
17 Darrell Waltrip	15.00	40.00
Parts America Green		
with white number/6000		
17 Darrell Waltrip	15.00	40.00
Parts America Orange/6000		
17 Darrell Waltrip	15.00	40.00
Parts America Red&White/6000		
17 Darrell Waltrip	15.00	40.00
Parts America		
Yellow&White/6000		
18 Bobby Labonte	25.00	50.00
Interstate Batteries Bank/3500		
22 Ward Burton	20.00	50.00
MBNA Gold/2500		
23 Jimmy Spencer	75.00	150.00
Camel Bank		
24 Jeff Gordon	40.00	100.00
DuPont Bank/3500		
24 Jeff Gordon	75.00	150.00
DuPont ChromaPremier/15,000		
24 Jeff Gordon	40.00	75.00
DuPont Million Dollar Date/15,000		
24 Jeff Gordon	60.00	120.00
Jurassic Park 3		
25 Ricky Craven	25.00	60.00
Budweiser/3500		
26 Rich Bickle	15.00	40.00
KFC/3500		
27 Kenny Irwin	30.00	60.00
Action/3500		
27 Kenny Irwin	30.00	60.00
G.I. Joe		
27 Kenny Irwin	25.00	50.00
Nerf Bank		
27 Kenny Irwin	25.00	50.00
Tonka Bank/3500		
27 Rusty Wallace	125.00	200.00
Miller Genuine Draft		
1990 Grand Prix/5000		
in plastic case		
29 Jeff Green	15.00	40.00
Tom & Jerry Bank/3500		
29 Elliott Sadler	25.00	60.00
Phillips 66		
31 Mike Skinner	15.00	40.00
Lowe's Bank/3500		
31 Mike Skinner	15.00	30.00
Lowe's Japan		
32 Dale Jarrett	20.00	50.00
White Rain		
33 Ken Schrader	50.00	90.00
Skoal		
36 Todd Bodine	20.00	50.00
Stanley		
36 Derrike Cope	15.00	40.00
Skittles/5000		
37 Mark Green	20.00	50.00
Timber Wolf Bank		
37 Jeremy Mayfield	30.00	80.00
K-Mart RC-Cola		
40 Robby Gordon	25.00	60.00
Coors Light/2500		
41 Steve Grissom	20.00	50.00
Kodiak/2500		
42 Joe Nemechek	20.00	40.00
BellSouth Bank		
46 Wally Dallenbach	20.00	40.00
First Union Bank		
60 Mark Martin	40.00	80.00
Winn Dixie/5500		
71 Dave Marcis	25.00	60.00
Realtree/2500		
71 Dave Marcis	25.00	60.00
Realtree Making of Champions/2500		
75 Rick Mast	15.00	40.00
Remington Bank/2500		
75 Rick Mast	20.00	45.00
Remington Camo Bank		
81 Kenny Wallace	15.00	40.00
Square D		
88 Dale Jarrett	20.00	50.00
Quality Care Bank/5000		
94 Bill Elliott	30.00	80.00
Mac Tonight Bank/7500		
94 Bill Elliott	35.00	70.00
McDonald's		
96 David Green	15.00	40.00
Caterpillar/3500		
97 Chad Little	20.00	60.00
John Deere		
97 Chad Little	15.00	40.00
John Deere Bank/2500		
97 Chad Little	30.00	60.00
John Deere 160th Anniversary		
97 Chad Little	25.00	55.00
John Deere		
160th Anniversary Bank/2500		
99 Jeff Burton	40.00	70.00
Exide Bank/2500		
00 Buckshot Jones	15.00	40.00
Aqua Fresh Bank/2500		

1997 Action/RCCA Elite 1:24

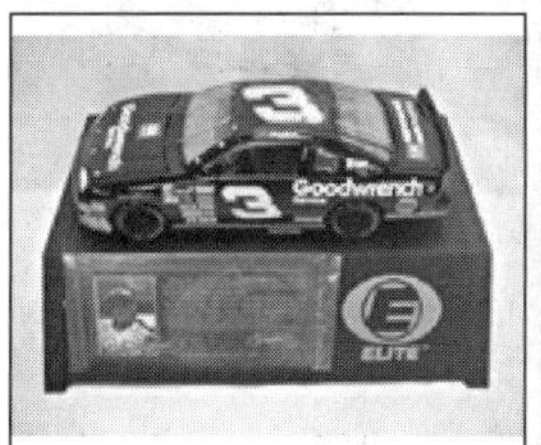

This series consists of upgraded versions of their standard production cars. It was started in 1997. The cars from this series contain serial number plates on the undercarriage at the end of the car.

Item	EX	NM-MT
2 Rusty Wallace	50.00	120.00
Miller Lite/5000		
2 Rusty Wallace	30.00	80.00
Miller Japan/5000		
2 Rusty Wallace	60.00	120.00
Miller Lite Texas/1500		
3 Dale Earnhardt	75.00	150.00
AC Delco/12,500		
3 Dale Earnhardt	250.00	400.00
Goodwrench/3500		
3 Dale Earnhardt	100.00	200.00
Goodwrench Plus/12,500		
3 Dale Earnhardt	250.00	400.00
Wheaties		
Gold number plate/5000		
3 Dale Earnhardt	150.00	300.00
Wheaties		
Brass number plate/8618		
3 Steve Park	125.00	200.00
AC Delco		
4 Sterling Marlin	30.00	80.00
Kodak/1500		
6 Mark Martin	60.00	120.00
Valvoline/2500		
9 Jeff Burton	25.00	60.00
Track Gear/1500		
10 Ricky Rudd	40.00	80.00
Tide/1500		
14 Steve Park	75.00	150.00
Burger King/3500		
17 Darrell Waltrip	40.00	100.00
Parts America/4008		
17 Darrell Waltrip	75.00	150.00
Parts America Chrome/3500		
18 Bobby Labonte	75.00	150.00
Interstate Batteries/1500		
22 Ward Burton	40.00	100.00
MBNA Gold/1500		
24 Jeff Gordon	125.00	250.00
DuPont/3500		
24 Jeff Gordon	100.00	175.00
DuPont Million Dollar Date/10,000		
24 Jeff Gordon	175.00	300.00
DuPont ChromaPremier/5000		
24 Jeff Gordon	150.00	300.00
Jurassic Park 3/7500		
25 Ricky Craven	40.00	80.00
Budweiser/1500		
29 Jeff Green	30.00	60.00
Tom & Jerry/3500		
29 No Driver Associated	60.00	120.00
Scooby-Doo		

29 Robert Pressley Scooby-Doo/1200	40.00	80.00
29 Elliot Sadler Phillips 66/1200	30.00	60.00
31 Mike Skinner Lowe's/5000	50.00	100.00
31 Mike Skinner Lowe's Japan	40.00	80.00
32 Dale Jarrett White Rain	75.00	150.00
36 Todd Bodine Stanley/1500	90.00	150.00
36 Derrike Cope Skittles/1200	25.00	60.00
37 Mark Green Timber Wolf	60.00	150.00
37 Jeremy Mayfield K-Mart RC-Cola	40.00	100.00
46 Wally Dallenbach First Union/1500	25.00	50.00
60 Mark Martin Winn Dixie/3500	60.00	120.00
75 Rick Mast Remington/2500	25.00	60.00
88 Dale Jarrett Quality Care/2000	50.00	120.00
94 Bill Elliott McDonald's/1500	75.00	150.00
94 Bill Elliott Mac Tonight/7500	40.00	80.00
96 David Green Caterpillar/2500	25.00	50.00
97 Chad Little John Deere	40.00	100.00
97 Chad Little John Deere 160th Anniversary/2500	40.00	100.00
99 Jeff Burton Exide/2500	50.00	120.00
00 Buckshot Jones Aqua Fresh/1200	30.00	80.00

1998 Action Racing Collectables 1:24

These 1:24 scale replicas were produced by Action Racing Collectibles. Most pieces were packaged in a blue box and have the Action Racing Collectibles logo or the Racing Collectibles Inc. logo on the box.

	EX	NM-MT
1 Dale Earnhardt Jr. Coke Bear	25.00	60.00
1 Dale Earnhardt Jr. Coke Bear Bank	25.00	60.00
1 Jeff Gordon Baby Ruth 1992 Thunderbird	50.00	100.00
1 Jeff Gordon Baby Ruth 1992 Thunderbird Bank/7500	40.00	80.00
1 Steve Park Pennzoil Black Roof/8500	25.00	60.00
1 Steve Park Pennzoil Black Roof Bank	30.00	80.00
1 Steve Park Pennzoil Yellow Roof	30.00	75.00
1 Steve Park Pennzoil Yellow Roof Bank/3000	20.00	50.00
1 Darrell Waltrip Pennzoil	35.00	75.00
1 Darrell Waltrip Pennzoil Bank	45.00	90.00
1/3 Dale Earnhardt Dale Earnhardt Jr. Coke Bear Snap-on 2-car set packaged with wrench	100.00	175.00
2 Rusty Wallace Adventures of Rusty	20.00	50.00
2 Rusty Wallace Miller Lite	20.00	50.00
2 Rusty Wallace Miller Lite Bank/2500	20.00	50.00
2 Rusty Wallace Miller Lite Elvis	25.00	50.00
2 Rusty Wallace Miller Lite Elvis Bank/15,996	20.00	50.00
2 Rusty Wallace Miller Lite TCB Elvis	25.00	50.00
2 Rusty Wallace Miller Lite TCB Elvis Bank/2508	20.00	50.00
3 Dale Earnhardt Coke	60.00	120.00
3 Dale Earnhardt Coke Bank	60.00	120.00
3 Dale Earnhardt Goodwrench Plus	50.00	100.00
3 Dale Earnhardt Goodwrench Plus Bank with Coke decal	50.00	100.00
3 Dale Earnhardt Goodwrench Plus Bank without Coke decal	75.00	150.00
3 Dale Earnhardt Goodwrench Plus Bass Pro	60.00	120.00
3 Dale Earnhardt Goodwrench Plus Bass Pro Black Window Promo	50.00	100.00
3 Dale Earnhardt Goodwrench Plus Bass Pro Bank	50.00	100.00
3 Dale Earnhardt Goodwrench Plus Daytona	75.00	150.00
3 Dale Earnhardt Goodwrench Plus Daytona Bank/15,000	60.00	120.00
3 Dale Earnhardt Goodwrench Plus Gold/500	500.00	1000.00
3 Dale Earnhardt Dale Earnhardt Jr. Goodwrench AC Delco Split/624	500.00	800.00
3 Dale Earnhardt Jr. AC Delco/15,000	75.00	150.00
3 Dale Earnhardt Jr. AC Delco Bank/2500	75.00	150.00
3 Dale Earnhardt Jr. AC Delco 1998 BGN Champ	50.00	100.00
3 Dale Earnhardt Jr. AC Delco 1998 BGN Champ Bank	50.00	100.00
3 Race Rock Promo/2504	15.00	30.00
4 Bobby Hamilton Kodak/5000	8.00	20.00
4 Bobby Hamilton Kodak Bank	25.00	50.00
5 Terry Labonte Blasted Fruit Loops/7500	20.00	50.00
5 Terry Labonte Blasted Fruit Loops Bank	25.00	60.00
5 Terry Labonte Kellogg's	30.00	60.00
5 Terry Labonte Kellogg's Bank	35.00	75.00
5 Terry Labonte Kellogg's Corny	30.00	80.00
5 Terry Labonte Kellogg's Corny Bank/3500	30.00	70.00
5 Terry Labonte Kellogg's Ironman	25.00	60.00
5 Terry Labonte Kellogg's Ironman Bank	25.00	60.00
8 Dale Earnhardt RPM 1975 Dodge/7500	60.00	150.00
8 Dale Earnhardt RPM 1975 Dodge Bank/10,000	50.00	100.00
8 Hut Stricklin Circuit City/5004	8.00	20.00
8 Hut Stricklin Circuit City Bank	15.00	30.00
9 Jerry Nadeau Power Puff/2508	100.00	175.00
9 Jerry Nadeau Scooby Zombie Island	30.00	70.00
9 Lake Speed Birthday Cake/6000	20.00	50.00
9 Lake Speed Birthday Cake Bank	25.00	50.00
9 Lake Speed Huckleberry Hound/7500	20.00	50.00
9 Lake Speed Huckleberry Hound Bank	30.00	70.00
10 Ricky Rudd Tide	35.00	60.00
10 Ricky Rudd Tide Bank	30.00	60.00
10 Ricky Rudd Tide Give Kids the World	30.00	80.00
12 Jeremy Mayfield Mobil 1/15,000	20.00	50.00
12 Jeremy Mayfield Mobil 1 Bank	20.00	50.00
12 Jimmy Spencer Zippo/2000	60.00	120.00
12 Jimmy Spencer Zippo Bank	150.00	200.00
14 Patty Moise Rhodes Xena/5004	35.00	80.00
14 Patty Moise Rhodes Xena Bank	30.00	80.00
18 Bobby Labonte Interstate Batteries/5000	30.00	80.00
18 Bobby Labonte Interstate Batteries Bank/2500	20.00	50.00
18 Bobby Labonte Interstate Batteries Hot Rod/10,992	40.00	100.00
18 Bobby Labonte Interstate Batteries Hot Rod Bank	40.00	80.00
18 Bobby Labonte Interstate Batteries Small Soldiers/2508	30.00	80.00
18 Bobby Labonte Interstate Batteries Small Soldiers Bank	30.00	80.00
21 Michael Waltrip Citgo/4008	15.00	30.00
21 Michael Waltrip Citgo Woody/2508	40.00	80.00
22 Ward Burton MBNA/5004	15.00	40.00
23 Jimmy Spencer No Bull	30.00	80.00
23 Jimmy Spencer No Bull Bank/2500	30.00	80.00
24 Jeff Gordon DuPont	40.00	80.00
24 Jeff Gordon DuPont Bank/7500	40.00	80.00
24 Jeff Gordon DuPont Brickyard Win/2508	75.00	125.00
24 Jeff Gordon DuPont Mac Tools	60.00	100.00
24 Jeff Gordon DuPont Chromalusion	60.00	120.00
24 Jeff Gordon DuPont Chromalusion Bank/15,000	50.00	100.00
24 Jeff Gordon DuPont Chromalusion Mac Tools	75.00	150.00
24 Jeff Gordon DuPont No Bull	50.00	80.00
24 Jeff Gordon DuPont No Bull Bank	40.00	80.00
28 Kenny Irwin Havoline/10,000	20.00	50.00
28 Kenny Irwin Havoline Joker	25.00	60.00
28 Kenny Irwin Havoline Joker Bank	25.00	60.00
30 Derrike Cope Gumout/3504	12.00	30.00
31 Dale Earnhardt Jr. Sikkens Blue 1997 Monte Carlo/5000	100.00	175.00
31 Dale Earnhardt Jr. Sikkens Blue Bank 1997 Monte Carlo/5004	60.00	150.00
31 Dale Earnhardt Jr. Wrangler 1997 Monte Carlo/10,008	100.00	200.00
31 Dale Earnhardt Jr. Wrangler Bank 1997 Monte Carlo/2508	60.00	150.00
31 Mike Skinner Lowe's/6000	20.00	50.00
31 Mike Skinner Lowe's Bank/2500	20.00	50.00
31 Mike Skinner Lowe's Special Olympics	25.00	60.00
31 Mike Skinner Lowe's Special Olympics Bank/2500	20.00	50.00
32 Dale Jarrett White Rain/6000	30.00	60.00
33 Tim Fedewa Kleenex/2000	25.00	60.00
33 Tim Fedewa Kleenex Bank	20.00	50.00
33 Ken Schrader Skoal/3504	40.00	80.00
34 Mike McLaughlin Goulds/2000	25.00	60.00
34 Mike McLaughlin Goulds Bank	25.00	60.00
35 Todd Bodine Tabasco Orange&White	15.00	40.00
35 Todd Bodine Tabasco Orange&White Bank	15.00	40.00
35 Todd Bodine Tabasco Red&Black	20.00	40.00
35 Todd Bodine Tabasco Red&Black Bank/2508	15.00	40.00
36 Ernie Irvan M&M's/10,008	50.00	100.00
36 Ernie Irvan M&M's Mac Tools Bank/4500	25.00	60.00
36 Ernie Irvan Skittles/10,008	20.00	50.00
36 Ernie Irvan Skittles Mac Tools Bank/4500	20.00	50.00
36 Ernie Irvan Wildberry Skittles/10,008	20.00	50.00
36 Ernie Irvan Wildberry Skittles Mac Tools Bank/4500	20.00	50.00
40 Sterling Marlin Coors Light	25.00	60.00
41 Steve Grissom Kodiak/3500	20.00	50.00
41 Steve Grissom Kodiak Bank/2500	20.00	50.00
42 Joe Nemechek BellSouth/4008	15.00	40.00
42 Joe Nemechek BellSouth Bank	20.00	50.00
42 Marty Robbins 1974 Dodge/6000	40.00	80.00
44 Tony Stewart Shell/5508	100.00	175.00
44 Tony Stewart Shell Bank/2508	50.00	100.00
44 Tony Stewart Shell Small Soldiers/10,992	50.00	100.00
44 Tony Stewart Shell Small Soldiers Bank/2508	45.00	80.00
50 Ricky Craven Budweiser	20.00	50.00
50 Ricky Craven Bud Bank	30.00	80.00
50 Ricky Craven Bud Mac Tools Bank/3500	30.00	80.00
50 No Driver Association Bud Louie	25.00	60.00
50 No Driver Association Bud Louie Bank	25.00	60.00
72 Mike Dillon Detroit Gasket/4008	12.50	30.00
81 Kenny Wallace Square D/2508	15.00	40.00
81 Kenny Wallace Square D Lightning/4008	20.00	50.00
88 Dale Jarrett Quality Care	40.00	70.00
88 Dale Jarrett Quality Care Bank	30.00	70.00
88 Dale Jarrett Batman	60.00	100.00
88 Dale Jarrett Batman Bank	40.00	80.00
90 Dick Trickle Heilig-Meyers/3500	25.00	50.00
96 David Green Caterpillar/6996	8.00	20.00
98 Greg Sacks Thorn Apple Valley/4008	12.50	30.00
98 Rich Bickle Thorn Apple Valley Go Grill Crazy/2508	12.50	30.00
300 Darrell Waltrip Flock Special/3500	30.00	80.00
300 Darrell Waltrip Tim Flock Special Bank	30.00	80.00
00 Buckshot Jones Alka Seltzer	15.00	40.00
K2 Dale Earnhardt Dayvault's '56 Ford Dark Roof/10,000	50.00	100.00
K2 Dale Earnhardt Dayvault's '56 Ford Dark Roof Bank	40.00	80.00
K2 Dale Earnhardt Dayvault's '56 Ford Pink Roof	50.00	100.00

1998 Action Racing Collectables NAPA 1:24

This set was only available thru participating NAPA dealers.

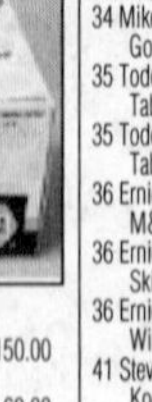

	EX	NM-MT
7 Alan Kulwicki Hooters 1992 Thunderbird	45.00	90.00
7 Alan Kulwicki Hooters Gold 1992 T-bird	100.00	175.00
11 Ned Jarrett Richmond Ford Gold 1965 Ford	100.00	175.00
11 Cale Yarborough Gold 1976 Monte Carlo	75.00	150.00
22 Red Byron Overseas Motors 1949 Hudson	30.00	60.00
22 Red Byron Overseas Motors Gold 1949 Hudson	100.00	175.00
28 Buddy Baker NAPA 1980 Olds	50.00	100.00
28 Buddy Baker NAPA Gold 1980 Olds	100.00	200.00
99 Curtis Turner Gold 1956 Ford	60.00	120.00

1998 Action/RCCA Banks 1:24

These cars were produced by Action and distributed through the club (RCCA). Each car has a slot in the back window for a coin bank. All banks have clear windows.

	EX	NM-MT
1 Dale Earnhardt Jr. Coke Bear/12,500	60.00	120.00
1 Jeff Gordon Baby Ruth 1992 Thunderbird	60.00	120.00
1 Steve Park Pennzoil/2000	75.00	150.00
1 Darrell Waltrip Pennzoil	60.00	100.00
2 Rusty Wallace Adventures of Rusty/3500	25.00	60.00
2 Rusty Wallace Miller Lite/6000	20.00	50.00
2 Rusty Wallace Miller Lite Elvis/20,000	20.00	50.00
2 Rusty Wallace Miller Lite TCB Elvis	15.00	40.00
3 Dale Earnhardt Coke/15,000	75.00	150.00
3 Dale Earnhardt Goodwrench Plus/12,500	75.00	150.00
3 Dale Earnhardt Goodwrench Plus Bass Pro/12,500	60.00	120.00
3 Dale Earnhardt Goodwrench Plus Daytona Win	75.00	150.00
3 Dale Earnhardt Jr. AC Delco/2500	75.00	150.00
4 Bobby Hamilton Kodak/3500	15.00	40.00
5 Terry Labonte Blasted Fruit Loops/5000	20.00	50.00
5 Terry Labonte Kellogg's/5000	20.00	50.00
5 Terry Labonte Kellogg's Corny/3500	25.00	60.00
5 Terry Labonte Kellogg's Ironman	40.00	100.00
8 Dale Earnhardt RPM 1975 Dodge/12,500	50.00	120.00
8 Hut Stricklin Circuit City	20.00	50.00
9 Jerry Nadeau Scooby Zombie Island/2500	30.00	80.00
9 Lake Speed Birthday Cake	25.00	60.00
9 Lake Speed Huckleberry Hound	30.00	60.00
10 Ricky Rudd Tide/2500	30.00	70.00
12 Jeremy Mayfield Mobil 1/3500	25.00	50.00
12 Jimmy Spencer Zippo/600	60.00	150.00
14 Patty Moise Rhodes Xena/2500	25.00	50.00
18 Bobby Labonte Interstate Batteries/1500	30.00	75.00
18 Bobby Labonte Interstate Batteries Small Soldiers/7500	25.00	60.00
23 Jimmy Spencer No Bull/2500	25.00	60.00
24 Jeff Gordon DuPont/12,500	40.00	80.00
24 Jeff Gordon DuPont No Bull	30.00	60.00
24 Jeff Gordon DuPont Chromalusion/10,000	50.00	100.00
28 Kenny Irwin Havoline/5000	30.00	80.00
28 Kenny Irwin Havoline Joker/5000	30.00	80.00
31 Dale Earnhardt Jr. Sikkens Blue 1997 Monte Carlo/3500	75.00	200.00
31 Mike Skinner Lowe's/3500	15.00	40.00
31 Mike Skinner Lowe's Special Olympic/3500	20.00	50.00
32 Dale Jarrett White Rain/2000	30.00	60.00
33 Tim Fedewa Kleenex	25.00	60.00
34 Mike McLaughlin Goulds/600	25.00	60.
35 Todd Bodine Tabasco Orange&White/1000	20.00	50.
35 Todd Bodine Tabasco Red&Black/4000	20.00	50.
36 Ernie Irvan M&M's	50.00	100.
36 Ernie Irvan Skittles	40.00	80.
36 Ernie Irvan Wildberry Skittles	40.00	100.
41 Steve Grissom Kodiak/2500	30.00	60
42 Joe Nemechek BellSouth	25.00	60.
42 Marty Robbins 1974 Dodge/2500	40.00	80
44 Tony Stewart Shell/1500	60.00	120.
44 Tony Stewart Shell Small Soldiers/5000	60.00	100.
50 Ricky Craven Budweiser	30.00	80.
50 No Driver Association Bud Louie/2000	40.00	80.
81 Kenny Wallace Square D/1500	25.00	60
81 Kenny Wallace Square D Lightning/2500	25.00	60
88 Dale Jarrett Quality Care/5000	30.00	75
88 Dale Jarrett Quality Care Batman/7500	30.00	75
88 Dale Jarrett Quality Care No Bull/2500	30.00	75
90 Dick Trickle Heilig-Meyers/1500	25.00	60
96 David Green Caterpillar/1500	15.00	40
98 Greg Sacks Thorn Apple Valley	15.00	40
300 Darrell Waltrip Flock Special/2000	40.00	100
K2 Dale Earnhardt Dayvault's Pink Roof 1956 Ford	50.00	100

1998 Action/RCCA Elite 1:2

This series was consists of upgraded versions of their sta production cars. The cars from this series contain serial nu plates on the undercarriage at the end of the car.

	EX	NM-
1 Dale Earnhardt Jr. Coke Bear/10,000	90.00	150
1 Steve Park Pennzoil Black Roof	60.00	120
1 Steve Park Pennzoil Yellow Roof/3200	50.00	100
1 Darrell Waltrip Pennzoil/1200	100.00	175
2 Rusty Wallace Adventures of Rusty/1320	60.00	120
2 Rusty Wallace Miller Lite/2500	50.00	100
2 Rusty Wallace Miller Lite Elvis/2500	50.00	100
2 Rusty Wallace Miller Lite TCB Elvis/1000	50.00	100
3 Dale Earnhardt Coke/12,500	150.00	250
3 Dale Earnhardt Goodwrench Plus/7500	125.00	250
3 Dale Earnhardt Goodwrench Plus Bass Pro/10,000	100.00	200
3 Dale Earnhardt Goodwrench Plus Daytona Win/9996 raced version with tire swatch	150.00	300
3 Dale Earnhardt Goodwrench Plus Gold/100	1200.00	1600
3 Dale Earnhardt Goodwrench 1995 Monte Carlo Silver/20,000	150.00	250
3 Dale Earnhardt Jr. AC Delco/1500	200.00	350
3 Dale Earnhardt Jr. AC Delco Gold Promo/100	800.00	1400
4 Bobby Hamilton Kodak	30.00	80
5 Terry Labonte Blasted Fruit Loops	50.00	120
5 Terry Labonte Kellogg's/3000	50.00	120
5 Terry Labonte Kellogg's Corny/1500	60.00	120
5 Terry Labonte Kellogg's Ironman/3500	50.00	100
8 Dale Earnhardt RPM 1975 Dodge/10,000	75.00	150
8 Hut Stricklin Circuit City	25.00	60
9 Jerry Nadeau Scooby Zombie Island	50.00	120
9 Lake Speed Birthday Cake	40.00	100
9 Lake Speed Huckleberry Hound	40.00	100
10 Ricky Rudd Tide	50.00	120
12 Jeremy Mayfield Mobil 1	40.00	80
12 Jimmy Spencer Zippo/400	100.00	200
14 Patty Moise Rhodes Xena	40.00	100
18 Bobby Labonte Interstate Batteries Hot Rod/1200	75.00	150
18 Bobby Labonte Interstate Batteries Small Soldiers/5000	75.00	150
22 Ward Burton MBNA/1200	30.00	80
23 Jimmy Spencer No Bull/1200	60.00	150
24 Jeff Gordon DuPont/3500	100.00	175

	EX	NM-MT
Jeff Gordon / DuPont No Bull/1500	125.00	225.00
Jeff Gordon / DuPont Chromalusion/7500	125.00	250.00
Kenny Irwin / Havoline	60.00	120.00
Kenny Irwin / Havoline Joker/3500	60.00	120.00
Dale Earnhardt Jr. / Sikkens Blue/2500 / 1997 Monte Carlo	125.00	250.00
Mike Skinner / Lowe's	30.00	80.00
Mike Skinner / Lowe's Special Olympics/2500	25.00	60.00
Tim Fedewa / Kleenex	100.00	175.00
Mike McLaughlin / Goulds	100.00	175.00
Todd Bodine / Tabasco Red&Black/1700	50.00	120.00
Ernie Irvan / M&M's	125.00	200.00
Ernie Irvan / Skittles	50.00	120.00
Ernie Irvan / Wildberry Skittles/2000	40.00	100.00
Steve Grissom / Kodiak/1200	40.00	80.00
Tony Stewart / Shell/1200	150.00	300.00
Tony Stewart / Shell Small Soldiers/3500	60.00	120.00
Ricky Craven / Budweiser	50.00	100.00
No Driver Association / Bud Louie/1000	60.00	120.00
Kenny Wallace / Square D	50.00	100.00
Kenny Wallace / Square D Lightning	50.00	100.00
Dale Jarrett / Batman/5000	60.00	120.00
Dale Jarrett / Quality Care Proto		
Dale Jarrett / Quality Care	60.00	120.00
Dale Jarrett / Quality Care No Bull/1200	60.00	120.00
David Green / Caterpillar/1200	25.00	60.00
Greg Sacks / Thorn Apple Valley/1000	25.00	60.00
) Darrell Waltrip / Flock Special/1200	50.00	100.00
Dale Earnhardt / Dayvault's/10,000	75.00	150.00

1998-00 Action Racing Collectables Crystal 1:24

	EX	NM-MT
ale Earnhardt Jr. / Coke Bear/9000 1999	25.00	50.00
eff Gordon / Baby Ruth / 1992 Thunderbird/4008 1999	25.00	50.00
ale Earnhardt / Coke/9000 1998	50.00	100.00
ale Earnhardt / Goodwrench 1999	60.00	100.00
ale Earnhardt / Goodwrench Taz/2500 '00	60.00	100.00
ale Earnhardt / Wrangler/5000 1999	60.00	100.00
ale Earnhardt Jr. / AC Delco Superman/4008 1999	25.00	50.00
ale Earnhardt Jr. / Bud 1999	25.00	50.00
Jeff Gordon / DuPont 1999	25.00	50.00
Jeff Gordon / DuPont Superman/6000 1999	30.00	60.00
Jeff Gordon / Pepsi/8000 1999	25.00	50.00

1998 Action Racing :ollectables Fan Fueler 1:24

s series of 1:24 cars was produced for mass retailers and kside sales by Action. Each piece is packaged in a clear dow box with the name "Fan Fueler" printed clearly on the s. No production run totals were given.

	EX	NM-MT
usty Wallace / Ford Motorsports	10.00	25.00
ale Earnhardt / Goodwrench Plus	15.00	30.00
Jeff Gordon / DuPont	12.50	25.00
Dale Jarrett / Quality Care	10.00	25.00

1999 Action Performance 1:24

se cars were issued in an "AP" or Action Performance clear dow or solid box. The red and black "AP" logo and a ckered flag design on both box varieties helps to identify year along with the obvious notation of "1999" at the om of the box.

	EX	NM-MT
ale Earnhardt Jr. / AC Delco	12.50	25.00
ale Earnhardt Jr. / Budweiser	15.00	30.00
20 Tony Stewart / Home Depot HO / Black Windows	90.00	150.00
20 Tony Stewart / Home Depot HO / Black Windows Rookie Stripes	40.00	80.00
20 Tony Stewart / Home Depot HO / Clear Windows Rookie Stripes	30.00	60.00
20 Tony Stewart / Home Depot not/HO / Clear Windows Rookie Stripes	12.50	30.00
20 Tony Stewart / Home Depot Habitat HO	20.00	50.00
20 Tony Stewart / Home Depot Habitat not/HO	12.50	30.00
22 Ward Burton / Caterpiller	15.00	25.00
24 Jeff Gordon / DuPont	15.00	30.00
28 Kenny Irwin / Havoline Flames	10.00	25.00
88 Dale Jarrett / Quality Care	10.00	25.00

1999 Action Racing Collectables 1:24

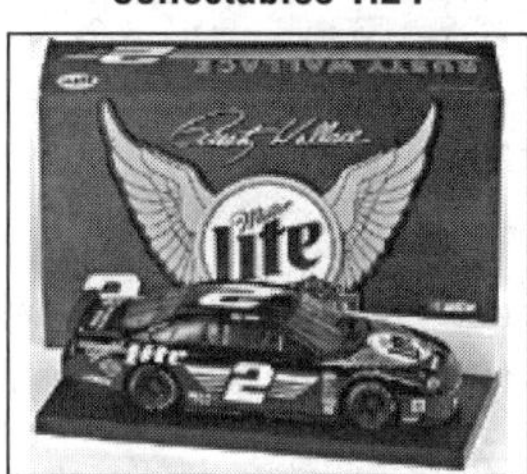

This year Action mounted their Alcohol and Tobacco cars on a base that resembles a pit wall and labeled them "For adults only" so as not to confuse their collectables with toys.

ALCOHOL/TOBACCO CARS ON PIT WALL BASE

	EX	NM-MT
1 Jeff Gordon / Carolina Ford 1991 Thunderbird	40.00	80.00
1 Jeff Gordon / Carolina Ford 1991 Thunderbird Bank	50.00	80.00
1 Jeff Gordon / Carolina '91 T-bird / Mac Tools	30.00	80.00
1 Steve Park / Pennzoil	30.00	60.00
1 Steve Park / Pennzoil Bank	25.00	60.00
1 Steve Park / Pennzoil Shark	30.00	60.00
2 Rusty Wallace / Miller Lite/15,000	30.00	70.00
2 Rusty Wallace / Miller Lite Bank/2508	40.00	80.00
2 Rusty Wallace / Miller Lite Harley/2508 / black windows	25.00	60.00
2 Rusty Wallace / Miller Lite Harley / clear windows	25.00	50.00
2 Rusty Wallace / Miller Lite Harley Bank/5004	25.00	60.00
2 Rusty Wallace / Miller Lite Last Lap/10,080	30.00	80.00
2 Rusty Wallace / Miller Lite Last Lap Bank	30.00	80.00
2 Rusty Wallace / Miller Lite Texas	40.00	75.00
3 Dale Earnhardt / Goodwrench	75.00	150.00
3 Dale Earnhardt / Goodwrench Bank/10,008	60.00	120.00
3 Dale Earnhardt / Goodwrench 25th Anniversary/2500	75.00	150.00
3 Dale Earnhardt / Goodwrench 25th Anniversary Bank	75.00	125.00
3 Dale Earnhardt / Goodwrench Crash 1997 Monte Carlo	250.00	400.00
3 Dale Earnhardt / Goodwrench Sign	60.00	120.00
3 Dale Earnhardt / Goodwrench Sign Last Lap/15,504	150.00	250.00
3 Dale Earnhardt / Goodwrench Sign / Last Lap Bank/2508	100.00	200.00
3 Dale Earnhardt / Wrangler/5004	75.00	150.00
3 Dale Earnhardt / Wrangler Bank/5004	60.00	120.00
3 Dale Earnhardt Jr. / AC Delco	30.00	80.00
3 Dale Earnhardt Jr. / AC Delco Bank/5004	50.00	100.00
3 Dale Earnhardt Jr. / AC Delco Last Lap/12,000	60.00	120.00
3 Dale Earnhardt Jr. / AC Delco / Last Lap Bank	70.00	120.00
3 Dale Earnhardt Jr. / AC Delco Superman	40.00	100.00
3 Dale Earnhardt Jr. / AC Delco Superman Bank	40.00	100.00
4 Bobby Hamilton / Advantix	15.00	40.00
4 Jeff Purvis / Lance/4008	12.50	30.00
5 Terry Labonte / Kellogg's	30.00	70.00
5 Terry Labonte / Kellogg's Bank/2508	25.00	60.00
5 Terry Labonte / Kellogg's Bank Mac Tools	20.00	50.00
5 Terry Labonte / Kellogg's NASCAR Racers/7500	25.00	60.00
5 Terry Labonte / K-Sentials	30.00	80.00
5 Terry Labonte / K-Sentials Bank/2508	25.00	60.00
5 Terry Labonte / Rice Krispies/10,080	25.00	60.00
5 Terry Labonte / Rice Krispies Bank/2508	25.00	60.00
8 Dale Earnhardt Jr. / Bud	60.00	120.00
8 Dale Earnhardt Jr. / Bud Bank/3000	50.00	100.00
8 Dale Earnhardt Jr. / Bud Atlanta/7008	60.00	120.00
8 Dale Earnhardt Jr. / Bud Michigan/6708	60.00	120.00
8 Dale Earnhardt Jr. / Bud New Hampshire/6708	60.00	120.00
8 Dale Earnhardt Jr. / Bud Richmond/6708	60.00	120.00
9 Jerry Nadeau / Dexter's Lab/7500	20.00	50.00
9 Jerry Nadeau / Dexter's Lab Bank/2508	20.00	50.00
9 Jerry Nadeau / Jetsons/5004	20.00	50.00
10 Ricky Rudd / Tide/4008	35.00	75.00
10 Ricky Rudd / Tide Mac Tools	30.00	75.00
10 Ricky Rudd / Tide Kids	30.00	80.00
11 Dale Jarrett / Green Bay Packers/6084	75.00	125.00
11 Dale Jarrett / Rayovac	20.00	50.00
12 Jeremy Mayfield / Mobil 1	25.00	60.00
12 Jeremy Mayfield / Mobil 1 Kentucky Derby	20.00	50.00
12 Jeremy Mayfield / Mobil 1 / Kentucky Derby Bank/5004	15.00	40.00
15 Ken Schrader / Oakwood Homes/3504	15.00	40.00
16 Ron Hornaday / NAPA SuperTruck/2940	30.00	80.00
16 Ron Hornaday / NAPA Superman / SuperTruck/7920	20.00	50.00
17 Matt Kenseth / DeWalt/4008	60.00	120.00
17 Matt Kenseth / DeWalt Bank/2508	50.00	100.00
18 Bobby Labonte / Interstate Batteries	40.00	75.00
18 Bobby Labonte / Interstate Batt.Bank	35.00	70.00
18 Bobby Labonte / Interstate Batteries / NASCAR Racers/7500	35.00	70.00
18 Bobby Labonte / MBNA/4608	30.00	80.00
19 Mike Skinner / Yellow Freight/4008	25.00	60.00
20 Tony Stewart / Home Depot/5004	125.00	250.00
20 Tony Stewart / Home Depot black windows	60.00	120.00
20 Tony Stewart / Home Depot Bank/2508	100.00	200.00
20 Tony Stewart / Home Depot Gold / QVC Race Fans/2508	100.00	200.00
20 Tony Stewart / Home Depot Fan Club AUTO	125.00	250.00
20 Tony Stewart / Home Depot Habitat	30.00	80.00
21 Elliott Sadler / Citgo/4008	25.00	60.00
22 Ward Burton / Caterpillar/3804	30.00	80.00
22 Ward Burton / Caterpillar Mac Tools/5004	30.00	80.00
23 Jimmy Spencer / No Bull	20.00	50.00
23 Jimmy Spencer / No Bull Bank/2508	20.00	50.00
23 Jimmy Spencer / Winston Lights	15.00	40.00
23 Jimmy Spencer / Winston Lights / Mac Tools	20.00	40.00
23 Jimmy Spencer / Winston Lights Bank/2508	20.00	50.00
24 Jeff Gordon / DuPont	25.00	60.00
24 Jeff Gordon / DuPont Black Window/7500	20.00	50.00
24 Jeff Gordon / DuPont Mac Tools	30.00	60.00
24 Jeff Gordon / DuPont Bank/7500	25.00	60.00
24 Jeff Gordon / DuPont Brickyard/2500	50.00	100.00
24 Jeff Gordon / DuPont Gold / 1998 3-Time Champ	100.00	200.00
24 Jeff Gordon / DuPont NASCAR Racers/7800	75.00	150.00
24 Jeff Gordon / DuPont Superman	50.00	100.00
24 Jeff Gordon / DuPont Superman / Mac Tools	50.00	100.00
24 Jeff Gordon / DuPont Superman Bank	50.00	100.00
24 Jeff Gordon / Pepsi	30.00	80.00
24 Jeff Gordon / Pepsi Bank/7500	25.00	60.00
24 Jeff Gordon / Pepsi Mac Tools	30.00	60.00
24 Jeff Gordon / Pepsi Star Wars	40.00	80.00
24 Jeff Gordon / Pepsi Star Wars Bank	40.00	80.00
24 Jeff Gordon / Pepsi Star Wars Mac Tools	25.00	60.00
25 Wally Dallenbach / Bud/5004	25.00	60.00
25 Wally Dallenbach / Bud Bank/2508	20.00	50.00
25 Wally Dallenbach / Bud Bank Mac Tools	20.00	50.00
27 Casey Atwood / Castrol/6312	20.00	50.00
27 Casey Atwood / Castrol Last Lap/5004	20.00	50.00
27 Casey Atwood / Castrol Last Lap Bank	25.00	60.00
28 Kenny Irwin / Havoline/5004	25.00	60.00
28 Kenny Irwin / Havoline Bank	35.00	65.00
30 Derrike Cope / Bryan/2508	12.00	30.00
30 Derrike Cope / Jimmy Dean	12.00	30.00
30 Dale Earnhardt / Army 1976 Malibu	75.00	150.00
30 Dale Earnhardt / Army '76 Malibu Bank/2508	75.00	150.00
31 Dale Earnhardt Jr. / Gargoyles 1997 Monte Carlo/8500	75.00	135.00
31 Dale Earnhardt Jr. / Gargoyles / 1997 Monte Carlo Bank/2508	60.00	110.00
31 Dale Earnhardt Jr. / Mom 'N' Pop's / 1996 Monte Carlo	40.00	100.00
31 Dale Earnhardt Jr. / Mom 'N' Pop's / 1996 Monte Carlo Bank/2508	40.00	100.00
31 Dale Earnhardt Jr. / Sikkens White / 1997 Monte Carlo/5000	50.00	100.00
31 Dale Earnhardt Jr. / Sikkens White / 1997 Monte Carlo Bank/6000	40.00	80.00
31 Mike Skinner / Lowe's/3504	15.00	40.00
32 Jeff Green / Kleenex 75th	25.00	50.00
33 Ken Schrader / Skoal/6000	40.00	75.00
33 Ken Schrader / Skoal Red/6000	40.00	75.00
36 Ernie Irvan / M&M's	30.00	60.00
36 Ernie Irvan / M&M's Mac Tools	20.00	50.00
36 Ernie Irvan / M&M's Countdown/9000	20.00	50.00
36 Ernie Irvan / M&M's Millennium	20.00	50.00
36 Ernie Irvan / M&M's Millennium Bank	15.00	40.00
36 Ernie Irvan / Crispy M&M's	20.00	50.00
36 Ernie Irvan / Crispy M&M's Bank/2508	25.00	60.00
36 Ernie Irvan / Pedigree/9012	20.00	50.00
36 Tim Fedewa / Stanley	15.00	40.00
36 Tim Fedewa / Stanley Bank/2508	15.00	40.00
37 Kevin Grubb / Timber Wolf/5004	20.00	50.00
40 Coca-Cola 600/4608	20.00	40.00
40 Kerry Earnhardt / Channellock/6504	30.00	75.00
40 Kerry Earnhardt / Channellock Mac Tools/5004	30.00	75.00
40 Sterling Marlin / Coors Light/600	25.00	60.00
40 Sterling Marlin / Coors Light/Brooks & Dunn	30.00	80.00
40 Sterling Marlin / Coors Light Brooks & Dunn Bank/2508	25.00	60.00
40 Sterling Marlin / Coors Light / John Wayne/11,364	25.00	60.00
40 Sterling Marlin / Coors Light / John Wayne Bank/2508	25.00	60.00
44 Justin Labonte / Slim Jim	20.00	50.00
45 Rich Bickle / 10-10-345	25.00	60.00
50 Mark Green / Dr Pepper	15.00	40.00
55 Kenny Wallace / Square D	25.00	60.00
55 Kenny Wallace / Square D NASCAR Racers/7764	20.00	50.00
59 Mike Dillon / Kingsford	15.00	40.00
66 Darrell Waltrip / Big K Route 66/8508	25.00	60.00
66 Darrell Waltrip / Big K Route 66 / Victory Tour/4008	25.00	60.00
71 Dave Marcis / Realtree/5004	25.00	60.00
77 Dale Earnhardt / Hy-Gain 1976 Malibu	75.00	150.00
77 Dale Earnhardt / Hy-Gain 1976 Malibu Bank	75.00	150.00
88 Dale Jarrett / Quality Care/14,508	30.00	60.00
88 Dale Jarrett / Quality Care Bank/2508	30.00	60.00
88 Dale Jarrett / Quality Care Mac Tools/5004	20.00	50.00
88 Dale Jarrett / Quality Care White/8208	50.00	80.00
88 Dale Jarrett / Quality Care White Bank	40.00	70.00
88 Dale Jarrett / Quality Care Last Lap/12,000	40.00	75.00
88 Dale Jarrett / Quality Care Last Lap Bank	40.00	80.00
88 Dale Jarrett / Quality Care Gold / QVC Race Fans/2508	50.00	100.00
99 Kevin Lepage / Red Man	20.00	50.00
00 Buckshot Jones / Crown Fiber/9012	15.00	40.00
00 Larry Pearson / Cheez-it/3000	15.00	40.00

1999 Action/RCCA Banks 1:24

These cars were available only through the club, and were very limited. All banks have clear windows.

	EX	NM-MT
1 Jeff Gordon / Carolina Ford 1991 Thunderbird	75.00	125.00
1 Steve Park / Pennzoil	70.00	110.00
1 Steve Park / Pennzoil Shark/2000	50.00	100.00
2 Rusty Wallace / Miller Lite/3500	40.00	100.00
2 Rusty Wallace / Miller Lite Harley-Davidson	40.00	100.00
2 Rusty Wallace / Miller Lite Last Lap/3000	25.00	60.00
2 Rusty Wallace / Miller Lite True to Texas/1500	50.00	100.00
3 Dale Earnhardt / Goodwrench	100.00	200.00
3 Dale Earnhardt / Goodwrench / 25th Anniversary/8000	75.00	125.00
3 Dale Earnhardt / Goodwrench Sign	75.00	150.00
3 Dale Earnhardt / Goodwrench Sign / Last Lap/10,000	75.00	150.00
3 Dale Earnhardt / Wrangler/10,020	60.00	120.00
3 Dale Earnhardt Jr. / AC Delco/4500	40.00	100.00
3 Dale Earnhardt Jr. / AC Delco Superman/15,000	40.00	100.00
3 Dale Earnhardt Jr. / AC Delco Last Lap/10,000	60.00	120.00
4 Bobby Hamilton / Advantix	30.00	80.00
5 Terry Labonte / Kellogg's/3500	25.00	60.00
5 Terry Labonte / Kellogg's NASCAR Racers/3500	25.00	60.00
5 Terry Labonte / K-Sentials	40.00	100.00
5 Terry Labonte / Rice Krispies/3500	40.00	100.00
8 Dale Earnhardt Jr. / Bud/5000	60.00	120.00
8 Dale Earnhardt Jr. / Bud Atlanta/2500	60.00	120.00
8 Dale Earnhardt Jr. / Bud Michigan/2500	60.00	120.00
8 Dale Earnhardt Jr. / Bud New Hamp./2500	60.00	120.00
8 Dale Earnhardt Jr. / Bud Richmond/2500	60.00	120.00
9 Jerry Nadeau / Dexter's Laboratory	50.00	100.00
9 Jerry Nadeau / Jetsons	50.00	100.00
10 Ricky Rudd / Tide	30.00	80.00
10 Ricky Rudd / Tide Peroxide/1500	30.00	80.00
11 Dale Jarrett / Green Bay Packers/1500	50.00	100.00
12 Jeremy Mayfield / Mobil 1/2500	25.00	60.00
12 Jeremy Mayfield / Mobil 1 Kentucky Derby	30.00	80.00
15 Ken Schrader / Oakwood Homes	30.00	80.00
16 Ron Hornaday / NAPA Superman / SuperTruck/3500	20.00	50.00
17 Matt Kenseth / DeWalt/2500	50.00	100.00
18 Bobby Labonte / Interstate Batteries	50.00	100.00
18 Bobby Labonte / Interstate Batteries / NASCAR Racers/3500	40.00	80.00
19 Mike Skinner / Yellow Freight	40.00	100.00
20 Tony Stewart / Home Depot/2500	100.00	200.00
20 Tony Stewart / Home Depot Habitat/8000	30.00	80.00
21 Elliott Sadler / Citgo/1000	30.00	80.00
22 Ward Burton / Caterpillar Proto		
23 Jimmy Spencer / No Bull/2508	30.00	80.00
23 Jimmy Spencer / Winston Lights/5000	30.00	80.00
24 Jeff Gordon / DuPont/8500	40.00	100.00
24 Jeff Gordon / DuPont NASCAR Racers/8500	75.00	150.00
24 Jeff Gordon / DuPont Superman	50.00	100.00
24 Jeff Gordon / Pepsi/5000	30.00	80.00
24 Jeff Gordon / Pepsi Star Wars/10,000	40.00	80.00
25 Wally Dallenbach / Budweiser	25.00	60.00
27 Casey Atwood / Castrol	25.00	60.00
27 Casey Atwood / Castrol Last Lap/3000	20.00	50.00
28 Kenny Irwin / Havoline/2500	20.00	50.00
30 Derrike Cope	20.00	50.00

	EX	NM-MT
Jimmy Dean		
30 Dale Earnhardt Army 1976 Malibu Bank/4000	75.00	150.00
31 Dale Earnhardt Jr. Gargoyles 1997 Monte Carlo/7500	60.00	100.00
31 Dale Earnhardt Jr. Mom 'N' Pop's 1996 Monte Carlo/7500	50.00	100.00
31 Dale Earnhardt Jr. Sikkens White 1997 Monte Carlo/7500	40.00	80.00
31 Dale Earnhardt Jr. Wrangler 1997 Monte Carlo/4500	50.00	100.00
31 Mike Skinner Lowe's	25.00	60.00
33 Ken Schrader Skoal/2000	40.00	80.00
33 Ken Schrader Skoal Red/2000	40.00	80.00
36 Ernie Irvan M&M's	30.00	80.00
36 Ernie Irvan Crispy M&M's/1800	30.00	80.00
36 Ernie Irvan Pedigree	25.00	60.00
40 Coca-Cola 600	25.00	60.00
40 Kerry Earnhardt Channellock	40.00	100.00
40 Sterling Marlin Coors Light	40.00	100.00
40 Sterling Marlin Coors Light Brooks & Dunn	40.00	100.00
40 Sterling Marlin Coors Light John Wayne	40.00	100.00
44 Justin Labonte Slim Jim	20.00	50.00
45 Rich Bickle 10-10-345	25.00	60.00
50 Mark Green Dr Pepper/2000	25.00	60.00
55 Kenny Wallace Square D	20.00	50.00
55 Kenny Wallace Square D NASCAR Racers/3500	20.00	50.00
66 Darrell Waltrip Big K Route 66/1500	25.00	60.00
71 Dave Marcis Realtree	25.00	60.00
77 Robert Pressley Jasper/2500	20.00	50.00
88 Dale Jarrett Quality Care/2500	25.00	60.00
88 Dale Jarrett Quality Care No Bull	30.00	80.00
88 Dale Jarrett Quality Care Last Lap	30.00	60.00
88 Dale Jarrett Quality Care White/2500	40.00	80.00
99 Kevin Lepage Red Man/2000	20.00	50.00
00 Buckshot Jones Crown Fiber	25.00	60.00
02 Mark Martin J-Mar Trucking/2500	45.00	80.00

1999 Action/RCCA Elite 1:24

	EX	NM-MT
1 Jeff Gordon Baby Ruth 1992 Thunderbird/2500	150.00	250.00
1 Jeff Gordon Carolina 1991 Thunderbird/1500	100.00	175.00
1 Steve Park Pennzoil	90.00	150.00
1 Steve Park Pennzoil Shark	60.00	120.00
2 Rusty Wallace Miller Lite	90.00	150.00
2 Rusty Wallace Miller Lite Last Lap/1500	75.00	150.00
2 Rusty Wallace Miller Lite Harley/2500	100.00	175.00
3 Dale Earnhardt Goodwrench/7500	125.00	200.00
3 Dale Earnhardt Goodwrench 25th Anniversary/7500	100.00	200.00
3 Dale Earnhardt Goodwrench Sign/5000	100.00	200.00
3 Dale Earnhardt Goodwrench Sign Last Lap/8500	150.00	250.00
3 Dale Earnhardt Wrangler/7500	125.00	250.00
3 Dale Earnhardt Jr. AC Delco/8500	100.00	200.00
3 Dale Earnhardt Jr. AC Delco Last Lap/8500	75.00	150.00
3 Dale Earnhardt Jr. AC Delco Platinum/300	350.00	650.00
3 Dale Earnhardt Jr. AC Delco Superman/10,000	75.00	150.00
4 Bobby Hamilton Advantix/800	30.00	80.00
5 Terry Labonte Kellogg's/2500	25.00	60.00
5 Terry Labonte Kellogg's NASCAR Racers/2500	40.00	100.00
5 Terry Labonte K-Sentials	75.00	150.00
5 Terry Labonte Rice Krispies	75.00	150.00
6 Mark Martin Jim Magill Green 1983 Monte Carlo/2500	75.00	125.00
8 Dale Earnhardt Jr. Bud/5004	100.00	200.00
8 Dale Earnhardt Jr. Bud Atlanta/1000	100.00	200.00
8 Dale Earnhardt Jr. Bud Michigan/1000	100.00	200.00
8 Dale Earnhardt Jr. Bud New Hampshire/1000	100.00	200.00
8 Dale Earnhardt Jr. Bud Richmond/1000	100.00	200.00
9 Jerry Nadeau Dexter's Lab/1000	40.00	100.00
9 Jerry Nadeau Jetsons/600	40.00	100.00
10 Ricky Rudd Tide	50.00	120.00
10 Ricky Rudd Tide Kids	50.00	120.00
11 Dale Jarrett Green Bay Packers	80.00	150.00
12 Jeremy Mayfield Mobil 1/1500	40.00	100.00
12 Jeremy Mayfield Mobil 1 Kentucky Derby/3500	30.00	80.00
17 Matt Kenseth DeWalt/1000	125.00	200.00
18 Bobby Labonte Interstate Batteries/1000	75.00	150.00
18 Bobby Labonte Interstate Batteries NASCAR Racers/2500	60.00	120.00
18 Bobby Labonte MBNA/800	60.00	120.00
19 Mike Skinner Yellow Freight/1000	40.00	100.00
20 Tony Stewart Home Depot/1000	275.00	450.00
20 Tony Stewart Home Depot Habitat/5000	75.00	150.00
22 Ward Burton Caterpiller	125.00	225.00
23 Jimmy Spencer No Bull	50.00	120.00
23 Jimmy Spencer Winston Lights/3500	40.00	100.00
24 Jeff Gordon DuPont/5000	75.00	150.00
24 Jeff Gordon DuPont NASCAR Racers/5500	100.00	200.00
24 Jeff Gordon DuPont Superman/10,000	75.00	150.00
24 Jeff Gordon Pepsi/3500	60.00	120.00
24 Jeff Gordon Pepsi Star Wars/7500	60.00	150.00
25 Wally Dallenbach Budweiser	40.00	100.00
27 Casey Atwood Castrol/1000	40.00	100.00
27 Casey Atwood Castrol Last Lap/1500	40.00	100.00
28 Kenny Irwin Havoline/1000	50.00	120.00
30 Derrike Cope Jimmy Dean/800	30.00	80.00
30 Dale Earnhardt Army 1976 Malibu/2500	150.00	250.00
31 Dale Earnhardt Jr. Gargoyles 1997 Monte Carlo/3500	125.00	225.00
31 Dale Earnhardt Jr. Mom 'N' Pop's 1996 Monte Carlo/5000	60.00	120.00
31 Dale Earnhardt Jr. Sikkens White 1997 Monte Carlo/4000	75.00	150.00
31 Dale Earnhardt Jr. Wrangler 1997 Monte Carlo/3500	75.00	150.00
31 Mike Skinner Lowe's/1000	40.00	100.00
33 Ken Schrader Skoal	125.00	200.00
33 Ken Schrader Skoal Red	125.00	200.00
36 Ernie Irvan M&M's	75.00	150.00
36 Ernie Irvan M&M's Countdown/1500	50.00	100.00
36 Ernie Irvan M&M's Millennium	50.00	100.00
36 Ernie Irvan Crispy M&M's/1000	60.00	120.00
36 Ernie Irvan Pedigree	50.00	100.00
40 Coca-Cola 600	80.00	125.00
40 Kerry Earnhardt Channellock/800	75.00	150.00
40 Sterling Marlin Coors Light	50.00	100.00
40 Sterling Marlin Coors Light Brooks & Dunn/800	60.00	120.00
40 Sterling Marlin Coors Light John Wayne	60.00	120.00
45 Rich Bickle 10-10-345/800	30.00	80.00
50 Mark Green Dr Pepper/1000	40.00	100.00
55 Kenny Wallace Square D/1000	25.00	60.00
55 Kenny Wallace Square D NASCAR Racers/2500	25.00	60.00
66 Darrell Waltrip Big K Route 66/1000	40.00	100.00
71 Dave Marcis Realtree	75.00	150.00
77 Dale Earnhardt Hy-Gain 1976 Malibu/2500	150.00	250.00
77 Robet Pressley Jasper/1000	25.00	60.00
88 Dale Jarrett Quality Care/1000	100.00	175.00
88 Dale Jarrett Quality Care White/1000	125.00	200.00
88 Dale Jarrett Quality Care Last Lap/1000	75.00	150.00
02 Mark Martin J-Mar Trucking/1000	100.00	200.00

1999 Action/RCCA SelectNet Banks 1:24

	EX	NM-MT
1 Jeff Gordon Carolina Ford 1991	50.00	100.00
3 Dale Earnhardt Jr. AC Delco	25.00	60.00
3 Dale Earnhardt Wrangler	30.00	80.00
8 Dale Earnhardt Jr. Bud	50.00	120.00
11 Dale Jarrett Green Bay Packers/2500	75.00	125.00
17 Matt Kenseth DeWalt	40.00	80.00
20 Tony Stewart Home Depot	125.00	200.00
20 Tony Stewart Home Depot Habitat for Humanity/1600	60.00	100.00
24 Jeff Gordon Pepsi/804	25.00	60.00
27 Casey Atwood Castrol/800	25.00	50.00
31 Dale Earnhardt Jr. Sikkens White 1997 Monte Carlo	30.00	80.00
31 Dale Earnhardt Jr. Wrangler 1997 Monte Carlo/600	40.00	100.00
33 Ken Schrader Skoal/250	25.00	60.00
36 Ernie Irvan M&M's	20.00	50.00

1999 Action/RCCA SelectNet Elite 1:24

	EX	NM-MT
1 Goracing.com	40.00	80.00
8 Dale Earnhardt Jr. Bud/1500	75.00	150.00
17 Matt Kenseth DeWalt/1000	75.00	150.00
20 Tony Stewart Home Depot/1500	150.00	250.00
20 Tony Stewart Home Depot Habitat/1600	50.00	100.00
24 Jeff Gordon Pepsi/600	40.00	100.00
27 Casey Atwood Castrol/800	30.00	60.00
31 Dale Earnhardt Jr. Sikkens White 1997/1000	75.00	150.00
31 Dale Earnhardt Jr. Wrangler 1997/500	75.00	150.00
33 Ken Schrader Skoal	40.00	80.00
36 Ken Schrader M&M's	30.00	80.00

2000 Action Performance 1:24

These cars were packaged in an "AP" Action Performance box. Many were issued in both the clear window box or solid box variety. The solid boxes are black and red with the year 2000 clearly printed on them. The window boxes are also black and red with the year notation except for a few pieces that were issued in a colorful promo style window box.

	EX	NM-MT
2 Kevin Harvick AC Delco	15.00	30.00
2 Rusty Wallace Rusty	12.50	25.00
3 Dale Earnhardt Goodwrench	25.00	50.00
3 Ron Hornaday NAPA	10.00	20.00
3 Ron Hornaday NAPA 75th Anniversary in Promo style packaging	10.00	20.00
8 Dale Earnhardt Jr. Dale Earnhardt Jr.	15.00	30.00
18 Bobby Labonte Interstate Batteries	15.00	30.00
20 Tony Stewart Home Depot solid box	15.00	30.00
20 Tony Stewart Home Depot window box	15.00	30.00
21 Mike Dillon Quantis	10.00	20.00
24 Jeff Gordon DuPont	15.00	30.00
24 Jeff Gordon Pepsi	15.00	30.00
28 Ricky Rudd Havoline	15.00	25.00
31 Mike Skinner Lowe's	10.00	20.00
36 Ken Schrader M&M's	10.00	20.00
37 Kevin Grubb Timber Wolf	12.50	25.00
88 Dale Jarrett Quality Care	12.50	25.00

2000 Action Racing Collectables 1:24

These 1:24 scale replicas were produced by Action Racing Collectibles. Most pieces were packaged in a blue box and have the Action Racing Collectibles logo or the Racing Collectibles Inc. logo on the box.

	EX	NM-MT
1 Randy LaJoie Bob Evan's	15.00	30.00
1 Randy LaJoie Bob Evan's Bank/608	12.50	25.00
1 Randy LaJoie Bob Evan's Monsters/4800	12.50	25.00
1 Randy LaJoie Bob Evan's Monsters Bank	20.00	40.00
1 Steve Park Pennzoil/7008	30.00	80.00
1 Steve Park Pennzoil Bank/1008	25.00	60.00
1 Steve Park Pennzoil Shark Snap-on Promo Black Window Promo	15.00	30.00
2 Kevin Harvick AC Delco/5004	100.00	200.00
2 Mark Martin G&G Trucking '83 ASA Firebird/5940	15.00	40.00
2 Mark Martin Hartley's 1979 ASA Camaro/5508	25.00	60.00
2 Rusty Wallace Miller Lite/10,500	20.00	50.00
2 Rusty Wallace Miller Lite Bank/2508	20.00	50.00
2 Rusty Wallace Miller Lite 10th Ann./6000	25.00	50.00
2 Rusty Wallace Miller Lite Harley/19,704	60.00	120.00
2 Rusty Wallace Miller Lite Harley Bank/3276	30.00	60.00
3 Dale Earnhardt Goodwrench/34,992	75.00	150.00
3 Dale Earnhardt Goodwrench Bank/3504	100.00	250.00
3 Dale Earnhardt Goodwrench Brickyard	75.00	150.00
3 Dale Earnhardt Goodwrench Clear	175.00	300.00
3 Dale Earnhardt Goodwrench No Bull raced version	50.00	100.00
3 Dale Earnhardt Goodwrench No Bull Bank raced version/13,333	40.00	80.00
3 Dale Earnhardt Goodwrench Peter Max/101,916	100.00	200.00
3 Dale Earnhardt Goodwr.Peter Max BW car/100,247	75.00	150.00
3 Dale Earnhardt Goodwrench Peter Max Snap-on black window car/7500	75.00	150.00
3 Dale Earnhardt Goodwrench Peter Max Bank/5004	100.00	200.00
3 Dale Earnhardt Goodwrench Platinum 75th Win/25,008	100.00	200.00
3 Dale Earnhardt Goodwrench Talladega Win No Bull/10.003	75.00	150.00
3 Dale Earnhardt Goodwrench Taz No Bull/16,008	100.00	200.00
3 Dale Earnhardt Goodwrench Taz No Bull black window/16,008	75.00	150.00
3 Dale Earnhardt Goodwrench Taz No Bull Bank	75.00	150.00
3 Ron Hornaday NAPA/4008	20.00	50.00
3 Ron Hornaday NAPA 75th Anniversary/4008	20.00	50.00
3 Ron Hornaday NAPA 75th Ann.Bank	20.00	40.00
3 Ron Hornaday NAPA Monsters/8004	20.00	40.00
3 Ron Hornaday NAPA Monsters Bank	20.00	40.00
4 Bobby Hamilton Kodak/3504	15.00	40.00
4 Bobby Hamilton Kodak Navy/12,252	25.00	50.00
4 Bobby Hamilton Kodak Navy Bank/2508	25.00	50.00
4 Ernie Irvan Kodak 1991 Lumina	30.00	60.00
4 Ernie Irvan Kodak 1991 Lumina Mac Tools/3000	20.00	50.00
4 Mark Martin Jim Magill Orange 1983 Monte Carlo	30.00	60.00
4 Jeff Purvis Porter Cable/3504	15.00	40.00
5 Terry Labonte Froot Loops/14,148	20.00	50.00
5 Terry Labonte Froot Loops Mac Tools/3000	20.00	50.00
5 Terry Labonte Froot Loops Bank/2508	20.00	50.00
5 Terry Labonte Frost.Flakes Bank/1008	20.00	50.00
5 Terry Labonte Kellogg's	25.00	60.00
5 Terry Labonte Kellogg's Mac Tools/3000	25.00	60.00
5 Terry Labonte Kellogg's Bank	25.00	60.00
5 Terry Labonte Kellogg's Grinch	30.00	60.00
5 Terry Labonte Rice Krispies	20.00	50.00
5 Terry Labonte Rice Krispies Mac Tools/3000	20.00	50.00
6 Ernie Irvan Kroger 1987 Monte Carlo Aero Coupe/3504	35.00	60.00
6 Mark Martin Jim Magill Green 1983 Monte Carlo/7008	25.00	60.00
6 Mark Martin Jim Magill Green 1983 Monte Carlo Bank/6500	25.00	60.00
7 Michael Waltrip Nations Rent	20.00	50.00
7 Michael Waltrip Nations Rent Bank	20.00	50.00
8 Jeff Burton Baby Ruth 1990 Thunderbird/8004	25.00	60.00
8 Dale Earnhardt Jr. Bud/30,000	100.00	200.00
8 Dale Earnhardt Jr. Bud Bank/3504	90.00	150.00
8 Dale Earnhardt Jr. Bud Brickyard/2508	150.00	250.00
8 Dale Earnhardt Jr. Bud Olympic/37,440	75.00	135.00
8 Bobby Hillin Kleenex/2508	15.00	40.00
10 Johnny Benson Aaron's/4008	20.00	40.00
10 Jeff Green Nesquik	25.00	60.00
11 Jason Jarrett Rayovac/3504	20.00	40.00
11 Jason Jarrett Rayovac Bank/1008	15.00	40.00
11 Darrell Waltrip Hodgdon 1984 Camaro/3000	20.00	50.00
11 Darrell Waltrip Pepsi '83 Firebird/4008	15.00	40.00
11 Darrell Waltrip Mountain Dew 1984 Camaro/3000	20.00	50.00
11 Cale Yarborough Holly Farms 1976 Malibu/5640	30.00	60.00
12 Jeremy Mayfield Mobil 1/5004	15.00	40.00
12 Jeremy Mayfield Mobil 1 Bank	20.00	50.00
12 Jeremy Mayfield Mobil 1 World Series/7896	15.00	40.00
12 Jeremy Mayfield Mobil 1 World Series Bank/1008	20.00	50.00
12 Bobby Allison Coke 1974 Malibu/3504	30.00	60.00
12 Bobby Allison Coke 1974 Malibu Bank/1008	25.00	60.00
13 Robby Gordon Menards Monsters/5712	20.00	50.00
13 Robby Gordon Menards Monsters Bank/1380	20.00	40.00
14 Rusty Wallace Southland 1981 Camaro/3000	100.00	200.00
15 Mike Skinner Albertsons/2508	15.00	40.00
15 Mike Skinner Albertsons Bank	20.00	40.00
15 Tony Stewart Vision3 1996 Grand Prix/10,536	40.00	80.00
18 Bobby Labonte Interstate Batteries	30.00	80.00
18 Bobby Labonte Interstate Batteries Bank	25.00	60.00
18 Bobby Labonte Interstate Batteries Clear/4008	20.00	50.00
18 Bobby Labonte Interstate Batteries All Star Game/15,482	25.00	60.00
18 Bobby Labonte Interstate Batteries All Star Game Bank/2808	25.00	60.00
18 Bobby Labonte Interstate Batteries Frankenstein/11,664	50.00	100.00
18 Jason Leffler MBNA/3504	20.00	50.00
18 Jason Leffler MBNA Monsters	15.00	40.00
18 Jason Leffler MBNA Monsters Bank	20.00	40.00
19 Casey Atwood Motorola	30.00	80.00
19 Dodge Show Car/49,900	20.00	40.00
20 Tony Stewart Home Depot/29,508	40.00	80.00
20 Tony Stewart Home Depot Bank/2508	30.00	80.00
20 Tony Stewart Home Depot Brushed Metal Autographed Fan Club Promo/4000	100.00	200.00
20 Tony Stewart Home Depot Brickyard	50.00	100.00
20 Tony Stewart Home Depot Kids/23,676	35.00	60.00
20 Tony Stewart Home Depot Kids Mac Tools/3000	30.00	60.00
20 Tony Stewart Home Depot Kids Bank/2400	25.00	60.00
21 Mike Dillon Quantis/1008	20.00	40.00
21 Mike Dillon Rockwell/3504	15.00	40.00
21 Mike Dillon Rockwell Bank	20.00	50.00
21 Dale Jarrett Citgo 1991 Thunderbird/3216	75.00	150.00
21 Elliott Sadler Citgo/3504	20.00	50.00
21 Elliott Sadler Citgo 1950's/2004 red car w/white numbers	20.00	50.00
21 Elliott Sadler Citgo 1970's Paint/2004 white car w/red roof	20.00	50.00
21 Elliott Sadler Citgo Virgina Tech/3504	30.00	60.00
24 Jeff Gordon DuPont/29,220	25.00	60.00
24 Jeff Gordon DuPont Mac Tools/3000	25.00	60.00
24 Jeff Gordon DuPont Bank/3504	25.00	60.00
24 Jeff Gordon DuPont Brickyard/2508	60.00	120.00

ff Gordon 40.00 100.00
uPont Millennium
ff Gordon 40.00 100.00
uPont Millennium Bank/5004
ff Gordon 75.00 150.00
uPont Sign
ff Gordon 60.00 125.00
uPont Peanuts/48,480
ff Gordon 75.00 135.00
uPont Peanuts
Mac Tools/3000
ff Gordon 50.00 100.00
uPont Winston
ff Gordon 25.00 60.00
Pepsi/27,282
ff Gordon 25.00 60.00
Pepsi Bank/5000
cky Hendrick 20.00 40.00
GMAC/2004
ck Sprague 20.00 50.00
GMAC SuperTruck/2508
rry Nadeau 25.00 50.00
Holigan
rry Nadeau 25.00 60.00
Holigan Bank
rry Nadeau 25.00 50.00
Holigan Coast Guard
rry Nadeau 20.00 50.00
Holigan Coast Guard Bank/2508
nny Wallace 20.00 50.00
ance/3504
mmy Spencer 25.00 50.00
ig K/4500
mmy Spencer 15.00 40.00
ig K Bank/1008
sey Atwood 20.00 50.00
Castrol Busch
sey Atwood 25.00 60.00
Castrol Bank
sey Atwood 20.00 50.00
Castrol Monsters
sey Atwood 20.00 50.00
Castrol Monsters Bank/1008
cky Rudd 25.00 60.00
Havoline/13,056
cky Rudd 25.00 60.00
Havoline Mac Tools/3000
cky Rudd 25.00 60.00
Havoline Bank/2736
cky Rudd 25.00 60.00
Havoline Marines
cky Rudd 25.00 50.00
Havoline Marines Bank/2508
cky Rudd 12.50 25.00
Havoline Silver Promo
n window box
ad Little 15.00 40.00
ittle Trees/1992
eve Park 75.00 125.00
Whelen/1180
ke Skinner 15.00 40.00
owe's/7500
ke Skinner 20.00 50.00
owe's Bank
ke Skinner 25.00 60.00
owe's Army/9456
ke Skinner 20.00 50.00
owe's Army Bank/2508
le Jarrett 50.00 80.00
Nestle 1990 Grand Prix/3000
ny Raines 15.00 40.00
lka Seltzer Plus/2508
vid Green 15.00 40.00
FG Glass
en Schrader 20.00 50.00
M&M's
n Schrader 20.00 50.00
M&M's Mac Tools/3000
n Schrader 20.00 50.00
M&M's Bank
n Schrader 25.00 60.00
M&M's Green/8004
n Schrader 25.00 50.00
M&M's Green Bank
n Schrader 30.00 60.00
M&M's Halloween/4680
n Schrader 30.00 60.00
M&M's Halloween
Mac Tools/3000
n Schrader 25.00 60.00
M&M's Keep Back/14,400
n Schrader 25.00 60.00
M&M's Keep Back
Mac Tools/3000
n Schrader 25.00 60.00
M&M's Keep Back Bank/2508
n Schrader 25.00 60.00
M&M's July 4th
evin Grubb 20.00 40.00
imber Wolf/3504
erling Marlin 25.00 60.00
oors Light/3504
erling Marlin 25.00 60.00
oors Light Black/4008
erling Marlin 25.00 50.00
oors Light Black Bank
erling Marlin 25.00 60.00
oors Light Brooks & Dunn/7560
nny Irwin 35.00 70.00
ellSouth/3504
rry Labonte 125.00 250.00
iedmont 1984
Monte Carlo/2508
stin Labonte 20.00 50.00
lim Jim/5004
stin Labonte 20.00 50.00
lim Jim Bank/1008
ke McLaughlin 10.00 25.00
oulds Pumps/2508
ny Roper 60.00 150.00
r. Pepper Busch
nk Parker Jr. 25.00 60.00
eam Marines/2508
nny Wallace 20.00 50.00
quare D/3504
nny Wallace 20.00 50.00
quare D Bank/2508
ie Irvan 25.00 50.00
arnhardt 1987 Monte Carlo
ilver/18,300
ie Irvan 25.00 50.00
Earnhardt 1987 Monte Carlo
White/16,836
60 Geoffrey Bodine 15.00 40.00
Power Team/5004
60 Geoff Bodine 20.00 40.00
Power Team Bank
66 Todd Bodine 15.00 40.00
Blue Light Special
66 Darrell Waltrip 25.00 50.00
Big K Route 66
66 Darrell Waltrip 15.00 40.00
Big K Route 66 Bank/2508
66 Darrell Waltrip 25.00 60.00
Big K Route 66 Flames/6996
66 Darrell Waltrip 15.00 40.00
Big K Route 66 Flames Bank/2508
66 Rusty Wallace 125.00 200.00
Alugard 1984 Camaro Black/3000
66 Rusty Wallace 40.00 80.00
Alugard 1984 Camaro
Red/Yellow/3000
67 Jeff Gordon 30.00 60.00
Outback Steakhouse
1990 Grand Prix/28,992
71 Dave Marcis 30.00 60.00
Realtree/3504
75 Wally Dallenbach 20.00 50.00
Powerpuff Girls
75 Wally Dallenbach 15.00 40.00
Powerpuff Girls Bank
77 Robert Pressley 15.00 40.00
Jasper/5004
77 Robert Pressley 15.00 40.00
Jasper Federal Red/2508
77 Robert Pressley 20.00 50.00
Jasper Federal Red Bank
87 Joe Nemechek 20.00 50.00
CellularOne/3504
88 Dale Jarrett 25.00 60.00
Quality Care
88 Dale Jarrett 25.00 60.00
Quality Care Bank/2508
88 Dale Jarrett 30.00 80.00
Quality Care Air Force
88 Dale Jarrett 25.00 60.00
Qual.Care Air Force Bank/2508
88 Dale Jarrett 30.00 80.00
Quality Care Last Ride/5008
88 Darrell Waltrip 25.00 60.00
Gatorade 1976 Malibu/5784
92 Jimmie Johnson 150.00 250.00
Alltel/3000
94 Bill Elliott 25.00 60.00
McDonald's/10,500
94 Bill Elliott 20.00 50.00
McDonald's Bank/2508
94 Bill Elliott 25.00 60.00
McDonald's 25th Anniversary/15,000
94 Bill Elliott 25.00 60.00
McDonald's 25th Anniversary Bank
94 Bill Elliott 25.00 60.00
McDonald's McFlurry
97 Alan Kulwicki 25.00 60.00
WLPX 1981 Firebird
Yellow/3504
97 Alan Kulwicki 25.00 60.00
WLPX '81 Firebird
White Prototype/3504
97 Alan Kulwicki 25.00 60.00
WLPX 1983 Firebird/3792
97 Alan Kulwicki 25.00 60.00
1983 Firebird Prototype
97 Alan Kulwicki 30.00 60.00
West Bend Tire
1983 Firebird/4500
98 Elton Sawyer 20.00 50.00
Lysol
01 Mark Martin 30.00 60.00
Activision 1983 Monte Carlo/6500
00 Buckshot Jones 20.00 40.00
Cheez-it/3504
2000 Jeff Gordon 200.00 350.00
Action Fantasy/1800

2000 Action QVC For Race Fans Only 1:24

The cars in this set were only available on QVC and are finished in either Color Chrome, 24k. Gold, or Platinum.

EX NM-MT
2 Rusty Wallace 100.00 200.00
Miller Lite Gold/2000
3 Dale Earnhardt 200.00 350.00
Goodwrench
Color Chrome/3504
3 Dale Earnhardt 200.00 400.00
Goodwrench Gold/2000
3 Dale Earnhardt 100.00 200.00
Goodwrench No Bull
Gold/5000
3 Dale Earnhardt 100.00 200.00
Goodwrench No Bull
Platinum/2508
3 Dale Earnhardt 200.00 350.00
Goodwrench Taz
No Bull Gold/2000
3 Dale Earnhardt 150.00 300.00
Goodwrench Taz
No Bull Color Chrome/3504
3 Dale Earnhardt 175.00 350.00
Goodwrench Peter Max
Gold/2000
5 Terry Labonte 75.00 150.00
Froot Loops Gold/2000
5 Terry Labonte 80.00 175.00
Kellogg's Gold
5 Terry Labonte 100.00 175.00
Kellogg's Grinch Gold/1000
8 Dale Earnhardt Jr. 100.00 200.00
Bud Color Chrome/3504
8 Dale Earnhardt Jr. 125.00 250.00
Bud Gold/2000
8 Dale Earnhardt Jr. 75.00 150.00
Bud Olympic Color Chrome/20,000
8 Dale Earnhardt Jr. 100.00 200.00
Bud Olympic Gold/2000
18 Bobby Labonte 75.00 150.00
Interstate Batteries
All-Star Game Color Chrome/1000
18 Bobby Labonte 75.00 150.00
Interstate Batteries
All-Star Gold/1000
18 Bobby Labonte 75.00 150.00
Interstate Batteries
Frankenstein Gold/2000
20 Tony Stewart 75.00 150.00
Home Depot Gold/2000
20 Tony Stewart 90.00 150.00
Home Depot Kids Gold/1000
20 Tony Stewart 60.00 120.00
Home Depot Kids
2-car set/2000
24 Jeff Gordon 100.00 200.00
DuPont Gold/2000
24 Jeff Gordon 125.00 250.00
DuPont Peanuts Gold/2000
24 Jeff Gordon 100.00 250.00
DuPont Winston Gold/2000
24 Jeff Gordon 100.00 200.00
Pepsi Gold
36 Ken Schrader 100.00 200.00
M&M's Gold
36 Ken Schrader 70.00 150.00
M&M's Green Gold
67 Jeff Gordon 80.00 150.00
Outback Steakhouse Gold
94 Bill Elliott 100.00 200.00
McDonald's Gold
94 Bill Elliott 100.00 200.00
McDonald's 25th Anniversary Platinum

2000 Action/RCCA Banks 1:24

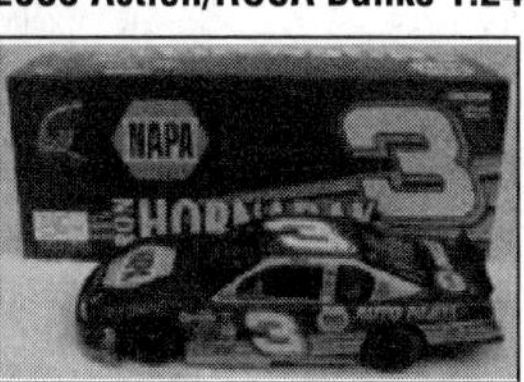

These banks are available solely through the RCCA club and feature clear windows.

EX NM-MT
1 Mark Martin 25.00 50.00
Activision 1983 Monte Carlo/6500
1 Steve Park 20.00 50.00
Pennzoil/2500
2 Dale Earnhardt 100.00 175.00
Curb '80 Olds/2004
2 Kevin Harvick 60.00 120.00
AC Delco/2004
2 Rusty Wallace 25.00 60.00
Miller Lite/2508
2 Rusty Wallace 25.00 60.00
Miller Lite 10th Anniversary
Color Chrome/2196
2 Rusty Wallace 50.00 100.00
Miller Lite Harley Davidson/2004
3 Dale Earnhardt 100.00 175.00
Goodwrench/7000
3 Dale Earnhardt 100.00 200.00
Goodwrench No Bull/5052
3 Dale Earnhardt 100.00 200.00
Goodwrench
Peter Max/7500
3 Dale Earnhardt 100.00 200.00
Goodwrench Taz
No Bull/13,500
3 Dale Earnhardt 250.00 400.00
Goodwrench Under
the Lights/2304
3 Dale Earnhardt 125.00 250.00
Wrangler
1987 Monte Carlo
Aerocoupe/2004
3 Ron Hornaday 20.00 50.00
NAPA/2508
4 Bobby Hamilton 20.00 50.00
Kodak Navy/2004
4 Ernie Irvan 20.00 50.00
Kodak 1991 Lumina/1500
4 Mark Martin 15.00 40.00
Jim Magill Orange
1983 Monte Carlo/6500
5 Terry Labonte 15.00 40.00
Kellogg's
6 Mark Martin 15.00 40.00
Jim Magill Green
1983 Monte Carlo/6500
7 Michael Waltrip 15.00 40.00
Nations Rent/1008
8 Jeff Burton 15.00 40.00
Baby Ruth
1990 Thunderbird/1500
8 Dale Earnhardt Jr. 90.00 150.00
Bud/7000
8 Dale Earnhardt Jr. 75.00 150.00
Bud No Bull/5052
8 Dale Earnhardt Jr. 90.00 150.00
Bud Olympic/7500
8 Bobby Hillin 20.00 50.00
Kleenex/504
12 Jeremy Mayfield 15.00 40.00
Mobil 1/1008
18 Bobby Labonte 30.00 80.00
Interstate Batteries/1500
20 Tony Stewart 30.00 80.00
Home Depot/3600
20 Tony Stewart 25.00 60.00
Home Depot Kids/2808
24 Jeff Gordon 30.00 60.00
DuPont/7500
24 Jeff Gordon 25.00 60.00
DuPont Millennium/10,992
24 Jeff Gordon 50.00 100.00
DuPont Peanuts
25 Jerry Nadeau 15.00 40.00
Holigan/2004
25 Jerry Nadeau 20.00 50.00
Holigan Coast Guard/2508
25 Kenny Wallace 20.00 40.00
Lance
27 Casey Atwood 15.00 40.00
Castrol
28 Ricky Rudd 20.00 50.00
Havoline/3504
28 Ricky Rudd 20.00 50.00
Havoline Marines/4500
30 Chad Little 20.00 40.00
Little Trees/804
31 Mike Skinner 20.00 40.00
Lowe's/1500
33 Tony Raines 15.00 40.00
Alka Seltzer Plus/996
36 Ken Schrader 15.00 40.00
M&M's/2508
40 Sterling Marlin 30.00 60.00
Coors Light/2508
40 Sterling Marlin 20.00 50.00
Coors Light Black/3504
44 Justin Labonte 15.00 40.00
Slim Jim/2004
44 Terry Labonte 125.00 200.00
Piedmont
1984 Monte Carlo/1009
53 Hank Parker Jr. 20.00 40.00
Team Marines/1008
55 Kenny Wallace 20.00 40.00
Square D
66 Darrell Waltrip 20.00 50.00
Big K Route 66/1008
66 Darrell Waltrip 20.00 50.00
Big K Route 66 Flames/1008
75 Wally Dallenbach 20.00 50.00
Powerpuff Girls
77 Robert Pressley 20.00 40.00
Jasper
88 Dale Jarrett 20.00 50.00
Quality Care Air Force/4500
94 Bill Elliott 20.00 50.00
McDonald's/3000
94 Bill Elliott 20.00 50.00
McDonald's 25th Ann./4500
00 Buckshot Jones 15.00 40.00
Cheez-it/804

2000 Action/RCCA Elite 1:24

These cars are available solely through the RCCA club and feature exacting detail.

EX NM-MT
1 Randy LaJoie 30.00 80.00
Bob Evan's Monsters/492
1 Mark Martin 60.00 120.00
Activision 1983 Monte Carlo/2500
1 Steve Park 60.00 120.00
Pennzoil/1008
2 Dale Earnhardt 300.00 500.00
Curb 1980 Olds/2700
2 Kevin Harvick 100.00 200.00
AC Delco/1008
2 Rusty Wallace 60.00 120.00
Miller Lite/1000
2 Rusty Wallace 50.00 120.00
Miller Lite 10th Ann./816
2 Rusty Wallace 100.00 200.00
Miller Lite Harley/1008
3 Dale Earnhardt 125.00 250.00
Goodwrench/5000
3 Dale Earnhardt 175.00 300.00
Goodwrench No Bull/3504
3 Dale Earnhardt 150.00 300.00
Goodwrench Peter Max/7500
3 Dale Earnhardt 150.00 300.00
Goodwrench Taz No Bull/9504
3 Dale Earnhardt 125.00 250.00
Goodwrench Test/3500
3 Dale Earnhardt 500.00 750.00
Goodwrench
Under the Lights/1200
3 Dale Earnhardt 200.00 350.00
Goodwrench 75th Win Platinum/3504
3 Dale Earnhardt 250.00 400.00
Wrangler 1987 Monte Carlo Aerocoupe/2700
3 Ron Hornaday 30.00 80.00
NAPA/1500
3 Ron Hornaday 30.00 80.00
NAPA 75th Anniv./1008
3 Ron Hornaday 30.00 80.00
NAPA Monsters/1200
4 Bobby Hamilton 25.00 60.00
Kodak Max/804
4 Mark Martin 40.00 100.00
Jim Magill Orange
1983 Monte Carlo/2500
5 Terry Labonte 100.00 150.00
Kellogg's
5 Terry Labonte 100.00 175.00
Froot Loops
5 Terry Labonte 70.00 120.00
Kellogg's Grinch/804
8 Jeff Burton 30.00 80.00
Baby Ruth
1990 Thunderbird/804
8 Dale Earnhardt Jr. 175.00 300.00
Bud/5000
8 Dale Earnhardt Jr. 100.00 200.00
Bud Test Gray/3500
8 Dale Earnhardt Jr. 125.00 250.00
Bud No Bull/3504
8 Dale Earnhardt Jr. 150.00 300.00
Bud Olympic/4992
10 Johnny Benson 25.00 60.00
Aaron's/492
11 Jason Jarrett 30.00 80.00
Rayovac/804
11 Cale Yarborough 80.00 150.00
Holly Farms 1976 Malibu/600
12 Bobby Allison 125.00 250.00
Coke 1974 Malibu/804
15 Tony Stewart 100.00 200.00
Vision 3/1992
18 Dale Jarrett 125.00 200.00
Freedlander
1987 Monte Carlo/492
18 Bobby Labonte 75.00 150.00
Interstate Batteries/1000
18 Bobby Labonte 60.00 120.00
Interstate Batteries
All-Star Game/1008
18 Bobby Labonte 60.00 100.00
Interstate Batteries
Frankenstein/696
20 Tony Stewart 125.00 200.00
Home Depot/5000
20 Tony Stewart 75.00 150.00
Home Depot ROY/5000
20 Tony Stewart 100.00 175.00
Home Depot Kids/1404
21 Dale Jarrett 50.00 90.00
Citgo 1991 Thunderbird/804
21 Elliott Sadler 40.00 70.00
Citgo/804
22 Bobby Allison 60.00 120.00
Miller High Life
1983 Monte Carlo
24 Jeff Gordon 75.00 150.00
DuPont/5000
24 Jeff Gordon 125.00 200.00
DuPont Test/3000
24 Jeff Gordon 60.00 150.00
DuPont Millennium/7500
24 Jeff Gordon 75.00 150.00
DuPont Peanuts/3456
24 Jeff Gordon 175.00 350.00
DuPont Winston/1008
24 Jeff Gordon 60.00 150.00
Pepsi/3504
24 Ricky Hendrick 25.00 60.00
GMAC/504
25 Jerry Nadeau 25.00 60.00
Holigan/1008
26 Jimmy Spencer 60.00 120.00
Big K/804
27 Casey Atwood 50.00 100.00
Castrol/1500
27 Casey Atwood 60.00 120.00
Castrol Monsters
28 Ricky Rudd 75.00 150.00
Havoline/1500
28 Ricky Rudd 50.00 100.00
Havoline Marines/2004
31 Mike Skinner 30.00 80.00
Lowe's Army/1500
32 Dale Jarrett 100.00 200.00
Nestle 1990 Grand Prix/492
36 Ken Schrader 100.00 150.00
M&M's Keep Back
40 Sterling Marlin 60.00 100.00
Coors Light/804
40 Sterling Marlin 40.00 100.00
Coors Light Black/1008
44 Justin Labonte 20.00 50.00
Slim Jim/1008
44 Terry Labonte 150.00 300.00
Piedmont 1984 Monte Carlo/800
53 Hank Parker Jr. 30.00 80.00
Team Marines/804
67 Jeff Gordon 50.00 100.00
Outback Steakhouse
1990 Grand Prix/3000
88 Dale Jarrett 100.00 150.00
Quality Care/1500
88 Dale Jarrett 75.00 150.00
Quality Care Air Force/2004
88 Dale Jarrett 75.00 150.00
Quality Care Last Ride/600
88 Dale Jarrett 70.00 120.00
UPS Test/2508
88 Darrell Waltrip 60.00 100.00
Gatorade 1976 Malibu/600
92 Jimmie Johnson 250.00 400.00
Alltel/492
94 Bill Elliott 60.00 150.00
McDonald's/1000
94 Bill Elliott 40.00 100.00
McDonald's 25th Ann.
2000 DEI Pit Practice/1008 175.00 300.00

2001 Action Performance 1:24

These "AP" or Action Performance cars were primarily distributed to mass retail and to trackside retailers. Unless noted below, each was packaged in a 2-sided clear window red and brown box with a white "AP" logo on the sides.

EX NM-MT
3 Dale Earnhardt 12.50 25.00
Goodwrench w/sonic logo
window box
3 Dale Earnhardt 45.00 80.00
Goodwrench Promo
without Sonic logo, solid box
8 Dale Earnhardt Jr. 20.00 35.00
Dale Jr.
15 Michael Waltrip 15.00 40.00
NAPA Daytona Win Promo
24 Jeff Gordon 20.00 35.00
DuPont Flames
88 Dale Jarrett 20.00 35.00
UPS

2001 Action Racing Collectables 1:24

EX NM-MT
1 Neil Bonnett 20.00 50.00
B&H Motors 1964 Chevelle/7836
1 Steve Park 40.00 80.00
Pennzoil
1 Steve Park 45.00 90.00
Pennzoil Bank/1008
1 Steve Park 25.00 60.00
Pennzoil Sylvester&Tweety/28,212
1 Steve Park 20.00 50.00
Pennzoil Sylvester
and Tweety Bank/1908
2 Kerry Earnhardt 35.00 60.00
Kannapolis Intimidators/2004
2 Kerry Earnhardt 25.00 50.00

	EX	NM-MT
Kannapolis Intimidators Bank/804		
2 Kerry Earnhardt Kannapolis Intimidators Clear/6000	30.00	60.00
2 Kevin Harvick AC Delco/3300	75.00	150.00
2 Kevin Harvick AC Delco 2001 Busch Champion/30,000	40.00	100.00
2 Kevin Harvick AC Delco Bank/600	75.00	150.00
2 Kevin Harvick AC Delco 2001 Busch Champ GM Dealers/2496	40.00	100.00
2 Rusty Wallace Miller Lite/12,036	35.00	75.00
2 Rusty Wallace Miller Lite Bank/1500	30.00	80.00
2 Rusty Wallace Miller Lite Harley/19,884	40.00	80.00
2 Rusty Wallace Miller Lite Harley Clear/6792	30.00	60.00
2/29 Kevin Harvick AC Delco/Goodwrench dual sponsor split paint/5004	75.00	150.00
3 Dale Earnhardt Goodwrench/33,504	150.00	250.00
3 Dale Earnhardt Goodwrench White Gold Promo/5000	125.00	250.00
3 Dale Earnhardt Goodwrench Bank/2508	150.00	300.00
3 Dale Earnhardt Goodwrench Oreo/55,008	150.00	300.00
3 Dale Earnhardt Goodwrench Oreo Bank/15,000	200.00	350.00
3 Dale Earnhardt Goodwrench Oreo Clear/6000	175.00	300.00
3 Dale Earnhardt Goodwrench Oreo GM Dealers White Gold/5000	150.00	250.00
3 Dale Earnhardt Goodwrench Clear/5004	200.00	400.00
3 Dale Earnhardt Goodwrench Talladega Win No Bull Bank/13,333	50.00	120.00
3 Dale Earnhardt Jr. Mom 'N' Pop's 1994 Camaro/10,008	125.00	225.00
5 Terry Labonte Kellogg's/7704	35.00	70.00
5 Terry Labonte Kellogg's Monster's Inc./6000	35.00	70.00
5 Terry Labonte Kellogg's Wile E./Road Runner/19,944	35.00	80.00
5 Terry Labonte Kellogg's Wile E./Road Runner Mac Tools/3000	35.00	80.00
5 Terry Labonte Kellogg's Wile E. and Road Runner Bank	30.00	80.00
7 Dale Earnhardt Jr. Church Brothers 1997 Monte Carlo/5028	125.00	200.00
8 Dale Earnhardt Docs Cycle Center 1964 Chevelle/86,924	50.00	100.00
8 Dale Earnhardt Docs 1964 Chevelle Bank	75.00	150.00
8 Dale Earnhardt Goodwrench 1987 Nova/10,008	150.00	250.00
8 Dale Earnhardt Jr. Bud/27,180	75.00	135.00
8 Dale Earnhardt Jr. Bud Bank/2088	60.00	120.00
8 Dale Earnhardt Jr. Bud Promo in plastic case/3750	50.00	100.00
8 Dale Earnhardt Jr. Bud w/Remington on deck lid	75.00	135.00
8 Dale Earnhardt Jr. Bud Van Camp's Promo	40.00	80.00
8 Dale Earnhardt Jr. Bud Talladega Win No Bull w/flag/64,676	50.00	100.00
8 Dale Earnhardt Jr. Bud MLB All-Star/54,408	150.00	300.00
8 Dale Earnhardt Jr. Bud All-Star Bank/2508	125.00	200.00
9 Bill Elliott Dodge/29,508	35.00	75.00
9 Bill Elliott Dodge Bank/4812	30.00	60.00
9 Bill Elliott Dodge Muhammad Ali/28,008	30.00	60.00
9 Bill Elliott Dodge Muhammad Ali Bank/1500	25.00	60.00
9 Bill Elliott Dodge Spider-Man/23,865	25.00	60.00
9 Bill Elliott Dodge Spider Man Bank/1836	25.00	60.00
9 Bill Elliott Dodge Spider Man Clear/4008	25.00	60.00
9 Bill Elliott Dodge Test black/5004	25.00	60.00
9 Bill Elliott Dahlonega 1976 Ford Torino/9000	25.00	60.00
10 Johnny Benson Valvoline James Dean/13,728	25.00	60.00
10 Johnny Benson Valvoline James Dean Bank	20.00	50.00
10 Jeff Green Nesquik/2376	20.00	50.00
10 Jeff Green Nesquik Bank/504	25.00	50.00
11 Darrell Waltrip Budweiser 1985 Monte Carlo/8508	35.00	75.00
12 Jeremy Mayfield Mobil 1/3732	20.00	50.00
12 Jeremy Mayfield Mobil 1 Bank/1008	30.00	80.00
14 Larry Foyt Harrah's/3504	30.00	60.00
15 Michael Waltrip NAPA/6228	50.00	120.00
15 Michael Waltrip NAPA Bank	40.00	100.00
15 Michael Waltrip NAPA Stars&Stripes/27,348	30.00	80.00
15 Michael Waltrip NAPA Stars&Stripes Bank/1008	30.00	60.00
18 Bobby Labonte Interstate Batteries	30.00	80.00
18 Bobby Labonte Interstate Batteries Bank	30.00	80.00
18 Bobby Labonte Interstate Batteries Color Chrome 2000 WC Champ/19,188	30.00	80.00
18 Bobby Labonte Interstate Batteries Cal Ripken/24,636	30.00	60.00
18 Bobby Labonte Interstate Batteries Coke Bear/25,320	30.00	60.00
18 Bobby Labonte Interstate Batteries Coke Bear Bank/2004	25.00	60.00
18 Bobby Labonte Interstate Batteries Coke Bear Mac Tools/3000	30.00	60.00
18 Bobby Labonte Interstate Batteries Coke Bear Clear	50.00	100.00
18 Bobby Labonte Interstate Batteries Jurassic Park 3/21,096	30.00	60.00
18 Bobby Labonte Interstate Batteries Jurassic Park 3 Bank/1788	25.00	60.00
18 Bobby Labonte Interstate Batteries Jurassic Park 3 Clear/6000	50.00	100.00
18 Jeff Purvis MBNA/2016	20.00	50.00
18 Bobby Labonte Interstate Batteries Jurassic Park 3 Mac Tools/3000	20.00	50.00
19 Casey Atwood Dodge/11,196	25.00	60.00
19 Casey Atwood Dodge Mountain Dew/16,104	25.00	60.00
19 Casey Atwood Dodge Mountain Dew Bank	25.00	60.00
19 Casey Atwood Dodge Spider-Man/18,924	25.00	60.00
19 Casey Atwood Dodge Spider-Man Mac Tools/3000	25.00	60.00
20 Tony Stewart Home Depot	30.00	80.00
20 Tony Stewart Home Depot Bank	25.00	60.00
20 Tony Stewart Home Depot Coke Bear/26,280	25.00	60.00
20 Tony Stewart Home Depot Coke Bear Bank/2004	25.00	60.00
20 Tony Stewart Home Depot Jurassic Park 3/22,128	30.00	80.00
20 Tony Stewart Home Depot Jurassic Park 3 Bank/1584	25.00	60.00
20 Tony Stewart Home Depot Jurassic Park 3 Clear/6000	25.00	60.00
22 Alan Kulwicki Miller 1984 Pontiac/4500	25.00	50.00
24 Jeff Gordon DuPont Flames/38,004	100.00	200.00
24 Jeff Gordon DuPont Flames Bank/1800	60.00	100.00
24 Jeff Gordon DuPont Flames Clear/6996	50.00	100.00
24 Jeff Gordon DuPont Flames Mac Tools Promo/3500	75.00	150.00
24 Jeff Gordon DuPont Flames Brickyard Win/3504	40.00	80.00
24 Jeff Gordon Gordon Foundation/36,528	20.00	50.00
24 Jeff Gordon DuPont Bugs Bunny/64,800	50.00	100.00
24 Jeff Gordon DuPont Bugs Bunny Bank/3300	50.00	100.00
24 Jeff Gordon DuPont Bugs Bunny Clear/6792	30.00	60.00
24 Jeff Gordon Pepsi/13,032	50.00	100.00
24 Jeff Gordon Pepsi Bank/1644	50.00	100.00
24 Jeff Gordon Pepsi Clear/3000	60.00	120.00
25 Jerry Nadeau UAW/3000	25.00	60.00
25 Jerry Nadeau UAW Bank/504	25.00	60.00
26 Jimmy Spencer K-Mart/2856	20.00	50.00
26 Jimmy Spencer K-Mart Bank	25.00	50.00
27 Jamie McMurray Williams Promo in window box	15.00	40.00
28 Alan Kulwicki Hardee's 1984 Pontiac/4752	25.00	50.00
28 Ricky Rudd Havoline/7308	30.00	80.00
28 Ricky Rudd Havoline Bank/1008	30.00	80.00
28 Ricky Rudd Havoline Bud Shoot Out	30.00	80.00
28 Ricky Rudd Havoline Bud Shoot Out Bank	30.00	80.00
28 Ricky Rudd Havoline Flag/9000	30.00	80.00
28 Ricky Rudd Havoline Need for Speed/10,296	30.00	60.00
28 Ricky Rudd Havoline Need for Speed Bank/1308	30.00	60.00
29 Kevin Harvick Goodwrench/102,432	75.00	150.00
29 Kevin Harvick Goodwrench Clear/8292	50.00	100.00
29 Kevin Harvick Goodwrench White Gold Promo/5000	50.00	100.00
29 Kevin Harvick Goodwrench Rookie of the Year/37,812	20.00	50.00
29 Kevin Harvick Goodwrench Van Camp's box Promo	40.00	80.00
29 Kevin Harvick Goodwrench Make-a-Wish/6816	40.00	80.00
29 Kevin Harvick Goodwrench AOL/46,500	30.00	80.00
29 Kevin Harvick Goodwrench AOL Bank/2004	30.00	60.00
29 Kevin Harvick Goodwrench AOL Col.Chrome	30.00	80.00
29 Kevin Harvick Goodwrench Oreo Show car/56,196	30.00	80.00
29 Kevin Harvick Goodwrench Taz/92,748	40.00	100.00
29 Kevin Harvick Goodwrench Taz Clear/7164	50.00	120.00
30 Jeff Green AOL Bank/504	25.00	50.00
30 Jeff Green AOL Daffy Duck/8496	30.00	80.00
30 Jeff Green AOL Daffy Duck Bank/1008	25.00	50.00
31 Mike Skinner Lowe's/4008	20.00	50.00
31 Mike Skinner Lowe's Bank	25.00	50.00
31 Mike Skinner Lowe's Yosemite Sam/4008	30.00	60.00
31 Mike Skinner Lowe's Yosemite Sam Bank	25.00	50.00
36 Hank Parker Jr. GNC Live Well/2280	20.00	50.00
36 Hank Parker Jr. GNC Live Well Bank	20.00	50.00
36 Hank Parker Jr. GNC Live Well Pearl/816	25.00	50.00
36 Ken Schrader M&M's	30.00	60.00
36 Ken Schrader M&M's Bank	30.00	60.00
36 Ken Schrader M&M's Halloween/9348	30.00	60.00
36 Ken Schrader M&M's July 4th/7788	30.00	60.00
36 Ken Schrader Pedigree/3252	30.00	60.00
36 Ken Schrader Pedigree Bank	30.00	60.00
36 Ken Schrader Snickers/5904	30.00	60.00
36 Ken Schrader Snickers Bank	30.00	60.00
40 Sterling Marlin Coors Light/12,852	30.00	80.00
40 Sterling Marlin Coors Light Kiss/27,108	30.00	80.00
40 Sterling Marlin Coors Light Kiss Bank/504	30.00	60.00
40 Sterling Marlin Proud to be American/16,000	30.00	80.00
55 Bobby Hamilton Square D Marvin the Martian/8196	30.00	60.00
55 Bobby Hamilton Square D Marvin the Martian Bank	25.00	50.00
66 Todd Bodine Big K	25.00	50.00
66 Todd Bodine Big K Blue Light/2964	20.00	50.00
66 Rusty Wallace Child's 1981 Camaro Red	25.00	50.00
72 Benny Parsons Kings Row 1976 Chevy Malibu/3000	60.00	120.00
88 Dale Jarrett UPS/28,524	40.00	80.00
88 Dale Jarrett UPS Bank	40.00	100.00
88 Dale Jarrett UPS Chrome/1020	50.00	100.00
88 Dale Jarrett UPS Clear/6792	30.00	80.00
88 Dale Jarrett UPS Employee Promo	40.00	100.00
88 Dale Jarrett UPS Flag/12,000	40.00	75.00
88 Dale Jarrett UPS Split Clear/3500	40.00	80.00
88 Dale Jarrett UPS Flames/48,780	40.00	100.00
88 Dale Jarrett UPS Flames Clear/7000	30.00	80.00
92 Jimmie Johnson Excedrin/2016	150.00	250.00
95 Davey Allison Miller 1986 Nova/5808	30.00	80.00
2001 DEI Pit Practice Car/2508	50.00	100.00
2001 DEI Pit Practice Car Snap-on Carolina Run	50.00	120.00
01 NDA/Brickyard 400 2001	25.00	50.00
02 Ryan Newman Alltel/2412	125.00	200.00
02 Ryan Newman Alltel Bank/600	75.00	125.00
NNO Monte Carlo 400 Looney Tunes/9504	50.00	100.00
NNO Monte Carlo 400 Looney Tunes Clear/5508	40.00	80.00
NNO Monte Carlo 400 Looney Tunes Color Chrome/504	100.00	175.00

2001 Action QVC For Race Fans Only 1:24

	EX	NM-MT
2 Kevin Harvick AC Delco Color Chrome/1000	75.00	150.00
2 Kevin Harvick AC Delco Gold/1000	100.00	175.00
2 Rusty Wallace Miller Lite Gold/1000	75.00	150.00
2 Rusty Wallace Miller Lite Harley Color Chrome/2508	60.00	120.00
2 Rusty Wallace Miller Lite Harley Gold/2000	90.00	150.00
2 Rusty Wallace Miller Lite Harley Platinum/624	100.00	200.00
3 Dale Earnhardt Goodwrench Gold/10,000	150.00	300.00
3 Dale Earnhardt Goodwrench Platinum/2508	200.00	400.00
3 Dale Earnhardt Goodwrench w/Sonic decal	125.00	250.00
3 Dale Earnhardt Goodwrench Oreo Gold/2000	150.00	300.00
3 Dale Earnhardt Goodwrench Oreo Platinum/624	200.00	400.00
8 Dale Earnhardt Jr. Bud Color Chrome/2508	100.00	200.00
8 Dale Earnhardt Jr. Bud Gold/2500	125.00	250.00
8 Dale Earnhardt Jr. Bud Platinum/624	150.00	300.00
8 Dale Earnhardt Jr. Bud MLB All-Star Gold/2000	135.00	225.00
8 Dale Earnhardt Jr. Bud MLB All-Star Platinum/624	150.00	300.00
9 Bill Elliott Dodge Muhammad Ali Gold/1000	70.00	135.00
18 Bobby Labonte Interstate Batteries Coke Bear Col.Chrome/1000	50.00	120.00
18 Bobby Labonte Interstate Batteries Coke Bear Gold/1000	60.00	120.00
18 Bobby Labonte Interstate Batteries Coke Bear Platinum/624	75.00	150.00
18 Bobby Labonte Interstate Batteries Jurassic Park 3 Gold/1000	50.00	120.00
18 Bobby Labonte Interstate Batteries Jurassic Park 3 Platinum/624	75.00	150.00
20 Tony Stewart Home Depot Coke Bear Color Chrome/1008	75.00	150.00
20 Tony Stewart Home Depot Coke Bear Gold/1000	75.00	150.00
20 Tony Stewart Home Depot Coke Bear Platinum/624	125.00	200.00
20 Tony Stewart Home Depot Jurassic Park 3 Gold/1000	90.00	150.00
20 Tony Stewart Home Depot Jurassic Park 3 Platinum/624	100.00	200.00
24 Jeff Gordon DuPont Bugs Bunny Gold/2000	125.00	250.00
24 Jeff Gordon DuPont Bugs Bunny Platinum/624	100.00	200.00
24 Jeff Gordon DuPont Flames Color Chrome/2508	60.00	120.00
24 Jeff Gordon DuPont Flames Gold/2000	125.00	250.00
24 Jeff Gordon DuPont Flames Color Chrome HMS 100th Win/2508	60.00	120.00
24 Jeff Gordon DuPont Flames Platinum/624	125.00	225.00
24 Jeff Gordon Pepsi Color Chrome/2508	60.00	120.00
24 Jeff Gordon Pepsi Gold/2000	100.00	200.00
24 Jeff Gordon Pepsi Platinum/624	125.00	250.00
29 Kevin Harvick Goodwrench Gold/10,000	75.00	150.00
29 Kevin Harvick Goodwrench Platinum/624	100.00	200.00
29 Kevin Harvick Goodwrench AOL Gold/1000	60.00	120.00
29 Kevin Harvick Goodwrench AOL Platinum/624	75.00	150.00
29 Kevin Harvick Goodwrench Oreo Platinum/624	75.00	150.00
29 Kevin Harvick Goodwrench Taz Chrome/3504	60.00	120.00
29 Kevin Harvick Goodwrench Taz Gold	75.00	150.00
29 Kevin Harvick Goodwrench Taz Platinum/624	90.00	150.00
29 Kevin Harvick Goodwrench Oreo Platinum/624	125.00	200.00
88 Dale Jarrett UPS Gold/2000	70.00	120.00
88 Dale Jarrett UPS Platinum/624	100.00	175.00
88 Dale Jarrett UPS Flames Color Chrome/2508	50.00	120.00
88 Dale Jarrett UPS Flames Gold./2000	70.00	120.00
88 Dale Jarrett UPS Flames Platinum/624	100.00	175.00

2001 Action/RCCA Banks 1:

	EX	NM-
2 Kevin Harvick AC Delco/1200	60.00	12
3 Dale Earnhardt Goodwrench/3996	125.00	25
3 Dale Earnhardt Goodwrench Oreo/4008	125.00	25
3 Dale Earnhardt Goodwrench 1988 Monte Carlo/2005	150.00	25
5 Terry Labonte Kellogg's Wile E. and Road Runner/720	40.00	80
8 Dale Earnhardt Goodwrench 1987 Nova Bank/2304	125.00	225
8 Dale Earnhardt Jr. Bud/1500	75.00	15
8 Dale Earnhardt Jr. Bud color chrome/3600	75.00	15
8 Dale Earnhardt Jr. Bud All-Star/5004	125.00	20
8 Dale Earnhardt Jr. Bud All-Star Raced/3504	90.00	15
9 Bill Elliott Dodge/2508	25.00	6
9 Bill Elliott Dodge Muhammad Ali/1008	25.00	6
15 Michael Waltrip NAPA/900	40.00	10
18 Bobby Labonte Interstate Batteries/1500	75.00	15
19 Casey Atwood Dodge	50.00	12
20 Tony Stewart Home Depot/3600	25.00	6
24 Jeff Gordon DuPont Flames/3456	40.00	7
24 Jeff Gordon DuPont Bugs Bunny/5004	30.00	8
24 Jeff Gordon Pepsi	50.00	12
25 Jerry Nadeau UAW/720	15.00	4
28 Ricky Rudd Havoline/1200	40.00	10
29 Kevin Harvick Goodwrench/3000	30.00	8
29 Kevin Harvick Goodwrench AOL/2504	25.00	6
29 Kevin Harvick Goodwrench Oreo Show car Bank/2004	40.00	10
29 Kevin Harvick Goodwrench Taz/3200	50.00	12
36 Ken Schrader M&M's Halloween/720	40.00	8
36 Ken Schrader Snickers	30.00	8
40 Sterling Marlin Coors Light/600	30.00	8
55 Bobby Hamilton Square D Marvin the Martian/600	25.00	5
66 Todd Bodine Big K Blue Light/360	15.00	4
88 Dale Jarrett UPS/2700	40.00	10
88 Dale Jarrett UPS Flames/1836	35.00	6
01 NDA/Brickyard 400/804	20.00	4
02 Ryan Newman Alltel/492	100.00	15

2001 Action/RCCA Elite 1:

	EX	NM-
1 Steve Park Pennzoil	150.00	25
1 Steve Park Pennzoil Sylvester&Tweety/1800	60.00	12
2 Kevin Harvick AC Delco/804	100.00	20
2 Kevin Harvick AC Delco Color Chrome/1200	100.00	17
2 Rusty Wallace Miller Lite/1008	100.00	20
2 Rusty Wallace Miller Lite Metal/3504	50.00	10
2 Rusty Wallace Miller Lite Harley/3996	100.00	17
3 Dale Earnhardt Goodwrench/2496	250.00	50
3 Dale Earnhardt Goodwrench Split Clear/3504	150.00	30
3 Dale Earnhardt Goodwr.Metal/7500	100.00	20
3 Dale Earnhardt Goodwrench Test/3504	175.00	30
3 Dale Earnhardt Goodwrench Oreo/5004	150.00	25
3 Dale Earnhardt Goodwrench 1988 Monte Carlo Aerocoupe/3205	250.00	40
5 Terry Labonte Kellogg's	50.00	12
5 Terry Labonte Kellogg's Wile E./Road Runner/1200	60.00	12
7 Dale Earnhardt Jr. Church Brothers 1997 Monte Carlo/1500	150.00	30
8 Dale Earnhardt Goodwrench 1987 Nova/2304	200.00	35

le Earnhardt Jr. 175.00 300.00
Bud/2004
le Earnhardt Jr. 150.00 250.00
Bud Color Chrome/2400
le Earnhardt Jr. 150.00 250.00
Bud Dover Win w/flag/2508
le Earnhardt Jr. 100.00 200.00
Bud Talladega
Win No Bull/2508
le Earnhardt Jr. 100.00 250.00
Bud Test/3504
le Earnhardt Jr. 175.00 300.00
Bud All-Star Game/5996
le Earnhardt Jr. 175.00 300.00
Bud All-Star
raced version/4008
ll Elliott 30.00 80.00
Dodge Spiderman/720
Johnny Benson 50.00 100.00
Valvoline James Dean/1008
eff Green 40.00 80.00
Nesquik/1008
arrell Waltrip 75.00 150.00
Budweiser 1985 Monte Carlo/720
Jeremy Mayfield 30.00 80.00
Mobil 1/720
Michael Waltrip 100.00 200.00
NAPA/1008
Michael Waltrip 75.00 135.00
NAPA Daytona Raced/2800
issued with tire swatch
obby Labonte 75.00 150.00
Interstate Batteries/1008
obby Labonte 50.00 100.00
Interstate Batteries Test/3504
obby Labonte 75.00 150.00
Interstate Batteries
Coke Bear/1008
obby Labonte 125.00 250.00
Interstate Batteries Cal Ripken Farwell/600
obby Labonte 50.00 100.00
Interstate Batteries
Jurassic Park 3/804
eff Purvis 50.00 100.00
MBNA/492
ony Stewart 125.00 200.00
Home Depot/2004
ony Stewart 75.00 125.00
Home Depot Test/3504
ony Stewart 90.00 150.00
Home Depot Coke Bear/1392
ony Stewart 100.00 175.00
Home Depot
Jurassic Park 3/1200
eff Gordon 150.00 300.00
DuPont Flames/3600
eff Gordon 125.00 225.00
DuPont Flames Metal/3504
eff Gordon 100.00 200.00
DuPont Flames Split Clear/5004
eff Gordon 100.00 200.00
DuPont Flames No Bull
Las Vegas Raced/3504
eff Gordon 150.00 300.00
DuPont Flames
Platinum HMS 100th Win/1800
eff Gordon 150.00 300.00
DuPont Test/2508
eff Gordon 100.00 175.00
DuPont Bugs Bunny/7500
eff Gordon 50.00 120.00
Gordon Foundation/3996
eff Gordon 150.00 300.00
Pepsi/1800
eff Gordon 75.00 150.00
Pepsi Color Chrome/3000
erry Nadeau 40.00 100.00
UAW/720
immy Spencer 25.00 60.00
K-Mart/720
icky Rudd 60.00 120.00
Havoline/804
icky Rudd 100.00 175.00
Havoline Bud Shoot Out/1200
icky Rudd 75.00 150.00
Havoline Need for Speed/720
evin Harvick 75.00 150.00
Goodwrench/4996
evin Harvick 50.00 100.00
Goodwrench Split Clear/5004
evin Harvick 75.00 150.00
Goodwrench
Make a Wish Foundation/2496
evin Harvick 60.00 120.00
Goodwrench Oreo Show car/4200
evin Harvick 60.00 120.00
Goodwrench Taz/5996
evin Harvick 60.00 120.00
Goodwrench AOL/4008
Jeff Green 50.00 100.00
AOL Daffy Duck/600
Mike Skinner 60.00 120.00
Lowe's Yosemite Sam/720
Ken Schrader 40.00 80.00
Snickers/1200
Ken Schrader 30.00 60.00
M&M's/804
en Schrader 50.00 100.00
M&M's Halloween/804
en Schrader 50.00 100.00
M&M's July 4th/1008
en Schrader 40.00 80.00
Pedigree/492
Sterling Marlin 90.00 150.00
Coors Light Kiss/1008
Bobby Hamilton 50.00 100.00
Square D
Marvin the Martian/600
Dale Jarrett 100.00 250.00
UPS/3204
ale Jarrett 60.00 120.00
UPS Chrome/2004
ale Jarrett 75.00 150.00
UPS Test/2508
ale Jarrett 70.00 120.00
UPS Flames/3000
immie Johnson 250.00 400.00
Excedrin/492
DEI Pit Practice Car/2796 125.00 250.00
rickyard 400/804 40.00 80.00
Looney Tunes/1800 125.00 200.00

2002 Action Performance 1:24

These "AP" or Action Performance cars were primarily distributed to mass retail and to trackside retailers. Unless noted below, each was packaged in a 2-sided clear window red and black box with a red "A" and white "P" AP logo on the sides.

	EX	NM-MT
1 Steve Park Pennzoil	15.00	30.00
3 Dale Earnhardt Goodwrench	25.00	40.00
8 Dale Earnhardt Jr. Dale Jr.	20.00	35.00
18 Bobby Labonte Interstate Batteries	15.00	30.00
20 Tony Stewart Home Depot	15.00	30.00
24 Jeff Gordon DuPont Flames	20.00	35.00
29 Kevin Harvick Goodwrench	20.00	35.00
40 Sterling Marlin Sterling	15.00	30.00
88 Dale Jarrett UPS	15.00	30.00
88 Dale Jarrett UPS Employee/5004	25.00	50.00

2002 Action Racing Collectables 1:24

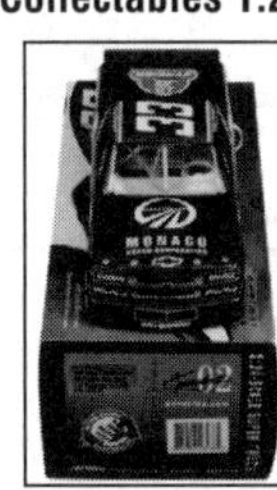

EX NM-MT
1 Dale Earnhardt 35.00 60.00
True Value 1999 IROC
1 Dale Earnhardt 35.00 60.00
True Value 2000 IROC Lt. Blue/39,960
1 Dale Earnhardt 35.00 60.00
True Value 2001 IROC Green/28,512
1 Jeff Gordon 35.00 60.00
Autolite 1989 T-bird/15,036
1 Jeff Gordon 35.00 60.00
Autolite 1989 T-bird Bank/1608
1 Kevin Harvick 25.00 50.00
True Value 2001 IROC/6996
1 Bobby Labonte 25.00 50.00
True Value '01 IROC/4668
1 Steve Park 20.00 50.00
Pennzoil/25,008
1 Steve Park 20.00 50.00
Pennzoil Bank/888
2 Dale Earnhardt 20.00 50.00
Wrangler 1979 Monte Carlo
Rookie of the Year car/68,016
2 Dale Earnhardt 20.00 50.00
Wrangler '79 MC Bank/4500
2 Dale Earnhardt 20.00 50.00
Coke 1980 Pontiac/64,836
2 Dale Earnhardt 20.00 50.00
Coke '80 Pontiac Bank/4044
2 Mark Martin 60.00 100.00
Amsoil 1980 ASA/3240
2 Mark Martin 30.00 60.00
Miller 1986 ASA/4656
2 Johnny Sauter 20.00 50.00
AC Delco/6000
2 Johnny Sauter 20.00 50.00
AC Delco Bank/504
2 Rusty Wallace 30.00 60.00
Miller Lite/21,024
2 Rusty Wallace 25.00 50.00
Miller Lite Bank/1200
2 Rusty Wallace 25.00 50.00
Miller Lite Elvis Bank/1800
2 Rusty Wallace 25.00 50.00
Miller Lite Elvis/23,696
2 Rusty Wallace 25.00 50.00
Miller Lite Elvis Clear/4884
2 Rusty Wallace 60.00 100.00
Miller Lite Harley Flames/18,072
2 Rusty Wallace 50.00 80.00
Miller Lite Harley
Flames Bank/672
2 Rusty Wallace 40.00 70.00
Miller Lite Flames/8592
2 Rusty Wallace 30.00 60.00
MGD 1991 Thunderbird/8940
2 Rusty Wallace 30.00 60.00
MGD 1995 Thunderbird
3 Dale Earnhardt Jr. 30.00 60.00
Nilla Wafers/91,512
3 Dale Earnhardt Jr. 30.00 60.00
Nilla Wafers Bank/2508
3 Dale Earnhardt Jr. 30.00 60.00
Nilla Wafers Clear/7008
3 Dale Earnhardt Jr. 30.00 60.00
Oreo/112,996
3 Dale Earnhardt Jr. 25.00 60.00
Oreo Bank/2508
3 Dale Earnhardt Jr. 30.00 60.00
Oreo Clear/7008
3 Dale Earnhardt Jr. 30.00 60.00
Oreo Snap-On
Black Window Car/21,012
3 Dale Earnhardt Jr. 30.00 60.00
Sun Drop 1994 Lumina/24,504
4 Mike Skinner 15.00 40.00
Kodak Max Yosemite Sam/9612
4 Mike Skinner 15.00 40.00
Kodak Max
Yosemite Sam Bank/612
5 Terry Labonte 25.00 60.00
Kellogg's/11,676
5 Terry Labonte 20.00 50.00
Cheez-It/6000
5 Terry Labonte 20.00 50.00
Kellogg's Bank/1008
5 Terry Labonte 20.00 50.00
Kellogg's Road Runner
and Wile E.Coyote/15,528
6 Mark Martin 30.00 60.00
Stroh's Light '89 T-bird/5004
7 Casey Atwood 20.00 50.00
Sirius/8652
7 Casey Atwood 20.00 50.00
Sirius Bank
7 Casey Atwood 20.00 50.00
Sirius Mac Tools/2172
7 Casey Atwood 20.00 50.00
Sirius Muppets/6552
7 Casey Atwood 20.00 50.00
Sirius Muppets Mac Tools/2172
7 Casey Atwood 20.00 50.00
Sirius Muppets Bank/504
8 Dale Earnhardt Jr. 50.00 100.00
Bud/70,068
8 Dale Earnhardt Jr. 40.00 100.00
Bud Bank/2508
8 Dale Earnhardt Jr. 75.00 150.00
Bud White Gold Promo/5004
8 Dale Earnhardt Jr. 60.00 100.00
Bud Clear/7008
8 Dale Earnhardt Jr. 20.00 50.00
Bud Champion
Spark Plug Promo
8 Dale Earnhardt Jr. 100.00 175.00
Bud Employee in acrylic case
8 Dale Earnhardt Jr. 35.00 70.00
Bud All-Star/103,152
8 Dale Earnhardt Jr. 45.00 80.00
Bud All-Star Bank/2652
8 Dale Earnhardt Jr. 25.00 60.00
Bud All-Star
Snap-On BW Car
8 Dale Earnhardt Jr. 35.00 60.00
Bud All-Star
Red Clear/5304
8 Dale Earnhardt Jr. 75.00 150.00
Bud All-Star
White Gold Promo/5004
8 Dale Earnhardt Jr. 40.00 80.00
Looney Tunes/79,992
8 Dale Earnhardt Jr. 35.00 70.00
Looney Tunes Bank/1980
9 Bill Elliott 30.00 60.00
Dodge/18,468
9 Bill Elliott 25.00 60.00
Dodge Clear/6792
9 Bill Elliott 30.00 60.00
Dodge Mac Tools/2172
9 Bill Elliott 20.00 50.00
Dodge Muppet/12,924
9 Bill Elliott 20.00 50.00
Dodge Muppet Bank/708
9 Bill Elliott 35.00 60.00
Dodge Viper/7008
10 Johnny Benson 20.00 50.00
Valvoline/6948
10 Johnny Benson 20.00 50.00
Valvoline Muppet/13,572
10 Johnny Benson 20.00 50.00
Valvoline Muppet Bank/1008
11 Dale Earnhardt Jr. 35.00 60.00
True Value 1999
IROC/33,876
11 Tony Stewart 35.00 60.00
True Value 2001 IROC/8456
12 Kerry Earnhardt 20.00 50.00
10-10-220/9624
12 Kerry Earnhardt 20.00 50.00
JaniKing Yosemite
Sam/10,368
12 Kerry Earnhardt 20.00 50.00
JaniKing Yosemite
Sam GM Dealers/444
12 Kerry Earnhardt 20.00 50.00
JaniKing Yosemite
Sam Bank/612
12 Kerry Earnhardt 20.00 50.00
Supercuts
12 Ryan Newman 35.00 70.00
Alltel/10,404
12 Ryan Newman 30.00 60.00
Mobil 1/11,292
15 Dale Earnhardt 20.00 50.00
Wrangler 1979 Pontiac
Ventura/58,716
15 Dale Earnhardt 20.00 50.00
Wrangler 1979 Pontiac
Ventura GM Dealers/3504
15 Dale Earnhardt 20.00 50.00
Wrangler 1979 Pontiac
Ventura Bank/2508
15 Michael Waltrip 25.00 50.00
NAPA/17,280
15 Michael Waltrip 25.00 50.00
NAPA Bank/1332
15 Michael Waltrip 15.00 40.00
NAPA Clear/4548
15 Michael Waltrip 25.00 50.00
NAPA Stars&Stripes/9650
15 Michael Waltrip 25.00 50.00
NAPA Stars&Stripes Bank/1008
17 Darrell Waltrip 25.00 50.00
Tide 1989 Monte Carlo/8340
17 Darrell Waltrip 30.00 60.00
Tide SuperTruck/4008
18 Bobby Labonte 75.00 125.00
3M 100th Anniversary
18 Bobby Labonte 30.00 60.00
Interstate Batteries/19,860
18 Bobby Labonte 30.00 60.00
Interstate Batteries Bank/1008
18 Bobby Labonte 20.00 50.00
Interstate Batteries Clear/5064
18 Bobby Labonte 30.00 60.00
Interstate Batteries Mac Tools/2172
18 Bobby Labonte 20.00 50.00
Interstate Batteries Muppet/17,076
18 Bobby Labonte 20.00 50.00
Interstate Batteries
Muppet Bank/960
18 Bobby Labonte 75.00 125.00
Let's Roll/11,158
18 Bobby Labonte 75.00 125.00
Let's Roll Bank/600
18 Bobby Labonte 75.00 125.00
Let's Roll Mac Tools/1798
18 Mike McLaughlin 20.00 50.00
MBNA/2004
19 Jeremy Mayfield 20.00 50.00
Dodge/13,344
19 Jeremy Mayfield 20.00 50.00
Dodge Bank/804
19 Jeremy Mayfield 20.00 50.00
Dodge Mac Tools/2172
19 Jeremy Mayfield 20.00 50.00
Dodge Muppet/12,612
19 Jeremy Mayfield 20.00 50.00
Dodge Muppet Bank/708
19 Jeremy Mayfield 20.00 50.00
Mountain Dew/11,508
19 Jeremy Mayfield 20.00 50.00
Mountain Dew Bank/804
19 Jeremy Mayfield 10.00 20.00
Mountain Dew Promo in can
20 Tony Stewart 90.00 150.00
Home Depot/26,508
20 Tony Stewart 60.00 100.00
Home Depot Bank/1624
20 Tony Stewart 40.00 75.00
Home Depot Clear/4008
20 Tony Stewart 90.00 150.00
Home Depot Mac Tools/2172
20 Tony Stewart 40.00 75.00
Home Depot 2002 Champion
Color Chrome/17,640
20 Tony Stewart 150.00 250.00
Home Depot
Maintenance Warehouse Promo/3504
20 Tony Stewart 50.00 90.00
Home Depot Peanuts
Black/22,928
20 Tony Stewart 40.00 75.00
Home Depot Peanuts
Black Bank/984
20 Tony Stewart 40.00 75.00
Home Depot Peanuts
Black Clear/2508
20 Tony Stewart 50.00 90.00
Home Depot Peanuts
Orange/20,866
20 Tony Stewart 40.00 75.00
Home Depot Peanuts
Orange Bank/1068
20 Tony Stewart 40.00 75.00
Home Depot Peanuts
Orange Clear/2508
20 Tony Stewart 50.00 90.00
Home Depot Peanuts
Orange Mac Tools/1860
21 Jeff Green 20.00 50.00
Jason Sauter
Rockwell Automation/2904
23 Davey Allison 30.00 60.00
Sims Bros. 1981 Camaro/3504
24 Jeff Gordon 25.00 50.00
DuPont 200th Anniversary/78,180
24 Jeff Gordon 25.00 50.00
DuPont 200th Anniversary Bank/3000
24 Jeff Gordon 25.00 50.00
DuPont 200th Anniversary Clear/7152
24 Jeff Gordon 30.00 60.00
DuPont Bugs Bunny/44,958
24 Jeff Gordon 30.00 50.00
DuPont Bugs Bunny
Bank/1644
24 Jeff Gordon 50.00 100.00
DuPont Flames/70,224
24 Jeff Gordon 30.00 60.00
DuPont Flames Bank/2508
24 Jeff Gordon 30.00 60.00
DuPont Flames Clear/7008
24 Jeff Gordon 35.00 60.00
Elmo/26,844
24 Jeff Gordon 30.00 60.00
Pepsi Daytona/37,836
24 Jeff Gordon 40.00 80.00
Pepsi Daytona Bank/1800
24 Jeff Gordon 30.00 60.00
Pepsi Talladega/19,020
24 Jeff Gordon 40.00 80.00
Pepsi Talladega Bank/1800
24 Jeff Gordon 60.00 100.00
Pepsi Talladega Color Chrome/2508
24 Jeff Gordon 50.00 100.00
Pepsi Talladega Color Chrome Bank/1008
25 Jerry Nadeau 20.00 50.00
UAW/4008
25 Jerry Nadeau 25.00 50.00
UAW Mac Tools/2172
25 Jerry Nadeau 20.00 50.00
UAW Bank/504
25 Joe Nemechek 20.00 50.00
UAW Speedy Gonzalez/9144
25 Joe Nemechek 15.00 40.00
UAW Speedy
Gonzalez Bank/600
28 Davey Allison 50.00 80.00
Havoline black&white
1987 Thunderbird/10,200
28 Davey Allison 35.00 70.00
Havoline 1990 Thunderbird/6936
28 Ricky Rudd 30.00 60.00
Havoline/17,436
28 Ricky Rudd 25.00 50.00
Havoline Bank/1500
28 Ricky Rudd 15.00 40.00
Havoline Clear/4512
28 Ricky Rudd 30.00 60.00
Havoline Iron Man/10,920
28 Ricky Rudd 30.00 60.00
Havoline Iron Man
Mac Tools/2172
28 Ricky Rudd 20.00 50.00
Havoline Muppet/15,744
28 Ricky Rudd 20.00 50.00
Havoline Muppet Bank/984
28 Cale Yarborough 35.00 60.00
Hardee's 1984 Monte
Carlo/4728
29 Kevin Harvick 20.00 50.00
Action ET/22,860
29 Kevin Harvick 25.00 50.00
Action ET Color Chrome Bank/1284
29 Kevin Harvick 175.00 300.00
Flag GM Dealers/3420
29 Kevin Harvick 20.00 50.00
Goodwrench/103,716
29 Kevin Harvick 20.00 50.00
Goodwrench Bank/3144
29 Kevin Harvick 20.00 50.00
Goodwrench Clear/4812
29 Kevin Harvick 20.00 50.00
Goodwrench GM Dealer/11,616
29 Kevin Harvick 20.00 50.00
Goodwrench ET/64,860
29 Kevin Harvick 20.00 50.00
Goodwrench ET
GM Dealers/8508
29 Kevin Harvick 20.00 50.00
Goodwrench ET Clear/6288
29 Kevin Harvick 20.00 50.00
Goodwrench ET
Color Chrome Bank/2700
29 Kevin Harvick 20.00 50.00
Goodwrench
Now Sell Tires/28,896
29 Kevin Harvick 20.00 50.00
Goodwrench Now Sell
Tires GM Dealers/2004
29 Kevin Harvick 20.00 50.00
Goodwrench Taz/21,684
29 Kevin Harvick 20.00 50.00
Goodwrench Taz Bank/1056
29 Kevin Harvick 20.00 50.00
Goodwrench Taz
GM Dealers/8508
29 Kevin Harvick 50.00 100.00
Goodwrench Taz
GM Dealers White Gold/2496
29 Kevin Harvick 300.00 450.00
Reese's Fastbreak/3504
29 Kevin Harvick 20.00 50.00
Sonic/21,768
29 Kevin Harvick 20.00 50.00
Sonic Bank/1008
29 Kevin Harvick 20.00 50.00
Sylvania/8016
29 Kevin Harvick 20.00 50.00
Sylvania Bank/504
29 Kevin Harvick 20.00 50.00
Sylvania GM Dealers/1008
29 Kevin Harvick 20.00 50.00
Snap-On/23,712
30 Jeff Green 15.00 40.00
AOL/9494
30 Jeff Green 25.00 50.00
AOL Bank/504
30 Jeff Green 15.00 40.00
AOL Daffy Duck/8796
30 Jeff Green 15.00 40.00
AOL Daffy Duck Bank/696
30 Jeff Green 20.00 50.00
AOL Scooby-Doo/9072
31 Robby Gordon 20.00 50.00
Cingular/7008
31 Robby Gordon 20.00 50.00
Cingular Bank/600
31 Robby Gordon 20.00 50.00
Cingular Pepe le Pew/9060
31 Robby Gordon 15.00 40.00
Cingular Pepe le Pew
Bank/1644
31 Mark Martin 30.00 60.00
Fat Boys BBQ
1987 Thunderbird/3444
33 Tony Stewart 35.00 60.00
Monaco SuperTruck/8652
36 Ken Schrader 25.00 50.00
M&M's/6744
36 Ken Schrader 25.00 60.00
M&M's Halloween/6684
36 Ken Schrader 25.00 60.00
M&M's Halloween Bank/600
36 Ken Schrader 20.00 50.00
M&M's July 4th/6936
40 Sterling Marlin 30.00 60.00
Coors Light/21,708
40 Sterling Marlin 30.00 60.00
Coors Original/15,804
40 Sterling Marlin 30.00 60.00
Coors Original Bank/804
41 Jimmy Spencer 20.00 50.00
Energizer/6168
41 Jimmy Spencer 20.00 50.00
Fujifilm/3480
41 Jimmy Spencer 20.00 50.00
Target/7764
41 Jimmy Spencer 20.00 50.00
Target Bank/900
41 Jimmy Spencer 20.00 50.00
Target Muppet/10,956
41 Jimmy Spencer 20.00 50.00
Target Muppet Bank/900
48 Jimmie Johnson 90.00 150.00
Lowe's/19,704
48 Jimmie Johnson 25.00 60.00
Lowe's Power of Pride/15,552
48 Jimmie Johnson 35.00 60.00
Lowe's Power of Pride
Bank
48 Jimmie Johnson 35.00 60.00
Lowe's Sylvester.&Tweety/25,212
48 Jimmie Johnson 35.00 60.00
Lowe's Sylvester
and Tweety Bank/1140
48 Darrell Waltrip 25.00 50.00
Crowell & Reed
1964 Chevelle/3840
48 Darrell Waltrip 25.00 50.00
Crowell & Reed
1964 Chevelle Bank/408
55 Bobby Hamilton 20.00 50.00

Square D Marvin/7128		
55 Bobby Hamilton Square D Marvin Bank/636	20.00	50.00
71 Dave Marcis Realtree Retirement/4008	40.00	75.00
88 Dale Jarrett UPS/42,052	25.00	60.00
88 Dale Jarrett UPS Clear/6180	20.00	50.00
88 Dale Jarrett UPS Color Chrome Bank/2508	30.00	60.00
88 Dale Jarrett UPS Muppet/28,140	20.00	50.00
88 Dale Jarrett UPS Muppet Bank/1200	20.00	50.00
91 Hank Parker Jr. USG Promo	30.00	60.00
97 Alan Kulwicki Prototype Engines '83 Pontiac Firebird/260	15.00	40.00
98 Kasey Kahne Channellock/3024	40.00	75.00
2002 DEI Pit Practice/2508	60.00	100.00
NNO Dale Earnhardt Legacy/58,212	35.00	60.00
NNO Looney Tunes Rematch/15,528	15.00	40.00
NNO Looney Tunes Rematch GM Dealers/504	15.00	40.00
NNO Muppet Show 25th Anniversary/18,204	15.00	40.00
NNO Muppet Show 25th Anniversary Clear/3384	15.00	40.00

2002 Action QVC For Race Fans Only 1:24

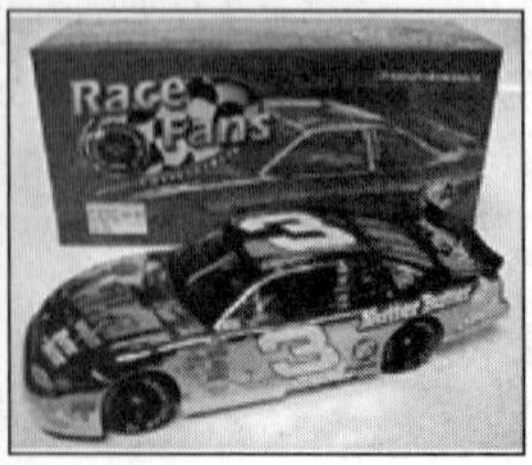

	EX	NM-MT
2 Rusty Wallace Miller Lite Harley Flames Color Chrome/1008	60.00	120.00
3 Dale Earnhardt Jr. Nilla Wafers Color Chrome/7500	60.00	100.00
3 Dale Earnhardt Jr. Nilla Wafers Gold/2508	125.00	200.00
3 Dale Earnhardt Jr. Nilla Wafers Platinum/624	125.00	250.00
3 Dale Earnhardt Jr. Oreo Color Chrome/2508	60.00	100.00
3 Dale Earnhardt Jr. Oreo Gold/2508	125.00	200.00
3 Dale Earnhardt Jr. Oreo Platinum/624	125.00	250.00
8 Dale Earnhardt Jr. Bud Color Chrome/2508	60.00	120.00
8 Dale Earnhardt Jr. Bud Gold/2508	100.00	175.00
8 Dale Earnhardt Jr. Bud Platinum/624	125.00	225.00
8 Dale Earnhardt Jr. Bud All-Star Gold/2508	75.00	150.00
8 Dale Earnhardt Jr. Bud All-Star Platinum/624	125.00	225.00
8 Dale Earnhardt Jr. Looney Tunes Color Chrome/5004	60.00	100.00
8 Dale Earnhardt Jr. Looney Tunes Gold/2508	100.00	175.00
8 Dale Earnhardt Jr. Looney Tunes Platinum/624	125.00	225.00
12 Ryan Newman Alltel ROY Gold/1008	100.00	200.00
12 Ryan Newman Alltel ROY Platinum/624	135.00	225.00
20 Tony Stewart Home Depot Color Chrome/2508	90.00	150.00
20 Tony Stewart Home Depot Peanuts Black Color Chrome/2508	75.00	150.00
20 Tony Stewart Home Depot Peanuts Black Platinum/624	150.00	250.00
20 Tony Stewart Home Depot Peanuts Orange Color Chrome/2508	75.00	150.00
20 Tony Stewart Home Depot Peanuts Orange Platinum/624	150.00	250.00
24 Jeff Gordon DuPont 200th Ann. Gold/2508	100.00	175.00
24 Jeff Gordon DuPont 200th Anniversary Platinum/624	125.00	200.00
24 Jeff Gordon DuPont Bugs Color Chrome/5004	60.00	100.00
24 Jeff Gordon DuPont Bugs Gold/2508	75.00	150.00
24 Jeff Gordon DuPont Bugs Platinum/624	125.00	200.00
24 Jeff Gordon DuPont Flames Color Chrome/22,424	50.00	80.00
24 Jeff Gordon DuPont Flames Gold/2508	100.00	175.00
24 Jeff Gordon DuPont Flames Platinum/624	125.00	225.00
24 Jeff Gordon Pepsi Daytona Color Chrome/7500	60.00	100.00
24 Jeff Gordon Pepsi Daytona Gold/2508	90.00	150.00
24 Jeff Gordon Pepsi Daytona Platinum/624	125.00	200.00
24 Jeff Gordon Pepsi Talladega Color Chrome/2508	60.00	120.00
24 Jeff Gordon Pepsi Talladega Gold/2508	70.00	135.00
24 Jeff Gordon Pepsi Talladega Platinum/624	125.00	200.00
29 Kevin Harvick Goodwrench Gold/2508	75.00	150.00
29 Kevin Harvick Goodwrench Platinum/624	125.00	200.00
29 Kevin Harvick Goodwrench ET Gold/2508	75.00	150.00
29 Kevin Harvick Goodwrench ET Chrome/3504	40.00	100.00
29 Kevin Harvick Goodwrench ET Platinum/624	75.00	150.00
29 Kevin Harvick Goodwrench Taz Color Chome/2508	40.00	80.00
88 Dale Jarrett UPS Color Chrome/1000	40.00	100.00
88 Dale Jarrett UPS Muppets Color Chrome/2508	70.00	120.00

2002 Action/RCCA 1:24

	EX	NM-MT
1 Jeff Gordon Autolite 1989 Thunderbird Bank/1800	35.00	60.00
1 Steve Park Pennzoil Bank/720	30.00	60.00
2 Dale Earnhardt Coke '80 Pontiac Bank/5004	30.00	60.00
2 Johnny Sauter AC Delco Bank/600	30.00	60.00
2 Rusty Wallace MGD 1995 Thunderbird Bank/600	35.00	60.00
2 Rusty Wallace Miller Lite Color Chrome Bank/1008	30.00	60.00
2 Rusty Wallace Miller Lite Split Clear/2508	35.00	60.00
2 Rusty Wallace Miller Lite Elvis Bank/1200	30.00	60.00
2 Rusty Wallace Miller Lite Harley Flames Bank/1008	40.00	80.00
2K2 Childress Racing Pit Practice Bank/1008	35.00	70.00
3 Dale Earnhardt Goodwrench Bank '90 Lumina/4008	35.00	60.00
3 Dale Earnhardt Jr. Nilla Wafers Bank/5004	35.00	60.00
3 Dale Earnhardt Jr. Nilla Wafers Split Clear/3000	35.00	60.00
3 Dale Earnhardt Jr. Oreo Bank/5004	40.00	70.00
3 Dale Earnhardt Jr. Oreo Split Clear/3000	40.00	75.00
4 Mike Skinner Kodak Max Yosemite Sam Bank/600	25.00	60.00
5 Terry Labonte Cheez-It Bank/720	30.00	60.00
5 Terry Labonte Kellogg's Road Runner & Wile E.Coyote Bank/600	35.00	60.00
7 Casey Atwood Sirius Bank/408	25.00	50.00
7 Casey Atwood Sirius Muppet Bank/408	25.00	50.00
8 Dale Earnhardt Docs '64 Chevelle Bank/3504	30.00	60.00
8 Dale Earnhardt Jr. Bud Bank/3504	40.00	75.00
8 Dale Earnhardt Jr. Bud Split Clear/4500	40.00	80.00
8 Dale Earnhardt Jr. Bud Color Chrome Bank/3600	40.00	75.00
8 Dale Earnhardt Jr. Bud All-Star Bank/4800	40.00	75.00
8 Dale Earnhardt Jr. Bud All-Star Split Clear/2508	40.00	75.00
8 Dale Earnhardt Jr. Bud Talladega April 2002 Win Raced/1008	40.00	75.00
8 Dale Earnhardt Jr. Looney Tunes Bank/4008	40.00	75.00
8 Dale Earnhardt Jr. Looney Tunes Split Clear/2508	40.00	75.00
9 Bill Elliott Dodge Bank/600	30.00	60.00
9 Bill Elliott Dodge Muppet Bank/720	30.00	60.00
9 Bill Elliott Dodge Viper Bank/600	30.00	60.00
10 Johnny Benson Valvoline Bank/408	30.00	60.00
12 Kerry Earnhardt 10-10-220 Bank/1008	25.00	50.00
12 Kerry Earnhardt JaniKing Yosemite Sam Bank/720	25.00	50.00
12 Kerry Earnhardt Supercuts Bank/1008	30.00	60.00
12 Ryan Newman Alltel Bank/1008	45.00	80.00
12 Ryan Newman Alltel Rookie of the Year Color Chrome/10,248	40.00	75.00
12 Ryan Newman Mobil 1 Bank/804	45.00	80.00
15 Dale Earnhardt Wrangler 1979 Pontiac Ventura Bank/3000	40.00	70.00
15 Michael Waltrip NAPA Bank/600	30.00	60.00
15 Michael Waltrip NAPA Stars and Stripes Bank/504	30.00	60.00
17 Darrell Waltrip Tide SuperTruck/504	45.00	80.00
18 Bobby Labonte Interstate Batteries Bank/804	30.00	60.00
18 Bobby Labonte Interstate Batteries Muppet Bank/720	30.00	60.00
18 Bobby Labonte Let's Roll Bank/600	60.00	120.00
19 Jeremy Mayfield Dodge Clear/3816	25.00	60.00
19 Jeremy Mayfield Dodge Muppet Bank/600	30.00	60.00
19 Jeremy Mayfield Mountain Dew Bank/492	30.00	60.00
20 Tony Stewart Home Depot Bank/720	75.00	125.00
20 Tony Stewart Home Depot Split Clear/2508	40.00	75.00
20 Tony Stewart Home Depot 2002 Champion Color Chrome Bank/1008	40.00	70.00
20 Tony Stewart Home Depot Peanuts Black Bank/1008	45.00	80.00
20 Tony Stewart Home Depot Peanuts Black Split Clear/504	40.00	75.00
20 Tony Stewart Home Depot Peanuts Orange Bank/1008	45.00	80.00
20 Tony Stewart Home Depot Peanuts Orange Split Clear/504	40.00	80.00
24 Jeff Gordon DuPont 200th Anniversary Bank/4008	35.00	70.00
24 Jeff Gordon DuPont 200th Anniversary Split Clear/2508	35.00	60.00
24 Jeff Gordon DuPont 200th Anniversary Clear/7152	30.00	60.00
24 Jeff Gordon DuPont Bugs Bunny Bank/4008	40.00	75.00
24 Jeff Gordon DuPont Flames Bank/2800	40.00	70.00
24 Jeff Gordon Elmo Bank/2004	30.00	60.00
24 Jeff Gordon Pepsi Daytona Bank/3012	40.00	70.00
24 Jeff Gordon Pepsi Talladega Split Clear/2508	35.00	60.00
24 Jeff Gordon Pepsi Talladega Color Chrome Bank/1800	30.00	60.00
28 Davey Allison Havoline 1990 Thunderbird Bank/1008	30.00	60.00
28 Ricky Rudd Havoline Bank/804	30.00	60.00
28 Ricky Rudd Havoline Iron Man Bank/720	30.00	60.00
28 Cale Yarborough Hardee's 1984 Monte Carlo Bank/504	30.00	60.00
29 Kevin Harvick Action ET Bank/1200	20.00	50.00
29 Kevin Harvick Goodwrench Bank/5004	20.00	50.00
29 Kevin Harvick Goodwrench Split Clear/2508	20.00	50.00
29 Kevin Harvick Goodwrench ET Bank/2004	20.00	50.00
29 Kevin Harvick Goodwrench Now Sell Tires Bank/1500	20.00	50.00
29 Kevin Harvick Sonic Bank/1008	20.00	50.00
29 Kevin Harvick Sylvania Bank/1008	20.00	50.00
30 Jeff Green AOL Bank/492	25.00	50.00
30 Jeff Green AOL Daffy Duck Bank/600	30.00	60.00
30 Jeff Green AOL Scooby-Doo Bank/720	25.00	50.00
31 Robby Gordon Cingular Bank/720	30.00	60.00
31 Robby Gordon Cingular Pepe le Pew Bank/600	30.00	60.00
31 Mark Martin Fat Boys BBQ 1987 Thunderbird Bank/600	30.00	50.00
36 Ken Schrader M&M's Halloween Bank/600	30.00	60.00
36 Ken Schrader M&M's July 4th Bank/504	30.00	60.00
40 Sterling Marlin Coors Light Bank/804	30.00	60.00
40 Sterling Marlin Coors Original Bank/900	30.00	60.00
41 Jimmy Spencer Energizer Bank/408	30.00	60.00
41 Jimmy Spencer Target Bank/600	30.00	60.00
41 Jimmy Spencer Target Muppet Bank/600	25.00	50.00
48 Jimmie Johnson Lowe's Bank/600	75.00	125.00
48 Jimmie Johnson Lowe's Power of Pride Bank/900	35.00	60.00
48 Jimmie Johnson Lowe's Sylv.&Tweety Bank/1500	35.00	60.00
48 Darrell Waltrip Crowell&Reed 1964 Chevelle Bank/720	30.00	60.00
55 Bobby Hamilton Square D Marvin the Martian Bank/600	30.00	60.00
88 Dale Jarrett UPS Bank/2004	30.00	60.00
88 Dale Jarrett UPS Muppet Bank/1500	30.00	60.00
98 Kasey Kahne Channellock Bank/408	30.00	60.00
NNO Dale Earnhardt Legacy Bank/2004	40.00	70.00
NNO Looney Tunes Rematch Bank/804	30.00	60.00

2002 Action/RCCA Elite 1:24

	EX	NM-MT
1 Steve Park Pennzoil/600	60.00	110.00
2 Dale Earnhardt Coke '80 Pontiac/5004	50.00	100.00
2 Rusty Wallace MGD 1995 Thunderbird/900	75.00	135.00
2 Rusty Wallace Miller Lite Color Chrome/1608	60.00	120.00
2 Rusty Wallace Miller Lite Elvis/2004	60.00	120.00
2 Rusty Wallace Miller Lite Harley Flames/1800	100.00	200.00
2 Rusty Wallace Miller Lite Test Flames/1488-A	60.00	120.00
2 Rusty Wallace Miller Lite Flames/1200	75.00	135.00
2K2 Childress Racing Pit Practice/1200	50.00	100.00
3 Dale Earnhardt Goodwrench Plus No Bull 76th Win/4500	100.00	175.00
3 Dale Earnhardt Jr. Nilla Wafers/6504	75.00	150.00
3 Dale Earnhardt Jr. Oreo/8988	75.00	150.00
3 Dale Earnhardt Jr. Oreo Raced Version/2004	70.00	135.00
3 Dale Earnhardt Jr. Oreo Test Gray/3504	75.00	135.00
4 Mike Skinner Kodak Max Yosemite Sam/600	60.00	100.00
5 Terry Labonte Cheez-It/540-A	50.00	100.00
5 Terry Labonte Kellogg's/600	60.00	100.00
5 Terry Labonte Kellogg's Road Runner & Wile E.Coyote/600	50.00	100.00
7 Casey Atwood Sirius/408	40.00	80.00
7 Casey Atwood Sirius Muppet/408	40.00	80.00
8 Dale Earnhardt Docs '64 Chevelle/3504	75.00	150.00
8 Dale Earnhardt Jr. Bud/1200	200.00	350.00
8 Dale Earnhardt Jr. Bud Color Chrome/4200	150.00	250.00
8 Dale Earnhardt Jr. Bud Talladega April 2002 Win Raced/1500	175.00	300.00
8 Dale Earnhardt Jr. Bud Test Red/5004	70.00	135.00
8 Dale Earnhardt Jr. Bud All-Star/6996	80.00	135.00
8 Dale Earnhardt Jr. Looney Tunes/6000	80.00	135.00
8 Dale Earnhardt Jr. Looney Tunes Raced Version Richmond/2004	70.00	120.00
9 Bill Elliott Dodge/600	70.00	120.00
9 Bill Elliott Dodge Muppet/804	70.00	120.00
9 Bill Elliott Dodge Raced Version Brickyard/600	70.00	120.00
9 Bill Elliott Dodge Viper/600	80.00	135.00
10 Johnny Benson Valvoline/600	60.00	100.00
10 Johnny Benson Valvoline Muppet/408	50.00	100.00
12 Kerry Earnhardt 10-10-220/1008	40.00	80.00
12 Kerry Earnhardt JaniKing Yosemite Sam/1008	40.00	80.00
12 Kerry Earnhardt Supercuts/1008	40.00	80.00
12 Ryan Newman Alltel/1392	100.00	200.00
12 Ryan Newman Alltel Rookie of the Year Color Chrome/1140	75.00	150.00
12 Ryan Newman Mobil 1/1008	75.00	150.00
15 Dale Earnhardt Wrangler 1979 Pontiac Ventura/4008	75.00	125.00
15 Michael Waltrip NAPA/600	70.00	110.00
15 Michael Waltrip NAPA Stars and Stripes/540A	70.00	120.00
18 Bobby Labonte Interstate Batteries/1008	70.00	110.00
18 Bobby Labonte Interstate Batteries Muppet/960	70.00	110.00
18 Bobby Labonte Let's Roll/900	125.00	250.00
19 Jeremy Mayfield Dodge/804	50.00	100.00
19 Jeremy Mayfield Dodge Muppet/600	50.00	100.00
19 Jeremy Mayfield Mountain Dew/600	50.00	100.00
20 Tony Stewart Home Depot/1404	150.00	300.00
20 Tony Stewart Home Depot 2002 Champion Color Chrome/2004	75.00	135.00
20 Tony Stewart Home Depot Metal/1800	100.00	175.
20 Tony Stewart Home Depot Peanuts Black/1500	90.00	150.
20 Tony Stewart Home Depot Peanuts Orange/1500	75.00	150.
24 Jeff Gordon DuPont 200th Anniversary/5004	60.00	110.
24 Jeff Gordon DuPont Flames/3204	100.00	175.
24 Jeff Gordon DuPont Test black/4500	60.00	110.
24 Jeff Gordon DuPont Bugs Bunny/6000	70.00	120.
24 Jeff Gordon Elmo/3600	70.00	120.
24 Jeff Gordon Pepsi Daytona/4500	80.00	135.
24 Jeff Gordon Pepsi Talladega/2504	80.00	135.
25 Joe Nemechek UAW Speedy Gonzalez/600	50.00	100.
28 Ricky Rudd Havoline/1008	50.00	100.
28 Ricky Rudd Havoline Iron Man/804	50.00	100.
28 Ricky Rudd Havoline Muppet/804	50.00	100.
29 Kevin Harvick Action ET/2004	40.00	80.
29 Kevin Harvick Goodwrench/7500	40.00	80.
29 Kevin Harvick Goodwrench ET/4212	40.00	80.
29 Kevin Harvick Goodwrench Now Sell Tires/3000	40.00	80.
29 Kevin Harvick Goodwrench Test Gray/3000	40.00	80.
29 Kevin Harvick Goodwrench Taz/1800	40.00	80.
29 Kevin Harvick Sonic/1008	40.00	80.
29 Kevin Harvick Sylvania/1500	40.00	80.
30 Jeff Green AOL/600	40.00	80.
30 Jeff Green AOL Daffy Duck/600	50.00	100.
30 Jeff Green AOL Scooby-Doo/720	40.00	80.
31 Robby Gordon Cingular/720	60.00	100.
31 Robby Gordon Cingular Pepe le Pew/600	60.00	100.
31 Mark Martin Fat Boys BBQ 1987 Thunderbird/600	70.00	110.
36 Ken Schrader M&M's Halloween/600	70.00	110.
36 Ken Schrader M&M's July 4th/1008	70.00	110.
40 Sterling Marlin Coors Light/1008	80.00	120.
40 Sterling Marlin Coors Original/1200	70.00	120.
40 Jamie McMurray Coors Light 1st Win raced version/600	50.00	100.
41 Jimmy Spencer Energizer/408	40.00	80.
41 Jimmy Spencer Target/600	50.00	100.
41 Jimmy Spencer Target Muppet/600	40.00	80.
48 Jimmie Johnson Lowe's/900	250.00	350.
48 Jimmie Johnson Lowe's California Raced/1008	150.00	250.
48 Jimmie Johnson Lowe's Power of Pride/1200	75.00	150.
48 Jimmie Johnson Lowe's Sylv.&Tweety/2220	75.00	150.
55 Bobby Hamilton Square D Marvin/600	50.00	100.
88 Dale Jarrett UPS/2800	50.00	100.
88 Dale Jarrett UPS Muppet/2004	50.00	100.
88 Dale Jarrett UPS Metal/1500	60.00	100.
98 Kasey Kahne Channellock/408	75.00	150.
2002 DEI Racing Pit Practice/2002	70.00	120.
02 Action Performance Gold/100	125.00	250.
NNO Dale Earnhardt Legacy/3000	125.00	200.
NNO Looney Tunes Rematch/1200	30.00	80.
NNO Muppet Show 25th Anniversary/600-A	30.00	80.

2003 Action Performance 1:24

	EX	NM-M
2 Rusty Wallace Rusty	15.00	25.
3 Dale Earnhardt Goodwrench Forever the Man window box	15.00	30.
8 Dale Earnhardt Jr. Dale Jr.	15.00	25.
8 Dale Earnhardt Jr. JR	15.00	25.
15 Michael Waltrip NAPA Daytona Win Promo	18.00	30.
15 Michael Waltrip NAPA Nilla Wafers Promo	12.50	25.
15 Michael Waltrip	10.00	25.

NAPA Stars&Stripes Promo
Bobby Labonte 12.50 25.00
Interstate Batteries
Tony Stewart 15.00 25.00
Home Depot
Jeff Gordon 15.00 25.00
DuPont Flames
Kevin Harvick 12.50 25.00
Goodwrench
Dale Jarrett 15.00 25.00
UPS

2003 Action Racing Collectables 1:24

EX NM-MT
Donnie Allison 50.00 100.00
Hawaiian Tropic 1977 Oldsmobile/3228
Jeff Green 20.00 50.00
Pennzoil Synthetic/4476
Mark Martin 30.00 60.00
True Value 1998 IROC/5976
Jamie McMurray 20.00 50.00
Yellow Freight/4104
Steve Park 35.00 60.00
Pennzoil/6300
Steve Park 35.00 60.00
Pennzoil GM Dealers/504
Kurt Busch 35.00 60.00
True Value IROC Lt.Blue/3540
Kurt Busch 40.00 75.00
True Value IROC
Light Blue AU/5004
Ron Hornaday 20.00 50.00
AC Delco/4152
Ron Hornaday 15.00 40.00
AC Delco
Black Window Bank/312
Ron Hornaday 20.00 50.00
AC Delco Franky Perez/2076
Ron Hornaday 20.00 50.00
AC Delco Franky Perez
GM Dealers/288
Jason Leffler 30.00 60.00
ASE Carquest SuperTruck
Promo in window box
Jason Leffler 20.00 50.00
Hulk SuperTruck/15,076
Mark Martin 35.00 60.00
SAI Roofing
1987 Thunderbird/3660
Rusty Wallace 50.00 80.00
Miller Lite/18,012
Rusty Wallace 40.00 70.00
Miller Lite
Black Window Bank/708
Rusty Wallace 60.00 100.00
Miller Lite Victory Lap/7476
Rusty Wallace 60.00 100.00
Miller Lite Victory Lap
Clear Window Bank/420
Rusty Wallace 40.00 75.00
Miller Lite 600th/9936
Rusty Wallace 40.00 70.00
Miller Lite 600th
Clear Window Bank/504
Rusty Wallace 40.00 70.00
Miller Time Live
Goo Goo Dolls/12,688
Rusty Wallace 30.00 60.00
Miller Time Live
Goo Goo Dolls
Clear Window Bank/856
Dale Earnhardt 25.00 50.00
Foundation/53,796
Dale Earnhardt 25.00 50.00
Foundation
Clear Window Bank/2004
Dale Earnhardt 40.00 70.00
Goodwrench
1990 Lumina/35,664
Dale Earnhardt 40.00 70.00
Goodwrench Silver Select
1995 Monte Carlo
Clear Window Bank/33,333
Dale Earnhardt 45.00 75.00
Goodwrench No Bull
2000 Monte Carlo/25,244
Dale Earnhardt 30.00 60.00
Goodwrench No Bull
2000 Monte Carlo
Clear Window Bank/1596
Dale Earnhardt 45.00 75.00
Goodwrench No Bull
2000 MC GM Dealers/3504
Dale Earnhardt 45.00 75.00
Goodwrench 2001 Monte Carlo
Clear Window Bank/15,360
Dale Earnhardt 35.00 60.00
Goodwrench
2001 Monte Carlo Clear/6108
Dale Earnhardt 35.00 60.00
Goodwrench 2001 Monte Carlo
Clear GM Dealers/300
Dale Earnhardt 40.00 70.00
Goodwrench Bass
Pro Bank/16,944
Dale Earnhardt 40.00 70.00
Victory Lap/29,628
Dale Earnhardt 40.00 70.00
Victory Lap
CW Bank/1260
Dale Earnhardt 40.00 70.00
Victory Lap
GM Dealers/3300
3 Dale Earnhardt 50.00 80.00
Victory Lap
Color Chrome/6012
3 Dale Earnhardt 50.00 80.00
Victory Lap
Color Chrome GM Dealers/744
3 Dale Earnhardt 45.00 75.00
Wheaties 1997 Monte Carlo
Clear Window Bank/9900
3 Dale Earnhardt Jr. 40.00 70.00
Goodwrench 1997 Monte Carlo/24,396
3 Dale Earnhardt Jr. 40.00 75.00
Goodwrench 1997 Monte Carlo
GM Dealers/1416
3 Dale Earnhardt Jr. 40.00 70.00
Prime Sirloin '95 Monte Carlo
brushed metal /3504
5 Terry Labonte 40.00 70.00
Kellogg's/4152
5 Terry Labonte 40.00 70.00
Kellogg'sGot Milk/4320
5 Terry Labonte 35.00 60.00
Kellogg's Victory Lap/5148
5 Terry Labonte 35.00 60.00
Kellogg's Victory Lap
Clear Window Bank/396
5 Terry Labonte 35.00 60.00
Kellogg's Victory Lap
GM Dealers/324
5 Brian Vickers 50.00 100.00
GMAC Raced Win AU/1908
6 Jeff Gordon 45.00 75.00
True Value 1998 IROC/900
6 Kevin Harvick 40.00 70.00
kevinharvick.com
SuperTruck 1st Win/3504
7 Greg Biffle 20.00 50.00
Kleenex Wolfman/1572
7 Greg Biffle 20.00 50.00
Kleenex Wolfman
Clear Window Bank/240
7 Jimmie Johnson 35.00 60.00
True Value IROC/2616
7 Jimmie Johnson 50.00 80.00
True Value IROC AU/3144
7 Alan Kulwicki 35.00 60.00
Hooters '93 T-bird/6010
7 Alan Kulwicki 40.00 70.00
Victory Lap/5700
7 Alan Kulwicki 40.00 70.00
Victory Lap
Clear Window Bank/372
7 Alan Kulwicki 20.00 50.00
Zerex 1987 T-Bird/4242
7 Alan Kulwicki 20.00 50.00
Zerex 1987 T-Bird
Clear Window Bank/972
7 Kyle Petty 35.00 60.00
7-11 1985 Thunderbird/2556
7 Jimmy Spencer 20.00 50.00
Sirius/3600
7 Jimmy Spencer 20.00 50.00
Sirius 3 Stooges/3444
8 Dale Earnhardt Jr. 50.00 80.00
Bud/105,248
8 Dale Earnhardt Jr. 40.00 80.00
Bud GM Dealer/8504
8 Dale Earnhardt Jr. 40.00 75.00
Bud Black Window Bank/3300
8 Dale Earnhardt Jr. 45.00 75.00
Bud No Bull
2000 Monte Carlo/28,764
8 Dale Earnhardt Jr. 45.00 75.00
Bud No Bull
2000 Monte Carlo Clear Window Bank/1536
8 Dale Earnhardt Jr. 45.00 75.00
Bud No Bull
'00 Mon.Carlo GM Dealers/3504
8 Dale Earnhardt Jr. 45.00 75.00
Bud Talladega '02/17,052
8 Dale Earnhardt Jr. 45.00 75.00
Bud Talladega '02 CW Bank/1008
8 Dale Earnhardt Jr. 45.00 75.00
Budweiser Talladega/45,024
8 Dale Earnhardt Jr. 45.00 75.00
Bud All-Star Game/60,456
8 Dale Earnhardt Jr. 45.00 75.00
Bud All-Star
Clear Window Bank/1475
8 Dale Earnhardt Jr. 30.00 60.00
Bud All-Star
Red Clear/4320
8 Dale Earnhardt Jr. 30.00 60.00
Bud All-Star
Red Clear GM Dealer/240
8 Dale Earnhardt Jr. 45.00 75.00
Bud StainD/60,204
8 Dale Earnhardt Jr. 40.00 75.00
Bud StainD
Clear Window Bank/1968
8 Dale Earnhardt Jr. 40.00 75.00
Bud StainD
GM Dealer/3504
8 Dale Earnhardt Jr. 40.00 70.00
Dirty Mo Posse/59,796
8 Dale Earnhardt Jr. 40.00 70.00
Dirty Mo Posse
Black Window Bank/2292
8 Dale Earnhardt Jr. 40.00 70.00
Dirty Mo Posse Clear/5304
8 Dale Earnhardt Jr. 40.00 70.00
Dirty Mo Posse GM Dealers/3504
8 Dale Earnhardt Jr. 40.00 70.00
E Concert/74,352
8 Dale Earnhardt Jr. 40.00 70.00
E Concert
Black Window Bank/2304
8 Dale Earnhardt Jr. 40.00 70.00
E Concert
GM Dealers/5004
8 Dale Earnhardt Jr. 40.00 75.00
Oreo Ritz/77,208
8 Dale Earnhardt Jr. 30.00 60.00
Oreo Ritz Bank/2268
8 Dale Earnhardt Jr. 35.00 60.00
Oreo Ritz Clear/6588
8 Dale Earnhardt Jr. 40.00 75.00
Oreo Ritz
GM Dealers/5004
8 Dale Earnhardt Jr. 75.00 125.00
Oreo Ritz
White Gold/2496
8 Kerry Earnhardt 20.00 50.00
Mom N' Pops 1996/5232
8 Mark Martin 35.00 60.00
True Value IROC Green/6748
8 Steve Park 35.00 60.00
Cheese Nips/5760
8 Steve Park 35.00 60.00
Cheese Nips Black Window Bank/516
8 Steve Park 40.00 70.00
Maxwell House/6540
8 Steve Park 40.00 70.00
Maxwell House
GM Dealers/240
8 Hank Parker Jr. 20.00 50.00
Remmington Bass
Pro Shops/3972
8 Hank Parker Jr. 20.00 50.00
Remmington Bass Pro
Shops GM Dealers/240
8 Hank Parker Jr. 20.00 50.00
Remmington
Bass Pro Shops
Clear Window Bank/420
8 Hank Parker Jr. 20.00 50.00
Remmington
Dick's Sporting Goods/3372
8 Tony Stewart 40.00 70.00
3 Doors Down/26,916
8 Tony Stewart 35.00 70.00
3 Doors Down
Clear Window Bank/1272
9 Bill Elliott 45.00 75.00
Coors 1984 T-bird/5592
9 Bill Elliott 45.00 75.00
Coors Winston Million
1985 Thunderbird/5508
9 Bill Elliott 45.00 75.00
Coors Winston Million
1985 Thunderbird
Clear Window Bank/432
9 Bill Elliott 45.00 75.00
Coors '87 Thunderbird/6864
9 Bill Elliott 40.00 70.00
Coors 1987 Thunderbird
Black Window Bank/636
9 Bill Elliott 40.00 70.00
Coors 1988 Thunderbird/6228
9 Bill Elliott 35.00 60.00
Dodge/8856
9 Bill Elliott 30.00 60.00
Dodge Black Window Bank/792
9 Bill Elliott 30.00 60.00
Dodge Clear/2748
9 Bill Elliott 35.00 60.00
Dodge Lion King/3612
9 Bill Elliott 35.00 60.00
Dodge Lion King
Clear Window Bank/324
9 Bill Elliott 35.00 60.00
Dodge 10th Anniversary Brickyard/6528
9 Bill Elliott 35.00 60.00
Dodge 10th Brickyard Clear Window Bank/540
9 Bill Elliott 40.00 60.00
Dodge Victory Lap/6132
9 Bill Elliott 40.00 60.00
Dodge Victory Lap
Clear Window Bank/420
9 Bill Elliott 30.00 60.00
Melling 1982 Thunderbird/5196
10 Johnny Benson 20.00 50.00
Valvoline/3048
11 Kevin Harvick 40.00 70.00
True Value IROC Yellow/7128
11 Dale Jarrett 45.00 70.00
True Value IROC Blue/6648
11 Darrell Waltrip 40.00 60.00
Victory Lap/6360
11 Darrell Waltrip 40.00 60.00
Victory Lap
Clear Window Bank/348
11 Cale Yarborough 35.00 60.00
Victory Lap/4044
11 Cale Yarborough 35.00 60.00
Victory Lap
Clear Window Bank/336
12 Kerry Earnhardt 20.00 50.00
Hot Tamales red/5232
15 Michael Waltrip 40.00 70.00
NAPA/8304
15 Michael Waltrip 40.00 70.00
NAPA Bank/480
15 Michael Waltrip 40.00 70.00
NAPA GM Dealer/504
15 Michael Waltrip 25.00 50.00
NAPA Hootie & the Blowfish/10,008
15 Michael Waltrip 25.00 50.00
NAPA Hootie & The Blowfish
Clear Window Bank/684
15 Michael Waltrip 25.00 50.00
NAPA Hootie
GM Dealers/504
15 Michael Waltrip 25.00 50.00
NAPA Nilla Wafers/7164
15 Michael Waltrip 25.00 50.00
NAPA Nilla Wafers
Clear Window Bank/456
15 Michael Waltrip 35.00 60.00
NAPA Stars & Stripes/8652
15 Michael Waltrip 35.00 60.00
NAPA Stars&Stripes
Clear Window Bank/492
17 Darrell Waltrip 35.00 60.00
Aaron's Rent 3 Stooges
SuperTruck/6108
17 Darrell Waltrip 75.00 125.00
Boogity Boogity AU/4356
17 Darrell Waltrip 75.00 125.00
Boogity Boogity GM Dealers AU/240
17 Darrell Waltrip 35.00 60.00
Tide Give Kids the
World SuperTruck/4512
18 Coy Gibbs 20.00 50.00
MBNA/1392
18 Bobby Labonte 40.00 75.00
Interstate Batteries/11,244
18 Bobby Labonte 40.00 70.00
Interstate Batteries
Black Window Bank/504
18 Bobby Labonte 40.00 75.00
Interstate Batteries GM Dealers/288
18 Bobby Labonte 40.00 70.00
Interstate Batteries
Advair Green/5784
18 Bobby Labonte 40.00 70.00
Interstate Batteries
Advair Purple/7068
18 Bobby Labonte 40.00 70.00
Interstate Batteries
Advair Purple GM Dealers/300
18 Bobby Labonte 40.00 70.00
Interstate Batteries Hulk/10,884
18 Bobby Labonte 40.00 70.00
Interstate Batteries
Clear Window Bank/720
18 Bobby Labonte 40.00 70.00
Interstate Batteries Victory Lap/6876
18 Bobby Labonte 40.00 70.00
Interstate Batteries Victory Lap
Clear Window Bank/420
18 Bobby Labonte 40.00 70.00
Interstate Batteries Victory Lap
GM Dealers/336
18 Bobby Labonte 40.00 70.00
Interstate Batteries
Victory Lap Mac Tools/288
18 Bobby Labonte 50.00 75.00
Interstate Batteries 3M Employee Promo/2700
19 Dale Earnhardt 35.00 60.00
Beldon Asphalt
1977 Malibu/24,716
19 Dale Earnhardt 35.00 60.00
Beldon Asphalt
1977 Malibu Clear
Window Bank/1884
19 Jeremy Mayfield 20.00 50.00
Dodge/4584
19 Jeremy Mayfield 20.00 50.00
Dodge Black Window Bank/696
19 Jeremy Mayfield 20.00 50.00
Dodge Lion King/2004
19 Jeremy Mayfield 20.00 50.00
Dodge Lion King
Clear Window Bank/288
19 Jeremy Mayfield 20.00 50.00
Mountain Dew/3612
19 Jeremy Mayfield 20.00 50.00
Mountain Dew
CW Bank/324
20 Mike Bliss 20.00 50.00
Rockwell Automation/2796
20 Mike Bliss 20.00 50.00
Rockwell Automation
Bell Tower/3504
20 Mike Bliss 20.00 50.00
Rockwell Automation Frankenstein/1780
20 Mike Bliss 20.00 50.00
Rockwell Automation Frankenstein
Clear Window Bank/240
20 Tony Stewart 40.00 75.00
Home Depot/29,700
20 Tony Stewart 40.00 70.00
Home Depot
Black Window Bank/1068
20 Tony Stewart 40.00 70.00
Home Depot
BW Bank Mac Tools/288
20 Tony Stewart 40.00 75.00
Home Depot GM Dealers/1008
20 Tony Stewart 35.00 60.00
Home Depot Declaration
of Independence/23,940
20 Tony Stewart 30.00 60.00
Home Depot Declaration of Independence
Clear Window Bank/1008
20 Tony Stewart 40.00 70.00
Home Depot Victory Lap/10,488
20 Tony Stewart 40.00 70.00
Home Depot Victory Lap
Clear Window Bank/492
20 Tony Stewart 40.00 70.00
Home Depot Victory Lap
GM Dealers/588
20 Tony Stewart 40.00 70.00
Home Depot
Victory Lap Mac Tools/288
21 Buddy Baker 20.00 50.00
Valvoline 1983 Thunderbird/2796
21 Kevin Harvick 40.00 65.00
Payday/12,888
21 Kevin Harvick 35.00 60.00
Payday Black Window Bank/720
21 Johnny Sauter 20.00 50.00
Payday/624
22 Bobby Allison 35.00 60.00
Victory Lap/4140
22 Bobby Allison 35.00 60.00
Victory Lap Clear Window Bank/324
22 Bobby Allison 35.00 60.00
Victory Lap GM Dealers/312
23 Scott Wimmer 20.00 40.00
Stacker 2
Dracula/1822
23 Scott Wimmer 20.00 40.00
Stacker 2 Dracula
Clear Window Bank/300
24 Jeff Gordon 40.00 70.00
Cookie Monster Foundation/21,552
24 Jeff Gordon 40.00 75.00
DuPont Flames/34,332
24 Jeff Gordon 40.00 75.00
DuPont Flames GM Dealers
24 Jeff Gordon 45.00 75.00
DuPont Victory Lap/14,592
24 Jeff Gordon 45.00 75.00
DuPont Victory Lap
Clear Window Bank/672
24 Jeff Gordon 40.00 70.00
DuPont Wright Bros./26,520
24 Jeff Gordon 30.00 60.00
DuPont Wright Bros
Clear Window Bank/1440
24 Jeff Gordon 30.00 60.00
DuPont Yosemite Sam/19,416
24 Jeff Gordon 25.00 50.00
DuPont Yosemite Sam Bank/1092
24 Jeff Gordon 40.00 70.00
Pepsi/22,752
24 Jeff Gordon 40.00 70.00
Pepsi Dark Window Bank/864
24 Jeff Gordon 40.00 70.00
Pepsi GM Dealers/1008
24 Jeff Gordon 40.00 70.00
Pepsi Mac Tools/288
24 Jeff Gordon 40.00 70.00
Pepsi Billion $/22,692
24 Jeff Gordon 30.00 60.00
Pepsi Billion $
Clear Window Bank/1272
24 Jeff Gordon 40.00 70.00
Pepsi Billion $
GM Dealers/648
24 Tim Richmond 35.00 60.00
Pepsi 1985 Firebird/2664
25 Joe Nemechek 20.00 50.00
UAW Delphi/2640
25 Joe Nemechek 20.00 50.00
UAW Delphi DW Bank/384
25 Joe Nemechek 20.00 50.00
UAW Delphi Bugs Bunny/5004
25 Joe Nemechek 20.00 50.00
UAW Delphi Bugs Bunny
Clear Window Bank/444
25 Joe Nemechek 20.00 50.00
UAW Delphi Uncle Kracker/3000
25 Joe Nemechek 20.00 50.00
UAW Delphi Uncle Kracker
Clear Window Bank/420
27 Kenny Irwin 30.00 60.00
Raybestos
1998 Thunderbird/2316
29 Kevin Harvick 40.00 70.00
Goodwrench/19,416
29 Kevin Harvick 25.00 50.00
Goodwrench Black Window Bank/804
29 Kevin Harvick 40.00 70.00
Goodwrench GM Dealers/2496
29 Kevin Harvick 100.00 150.00
Goodwrench Raced/8532
29 Kevin Harvick 100.00 150.00
Goodwrench Raced
GM Dealers/1644
29 Kevin Harvick 35.00 60.00
Goodwrench Red
GM Dealers/12,000
29 Kevin Harvick 35.00 60.00
Goodwrench Sugar Ray/8520
29 Kevin Harvick 35.00 60.00
Goodwrench Sugar Ray
Clear Window Bank/624
29 Kevin Harvick 40.00 70.00
Snap-On/20,004
29 Kevin Harvick 40.00 70.00
Snap-On GM Dealers/1440
30 Jeff Green 20.00 50.00
AOL/3180
30 Steve Park 35.00 60.00
GM Card/1908
30 Steve Park 20.00 50.00
AOL Kraft 100th Anniversary/4008
30 Steve Park 20.00 50.00
AOL Daffy/3576
30 Steve Park 20.00 50.00
AOL Daffy
Clear Window Bank/408
30 Steve Park 35.00 60.00
AOL Daffy
GM Dealers/60
30 Steve Park 35.00 60.00
AOL Third Eye Blind/4596
30 Steve Park 35.00 60.00
AOL Third Eye Blind
Clear Window Bank/456
30 Steve Park 35.00 60.00
AOL Third Eye Blind
GM Dealers/504
31 Robby Gordon 25.00 50.00
Cingular black/4836
31 Robby Gordon 20.00 50.00
Cingular black
Black Window Bank/648
31 Robby Gordon 25.00 50.00
Cingular black GM Dealers/120
31 Robby Gordon 25.00 50.00
Cingular orange/6000
31 Robby Gordon 20.00 50.00
Cingular oranget
Black Window Bank/408
31 Robby Gordon 25.00 50.00
Cingular Charlie's Angels 2/3956
31 Robby Gordon 25.00 50.00
Cingular FDNY/6420
31 Robby Gordon 20.00 50.00
Cingular FDNY
Clear Window Bank/532
31 Robby Gordon 25.00 50.00
Cingular TRAPT/6000
31 Robby Gordon 20.00 50.00
Cingular TRAPT
Clear Window Bank
32 Ricky Craven 20.00 50.00
Tide/3996
32 Ricky Craven 20.00 50.00
Tide Clear Window Bank/480
33 Tony Stewart 35.00 60.00
Monaco Diamond Rio
SuperTruck/9424
33 Tony Stewart 35.00 60.00
Monaco Diamond Rio
SuperTruck GM Dealers/360
33 Tony Stewart 35.00 60.00
Monaco Diamond Rio
SuperTruck Mac Tools/288
35 Alan Kulwicki 35.00 60.00
Quincy's Steakhouse
1986 Thunderbird/3780
38 Elliott Sadler 20.00 50.00
Combos/4932
38 Elliott Sadler 25.00 50.00
M&M's/8712
38 Elliott Sadler 25.00 40.00
M&M's Mac Tools/288
38 Elliott Sadler 20.00 50.00
M&M's Groovy/9312
38 Elliott Sadler 20.00 50.00
M&M's Groovy
Clear Window Bank/792
38 Elliott Sadler 25.00 50.00
M&M's Halloween/6504
38 Elliott Sadler 25.00 50.00
M&M's Halloween
Clear Window Bank/480

38 Elliott Sadler M&M's Pedigree/3984	20.00	50.00
40 Sterling Marlin Coors Light/10,152	35.00	60.00
40 Sterling Marlin Coors Light Black Window Bank/792	30.00	60.00
40 Sterling Marlin Coors Light Clear/2808	30.00	60.00
40 Sterling Marlin Coors Light Scary Movie 3 Twins/3384	35.00	60.00
40 Sterling Marlin Coors Light Target 2001 Dodge/3504	35.00	60.00
40 Sterling Marlin Coors Original 2001/4428	40.00	70.00
41 Casey Mears Fuji Film/2040	20.00	50.00
41 Casey Mears Fuji Film Clear Window Bank/384	20.00	50.00
41 Casey Mears Target/4536	20.00	50.00
41 Casey Mears Target House/1932	20.00	50.00
41 Casey Mears Target House Clear Window Bank/228	20.00	50.00
42 Jamie McMurray Havoline/11,100	35.00	60.00
42 Jamie McMurray Havoline Black Window Bank/792	20.00	50.00
42 Jamie McMurray Havoline ROY/4404	25.00	50.00
42 Jamie McMurray Havoline ROY Clear Window Bank/360	25.00	50.00
42 Jamie McMurray Havoline Terminator 3/10,260	20.00	50.00
42 Jamie McMurray Havoline Terminator 3 Clear Window Bank/812	20.00	50.00
42 Jamie McMurray Havoline White/7608	30.00	60.00
42 Jamie McMurray Havoline White Clear Window Bank/552	30.00	60.00
42 Jamie McMurray Havoline White Mac Tools/288	30.00	60.00
43 John Andretti Cheerios/4092	20.00	50.00
43 John Andretti Cheerios Berry Burst/3624	20.00	50.00
43 John Andretti Cheerios Berry Burst Clear Window Bank/408	20.00	50.00
43 Richard Petty Victory Lap/7440	40.00	70.00
43 Richard Petty Victory Lap Clear Window Bank/468	40.00	70.00
43 Richard Petty Yankees 100th Anniversary/5700	40.00	70.00
43 Richard Petty Yankees 100th Anniversary AUTO/6100	60.00	100.00
43 Richard Petty STP 1975 Dodge Charger/8268	150.00	250.00
43 Richard Petty STP 1975 Charger Clear Window Bank/619	125.00	200.00
44 Christian Fittipaldi Yankees 100th Anniversary/4836	20.00	50.00
44 Christian Fittipaldi Yankees 100th Anniversary Clear Window Bank/588	20.00	50.00
45 Kyle Petty Georgia Pacific/4608	20.00	50.00
45 Kyle Petty Hands to Victory/2868	20.00	50.00
45 Kyle Petty Hands to Victory Clear Window Bank/252	20.00	50.00
45 Kyle Petty Georgia Pacific Garfield/4296	20.00	50.00
48 Jimmie Johnson Lowe's/30,070	35.00	60.00
48 Jimmie Johnson Lowe's Black Window Bank/936	35.00	60.00
48 Jimmie Johnson Lowe's GM Dealers/1008	35.00	60.00
48 Jimmie Johnson Lowe's Power of Pride/13,728	30.00	60.00
48 Jimmie Johnson Lowe's Power of Pride Clear Window Bank/648	25.00	60.00
48 Jimmie Johnson Lowe's SpongeBob/15,672	35.00	60.00
48 Jimmie Johnson Lowe's SpongeBob GM Dealer/504	35.00	60.00
48 Jimmie Johnson Lowe's SpongeBob Clear Window Bank/948	35.00	60.00
54 Todd Bodine National Guard/3252	30.00	60.00
66 Rusty Wallace Motion 1985 Thunderbird/4356	40.00	70.00
72 Benny Parsons Victory Lap/3768	35.00	60.00
72 Benny Parsons Victory Lap Clear Window Bank/324	35.00	60.00
72 Benny Parsons Victory Lap GM Dealers/252	35.00	60.00
77 Dave Blaney Jasper/4008	20.00	50.00
81 Jason Keller Kraft 100 Years/3372	20.00	50.00
81 Martin Truex Jr. Chance 2/3504	35.00	60.00
81 Martin Truex Jr. Chance 2 GM Dealers/180	35.00	60.00
83 Kerry Earnhardt Hot Tamales black/7692	20.00	50.00
87 Kyle Busch ditech.com AU/2400	75.00	125.00
87 Kyle Busch ditech.com GM Dealers AU/120	75.00	125.00
87 Kyle Busch ditech.com Mummy/3372	25.00	60.00
87 Kyle Busch ditech.com Mummy Clear Window Bank/516	25.00	60.00
88 Dale Jarrett UPS Brown Logo/11,184	35.00	60.00
88 Dale Jarrett UPS Brown Logo Black Window Bank/780	35.00	60.00
88 Dale Jarrett UPS Brown Yellow Logo/11,832	40.00	70.00
88 Dale Jarrett UPS Brown&Yellow Logo Black Window Bank/790	35.00	60.00
88 Dale Jarrett UPS Brown Yellow Logo Clear/1752	35.00	60.00
88 Dale Jarrett UPS Store/5028	40.00	70.00
88 Dale Jarrett UPS Store Clear Window Bank/396	40.00	70.00
88 Dale Jarrett UPS Store Mac Tools/288	40.00	70.00
88 Dale Jarrett UPS Victory Lap/6252	40.00	70.00
88 Dale Jarrett UPS Victory Lap Clear Window Bank/372	40.00	70.00
88 Darrell Waltrip Gatorade '79 Monte Carlo/4164	35.00	60.00
91 Casey Atwood Mountain Dew Live Wire/2604	20.00	50.00
91 Casey Atwood Mountain Dew Live Wire Clear Window Bank/288	20.00	50.00
91 Hank Parker Jr. USG Promo	50.00	100.00
99 Michael Waltrip Aaron's Rent/3504	25.00	50.00
99 Michael Waltrip Aaron's Rent Cat in the Hat/4968	25.00	50.00
99 Michael Waltrip Aaron's Rent Three Stooges/7584	25.00	50.00
99 Michael Waltrip Aaron's Rent Terminator 3/8004	20.00	50.00
99 Michael Waltrip Aaron's Rent T3 Clear Window Bank/692	20.00	50.00
99 Michael Waltrip Aaron's Rent T3 GM Dealers/360	20.00	50.00
01 Jerry Nadeau Army/4404	25.00	50.00
03 Cat in the Hat Event Car/1428	20.00	40.00
03 Cat in the Hat Event Car Clear Window Bank/216	20.00	40.00
03 Hulk Event Car/4632	20.00	40.00
03 Terminator 3 Event Car Color Chrome/3432	20.00	40.00
06 Mark Martin Carolina Ford Dealers 1986 Thunderbird/2736	40.00	70.00
06 Mark Martin Carolina Ford Dealers '86 Thunderbird Clear Window Bank/600	40.00	70.00
2003 DEI Pit Practice/2508	40.00	70.00
2003 Hendrick Motor Sports Pit Practice/2424	35.00	60.00
NNO Chevy Rock & Roll Event Car/3504	20.00	40.00
NNO Looney Tunes Event Car/4631	20.00	40.00
NNO Looney Tunes Event Car GM Dealers/564	20.00	40.00

2003 Action QVC For Race Fans Only 1:24

	EX	NM-MT
2 Rusty Wallace Miller Lite Color Chrome/1008	90.00	150.00
2 Rusty Wallace Miller Lite Gold/1000	100.00	150.00
2 Rusty Wallace Miller Lite Platinum/624	125.00	200.00
2 Rusty Wallace Miller Lite 600th Consecutive Start Col.Chrome/1008	90.00	150.00
2 Rusty Wallace Miller Time Live Goo Goo Dolls Color Chrome/1000	90.00	150.00
3 Dale Earnhardt Foundation Gold/3333	125.00	175.00
3 Dale Earnhardt Foundation Platinum/1008	125.00	200.00
3 Dale Earnhardt Goodwrench 1990 Lumina Gold/2508	75.00	150.00
3 Dale Earnhardt Goodwrench 1990 Lumina Pearlized/2508	60.00	100.00
3 Dale Earnhardt Goodwrench 1990 Lumina Platinum/1008	150.00	225.00
8 Dale Earnhardt Jr. Bud Gold/2508	100.00	150.00
8 Dale Earnhardt Jr. Bud Platinum/624	150.00	250.00
8 Dale Earnhardt Jr. Bud All-Star Color Chrome/2508	75.00	135.00
8 Dale Earnhardt Jr. Bud All-Star Gold/2508	100.00	150.00
8 Dale Earnhardt Jr. Bud All-Star Platinum/624	150.00	225.00
8 Dale Earnhardt Jr. Bud StainD Brushed Metal/2508	60.00	100.00
8 Dale Earnhardt Jr. Bud StainD Color Chrome/3504	75.00	125.00
8 Dale Earnhardt Jr. Bud StainD Gold/1000	75.00	125.00
8 Dale Earnhardt Jr. Bud StainD Platinum/624	100.00	150.00
8 Dale Earnhardt Jr. DMP Gold/2508	100.00	150.00
8 Dale Earnhardt Jr. DMP Platinum/624	150.00	225.00
8 Dale Earnhardt Jr. E Concert Color Chrome/3508	70.00	120.00
8 Dale Earnhardt Jr. E Concert Gold/2508	75.00	125.00
8 Dale Earnhardt Jr. E Concert Platinum/624	125.00	225.00
8 Dale Earnhardt Jr. Oreo Ritz Gold/2508	90.00	150.00
8 Dale Earnhardt Jr. Oreo Ritz Platinum/624	150.00	225.00
8 Tony Stewart 3 Doors Down Color Chrome/2508	50.00	100.00
8 Tony Stewart 3 Doors Down Gold	75.00	125.00
20 Tony Stewart Home Depot Declaration of Independence Color Chrome/1008	50.00	100.00
20 Tony Stewart Home Depot Declaration of Independence Platinum/624	100.00	175.00
24 Jeff Gordon DuPont Flames Gold/1000	90.00	150.00
24 Jeff Gordon DuPont Flames Platinum/624	125.00	200.00
24 Jeff Gordon DuPont Flames Yosemite Sam Color Chrome/1008	90.00	150.00
24 Jeff Gordon Pepsi Billion $ Color Chrome/2508	90.00	150.00
24 Jeff Gordon Pepsi Billion $ Gold/1000	100.00	150.00
24 Jeff Gordon Pepsi Billion $ Platinum/674	100.00	175.00
24 Jeff Gordon DuPont Wright Brothers Gold/1008	90.00	135.00
24 Jeff Gordon Wright Brothers Platinum/624	125.00	200.00
43 Richard Petty Yankees 100th Anniversary Color Chrome/1008	75.00	125.00
48 Jimmie Johnson Lowe's Power of Pride Gold/504	75.00	125.00
48 Jimmie Johnson Lowe's Power of Pride Platinum/624	125.00	200.00
48 Jimmie Johnson Lowe's SpongeBob Color Chrome/1008	75.00	125.00
NNO Dale Earnhardt Legacy Gold/3333	90.00	135.00
NNO Dale Earnhardt Legacy Platinum/1008	100.00	175.00

2003 Action/RCCA 1:24

	EX	NM-MT
1 Jeff Green Pennzoil Synthetic/400	20.00	50.00
1 Jamie McMurray Yellow Freight/360	20.00	50.00
1 Steve Park Pennzoil Clear Window Bank/504	20.00	50.00
2 Ron Hornaday AC Delco Bank/408	20.00	50.00
2 Jason Leffler Hulk SuperTruck/580	20.00	50.00
2 Mark Martin SAI Roofing 1987 Thunderbird/504	30.00	60.00
2 Rusty Wallace Miller Lite Clear Window Bank/1200	40.00	75.00
2 Rusty Wallace Miller Lite 600 Starts/600	40.00	70.00
2 Rusty Wallace Miller Time Live Goo Goo Dolls/1204	40.00	70.00
3 Dale Earnhardt Earnhardt Foundation/3100	50.00	75.00
3 Dale Earnhardt Goodwrench 1990 Lumina/4008	50.00	80.00
3 Dale Earnhardt Goodwrench No Bull 2000 Monte Carlo/2508	50.00	80.00
3 Dale Earnhardt Goodwrench '01 Monte Carlo/3333	50.00	80.00
3 Dale Earnhardt Goodwrench Bass Pro Shops/4500	40.00	70.00
3 Dale Earnhardt Goodwrench Silver 1995 Monte Carlo/4800	50.00	80.00
3 Dale Earnhardt Victory Lap/2400	45.00	75.00
3 Dale Earnhardt Jr. Mom 'n' Pops Prime Sirloin/4800	50.00	75.00
3 Dale Earnhardt Jr. Sundrop 1994 Lumina/4800	50.00	75.00
5 Terry Labonte Kellogg's Bank/444	20.00	50.00
5 Terry Labonte Got Milk Clear Window Bank/496	20.00	50.00
5 Brian Vickers GMAC Raced Win AU/300	60.00	120.00
7 Alan Kulwicki Hooters Bank 1993 Thunderbird/504	40.00	70.00
7 Alan Kulwicki Victory Lap/504	40.00	70.00
7 Jimmy Spencer Sirius/444	20.00	50.00
8 Dale Earnhardt Jr. Bud Bank/3300	50.00	80.00
8 Dale Earnhardt Jr. Bud No Bull 2000 Monte Carlo/2508	50.00	80.00
8 Dale Earnhardt Jr. Bud Talladega Raced/1300	50.00	80.00
8 Dale Earnhardt Jr. Bud Talladega October 2002 Win, Raced Clear Window Bank/1008	50.00	75.00
8 Dale Earnhardt Jr. Bud MLB All-Star Game/3300	50.00	80.00
8 Dale Earnhardt Jr. Bud StainD/3100	50.00	80.00
8 Dale Earnhardt Jr. Dirty Mo Posse Bank/3204	45.00	75.00
8 Dale Earnhardt Jr. Dirty Mo Posse Split Clear/1008	45.00	75.00
8 Dale Earnhardt Jr. E Concert Bank/3600	45.00	75.00
8 Dale Earnhardt Jr. E Concert Raced/600	60.00	120.00
8 Dale Earnhardt Jr. Oreo Ritz Clear Window Bank/3600	45.00	75.00
8 Dale Earnhardt Jr. Oreo Ritz Split Clear/1008	45.00	75.00
8 Steve Park Cheese Nips Clear Window Bank/504	20.00	50.00
8 Steve Park Maxwell House Bank/504	20.00	50.00
8 Hank Parker Jr. Dick's Sporting Goods/520	20.00	50.00
8 Tony Stewart 3 Doors Down/1200	40.00	65.00
9 Bill Elliott Coors 1984 Thunderbird/804	45.00	75.00
9 Bill Elliott Coors 1987 Thunderbird Bank/804	50.00	80.00
9 Bill Elliott Coors 1988 Thunderbird/804	45.00	75.00
9 Bill Elliott Dodge Clear Window Bank/444	30.00	60.00
9 Bill Elliott Dodge Split Clear/408	35.00	60.00
11 Dale Jarrett True Value 2002 IROC Blue/360	35.00	60.00
11 Darrell Waltrip Victory Lap/804	35.00	60.00
12 Kerry Earnhardt Hot Tamales red/504	20.00	50.00
15 Michael Waltrip NAPA Bank/504	20.00	50.00
15 Michael Waltrip NAPA Nilla Wafers Clear Window Bank/504	20.00	50.00
15 Michael Waltrip NAPA Stars&Stripes/504	20.00	50.00
18 Bobby Labonte Interstate Batteries Clear Window Bank/504	35.00	60.00
18 Bobby Labonte Interstate Batt. Advair Green/360	40.00	65.00
18 Bobby Labonte Interstate Batteries Advair Purple/444	40.00	65.00
18 Bobby Labonte Interstate Batteries Hulk Clear Window Bank/600	40.00	65.00
19 Jeremy Mayfield Dodge Bank/504	20.00	50.00
19 Jeremy Mayfield Dodge Lion King/400	20.00	50.00
20 Mike Bliss Rockwell Automation Frankenstein/300	20.00	50.00
20 Tony Stewart Home Depot Clear Window Bank/1500	30.00	60.00
20 Tony Stewart Home Depot Pocono Raced/504	30.00	60.00
20 Tony Stewart Home Depot Declaration of Independence/1600	30.00	60.00
21 Kevin Harvick Payday Clear Window Bank/1008	30.00	60.00
21 Johnny Sauter Payday Clear Window Bank/300	20.00	50.00
23 Scott Wimmer Stacker 2 Dracula/300	20.00	50.00
24 Jeff Gordon Cookie Monster/1800	45.00	70.00
24 Jeff Gordon DuPont Flames Clear Window Bank/2124	40.00	70.00
24 Jeff Gordon DuPont Flames Martinsville Raced/604	45.00	75.00
24 Jeff Gordon DuPont Victory Lap/1500	45.00	75.00
24 Jeff Gordon DuPont Wright Brothers/2404	40.00	70.00
24 Jeff Gordon DuPont Yosemite Sam/1900	40.00	70.00
24 Jeff Gordon Pepsi Bank/1524	40.00	70.00
24 Jeff Gordon Pepsi Billion $/2224	40.00	70.00
25 Joe Nemechek UAW Delphi Clear Window Bank/408	20.00	50.00
29 Kevin Harvick Goodwrench Bank/1300	40.00	70.00
29 Kevin Harvick Goodwrench Raced/444	100.00	150.00
29 Kevin Harvick Goodwrench Sugar Ray/600	35.00	60.00
29 Kevin Harvick Snap-On Clear Window Bank/2004	40.00	65.00
30 Jeff Green AOL Clear Window Bank/600	20.00	50.00
30 Jeff Green AOL Kraft 100 Years/460	20.00	50.00
31 Robby Gordon Cingular Bank/444	20.00	50.00
31 Robby Gordon Cingular Orange Reverse Paint Clear Window Bank/444	20.00	50.00
31 Robby Gordon Cingular FDNY Special Olympics/400	20.00	50.0
31 Robby Gordon Cingular TRAPT/300	20.00	50.0
35 Alan Kulwicki Quincy's Steakhouse 1986 Thunderbird/504	20.00	50.0
38 Elliott Sadler Combos/604	20.00	50.0
38 Elliott Sadler M&M's Clear Window Bank/600	20.00	50.0
38 Elliott Sadler M&M's Groovy/504	20.00	50.0
40 Sterling Marlin Coors Light Bank/804	35.00	60.0
40 Sterling Marlin Coors Light Split Clear/2808	30.00	60.0
40 Sterling Marlin Coors Original 2001/408	30.00	60.0
40 Sterling Marlin Target '01 Dodge/400	30.00	60.0
41 Casey Mears Target Clear Window Bank/400	20.00	50.0
42 Jamie McMurray Havoline Clear Window Bank/804	30.00	60.0
42 Jamie McMurray Havoline White/600	40.00	70.0
43 John Andretti Cheerios Clear Window Bank/600	20.00	50.0
43 John Andretti Cheerios Berry Burst/580	20.00	50.0
43 Richard Petty STP 1975 Charger/1000	150.00	250.0
43 Richard Petty Yankees 100th Anniversary/500	35.00	60.0
43 Richard Petty Yankees 100th Anniversary AUTO/700	75.00	125.0
44 Christian Fittipaldi 100th Anniversary Yankees/600	20.00	50.0
48 Jimmie Johnson Lowe's Power of Pride/1444	50.00	75.0
48 Jimmie Johnson Lowe's SpongeBob/1300	40.00	65.0
54 Todd Bodine National Guard/300	30.00	60.0
77 Dave Blaney Jasper Clear Window Bank/400	20.00	50.0
81 Jason Keller Kraft 100 Years/460	20.00	50.0
81 Martin Truex Jr. Chance 2/400	35.00	60.0
83 Kerry Earnhardt Hot Tamales black/460	20.00	50.0
87 Kyle Busch Ditech.com AU/240	100.00	150.0
88 Dale Jarrett UPS Brown Logo Clear Window Bank/600	35.00	60.0
88 Dale Jarrett UPS Brown Yellow Logo Split Clear/504	35.00	60.0
88 Darrell Waltrip Gatorade Bank 1979 Monte Carlo/600	20.00	50.0
91 Casey Atwood Mountain Dew Live Wire/300	20.00	50.0
99 Michael Waltrip Aaron's Rent/444	20.00	50.0
99 Michael Waltrip Aaron's Rent Terminator 3/504	20.00	50.0
03 Hulk Event Car/408	20.00	50.0
06 Mark Martin Carolina Ford Dealers Bank '86 Thunderbird/600	35.00	60.0

2003 Action/RCCA Elite 1:24

	EX	NM-M
1 Steve Park Pennzoil/504	60.00	100.0
2 Ron Hornaday AC Delco/408	50.00	100.0
2 Mark Martin SAI Roofing 1987 Thunderbird/504	60.00	100.0
2 Rusty Wallace Miller Lite/2004	60.00	100.0
2 Rusty Wallace Miller Lite Color Chrome/408	75.00	125.0
2 Rusty Wallace Miller Lite Victory Lap/600	75.00	125.0
2 Rusty Wallace Miller Lite 600 Starts/900	75.00	125.0
2 Rusty Wallace Miller Time Live Goo Goo Dolls/804	60.00	100.0
3 Dale Earnhardt Earnhardt Foundation/4300	75.00	150.0
3 Dale Earnhardt Goodwrench No Bull 2000 Monte Carlo/4500	90.00	150.0
3 Dale Earnhardt Victory Lap/3000	90.00	135.0
5 Terry Labonte Got Milk/496	60.00	120.0
7 Greg Biffle Kleenex Wolfman/300	50.00	100.0
8 Dale Earnhardt Jr. Bud/5700	100.00	175.0
8 Dale Earnhardt Jr. Bud Color Chrome/2004	90.00	150.0
8 Dale Earnhardt Jr. Bud/4000	90.00	135.0
8 Dale Earnhardt Jr.	125.00	200.0

ɜud Talladega)ctober '02 Win Raced/1500		
e Earnhardt Jr. Bud Talladega 2003 Vin Raced/2200	125.00	200.00
e Earnhardt Jr. ɜud Test/4800	80.00	135.00
e Earnhardt Jr. ɜud All-Star Game/5544	80.00	135.00
le Earnhardt Jr. ɜud StainD/5500	90.00	150.00
e Earnhardt Jr. ɜusch Test/1600	90.00	135.00
e Earnhardt Jr.)irty Mo Posse/5004	50.00	100.00
e Earnhardt Jr. :arnhardt Tribute Concert/6300	75.00	125.00
le Earnhardt Jr. : Concert Raced/1008	90.00	150.00
e Earnhardt Jr.)reo Ritz/6000	50.00	100.00
le Earnhardt Jr.)reo Ritz Raced/1000	50.00	100.00
ve Park :heese Nips/504	60.00	100.00
ve Park Maxwell House/504	60.00	100.00
ınk Parker Jr.)ick's Sporting Goods/520	40.00	80.00
ınk Parker Jr. Remmington Bass Pro Shops/520	40.00	80.00
ıy Stewart 3 Doors Down/1800	75.00	125.00
Elliott :oors Winston Million 85 t-bird/600	70.00	120.00
Elliott)odge/600	60.00	100.00
Elliott)odge Color Chrome/408	75.00	125.00
l Elliott)odge Lion King/600	60.00	100.00
Elliott)odge Victory Lap/408	75.00	125.00
l Elliott)odge 10th Brickyard/604	60.00	100.00
ərry Earnhardt Hot Tamales red/504	60.00	100.00
lichael Waltrip NAPA/604	75.00	125.00
lichael Waltrip NAPA Raced/604	60.00	100.00
lichael Waltrip NAPA Hootie & The Blowfish/496	40.00	80.00
lichael Waltrip NAPA Nilla Wafers/804	40.00	80.00
lichael Waltrip NAPA Stars & Stripes/804	60.00	100.00
arrell Waltrip Boogity Boogity AU/528	100.00	200.00
obby Labonte nterstate Batteries/720	75.00	125.00
obby Labonte nterstate Batteries Advair Purple/444	60.00	100.00
obby Labonte nterstate Batteries Hulk/900	60.00	100.00
obby Labonte nterstate Batteries Victory Lap/600	60.00	100.00
ale Earnhardt Beldon Asphalt 1976 Malibu/3600	60.00	120.00
eremy Mayfield)odge Mountain Dew/400	50.00	100.00
ike Bliss Rockwell Automation Frankenstein/300	40.00	80.00
ɔny Stewart Home Depot/1500	75.00	125.00
ɔny Stewart Home Depot Color Chrome/1008	60.00	120.00
ɔny Stewart Home Depot Pocono Raced/504	90.00	135.00
ɔny Stewart Home Depot Test/1300	80.00	125.00
ɔny Stewart Home Depot Declaration of Independence/2800	100.00	135.00
ɔny Stewart Home Depot Victory Lap/1200	90.00	135.00
evin Harvick Payday/1500	50.00	100.00
cott Wimmer Stacker 2 Dracula/300	40.00	80.00
eff Gordon Cookie Monster/3000	60.00	100.00
eff Gordon DuPont Flames/3624	90.00	135.00
eff Gordon DuPont Flames Color Chrome/804	125.00	250.00
eff Gordon DuPont Flames Martinsville Raced/1000	90.00	135.00
eff Gordon DuPont Victory Lap/2004	100.00	150.00
eff Gordon DuPont Wright Brothers/4024	75.00	125.00
eff Gordon DuPont Yosemite Sam/3000	75.00	125.00
eff Gordon Pepsi/2724	90.00	135.00
eff Gordon Pepsi Billion $/3724	60.00	100.00
enny Irwin Raybestos 1998 Thunderbird/600	60.00	100.00
evin Harvick Goodwrench/2500	75.00	125.00
evin Harvick Goodwrench Raced/444	150.00	300.00
evin Harvick Goodwrench Sugar Ray/1008	60.00	100.00
evin Harvick Snap-On/2004	60.00	100.00
eff Green AOL Kraft 100 Years/600	50.00	100.00
eve Park AOL Kraft 100 Years/600	50.00	100.00
obby Gordon Cingular black/444	50.00	100.00
obby Gordon Cingular orange/444	50.00	100.00
31 Robby Gordon Cingular Charlie's Angels 2/400	50.00	100.00
31 Robby Gordon Cingular FDNY Special Olympics/400	50.00	100.00
35 Alan Kulwicki Quincy's Steakhouse 1986 Thunderbird/504	50.00	100.00
38 Elliott Sadler Combos/400	50.00	100.00
38 Elliott Sadler M&M's/900	50.00	100.00
38 Elliott Sadler M&M's Groovy/720	50.00	100.00
38 Elliott Sadler M&M's Halloween/504	50.00	100.00
40 Sterling Marlin Coors Light/1200	60.00	120.00
40 Sterling Marlin Coors Light Test/1008	50.00	100.00
40 Sterling Marlin Coors Light Scary Movie 3/408	50.00	100.00
40 Sterling Marlin Coors Original 2001/400	50.00	100.00
40 Sterling Marlin Target '01 Dodge/400	50.00	100.00
42 Jamie McMurray Havoline/804	60.00	100.00
42 Jamie McMurray Havoline Terminator 3/700	50.00	100.00
42 Jamie McMurray Havoline White/804	60.00	100.00
43 Richard Petty STP 1975 Charger/1300	175.00	300.00
43 Richard Petty Victory Lap/1200	60.00	100.00
43 Richard Petty Yankees 100th Anniversary/520	60.00	120.00
43 Richard Petty Yankees 100th Anniversary AUTO/700	100.00	150.00
45 Kyle Petty Georgia Pacific Hands to Victory/288	50.00	100.00
45 Kyle Petty Georgia Pacific Garfield/300	40.00	80.00
48 Jimmie Johnson Lowe's/2400	50.00	100.00
48 Jimmie Johnson Lowe's Color Chrome/804	75.00	125.00
48 Jimmie Johnson Lowe's/1600	75.00	125.00
48 Jimmie Johnson Lowe's Test/1900	50.00	100.00
48 Jimmie Johnson Lowe's Power of Pride/2200	50.00	100.00
48 Jimmie Johnson Lowe's SpongeBob/1648	50.00	100.00
54 Todd Bodine National Guard/300	50.00	100.00
87 Kyle Busch Ditech.com AU/240	125.00	200.00
87 Kyle Busch Ditech.com Mummy/300	60.00	120.00
88 Dale Jarrett UPS/1008	50.00	100.00
88 Dale Jarrett UPS Color Chrome/408	60.00	120.00
88 Dale Jarrett UPS Store/504	50.00	100.00
88 Dale Jarrett UPS Victory Lap/408	60.00	120.00
99 Michael Waltrip Aaron's Rent/444	50.00	100.00
99 Michael Waltrip Aaron's Rent Cat in the Hat/444	50.00	100.00
99 Michael Waltrip Aaron's Rent Three Stooges/460	50.00	100.00
99 Michael Waltrip Aaron's Rent T3/804	50.00	100.00
2003 DEI Pit Practice/1008	75.00	125.00
03 Hulk Event Car/600	50.00	100.00
06 Mark Martin Carolina Ford Dealers 1986 Thunderbird/600	60.00	120.00
NNO HMS Pit Practice Car/496	75.00	125.00
NNO Looney Tunes Event Car/408	60.00	120.00
NNO Victory Lap Color Chrome Event Car/360	100.00	175.00

2004 Action Performance 1:24

	EX	NM-MT
2 Rusty Wallace Miller Lite Last Call	30.00	60.00
9 Kasey Kahne Dodge refresh	25.00	50.00
20 Tony Stewart Home Depot Shrek 2	20.00	40.00
24 Jeff Gordon DuPont Flames	20.00	40.00

2004 Action Racing Collectables 1:24

	EX	NM-MT
1 John Andretti Coke C2/1584	35.00	60.00
1 John Andretti Coke C2 Clear Window Bank/240	35.00	60.00
1 John Andretti Post Maxwell House/3792	35.00	60.00
1 John Andretti Legacy Snap-On/3468	40.00	60.00
2 Ron Hornaday AC Delco/1260	35.00	60.00
2 Ron Hornaday AC Delco Clear Window bank/204	35.00	60.00
2 Ron Hornaday AC Delco KISS/1716	40.00	60.00
2 Ron Hornaday AC Delco KISS Clear Window Bank/228	40.00	60.00
2 Ron Hornaday AC Delco RCR35th Anniversary/1332	35.00	60.00
2 Ron Hornaday AC Delco RCR35th Anniversary Clear Window Bank/264	35.00	60.00
2 Rusty Wallace Kodak/4836	40.00	70.00
2 Rusty Wallace Kodak Clear Window Bank/324	40.00	70.00
2 Rusty Wallace Miller Lite/12,420	40.00	70.00
2 Rusty Wallace Miller Lite Clear Window Bank/384	40.00	70.00
2 Rusty Wallace Miller Lite Mac Tools/288	40.00	70.00
2 Rusty Wallace Miller Lite Martinsville Raced w/tire/4188	45.00	75.00
2 Rusty Wallace Miller Lite Nextel Incentive/2004	50.00	100.00
2 Rusty Wallace Miller Lite Father's Day/4188	40.00	70.00
2 Rusty Wallace Miller Lite Father's Day Clear Window Bank/384	40.00	70.00
2 Rusty Wallace Miller Lite Miller Can/2560	40.00	70.00
2 Rusty Wallace Miller Lite Last Call	75.00	150.00
2 Rusty Wallace Miller Lite Last Call Clear Window Bank/228	60.00	100.00
2 Rusty Wallace Miller Lite Last Call Color Chrome/2004	75.00	150.00
2 Rusty Wallace Miller Lite President of Beers/5412	40.00	70.00
2 Rusty Wallace Miller Lite President of Beers Clear Window Bank/384	40.00	70.00
2 Rusty Wallace Miller Lite Puddle of Mudd/4884	40.00	70.00
2 Rusty Wallace Miller Lite Puddle of Mudd Clear Window Bank/336	40.00	70.00
2 Rusty Wallace Miller Lite Penske 50th/5628	40.00	70.00
2 Rusty Wallace Miller Lite Penske 50th Clear Window Bank/348	40.00	70.00
5 Kyle Busch Lowe's/2328	45.00	75.00
5 Kyle Busch Lowe's Clear Window Bank/264	40.00	70.00
5 Kyle Busch Lowe's SpongeBob/3396	40.00	70.00
5 Kyle Busch Lowe's SpongeBob Clear Window Bank	40.00	70.00
5 Terry Labonte Delphi/2508	40.00	70.00
5 Terry Labonte Delphi Clear Window Bank/264	40.00	70.00
5 Terry Labonte Kellogg's/3816	40.00	70.00
5 Terry Labonte Kellogg's Clear Window Bank/288	40.00	70.00
5 Terry Labonte Kellogg's GM Dealers/276	40.00	70.00
5 Terry Labonte Kellogg's Mac Tools/288	40.00	70.00
5 Terry Labonte Kellogg's Father's Day/2640	40.00	70.00
5 Terry Labonte Kellogg's Father's Day Clear Window Bank	40.00	70.00
5 Terry Labonte Kellogg's HMS 20th Anniversary/2412	40.00	70.00
5 Terry Labonte Kellogg's HMS 20th Anniversary Clear Window Bank/300	40.00	70.00
5 Terry Labonte Kellogg's HMS 20th GM Dealers/168	40.00	70.00
5 Terry Labonte Kellogg's Incredibles/1236	40.00	70.00
5 Terry Labonte Kellogg's Incredibles Clear Window Bank/228	40.00	70.00
5 Terry Labonte Kellogg's Olympics/3048	40.00	70.00
5 Terry Labonte Kellogg's Olympics Clear Window Bank/336	40.00	70.00
6 Matt Crafton Goodwrench SuperTruck/1428	40.00	70.00
6 Matt Crafton Goodwrench KISS/1752	45.00	75.00
6 Matt Crafton Goodwrench KISS QVC/120		
6 Bill Elliott Lucas Oil Elvis/4248	45.00	75.00
6 Bill Elliott Lucas Oil Elvis Clear Window Bank/384	45.00	75.00
8 Dale Earnhardt Jr. Bud/72,072	40.00	70.00
8 Dale Earnhardt Jr. Bud Clear Window Bank/1260	40.00	70.00
8 Dale Earnhardt Jr. Bud GM Dealers/7548	40.00	70.00
8 Dale Earnhardt Jr. Bud Mac Tools/288	40.00	70.00
8 Dale Earnhardt Jr. Bud Bristol Raced/8808	50.00	80.00
8 Dale Earnhardt Jr. Bud Talladega Raced/7368	50.00	80.00
8 Dale Earnhardt Jr. Bud Born On Feb.7/16,392	75.00	125.00
8 Dale Earnhardt Jr. Bud Born On Feb.7 Clear Window Bank/888	75.00	125.00
8 Dale Earnhardt Jr. Bud Born On Feb.7 GM Dealers/1500	75.00	125.00
8 Dale Earnhardt Jr. Bud Born On Feb.12 Raced/28,884	60.00	100.00
8 Dale Earnhardt Jr. Bud Born On Feb.12 Raced GM Dealers/3504	60.00	100.00
8 Dale Earnhardt Jr. Bud Born On Feb.15/5004	175.00	300.00
8 Dale Earnhardt Jr. Bud Born On Feb.15 Raced GM Dealers/4008	60.00	100.00
8 Dale Earnhardt Jr. Bud Born On Feb.15 Raced/68,808	60.00	100.00
8 Dale Earnhardt Jr. Bud Born On Feb.15 Raced w/tire CW Bank/5004	60.00	100.00
8 Dale Earnhardt Jr. Bud Dave Matthews Band/20,700	40.00	70.00
8 Dale Earnhardt Jr. Bud Dave Matthews Band Clear Window Bank/600	40.00	70.00
8 Dale Earnhardt Jr. Bud Father's Day/41,880	60.00	100.00
8 Dale Earnhardt Jr. Bud Father's Day Clear Window Bank/1008	60.00	100.00
8 Dale Earnhardt Jr. Bud Father's Day GM Dealers/4008	60.00	100.00
8 Dale Earnhardt Jr. Bud World Series/21,324	40.00	70.00
8 Dale Earnhardt Jr. Bud World Series Clear Window Bank/900	40.00	70.00
8 Dale Earnhardt Jr. Bud World Series Liquid Metal/4008	75.00	125.00
8 Dale Earnhardt Jr. Oreo/34,828	40.00	70.00
8 Dale Earnhardt Jr. Oreo Clear Window Bank/1008	40.00	70.00
8 Dale Earnhardt Jr. Oreo GM Dealers/2496	40.00	70.00
8 Dale Earnhardt Jr. Oreo Mac Tools/288	40.00	65.00
8 Martin Truex Jr. Bass Pro Shops/6384	50.00	75.00
8 Martin Truex Jr. Bass Pro Shops Clear Window Bank/288	50.00	75.00
8 Martin Truex Jr. Bass Pro Shops GM Dealers/360	50.00	75.00
8 Martin Truex Jr. Bass Pro Shops Talladega Raced/2904	50.00	75.00
8 Martin Truex Jr. Bass Pro Shops Talladega Raced GM Dealers/144	50.00	75.00
8 Martin Truex Jr. Bass Pro Shops '04 Champion Color Chrome/5004	60.00	100.00
8 Martin Truex Jr. Chance 2 Ralph Earnhardt/5016	40.00	70.00
8 Martin Truex Jr. Chance 2 Ralph Earnhardt GM Dealers/396	40.00	70.00
8 Martin Truex Jr. Chance 2 Richie Evans/2940	40.00	70.00
8 Martin Truex Jr. Chance 2 Richie Evans GM Dealers/144	40.00	70.00
8 Martin Truex Jr. Chance 2 Tear Away/3216	40.00	70.00
8 Martin Truex Jr. Chance 2 Tear Away GM Dealers/144	40.00	70.00
8 Martin Truex Jr. KFC Dover Raced/1896	50.00	75.00
8 Martin Truex Jr. KFC Dover Raced GM Dealers/348	50.00	75.00
8 Martin Truex Jr. Long John Silvers/3948	40.00	70.00
8 Martin Truex Jr. Long John Silvers CW Bank/264	40.00	70.00
8 Martin Truex Jr. Taco Bell Bristol Raced/6576	40.00	70.00
8 Martin Truex Jr. Taco Bell Bristol Raced GM Dealers/240	40.00	70.00
8 Martin Truex Jr. Wrangler/6000	45.00	75.00
8 Martin Truex Jr. Wrangler Clear Window Bank/396	45.00	75.00
8 Martin Truex Jr. Wrangler GM Dealers/456	45.00	75.00
8 Martin Truex Jr. Wrangler Retro Darlington Raced/5616	45.00	75.00
9 Bill Elliott Milestones/1872	40.00	70.00
9 Bill Elliott Milestones Clear Window Bank/216	40.00	70.00
9 Kasey Kahne Dodge/3936	100.00	200.00
9 Kasey Kahne Dodge Clear Window Bank/264	75.00	150.00
9 Kasey Kahne Dodge refresh/12,564	50.00	80.00
9 Kasey Kahne Dodge refresh liquid chrome ROY AU/4596	100.00	150.00
9 Kasey Kahne Dodge refresh QVC/360	50.00	80.00
9 Kasey Kahne Dodge Mad Magazine/9024	50.00	80.00
9 Kasey Kahne Dodge Mad Magazine Clear Window Bank/456	50.00	80.00
9 Kasey Kahne Dodge Mopar/8592	50.00	80.00
9 Kasey Kahne Dodge Mopar Color Chrome/1248	60.00	120.00
9 Kasey Kahne Dodge Pit Cap/7752	50.00	80.00
9 Kasey Kahne Dodge Pit Cap Clear Window Bank/384	50.00	80.00
9 Kasey Kahne Dodge Pit Cap QVC/504	50.00	80.00
9 Kasey Kahne Dodge Popeye 75th Anniversary/3780	60.00	100.00
9 Kasey Kahne Dodge Popeye 75th Anniversary Clear Window Bank/324	50.00	80.00
9 Kasey Kahne Mountain Dew/6216	75.00	125.00
9 Kasey Kahne Mountain Dew Clear Window Bank/480	75.00	125.00
10 Scott Riggs Valvoline/2532	35.00	60.00
10 Scott Riggs Valvoline Clear Window Bank/288	35.00	60.00
10 Scott Riggs Valvoline Wizard of Oz/1668	35.00	60.00
10 Scott Riggs Valvoline Wizard of Oz Clear Window Bank/252	35.00	60.00
12 Ryan Newman Crown Royal IROC/5004	40.00	70.00
15 Michael Waltrip NAPA/13,596	40.00	70.00
15 Michael Waltrip NAPA Clear Window Bank/396	40.00	70.00
15 Michael Waltrip NAPA GM Dealers/2004	40.00	70.00
15 Michael Waltrip NAPA Mac Tools/288	40.00	70.00
15 Michael Waltrip NAPA Nextel Incentive/2304	45.00	70.00
15 Michael Waltrip NAPA Father's Day/5184	40.00	70.00
15 Michael Waltrip NAPA Father's Day Clear Window Bank/324	40.00	70.00
15 Michael Waltrip NAPA Stars&Stripes/4488	40.00	70.00
15 Michael Waltrip NAPA Stars&Stripes Clear Window Bank/252	40.00	70.00
15 Michael Waltrip NAPA Stars&Stripes GM Dealers/288	40.00	70.00
16 Jack Sprague SilveradoTrucks SuperTruck/2300	35.00	60.00
17 Matt Kenseth Crown Royal IROC/4500	40.00	70.00
17 Matt Kenseth Crown Royal IROC '04 Champion pearl/1368	40.00	70.00
17 Darrell Waltrip King of Bristol AU/2508	75.00	125.00
18 Bobby Labonte Interstate Batteries/12,612	40.00	60.00
18 Bobby Labonte Interstate Batteries Clear Window Bank/372	40.00	60.00
18 Bobby Labonte Interstate Batteries GM Dealers/1896	40.00	60.00
18 Bobby Labonte Interstate Batteries Mac Tools/288	40.00	60.00
18 Bobby Labonte Interstate Batteries Nextel Incentive/2304	50.00	100.00
18 Bobby Labonte Interstate Batteries D-Day/6060	40.00	70.00
18 Bobby Labonte Interstate Batteries D-Day CW Bank/360	40.00	70.00
18 Bobby Labonte Interstate Batteries D-Day GM Dealers/432	40.00	70.00
18 Bobby Labonte Interstate Batteries Father's Day/3528	40.00	60.00
18 Bobby Labonte Interstate Batteries Father's Day Clear Window Bank/360	40.00	60.00
18 Bobby Labonte Interstate Batteries Father's Day GM Dealers/180	40.00	60.00
18 Bobby Labonte Interstate Batteries Shrek 2/8292	40.00	60.00
18 Bobby Labonte Interstate Batteries Shrek 2 Clear Window Bank/336	40.00	60.00
18 Bobby Labonte Interstate Batteries Shrek 2 GM Dealers/548	40.00	60.00
18 Bobby Labonte Interstate Batteries Shrek 2 Mac Tools/288	40.00	60.00
18 Bobby Labonte Wellbutrin/2784	40.00	70.00
18 Bobby Labonte Wellbutrin Clear Window Bank/288	40.00	70.00
18 Bobby Labonte Wellbutrin GM Dealers/108	40.00	70.00
18 J.J. Yeley Vigoro/2400	35.00	60.00
19 Bobby Labonte Banquet/1608	40.00	60.00
19 Bobby Labonte Banquet Clear Window Bank/240	40.00	60.00
19 Bobby Labonte Banquet GM Dealers/24	40.00	60.00
19 Jeremy Mayfield Dodge/2808	35.00	60.00
19 Jeremy Mayfield Dodge Clear Window Bank/240	35.00	60.00
19 Jeremy Mayfield Dodge HEMI/2508	35.00	60.00

19 Jeremy Mayfield Dodge HEMI Clear Window Bank/216	35.00	60.00
19 Jeremy Mayfield Dodge Mad Magazine/1956	35.00	60.00
19 Jeremy Mayfield Dodge Mad Magazine Mac Tools/204	35.00	60.00
19 Jeremy Mayfield Dodge NHL All Star/2376	35.00	60.00
19 Jeremy Mayfield Dodge NHL All Star Clear Window Bank/276	35.00	60.00
19 Jeremy Mayfield Dodge Popeye 75th Anniversary/2304	40.00	70.00
19 Jeremy Mayfield Dodge Popeye 75th Anniversary Clear Window Bank/300	35.00	60.00
19 Jeremy Mayfield Mountain Dew/2220	40.00	70.00
20 Tony Stewart Coke C2/4728	45.00	75.00
20 Tony Stewart Coke C2 Clear Window Bank/336	40.00	70.00
20 Tony Stewart Coke C2 GM Dealers/456	40.00	70.00
20 Tony Stewart Coke C2 Mac Tools/468	40.00	70.00
20 Tony Stewart Coke C2 QVC/504	40.00	70.00
20 Tony Stewart Home Depot/17,460	40.00	70.00
20 Tony Stewart Home Depot Clear Window Bank/516	40.00	70.00
20 Tony Stewart Home Depot GM Dealers/2244	40.00	70.00
20 Tony Stewart Home Depot Mac Tools/288	40.00	70.00
20 Tony Stewart Home Depot Nextel Incentive/3704	60.00	100.00
20 Tony Stewart Home Depot Reverse Paint Black/9756	40.00	70.00
20 Tony Stewart Home Depot Reverse Paint Black Clear Window Bank/432	40.00	70.00
20 Tony Stewart Home Depot Reverse Paint Black Mac Tools/288	40.00	70.00
20 Tony Stewart Home Depot Father's Day/5916	40.00	70.00
20 Tony Stewart Home Depot Father's Day Clear Window Bank/420	40.00	70.00
20 Tony Stewart Home Depot Father's Day Hamilton/156	40.00	70.00
20 Tony Stewart Home Depot Father's Day QVC/504	40.00	70.00
20 Tony Stewart Home Depot Olympics/4008	40.00	70.00
20 Tony Stewart Home Depot Olympics Clear Window Bank/252	40.00	70.00
20 Tony Stewart Home Depot Olympics Mac Tools/468	40.00	70.00
20 Tony Stewart Home Depot Olympics QVC/288	40.00	70.00
20 Tony Stewart Home Depot Shrek 2/10,836	40.00	70.00
20 Tony Stewart Home Depot Shrek 2 Clear Window Bank/348	40.00	70.00
20 Tony Stewart Home Depot Shrek 2 GM Dealers/576	40.00	70.00
20 Tony Stewart Home Depot 25th Anniversary/8664	40.00	70.00
20 Tony Stewart Home Depot 25th Anniversary Clear Window Bank	40.00	70.00
20 Tony Stewart 25 Years of Hard Nosed Racing/3504	40.00	70.00
21 Clint Bowyer Reese's/1008	40.00	70.00
21 Clint Bowyer Reese's GM Dealers/144	40.00	70.00
21 Kevin Harvick Hershey's Kisses/8004	40.00	70.00
21 Kevin Harvick Hershey's Kisses Clear Window Bank/408	40.00	70.00
21 Kevin Harvick Hershey's Kisses GM Dealers/1224	40.00	70.00
21 Kevin Harvick Meijer Reese's White Chocolate/3744	40.00	70.00
21 Kevin Harvick Meijer Reese's White Chocolate CW Bank/228	40.00	70.00
21 Kevin Harvick Reese's/11,376	35.00	60.00
21 Kevin Harvick Reese's Clear Window Bank/384	35.00	60.00
21 Kevin Harvick Reese's GM Dealers/1224	35.00	60.00
21 Kevin Harvick Reese's Mac Tools/288	35.00	60.00
21 Kevin Harvick Reese's Las Vegas Raced/3000	35.00	60.00
21 Kevin Harvick Reese's RCR 35th Anniversary/4812	40.00	70.00
21 Kevin Harvick Reese's RCR 35th Anniversary Clear Window Bank/324	40.00	70.00
22 Jason Keller Miller High Life/2640	35.00	60.00
22 Jason Keller Miller High Life Clear Window Bank/264	35.00	60.00
23 Kenny Wallace Stacker 2/1560	40.00	60.00
23 Kenny Wallace Stacker 2 Clear Window Bank/240	30.00	60.00
24 Jeff Gordon Big Bird/9612	45.00	75.00
24 Jeff Gordon DuPont Flames/22,716	45.00	75.00
24 Jeff Gordon DuPont Flames Clear Window Bank/636	45.00	75.00
24 Jeff Gordon DuPont Flames GM Dealers/2796	45.00	75.00
24 Jeff Gordon DuPont Flames Mac Tools/288	50.00	80.00
24 Jeff Gordon DuPont Flames Nextel Incentive/4704	75.00	125.00
24 Jeff Gordon DuPont Flames Brickyard Raced/6612	50.00	80.00
24 Jeff Gordon DuPont Flames Brickyard Raced w/tire/1596	60.00	100.00
24 Jeff Gordon DuPont Flames California Raced/3012	45.00	75.00
24 Jeff Gordon DuPont Flames HMS 20th Anniversary/8232	45.00	75.00
24 Jeff Gordon DuPont Flames HMS 20th Anniversary Clear Window Bank/528	45.00	75.00
24 Jeff Gordon DuPont Flames HMS 20th Anniversary GM Dealers/420	45.00	75.00
24 Jeff Gordon DuPont Flames HMS 20th Anniversary Mac Tools/468	45.00	75.00
24 Jeff Gordon DuPont Racing Stripes/4920	45.00	75.00
24 Jeff Gordon DuPont Racing Stripes GM Dealers/468	45.00	75.00
24 Jeff Gordon DuPont Rainbow/12,900	50.00	80.00
24 Jeff Gordon DuPont Rainbow Clear Window Bank/552	50.00	80.00
24 Jeff Gordon DuPont Rainbow GM Dealers/960	50.00	80.00
24 Jeff Gordon DuPont Wizard of Oz/14,088	45.00	75.00
24 Jeff Gordon DuPont Wizard of Oz Clear Window Bank/528	45.00	75.00
24 Jeff Gordon Pepsi Billion/9564	45.00	75.00
24 Jeff Gordon Pepsi Billion Clear Window Bank/1008	45.00	75.00
24 Jeff Gordon Pepsi Billion GM Dealers/312	50.00	75.00
24 Jeff Gordon Pepsi Billion Daytona Raced/2892	45.00	75.00
24 Jeff Gordon Pepsi Billion Daytona Raced QVC/504	45.00	75.00
24 Jeff Gordon Pepsi Shards/11,028	50.00	75.00
24 Jeff Gordon Pepsi Shards Clear Window Bank/576	50.00	75.00
24 Jeff Gordon Pepsi Shards GM Dealers/504	50.00	75.00
24 Jeff Gordon Pepsi Shards Talladega Raced/4524	50.00	75.00
24 Jeff Gordon Pepsi Shards Talladega Raced Mac Tools/468	50.00	75.00
24 Jeff Gordon Santa/6132	45.00	75.00
24 Jeff Gordon Santa QVC	45.00	75.00
24 Jeff Gordon 400 Career Starts/3504	45.00	75.00
24 Jeff Gordon 400 Career Starts GM Dealers/408	45.00	75.00
25 Brian Vickers Ditech/5976	40.00	70.00
25 Brian Vickers Ditech Clear Window Bank/300	40.00	70.00
25 Brian Vickers Ditech GM Dealers/288	40.00	70.00
25 Brian Vickers Ditech Father's Day/2868	35.00	60.00
25 Brian Vickers Ditech Father's Day Clear Window Bank/312	35.00	60.00
25 Brian Vickers Ditech Father's Day GM Dealers/144	35.00	60.00
25 Brian Vickers Ditech HMS 20th Anniversary/2448	35.00	60.00
25 Brian Vickers Ditech HMS 20th Anniversary Clear Window Bank/276	35.00	60.00
25 Brian Vickers Ditech HMS 20th GM Dealers/144	35.00	60.00
29 Ricky Craven ESGR Navy/1788	40.00	60.00
29 Ricky Craven ESGR Navy Clear Window Bank/276	40.00	60.00
29 Ricky Craven ESGR Navy GM Dealers/156	40.00	60.00
29 Kerry Earnhardt ESGR Air Force/2052	40.00	60.00
29 Kerry Earnhardt ESGR Air Force Clear Window Bank/252	40.00	60.00
29 Kevin Harvick Coke C2/5472	45.00	75.00
29 Kevin Harvick Coke C2 Clear Window Bank/288	40.00	70.00
29 Kevin Harvick Coke C2 GM Dealers/288	45.00	75.00
29 Kevin Harvick Coke C2 Mac Tools/468	40.00	70.00
29 Kevin Harvick Crown Royal IROC/4776	40.00	70.00
29 Kevin Harvick ESGR Coast Guard/4824	40.00	70.00
29 Kevin Harvick ESGR Coast Guard Clear Window Bank/348	40.00	70.00
29 Kevin Harvick Goodwrench/13,884	40.00	70.00
29 Kevin Harvick Goodwrench Clear Window Bank/432	40.00	70.00
29 Kevin Harvick Goodwrench GM Dealers/2280	40.00	70.00
29 Kevin Harvick Goodwrench Mac Tools/288	40.00	70.00
29 Kevin Harvick Goodwrench Nextel Incentive/2904	60.00	120.00
29 Kevin Harvick Goodwrench KISS/8148	60.00	100.00
29 Kevin Harvick Goodwrench KISS Clear Window Bank/420	60.00	100.00
29 Kevin Harvick Goodwrench RCR 35th Anniversary/7596	40.00	70.00
29 Kevin Harvick Goodwrench RCR 35th Ann. Clear Window Bank/444	40.00	70.00
29 Kevin Harvick Goodwrench Realtree/7572	40.00	70.00
29 Kevin Harvick Goodwrench Realtree Clear Window Bank/432	40.00	70.00
29 Kevin Harvick Goodwrench Realtree GM Dealers/1092	40.00	70.00
29 Kevin Harvick Ice Breakers Liquid Ice/8748	40.00	70.00
29 Kevin Harvick Ice Breakers Liquid Ice Clear Window Bank/444	40.00	70.00
29 Kevin Harvick Powerade/3288	40.00	70.00
29 Kevin Harvick Powerade Clear Window Bank/336	40.00	70.00
29 Kevin Harvick Snap-On/8652	40.00	70.00
29 Kevin Harvick Snap-On Clear Window Bank/432	40.00	70.00
29 Kevin Harvick Snap-On GM Dealers/1080	40.00	70.00
29 Bobby Labonte ESGR Army/4824	40.00	60.00
29 Bobby Labonte ESGR Army Clear Window Bank/300	40.00	60.00
29 Bobby Labonte ESGR Army GM Dealers/300	40.00	60.00
29 Tony Stewart ESGR Marines/7308	40.00	70.00
29 Tony Stewart ESGR Marines Clear Window Bank/384	40.00	70.00
29 Tony Stewart ESGR Marines GM Dealers/372	40.00	70.00
29 Tony Stewart Kid Rock/14,076	40.00	70.00
29 Tony Stewart Kid Rock Clear Window Bank/636	40.00	70.00
29 Tony Stewart Kid Rock GM Dealers/1044	40.00	70.00
30 Jeff Burton AOL RCR 35th Ann./1848	40.00	60.00
30 Johnny Sauter AOL/2532	40.00	70.00
30 Johnny Sauter AOL Clear Window Bank/252	40.00	70.00
30 Johnny Sauter AOL IMAX/2592	40.00	70.00
30 Johnny Sauter AOL IMAX Clear Window Bank/228	40.00	70.00
30 Johnny Sauter AOL IMAX GM Dealers/156	40.00	70.00
30 Johnny Sauter AOL RCR 35th Anniversary/1848	40.00	60.00
30 Johnny Sauter AOL RCR 35th Anniversary Clear Window Bank	40.00	60.00
31 Robby Gordon Cingular/3804	35.00	60.00
31 Robby Gordon Cingular Clear Window Bank/276	35.00	60.00
31 Robby Gordon Cingular Black/2844	40.00	70.00
31 Robby Gordon Cingular Black Clear Window Bank/240	40.00	70.00
31 Robby Gordon Cingular RCR 35th Anniversary/2508	40.00	60.00
31 Robby Gordon Cingular RCR 35th Anniversary Clear Window Bank/276	40.00	60.00
32 Ricky Craven Tide/2988	35.00	60.00
32 Ricky Craven Tide Clear Window Bank/276	35.00	60.00
33 Kerry Earnhardt Bass Pro Shops/4548	40.00	70.00
33 Kerry Earnhardt Bass Pro Shops Clear Window Bank/288	40.00	70.00
33 Kerry Earnhardt Bass Pro Shops Father's Day/7836	40.00	70.00
33 Kerry Earnhardt Bass Pro Shops Father's Day Clear Window Bank/396	40.00	70.00
33 Kerry Earnhardt Bass Pro Shops NRA/2448	35.00	60.00
33 Kerry Earnhardt Bass Pro Shops NRA Clear Window Bank/252	35.00	60.00
38 Kasey Kahne Great Clips/6636	50.00	80.00
38 Kasey Kahne Great Clips Shark Tales/5004	40.00	65.00
38 Kasey Kahne Great Clips Shark Tales Clear Window Bank/336	40.00	65.00
38 Elliott Sadler M&M's/9000	35.00	60.00
38 Elliott Sadler M&M's Clear Window Bank/360	35.00	60.00
38 Elliott Sadler M&M's Mac Tools/288	35.00	60.00
38 Elliott Sadler M&M's Texas Raced w/tire swatch/3504	45.00	75.00
38 Elliott Sadler M&M's Black&White/5880	60.00	100.00
38 Elliott Sadler M&M's Black&White Clear Window Bank/336	45.00	75.00
38 Elliott Sadler M&M's Black&White Raced with tire swatch/2484	60.00	100.00
38 Elliott Sadler M&M's Black&White Raced Clear Window Bank/408	40.00	70.00
38 Elliott Sadler M&M's Halloween/2556	35.00	60.00
38 Elliott Sadler M&M's Halloween Clear Window Bank/204	35.00	60.00
38 Elliott Sadler M&M's Halloween Mac Tools/204	35.00	60.00
38 Elliott Sadler M&M's Halloween QVC/288	35.00	60.00
38 Elliott Sadler M&M's July 4th/4644	35.00	60.00
38 Elliott Sadler Pedigree Wizard of Oz/3540	35.00	60.00
38 Elliott Sadler Pedigree Wizard of Oz Clear Window Bank/252	35.00	60.00
40 Sterling Marlin Aspen Edge/2472	40.00	70.00
40 Sterling Marlin Aspen Edge Clear Window Bank/264	40.00	70.00
40 Sterling Marlin Coors Light/4644	40.00	70.00
40 Sterling Marlin Coors Light Clear Window Bank/312	40.00	70.00
40 Sterling Marlin Coors Light Nextel Incentive/2004	50.00	75.00
40 Sterling Marlin Coors Light Father's Day/2808	40.00	70.00
40 Sterling Marlin Coors Light Father's Day Clear Window Bank/324	40.00	70.00
40 Sterling Marlin Coors Light Kentucy Derby/2988	40.00	70.00
40 Sterling Marlin Coors Light Kentucy Derby Clear Window Bank/216	35.00	60.00
40 Sterling Marlin Prilosec OTC/2100	35.00	60.00
40 Sterling Marlin Prilosec OTC Clear Window Bank/204	35.00	60.00
41 Jamie McMurray Discount Tire Phoenix Raced/4152	45.00	75.00
41 Casey Mears Target/2832	35.00	60.00
41 Casey Mears Target Clear Window Bank/240	35.00	60.00
41 Casey Mears Target Father's Day/1452	35.00	60.00
41 Casey Mears Target Father's Day Clear Window Bank	35.00	60.00
41 Casey Mears Target SpongeBob/2832	35.00	60.00
41 Casey Mears Target SpongeBob Clear Window Bank/240	35.00	60.00
42 Jamie McMurray Havoline/8976	40.00	60.00
42 Jamie McMurray Havoline Clear Window Bank/300	40.00	60.00
42 Jamie McMurray Havoline Mac Tools/288	40.00	60.00
42 Jamie McMurray Havoline Mac Tools/288	40.00	60.00
42 Jamie McMurray Havoline Nextel Incentive/2004	50.00	100.00
42 Jamie McMurray Havoline Father's Day/3408	40.00	60.00
42 Jamie McMurray Havoline Father's Day Clear Window Bank	40.00	60.00
42 Jamie McMurray Havoline Texaco/2700	40.00	60.00
42 Jamie McMurray Havoline Walk of Fame	40.00	60.00
43 Jeff Green Cheerios/1788	35.00	60.00
43 Jeff Green Cheerios Clear Window Bank/228	35.00	60.00
45 Kyle Petty Brawny/1920	40.00	60.00
45 Kyle Petty Brawny Clear Window Bank/228	40.00	60.00
45 Kyle Petty Geogia Pacific/2040	40.00	60.00
45 Kyle Petty Georgia Pacific Clear Window Bank/264	40.00	60.00
45 Kyle Petty Georgia Pacific Father's Day/2844	40.00	60.00
45 Kyle Petty Georgia Pacific Father's Day Clear Window Bank/216	40.00	60.00
46 Dennis Setzer Silverado Trucks SuperTruck/2300	40.00	60.00
47 Ward Burton Silverado Joe Nichols SuperTruck/1932	40.00	70.00
47 Tony Stewart Silverado Sara Evans SuperTruck/4308	40.00	70.00
47 Tony Stewart Sara Evans SuperTruck QVC/504	40.00	70.00
47 Michael Waltrip Silverado Sheryl Crow SuperTruck/4344	40.00	70
48 Jimmie Johnson Crown Royal IROC/3792	40.00	70
48 Jimmie Johnson Lowe's/9300	40.00	70
48 Jimmie Johnson Lowe's Clear Window Bank/384	35.00	60
48 Jimmie Johnson Lowe's GM Dealers/1896	40.00	70
48 Jimmie Johnson Lowe's Mac Tools/288	40.00	70
48 Jimmie Johnson Lowe's Nextel Incentive/2004	60.00	100
48 Jimmie Johnson Lowe's Atlanta Raced GM Dealers/852	50.00	75
48 Jimmie Johnson Lowe's Atlanta Raced QVC/804 w/Bracelet	50.00	75
48 Jimmie Johnson Lowe's Father's Day/3372	40.00	70
48 Jimmie Johnson Lowe's Father's Day Clear Window Bank/348	40.00	70
48 Jimmie Johnson Lowe's HMS20th Anniversary/10,008	40.00	70
48 Jimmie Johnson Lowe's HMS20th Anniversary Clear Window Bank/300	40.00	70
48 Jimmie Johnson Lowe's HMS20th GM Dealers/180	40.00	70
48 Jimmie Johnson Lowe's SpongeBob/2364	40.00	70
48 Jimmie Johnson Lowe's SpongeBob Clear Window Bank	40.00	70
48 Jimmie Johnson Lowe's Tool World/2508	40.00	70
48 Jimmie Johnson Lowe's Tool World Clear Window Bank/240	40.00	70
49 Ken Schrader Schwan's Foods/2928	40.00	60
55 Robby Gordon Fruit of the Loom/2172	40.00	60
55 Robby Gordon Fruit of the Loom CW Bank/216	40.00	60
66 Jamie McMurray Duraflame Darlington Raced/1356	40.00	65
66 Billy Parker Jr. Duraflame/1200	40.00	60
66 Rusty Wallace Duraflame/2340	40.00	70
66 Rusty Wallace Duraflame Clear Window Bank/204	40.00	70
74 Kerry Earnhardt Smith & Wesson/2364	40.00	60
74 Kerry Earnhardt Smith & Wesson Clear Window Bank/300	40.00	60
77 Brendan Gaughan Kodak/3312	45.00	70
77 Brendan Gaughan Kodak Clear Window Bank/240	35.00	60
77 Brendan Gaughan Kodak Jasper Engines/2628	40.00	70
77 Brendan Gaughan Kodak Jasper Engines Clear Window Bank/288	40.00	70
77 Brendan Gaughan Kodak Punisher/2844	35.00	60
77 Brendan Gaughan Kodak Punisher Clear Window Bank/276	35.00	60
77 Brendan Gaughan Kodak Wizard of Oz/2496	35.00	60
77 Brendan Gaughan Kodak Wizard of Oz Clear Window Bank/264	35.00	60
80 J.J. Yeley Crown Royal IROC/2856	45.00	75
80 J.J. Yeley Crown Royal IROC Chrome/204	50.00	75
81 Dale Earnhardt Jr. KFC/24,828	40.00	65
81 Dale Earnhardt Jr. KFC Clear Window Bank/1068	40.00	65
81 Dale Earnhardt Jr. KFC GM Dealers/1944	40.00	65
81 Dale Earnhardt Jr. Menards Bristol Raced/8808	40.00	65
81 Dale Earnhardt Jr. Taco Bell/28,656	40.00	65
81 Dale Earnhardt Jr. Taco Bell Clear Window Bank/1092	40.00	65
81 Dale Earnhardt Jr. Taco Bell GM Dealers/1584	40.00	65
81 Tony Stewart Bass Pro Shops	40.00	70
81 Tony Stewart Bass Pro Shops Clear Window Bank/408	40.00	70
81 Martin Truex Jr. Chance 2/4092	40.00	70
81 Martin Truex Jr. Chance 2 GM Dealers/180	40.00	70
81 Martin Truex Jr. Chance 2 Robert Gee/2880	40.00	70
81 Martin Truex Jr. Chance 2 Robert Gee GM Dealers/144	40.00	70
84 Kyle Busch Carquest/3084	45.00	75
84 Kyle Busch Carquest CW Bank/276	45.00	70
84 Kyle Busch Carquest GM Dealers/144	45.00	75
88 Dale Jarrett UPS/7440	40.00	70
88 Dale Jarrett UPS Clear Window Bank/324	40.00	70
88 Dale Jarrett	50.00	100

UPS Nextel Incentive/2004
Dale Jarrett 45.00 75.00
UPS Arnold Palmer/6024
Dale Jarrett 45.00 75.00
UPS Arnold Palmer
Clear Window Bank/312
Dale Jarrett 50.00 75.00
UPS Bud Shootout Raced
w/tire/4188
Dale Jarrett 45.00 75.00
UPS Monsters/3000
Dale Jarrett 45.00 75.00
UPS Monsters
Clear Window Bank/240
Dale Jarrett 45.00 75.00
UPS Monsters
Mac Tools/204
Bill Elliott 50.00 75.00
UAW Daimler Chrysler
w/tire swatch/5148
Bill Elliott 40.00 70.00
Visteon/2400
Bill Elliott 40.00 70.00
Visteon Clear Window Bank
Kevin Harvick 45.00 75.00
Goodwrench SuperTruck/3480
Kevin Harvick 40.00 70.00
Snap On SuperTruck/4062
Tony Stewart 45.00 75.00
McDonald's/3516
Tony Stewart 45.00 75.00
McDonald's
Clear Window Bank/288
Tony Stewart 45.00 75.00
McDonald's QVC/444
Kurt Busch 40.00 70.00
Crown Royal IROC/2940
Kurt Busch 50.00 75.00
Crown Royal IROC
Chrome/288
Bill Elliott 40.00 70.00
Coke C2/2520
Bill Elliott 40.00 70.00
Coke C2 Clear Window Bank/276
Bill Elliott 40.00 70.00
McDonald's/2376
Bill Elliott 40.00 70.00
McDonald's Clear Window Bank/216
Michael Waltrip/Aaron's/2664 35.00 60.00
Michael Waltrip 35.00 60.00
Aaron's Clear Window Bank/240
Michael Waltrip 35.00 60.00
Aaron's Mac Tools/288
Michael Waltrip 40.00 70.00
Aaron's LeAnn Rimes/2124
Michael Waltrip 40.00 70.00
Aaron's LeAnn Rimes
Clear Window Bank/192
Michael Waltrip 40.00 70.00
Aaron's LeAnn Rimes
GM Dealers/240
Michael Waltrip 40.00 60.00
Aaron's Mad Magazine/2364
Michael Waltrip 40.00 60.00
Aaron's Mad Magazine
Clear Window Bank/240
Michael Waltrip 40.00 60.00
Aaron's Mad Magazine
Mac Tools/204
Michael Waltrip 40.00 60.00
Aaron's Mad Magazine
QVC/288
Michael Waltrip 40.00 60.00
Aaron's
Operation Marathon/1296
Michael Waltrip 35.00 60.00
Best Western/2748
Michael Waltrip 35.00 60.00
Best Western
Clear Window Bank
Michael Waltrip 35.00 60.00
Domino's Pizza/2100
Ward Burton 40.00 70.00
NetZero/2244
Ward Burton 40.00 70.00
NetZero Clear Window Bank/216
Ward Burton 40.00 70.00
NetZero GM Dealers/144
Ward Burton 40.00 70.00
NetZero Shark Tales/1956
Ward Burton 40.00 70.00
NetZero Shark Tales
Clear Window Bank/288
Ward Burton 40.00 70.00
NetZero Shark Tales
GM Dealers/60
Jason Leffler 40.00 60.00
Haas/1200
Jason Leffler 35.00 60.00
Haas Clear Window Bank/240
Kenny Wallace 40.00 60.00
Aaron's Rent Mad Magazine/1860
Kenny Wallace 40.00 60.00
Aaron's Rent Mad Magaine
Clear Window Bank/216
Joe Nemechek 40.00 70.00
Army/2064
Joe Nemechek 40.00 70.00
Army Clear Window Bank/276
Joe Nemechek 35.00 60.00
Army GI Joe/2496
Joe Nemechek 35.00 60.00
Army GI Joe
Clear Window Bank/240
Joe Nemechek 40.00 70.00
Army Time Magazine/2376
Joe Nemechek 40.00 70.00
Army Time Magazine
Clear Window Bank/300
Joe Nemechek 40.00 70.00
Army Time Magazine
GM Dealers/144
Chase for the Nextel Cup 40.00 70.00
brushed metal/1956
Nextel Inaugural Event Car/5112 40.00 70.00
Nextel Inaugural Event Car 40.00 70.00
GM Dealers/288
Victory Junction Gang 40.00 60.00
Event Car/2292
Victory Junction Event Car 30.00 60.00
Clear Window Bank/240
04 Wizard of Oz Event Car/1836 30.00 60.00
04 Wizard of Oz Event 30.00 60.00
GM Dealers/228
35th RCR 35th Anniversary/2520 40.00 60.00
35th RCR 35th Anniversary 40.00 60.00
Clear Window Bank/276
35th RCR 35th Anniversary GM Dealers/348 40.00 60.00
NNO Chevy Rock & Roll 35.00 60.00
Event Car/1656
NNO Chevy Rock & Roll Event Car 35.00 60.00
GM Dealers/216
NNO HMS 20th Anniversary 40.00 60.00
Event Car/1728
NNO Shrek 2 Event Car/1788 35.00 60.00

2004 Action Racing Collectables Historical Series 1:24

EX NM-MT
1 Dale Earnhardt 40.00 70.00
True Value
1999 IROC Orange/6372
2 Dale Earnhardt 50.00 80.00
Mello Yello
1979 Pontiac Ventura/11,664
2 Dale Earnhardt 50.00 80.00
Mello Yello '79 Pontiac Ventura
GM Dealers/984
3 Dale Earnhardt 50.00 80.00
Goodwrench Olympic 1996 Monte Carlo
Clear Window Bank/6696
3 Dale Earnhardt 40.00 75.00
Wrangler 1985 Camaro/21,000
3 Dale Earnhardt 40.00 75.00
Wrangler 1985 Camaro
GM Dealers/1092
3 Dale Earnhardt Jr. 50.00 75.00
Sun Drop 1994 Lumina
Color Chrome/11,136
3 Dale Earnhardt Jr. 50.00 80.00
Sun Drop '94 Lum.
Color Chrome Mac Tools/288
7 Dale Earnhardt Jr. 40.00 75.00
Church Brothers 1997 Monte Carlo
Clear Window Bank/7008
8 Dale Earnhardt Jr. 50.00 75.00
Bud Olympics 2000 Monte Carlo
CW Bank/6138
8 Dale Earnhardt Jr. 60.00 100.00
Bud 2003 Phoenix Raced/7116
8 Dale Earnhardt Jr. 60.00 100.00
Bud '03 Phoenix Raced
GM Dealers/324
9 Bill Elliott 45.00 75.00
Coors '85 t-bird/3660
9 Bill Elliott 45.00 75.00
Coors '85 t-bird
Clear Window Bank/348
9 Bill Elliott 45.00 75.00
Coors Light '91 t-bird/4032
9 Bill Elliott 45.00 75.00
Coors Light 1991 t-bird
Clear Window Bank/348
17 Darrell Waltrip 40.00 70.00
Tide 1987 400 Chevy Wins
Color Chrome/3132
24 Jeff Gordon 50.00 80.00
DuPont 1996 Monte Carlo
400 Chevy Wins Color Chrome/6192
28 Davey Allison 45.00 75.00
Texaco 1993 Thunderbird/2988
28 Davey Allison 45.00 75.00
Texaco 1993 Thunderbird
Clear Window Bank/360
29 Kevin Harvick 50.00 80.00
Goodwrench Service Plus
2001 Monte Carlo
black numbers/33,000
29 Kevin Harvick 50.00 80.00
Goodwrench Service Plus
2001 Monte Carlo
Clear Window Bank/240
38 Kelley Earnhardt 40.00 70.00
Mom & Pop's
1995 Camaro/3588
43 Richard Petty 50.00 80.00
STP 1980 400 Chevy Wins
Color Chrome/3924
43 Richard Petty 50.00 80.00
STP 200th Win
1984 Grand Prix/4992
43 Richard Petty 40.00 70.00
STP 200th Win
1984 Tribute/3768
48 Jimmie Johnson 60.00 100.00
Lowe's 2003 Monte Carlo
400 Chevy Wins Color Chrome/3204

2004 Action QVC For Race Fans Only 1:24

EX NM-MT
2 Rusty Wallace 75.00 150.00
Miller Lite Martinsville Raced
Color Chrome AU/504
2 Rusty Wallace 75.00 125.00
Miller Lite Last Call
Color Chrome/1500
3 Dale Earnhardt 60.00 100.00
Goodwrench Olympic
1996 Monte Carlo Color Chrome/5004
3 Dale Earnhardt 100.00 200.00
Goodwrench Crash
'97 Daytona Raced Color Chrome/5004
3 Dale Earnhardt 100.00 200.00
Goodwrench Crash
'97 Daytona Raced Gold/504
3 Dale Earnhardt 75.00 150.00
Goodwrench Peter Max
'00 Monte Carlo Color Chrome/504
8 Dale Earnhardt Jr. 125.00 200.00
Bud Brushed Metal/1008
8 Dale Earnhardt Jr. 60.00 100.00
Bud Color Chrome/5016
8 Dale Earnhardt Jr. 80.00 130.00
Bud Gold/1008
8 Dale Earnhardt Jr. 150.00 250.00
Bud Platinum/504
8 Dale Earnhardt Jr. 90.00 150.00
Bud Born On Feb.7
Color Chrome/5004
8 Dale Earnhardt Jr. 100.00 175.00
Bud Born On
Feb.7 Gold/504
8 Dale Earnhardt Jr. 200.00 350.00
Bud Born On
Feb.7 Platinum/300
8 Dale Earnhardt Jr. 75.00 125.00
Bud Born On Feb.15
Raced Color Chrome/7500
8 Dale Earnhardt Jr. 75.00 125.00
Bud Dave Matthews Band
Color Chrome/6000
8 Dale Earnhardt Jr. 60.00 100.00
Bud Father's Day
Brushed Metal/504
8 Dale Earnhardt Jr. 75.00 125.00
Bud World Series
Color Chrome/6000
8 Dale Earnhardt Jr. 75.00 125.00
Bud World Series
Gold/500
8 Dale Earnhardt Jr. 75.00 125.00
Oreo Brushed Metal/504
8 Dale Earnhardt Jr. 75.00 125.00
Oreo Color Chrome/5016
8 Dale Earnhardt Jr. 100.00 175.00
Oreo Gold/504
8 Dale Earnhardt Jr. 175.00 300.00
Oreo Platinum/300
8 Martin Truex Jr. 125.00 200.00
Wrangler
Color Chrome AU/408
9 Kasey Kahne 60.00 100.00
Dodge Refresh Color Chrome/504
9 Kasey Kahne 150.00 250.00
Dodge Refresh Gold/300
9 Kasey Kahne 150.00 250.00
Dodge Refresh
Platinum/300
9 Kasey Kahne 50.00 75.00
Dodge ROY Brushed Metal/504
9 Kasey Kahne 50.00 75.00
Dodge Mad Magazine
Color Chrome/408
9 Kasey Kahne 100.00 175.00
Dodge Popeye
Color Chrome/504
9 Kasey Kahne 60.00 100.00
Mopar Color Chrome/1008
9 Kasey Kahne 125.00 200.00
Mountain Dew Color Chrome/408
24 Jeff Gordon 60.00 100.00
DuPont Flames
Brushed Metal/1008
24 Jeff Gordon 90.00 150.00
DuPont Flames
Color Chrome/504
24 Jeff Gordon 100.00 175.00
DuPont Flames Platinum/300
24 Jeff Gordon 100.00 175.00
DuPont Flames
Wizard of Oz Platinum/300
24 Jeff Gordon 60.00 100.00
DuPont Rainbow
Color Chrome/504
81 Dale Earnhardt Jr. 60.00 100.00
Chance 2 KFC
Color Chrome/5004
81 Dale Earnhardt Jr. 60.00 100.00
Chance 2 Taco Bell
Color Chrome/5004

2004 Action/RCCA 1:24

EX NM-MT
1 John Andretti 30.00 60.00
Coke C2/288
1 John Andretti 40.00 70.00
Legacy Snap-On/288
1 John Andretti 30.00 60.00
Post Maxwell House/300
2 Ron Hornaday 40.00 60.00
AC Delco KISS/288
2 Rusty Wallace 40.00 70.00
Kodak/600
2 Rusty Wallace 40.00 70.00
Miller Lite/1200
2 Rusty Wallace 40.00 70.00
Miller Lite
Can Promotion/408
2 Rusty Wallace 40.00 70.00
Miller Lite
Father's Day/240
2 Rusty Wallace 60.00 100.00
Miller Lite
Last Call/600
2 Rusty Wallace 45.00 75.00
Miller Lite
Martinsville Raced w/tire/240
2 Rusty Wallace 40.00 70.00
Miller Lite
Penske 50th/504
2 Rusty Wallace 40.00 70.00
Miller Lite
President of Beers/600
2 Rusty Wallace 40.00 70.00
Miller Lite
Puddle of Mudd/504
5 Kyle Busch 45.00 75.00
Lowe's/288
5 Kyle Busch 40.00 70.00
Lowe's SpongeBob/360
5 Terry Labonte 40.00 60.00
Kellogg's/300
5 Terry Labonte 40.00 60.00
Kellogg's Father's Day/240
5 Terry Labonte 40.00 60.00
Kellogg's HMS 20th Anniversary/288
5 Terry Labonte 40.00 60.00
Kellogg's Incredibles/408
5 Terry Labonte 40.00 60.00
Kellogg's UAW Delphi/288
6 Bill Elliott 45.00 75.00
Lucas Oil Elvis/540
8 Dale Earnhardt Jr. 40.00 70.00
Bud/3600
8 Dale Earnhardt Jr. 50.00 80.00
Bud Born On
Feb.12 Raced/3000
8 Dale Earnhardt Jr. 75.00 125.00
Bud Born On
Feb.7/3000
8 Dale Earnhardt Jr. 60.00 100.00
Bud Born On
Feb.15 Raced/4800
8 Dale Earnhardt Jr. 40.00 70.00
Bud Dave Matthews Band/2388
8 Dale Earnhardt Jr. 60.00 100.00
Bud Father's Day/1200
8 Dale Earnhardt Jr. 40.00 70.00
Bud World Series/2508
8 Dale Earnhardt Jr. 40.00 65.00
Oreo/3000
8 Martin Truex Jr. 45.00 75.00
Bass Pro Shops/444
8 Martin Truex Jr. 60.00 100.00
Bass Pro Shops
'04 Champion Color Chrome/600
8 Martin Truex Jr. 45.00 75.00
Chance 2 Ralph Earnhardt/444
8 Martin Truex Jr. 40.00 70.00
Chance 2 Richie Evans/360
8 Martin Truex Jr. 40.00 70.00
Chance 2 Tear Away/444
8 Martin Truex Jr. 40.00 70.00
KFC Dover Raced/300
8 Martin Truex Jr. 45.00 75.00
Long John Silver's/360
8 Martin Truex Jr. 50.00 75.00
Taco Bell
Bristol Raced/540
8 Martin Truex Jr. 45.00 75.00
Wrangler/444
9 Bill Elliott 40.00 70.00
Milestones/408
9 Kasey Kahne 125.00 200.00
Dodge/288
9 Kasey Kahne 100.00 175.00
Dodge refresh ROY AU/504
9 Kasey Kahne 50.00 75.00
Dodge Mad Magazine/600
9 Kasey Kahne 60.00 100.00
Dodge Mopar/444
9 Kasey Kahne 50.00 80.00
Dodge Pit Cap/600
9 Kasey Kahne 50.00 75.00
Dodge Popeye/576
9 Kasey Kahne 75.00 125.00
Mountain Dew/540
10 Scott Riggs 40.00 60.00
Valvoline/360
10 Scott Riggs 40.00 60.00
Valvoline Wizard of Oz/288
12 Ryan Newman 50.00 75.00
Crown Royal IROC
Color Chrome/288
15 Michael Waltrip 40.00 70.00
NAPA/600
15 Michael Waltrip 40.00 70.00
NAPA Father's Day/240
15 Michael Waltrip 40.00 70.00
NAPA Stars & Stripes/288
17 Matt Kenseth 50.00 75.00
Crown Royal IROC Color Chrome/288
17 Matt Kenseth 50.00 75.00
Crown Royal IROC
'04 Champion Pearl/360
17 Darrell Waltrip 50.00 100.00
King of Bristol AU/360
18 Bobby Labonte 40.00 60.00
Interstate Batteries/504
18 Bobby Labonte 40.00 60.00
Interstate Batteries
Father's Day/240
18 Bobby Labonte 40.00 70.00
Interstate Batteries
D-Day/504
18 Bobby Labonte 40.00 60.00
Interstate Batteries Shrek 2/600
18 Bobby Labonte 40.00 60.00
Wellbutrin/360
18 J.J. Yeley 35.00 60.00
Vigoro/204
19 Bobby Labonte 40.00 60.00
Banquet/288
19 Jeremy Mayfield 40.00 60.00
Dodge HEMI/288
19 Jeremy Mayfield 40.00 60.00
Dodge Mad Magazine/288
19 Jeremy Mayfield 40.00 60.00
Dodge NHL All Star Game/288
19 Jeremy Mayfield 40.00 60.00
Dodge Popeye/360
20 Tony Stewart 40.00 70.00
Coke C2/600
20 Tony Stewart 40.00 70.00
Home Depot/1500
20 Tony Stewart 40.00 70.00
Home Depot Black Reverse/1008
20 Tony Stewart 40.00 70.00
Home Depot
Father's Day/204
20 Tony Stewart 40.00 70.00
Home Depot
Olympic/600
20 Tony Stewart 40.00 70.00
Home Depot Shrek 2/1008
20 Tony Stewart 40.00 70.00
Home Depot 25th Anniversary
21 Clint Bowyer 40.00 70.00
Reese's/144
21 Kevin Harvick 40.00 70.00
Hershey's Kisses/720
21 Kevin Harvick 40.00 70.00
Meijer Reese's White Chocolate/288
21 Kevin Harvick 40.00 70.00
Reese's/900
21 Kevin Harvick 40.00 60.00
Reese's RCR 35th Anniversary/444
22 Jason Keller 40.00 60.00
Miller High Life/288
23 Kenny Wallace 30.00 60.00
Stacker 2/288
24 Jeff Gordon 45.00 75.00
Big Bird/1500
24 Jeff Gordon 50.00 80.00
DuPont Flames/1800
24 Jeff Gordon 60.00 100.00
DuPont Flames
Brickyard Raced/524
24 Jeff Gordon 45.00 75.00
DuPont Flames
Wizard of Oz/1800
24 Jeff Gordon 50.00 80.00
DuPont Flames HMS 20th Anniversary/1500
24 Jeff Gordon 45.00 75.00
DuPont Racing Stripes/660
24 Jeff Gordon 50.00 80.00
DuPont Rainbow/1200
24 Jeff Gordon 45.00 75.00
Pepsi Billion/1200
24 Jeff Gordon 45.00 75.00
Pepsi Billion
Daytona Raced/444
24 Jeff Gordon 50.00 80.00
Pepsi Shards/720
24 Jeff Gordon 50.00 80.00
Pepsi Shards
Talladega Raced/300
25 Brian Vickers 40.00 70.00
ditech/288
25 Brian Vickers 35.00 60.00
ditech Father's Day/240
25 Brian Vickers 35.00 60.00
ditech HMS 20th Anniversary/288
29 Kevin Harvick 40.00 70.00
Coke C2/600
29 Kevin Harvick 50.00 75.00
Crown Royal IROC
Color Chrome/288
29 Kevin Harvick 40.00 70.00
ESGR Coast Guard/600
29 Kevin Harvick 40.00 70.00
Goodwrench/1008
29 Kevin Harvick 60.00 100.00
Goodwrench KISS/1008
29 Kevin Harvick 40.00 70.00
Goodwrench RCR
35th Anniversary/900
29 Kevin Harvick 40.00 70.00
Goodwrench Realtree/1200
29 Kevin Harvick 40.00 70.00
Ice Breakers/504
29 Kevin Harvick 40.00 70.00
Powerade/600
29 Kevin Harvick 40.00 70.00
Snap-On/804
29 Bobby Labonte 40.00 60.00
ESGR Army/600
29 Tony Stewart 40.00 70.00
ESGR Marines/1008
29 Tony Stewart 40.00 70.00
Kid Rock/1200
30 Johnny Sauter 40.00 70.00
AOL/288
30 Johnny Sauter 40.00 70.00
AOL IMAX/288
31 Robby Gordon 35.00 60.00
Cingular Black/300
31 Robby Gordon 35.00 60.00
Cingular RCR 35th Ann./288
32 Ricky Craven 35.00 60.00
Tide/300
33 Kerry Earnhardt 35.00 60.00
Bass Pro Shops/504
38 Kasey Kahne 50.00 80.00
Great Clips/360
38 Kasey Kahne 35.00 60.00
Great Clips Shark Tale/560
38 Elliott Sadler 40.00 70.00
M&M's/300
38 Elliott Sadler 40.00 70.00
M&M's Texas Raced/240
38 Elliott Sadler 40.00 70.00
M&M's Black&White/360
38 Elliott Sadler 60.00 100.00
M&M's Black&White
Raced w/tire/240
38 Elliott Sadler 35.00 60.00
M&M's Halloween/408
38 Elliott Sadler 35.00 60.00
M&M's July 4/288
38 Elliott Sadler 35.00 60.00
Pedigree
Wizard of Oz/360
40 Sterling Marlin 40.00 70.00
Aspen Edge/288
40 Sterling Marlin 40.00 70.00
Coors Light/300
40 Sterling Marlin 35.00 60.00
Coors Light Father's Day/240
40 Sterling Marlin 40.00 60.00
Coors Light
Kentucky Derby/204
40 Sterling Marlin 40.00 60.00
Prilosec/288
41 Casey Mears 35.00 60.00
Target/408
41 Casey Mears 35.00 60.00
Target SpongeBob/288
42 Jamie McMurray 40.00 60.00
Havoline Father's Day/240
42 Jamie McMurray 40.00 60.00
Havoline Texaco Rising Star/360
43 Jeff Green 40.00 60.00
Cheerios/288
45 Kyle Petty 35.00 60.00
Brawny/300
45 Kyle Petty 35.00 60.00
Georgia Pacific/300
45 Kyle Petty 40.00 60.00
Georgia Pacific Father's Day/240
48 Jimmie Johnson 50.00 75.00

Crown Royal IROC
Color Chrome/288
48 Jimmie Johnson 40.00 70.00
Lowe's/804
48 Jimmie Johnson 35.00 60.00
Lowe's Father's Day/240
48 Jimmie Johnson 40.00 70.00
Lowe's HMS 20th Anniversary/600
48 Jimmie Johnson 40.00 70.00
Lowe's SpongeBob/504
48 Jimmie Johnson 40.00 70.00
Lowe's Tool World/600
55 Robby Gordon 35.00 60.00
Fruit of the Loom/336
66 Billy Parker 40.00 60.00
Duraflame/300
66 Rusty Wallace 40.00 70.00
Duraflame/408
77 Brendan Gaughan 45.00 70.00
Kodak/288
77 Brendan Gaughan 35.00 60.00
Kodak Punisher/288
77 Brendan Gaughan 35.00 60.00
Kodak Wizard of Oz/288
77 Brendan Gaughan 40.00 70.00
Jasper/288
81 Dale Earnhardt Jr. 40.00 65.00
KFC/3000
81 Dale Earnhardt Jr. 40.00 65.00
Menards Bristol Raced/1008
81 Dale Earnhardt Jr. 40.00 65.00
Taco Bell/1800
81 Tony Stewart 45.00 75.00
Bass Pro Shops/600
81 Martin Truex Jr. 40.00 70.00
Chance 2
Robert Gee/360
84 Kyle Busch 40.00 70.00
CarQuest/360
88 Dale Jarrett 40.00 70.00
UPS/300
88 Dale Jarrett 50.00 75.00
UPS Raced w/tire/240
88 Dale Jarrett 40.00 70.00
UPS Monsters/540
91 Bill Elliott 50.00 75.00
UAW Daimler Chrysler
w/tire swatch/288
91 Bill Elliott 40.00 70.00
Visteon/360
92 Kevin Harvick 40.00 70.00
Goodwrench
SuperTruck/444
92 Tony Stewart 40.00 70.00
McDonald's/600
97 Kurt Busch 50.00 75.00
Crown Royal IROC
Color Chrome/288
98 Bill Elliott 40.00 70.00
Coke C2/360
98 Bill Elliott 40.00 70.00
McDonald's/360
99 Michael Waltrip 40.00 60.00
Aaron's Dream Machine
LeAnn Rimes/288
99 Michael Waltrip 35.00 60.00
Aaron's Dream Machine
Mad Magazine/288
99 Michael Waltrip 35.00 60.00
Aaron's Dream Machine
Operation Marathon/360
99 Michael Waltrip 35.00 60.00
Domino's Pizza/360
0 Ward Burton 40.00 60.00
NetZero Hi Speed/204
0 Ward Burton 40.00 60.00
NetZero Hi Speed
Shark Tale/444
0 Jason Leffler 30.00 60.00
HAAS/288
0 Kenny Wallace 30.00 60.00
Aaron's Mad Magazine/288
01 Joe Nemechek 40.00 70.00
Army/288
01 Joe Nemechek 40.00 70.00
Army GI Joe/288
01 Joe Nemechek 40.00 70.00
Army Time Magazine/360
04 Nextel Inaugural Event Car/444 40.00 80.00
04 Victory Junction Gang 30.00 60.00
Event Car/360
04 Wizard of Oz Event Car/396 35.00 60.00
35th RCR 35th Anniversary 35.00 60.00
Event Car/288
NNO Chevy Rock&Roll 35.00 60.00
Event Car/288
NNO HMS 20th Anniversary 40.00 60.00
Event Car/288
NNO Shrek 2 Event Car/300 40.00 60.00

2004 Action/RCCA Elite 1:24

EX NM-MT
1 John Andretti 70.00 110.00
Legacy Snap-On/288
1 John Andretti 70.00 110.00
Post Maxwell House/300
2 Rusty Wallace 75.00 125.00
Kodak/600
2 Rusty Wallace 250.00 350.00
Kodak White Gold/25
2 Rusty Wallace 75.00 125.00
Miller Lite/1500
2 Rusty Wallace 75.00 125.00
Miller Lite Color Chrome/408
2 Rusty Wallace 90.00 135.00
Miller Lite
Martinsville Raced/240
2 Rusty Wallace 75.00 125.00
Miller Lite
Can Promotion/504
2 Rusty Wallace 90.00 150.00
Miller Lite Last Call/804
2 Rusty Wallace 250.00 350.00
Miller Lite Last Call
Platinum/204
2 Rusty Wallace 350.00 500.00
Miller Lite Last Call
White Gold/25
2 Rusty Wallace 80.00 135.00
Miller Lite
Penske 50th/504
2 Rusty Wallace 70.00 110.00
Miller Lite
Puddle of Mudd/504
2 Rusty Wallace 80.00 125.00
Miller Lite
President of Beers/600
5 Kyle Busch 100.00 175.00
Lowe's/288
5 Kyle Busch 75.00 125.00
Lowe's SpongeBob/300
5 Kyle Busch 200.00 300.00
Lowe's SpongeBob
White Gold/25
5 Terry Labonte 75.00 120.00
Kellogg's/300
5 Terry Labonte 75.00 120.00
Kellogg's HMS 20th Ann/288
5 Terry Labonte 75.00 125.00
Kellogg's Incredibles/408
5 Terry Labonte 300.00 450.00
Kellogg's Incredibles
White Gold/25
5 Terry Labonte 75.00 120.00
Kellogg's Olympic/360
5 Terry Labonte 75.00 120.00
Kellogg's UAW Delphi/288
6 Bill Elliott 70.00 110.00
Lucas Oil Elvis/540
6 Bill Elliott 200.00 350.00
Lucas Oil Elvis
White Gold/25
8 Dale Earnhardt Jr. 90.00 150.00
Bud/5004
8 Dale Earnhardt Jr. 90.00 150.00
Bud Color Chrome/2400
8 Dale Earnhardt Jr. 200.00 350.00
Bud Platinum/408
8 Dale Earnhardt Jr. 90.00 135.00
Bud Bristol Raced/1200
8 Dale Earnhardt Jr. 90.00 135.00
Bud Talladega Raced/804
8 Dale Earnhardt Jr. 100.00 175.00
Bud Born On
Feb.7/4008
8 Dale Earnhardt Jr. 250.00 400.00
Bud Born On Feb.7
Platinum/408
8 Dale Earnhardt Jr. 90.00 150.00
Bud Born On
Feb.12 Raced/2400
8 Dale Earnhardt Jr. 125.00 200.00
Bud Born On
Feb.15 Raced/6996
8 Dale Earnhardt Jr. 250.00 400.00
Bud Born On Feb.15
Raced Platinum/408
8 Dale Earnhardt Jr. 75.00 125.00
Bud
Dave Matthews Band/3888
8 Dale Earnhardt Jr. 100.00 200.00
Bud Dave Matthews Band
Platinum/360
8 Dale Earnhardt Jr. 300.00 450.00
Bud Dave Matthews Band
White Gold/25
8 Dale Earnhardt Jr. 90.00 150.00
Bud Father's Day/2200
8 Dale Earnhardt Jr. 150.00 300.00
Bud Father's Day
Platinum/300
8 Dale Earnhardt Jr. 90.00 150.00
Bud World Series/2888
8 Dale Earnhardt Jr. 175.00 300.00
Bud World Series
Platinum/300
8 Dale Earnhardt Jr. 300.00 450.00
Bud World Series
White Gold/50
8 Dale Earnhardt Jr. 75.00 125.00
Oreo/4800
8 Dale Earnhardt Jr. 175.00 300.00
Oreo Platinum/300
8 Dale Earnhardt Jr. 75.00 125.00
Test/4000
8 Martin Truex Jr. 90.00 150.00
Bass Pro Shops/444
8 Martin Truex Jr. 100.00 175.00
Bass Pro Shops
'04 Champion Color Chrome/600
8 Martin Truex Jr. 75.00 120.00
Chance 2 Ralph Earnhardt/444
8 Martin Truex Jr. 70.00 110.00
Chance 2 Richie Evans/360
8 Martin Truex Jr. 70.00 110.00
Chance 2 Tear Away/360
8 Martin Truex Jr. 90.00 135.00
KFC Dover Raced/300
8 Martin Truex Jr. 70.00 110.00
Long John Silver's/360
8 Martin Truex Jr. 90.00 150.00
Taco Bell
Bristol Raced/540
8 Martin Truex Jr. 70.00 110.00
Wrangler/444
9 Bill Elliott 80.00 125.00
Milestones/408
9 Bill Elliott 250.00 400.00
Milestones White Gold/40
9 Kasey Kahne 300.00 450.00
Dodge/288
9 Kasey Kahne 100.00 200.00
Dodge Refresh Color Chrome/444
9 Kasey Kahne 175.00 300.00
Dodge refresh ROY AU/600
9 Kasey Kahne 150.00 300.00
Dodge refresh ROY
liquid metal/100
9 Kasey Kahne 100.00 175.00
Dodge Mad Magazine/804
9 Kasey Kahne 300.00 450.00
Dodge Mad Magazine
White Gold/50
9 Kasey Kahne 100.00 175.00
Dodge Mopar/444
9 Kasey Kahne 100.00 200.00
Dodge Pit Cap/600
9 Kasey Kahne 300.00 500.00
Dodge Pit Cap
White Gold/50
9 Kasey Kahne 100.00 175.00
Dodge Popeye/576
9 Kasey Kahne 125.00 250.00
Mountain Dew/540
10 Scott Riggs 70.00 110.00
Valvoline Wizard of Oz/288
15 Michael Waltrip 70.00 110.00
NAPA/800
15 Michael Waltrip 75.00 120.00
NAPA Color Chrome/300
15 Michael Waltrip 70.00 110.00
NAPA Test Daytona/504
15 Michael Waltrip 70.00 110.00
NAPA Stars & Stripes/288
17 Darrell Waltrip 75.00 125.00
King of Bristol AU/360
18 Bobby Labonte 70.00 120.00
Interstate Batteries/720
18 Bobby Labonte 75.00 125.00
Interstate Batteries Color Chrome/300
18 Bobby Labonte 70.00 110.00
Interstate Batteries D-Day/504
18 Bobby Labonte 70.00 110.00
Interstate Batteries Shrek 2/600
18 Bobby Labonte 70.00 110.00
Wellbutrin/360
18 J.J. Yeley 70.00 110.00
Vigoro/204
19 Bobby Labonte 70.00 110.00
Banquet/288
19 Jeremy Mayfield 70.00 110.00
Dodge HEMI/288
20 Tony Stewart 80.00 125.00
Coke C2/600
20 Tony Stewart 80.00 125.00
Home Depot/1800
20 Tony Stewart 90.00 150.00
Home Depot Color Chrome/600
20 Tony Stewart 75.00 125.00
Home Depot Black Reverse/1500
20 Tony Stewart 75.00 125.00
Home Depot
Olympic/900
20 Tony Stewart 400.00 600.00
Home Depot Olympic
White Gold/25
20 Tony Stewart 75.00 125.00
Home Depot Shrek 2/1500
20 Tony Stewart 75.00 125.00
Home Depot Test/1200
20 Tony Stewart 75.00 125.00
Home Depot 25th Anniversary/1008
21 Kevin Harvick 75.00 125.00
Hershey's Kisses/1008
21 Kevin Harvick 75.00 120.00
Meijer Reese's White Chocolate/288
21 Kevin Harvick 75.00 120.00
Reese's/1200
21 Kevin Harvick 75.00 125.00
Reese's Las Vegas Raced/240
21 Kevin Harvick 75.00 120.00
Reese's RCR
35th Anniversary/444
24 Jeff Gordon 80.00 125.00
Big Bird/2004
24 Jeff Gordon 90.00 150.00
DuPont Flames/2400
24 Jeff Gordon 100.00 175.00
DuPont Flames Color Chrome/804
24 Jeff Gordon 100.00 175.00
DuPont Flames
Brickyard Raced/524
24 Jeff Gordon 90.00 135.00
DuPont Flames
HMS 20th Anniversary/1800
24 Jeff Gordon 200.00 300.00
DuPont Flames HMS 20th Ann.
Platinum/300
24 Jeff Gordon 80.00 125.00
DuPont Flames
Wizard of Oz/2700
24 Jeff Gordon 125.00 250.00
DuPont Flames
Wizard of Oz Platinum/360
24 Jeff Gordon 500.00 750.00
DuPont Flames
Wizard of Oz White Gold/25
24 Jeff Gordon 80.00 125.00
DuPont HMS20 Years Test/1824
24 Jeff Gordon 90.00 135.00
DuPont Racing Stripes/660
24 Jeff Gordon 100.00 200.00
DuPont Rainbow/1800
24 Jeff Gordon 80.00 135.00
Pepsi Billion/1500
24 Jeff Gordon 90.00 135.00
Pepsi Billion
Daytona Raced/444
24 Jeff Gordon 90.00 135.00
Pepsi Shards/1008
24 Jeff Gordon 90.00 135.00
Pepsi Shards
Talladega Raced/480
24 Jeff Gordon 80.00 125.00
Santa/900
24 Jeff Gordon 150.00 250.00
400 Career Starts/624
25 Brian Vickers 80.00 135.00
ditech.com/444
25 Brian Vickers 70.00 110.00
ditech HMS 20th Ann/288
29 Ricky Craven 70.00 110.00
ESGR Navy/288
29 Kerry Earnhardt 70.00 110.00
ESGR Air Force/504
29 Kevin Harvick 80.00 125.00
Coke C2/600
29 Kevin Harvick 70.00 110.00
ESGR Coast Guard/600
29 Kevin Harvick 80.00 125.00
Goodwrench/1500
29 Kevin Harvick 100.00 175.00
Goodwrench Color Chrome/600
29 Kevin Harvick 100.00 150.00
Goodwrench KISS/1500
29 Kevin Harvick 80.00 135.00
Goodwrench RCR
35th Anniversary/1200
29 Kevin Harvick 70.00 110.00
Goodwrench Realtree/1500
29 Kevin Harvick 80.00 125.00
Ice Breakers/804
29 Kevin Harvick 80.00 125.00
Powerade/600
29 Kevin Harvick 70.00 110.00
Snap-On/1200
29 Bobby Labonte 80.00 125.00
ESGR Army/600
29 Tony Stewart 75.00 120.00
ESGR Marines/1500
29 Tony Stewart 80.00 125.00
Kid Rock/1500
30 Johnny Sauter 75.00 120.00
AOL IMAX/288
31 Robby Gordon 70.00 100.00
Cingular/408
31 Robby Gordon 75.00 125.00
Cingular Color Chrome/288
31 Robby Gordon 70.00 100.00
Cingular Black/288
31 Robby Gordon 70.00 100.00
Cingular RCR
35th Ann./288
33 Kerry Earnhardt 80.00 125.00
Bass Pro Shops/504
33 Kerry Earnhardt 80.00 125.00
Bass Pro Shops
Father's Day/360
33 Kerry Earnhardt 80.00 125.00
Bass Pro Shops NRA/288
38 Kasey Kahne 75.00 125.00
Great Clips/360
38 Kasey Kahne 60.00 100.00
Great Clips Shark Tale/560
38 Kasey Kahne 275.00 400.00
Great Clips Shark Tale
White Gold/25
38 Elliott Sadler 80.00 125.00
M&M's/300
38 Elliott Sadler 90.00 135.00
M&M's Texas Raced/240
38 Elliott Sadler 80.00 135.00
M&M's Black&White/360
38 Elliott Sadler 90.00 150.00
M&M's Black&White
Raced w/tire/240
38 Elliott Sadler 70.00 110.00
M&M's Halloween/408
38 Elliott Sadler 70.00 110.00
M&M's July 4/288
38 Elliott Sadler 70.00 110.00
Pedigree Wizard of Oz/360
40 Sterling Marlin 75.00 120.00
Aspen Edge/288
40 Sterling Marlin 70.00 110.00
Coors Light Kentucky Derby/204
41 Casey Mears 70.00 110.00
Target SpongeBob/240
42 Jamie McMurray 75.00 120.00
Havoline/900
42 Jamie McMurray 70.00 110.00
Havoline Texaco
Rising Star/360
43 Jeff Green 70.00 110.00
Cheerios
45 Kyle Petty 70.00 110.00
Brawny/300
45 Kyle Petty 75.00 120.00
Georgia Pacific/300
45 Kyle Petty 75.00 120.00
Georgia Pacific Father's Day/240
48 Jimmie Johnson 75.00 125.00
Lowe's/1200
48 Jimmie Johnson 90.00 135.00
Lowe's Color Chrome/480
48 Jimmie Johnson 90.00 135.00
Lowe's HMS 20th Anniversary/900
48 Jimmie Johnson 75.00 125.00
Lowe's SpongeBob/504
48 Jimmie Johnson 300.00 450.00
Lowe's SpongeBob
White Gold/25
48 Jimmie Johnson 75.00 125.00
Lowe's Tool World/900
48 Jimmie Johnson 300.00 450.00
Lowe's Tool World
White Gold/25
55 Robby Gordon 70.00 110.00
Fruit of the Loom/336
66 Rusty Wallace 70.00 110.00
Duraflame/600
74 Kerry Earnhardt 70.00 110.00
Smith & Wesson/288
77 Brendan Gaughan 80.00 125.00
Kodak/288
77 Brendan Gaughan 70.00 110.00
Kodak Punisher/288
77 Brendan Gaughan 70.00 110.00
Kodak Wizard of Oz/288
81 Dale Earnhardt Jr. 75.00 125.00
KFC/4440
81 Dale Earnhardt Jr. 75.00 125.00
Menards Bristol Raced/1500
81 Dale Earnhardt Jr. 200.00 350.00
Menards Bristol Raced
White Gold/48
81 Dale Earnhardt Jr. 75.00 125.00
Taco Bell/3000
81 Dale Earnhardt Jr. 175.00 300.00
Taco Bell
Platinum/300
81 Tony Stewart 80.00 125.00
Bass Pro Shops/900
81 Martin Truex Jr. 70.00 110.00
Chance 2
Robert Gee/360
84 Kyle Busch 60.00 120.00
CarQuest/360
88 Dale Jarrett 80.00 125.
UPS/300
88 Dale Jarrett 90.00 135.
UPS Color Chrome/300
88 Dale Jarrett 90.00 135.
UPS Raced w/tire/240
88 Dale Jarrett 90.00 135.
UPS Arnold Palmer/492
88 Dale Jarrett 75.00 125.
UPS Monsters/540
88 Dale Jarrett 250.00 400.
UPS Monsters White Gold/25
91 Bill Elliott 90.00 135.
UAW Daimler Chrysler
w/tire swatch/288
91 Bill Elliott 80.00 125.
Visteon/360
92 Tony Stewart 70.00 110.
McDonald's/600
98 Bill Elliott 75.00 120.
Coke C2/360
98 Bill Elliott 70.00 110.
McDonald's/360
99 Michael Waltrip 70.00 110.
Aaron's Dream Machine
LeAnn Rimes/288
99 Michael Waltrip 70.00 110.
Best Western/228
0 Ward Burton 70.00 110.
NetZero Hi Speed/204
0 Ward Burton 70.00 110.
NetZero Hi Speed
Shark Tale/444
01 Joe Nemechek 70.00 110.
Army GI Joe/288
01 Joe Nemechek 70.00 110.
Army Time Magazine/360
04 Nextel Inaugural Event Car/444 90.00 150.

2004 Action/RCCA Historica Series 1:24

EX NM-M
2 Dale Earnhardt 40.00 70.
Mello Yello
'80 Ventura/1800
3 Dale Earnhardt 45.00 75.
AC Delco
'96 Monte Carlo/1500
3 Dale Earnhardt 45.00 75.
Goodwrench Olympic
'96 Monte Carlo/2700
3 Dale Earnhardt 60.00 100.
Goodwrench Peter Max
'00 Monte Carlo/2400
3 Dale Earnhardt 50.00 80.
Wheaties 1997 Monte Carlo/2508
3 Dale Earnhardt 45.00 75.
Wrangler 1985 Camaro/2400
7 Dale Earnhardt Jr. 50.00 75.
Church Brothers 1997 Monte Carlo/2508
7 Kyle Petty 40.00 60.
7-Eleven 1985 T-bird/408
8 Dale Earnhardt Jr. 50.00 75.
Bud Olympic
'00 Monte Carlo/2508
8 Dale Earnhardt Jr. 50.00 75.
Bud 2003 Monte Carlo
Phoenix Raced/504
9 Bill Elliott 50.00 80.
Coors 1985 T-bird/504
9 Bill Elliott 45.00 75.
Coors Light 1991 Thunderbird/504
17 Darrell Waltrip 40.00 60.
Tide 200th Chevy Win
'87 Monte Carlo/600
24 Jeff Gordon 45.00 75.
DuPont 300th Chevy Win
'96 Monte Carlo Chrome/900
28 Davey Allison 35.00 60.
Havoline 1993 Thunderbird/600
29 Kevin Harvick 50.00 80.
Goodwrench Service Plus
'01 Monte Carlo black numbers/1008
43 Richard Petty 45.00 75.
STP 100th Chevy Win
1980 Monte Carlo Chrome/600
43 Richard Petty 60.00 100.
STP 200th Win 1984 Grand Prix/444
43 Richard Petty 45.00 75.
STP 200th Win '84 Grand Prix
Brushed Metal/444
43 Richard Petty 45.00 75.
STP 200th Win '84 Grand Prix Brushed Metal
Clear Window Bank/504
43 Richard Petty 35.00 60.
STP 20th Anniversary 200th Win/444
48 Jimmie Johnson 45.00 75.
Lowe's 400th Chevy Win
2003 Monte Carlo Chrome/600

2004 Action/RCCA Historica Series Elite 1:24

EX NM-M
2 Dale Earnhardt 70.00 110.0
Mello Yello
'80 Ventura/2508
3 Dale Earnhardt 100.00 175.0
AC Delco
'96 Monte Carlo Platinum/408
3 Dale Earnhardt 250.00 400.0
Goodwrench Crash '97 Daytona Raced/10,000

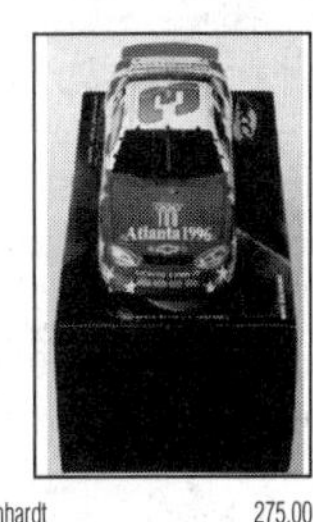

Dale Earnhardt 275.00 450.00
Goodwrench Crash
1997 Daytona Raced Platinum/504
Dale Earnhardt 75.00 125.00
Goodwrench Olympic
1996 Monte Carlo/3996
Dale Earnhardt 200.00 300.00
Goodwrench Olympic
1996 Monte Carlo Platinum/408
Dale Earnhardt 125.00 200.00
Goodwrench Peter Max
'00 Monte Carlo Plat./408
Kyle Petty 80.00 125.00
7-Eleven 1985 T-bird/408
Dale Earnhardt Jr. 90.00 150.00
Bud 2003 Monte Carlo
Phoenix Raced/1008
Dale Earnhardt Jr. 125.00 250.00
Bud Olympic 2000 Monte Carlo
Platinum/408
Bill Elliott 80.00 125.00
Coors 1985 T-bird/504
Bill Elliott 90.00 135.00
Coors Light '91 Thunderbird/504
Davey Allison 90.00 135.00
Havoline 1993 Thunderbird/600
Kevin Harvick 90.00 150.00
Goodwrench Service Plus
2001 Monte Carlo black numbers/1500
Kevin Harvick 100.00 175.00
Goodwrench Service Plus
2001 Monte Carlo black numbers Platinum/300
Richard Petty 150.00 250.00
STP 20th Anniversary
200th Win AU/444

2004 Action/RCCA Metal Elite 1:24

EX NM-MT
Michael Waltrip 60.00 120.00
NAPA/800
Kevin Harvick 60.00 120.00
Goodwrench/1200

2005 Action Clearly Collectibles 1:24

SOME CARS NOT PRICED DUE TO SCARCITY
EX NM-MT
Rusty Wallace
Atlanta Raced Spark Plug/8
Rusty Wallace
Bristol Raced Spark Plug/8
Rusty Wallace
Daytona Raced Spark Plug/8
Rusty Wallace
Talladega Raced Spark Plug/8
Rusty Wallace
Texas Raced Spark Plug/8
Kasey Kahne 60.00 120.00
Richmond Raced Tire/650
Jeff Gordon 75.00 150.00
Daytona Raced Tire/2000
Jimmie Johnson 60.00 120.00
Daytona Raced Lugnut/100
Jimmie Johnson 60.00 120.00
Las Vegas Raced Lugnut/100
Jimmie Johnson
Las Vegas Raced Spark Plug/8
Dale Jarrett 60.00 120.00
Raced Sheet Metal/200

2005 Action Performance 1:24

EX NM-MT
Rusty Wallace 35.00 60.00
Miller Lite Hometown Saint Louis
Rusty Wallace 25.00 50.00
Miller Lite Last Call
Kasey Kahne 35.00 60.00
Dodge Hometown Enumclaw
9/43 Kasey Kahne 50.00 100.00
Richard Petty
Dodge '75 Charger
STP '05 Charger/1896
9/43 Kasey Kahne 50.00 100.00
Richard Petty
Dodge/STP QVC/504
20 Tony Stewart 35.00 60.00
Home Depot Hometown Columbus
20 Tony Stewart 20.00 40.00
Home Depot Madagascar
Promo
20 DeAngelo Williams 125.00 175.00
Memphis Tigers Promo
The Race is On
24 Jeff Gordon 50.00 100.00
Halston Z-14 Promo in window box
24 Jeff Gordon 40.00 80.00
Milestones '94 Charlotte Win/6000
24 Jeff Gordon 40.00 80.00
Milestones
3-Time Daytona Winner/6000
24 Jeff Gordon 40.00 80.00
Milestones 4-Time Champion/6000
24 Jeff Gordon 40.00 80.00
Milestones 4-Time Brickyard Winner/6000
27 Rusty Wallace 40.00 80.00
Milestones '89 Champion/4008
29 Kevin Harvick 35.00 60.00
Goodwrench
Hometown Bakersfield
31 Jeff Burton 25.00 40.00
Cingular
31 Jeff Burton 20.00 35.00
Cingular black AP box
38 Elliott Sadler 35.00 60.00
M&M's Hometown Emporia
88 Dale Jarrett 35.00 60.00
UPS Hometown Conover
88 Dale Jarrett 20.00 40.00
UPS Herbie
07 Dave Blaney 25.00 50.00
Jack Daniel's
07 Dave Blaney 20.00 40.00
Jack Daniel's in plain black AP box

2005 Action President's Platinum Series 1:24

EX NM-MT
2 Rusty Wallace 125.00 225.00
Miller Lite AU/1100
w/Fred Wagenhals AU

2005 Action Racing Collectables 1:24

EX NM-MT
1 Martin Truex Jr. 45.00 70.00
Bass Pro Shops/6120
1 Martin Truex Jr. 45.00 70.00
Bass Pro Shops
Clear Window Bank/228
1 Martin Truex Jr. 45.00 70.00
Bass Pro Shops GM Dealers/768
1 Martin Truex Jr. 45.00 70.00
Bass Pro Shops
Matco/72
1 Martin Truex Jr. 45.00 70.00
Bass Pro Shops
QVC/400
1 Martin Truex Jr. 60.00 100.00
Bass Pro Shops Black/3000
1 Martin Truex Jr. 60.00 100.00
Bass Pro Shops Black
GM Dealers/204
1 Martin Truex Jr. 60.00 100.00
Bass Pro Shops Black
QVC/288
1 Martin Truex Jr. 100.00 250.00
Enterprise RAC/5808
2 Clint Bowyer 35.00 60.00
AC Delco/2148
2 Clint Bowyer 35.00 60.00
AC Delco Chris Cagle/816
2 Clint Bowyer 35.00 60.00
AC Delco Chris Cagle
GM Dealers/156
2 Jimmy Spencer 40.00 65.00
Snap-On 85th Anniversary/732
2 Jimmy Spencer 40.00 65.00
Snap-On 85th Anniversary
Snap-On/3000
2 Rusty Wallace 45.00 70.00
Kodak/5568
2 Rusty Wallace 45.00 70.00
Kodak Clear Window Bank/228
2 Rusty Wallace 60.00 100.00
Kodak Liquid Metal/708
2 Rusty Wallace 45.00 70.00
Kodak Matco/48
2 Rusty Wallace 45.00 70.00
Kodak QVC/504
2 Rusty Wallace 45.00 70.00
Miller Genuine Draft/9012
2 Rusty Wallace 45.00 70.00
Miller Genuine Draft
Clear Window Bank/264
2 Rusty Wallace 45.00 70.00
Miller Genuine Draft
Matco/72
2 Rusty Wallace 60.00 100.00
Miller Genuine Draft
Pearl Chrome/720
2 Rusty Wallace 45.00 70.00
Miller Genuine Draft
QVC/1008
2 Rusty Wallace 45.00 70.00
Miller Lite/7584
2 Rusty Wallace 45.00 70.00
Miller Lite Clear Window Bank/276
2 Rusty Wallace 75.00 125.00
Miller Lite Color Chrome/2004
2 Rusty Wallace 60.00 100.00
Miller Lite
Liquid Metal/2004
2 Rusty Wallace 45.00 70.00
Miller Lite Mac Tools/108
2 Rusty Wallace 45.00 70.00
Miller Lite Matco/180
2 Rusty Wallace 45.00 70.00
Miller Lite QVC/1008
2 Rusty Wallace 45.00 70.00
Miller Lite Flames
Bristol/4008
2 Rusty Wallace 45.00 70.00
Miller Lite Flames
Bristol QVC/1008
2 Rusty Wallace 50.00 75.00
Miller lite Last Call
Daytona Shootout/4476
2 Rusty Wallace 50.00 75.00
Miller Lite Last Call
Daytona Shootout
Clear Window Bank/204
2 Rusty Wallace 75.00 125.00
Miller Lite Last Call
Daytona Shootout Liquid Metal/2004
2 Rusty Wallace 50.00 75.00
Miller Lite Last Call
Daytona Shootout QVC/504
2 Rusty Wallace 50.00 75.00
Miller Lite Last Call Test/2484
2 Rusty Wallace 50.00 75.00
Miller Lite Last Call Test
QVC/288
2 Rusty Wallace 50.00 75.00
Miller Lite Last Race/3504
2 Rusty Wallace 50.00 75.00
Miller Lite Last Race
Mac Tools/120
2 Rusty Wallace 50.00 75.00
Miller Lite Last Race
Matco/98
2 Rusty Wallace 50.00 75.00
Miller Lite Last Race
QVC/2004
2 Rusty Wallace 50.00 75.00
Miller Lite Sirius/2508
2 Rusty Wallace 50.00 75.00
Miller Lite Sirius QVC/288
2 Rusty Wallace 50.00 75.00
Miller Lite 500 Consecutive Starts/2508
2 Rusty Wallace 45.00 70.00
Mobil/5676
2 Rusty Wallace 45.00 70.00
Mobil Clear Window Bank/276
2 Rusty Wallace 45.00 70.00
Mobil QVC/504
2 Rusty Wallace 45.00 70.00
Snap-On 85th Anniversary/5508
2 Rusty Wallace 45.00 70.00
Snap-On 85th Anniversary
Clear Window Bank/252
2 Rusty Wallace 60.00 100.00
Snap-On 85th Anniversary
Pearl Chrome/720
2 Rusty Wallace 60.00 100.00
700 Starts/3816
2 Rusty Wallace 60.00 100.00
700 Starts Matco/48
2 Rusty Wallace 60.00 100.00
700 Starts QVC/504
5 Kyle Busch 50.00 75.00
CarQuest/1284
5 Kyle Busch 60.00 100.00
Kellogg's/2340
5 Kyle Busch 60.00 100.00
Kellogg's Clear Window Bank/192
5 Kyle Busch 60.00 100.00
Kellogg's GM Dealers/144
5 Kyle Busch 60.00 100.00
Kellogg's Matco/36
5 Kyle Busch 60.00 100.00
Kellogg's QVC/144
5 Kyle Busch 60.00 100.00
Kellogg's California Raced/2508
5 Kyle Busch 60.00 100.00
Kellogg's California Raced QVC/120
5 Kyle Busch 75.00 125.00
Kellogg's Rookie of the Year
Color Chrome/5004
5 Kyle Busch 75.00 125.00
Kellogg's ROY
Color Chrome GM Dealers/288
5 Kyle Busch 75.00 125.00
Kellogg's Rookie of the Year
Color Chrome QVC/504
5 Kyle Busch 50.00 75.00
Kellogg's Star Wars/2484
5 Kyle Busch 50.00 75.00
Kellogg's Star Wars
Clear Window Bank/204
5 Blake Feese 40.00 65.00
Lowe's AU/900
5 Adrian Fernandez 40.00 65.00
Lowe's/1500
5 Adrian Fernandez 40.00 65.00
Lowe's GM Dealers/60
5 Boston Reid 40.00 65.00
Lowe's AU/824
6 Bill Elliott 50.00 75.00
Charlie Brown Christmas/4008
6 Bill Elliott 50.00 75.00
Charlie Brown Christmas
QVC/288
6 Ron Hornaday 40.00 65.00
Goodwrench SuperTruck/812
6 Mark Martin 75.00 125.00
Crown Royal IROC/2232
6 Mark Martin 100.00 150.00
Crown Royal IROC
Brushed Metal/360
6 Mark Martin 75.00 125.00
Crown Royal IROC
GM Dealers/84
6 Mark Martin 75.00 125.00
Crown Royal IROC
QVC/504
7 Robby Gordon 50.00 75.00
Jim Beam/4752
7 Robby Gordon 50.00 75.00
Jim Beam Clear Window Bank/144
7 Robby Gordon 50.00 75.00
Jim Beam GM Dealers/312
7 Robby Gordon 60.00 100.00
Jim Beam Liquid Metal/720
7 Robby Gordon 50.00 75.00
Jim Beam QVC/288
8 Dale Earnhardt Jr. 40.00 70.00
Bud/33,960
8 Dale Earnhardt Jr. 40.00 70.00
Bud Clear Window Bank/612
8 Dale Earnhardt Jr. 40.00 70.00
Bud
GM Dealers/5004
8 Dale Earnhardt Jr. 60.00 100.00
Bud Liquid Metal/3504
8 Dale Earnhardt Jr. 40.00 70.00
Bud Mac Tools/300
8 Dale Earnhardt Jr. 40.00 70.00
Bud Matco/492
8 Dale Earnhardt Jr. 40.00 70.00
Bud QVC/7500
8 Dale Earnhardt Jr. 75.00 125.00
Bud Born On
Feb.12/5004
8 Dale Earnhardt Jr. 50.00 75.00
Bud Born On Feb.12
Clear Window Bank/708
8 Dale Earnhardt Jr. 75.00 125.00
Bud Born On
Feb.12 GM Dealers/2640
8 Dale Earnhardt Jr. 75.00 125.00
Bud Born On Feb.12 Matco/480
8 Dale Earnhardt Jr. 75.00 125.00
Bud Born On Feb.12 QVC/504
8 Dale Earnhardt Jr. 60.00 100.00
Bud Born On Feb.17/13,752
8 Dale Earnhardt Jr. 50.00 75.00
Bud Born On Feb.17
Clear Window Bank/648
8 Dale Earnhardt Jr. 60.00 100.00
Bud Born On
Feb.17 GM Dealers/2280
8 Dale Earnhardt Jr. 75.00 125.00
Bud Born On
Feb.17 GM Dealers Chrome/1512
8 Dale Earnhardt Jr. 60.00 100.00
Bud Born On
Feb.17 Matco/480
8 Dale Earnhardt Jr. 60.00 100.00
Bud Born On
Feb.17 QVC/600
8 Dale Earnhardt Jr. 60.00 100.00
Bud Born On Feb.20/22,668
8 Dale Earnhardt Jr. 50.00 75.00
Bud Born On Feb.20
Clear Window Bank/900
8 Dale Earnhardt Jr. 60.00 100.00
Bud Born On Feb.20
GM Dealers/3588
8 Dale Earnhardt Jr. 60.00 100.00
Bud Born On
Feb.20 Mac Tools/300
8 Dale Earnhardt Jr. 60.00 100.00
Bud Born On
Feb.20 Matco/480
8 Dale Earnhardt Jr. 60.00 100.00
Bud Born On
Feb.20 QVC/2004
8 Dale Earnhardt Jr. 40.00 70.00
Bud MLB All Star Game/15,804
8 Dale Earnhardt Jr. 50.00 75.00
Bud MLB All Star Game
Clear Window Bank/600
8 Dale Earnhardt Jr. 60.00 100.00
Bud MLB All Star Game
GM Dealers Chrome/1992
8 Dale Earnhardt Jr. 50.00 75.00
Bud MLB All Star Game
Matco/96
8 Dale Earnhardt Jr. 50.00 75.00
Bud MLB All Star Game
QVC/2004
8 Dale Earnhardt Jr. 50.00 75.00
Bud MLB All Star Game
Chicago Raced/2880
8 Dale Earnhardt Jr. 50.00 75.00
Bud MLB All Star Game
Chicago Raced QVC/2004
8 Dale Earnhardt Jr. 60.00 100.00
Bud Test w/Tony Eury AU/5016
8 Dale Earnhardt Jr. 40.00 70.00
Bud 3 Doors Down/15,468
8 Dale Earnhardt Jr. 40.00 70.00
Bud 3 Doors Down
Clear Window Bank/636
8 Dale Earnhardt Jr. 40.00 70.00
Bud 3 Doors Down
GM Dealers/2160
8 Dale Earnhardt Jr. 40.00 70.00
Bud 3 Doors Down
QVC/2004
8 Martin Truex Jr. 40.00 65.00
Bass Pro/5004
8 Martin Truex Jr. 40.00 65.00
Bass Pro Clear Window Bank/204
8 Martin Truex Jr. 40.00 65.00
Bass Pro GM Dealers/552
8 Martin Truex Jr. 40.00 65.00
Bass Pro QVC/504
8 Martin Truex Jr. 50.00 75.00
Bass Pro Indy Raced/1812
8 Martin Truex Jr. 50.00 75.00
Bass Pro Indy Raced QVC/288
8 Martin Truex Jr. 40.00 65.00
Bass Pro
Mexico City Raced/2028
8 Martin Truex Jr. 40.00 65.00
Bass Pro Mexico City Raced
GM Dealers/360
8 Martin Truex Jr. 40.00 65.00
Bass Pro
Talladega Raced/2652
8 Martin Truex Jr. 40.00 65.00
Bass Pro Talladega Raced
GM Dealers/444
8 Martin Truex Jr. 40.00 65.00
Bass Pro
Talladega Raced QVC/288
8 Martin Truex Jr. 40.00 65.00
Crown Royal IROC/2172
8 Martin Truex Jr. 40.00 65.00
Crown Royal IROC QVC/288
8 Martin Truex Jr. 40.00 65.00
Chance 2 Test/1848
8 Martin Truex Jr. 40.00 65.00
Chance 2 Test
GM Dealers/252
8 Martin Truex Jr. 40.00 65.00
Chance 2 Test QVC/288
9 Kasey Kahne 50.00 75.00
Dodge/13,284
9 Kasey Kahne 50.00 75.00
Dodge Clear Window Bank/396
9 Kasey Kahne 60.00 100.00
Dodge Liquid Metal/2508
9 Kasey Kahne 50.00 75.00
Dodge Mac Tools/300
9 Kasey Kahne 50.00 75.00
Dodge Matco/108
9 Kasey Kahne 50.00 75.00
Dodge QVC/1500
9 Kasey Kahne 50.00 75.00
Dodge Richmond Raced/9420
9 Kasey Kahne 60.00 100.00
Dodge Richmond Raced
Liquid Metal/1056
9 Kasey Kahne 50.00 75.00
Dodge
Richmond Raced QVC/1008
9 Kasey Kahne 50.00 75.00
Dodge Longest Yard/4344
9 Kasey Kahne 50.00 75.00
Dodge Longest Yard
QVC/288
9 Kasey Kahne 50.00 75.00
Dodge Mega Cab/2520
9 Kasey Kahne 50.00 75.00
Dodge Mega Cab QVC/288
9 Kasey Kahne 50.00 75.00
Dodge Pit Cap White/7476
9 Kasey Kahne 50.00 75.00
Dodge Pit Cap White
Clear Window Bank/336
9 Kasey Kahne 50.00 75.00
Dodge Pit Cap White
QVC/504
9 Kasey Kahne 50.00 75.00
Dodge Retro
Bud Shootout/6000
9 Kasey Kahne 50.00 75.00
Dodge Retro Bud Shootout
Clear Window Bank/300
9 Kasey Kahne 60.00 100.00
Dodge Retro Bud Shootout
Liquid Metal/1008
9 Kasey Kahne 50.00 75.00
Dodge Retro
Bud Shootout QVC/1008
9 Kasey Kahne 50.00 75.00
Dodge Test/1452
9 Kasey Kahne 60.00 100.00
Mopar/4500
9 Kasey Kahne 60.00 100.00
Mopar QVC/288
9 Kasey Kahne 50.00 75.00
Mountain Dew/8016
9 Kasey Kahne 50.00 75.00
Mountain Dew
Clear Window Bank/348
9 Kasey Kahne 50.00 75.00
Mountain Dew QVC/600
10 Scott Riggs 40.00 65.00
Valvoline/696
10 Scott Riggs 40.00 65.00
Valvoline QVC/120
10 Scott Riggs 40.00 65.00
Valvoline Herbie Fully Loaded/1140
10 Scott Riggs 40.00 65.00
Valvoline Herbie
Clear Window Bank/144
10 Scott Riggs 40.00 65.00
Valvoline Nickelback/1152
10 Scott Riggs 40.00 65.00
Valvoline Nickelback
GM Dealers/60
10 Scott Riggs 40.00 65.00
Valvoline Nickelback QVC/120
11 Steve Kinser 40.00 65.00
Crown Royal IROC/1464
11 Jason Leffler 40.00 65.00
FedEx/3960
11 Jason Leffler 40.00 65.00
FedEx QVC/120
11 Jason Leffler 40.00 65.00
FedEx Freight/5352
11 Jason Leffler 40.00 65.00
FedEx Ground/2208
11 Jason Leffler 40.00 65.00
FedEx Ground
GM Dealers/48
11 Jason Leffler 40.00 65.00
FedEx Kinkos/2448
12 Darrell Waltrip 50.00 75.00
Tundra One & Done/3504
12 Darrell Waltrip 50.00 75.00
Tundra One & Done
BD&A/1752
15 Kyle Busch 40.00 70.00
ditech.com SuperTruck
Charlotte Raced w/tire/1956
15 Kyle Busch 40.00 70.00
ditech.com SuperTruck
Charlotte Raced w/tire QVC/144
15 Michael Waltrip 40.00 65.00
Napa/4512
15 Michael Waltrip 40.00 65.00
Napa Clear Window Bank/192
15 Michael Waltrip 40.00 65.00
Napa Matco/72
15 Michael Waltrip 40.00 65.00
Napa QVC/360
15 Michael Waltrip 40.00 65.00
Napa Stars & Stripes/1440

15 Michael Waltrip Napa Stars & Stripes GM Dealers/84	40.00	65.00
17 Matt Kenseth Crown Royal IROC/1272	40.00	65.00
18 Bobby Labonte Boniva/996	60.00	100.00
18 Bobby Labonte FedEx/2508	60.00	100.00
18 Bobby Labonte FedEx GM Dealers/180	60.00	100.00
18 Bobby Labonte FedEx Mac Tools/120	60.00	100.00
18 Bobby Labonte Interstate Batteries/4872	40.00	65.00
18 Bobby Labonte Interstate Batteries Clear Window Bank/204	40.00	65.00
18 Bobby Labonte Interstate Batteries GM Dealers/360	40.00	65.00
18 Bobby Labonte Interstate Batteries Matco/84	40.00	65.00
18 Bobby Labonte Interstate Batteries QVC/288	40.00	65.00
18 Bobby Labonte Interstate Batteries Madagascar/3864	40.00	65.00
18 Bobby Labonte Interstate Batteries Madagascar Clear Window Bank/144	40.00	65.00
18 Bobby Labonte Interstate Batteries Madagascar GM Dealers/144	40.00	65.00
18 Bobby Labonte Interstate Batteries Madagascar Matco/84	40.00	65.00
18 Bobby Labonte Interstate Batteries Madagascar QVC/408	40.00	65.00
18 J.J. Yeley Vigoro AU/2832	50.00	75.00
18 J.J. Yeley Vigoro Clear Window Bank AU/120	50.00	75.00
18 J.J. Yeley Vigoro Matco AU/36	50.00	75.00
19 Jeremy Mayfield Dodge/2304	35.00	60.00
19 Jeremy Mayfield Dodge Clear Window Bank/156	35.00	60.00
19 Jeremy Mayfield Dodge Matco/60	35.00	60.00
19 Jeremy Mayfield Dodge QVC/144	35.00	60.00
19 Jeremy Mayfield Dodge Bad News Bears/1884	35.00	60.00
19 Jeremy Mayfield Dodge Black Reverse/2880	35.00	60.00
19 Jeremy Mayfield Dodge Retro Bud Shootout/1356	35.00	60.00
19 Jeremy Mayfield Dodge Retro Bud Shootout Clear Window Bank/240	35.00	60.00
19 Jeremy Mayfield Dodge Retro Bud Shootout QVC/144	35.00	60.00
19 Jeremy Mayfield Mountain Dew Pitch Black/5004	40.00	65.00
19 Jeremy Mayfield Mountain Dew Pitch Black QVC/120	40.00	65.00
20 Danny Lasoski Crown Royal IROC/1344	40.00	65.00
20 Tony Stewart Home Depot/9000	75.00	125.00
20 Tony Stewart Home Depot Clear Window Bank/264	60.00	100.00
20 Tony Stewart Home Depot GM Dealers/1008	75.00	125.00
20 Tony Stewart Home Depot Matco/300	75.00	125.00
20 Tony Stewart Home Depot QVC/720	75.00	125.00
20 Tony Stewart Home Depot Brickyard Raced/3012	100.00	175.00
20 Tony Stewart Home Depot Champion Color Chrome/8492	75.00	125.00
20 T.Stewart/Home Depot Champion Color Chrome Mac Tools/504	75.00	125.00
20 Tony Stewart Home Depot Champion Color Chrome QVC/2508	75.00	125.00
20 Tony Stewart Home Depot Brickyard Raced GM Dealers/288	75.00	125.00
20 Tony Stewart Home Depot Brickyard Raced QVC/504	75.00	125.00
20 Tony Stewart Home Depot Daytona Raced/2700	75.00	125.00
20 Tony Stewart Home Depot Daytona Raced QVC/288	75.00	125.00
20 Tony Stewart Home Depot KaBOOM/3000	50.00	75.00
20 Tony Stewart Home Depot KaBOOM GM Dealers/168	50.00	75.00
20 Tony Stewart Home Depot KaBOOM QVC/288	50.00	75.00
20 Tony Stewart Home Depot Madagascar/4752	50.00	75.00
20 Tony Stewart Home Depot Madagascar Clear Window Bank/216	50.00	75.00
20 Tony Stewart Home Depot Madagascar GM Dealers/204	50.00	75.00
20 Tony Stewart Home Depot Madagascar Liquid Metal/600	60.00	100.00
20 Tony Stewart Home Depot Madagascar Mac Tools/300	50.00	75.00
20 Tony Stewart Home Depot Madagascar Matco/144	50.00	75.00
20 Tony Stewart Home Depot Madagascar QVC/504	50.00	75.00
20 Tony Stewart Home Depot Test Greg Zipadelli AU/2508	75.00	125.00
21 Kevin Harvick Hershey's Take 5/4872	35.00	60.00
21 Kevin Harvick Hershey's Take 5 GM Dealers/468	35.00	60.00
21 Kevin Harvick Hershey's Take 5 QVC/288	35.00	60.00
21 Kevin Harvick Pelon Pelo Rico/2400	35.00	60.00
21 Kevin Harvick Pelon Pelo Rico Clear Window Bank/168	35.00	60.00
21 Kevin Harvick Pelon Pelo Rico GM Dealers/228	35.00	60.00
21 Kevin Harvick Reese's/6144	40.00	65.00
21 Kevin Harvick Reese's GM Dealers/600	40.00	65.00
21 Kevin Harvick Reese's QVC/288	40.00	65.00
21 Kevin Harvick Reese's Honey Roasted/2340	40.00	65.00
21 Kevin Harvick Reese's Honey Roasted Liquid Metal/1164	50.00	75.00
21 Kevin Harvick Twizzlers/1680	35.00	60.00
21 Kevin Harvick Twizzlers GM Dealers/168	35.00	60.00
21 Brandon Miller Reese's/804	40.00	65.00
24 Jeff Gordon DuPont Flames/12,744	50.00	75.00
24 Jeff Gordon DuPont Flames Clear Window Bank/408	50.00	75.00
24 Jeff Gordon DuPont Flames GM Dealers/2700	50.00	75.00
24 Jeff Gordon DuPont Flames Matco/204	50.00	75.00
24 Jeff Gordon DuPont Flames QVC/1500	50.00	75.00
24 Jeff Gordon DuPont Flames Daytona Raced/8856	50.00	75.00
24 Jeff Gordon DuPont Flames Daytona Raced GM Dealers/638	50.00	75.00
24 Jeff Gordon DuPont Flames Daytona Raced QVC/624	50.00	75.00
24 Jeff Gordon DuPont Flames Martinsville Raced/3528	50.00	75.00
24 Jeff Gordon DuPont Flames Martinsville Raced GM Dealers/180	50.00	75.00
24 Jeff Gordon DuPont Flames Martinsville Raced QVC/288	50.00	75.00
24 Jeff Gordon DuPont Flames Performance Alliance Reverse/10,020	50.00	75.00
24 Jeff Gordon DuPont Flames Performance Alliance Reverse Clear Window Bank/402	50.00	75.00
24 Jeff Gordon DuPont Flames Performance Alliance Reverse GM Dealers/768	50.00	75.00
24 Jeff Gordon DuPont Flames Performance Alliance Reverse Liquid Metal/1008	75.00	125.00
24 Jeff Gordon DuPont Flames Performance Alliance Reverse QVC/1500	50.00	75.00
24 Jeff Gordon DuPont Test Robbie Loomis AU/2508	50.00	75.00
24 Jeff Gordon Mighty Mouse/7356	50.00	75.00
24 Jeff Gordon Mighty Mouse Clear Window Bank/432	50.00	75.00
24 Jeff Gordon Mighty Mouse GM Dealers/648	50.00	75.00
24 Jeff Gordon Mighty Mouse Liquid Metal/1008	60.00	100.00
24 Jeff Gordon Mighty Mouse QVC/1800	50.00	75.00
24 Jeff Gordon Pepsi Daytona/8160	50.00	75.00
24 Jeff Gordon Pepsi Daytona Clear Window Bank/360	50.00	75.00
24 Jeff Gordon Pepsi Daytona GM Dealers/720	50.00	75.00
24 Jeff Gordon Pepsi Daytona Mac Tools/300	50.00	75.00
24 Jeff Gordon Pepsi Daytona QVC/504	50.00	75.00
24 Jeff Gordon Pepsi Star Wars/10,896	50.00	75.00
24 Jeff Gordon Pepsi Star Wars Clear Window Bank/468	50.00	75.00
24 Jeff Gordon Pepsi Star Wars GM Dealers/720	50.00	75.00
24 Jeff Gordon Pepsi Star Wars Mac Tools/300	50.00	75.00
24 Jeff Gordon Pepsi Star Wars Matco/84	50.00	75.00
24 Jeff Gordon Pepsi Star Wars QVC/2508	50.00	75.00
24 Jeff Gordon Pepsi Star Wars Talladega Raced/6756	50.00	75.00
24 Jeff Gordon Pepsi Star Wars Talladega Raced GM Dealers/608	50.00	75.00
24 Jeff Gordon Pepsi Star Wars Talladega Raced QVC/1008	50.00	75.00
24 Jeff Gordon Santa Holiday/3504	50.00	75.00
25 Brian Vickers GMAC/1488	40.00	65.00
25 B.Vickers/GMAC QVC/288	40.00	65.00
25 Brian Vickers GMAC Green Day/1272	40.00	65.00
25 Brian Vickers GMAC Green Day GM Dealers/72	40.00	65.00
29 Kevin Harvick Goodwrench/6564	40.00	65.00
29 Kevin Harvick Goodwrench Clear Window Bank/216	40.00	65.00
29 Kevin Harvick Goodwrench GM Dealers/1200	40.00	65.00
29 Kevin Harvick Goodwrench Matco/120	40.00	65.00
29 Kevin Harvick Goodwrench QVC/504	40.00	65.00
29 Kevin Harvick Goodwrench Bristol Raced/2400	40.00	65.00
29 Kevin Harvick Goodwrench Bristol Raced GM Dealers/276	40.00	65.00
29 Kevin Harvick Goodwrench Atlanta/6000	40.00	65.00
29 Kevin Harvick Goodwrench Atlanta Clear Window Bank/240	40.00	65.00
29 Kevin Harvick Goodwrench Atlanta GM Dealers/492	40.00	65.00
29 Kevin Harvick Goodwrench Atlanta GM Dealers Chrome/2508	60.00	100.00
29 Kevin Harvick Goodwrench Brickyard/4032	40.00	65.00
29 Kevin Harvick Goodwrench Brickyard Clear Window Bank/204	40.00	65.00
29 Kevin Harvick Goodwrench Brickyard GM Dealers/720	40.00	65.00
29 Kevin Harvick Goodwrench Brickyard GM Dealers Chrome/1500	60.00	100.00
29 Kevin Harvick Goodwrench Brickyard QVC/504	40.00	65.00
29 Kevin Harvick Goodwrench Daytona/5304	40.00	65.00
29 Kevin Harvick Goodwrench Daytona Clear Window Bank/216	40.00	65.00
29 Kevin Harvick Goodwrench Daytona GM Dealers/2004	40.00	65.00
29 Kevin Harvick Goodwrench Daytona GM Dealers Chrome/2508	60.00	100.00
29 Kevin Harvick Goodwrench Daytona QVC/504	40.00	65.00
29 Kevin Harvick Goodwrench Gretchen Wilson/3480	40.00	65.00
29 Kevin Harvick Goodwrench Gretchen Wilson GM Dealers/1200	40.00	65.00
29 Kevin Harvick Goodwrench Gretchen Wilson QVC/120	40.00	65.00
29 Kevin Harvick Goodwrench Quicksilver/5004	40.00	65.00
29 Kevin Harvick Goodwrench Quicksilver CW Bank/168	40.00	65.00
29 Kevin Harvick Goodwrench Quicksilver GM Dealers Chrome/1500	60.00	100.00
29 Kevin Harvick Goodwrench Quicksilver QVC/288	40.00	65.00
29 Kevin Harvick Goodwrench Test Todd Berrier AU/2508	50.00	75.00
29 Kevin Harvick Reese's Big Cup/1632	40.00	65.00
29 Kevin Harvick Reese's Big Cup GM Dealers/336	40.00	65.00
29 Kevin Harvick Snap-On/2508	45.00	70.00
29 Kevin Harvick Snap-On Snap On/3000	45.00	70.00
31 Jeff Burton Cingular/2438	50.00	75.00
31 Jeff Burton Cingular Clear Window Bank/144	50.00	75.00
31 Jeff Burton Cingular Cingular/30,000	50.00	75.00
31 Jeff Burton Cingular Beneficial/1164	50.00	75.00
31 Jeff Burton Cingular GM Dealers/144	50.00	75.00
31 Jeff Burton Cingular Matco/36	50.00	75.00
31 Jeff Burton Cingular QVC/144	50.00	75.00
31 Jeff Burton Cingular Big & Rich/1452	40.00	65.00
31 Jeff Burton Cingular Big & Rich QVC/120	40.00	65.00
33 Tony Raines The Outdoor Channel/250	35.00	60.00
33 Tony Raines Yardman/250	35.00	60.00
33 Tony Stewart James Dean 50th Anniversary/5244	40.00	65.00
33 Tony Stewart James Dean 50th Anniversary GM Dealers/432	40.00	65.00
33 Tony Stewart James Dean 50th Anniversary QVC/504	40.00	65.00
33 Tony Stewart Mr.Clean AutoDry/2364	40.00	65.00
33 Tony Stewart Mr.Clean AutoDry Clear Window Bank/144	40.00	65.00
33 Tony Stewart Mr.Clean AutoDry Daytona Raced/4284	40.00	65.00
33 Tony Stewart Mr.Clean AutoDry Daytona Raced GM Dealers/240	40.00	65.00
33 Tony Stewart Mr.Clean AutoDry Daytona Raced QVC/288	40.00	65.00
33 Tony Stewart Old Spice/2760	40.00	65.00
33 Tony Stewart Old Spice Clear Window Bank/180	40.00	65.00
33 Tony Stewart Old Spice GM Dealers/144	40.00	65.00
38 Kasey Kahne Great Clips/2820	35.00	60.00
38 Kasey Kahne Great Clips Clear Window Bank/144	35.00	60.00
38 Kasey Kahne Great Clips QVC/144	35.00	60.00
38 Kasey Kahne Great Clips Spy v. Spy Kids/3504	35.00	60.00
38 Kasey Kahne Great Clips Spy v. Spy Kids QVC/120	35.00	60.00
38 Elliott Sadler Combos/1524	35.00	60.00
38 Elliott Sadler M&M's/5856	40.00	65.00
38 Elliott Sadler M&M's Matco/72	40.00	65.00
38 Elliott Sadler M&M's QVC/504	40.00	65.00
38 Elliott Sadler M&M's Halloween/4008	40.00	65.00
38 Elliott Sadler M&M's Halloween QVC/288	40.00	65.00
38 Elliott Sadler M&M's July 4th/3204	40.00	65.00
38 Elliott Sadler M&M's July 4th Clear Window Bank/144	40.00	65.00
38 Elliott Sadler M&M's July 4th QVC/144	40.00	65.00
38 Elliott Sadler M&M's Star Wars/4332	40.00	65.00
38 Elliott Sadler M&M's Star Wars Clear Window Bank/204	40.00	65.00
38 Elliott Sadler M&M's Star Wars Matco/48	40.00	65.00
38 Elliott Sadler M&M's Star Wars QVC/408	40.00	65.00
38 Elliott Sadler M&M's Test/792	40.00	65.00
38 Elliott Sadler M&M's Test QVC/144	40.00	65.00
38 Elliott Sadler Pedigree/1488	35.00	60.00
38 Elliott Sadler Pedigree Matco/12	35.00	60.00
38 Elliott Sadler Pedigree QVC/144	35.00	60.00
38 Elliott Sadler 30th Birthday Fantasy/2640	35.00	60.00
38 Elliott Sadler 30th Birthday Fantasy Matco/12	35.00	60.00
39 Bill Elliott Coors Retro Bud Shootout/3528	50.00	75.00
39 Bill Elliott Coors Retro Bud Shootout Liquid Metal/1500	75.00	125.00
39 Bill Elliott Coors Retro Bud Shootout QVC/120	50.00	75.00
39 Reed Sorenson Discount Tire/1908	50.00	75.00
39 David Stremme Committ/3216	50.00	75.00
40 Sterling Marlin Coors Light/3036	40.00	65.00
40 Sterling Marlin Coors Light Clear Window Bank/168	40.00	65.00
40 Sterling Marlin Coors Light Matco/72	40.00	65.00
40 Sterling Marlin Coors Light QVC/288	40.00	65.00
41 Casey Mears Nicorette/2676	40.00	65.00
41 Casey Mears Target/2064	40.00	65.00
41 Casey Mears Target Clear Window Bank/144	40.00	65.00
41 Casey Mears Target Matco/24	40.00	65.00
41 Casey Mears Target QVC/144	40.00	65.00
41 Casey Mears Target Pink/2240	50.00	75.00
41 Reed Sorenson Discount Tire/3228	50.00	75.00
41 Reed Sorenson Discount Tire Clear Window Bank/168	50.00	75.00
41 Reed Sorenson Discount Tire Coats Nashville Raced/3036	50.00	75.00
41 Reed Sorenson Home 123/2508	40.00	65.00
42 Jamie McMurray Havoline/4392	35.00	60.00
42 Jamie McMurray Havoline Clear Window Bank/180	35.00	60.00
42 Jamie McMurray Havoline Matco/48	35.00	60.00
42 Jamie McMurray Havoline QVC/288	35.00	60.00
42 Jamie McMurray Havoline Autism Society/1440	35.00	60.00
42 Jamie McMurray Havoline Autism Society Clear Window Bank/144	35.00	60.00
42 Jamie McMurray Havoline Autism Society Matco/48	35.00	60.00
42 Jamie McMurray Havoline Autism Society QVC/120	35.00	60.00
42 Jamie McMurray Havoline Shine On Charlotte/2052	35.00	60.00
42 Jamie McMurray Havoline Shine On Charlotte Matco/24	35.00	60.00
42 Jamie McMurray Havoline Shine On Charlotte QVC/144	35.00	60.00
42 Jamie McMurray Havoline Shine On Sonoma/1848	35.00	60.00
42 Jamie McMurray Havoline Shine On Sonoma QVC/120	35.00	60.00
42 Jamie McMurray Havoline Shine On Talladega/1896	35.00	60.00
42 Jamie McMurray Havoline Shine On Talladega QVC/120	35.00	60.00
42 Jamie McMurray Havoline Shine On Texas/2592	35.00	60.00
42 Jamie McMurray Havoline Shine On Texas Matco/48	35.00	60.00
42 Jamie McMurray Havoline Shine On Texas QVC/120	35.00	60.00
43 Jeff Green Cheerios Narnia/2160	40.00	65.00
44 Terry Labonte Kellogg's/2172	40.00	65.00
44 Terry Labonte Kellogg's Clear Window Bank/204	40.00	65.00
44 Terry Labonte Kellogg's GM Dealers/108	40.00	65.00
44 Terry Labonte Kellogg's QVC/288	40.00	65.00
44 Terry Labonte Pizza Hut/1188	40.00	65.00
45 Kyle Petty Georgia Pacific/612	40.00	65.00
45 Kyle Petty Georgia Pacific Clear Window Bank/144	40.00	65.00
45 Kyle Petty Georgia Pacific QVC/120	40.00	65.00
45 Kyle Petty Georgia Pacific Mother's Day/1884	40.00	65.00
45 Kyle Petty Georgia Pacific Mother's Day Clear Window Bank/204	40.00	65.00
45 Kyle Petty Georgia Pacific Mother's Day Matco/12	40.00	65.00
45 Kyle Petty Georgia Pacific Mother's Day QVC/288	40.00	65.00
45 Kyle Petty Georgia Pacific Narnia/2160	40.00	60.00
47 Bobby Labonte Silverado Trick Pony SuperTruck Martinsville Raced w/tire/1416	60.00	100.00
48 Jimmie Johnson Lowe's/3660	40.00	65.00
48 Jimmie Johnson Lowe's GM Dealers/780	40.00	65.00
48 Jimmie Johnson Lowe's Matco/84	40.00	65.00
48 Jimmie Johnson Lowe's QVC/504	40.00	65.00
48 Jimmie Johnson Lowe's Las Vegas Raced/2772	40.00	65.00
48 Jimmie Johnson Lowe's Las Vegas Raced QVC/144	40.00	65.00
48 Jimmie Johnson Lowe's Kobalt/1848	45.00	70.00
48 Jimmie Johnson Lowe's Kobalt GM Dealers/180	45.00	70.00
48 Jimmie Johnson Lowe's Test Chad Knaus AU/2508	50.00	75.00
48 Jimmie Johnson Lowe's '06 Preview/6000	50.00	100.00
48 Jimmie Johnson Lowe's '06 Preview GM Dealers/360	50.00	100.00
48 Jimmie Johnson Lowe's '06 Preview QVC/288	50.00	100.00
64 Jeremy Mayfield Miller High Life Light/1116	35.00	60.00
64 Jamie McMurray Top Flite Golf/1512	35.00	60.00
64 Jamie McMurray Top Flite Golf Clear Window Bank/204	35.00	60.00
64 Rusty Wallace Bell Helicopter/6192	40.00	65.00
64 Rusty Wallace Bell Helicopter Clear Window Bank/204	40.00	65.00
64 Rusty Wallace Bell Helicopter QVC/504	40.00	65.00
64 Rusty Wallace Miller High Life Saint Louis Family Tribute/5280	40.00	65.00
64 Rusty Wallace Miller High Life Saint Louis Family Tribute Clear Window Bank/228	40.00	65.00
64 Rusty Wallace Miller High Life St. Louis Family Tribute QVC/600	40.00	65.00
64 Rusty Wallace Top Flite/2652	40.00	65.00
64 Rusty Wallace Top Flite QVC/288	40.00	65.00
77 Travis Kvapil Kodak/2832	40.00	65.00
77 Travis Kvapil Mobil Clean/936	40.00	65.00
79 Jeremy Mayfield Auto Value/576	35.00	60.00
79 Jeremy Mayfield Auto Value	35.00	60.00

lear Window Bank/204
sey Kahne 35.00 60.00
uto Value/2532
asey Kahne 35.00 60.00
uto Value Clear Window Bank/168
sey Kahne 40.00 80.00
us Joist/2004
ale Earnhardt Jr. 40.00 65.00
hance 2 Test/2616
le Earnhardt Jr. 40.00 65.00
hance 2 Test
M Dealers/288
ale Earnhardt Jr. 40.00 65.00
hance 2 Test QVC/288
ale Earnhardt Jr. 40.00 65.00
enards/7668
le Earnhardt Jr. 40.00 65.00
enards GM Dealers/1008
ale Earnhardt Jr. 40.00 65.00
enards QVC/1508
le Earnhardt Jr. 40.00 65.00
reo Ritz/15,516
le Earnhardt Jr. 40.00 65.00
reo Ritz
lear Window Bank/564
le Earnhardt Jr. 40.00 65.00
reo Ritz
M Dealers/2016
ale Earnhardt Jr. 40.00 65.00
reo Ritz QVC/3000
le Jarrett 50.00 75.00
PS/2664
le Jarrett 50.00 75.00
PS Matco/96
ale Jarrett 50.00 75.00
PS QVC/360
le Jarrett 60.00 100.00
PS Talladega Raced w/tire/1500
le Jarrett 40.00 65.00
PS Herbie Fully Loaded/3624
le Jarrett 40.00 65.00
PS Herbie Clear Window Bank/192
le Jarrett 40.00 65.00
PS Herbie Matco/24
ale Jarrett 40.00 65.00
PS Herbie QVC/504
le Jarrett 40.00 65.00
PS Mother's Day/2664
le Jarrett 40.00 65.00
PS Mother's Day
lear Window Bank/168
le Jarrett 40.00 65.00
PS Mother's Day
ac Tools/108
le Jarrett 40.00 65.00
PS Mother's Day
atco/24
ale Jarrett 40.00 65.00
PS Mother's Day QVC/288
le Jarrett 40.00 65.00
PS Star Wars/4908
le Jarrett 40.00 65.00
PS Star Wars
lear Window Bank/192
le Jarrett 40.00 65.00
PS Star Wars Matco/48
le Jarrett 50.00 75.00
PS Store Toys for Tots/4008
le Jarrett 40.00 65.00
PS Test/612
ale Jarrett 40.00 65.00
PS Test QVC/144
ve Wallace 60.00 100.00
ast Call Action Scheck
RCA AU/2364
le Jarrett 35.00 60.00
itifinancial
ephen Leicht 40.00 65.00
ction
ott Sadler 35.00 60.00
itifinancial/864
Elliott 50.00 75.00
uto Value/1224
Elliott 50.00 75.00
uto Value Clear Window Bank/168
ll Elliott 45.00 70.00
cDonald's 50th Anniversary/2340
Elliott 45.00 70.00
cDonald's 50th Anniversary
lear Window Bank/168
ll Elliott 45.00 70.00
cDonald's 50th Anniversary
VC/288
Elliott 45.00 70.00
tanley Tools/1764
ll Elliott 45.00 70.00
tanley Tools
lear Window Bank/216
ll Elliott 45.00 70.00
tanley Tools QVC/144
vin Harvick 40.00 65.00
oodwrench SuperTruck/1452
vin Harvick 35.00 60.00
ard-Man SuperTruck/1440
vin Harvick 35.00 60.00
ard-Man SuperTruck
M Dealers/96
vin Harvick 60.00 100.00
ard-Man SuperTruck
quid Metal/300
rt Busch 25.00 50.00
rown Royal IROC/1152
chael Waltrip 40.00 65.00
aron's/1200
chael Waltrip 40.00 65.00
aron's 50th Anniversary/3660
chael Waltrip 40.00 65.00
aron's 50th Anniversary
M Dealers/24
chael Waltrip 40.00 65.00
aron's 50th Anniversary Matco/24
chael Waltrip 40.00 65.00
omino's Pizza/2508
chael Waltrip 40.00 65.00
omino's Pizza
M Dealers/36
nny Wallace 40.00 65.00
aron's 50th Anniversary/1764
nny Wallace 40.00 65.00
aron's 50th Anniversary Matco/12
Nemechek 60.00 100.00
Army Camo
Call to Duty/2220
01 Joe Nemechek 60.00 100.00
Army Camo
Call to Duty GM Dealers/96
05 Star Wars Event 25.00 50.00
05 Star Wars Event GM Dealers/144 25.00 50.00
05 Star Wars Event Matco/24 25.00 50.00
07 Dave Blaney 50.00 75.00
Jack Daniel's/10,464
07 Dave Blaney 60.00 100.00
Jack Daniel's Color Chrome/1440
07 Dave Blaney 50.00 75.00
Jack Daniel's
GM Dealers/960
07 Dave Blaney 40.00 70.00
Jack Daniel's Country Cocktails/5904
07 Dave Blaney 40.00 70.00
Jack Daniel's Country Cocktails
GM Dealers/444
07 Dave Blaney 40.00 70.00
Jack Daniel's Country Cocktails
QVC/504
07 Dave Blaney 40.00 70.00
Jack Daniel's
Drive-By Truckers/3468
07 Dave Blaney 40.00 70.00
Jack Daniel's Drive-By Truckers
GM Dealers/156
07 Dave Blaney 40.00 70.00
Jack Daniel's
Drive-By Truckers QVC/504
07 Dave Blaney 40.00 70.00
Jack Daniel's
Happy Birthday/4740
07 Dave Blaney 50.00 75.00
Jack Daniel's Happy Birthday
Black Pearl/720
07 Dave Blaney 40.00 70.00
Jack Daniel's Happy Birthday
GM Dealers/528
07 Dave Blaney 40.00 70.00
Jack Daniel's
Happy Birthday QVC/504
NNO Chevy Rock&Roll Event/1692 25.00 50.00
NNO Chevy Rock&Roll Event 25.00 50.00
GM Dealers/144

2005 Action Racing Collectables Historical Series 1:24

EX NM-MT
2 Rusty Wallace 40.00 65.00
Aluguard '85 Grand Prix/2376
2 Rusty Wallace 40.00 65.00
Aluguard '85 Grand Prix
GM Dealers/144
2 Rusty Wallace 40.00 65.00
Aluguard '85 Grand Prix QVC/288
3 Dale Earnhardt 60.00 100.00
Goodwrench '91 Lumina/5004
3 Dale Earnhardt 60.00 100.00
Goodwrench '91 Lumina QVC/1008
11 Darrell Waltrip 40.00 65.00
Pepsi '83 Monte Carlo/1332
12 Dale Earnhardt 60.00 100.00
Budweiser IROC
'87 Camaro/3276
12 Dale Earnhardt 60.00 100.00
Budweiser IROC
'87 Camaro GM Dealers/360
12 Dale Earnhardt 60.00 100.00
Budweiser IROC '87 Camaro
GM Dealers Chrome/564
12 D.Earnhardt/Budweiser IROC 60.00 100.00
'87 Camaro Liquid Metal/6684
14 Dale Earnhardt 50.00 75.00
Budweiser IROC
Lime Green '88 Camaro/5844
24 Jeff Gordon 60.00 100.00
DuPont '93 Lumina ROY/5004
43 Richard Petty 50.00 75.00
STP '79 Olds/2952
43 Richard Petty 125.00 175.00
STP '92 Grand Prix AU/1716
43 Richard Petty 125.00 175.00
STP '92 Grand Prix AU QVC/504

2005 Action QVC For Race Fans Only 1:24

EX NM-MT
2 Rusty Wallace 50.00 75.00
Kodak Color Chrome/2004
2 Rusty Wallace 50.00 75.00
Miller Genuine Draft
Brushed Metal/504
2 Rusty Wallace 75.00 125.00
Miller Genuine Draft
Color Chrome/2004
2 Rusty Wallace 100.00 200.00
Miller Genuine Draft
Color Chrome/Chrome 2-car set/504
2 Rusty Wallace 100.00 150.00
Miller Genuine Draft
Gold/300
2 Rusty Wallace 100.00 150.00
Miller Genuine Draft
Platinum/144
2 Rusty Wallace 75.00 125.00
Miller Lite Color Chrome/1008
2 Rusty Wallace 100.00 150.00
Miller Lite Gold/300
2 Rusty Wallace 75.00 125.00
Mobil Color Chrome/960
2 Rusty Wallace 60.00 100.00
Snap On Miller Lite
Brushed Metal/288
2 Rusty Wallace 100.00 175.00
Snap On Miller Lite
Gold/204
2 Rusty Wallace 150.00 250.00
Snap On Miller Lite
Platinum/108
2 Rusty Wallace 60.00 100.00
700 Starts Color Chrome
3 Dale Earnhardt 75.00 150.00
Goodwrench Plus
'98 MC Daytona Win Color Chrome/5004
8 Dale Earnhardt Jr. 50.00 75.00
Bud Brushed Metal/504
8 Dale Earnhardt Jr. 60.00 100.00
Bud Color Chrome/3504
8 Dale Earnhardt Jr. 175.00 300.00
Bud Platinum/300
8 Dale Earnhardt Jr. 50.00 75.00
Bud Born On Feb.20
Brushed Metal/504
8 Dale Earnhardt Jr. 60.00 100.00
Bud Born On Feb.20
Color Chrome/3504
8 Dale Earnhardt Jr. 50.00 75.00
Bud MLB All Star
Brushed Metal/288
8 Dale Earnhardt Jr. 75.00 125.00
Bud MLB All Star
Gold/204
8 Dale Earnhardt Jr. 50.00 75.00
Bud 3 Doors Down
Brushed Metal/288
8 Dale Earnhardt Jr. 100.00 150.00
Bud 3 Doors Down
Color Chrome/2004
8 Dale Earnhardt Jr. 60.00 100.00
Milestones '04 Daytona 500
Color Chrome/5004
9 Kasey Kahne 60.00 100.00
Dodge Brushed Metal/504
9 Kasey Kahne 100.00 175.00
Dodge Gold/300
9 Kasey Kahne 100.00 175.00
Dodge Pit Cap Reverse
Brushed Metal AU/900
9 Kasey Kahne 75.00 125.00
Dodge Pit Cap Reverse
Gold/300
9 Kasey Kahne 100.00 175.00
Dodge Pit Cap Reverse Platinum/144
9 Kasey Kahne 75.00 125.00
Dodge Retro Bud Shootout
Color Chrome/1008
9 Kasey Kahne 100.00 150.00
Dodge Retro Bud Shootout
Gold/288
9 Kasey Kahne 100.00 175.00
Dodge Retro Bud Shootout
Platinum/144
9 Kasey Kahne 100.00 175.00
Mountain Dew Brushed Metal AU/504
9 Kasey Kahne 60.00 100.00
Mountain Dew Color Chrome/1008
9/43 Kasey Kahne 100.00 150.00
Richard Petty
Dodge '75 Charger/STP Color Chrome/1008
12 Dale Earnhardt 75.00 125.00
Budweiser IROC
'87 Camaro Color Chrome/504
20 Tony Stewart 100.00 175.00
Home Depot Brickyard Raced
Color Chrome/1008
20 Tony Stewart 60.00 100.00
Home Depot Madagascar
Color Chrome/300
24 Jeff Gordon 50.00 75.00
DuPont Flames Brushed Metal/504
24 Jeff Gordon 100.00 150.00
DuPont Flames Performance Alliance
Reverse Color Chrome/3504
24 Jeff Gordon 60.00 100.00
Mighty Mouse Color Chrome/3504
24 Jeff Gordon 75.00 125.00
Pepsi Daytona Color Chrome/3456
24 Jeff Gordon 75.00 125.00
Pepsi Star Wars
Color Chrome/3504
24 Jeff Gordon 100.00 175.00
Pepsi Star Wars
Gold/300
24 Jeff Gordon 175.00 300.00
Pepsi Star Wars
Platinum/144
24 Jeff Gordon 100.00 200.00
Pepsi Star Wars
Talladega Raced Brushed Copper/288
24 Jeff Gordon 100.00 200.00
Pepsi Star Wars
Talladega Raced Silver/624
29 Kevin Harvick 75.00 125.00
Goodwrench Color Chrome/360
29 Kevin Harvick 75.00 125.00
Goodwrench Quicksilver
Color Chrome/360
33 Tony Stewart 50.00 75.00
James Dean 50th Anniversary
Color Chrome/300
38 Elliott Sadler 50.00 75.00
M&M's Color Chrome/360
81 Dale Earnhardt Jr. 75.00 125.00
Oreo Color Chrome/3508
81 Dale Earnhardt Jr. 100.00 200.00
Oreo Ritz Platinum/300

2005 Action/RCCA 1:24

EX NM-MT
1 Martin Truex Jr. 40.00 65.00
Bass Pro Shops/408
2 Clint Bowyer 35.00 60.00
AC Delco/288
2 Jimmy Spencer 50.00 75.00
Snap-On 85th Anniversary
Color Chrome/288
2 Rusty Wallace 35.00 60.00
Kodak/408
2 Rusty Wallace 50.00 75.00
Milestones Last Call/502
2 Rusty Wallace
Milestones 700th Start/602
2 Rusty Wallace 60.00 100.00
Milestones 9X Bristol Winner/502
2 Rusty Wallace 50.00 75.00
Miller Lite/480
2 Rusty Wallace 60.00 100.00
Miller Lite Color Chrome/288
2 Rusty Wallace 50.00 75.00
Miller Lite Last Call
Daytona Shootout/600
2 Rusty Wallace 50.00 75.00
Miller Lite Last Call Test/360
2 Rusty Wallace 50.00 75.00
Mobil/444
2 Rusty Wallace 40.00 65.00
Snap-On Miller Lite/540
3 Dale Earnhardt Jr. 50.00 75.00
Milestones
'98-'99 BGN Champ/1500
5 Kyle Busch 50.00 75.00
CarQuest/288
5 Kyle Busch 50.00 75.00
Kellogg's/444
5 Kyle Busch 60.00 100.00
Kellogg's Color Chrome/144
5 Kyle Busch 75.00 125.00
Kellogg's Liquid Metal/144
5 Kyle Busch
Kellogg's California Raced/240
5 Kyle Busch 50.00 75.00
Kellogg's Star Wars/408
6 Mark Martin 50.00 75.00
Crown Royal IROC
Brushed Metal/360
7 Robby Gordon 50.00 75.00
Jim Beam/408
8 Dale Earnhardt Jr. 35.00 60.00
Bud/1500
8 Dale Earnhardt Jr. 50.00 75.00
Bud Color Chrome/804
8 Dale Earnhardt Jr. 50.00 75.00
Bud Born On Feb.20/2400
8 Dale Earnhardt Jr. 50.00 75.00
Bud MLB All-Star/1800
8 Dale Earnhardt Jr. 40.00 70.00
Bud MLB All-Star
Chicago Raced/444
8 Dale Earnhardt Jr. 40.00 70.00
Bud Test/804
8 Dale Earnhardt Jr.
Milestones '00 All-Star Win/999
8 Dale Earnhardt Jr. 60.00 100.00
Milestones '01 Daytona Win/1200
8 Dale Earnhardt Jr. 60.00 100.00
Milestones '04 Daytona Win/1800
8 Martin Truex Jr. 40.00 65.00
Bass Pro/408
8 Martin Truex Jr. 40.00 65.00
Bass Pro Mexico City Raced/424
8 Martin Truex Jr. 40.00 65.00
Bass Pro Talladega Raced/144
8 Martin Truex Jr. 40.00 65.00
Chance 2 Test/288
9 Kasey Kahne 50.00 75.00
Dodge/600
9 Kasey Kahne 75.00 125.00
Dodge Color Chrome/408
9 Kasey Kahne 75.00 125.00
Dodge Liquid Metal/408
9 Kasey Kahne 50.00 75.00
Dodge Richmond Raced/499
9 Kasey Kahne 50.00 75.00
Dodge Longest Yard/504
9 Kasey Kahne 50.00 75.00
Dodge Pit Cap White/504
9 Kasey Kahne 50.00 75.00
Dodge Retro Bud Shootout/600
9 Kasey Kahne 50.00 80.00
Dodge Test/408
9 Kasey Kahne 50.00 75.00
Mountain Dew/444
10 Scott Riggs 35.00 60.00
Valvoline/240
11 Jason Leffler 40.00 65.00
Fed Ex/288
15 Kyle Busch 40.00 70.00
ditech.com SuperTruck
Charlotte Raced w/tire/360
15 Michael Waltrip 35.00 60.00
Napa/288
18 Bobby Labonte 40.00 65.00
Interstate Batteries/288
18 Bobby Labonte 50.00 75.00
Interstate Batteries
Color Chrome/204
18 Bobby Labonte 40.00 65.00
Interstate Batteries Test/360
18 J.J. Yeley 40.00 65.00
Vigoro AU/240
19 Jeremy Mayfield 35.00 60.00
Dodge/288
20 Tony Stewart 75.00 125.00
Home Depot/600
20 Tony Stewart 60.00 100.00
Home Depot Color Chrome/288
20 Tony Stewart 100.00 175.00
Home Depot
Brickyard Raced/288
20 Tony Stewart 75.00 125.00
Home Depot
Daytona Raced/204
20 Tony Stewart 50.00 75.00
Home Depot Hometown Columbus
Brushed Bronze/204
20 Tony Stewart 40.00 65.00
Home Depot Madagascar/504
20 Tony Stewart 40.00 65.00
Home Depot Test/600
20 Tony Stewart 50.00 75.00
Milestones First Win/600
20 Tony Stewart 50.00 75.00
Milestones ROY/600
20 Tony Stewart 50.00 75.00
Milestones '05 Brickyard Win/550
20 Tony Stewart 50.00 75.00
Milestones 2X Champion/450
21 Kevin Harvick 40.00 65.00
Hershey's Take 5/504
21 Kevin Harvick 40.00 65.00
Pelon Pelo Rico/360
21 Kevin Harvick 40.00 65.00
Reese's/288
21 Kevin Harvick 40.00 65.00
Twizzlers/144
21 Brandon Miller 25.00 50.00
Reese's/204
24 Jeff Gordon 50.00 75.00
DuPont Flames/1008
24 Jeff Gordon 60.00 100.00
DuPont Flames Color Chrome/408
24 Jeff Gordon 50.00 75.00
DuPont Flames Daytona Raced/824
24 Jeff Gordon 50.00 75.00
DuPont Flames
Martinsville Raced/424
24 Jeff Gordon 50.00 75.00
DuPont Test/804
24 Jeff Gordon 50.00 75.00
Mighty Mouse/900
24 Jeff Gordon 50.00 75.00
Milestones First Win/1008
24 Jeff Gordon
Milestones 4X Brickyard Winner/900
24 Jeff Gordon 50.00 75.00
Milestones 4X Champion/1800
24 Jeff Gordon
Milestones 4X Daytona Winner/1800
24 Jeff Gordon 50.00 75.00
Pepsi Star Wars/1200
27 Rusty Wallace 50.00 75.00
Milestones '89 Champ/802
29 Kevin Harvick 40.00 65.00
Goodwrench/600
29 Kevin Harvick 50.00 75.00
Goodwrench Color Chrome/288
29 Kevin Harvick 40.00 65.00
Goodwrench Bristol Raced/204
29 Kevin Harvick 35.00 60.00
Goodwrench Daytona/804
29 Kevin Harvick 40.00 65.00
Goodwrench Test/408
33 Tony Stewart 40.00 65.00
James Dean 50th Anniversary/504
33 Tony Stewart 40.00 65.00
Mr.Clean AutoDry
Daytona Raced/288
33 Tony Stewart 40.00 65.00
Old Spice/252
38 Elliott Sadler 35.00 60.00
Combos/204
38 Elliott Sadler 40.00 65.00
M&M's/408
38 Elliott Sadler 50.00 75.00
M&M's Color Chrome/204
38 Elliott Sadler 40.00 65.00
M&M's Star Wars/408
38 Elliott Sadler 40.00 65.00
M&M's Test/360
38 Elliott Sadler 35.00 60.00
Pedigree/288
38 Elliott Sadler 40.00 65.00
30th Birthday Fantasy/300
41 Reed Sorenson 75.00 125.00
Discount Tire/288
41 Reed Sorenson 75.00 125.00
Discount Tire Nashville Raced/144
42 Jamie McMurray 35.00 60.00
Havoline Shine On Charlotte/240
44 Terry Labonte 50.00 75.00
Kellogg's/408
47 Bobby Labonte 50.00 75.00
Silverado Trick Pony
Martinsville Raced w/tire/288
48 Jimmie Johnson 40.00 65.00
Lowe's/444
48 Jimmie Johnson 60.00 100.00
Lowe's Color Chrome/240
48 Jimmie Johnson 50.00 75.00
Lowe's Las Vegas Raced/144
48 Jimmie Johnson 50.00 75.00
Lowe's Kobalt Truck Boxes/240
48 Jimmie Johnson 40.00 65.00
Lowe's Test/408
64 Rusty Wallace 40.00 65.00
Bell Helicopter/408
77 Travis Kvapil 35.00 60.00
Kodak/288
79 Kasey Kahne 35.00 60.00
Auto Value/360
79 Kasey Kahne 50.00 75.00
Trus Joist/204
81 Dale Earnhardt Jr. 40.00 65.00
Chance 2 Test/408
81 Dale Earnhardt Jr. 40.00 65.00
Oreo Ritz/1800
88 Dale Jarrett 40.00 65.00
UPS/444
88 Dale Jarrett 50.00 75.00
UPS Color Chrome/204
88 Dale Jarrett 40.00 65.00
UPS Mother's Day/288
88 Dale Jarrett 40.00 65.00
UPS Star Wars/444
88 Dale Jarrett 40.00 65.00
UPS Test/360
05 Star Wars Event/408 40.00 60.00
07 Dave Blaney 60.00 100.00
Jack Daniel's/408

2005 Action/RCCA Elite 1:24

EX NM-MT
1 Martin Truex Jr. 60.00 100.00
Bass Pro Shops/504
1 Martin Truex Jr. 75.00 125.00
Bass Pro Black/288
2 Rusty Wallace 75.00 125.00
Kodak/408
2 Rusty Wallace 250.00 400.00
Kodak White Gold/25
2 Rusty Wallace 75.00 125.00
Milestones Last Call/502
2 Rusty Wallace 100.00 150.00
Milestones 700th Start/602
2 Rusty Wallace 100.00 150.00
Milestones 9X Bristol Winner/502
2 Rusty Wallace 75.00 125.00
Miller Genuine Draft/720
2 Rusty Wallace 250.00 400.00
Miller Genuine Draft
White Gold/30
2 Rusty Wallace 75.00 125.00
Miller Lite/720
2 Rusty Wallace 90.00 135.00
Miller Lite
Color Chrome/480
2 Rusty Wallace 300.00 500.00
Miller Lite White Gold/30
2 Rusty Wallace 100.00 150.00
Miller Lite Bristol/600
2 Rusty Wallace 300.00 500.00
Miller Lite Bristol
White Gold/25
2 Rusty Wallace 100.00 150.00
Miller Lite Hometown Saint Louis

Brushed Bronze/288
2 Rusty Wallace Miller Lite Last Call Daytona Shootout/600 125.00 250.00
2 Rusty Wallace Miller Lite Last Call Daytona Shootout White Gold/25 250.00 400.00
2 Rusty Wallace Miller Lite Last Call Test/444 100.00 150.00
2 Rusty Wallace Mobil/540 90.00 135.00
2 Rusty Wallace Mobil White Gold/25 250.00 400.00
2 Rusty Wallace Snap-On Miller Lite/540 100.00 150.00
2 Rusty Wallace Snap-On Miller Lite White Gold/25 250.00 400.00
3 Dale Earnhardt Jr. Milestones '98-'99 Busch Champion/1500 100.00 150.00
5 Kyle Busch CarQuest/288 100.00 150.00
5 Kyle Busch CarQuest White Gold/25 250.00 400.00
5 Kyle Busch Kellogg's/444 125.00 200.00
5 Kyle Busch Kellogg's Color Chrome/144 100.00 150.00
5 Kyle Busch Kellogg's White Gold/25 300.00 500.00
5 Kyle Busch Kellogg's California Raced/240 150.00 250.00
5 Kyle Busch Kellogg's Star Wars/408 75.00 125.00
5 Kyle Busch Kellogg's Star Wars White Gold/25 275.00 400.00
7 Robby Gordon Jim Beam/408 75.00 125.00
7 Robby Gordon Jim Beam White Gold/25 275.00 400.00
8 Dale Earnhardt Jr. Bud/2400 90.00 135.00
8 Dale Earnhardt Jr. Bud Color Chrome/1200 75.00 125.00
8 D.Earnhardt Jr./Bud White Gold/50 450.00 650.00
8 Dale Earnhardt Jr. Bud Born On Feb.12/600 75.00 125.00
8 Dale Earnhardt Jr. Bud Born On Feb.12 Platinum/140 200.00 350.00
8 Dale Earnhardt Jr. Bud Born On Feb.12 White Gold/33 350.00 600.00
8 Dale Earnhardt Jr. Bud Born On Feb.17 Platinum/88 150.00 300.00
8 Dale Earnhardt Jr. Bud Born On Feb.17 White Gold/25 400.00 600.00
8 Dale Earnhardt Jr. Bud Born On Feb.20/3300 90.00 135.00
8 Dale Earnhardt Jr. Bud Born On Feb.20 Platinum/200 150.00 300.00
8 Dale Earnhardt Jr. Bud Born On Feb.20 White Gold/50 350.00 600.00
8 Dale Earnhardt Jr. Bud MLB All-Star/2400 75.00 125.00
8 Dale Earnhardt Jr. Bud MLB All-Star Platinum/144 125.00 250.00
8 Dale Earnhardt Jr. Bud MLB All-Star White Gold/44 350.00 600.00
8 Dale Earnhardt Jr. Bud Test/2005 75.00 125.00
8 Dale Earnhardt Jr. Bud 3 Doors Down/2100 75.00 125.00
8 Dale Earnhardt Jr. Bud 3 Doors Down Platinum/144 150.00 250.00
8 Dale Earnhardt Jr. Bud 3 Doors Down White Gold/50 350.00 600.00
8 Dale Earnhardt Jr. Milestones '00 All-Star Win/999 100.00 150.00
8 Dale Earnhardt Jr. Milestones '01 Daytona Win/1000 100.00 150.00
8 Dale Earnhardt Jr. Milestones '04 Daytona Win/1800 100.00 150.00
8 Martin Truex Jr. Bass Pro/600 75.00 125.00
8 Martin Truex Jr. Bass Pro White Gold/25 250.00 400.00
8 Martin Truex Jr. Bass Pro Mexico City Raced/200 75.00 125.00
8 Martin Truex Jr. Bass Pro Talladega Raced/144 75.00 125.00
8 Martin Truex Jr. Chance 2 Test/408 60.00 100.00
9 Kasey Kahne Dodge/900 100.00 150.00
9 Kasey Kahne Dodge Color Chrome/600 100.00 150.00
9 Kasey Kahne Dodge Color Chrome AU/132 125.00 200.00
9 Kasey Kahne Dodge Platinum/144 150.00 250.00
9 Kasey Kahne Dodge White Gold/30 350.00 600.00
9 Kasey Kahne Dodge Richmond Raced/899 100.00 150.00
9 Kasey Kahne Dodge Richmond Raced AU/144 125.00 200.00
9 Kasey Kahne Dodge Richmond Raced Platinum/99 200.00 350.00
9 Kasey Kahne Dodge Hometown Enumclaw Brushed Bronze/288 75.00 125.00
9 Kasey Kahne Dodge Longest Yard/600 75.00 125.00
9 Kasey Kahne Dodge Longest Yard White Gold/25 250.00 400.00
9 Kasey Kahne Dodge Pit Cap White/600 90.00 135.00
9 Kasey Kahne Dodge Pit Cap White White Gold/30 250.00 500.00
9 Kasey Kahne Dodge Retro Bud Shootout/900 100.00 150.00
9 Kasey Kahne Dodge Retro Bud Shootout Platinum/144 150.00 250.00
9 Kasey Kahne Dodge Retro Bud Shootout White Gold/50 250.00 400.00
9 Kasey Kahne Mopar/480 100.00 150.00
9 Kasey Kahne Mopar White Gold/25 250.00 400.00
9 Kasey Kahne Mountain Dew/804 100.00 150.00
9 Kasey Kahne Mountain Dew AU/138 125.00 200.00
9 Kasey Kahne Mountain Dew White Gold/30 300.00 500.00
12 Darrell Waltrip Tundra Last Race SuperTruck White Gold/25
15 Michael Waltrip Napa/408 60.00 100.00
15 Michael Waltrip Napa Color Chrome/204 75.00 125.00
15 Michael Waltrip Napa White Gold/25 150.00 300.00
15 Michael Waltrip Napa Stars & Stripes/288 60.00 100.00
18 Bobby Labonte FedEx Freight/240 100.00 175.00
18 Bobby Labonte Interstate Batteries/408 60.00 100.00
18 Bobby Labonte Interstate Batteries Color Chrome/204 75.00 125.00
18 Bobby Labonte Interstate Batteries White Gold/25 200.00 400.00
18 Bobby Labonte Interstate Batteries Madagascar/408 60.00 100.00
18 Bobby Labonte Interstate Batteries Test/408 60.00 100.00
19 Jeremy Mayfield Dodge/288 60.00 100.00
19 Jeremy Mayfield Mountain Dew Pitch Black/360 60.00 100.00
19 Jeremy Mayfield Mountain Dew Pitch Black White Gold/25 200.00 350.00
19 Jeremy Mayfield Dodge Retro Bud Shootout/288 60.00 100.00
19 Jeremy Mayfield Dodge Retro Bud Shootout White Gold/25 200.00 350.00
20 Tony Stewart Home Depot/804 150.00 250.00
20 Tony Stewart Home Depot Color Chrome/360 125.00 200.00
20 Tony Stewart Home Depot White Gold/30 500.00 650.00
20 Tony Stewart Home Depot '05 Champion Liquid Color/620 200.00 350.00
20 Tony Stewart Home Depot Hometown Columbus Brushed Bronze/204 100.00 150.00
20 Tony Stewart Home Depot KaBOOM/504 100.00 150.00
20 Tony Stewart Home Depot Lithium Ion/408 200.00 350.00
20 Tony Stewart Home Depot Lithium Ion Platinum/8 200.00 350.00
20 Tony Stewart Home Depot Lithium Ion White Gold/25 200.00 350.00
20 Tony Stewart Home Depot Madagascar/600 100.00 150.00
20 Tony Stewart Home Depot Test/600 100.00 150.00
20 Tony Stewart Milestones First Win/600 75.00 125.00
20 Tony Stewart Milestones ROY/600 75.00 125.00
20 Tony Stewart Milestones '05 Brickyard Win/550 100.00 150.00
20 Tony Stewart Milestones 2X Champion/450 100.00 150.00
21 Kevin Harvick Hershey's Take 5/504 75.00 125.00
21 Kevin Harvick Pelon Pelo Rico/360 60.00 100.00
21 Kevin Harvick Reese's/288 60.00 100.00
24 Jeff Gordon DuPont Flames/1500 100.00 150.00
24 Jeff Gordon DuPont Flames Color Chrome/600 100.00 150.00
24 Jeff Gordon DuPont Flames Platinum/144 175.00 300.00
24 Jeff Gordon DuPont Flames White Gold/50 600.00 800.00
24 Jeff Gordon DuPont Flames Daytona Raced/1524 100.00 150.00
24 Jeff Gordon DuPont Flames Daytona Raced White Gold/40 500.00 750.00
24 Jeff Gordon DuPont Flames Martinsville Raced/524 100.00 150.00
24 Jeff Gordon DuPont Flames Reverse Performance Alliance/1500 100.00 150.00
24 Jeff Gordon DuPont Flames Performance Alliance Reverse White Gold/30 500.00 750.00
24 Jeff Gordon DuPont Test/1200 75.00 125.00
24 Jeff Gordon Foundation Holiday/600 100.00 175.00
24 Jeff Gordon Mighty Mouse/1500 100.00 150.00
24 Jeff Gordon Mighty Mouse Platinum/144 175.00 300.00
24 Jeff Gordon Mighty Mouse White Gold/30 400.00 650.00
24 Jeff Gordon Milestones First Win/1008 100.00 150.00
24 Jeff Gordon Milestones 4X Brickyard Winner/900 100.00 150.00
24 Jeff Gordon Milestones 4X Champion/1200 100.00 150.00
24 Jeff Gordon Milestones 4X Daytona Winner/1800 100.00 150.00
24 Jeff Gordon Pepsi Daytona/1224 100.00 150.00
24 Jeff Gordon Pepsi Daytona Platinum/144 175.00 300.00
24 Jeff Gordon Pepsi Daytona White Gold/34 500.00 750.00
24 Jeff Gordon Pepsi Star Wars/2004 100.00 150.00
24 Jeff Gordon Pepsi Star Wars White Gold/44 600.00 800.00
24 Jeff Gordon Pepsi Star Wars Talladega Raced/624 100.00 150.00
25 Brian Vickers GMAC Green Day AU/144
27 Rusty Wallace Milestones '89 Champion/802 100.00 150.00
29 Kevin Harvick Goodwrench/804 75.00 125.00
29 Kevin Harvick Goodwrench AU/144 100.00 150.00
29 Kevin Harvick Goodwrench Color Chrome/360 75.00 125.00
29 Kevin Harvick Goodwrench White Gold/30 250.00 400.00
29 Kevin Harvick Goodwrench Bristol Raced/204 60.00 100.00
29 Kevin Harvick Goodwrench Atlanta/600 75.00 125.00
29 Kevin Harvick Goodwrench Atlanta AU/144 100.00 150.00
29 Kevin Harvick Goodwrench Atlanta White Gold/29 175.00 350.00
29 Kevin Harvick Goodwrench Brickyard/504 60.00 100.00
29 Kevin Harvick Goodwrench Brickyard White Gold/30 175.00 350.00
29 Kevin Harvick Goodwrench Daytona/900 75.00 125.00
29 Kevin Harvick Goodwrench Daytona AU/144 100.00 150.00
29 Kevin Harvick Goodwrench Daytona White Gold/48 175.00 350.00
29 Kevin Harvick Goodwrench Gretchen Wilson/444 75.00 125.00
29 Kevin Harvick Goodwrench Hometown Brushed Bronze/144 75.00 125.00
29 Kevin Harvick Goodwrench Quicksilver 60.00 100.00
29 Kevin Harvick Goodwrench Quicksilver White Gold/25 200.00 350.00
29 Kevin Harvick Goodwrench Test/600 60.00 100.00
29 Kevin Harvick Reese's Big Cup/204 60.00 100.00
31 Jeff Burton Cingular/288 60.00 100.00
31 Jeff Burton Cingular AU/150 75.00 150.00
31 Jeff Burton Cingular White Gold/25 300.00 450.00
31 Jeff Burton Cingular Big & Rich AU/121 75.00 150.00
33 Tony Stewart James Dean 50th Anniversary/600 75.00 125.00
33 Tony Stewart James Dean 50th Anniversary White Gold/30 400.00 600.00
33 Tony Stewart Mr.Clean AutoDry Daytona Raced/288 75.00 125.00
33 Tony Stewart Old Spice/252 60.00 100.00
38 Elliott Sadler M&M's/408 75.00 125.00
38 Elliott Sadler M&M's Color Chrome/204 75.00 125.00
38 Elliott Sadler M&M White Gold/25 200.00 350.00
38 Elliott Sadler M&M's Halloween White Gold/25 200.00 350.00
38 Elliott Sadler M&M's July 4/288 60.00 100.00
38 Elliott Sadler M&M's Star Wars/480 75.00 125.00
38 Elliott Sadler M&M's Star Wars AU/141 75.00 150.00
38 Elliott Sadler M&M's Test/408 75.00 125.00
38 Elliott Sadler 30th Birthday Fantasy/204 75.00 125.00
39 Bill Elliott Coors Daytona Shootout/300 60.00 100.00
39 Bill Elliott Coors Daytona Shootout White Gold/25 250.00 400.00
39 Reed Sorenson Discount Tire/144 125.00 200.00
39 Reed Sorenson Discount Tire White Gold/25
40 Sterling Marlin Coors Light White Gold/25 200.00 350.00
41 Reed Sorenson Coats Discount Tire Nashville Raced/144 100.00 175.00
41 Reed Sorenson Home 123 White Gold/25 200.00 350.00
42 Jamie McMurray Havoline/288 75.00 125.00
42 Jamie McMurray Havoline White Gold/25 250.00 400.00
42 Jamie McMurray Havoline Autism Society of America/360 75.00 125.00
42 Jamie McMurray Havoline Shine On Texas/240 60.00 100.00
44 Terry Labonte Kellogg's/408 75.00 125.00
44 Terry Labonte Kellogg's White Gold/25 250.00 400.00
48 Jimmie Johnson Lowe's/504 100.00 150.00
48 Jimmie Johnson Lowe's Color Chrome/288 90.00 135.00
48 Jimmie Johnson Lowe's White Gold/25 500.00 750.00
48 Jimmie Johnson Lowe's Las Vegas Raced/204 60.00 100.00
48 Jimmie Johnson Lowe's Test/504 75.00 125.00
48 Jimmie Johnson Lowe's '06 Preview White Gold/25 350.00 500.00
64 Rusty Wallace Bell Helicopter/408 60.00 100.00
64 Rusty Wallace Bell Helicopter White Gold/25 275.00 400.00
64 Rusty Wallace Miller High Life Saint Louis Family Tribute/600 60.00 100.00
64 Rusty Wallace Miller High Life Saint Louis Family Tribute White Gold/25 300.00 450.00
79 Kasey Kahne Auto Value/360 100.00 150.00
79 Kasey Kahne Trus Joist/204 100.00 150.00
81 Dale Earnhardt Jr. Chance 2 Test/1008 60.00 100.00
81 Dale Earnhardt Jr. Menards/1200 60.00 100.00
81 Dale Earnhardt Jr. Menards White Gold/25 300.00 450.00
81 Dale Earnhardt Jr. Oreo Ritz/2400 75.00 125.00
81 Dale Earnhardt Jr. Oreo Ritz Platinum/240 150.00 250.00
81 Dale Earnhardt Jr. Oreo Ritz White Gold/48 250.00 400.00
88 Dale Jarrett UPS/504 60.00 100.00
88 Dale Jarrett UPS Color Chrome/240 75.00 125.00
88 Dale Jarrett UPS Color Chrome AU/59 100.00 175.00
88 Dale Jarrett UPS White Gold/25 275.00 400.00
88 Dale Jarrett UPS Herbie Fully Loaded/600 60.00 100.00
88 Dale Jarrett UPS Herbie AU/144 75.00 125.00
88 Dale Jarrett UPS Herbie Fully Loaded White Gold/28 200.00 350.00
88 Dale Jarrett UPS Hometown Conover Brushed Bronze/144 90.00 135.00
88 Dale Jarrett UPS Mother's Day/288 60.00 100.00
88 Dale Jarrett UPS Star Wars/600 60.00 100.00
88 Dale Jarrett UPS Star Wars White Gold/25 300.00 450.00
88 Dale Jarrett UPS Store Toys for Tots White Gold/25 250.00 400.00
88 Dale Jarrett UPS Test/408 75.00 125.00
91 Bill Elliott McDonald's White Gold/25 200.00 350.00
91 Bill Elliott Stanley Tools/288 75.00 125.00
07 Dave Blaney Jack Daniel's/444 100.00 175.00
07 Dave Blaney Jack Daniel's White Gold/25 350.00 500.00
07 Dave Blaney Jack Daniel's Country Cocktails/504 100.00 150.00
07 Dave Blaney Jack Daniel's Country Cocktails White Gold/33 200.00 350.00
07 Dave Blaney Jack Daniel's Happy Birthday Jack White Gold/25 200.00 350.00

2005 Action/RCCA Historical Series 1:24

EX NM-MT
3 Dale Earnhardt Coke '98 Monte Carlo/903 50.00 75.00
3 Dale Earnhardt Goodwrench Service Plus Daytona Win '98 Monte Carlo/903 50.00 75.00
3 Dale Earnhardt Goodwrench Service Plus Talladega Win '00 Monte Carlo/903 50.00 75.00
3 Dale Earnhardt Wrangler '99 Monte Carlo/903 50.00 75.00
11 Darrell Waltrip Pepsi '83 Monte Carlo/444 40.00 65.00
12 Dale Earnhardt Bud '87 Camaro/804 50.00 75.00
14 Dale Earnhardt Budweiser IROC Lime Green '88 Camaro Color Chrome/504 60.00 100.00
43 Richard Petty STP '79 Olds/480 50.00 75.00

2005 Action/RCCA Historical Series Elite 1:24

EX NM-MT
3 Dale Earnhardt Coke '98 Monte Carlo Color Chrome/603 90.00 135.00
3 Dale Earnhardt Coke '98 Monte Carlo Platinum/203 175.00 30(
3 Dale Earnhardt Coke '98 Monte Carlo White Gold/33 400.00 65(
3 Dale Earnhardt Goodwrench Service Plus '98 Daytona Raced Color Chrome/603 90.00 13
3 Dale Earnhardt Goodwrench Service Plus Daytona Raced '98 Monte Carlo Platinum/203 175.00 30
3 Dale Earnhardt Goodwrench Service Plus '98 Daytona Raced White Gold/33 400.00 65
3 Dale Earnhardt Goodwrench Service Plus '00 Talladega Raced Color Chrome/603 90.00 13
3 Dale Earnhardt Goodwrench Service Plus Talladega Raced '00 Monte Carlo Platinum/203 175.00 30
3 Dale Earnhardt Goodwrench Service Plus '00 Talladega Raced White Gold/33 400.00 65
3 Dale Earnhardt Wrangler '99 Monte Carlo Color Chrome/603 90.00 13
3 Dale Earnhardt Wrangler '99 Monte Carlo Platinum/203 175.00 30
3 Dale Earnhardt Wrangler '99 Monte Carlo White Gold/33 400.00 65
11 Darrell Waltrip Pepsi '83 Monte Carlo/288 75.00 12
24 Jeff Gordon DuPont '93 Lumina/1224 125.00 20
43 Richard Petty STP '79 Olds/480 60.00 10
43 Richard Petty STP '79 Olds White Gold/25 250.00 40
43 Richard Petty STP '92 Grand Prix/408 100.00 15

2005 Action/RCCA Metal El
1:24

EX NM
9 Kasey Kahne Dodge/600 75.00 12
18 Bobby Labonte Interstate Batteries/408 60.00 10
38 Elliott Sadler M&M's/408 60.00 10
38 Elliott Sadler M&M's AU/144 75.00 15

2006 Action Performance
1:24

EX NM
22 Kenny Wallace Auto Zone Promo in window box 15.00 3
29 Jeff Burton Holiday Inn Promo in split window box 20.00 4
66 Jeff Green Best Buy Promo in window box 20.00 4
88 Dale Jarrett UPS in AP box 20.00 4

2006 Action Racing Collectables 1:24

* DENOTES TOTAL PRODUCTION RUNS LISTED ON BASIC ARC PIECE

EX NM
1 Martin Truex Jr. Bass Pro Shops/6000 50.00 7
1 Martin Truex Jr. Bass Pro Shops Clear Window Bank/204 50.00 7
1 Martin Truex Jr. Bass Pro Shops GM Dealers/1008 50.00 7
1 Martin Truex Jr. Bass Pro Shops Mac Tools/300 50.00 7
1 Martin Truex Jr. Bass Pro Shops Matco/72 50.00 7
1 Martin Truex Jr. Bass Pro Shops QVC/288 50.00 7
1 Martin Truex Jr. Bass Pro Shops 3 Days of Dale Tribute/3504 60.00 10
1 Martin Truex Jr. Bass Pro Shops 3 Days of Dale Tribute GM Dealers/1488 60.00 10
1 Martin Truex Jr. Bass Pro Shops Test/3504 50.00 7
1 Martin Truex Jr. Bass Pro Shops Test GM Dealers/504 50.00 7
2 Clint Bowyer AC Delco/2052 40.00 6
2 Clint Bowyer AC Delco Clear Window Bank/144 40.00 6
2 Clint Bowyer AC Delco GM Dealers/504 40.00 6
2 Rusty Wallace Legendary/4220 50.00 7
5 Kyle Busch Carquest/2508 50.00 7
5 Kyle Busch Carquest 50.00 7

GM Dealers/72
le Busch 50.00 75.00
Delphi/1356
le Busch 50.00 75.00
Delphi GM Dealers/96
le Busch 50.00 75.00
Kellogg's/3864
le Busch 50.00 75.00
Kellogg's GM Dealers/360
le Busch 50.00 75.00
Kellogg's QVC/120
le Busch 50.00 75.00
Kellogg's Cars/3000
le Busch 50.00 75.00
Kellogg's Ice Age/2556
le Busch 50.00 75.00
Kellogg's Ice Age
Clear Window Bank
le Busch 50.00 75.00
Kellogg's Ice Age
GM Dealers/288
le Busch 50.00 75.00
Lowe's
ark Martin 50.00 75.00
AAA Holiday/1584*
ark Martin 50.00 75.00
AAA Holiday QVC*
ark Martin 50.00 75.00
Crown Royal IROC/2316
ark Martin 50.00 75.00
Crown Royal IROC
GM Dealers/192
le Earnhardt Jr. 60.00 100.00
Bud/30,000
le Earnhardt Jr. 60.00 100.00
Bud AB/600
le Earnhardt Jr. 60.00 100.00
Bud Clear Window Bank/504
le Earnhardt Jr. 60.00 100.00
Bud GM Dealers/2508
le Earnhardt Jr. 60.00 100.00
Bud Mac Tools/504
le Earnhardt Jr. 60.00 100.00
Bud Matco/228
le Earnhardt Jr. 60.00 100.00
Bud QVC/6500
le Earnhardt Jr. 75.00 125.00
Bud Richmond Raced/8556
le Earnhardt Jr. 75.00 125.00
Bud Richmond Raced
GM Dealers/2652
le Earnhardt Jr. 75.00 125.00
Bud 3 Days of Dale Tribute/44,169*
le Earnhardt Jr. 75.00 125.00
Bud 3 Days of Dale Tribute
Anheuser Busch*
le Earnhardt Jr. 75.00 125.00
Bud Dale Tribute
GM Dealers/7392
le Earnhardt Jr. 75.00 125.00
Bud 3 Days of Dale Tribute
Hamilton*
le Earnhardt Jr. 75.00 125.00
Bud 3 Days of Dale Tribute
Mac Tools*
le Earnhardt Jr. 75.00 125.00
Bud 3 Days of Dale Tribute
QVC*
le Earnhardt Jr. 75.00 125.00
Bud 3 Days of Dale Tribute
Snap On*
le Earnhardt Jr. 75.00 125.00
Bud Father's Day/30,456*
le Earnhardt Jr. 75.00 125.00
Bud Father's Day
Anheuser Busch*
le Earnhardt Jr. 75.00 125.00
Bud Father's Day
Clear Window Bank/492
le Earnhardt Jr. 75.00 125.00
Bud Father's Day
GM Dealers/3792
le Earnhardt Jr. 75.00 125.00
Bud Father's Day
Hamilton*
le Earnhardt Jr. 75.00 125.00
Bud Father's Day
Mac Tools*
le Earnhardt Jr. 75.00 125.00
Bud Father's Day
QVC*
le Earnhardt Jr. 75.00 125.00
Bud Father's Day
Snap-On*
le Earnhardt Jr. 50.00 75.00
Bud Test/5196*
le Earnhardt Jr. 50.00 75.00
Bud Test GM Dealers/720
le Earnhardt Jr. 50.00 75.00
Bud Test Mac Tools*
le Earnhardt Jr. 50.00 75.00
Bud Test Matco*
le Earnhardt Jr. 50.00 75.00
Bud Test QVC*
le Earnhardt Jr. 50.00 75.00
Oreo/6000
le Earnhardt Jr. 50.00 75.00
Oreo Clear Window Bank/480
le Earnhardt Jr. 60.00 100.00
Oreo GM Dealers
Brushed Metal/504
le Earnhardt Jr. 50.00 75.00
Oreo Mac Tools/360
le Earnhardt Jr. 50.00 75.00
Oreo QVC/1008
le Earnhardt Jr. 50.00 75.00
250 Starts/7812*
le Earnhardt Jr. 50.00 75.00
250 Starts GM Dealers/1980
le Earnhardt Jr. 50.00 75.00
250 Starts Hamilton*
ny Stewart 50.00 75.00
Goody's/1644
artin Truex Jr. 50.00 75.00
Bass Pro Shops '05 BGN Champ
Color Chrome/4680*
artin Truex Jr. 50.00 75.00
Bass Pro Shops '05 BGN Champ
Color Chrome GM Dealers/504
artin Truex Jr. 50.00 75.00
Bass Pro Shops '05 BGN Champ
Color Chrome QVC*
8 Martin Truex Jr. 60.00 100.00
Bass Pro Shops 3 Days of Dale Tribute
Talladega Raced/3900
8 Martin Truex Jr. 60.00 100.00
Bass Pro Shops 3 Days of Dale Tribute
Talladega Raced GM Dealers/1104
8 Martin Truex Jr. 50.00 75.00
Crown Royal IROC/1404
8 Martin Truex Jr. 50.00 75.00
Crown Royal IROC
GM Dealers/204
9 Kasey Kahne 50.00 75.00
Click Michigan Raced/2388
9 Kasey Kahne 60.00 100.00
Dodge/10,000
9 Kasey Kahne 60.00 100.00
Dodge Clear Window Bank/360
9 Kasey Kahne 60.00 100.00
Dodge Mac Tools/504
9 Kasey Kahne 60.00 100.00
Dodge Matco/72
9 Kasey Kahne 60.00 100.00
Dodge QVC/504
9 Kasey Kahne 50.00 75.00
Dodge Holiday/1296*
9 Kasey Kahne 50.00 75.00
Dodge Holiday QVC*
9 Kasey Kahne 50.00 75.00
Dodge SRT/1728
9 Kasey Kahne 50.00 75.00
Dodge Test/3504
9 Kasey Kahne 50.00 75.00
Dodge UAW Daimler Chrysler 400/1500
9 Kasey Kahne 50.00 75.00
Dodge UAW Daimler Chrysler 400
Clear Window Bank/144
9 Kasey Kahne 50.00 75.00
Mopar/1980
9 Kasey Kahne 50.00 75.00
McDonald's/1644
9 Kasey Kahne 50.00 75.00
McDonald's Clear Window Bank/132
9 Kasey Kahne 50.00 75.00
Ragu/2580
9 Kasey Kahne 50.00 75.00
Vitamin Water/2232
9 Boris Said 50.00 75.00
Ingersoll Rand Clear Window Bank/144
10 Scott Riggs 40.00 70.00
Advance Auto
Bumper to Bumper
10 Scott Riggs 50.00 75.00
Stanley Tools/2220
10 Scott Riggs 50.00 75.00
Valvoline/3504
10 Scott Riggs 50.00 75.00
Valvoline Cars/2508
11 Denny Hamlin 75.00 125.00
Fed Ex Express/7728
11 Denny Hamlin 75.00 125.00
Fed Ex Express Daytona
Shootout Raced/2208
11 Denny Hamlin 75.00 125.00
Fed Ex Express
Daytona Shootout Raced
GM Dealers/552
11 Denny Hamlin 75.00 125.00
Fed Ex Express
2006 Rookie of the Year/LE
11 Denny Hamlin 75.00 125.00
Fed Ex Express
2006 Rookie of the Year
GM Dealers/504
11 Denny Hamlin 60.00 100.00
Fed Ex Freight/5208
11 Denny Hamlin 60.00 100.00
Fed Ex Ground/3000
11 Denny Hamlin 60.00 100.00
Fed Ex Ground
Clear Window Bank/240
11 Denny Hamlin 60.00 100.00
Fed Ex Ground
GM Dealers/300
11 Denny Hamlin 60.00 100.00
Fed Ex Ground
Pocono Raced/2952
11 Denny Hamlin 60.00 100.00
Fed Ex Ground
Pocono Raced GM Dealers/636
11 Denny Hamlin 60.00 100.00
Fed Ex Home Delivery/2209*
11 Denny Hamlin 60.00 100.00
Fed Ex Home Delivery
Clear Window Bank/300
11 Denny Hamlin 60.00 100.00
Fed Ex Home Delivery
GM Dealers/648
11 Denny Hamlin 60.00 100.00
Fed Ex Home Delivery QVC*
11 Denny Hamlin 60.00 100.00
Fed Ex Kinko's
Clear Window Bank/144
11 Denny Hamlin 60.00 100.00
Fed Ex Kinko's
GM Dealers/300
11 Steve Kinser 50.00 75.00
Crown Royal IROC/804
11 Steve Kinser 50.00 75.00
Crown Royal IROC
GM Dealers/72
11 Paul Menard 60.00 100.00
Menard's 3 Days of Dale Tribute/3333
11 Paul Menard 60.00 100.00
Menard's 3 Days of Dale Tribute
GM Dealers/1272
11 Paul Menard 50.00 75.00
Menard's Johns Manville/2090
12 Ryan Newman 50.00 75.00
Crown Royal IROC/1056
12 Ryan Newman 50.00 75.00
Crown Royal IROC
GM Dealers/132
14 Sterling Marlin 50.00 75.00
Waste Management/2280
15 Paul Menard 50.00 75.00
Quaker State/1284
17 Matt Kenseth 50.00 75.00
Crown Royal IROC/1128
17 Matt Kenseth 50.00 75.00
Crown Royal IROC
GM Dealers/132
18 J.J. Yeley 50.00 75.00
Husqvarna/1992
18 J.J. Yeley 50.00 75.00
Husqvarna GM Dealers/108
18 J.J. Yeley 50.00 75.00
Interstate Batteries/3000
no rookie stripes
18 J.J. Yeley 50.00 75.00
Interstate Batteries
GM Dealers/144
no rookie stripes
19 Jeremy Mayfield 40.00 70.00
Dodge/5004
19 Jeremy Mayfield 40.00 70.00
Dodge Mac Tools/300
19 Jeremy Mayfield 40.00 70.00
Dodge QVC/60
19 Elliott Sadler 50.00 75.00
Dodge Holiday/576*
19 Elliott Sadler 50.00 75.00
Dodge Holiday QVC*
20 Denny Hamlin 50.00 75.00
Rockwell Automation/2508
20 Tony Stewart 50.00 75.00
Crown Royal IROC/3024
20 Tony Stewart 50.00 75.00
Crown Royal IROC
GM Dealers/204
20 Tony Stewart 60.00 100.00
Home Depot/9000
20 Tony Stewart 60.00 100.00
Home Depot
GM Dealers/1200
20 Tony Stewart 60.00 100.00
Home Depot Mac Tools/504
20 Tony Stewart 60.00 100.00
Home Depot Matco/156
20 Tony Stewart 60.00 100.00
Home Depot QVC/504
20 Tony Stewart 60.00 100.00
Home Depot
Martinsville Raced/2520*
20 Tony Stewart 60.00 100.00
Home Depot Martinsville Raced
GM Dealers/360
20 Tony Stewart 60.00 100.00
Home Depot
Martinsville Raced QVC*
20 Tony Stewart 50.00 75.00
Home Depot Holiday/1551*
20 Tony Stewart 50.00 75.00
Home Depot Holiday
GM Dealers/432
20 Tony Stewart 50.00 75.00
Home Depot Holiday QVC*
20 Tony Stewart 50.00 75.00
Home Depot Lithium-Ion/2508
20 Tony Stewart 50.00 75.00
Home Depot Lithium-Ion
GM Dealers/504
20 Tony Stewart 50.00 75.00
Home Depot Test/3588*
20 Tony Stewart 50.00 75.00
Home Depot Test
GM Dealers/288
20 Tony Stewart 50.00 75.00
Home Depot Test
Matco*
20 Tony Stewart 50.00 75.00
Powerade/3852*
20 Tony Stewart 50.00 75.00
Powerade Clear Window Bank/204
20 Tony Stewart 50.00 75.00
Powerade GM Dealers/696
20 Tony Stewart 50.00 75.00
Powerade Mac Tools*
20 Tony Stewart 50.00 75.00
Powerade QVC*
21 Jeff Burton 50.00 75.00
Coast Guard/804
21 Jeff Burton 50.00 75.00
Coast Guard
GM Dealers/288
21 Kevin Harvick 75.00 125.00
Coast Guard/2004
21 Kevin Harvick 75.00 125.00
Coast Guard
Clear Window Bank/144
21 Kevin Harvick 75.00 125.00
Coast Guard
2006 Busch Series Champion/LE
21 Kevin Harvick 75.00 125.00
Coast Guard 2006 Busch Champion
GM Dealers/384
21 Kevin Harvick 75.00 125.00
Coast Guard Reserve
Richmond Raced/1056
21 Kevin Harvick 75.00 125.00
Coast Guard Reserve
Richmond Raced GM Dealers/72
24 Jeff Gordon 60.00 100.00
DuPont Flames/10,008
24 Jeff Gordon 60.00 100.00
DuPont Flames
GM Dealers/1008
24 Jeff Gordon 60.00 100.00
DuPont Flames Mac Tools/504
24 Jeff Gordon 60.00 100.00
DuPont Flames Matco/216
24 Jeff Gordon 60.00 100.00
DuPont Flames QVC/504
24 Jeff Gordon 100.00 175.00
DuPont Flames
Chicagoland Raced/2475
24 Jeff Gordon 800.00 1200.00
DuPont Flames
Chicagoland Raced Platinum/75
24 Jeff Gordon 350.00 600.00
DuPont Flames
Chicagoland Raced Platinum/125
24 Jeff Gordon 50.00 75.00
DuPont Flames
Performance Alliance/6528*
24 Jeff Gordon 50.00 75.00
DuPont Flames
Performance Alliance Clear Window Bank/240
24 Jeff Gordon 50.00 75.00
DuPont Flames Performance Alliance
GM Dealers/696
24 Jeff Gordon 50.00 75.00
DuPont Flames
Performance Alliance QVC*
24 Jeff Gordon 300.00 400.00
DuPont Flames
Sonoma Raced/678
24 Jeff Gordon 60.00 100.00
DuPont Flames Test/4584*
24 Jeff Gordon 60.00 100.00
DuPont Flames Test Matco*
24 Jeff Gordon 60.00 100.00
DuPont Flames Test QVC*
24 Jeff Gordon 60.00 100.00
DuPont Hot Hues
Foose Design/18,240
24 Jeff Gordon 60.00 100.00
DuPont Hot Hues
Foose Design Mac Tools/504
24 Jeff Gordon 60.00 100.00
DuPont Hot Hues
Foose Design Matco/84
24 Jeff Gordon 60.00 100.00
DuPont Hot Hues
Foose Design QVC/1500
24 Jeff Gordon 50.00 75.00
Holiday Jeff Gordon Foundation/3252*
24 Jeff Gordon 50.00 75.00
Holiday JG Foundation
GM Dealers/2478
24 Jeff Gordon 50.00 75.00
Holiday Jeff Gordon Foundation QVC*
24 Jeff Gordon 50.00 75.00
Mighty Mouse/6072*
24 Jeff Gordon 50.00 75.00
Mighty Mouse Clear Window Bank/360
24 Jeff Gordon 50.00 75.00
Mighty Mouse GM Dealers/708
24 Jeff Gordon 50.00 75.00
Mighty Mouse Matco*
24 Jeff Gordon 60.00 100.00
Nicorette/7512*
24 Jeff Gordon 60.00 100.00
Nicorette Clear Window Bank/360
24 Jeff Gordon 60.00 100.00
Nicorette QVC*
24 Jeff Gordon 60.00 100.00
Pepsi/8868*
24 Jeff Gordon 60.00 100.00
Pepsi Clear Window Bank/240
24 Jeff Gordon 60.00 100.00
Pepsi GM Dealers/900
24 Jeff Gordon 60.00 100.00
Pepsi Mac Tools*
24 Jeff Gordon 60.00 100.00
Pepsi Matco*
24 Jeff Gordon 60.00 100.00
Pepsi QVC*
24 Jeff Gordon 60.00 100.00
Superman/9823*
24 Jeff Gordon 60.00 100.00
Superman GM Dealers/1356
24 Jeff Gordon 75.00 125.00
Superman
GM Dealers Brushed Metal/504
24 Jeff Gordon 60.00 100.00
Superman Mac Tools*
24 Jeff Gordon 60.00 100.00
Superman Matco*
24 Jeff Gordon 60.00 100.00
Superman QVC*
24 Jeff Gordon 60.00 100.00
World Series of Poker
Jeff Gordon Foundation/9828
24 Jeff Gordon 60.00 100.00
World Series of Poker Jeff Gordon Foundation
Clear Window Bank/240
24 Jeff Gordon 60.00 100.00
World Series of Poker Jeff Gordon Foundation
GM Dealers/804
25 Brian Vickers 50.00 75.00
GMAC/3744
25 Brian Vickers 50.00 75.00
GMAC QVC/60
26 Ricky Bobby 35.00 60.00
Laughing Clown Malt Liquor/2508
26 Ricky Bobby 35.00 60.00
Wonder Bread/2508
29 Jeff Burton 50.00 75.00
Holiday Inn/1356
29 Jeff Burton 60.00 100.00
Holiday Inn AU
29 Kevin Harvick 50.00 75.00
Goodwrench/5004
29 Kevin Harvick 50.00 75.00
Goodwrench
Clear Window Bank/204
29 Kevin Harvick 50.00 75.00
Goodwrench
GM Dealers/1200
29 Kevin Harvick 50.00 75.00
Goodwrench Mac Tools/504
29 Kevin Harvick 50.00 75.00
Goodwrench Matco/72
29 Kevin Harvick 50.00 75.00
Goodwrench QVC/144
29 Kevin Harvick 50.00 75.00
Goodwrench Holiday/1044*
29 Kevin Harvick 50.00 75.00
Goodwrench Holiday
GM Dealers/437
29 Kevin Harvick 50.00 75.00
Goodwrench Holiday QVC*
29 Kevin Harvick 50.00 75.00
Hershey's/2940*
29 Kevin Harvick 50.00 75.00
Hershey's Clear Window Bank/204
29 Kevin Harvick 50.00 75.00
Hershey's GM Dealers/600
29 Kevin Harvick 50.00 75.00
Hershey's Mac Tools*
29 Kevin Harvick 50.00 75.00
Hershey's QVC*
29 Kevin Harvick 50.00 75.00
Hershey's Kissables/4008
29 Kevin Harvick 50.00 75.00
Hershey's Kissables
Clear Window Bank/204
29 Kevin Harvick 50.00 75.00
Reese's/5244
29 Kevin Harvick 50.00 75.00
Reese's Clear Window Bank/204
29 Kevin Harvick 50.00 75.00
Reese's Caramel/2508
29 Kevin Harvick 50.00 75.00
Reese's Caramel
GM Dealers/288
31 Jeff Burton 50.00 75.00
Cingular/3504
31 Jeff Burton
Cingular AU/50
31 Jeff Burton 50.00 75.00
Cingular Clear Window Bank
31 Jeff Burton 50.00 75.00
Cingular QVC/48
31 Jeff Burton 50.00 75.00
Cingular Dover Raced/836
33 Tony Stewart 50.00 75.00
Old Spice/3504
33 Tony Stewart 50.00 75.00
Old Spice GM Dealers/204
38 David Gilliland 60.00 100.00
M&M's Halloween/1896
38 Elliott Sadler 50.00 75.00
M&M's/5244
38 Elliott Sadler 50.00 75.00
M&M's Clear Window Bank/252
38 Elliott Sadler 50.00 75.00
M&M's Mac Tools/504
38 Elliott Sadler 50.00 75.00
M&M's Matco/48
38 Elliott Sadler 50.00 75.00
M&M's QVC/96
38 Elliott Sadler 50.00 75.00
M&M's Pirates of the Caribbean/7560*
38 Elliott Sadler 50.00 75.00
M&M's Pirates of the Caribbean
Clear Window Bank/300
38 Elliott Sadler 50.00 75.00
M&M's Pirates of the Caribbean
Mac Tools*
38 Elliott Sadler 50.00 75.00
M&M's Pirates of the Caribbean
Matco*
38 Elliott Sadler 50.00 75.00
Pedigree/2508
38 Elliott Sadler 50.00 75.00
Snickers/2868*
38 Elliott Sadler 50.00 75.00
Snickers Clear Window Bank/144
38 Elliott Sadler 50.00 75.00
Snickers Mac Tools*
40 David Stremme 60.00 100.00
Coors Light/4008
40 David Stremme 50.00 75.00
Lone Star Steakhouse/3504
40 David Stremme
Lone Star Steakhouse
Clear Window Bank/144
41 Reed Sorenson 60.00 100.00
Discount Tire/3012
41 Reed Sorenson 50.00 75.00
Discount Tire
Clear Window Bank/204
41 Reed Sorenson 60.00 100.00
Target/5004
41 Reed Sorenson 50.00 75.00
Target Clear Window Bank/240
42 Casey Mears 50.00 75.00
Havoline/2754*
42 Casey Mears 50.00 75.00
Havoline QVC*
43 Bobby Labonte 50.00 75.00
Gogurt/1296
43 Bobby Labonte 50.00 75.00
STP/2616
44 Terry Labonte 50.00 75.00
Kellogg's
44 Terry Labonte 50.00 75.00
Kellogg's Clear Window Bank/144
44 Terry Labonte 175.00 300.00
Kellogg's Farewell Tribute/1008
45 Kyle Petty 75.00 125.00
Wells Fargo/1356
47 Cal Naughton Jr. 35.00 60.00
Old Spice/1500
48 Jimmie Johnson 75.00 125.00
Lowe's/5484
48 Jimmie Johnson 75.00 125.00
Lowe's Mac Tools/504
48 Jimmie Johnson 75.00 125.00
Lowe's Matco/120
48 Jimmie Johnson 75.00 125.00
Lowe's QVC/96
48 Jimmie Johnson 150.00 250.00
Lowe's Daytona Raced Employee/280
48 Jimmie Johnson 150.00 300.00
Lowe's Daytona Raced w/tire/1872
48 Jimmie Johnson 150.00 300.00
Lowe's Daytona Raced
w/tire GM Dealers/336
48 Jimmie Johnson 60.00 100.00
Lowe's Flames Test/3552*
48 Jimmie Johnson 60.00 100.00
Lowe's Flames Test
GM Dealers/216
48 Jimmie Johnson 60.00 100.00
Lowe's Flames Test Matco*
48 Jimmie Johnson 50.00 75.00
Lowe's Holiday/840
48 Jimmie Johnson 50.00 75.00
Lowe's Holiday
GM Dealers/288
48 Jimmie Johnson 60.00 100.00
Lowe's Jimmie Johnson Foundation/1500*
48 Jimmie Johnson 60.00 100.00
Lowe's Jimmie Johnson Foundation
GM Dealers/1500
48 Jimmie Johnson 50.00 75.00
Lowe's Sea World/8556*
48 Jimmie Johnson 50.00 75.00
Lowe's Sea World
GM Dealers/552
48 Jimmie Johnson 50.00 75.00
Lowe's Sea World Matco*
48 Jimmie Johnson 50.00 75.00
Lowe's Sea World QVC*
48 Jimmie Johnson 60.00 100.00
Lowe's 60th Anniversary/3036
48 Jimmie Johnson 60.00 100.00
Lowe's 60th Anniversary
GM Dealers/564
48 Jimmie Johnson 75.00 125.00
Lowe's 2006 Nextel Champion/LE

48 Jimmie Johnson Lowe's 2006 Nextel Champion GM Dealers/696	75.00	125.00
55 Jean Girard Perrier/1500	35.00	60.00
57 Brian Vickers Mountain Dew/2832	35.00	60.00
57 Brian Vickers Mountain Dew Clear Window Bank/144	35.00	60.00
57 Brian Vickers Mountain Dew GM Dealers/144	35.00	60.00
57 Brian Vickers Ore-Ida/2544	35.00	60.00
57 Brian Vickers Ore-Ida GM Dealers/72	35.00	60.00
62 Ricky Bobby ME/1500	35.00	60.00
85 Dennis Setzer Flex Fuel SuperTruck/1212	50.00	75.00
88 Dale Jarrett UPS/5244	50.00	75.00
88 Dale Jarrett UPS Mac Tools/300	50.00	75.00
88 Dale Jarrett UPS Matco/48	50.00	75.00
88 Dale Jarrett UPS QVC/504	50.00	75.00
88 Dale Jarrett UPS Freight/3104	50.00	75.00
88 Mark McFarland Navy/2004	40.00	65.00
88 Mark McFarland Navy Clear Window Bank/180	40.00	65.00
90 Elliott Sadler Citifinancial/2004	50.00	75.00
96 Terry Labonte HDTV DLP/2004	50.00	75.00
96 Terry Labonte HDTV DLP Clear Window Bank/144	50.00	75.00
96 Tony Raines HDTV DLP/1008	50.00	75.00
96 Tony Raines HDTV DLP Troy Aikman HOF/1500	50.00	75.00
96 Tony Raines HDTV DLP Hall of Fame GM Dealers/144	50.00	75.00
98 Erin Crocker Cheerios/2988*	50.00	75.00
98 Erin Crocker Cheerios QVC*	50.00	75.00
99 Carl Edwards Office Depot Holiday/1075*	50.00	75.00
99 Carl Edwards Office Depot Holiday QVC*	50.00	75.00
01 Joe Nemechek Army/2076	50.00	75.00
06 Sam Bass Holiday/987*	50.00	75.00
06 Sam Bass Holiday GM Dealers/288	40.00	65.00
06 Sam Bass Holiday QVC*	40.00	65.00
07 Clint Bowyer Jack Daniel's/4488	60.00	100.00
07 Clint Bowyer Jack Daniel's GM Dealers/760	60.00	100.00
07 Clint Bowyer Jack Daniel's QVC/288	60.00	100.00
07 Clint Bowyer Jack Daniel's Country Cocktails/3504	50.00	75.00
07 Clint Bowyer Jack Daniel's Country Cocktails GM Dealers/504	50.00	75.00
07 Clint Bowyer Jack Daniel's Directv/2328	50.00	75.00
07 Clint Bowyer Jack Daniel's Directv GM Dealers/456	50.00	75.00
07 Clint Bowyer Jack Daniel's Happy Birthday Jack/876	50.00	75.00
07 Clint Bowyer Jack Daniel's Happy B-Day GM Dealers/372	50.00	75.00
07 Clint Bowyer Jack Daniel's Sopranos/2580	60.00	100.00
07 Clint Bowyer Jack Daniel's Texas/600	50.00	75.00
07 Clint Bowyer Jack Daniel's Texas GM Dealers/504	50.00	75.00
NNO Dale Earnhardt Hall of Fame/33,333	50.00	75.00
NNO Dale Earnhardt Hall of Fame GM Dealers/2004	50.00	75.00

2006 Action Racing Collectables Historical Series 1:24

	EX	NM-MT
3 Dale Earnhardt Bud IROC '89 Camaro/8500*	50.00	75.00
3 Dale Earnhardt Bud IROC '89 Camaro GM Dealers/792	50.00	75.00
3 Dale Earnhardt Bud IROC '89 Camaro QVC*	50.00	75.00
5 Darrell Waltrip Bud IROC '84 Camaro/2916*	40.00	70.00
5 Darrell Waltrip Bud IROC '84 Camaro GM Dealers/228	40.00	70.00
5 Darrell Waltrip Bud IROC '84 Camaro QVC*	40.00	70.00
11 Darrell Waltrip Mountain Dew '81 Buick Liquid Chrome/1500	50.00	75.00

2006 Action QVC For Race Fans Only 1:24

	EX	NM-MT
6 Mark Martin Crown Royal IROC Color Chrome/504	50.00	75.00
8 Dale Earnhardt Jr. Bud Color Chrome/3504	75.00	125.00
8 Dale Earnhardt Jr. Bud Gold/504	100.00	150.00
8 Dale Earnhardt Jr. Bud Richmond Raced Color Chrome/2508	75.00	125.00
8 Dale Earnhardt Jr. Bud Richmond Raced Silver/504	125.00	200.00
8 Dale Earnhardt Jr. Bud 3 Days of Dale Tribute Platinum/411	125.00	200.00
8 Dale Earnhardt Jr. Bud 3 Days of Dale Tribute Silver/504	100.00	150.00
8 Dale Earnhardt Jr. Bud Father's Day Platinum/288	100.00	150.00
8 Dale Earnhardt Jr. Oreo Color Chrome/3504	60.00	100.00
9 Kasey Kahne Dodge Color Chrome/504	60.00	100.00
9 Kasey Kahne Dodge Mesma Chrome/288	60.00	100.00
11 Denny Hamlin Fed Ex Ground Pocono Raced Color Chrome AU/504	100.00	175.00
20 Tony Stewart Home Depot Color Chrome/504	60.00	100.00
20 Tony Stewart Home Depot Platinum/108	75.00	125.00
24 Jeff Gordon DuPont Flames Mesma Chrome/408	75.00	125.00
24 Jeff Gordon DuPont Hot Hues Foose Design Gold/108	100.00	150.00
24 Jeff Gordon Mighty Mouse Copper/288	60.00	100.00
24 Jeff Gordon Superman Copper/408	60.00	100.00
24 Jeff Gordon Superman Gold/144	100.00	150.00
24 Jeff Gordon Superman Platinum/144	100.00	175.00
24 Jeff Gordon Superman Silver/288	100.00	150.00
48 Jimmie Johnson Lowe's SeaWorld Color Chrome/504	60.00	100.00
NNO Dale Earnhardt Hall of Fame Mesma Chrome/1008	60.00	100.00

2006 Action/RCCA 1:24

	EX	NM-MT
1 Martin Truex Jr. Bass Pro Shops Color Chrome/180	60.00	100.00
1 Martin Truex Jr. Bass Pro 3 Days of Dale Tribute/250	60.00	100.00
1 Martin Truex Jr. Bass Pro Test/250	50.00	75.00
5 Kyle Busch Kellogg's/120	50.00	75.00
5 Kyle Busch Kellogg's Ice Age/288	50.00	75.00
5 Kyle Busch Lowe's/120	50.00	75.00
6 Mark Martin Crown Royal White Pearl/288	50.00	75.00
8 Dale Earnhardt Jr. Bud/1008	50.00	75.00
8 Dale Earnhardt Jr. Bud Color Chrome/288	75.00	125.00
8 Dale Earnhardt Jr. Bud Richmond Raced/888	60.00	100.00
8 Dale Earnhardt Jr. Bud 3 Days of Dale Tribute/3333	60.00	100.00
8 Dale Earnhardt Jr. Bud Father's Day/2333	60.00	100.00
8 Dale Earnhardt Jr. Bud Test/700	50.00	75.00
8 Dale Earnhardt Jr. 250th Start/1008	50.00	75.00
9 Kasey Kahne Click Michigan Raced/350	50.00	75.00
9 Kasey Kahne Dodge/408	50.00	75.00
9 Kasey Kahne Dodge SRT/200	50.00	75.00
9 Kasey Kahne Dodge UAW Daimler Chrysler 400/250	50.00	75.00
9 Kasey Kahne Mopar/200	50.00	75.00
9 Kasey Kahne McDonald's/250	50.00	75.00
9 Kasey Kahne Vitamin Water/100	50.00	75.00
11 Denny Hamlin Fed Ex Express/311	75.00	125.00
11 Denny Hamlin Fed Ex Express Daytona Shootout Raced/311	75.00	125.00
11 Denny Hamlin Fed Ex Freight/211	75.00	125.00
11 Denny Hamlin Fed Ex Ground/311	75.00	125.00
11 Denny Hamlin Fed Ex Ground Pocono Raced/299	75.00	125.00
11 Denny Hamlin Fed Ex Home Delivery/211	75.00	125.00
11 Denny Hamlin Fed Ex Kinko's/211	75.00	125.00
11 Paul Menard Menard's Johns Manville/144	50.00	75.00
11 Paul Menard Turtle Wax/144	50.00	75.00
11 Paul Menard Turtle Wax 3 Days of Dale Tribute/203	60.00	100.00
20 Tony Stewart Crown Royal White Pearl/288	40.00	65.00
20 Tony Stewart Home Depot/600	50.00	75.00
20 Tony Stewart Home Depot Color Chrome/160	75.00	125.00
20 Tony Stewart Home Depot Martinsville Raced/150	50.00	75.00
21 Jeff Burton Coast Guard/120	50.00	75.00
21 Kevin Harvick Coast Guard/120	60.00	100.00
24 Jeff Gordon DuPont Flames Color Chrome/288	60.00	100.00
24 Jeff Gordon DuPont Hot Hues Foose Designs/1400	60.00	100.00
24 Jeff Gordon Superman/1500	60.00	100.00
24 Jeff Gordon World Series of Poker JG Foundation/600	60.00	100.00
26 Ricky Bobby Laughing Clown/200	40.00	65.00
26 Ricky Bobby Wonderbread/200	40.00	65.00
29 Kevin Harvick Goodwrench/288	50.00	75.00
29 Kevin Harvick Goodwrench Color Chrome/120	60.00	100.00
29 Kevin Harvick Hershey's/360	40.00	65.00
29 Kevin Harvick Reese's/240	50.00	75.00
31 Jeff Burton Cingular/204	50.00	75.00
38 David Gilliland M&M's Halloween/200	60.00	100.00
38 Elliott Sadler M&M's Pirates of the Caribbean/300	50.00	75.00
43 Bobby Labonte Gogurt/200	50.00	75.00
45 Kyle Petty Wells Fargo/144	60.00	100.00
48 Jimmie Johnson Lowe's/288	60.00	100.00
48 Jimmie Johnson Lowe's Color Chrome/144	60.00	100.00
48 Jimmie Johnson Lowe's Daytona Raced w/tire/248	75.00	125.00
48 Jimmie Johnson Lowe's Sea World/448	50.00	75.00
88 Dale Jarrett UPS/288	50.00	75.00
96 Terry Labonte DLP/144	50.00	75.00
96 Tony Raines DLP HOF Color Chrome/100	60.00	100.00
98 Erin Crocker Cheerios/120	50.00	75.00
07 Clint Bowyer Directv/277	50.00	75.00
07 Clint Bowyer Jack Daniel's/222	60.00	100.00

2006 Action/RCCA Elite 1:24

SOME DC NOT PRICED
DUE TO SCARCITY

	EX	NM-MT
1 Martin Truex Jr. Bass Pro Shops/408	60.00	120.00
1 Martin Truex Jr. Bass Pro Shops Color Chrome/200	75.00	125.00
1 Martin Truex Jr. Bass Pro Shops Platinum/8		
1 Martin Truex Jr. Bass Pro Shops White Gold/25	250.00	400.00
1 Martin Truex Jr. Bass Pro Shops Test/300	75.00	125.00
1 Martin Truex Jr. Bass Pro Shops Test Platinum/6		
2 Clint Bowyer AC Delco/144	60.00	120.00
2 Clint Bowyer AC Delco Platinum/2		
2 Rusty Wallace Legendary/444	75.00	125.00
2 Rusty Wallace Legendary Platinum/8		
2 Rusty Wallace Legendary White Gold/25	250.00	400.00
5 Kyle Busch Carquest/120	60.00	120.00
5 Kyle Busch Carquest Platinum/2		
5 Kyle Busch Kellogg's/288	75.00	125.00
5 Kyle Busch Kellogg's Color Chrome/108	75.00	125.00
5 Kyle Busch Kellogg's Platinum/5	450.00	600.00
5 Kyle Busch Kellogg's White Gold/25	200.00	350.00
5 Kyle Busch Kellogg's Cars White Gold/25	250.00	400.00
5 Kyle Busch Kellogg's Ice Age 2/288	60.00	120.00
5 Kyle Busch Kellogg's Ice Age 2 Platinum/5		
6 Mark Martin AAA Holiday/250	100.00	150.00
6 Mark Martin AAA Holiday Platinum/5		
8 Dale Earnhardt Jr. Bud/1500	90.00	150.00
8 Dale Earnhardt Jr. Bud Color Chrome/444	100.00	175.00
8 Dale Earnhardt Jr. Bud Platinum/30	600.00	800.00
8 Dale Earnhardt Jr. Bud White Gold/30	600.00	800.00
8 Dale Earnhardt Jr. Bud Richmond Raced/1388	125.00	200.00
8 Dale Earnhardt Jr. Bud Richmond Raced Platinum/27		
8 Dale Earnhardt Jr. Bud 3 Days of Dale Tribute/3333	150.00	250.00
8 Dale Earnhardt Jr. Bud Dale Tribute Platinum/66	400.00	600.00
8 Dale Earnhardt Jr. Bud 3 Days of Dale Tribute White Gold/33	600.00	900.00
8 Dale Earnhardt Jr. Bud Father's Day/3333	100.00	175.00
8 Dale Earnhardt Jr. Bud Father's Day Platinum/50	350.00	500.00
8 Dale Earnhardt Jr. Bud Father's Day White Gold/33	500.00	750.00
8 Dale Earnhardt Jr. Bud Test/1000	90.00	150.00
8 Dale Earnhardt Jr. Bud Test Platinum/20		
8 Dale Earnhardt Jr. Oreo/1200	75.00	125.00
8 Dale Earnhardt Jr. Oreo Platinum/24		
8 Dale Earnhardt Jr. Oreo White Gold/30	250.00	400.00
8 Dale Earnhardt Jr. 250th Start/1500	90.00	150.00
8 Dale Earnhardt Jr. 250th Start Platinum/30		
8 Dale Earnhardt Jr. 250th Start White Gold/33	350.00	500.00
8 Martin Truex Jr. Bass Pro 3 Days of Dale Tribute Talladega Raced/250	100.00	150.00
8 Martin Truex Jr. Bass Pro Shops Dale Tribute Talladega Raced Platinum/5		
9 Kasey Kahne Click Michigan Raced/350	75.00	125.00
9 Kasey Kahne Click Michigan Raced Platinum/7		
9 Kasey Kahne Dodge/600	75.00	125.00
9 Kasey Kahne Dodge Color Chrome/144	90.00	150.00
9 Kasey Kahne Dodge Platinum/12	650.00	900.00
9 Kasey Kahne Dodge White Gold/25	400.00	600.00
9 Kasey Kahne Dodge Holiday/250	75.00	125.00
9 Kasey Kahne Dodge Holiday Platinum/5		
9 Kasey Kahne Dodge SRT/250	75.00	125.00
9 Kasey Kahne Dodge SRT Platinum/6		
9 Kasey Kahne Dodge SRT White Gold/25	250.00	400.00
9 Kasey Kahne Dodge Test/400	75.00	125.00
9 Kasey Kahne Dodge Test Platinum/8		
9 Kasey Kahne Dodge UAW Daimler Chrysler 400/300	75.00	125.00
9 Kasey Kahne Dodge UAW Daimler Chrysler 400 Platinum/6		
9 Kasey Kahne Dodge UAW Daimler Chrysler 400 White Gold/25	250.00	500.00
9 Kasey Kahne Mopar/250	75.00	125.00
9 Kasey Kahne Mopar Platinum/5		
9 Kasey Kahne Mopar White Gold/25	300.00	450.00
9 Kasey Kahne McDonald's/250	75.00	125.00
9 Kasey Kahne McDonald's Platinum/5		
9 Kasey Kahne Ragu/204	75.00	125.00
9 Kasey Kahne Ragu Platinum/4		
10 Scott Riggs Valvoline White Gold/25	125.00	250.00
11 Denny Hamlin FedEx Express/411	100.00	175.00
11 Denny Hamlin Fed Ex Express Platinum/8		
11 Denny Hamlin FedEx Express Daytona Shootout Raced/311	125.00	200.00
11 Denny Hamlin Fed Ex Express Daytona Shootout Raced Platinum/4		
11 Denny Hamlin FedEx Freight/299	100.00	175.00
11 Denny Hamlin Fed Ex Freight Platinum/5		
11 Denny Hamlin FedEx Ground/411	100.00	175.00
11 Denny Hamlin Fed Ex Ground Platinum/8	400.00	600.00
11 Denny Hamlin FedEx Ground White Gold/25	400.00	600.00
11 Denny Hamlin Fed Ex Ground Pocono Raced/299	100.00	175.00
11 Denny Hamlin Fed Ex Ground Pocono Raced Platinum/5		
11 Denny Hamlin Fed Ex Home Delivery/411	100.00	150.
11 Denny Hamlin Fed Ex Home Delivery Platinum/8		
11 Denny Hamlin Fed Ex Home Delivery White Gold/25	400.00	600.
11 Denny Hamlin FedEx Kinko's/299	100.00	175.
11 Denny Hamlin Fed Ex Kinko's Platinum/5		
11 Denny Hamlin Fed Ex PGA Cup White Gold/25	400.00	600.
11 Paul Menard Menard's Johns Manville/144	60.00	120.
11 Paul Menard Menard's Johns Manville Platinum/2		
11 Paul Menard Turtle Wax 3 Days of Dale Tribute/203	90.00	150.
11 Paul Menard Turtle Wax Dale Tribute Platinum/4		
15 Paul Menard Quaker State/120	60.00	120.
15 Paul Menard Quaker State Platinum/2		
18 J.J. Yeley Interstate Batteries/200	90.00	150.
18 J.J. Yeley Interstate Batteries Platinum/4		
18 J.J. Yeley Interstate Batteries White Gold/25	250.00	400.
19 Jeremy Mayfield Dodge/288	50.00	100.
19 Jeremy Mayfield Dodge Platinum/5		
19 Jeremy Mayfield Dodge White Gold/25	200.00	350.
19 Elliott Sadler Dodge Holiday White Gold/25	175.00	350.
20 Denny Hamlin Rockwell Automation/144	75.00	125.
20 Denny Hamlin Rockwell Automation Platinum/2		
20 Tony Stewart Home Depot/800	90.00	150.
20 Tony Stewart Home Depot Color Chrome/220	90.00	150.
20 Tony Stewart Home Depot Platinum/16		
20 Tony Stewart Home Depot White Gold/30	400.00	600.
20 Tony Stewart Home Depot Martinsville Raced/200	75.00	125.
20 Tony Stewart Home Depot Martinsville Raced Platinum/4		
20 Tony Stewart Home Depot Holiday/250	100.00	150.
20 Tony Stewart Home Depot Holiday Platinum/5		
20 Tony Stewart Home Depot Holiday White Gold/25	400.00	600.
20 Tony Stewart Home Depot Test/600	75.00	125.
20 Tony Stewart Home Depot Test Platinum/5		
20 Tony Stewart Powerade/400	75.00	125.
20 Tony Stewart Powerade Platinum/8		
20 Tony Stewart Powerade White Gold/25	400.00	600.
21 Kevin Harvick Coast Guard/120	125.00	200.
21 Kevin Harvick Coast Guard Platinum/2		
24 Jeff Gordon DuPont Flames/1008	75.00	125.
24 Jeff Gordon DuPont Flames Color Chrome/288	100.00	175.
24 Jeff Gordon DuPont Flames Platinum/20	700.00	1000.
24 Jeff Gordon DuPont Flames White Gold/30	500.00	750.
24 Jeff Gordon DuPont Flames Performance Alliance/416	75.00	125.
24 Jeff Gordon DuPont Flames Performance Alliance Platinum/12		
24 Jeff Gordon DuPont Flames Test/724	75.00	125.
24 Jeff Gordon DuPont Flames Test Platinum/14	700.00	1000.
24 Jeff Gordon DuPont Hot Hues Chip Foose/1900	90.00	150.
24 Jeff Gordon DuPont Hot Hues Chip Foose Designs AU/200	125.00	200.
24 Jeff Gordon DuPont Hot Hues Chip Foose Designs Platinum/38	600.00	900.
24 Jeff Gordon Holiday JG Foundation Color Chrome/494	100.00	150.
24 Jeff Gordon Holiday JG Foundation Platinum/10		
24 Jeff Gordon Holiday JG Foundation	500.00	750.

White Gold/25
Jeff Gordon 75.00 125.00
Mighty Mouse
Jeff Gordon Foundation/900
Jeff Gordon
Mighty Mouse
Jeff Gordon Foundation Platinum/18
Jeff Gordon 500.00 750.00
Mighty Mouse Jeff Gordon Foundation
White Gold/30
Jeff Gordon 75.00 125.00
Nicorette/999
Jeff Gordon 400.00 600.00
Nicorette Platinum/19
Jeff Gordon 500.00 750.00
Nicorette White Gold/30
Jeff Gordon 90.00 150.00
Pepsi/900
Jeff Gordon
Pepsi Platinum/18
Jeff Gordon 400.00 650.00
Pepsi White Gold/40
Jeff Gordon 90.00 150.00
Superman/1800
Jeff Gordon 500.00 750.00
Superman Platinum/36
Jeff Gordon 400.00 600.00
Superman White Gold/40
Jeff Gordon 75.00 125.00
World Series of Poker
Jeff Gordon Foundation/600
Jeff Gordon
WSOP
JG Foundation Platinum/18
Jeff Gordon 500.00 750.00
WSOP JG Foundation
White Gold/33
Kevin Harvick 75.00 125.00
Goodwrench/408
Kevin Harvick 90.00 150.00
Goodwrench
Color Chrome/144
Kevin Harvick
Goodwrench Platinum/8
Kevin Harvick 250.00 400.00
Goodwrench White Gold/25
Kevin Harvick 75.00 125.00
Goodwrench Holiday/250
Kevin Harvick
Goodwrench Holiday
Platinum/5
Kevin Harvick 200.00 350.00
Goodwrench Holiday
White Gold/25
Kevin Harvick 60.00 120.00
Hershey's/429
Kevin Harvick
Hershey's Platinum/8
Kevin Harvick 250.00 400.00
Hershey's White Gold/25
Kevin Harvick 60.00 120.00
Hershey's Kissables/240
Kevin Harvick
Hershey's Kissables
Platinum/4
Kevin Harvick 200.00 350.00
Hershey's Kissables
White Gold/25
Kevin Harvick 60.00 120.00
Reese's/240
Kevin Harvick
Reese's Platinum/4
Kevin Harvick 250.00 400.00
Reese's White Gold/25
Kevin Harvick 60.00 120.00
Reese's Caramel/240
Kevin Harvick
Reese's Caramel Platinum/4
Jeff Burton 75.00 125.00
Cingular/204
Jeff Burton 600.00 800.00
Cingular Platinum/4
Jeff Burton 200.00 350.00
Cingular White Gold/25
Tony Stewart 75.00 125.00
Old Spice/288
Tony Stewart
Old Spice Platinum/5
David Gilliland 100.00 150.00
M&M's Halloween/200
David Gilliland
M&M's Halloween Platinum/4
David Gilliland 250.00 400.00
M&M's Halloween
White Gold/25
Elliott Sadler 90.00 150.00
M&M's Color Chrome/120
Elliott Sadler 250.00 400.00
M&M's White Gold/25
Elliott Sadler 200.00 350.00
M&M's Pirates of the Caribbean
White Gold/25
Elliott Sadler 75.00 125.00
Snickers/250
Elliott Sadler
Snickers Platinum/5
Elliott Sadler 200.00 350.00
Snickers White Gold/25
David Stremme 90.00 150.00
Coors Light/120
David Stremme
Coors Light
Platinum/2
David Stremme 200.00 350.00
Coors Light
White Gold/25
David Stremme 75.00 125.00
Lonestar Steakhouse/120
David Stremme
Lone Star Steakhouse
Platinum/2
Reed Sorenson 60.00 120.00
Discount Tire/144
Reed Sorenson
Discount Tire
Platinum/2
Reed Sorenson 90.00 150.00
Target/240
Reed Sorenson
Target Platinum/4
Reed Sorenson 250.00 400.00
Target White Gold/25
43 Bobby Labonte 75.00 125.00
Cheerios/200
43 Bobby Labonte
Cheerios Platinum/4
43 Bobby Labonte 250.00 400.00
Cheerios White Gold/25
43 Bobby Labonte 90.00 150.00
Gogurt/200
43 Bobby Labonte
Gogurt Platinum/4
43 Bobby Labonte 250.00 400.00
Gogurt White Gold/25
43 Bobby Labonte 75.00 125.00
STP/300
43 Bobby Labonte
STP Platinum/6
43 Bobby Labonte 250.00 400.00
STP White Gold/25
44 Terry Labonte 200.00 350.00
Kellogg's White Gold/25
48 Jimmie Johnson 125.00 200.00
Lowe's/408
48 Jimmie Johnson 125.00 200.00
Lowe's Brickyard Raced/240
48 Jimmie Johnson 125.00 200.00
Lowe's Color Chrome/144
48 Jimmie Johnson
Lowe's Platinum/8
48 Jimmie Johnson 400.00 600.00
Lowe's White Gold/25
48 Jimmie Johnson 350.00 500.00
Lowe's Daytona Raced AU/200
48 Jimmie Johnson 200.00 350.00
Lowe's Daytona Raced w/tire/248
48 Jimmie Johnson
Lowe's Daytona Raced
Platinum/4
48 Jimmie Johnson 100.00 150.00
Lowe's Flames Test/200
48 Jimmie Johnson
Lowe's Flames Test
Platinum/4
48 Jimmie Johnson 100.00 150.00
Lowe's Holiday/250
48 Jimmie Johnson
Lowe's Holiday
Platinum/5
48 Jimmie Johnson 300.00 450.00
Lowe's Holiday
White Gold/25
48 Jimmie Johnson 100.00 150.00
Lowe's Jimmie Johnson Foundation/120
48 Jimmie Johnson
Lowe's JJ Foundation
Platinum/2
48 Jimmie Johnson 75.00 125.00
Lowe's SeaWorld/548
48 Jimmie Johnson 125.00 200.00
Lowe's SeaWorld AU/100
48 Jimmie Johnson
Lowe's SeaWorld
Platinum/10
48 Jimmie Johnson 300.00 500.00
Lowe's SeaWorld
White Gold/25
48 Jimmie Johnson 75.00 125.00
Lowe's 60th Anniversary/300
48 Jimmie Johnson
Lowe's 60th Anniversary
Platinum/6
48 Jimmie Johnson 350.00 600.00
Lowe's 60th Anniversary
White Gold/25
64 Steve Wallace 60.00 100.00
Top Flite/120
64 Steve Wallace
Top Flite Platinum/2
88 Dale Jarrett 90.00 150.00
UPS Color Chrome/120
88 Dale Jarrett 350.00 500.00
UPS White Gold/25
88 Dale Jarrett 100.00 175.00
UPS Freight/200
88 Dale Jarrett
UPS Freight
Platinum/4
88 Mark McFarland 75.00 125.00
Navy/144
88 Mark McFarland
Navy Platinum/2
90 Stephen Leicht 75.00 125.00
Citifinancial/60
90 Stephen Leicht
Citifinancial Platinum/1
90 Matt McCall 75.00 125.00
Citifinancial/60
90 Matt McCall
Citifinancial Platinum/1
96 Terry Labonte 200.00 350.00
DLP White Gold/25
98 Erin Crocker 75.00 125.00
Cheerios/120
98 Erin Crocker
Cheerios Platinum/2
99 Carl Edwards 100.00 150.00
Office Depot Holiday/200
99 Carl Edwards
Office Depot Holiday
Platinum/4
99 Carl Edwards 250.00 400.00
Office Depot Holiday
White Gold/25
06 Holiday Event Car White Gold/25 175.00 300.00
07 Clint Bowyer 90.00 150.00
Directv/277
07 Clint Bowyer
Directv Platinum/5
07 Clint Bowyer 300.00 450.00
Directv White Gold/25
07 Clint Bowyer 90.00 150.00
Jack Daniel's/333
07 Clint Bowyer
Jack Daniel's Platinum/6
07 Clint Bowyer 300.00 450.00
Jack Daniel's White Gold/25
07 Clint Bowyer 90.00 150.00
Jack Daniel's
Country Cocktails/250
07 Clint Bowyer
Jack Daniel's
Country Cocktails Platinum/5
07 Clint Bowyer 300.00 450.00
Jack Daniel's Country Cocktails
White Gold/25
07 Clint Bowyer 90.00 150.00
Jack Daniel's Happy Birthday/203
07 Clint Bowyer
Jack Daniel's Happy B-Day
Platinum/5
07 Clint Bowyer 300.00 450.00
Jack Daniel's Happy Birthday
White Gold/25
07 Clint Bowyer 90.00 150.00
Jack Daniel's Sopranos/277
07 Clint Bowyer
Jack Daniel's Sopranos Platinum/5
07 Clint Bowyer 300.00 450.00
Jack Daniel's Sopranos
White Gold/25
07 Clint Bowyer 90.00 150.00
Jack Daniel's Texas/250
07 Clint Bowyer
Jack Daniel's Texas
Platinum/5
07 Clint Bowyer 300.00 450.00
Jack Daniel's Texas
White Gold/25
NNO Dale Earnhardt 60.00 100.00
HOF/2333
NNO Dale Earnhardt
HOF Platinum/46

2006 Action/RCCA Elite Historical 1:24

EX NM-MT
3 Dale Earnhardt 100.00 150.00
GM Goodwrench '91 Lumina/1333
3 Dale Earnhardt
GM Goodwrench '91 Lumina
White Gold/33

2008 Action Racing Collectables Advanced Production 1:24

EX NM-MT
3 Dale Earnhardt 400.00 600.00
Goodwrench '98 Daytona COT/333
3 Dale Earnhardt 125.00 200.00
Enduring Legends Johnny Cash/333
29 Kevin Harvick 100.00 200.00
Pennzoil Platinum/144
44 Dale Jarrett 125.00 250.00
UPS All-Star/144
83 Dale Earnhardt Jr. 100.00 200.00
Navy JR Motorsports/383
88 Dale Earnhardt Jr. 150.00 250.00
National Guard Salute the Troops/888
88 Dale Earnhardt Jr. 150.00 250.00
Mountian Dew Retro/888
88 Dale Earnhardt Jr. 125.00 250.00
National Guard Citizen Soldier/888
88 Dale Earnhardt Jr. 150.00 250.00
National Guard Camo/888

2008 Action Racing Collectables Platinum 1:24

1 Martin Truex Jr. 50.00 75.00
Bass Pro Shops/4956
2 Kurt Busch 50.00 75.00
Miller Lite/3408
5 Casey Mears 50.00 75.00
Carquest1224
5 Casey Mears 50.00 75.00
Kellogg's/3564
5 Dale Earnhardt Jr. 75.00 125.00
All Star Test/9204
8 Mark Martin 60.00 100.00
U.S. Army/8004
9 Kasey Kahne 50.00 75.00
Bud/24,600
11 Denny Hamlin 50.00 75.00
Fed Ex Express/5148
11 Denny Hamlin 50.00 75.00
Fed Ex Freight/2117
11 Denny Hamlin 50.00 75.00
Fed Ex Ground/2160
11 Denny Hamlin 50.00 75.00
Fed Ex Kinko's/1860
12 Ryan Newman 60.00 100.00
Alltel/3276
15 Paul Menard 50.00 75.00
Menards/816
16 Greg Biffle 50.00 75.00
3M/2928
17 Matt Kenseth 50.00 75.00
Carhartt/3144
17 Matt Kenseth 50.00 75.00
DeWalt/6672
18 Kyle Busch 60.00 120.00
Interstate Batteries
18 Kyle Busch 75.00 125.00
M&M's/5448
20 Tony Stewart 50.00 75.00
Home Depot/26,880
26 Jamie McMurray 50.00 75.00
Crown Royal/2532
24 Jeff Gordon 50.00 75.00
Nicorette/21,468
24 Jeff Gordon 50.00 75.00
Pepsi
24 Jeff Gordon 50.00 75.00
DuPont Flames/37,032
26 Jamie McMurray 50.00 75.00
Irwin Tools/1416
29 Kevin Harvick 50.00 75.00
Shell Pennzoil/11,736
31 Jeff Burton 50.00 75.00
AT&T/8396
42 Juan Pablo Montoya 50.00 75.00
Big Red/1092
42 Juan Pablo Montoya 50.00 75.00
Texaco Havoline '07 ROY w/tire/708
43 Bobby Labonte 50.00 75.00
Cheerios/3300
45 Kyle Petty 50.00 75.00
Wells Fargo/1284
48 Jimmie Johnson 50.00 75.00
Lowe's/15,292
48 Jimmie Johnson 50.00 75.00
Lowe's Kobalt/2237
55 Michael Waltrip 50.00 75.00
Napa/5388
77 Sam Hornish Jr. 50.00 75.00
Mobil 1/1284
88 Dale Earnhardt Jr. 50.00 75.00
AMP Mac Tools/1200
88 Dale Earnhardt Jr. 60.00 100.00
AMP/108,088
88 D.Earnardt Jr. 175.00 300.00
Mountain Dew Retro
Pre-Production/888
42 Juan Pablo Montoya 50.00 75.00
Texaco Havoline/3612
88 Dale Earnhardt Jr./National Guard/80,488 50.00 75.00
88 Dale Earnhardt Jr. 50.00 75.00
National Guard Mac Tools/1200
88 Dale Earnhardt Jr. 50.00 75.00
National Guard QVC/22,752
99 Carl Edwards 50.00 75.00
Office Depot/7248
07 Clint Bowyer 50.00 75.00
Jack Daniel's/10,740

2008 Action Racing Collectables Platinum Daytona 1:24

EX NM-MT
3 Dale Earnhardt 60.00 100.00
Goodwrench Plus
'98 Monte Carlo/7104
4 Sterling Marlin 40.00 70.00
Kodak '94 Lumina/324
8 Dale Earnhardt Jr. 50.00 75.00
Bud Born On Feb. 15
'04 Monte Carlo/6180
24 Jeff Gordon 40.00 70.00
DuPont '97 Monte Carlo/2832
48 Jimmie Johnson 40.00 70.00
Lowe's '06 Monte Carlo/1068

2008 RCCA Club 1:24

EX NM-MT
1 Martin Truex Jr. 50.00 75.00
Bass Pro Shops/156
2 Kurt Busch 50.00 75.00
Miller Lite/150
3 Dale Earnhardt 75.00 125.00
Goodwrench '98 Daytona COT/700
5 Casey Mears 50.00 75.00
Kellogg's/150
6 David Ragan 50.00 75.00
AAA/150
8 Aric Almirola 50.00 75.00
U.S. Army/120
8 Mark Martin 50.00 75.00
U.S. Army/204
8 Mark Martin 50.00 75.00
U.S. Army
Salute the Troops/150
9 Kasey Kahne 50.00 75.00
Bud/504
10 Patrick Carpentier 50.00 75.00
Valvoline/150
11 Denny Hamlin 50.00 75.00
Fed Ex Express/252
11 Denny Hamlin 50.00 75.00
Fed Ex Freight/150
11 Denny Hamlin 50.00 75.00
Fed Ex Ground/150
12 Ryan Newman 50.00 75.00
Alltel/150
15 Paul Menard 50.00 75.00
Menards/300
16 Greg Biffle 50.00 75.00
3M/150
17 Matt Kenseth 50.00 75.00
Carhartt/150
17 Matt Kenseth 50.00 75.00
DeWalt/150
18 Kyle Busch 100.00 150.00
M&M's/250
19 Elliott Sadler 50.00 75.00
Best Buy/150
20 Tony Stewart 50.00 75.00
Home Depot/408
20 Tony Stewart 50.00 75.00
Home Depot
10th Anniversary/300
20 Tony Stewart 50.00 75.00
Smoke/300
20 Tony Stewart 50.00 75.00
Subway/200
24 Jeff Gordon 50.00 75.00
DuPont Flames/700
24 Jeff Gordon 50.00 75.00
DuPont Flames
Salute the Troops/500
24 Jeff Gordon 50.00 75.00
Nicorette/500
24 Jeff Gordon 50.00 75.00
Pepsi/500
24 Jeff Gordon 50.00 75.00
Pepsi Stuff/500
24 Jeff Gordon 50.00 75.00
Speed Racer/500
26 Jamie McMurray 50.00 75.00
Crown Royal/150
26 Jamie McMurray 50.00 75.00
Irwin Tools/150
29 Kevin Harvick 50.00 75.00
Pennzoil Platinum/150
29 Kevin Harvick 50.00 75.00
Shell/300
31 Jeff Burton 50.00 75.00
AT&T/156
41 Reed Sorenson 50.00 75.00
Target/156
42 Juan Pablo Montoya 50.00 75.00
Texaco/252
43 Bobby Labonte 50.00 75.00
Cheerios/150
44 Dale Jarrett 50.00 75.00
UPS/300
44 Dale Jarrett 50.00 75.00
UPS All Star/150
44 David Reutimann 50.00 75.00
UPS Kentucky Derby/150
48 Jimmie Johnson 50.00 75.00
Lowe's/300
55 Michael Waltrip 50.00 75.00
Napa/120
88 Dale Earnhardt Jr. 60.00 100.00
AMP/2100
88 Dale Earnhardt Jr. 60.00 100.00
Mountian Dew Retro/1200
88 Dale Earnhardt Jr. 60.00 100.00
National Guard/1000
88 Dale Earnhardt Jr. 60.00 100.00
National Guard
Citizen Soldier/1200
88 Dale Earnhardt Jr. 60.00 100.00
National Guard
Salute the Troops/500
07 Clint Bowyer 50.00 75.00
Jack Daniel's/150
07 Clint Bowyer 50.00 75.00
Jack Daniel's
Salute the Troops/250

2008 RCCA Elite 1:24

EX NM-MT
1 Martin Truex Jr. 75.00 125.00
Bass Pro Shops/300
1 Martin Truex Jr. 175.00 300.00
Bass Pro Shops
Platinum/25
1 Martin Truex Jr. 175.00 300.00
Bass Pro Shops
White Gold/50
2 Kurt Busch 75.00 125.00
Miller Lite/300
2 Kurt Busch 175.00 300.00
Miller Lite Platinum/25
2 Kurt Busch 175.00 300.00
Miller Lite White Gold/50
3 Dale Earnhardt 100.00 175.00
Goodwrench '98 Daytona COT/1000
3 Dale Earnhardt 300.00 500.00
Goodwrench '98 Daytona COT Platinum/53
3 Dale Earnhardt 300.00 500.00
Goodwrench '98 Daytona COT White Gold/103
5 Dale Earnhardt Jr. 100.00 150.00
City Chevrolet Test/1200
5 Casey Mears 75.00 125.00
Kellogg's/300
5 Casey Mears 175.00 300.00
Kellogg's Platinum/25
5 Casey Mears 175.00 300.00
Kellogg's White Gold/50
8 Mark Martin 75.00 125.00
U.S. Army/408
8 Mark Martin 200.00 350.00
U.S. Army Platinum/25
8 Mark Martin 200.00 350.00
U.S. Army White Gold/50
8 Mark Martin 100.00 150.00
U.S. Army
Salute the Troops/300
8 Mark Martin 200.00 350.00
U.S. Army
Salute the Troops Platinum/25
8 Mark Martin 200.00 350.00
U.S. Army
Salute the Troops White Gold/50
9 Kasey Kahne 100.00 150.00
Bud/1500
9 Kasey Kahne 250.00 400.00
Bud Platinum/25
9 Kasey Kahne 250.00 400.00
Bud White Gold/50
11 Denny Hamlin 75.00 125.00
Fed Ex Express/408
11 Denny Hamlin 200.00 350.00
Fed Ex Express Platinum/25
11 Denny Hamlin 200.00 350.00
Fed Ex Express White Gold/50
11 Denny Hamlin 75.00 125.00
Fed Ex Ground/300
11 Denny Hamlin 75.00 125.00
Fed Ex Kinko's/300
11 Denny Hamlin 200.00 350.00
Fed Ex Kinko's Platinum/25
11 Denny Hamlin 200.00 350.00
Fed Ex Kinko's White Gold/50
12 Ryan Newman 100.00 150.00
Alltel/300
12 Ryan Newman 200.00 350.00
Alltel Platinum/25
12 Ryan Newman 200.00 350.00
Alltel White Gold/50
12 Ryan Newman 75.00 125.00
Alltel Mummy 3/400
12 Ryan Newman 175.00 300.00
Alltel Mummy 3
Platinum/25
12 Ryan Newman 175.00 300.00
Alltel Mummy 3
White Gold/50
16 Greg Biffle 75.00 125.00
3M/300
16 Greg Biffle 175.00 300.00
3M Platinum/25
16 Greg Biffle 175.00 300.00
3M White Gold/50
17 Matt Kenseth 75.00 125.00
DeWalt/300
18 Kyle Busch 125.00 200.00
M&M's/408

	EX	NM-MT
18 Kyle Busch M&M's Platinum/25	350.00	600.00
18 Kyle Busch M&M's White Gold/50	350.00	600.00
18 Kyle Busch M&M's Red White Blue/504	100.00	175.00
18 Kyle Busch M&M's Red White Blue Platinum/25	275.00	400.00
18 Kyle Busch M&M's Red White Blue White Gold/50	275.00	400.00
19 Elliott Sadler Best Buy/300	75.00	125.00
19 Elliott Sadler McDonald's/300	75.00	125.00
20 Tony Stewart Home Depot/1200	100.00	150.00
20 Tony Stewart Home Depot Platinum/25	250.00	400.00
20 Tony Stewart Home Depot White Gold/50	250.00	400.00
20 Tony Stewart Home Depot 10th Anniversary/1000	100.00	150.00
20 Tony Stewart Home Depot 10th Anniversary Platinum/25	250.00	400.00
20 Tony Stewart Home Depot 10th Anniversary White Gold/50	250.00	400.00
20 Tony Stewart Smoke/504	100.00	150.00
20 Tony Stewart Subway/504	75.00	125.00
20 Tony Stewart Subway Platinum/25	200.00	350.00
20 Tony Stewart Subway White Gold/50	200.00	350.00
24 Jeff Gordon DuPont Flames/1200	100.00	150.00
24 Jeff Gordon DuPont Flames Platinum/25	350.00	600.00
24 Jeff Gordon DuPont Flames White Gold/50	350.00	600.00
24 Jeff Gordon DuPont Flames Salute the Troops/1000	100.00	150.00
24 Jeff Gordon DuPont Test/504	100.00	150.00
24 Jeff Gordon Nicorette/700	75.00	125.00
24 Jeff Gordon Nicorette Platinum/25	250.00	400.00
24 Jeff Gordon Nicorette White Gold/50	250.00	400.00
24 Jeff Gordon Pepsi/700	75.00	125.00
24 Jeff Gordon Pepsi Platinum/25	250.00	400.00
24 Jeff Gordon Pepsi White Gold/50	250.00	400.00
24 Jeff Gordon Pepsi Stuff/1000	75.00	125.00
24 Jeff Gordon Pepsi Stuff Platinum/25	250.00	400.00
24 Jeff Gordon Pepsi Stuff White Gold/50	250.00	400.00
24 Jeff Gordon Speed Racer/1000	75.00	125.00
24 Jeff Gordon Speed Racer Platinum/25	250.00	400.00
24 Jeff Gordon Speed Racer White Gold/50	250.00	400.00
26 Jamie McMurray Crown Royal/300	75.00	125.00
26 Jamie McMurray Crown Royal Platinum/25	175.00	300.00
26 Jamie McMurray Crown Royal White Gold/50	175.00	300.00
29 Kevin Harvick Penzoil Platinum/300	75.00	125.00
29 Kevin Harvick Penzoil Platinum Platinum/25	175.00	300.00
29 Kevin Harvick Penzoil Platinum White Gold/50	175.00	300.00
29 Kevin Harvick Reese's/708	75.00	150.00
29 Kevin Harvick Shell/708	75.00	125.00
29 Kevin Harvick Shell Platinum/25	200.00	350.00
29 Kevin Harvick Shell White Gold/50	200.00	350.00
31 Jeff Burton AT&T/300	75.00	125.00
42 Juan Pablo Montoya Texaco/504	75.00	125.00
42 Juan Pablo Montoya Texaco Platinum/25	200.00	350.00
42 Juan Pablo Montoya Texaco White Gold/50	200.00	350.00
43 Bobby Labonte Cheerios/300	75.00	125.00
43 Bobby Labonte Cheerios Platinum/25	175.00	300.00
43 Bobby Labonte Cheerios White Gold/50	175.00	300.00
44 Dale Jarrett UPS/600	75.00	150.00
44 Dale Jarrett UPS Platinum/25	250.00	400.00
44 Dale Jarrett UPS White Gold/50	250.00	400.00
44 Dale Jarrett/UPS All Star/444	75.00	125.00
44 Dale Jarrett UPS All Star Platinum/25	250.00	400.00
44 Dale Jarrett UPS All Star White Gold/50	250.00	400.00
44 David Reutimann UPS Kentucky Derby/300	75.00	125.00
44 David Reutimann UPS Kentucky Derby Platinum/25	175.00	300.00
44 David Reutimann UPS Kentucky Derby White Gold/50	175.00	300.00
45 Kyle Petty Wells Fargo/300	75.00	125.00
48 Jimmie Johnson Lowe's/500	100.00	150.00
48 Jimmie Johnson Lowe's Platinum/25	250.00	400.00
48 Jimmie Johnson Lowe's White Gold/50	250.00	400.00
55 Michael Waltrip Napa/300	75.00	125.00
55 Michael Waltrip Napa Platinum/25	175.00	350.00
55 Michael Waltrip Napa White Gold/50	175.00	350.00
88 Dale Earnhardt Jr. AMP/5000	100.00	150.00
88 Dale Earnhardt Jr. AMP Platinum/25	350.00	600.00
88 Dale Earnhardt Jr. AMP White Gold/50	350.00	600.00
88 Dale Earnhardt Jr. AMP Test/504	100.00	150.00
88 Dale Earnhardt Jr. Mountian Dew Retro/3000	100.00	150.00
88 Dale Earnhardt Jr. Mountian Dew Retro Platinum/25	300.00	500.00
88 Dale Earnhardt Jr. Mountian Dew Retro White Gold/50	300.00	500.00
88 Dale Earnhardt Jr. National Guard/3000	100.00	150.00
88 Dale Earnhardt Jr. National Guard Platinum/25	350.00	600.00
88 Dale Earnhardt Jr. National Guard White Gold/50	350.00	600.00
88 Dale Earnhardt Jr. National Guard Citizen Soldier/3000	100.00	150.00
88 Dale Earnhardt Jr. National Guard Citizen Soldier Platinum/25	300.00	500.00
88 Dale Earnhardt Jr. National Guard Citizen Soldier White Gold/50	300.00	500.00
88 Brad Keselowski Navy Salute the Troops/300	75.00	125.00
88 Brad Keselowski Navy Salute the Troops Platinum/25	175.00	300.00
88 Brad Keselowski Navy Salute the Troops White Gold/50	175.00	300.00
88 Dale Earnhardt Jr. National Guard Salute the Troops/1000	100.00	150.00
88 Dale Earnhardt Jr. National Guard Test/708	100.00	150.00
99 Carl Edwards Office Depot/300	75.00	125.00
99 Carl Edwards Office Depot Platinum/25	200.00	350.00
99 Carl Edwards Office Depot White Gold/50	200.00	350.00
07 Clint Bowyer Jack Daniel's/300	75.00	125.00
07 Clint Bowyer Jack Daniel's Platinum/25	175.00	300.00
07 Clint Bowyer Jack Daniel's White Gold/50	175.00	300.00
07 Clint Bowyer Jack Daniel's Salute the Troops/500	100.00	150.00
07 Clint Bowyer Jack Daniel's Salute the Troops White Gold/50	175.00	300.00
07 Clint Bowyer Jack Daniel's Salute the Troops Platinum/25	175.00	300.00
08 Daytona 500 50th Anniversary Red/504	100.00	150.00
08 Daytona 500 50th Anniversary White/504	100.00	150.00

1998-01 Action Racing Collectables 1:32

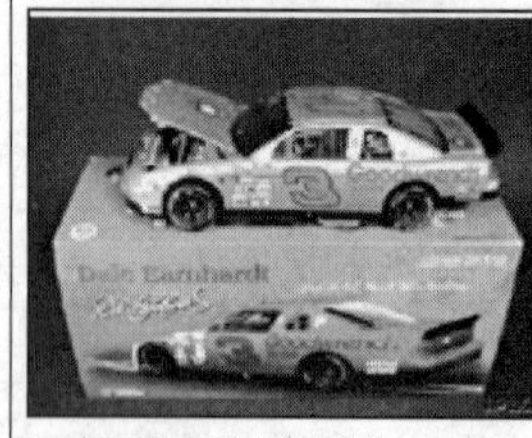

These 1:32 scale cars debuted in 1998. These cars were sold through GM and Ford dealerships as well as through various TV outlets.

	EX	NM-MT
2 Rusty Wallace Miller Lite 1998	15.00	40.00
3 Dale Earnhardt Goodwrench Sign Last Lap/3504	30.00	60.00
3 Dale Earnhardt Goodwrench 25th Anniversary	30.00	60.00
3 Dale Earnhardt Goodwrench Plus Bass Pro/5000	30.00	80.00
3 Dale Earnhardt Goodwrench Plus Daytona Win/20,000 1998	30.00	60.00
3 Dale Earnhardt Goodwrench Silver 1995 Monte Carlo/5000	40.00	80.00
3 Dale Earnhardt Goodwrench Taz No Bull	60.00	120.00
3 Dale Earnhardt Jr. AC Delco/12,000 1998	30.00	70.00
3 Dale Earnhardt Jr. AC Delco Last Lap 1999	20.00	50.00
5 Terry Labonte Corny/Blasted Froot Loops 2-car set in tin/4500 1998	20.00	40.00
5 Terry Labonte Kellogg's Ironman/5000 1998	15.00	40.00
5 Terry Labonte Kellogg's Ironman II		
5/18 Terry Labonte Bobby Labonte Kelloggs/Interstate Batteries 2-car set 1998	25.00	60.00
8 Dale Earnhardt Jr. Bud/12,000 1999	25.00	50.00
12 Jeremy Mayfield Mobil 1/3500 '98	12.50	30.00
12 Jeremy Mayfield Mobil 1 Kentucky Derby/3504 1999	15.00	40.00
18/44 Bobby Labonte Tony Stewart Small Soldiers 2-cars/4500 1998	20.00	40.00
24 Jeff Gordon DuPont Chromalusion/3500 1998	25.00	50.00
24 Jeff Gordon DuPont Superman/3504 1999	25.00	50.00
24 Jeff Gordon Pepsi/12,000 w/helmet	20.00	50.00
28 Kenny Irwin Havoline '98	15.00	40.00
28 Kenny Irwin Havoline Joker 1998	15.00	40.00
31 Dale Earnhardt Jr. Gargoyles 1997 Monte Carlo	20.00	50.00
88 Dale Jarrett Batman 1998	20.00	50.00
88 Dale Jarrett Quality Care 1998	12.50	30.00
88 Dale Jarrett UPS Flames Van/4008	40.00	75.00

1998 Action/RCCA Gold 1:32

These 1:32 scale cars were distributed by Action through RCCA.

	EX	NM-MT
1 Steve Park Pennzoil/1500	25.00	60.00
2 Rusty Wallace Miller Lite	25.00	60.00
3 Dale Earnhardt Goodwrench Bass Pro	75.00	150.00
3 Dale Earnhardt Jr. AC Delco/5000	50.00	100.00
5 Terry Labonte Kellogg's	25.00	60.00
12 Jeremy Mayfield Mobil 1/1000	25.00	60.00
18 Bobby Labonte Interstate Batteries	40.00	100.00
23 Jimmy Spencer No Bull	25.00	60.00
24 Jeff Gordon DuPont/3500	50.00	100.00
28 Kenny Irwin Havoline	25.00	60.00
36 Ernie Irvan M&M's	25.00	60.00
88 Dale Jarrett Quality Care/700	25.00	60.00

1999-00 Action/RCCA 1:32

	EX	NM-MT
3 Dale Earnhardt Wrangler/3500	30.00	60.00
19 Dodge Red Show Ceramic Pit Scene/2592 2000	20.00	40.00
20 Tony Stewart Home Depot/7500	20.00	50.00
27 Casey Atwood Castrol/3500	12.50	30.00

2002 Action/RCCA 1:32

	EX	NM-MT
1 Dale Earnhardt Jr. Coke '98 Monte Carlo in vending machine tin/2004	30.00	60.00
2/29 Kevin Harvick AC Delco Goodwrench 2-car set/3000	30.00	60.00
3 Dale Earnhardt Coke 1998 Monte Carlo in vending machine tin/2004	30.00	60.00
3 Dale Earnhardt Goodwrench/3600 2001 Monte Carlo	35.00	60.00
3 Dale Earnhardt Goodwrench Gold/720 2001 Monte Carlo	60.00	120.00
3 Dale Earnhardt Goodwrench Oreo 2001 Monte Carlo/3000	35.00	60.00
3 Dale Earnhardt Goodwrench Oreo Gold 2001 Monte Carlo/600	35.00	60.00
3 Dale Earnhardt Goodwrench Peter Max 2000 Monte Carlo/3600	35.00	60.00
3 Dale Earnhardt Goodwrench Gold Peter Max 2000 Monte Carlo/960	50.00	100.00
3 Dale Earnhardt Jr. Nilla Wafers/Oreo 2-car set/2016	35.00	60.00
8 Dale Earnhardt Jr. Bud/3000 with Fan Scan card	30.00	50.00
8 Dale Earnhardt Jr. Bud Gold/652	50.00	100.00
8 Dale Earnhardt Jr. Bud 2001 All-Star/1416	35.00	60.00
8 Dale Earnhardt Jr. Bud 2001 All-Star Gold/600	40.00	80.00
8 Dale Earnhardt Jr. Bud '02 All-Star/1416	35.00	60.00
8 Dale Earnhardt Jr. Bud '02 All-Star Gold/600	40.00	80.00
8 Dale Earnhardt Jr. Looney Tunes/1416	25.00	50.00
8 Dale Earnhardt Jr. Looney Tunes Gold/600	40.00	80.00
24 Jeff Gordon DuPont Flames 2001 WC Champ/3600	25.00	50.00
24 Jeff Gordon DuPont Bugs/1416	25.00	40.00
24 Jeff Gordon DuPont Bugs Gold/600	40.00	80.00
24 Jeff Gordon Pepsi Daytona/2280	25.00	40.00
24 Jeff Gordon Pepsi Daytona Gold/720	45.00	80.00
29 Kevin Harvick Goodwrench with Fan Scan card/2280	20.00	40.00
29 Kevin Harvick Goodwrench Gold/532	30.00	60.00
29 Kevin Harvick Goodwrench '01/AC Delco '01 set/3000	35.00	60.00
48 Jimmie Johnson Lowe's/1536	30.00	60.00
48 Jimmie Johnson Lowe's Gold/480	50.00	100.00
NNO Dale Earnhardt Legacy/2004	40.00	80.00

2003 Action/RCCA 1:32

	EX	NM-MT
3 Dale Earnhardt Earnhardt Foundation/1012	25.00	50.00
3 Dale Earnhardt Goodwrench Bass Pro Shops	20.00	40.00
8 Dale Earnhardt Jr. Bud/1572	25.00	50.00
8 Dale Earnhardt Jr. Bud 24K/444	35.00	60.00
8 Dale Earnhardt Jr. Bud MLB All-Star Game 24K/316	35.00	60.00
8 Dale Earnhardt Jr. Bud MLB All-Star Game/844	25.00	50.00
8 Dale Earnhardt Jr. Bud StainD/844	25.00	50.00
8 Dale Earnhardt Jr. Oreo Ritz/2004	30.00	50.00
8 Dale Earnhardt Jr. Oreo Ritz Gold/588	35.00	60.00
8 Dale Earnhardt Jr. Dirty Mo Posse/1572	25.00	50.00
8 Dale Earnhardt Jr. Dirty Mo Posse 24K/444	35.00	60.00
8 Dale Earnhardt Jr. E Concert/1572	30.00	50.00
8 Dale Earnhardt Jr. E Concert 24K/444	35.00	60.00
20 Tony Stewart Home Depot/1572	25.00	50.00
20 Tony Stewart Home Depot Gold/444	30.00	60.00
20 Tony Stewart Home Depot/Peanuts Orange/Peanuts Black 3-car set/2004	50.00	90.00
24 Jeff Gordon DuPont Flames/1572	25.00	50.00
24 Jeff Gordon DuPont Flames 24K/444	35.00	60.00
24 Jeff Gordon DuPont Wright Brothers/844	25.00	50.00
24 Jeff Gordon DuPont Wright Bros. 24K/316	35.00	60.00
24 Jeff Gordon Pepsi in Vending Machine/2004	35.00	60.00
24 Jeff Gordon Pepsi Billion $/844	25.00	50.00
24 Jeff Gordon Pepsi Billion $ 24K/316	35.00	60.00
88 Dale Jarrett Race For a Cure	30.00	60.00

2003 Action/RCCA Elite 1:32

	EX	NM-MT
3 Dale Earnhardt Earnhardt Foundation/1012	30.00	50.00
3 Dale Earnhardt Goodwrench No Bull 2000 Monte Carlo/1008	30.00	50.00
3 Dale Earnhardt Goodwrench Bass Pro Shops/1800	25.00	50.00
3 Dale Earnhardt Goodwrench Silver Select 1995 Monte Carlo/1800	35.00	50.00
8 Dale Earnhardt Jr. Bud/1500	30.00	50.00
8 Dale Earnhardt Jr. Bud No Bull 2000 Monte Carlo/1008	30.00	50.00
8 Dale Earnhardt Jr. Bud MLB All-Star Game/844	30.00	50.00
8 Dale Earnhardt Jr. Bud StainD/844	30.00	50.00
8 Tony Stewart 3 Doors Down/844	30.00	50.00
20 Tony Stewart Home Depot/1008	30.00	50.00
24 Jeff Gordon DuPont Flames/1008	30.00	50.00
24 Jeff Gordon DuPont Wright Brothers/804	30.00	50.00
24 Jeff Gordon Pepsi Billion $/844	30.00	50.00

2004 Action Racing Collectables 1:32

	EX	NM-MT
8 Dale Earnhardt Jr. Bud/2508	35.00	60.00
8 Dale Earnhardt Jr. Bud Born On Feb.7/1764	35.00	60.0
8 Dale Earnhardt Jr. Oreo/1584	30.00	60.0
20 Tony Stewart Home Depot/1488	25.00	50.0
24 Jeff Gordon DuPont Flames/1512	30.00	50.0
29 Tony Stewart Kid Rock/1308	25.00	50.0

2004 Action Racing Collectables Historical Serie 1:32

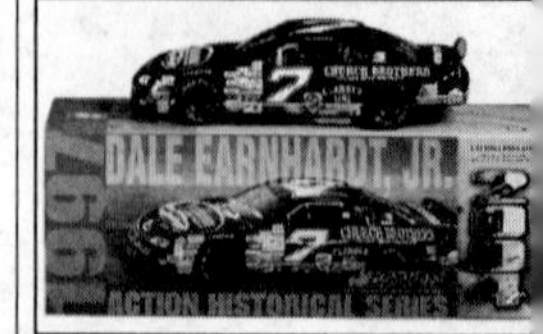

	EX	NM-M
3 Dale Earnhardt Wheaties 1997 Monte Carlo/2200	30.00	50.0
3 Dale Earnhardt Wheaties '97 Monte Carlo Mac Tools/288	30.00	50.0
3 Dale Earnhardt Jr. AC Delco Last Lap of the Century Color Chrome/1452	35.00	60.0
7 Dale Earnhardt Jr. Church Bros 1997 Monte Carlo/2316	30.00	50.0
8 Dale Earnhardt Jr. Bud Olympics '00 Monte Carlo/1304	30.00	50.0
8 Dale Earnhardt Jr. Bud Olympics '00 Monte Carlo QVC/216	30.00	50.0

2004 Action/RCCA 1:32

	EX	NM-M
8 Dale Earnhardt Jr. Bud/600	30.00	50.0
8 Dale Earnhardt Jr. Bud Born On Feb.7/408	30.00	50.0
8 Dale Earnhardt Jr. Bud Born On Feb.15/960	30.00	50.0
8 Dale Earnhardt Jr. Oreo/600	30.00	50.0
20 Tony Stewart Home Depot/600	25.00	50.0
24 Jeff Gordon DuPont Flames/600	30.00	50.0
29 Tony Stewart Kid Rock/408	30.00	50.0

2004 Action/RCCA Elite 1:32

	EX	NM-M
8 Dale Earnhardt Jr. Bud/600	40.00	60.0
8 Dale Earnhardt Jr. Bud Born On Feb.7/408	40.00	80.0
8 Dale Earnhardt Jr. Bud Born On Feb.15/960	40.00	80.0
8 Dale Earnhardt Jr. Oreo/600	40.00	60.0
20 Tony Stewart Home Depot/844	35.00	60.0
24 Jeff Gordon DuPont Flames/600	35.00	60.0
29 Tony Stewart Kid Rock/408	30.00	60.0

2004 Action/RCCA Historica Series 1:32

	EX	NM-M
3 Dale Earnhardt Wheaties '97 Monte Carlo/804	25.00	50.0
3 Dale Earnhardt Jr. AC Delco Last Lap 1999 Monte Carlo/480	25.00	50.0
7 Dale Earnhardt Jr. Church Brothers 1997 Monte Carlo/600	25.00	50.0
8 Dale Earnhardt Jr. Bud Olympic 2000 Monte Carlo/408	25.00	50.0

2004 Action/RCCA Historica Series Elite 1:32

	EX	NM-M
3 Dale Earnhardt Wheaties 1997 Monte Carlo/804	35.00	60.0
3 Dale Earnhardt Jr. AC Delco Last Lap 1999 Monte Carlo/480	35.00	60.0
7 Dale Earnhardt Jr. Church Brothers 1997 Monte Carlo/600	35.00	60.0
8 Dale Earnhardt Jr. Bud Olympic 2000 Monte Carlo/408	40.00	60.0

2004 Action RCR 1:32

These 1:32 scale cars were produced and released May thro December of 2004. They were available via distributors through Action/RCCA. Each car was individually se numbered on the rear window deck using the ink jet meth All cars have RCR molded into the chasis. All packaging is generic RCR skybox with a special sleeve. The first 2500 s numbered copies are only available through Action/RCCA remaining copies are Action Racing Collectables pieces.

	EX	NM-M
3 Dale Earnhardt AC Delco Japan 1997 Monte Carlo/4296	25.00	50.0

	EX	NM-MT
Earnhardt Delco Japan Monte Carlo GM Dealers/624	25.00	50.00
Earnhardt ca Cola Japan 98 Monte Carlo/3672	25.00	50.00
Earnhardt ca Cola Japan Monte Carlo GM Dealers/528	25.00	50.00
Earnhardt odwrench 96 Monte Carlo/4296	25.00	50.00
Earnhardt odwrench 1996 Monte Carlo Dealers/504	25.00	50.00
Earnhardt odwrench Olympics 96 Monte Carlo/4344	25.00	50.00
Earnhardt odwrench Olympics 96 Monte Carlo GM Dealers/408	25.00	50.00
Earnhardt odwrench Crash 97 Monte Carlo/15,516	35.00	60.00
Earnhardt odwrench Crash MC GM Dealers/936	35.00	60.00
Earnhardt odwrench Service Plus Daytona Win 98 Monte Carlo/3168	25.00	50.00
Earnhardt odwrench Plus Daytona n '98 MC GM Dealers/264	25.00	50.00
Earnhardt odwrench Sign 99 Monte Carlo/4008	25.00	50.00
Earnhardt odwrench Sign 99 Monte Carlo GM Dealers/648	25.00	60.00
Earnhardt odwrench Talladega 00 Monte Carlo/3432	30.00	50.00
Earnhardt odwrench Peter Max 00 Monte Carlo/5784	30.00	50.00
Earnhardt odwrench Peter Max 00 Monte Carlo GM Dealers/888	30.00	50.00
Earnhardt odwrench Taz '00 Monte Carlo	30.00	50.00
Earnhardt angler 1999 Monte Carlo/4380	25.00	50.00
Earnhardt angler 1999 Monte Carlo Dealers/648	25.00	50.00

04 Action/RCCA RCR 1:32

:32 scale cars were produced and released May through ber of 2004. They were available via distributors and h Action/RCCA. Each car was individually serial ed on the rear window deck using the ink jet method. have RCR molded into the chassis. All packaging is in a RCR skybox with a special sleeve. The first 2500 serial ed copies are only available through Action/RCCA the ng copies are Action Racing Collectables pieces.

	EX	NM-MT
Earnhardt ca Cola Japan 98 Monte Carlo/1500	35.00	60.00
Earnhardt odwrench 96 Monte Carlo/1500	35.00	60.00
Earnhardt odwrench Olympics 96 Monte Carlo/1500	35.00	60.00
Earnhardt odwrench Crash '97 Monte Carlo ytona Raced/1500	40.00	70.00
Earnhardt odwrench Peter Max 00 Monte Carlo/1500	35.00	60.00
Earnhardt angler 99 Monte Carlo/1500	35.00	60.00

2005 Action RCR 1:32

	EX	NM-MT
Earnhardt ss Pro Monte Carlo/2604	25.00	50.00
Earnhardt odwrench 25th Anniversary Monte Carlo/1728	25.00	50.00
Earnhardt odwrench Under the Lights Monte Carlo/3504	25.00	50.00
Earnhardt	25.00	50.00

	EX	NM-MT
Goodwrench Under the Lights '00 Monte Carlo GM Dealers/312		
3 Dale Earnhardt Goodwrench Under the Lights '00 Monte Carlo QVC/1200	25.00	50.00
3 Dale Earnhardt Oreo '01 Monte Carlo/1740	25.00	50.00
3 Dale Earnhardt Oreo '01 Monte Carlo GM Dealers/312	25.00	50.00
3 Dale Earnhardt Oreo '01 Monte Carlo QVC/1500	25.00	50.00
3 Dale Earnhardt Wheaties '97 Monte Carlo/1776	25.00	50.00

2005 Action/RCCA RCR 1:32

	EX	NM-MT
3 Dale Earnhardt Goodwrench Under the Lights '00 Monte Carlo/1008	25.00	50.00

2000-01 Action Road Racing 1:43

	EX	NM-MT
3 Dale Earnhardt Dale Earnhardt Jr Andy Pilgrim Kelly Collins C5-R Corvette/12,024 2001	40.00	100.00
3 Dale Earnhardt Dale Earnhardt Jr Andy Pilgrim Kelly Collins C5-R Corvette raced version/2424 2001	30.00	75.00
3 Ron Fellows Justan Bell Chris Kneifel Goodwrench C5-R/2352 2000	15.00	40.00

2004 Action Road Racing 1:43

	EX	NM-MT
8 Dale Earnhardt Jr. Boris Said Corvette C-5R/3198	20.00	40.00

2003 Action Racing Collectables 1:43

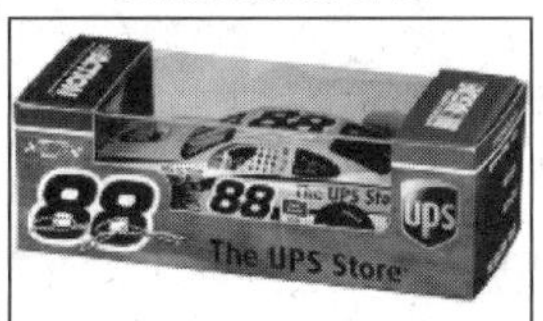

	EX	NM-MT
88 Dale Jarrett UPS Store promo in window box	7.50	20.00

2005 Action Racing Collectables 1:43

	EX	NM-MT
11 Paul Menard Menards Promo in window box	15.00	30.00
81 Dale Earnhardt Jr. Menards Promo in window box	15.00	30.00
88 Dale Jarrett UPS Store Toys for Tots Promo in wind.box	10.00	20.00

1991-92 Action/RCCA Revell 1:64

This set marks the first issue of current NASCAR drivers released by Racing Collectables, Inc. which soon was purchased by Action to become Action/RCCA. The cars themselves were produced by Revell but distributed by RCI, therefore they are often referred to as Revell pieces. Each was issued in a white clear window cardboard box. The name "Racing Collectibles, Inc." is printed on the front along with the car number and model and sometimes the sponsor noted at the bottom below the window. Either a 1991 or 1992 date is included on the copyright line on the box bottoms.

	EX	NM-MT
1 Jeff Gordon Baby Ruth Revell	25.00	60.00
2 Rusty Wallace Pontiac Excitement Revell	4.00	8.00
3 Dale Earnhardt Goodwrench	20.00	40.00
5 Ricky Rudd Tide Promo	6.00	12.00
6 Mark Martin Valvoline	6.00	12.00
7 Mac Tools/7500	10.00	20.00
10 Derrike Cope Purolator	4.00	10.00
15 Ricky Rudd Motorcraft red	5.00	12.00
17 Darrell Waltrip Western Auto	6.00	15.00
18 Dale Jarrett Interstate Batteries	4.00	8.00
20 Rob Moroso Swisher Sweets Promo '89 Rookie of the Year red car	6.00	15.00
20 Rob Moroso Swisher Sweets Promo 1989 Rookie of the Year red car w/yellow stripe	6.00	15.00
20/25 Rob Moroso Swisher Sweets 2-car Promo set in box/13,628	15.00	30.00
21 Morgan Shepherd Citgo	2.00	5.00
22 Sterling Marlin Maxwell House	3.00	6.00
25 Bill Venturini Rain-X	2.00	5.00
26 Brett Bodine Quaker State	1.50	5.00
28 Davey Allison Havoline black	10.00	25.00
30 Michael Waltrip Pennzoil	2.00	5.00
33 Harry Gant Skoal with Mug Promo	15.00	30.00
36 Kenny Wallace Cox Lumber	2.00	5.00
36 Kenny Wallace Dirt Devil	2.00	5.00
42 Kyle Petty Mello Yello	2.00	5.00
43 Richard Petty STP	10.00	25.00
44 Larry Caudill Army	2.00	5.00
63 Chuck Bown Nescafe Promo blister/15,000	5.00	12.00
66 Jimmy Hensley TropArtic Phillips 66	2.00	5.00
68 Bobby Hamilton Country Time	2.00	5.00
87 Joe Nemechek Texas Pete	3.00	8.00
89 Jim Sauter Evinrude	2.00	5.00
90 Mike Wallace Heilig-Meyers Promo	5.00	10.00
91 Clifford Allison Mac Tools Promo/20,160	15.00	30.00
93 Mike Wallace Racing Collectables Inc.	2.00	5.00
99 Ricky Craven DuPont	2.00	5.00

1991-92 Action/RCCA Legends, Oldsmobiles and T-Birds 1:64

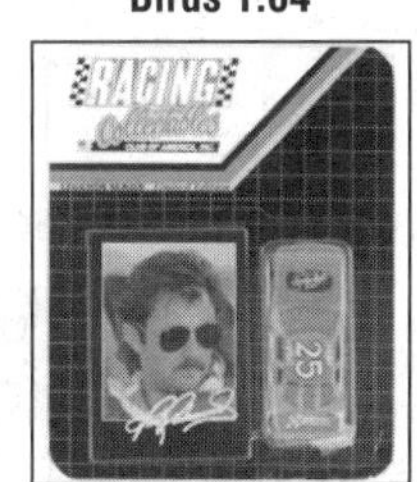

These 1:64 die cast cars were issued between 1990 and 1992 and feature past legends of NASCAR as well as replicas of 1991 Oldsmobiles and Thunderbirds that were driven between 1983-1986. We've included all of these cars into one listing for ease in cataloging. All were produced by a variety of manufacturers for RCCA and can be found inside one of three different cardboard window box designs with some being released in more than one type of box at different times: white Racing Collectables Club of America Inc. Legend Series, black Racing Collectables Inc. Collector's Series, or black Racing Collectables Inc. Legend Series 1 of 16 box. The last box also had the year and car model listed on the front of the box along with an announced print run of 15,000. The #25 Tim Richmond Fan Club Promo piece was issued on a Legends Series blister along with a Tim Richmond trading card. It was produced for RCCA by Racing Champions before RCCA was acquired by Action.

	EX	NM-MT
1 Paul Goldsmith Packer Pontiac 1962	8.00	20.00
3 David Pearson Gerry Earl Pontiac 1962	10.00	20.00
4 Rex White Sherwood Chevy '63	6.00	15.00
6 Cotton Owens Hines Pontiac 1962	6.00	15.00
7 Kyle Petty 7-Eleven	15.00	40.00
8 Elmo Langley 1957 Chevy Convertible	6.00	15.00
8 Joe Weatherly Gillman Pontiac 1962	15.00	40.00
9 Bill Elliott Melling	15.00	30.00
13 Johnny Rutherford 1963 Chevy	6.00	15.00
15 Dale Earnhardt Wrangler	40.00	80.00
15 Ricky Rudd Motorcraft red&white	10.00	20.00
16 Tom Pistone S&K 1957	6.00	15.00
21 Buddy Baker Valvoline with V logo on deck lid	5.00	10.00
21 Buddy Baker Valvoline with Valvoline on deck lid	10.00	20.00
21 Tiny Lund English Motors 1963	8.00	20.00
21 Marvin Panch English Motors 1963	6.00	15.00
21 Marvin Panch Augusta Motors '65	8.00	20.00
21 David Pearson Pearson Racing white&black	20.00	40.00
21 David Pearson Pearson Racing white&brown	15.00	30.00
22 Bobby Allison Gold Wheels	20.00	40.00
22 Ed Berrier Greased Lightning	3.00	6.00
22 Bobby Allison Silver Wheels	15.00	30.00
22 Fireball Roberts Stephens Pontiac 1962	10.00	20.00
22 Firebell Roberts Young Ford dark purple 1963	8.00	20.00
22 Fireball Roberts Young Ford light purple 1963	8.00	20.00
24 Larry Frank 1957 Chevy	6.00	15.00
25 Rob Moroso Swisher Sweets	6.00	15.00
25 Tim Richmond Fan Club Promo blister black bordered card (1990 car made by Racing Champions)	10.00	20.00
25 Tim Richmond Fan Club Promo blister tan bordered serial #'d card	10.00	20.00
26 Curtis Turner Ed Martin Ford 1963	6.00	15.00
27 A.J. Foyt Sheraton Thompson Ford 1965	8.00	20.00
27 Junior Johnson Hansford Pontiac 1962	10.00	20.00
28 Davey Allison Havoline black&white	15.00	30.00
28 Dan Gurney LaFayette Ford 1963	6.00	15.00
28 Fred Lorenzen LaFayette Ford 1963	6.00	15.00
28 Fred Lorenzen LaFayette Ford 1965 Fastback	6.00	15.00
28 Cale Yarborough Hardee's	15.00	30.00
29 Nelson Stacy Ron's Ford 1963	6.00	15.00
31 Ralph Earnhardt Jimmy Rivers Body Shop Ford	25.00	60.00
32 Bristol Food City 500 promo blister/15,000 1963 Ford	5.00	10.00
34 Wendell Scott 1963 Orange Ford	8.00	20.00
34 Wendell Scott 1965 Blue Ford	8.00	20.00
35 Alan Kulwicki Quincy's Steakhouse	25.00	60.00
35 Dick May Hanover Printing	5.00	10.00
39 Lee Roy Yarborough H&B Auto Parts 1962	10.00	25.00
41 Curtis Turner Harvest Motors '65 Fastback	8.00	20.00
44 Bobby Labonte Penrose	20.00	50.00
44 Sterling Marlin Piedmont	10.00	20.00
44 Bob Welborn Frizzle Pontiac 1962	10.00	20.00
46 Johnny Allen Hansford Pontiac 1962	6.00	15.00
47 Buck Baker Miller Pontiac 1962	8.00	20.00
49 Bob Welborn Nalley Chevrolet 1957 Chevy Convertible	6.00	15.00
54 Ralph Earnhardt Adamson Motors Ford	15.00	40.00
54 Jimmy Pardue Scenic Motors 1963	6.00	15.00
57 Dick May McClure Motors 1963	6.00	15.00
57 Jody Ridley Nationwise	5.00	10.00
64 Rodney Combs Sunny King small numbers on roof	5.00	10.00
64 Rodney Combs Jr. Sunny King large numbers on roof	5.00	10.00
66 Johnny Allen Commonwealth Ford 1963	6.00	15.00
67 Buddy Arrington Arrington Racing	5.00	10.00
70 J.D. McDuffie Lockhart	5.00	10.00
71 Dave Marcis Shoney's	20.00	50.00
71 Lee Roy Yarborough Harison&Gulley '63	6.00	15.00
73 Phil Barkdoll XR-1	4.00	8.00
77 Joe Lee Johnson 1957 Chevy	6.00	15.00
87 Curtis Turner Blanket Order 1963	6.00	15.00
88 Buddy Baker Red Baron Pizza	15.00	30.00
90 Junie Donlavey Chameleon	5.00	10.00
90 Ken Schrader Red Baron Pizza	15.00	40.00
90 Ken Schrader Sunny King	10.00	20.00
92 Daytona Circle Track Show promo blister/15,000 1992	5.00	10.00
94 Banjo Mathews Warrior Motel 1962	6.00	15.00
121 Dan Gurney Harvest Motors 1965	6.00	15.00
0 Dan Gurney LaFayette Ford 1963	6.00	15.00
0 Tiny Lund Pulliam Motor Co. 1963	6.00	15.00
03 G.C. Spencer Cottrell Bakery '63	6.00	15.00
03 Red Wickersham Bailey's Used Cars '65	6.00	15.00
06 Larry Frank Schwister Ford 1963	6.00	15.00
06 Larry Frank Schwister 1963 Ford/10,000 Southern 500 30-year Anniversary promo blister	5.00	10.00

1993 Action Racing Collectables 1:64

	EX	NM-MT
3/24 Dale Earnhardt Jeff Gordon Dual package Kellogg's Promo	40.00	80.00
5/24 Terry Labonte Jeff Gordon Dual package Kellogg's Promo	25.00	50.00
6 Tommy Houston Roses promo/10,000	4.00	8.00
7 Alan Kulwicki Army Promo blister/10,000 black window car	20.00	50.00
7 Alan Kulwicki Hooters 1992 Ford Thunderbird	25.00	50.00
7 Alan Kulwicki Hooters AK Racing blister/10,000	15.00	30.00

1993 Action Racing Collectables AC Racing 1:64

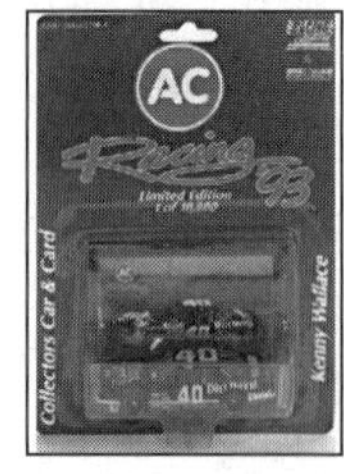

Each car in this set of 1:64 die cast were issued in a blue promo AC Racing blister pack. Total print run figure of 10,000 was also printed on the front.

	EX	NM-MT
2 Rusty Wallace Pontiac Excitement	4.00	10.00
3 Dale Earnhardt Goodwrench	12.50	25.00
4 Ernie Irvan Kodak	4.00	8.00
17 Darrell Waltrip Western Auto	6.00	15.00
24 Jeff Gordon DuPont	15.00	40.00
25 Ken Schrader GMAC	4.00	8.00
40 Kenny Wallace Dirt Devil	4.00	8.00
41 Phil Parsons AC Racing	4.00	8.00
42 Kyle Petty Mello Yello	4.00	8.00

1993 Action Racing Collectables Delco Remy 1:64

Action issued each car in this set in a black and yellow Delco Remy promo blister. The total print run figure of 10,000 was also printed on the front.

	EX	NM-MT
2 Rusty Wallace Pontiac Excitement	6.00	10.00
4 Ernie Irvan Kodak	5.00	8.00
17 Darrell Waltrip Western Auto	10.00	20.00

1993 Action Racing Collectables Valvoline Team 1:64

Each car in this set of 1:64 die cast were issued in a light blue checkerboard promo blister pack. The total print run figure of 10,000 was also printed on the front.

	EX	NM-MT
6 Mark Martin Valvoline	5.00	8.00
16 Wally Dallenbach Jr. Roush Racing	25.00	50.00
24 Jeff Gordon DuPont	20.00	35.00
25 Ken Schrader GMAC	3.00	8.00
46 Al Unser Jr. Valvoline	15.00	40.00

1993 Action/RCCA 1:64

These 1:64 scale cars were made by Action and distributed through the RCCA club. Most were distributed in a small cardboard window box printed in yellow, orange, and black with the name "Stock Car H.O. Collector Series" on it with gold foil printing on the plastic window that includes the year model and make of the car and the production run.

	EX	NM-MT
2 Mark Martin Miller Acrylic	7.50	15.00
2 Rusty Wallace Miller Genuine Draft Club Only	9.00	18.00
3 Richard Childress CRC Chemical 1980 Olds	6.00	12.00
6 Mark Martin Folgers Promo blister	15.00	40.00
6 Mark Martin Stroh's Light 2 car combo/15,000	30.00	50.00

	EX	NM-MT
6 Mark Martin Valvoline/15,000	6.00	15.00
9 Bill Elliott Melling Club Only	10.00	20.00
11 Darrell Waltrip Budweiser 1984 Monte Carlo notchback/10,080	8.00	20.00
12 Neil Bonnett Budweiser 1984 Monte Carlo notchback/16,128	7.50	15.00
12 Hut Stricklin Raybestos	2.00	5.00
17 Darrell Waltrip Superflo ASA Camaro	6.00	15.00
21 Morgan Shepherd Cheerwine Morema	5.00	12.00
24 Jeff Gordon DuPont/15,000	15.00	40.00
24 Jeff Gordon DuPont in gray box	10.00	25.00
25 Ricky Craven 1991 BGN Champion Promo	7.50	15.00
27 Rusty Wallace Kodiak 1989 Pontiac in plastic case	18.00	30.00
28 Davey Allison Havoline/28,000	12.50	25.00
28 Davey Allison Mac Tools Promo	12.50	25.00
35 Shawna Robinson Polaroid Captiva Promo blister/10,000	12.50	30.00
42 Kyle Petty Mello Yello/15,000	5.00	12.00
88 Darrell Waltrip Gatorade 1980 Monte Carlo/10,080	7.50	15.00
90 Bobby Hillin Jr. Heilig-Meyers Promo	6.00	12.00
93 Action Platinum Series Promo blister/15,000	5.00	10.00
93 RCCA/Christmas Car	10.00	20.00
93 RCCA/Lumina Primer/10,000	5.00	10.00
93 RCCA/Pontiac Primer/10,000	5.00	10.00
93 RCCA/Thunderbird Primer/10,000	5.00	10.00
94 Casey Elliott RCCA/10,000	5.00	12.00
94 Casey Elliott RCCA in a gray Grand National Series box	5.00	12.00

1994 Action Racing Collectables 1:64

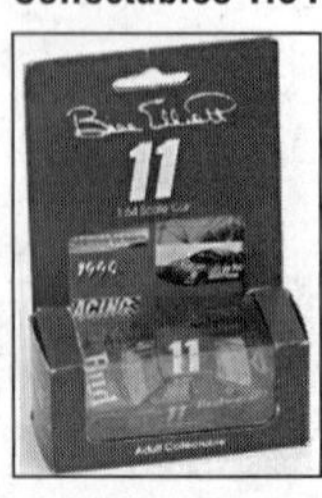

These 1:64 scale cars feature some of the top cars in NASCAR racing. Action used the "Platinum Series" clamshell packaging for the first time in 1994 on this series of cars. Most pieces also include an Action trading card.

	EX	NM-MT
2 Ricky Craven DuPont	10.00	20.00
2 Rusty Wallace Ford Motorsports	5.00	10.00
3 Dale Earnhardt Goodwrench/16,128	15.00	40.00
3 Dale Earnhardt Goodwrench 1988 Monte Carlo Aerocoupe	30.00	60.00
3 Dale Earnhardt Wrangler 1984 Monte Carlo	25.00	60.00
3 Dale Earnhardt 16-car set	125.00	250.00
4 Sterling Marlin Kodak	5.00	12.00
5 Terry Labonte Kellogg's/10,000	4.00	10.00
11 Bill Elliott Budweiser	12.50	25.00
11 Darrell Waltrip Budweiser 1987 Monte Carlo	20.00	40.00
12 Neil Bonnett Budweiser 1987 Monte Carlo	12.00	20.00
15 Lake Speed Quality Care/10,080	3.00	8.00
16 Ted Musgrave Family Channel	3.00	8.00
24 Jeff Gordon DuPont	25.00	40.00
26 Sammy Swindell Bull Hannah	3.00	8.00
28 Ernie Irvan Havoline	6.00	12.00
41 Joe Nemechek Meineke/10,080	3.00	8.00
42 Kyle Petty Mello Yello/10,080	3.00	8.00
51 Neil Bonnett Country Time	7.50	20.00
93 Lumina Prototype	4.00	8.00
93 Pontiac Prototype	4.00	8.00
93 Thunderbird Prototype	4.00	8.00
98 Derrike Cope Fingerhut	3.00	8.00
07 George Crenshaw Campbell's Promo/10,000	20.00	35.00

1994 Action/RCCA 1:64

These 1:64 scale cars were made by Action and distributed through the RCCA club. Each was distributed in a small cardboard window box printed in yellow, orange, and black with the name "Stock Car H.O. Collector Series" on it (the same as the 1993 box) or a red checkerboard pattern RCCA box with the year printed on it. All box varieties have gold foil printing on the

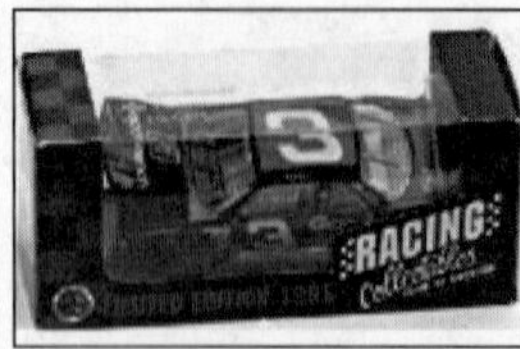

plastic window that includes the driver's name, the year model and make of the car, and the production run.

	EX	NM-MT
3 Dale Earnhardt Goodwrench/16,128	25.00	50.00
3 Dale Earnhardt Goodwrench 1994 Club Only	25.00	50.00
3 Dale Earnhardt Wrangler 1985 Monte Carlo Notchback	30.00	60.00
3 Dale Earnhardt Wrangler 1987 Monte Carlo Fastback	30.00	60.00
3 Dale Earnhardt Jr. Mom 'N' Pop's/10,080	50.00	80.00
5 Terry Labonte Kellogg's	15.00	30.00
8 Kerry Earnhardt Mom-n-Pop's/10,080	10.00	20.00
11 Bill Elliott Budweiser/10,080	7.50	15.00
15 Lake Speed Quality Care/10,080	7.50	15.00
16 Ted Musgrave Family Channel/10,000	7.50	15.00
17 Darrell Waltrip Western Auto	6.00	12.00
18 Dale Jarrett Interstate Batteries/10,000	12.50	25.00
21 David Pearson Chattanooga Chew 1985 Monte Carlo/16,128	5.00	12.00
24 Jeff Gordon DuPont	18.00	30.00
27 Tim Richmond Old Milwaukee/16,128 1985 Pontiac Grand Prix	6.00	15.00
28 Davey Allison Havoline black&gold	10.00	20.00
28 Davey Allison Havoline black&orange	10.00	20.00
30 Michael Waltrip Pennzoil/10,000	6.00	12.00
38 Kelley Earnhardt Mom-n-Pop's/10,080	7.50	15.00
41 Joe Nemechek Meineke	2.00	5.00
42 Kyle Petty Mello Yello	6.00	12.00
51 Neil Bonnett Country Time	30.00	50.00
51 Neil Bonnett Country Time Promo blister	6.00	15.00
98 Derrike Cope Fingerhut	5.00	12.00

1995 Action Racing Collectables 1:64

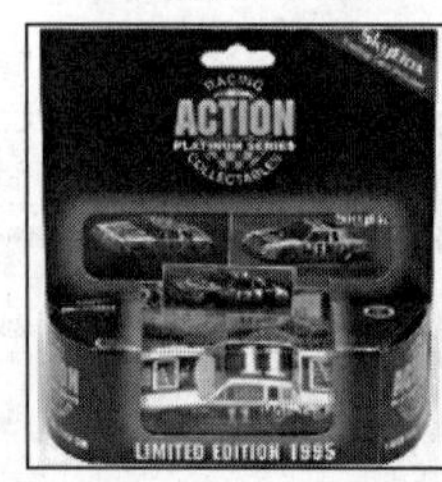

These 1:64 scale cars feature the top cars in NASCAR racing and were issued in a cardboard window box "Platinum Series" packaging including a cardboard backer used for retail display racks. Most of the 1995 Platinum Series cars were issued with an oversized SkyBox card. In most cases, the SkyBox card was specifically made for those Platinum Series pieces and was not distributed in any other method. Action also produced their own cards for inclusion with some die-cast pieces.

	EX	NM-MT
2 Dale Earnhardt Wrangler 1981 Pontiac/24,912	20.00	50.00
2 Rusty Wallace Miller Geniune Draft in acrylic display case	8.00	20.00
2/43 Dale Earnhardt Goodwrench Richard Petty STP 7&7 Championship 2-car blister	25.00	50.00
3 Richard Childress Black Gold 1979	5.00	10.00
3 Dale Earnhardt Goodwrench	20.00	40.00
3 Dale Earnhardt Goodwrench Brickyard/30,000	20.00	50.00
3 Dale Earnhardt Goodwrench Silver Platinum Series	35.00	75.00
3 Dale Earnhardt Goodwrench Silver Winston Select blister	35.00	75.00
3 Dale Earnhardt Goodwrench Silver Race World blister	15.00	40.00
3 Jeff Green Goodwrench	5.00	10.00
3/24 Dale Earnhardt Jeff Gordon Brickyard Special 2-car set/20,000	25.00	60.00
4 Sterling Marlin Kodak/24,912	5.00	12.00
6 Mark Martin Folgers/24,912	20.00	40.00
6 Mark Martin Valvoline	5.00	10.00
6 Mark Martin Valvoline Brickyard Platinum Series	6.00	12.00
6 Mark Martin Valvoline Brickyard blister	5.00	12.00
7 Geoff Bodine Exide/26,928	3.00	8.00
7 Alan Kulwicki Zerex ASA Camaro/24,912	8.00	20.00
8 Dale Earnhardt ASA Camaro 1985	20.00	40.00
11 Brett Bodine Lowe's/24,912	3.00	8.00
11 Darrell Waltrip Mountain Dew 1982 Buick/20,000	7.50	20.00
11 Darrell Waltrip Pepsi Camaro ASA/16,128	5.00	10.00
17 Darrell Waltrip Tide ASA Camaro	12.50	25.00
17 Darrell Waltrip Western Auto/24,912	6.00	15.00
21 Neil Bonnett Hodgdon/16,128 1982 Thunderbird	7.50	15.00
22 Bobby Allison Miller High Life/24,912 1983 Buick in acrylic case	8.00	20.00
23 Jimmy Spencer Smokin' Joe's in acrylic case	20.00	40.00
24 Jeff Gordon DuPont	10.00	25.00
24 Jeff Gordon DuPont 1995 Champion in blister package	10.00	25.00
25 Ken Schrader Budweiser/24,912	5.00	12.00
27 Tim Richmond Old Milwaukee/16,128	5.00	12.00
28 Dale Jarrett Havoline/29,808	8.00	20.00
42 Kyle Petty Coors Light in acrylic case	6.00	15.00
52 Ken Schrader AC Delco/24,912	4.00	10.00
52 Ken Schrader AC Delco Busch Promo	5.00	10.00
88 Ernie Irvan Havoline	4.00	10.00
88 Darrell Waltrip Gatorade 1980 Olds/16,128	6.00	15.00
94 Bill Elliott McDonald's	4.00	10.00
94 Bill Elliott Thunderbat	18.00	30.00
95 David Green Busch Beer	3.00	8.00

1995 Action/RCCA 1:64

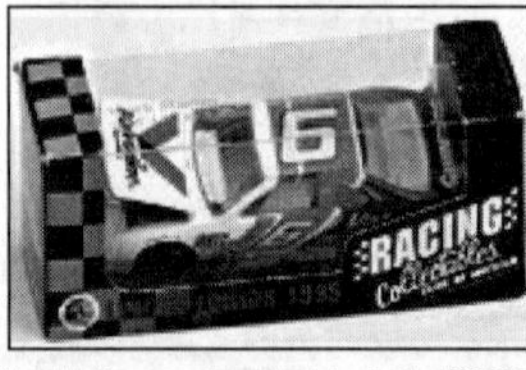

These "club" cars were issued by Action for the 1995 RCCA collector's club. Each is packaged in a small cardboard window box clearly marked with the Racing Collector's Club of America notation. Some boxes were serial numbered and all cars feature opening hoods. A few were issued in acrylic, or plastic, display cases as noted below.

	EX	NM-MT
1 Winston Cup show car in acrylic case	8.00	20.00
2 Mark Martin Miller American 1985 ASA/10,000	10.00	20.00
2 Rusty Wallace Miller Genuine Draft in acrylic case	7.50	15.00
3 Richard Childress CRC Chemical/10,080 1980 Oldsmobile	6.00	15.00
3 Dale Earnhardt Goodwrench 1994 Lumina/16,128	15.00	40.00
3 Dale Earnhardt Goodwrench Silver	50.00	100.00
3 Dale Earnhardt Wrangler 1981 Pontiac/16,128	25.00	50.00
4 Sterling Marlin Kodak/10,080	4.00	10.00
6 Mark Martin Valvoline/10,080	6.00	15.00
6 Mark Martin Valvoline Brickyard	5.00	12.00
7 Geoff Bodine Exide/10,080	4.00	10.00
7 Alan Kulwicki Hooters/10,000	15.00	30.00
7 Alan Kulwicki Zerex/10,080	12.50	30.00
9 Ted Musgrave RCCA/10,080	4.00	10.00
10 Ricky Rudd Tide/10,080	5.00	12.00
11 Brett Bodine Lowe's/10,080	4.00	10.00
17 Darrell Waltrip Superflo Camaro ASA/10,080	6.00	15.00
17 Darrell Waltrip Western Auto/10,080	6.00	15.00
23 Jimmy Spencer Smokin' Joe's/10,080 in acrylic case	25.00	50.00
24 Jeff Gordon DuPont 1994 Lumina/16,128	10.00	20.00
25 Ken Schrader Budweiser	7.50	15.00
26 Steve Kinser Quaker State	6.00	15.00
27 Rusty Wallace Kodiak 1989 Grand Prix in plastic case/20,000	20.00	35.00
28 Dale Jarrett Havoline	6.00	15.00
42 Kyle Petty Coors Light/15,000 in acrylic case	5.00	12.00
42 Kyle Petty Coors Light Pumpkin in acrylic case/15,000	30.00	60.00
88 Ernie Irvan Havoline/15,000	5.00	10.00
88 Darrell Waltrip Gatorade/10,080	6.00	15.00
94 Bill Elliott McDonald's/16,128	6.00	15.00
94 Bill Elliott McDonald's Thunderbat	8.00	20.00
95 David Green Busch Beer	6.00	15.00

1995-96 Action Racing Collectables SuperTrucks 1:64

These pieces are 1:64 scale replicas of the SuperTrucks that race in the NASCAR SuperTruck Series. Each was issued in a blister pack.

	EX	NM-MT
3 Mike Skinner Goodwrench 1995	5.00	12.00
3 Mike Skinner Goodwrench 1996	5.00	10.00
6 Rick Carelli Total Petroleum 1995	4.00	8.00
7 Geoff Bodine Exide	3.00	8.00
7 Geoff Bodine Exide	20.00	45.00
16 Ron Hornaday Action '95	5.00	10.00
16 Ron Hornaday NAPA '96	5.00	10.00
16 Ron Hornaday Papa John's Pizza 1995	6.00	15.00
24 Scott Lagasse DuPont/24,912 1995	6.00	15.00
24 Jack Sprague Quaker State 1996	5.00	12.00
28 Ernie Irvan NAPA/18,000	6.00	12.00
52 Ken Schrader AC Delco	3.00	8.00
71 Kenji Momota Action/18,000	3.00	6.00
84 Joe Ruttman Mac Tools/18,000	3.00	6.00
98 Butch Miller Raybestos/24,912	3.00	6.00

1996 Action Racing Collectables 1:64

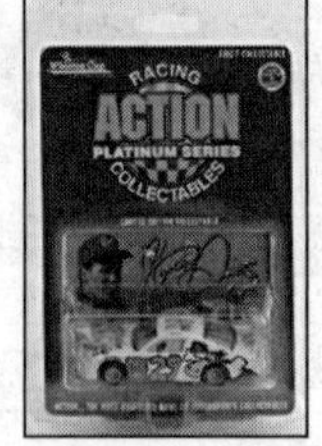

Most of these 1:64 scale cards were issued as part of the Platinum Series. Cars with alcohol and/or tobacco sponsorship were packaged in clear plastic cases.

	EX	NM-MT
2 Mark Martin Miller American 1985 ASA/20,000	5.00	12.00
2 Rusty Wallace Miller Genuine Draft	6.00	15.00
2 Rusty Wallace Miller Genuine Draft Silver 25th Anniversary	6.00	15.00
3 Dale Earnhardt AC-Delco Japan	12.50	30.00
3 Dale Earnhardt Goodwrench	12.50	30.00
3 Dale Earnhardt Goodwrench Race Day Blister	10.00	25.00
3 Dale Earnhardt Goodwrench Pit Stop blister	6.00	15.00
3 Dale Earnhardt Olympic Hood Open clear windows blister	12.50	30.00
3 Dale Earnhardt Olympic black windows blister	10.00	25.00
3 Dale Earnhardt Olympic HO clear windows blue box	20.00	50.00
5 Terry Labonte Kellogg's Iron Man Silver	6.00	
5 Terry Labonte Kellogg's Japan	6.00	
6 Mark Martin Valvoline	4.00	
6 Mark Martin Valvoline Race Day blister	4.00	
7 Geoff Bodine Exide	2.50	
10 Ricky Rudd Tide	3.00	
14 Jeff Green Racing For Kids	5.00	
18 Bobby Labonte Interstate Batteries	3.00	
18 Bobby Labonte Interstate Batteries Pro Football Hall of Fame	7.50	
21 Michael Waltrip Citgo	3.00	
21 Michael Waltrip Citgo Star Trek	6.00	
22 Bobby Allison Miller American/10,080 1985 Monte Carlo	6.00	
22 Ward Burton MBNA	3.00	
24 Jeff Gordon DuPont Monte Carlo	7.50	
24 Jeff Gordon DuPont Race Day blister	5.00	
25 Tim Richmond Folgers 1987 Monte Carlo	6.00	
28 Davey Allison Vinyl Tech 1987	5.00	
28 Ernie Irvan Havoline	5.00	
29 Steve Grissom Flintstones	4.00	
29 Steve Grissom WCW	4.00	
29 No Driver Association Scooby-Doo	5.00	
30 Johnny Benson Pennzoil	4.00	
42 Kyle Petty Coors Light	6.00	
42 Kyle Petty Coors Light Black	10.00	
43 Bobby Hamilton STP '72 Blue	4.00	
43 Bobby Hamilton STP '72 Blue&Red	4.00	
43 Bobby Hamilton STP '79 Blue&Red red sides/blue roof	4.00	
43 Bobby Hamilton STP '84 Blue&Red blue sides w/red stripes	4.00	
43 Bobby Hamilton STP Silver 25th Anniversary	6.00	
57 Jason Keller Halloween Havoc	3.00	
88 Ernie Irvan Havoline	5.00	
88 Dale Jarrett Quality Care	5.00	
94 Bill Elliott McDonald's	4.00	
96 David Green Caterpillar	3.00	

1996 Action/RCCA 1:64

These 1:64 scale cars were made by Action and dis through their club -- RCCA. Most of the cars were prod hood open models and packaged in boxes in contrast basic issue Action counterparts which are typically is blister packs.

	EX	NM
2 Rusty Wallace Miller Genuine Draft	7.50	
2 Rusty Wallace Miller Genuine Draft Silver 25th Anniversary in plastic case	10.00	
3 Dale Earnhardt AC Delco	10.00	
3 Dale Earnhardt Goodwrench/20,000	12.50	
4 Sterling Marlin Kodak	6.00	
5 Terry Labonte Kellogg's Iron Man Silver/10,000	10.00	
5 Terry Labonte Kellogg's Japan	7.50	
6 Mark Martin Valvoline/10,000	5.00	
7 Geoff Bodine Exide	5.00	
14 Jeff Green Racing For Kids/10,000	5.00	
15 Dale Earnhardt Wrangler 1982 Thunderbird/20,000	10.00	
17 Darrell Waltrip Tide 1988 Monte Carlo/10,080	5.00	
18 Bobby Labonte Interstate Batteries/10,000	6.00	
18 Bobby Labonte Interstate Batteries Pro Football Hall of Fame/10,000	10.00	
21 Michael Waltrip	6.00	

itgo Star Trek/10,000
eff Gordon 10.00 20.00
DuPont/15,000
m Richmond 10.00 20.00
Folgers 1987
Monte Carlo/10,000
nie Irvan 6.00 15.00
Havoline/10,000
eve Grissom 7.50 15.00
Flintstones
o Driver Association 7.50 15.00
Scooby-Doo
hnny Benson 5.00 12.00
Pennzoil/10,000
yle Petty 5.00 12.00
Coors Light
yle Petty 10.00 20.00
Coors Light Black
n plastic case/10,000
obby Hamilton 6.00 15.00
STP Silver/10,000
son Keller 5.00 12.00
Halloween Havoc/8000
ale Jarrett 6.00 15.00
Quality Care
ll Elliott 6.00 15.00
McDonald's/10,000

1997 Action Racing Collectables 1:64

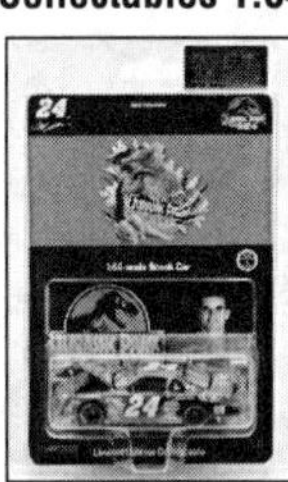

of these 1:64 scale cards were issued as part of the um Series. Cars with alcohol and/or tobacco sponsorship ackaged in acrylic cases.

EX NM-MT
sty Wallace 6.00 12.00
Miller Lite
sty Wallace 6.00 15.00
Miller Japan/12,000
sty Wallace 7.50 15.00
Miller Lite Texas
e Earnhardt 12.50 25.00
AC Delco
e Earnhardt 10.00 25.00
AC Delco
Black Window blister
e Earnhardt 10.00 25.00
Goodwrench
e Earnhardt 12.50 25.00
Goodwrench
Brickyard/14,256
le Earnhardt 12.50 30.00
Goodwrench Plus in blister
e Earnhardt 20.00 40.00
Goodwrench Plus in box
e Earnhardt 20.00 40.00
Wheaties
e Earnhardt 12.50 25.00
Wheaties
Black Window blister
e Earnhardt 25.00 60.00
Wheaties Hood Open
Sports Image
e Earnhardt 12.50 25.00
Wheaties Mail-In
ve Park 10.00 20.00
AC Delco/12,024
ky Rudd 10.00 20.00
Piedmont 1983 Monte Carlo/10,080
rling Marlin 5.00 12.00
Kodak
rk Martin 5.00 10.00
Valvoline
Burton 4.00 8.00
Track Gear
cky Rudd 5.00 10.00
Tide/9000
cky Rudd 5.00 10.00
Tide Mac Tools/1000
ett Bodine 2.50 6.00
Close Call/10,944
nny Wallace 3.00 8.00
Gray Bar
eve Park 12.00 20.00
Burger King
ed Musgrave 3.00 6.00
Primestar/12,080
arrell Waltrip 4.00 10.00
Parts America Blue&White
arrell Waltrip 6.00 15.00
Parts America Chrome Box
arrell Waltrip 4.00 10.00
Parts America Green
with green number
arrell Waltrip 4.00 10.00
Parts America Green
with white number
arrell Waltrip 4.00 10.00
Parts America Orange
arrell Waltrip 4.00 10.00
Parts America Red&White
arrell Waltrip 4.00 10.00
Parts America Yellow&White
obby Labonte 5.00 12.00
Interstate Batteries
ard Burton 4.00 10.00
MBNA
ard Burton 5.00 12.00
MBNA Gold/11,016
mmy Spencer 12.50 25.00
Camel
ff Gordon 8.00 20.00
DuPont
ff Gordon 8.00 20.00
DuPont Bickyard/14,256
24 Jeff Gordon 8.00 20.00
DuPont Million Dollar Date
24 Jeff Gordon 8.00 20.00
DuPont Million Dollar Date
black windows
24 Jeff Gordon 8.00 20.00
DuPont Million Dollar Date
Mac Tools black window
24 Jeff Gordon 15.00 40.00
DuPont ChromaPremier/25,000
24 Jeff Gordon 10.00 25.00
Jurassic Park 3
24 Jeff Gordon 8.00 20.00
Jurassic Park 3
black window blister
24 Jeff Gordon 15.00 40.00
Jurassic Park 3
Hood Open Sports Image
24 Jeff Gordon 10.00 20.00
3-Car Promo blister
DuPont car
DuPont Million Dollar
Jurassic Park 3
25 Ricky Craven 4.00 10.00
Budweiser
26 Rich Bickle 4.00 10.00
KFC
27 Kenny Irwin 7.50 15.00
G.I. Joe
27 Kenny Irwin 6.00 15.00
Tonka/10,080
27 Rusty Wallace 35.00 60.00
Miller Genuine Draft
1990 Grand Prix/10,080
29 Jeff Green 5.00 12.00
Tom & Jerry/12,888
29 Elliott Sadler 4.00 10.00
Phillips 66
31 Mike Skinner 4.00 10.00
Lowe's
31 Mike Skinner 4.00 10.00
Lowe's Blister Pack
31 Mike Skinner 4.00 10.00
Lowe's Japan
32 Dale Jarrett 5.00 12.00
White Rain/10,080
36 Todd Bodine 4.00 10.00
Stanley
36 Derrike Cope 3.00 8.00
Skittles
37 Mark Green 5.00 12.00
Timber Wolf
37 Jeremy Mayfield 4.00 10.00
K-Mart RC-Cola
40 Robby Gordon 5.00 12.00
Coors Light/12,024
41 Steve Grissom 5.00 12.00
Kodak/7500
46 Wally Dallenbach 3.00 8.00
First Union/10,080
60 Mark Martin 5.00 12.00
Winn Dixie
71 Dave Marcis 6.00 15.00
Realtree
75 Rick Mast 4.00 10.00
Remington/10,080
75 Rick Mast 4.00 10.00
Remington Camo
77 Bobby Hillin Jr. 4.00 10.00
Jasper
81 Kenny Wallace 4.00 10.00
Square D/16,488
88 Dale Jarrett 4.00 10.00
Quality Care
88 Dale Jarrett 4.00 10.00
Quality Care
Brickyard/14,256
94 Bill Elliott 5.00 12.00
McDonald's
94 Bill Elliott 4.00 10.00
Mac Tonight
96 David Green 3.00 10.00
Caterpillar
99 Jeff Burton 4.00 10.00
Exide
00 Buckshot Jones 3.00 8.00
Aqua Fresh

1997 Action/RCCA 1:64

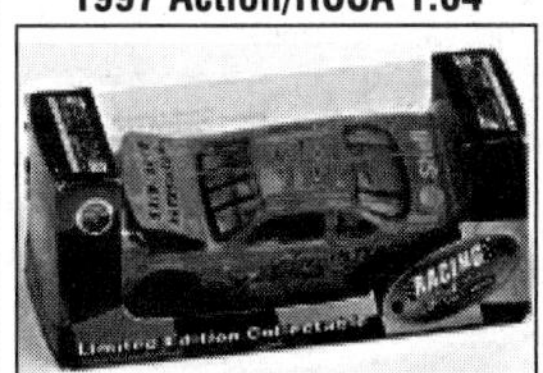

These 1:64 scale cars were made by Action and distributed through their collector's club (RCCA). All cars have opening hoods and were packaged in small clear window boxes.

EX NM-MT
1 Gargoyles 300 Promo/5000 3.00 6.00
2 Rusty Wallace 8.00 16.00
Miller Lite
2 Rusty Wallace 9.00 18.00
Miller Japan
2 Rusty Wallace 9.00 18.00
Miller Lite Texas
3 Dale Earnhardt 20.00 40.00
AC Delco/20,000
3 Dale Earnhardt 30.00 50.00
Goodwrench/5000
3 Dale Earnhardt 10.00 25.00
Goodwrench Plus/25,000
3 Dale Earnhardt 30.00 60.00
Lowes Foods
3 Dale Earnhardt 30.00 60.00
Wheaties
3 Steve Park 15.00 30.00
AC Delco
4 Sterling Marlin 5.00 12.00
Kodak/5000
6 Mark Martin 6.00 15.00
Valvoline/5000
9 Jeff Burton 7.50 15.00
Track Gear/3500
10 Ricky Rudd 8.00 16.00
Tide
11 Brett Bodine 4.00 10.00
Close Call/5000
12 Kenny Wallace 5.00 12.00
Gray Bar/3500
14 Steve Park 15.00 30.00
Burger King
16 Ted Musgrave 4.00 10.00
Primestar/5000
17 Darrell Waltrip 5.00 12.00
Parts America
Blue&White/5000
17 Darrell Waltrip 10.00 20.00
Parts America Chrome/5000
17 Darrell Waltrip 5.00 12.00
Parts America Green
with green number/5000
17 Darrell Waltrip 5.00 12.00
Parts America Green
with white number/5000
17 Darrell Waltrip 5.00 12.00
Parts America Orange/5000
17 Darrell Waltrip 5.00 12.00
Parts America
Red&White/5000
17 Darrell Waltrip 5.00 12.00
Parts America
Yellow&White/5000
18 Bobby Labonte 10.00 20.00
Interstate Batteries/5000
22 Ward Burton 8.00 16.00
MBNA
22 Ward Burton 8.00 16.00
MBNA Gold
23 Jimmy Spencer 25.00 40.00
Camel/5000
24 Jeff Gordon 18.00 30.00
DuPont/5000
24 Jeff Gordon 12.50 25.00
DuPont Million
Dollar Date/25,000
24 Jeff Gordon 25.00 50.00
DuPont ChromaPremier
24 Jeff Gordon 18.00 30.00
Jurassic Park 3
24 Jeff Gordon 30.00 50.00
Jurassic Park 3 w/card set
25 Ricky Craven 6.00 15.00
Budweiser
26 Rich Bickle 6.00 15.00
KFC/5000
27 Kenny Irwin 8.00 20.00
G.I. Joe/7500
27 Kenny Irwin 8.00 20.00
Tonka
29 Jeff Green 6.00 15.00
Tom & Jerry/5000
29 Elliott Sadler 5.00 12.00
Phillips 66/3500
31 Mike Skinner 6.00 15.00
Lowe's
31 Mike Skinner 6.00 15.00
Lowe's Japan
32 Dale Jarrett 5.00 12.00
White Rain/3500
36 Todd Bodine 5.00 10.00
Stanley/5000
36 Derrike Cope 5.00 12.00
Skittles
37 Mark Green 5.00 12.00
Timber Wolf/5000
37 Jeremy Mayfield 5.00 12.00
K-Mart RC-Cola/5000
41 Steve Grissom 5.00 12.00
Kodiak/5000
46 Wally Dallenbach 5.00 12.00
First Union/3500
60 Mark Martin 8.00 16.00
Winn Dixie
71 Dave Marcis 10.00 25.00
Realtree
75 Rick Mast 5.00 12.00
Remington/5000
75 Rick Mast 6.00 12.00
Remington Camo
77 Bobby Hillin Jr. 5.00 12.00
Jasper/5000
81 Kenny Wallace 5.00 12.00
Square D/5000
88 Dale Jarrett 10.00 20.00
Quality Care/5000
93 Mike Skinner 12.50 25.00
Llumar SuperTruck Promo
94 Bill Elliott 8.00 16.00
McDonald's/5000
94 Bill Elliott 10.00 20.00
Mac Tonight
96 David Green 5.00 12.00
Caterpillar
97 Chad Little 5.00 12.00
John Deere
97 Chad Little 8.00 16.00
John Deere
160th Anniversary/10,080
99 Jeff Burton 5.00 12.00
Exide/5000
00 Buckshot Jones 5.00 12.00
Aqua Fresh/3500

1998 Action Racing Collectables 1:64

Most of these 1:64 scale cards were issued as part of the Platinum Series. Cars with alcohol and/or tobacco sponsorship are packaged in acrylic cases.

EX NM-MT
1 Dale Earnhardt Jr. 6.00 15.00
Coke Bear
1 Steve Park 6.00 15.00
Pennzoil Black Roof/15,000
1 Steve Park 6.00 15.00
Pennzoil Yellow Roof
1 Steve Park 10.00 20.00
Darrell Watrip
Pennzoil
2-car set in tin
1 Darrell Waltrip 6.00 15.00
Pennzoil
2 Rusty Wallace 6.00 15.00
Adventures of Rusty
2 Rusty Wallace 6.00 15.00
Miller Lite
2 Rusty Wallace 6.00 15.00
Miller Lite Elvis
2 Rusty Wallace 6.00 15.00
Miller Lite TCB Elvis
2/12 Rusty Wallace 8.00 20.00
Jeremy Mayfield
2-car set
on pit wall base
3 Dale Earnhardt 12.50 30.00
Coke/10,000
3 Dale Earnhardt 12.50 30.00
Goodwrench Plus
3 Dale Earnhardt 15.00 30.00
Goodwrench Plus Blister Pack
3 Dale Earnhardt 10.00 25.00
Goodwrench Plus Daytona Win
3 Dale Earnhardt 20.00 40.00
Goodwrench Plus Bass Pro
3 Dale Earnhardt Jr. 15.00 25.00
AC Delco
3 Dale Earnhardt Jr. 12.00 20.00
AC Delco
1998 BGN Champ blister
4 Bobby Hamilton 3.00 8.00
Kodak
5 Terry Labonte 5.00 12.00
Kellogg's/9000
5 Terry Labonte 5.00 12.00
Blasted Fruit Loops
5 Terry Labonte 5.00 12.00
Kellogg's Corny/15,000
5 Terry Labonte 5.00 12.00
Kellogg's Ironman
8 Dale Earnhardt 10.00 25.00
10,000 RPM 1975 Dodge
8 Hut Stricklin 3.00 8.00
Circuit City/10,080
9 Jerry Nadeau 15.00 30.00
Power Puff/7560
9 Jerry Nadeau 6.00 12.00
Scooby Zombie Island
9 Lake Speed 5.00 12.00
Birthday Cake/12,000
9 Lake Speed 5.00 12.00
Huckleberry Hound/15,000
10 Ricky Rudd 5.00 10.00
Tide/9000
10 Ricky Rudd 5.00 12.00
Tide Mac Tools/1000
10 Ricky Rudd 5.00 10.00
Give Kids the World
12 Jeremy Mayfield 4.00 10.00
Mobil 1
14 Patty Moise 5.00 12.00
Rhodes Xena/12,024
18 Bobby Labonte 5.00 12.00
Interstate Batteries
18 Bobby Labonte 5.00 12.00
Interstate Batteries Hot Rod
18 Bobby Labonte 5.00 12.00
Interstate Batteries Small Soldiers
22 Ward Burton 4.00 10.00
MBNA/10,080
23 Jimmy Spencer 7.50 15.00
No Bull
24 Jeff Gordon 7.50 15.00
DuPont
24 Jeff Gordon 7.50 15.00
DuPont Brickyard Winner/10,024
24 Jeff Gordon 10.00 25.00
DuPont Chromalusion
24 Jeff Gordon 7.50 15.00
DuPont No Bull
28 Kenny Irwin 4.00 8.00
Havoline
28 Kenny Irwin 7.50 15.00
Havoline Joker
30 Derrike Cope 3.00 8.00
Gumout/10,080
31 Dale Earnhardt Jr. 15.00 25.00
Sikkens Blue
1997 Monte Carlo
31 Mike Skinner 4.00 10.00
Lowe's
31 Mike Skinner 4.00 10.00
Lowe's Special Olympic
32 Dale Jarrett 4.00 8.00
White Rain
32 Dale Jarrett 6.00 15.00
White Rain Promo
in die cut blister
35 Todd Bodine 6.00 12.00
Tabasco Orange
35 Todd Bodine 6.00 12.00
Tabasco Red
36 Ernie Irvan 9.00 18.00
M&M's
36 Ernie Irvan 6.00 12.00
Skittles/10,080
36 Ernie Irvan 7.50 15.00
Wildberry Skittles
40 Sterling Marlin 6.00 15.00
Coors Light/7560
41 Steve Grissom 7.50 15.00
Kodiak
44 Tony Stewart 12.50 25.00
Shell/10,080
44 Tony Stewart 12.50 25.00
Shell Small Soldiers/16,992
50 Ricky Craven 5.00 10.00
Budweiser
50 NDA 6.00 12.00
Bud Louie
72 Mike Dillon 5.00 10.00
Detroit Gasket
75 Rick Mast 3.00 8.00
Remington/12,024
75 Rick Mast 4.00 8.00
Remington Mac Tools/1000
81 Kenny Wallace 4.00 8.00
Square D
81 Kenny Wallace 4.00 8.00
Square D Lightning
88 Dale Jarrett 6.00 12.00
Quality Care
88 Dale Jarrett 8.00 20.00
Batman
90 Dick Trickle 4.00 10.00
Heilig-Meyers/12,024
96 David Green 3.00 8.00
Caterpillar/10,080
300 Darrell Waltrip 6.00 12.00
Flock Special
00 Buckshot Jones 4.00 10.00
Alka Seltzer/11,016
K2 Dale Earnhardt 12.50 30.00
Dayvault's Dark Roof
1956 Ford
K2 Dale Earnhardt 12.50 30.00
Dayvault's Pink Roof
1956 Ford

1998 Action/RCCA 1:64

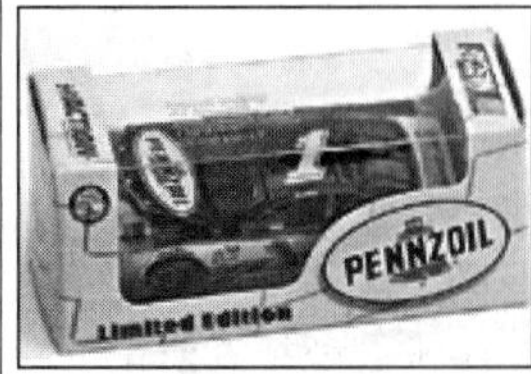

These were the 1:64 scale cars that were made by Action and distributed through the club (RCCA). All cars have open hoods. These cars are packaged in boxes in contrast to their ARC counterparts.

EX NM-MT
1 Dale Earnhardt Jr. 15.00 30.00
Coke Bear
1 Jeff Gordon 20.00 35.00
Baby Ruth 1992 Thunderbird
1 Steve Park 18.00 30.00
Pennzoil Black Roof
1 Darrell Waltrip 9.00 18.00
Pennzoil
2 Rusty Wallace 10.00 20.00
Adventures of Rusty
2 Rusty Wallace 6.00 15.00
Miller Lite/7500
2 Rusty Wallace 10.00 20.00
Miller Lite Elvis
2 Rusty Wallace 10.00 20.00
Miller Lite TCB Elivs
3 Dale Earnhardt 25.00 50.00
Coke
3 Dale Earnhardt 15.00 40.00
Goodwrench Plus
3 Dale Earnhardt 40.00 80.00
Goodwrench Plus Bass Pro
3 Dale Earnhardt 12.50 25.00
Goodwrench Plus
Fan Club box
3 Dale Earnhardt Jr. 20.00 40.00
AC Delco/3500
3 Race Rock Promo/10,080 6.00 12.00
4 Bobby Hamilton 6.00 15.00
Kodak/5000
5 Terry Labonte 6.00 15.00
Blasted Fruit Loops/7500
5 Terry Labonte 6.00 15.00
Kellogg's/5000
5 Terry Labonte 7.50 15.00
Kellogg's Corny
5 Terry Labonte 7.50 15.00
Kellogg's Ironman/10,000
8 Dale Earnhardt 12.50 30.00
RPM 1975 Dodge/12,500
8 Hut Stricklin 6.00 15.00
Circuit City/2500
9 Jerry Nadeau 7.50 15.00
Scooby Zombie Island/3550
9 Lake Speed 6.00 15.00
Birthday Cake
9 Lake Speed 6.00 15.00
Huckleberry Hound/5000
10 Ricky Rudd 6.00 15.00
Tide/3500
12 Jeremy Mayfield 6.00 15.00
Mobil 1/5000
14 Patty Moise 6.00 15.00
Rhodes Xena/3500
18 Bobby Labonte 7.50 15.00
Interstate Batteries
18 Bobby Labonte 15.00 30.00
Interstate Batteries Hot Rod
18 Bobby Labonte 7.50 15.00
Interstate Batteries
Small Soldiers/10,000
24 Jeff Gordon 10.00 20.00
DuPont
24 Jeff Gordon 20.00 40.00
DuPont Chromalusion/15,000
24 Jeff Gordon 15.00 25.00
DuPont No Bull
28 Kenny Irwin 6.00 15.00
Havoline/7500
28 Kenny Irwin 6.00 15.00
Havoline Joker/7500
31 Dale Earnhardt Jr. 20.00 40.00
Sikkens Blue
1997 Monte Carlo
31 Mike Skinner 6.00 15.00
Lowe's/5000
31 Mike Skinner 7.50 15.00
Lowe's Special Olympics

	EX	NM-MT
32 Dale Jarrett White Rain/2500	7.50	15.00
35 Todd Bodine Tabasco Orange&White	6.00	15.00
35 Todd Bodine Tabasco Red&Black/7500	6.00	15.00
36 Ernie Irvan Skittles	7.50	15.00
36 Ernie Irvan Wildberry Skittles/5000	7.50	15.00
41 Steve Grissom Kodiak/3500	7.50	15.00
44 Tony Stewart Shell/3500	15.00	30.00
44 Tony Stewart Shell Small Soldiers/7500	12.50	25.00
50 Ricky Craven Bud/3500	6.00	15.00
81 Kenny Wallace Square D/3500	6.00	15.00
81 Kenny Wallace Square D Lightning	7.50	15.00
88 Dale Jarrett Quality Care/5000	7.50	15.00
88 Dale Jarrett Batman	7.50	15.00
90 Dick Trickle Heilig-Meyers	6.00	15.00
98 Greg Sacks Thorn Apple Valley/2500	6.00	15.00
300 Darrell Waltrip Tim Flock Special	8.00	18.00
K2 Dale Earnhardt Dayvault's Pink Roof 1956 Ford	12.50	30.00
NNO NASCAR 50th Anniversary SuperTruck/7500	5.00	12.00

1999 Action Performance 1:64

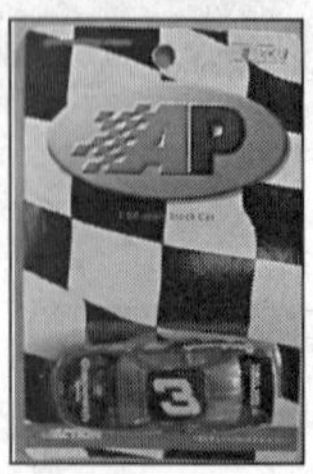

These cars were issued in an "AP" Action Performance blister packs. Each package includes the year on the front along with a checkered flag background design and a black and red AP logo.

	EX	NM-MT
3 Dale Earnhardt Goodwrench	10.00	20.00
3 Dale Earnhardt Jr. AC Delco in AP box	5.00	12.00
3 Dale Earnhardt Jr. AC Delco Promo Blister	5.00	10.00
20 Tony Stewart Home Depot HO in box	10.00	20.00
24 Jeff Gordon DuPont	5.00	10.00
28 Andy Kirby Williams Promo	3.00	8.00
36 Ken Schrader M&M's Promo	3.00	6.00
88 Dale Jarrett Quality Care	4.00	8.00

1999 Action Racing Collectables 1:64

These 1:64 scale cards were issued as part of the Platinum Series. The Alcohol/Tobacco cars were released on a pit wall base.

	EX	NM-MT
1 Jeff Gordon Carolina 1991 Thunderbird	7.50	15.00
1 Jeff Gordon Baby Ruth 1992 Thunderbird	6.00	12.00
1 Steve Park Pennzoil/9000	5.00	12.00
1 Steve Park Pennzoil Shark/9000	5.00	12.00
2 Rusty Wallace Miller Lite	6.00	15.00
2 Rusty Wallace Miller Lite Harley	5.00	12.00
2 Rusty Wallace Miller Lite Last Lap	6.00	15.00
2 Rusty Wallace Miller Lite Texas	6.00	12.00
3 Dale Earnhardt Goodwrench	12.50	30.00
3 Dale Earnhardt Goodwrench 25th Anniversary	12.50	30.00
3 Dale Earnhardt Goodwrench Sign	15.00	40.00
3 Dale Earnhardt Goodwrench Last Lap	12.50	30.00
3 Dale Earnhardt Wrangler	15.00	40.00
3 Dale Earnhardt Jr. AC Delco	6.00	15.00
3 Dale Earnhardt Jr. AC Delco Promo/10,080	6.00	15.00
3 Dale Earnhardt Jr. AC Delco Last Lap	7.50	20.00
3 Dale Earnhardt Jr. AC Delco Superman	7.50	20.00
4 Bobby Hamilton Advantix	4.00	10.00
5 Terry Labonte Kellogg's/10,080	6.00	15.00
5 Terry Labonte Kellogg's Mac Tools/1008	6.00	15.00
5 Terry Labonte K-Sentials	6.00	15.00
5 Terry Labonte Kellogg's NASCAR Racers	7.50	20.00
5 Terry Labonte Rice Krispies	5.00	12.00
8 Dale Earnhardt Jr. Bud	12.50	25.00
8 Dale Earnhardt Jr. Bud Atlanta/10,080	10.00	20.00
8 Dale Earnhardt Jr. Bud Michigan/10,080	10.00	20.00
8 Dale Earnhardt Jr. Bud New Hampshire/10,080	10.00	20.00
8 Dale Earnhardt Jr. Bud Richmond/10,080	10.00	20.00
9 Jerry Nadeau Dexter's Lab/12,024	5.00	12.00
9 Jerry Nadeau Jetsons/12,024	5.00	12.00
10 Ricky Rudd Tide Kids blister package	4.00	10.00
11 Dale Jarrett Rayovac	5.00	12.00
11 Dale Jarrett Green Bay	5.00	12.00
12 Jeremy Mayfield Mobil 1	4.00	10.00
12 Jeremy Mayfield Mobil 1 Kentucky Derby	4.00	10.00
12 Jeremy Mayfield Mobil 1 Kentucky Derby 2-car Promo blister	5.00	12.00
15 Ken Schrader Oakwood Homes/7056	4.00	10.00
16 Ron Hornaday NAPA Superman SuperTruck	6.00	12.00
17 Matt Kenseth DeWalt 1997 Monte Carlo/7056	7.50	15.00
18 Bobby Labonte Interstate Batteries	6.00	15.00
18 Bobby Labonte Interstate Batteries NASCAR Racers	7.50	20.00
18 Bobby Labonte MBNA/7488	6.00	15.00
20 Tony Stewart Home Depot/10,080	25.00	50.00
20 Tony Stewart Home Depot Promo blister	5.00	12.00
20 Tony Stewart Home Depot Habitat	10.00	25.00
20 Tony Stewart Home Depot/Habitat 2-car promo set	6.00	15.00
21 Elliott Sadler Citgo	4.00	10.00
22 Ward Burton Caterpillar/8280	6.00	15.00
23 Jimmy Spencer No Bull	6.00	15.00
23 Jimmy Spencer No Bull Mac Tools	6.00	15.00
23 Jimmy Spencer Winston Lights	6.00	15.00
24 Jeff Gordon DuPont	6.00	15.00
24 Jeff Gordon DuPont NASCAR Racers	15.00	30.00
24 Jeff Gordon DuPont Superman	6.00	15.00
24 Jeff Gordon Pepsi/10,000	8.00	20.00
24 Jeff Gordon Pepsi Star Wars	8.00	20.00
25 W.Dallenbach/Budweiser	4.00	10.00
27 Casey Atwood Castrol/8064	6.00	15.00
27 Casey Atwood Castrol Last Lap/12,024	6.00	15.00
28 Kenny Irwin Havoline/10,080	5.00	10.00
28 Kenny Irwin Havoline Mac Tools/1008	5.00	10.00
28/88 Kenny Irwin Dale Jarrett Batman & Joker	15.00	30.00
30 Dale Earnhardt Army '76 Malibu	15.00	30.00
31 Dale Earnhardt Jr. Gargoyles 1997 Monte Carlo/10,080	8.00	18.00
31 Dale Earnhardt Jr. Sikkens White 1997 Monte Carlo	10.00	20.00
31 Dale Earnhardt Jr. Wrangler 1997 Monte Carlo	18.00	30.00
31 Mike Skinner Lowe's	4.00	10.00
33 Ken Schrader Skoal	6.00	15.00
36 Ernie Irvan M&M's/13,032	6.00	15.00
36 Ernie Irvan M&M's Millennium Red on package	10.00	20.00
36 Ernie Irvan M&M's Millennium Yellow on package	10.00	20.00
36 Ernie Irvan M&M's Millennium Countdown/14,040	6.00	15.00
36 Ernie Irvan Crispy M&M's	5.00	12.00
36 Ernie Irvan Pedigree/7056	6.00	15.00
36 Tim Fedewa Stanley	4.00	10.00
40 Coca-Cola 600	3.00	8.00
40 Kerry Earnhardt Channellock	6.00	15.00
40 Sterling Marlin Coors Light	5.00	12.00
40 Sterling Marlin Coors Light Brooks & Dunn	5.00	12.00
40 Sterling Marlin Coors Light John Wayne	5.00	12.00
55 Kenny Wallace Square D	4.00	10.00
55 Kenny Wallace Square D NASCAR Racers	6.00	15.00
66 Darrell Waltrip Big K Route 66 Victory Tour/10,080	5.00	12.00
71 Dave Marcis Realtree	8.00	20.00
77 Dale Earnhardt HyGain 1976 Malibu	12.50	25.00
88 Dale Jarrett Quality Care/14,876	5.00	12.00
88 Dale Jarrett Quality Care White/14,976	8.00	20.00
88 Dale Jarrett Quality Care and Quality Care White 2 Car Tin	25.00	50.00
88 Dale Jarrett Quality Care Last Lap	7.50	15.00
99 Cracker Barrel 500 Promo in clear box	6.00	12.00
00 Buckshot Jones Crown Fiber/9000	4.00	10.00
NNO Superman 9-car set in tin	60.00	110.00

1999 Action/RCCA 1:64

These car were available only through the club, and were very limited. All cars have opening hoods.

	EX	NM-MT
1 Jeff Gordon Carolina 1991 Thunderbird	12.00	20.00
1 Steve Park Pennzoil/5000	8.00	18.00
1 Steve Park Pennzoil Shark/3500	10.00	20.00
2 Rusty Wallace Miller Lite/5000	7.50	20.00
2 Rusty Wallace Miller Lite Last Lap/3000	7.50	20.00
2 Rusty Wallace Miller Lite Harley/7500	6.00	15.00
2 Rusty Wallace Wallace Fan Club	6.00	15.00
3 Dale Earnhardt Goodwrench/10,000	15.00	40.00
3 Dale Earnhardt Goodwrench 25th Anniversary/10,000	15.00	40.00
3 Dale Earnhardt Goodwrench Sign/10,000	15.00	40.00
3 Dale Earnhardt Goodwrench Sign Last Lap/15,000	12.50	30.00
3 Dale Earnhardt Wrangler/15,192	20.00	50.00
3 Dale Earnhardt Jr. AC Delco/10,000	12.50	25.00
3 Dale Earnhardt Jr. AC Delco Last Lap	7.50	20.00
3 Dale Earnhardt Jr. AC Delco Superman	10.00	20.00
4 Bobby Hamilton Advantix	7.50	15.00
5 Terry Labonte Kellogg's/4500	7.50	15.00
5 Terry Labonte K-Sentials	7.50	15.00
5 NASCAR Cafe Promo/10,000	10.00	20.00
8 Dale Earnhardt Jr. Bud	12.50	30.00
8 Dale Earnhardt Jr. Bud Atlanta/3500	10.00	20.00
8 Dale Earnhardt Jr. Bud Michigan/3500	10.00	20.00
8 Dale Earnhardt Jr. Bud New Hampshire/3500	10.00	20.00
8 Dale Earnhardt Jr. Bud Richmond/3500	10.00	20.00
9 Jerry Nadeau Dexter's Lab/3500	7.50	15.00
9 Jerry Nadeau Jetsons/3500	7.50	15.00
10 Ricky Rudd Tide/2500	10.00	20.00
11 Dale Jarrett Green Bay Packers/2500	25.00	50.00
12 Jeremy Mayfield Mobil 1/3500	7.50	15.00
12 Jeremy Mayfield Mobil 1 Kentucky Derby	7.50	15.00
17 Matt Kenseth DeWalt 1997 Monte Carlo/3000	12.00	20.00
18 Bobby Labonte Interstate Batteries	8.00	18.00
20 Tony Stewart Home Depot/3500	35.00	60.00
20 Tony Stewart Home Depot Habitat	15.00	30.00
21 Elliott Sadler Citgo/2500	7.50	15.00
23 Jimmy Spencer No Bull/5000	6.00	15.00
23 Jimmy Spencer Winston Lights/5000	6.00	15.00
24 Jeff Gordon DuPont/15,000	7.50	20.00
24 Jeff Gordon DuPont NASCAR Racers/10,000	20.00	40.00
24 Jeff Gordon DuPont Superman	7.50	20.00
24 Jeff Gordon Pepsi/10,000	7.50	20.00
24 Jeff Gordon Pepsi Star Wars/15,000	10.00	25.00
25 Wally Dallenbach Bud/2508	6.00	15.00
25 Dura Lube Promo	5.00	10.00
27 Casey Atwood Castrol/2500	7.50	20.00
27 Casey Atwood Castrol Last Lap/3000	7.50	20.00
28 Kenny Irwin Havoline/3500	6.00	15.00
30 Dale Earnhardt Army 1976 Malibu/5000	25.00	50.00
31 Dale Earnhardt Jr. Gargoyles 1997 Monte Carlo/12,000	12.50	25.00
31 Dale Earnhardt Jr. Sikkens White 1997 Monte Carlo/10,000	15.00	25.00
31 Dale Earnhardt Jr. Wrangler 1997 Monte Carlo/7500	15.00	25.00
31 Mike Skinner Lowe's/2500	6.00	15.00
33 Ken Schrader Skoal/3500	12.50	25.00
36 Ernie Irvan M&M's	6.00	15.00
36 Ernie Irvan M&M's Countdown/6500	6.00	15.00
36 Ernie Irvan Crispy M&M's/3500	7.50	20.00
40 Kerry Earnhardt Channellock/5000	7.50	20.00
40 Sterling Marlin Coors Light/2500	6.00	15.00
55 Kenny Wallace Square D/2500	6.00	15.00
55 Kenny Wallace Square D NASCAR Racers/4500	6.00	15.00
71 Dave Marcis Realtree	7.50	20.00
77 Dale Earnhardt Hy-Gain 1976 Malibu	15.00	30.00
88 Dale Jarrett Quality Care White	12.50	25.00
00 Buckshot Jones Crown Fiber	6.00	15.00

2000 Action Performance 1:64

These 1:64 cars were issued in a black and red AP "Action Performance" blister with cardboard backer. The year of issue is clearly printed on the backer board. The cars were distributed primarily by mass retailers.

	EX	NM-MT
1 Steve Park Pennzoil	3.00	8.00
2 Rusty Wallace Rusty Red Cell Batteries Promo	5.00	12.00
3 Dale Earnhardt Goodwrench	6.00	15.00
3 Dale Earnhardt Goodwrench Red Call Batteries Promo	10.00	20.00
4 Jeff Purvis Porter-Cable	30.00	50.00
5 Terry Labonte Kellogg's	3.00	8.00
5 Terry Labonte Kellogg's Red Cell Batteries Promo	4.00	8.00
18 Bobby Labonte Interstate Batteries	3.00	8.00
20 Tony Stewart Home Depot	4.00	8.00
24 Jeff Gordon DuPont	4.00	8.00
25 Jerry Nadeau Holigan	3.00	6.00
28 Ricky Rudd Havoline	3.00	6.00
28 Ricky Rudd Havoline Red Cell Batteries Promo	4.00	8.00
36 Ken Schrader M&M's	3.00	6.00
75 Wally Dallenbach Red Cell Batteries Promo	4.00	8.00
88 Dale Jarrett Quality Care	3.00	6.00

2000 Action Racing Collectables 1:64

These 1:64 scale cards were issued as part of the Platinum Series. The Alcohol/Tobacco sponsored cars were released on a pit wall base and packaged in a clear window box similar to the RCCA releases. The rest were packaged in a plastic clam-shell blister.

	EX	NM-MT
1 Coca-Cola in a can	6.00	15.00
1 Randy LaJoie Bob Evan's/7560	4.00	8.00
1 Randy LaJoie Bob Evan's Monsters	4.00	8.00
1 Steve Park Pennzoil/10,080	5.00	12.00
2 Rusty Wallace Miller Lite/15,048	5.00	12.00
3 Dale Earnhardt Goodwrench/30,024	12.50	25.00
3 Dale Earnhardt Goodwrench No Bull raced/76,003	10.00	25.00
3 Dale Earnhardt Goodwrench Taz No Bull	15.00	30.00
3 Ron Hornaday NAPA/7560	4.00	10.00
3 Ron Hornaday NAPA 75th Anniv./7560	4.00	10.00
3 Ron Hornaday NAPA Monsters/7560	4.00	10.00
4 Bobby Hamilton Kodak	4.00	8.00
4 Bobby Hamilton Kodak Navy/10,080	4.00	10
5 Terry Labonte Froot Loops/16,272	5.00	10
5 Terry Labonte Kellogg's	5.00	12
7 Michael Waltrip Nations Rent	4.00	8
8 Jeff Burton Baby Ruth '90 T-bird/9720	4.00	8
8 Dale Earnhardt Jr. Bud	12.50	25
10 Jeff Green Nesquik	4.00	8
11 Jason Jarrett Rayovac/7560	4.00	8
11 Jason Jarrett Rayovac Promo blister	5.00	10
12 Jeremy Mayfield Mobil 1/9000	4.00	8
12 Jeremy Mayfield Mobil 1 World Series/8712	4.00	8
13 Robby Gordon Menards Monsters/7056	5.00	10
15 Tony Stewart Vision3 1996 Grand Prix/9720	5.00	10
15 Michael Waltrip Nations Rent/7560	4.00	8
18 Bobby Labonte Interstate Batteries	5.00	10
18 Bobby Labonte Interstate Batteries Frankenstein/9360	5.00	10
18/20 Bobby Labonte Interstate Batteries Tony Stewart Home Depot Chef Boyardee blister 2-car promo set	12.50	25
19 Dodge Show Car	4.00	10
20 Tony Stewart Home Depot	5.00	12
20 Tony Stewart Home Depot Brickyard/7500	5.00	15
20 Tony Stewart Home Depot Kids	6.00	15
24 Jeff Gordon DuPont/34,272	5.00	12
24 Jeff Gordon DuPont Millennium	7.50	15
24 Jeff Gordon Pepsi/22,752	6.00	12
25 Jerry Nadeau Holigan/7560	4.00	10
25 Jerry Nadeau Holigan Coast Guard/10,008	4.00	10
25 Kenny Wallace Lance	4.00	8
26 Jimmy Spencer Big K	4.00	10
27 Casey Atwood Castrol	4.00	10
28 Ricky Rudd Havoline	5.00	12
28 Ricky Rudd Havoline Marines/20,016	5.00	12
31 Dale Earnhardt Jr. Mom 'N' Pop's 1996 Monte Carlo	7.50	15
31 Mike Skinner Lowe's	4.00	10
31 Mike Skinner Lowe's Army	4.00	10
34 David Green AFG Busch Promo	3.00	8
36 Ken Schrader M&M's/10,896	5.00	10
36 Ken Schrader M&M's Green	6.00	12
36 Ken Schrader M&M's Keep Back	5.00	10
36 Ken Schrader M&M's Promo blister	5.00	10
40 Sterling Marlin Coors/7560	6.00	15
40 Sterling Marlin Coors Brooks & Dunn/7560	5.00	12
40 Sterling Marlin Coors Light/7560	5.00	12
40 Sterling Marlin Coors Light Black	5.00	12
42 Kenny Irwin BellSouth/7560	5.00	12
53 Hank Parker Jr. Team Marines/6552	4.00	10
55 Kenny Wallace Square D	4.00	10
55 Kenny Wallace Square D NASCAR Racers/4500	4.00	10
60 Geoffery Bodine Power Team	4.00	10
66 Darrell Waltrip Big K Route 66/9000	4.00	8
66 Darrell Waltrip Big K Route 66 Flames/12,744	4.00	8
67 Jeff Gordon Outback Steakhouse 1990 Grand Prix	6.00	12
71 Dave Marcis Realtree	5.00	10
75 Wally Dallenbach Powerpuff Girls/9000	4.00	8
77 Robert Pressley Jasper	4.00	10
88 Dale Jarrett Quality Care/20,016	6.00	12
88 Dale Jarrett Quality Care Air Force	6.00	12
94 Bill Elliott McDonald's/18,216	5.00	12
94 Bill Elliott McDonald's 25th Ann./20,016	5.00	12
00 Buckshot Jones Cheez-It	4.00	10
2000 NAPA Atlanta Promo in PVC box	2.00	5
2000 Sam Bass Promo in PVC box	4.00	10
NNO Armed Forces 5-car set in Promo blister 4. Bobby Hamilton/Navy 25. Jerry Nadeau/Coast Guard 28. Ricky Rudd/Marines	15.00	30

31. Mike Skinner/Army		
88. Dale Jarrett/Air Force		
) Armed Forces 5-car set Gold	40.00	100.00

2000 Action/RCCA 1:64

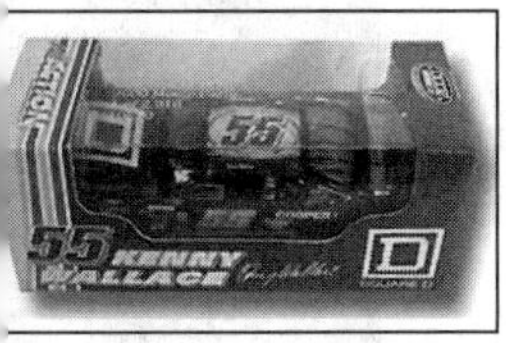

e cars are available solely through the club. Alcohol and cco sponsored cars were mounted on a clear base.

	EX	NM-MT
indy LaJoie Bob Evan's/2016	4.00	10.00
indy LaJoie Bob Evan's Monsters/1500	4.00	10.00
teve Park Pennzoil/3523	5.00	10.00
isty Wallace Miller Lite	12.00	20.00
ale Earnhardt Goodwrench/10,008	12.50	25.00
ale Earnhardt Goodwrench Peter Max/5544	35.00	60.00
ale Earnhardt Goodwrench Taz No Bull/17,000	20.00	50.00
n Hornaday NAPA/3528	4.00	10.00
n Hornaday NAPA Monsters/2736	5.00	10.00
Dale Earnhardt Dale Earnhardt Jr. No Bull 2-cars in tin/6504	45.00	80.00
obby Hamilton Kodak/3528	5.00	12.00
ark Martin Jim Magill Green 1983 Monte Carlo/7560	5.00	10.00
ichael Waltrip Nations Rent/2016	5.00	10.00
ff Burton Baby Ruth '90 T-bird/2520	5.00	10.00
ale Earnhardt Jr. Bud/10,000	15.00	30.00
ale Earnhardt Jr. Bud Olympic/5040	20.00	40.00
Jason Jarrett Rayovac/1512	4.00	10.00
obby Gordon Menards Monsters/1500	5.00	10.00
obby Labonte Interstate Batteries/2520	7.50	15.00
obby Labonte Interstate Batteries All Star Game/2880	10.00	20.00
obby Labonte Interstate Batteries NASCAR Racers/4500	7.50	15.00
ony Stewart Home Depot/10,000	6.00	15.00
ony Stewart Home Depot Kids	10.00	20.00
Jeff Gordon DuPont/10,008	10.00	20.00
eff Gordon DuPont Millennium/8496	12.50	25.00
eff Gordon DuPont Peanuts in lunch box/3800	50.00	100.00
eff Gordon DuPont Winston/1500	12.50	25.00
erry Nadeau Holigan/3528	5.00	12.00
Kenny Wallace Lance/2520	5.00	10.00
Jimmy Spencer Big K/1500	5.00	10.00
Casey Atwood Castrol/3500	6.00	15.00
Ricky Rudd Havoline/2520	6.00	15.00
Dale Earnhardt Jr. Mom 'N' Pop's 1996 Monte Carlo/10,000	12.50	25.00
Mike Skinner Lowe's/2520	5.00	10.00
Ken Schrader M&M's/3528	5.00	10.00
Ken Schrader M&M's July 4th/2520	5.00	12.00
Sterling Marlin Coors	12.50	25.00
Sterling Marlin Coors Light/2016	6.00	15.00
Sterling Marlin Coors Light Black/3528	6.00	15.00
Kenny Irwin BellSouth	12.00	20.00
Hank Parker Jr. Team Marines/1512	4.00	10.00
Kenny Wallace Square D/2016	4.00	10.00
Geoff Bodine Power Team/2520	5.00	10.00
Darrell Waltrip Big K Route 66/2520	5.00	10.00
Darrell Waltrip Big K Route 66 Flames/2520	5.00	10.00
Jeff Gordon Outback Steakhouse 1990 Grand Prix	6.00	15.00
Dave Marcis Realtree/1584	5.00	10.00
Wally Dallenbach Powerpuff Girls	5.00	10.00
Dale Jarrett Quality Care	6.00	15.00
Aaron's 312 Promo	10.00	20.00
Bill Elliott McDonald's/3042	6.00	15.00
Bill Elliott McDonald's 25th Ann./3528	6.00	15.00

00 Buckshot Jones Cheez-it Promo/1512	5.00	12.00
00 Atlanta Cracker Barrel 500 Promo/22,500	5.00	12.00

2000 Action/RCCA Total View 1:64

This set marks the debut of Total View, Actions top of the line 1:64. This car features a removable die-cast body that can be lifted from an authentically constructed roll cage and chassis, and snaps back on.

	EX	NM-MT
2 Rusty Wallace Miller Lite Harley-Davidson	12.50	25.00
3 Dale Earnhardt Goodwrench No Bull	40.00	80.00
3 Dale Earnhardt Goodwrench Peter Max/5760	50.00	100.00
4 Bobby Hamilton Kodak Navy	6.00	15.00
8 Dale Earnhardt Jr. Bud No Bull	18.00	30.00
8 Dale Earnhardt Jr. Bud Olympic/4032	20.00	40.00
24 Jeff Gordon DuPont Millennium	15.00	35.00
24 Jeff Gordon DuPont Peanuts/3024	12.50	25.00
24 Jeff Gordon Pepsi	15.00	25.00
25 Jerry Nadeau Holigan Coast Guard	6.00	15.00
28 Ricky Rudd Havoline/2544	6.00	15.00
28 Ricky Rudd Havoline Marines/2016	6.00	15.00
31 Mike Skinner Lowe's Army	6.00	15.00
88 Dale Jarrett Quality Care Air Force	12.00	25.00

2000 Action Total Concept 1:64

	EX	NM-MT
1 Randy LaJoie Bob Evan's Monsters/5832	6.00	15.00
2 Rusty Wallace Miller Lite Harley/20,808	10.00	20.00
3 Dale Earnhardt Goodwrench Peter Max paint/69,480	20.00	50.00
3 Ron Hornaday NAPA Monsters	6.00	15.00
4 Bobby Hamilton Kodak Navy	5.00	12.00
5 Terry Labonte Kellogg's Grinch	7.50	15.00
8 Dale Earnhardt Jr. Bud Olympic/26,568	10.00	20.00
13 Robby Gordon Menards Monsters	6.00	15.00
18 Bobby Labonte Interstate Batteries All Star Game/15,336	10.00	20.00
18 Bobby Labonte Interstate Batteries Monsters	10.00	20.00
19 Dodge Show Car	6.00	15.00
20 Tony Stewart Home Depot Kids/11,367	10.00	20.00
24 Jeff Gordon DuPont Peanuts/21,456	8.00	20.00
24 Jeff Gordon DuPont Winston/41,400	8.00	20.00
25 Jerry Nadeau Holigan Coast Guard	6.00	15.00
27 Casey Atwood Castrol Monsters	6.00	15.00
28 Ricky Rudd Havoline/5040	6.00	15.00
28 Ricky Rudd Havoline Marines/8712	6.00	15.00
31 Mike Skinner Lowe's Army/7128	5.00	12.00
36 Ken Schrader M&M's Halloween/7560	6.00	15.00
88 Dale Jarrett Quality Care Air Force	6.00	15.00
94 Bill Elliott McDonald's	6.00	15.00
94 Bill Elliott McDonald's McFlurry/7920	6.00	15.00

2001 Action Performance 1:64

These cars are packaged in an Action "AP" blister. The cardboard backer is red and black with a blueprint type drawing of a car in the background. The 2001 pieces look very similar to the 2002 releases, but can be identified by the copyright year found on the backs. Most of the 2001 cars also include the "Action Sports Image" logo on the front below the car.

	EX	NM-MT
3 Dale Earnhardt Goodwrench BP	5.00	12.00
3 Dale Earnhardt Goodwrench w/Sonic decal	15.00	30.00
3 Dale Earnhardt Goodwrench Promo in clear plastic box	12.50	25.00
24 Jeff Gordon DuPont Flames	4.00	8.00
29 Kevin Harvick Goodwrench	4.00	8.00
88 Dale Jarrett UPS	4.00	8.00

2001 Action Racing Collectables 1:64

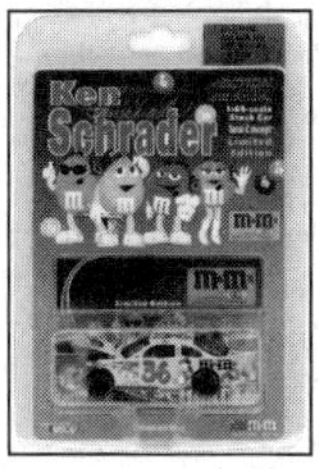

This series was issued in a clamshell type packaging with many pieces including the typical silver Action sticker with the car model information and production run total. Both Total Concept and regular issue pieces are included in the listing below. The Total Concept cars are hood open with a removable body.

	EX	NM-MT
1 Steve Park Pennzoil in Can/8688	15.00	25.00
1 Steve Park Pennzoil Sylvester&Tweety/24,912	10.00	20.00
2 Kerry Earnhardt Kannapolis Intimidators/20,016	7.50	15.00
2 Rusty Wallace Miller Lite in Can	15.00	25.00
2 Rusty Wallace Miller Lite Harley/14,592	7.50	15.00
2 Rusty Wallace Miller Light Harley in Can	15.00	25.00
2/29 Kevin Harvick AC Delco/Goodwrench 2-cars in tin/35,040	15.00	30.00
3 Dale Earnhardt Goodwrench/20,880	15.00	30.00
3 Dale Earnhardt Goodwrench Oreo/55,040	15.00	30.00
3 Dale Earnhardt Goodwrench Oreo Tin/34,161	20.00	40.00
3 Dale Earnhardt Goodwrench Talladega No Bull Win	12.50	25.00
5 Terry Labonte Kellogg's/7560	10.00	20.00
5 Terry Labonte Kellogg's Wile E. Coyote and Road Runner/10,080	12.50	25.00
8 Dale Earnhardt Jr. Bud in can/30,768	30.00	60.00
8 Dale Earnhardt Jr. Bud MLB All-Star/30,060	25.00	40.00
9 Bill Elliott Dodge/21,024	6.00	12.00
9 Bill Elliott Dodge Muhammad Ali/24,984	5.00	12.00
9 Bill Elliott Dodge Spider-Man Lunch Box	10.00	20.00
9 Bill Elliott Dodge Spider-Man Promo in blister	6.00	12.00
10 Johnny Benson Valvoline James Dean/10,080	6.00	12.00
11 Darrell Waltrip Bud '85MC in a can/21,000	6.00	15.00
15 Michael Waltrip NAPA	10.00	20.00
15 Michael Waltrip NAPA Stars&Stripes/22,104	10.00	20.00
18 Bobby Labonte Interstate Batteries/10,500	10.00	20.00
18 Bobby Labonte Interstate Batteries in a Coke Bottle/21,524	10.00	25.00
18 Bobby Labonte Interstate Batteries Jurassic Park 3/16,128	10.00	20.00
18/20 Bobb Labonte Tony Stewart Coke Bear 2-car promo blister	7.50	15.00
19 Casey Atwood Dodge	6.00	12.00
19 Casey Atwood Dodge Mountain Dew in a can/16,128	12.00	25.00
19 Casey Atwood Dodge Spider-Man/14,112	7.50	15.00
20 Tony Stewart Home Depot/14,472	10.00	20.00
20 Tony Stewart Home Depot Coke Bear in Coke bottle/20,516	12.50	25.00
20 Tony Stewart Home Depot Jurassic Park 3/19,128	10.00	20.00
24 Jeff Gordon DuPont Bugs Bunny/50,496	15.00	30.00
24 Jeff Gordon DuPont Flames	15.00	30.00
24 Jeff Gordon DuPont Flames 2001 Championship in tin/37,560	10.00	20.00
24 Jeff Gordon Pepsi in Can	12.50	25.00
28 Ricky Rudd Havoline in oil bottle/9024	10.00	25.00
28 Ricky Rudd Havoline Bud Shoot Out/8712	12.00	20.00
28 Ricky Rudd Havoline Need for Speed Regular Promo	4.00	10.00
28 Ricky Rudd Havoline Need for Speed Custom Promo	4.00	10.00
28 Ricky Rudd Havoline Need for Speed Special Promo	4.00	10.00
29 Kevin Harvick Goodwrench/44,568	10.00	25.00
29 Kevin Harvick Goodwrench AOL/30,456	10.00	20.00
29 Kevin Harvick Goodwrench Taz/52,704	10.00	20.00
29 Kevin Harvick Goodwrench Taz QVC 4-car set in tin/2000	25.00	50.00
30 Jeff Green AOL Daffy Duck/8568	7.50	15.00
31 Mike Skinner Lowe's Yosemite Sam/12,888	6.00	12.00
36 Ken Schrader M&M's/9576	6.00	12.00
36 Ken Schrader M&M's Halloween/12,096	6.00	12.00
36 Ken Schrader M&M's July 4th/7776	6.00	12.00
36 Ken Schrader Snickers/8784	6.00	12.00
40 Sterling Marlin Coors Light in a can/15,408	12.50	25.00
40 Sterling Marlin Coors Light Kiss/24,672	7.50	15.00
55 Bobby Hamilton Square D Marvin Martian	6.00	15.00
88 Dale Jarrett UPS/23,112	12.00	20.00
88 Dale Jarrett UPS Flames/37,224	10.00	20.00
NNO Hendrick 100th Win 8-car set in tin/7560	30.00	80.00

2001 Action/RCCA 1:64

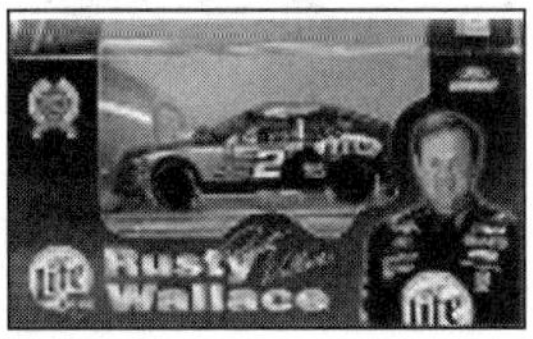

	EX	NM-MT
2 Kerry Earnhardt Kannapolis Intimidators/1584	12.50	25.00
2 Rusty Wallace Miller Lite/1584	15.00	30.00
2 Rusty Wallace Miller Lite Harley/3600	10.00	20.00
3 Dale Earnhardt Goodwrench/3024	40.00	80.00
3 Dale Earnhardt Goodwrench Platinum 7-car set/5004	50.00	100.00
3 Dale Earnhardt Goodwrench Oreo/3168	40.00	60.00
5 Terry Labonte Kellogg's/1584	15.00	30.00
5 Terry Labonte Kellogg's Wile E./Road Runner	12.50	25.00
8 Dale Earnhardt Jr. Bud/2016	25.00	50.00
8 Dale Earnhardt Jr. Bud MLB All-Star/5040	25.00	50.00
9 Bill Elliott Dodge/3600	15.00	30.00
9 Bill Elliott Dodge Muhammad Ali/1776	15.00	30.00
9 Bill Elliott Dodge Spider-Man/2160	15.00	30.00
10 Johnny Benson Valvoline James Dean	10.00	20.00
15 Michael Waltrip NAPA/1584	15.00	30.00
15 Michael Waltrip NAPA Stars&Stripes/1104	12.50	25.00
18 Bobby Labonte Interstate Batteries/1584	15.00	30.00
18 Bobby Labonte Interstate Batteries Coke Bear/1800	10.00	20.00
18 Bobby Labonte Interstate Batteries Jurassic Park 3/1484	10.00	20.00
19 Casey Atwood Dodge/1584	10.00	25.00
19 Casey Atwood Dodge Mountain Dew Color Chrome/1800	15.00	30.00
19 Casey Atwood Dodge Spider-Man/1584	12.50	25.00
20 Tony Stewart Home Depot/2594	12.50	25.00
20 Tony Stewart Home Depot Coke Bear/1800	10.00	20.00
20 Tony Stewart Home Depot Jurassic Park 3/1584	20.00	40.00
24 Jeff Gordon DuPont/3312	25.00	40.00
24 Jeff Gordon DuPont Bugs Bunny in lunch box/5004	20.00	40.00
24 Jeff Gordon Pepsi/1584	25.00	40.00
28 Ricky Rudd Havoline	15.00	30.00
28 Ricky Rudd Havoline Bud Shoot Out/1584	10.00	25.00
29 Kevin Harvick Goodwrench/4272	12.50	25.00
29 Kevin Harvick Goodwrench AOL/3888	10.00	20.00
29 Kevin Harvick Goodwrench Taz in lunch box/4008	18.00	30.00
29 Kevin Harvick Goodwrench Nilla Wafers Promo	6.00	15.00
31 Mike Skinner Lowe's Yosemite Sam/1584	10.00	20.00
36 Ken Schrader M&M's July 4th/1584	10.00	20.00
36 Ken Schrader Snickers	6.00	15.00
40 Sterling Marlin Coors Light/1584	12.50	25.00
40 Sterling Marlin Coors Light Kiss/1584	12.50	25.00
88 Dale Jarrett UPS	12.50	25.00

2001 Action/RCCA Elite 1:64

New detail for this year includes opening hood and trunk, better engine and chassis detail. Alcohol cars are on a clear base.

	EX	NM-MT
1 Steve Park Pennzoil Sylvester&Tweety/1584	15.00	30.00
2 Kerry Earnhardt Kannapolis Intimidators/1584	15.00	30.00
2 Rusty Wallace Miller Lite/1104	25.00	50.00
2 Rusty Wallace Miller Lite Harley-Davidson	30.00	60.00
3 Dale Earnhardt Goodwrench/2976	50.00	100.00
3 Dale Earnhardt Goodwrench Metal/7500	75.00	150.00
3 Dale Earnhardt Goodwrench Oreo/3168	50.00	100.00
5 Terry Labonte Kellogg's	20.00	40.00
8 Dale Earnhardt Jr. Bud/2016	30.00	80.00
8 Dale Earnhardt Jr. Bud All-Star/2976	50.00	100.00
15 Michael Waltrip NAPA Stars&Stripes/1104	15.00	30.00
18 Bobby Labonte Interstate Batteries	15.00	40.00
18 Bobby Labonte Interstate Batteries Coke Bear/1296	15.00	30.00
18 Bobby Labonte Interstate Batteries Jurassic Park 3/1104	15.00	30.00
20 Tony Stewart Home Depot/1824	15.00	40.00
20 Tony Stewart Home Depot Coke Bear/1296	15.00	40.00
20 Tony Stewart Home Depot Jurassic Park 3/1104	15.00	40.00
24 Jeff Gordon DuPont Flames/2688	30.00	60.00
24 Jeff Gordon DuPont Bugs Bunny/3960	20.00	40.00
24 Jeff Gordon Pepsi/1104	30.00	60.00
28 Ricky Rudd Havoline	15.00	30.00
29 Kevin Harvick Goodwrench/2160	40.00	75.00
29 Kevin Harvick Goodwrench AOL/3000	15.00	30.00
29 Kevin Harvick Goodwrench Taz/3024	15.00	30.00
36 Ken Schrader M&M's/1584	12.50	30.00
88 Dale Jarrett UPS	25.00	50.00
88 Dale Jarrett UPS Flames/1800	15.00	30.00
NNO Looney Tunes/1800	20.00	40.00

2002 Action Performance 1:64

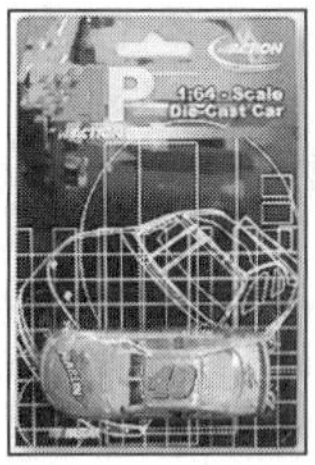

These cars are packaged in an Action "AP" blister. The cardboard backer is red and black with a larger blueprint type drawing of a car in the background versusu the 2001 release. The 2002 releases can be identified by the copyright year found on the backs and the lack of the "Action Sports Image" logo on the front.

	EX	NM-MT
2 Rusty Wallace Rusty	3.00	6.00
3 Dale Earnhardt Goodwrench	4.00	8.00
8 Dale Earnhardt Jr Dale Jr.	4.00	8.00
18 Bobby Labonte Interstate Batteries	3.00	6.00
20 Tony Stewart Home Depot	3.00	6.00
24 Jeff Gordon DuPont Flames	4.00	8.00
28 Ricky Rudd Havoline	3.00	6.00
29 Kevin Harvick Goodwrench	3.00	6.00
40 Sterling Marlin	3.00	6.00

	EX	NM-MT
Sterling		
88 Dale Jarrett UPS	3.00	6.00

2002 Action Racing Collectables 1:64

	EX	NM-MT
1 Dale Earnhardt Jr. Coke '98 Monte Carlo in vending machine tin/25,883	15.00	30.00
1 Jeff Gordon Autolite '89 T-bird/13,464	6.00	12.00
1 Steve Park Pennzoil in oil filter/16,716	10.00	20.00
2 Dale Earnhardt Coke '80 Pontiac in a Coke can/61,680	6.00	15.00
2 Dale Earnhardt Wrangler '79 Monte Carlo/30,744	6.00	15.00
2 Rusty Wallace MGD 1991 Thunderbird in a can/16,272	10.00	20.00
2 Rusty Wallace Miller Lite in a bottle/39,288	10.00	20.00
2 Rusty Wallace Miller Lite Elvis/24,864 in a tin box	10.00	20.00
2 Rusty Wallace Miller Lite Harley Flames/16,680	10.00	20.00
2 Rusty Wallace Miller Lite Flames/9000	10.00	20.00
3 Dale Earnhardt Coke '98 Monte Carlo in vending machine tin/25,883	15.00	30.00
3 Dale Earnhardt Jr. Nilla Wafers/57,600	10.00	20.00
3 Dale Earnhardt Jr. Nilla Wafers/Oreo Color Chrome set/8333	20.00	35.00
3 Dale Earnhardt Jr. Oreo/66,096	10.00	20.00
3 Dale Earnhardt Jr. Oreo Promo in box	10.00	20.00
3/3 Dale Earnhardt Dale Earnhardt Jr. Oreo White Gold 2-car set in tin/7560	35.00	60.00
4 Mike Skinner Kodak Max Yosemite Sam/8568	5.00	12.00
5 Terry Labonte Cheez-It/7056	7.50	15.00
5 Terry Labonte Kellogg's in cereal box/15,360	5.00	12.00
5 Terry Labonte Kellogg's Road Runner and Wile E.Coyote/10,872	5.00	12.00
7 Casey Atwood Sirius/8640	5.00	12.00
7 Casey Atwood Sirius Muppets/8064	5.00	12.00
8 Dale Earnhardt Jr. Bud in bottle/80,016	12.50	25.00
8 Dale Earnhardt Jr. Bud MLB All-Star/51,984	10.00	20.00
8 Dale Earnhardt Jr. Bud All-Star 2001 and 2002 2-car Color Chrome set/8888	20.00	35.00
8 Dale Earnhardt Jr. Looney Tunes/41,688	10.00	20.00
9 Bill Elliott Dodge in tin/15,120	6.00	15.00
9 Bill Elliott Dodge Muppet/14,040	7.50	15.00
10 Johnny Benson Vavoline in oil can/7656	6.00	12.00
10 Johnny Benson Valvoline Muppet/11,664	5.00	12.00
12 Kerry Earnhardt JaniKing Yosemite Sam/10,008	5.00	12.00
12 Kerry Earnhardt Supercuts	6.00	12.00
12 Kerry Earnhardt Supercuts Promo in clear box	5.00	10.00
12 Ryan Newman Alltel/11,664	6.00	15.00
12 Ryan Newman Alltel ROY/6640	7.50	15.00
12 Ryan Newman Mobil 1/9936	6.00	15.00
15 Dale Earnhardt Wrangler 1979 Pontiac Ventura/30,744	6.00	15.00
15 Michael Waltrip NAPA/16,920	7.50	15.00
15 Michael Waltrip NAPA Stars&Stripes/10,388	7.50	15.00
18 Bobby Labonte Interstate Batteries/18,864	7.50	15.00
18 Bobby Labonte Interstate Batteries Muppet/14,544	7.50	15.00
18 Bobby Labonte Let's Roll/8856	12.50	25.00
18 Bobby Labonte Let's Roll in tin/4464	15.00	30.00
19 Jeremy Mayfield Dodge/11,448	6.00	12.00
19 Jeremy Mayfield Dodge Muppet/11,952	5.00	12.00
19 Jeremy Mayfield Mountain Dew in vending machine/12,660	12.50	25.00
20 Tony Stewart Home Depot/23,040	10.00	20.00
20 Tony Stewart Home Depot 2002 Winston Cup Champion/17,640	6.00	15.00
20 Tony Stewart Home Depot Promo Old Spice window box	5.00	12.00
20 Tony Stewart Home Depot Promo Maintenance Warehouse blister	10.00	20.00
20 Tony Stewart Home Depot Peanuts Black/15,048	10.00	20.00
20 Tony Stewart Home Depot Peanuts Orange/15,048	10.00	20.00
20 Tony Stewart Home Depot Peanuts 2-car set promo blister	7.50	15.00
20 Tony Stewart Old Spice Promo in box	18.00	30.00
21 Jy Sauter Jeff Green Rockwell Promo blister	10.00	20.00
24 Jeff Gordon DuPont in paint can/62,016	6.00	15.00
24 Jeff Gordon DuPont 4-cars/2000	45.00	80.00
24 Jeff Gordon DuPont 200th Anniversary/52,056	10.00	20.00
24 Jeff Gordon DuPont Bugs Bunny/24,312	10.00	20.00
24 Jeff Gordon Elmo/17,424	10.00	20.00
24 Jeff Gordon Pepsi Daytona in vending machine/35,952	12.50	25.00
24 Jeff Gordon Pepsi Talladega in a can/23,712	12.50	25.00
25 Joe Nemechek UAW Speedy Gonzalez/8640	5.00	12.00
28 Ricky Rudd Havoline/16,272	6.00	12.00
28 Ricky Rudd Havoline Iron Man/9000	7.50	15.00
28 Ricky Rudd Havoline Muppet/14,832	5.00	12.00
29 Kevin Harvick Action ET/18,000	7.50	15.00
29 Kevin Harvick Goodwrench/68,112	7.50	15.00
29 Kevin Harvick Goodwrench ET/40,032	7.50	15.00
29 Kevin Harvick Goodwrench Now Sell Tires/15,408	7.50	15.00
29 Kevin Harvick Goodwrench Taz/12,024	7.50	20.00
29 Kevin Harvick Sylvania/9000	6.00	15.00
30 Jeff Green AOL/12,096	7.50	15.00
30 Jeff Green AOL Daffy Duck/9720	7.50	15.00
30 Jeff Green AOL Scooby-Doo/10,296	7.50	15.00
31 Robby Gordon Cingular/7992	7.50	15.00
31 Robby Gordon Cingular Pepe le Pew/10,224	5.00	12.00
36 Ken Schrader M&M's/10,008	7.50	15.00
36 Ken Schrader M&M's Halloween/8640	5.00	12.00
36 Ken Schrader M&M's July 4th/5976	5.00	12.00
40 Sterling Marlin Coors Light in a bottle/32,784	12.50	25.00
40 Sterling Marlin Coors Original in a can/18,288	12.50	25.00
41 Jimmy Spencer Energizer/7560	5.00	12.00
41 Jimmy Spencer Target/10,080	7.50	15.00
41 Jimmy Spencer Target Muppet/12,240	10.00	20.00
48 Jimmie Johnson Lowe's/13,608	12.50	25.00
48 Jimmie Johnson Lowe's Sylvester and Tweety/19,689	10.00	20.00
55 Bobby Hamilton Square D Marvin/8064	5.00	12.00
88 Dale Jarrett UPS/38,088	6.00	15.00
88 Dale Jarrett UPS Muppet/22,824	5.00	12.00
88 Dale Jarrett UPS Van Color Chrome/22,752	7.50	20.00
02 Tropicana 400 Promo blister	3.00	8.00
NNO Dale Earnhardt Legacy/29,088	7.50	15.00
NNO Looney Tunes Rematch/13,464	6.00	15.00
NNO Muppet Show 25th Anniversary/19,152	5.00	12.00

2002 Action/RCCA 1:64

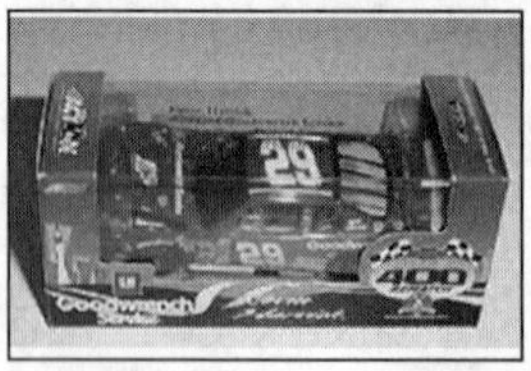

	EX	NM-MT
1 Dale Earnhardt Jr. Coke 1998 Monte Carlo in vending machine/3000	12.50	25.00
1 Steve Park Pennzoil/1584	7.50	15.00
2 Dale Earnhardt Coke '80 Pontiac/6480	10.00	20.00
2 Rusty Wallace Miller Lite/1584	15.00	25.00
2 Rusty Wallace Miller Lite Elvis/1800	10.00	25.00
2 Rusty Wallace Miller Lite Harley Flames/1800	15.00	30.00
2 Rusty Wallace Miller Lite Flames/1596	12.50	25.00
2/3 Dale Earnhardt 7-car set Gold/10,000 1980 Mike Curb car 1986 Wrangler car 1987 Wrangler car 1990 Goodwrench car 1991 Goodwrench car 1993 Goodwrench car 1994 Goodwrench car	90.00	150.00
2K2 Childress Racing Pit Practice/2448	7.50	15.00
3 Dale Earnhardt Goodwrench Plus No Bull 76th Win/6048	12.50	25.00
3 Dale Earnhardt Jr. Nilla Wafers/6000	12.50	25.00
3 Dale Earnhardt Jr. Nilla Wafers Promo	4.00	10.00
3 Dale Earnhardt Jr. Oreo/6000	12.50	25.00
3 Dale Earnhardt Jr. Oreo Promo	4.00	10.00
4 Mike Skinner Kodak Max Yosemite Sam/1584	7.50	15.00
5 Terry Labonte Cheez-It/1584	10.00	20.00
5 Terry Labonte Kellogg's/1584	10.00	20.00
5 Terry Labonte Kellogg's Road Runner & Wile E.Coyote/1584	10.00	20.00
7 Casey Atwood Sirius/1584	10.00	20.00
8 Dale Earnhardt Jr. Bud Color Chrome/5040	12.50	25.00
8 Dale Earnhardt Jr. Bud All-Star/6000	12.50	25.00
8 Dale Earnhardt Jr. Looney Tunes/6000	12.50	25.00
9 Bill Elliott Dodge/1584	10.00	20.00
9 Bill Elliott Dodge Muppet/1800	10.00	20.00
10 Johnny Benson Valvoline/1584	10.00	20.00
12 Kerry Earnhardt 10-10-220/1584	10.00	20.00
12 Kerry Earnhardt JaniKing Yosemite Sam/1584	10.00	20.00
12 Kerry Earnhardt Supercuts/1584	10.00	20.00
12 Ryan Newman Alltel/1584	15.00	30.00
12 Ryan Newman Mobil 1/1584	15.00	30.00
15 Dale Earnhardt Wrangler 1979 Pontiac Ventura/4200	10.00	20.00
15 Michael Waltrip NAPA/1584	10.00	20.00
15 Michael Waltrip NAPA Stars and Stripes/1584	7.50	15.00
18 Bobby Labonte Interstate Batteries/1584	10.00	20.00
18 Bobby Labonte Interstate Batteries Muppet/1584	10.00	20.00
18 Bobby Labonte Let's Roll/1584	15.00	25.00
19 Jeremy Mayfield Dodge/1584	10.00	20.00
19 Jeremy Mayfield Mountain Dew/1584	10.00	20.00
20 Tony Stewart Home Depot/1584	15.00	30.00
20 Tony Stewart Home Depot 2002 Champion Color Chrome/1212	12.00	20.00
20 Tony Stewart Home Depot Peanuts Black/1800	12.50	25.00
20 Tony Stewart Home Depot Peanuts Orange/1800	12.50	25.00
24 Jeff Gordon DuPont 200th Anniversary/3312	12.50	25.00
24 Jeff Gordon DuPont Bugs Bunny/4032	10.00	20.00
24 Jeff Gordon DuPont Flames/2856	12.50	25.00
24 Jeff Gordon Elmo/4032	15.00	25.00
24 Jeff Gordon Pepsi Daytona/3600	12.00	20.00
24 Jeff Gordon Pepsi Talladega Color Chrome/1584	12.00	20.00
25 Joe Nemechek UAW Speedy Gonzalez/1584	7.50	15.00
28 Ricky Rudd Havoline/1584	10.00	20.00
28 Ricky Rudd Havoline Iron Man/1584	10.00	20.00
28 Ricky Rudd Havoline Muppet/1584	10.00	20.00
29 Kevin Harvick Action ET/2304	10.00	20.00
29 Kevin Harvick Goodwrench/4500	10.00	20.00
29 Kevin Harvick Goodwrench ET/4008	10.00	20.00
29 Kevin Harvick Goodwrench Now Sell Tires/2304	10.00	20.00
29 Kevin Harvick Goodwrench Taz/1584	10.00	20.00
29 Kevin Harvick Sonic/1584	10.00	20.00
29 Kevin Harvick Sylvania/1800	12.50	25.00
30 Jeff Green AOL/1584	7.50	15.00
30 Jeff Green AOL Daffy Duck/1584	6.00	12.00
30 Jeff Green AOL Scooby-Doo/1584	10.00	20.00
31 Robby Gordon Cingular/1584	7.50	15.00
31 Robby Gordon Cingular Pepe le Pew/1584	6.00	12.00
36 Ken Schrader M&M's Halloween/1584	10.00	20.00
36 Ken Schrader M&M's July 4th/1584	10.00	20.00
40 Sterling Marlin Coors Light/1800	10.00	20.00
40 Sterling Marlin Coors Original/1800	10.00	20.00
41 Jimmy Spencer Energizer/1584	7.50	15.00
41 Jimmy Spencer Target/1584	7.50	15.00
48 Jimmie Johnson Lowe's/1584	10.00	20.00
48 Jimmie Johnson Lowe's Power of Pride/5928	10.00	20.00
48 Jimmie Johnson Lowe's Sylv.&Tweety/2016	10.00	20.00
55 Bobby Hamilton Square D Marvin/1584	10.00	20.00
88 Dale Jarrett UPS/2880	10.00	20.00
88 Dale Jarrett UPS Muppet/2196	10.00	20.00
91 Hank Parker Jr. USG Promo	15.00	30.00
NNO Dale Earnhardt Legacy/3036	10.00	20.00
NNO Looney Tunes Rematch/1584	7.50	15.00
NNO Muppet Show 25th Ann./2016	7.50	15.00

2002 Action/RCCA Elite 1:64

	EX	NM-MT
1 Steve Park Pennzoil/1200	12.50	25.00
2 Rusty Wallace Miller Lite/1584	18.00	30.00
2 Rusty Wallace Miller Lite Elvis/1800	18.00	30.00
2 Rusty Wallace Miller Lite Harley Flames/1800	20.00	35.00
2 Rusty Wallace Miller Lite Flames/1212	18.00	30.00
2K2 Childress Racing Pit Practice/2160	15.00	25.00
3 Dale Earnhardt Jr. Nilla Wafers/4000	18.00	30.00
3 Dale Earnhardt Jr. Oreo/4000	18.00	30.00
5 Terry Labonte Kellogg's/1200	12.50	25.00
8 Dale Earnhardt Jr. Bud Color Chrome/3600	20.00	35.00
8 Dale Earnhardt Jr. Bud All-Star/4612	15.00	30.00
8 Dale Earnhardt Jr. Looney Tunes/4008	15.00	30.00
12 Kerry Earnhardt 10-10-220/1200	10.00	20.00
12 Kerry Earnhardt JaniKing Yosemite Sam/1200	10.00	20.00
12 Kerry Earnhardt Supercuts/1584	12.50	25.00
12 Ryan Newman Alltel/1584	15.00	30.00
12 Ryan Newman Mobil 1/1584	15.00	30.00
15 Michael Waltrip NAPA Stars and Stripes/1152A	12.50	25.00
18 Bobby Labonte Interstate Batteries/1200	12.50	25.00
18 Bobby Labonte Interstate Batteries Muppet/1200	15.00	25.00
20 Tony Stewart Home Depot/1200	20.00	40.00
20 Tony Stewart Home Depot 2002 Champion Color Chrome/1212	15.00	30.00
20 Tony Stewart Home Depot Peanuts Black/1584	18.00	30.00
20 Tony Stewart Home Depot Peanuts Orange/1584	18.00	30.00
24 Jeff Gordon DuPont 200th Anniversary/3000	15.00	30.00
24 Jeff Gordon DuPont Flames/2160	15.00	30.00
24 Jeff Gordon DuPont Bugs Bunny/4008	15.00	30.00
24 Jeff Gordon Elmo/2016	15.00	30.00
24 Jeff Gordon Pepsi Daytona/3000	15.00	30.00
24 Jeff Gordon Pepsi Talladega/1200	15.00	30.00
28 Ricky Rudd Havoline/1200	12.50	25.00
28 Ricky Rudd Havoline Iron Man/1200	12.50	25.00
28 Ricky Rudd Havoline Muppet/1200	12.50	25.00
29 Kevin Harvick Action ET/2016	15.00	25.00
29 Kevin Harvick Goodwrench/4000	12.50	25.00
29 Kevin Harvick Goodwrench Now Sell Tires/2004	12.50	25.00
29 Kevin Harvick Goodwrench ET/3400	15.00	25.00
29 Kevin Harvick Goodwrench Taz/1200	15.00	25.00
29 Kevin Harvick Sonic/1536-A	15.00	30.00
29 Kevin Harvick Sylvania/1200	15.00	30.00
30 Jeff Green AOL Scooby-Doo/1200	15.00	25.00
31 Robby Gordon Cingular/1584	10.00	20.00
48 Jimmie Johnson Lowe's/1584	20.00	40.00
48 Jimmie Johnson Lowe's Power of Pride/1584	12.50	30.00
48 Jimmie Johnson Lowe's Sylvester and Tweety/1584	15.00	30.00
88 Dale Jarrett UPS/1584	12.50	25.00
88 Dale Jarrett UPS Muppet/1800	12.50	25.00
NNO Dale Earnhardt Legacy/2028	18.00	30.00
NNO Looney Tunes Rematch/1200	10.00	20.00

2003 Action Performance 1:64

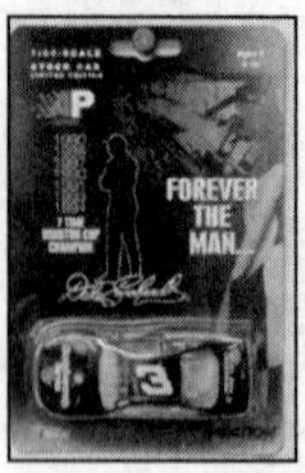

	EX	NM-M
2 Rusty Wallace Rusty	3.00	6.
3 Dale Earnhardt Goodwrench Forever the Man blister	4.00	8.
8 Dale Earnhardt Jr. Dale Jr.	4.00	8.
8 Dale Earnhardt Jr. JR	4.00	8.
18 Bobby Labonte Interstate Batteries	3.00	6.
20 Tony Stewart Home Depot	4.00	8.
24 Jeff Gordon DuPont Flames	4.00	8.
29 Kevin Harvick Goodwrench	4.00	8.
88 Dale Jarrett UPS	3.00	6.

2003 Action Racing Collectables 1:64

	EX	NM-M
1 Dale Earnhardt True Value '99 IROC Blue/12,096	7.50	15.
1 Dale Earnhardt True Value '00 IROC Lt.Blue/11,736	7.50	15.
1 Dale Earnhardt True Value '01 IROC Green/11,736	7.50	15.
1 Steve Park Pennzoil/6912	5.00	12.
2 Rusty Wallace Miller Lite/15,360	10.00	20.
2 Rusty Wallace Miller Lite Victory Lap/5976	7.50	15.
2 Rusty Wallace Miller Lite 600th/9936	10.00	20.
2 Rusty Wallace Miller Time Live Goo Goo Dolls/9360	6.00	15.
3 Dale Earnhardt Foundation/30,888	7.50	15.
3 Dale Earnhardt Goodwrench No Bull 2000 Monte Carlo/15,264	10.00	20.
3 Dale Earnhardt Victory Lap/14,040	7.50	15.
5 Terry Labonte Kellogg's/5808	6.00	15.
5 Terry Labonte Kellogg's Victory Lap/8532	6.00	15.
7 Alan Kulwicki Victory Lap/8676	5.00	12.
8 Dale Earnhardt Jr. Bud/36,288	10.00	20.
8 Dale Earnhardt Jr. Bud All-Star Game/12,984	10.00	20.
8 Dale Earnhardt Jr. Bud No Bull 2000 Monte Carlo/15,264	10.00	20.
8 Dale Earnhardt Jr. Bud StainD/20,520	7.50	15.
8 Dale Earnhardt Jr. Dirty Mo Posse/38,936	6.00	15.
8 Dale Earnhardt Jr. Earnhardt Tribute Concert/35,568	7.50	15.
8 Dale Earnhardt Jr. Oreo Ritz/46,944	7.50	15.
8 Steve Park Cheese Nips/5400	5.00	12.
8 Steve Park Maxwell House/6120	5.00	12.
8 Tony Stewart 3 Doors Down/14,976	7.50	15.
9 Bill Elliott Coors Winston Million 1985 Thunderbird in can/6088	10.00	20.
9 Bill Elliott Coors 1987 Thunderbird/6912	7.50	15.
9 Bill Elliott Coors 1988 Thunderbird in can	10.00	20.
9 Bill Elliott Dodge/9432	7.50	15.
9 Bill Elliott Dodge Lion King/3456	7.50	15.
9 Bill Elliott Dodge Victory Lap/5472	7.50	15.
9 Bill Elliott Dodge 10th Anniversary Brickyard/5292	7.50	15.
11 Dale Earnhardt Jr. True Value 1999 IROC Orange/10,728	7.50	15.

ell Waltrip 7.50 15.00
tory Lap/8856
Yarborough 5.00 12.00
tory Lap/4320
hael Waltrip 5.00 12.00
PA/9072
hael Waltrip 5.00 12.00
PA Hootie & the Blowfish/7200
ael Waltrip 5.00 12.00
PA Nilla Wafers
hael Waltrip 5.00 12.00
PA Stars & Stripes/7992
by Labonte 7.50 15.00
erstate Batteries/10,728
by Labonte 7.50 15.00
erstate Batteries Hulk/5256
by Labonte 7.50 15.00
erstate Batteries
tory Lap/9324
Earnhardt 7.50 15.00
don Asphalt
7 Malibu/11,376
my Mayfield 5.00 12.00
dge/5760
Bliss 12.50 25.00
ckwell Automation Promo
blister package
Stewart 7.50 15.00
me Depot/21,384
Stewart 7.50 15.00
me Depot Declaration
Independence/16,344
in Harvick 7.50 15.00
yday/6912
nny Sauter 5.00 12.00
yday/1440
by Allison 5.00 12.00
tory Lap/4608
Gordon 7.50 15.00
okie Monster Foundation/14,976
Gordon 7.50 15.00
Pont Flames/24,696
Gordon 8.00 20.00
Pont Flames Victory Lap/13,212
Gordon 7.50 15.00
Pont Wright Bros./17,856
Gordon 7.50 15.00
Pont Yosemite Sam/11,544
Gordon 7.50 15.00
psi
Gordon 7.50 15.00
psi Billion $/13,752
Davey Allison 15.00 30.00
aco
nie McMurray
voline 2-car set/6480
in Harvick 7.50 15.00
odwrench/13,968
in Harvick 7.50 15.00
odwrench Sugar Ray/6192
in Harvick 7.50 15.00
ap-On/12,528
Green 5.00 12.00
L
Driver Association 10.00 20.00
L Promo in PVC box
by Gordon 5.00 12.00
gular black/6984
by Gordon 5.00 12.00
gular orange/5976
y Stewart 7.50 15.00
naco Diamond Rio
perTruck
ott Sadler 5.00 12.00
M's/9576
ott Sadler 5.00 12.00
M's Groovy/8424
ott Sadler 5.00 12.00
M's Halloween/6696
ey Mears 5.00 12.00
get/5832
ie McMurray 10.00 20.00
voline/9648
ie McMurray 5.00 12.00
voline Terminator 3/8784
hard Petty 7.50 15.00
1975 Dodge Charger/6294
hard Petty 7.50 15.00
nkees 100th
niversary/6408
hard Petty 7.50 15.00
tory Lap/10,620
istian Fittipaldi 5.00 12.00
nkees 100th Ann/4248
e Petty 5.00 12.00
orgia Pacific/6264
e Petty 5.00 12.00
nds to Victory/3240
k Kimmel 5.00 12.00
vance Auto Parts Promo
blister pack
mie Johnson 7.50 15.00
we's/19,008
mie Johnson 7.50 15.00
we's Power of Pride
nie Johnson 10.00 20.00
we's SpongeBob/11,532
ny Parsons 5.00 12.00
tory Lap/4320
n Keller 20.00 40.00
ft 100 Years
omo in window box
y Earnhardt 5.00 12.00
Tamales black/10,584
e Jarrett 7.50 15.00
S/10,584
e Jarrett 7.50 15.00
S Store/4320
Jarrett 7.50 15.00
S Victory Lap/8820
hael Waltrip 5.00 12.00
ron's Rent
in the Hat/3888
hael Waltrip 5.00 12.00
ron's Rent Terminator 3/6912
hael Waltrip 5.00 12.00
ron's Rent 3 Stooges/6408
y Nadeau 5.00 12.00
my/5616
k Event Car/5256 7.50 15.00
icana 400 Promo in bottle 15.00 25.00

NNO Winston Cup Champions 125.00 200.00
14-car set in oak case
Bobby Allison
Dale Earnhardt
Bill Elliott
Jeff Gordon
Dale Jarrett
Alan Kulwicki
Bobby Labonte
Terry Labonte
Benny Parsons
Richard Petty
Tony Stewart
Rusty Wallace
Darrell Waltrip
Cale Yarborough/3492

2003 Action/RCCA 1:64

EX NM-MT
1 Steve Park 7.50 15.00
Pennzoil/1020
2 Rusty Wallace 10.00 20.00
Miller Lite/1500
2 Rusty Wallace 8.00 20.00
Miller Lite 600 Starts/1012
2 Rusty Wallace 8.00 20.00
Miller Time Live
Goo Goo Dolls/1444
3 Dale Earnhardt 10.00 20.00
Earnhardt Foundation/3604
3 Dale Earnhardt 12.50 25.00
Victory Lap/1500
5 Terry Labonte 7.50 15.00
Kellogg's/1020
8 Dale Earnhardt Jr. 15.00 30.00
Bud/3748
8 Dale Earnhardt Jr. 12.50 25.00
Bud All-Star Game/3316
8 Dale Earnhardt Jr. 20.00 35.00
Bud All-Star Game
in baseball tin/2340
8 Dale Earnhardt Jr. 10.00 20.00
Bud StainD/4036
8 Dale Earnhardt Jr. 10.00 20.00
Dirty Mo Posse/4670
8 Dale Earnhardt Jr. 15.00 30.00
E Concert/3300
8 Dale Earnhardt Jr. 10.00 20.00
Oreo Ritz/6060
8 Steve Park 7.50 15.00
Cheese Nips/1020
8 Steve Park 7.50 15.00
Cheese Nips Promo
8 Steve Park 7.50 15.00
Maxwell House/1020
8 Hank Parker Jr. 12.50 25.00
Bass Pro Promo
8 Tony Stewart 8.00 20.00
3 Doors Down/2016
9 Bill Elliott 8.00 20.00
Coors '87 Thunderbird/1164
9 Bill Elliott 8.00 20.00
Dodge/1012
9 Bill Elliott 8.00 20.00
Dodge 10th Brickyard/1012
15 Michael Waltrip 7.50 15.00
NAPA/1020
15 Michael Waltrip 7.50 15.00
NAPA Hootie & the Blowfish/1012
15 Michael Waltrip 7.50 15.00
NAPA Nilla Wafers/1020
15 Michael Waltrip 7.50 15.00
NAPA Stars&Stripes/1020
18 Bobby Labonte 8.00 20.00
Interstate Batteries/1212
18 Bobby Labonte 8.00 20.00
Interstate Batteries Hulk/1020
19 Dale Earnhardt 10.00 20.00
Beldon Asphalt 1976 Malibu/3460
19 Jeremy Mayfield 7.50 15.00
Dodge/1452
20 Tony Stewart 8.00 20.00
Home Depot/2308
20 Tony Stewart 8.00 20.00
Home Depot Declaration
of Independence/2020
21 Kevin Harvick 8.00 20.00
Payday/1300
21 Johnny Sauter 7.50 15.00
Payday/504
24 Jeff Gordon 10.00 20.00
Cookie Monster/2596
24 Jeff Gordon 12.50 25.00
DuPont Flames/2172
24 Jeff Gordon 12.50 25.00
DuPont Victory Lap/1008
24 Jeff Gordon 10.00 20.00
DuPont Wright Brothers/3328
24 Jeff Gordon 10.00 20.00
DuPont Yosemite Sam/2448
24 Jeff Gordon 10.00 20.00
Pepsi/2460
24 Jeff Gordon 10.00 20.00
Pepsi Billion $/3040
28/42 Davey Allison 25.00 50.00
Jamie McMurray
Havoline White/1080
29 Kevin Harvick 8.00 20.00
Goodwrench/2028
29 Kevin Harvick 8.00 20.00
Goodwrench Sugar Ray/1300
29 Kevin Harvick 8.00 20.00
Snap-On/1588
30 Jeff Green 7.50 15.00
AOL/1492
30 Steve Park 15.00 30.00
GM Card Promo
31 Robby Gordon 7.50 15.00
Cingular black/1596
31 Robby Gordon 7.50 15.00
Cingular orange/1020
38 Elliott Sadler 7.50 15.00
M&M's/1300
38 Elliott Sadler 8.00 20.00
M&M's Groovy/1012
38 Elliott Sadler 7.50 15.00
M&M's Halloween/1012
40 Sterling Marlin 15.00 30.00
Coors Light in a keg/12,144
42 Jamie McMurray 7.50 15.00
Havoline/1596
42 Jamie McMurray 7.50 15.00
Havoline Terminator 3/1300
43 Richard Petty 8.00 20.00
STP 1975 Charger/1444
43 Richard Petty 8.00 20.00
Victory Lap/1008
44 Christian Fittipaldi 7.50 15.00
100th Ann.Yankees/1020
45 Kyle Petty 7.50 15.00
Georgia Pacific/1020
48 Jimmie Johnson 8.00 20.00
Lowe's/2460
48 Jimmie Johnson 8.00 20.00
Lowe's Power of Pride/2460
48 Jimmie Johnson 8.00 20.00
Lowe's SpongeBob/1588
88 Dale Jarrett 8.00 20.00
UPS/1184
88 Dale Jarrett 8.00 20.00
UPS Store/1008
99 Michael Waltrip 7.50 15.00
Aaron's Rent
Cat in the Hat/1020
99 Michael Waltrip 7.50 15.00
Aaron's Rent Three Stooges/1020
99 Michael Waltrip 7.50 15.00
Aaron's Rent Terminator 3/1020
01 Jerry Nadeau 7.50 15.00
Army/1300
03 Hulk Event Car/1212 7.50 15.00

2003 Action/RCCA Elite 1:64

EX NM-MT
1 Steve Park 10.00 20.00
Pennzoil/1020
2 Rusty Wallace 15.00 30.00
Miller Lite/1500
2 Rusty Wallace 15.00 30.00
Miller Lite 600 Starts/1012
2 Rusty Wallace 15.00 30.00
Miller Time Live
Goo Goo Dolls/1204
3 Dale Earnhardt 12.50 30.00
Earnhardt Foundation/2500
8 Dale Earnhardt Jr. 20.00 35.00
Bud/3660
8 Dale Earnhardt Jr. 20.00 35.00
Bud MLB All-Star Game/3300
8 Dale Earnhardt Jr. 20.00 35.00
Bud StainD/2980
8 Dale Earnhardt Jr. 20.00 35.00
Dirty Mo Posse/2988
8 Dale Earnhardt Jr. 20.00 35.00
E Concert/3300
8 Dale Earnhardt Jr. 15.00 30.00
Oreo Ritz/4380
8 Steve Park 10.00 20.00
Cheese Nips/1020
8 Steve Park 10.00 20.00
Maxwell House/1020
8 Tony Stewart 15.00 30.00
3 Doors Down/2028
9 Bill Elliott 10.00 20.00
Dodge/1012
9 Bill Elliott 15.00 30.00
Dodge Lion King/1012
9 Bill Elliott 10.00 20.00
Dodge 10th Brickyard/1012
15 Michael Waltrip 10.00 20.00
NAPA/1020
15 Michael Waltrip 10.00 20.00
NAPA Hootie & the Blowfish/1012
15 Michael Waltrip 10.00 20.00
NAPA Nilla Wafers/1020
15 Michael Waltrip 10.00 20.00
NAPA Stars&Stripes/1020
18 Bobby Labonte 10.00 20.00
Interstate Batteries/1212
18 Bobby Labonte 12.50 25.00
Interstate Batteries Hulk/1200
20 Tony Stewart 15.00 30.00
Home Depot/2220
20 Tony Stewart 15.00 30.00
Home Depot Declaration
of Independence/2020
21 Kevin Harvick 12.50 25.00
Payday/1156
24 Jeff Gordon 15.00 30.00
Cookie Monster/1588
24 Jeff Gordon 20.00 40.00
DuPont Flames/2124
24 Jeff Gordon 15.00 30.00
DuPont Wright Brothers/2128
24 Jeff Gordon 20.00 40.00
DuPont Yosemite Sam/1924
24 Jeff Gordon 15.00 30.00
Pepsi/1824
24 Jeff Gordon 15.00 30.00
Pepsi Billion $/2128
29 Kevin Harvick 12.50 25.00
Goodwrench/1588
29 Kevin Harvick 20.00 35.00
Goodwrench Sugar Ray/1012
29 Kevin Harvick 12.50 25.00
Snap-On/1300
31 Robby Gordon 10.00 20.00
Cingular/1012
38 Elliott Sadler 12.50 25.00
M&M's Groovy/1012
38 Elliott Sadler 10.00 20.00
M&M's Halloween/1012
40 Sterling Marlin 12.50 25.00
Coors Light/1012
42 Jamie McMurray 12.50 25.00
Havoline/1212
42 Jamie McMurray 12.50 25.00
Havoline Terminator 3/1212
42 Jamie McMurray 12.50 25.00
Havoline White/1012
43 Richard Petty 15.00 30.00
Yankees 100th Anniversary/1012
48 Jimmie Johnson 15.00 30.00
Lowe's/1500
48 Jimmie Johnson 15.00 30.00
Lowe's Power of Pride/1548
48 Jimmie Johnson 15.00 30.00
Lowe's SpongeBob/1300
88 Dale Jarrett 12.50 25.00
UPS/1020
99 Michael Waltrip 10.00 20.00
Aaron's Rent Terminator 3/1020

2004 Action Performance 1:64

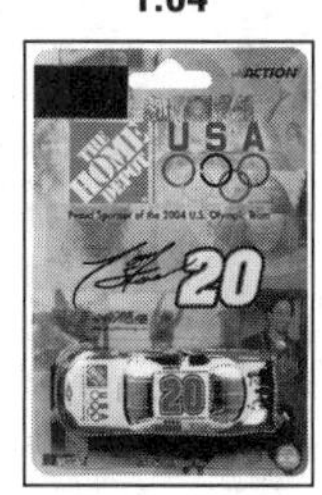

EX NM-MT
8 Dale Earnhardt Jr. 25.00 40.00
Nextel Cup 6-car set
Bud
Bud Born On Feb. 8
Bud Born On Feb. 15 raced
Bud Father's Day
Bud Dave Matthews Band
Bud World Series
8 Martin TruexJr. 25.00 40.00
Busch Series 6-car set
Bass Pro Shops
KFC
Long John Silvers
Oreo Ritz
Taco Bell
Wrangler
9 Kasey Kahne 25.00 40.00
Nextel Cup 6-car set
Dodge
Dodge Refresh
Dodge Mad Magazine
Dodge Pit Cap
Dodge Popeye
Mountain Dew
18 Bobby Labonte 3.00 6.00
Interstate Batteries
20 Tony Stewart 5.00 10.00
Home Depot Olympic
20 Tony Stewart 5.00 10.00
Home Depot Shrek 2
20 Tony Stewart 25.00 40.00
Nextel Cup 6-car set
Coke C2
Home Depot
Home Depot Black
Home Depot Olympic
Home Depot Shrek 2
Home Depot 25th Anniversary
24 Jeff Gordon 25.00 40.00
Nextel Cup 6-car set
Dupont Flames
DuPont Flames HMS 20th Anniversary
DuPont Flames Wizard of Oz
DuPont Rainbow
Pepsi Billion $
Pepsi Shards
29 Kevin Harvick 25.00 40.00
Nextel Cup 6-car set
Coke C2
Goodwrench
Goodwrench KISS
Ice Breakers
Realtree
Snap-On
32 Ricky Craven 2.00 5.00
Tide
66 Billy Parker Jr. 60.00 100.00
Duraflame Promo

2004 Action Racing Collectables 1:64

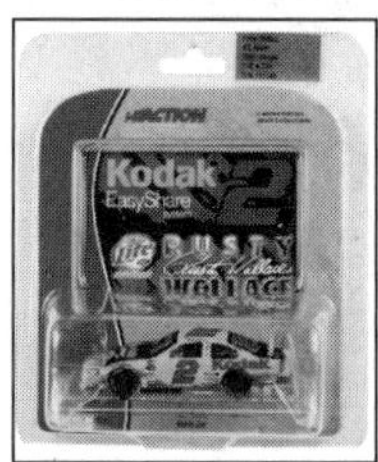

EX NM-MT
2 Rusty Wallace 7.50 15.00
Kodak/4128
2 Rusty Wallace 7.50 15.00
Miller Lite/8496
2 Rusty Wallace 12.50 25.00
Miller Lite in keg
2 Rusty Wallace 10.00 20.00
Miller Lite Last Call/3936
2 Rusty Wallace 7.50 15.00
Miller Lite
Puddle of Mudd/4464
3 Dale Earnhardt 40.00 80.00
Goodwrench Olympics '96 MC
Goodwrench '97 MC
AC Delco Japan '97 MC
Goodwrench Crash '97 MC
Coke Japan '98 MC
Goodwrench Talladega Win '98 MC
Goodwrench Sign '99 MC
Wrangler '99 MC
Goodwrench Peter Max '00 MC
9-car set/5004 w/case
3/8/8 Dale Earnhardt Jr. 20.00 40.00
3-car set in tin/7128
2002 Oreo 2003 Oreo Ritz 2004 Oreo
5 Terry Labonte 6.00 12.00
Kellogg's/9168
6 Bill Elliott 7.50 15.00
Lucas Oil Elvis/4224
8 Dale Earnhardt Jr. 10.00 20.00
Bud/30,480
on a base
8 Dale Earnhardt Jr. 10.00 20.00
Bud Born On Feb.7/13,296
8 Dale Earnhardt Jr. 10.00 20.00
Bud Born On Feb.12
Raced/15,000
8 Dale Earnhardt Jr. 10.00 20.00
Bud Born On
Feb.15 Raced/22,004
8 Dale Earnhardt Jr. 7.50 15.00
Bud Dave Matthews Band
8 Dale Earnhardt Jr. 10.00 20.00
Bud World Series
8 Dale Earnhardt Jr. 7.50 15.00
Oreo/18,288
8 Martin Truex Jr. 7.50 15.00
Bass Pro Shops/8496
8 Martin Truex Jr. 7.50 15.00
Wrangler/5040
8/33 Dale Earnhardt Jr. 15.00 30.00
Bud Father's Day
Kerry Earnhardt
Bass Pro Shop Father's Day
2-car set/12,288
8/81 Dale Earnhardt Jr. 25.00 40.00
Bristol Raced 2-car set
Bud Bristol Raced
Menards Bristol Raced
9 Kasey Kahne 15.00 25.00
Dodge/4128
9 Kasey Kahne 10.00 20.00
Dodge refresh/9120
9 Kasey Kahne 10.00 20.00
Dodge refresh Rookie of the Year
Color Chrome
9 Kasey Kahne 7.50 15.00
Dodge Mopar
9 Kasey Kahne 25.00 40.00
Mountain Dew in vending tin/5124
15 Michael Waltrip 6.00 12.00
NAPA/8976
15 Michael Waltrip 6.00 12.00
NAPA Stars&Stripes/3792
18 Bobby Labonte 6.00 12.00
Interstate Batteries/8640
18 Bobby Labonte 6.00 12.00
Interstate Batteries D-Day/5568
18 Bobby Labonte 6.00 12.00
Interstate Batteries
Shrek 2/5712
20 Tony Stewart 7.50 15.00
Home Depot/13,584
20 Tony Stewart 10.00 20.00
Home Depot in tool box/3540
20 Tony Stewart 7.50 15.00
Home Depot Reverse Paint
Black/6576
20 Tony Stewart 7.50 15.00
Home Depot
Shrek 2/7728
20 Tony Stewart 7.50 15.00
Home Depot 25th Anniversary/6336
21 Kevin Harvick 6.00 12.00
Hershey's Kisses/6884
21 Kevin Harvick 6.00 12.00
Reese's/7248
24 Jeff Gordon 7.50 15.00
Big Bird/7440
24 Jeff Gordon 7.50 15.00
DuPont Flames/22,848
24 Jeff Gordon 10.00 20.00
DuPont Flames
Brickyard Raced/5040
24 Jeff Gordon 10.00 20.00
DuPont Flame
HMS 20th Anniversary/5952
24 Jeff Gordon 10.00 20.00
DuPont Rainbow/8400
24 Jeff Gordon 7.50 15.00
DuPont Wizard of Oz/9024
24 Jeff Gordon 7.50 15.00
Pepsi Billion/7776
24 Jeff Gordon 7.50 15.00
Pepsi Shards/8064
24 Jeff Gordon 7.50 15.00
Santa/5040
25 Brian Vickers 6.00 12.00
ditech/5040
29 Kevin Harvick 6.00 12.00
Goodwrench/10,752
29 Kevin Harvick 7.50 15.00
Goodwrench KISS/5280
29 Kevin Harvick 6.00 12.00
Goodwrench RCR 35th Anniversary/5568
29 Kevin Harvick 6.00 12.00
Goodwrench Realtree/5568
29 Kevin Harvick 6.00 12.00
Ice Breakers Liquid Ice/5328
29 Kevin Harvick 6.00 12.00
Snap-On/5616
29 Tony Stewart 6.00 12.00
Kid Rock/7488
31 Robby Gordon 6.00 12.00
Cingular/4080
33 Kerry Earnhardt 6.00 12.00
Bass Pro Shops/5376
38 Kasey Kahne 7.50 15.00
Great Clips Shark Tales/4464
38 Elliott Sadler 6.00 12.00
M&M's/6576
38 Elliott Sadler 7.50 15.00
M&M's Black&White/5184

38 Elliott Sadler 6.00 12.00
M&M's Halloween
38 Elliott Sadler 6.00 12.00
Pedigree Wizard of Oz/4560
40 Sterling Marlin 6.00 12.00
Coors Light/4944
40 Sterling Marlin 15.00 30.00
Coors Light Keg tin/2952
on a base
42 Jamie McMurray 6.00 12.00
Havoline/10,272
45 Kyle Petty 6.00 12.00
Georgia Pacific/6264
48 Jimmie Johnson 7.50 15.00
Lowe's/12,960
48 Jimmie Johnson 7.50 15.00
Lowe's HMS 20th Anniversary/3408
48 Jimmie Johnson 7.50 15.00
Lowe's Power of Pride/11,616
48 Jimmie Johnson 6.00 12.00
Lowe's SpongeBob/3984
77 Brendan Gaughan 7.50 15.00
Kodak/4512
77 Brendan Gaughan 6.00 12.00
Kodak Wizard of Oz/3504
81 Dale Earnhardt Jr. 7.50 15.00
KFC/12,288
81 Dale Earnhardt Jr. 7.50 15.00
Taco Bell/11,664
81 Tony Stewart 6.00 12.00
Bass Pro/5088
88 Dale Jarrett 7.50 15.00
UPS/6144
88 Dale Jarrett 7.50 15.00
UPS Arnold Palmer/8400
88 Dale Jarrett 12.50 25.00
UPS Arnold Palmer/8400
with golf ball
01 Joe Nemechek 6.00 12.00
Army GI Joe/3168

2004 Action Racing Collectables Historical Series 1:64

EX NM-MT
2 Dale Earnhardt 10.00 20.00
Mello Yello
1979 Pontiac Ventura/6960
9 Bill Elliott 7.50 15.00
Coors Light 1991 t-bird/3984
29 Kevin Harvick 8.00 20.00
Goodwrench Service Plus
2001 Monte Carlo black numbers/10,944

2004 Action/RCCA 1:64

EX NM-MT
1 John Andretti 7.50 15.00
Post Maxwell House Promo
2 Rusty Wallace 7.50 15.00
Kodak/576
2 Rusty Wallace 7.50 15.00
Miller Lite/1588
2 Rusty Wallace 12.50 25.00
Miller Lite Last Call/576
3/8/8 Dale Earnhardt Jr. 20.00 35.00
2002 Oreo 2003 Oreo Ritz 2004 Oreo Ritz
3-car set in tin
5 Terry Labonte 7.50 15.00
Kellogg's/720
8 Dale Earnhardt Jr. 12.50 25.00
Bud/3024
8 Dale Earnhardt Jr. 12.50 25.00
Bud Born On
Feb.7/3024
8 D.Earnhardt Jr./Bud Born On 20.00 35.00
Feb.12&15 Raced 2-car set/4008
8 Dale Earnhardt Jr. 10.00 20.00
Bud Dave Matthews Band/2880
8 Dale Earnhardt Jr. 12.50 25.00
Bud World Series/2448
8 Dale Earnhardt Jr. 10.00 20.00
Oreo/4032
8 Martin Truex Jr. 7.50 15.00
Bass Pro Shops/720
8/33 Dale Earnhardt Jr. 20.00 35.00
Bud Father's Day
Kerry Earnhardt
Bass Pro Shops Father's Day/1500
2-car set
8/81 Dale Earnhardt Jr. 25.00 40.00
Bristol Raced 2-car set/960
Bud Bristol Raced
Menards Bristol Raced
9 Kasey Kahne 25.00 40.00
Dodge/576
9 Kasey Kahne 20.00 35.00
Dodge Mopar/576
9 Kasey Kahne 25.00 40.00
Mountain Dew in vending tin/600
15 Michael Waltrip 7.50 15.00
NAPA/1008
15 Michael Waltrip 7.50 15.00
NAPA Stars & Stripes/720
18 Bobby Labonte 7.50 15.00
Interstate Batteries
D-Day/576
18 Bobby Labonte 7.50 15.00
Interstate Batteries Shrek 2/1008
18 Bobby Labonte 7.50 15.00
Wellbutrin
20 Tony Stewart 10.00 20.00
Coke C2/576
20 Tony Stewart 15.00 30.00
Home Depot
in tool box/1500
20 Tony Stewart 10.00 20.00
Home Depot Black Reverse/1152
20 Tony Stewart 10.00 20.00
Home Depot Shrek 2/1008
20 Tony Stewart 10.00 20.00
Home Depot 25th Anniversary/1008
21 Kevin Harvick 10.00 20.00
Reese's/1008
24 Jeff Gordon 12.50 25.00
DuPont Flames
HMS 20th Anniversary/1440
24 Jeff Gordon 10.00 20.00
Pepsi Billion/1008
24 Jeff Gordon 12.50 25.00
Pepsi Shards/1296
24 Jeff Gordon 12.50 25.00
Santa/576
25 Brian Vickers 7.50 15.00
ditech.com/504
29 Kevin Harvick 10.00 20.00
Goodwrench
KISS/1584
29 Kevin Harvick 10.00 20.00
Goodwrench
RCR 35th Ann/1008
29 Kevin Harvick 10.00 20.00
Ice Breakers/720
29 Kevin Harvick 10.00 20.00
Snap-On/1008
29 Tony Stewart 10.00 20.00
Kid Rock/1200
31 Robby Gordon 7.50 15.00
Cingular/720
33 Kerry Earnhardt 7.50 15.00
Bass Pro Shops/576
38 Kasey Kahne 10.00 20.00
Great Clips Shark Tale/576
38 Elliott Sadler 7.50 15.00
M&M's/720
38 Elliott Sadler 7.50 15.00
M&M's Black&White/1008
40 Sterling Marlin 7.50 15.00
Coors Light/504
42 Jamie McMurray 7.50 15.00
Havoline/1008
48 Jimmie Johnson 10.00 20.00
Lowe's/1008
48 Jimmie Johnson 10.00 20.00
Lowe's HMS 20th Anniversary/720
48 Jimmie Johnson 10.00 20.00
Lowe's SpongeBob/576
81 Dale Earnhardt Jr. 10.00 20.00
KFC/3600
81 Dale Earnhardt Jr. 12.50 25.00
Menards Bristol Raced/720
81 Dale Earnhardt Jr. 10.00 20.00
Taco Bell/1800
81 Tony Stewart 10.00 20.00
Bass Pro Shops/720
88 Dale Jarrett 7.50 15.00
UPS/504
88 Dale Jarrett 15.00 30.00
UPS Arnold Palmer
with golf ball/720
99 Michael Waltrip 7.50 15.00
Aaron's Dream Machine Promo

2004 Action/RCCA Elite 1:64

EX NM-MT
2 Rusty Wallace 12.50 25.00
Kodak/576
2 Rusty Wallace 15.00 30.00
Miller Lite/1500
2 Rusty Wallace 20.00 35.00
Miller Lite Last Call/528
2 Rusty Wallace 15.00 30.00
Miller Lite
Puddle of Mudd/528
6 Bill Elliott 12.50 25.00
Lucas Oil Elvis/480
8 Dale Earnhardt Jr. 20.00 40.00
Bud/2400
8 Dale Earnhardt Jr. 20.00 40.00
Bud Born On
Feb.7/2016
8 Dale Earnhardt Jr. 20.00 40.00
Bud Dave Matthews Band/1968
8 Dale Earnhardt Jr. 20.00 40.00
Bud World Series/1824
8 Dale Earnhardt Jr. 20.00 40.00
Oreo/2880
9 Kasey Kahne 25.00 50.00
Dodge/576
9 Kasey Kahne 25.00 40.00
Dodge Refresh Color Chrome/528
9 Kasey Kahne 15.00 30.00
Dodge refresh ROY/480
9 Kasey Kahne 20.00 40.00
Dodge Mopar/480
9 Kasey Kahne 25.00 50.00
Mountain Dew/528
15 Michael Waltrip 12.50 25.00
NAPA/720
18 Bobby Labonte 12.50 25.00
Interstate Batteries/1008
18 Bobby Labonte 12.50 25.00
Interstate Batteries D-Day/528
18 Bobby Labonte 12.50 25.00
Interstate Batteries
Shrek 2/720
20 Tony Stewart 15.00 30.00
Home Depot/1440
20 Tony Stewart 15.00 30.00
Home Depot
Black Reverse/1008
20 Tony Stewart 15.00 30.00
Home Depot Shrek 2/1008
20 Tony Stewart 15.00 30.00
Home Depot 25th Anniversary/720
21 Kevin Harvick 12.50 25.00
Hershey's Kisses/720
21 Kevin Harvick 12.50 25.00
Reese's/720
24 Jeff Gordon 15.00 30.00
Big Bird/1200
24 Jeff Gordon 20.00 35.00
DuPont Flames/1440
24 Jeff Gordon 15.00 30.00
DuPont Flames
Wizard of Oz/1200
24 Jeff Gordon 20.00 35.00
DuPont Rainbow/1008
24 Jeff Gordon 12.50 25.00
Pepsi Billion/1008
24 Jeff Gordon 15.00 30.00
Pepsi Shards/1008
24 Jeff Gordon 15.00 30.00
Santa/480
29 Kevin Harvick 15.00 30.00
Goodwrench/1008
29 Kevin Harvick 15.00 30.00
Goodwrench KISS/1008
29 Kevin Harvick 15.00 30.00
Goodwrench RCR 35th Anniversary/576
29 Kevin Harvick 12.50 25.00
Goodwrench Realtree/1008
29 Kevin Harvick 12.50 25.00
Ice Breakers/528
29 Kevin Harvick 12.50 25.00
Snap-On/720
29 Tony Stewart 12.50 25.00
Kid Rock/1008
31 Robby Gordon 12.50 25.00
Cingular Black/1584
33 Kerry Earnhardt 12.50 25.00
Bass Pro Shops/528
38 Elliott Sadler 15.00 30.00
M&M's/504
42 Jamie McMurray 15.00 30.00
Havoline/1008
48 Jimmie Johnson 15.00 30.00
Lowe's/720
48 Jimmie Johnson 15.00 30.00
Lowe's HMS 20th Anniversary/624
48 Jimmie Johnson 12.50 25.00
Lowe's SpongeBob/480
81 Dale Earnhardt Jr. 15.00 30.00
KFC/2400
81 Dale Earnhardt Jr. 15.00 30.00
Taco Bell/1200
81 Tony Stewart 12.50 25.00
Bass Pro Shops/528
88 Dale Jarrett 15.00 30.00
UPS/504
88 Dale Jarrett 15.00 30.00
UPS Arnold Palmer/528

2004 Action/RCCA Historical Series 1:64

EX NM-MT
29 Kevin Harvick 10.00 20.00
Goodwrench Service Plus
2001 MC black numbers/1296
43 Richard Petty 15.00 30.00
STP '72 Charger Promo
43 Richard Petty 15.00 30.00
STP '04 Fantasy Promo
43 Richard Petty 10.00 20.00
STP '84 Grand Prix Promo
NNO Jeff Gordon 30.00 60.00
DuPont '96 Monte Carlo
Jimmie Johnson
Lowe's 2003 Monte Carlo
Richard Petty
STP 1980 Monte Carlo
Darrell Waltrip
Tide 1987 Monte Carlo
Chevy Wins 4-car tin set

2004 Action/RCCA Historical Series Elite 1:64

EX NM-MT
29 Kevin Harvick 12.50 25.00
Goodwrench Service Plus
2001 MC black numbers/720

2005 Action Performance 1:64

EX NM-MT
2/64 Rusty Wallace 25.00 40.00
Nextel Cup 6-car set series 1
64.Bell Helicopter
2.Kodak
2.Miller Lite
2.Miller Lite Last Call
2.Mobil Clean 7500
2.Snap-On 85th Anniversary
2/64 Rusty Wallace 25.00 40.00
Nextel Cup 6-car set series 2
64.Miller High Life
64.Top Flite
2.Miller Lite Last Race
2.Miller Lite Bristol
2.Miller Lite Sirius
2.Miller Genuine Draft
3 Dale Earnhardt 4.00 8.00
Goodwrench '00 MC
8 Dale Earnhardt Jr. 4.00 8.00
JR
9 Kasey Kahne 4.00 8.00
Dodge
9 Kasey Kahne 25.00 40.00
Nextel Cup 6-car set
Dodge
Dodge Pit Cap White
Mountain Dew
Dodge Mega Cab
Dodge Mopar
Dodge Retro
15 Michael Waltrip 4.00 8.00
Napa
18 Bobby Labonte 4.00 8.00
Interstate Batteries
19 Jeremy Mayfield 25.00 40.00
Nextel Cup 6-car set
Dodge
Dodge Black Reverse
Dodge Retro Daytona Shootout
Mountain Dew Pitch Black
79.AutoValue
20 Tony Stewart 4.00 8.00
Home Depot
20 Tony Stewart 25.00 40.00
Nextel Cup 6-car set
20.Home Depot
20.Home Depot Test
20.Home Depot Madagascar
20.Home Depot Daytona
20.Home Depot KaBOOM
20.Home Depot Brickyard
38 Elliott Sadler 4.00 8.00
M&M's
88 Dale Jarrett 4.00 8.00
UPS

2005 Action Promos 1:64

EX NM-MT
11 Jason Leffler 12.50 25.00
FedEx Express
11 Jason Leffler 12.50 25.00
FedEx Freight
11 Jason Leffler 12.50 25.00
FedEx Ground
11 Jason Leffler 12.50 25.00
FedEx Kinko's
31 Jeff Burton 10.00 20.00
Cingular in window box
43 Richard Petty 12.50 25.00
STP '72 Charger
in window box
43 Richard Petty 12.50 25.00
STP '84 Grand Prix
in window box
43 Richard Petty 10.00 20.00
STP Fantasy
in window box
96 DLP Hall of Fame Racing Promo 40.00 60.00
in bag

2005 Action Racing Collectables 1:64

EX NM-MT
1 Martin Truex Jr. 6.00 12.00
Bass Pro Shops
2 Rusty Wallace 15.00 25.00
Miller Genuine Draft
in can/4068
2 Rusty Wallace 6.00 12.00
Miller Lite
2 Rusty Wallace 15.00 25.00
Miller Lite in a can
2 Rusty Wallace 6.00 12.00
Miller Lite Last Call
Daytona Shootout
6 Bill Elliott 10.00 20.00
Charlie Brown Christmas
6/22/64 Wallace Family Tribute 3-car tin/3000 15.00 30.00
4.Mike Wallace
Ragu
23.Kenny Wallace
Whelen
64.Rusty Wallace
Miller High Life
8 Dale Earnhardt Jr. 7.50 15.00
Bud
8 Dale Earnhardt Jr. 7.50 15.00
Bud MLB All Star Game
8 Dale Earnhardt Jr. 7.50 15.00
Bud 3 Doors Down
8 Dale Earnhardt Jr. 25.00 40.00
Bud Born On Feb.12th
Bud Born On Feb.17
Bud Born On Feb.20
3-car set in tin/8000
8 Martin Truex Jr. 6.00 12.00
Bass Pro
9 Kasey Kahne 6.00 12.00
Dodge
9 Kasey Kahne 6.00 12.00
Dodge Pit Cap White
9 Kasey Kahne 6.00 12.00
Dodge Retro
Bud Shootout
9 Kasey Kahne 6.00 12.00
Mopar
9 Kasey Kahne 6.00
Mountain Dew
9 Kasey Kahne 12.50
Mountain Dew in can
15 Michael Waltrip 6.00
Napa
18 Bobby Labonte 6.00
Interstate Batteries
18 Bobby Labonte 6.00
Interstate Batteries Madagascar
19 Jeremy Mayfield 5.00
Dodge
20 Tony Stewart 6.00
Home Depot
20 Tony Stewart 6.00
Home Depot KaBOOM
20 Tony Stewart 6.00
Home Depot Madagascar
21 Kevin Harvick 6.00
Hershey's Take 5
21 Kevin Harvick 6.00
Pelon Pelo Rico
21 Kevin Harvick 6.00
Reese's
24 Jeff Gordon 7.50
DuPont Flames
24 Jeff Gordon 7.50
DuPont Flames Performance Alliance
Reverse
24 Jeff Gordon 7.50
Mighty Mouse
24 Jeff Gordon 7.50
Pepsi Daytona
24 Jeff Gordon 7.50
Pepsi Star Wars
24 Jeff Gordon 7.50
Santa Holiday
29 Kevin Harvick 6.00
Goodwrench
29 Kevin Harvick 6.00
Goodwrench Atlanta
29 Kevin Harvick 6.00
Goodwrench Brickyard
29 Kevin Harvick 6.00
Goodwrench Daytona
29 Kevin Harvick 6.00
Goodwrench Quicksilver
33 Tony Stewart 6.00
James Dean 50th Anniversary
38 Kasey Kahne 6.00
Great Clips
38 Elliott Sadler 6.00
M&M's
38 Elliott Sadler 6.00
M&M's Halloween
38 Elliott Sadler 6.00
M&M's July 4th
40 Sterling Marlin 6.00
Coors Light
41 Casey Mears 6.00
Target
42 Jamie McMurray 6.00
Havoline
44 Terry Labonte 6.00
Kellogg's
48 Jimmie Johnson 6.00
Lowe's
48 Jimmie Johnson 7.50
Lowe's '06 Preview
77 Travis Kvapil 6.00
Kodak
79 Kasey Kahne 6.00
Auto Value
81 Dale Earnhardt Jr. 6.00
Menards
81 Dale Earnhardt Jr. 6.00
Oreo Ritz
88 Dale Jarrett 6.00
UPS
88 Dale Jarrett 6.00
UPS Herbie Fully Loaded
88 Dale Jarrett 6.00
UPS Store Toys for Tots
91 Bill Elliott 6.00
Auto Value
91 Bill Elliott 6.00
McDonald's 50th Anniversary
99 Michael Waltrip 6.00
Aaron's
99/00 Michael Waltrip 12.50
Kenny Wallace
Aaron's 50th Anniversary
2-car set in tin

2005 Action Racing Collectables Historical Se[ries] 1:64

EX N[M-MT]
3 Dale Earnhardt 7.50
Goodwrench Daytona Crash
'97 Monte Carlo
9 Bill Elliott 7.50
Mel Gear '81 T-bird
1st Pole

2005 Action/RCCA 1:64

EX N[M-MT]
1 Martin Truex Jr. 10.00
Bass Pro Shops/576
2 Rusty Wallace 10.00
Miller Genuine Draft/576

ty Wallace 10.00 20.00
Miller Lite/576
sty Wallace 10.00 20.00
Miller Lite Last Call
Daytona Shootout/576
e Earnhardt Jr. 10.00 20.00
ud/1584
e Earnhardt Jr. 10.00 20.00
ud MLB All-Star/2016
e Earnhardt Jr. 10.00 20.00
ud 3 Doors Down/1584
artin Truex Jr. 10.00 20.00
ass Pro/576
ey Kahne 10.00 20.00
Dodge/720
ey Kahne 10.00 20.00
Dodge Pit Cap White/576
sey Kahne 10.00 20.00
Dodge Retro Bud Shootout/720
sey Kahne 10.00 20.00
Mountain Dew/720
ey Kahne 12.50 25.00
Mountain Dew
n can/504
bby Labonte 10.00 20.00
nterstate Batteries/576
ony Stewart 10.00 20.00
Home Depot/864
ony Stewart 12.50 25.00
Home Depot KaBOOM/480
ny Stewart 7.50 15.00
Home Depot Madagascar/576
eff Gordon 10.00 20.00
DuPont Flames/1008
eff Gordon 12.50 25.00
Foundation Holiday/432
ff Gordon 10.00 20.00
Mighty Mouse/1296
eff Gordon 10.00 20.00
Pepsi Star Wars/1584
evin Harvick 7.50 15.00
Goodwrench/864
evin Harvick 7.50 15.00
Goodwrench Atlanta/720
evin Harvick 7.50 15.00
Goodwrench Daytona/864
ony Stewart 7.50 15.00
ames Dean 50th Anniversary
liott Sadler 7.50 15.00
M&M's/576
liott Sadler 7.50 15.00
M&M's July 4/432
mmie Johnson 10.00 20.00
owe's/576
mmie Johnson 10.00 20.00
owe's '06 Preview/288
ale Earnhardt Jr. 10.00 20.00
Oreo Ritz/2016
ale Jarrett 10.00 20.00
UPS/576
ale Jarrett 10.00 20.00
UPS Herbie Fully Loaded/720
ale Jarrett 10.00 20.00
UPS Store
oys for Tots/408
l Elliott 10.00 20.00
McDonald's/432

005 Action/RCCA Elite 1:64

EX NM-MT
ty Wallace 12.50 25.00
Miller Lite/480
ty Wallace 12.50 25.00
Miller Lite Last Call
Daytona Shootout/480
e Earnhardt Jr. 15.00 30.00
ud/1200
e Earnhardt Jr. 15.00 30.00
ud MLB All-Star/1440
ey Kahne 15.00 30.00
Dodge/576
ey Kahne 12.50 25.00
Dodge Pit Cap White/480
sey Kahne 12.50 25.00
Dodge Retro Bud Shootout/528
sey Kahne 15.00 30.00
Mountain Dew/528
ony Stewart 12.50 25.00
Home Depot/576
ony Stewart 12.50 25.00
Home Depot Madagascar/480
ff Gordon 15.00 30.00
DuPont Flames/864
eff Gordon 25.00 50.00
oundation Holiday/288
eff Gordon 15.00 30.00
Mighty Mouse/816
eff Gordon 15.00 30.00
Pepsi Star Wars/1200
ony Stewart 12.50 25.00
ames Dean 50th Anniversary/528
rry Labonte 15.00 30.00
ellogg's/480
mmie Johnson 15.00 30.00
owe's/480
mmie Johnson 25.00 50.00
owe's '06 Preview/240
ale Earnhardt Jr. 12.50 25.00
reo Ritz/1584
ale Jarrett 20.00 40.00
UPS Store
oys for Tots/240

2006 Action Performance 1:64

EX NM-MT
tin Truex Jr. 5.00 10.00
ass Pro Shops
ey Kahne 5.00 10.00
Dodge
ny Stewart 5.00 10.00
Home Depot
ff Gordon 5.00 10.00
uPont Flames
/55 Talladega Nights 5-car set 15.00 30.00
6 Ricky Bobby
aughing Clown Malt Liquor
6 Ricky Bobby
ME

26 Ricky Bobby
Wonderbread
47 Cal Naughton Jr.
Old Spice
55 Jean Girard
Perrier
48 Jimmie Johnson 5.00 10.00
Lowe's

2006 Action Promos 1:64

EX NM-MT
11 Denny Hamlin 10.00 20.00
Fed Ex Express in blister
11 Denny Hamlin 10.00 20.00
Fed Ex Freight in blister
11 Denny Hamlin 10.00 20.00
Fed Ex Ground in blister
11 Denny Hamlin 10.00 20.00
Fed Ex Kinko's in blister
22 Kenny Wallace 5.00 10.00
Auto Zone in blister
38 Elliott Sadler 10.00 20.00
M&M's & Snicker's 2-car blister pack
64 Jamie McMurray 7.50 15.00
USG Sheetrock in window box
66 Jeff Green 10.00 20.00
Best Buy in blister

2006 Action Racing Collectables 1:64

EX NM-MT
1 Martin Truex Jr. 6.00 12.00
Bass Pro Shops
1 Martin Truex Jr. 7.50 15.00
Bass Pro Shops
3 Days of Dale Tribute
5 Kyle Busch 6.00 12.00
Kellogg's
5 Kyle Busch 6.00 12.00
Kellogg's Cars
5 Kyle Busch 6.00 12.00
Kellogg's Ice Age
6 Mark Martin 7.50 15.00
AAA Holiday
8 Dale Earnhardt Jr. 7.50 15.00
Bud
8 Dale Earnhardt Jr. 7.50 15.00
Bud Richmond Raced
8 Dale Earnhardt Jr. 10.00 20.00
Bud 3 Days of Dale Tribute
8 Dale Earnhardt Jr. 10.00 20.00
Bud Father's Day
8 Dale Earnhardt Jr. 7.50 15.00
Oreo
8 Dale Earnhardt Jr. 7.50 15.00
250 Starts
8 Martin Truex Jr. 7.50 15.00
Bass Pro 3 Days of Dale Tribute
Talladega Raced
9 Kasey Kahne 7.50 15.00
Dodge
10 Scott Riggs 6.00 12.00
Stanley Tools
10 Scott Riggs 6.00 12.00
Valvoline
10 Scott Riggs 6.00 12.00
Valvoline Cars
11 Denny Hamlin 10.00 20.00
Fed Ex Express
11 Denny Hamlin 10.00 20.00
Fed Ex Freight
11 Denny Hamlin 10.00 20.00
Fed Ex Ground
11 Denny Hamlin 10.00 20.00
Fed Ex Kinko's
11 Paul Menard 7.50 15.00
Turtle Wax 3 Days of Dale Tribute
19 Jeremy Mayfield 5.00 10.00
Dodge
20 Denny Hamlin 6.00 12.00
Rockwell Automation
20 Tony Stewart 7.50 15.00
Home Depot
24 Jeff Gordon 7.50 15.00
DuPont Flames
24 Jeff Gordon 7.50 15.00
DuPont Flames
Performance Alliance
24 Jeff Gordon 7.50 15.00
DuPont Hot Hues
Foose Design
24 Jeff Gordon 6.00 12.00
Holiday Jeff Gordon Foundation
24 Jeff Gordon 6.00 12.00
Mighty Mouse
Jeff Gordon Foundation
24 Jeff Gordon 7.50 15.00
Nicorette
24 Jeff Gordon 7.50 15.00
Pepsi
24 Jeff Gordon 7.50 15.00
Superman
24 Jeff Gordon 7.50 15.00
World Series of Poker
Jeff Gordon Foundation
25 Brian Vickers 6.00 12.00
GMAC
29 Kevin Harvick 6.00 12.00
Goodwrench
29 Kevin Harvick 6.00 12.00
Hershey's
29 Kevin Harvick 6.00 12.00
Hershey's Kissables
29 Kevin Harvick 6.00 12.00
Reese's
31 Jeff Burton 6.00 12.00
Cingular
38 David Gilliland 7.50 15.00
M&M's Halloween
38 Elliott Sadler 6.00 12.00
M&M's
38 Elliott Sadler 6.00 12.00
M&M's Pirates of the Caribbean
38 Elliott Sadler 6.00 12.00
Snickers
40 David Stremme 7.50 15.00
Coors Light
41 Reed Sorenson 7.50 15.00
Target
43 Bobby Labonte 6.00 12.00
Cheerios
43 Bobby Labonte 6.00 12.00
STP
44 Terry Labonte 6.00 12.00
Kellogg's
48 Jimmie Johnson 7.50 15.00
Lowe's
48 Jimmie Johnson 15.00 30.00
Lowe's Dover Win w/Monster/3948
48 Jimmie Johnson 6.00 12.00
Lowe's SeaWorld
48 Jimmie Johnson 7.50 15.00
Lowe's 60th Anniverary
88 Dale Jarrett 6.00 12.00
UPS
90 Elliott Sadler 6.00 12.00
Citifinancial
06 Sam Bass Holiday 5.00 10.00
NNO Dale Earnhardt 7.50 15.00
Hall of Fame

2006 Action/RCCA 1:64

EX NM-MT
5 Kyle Busch 10.00 20.00
Kellogg's Cars/288
5 Kyle Busch 10.00 20.00
Kellogg's Ice Age/288
8 Dale Earnhardt Jr. 12.50 25.00
Bud/936
8 Dale Earnhardt Jr. 15.00 30.00
Bud 3 Days of Dale Tribute/2133
8 Dale Earnhardt Jr. 12.50 25.00
Bud Father's Day/2008
8 Dale Earnhardt Jr. 10.00 20.00
250th Start/1008
11 Denny Hamlin 12.50 25.00
Fed Ex Express/384
11 Denny Hamlin 12.50 25.00
Fed Ex Freight/288
11 Denny Hamlin 12.50 25.00
Fed Ex Ground/360
11 Denny Hamlin 12.50 25.00
Fed Ex Kinko's/288
20 Denny Hamlin 10.00 20.00
Rockwall Automation/288
20 Tony Stewart 10.00 20.00
Home Depot/600
24 Jeff Gordon 12.50 25.00
DuPont Flames/720
24 Jeff Gordon 10.00 20.00
DuPont Hot Hues Foose/1008
24 Jeff Gordon 10.00 20.00
DuPont Flames
Performance Alliance/600
24 Jeff Gordon 10.00 20.00
Holiday Jeff Gordon Foundation/432
24 Jeff Gordon 10.00 20.00
Mighty Mouse
Jeff Gordon Foundation/576
24 Jeff Gordon 10.00 20.00
Nicorette/720
24 Jeff Gordon 10.00 20.00
Pepsi/864
24 Jeff Gordon 10.00 20.00
Superman/1296
24 Jeff Gordon 12.50 25.00
World Series of Poker
Jeff Gordon Foundation/720
29 Kevin Harvick 10.00 20.00
Goodwrench/432
29 Kevin Harvick 10.00 20.00
Hershey's/360
29 Kevin Harvick 10.00 20.00
Hershey's Kissables/432
29 Kevin Harvick 10.00 20.00
Reese's/288
38 David Gilliland 12.50 25.00
M&M's Halloween/288
38 Elliott Sadler 10.00 20.00
M&M's Pirates of the Caribbean/240
41 Reed Sorenson 12.50 25.00
Target/288
43 Bobby Labonte 10.00 20.00
STP/288
48 Jimmie Johnson 10.00 20.00
Lowe's/528
48 Jimmie Johnson 10.00 20.00
Lowe's Sea World/408
48 Jimmie Johnson 10.00 20.00
Lowe's 60th Anniversary/432
NNO Dale Earnhardt 10.00 20.00
Dale Tribute Hall Of Fame/1584

2006 Action/RCCA Elite 1:64

EX NM-MT
8 Dale Earnhardt Jr. 20.00 40.00
Bud 3 Days of Dale Tribute/1533
8 Dale Earnhardt Jr. 20.00 40.00
Bud Father's Day/1508
8 Dale Earnhardt Jr. 15.00 30.00
250th Start/720
9 Kasey Kahne 15.00 30.00
Dodge/288
11 Denny Hamlin 25.00 50.00
Fed Ex Express/144
20 Denny Hamlin 15.00 30.00
Rockwall Automation/288
20 Tony Stewart 15.00 30.00
Home Depot/384
24 Jeff Gordon 20.00 40.00
DuPont Flames/432
24 Jeff Gordon 15.00 30.00
DuPont Flames
Performance Alliance/240
24 Jeff Gordon 20.00 40.00
DuPont Hot Hues
Foose Designs/720
24 Jeff Gordon 15.00 30.00
Holiday JG Foundation/288
24 Jeff Gordon 15.00 30.00
Nicorette/480
24 Jeff Gordon 20.00 40.00
Pepsi/528
24 Jeff Gordon 20.00 40.00
Superman/720
24 Jeff Gordon 20.00 40.00
WSOP
JG Foundation/480
29 Kevin Harvick 15.00 30.00
Goodwrench/240
29 Kevin Harvick 12.50 25.00
Hershey's/240
29 Kevin Harvick 12.50 25.00
Reese's/144
31 Jeff Burton 12.50 25.00
Cingular/144
38 David Gilliland 20.00 40.00
M&M's Halloween/144
38 Elliott Sadler 12.50 25.00
M&M's
Pirates of the Caribbean/240
43 Bobby Labonte 12.50 25.00
STP/204
48 Jimmie Johnson 20.00 40.00
Lowe's/288
48 Jimmie Johnson 20.00 40.00
Lowe's SeaWorld/240
48 Jimmie Johnson 20.00 40.00
Lowe's 60th Anniversary/240
NNO Dale Earnhardt 20.00 40.00
HOF/933

2008 Action Racing Collectables 1:64

EX NM-MT
1 Martin Truex Jr. 4.00 8.00
Bass Pro Shops
6 David Ragan 4.00 8.00
AAA Insurance
6 David Ragan 4.00 8.00
AAA Show Your Card
6 David Ragan 4.00 8.00
AAA Travel
16 Greg Biffle 4.00 8.00
3M
17 Matt Kenseth 4.00 8.00
DeWalt
18 Kyle Busch 4.00 8.00
M&M's
24 Jeff Gordon 5.00 10.00
DuPont Flames
26 Jamie McMurray 4.00 8.00
Irwin Tools
42 Juan Pablo Montoya 4.00 8.00
Texaco Havoline
43 Bobby Labonte 4.00 8.00
Cheerios
99 Carl Edwards 4.00 8.00
Office Depot

2008 Action Racing Collectables Platinum 1:64

EX NM-MT
17 Matt Kenseth 7.50 15.00
DeWalt/3024
18 Kyle Busch 7.50 15.00
M&M's/6192
24 Jeff Gordon 10.00 20.00
DuPont Flames/13,824
48 Jimmie Johnson 7.50 15.00
Lowe's/8208
99 Carl Edwards 7.50 15.00
Office Depot/3504

1997-99 Brookfield 1:24

EX NM-MT
3 Dale Earnhardt 25.00 60.00
AC Delco/15,000 1997

1999 Brookfield 1:24

EX NM-MT
3 Dale Earnhardt 60.00 120.00
Goodwrench/Wrangler/7500
2-car set
3 Dale Earnhardt 50.00 100.00
Wrangler Silver Incentive/624
3 Dale Earnhardt Jr. 125.00 200.00
AC Delco Superman
Silver/624 1999

1994-03 Brookfield Sets 1:24

EX NM-MT
1/3 Dale Earnhardt 50.00 100.00
Dale Earnhardt Jr.
Coke/Coke Bear
2-car set/5000 1998
3 Dale Earnhardt 75.00 125.00
Foundation Black/Brushed Metal
2-car set/55,000
3 Dale Earnhardt 50.00 100.00
Goodwrench/Coke
2-car set/10,000 1996
3/24 Dale Earnhardt 125.00 225.00
Jeff Gordon
Brickyard 400
2-car set/5000 1995
8 Dale Earnhardt Jr. 125.00 200.00
Bud First Win QVC
2-car set/2000 2000
8 Dale Earnhardt Jr. 75.00 150.00
Bud All-Star QVC
2-car set/5004 2001
8 Dale Earnhardt Jr. 125.00 225.00
Bud All-Star QVC 2001 and 2002
2-car set/20,004 2002
24 Jeff Gordon 50.00 100.00
DuPont Brickyard
2-car set with Pace Car 1994
24 Jeff Gordon 75.00 150.00
DuPont Charlotte QVC
regular and brushed metal
2-car set/2000 2000
24 Jeff Gordon 60.00 120.00
DuPont Peanuts QVC
regular and chrome
2-car set/20,000 2000
29 Kevin Harvick 60.00 100.00
Goodwrench QVC 2001
2-car set/2000
white car and brushed metal
36 Ken Schrader 40.00 80.00
M&M's QVC
2-car set/2000 2000
88 Dale Jarrett 75.00 135.00
Quality Care QVC
2-car set/2000 2000

2005 Brookfield 1:24

EX NM-MT
1 Martin Truex Jr. 20.00 40.00
Bass Pro Shops/204
2 Rusty Wallace 25.00 50.00
Miller Lite/444
5 Kyle Busch 20.00 40.00
Kellogg's/204
8 Dale Earnhardt Jr. 25.00 50.00
Bud/804
8 Dale Earnhardt Jr. 25.00 50.00
Bud Born On Feb.12/408
8 Dale Earnhardt Jr. 25.00 50.00
Bud Born On Feb.17/300
8 Dale Earnhardt Jr. 25.00 50.00
Bud Born On Feb.20/900
8 Martin Truex Jr. 20.00 40.00
Bass Pro Shops/204
9 Kasey Kahne 25.00 40.00
Dodge Pit Cap White/240
9 Kasey Kahne 25.00 50.00
Mountain Dew/288
15 Michael Waltrip 20.00 40.00
Napa/204
20 Tony Stewart 20.00 40.00
Home Depot/360
20 Tony Stewart 20.00 40.00
Home Depot Madagascar/204
24 Jeff Gordon 25.00 50.00
DuPont Flames/600
24 Jeff Gordon 25.00 50.00
Mighty Mouse/408
24 Jeff Gordon 25.00 50.00
Pepsi Star Wars/600
29 Kevin Harvick 20.00 40.00
Goodwrench/360
29 Kevin Harvick 20.00 40.00
Goodwrench Atlanta/300
31 Jeff Burton 20.00 40.00
Cingular/288
44 Terry Labonte 20.00 40.00
Kellogg's/204
48 Jimmie Johnson 20.00 40.00
Lowe's/300
81 Dale Earnhardt Jr. 25.00 40.00
Oreo Ritz/804
05 Star Wars Event/900 20.00 40.00
07 Dave Blaney 30.00 50.00
Jack Daniel's/444

2006 Brookfield 1:24

EX NM-MT
8 Dale Earnhardt Jr. 50.00 75.00
Bud/300
8 Dale Earnhardt Jr. 60.00 100.00
Bud 3 Days of Dale Tribute/833
8 Dale Earnhardt Jr. 75.00 125.00
Bud 3 Days of Dale Tribute
Color Chrome/Chrome 2-car set/2004
8 Dale Earnhardt Jr. 60.00 100.00
Bud Father's Day/508
8 Dale Earnhardt Jr. 50.00 75.00
Oreo/300
24 Jeff Gordon 60.00 100.00
DuPont Hot Hues
Foose Designs/300
24 Jeff Gordon 50.00 75.00
Nicorette/222
24 Jeff Gordon 50.00 75.00
Superman/300
24 Jeff Gordon 60.00 100.00
WSOP
JG Foundation/200
48 Jimmie Johnson 50.00 75.00
Lowe's/144
NNO Dale Earnhardt 30.00 60.00
HOF/333

1995 Brookfield Sets 1:64

EX NM-MT
3 Dale Earnhardt 40.00 80.00
Goodwrench/Olympic
3-car set/10,000 1995

2007 Checkered Flag Sports Champions 1:24

EX NM-MT
4 Ward Burton 40.00 65.00
State Water Heaters
7 Robby Gordon 50.00 75.00
Jim Beam/3120
7 Robby Gordon 50.00 75.00
Jim Beam
Car of Tomorrow/3000
7 Robby Gordon 50.00 75.00
Jim Beam Black/3000
7 Robby Gordon 50.00 75.00
Jim Beam Black
Car of Tomorrow/3000
14 Sterling Marlin 40.00 65.00
Waste Management/3504
22 Dave Blaney 40.00 65.00
CAT
83 Shane Huffman 40.00 65.00
Make A Wish/2508
01 Mark Martin 50.00 75.00
U.S. Army/10,000

	EX	NM-MT
01 Mark Martin U.S. Army Car of Tomorrow/10,000	60.00	100.00
07 Dodge Program/2400	40.00	60.00
07 Dodge Program Test/2400	40.00	60.00
07 Dodge Program Test Car of Tomorrow/2400	40.00	60.00
07 JR Motorsports Grand Opening/3883	40.00	60.00
07 Toyota Program/2400	40.00	60.00
07 Toyota Program Car of Tomorrow/2400	40.00	60.00
07 Toyota Program Test/2400	40.00	60.00
07 Toyota Program Test Car of Tomorrow/2400	40.00	60.00

2007 Checkered Flag Sports Champions Black Liquid Chrome 1:24

	EX	NM-MT
4 Ward Burton State Water Heaters	50.00	75.00
7 Robby Gordon Jim Beam/390	75.00	125.00
7 Robby Gordon Jim Beam Car of Tomorrow/375	75.00	125.00
7 Robby Gordon Jim Beam Black/375	75.00	125.00
7 Robby Gordon Jim Beam Black Car of Tomorrow/375	75.00	125.00
14 Sterling Marlin Waste Management/438	50.00	75.00
22 Dave Blaney CAT	50.00	75.00
88 Shane Huffman Make A Wish	50.00	75.00
01 Mark Martin U.S. Army/1250	75.00	125.00
01 Mark Martin U.S. Army COT	100.00	150.00
07 JR Motorsports/833	50.00	75.00
07 JR Motorsports AU/833	100.00	150.00
07 JR Motorsports 24K/283	75.00	125.00

2007 Checkered Flag Sports Contender 1:24

	EX	NM-MT
4 Ward Burton State Water Heaters	10.00	20.00
7 Robby Gordon Jim Beam	15.00	25.00
7 Robby Gordon Jim Beam Car of Tomorrow	15.00	30.00
7 Robby Gordon Jim Beam Black	15.00	25.00
7 Robby Gordon Jim Beam Black Car of Tomorrow	15.00	30.00
7 Robby Gordon Mapei Menards Car of Tomorrow	15.00	25.00
7 Robby Gordon Monster Car of Tomorrow	15.00	25.00
7 Robby Gordon Motorola	15.00	25.00
14 Sterling Marlin Waste Management	10.00	20.00
21 Ken Schrader Motorcraft	15.00	30.00
21 Jon Wood Air Force no rookie stripes	20.00	40.00
22 Dave Blaney CAT Car of Tomorrow	15.00	25.00
55 Robby Gordon Verizon	15.00	25.00
66 Jeff Green Best Buy	15.00	25.00
66 Jeff Green Comcast	15.00	25.00
66 Jeff Green Garmin	15.00	25.00
01 Mark Martin U.S. Army	15.00	30.00
01 Mark Martin U.S. Army Car of Tomorrow	20.00	40.00
07 Dodge Program	15.00	25.00
07 Dodge Program Test	15.00	25.00
07 Ford Program	15.00	25.00
07 Ford Program Car of Tomorrow	15.00	25.00
07 NASCAR on FOX Car of Tomorrow	15.00	25.00
07 Toyota Program	15.00	25.00
07 Toyota Program Car of Tomorrow	15.00	25.00
07 Toyota Program Test	15.00	25.00
07 Toyota Program Test Car of Tomorrow	15.00	25.00

2008 Checkered Flag Sports Champion 1:24

	EX	NM-MT
1 Martin Truex Jr. Bass Pro Shops	40.00	65.00
7 Robby Gordon Jim Beam	40.00	65.00
8 Mark Martin U.S. Army	40.00	65.00
8 Mark Martin Steak-Umm	40.00	65.00
22 Dave Blaney Cat	40.00	65.00
96 Tony Raines DLP	40.00	65.00
08 Toyota Camry	40.00	65.00
08 Dodge Charger	40.00	65.00

2008 Checkered Flag Sports Contender 1:24

	EX	NM-MT
1 Martin Truex Jr. Bass Pro Shops	25.00	50.00
7 Robby Gordon Jim Beam	25.00	50.00
8 Mark Martin U.S. Army	25.00	50.00
15 Paul Menard Menards	25.00	50.00
22 Dave Blaney Cat	25.00	50.00
96 Tony Raines DLP	25.00	50.00

2007 Checkered Flag Sports Contender 1:64

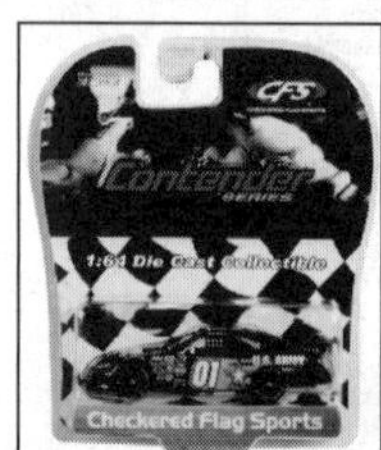

	EX	NM-MT
4 Ward Burton State Water Heaters	3.00	6.00
14 Sterling Marlin Waste Management	3.00	6.00
14 Sterling Marlin Waste Management Car of Tomorrow	4.00	8.00
21 Ken Schrader Motorcraft	3.00	6.00
21 Jon Wood Air Force no rookie stripes	4.00	8.00
22 Dave Blaney CAT	3.00	6.00
66 Jeff Green Best Buy	3.00	6.00
96 Tony Raines DLP Car of Tomorrow	4.00	8.00
01 Mark Martin U.S. Army	4.00	8.00
01 Mark Martin U.S. Army Car of Tomorrow	5.00	10.00
07 Dodge Program	2.50	5.00
07 Dodge Program Car of Tomorrow	3.00	6.00
07 Ford Program	2.50	5.00
07 Ford Program Car of Tomorrow	3.00	6.00
07 NASCAR on FOX COT	3.00	6.00
07 Toyota Program	2.50	5.00
07 Toyota Program Car of Tomorrow	3.00	6.00
07 Toyota Program Test	2.50	5.00
07 Toyota Program Test Car of Tomorrow	3.00	6.00

2008 Checkered Flag Sports Contender 1:64

	EX	NM-MT
1 Martin Truex Jr. Bass Pro Shops	3.00	6.00
22 Dave Blaney Cat	3.00	6.00
96 Tony Raines DLP	3.00	6.00

1992 Ertl 1:18

	EX	NM-MT
3 Dale Earnhardt Goodwrench/40,000	60.00	150.00
4 Ernie Irvan Kodak	20.00	40.00
6 Mark Martin Valvoline	25.00	50.00
10 Derrike Cope Purolator	20.00	40.00
15 Geoff Bodine Motorcraft	60.00	125.00
17 Darrell Waltrip Western Auto Parts America	25.00	50.00
18 Dale Jarrett Interstate Batteries	25.00	40.00
30 Michael Waltrip Pennzoil	12.50	25.00
42 Kyle Petty Mello Yello	20.00	40.00
43 Richard Petty STP	20.00	50.00
59 Robert Pressley Alliance/2502	60.00	150.00

1993 Ertl 1:18

Cars in this series were packaged in clear window boxes that typically included the year of issue on the box bottom. Many of the 1:18 scale cars are commonly referred to as American Muscle since that name is often found on the packaging. Some of the newer pieces were issued in 2-car or 3-car sets. Ertl no longer produces a line of 1:18 scale racing cars to be distributed by themselves but does produce 1:18 cars for other companies.

	EX	NM-MT
11 Bill Elliott Budweiser	20.00	40.00
12 Jimmy Spencer Meineke Bank/2500 White Rose Collectibles	40.00	100.00
20 Bobby Hamilton Fina Lube Bank/5000	20.00	50.00
21 Bobby Bowsher Quality Farm	20.00	50.00
28 Davey Allison Havoline	30.00	60.00
42 Andy Hillenburg Budget Gourmet Promo Bank	40.00	75.00
87 Joe Nemechek Dentyne Bank/2500 White Rose Collectibles	60.00	150.00

1994 Ertl 1:18

	EX	NM-MT
6 Mark Martin Valvoline/30,000	20.00	50.00
7 Alan Kulwicki Army Buck Fever/5000	60.00	120.00
7 Alan Kulwicki Hooters Buck Fever/5000	100.00	175.00
7 Alan Kulwicki Zerex Buck Fever/5000	60.00	120.00
14 John Andretti Kanawaha	20.00	40.00
16 Chad Chaffin 31W Insulation	30.00	50.00
21 Morgan Shepherd Cheerwine	35.00	60.00
24 Jeff Gordon DuPont raced version/5000	40.00	80.00
24 Jeff Gordon DuPont Bank White Rose Collectibles with serial # on bottom of 5000	150.00	300.00
24 Jeff Gordon DuPont Bank White Rose Collectibles without serial number on bottom	50.00	120.00
33 Brad Loney Winnebago Promo	20.00	50.00
59 Andy Belmont Dr. Die Cast Bank/3500	20.00	50.00
59 Dennis Setzer Alliance/5000	40.00	75.00
59 Dennis Setzer Alliance 2-car set	125.00	225.00
60 Mark Martin Winn Dixie GMP/3500	45.00	80.00
84 Benny Senneker Lane Automotive/2500	20.00	50.00

1995 Ertl 1:18

	EX	NM-MT
1 Davey Allison Lancaster/4000	35.00	60.00
1 Jeff Gordon Baby Ruth 1992 T-bird Buck Fever/5000	50.00	100.00
1 Rick Mast Skoal black&green	30.00	60.00
1 Rick Mast Skoal black&white Hoosier Tires	30.00	60.00
1 Rick Mast Skoal black&white Goodyear Tires	20.00	50.00
2 Rusty Wallace Miller Genuine Draft/5000	40.00	80.00
3 Dale Earnhardt Goodwrench 7-Time Champion/10,000	60.00	150.00
3 Dale Earnhardt Goodwrench Silver Buck Fever/15,000	60.00	150.00
3 Jeff Green Goodwrench Buck Fever/3500	25.00	45.00
3 Mike Skinner Goodwrench SuperTruck	25.00	45.00
4 Sterling Marlin Kodak Funsaver	25.00	60.00
4 Jeff Purvis Kodak Funsaver	20.00	50.00
4 Dennis Sensiba Lane Automotive/2500	20.00	50.00
6 Mark Martin Valvoline/15,000	20.00	50.00
7 Geoff Bodine Exide GMP	30.00	60.00
7 Harry Gant Manheim/2502	20.00	50.00
8 Jeff Burton Raybestos	20.00	40.00
10 Ricky Rudd Tide GMP	30.00	60.00
11 Brett Bodine Lowe's White Rose/2500	20.00	50.00
21 Morgan Shepherd Citgo/3500	20.00	40.00
23 Davey Allison Miller American Bank/5000	25.00	60.00
23 Davey Allison Miller High Life Bank/5000	25.00	60.00
23 Jimmy Spencer Smokin' Joe's	90.00	150.00
24 Jeff Gordon DuPont Buck Fever/5000	40.00	80.00
24 Jeff Gordon DuPont GMP/3500	40.00	80.00
26 Steve Kinser Quaker State/3864	40.00	80.00
27 Tim Richmond Old Milwaukee	25.00	50.00
27 Rusty Wallace Kodiak 1989 Grand Prix/3500	100.00	175.00
28 Ernie Irvan Havoline/7500	25.00	60.00
28 Dale Jarrett Havoline/4000	25.00	60.00
32 Dale Jarrett Mac Tools/5000	30.00	60.00
33 Harry Gant Manheim/2502	20.00	50.00
33 Harry Gant Skoal/5004	35.00	60.00
33 Harry Gant Skoal Bandit/5004	35.00	60.00
33 Robert Pressley Skoal	25.00	60.00
41 Ricky Craven Kodiak GMP/2800	25.00	60.00
43 Rodney Combs Jr. French's	50.00	90.00
43 Richard Petty STP 7-Time Champion/10,000	40.00	75.00
43 Robert Pressley French's/1250	50.00	90.00
44 David Green Slim Jim/2500	20.00	50.00
52 Butch Miller Liberty Ford/5000	20.00	50.00
52 Ken Schrader AC Delco	30.00	50.00
52 Ken Schrader AC Delco Bank GMP	20.00	50.00
52 Ken Schrader AC Delco SuperTruck	30.00	50.00
54 Robert Pressley Manheim/2502	20.00	50.00
59 Chad Chaffin Dr. Die Cast	30.00	45.00
59 Dennis Setzer Alliance/2500	30.00	60.00
71 Dave Marcis Olive Garden/2502	20.00	50.00
90 Ernie Irvan Bulls Eye	25.00	60.00
94 Bill Elliott McDonald's	20.00	45.00
94 Bill Elliott McDonald's Thunderbat	30.00	50.00
95 Andy Belmont Old Milwaukee	25.00	45.00
98 Jeremy Mayfield Fingerhut/3500	20.00	40.00
99 Dick Trickle Articat/5000	30.00	50.00

1996 Ertl 1:18

	EX	NM-MT
1 Rick Mast Hooters	30.00	50.00
2 Rusty Wallace Miller Silver/10,000	25.00	60.00
3 Dale Earnhardt Goodwrench '95 Monte Carlo Buck Fever/15,000	40.00	100.00
4 Sterling Marlin Kodak 1995 Monte Carlo Buck Fever/3500	20.00	50.00
5 Terry Labonte Kellogg's	20.00	50.00
5 Terry Labonte Kellogg's Silver	25.00	60.00
6 Mark Martin Valvoline/10,000	30.00	50.00
7 Gary St.Amant Wynn's ASA	30.00	60.00
8 Bobby Dotter Lubteck ASA	30.00	60.00
8 Kenny Wallace Red Dog/3000	20.00	50.00
8 Kenny Wallace Red Dog Bank	30.00	60
9 Lake Speed SPAM	25.00	50
16 Ted Musgrave Family Channel Primestar	20.00	40
17 Bill Sedgwick Die Hard SuperTruck	25.00	50
21 Doug George Ortho SuperTruck	20.00	40
23 Chad Little John Deere in plastic case	25.00	60
23 Chad Little John Deere Autographed	150.00	300
25 Ken Schrader Budweiser	20.00	40
27 Rusty Wallace Miller Genuine Draft	45.00	80
28 Davey Allison Havoline Black&Gold	40.00	70
28 Davey Allison Havoline Black&White	40.00	70
33 Brad Loney Winnebago	35.00	60
42 Kyle Petty Coors Light GMP	30.00	60
42 Kyle Petty Coors Light White Rose	30.00	60
43 Rodney Combs Jr. Hulk Hogan Bank	40.00	75
43 Bobby Hamilton 1972 STP Blue paint	15.00	40
43 Bobby Hamilton 1972 STP Blue/Red paint	15.00	40
43 Bobby Hamilton 1979 STP paint	15.00	40
43 Bobby Hamilton 1984 STP paint	15.00	40
43 Bobby Hamilton STP Silver	20.00	50
75 Todd Bodine Factory Stores Buck Fever	15.00	40
87 Joe Nemechek Burger King GMP	20.00	50
88 Dale Jarrett Quality Care	25.00	45
90 Mike Wallace Heilig-Meyers/2500	20.00	40
94 Bill Elliott McDonald's	25.00	45
95 David Green Busch/1500	30.00	60
95 David Green Busch Bank/1500	30.00	60
95 David Green Caterpillar GMP	25.00	60
95 David Green Caterpillar White Rose Bank	25.00	60
98 Kenny Irwin Raybestos	25.00	50

1997 Ertl 1:18

	EX	NM-
4 Sterling Marlin Kodak	20.00	50
5 Terry Labonte Honey Crunch GMP	100.00	175
6 Mark Martin Valvoline/10,000	20.00	50
7 Geoff Bodine QVC	20.00	45
16 Ted Musgrave Family Channel Primestar	20.00	40
24 Jack Sprague Quaker State SuperTruck	20.00	40
30 Johnny Benson Jr. Pennzoil	20.00	40
36 Derrike Cope Skittles	15.00	40
37 Jeremy Mayfield K-Mart GMP	25.00	60
94 Ron Barfield New Holland	25.00	60
94 Bill Elliott McDonald's	30.00	60
96 David Green Caterpillar/5000	25.00	60
97 Chad Little John Deere Autographed Box	40.00	100

1997 Ertl Prestige Series 1:

	EX	NM-
5 Terry Labonte Honey Crunch/2898	40.00	100
5 Terry Labonte Kellogg's Tony/2898	40.00	100
25 Ricky Craven Budweiser/2502	25.00	60
37 Jeremy Mayfield K-Mart RC-Cola/2502	25.00	60
94 Bill Elliott Mac Tonight/2898	30.00	80

1998 Ertl 1:18

	EX	NM-
26 Johnny Benson Cheerios	15.00	40
40 Sterling Marlin Coors	20.00	50
43 John Andretti STP	20.00	50

1999 Ertl 1:18

	EX	NM-
22 Fireball Roberts Aiken-Mitchell Motors 1957 Chevy Hardtop	15.00	40

reball Roberts	15.00	40.00
Atlanta Tune-Up		
1957 Chevy Convertible		
had Little	25.00	50.00
John Deere Promo		

2000 Ertl Proshop 1:18

	EX	NM-MT
rk Martin	50.00	100.00
Valvoline		
eremy Mayfield	25.00	60.00
Mobil 1		
Mike Bliss	25.00	60.00
Conseco		
Matt Kenseth	50.00	100.00
DeWalt		
Ward Burton	35.00	75.00
Caterpillar Dealers		
Ward Burton	35.00	75.00
Caterpillar Bud Shoot Out		
ave Blaney	25.00	60.00
Amoco		
ill Elliott	35.00	75.00
McDonald's		
eff Burton	30.00	80.00
Exide		

003 Ertl 75 Years of Pontiac 1:18

TED PRODUCTION RUN 2500

	EX	NM-MT
ireball Roberts	40.00	75.00
Stephens 1962 Catalina		
Arnie Beswick	40.00	75.00
Seltzer 1962 Catalina		
Packer Pontiac	40.00	75.00

2000 Ertl Proshop 1:24

	EX	NM-MT
rry Labonte	15.00	30.00
Kellogg's		
rk Martin	15.00	30.00
Valvoline		
Matt Kenseth	20.00	40.00
DeWalt		
Ward Burton	12.50	25.00
Caterpillar Dealers		
Ward Burton	15.00	30.00
Caterpillar Bud Shoot Out		
Ward Burton	30.00	60.00
Wildlife Foundation		
Wally Dallenbach	12.50	25.00
Powerpuff Girls		
ave Blaney	10.00	25.00
Amoco		
Chad Little	12.50	25.00
John Deere		

1982-84 Ertl 1:25

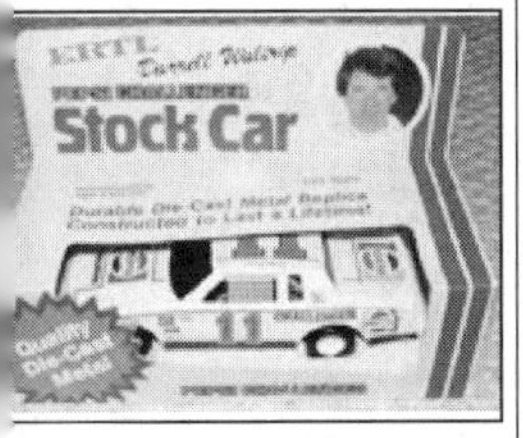

series of cars was released in the early to mid-1980s. Each ackaged in an Ertl window display box with either a erstock Race Car" or "Stock Car" notation at the top of the ge. A small photo of the featured driver was also included e right side of the package.

	EX	NM-MT
Darrell Waltrip	125.00	200.00
Mountain Dew Caprice		
Superstock package		
arrell Waltrip	125.00	200.00
Pepsi Challenger		
Stock Car Package		
ichard Petty	100.00	200.00
STP Stock Car Package		
ichard Petty	100.00	200.00
STP Superstock Package		
arrell Waltrip	125.00	200.00
Gatorade Caprice		
Superstock package		

982 Ertl Motorized Pullback 1:43

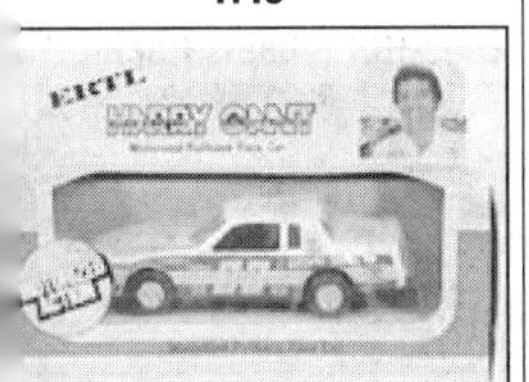

e cars was released in the early 1980s. Each was packaged Ertl window display box with "Motorized Pullback Race printed at the top of the package. A small photo of the red driver was also included on the right side of the age. The back features a short write-up on the driver.

	EX	NM-MT
arrell Waltrip	25.00	50.00
Mountain Dew		
Harry Gant	20.00	40.00
Skoal		
ichard Petty	40.00	80.00
STP		

1981 Ertl Superstock 1:64

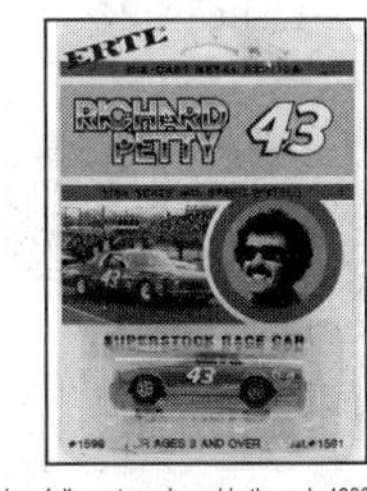

This series of die-cast was issued in the early 1980s by Ertl and is one of the earliest 1:64 NASCAR racing die-cast series. Each car was included on a blister pack that featured a photo of the driver's car on the left and a photo of the driver on the right within a circle design. The driver's name and car number were included above the photos along with the Ertl logo and the die-cast piece was attached below the photos.

	EX	NM-MT
11 Darrell Waltrip	10.00	20.00
Mountain Dew 1980 Chevy		
(issue #1598)		
11 Darrell Waltrip	10.00	20.00
Mountain Dew Buick		
(issue #1946)		
27 Cale Yarborough	10.00	20.00
Valvoline		
(issue #1943)		
43 Richard Petty	12.50	25.00
STP 1980 Chevy blue above		
and below red stripe on sides		
(issue #1599)		
43 Richard Petty	12.50	25.00
STP Buick red above		
and blue below on sides		
(issue #1942)		
88 Bobby Allison	10.00	20.00
Gatorade Buick		
(issue #1944)		
88 Darrell Waltrip	10.00	20.00
Gatorade 1980 Chevy		
(issue #1598)		

1984 Ertl Pow-R Pull 1:64

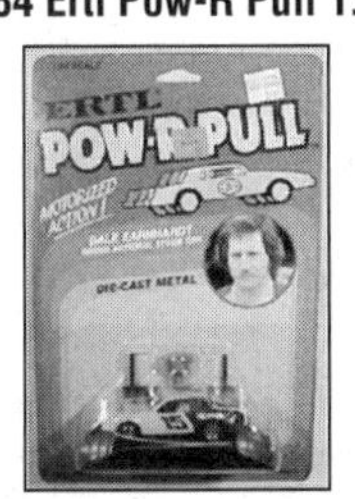

Ertl issued this series of 1:64 die-cast cars in the mid-1980s. Each car was packaged on a large green blister with a photo of the featured driver. A mechanism was also included to be used to provide power to the car so that it could propel itself across the ground.

	EX	NM-MT
7 Kyle Petty	40.00	80.00
Seven-Eleven		
15 Dale Earnhardt	175.00	300.00
Wrangler		
28 Cale Yarborough	40.00	80.00
Hardee's		
43 Richard Petty	60.00	120.00
STP		

1986-93 Ertl 1:64

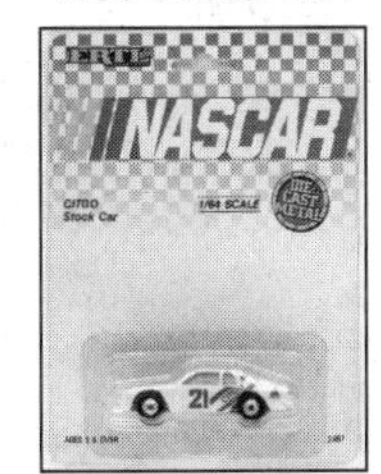

These cars were distributed by Ertl in the late 1980s and early 1990s. Each was packaged in either a white checkered flag designed blister pack or a promo design blister with sponsor logos and artwork. The year of issue is included on the back of the packaging. Some drivers are not specifically identified on the car or the packaging. However, we've included the names below of the driver's on those cars for the year of issue.

	EX	NM-MT
4 NDA/Kodak 1990	5.00	12.00
(Rick Wilson's Car)		
15 Brett Bodine/Crisco 1988	5.00	12.00
15 No Driver Association	5.00	12.00
Crisco Promo 1990		
(Brett Bodine's Car)		
15 Dale Earnhardt	200.00	350.00
Wrangler Promo		
17 Sterling Marlin	7.50	15.00
Hesco 1983 Monte		
Carlo/15,000 1993		
21 NDA/Citgo 1990	5.00	12.00
(Dale Jarrett's Car)		
21 Kyle Petty	6.00	15.00
Citgo 1988		
21 Kyle Petty	6.00	15.00
Citgo Promo 1987		
25 NDA/Folgers 1990	5.00	12.00
(Tim Richmond's Car)		
25 Tim Richmond	7.50	20.00
Folgers Promo 1986		
with T.G. Shephard on package		
30 NDA/Country Time	5.00	12.00
Maxwell House 1990		
(Michael Waltrip's Car)		
43 NDA/STP 1990	7.50	20.00
(Richard Petty's Car)		
49 Buddy Baker	5.00	12.00
Six Pack Camaro Promo		
49 Buddy Baker	5.00	12.00
Six Pack Thunderbird Promo		
55 Phil Parsons	5.00	12.00
Crown Promo 1989		
59 Robert Pressley	4.00	10.00
Alliance Promo 1991		
59 Robert Pressley	4.00	10.00
Alliance Promo/10,000 1992		
Pressley's picture on blister		
88 Buddy Baker	15.00	30.00
Crisco Promo 1986		
00 Sam Ard	4.00	10.00
Thomas Bros.Country Ham 1991		
1984 BGN Championship car		

1992-93 Ertl 1930s Stock Cars 1:64

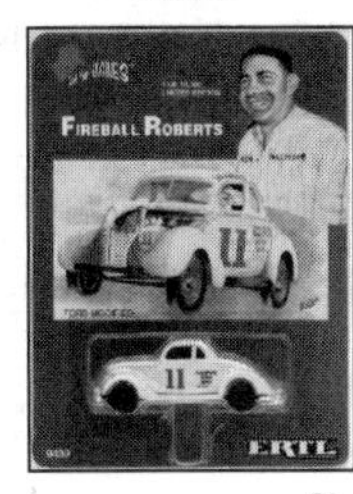

	EX	NM-MT
9 Curtis Crider	5.00	12.00
Fathers of Racing/10,000		
11 Fireball Roberts	5.00	12.00
Roquemore Motor Supply		
Start Your Engines Promo/10,000 1993		
70 Cotton Owens	5.00	12.00
Founding Fathers Promo/10,000 1992		
94 Louise Smith	5.00	12.00
First Ladies of Racing/10,000		

2000 Ertl Proshop 1:64

This series was issued in a large black box that includes a picture of the featured driver and his car. Each box also includes the year of issue and the production run of 10,000.

	EX	NM-MT
5 Terry Labonte	5.00	12.00
Kellogg's		
6 Mark Martin	6.00	12.00
Valvoline		
12 Jermey Mayfield	4.00	10.00
Mobil 1		
17 Matt Kenseth	6.00	15.00
DeWalt		
22 Ward Burton	4.00	10.00
Caterpillar Dealers		
22 Ward Burton	5.00	12.00
Caterpillar Bud Shoot Out		
97 Chad Little	4.00	10.00
John Deere		
99 Jeff Burton	4.00	10.00
Exide		

1992 Funstuf Pit Row 1:43

These 1:43 scale cars were distributed through retail outlets and packaged in standard blister packs. The series features an early Jeff Gordon Baby Ruth BGN car.

	EX	NM-MT
1 Jeff Gordon	15.00	30.00
Baby Ruth		
6 Mark Martin	2.50	5.00
Valvoline		
11 Bill Elliott	2.50	5.00
Amoco		
12 Hut Stricklin	2.50	5.00
Raybestos		
16 Wally Dallenbach Jr.	3.00	6.00
Roush Racing		
18 Dale Jarrett	2.50	5.00
Interstate Batteries		
21 Morgan Shepherd	2.50	5.00
Citgo		
22 Sterling Marlin	2.50	6.00
Maxwell House		
33 Harry Gant	2.50	5.00
Leo Jackson Motors		
41 Greg Sacks	3.00	6.00
Kellogg's		
49 Stanley Smith	2.50	5.00
Ameritron Batteries		
66 Jimmy Hensley	2.50	5.00
TropArtic		
66 Chad Little	2.00	5.00
TropArtic		
75 Joe Ruttman	2.50	5.00
Dinner Bell		
83 Jeff McClure	3.00	6.00
Collector's World		
98 Jimmy Spencer	2.50	5.00
Moly Black Gold		

1992 Funstuf Pit Row 1:64

This series of 1:64 cars was produced by Pit Row and distributed through retail outlets. The series features an early Jeff Gordon Baby Ruth BGN car. A variation of the #94 Terry Labonte car exists as well as variations on some cars with or without a "Winston" decal on the fender.

	EX	NM-MT
1 Jeff Gordon	12.00	20.00
Baby Ruth		
11 Bill Elliott	1.00	3.00
Amoco on the Deck Lid		
11 Bill Elliott	1.00	3.00
Amoco on the Hood		
11 No Driver Association	1.00	3.00

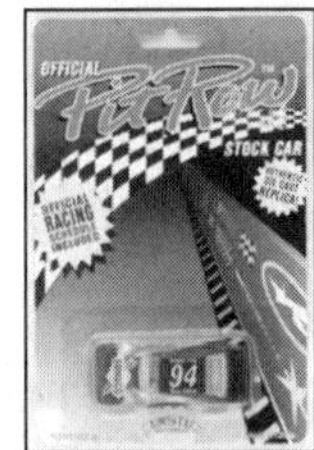

Baby Ruth		
12 Ken Schulz	2.00	5.00
Piggly Wiggly		
15 Morgan Shepherd	1.00	3.00
Motorcraft		
15 Morgan Shepherd	3.00	7.00
Motorcraft with		
Winston Decal on Fender		
15 No Driver Association	1.00	3.00
Motorcraft		
18 Dale Jarrett	1.00	3.00
Interstate Batteries		
18 No Driver Association	1.00	3.00
Interstate Batteries		
20 Michael Waltrip	2.00	5.00
Orkin		
21 Dale Jarrett	1.00	3.00
Citgo		
21 Dale Jarrett	3.00	7.00
Citgo		
with Winston Decal on Fender		
21 Morgan Shepherd	1.00	3.00
Citgo		
23 Eddie Bierschwale	2.00	5.00
AutoFinders		
27 Ward Burton	2.00	5.00
Gaultney		
27 Jeff McClure	2.00	5.00
Race For Life		
41 Greg Sacks	2.00	5.00
Kellogg's		
43 Richard Petty	1.00	3.00
STP		
43 Richard Petty	3.00	7.00
STP		
with Winston Decal on Fender		
49 Stanley Smith	2.00	5.00
Ameritron Batteries		
66 Jimmy Hensley	1.00	3.00
TropArtic		
66 Chad Little	1.25	3.00
TropArtic		
66 Lake Speed	1.00	3.00
TropArtic		
75 No Driver Association	1.00	3.00
Dinner Bell		
75 Joe Ruttman	1.00	3.00
Dinner Bell		
83 Jeff McClure	2.00	5.00
Collector's World		
94 Terry Labonte	1.00	3.00
Sunoco		
94 Terry Labonte	2.00	5.00
Sunoco with Busch decal		
NNO 6-Car Set	6.00	15.00
11. Baby Ruth		
22. S.Marlin/Maxwell Huse		
43. R.Petty/STP		
71. D.Marcis/Big Apple		
94. T.Labonte/Sunoco		
Pit Row Pace Car		

1992 Funstuf Trackside 1:64

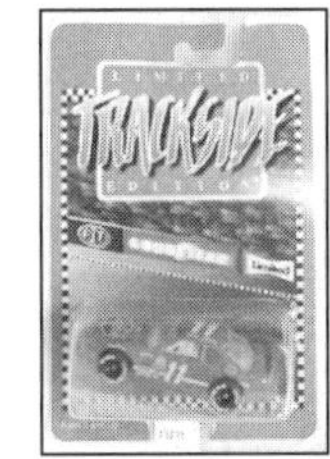

	EX	NM-MT
8 Jeff Burton	1.50	4.00
TIC Financial		
9 Chad Little	1.50	4.00
Melling		
11 Bill Elliott	1.50	4.00
Amoco		
16 Wally Dallenbach	1.50	4.00
Roush Racing		
20 Mike Wallace	1.50	4.00
First Ade		
27 Hut Stricklin	1.50	4.00
McDonald's		
36 Kenny Wallace	1.50	4.00
Dirt Devil		
41 Greg Sacks	1.50	4.00
Kellogg's		
55 Ted Musgrave	1.50	4.00
Jasper		
83 Lake Speed	1.50	4.00
Purex		

2002-04 General Mills Petty Promos 1:64

These 1:64 scale cars were released in 2002 and 2003 in various General Mills products. Each includes black windows and was packaged in either a clear promo style bag or shrinked wrapped on a thin backer board with the copyright "2002 General Mills" on the back. The year the car model ran is also printed on the fronts of the 4-shrinked wrapped die-cast. Those four were initially released in early 2003.

	EX	NM-MT
43 John Andretti	2.00	5.00

2003 Cheerios on card		
43 John Andretti	2.00	5.00
2002 Chex Party Mix on card		
43 John Andretti	2.00	5.00
2001 Honey Nut Cheerios		
on card		
43 John Andretti	2.00	5.00
Pop Secret on card		
43 John Andretti	2.00	5.00
2002 Honey Nut Cheerios		
in bag		
43 John Andretti	2.00	5.00
2000 Wheaties on card		
43 Berry Burst Cheerios in bag 2003	10.00	20.00
43 Betty Crocker in bag	2.50	6.00
43 Box Tops Education in bag 2004	6.00	15.00
43 Cheerios in bag 2003	2.00	5.00
43 Fruit Roll-Ups in bag 2004	4.00	10.00
43 Hamburger Helper in bag 2003	3.00	8.00
43 LeSueur Peas in bag 2004	6.00	15.00
43 Old El Paso in bag 2003	2.50	6.00
43 Pillsbury Grands in bag 2003	2.50	6.00
43 Pop Secret in bag 2003	2.00	5.00
43 Star Wars Attack of the Clones in bag 2002	6.00	15.00
43 Star Wars Phantom Menace in bag 2002	6.00	15.00
43 Star Wars Trilogy in bag 2002	6.00	15.00
43/44/45 John Andretti/Cheerios	10.00	20.00
Petty Enterprises		
Kyle Petty/Sprint		
3-car gold set in bag		
44 Brawny in bag 2004	2.00	5.00
44 Bugles in bag 2004	3.00	8.00
45 Kyle Petty	2.00	5.00
Sprint in bag 2003		

2004 General Mills Hot Wheels Petty Promos 1:64

These 10-die-cast cars were issued inside specially marked boxes of General Mills cereals in 2004. The cars consist of models of actual Richard Petty stock cars over the course of his career as well as a few "fantasy" cars featuring new cereal paint schemes on vintage stock cars. Each car was manufactured by Hot Wheels and issued in an oversized clear plastic wrapper.

	EX	NM-MT
43 Cheerios 1974 Charger	2.50	6.00
43 Cheerios 2004 Dodge Intrepid	2.50	6.00
43 Chex 1970 Barracuda	2.50	6.00
43 Honey Nut Cheerios 1970 Roadrunner	2.50	6.00
43 Lucky Charms 1971 Plymouth GTX	2.50	6.00
43 Lucky Charms 2004 Dodge Intrepid	2.50	6.00
43 Pop Secret 1964 Plymouth	2.50	6.00
43 Pop Secret 1970 Barracuda	2.50	6.00
43 Pop Secret 1974 Charger	2.50	6.00
43 Pop Secret 1984 Grand Prix	2.50	6.00
43 Wheaties 1967 GTO	2.50	6.00
43 Richard Petty	3.00	8.00
STP 1964 Plymouth		
43 Richard Petty	3.00	8.00
STP 1974 Charger		

2003 GreenLight 1:24

	EX	NM-MT
10 Brickyard 400 10th Anniversary	12.50	25.00
Event Car/2003		

2003 GreenLight 1:64

	EX	NM-MT
03 Brickyard 400 Event Car Orange	4.00	8.00
with Silver Hood/4080		
03 Brickyard 400 Event Car Silver	6.00	12.00
with Oragne Hood/4080		

2002 Hot Wheels Thunder Series Motorcycles 1:18

	EX	NM-MT
5 Terry Labonte	5.00	10.00
Kellogg's		
6 Mark Martin	5.00	10.00
Pfizer		
10 Johnny Benson	5.00	10.00
Valvoline		
10 Scott Riggs	5.00	10.00
Nesquik		
12 Ryan Nemwan	5.00	10.00
Alltel		
14 Larry Foyt	5.00	10.00
Harrah's		

	EX	NM-MT
17 Matt Kenseth DeWalt	5.00	10.00
22 Ward Burton Caterpillar	5.00	10.00
25 Randy Tolsma Marines Red/Black	5.00	10.00
36 Ken Schrader M&M's	5.00	10.00
40 Sterling Marlin Silver	5.00	10.00
43 John Andretti Cheerios	5.00	10.00
45 Kyle Petty Sprint	5.00	10.00
99 Jeff Burton Citgo	5.00	10.00

2004 Hot Wheels Racing Justice League Thunder Rides 1:18

	EX	NM-MT
6 Mark Martin Batman	7.50	15.00
16 Greg Biffle Flash	6.00	12.00
17 Matt Kenseth Martian Manhunter	6.00	12.00
21 Ricky Rudd Wonder Woman	6.00	12.00
97 Kurt Busch Superman	6.00	12.00
99 Jeff Burton Green Lantern	6.00	12.00

1998 Hot Wheels Legends 1:24

	EX	NM-MT
44 Kyle Petty Blues Brothers	25.00	50.00
44 Kyle Petty Hot Wheels	25.00	50.00

1998 Hot Wheels Racing 1:24

This series of 1:24 scale cars was released in 1998. Each was packaged in a Hot Wheels Racing black window box. Note that a similar box was also used in 1999, but that series was entitled "Hot Wheels Pro Racing."

	EX	NM-MT
6 Mark Martin Valvoline	10.00	25.00
12 Jeremy Mayfield Mobil 1	8.00	20.00
26 Johnny Benson Cheerios	8.00	20.00
35 Todd Bodine Tabasco	8.00	20.00
36 Ernie Irvan Skittles	8.00	20.00
42 Joe Nemechek Bell South	8.00	20.00
44 Kyle Petty Blues Brothers	10.00	25.00
44 Kyle Petty Hot Wheels	10.00	25.00
58 Ricky Craven Turbine Solutions	20.00	40.00
97 Chad Little John Deere	8.00	20.00

1998 Hot Wheels Racing 2-Car Sets 1:24/1:64

	EX	NM-MT
6 Mark Martin Eagle One w/Valvoline 1:64	10.00	25.00
43 John Andretti STP	8.00	20.00
44 Kyle Petty Hot Wheels	10.00	25.00

1998 Hot Wheels Racing Electronic Fast Facts 1:24

This series was prodcued with each car acting as an electonic trivia game complete with questions and answers about the specific driver featured. Each was packaged in a black "Hot Wheels Racing Electonic Fast Facts" window box.

	EX	NM-MT
12 Jeremy Mayfield Mobil One	10.00	20.00
44 Kyle Petty Hot Wheels	10.00	20.00

1999 Hot Wheels Crew's Choice 1:24

These 1:24 scale cars feature bodies that are detachable from the chassis. Each was packaged in a solid black Hot Wheels Crew's Choice box.

	EX	NM-MT
10 Ricky Rudd Tide	8.00	20.00
12 Jeremy Mayfield Mobil 1	8.00	20.00
14 Sterling Marlin Tennessee	20.00	35.00
17 Matt Kenseth DeWalt	20.00	40.00
22 Ward Burton Caterpillar	8.00	20.00
26 Jimmy Spencer Big K	8.00	20.00
36 Ernie Irvan M&M's	15.00	30.00
40 Sterling Marlin Coors	15.00	40.00
43 John Andretti STP	8.00	20.00
44 Kyle Petty Hot Wheels	12.50	30.00
45 Adam Petty Spree	30.00	60.00
55 Kenny Wallace Square D Aerosmith	8.00	20.00
94 Bill Elliott McDonald's	10.00	25.00
94 Bill Elliott Toy Story 2	75.00	125.00
99 Jeff Burton Exide	8.00	20.00

1999 Hot Wheels Deluxe 1:24

This series of cars was isued through retail outlets in a black and blue window box. The box features the title "Deluxe" in the lower right hand corner. Please note that the same box was also used in 2000 with the addition of the words "Race Day" to the Deluxe title.

	EX	NM-MT
5 Terry Labonte Kellogg's	10.00	25.00
6 Mark Martin Valvoline Black Chrome	10.00	25.00
17 Matt Kenseth DeWalt	10.00	25.00
22 Ward Burton Caterpillar Black Chrome	8.00	20.00
32 Scott Pruett Tide	8.00	20.00
36 John Andretti Cheerios	8.00	20.00
42 Joe Nemechek BellSouth	8.00	20.00
45 Adam Petty Sprint	15.00	40.00
94 Bill Elliott McDonald's Drive Thru	8.00	20.00

1999 Hot Wheels Fresh Paint 1:24

These 1:24 scale die-casts were issued in Hot Wheels Fresh Paint window box. Each box includes the notation "Speedway Special Edition" on the front along with the stated production run of 7998.

	EX	NM-MT
5 Terry Labonte K-Sentials	5.00	10.00
6 Mark Martin Zerex	5.00	10.00
7 Michael Waltrip Sealy	4.00	8.00
99 Jeff Burton Citgo	4.00	8.00

1999 Hot Wheels Pro Racing 1:24

These 1:24 scale cars were available primarily through retail outlets. Each was packaged in a solid black Hot Wheels Pro Racing window box. Note that a similar box was used in 1998, but that series was called "Hot Wheels Racing."

	EX	NM-MT
5 Terry Labonte Kellogg's	15.00	30.00
6 Mark Martin Valvoline	15.00	30.00
10 Ricky Rudd Tide	8.00	20.00
12 Jeremy Mayfield Mobil 1	8.00	20.00
14 Sterling Marlin Tennessee	35.00	60.00
26 Johnny Benson Betty Crocker	8.00	20.00
26 Johnny Benson Cheerios	8.00	20.00
35 Todd Bodine Tabasco Red	8.00	20.00
36 Ernie Irvan M&M's	15.00	30.00
42 Joe Nemechek BellSouth	8.00	20.00
43 Richard Petty STP '81 Buick	15.00	40.00
44 Kyle Petty Blues Brothers	12.50	30.00
44 Kyle Petty Hot Wheels	12.50	30.00
44 Kyle Petty Players Inc.	12.50	30.00
94 Bill Elliott McDonald's Drive Thru	8.00	20.00
97 Chad Little John Deere	8.00	20.00

1999 Hot Wheels Racing NASCAR Rocks 1:24

Each of these 1:24 scale cars were issued in a black Hot Wheels window box. A small plastic guitar was also packaged with each car. The cars were produced with a production run of 15,000.

	EX	NM-MT
5 Terry Labonte Kellogg's	10.00	25.00
6 Mark Martin Valvoline	12.50	25.00
9 Jerry Nadeau Dexter's Lab	10.00	25.00
10 Ricky Rudd Tide	10.00	25.00
12 Jeremy Mayfield Mobil 1	10.00	25.00
22 Ward Burton Caterpillar	10.00	25.00
26 Johnny Benson Cheerios	10.00	25.00
44 Kyle Petty Hot Wheels	10.00	25.00
66 Darrell Waltrip Big K	10.00	25.00
94 Bill Elliott McDonald's Drive Thru	10.00	25.00
97 Chad Little John Deere	10.00	25.00
99 Jeff Burton Exide	10.00	25.00

1999 Hot Wheels Racing Select 1:24

These 1:24 scale die-cast cars were issued by Hot Wheels in a black window box. The "Select" name appears in red in the lower right hand corner of the box. The stated production run was 10,000. A few pieces were also issued in a Toy Story 2 promo window box. The Toy Story logo appears in the lower right hand corner with the Select name on the top of the box.

STATED PRODUCTION RUN 10,000

	EX	NM-MT
4 Bobby Hamilton Kodak Advantix	8.00	20.00
5 Terry Labonte Kellogg's	10.00	25.00
6 Mark Martin Valvoline	10.00	25.00
26 Johnny Benson Cheerios	8.00	20.00
26 Johnny Benson Cheerios Toy Story 2	8.00	20.00
36 Ken Schrader M&M's	8.00	20.00
43 John Andretti STP	8.00	20.00
44 Kyle Petty Hot Wheels	8.00	20.00
44 Kyle Petty Hot Wheels Toy Story 2	8.00	20.00
94 Bill Elliott McDonald's Drive Thru	8.00	20.00
97 Chad Little John Deere	8.00	20.00
99 Jeff Burton Exide	8.00	20.00

1999 Hot Wheels Select Clear 1:24

These 1:24 scale plastic body cars were issued by Hot Wheels primarily to the hobby. Each was packaged in a blue and black window box with the driver's photo and the "Select Clear" name in the lower right hand corner of the box. Each was produced with a clear plastic body.

	EX	NM-MT
6 Mark Martin Valvoline	8.00	20.00
21 Elliott Sadler Citgo	8.00	20.00
43 John Andretti STP	8.00	20.00
44 Kyle Petty Hot Wheels	8.00	20.00
60 Geoff Bodine Power Team	8.00	20.00
66 Darrell Waltrip Big K	8.00	20.00
94 Bill Elliott McDonald's Drive Thru	8.00	20.00
99 Jeff Burton Exide	8.00	20.00

1999 Hot Wheels Trading Paint 1:24

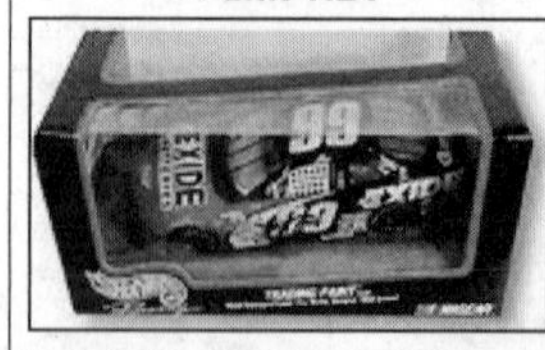

These 1:24 scale cars feature painting detail that creates a race damaged look. Each car was packaged in a black Hot Wheels window box.

	EX	NM-MT
7 Michael Waltrip Phillips	8.00	20.00
12 Jeremy Mayfield Mobil 1	8.00	20.00
22 Ward Burton Caterpillar	8.00	20.00
43 John Andretti STP	8.00	20.00
44 Kyle Petty Hot Wheels	8.00	20.00
66 Darrell Waltrip Big K	8.00	20.00
94 Bill Elliott McDonald's	10.00	20.00
99 Jeff Burton Exide	8.00	20.00

2000 Hot Wheels Crew's Choice 1:24

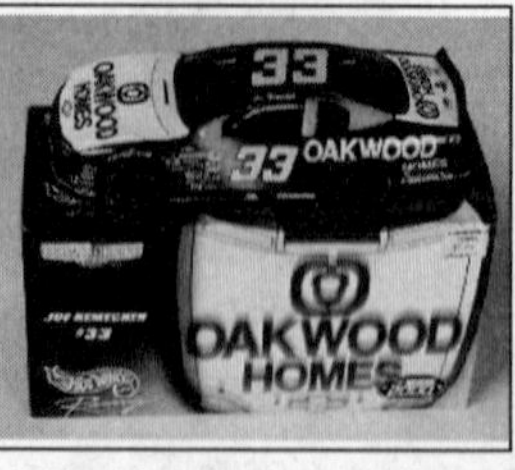

The Hot Wheels Crew's Choice brand was produced as the company's highest quality 1:24 die-cast. Each car was built with more than 25-detailed parts and a removable body. They were packaged in a solid box (in the colors of the driver's car) with the "Crew's Choice" name and year of issue clearly defined. Each car also included a certificate of authenticity that noted a production run of 4998 of each piece.

	EX	NM-MT
4 Bobby Hamilton Kodak	8.00	20.00
6 Mark Martin Valvoline	10.00	25.00
7 Michael Waltrip Nations Rent	8.00	20.00
12 Jeremy Mayfield Mobil 1	8.00	20.00
14 Mike Bliss Conseco	8.00	20.00
17 Matt Kenseth DeWalt	15.00	30.00
22 Ward Burton Caterpillar	8.00	20.00
26 Jimmy Spencer Big K	8.00	20.00
32 Scott Pruett Tide	8.00	20.00
33 Joe Nemechek Oakwood Homes	8.00	20.00
40 Sterling Marlin Coors Light	15.00	30.00
42 Kenny Irwin BellSouth	15.00	30.00
43 John Andretti STP 1972 paint scheme	8.00	20.00
43 John Andretti STP	8.00	20.00
43 John Andretti Cheerios	8.00	20.00
43 John Andretti STP Texas	8.00	20.00
43 John Andretti Wheaties	10.00	25.00
44 Kyle Petty Hot Wheels	10.00	25.00
45 Adam Petty Sprint PCS	15.00	40.00
55 Kenny Wallace Square D	8.00	20.00
60 Geoff Bodine Power Team	8.00	20.00
66 Darrell Waltrip Big K Route 66	8.00	20.00
77 Robert Pressley Jasper	8.00	20.00
94 Bill Elliott McDonald's	10.00	25.00
97 Chad Little John Deere	8.00	20.00
97 Anthony Lazzaro McDonald's	8.00	20.00
99 Jeff Burton Exide	8.00	20.00

2000 Hot Wheels Race Day Deluxe 1:24

These cars were available through retail outlets, in a black and blue box with a window to let you see the driver side and top of the car. The box features the title "Race Day Deluxe" in the lower right hand corner. Please note that the same box was also used in 1999 without the words "Race Day" in the Deluxe title.

	EX	NM-MT
4 Bobby Hamilton Kodak	8.00	20.00
5 Terry Labonte Kellogg's	10.00	25.00
6 Mark Martin Valvoline	10.00	25.00
7 Michael Waltrip NationsRent	8.00	20.00
12 Jeremy Mayfield Mobil 1	8.00	20.00
14 Mike Bliss Conseco	8.00	20.00
17 Matt Kenseth DeWalt	15.00	30.00
21 Elliott Sadler Citgo	8.00	20.00
22 Ward Burton Caterpillar	8.00	20.00
25 Jerry Nadeau Holigan	8.00	20.00
26 Jimmy Spencer Big K	8.00	20.00
32 Scott Pruett Tide	8.00	20.00
33 Joe Nemechek Oakwood Homes	8.00	20.00
42 Kenny Irwin BellSouth	15.00	40.00
43 John Andretti Cheerios	8.00	20.00
43 John Andretti STP	8.00	20.00
43 John Andretti Wheaties	8.00	20.00
44 Kyle Petty Hot Wheels	10.00	25.00
45 Adam Petty Sprint	15.00	40.00
55 Kenny Wallace Aerosmith	8.00	20
60 Geoffery Bodine Power Team	8.00	20
94 Bill Elliott McDonald's Drive Thru	10.00	25.
97 Anthony Lazzaro McDonald's	8.00	20
97 Chad Little John Deere	8.00	20
99 Jeff Burton Exide	8.00	20.

2000 Hot Wheels Select 1:

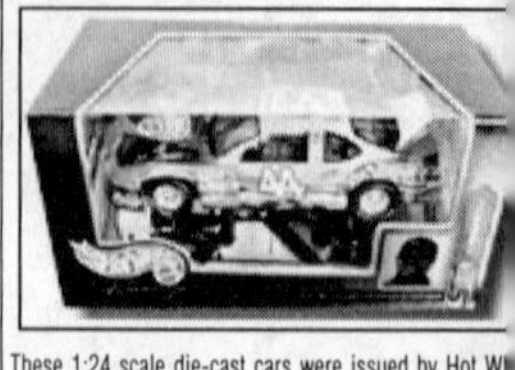

These 1:24 scale die-cast cars were issued by Hot W primarily to the hobby. Each was packaged in a blue and window box with the driver's photo and the "Select 2000" in the lower right hand corner of the box. The stated produ run was 9998 of each car.

	EX	NM-MT
12 Jeremy Mayfield Mobil 1	8.00	20.
17 Matt Kenseth DeWalt	10.00	25.
22 Ward Burton Caterpillar	8.00	20.
43 John Andretti STP	8.00	20.
44 Kyle Petty Hot Wheels	8.00	20.

2001 Hot Wheels Racing 1:

	EX	NM-MT
5 Terry Labonte Kellogg's Tony	10.00	25.
6 Mark Martin Pfizer	10.00	25.
10 Johnny Benson Valvoline	8.00	20.
10 Jeff Green Nesquik	8.00	20.
12 Jeremy Mayfield Mobil 1	8.00	20.
17 Matt Kenseth DeWalt Yellow&Black	12.00	30.
17 Matt Kenseth DeWalt Black	12.00	30.
21 Elliott Sadler Motorcraft	8.00	20.
22 Ward Burton Caterpillar	8.00	20.
25 Jerry Nadeau UAW Delphi	8.00	20.
32 Scott Pruett Tide	8.00	20.
32 Scott Pruett Tide Alabama	12.50	30.
32 Ricky Craven Tide Downy Promo	6.00	15.
33 Joe Nemechek Oakwood Homes	8.00	20.
36 Ken Schrader M&M's	10.00	25.
43 John Andretti Cheerios	8.00	20.
44 Buckshot Jones Four Generations of Petty	8.00	20.
44 Buckshot Jones Georgia Pacific	8.00	20.
45 Kyle Petty Sprint PCS	8.00	20.
45 Kyle Petty Sprint Charity Ride	8.00	20.
60 Greg Biffle Grainger	8.00	20.
96 Andy Houston McDonald's	8.00	20.
99 Jeff Burton Citgo	8.00	20.
02 Ryan Newman Alltel	12.50	25.

2002 Hot Wheels Racing 1:

	EX	NM-M
5 Terry Labonte Kellogg's	10.00	20.
5 Terry Labonte Monster's Inc.	12.50	25.
6 Mark Martin Pfizer	10.00	20.
10 Johnny Benson Eagle One	10.00	20.
10 Scott Riggs Nesquik	10.00	20.
12 Ryan Newman Alltel	12.50	25.
14 Larry Foyt	10.00	20.

	EX	NM-MT
rah's		
Kenseth Walt	10.00	20.00
d Burton erpillar	10.00	20.00
dy Tolsma rines red/black	10.00	20.00
dy Tolsma rines red/white/blue	12.50	25.00
Schrader M's	10.00	20.00
Andretti eerios	10.00	20.00
Andretti mburger Helper	10.00	20.00
Andretti ney Nut Cheerios	10.00	20.00
Andretti o Secret	10.00	20.00
Petty int	10.00	20.00
Busch bermaid	10.00	20.00
Burton go	10.00	20.00

3 Hot Wheels Racing 1:24

	EX	NM-MT
Martin zer	12.50	25.00
t Riggs squik	12.50	25.00
Newman el	15.00	25.00
Newman bil 1	12.50	25.00
Newman bil 1 First Win/1212	15.00	30.00
Biffle inger	12.50	25.00
Kenseth Walt	15.00	25.00
y Rudd torcraft	12.50	25.00
by Hamilton Jr. rines	15.00	25.00
Schrader M's Haloween	12.50	25.00
Andretti erios	12.50	25.00
Andretti Secret	12.50	25.00
Petty rgia Pacific Brawny	12.50	25.00
Busch bermaid	15.00	25.00
Busch bermaid Little Tikes	15.00	25.00
Burton go	12.50	25.00
Burton go Bass Masters	12.50	25.00
Nadeau ny	12.50	25.00

3 Hot Wheels Racing Matt nseth Championship 1:24

	EX	NM-MT
Kenseth Walt	12.50	25.00
Kenseth Walt/10,000	18.00	30.00

003 Hot Wheels Racing Stock Car Cruisers 1:24

	EX	NM-MT
Martin er	12.50	25.00
Newman el	12.50	25.00
Kenseth Walt	12.50	25.00
Busch bermaid	12.50	25.00

004 Hot Wheels Racing lternative Paint Scheme 1:24

	EX	NM-MT
Martin ar Mayer	10.00	20.00
y Rudd Force	10.00	20.00
Petty wny	10.00	20.00

004 Hot Wheels Racing Artist Collection 1:24

	EX	NM-MT
Martin er	15.00	30.00
Newman el	12.50	25.00
Biffle	12.50	25.00

	EX	NM-MT
Grainger		
17 Matt Kenseth DeWalt	15.00	30.00
21 Ricky Rudd Motorcraft	12.50	25.00
97 Kurt Busch Rubbermaid	12.50	25.00
99 Jeff Burton Citgo	12.50	25.00

2004 Hot Wheels Racing Chase for the Cup 1:24

	EX	NM-MT
6 Mark Martin Viagra/6000	15.00	30.00
12 Ryan Newman Alltel/6000	12.50	25.00
17 Matt Kenseth DeWalt/6000	15.00	30.00
97 Kurt Busch Irwin Tools/6000	12.50	25.00

2004 Hot Wheels Racing Justice League 1:24

	EX	NM-MT
6 Mark Martin Batman	15.00	30.00
9 Mark Martin Batman	15.00	30.00
16 Greg Biffle Flash	10.00	20.00
21 Ricky Rudd Wonder Woman	10.00	20.00
60 Greg Biffle Flash	10.00	20.00
97 Kurt Busch Superman	15.00	25.00
99 Jeff Burton Green Lantern	10.00	20.00
04 Justice League Super Heroes	10.00	20.00
04 Justice League Villains	10.00	20.00

2004 Hot Wheels Racing Race Day 1:24

	EX	NM-MT
6 Mark Martin Viagra	15.00	25.00
12 Ryan Newman Alltel	10.00	20.00
17 Matt Kenseth DeWalt	15.00	25.00
21 Ricky Rudd Motorcraft	10.00	20.00
45 Kyle Petty Georgia Pacific	10.00	20.00
97 Kurt Busch Sharpie	10.00	20.00

2004 Hot Wheels Racing Stockerz 1:24

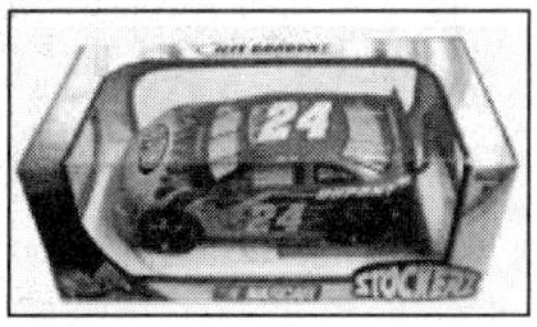

	EX	NM-MT
6 Mark Martin Oscar Mayer	12.50	25.00
6 Mark Martin Pfizer	12.50	25.00
12 Ryan Newman Alltel	12.50	25.00
17 Matt Kenseth DeWalt	18.00	30.00
21 Ricky Rudd Motorcraft	12.50	25.00
24 Jeff Gordon DuPont Flames	18.00	30.00
29 Kevin Harvick Goodwrench	12.50	25.00
97 Kurt Busch Rubbermaid	10.00	20.00
97 Kurt Busch Sharpie	10.00	20.00

2004 Hot Wheels Racing Test Track 1:24

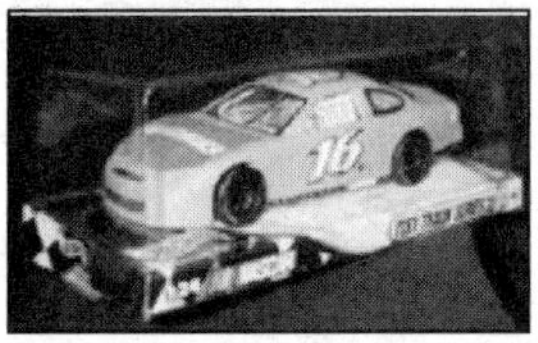

	EX	NM-MT
6 Mark Martin Pfizer	12.50	25.00
12 Ryan Newman Alltel	10.00	20.00
16 Greg Biffle Grainger	10.00	20.00
17 Matt Kenseth DeWalt	12.50	25.00
43 Richard Petty STP	12.50	25.00
97 Kurt Busch Sharpie	10.00	20.00

2005 Hot Wheels Alternative Paint Scheme 1:24

	EX	NM-MT
17 Matt Kenseth Trex	10.00	20.00

	EX	NM-MT
21 Ricky Rudd Air Force	10.00	20.00
97 Kurt Busch Irwin Tools	10.00	20.00
99 Carl Edwards Office Depot	15.00	30.00

2005 Hot Wheels Batman Begins 1:24

	EX	NM-MT
6 Mark Martin Batman	15.00	30.00

2005 Hot Wheels Race Day 1:24

	EX	NM-MT
16 Greg Biffle National Guard	10.00	20.00
21 Ricky Rudd Motorcraft	10.00	20.00
97 Kurt Busch Sharpie	10.00	20.00
99 Carl Edwards AAA	15.00	30.00

1998 Hot Wheels Racing 1:43

These 1:43 scale cars were produced by Hot Wheels and marks their introduction in the NASCAR market. These cars were distributed through hobby, retail and trackside outlets.

	EX	NM-MT
5 Terry Labonte Kellogg's	6.00	15.00
6 Mark Martin Valvoline	6.00	15.00
7 Michael Waltrip Phillips	5.00	12.00
10 Ricky Rudd Tide	5.00	12.00
12 Jeremy Mayfield Mobil 1	5.00	12.00
35 Todd Bodine Tabasco	5.00	12.00
43 John Andretti STP	5.00	12.00
44 Kyle Petty Hot Wheels	5.00	12.00
99 Jeff Burton Exide	5.00	12.00

1999 Hot Wheels Crew's Choice 1:43

These 1:43 scale cars feature bodies that are detachable from the chassis.

	EX	NM-MT
6 Mark Martin Valvoline	10.00	20.00
36 Ernie Irvan M&M's	8.00	20.00
44 Kyle Petty Hot Wheels	8.00	20.00
66 Darrell Waltrip Big K	8.00	20.00
94 Bill Elliott McDonald's	8.00	20.00

1999 Hot Wheels Deluxe Black Chrome 1:43

	EX	NM-MT
4 Bobby Hamilton Kodak Max	4.00	10.00
5 Terry Labonte Kellogg's	5.00	10.00
6 Mark Martin Valvoline	5.00	10.00
12 Jeremy Mayfield Mobil 1	4.00	10.00
21 Elliott Sadler Citgo	4.00	10.00
22 Ward Burton Caterpillar	4.00	10.00
43 John Andretti STP	4.00	10.00
44 Kyle Petty Hot Wheels	4.00	10.00
60 Geoff Bodine Power Team	4.00	10.00
97 Chad Little John Deere	4.00	10.00
99 Jeff Burton Exide	4.00	10.00

1999 Hot Wheels Pro Racing 1:43

These 1:43 scale cars were available through retail outlets.

	EX	NM-MT
5 Terry Labonte Kellogg's	6.00	15.00
6 Mark Martin Vavoline	6.00	15.00
6 Mark Martin Synpower	6.00	15.00
10 Ricky Rudd Tide	5.00	12.00
12 Jeremy Mayfield Mobil 1	5.00	12.00
22 Ward Burton Caterpillar	5.00	12.00
26 Johnny Benson Cheerios	5.00	12.00
36 Ernie Irvan M&M's	5.00	12.00
36 Ernie Irvan Skittles	5.00	12.00
43 John Andretti STP	5.00	12.00
44 Kyle Petty Hot Wheels	5.00	12.00
94 Bill Elliott McDonald's	6.00	15.00
97 Chad Little John Deere	5.00	12.00

1999 Hot Wheels Radical Rides 1:43

This series features a highly exaggerated modified stock car with an oversized driver figure on top. The scale is roughly 1:43 and each was packaged in a Hot Wheels blister with the title "Radical Rides" printed in blue and yellow in the upper right hand corner.

	EX	NM-MT
6 Mark Martin Valvoline	6.00	12.00
17 Matt Kenseth DeWalt	6.00	12.00
43 John Andretti Cheerios	5.00	10.00
43 Richard Petty STP	6.00	12.00
44 Kyle Petty Hot Wheels	5.00	10.00
45 Adam Petty Sprint	10.00	20.00
66 Darrell Waltrip K-Mart Route 66	5.00	10.00
97 Chad Little John Deere	5.00	10.00
99 Jeff Burton Exide	5.00	10.00

1999 Hot Wheels Select 1:43

These 1:43 scale die-cast cars were issued by Hot Wheels in a black window box. The "Select" name appears in red in the lower right hand corner of the box. The stated production run was 10,000.

	EX	NM-MT
12 Jeremy Mayfield Mobil 1	4.00	10.00
22 Ward Burton Caterpillar	4.00	10.00
36 Ken Schrader M&M's	6.00	12.00
44 Kyle Petty Hot Wheels	4.00	10.00
99 Jeff Burton Exide	4.00	10.00

1999 Hot Wheels Select Clear 1:43

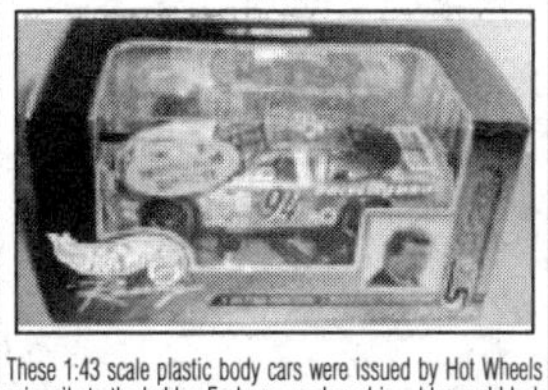

These 1:43 scale plastic body cars were issued by Hot Wheels primarily to the hobby. Each was packaged in a blue and black window box with the driver's photo and the "Select Clear" name in the lower right hand corner of the box. Each was produced with a clear plastic body.

	EX	NM-MT
6 Mark Martin Valvoline	6.00	12.00
12 Jeremy Mayfield Mobil 1	4.00	10.00
21 Elliott Sadler Citgo	4.00	10.00
43 John Andretti STP	4.00	10.00
55 Kenny Wallace Square D	4.00	10.00
66 Darrell Waltrip Big K	4.00	10.00
94 Bill Elliott McDonald's	5.00	12.00
94 Bill Elliott McDonald's Drive Thru	5.00	10.00
98 No Driver Association Woody Woodpecker	4.00	10.00
99 Jeff Burton Exide	4.00	10.00

1999 Hot Wheels Track Edition 1:43

The track edition set comes with a 1:64 scale car.

	EX	NM-MT
12 Jeremy Mayfield Mobil 1	6.00	15.00
16 Kevin Lepage Primestar	6.00	15.00

	EX	NM-MT
36 Ernie Irvan M&M's	6.00	15.00
94 Bill Elliott Drive Thru	6.00	15.00
97 Chad Little John Deere	6.00	15.00

2000 Hot Wheels Deluxe 1:43

	EX	NM-MT
4 Bobby Hamilton Kodak	4.00	10.00
22 Ward Burton Caterpillar	4.00	10.00
33 Joe Nemechek Oakwood Homes	4.00	10.00
43 John Andretti STP	4.00	10.00
44 Kyle Petty Hot Wheels	4.00	10.00

2000 Hot Wheels Select 1:43

These 1:43 scale die-cast cars were issued by Hot Wheels primarily to the hobby. Each was packaged in a blue and black window box with the driver's photo and the "Select" name in the lower right hand corner of the box.

	EX	NM-MT
43 John Andretti STP	4.00	10.00
44 Kyle Petty Hot Wheels	4.00	10.00
94 Bill Elliott McDonald's Drive Thru	4.00	10.00

2001 Hot Wheels Racing Radical Rods 1:43

	EX	NM-MT
6 Mark Martin Valvoline	5.00	12.00
12 Jeremy Mayfield Mobil 1	4.00	10.00
17 Matt Kenseth DeWalt	6.00	12.00
22 Ward Burton Caterpillar	4.00	10.00
32 Scott Pruett Tide	4.00	10.00
33 Joe Nemechek Oakwood Homes	4.00	10.00
43 John Andretti Cheerios	4.00	10.00
43 Richard Petty STP	4.00	10.00
45 Kyle Petty Hot Wheels	4.00	10.00
45 Kyle Petty Sprint	4.00	10.00
99 Jeff Burton Citgo	4.00	10.00

1992 Hot Wheels Pro Circuit 1:64

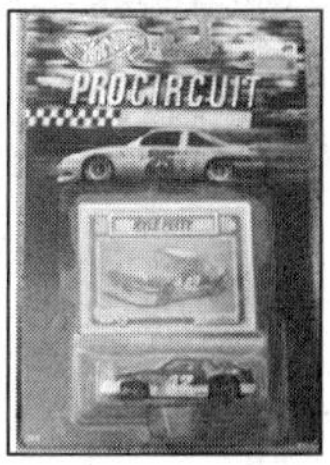

These 1:64 cars were issued in 1992 was part of the Hot Wheels Pro Circuit series. Each car was packaged in a "Pro Circuit" blister along with a silver bordered foil trading card.

	EX	NM-MT
2 Rusty Wallace Pontiac	3.00	6.00
6 Mark Martin Valvoline	3.00	6.00
21 Morgan Shepherd Citgo	2.00	5.00
26 Brett Bodine Quaker State	2.00	5.00
42 Kyle Petty Mello Yello	2.00	5.00
43 Richard Petty STP	3.00	6.00

1995-96 Hot Wheels 1:64

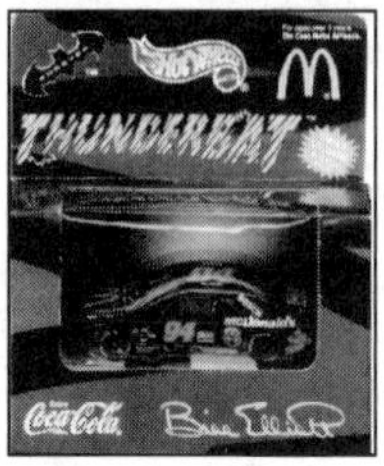

Each of these 1:64 cars were issued in a Hot Wheels window display box. The boxes also included a backer board and a copyright date on the bottoms.

	EX	NM-MT
44 Kyle Petty Hot Wheels in blue box 1996	3.00	6.00
94 Bill Elliott McDonald's Thunderbat 1995	4.00	10.00

1997 Hot Wheels First Edition 1:64

This series was produced by Hot Wheels in blister packs that featured the title "First Edition 1997." Each 1:64 car was packaged with a Hot Wheels trading card.

	EX	NM-MT
4 Sterling Marlin Kodak	3.00	8.00
5 Terry Labonte Kellogg's	3.00	6.00
6 Mark Martin Valvoline	3.00	6.00
7 Geoff Bodine QVC	2.00	4.00
8 Hut Stricklin Circuit City	2.00	4.00
10 Ricky Rudd Tide	2.00	4.00
16 Ted Musgrave Primestar	2.00	4.00
21 Michael Waltrip Citgo	2.00	4.00
28 Ernie Irvan Havoline	3.00	6.00
30 Johnny Benson Pennzoil	2.00	4.00
43 Bobby Hamilton STP	2.00	4.00
44 Kyle Petty Hot Wheels (with signature on card)	3.00	6.00
44 Kyle Petty Hot Wheels (no signature on card)	4.00	10.00
94 Bill Elliott McDonald's	2.00	4.00
98 John Andretti RCA	3.00	6.00
99 Jeff Burton Exide	2.00	4.00

1997 Hot Wheels Short Track 1:64

	EX	NM-MT
4 Sterling Marlin Kodak	1.50	4.00
5 Terry Labonte Kellogg's	3.00	6.00
5 Terry Labonte Kellogg's Tony	4.00	8.00
6 Mark Martin Valvoline	3.00	6.00
7 Geoff Bodine QVC	1.50	4.00
8 Hut Stricklin Circuit City	1.50	4.00
10 Ricky Rudd Spring Fresh	1.50	4.00
10 Ricky Rudd Tide	1.50	4.00
16 Ted Musgrave Primestar	1.50	4.00
21 Michael Waltrip Citgo	1.50	4.00
21 Michael Waltrip Citgo Red top	1.50	4.00
28 Ernie Irvan Havoline	1.50	4.00
30 Johnny Benson Pennzoil	1.50	4.00
37 Jeremy Mayfield K-Mart	1.50	4.00
43 Bobby Hamilton STP	1.50	4.00
44 Kyle Petty Hot Wheels	3.00	6.00
91 Mike Wallace Spam	1.50	4.00
94 Bill Elliott McDonald's	2.00	4.00
94 Bill Elliott Mac Tonight	3.00	6.00
96 David Green Caterpillar	1.50	4.00
99 Jeff Burton Exide	1.50	4.00

1997 Hot Wheels Pro Racing Superspeedway 1:64

This series of 1:64 cars marks Hot Wheels second mass-market venture into NASCAR. These cars are the upgraded versions of those cars available in the Pro Racing series.

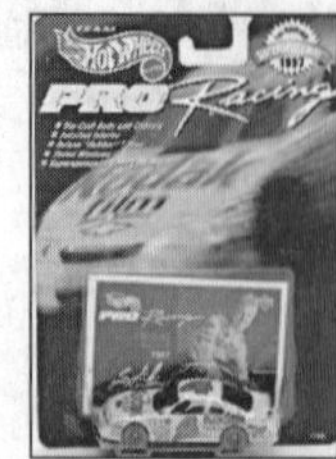

	EX	NM-MT
4 Sterling Marlin Kodak	2.00	4.00
5 Terry Labonte Kellogg's	3.00	6.00
6 Mark Martin Valvoline	3.00	6.00
7 Geoff Bodine QVC	2.00	4.00
8 Hut Stricklin Circuit City	2.00	4.00
10 Ricky Rudd Tide	2.00	4.00
16 Ted Musgrave Primestar	2.00	4.00
21 Michael Waltrip Citgo	2.00	4.00
28 Ernie Irvan Havoline	2.00	4.00
30 Johnny Benson Pennzoil	2.00	4.00
37 Jeremy Mayfield K-Mart	2.00	4.00
43 Bobby Hamilton STP	2.00	4.00
44 Kyle Petty Hot Wheels	3.00	6.00
91 Mike Wallace Spam	2.00	4.00
94 Bill Elliott McDonald's	2.00	4.00
96 David Green Caterpillar	2.00	4.00
98 John Andretti RCA	2.00	4.00
99 Jeff Burton Exide	2.00	4.00

1997 Hot Wheels Track Edition 1:64

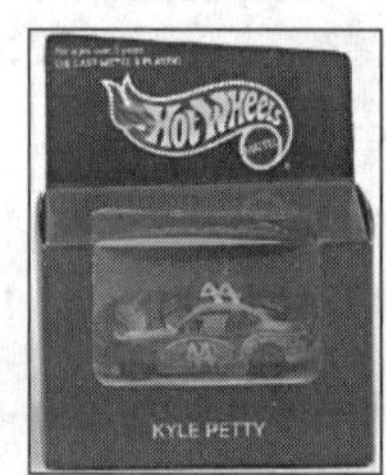

	EX	NM-MT
4 Sterling Marlin Kodak	5.00	12.00
28 Ernie Irvan Havoline	5.00	10.00
28 Ernie Irvan Hot Wheels SuperTruck	25.00	40.00
43 Bobby Hamilton STP with yellow nose	25.00	40.00
43 Bobby Hamilton STP with blue nose	5.00	10.00
44 Kyle Petty Hot Wheels Blue Box	10.00	25.00
44 Kyle Petty Hot Wheels White Box	150.00	250.00

1997 Hot Wheels Pro Racing 1:64

This series of 1:64 cars marks Hot Wheels first mass-market venture into NASCAR. These cars are packaged with cardboard backing shaped like a number one.

	EX	NM-MT
4 Sterling Marlin Kodak	1.50	4.00
5 Terry Labonte Kellogg's	1.50	4.00
6 Mark Martin Valvoline	1.50	4.00
7 Geoff Bodine QVC	1.50	4.00
8 Hut Stricklin Circuit City	1.50	4.00
10 Ricky Rudd Tide	1.50	4.00
16 Ted Musgrave Primestar	1.50	4.00
21 Michael Waltrip Citgo	1.50	4.00
28 Ernie Irvan Havoline	1.50	4.00
30 Johnny Benson Pennzoil	1.50	4.00
37 Jeremy Mayfield K-Mart	1.50	4.00
43 Bobby Hamilton STP	1.50	4.00
44 Kyle Petty Hot Wheels	1.50	4.00
91 Mike Wallace Spam	1.50	4.00
94 Bill Elliott McDonald's	1.50	4.00
96 David Green Caterpillar	1.50	4.00
98 John Andretti RCA	1.50	4.00
99 Jeff Burton Exide	1.50	4.00

1998 Hot Wheels First Edition 1:64

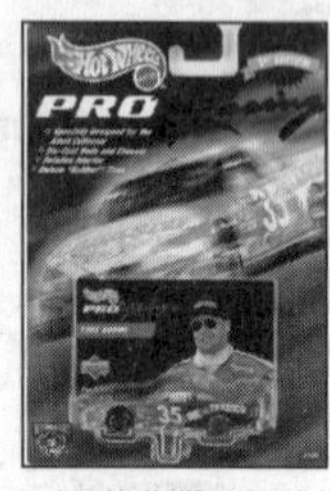

This series was released by Hot Wheels in early 1998. Each car was packaged in a Hot Wheels blister with a "1st Edition" logo in the upper right hand corner.

	EX	NM-MT
4 Bobby Hamilton Kodak	2.00	5.00
5 Terry Labonte Kellogg's	2.50	6.00
6 Mark Martin Eagle One	2.50	6.00
6 Mark Martin Eagle One Promo with bottle of car wax	5.00	12.00
6 Mark Martin Synpower	2.50	6.00
6 Mark Martin Valvoline	2.50	6.00
8 Hut Stricklin Circuit City	2.00	5.00
10 Ricky Rudd Tide	2.00	5.00
11 Brett Bodine Paychex	2.00	5.00
12 Jeremy Mayfield Mobil One	2.00	5.00
13 Jerry Nadeau First Plus	2.00	5.00
21 Michael Waltrip Citgo	2.00	5.00
26 Johnny Benson Cheerios	2.00	5.00
30 Derrike Cope Gumout	2.00	5.00
35 Todd Bodine Tabasco Green	2.00	5.00
35 Todd Bodine Tabasco Red	2.00	5.00
35 Todd Bodine Tabasco Orange	2.00	5.00
36 Ernie Irvan Skittles	2.00	5.00
40 Sterling Marlin Marlin	2.50	6.00
42 Joe Nemechek BellSouth blue	2.00	5.00
42 Joe Nemechek BellSouth Yellow Pages	2.00	5.00
43 John Andretti STP	2.00	5.00
44 Kyle Petty Blues Brothers	2.00	5.00
44 Kyle Petty Hot Wheels	2.00	5.00
44 Kyle Petty Hot Wheels Players Inc.	2.00	5.00
46 Wally Dallenbach First Union	2.00	5.00
46 Wally Dallenbach Tampa Bay Devil Rays	2.00	5.00
50 Ricky Craven Hendrick	2.00	5.00
89 Bill Elliott McRib	2.50	6.00
90 Dick Trickle Heilig-Meyers	2.00	5.00
94 Bill Elliott McDonald's	2.50	6.00
96 David Green Caterpillar	2.00	5.00
97 Chad Little John Deere	2.00	5.00
99 Jeff Burton Exide	2.00	5.00

1998 Hot Wheels Preview Edition 1:64

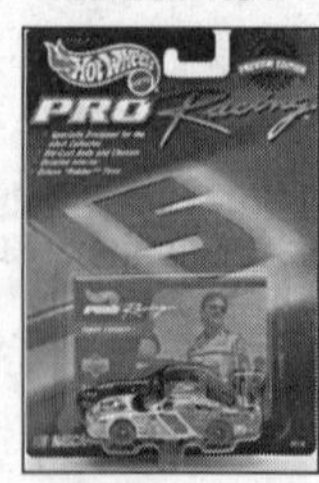

These cars came out before the start of the 1998 season and are painted to reflect the '97 paint jobs. The cars were sold in blister packs with a "Preview Edition" logo in the upper right hand corner.

	EX	NM-MT
4 Bobby Hamilton Kodak	4.00	8.00
5 Terry Labonte Kellogg's	4.00	8.00
6 Mark Martin Eagle One	5.00	10.00
6 Mark Martin Syntec	5.00	10.00
6 Mark Martin Valvoline	4.00	8.00
8 Hut Stricklin Circuit City	4.00	8.00
10 Ricky Rudd Tide	5.00	10.00
12 Jeremy Mayfield Mobil 1	4.00	8.00
13 Jerry Nadeau First Plus	4.00	8.00
16 Ted Musgrave Primestar	4.00	8.00
21 Michael Waltrip Citgo	4.00	8.00
26 Johnny Benson Cheerios	4.00	8.00
30 Derrike Cope Gumout	4.00	8.00
35 Todd Bodine Tabasco	4.00	8.00
35 Todd Bodine Tabasco Green	4.00	8.00
35 Todd Bodine Tabasco Red	4.00	8.00
36 Ernie Irvan Skittles	4.00	8.00
40 Sterling Marlin Sabco	4.00	8.00
42 Joe Nemechek BellSouth	4.00	8.00
42 Joe Nemechek BellSouth Black	4.00	8.00
43 John Andretti STP	4.00	8.00
43 John Andretti STP Players Inc.	4.00	8.00
44 Kyle Petty Blues Brothers 2000	4.00	10.00
44 Kyle Petty Hot Wheels	4.00	10.00
44 Kyle Petty Players Inc.	4.00	10.00
50 Ricky Craven Hendrick	4.00	8.00
89 Dennis Setzer McRib	6.00	12.00
90 Dick Trickle Heilig-Meyers	4.00	8.00
94 Bill Elliott McDonalds	4.00	8.00
96 David Green Caterpillar	4.00	8.00
97 Chad Little John Deere	4.00	8.00
99 Jeff Burton Exide	4.00	8.00

1998 Hot Wheels Pro Racing 1:64

This was Hot Wheels basic issue NASCAR brand for 1998. Each car was issued in a blue and red blister package in the shape of the #1.

	EX	NM-MT
4 Bobby Hamilton Kodak	1.50	4.00
5 Terry Labonte Kellogg's	2.00	5.00
6 Mark Martin Valvoline	2.00	5.00
10 Ricky Rudd Tide	1.50	4.00
12 Jeremy Mayfield Mobil 1	1.50	4.00
16 Kevin Lepage Primestar	1.50	4.00
26 Johnny Benson Cheerios	1.50	4.00
35 Todd Bodine Tabasco	1.50	4.00
36 Ernie Irvan Skittles	1.50	4.00
43 John Andretti STP	1.50	4.00
43/44/45 John Andretti Kyle Petty Adam Petty Generations Target	12.50	25.00
44 Kyle Petty Hot Wheels	1.50	4.00
94 Bill Elliott McDonald's	2.00	5.00
96 Steve Grissom Caterpillar	1.50	4.00
97 Chad Little John Deere	1.50	4.00

1998 Hot Wheels Pro Racing Pit Crew 1:64

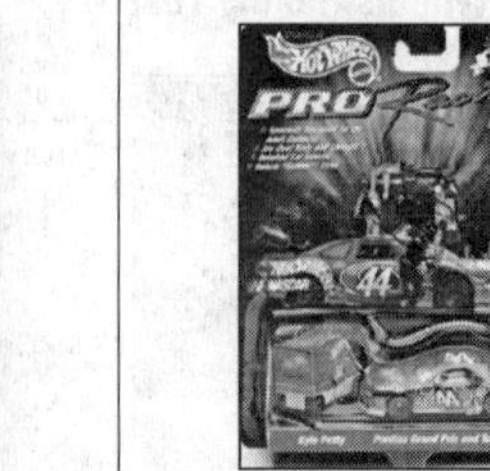

These 1:64 scale cars were produced by Hot Wheels and were packaged in blister packs with their corresponding pit wagon. They were distributed through hobby, retail and trackside outlets. The blister reads "1998 Pit Crew" in the upper right hand corner and the driver's name appears on the cardboard base. A Gold version of some drivers was made. These were packaged in a similar blister with the words "Limited Edition Series" on the front. The driver's name is not included on the base for the Gold version.

	EX	NM-MT
4 Sterling Marlin Kodak	4.00	10.00
5 Terry Labonte Kellogg's	4.00	10.00
6 Mark Martin Valvoline	4.00	10.00
8 Hut Stricklin	4.00	8.00

10 Ricky Rudd Tide	4.00
12 Jeremy Mayfield Mobil 1	4.00
13 Jerry Nadeau First Plus	4.00
16 Ted Musgrave Primestar	4.00
21 Michael Waltrip Citgo	4.00
28 Ernie Irvan Havoline	4.00
30 Derrike Cope Gumout	4.00
33 Tim Fedewa Kleenex	4.00
35 Todd Bodine Tabasco	4.00
36 Matt Hutter Stanley	4.00
36 Ernie Irvan Skittles	4.00
40 Sterling Marlin Sabco	4.00
43 Bobby Hamilton STP	4.00
44 Kyle Petty Hot Wheels	4.00
74 Randy LaJoie Fina	4.00
94 Bill Elliott McDonald's	4.00
96 David Green Caterpillar	4.00
97 Chad Little John Deere	4.00
99 Jeff Burton Exide	4.00

1998 Hot Wheels Pro Rac Pit Crew Gold 1:64

	EX
4 Sterling Marlin Kodak	5.00
5 Terry Labonte Kellogg's	5.00
6 Mark Martin Valvoline	5.00
8 Hut Stricklin	5.00
10 Ricky Rudd Tide Gold	5.00
12 Jeremy Mayfield Mobil 1	5.00
13 Jerry Nadeau First Plus	5.00
16 Ted Musgrave Primestar	5.00
21 Michael Waltrip Citgo	5.00
28 Ernie Irvan Havoline	5.00
33 Tim Fedewa Kleenex	5.00
35 Todd Bodine Tabasco	5.00
36 Matt Hutter Stanley	5.00
36 Ernie Irvan Skittles	5.00
40 Sterling Marlin Sabco	5.00
43 Bobby Hamilton STP	5.00
44 Kyle Petty Hot Wheels	5.00
74 Randy LaJoie Fina	5.00
94 Bill Elliott McDonald's	5.00
96 David Green Caterpillar	5.00
97 Chad Little John Deere	5.00
99 Jeff Burton Exide	5.00

1998 Hot Wheels Test Tr 1:64

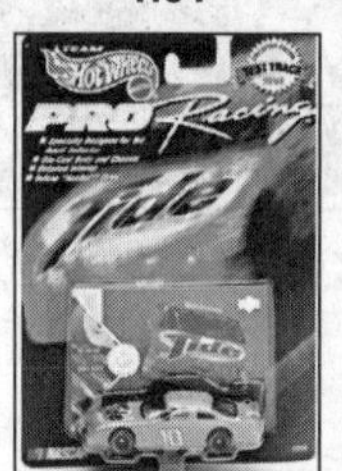

These 1:64 scale cars were produced by Hot Wheels. packaged in blister packs and have primer coating as cars do. These cars were distributed through hobby and

	EX
4 Bobby Hamilton Kodak	2.50
5 Terry Labonte Kellogg's	2.50
6 Mark Martin Valvoline	2.50
10 Ricky Rudd Tide	2.50
21 Michael Waltrip Citgo	2.50
28 Ernie Irvan Havoline	2.50
43 John Andretti STP	2.50
44 Kyle Petty Hot Wheels	2.50
99 Jeff Burton Exide	2.50

1998 Hot Wheels Track Edition 1:64

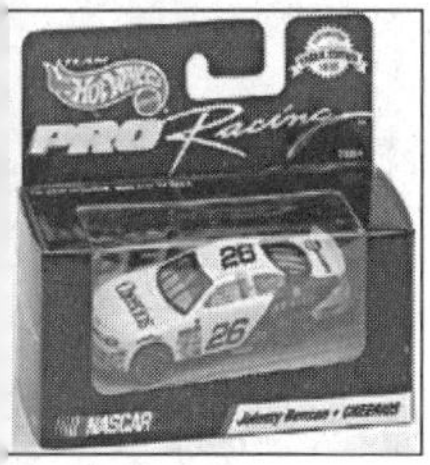

:64 scale cars are in a black box and were only available
bby or trackside sale.

	EX	NM-MT
jy Hamilton dak	6.00	15.00
Labonte llogg's	8.00	20.00
Martin lvoline	8.00	20.00
Martin gle One	10.00	25.00
Martin npower	8.00	20.00
Stricklin cuit City	6.00	15.00
ky Rudd le	6.00	15.00
emy Mayfield bil 1	6.00	15.00
y Nadeau st Plus	6.00	15.00
chael Waltrip igo	6.00	15.00
nny Benson eerios	6.00	15.00
rike Cope mout	6.00	15.00
ld Bodine oasco Orange	6.00	15.00
ld Bodine oasco Green	6.00	15.00
ld Bodine oasco Red	6.00	15.00
ie Irvan ttles	6.00	15.00
ling Marlin oco	6.00	15.00
Nemechek lSouth	6.00	15.00
Nemechek lSouth Black	6.00	15.00
n Andretti P	6.00	15.00
n Andretti yers Inc.	6.00	15.00
e Petty t Wheels	6.00	15.00
e Petty ies Brothers 2000	6.00	15.00
e Petty yers Inc.	6.00	15.00
ky Craven ndrick	6.00	15.00
Driver Association y Scouts	6.00	15.00
nis Setzer Rib	10.00	25.00
k Trickle lig-Meyers	6.00	15.00
Elliott Donald's	8.00	20.00
id Green erpiller	6.00	15.00
id Little n Deere	6.00	15.00
Burton de	6.00	15.00

98 Hot Wheels Pro Racing Trading Paint 1:64

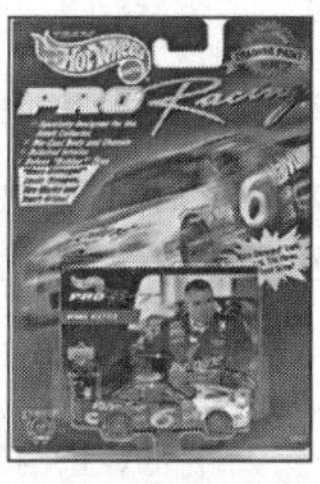

:64 scale cars show the wear and tear a NASCAR is
d to during a 500 mile race including road grime, paint
and wheel rub marks.

	EX	NM-MT
Martin voline	6.00	15.00
my Mayfield bil 1	3.00	8.00
y Nadeau st Plus	5.00	12.00
Musgrave mestar	3.00	8.00
hael Waltrip go	3.00	8.00
d Bodine oasco	6.00	15.00
ling Marlin abco	3.00	8.00
Nemechek ellSouth	3.00	8.00
n Andretti P	5.00	12.00
Petty	5.00	12.00

Hot Wheels		
46 Wally Dallenbach First Union	3.00	8.00
96 David Green Caterpillar	3.00	8.00
99 Jeff Burton Exide	4.00	10.00

1999 Hot Wheels Racing Daytona 500 1:64

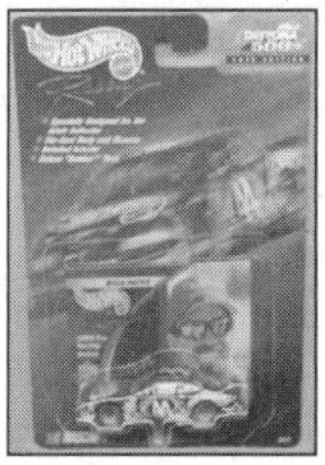

	EX	NM-MT
4 Bobby Hamilton Adantix	2.00	5.00
6 Mark Martin Valvoline	2.50	6.00
7 Michael Waltrip Phillips	2.00	5.00
10 Ricky Rudd Tide	2.00	5.00
11 Brett Bodine Paychex	2.00	5.00
12 Jeremy Mayfield Mobil 1	2.00	5.00
16 Kevin Lepage Primestar	2.00	5.00
21 Michael Waltrip Citgo	2.00	5.00
22 Ward Burton Caterpillar	2.00	5.00
26 Johnny Benson Cheerios	2.00	5.00
30 Derrike Cope Bryan	2.00	5.00
30 Derrike Cope State Fair	2.00	5.00
36 Ernie Irvan M&M's	2.00	5.00
40 Sterling Marlin Marlin Racing	2.00	5.00
42 Joe Nemechek BellSouth	2.00	5.00
43 John Andretti STP	2.00	5.00
44 Kyle Petty Hot Wheels	2.00	5.00
66 Darrell Waltrip K-Mart	2.00	5.00
94 Bill Elliott McDonald's	2.50	6.00
97 Chad Little John Deere	2.00	5.00
99 Jeff Burton Exide	2.00	5.00

1999 Hot Wheels Racing Deluxe 1:64

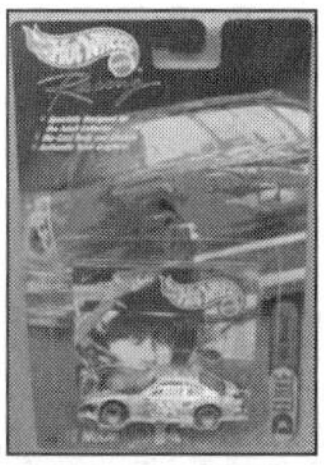

This series was issued in a Hot Wheels Racing blister with the word "Deluxe" printed in red at the lower right hand corner. A Hot Wheels trading card was packaged with each car.

	EX	NM-MT
44 Kyle Petty Hot Wheels	3.00	6.00
45 Adam Petty Sprint	5.00	12.00

1999 Hot Wheels Racing NASCAR Rocks 1:64

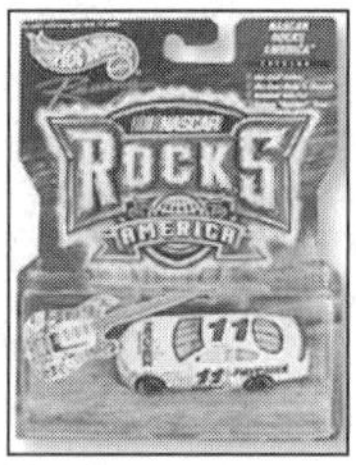

Each of these 1:64 scale cars was packaged with a miniature guitar painted in the color scheme of the driver's car. Both were packaged in a NASCAR Rocks America blister package.

	EX	NM-MT
6 Mark Martin Valvoline	5.00	10.00
11 Brett Bodine Paychex	4.00	8.00
12 Jeremy Mayfield Mobil 1	4.00	8.00
43 John Andretti	4.00	8.00

STP		
44 Kyle Petty Hot Wheels	4.00	8.00
66 Darrell Waltrip Big K	4.00	8.00

1999 Hot Wheels Pro Racing 1:64

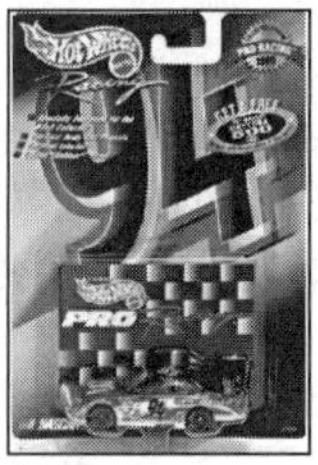

These black box cars were available at the track or through hobby dealers.

	EX	NM-MT
4 Bobby Hamilton Kodak	2.00	4.00
5 Terry Labonte Kellogg's	2.00	4.00
6 Mark Martin Valvoline	2.00	4.00
7 Geoffery Bodine Philips	2.00	4.00
7 Geoff Bodine Klaussner	2.00	4.00
9 Jerry Nadeau Jetsons	2.00	4.00
10 Ricky Rudd Tide	2.00	4.00
11 Brett Bodine Paychex	2.00	4.00
12 Jeremy Mayfield Mobil 1	2.00	4.00
16 Kevin Lepage Primestar	2.00	4.00
22 Ward Burton Caterpillar	2.00	4.00
25 Wally Dallenbach Dallenbach	2.00	4.00
26 Johnny Benson Betty Crocker	2.00	4.00
28 Davey Allison Havoline	3.00	8.00
36 Ernie Irvan M&M's	2.00	4.00
40 Sterling Marlin Sabco	2.00	4.00
42 Joe Nemechek BellSouth	2.00	4.00
43 Richard Petty STP '64	3.00	8.00
43 Richard Petty STP '67	3.00	8.00
43 Richard Petty STP '72	3.00	8.00
43 John Andretti STP	2.00	4.00
43/44/45 John Andretti Jimmy Hensley Kyle Petty Adam Petty 50th Anniversary 4-car set	10.00	25.00
43/44/45 John Andretti Kyle Petty Adam Petty Generations Father's Day 1999	10.00	25.00
44 Kyle Petty Hot Wheels	2.00	4.00
66 Darrell Waltrip Big K	2.00	4.00
94 Bill Elliott Drive Thru	2.00	4.00
97 Chad Little John Deere	2.00	4.00
99 Jeff Burton Exide	2.00	4.00

1999 Hot Wheels Racing Pit Crew 1:64

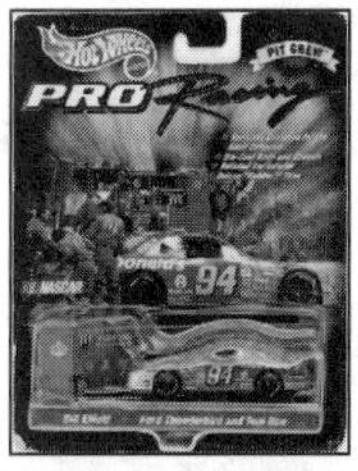

These 1:64 scale cars were packaged with a replica pit wagon tool box. There were two different blister packages used. One blister included the title Hot Wheels Racing with "Pit Crew" within a green box in the upper right hand corner. The other included the title Hot Wheels Pro Racing with "Pit Crew 1999" within a gold seal in the upper right corner similar to the 1998 set. The name of the team, not the driver's name, appears on the cardboard base. The stated production run was 20,000. A Gold version was also created for a select number of pieces, with both the pit wagon and car being detailed in gold paint.

	EX	NM-MT
4 Bobby Hamilton Kodak Advantix	4.00	8.00
5 Terry Labonte Kellogg's	4.00	8.00
5 Terry Labonte Kellogg's Gold	4.00	8.00
6 Mark Martin Valvoline	5.00	10.00
6 Mark Martin	5.00	10.00

Valvoline Gold		
7 Michael Waltrip Phillips	4.00	8.00
9 Jerry Nadeau Dexter's Laboratory	4.00	8.00
9 Jerry Nadeau Jetsons with Dexter's Lab pit wagon	4.00	8.00
10 Ricky Rudd Tide	4.00	8.00
10 Ricky Rudd Tide Gold	4.00	8.00
11 Brett Bodine Paychex	4.00	8.00
12 Jeremy Mayfield Mobil 1	4.00	8.00
12 Jeremy Mayfield Mobil 1 Gold	4.00	8.00
17 Matt Kenseth DeWalt	5.00	12.00
21 Michael Waltrip Citgo	4.00	8.00
25 Wally Dallenbach Hendrick	4.00	8.00
26 Johnny Benson Cheerios	4.00	8.00
30 Derrike Cope Jimmy Dean	4.00	8.00
30 Derrike Cope State Fair	4.00	8.00
34 Mike McLaughlin Goulds Pumps	4.00	8.00
36 Tim Fedewa Stanley	4.00	8.00
36 Ernie Irvan M&M's	4.00	8.00
40 Sterling Marlin Sabco	4.00	8.00
43 John Andretti STP	4.00	8.00
43 John Andretti STP Gold	4.00	8.00
44 Kyle Petty Hot Wheels	4.00	8.00
44 Kyle Petty Hot Wheels Gold	4.00	8.00
44 Kyle Petty Players Inc.	4.00	8.00
58 Ricky Craven Turbine	10.00	20.00
60 Mark Martin Winn Dixie	5.00	10.00
66 Todd Bodine Phillips 66	4.00	8.00
66 Darrell Waltrip Big K	4.00	8.00
94 Bill Elliott McDonald's	4.00	8.00
94 Bill Elliott Drive Thru Gold	4.00	8.00
97 Chad Little John Deere	4.00	8.00
97 Chad Little John Deere Gold	4.00	8.00
99 Jeff Burton Exide	4.00	8.00
99 Jeff Burton Exide Gold	4.00	8.00

1999 Hot Wheels Racing Pit Cruisers 1:64

These 1:64 scale die-casts were NASCAR versions of miniature golf carts. Each was limited to 15,000 pieces.

	EX	NM-MT
6 Mark Martin Valvoilne	5.00	12.00
10 Rudd Rudd Tide	4.00	10.00
43 John Andretti STP	4.00	10.00
44 Kyle Petty Hot Wheels	4.00	10.00

1999 Hot Wheels Racing Promos 1:64

	EX	NM-MT
6 Mark Martin 1995 Valvoline (packaged with Valvoline fuel treatment)	6.00	15.00
6 Mark Martin 1997 Valvoline (packaged with Valvoline fuel treatment)	6.00	15.00
6 Mark Martin 1999 Valvoline (packaged with Valvoline fuel treatment)	6.00	15.00
26/44 Johnny Benson Kyle Petty Cheerios/Hot Wheels Promo	3.00	8.00
64 VISA Promo	3.00	8.00

1999 Hot Wheels Racing Speed and Thunder 1:64

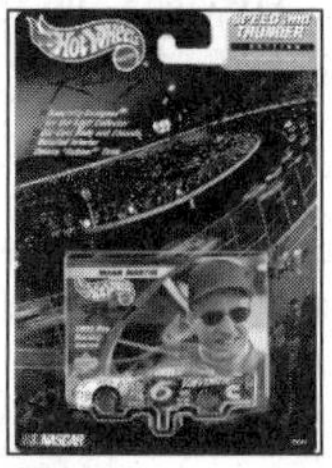

Each 1:64 scale car in this series was packaged in a Hot Wheels Speed and Thunder blister. The stated production run was 25,000 of each piece.

	EX	NM-MT
6 Mark Martin	2.50	6.00

Valvoline		
9 Jerry Nadeau Dexter's Lab	2.00	5.00
11 Brett Bodine Paychex	2.00	5.00
30 Michael Waltrip State Fair	2.00	5.00
36 Ernie Irvan M&M's	2.00	5.00
42 Joe Nemechek BellSouth	2.00	5.00
44 Kyle Petty Hot Wheels	2.00	5.00

1999 Hot Wheels Racing Track Edition 1:64

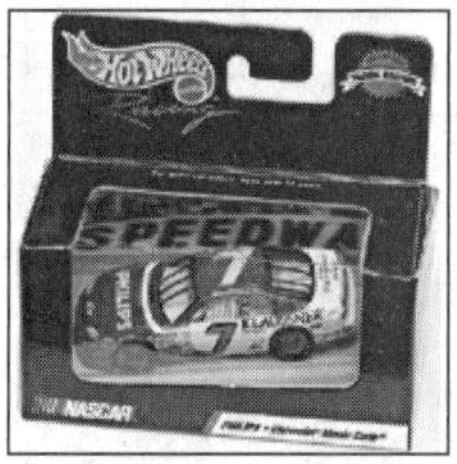

These 1:64 scale black box cars were available at the track or through a hobby dealer.

	EX	NM-MT
4 Bobby Hamilton Kodak	6.00	15.00
5 Terry Labonte Kellogg's	8.00	20.00
6 Mark Martin Valvoline	8.00	20.00
7 Michael Waltrip Klaussner/Philips	6.00	15.00
10 Ricky Rudd Tide	6.00	15.00
11 Brett Bodine Paychex	6.00	15.00
12 Jeremy Mayfield Mobil 1	6.00	15.00
14 Sterling Marlin Tennessee	12.00	25.00
21 Elliott Sadler Citgo	6.00	15.00
22 Ward Burton Caterpillar	6.00	15.00
25 Wally Dallenbach Dallenbach	6.00	15.00
26 Johnny Benson Cheerios	6.00	15.00
28 Davey Allison Havoline	10.00	20.00
36 Ernie Irvan M&M's	6.00	15.00
40 Sterling Marlin Sabco	6.00	15.00
42 Joe Nemechek BellSouth	6.00	15.00
43 Richard Petty STP '64	10.00	20.00
43 Richard Petty STP '67	10.00	20.00
43 Richard Petty STP '72	10.00	20.00
43 John Andretti STP	6.00	15.00
44 Kyle Petty Hot Wheels	6.00	15.00
66 Darrell Waltrip Big K	6.00	15.00
94 Bill Elliott Drive Thru	6.00	15.00
97 Chad Little John Deere	6.00	15.00

1999 Hot Wheels Racing Test Track 1:64

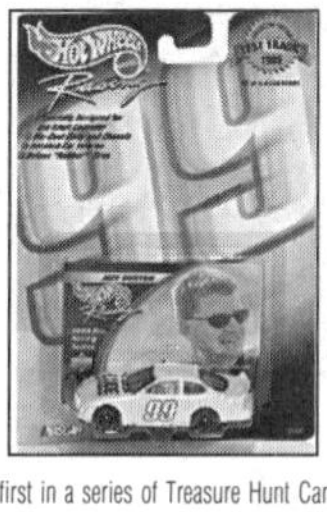

This is the first in a series of Treasure Hunt Cars limited to 15,000

	EX	NM-MT
10 Ricky Rudd Tide	6.00	15.00
12 Jeremy Mayfield Mobil 1	6.00	15.00
44 Kyle Petty Hot Wheels	6.00	15.00
99 Jeff Burton Exide	6.00	15.00

1999 Hot Wheels Racing Trading Paint 1:64

This is the second in a series of Treasure Hunt Cars with each limited in production to 15,000.

	EX	NM-MT
5 Terry Labonte Kellogg's	8.00	20.00
6 Mark Martin Valvoline	8.00	20.00
44 Kyle Petty Hot Wheels	6.00	15.00

	EX	NM-MT
97 Chad Little John Deere	6.00	15.00

2000 Hot Wheels Deluxe 1:64

These cars are available through retail outlets.

	EX	NM-MT
4 Bobby Hamilton Kodak	2.00	4.00
5 Terry Labonte Kellogg's	3.00	6.00
6 Mark Martin Valvoline	3.00	6.00
7 Michael Waltrip NationsRent	3.00	6.00
10 Jeff Green Nesquik Promo	4.00	8.00
12 Jeremy Mayfield Mobil 1	2.00	4.00
14 Mike Bliss Conseco	2.00	4.00
17 Matt Kenseth DeWalt	3.00	6.00
21 Elliott Sadler Citgo	2.00	4.00
22 Ward Burton Caterpillar	2.00	4.00
25 Jerry Nadeau Holigan	2.00	4.00
26 Jimmy Spencer Big K	2.00	4.00
26/44/94 Johnny Benson Kyle Petty Bill Elliott Toy Story 2	12.50	25.00
32 Scott Pruett Tide	5.00	10.00
33 Joe Nemechek Oakwood Homes	2.00	4.00
40 Sterling Marlin Marlin	2.00	5.00
42 Kenny Irwin BellSouth	2.00	5.00
43 John Andretti Cheerios	2.00	4.00
43 John Andretti STP	2.00	4.00
43 John Andretti STP Historic Paint	4.00	8.00
43 John Andretti Wheaties	2.50	5.00
44 Kyle Petty Hot Wheels	2.00	4.00
44 Kyle Petty Hot Wheels Chrome	3.00	6.00
45 Adam Petty Sprint PCS	10.00	25.00
55 Kenny Wallace Aerosmith	5.00	10.00
55 Kenny Wallace Square D	2.00	4.00
60 Geoffery Bodine Power Team	2.00	4.00
66 Darrell Waltrip Big K	2.00	4.00
75 Wally Dallenbach Cartoon Network	2.00	4.00
77 Robert Pressley Jasper	2.00	4.00
94 Bill Elliott McDonald's Drive Thru	3.00	6.00
97 Chad Little John Deere	2.00	4.00
97 Anthony Lazzaro McDonald's	2.00	4.00
99 Jeff Burton Exide	2.00	4.00

2000 Hot Wheels Deluxe Draggin' Wagon 1:64

	EX	NM-MT
5 Terry Labonte Kellogg's	2.00	5.00
33 Joe Nemechek Oakwood Homes	2.00	5.00
43 John Andretti Cheerios	2.00	5.00
75 Wally Dallenbach Cartoon Network	2.00	5.00

2000 Hot Wheels Deluxe Go Kart 1:64

	EX	NM-MT
4 Bobby Hamilton Kodak	4.00	10.00
6 Mark Martin Valvoline	5.00	12.00
98 Rick Mast Woody	4.00	10.00
99 Jeff Burton Exide	4.00	10.00

2000 Hot Wheels Deluxe Helicopter 1:64

	EX	NM-MT
22 Ward Burton Caterpillar	3.00	6.00
32 Scott Pruett Tide	3.00	6.00
33 Joe Nemechek Oakwood Homes	3.00	6.00
99 Jeff Burton Exide	3.00	6.00

2000 Hot Wheels Deluxe Hot Rod 1:64

	EX	NM-MT
21 Elliott Sadler Citgo	4.00	10.00
32 Scott Pruett Tide	4.00	10.00
66 Darrell Waltrip Big K	4.00	10.00
94 Bill Elliott McDonald's	4.00	10.00

2000 Hot Wheels Deluxe Hydroplane 1:64

	EX	NM-MT
4 Bobby Hamilton Kodak	2.00	5.00
7 Michael Waltrip Nations Rent	2.00	5.00
12 Jeremy Mayfield Mobil 1	2.00	5.00
44 Kyle Petty Hot Wheels	2.00	5.00

2000 Hot Wheels Deluxe Pit Crew 1:64

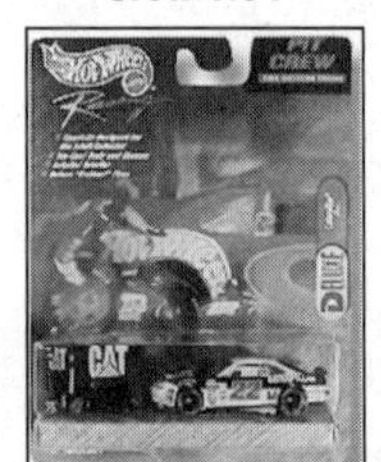

Each of these 1:64 scale cars was packaged with a replica pit wagon. Both pieces were packaged together in a blister that included the name "Pit Crew" in the upper right in red and the word "Deluxe" in the lower right.

	EX	NM-MT
4 Bobby Hamilton Kodak	3.00	6.00
5 Terry Labonte Kellogg's	4.00	8.00
6 Mark Martin Valvoline	4.00	8.00
12 Jeremy Mayfield Mobil 1	3.00	6.00
14 Mike Bliss Conseco	3.00	6.00
17 Matt Kenseth DeWalt	5.00	10.00
22 Ward Burton Caterpillar	3.00	6.00
33 Joe Nemechek Oakwood Homes	3.00	6.00
40 Sterling Marlin Sabco	3.00	6.00
43 John Andretti STP	3.00	6.00
44 Kyle Petty Hot Wheels	3.00	6.00
55 Kenny Wallace Square D	3.00	6.00
60 Geoffery Bodine Power Team	3.00	6.00
66 Darrell Waltrip Big K	3.00	6.00
75 Wally Dallenbach Power Puff Girls	3.00	6.00
94 Bill Elliott McDonald's	4.00	8.00
97 Chad Little John Deere	3.00	6.00
98 Rick Mast Woody	3.00	6.00

2000 Hot Wheels Deluxe Pit Crew Daytona 500 1:64

Each 1:64 scale car in this series was issued with a Daytona 500 commemorative pit wagon. The packaging is identical to the basic issue 2000 Deluxe Pit Crew series, but the pit wagon has been switched from the driver's team version to the Daytona version.

	EX	NM-MT
4 Bobby Hamilton Kodak	3.00	6.00
5 Terry Labonte Kellogg's	4.00	8.00
12 Jeremy Mayfield Mobil 1	3.00	6.00
22 Ward Burton Caterpillar	3.00	6.00
43 John Andretti STP	3.00	6.00
44 Kyle Petty Hot Wheels	3.00	6.00
55 Kenny Wallace Square D	3.00	6.00
60 Geoffery Bodine Power Team	3.00	6.00
98 Rick Mast Woody	3.00	6.00

2000 Hot Wheels Deluxe RV 1:64

	EX	NM-MT
14 Mike Bliss Conseco	2.00	5.00
44 Kyle Petty Hot Wheels	2.00	5.00
77 Robert Pressley Jasper	2.00	5.00
97 Anthony Lazzaro McDonald's	2.00	5.00

2000 Hot Wheels Deluxe School Bus 1:64

	EX	NM-MT
22 Ward Burton Caterpillar	4.00	10.00
44 Kyle Petty Hot Wheels	4.00	10.00
94 Bill Elliott McDonald's	4.00	10.00

2000 Hot Wheels Deluxe Scorchin Scooter 1:64

These are from the Hot Wheels mainline release, and are limited.

	EX	NM-MT
4 Bobby Hamilton Kodak	4.00	10.00
5 Terry Labonte Kellogg's	5.00	12.00
6 Mark Martin Valvoline	5.00	12.00
12 Jeremy Mayfield Mobil 1	4.00	10.00
21 Elliott Sadler Citgo	4.00	10.00
22 Ward Burton Caterpillar	4.00	10.00
43 John Andretti STP	4.00	10.00
44 Kyle Petty Hot Wheels	4.00	10.00
45 Adam Petty Sprint	10.00	25.00
55 Kenny Wallace Square D	4.00	10.00
60 Geoffery Bodine Power Team	4.00	10.00
66 Darrell Waltrip Big K	4.00	10.00
94 Bill Elliott McDonald's	5.00	12.00
97 Chad Little John Deere	4.00	10.00
98 Rick Mast Woody Woodpecker	4.00	10.00
99 Jeff Burton Exide	4.00	10.00
NNO Complete Factory Set	50.00	100.00

2000 Hot Wheels Deluxe Suburban 1:64

	EX	NM-MT
5 Terry Labonte Kellogg's	4.00	8.00
40 Sterling Marlin Sabco	4.00	8.00
55 Kenny Wallace Square D	4.00	8.00
60 Geoffery Bodine Power Team	3.00	8.00

2000 Hot Wheels Deluxe Treasure Hunt 1:64

	EX	NM-MT
44 California	10.00	25.00
44 Darlington	10.00	25.00
44 Daytona	15.00	30.00
44 Daytona Night Race	15.00	30.00
44 Miami	10.00	25.00
44 Michigan	10.00	25.00
44 Phoenix	15.00	30.00
44 Talladega Spring Race	15.00	30.00
44 Talladega Fall Race	15.00	30.00
44 Watkins Glen	10.00	25.00

2000 Hot Wheels Racing 1:64

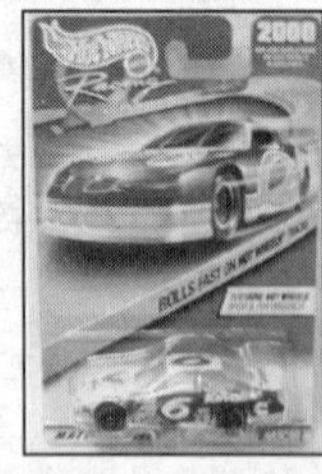

	EX	NM-MT
4 Bobby Hamilton Kodak	2.00	5.00
5 Terry Labonte Kellogg's	2.00	5.00
6 Mark Martin Valvoline	2.50	6.00
32 Scott Pruett Tide	2.00	5.00
43 John Andretti STP	2.00	5.00
44 Kyle Petty Hot Wheels	2.00	5.00
45 Adam Petty Sprint	4.00	10.00
97 Chad Little John Deere	2.00	5.00
98 Rick Mast Woody Woodpecker	2.00	5.00
99 Jeff Burton Exide Batteries	2.00	5.00

2000 Hot Wheels Racing Crew's Choice 1:64

The cars in this series feature bodies that are removable from the chassis. Each was packaged within a styrofoam shell within a solid Hot Wheels Racing Crew's Choice box. A small certificate of authenticity was also issued that featured a stated production run total of 9998 for each die-cast piece.

	EX	NM-MT
4 Bobby Hamilton Kodak	5.00	12.00
6 Mark Martin Valvoline	10.00	20.00
17 Matt Kenseth DeWalt	10.00	20.00
22 Ward Burton Caterpillar	5.00	12.00
32 Scott Pruett Tide	5.00	12.00
33 Joe Nemechek Oakwood Homes	5.00	12.00
40 Sterling Marlin Sterling	6.00	15.00
43 John Andretti STP	5.00	12.00
43 John Andretti Cheerios	5.00	12.00
43 John Andretti STP 1972 paint	6.00	15.00
44 Kyle Petty Hot Wheels	5.00	12.00
45 Adam Petty Sprint PCS	20.00	50.00
55 Kenny Wallace Square D	5.00	12.00
60 Geoffery Bodine Power Team	5.00	12.00
66 Darrell Waltrip Big K	5.00	12.00
97 Anthony Lazzaro McDonald's	5.00	12.00
99 Jeff Burton Exide	5.00	12.00

2000 Hot Wheels Racing Promos 1:64

	EX	NM-MT
32 Scott Pruett Tide Promo	2.00	5.00
32 Scott Pruett Tide Kids Promo	3.00	6.00

2000 Hot Wheels Racing Radical Rides 1:64

	EX	NM-MT
6 Mark Martin Valvoline	5.00	12.00
7 Michael Waltrip Nations Rent	4.00	10.00
12 Jeremy Mayfield Mobil 1	4.00	10.00
17 Matt Kenseth DeWalt	4.00	10.00
43 Richard Petty STP	4.00	10.00
43 John Andretti STP	4.00	10.00
44 Kyle Petty Hot Wheels	4.00	10.00
45 Adam Petty Sprint	10.00	20.00
66 Darrell Waltrip Big K	4.00	10.00
97 Chad Little John Deere	4.00	10.00
99 Jeff Burton Exide	4.00	10.00

2000 Hot Wheels Racing Track Edition 1:64

This series of 1:64 cars was issued in a Hot Wheels Track Edition 2000 clear window box. The blue and black box featured a backer board that could be used to hang the car on a retail sales rack.

	EX	NM-MT
4 Bobby Hamilton Kodak	4.00	8.00
6 Mark Martin Valvoline	5.00	10.00
7 Michael Waltrip Nations Rent	4.00	8.00
12 Jeremy Mayfield Mobil 1	4.00	8.00
14 Mike Bliss Conseco	4.00	8.00
17 Matt Kenseth DeWalt	5.00	10.00
22 Ward Burton Caterpillar	4.00	8.00
32 Scott Pruett Tide	10.00	20.00
33 Joe Nemechek Oakwood Homes	4.00	8.00
42 Kenny Irwin BellSouth	4.00	10.00
43 John Andretti STP	4.00	8.00
43 John Andretti Cheerios	4.00	8.00
43 John Andretti STP Texas	5.00	10.00
43 John Andretti STP 1972 paint	5.00	10.00
44 Kyle Petty Hot Wheels	4.00	8.00
45 Adam Petty Sprint	12.50	30.00
55 Kenny Wallace Square D		
60 Geoffery Bodine Power Team	4.00	
66 Jimmy Spencer Big K-Mart		
66 Darrell Waltrip Big K	4.00	
77 Robert Pressley Jasper	4.00	
94 Bill Elliott McDonald's Drive Thru	5.00	
97 Chad Little John Deere	4.00	
97 Anthony Lazzaro McDonald's	4.00	
99 Jeff Burton Exide	4.00	

2000 Hot Wheels Select 1

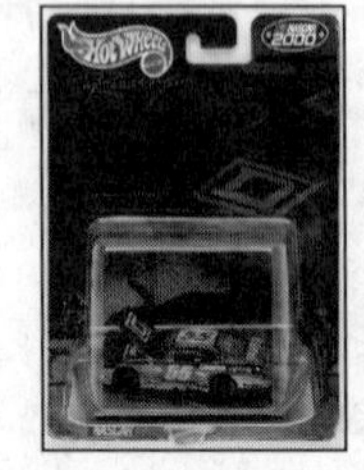

This is the first year of the high end Select series in 1:6 It was sold in a blister pack featuring a display stan resembles a track wall complete with fence and tire ma stated production run was 24,998.

	EX	NM
4 Bobby Hamilton Kodak	3.00	
6 Mark Martin Valvoline	4.00	
12 Jeremy Mayfield Mobil 1	3.00	
14 Mike Bliss Conseco	3.00	
17 Matt Kenseth DeWalt	4.00	
21 Elliott Sadler Citgo	3.00	
22 Ward Burton Caterpillar	3.00	
26 Jimmy Spencer Big K	3.00	
32 Scott Pruett Tide	3.00	
33 Joe Nemechek Oakwood Homes	3.00	
40 Sterling Marlin Sterling	3.00	
42 Kenny Irwin BellSouth	5.00	
43 John Andretti Cheerios	3.00	
43 John Andretti STP	3.00	
43 John Andretti Wheaties	3.00	
44 Kyle Petty Hot Wheels	3.00	
45 Adam Petty Sprint PCS	8.00	
55 Kenny Wallace Square D	3.00	
60 Geoffery Bodine Power Team	3.00	
66 Darrell Waltrip Big K	3.00	
77 Robert Pressley Jasper	3.00	
94 Bill Elliott McDonald's Drive Thru	4.00	
96 Anthony Lazzaro McDonald's	3.00	
97 Chad Little John Deere	3.00	
99 Jeff Burton Exide	3.00	

2000 Hot Wheels Valvoli 10 Years Promos 1:64

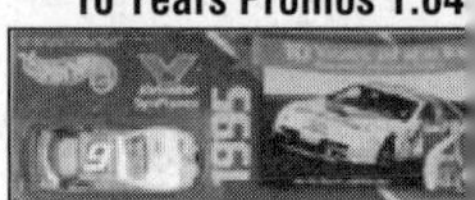

Cars in this series were issued to commemorate Va 10th Year of sponsoring Winston Cup Racing. Each packaged on an oversized blister that included a pho car.

	EX	N
6 Mark Martin Valvoline 1995	3.00	
6 Mark Martin Valvoline 1997	3.00	
6 Mark Martin Valvoline 1999	3.00	

2001 Hot Wheels Racin Anglia 1:64

	EX	N
5 Terry Labonte Kellogg's Tony	5.00	
6 Mark Martin Pfizer		
36 Ken Schrader M&M's	6.00	
44 Buckshot Jones Georgia Pacific		

2001 Hot Wheels Racing Blimp 1:64

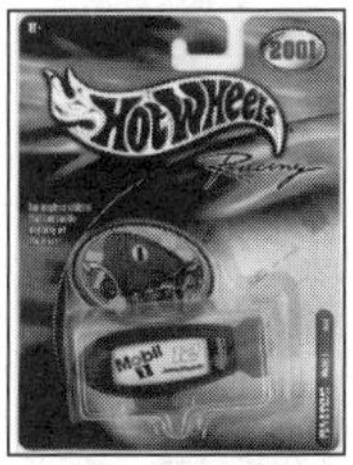

	EX	NM-MT
eremy Mayfield Mobil 1 1/4	6.00	12.00
latt Kenseth DeWalt 2/4	6.00	12.00
cott Pruett Tide 3/4	5.00	10.00
eff Burton Citgo 4/4	7.50	15.00

2001 Hot Wheels Racing oush Commemorative 1:64

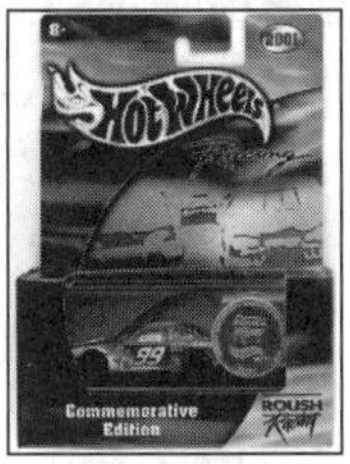

set of 5-cars was issued to commemorate the Roush ng team and its 50th Winston Cup win. Each car is aged in a hard plastic clear box inside a cardboard vrap along with a small metal medallion.

	EX	NM-MT
rk Martin Pfizer	6.00	15.00
Matt Kenseth DeWalt	6.00	15.00
reg Biffle Grainger	5.00	12.00
Kurt Busch Sharpie	6.00	15.00
eff Burton Citgo	5.00	12.00

2001 Hot Wheels Racing Deora 1:64

	EX	NM-MT
eremy Mayfield Mobil 1 3/4	4.00	8.00
latt Kenseth DeWalt 2/4	5.00	10.00
ohn Andretti STP 4/4	5.00	10.00
ff Burton Citgo 1/4	4.00	8.00

001 Hot Wheels Racing Pit Board 1:64

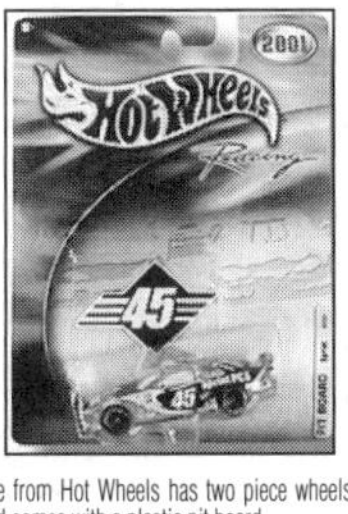

release from Hot Wheels has two piece wheels, a plastic sis, and comes with a plastic pit board.

	EX	NM-MT
ry Labonte Kellogg's Tony	3.00	6.00
rk Martin Pfizer	3.00	6.00
ohnny Benson Valvoline	2.00	4.00
ff Green Nesquik	2.00	4.00
eremy Mayfield Mobil 1	2.00	4.00
att Kenseth DeWalt	3.00	6.00
liott Sadler Motorcraft	2.00	4.00
ard Burton Caterpillar	2.00	4.00
erry Nadeau UAW	2.00	4.00
mmy Spencer K-Mart	2.00	4.00
cott Pruett Tide	2.00	4.00
cky Craven Tide	2.00	4.00
e Nemechek Oakwood Homes	2.00	4.00
en Schrader M&M's	2.00	4.00
en Schrader M&M'S Halloween	2.00	5.00
36 Ken Schrader M&M'S July 4th	3.00	6.00
40 Sterling Marlin Sterling Marlin	2.00	5.00
43 John Andretti Cheerios	2.00	4.00
44 Buckshot Jones Four Generations of Petty	4.00	8.00
44 Buckshot Jones Georgia Pacific	4.00	8.00
45 Kyle Petty Sprint PCS	3.00	6.00
45 Kyle Petty Sprint Charity Ride	4.00	8.00
60 Greg Biffle Grainger	2.50	6.00
96 Andy Houston McDonald's	2.00	4.00
99 Jeff Burton Citgo	4.00	8.00
99 Jeff Burton Exide	3.00	6.00
02 Ryan Newman Alltel	7.50	15.00

2001 Hot Wheels Racing Promos 1:64

	EX	NM-MT
32 Scott Pruett Tide Downy	2.50	6.00
32 Scott Pruett Tide Downy with French language sticker	3.00	8.00
01 Daytona Speed of Light	6.00	12.00
01 VISA in blister	10.00	20.00

2001 Hot Wheels Racing Select 1:64

The Hot Wheels Select brand was produced as a higher end 1:64 die-cast complete with opening hoods and more detailed engine and underbody work. They were packaged in a blister pack on a mirrored base designed to display the underbody of the car. The year of issue was printed on the front of the packaging in the lower right hand corner.

	EX	NM-MT
5 Terry Labonte Kellogg's	5.00	10.00
6 Mark Martin Pfizer	5.00	10.00
10 Johnny Benson Valvoline	4.00	8.00
11 Darrell Waltrip Mountain Dew	4.00	8.00
12 Jeremy Mayfield Mobil 1	4.00	8.00
17 Matt Kenseth DeWalt	5.00	10.00
17 Matt Kenseth DeWalt Black	5.00	10.00
21 Elliott Sadler Motorcraft	4.00	8.00
22 Ward Burton Caterpillar	4.00	8.00
25 Jerry Nadeau UAW	4.00	8.00
32 Scott Pruett Tide	4.00	8.00
33 Joe Nemechek Oakwood Homes	4.00	8.00
36 Ken Schrader M&M's	4.00	8.00
40 Sterling Marlin Sterling	4.00	8.00
40 Pete Hamilton 7-up 1970 Plymouth	6.00	15.00
42 Lee Petty 1957 Olds	6.00	15.00
43 John Andretti Cheerios	4.00	8.00
43 Richard Petty 1957 Olds	7.50	15.00
43 Richard Petty 1963 Plymouth	12.00	25.00
43 Richard Petty 1967 Plymouth	12.00	25.00
43 Richard Petty 1970 Plymouth Superbird	8.00	20.00
44 Buckshot Jones 4- Generations of Petty	5.00	12.00
45 Kyle Petty Sprint PCS	6.00	12.00
99 Jeff Burton Citgo	4.00	8.00

2001 Hot Wheels Racing Tail Draggers 1:64

These are labeled as 2001 Hot Wheels series but are painted in the 2000 season colors.

	EX	NM-MT
5 Terry Labonte Kellogg's	4.00	10.00
6 Mark Martin Valvoline	6.00	15.00
7 Micheal Waltrip Nations Rent	4.00	10.00
12 Jeremy Mayfield Mobil 1	4.00	10.00
17 Matt Kenseth DeWalt	7.50	15.00
22 Ward Burton Caterpillar	4.00	10.00
33 Joe Nemechek Oakwood Homes	4.00	8.00
43 John Andretti STP	4.00	8.00
44 Kyle Petty Hot Wheels	5.00	12.00
45 Adam Petty Sprint PCS	10.00	25.00
55 Kenny Wallace Square D	4.00	8.00
99 Jeff Burton Exide	4.00	8.00

2001 Hot Wheels Racing Tail Gunner 1:64

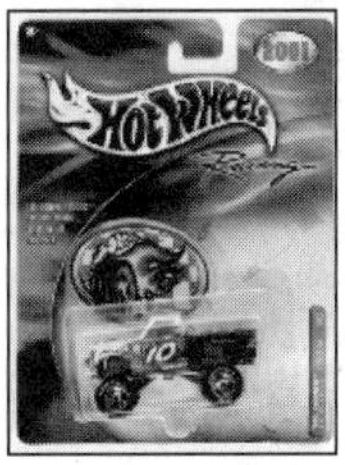

	EX	NM-MT
10 Johnny Benson Valvoline	4.00	8.00
33 Joe Nemechek Oakwood Homes	4.00	8.00
45 Kyle Petty Sprint	4.00	8.00
96 Andy Houston McDonald's	4.00	8.00

2001 Hot Wheels Racing The Demon 1:64

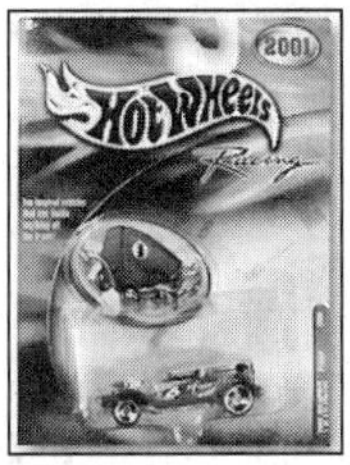

	EX	NM-MT
6 Mark Martin Pfizer	4.00	8.00
21 Elliott Sadler Motorcraft	3.00	6.00
22 Ward Burton Caterpillar	3.00	6.00
40 Sterling Marlin Sterling Marlin	3.00	6.00

2001 Hot Wheels Racing Treasure Hunt 1:64

Each of these die-casts were issued in a Hot Wheels Treasure Hunt blister. The model is wrecker truck with each being painted in the colors of a NASCAR track.

	EX	NM-MT
NNO California	12.50	25.00
NNO Darlington	10.00	25.00
NNO Daytona 500	10.00	25.00
NNO Daytona Night Race	12.50	25.00
NNO Homestead Miami	10.00	25.00
NNO Kansas	12.50	25.00
NNO Phoenix	10.00	25.00
NNO Talladega 500	12.50	25.00
NNO Talladega Superspeedway	12.50	25.00
NNO Watkins Glen	10.00	25.00
NNO Complete J.C.Penney Set/1500	90.00	150.00

2001 Hot Wheels Racing Twin Mill 1:64

	EX	NM-MT
10 Johnny Benson Valvoline 2/4	3.00	6.00
22 Ward Burton Caterpillar 1/4	3.00	6.00
32 Scott Pruett Tide 4/4	3.00	6.00
99 Jeff Burton Citgo 3/4	3.00	6.00

2001 Hot Wheels Racing Way 2 Fast 1:64

	EX	NM-MT
12 Jeremy Mayfield Mobil 1	3.00	6.00
36 Ken Schrader M&M's	3.00	6.00
45 Kyle Petty Sprint	3.00	6.00
96 Andy Houston McDonald's	3.00	6.00

2002 Hot Wheels Racing Sticker 1:64

	EX	NM-MT
5 Terry Labonte Kellogg's	3.00	6.00
5 Terry Labonte Monster's Inc.	3.00	6.00
6 Mark Martin Pfizer	3.00	6.00
10 Scott Riggs Nesquik	3.00	6.00
12 Ryan Newman Alltel	3.00	8.00
14 Larry Foyt Harrah's	3.00	6.00
17 Matt Kenseth DeWalt	4.00	10.00
21 Elliott Sadler Motorcraft	3.00	6.00
22 Ward Burton Caterpillar	3.00	6.00
25 Randy Tolsma Marines red/black	3.00	6.00
25 Randy Tolsma Marines red/white/blue	3.00	6.00
32 Ricky Rudd Tide	3.00	6.00
36 Ken Schrader M&M's	3.00	6.00
36 Ken Schrader M&M's Promo w/o Sticker	5.00	10.00
36 Ken Schrader M&M's Halloween	3.00	6.00
36 Ken Schrader M&M's Vote Aqua #1	8.00	20.00
36 Ken Schrader M&M's Vote Purple #2	8.00	20.00
36 Ken Schrader M&M's Vote Pink #3	15.00	40.00
36 Ken Schrader M&M's Vote Campaign #4	4.00	10.00
40 Sterling Marlin Sterling	3.00	6.00
43 John Andretti Cheerios	3.00	6.00
43 John Andretti Honey Nut Cheerios	3.00	6.00
43 John Andretti Pop Secret	3.00	6.00
43 Carlos Contreras Hot Wheels SuperTruck	3.00	6.00
44 Buckshot Jones Georgia-Pacific	3.00	6.00
45 Kyle Petty Sprint	3.00	6.00
60 Greg Biffle Grainger	3.00	6.00
97 Kurt Busch Rubbermaid	4.00	10.00
99 Jeff Burton Citgo	3.00	6.00

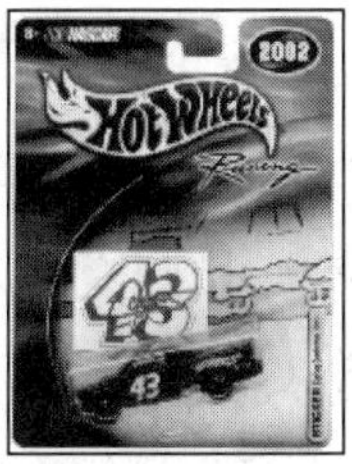

2002 Hot Wheels Racing '33 Roadster 1:64

	EX	NM-MT
99 Jeff Burton Citgo 1	3.00	6.00

2002 Hot Wheels Racing '57 Chevy 1:64

	EX	NM-MT
5 Terry Labonte Kellogg's	3.00	6.00
25 Jerry Nadeau UAW	3.00	6.00
55 Bobby Hamilton Square D 3	3.00	6.00

2002 Hot Wheels Racing '57 T-Bird 1:64

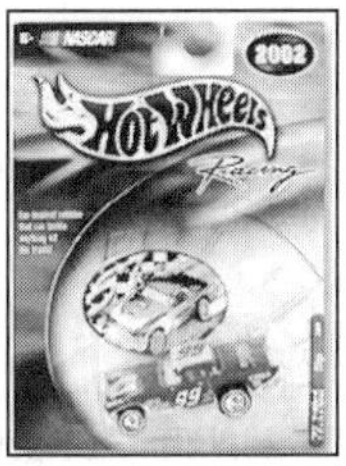

	EX	NM-MT
6 Mark Martin Pfizer 1	3.00	8.00
10 Scott Riggs Nesquik 4	2.50	6.00
12 Ryan Newman Alltel 3	4.00	10.00
99 Jeff Burton Citgo 2	3.00	8.00

2002 Hot Wheels Racing Hooligan 1:64

	EX	NM-MT
45 Kyle Petty Sprint	2.00	5.00

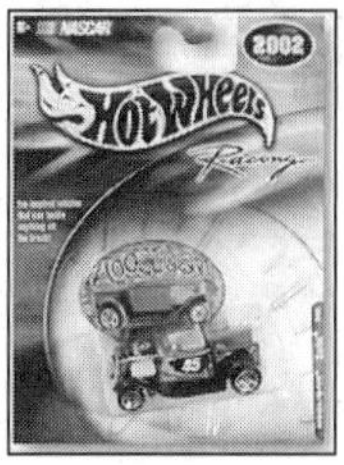

2002 Hot Wheels Racing Limozeen 1:64

	EX	NM-MT
10 Johnny Benson Vavoline 1	3.00	8.00
36 Ken Schrader M&M's 2	6.00	15.00
45 Kyle Petty Sprint 3	3.00	8.00

2002 Hot Wheels Racing Phaeton 1:64

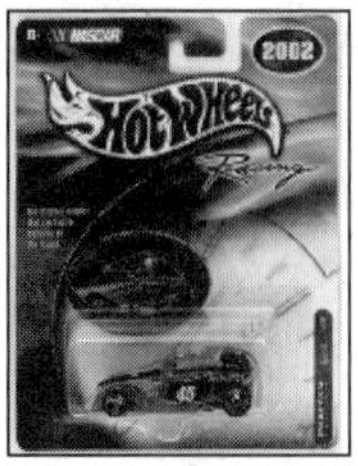

	EX	NM-MT
5 Terry Labonte Kellogg's 7	3.00	6.00
6 Mark Martin Pfizer 2	3.00	8.00
10 Scott Riggs Nesquik 8	3.00	6.00
25 Jerry Nadeau UAW 10	3.00	6.00
36 Ken Schrader M&M's 6	3.00	8.00
40 Sterling Marlin Sterling 9	3.00	6.00
43 John Andretti Cheerios 4	3.00	6.00
45 Kyle Petty Sprint 3	3.00	6.00
99 Jeff Burton Citgo 1	3.00	6.00
02 Ryan Newman Alltel 5	3.00	8.00

2002 Hot Wheels Racing Promos 1:64

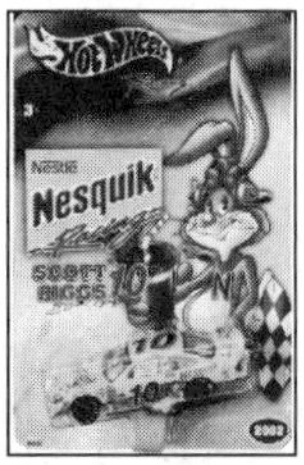

	EX	NM-MT
6 Mark Martin Kraft blister	12.50	25.00
10 Scott Riggs Nesquik blister	7.50	15.00
36 Ken Schrader M&M's blister	6.00	12.00
44 Brawny blister	10.00	20.00
92 Todd Bodine Excedrin in box	6.00	15.00

2002 Hot Wheels Racing Record Times 1:64

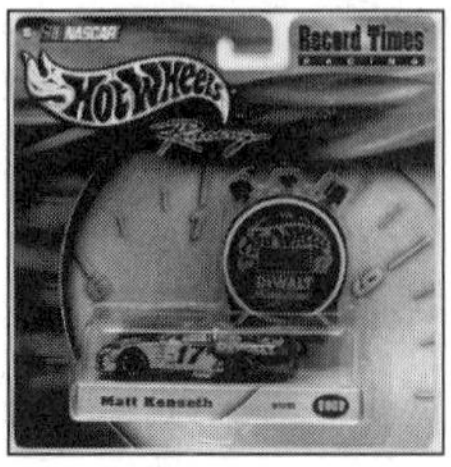

Record Times was a series created by Hot Wheels that combined a 1:64 scale die-cast car with a stop watch produced in the racing team's colors. Each car and stop watch combination was packaged together in an oversized blister pack.

	EX	NM-MT
5 Terry Labonte Kellogg's	4.00	10.00
6 Mark Martin Pfizer	4.00	10.00
10 Johnny Benson	4.00	10.00

	EX	NM-MT
Valvoline		
17 Matt Kenseth DeWalt	5.00	12.00
25 Jerry Nadeau UAW	4.00	10.00
36 Ken Schrader M&M's	4.00	10.00
43 John Andretti Cheerios	4.00	10.00
44 Buckshot Jones Georgia Pacific	4.00	10.00
45 Kyle Petty Sprint	4.00	10.00
99 Jeff Burton Citgo	4.00	10.00

2002 Hot Wheels Racing Treasure Hunt 1:64

	EX	NM-MT
NNO California	10.00	25.00
NNO Darlington	10.00	25.00
NNO Daytona	10.00	25.00
NNO Daytona Night	10.00	25.00
NNO Kansas	10.00	25.00
NNO Miami	10.00	25.00
NNO Phoenix	10.00	25.00
NNO Talladega Red and Blue	10.00	25.00
NNO Talladega Superspeedway	10.00	25.00
NNO Watkins Glen	10.00	25.00
NNO 10-Car Set/1500	125.00	250.00

2002 Hot Wheels Daytona Set-Up 1:64

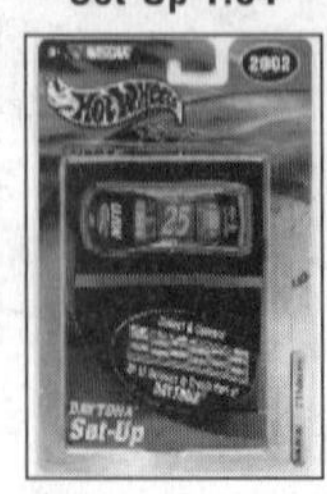

This series was produced by Hot Wheels and packaged in a large blister. Each included a 1:64 car along with a portion of plastic race track. The 12-cars and track pieces could be assembled to represent a section of track from Daytona International Speedway.

	EX	NM-MT
5 Terry Labonte Kellogg's	4.00	8.00
6 Mark Martin Pfizer	4.00	10.00
10 Johnny Benson Valvoline	4.00	8.00
17 Matt Kenseth DeWalt	4.00	10.00
21 Elliott Sadler Motorcraft	4.00	8.00
25 Jerry Nadeau UAW	4.00	8.00
36 Ken Schrader M&M's	4.00	10.00
40 Sterling Marlin Sterling	4.00	10.00
43 John Andretti Cheerios	4.00	8.00
45 Kyle Petty Sprint	4.00	8.00
99 Jeff Burton Citgo	4.00	8.00
02 Ryan Newman Alltel	6.00	12.00

2003 Hot Wheels Racing Color Change 1:64

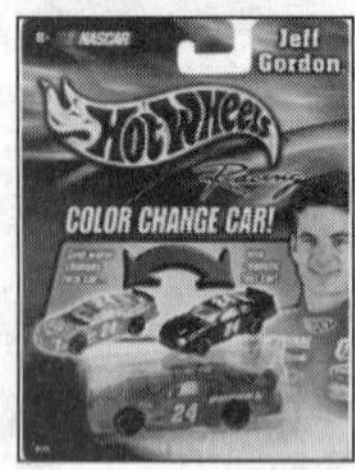

	EX	NM-MT
5 Terry Labonte Kellogg's	4.00	8.00
12 Ryan Newman Alltel	5.00	10.00
12 Ryan Newman Sony Wega	5.00	10.00
17 Matt Kenseth DeWalt	5.00	10.00
18 Bobby Labonte Interstate Batteries	4.00	8.00
20 Tony Stewart Home Depot	5.00	12.00
24 Jeff Gordon DuPont Flames	5.00	12.00
24 Jeff Gordon Pepsi	5.00	12.00
29 Kevin Harvick Goodwrench	5.00	10.00
29 Kevin Harvick Snap-On	5.00	10.00
45 Kyle Petty Georgia Pacific	4.00	8.00
48 Jimmie Johnson Lowe's	5.00	10.00
48 Jimmie Johnson Lowe's Power of Pride	5.00	10.00

2003 Hot Wheels Racing Luxury Rides 1:64

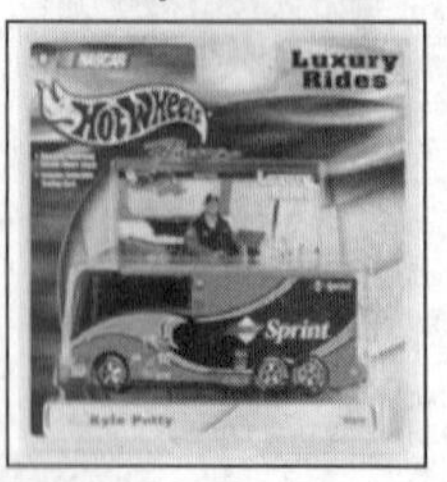

	EX	NM-MT
4 Mike Skinner Kodak	7.50	15.00
6 Mark Martin Pfizer	7.50	15.00
10 Johnny Benson Valvoline	7.50	15.00
10 Scott Riggs Nesquik	7.50	15.00
12 Ryan Newman Alltel	8.00	20.00
17 Matt Kenseth DeWalt	7.50	15.00
21 Ricky Rudd Motorcraft	8.00	20.00
36 Ken Schrader M&M's	8.00	20.00
43 John Andretti Cheerios	7.50	15.00
43 Richard Petty STP	8.00	20.00
45 Kyle Petty Sprint	7.50	15.00
97 Kurt Busch Rubbermaid	7.50	15.00
99 Jeff Burton Citgo	7.50	15.00

2003 Hot Wheels Racing Matt Kenseth Championship 1:64

	EX	NM-MT
17 Matt Kenseth DeWalt	4.00	8.00
17 Matt Kenseth DeWalt Color Change	5.00	10.00

2003 Hot Wheels Racing Power Launchers 1:64

	EX	NM-MT
5 Terry Labonte Kellogg's	5.00	10.00
17 Matt Kenseth DeWalt	5.00	10.00
24 Jeff Gordon DuPont Flames	6.00	12.00
48 Jimmie Johnson Lowe's	5.00	10.00

2003 Hot Wheels Racing Promos 1:64

	EX	NM-MT
1 Land o' Frost blue nose blister	3.00	8.00
1 Land o' Frost red nose blister	3.00	8.00
17 Matt Kenseth DeWalt Oscar Mayer Wienermobile	20.00	40.00

2003 Hot Wheels Racing Race Day 1:64

	EX	NM-MT
6 Mark Martin Pfizer	4.00	8.00
10 Johnny Benson Valvoline	4.00	8.00
10 Scott Riggs Nesquik	4.00	8.00
12 Ryan Newman Alltel	4.00	10.00
16 Greg Biffle Grainger	4.00	8.00
17 Matt Kenseth DeWalt	4.00	10.00
21 Ricky Rudd Motorcraft	4.00	8.00
25 Bobby Hamilton Jr. Marines	4.00	8.00
25 Joe Nemechek UAW-Delphi	4.00	8.00
43 John Andretti Cheerios	4.00	8.00
45 Kyle Petty Georgia Pacific Brawny	4.00	8.00
97 Kurt Busch Rubbermaid	4.00	8.00
01 Jerry Nadeau Army	4.00	8.00

2003 Hot Wheels Racing Recreational Vehicles ATV 1:64

	EX	NM-MT
5 Terry Labonte Kellogg's	5.00	10.00
6 Mark Martin Pfizer	5.00	10.00
17 Matt Kenseth DeWalt	5.00	10.00
45 Kyle Petty Georgia Pacific Brawny	5.00	10.00
97 Kurt Busch Rubbermaid	5.00	10.00

2003 Hot Wheels Racing Recreational Vehicles Bass Boat 1:64

	EX	NM-MT
6 Mark Martin Pfizer	5.00	10.00
12 Ryan Newman Alltel	5.00	10.00
17 Matt Kenseth DeWalt	5.00	10.00
45 Kyle Petty Georgia Pacific Brawny	4.00	8.00
45 Kyle Petty Sprint	4.00	8.00
97 Kurt Busch Rubbermaid	5.00	10.00
99 Jeff Burton Citgo	4.00	8.00

2003 Hot Wheels Racing Recreational Vehicles Motorcycle 1:64

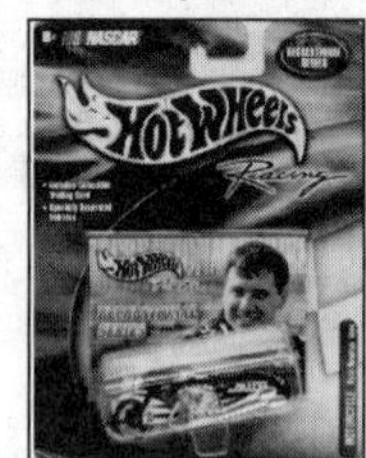

	EX	NM-MT
6 Mark Martin Pfizer	5.00	10.00
12 Ryan Newman Alltel	4.00	10.00
16 Greg Biffle Grainger	5.00	10.00
17 Matt Kenseth DeWalt	4.00	10.00
45 Kyle Petty Georgia Pacific Brawny	5.00	10.00
97 Kurt Busch Rubbermaid	4.00	10.00

2003 Hot Wheels Racing Recreational Vehicles Truck 1:64

	EX	NM-MT
5 Terry Labonte Kellogg's	4.00	8.00
6 Mark Martin Pfizer	4.00	8.00
12 Ryan Newman Alltel	4.00	10.00
97 Kurt Busch Rubbermaid	4.00	8.00

	EX	NM-MT
99 Jeff Burton Citgo	4.00	8.00

2003 Hot Wheels Racing Special Paint 1:64

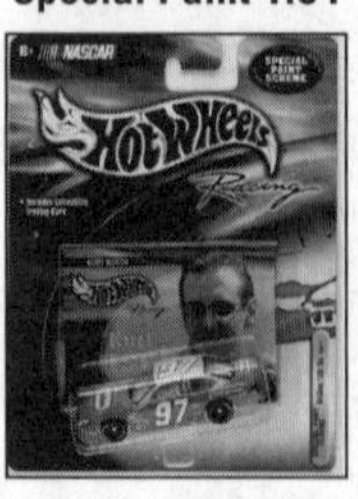

This series is entitled "Special Paint Scheme" as noted in the upper right hand corner of the blister. Each car is accompanied by a Hot Wheels standard sized trading card of the driver. The Mattel copyright line year on the back is 2000. However, they were initally released in late 2002 and all of 2003 therefore are considered the first of the 2003 Hot Wheels Racing releases.

	EX	NM-MT
6 Mark Martin Pfizer White	5.00	10.00
12 Ryan Newman Mobil 1	3.00	8.00
12 Ryan Newman Mobil 1 First Win/1212	7.50	15.00
12 Ryan Newman Sony Wega	4.00	8.00
21 Ricky Rudd Air Force	4.00	8.00
25 Bobby Hamilton Jr. Marines	4.00	8.00
36 Ken Schrader M&M's Halloween	5.00	10.00
43 John Andretti Pop Secret	4.00	8.00
97 Kurt Busch Rubbermaid Little Tikes	4.00	8.00
97 Kurt Busch Sharpie	4.00	8.00
99 Jeff Burton Bass Masters	4.00	8.00

2003 Hot Wheels Racing Treasure Hunt 1:64

	EX	NM-MT
5 Terry Labonte Kellogg's 6	6.00	12.00
6 Mark Martin Pfizer 2	10.00	25.00
12 Ryan Newman Alltel 1	5.00	10.00
16 Greg Biffle Grainger 7	10.00	20.00
21 Ricky Rudd Motorcraft 10	10.00	20.00
43 Richard Petty STP 9	20.00	40.00
45 Kyle Petty GP Brawny 8	15.00	30.00
97 Kurt Busch Sharpie 4	6.00	12.00
99 Jeff Burton Citgo 3	6.00	12.00

2003 Hot Wheels Racing Wrenchin' and Racin' 1:64

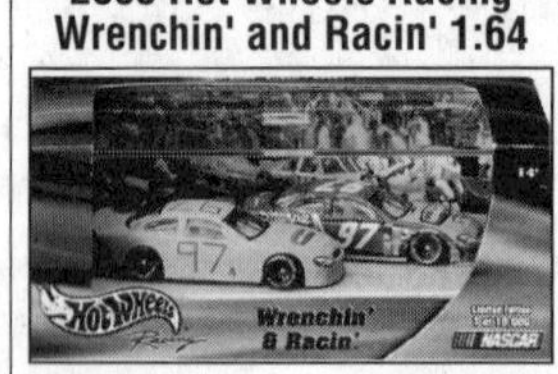

	EX	NM-MT
4 Mike Skinner Kodak	8.00	20.00
6 Mark Martin Pfizer	8.00	20.00
10 Johnny Benson Valvoline	8.00	20.00
12 Ryan Newman Alltel	10.00	20.00
16 Greg Biffle Grainger	8.00	20.00
17 Matt Kenseth DeWalt	10.00	20.00
21 Ricky Rudd Motorcraft	8.00	20.00
25 Bobby Hamilton Jr. Marines	12.50	25.00
43 John Andretti Cheerios	8.00	20.00
45 Kyle Petty Sprint	12.50	25.00
97 Kurt Busch Rubbermaid	10.00	20.00
99 Jeff Burton Citgo	8.00	20.00

2004 Hot Wheels Racing Alternative Paint Scheme 1:64

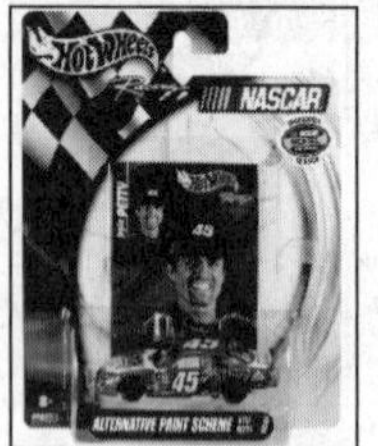

	EX	NM-
6 Mark Martin Oscar Mayer	5.00	10
21 Ricky Rudd Air Force	4.00	8
21 Ricky Rudd Rent-A-Center	4.00	8
45 Kyle Petty Brawny	4.00	8

2004 Hot Wheels Racing Artist Collection 1:64

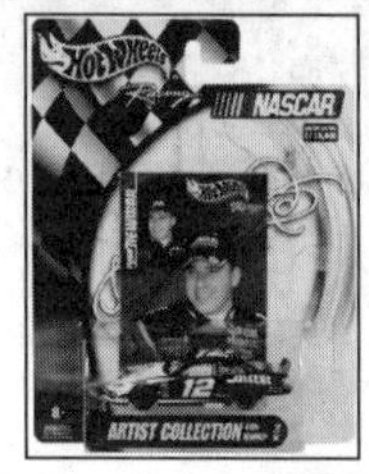

	EX	NM-
6 Mark Martin Pfizer	5.00	10
12 Ryan Newman Alltel	4.00	8
16 Greg Biffle Grainger	4.00	8
17 Matt Kenseth DeWalt	5.00	10
21 Ricky Rudd Motorcraft	4.00	8

2004 Hot Wheels Racing Chase for the Cup 1:64

	EX	NM-
6 Mark Martin Viagra	7.50	15
17 Matt Kenseth DeWalt	7.50	15
97 Kurt Busch Irwin Tools	5.00	10
97 Kurt Busch Sharpie	5.00	10

2004 Hot Wheels Racing Color Change 1:64

	EX	NM-
6 Mark Martin Oscar Mayer	5.00	10
12 Ryan Newman Alltel	5.00	10
17 Matt Kenseth DeWalt	5.00	10
45 Kyle Petty Brawny	4.00	8
45 Kyle Petty Georgia Pacific	4.00	8
97 Kurt Busch Rubbermaid	4.00	8
97 Kurt Busch Sharpie	4.00	8

2004 Hot Wheels Racing Goodyear Showcase 1:64

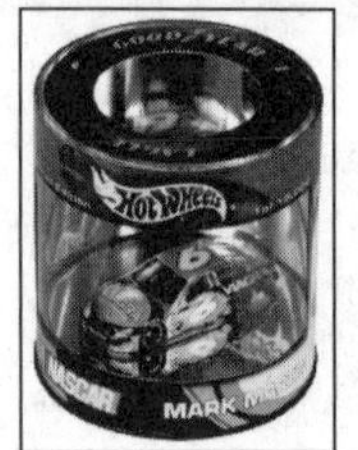

	EX	NM
6 Mark Martin Batman/15,000	10.00	20
6 Mark Martin Viagra/15,000	12.50	25
6 Mark Martin Viagra White/15,000	10.00	20
12 Ryan Newman Mobil 1/15,000	7.50	15
16 Greg Biffle National Guard/15,000	7.50	15
17 Matt Kenseth DeWalt/15,000	10.00	20
21 Ricky Rudd Motorcraft/15,000	7.50	15
21 Ricky Rudd	7.50	15

otorcraft Parts & Service/15,000		
t Busch vin Tools/15,000	7.50	15.00
t Busch arpie/15,000	7.50	15.00
t Busch perman/15,000	7.50	15.00

2004 Hot Wheels Racing Justice League 1:64

	EX	NM-MT
Martin tman	10.00	20.00
Martin tman	10.00	20.00
n Newman stice League	10.00	20.00
g Biffle ish	7.50	15.00
t Kenseth artian Manhunter	10.00	20.00
ky Rudd onder Woman	7.50	15.00
g Biffle ish	7.50	15.00
Busch perman	7.50	15.00
Burton een Lantern	7.50	15.00
ic League Super Heroes	6.00	12.00
ic League Villains	6.00	12.00

2004 Hot Wheels Racing tice League w/Figure 1:64

	EX	NM-MT
Martin tman	12.50	25.00
g Biffle ish	10.00	20.00
tt Kenseth artian Manhunter	12.50	25.00
ky Rudd onder Woman	12.50	25.00
t Busch perman	12.50	25.00
Burton een Lantern	10.00	20.00

04 Hot Wheels Racing Pit Cruisers 1:64

	EX	NM-MT
Martin tman	30.00	60.00
tt Kenseth Walt	5.00	10.00

2004 Hot Wheels Racing Promos 1:64

	EX	NM-MT
Burton t Wheels Back in Black/10,000	15.00	30.00

2004 Hot Wheels Racing Race Day 1:64

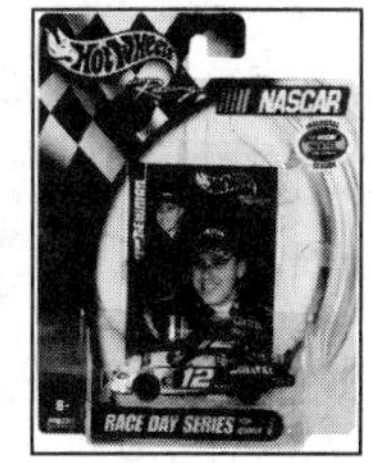

	EX	NM-MT
Martin gra	5.00	12.00
Newman tel	4.00	8.00
Kenseth Walt	4.00	8.00
y Rudd torcraft	4.00	8.00
y Craven e	4.00	8.00
Green eerios	4.00	8.00
Petty orgia Pacific	4.00	8.00

2004 Hot Wheels Racing Stockerz 1:64

	EX	NM-MT
Martin car Mayer	4.00	8.00
Martin zer	4.00	8.00
Newman tel	4.00	8.00
Kenseth Walt	4.00	8.00

21 Ricky Rudd Motorcraft	4.00	8.00
24 Jeff Gordon DuPont Flames	5.00	10.00
29 Kevin Harvick Goodwrench	4.00	8.00
45 Kyle Petty Brawny	4.00	8.00
97 Kurt Busch Rubbermaid	4.00	8.00
97 Kurt Busch Sharpie	4.00	8.00

2004 Hot Wheels Racing Test Track 1:64

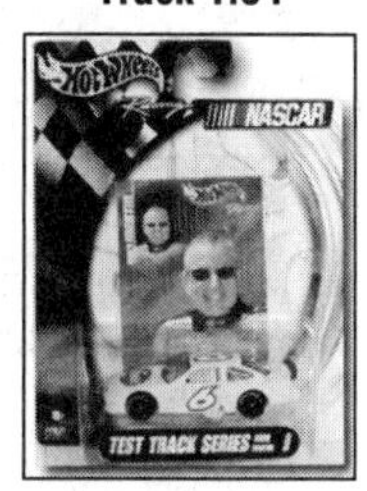

	EX	NM-MT
6 Mark Martin Pfizer	4.00	8.00
12 Ryan Newman Alltel	5.00	10.00
16 Greg Biffle Grainger	4.00	8.00
17 Matt Kenseth DeWalt	6.00	12.00
21 Ricky Rudd Motorcraft	4.00	8.00
43 Richard Petty STP	5.00	10.00
45 Kyle Petty Petty Racing	4.00	8.00
97 Kurt Busch Sharpie	4.00	8.00

2004 Hot Wheels Racing Treasure Hunt 1:64

99 Jeff Burton Hot Wheels/10,000	12.50	25.00

2005 Hot Wheels Alternative Paint Scheme 1:64

	EX	NM-MT
6 Mark Martin Kraft	4.00	8.00
12 Ryan Newman Mobil 1	4.00	8.00
16 Greg Biffle Post-It	4.00	8.00
17 Matt Kenseth Trex	4.00	8.00
21 Ricky Rudd Air Force	4.00	8.00
97 Kurt Busch Irwin Tools	4.00	8.00
99 Carl Edwards Office Depot	7.50	15.00

2005 Hot Wheels Batman Begins 1:64

	EX	NM-MT
6 Mark Martin Batman	6.00	12.00

2005 Hot Wheels Race Day 1:64

	EX	NM-MT
6 Mark Martin Pfizer	4.00	8.00
16 Greg Biffle National Guard	4.00	8.00
17 Matt Kenseth DeWalt	4.00	8.00
21 Ricky Rudd Motorcraft	3.00	6.00
43 Jeff Green Cheerios	3.00	6.00
43 Richard Petty '67 Plymouth	4.00	8.00

2006 Hot Wheels Promos 1:64

	EX	NM-MT
10 Scott Riggs Valvoline Cars in blister	5.00	10.00

1998 Johnny Lightning Stock Car Legends 1:64

These 1:64 scale cars take a look back at some of the most successful drivers in NASCAR history along with their top rides. Each car was produced as a hood open model.

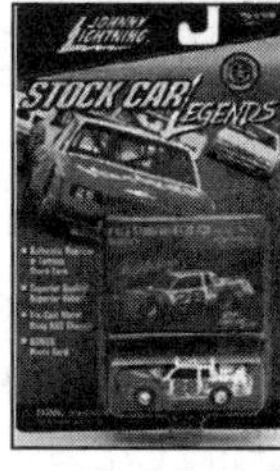

	EX	NM-MT
5 Neil Bonnett Jim Stacy 1977 Dodge	6.00	12.00
6 Buddy Baker Dodge Daytona 1969	6.00	12.00
6 Pete Hamilton American Brakeblok 1971 Plymouth GTX	6.00	12.00
11 Mario Andretti Bunnell Motor 1967 Ford Fairlane	6.00	12.00
11 Darrell Waltrip Pepsi 1983 Monte Carlo	6.00	12.00
11 Cale Yarborough First American City Travelers Checks 1978 Oldsmobile 442	6.00	12.00
17 David Pearson East Tennessee Motors 1969 Ford Torino	6.00	12.00
17 David Pearson 1967 Ford Fairlane	6.00	12.00
21 Donnie Allison Purolator 1971 Mercury Cylone	6.00	12.00
21 Buddy Baker Vavoline 1984 Thunderbird	6.00	12.00
27 Benny Parsons Melling 1980 Monte Carlo	6.00	12.00
28 Cale Yarborough Hardee's 1984 Monte Carlo	6.00	12.00
32 Dick Brooks Bestline 1970	6.00	12.00
40 Pete Hamilton 7-up 1970 Plymouth	6.00	12.00
42 Marty Robbins 1973 Dodge Charger	6.00	12.00
50 Geoff Bodine Spectrum 1982 Grand Prix	6.00	12.00
51 A.J. Foyt Valvoline 1979 Olds	10.00	20.00
71 Bobby Isaac K&K Insurance 1970 Dodge Daytona	6.00	12.00
88 Rusty Wallace Gatorade 1984 Grand Prix	6.00	12.00
88 Darrell Waltrip Gatorade 1979 Monte Carlo	6.00	12.00
98 Lee Roy Yarborough 1969 Ford Torino	6.00	12.00
99 Fred Lorenzen STP 1971 Plymouth	6.00	12.00

1997 Lindberg ARCA 1:64

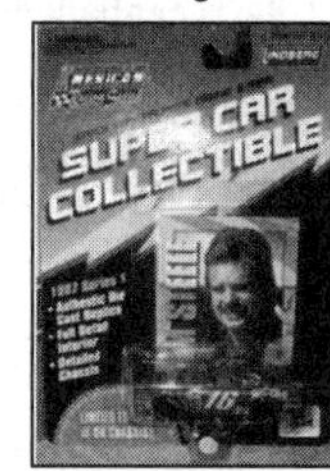

Die-cast in this series feature drivers from the ARCA racing circuit. Each is packaged on a blister that reads "Super Car Collectible" and includes a trading card. The blister also features the Lindberg logo, the American Racing Series logo, and the year of issue on the front.

	EX	NM-MT
16 Tim Steele Craft House	2.00	5.00

1990-92 Matchbox White Rose Super Stars 1:64

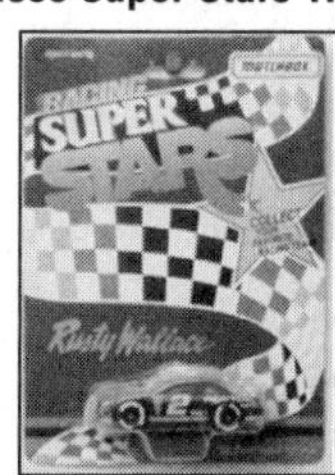

These were the first series of NASCAR replica cars distributed by White Rose. The cars were produced by Matchbox and were issued in either a blister package, a small window box or a promo style polybag.

	EX	NM-MT
1 Jeff Gordon Baby Ruth Orange Lettering '92 BX	10.00	20.00
1 Jeff Gordon Baby Ruth Red Lettering '92 BX	6.00	12.00
2 Rusty Wallace Pontiac Excitement '92 BL	2.00	5.00
3 Dale Earnhardt GM '90 BX	35.00	75.00
3 Dale Earnhardt GM Parts '91 BX	25.00	50.00
3 Dale Earnhardt Goodwrench '92 BL	10.00	25.00
3 Dale Earnhardt Mom-n-Pop's '92 polly bag	10.00	20.00
4 Ernie Irvan Kodak '92 BL	2.00	5.00
7 Harry Gant Mac Tools '92 BX	4.00	8.00
7 Jimmy Hensley White Rose Collectibles '92 BX	4.00	8.00
7 Alan Kulwicki Hooters '92 BL	15.00	30.00
7 Alan Kulwicki Hooters Naturally Fresh '92 BL	10.00	20.00
8 Jeff Burton TIC Financial '92 BX	1.50	4.00
8 Dick Trickle Snicker's '92 BL	1.50	4.00
9 No Driver Association Melling 1992 BL	1.50	4.00
10 Derrike Cope Purolator '92 BL	1.50	4.00
10 Ernie Irvan Mac Tools '91 BX	10.00	20.00
11 Bill Elliott Amoco '92 BL	1.50	4.00
12 Hut Stricklin Raybestos '92 BL	1.50	4.00
15 No Driver Association Motorcraft '92 BL	1.50	4.00
15 Morgan Shepherd Motorcraft '92 BL	1.50	4.00
18 Dale Jarrett Interstate Batteries '92 BL	2.00	5.00
22 Sterling Marlin Maxwell House '92 BL	2.00	5.00
26 Brett Bodine Quaker State '92 BL	1.50	4.00
28 Davey Allison Havoline '92 BL	7.50	15.00
28 Davey Allison Havoline Mac Tools '92 BL	7.50	15.00
29 No Driver Association Matchbox Racing White Rose Collectibles '92 BX	2.50	5.00
29 Phil Parsons Parsons Racing '92 BX	10.00	20.00
30 Michael Waltrip Pennzoil '92 BL	1.50	4.00
41 James Smith White House Apple Juice '92 BL	1.50	4.00
42 Kyle Petty Mello Yello '92 BL	1.50	4.00
43 Richard Petty STP '92 BL	1.50	4.00
44 Bobby Labonte Penrose '92 BX	4.00	8.00
44 Bobby Labonte Slim Jim '92 BX	4.00	8.00
48 James Hylton Valtrol '92 BL	1.50	4.00
49 Ed Ferree Fergaed Racing '92 BX	1.50	4.00
55 Ted Musgrave Jasper Engines	1.50	4.00
66 Chad Little Phillips 66 red car '92 BL	1.50	4.00
66 No Driver Association Phillips 66 black car '92 BL	1.50	4.00
68 Bobby Hamilton Country Time '92 BL	1.50	4.00
87 Joe Nemechek Texas Pete '92 BX	1.50	4.00
89 Jim Sauter Evinrude '92 BL	1.50	4.00
92 No Driver Association White Rose Collectibles '92 BL	25.00	35.00
92 Hut Stricklin Stanley Tools '92 BX	1.50	4.00

1993 Matchbox White Rose Super Stars 1:64

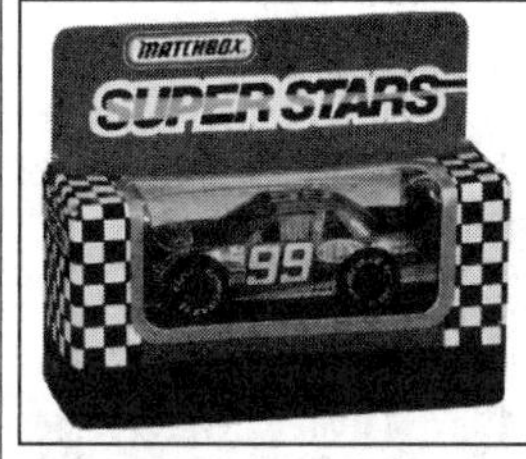

This series features six Jimmy Hensley cars honoring many of the sponsors of the number 7 car. Each piece either comes in a blister package or a small window box. The year is on the end of each of the box packages.

	EX	NM-MT
1 Rodney Combs Jr. Luxaire Promo blister/5000	10.00	18.00
1 Rodney Combs Jr. Goody's BX	9.00	16.00
6 Mark Martin Valvoline BX	3.00	5.00
7 Jimmy Hensley Bobsled BX	5.00	9.00
7 Jimmy Hensley Bojangles BL	5.00	9.00
7 Jimmy Hensley Cellular One BX	5.00	9.00
7 Jimmy Hensley Family Channel BX	5.00	9.00
7 Jimmy Hensley Hanes BX	5.00	9.00
7 Jimmy Hensley Matchbox BX	5.00	9.00
8 Jeff Burton TIC Financal BX	1.50	4.00
8 Jeff Burton Baby Ruth BX	1.50	4.00
8 Sterling Marlin Raybestos BL	2.00	5.00
8 Bobby Dotter Dewalt BX	1.50	4.00
9 Mike Wallace FDP Brakes BX	1.50	4.00
12 Jimmy Spencer Meineke BL	1.50	4.00
14 Terry Labonte MW Windows BX	2.00	5.00
21 Morgan Shepherd Citgo BL	1.50	4.00
22 Bobby Labonte Maxwell House BL	3.00	6.00
24 Jeff Gordon DuPont BL	6.00	10.00
25 Hermie Sadler VA is for Lovers BX	1.50	4.00
28 Davey Allison Havoline BL	10.00	18.00
29 Phil Parsons Matchbox BL	1.50	4.00
31 Bobby Hillin Jr. Team Ireland BL	1.50	4.00
32 Jimmy Horton Active Racing BL	1.50	4.00
32 Dale Jarrett Pic-N-Pay BX	2.00	5.00
40 Kenny Wallace Dirt Devil BL	1.50	4.00
41 Phil Parsons Manheim BL	1.50	4.00
48 Sterling Marlin Cappio BX	2.00	5.00
69 Jeff Sparker WFE Challenge BL	6.00	12.00
71 Dave Marcis Enick's Catering BL	1.50	4.00
83 Lake Speed Purex	1.50	4.00
87 Joe Nemechek Dentyne	1.50	4.00
93 No Driver Association White Rose Collectibles BL	20.00	35.00
93 No Driver Association American Zoom poly bag	4.00	8.00
94 Terry Labonte Sunoco BL	3.00	6.00
98 Derrike Cope Bojangles BL	1.50	4.00
98 Jimmy Spencer Moly Black Gold BL	1.50	4.00
99 Ricky Craven DuPont BX	1.50	4.00

1994 Matchbox White Rose Super Stars 1:64

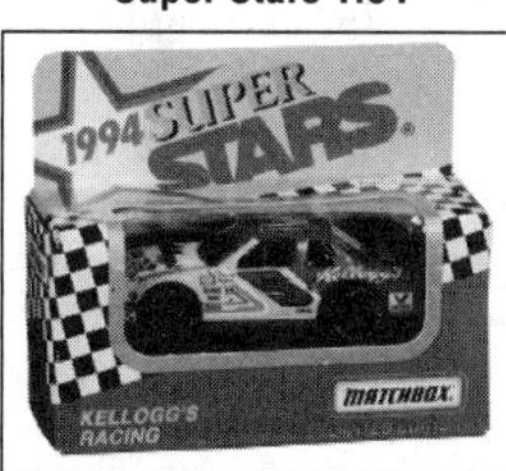

This is considered the second Super Stars Series distributed by White Rose Collectibles. Each standard car was issued in a small window box. There were special cars released that featured "Future Cup Stars" and drivers who won "Super Star Awards." The Super Star Awards cars came in a jewelry type box with the car being painted in gold.

	EX	NM-MT
2 Ricky Craven DuPont BX	1.50	4.00
2 Rusty Wallace Ford Motorsports BX	1.50	4.00
3 Dale Earnhardt Gold Lumina Super Star Awards	25.00	50.00
4 Sterling Marlin Kodak BX	1.50	4.00
4 Sterling Marlin Kodak FunSaver BX	1.50	4.00
5 Terry Labonte Kellogg's BX	2.00	4.00
6 Mark Martin Valvoline BX	2.00	4.00
7 Geoff Bodine Exide BX	3.00	8.00
7 Harry Gant Manheim BX	1.50	4.00
8 Jeff Burton Raybestos BX	1.50	4.00
12 Derrike Cope Straight Arrow BX	1.50	4.00
15 Lake Speed Quality Care BX	1.50	4.00
16 Ted Musgrave Family Channel BX	1.50	4.00
17 Darrell Waltrip Western Auto BX	1.50	4.00
19 Loy Allen Jr. Hooters BX	1.50	4.00
23 Hut Stricklin Smokin' Joe's BX	10.00	20.00
24 Jeff Gordon DuPont BX	5.00	10.00
26 Brett Bodine Quaker State BX	1.50	4.00
29 Phil Parsons Baltimore Colts BL Promo/5000	6.00	15.00
29 Phil Parsons Matchbox White Rose Collectibles BX	1.50	4.00
30 Michael Waltrip Pennzoil BX	1.50	4.00
32 Dale Jarrett Pic-N-Pay BX	2.00	4.00
33 Harry Gant Gold Lumina Super Star Awards in box	12.50	25.00
34 Mike McLaughlin Fiddle Faddle BL	1.50	4.00
37 Loy Allen Jr. Naturally Fresh Future Cup Stars '94 BX	3.00	8.00
40 Bobby Hamilton Kendall BX	1.50	4.00
41 Joe Nemechek Meineke BX	1.50	4.00

	EX	NM-MT
43 Rodney Combs Jr. Black Flag BX	3.00	8.00
43 Rodney Combs Jr. French's Black Flag BL	12.50	25.00
43 Rodney Combs Jr. French's BX	3.00	8.00
46 Shawna Robinson Polaroid BL	12.50	25.00
52 Ken Schrader AC Delco BX	1.50	4.00
55 Jimmy Hensley Petron Plus BL Promo/5000	7.50	15.00
60 Mark Martin Winn Dixie BX	5.00	10.00
66 Mike Wallace Duron Paint Future Cup Stars '94 BX	3.00	8.00
75 Todd Bodine Factory Stores of America BX	1.50	4.00
87 Joe Nemechek Cintas Future Cup Stars '94 BX	3.00	8.00
92 Burn Foundation promo blister	2.00	4.00
92 Larry Pearson Stanley Tools BX	1.50	4.00
94 No Driver Association Matchbox White Rose Collectibles BL	12.50	25.00
94 No Driver Association Series 2 preview BX	4.00	8.00
98 Derrike Cope Fingerhut BX	1.50	4.00
0 Jeff Burton TIC Financial Future Cup Stars '94 BX	5.00	10.00

1995 Matchbox White Rose Super Stars 1:64

This is the continuation of the second Super Stars Series. The Super Star Awards cars again come in a special box and are gold.

	EX	NM-MT
1 Mike Chase Sears Diehard SuperTruck	3.00	5.00
1 Hermie Sadler DeWalt	3.00	5.00
2 Ricky Craven DuPont	3.00	5.00
3 Dale Earnhardt Gold 7-Time Champion Super Star Awards	20.00	40.00
3 Dale Earnhardt Goodwrench	10.00	20.00
3 Mike Skinner Goodwrench SuperTruck	3.00	5.00
5 Terry Labonte Kellogg's	3.00	5.00
6 Rick Carelli Total SuperTruck	3.00	5.00
6 Mark Martin Valvoline	3.00	5.00
7 Geoff Bodine Exide	3.00	5.00
8 Jeff Burton Raybestos	3.00	5.00
8 Jeff Burton Raybestos Super Star Awards	10.00	20.00
8 Bobby Dotter Hyde Tools	3.00	5.00
11 Brett Bodine Lowe's	3.00	5.00
12 Derrike Cope Straight Arrow	3.00	5.00
18 Bobby Labonte Interstate Batteries	3.00	5.00
24 Jeff Gordon DuPont	4.00	8.00
24 Scott Lagasse DuPont SuperTruck	3.00	5.00
24 Mickey York Cobra Promo/7000	4.00	10.00
25 Ken Schrader Budweiser in acrylic Case	7.50	15.00
26 Steve Kinser Quaker State	3.00	5.00
28 Dale Jarrett Havoline	3.00	5.00
40 Patty Moise Dial Purex	3.00	5.00
42 Kyle Petty Coors Light in acrylic Case	7.50	15.00
57 Jason Keller Budget Gourmet	3.00	5.00
71 Kevin Lepage Vermont Teddy Bear	3.00	5.00
72 Tracy Leslie Detroit Gasket	3.00	5.00
74 Johnny Benson Jr. Lipton Tea	3.00	5.00
87 Joe Nemechek BellSouth Mobility Promo/7000	7.50	15.00
87 Joe Nemechek Burger King	3.00	5.00
90 Mike Wallace Heilig-Meyers	3.00	5.00
94 Bill Elliott Gold Thunderbird SuperStars Awards	10.00	20.00
94 Bill Elliott McDonald's	3.00	5.00
94 Bill Elliott McDonald's Thunderbat Promo	7.50	15.00
95 John Tanner Caterpillar	3.00	5.00
99 Phil Parsons Luxaire	3.00	5.00

1996 Matchbox White Rose Super Stars 1:64

This series of 1:64 replicas were packaged in a small clear window box featuring the name "Racing SuperStars." They were manufactured by Matchbox and licensed and distributed by White Rose Collectibles. A production run of 10,000 was noted on the outside of the box as well. The listings below also include four special issue SuperStar Awards cars that were produced in gold chrome and feature winners of the Winston Cup Series, the SuperTruck Series, the Winston Cup Rookie of

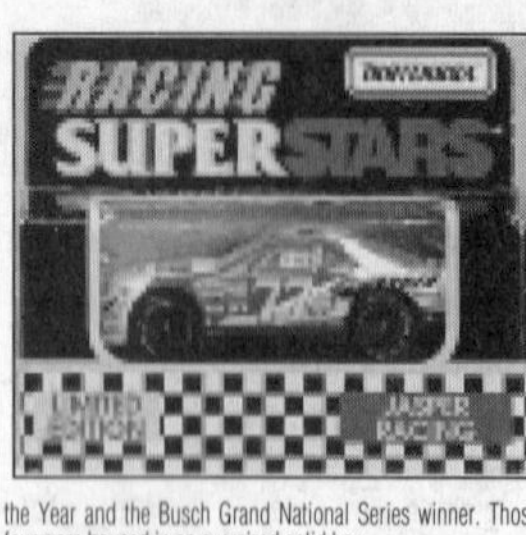

the Year and the Busch Grand National Series winner. Those four were housed in an oversized solid box.

	EX	NM-MT
2 Mike Bliss ASE SuperTruck	3.00	5.00
3 Mike Skinner Gold SuperStars Awards SuperTruck	10.00	18.00
4 Sterling Marlin Kodak	3.00	5.00
5 Terry Labonte Kellogg's	3.00	5.00
6 Mark Martin Valvoline	3.00	5.00
9 Lake Speed SPAM	3.00	5.00
10 Phil Parsons Channellock SuperTruck	3.00	5.00
10 Ricky Rudd Tide	3.00	5.00
12 Derrike Cope Badcock Promo/5000	6.00	15.00
15 Wally Dallenbach Hayes Modems Promo/5000	6.00	15.00
16 Ted Musgrave Family Channel	3.00	5.00
21 Tobey Butler Ortho SuperTruck	3.00	5.00
21 Michael Waltrip Citgo	3.00	5.00
22 Ward Burton MBNA	3.00	5.00
24 Jeff Gordon DuPont	4.00	8.00
24 Jeff Gordon DuPont Gold SuperStars Awards	15.00	25.00
24 Jack Sprague Quaker State SuperTruck	3.00	5.00
25 White Rose Santa Promo/2500	3.00	8.00
34 Mike McLaughlin Royal Oak	3.00	5.00
37 John Andretti K-Mart	3.00	5.00
40 Tim Fedewa Kleenex	3.00	5.00
41 Ricky Craven Kodiak	3.00	5.00
41 Ricky Craven Rookie of the Year Gold SuperStars Awards	10.00	18.00
43 Rodney Combs Lance	3.00	5.00
74 Johnny Benson Jr. Lipton Tea Gold SuperStar Awards	10.00	18.00
77 Bobby Hillin Jr. Jasper	3.00	5.00
87 Joe Nemechek BellSouth Promo	5.00	10.00
87 Joe Nemechek Burger King	3.00	5.00
87 Joe Nemechek Burger King Promo/5000	3.00	8.00
88 Dale Jarrett Quality Care	3.00	5.00
94 Ron Barfield New Holland	3.00	5.00
94 Bill Elliott McDonald's Monopoly Promo/5000	4.00	10.00
94 Bill Elliott McDonald's	3.00	5.00
95 David Green Caterpillar	3.00	5.00
99 Jeff Burton Exide	3.00	5.00
0 Rick Eckert Ray-Vest SuperTruck Promo	4.00	8.00

1997 Matchbox White Rose Super Stars 1:64

This series of 1:64 replicas were issued in a Matchbox by White Rose window box. In addition the release also features two Super Star Awards cars and three other cars packaged in glass bottles. The most unique car from this series is that of Rick Mast which is packaged in a glass replica of a shotgun shell.

	EX	NM-MT
2 Rusty Wallace Miller Lite packaged in a bottle	50.00	75.00
5 Terry Labonte Kellogg's	3.00	6.00
5 Terry Labonte Kellogg's SSA Gold	15.00	25.00
25 Ricky Craven Budweiser packaged in a bottle	40.00	60.00
36 Derrike Cope Skittles	2.50	5.00
40 Robby Gordon Coors Light packaged in a bottle	40.00	60.00
74 Randy LaJoie Fina	2.50	5.00
74 Randy LaJoie Fina SSA Gold	10.00	20.00
75 Rick Mast Remington packaged in a shotgun shell	35.00	50.00
75 Rick Mast Remington Camo in a shotgun shell	30.00	50.00
75 Rick Mast Stren in a shotgun shell	30.00	50.00
88 Kevin Lepage Hype	2.50	5.00
94 Bill Elliott McDonald's	2.50	5.00
94 Bill Elliott Mac Tonight Promo blister	4.00	10.00
96 David Green Caterpillar	2.50	5.00

1996 Miscellaneous Promos 1:24

	EX	NM-MT
5 Terry Labonte Kellogg's Korny Bank 1998 produced by Nevins&Garner	12.50	25.00
5 Terry Labonte Kellogg's Tony Food City produced by Nevins&Garner	15.00	25.00
32 Dale Jarrett Band-Aid DAJ Racing/5000	60.00	120.00
44 Bobby Labonte Shell 1996 EPI	30.00	50.00

1991-03 Miscellaneous Promos 1:43

	EX	NM-MT
5 Terry Labonte Kellogg's Bi-lo 2003	12.50	25.00
5 Terry Labonte Kellogg's Giant 2003	10.00	25.00
5 Terry Labonte Kellogg's Tops 2003	6.00	15.00
8 Bobby Hillin Snickers Promo 1991 issued w/candy bars	6.00	15.00
8 Dick Trickle Snickers Promo 1992 issued w/candy bars	6.00	15.00

1991-04 Miscellaneous Promos 1:64

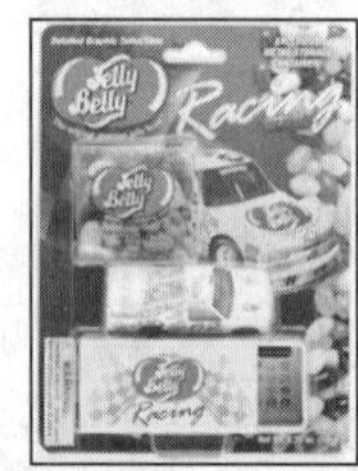

These 1:64 die-cast pieces were issued as promotional itmes for various businesses and other entities. Most were issued in blister packs or in separate poly bags. There is no definative die-cast manufacturer noted on the cars or boxes.

	EX	NM-MT
1 Jeff Gordon Baby Ruth First BGN Win Motorsports Properties blister/20,000 1993	12.50	25.00
5 Terry Labonte Apple Jacks black windows in bag '=1999	5.00	12.00
5 Terry Labonte Honey Frosted Mini-Wheats in bag 2002	4.00	10.00
5 Terry Labonte Kellogg's Promo 1995 black windows produced by Nevin International	4.00	10.00
5 Terry Labonte Kellogg's Promo 1996 black windows produced by Nevin International	4.00	10.00
5 Terry Labonte Kellogg's Promo 2000 black windows Garner and Nevin	2.00	5.00
5 Terry Labonte Mini-Wheats Red in bag 2001	5.00	12.00
6 Mark Martin Stroh Light Trackside Souvenirs	20.00	35.00
9 Bill Elliott Melling Trackside Souvenirs	20.00	35.00
18 Bobby Labonte Banquet in bag 2002	5.00	12.00
18 Bobby Labonte Interstate Batteries EPI Motorsports blister 1996	3.00	8.00
22 Rob Moroso Moroso Racing blister 1991	3.00	8.00
22 Rob Moroso Prestone blister 1991	3.00	8.00
27 Ward Burton Gwaltney Promo in blister/20,000 1992	10.00	20.00
44 Bobby Labonte Shell EPI Motorsports blister 1996	3.00	8.00
54 Rich Bickle Kleenex in bag	15.00	25.00
54 Kevin Grubb Toys 'R' Us blister 2002	7.50	15.00
64 Elmo Langley Start Your Engines promo 1992	4.00	10.00
91 Rich Bickle Aqua Velva in J.B. Williams clamshell 2000	10.00	20.00
92 Jimmie Johnson Alltel blister/20,000 2000	30.00	50.00
92 Jimmie Johnson Alltel window box/10,000 2000	30.00	60.00
93 Dave Blaney Amoco in bag 2001	1.50	3.00
94 Bill Elliott McDonald's Mac Tonight 2-car Promo blister 1997	5.00	12.00
97 Energizer Bunny Promo in bag 1997	5.00	10.00
02 Jim Inglebright Jelly Belly SuperTruck 2000 packaged with jelly beans on blister	3.00	8.00

2006 Motorsports Authentics Steel 1:16

	EX	NM-MT
8 Dale Earnhardt Jr. Bud Dale Tribute/2133	175.00	300.00
8 Dale Earnhardt Jr. Bud Father's Day/1800	175.00	300.00

2007 Motorsports Authentics Driver's Select 1:18

SOME PRINT RUNS LISTED ON PACKAGE
SOME PRINT RUNS PROVIDED BY MA

	EX	NM-MT
8 Dale Earnhardt Jr. Bud/2004	60.00	100.00

2007 Motorsports Authentics Dale The Movie 1:24

	EX	NM-MT
2 Dale Earnhardt Mike Curb '80 Olds 1st Championship/7003	75.00	125.00
2 Dale Earnhardt Wrangler '81 Pontiac 1st Wrangler Win/7003	75.00	125.00
3 Dale Earnhardt Wrangler '86 Monte Carlo Muddy Windshield/7003	75.00	125.00
3 Dale Earnhardt Wrangler '87 Monte Carlo Pass in the Grass/7003	75.00	125.00
3 Dale Earnhardt Goodwrench '88 Monte Carlo 1st Goodwrench Win/7003	75.00	125.00
3 Dale Earnhardt Goodwrench '90 Lumina Engine Change/7003	75.00	125.00
3 Dale Earnhardt Goodwrench '94 Lumina Four Tire Stop/7003	75.00	125.00
3 Dale Earnhardt Goodwrench '94 Lumina Number 7/7003	75.00	125.00
3 Dale Earnhardt Goodwrench Silver '95 Monte Carlro Silver Select/7003	75.00	125.00
3 Dale Earnhardt Goodwrench '95 Monte Carlo Bricks/7003	75.00	125.00
3 Dale Earnhardt Goodwrench '96 Monte Carlo Starting in Front/7003	75.00	125.00
3 Dale Earnhardt Goodwrench Plus '98 Monte Carlo The 500/7003	75.00	125.00

2007 Motorsports Authentics Driver's Select 1:24

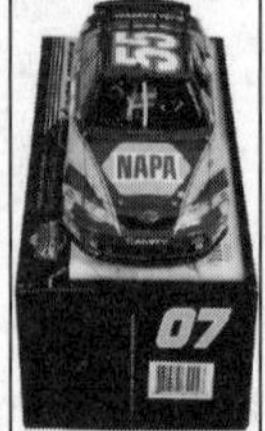

SOME PRINT RUNS LISTED ON PACKAGE
*SOME PRINT RUNS PROVIDED BY MA

	EX	NM-MT
1 Martin Truex Jr. Bass Pro Shops/4800*	40.00	70.00
1 Martin Truex Jr. Bass Pro Shops COT/1570*	40.00	70.00
1 Martin Truex Jr. Bass Pro Shops COT Dover Raced/2248*	40.00	70.00
1 Martin Truex Jr. Bass Pro Shops National Wild Turkey Foundation/1704*	40.00	70.00
1 Martin Truex Jr. Bass Pro Shops 35th Anniversary/1404*	40.00	
1 Martin Truex Jr. Bass Pro Shops '57 Chevy/1536*	40.00	
2 Clint Bowyer BB&T/2176*	40.00	
2 Kurt Busch Miller Lite/4008*	40.00	
2 Kurt Busch Miller Lite COT/1104*	50.00	
2 Kurt Busch Miller Lite Wolrd Beer Challenge/1176*	40.00	
4 Ward Burton Air Force American Heroes/1056	40.00	
5 Kyle Busch Carquest/1800*	35.00	
5 Kyle Busch Carquest COT Bristol Raced/1368*	40.00	
5 Kyle Busch Kellogg's/1800*	35.00	
5 Kyle Busch Kellogg's COT/1163*	40.00	
6 David Ragan AAA/6624*	40.00	
6 David Ragan AAA COT/708*	50.00	
6 David Ragan AAA Insurance/804*	40.00	
6 David Ragan AAA Show Your Card/852*	40.00	
6 David Ragan AAA Travel/804*	40.00	
6 David Ragan Discount Tire/1200*	35.00	
7 Mike Wallace Geico/1000*	40.00	
8 Dale Earnhardt Jr. Bud/26,904*	75.00	
8 Dale Earnhardt Jr. Bud COT/33,934*	75.00	
8 Dale Earnhardt Jr. Bud Camo American Heroes/41,520	50.00	
8 Dale Earnhardt Jr. Bud Elvis COT/35,816*	50.00	
8 Dale Earnhardt Jr. Bud Stars & Stripes31,272*	50.00	
8 Dale Earnhardt Jr. Bud '57 Chevy/19,504*	40.00	
8 Dale Earnhardt Jr. JM Menards/2232*	30.00	
8 Dale Earnhardt Jr. Sharpie/13,182*	30.00	
8 Dale Earnhardt Jr. Veritas/1896*	40.00	
8 Martin Truex Jr. Ritz Oreo	35.00	
9 Kasey Kahne Dodge Dealers/9504*	40.00	
9 Kasey Kahne Dodge Dealers COT/2616*	50.00	
9 Kasey Kahne Dodge Dealers Holiday Sam Bass/894*	40.00	
9 Kasey Kahne Doublemint/1704*	35.00	
9 Kasey Kahne Hellmann's/2208*	35.00	
9 Kasey Kahne McDonald's/1296*	40.00	
9 Kasey Kahne Mopar/1608*	40.00	
9 Kasey Kahne Vitamin Water/1674*	40.00	
10 Scott Riggs Stanley Tools/1008*	35.00	
10 Scott Riggs Stanley Tools COT/708*	40.00	
10 Scott Riggs Valvoline/1404*	35.00	
10 Scott Riggs Valvoline COT/708*	40.00	
11 Denny Hamlin Fed Ex Express/9000*	40.00	
11 Denny Hamlin Fed Ex Express COT/1408*	50.00	
11 Denny Hamlin Fed Ex Express Sam Bass Holiday/1020*	50.00	
11 Denny Hamlin Fed Ex Freight/7008*	40.00	
11 Denny Hamlin Fed Ex Freight COT/1152*	50.00	
11 Denny Hamlin Fed Ex Freight Marines American Heroes/3240	40.00	
11 Denny Hamlin Fed Ex Ground/3756*	40.00	
11 Denny Hamlin Fed Ex Ground COT/1260*	50.00	
11 Denny Hamlin Fed Ex Ground COT New Hampshire Raced/888	50.00	
11 Denny Hamlin Fed Ex Kinko's/3216*	40.00	
11 Denny Hamlin Fed Ex Kinko's COT/1372*	50.00	
12 Kurt Busch Penske/1000*	40.00	
12 Sam Hornish Jr. Mobil 1/1200*	50.00	
12 Ryan Newman Alltel/3700*	40.00	
12 Ryan Newman Alltel COT/2488*	40.00	
12 Ryan Newman Alltel My Circle/800*	40.00	
12 Ryan Newman Kodak/1852*	40.00	
12 Ryan Newman Mobil 1/1400*	40.00	
14 Sterling Marlin Waste Management/1236*	40.00	
15 Paul Menard JM Menards/2208*	40.00	
15 Paul Menard JM Menards COT/514*	40.00	

ıl Menard	40.00	70.00
M Menards		
7 Chevy/348		
eg Biffle	40.00	70.00
flac COT/1086*		
eg Biffle	30.00	60.00
meriquest/3000*		
eg Biffle	40.00	70.00
meriquest COT/700*		
eg Biffle	40.00	70.00
ish Network COT/700*		
eg Biffle	30.00	60.00
ackson Hewitt/700*		
eg Biffle	40.00	70.00
M/2100*		
eg Biffle	50.00	75.00
M Blue Tape/600*		
eg Biffle	50.00	75.00
M Coast Guard		
merican Heroes/2568		
eg Biffle	60.00	100.00
M Finishmast/60*		
tt Kenseth	40.00	70.00
lac/1452*		
tt Kenseth	50.00	75.00
by's/2240*		
tt Kenseth	40.00	70.00
arhartt/1900*		
tt Kenseth	50.00	75.00
arhartt California Raced/1200*		
tt Kenseth	40.00	70.00
arhartt for Women/700*		
tt Kenseth	50.00	75.00
arhartt COT/900*		
tt Kenseth	50.00	75.00
eWalt/3708*		
tt Kenseth	50.00	75.00
eWalt		
omestead-Miami Raced/864*		
tt Kenseth	50.00	75.00
eWalt COT/2182*		
tt Kenseth	40.00	70.00
eWalt Holiday		
am Bass/780*		
tt Kenseth	40.00	70.00
sh Network/1116*		
tt Kenseth	40.00	70.00
evel Wayerhouser/948*		
tt Kenseth	40.00	70.00
&L Carriers/1900*		
tt Kenseth	50.00	75.00
&L Carriers COT/756*		
tt Kenseth	40.00	70.00
SG Sheetrock/3434*		
Yeley	50.00	75.00
terstate Batteries/2508*		
Yeley	40.00	70.00
terstate Batteries COT/708*		
Yeley	40.00	70.00
terstate Batteries		
7 Chevy/456*		
ott Sadler	40.00	70.00
odge Dealers/4508*		
ott Sadler	50.00	75.00
odge Dealers COT/1104*		
ott Sadler	40.00	70.00
odge Dealers Holiday		
am Bass/387*		
ott Sadler	50.00	75.00
emen's COT/1212*		
y Logano	200.00	350.00
Racing Oil/720*		
y Stewart	40.00	70.00
ome Depot/8508*		
y Stewart	50.00	75.00
ome Depot		
ickyard Raced/3744*		
y Stewart	50.00	75.00
ome Depot		
hicagoland Raced/1248*		
y Stewart	50.00	75.00
ome Depot		
d Shootout Daytona Raced/2007*		
y Stewart	50.00	75.00
ome Depot		
vin 150s Daytona Raced/2028*		
y Stewart	50.00	75.00
ome Depot		
atkins Glen Raced/1116*		
y Stewart	50.00	75.00
ome Depot COT/7392*		
y Stewart	40.00	70.00
ome Depot Holiday		
m Bass/1572*		
y Stewart	50.00	75.00
ome Depot '57 Chevy/300*		
in Harvick	40.00	70.00
to Zone/2208*		
in Harvick	50.00	75.00
to Zone Daytona Raced/1908*		
Wood	50.00	75.00
Force		
merican Heroes/1548*		
Kevin Harvick	75.00	125.00
to Zone Daytona Raced		
ell Pennzoil Daytona Raced		
car set		
e Blaney	40.00	70.00
T/1978*		
e Blaney	40.00	70.00
T COT/708*		
e Blaney	40.00	70.00
T D6T/1408*		
e Blaney	40.00	70.00
T M-Series/960*		
e Blaney	40.00	70.00
Tused.com/792*		
Gordon	50.00	75.00
Pont Department of Defense		
merican Heroes/7008		
Gordon	50.00	75.00
Pont Flames/13,500*		
Gordon	50.00	75.00
Pont Flames		
in 150s Daytona Raced/2256*		
Gordon	60.00	100.00
Pont Flames		
cono Raced/1576*		
Gordon	50.00	75.00
Pont Flames		
lladega Raced/7777*		

24 Jeff Gordon	200.00	350.00
DuPont Flames		
Cromax Pro Employee/711		
24 Jeff Gordon	60.00	100.00
DuPont Flames Car of Tomorrow/19,228*		
24 Jeff Gordon	60.00	100.00
DuPont Flames COT		
Darlington Raced/2892*		
24 Jeff Gordon	50.00	75.00
DuPont Flames COT		
Phoenix Raced/7676*		
24 Jeff Gordon	250.00	350.00
DuPont Flames COT		
Pioneer Employee/711		
24 Jeff Gordon	50.00	75.00
DuPont Flames '57 Chevy/6180*		
24 Jeff Gordon	40.00	70.00
Hoiliday Sam Bass		
Jeff Gordon Foundation/3288*		
24 Jeff Gordon	50.00	75.00
Nicorette/5704*		
24 Jeff Gordon	50.00	75.00
Nicorette COT/4662*		
24 Jeff Gordon	50.00	75.00
Pepsi/5704*		
24 Jeff Gordon	50.00	75.00
Pepsi COT/5788*		
24 Jeff Gordon	60.00	100.00
Pepsi COT		
Talladega Raced/3192*		
24 Jeff Gordon	50.00	75.00
Underdog JG Foundation/5180*		
25 Casey Mears	50.00	75.00
National Guard/2758*		
25 Casey Mears	40.00	70.00
National Guard COT/2016*		
25 Casey Mears	40.00	70.00
National Guard Camo		
American Heroes/912*		
25 Casey Mears	40.00	70.00
National Guard Camo		
American Heroes Charlotte Raced/1190*		
26 Jamie McMurray	40.00	70.00
Aflac/1008*		
26 Jamie McMurray	50.00	75.00
Crown Royal/2256*		
26 Jamie McMurray	50.00	75.00
Crown Royal COT/1152*		
26 Jamie McMurray	40.00	70.00
Dish Network/700*		
26 Jamie McMurray	40.00	70.00
Irwin Tools/1200*		
29 Jeff Burton	40.00	70.00
Holiday Inn/816*		
29 Kevin Harvick	40.00	70.00
Pennzoil Platinum All Star		
Charlotte Raced/3255*		
29 Kevin Harvick	50.00	75.00
Pennzoil Platinum COT/2700*		
29 Kevin Harvick	50.00	75.00
Reese's/3000*		
29 Kevin Harvick	500.00	750.00
Reese's Elvis/723*		
29 Kevin Harvick	50.00	75.00
Shell Pennzoil/13,924*		
29 Kevin Harvick	60.00	100.00
Shell Pennzoil		
Daytona Raced/7029*		
29 Kevin Harvick	50.00	75.00
Shell Pennzoil		
Daytona Raced Liquid Chrome/729		
29 Kevin Harvick	50.00	75.00
Shell Pennzoil COT/10,008*		
29 Kevin Harvick	40.00	70.00
Shell Pennzoil Holiday		
Sam Bass/1129*		
29 Scott Wimmer	40.00	70.00
Holiday Inn/144*		
31 Jeff Burton	40.00	70.00
AT&T COT/2135*		
31 Jeff Burton	50.00	75.00
Cingular/3264*		
31 Jeff Burton	40.00	70.00
Lenox/708*		
31 Jeff Burton	40.00	70.00
Prilosec/2264*		
31 Jeff Burton	50.00	75.00
Prilosec Texas Raced/840		
33 Kevin Harvick	40.00	70.00
Road Loans/1120*		
33 Tony Stewart	40.00	70.00
Old Spice/1320*		
38 David Gilliland	50.00	75.00
M&M's/4404*		
38 David Gilliland	50.00	75.00
M&M's COT/1428*		
38 David Gilliland	40.00	70.00
M&M's Holiday		
Sam Bass/396*		
38 David Gilliland	30.00	60.00
M&M's July 4/1020*		
38 David Gilliland	40.00	70.00
M&M's Pink		
Susan G. Komen/1318*		
38 David Gilliland	50.00	75.00
M&M's Shrek/2424*		
39 Sam Hornish Jr.	40.00	70.00
Mobil 1/639*		
40 David Stremme	50.00	75.00
Coors Light/1500*		
40 David Stremme	50.00	75.00
Coors Light COT/708*		
40 David Stremme	25.00	50.00
Lone Star Steakhouse/1104*		
41 Bryan Clauson	40.00	70.00
Memorex/708*		
41 Reed Sorenson	40.00	70.00
Fuji Film/708*		
41 Reed Sorenson	40.00	70.00
Juicy Fruit/778*		
41 Reed Sorenson	40.00	70.00
Target/2004*		
41 Reed Sorenson	50.00	75.00
Target COT/708*		
42 Dario Franchitti	50.00	75.00
Target/708*		
42 Juan Pablo Montoya	40.00	70.00
Big Red/3464*		
42 Juan Pablo Montoya	60.00	100.00
Texaco Havoline/6504*		
42 Juan Pablo Montoya	50.00	75.00
Texaco Havoline		
Mexico City Raced/1366*		
42 Juan Pablo Montoya	60.00	100.00
Texaco Havoline COT1752*		
42 Juan Pablo Montoya	50.00	75.00
Texaco Havoline COT		
Infineon Raced/828*		
42 Juan Pablo Montoya	40.00	70.00
Texaco Havoline Holiday		
Sam Bass/381*		
43 Bobby Labonte	50.00	75.00
Cheerios/4204*		
43 Bobby Labonte	50.00	75.00
Cheerios COT/960*		
43 Bobby Labonte	40.00	70.00
Cheerios Pink		
Susan G. Komen/1056*		
43 Bobby Labonte	40.00	70.00
Cheerios Spiderman/2032*		
43 Bobby Labonte	40.00	70.00
Cheerios 500 Starts COT/840*		
43 Bobby Labonte	40.00	70.00
General Mills COT/1140*		
44 Dale Jarrett	40.00	70.00
UPS/9504*		
44 Dale Jarrett	40.00	70.00
UPS COT/2208*		
44 Dale Jarrett	50.00	75.00
UPS Kentucky Derby/3540*		
44 Dale Jarrett	40.00	70.00
UPS Toys for Tots/876*		
44 Dale Jarrett	40.00	70.00
UPS 100th Anniversary COT/1794*		
45 Kyle Petty	40.00	70.00
Marathon Oil/1404*		
45 Kyle Petty	40.00	70.00
Marathon Oil COT/708*		
45 Kyle Petty	40.00	70.00
Wells Fargo1896*		
45 Kyle Petty	40.00	70.00
Wells Fargo COT/2200*		
48 Jimmie Johnson	50.00	75.00
Lowe's/7500*		
48 Jimmie Johnson	50.00	75.00
Lowe's Las Vegas Raced/1380*		
48 Jimmie Johnson	50.00	75.00
Lowe's		
Fall Martinsville Raced/792*		
48 Jimmie Johnson	60.00	100.00
Lowe's Car of Tomorrow/6012*		
48 Jimmie Johnson	50.00	75.00
Lowe's COT		
Martinsville Raced/1320*		
48 Jimmie Johnson	50.00	75.00
Lowe's COT		
Richmond Raced/1320*		
48 Jimmie Johnson	40.00	70.00
Lowe's Holiday		
Sam Bass/1166*		
48 Jimmie Johnson	50.00	75.00
Lowe's Jimmie Johnson Foundation/708*		
48 Jimmie Johnson	50.00	75.00
Lowe's Kobalt/1572*		
48 Jimmie Johnson	60.00	100.00
Lowe's Kobalt		
Atlanta Raced/1537*		
48 Jimmie Johnson	50.00	75.00
Lowe's Kobalt		
Fall Atlanta Raced/853*		
48 Jimmie Johnson	50.00	75.00
Lowe's Kobalt		
Texas Raced/792*		
48 Jimmie Johnson	50.00	75.00
Lowe's Power of Pride		
American Heroes/4164		
48 Jimmie Johnson	50.00	75.00
Lowe's '57 Chevy/1906*		
55 Michael Waltrip	40.00	70.00
NAPA/10,404*		
55 Michael Waltrip	40.00	70.00
NAPA COT/1416*		
60 Carl Edwards	40.00	70.00
Aflac/1116*		
60 Carl Edwards	40.00	70.00
Scotts/1608*		
60 Carl Edwards	40.00	70.00
Scotts '07 BGN Champion/1084*		
60 Carl Edwards	40.00	70.00
World Financial/708*		
66 Steve Wallace	40.00	70.00
Home Life/700*		
83 Brian Vickers	50.00	75.00
Red Bull/2460*		
83 Brian Vickers	40.00	70.00
Red Bull COT/804*		
84 A.J. Allmendinger	50.00	75.00
Red Bull/1308*		
84 A.J. Allmendinger	40.00	70.00
Red Bull COT/700*		
88 Shane Huffman	40.00	70.00
Navy/1400*		
88 Shane Huffman	50.00	75.00
Navy American Heroes/840		
88 Shane Huffman	60.00	100.00
Navy SEALS/1092*		
88 Ricky Rudd	40.00	70.00
Combos COT/708*		
88 Ricky Rudd	40.00	70.00
Pedigree COT/852*		
88 Ricky Rudd	35.00	60.00
Snickers/2832*		
88 Ricky Rudd	50.00	75.00
Snickers COT/1017*		
88 Ricky Rudd	40.00	70.00
Snickers Dark/708*		
90 Stephen Leicht	40.00	70.00
Citifinancial/1000*		
96 Tony Raines	40.00	70.00
DLP/1200*		
96 Tony Raines	40.00	70.00
DLP COT/700*		
96 Tony Raines	50.00	75.00
DLP Shrek		
Car of Tomorrow/1440*		
96 Tony Raines	40.00	70.00
DLP '57 Chevy/312*		
99 Carl Edwards	40.00	70.00
Boston Red Sox COT/1764*		
99 Carl Edwards	50.00	75.00
Office Depot/3756*		
99 Carl Edwards	40.00	70.00
Office Depot COT/1056*		
99 Carl Edwards	40.00	70.00
Office Depot Holiday		
Sam Bass/520*		
99 David Reutimann	50.00	75.00
Aaron's/3488*		
00 David Reutimann	50.00	75.00
Burger King/2200*		
00 David Reutimann	40.00	70.00
Burger King COT/708*		
00 David Reutimann	40.00	70.00
Domino's Pizza/2508*		
00 David Reutimann	50.00	75.00
Domino's Pizza COT/700*		
00 Josh Wise	40.00	70.00
Aaron's SuperTruck/1704*		
01 Mark Martin	40.00	70.00
Principal Financial Group/1224*		
01 Mark Martin	40.00	70.00
U.S. Army/11,340*		
01 Mark Martin	50.00	75.00
U.S. Army COT/2508*		
01 Mark Martin	40.00	70.00
U.S. Army American Heroes/3204		
01 Mark Martin	40.00	70.00
U.S. Army Holiday		
Sam Bass/912*		
01 Mark Martin	40.00	70.00
U.S. Army '57 Chevy/1248*		
01 Regan Smith	60.00	100.00
U.S. Army/1004*		
06 Mark Martin	40.00	70.00
Dish Network/756*		
07 Clint Bowyer	40.00	70.00
Directv/708*		
07 Clint Bowyer	50.00	75.00
Jack Daniel's/5412*		
07 Clint Bowyer	50.00	75.00
Jack Daniel's COT/3448*		
07 Clint Bowyer	50.00	75.00
Jack Daniel's COT		
New Hamshire Raced/1224*		

2007 Motorsports Authentics Driver's Select GM Dealers 1:24

	EX	NM-MT
1 Martin Truex Jr.	50.00	75.00
Bass Pro Shops/600		
1 Martin Truex Jr.	50.00	75.00
Bass Pro Shops		
Car of Tomorrow/360		
2 Clint Bowyer	50.00	75.00
BB&T/72		
5 Kyle Busch	50.00	75.00
Carquest/144		
5 Kyle Busch	50.00	75.00
Carquest COT		
Bristol Raced/1368		
5 Kyle Busch	50.00	75.00
Kellogg's/288		
5 Kyle Busch	50.00	75.00
Kellogg's Car of Tomorrow/240		
5 Mark Martin	50.00	75.00
Autoguard/1152		
8 Dale Earnhardt Jr.	75.00	125.00
Bud/3792		
8 Dale Earnhardt Jr.	75.00	125.00
Bud Car of Tomorrow/3630		
8 Dale Earnhardt Jr.	50.00	75.00
Bud Stars & Stripes/31,272		
8 Dale Earnhardt Jr.	50.00	75.00
JM Memards/600		
8 Dale Earnhardt Jr.	50.00	75.00
Sharpie/1500		
11 Denny Hamlin	50.00	75.00
Fed Ex Express/360		
11 Denny Hamlin	50.00	75.00
Fed Ex Express		
Car of Tomorrow/360		
11 Denny Hamlin	50.00	75.00
Fed Ex Freight/432		
11 Denny Hamlin	50.00	75.00
Fed Ex Freight		
Car of Tomorrow/288		
11 Denny Hamlin	50.00	75.00
Fed Ex Ground/432		
11 Denny Hamlin	50.00	75.00
Fed Ex Ground		
Car of Tomorrow/288		
11 Denny Hamlin	50.00	75.00
Fed Ex Kinko's/432		
11 Denny Hamlin	50.00	75.00
Fed Ex Kinko's		
Car of Tomorrow/288		
14 Sterling Marlin	50.00	75.00
Waste Management/144		
15 Paul Menard	50.00	75.00
Menards/288		
15 Paul Menard	50.00	75.00
Menards Car of Tomorrow/288		
18 J.J. Yeley	50.00	75.00
Interstate Batteries/144		
18 J.J. Yeley	50.00	75.00
Interstate Batteries		
Car of Tomorrow/96		
20 Tony Stewart	60.00	100.00
Home Depot/1152		
20 Tony Stewart	60.00	100.00
Home Depot		
Car of Tomorrow/1128		
21 Kevin Harvick	50.00	75.00
Auto Zone/396		
24 Jeff Gordon	50.00	75.00
DuPont Flames/2400		
24 Jeff Gordon	50.00	75.00
DuPont Flames		
Talladega Raced		
24 Jeff Gordon	60.00	100.00
DuPont Flames		
Car of Tomorrow/1200		
24 Jeff Gordon	60.00	100.00
DuPont Flames COT		
Phoenix Raced/7676		
24 Jeff Gordon	50.00	75.00
Nicorette/876		
24 Jeff Gordon	60.00	100.00
Nicorette		
Car of Tomorrow/876		
24 Jeff Gordon	50.00	75.00
Pepsi/876		
25 Casey Mears	50.00	75.00
National Guard/576		
25 Casey Mears	50.00	75.00
National Guard		
Car of Tomorrow/288		
29 Jeff Burton	50.00	75.00
Holiday Inn/144		
29 Kevin Harvick	50.00	75.00
Pennzoil Platinum COT/2700		
29 Kevin Harvick	60.00	100.00
Reese's Car of Tomorrow/720		
29 Kevin Harvick	50.00	75.00
Shell Pennzoil/2004		
29 Kevin Harvick	50.00	75.00
Shell Pennzoil		
Car of Tomorrow/1500		
31 Jeff Burton	50.00	75.00
AT&T COT		
31 Jeff Burton	50.00	75.00
Cingular/360		
31 Jeff Burton	50.00	75.00
Lenox Tools/156		
31 Jeff Burton	50.00	75.00
Prilosec/360		
31 Jeff Burton	50.00	75.00
Prilosec Texas Raced/840		
33 Kevin Harvick	50.00	75.00
Road Loans/288		
33 Tony Stewart	50.00	75.00
Old Spice/288		
48 Jimmie Johnson	60.00	100.00
Lowe's/480		
48 Jimmie Johnson	60.00	100.00
Lowe's		
Car of Tomorrow/840		
48 Jimmie Johnson	50.00	75.00
Lowe's Kobalt/432		
48 Jimmie Johnson	50.00	75.00
Lowe's JJ Foundation/804		
88 Shane Huffman	50.00	75.00
Navy/288		
88 Shane Huffman	50.00	75.00
Navy SEALS/84		
96 Tony Raines	50.00	75.00
DLP/144		
96 Tony Raines	50.00	75.00
DLP Car of Tomorrow/96		
01 Mark Martin	60.00	100.00
U.S. Army/1008		
01 Mark Martin	60.00	100.00
U.S. Army Car of Tomorrow/996		
01 Mark Martin	60.00	100.00
U.S. Army		
American Heroes/3204		
01 Regan Smith	50.00	75.00
U.S. Army/96		
07 Clint Bowyer	50.00	75.00
Directv/180		
07 Clint Bowyer	60.00	100.00
Jack Daniel's/1200		
07 Clint Bowyer	60.00	100.00
Jack Daniel's Car of Tomorrow/696		

2007 Motorsports Authentics Owner's Elite 1:24

*ACTUAL PRINT RUNS PROVIDED BY MA

	EX	NM-MT
1 Martin Truex Jr.	75.00	125.00
Bass Pro Shops/708*		
1 Martin Truex Jr.	100.00	150.00
Bass Pro Shops COT/504		
1 Martin Truex Jr.	100.00	150.00
Bass Pro Shops COT		
Dover Raced/504		
2 Kurt Busch	75.00	125.00
Miller Lite/1500*		
2 Kurt Busch	100.00	175.00
Miller Lite AU/504		
2 Kurt Busch	100.00	150.00
Miller Lite COT/504*		
4 Ward Burton	75.00	125.00
Air Force American Heroes/504*		
5 Kyle Busch	75.00	125.00
Kellogg's/504		
5 Kyle Busch	100.00	150.00
Kellogg's COT/504		
6 David Ragan	100.00	150.00
AAA/504*		
8 Dale Earnhardt Jr.	100.00	175.00
Bud/2007		
8 Dale Earnhardt Jr.	600.00	800.00
Bud Platinum/25		
8 Dale Earnhardt Jr.	275.00	400.00
Bud White Gold/100		
8 Dale Earnhardt Jr.	150.00	250.00
Bud Car of Tomorrow/2007		
8 Dale Earnhardt Jr.	500.00	750.00
Bud COT Platinum/25		
8 Dale Earnhardt Jr.	300.00	500.00
Bud COT White Gold/50*		
8 Dale Earnhardt Jr.	100.00	175.00
Bud Camo American Heroes/2007		
8 Dale Earnhardt Jr.	100.00	175.00
Bud Camo American Heroes		
Color Chrome/2007		
8 Dale Earnhardt Jr.	400.00	600.00
Bud Camo American Heroes		
Platinum/25		
8 Dale Earnhardt Jr.	250.00	400.00
Bud Camo American Heroes		
White Gold/50*		
8 Dale Earnhardt Jr.	125.00	200.00
Bud Elvis COT/2007		
8 Dale Earnhardt Jr.	400.00	600.00
Bud Elvis COT		
Platinum/25		
8 Dale Earnhardt Jr.	250.00	450.00
Bud Elvis COT White Gold/50*		
8 Dale Earnhardt Jr.	100.00	175.00
Bud Stars & Stripes/2007		
8 Dale Earnhardt Jr.	100.00	175.00
Bud Stars & Stripes		
Color Chrome/2007		
8 Dale Earnhardt Jr.	350.00	600.00
Bud Stars & Stripes		
Platinum/25		
8 Dale Earnhardt Jr.	200.00	350.00

Bud Stars & Stripes White Gold/50*
8 Dale Earnhardt Jr. Bud Test/2007 100.00 150.00
8 Dale Earnhardt Jr. Bud '57 Chevy/1008 100.00 150.00
8 Dale Earnhardt Jr. Bud '57 Chevy Platinum/25 600.00 800.00
8 Dale Earnhardt Jr. Bud '57 Chevy White Gold/50 350.00 500.00
8 Dale Earnhardt Jr. JM Menards/1008* 75.00 125.00
8 Dale Earnhardt Jr. Sharpie/2007 75.00 125.00
8 Dale Earnhardt Jr. Sharpie Platinum/25 400.00 600.00
8 Dale Earnhardt Jr. Sharpie White Gold/100 200.00 350.00
9 Kasey Kahne Dodge Dealers/1212* 75.00 125.00
9 Kasey Kahne Dodge Dealers Platinum/25 300.00 500.00
9 Kasey Kahne Dodge Dealers White Gold/100 250.00 500.00
9 Kasey Kahne Dodge Dealers COT/708* 100.00 150.00
9 Kasey Kahne Dodge Dealers Test/708* 75.00 125.00
9 Kasey Kahne Doublemint/504* 75.00 125.00
9 Kasey Kahne Doublemint Platinum/25 200.00 400.00
9 Kasey Kahne Doublemint White Gold/50* 250.00 400.00
10 Scott Riggs Valvoline/504* 75.00 125.00
11 Denny Hamlin Fed Ex Express/1200* 75.00 125.00
11 Denny Hamlin Fed Ex Express Platinum/25 300.00 500.00
11 Denny Hamlin Fed Ex Express White Gold/100 150.00 300.00
11 Denny Hamlin Fed Ex Express COT/708 100.00 150.00
11 Denny Hamlin Fed Ex Express 2006 Rookie of the Year/1011 75.00 125.00
11 Denny Hamlin Fed Ex Express 2006 Rookie of the Year Color Chrome/100 200.00 300.00
11 Denny Hamlin Fed Ex Express '06 ROY w/tire/111 125.00 200.00
11 Denny Hamlin Fed Ex Express '06 ROY White Gold/100 150.00 300.00
11 Denny Hamlin Fed Ex Freight/504* 75.00 125.00
11 Denny Hamlin Fed Ex Freight Marines Heroes/1200* 75.00 125.00
11 Denny Hamlin Fed Ex Freight Marines American Heroes Platinum/25 275.00 400.00
11 Denny Hamlin Fed Ex Freight Marines American Heroes White Gold/50* 250.00 400.00
11 Denny Hamlin Fed Ex Ground/504* 75.00 125.00
11 Denny Hamlin Fed Ex Kinko's/504* 75.00 125.00
11 Denny Hamlin Fed Ex Kinko's Platinum/25 275.00 400.00
11 Denny Hamlin Fed Ex Kinko's White Gold/50* 175.00 350.00
11 Denny Hamlin Fed Ex Test/1200* 75.00 125.00
12 Ryan Newman Alltel/708* 75.00 125.00
12 Ryan Newman Alltel COT/504* 75.00 125.00
14 Sterling Marlin Waste Management/504* 75.00 125.00
15 Paul Menard JM Menards/504* 75.00 125.00
16 Greg Biffle Ameriquest/708* 75.00 125.00
16 Greg Biffle 3M Coast Guard/504* 75.00 125.00
17 Matt Kenseth DeWalt/708* 90.00 150.00
17 Matt Kenseth DeWalt COT/504 100.00 175.00
18 J.J. Yeley Interstate Batteries/504* 75.00 125.00
19 Elliott Sadler Dodge Dealers/504* 75.00 125.00
19 Elliott Sadler Dodge Dealers COT/504* 75.00 125.00
20 Tony Stewart Home Depot/1212* 90.00 150.00
20 Tony Stewart Home Depot Platinum/25 400.00 600.00
20 Tony Stewart Home Depot White Gold/100 250.00 400.00
20 Tony Stewart Home Depot Brickyard Raced/504* 75.00 125.00
20 Tony Stewart Home Depot Daytona Shootout Raced/2007 100.00 150.00
20 Tony Stewart Home Depot COT/1212 100.00 150.00
20 Tony Stewart Home Depot COT Platinum/25 400.00 600.00
20 Tony Stewart Home Depot COT White Gold/50* 250.00 400.00
20 Tony Stewart Home Depot Holiday Sam Bass/504* 75.00 125.00
20 Tony Stewart Home Depot Holiday Sam Bass Platinum/25 400.00 600.00
20 Tony Stewart Home Depot Holiday Sam Bass White Gold/50* 250.00 400.00
20 Tony Stewart Home Depot Test/1200* 75.00 125.00
21 Kevin Harvick Coast Guard '06 NBS Champion Liquid Color/541 100.00 175.00
21 Jon Wood Air Force American Heroes/708* 75.00 125.00
22 Dave Blaney CAT/504* 75.00 125.00
24 Jeff Gordon DuPont Department of Defense American Heroes/1200* 75.00 125.00
24 Jeff Gordon DuPont Holiday Sam Bass/504* 75.00 125.00
24 Jeff Gordon DuPont Holiday Sam Bass Platinum/25 350.00 500.00
24 Jeff Gordon DuPont Holiday Sam Bass White Gold/50* 250.00 400.00
24 Jeff Gordon DuPont Flames/2007 100.00 175.00
24 Jeff Gordon DuPont Flames Platinum/25 750.00 1000.00
24 Jeff Gordon DuPont Flames White Gold/50* 275.00 400.00
24 Jeff Gordon DuPont Flames COT/2007 100.00 175.00
24 Jeff Gordon DuPont Flames COT Platinum/25 600.00 800.00
24 Jeff Gordon DuPont Flames COT Phoenix Raced/1492* 100.00 150.00
24 Jeff Gordon DuPont Flames COT Phoenix Raced Platinum/25 450.00 650.00
24 Jeff Gordon DuPont Flames COT Phoenix Raced White Gold/50* 250.00 500.00
24 Jeff Gordon DuPont Flames Test/2007 100.00 175.00
24 Jeff Gordon DuPont Flames '57 Chevy/504 100.00 150.00
24 Jeff Gordon Milestones 77th Win/1200 75.00 125.00
24 Jeff Gordon Nicorette/2007 75.00 125.00
24 Jeff Gordon Nicorette Platinum/25 450.00 600.00
24 Jeff Gordon Nicorette White Gold/50* 200.00 350.00
24 Jeff Gordon Nicorette COT/1142* 75.00 125.00
24 Jeff Gordon Nicorette COT Platinum/25 100.00 150.00
24 Jeff Gordon Pepsi/1504* 75.00 125.00
24 Jeff Gordon Pepsi COT Talladega Raced/504* 75.00 125.00
24 Jeff Gordon Underdog JG Foundation/708* 75.00 125.00
25 Casey Mears National Guard AU/504* 75.00 125.00
25 Casey Mears National Guard Camo American Heroes/504* 75.00 125.00
26 Jamie McMurray Crown Royal/504* 75.00 125.00
26 Jamie McMurray Crown Royal COT/504* 75.00 125.00
29 Kevin Harvick Pennzoil Platinum All Star Win/708* 75.00 125.00
29 Kevin Harvick Pennzoil Platinum COT/504* 75.00 125.00
29 Kevin Harvick Shell Pennzoil/1008* 100.00 150.00
29 Kevin Harvick Shell Pennzoil Platinum/25 350.00 500.00
29 Kevin Harvick Shell Pennzoil White Gold/100 175.00 350.00
29 Kevin Harvick Shell Pennzoil Daytona Raced/1200* 100.00 150.00
29 Kevin Harvick Shell Pennzoil Daytona Raced Platinum/25 300.00 500.00
29 Kevin Harvick Shell Pennzoil Daytona Raced White Gold/50* 175.00 350.00
29 Kevin Harvick Shell Pennzoil COT/1008 100.00 150.00
29 Kevin Harvick Shell Pennzoil COT Platinum/25 350.00 500.00
29 Kevin Harvick Shell Pennzoil COT White Gold/50* 175.00 350.00
29 Kevin Harvick Shell Pennzoil Holiday Sam Bass/504 75.00 125.00
29 Kevin Harvick Shell Pennzoil Test/1008* 75.00 125.00
31 Jeff Burton AT&T COT/504* 75.00 125.00
31 Jeff Burton Cingular/504* 100.00 150.00
31 Jeff Burton Prilosec Texas Raced/504 75.00 125.00
31 Jeff Burton Prilosec Texas Raced Platinum/25 200.00 350.00
31 Jeff Burton Prilosec Texas Raced White Gold/50* 150.00 300.00
38 David Gilliland M&M's/1008* 75.00 125.00
38 David Gilliland M&M's COT/504 75.00 125.00
38 David Gilliland M&M's July 4/504 75.00 125.00
38 David Gilliland M&M's Pink Susan G. Komen Foundation/504 75.00 125.00
38 David Gilliland M&M's Pink Platinum/25 250.00 400.00
38 David Gilliland M&M's Pink White Gold/100 175.00 350.00
38 David Gilliland M&M's Shrek/504 75.00 125.00
40 David Stremme Coors Light/504* 75.00 125.00
41 Reed Sorenson Target/504* 75.00 125.00
42 Juan Pablo Montoya Big Red/1008 75.00 125.00
42 Juan Pablo Montoya Big Red Platinum/25 300.00 500.00
42 Juan Pablo Montoya Big Red White Gold/50* 175.00 300.00
42 Juan Pablo Montoya Texaco Havoline/1008* 100.00 175.00
42 Juan Pablo Montoya Texaco Havoline Platinum/25 300.00 500.00
42 Juan Pablo Montoya Texaco Havoline White Gold/100 175.00 350.00
42 Juan Pablo Montoya Texaco Havoline Sonoma Raced/504* 100.00 150.00
42 Juan Pablo Montoya Texaco Havoline COT/504* 125.00 200.00
42 Juan Pablo Montoya Texaco Havoline Test/708* 75.00 125.00
43 Bobby Labonte Cheerios/504* 75.00 125.00
43 Bobby Labonte Cheerios COT/504 100.00 150.00
43 Bobby Labonte Cheerios COT Platinum/25 300.00 450.00
43 Bobby Labonte Cheerios COT White Gold/50 150.00 300.00
44 Dale Jarrett UPS/1008* 75.00 125.00
44 Dale Jarrett UPS Platinum/25 300.00 450.00
44 Dale Jarrett UPS White Gold/50* 175.00 350.00
44 Dale Jarrett UPS COT/504 100.00 150.00
44 Dale Jarrett UPS 100th Anniversary COT/708* 75.00 125.00
48 Jimmie Johnson Lowe's/1200* 100.00 175.00
48 Jimmie Johnson Lowe's Platinum/25 450.00 600.00
48 Jimmie Johnson Lowe's White Gold/50* 250.00 400.00
48 Jimmie Johnson Lowe's COT/1008 100.00 175.00
48 Jimmie Johnson Lowe's Holiday Sam Bass/504* 75.00 125.00
48 Jimmie Johnson Lowe's Kobalt/708 100.00 150.00
48 Jimmie Johnson Lowe's Power of Pride American Heroes/708* 75.00 125.00
48 Jimmie Johnson Lowe's Test/708 100.00 150.00
48 Jimmie Johnson Lowe's '57 Chevy/504 75.00 125.00
55 Michael Waltrip NAPA/1008* 75.00 125.00
55 Michael Waltrip NAPA COT/504* 75.00 125.00
84 A.J. Allmendinger Red Bull/504* 75.00 125.00
88 Shane Huffman Navy American Heroes/708 75.00 125.00
88 Shane Huffman Navy American Heroes Platinum/25 250.00 450.00
88 Shane Huffman Navy American Heroes White Gold/96* 150.00 300.00
88 Shane Huffman Navy Test/708* 75.00 125.00
88 Shane Huffman Navy SEALS/504* 75.00 125.00
88 Ricky Rudd Pedigree COT/504* 75.00 125.00
88 Ricky Rudd Pedigree COT Platinum/25 250.00 400.00
88 Ricky Rudd Pedigree COT White Gold/50* 150.00 300.00
88 Ricky Rudd Snickers/708* 75.00 125.00
88 Ricky Rudd Snickers Platinum/25 250.00 400.00
88 Ricky Rudd Snickers White Gold/100 175.00 300.00
88 Ricky Rudd Snickers COT/504* 75.00 125.00
96 Tony Raines DLP/504* 75.00 125.00
99 Carl Edwards Office Depot/1008* 75.00 125.00
99 Carl Edwards Office Depot Platinum/25 300.00 500.00
99 Carl Edwards Office Depot White Gold/50* 175.00 350.00
99 Carl Edwards Office Depot COT/504* 100.00 150.00
00 David Reutimann Burger King/504* 75.00 125.00
00 David Reutimann Burger King COT/504* 75.00 125.00
00 David Reutimann Domino's/504* 75.00 125.00
00 David Reutimann Domino's COT/504* 100.00 150.00
01 Mark Martin U.S. Army/1200* 100.00 150.00
01 Mark Martin U.S. Army Platinum/25 200.00 400.00
01 Mark Martin U.S. Army White Gold/100 150.00 300.00
01 Mark Martin U.S. Army American Heroes/708* 75.00 125.00
01 Mark Martin U.S. Army Car of Tomorrow/708* 100.00 150.00
07 Clint Bowyer Jack Daniel's/504* 75.00 125.00
07 Clint Bowyer Jack Daniel's Platinum/25 275.00 400.00
07 Clint Bowyer Jack Daniel's White Gold/50* 175.00 350.00
07 Clint Bowyer Jack Daniel's COT/504 100.00 150.00
07 Clint Bowyer Jack Daniel's COT Platinum/25 275.00 400.00
07 Clint Bowyer Jack Daniel's COT White Gold/50* 175.00 350.00
08 Daytona 500 50th Anniversary COT Red/504* 75.00 125.00
08 Daytona 500 50th Anniversary COT White/504* 75.00 125.00
08 Daytona 500 50th Anniversary COT Platinum/25 150.00 300.00
08 Daytona 500 50th Anniversary COT White Gold/50* 150.00 300.00

2007 Motorsports Authentics Owner's Elite Trackside 1:24

PACKAGE STATES MAXIMUM OF 2007
*ACTUAL PRINTS RUNS PROVIDED BY MA

EX NM-MT
1 Martin Truex Jr. Bass Pro Shops/408* 60.00 100.00
2 Kurt Busch Miller Lite/708* 60.00 100.00
5 Kyle Busch Carquest/204* 40.00 80.00
5 Kyle Busch Kellogg's/204* 60.00 100.00
6 David Ragan AAA/1500* 100.00 150.00
6 David Ragan Discount Tire/144* 100.00 150.00
7 Mike Wallace Geico/144* 75.00 125.00
8 Dale Earnhardt Jr. Bud/2007* 125.00 175.00
8 Dale Earnhardt Jr. Bud Camo American Heroes/708* 100.00 150.00
8 Dale Earnhardt Jr. Sharpie/576* 60.00 100.00
9 Kasey Kahne Dodge Dealers/408* 100.00 150.00
9 Kasey Kahne Doublemint/504* 60.00 100.00
10 Scott Riggs Stanley Tools/334* 40.00 80.00
10 Scott Riggs Valvoline/204* 60.00 100.00
11 Denny Hamlin Fed Ex Express/504* 75.00 125.00
11 Denny Hamlin Fed Ex Express '06 ROY Color Chrome/96* 60.00 100.00
11 Denny Hamlin Fed Ex Freight/504* 75.00 125.00
11 Denny Hamlin Fed Ex Freight Marines American Heroes/100* 60.00 100.00
11 Denny Hamlin Fed Ex Ground/400* 75.00 125.00
11 Denny Hamlin Fed Ex Kinko's/404* 60.00 100.00
12 Kurt Busch Penske/144* 60.00 100.00
12 Ryan Newman Mobil 1/204* 60.00 100.00
12 Ryan Newman Alltel/800* 75.00 125.00
12 Ryan Newman Kodak/144* 75.00 125.00
15 Paul Menard JM Menards/204* 75.00 125.00
16 Greg Biffle Ameriquest/408* 75.00 125.00
16 Greg Biffle 3M Coast Guard American Heroes/100* 60.00 100.00
17 Matt Kenseth Carhartt/408* 75.00 125.00
17 Matt Kenseth DeWalt/908* 100.00 150.00
18 J.J. Yeley Interstate Batteries/504* 75.00 125.00
19 Elliott Sadler Dodge Dealers/1716* 60.00 120.00
20 Tony Stewart Home Depot/1704* 75.00 125.00
21 Kevin Harvick Coast Guard '06 BGN Champ Color Chrome/96* 60.00 100.00
21 Jon Wood Air Force American Heroes/100* 40.00 80.00
22 Dave Blaney CAT/204* 75.00 125.00
24 Jeff Gordon DuPont Dept. of Defense American Heroes/100* 75.00 125.00
24 Jeff Gordon DuPont Flames/1008* 100.00 150.00
24 Jeff Gordon Nicorette/504* 75.00 125.00
24 Jeff Gordon Pepsi/1008* 75.00 125.00
25 Casey Mears National Guard/904* 75.00 125.00
26 Jamie McMurray Crown Royal/300* 75.00 12
26 Jamie McMurray Irwin Tools/204* 60.00 10
29 Kevin Harvick Shell Pennzoil/1500* 125.00 17
29 Kevin Harvick Shell Pennzoil Daytona Raced/729* 60.00 10
31 Jeff Burton Cingular/300* 100.00 15
38 David Gilliland M&M's/1008* 100.00 15
39 Sam Hornish Jr. Mobil 1/144* 60.00 10
40 David Stremme Coors Light/204* 40.00 8
40 David Stremme Lonestar Steakhouse/204* 40.00 8
41 Reed Sorenson Target/204* 75.00 12
42 Juan Pablo Montoya Big Red/432* 60.00 10
42 Juan Pablo Montoya Texaco Havoline/708* 75.00 12
43 Bobby Labonte Cheerios/204* 75.00 12
44 Dale Jarrett UPS/1000* 75.00 12
45 Kyle Petty Wells Fargo/204* 50.00 10
48 Jimmie Johnson Lowe's/1008* 100.00 15
48 Jimmie Johnson Lowe's Power of Pride American Heroes/96* 100.00 15
48 Jimmie Johnson Lowe's '57 Chevy/100* 40.00 8
55 Michael Waltrip NAPA/1000* 75.00 12
83 Brian Vickers Red Bull/304* 60.00 10
84 A.J. Allmendinger Red Bull/304* 60.00 10
88 Shane Huffman Navy/144* 50.00 10
88 Ricky Rudd Snickers/504* 50.00 10
90 Stephen Leicht CitiFinancial/144* 50.00 10
96 Tony Raines DLP/204* 40.00 8
99 Carl Edwards Office Depot/708* 75.00 12
99 David Reutimann Aaron's/144* 60.00 10
00 David Reutimann Burger King/300* 40.00 8
00 David Reutimann Domino's Pizza/300* 75.00 12
01 Mark Martin U.S.Army/504* 50.00 10
01 Mark Martin U.S.Army American Heroes/100* 50.00 10
07 Clint Bowyer Jack Daniels/1068* 60.00 10

2007 Motorsports Authent Pit Stop 1:24

EX NM
25 Casey Mears National Guard 15.00 2

2007 Motorsports Authent QVC For Race Fans Only 1

EX NM
1 Martin Truex Jr. Bass Pro Shops '57 Chevy Color Chrome/1500 100.00 17
2 Kurt Busch Miller Lite Chrome/288 125.00 20
2 Kurt Busch Miller Lite Color Chrome/96 100.00 17
5 Kyle Busch Carquest Chrome/96 125.00 20
5 Kyle Busch Carquest Color Chrome/96 100.00 17
5 Kyle Busch Kellogg's Chrome/96 125.00 20
5 Kyle Busch Kellogg's Color Chrome/96 100.00 17
8 Dale Earnhardt Jr. Bud Chrome/2004 125.00 20
8 Dale Earnhardt Jr. Bud Color Chrome/2508 100.00 17
8 Dale Earnhardt Jr. Bud Gold/288 100.00 17
8 Dale Earnhardt Jr. Bud Gold Chrome/3888 75.00 12
8 Dale Earnhardt Jr. Bud Mesma Chrome/2508 75.00 12
8 Dale Earnhardt Jr. Bud Platinum/144 125.00 20
8 Dale Earnhardt Jr. Bud COT Chrome/504 125.00 20
8 Dale Earnhardt Jr. Bud COT Color Chrome/2508 100.00 17
8 Dale Earnhardt Jr. Bud COT Gold/288 100.00 17
8 Dale Earnhardt Jr. Bud COT Gold Chrome/3888 75.00 12
8 Dale Earnhardt Jr. Bud COT Mesma Chrome/2508 75.00 12
8 Dale Earnhardt Jr. Bud COT Platinum/204 125.00 20
8 Dale Earnhardt Jr. Bud Camo Heroes 125.00 2

Chrome/504
le Earnhardt Jr. 60.00 100.00
Bud Camo American Heroes
Color Chrome/3888
le Earnhardt Jr. 75.00 125.00
Bud Camo American Heroes
Gold/288
le Earnhardt Jr. 100.00 150.00
Bud Camo Heroes
Mesma Chrome/2508
le Earnhardt Jr. 150.00 250.00
Bud Camo Heroes
Platinum/144
le Earnhardt Jr. 100.00 150.00
Bud Elvis COT
Chrome/3888
le Earnhardt Jr. 125.00 200.00
Bud Elvis COT
Gold/188
le Earnhardt Jr. 60.00 100.00
Bud Elvis COT
Gold Chrome/3888
le Earnhardt Jr. 100.00 175.00
Bud Elvis COT
Mesma Chrome/888
le Earnhardt Jr. 60.00 100.00
Bud Elvis COT
Mesma Chrome/888
le Earnhardt Jr. 125.00 200.00
Bud Elvis COT
Platinum/108
le Earnhardt Jr. 100.00 150.00
Bud Stars & Stripes
Chrome/504
le Earnhardt Jr. 75.00 125.00
Bud Stars & Stripes
Color Chrome/2508
le Earnhardt Jr. 60.00 100.00
Bud Stars & Stripes
Gold Chrome/3888
le Earnhardt Jr. 60.00 100.00
Bud Stars & Stripes
Mesma Chrome/2508
le Earnhardt Jr. 125.00 200.00
Bud Stars & Stripes
Platinum/108
le Earnhardt Jr. 75.00 125.00
Bud '57 Chevy
Chrome/504
le Earnhardt Jr. 60.00 100.00
Bud '57 Chevy
Color Chrome/3888
le Earnhardt Jr. 75.00 125.00
Bud '57 Chevy
Gold/188
le Earnhardt Jr. 60.00 100.00
Bud '57 Chevy
Mesma Chrome/888
le Earnhardt Jr. 125.00 200.00
Bud '57 Chevy
Platinum/108
le Earnhardt Jr. 75.00 125.00
Sharpie Chrome/288
le Earnhardt Jr. 75.00 125.00
Sharpie Color Chrome/2508
le Earnhardt Jr. 75.00 150.00
Sharpie Gold/108
le Earnhardt Jr. 75.00 125.00
Sharpie Mesma Chrome/2508
le Earnhardt Jr. 100.00 175.00
Sharpie Platinum/108
sey Kahne 100.00 150.00
Dodge Dealers
Chrome/288
sey Kahne 100.00 150.00
Dodge Dealers
Color Chrome/288
sey Kahne 75.00 125.00
Dodge Dealers Copper/288
sey Kahne 60.00 100.00
Dodge Dealers
Mesma Chrome/288
enny Hamlin 100.00 150.00
Fed Ex Express
Color Chrome/108
enny Hamlin 60.00 100.00
Fed Ex Express
Copper/108
yan Newman 60.00 100.00
Alltel Chrome/204
reg Biffle 125.00 200.00
Ameriquest Chrome/96
att Kenseth 150.00 300.00
R&L Carriers Chrome/96
liott Sadler 100.00 150.00
Dodge Dealers
Color Chrome/96
ony Stewart 100.00 175.00
Home Depot Brickyard Raced
Color Chrome/288
ony Stewart 100.00 150.00
Home Depot Brickyard Raced
Copper/288
ony Stewart 100.00 175.00
Home Depot Daytona Shootout Raced
Color Chrome/288
ony Stewart 100.00 150.00
Home Depot Daytona Shootout Raced
Copper/288
ony Stewart 100.00 175.00
Home Depot COT
Color Chrome/504
ony Stewart 100.00 150.00
Home Depot COT
Gold/108
ony Stewart 60.00 100.00
Home Depot COT
Copper/504
ony Stewart 100.00 150.00
Home Depot COT
Mesma Chrome/288
ony Stewart 125.00 200.00
Home Depot COT
Platinum/108
ff Gordon 100.00 175.00
DuPont Department of Defense
Chrome/504
ff Gordon 75.00 150.00
DuPont Dept.of Defense
Color Chrome/1008
ff Gordon 60.00 100.00
DuPont Department of Defense
Copper/504
24 Jeff Gordon 125.00 200.00
DuPont Department of Defense
Gold/108
24 Jeff Gordon 75.00 125.00
DuPont Department of Defense
Mesma Chrome/504
24 Jeff Gordon 175.00 350.00
DuPont Department of Defense
American Heroes Platinum/108
24 Jeff Gordon 75.00 150.00
DuPont Flames
Talladega Raced Color Chrome/1500
24 Jeff Gordon 60.00 100.00
DuPont Flames
Talladega Raced Copper/504
24 Jeff Gordon 75.00 125.00
DuPont Flames
Talladega Raced Mesma Chrome/324
24 Jeff Gordon 100.00 175.00
DuPont Flames COT
Chrome/288
24 Jeff Gordon 75.00 125.00
DuPont Flames COT
Color Chrome/1008
24 Jeff Gordon 60.00 100.00
DuPont Flames COT
Copper/504
24 Jeff Gordon 75.00 125.00
DuPont Flames COT
Gold/144
24 Jeff Gordon 60.00 100.00
DuPont Flames COT
Mesma Chrome/324
24 Jeff Gordon 125.00 200.00
DuPont Flames COT
Platinum/108
24 Jeff Gordon 100.00 175.00
DuPont Flames '57 Chevy
Chrome/288
24 Jeff Gordon 75.00 125.00
DuPont Flames COT
Phoenix Raced Color Chrome/1500
24 Jeff Gordon 75.00 125.00
DuPont Flames COT
Phoenix Raced Copper/504
24 Jeff Gordon 75.00 125.00
DuPont Flames Holiday
Sam Bass Color Chrome/1500
24 Jeff Gordon 75.00 125.00
DuPont Flames '57 Chevy
Color Chrome/1500
24 Jeff Gordon 60.00 100.00
DuPont Flames '57 Chevy
Copper/504
24 Jeff Gordon 75.00 125.00
DuPont Flames '57 Chevy
Gold/108
24 Jeff Gordon 60.00 100.00
DuPont Flames '57 Chevy
Gold Chrome/1008
24 Jeff Gordon 60.00 100.00
DuPont Flames '57 Chevy
Mesma Chrome/324
24 Jeff Gordon 125.00 200.00
DuPont Flames '57 Chevy
Platinum/144
24 Jeff Gordon 75.00 125.00
Nicorette Color Chrome/1008
24 Jeff Gordon 60.00 100.00
Nicorette Mesma Chrome/504
24 Jeff Gordon 75.00 125.00
Nicorette COT
Color Chrome/1500
24 Jeff Gordon 60.00 100.00
Nicorette COT
Copper/504
24 Jeff Gordon 100.00 150.00
Nicorette COT
Mesma Chrome/504
24 Jeff Gordon 75.00 125.00
Pepsi Color Chrome/1008
24 Jeff Gordon 75.00 125.00
Pepsi Mesma Chrome/504
25 Casey Mears 50.00 75.00
National Guard Camo
American Heroes/504
29 Kevin Harvick 50.00 75.00
Reese's/1008
29 Kevin Harvick 60.00 100.00
Reese's Color Chrome/504
29 Kevin Harvick 75.00 150.00
Shell Pennzoil
Chrome/504
29 Kevin Harvick 75.00 125.00
Shell Pennzoil Color Chrome/1500
29 Kevin Harvick 60.00 100.00
Shell Pennzoil
Copper/504
29 Kevin Harvick 75.00 150.00
Shell Pennzoil
Gold/108
29 Kevin Harvick 60.00 100.00
Shell Pennzoil
Mesma Chrome/504
29 Kevin Harvick 100.00 175.00
Shell Pennzoil Platinum/108
29 Kevin Harvick 75.00 125.00
Shell Pennzoil
Daytona Raced Color Chrome/1500
29 Kevin Harvick 60.00 100.00
Shell Pennzoil
Daytona Raced Copper/504
29 Kevin Harvick 50.00 75.00
Shell Pennzoil COT
29 Kevin Harvick 75.00 125.00
Shell Pennzoil COT
Color Chrome/1500
29 Kevin Harvick 60.00 100.00
Shell Pennzoil Car of Tomorrow
Copper/504
29 Kevin Harvick 125.00 200.00
Shell Pennzoil COT
Gold/108
29 Kevin Harvick 60.00 100.00
Shell Pennzoil COT
Mesma Chrome/288
29 Kevin Harvick 150.00 250.00
Shell Pennzoil Car of Tomorrow
Platinum/108
44 Dale Jarrett 75.00 125.00
UPS Chrome/288
44 Dale Jarrett 60.00 100.00
UPS Copper/108
44 Dale Jarrett 60.00 100.00
UPS Mesma Chrome/504
48 Jimmie Johnson 75.00 125.00
Lowe's Color Chrome/288
48 Jimmie Johnson 100.00 175.00
Lowe's Gold/108
48 Jimmie Johnson 60.00 100.00
Lowe's Copper/288
48 Jimmie Johnson 60.00 100.00
Lowe's Mesma Chrome/288
48 Jimmie Johnson 125.00 200.00
Lowe's Platinum/108
48 Jimmie Johnson 100.00 175.00
Lowe's COT
Color Chrome/288
48 Jimmie Johnson 100.00 175.00
Lowe's COT Copper/288
48 Jimmie Johnson
Lowe's COT Copper/288
48 Jimmie Johnson 100.00 150.00
Lowe's '06 Champ
Mesma Chrome/504
99 Carl Edwards 75.00 125.00
Office Depot Chrome/204
01 Mark Martin 100.00 150.00
U.S. Army
Chrome/504
01 Mark Martin 75.00 125.00
U.S. Army
Color Chrome/504
01 Mark Martin 125.00 200.00
U.S. Army
Color Chrome AU/504
01 Mark Martin 125.00 200.00
U.S. Army Copper AU/288
01 Mark Martin 100.00 175.00
U.S. Army Gold/288
01 Mark Martin 125.00 200.00
U.S. Army Mesma Chrome AU/504
01 Mark Martin 75.00 125.00
U.S. Army American Heroes
Color Chrome/504
01 Mark Martin 60.00 100.00
U.S. Army American Heroes
Copper/504
01 Mark Martin 125.00 200.00
U.S. Army American Heroes
Gold/288
01 Mark Martin 60.00 100.00
U.S. Army American Heroes
Mesma Chrome/288
07 Clint Bowyer 75.00 125.00
Jack Daniel's
Color Chrome/108
07 Clint Bowyer 60.00 100.00
Jack Daniel's
Copper/108

2007 Motorsports Authentics/RCCA Owner's Club Select 1:24

EX NM-MT
8 Dale Earnhardt Jr. 100.00 175.00
Bud/3000*
8 Dale Earnhardt Jr. 50.00 75.00
Bud Camo
American Heroes/2007*
8 Dale Earnhardt Jr. 50.00 75.00
Bud Stars & Stripes/3000*
8 Dale Earnhardt Jr. 50.00 75.00
Bud '57 Chevy/1008*
9 Kasey Kahne 50.00 75.00
Dodge Dealers/1500*
9 Kasey Kahne 40.00 65.00
Dodge Dealers Holiday
Sam Bass/96*
11 Denny Hamlin 50.00 75.00
Fed Ex Express/708*
11 Denny Hamlin 40.00 65.00
Fed Ex Express Holiday
Sam Bass/144*
11 Denny Hamlin 40.00 65.00
Fed Ex Freight/708*
11 Denny Hamlin 50.00 75.00
Fed Ex Freight Marines
American Heroes/708*
11 Denny Hamlin 40.00 65.00
Fed Ex Ground/708*
11 Denny Hamlin 40.00 65.00
Fed Ex Kinko's/708*
17 Matt Kenseth 50.00 75.00
DeWalt/1200*
17 Matt Kenseth 40.00 65.00
DeWalt Holiday
Sam Bass/96*
19 Elliott Sadler 40.00 65.00
Dodge Dealers Holiday
Sam Bass/96*
20 Tony Stewart 50.00 75.00
Home Depot/2100*
24 Jeff Gordon 50.00 75.00
DuPont Flames/1500*
24 Jeff Gordon 50.00 75.00
DuPont Flames '57 Chevy/288
24 Jeff Gordon 40.00 65.00
Nicorette/1500*
24 Jeff Gordon 40.00 65.00
Pepsi/1500*
29 Kevin Harvick 50.00 75.00
Shell Pennzoil/1500*
38 David Gilliland 40.00 65.00
M&M's/708*
38 David Gilliland 40.00 65.00
M&M's Holiday
Sam Bass/96*
42 Juan Pablo Montoya 40.00 65.00
Big Red/708*
42 Juan Pablo Montoya 60.00 100.00
Texaco Havoline/708*
42 Juan Pablo Montoya 40.00 65.00
Texaco Havoline Holiday
Sam Bass/96*
43 Bobby Labonte 40.00 65.00
Cheerios/708*
44 Dale Jarrett 40.00 65.00
UPS/504*
48 Jimmie Johnson 60.00 100.00
Lowe's/1500*
48 Jimmie Johnson 50.00 75.00
Lowe's '57 Chevy/288*
55 Michael Waltrip 40.00 65.00
NAPA/708*
88 Shane Huffman 40.00 65.00
Navy/708*
88 Ricky Rudd 40.00 65.00
Snickers/708*
99 Carl Edwards 40.00 65.00
Office Depot/1200*
99 Carl Edwards 40.00 65.00
Office Depot Holiday
Sam Bass/96*
01 Mark Martin 50.00 75.00
U.S. Army/1200*
01 Mark Martin 50.00 75.00
U.S. Army Holiday
Sam Bass/96*
07 Clint Bowyer 40.00 65.00
Jack Daniels/1200

2007 Motorsports Authentics Driver's Select 1:64

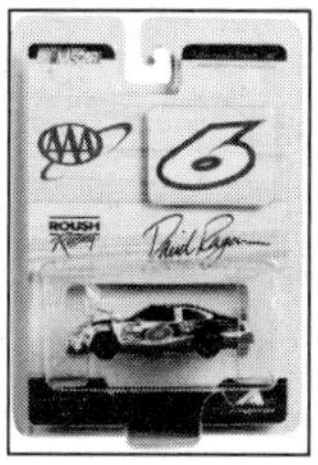

EX NM-MT
2 Kurt Busch 5.00 10.00
Miller Lite
2 Kurt Busch 6.00 12.00
Miller Lite COT
5 Kyle Busch 5.00 10.00
Kellogg's
5 Kyle Busch 6.00 12.00
Kellogg's COT
6 David Ragan 7.50 15.00
AAA
6 David Ragan 7.50 15.00
AAA COT
6 David Ragan 6.00 12.00
AAA Insurance
6 David Ragan 6.00 12.00
AAA Show Your Card
6 David Ragan 6.00 12.00
AAA Travel
6 David Ragan 6.00 12.00
Discount Tire
8 Dale Earnhardt Jr. 7.50 15.00
Bud
8 Dale Earnhardt Jr. 6.00 12.00
Bud Stars & Stripes
9 Kasey Kahne 5.00 10.00
Dodge Dealers
9 Kasey Kahne 6.00 12.00
Dodge Dealers COT
9 Kasey Kahne 5.00 10.00
Hellmann's
9 Kasey Kahne 5.00 10.00
McDonald's
10 Scott Riggs 4.00 8.00
Stanley Tools
10 Scott Riggs 4.00 8.00
Valvoline
11 Denny Hamlin 5.00 10.00
Fed Ex Express
11 Denny Hamlin 6.00 12.00
Fed Ex Express COT
11 Denny Hamlin 5.00 10.00
Fed Ex Freight
11 Denny Hamlin 6.00 12.00
Fed Ex Freight COT
11 Denny Hamlin 6.00 12.00
Fed Ex Freight Marines
American Heroes
11 Denny Hamlin 5.00 10.00
Fed Ex Ground
11 Denny Hamlin 6.00 12.00
Fed Ex Ground COT
11 Denny Hamlin 5.00 10.00
Fed Ex Kinko's
11 Denny Hamlin 6.00 12.00
Fed Ex Kinko's COT
12 Kurt Busch 6.00 12.00
Penske
12 Sam Hornish Jr. 6.00 12.00
Mobil 1
12 Ryan Newman 5.00 10.00
Alltel
12 Ryan Newman 5.00 10.00
Alltel My Circle
16 Greg Biffle 4.00 8.00
Ameriquest
16 Greg Biffle 4.00 8.00
Jackson Hewitt
16 Greg Biffle 5.00 10.00
3M Coast Guard
American Heroes
17 Matt Kenseth 6.00 12.00
Carhartt COT
17 Matt Kenseth 6.00 12.00
iLevel Weyerhouser
18 J.J. Yeley 6.00 12.00
Interstate Batteries
19 Elliott Sadler 5.00 10.00
Dodge Dealers
19 Elliott Sadler 6.00 12.00
Siemen's COT
20 Tony Stewart 6.00 12.00
Home Depot
20 Tony Stewart 6.00 12.00
Home Depot COT
21 Kevin Harvick 6.00 12.00
Auto Zone
21 Jon Wood 6.00 12.00
Air Force American Heroes
22 Dave Blaney 6.00 12.00
CAT COT
24 Jeff Gordon 7.50 15.00
DuPont Department of Defense
American Heroes
24 Jeff Gordon 7.50 15.00
DuPont Flames
24 Jeff Gordon 7.50 15.00
DuPont Flames COT
24 Jeff Gordon 6.00 12.00
DuPont Flames '57 Chevy
24 Jeff Gordon 6.00 12.00
Pepsi
24 Jeff Gordon 6.00 12.00
Nicorette COT
25 Casey Mears 5.00 10.00
National Guard
26 Jamie McMurray 5.00 10.00
Dish Network
29 Kevin Harvick 6.00 12.00
Pennzoil Platinum COT
29 Kevin Harvick 5.00 10.00
Shell Pennzoil
29 Kevin Harvick 6.00 12.00
Shell Pennzoil COT
31 Jeff Burton 6.00 12.00
Cingular
33 Tony Stewart 6.00 12.00
Old Spice
38 David Gilliland 6.00 12.00
M&M's
38 David Gilliland 4.00 8.00
M&M's July 4
40 David Stremme 3.00 6.00
Lone Star Steakhouse
41 Reed Sorenson 6.00 12.00
Target
42 Juan Pablo Montoya 5.00 10.00
Big Red
42 Juan Pablo Montoya 6.00 12.00
Texaco Havoline
42 Juan Pablo Montoya 6.00 12.00
Texaco Havoline COT
43 Bobby Labonte 6.00 12.00
Cheerios
48 Jimmie Johnson 6.00 12.00
Lowe's
48 Jimmie Johnson 6.00 12.00
Lowe's COT
48 Jimmie Johnson 6.00 12.00
Lowe's Power of Pride
American Heroes
48 Jimmie Johnson 5.00 10.00
Lowe's '57 Chevy
48 Jimmie Johnson 6.00 12.00
Lowe's '06 Nextel Champ
88 Shane Huffman 6.00 12.00
Navy American Heroes
88 Ricky Rudd 3.00 6.00
Snickers
88 Ricky Rudd 3.00 6.00
Snickers COT
88 Ricky Rudd 3.00 6.00
Snickers Dark
96 Tony Raines 6.00 12.00
DLP
99 Carl Edwards 6.00 12.00
Office Depot
01 Mark Martin 6.00 12.00
U.S. Army
01 Mark Martin 6.00 12.00
U.S. Army American Heroes

2007 Motorsports Authentics Owner's Elite 1:64

EX NM-MT
1 Martin Truex Jr. 15.00 30.00
Bass Pro Shops/1008*
4 Ward Burton 15.00 30.00
Air Force American Heroes/504*
8 Dale Earnhardt Jr. 20.00 40.00
Bud/2007*
8 Dale Earnhardt Jr. 20.00 40.00
Bud Camo
American Heroes/1500*
8 Dale Earnhardt Jr. 20.00 40.00
Bud Stars & Stripes/2007
8 Dale Earnhardt Jr. 15.00 30.00
Sharpie/2007
9 Kasey Kahne 20.00 40.00
Dodge Dealers/2007*
11 Denny Hamlin 15.00 30.00
Fed Ex Express/2007*
11 Denny Hamlin 15.00 30.00
Fed Ex Freight Marines
American Heroes/1507*
11 Denny Hamlin 15.00 30.00
Fed Ex Kinko's/1008*
16 Greg Biffle 15.00 30.00
3M Coast Guard/504*
17 Matt Kenseth 15.00 30.00
DeWalt/2007*
20 Tony Stewart 20.00 40.00
Home Depot/2007*
21 Jon Wood 15.00 30.00
Air Force American Heroes/504*
24 Jeff Gordon 20.00 40.00
DuPont Department of Defense
American Heroes/504*
24 Jeff Gordon 20.00 40.00
DuPont Flames/2007*
24 Jeff Gordon 15.00 30.00
Nicorette/1008*
24 Jeff Gordon 15.00 30.00
Pepsi/2007*
29 Kevin Harvick 20.00 40.00
Shell Pennzoil/2007*
38 David Gilliland 15.00 30.00
M&M's/1008*
42 Juan Pablo Montoya 20.00 40.00
Texaco Havoline/1008*
43 Bobby Labonte 15.00 30.00
Cheerios/1008*
44 Dale Jarrett 15.00 30.00
UPS/2007*
48 Jimmie Johnson 15.00 30.00
Lowe's/2007*

48 Jimmie Johnson Lowe's Power of Pride American Heroes/504*	15.00	30.00
55 Michael Waltrip NAPA/1008*	15.00	30.00
88 Shane Huffman Navy American Heroes/1008*	15.00	30.00
88 Ricky Rudd Snickers/1008*	15.00	30.00
99 Carl Edwards Office Depot/2007*	15.00	30.00
00 David Reutimann Domino's/1008*	15.00	30.00
01 Mark Martin U.S. Army/1008*	15.00	30.00
01 Mark Martin U.S. Army American Heroes/1008*	15.00	30.00

2007 Motorsports Authentics Pit Stop 1:64

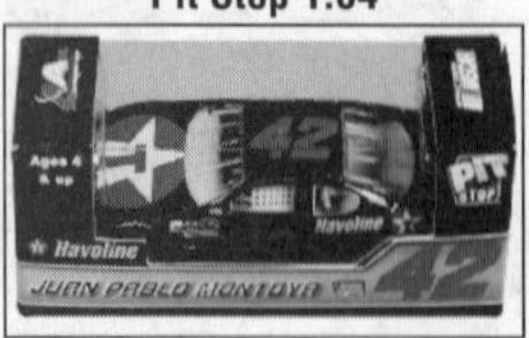

	EX	NM-MT
1 Martin Truex Jr. Bass Pro Shops	3.00	6.00
1 Martin Truex Jr. Bass Pro Shops COT	4.00	8.00
2 Kurt Busch Kurt	3.00	6.00
2 Kurt Busch Kurt COT	4.00	8.00
5 Kyle Busch Kellogg's	5.00	10.00
6 David Ragan AAA	4.00	8.00
6 David Ragan AAA COT	4.00	8.00
6 David Ragan AAA Insurance	4.00	8.00
6 David Ragan AAA Show Your Card	4.00	8.00
6 David Ragan AAA Travel	4.00	8.00
6 David Ragan Discount Tire	4.00	8.00
7 Mike Wallace Geico	5.00	10.00
8 Dale Earnhardt Jr. DEI	3.00	6.00
8 Dale Earnhardt Jr. DEI Camo American Heroes	4.00	8.00
8 Dale Earnhardt Jr. DEI Elvis Car of Tomorrow	5.00	10.00
8 Dale Earnhardt Jr. DEI Stars & Stripes	5.00	10.00
8 Dale Earnhardt Jr. DEI '57 Chevy	3.00	6.00
8 Dale Earnhardt Jr. JM Menards	3.00	6.00
8 Dale Earnhardt Jr. Sharpie	3.00	6.00
9 Kasey Kahne Dodge Dealers	4.00	8.00
9 Kasey Kahne Doublemint	4.00	8.00
10 Scott Riggs Stanley Tools	3.00	6.00
10 Scott Riggs Valvoline	3.00	6.00
11 Denny Hamlin Fed Ex Express	3.00	6.00
11 Denny Hamlin Fed Ex Express Car of Tomorrow	5.00	10.00
11 Denny Hamlin Fed Ex Freight	3.00	6.00
11 Denny Hamlin Fed Ex Freight Car of Tomorrow	5.00	10.00
11 Denny Hamlin Fed Ex Freight Marines American Heroes	3.00	6.00
11 Denny Hamlin Fed Ex Ground	3.00	6.00
11 Denny Hamlin Fed Ex Ground Car of Tomorrow	5.00	10.00
11 Denny Hamlin Fed Ex Kinko's	3.00	6.00
11 Denny Hamlin Fed Ex Kinko's Car of Tomorrow	5.00	10.00
12 Ryan Newman Alltel	5.00	10.00
12 Ryan Newman Kodak	5.00	10.00
12 Ryan Newman Mobil 1	5.00	10.00
14 Sterling Marlin Waste Management	3.00	6.00
15 Paul Menard JM Menards	4.00	8.00
16 Greg Biffle Ameriquest	3.00	6.00
16 Greg Biffle Jackson Hewitt	3.00	6.00
16 Greg Biffle 3M	4.00	8.00
16 Greg Biffle 3M Coast Guard American Heroes	4.00	8.00
17 Matt Kenseth Arby's	4.00	8.00
17 Matt Kenseth DeWalt	5.00	10.00
17 Matt Kenseth DeWalt Car of Tomorrow	5.00	10.00
17 Matt Kenseth Dish Network	4.00	8.00
17 Matt Kenseth R&L Carriers COT	4.00	8.00
17 Matt Kenseth USG Sheetrock	4.00	8.00
18 J.J. Yeley Interstate Batteries	5.00	10.00
19 Elliott Sadler Dodge Dealers	4.00	8.00
19 Elliott Sadler Siemen's COT	5.00	10.00
20 Tony Stewart Home Depot	4.00	8.00
20 Tony Stewart Home Depot COT	5.00	10.00
21 Kevin Harvick Auto Zone	3.00	6.00
21 Jon Wood Air Force American Heroes	4.00	8.00
22 Dave Blaney CAT	4.00	8.00
22 Dave Blaney CAT D6T	4.00	8.00
22 Dave Blaney CAT M-Series	4.00	8.00
24 Jeff Gordon DuPont Department of Defense American Heroes	5.00	10.00
24 Jeff Gordon DuPont Flames	5.00	10.00
24 Jeff Gordon DuPont Flames Car of Tomorrow	6.00	12.00
24 Jeff Gordon Nicorette	4.00	8.00
24 Jeff Gordon Nicorette Car of Tomorrow	5.00	10.00
24 Jeff Gordon Pepsi	5.00	10.00
24 Jeff Gordon Underdog JG Foundation	5.00	10.00
25 Casey Mears National Guard	4.00	8.00
26 Jamie McMurray Irwin Tools	4.00	8.00
29 Kevin Harvick Reese's	5.00	10.00
29 Kevin Harvick Shell Pennzoil	5.00	10.00
29 Kevin Harvick Shell Pennzoil Car of Tomorrow	6.00	12.00
29 Kevin Harvick Pennzoil Platinum COT	5.00	10.00
31 Jeff Burton Cingular	5.00	10.00
38 David Gilliland M&M's	5.00	10.00
38 David Gilliland M&M's Car of Tomorrow	5.00	10.00
38 David Gilliland M&M's July 4	3.00	6.00
38 David Gilliland M&M's Pink	3.00	6.00
38 David Gilliland M&M's Shrek	3.00	6.00
41 Reed Sorenson Juicy Fruit	4.00	8.00
41 Reed Sorenson Target	4.00	8.00
42 Juan Pablo Montoya Big Red	4.00	8.00
42 Juan Pablo Montoya Texaco Havoline	5.00	10.00
42 Juan Pablo Montoya Texaco Havoline COT	5.00	10.00
43 Bobby Labonte Cheerios	5.00	10.00
44 Dale Jarrett UPS	5.00	10.00
44 Dale Jarrett UPS Kentucky Derby	5.00	10.00
45 Kyle Petty Wells Fargo	5.00	10.00
48 Jimmie Johnson Lowe's	5.00	10.00
48 Jimmie Johnson Lowe's Car of Tomorrow	6.00	12.00
48 Jimmie Johnson Lowe's Kobalt	5.00	10.00
48 Jimmie Johnson Lowe's Power of Pride American Heroes	5.00	10.00
48 Jimmie Johnson Lowe's Sam Bass Holiday	5.00	10.00
55 Michael Waltrip NAPA	5.00	10.00
60 Carl Edwards Scotts	4.00	8.00
83 Brian Vickers Red Bull	4.00	8.00
88 Shane Huffman Navy	5.00	10.00
88 Shane Huffman Navy American Heroes	5.00	10.00
88 Shane Huffman Navy SEALS	4.00	8.00
88 Ricky Rudd Pedigree COT	3.00	6.00
88 Ricky Rudd Snickers	3.00	6.00
88 Ricky Rudd Snickers COT	3.00	6.00
88 Ricky Rudd Snickers Dark	3.00	6.00
90 Stephen Leicht Citifinancial	5.00	10.00
96 Tony Raines DLP	5.00	10.00
96 Tony Raines DLP Shrek Car of Tomorrow	4.00	8.00
99 Carl Edwards Office Depot	5.00	10.00
99 Carl Edwards Scotts	5.00	10.00
99 David Reutimann Aaron's	5.00	10.00
00 David Reutimann Burger King	5.00	10.00
00 David Reutimann Domino's Pizza	5.00	10.00
01 Mark Martin U.S. Army	3.00	6.00
01 Mark Martin U.S. Army Car of Tomorrow	4.00	8.00
01 Mark Martin U.S. Army American Heroes	3.00	6.00
07 Daytona 500 Event Car	3.00	6.00

2007 Motorsports Authentics Pit Stop Blister 1:64

	EX	NM-MT
8 Dale Earnhardt Jr. DEI	4.00	8.00
9 Kasey Kahne Dodge Dealers	3.00	6.00
19 Elliott Sadler Dodge Dealers	3.00	6.00
20 Tony Stewart Home Depot	3.00	6.00
24 Jeff Gordon DuPont Flames	4.00	8.00
29 Kevin Harvick Shell Pennzoil	4.00	8.00
48 Jimmie Johnson Lowe's	3.00	6.00

1991-92 Pole Position 1:64

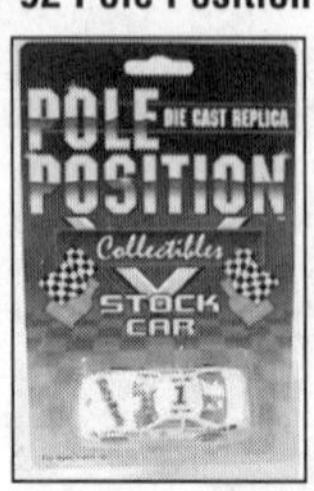

These 1:64 die-cast pieces were issued in a Pole Position blister pack. The bottom half of the package was printed in a red and orange checkered flag design and the top of the package is black and dark purple. The cars were released over a 2-year period from 1991-1992.

	EX	NM-MT
1 Jeff Gordon Baby Ruth	7.50	15.00
4 Ernie Irvan Kodak	3.00	6.00
7 Harry Gant Mac Tools	3.00	6.00
11 Bill Elliott Amoco	3.00	6.00
21 Morgan Shepherd Citgo	3.00	6.00
21 Morgan Shepherd Motorcraft	3.00	6.00
22 Sterling Marlin Maxwell House	3.00	8.00
33 Harry Gant Leo Jackson	3.00	6.00
36 Kenny Wallace Dirt Devil	3.00	6.00
43 Richard Petty STP	4.00	10.00
52 Jimmy Means Taco Bell	3.00	6.00
66 Jimmy Hensley Trop Artic	3.00	6.00
68 Bobby Hamilton Country Time	3.00	6.00
71 Dave Marcis Big Apple	3.00	6.00
73 Phil Barkdoll X-1R	3.00	6.00
75 Butch Miller Food Country	3.00	6.00
75 Joe Ruttman Dinner Bell	3.00	6.00
94 Terry Labonte Sunoco	3.00	8.00
98 Jimmy Spencer Food City	3.00	6.00
98 Jimmy Spencer Moly Black Gold	3.00	6.00

1993 Pole Position 1:64

	EX	NM-MT
14 Donnie Neuenberger Promo Blister	4.00	8.00

1996 Press Pass Sets 1:24/64

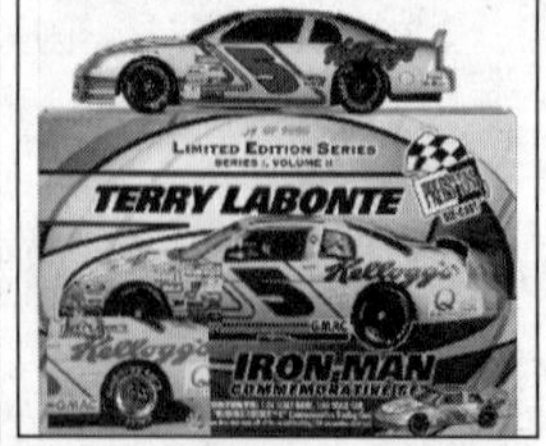

Card manufacturer Press Pass ventured into die-cast with these three pieces. Each piece is a boxed set containing a 1:24 bank or Hauler, a 1:64 car and one Burning Rubber card produced by Press Pass. Each piece was also serial numbered on the outside of the box.

	EX	NM-MT
2 Rusty Wallace Miller 25th Anniversary/1996 1:24 Revell Bank, 1:64 Revell car and Press Pass Burning Rubber I card	40.00	100.00
5 Terry Labonte Kellogg's Silver/1996 1:24 Action black window bank, 1:64 car, and Burning Rubber II card	50.00	120.00
18 Bobby Labonte Interstate Batteries/1008 1:64 Revell car, 1:64 GMP hauler, and Press Pass Burning Rubber card	50.00	120.00

1997 Race Image 1:43

	EX	NM-MT
6 Mark Martin Valvoline	5.00	12.00
9 Jeff Burton Track Gear	4.00	10.00
21 Michael Waltrip Citgo	4.00	10.00
99 Jeff Burton Exide	4.00	10.00

1998 Race Image 1:43

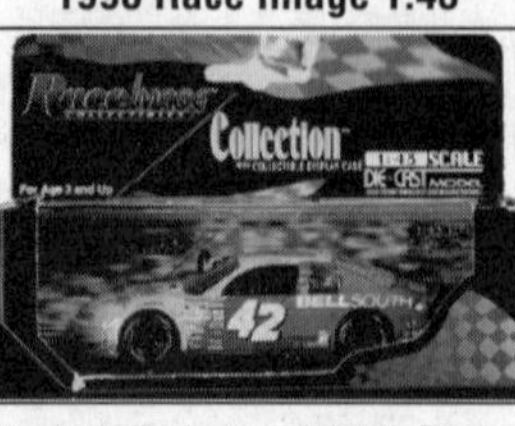

This series of 1:43 scale cars was distributed by Dimension 4 and entitled "Race Image." Each car was packaged in a window display box.

	EX	NM-MT
4 Bobby Hamilton Kodak Gold	4.00	10.00
6 Mark Martin Eagle One	5.00	12.00
6 Mark Martin Valvoline	5.00	12.00
6 Mark Martin Valvoline SynPower	5.00	12.00
8 Hut Stricklin Circuit City	4.00	10.00
16 Ted Musgrave Primestar	4.00	10.00
18 Bobby Labonte Interstate Batteries	5.00	12.00
21 Michael Waltrip Citgo	4.00	10.00
26 Johnny Benson Cheerios	4.00	10.00
35 Todd Bodine Tabasco Orange&White	5.00	12.00
35 Todd Bodine Tabasco Red&Black	5.00	12.00
40 Sterling Marlin Coors Light	5.00	12.00
41 Steve Grissom Grissom Racing	4.00	10.00
41 Steve Grissom Kodiak Chrome	12.50	30.00
42 Joe Nemechek BellSouth	4.00	10.00
42 Joe Nemechek Yellow Pages	4.00	10.00
43 John Andretti STP	4.00	10.00
50 Mark Green Diet Dr.Pepper	4.00	10.00
55 Brad Leighton Coed Naked	4.00	10.00
90 Dick Trickle Heilig-Meyers	4.00	10.00
97 Chad Little John Deere	5.00	12.00
98 Rich Bickle Thorn Apple Valley	4.00	10.00

1998 Race Image Service Kit 1:43

These 1:43 scale cars were issued in a black Race Image blister pack and distributed by Dimension 4. Each car included a group of race day supplies, such as extra tires, a gas can, and jack.

	EX	NM-MT
6 Mark Martin Eagle One	5.00	12.00
6 Mark Martin Zerex	5.00	12.00
17 Matt Kenseth DeWalt	7.50	15.00
21 Michael Waltrip Citgo	4.00	10.00
41 Steve Grissom Grissom Racing	4.00	10.00
57 Andy Santerre Monroe	4.00	10.00
90 Dick Trickle Heilig-Meyers	4.00	10.00
98 Rich Bickle Thorn Apple Valley	4.00	10.00

1992-97 Raceway Replicas 1:24

This manufacturer of high end 1:24 scale die cast replicas has produced this series of cars. The cars are sold directly to the public usually through ads in racing publications.

	EX	NM-MT
4 Sterling Marlin Kodak 1996	100.00	150.00
6 Mark Martin Valvoline 1994	100.00	175.00
11 Bill Elliott Budweiser 1992	100.00	175.00
27 Hut Stricklin McDonald's 1993	90.00	130.
28 Davey Allison Havoline 1993	100.00	175.
96 David Green Caterpillar 1997	80.00	130.

1995 Racing Champions Premier 1:18

	EX	NM-
4 Sterling Marlin Kodak	15.00	40.
17 Darrell Waltrip Western Auto	15.00	30.
18 Bobby Labonte Interstate Batteries	25.00	50.
24 Jeff Gordon DuPont	25.00	50.
25 Ken Schrader Budweiser	15.00	30.
74 Johnny Benson Lipton Tea	15.00	30.
87 Joe Nemechek Burger King	15.00	40.

1995-96 Racing Champion SuperTrucks 1:18

This is a 1:18 scale series of SuperTrucks. The Mike Sk piece is available both in a hood open version and the re hood sealed version.

	EX	NM-
2 Mike Bliss ASE	12.50	30.
3 Mike Skinner Goodwrench 1995	25.00	45.
3 Mike Skinner Goodwrench 1995 Craftsman Truck Series Champion	20.00	40.
6 Rick Carelli Total	12.50	30.
7 Geoff Bodine QVC	12.50	30.
9 Joe Bessey New Hampshire Speedway	12.50	30.
14 Butch Gilliland Stroppe	12.50	30.
17 Bill Sedgwick Die Hard	12.50	30.
17 Darrell Waltrip Western Auto	12.50	30.
20 Walker Evans Dana	12.50	30.
21 Doug George Ortho	12.50	30.
24 Jack Sprague Quaker State	12.50	30.
29 Bob Keselowski Winnebago	12.50	30.
30 Jimmy Hensley Mopar	12.50	30.
35 Bill Venturini Rain X	12.50	30
43 Rich Bickle Cummins	12.50	30.
52 Ken Schrader AC Delco 1995	25.00	40
75 Bobby Gill Spears	12.50	30.
83 Steve Portenga Coffee Critic	12.50	30
98 Butch Miller Raybestos	12.50	30.

1996 Racing Champions Premier 1:18

This series of cars was the first entry into the 1:18 scale s manufacturer Racing Champions. The cars were sold th retail outlets and through hobby shops packaged in Racing Champions window box.

	EX	NM-
1 Rick Mast Hooters	20.00	40
2 Ricky Craven DuPont	25.00	50
2 Rusty Wallace MGD	20.00	40
5 Terry Labonte Bayer	25.00	50
7 Geoff Bodine QVC	15.00	40
9 Joe Bessey Delco Remy	15.00	30
15 Wally Dallenbach Hayes Modems	20.00	40
16 Ted Musgrave Primestar	10.00	25
22 Ward Burton MBNA	15.00	30
24 Jeff Gordon DuPont	20.00	50
24 Jeff Gordon DuPont Signature Series	25.00	50
24 Jeff Gordon DuPont 1995 WC Champ	25.00	50
25 Ken Schrader Budweiser	20.00	50
25 Ken Schrader Bud Olympic/1826	20.00	40
25 Ken Schrader Budweiser Olympic Chrome	150.00	300
29 Steve Grissom Scooby Doo	15.00	30
30 Johnny Benson Pennzoil	15.00	30
31 Mike Skinner Realtree	30.00	60
34 Mike McLaughlin Royal Oak	15.00	30
43 Bobby Hamilton STP Anniversary/2496 1972 Red/Blue	15.00	30
43 Bobby Hamilton STP Anniversary/2496 1972 Blue	15.00	30
43 Bobby Hamilton	15.00	30

TP Anniversary/2496		
979 Red/Blue		
obby Hamilton	15.00	30.00
TP Anniversary/2496		
984 Red/Blue		
obby Hamilton	20.00	35.00
TP Anniversary 1996 Silver		
ff Fuller	15.00	30.00
unoco		
uck Bown	15.00	30.00
ucks		
en Schrader	15.00	30.00
C Delco		
n Bown	20.00	40.00
latco		
son Keller	15.00	30.00
alloween Havoc		
son Keller	15.00	30.00
lim Jim		
ale Jarrett	15.00	30.00
uality Care		
ll Elliott	15.00	30.00
cDonald's Monopoly		
ad Little	12.00	30.00
terling Cowboy		

1997 Racing Champions Premier 1:18

eries of 1:18 scale cars was distributed primarily through outlets. Each basic issue car carried a production run of 0. A Gold version of most cars was also produced with old being produced in quantities of 166-200.

	EX	NM-MT
y Wallace	30.00	60.00
iller Lite		
y Wallace	100.00	200.00
iller Lite Gold		
y Labonte	25.00	50.00
ellogg's Tony/800		
y Labonte	75.00	150.00
ellogg's Tony Gold/200		
k Martin	30.00	60.00
alvoline		
k Martin	100.00	200.00
alvoline Gold		
ky Rudd	20.00	50.00
de/830		
ky Rudd	75.00	150.00
de Gold/166		
rrell Waltrip	35.00	60.00
arts America Chrome		
bby Labonte	25.00	50.00
terstate Batteries		
bby Labonte	75.00	150.00
terstate Batteries Gold		
rike Cope	20.00	50.00
kittles/830		
rike Cope	60.00	120.00
kittles Gold/166		
k Mast	25.00	50.00
emington/830		
k Mast	75.00	150.00
emington Gold/166		
Elliott	25.00	50.00
cDonald's/830		
Elliott	75.00	150.00
cDonald's Gold/166		
Elliott	25.00	50.00
ac Tonight/800		
Elliott	75.00	150.00
ac Tonight Gold/200		
vid Green	15.00	40.00
aterpillar Promo		

1997 Racing Champions SuperTrucks 1:18

s the series edition of 1:18 SuperTrucks released by Champions.

	EX	NM-MT
e Bliss	12.50	30.00
eam ASE		
ke Cope	12.50	30.00
enrose		
ke Dokken	12.50	30.00
ana		
ck Sprague	12.50	30.00
uaker State		
ris Said	12.50	30.00
ederated Auto		
yan Refner	12.50	30.00
arlin		
n Press	12.50	30.00
ears		
e Ruttman	12.50	30.00
CI		
e Nemechek	12.50	30.00
ellSouth		
mmy Jo Kirk	12.50	30.00
oveable		

98 Racing Champions Gold Hood Open 1:18

s a special series produced by Racing Champions to ate NASCAR's 50th anniversary. Each car is a limited of 1,998. Each car is also plated in gold chrome and s a serial number on its chassis.

	EX	NM-MT
by Hamilton	25.00	60.00
odak		
Labonte	60.00	100.00
ellogg's		
Stricklin	25.00	60.00
rcuit City		
rike Cope	25.00	60.00

Gumout		
33 Ken Schrader	25.00	60.00
Petree		
35 Todd Bodine	25.00	60.00
Tabasco		
36 Ernie Irvan	40.00	80.00
Skittles		

1998 Racing Champions Premier 1:18

	EX	NM-MT
92 Derrike Cope	40.00	75.00
Kraft Promo/5000		

1998 Racing Champions Stock Rods 1:18

	EX	NM-MT
93 Dave Blaney	20.00	40.00
Amoco Ultimate Promo		
1968 Dodge Charger		

2000 Racing Champions 1:18

	EX	NM-MT
22 Ward Burton	20.00	40.00
Caterpillar		

2002 Racing Champions Stock Rods 1:18

	EX	NM-MT
5 Terry Labonte	30.00	60.00
Kellogg's/999		
5 Terry Labonte	40.00	80.00
Kellogg's Chrome/199		
10 Johnny Benson	25.00	50.00
Valvoline/999		
10 Johnny Benson	40.00	80.00
Valvoline Chrome/199		
22 Ward Burton	25.00	50.00
Caterpillar/999		
22 Ward Burton	40.00	80.00
Caterpillar Chrome/199		
36 Ken Schrader	35.00	70.00
M&M's/999		
36 Ken Schrader	60.00	100.00
M&M's Chrome/199		
48 Jimmie Johnson	40.00	75.00
Lowe's/999		
48 Jimmie Johnson	60.00	120.00
Lowe's 1970 Chevelle		
Chrome/199		

2003 Racing Champions Stock Rods 1:18

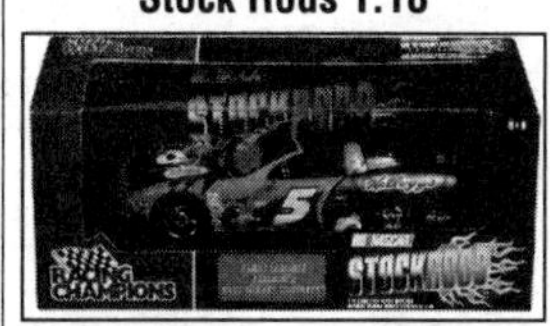

	EX	NM-MT
5 Terry Labonte	25.00	40.00
Kellogg's Corvette		
5 Terry Labonte	25.00	60.00
Kellogg's Mach V		
10 Johnny Benson	25.00	40.00
Valvoline 1996 Firebird		
22 Ward Burton	25.00	40.00
Cat 1970 Challenger		
22 Ward Burton	25.00	40.00
Cat 1971 GTX		
22 Ward Burton	25.00	40.00
Cat 1969 Charger		
32 Ricky Craven	25.00	40.00
Tide 1969 GTO		
48 Jimmie Johnson	25.00	40.00
Lowe's 1955 Chevy		
48 Jimmie Johnson	25.00	40.00
Lowe's 1966 Nova		
48 Jimmie Johnson	25.00	40.00
Lowe's '69 Camaro		
01 Jerry Nadeau	25.00	40.00
Army 1966 GTO		

2004 Racing Champions Stock Rods 1:18

	EX	NM-MT
5 Terry Labonte	25.00	40.00
Kellogg's '70 Chevelle		
22 Scott Wimmer	25.00	50.00
Caterpillar '71 Dodge Demon		
25 Brian Vickers	25.00	40.00
Ditech.com '67 Chevelle		
25 Brian Vickers	25.00	40.00
Ditech.com '69 Nova		
48 Jimmie Johnson	25.00	40.00
Lowe's '64 Impala SS		

1991-92 Racing Champions 1:24

This series of 1:24 cars features some of the most expensive and toughest to find die cast pieces. The pieces were packaged in a black box and were distributed through retail outlets and hobby shops. The Kenny Wallace Dirt Devil car and the Cox Lumber car are the two toughest to come by.

	EX	NM-MT
1 Jeff Gordon	300.00	600.00
Baby Ruth 1992		
1 Rick Mast	15.00	30.00
Majik Market		
2 Rusty Wallace	30.00	60.00
AC Delco		
2 Rusty Wallace	20.00	40.00
Pontiac Excitement		
3 Dale Earnhardt	75.00	150.00
Goodwrench with		
fender stickers 1992		
3 Dale Earnhardt	60.00	150.00
Goodwrench with		
tampo decals 1992		
4 Ernie Irvan	10.00	20.00
Kodak		
5 Ricky Rudd	20.00	40.00
Tide		
6 Mark Martin	25.00	50.00
Valvoline		
7 Harry Gant	30.00	50.00
Morema		
7 No Driver Association	30.00	50.00
Easy Off		
7 No Driver Association	35.00	60.00
French's		
7 No Driver Association	35.00	60.00
Gulf Lite		
7 Jimmy Hensley	30.00	50.00
Bojangles		
7 Tommy Kendall	20.00	60.00
Family Channel		
7 Alan Kulwicki	50.00	120.00
Hooters 1992		
9 Joe Bessey	400.00	600.00
AC Delco		
9 Bill Elliott	40.00	80.00
Melling		
10 Derrike Cope	8.00	20.00
Purolator		
11 Bill Elliott	10.00	25.00
Amoco		
15 Geoff Bodine	8.00	20.00
Motorcraft		
15 Morgan Shepherd	8.00	20.00
Motorcraft		
16 Wally Dallenbach Jr.	40.00	80.00
Roush Racing 1992		
17 Darrell Waltrip	10.00	25.00
Western Auto with fender stickers		
17 Darrell Waltrip	12.50	30.00
Western Auto with tampo decals		
18 Dale Jarrett	30.00	70.00
Interstate Batteries		
18 Gregory Trammell	8.00	20.00
Melling		
21 Dale Jarrett	50.00	90.00
Citgo 1991		
21 Morgan Shepherd	10.00	20.00
Citgo		
22 Sterling Marlin	35.00	60.00
Maxwell House 1991		
25 Ken Schrader	15.00	30.00
No Sponsor		
with Large K on roof		
25 Ken Schrader	8.00	20.00
No Sponsor		
25 Bill Venturini	300.00	500.00
Rain X		
28 Davey Allison	50.00	125.00
Havoline 1992		
30 Michael Waltrip	8.00	20.00
Pennzoil		
33 Harry Gant	20.00	40.00
No Sponsor Oldsmobile		
33 Harry Gant	15.00	30.00
No Sponsor Chevrolet		
36 Kenny Wallace	100.00	200.00
Cox Lumber		
36 Kenny Wallace	150.00	300.00
Dirt Devil		
42 Bobby Hillin Jr.	20.00	40.00
Mello Yello 1991		
42 Kyle Petty	15.00	30.00
Mello Yello		
42/43 Kyle Petty	60.00	100.00
Mello Yello		
Richard Petty		
STP		
2-cars 1:24		
43 Richard Petty	30.00	50.00
STP 1991		
43 Richard Petty	15.00	25.00
STP with Blue Wheels 1992		
49 Stanley Smith	125.00	250.00
Ameritron Batteries		
51 No Driver Association	90.00	160.00
Racing Champions		
55 Ted Musgrave	500.00	800.00
Jasper		
59 Andy Belmont	300.00	500.00
FDP Brakes		
60 Mark Martin	100.00	175.00
Winn Dixie with Red Numbers		
60 Mark Martin	60.00	100.00
Winn Dixie with White Numbers		
63 Chuck Bown	500.00	800.00
Nescafe		
66 Jimmy Hensley	10.00	22.00
TropArtic		
66 Chad Little	8.00	20.00
TropArtic		
66 No Driver Association	12.50	25.00
TropArtic Red Car		
66 Cale Yarborough	15.00	40.00
TropArtic		
68 Bobby Hamilton	20.00	40.00
Country Time		
70 J.D. McDuffie	8.00	20.00
Son's Auto		
71 Dave Marcis	25.00	60.00
Big Apple Market		
75 Butch Miller	250.00	400.00
Food Country		
83 Lake Speed	125.00	175.00
Purex		
87 Joe Nemechek	250.00	400.00
Texas Pete		
94 Terry Labonte	50.00	120.00
Sunoco		
94 Terry Labonte	75.00	150.00
Sunoco		
Arrow on decal points to tire		

1992 Racing Champions IROC 1:24

	EX	NM-MT
11 True Value IROC Black		
19 Rusty Wallace	60.00	100.00
True Value IROC Purple		

1992 Racing Champions Pit Stop 1:24

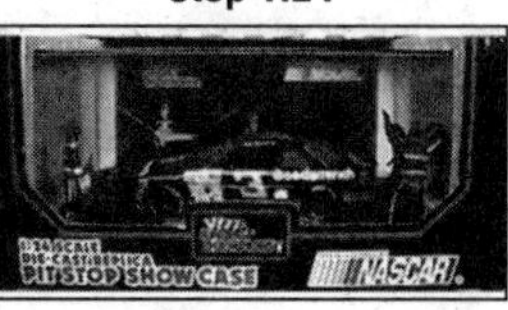

Each if these "Pit Stop Show Case" scenes were packaged in a hard plastic case inside a Racing Champions black window box or promo box printed in sponsor colors. Each car was mounted on a black base with plastic crew members surrounding the car as if it were in a pit stall during a race.

	EX	NM-MT
3 Dale Earnhardt	50.00	100.00
Goodwrench		
5 Ricky Rudd	20.00	40.00
Tide		
7 Alan Kulwicki	45.00	80.00
Hooters		
9 Bill Elliott	20.00	40.00
Melling blue		
17 Darrell Waltrip	10.00	25.00
Western Auto Promo		
42 Kyle Petty	20.00	40.00
Mello Yello		
43 Richard Petty	20.00	40.00
STP		

1992-94 Racing Champions Super Collector's Set 1:24/43/64

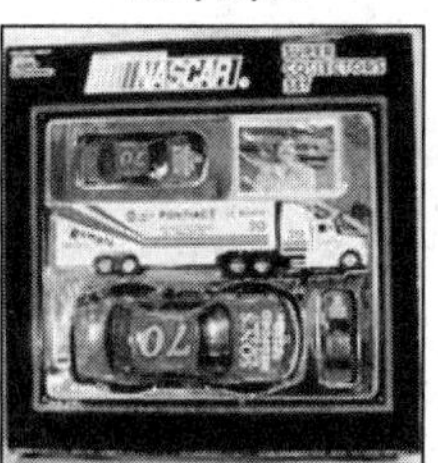

Each boxed set consists of a grouping of 1:24, 1:43, and/or 1:64 scale die-cast cars. A 1:64 and/or 1:87 die-cast Transporter was also included in some sets to round out the package. Each set was packaged together in a black clear window box.

	EX	NM-MT
3 Dale Earnhardt	30.00	60.00
Goodwrench		
2-cars 1:24, 1:64		
and 2-Transporters 1:64, 1:87		
3 Dale Earnhardt	35.00	60.00
Goodwrench 3-cars		
1:24, 1:43, 1:64 and		
a 1:64 Transporter		
5 Ricky Rudd	12.50	30.00
Tide 2-cars 1:24 and 1:64		
and 2-Transporters 1:64, 1:87		
7 Alan Kulwicki	40.00	80.00
Hooters 3-cars		
1:24, 1:43, 1:64		
and a 1:64 Transporter		
28 Davey Allison	15.00	40.00
Havoline 2-cars		
1:24, 1:64 and 2-Transporters		
28 Davey Allison	25.00	50.00
Havoline 3-cars		
1:24, 1:43, 1:64 and		
a 1:64 Transporter		
30 Michael Waltrip	20.00	40.00
Pennzoil 3-cars 1:24/64/87		
and 2-Transporters		
33 Harry Gant	15.00	40.00
Leo Jackson 3-cars:		
1:24/43/64 & Transporter 1994		
43 Richard Petty	10.00	25.00
STP Fan Tour 2-cars		
1:24, 1:43 & Transporter 1992		
43 Richard Petty	20.00	50.00
STP 3-cars		
1:24, 1:43, 1:64		
and a 1:64 Transporter 1992		
66 Cale Yarborough	20.00	40.00
Phillips 66		
3-cars 1:24/64/87		
and 2-Transporters		
70 J.D. McDuffie	20.00	40.00
Son's Auto Supply		
3-cars 1:24, 1:43, 1:64		
and 1:64 transporter		

1992-94 Racing Champions Banks 1:24

These 1:24 scale cars were prodcued as banks with a slot in the back window to slip your money into. The cars, as with most die cast banks, have blacked in windows. Most were issued in a small solid red box with a black #51 car pictured on the outside. A sticker can often be found on the bottom of the box with a brief description of the car found inside along with the production run total.

	EX	NM-MT
0 Dick McCabe	18.00	30.00
Fisher Snow Plows		
1 Ford Manufacturers/5000 1992	10.00	20.00
1 Rick Mast	12.50	25.00
Precision Products		
2 Ward Burton	20.00	35.00
Hardee's/5000 1992		
2 Ricky Craven	15.00	25.00
DuPont		
2 Rusty Wallace	20.00	35.00
Ford Motorsports		
2 Rusty Wallace	100.00	200.00
Pontiac Excitement/2500		
3 Dale Earnhardt	50.00	120.00
Goodwrench 1993		
Mom-n-Pop's rear fender		
3 Dale Earnhardt	75.00	150.00
Goodwrench Western		
Steer on fender/10,000 1993		
3 Dale Earnhardt	75.00	150.00
Goodwrench/10,000		
with numbered box 1992		
3 Dale Earnhardt	40.00	100.00
Goodwrench		
no serial #'d box 1992		
3 Dale Earnhardt	75.00	150.00
Goodwrench with Snap On		
3 Dale Earnhardt	50.00	120.00
Goodwrench Sports Image		
Mom-n-Pop's on rear fender 1994		
4 Ernie Irvan	20.00	35.00
Kodak		
4 Sterling Marlin	18.00	30.00
Kodak		
4 Sterling Marlin	18.00	30.00
Kodak Fun Saver		
5 Terry Labonte	25.00	50.00
Kellogg's		
5 Ricky Rudd	25.00	50.00
Tide/7500 1992		
6 Mark Martin	18.00	30.00
Valvoline		
6 Mark Martin	18.00	30.00
Valvoline Reese's		
7 Geoff Bodine	10.00	25.00
Exide		
7 Harry Gant	30.00	45.00
Black Flag/2500 1994		
7 Harry Gant	25.00	45.00
Easy Off/2500 1993		
7 Harry Gant	30.00	45.00
French's/1994		
7 Harry Gant	30.00	45.00
Gulf Lite		
7 Harry Gant	30.00	45.00
Manheim		
7 Harry Gant	30.00	45.00
Morema		
7 Harry Gant	25.00	45.00
Woolite/2500 1993		
7 Jimmy Hensley	15.00	25.00
Bojangles		
7 Tommy Kendall	18.00	30.00
Family Channel		
7 Alan Kulwicki	30.00	80.00
Army 1994		
7 Alan Kulwicki	100.00	200.00
Hooters/10,000 1992		
7 Alan Kulwicki	50.00	100.00
Zerex/5000 1993		
8 Sterling Marlin	12.50	25.00
Raybestos		
8 Kenny Wallace	12.50	25.00
TIC Financial		
10 Ricky Rudd	20.00	35.00
Tide		
10 Jimmy Spencer	50.00	100.00
Kleenex/2825 1992		
11 Bill Elliott	25.00	40.00
Amoco		
11 Bill Elliott	30.00	50.00
Bud/7500 1993		
11 Bill Elliott	25.00	50.00
Bud Busch/5000 1993		
11 Bill Elliott	25.00	40.00
Budweiser Hardy Boys car		
12 Clifford Allison	25.00	40.00
Sports Image		
12 Jimmy Spencer	35.00	60.00
Meineke		
14 John Andretti	18.00	30.00
Kanawaha		
14 Terry Labonte	60.00	100.00
MW Windows/2500 1994		
15 Geoff Bodine	10.00	25.00
Motorcraft		
15 Lake Speed	12.50	25.00
Quality Care		
16 Chad Chaffin	15.00	25.00
Dr. Die Cast		
16 Ted Musgrave	15.00	25.00
Family Channel		
17 Darrell Waltrip	30.00	50.00
Tide Orange paint scheme		
17 Darrell Waltrip	20.00	40.00
Tide Primer gray car		
17 Darrell Waltrip	90.00	150.00
Western Auto		
18 Dale Jarrett	40.00	75.00
Interstate Batteries/10,000 1993		
20 Randy LaJoie	15.00	30.00
Fina/2500 1994		
20 Joe Ruttman	20.00	35.00
Fina		
20 Joe Ruttman	25.00	40.00
Fina 520 made		

21 Morgan Shepherd Cheerwine	18.00	30.00
21 Morgan Shepherd Citgo	12.50	25.00
22 Bobby Labonte Maxwell House/7500 1993	50.00	100.00
23 Chad Little Bayer	8.00	20.00
24 Jeff Gordon DuPont/10,000 1993	75.00	150.00
24 Jeff Gordon DuPont Brickyard Win/5024 1994	60.00	120.00
24 Jeff Gordon DuPont Coca-Cola 600 Win 1994	100.00	200.00
24 Jeff Gordon DuPont Snickers on deck lid 1994	40.00	80.00
25 Hermie Sadler Virginia is for Lovers	12.50	25.00
26 Brett Bodine Quaker State	10.00	25.00
27 Hut Stricklin McDonald's	18.00	30.00
28 Davey Allison Havoline black and white/28,000 1992	30.00	50.00
28 Davey Allison Havoline black&white and gold/5000 1993	40.00	80.00
28 Davey Allison Havoline black 1993	50.00	120.00
28 Ernie Irvan Havoline	25.00	40.00
28 Ernie Irvan Mac Tools/7541 1993	25.00	40.00
28 Davey Allison Havoline Mac Tools/5000 1992	50.00	120.00
30 Michael Waltrip Pennzoil	12.50	25.00
31 Steve Grissom Channellock	12.50	25.00
31 Tom Peck Channellock	12.50	25.00
33 Harry Gant Farewell Tour	20.00	35.00
33 Harry Gant Leo Jackson	15.00	25.00
33 Harry Gant Manheim Auctions	50.00	75.00
33 Harry Gant Manheim Auctions Autographed	75.00	125.00
33 Bobby Labonte Dentyne/2500 1994	40.00	80.00
34 Mike McLaughlin Fiddle Faddle	12.50	25.00
35 Shawna Robinson Polaroid Captiva	30.00	80.00
38 Elton Sawyer Ford Credit	15.00	25.00
41 Ernie Irvan Mac Tools	25.00	40.00
42 Kyle Petty Mello Yello/5000 1993	25.00	40.00
43 Rodney Combs French's Black Flag 1994	40.00	80.00
43 Wally Dallenbach Jr. STP	12.50	25.00
43 Richard Petty STP	30.00	50.00
44 David Green Slim Jim/2500 1994	15.00	30.00
44 Bobby Hillin Jr. Buss Fuses	15.00	25.00
44 Rick Wilson STP	15.00	25.00
46 Shawna Robinson Polaroid	25.00	60.00
51 Racing Champions/3000 1992	50.00	100.00
52 Ken Schrader AC Delco	15.00	25.00
52 Ken Schrader Morema	20.00	35.00
54 Robert Pressley Manheim Auctions	20.00	35.00
55 Ted Musgrave US Air/2500 1993	30.00	50.00
59 Andy Belmont Metal Arrester	15.00	30.00
59 Robert Pressley Alliance	45.00	70.00
59 Dennis Setzer Alliance	30.00	45.00
60 Mark Martin Winn Dixie of 5000 1993	45.00	75.00
60 Mark Martin Winn Dixie of 10,000	20.00	35.00
63 Jim Bown Lysol	12.50	25.00
70 J.D. McDuffie Son's Auto/2500 1994	12.50	25.00
71 Dave Marcis Earnhardt Chevrolet/2500 1993	35.00	60.00
75 Todd Bodine Factory Stores	12.50	25.00
77 Greg Sacks US Air	20.00	35.00
83 Sherry Blakely Ramses	18.00	30.00
87 Joe Nemechek Dentyne	15.00	25.00
92 Larry Pearson Stanley Tools	12.50	25.00
93 Racing Champions Collector's Club/1440 1993	50.00	100.00
93 Rockingham/2500 1993	20.00	35.00
94 Brickyard 400 Special	20.00	35.00
97 Joe Bessey Auto Palace	18.00	30.00
97 Joe Bessey Johnson AC Delco	18.00	30.00
98 Derrike Cope Bojangles Black car	20.00	35.00
98 Derrike Cope Bojangles Yellow car	20.00	35.00
98 Jody Ridley Ford Motorsports	25.00	40.00

1993 Racing Champions 1:24

These 1:24 scale cars come in a Red box and feature some of the top names in racing.

	EX	NM-MT
2 Davey Allison True Value IROC/5000	60.00	150.00
2 Rusty Wallace Pontiac Excitement	15.00	25.00
3 Dale Earnhardt Goodwrench Goodyear in White	60.00	120.00
3 Dale Earnhardt Goodwrench Goodyear in Yellow	40.00	100.00
3 Dale Earnhardt Goodwrench Mom-n-Pop's on fender	60.00	150.00
4 Ernie Irvan Kodak Gold Film	8.00	20.00
4 Ernie Irvan Kodak Gold Film Promo sticker decals	50.00	100.00
4 Ernie Irvan Kodak Gold Plus	8.00	20.00
4 Ernie Irvan Kodak Gold Plus Promo sticker decals	50.00	100.00
5 Ricky Rudd Tide Exxon	8.00	20.00
5 Ricky Rudd Tide Valvoline	8.00	20.00
6 Mark Martin Valvoline	15.00	30.00
7 Alan Kulwicki Hooters	50.00	100.00
7/42 Alan Kulwick Hooters Kyle Petty Mello Yello 2-Car set	90.00	150.00
8 Sterling Marlin Raybestos	8.00	20.00
8 Sterling Marlin Raybestos Douglas Batteries	12.00	22.00
10 Bill Elliott True Value IROC/5000	40.00	75.00
11 Bill Elliott Amoco	12.00	20.00
12 Jimmy Spencer Meineke	8.00	20.00
14 Terry Labonte Kellogg's	60.00	120.00
15 Geoff Bodine Motorcraft	8.00	20.00
17 Darrell Waltrip Western Auto	8.00	20.00
18 Dale Jarrett Interstate Batteries	20.00	40.00
21 Morgan Shepherd Citgo red pillar post	8.00	20.00
21 Morgan Shepherd Citgo Tri-color Pillar Post	8.00	20.00
22 Bobby Labonte Maxwell House	75.00	150.00
24 Jeff Gordon DuPont	60.00	150.00
25 Ken Schrader No Sponsor	20.00	40.00
26 Brett Bodine Quaker State	8.00	20.00
27 Hut Stricklin McDonald's	8.00	20.00
28 Davey Allison Havoline Black and Gold paint scheme	40.00	80.00
28 Davey Allison Havoline Black/Orange	25.00	60.00
28 Davey Allison Havoline Black and White paint scheme	60.00	120.00
30 Michael Waltrip Pennzoil	15.00	35.00
42 Kyle Petty Mello Yello	15.00	30.00
44 Rick Wilson STP	15.00	30.00
49 Stanley Smith Ameritron Batteries	75.00	125.00
59 Andy Belmont FDP Brakes	60.00	100.00
60 Mark Martin Winn Dixie	20.00	50.00
75 No Driver Association Auto Value	15.00	25.00
75 No Driver Association Factory Stores	8.00	20.00
87 Joe Nemechek Dentyne	20.00	40.00
96 Auto Value Promo	10.00	25.00
98 Derrike Cope Bojangles	12.50	25.00

1993 Racing Champions Pit Stop 1:24

Each if these "Pit Stop Show Case" scenes were packaged in a hard plastic case inside a Racing Champions red window box. Each car was mounted on a black base with plastic crew members surrounding the car as if it were in a pit stall during a race.

	EX	NM-MT
7 A.Kulwicki/Hooters	45.00	80.00
24 Jeff Gordon DuPont	45.00	80.00
27 Hut Stricklin McDonald's	15.00	30.00

1994 Racing Champions 1:24

These 1:24 scale cars were issued primarily in red clear window display boxes but a few could be found in race team colors. The year of issue can be found on the back of the box and most were distributed through hobby and retail outlets.

	EX	NM-MT
1 Rick Mast Percision Products	7.50	15.00
2 Ricky Craven DuPont	20.00	40.00
2 Rusty Wallace Ford Motorsports Black Ford Oval	10.00	20.00
2 Rusty Wallace Ford Motorsports Blue Ford Oval	10.00	20.00
3 Dale Earnhardt Goodwrench	100.00	200.00
4 Sterling Marlin Kodak	8.00	20.00
5 Terry Labonte Kellogg's	40.00	80.00
6 Mark Martin Valvoline Reese's	20.00	40.00
7 Geoff Bodine Exide	7.50	15.00
7 Harry Gant Manheim	15.00	25.00
7 Alan Kulwicki Zerex	40.00	80.00
8 Jeff Burton Raybestos with Goodyear tires	20.00	40.00
8 Jeff Burton Raybestos with Hoosier tires	15.00	40.00
8 Kenny Wallace TIC Financial	7.50	15.00
12 Clifford Allison Sports Image	30.00	60.00
14 John Andretti Kanawaha	20.00	40.00
14 Terry Labonte MW Windows	60.00	125.00
15 Lake Speed Quality Care	7.50	15.00
16 Chad Chaffin Dr. Die Cast	7.50	15.00
16 Ted Musgrave Family Channel	7.50	15.00
17 Darrell Waltrip Western Auto	7.50	15.00
18 Dale Jarrett Interstate Batteries	35.00	60.00
19 Loy Allen Hooters	12.50	25.00
20 Bobby Hillin Jr. Fina	7.50	15.00
20 Randy LaJoie Fina	7.50	15.00
21 Morgan Shepherd Citgo	7.50	15.00
22 Bobby Labonte Maxwell House	60.00	100.00
23 Chad Little Bayer	7.50	15.00
23 Hut Stricklin Smokin' Joe's in plastic case	50.00	120.00
24 Jeff Gordon DuPont with plain red deck lid	75.00	125.00
24 Jeff Gordon DuPont Snickers on deck lid	75.00	125.00
24 Jeff Gordon DuPont Coca-Cola 600 Win in plastic case/2000	90.00	150.00
24 Jeff Gordon DuPont Brickyard Special in purple box/10,024	40.00	80.00
25 Ken Schrader GMAC	25.00	40.00
26 Brett Bodine Quaker State	7.50	15.00
27 Jimmy Spencer McDonald's	30.00	75.00
28 Ernie Irvan Havoline	12.00	22.00
30 Michael Waltrip Pennzoil	12.50	25.00
31 Steve Grissom Channellock	7.50	15.00
31 Tom Peck Channellock	7.50	15.00
33 Harry Gant No Sponsor	7.50	15.00
33 Harry Gant Leo Jackson Motorsports	7.50	15.00
33 Harry Gant Manheim Auctions	20.00	40.00
33 Bobby Labonte Dentyne	90.00	150.00
34 Mike McLaughlin Fiddle Faddle	7.50	15.00
35 Shawna Robinson Polaroid Captiva	20.00	35.00
38 Elton Sawyer Ford Credit	7.50	15.00
40 Bobby Hamilton Kendall	7.50	15.00
42 Kyle Petty Mello Yello	10.00	20.00
44 David Green Slim Jim	7.50	15.00
44 Bobby Hillin Jr. Buss Fuses	7.50	15.00
46 Shawna Robinson Polaroid	20.00	35.00
52 Ken Schrader AC Delco	7.50	15.00
54 Robert Pressley Manheim	7.50	15.00
59 Andy Belmont Metal Arrester	7.50	15.00
59 Dennis Setzer Alliance	18.00	30.00
60 Mark Martin Winn Dixie	20.00	40.00
63 Jim Bown Lysol	7.50	15.00
70 J.D. McDuffie Son's Auto	7.50	15.00
75 Todd Bodine Factory Stores of America	7.50	15.00
79 Dave Rezendes Lipton Tea	7.50	15.00
83 Sherry Blakely Ramses	15.00	40.00
92 Larry Pearson Stanley Tools	7.50	15.00
94 No Driver Association Auto Value	15.00	25.00
94 No Driver Association Brickyard 400 Purple Box	15.00	30.00
97 Joe Bessey Johnson	7.50	15.00
98 Derrike Cope Fingerhut	7.50	15.00
0 Dick McCabe Fisher Snow Plows	12.00	20.00

1995 Racing Champions Preview 1:24

This is the first time Racing Champions did a preview series for its 1:24 scale series. The cars were a preview of some of the cars that raced in the 1995 season.

	EX	NM-MT
2 Rusty Wallace Ford Motorsports	10.00	18.00
6 Mark Martin Valvoline	10.00	18.00
7 Geoff Bodine Exide with Goodyear tires	6.00	15.00
7 Geoff Bodine Exide with Hoosier tires	6.00	15.00
10 Ricky Rudd Tide	12.50	25.00
57 Jason Keller Budget Gourmet	9.00	18.00
63 Curtis Markham Lysol	9.00	18.00
94 Bill Elliott McDonald's	10.00	18.00
98 Jeremy Mayfield Fingerhut	25.00	50.00

1995 Racing Champions 1:24

This series of 1:24 cars features both Winston Cup cars and Busch Grand National cars. Featured in the series is Bill Elliott's Thunderbat car. The car was a promotion done in conjunction with the movie Batman Forever.

	EX	NM-MT
2 Ricky Craven DuPont	15.00	30.00
2 Rusty Wallace Ford Motorsports	10.00	20.00
4 Sterling Marlin Kodak	10.00	25.00
4 Jeff Purvis Kodak Fun Saver	7.50	15.00
5 Terry Labonte Kellogg's	15.00	30.00
6 Tommy Houston Red Devil	7.50	15.00
6 Mark Martin Valvoline	10.00	20.00
7 Geoff Bodine Exide	7.50	15.00
7 Stevie Reeves Clabber Girl	7.50	15.00
8 Jeff Burton Raybestos	20.00	40.00
8 Kenny Wallace Red Dog Promo	40.00	80.00
8 Bobby Dotter Hyde Tools	7.50	15.00
10 Ricky Rudd Tide	7.50	15.00
12 Derrike Cope Mane N' Tail	7.50	15.00
15 Dick Trickle Quality Care	7.50	15.00
16 Ted Musgrave Family Channel	7.50	15.00
17 Darrell Waltrip Western Auto	10.00	20.00
18 Bobby Labonte Interstate Batteries	30.00	60.00
21 Morgan Shepherd Citgo	7.50	15.00
23 Chad Little Bayer	7.50	15.00
24 Jeff Gordon DuPont	40.00	80.00
24 Jeff Gordon DuPont Signature Series	45.00	90.00
24 Jeff Gordon DuPont Signature Series Hood Open	60.00	150.00
25 Johnny Rumley Big Johnson	12.50	25.00
25 Ken Schrader Budweiser	10.00	20
26 Steve Kinser Quaker State	15.00	30
27 Loy Allen Hooters	15.00	3
28 Dale Jarrett Havoline	35.00	60
29 Steve Grissom Meineke	7.50	15
34 Mike McLaughlin French's	18.00	30
37 John Andretti K-Mart	15.00	30
38 Elton Sawyer Red Carpet Lease	7.50	15
40 Patty Moise Dial Purex	15.00	3
41 Ricky Craven Larry Hedrick Mtrsprts.	7.50	15
44 David Green Slim Jim	7.50	15
44 Jeff Purvis Jackaroo	7.50	15
51 Jim Bown Luck's	7.50	15
60 Mark Martin Winn Dixie	12.50	25
71 Kevin Lepage Vermont Teddy Bear	15.00	3
71 Dave Marcis Olive Garden	30.00	75
75 Todd Bodine Factory Stores of America	7.50	15
81 Kenny Wallace TIC Financial	7.50	15
87 Joe Nemechek Burger King	7.50	15
88 Ernie Irvan Havoline	15.00	2
90 Mike Wallace Heilig-Meyers	7.50	1
94 Bill Elliott McDonald's	10.00	2
94 Bill Elliott McDonald's Thunderbat Promo	25.00	5
95 Auto Value Promo	7.50	1

1995 Racing Champions Banks 1:24

This series of 1:24 cars offers the collector the option them as bank. Each car has a slot in the rear window or i cases the deck lid.

	EX	NM
2 Rusty Wallace Ford Motorsports	15.00	2
4 Sterling Marlin Kodak	15.00	3
5 Terry Labonte Kellogg's	15.00	2
6 Mark Martin Valvoline	15.00	2
7 Geoff Bodine Exide	12.00	2
8 Jeff Burton Raybestos	15.00	2
8 Kenny Wallace Red Dog Hood Open Promo	25.00	4
12 Derrike Cope Straight Arrow	15.00	2
16 Ted Musgrave Family Channel	16.00	2
24 Jeff Gordon DuPont/10,000	30.00	6
24 Jeff Gordon DuPont Signature Series Hood Open	40.00	8
24 Jeff Gordon DuPont Signature Series 1995 Champion Hood Open	40.00	8
25 Ken Schrader Budweiser	16.00	2
25 Ken Schrader Budweiser Hood Open	15.00	3
27 Loy Allen Hooters	16.00	2
28 Dale Jarrett Havoline Hood Open	30.00	5
32 Dale Jarrett Mac Tools/4000	30.00	5
37 John Andretti K-Mart Hood Open Promo	20.00	3
44 David Green Slim Jim	10.00	2
59 Dennis Setzer Alliance	15.00	3
60 Mark Martin Winn Dixie/10,000	20.00	3
74 Johnny Benson Lipton Tea Hood Open	25.00	4
88 Ernie Irvan Texaco Hood Open	25.00	4
94 Bill Elliott McDonald's	15.00	3
94 Bill Elliott McDonald's Thunderbat	25.00	5

1995 Racing Champions P Stop 1:24

	EX	NM
24 Jeff Gordon DuPont Signature Series	30.00	6
74 Johnny Benson Lipton 1995 BGN Champion	15.00	4

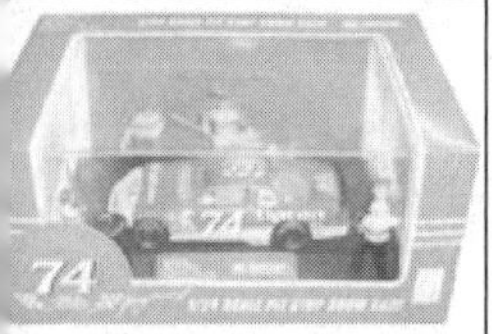

1995 Racing Champions SuperTrucks 1:24

:24 scale series is representitive of the many different that raced in the inaugural SuperTruck series. Each was ged in a red and white clear window display box with the f issue printed on the top.

	EX	NM-MT
. Jones ears Diehard Chevrolet	7.50	15.00
. Jones essells Ford	7.50	15.00
vid Ashley outhern California Ford	7.50	15.00
e Skinner oodwrench	10.00	25.00
ke Bliss ltra Wheels	7.50	15.00
ch Gilliland ltra Wheels	7.50	15.00
k Carelli otal Petroleum	7.50	15.00
ff Bodine xide	7.50	15.00
ff Bodine xide Salsa	7.50	15.00
ve Rezendes xide	7.50	15.00
ke Bliss ltra Wheels	7.50	15.00
an Fox lade for You	7.50	15.00
andy MacCachren enable	7.50	15.00
hnny Benson ella Lights	7.50	15.00
bey Butler rtho with Green Nose piece	7.50	15.00
bey Butler rtho with Yellow Nose piece	7.50	15.00
J. Clark SE with Blue scheme	7.50	15.00
J. Clark SE with White scheme	7.50	15.00
f Gordon uPont	20.00	40.00
f Gordon uPont Signature Series	15.00	30.00
ott Lagasse uPont	10.00	20.00
ott Lagasse uPont Bank	12.00	25.00
b Strait arget Expediting	7.50	15.00
ammy Swindell hannellock	7.50	15.00
rry Teague osenblum Racing	7.50	15.00
en Schrader C Delco	7.50	15.00
eve McEachern lcEachern Racing	7.50	15.00
dd Bodine oush Racing	7.50	15.00
ll Sedgwick pears Motorsports	7.50	15.00
eve Portenga offee Critic	7.50	15.00
Driver Association rickyard 400 Special	10.00	20.00
Driver Association rickyard 400 Special Bank	15.00	25.00
tch Miller aybestos	7.50	15.00

1996 Racing Champions Preview 1:24

eries of 1:24 die cast replicas featured a preview of some new paint jobs to run in the 1996 season. The Terry te Bayer car is one of the first for this new car.

	EX	NM-MT
ky Craven uPont	7.50	15.00
ling Marlin odak	8.00	20.00
ry Labonte ellogg's	8.00	20.00
y Labonte ayer	8.00	20.00
k Martin alvoline	8.00	20.00
vie Reeves labber Girl	7.50	15.00
Bessey elco Remy	7.50	15.00
e Speed PAM	7.50	15.00
cky Rudd ide	7.50	15.00
ett Bodine owe's	7.50	15.00
errike Cope lane N' Tail	7.50	15.00
tty Moise ial Purex	7.50	15.00
d Musgrave Family Channel	7.50	15.00
17 Darrell Waltrip Western Auto	7.50	15.00
18 Bobby Labonte Interstate Batteries	10.00	25.00
22 Ward Burton MBNA	7.50	15.00
24 Jeff Gordon DuPont	15.00	40.00
30 Johnny Benson Pennzoil	7.50	15.00
40 Tim Fedewa Kleenex	7.50	15.00
41 Ricky Craven Kodiak	10.00	25.00
47 Jeff Fuller Sunoco	7.50	15.00
51 Chuck Bown Lucks	7.50	15.00
52 Ken Schrader AC Delco	7.50	15.00
57 Jason Keller Slim Jim	7.50	15.00
74 Johnny Benson Lipton Tea	7.50	15.00
87 Joe Nemechek Burger King	10.00	25.00
90 Mike Wallace Heilig-Meyers	7.50	15.00
94 Bill Elliott McDonald's	8.00	20.00

1996 Racing Champions 1:24

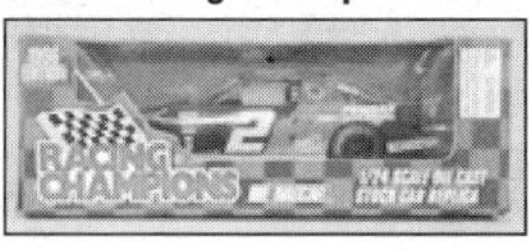

The 1:24 scale cars that appear in this series are replicas of many of the cars that ran during the 1996 season. The Rusty Wallace Miller Genuine Draft car is one of the few times that Racing Champions has offered a collectible die cast that included a beer logo.

	EX	NM-MT
1 Rick Mast Hooter's	15.00	30.00
2 Ricky Craven DuPont	7.50	15.00
2 Rusty Wallace Miller Genuine Draft	18.00	30.00
2 Rusty Wallace Miller Splash Promo	12.50	25.00
2 Rusty Wallace Penske Racing	25.00	40.00
3 Mike Skinner Goodwrench	12.50	25.00
4 Sterling Marlin Kodak Back to Back Special	12.50	25.00
5 Terry Labonte Kellogg's	10.00	20.00
5 Terry Labonte Kellogg's Silver car	25.00	40.00
6 Tommy Houston Suburban Propane	7.50	15.00
6 Mark Martin Valvoline	12.50	25.00
6 Mark Martin Valvoline DuraBlend	50.00	90.00
7 Geoff Bodine QVC	7.50	15.00
8 Hut Stricklin Circuit City	7.50	15.00
9 Joe Bessey Delco Remy	7.50	15.00
9 Lake Speed SPAM	7.50	15.00
10 Ricky Rudd Tide	7.50	15.00
11 Brett Bodine Lowe's	7.50	15.00
11 Brett Bodine Lowe's 50th Anniversary Paint Scheme	15.00	40.00
14 Patty Moise Purex	7.50	15.00
15 Wally Dallenbach Hayes Modems	30.00	50.00
16 Ted Musgrave Primestar	7.50	15.00
17 Darrell Waltrip Parts America	7.50	15.00
18 Bobby Labonte Interstate Batteries	20.00	40.00
19 Loy Allen Healthsource	7.50	15.00
21 Michael Waltrip Citgo	7.50	15.00
22 Ward Burton MBNA	7.50	15.00
23 Chad Little John Deere	15.00	30.00
23 Chad Little John Deere in a John Deere Box	15.00	40.00
24 Jeff Gordon DuPont	30.00	60.00
24 Jeff Gordon DuPont 1995 Champion	30.00	60.00
24 Jeff Gordon DuPont Bristol Win in plastic case/2424	50.00	100.00
24 Jeff Gordon DuPont Darlington in plastic case/2424	50.00	100.00
24 Jeff Gordon DuPont The Kid in plastic case/2424	50.00	100.00
24 Jeff Gordon DuPont Pocono Win in plastic case/2424	50.00	100.00
25 Ken Schrader Budweiser	25.00	40.00
25 Ken Schrader Bud Olympic Chrome/400	125.00	250.00
25 Ken Schrader Hendrick Motorsports	7.50	15.00
28 Ernie Irvan Havoline	7.50	15.00
29 Steve Grissom Cartoon Network	7.50	15.00
29 Steve Grissom WCW	10.00	25.00
29 No Driver Association Scooby-Doo in Scooby Box	7.50	15.00
29 No Driver Association WCW Sting	7.50	15.00
30 Johnny Benson Pennzoil	7.50	15.00
31 Mike Skinner Realtree	30.00	80.00
34 Mike McLaughlin Royal Oak	7.50	15.00
37 John Andretti K-Mart	7.50	15.00
38 Dennis Setzer Lipton	7.50	15.00
40 Tim Fedewa Kleenex	7.50	15.00
40 Jim Sauter First Union	7.50	15.00
41 Ricky Craven Larry Hedrick Racing	7.50	15.00
41 Ricky Craven Kodiak in Acrylic case	25.00	50.00
41 Ricky Craven Manheim	7.50	15.00
43 Bobby Hamilton STP Anniversary 1972 Red/Blue	10.00	20.00
43 Bobby Hamilton STP Anniversary 1972 Blue	10.00	20.00
43 Bobby Hamilton STP Anniversary 1979 Red/Blue	10.00	20.00
43 Bobby Hamilton STP Anniversary 1984 Red/Blue	10.00	20.00
43 Bobby Hamilton STP Anniversary 1996 Silver	12.50	25.00
43 Bobby Hamilton STP 5-trailer set	75.00	150.00
44 Bobby Labonte Shell	25.00	50.00
52 Ken Schrader AC Delco	7.50	15.00
57 Jason Keller Halloween Havoc	7.50	15.00
60 Mark Martin Winn Dixie	15.00	30.00
63 Curtis Markham Lysol	7.50	15.00
74 Johnny Benson Lipton Tea 1995 BGN Champion	7.50	15.00
75 Morgan Shepherd Remington	15.00	30.00
77 Bobby Hillin Jr. Jasper Engines	7.50	15.00
81 Kenny Wallace Square D	7.50	15.00
87 Joe Nemechek Burger King	30.00	60.00
88 Dale Jarrett Quality Care	7.50	15.00
90 Mike Wallace Duron	7.50	15.00
94 Ron Barfield New Holland	7.50	15.00
94 Bill Elliott McDonald's	8.00	18.00
94 Bill Elliott McDonald's Monopoly	10.00	20.00
96 Auto Value Promo	7.50	15.00
96 David Green Busch Chrome	100.00	250.00
96 David Green Busch Hobby	15.00	35.00
97 Chad Little Sterling Cowboy	7.50	15.00
99 Glenn Allen Luxaire	7.50	15.00
99 Jeff Burton Exide	7.50	15.00

1996 Racing Champions Banks 1:24

This series of 1:24 cars offers the collector the option to use them as bank. Each car has a slot in the rear window or in some cases the deck lid. These banks have blacked in windows.

	EX	NM-MT
6 Mark Martin Valvoline	16.00	25.00
23 Chad Little John Deere	20.00	40.00
29 Steve Grissom Cartoon Network	15.00	30.00
32 Dale Jarrett Band-Aid	30.00	60.00
47 Jeff Fuller Sunoco	16.00	25.00
51 Chuck Bown Lucks	10.00	25.00
94 Bill Elliott McDonald's	16.00	25.00
94 Bill Elliott McDonald's Monopoly	15.00	30.00

1996 Racing Champions Premier Banks 1:24

These 1:24 scale banks were distributed with the chrome banks through hobby outlets.

	EX	NM-MT
2 Rusty Wallace Penske	20.00	40.00
2 Rusty Wallace Penske Chrome/166	75.00	150.00
4 Sterling Marlin Kodak	20.00	50.00
4 Sterling Marlin Kodak Chrome/166	60.00	120.00
5 Terry Labonte Kellogg's	20.00	40.00
5 Terry Labonte Kellogg's Silver Chrome/166	200.00	400.00
6 Mark Martin Valvoline	20.00	40.00
6 Mark Martin Valvoline Chrome/166	175.00	350.00
10 Ricky Rudd Tide	20.00	40.00
10 Ricky Rudd Tide Chrome/166	60.00	120.00
11 Brett Bodine Lowe's 50th Anniversary	12.00	35.00
17 Darrell Waltrip Parts America	20.00	40.00
17 Darrell Waltrip Parts America Chrome/166	60.00	120.00
18 Bobby Labonte Interstate Batteries/1826	20.00	40.00
18 Bobby Labonte Interstate Batteries Chrome/166	60.00	120.00
24 Jeff Gordon DuPont/1830	25.00	50.00
24 Jeff Gordon DuPont Chrome/166	1000.00	1400.00
25 Ken Schrader Bud Olympic	25.00	50.00
25 Ken Schrader Bud Chrome/166	75.00	150.00
29 Steve Grissom Cartoon Network	20.00	40.00
29 Steve Grissom Cartoon Network Chrome/166	60.00	120.00
29 No Driver Association Scooby-Doo	20.00	40.00
29 No Driver Association Scooby-Doo Chrome/166	60.00	120.00
37 John Andretti K-Mart	20.00	40.00
37 John Andretti K-Mart Chrome/166	60.00	120.00
88 Dale Jarrett Quality Care	20.00	40.00
88 Dale Jarrett Quality Care Chrome/166	75.00	150.00
94 Bill Elliott McDonald's	20.00	40.00
94 Bill Elliott McDonald's Chrome/166	75.00	150.00
96 David Green Busch	15.00	40.00
96 David Green Busch Chrome/166	60.00	120.00

1996 Racing Champions Premier Hood Open 1:24

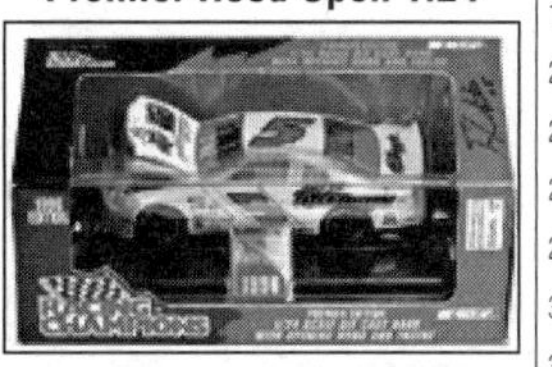

	EX	NM-MT
1 Rick Mast Hooter's	18.00	30.00
2 Ricky Craven DuPont	15.00	25.00
2 Rusty Wallace Miller Genuine Draft	25.00	40.00
5 Terry Labonte Bayer	30.00	60.00
5 Terry Labonte Kellogg's	25.00	35.00
5 Terry Labonte Kellogg's Silver Ironman	20.00	40.00
6 Mark Martin Valvoline	25.00	35.00
9 Joe Bessey Delco Remy	15.00	25.00
11 Brett Bodine Lowe's	10.00	25.00
11 Brett Bodine Lowe's 50th Anniversary Paint Scheme	8.00	20.00
15 Wally Dallenbach Hayes Modems	20.00	35.00
21 Michael Waltrip Citgo	15.00	30.00
23 Chad Little John Deere	15.00	40.00
24 Jeff Gordon DuPont 1995 Champion	30.00	60.00
28 Ernie Irvan Havoline	15.00	30.00
29 Steve Grissom Cartoon Network	12.50	25.00
29 Steve Grissom WCW	12.50	30.00
30 Johnny Benson Pennzoil	25.00	45.00
31 Mike Skinner Realtree	60.00	90.00
47 Jeff Fuller Sunoco	15.00	25.00
51 Jim Bown Lucks	15.00	25.00
52 Ken Schrader AC Delco	15.00	25.00
57 Jason Keller Slim Jim	15.00	30.00
60 Mark Martin Winn Dixie	25.00	35.00
74 Johnny Benson Lipton Tea 1995 BGN Champion	15.00	30.00
75 Morgan Shepherd Remington	20.00	35.00
88 Dale Jarrett Quality Care	15.00	30.00
94 Bill Elliott McDonald's	15.00	30.00
94 Bill Elliott McDonald's Monopoly	15.00	30.00
96 David Green Busch/1859	10.00	25.00

1996 Racing Champions Hood Open Banks 1:24

These 1:24 scale banks have open hood and were distributed through hobby and retail outlets.

	EX	NM-MT
2 Rusty Wallace Miller Genuine Draft	20.00	35.00
5 Terry Labonte Kellogg's Silver	20.00	35.00
21 Michael Waltrip Citgo	20.00	35.00
23 Chad Little John Deere	20.00	50.00
25 Ken Schrader Budweiser	20.00	35.00
57 Steve Seligman Matco Tools/5000	20.00	40.00
60 Mark Martin Winn Dixie Promo/10,000	25.00	40.00
75 Morgan Shepherd Remington	20.00	35.00
88 Dale Jarrett Quality Care	20.00	35.00
94 Bill Elliott McDonald's Monopoly	20.00	35.00

1996 Racing Champions SuperTrucks 1:24

Racing Champions continued their line of 1:24 SuperTrucks in 1996. This series features many of the circuit's first-time drivers.

	EX	NM-MT
2 Mike Bliss ASE	10.00	20.00
2 Mike Bliss Super Wheels	10.00	20.00
3 Mike Skinner Goodwrench Premier	12.50	25.00
3 Mike Skinner Goodwrench Snap-On Promo/10,000	10.00	25.00
6 Rick Carelli Chesrown	10.00	20.00
7 Geoff Bodine QVC	10.00	20.00
14 Butch Gilliland Stropps	10.00	20.00
17 Bill Sedgwick Die Hard	10.00	20.00
19 Lance Norick Macklenburg-Duncan	10.00	20.00
20 Walker Evans Dana	10.00	20.00
21 Doug George Ortho	10.00	20.00
24 Jack Sprague Quaker State	10.00	20.00
29 Bob Keselowski Winnebago	10.00	20.00
30 Jimmy Hensley Mopar	10.00	20.00
34 Bob Brevak Concor	10.00	20.00
43 Rich Bickle Cummins	10.00	20.00
44 Bryan Refner 1-800-Collect	10.00	20.00
52 Ken Schrader AC Delco	10.00	20.00
57 Robbie Pyle Aisyn	10.00	20.00
75 Bobby Gill Spears	10.00	20.00
78 Mike Chase Petron Plus	10.00	20.00
83 Steve Portenga Coffee Critic	10.00	20.00
96 DeVilbiss Superfinish 200 Promo	15.00	30.00
98 Butch Miller Raybestos	10.00	20.00

1997 Racing Champions Preview 1:24

This series of 1:24 die cast replicas featured a preview at some of the new paint jobs to run in the 1997 season. The Rick Mast Remington car and the Robert Pressley Scooby Doo car features two of the numerous driver changes for the 97 Winston Cup season.

	EX	NM-MT
4 Sterling Marlin Kodak	8.00	18.00
5 Terry Labonte Kellogg's	8.00	18.00
6 Mark Martin Valvoline	8.00	18.00
10 Ricky Rudd Tide	7.50	15.00
18 Bobby Labonte Interstate Batteries	8.00	18.00
21 Michael Waltrip Citgo	7.50	15.00
24 Jeff Gordon DuPont	10.00	20.00
28 Ernie Irvan Havoline	7.50	15.00
29 Robert Pressley Scooby-Doo	7.50	15.00
30 Johnny Benson Pennzoil	7.50	15.00
75 Rick Mast Remington	7.50	15.00
94 Bill Elliott McDonald's	8.00	18.00

1997 Racing Champions 1:24

The 1:24 scale cars that appear in this series are replicas of many of the cars that ran in the 1996 season. The series is highlighted by the Terry Labonte Kellogg's car commemorating his 1996 Winston Cup Championship. This car is available in two variations: standard and hood open. The Lake Speed University of Nebraska car is believed to be in short supply because of the dissolved team sponsorship. It is also believed to be available in a red tampo and black tampo version.

	EX	NM-MT
1 Hermie Sadler	7.50	15.00

	EX	NM-MT
DeWalt		
1 Morgan Shepherd Delco Remy Crusin' America	7.50	15.00
1 Morgan Shepherd R&L Carriers	7.50	15.00
2 Ricky Craven Raybestos	7.50	15.00
2 Rusty Wallace Penske	7.50	15.00
4 Sterling Marlin Kodak	8.00	20.00
5 Terry Labonte Bayer	15.00	25.00
5 Terry Labonte Kellogg's	8.00	20.00
5 Terry Labonte Kellogg's 1996 Champion Premier/9996	15.00	25.00
5 Terry Labonte Kellogg's 1996 Champion Hood Open	25.00	40.00
5 Terry Labonte Kellogg's 1996 Champion Bank	30.00	45.00
5 Terry Labonte Kellogg's '96 Champion Chrome Bank/166	250.00	400.00
5 Terry Labonte Kellogg's Tony	15.00	30.00
6 Tommy Houston Suburban Propane	7.50	15.00
6 Mark Martin Valvoline	8.00	20.00
7 Geoff Bodine QVC	7.50	15.00
7 Geoff Bodine QVC Gold Rush	10.00	25.00
8 Hut Stricklin Circuit City	7.50	15.00
9 Lake Speed University of Nebraska	40.00	80.00
9 Joe Bessey Power Team	7.50	15.00
9 Jeff Burton Track Gear	7.50	15.00
10 Phil Parsons Channellock	7.50	15.00
10 Ricky Rudd Tide	7.50	15.00
10 Ricky Rudd Tide Brickyard Win/2800 in solid box	30.00	50.00
11 Brett Bodine Close Call	7.50	15.00
11 Jimmy Foster Speedvision	7.50	15.00
16 Ted Musgrave Primestar	7.50	15.00
17 Darrell Waltrip Parts America	8.00	18.00
17 Darrell Waltrip Parts America Chrome	12.50	25.00
17 Darrell Waltrip Parts America Chrome Promo	15.00	25.00
18 Bobby Labonte Interstate Batt.	7.50	15.00
19 Gary Bradberry CSR	7.50	15.00
21 Michael Waltrip Citgo	7.50	15.00
24 Jeff Gordon DuPont	12.50	25.00
25 Ricky Craven Bud Lizard	15.00	30.00
25 Ricky Craven Bud Lizard 3-car set	50.00	75.00
25 Ricky Craven Hendrick	7.50	15.00
28 Ernie Irvan Havoline	7.50	15.00
28 Ernie Irvan Havoline 10th Anniversary Promo in solid box	15.00	30.00
28 Ernie Irvan Havoline 10th Anniversary Promo in window box	15.00	30.00
28 Ernie Irvan Havoline 10th Anniv.Chrome	125.00	250.00
28 Ernie Irvan Havoline 10th Anniversary Bank	25.00	40.00
28 Ernie Irvan Havoline 10th Anniversary Texaco Marketing Consultant Promo Bank/144	50.00	100.00
29 Jeff Green Tom and Jerry	7.50	15.00
29 Robert Pressley Cartoon Network	7.50	15.00
29 Elliott Sadler Phillips 66	12.50	25.00
30 Johnny Benson Pennzoil	7.50	15.00
32 Dale Jarrett White Rain	8.00	20.00
32 Dale Jarrett Gillette	8.00	20.00
33 Ken Schrader Petree Racing	7.50	15.00
34 Mike McLaughlin Royal Oak	7.50	15.00
36 Todd Bodine Stanley Tools	7.50	15.00
36 Derrike Cope Skittles	7.50	15.00
37 Jeremy Mayfield K-Mart	7.50	15.00
38 Elton Sawyer Barbasol	7.50	15.00
40 Robby Gordon Sabco Racing	7.50	15.00
41 Steve Grissom Larry Hedrick Racing	7.50	15.00
42 Joe Nemechek Bell South	7.50	15.00
46 Wally Dallenbach First Union	7.50	15.00
47 Jeff Fuller Sunoco	7.50	15.00
49 Kyle Petty nWo	15.00	30.00
57 Jason Keller Slim Jim	7.50	15.00
60 Mark Martin Winn Dixie Promo	15.00	35.00
72 Mike Dillon Detroit Gasket	7.50	15.00
74 Randy LaJoie Fina	7.50	15.00
74 Randy LaJoie Fina 1996 Busch Champion	15.00	30.00
75 Rick Mast Remington	7.50	15.00
75 Rick Mast Remington Camo	7.50	15.00
75 Rick Mast Remington Stren	7.50	15.00
87 Joe Nemechek Bell South	7.50	15.00
88 Kevin Lepage Hype	7.50	15.00
90 Dick Trickle Heilig-Meyers	7.50	15.00
91 Mike Wallace Spam	7.50	15.00
94 Bill Elliott McDonald's	8.00	18.00
94 Ron Barfield New Holland	7.50	15.00
94 Bill Elliott Mac Tonight	8.00	18.00
94 Bill Elliott Mac Tonight Bank	35.00	50.00
94 Bill Elliott Mac Tonight 3-car set	50.00	80.00
96 David Green Caterpillar	7.50	15.00
96 David Green Caterpillar Bank	20.00	40.00
96 David Green Caterpillar Promo	8.00	20.00
97 Donnie Allison Auto Value Promo	6.00	15.00
97 Chad Little John Deere	7.50	15.00
97 Chad Little John Deere Promo	12.50	30.00
97 No Driver Association Brickyard 500	12.00	20.00
99 Glenn Allen Luxaire	7.50	15.00
99 Jeff Burton Exide	7.50	15.00
00 Buckshot Jones Aqua Fresh Promo/1250	7.50	15.00

1997 Racing Champions Premier Banks 1:24

These 1:24 scale banks were distributed through hobby outlets.

	EX	NM-MT
2 Rusty Wallace Miller Lite/1992	20.00	40.00
2 Rusty Wallace Miller Lite Gold/166	100.00	200.00
6 Mark Martin Valvoline	20.00	40.00
6 Mark Martin Valvoline Gold/166	100.00	200.00
10 Ricky Rudd Tide/1992	20.00	40.00
10 Ricky Rudd Tide Gold/166	50.00	120.00
18 Bobby Labonte Interstate Batteries/4992	20.00	40.00
18 Bobby Labonte Interstate Batteries Gold/166	75.00	150.00
36 Derrike Cope Skittles	15.00	40.00
36 Derrike Cope Skittles Gold/166	40.00	100.00
40 Robby Gordon Coors Light	15.00	40.00
40 Robby Gordon Coors Light Gold/166	30.00	80.00
75 Rick Mast Remington	20.00	40.00
75 Rick Mast Remington Gold/166	40.00	100.00
94 Bill Elliott McDonald's	20.00	40.00
94 Bill Elliott McDonald's Gold/166	50.00	120.00

1997 Racing Champions Hood Open Banks 1:24

These 1:24 scale banks were distributed through retail outlets. Each car features an opening hood and was individually serial numbered.

	EX	NM-MT
2 Rusty Wallace Miller Lite Matco	35.00	60.00
2 Rusty Wallace Miller Lite Matco Chrome	75.00	150.00
5 Terry Labonte Kellogg's/4992	20.00	35.00
6 Mark Martin Valvoline/4992	20.00	35.00
10 Ricky Rudd Tide/4992	15.00	30.00
28 Ernie Irvan Havoline/4992	20.00	35.00
29 Robert Pressley Scooby-Doo/4992	15.00	30.00
36 Derrike Cope Skittles/4992	15.00	30.00
60 Mark Martin Winn Dixie Promo/5000	25.00	40.00
75 Rick Mast Remington/4992	15.00	30.00
94 Bill Elliott McDonald's/4992	20.00	35.00
96 David Green Caterpillar/4992	15.00	30.00
97 Chad Little John Deere/4992	15.00	30.00

1997 Racing Champions Stock Rods 1:24

These 1:24 scale cars are replicas of vintage stock rods with NASCAR paint schemes. Cars are listed by issue number instead of car number.

	EX	NM-MT
1 Darrell Waltrip Parts America	8.00	20.00
2 Sterling Marlin Kodak	8.00	20.00
3 Steve Grissom Larry Hedrick Racing	8.00	20.00
4 Ken Schrader Petree	8.00	20.00
5 Dennis Setzer Lance	8.00	20.00
6 Ricky Craven Hendrick	8.00	20.00
7 Ricky Rudd Tide	8.00	20.00
8 Rusty Wallace Penske	8.00	20.00
9 Rick Mast Remington	8.00	20.00
10 Terry Labonte Spooky Loops	25.00	40.00
11 Bill Elliott Mac Tonight	10.00	25.00
12 Bobby Hamilton Kodak	8.00	20.00
13 Terry Labonte Spooky Loops	10.00	25.00
14 Terry Labonte Kellogg's	10.00	25.00

1997 Racing Champions SuperTrucks 1:24

Racing Champions continued their line of 1:24 SuperTrucks in 1997. This series features many of the circuit's first-time drivers and Winston Cup regulars.

	EX	NM-MT
1 Michael Waltrip MW Windows	10.00	20.00
2 Mike Bliss Team ASE	6.00	15.00
4 Bill Elliott Team ASE	7.50	15.00
6 Rick Carelli ReMax	6.00	15.00
7 Tammy Kirk Loveable	6.00	15.00
15 Mike Cope Penrose	6.00	15.00
15 Mike Colabucci VISA	6.00	15.00
18 Johnny Benson Pennzoil	6.00	15.00
18 Mark Dokken Dana	6.00	15.00
19 Tony Raines Pennzoil	6.00	15.00
24 Jack Sprague Quaker State	6.00	15.00
29 Bob Keselowski Mopar	6.00	15.00
35 Dave Rezendes Ortho	6.00	15.00
49 Rodney Combs Lance	6.00	15.00
52 Tobey Butler Purolator	6.00	15.00
66 Bryan Refner Carlin	6.00	15.00
75 Dan Press Spears	6.00	15.00
80 Joe Ruttman LCI	6.00	15.00
86 Stacy Compton Valvoline	6.00	15.00
87 Joe Nemechek Bell South	6.00	15.00
92 Mark Kinser Rotary	6.00	15.00
98 Kenny Irwin Raybestos	10.00	25.00
99 Chuck Bown Exide	6.00	15.00
99 Jeff Burton Exide	6.00	15.00
99 Mark Martin Exide	100.00	175.00

1998 Racing Champions 1:24

The 1:24 scale cars that appear in this series are replicas of many of the cars that ran in the 1998 season. The Mark Martin Kosei car is one of the cars that highlights this series.

	EX	NM-MT
1 Little Debbie Promo/5000	20.00	40.00
4 Bobby Hamilton Kodak	7.50	15.00
5 Terry Labonte Blasted Fruit Loops	10.00	20.00
5 Terry Labonte Kellogg's	10.00	20.00
5 Terry Labonte Kellogg's Corny	10.00	20.00
5 Terry Labonte Kellogg's Corny Bank Promo	10.00	20.00
6 Joe Bessey Power Team	7.50	15.00
6 Mark Martin Eagle One	15.00	30.00
6 Mark Martin Kosei Promo/2500	125.00	200.00
6 Mark Martin Synpower	15.00	30.00
6 Mark Martin Valvoline	10.00	25.00
6 Mark Martin 3-car set/5000 Eagle One/Synpower/Valvoline	30.00	60.00
7 Geoff Bodine Phillips	10.00	25.00
8 Bobby Hillin Jr. Clean Shower Mac Attack Promo/10,000	12.50	25.00
8 Hut Stricklin Circuit City	7.50	15.00
9 Jeff Burton Track Gear	7.50	15.00
9 Lake Speed Birthday Cake	7.50	15.00
9 Lake Speed Huckleberry Hound	7.50	15.00
10 Ricky Rudd Tide	7.50	15.00
10 Ricky Rudd Tide Give Kids The World	7.50	15.00
11 Brett Bodine Paychex	7.50	15.00
13 Ted Christopher Whelen Promo	25.00	40.00
13 Jerry Nadeau First Plus	12.50	25.00
16 Ted Musgrave Primestar	7.50	15.00
17 Matt Kenseth Lycos	35.00	60.00
17 Darrell Waltrip Builders' Square	20.00	50.00
19 Tom Hubert Bradford White Water Heaters Promo	35.00	60.00
19 Tony Raines Yellow Freight Promo	15.00	40.00
20 Blaise Alexander Rescue Engine	12.50	30.00
20 Jimmy Spencer All Pro Stores Promo	25.00	50.00
21 Michael Waltrip Citgo	7.50	15.00
23 Jimmy Spencer No Bull in plastic case	40.00	100.00
26 Johnny Benson Betty Crocker	15.00	30.00
26 Johnny Benson Cheerios	10.00	20.00
28 Kenny Irwin Havoline	20.00	35.00
28 Kenny Irwin Havoline Bank Promo	10.00	25.00
29 Hermie Sadler DeWalt	7.50	15.00
30 Derrike Cope Gumout	7.50	15.00
30 Mike Cope Slim Jim	7.50	15.00
33 Tim Fedewa Kleenex Promo	7.50	15.00
33 Ken Schrader Petree	7.50	15.00
35 Todd Bodine Tabasco	10.00	20.00
36 Ernie Irvan M&M's	10.00	25.00
36 Ernie Irvan Skittles	8.00	18.00
36 Ernie Irvan Wildberry Skittles	7.50	15.00
40 Andy Belmont AOL Promo	30.00	50.00
40 Sterling Marlin Sabco	7.50	15.00
41 Steve Grissom Larry Hedrick Racing	7.50	15.00
42 Joe Nemechek BellSouth	7.50	15.00
43 John Andretti STP Firefighters Promo 2-car set w/gold car/4343	15.00	40.00
46 Wally Dallenbach First Union	7.50	15.00
46 Deka Batteries Promo	15.00	30.00
50 NDA Budweiser Promo	12.50	25
50 Ricky Craven Hendrick	7.50	15
50 NASCAR 50th Anniversary	7.50	15
50 NDA Dr. Pepper	7.50	15
59 Robert Pressley Kingsford	7.50	15
60 Mark Martin Winn Dixie Most BGN Wins Promo/5000	40.00	75
64 Dick Trickle Schneider	25.00	50
66 Elliott Sadler Phillips 66	7.50	15
72 Mike Dillon Detroit Gasket	7.50	15
75 Rick Mast Remington	7.50	15
78 Gary Bradberry Pilot	7.50	15
84 North American Insurance Promo/2004	30.00	50
87 Joe Nemechek Bell South	7.50	15
88 Kevin Schwantz Ryder	7.50	15
90 Dick Trickle Heilig-Meyers	7.50	15
91 Dick Trickle Invinca-Shield Promo	10.00	20
94 Bill Elliott Big Mac/5000	40.00	100
94 Bill Elliott Happy Meal	7.50	15
94 Bill Elliott Mac Tonight	7.50	15
94 Bill Elliott McDonald's	7.50	15
94 Bill Elliott McDonald's with NASCAR 50th Anniv.logo on hood	7.50	15
96 David Green Caterpiller	7.50	15
96 David Green Caterpillar Promo	10.00	25
98 Rich Bickle Thorn Apple Valley	7.50	15
98 Marathon Oil Promo/5000	10.00	25
98 Greg Sacks Thorn Apple Valley	7.50	15
99 Glenn Allen Luxaire	7.50	15
99 Jeff Burton Exide	7.50	15
300 Darrell Waltrip { Tim Flock Special	7.50	15
00 Buckshot Jones Bayer	7.50	15

1998 Racing Champions Authentics 1:24

These 1:24 scale cars mark the first in a series by [Racing] Champions. These cars and banks were distributed th[rough] hobby and trackside outlets. Each car is packaged in a [...] black snap case.

	EX	NM
6 Mark Martin Eagle One/7100	25.00	6
6 Mark Martin Eagle One Bank	25.00	6
6 Mark Martin Synpower/7000	25.00	6
6 Mark Martin Synpower Mac Tools/4000	25.00	6
6 Mark Martin Synpower Bank/2500	25.00	6
6 Mark Martin Valvoline/7000	25.00	6
6 Mark Martin Valvoline Bank	25.00	6
16 Kevin Lepage Primestar/3100	15.00	4
16 Kevin Lepage Primestar Bank/1400	15.00	4
26 Johnny Benson Betty Crocker/4500	20.00	5
26 Johnny Benson Betty Crocker Bank/1700	15.00	4
26 Johnny Benson Cheerios/4500	15.00	4
26 Johnny Benson Cheerios Bank/1700	15.00	4
26 Johnny Benson Trix/4600	20.00	5
26 Johnny Benson Trix Bank	25.00	6
97 Chad Little John Deere/4000	25.00	6
97 Chad Little John Deere Bank/1700	20.00	5
99 Jeff Burton Bruce Lee	25.00	6
99 Jeff Burton Bruce Lee Bank/500	60.00	12
99 Jeff Burton Exide/4300	25.00	6
99 Jeff Burton Exide Bank	40.00	8

1998 Racing Champions Driver's Choice Banks 1:2

These 1:24 scale banks were distributed through tracks[ide and] hobby outlets.

	EX	NM
5 Terry Labonte Kellogg's	30.00	5
6 Mark Martin Valvoline	30.00	5
10 Ricky Rudd Tide	30.00	4
94 Bill Elliott McDonald's	30.00	5

998 Racing Champions Gold 1:24

s is a special series produced by Racing Champions to brate NASCAR's 50th anniversary. Each car or bank was ed in gold chrome and the numbered versions contained the al number on its chassis. Some cars were also issued in red low boxes or white solid boxes which were not not serial bered. Unless noted below, the cars were packaged in a d Racing Champions window box that included the duction run notation of 2500 cars produced.

	EX	NM-MT
on Barfield New Holland	10.00	25.00
obby Hamilton Kodak	10.00	25.00
erry Labonte Blasted Fruit Loops	12.00	30.00
erry Labonte Kellogg's	12.00	30.00
erry Labonte Kellogg's Corny	12.00	30.00
oe Bessey Power Team	10.00	25.00
ark Martin Eagle One	12.00	30.00
ark Martin Syntec	12.00	30.00
ark Martin Valvoline	12.00	30.00
ark Martin Valvoline Bank	15.00	40.00
ut Stricklin Circuit City	10.00	25.00
ff Burton Track Gear	10.00	25.00
erry Nadeau Zombie Island	10.00	25.00
ake Speed Huckleberry Hound	10.00	25.00
ake Speed Birthday Cake	10.00	25.00
ake Speed Huckleberry Hound Bank	10.00	25.00
Phil Parsons Duralube	10.00	25.00
Ricky Rudd Tide	10.00	25.00
Ricky Rudd Tide Bank	10.00	25.00
Brett Bodine Paychex	10.00	25.00
Brett Bodine Paychex	10.00	25.00
Jerry Nadeau First Plus	10.00	25.00
Patty Moise Rhodes	10.00	25.00
ed Musgrave Primestar	10.00	25.00
Matt Kenseth Lycos	60.00	100.00
Darrell Waltrip HQ Builders' Square	10.00	25.00
ony Raines Yellow Freight	10.00	25.00
Blaise Alexander Rescue Engine	10.00	25.00
Michael Waltrip Citgo	10.00	25.00
Michael Waltrip Citgo Bank	10.00	25.00
ance Hooper WCW	10.00	25.00
Jimmy Spencer No Bull	90.00	150.00
Johnny Benson Cheerios	10.00	25.00
Johnny Benson Cheerios Bank	10.00	25.00
Kenny Irwin Havoline Mac Tools	50.00	100.00
Hermie Sadler DeWalt	10.00	25.00
Derrike Cope Gumout	10.00	25.00
Mike Cope Slim Jim	10.00	25.00
im Fedewa Kleenex	10.00	25.00
Ken Schrader Petree	10.00	25.00
Mike McLaughlin Goulds	10.00	25.00
Todd Bodine Tabasco	10.00	25.00
Matt Hutter Stanley	10.00	25.00
Ernie Irvan M&M's	12.00	30.00
Ernie Irvan Skittles	10.00	25.00
Ernie Irvan Wildberry Skittles	12.00	30.00
Rick Fuller Channellock	10.00	25.00
Kevin Lepage Channellock	10.00	25.00
Sterling Marlin Sabco	12.00	30.00
Steve Grissom Larry Hedrick Racing	10.00	25.00
Joe Nemechek BellSouth	10.00	25.00
Wally Dallenbach First Union	10.00	25.00
47 Andy Santerie Monroe	10.00	25.00
50 Ricky Craven Hendrick	10.00	25.00
50 No Driver Association 50th Anniversary	10.00	25.00
59 Robert Pressley Kingsford	10.00	25.00
60 Mark Martin Winn Dixie	12.00	30.00
64 Dick Trickle Schneider	10.00	25.00
66 Eliott Sadler Phillips 66	10.00	25.00
72 Mike Dillon Detroit Gasket	10.00	25.00
74 Randy LaJoie Fina	10.00	25.00
75 Rick Mast Remington	10.00	25.00
77 Robert Pressley Jasper	10.00	25.00
78 Gary Bradberry Pilot	10.00	25.00
87 Joe Nemechek BellSouth	10.00	25.00
88 Kevin Schwantz Ryder	10.00	25.00
90 Dick Trickle Helig-Meyers	10.00	25.00
94 Bill Elliott Big Mac/4998	12.00	30.00
94 Bill Elliott Happy Meal	12.00	30.00
94 Bill Elliott Mac Tonight with Super 8 logo on side	10.00	25.00
94 Bill Elliott McDonald's/5000	12.00	30.00
94 Bill Elliott McDonald's Bank	12.00	30.00
94 Bill Elliott McDonald's with NASCAR 50th Anniv.logo on hood	12.00	30.00
96 David Green Caterpiller	10.00	25.00
97 Chad Little John Deere P	50.00	100.00
98 Rich Bickle Go Grill Crazy	10.00	25.00
98 Greg Sacks Thorn Apple Valley	10.00	25.00
99 Glen Allen Luxaire	10.00	25.00
99 Jeff Burton Exide	10.00	25.00
99 Jeff Burton Exide Bank	10.00	25.00
300 Darrell Waltrip Flock Special	12.00	30.00
400 No Driver Association Brickyard 400	10.00	25.00
00 Buckshot Jones Alka Seltzer	10.00	25.00
00 Buckshot Jones Aqua Fresh	10.00	25.00
00 Buckshot Jones Bayer	10.00	25.00

1998 Racing Champions Gold Hood Open 1:24

This is a special series produced by Racing Champions to celebrate NASCAR's 50th anniversary. The cars all have opening hoods and were issued in red window boxes unless noted below. Each car or bank was plated in gold chrome.

	EX	NM-MT
4 Bobby Hamilton Kodak	12.00	30.00
5 Terry Labonte Blasted Fruit Loops	15.00	40.00
5 Terry Labonte Blasted Froot Loops Bank	15.00	40.00
5 Terry Labonte Kellogg's	15.00	40.00
5 Terry Labonte Kellogg's Corny	15.00	40.00
5 Terry Labonte Kellogg's Corny Bank/1998 in gold box	15.00	40.00
6 Joe Bessey Power Team	12.00	30.00
6 Mark Martin Eagle One Bank	15.00	40.00
6 Mark Martin Synpower	15.00	40.00
6 Mark Martin Synpower Bank	15.00	40.00
6 Mark Martin Valvoline	15.00	40.00
6 Mark Martin Valvoline Bank	15.00	40.00
8 Hut Stricklin Circuit City	12.00	30.00
9 Lake Speed Huckleberry Hound	12.00	30.00
10 Ricky Rudd Tide	12.00	30.00
10 Ricky Rudd Tide Bank	12.00	30.00
11 Brett Bodine Paychex	12.00	30.00
16 Ted Musgrave Primestar	12.00	30.00
17 Darrell Waltrip Builders' Square	15.00	40.00
19 Tony Raines Yellow Freight	12.00	30.00
21 Michael Waltrip Goodwill Games	12.00	30.00
30 Derrike Cope Gumout	12.00	30.00
33 Ken Schrader Petree	12.00	30.00
35 Todd Bodine Tabasco	12.00	30.00
36 Ernie Irvan M&M's Bank	12.00	30.00
36 Ernie Irvan Skittles	12.00	30.00
36 Ernie Irvan Skittles Bank	12.00	30.00
36 Ernie Irvan Wildberry Skittles	12.00	30.00
36 Ernie Irvan Wildberry Skittles Bank	12.00	30.00
40 Sterling Marlin Sabco	15.00	40.00
50 Ricky Craven Hendrick	12.00	30.00
50 50th Anniversary Chevy/5000	12.00	30.00
50 50th Anniversary Ford/5000	12.00	30.00
50 50th Anniversary Pontiac/5000	12.00	30.00
77 Robert Pressley Jasper	12.00	30.00
78 Gary Bradberry Pilot	12.00	30.00
90 Dick Trickle Heilig-Meyers	12.00	30.00
94 Bill Elliott Big Mac white box	10.00	25.00
94 Bill Elliott Happy Meal gold box/1998	15.00	40.00
94 Bill Elliott Happy Meal Bank	15.00	40.00
94 Bill Elliott Mac Tonight red box with New Holland logo on side	10.00	25.00
94 Bill Elliott Mac Tonight white box with Super 8 logo on side	10.00	25.00
94 Bill Elliott Mac Tonight white box with New Holland logo on side	10.00	25.00
94 Bill Elliott McDonald's red box	15.00	40.00
94 Bill Elliott McDonald's white box New Holland logo on side	10.00	25.00
94 Bill Elliott McDonald's with NASCAR 50th Anniv.logo on hood	15.00	40.00
98 Greg Sacks Thorn Apple Valley	12.00	30.00
99 Jeff Burton Exide	12.00	30.00
99 Jeff Burton Exide Bank	12.00	30.00
400 No Driver Association Brickyard 400	12.00	30.00

1998 Racing Champions Gold NASCAR Fans Hood Open 1:24

Each car in this special series was produced by Racing Champions and packaged in a gold "NASCAR Fans" window box. The cars all have opening hoods and were plated in gold chrome. The stated production run was 1998 of each car.

	EX	NM-MT
5 Terry Labonte Kellogg's Corny green roof	15.00	40.00
5 Terry Labonte Kellogg's Corny white hood	15.00	40.00
6 Mark Martin Valvoline Synpower	15.00	40.00
40 Sterling Marlin Sabco	15.00	40.00
98 Greg Sacks Thorn Apple Valley	12.00	30.00

1998 Racing Champions 24K Gold 1:24

This is a special series produced by Racing Champions to celebrate NASCAR's 50th anniversary. Each was packaged in a black and gold window box with the notation "Reflections in Gold 24K Gold" on the front. Each car was limited to a production run of 4998 and was produced in an all-gold plated finish. Each also included a serial number on its chassis.

	EX	NM-MT
4 Bobby Hamilton Kodak	12.50	25.00
5 Terry Labonte Kellogg's Corny	25.00	50.00
6 Joe Bessey Power Team	12.50	25.00
6 Mark Martin Eagle One	25.00	60.00
6 Mark Martin Valvoline	25.00	60.00
8 Hut Stricklin Circuit City	12.50	25.00
9 Lake Speed Huckleberry Hound	12.50	25.00
10 Phil Parsons Duralube	12.50	25.00
10 Ricky Rudd Tide	12.50	25.00
11 Brett Bodine Paychex	12.50	25.00
13 Jerry Nadeau First Plus	25.00	50.00
16 Ted Musgrave Primestar	12.50	25.00
20 BlaisÃ© Alexander Rescue Engine	15.00	40.00
21 Michael Waltrip Citgo	12.50	25.00
23 Lance Hooper WCW	12.50	25.00
26 Johnny Benson Cheerios	12.50	25.00
29 Hermie Sadler DeWalt	12.50	25.00
30 Derrike Cope Gumout	12.50	25.00
33 Tim Fedewa Kleenex	12.50	25.00
33 Ken Schrader Petree	12.50	25.00
34 Mike McLaughlin Goulds	12.50	25.00
35 Todd Bodine Tabasco	12.50	25.00
36 Ernie Irvan Skittles	15.00	40.00
40 Sterling Marlin Sabco	15.00	30.00
41 Steve Grissom Larry Hedrick Racing	12.50	25.00
42 Joe Nemechek Bell South	12.50	25.00
46 Wally Dallenbach First Union	12.50	25.00
47 Andy Santerie Monroe	12.50	25.00
50 Ricky Craven Budweiser	15.00	40.00
59 Robert Pressley Kingsford	12.50	25.00
60 Mark Martin Winn Dixie	25.00	50.00
63 Tracy Leslie Lysol	12.50	25.00
64 Dick Trickle Schneider	12.50	25.00
72 Mike Dillon Detroit Gasket	12.50	25.00
74 Randy LaJoie Fina	12.50	25.00
75 Rick Mast Remington	12.50	25.00
90 Dick Trickle Heilig-Meyers	12.50	25.00
94 Bill Elliott McDonald's	25.00	50.00
97 Chad Little John Deere in black case	20.00	50.00
99 Jeff Burton Exide	15.00	40.00
00 Buckshot Jones Aqua Fresh	12.50	25.00

1998 Racing Champions Race Day 1:24

	EX	NM-MT
16 Ted Musgrave Primestar	1.50	4.00
41 Steve Grissom Kodak	1.50	4.00
00 Buckshot Jones Aqua Fresh	1.50	4.00

1998 Racing Champions Signature Series 1:24

This is a special series produced by Racing Champions to celebrate NASCAR's 50th anniversary. It parallels the regular 1998 1:24 scale series. Each car is a packaged in a decorative box with the driver's facsimile autograph on the front.

	EX	NM-MT
5 Terry Labonte Kellogg's	10.00	20.00
6 Mark Martin Valvoline	10.00	20.00
9 Jeff Burton Track Gear	8.00	20.00
9 Lake Speed Huckleberry Hound	8.00	20.00
10 Phil Parsons Duralube	8.00	20.00
10 Ricky Rudd Tide	8.00	20.00
11 Brett Bodine Paychex	8.00	20.00
13 Jerry Nadeau First Plus	8.00	20.00
16 Ted Musgrave Primestar	8.00	20.00
26 Johnny Benson Cheerios	8.00	20.00
30 Derrike Cope Gumout	8.00	20.00
33 Ken Schrader Petree	8.00	20.00
35 Todd Bodine Tabasco	8.00	20.00
36 Ernie Irvan Skittles	8.00	20.00
50 Ricky Craven Hendrick	8.00	20.00
75 Rick Mast Remington	8.00	20.00
94 Bill Elliott McDonald's	10.00	20.00
98 Greg Sacks Thorn Apple Valley	8.00	20.00

1998 Racing Champions Stock Rods 1:24

These 1:24 scale cars are replicas of vintage stock rods with NASCAR paint schemes. Cars are listed by issue number instead of car number.

	EX	NM-MT
15 Jeff Green Cartoon Network	6.00	15.00
16 Kevin Schwantz Ryder	6.00	15.00
17 Glen Allen Luxaire	6.00	15.00
18 Jeff Burton Exide	6.00	15.00
19 Michael Waltrip Citgo	6.00	15.00
20 Robert Pressley Kingsford	6.00	15.00
21 Kevin Schwantz Ryder	6.00	15.00
22 Ken Schrader Petree	6.00	15.00
23 Dick Trickle Heilig-Meyers	6.00	15.00
24 Joe Bessey Power Team	6.00	15.00
25 Glen Allen Luxaire	6.00	15.00
26 Jerry Nadeau First Plus	6.00	15.00
27 Hut Stricklin Circuit City	6.00	15.00
28 Terry Labonte Kellogg's	8.00	20.00
29 Wally Dallenbach First Union	6.00	15.00
30 Joe Nemechek BellSouth	6.00	15.00
31 Robert Pressley Kingsford	6.00	15.00
32 Hut Stricklin Circuit City	6.00	15.00
33 Elliot Sadler Phillips 66	6.00	15.00
34 Hermie Sadler DeWalt	6.00	15.00
35 Steve Grissom Hedrick Racing Gold	8.00	20.00
36 Lake Speed Huckleberry Hound	6.00	15.00
37 Bill Elliott McDonald's Gold	15.00	40.00
38 Michael Waltrip Citgo	6.00	15.00
39 Jeff Burton Track Gear	6.00	15.00
40 Mark Martin Valvoline	8.00	20.00
41 Bill Elliott McDonald's	8.00	20.00
42 Jeff Burton Exide Gold	10.00	25.00
43 Jerry Nadeau First Plus Gold	8.00	20.00
44 Jeff Burton Exide	6.00	15.00
45 Rick Fuller Channellock	6.00	15.00
46 Ted Musgrave Primestar	6.00	15.00
47 Ricky Craven Hendrick	6.00	15.00
48 Terry Labonte Kellogg's Gold	15.00	40.00
49 Hut Stricklin Circuit City Gold	8.00	20.00
50 NDA NASCAR 50th Anniversary	6.00	15.00
51 Wally Dallenbach First Union	6.00	15.00
52 Terry Labonte Kellogg's Corny	8.00	20.00
53 Elliot Sadler Phillips 66	6.00	15.00
54 Bill Elliott McDonald's Gold	15.00	40.00
55 Steve Grissom Hedrick Racing Gold	8.00	20.00
56 Terry Labonte Kellogg's	8.00	20.00
57 Bobby Hamilton Kodak	6.00	15.00
58 Bill Elliott McDonald's Gold	15.00	40.00
59 Mark Martin Valvoline	8.00	20.00
60 Hut Stricklin Circuit City Gold	8.00	20.00
61 Ricky Rudd Tide	6.00	15.00
62 Johnny Benson Cheerios	6.00	15.00
63 Ricky Craven Hendrick Gold	10.00	25.00
64 Michael Waltrip Citgo	6.00	15.00
65 Hermie Sadler DeWalt	6.00	15.00
66 Ken Schrader Petree	6.00	15.00
67 Bill Elliott McDonald's Gold	15.00	40.00
68 Joe Nemechek Bell South Gold	8.00	20.00
69 Bill Elliott McDonald's	8.00	20.00
70 Steve Grissom Larry Hedrick Racing	6.00	15.00
71 Mark Martin Valvoline	8.00	20.00
72 Ken Schrader Petree	6.00	15.00
73 Michael Waltrip Citgo Gold	8.00	20.00

1998 Racing Champions Stock Rods 24K Gold 1:24

These 1:24 scale cars are replicas of vintage stock rods with NASCAR paint schemes and gold plating. Cars are listed by issue number instead of car number.

	EX	NM-MT
1 Bill Elliott McDonald's	20.00	40.00
2 Todd Bodine Tabasco	10.00	25.00
3 Terry Labonte Kellogg's	20.00	40.00
4 Bobby Hamilton Kodak	10.00	25.00
5 Mark Martin Valvoline	20.00	40.00
6 Jeff Burton Exide	15.00	30.00
7 Ernie Irvan Skittles	15.00	35.00
8 Ted Musgrave Primestar	10.00	25.00
9 Terry Labonte Kellogg's	20.00	40.00
10 Ken Schrader Petree	10.00	25.00
11 Dick Trickle Schneider	10.00	25.00
12 Michael Waltrip Citgo	10.00	25.00

1998 Racing Champions SuperTrucks 1:24

Racing Champions continued their line of 1:24 SuperTrucks in 1998. This series features many of the circuit's first-time drivers and Winston Cup regulars.

	EX	NM-MT
2 Mike Bliss Team ASE	8.00	20.00
6 Rick Carelli Remax	8.00	20.00
18 No Driver Association Dana	8.00	20.00
19 Tony Raines Pennzoil	8.00	20.00
29 Bob Keselowski Mopar	8.00	20.00
31 Tony Roper Concor Tools	8.00	20.00
35 Ron Barfield Ortho	8.00	20.00
44 Boris Said Federated	8.00	20.00
50 Greg Biffle Grainger	75.00	150.00
52 Mike Wallace Pure One	8.00	20.00
66 Bryan Refner Carlin	8.00	20.00
84 Wayne Anderson Porter Cable	8.00	20.00
86 Stacy Compton RC Cola	8.00	20.00
87 Joe Nemechek BellSouth	8.00	20.00
90 Lance Norick National Hockey League	8.00	20.00
94 Bill Elliott Team ASE	8.00	20.00

1998 Racing Champions SuperTrucks Gold 1:24

This is a special series produced by Racing Champions to celebrate NASCAR's 50th anniversary. It parallels the regular 1998 1:24 scale series. Each truck is a limited edition of 2,500. Each truck is also plated in gold chrome and contains a serial number on its chassis.

	EX	NM-MT
2 Mike Bliss Team ASE	10.00	25.00
6 Rick Carelli Remax	10.00	25.00
29 Bob Keselowski Mopar	10.00	25.00
50 Greg Biffle Grainger	60.00	100.00
66 Bryan Refner Carlin	10.00	25.00
86 Stacy Compton RC Cola	10.00	25.00

1999 Racing Champions 1:24

The 1:24 scale cars that appear in this series are replicas of many of the cars that ran in the 1999 season.

	EX	NM-MT
1 Iowa Hawkeyes Promo	15.00	30.00
1 Mac Tools Promo	10.00	20.00
4 Don Thomas Jr. Home Hardware Promo	35.00	60.00
4 Bobby Hamilton Kodak	7.50	15.00
4 Bobby Hamilton Kodak Advantix	7.50	15.00
5 HK Fabarm Promo	30.00	50.00
5 Terry Labonte Kellogg's	7.50	15.00
5 Terry Labonte Kellogg's Chrome/2499	20.00	50.00
5 Dick Trickle Schneider Promo	10.00	25.00
6 Mark Martin Valvoline	7.50	15.00
6 Mark Martin Valvoline Chrome/2499	25.00	60.00
6 Mark Martin Zerex	15.00	35.00
6 Mark Martin Zerex Chrome/2499	25.00	60.00
7 Michael Waltrip Philips	15.00	35.00
9 Jerry Nadeau Dexter's Laboratory	7.50	15.00
9 Jerry Nadeau WCW nWo	7.50	15.00
9 Jerry Nadeau Goldberg	12.50	25.00
10 Racing Champions Silver	10.00	25.00
10 Ricky Rudd Tide	7.50	15.00
10 Ricky Rudd Tide Peroxide	7.50	15.00
11 Brett Bodine Paychex	7.50	15.00
12 Jeremy Mayfield Mobil 1	7.50	15.00
12 Jimmy Spencer Zippo	15.00	30.00
12 Jeremy Mayfield Mobil 1 Chrome/2499	20.00	40.00
14 Rick Crawford Circle Bar Super Truck	7.50	15.00
15 Ken Schrader Oakwood Homes Promo box shaped like mobile home	15.00	30.00
16 Kevin Lepage Primestar	7.50	15.00
17 Matt Kenseth DeWalt	15.00	30.00
17 Matt Kenseth Luxaire Promo	35.00	70.00
18 Butch Miller Dana SuperTruck Promo	12.50	25.00
20 Tony Stewart Arvin Racing Promo/5000	15.00	40.00
21 Elliott Sadler Citgo	7.50	15.00
21 Elliott Sadler Citgo Chrome/2499	20.00	40.00
23 Jimmy Spencer TCE	7.50	15.00
23 Jimmy Spencer TCE Chrome/2499	20.00	50.00
24 Jack Sprague GMAC Super Truck	7.50	15.00
25 Wally Dallenbach Hendrick	7.50	15.00
26 Johnny Benson Cheerios	7.50	15.00
30 Derrike Cope Bryan Foods	7.50	15.00
30 Derrike Cope Rudy's Farm	35.00	50.00
32 Jeff Green Kleenex	7.50	15.00
33 Ken Schrader Petree	7.50	15.00
34 Mike McLaughlin Goulds Pumps	7.50	15.00
36 Ernie Irvan Crispy M&M's	12.50	25.00
36 Ernie Irvan M&M's	12.50	25.00
36 Ernie Irvan M&M's Chrome/2499	20.00	50.00
36 Ernie Irvan M&M's Promo	15.00	30.00
36 Ernie Irvan Pedigree Promo	15.00	30.00
38 Glen Allen Barbasol	7.50	15.00
40 Sterling Marlin John Wayne	15.00	40.00
40 Sterling Marlin Brooks & Dunn Promo	10.00	25.00
42 Joe Nemechek BellSouth	7.50	15.00
42 Joe Nemechek BellSouth Promo	15.00	30.00
43 John Andretti STP	7.50	15.00
44 Justin Labonte Slim Jim	7.50	15.00
44 Tery Labonte Justin Labonte Slim Jim/Penrose 2-car Promo set	12.50	25.00
45 Adam Petty Spree	30.00	60.00
45 Polaris Promo	15.00	30.00
50 Greg Biffle Grainger SuperTruck Promo	75.00	135.00
50 Mark Green Dr.Pepper	7.50	15.00
55 No Driver Association Florida Gators Promo	18.00	30.00
55 Kenny Wallace Square D	7.50	15.00
59 Mike Dillon Kingsford	7.50	15.00
60 Mark Martin Winn Dixie	15.00	35.00
60 Mark Martin Winn Dixie Beef People Promo	18.00	30.00
63 NDA/Exxon SuperFlo	25.00	40.00
66 Todd Bodine Phillips 66 Promo	10.00	25.00
66 Darrell Waltrip Big K	7.50	15.00
75 Ted Musgrave Polaris ATVs Promo	12.50	25.00
75 Ted Musgrave Remington	7.50	15.00
77 Robert Pressley Jasper	7.50	15.00
86 Stacy Compton RC Cola SuperTruck	7.50	15.00
90 Hills Bros. Nesquik Promo	20.00	35.00
94 Bill Elliott Drive Thru	8.00	20.00
94 Bill Elliott McDonald's Name Game Promo	15.00	30.00
97 Chad Little John Deere	7.50	15.00
98 Kevin Harvick Porter-Cable SuperTruck Promo	200.00	300.00
99 Auto Value Promo	15.00	30.00
99 Jeff Burton Exide	7.50	15.00
99 Jeff Burton Exide Bruce Lee	7.50	15.00
99 Snap-On Southern Thunder Promo/10,000	12.50	25.00
00 Cheez-It Promo (driven by Larry Pearson)	30.00	50.00
00 Connectiv Promo	12.50	25.00
NNO Jeg's SuperTruck Promo	15.00	30.00

1999 Racing Champions 2-Car Sets 1:24

These 1:24 scale die-cast cars were packaged together in a large Racing Champions window box. Each regular version car was issued with a silver or gold chrome version.

	EX	NM-MT
4 Bobby Hamilton Kodak Advantix	10.00	20.00
36 Ernie Irvan M&M's	10.00	20.00
94 Bill Elliott McDonald's/5000	10.00	20.00
99 Jeff Burton Bruce Lee/4000	10.00	25.00

1999 Racing Champions 2-Car Sets 1:24/1:64

	EX	NM-MT
6 Mark Martin Valvoline/9999	10.00	20.00
6 Mark Martin Zerex Chrome 3-piece set with 1:24 car, 1:64 car and 1:64 Valvoline transporter	20.00	40.00
7 Michael Waltrip Phillips Promo	10.00	20.00
40 Sterling Marlin John Wayne	20.00	40.00
50 Mark Green Dr.Pepper Chrome 3-piece set with 1:24 car, 1:64 car and 1:64 transporter	20.00	40.00
77 Robert Pressley Jasper/9999	7.50	20.00

1999 Racing Champions 3-Car Sets 1:24

	EX	NM-MT
5/6/94 Terry Labonte Kellogg's Mark Martin Valvoline Bill Elliott McDonald's	25.00	50.00

1999 Racing Champions Authentics 1:24

	EX	NM-MT
6 Mark Martin Eagle One/8500	40.00	75.00
6 Mark Martin Valvoline/8500	40.00	75.00
6 Mark Martin Zerex/8500	40.00	75.00
9 Jeff Burton Track Gear/2000	20.00	50.00
9 Jerry Nadeau Jetsons/5000	12.50	30.00
10 Ricky Rudd Tide/2500	25.00	50.00
10 Ricky Rudd Tide Peroxide/5000	20.00	50.00
16 Kevin Lepage TV Guide/2000	25.00	50.00
23 Jimmy Spencer Winston/5000 in black case	25.00	50.00
26 Johnny Benson Cheerios/2000	20.00	50.00
55 No Driver Association Florida Gators Promo/1008	30.00	50.00
60 Mark Martin Winn Dixie/2000	25.00	50.00
94 Bill Elliott McDonald's Drive Thru/7500	25.00	50.00
94 Bill Elliott McDonald's Win $1 Million/5000	30.00	80.00
97 Chad Little John Deere/3500	25.00	50.00
97 Chad Little John Deere FFA/7500	25.00	50.00
99 Jeff Burton Exide/5000	25.00	50.00

1999 Racing Champions Gold 1:24

This is a special series produced by Racing Champions to celebrate their 10th anniversary. Each car was produced in a limited edition of 4,999 and featured a gold chrome finish as well as a serial number on its chassis. A few cars were also produced in an upgraded Hood Open model that carried a production run of 1999.

	EX	NM-MT
4 Bobby Hamilton Kodak	12.50	25.00
5 Terry Labonte Kellogg's	20.00	40.00
6 Mark Martin Valvoline	20.00	40.00
9 Jerry Nadeau Dexter's Laboratory	12.50	25.00
10 Ricky Rudd Tide	12.50	25.00
11 Brett Bodine Paychex	12.50	25.00
15 Ken Schrader Oakwood Homes	12.50	25.00
25 Wally Dallenbach Hendrick	12.50	25.00
26 Johnny Benson Cheerios	12.50	25.00
33 Ken Schrader Petree	12.50	25.00
36 Ernie Irvan M&M's	15.00	30.00
45 Adam Petty Spree Hood Open/1999	40.00	75.00
55 Kenny Wallace Square D	12.50	25.00
60 Mark Martin Winn Dixie	20.00	40.00
66 Darrell Waltrip Big K	12.50	25.00
77 Robert Pressley Jasper	12.50	25.00
94 Bill Elliott McDonald's Drive Thru	15.00	40.00
99 Jeff Burton Exide	12.50	25.00
99 Jeff Burton Exide Bruce Lee	12.50	25.00
00 Larry Pearson Cheez-It	12.50	25.00

1999 Racing Champions Petty Collection 1:24

These 1:24 cars were issued to commemorate the racing history of the Petty Family. Each was packaged in an STP blue clear window box with the Petty Racing 50th Anniversary logo.

	EX	NM-MT
42 Lee Petty 1949 Plymouth	50.00	90.00
42 Richard Petty 1957 Oldsmobile	150.00	225.00
43 Richard Petty 1964 Plymouth	90.00	150.00
43 Richard Petty 1970 Superbird	40.00	80.00
43 Richard Petty 1981 Buick	30.00	70.00
43 John Andretti 1999 Pontiac	25.00	40.00

1999 Racing Champions Platinum 1:24

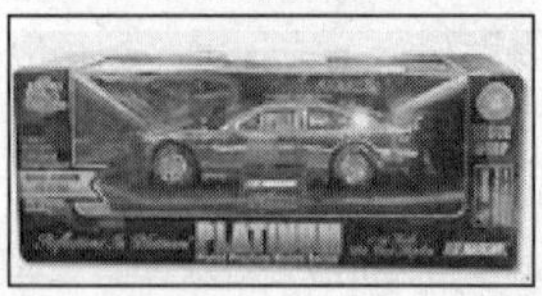

This is a special series produced by Racing Champions to celebrate their 10th anniversary. It parallels the regular 1999 1:24 scale series. Each car is a limited edition of 4,999. Each car is also plated in platinum chrome and contains a serial number on its chassis.

	EX	NM-MT
4 Bobby Hamilton Kodak	20.00	40.00
5 Terry Labonte Kellogg's	30.00	75.00
6 Mark Martin Valvoline	30.00	75.00
9 Jerry Nadeau Dexter's Laboratory	20.00	40.00
9 Jeff Burton Track Gear	20.00	40.00
10 Ricky Rudd Tide	20.00	40.00
11 Brett Bodine Paychex	20.00	40.00
16 Kevin Lepage Primestar	20.00	40.00
25 Wally Dallenbach Hendrick	20.00	40.00
26 Johnny Benson Cheerios	20.00	40.00
33 Ken Schrader Petree	20.00	40.00
36 Ernie Irvan M&M's	20.00	40.00
42 Joe Nemechek BellSouth	20.00	40.00
55 Kenny Wallace Square D	20.00	40.0
77 Robert Pressley Jasper	20.00	40.0
94 Bill Elliott Drive Thru	30.00	75.0
97 Chad Little John Deere	20.00	40.0
99 Jeff Burton Exide	20.00	40.0

1999 Racing Champions Premier 1:24

Each of these 1:24 scale die-cast pieces were issued in a s (not window) Racing Champions Premier box.

	EX	NM-M
6 Mark Martin Eagle One Mac Tools/5000	25.00	50.0
6 Mark Martin Valvoline/3000	20.00	50.0
6 Mark Martin Valvoline Bank/500	30.00	60.0
6 Mark Martin Zerex Mac Tools/5000	15.00	40.0
9 Jeff Burton Track Gear Bank/500	20.00	50.0
60 Mark Martin Winn Dixie/3000	20.00	50.0
60 Mark Martin Winn Dixie Bank/500	30.00	60.0
97 Chad Little John Deere	10.00	25.0
97 Chad Little John Deere Bank/500	25.00	50.0
99 Jeff Burton Exide/3000	12.50	30.0
99 Jeff Burton Exide Bank/500	20.00	50.0

1999 Racing Champions Signature Series 1:24

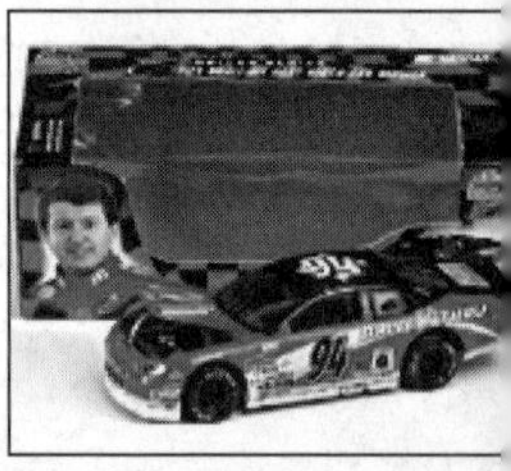

This is a special series produced by Racing Champion celebrate their 10th anniversary. It parallels the regular 1 1:24 scale series. Each car is a packaged in a decorative with the driver's facsimile autograph on the front.

	EX	NM-M
4 Bobby Hamilton Kodak	8.00	20.
4 Bobby Hamilton Kodak Chrome	20.00	40.
5 Terry Labonte Kellogg's	10.00	20.
5 Terry Labonte Kellogg's Chrome	35.00	60.
6 Joe Bessey Power Team	8.00	20.
6 Mark Martin Valvoline	10.00	20.
6 Mark Martin Valvoline Chrome	35.00	60.
9 Jerry Nadeau Dexter's Laboratory	8.00	20.
9 Jerry Nadeau Dexter's Laboratory Chrome	30.00	60.
10 Ricky Rudd Tide	8.00	20.
11 Brett Bodine Paychex	8.00	20.
12 Jeremy Mayfield Mobil 1	8.00	20.
12 Jeremy Mayfield Mobil 1 Chrome	20.00	40.
16 Kevin Lepage Primestar	8.00	20.
16 Kevin Lepage Primestar Chrome	20.00	40.
25 Wally Dallenbach Hendrick	8.00	20.
25 Wally Dallenbach Hendrick Chrome	20.00	40.
26 Johnny Benson Cheerios	8.00	20.
32 Jeff Green Kleenex	8.00	20.
34 Mike McLaughlin Goulds Pump	8.00	20.
36 Ernie Irvan M&M's	10.00	20.
36 Ernie Irvan M&M's Chrome	30.00	60.
40 Sterling Marlin John Wayne	10.00	25.
77 Robert Pressley Jasper	8.00	20.
77 Robert Pressley Jasper Chrome	20.00	40.
94 Bill Elliott McDonald's Drive Thru	10.00	20.
94 Bill Elliott McDonald's Drive Thru Chrome	35.00	60.
99 Jeff Burton Exide	8.00	20.

1999 Racing Champions Stock Rods 1:24

These 1:24 scale cars are replicas of various types vintage s hot rods with NASCAR paint schemes. Since some p schemes were issued more than once (in different car moc we've listed them below by issue number instead of car num

	EX	NM-MT
ff Burton	6.00	15.00
Exide		
vin Lepage	6.00	15.00
Primestar		
rry Labonte	8.00	20.00
Kellogg's Iron Man		
bby Hamilton	6.00	15.00
Kodak		
rry Labonte	8.00	20.00
Blasted Fruit Loops		
ck Mast	6.00	15.00
Remington		
vin Lepage	8.00	20.00
Primestar Gold		
bby Hamilton	8.00	20.00
Kodak Gold		
obby Hamilton	6.00	15.00
Kodak		
erry Labonte	8.00	20.00
Kellogg's Iron Man		
ark Martin	8.00	20.00
Valvoline		
ff Burton	6.00	15.00
Exide		
obby Hamilton	6.00	15.00
Kodak		
rett Bodine	6.00	15.00
Paychex		
ally Dallenbach	6.00	15.00
Hendrick		
ally Dallenbach	8.00	20.00
Hendrick Gold		
rnie Irvan	8.00	20.00
M&M's		
rnie Irvan	12.00	30.00
M&M's Gold		
obby Hamilton	8.00	20.00
Kodak Gold		
rett Bodine	6.00	15.00
Paychex Gold		
ill Elliott	15.00	40.00
Drive Thru Gold		
ill Elliott	8.00	20.00
Drive Thru		
rry Nadeau	6.00	15.00
Dexter's Laboratory		
terling Marlin	8.00	20.00
John Wayne		
obert Pressley	6.00	15.00
Jasper		
Robert Pressley	8.00	20.00
Jasper Gold		
Ken Schrader	6.00	15.00
Andy Petree Racing		
Serling Marlin	8.00	20.00
John Wayne		
Jeff Burton	6.00	15.00
Bruce Lee		
Terry Labonte	8.00	20.00
Kellogg's		
Ricky Rudd	6.00	15.00
Tide		
Derrike Cope	6.00	15.00
Bryan Foods		
Ken Schrader	6.00	15.00
APR Blue		
Jimmy Spencer	6.00	15.00
TCE		

1999 Racing Champions Trackside 1:24

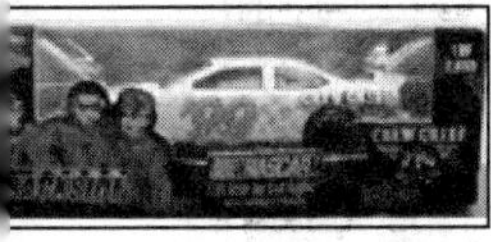

1:24 cars were primarily available at the race track. Each ackaged in a "Trackside" labeled window box with each ling the production run total of 2499.

	EX	NM-MT
ry Nadeau	20.00	40.00
Atlanta Braves		
ry Nadeau	12.50	30.00
Dexter's Lab		
ry Nadeau	15.00	40.00
Dexter's Lab Platinum		
ry Nadeau	12.50	30.00
WCW nWo		
mmy Spencer	15.00	40.00
No Bull		
hn Andretti	12.50	30.00
STP		
am Petty	40.00	80.00
Spree		
ll Elliott	15.00	40.00
McDonald's Drive Thru Platinum		
hevrolet Racing Platinum	10.00	25.00
ew Chief Club	10.00	20.00
ord Racing Platinum	10.00	25.00

1999 Racing Champions Under the Lights 1:24

	EX	NM-MT
nny Benson	8.00	20.00
Kodak Max		
ry Labonte	8.00	20.00
Kellogg's K-Sentials/5000		
rk Martin	10.00	25.00
Valvoline		
rk Martin	12.50	25.00
Zerex/7500		
cky Rudd	8.00	20.00
Tide		
remy Mayfield	8.00	20.00
Mobil 1		
liott Sadler	8.00	20.00
Citgo		
ard Burton	8.00	20.00
Caterpillar		
hn Andretti	10.00	25.00
STP		
ark Martin	10.00	25.00
Winn Dixie		
arrell Waltrip	8.00	20.00
Big K		
94 Bill Elliott	10.00	25.00
McDonald's Drive Thru/5000		
99 Jeff Burton	8.00	20.00
Exide		

1999 Racing Champions 24K Gold 1:24

This is a special series produced by Racing Champions to celebrate their 10th anniversary. It parallels the regular 1998 1:24 scale series. Each car is a limited edition of 4,999. Each car is also plated in gold chrome and contains a serial number on its chassis.

	EX	NM-MT
4 Bobby Hamilton	20.00	40.00
Kodak		
5 Terry Labonte	30.00	75.00
Kellogg's		
6 Joe Bessey	20.00	40.00
Power Team		
6 Mark Martin	30.00	75.00
Valvoline		
9 Jerry Nadeau	30.00	50.00
Dexter's Laboratory		
9 Jeff Burton	20.00	40.00
Track Gear		
10 Ricky Rudd	20.00	40.00
Tide		
11 Brett Bodine	20.00	40.00
Paychex		
16 Kevin Lepage	20.00	40.00
Primestar		
26 Johnny Benson	20.00	40.00
Cheerios		
42 Joe Nemechek	20.00	40.00
BellSouth		
77 Robert Pressley	20.00	40.00
Jasper		
97 Chad Little	20.00	40.00
John Deere		
99 Jeff Burton	20.00	40.00
Exide		

2000 Racing Champions Preview 1:24

	EX	NM-MT
5 Terry Labonte	10.00	20.00
Kellogg's		
6 Mrak Martin	10.00	20.00
Valvoline		
7 Michael Waltrip	7.50	15.00
Nation's Rent		
12 Jeremy Mayfield	7.50	15.00
Mobil 1		
17 Matt Kenseth	10.00	20.00
DeWalt		
22 Ward Burton	7.50	15.00
Caterpillar		
22 Ward Burton	8.00	20.00
Caterpillar Bud Shoot Out		
33 Joe Nemechek	7.50	15.00
Oakwood Homes		
66 Darrell Waltrip	7.50	15.00
Big K Flames		
75 Wally Dallenbach	7.50	15.00
Cartoon Network		
77 Robert Pressley	7.50	15.00
Jasper		
99 Jeff Burton	7.50	15.00
Exide		
99 Jeff Burton	12.50	25.00
Exide Chrome/999		

2000 Racing Champions Premier Preview 1:24

	EX	NM-MT
6 Mark Martin	10.00	25.00
Valvoline		
17 Matt Kenseth	10.00	25.00
DeWalt		
99 Jeff Burton	10.00	25.00
Exide		

2000 Racing Champions 1:24

	EX	NM-MT
1 MSD Ignition Syst.Promo/2508	20.00	40.00
1 Peter Gibbons	15.00	40.00
Candian Tire Promo		
4 Bobby Hamilton	20.00	35.00
Dana SuperTruck Promo		
5 Terry Labonte	10.00	25.00
Kellogg's		
5 Terry Labonte	20.00	50.00
Kellogg's Chrome/999		
6 Mark Martin	10.00	25.00
Valvoline		
6 Mark Martin	25.00	50.00
Valvoline Chrome/999		
7 Michael Waltrip	7.50	15.00
Nation's Rent		
7 Michael Waltrip	15.00	40.00
Nations Rent Chrome/999		
9 Stacy Compton	10.00	20.00
Kodiak Promo		
9 Jeff Burton	7.50	15.00
NorthernLight.com		
12 Jeremy Mayfield	7.50	15.00
Mobil 1		
14 Mike Bliss	7.50	15.00
Conseco		
14 Rick Crawford	10.00	20.00
Milwaukee Tools		
SuperTruck Promo		
17 Matt Kenseth	10.00	20.00
DeWalt		
20 Arvin Racing Promo	15.00	25.00
22 Ward Burton	7.50	15.00
Caterpillar		
22 Ward Burton	10.00	25.00
Caterpillar Promo		
22 Ward Burton	10.00	20.00
Caterpillar Bud Shoot Out		
22 Ward Burton	10.00	25.00
Cat Dealers Promo		
22 Ward Burton	10.00	25.00
Caterpillar Bosch Promo		
25 Jerry Nadeau	7.50	15.00
Holigan		
33 Joe Nemechek	7.50	15.00
Oakwood Bud Shoot Out		
39 Schaeffer's Racing Oil Promo	25.00	40.00
40 Sterling Marlin	7.50	15.00
Sabco		
42 Kenny Irwin	10.00	25.00
BellSouth		
44 Doc Brewer	25.00	50.00
Pabst Blue Ribbon Promo		
48 Mike McGlaughlin	60.00	100.00
Goulds Pumps Promo		
50 Greg Biffle	75.00	135.00
Grainger SuperTruck Promo		
50 Tony Roper	30.00	60.00
Dr. Pepper Promo		
59 Mark Gibson	30.00	50.00
Cornwell Tools Promo		
64 Mark Dilley	30.00	50.00
NTN Promo		
66 Darrell Waltrip	7.50	15.00
Big K		
66 Darrell Waltrip	7.50	15.00
Big K Flames		
66 Darrell Waltrip	25.00	50.00
Big K 500 Promo		
in solid box		
75 Wally Dallenbach	25.00	40.00
Rotozip Promo		
75 Wally Dallenbach	7.50	15.00
Scooby Doo		
77 Robert Pressley	10.00	20.00
Federal Mogul Red		
Promo		
77 Robert Pressley	7.50	15.00
Jasper		
77 Robert Pressley	10.00	25.00
Jasper Blue Promo		
77 Robert Pressley	10.00	25.00
Jasper Teal Promo		
90 Ed Berrier	35.00	60.00
Hills Bros.Promo		
set with two 1:64 cars		
91 Rich Bickle	10.00	25.00
Aqua Velva Promo/2508		
91 Rich Bickle	12.50	25.00
Popeyes Promo		
93 Dave Blaney	10.00	25.00
Amoco		
93 Dave Blaney	15.00	30.00
Amoco Ultimate Promo		
97 Chad Little	7.50	15.00
John Deere		
99 Jeff Burton	7.50	15.00
Exide		
99 Jeff Burton	20.00	50.00
Exide Chrome/999		
99 Kurt Busch	150.00	250.00
Exide SuperTruck Promo		
99 Michael Waltrip	20.00	35.00
Aaron's Promo		
2000 Kroger Fred Meyer Promo/4700	15.00	30.00
00 Auto Value Gold Chrome Promo	15.00	30.00
00 Ryan McGlynn	25.00	40.00
Howes Lubricator		
80th Anniversary		
SuperTruck Promo		
00 Snap-On Racing Promo/5000	7.50	20.00

2000 Racing Champions Authentics 1:24

	EX	NM-MT
6 Mark Martin	25.00	50.00
Eagle One/4000		
6 Mark Martin	25.00	50.00
Valvoline		
7 Michael Waltrip	40.00	80.00
Nations Rent Matco Tools/3100		
22 Ward Burton	15.00	40.00
Caterpillar		
22 Ward Burton	30.00	50.00
Cat Dealers/2000		
22 Ward Burton	25.00	50.00
Caterpillar No Bull		
40 Sterling Marlin	50.00	100.00
Coors Light Matco Tools		
42 Kenny Irwin	60.00	100.00
BellSouth Matco Tools		
75 Wally Dallenbach	20.00	45.00
Power Puff Girls/1000		
82 Sterling Marlin	35.00	75.00
Channellock Matco Tools		
87 Joe Nemechek	35.00	75.00
Cellularone Matco Tools		
93 Dave Blaney	15.00	40.00
Amoco		

2000 Racing Champions Model Kits 1:24

Cars in this series were issued in a large Racing Champions window box with the title "Die Cast Model Kit" on the front and top along with the NASCAR2000 logo. The kit is essentially a metal die-cast model that was to be assembled by the collector. The car came complete with a small screwdriver and model glue.

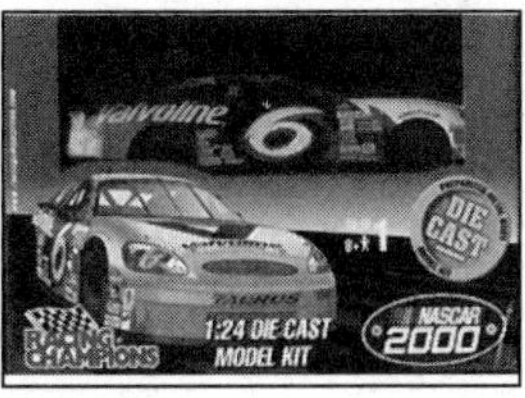

	EX	NM-MT
5 Terry Labonte	8.00	20.00
Kellogg's		
6 Mark Martin	8.00	20.00
Valvoline		
22 Ward Burton	6.00	15.00
Caterpillar		
99 Jeff Burton	6.00	15.00
Exide		

2000 Racing Champions Premier 1:24

	EX	NM-MT
4 Bobby Hamilton	10.00	20.00
Kodak		
5 Terry Labonte	12.50	25.00
Froot Loops CherryBerry		
5 Terry Labonte	12.50	25.00
Kellogg's Tony		
6 Mark Martin	12.50	25.00
Valvoline		
6 Mark Martin	12.50	25.00
Valvoline No Bull		
12 Jeremy Mayfield	10.00	20.00
Mobil 1		
17 Matt Kenseth	15.00	30.00
DeWalt		
17 Matt Kenseth	15.00	30.00
DeWalt 24 Volt		
22 Ward Burton	10.00	20.00
Caterpillar		
22 Ward Burton	12.50	25.00
Caterpillar No Bull		
42 Kenny Irwin	10.00	20.00
BellSouth		
42 Kenny Irwin	15.00	30.00
BellSouth Chrome/999		
60 Mark Martin	75.00	125.00
Winn Dixie Farewell Tour		
Promo in solid box		
60 Mark Martin	75.00	125.00
Winn Dixie Flag		
in window box		
99 Jeff Burton	12.50	25.00
Exide		
99 Jeff Burton	20.00	40.00
Exide Chrome/999		

2000 Racing Champions Stock Rods 1:24

	EX	NM-MT
1 Mark Martin	7.50	15.00
Valvoline 1937 Ford		
2 Jeff Burton	7.50	15.00
Exide 1932 Ford		
3 Bobby Hamilton	6.00	12.00
Kodak 1967 Chevelle		

2000 Racing Champions Time Trial 2000 1:24

New for 2000, Racing Champions introduced a series that focuses on the testing and development of NASCAR stock cars rather than the final race-ready car - Time Trial stock car replicas. Sporting just a coat of gray primer and the team number.

	EX	NM-MT
6 Mark Martin	12.00	20.00
Valvoline		
17 Matt Kenseth	50.00	100.00
DeWalt		
97 Chad Little	10.00	20.00
John Deere		
99 Jeff Burton	12.00	20.00
Exide		

2000 Racing Champions Under the Lights 1:24

	EX	NM-MT
5 Terry Labonte	12.50	25.00
Kellogg's K-Sentials/5000		
6 Mark Martin	12.50	30.00
Zerex		
22 Ward Burton	15.00	40.00
Caterpillar/2288		
99 Jeff Burton	12.50	25.00
Exide 2-car set/2500		
regular issue car and		
chrome hood car		
2K Ford Chrome/10,000	10.00	20.00
Y2K Chevy Chrome/10,000	10.00	20.00

2000 Racing Champions War Paint 1:24

	EX	NM-MT
5 Terry Labonte	10.00	20.00
Kellogg's		
5 Terry Labonte	10.00	20.00
Kellogg's Hood Open		
6 Mark Martin	12.50	25.00
Valvoline		
6 Mark Martin	12.50	25.00
Valvoline Hood Open		
22 Ward Burton	10.00	20.00
Caterpillar		
22 Ward Burton	10.00	20.00
Caterpillar Hood Open		
99 Jeff Burton	10.00	20.00
Exide		
99 Jeff Burton	10.00	20.00
Exide Hood Open		

2001 Racing Champions Preview 1:24

	EX	NM-MT
5 Terry Labonte	10.00	20.00
Kellogg's Tony		
5 Terry Labonte	25.00	50.00
Kellogg's Tony Chrome		
10 Johnny Benson	8.00	20.00
Valvoline		
12 Jeremy Mayfield	10.00	20.00
Mobil 1		
12 Jeremy Mayfield	15.00	40.00
Mobil 1 Layin' Rubber		
14 Ron Hornaday	8.00	20.00
Conseco		
22 Ward Burton	8.00	20.00
Caterpillar		
22 Ward Burton	40.00	80.00
Caterpillar Autographed		
22 Ward Burton	20.00	50.00
Caterpillar Chrome		
22 Ward Burton	20.00	50.00
Caterpillar Layin' Rubber		
36 Ken Schrader	8.00	20.00
M&M's		
36 Ken Schrader	25.00	50.00
M&M's Chrome		
55 Bobby Hamilton	8.00	20.00
Square D		
55 Bobby Hamilton	20.00	40.00
Square D Chrome/1500		
92 Stacy Compton	8.00	20.00
Compton		
92 Stacy Compton	20.00	40.00
Compton Chrome		
93 Dave Blaney	8.00	20.00
Amoco		
93 Dave Blaney	15.00	40.00
Amoco Chrome		
NNO Dodge Test Car	10.00	25.00

2001 Racing Champions Premier Preview 1:24

	EX	NM-MT
5 Terry Labonte	12.50	25.00
Frosed Flakes 2000		
5 Terry Labonte	20.00	35.00
Kellogg's Tony		
10 Johnny Benson	12.50	25.00
Valvoline		
12 Jeremy Mayfield	12.50	25.00
Mobil 1		
12 Jeremy Mayfield	20.00	50.00
Mobil 1 Layin' Rubber		

2001 Racing Champions 1:24

	EX	NM-MT
1 Justice Bros. Promo	25.00	40.00
1 Ted Musgrave	15.00	40.00
Mopar SuperTruck Promo		
1 Racing Experience Promo	30.00	50.00
2 Scott Riggs	25.00	50.00
ASE SuperTruck		
4 Graybar Lutron Promo/3600	20.00	35.00
5 Terry Labonte	12.00	30.00
Kellogg's Tony		
5 Terry Labonte	25.00	50.00
Kellogg's Tony Chrome/1500		
5 Terry Labonte	15.00	40.00
Kellogg's		
5 Terry Labonte		
Kellogg's Autographed		
5 Terry Labonte	15.00	30.00
Monsters Inc.Promo		
7 Randy LaJoie	10.00	20.00
Kleenex Promo		
8 Willie T. Ribbs	12.50	25.00
Dodge SuperTruck		
10 Johnny Benson	8.00	20.00
Valvoline		
12 Jeremy Mayfield	8.00	20.00
Mobil 1		
12 Jeremy Mayfield		
Mobil Autographed		
12 Jeremy Mayfield	20.00	40.00
Mobil Layin' Rubber		
12 Jeremy Mayfield	20.00	45.00
Mobil Race Rubber		
12 Jeremy Mayfield	12.00	30.00
Sony-Mobil 1		
12 Jeremy Mayfield	15.00	30.00
Sony Chrome/1500		
13 Hermie Sadler	15.00	30.00
Virginia Lottery Promo		
14 Rick Crawford	5.00	10.00
Milwaukee Tools SuperTruck Promo		
14 Ron Hornaday	8.00	20.00
Conseco		
16 Brendan Gaughan	30.00	50.00
NAPA Promo		
16 Wisconsin Cheese Promo	15.00	30.00
18 Dave Heitzhaus	8.00	20.00
Pro Hardware Promo in blister		
21 Elliott Sadler	12.00	30.00
Motorcraft		
21 Elliott Sadler	20.00	40.00
Motorcraft Layin' Rubber		
22 Ward Burton	8.00	20.00
Caterpillar		
22 Ward Burton		
Caterpillar Autographed		
22 Ward Burton	25.00	50.00
Caterpillar Chrome/1500		
22 Ward Burton	25.00	50.00
Caterpillar 24kt.Gold Promo		
22 Ward Burton	15.00	40.00
Caterpillar Layin' Rubber		
22 Ward Burton	25.00	50.00
Caterpillar Race Rubber		
22 Ward Burton	12.50	25.00
Cat Black Time Trial		

22 Ward Burton 25.00 50.00
Cat Black Time Trial Chrome/1500
22 Ward Burton 25.00 50.00
Caterpillar War Chrome/1500
22 Ward Burton 15.00 25.00
Caterpillar Promo
22 Ward Burton 20.00 50.00
Cat Tractor
22 Ward Burton 40.00 75.00
Cat Tractor Layin' Rubber/500
25 Jerry Nadeau 8.00 20.00
UAW
25 Jerry Nadeau 20.00 40.00
UAW Chrome/1500
25 Jerry Nadeau 25.00 40.00
UAW Promo
Mac Tools box/3000
26 Bobby Hamilton Jr. 15.00 30.00
Dr.Pepper Promo
26 Jimmy Spencer 8.00 20.00
K-Mart
26 Jimmy Spencer 15.00 30.00
K-Mart Grinch
28 Brad Baker 18.00 30.00
Whitetails Unlimited
36 Hank Parker Jr. 45.00 80.00
GNC Live Well
36 Ken Schrader 8.00 20.00
M&M's
36 Ken Schrader 25.00 50.00
M&M's Layin' Rubber
36 Ken Schrader 25.00 40.00
M&M's Promo
Mac Tools box/3000
36 Ken Schrader 8.00 20.00
M&M's July 4th
36 Ken Schrader 25.00 50.00
M&M's July 4th
Race Rubber
36 Ken Schrader 25.00 50.00
Snickers
36 Ken Schrader 20.00 40.00
Snickers Chrome/1500
38 Christian Elder 18.00 30.00
Deka Batteries Promo
38 Christian Elder 18.00 30.00
Great Clips Promo
40 Sterling Marlin 25.00 50.00
Coors Light 24K Gold Promo
40 Sterling Marlin 12.00 30.00
Marlin
43 Jay Sauter 30.00 50.00
Morton's Salt Promo
43 Jay Sauter 35.00 60.00
Quality Farm Promo
55 Bobby Hamilton 8.00 20.00
Square D
55 Bobby Hamilton 15.00 30.00
Square D Chrome/1500
55 Bobby Hamilton 15.00 40.00
Square D Lightning
Layin' Rubber/500
55 Bobby Hamilton 30.00 50.00
Square D Encompass
57 Jason Keller 8.00 20.00
Albertsons Promo
60 Travis Kvapil 15.00 30.00
Cat Rental SuperTruck Promo
66 Todd Bodine 8.00 20.00
Phillips 66
66 Todd Bodine 15.00 30.00
Phillips 66 Chrome/1500
92 Stacy Compton 12.00 30.00
Compton
92 Stacy Compton 10.00 20.00
Kodiak Promo/2500
92 Stacy Compton 15.00 30.00
Compton Chrome/1500
93 Dave Blaney 8.00 20.00
Amoco
93 Dave Blaney 15.00 30.00
Amoco Chrome/1500
93 Dave Blaney 20.00 40.00
Amoco Layin' Rubber
93 Dave Blaney 15.00 40.00
Amoco 24kt. Gold Promo
93 Dave Blaney 8.00 20.00
Amoco BP
93 Dave Blaney 15.00 40.00
Amoco BP Race Rubber
93 Dave Blaney 6.00 15.00
Amoco Siemens Promo
93 Dave Blaney 12.00 30.00
Mac Tools/4000
98 Elton Sawyer 25.00 40.00
Auburn U. Promo
98 Elton Sawyer 25.00 40.00
Georgia U. Promo/1250
98 Elton Sawyer 25.00 40.00
Miami U. Promo/1250
98 Elton Sawyer 25.00 40.00
Michigan University
Promo/1250
98 Elton Sawyer 25.00 40.00
North Carolina University
Promo/1250
98 Elton Sawyer 25.00 40.00
Tennessee University
Promo/1250
01 All-Pro Auto Value Promo 15.00 30.00
01 Chik-fil-a Peach Bowl Promo 7.50 15.00
01 Jason Leffler 12.00 30.00
Cingular
01 Jason Leffler 20.00 40.00
Cingular Layin' Rubber/500
01 Jason Leffler 15.00 30.00
Cingular Special Olympics Promo
01 Jason Leffler 15.00 40.00
Cingular Promo
01 Michigan International Speedway 15.00 30.00
01 Mountain Dew 25.00 40.00
Tropicana 400 Promo
01 Ratheon Six Sigma Promo 20.00 40.00
01 Shop 'n Save Promo 10.00 20.00
NNO NDA/Dodge Test Team 12.00 30.00

2001 Racing Champions Premier 1:24

EX NM-MT
5 Terry Labonte 15.00 40.00
Frosted Flakes 2000
5 Terry Labonte 15.00 40.00
Kellogg's
5 Terry Labonte 30.00 60.00
Kellogg's Chrome
10 Johnny Benson 12.00 30.00
Valvoline
10 Johnny Benson 15.00 40.00
Valvoline Layin Rubber
12 Jeremy Mayfield 12.00 30.00
Mobil 1
12 Jeremy Mayfield
Mobil Autographed
12 Jeremy Mayfield 25.00 50.00
Mobil Chrome
12 Jeremy Mayfield 25.00 50.00
Mobil Firesuit
12 Jeremy Mayfield 25.00 50.00
Mobil Layin Rubber
12 Jeremy Mayfield 25.00 50.00
Mobil Race Rubber
12 Jeremy Mayfield 40.00 80.00
Mobil Real Steel
21 Elliott Sadler 12.00 30.00
Motorcraft
21 Elliott Sadler 15.00 40.00
Motorcraft Chrome/1500
21 Elliott Sadler 25.00 50.00
Motorcraft Layin Rubber
22 Ward Burton 12.00 30.00
Caterpillar
22 Ward Burton
Caterpillar Autographed
22 Ward Burton 30.00 60.00
Caterpillar Race Rubber
22 Ward Burton 40.00 80.00
Caterpillar Real Steel
25 Jerry Nadeau 12.00 30.00
UAW
25 Jerry Nadeau 20.00 40.00
UAW Chrome/1500
25 Jerry Nadeau 20.00 50.00
UAW Layin Rubber
26 Jimmy Spencer 12.00 30.00
K-Mart
26 Jimmy Spencer 15.00 40.00
K-Mart Layin Rubber
36 Ken Schrader 12.00 30.00
M&M's
36 Ken Schrader 20.00 40.00
M&M's Chrome
36 Ken Schrader 25.00 50.00
M&M's Firesuit
36 Ken Schrader 40.00 80.00
M&M's Real Steel
93 Dave Blaney 12.00 30.00
Amoco
93 Dave Blaney 20.00 50.00
Amoco Firesuit
98 Elton Sawyer 20.00 35.00
Huskers

2001 Racing Champions Authentics 1:24

EX NM-MT
5 Terry Labonte 20.00 50.00
Kellogg'sTony
Mac Tools Promo/3000
10 Johnny Benson 20.00 40.00
Valvoline Firesuit/1200
10 Johnny Benson 20.00 40.00
Valvoline Sheetmetal/1200
11 Smuckers Promo/8000 25.00 50.00
22 Ward Burton 30.00 60.00
Caterpillar Firesuit/1500
22 Ward Burton 100.00 175.00
Cat Tractors
22 Ward Burton 125.00 200.00
Cat Tractors Chrome/250
36 Ken Schrader 20.00 40.00
M&M's Firesuit/1200
36 Ken Schrader 20.00 40.00
M&M's Race Rubber/1200
36 Ken Schrader 20.00 40.00
M&M's Sheetmetal/1200
40 Sterling Marlin 75.00 135.00
Coors Firesuit
40 Sterling Marlin 70.00 120.00
Coors Chrome/250
40 Sterling Marlin 50.00 100.00
Coors Light Firesuit/1200
93 Dave Blaney 15.00 40.00
Amoco Firesuit/1200
93 Dave Blaney 15.00 40.00
Amoco Sheetmetal/1200
01 Dave Blaney 7.50 20.00
Amoco Ultimate Promo
without Firesuit
01 Dave Blaney 15.00 30.00
Amoco Ultimate Promo Firesuit/1200

2002 Racing Champions 1:24

EX NM-MT
1 Jimmy Spencer 10.00 20.00
Yellow Freight
1 Jimmy Spencer 20.00 50.00
Yellow Freight Tire
2 Jason Leffler 15.00 30.00
CarQuest SuperTruck
Promo w/1:64 car
4 Mike Skinner 10.00 20.00
Kodak
5 Terry Labonte 12.50 25.00
Cheez-it
5 Terry Labonte 30.00 60.00
Cheez-it Car Cover/500
5 Terry Labonte 60.00 100.00
Cheez-it Firesuit
5 Terry Labonte 15.00 25.00
Got Milk
5 Terry Labonte 40.00 80.00
Got Milk AUTO
5 Terry Labonte 10.00 25.00
Kellogg's
5 Terry Labonte 30.00 60.00
Kellogg's Cover/500
5 Terry Labonte 50.00 100.00
Kellogg's Firesuit
10 Johnny Benson 10.00 25.00
Eagle One
10 Johnny Benson 30.00 80.00
Eagle One AUTO
10 Johnny Benson 40.00 80.00
Eagle One Firesuit
10 Johnny Benson 10.00 25.00
Valvoline
10 Johnny Benson 50.00 100.00
Valvoline Steel
10 Johnny Benson 10.00 20.00
Zerex
10 Johnny Benson 50.00 100.00
Zerex Firesuit/25
10 Johnny Benson 25.00 50.00
Zerex Tire
10 Johnny Benson 25.00 40.00
100 Years of Kentucky BK
10 Johnny Benson 35.00 60.00
100 Years of Kentucky
Basketball Promo/835
10 Johnny Benson 60.00 100.00
100 Years of Kentucky
Basketball Color Chrome Promo/167
10 Scott Riggs 15.00 30.00
Nestea Promo
10 Scott Riggs 15.00 30.00
Nestle Toll House
Halloween Promo
10 Scott Riggs 10.00 25.00
Nesquik
11 Brett Bodine 15.00 30.00
Hooters
12 Carey Heath 12.50 25.00
Aubuchon Hardware Promo
14 Stacy Compton 10.00 25.00
Conseco
15 Robin Buck 20.00 35.00
NAPA Promo
19 Tim Sauter 18.00 30.00
Motorsports Park 131
21 Elliott Sadler 20.00 40.00
Motorcraft
22 Ward Burton 12.50 25.00
Caterpillar Daytona Win
22 Ward Burton 40.00 80.00
Caterpillar Daytona Win AUTO
22 Ward Burton 20.00 40.00
Caterpillar Daytona Win Chrome/1500
22 Ward Burton 20.00 35.00
Cat Dealers '02 packaging
22 Ward Burton 12.50 25.00
Cat Dealers '03 packaging
22 Ward Burton 25.00 40.00
Cat Dealers Chrome/1500
2003 packaging
22 Ward Burton 50.00 80.00
Wildlife Foundation Promo
23 Hut Stricklin 15.00 30.00
Hills Bros.
24 Jack Sprague 10.00 20.00
NETZERO
25 Jerry Nadeau 10.00 20.00
UAW
26 Lyndon Amick 15.00 30.00
Dr.Pepper Spider-Man
26 Ron Hornaday 20.00 35.00
Dr.Pepper Promo Error
Bobby Hamilton Jr. name on car
26 Ron Hornaday 20.00 35.00
Red Fusion Promo
26 Ron Hornaday 30.00 50.00
Red Fusion Color
Chrome Promo
26 Joe Nemechek 10.00 20.00
K-Mart
27 Scott Wimmer 25.00 50.00
Siemens Promo/625
27 Scott Wimmer 30.00 60.00
Siemens Brushed
Metal Promo/125
28 Brad Baker 15.00 30.00
Whitetails Unlimited
30 Christian Fittipaldi 25.00 40.00
Mike's Hard Lemonade
Promo/625
30 Christian Fittipaldi 30.00 50.00
Mike's Hard Lemonade
Brushed Metal Promo/125
32 Ricky Craven 10.00 20.00
Tide
32 Ricky Craven 15.00 40.00
Tide Chrome/1500
32 Ricky Craven 12.50 25.00
Tide Promo
32 Ricky Craven 10.00 25.00
Tide First Win Raced
32 Ricky Craven 10.00 25.00
Tide Kids
32 Ricky Craven
Tide Kids AUTO
33 John Komarinski 30.00 60.00
Rolling Rock Promo/1333
33 Kenny Wallace 30.00 50.00
1-800-CALL-ATT Promo
33 Mike Wallace 30.00 60.00
Preen Promo
36 Hank Parker Jr 10.00 25.00
GNC
36 Ken Schrader 60.00 120.00
Combos Promo
36 Ken Schrader 12.50 25.00
M&M's
36 Ken Schrader 30.00 60.00
M&M's AUTO
36 Ken Schrader 15.00 40.00
M&M's Chrome/1500
36 Ken Schrader 30.00 60.00
M&M's Car Cover/500
36 Ken Schrader 50.00 100.00
M&M's Firesuit
36 Ken Schrader 50.00 100.00
M&M's Steel
36 Ken Schrader 12.50 25.00
M&M's Halloween
2003 packaging
36 Ken Schrader 12.50 25.00
M&M's July 4th
36 Ken Schrader 12.50 25.00
Pedigree
36 Ken Schrader
Pedigree Firesuit
40 Brian Vickers 75.00 150.00
EMP Promo
43 Jay Sauter 25.00 40.00
Morton Salt Promo
44 Pabst Blue Ribbon Promo 20.00 35.00
46 Ashton Lewis 20.00 40.00
Civil Air Patrol Promo
47 Shane Hmiel 25.00 40.00
Mike's Hard Cranberry
Promo/625
47 Shane Hmiel 30.00 50.00
Mike's Hard Cranberry
Brushed Metal Promo/125
47 Shane Hmiel 25.00 40.00
Mike's Hard Lemonade
Promo/625
47 Shane Hmiel 30.00 50.00
Mike's Hard Lemonade
Brushed Metal Promo/125
47 Shane Hmiel 25.00 40.00
Mike's Hard Iced Tea
Promo/625
47 Shane Hmiel 30.00 50.00
Mike's Hard Iced Tea
Brushed Metal Promo/125
48 Jimmie Johnson 15.00 30.00
Lowe's
48 Jimmie Johnson 50.00 80.00
Lowe's Chrome/1500
48 Jimmie Johnson 40.00 80.00
Lowe's Car Cover/500
48 Jimmie Johnson 100.00 175.00
Lowe's Steel/25
48 Jimmie Johnson 10.00 20.00
Lowe's with Press Pass card
48 Jimmie Johnson 15.00 30.00
Lowe's Power of Pride
48 Jimmie Johnson 25.00 60.00
Lowe's Power of Pride Chrome/1500
48 Jimmie Johnson 10.00 20.00
Lowe's Power of Pride
with Press Pass card
49 Shawna Robinson 25.00 50.00
BAM Promo
54 Kevin Grubb 12.50 25.00
Toys 'R' Us Promo
55 Bobby Hamilton 10.00 20.00
Schneider
55 Bobby Hamilton 15.00 30.00
Schneider Chrome/1500
55 Bobby Hamilton 20.00 40.00
Schneider Car Cover/500
55 Bobby Hamilton 25.00 60.00
Schneider Tire/250
57 Jason Keller 10.00 20.00
Albertsons Flag
57 Jason Keller 12.00 20.00
Albertson's Promo
66 Casey Mears 25.00 40.00
Phillips 66
66 Robin Buck 18.00 30.00
UAP NAPA Promo
box in French&English
77 Dave Blaney 10.00 20.00
Jasper
77 Dave Blaney 20.00 40.00
Jasper Car Cover/500
77 Dave Blaney 15.00 30.00
Jasper Promo
93 Travis Benjamin 18.00 30.00
Irving Promo
98 Kenny Wallace 15.00 30.00
Stacker 2 in 2003 packaging
99 Michael Waltrip 10.00 20.00
Aaron's Rent
01 K-Resin Promo 18.00 30.00
02 All Pro Auto Value Flames Promo 18.00 30.00
02 Cabela's 250 Promo 18.00 30.00
02 Foodland Super Market Promo 15.00 30.00
02 Nebraska Blackshirts Promo 25.00 40.00
02 Snap-On Promo 25.00 40.00
02 Timken Store Promo 35.00 60.00

2002 Racing Champions Premier 1:24

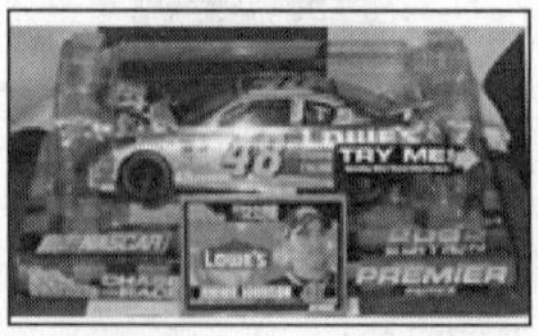

EX NM-MT
1 Snap-On Team Memphis Promo 18.00 30.00
in a box
5 Terry Labonte 15.00 30.00
Kellogg's
5 Terry Labonte
Kellogg's Firesuit
5 Terry Labonte
Kellogg's Steel
10 Johnny Benson 15.00 30.00
Eagle One
10 Johnny Benson 30.00 80.00
Eagle One AUTO
10 Johnny Benson 15.00 30.00
Valvoline Maxlife
10 Johnny Benson 15.00 30.00
Zerex
10 Johnny Benson
Zerex AUTO
10 Johnny Benson 25.00 50
Zerex Car Cover/500
10 Johnny Benson 50.00 100
Zerex Firesuit/25
22 Ward Burton 15.00 30
Caterpillar Daytona Win
22 Ward Burton 50.00 100
Caterpillar Daytona Win AU/100
22 Ward Burton 20.00 40
Caterpillar Daytona
Win Chrome/1500
22 Ward Burton 15.00 30
Cat Dealers
in 2003 packaging
22 Ward Burton 20.00 40
Cat Dealers Chrome/1500
in 2003 packaging
32 Ricky Craven 15.00 30
Tide
32 Ricky Craven 25.00 50
Tide Car Cover/500
32 Ricky Craven 20.00 40
Tide Chrome/1500
32 Ricky Craven 15.00 30
Tide Kids
40 Sterling Marlin 15.00 30
Flag
48 Jimmie Johnson 20.00 40
Lowe's
48 Jimmie Johnson 50.00 100
Lowe's Car Cover/500
48 Jimmie Johnson 15.00 40
Lowe's First Win
48 Jimmie Johnson 25.00 60
Lowe's First Win
Car Cover/500
48 Jimmie Johnson 15.00 40
Lowe's Power of Pride
48 Jimmie Johnson 30.00 80
Lowe's Power of Pride#[Chrome/1500
48 Jimmie Johnson 15.00 30
Lowe's Press Pass/2500
55 Bobby Hamilton 15.00 30
Schneider
77 Dave Blaney 15.00 30
Jasper

2002 Racing Champions American Muscle Body Sh 1:24

EX NM-
32 Scott Pruett 7.50 15
Tide SuperTruck
64 Chuck Erdman 7.50 15
1964 Plymouth Belvedere

2002 Racing Champions Premier Preview 1:24

EX NM-
5 Terry Labonte 12.50 30
Kellogg's
5 Terry Labonte 20.00 50
Kellogg's Chrome/1500
5 Terry Labonte
Kellogg's Tire
10 Johnny Benson 12.50 30
Valvoline
10 Johnny Benson 40.00 80
Valvoline Firesuit
10 Johnny Benson
Valvoline Firesuit/Tire
10 Johnny Benson 25.00 50
Valvoline Tire
22 Ward Burton 12.50 30
Caterpillar
22 Ward Burton 20.00 40
Caterpillar Car Cover/500
22 Ward Burton 40.00 80
Caterpillar Firesuit
22 Ward Burton
Caterpillar Steel
25 Jerry Nadeau 12.50 30
UAW
25 Jerry Nadeau 15.00 40
UAW Car Cover/500
25 Jerry Nadeau 20.00 40
UAW Chrome
36 Ken Schrader 12.50 30
M&M's
40 Sterling Marlin 15.00 35
Marlin Flag

2002 Racing Champions Preview 1:24

EX NM-
5 Terry Labonte 12.50 25
Kellogg's
5 Terry Labonte 15.00 40
Kellogg's Chrome/1500
10 Johnny Benson 12.50 25
Valvoline
10 Johnny Benson 15.00 40

	EX	NM-MT
'alvoline Chrome/1500		
hnny Benson 'alvoline Firesuit	40.00	80.00
hnny Benson 'alvoline Tire	25.00	50.00
ard Burton aterpillar	12.50	25.00
ard Burton aterpillar Car Cover/500	20.00	50.00
ard Burton aterpillar Firesuit	40.00	80.00
ard Burton aterpillar Steel		
rry Nadeau AW	12.50	25.00
rry Nadeau AW Tire		
mmy Spencer -Mart Shrek	15.00	30.00
cky Craven ide	12.50	25.00
cky Craven ide Car Cover/500	20.00	40.00
n Schrader M&M's	12.50	25.00
erling Marlin arlin Flag	12.50	30.00
son Keller lbertsons Flag Promo	7.50	15.00

2002 Racing Champions Authentics 1:24

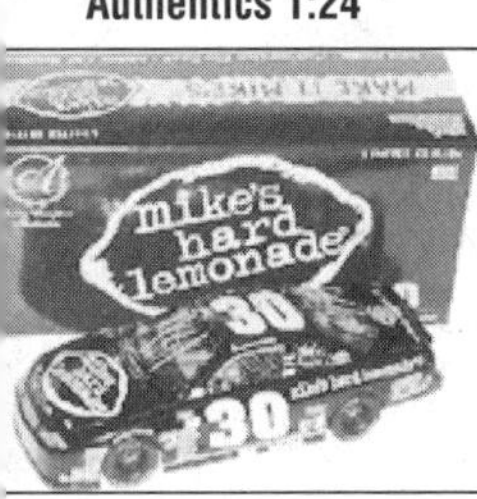

	EX	NM-MT
my Spencer ellow Freight	25.00	50.00
my Spencer ellow Freight Chrome/139	30.00	80.00
e Skinner odak/999	25.00	50.00
e Skinner odak Chrome/199	30.00	80.00
y Labonte ot Milk/999	30.00	60.00
y Labonte ot Milk Chrome/199	30.00	80.00
dy LaJoie leenex	30.00	60.00
hnny Benson agle One/999	25.00	50.00
hnny Benson agle One Chrome/199	50.00	100.00
hnny Benson alvoline/999	25.00	50.00
hnny Benson alvoline Chrome/199	50.00	120.00
ett Bodine ooters/699	30.00	60.00
ett Bodine ooters Chrome/199	50.00	100.00
ett Bodine ells Fargo Promo/2000	45.00	80.00
iott Sadler ir Force/999	25.00	50.00
iott Sadler ir Force Chrome/199	30.00	80.00
iott Sadler otorcraft/999	20.00	40.00
iott Sadler otorcraft Chrome/199	25.00	60.00
ard Burton aterpillar/999	25.00	60.00
ard Burton aterpillar Chrome/199	60.00	120.00
ard Burton aterpillar Daytona Win	40.00	80.00
ard Burton aterpillar Flag	30.00	60.00
ard Burton at Dealers/999	60.00	100.00
ard Burton at Dealers Chrome/199	75.00	125.00
t Stricklin ills Bros./999	25.00	50.00
t Stricklin ills Bros.Chrome/199	40.00	80.00
ck Sprague ETZERO/699	20.00	50.00
ck Sprague ETZERO Chrome/139	30.00	80.00
e Nemechek AW/999	25.00	50.00
e Nemechek AW Chrome	50.00	100.00
ndon Amick r.Pepper Spider-Man/699	25.00	50.00
ndon Amick r.Pepper Spider-Man hrome/149	40.00	80.00
istian Fittipaldi ike's Hard Lemonade/585	50.00	80.00
ristian Fittipaldi ike's Hard Lemonade hrome/117	60.00	100.00
cky Craven ide/999	25.00	50.00
cky Craven ide Chrome/199	40.00	80.00
cky Craven ide Kids/999	25.00	50.00
cky Craven ide Kids Chrome/199	40.00	80.00
n Schrader M&M's/999	25.00	60.00
36 Ken Schrader M&M's Chrome/199	50.00	100.00
36 Ken Schrader M&M's July 4th/999	25.00	60.00
36 Ken Schrader M&M's July 4th Chrome/199	50.00	100.00
36 Hank Parker Jr. GNC/699	25.00	50.00
36 Hank Parker Jr. GNC Chrome/139	40.00	80.00
37 Jeff Purvis Timberwolf/699	25.00	50.00
37 Jeff Purvis Timberwolf Chrome/149	30.00	60.00
40 Sterling Marlin Proud to be American	40.00	80.00
43 Richard Petty Garfield/999	30.00	60.00
48 Jimmie Johnson Lowe's/999	75.00	150.00
48 Jimmie Johnson Lowe's Chrome/199	150.00	300.00
48 Jimmie Johnson Lowe's First Win/2555	40.00	80.00
48 Jimmie Johnson Lowe's First Win Chrome/511	75.00	150.00
48 Jimmie Johnson Lowe's Sylvester and Tweety/4167	30.00	60.00
48 Jimmie Johnson Lowe's Sylvester and Tweety Chrome/833	50.00	100.00
48 Jimmie Johnson Lowe's 2001 Power of Pride/999	60.00	120.00
48 Jimmie Johnson Lowe's Power of Pride/999	75.00	150.00
48 Jimmie Johnson Lowe's Power of Pride Chrome/199	100.00	200.00
48 Jimmie Johnson Lowe's Power of Pride Employee/10,000	50.00	120.00
49 Shawna Robinson BAM/699	35.00	60.00
49 Shawna Robinson BAM Chrome/139	60.00	100.00
52 Donnie Neuenberger Maryland University Promo	30.00	60.00
66 Casey Mears Kansas Jayhawks Promo	40.00	75.00

2002 Racing Champions Ironman 1:24

	EX	NM-MT
5 Terry Labonte Kellogg's/504	30.00	50.00
10 Johnny Benson Valvoline/504	25.00	50.00
22 Ward Burton Caterpillar/504	25.00	50.00
32 Ricky Craven Tide/504	30.00	50.00
48 Jimmie Johnson Lowe's/504	60.00	100.00

2002 Racing Champions Under the Lights 1:24

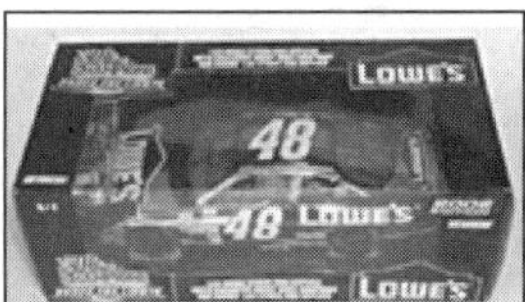

Racing Champions issued this series of 1:24 die-cast cars packaged along with the counterpart 1:64 car. Each was produced in a chrome finish to give the car the appearance of a night race event.

	EX	NM-MT
48 Jimmie Johnson Lowe's	30.00	50.00

2002 Racing Champions War Paint 1:24

Racing Champions issued this series of 1:24 die-cast cars packaged along with the counterpart 1:64 car. Each was produced with tire marks on the sides to give the car a post-race appearance.

	EX	NM-MT
48 Jimmie Johnson Lowe's	25.00	50.00

2003 Racing Champions 1:24

	EX	NM-MT
1 Jamie McMurray Yellow Freight	10.00	20.00
1 Ted Musgrave Mopar SuperTruck Promo measures slightly larger than 1:24 scale	40.00	80.00
4 Mike Skinner Kodak	10.00	20.00
4 Mike Skinner Kodak Rain Delay/500	20.00	40.00
4 Square D SuperTruck Promo	15.00	30.00
5 Terry Labonte Kellogg's	10.00	20.00
5 Terry Labonte Finding Nemo	10.00	25.00
5 Terry Labonte Finding Nemo AU/100	50.00	100.00
5 Terry Labonte Power of Cheese	10.00	20.00
5 Terry Labonte Power of Cheese AU/100	50.00	100.00
5 Brian Vickers GMAC	15.00	25.00
7 Alan Kulwicki Hooters 20th Anniv. Chrome Promo	35.00	60.00
7 Randy LaJoie Kleenex Promo	18.00	30.00
7 Jimmy Spencer Sirius	15.00	30.00
8 Bill Lester Dodge SuperTruck Promo measures slightly larger than 1:24 scale	15.00	40.00
10 Johnny Benson Valvoline	10.00	20.00
10 Johnny Benson Valvoline Firesuit/50	30.00	50.00
10 Johnny Benson Valvoline Steel/50	40.00	80.00
11 Brett Bodine Hooters	10.00	20.00
11 Brett Bodine Hooters 20th Anniversary	10.00	25.00
11 Brett Bodine US Micro Brick Promo	30.00	50.00
12 Shane Riffel USS Hornet SuperTruck Promo	20.00	40.00
14 Rick Crawford Strategic Air Command Promo	18.00	30.00
18 Chad Chaffin Dickies SuperTruck Promo measures slightly larger than 1:24 scale	15.00	30.00
22 Ward Burton Caterpillar	10.00	20.00
22 Ward Burton Caterpillar Chrome/1500	18.00	30.00
22 Ward Burton Caterpillar Firesuit/50	40.00	80.00
22 Ward Burton Caterpillar Rain Delay/500	18.00	30.00
22 Ward Burton Caterpillar Steel/50	40.00	80.00
22 Ward Burton Caterpillar Time Trial/5000	15.00	25.00
22 Ward Burton Cat Acert	15.00	25.00
22 Ward Burton Cat Acert Promo	20.00	35.00
23 Scott Wimmer Stacker 2 Fast & Furious	10.00	25.00
25 Joe Nemechek UAW Delphi	12.50	25.00
25 Joe Nemechek UAW Delphi AU/100	25.00	50.00
25 Joe Nemechek UAW Delphi Chrome/1500	12.50	30.00
25 Joe Nemechek UAW Delphi Rain Delay/500	15.00	30.00
26 Todd Bodine Discover	12.50	25.00
26 Kevin Grubb Dr.Pepper	20.00	35.00
31 Tina Gordon Scotch Transparent Duct Tape Promo	15.00	30.00
31 Tina Gordon 3M Post-it Promo	15.00	30.00
32 Ricky Craven Tide	10.00	20.00
32 Ricky Craven Tide Rain Delay/500	20.00	40.00
32 Ricky Craven Tide TCF Bank Promo	25.00	40.00
33 John Komarinski Rock Light Promo/1033	20.00	40.00
33 Tony Raines Outdoor Channel Promo	25.00	50.00
37 Derrike Cope Friendly's Promo	30.00	50.00
37 David Green Timberwolf Promo Adult Collectible box	15.00	40.00
37 David Green Timberwolf Promo Age 8+ box	20.00	50.00
48 Shane Hmiel Thomas Automotive	25.00	50.00
48 Jimmie Johnson Lowe's	15.00	25.00
48 Jimmie Johnson Lowe's Chrome/1500 with Press Pass card	20.00	35.00
48 Jimmie Johnson Lowe's Firesuit/50	60.00	120.00
48 Jimmie Johnson Lowe's Rain Delay/500	25.00	50.00
48 Jimmie Johnson Lowe's Steel/50	75.00	150.00
48 Jimmie Johnson Lowe's Power of Pride with Ultra Series card	15.00	25.00
48 Jimmie Johnson Lowe's Power of Pride Chrome/1500	15.00	30.00
48 Jimmie Johnson Lowe's Power of Pride Firesuit/50	60.00	120.00
48 Jimmie Johnson Lowe's Power of Pride Rain Delay	20.00	40.00
48 Jimmie Johnson Lowe's Power of Pride Steel/50	60.00	120.00
48 Jimmie Johnson Lowe's SpongeBob	15.00	25.00
48 Jimmie Johnson Lowe's SpongeBob Chrome/1500	25.00	40.00
49 Ken Schrader 1-800-CALL-ATT Promo	25.00	60.00
50 Scooby-Doo SD Racing	15.00	30.00
54 Todd Bodine National Guard Promo	20.00	40.00
57 Jason Keller Albertson's	10.00	20.00
62 Brendan Gaughan American Racing SuperTruck Promo in solid box measures slightly larger than 1:24 scale	30.00	50.00
77 Dave Blaney First Tennessee Promo	30.00	50.00
77 Dave Blaney Jasper Fast&Furious	10.00	25.00
90 Lance Norick Express Personnel Promo	20.00	40.00
01 Jerry Nadeau Army	12.50	25.00
01 Jerry Nadeau Army Chrome/1500	15.00	40.00
01 Jerry Nadeau Army Camo	12.50	25.00
01 Jerry Nadeau Army Camo Chrome/1500	15.00	40.00
03 Ward Burton CertainTeed Promo	25.00	50.00
03 Dana Fantasy Racing Promo	30.00	50.00
03 Parts Master Promo/7500	15.00	30.00
03 Jay Sauter Timken SuperTruck Promo	15.00	30.00
G3 Goodyear G3Xpress Promo	15.00	30.00

2003 Racing Champions Premier 1:24

	EX	NM-MT
11 Brett Bodine Hooters	20.00	35.00
11 Brett Bodine Hooters 20th Anniversary	20.00	35.00
22 Ward Burton Caterpillar	15.00	30.00
22 Ward Burton Caterpillar Chrome/1500	25.00	40.00
22 Ward Burton Caterpillar Rain Delay/500	20.00	40.00
57 Jason Keller Albertsons	18.00	30.00

2003 Racing Champions Premier Preview 1:24

	EX	NM-MT
22 Ward Burton Caterpillar	18.00	30.00
22 Ward Burton Caterpillar Firesuit/50	40.00	80.00
22 Ward Burton Caterpillar Rain Delay/500	20.00	40.00
22 Ward Burton Cat Rental	18.00	30.00
22 Ward Burton Cat Rental Chrome/1500	25.00	40.00
22 Ward Burton Cat Rental Firesuit/50	45.00	80.00
22 Ward Burton Cat Rental Firesuit/Steel/50	50.00	100.00
22 Ward Burton Cat Rental Rain Delay/500	12.50	25.00
26 Todd Bodine Discover	18.00	30.00
48 Jimmie Johnson Lowe's 2002 Season to Remember	18.00	30.00

2003 Racing Champions Preview 1:24

	EX	NM-MT
5 Terry Labonte Kellogg's	10.00	20.00
22 Ward Burton Caterpillar	12.50	25.00
22 Ward Burton Caterpillar Firesuit/50	50.00	100.00
22 Ward Burton Caterpillar Rain Delay/500	18.00	30.00
22 Ward Burton Caterpillar Steel/50	40.00	100.00
22 Ward Burton Cat Rental	12.50	25.00
22 Ward Burton Cat Rental Chrome/1500	20.00	40.00
22 Ward Burton Cat Rental Firesuit/50	40.00	100.00
22 Ward Burton Cat Rental Rain Delay/500	18.00	30.00
26 Todd Bodine Discover	10.00	25.00
32 Ricky Craven Tide	10.00	20.00
48 Jimmie Johnson Lowe's 2002 Season to Remember	10.00	25.00

2003 Racing Champions Authentics 1:24

	EX	NM-MT
1 Jamie McMurray Yellow Freight/700	30.00	60.00
1 Jamie McMurray Yellow Freight Chrome/140	75.00	135.00
11 Brett Bodine Hooters/1585	40.00	70.00
11 Brett Bodine Hooters Chrome/317	50.00	90.00
11 Brett Bodine Hooters 20th Anniv./700	40.00	70.00
11 Brett Bodine Hooters 20th Anniv. Chrome/140	60.00	100.00
22 Ward Burton Caterpillar/3690	25.00	50.00
22 Ward Burton Caterpillar Chrome/738	45.00	80.00
22 Ward Burton Cat Acert/1685	30.00	60.00
22 Ward Burton Cat Acert Chrome/337	50.00	90.00
22 Ward Burton Cat Rental/3140	25.00	50.00
22 Ward Burton Cat Rental Chrome/628	40.00	75.00
48 Jimmie Johnson Lowe's/4540	30.00	60.00
48 Jimmie Johnson Lowe's Chrome/908	50.00	100.00
48 Jimmie Johnson Lowe's Power of Pride/3470	30.00	60.00
48 Jimmie Johnson Lowe's Power of Pride Chrome/694	50.00	100.00
48 Jimmie Johnson Lowe's SpongeBob/2020	35.00	60.00
48 Jimmie Johnson Lowe's Spongebob Chrome/404	60.00	100.00

2004 Racing Champions 1:24

	EX	NM-MT
1 Johnny Benson Yellow Freight Promo	20.00	35.00
11 Darrell Waltrip Toyota TRD SuperTruck Promo	25.00	40.00
17 David Reutimann NTN Bearings SuperTruck Promo	35.00	60.00
27 Johnny Sauter Kleenex Promo	25.00	40.00
35 Brad Leighton Irving Oil Promo	15.00	30.00
38 Kasey Kahne Great Clips Promo	25.00	40.00
38 Elliott Sadler Combos Promo	12.50	25.00
38 Elliott Sadler M&M's Promo	15.00	30.00
38 Brandon Whitt Werner Ladders SuperTruck Promo	40.00	80.00
42 Mike Skinner Toyota TRD SuperTruck Promo	15.00	30.00
43 Aaron Fike Ollie's Bargain Outlet	12.50	25.00
49 Ken Schrader Red Baron Promo	30.00	60.00
49 Ken Schrader Schwan's Promo	30.00	60.00
67 Jason Jarrett Gladiator Bennigan's Promo	40.00	70.00
74 Tony Raines The Outdoor Channel Promo	15.00	30.00

2004 Racing Champions Authentics 1:24

	EX	NM-MT
5 Terry Labonte Kellogg's	30.00	50.00
22 Scott Wimmer Cat/2400	25.00	50.00
22 Scott Wimmer Cat Chrome/480	60.00	100.00
25 Brian Vickers Ditech	30.00	50.00
25 Brian Vickers Ditech.com Matco Promo	20.00	40.00
43 Richard Petty Blue 1957 Oldsmobile/800	100.00	175.00
43 Richard Petty Blue 1957 Oldsmobile Chrome/200	150.00	225.00
48 Jimmie Johnson Lowe's/2400	30.00	50.00
48 Jimmie Johnson Lowe's Chrome	50.00	80.00
48 Jimmie Johnson Lowe's HMS 20th Anniversary/2500	30.00	50.00
48 Jimmie Johnson Lowe's HMS 20th Anniversary Chrome/500	40.00	70.00
48 Jimmie Johnson Lowe's SpongeBob/2500	25.00	50.00
48 Jimmie Johnson Lowe's SpongeBob Chrome/500	35.00	60.00
48 Jimmie Johnson Lowe's Tool World	30.00	50.00
48 Jimmie Johnson Lowe's Tool World Chrome/500	40.00	70.00
0 Ward Burton NetZero	30.00	50.00
0 Ward Burton NetZero Chrome/168	35.00	60.00

2004 Racing Champions Ultra Previews 1:24

	EX	NM-MT
10 Scott Riggs Valvoline	10.00	25.00
48 Jimmie Johnson Lowe's	10.00	25.00
48 Jimmie Johnson Lowe's Chrome/1500	20.00	40.00

2004 Racing Champions Ultra 1:24

	EX	NM-MT
5 Kyle Busch Lowe's	15.00	30.00
5 Kyle Busch Lowe's SpongeBob	10.00	20.00
5 Terry Labonte	10.00	20.00

	EX	NM-MT
Delphi		
5 Terry Labonte Kellogg's	10.00	20.00
5 Terry Labonte Kellogg's Chrome/1500	20.00	40.00
5 Terry Labonte Kellogg's HMS 20th Ann. in '05 packaging	10.00	20.00
5 Terry Labonte Kellogg's Incredibles in '05 packaging	10.00	20.00
10 Scott Riggs Harlem Globetrotters	10.00	20.00
10 Scott Riggs Valvoline	10.00	20.00
10 Scott Riggs Valvoline Firesuit/50	25.00	50.00
10 Scott Riggs Valvoline Steel/50	30.00	60.00
22 Scott Wimmer Caterpillar	10.00	20.00
22 Scott Wimmer Caterpillar Chrome	20.00	40.00
22 Scott Wimmer Cat Dealer	10.00	20.00
22 Scott Wimmer Cat Rental	10.00	20.00
25 Brian Vickers ditech.com	10.00	20.00
48 Jimmie Johnson Lowe's	10.00	20.00
48 Jimmie Johnson Lowe's HMS 20th Ann. in '05 packaging	12.50	25.00
48 Jimmie Johnson Lowe's HMS 20th Anniversary Chrome/500	20.00	40.00
48 Jimmie Johnson Lowe's SpongeBob	10.00	20.00
48 Jimmie Johnson Lowe's Tool World	10.00	20.00
48 Jimmie Johnson Lowe's Tool World in '05 packaging	10.00	20.00
0 Ward Burton NetZero	15.00	30.00
0 Ward Burton NetZero Chrome/1500	25.00	50.00
0 Ward Burton NetZero Rain Delay/500	20.00	40.00
01 Joe Nemechek Army	10.00	20.00

2005 Racing Champions 1:24

	EX	NM-MT
1 Johnny Sauter Yellow Promo	20.00	35.00
5 Mike Skinner Toyota TRD SuperTruck Promo	25.00	40.00
10 Terry Cook Powerstroke Diesel SuperTruck Promo	25.00	40.00
12 Robert Huffman Toyota TRD SuperTruck Promo	25.00	40.00
17 David Reutimann Toyota TRD SuperTruck Promo	25.00	40.00
27 David Green Kleenex Promo	15.00	30.00
34 Randy Lajoie Dollar General Promo	15.00	30.00
66 Greg Biffle Royal Office Products Promo	20.00	40.00
66 Matt Martin Gatorade SuperTruck Promo	25.00	50.00

2005 Racing Champions Authentics 1:24

	EX	NM-MT
40 Pete Hamilton '70 Superbird/1002	35.00	60.00
40 Pete Hamilton '70 Superbird Black Chrome/72	50.00	100.00
40 Pete Hamilton '70 Superbird Silver Chrome/72	50.00	100.00
41 Lee Petty '64 Belvedere/630	60.00	120.00
42 Lee Petty '57 Hardtop/630	75.00	125.00
42 Lee Petty '57 Hardtop Chrome/126	100.00	175.00
43 Richard Petty '64 Plymouth Belvedere/800	50.00	75.00
43 Richard Petty '64 Plymouth Belvedere Black Chrome/200	100.00	150.00
43 Richard Petty '70 Superbird/1002	60.00	100.00
43 Richard Petty '70 Superbird Black Chrome/72	100.00	150.00
43 Richard Petty '70 Superbird Silver Chrome/72	100.00	150.00
43 Richard Petty '70 Superbird Marc Times/1002	60.00	100.00
43 Richard Petty '70 Superbird Marc Times Black Chrome/72	100.00	150.00
43 Richard Petty '70 Superbird Marc Times Silver Chrome/72	100.00	150.00
43 Richard Petty '70 Superbird Southern Chrysler/1002	60.00	100.00
43 Richard Petty '70 Superbird Southern Chrysler Black Chrome/72	100.00	150.00
43 Richard Petty '70 Superbird Southern Chrysler Silver Chrome/72	100.00	150.00
48 Jimmie Johnson Lowe's/2400	40.00	65.00
48 Jimmie Johnson Lowe's Chrome/480	50.00	80.00

2005 Racing Champions Ultra Previews 1:24

	EX	NM-MT
22 Scott Wimmer Cat Chrome	15.00	30.00

2005 Racing Champions Ultra 1:24

	EX	NM-MT
5 Kyle Busch Kellogg's	10.00	20.00
5 Blake Feese Boston Reid Lowe's	12.50	25.00
10 Scott Riggs Valvoline	10.00	20.00
14 John Andretti JA	10.00	20.00
25 Brian Vickers GMAC	10.00	20.00
36 Boris Said Centex Financial	12.50	25.00
44 Terry Labonte Kellogg's	10.00	20.00
44 Terry Labonte Kellogg's Chrome	15.00	30.00
48 Jimmie Johnson Lowe's	10.00	20.00
48 Jimmie Johnson Lowe's Chrome	15.00	30.00
57 Brian Vickers Ore Ida	10.00	20.00
57 Brian Vickers Ore Ida Chrome	15.00	30.00
66 Greg Biffle Duraflame	10.00	20.00
0 Mike Bliss NetZero Best Buy	10.00	20.00
01 Joe Nemechek Army Chrome	12.50	25.00

2006 Racing Champions 1:24

	EX	NM-MT
9 Ted Musgrave Toyota Team ASE SuperTruck Promo	100.00	150.00
23 Johnny Benson Toyota Certified SuperTruck Promo	75.00	150.00
23 Johnny Benson Toyota Exide SuperTruck Promo	150.00	225.00
30 Todd Bodine Germain Toyota SuperTruck Promo	40.00	70.00
51 Mike Garvey Marathon Oil Promo in window box	12.50	25.00
66 Greg Biffle Cub Cadet Promo	20.00	40.00

2006 Racing Champions Authentics 1:24

	EX	NM-MT
43 Richard Petty '64 Belvedere 1st Championship 1st Daytona/5004 series 2 on box	50.00	75.00

1991 Racing Champions 1:43

This was the first 1:43 scale size series from Racing Champions. Each piece was issued in a black clear-window style box with a dated copyright line on the back.

	EX	NM-MT
2 Rusty Wallace Pontiac Excitement	5.00	12.00
4 Ernie Irvan Kodak	3.00	6.00
6 Mark Martin Valvoline	5.00	12.00
9 Bill Elliott Melling	5.00	12.00
11 Geoff Bodine No Sponsor	3.00	6.00
15 Morgan Shepherd Motorcraft	3.00	6.00
18 Gregory Trammell Melling	3.00	6.00
21 Dale Jarrett Citgo	5.00	12.00
22 Sterling Marlin Maxwell House	3.00	8.00
25 Ken Schrader No Sponsor	3.00	6.00
36 Kenny Wallace Cox Lumber	3.00	6.00
42 Kyle Petty Mello Yello	3.00	6.00
43 Richard Petty STP	3.00	6.00
66 Cale Yarborough TropArtic	3.00	6.00
70 J.D. McDuffie Son's Auto	4.00	10.00
72 Ken Bouchard ADAP	3.00	6.00
89 Jim Sauter Evinrude	3.00	6.00

1991 Racing Champions 2-Car Sets 1:43

	EX	NM-MT
9/9 Bill Elliott Melling/25,000	7.50	20.00
9/15 Bill Elliott/Melling Blue Morgan Shepherd/Motorcraft	6.00	15.00
9/90 Bill Elliott/Melling Wally Dallenbach/Ford Motorsport	6.00	15.00
11/22 Geoff Bodine Sterling Marlin/Maxwell House	6.00	15.00
11/98 Bil Elliott/Bud Jody Ridley/Ford Motorsport	6.00	15.00
15/26 Geoff Bodine/Motorcraft Brett Bodine/Quaker State	6.00	15.00
18/21 Greg Trammell/Melling Dale Jarrett/Citgo	6.00	15.00
25/43 Ken Schrader Richard Petty/STP	7.50	20.00
25/89 Ken Schrader Jim Sauter	6.00	15.00
84/84 Bill Elliott Ford Motorsport/25,000	7.50	20.00

1992 Racing Champions 1:43

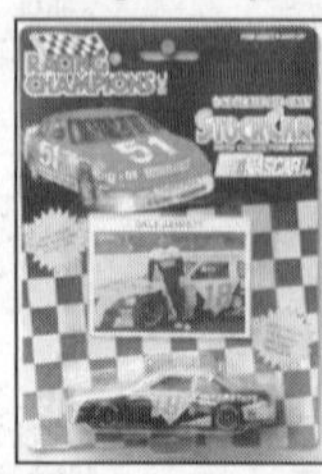

This series of 1:43 scale cars was issued in black boxes or on blister packages. They were distributed through both hobby stores and retail outlets.

	EX	NM-MT
1 Jeff Gordon Baby Ruth	45.00	75.00
1 Rick Mast Majik Market	3.00	6.00
3 Dale Earnhardt Goodwrench	40.00	80.00
5 Ricky Rudd Tide	3.00	6.00
7 Alan Kulwicki Hooters	20.00	40.00
11 Bill Elliott Amoco	5.00	10.00
17 Darrell Waltrip Western Auto	3.00	6.00
17 Darrell Waltrip Western Auto Promo	4.00	8.00
18 Dale Jarrett Interstate Batteries	5.00	10.00
28 Davey Allison Havoline	10.00	20.00
30 Michael Waltrip Pennzoil	3.00	6.00
33 Harry Gant NS	15.00	30.00
43 Richard Petty STP 1970 Superbird	15.00	30.00
66 Chad Little TropArtic	3.00	6.00
72 Ken Bouchard Auto Palace	3.00	6.00

1992 Racing Champions Pit Stop 1:43

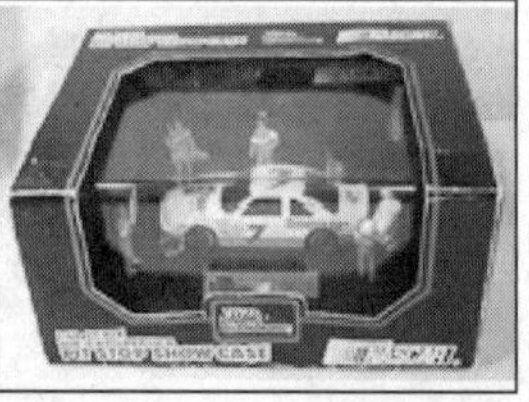

Each if these 1:43 scale "Pit Stop Show Case" scenes were packaged in a hard plastic case inside a Racing Champions black window box. Each car was mounted on a black base with plastic crew members surrounding the car as if it were in a pit stall during a race.

	EX	NM-MT
3 Dale Earnhardt Goodwrench	25.00	50.00
4 Ernie Irvan Kodak	12.50	30.00
7 Alan Kulwicki Hooters	25.00	50.00
11 Bill Elliott Bud	20.00	40.00
98 Jody Ridley Ford	10.00	25.00

1992 Racing Champions Racing Relatives 1:43

Cars from this series were issued in black window box. Each box included 2-1:43 scale cars of "Racing Relatives" or family members who both raced in the NASCAR circuit.

	EX	NM-MT
2/36 Rusty Wallace Pontiac Excitement Kenny Wallace Cox Lumber	7.50	20.00
15/26 Geoff Bodine Motorcraft Brett Bodine Quaker State	6.00	15.00
42/43 Kle Petty Mello Yello Richard Petty STP	7.50	20.00

1993 Racing Champions 1:43

	EX	NM-MT
2 Rusty Wallace Pontiac Excitement	4.00	8.00
3 Dale Earnhardt Goodwrench	25.00	60.00
4 Ernie Irvan Kodak	3.00	6.00
5 Ricky Rudd Tide	3.00	6.00
6 Mark Martin Valvoline	4.00	8.00
7 Alan Kulwicki Hooters blister	12.50	25.00
7 Alan Kulwicki Hooters in Box	12.00	25.00
8 Sterling Marlin Raybestos	12.00	20.00
11 Bill Elliott Amoco	4.00	8.00
14 Terry Labonte Kellogg's	4.00	8.00
15 Geoff Bodine Motorcraft	3.00	6.00
17 Darrell Waltrip Western Auto	3.00	6.00
21 Morgan Shepherd Citgo	3.00	6.00
24 Jeff Gordon DuPont	20.00	40.00
25 Bill Venturini Rain X	6.00	12.00
26 Brett Bodine Quaker State	3.00	6.00
27 Hut Stricklin McDonald's	3.00	6.00
28 Davey Allison Havoline	6.00	12.00
33 Harry Gant No Sponsor	3.00	6.00
42 Kyle Petty Mello Yello	3.00	6.00
44 Rick Wilson STP	3.00	6.00
51 No Driver Association Chevrolet with Primer paint	6.00	12.00
51 No Driver Association Ford with Primer paint	6.00	12.00
51 No Driver Association Pontiac with Primer paint	6.00	12.00
59 Andy Belmont FDP Brakes	6.00	12.00
60 Mark Martin Winn Dixie	5.00	10.00

1993 Racing Champions 1964 Ford Legends 1:43

Each 1:43 scale car in this series was issued in a clear plastic (PVC) box with gold foil lettering. The title "Racing Champions 1964 Ford" is printed on the top of the box along with "Limited Edition of 5000."

	EX	NM-MT
1 Dick Hutcherson Ford	15.00	30.00
21 Marvin Panch Augusta Motors	20.00	35.00
26 Curtis Turner Ed Martin Ford	12.50	25.00
27 Junior Johnson Ford	12.50	25.00
28 Fred Lorenzen LaFayette Ford	20.00	35.00
29 Nelson Stacy Ron's Ford	20.00	35.00
31 Ralph Earnhardt Ford	15.00	30.00
32 Tiny Lund Ford	12.50	25.00
49 G.C. Spencer Ford	15.00	30.00
51 Racing Champions Primer	12.50	25.00
59 Tom Pistone Ford	12.50	25.00
70 J.D. McDuffie Ford	12.50	25.00
73 Buddy Arrington Ford	15.00	30.00
76 Larry Frank Ford	12.50	25.00
99 Bobby Isaac Ford	12.50	25.00
06 Cale Yarborough Ford	12.50	25.00

1993 Racing Champions Pit Stop 1:43

Each if these "Pit Stop Show Case" scenes were packaged in a hard plastic case inside a Racing Champions red window box. Each car was mounted on a black base with plastic crew members surrounding the car as if it were in a pit stall during a race.

	EX	NM-MT
3 Dale Earnhardt Goodwrench	25.00	50.00
5 Ricky Rudd Tide	12.50	25.00
7 Alan Kulwicki Hooters	20.00	40.00
16 Ted Musgrave Family Channel	12.50	25.00
24 Jeff Gordon DuPont	25.00	50.00
27 Hut Stricklin McDonald's	12.50	25

1993 Racing Champions Premier 1:43

This is the first year that Racing Champions did a P
series for its 1:43 scale size.

	EX	NM
2 Ward Burton Hardee's	6.00	15
3 Dale Earnhardt Goodwrench/10,000	40.00	80
5 Ricky Rudd Tide	6.00	15
6 Mark Martin Valvoline/10,000	10.00	20
7 Alan Kulwicki Hooters/10,000	30.00	60
8 Sterling Marlin Raybestos	6.00	15
11 Bill Elliott Amoco	7.50	15
11 Bill Elliott Budweiser/10,000	12.00	22
17 Darrell Waltrip Western Auto/10,000	6.00	15
24 Jeff Gordon DuPont/10,000	40.00	80
27 Hut Stricklin McDonald's	6.00	15
28 Davey Allison Havoline Black&Orange/10,000	20.00	35
28 Davey Allison Havoline Black&White/10,000	15.00	30
28 Ernie Irvan Havoline	15.00	30
33 Harry Gant No Sponsor	6.00	15
42 Kyle Petty Mello Yello	6.00	15
59 Robert Pressley Alliance	25.00	45
60 Mark Martin Winn Dixie/5000	15.00	25
87 Joe Nemechek Dentyne	20.00	60
97 Joe Bessey AC Delco	6.00	15
98 Derrike Cope Bojangles by RCCC	40.00	75

1994 Racing Champions 1:

This was one of the last years that Racing Champions
regular issue 1:43 scale series. Each car was packaged in
clear window box with the year of issue printed on the
checklist of drivers appears on the bottom of the box, but
drivers were issued for this series.

	EX	NM
1 Rick Mast Precision Products	2.00	5
4 Sterling Marlin Kodak	2.00	5
5 Terry Labonte Kellogg's	3.00	6
10 Ricky Rudd Tide	2.00	5
19 Loy Allen Hooters	2.00	5
24 Jeff Gordon DuPont	20.00	40
24 Jeff Gordon DuPont Coca-Cola 600 Win in plastic case	25.00	50
26 Brett Bodine Quaker State	2.00	5
33 Harry Gant Farewell Tour	8.00	16
33 Harry Gant Leo Jackson	2.00	5
42 Kyle Petty Mello Yello	2.00	5
60 Mark Martin Winn Dixie	4.00	10

1994 Racing Champions P Stop 1:43

Each if these "Pit Stop Show Case" scenes were package
hard plastic case inside a Racing Champions yellow w
box. Each car was mounted on a black base with plasti
members surrounding the car as if it were in a pit stall du
race.

	EX	NM-
28 Ernie Irvan Havoline	12.50	25
28 Ernie Irvan Mac Tools	12.50	25

1994 Racing Champions Premier 1:43

This was the second year that Racing Champions did
Premier series. Highlighting the series are two Alan Ku
cars (Zerex and Army).

	EX	NM
1 Rick Mast Precision Products	7.50	15
2 Rusty Wallace Ford Motorsports	10.00	18
3 Dale Earnhardt Goodwrench	50.00	10

	EX	NM-MT
Sterling Marlin Kodak	8.00	20.00
Terry Labonte Kellogg's	10.00	20.00
Mark Martin Valvoline	10.00	18.00
Harry Gant Manheim	15.00	25.00
Jimmy Hensley Bojangles	7.50	15.00
Tommy Kendall Family Channel	7.50	15.00
Alan Kulwicki Army	15.00	30.00
Alan Kulwicki Zerex	15.00	30.00
Clifford Allison Sports Image	12.00	20.00
Lake Speed Quality Care	7.50	15.00
Ted Musgrave Family Channel	7.50	15.00
Morgan Shepherd Cheerwine	7.50	15.00
Bobby Labonte Maxwell House/5000	15.00	30.00
Jeff Gordon DuPont Snickers	30.00	60.00
Ken Schrader GMAC	7.50	15.00
Brett Bodine Quaker State	7.50	15.00
Ernie Irvan Havoline	12.00	20.00
Ernie Irvan Mac Tools/7500	15.00	25.00
Michael Waltrip Pennzoil	7.50	15.00
Harry Gant Farewell Tour	7.50	15.00
Harry Gant Leo Jackson Motorsports	7.50	15.00
Dennis Setzer Alliance	7.50	15.00
Mark Martin Winn Dixie	12.00	20.00
Greg Sacks US Air	7.50	15.00

1995 Racing Champions Premier 1:43

1995, Racing Champions only produced 1:43 size cars for ecial circumstances. The Jeff Gordon was a salute to the ugural Brickyard Winner and the Mark Martin was done as a mo. The Martin piece was available through Winn Dixie res.

	EX	NM-MT
Jeff Gordon Brickyard Win in plastic case	25.00	60.00
Mark Martin Winn Dixie	10.00	20.00

1997 Racing Champions 1:43

	EX	NM-MT
Ricky Rudd Tide Mountain Spring Promo	4.00	10.00

1998 Racing Champions 1:43

	EX	NM-MT
Ricky Rudd Tide Kids Promo	5.00	10.00

1999 Racing Champions Petty Collection 1:43

	EX	NM-MT
Richard Petty 1970 Superbird	6.00	12.00
R.Petty/'70 Superbird 3-car set	12.50	25.00

1999 Racing Champions Under the Lights 1:43

ese 1:43 scale cars feature special anodized paint to give that der the lights appearance.

	EX	NM-MT
Terry Labonte Kellogg's	5.00	10.00
Jeremy Mayfield Mobil 1	4.00	8.00
Bill Elliott Drive Thru	8.00	20.00

1989 Racing Champions Flat Bottom 1:64

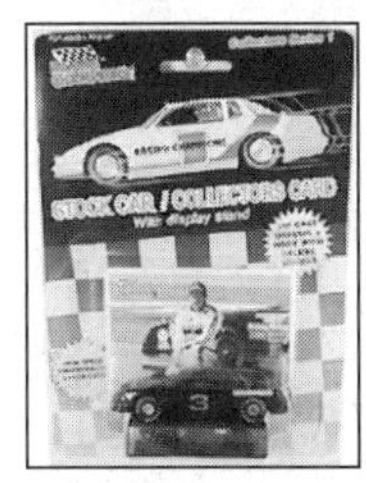

s was the first series of NASCAR die cast cars produced by cing Champions. The series is commonly referred to as flat ttoms because the blister package the car came in was flat oss the bottom. In all subsequent years there was a bubble oss the bottom to help the package freely stand up.

	EX	NM-MT
Dale Earnhardt Goodwrench	75.00	150.00
Bill Elliott Motorcraft Melling Ford	50.00	100.00
Larry Pearson No Sponsor	30.00	60.00
Davey Allison Havoline	70.00	120.00
30 Michael Waltrip Country Time	30.00	60.00
94 Sterling Marlin Sunoco	30.00	60.00

1990 Racing Champions 1:64

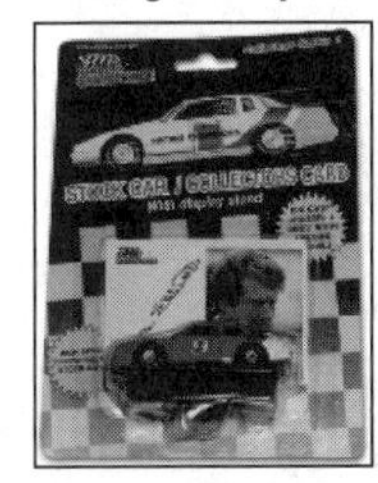

This was the first full series of 1:64 scale cars produced by Racing Champions. Many of the cars came with rubber tires as opposed to plastic. Cars with rubber tires usually carry a $5.00 to $10.00 premium. The cars used many different body styles.

	EX	NM-MT
1 Terry Labonte Majik Market Oldsmobile	30.00	60.00
3 Dale Earnhardt Goodwrench	75.00	150.00
3 Dale Earnhardt GM Performance Parts	20.00	50.00
9 Bill Elliott Orange and Blue Stripe No Melling on the car	60.00	100.00
9 Bill Elliott Orange and Blue Stripe with Melling on the car	35.00	60.00
9 Bill Elliott Red and Blue Stripe with Melling on the car	30.00	50.00
10 Derrike Cope Lumina	50.00	100.00
14 A.J. Foyt Buick	75.00	125.00
14 A.J. Foyt Lumina	60.00	120.00
14 A.J. Foyt Old Pontiac body style	30.00	60.00
14 A.J. Foyt Oldsmobile	25.00	50.00
14 A.J. Foyt Pontiac	20.00	40.00
15 Morgan Shepherd Red and White color scheme	20.00	40.00
15 Morgan Shepherd Red and Cream color scheme	15.00	30.00
16 Larry Pearson Buick with White Bumper	75.00	125.00
16 Larry Pearson Buick with brown bumper driver name in script	18.00	35.00
16 Larry Pearson Buick with Brown Bumper driver name in print	15.00	30.00
16 Larry Pearson Lumina with Brown Bumper	40.00	75.00
16 Larry Pearson Old Pontiac with Brown Bumper	40.00	75.00
16 Larry Pearson Oldsmobile with Brown Bumper	40.00	75.00
16 Larry Pearson Pontiac with Brown Bumper	12.50	25.00
18 Greg Sacks Slim Fast	18.00	30.00
20 Rob Moroso Red Stripe	15.00	30.00
21 Neil Bonnett Citgo	20.00	50.00
25 Tim Richmond Fan Club Promo in bag and PVC Box	4.00	10.00
26 Kenny Bernstein Buick	20.00	40.00
26 Kenny Bernstein Lumina	25.00	50.00
26 Kenny Bernstein Old Pontiac body style	25.00	50.00
26 Kenny Bernstein Oldsmobile	20.00	40.00
27 Rusty Wallace Old Pontiac Miller Genuine Draft	40.00	80.00
27 Rusty Wallace Oldsmobile	60.00	100.00
27 Rusty Wallace Pontiac Miller Genuine Draft	30.00	60.00
27 Rusty Wallace Pontiac Miller	30.00	60.00
27 Rusty Wallace Pontiac with Silver Decals	40.00	80.00
27 Rusty Wallace 1989 Champion Promo/30,000	8.00	20.00
28 Davey Allison Black and White paint scheme	30.00	80.00
28 Davey Allison Black and Gold paint scheme	25.00	50.00
30 Michael Waltrip Country Time	35.00	70.00
30 Michael Waltrip Country Time Promo	4.00	10.00
30 Michael Waltrip Maxwell House	12.50	30.00
30 Michael Waltrip Maxwell House Promo	4.00	10.00
33 Harry Gant Pontiac	20.00	40.00
42 Kyle Petty Buick with Blue and White paint	50.00	100.00
42 Kyle Petty Lumina with Blue and White paint	50.00	100.00
42 Kyle Petty Old Pontiac with Blue and White paint	30.00	60.00
42 Kyle Petty Oldsmobile with Blue and White paint	50.00	100.00
42 Kyle Petty Peak with Sabco on deck lid	15.00	30.00
42 Kyle Petty Peak without Sabco on deck lid Blue and Pink paint scheme	15.00	30.00
43 Richard Petty Pontiac	20.00	40.00
94 Sterling Marlin Buick	50.00	120.00
94 Sterling Marlin Lumina	40.00	80.00
94 Sterling Marlin Old Pontiac	50.00	90.00
94 Sterling Marlin Oldsmobile	20.00	40.00
NNO 12-car set in case each car issued in plastic bag 3. Dale Earnhardt/Goodwrench 9. Bill Elliott/Melling Red 14. A.J. Foyt 15. Morgan Shepherd/Motorcraft 16. Larry Pearson#21. Neil Bonnett/Citgo 26. Kenny Bernstein/Quaker State 27. Rusty Wallace/MGD 28. Davey Allison/Havoline 30. Michael Waltrip/Maxwell House 42. Kyle Petty/Peak 94. Sterling Marlin/Sunoco	40.00	80.00

1990-91 Racing Champions Roaring Racers 1:64

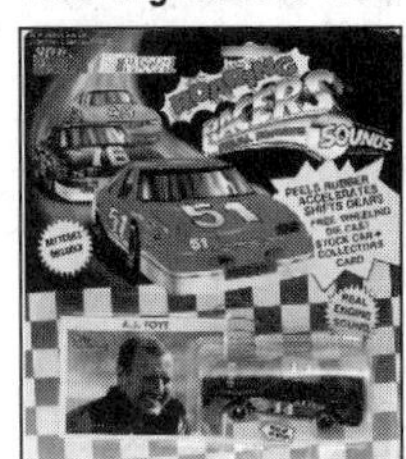

	EX	NM-MT
2 Rusty Wallace No sponsor BW 1991	4.00	10.00
3 Dale Earnhardt Goodwrench SW '90	12.50	25.00
9 Bill Elliott Melling Blue BW 1991	4.00	10.00
9 Bill Elliott Melling Red SW 1990	4.00	10.00
9 Bill Elliott Melling Red BW 1991	4.00	10.00
9 Bill Elliott Melling Red SW 1991	4.00	10.00
10 Derrike Cope Purolator BW 1991	3.00	8.00
10 Derrike Cope Purolator SW 1991	3.00	8.00
11 Geoff Bodine Bodine Racing BW 1991	3.00	8.00
11 Geoff Bodine Bodine Racing SW 1991	3.00	8.00
14 Bobby Allison No Sponsor SW 1991	3.00	8.00
14 A.J. Foyt Foyt Racing 1991	3.00	8.00
14 A.J.Foyt Foyt Racing SW 1991	3.00	8.00
15 Morgan Shepherd Motorcraft 1990	3.00	8.00
15 Morgan Shepherd Motorcraft SW 1991	3.00	8.00
18 Greg Trammell Melling SW 1991	3.00	8.00
21 Dale Jarrett Citgo BW 1991	4.00	10.00
21 Dale Jarrett Citgo SW 1991	4.00	10.00
22 Sterling Marlin Maxwell House BW 1991	4.00	10.00
25 Ken Schrader Schrader Racing 1991	3.00	8.00
26 Kenny Bernstein Quaker State SW 1991	3.00	8.00
28 Davey Allison Havoline SW 1990	6.00	15.00
28 Davey Allison Havoline SW 1991	6.00	15.00
30 Michael Waltrip Pennzoil 1990	3.00	8.00
33 Harry Gant Gant Racing SW 1991	3.00	8.00
36 Kenny Wallace Cox Lumber BW 1991	3.00	8.00
42 Kyle Petty Mello Yello BW 1991	3.00	8.00
42 Kyle Petty Peak SW 1990	3.00	8.00
42 Kyle Petty Peak SW 1991	3.00	8.00
43 Richard Petty STP BW 1991	5.00	12.00
43 Richard Petty STP SW 1991	5.00	12.00
52 Jimmy Means No sponsor 1991	3.00	8.00
66 Cale Yarborough Phillips 66 BW 1991	4.00	10.00
66 Cale Yarborough Phillips 66 SW 1991	4.00	10.00
68 Bobby Hamilton Country Time SW 1991	3.00	8.00
71 Dave Marcis Big Apple 1991	3.00	8.00
72 Ken Bouchard ADAP BW 1991	3.00	8.00
72 Tracy Leslie Detroit Gasket BW 1991	3.00	8.00

1990-92 Racing Champions 3-Pack 1:64

These Racing Champions 1:64 cars were packaged 3-per large blister and were issued over a period of years. Some included a theme, such as the Daytona 500, while others included 10-bonus cards in each pack.

	EX	NM-MT
1/68/96 Rick Mast Bobby Hamilton Tom Peck 1992 with 10-extra cards	7.50	15.00
3/15/43 Dale Earnhardt Goodwrench Morgan Shepherd Motorcraft Richard Petty STP 1990 with 10-extra cards	25.00	50.00
10/15/43 Derrike Cope Puralator Morgan Shepherd Motorcraft Richard Petty STP 1990 with 10-extra cards	10.00	20.00
15/21/28 1992 Daytona 500 Top 3 Davey Allison Morgan Shepherd Geoff Bodine	7.50	20.00
16/20/26 Larry Pearson Buick Rob Moroso Crown Xtra Kenny Bernstein Quaker State 1990 with 10-extra cards	6.00	15.00
26/52/66 Brett Bodine/Quaker State Jimmy Means Cale Yarborough/Phillips 66 1991 with 10-extra cards	6.00	15.00
28/30/94 Davey Allison Michael Waltrip Sterling Marlin 1990 with 10-extra cards	10.00	20.00

1991 Racing Champions 1:64

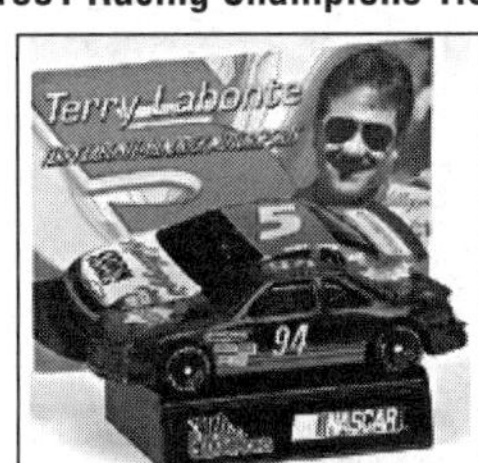

This series of 1:64 scale Racing Champion cars has many different package variations, although all were issued in the typical cardboard and plastic blister pack. The front of the backer board featured a red #51 car, while the backs were printed with up to three different variations. One has Dale Earnhardt on the back of the package (abbreviated EB in the listing). Another has Richard Petty on the back of the package (abbreviated PB). Finally a third variation comes with NASCAR Properties on the stand the car sits on. Additionally, some cars were produced in different body styles as well.

	EX	NM-MT
1 Terry Labonte Oldsmobile EB	15.00	30.00
1 Terry Labonte Oldsmobile NP	20.00	40.00
1 Terry Labonte Oldsmobile PB	15.00	30.00
1 Rick Mast Buick PB	3.00	6.00
1 Rick Mast Oldsmobile PB	2.00	5.00
2 Rusty Wallace Pontiac EB	7.50	15.00
2 Rusty Wallace Pontiac PB	5.00	10.00
2 Rusty Wallace Mobil 1 Promo	5.00	12.00
3 Dale Earnhardt Lumina EB	30.00	80.00
3 Dale Earnhardt Lumina NP	75.00	150.00
3 Dale Earnhardt Lumina PB	25.00	60.00
4 Ernie Irvan Kodak PB	2.00	5.00
5 Jay Fogleman Lumina PB	6.00	12.00
9 Bill Elliott Ford PB	2.00	5.00
9 Bill Elliott Ford EB Car is 1/2 blue	12.50	25.00
9 Bill Elliott Ford EB Car is 3/4 blue	9.00	18.00
9 Bill Elliott Old Ford body style EB Orange and White paint scheme	15.00	30.00
9 Bill Elliott Old Ford body style NP Orange and White paint scheme	18.00	35.00
10 Derrike Cope Purolator EB with 2 rows of checkers	3.00	6.00
10 Derrike Cope Purolator EB with 3 rows of checkers	12.50	25.00
10 Derrike Cope Purolator PB with 2 rows of checkers	2.00	5.00
10 Derrike Cope Purolator PB with 3 rows of checkers	7.50	15.00
11 Geoff Bodine Ford EB	2.00	5.00
11 Geoff Bodine Ford PB	2.00	5.00
12 Bobby Allison Buick PB	2.00	5.00
12 Hut Stricklin Buick PB	2.00	5.00
12 Hut Stricklin Lumina PB	2.00	5.00
14 A.J. Foyt Buick PB	25.00	50.00
14 A.J. Foyt Oldsmobile EB	15.00	30.00
14 A.J. Foyt Oldsmobile NP	25.00	60.00
14 A.J. Foyt Oldsmobile PB	8.00	16.00
15 Morgan Shepherd Ford with Red paint scheme EB	5.00	10.00
15 Morgan Shepherd Ford EB with Red and White paint scheme	7.50	15.00
15 Morgan Shepherd Ford PB	2.00	5.00
15 Morgan Shepherd Old Ford EB	5.00	10.00
15 Morgan Shepherd Old Ford NP	30.00	60.00
16 Larry Pearson Buick EB	3.00	6.00
16 Larry Pearson Buick NP	30.00	60.00
16 Larry Pearson Buick PB	2.00	5.00
16 Larry Pearson Lumina PB	12.50	25.00
18 Gregory Trammell Melling PB	2.00	5.00
20 Rob Moroso Crown Oldsmobile EB	15.00	30.00
20 Rob Moroso Crown Oldsmobile with STP decal NP	25.00	50.00
21 Neil Bonnett Old Ford EB	15.00	30.00
21 Neil Bonnett Old Ford NP	50.00	90.00
21 Dale Jarrett Ford EB	10.00	20.00
21 Dale Jarrett Ford PB	4.00	8.00
22 Sterling Marlin Ford with Black wheels PB	2.00	5.00
22 Sterling Marlin Ford with Silver Wheels PB	15.00	40.00
25 Ken Schrader Lumina PB	2.00	5.00
26 Kenny Bernstein Buick EB	3.00	6.00
26 Kenny Bernstein Buick Quaker State NP	30.00	60.00
26 Kenny Bernstein Buick PB	2.00	5.00
26 Kenny Bernstein Oldsmobile PB	5.00	10.00
26 Brett Bodine Buick Quaker State PB	2.00	5.00
26 Brett Bodine Lumina PB	1.50	4.00
27 Rusty Wallace Pontiac Miller Genuine Draft EB	30.00	60.00
27 Rusty Wallace Pontiac Miller Genuine Draft NP	50.00	90.00
27 Rusty Wallace Pontiac no MGD EB	25.00	50.00
27 Rusty Wallace Pontiac Miller EB	20.00	40.00
28 Davey Allison Ford EB	25.00	50.00
28 Davey Allison Ford PB	18.00	35.00
28 Davey Allison Old Ford EB	20.00	40.00
28 Davey Allison Old Ford NP	50.00	90.00
28 Davey Allison Old Ford PB	15.00	30.00
30 Michael Waltrip Pontiac Country Time EB	12.50	25.00
30 Michael Waltrip Pontiac Pennzoil EB with STP decal	6.00	12.00
30 Michael Waltrip Pontiac Pennzoil EB without STP decal	6.00	12.00
30 Michael Waltrip Pontiac NP	30.00	60.00
30 Michael Waltrip Pontiac PB	2.00	5.00
33 Harry Gant Buick PB	10.00	20.00
33 Harry Gant Oldsmobile EB	7.50	15.00
33 Harry Gant Oldsmobile PB	6.00	12.00
33 Harry Gant Pontiac EB	7.50	15.00
33 Harry Gant Pontiac NP	30.00	60.00
34 Todd Bodine Welco	2.00	5.00
36 Kenny Wallace Cox Lumber	2.00	5.00
41 No Driver Association Kellogg's Promo in bag	2.50	6.00
42 Kyle Petty Mello Yello PB	4.00	8.00
42 Kyle Petty Peak EB	7.50	15.00
42 Kyle Petty Peak NB	18.00	35.00
42 Kyle Petty Peak PB	10.00	20.00
43 Richard Petty STP EB	7.50	15.00
43 Richard Petty STP NP	30.00	60.00
43 Richard Petty STP PB	4.00	8.00
52 Jimmy Means Pontiac PB	2.00	5.00
59 Robert Pressley Alliance	2.00	5.00
66 Cale Yarborough Pontiac PB	4.00	8.00
68 Bobby Hamilton Oldsmobile PB	2.00	5.00
68 NDA Country Time Promo	4.00	8.00
68 Bobby Hamilton	10.00	20.00

	EX	NM-MT
Buick PB		
70 J.D. McDuffie Son's Auto	2.00	5.00
71 Dave Marcis Lumina PB	8.00	20.00
72 Ken Bouchard ADAP PB	10.00	20.00
72 Tracy Leslie Detroit Gaskets PB	2.00	5.00
84 Mike Alexander Nashville Ford	2.00	5.00
84 NDA/Miller High Life in plastic box	30.00	50.00
84 Dick Trickle Miller High Life in plastic box	45.00	80.00
89 Jim Sauter Pontiac PB	2.00	5.00
89 Jim Sauter Pontiac Day Glow PB	5.00	10.00
91 Phoenix International November 3 Promo	3.00	6.00
91 Racing Champions Club Promo	5.00	12.00
94 Terry Labonte Buick PB	6.00	12.00
94 Terry Labonte Oldsmobile PB	4.00	8.00
94 Sterling Marlin Oldsmobile EB	5.00	10.00
94 Sterling Marlin Oldsmobile NP	12.50	25.00
96 Tom Peck Lumina PB	18.00	35.00
96 Tom Peck Oldsmobile PB	2.00	5.00
S1 Robert Griggs Winston Cup Scene	4.00	10.00
NNO Collectors Edition 12-car set	15.00	40.00
4. Ernie Irvan		
5. Jay Fogleman		
9. Bill Elliott		
12. Bobby Allison		
22. Sterling Marlin		
34. Todd Bodine		
36. Kenny Wallace		
66. Cale Yarborough		
68. Bobby Hamilton		
71. Dave Marcis		
72. Tracy Leslie		
96. Tom Peck		
NNO Collectors Edition 12-car set	15.00	40.00
1. Rick Mast/Majik Market		
9. Bill Elliott/Melling Blue		
10. Derrike Cope/Purolator		
18. Greg Trammell		
22. Sterling Marlin/Maxwell House		
25. Ken Schrader		
33. Harry Gant		
43. Richard Petty/STP		
52. Jimmy Means		
66. Cale Yarborough/Phillips 66		
71. Dave Marcis		
94. Terry Labonte/Sunoco		
NNO Daytona 5-car Military set We Support Our Troops	10.00	25.00
7. Alan Kulwicki/Army		
18. Dale Jarrett/Navy		
24. Air Force		
71. Dave Marcis/Coast Guard		
88. Marines		
NNO Sears 13-car set	15.00	40.00
1. Rick Mast/Majik Market		
2. Rusty Wallace		
9. Bill Elliott/Melling Blue		
12. Hut Stricklin/Raybestos		
14. A.J. Foyt		
22. Sterling Marlin/Maxwell House		
36. Kenny Wallace/Cox Lumber		
42. Kyle Petty/Mello Yello		
43. Richard Petty/STP		
66. Cale Yarborough/Phillips 66		
68. Bobby Hamilton/Country Time		
89. Jim Sauter/Evinrude		
91. Racing Champions		

1991 Racing Champions with Figure 1:64

Each 1:64 car in this series was packaged with a plastic collectible figurine of the featured driver. A die-cast piece, card and driver statue were all issued in a large "Racing Superstars" blister pack.

	EX	NM-MT
9 Bill Elliott Melling	5.00	12.00
10 Derrike Cope Purolator	4.00	10.00
22 Sterling Marlin Maxwell House	5.00	12.00
25 Ken Schrader	4.00	10.00
43 Richard Petty STP	6.00	15.00
68 Bobby Hamilton Country Time	4.00	10.00

1991-92 Racing Champions Legends 1:64

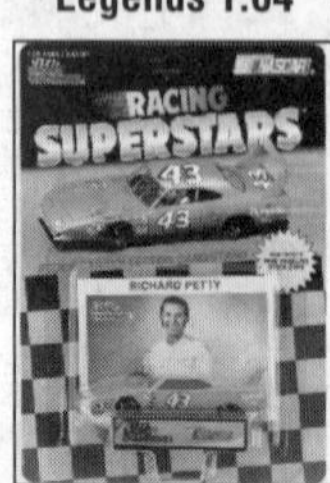

This series of NASCAR legends was issued in 1991 and 1992. Each car was packaged in one of two different blisters: "Racing Superstars" packaged with a white bordered trading card, or simply "Racing Champions" packaged with a "Collector's Series" black bordered card.

	EX	NM-MT
1 Bud Moore 1969 Dodge Daytona	4.00	10.00
3 Don White 1969 Dodge Daytona	4.00	10.00
4 John Sears 1964 Ford	4.00	10.00
4 John Sears 1969 Ford Torino	4.00	10.00
5 Buddy Arrington 1969 Dodge Daytona	4.00	10.00
5 Pete Hamilton 1969 Ford Torino	4.00	10.00
7 Ramo Stott 1970 Plymouth Superbird	4.00	10.00
10 Buddy Baker 1964 Ford	4.00	10.00
11 Ned Jarrett 1964 Ford	4.00	10.00
14 Bill Ellis 1970 Plymouth Superbird	4.00	10.00
17 David Pearson 1969 Ford Torino	4.00	10.00
18 Joe Frasson 1969 Dodge Daytona	4.00	10.00
21 Marvin Panch 1964 Ford	4.00	10.00
21 Cale Yarborough 1969 Ford Torino	4.00	10.00
22 Dick Brooks 1969 Dodge Daytona	4.00	10.00
22 Fireball Roberts 1964 Ford	4.00	10.00
27 Donnie Allison 1969 Ford Torino	4.00	10.00
28 Fred Lorenzen 1964 Ford Fastback	4.00	10.00
29 Bobby Allison 1969 Ford Torino	4.00	10.00
29 Bud Moore 1969 Ford Torino	4.00	10.00
30 Dave Marcis 1969 Dodge Daytona	4.00	10.00
31 Ralph Earnhardt 1964 Ford	15.00	30.00
32 Dick Brooks 1970 Plymouth Superbird 1969 Rookie of the Year	4.00	10.00
34 Wendell Scott 1964 Ford	4.00	10.00
40 Pete Hamilton Plymouth only on fender 1970 Superbird Racing Superstars blister	5.00	12.00
40 Pete Hamilton Plymouth by Petty on fender 1970 Superbird Racing Superstars blister	4.00	10.00
42 Marty Robbins	25.00	40.00
43 Richard Petty 1969 Ford Torino	5.00	12.00
43 Richard Petty 1970 Plymouth Superbird Racing Superstars blister	5.00	12.00
48 James Hylton 1969 Dodge Daytona	4.00	10.00
55 Tiny Lund 1969 Dodge Daytona	4.00	10.00
61 Hoss Ellington 1969 Ford Torino	4.00	10.00
64 Elmo Langley 1964 Ford	4.00	10.00
70 J.D. McDuffie 1964 Ford	4.00	10.00
70 J.D. McDuffie 1969 Ford Torino	4.00	10.00
71 Bobby Isaac 1969 Dodge Daytona	4.00	10.00
73 Buddy Arrington 1964 Ford	4.00	10.00
88 Benny Parsons 1969 Ford Torino	4.00	10.00
99 Charlie Glotzbach 1969 Dodge Daytona	4.00	10.00
06 Neil Castles 1969 Dodge Daytona	4.00	10.00
06 Cale Yarborough 1964 Ford	4.00	10.00

1992 Racing Champions 1:64

Every regular issue piece in this series was produced with both a photo of Richard Petty on the back of the blister card and a checklist on the back. The blister pack fronts feature a checkered flag design on the bottom half and artwork for a red car #51 on the top half of the package. A trading card was also packaged with each car. The promo pieces were issued with sponsor logos and artwork on the fronts of the blisters. This was Jeff Gordon's first appearance in a Racing Champions die cast series.

	EX	NM-MT
1 Ford Motorsport Promo/10,000	3.00	8.00
1 Jeff Gordon Baby Ruth	25.00	60.00
1 Jeff Gordon Baby Ruth Promo black windows	8.00	20.00
1 Rick Mast Majik Market	1.50	4.00
2 Rusty Wallace Pontiac Excitement	6.00	12.00
3 Dale Earnhardt Goodwrench 5-Time Champion card	30.00	60.00
4 Ernie Irvan Kodak	4.00	8.00
4U Boyd Adams Nashville Raceway Promo	4.00	10.00
5 Jay Fogleman Inn Keeper	1.50	4.00
5 Ricky Rudd Tide	1.50	4.00
5 Ricky Rudd Tide Promo black windows	5.00	10.00
6 Mark Martin Valvoline	12.00	20.00
6 Mark Martin Valvoline 2-car set	15.00	30.00
7 Harry Gant Mac Tools	10.00	20.00
7 Alan Kulwicki Hooters	15.00	40.00
8 Jeff Burton TIC Financial Promo/15,000	2.50	6.00
8 Bobby Dotter Team R	1.50	4.00
9 Joe Bessey AC Delco	6.00	12.00
9 Bill Elliott Coors Light Promo in bag	20.00	40.00
9 Bill Elliott Melling	5.00	12.00
9 Bill Elliott Melling Motorcraft 500 Promo black windows	5.00	10.00
9 Chad Little Melling Performance	4.00	10.00
9/14 Joe Bessey Mike Stefanik Auto Palace Promo 2-car set	3.00	8.00
10 No Driver Association Bull Frog Promo/20,000 (Derrike Cope's Car)	4.00	10.00
10 Derrike Cope Purolator Adam's Mark	2.00	5.00
10 Derrike Cope Purolator with name in Blue	2.00	5.00
10 Derrike Cope Purolator with name in White	6.00	15.00
10 Sterling Marlin Maxwell House	5.00	12.00
11 Geoff Bodine No Sponsor	1.50	4.00
11 Bill Elliott Amoco	6.00	12.00
11 Bill Elliott Amoco Jan.2, 1992	6.00	12.00
12 Bobby Allison No Sponsor	1.50	4.00
12 Karen Schulz Piggly Wiggly Promo/10,000	6.00	15.00
12 Hut Stricklin Raybestos	1.50	4.00
14 A.J. Foyt No Sponsor	10.00	20.00
15 Geoff Bodine Motorcraft	1.50	4.00
15 Chad Chaffin N&S Parts Promo/15,000	6.00	12.00
15 Chad Chaffin Shoney's Promo/15,000	10.00	20.00
16 Wally Dallenbach Jr. Roush Racing	7.50	15.00
17 Darrell Waltrip Western Auto	1.50	4.00
17 Darrell Waltrip Western Auto Promo	4.00	10.00
18 Dale Jarrett Interstate Batteries	4.00	8.00
18 Gregory Trammell Melling	1.50	4.00
19 Chad Little Tyson	1.50	4.00
20 Mike Wallace First Aide	4.00	8.00
21 Dale Jarrett Citgo	4.00	8.00
21 Morgan Shepherd Citgo	1.50	4.00
22 Sterling Marlin Maxwell House	1.25	3.00
25 Ken Schrader Hendrick Motorsports	2.00	5.00
25 Bill Venturini Amoco Rain X	2.00	5.00
26 Brett Bodine Quaker State	1.50	4.00
27 Hut Stricklin McDonald's Promo	4.00	10.00
28 Davey Allison Havoline	7.50	15.00
28 Davey Allison Havoline 7-Up Promo	7.50	15.00
28 Bobby Hillin Jr. Havoline	7.50	15.00
30 Michael Waltrip Pennzoil	1.50	4.00
31 Steve Grissom Big Mama Promo	20.00	50.00
31 Steve Grissom Roddenbery's Promo	4.00	10.00
31 Bobby Hillin Jr. Team Ireland	2.00	5.00
33 Harry Gant No Sponsor	1.50	4.00
34 Todd Bodine Welco Quick Stop	2.00	5.00
36 Kenny Wallace Cox Lumber	2.00	5.00
36 Kenny Wallace Dirt Devil	3.00	6.00
42 Bobby Hillin Jr. Mello Yello	9.00	18.00
42 Kyle Petty Mello Yello	4.00	8.00
43 Richard Petty STP with Black wheels	6.00	12.00
43 Richard Petty STP with Blue wheels	6.00	12.00
44 Bill Caudill Army	1.50	4.00
49 Stanley Smith Ameritron	5.00	10.00
55 Ted Musgrave Jasper Engines	5.00	10.00
56 Jerry Glanville Atlanta Falcons Promo	3.00	6.00
59 Andy Belmont FDP Brakes	3.00	6.00
59 Robert Pressley Alliance Promo	5.00	12.00
60 Mark Martin Winn Dixie	4.00	8.00
63 Chuck Bown Nescafe	1.50	4.00
66 Jimmy Hensley TropArtic	1.50	4.00
66 Chad Little TropArtic	1.50	4.00
66 Cale Yarborough TropArtic Ford	3.00	6.00
66 Cale Yarborough TropArtic Pontiac	1.50	4.00
68 Bobby Hamilton Country Time	1.50	4.00
70 J.D. McDuffie Son's Auto	1.50	4.00
71 Dave Marcis Big Apple Market	3.00	8.00
72 Ken Bouchard ADAP	4.00	8.00
72 Tracy Leslie Detroit Gasket	1.50	4.00
75 Butch Miller Food Country	1.50	4.00
83 Lake Speed Purex	3.00	6.00
83 Lake Speed Purex Promo/20,000	5.00	10.00
87 Joe Nemechek Texas Pete	1.50	4.00
89 Jim Sauter Evinrude	1.50	4.00
92 NDA Hungry Jack Promo in bag	1.50	4.00
92 Racing Champions Club Promo	4.00	10.00
92 Sam Bass Promo	3.00	8.00
94 Terry Labonte Sunoco with blue bumper	6.00	12.00
94 Terry Labonte Sunoco with yellow bumper	10.00	20.00
96 Tom Peck Thomas Brothers	1.50	4.00
98 Jody Ridley Ford Motorsport Promo/10,000	3.00	8.00
NNO Collectors Edition 4-car set	6.00	15.00
15. Geoff Bodine/Motorcraft		
30. Michael Waltrip/Pennzoil		
68. Bobby Hamilton/Country Time		
70. J.D. McDuffie/Son's Auto		
NNO Collectors Edition 6-car set	10.00	25.00
5. Ricky Rudd/Tide		
8. Bobby Dotter		
15. Geoff Bodine/Motorcraft		
28. Davey Allison/Havoline		
70. J.D. McDuffie/Son's Automotive		
94. Terry Labonte/Sunoco		
NNO Collectors Edition 12-car set	15.00	40.00
1. Rick Mast/Majik Markets		
10. Derrike Cope/Purolator		
12. Hut Stricklin/Raybestos		
22. Sterling Marlin/Maxwell House		
33. Harry Gant/No sponsor		
34. Todd Bodine/Wellco		
42. Kyle Petty/Mello Yello		
68. Bobby Hamilton/Country Time		
92. Racing Champions		
96. Tom Peck/Thomas		
98. Jody Ridley		
0. Dick McCabe/Fisher Snowplows		
NNO Collectors Edition 12-car set	15.00	40.00
2. Rusty Wallace/Pontiac Excite.		
4. Ernie Irvan/Kodak Film		
5. Ricky Rudd/Tide		
6. Mark Martin/Valvoline#11. Bill Elliott		
17. Darrell Waltrip/Western Auto		
21. Morgan Shepherd/Citgo		
28. Davey Allison/Havoline		
30. Michael Waltrip/Pennzoil		
43. Richard Petty/STP		
70. J.D. McDuffie/Son's Auto		
92. Racing Champions		
NNO Sears 12-car set	15.00	40.00
2. Rusty Wallace/Pontiac Excite.		
4. Ernie Irvan/Kodak		
5. Ricky Rudd/Tide		
6. Mark Martin/Valvoline		
11. Geoff Bodine		
17. Darrell Waltrip/Western Auto		
21. Morgan Shepherd/Citgo		
28. Davey Allison/Havoline		
30. Michael Waltrip/Pennzoil		
43. Richard Petty/STP		
70. J.D.McDuffie/Son's Auto		
92. Racing Champions		

1992 Racing Champions AC Racing Promos 1:64

	EX	NM-MT
2 Rusty Wallace Pontiac Excitement	4.00	8.00
3 Dale Earnhardt Goodwrench	6.00	15.00
4 Ernie Irvan Kodak	3.00	6.00
5 Ricky Rudd Tide	3.00	6.00
12 Hut Stricklin Raybestos	3.00	6.00
17 Darrell Waltrip Western Auto	3.00	6.00
25 Ken Schrader Hendrick	3.00	6.00
42 Kyle Petty Mello Yello	3.00	6.00

1992 Racing Champions Milkhouse Cheese Promos 1:64

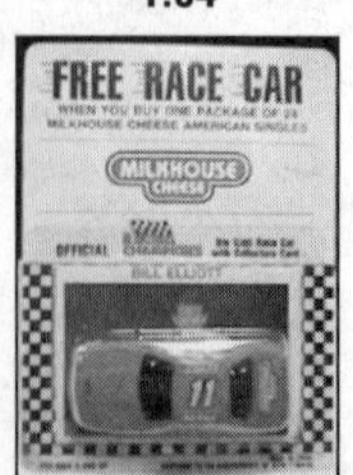

This series of die-cast cars was produced by Racing Champions for promotional use and distributed by Milkhouse Cheese. Each car was packaged on a yellow and checkered flag designed blister with the Milkhouse Cheese logo on the package Racing Champions card was also included in the blister pa The stated production run of each piece was 14,400.

	EX	NM-M
2 Rusty Wallace Miller Genuine Draft	6.00	15.0
6 Mark Martin Valvoline	10.00	20.0
7 Alan Kulwicki Hooters	7.50	20.0
11 Bill Elliott Milkhouse Cheese	6.00	15.0
17 Darrell Waltrip Western Auto	6.00	15.0

1992 Racing Champions NF 1:64

	EX	NM-M
18 Dale Jarrett Interstate Batteries Atlanta Falcons	6.00	12.0
18 Dale Jarrett Interstate Batteries Cincinnati Bengals	6.00	12.0
18 Dale Jarrett Interstate Batteries Cleveland Browns	6.00	12.0
18 Dale Jarrett Interstate Batteries Los Angeles Raiders	6.00	12.0
18 Dale Jarrett Interstate Batteries Los Angeles Rams	6.00	12.0
18 Dale Jarrett Interstate Batteries Miami Dolphins	6.00	12.0
18 Dale Jarrett Interstate Batteries New York Giants	6.00	12.0
18 Dale Jarrett Interstate Batteries New York Jets	6.00	12.0
18 Dale Jarrett Interstate Batteries Seattle Seahawks	6.00	12.0
18 Dale Jarrett Interstate Batteries St. Louis Cardinals	6.00	12.0

1992 Racing Champions Pet Fan Appreciation Tour 1:64

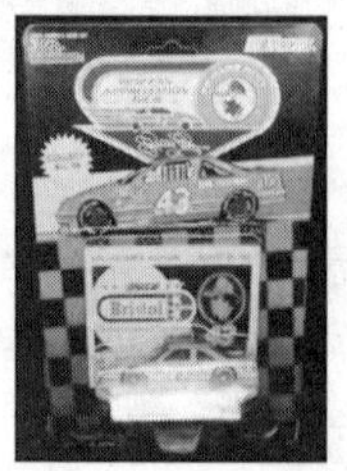

Racing Champions issued this series to commemorate Ric Petty's 1992 farewell tour. Each car was packaged in a Ra Champions blister along with a card commemorating one t event for 1992. Only the trading cards are different in e package.

	EX	NM-M
43 Richard Petty Atlanta Motor Speedway March 15	5.00	12.0
43 Richard Petty Atlanta Hooters 500 November 15	5.00	12.0
43 Richard Petty Bristol April 3	5.00	12.0
43 Richard Petty Bristol August 29	5.00	12.0
43 Richard Petty Charlotte One Hot Night May 16	5.00	12.0
43 Richard Petty Charlotte May 24	5.00	12.0
43 Richard Petty Charlotte October 11	5.00	12.0
43 Richard Petty Darlington March 29	5.00	12.0
43 Richard Petty Darlington September 6	5.00	12.0
43 Richard Petty Daytona 500 Feb.16	5.00	12.0
43 Richard Petty Daytona July 4	5.00	12.0
43 Richard Petty Dover Downs May 31	5.00	12.0
43 Richard Petty Dover Downs Sept.20	5.00	12.0
43 Richard Petty Martinsville April 26	5.00	12.0
43 Richard Petty Martinsville Sept.27	5.00	12.0
43 Richard Petty Michigan June 21	5.00	12.0
43 Richard Petty Michigan Aug.16	5.00	12.0
43 Richard Petty North Wilkesboro April 12	5.00	12.0
43 Richard Petty North Wilkesboro Oct.4	5.00	12.0
43 Richard Petty Phoenix Nov.1	5.00	12.0
43 Richard Petty Pocono Raceway June 14	5.00	12.0
43 Richard Petty Pocono July 19	5.00	12.0
43 Richard Petty Richmond March 8	5.00	12.0
43 Richard Petty Richmond September 12	5.00	12.0
43 Richard Petty Rockingham March 1	5.00	12.0
43 Richard Petty Rockingham October 25	5.00	12.0

chard Petty	5.00	12.00
ears Point June 7		
chard Petty	5.00	12.00
alladega May 3		
chard Petty	5.00	12.00
alladega July 26		
chard Petty	5.00	12.00
Vatkins Glen August 9		

1992 Racing Champions Premier 1:64

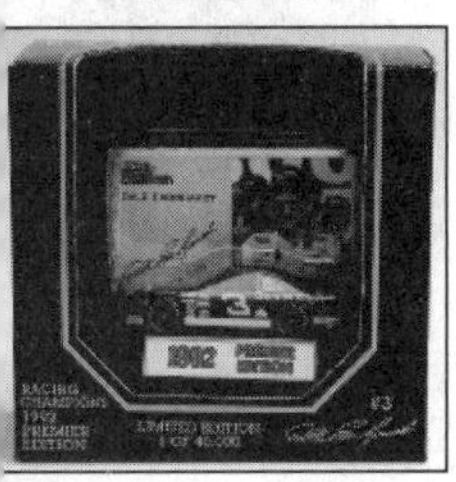

-piece series was the first time Racing Champions did a er Series. Each piece comes in a black shadow box with antity produced on the front of the box.

	EX	NM-MT
e Earnhardt	20.00	50.00
oodwrench/40,000		
ll Elliott	7.50	15.00
moco/20,000		
rrell Waltrip	6.00	14.00
Vestern Auto/20,000		
avey Allison	18.00	30.00
avoline/20,000		
chard Petty	10.00	20.00
TP/20,000		
ack Lumina Club Promo/5000	8.00	20.00
n clear box		
hite Lumina Promo/5000	8.00	20.00
n clear box		

1992 Racing Champions Track Promos 1:64

	EX	NM-MT
lanta March 15	1.50	4.00
istol August 29	1.50	4.00
harlotte October 11	1.50	4.00
arlington March 29	1.50	4.00
arlington September 6	1.50	4.00
ayona 500 February 16	1.50	4.00
aytona Pepsi 400 July 4	1.50	4.00
over May 31	1.50	4.00
artinsville 45th Anniversary	1.50	4.00
ichigan International June 21	1.50	4.00
orth Wilkesboro April 12	1.50	4.00
ocono June 14	1.50	4.00
ocono July 19	1.50	4.00
chmond March 8	1.50	4.00
chmond September 12	1.50	4.00
ockingham March 1	1.50	4.00
ockingham October 25	1.50	4.00
ears Point June 7	1.50	4.00
alladega May 3	1.50	4.00
alladega July 26	1.50	4.00
atkins Glen August 9	1.50	4.00

92 Racing Champions with Figure 1:64

1:64 car in this series was packaged with a plastic ible figurine of the featured driver. Both the die-cast and statue were issued with a card in a large "Racing pions" blister pack.

	EX	NM-MT
ty Wallace	6.00	15.00
ontiac Excitement		
e Irvan	5.00	12.00
odak		
t Stricklin	4.00	10.00
aybestos		
rry Gant	4.00	10.00
e Petty	5.00	12.00
ello Yello		

93 Racing Champions 1:64

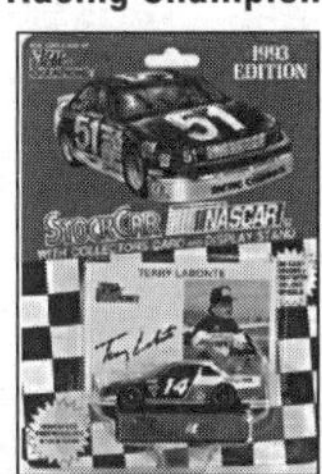

eries of 1:64 scale cars features the top names in racing. ars came in a blister pack and were sold through both and retail outlets.

	EX	NM-MT
k McCabe	1.50	4.00
isher Snow Plows		
ff Gordon	12.50	25.00
ark Martin		
arolina Ford		
-car promo set		
rd Burton	3.00	8.00
ardee's Promo		
ty Wallace	2.00	5.00
ontiac Excitement		
e Earnhardt	30.00	80.00
oodwrench		
e Earnhardt	25.00	60.00
oodwrench		
om-n-Pop's blister Promo		
e Earnhardt	10.00	20.00

Goodwrench 1988		
Monte Carlo Promo blister		
3 Dale Earnhardt	10.00	20.00
Goodwrench 1989		
Monte Carlo Promo blister		
4 Ernie Irvan	2.00	5.00
Kodak		
5 Terry Labonte	4.00	8.00
Kellogg's Promo black windows		
5 Ricky Rudd	1.50	4.00
Tide		
6 Mark Martin	5.00	10.00
Valvoline		
7 Harry Gant	5.00	12.00
Black Flag Promo/15,000		
7 Harry Gant	5.00	12.00
Easy-Off Promo/15,000		
7 Harry Gant	5.00	12.00
French's Promo/15,000		
7 Harry Gant	5.00	12.00
Gulf Lite Promo/15,000		
7 Harry Gant	5.00	12.00
Woolite Promo/15,000		
7 Alan Kulwicki	6.00	15.00
Hooters 1992 Champ card		
8 Sterling Marlin	1.50	4.00
Raybestos		
11 Bill Elliott	2.00	5.00
Amoco		
12 Jimmy Spencer	1.50	4.00
Meineke		
14 Terry Labonte	12.50	25.00
Kellogg's		
15 Geoff Bodine	1.50	4.00
Motorcraft		
17 Darrell Waltrip	1.50	4.00
Western Auto		
18 Dale Jarrett	5.00	10.00
Interstate Batteries		
20 Joe Ruttman	3.00	8.00
Fina Promo		
21 Morgan Shepherd	1.50	4.00
Citgo		
21 Morgan Shepherd	2.50	6.00
Citgo Promo		
22 Bobby Labonte	25.00	50.00
Maxwell House		
24 Jeff Gordon	40.00	80.00
DuPont		
25 Ken Schrader	5.00	10.00
Kodiak		
25 Bill Venturini	1.50	4.00
Rain X		
26 Brett Bodine	1.50	4.00
Quaker State		
27 Hut Stricklin	1.50	4.00
McDonald's		
28 Davey Allison	5.00	12.00
Havoline		
28 Davey Allison	6.00	15.00
Havoline		
with Black and White paint scheme		
28 Ernie Irvan	5.00	10.00
Havoline		
31 Steve Grissom	3.00	8.00
Channellock Promo		
33 Harry Gant	1.50	4.00
No Sponsor Lumina		
33 Harry Gant	1.50	4.00
No Sponsor Oldsmobile		
42 Kyle Petty	1.50	4.00
Mello Yello		
44 Rick Wilson	1.50	4.00
STP		
59 Andy Belmont	4.00	8.00
FDP Brakes		
59 Robert Pressley	4.00	8.00
Alliance		
60 Mark Martin	4.00	8.00
Winn Dixie		
71 Dave Marcis	4.00	10.00
STG		
75 Butch Mock	1.50	4.00
Factory Stores of America		
87 Joe Nemechek	1.50	4.00
Dentyne		
98 Derrike Cope	1.50	4.00
Bojangles		

1993 Racing Champions Craftsman Motorsports Promos 1:64

	EX	NM-MT
8 Sterling Marlin	2.50	6.00
Raybestos		
11 Bill Elliott	2.50	6.00
Amoco		
14 Terry Labonte	2.50	6.00
Kellogg's		
15 Geoff Bodine	2.50	6.00
Motorcraft		
17 Darrell Waltrip	2.50	6.00
Western Auto		
33 Harry Gant	2.50	6.00
No Sponsor		

1993 Racing Champions Mercury Cyclones 1:64

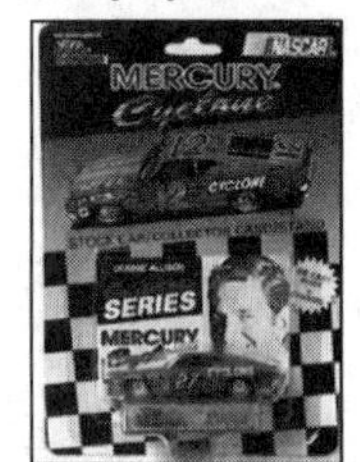

	EX	NM-MT
12 Bobby Allison	4.00	10.00
1969 Mercury Cyclone		
16 Tiny Lund	4.00	10.00
1969 Mercury Cyclone red		
21 Donnie Allison	4.00	10.00
1969 Mercury Cyclone white		
21 A.J. Foyt	4.00	10.00
1969 Mercury Cyclone		
21 Cale Yarborough	4.00	10.00
1969 Mercury Cyclone		
24 Cecil Gordon	4.00	10.00
1969 Mercury Cyclone		
26 Lee Roy Yarborough	4.00	10.00
1969 Mercury Cyclone		
27 Donnie Allison	4.00	10.00
1969 Mercury Cyclone red		
52 A.J. Foyt	4.00	10.00
1969 Mercury Cyclone		
55 Tiny Lund	4.00	10.00
1969 Mercury Cyclone blue		
64 Elmo Langley	4.00	10.00
1969 Mercury Cyclone		

1993 Racing Champions Premier 1:64

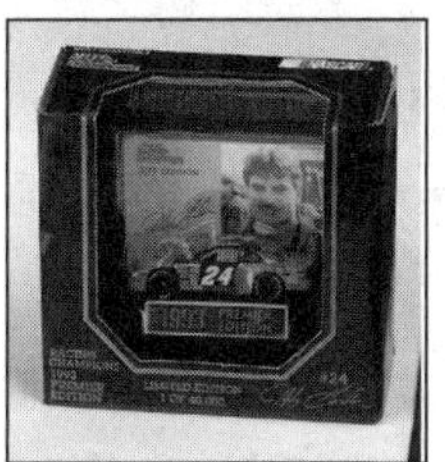

This was the second year of the 1:64 scale Premier series. The series is highlighted by the Alan Kulwicki Hooters car and the three different Champion Forever Davey Allison pieces.

	EX	NM-MT
1 Rodney Combs	3.00	8.00
Jebco Clocks		
2 Ward Burton	6.00	15.00
Hardee's/10,000		
2 Rusty Wallace	5.00	12.00
Pontiac Excitement/40,000		
3 Dale Earnhardt	30.00	80.00
Goodwrench/20,000		
3 Dale Earnhardt	30.00	80.00
Goodwrench/20,000		
DEI on package		
4 Ernie Irvan	3.00	8.00
Kodak/60,000		
4 Jeff Purvis	7.50	15.00
Kodak		
5 Ricky Rudd	3.00	8.00
Tide/40,000		
6 Mark Martin	4.00	10.00
Valvoline		
6 Mark Martin	7.00	15.00
Valvoline		
Four in a Row Promo		
6 Mike Stefanik	5.00	10.00
Valvoline Auto Palace		
7 Jimmy Hensley	15.00	30.00
Alan Kulwicki Racing		
7 Alan Kulwicki	20.00	50.00
Hooters/60,000		
1992 Champion card		
7 Alan Kulwicki	15.00	30.00
Zerex/10,000		
8 Sterling Marlin	3.00	8.00
Raybestos		
11 Bill Elliott	8.00	20.00
Budweiser Promo		
12 Jimmy Spencer	3.00	8.00
Meineke/40,000		
14 Terry Labonte	12.50	25.00
Kellogg's		
15 Geoff Bodine	3.00	8.00
Motorcraft/40,000		
18 Dale Jarrett	5.00	10.00
Interstate Batteries/20,000		
21 Morgan Shepherd	3.00	8.00
Citgo/40,000		
24 Jeff Gordon	20.00	50.00
DuPont/40,000		
26 Brett Bodine	3.00	8.00
Quaker State/40,000		
27 Hut Stricklin	3.00	8.00
McDonald's/40,000		
27 Hut Stricklin	3.00	8.00
Mr. Pibb		
28 Davey Allison	10.00	20.00
Havoline Black paint scheme		
28 Davey Allison	7.50	15.00
Havoline Black and Gold		
Champion Forever/28,000		
28 Davey Allison	10.00	20.00
Havoline Black and Orange		
Champion Forever/28,000		
28 Davey Allison	10.00	20.00
Havoline Black and White		
Champion Forever/28,000		
28 Ernie Irvan	10.00	20.00
Havoline		
31 Neil Bonnett	25.00	50.00
Mom-n-Pop's/10,000		
33 Harry Gant	3.00	8.00
No Sponsor		
41 Ernie Irvan	6.00	15.00
Mac Tools/16,041		
42 Kyle Petty	3.00	8.00
Mello Yello/40,000		
44 Jimmy Hensley	3.00	8.00
STP		
59 Robert Pressley	8.00	20.00
Alliance		
59 Dennis Setzer	7.50	15.00
Alliance		
60 Mark Martin	10.00	20.00
Winn Dixie		
87 Joe Nemechek	3.00	8.00
Dentyne/20,000		
93 DCD Anniversary/5000	3.00	8.00
97 Joe Bessey	3.00	8.00
Auto Palace		
98 Derrike Cope	3.00	8.00
Bojangles with Black paint scheme		
98 Derrike Cope	3.00	8.00
Bojangles with Yellow paint scheme		
02 Frank Kimmel	20.00	40.00
Harley Davidson		

1993 Racing Champions PVC Box 1:64

Most die-casts in this series were produced for a special race occasion. Each piece comes packaged in a clear PVC box featuring the driver's name, what the occasion was, and the quantity produced all printed in gold foil.

	EX	NM-MT
2 Rusty Wallace	5.00	10.00
Pontiac Excitement		
Feb.28th Win/5000		
2 Rusty Wallace	5.00	10.00
Pontiac Excitement		
April 4th Win/5000		
2 Rusty Wallace	5.00	10.00
Pontiac Excitement		
April 18th Win/5000		
2 Rusty Wallace	5.00	10.00
Pontiac Excitement		
April 25th Win/5000		
2 Rusty Wallace	5.00	10.00
Pontiac Excitement		
July 11th Win		
2 Rusty Wallace	5.00	10.00
Pontiac Excitement		
September 11th Win		
2 Rusty Wallace	5.00	10.00
Pontiac Excitement		
September 19th Win		
2 Rusty Wallace	5.00	10.00
Pontiac Excitement		
October 3rd Win		
2 Rusty Wallace	5.00	10.00
Pontiac Excitement		
October 24th Win		
2 Rusty Wallace	5.00	10.00
Pontiac Excitement		
November 14th Win		
3 Dale Earnhardt	25.00	60.00
1993 WC Champ/5000		
3 Dale Earnhardt	30.00	60.00
1993 WC Champ		
with Red Flags in box		
3 Dale Earnhardt	25.00	60.00
Back in Black/5000		
3 Dale Earnhardt	25.00	60.00
Busch Clash Win/5000		
3 Dale Earnhardt	25.00	60.00
Coca-Cola 600 Win/7500		
3 Dale Earnhardt	25.00	60.00
Pepsi 400 Win		
3 Dale Earnhardt	25.00	60.00
June 6th Win/5000		
3 Dale Earnhardt	25.00	60.00
One Hot Night Win/7500		
3 Dale Earnhardt	25.00	60.00
Die Hard 500 Win/5000		
4 Ernie Irvan	4.00	10.00
Kodak Talladega Win		
5 Max Dumesny	4.00	10.00
Valvoline		
5 Ricky Rudd	4.00	10.00
Tide June 20th Win/1000		
6 Mark Martin	5.00	10.00
Valvoline Aug.8 Win/5000		
6 Mark Martin	5.00	10.00
Valvoline Aug.15 Win/5000		
7 Harry Gant	4.00	10.00
Morema/5000		
7 Jimmy Hensley	4.00	10.00
Hanes		
7 Jimmy Hensley	4.00	10.00
Purolator		
8 Sterling Marlin	15.00	30.00
Raybestos Winston Open/2500		
12 David Bonnett	4.00	10.00
Plasti-Kote		
16 Wally Dallenbach	15.00	25.00
Keystone Promo		
18 Dale Jarrett	5.00	10.00
Interstate Batteries		
Daytona Win/10,000		
20 Pocono 20th Anniversary/7500	4.00	10.00
21 Morgan Shepherd	4.00	10.00
Cheerwine		
24 Jeff Gordon	20.00	50.00
DuPont/5000		
24 Jeff Gordon	30.00	60.00
DuPont Fan Club		
24 Jeff Gordon	20.00	50.00
DuPont Daytona/5000		
24 Jeff Gordon	20.00	50.00
DuPont Twin 125 Win/5000		
27 Hut Stricklin	4.00	10.00
McDonald's All-American		
27 Hut Stricklin	10.00	20.00
McDonald's Daytona		
27 Hut Stricklin	25.00	50.00
McDonald's 250 produced		
27 Hut Stricklin	4.00	10.00
McDonald's Taylorsville		
April 19, 1993		
28 Alan Kulwicki	25.00	50.00
Hardee's		
28 Davey Allison	10.00	20.00
Havoline race win/5000		
28 Ernie Irvan	10.00	20.00
Havoline		
28 Ernie Irvan	10.00	20.00
Havoline Charlotte		
40 Kenny Wallace	8.00	20.00
Dirt Devil/5000		
42 Kyle Petty	10.00	20.00
Mello Yello Daytona Pole/5000		
44 David Green	8.00	20.00
Slim Jim		
44 Rick Wilson	4.00	10.00
STP/5000		
46 Al Unser Jr.	12.50	25.00
Valvoline/5000		
51 Lumina Racing Champions	20.00	40.00
51 Pontiac Racing Champions	20.00	40.00
51 Thunderbird Racing Champions	20.00	40.00
51 Racing Champions Mascot	20.00	40.00
52 Ken Schrader	4.00	10.00
Morema/5000		
55 Ted Musgrave	4.00	10.00
Jasper/5000		
56 Ernie Irvan	25.00	60.00
Earnhardt Chevrolet		
1987 Monte Carlo/5000		
59 Robert Pressley	10.00	20.00
Alliance Fan Club		
59 Robert Pressley	10.00	20.00
Alliance Pressley		
59 Robert Pressley	18.00	35.00
Alliance September 1993		
60 Mark Martin	7.50	15.00
Winn Dixie		
68 Bobby Hamilton	40.00	80.00
Country Time/1000		
February 14, 1993		
82 Derrike Cope	12.50	25.00
Zook Racing/2000		
89 Jeff McClure	4.00	10.00
Bero Motors		
93 Bristol April 4	5.00	12.00
93 Bristol August 28/5000	4.00	10.00
93 Bud 500/5000	5.00	12.00
93 Racing Champions Club	5.00	12.00
93 Slick 50 300	5.00	12.00
98 Derrike Cope	4.00	10.00
Bojangles/5000		

1994 Racing Champions 1:64

These 1:64 scale pieces were mainly packaged in a red blister pack and distributed through hobby shops and retail outlets. The year of issue is printed on the blister for the regular issue pieces. Most promo die-casts were issued in blisters printed in the sponsor's colors.

	EX	NM-MT
1 Rick Mast	1.50	4.00
Precision Products		
1/24 Jeff Gordon	20.00	40.00
Frosted Mini-Wheats Promo		
Baby Ruth & DuPont cars		
with Sprint car in blister		
2 Ricky Craven	3.00	6.00
DuPont		
2 Rusty Wallace	4.00	8.00
Ford Motorsports		
2 Rusty Wallace	4.00	8.00
Ford Motorsports with no Blue		
4 Sterling Marlin	1.50	4.00
Kodak		
5 Terry Labonte	3.00	6.00
Kellogg's		
5 Terry Labonte	4.00	10.00
Kellogg's Promo black windows		
5/10/17 Ricky Rudd	4.00	10.00
Darrell Waltrip		
Tide 3-car Promo set		
6 Mark Martin	2.00	5.00
Valvoline		
7 Geoff Bodine	1.50	4.00
Exide		
7 Harry Gant	4.00	8.00
Manheim		
8 Jeff Burton	4.00	8.00
Raybestos		
8 Kenny Wallace	1.50	4.00
TIC Financial		
10 Ricky Rudd	1.50	4.00
Tide		
10 Ricky Rudd	4.00	10.00
Tide Promo black windows		
12 Clifford Allison	5.00	10.00
Sports Image		
14 John Andretti	1.50	4.00
Kanawaha		
15 Lake Speed	1.50	4.00
Quality Care		
16 Ted Musgrave	1.50	4.00
Family Channel		
17 Darrell Waltrip	1.50	4.00
Western Auto		
18 Dale Jarrett	6.00	15.00
Interstate Batteries		
19 Loy Allen	4.00	8.00
Hooters		
20 Randy LaJoie	1.50	4.00
Fina		
21 Morgan Shepherd	1.50	4.00
Citgo		
22 Bobby Labonte	10.00	20.00
Maxwell House		
23 Hut Stricklin	5.00	10.00
Smokin' Joe's in plastic case		
24 Jeff Gordon	25.00	50.00
DuPont		
24 Jeff Gordon	20.00	40.00
DuPont Coca-Cola 600 Win		
in plastic case		
24 Jeff Gordon	20.00	40.00
DuPont Brickyard		
25 Hermie Sadler	1.50	4.00
Virginia is for Lovers		
25 Ken Schrader	1.50	4.00
GMAC		
26 Brett Bodine	1.50	4.00
Quaker State		
27 Jimmy Spencer	1.50	4.00
McDonald's		
27 Jimmy Spencer	4.00	8.00
McDonald's Promo		

black windows		
28 Ernie Irvan Havoline	2.00	5.00
28 Ernie Irvan Havoline Promo	4.00	10.00
30 Michael Waltrip Pennzoil	1.50	4.00
31 Ward Burton Hardees Promo	10.00	20.00
31 Tom Peck Channellock	1.50	4.00
33 Harry Gant No Sponsor	20.00	40.00
33 Bobby Labonte Dentyne	40.00	80.00
38 Elton Sawyer Ford Credit	1.50	4.00
40 Bobby Hamilton Kendall	1.50	4.00
42 Kyle Petty Mello Yello	1.50	4.00
44 Bobby Hillin Jr. Buss Fuses	1.50	4.00
46 Shawna Robinson Polaroid	5.00	10.00
52 Ken Schrader AC Delco	3.00	6.00
54 Robert Pressley Manheim	1.50	4.00
60 Mark Martin Winn Dixie	5.00	12.00
63 Jim Bown Lysol	1.50	4.00
63 NDA/Lysol Promo	10.00	20.00
75 Todd Bodine Factory Stores of America	1.50	4.00
79 Dave Rezendes Lipton Tea	4.00	10.00
83 Sherry Blakely Ramses	1.50	4.00
92 Larry Pearson Stanley Tools	1.50	4.00
94 Brickyard 400 Promo	1.50	4.00
94 McDonald's All-Star Promo 3/24/2 car numbers on deck lid	1.50	4.00
94 Sunoco Ultra 94 Promo black windows	3.00	8.00
97 Joe Bessey Johnson	1.50	4.00
98 Derrike Cope Fingerhut	1.50	4.00
00 Johnny Rumley Big Dog Coal	4.00	8.00

1994 Racing Champions Hobby Yellow Box 1:64

This series was distributed through hobby channels. Each piece came in a yellow box.

	EX	NM-MT
1 Rick Mast Precision Products	1.50	4.00
2 Ricky Craven DuPont	1.50	4.00
2 Rusty Wallace Ford Motorsports	2.00	5.00
4 Sterling Marlin Kodak	1.50	4.00
4 Sterling Marlin Kodak Funsaver	1.50	4.00
5 Terry Labonte Kellogg's	3.00	6.00
6 Mark Martin Valvoline	4.00	8.00
7 Geoff Bodine Exide	1.50	4.00
8 Jeff Burton Raybestos	1.50	4.00
14 Terry Labonte MW Windows	8.00	20.00
15 Lake Speed Quality Care	1.50	4.00
16 Ted Musgrave Family Channel	1.50	4.00
17 Darrell Waltrip Western Auto	1.50	4.00
18 Dale Jarrett Interstate Batteries	6.00	15.00
19 Loy Allen Hooters	1.50	4.00
22 Brett Bodine Maxwell House	4.00	10.00
23 Chad Little Bayer	5.00	12.00
24 Jeff Gordon DuPont	20.00	40.00
25 Hermie Sadler Virginia is for Lovers	1.50	4.00
26 Brett Bodine Quaker State	1.50	4.00
27 Jimmy Spencer McDonald's	1.50	4.00
30 Michael Waltrip Pennzoil	1.50	4.00
31 Tom Peck Channellock	1.50	4.00
33 Harry Gant No Sponsor	1.50	4.00
34 Mike McLaughlin Fiddle Faddle	1.50	4.00
38 Elton Sawyer Ford Credit	1.50	4.00
40 Bobby Hamilton Kendall	1.50	4.00
42 Kyle Petty Mello Yello	1.50	4.00
46 Shawna Robinson Polaroid	4.00	10.00
63 Jim Bown Lysol	1.50	4.00
75 Todd Bodine Factory Stores of America	1.50	4.00
92 Larry Pearson Stanley Tools	1.50	4.00
94 No Driver Association Brickyard 400	1.50	4.00
98 Derrike Cope Fingerhut	1.50	4.00

1994 Racing Champions Country Time Legends Promos 1:64

This series of die-cast cars was produced by Racing Champions and distributed through a promotional offer from Kraft General Foods and Country Time Drink Mix in 1994. Note that each car features a retired legendary NASCAR driver in a vintage car with a 1991 copyright date on the bottom. Each was also issued in a "Legends of Racing" black and checkered box with the Country Time logo and driver checklist present.

	EX	NM-MT
11 Ned Jarrett Bowani 1963 Ford	6.00	15.00
21 Cale Yarborough 1969 Ford	6.00	15.00
22 Fireball Roberts Young Ford 1963 Ford	5.00	12.00
28 Fred Lorenzen LaFayette Ford 1963 Ford	5.00	12.00
29 Bobby Allison 1969 Ford	6.00	15.00
51 Neil Bonnett Country Time	6.00	15.00

1994 Racing Champions Premier 1:64

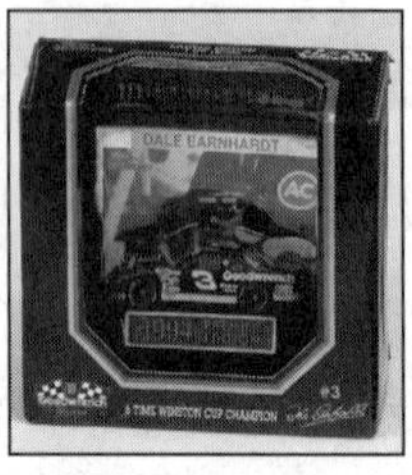

This series of 1:64 Premier series was issued by Racing Champions through retail outlets and hobby dealers. The pieces come in a black shadow box and have the quantity produced stamped in gold on the front of the box.

	EX	NM-MT
1 Davey Allison Lancaster	10.00	20.00
2 Ricky Craven DuPont	3.00	6.00
2 Rusty Wallace Miller Genuine Draft/20,000	6.00	12.00
2 Rusty Wallace Mac Tools	10.00	20.00
3 Dale Earnhardt Goodwrench 6-time champ/10,000	25.00	60.00
4 Sterling Marlin Kodak	3.00	8.00
4 Sterling Marlin Kodak Funsaver	5.00	12.00
5 Terry Labonte Kellogg's/20,000	15.00	30.00
6 Mark Martin Valvoline	3.00	6.00
6 Mark Martin Valvoline four in a row special	7.00	14.00
7 Geoff Bodine Exide	3.00	6.00
7 Harry Gant Manheim	7.50	15.00
7 Alan Kulwicki Army	15.00	30.00
7 Alan Kulwicki Zerex Promo blister/20,000	7.50	15.00
8 Jeff Burton Raybestos/20,000	3.00	6.00
8 Kenny Wallace TIC Financial	3.00	6.00
12 Clifford Allison Sports Image/10,000	10.00	20.00
15 Lake Speed Quality Care	3.00	6.00
16 Chad Chaffin 31W Insulation	6.00	12.00
16 Ted Musgrave Family Channel	3.00	6.00
18 Dale Jarrett Interstate Batteries	5.00	10.00
19 Loy Allen Hooters	3.00	6.00
20 Randy LaJoie Fina	3.00	6.00
21 Johnny Benson Berger	7.50	15.00
24 Jeff Gordon DuPont/20,000	12.50	30.00
24 Jeff Gordon DuPont 1993 Rookie of the Year/20,000	12.50	30.00
25 Hermie Sadler Virgina is for Lovers	6.00	12.00
25 Ken Schrader Kodiak	3.00	6.00
26 Brett Bodine Quaker State	3.00	6.00
27 Jimmy Spencer McDonald's	3.00	6.00
28 Ernie Irvan Mac Tools in Yellow box/25,028	9.00	18.00
31 Steve Grissom Channellock	6.00	12.00
33 Bobby Labonte Dentyne/10,000	30.00	50.00
34 Mike McLaughlin Fiddle Faddle	3.00	6.00
35 Shawna Robinson Polaroid Captiva/10,000	12.50	25.00
40 Bobby Hamilton Kendall	3.00	6.00
43 Rodney Combs French's	7.50	15.00
43 Wally Dallenbach Jr. STP	7.50	15.00
46 Shawna Robinson Polaroid	7.50	15.00
54 Robert Pressley Alliance	6.00	12.00
59 Andy Belmont Metal Arrester	3.00	6.00
59 Dennis Setzer Alliance	6.00	12.00
59 Dennis Setzer Alliance 2000 produced	12.50	25.00
60 Mark Martin Winn Dixie	7.50	15.00
70 J.D. McDuffie Son's Auto	7.50	15.00
71 Dave Marcis Earnhardt Chevrolet	12.00	30.00
75 Todd Bodine Factory Stores of America	3.00	6.00
77 Greg Sacks US Air Jasper Engines	7.50	15.00
85 Jim Sauter Rheem AC	5.00	10.00
89 Jeff McClure FSU Seminoles	5.00	10.00
89 Jeff McClure NC State Wolfpack/7500	10.00	20.00
89 Jeff McClure UNLV Runnin' Rebels/7500	10.00	20.00
94 Charlotte Promo/8000	6.00	12.00
98 Jody Ridley Ford Motorsports	3.00	6.00
0 Dick McCabe Fisher Snow Plows	5.00	10.00

1994 Racing Champions Premier Brickyard 400 1:64

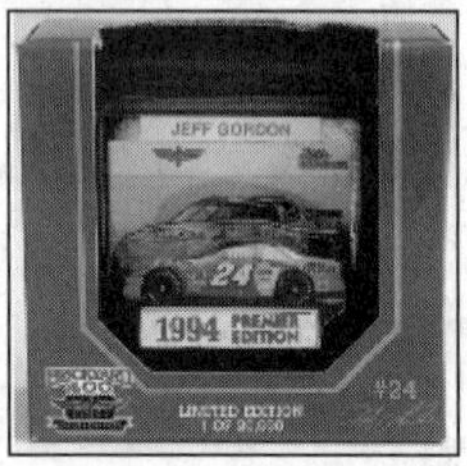

This series was issued in conjunction with the first Brickyard 400 race. The boxes are the usual shadow box style, but are easily distinguishable due to their purple color. Each piece included a gold bordered Brickyard 400 photo card that included a facsimile driver's signature. The outside of the box featured the production run total of 20,000.

	EX	NM-MT
3 Dale Earnhardt Goodwrench	20.00	50.00
6 Mark Martin Valvoline	5.00	12.00
18 Dale Jarrett Interstate Batteries	7.50	15.00
21 Morgan Shepherd Citgo	3.00	8.00
24 Jeff Gordon DuPont	40.00	75.00
26 Brett Bodine Quaker State	3.00	8.00
27 Jimmy Spencer McDonald's	3.00	8.00
30 Michael Waltrip Pennzoil	3.00	8.00
42 Kyle Petty Mello Yello	3.00	8.00

1994 Racing Champions PVC Box 1:64

	EX	NM-MT
24 Jeff Gordon DuPont Fan Club/3000		
24 Jeff Gordon DuPont ROY/5000	10.00	20.00

1994 Racing Champions Short Track Champions 1:64

	EX	NM-MT
2 Mark Martin RECO	4.00	10.00
5 Ernie Irvan Terminal Trucking	3.00	8.00
23 Davey Allison No sponsor	4.00	10.00
33 Harry Gant Dillon	3.00	8.00
52 Butch Miller Lane	3.00	8.00
66 Rusty Wallace Alugard	4.00	10.00
99 Dick Trickle Prototype	3.00	8.00

1994 Racing Champions To the Maxx 1:64

This was the first series issued by Racing Champions that included a Maxx Premier Plus card.

	EX	NM-MT
2 Rusty Wallace Ford Motorsports	4.00	8.00
4 Sterling Marlin Kodak	4.00	10.00
5 Terry Labonte Kellogg's	5.00	10.00
6 Mark Martin Valvoline	4.00	8.00
16 Ted Musgrave Family Channel	4.00	7.00
24 Jeff Gordon DuPont	15.00	25.00
28 Ernie Irvan Havoline	4.00	8.00
42 Kyle Petty Mello Yello	4.00	7.00

1995 Racing Champions Preview 1:64

This series of 1:64 replica cars was a Preview to many of the cars that raced in the 1995 season. The packaging is a cardboard and plastic blister with a black #51 car printed on the backer board. A Racing Champions Preview card was also packaged with each car. The Geoff Bodine Exide car can be found with either Hoosier or Goodyear tires.

	EX	NM-MT
1 Rick Mast Precision Products	1.50	4.00
2 Ricky Craven DuPont	1.50	4.00
2 Rusty Wallace Ford Motorsports	2.00	5.00
4 Sterling Marlin Kodak	2.00	5.00
6 Mark Martin Valvoline	2.00	4.00
7 Geoff Bodine Exide with Goodyear tires	1.50	4.00
7 Geoff Bodine Exide with Hoosier tires	1.50	4.00
10 Ricky Rudd Tide	1.50	4.00
14 Terry Labonte MW Windows	6.00	12.00
16 Ted Musgrave Family Channel	1.50	4.00
21 Morgan Shepherd Citgo	1.50	4.00
23 Chad Little Bayer	1.50	4.00
24 Jeff Gordon DuPont	7.50	15.00
25 Kirk Shelmerdine Big Johnson	3.00	6.00
26 Steve Kinser Quaker State	1.50	4.00
28 Dale Jarrett Havoline	2.50	5.00
30 Michael Waltrip Pennzoil	1.50	4.00
38 Elton Sawyer Ford Credit	1.50	4.00
40 Bobby Hamilton Kendall	1.50	4.00
40 Patty Moise Dial Purex	1.50	4.00
52 Ken Schrader AC Delco	1.50	4.00
57 Jason Keller Budget Gourmet	1.50	4.00
63 Curtis Markham Lysol	1.50	4.00
75 Todd Bodine Factory Stores of America	1.50	4.00
92 Larry Pearson Stanley Tools	1.50	4.00
94 Bill Elliott McDonald's	2.00	4.00
98 Jeremy Mayfield Fingerhut	1.50	4.00

1995 Racing Champions 1:

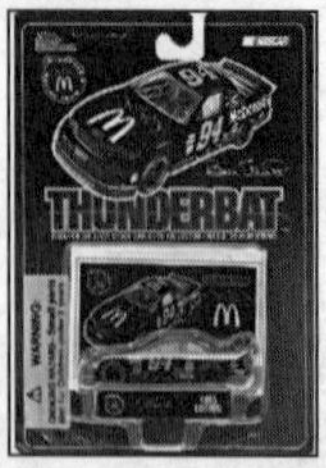

This is the regular issued of the 1:64 scale 1995 F Champions series. The Bobby Labonte car comes wi without roof flaps. This was one of the first cars to incor the new NASCAR safety feature into a die cast.

	EX	NM
1 Rick Mast Precision	1.50	
2 Ricky Craven DuPont	1.50	
2 Rusty Wallace Ford Motorsports	2.00	
4 Sterling Marlin Kodak	1.50	
4 Jeff Purvis Kodak Funsaver	1.50	
5 Terry Labonte Kellogg's	2.50	
6 Tommy Houston Red Devil	1.50	
6 Mark Martin Valvoline	2.00	
7 Geoff Bodine Exide	1.50	
7 Stevie Reeves Clabber Girl	1.50	
8 Jeff Burton Raybestos	1.50	
8 Jeff Burton Raybestos with Blue numbers	1.50	
8 Bobby Dotter Hyde Tools	1.50	
8 Kenny Wallace Red Dog	4.00	
10 Ricky Rudd Tide	1.50	
10 Ricky Rudd Tide Promo black windows	4.00	1
12 Derrike Cope Straight Arrow	1.50	
14 Terry Labonte MW Windows	15.00	3
15 Jack Nadeau Buss Fuses	1.50	
15 Jerry Nadeau Buss Fuses Promo packaged with fuses	3.00	
15 Dick Trickle Ford Quality	1.50	
16 Stub Fadden NAPA Promo in bag	4.00	1
16 Ted Musgrave Family Channel	1.50	
17 Darrell Waltrip Western Auto	1.50	
18 Bobby Labonte Interstate Batteries with roof flaps	4.00	
18 Bobby Labonte Interstate Batteries without roof flaps	3.00	
21 Morgan Shepherd Citgo	1.50	
22 Randy LaJoie MBNA	1.50	
23 Chad Little Bayer	1.50	
24 Jeff Gordon DuPont	15.00	3
24 Jeff Gordon DuPont Coca-Cola	15.00	3
24 Jeff Gordon DuPont Fan Club/2000 in PVC box	20.00	3
25 Johnny Rumley Big Johnson	2.50	
25 Ken Schrader Hendrick	1.50	
25 Kirk Shelmerdine Big Johnson	1.50	
26 Steve Kinser Quaker State	1.50	
27 Loy Allen Hooters	1.50	
28 Dale Jarrett Havoline	2.00	
29 Steve Grissom Meineke	1.50	
30 Michael Waltrip Pennzoil	1.50	
34 Mike McLaughlin French's	1.50	
37 John Andretti K-Mart	1.50	
40 Patty Moise Dial Purex	1.50	
41 Ricky Craven Larry Hedrick Racing	1.50	
44 David Green Slim Jim	1.50	
44 Jeff Purvis Jackaroo	1.50	
47 Jeff Fuller Sunoco	1.50	
51 Jim Bown Luck's	1.50	
52 Ken Schrader AC Delco	1.50	
57 Jason Keller Budget Gourmet	1.50	
60 Mark Martin Winn Dixie	2.00	
60 Mark Martin	5.00	1

Winn Dixie Promo
Kevin Lepage 4.00 10.00
Vermont Teddy Bear
Dave Marcis 5.00 15.00
Olive Garden
Todd Bodine 1.50 4.00
Factory Stores of America
Kenny Wallace 1.50 4.00
TIC Financial
Derrike Cope 1.50 4.00
FDP Brakes
Bob Senneker 12.00 20.00
Jacksonville
Bratwurst Promo/10,000
Joe Nemechek 1.50 4.00
Burger King
Mike Wallace 1.50 4.00
Heilig-Meyers
Larry Pearson 1.50 4.00
Stanley Tools
Bill Elliott 4.00 8.00
McDonald's
Bill Elliott 4.00 8.00
McDonald's Upper Deck Promo
Bill Elliott 5.00 10.00
McDonald's Thunderbat Promo
Phil Parsons 1.50 4.00
Luxaire

1995 Racing Champions Matched Serial Numbers 1:64

...s series features cards and die cast whose serial numbers ...ch. The cars come in a black blister pack with a card. The ... has a gold border and features the driver of the car.

EX NM-MT
usty Wallace 4.00 7.00
Ford
erry Labonte 5.00 10.00
Kellogg's
ark Martin 5.00 10.00
Valvoline
eoff Bodine 2.50 6.00
Exide
Bobby Labonte 5.00 10.00
Interstate Batteries
Jeff Gordon 12.50 25.00
DuPont

1995 Racing Champions Premier 1:64

...is the 1995 series of the 1:64 Premier pieces. The cars are ...n packaged in a black shadow box and feature a gold foil ...ber on the front of the box that states how many pieces ... made. The cars were distributed through both hobby and ...il.

EX NM-MT
usty Wallace 3.50 8.00
Ford Motorsports
terling Marlin 3.00 8.00
Kodak
ark Martin 3.50 8.00
Valvoline
eff Burton 3.00 6.00
Raybestos
enny Wallace 60.00 120.00
Red Dog Promo
Bobby Labonte 3.00 6.00
Interstate Batteries
Jeff Gordon 20.00 35.00
DuPont/20,000
Jeff Gordon 15.00 30.00
DuPont Signature Series
Jeff Gordon 15.00 30.00
DuPont Signature Series
combo with SuperTruck
Ken Schrader 3.00 6.00
Budweiser
Steve Kinser 3.00 6.00
Quaker State
Loy Allen 3.00 6.00
Hooters
Dale Jarrett 3.00 8.00
Havoline
Bobby Hamilton 3.00 6.00
Kendall
Patty Moise 3.00 6.00
Dial Purex
Dennis Setzer 3.00 6.00
Alliance
Mark Martin 5.00 10.00
Winn Dixie
Todd Bodine 3.00 6.00
Factory Stores of America
Kenny Wallace 3.00 6.00
TIC Financial

94 Bill Elliott 10.00 20.00
McDonald's

1995 Racing Champions PVC Box 1:64

EX NM-MT
95 Charlotte October 8/36,000 5.00 12.00
95 Richmond Sept.9 5.00 12.00
SuperTruck/18,000

1995 Racing Champions To the Maxx 1:64

These pieces represent the second through fifth series of Racing Champions To the Maxx line. Each package includes a Maxx Premier Plus card that is only available with the die cast piece and was not inserted in any packs of the Premier Plus product.

EX NM-MT
2 Rusty Wallace 5.00 10.00
Ford Motorsports
4 Sterling Marlin 3.00 8.00
Kodak
4 Jeff Purvis 3.00 8.00
Kodak
6 Tommy Houston 3.00 8.00
Dirt Devil
6 Mark Martin 5.00 10.00
Valvoline
7 Geoff Bodine 3.00 8.00
Exide
7 Stevie Reeves 3.00 8.00
Clabber Girl
8 Jeff Burton 3.00 8.00
Raybestos
10 Ricky Rudd 3.00 8.00
Tide
12 Derrike Cope 3.00 8.00
Mane N Tail
14 Terry Labonte 3.00 8.00
MW Windows
15 Dick Trickle 3.00 8.00
Quality Care
17 Darrell Waltrip 3.00 8.00
Western Auto
18 Bobby Labonte 3.00 8.00
Interstate Batteries
21 Morgan Shepherd 3.00 8.00
Citgo
22 Randy LaJoie 3.00 8.00
MBNA
23 Chad Little 3.00 8.00
Bayer
24 Jeff Gordon 5.00 10.00
DuPont
26 Steve Kinser 3.00 8.00
Quaker State
28 Dale Jarrett 5.00 10.00
Havoline
29 Steve Grissom 3.00 8.00
Meineke
34 Mike McLaughlin 3.00 8.00
French's
38 Elton Sawyer 3.00 8.00
Ford Credit
44 David Green 3.00 8.00
Slim Jim
44 Jeff Purvis 3.00 8.00
Jackaroo
52 Ken Schrader 3.00 8.00
AC Delco
57 Jason Keller 3.00 8.00
Budget Gourmet
75 Todd Bodine 3.00 8.00
Factory Stores of America
81 Kenny Wallace 3.00 8.00
TIC Financial
90 Mike Wallace 3.00 8.00
Heilig-Meyers
92 Larry Pearson 3.00 8.00
Stanley Tools
94 Bill Elliott 3.00 8.00
McDonald's

1995 Racing Champions SuperTrucks 1:64

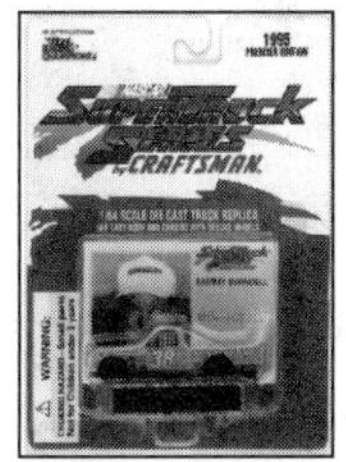

This series of 1:64 SuperTrucks includes a good sampling of many of the trucks that competed in the first NASCAR SuperTruck series. Each was packaged in a white and red blister that included a Racing Champions collector card.

EX NM-MT
1 P.J. Jones 3.00 6.00
Sears Diehard
1 P.J. Jones 5.00 10.00
Vessells Ford
1 Richmond Night Race Special 10.00 20.00
1 Tucson April 8 Race 12.50 25.00
2 David Ashley 3.00 6.00
Southern California Ford
3 Mike Skinner 3.00 6.00
Goodwrench
6 Mike Bliss 3.00 6.00
Ultra Wheels
6 Butch Gilliland 3.00 6.00
Ultra Wheels
6 Rick Carelli 3.00 6.00
Total Petroleum
7 Geoff Bodine 3.00 6.00
Exide
7 Geoff Bodine 3.00 6.00
Exide Salsa
7 Dave Rezendes 3.00 6.00
Exide
8 Mike Bliss 3.00 6.00
Ultra Wheels
8 Craig Huartson 3.00 6.00
AC Delco
10 Stan Fox 3.00 6.00
Made for You
12 Randy MacCachren 3.00 6.00
Venable
18 Johnny Benson 3.00 6.00
Hella Lights
21 Tobey Butler 3.00 6.00
Ortho with Green Nose
21 Tobey Butler 3.00 6.00
Ortho with Yellow Nose
23 T.J. Clark 3.00 6.00
ASE with Blue paint scheme
23 T.J. Clark 3.00 6.00
ASE with White paint scheme
24 No Driver Association 3.00 6.00
DuPont Gordon Signature Series
24 No Driver Association 4.00 8.00
DuPont with Gordon on the card
37 Bob Strait 3.00 6.00
Target Expediting
38 Sammy Swindell 3.00 6.00
Channellock
with White Goodyear on tires
38 Sammy Swindell 3.00 6.00
Channellock
with Yellow Goodyear on tires
51 Kerry Teague 3.00 6.00
Rosenblum Racing
52 Ken Schrader 3.00 6.00
AC Delco
54 Steve McEachern 3.00 6.00
McEachern Racing
61 Todd Bodine 3.00 6.00
Roush Racing
75 Bill Sedgwick 3.00 6.00
Spears Motorsports
83 Steve Portenga 3.00 6.00
Coffee Critic
95 Brickyard 400 special 3.00 6.00
95 Brickyard 400 Premier/20,000 4.00 10.00
98 Butch Miller 3.00 6.00
Raybestos

1995 Racing Champions SuperTrucks Matched Serial Numbers 1:64

This series features trucks and cards with matching serial numbers. The truck has a serial number stamp on the bottom of it. The card has a black serial number stamped on the front of it. The truck sits on a stand that also has a serial number that matches.

EX NM-MT
1 Mike Chase 4.00 7.00
Sears Diehard
3 Mike Skinner 4.00 7.00
Goodwrench
6 Rick Carelli 4.00 7.00
Total Petroleum
24 Scott Lagasse 4.00 7.00
DuPont
75 Bill Sedgwick 4.00 7.00
Spears Motorsports
98 Butch Miller 4.00 7.00
Raybestos

1995 Racing Champions SuperTrucks To the Maxx 1:64

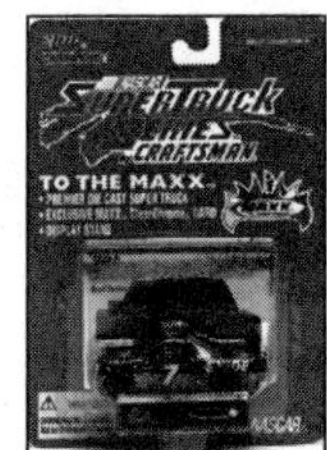

This is the first series of SuperTruck To the Maxx pieces. Each piece is packaged in a red blister pack and comes with a Crown Chrome acetate card.

EX NM-MT
1 P.J. Jones 3.00 6.00
Sears Diehard
3 Mike Skinner 4.00 8.00
Goodwrench
6 Rick Carelli 3.00 6.00
Total Petroleum
7 Geoff Bodine 3.00 6.00
Exide
21 Tobey Butler 3.00 6.00
Ortho
24 Jeff Gordon 5.00 10.00
DuPont
38 Sammy Swindell 3.00 6.00
Channellock
98 Butch Miller 3.00 6.00
Raybestos

1996 Racing Champions Preview 1:64

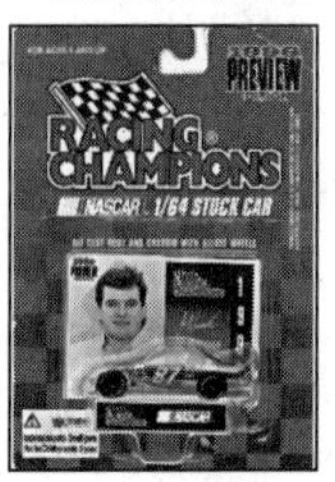

This series features some of the new paint schemes and driver changes for the 1996 season. The cars again come in a red blister with the word preview appearing below the year in the upper right hand corner.

EX NM-MT
2 Ricky Craven 1.50 4.00
DuPont
4 Sterling Marlin 2.00 5.00
Kodak
5 Terry Labonte 2.00 4.00
Kellogg's
6 Mark Martin 2.00 4.00
Valvoline
7 Stevie Reeves 1.50 4.00
Clabber Girl
9 Joe Bessey 1.50 4.00
Delco Remy
9 Lake Speed 1.50 4.00
SPAM
10 Ricky Rudd 1.50 4.00
Tide
11 Brett Bodine 1.50 4.00
Lowe's
12 Derrike Cope 1.50 4.00
Mane N' Tail
14 Patty Moise 1.50 4.00
Dial Purex
16 Ted Musgrave 1.50 4.00
Family Channel
17 Darrell Waltrip 1.50 4.00
Western Auto
18 Bobby Labonte 1.50 4.00
Interstate Batteries
22 Ward Burton 1.50 4.00
MBNA
24 Jeff Gordon 6.00 15.00
DuPont
30 Johnny Benson 1.50 4.00
Pennzoil
40 Tim Fedewa 1.50 4.00
Kleenex
41 Ricky Craven 1.50 4.00
Kodiak
47 Jeff Fuller 1.50 4.00
Sunoco
52 Ken Schrader 1.50 4.00
AC Delco
57 Jason Keller 1.50 4.00
Slim Jim
74 Johnny Benson 1.50 4.00
Lipton Tea
87 Joe Nemechek 1.50 4.00
Burger King
90 Mike Wallace 1.50 4.00
Heilig-Meyers
94 Bill Elliott 2.00 4.00
McDonald's

1996 Racing Champions 1:64

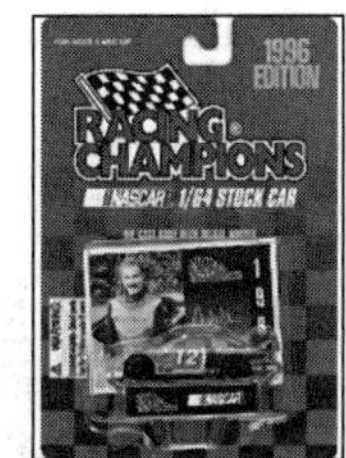

This set features some unique pieces that Racing Champions had never issued before. Some pieces came with a metal and plastic medallion in the blister package with the car. The Rusty Wallace was also available in both the Penske Racing and the MGD car.

EX NM-MT
1 Rick Mast 12.00 20.00
Hooters
1 Rick Mast 30.00 50.00
Hooter's Chrome/1996
2 Ricky Craven 2.00 4.00
DuPont
2 Rusty Wallace 8.00 15.00
Miller Genuine Draft
2 Rusty Wallace 50.00 100.00
Miller Genuine Draft Chrome/1996
2 Rusty Wallace 2.00 4.00
Penske Racing
4 Sterling Marlin 1.50 4.00
Kodak
4 Sterling Marlin 35.00 75.00
Kodak Chrome/1996
5 Terry Labonte 2.00 4.00
Kellogg's
5 Terry Labonte 40.00 100.00
Kellogg's Chrome/1996
5 Terry Labonte 4.00 10.00
Kellogg's Honey Crunch
Promo black windows
5 Terry Labonte 6.00 15.00
Kellogg's with Iron Man card
5 Terry Labonte 4.00 10.00
Kellogg's Iron Man
Promo in large box
5 Terry Labonte 4.00 8.00
Kellogg's Silver car
6 Tommy Houston 2.00 4.00
Suburban Propane
6 Mark Martin 2.00 4.00
Valvoline
6 Mark Martin 50.00 100.00
Valvoline Chrome/1996
6 Mark Martin 10.00 20.00
Valvoline Dura Blend
6 Mark Martin 7.00 12.00
Roush Box Promo
7 Geoff Bodine 2.00 4.00
QVC
8 Hut Stricklin 2.00 4.00
Circuit City
10 Phil Parsons 2.00 4.00
Channellock
10 Ricky Rudd 2.00 4.00
Tide
10 Ricky Rudd 25.00 50.00
Tide Chrome/1996
10 Ricky Rudd 4.00 10.00
Tide Promo black windows
11 Brett Bodine 2.00 4.00
Lowe's
11 Brett Bodine 6.00 15.00
Lowe's 50th Anniversary
12 Derrike Cope 7.50 15.00
Badcock
12 Michael Waltrip 3.00 6.00
MW Windows
14 Patty Moise 2.00 4.00
Dial Purex
16 Ted Musgrave 2.00 4.00
Family Channel
17 Darrell Waltrip 2.00 4.00
Parts America
17 Darrell Waltrip 25.00 50.00
Parts America Chrome/1996
17 Darrell Waltrip 4.00 8.00
Parts America Promo
18 Bobby Labonte 2.00 4.00
Interstate Batteries
18 Bobby Labonte 30.00 60.00
Interstate Batteries Chrome/1996
19 Loy Allen 7.50 15.00
Healthsource
21 Michael Waltrip 2.00 4.00
Citgo
21 Michael Waltrip 4.00 8.00
Citgo Promo
22 Ward Burton 7.50 15.00
MBNA
23 Chad Little 2.50 6.00
John Deere
23 Chad Little 5.00 12.00
John Deere Promo
24 Jeff Gordon 15.00 30.00
DuPont
24 Jeff Gordon 125.00 200.00
DuPont Chrome/1996
24 Jeff Gordon 20.00 40.00
DuPont Fan Club
in PVC box/1500
24 Jeff Gordon 7.50 15.00
DuPont Union 76 Promo
28 Ernie Irvan 2.00 4.00
Havoline
28 Ernie Irvan 30.00 80.00
Havoline Chrome/1996
28 Ernie Irvan 3.00 8.00
Havoline Promo
29 Steve Grissom 5.00 10.00
Cartoon Network
29 Steve Grissom 5.00 12.00
WCW
29 No Driver Association 4.00 8.00
Scooby-Doo
29 No Driver Association 6.00 12.00
WCW Sting
30 Johnny Benson 2.00 4.00
Pennzoil
31 Mike Skinner 15.00 30.00
Realtree
32 Dale Jarrett 4.00 10.00
Band-Aid Promo
34 Mike McLaughlin 6.00 12.00
Royal Oak
37 John Andretti 2.00 4.00
K-Mart
37 John Andretti 4.00 8.00
K-Mart Promo
38 Dennis Setzer 2.00 4.00
Lipton Tea
40 Tim Fedewa 2.00 4.00
Kleenex
40 Jim Sauter 3.00 6.00
First Union
41 Ricky Craven 2.00 4.00
Larry Hedrick Racing
41 Ricky Craven 2.00 4.00
Manheim
41 Ricky Craven 18.00 30.00
Team Hedrick Promo
43 Rodney Combs 2.00 4.00
Lance
43 Bobby Hamilton 60.00 100.00
5-trailer set 25th Anniversary
43 Bobby Hamilton 15.00 30.00
5-car set 25th Anniversary
43 Bobby Hamilton 20.00 50.00
STP 25th Anniversary set
Hood Open 5-STP cars and bonus
#5 Terry Labonte/Kellogg's Silver
43 Bobby Hamilton 3.00 8.00
STP Anniversary
1972 Red/Blue
43 Bobby Hamilton 3.00 8.00
STP Anniversary 1972 Blue
43 Bobby Hamilton 3.00 8.00
STP Anniversary
1979 Red/Blue
43 Bobby Hamilton 3.00 8.00
STP Anniversary
1984 Blue/Red
43 Bobby Hamilton 7.50 15.00
STP Anniversary 1996 Silver
43 Bobby Hamilton 9.00 18.00
STP Anniversary 1996 Silver
in Red and Blue Box

	EX	NM-MT
43 Bobby Hamilton STP Anniversary Promo/5000	5.00	12.00
44 Bobby Labonte Shell	5.00	10.00
47 Jeff Fuller Sunoco	2.00	4.00
47 Jeff Fuller Sunoco Diamond Car Promo	4.00	10.00
51 Jim Bown Lucks	2.00	4.00
51 Mike Stefanik Burnham Boilers Promo	20.00	35.00
57 Jim Bown Matco Tools	5.00	10.00
57 Jason Keller Halloween Havoc	2.00	4.00
57 Jason Keller Slim Jim	2.00	4.00
58 Mike Cope Penrose	2.00	4.00
60 Mark Martin Winn Dixie Promo	4.00	8.00
61 Mike Olsen Little Trees Promo in bag	4.00	10.00
63 Curtis Markham Lysol	2.00	4.00
74 Randy LaJoie Fina	2.00	4.00
75 Morgan Shepherd Remington	4.00	8.00
81 Kenny Wallace TIC Financial	7.50	15.00
87 Joe Nemechek BellSouth	6.00	12.00
87 Joe Nemechek Burger King	12.50	25.00
88 Dale Jarrett Quality Care	5.00	10.00
88 Dale Jarrett Quality Care Chrome/1996	30.00	80.00
90 Mike Wallace Duron	2.00	4.00
92 David Pearson Stanley Tools	2.00	4.00
94 Ron Barfield New Holland	2.00	4.00
94 Bill Elliott McDonald's	2.00	4.00
94 Bill Elliott McDonald's Chrome/1996	25.00	60.00
94 Bill Elliott McDonald's Monopoly	2.00	4.00
94 Bill Elliott 10-Time Most Popular Driver Silver	40.00	70.00
94 Harry Gant McDonald's	3.00	6.00
96 David Green Busch	4.00	10.00
96 Stevie Reeves Clabber Girl	2.00	4.00
97 Chad Little Sterling Cowboy	5.00	12.00
99 Glenn Allen Luxaire	2.00	4.00
99 Jeff Burton Exide	2.00	4.00
NNO Kellogg's 6-car 1990-96 Promo #97 Chuck Bown (1990) #41 (1991-92) #14 Terry Labonte (1993) #5 Terry Labonte (1994) #5 Terry Labonte (1995) #5 Terry Labonte Silver (1996)	10.00	20.00
NNO 12-Car set in case 2. Rusty Wallace/Penske 4. Sterling Marlin/Kodak 5. Terry Labonte/Kellogg's Red and Yellow 5. Terry Labonte/Kellogg's Red and Gray 6. Mark Martin/Valvoline 10. Ricky Rudd/Tide 12. Michael Waltrip/MW Windows 16. Ted Musgrave/Primestar 17. Darrell Waltrip/Parts America 24. Jeff Gordon/DuPont 28. Ernie Irvan/Havoline 29 Steve Grissom/Cartoon Network 29. NDA/WCW Sting 30. Johnny Benson/Pennzoil 37. John Andretti/K-Mart 57. Jason Keller/Slim Jim Halloween 75. Morgan Shepherd/Remington 88. Dale Jarrett/Quality Care 94. Bill Elliott/McDonald's 94. Bill Elliott/McDonald's Monopoly	25.00	50.00

1996 Racing Champions Classics 1:64

	EX	NM-MT
1 Bud Moore 1969 Dodge Daytona	2.00	5.00
1 Dick Hutcherson 1964 Ford	2.00	5.00
3 Don White 1969 Dodge Daytona	2.00	5.00
3 Fred Lorenzen 1969 Dodge Daytona	2.00	5.00
4 John Sears 1964 Ford	2.00	5.00
5 Pete Hamilton 1969 Ford Talladega	2.00	5.00
6 Buddy Baker 1969 Dodge Daytona	2.00	5.00
10 Buddy Baker 1964 Ford	2.00	5.00
11 Ned Jarrett Bowani Inc. 1964 Ford	2.00	5.00
12 Bobby Allison 1969 Mercury Cyclone	2.50	6.00
16 Tiny Lund 1969 Mercury Cyclone	2.00	5.00
17 David Pearson 1969 Ford Talladega	2.50	6.00
17 David Pearson 1969 Mercury Cyclone	2.50	6.00
21 Donnie Allison 1969 Mercury Cyclone	2.00	5.00
21 Marvin Panch 1964 Ford	2.00	5.00
21 Jack Bowsher 1969 Ford Torino	2.00	5.00
22 Bobby Allison 1969 Dodge Daytona	2.50	6.00
22 Fireball Roberts Young Ford 1964 Ford	2.00	5.00
22 Dick Brooks 1969 Dodge Daytona	2.00	5.00
24 Cecil Gordon 1969 Mercury Cyclone	2.00	5.00
27 Donnie Allison 1969 Ford Talladega	2.00	5.00
27 Banjo Mathews 1964 Ford	2.00	5.00
28 Fred Lorenzen 1969 Dodge Daytona	2.00	5.00
29 Bud Moore 1969 Ford Talladega	2.00	5.00
29 Bobby Allison 1969 Ford Talladega	2.50	6.00
31 Jim Vandiver 1969 Dodge Daytona	2.00	5.00
32 Dick Brooks 1970 Plym.Superbird	2.00	5.00
34 Wendell Scott 1969 Ford Talladega	2.00	5.00
48 James Hylton 1969 Ford Talladega	2.00	5.00
48 James Hylton 1969 Mercury Cyclone	2.00	5.00
55 Tiny Lund 1969 Dodge Daytona	2.00	5.00
57 Dick May 1964 Ford	2.00	5.00
57 Dick May 1969 Ford Talladega	2.00	5.00
64 Elmo Langley 1964 Ford	2.00	5.00
64 Elmo Langley 1969 Ford Talladega	2.00	5.00
64 Elmo Langley 1969 Mercury Cyclone	2.00	5.00
71 Bobby Isaac K&K Insurance 1969 Dodge Daytona	2.00	5.00
73 Buddy Arrington 1964 Ford	2.00	5.00
76 Larry Frank 1964 Ford	2.00	5.00
88 Benny Parsons 1969 Ford Talladega	2.00	5.00
98 Lee Roy Yarborough 1969 Ford Talladega	2.00	5.00
99 Charlie Glotzbach 1969 Dodge Daytona	2.00	5.00
99 Bobby Isaac 1964 Ford	2.00	5.00
06 Neil Castles 1969 Dodge Daytona	2.00	5.00

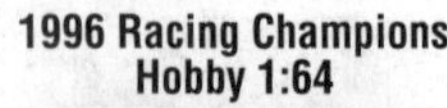

1996 Racing Champions Hobby 1:64

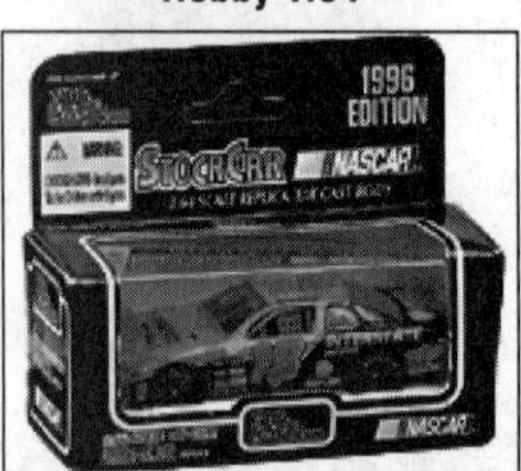

These pieces were released through Hobby outlets only. Each car was issued in a 1996 Edition window box.

	EX	NM-MT
4 Sterling Marlin Kodak	3.00	8.00
6 Mark Martin Valvoline	3.00	6.00
18 Bobby Labonte Interstate Batteries	3.00	6.00
24 Jeff Gordon DuPont	3.00	6.00
47 Jeff Fuller Sunoco	3.00	6.00
81 Kenny Wallace Square D	3.00	6.00

1996 Racing Champions Premier with Medallion 1:64

These pieces are the same as the standard Racing Champions 1:64 1996 pieces with the exception of the packaging. Each car is packaged with a medallion instead of a card.

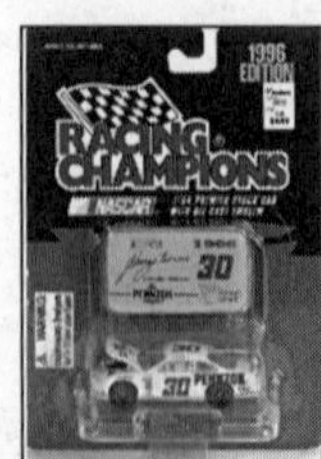

	EX	NM-MT
1 Rick Mast Hooters Hood Open	6.00	12.00
1 Hermie Sadler DeWalt	3.00	8.00
2 Ricky Craven DuPont	3.00	8.00
2 Ricky Craven DuPont Hood Open	5.00	10.00
2 Rusty Wallace Miller Genuine Draft Hood Open In Miller Package	6.00	12.00
3 Mike Skinner Goodwrench	3.00	8.00
4 Sterling Marlin Kodak	4.00	10.00
5 Terry Labonte Bayer Hood Open	5.00	10.00
5 Terry Labonte Kellogg's Silver car Hood Open	5.00	10.00
6 Mark Martin Valvoline Dura Blend Hood Open	5.00	10.00
7 Geoff Bodine QVC	3.00	8.00
10 Ricky Rudd Tide Hood Open	5.00	10.00
11 Brett Bodine Lowe's	3.00	8.00
15 Wally Dallenbach Hayes Modems	10.00	20.00
16 Ted Musgrave Family Channel	3.00	8.00
18 Bobby Labonte Interstate Batteries	3.00	8.00
18 Bobby Labonte Interstate Batteries Hood Open	5.00	10.00
22 Ward Burton MBNA	3.00	8.00
23 Chad Little John Deere Hood Open	4.00	10.00
23 Chad Little John Deere Hood Open Promo	6.00	15.00
24 Jeff Gordon DuPont	6.00	12.00
24 Jeff Gordon DuPont Hood Open	7.50	15.00
24 Jeff Gordon DuPont 1995 Champion	6.00	12.00
25 Ken Schrader Budweiser	6.00	15.00
25 Ken Schrader Budweiser Silver	50.00	90.00
25 Ken Schrader Hendrick	3.00	8.00
28 Ernie Irvan Havoline Hood Open	5.00	10.00
29 Steve Grissom Cartoon Network	3.00	8.00
29 Steve Grissom Cartoon Network Hood Open	6.00	12.00
29 Steve Grissom Cartoon Network 5-car set	25.00	50.00
29 No Driver Association Scooby-Doo	3.00	8.00
29 No Driver Association Shaggy	3.00	8.00
30 Johnny Benson Pennzoil	3.00	8.00
31 Mike Skinner Realtree	20.00	35.00
34 Mike McLaughlin Royal Oak	3.00	8.00
37 John Andretti K-Mart	3.00	8.00
41 Ricky Craven Larry Hedrick Racing	3.00	8.00
43 Bobby Hamilton STP Hood Open	6.00	12.00
43 Bobby Hamilton STP Silver Hood Open	6.00	12.00
43 Bobby Hamilton STP 5-car set	30.00	55.00
44 Bobby Labonte Shell	10.00	20.00
52 Ken Schrader AC Delco	3.00	8.00
52 Ken Schrader AC Delco Hood Open	5.00	10.00
57 Chuck Bown Matco	3.00	8.00
71 Dave Marcis Prodigy	10.00	25.00
74 Johnny Benson Lipton Tea	3.00	8.00
87 Joe Nemechek Burger King	6.00	15.00
88 Dale Jarrett Quality Care	3.00	8.00
92 Larry Pearson Stanley Tools	3.00	8.00
94 Bill Elliott McDonald's Hood Open	5.00	10.00
94 Bill Elliott McDonald's Monopoly Hood Open	5.00	10.00
94 Bill Elliott McDonald's Monopoly Hood Open Promo	4.00	8.00
96 David Green Busch	3.00	8.00
97 Chad Little Sterling Cowboy	3.00	8.00

1996 Racing Champions PVC Box 1:64

	EX	NM-MT
96 Charlotte Coca-Cola 500	4.00	10.00
96 Charlotte October 6	4.00	10.00
96 Richmond March 3	4.00	10.00
96 David Green Busch Spencer Gifts Promo/800	50.00	100.00

1996 Racing Champions SuperTrucks 1:64

Racing Champions continued their line of 1:64 SuperTrucks in 1996. Each truck was packaged in a small red and black window box with an extra backer board so the piece could be hung on a peg board retail display.

	EX	NM-MT
2 Mike Bliss Team ASE	2.00	4.00
3 Mike Skinner Goodwrench	2.00	4.00
5 Darrell Waltrip Die Hard	2.00	4.00
6 Rick Carelli Chesrown	2.00	4.00
6 Rick Carelli Total	2.00	4.00
9 Joe Bessey New Hampshire Speedway	2.00	4.00
14 Butch Gilliland Stroppe	2.00	4.00
17 Bill Sedgwick Die Hard	2.00	4.00
17 Darrell Waltrip Western Auto	2.00	4.00
19 Lance Norick Macklenburg-Duncan	2.00	4.00
20 Walker Evans Dana	2.00	4.00
21 Doug George Ortho	2.00	4.00
24 Jack Sprague Quaker State	2.00	4.00
29 Bob Keselowski Winnebago	2.00	4.00
30 Jimmy Hensley Mopar	2.00	4.00
52 Ken Schrader AC Delco	2.00	4.00
57 Robbie Pyne Aisyn	2.00	4.00
75 Bobby Gill Spears	2.00	4.00
78 Mike Chase Petron Plus	2.00	4.00
80 Joe Ruttman J.R.Garage	2.00	4.00
83 Steve Portenga Coffee Critic	2.00	4.00
98 Butch Miller Raybestos	2.00	4.00

1997 Racing Champions Preview 1:64

This series of 1:64 die cast replicas featured a preview of some of the new paint jobs to run in the 1997 season. The Rick Mast Remington car and the Robert Pressley Scooby Doo car feature two of the numerous driver changes for the 97 Winston Cup season.

	EX	NM-MT
4 Sterling Marlin Kodak	2.00	5.00
5 Terry Labonte Kellogg's	2.00	4.00
6 Mark Martin Valvoline	2.00	4.00
18 Bobby Labonte Interstate Batteries	1.50	4.00
21 Michael Waltrip Citgo	1.50	4.00
24 Jeff Gordon DuPont	2.50	5.00
28 Ernie Irvan Havoline	1.50	4.00
29 Robert Pressley Scooby-Doo	1.50	4.00
30 Johnny Benson Pennzoil	1.50	4.00
75 Rick Mast Remington	1.50	4.00
94 Bill Elliott McDonald's	2.00	4.00
99 Jeff Burton Exide	1.50	4.00

1997 Racing Champions Premier Preview with Medallion 1:64

This is the first time Racing Champions has issued a Preview of their Premier. Each car comes with a medallion like the standard Premier cars.

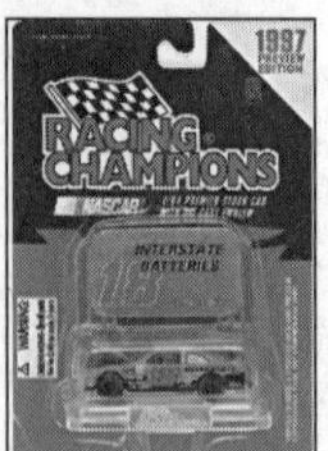

	EX	NM-MT
4 Sterling Marlin Kodak	3.00	8.00
5 Terry Labonte Kellogg's	4.00	8.0
6 Mark Martin Valvoline	3.00	6.0
18 Bobby Labonte Interstate Batteries	3.00	6.0
24 Jeff Gordon DuPont	4.00	10.0
29 Robert Pressley Scooby-Doo	3.00	6.0
94 Bill Elliott McDonald's	3.00	6.0

1997 Racing Champions 1:6

The 1:64 scale cars that appear in this series are replica many of the cars that ran in the 1997 season. The serie highlighted by the Terry Labonte Kellogg's car commemora his 1996 Winston Cup Championship. This car is availabl two variations: standard and hood open.

	EX	NM-M
1 Andy Hillenburg Gravy Train Promo	12.50	25.0
1 Hermie Sadler DeWalt	2.00	4.0
1 Morgan Shepherd R&L Carriers	2.00	4.0
1 Morgan Shepherd R&L Carriers Promo	10.00	20.0
2 Ricky Craven Raybestos	2.00	4.0
2 Rusty Wallace Miller Lite Matco Promo/20,000	5.00	10.0
2 Rusty Wallace Penske Racing	2.00	4.0
4 Sterling Marlin Kodak	2.00	5.0
5 Terry Labonte Bayer	2.00	4.0
5 Terry Labonte Kellogg's 1996 Champion	3.00	8.0
5 Terry Labonte Kellogg's 1996 Champion Chrome/1997	75.00	125.0
5 Terry Labonte Kellogg's 2-car Promo Set	6.00	15.0
5 Terry Labonte Kellogg's 3-car Promo 1996 Champion blister	6.00	15.0
5 Terry Labonte Kellogg's Tony	3.00	6.0
5 Terry Labonte Kellogg's Tony Promo black windows	4.00	10.0
6 Joe Bessey Power Team	2.00	4.0
6 Mark Martin Valvoline	2.00	4.0
6 Mark Martin Valvoline Kosei Promo/5000	40.00	75.0
7 Geoff Bodine QVC	2.00	4.0
7 Geoff Bodine QVC Chrome/1997	15.00	40.0
7 Geoff Bodine QVC Gold Rush	3.00	8.0
8 Hut Stricklin Circuit City	2.00	4.0
9 Joe Bessey Power Team	2.00	4.0
9 Jeff Burton Track Gear	2.00	4.0
10 Phil Parsons Channellock	2.00	4.0
10 Ricky Rudd Tide	2.00	4.0
10 Ricky Rudd Tide Promo	4.00	10.0
11 Jimmy Foster Speedvision	2.00	4.0
11 Brett Bodine Close Call	2.00	4.0
15 C.Long Austin Crackers Promo	60.00	100.0
16 Ted Musgrave Primestar	2.00	4.0
16 Ted Musgrave Primestar Chrome/1997	20.00	40.0
17 Tim Bender Kraft Singles promo in bag	10.00	20.0
17 Darrell Waltrip Parts America	2.00	4.0
17 Darrell Waltrip Parts America Chrome	3.00	8.0
18 Bobby Labonte Interstate Batteries	2.00	4.0
19 Gary Bradberry	2.00	4.0

CSR		
Michael Waltrip Citgo	2.00	4.00
Michael Waltrip Citgo Chrome/1997	20.00	40.00
Jeff Gordon DuPont	4.00	8.00
Ricky Craven Bud Lizard	6.00	12.00
Ricky Craven Bud Lizard Chrome/1997	20.00	40.00
Ricky Craven Hendrick	2.00	4.00
Ernie Irvan Havoline	2.00	4.00
Ernie Irvan Havoline 10th Anniversary	2.00	4.00
Robert Pressley Cartoon Network	2.00	4.00
Jeff Green Tom and Jerry	2.00	4.00
Elliott Sadler Phillips 66	2.00	4.00
Johnny Benson Pennzoil	2.00	4.00
Johnny Benson Pennzoil Chrome/1997	15.00	40.00
Dale Jarrett White Rain	2.00	4.00
Ken Schrader Petree Racing	2.00	4.00
Mike McLaughlin Royal Oak	2.00	4.00
Todd Bodine Stanley Tools	2.00	4.00
Derrike Cope Skittles	2.00	4.00
Derrike Cope Skittles Chrome/1997	15.00	40.00
Derrike Cope Skittles Promo in box	2.00	5.00
Jeremy Mayfield K-Mart	2.00	4.00
Elton Sawyer Barbasol	2.00	4.00
Tim Fedewa Kleenex	2.00	4.00
Robby Gordon Sabco Racing	2.00	4.00
Robby Gordon Sabco Chrome/1997	20.00	40.00
Steve Grissom Larry Hedrick Racing	2.00	4.00
Joe Nemechek BellSouth	2.00	4.00
Joe Nemechek BellSouth Chrome/1997	20.00	40.00
Rodney Combs Lance	2.00	4.00
Dennis Setzer Lance	2.00	4.00
Wally Dallenbach First Union	2.00	4.00
Wally Dallenbach First Union Chrome/1997	20.00	40.00
Jeff Fuller Sunoco	2.00	4.00
Kyle Petty NWO	4.00	8.00
Jason Keller Slim Jim	2.00	4.00
Lou Rettenmeier Mobil Promo	18.00	30.00
Mark Martin Winn Dixie	4.00	8.00
Mike Dillon Detriot Gasket	2.00	4.00
Randy LaJoie Fina	2.00	4.00
Randy LaJoie Fina Promo	4.00	8.00
Rick Mast Remington	2.00	4.00
Rick Mast Remington Camo	2.00	4.00
Rick Mast Remington Stren	2.00	4.00
Rick Mast Remington Chrome/1997	20.00	40.00
NASCAR Thunder TNN Promo/4000	6.00	15.00
Shane Hall Luck's Beans Promo	12.50	25.00
Kevin Lepage Hype	2.00	4.00
Dick Trickle Heilig-Meyers	2.00	4.00
Mike Wallace Spam	2.00	4.00
Ron Barfield New Holland	2.00	4.00
Bill Elliott McDonald's	2.00	4.00
Bill Elliott Mac Tonight	2.00	4.00
Bill Elliott Mac Tonight Chrome/1997	25.00	50.00
David Green Caterpillar	2.00	4.00
David Green Caterpillar Chrome/1997	15.00	40.00
David Green Caterpillar Promo	3.00	8.00
No Driver Association Brickyard 400	3.00	6.00
No Driver Association www.racingchamps.com	10.00	18.00
Chad Little John Deere	2.00	4.00
Chad Little John Deere Chrome/1997	15.00	40.00
Chad Little John Deere Promo	3.00	8.00
No Driver Association EA Sports	2.00	4.00
Glenn Allen Luxaire	2.00	4.00
Jeff Burton Exide	2.00	4.00
Jeff Burton Exide Chrome/1997	25.00	50.00
00 Buckshot Jones Aqua Fresh	2.00	4.00
NNO 12-Car set in black case	15.00	40.00

4. Sterling Marlin/Kodak
5. Terry Labonte/Kellogg's Tony
6. Mark Martin/Valvoline
7. Geoff Bodine/QVC
10. Ricky Rudd/Tide
16. Ted Musgrave/Primestar
18. Bobby Labonte/Inter.Batteries
28. Ernie Irvan/Havoline
29. NDA/Cartoon Network
30. Johnny Benson/Pennzoil
94. Bill Elliott/Mac Tonight
96. David Green/Caterpillar

1997 Racing Champions Pinnacle Series 1:64

This marks the second time Racing Champions have teamed up with a card manufacturer to product a line of die cast car with trading cards. Each car is boxed in similar packaging as the standard cars, but Pinnacle cards are featured in place of Racing Champions generic cards.

	EX	NM-MT
4 Sterling Marlin Kodak	4.00	10.00
5 Terry Labonte Kellogg's	5.00	10.00
6 Mark Martin Valvoline	4.00	8.00
7 Geoff Bodine QVC	3.00	8.00
8 Hut Stricklin Circuit City	3.00	8.00
10 Ricky Rudd Tide	3.00	8.00
16 Ted Musgrave Primestar	3.00	8.00
18 Bobby Labonte Interstate Batteries	3.00	8.00
21 Michael Waltrip Citgo	3.00	8.00
28 Ernie Irvan Havoline	3.00	8.00
29 Robert Pressley Cartoon Network	3.00	8.00
30 Johnny Benson Pennzoil	3.00	8.00
36 Derrike Cope Skittles	3.00	8.00
37 Jeremy Mayfield K-Mart	3.00	8.00
75 Rick Mast Remington	3.00	8.00
87 Joe Nemechek BellSouth	3.00	8.00
94 Bill Elliott McDonald's	4.00	8.00
96 David Green Caterpillar	3.00	8.00
97 Chad Little John Deere	3.00	8.00
99 Jeff Burton Exide	3.00	8.00

1997 Racing Champions Premier Gold 1:64

These 1:64 scale cars were distributed primarily through hobby outlets in a Racing Champions' Premier Gold' solid black box. The total production run was 4800 of each car with 4600 of those being produced with a standard paint scheme and 200 in gold chrome paint.

	EX	NM-MT
2 Rusty Wallace Miller Lite	4.00	8.00
6 Mark Martin Valvoline	4.00	8.00
10 Ricky Rudd Tide	4.00	8.00
18 Bobby Labonte Interstate Batteries	4.00	8.00
36 Derrike Cope Skittles	3.00	8.00
40 Robby Gordon Coors Light	4.00	8.00
75 Rick Mast Remington	4.00	8.00
94 Bill Elliott McDonald's	4.00	8.00

1997 Racing Champions Premier Gold Chrome 1:64

These 1:64 scale cars were distributed through hobby outlets in a Racing Champions' Premier Gold' solid black box. The total production run was 4800 of each car with 200 of those being produced with a gold chrome finish.

	EX	NM-MT
2 Rusty Wallace Miller Lite	50.00	100.00
6 Mark Martin Valvoline	50.00	100.00
10 Ricky Rudd Tide	40.00	80.00
18 Bobby Labonte Interstate Batteries	40.00	80.00
36 Derrike Cope Skittles	30.00	80.00
40 Robby Gordon Coors Light	40.00	80.00
75 Rick Mast Remington	40.00	80.00
94 Bill Elliott McDonald's	50.00	100.00

1997 Racing Champions Premier with Medallion 1:64

These pieces are the same as the standard Racing Champions 1:64 1997 pieces with the exception of the packaging. Each car is packaged with a medallion instead of a card. A few cars were produced in a limited silver parallel version as well.

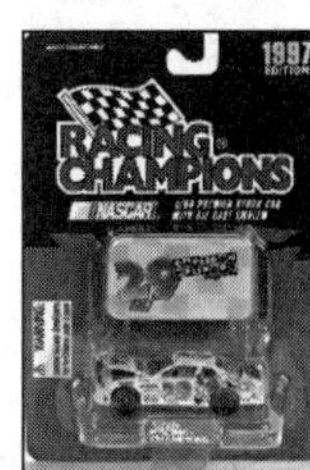

	EX	NM-MT
1 Morgan Shepherd Crusin' America	3.00	8.00
2 Rusty Wallace Penske	4.00	8.00
5 Terry Labonte Kellogg's Tony	5.00	10.00
5 Terry Labonte Kellogg's Tony Chrome/997	25.00	60.00
6 Mark Martin Valvoline	4.00	8.00
7 Geoff Bodine QVC	3.00	8.00
7 Geoff Bodine QVC Chrome/997	20.00	50.00
8 Hut Stricklin Circuit City	3.00	8.00
9 Lake Speed University of Nebraska	15.00	30.00
10 Ricky Rudd Tide	3.00	8.00
10 Ricky Rudd Tide Chrome/997	20.00	50.00
11 Brett Bodine Close Call	3.00	8.00
16 Ted Musgrave Primestar	3.00	8.00
16 Ted Musgrave Primestar Chrome/997	20.00	50.00
17 Darrell Waltrip Parts America	3.00	8.00
17 Darrell Waltrip Parts America Chrome/997	5.00	10.00
18 Bobby Labonte Interstate Batteries	3.00	8.00
18 Bobby Labonte Intertstate Batteries Silver/997	20.00	50.00
21 Michael Waltrip Citgo	3.00	8.00
28 Ernie Irvan Havoline	3.00	8.00
28 Ernie Irvan Havoline Chrome/997	20.00	50.00
28 Ernie Irvan Havoline 10th Anniversary	5.00	10.00
29 Robert Pressley Scooby-Doo	3.00	8.00
29 No Driver Assocation Tom and Jerry	3.00	8.00
30 Johnny Benson Pennzoil	3.00	8.00
36 Derrike Cope Skittles	3.00	8.00
37 Jeremy Mayfield K-Mart	3.00	8.00
75 Rick Mast Remington	3.00	8.00
75 Rick Mast Remington Camo	3.00	8.00
75 Rick Mast Remington Stren	3.00	8.00
94 Bill Elliott Mac Tonight	4.00	8.00
96 David Green Caterpillar	3.00	8.00
96 David Green Caterpillar Promo	5.00	12.00
97 Chad Little John Deere	3.00	8.00
97 Chad Little John Deere Promo	5.00	12.00
99 Jeff Burton Exide	3.00	8.00

1997 Racing Champions Roaring Racers 1:64

	EX	NM-MT
4 Sterling Marlin Kodak	5.00	12.00
5 Terry Labonte Kellogg's	5.00	12.00
5 Terry Labonte Kellogg's Tony	5.00	12.00
6 Mark Martin Valvoline	5.00	12.00
16 Ted Musgrave Primestar	4.00	10.00
18 Bobby Labonte Interstate Batteries	5.00	12.00
21 Michael Waltrip Citgo	4.00	10.00
28 Ernie Irvan Havoline	4.00	10.00
29 Robert Pressley Cartoon Network	4.00	10.00
36 Derrike Cope Skittles	4.00	10.00
94 Bill Elliott Mac Tonight	5.00	12.00
97 Chad Little John Deere	4.00	10.00

1997 Racing Champions Stock Rods 1:64

These 1:64 scale cars are replicas of vintage stock rods with NASCAR paint schemes. Cars are listed by issue number instead of car number.

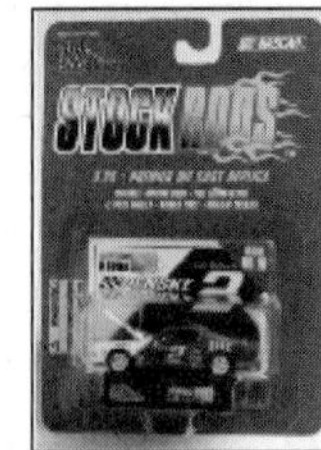

	EX	NM-MT
1 Terry Labonte Kellogg's	6.00	15.00
2 Bill Elliott McDonald's	5.00	12.00
3 Mark Martin Valvoline	5.00	12.00
4 Robert Pressley Scooby-Doo	3.00	8.00
5 Ted Musgrave Primestar	3.00	8.00
6 Jeff Burton Exide	3.00	8.00
7 Bobby Labonte Interstate Batteries	3.00	8.00
8 Ricky Craven Hendrick	3.00	8.00
9 Darrell Waltrip Parts America	3.00	8.00
10 Rusty Wallace Miller Lite	60.00	120.00
11 Derrike Cope Skittles	3.00	8.00
12 Ricky Rudd Tide	3.00	8.00
13 Rick Mast Remington	3.00	8.00
14 Ricky Craven Hendrick	3.00	8.00
15 Jeff Green Tom & Jerry	3.00	8.00
16 Bill Elliott Mac Tonight	3.00	8.00
17 Mark Martin Valvoline	3.00	8.00
18 Rusty Wallace Penske	3.00	8.00
19 Ted Musgrave Primestar	3.00	8.00
20 Jeff Burton Exide	3.00	8.00
21 Darrell Waltrip Parts America	3.00	8.00
22 Ricky Rudd Tide	3.00	8.00
23 Rick Mast Remington	3.00	8.00
24 Steve Grissom Larry Hedrick Racing	3.00	8.00
25 Bill Elliott Mac Tonight	3.00	8.00
26 Glen Allen Luxaire	3.00	8.00
27 Dennis Setzer Lance	3.00	8.00
28 Bill Elliott McDonald's	3.00	8.00
29 Ricky Craven Hendrick	3.00	8.00
30 Sterling Marlin Sabco	3.00	8.00
31 Jeff Green Cartoon Network	3.00	8.00
32 Joe Nemechek Bell South	3.00	8.00
33 Ernie Irvan Havoline	3.00	8.00
34 Ricky Rudd Tide	3.00	8.00
35 Rusty Wallace Penske	3.00	8.00
36 Ernie Irvan Havoline	3.00	8.00
37 Mark Martin Valvoline	3.00	8.00
38 Terry Labonte Spooky Loops	5.00	10.00
39 Terry Labonte Spooky Loops	5.00	10.00
40 Derrike Cope Skittles	3.00	8.00
41 Steve Grissom Larry Hedrick Racing	3.00	8.00
42 Terry Labonte Spooky Loops Chrome	30.00	50.00
43 Terry Labonte Spooky Loops	7.50	15.00
44 Jeff Burton Exide	3.00	8.00
45 Bill Elliott McDonald's	3.00	8.00
46 Ted Musgrave Primestar	3.00	8.00
47 Mark Martin Valvoline	3.00	8.00
48 Ricky Rudd Tide	3.00	8.00
49 Glen Allen Luxaire	3.00	8.00
50 Terry Labonte Spooky Loops	3.00	8.00
51 Joe Bessey Power Team	3.00	8.00
52 Terry Labonte Kellogg's	3.00	8.00
53 Wally Dallenbach First Union	3.00	8.00
54 Ricky Craven Hendrick	3.00	8.00
55 Ricky Craven Hendrick	3.00	8.00

1997 Racing Champions SuperTrucks 1:64

Racing Champions continued their line of 1:64 SuperTrucks in 1997. This series features many of the circuit's first-time drivers and Winston Cup regulars.

	EX	NM-MT
1 Michael Waltrip MW Windows	2.00	4.00
2 Mike Bliss Team ASE	2.00	4.00
4 Bill Elliott Team ASE	2.00	4.00
6 Rick Carelli Remax	2.00	4.00
7 Tammy Kirk Loveable	2.00	4.00
13 Mike Colabucci VISA	2.00	4.00
15 Mike Colabucci VISA	2.00	4.00
15 Mike Cope Penrose	2.00	4.00
18 Johnny Benson Pennzoil	2.00	4.00
18 Mike Dokken Dana	2.00	4.00
19 Tony Raines Pennzoil	2.00	4.00
20 Butch Miller The Orleans	2.00	4.00
23 T.J. Clark CRG Motorsports	2.00	4.00
24 Jack Sprague Quaker State	2.00	4.00
29 Bob Keselowski Mopar	2.00	4.00
35 Dave Rezendes Ortho	2.00	4.00
44 Boris Said Federated Auto	2.00	4.00
49 Rodney Combs Lance	2.00	4.00
52 Tobey Butler Purolater	2.00	4.00
66 Bryan Refner Carlin	2.00	4.00
75 Dan Press Spears	2.00	4.00
80 Joe Ruttman LCI	2.00	4.00
86 Stacy Compton Valvoline	2.00	4.00
87 Joe Nemechek Bell South	2.00	4.00
92 Mark Kinser Rotary	2.00	4.00
94 Ron Barfield Super 8	2.00	4.00
99 Chuck Bown Exide	2.00	4.00
99 Jeff Burton Exide	2.00	4.00
99 Mark Martin Exide	12.50	25.00

1998 Racing Champions 1:64

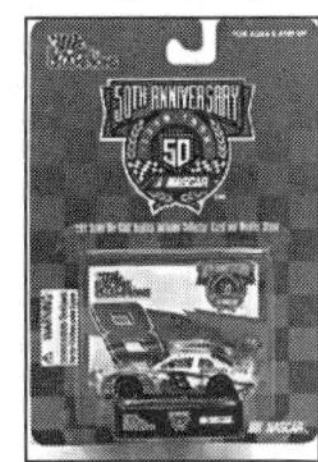

The 1:64 scale cars that appear in this series are replicas of many of the cars that ran in the 1997 season, but also include some cars slated to appear in 1998. They were packaged in red blister packs that display the NASCAR 50th anniversary logo. A yellow bordered card was also inserted into each regular issue piece. Chrome versions were produced of some cars with Winston Cup driver's die-casts being numbered of 5050 and Busch Series cars of 1000 produced. Most promo pieces were issued without the card and in a blister pack that more closely follows the paint scheme of the featured driver's car or die-cast sponsor.

	EX	NM-MT
4 Bobby Hamilton Kodak	2.00	4.00
4 Jeff Purvis Lance	2.00	4.00
5 Terry Labonte Kellogg's	2.00	5.00
5 Terry Labonte Kellogg's Chrome/5050	20.00	50.00
5 Terry Labonte Kellogg's Corny	2.00	5.00
5 Terry Labonte Kellogg's Corny Chrome/5050	20.00	50.00
6 Joe Bessey Power Team	2.00	4.00
6 Mark Martin Eagle One	2.00	4.00
6 Mark Martin Eagle One Chrome/5050	20.00	50.00
6 Mark Martin Kosei Promo/5000	30.00	50.00
6 Mark Martin Valvoline	2.00	4.00
6 Mark Martin Valvoline Chrome/5050	20.00	50.00
8 Hut Stricklin Circuit City 4th of July	2.00	4.00
8 Hut Stricklin Circuit City Chrome/5050	15.00	40.00
9 Jeff Burton	2.00	4.00

Track Gear
9 Jeff Burton 15.00 40.00
Track Gear Chrome/1000
9 Lake Speed 2.00 4.00
Birthday Cake
10 Ricky Rudd 2.00 4.00
Tide
10 Ricky Rudd 15.00 40.00
Tide Chrome/5050
10 Ricky Rudd 4.00 10.00
Tide Promo
10 Ricky Rudd 4.00 10.00
Tide 5th Anniversary Promo
10 Ricky Rudd 4.00 10.00
Tide Kids Promo
11 Brett Bodine 2.00 4.00
Paychex
12 Jeremy Mayfield 2.00 4.00
Mobil 1
13 Jerry Nadeau 2.00 4.00
First Plus
16 Ted Musgrave 2.00 4.00
Primestar
16 Ted Musgrave 15.00 40.00
Primestar Chrome
17 Matt Kenseth 10.00 20.00
Lycos
17 Darrell Waltrip 3.00 6.00
Builder's Square
19 Tony Raines 2.00 4.00
Yellow Freight
19 Tony Raines 4.00 8.00
Yellow Freight Promo
20 Blaise Alexander 4.00 8.00
Rescue Engine
20 Blaise Alexander 15.00 40.00
Rescue Engine Chrome/1000
21 Michael Waltrip 2.00 4.00
Citgo
21 Michael Waltrip 2.00 4.00
Goodwill Games
23 Lance Hooper 2.00 4.00
WCW
23 Lance Hooper 15.00 40.00
WCW Chrome/1000
23 Jimmy Spencer 8.00 20.00
No Bull Promo box on blister
23 Jimmy Spencer 10.00 25.00
No Bull Gold
Promo box on blister
23 Jimmy Spencer 8.00 20.00
No Bull Stock Rod
Promo box on blister
23 Jimmy Spencer 10.00 25.00
No Bull Stock Rod Gold
Promo box on blister
25 David Morgan 15.00 30.00
Austin Crackers
26 Johnny Benson 25.00 50.00
Betty Crocker
26 Johnny Benson 2.00 4.00
Cheerios
26 Johnny Benson 15.00 40.00
Cheerios Chrome/5050
26 Johnny Benson 4.00 8.00
Lucky Charms
28 Tony's Pizza Promo 5.00 10.00
29 Hermie Sadler 2.00 4.00
DeWalt
30 Derrike Cope 2.00 4.00
Gumout
30 Mike Cope 2.00 4.00
Slim Jim
33 Tim Fedewa 15.00 40.00
Kleenex Chrome
33 Tim Fedewa 2.00 4.00
Kleenex
33 Ken Schrader 2.00 4.00
Petree
33 Ken Schrader 18.00 30.00
Skoal Promo in box/1992
34 Mike McLaughlin 15.00 40.00
Goulds Chrome/1000
35 Todd Bodine 2.00 4.00
Tabasco Orange
35 Todd Bodine 15.00 40.00
Tabasco Chrome/5050
36 Matt Hutter 2.00 4.00
Stanley
36 Matt Hutter 15.00 40.00
Stanley Chrome
36 Ernie Irvan 2.00 4.00
Skittles
36 Ernie Irvan 15.00 40.00
Skittles Chrome/5050
38 Elton Sawyer 20.00 40.00
Barbasol Chrome/1000
40 Kevin Lepage 2.00 4.00
Chanellock
40 Kevin Lepage 15.00 40.00
Channellock Chrome/1000
40 Sterling Marlin 5.00 12.00
Coors Light Promo
box on blister
40 Sterling Marlin 6.00 15.00
Coors Light Chrome
Promo box on blister
40 Sterling Marlin 15.00 40.00
Coors Light Gold
Promo box on blister
40 Sterling Marlin 6.00 15.00
Coors Light Stock Rod/5000
Promo in box on blister
40 Sterling Marlin 2.00 4.00
Sabco
41 Steve Grissom 2.00 4.00
Larry Hedrick Racing
42 Joe Nemechek 2.00 4.00
BellSouth
43 Shane Hall 15.00 25.00
Tecumseh Promo in bag
46 Wally Dallenbach 2.00 4.00
First Union
50 Ricky Craven 2.00 4.00
Hendrick
50 Ricky Craven 6.00 12.00
Bud Promo box
on blister/5000
50 Ricky Craven 6.00 12.00
Bud Stock Rod/5000
Promo box on blister
50 Ricky Craven 8.00 20.00
Bud Stock Rod Gold/5000
Promo box on blister
50 NASCAR 50th Anniversary 5.00 10.00
Gold Chrome
in clear plastic box
50 TBS Promo in PVC Box 10.00 20.00
54 Kathryn Teasdale 18.00 30.00
IGA
59 Robert Pressley 2.00 4.00
Kingsford
60 Mark Martin 2.00 4.00
Winn Dixie
60 Mark Martin 20.00 50.00
Winn Dixie Chrome/1000
60 Mark Martin 3.00 8.00
Winn Dixie Promo
64 Dick Trickle 2.00 4.00
Schneider
64 Dick Trickle 15.00 40.00
Schneider Chrome
66 Elliot Sadler 2.00 4.00
Phillips 66
74 Randy LaJoie 2.00 4.00
Fina
74 Randy LaJoie 15.00 40.00
Fina Chrome
75 Rick Mast 2.00 4.00
Remington
78 Gary Bradberry 2.00 4.00
Pilot
85 Shane Hall 50.00 100.00
Big A Auto Parts Promo
94 Bill Elliott 15.00 30.00
Big Mac Promo
in Happy Meal Box
94 Bill Elliott 2.00 4.00
McDonald's
94 Bill Elliott 20.00 50.00
McDonald's Chrome/5050
94 Bill Elliott 7.50 20.00
McDonald's Gold
2-car promo set/2500
96 David Green 2.00 4.00
Caterpiller
97 Chad Little 3.00 8.00
John Deere Promo
99 Glen Allen 2.00 4.00
Luxaire
99 Jeff Burton 2.00 4.00
Exide
99 Jeff Burton 15.00 40.00
Exide Chrome/5050
300 Darrell Waltrip 3.00 6.00
Flock Special
0 Steven Christian 15.00 40.00
BellSouth Promo
00 Buckshot Jones 2.00 4.00
Alka Seltzer
00 Buckshot Jones 15.00 40.00
Alka Seltzer Chrome/1000
00 Buckshot Jones 2.00 4.00
Aqua Fresh
NNO Collector's Set 1/5000 12-car set 10.00 20.00
NNO Collector's Set 2/5000 12-car set 10.00 20.00
5.Terry Labonte/Kellogg's
5.Terry Labonte/Blasted Froot Loops
9.Jerry Nadeau/Cartoon Network
9.Jerry Nadeau/Scooby Doo
26.Johnny Benson/Trix
36.Ernie Irvan/M&M's
26.Ernie Irvan/Skittles
94.Bill Elliott/Happy Meal
94.Bill Elliott/McDonald's
Bill Elliott/Mac Tonight
Darrell Waltrip/Flock Special
50th Anniversary Gold
NNO Chrome 12-car set/3000 40.00 80.00
NNO Roush Racing 5-Pack 6.00 15.00
97. Chad Little/John Deere
6. Mark Martin/Valvoline
16. Kevin LePage/Primestar
99. Jeff Burton/Exide
26. Johnny Benson/Cheerios
NNO Roush Racing AUTO Gold/1000 40.00 80.00
5-cars: 6/16/26/97/99
Mark Martin, Kevin Lepage
Johnny Benson, Chad Little
and Jeff Burton with
Certificate signed by all
5-drivers and Jack Roush

1998 Racing Champions 50 Years of NASCAR 1:64

	EX	NM-MT
1 1949	1.50	4.00
2 1950	1.50	4.00
3 1951	1.50	4.00
4 1952	1.50	4.00
5 1953	1.50	4.00
6 1954	1.50	4.00
7 1955	1.50	4.00
8 1956	1.50	4.00
9 1957	1.50	4.00
10 1958	1.50	4.00
11 1959	1.50	4.00
12 1960	1.50	4.00
13 1961	1.50	4.00
14 1962	1.50	4.00
15 1963	1.50	4.00
16 1964	1.50	4.00
17 1965	1.50	4.00
18 1966	1.50	4.00
19 1967	1.50	4.00
20 1970	1.50	4.00
21 1971	1.50	4.00
22 1972	1.50	4.00
23 1973	1.50	4.00
24 1974	1.50	4.00
25 1975	1.50	4.00
26 1976	1.50	4.00
27 1977	1.50	4.00
28 1978	1.50	4.00
29 1979	1.50	4.00
30 1980	1.50	4.00
31 1981	1.50	4.00
32 1982	1.50	4.00
33 1983	1.50	4.00
34 1984	1.50	4.00
35 1985	1.50	4.00
36 1986	1.50	4.00
37 1987	1.50	4.00
38 1988	1.50	4.00
39 1989	1.50	4.00
40 1990	1.50	4.00
41 1991	1.50	4.00
42 1992	1.50	4.00
43 1993	1.50	4.00
44 1994	1.50	4.00
45 1995	1.50	4.00
46 1996	1.50	4.00
47 1997	1.50	4.00
48 1998	1.50	4.00

1998 Racing Champions Fan Appreciation 5-Pack 1:64

This set was issued 5-cars at a time in Racing Champions 5-Pack blister and box combinations. Each package was entitled "Fan Appreciation" at the bottom and issued to commemorate the 50th Anniversary of NASCAR. A special 50th Anniversary NASCAR Gold Chrome die-cast was one of the five cars in each package. Some cars were only issued in these special 5-packs. An issue number was assigned to each package near the upper right hand corner. We've cataloged the pieces below by the reported issue number.

EX NM-MT
1 4. Bobby Hamilton/Kodak Max 6.00 15.00
5. Terry Labonte/Kellogg's
50. NASCAR Rivalries Gold Chrome
50. No Driver Assoc./Dr.Pepper
26. Johnny Benson/Trix Lucky Charms
2 6. Mark Martin/Valvoline 6.00 15.00
13. Jerry Nadeau/First Plus
50. NASCAR Gold Chrome
9. Lake Speed/Cartoon Network
94. Bill Elliott/McDonald's Gold Chrome
3 10. Ricky Rudd/Tide 6.00 15.00
96. David Green/Caterpillar
50. NASCAR Fans Gold Chrome
14. Patty Moise/Rhodes
11. Brett Bodine/Paycheck
4 23. Lance Hooper/WCW 6.00 15.00
5. Terry Labonte/Blasted Froot Loops
50. NASCAR Country Gold Chrome
19. Tony Raines/Yellow Freight
36. Ernie Irvan/Skittles
5 33. Ken Schrader/APR 6.00 15.00
26. Johnny Benson/Cheerios
50. NASCAR Rivalries Chrome
63. Tracy Leslie/Lysol
10. Ricky Rudd/Tide Kids
6 35. NDA/Tabasco Orange & White 6.00 15.00
26. Johnny Benson/Trix Lucky Charms
50. NASCAR Fans Chrome
21. Michael Waltrip/Citgo
21. Michael Waltrip/Citgo
Goodwill Games
7 94. Bill Elliott/McDonald's 6.00 15.00
36. Ernie Irvan/Skittles WildBerry
50. NASCAR Country Chrome
10. Phil Parsons/Dura Lube
26. Johnny Benson/Betty Crocker
8 16. Kevin Lepage/Primestar 6.00 15.00
30. Derrike Cope/Gumout
50. NASCAR Legends Chrome
94. Bill Elliott/Mac Tonight
99. Jeff Burton/Exide

1998 Racing Champions Gold with Medallion 1:64

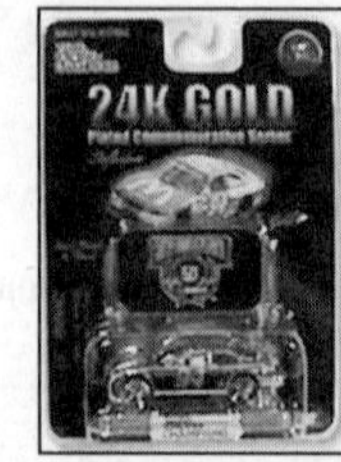

This is a special series produced by Racing Champions to celebrate NASCAR's 50th anniversary. It parallels the regular 1998 1:64 scale series. Each car is a limited edition of 5,000. Each car is also plated in gold chrome and contains a serial number on its chassis. This series is packaged with medallion sponsor emblems in blister packs.

EX NM-MT
2 Ron Barfield 6.00 15.00
New Holland
4 Bobby Hamilton 6.00 15.00
Kodak
4 Jeff Purvis 6.00 15.00
Lance
5 Terry Labonte 12.00 30.00
Blasted Fruit Loops
5 Terry Labonte 12.00 30.00
Kellogg's
5 Terry Labonte 12.00 30.00
Kellogg's Corny
6 Joe Bessey 6.00 15.00
Power Team
6 Mark Martin 12.00 30.00
Eagle One
6 Mark Martin 12.00 30.00
Syntec
6 Mark Martin 12.00 30.00
Valvoline
8 Hut Stricklin 6.00 15.00
Circuit City
9 Jeff Burton 6.00 15.00
Track Gear
9 Jerry Nadeau 6.00 15.00
Zombie Island
9 Lake Speed 6.00 15.00
Birthday Cake
9 Lake Speed 6.00 15.00
Huckleberry Hound
10 Phil Parsons 6.00 15.00
Duralube
10 Ricky Rudd 6.00 15.00
Tide
11 Brett Bodine 6.00 15.00
Paychex
13 Jerry Nadeau 8.00 20.00
First Plus
14 Patty Moise 6.00 15.00
Rhodes
16 Ted Musgrave 6.00 15.00
Primestar
17 Matt Kenseth 12.50 30.00
Lycos.com
19 Tony Raines 6.00 15.00
Yellow Freight
20 Blaise Alexander 15.00 30.00
Rescue Engine
21 Michael Waltrip 6.00 15.00
Citgo
23 Lance Hooper 6.00 15.00
WCW
26 Johnny Benson 6.00 15.00
Cheerios
29 Hermie Sadler 6.00 15.00
DeWalt
30 Derrike Cope 6.00 15.00
Gumout
30 Mike Cope 6.00 15.00
Slim Jim
33 Tim Fedewa 6.00 15.00
Kleenex
33 Ken Schrader 6.00 15.00
Petree
34 Mike McLaughlin 6.00 15.00
Goulds
35 Todd Bodine 6.00 15.00
Tabasco
36 Matt Hutter 6.00 15.00
Stanley
36 Ernie Irvan 10.00 25.00
M&M's
36 Ernie Irvan 6.00 15.00
Skittles
36 Ernie Irvan 8.00 20.00
Wildberry Skittles
38 Elton Sawyer 6.00 15.00
Barbasol
40 Rick Fuller 6.00 15.00
Channellock
40 Kevin Lepage 6.00 15.00
Channellock
40 Sterling Marlin 6.00 15.00
Sabco
41 Steve Grissom 6.00 15.00
Larry Hedrick Racing
42 Joe Nemechek 6.00 15.00
BellSouth
46 Wally Dallenbach 6.00 15.00
First Union
50 Ricky Craven 6.00 15.00
Hendrick
50 NDA 6.00 15.00
Dr.Pepper
59 Robert Pressley 6.00 15.00
Kingsford
60 Mark Martin 12.00 30.00
Winn Dixie
63 Tracy Leslie 6.00 15.00
Lysol
64 Dick Trickle 6.00 15.00
Schneider
66 Elliot Sadler 6.00 15.00
Phillips 66
72 Mike Dillon 6.00 15.00
Detroit Gasket
74 Randy LaJoie 6.00 15.00
Fina
75 Rick Mast 6.00 15.00
Remington
78 Gary Bradberry 6.00 15.00
Pilot
87 Joe Nemechek 6.00 15.00
BellSouth
88 Kevin Schwantz 6.00 15.00
Ryder
90 Dick Trickle 6.00 15.00
Heilig-Meyers
94 Bill Elliott 10.00 30.00
Happy Meal
94 Bill Elliott 10.00 30.00
McDonald's
96 David Green 6.00 15.00
Caterpillar
97 Chad Little 12.50 30.00
John Deere Promo/20,000
98 Greg Sacks 6.00 15.00
Thorn Apple Valley
99 Glen Allen 6.00 15.00
Luxaire
99 Jeff Burton 6.00 15.00
Exide
300 Darrell Waltrip 10.00 25.
Flock Special
00 Buckshot Jones 6.00 15.
Alka Seltzer
00 Buckshot Jones 6.00 15.
Aqua Fresh

1998 Racing Champions NASCAR Legends 1:64

EX NM-M
1 Dick Hutcherson 2.00 5.
1964 Ford
1 Bud Moore 2.00 5.
1969 Dodge Daytona
4 John Sears 2.00 5.
1964 Ford
4 John Sears 2.00 5.
1969 Ford Talladega
5 Buddy Arrington 2.00 5.
1969 Dodge Daytona
5 Pete Hamilton 2.00 5.
1969 Ford Talladega
6 Buddy Baker 2.00 5.
1969 Dodge Daytona
7 Ramo Stott 2.50 6.
1970 Plymouth Superbird
10 Buddy Baker 2.00 5.
1964 Ford
11 Ned Jarrett 2.00 5.
1964 Ford
11 Ned Jarrett 2.00 5.
1969 Ford Talladega
12 Bobby Allison 2.50 6.
1969 Mercury Cyclone
13 Smokey Yunick 2.00 5.
1964 Ford
16 Tiny Lund 2.00 5.
1969 Mercury Cyclone
17 Fred Lorenzen 2.00 5.
1969 Dodge Daytona
17 Fred Lorenzen 2.50 6.
1969 Ford Talladega
17 David Pearson 2.50 6.
1969 Mercury Cyclone
18 Joe Frasson 2.00 5.
1969 Dodge Daytona
21 Donnie Allison 2.00 5.
1969 Mercury Cyclone
21 Jack Bowsher 2.00 5.
1969 Ford Talladega
21 Jack Bowsher 2.00 5.
1969 Dodge Daytona
21 Marvin Panch 2.00 5.
1964 Ford
21 Marvin Panch 2.00 5.
1969 Ford Talladega
22 Bobby Allison 2.50 6.
1969 Dodge Daytona
22 Fierball Roberts 2.00 5.
1964 Ford
24 Cecil Gordon 2.00 5.
1969 Mercury Cyclone
26 Curtis Turner 2.00 5.
1964 Ford
27 Donnie Allison 2.00 5.
1969 Ford Talladega
27 Donnie Allison 2.00 5.
1969 Mercury Cyclone
27 Banjo Mathews 2.00 5.
1964 Ford
28 Fred Lorenzen 2.00 5.
1964 Ford
29 Bobby Allison 2.50 6.
1969 Ford Talladega
29 Bud Moore 2.00 5.
1969 Ford Talladega
31 Jim Vandiver 2.00 5.
1969 Dodge Daytona
32 Dick Brooks 2.00 5.
1970 Plymouth Superbird
48 James Hylton 2.00 5.
1969 Dodge Daytona
48 James Hylton 2.00 5.
1969 Mercury Cyclone
49 G.C. Spencer 2.00 5.
1964 Ford
55 Tiny Lund 2.00 5.
1969 Dodge Daytona
57 Dick May 2.00 5.
1964 Ford
59 Tom Pistone 2.00 5.
1964 Ford
61 Hoss Ellington 2.00 5.
1969 Ford Talladega
64 Elmo Langley 2.00 5.
1969 Ford Talladega
64 Elmo Langley 2.00 5.
1969 Mercury Cyclone
67 Dick May 2.00 5.
1969 Ford Talladega
71 Bobby Isaac 2.00 5.
1969 Dodge Daytona
72 Benny Parsons 2.00 5.
1969 Mercury Cyclone
73 Buddy Arrington 2.00 5.
1964 Ford
76 Larry Frank 2.00 5.
1964 Ford
99 Bobby Isaac 2.00 5.
1964 Ford
99 Charlie Glotzbach 2.00 5.
1969 Dodge Daytona
06 Neil Castles 2.00 5.
1969 Dodge Daytona

1998 Racing Champions Pinnacle Series 1:64

This marks the second year Racing Champions teamed up Pinnacle to produce a line of die cast cars with trading c Each car is boxed in similar packaging as the standard cars Pinnacle cards are featured in place of Racing Champ generic cards.

EX NM-M
4 Bobby Hamilton 3.00 6.
Kodak
5 Terry Labonte 3.00 6.
Kellogg's
6 Mark Martin 3.00 6.

alvoline		
Stricklin ircuit City	3.00	6.00
Burton ack Gear	3.00	6.00
cky Rudd de	3.00	6.00
chael Waltrip itgo	3.00	6.00
n Fedewa eenex	3.00	6.00
n Schrader etree Racing	3.00	6.00
dd Bodine abasco	3.00	6.00
ie Irvan kittles	3.00	6.00
erling Marlin abco Racing	3.00	6.00
e Nemechek ell South	3.00	6.00
ally Dallenbach irst Union	3.00	6.00
cky Craven endrick	3.00	6.00
ndy LaJoie na	3.00	6.00
ck Mast emington	3.00	6.00
ck Trickle eilig Meyers	3.00	6.00
l Elliott cDonald's	3.00	6.00
vid Green aterpiller	3.00	6.00

1998 Racing Champions Press Pass Series 1:64

eries is a continuation of the Pinnacle series that was ed when Press Pass was purchased by Racing ions. Each car is packaged in a typical blister pack along e Press Pass/Racing Champions card. The backer board blister pack was printed in gold with a large NASCAR nniversary logo. The cars are hood open with each being umbered of 19,998 produced.

by Hamilton odak	3.00	6.00
y Labonte ellogg's	3.00	6.00
k Martin gle One	3.00	6.00
k Martin alvoline	3.00	6.00
Burton ack Gear	3.00	6.00
cky Rudd de	3.00	6.00
ett Bodine aychex	3.00	6.00
ry Nadeau rst Plus	3.00	6.00
d Musgrave imestar	3.00	6.00
rrell Waltrip uilders' Square	3.00	6.00
chael Waltrip oodwill Games	3.00	6.00
nny Benson heerios	3.00	6.00
rrike Cope umout	3.00	6.00
n Fedewa eenex	3.00	6.00
n Schrader etree	3.00	6.00
dd Bodine basco	3.00	6.00
ie Irvan &M's	3.00	6.00
erling Marlin abco	3.00	6.00
eve Grissom rry Hedrick Racing	3.00	6.00
e Nemechek ll South	3.00	6.00
cky Craven endrick	3.00	6.00
bert Pressley ngsford	3.00	6.00
rk Martin inn Dixie	3.00	6.00
iott Sadler illips 66	3.00	6.00
ck Mast emington	3.00	6.00
ck Trickle eilig-Meyers	3.00	6.00

94 Bill Elliott McDonald's	3.00	6.00
94 Bill Elliott Happy Meal	3.00	6.00
96 David Green Caterpillar	3.00	6.00
97 Chad Little John Deere	3.00	6.00
98 Greg Sacks Thorn Apple Valley	3.00	6.00
99 Jeff Burton Exide	3.00	6.00
0 Buckshot Jones Aqua Fresh	3.00	6.00

1998 Racing Champions Race Day 1:64

	EX	NM-MT
10 Ricky Rudd Tide	2.50	6.00
21 Michael Waltrip Citgo	2.50	6.00
46 Wally Dallenbach First Union	2.00	5.00
90 Dick Trickle Heilig Meyers	2.00	5.00
99 Glenn Allen Luxaire	2.00	5.00
00 Buckshot Jones Aquafresh	2.00	5.00

1998 Racing Champions 24K Gold 1:64

This is a special series produced by Racing Champions to celebrate NASCAR's 50th anniversary. Each car is packaged in a "Reflections in Gold 24K Gold" blister with a limited edition of 9,998. Each car was plated in gold chrome and contains a serial number on its chassis.

	EX	NM-MT
4 Bobby Hamilton Kodak	6.00	15.00
4 Jeff Purvis Lance	6.00	15.00
5 Terry Labonte Kellogg's	12.00	30.00
6 Joe Bessey Power Team	6.00	15.00
6 Mark Martin Valvoline	12.00	30.00
8 Hut Stricklin Circuit City	6.00	15.00
9 Jeff Burton Track Gear	6.00	15.00
9 Lake Speed Huckleberry Hound	6.00	15.00
10 Phil Parsons Duralube	6.00	15.00
10 Ricky Rudd Tide	6.00	15.00
11 Brett Bodine Paychex	6.00	15.00
13 Jerry Nadeau First Plus	6.00	15.00
16 Ted Musgrave Primestar	6.00	15.00
20 Blaise Alexander Rescue	12.50	25.00
21 Michael Waltrip Citgo	6.00	15.00
26 Johnny Benson Cheerios	6.00	15.00
29 Hermie Sadler DeWalt	6.00	15.00
30 Derrike Cope Gumout	6.00	15.00
30 Mike Cope Slim Jim	6.00	15.00
33 Tim Fedewa Kleenex	6.00	15.00
33 Ken Schrader Petree	6.00	15.00
34 Mike McLaughlin Goulds	6.00	15.00
35 Todd Bodine Tabasco	6.00	15.00
36 Ernie Irvan Skittles	6.00	15.00
38 Elton Sawyer Barbasol	6.00	15.00
40 Sterling Marlin Sabco	6.00	15.00
41 Steve Grissom Larry Hedrick Racing	6.00	15.00
42 Joe Nemechek Bell South	6.00	15.00
43 Richard Petty STP 4-car set w/transporter 1964 Plymouth 1964 Ford 1970 Plymouth Superbird 1981 Buick	20.00	40.00
46 Wally Dallenbach First Union	6.00	15.00
47 Andy Santerre Monroe	6.00	15.00
50 Ricky Craven Hendrick	6.00	15.00
59 Robert Pressley Kingsford	6.00	15.00
60 Mark Martin Winn Dixie	12.00	30.00
63 Tracy Leslie Lysol	6.00	15.00
75 Rick Mast Remington	6.00	15.00
77 Robert Pressley Jasper	6.00	15.00
90 Dick Trickle Heilig-Meyers	6.00	15.00
94 Bill Elliott McDonald's	12.00	30.00
98 Rich Bickle Go Grill Crazy	6.00	15.00
98 Greg Sacks Thorn Apple Valley	6.00	15.00
99 Glen Allen Luxaire	6.00	15.00
99 Jeff Burton Exide	6.00	15.00
00 Buckshot Jones Aqua Fresh	6.00	15.00

1998 Racing Champions Signature Series 1:64

This is a special series produced by Racing Champions to celebrate NASCAR's 50th anniversary. It parallels the regular 1998 1:64 scale series. Each car is packaged in a decorative box with the driver's facsimile autograph on the front.

	EX	NM-MT
4 Bobby Hamilton Kodak	2.00	5.00
5 Terry Labonte Kellogg's	3.00	6.00
6 Mark Martin Valvoline	3.00	6.00
8 Hut Stricklin Circuit City	2.00	5.00
9 Jeff Burton Track Gear	2.00	5.00
9 Lake Speed Huckleberry Hound	2.00	5.00
10 Ricky Rudd Tide	2.00	5.00
11 Brett Bodine Paychex	2.00	5.00
13 Jerry Nadeau First Plus	2.00	5.00
16 Ted Musgrave Family Channel Primestar	2.00	5.00
21 Michael Waltrip Citgo	2.00	5.00
26 Johnny Benson Cheerios	2.00	5.00
30 Mike Cope Slim Jim	2.00	5.00
33 Ken Schrader Petree	2.00	5.00
35 Todd Bodine Tabasco	2.00	5.00
36 Ernie Irvan Skittles	2.00	5.00
38 Elton Sawyer Barbasol	2.00	5.00
40 Sterling Marlin Sabco	2.00	6.00
42 Joe Nemechek Bell South	2.00	5.00
46 Wally Dallenbach First Union	2.00	5.00
50 Ricky Craven Hendrick	2.00	5.00
59 Robert Pressley Kingsford	2.00	5.00
75 Rick Mast Remington	2.00	5.00
90 Dick Trickle Helig-Meyers	2.00	5.00
94 Bill Elliott Happy Meal	3.00	6.00
94 Bill Elliott McDonald's	3.00	6.00
97 Chad Little John Deere	2.00	5.00
98 Greg Sacks Thorn Apple Valley	2.00	5.00
99 Jeff Burton Exide	2.00	5.00
00 Buckshot Jones Aqua Fresh	2.00	5.00

1998 Racing Champions Stock Rods 1:64

These 1:64 scale cars are replicas of vintage stock rods with NASCAR paint schemes. Cars are listed by issue number instead of car number.

	EX	NM-MT
56 Terry Labonte Spooky Loops	4.00	8.00
57 Terry Labonte Kellogg's	4.00	8.00
58 Glen Allen Luxaire	3.00	6.00
59 Bobby Hamilton Kodak	3.00	6.00
60 Dick Trickle Heilig-Meyers	3.00	6.00
61 Robert Pressley Kingsford	3.00	6.00
62 Ted Musgrave Primestar	3.00	6.00
63 Hut Stricklin Circuit City	3.00	6.00
64 Kevin Schwantz Ryder	3.00	6.00
65 Michael Waltrip Citgo	3.00	6.00
66 Buckshot Jones Alka Seltzer	3.00	6.00
67 Ken Schrader Petree	3.00	6.00
68 Bobby Hamilton Kodak	3.00	6.00
69 Hut Stricklin Circuit City	3.00	6.00
70 Terry Labonte Kellogg's	4.00	8.00
71 Rick Mast Remington	3.00	6.00
72 Joe Nemechek Bell South	3.00	6.00
73 Ricky Rudd Tide	3.00	6.00
74 Bill Elliott McDonald's	4.00	8.00
75 Ernie Irvan M&M's	3.00	6.00
76 Terry Labonte Kellogg's	4.00	8.00
77 Michael Waltrip Citgo	3.00	6.00
78 Ricky Rudd Tide Gold	4.00	8.00
79 Bill Elliott McDonald's Gold	12.00	20.00
80 Bobby Hamilton Kodak Gold	4.00	8.00
81 Hut Stricklin Circuit City Gold	4.00	8.00
82 Mark Martin Valvoline	4.00	8.00
83 Ted Musgrave Primestar	3.00	6.00
84 Jeff Burton Exide	3.00	6.00
85 Mark Martin Winn Dixie	4.00	8.00
86 Jeff Burton Exide Gold	6.00	12.00
87 Bill Elliott McDonald's Gold	12.00	20.00
88 Todd Bodine Tabasco	3.00	6.00
89 Lake Speed Huckleberry Hound	3.00	6.00
90 Jeff Burton Exide	3.00	6.00
91 Bill Elliott McDonald's	4.00	8.00
92 Mark Martin Winn Dixie	4.00	8.00
93 Mark Martin Valvoline	4.00	8.00
94 Lake Speed Cartoon Network	3.00	6.00
95 Terry Labonte Kellogg's Corny	4.00	8.00
96 Terry Labonte Kellogg's Corny Gold	12.00	20.00
97 Jeff Burton Exide Gold	6.00	15.00
98 Rick Mast Remington	3.00	6.00
99 Terry Labonte Kellogg's	4.00	8.00
100 Joe Nemechek Bell South	3.00	6.00
101 Robert Pressley Kingsford	3.00	6.00
102 Bill Elliott McDonald's	4.00	8.00
103 Mark Martin Winn Dixie	4.00	8.00
104 Jeff Burton Exide Gold	6.00	15.00
105 Bobby Hamilton Kodak Gold	4.00	8.00
106 Terry Labonte Kellogg's	4.00	8.00
107 Bill Elliott McDonald's	4.00	8.00
108 Mark Martin Valvoline	4.00	8.00
109 Jeff Burton Track Gear	3.00	6.00
110 Ted Musgrave Primestar	3.00	6.00
111 Lake Speed Huckleberry Hound	3.00	6.00
112 Terry Labonte Kellogg's Corny Gold	12.00	20.00
113 Ricky Rudd Tide Gold	4.00	8.00
114 Bobby Hamilton Kodak	3.00	6.00
115 Ken Schrader Petree	3.00	6.00
116 Dick Trickle Heilig-Meyers	3.00	6.00
117 Todd Bodine Tabasco	3.00	6.00
118 Terry Labonte Kellogg's	4.00	8.00
119 Terry Labonte Kellogg's	4.00	8.00
120 Joe Nemechek Bell South	3.00	6.00
121 Kevin Schwantz Ryder	3.00	6.00
122 Robert Pressley Kingsford	3.00	6.00
123 Bill Elliott McDonald's	4.00	8.00
124 Mark Martin Valvoline	4.00	8.00
125 Michael Waltrip Citgo	3.00	6.00
126 Dick Trickle Heilig-Meyers	3.00	6.00
127 Ted Musgrave Primestar	3.00	6.00
128 Michael Waltrip Citgo	3.00	6.00
129 Bobby Hamilton Kodak	3.00	6.00
130 Bill Elliott McDonald's	4.00	8.00
131 Terry Labonte Kellogg's	4.00	8.00
132 Rick Mast Remington Gold	4.00	8.00
133 Robert Pressley Kingsford	3.00	6.00
134 Michael Waltrip Citgo	3.00	6.00
135 Ken Schrader Petree Gold	4.00	8.00
136 Mark Martin Valvoline	4.00	8.00
137 Jeff Burton Track Gear	3.00	6.00
138 Bill Elliott McDonald's	4.00	8.00
139 Terry Labonte Kellogg's Corny	4.00	8.00
140 Rick Mast Remington	3.00	6.00
141 Terry Labonte Blasted Fruit Loops	4.00	8.00
142 Michael Waltrip Citgo Gold	4.00	8.00
143 Terry Labonte Kellogg's Gold	12.00	20.00

1998 Racing Champions Stock Rods Reflections of Gold 1:64

These 1:64 scale cars are replicas of vintage stock rods with NASCAR paint schemes and gold plating. Cars are listed by issue number instead of car number.

	EX	NM-MT
1 Terry Labonte Kellogg's	12.00	30.00
2 Jerry Nadeau First Plus	6.00	15.00
3 Bobby Hamilton Kodak	6.00	15.00
4 Todd Bodine Tabasco	6.00	15.00
5 Mark Martin Valvoline	12.00	30.00
6 Bill Elliott McDonald's	12.00	30.00
7 Ted Musgrave Primestar	6.00	15.00
8 Jeff Burton Exide	8.00	20.00

1998 Racing Champions Toys 'R Us Gold 1:64

This is a special series produced by Racing Champions to celebrate NASCAR's 50th anniversary. Each car is a limited edition of 19,998. Each car is also plated in gold chrome. These cars were distributed in Toys 'R Us stores.

	EX	NM-MT
5 Terry Labonte Blasted Fruit Loops	5.00	12.00
5 Terry Labonte Kellogg's Corny	5.00	12.00
6 Joe Bessey Power Team	3.00	8.00
6 Mark Martin Eagle One	5.00	12.00
6 Mark Martin Valvoline	5.00	12.00
9 Jerry Nadeau Zombie Island	2.50	6.00
9 Lake Speed Birthday Cake	2.50	6.00
10 Phil Parsons Duralube	2.50	6.00
10 Ricky Rudd Give Kids The World	2.50	6.00
11 Brett Bodine Paychex	2.50	6.00
13 Jerry Nadeau First Plus	2.50	6.00
17 Matt Kenseth Lycos	15.00	25.00
17 Darrell Waltrip Builders' Square	2.50	6.00
19 Tony Raines Yellow Freight	2.50	6.00
20 Blaise Alexander Rescue Engine	2.50	6.00
21 Michael Waltrip Goodwill Games	2.50	6.00
23 Lance Hooper WCW	2.50	6.00
26 Johnny Benson Betty Crocker	2.50	6.00
26 Johnny Benson Cheerios	2.50	6.00
33 Tim Fedewa Kleenex	2.50	6.00
33 Ken Schrader Petree	2.50	6.00
35 Todd Bodine Tabasco	2.50	6.00
36 Ernie Irvan Wildberry Skittles	3.00	8.00
42 Joe Nemechek Bell South	2.50	6.00
50 NDA Dr. Pepper	2.50	6.00
60 Mark Martin Winn Dixie	4.00	10.00
63 Tracy Leslie Lysol	2.50	6.00
64 Dick Trickle Schneider	2.50	6.00
74 Randy LaJoie Fina	2.50	6.00
77 Robert Pressley Jasper	2.50	6.00
87 Joe Nemechek Bell South	2.50	6.00
94 Bill Elliott Happy Meal	5.00	12.00
98 Greg Sacks Thorn Apple Valley	2.50	6.00
99 Jeff Burton Exide	2.50	6.00
300 Darrell Waltrip Flock Special	3.00	8.00

1998 Racing Champions SuperTrucks 1:64

Racing Champions continued their line of 1:64 SuperTrucks in 1998. This series features many of the circuit's first-time drivers and Winston Cup regulars.

	EX	NM-MT
2 Mike Bliss Team ASE	2.00	4.00
6 Rick Carelli Remax	2.00	4.00
18 No Driver Association Dana	2.00	4.00
19 Tony Raines Pennzoil	2.00	4.00
29 Bob Keselowski Mopar	2.00	4.00
31 Tony Roper Concor Tools	2.00	4.00
35 Ron Barfield Ortho	2.00	4.00
44 Boris Said Federated	2.00	4.00
52 Mike Wallace	2.00	4.00

	EX	NM-MT
Pure One		
66 Bryan Refner Carlin	2.00	4.00
75 Kevin Harvick Spears	50.00	100.00
84 Wayne Anderson Porter Cable	2.00	4.00
86 Stacy Compton RC Cola	2.00	4.00
87 Joe Nemechek BellSouth	2.00	4.00
90 Lance Norick National Hockey League	2.00	4.00
94 Bill Elliott Team ASE	2.00	4.00

1998 Racing Champions SuperTrucks Gold 1:64

This is a special series produced by Racing Champions to celebrate NASCAR's 50th anniversary. It parallels the regular 1998 1:24 scale series. Each truck is a limited edition of 5,000. Each truck is also plated in gold chrome and contains a serial number on its chassis.

	EX	NM-MT
2 Mike Bliss Team ASE	10.00	20.00
6 Rick Carelli Remax	10.00	20.00
29 Bob Keselowski Mopar	10.00	20.00
66 Bryan Refner Carlin	10.00	20.00
84 Wayne Anderson Porter Cable	10.00	20.00
86 Stacy Compton RC Cola	10.00	20.00

1999 Racing Champions 1:64

The 1:64 scale cars that appear in this series are replicas of many of the cars that ran in the 1998 season, but also cars slated to appear in the 1999 season. They were packaged in blister packs that display the "Racing Champions The Originals" 10th anniversary logo along with an oversized die cut card. A Chrome parallel version (production of 9999) was also created for some cars.

	EX	NM-MT
1 Tecumseh Promo in PVC box	7.50	15.00
4 Brad Baker Logan's Roadhouse Promo	20.00	40.00
4 Bobby Hamilton Kodak	2.00	4.00
4 Bobby Hamilton Kodak Advantix	2.00	4.00
5 Terry Labonte Kellogg's	2.00	4.00
5 Terry Labonte Kellogg's Chrome/9999	8.00	15.00
5 Terry Labonte Kellogg's Promo black windows	4.00	10.00
5 Terry Labonte Rice Krispies Treats Promo black windows	4.00	10.00
6 Mark Martin Valvoline	2.00	4.00
6 Mark Martin Valvoline Chrome/9999	8.00	15.00
6 Mark Martin Zerex	6.00	10.00
6 Mark Martin Zerex Chrome/9999	10.00	20.00
7 Michael Waltrip Philips	2.00	4.00
9 Jerry Nadeau Goldberg	4.00	8.00
9 Jerry Nadeau Dexter's Laboratory	2.00	4.00
9 Jerry Nadeau Dexter's Lab Chrome/9999	6.00	12.00
10 Ricky Rudd Tide	2.00	4.00
10 Ricky Rudd Tide Peroxide	2.00	4.00
10 Ricky Rudd Tide Promo	4.00	10.00
11 Brett Bodine Paychex	2.00	4.00
12 Jeremy Mayfield Mobil 1	2.00	4.00
12 Jeremy Mayfield Mobil 1 Chrome/9999	6.00	12.00
14 Rick Crawford Circle Bar SuperTruck	2.00	4.00
14 Donnie Neuenberger Cofab Steel Promo	10.00	25.00
15 Ken Schrader Oakwood Homes	2.00	4.00
15 Ken Schrader Oakwood Homes Chrome/9999	6.00	12.00
16 Kevin Lepage Primestar	2.00	4.00
16 Kevin Lepage Primestar Chrome/9999	6.00	12.00
16 Kevin Lepage TV Guide	2.00	4.00
17 Matt Kenseth DeWalt	5.00	12.00
17 Matt Kenseth DeWalt Chrome/9999	10.00	25.00
17 Matt Kenseth DeWalt Kraft Promo	5.00	12.00
17 Matt Kenseth Visine Kraft Promo/10,000	6.00	15.00
21 Elliott Sadler Citgo	2.00	4.00
21 Elliott Sadler Citgo Chrome/9999	6.00	12.00
23 Jimmy Spencer TCE	2.00	4.00
23 Jimmy Spencer TCE Chrome/9999	6.00	12.00
23 Jimmy Spencer TCE Lights	2.00	4.00
24 Jack Sprague GMAC SuperTruck	2.00	4.00
25 Wally Dallenbach Budweiser	2.00	4.00
25 Wally Dallenbach Hendrick Chrome/9999	6.00	12.00
26 Johnny Benson Cheerios	2.00	4.00
30 Derrike Cope Bryan	2.00	4.00
30 Derrike Cope Bryan Chrome/9999	6.00	12.00
32 Jeff Green Kleenex	2.00	4.00
32 Jeff Green Kleenex Chrome/9999	6.00	12.00
33 Ken Schrader Petree	2.00	4.00
34 Mike McLaughlin Goulds Pumps	2.00	4.00
35 Lyndon Amick Powertel Scana Promo	35.00	60.00
36 Ernie Irvan M&M's	2.00	4.00
36 Ernie Irvan M&M's Chrome/9999	10.00	20.00
37 Bob Huffman White House Promo	20.00	35.00
38 Glen Allen Barbersol	2.00	4.00
40 Andy Belmont AOL Promo in window box	5.00	12.00
40 Sterling Marlin Brooks & Dunn	2.00	5.00
40 Sterling Marlin John Wayne	2.00	5.00
42 Joe Nemechek BellSouth	2.00	4.00
43 John Andretti STP	2.00	4.00
43 John Andretti STP Chrome/9999	8.00	15.00
43 Shane Hall Tecumseh CT Promo	20.00	40.00
43 NDA/Richard Petty Driving Experience Promo	5.00	10.00
43 Richard Petty STP 7-car Championship set with transporter	40.00	80.00
45 Adam Petty Spree	10.00	25.00
50 Mark Green Dr. Pepper	2.00	4.00
55 Kenny Wallace Square D	2.00	4.00
59 Mike Dillon Kingsford	2.00	4.00
59 Mike Dillon Kingsford Chrome/9999	6.00	12.00
60 Mark Martin Winn Dixie	2.00	5.00
60 Mark Martin Winn Dixie Chrome/9999	10.00	20.00
66 Darrell Waltrip Big K	2.00	4.00
75 Ted Musgrave Remington	2.00	4.00
77 Robert Pressley Jasper	2.00	4.00
86 Stacy Compton RC Cola SuperTruck	2.00	4.00
93 Dave Blaney Amoco Promo box	5.00	10.00
94 Bill Elliott McDonald's	2.00	4.00
94 Bill Elliott Drive Thru Chrome/9999	8.00	15.00
94 Bill Elliott QPC	3.00	8.00
97 Chad Little John Deere	2.00	4.00
97 Chad Little John Deere Promo with Medallion	3.00	8.00
98 Kevin Harvick Porter-Cable SuperTruck Promo	40.00	75.00
99 Jeff Burton Exide	2.00	4.00
99 Jeff Burton Exide Bruce Lee	2.00	4.00
00 Buckshot Jones Crown Fiber	2.00	4.00
00 Larry Pearson Cheez-It	2.00	4.00
00 Larry Pearson Cheez-it Chrome/9999	6.00	12.00
02 Ward Burton Siemens Promo	6.00	15.00
NNO Roush Racing AUTO Gold set/3000 5-cars: 6/16/26/97/99 Mark Martin, Kevin Lepage Johnny Benson, Chad Little and Jeff Burton with Certificate signed by all 5-drivers and Jack Roush	25.00	50.00
NNO Roush Racing AUTO Platinum set/2000 5-cars: 6/16/26/97/99 Mark Martin, Kevin Lepage Johnny Benson, Chad Little and Jeff Burton with Certificate signed by all 5-drivers and Jack Roush	40.00	80.00

1999 Racing Champions 2-Car Sets 1:64

	EX	NM-MT
5 Terry Labonte Kellogg's with Gold car/2499	15.00	30.00
6 Mark Martin Eagle One with Chrome car/1999	15.00	30.00
6 Mark Martin Valvoline with Chrome car/5000	15.00	30.00
6 Mark Martin Zerex with Chrome car/2999	15.00	30.00
36 Ernie Irvan M&M's with Chrome car/2998	15.00	30.00
36 Ernie Irvan Skittles with Gold car/5000	15.00	30.00
43 Richard Petty STP 1966 Pontiac with Gold car/4343	15.00	30.00
94 Bill Elliott McDonald's with Chrome car/2499	15.00	30.00
94 Bill Elliott McDonald's with Gold car/2499	15.00	30.00
99 Jeff Burton Exide with Gold car/5000	15.00	30.00

1999 Racing Champions 12-Car Sets 1:64

	EX	NM-MT
1 12-Car Set 1 4. Bobby Hamilton/Kodak Adventure 4. Jeff Purvis/Lance 5. Terry Labonte/Kellogg's 10. Ricky Rudd/Tide 12. Jeremy Mayfield/Mobil 1 30. Derrike Cope/Bryan Gold 33. Jason Jarrett/Bayer 33. Ken Schrader/Kenny 40. Sterling Marlin/Sabco 45. Adam Petty/Spree 59. Mike Dillon/Kingsford 00. Buckshot Jones/Crown Fiber	12.50	30.00
2 12-Car Set 2 4. Bobby Hamilton/Kodak Gold 6. Mark Martin/Valvoline#10. Phil Parsons/Alltel 16. Kevin Lepage/Primestar 17. Matt Kenseth/DeWalt 23. Jimmy Spencer/TCE 30. Derrike Cope/Jimmy Dean 42. Joe Nemechek/BellSouth 66. Darrell Waltrip/Big K 72. Hermie Sadler/MGM Brakes 99. Jeff Burton/Bruce Lee 00. Larry Pearson/Cheez-it	12.50	30.00
3 12-Car Set 3 9. Jerry Nadeau/Cartoon Network 15. Kenny Schrader/Oakwood Homes 21. Elliott Sadler/Citgo 25. Wally Dallenbach/Hendrick 30. Derrike Cope/State Fair 33. Jason Jarrett/Alka-Seltzer 33. Ken Schrader/Schrader Gold 34. Mike McLaughlin/Gould Pumps 36. Ernie Irvan/M&M's 40. Sterling Marlin/John Wayne 77. Robert Pressley/Jasper 99. Jeff Burton/Exide	12.50	30.00
4 12-Car Set 4 5. Dick Trickle/Schneider 11. Brett Bodine/Paychex 30. Derrike Cope/Rudy's Farm 32. Jeff Green/Kleenex 33. Ken Schrader/Schrader Red 43. John Andretti/STP 55. Kenny Wallace/Square D 60. Geoff Bodine/Power Team 77. Robert Pressley/Jasper Yellow 94. Bill Elliott McDonald's Gold 97. Chad Little/John Deere 98. Elton Sawyer/Lysol	12.50	30.00
NNO Chase Car Collection 12-car set/2000 5. Terry Labonte/Kellogg's 6. Mark Martin/Valvoline 6. Mark Martin/Zerex 9. Jerry Nadeau/Cartoon Network 12. Jeremy Mayfield/Mobil 1 16. Kevin Lepage/Primestar 22. Jimmy Spencer/TCE 25. Wally Dallenbach/Hendrick 30. Derrike Cope/Bryan 36. Ernie Irvan/M&M's 43. John Andretti/STP 94. Bill Elliott/McDonald's	25.00	50.00
NNO NASCAR Introductory Chrome 12-car set/25,000 4. Bobby Hamilton/Kodak 5. Terry Labonte/Kellogg's 6. Mark Martin/Valvoline 9. Jerry Nadeau/WCW 10. Ricky Rudd/Tide 36. Ernie Irvan/M&M's 60. Mark Martin/Winn Dixie Most Wins 94. Bill Elliott/Drive Thru 97. Chad Little/John Deere 99. Jeff Burton/Exide 99. Jeff Burton/Bruce Lee 99. NASCAR Anniversary	15.00	40.00
NNO Richard Petty Dodge Motorsports 11-historical Petty cars and one gold Dodge truck	60.00	100.00

1999 Racing Champions Buss Fuses Promos 1:64

Each car in this series was packaged with two small boxes of fuses in a clam-shell type package. Buss Fuses sponsored the promo cars produced by Racing Champions.

	EX	NM-MT
1 Ted Musgrave Mopar SuperTruck	10.00	25.00
5 Terry Labonte Kellogg's	5.00	12.00
6 Mark Martin Valvoline	5.00	12.00
10 Ricky Rudd Tide	4.00	10.00
94 Bill Elliott McDonald's Drive Thru	4.00	10.00
99 Jeff Burton Exide	4.00	10.00

1999 Racing Champions Fan Appreciation 5-Pack 1:64

This set was issued 5-cars at a time in Racing Champions 5-Pack blister and box combinations. Each package was entitled "Fan Appreciation" at the bottom and issued to commemorate the 10th Anniversary of Racing Champions. A special 10th Anniversary die-cast was one of the five cars in each package with each package also including an issue number at the top. Some cars were only issued in these special 5-packs. The total print run of 19,999 was included on each package as well. We've cataloged the pieces below by the reported issue number.

	EX	NM-MT
1 4. Bobby Hamilton/Kodak 6. Mark Martin/Valvoline 36. Ken Schrader/M&M's 10. 10th Anniv.Maroon Chrome 99. Jeff Burton/Bruce Lee Gold Chrome	6.00	15.00
2 5. Terry Labonte/Kellogg's 9. No Driver Assoc./Melling WCW 97. Chad Little/John Deere 99. 10th Anniv.Blue Chrome 40. Sterling Marlin/John Wayne	6.00	15.00
3 10. Ricky Rudd/Tide 33. Ken Schrader/APR 43. John Andretti/STP 10th Anniversary Red & Black 94. Bill Elliott/McDonald's Drive Thru	6.00	15.00
4 11. Brett Bodine/Paycheck 30. Derrike Cope/Bryan 33. Ken Schrader/APR Blue & White 99. 10th Anniv.Yellow Chrome 4. Bobby Hamilton/Kodak Advantix Chrome	6.00	15.00
5 16. Kevin Lepage/Primestar 23. Jimmy Spencer/TCE 40. Sterling Marlin/Team Sabco 99. 10th Anniv.Black & Purple 12. Jeremy Mayfield/Mobil 1 Chrome	6.00	15.00
6 21. Elliott Sadler/Citgo 26. Johnny Benson/Cheerios 77. Robert Pressley/Jasper Black Panther 99. 10th Anniversary White & Rose 42. Joe Nemecheck/BellSouth Gold Chrome	6.00	15.00
7 00. Buckshot Jones/Crown Fiber 6. Mark Martin/Valvoline 7. Michael Waltrip/Klaussner 10th Anniversary Blue & White 9. No Driver Assoc./Melling/ WCW Gold Chrome	6.00	15.00
8 12. Jeremy Mayfield/Mobil One 36. Ernie Irvan/Pedigree 9. Jerry Nadeau/Cartoon Network 10. 10th Anniversary Red 25. Wally Dallenbach/Gold	6.00	15.00
9 30. Derrike Cope/Jimmy Dean 77. Robert Pressley/Jasper 99. Jeff Burton/Exide 10. 10th Anniversary Green Chrome 55. Kenny Wallace/Square D Chrome	6.00	15.00
10 36. Ernie Irvan/M&M's Blue 75. Ted Musgrave/Remington 00. Buckshot Jones/Crown Fiber 10. 10th Anniversary Red 94. Bill Elliott/McDonald's Gold	6.00	15.00
11 10. Ricky Rudd/Tide Hydrogen Peroxide 9. Jerry Nadeau/Goldberg WCW 40. Sterling Marlin/Brooks&Dunn 10. 10th Anniv.Purple&Yellow Chrome 16. No Driver Association/TV Guide Gold Chrome	6.00	15.00
12 9. Jerry Nadeau/Cartoon Network 6. Mark Martin/Eagle One 1. Randy LaJoie/Bob Evans 10. 10th Anniv.Blue & Yellow 5. Terry Labonte/Kellogg's Gold	6.00	15.00

1999 Racing Champions Gold with Medallion 1:64

This is a special series produced by Racing Champions to celebrate their 10th anniversary. Each car is also plated in gold chrome.

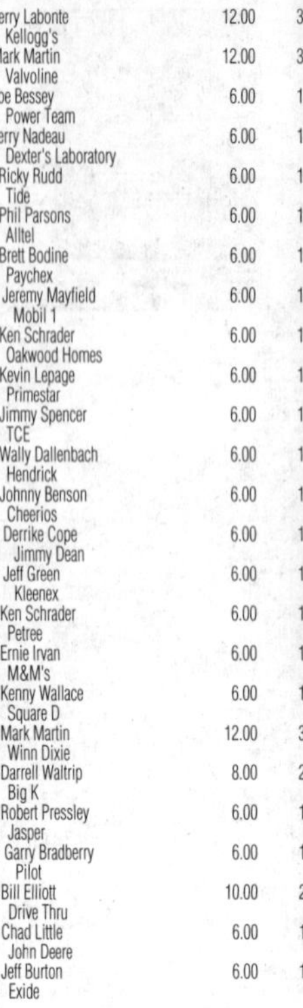

	EX	NM-MT
4 Bobby Hamilton Kodak	6.00	12.00
4 Bobby Hamilton Kodak Advantix	6.00	12.00
5 Terry Labonte Kellogg's	12.00	3
6 Mark Martin Valvoline	12.00	3
6 Joe Bessey Power Team	6.00	1
9 Jerry Nadeau Dexter's Laboratory	6.00	1.
10 Ricky Rudd Tide	6.00	1.
10 Phil Parsons Alltel	6.00	1
11 Brett Bodine Paychex	6.00	1
12 Jeremy Mayfield Mobil 1	6.00	1
15 Ken Schrader Oakwood Homes	6.00	1
16 Kevin Lepage Primestar	6.00	1
23 Jimmy Spencer TCE	6.00	1
25 Wally Dallenbach Hendrick	6.00	1
26 Johnny Benson Cheerios	6.00	1
30 Derrike Cope Jimmy Dean	6.00	1
32 Jeff Green Kleenex	6.00	1
33 Ken Schrader Petree	6.00	1
36 Ernie Irvan M&M's	6.00	1
55 Kenny Wallace Square D	6.00	1
60 Mark Martin Winn Dixie	12.00	3
66 Darrell Waltrip Big K	8.00	2
77 Robert Pressley Jasper	6.00	1
78 Garry Bradberry Pilot	6.00	1
94 Bill Elliott Drive Thru	10.00	2
97 Chad Little John Deere	6.00	1
99 Jeff Burton Exide	6.00	1

1999 Racing Champions NASCAR Rules 1:64

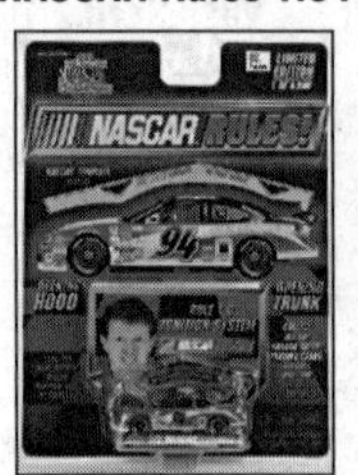

Packaged with a display stand and collector card that e some of the technical rules that govern NASCAR, the scale replicas have an opening hood with detailed opening trunk with fuel cell, and a replica NASCAR te The stated production run was 9999.

	EX	NM
6 Mark Martin Eagle One	10.00	2
6 Mark Martin Valvoline	10.00	2
6 Mark Martin Zerex	10.00	2
9 Jerry Nadeau WCW nWo	5.00	
9 Jeff Burton Track Gear	5.00	
10 Ricky Rudd Tide	5.00	
12 Jeremy Mayfield Mobil 1	5.00	
16 Kevin LePage Primestar	5.00	
21 Elliott Sadler Citgo	5.00	
23 Jimmy Spencer TCE	5.00	
26 Johnny Benson Cheerios	5.00	
43 John Andretti STP	5.00	
60 Mark Martin Winn Dixie	10.00	2
66 Darrell Waltrip Big K	5.00	
94 Bill Elliott Drive Thru	6.00	
97 Chad Little John Deere	5.00	
99 Jeff Burton Exide	6.00	
99 Jeff Burton Bruce Lee	6.00	

1999 Racing Champions P Collection 1:64

Racing Champions issued one car for each of 50-years Racing in 1999. Each car was packaged in a commer blister with the year that car represents noted on the each car along with a stated production run of 19,04 series remains one of the most collected of all 1:6 Racing Champions releases. Note that we've cataloged by year of issue and that the first 3-year's of Lee P models do not match the exact year in which that car wa There was also a 50-car factory complete set issued by Champions. Each card in the factory set was inserte plastic bag and placed into one of two 25-car trays larger box.

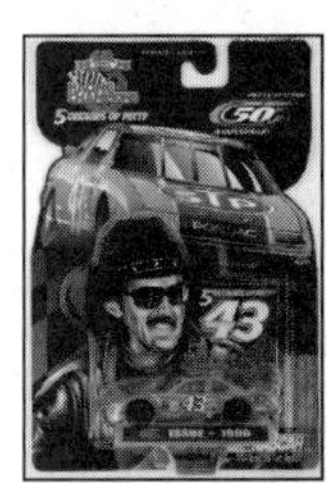

	EX	NM-MT
.ee Petty 1949 Plymouth	30.00	60.00
.ee Petty 1949 Plymouth	40.00	75.00
.ee Petty 1950 Plymouth	35.00	60.00
ee Petty 1953 Dodge Coronet	7.50	20.00
.ee Petty 1954 Dodge Coronet	7.50	20.00
ee Petty 1955 Chrysler 300-B	7.50	20.00
ee Petty 1956 Dodge Coronet	12.50	30.00
ee Petty 1957 Oldsmobile	30.00	60.00
ichard Petty 1958 Oldsmobile 1958 on package	40.00	75.00
ichard Petty 1959 Plymouth Plaza	20.00	35.00
ichard Petty 1960 Plymouth Fury	7.50	20.00
ichard Petty 1961 Plymouth Fury	7.50	20.00
ichard Petty 1962 Plymouth Savoy	7.50	20.00
ichard Petty 1963 Plymouth Savoy	7.50	20.00
ichard Petty 1964 Plymouth Belvedere	7.50	20.00
ichard Petty 1965 Plymouth Barracuda	7.50	20.00
ichard Petty 1966 Plymouth Belvedere	7.50	20.00
ichard Petty 1967 Plymouth Belvedere GTX	7.50	20.00
ichard Petty 1968 Plymouth Roadrunner	7.50	20.00
ichard Petty 1969 Ford Torino	7.50	20.00
ichard Petty 1970 Plymouth Superbird	7.50	20.00
ichard Petty Pepsi 1971 Plymouth Roadrunner	5.00	12.00
ichard Petty STP 1972 Plymouth Roadrunner	6.00	15.00
ichard Petty STP 1973 Dodge Charger	6.00	15.00
ichard Petty STP 1974 Dodge Charger	6.00	15.00
ichard Petty STP 1975 Dodge Charger	6.00	15.00
ichard Petty STP 1976 Dodge Charger	6.00	15.00
ichard Petty STP 1977 Dodge Charger	6.00	15.00
ichard Petty STP 1977 Monte Carlo 1978 on package	5.00	12.00
ichard Petty STP 1977 Monte Carlo 1979 on package	5.00	12.00
ichard Petty STP 1977 Monte Carlo 1980 on package	5.00	12.00
ichard Petty STP 1981 Buick Regal	12.50	25.00
ichard Petty STP 1982 Pontiac Grand Prix	6.00	15.00
ichard Petty STP 1982 Pontiac Grand Prix 1983 on package	5.00	12.00
ichard Petty STP '82 Pontiac Grand Prix 1984 on package	5.00	12.00
ichard Petty STP 1985 Pontiac Grand Prix	5.00	12.00
ichard Petty STP 1985 Pontiac Grand Prix 1986 on package	5.00	12.00
ichard Petty STP 1987 Pontiac Grand Prix	5.00	12.00
ichard Petty STP 1988 Pontiac Grand Prix	5.00	12.00
ichard Petty STP 1989 Pontiac Grand Prix	5.00	12.00
ichard Petty STP 1990 Pontiac Grand Prix	5.00	12.00
ichard Petty STP 1991 Pontiac Grand Prix	10.00	20.00
ichard Petty STP 1992 Pontiac Grand Prix	8.00	20.00
ick Wilson STP 1993 Pontiac Grand Prix	5.00	12.00
ohn Andretti STP 1994 Pontiac Grand Prix	5.00	12.00
obby Hamilton STP 1995 Grand Prix	5.00	12.00
obby Hamilton STP 1996 Grand Prix	5.00	12.00
obby Hamilton STP 1997 Grand Prix	5.00	12.00
ohn Andretti STP 1998 Grand Prix	5.00	12.00
ohn Andretti STP 1999 Grand Prix	5.00	12.00
Complete 50-Car Factory Set	150.00	250.00

1999 Racing Champions Platinum 1:64

This is a special series produced by Racing Champions to celebrate their 10th anniversary. It parallels the regular 1999 1:24 scale series. Each car is a limited edition of 9,999. Each car is also plated in platinum chrome and contains a serial number on its chassis.

	EX	NM-MT
4 Bobby Hamilton Kodak	6.00	12.00
4 Bobby Hamilton Kodak Max	6.00	12.00
5 Terry Labonte Kellogg's	10.00	20.00
6 Joe Bessey Power Team	6.00	12.00
6 Mark Martin Valvoline	12.00	20.00
9 Jerry Nadeau Dexter's Laboratory	6.00	12.00
9 Jeff Burton Track Gear	6.00	12.00
10 Ricky Rudd Tide	6.00	12.00
10 Ricky Rudd Tide Happy Holiday	6.00	12.00
11 Brett Bodine Paychex	6.00	12.00
16 Kevin Lepage Primestar	6.00	12.00
25 Wally Dallenbach Hendrick	6.00	12.00
26 Johnny Benson Cheerios	6.00	12.00
32 Jeff Green Kleenex	6.00	12.00
33 Ken Schrader Petree	6.00	12.00
36 Ernie Irvan M&M's	6.00	15.00
42 Joe Nemechek BellSouth	6.00	12.00
55 Kenny Wallace Square D	6.00	12.00
77 Robert Pressley Jasper	6.00	12.00
94 Bill Elliott Drive Thru	6.00	15.00
97 Chad Little John Deere	6.00	12.00
99 Jeff Burton Exide	6.00	12.00

1999 Racing Champions Platinum Stock Rods 1:64

	EX	NM-MT
1P Bobby Hamiltion Valvoline	5.00	10.00
2P Terry Labonte Kellogg's	5.00	10.00
3P Mark Martin Valvoline	5.00	10.00
4P Ricky Rudd Tide	5.00	10.00
5P Bill Elliott Drive Thru	5.00	10.00
6P Ernie Irvan M&M's	5.00	10.00

1999 Racing Champions Precious Metals Team Colors 1:64

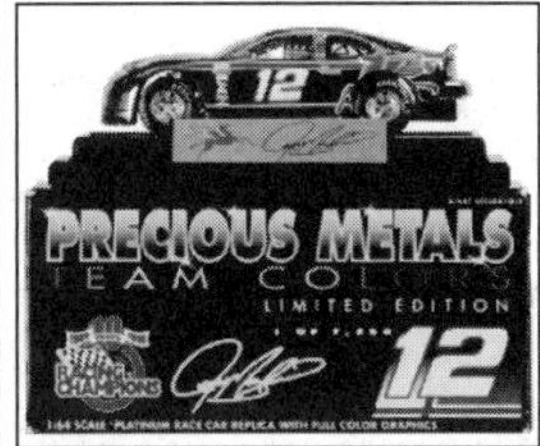

	EX	NM-MT
6 Mark Martin Valvoline/9500	5.00	12.00
12 Jeremy Mayfield Mobil	4.00	10.00
94 Bill Elliott McDonald's/7500	4.00	10.00

1999 Racing Champions Press Pass Series 1:64

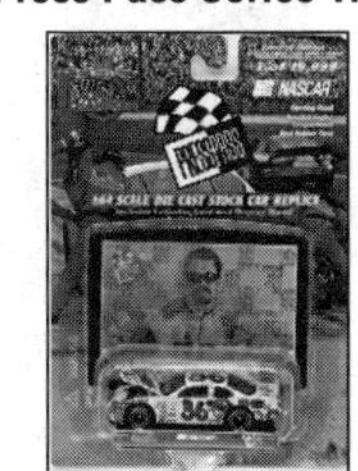

These 1:64 scale cars come packaged with a Press Pass card and feature opening hoods and two piece tires.

	EX	NM-MT
4 Bobby Hamilton Kodak	3.00	6.00
4 Bobby Hamilton Advantix	3.00	6.00
5 Terry Labonte Kellogg's	3.00	6.00
6 Mark Martin Valvoline	3.00	6.00
6 Joe Bessey Power Team	3.00	6.00
7 Michael Waltrip Philips	3.00	6.00
9 Jerry Nadeau Dexter's Laboratory	3.00	6.00
9 Jeff Burton Track Gear	3.00	6.00
10 Ricky Rudd Tide	3.00	6.00
11 Brett Bodine Paychex	3.00	6.00
15 Ken Schrader Oakwood Homes	3.00	6.00
16 Kevin Lepage Primestar	3.00	6.00
21 Elliott Sadler Citgo	3.00	6.00
25 Wally Dallenbach Hendrick	3.00	6.00
26 Johnny Benson Cheerios	3.00	6.00
30 Derrike Cope Bryan Foods	3.00	6.00
32 Jeff Green Kleenex	3.00	6.00
33 Elton Sawyer Lysol	3.00	6.00
33 Ken Schrader Petree	3.00	6.00
33 Ken Schrader APR Blue	3.00	6.00
34 Mike McLaughlin Goulds Pumps	3.00	6.00
36 Ernie Irvan M&M's	3.00	6.00
40 Sterling Marlin John Wayne	4.00	8.00
42 Joe Nemechek BellSouth	3.00	6.00
55 Kenny Wallace Square D	3.00	6.00
60 Geoffery Bodine Power Team	3.00	6.00
66 Darrell Waltrip Big K	3.00	6.00
66 Todd Bodine Phillips 66	3.00	6.00
72 Hermie Sadler MGM Brakes	3.00	6.00
77 Robert Pressley Jasper	3.00	6.00
78 Gary Bradberry Pilot	3.00	6.00
94 Bill Elliott Drive Thru	3.00	6.00
97 Chad Little John Deere	3.00	6.00
98 Elton Sawyer Lysol	3.00	6.00
99 Jeff Burton Exide	3.00	6.00
00 Buckshot Jones Crown Fiber	3.00	6.00

1999 Racing Champions Radio Controled Die Cast 1:64

These cars are touted as the smallest RC cars available. They came with a pit box remote and a pit stop recharging base. These remote control cars were capable of forward and reverse only.

	EX	NM-MT
5 Terry Labonte Kellogg's	15.00	30.00
6 Mark Martin Valvoline	15.00	30.00
12 Jeremy Mayfield Mobil 1	15.00	30.00
36 Ernie Irvan M&M's	20.00	40.00
43 John Andretti STP	20.00	40.00
94 Bill Elliott Drive Thru	15.00	30.00

1999 Racing Champions Signature Series 1:64

This is a special series produced by Racing Champions to celebrate their 10th anniversary. Each car was packaged in a decorative box and wrapped inside a blister pack. Some cars were also issued in a Chrome version with each carrying a production run of 4999.

	EX	NM-MT
4 Bobby Hamilton Kodak	2.00	5.00
4 Bobby Hamilton Kodak Chrome/4999	7.50	15.00
4 Jeff Purvis Lance Snacks	2.00	5.00
5 Terry Labonte Kellogg's	2.50	6.00
6 Joe Bessey Power Team	2.00	5.00
6 Mark Martin Valvoline	2.50	6.00
6 Mark Martin Valvoline Chrome/4999	15.00	30.00
6 Mark Martin Zerex Chrome/4999	15.00	30.00
7 Michael Waltrip Philips	2.00	5.00
9 Jerry Nadeau Dexter's Laboratory	2.00	5.00
9 Jerry Nadeau Dexter's Lab Chrome/4999	10.00	20.00
10 Ricky Rudd Tide	2.00	5.00
11 Brett Bodine Paychex	2.00	5.00
12 Jeremy Mayfield Mobil 1	2.00	5.00
12 Jeremy Mayfield Mobil 1 Chrome/4999	7.50	15.00
16 Kevin Lepage Primestar	2.00	5.00
16 Kevin Lepage Primestar Chrome/4999	7.50	15.00
17 Matt Kenseth DeWalt	3.00	8.00
23 Jimmy Spencer TCE	2.00	5.00
23 Jimmy Spencer TCE Chrome/4999	7.50	15.00
25 Wally Dallenbach Hendrick	2.00	5.00
25 Wally Dallenbach Hendrick Chrome/4999	7.50	15.00
26 Johnny Benson Cheerios	2.00	5.00
32 Jeff Green Kleenex	2.00	5.00
34 Mike McLaughlin Goulds Pump	2.00	5.00
36 Ernie Irvan M&M's	2.50	6.00
36 Ernie Irvan M&M's Chrome/4999	7.50	15.00
40 Sterling Marlin John Wayne	2.00	5.00
60 Mark Martin Winn Dixie	2.50	6.00
77 Robert Pressley Jasper	2.00	5.00
77 Robert Pressley Jasper Chrome/4999	7.50	15.00
94 Bill Elliott Drive Thru	2.50	6.00
94 Bill Elliott Drive Thru Chrome/4999	15.00	30.00
99 Jeff Burton Exide	2.00	5.00
00 Buckshot Jones Crown Fiber	2.00	5.00

1999 Racing Champions Stock Rods 1:64

These 1:64 scale cars are replicas of vintage stock rods with NASCAR paint schemes. Cars are listed by issue number instead of car number.

	EX	NM-MT
144 Terry Labonte Kellogg's Iron Man	4.00	8.00
145 Rick Mast Remington	3.00	6.00
146 Terry Labonte Kellogg's	4.00	8.00
147 Ricky Rudd Tide	3.00	6.00
148 Kevin Lepage Primestar	3.00	6.00
149 Terry Labonte Kellogg's Corny	4.00	8.00
150 Terry Labonte Iron Man Gold	4.00	8.00
151 Ricky Rudd Tide Gold	4.00	8.00
152 Bobby Hamilton Kodak	3.00	6.00
153 Terry Labonte Kellogg's Iron Man	4.00	8.00
154 Mark Martin Valvoline	4.00	8.00
155 Ricky Rudd Tide	3.00	6.00
156 Kevin Lepage Primestar	3.00	6.00
157 Jeff Burton Exide	3.00	6.00
158 Jeff Burton Exide Gold	6.00	15.00
159 Bobby Hamilton Kodak	3.00	6.00
160 Wally Dallenbach Hendrick	3.00	6.00
161 Wally Dallenbach Hendrick Gold	4.00	8.00
162 Ernie Irvan M&M's	4.00	8.00
163 Ernie Irvan M&M's Gold	8.00	12.00
164 Bobby Hamilton Kodak	3.00	6.00
165 Brett Bodine Paychex	3.00	6.00
166 Brett Bodine Paychex	3.00	6.00
167 Ken Schrader Petree	3.00	6.00
168 Ken Schrader Petree Gold	4.00	8.00
169 Bill Elliott Drive Thru	4.00	8.00
170 Bill Elliott Drive Thru Gold	10.00	15.00
171 Jerry Nadeau Dexter's Laboratory	4.00	8.00
172 Brett Bodine Paychex	3.00	6.00
173 Brett Bodine Paychex Gold	3.00	6.00
174 Wally Dallenbach Hendrick	3.00	6.00
175 Ernie Irvan M&M's	3.00	6.00
176 Kenny Wallace Square D	3.00	6.00
177 Kenny Wallace Square D Gold	4.00	8.00
178 Robert Pressley Jasper	3.00	6.00
179 Sterling Marlin John Wayne	5.00	10.00
180 Sterling Marlin John Wayne Gold	10.00	25.00
181 Bobby Hamilton Kodak	3.00	6.00
182 Ricky Rudd Tide	4.00	8.00
183 Jimmy Spencer TCE	3.00	6.00
184 Jerry Nadeau Dexter's Laboratory	3.00	6.00
185 Robert Pressly Jasper	3.00	6.00
186 Mark Martin Valvoline	4.00	8.00
187 Derrike Cope Bryan	4.00	8.00
188 Ken Schrader APR Blue	3.00	6.00
189 Sterling Marlin Sabco	3.00	6.00
190 Darrell Waltrip Big K	4.00	8.00
191 Jeff Burton Exide	4.00	8.00
192 Darrell Waltrip Big K Gold	10.00	15.00
193 Ken Schrader APR Maroon	3.00	6.00
194 Wally Dallenbach Hendrick	3.00	6.00
195 Ernie Irvan M&M's	4.00	8.00
196 Sterling Marlin John Wayne	5.00	10.00
197 Darrell Waltrip Big K	4.00	8.00

1999 Racing Champions Toys R Us Chrome Chase 1:64

These Chrome plated cars were packaged in special Toys "R" Us blister pack and were only available at Toys "R" Us.

	EX	NM-MT
4 Bobby Hamilton Kodak	2.00	5.00
5 Terry Labonte Kellogg's	4.00	8.00
6 Mark Martin Valvoline	4.00	8.00
9 Jerry Nadeau Dexter's Laboratory	2.00	5.00
10 Ricky Rudd Tide	2.00	5.00
11 Brett Bodine Paychex	2.00	5.00
23 Jimmy Spencer TCE	2.00	5.00
25 Wally Dallenbach Hendrick	2.00	5.00
33 Ken Schrader Petree	2.00	5.00
36 Ernie Irvan M&M's	4.00	8.00
55 Kenny Wallace Square D	2.00	5.00
94 Bill Elliott Drive Thru	4.00	8.00
99 Jeff Burton Exide	2.50	6.00

1999 Racing Champions Trackside 1:64

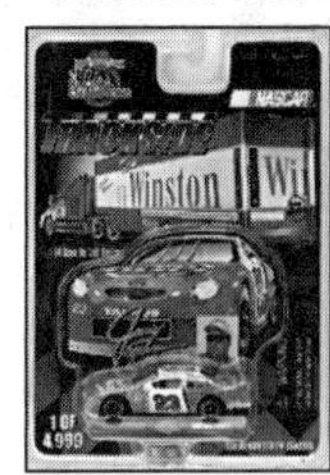

These 1:64 cars came in a special "Trackside" clamshell type package. They were distributed primarily at race events at the track. The production run for each was 4999 pieces.

	EX	NM-MT
9 Jerry Nadeau Atlanta Braves	7.50	20.00
9 Jerry Nadeau Dexter's Laboratory	10.00	20.00
9 Jerry Nadeau WCW nWo	10.00	20.00
23 Jimmy Spencer No Bull	12.50	25.00
43 John Andretti STP	10.00	20.00
45 Adam Petty Spree	10.00	25.00
94 Bill Elliott McDonald's Drive Thru	12.50	25.00
99 Crew Chief Club	7.50	15.00

1999 Racing Champions Trackside Platinum 1:64

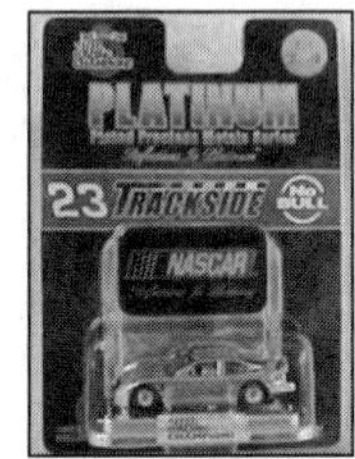

The Platinum Trackside cars were packaged in a clamshell with the name "Trackside Platinum" clearly printed on the packaging. Each carried an announced print run of 2499.

	EX	NM-MT
9 Jerry Nadeau Dexter's Lab	12.50	25.00
9 Jerry Nadeau WCW nWo	12.50	25.00
23 Jimmy Spencer No Bull	15.00	30.00

1999 Racing Champions Under the Lights 1:64

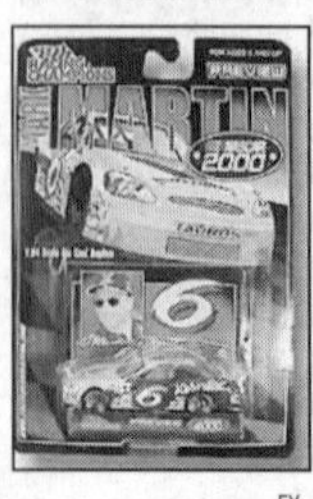

These 1:64 scale cars feature special color chrome paint to give that "Under the Lights" appearance. Most were issued in a clear clamshell packaging along with a trading card featuring foil highlights. Some were also issued as 2-car sets instead of just one.

	EX	NM-MT
4 Bobby Hamilton Kodak	4.00	8.00
5 Terry Labonte Kellogg's	8.00	12.00
6 Mark Martin Valvoline	8.00	12.00
6 Mark Martin Valvoline 2-car set	12.00	20.00
6 Mark Martin Valvoline Ames/5000	4.00	10.00
6 Mark Martin Valvoline Eagle One 2-car set	12.00	20.00
6 Mark Martin Valvoline Zerex 2-car set	12.00	20.00
10 Ricky Rudd Tide	4.00	8.00
12 Jeremy Mayfield Mobil 1	4.00	8.00
21 Elliott Sadler Citgo	4.00	8.00
43 John Andretti STP	4.00	8.00
94 Bill Elliott McDonald's Drive Thru	8.00	12.00
94 Bill Elliott McDonald's Drive Thru 2-car set	12.00	20.00
99 Jeff Burton Exide	8.00	12.00
99 Jeff Burton Exide 2-car set	12.00	20.00

1999 Racing Champions 24K Gold 1:64

This is a special series produced by Racing Champions to celebrate their 10th anniversary. It parallels the regular 1998 1:64 scale series. Each car is a limited edition of 9,999. Each car is also plated in gold chrome and contains a serial number on its chassis.

	EX	NM-MT
4 Bobby Hamilton Kodak Advantix	7.50	15.00
5 Terry Labonte Kellogg's	10.00	25.00
6 Joe Bessey Power Team	7.50	15.00
6 Mark Martin Valvoline	15.00	30.00
9 Jerry Nadeau Dexter's Laboratory	7.50	15.00
9 Jeff Burton Track Gear	7.50	15.00
10 Ricky Rudd Tide	7.50	15.00
10 Ricky Rudd Tide Happy Holiday	7.50	15.00
11 Brett Bodine Paychex	5.00	12.00
16 Kevin Lepage Primestar	7.50	15.00
25 Wally Dallenbach Hendrick	7.50	15.00
26 Johnny Benson Cheerios	7.50	15.00
33 Ken Schrader Petree	7.50	15.00
36 Ernie Irvan M&M's	10.00	20.00
42 Joe Nemechek BellSouth	7.50	15.00
77 Robert Pressley Jasper	7.50	15.00
97 Chad Little John Deere	6.00	15.00
99 Jeff Burton Exide	7.50	15.00

1999 Racing Champions 24K Gold Stock Rods 1:64

	EX	NM-MT
1G Bobby Hamilton Kodak	4.00	8.00
2G Terry Labonte Kellogg's	6.00	15.00
3G Mark Martin Valvoline	6.00	15.00
4G Ricky Rudd Tide	6.00	15.00
5G Bill Elliott Drive Thru	6.00	15.00
6G Ernie Irvan M&M's	6.00	15.00

1999 Racing Champions 3-D Originals 1:64

This set features a hood open car with a 3-D card.

	EX	NM-MT
5 Terry Labonte Kellogg's	6.00	15.00
6 Mark Martin Valvoline	6.00	15.00
12 Jeremy Mayfield Mobil 1	4.00	8.00
94 Bill Elliott Drive Thru	6.00	15.00

2000 Racing Champions Preview 1:64

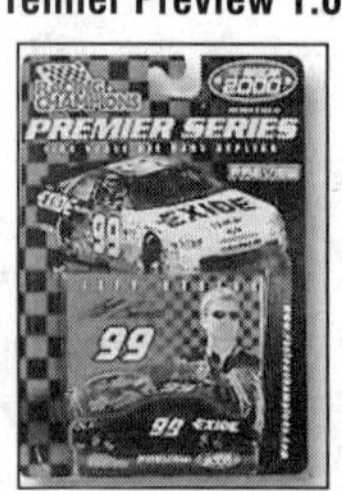

	EX	NM-MT
6 Mark Martin Valvoline	3.00	6.00
7 Michael Waltrip Nation's Rent	3.00	6.00
17 Matt Kenseth DeWalt	4.00	8.00
22 Ward Burton Caterpillar	3.00	6.00
22 Ward Burton Cat Dealers	3.00	6.00
33 Joe Nemechek Oakwood Homes	3.00	6.00
36 Ernie Irvan M&M's '99	3.00	6.00
66 Darrell Waltrip Big K Flames	3.00	6.00
75 Wally Dallenbach Power Puff Girls	3.00	6.00
99 Jeff Burton Exide	3.00	6.00
Y2K NDA Ford Taurus	3.00	6.00

2000 Racing Champions Premier Preview 1:64

This series was issued in a red and black checkered blister pack design with the NASCAR 2000 logo. A Racing Champions collector's card was also packaged with the car as well as a rain delay car cover. Each car features an opening hood and two-piece wheels.

	EX	NM-MT
5 Terry Labonte Kellogg's	5.00	10.00
6 Mark Martin Valvoline	5.00	10.00
14 Mike Bliss Conseco	5.00	10.00
17 Matt Kenseth DeWalt	5.00	12.00
22 Ward Burton Caterpillar	5.00	10.00
66 Darrell Waltrip Big K	4.00	8.00
66 Darrell Waltrip Big K Flames	5.00	10.00
99 Jeff Burton Exide	5.00	10.00

2000 Racing Champions 1:64

	EX	NM-MT
1 Dennis Setzer Mopar SuperTruck Promo in PVC Box	7.50	15.00
4 Bobby Hamilton Kodak	2.00	4.00
5 Terry Labonte Kellogg's	2.50	5.00
5 Wix Filters 3-car Promo set in box stock car, dragster and supertruck	20.00	40.00
5 Terry Labonte Froot Loops CherryBerry	2.50	5.00
5 Terry Labonte Froot Loops CherryBerry Chrome/999	10.00	25.00
6 Mark Martin Eagle One	2.50	5.00
6 Mark Martin Valvoline	2.50	5.00
6 Mark Martin Valvoline Chrome/999	15.00	30.00
6 Mark Martin Valvoline No Bull	2.50	5.00
6 Mark Martin Valvoline Promo in bag	2.00	5.00
6 Mark Martin Valvoline Stars&Stripes	2.50	5.00
6 Mark Martin Zerex	2.50	5.00
7 Michael Waltrip Nation's Rent	2.00	4.00
8 Bobby Hillin Kleenex Promo	6.00	10.00
9 Jeff Burton Exide Promo in clear box	2.00	5.00
9 Jeff Burton Northern Light Promo	20.00	35.00
9 Stacy Compton Compton Promo in PVC Box	7.50	15.00
12 Jeremy Mayfield Mobil 1	2.00	4.00
13 Robby Gordon Turtle Wax Promo in bag	10.00	25.00
14 Mike Bliss Conseco	2.00	4.00
14 Rick Crawford Milwaukee Electric SuperTruck Promo	5.00	10.00
16 Kevin Lepage familyclick.com	2.50	5.00
17 Matt Kenseth DeWalt	4.00	8.00
17 Matt Kenseth DeWalt 24 Volt	4.00	8.00
18 Joe Ruttman Dana SuperTruck Promo in PVC box	7.50	15.00
20 Scott Wimmer AT&T Promo	25.00	40.00
22 Ward Burton Caterpillar	2.00	4.00
22 Ward Burton Caterpillar Chrome/999	15.00	30.00
22 Ward Burton Caterpillar Promo in large window box	2.00	5.00
25 Jerry Nadeau Holigan	2.00	4.00
25 Randy Tolsma SuperGard SuperTruck Promo in PVC box	6.00	15.00
26 Jimmy Spencer Big K	2.00	4.00
40 Sterling Marlin Coors Light Brooks & Dunn	2.00	5.00
40 Sterling Marlin Sabco	2.00	4.00
42 Kenny Irwin BellSouth	2.00	4.00
43 Steve Grissom Dodge SuperTruck Promo in PVC box	7.50	15.00
43 Pro-Cuts Promo in window box	15.00	25.00
50 Tony Roper Dr.Pepper 2-car promo set in box	7.50	20.00
57 Jason Keller Excedrin Promo box	4.00	8.00
57 Jason Keller Excedrin Migraine Promo box	3.00	6.00
60 Mark Martin Winn Dixie	2.50	5.00
60 Mark Martin Winn Dixie Chrome/999	15.00	30.00
60 Mark Martin Winn Dixie Farewell Promo	10.00	20.00
75 Wally Dallenbach Rotozip Promo	15.00	25.00
75 Wally Dallenbach Scooby Doo	2.50	5.00
75 Wally Dallenbach WCW	2.50	5.00
77 Robert Pressley Jasper Promo	8.00	12.00
77 Robert Pressley Jasper Federal Mogul 3-Car Promo set	10.00	25.00
86 Stacy Compton RC Cola SuperTruck promo in PVC box	6.00	15.00
87 Joe Nemechek CellularOne Promo	5.00	12.00
90 Ed Berrier Hills Bros Promo	8.00	20.00
91 Rich Bickle Popeyes Promo in window box	6.00	12.00
93 Dave Blaney Amoco Promo in box	1.50	4.00
93 Dave Blaney Amoco Sprint Car Promo in box	2.50	6.00
93 Dave Blaney Amoco Pontiac Promo in box	2.50	6.00
93 Dave Blaney Siemens Promo	5.00	12.00
97 Chad Little John Deere	1.50	4.00
98 Elton Sawyer Lysol Promo	6.00	10.00
99 Jeff Burton Exide Chrome/999	15.00	30.00
99 Michael Waltrip Aaron's Promo	2.50	6.00
544 Terry Labonte Fan Club Promo	18.00	30.00
00 Buckshot Jones Cheez-It	1.50	4.00
02 Kelly Sutton Copaxone Promo	12.50	30.00
NNO Boxed 12-car set/2500	20.00	40.00
4. Bobby Hamilton/Kodak Max		
5. Terry Labonte/Kellogg's		
6. Mark Martin/Valvoline		
7. Michael Waltrip/Nation's Rent		
12. Jeremy Mayfield/Mobil One		
14. Mike Bliss/Conseco		
17. Matt Kenseth/DeWalt		
22. Ward Burton/Caterpillar		
22. Ward Burton/Cat Dealers		
33. Joe Nemechek/Oakwood Homes		
75. Wally Dallenbach/Cartoon Network		
99. Jeff Burton/Exide		
NNO Boxed 12-car set/2500 Time Trials	20.00	50.00
4. Bobby Hamilton/Kodak Max		
14. Mike Bliss/Conseco		
77. Robert Pressley/Jasper		
97. Chad Little/John Deere		
Young Guns		
17. Matt Kenseth/DeWalt		
21. Elliott Sadler/Citgo		
42. Kenny Irwin/BellSouth		
93. Dave Blaney/Amoco		
War Paint		
5. Terry Labonte/Kellogg's		
6. Mark Martin/Valvoline		
22. Ward Burton/Caterpillar		
99. Jeff Burton/Exide		

2000 Racing Champions 5-Pack 1:64

These 5-packs were issued in the usual blister and box combination just like the Fan Appreciation sets. However, the packaging was printed with a brown and white photograph of a race scene. Some sets included the NASCAR 2000 logo while others feature the older NASCAR logo. Some cars were only issued in these 5-packs. We've cataloged each set in order starting with the top car down to the bottom. No issue numbers were used for 2000.

	EX	NM-MT
NNO 5. Terry Labonte/Froot Loops	7.50	20.00
40. Sterling Marlin/Brooks&Dunn		
6. Mark Martin/Valvoline		
40. Sterling Marlin/Team Sabco		
6. Mark Martin/Eagle One		
NNO 6. Mark Martin/Eagle One	7.50	20.00
6. Mark Martin/Valvoline		
99. Jeff Burton/Bruce Lee		
36. Ernie Irvan/M&M's		
99. Jeff Burton/No Bull		
NNO 6. Mark Martin/Valvoline	6.00	15.00
33. Joe Nemechek/Oakwood Homes		
93. Dave Blaney/Ultimate		
77. Robert Pressley/Jasper		
75. Wally Dallenbach/Cartoon Network		
NNO 6. Mark Marttin/Valvoline	6.00	15.00
33. Joe Nemecheck.Oakwood Homes		
99. Jeff Burton/Citgo		
2K Ford		
55. Kenny Wallace/Square D		
NNO 6. Mark Martin/Valvoline	7.50	20.00
99. Jeff Burton/Citgo		
75. Wally Dallenbach/WCW		
7. Michael Waltrip/Nation's Rent		
40. Sterling Marlin/Brooks&Dunn		
NNO 9. Jerry Nadeau/Dexter's Lab	6.00	15.00
9. No Driver/Cartoon Network Pink		
9. Jerry Nadeau/Jetsons		
9. Jerry Nadeau/Goldberg/WCW		
2K. Red,White & Blue Ford		
NNO 21. Elliott Sadler Citgo 5-car set Five different paint schemes	10.00	20.00
NNO 22. Ward Burton/Caterpillar	6.00	15.00
17 Matt Kenseth/DeWalt		
5 Terry Labonte/Kellogg's		
12 Jeremy Mayfield/Mobil 1		
40. Sterling Marlin/John Wayne		
NNO 42. Kenny Irwin/BellSouth	10.00	25.00
21. Elliott Sadler/Citgo		
9. Stacy Compton/Compton		
34. No Driver Association		
50. Tony Roper/Dr.Pepper		
NNO 57. Jason Keller/Excedrin	6.00	15.00
60. Geoff Bodine/Power Team		
36. No Driver Assoc./Stanley		
60. Mark Martin/Winn Dixie Flames		
22. Ward Burton/Caterpillar		
NNO NASCAR SuperTrucks	6.00	15.00
86. Stacy Compton/Royal Crown		
43. Jimmy Hensley/Dodge		
24. Jack Sprague/GMAC		
50. Greg Biffle/Grainger		
2. No Driver Association/ASE		
NNO 99. Jeff Burton/Citgo	6.00	15.00
14. Mike Bliss/Conseco		
66. Darrell Waltrip/K-mart Route 66		
97. Chad Little/John Deere		
4. Bobby Hamilton/Kodak		

2000 Racing Champions Buss Fuses Promos 1:64

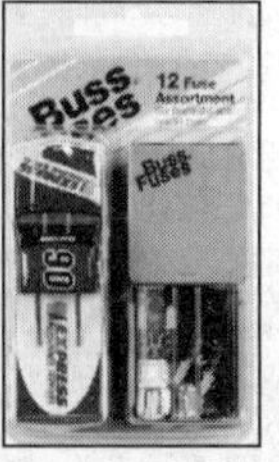

For the second year Buss Fuses sponsored a set of die-cast cars issued in clam-shell packages with two small boxes of fuses. Racing Champions produced the cars and the cardboard backing was printed in yellow for the basic promos and printed in white for NAPA promos.

	EX	NM-MT
5 Terry Labonte Kellogg's	4.00	8.00
6 Mark Martin Valvoline NAPA	5.00	10.00
8 Bill Lester Dodge SuperTruck	4.00	10.00
10 Johnny Benson Valvoline	3.00	6.00
12 Jeremy Mayfield Mobil 1	3.00	6.00
18 Dana SuperTruck	4.00	10.00
18 Robert Pressley Dodge SuperTruck	4.00	10.00
22 Ward Burton Caterpillar	3.00	6.
22 Ward Burton Cat Rental	4.00	10.
36 Ken Schrader M&M's	4.00	8.
43 Steve Grissom Dodge SuperTruck	4.00	10.
86 RC Cola SuperTruck	4.00	10.
90 Lance Norick Express SuperTruck	4.00	10.
99 Jeff Burton Exide NAPA	4.00	10.

2000 Racing Champions Hi Octane 1:64

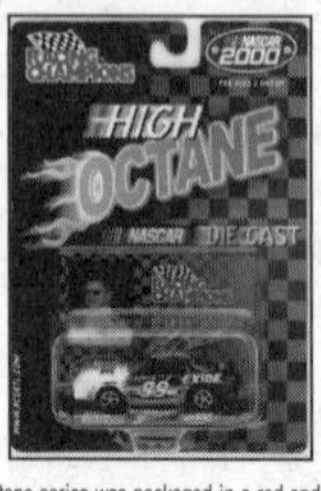

The High Octane series was packaged in a red and black b with a Racing Champions card. Each car is painted in the team colors, but is a replica of a typical street car not a NAS Winston Cup car.

	EX	NM-
5 Terry Labonte Kellogg's	2.00	5.
12 Jeremy Mayfield Mobil 1	2.00	5
17 Matt Kenseth DeWalt	4.00	8
25 Jerry Nadeau Holligan Homes	2.00	5.
99 Jeff Burton Exide	2.00	5.

2000 Racing Champions Model Kits 1:64

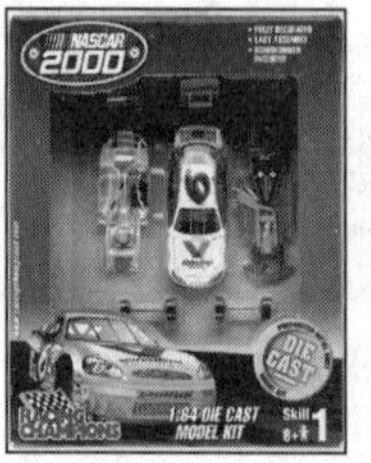

This set was issued in a large box with a clear blister pa inside. The car had to be assembled by the collector an package comes complete with all parts and even the ne screwdriver.

	EX	NM-
5 Terry Labonte Kellogg's	6.00	12
6 Mark Martin Valvoline	6.00	12
22 Ward Burton Caterpillar	6.00	12
99 Jeff Burton Exide	6.00	12

2000 Racing Champions Nascar Rules 1:64

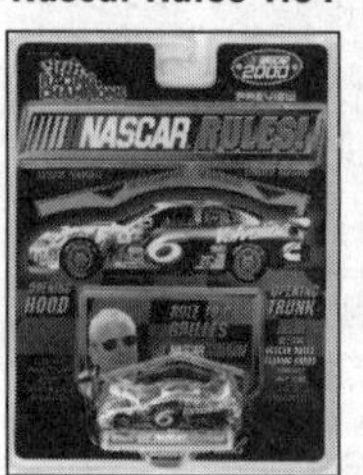

Introduced in 1999, NASCAR Rules returned in 2000 wi new Ford, Pontiac, and Chevy body styles featuring exactin detail and complete team graphics. Packaged in a larg plastic clamshell, each piece included a display stand collector card that explains some of the technical rules govern NASCAR. These 1:64 scale replicas have an op hood with detailed engine, opening trunk with fuel cell, replica NASCAR template.

	EX	NM-
5 Terry Labonte Kellogg's Preview	6.00	12
6 Mark Martin Valvoline	6.00	12
6 Mark Martin Valvoline Chrome/999	20.00	40
6 Mark Martin Valvoline Preview	6.00	12
7 Michael Waltrip Nation's Rent	5.00	10
14 Mike Bliss Conseco	5.00	10
17 Matt Kenseth DeWalt	10.00	20
22 Ward Burton Caterpillar Preview	5.00	10
22 Ward Burton	10.00	25

Caterpillar Chrome/999		
Vard Burton Cat Dealers	6.00	12.00
Vard Burton Cat Dealers Chrome/999	12.50	30.00
oe Nemechek Oakwood Homes	5.00	10.00
enny Wallace Square D	5.00	10.00
ave Blaney Amoco	4.00	10.00
had Little John Deere	4.00	10.00
eff Burton Exide	5.00	10.00

000 Racing Champions Pit Crew 1:64

Pit Crew series is a look at what it is like on NASCAR's pit. Each blister pack features a 1:64 scale car with replica pit n and small pit crew figures. All are mounted to a pit row that electronically simulates the sounds heard in the pits g a pit stop.

	EX	NM-MT
bby Hamilton Kodak	6.00	15.00
rry Labonte Kellogg's	8.00	20.00
ark Martin Valvoline	8.00	20.00
ark Martin Valvoline Chrome/999	10.00	20.00
chael Waltrip Naions Rent	6.00	15.00
eremy Mayfield Mobil 1	6.00	15.00
latt Kenseth DeWalt	8.00	20.00
latt Kenseth DeWalt 24 Volt	10.00	20.00
latt Kenseth DeWalt 24 Volt Chrome/999	15.00	25.00
enny Wallace Square D	6.00	15.00
had Little John Deere	6.00	15.00
eff Burton Exide	8.00	20.00
eff Burton Exide Chrome/999	10.00	20.00

2000 Racing Champions Premier 1:64

	EX	NM-MT
bby Hamilton Kodak	3.00	6.00
rry Labonte Froot Loops CherryBerry	4.00	8.00
rry Labonte Kellogg's	4.00	8.00
rk Martin Valvoline	4.00	8.00
rk Martin Valvoline No Bull	4.00	8.00
rk Martin Zerex	4.00	8.00
ichael Waltrip Nation's Rent	3.00	6.00
eremy Mayfield Mobil 1	3.00	6.00
ike Bliss Conseco	3.00	6.00
evin Lepage FamilyClick.com	3.00	6.00
latt Kenseth DeWalt	4.00	10.00
latt Kenseth DeWalt 24 Volt	5.00	10.00
ard Burton Caterpillar	3.00	6.00
ard Burton Caterpillar No Bull	3.00	6.00
ard Burton Caterpillar Bud Shoot Out	4.00	8.00
ard Burton Caterpillar Dealers Bud Shoot Out Chrome	12.50	25.00
erling Marlin Sabco	3.00	6.00
enny Irwin BellSouth	3.00	6.00
ave Blaney Amoco	2.50	6.00
had Little John Deere	2.50	6.00
ff Burton Exide	4.00	8.00
ff Burton Exide No Bull	4.00	8.00

2000 Racing Champions Stock Rods 1:64

	EX	NM-MT
ark Martin Valvoline 1968 Mustang	3.00	8.00
ff Burton Exide 1969 Cougar	3.00	8.00
att Kenseth DeWalt 1956 Ford	3.00	8.00
ark Martin Valvoline 1940 Ford	3.00	8.00
ff Burton Exide 1967 Mustang	3.00	8.00
rry Labonte Kellogg's 1950 Oldsmobile	3.00	8.00
ard Burton Caterpillar Bud Shoot Out 1967 Firebird	3.00	8.00
ard Burton Caterpillar 1966 Pontiac GTO	3.00	8.00
had Little John Deere Promo 1941 Lincoln	5.00	12.00

2000 Racing Champions Time Trial 1:64

New for 2000, Racing Champions introduced a series that focuses on the testing and development of NASCAR stock cars rather than the final race-ready cars. These Time Trial stock car replicas sport just a coat of gray primer and the team number and sponsor. They also feature opening hoods and two piece tires. Each was packaged in a blister along with a die cut card.

	EX	NM-MT
5 Terry Labonte Kellogg's	5.00	10.00
6 Mark Martin Valvoline	5.00	10.00
17 Matt Kenseth DeWalt	6.00	12.00
22 Ward Burton Caterpillar	4.00	8.00
99 Jeff Burton Exide	5.00	10.00

2000 Racing Champions Under the Lights 1:64

Each of these "Under the Lights" die-cast pieces were issued in a Racing Champions solid box as 2-car sets - one car in regular paint and the other in chrome. A small car cover was also included with each set.

	EX	NM-MT
2K Ford Silver Chrome Chevy Red Chrome	5.00	12.00
5 Terry Labonte Kellogg's	6.00	15.00
6 Mark Martin Valvoline/2288	6.00	15.00
99 Jeff Burton Exide/2596	6.00	15.00

2000 Racing Champions War Paint 1:64

	EX	NM-MT
5 Terry Labonte Kellogg's 2-car set	10.00	25.00
6 Mark Martin Valvoline	4.00	8.00
6 Mark Martin Valvoline 2-car set	10.00	25.00
7 Michael Waltrip Nations Rent	4.00	8.00
22 Ward Burton Caterpillar 2-car set	8.00	20.00
22 Ward Burton Caterpillar	4.00	8.00
42 Kenny Irwin BellSouth	4.00	8.00
93 Dave Blaney Amoco	3.00	8.00
99 Jeff Burton Exide	4.00	8.00
99 Jeff Burton Exide 2-car set	8.00	20.00

2001 Racing Champions Preview 1:64

	EX	NM-MT
5 Terry Labonte Kellogg's	5.00	10.00
5 Terry Labonte Kellogg's Chrome	10.00	20.00
5 Terry Labonte Frosted Flakes 2000	5.00	10.00
10 Johnny Benson Valvoline	5.00	10.00
10 Johnny Benson Valvoline Chrome	10.00	20.00
12 Jeremy Mayfield Mobil 1	5.00	10.00
12 Jeremy Mayfield Mobil 1 Chrome	10.00	20.00
12 Jeremy Mayfield Mobil 1 Autographed	25.00	50.00
12 Jeremy Mayfield Mobil 1 Layin' Rubber	10.00	25.00
12 Jeremy Mayfield Mobil 1 Race Rubber	15.00	30.00
14 Ron Hornaday Conseco	5.00	10.00
22 Ward Burton Caterpillar	5.00	10.00
22 Ward Burton Caterpillar Chrome	10.00	20.00
22 Ward Burton Caterpillar Autographed	25.00	50.00
22 Ward Burton Caterpillar Layin' Rubber	10.00	25.00
36 Ken Schrader M&M's	4.00	8.00
36 Ken Schrader M&M's Layin' Rubber	10.00	25.00
55 Bobby Hamilton Square D	4.00	8.00
55 Bobby Hamilton Square D Autographed	20.00	50.00
55 Bobby Hamilton Square D Layin' Rubber	10.00	20.00
55 Bobby Hamilton Square D Lightning	4.00	8.00
92 Stacy Compton Compton	4.00	8.00
92 Stacy Compton Compton Chrome	10.00	20.00
93 Dave Blaney Amoco	3.00	8.00
93 Dave Blaney Amoco Chrome	8.00	20.00
NNO Dodge Test Car	5.00	10.00

2001 Racing Champions Premier Preview 1:64

	EX	NM-MT
5 Terry Labonte Kellogg's	6.00	12.00
5 Terry Labonte Kellogg's Chrome	12.50	25.00
5 Terry Labonte Kellogg's Tony	6.00	12.00
5 Terry Labonte Kellogg's Tony Layin' Rubber	15.00	40.00
6 Mark Martin Zerex 2000	6.00	12.00
10 Johnny Benson Valvoline	6.00	12.00
12 Jeremy Mayfield Mobil 1	6.00	12.00
12 Jeremy Mayfield Mobil 1 Autograph	25.00	50.00
12 Jeremy Mayfield Mobil 1 Chrome	12.50	25.00
12 Jeremy Mayfield Mobil 1 Race Rubber	20.00	40.00
12 Jeremy Mayfield Mobil 1 Real Steel	40.00	80.00
12 Jeremy Mayfield Mobil 1 Layin' Rubber	12.50	30.00
17 Matt Kenseth DeWalt 2000	6.00	12.00

2001 Racing Champions 1:64

	EX	NM-MT
1 Ted Musgrave Mopar SuperTruck in Tomar PVC box	7.50	15.00
2 Scott Riggs ASE SuperTruck in Tomar Motorsports PVC box	15.00	30.00
5 Terry Labonte Frosted Flakes 2000	3.00	8.00
5 Terry Labonte Frosted Flakes Promo black windows	3.00	8.00
5 Terry Labonte Kellogg's	3.00	8.00
5 Terry Labonte Kellogg's Autographed	40.00	80.00
5 Terry Labonte Kellogg's Chrome/1500	7.50	15.00
5 Terry Labonte Monsters Inc.Promo	4.00	10.00
7 Randy LaJoie Kleenex Busch	3.00	6.00
7 Randy LaJoie Kleenex Promo	4.00	8.00
8 Willy T. Ribbs Dodge SuperTruck in Tomar PVC box	15.00	30.00
10 Johnny Benson Valvoline	3.00	8.00
10 Johnny Benson Valvoline AUTO	25.00	60.00
10 Johnny Benson Valvoline Chrome/1500	6.00	12.00
10 Johnny Benson Valvoline Race Rubber	7.50	15.00
10 Johnny Benson Valvoline Mrs.Smith's Promo	5.00	10.00
11 Brett Bodine Ralph's	4.00	10.00
12 Jeremy Mayfield Mobil 1	2.50	6.00
12 Jeremy Mayfield Mobil Autographed	40.00	80.00
12 Jeremy Mayfield Mobil Chrome/1500	6.00	12.50
12 Jeremy Mayfield Mobil Layin' Rubber	7.50	15.00
12 Jeremy Mayfield Mobil Race Rubber	10.00	20.00
12 Jeremy Mayfield Mobil 1 Sony	4.00	10.00
13 Hermie Sadler Virginia Lottery Promo	15.00	30.00
14 Ron Hornaday Conseco	2.50	6.00
14 Ron Hornaday Conseco Layin' Rubber/500	6.00	12.00
18 Dave Heitzhaus Pro Hardware Promo	6.00	12.00
21 Elliott Sadler Motorcraft	3.00	8.00
21 Elliott Sadler Motorcraft Layin' Rubber	7.50	15.00
22 Ward Burton Caterpillar	3.00	8.00
22 Ward Burton Caterpillar Autographed		
22 Ward Burton Caterpillar Chrome/1500	7.50	15.00
22 Ward Burton Caterpillar Layin' Rubber	10.00	20.00
22 Ward Burton Caterpillar Race Rubber	10.00	20.00
22 Ward Burton Caterpillar Promo	5.00	12.00
22 Ward Burton Caterpillar War-Chrome/1500	7.50	15.00
22 Ward Burton Caterpillar The Winston	3.00	8.00
22 Ward Burton Caterpillar Winston Autographed		
22 Ward Burton Cat WB Fan Club Promo in PVC Box	5.00	10.00
25 Jerry Nadeau UAW	3.00	8.00
25 Jerry Nadeau UAW Chrome/1500	6.00	12.00
25 Jerry Nadeau UAW Race Rubber	7.50	15.00
26 Jimmy Spencer K-Mart	2.50	6.00
26 Jimmy Spencer K-Mart Layin' Rubber	6.00	15.00
26 Jimmy Spencer K-Mart Race Rubber	7.50	20.00
26 Jimmy Spencer K-Mart Grinch	10.00	20.00
28 Brad Baker Whitetails Unlimited Promo	7.50	15.00
34 David Green AFG Glass	2.50	6.00
36 Hank Parker Jr. GNC	3.00	8.00
36 Hank Parker Jr. GNC Promo in box	3.00	8.00
36 Ken Schrader M&M's	3.00	8.00
36 Ken Schrader M&M's AUTO	40.00	80.00
36 Ken Schrader M&M's Layin' Rubber	7.50	15.00
36 Ken Schrader M&M's July 4th	4.00	10.00
36 Ken Schrader M&M's July 4th Race Rubber	10.00	20.00
36 Ken Schrader Snickers	4.00	10.00
36 Ken Schrader Snickers Chrome/1500	5.00	10.00
36 Ken Schrader Snickers Cruncher Promo	5.00	10.00
38 Christian Elder Great Clips Promo	6.00	15.00
40 Sterling Marlin Sterling	2.50	6.00
40 Sterling Marlin Sterling Chrome/1500	7.50	20.00
43 Jay Sauter Morton Salt Promo	18.00	30.00
43 Jay Sauter Quality Farm Promo	5.00	12.00
48 Kenny Wallace Goulds Pumps Promo	20.00	50.00
51 Donnie Neuenberger IHOP SuperTruck Promo	7.50	15.00
55 Bobby Hamilton Square D	2.50	6.00
55 Bobby Hamilton Square D Chrome/1500	5.00	10.00
55 Bobby Hamilton Square D AUTO	25.00	60.00
55 Bobby Hamilton Square D Lightning	2.50	6.00
55 Bobby Hamilton Square D Lightning Autographed	25.00	60.00
55 Bobby Hamilton Square D Lightning Layin' Rubber	6.00	15.00
55 Brad Leighton Burnham Boilers Promo	5.00	10.00
57 Jason Keller Albertsons	2.50	6.00
57 Jason Keller Albertsons Promo	3.00	6.00
59 Rich Bickle Kingsford Trail's Best Promo	5.00	12.00
60 Travis Kvapil Cat Rental SuperTruck Promo in window box	6.00	15.00
63 Shane Hall Lance's Promo in box	4.00	8.00
66 Todd Bodine K-Mart	2.50	6.00
66 Todd Bodine K-Mart Chrome/1500	5.00	10.00
66 Tim Fedewa Phillips 66	2.50	6.00
77 Robert Pressley Jasper Promo box	4.00	10.00
87 Joe Nemechek Cellular	2.50	6.00
90 Lance Norick AB Chioce SuperTruck Promo	20.00	35.00
90 Hut Stricklin Hills Bros.Promo	20.00	35.00
92 Stacy Compton Compton	2.50	6.00
92 Stacy Compton Compton Autographed		
92 Stacy Compton Compton Chrome/1500	5.00	10.00
92 Stacy Compton Compton Race Rubber	7.50	20.00
92 Stacy Compton Kodiak Promo	6.00	15.00
92 Jimmie Johnson Excedrin Cooling Pads Promo BX	12.50	25.00
92 Jimmie Johnson Excedrin PM Promo in box	4.00	10.00
93 Dave Blaney Amoco	2.50	6.00
93 Dave Blaney Amoco Chrome/1500	5.00	12.00
93 Dave Blaney Amoco Layin' Rubber	7.50	15.00
93 Dave Blaney Amoco Race Rubber	7.50	20.00
93 Dave Blaney Amoco Avenger Promo in box	3.00	6.00
93 Dave Blaney Amoco Charger Promo in box	3.00	6.00
93 Dave Blaney Amoco Pick-up Promo in box	3.00	6.00
93 Dave Blaney Amoco Viper Promo in box	3.00	6.00
93 Dave Blaney Amoco Siemens Promo	5.00	10.00
98 Elton Sawyer Auburn U. Promo	7.50	15.00
98 Elton Sawyer U.Connecticut Promo	7.50	15.00
98 Elton Sawyer East Carolina U. Promo	7.50	15.00
98 Elton Sawyer Georgia U. Promo	7.50	15.00
98 Elton Sawyer Illinois U. Promo	7.50	15.00
98 Elton Sawyer Kansas St.U. Promo	7.50	15.00
98 Elton Sawyer Michigan Promo	7.50	15.00
98 Elton Sawyer Miami U. Promo	7.50	15.00
98 Elton Sawyer Nebraska U. Promo	7.50	15.00
98 Elton Sawyer N.Carolina Promo	7.50	15.00
98 Elton Sawyer N.Carolina St. Promo	7.50	15.00
98 Elton Sawyer Purdue U. Promo	7.50	15.00
98 Elton Sawyer Tennessee U. Promo	7.50	15.00
98 Elton Sawyer Wisconsin U. Promo	7.50	15.00
98 Elton Sawyer Starter	7.50	15.00
01 Bell South Peach Bowl Promo/5000	12.50	30.00
01 Jason Leffler Cingular	4.00	10.00
01 Jason Leffler Cingular Layin' Rubber/500	10.00	20.00
01 Jason Leffler Cingular Special Olympics Promo	4.00	10.00
NNO Dodge Inaugural Season/1200 10-car set: 9. Bill Elliott/Dodge; 19. Casey Atwood/Dodge; 22. Ward Burton/Caterpillar; 40. Sterling Marlin/Coors Light; 43. John Andretti/Cheerios; 44. Buckshot Jones/Georgia Pacific; 45. Kyle Petty/Sprint; 93. Dave Blaney/Amoco; 92. Stacy Compton/Kodiak; 01. Jason Leffler/Cingular	50.00	80.00
NNO Dodge Test Car Black	3.00	8.00
NNO Dodge Test Car Gray	3.00	8.00

2001 Racing Champions Premier 1:64

	EX	NM-MT
5 Terry Labonte Frosted Flakes 2000	4.00	10.00
5 Terry Labonte Kellogg's	4.00	10.00
5 Terry Labonte Kellogg's Autographed		
5 Terry Labonte Kellogg's Chrome/1500	12.00	25.00
5 Terry Labonte Kellogg's Layin' Rubber	10.00	25.00
6 Mark Martin Zerex 2000	4.00	10.00
10 Johnny Benson Valvoline	4.00	10.00
10 Johnny Benson Valvoline Layin' Rubber	10.00	20.00
10 Johnny Benson Valvoline Race Rubber	10.00	20.00
12 Jeremy Mayfield Mobil 1	4.00	10.00
12 Jeremy Mayfield Mobil 1 Autographed	40.00	80.00
12 Jeremy Mayfield Mobil 1 Chrome/1500	7.50	15.00
12 Jeremy Mayfield Mobil 1 Layin' Rubber	10.00	20.00
12 Jeremy Mayfield Mobil 1 Race Rubber	15.00	30.00
12 Jeremy Mayfield Mobil Real Steel	40.00	80.00
17 Matt Kenseth DeWalt Black	4.00	10.00
21 Elliott Sadler Motorcraft	4.00	10.00
22 Ward Burton Caterpillar	4.00	10.00
22 Ward Burton Caterpillar Autographed		
22 Ward Burton Caterpillar Race Rubber	12.00	25.00
22 Ward Burton Caterpillar Real Steel	40.00	80.00
22 Ward Burton Caterpillar The Winston	5.00	12.00
25 Jerry Nadeau Uaw	4.00	10.00
25 Jerry Nadeau UAW Chrome/1500	8.00	20.00
25 Jerry Nadeau UAW Layin' Rubber	10.00	25.00
26 Jimmy Spencer K-Mart	4.00	10.00
26 Jimmy Spencer K-Mart Layin' Rubber	7.50	20.00
36 Ken Schrader M&M's	5.00	12.00
36 Ken Schrader M&M's Chrome/1500	8.00	20.00
36 Ken Schrader Snickers	5.00	12.00
36 Ken Schrader Snickers Chrome/1500	7.50	15.00
55 Bobby Hamilton Square D	4.00	10.00
55 Bobby Hamilton Square D Layin' Rubber	7.50	20.00
93 Dave Blaney Amoco	3.00	10.00
93 Dave Blaney		

	EX	NM-MT
Amoco Firesuit		
93 Dave Blaney Amoco BP	5.00	12.00
93 Dave Blaney Amoco BP Chrome/1500	6.00	15.00
93 Dave Blaney Amoco BP Race Rubber	12.50	25.00
NNO Dodge Test Car Red	5.00	12.00

2001 Racing Champions 5-Pack 1:64

These cars were issued five at a time together in one large blister package wrapped inside a box. A selection of 5-random 1:64 cars was included in each package which was printed in red and black. We've listed each below beginning with the top car in the package down to the bottom car. No issue numbers were used for 2001. Some cars were only released in these 5-packs.

	EX	NM-MT
NNO 10. Johnny Benson/Valvoline 22. Ward Burton/Caterpillar 93. Dave Blaney/Amoco NNO Black Dodge Show car 26. Bobby Hamilton/Dr.Pepper	6.00	15.00
NNO 22. Ward Burton/Caterpillar 17. Matt Kenseth/DeWalt 5. Terry Labonte/Kellogg's 12. Jeremy Mayfield/Mobil 1 40. Sterling Marlin/John Wayne	7.50	20.00
NNO 36. Ken Schrader/Snickers 55. Bobby Hamilton/Square D 25. Jerry Nadeau/UAW 11. Ralph's 7. Cottonelle	6.00	15.00
NNO 55. Bobby Hamilton/Square D 66. Todd Bodine/Big K Route 66 36. Ken Schrader/July 4th 12. Jeremy Mayfield/Mobil 1 Sony Wega 25. Jerry Nadeau/UAW	6.00	15.00
NNO 92. Jimmie Johnson/Excedrin 77. Dave Blaney/Jasper 22. Ward Burton/Caterpillar 25. Jerry Nadeau/UAW 5. Terry Labonte/Kellogg's Tony	15.00	40.00

2001 Racing Champions Model Kits 1:64

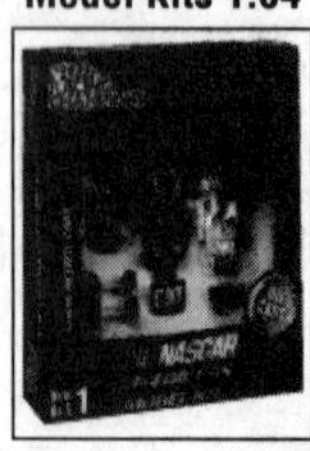

	EX	NM-MT
5 Terry Labonte Kellogg's	5.00	10.00
10 Johnny Benson Valvoline	5.00	10.00
12 Jeremy Mayfield Mobil 1	4.00	8.00
22 Ward Burton Caterpillar	5.00	10.00
25 Jerry Nadeau Uaw	4.00	8.00
36 Ken Schrader M&M's	4.00	8.00
40 Sterling Marlin Sterling	4.00	8.00
55 Bobby Hamilton Square D	4.00	8.00
99 Jeff Burton Exide	4.00	8.00

2002 Racing Champions 1:64

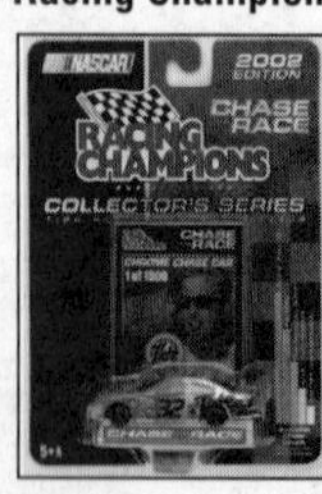

These cars were issued in a red and black blister package along with a Racing Champions card. It is a continuation of the Chase the Race theme with many cars being issued in chase versions of chrome paint or ones packaged with race used material. The autographed (AUTO below) pieces feature the driver's signature on the card but not the die cast car.

	EX	NM-MT
1 Ted Musgrave Mopar Chrysler Financial SuperTruck Promo in bag	5.00	12.00
1 Jimmy Spencer Yellow Freight	2.50	5.00
1 Jimmy Spencer Yellow Freight Tire	10.00	20.00
4 Mike Skinner Kodak Max	3.00	6.00
4 Mike Skinner Kodak Max AUTO	30.00	60.00
5 Ricky Hendrick GMAC	4.00	8.00
5 Terry Labonte Cheez-it	3.00	6.00
5 Terry Labonte Cheez-it AUTO	30.00	80.00
5 Terry Labonte Cheez-it Firesuit/25	60.00	120.00
5 Terry Labonte Cheez-it Promo in plastic bag	5.00	12.00
5 Terry Labonte Got Milk	4.00	10.00
5 Terry Labonte Kellogg's	3.00	6.00
5 Terry Labonte Kellogg's Firesuit	60.00	120.00
5 Terry Labonte Kellogg's Steel	75.00	150.00
5 Shane Riffel Race Cow Promo	7.50	15.00
7 Randy LaJoie Kleenex Promo	5.00	10.00
10 Johnny Benson Eagle One	3.00	6.00
10 Johnny Benson Eagle One AUTO		
10 Johnny Benson Eagle One Firesuit	40.00	80.00
10 Johnny Benson Valvoline	2.00	5.00
10 Johnny Benson Valvoline Car Cover/500	12.50	25.00
10 Johnny Benson Valvoline Steel	30.00	60.00
10 Johnny Benson Valvoline Maxlife	3.00	6.00
10 Johnny Benson Zerex	2.50	6.00
10 Johnny Benson Zerex AUTO	50.00	100.00
10 Johnny Benson Zerex Firesuit/25	60.00	120.00
10 Johnny Benson 100 Yrs.Kentucky BK in 2003 packaging	6.00	15.00
10 Scott Riggs Nesquik	3.00	6.00
10 Scott Riggs Nestle Toll House Halloween in '03 packaging	3.00	8.00
11 Brett Bodine Hooters	8.00	20.00
11 Josh Richeson Smucker's Promo in box	10.00	20.00
11 Brett Bodine Wells Fargo Promo in box	12.50	30.00
14 Stacy Compton Conseco	3.00	6.00
21 Elliott Sadler Motorcraft	5.00	10.00
22 Ward Burton Caterpillar	2.00	5.00
22 Ward Burton Caterpillar Chrome/1500	6.00	15.00
22 Ward Burton Caterpillar Flag	4.00	8.00
22 Ward Burton Caterpillar Daytona Win	4.00	8.00
22 Ward Burton Caterpillar Daytona Win AU/100	30.00	60.00
22 Ward Burton Caterpillar Daytona Win Chrome/1500	8.00	20.00
22 Ward Burton Cat Dealers '03 packaging	3.00	8.00
22 Ward Burton Cat Dealers Chrome/1500 in 2003 packaging	12.50	25.00
22 Ward Burton Caterpillar Daytona Win Promo w/Track Section	12.50	25.00
23 Hut Stricklin Hills Bros.	4.00	10.00
23 Hut Stricklin Hills Bros.Car Cover/500	25.00	50.00
23 Scott Wimmer Siemens	4.00	10.00
24 Jack Sprague NETZERO	2.50	6.00
25 Jerry Nadeau UAW	2.50	6.00
25 Jerry Nadeau UAW AUTO	40.00	80.00
25 Jerry Nadeau UAW Steel/25	40.00	80.00
26 Lyndon Amick Dr.Pepper Spider-Man	4.00	10.00
26 Ron Hornaday Dr.Pepper Promo Error Bobby Hamilton Jr. name on car	15.00	30.00
26 Joe Nemechek K-Mart	2.00	5.00
27 Jamie McMurray Williams	5.00	12.00
32 Ricky Craven Tide	2.00	5.00
32 Ricky Craven Tide AUTO	25.00	60.00
32 Ricky Craven Tide Car Cover/500	12.50	30.00
32 Ricky Craven Tide Chrome/1500	10.00	20.00
32 Ricky Craven Tide Promo	2.50	5.00
32 Ricky Craven Tide Clean Breeze	3.00	8.00
32 Ricky Craven Tide Kids Promo	6.00	15.00
33 Mike Wallace AutoLiv	4.00	10.00
33 Mike Wallace Preen Promo	15.00	30.00
36 Hank Parker Jr. GNC	2.50	5.00
36 Ken Schrader Combos	3.00	8.00
36 Ken Schrader Combos AUTO	50.00	80.00
36 Ken Schrader Combos Firesuit/25	60.00	120.00
36 Ken Schrader M&M's	3.00	6.00
36 Ken Schrader M&M's AUTO		
36 Ken Schrader M&M's Chrome/1500	7.50	20.00
36 Ken Schrader M&M's Car Cover/500	20.00	40.00
36 Ken Schrader M&M's Firesuit	50.00	100.00
36 Ken Schrader M&M's Steel	50.00	100.00
36 Ken Schrader M&M's Promo box	4.00	10.00
36 Ken Schrader M&M's Halloween in 2003 packaging	3.00	8.00
36 Ken Schrader M&M's July 4th	4.00	10.00
36 Ken Schrader M&M's July 4th Promo	4.00	8.00
36 Ken Schrader Pedigree	3.00	8.00
36 Ken Schrader Pedigree Firesuit/25	60.00	120.00
37 Jeff Purvis Purvis	3.00	8.00
40 Sterling Marlin Stars and Stripes Flag	3.00	6.00
43 Richard Petty Garfield	5.00	12.00
46 Frank Kimmel Advance Auto Parts Promo	7.50	15.00
46 Ashton Lewis Civil Air Patrol Promo	8.00	20.00
48 Jimmie Johnson Lowe's	5.00	12.00
48 Jimmie Johnson Lowe's Cover/500	25.00	50.00
48 Jimmie Johnson Lowe's Steel/25		
48 Jimmie Johnson Lowe's First Win	4.00	10.00
48 Jimmie Johnson Lowe's First Win Car Cover/500	20.00	40.00
48 Jimmie Johnson Lowe's Promo w/o card	12.50	25.00
48 Jimmie Johnson Lowe's Power of Pride	5.00	12.00
48 Jimmie Johnson Lowe's Power of Pride AUTO		
48 Jimmie Johnson Lowe's Power of Pride Chrome/1500	20.00	35.00
48 Kenny Wallace Stacker 2	4.00	10.00
49 Shawna Robinson BAM	6.00	15.00
55 Bobby Hamilton Schneider White	2.00	5.00
55 Bobby Hamilton Schneider White Chrome/1500	10.00	20.00
55 Bobby Hamilton Schneider White Tire	20.00	40.00
55 Bobby Hamilton Square D	4.00	10.00
55 Bobby Hamilton Square D AUTO	15.00	40.00
55 Bobby Hamilton Square D Flag	2.50	6.00
55 Bobby Hamilton Square D Flag Autographed	25.00	50.00
57 Jason Keller Albertsons	2.50	6.00
57 Jason Keller Albertsons Flag	2.00	5.00
57 Jason Keller Albertsons Flag Promo	2.50	6.00
59 Stacy Compton Johnsonville Promo	7.50	15.00
59 Stacy Compton Kingsford Promo	7.50	15.00
60 Andy Houston Cat Rental SuperTruck Promo in box	10.00	20.00
66 Todd Bodine K-Mart	2.50	6.00
66 Casey Mears Kansas Jayhawks Promo/2500	10.00	20.00
66 Casey Mears Phillips 66	3.00	8.00
77 Dave Blaney Jasper	2.00	5.00
77 Donnie Neuenberger Maryland University Promo in window box	10.00	20.00
77 Dave Blaney Jasper Promo	6.00	12.00
77 Robert Pressley Jasper Flag	2.50	6.00
87 Joe Nemechek Cellular One	2.00	5.00
90 Lance Norick Express SuperTruck Promo	10.00	20.00
93 Bill Hoff Mike's Famous Harley Promo	10.00	20.00
98 Kenny Wallace Stacker 2 in 2003 packaging	5.00	10.00
99 Michael Waltrip Aaron's	2.00	5.00
300 Tim Flock Hagood Bros. Mercury Outboards	5.00	12.00
02 Bristol Motor Speedway Promo in clear box	10.00	20.00
02 Cabela's 250 Promo	5.00	12.00
02 Cabela's Kansas City Promo	6.00	12.00
02 Cabela's Outfitters Promo	6.00	12.00
02 Ricky Craven Milk Chug Promo in clear box	15.00	40.00
02 Kroger 300 SuperTruck Promo	7.50	15.00
02 Kelly Sutton Copaxone Promo box	6.00	15.00

2002 Racing Champions 5-Pack 1:64

	EX	NM-MT
1 33. Mike Wallace/Autoliv 36. Ken Schrader/Combos 23. Scott Wimmer/Seimens 22. Ward Burton/Caterpillar 5. Terry Labonte/Cheez-it	7.50	15.00
2 36. Ken Schrader/Combos 22. Ward Burton/Caterpillar 55. Bobby Hamilton/Scheider 4. Mike Skinner/Kodak 5. Terry Labonte/Cheez-it	7.50	15.00

2002 Racing Champions Premier 1:64

	EX	NM-MT
1 Jimmy Spencer Yellow Freight	4.00	8.00
1 Jimmy Spencer Yellow Freight Steel	40.00	80.00
1 Jimmy Spencer Yellow Freight Tire	20.00	50.00
4 Mike Skinner Kodak	4.00	8.00
5 Terry Labonte Cheez-it	4.00	10.00
5 Terry Labonte Cheez-it AUTO	40.00	100.00
5 Terry Labonte Cheez-it Firesuit	40.00	80.00
5 Terry Labonte Got Milk	6.00	12.00
5 Terry Labonte Kellogg's	4.00	10.00
5 Terry Labonte Kellogg's Firesuit		
5 Terry Labonte Kellogg's Steel		
5 Jack Sprague NetZero	5.00	10.00
10 Johnny Benson Eagle One	4.00	8.00
10 Johnny Benson Eagle One AUTO	40.00	80.00
10 Johnny Benson Eagle One Chrome/1500	10.00	20.00
10 Johnny Benson Eagle One Firesuit	60.00	100.00
10 Johnny Benson Valvoline	4.00	8.00
10 Johnny Benson Valvoline Car Cover/500	20.00	40.00
10 Johnny Benson Zerex	4.00	8.00
10 Johnny Benson Zerex AUTO		
10 Johnny Benson Zerex Cover		
10 Johnny Benson Zerex Firesuit		
10 Johnny Benson 100 Yrs.Kentucky BK in 2003 packaging	6.00	15.00
10 Scott Riggs Nesquik	4.00	8.00
14 Stacy Compton Conseco	4.00	8.00
22 Ward Burton Caterpillar	4.00	8.00
22 Ward Burton Caterpillar Chrome/1500	10.00	20.00
22 Ward Burton Caterpillar Flag	6.00	12.00
22 Ward Burton Caterpillar Promo	5.00	12.00
22 Ward Burton Caterpillar Daytona Win	5.00	10.00
22 Ward Burton Caterpillar Daytona Win AUTO/100	30.00	80.00
22 Ward Burton Caterpillar Daytona Chrome/1500	10.00	20.00
22 Ward Burton Cat Dealers in 2003 packaging	5.00	10.00
23 Hut Stricklin Hills Bros.	7.50	15.00
23 Hut Stricklin Hills Bros. Car Cover/500	15.00	40.00
24 Jack Sprague NETZERO	4.00	8.00
25 Jerry Nadeau UAW	4.00	8.00
25 Jerry Nadeau UAW Steel/25	40.00	80.00
26 Joe Nemechek K-Mart	4.00	8.00
32 Ricky Craven Tide	4.00	8.00
32 Ricky Craven Tide Chrome	10.00	20.00
36 Hank Parker Jr. GNC	4.00	8.00
36 Ken Schrader M&M's	4.00	8.00
36 Ken Schrader M&M's Car Cover/500	20.00	40.00
36 Ken Schrader M&M's Steel	40.00	80.00
36 Ken Schrader M&M's Halloween in '03 packaging	3.00	8.00
36 Ken Schrader M&M's July 4th	5.00	10.00
36 Ken Schrader Pedigree	4.00	10.00
36 Ken Schrader Pedigree AUTO	40.00	80.00
36 Ken Schrader Pedigree Firesuit	40.00	80.00
40 Sterling Marlin Marlin Flag	5.00	10.00
48 Jimmie Johnson Lowe's	6.00	15.00
48 Jimmie Johnson Lowe's Chrome/1500	20.00	50.00
48 Jimmie Johnson Lowe's Car Cover/500	25.00	60.00
48 Jimmie Johnson Lowe's First Win	5.00	12.00
48 Jimmie Johnson Lowe's First Win Car Cover/500	25.00	50.00
48 Jimmie Johnson Lowe's Power of Pride	6.00	15.00
48 Jimmie Johnson Lowe's Power of Pride Chrome/1500	25.00	50.00
48 Jimmie Johnson Lowe's 3-car set	12.50	25.00
55 Bobby Hamilton Schneider White	4.00	8.00
55 Bobby Hamilton Schneider Black	4.00	8.00
55 Bobby Hamilton Schneider Black AUTO		
66 Todd Bodine K-Mart	5.00	12.
77 Dave Blaney Jasper	4.00	8.
77 Dave Blaney Jasper Tire	25.00	50.
98 Kenny Wallace Stacker 2 in 2003 packaging	6.00	12.
99 Michael Waltrip Aaron's	4.00	8.

2002 Racing Champions Premier Preview 1:64

This series was issued in a newly designed "wind tunnel" t pack that actually allows the collector to rotate the car wi opening the package. A Racing Champions card was inc and some cars were produced with various "chase" versio keeping with the Chase the Race theme. Each car featur opening hood.

	EX	NM-
5 Terry Labonte Kellogg's	5.00	10.
5 Terry Labonte Kellogg's Cover/500	15.00	40.
5 Terry Labonte Kellogg's Tire	25.00	50.
10 Johnny Benson Valvoline	4.00	8
10 Johnny Benson Valvoline Chrome/1500	7.50	15
10 Johnny Benson Valvoline Firesuit		
22 Ward Burton Caterpillar	4.00	8
22 Ward Burton Caterpillar Cover/500	12.50	30
22 Ward Burton Caterpillar Firesuit		
22 Ward Burton Caterpillar Steel		
25 Jerry Nadeau UAW	4.00	8
25 Jerry Nadeau UAW Tire	12.50	30
32 Ricky Craven Tide	4.00	8
36 Ken Schrader M&M's	5.00	10

2002 Racing Champions Preview 1:64

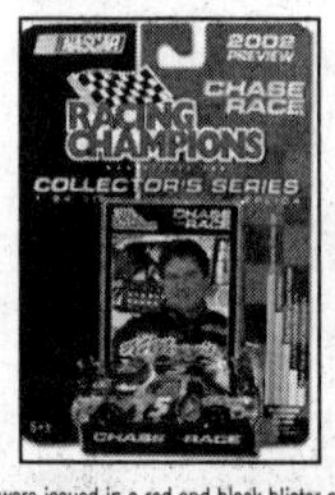

These cars were issued in a red and black blister pack wi name "Chase the Race" and the year clearly printed on the of the packaging. A Racing Champions card was also pac with each 1:64 car. None feature opening hoods.

	EX	NM-
4 Mike Skinner Kodak	2.00	5
5 Terry Labonte Kellogg's	2.50	5
5 Terry Labonte Kellogg's Chrome/1500	7.50	20
5 Terry Labonte Kellogg's Car Cover/500	15.00	30
5 Terry Labonte Kellogg's Tire	15.00	40
10 Johnny Benson Valvoline	2.00	4
10 Johnny Benson Valvoline Firesuit	20.00	50
22 Ward Burton Caterpillar	2.00	5
22 Ward Burton Caterpillar Car Cover/500	15.00	30
22 Ward Burton Caterpillar Firesuit	40.00	80
22 Ward Burton Caterpillar Steel		
25 Jerry Nadeau UAW	2.00	5
25 Jerry Nadeau UAW Chrome/1500	7.50	15
25 Jerry Nadeau UAW Tire	12.50	30
26 Jimmy Spencer Shrek	5.00	10
32 Ricky Craven Tide	2.00	5
36 Ken Schrader M&M's	2.50	5

2002 Racing Champions Stock Rods 1:64

ARE LISTED BY RELEASE NUMBER

Dunn Mooneyes	3.00	6.00
ny Benson alvoline 1969 Firebird	3.00	6.00
d Burton aterpillar 1971 Barracuda	3.00	6.00
e Skinner odak	3.00	6.00
nny Benson alvoline 1969 GTO	3.00	8.00
Schrader &M's 1937 Rapide	3.00	8.00
ry Labonte ellogg's 1969 Corvette	3.00	8.00

2002 Racing Champions Stock Rods Preview 1:64

ARE LISTED BY RELEASE NUMBER

	EX	NM-MT
Labonte ellogg's Monsters Inc. Monster Truck)	4.00	10.00
d Burton aterpillar	3.00	6.00
ny Benson alvoline (1978 Firebird)	3.00	6.00
Force astrol (1997 Mustang)	3.00	8.00
d Burton aterpillar 1968 Plymouth	3.00	6.00
y Craven de	3.00	6.00

03 Racing Champions 1:64

ries features 1:64 scale die-cast cars packaged with a oughly 2 /14" by 3") sized Racing Champions trading ach card features the year and an issue number on the ll pieces were issued with the "2003 Edition" notation on side of the blister while some pieces were also issued on variations without the "2003 Edition" designation.

	EX	NM-MT
Belmont rizon Promo	12.50	25.00
e McMurray llow Freight	3.00	8.00
Musgrave opar SuperTruck Promo easures slightly larger than 1:64 scale	7.50	20.00
re D SuperTruck Promo window box	10.00	25.00
Skinner dak	3.00	6.00
Skinner dak Rain Delay/500	7.50	20.00
Wallace ico Promo	12.50	25.00
Labonte eez-It Promo in bag	3.00	8.00
Labonte llogg's	4.00	10.00
Labonte llogg's Firesuit/50	50.00	100.00
Labonte llogg's Steel/50	50.00	100.00
Labonte wer of Cheese omo in box	10.00	20.00
Santerre stle Promo	10.00	25.00
dy LaJoie eenex Promo	7.50	20.00
dy LaJoie eenex Cub Foods Promo	10.00	20.00
dy LaJoie eenex Food City Promo	7.50	20.00
dy LaJoie eenex Meijer Promo	15.00	40.00
y Spencer ius	5.00	10.00
ester dge SuperTruck Promo asures slightly larger than 1:64 scale	7.50	20.00
nny Benson lvoline w/year on blister	3.00	6.00
nny Benson lvoline without ar on blister	3.00	6.00
nny Benson lvoline Firesuit/50	40.00	80.00
nny Benson lvoline Time Trial/5000	5.00	10.00
tt Riggs squik	4.00	8.00
tt Riggs squik Cub Foods Promo	6.00	15.00
tt Bodine oters	3.00	8.00
tin Cameron PA Promo in box	6.00	12.00
Austin Cameron PA	15.00	30.00
n Inglebright ly Belly 2-car Promo		
d Chaffin kies SuperTruck Promo asures slightly larger n 1:24 scale	7.50	20.00
Inglebright Jelly Belly Promo in window box	7.50	15.00
22 Ward Burton Caterpillar with year on blister	3.00	8.00
22 Ward Burton Caterpillar without year on blister	3.00	8.00
22 Ward Burton Caterpillar Chrome/1500	7.50	15.00
22 Ward Burton Caterpillar Steel/50	40.00	80.00
22 Ward Burton Cat Acert	4.00	10.00
22 Ward Burton Cat Acert Promo	10.00	25.00
23 Scott Wimmer Stacker 2	4.00	8.00
23 Scott Wimmer Stacker 2 Fast&Furious Promo	3.00	8.00
25 Joe Nemechek UAW Delphi	4.00	8.00
30 Jimmy Vasser Aventis Promo blister	30.00	50.00
30 Jimmy Vasser Aventis Promo in window box	12.50	30.00
32 Ricky Craven Tide with year on blister	3.00	8.00
32 Ricky Craven Tide without year on blister	3.00	8.00
32 Ricky Craven Tide w/o year on blister Rain Delay/500	7.50	20.00
32 Ricky Craven Tide Downy Promo	4.00	10.00
32 Ricky Craven Tide Kids Promo	6.00	12.00
33 Paul Menard Turtle Wax Promo in window box	12.50	30.00
38 Elliott Sadler Combos Promo in window box	25.00	40.00
38 Elliott Sadler M&M's Groovy Summer Promo in window box	10.00	20.00
48 Jimmie Johnson Lowe's	3.00	8.00
48 Jimmie Johnson Lowe's '02 Season to Remember	4.00	8.00
48 Jimmie Johnson Lowe's Chrome/500	10.00	20.00
48 Jimmie Johnson Lowe's Firesuit/50	40.00	100.00
48 Jimmie Johnson Lowe's Rain Delay/1500	10.00	25.00
48 Jimmie Johnson Lowes Steel/50	40.00	80.00
48 Jimmie Johnson Lowe's SpongeBob Promo in Signature Colors box	25.00	60.00
49 Ken Schrader 1-800-CALL-ATT Promo	12.50	30.00
54 Todd Bodine National Guard	6.00	15.00
54 Todd Bodine National Guard Promo	5.00	12.00
55 Mike Stefanik Burnham Boilers Promo	7.50	15.00
57 Jason Keller Albertsons with year on blister	3.00	8.00
57 Jason Keller Albertsons without year on blister	3.00	8.00
77 Dave Blaney Jasper	3.00	8.00
77 Dave Blaney Jasper Fast&Furious Promo	3.00	8.00
77 Dave Blaney Jasper Fast&Furious Promo AUTO/100	25.00	50.00
77 University of Maryland Promo in box	7.50	20.00
90 Lance Norick Express Personnel Promo	15.00	30.00
01 Jerry Nadeau Army	4.00	10.00
01 Jerry Nadeau Army Chrome/1500	6.00	15.00
01 Jerry Nadeau Army Time Trial/5000	5.00	12.00
01 Jery Nadeau Tony Schumacher Dragster Army Camo Promo 2-car blister	6.00	15.00
01 Jerry Nadeau USG promo in box	7.50	15.00
03 Ward Burton Certainteed Promo	10.00	20.00
03 Sharpie Bristol Food City 400 Promo in PVC box	10.00	20.00
03 Tanimura&Antle Promo in window box	10.00	20.00

2003 Racing Champions 5-Pack 1:64

	EX	NM-MT
NNO 5. Brian Vickers/GMAC 48. Jimmie Johnson/Lowe's POP 01. Jerry Nadeau/Army 22. Ward Burton/Cat 10. Johnny Benson/Valvoline	10.00	20.00
NNO 22. Ward Burton/CAT Acert 54. Todd Bodine/National Guard 7. Jimmy Spencer/Sirius 5. Terry Labonte/Kellogg's 48. Jimmie Johnson/Lowe's	7.50	15.00
NNO 48. Jimmie Johnson/Lowe's 10. Johnny Benson/Eagle One 11. Brett Bodine/Hooters Anniv. 01. Jerry Nadeau/USG 5. Terry Labonte/Finding Nemo	7.50	15.00
NNO 48. Jimmy Johnson/Lowe's Power of Pride 23. Scott Wimmer/Stacker 2 Fast&Furious 30. Jimmy Vasser/Aventis 33. Paul Menard/Turtle Wax 45. Kyle Petty/GP Garfied	7.50	15.00

2003 Racing Champions Preview 1:64

Racing Champions created a smaller more narrow blister pack for 2003. This series features the title "2003 Preview" on the left side of the blister. Each die-cast car was packaged with a mini (roughly 2 /14" by 3") sized Press Pass card.

	EX	NM-MT
22 Ward Burton Caterpillar	3.00	8.00
22 Ward Burton Caterpillar Firesuit/50	45.00	80.00
22 Ward Burton Caterpillar Rain Delay/500	7.50	20.00
22 Ward Burton Cat Rental	3.00	8.00
22 Ward Burton Cat Rental Chrome/1500	6.00	15.00
22 Ward Burton Cat Rental Firesuit/50	45.00	80.00
22 Ward Burton Cat Rental Rain Delay/500	7.50	20.00
22 Ward Burton Caterpillar Steel/50	40.00	80.00
22 Ward Burton Cat Time Trial/5000	4.00	10.00
22 Ward Burton Cat Time Trial Rain Delay/500	10.00	20.00
22 Ward Burton Caterpillar War Paint/5000	4.00	10.00
26 Todd Bodine Discover	3.00	8.00
48 Jimmie Johnson Lowe's 2002 A Season to Remember	3.00	8.00

2003 Racing Champions Premier 1:64

	EX	NM-MT
4 Mike Skinner Kodak	4.00	8.00
4 Mike Skinner Kodak Rain Delay/500	12.50	25.00
5 Terry Labonte Kellogg's	4.00	8.00
7 Jimmy Spencer Sirius	4.00	8.00
10 Johnny Benson Valvoline	4.00	8.00
10 Johnny Benson Valvoline Firesuit/50	40.00	80.00
10 Johnny Benson Valvoline Firesuit Steel/50	50.00	100.00
10 Johnny Benson Valvoline Steel/50	45.00	80.00
11 Brett Bodine Hooters	4.00	8.00
11 Brett Bodine Hooters Chrome/1500	12.50	25.00
22 Ward Burton Caterpillar	3.00	6.00
22 Ward Burton Cat Acert	4.00	8.00
25 Joe Nemechek UAW Delphi	4.00	8.00
32 Ricky Craven Tide	4.00	8.00
32 Ricky Craven Tide Rain Delay/500	8.00	20.00
48 Jimmie Johnson Lowe's	5.00	12.00
48 Jimmie Johnson Lowe's Chrome/1500	12.50	25.00
48 Jimmie Johnson Lowe's Firesuit Steel/50	60.00	120.00
57 Jason Keller Albertson's	4.00	8.00
01 Jerry Nadeau Army	6.00	15.00
01 Jerry Nadeau Army Chrome/1500	15.00	30.00

2003 Racing Champions Premier Preview 1:64

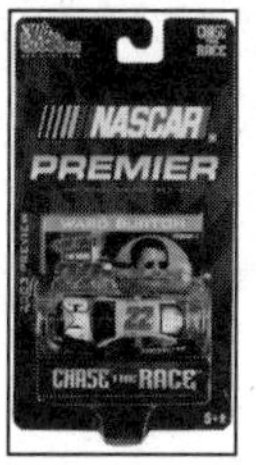

	EX	NM-MT
22 Ward Burton Caterpillar	4.00	10.00
22 Ward Burton Caterpillar Chrome/1500	8.00	20.00
22 Ward Burton Caterpillar Firesuit/50	60.00	120.00
22 Ward Burton Caterpillar Rain Delay/500	12.50	25.00
22 Ward Burton Cat Time Trial/5000	5.00	12.00
22 Ward Burton Cat Time Trial Rain Delay/500	12.50	25.00
22 Ward Burton Caterpillar War Paint/5000	5.00	12.00
22 Ward Burton Cat Rental	4.00	10.00
22 Ward Burton Caterpillar Rental Chrome/1500	8.00	20.00
22 Ward Burton Cat Rental Firesuit/50	40.00	80.00
22 Ward Burton Cat Rental Firesuit and Sheet Metal/50	60.00	120.00
22 Ward Burton Cat Rental Rain Delay/500	25.00	50.00
26 Todd Bodine Discover	4.00	10.00
48 Jimmie Johnson Lowe's 2002 Season to Remember	5.00	12.00

2003 Racing Champions Slammers 1:64

	EX	NM-MT
5 Terry Labonte Kellogg's	6.00	12.00
10 Johnny Benson Valvoline	6.00	12.00
22 Ward Burton Caterpillar	6.00	12.00
32 Ricky Craven Tide	6.00	12.00
45 Kyle Petty GP Garfield	6.00	12.00
48 Jimmie Johnson Lowe's	6.00	12.00
48 Jimmie Johnson Lowe's Power of Pride	6.00	12.00
48 Jimmie Johnson Lowe's SpongeBob Squarepants	6.00	12.00
01 Jerry Nadeau Army	6.00	12.00

2003 Racing Champions Stock Rods Preview 1:64

Racing Champions created a smaller more narrow blister pack for 2003. This series features the title "2003 Preview" on the left side of the blister. Each vintage car replica die-cast was packaged with a mini (roughly 2 /14" by 3") sized Racing Champions trading card.

	EX	NM-MT
5 Terry Labonte Kellogg's '55 Chevy (card reads "1970 Chevelle in error)	3.00	8.00
22 Ward Burton Caterpillar 1941 Willys	3.00	8.00
32 Ricky Craven Tide '69 GTO	3.00	8.00
48 Jimmie Johnson Lowe's 1970 Chevelle	4.00	10.00

2003 Racing Champions Stock Rods 1:64

This series is a continuation of the 2003 Preview release. Each vintage car replica die-cast was packaged with a mini (roughly 2 /14" by 3") sized Racing Champions trading card which features just the car number and Stock Rods logo. Each card also contains an issue number. All pieces were issued with the "2003 Edition" notation on the left side of the blister. Some pieces were also issued on blister variations without the "2003 Edition" designation.

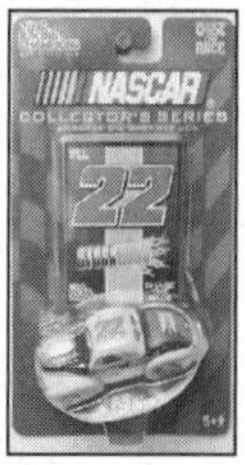

	EX	NM-MT
22 Ward Burton Cat Rental 1941 Willys with year on package	3.00	8.00
22 Ward Burton Cat Rental 1941 Willys no year on package	3.00	8.00
01 Jerry Nadeau Army 1968 Camaro	4.00	8.00

2003 Racing Champions Ultra 1:64

	EX	NM-MT
4 Mike Skinner Kodak Easyshare	5.00	10.00
4 Mike Skinner Kodak Easyshare AU/100	25.00	50.00
5 Terry Labonte Cheez-It	4.00	8.00
5 Terry Labonte Cheez-It AU/100	30.00	80.00
5 Terry Labonte Finding Nemo	5.00	10.00
5 Terry Labonte Power of Cheese	4.00	8.00
5 Terry Labonte Power of Cheese AU/100	40.00	80.00
5 Brian Vickers GMAC	6.00	12.00
10 Johnny Benson Eagle One	4.00	8.00
10 Johnny Benson Eagle One Chrome/1500	7.50	20.00
10 Johnny Benson Valvoline	3.00	6.00
10 Johnny Benson Valvoline Chrome/1500	10.00	20.00
10 Johnny Benson Valvoline Firesuit/50	40.00	80.00
10 Johnny Benson Valvoline Rain Delay/500	6.00	15.00
10 Johnny Benson Valvoline Steel/50	50.00	100.00
11 Brett Bodine Hooters 20th Anniversary	5.00	10.00
22 Ward Burton Caterpillar	3.00	6.00
22 Ward Burton Caterpillar Firesuit/50	50.00	100.00
25 Joe Nemechek UAW Delphi	4.00	8.00
25 Joe Nemechek UAW Delphi Rain Delay/500	10.00	20.00
45 Kyle Petty GP Garfield	6.00	12.00
45 Ken Schrader 1-800-CALLATT	6.00	12.00
48 J.Johnson/Lowe's	4.00	8.00
48 Jimmie Johnson Lowe's Steel/50	40.00	80.00
48 Jimmie Johnson Lowe's Power of Pride	4.00	8.00
48 Jimmie Johnson Lowe's Power of Pride Chrome/1500	10.00	20.00
48 Jimmie Johnson Lowe's SpongeBob Promo	5.00	12.00
48 Jimmie Johnson Lowe's SpongeBob Chrome Promo/1500	10.00	20.00
60 Brian Vickers HAAS	6.00	12.00
87 Kyle Busch Ditech.com	4.00	8.00
87 Joe Nemechek Cellular One	3.00	6.00
0 Jack Sprague NetZero	7.50	20.00
01 Jerry Nadeau Army	4.00	8.00
01 Jerry Nadeau Army Rain Delay/500	15.00	30.00
01 Jerry Nadeau Army Camo	4.00	10.00
01 Jerry Nadeau USG Sheet Rock	4.00	8.00

2004 Racing Champions 1:64

	EX	NM-MT
1 Johnny Benson Yellow Freight Promo	10.00	20.00
2 Kelly Sutton Team Copaxone Promo	15.00	30.00
4 Bobby Hamilton Square D SuperTruck Promo in wind.box	10.00	20.00
5 Terry Labonte Incredibles Promo in bag	25.00	50.00
27 Johnny Sauter Kleenex Promo	6.00	12.00
27 Johnny Sauter Kleenex Aldi Promo	6.00	12.00

27 Johnny Sauter 12.50 25.00
Kleenex Cub Foods Promo
27 Johnny Sauter 20.00 35.00
Kleenex Dollar General Promo
27 Johnny Sauter 25.00 40.00
Kleenex Food World Promo
35 Brad Leighton 10.00 20.00
Irving Oil Promo
In wind.box
38 Elliott Sadler 15.00 30.00
M&M's Yellow Promo
38 Elliott Sadler 12.50 25.00
M&M's Black&White Promo
43 Aaron Fike 30.00 60.00
Ollie's Bargain Outlet
44 Justin Labonte 10.00 20.00
Coast Guard Promo
49 Ken Schrader 35.00 60.00
Red Baron Promo in wind.box
49 Ken Schrader 30.00 50.00
Schwan's Promo
in wind.box
01 Joe Nemechek 12.50 25.00
USG Promo in window box

2004 Racing Champions Bare Metal Previews 1:64

EX NM-MT
10 Scott Riggs 4.00 8.00
Valvoline
22 Scott Wimmer 4.00 8.00
Caterpillar
48 Jimmie Johnson 3.00 6.00
Lowe's

2004 Racing Champions 5-Pack 1:64

EX NM-MT
NNO 01. Joe Nemechek/USG 10.00 20.00
5. Terry Labonte/Kellogg's
10. Scott Riggs/Harlem Globetrotters
25. Brian Vickers/ditech.com
59. Stacy Compton/Kingsford
NNO 01. Joe Nemechek/Army 12.50 25.00
5. Terry Labonte/Kellogg's Incredibles
22. Scott Wimmer/Cat Acert
38. Kasey Kahne/Great Clips
84. Kyle Busch/Carquest
in '05 packaging
NNO 01. Joe Nemechek/Army 12.50 25.00
22. Scott Wimmer/Cat
44. Justin Labonte/Coast Guard
48. Jimmie Johnson/Lowe's Tool World
49. Ken Schrader/Schwan's
in '05 packaging
NNO 10. Scott Riggs/Valvoline 10.00 20.00
22. Scott Wimmer/Caterpillar
25. Brian Vickers/ditech.com
27. Johnny Sauter/Kleenex
48. Jimmie Johnson/Lowe's
NNO 10. Scott Riggs/Valvoline 10.00 20.00
22. Scott Wimmer/Caterpillar
48. Jimmie Johnson/Lowe's
60. Brian Vickers/Hendrick's Team
87. Kyle Busch/Ditech.com

2004 Racing Champions Real Steel 1:64

EX NM-MT
5 Terry Labonte 5.00 12.00
Kellogg's
10 Scott Riggs 5.00 12.00
Valvoline
22 Scott Wimmer 5.00 12.00
Cat
25 Brian Vickers 5.00 12.00
Ditech.com
48 Jimmie Johnson 5.00 12.00
Lowe's
0 Ward Burton 5.00 12.00
NetZero
01 Joe Nemechek 5.00 12.00
Army

2004 Racing Champions Ultra Previews 1:64

EX NM-MT
10 Scott Riggs 3.00 8.00
Valvoline
22 Scott Wimmer 3.00 8.00
Cat
48 Jimmie Johnson 3.00 6.00
Lowe's
48 Jimmie Johnson 12.50 25.00
Lowe's Chrome

2004 Racing Champions Ultra 1:64

EX NM-MT
5 Kyle Busch 5.00 12.00
Lowe's
5 Kyle Busch 5.00 10.00
Lowe's SpongeBob
5 Terry Labonte 4.00 8.00
Delphi
5 Terry Labonte 4.00 8.00
Kellogg's
5 Terry Labonte 10.00 20.00
Kellogg's Chrome
5 Terry Labonte 4.00 8.00
Kellogg's HMS 20th Ann.
in 05 packaging
5 Terry Labonte 4.00 8.00
Kellogg's Incredibles
in '05 packaging
10 Scott Riggs 5.00 10.00
Harlem Globetrotters
10 Scott Riggs 3.00 8.00
Valvoline
22 Scott Wimmer 4.00 8.00
Cat
22 Scott Wimmer 7.50 15.00
Cat Chrome
22 Scott Wimmer 4.00 8.00
Cat Dealer
22 Scott Wimmer 4.00 8.00
Cat Rental
23 Kenny Wallace 4.00 8.00
Stacker 2
25 Brian Vickers 5.00 10.00
ditech.com
25 Brian Vickers 4.00 8.00
Ditech.com HMS 20 Ann.
in '05 packaging
27 Johnny Sauter 4.00 8.00
Kleenex
47 Robert Pressley 5.00 12.00
Clorox
48 Jimmie Johnson 3.00 8.00
Lowe's
48 Jimmie Johnson 4.00 8.00
Lowe's HMS 20th Anniversary
48 Jimmie Johnson 4.00 8.00
Lowe's HMS 20th Ann.
in '05 packaging
48 Jimmie Johnson 4.00 8.00
Lowe's SpongeBob
48 Jimmie Johnson 4.00 8.00
Lowe's Tool World
48 Jimmie Johnson 4.00 8.00
Lowe's Tool World
in '05 packaging
84 Kyle Busch 4.00 8.00
Carquest in '05 packaging
0 Ward Burton 5.00 10.00
NetZero
0 Ward Burton 8.00 20.00
NetZero Chrome
01 Joe Nemechek 5.00 10.00
Army
01 Joe Nemechek 5.00 10.00
USG
04 Nextel Cup Chevy 4.00 8.00
04 Nextel Cup Dodge 4.00 8.00

2004 Racing Champions Window Cling 1:64

EX NM-MT
5 Terry Labonte 4.00 8.00
Kellogg's
10 Scott Riggs 4.00 8.00
Valvoline
22 Scott Wimmer 4.00 8.00
Cat
25 Brian Vickers 4.00 8.00
Ditech
48 Jimmie Johnson 4.00 8.00
Lowe's
01 Joe Nemechek 4.00 8.00
Army

2005 Racing Champions 1:64

EX NM-MT
1 Johnny Sauter 6.00 12.00
Yellow Fleet Pride Promo
9 Shigeaki Hattori 15.00 30.00
Toyota TRD SuperTruck
Promo
10 Scott Riggs 6.00 12.00
Valvoline Promo
in window box
22 Bill Lester 30.00 60.00
Rally's Checker's SuperTruck
Promo
25 Brad Leighton 7.50 15.00
Irving Oil Promo
in window box
25 Ashton Lewis 20.00 35.00
Team Marines Promo
27 David Green 7.50 15.00
Kleenex Promo
27 David Green 7.50 15.00
Kleenex Bi-Lo Promo
27 David Green 7.50 15.00
Kleenex Cub Foods Promo
32 Bobby Hamilton Jr. 5.00 10.00
Tide Promo
34 Randy Lajoie 6.00 12.00
Dollar General Promo
35 Jason Keller 10.00 20.00
McDonald's Promo
36 Boris Said 12.50 25.00
USG Durock Promo
in window box
66 Greg Biffle 15.00 30.00
Royal Office Products Promo

2005 Racing Champions Ultra Previews 1:64

EX NM-MT
22 Scott Wimmer 4.00 8.00
Cat
22 Scott Wimmer 6.00 12.00
Cat Chrome

2005 Racing Champions Ultra 1:64

EX NM-MT
5 Kyle Busch 4.00 8.00
Delphi
5 Kyle Busch 5.00 10.00
Kellogg's
5 Blake Feese 6.00 12.00
Boston Reid
Lowe's
7 Robby Gordon 5.00 10.00
Fruit of the Loom
7 Robby Gordon 5.00 10.00
Harrah's
10 Scott Riggs 4.00 8.00
Valvoline
14 John Andretti 4.00 8.00
JA
22 Kenny Wallace 4.00 8.00
Stacker 2
22 Scott Wimmer 4.00 8.00
CAT
22 Scott Wimmer 6.00 12.00
CAT Chrome
25 Brian Vickers 4.00 8.00
GMAC
36 Boris Said 5.00 10.00
Centex Financial
40 Sterling Marlin 4.00 8.00
Cottman
44 Terry Labonte 4.00 8.00
GMAC
44 Terry Labonte 5.00 10.00
GMAC Chrome
44 Terry Labonte 4.00 8.00
Kellogg's
44 Terry Labonte 7.50 15.00
Kellogg's Chrome
44 Terry Labonte 5.00 10.00
Kellogg's Ironman
48 Jimmie Johnson 4.00 8.00
Lowe's
48 Jimmie Johnson 7.50 15.00
Lowe's Chrome
48 Jimmie Johnson 25.00 50.00
Lowe's Firesuit/50
48 Jimmie Johnson 4.00 8.00
Lowe's Kobalt
49 Ken Schrader 6.00 12.00
Schwan's
57 Brian Vickers 4.00 8.00
Ore Ida
66 Greg Biffle 4.00 8.00
Duraflame
87 Joe Nemechek 4.00 8.00
Cellular One
0 Mike Bliss 4.00 8.00
NetZero Best Buy
01 Joe Nemechek 4.00 8.00
Army
01 Joe Nemechek 6.00 12.00
Army Chrome

2006 Racing Champions Promos 1:64

EX NM-MT
17 David Reutimann 5.00 10.00
Tundra SuperTruck in blister
32 Travis Kvapil 4.00 8.00
Tide in blister
58 Donnie Neuenberger 5.00 10.00
Cayman Islands
in window box
66 Jeff Green 4.00 8.00
Certain Teed in blister

1991 Racing Champions 5-Pack 1:144

These 1:144 scale cars were issued in a Racing Champions "Mini Stock Cars" blister package.

EX NM-MT
NNO 3. Dale Earnhardt/Goodwrench 10.00 20.00
27. Rusty Wallace/
28. Davey Allison/Havoline
30. Bobby Hamilton/Max.House
43. Richard Petty/STP
NNO 9. Bill Elliott/Melling 7.50 15.00
27. Rusty Wallace
30. Bobby Hamilton/Max.House
33. Harry Gant
94. Sterling Marlin/Sunoco

1996 Racing Champions 1:144

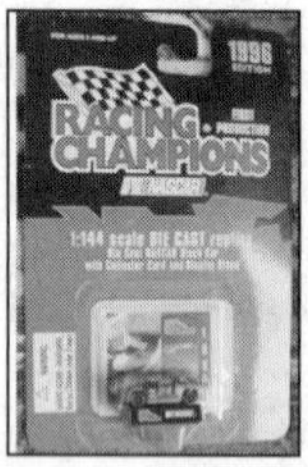

These 1:144 scale mini cars were issued in a red and black Racing Champions blister package. The blister reads "1996 Edition, First Production" on the front. Each was also packaged with a yellow bordered trading card.

EX NM-MT
2 Rusty Wallace 5.00 12.00
MGD
4 Sterling Marlin 4.00 10.00
Kodak
6 Mark Martin 5.00 12.00
Valvoline
17 Darrell Waltrip 4.00 10.00
Parts America
18 Bobby Labonte 4.00 10.00
Interstate Batteries
21 Michael Waltrip 4.00 10.00
Citgo
24 Jeff Gordon 5.00 12.00
DuPont
28 Ernie Irvan 4.00 10.00
Havoline
29 No Driver Association 4.00 10.00
Scooby-Doo
87 Joe Nemechek 4.00 10.00
BellSouth
88 Dale Jarrett 5.00 12.00
Quality Care
94 Bill Elliott 4.00 10.00
McDonald's

1997 Racing Champions Preview 1:144

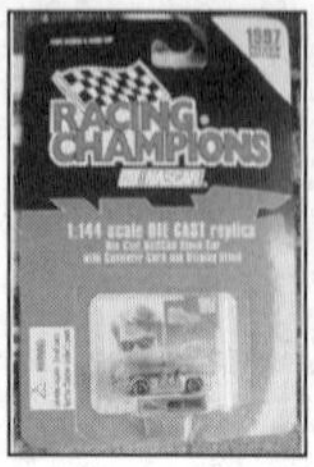

EX NM-MT
4 Sterling Marlin 2.50 6.00
Kodak
5 Terry Labonte 2.00 5.00
Kellogg's
6 Mark Martin 2.50 6.00
Valvoline
9 Joe Bessey 2.00 5.00
Power Team
18 Bobby Labonte 2.50 6.00
Interstate Batteries
21 Michael Waltrip 2.00 5.00
Citgo
24 Jeff Gordon 3.00 8.00
DuPont
28 Ernie Irvan 2.00 5.00
Havoline
29 Robert Pressley 2.00 5.00
Cartoon Network
30 Johnny Benson 2.00 5.00
Pennzoil
75 Rick Mast 2.00 5.00
Remington
94 Bill Elliott 2.50 6.00
McDonald's
99 Jeff Burton 2.00 5.00
Exide

1997 Racing Champions 1:144

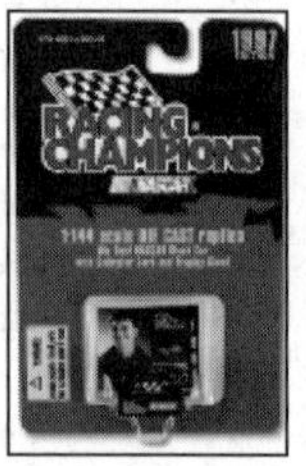

These 1:144 scale mini Transporters were issued in a red and black Racing Champions blister package. The blister reads "1997 Edition" on the front. Each was also packaged with a yellow bordered trading card.

EX NM-MT
1 Hermie Sadler 2.00 5.00
DeWalt
2 Rusty Wallace 2.50 6.00
Penske
2 Ricky Craven 2.00 5.00
Raybestos
4 Sterling Marlin 2.50 6.00
Kodak
5 Terry Labonte 2.50 6.00
Bayer
5 Terry Labonte 2.50 6.00
Kellogg's
5 Terry Labonte 2.50 6.00
Kellogg's Tony
5 Terry Labonte 2.50 6.00
Kellogg's 1996 Champ
6 Mark Martin 2.50 6.00
Valvoline
7 Geoff Bodine 2.00 5.00
QVC
8 Hut Stricklin 2.00 5.00
Circuit City
9 Joe Bessey 2.00 5.00
Power Team
10 Phil Parsons 2.00 5.00
Channellock
11 Jimmy Foster 2.00 5.00
SpeedVision
11 Brett Bodine 2.00 5.00
Close Call
16 Ted Musgrave 2.00 5.00
Family Channel
17 Darrell Waltrip 2.00 5.00
Parts America
17 Darrell Waltrip 2.00 5.00
Parts America Chrome
18 Bobby Labonte 2.50 6.00
Interstate Batteries
19 Gary Bradberry 2.00 5.00
Child Support
21 Michael Waltrip 2.00 5.00
Citgo
24 Jeff Gordon 3.00 8.00
DuPont
25 Ricky Craven 2.00 5.00
Hendrick
28 Ernie Irvan 2.00 5.00
Havoline black&orange
28 Ernie Irvan 2.00 5.00
Havoline black&white
29 Elliott Sadler 2.00 5.00
Phillips 66
29 Robert Pressley 2.00 5.00
Cartoon Network
29 Jeff Green 2.00
Tom&Jerry
30 Johnny Benson 2.00
Pennzoil
32 Dale Jarrett 2.00
White Rain
33 Ken Schrader 2.00
Petree Racing
36 Todd Bodine 2.00
Stanley
36 Derrike Cope 2.00
Skittles
37 Jeremy Mayfield 2.00
K-Mart
38 Elton Sawyer 2.00
Barbasol
40 Robby Gordon 2.00
Sabco
42 Joe Nemechek 2.00
BellSouth
43 Dennis Setzer 2.00
Lance
46 Wally Dallenbach 2.00
First Union
47 Jeff Fuller 2.00
Sunoco
49 Kyle Petty 2.00
NWO
57 Jason Keller 2.00
Slim Jim
60 Mark Martin 2.50
Winn Dixie
74 Randy LaJoie 2.00
Fina
75 Rick Mast 2.00
Remington
75 Rick Mast 2.00
Remington Camo
75 Rick Mast 2.00
Remington Stren
87 Joe Nemechek 2.00
BellSouth
88 Kevin Lepage 2.00
Hype
90 Dick Trickle 2.00
Heilig-Meyers
91 Mike Wallace 2.00
Spam
94 Ron Barfield 2.00
New Holland
94 Bill Elliott 2.50
McDonald's
94 Bill Elliott 2.50
Mac Tonight
96 David Green 2.00
Caterpillar
97 Chad Little 2.00
John Deere
99 Glenn Allen 2.00
Luxaire
99 Jeff Burton 2.00
Exide
00 Buckshot Jones 2.00
Aquafresh

1997 Racing Champions Pack 1:144

EX N[…]
NNO 24. Jeff Gordon/DuPont 4.00
32. Dale Jarrett/White Rain
40. Sterling Marlin
94. Bill Elliott/McDonld's
97. Chad Little/John Deere

1997 Racing Champions Pack Preview 1:144

These 1:144 scale cars were issued in a Racing Cha[…] 1997 Preview blister. The cars came with a card for eac[…] and a black display stand for the set.

EX N[…]
NNO 4. Sterling Marlin/Kodak 4.00
5. Terry Labonte/Kellogg's
9. Joe Bessey/Power Team
24. Jeff Gordon/DuPont
29. Robert Pressley/Cartoon Network
NNO 5. Terry Labonte/Kellogg's 4.00
6. Mark Martin/Valvoline
21. Michael Waltrip/Citgo
24. Jeff Gordon/DuPont
28. Ernie Irvan/Havoline
NNO 5. Terry Labonte/Kellogg's 4.00
24. Jeff Gordon/DuPont
30. Johnny Benson/Pennzoil
94. Bill Elliott/McDonald's
99. Jeff Burton/Exide
NNO 10. Phil Parsons/Channellock 4.00
36. Todd Bodine/Stanley Tools
42. Joe Nemechek/BellSouth
46. Wally Dallenbach/First Union
94. Bill Elliott/Mac Tonight

1997 Racing Champion[…] SuperTrucks 5-Pack 1:14[…]

NNO 99. Mark Martin/Exide
99. Jeff Burton/Exide
1. Michael Waltrip/MW Windows
15. Ernie Irvan/VISA
18. Johnny Benson/Valvoline

1997 Racing Champion[…] SuperTrucks 1:144

These 1:144 scale mini dragsters were issued in a red a[…] Racing Champions NASCAR Craftsman Truck blister p[…] The blister reads "1997 Edition" on the front. Each w[…] packaged with a yellow bordered trading card.

EX N[…]
1 Michael Waltrip 2.00
MW Windows
2 Mike Bliss 2.00
ASE
4 Bill Elliott 2.50
Wagner
6 Rick Carelli 2.00
Remax
15 Mike Colabucci 2.00

	EX	NM-MT
/ISA		
/ike Cope	2.00	5.00
Pennrose		
/ike Dokken	2.00	5.00
Dana		
ohnny Benson	2.00	5.00
Pennzoil		
ony Raines	2.00	5.00
Pennzoil		
J. Clark	2.00	5.00
CRG Motorsports		
ack Sprague	2.00	5.00
Quaker State		
ob Keselowski	2.00	5.00
Mopar		
ave Rezendes	2.00	5.00
Ortho		
oris Said	2.00	5.00
Federated		
obey Butler	2.00	5.00
Pure One		
ryan Refner	2.00	5.00
Carlin		
an Press	2.00	5.00
Spears		
oe Ruttman	2.00	5.00
LCI		
Stacy Compton	2.00	5.00
Valvoline		
oe Nemechek	2.00	5.00
BellSouth		
Mark Kinser	2.00	5.00
Rotary		
on Barfield	2.00	5.00
Super 8		
enny Irwin	3.00	8.00
Raybestos		
eff Burton	2.00	5.00
Exide		
ark Martin	2.50	6.00
Exide		
Billy Ogle	2.00	5.00
DCD		
ammy Kirk	2.00	5.00
Lovable		

1998 Racing Champions 1:144

e 1:144 scale mini Transporters were issued in a red g Champions blister package that reads "1998 Edition." was also packaged with a trading card.

	EX	NM-MT
ry Labonte	2.50	5.00
Kellogg's		
e Bessey	2.00	5.00
Power Team		
rk Martin	2.50	6.00
Valvoline		
t Stricklin	2.00	5.00
Circuit City		
ke Speed	2.00	5.00
Birthday Cake		
ke Speed	2.00	5.00
Huckleberry Hound		
eremy Mayfield	2.00	5.00
K-Mart		
erry Nadeau	2.00	5.00
First Plus		
Michael Waltrip	2.00	5.00
Citgo		
ohnny Benson	2.00	5.00
Cheerios		
Hermie Sadler	2.00	5.00
DeWalt		
errike Cope	2.00	5.00
Gumout		
odd Bodine	2.00	5.00
Tabasco Black		
odd Bodine	2.00	5.00
Tabasco Orange		
nie Irvan	2.00	5.00
M&M's		
erling Marlin	2.50	6.00
Sabco		
Steve Grissom	2.00	5.00
Larry Hedrick Racing		
oe Nemechek	2.00	5.00
BellSouth		
obert Pressley	2.00	5.00
Kingsford		
ick Trickle	2.00	5.00
Schneider		
lliott Sadler	2.00	5.00
Phillips 66		
ick Mast	2.00	5.00
Remington		
ll Elliott	2.50	6.00
McDonald's		
avid Green	2.00	5.00
Caterpillar		
had Little	2.00	5.00
John Deere Promo		
lenn Allen	2.00	5.00
Luxaire		
ff Burton	2.00	5.00
Exide		
uckshot Jones	2.00	5.00
Alka Seltzer		
uckshot Jones	2.00	5.00
Aqua Fresh		

998 Racing Champions 5-Pack 1:144

	EX	NM-MT
5. Terry Labonte/Kellogg's	3.00	8.00
3. Hut Stricklin/Circuit City		
35. Todd Bodine/Tabasco		
50. Ricky Craven/Hendrick		
59. Robert Pressley/Kingsford		
5. Terry Labonte/Kellogg's	3.00	8.00
30. Mike Cope/Slim Jim		
35. Todd Bodine/Tabasco		
36. Ernie Irvan/Skittles		
50. NASCAR 50th Anniversary		
5. Terry Labonte/Kellogg's	3.00	8.00
30.Mike Cope/Slim Jim		
36. Ernie Irvan/Skittles		
50. Ricky Craven/Hendrick		
50. NASCAR 50th Anniversary		
NNO 5. Terry Labonte/Kellogg's	3.00	8.00
35. Todd Bodine/Tabasco		
40. Sterling Marlin		
99. Glenn Allen/Luxaire		
00. Buckshot Jones/Bayer		

1998 Racing Champions Stock Rods 1:144

	EX	NM-MT
23 Hut Stricklin	2.50	6.00
Circuit City		
38 Wally Dallenbach	2.50	6.00
First Union		
42 Buckshot Jones	2.50	6.00
Aqua Fresh		
43 Michael Waltrip	2.50	6.00
Pennzoil		
44 Wally Dallenbach	2.50	6.00
First Union		

1998 Racing Champions Stock Rods 5-Pack 1:144

	EX	NM-MT
NNO 50. Ricky Craven/Hendrick	3.00	8.00
59. Robert Pressley/Kingsford		
90. Dick Trickle/Heilig Meyers		
99. Jeff Burton/Exide		
99. Glenn Allen/Luxaire		

1997 Revell Club 1:18

These 1:18 scale cars were from the same production run as the Collection cars. Each car distributed by the club has a serial number on the chassis. The boxes were uniquely colored to match the colors on the car.

	EX	NM-MT
1 Coca-Cola 600	50.00	100.00
5 Terry Labonte	90.00	150.00
Spooky Loops		
5 Terry Labonte	100.00	175.00
Kellogg's Tony		
23 Jimmy Spencer	100.00	175.00
Camel/504		
33 Ken Schrader	90.00	150.00
Skoal		
46 Wally Dallenbach	50.00	120.00
Woody Woodpecker		
88 Dale Jarrett	80.00	120.00
Quality Care		
97 Chad Little	60.00	150.00
John Deere/504		

1997 Revell Collection 1:18

This series marks Revell's first attempt to produce a 1:18 scale car. It was distributed to hobby dealers as part of Revell's Collection line.

	EX	NM-MT
1 Coca-Cola 600/3624	25.00	60.00
2 Rusty Wallace	40.00	100.00
Miller Lite/11,766		
3 Dale Earnhardt	60.00	120.00
Wheaties/10,008		
4 Sterling Marlin	40.00	80.00
Kodak		
5 Terry Labonte	50.00	100.00
Kellogg's		
5 Terry Labonte	40.00	100.00
Spooky Loops/6006		
5 Terry Labonte	40.00	100.00
Kellogg's Tony/6012		
6 Mark Martin	50.00	80.00
Valvoline		
10 Ricky Rudd	40.00	80.00
Tide/3120		
18 Bobby Labonte	40.00	80.00
Interstate Batteries		
18 Bobby Labonte	40.00	80.00
Interstate Batteries		
Texas/3120		
21 Michael Waltrip	25.00	60.00
Citgo Top Dog/3120		
23 Jimmy Spencer	60.00	120.00
Camel/5004		
24 Jeff Gordon	60.00	120.00
Jurassic Park 3/5004		
25 Ricky Craven	40.00	100.00
Bud Lizard		
28 Ernie Irvan	40.00	100.00
Havoline 10th Anniversary		
white and black		
29 Jeff Green	30.00	80.00
Scooby-Doo		
29 Jeff Green	30.00	80.00
Tom & Jerry		
29 Steve Grissom	30.00	80.00
Flintstones		
33 Ken Schrader	30.00	80.00
Skoal/3624		
35 Todd Bodine	40.00	80.00
Tabasco		
37 Jeremy Mayfield	40.00	80.00
K-Mart RC-Cola		
40 Robby Gordon	40.00	75.00
Coors Light/5004		
41 Steve Grissom	40.00	80.00
Kodiak		
43 Bobby Hamilton	40.00	80.00
STP Goody's		
46 Wally Dallenbach	40.00	80.00
Woody Woodpecker		
60 Mark Martin	50.00	90.00
Winn Dixie		
88 Dale Jarrett	40.00	80.00
Ford Credit		
94 Bill Elliott	40.00	80.00
McDonald's		
94 Bill Elliott	40.00	80.00
Mac Tonight		
97 Chad Little	40.00	90.00
John Deere AUTO/2616		
97 Texas Motor Speedway/5004	35.00	70.00

1998 Revell Club 1:18

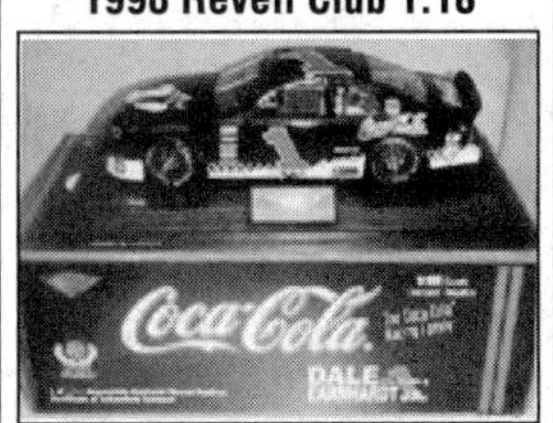

These 1:18 scale cars were from the same production run as the Collection cars. Each car distributed by the club has a serial number on the chassis. The boxes were uniquely colored to match the colors on the car.

	EX	NM-MT
1 Dale Earnhardt Jr.	50.00	100.00
Coke Bear/2004		
1 Steve Park	40.00	100.00
Pennzoil Black Roof		
1 Steve Park	30.00	80.00
Pennzoil Yellow Roof/504		
2 Rusty Wallace	60.00	120.00
Adventures of Rusty		
2 Rusty Wallace	60.00	120.00
Miller Lite Elvis/1002		
3 Dale Earnhardt	75.00	150.00
Coke/2004		
3 Dale Earnhardt	150.00	250.00
Goodwrench Plus		
3 Dale Earnhardt	200.00	300.00
Goodwrench Plus Bass Pro/504		
3 Dale Earnhardt	200.00	250.00
Goodwrench Plus		
Daytona Win/504		
3 Dale Earnhardt Jr.	75.00	150.00
AC Delco		
5 Terry Labonte	60.00	120.00
Blasted Fruit Loops/504		
5 Terry Labonte	60.00	120.00
Kellogg's Corny		
9 Lake Speed	40.00	100.00
Birthday Cake		
9 Lake Speed	40.00	100.00
Huckleberry Hound/504		
18 Bobby Labonte	50.00	100.00
Interstate Batteries Hot Rod/504		
18 Bobby Labonte	50.00	100.00
Interstate Batteries		
Small Soldiers/1002		
23 Jimmy Spencer	125.00	200.00
No Bull/504		
24 Jeff Gordon	60.00	150.00
DuPont/1008		
24 Jeff Gordon	100.00	200.00
DuPont Chromalusion		
28 Kenny Irwin	60.00	120.00
Havoline/504		
28 Kenny Irwin	60.00	120.00
Havoline Joker/504		
31 Mike Skinner	40.00	100.00
Lowe's		
35 Todd Bodine	50.00	100.00
Tabasco		
36 Ernie Irvan	60.00	120.00
M&M's/504		
36 Ernie Irvan	60.00	120.00
Wildberry Skittles		
44 Tony Stewart	90.00	150.00
Shell/504		
44 Tony Stewart	90.00	150.00
Shell Small Soldiers/1002		
50 Ricky Craven	50.00	100.00
Bud/504		
81 Kenny Wallace	30.00	80.00
Square D Lightning/504		
88 Dale Jarrett	75.00	150.00
Batman/1002		
88 Dale Jarrett	50.00	120.00
Quality Care/504		

1998 Revell Collection 1:18

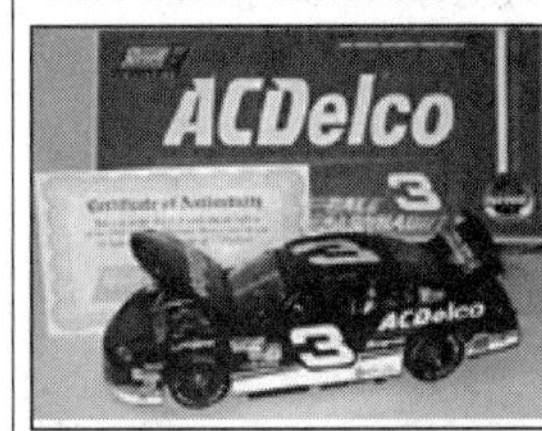

This series marks Revell's second year producing a 1:18 scale car. It was distributed to hobby dealers are part of Revell's Collection line.

	EX	NM-MT
1 Dale Earnhardt Jr.	40.00	100.00
Coke Bear/4002		
1 Steve Park	40.00	100.00
Pennzoil Black Roof/3120		
1 Steve Park	30.00	80.00
Pennzoil Yellow Roof/2508		
2 Rusty Wallace	30.00	80.00
Adventures of Rusty/5004		
2 Rusty Wallace	30.00	80.00
Miller Lite/5004		
2 Rusty Wallace	25.00	60.00
Miller Lite Elvis/5004		
2 Rusty Wallace	30.00	80.00
Miller Lite TCB Elvis		
3 Dale Earnhardt	60.00	120.00
Coke/4008		
3 Dale Earnhardt	60.00	120.00
Goodwrench Plus Bass Pro/8010		
3 Dale Earnhardt	60.00	120.00
Goodwrench Plus		
Daytona Win/5004		
3 Dale Earnhardt	150.00	250.00
Goodwrench Plus Brickyard Win		
5 Terry Labonte	30.00	80.00
Blasted Fruit Loops		
5 Terry Labonte	30.00	80.00
Kellogg's Corny/3120		
5 Terry Labonte	30.00	60.00
Kellogg's Ironman		
9 Lake Speed	40.00	80.00
Birthday Cake		
9 Lake Speed	40.00	80.00
Huckleberry Hound/3624		
18 Bobby Labonte	30.00	80.00
Interstate Batteries Hot Rod/3120		
18 Bobby Labonte	30.00	80.00
Interstate Batteries Small Soldiers		
23 Jimmy Spencer	50.00	100.00
No Bull		
24 Jeff Gordon	40.00	100.00
DuPont/5004		
24 Jeff Gordon	50.00	100.00
DuPont Brickyard Win		
24 Jeff Gordon	60.00	120.00
DuPont Chromalusion/5004		
28 Kenny Irwin	30.00	80.00
Havoline/3120		
31 Dale Earnhardt Jr.	40.00	80.00
Sikkens Blue 1997 Monte Carlo		
31 Dale Earnhardt Jr.	60.00	150.00
Wrangler		
1997 Monte Carlo/3120		
31 Mike Skinner	25.00	60.00
Lowe's/3120		
35 Todd Bodine	40.00	80.00
Tabasco		
36 Ernie Irvan	40.00	80.00
M&M's/3120		
36 Ernie Irvan	30.00	80.00
Wildberry Skittles		
44 Tony Stewart	40.00	80.00
Shell/3120		
44 Tony Stewart	30.00	60.00
Shell Small Soldiers/3120		
46 Jeff Green	25.00	60.00
First Union Devil Rays/3120		
50 Ricky Craven	30.00	60.00
Budweiser		
50 No Driver Association	30.00	80.00
Bud Louie		
81 Kenny Wallace	25.00	60.00
{ Square D Lightning/3120		
88 Dale Jarrett	40.00	80.00
Batman/3120		
88 Dale Jarrett	30.00	80.00
Quality Care/3120		

1999 Revell Club 1:18

These 1:18 scale cars were produced in very small numbers and were only available through the club.

	EX	NM-MT
3 Dale Earnhardt	150.00	250.00
Goodwrench		
20 Tony Stewart	30.00	80.00
Home Depot Habitat/2508		
23 Jimmy Spencer	60.00	120.00
No Bull		
24 Jeff Gordon	40.00	100.00
DuPont/1008		
24 Jeff Gordon	50.00	120.00
DuPont Superman		
24 Jeff Gordon	40.00	100.00
Pepsi/1008		
31 Dale Earnhardt Jr.	100.00	175.00
Gargoyles 1997 Monte Carlo		
36 Ernie Irvan	30.00	80.00
M&M's Millennium		

1999 Revell Collection 1:18

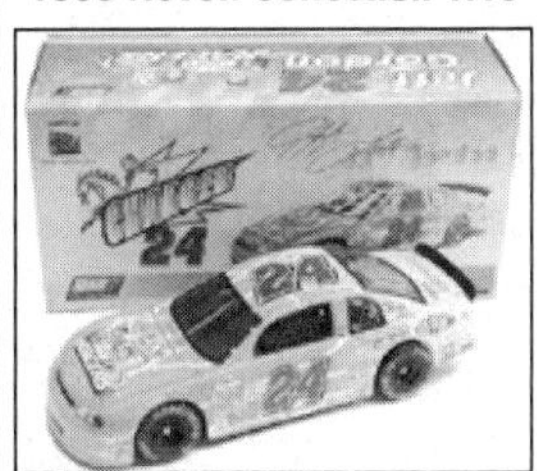

This series marks Revell's third year producing a 1:18 scale car. It was distributed to hobby dealers as part of Revell's Collection line.

	EX	NM-MT
2 Rusty Wallace	25.00	60.00
Miller Lite		
2 Rusty Wallace	30.00	80.00
Miller Lite Harley/2508		
3 Dale Earnhardt	100.00	200.00
Goodwrench		
3 Dale Earnhardt	50.00	120.00
Goodwrench		
25th Anniversary/2508		
3 Dale Earnhardt	50.00	120.00
Wrangler/6000		
3 Dale Earnhardt Jr.	40.00	100.00
AC Delco Superman/4800		
8 Dale Earnhardt Jr.	50.00	120.00
Bud/5004		
12 Jeremy Mayfield	30.00	80.00
Mobil 1 Kentucky Derby		
18 Bobby Labonte	30.00	80.00
Interstate Batteries/2508		
20 Tony Stewart	100.00	175.00
Home Depot		
23 Jimmy Spencer	25.00	60.00
No Bull/2508		
23 Jimmy Spencer	25.00	60.00
Winston Lights/2508		
24 Jeff Gordon	40.00	100.00
DuPont/2508		
24 Jeff Gordon	40.00	100.00
DuPont NASCAR Racers/2508		
24 Jeff Gordon	30.00	80.00
DuPont Superman/7500		
24 Jeff Gordon	40.00	100.00
Pepsi		
24 Jeff Gordon	40.00	100.00
Pepsi Star Wars		
28 Kenny Irwin	25.00	60.00
Havoline/2508		
31 Dale Earnhardt Jr.	40.00	80.00
Gargoyles 1997 Monte Carlo/2508		
31 Dale Earnhardt Jr.	40.00	80.00
Sikkens White		
1997 Monte Carlo/2508		
36 Ernie Irvan	25.00	60.00
M&M's TBS/2508		
40 Coca-Cola 600	30.00	60.00
40 Sterling Marlin	30.00	80.00
Coors Light Brooks & Dunn		
40 Sterling Marlin	30.00	80.00
Coors Light John Wayne/2508		

2000 Revell Club 1:18

	EX	NM-MT
3 Dale Earnhardt	75.00	150.00
Goodwrench Taz No Bull/2508		
8 Dale Earnhardt Jr.	40.00	100.00
Bud/2508		
20 Tony Stewart	30.00	80.00
Home Depot/2508		
20 Tony Stewart	30.00	80.00
Home Depot ROY/2508		
24 Jeff Gordon	30.00	80.00
DuPont Millennium/2508		

2000 Revell Collection 1:18

	EX	NM-MT
3 Dale Earnhardt	175.00	300.00
Goodwrench Peter Max/2508		
3 Dale Earnhardt	75.00	150.00
Goodwrench Taz No Bull/2508		
8 Dale Earnhardt Jr.	90.00	150.00
Bud		
18 Bobby Labonte	75.00	125.00
Interstate Batteries		
20 Tony Stewart	90.00	150.00
Home Depot/2508		
20 Tony Stewart	75.00	150.00
Home Depot Rookie of the Year		
24 Jeff Gordon	40.00	100.00
DuPont Peanuts		
94 Bill Elliott	30.00	80.00
McDonald's Drive Thru/2508		

2001 Revell Collection 1:18

	EX	NM-MT
3 Dale Earnhardt	150.00	250.00
Goodwrench with Sonic decal		

1991-95 Revell 1:24

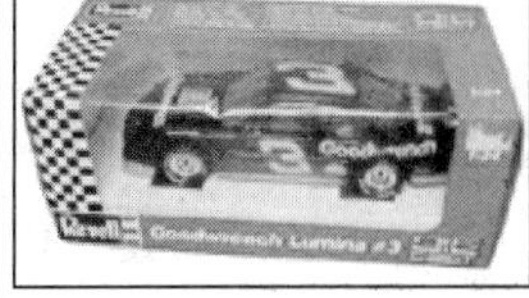

This set features many NASCAR's top drivers. Many of the pieces were issued through retail outlets but some were distributed through each driver's souvenir trailer.

	EX	NM-MT
1 Jeff Gordon	250.00	500.00
Baby Ruth produced for RCI		
3 Dale Earnhardt	100.00	175.00
Goodwrench Kellogg's Promo		
3 Dale Earnhardt	100.00	200.00
Goodwrench Black Wheels		
Sports Image 1993		
3 Dale Earnhardt	75.00	125.00
Goodwrench Silver Wheels		
Sports Image 1991		
3 Dale Earnhardt	60.00	120.00
Goodwrench Sports Image 1995		
3 Dale Earnhardt	100.00	250.00
Goodwrench 6-Time Champion		
4 Rick Wilson	15.00	30.00
Kodak produced for GMP		
6 Mark Martin	20.00	40.00
Valvoline		
7 Harry Gant	35.00	60.00
Mac Tools Morema/5000 1993		
7 Harry Gant	25.00	40.00
Morema		
7 No Driver Association	10.00	20.00
Mac Tools RCCA/7500 1992		
8 Dick Trickle	20.00	40.00
Snickers		
8 1/2 No Driver Association	8.00	20.00
Racing For Kids		
10 Derrike Cope	8.00	20.00
Purolator Flag 1991		
15 Geoff Bodine	15.00	35.00
Ford Motorsports		
17 Darrell Waltrip	20.00	40.00
Western Auto		
18 Dale Jarrett	35.00	60.00
Interstate Batteries		
21 Morgan Shepherd	15.00	30.00
Cheerwine		
21 Morgan Shepherd	12.00	20.00
Citgo		
22 Sterling Marlin	15.00	40.00
Maxwell House		
26 Brett Bodine	8.00	20.00
Quaker State		
28 Davey Allison	50.00	100.00
Havoline 1992		

	EX	NM-MT
28 Davey Allison Mac Tools	60.00	120.00
28 Ernie Irvan Mac Tools	50.00	100.00
28 Ernie Irvan Mac Tools Promo	12.50	25.00
30 Michael Waltrip Pennzoil 1991	15.00	30.00
32 Dale Jarrett Mac Tools	40.00	80.00
33 Harry Gant Farewell Tour	25.00	50.00
42 Kyle Petty Mello Yello	20.00	40.00
52 Ken Schrader Morema/5000 1993	20.00	30.00
57 No Driver Association Heinz 57	15.00	30.00
59 Robert Pressley Alliance produced RCI	30.00	55.00
60 Mark Martin Winn Dixie produced for GMP 1995	30.00	60.00
66 No Driver Association Phillips 66 TropArtic	10.00	20.00
66 Dick Trickle Phillips 66 TropArtic	25.00	50.00
68 Bobby Hamilton Country Time	25.00	50.00
75 Joe Ruttman Dinner Bell	10.00	20.00
83 Lake Speed Purex produced for GMP 1994	15.00	30.00
90 Bobby Hillin Jr. Heilig-Meyers	15.00	30.00
94 Binney&Smith Crayola Promo 1994	15.00	30.00
94 Terry Labonte Sunoco 1992	75.00	125.00

1994 Revell Hobby 1:24

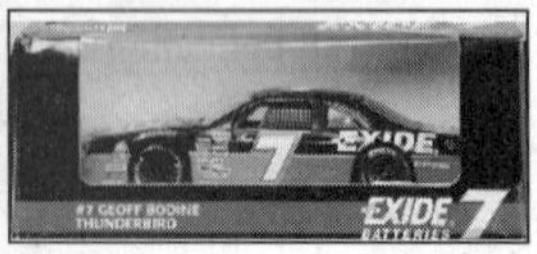

These pieces were distributed through hobby outlets. Each piece came in a black or yellow clear window box with a few additional colors that matched the driver's car. No piece was numbered and there were no announced production runs.

	EX	NM-MT
4 Sterling Marlin Kodak	20.00	50.00
5 Terry Labonte Kellogg's	40.00	80.00
7 Geoff Bodine Exide	12.50	30.00
15 Lake Speed Quality Care	15.00	30.00
24 Jeff Gordon DuPont	50.00	100.00
31 Ward Burton Hardee's	40.00	80.00
41 Joe Nemechek Meineke	20.00	40.00
43 Wally Dallenbach Jr. STP	20.00	40.00

1995 Revell Retail 1:24

These die-cast pieces were part of the continued growth of Revell's presence in the NASCAR market. The 1995 pieces were updated with driver and sponsor changes. The boxes were black with a stripe of color to match the predominant color on the car.

	EX	NM-MT
4 Sterling Marlin Kodak	10.00	25.00
6 Mark Martin Valvoline	20.00	40.00
7 Geoff Bodine Exide Promo	10.00	20.00
15 Dick Trickle Ford Quality Care	15.00	30.00
16 Ted Musgrave Family Channel	8.00	20.00
18 Bobby Labonte Interstate Batteries	40.00	80.00
21 Morgan Shepherd Citgo	10.00	20.00
23 Chad Little Bayer	10.00	25.00
24 Jeff Gordon DuPont	40.00	80.00
24 Jeff Gordon DuPont Coke deck lid	15.00	30.00
24 Jeff Gordon DuPont Dealer Promo Coke logo on deck lid issued in plain white box	30.00	60.00
24 Jeff Gordon DuPont Dealer Promo DuPont logo on deck lid issued in plain white box	30.00	60.00
25 Ken Schrader Budweiser	12.00	20.00
26 Steve Kinser Quaker State	10.00	20.00
31 Ward Burton Hardee's Promo/5000	30.00	60.00
32 Dale Jarrett Mac Tools Promo/5000	40.00	80.00
44 David Green Slim Jim	8.00	20.00
71 Kevin Lepage Vermont Teddy Bear	20.00	40.00
71 Dave Marcis Olive Garden Promo/5000	40.00	75.00
75 Todd Bodine Factory Stores of America	10.00	20.00
87 Joe Nemechek Burger King	20.00	40.00
95 DANA Perfect Circle Promo/5000	12.50	25.00

1996 Revell Retail 1:24

This series was distributed in retail outlets. These cars were packaged in colored boxes that matched the color schemes of the cars.

	EX	NM-MT
2 Rusty Wallace Miller Silver	12.50	25.00
2 Rusty Wallace Penske Motorsports	12.00	20.00
3 Dale Earnhardt Goodwrench	40.00	100.00
3 Dale Earnhardt Olympic car	30.00	80.00
4 Sterling Marlin Kodak	12.00	20.00
5 Terry Labonte Kellogg's	15.00	40.00
6 Mark Martin Valvoline	20.00	50.00
7 Geoff Bodine QVC in solid box	12.00	30.00
10 Ricky Rudd Tide	15.00	30.00
11 Brett Bodine Lowe's	8.00	20.00
16 Ron Hornaday Smith Wesson	25.00	50.00
16 Ted Musgrave Family Channel Primestar	8.00	20.00
17 Darrell Waltrip Parts America	15.00	30.00
18 Bobby Labonte Interstate Batteries	20.00	50.00
21 Michael Waltrip Citgo	10.00	20.00
24 Jeff Gordon DuPont	25.00	60.00
28 Ernie Irvan Havoline	20.00	40.00
37 John Andretti K-Mart Little Caesars	10.00	20.00
75 Morgan Shepherd Remington	10.00	20.00
75 Morgan Shepherd Remington Camouflage	12.50	25.00
75 Morgan Shepherd Stren	10.00	22.00
77 Bobby Hillin Jr. Jasper Engines	15.00	25.00
87 Joe Nemechek Burger King	20.00	50.00
88 Dale Jarrett Quality Care	20.00	40.00
96 Lawson Products Promo	18.00	30.00
99 Jeff Burton Exide	20.00	40.00

1996 Revell Collection 1:24

This series was produced for and distributed in hobby outlets. These cars have significant upgrades in comparison to the standard Revell Retail 1:24 pieces. Each car is packaged mounted to a black plastic base. The Terry Labonte Honey Crunch car saw a large portion of the production run sold to the general public before they were distributed to hobby distributors.

	EX	NM-MT
2 Rusty Wallace Miller Genuine Draft Silver 25th Anniversary	25.00	45.00
2 Rusty Wallace Penske	20.00	35.00
3 Dale Earnhardt Olympic	40.00	100.00
4 Sterling Marlin Kodak	20.00	40.00
5 Terry Labonte Honey Crunch/5004	150.00	300.00
5 Terry Labonte Honey Crunch Promo Sports Impressions	125.00	200.00
5 Terry Labonte Kellogg's/4020	25.00	60.00
5 Terry Labonte Kellogg's Iron Man Silver/10,008	30.00	80.00
6 Mark Martin Valvoline	20.00	35.00
8 Kenny Wallace Red Dog	25.00	50.00
10 Ricky Rudd Tide	25.00	40.00
11 Brett Bodine Lowe's 50th Anniversary	12.00	30.00
16 Ted Musgrave Family Channel Primestar	20.00	35.00
17 Darrell Waltrip Parts America	20.00	35.00
18 Bobby Labonte Interstate Batteries/2700	20.00	35.00
22 Rusty Wallace Miller Genuine Draft Suzuka Thunder SuperTruck/3120	40.00	60.00
22 Rusty Wallace Miller Genuine Draft Silver 25th Anniversary SuperTruck/2504	100.00	200.00
22 Rusty Wallace Miller Splash SuperTruck/2508	125.00	200.00
23 Chad Little John Deere	30.00	60.00
23 Chad Little John Deere Autographed signed box	40.00	80.00
23 Chad Little John Deere Bank set w/1:64 car	25.00	60.00
23 Chad Little John Deere Bank set with 1:64 car/2508 Autographed box	40.00	80.00
24 Jeff Gordon DuPont/8292	30.00	50.00
24 Jack Sprague Quaker State	20.00	35.00
25 Ken Schrader Bud/5004	20.00	35.00
25 Ken Schrader Budweiser Olympic car	20.00	35.00
28 Ernie Irvan Havoline	20.00	35.00
30 Johnny Benson Pennzoil/7008	15.00	35.00
37 Jeremy Mayfield K-Mart Little Caesars/5004	20.00	35.00
52 Jack Sprague Pedigree	20.00	35.00
75 Morgan Shepherd Remington	20.00	35.00
75 Morgan Shepherd Remington Camo/5004	30.00	50.00
75 Morgan Shepherd Stren/3120	20.00	35.00
76 David Green Smith and Wesson	15.00	35.00
77 Bobby Hillin Jr. Jasper Engines/3120	20.00	35.00
87 Joe Nemechek Burger King/3120	20.00	40.00
88 Dale Jarrett Quality Care/5004	30.00	50.00
96 Revell Collection SuperTruck Promo	15.00	30.00
99 Jeff Burton Exide	20.00	35.00

1997 Revell Club 1:24

These pieces were also a part of the continued growth of Revell's presence in the die cast market. In the last quarter of 1997, Revell formed a collector's club to which they distributed cars in this series. The actual cars themselves were from the same production run as the Collection cars and banks. Each car distributed by the club has a serial number on the chassis. The boxes were uniquely colored to match the colors on the car and feature the name "Revell Collection Club." Each piece is housed inside a clear plastic or acrylic box.

	EX	NM-MT
1 Coca-Cola 600/1596	30.00	60.00
1 Revell Club/10,002	15.00	40.00
2 Rusty Wallace Miller Lite	40.00	80.00
4 Sterling Marlin Kodak/1596	20.00	50.00
5 Terry Labonte Kellogg's/1596	30.00	80.00
5 Terry Labonte Kellogg's Tony/1596	50.00	100.00
5 Terry Labonte Kellogg's Tony Bank set w/1:64 car	60.00	150.00
5 Terry Labonte Spooky Loops	125.00	200.00
5 Terry Labonte Spooky Loops Bank	100.00	200.00
6 Mark Martin Valvoline/1596	40.00	100.00
10 Ricky Rudd Tide/1596	25.00	60.00
18 Bobby Labonte Interstate Batteries/1596	20.00	50.00
18 Bobby Labonte Interstate Batteries Texas/1596	50.00	100.00
21 Michael Waltrip Citgo Pearson white&red/1596	20.00	50.00
21 Michael Waltrip Citgo Top Dog/1596	25.00	60.00
23 Jimmy Spencer Camel/1596	60.00	150.00
23 Jimmy Spencer Winston/2300	150.00	300.00
25 Ricky Craven Budweiser/1596	25.00	60.00
28 Ernie Irvan Havoline black	70.00	120.00
28 Ernie Irvan Havoline 10th Anniversary white and black	90.00	150.00
28 Ernie Irvan Havoline 10th Anniversary white and black Bank set w/1:64 car	60.00	150.00
33 Ken Schrader Skoal/1596	25.00	60.00
35 Todd Bodine Tabasco/1596	20.00	50.00
36 Derrike Cope Skittles/1596	20.00	50.00
37 Jeremy Mayfield K-Mart RC-Cola/1596	40.00	80.00
40 Robby Gordon Coors Light/1596	30.00	60.00
41 Steve Grissom Kodiak/1596	20.00	50.00
43 Bobby Hamilton STP Goody's/1596	25.00	60.00
43 Jimmy Hensley Cummins SuperTruck/1596	20.00	50.00
46 Wally Dallenbach Woody Woodpecker	25.00	60.00
75 Rick Mast Remington	40.00	80.00
94 Bill Elliott McDonald's/1596	25.00	60.00
96 David Green Caterpillar/1596	20.00	50.00
97 California 500/1596	15.00	40.00
97 Chad Little John Deere/1596	40.00	100.00
97 Chad Little John Deere 160th Anniversary/1596	50.00	100.00
97 Texas Motor Speedway/1596	20.00	50.00

1997 Revell Collection 1:24

This series is the continuation of the 1996 Revell Collection. It signals Revell's continued expansion into the die cast market by its larger number of cars and banks. Each is packaged in a clear acrylic Revell Collection box which is wrapped inside a colorful outer cardboard box.

	EX	NM-MT
1 Coca-Cola 600	12.00	30.00
2 Rusty Wallace Miller Japan/5496	25.00	60.00
2 Rusty Wallace Miller Lite/25,000	20.00	50.00
2 Rusty Wallace Miller Lite Texas	30.00	60.00
4 Sterling Marlin Kodak/3120	25.00	60.00
5 Terry Labonte Kellogg's/5004	25.00	60.00
5 Terry Labonte Kellogg's distributed by Mac Tools	50.00	80.00
5 Terry Labonte Kellogg's 1996 Champion/5004	50.00	90.00
5 Terry Labonte Kellogg's Texas Motor Speedway	70.00	120.00
5 Terry Labonte Spooky Loops	30.00	80.00
5 Terry Labonte Spooky Loops Bank set with 1:64 car/1506	25.00	60.00
5 Terry Labonte Kellogg's Tony/6600	50.00	100.00
5 Terry Labonte Kellogg's Tony Bank set w/1:64 car/1506	40.00	100.00
6 Mark Martin Valvoline	35.00	50.00
7 Geoff Bodine QVC/5004	15.00	40.00
8 Hut Stricklin Circuit City	15.00	40.00
10 Ricky Rudd Tide/3120	25.00	45.00
11 Brett Bodine Close Call/3120	12.00	30.00
15 Mike Colabucci VISA SuperTruck	25.00	45.00
16 Ted Musgrave Primestar	15.00	40.00
17 Rich Bickle Die Hard SuperTruck/3120	15.00	40.00
17 Darrell Waltrip Parts America	30.00	45.00
18 Bobby Labonte Interstate Batteries/5004	30.00	50.00
18 Bobby Labonte Interstate Batteries Texas/8598	60.00	100.00
18 Bobby Labonte Interstate Batteries Texas Motor Speedway Bank	90.00	150.00
19 Tony Raines Pennzoil SuperTruck/3120	25.00	45.00
21 Michael Waltrip Citgo Orange/4122	15.00	40.00
21 Michael Waltrip Citgo Pearson white&red	20.00	40.00
21 Michael Waltrip Citgo Top Dog/5004	15.00	40.00
23 Jimmy Spencer Camel/5004	50.00	100.00
23 Jimmy Spencer Winston/3323	100.00	200.00
25 Ricky Craven Budweiser	20.00	50.00
25 Ricky Craven Budweiser Lizard	20.00	50.00
28 Ernie Irvan Havoline black	20.00	50.00
28 Ernie Irvan Havoline Bank black	50.00	80.00
28 Ernie Irvan Havoline 10th Anniversary white and black/5004	25.00	60.00
28 Ernie Irvan Havoline 10th Anniversary white and black Bank set w/1:64 car	20.00	50.00
29 Jeff Green Scooby-Doo	25.00	40.00
29 Jeff Green Scooby-Doo Bank	50.00	80.00
29 Steve Grissom Flintstones	15.00	40.00
29 Robert Pressley Scooby-Doo	25.00	50.00
29 Robert Pressley Tom & Jerry	25.00	40.00
30 Johnny Benson Pennzoil/6630	25.00	45.00
32 Dale Jarrett White Rain	25.00	40.00
33 Ken Schrader Skoal/5004	20.00	50.00
35 Todd Bodine Tabasco/5004	20.00	40.00
35 Todd Bodine Tabasco Bank set w/1:64 car/1002	15.00	40.00
36 Todd Bodine Stanley/3120	15.00	40.00
36 Derrike Cope Skittles/6636	15.00	40.00
37 David Green Jeff Green Red Man SuperTruck	15.00	40
37 Mark Green Timber Wolf/3120	15.00	40
37 Jeremy Mayfield K-Mart Kids/5004	15.00	40
37 Jeremy Mayfield K-Mart Lady Luck	25.00	45
37 Jeremy Mayfield K-Mart RC-Cola	15.00	40
40 Robby Gordon Coors Light/5004	25.00	40
41 Steve Grissom Kodiak/5004	15.00	40
42 Joe Nemechek BellSouth	15.00	40
43 Bobby Hamilton STP Goody's/5004	15.00	40
43 Jimmy Hensley Cummins SuperTruck	15.00	40
46 Wally Dallenbach First Union Bank	35.00	70
46 Wally Dallenbach Woody Woodpecker/5004	20.00	40
46 Wally Dallenbach Woody Woodpecker Bank	50.00	80
55 Michael Waltrip Sealy	15.00	40
60 Mark Martin Winn Dixie	35.00	50
75 Rick Mast Remington/4716	15.00	40
88 Dale Jarrett Quality Care	15.00	40
90 Dick Trickle Heilig-Meyers/3120	15.00	40
91 Mike Wallace Spam/6600	15.00	40
91 Mike Wallace Spam Bank	25.00	60
94 Ron Barfield New Holland/3120	15.00	40
94 Bill Elliott McDonald's	20.00	40
94 Bill Elliott Mac Tonight	15.00	40
96 David Green Caterpillar/5004	15.00	40
97 California 500/25,000	12.50	30
97 California 500 Bank set w/1:64 car	12.50	30
97 Chad Little John Deere Autographed box	30.00	80
97 Chad Little John Deere Bank Autographed box	30.00	70
97 Chad Little John Deere 160th Anniversary/5004	35.00	70
97 Chad Little John Deere 160th Anniversary Bank autographed box	50.00	80
97 Texas Motor Speedway/6000	20.00	40
98 John Andretti RCA/3120	20.00	40
99 Chuck Bown Exide SuperTruck/3120	15.00	40
99 Jeff Burton Exide/2502	20.00	40
99 Jeff Burton Exide Texas	25.00	60

1997 Revell Select 1:24

These cars were produced to appease those collector wanted an upgraded production die cast without the up price. The cars themselves appear to have similar prod qualities as the Collection cars, but were priced much intially and were packaged in black window boxes. Althou box does not include the "Select" name, this series in boxes is considered the first of the new Select line by Reve

	EX	NM-
2 Rusty Wallace Miller Lite	25.00	40
4 Sterling Marlin Kodak	20.00	40
5 Terry Labonte Kellogg's	20.00	35
5 Terry Labonte Kellogg's Texas	20.00	35
5 Terry Labonte Spooky Loops	30.00	60
5 Terry Labonte Tony the Tiger	20.00	40
6 Mark Martin Valvoline	20.00	35
10 Ricky Rudd Tide	20.00	35
17 Darrell Waltrip Parts America	20.00	35
18 Bobby Labonte Interstate Batteries	15.00	30
18 Bobby Labonte Interstate Batteries Texas	40.00	70
21 Michael Waltrip Citgo Top Dog paint scheme	20.00	35
23 Jimmy Spencer Camel	25.00	50
23 Jimmy Spencer No Bull	15.00	40
25 Ricky Craven Budweiser Lizard	20.00	40
28 Ernie Irvan Havoline black	20.00	35
28 Ernie Irvan Havoline 10th Anniversary white and black	25.00	40
29 Jeff Green Tom & Jerry	15.00	30

eve Grissom	15.00	30.00
lintstones		
obert Pressley	15.00	30.00
Scooby-Doo		
obert Pressley	15.00	30.00
Tom & Jerry		
en Schrader	25.00	40.00
Skoal		
errike Cope	15.00	35.00
Skittles		
remy Mayfield	20.00	35.00
K-Mart Kids Against Drugs		
obby Gordon	20.00	35.00
Coors Light		
eve Grissom	15.00	30.00
Kodiak		
oe Nemechek	15.00	30.00
Bell South		
obby Hamilton	15.00	30.00
STP Goody's		
ally Dallenbach	30.00	50.00
First Union Bank		
ally Dallenbach	15.00	30.00
Woody Woodpecker		
ick Mast	20.00	35.00
Remington		
Mike Wallace	15.00	30.00
Spam		
ll Elliott	20.00	35.00
McDonald's		
ll Elliott	20.00	35.00
Mac Tonight		
had Little	30.00	35.00
John Deere		
60th Anniversary paint scheme		
exas Motor Speedway	15.00	30.00
hn Andretti	15.00	30.00
RCA		
ff Burton	20.00	35.00
Exide		

1997 Revell Retail 1:24

series, Revell Racing, was produced for and distributed to ass-market. Each piece was packaged in a colorful clear w box with the sponsor logos and designs on the box. No ction run numbers were given for the retail version.

	EX	NM-MT
ca-Cola 600	10.00	20.00
c Tools	45.00	75.00
packaged in collectible tin		
sty Wallace	12.50	25.00
Penske		
erling Marlin	15.00	40.00
Kodak		
ry Labonte	12.50	25.00
Kellogg's Texas Motor Speedway		
ry Labonte	12.50	30.00
Spooky Loops		
ry Labonte	15.00	30.00
Tony The Tiger		
packaged in Food City box		
rk Martin	12.50	25.00
Valvoline		
icky Rudd	15.00	30.00
Tide		
ed Musgrave	15.00	30.00
Primestar		
arrell Waltrip	10.00	20.00
Parts America blue&white		
arrell Waltrip	15.00	30.00
Parts America Chrome Box		
arrell Waltrip	10.00	20.00
Parts America Green		
with green number		
arrell Waltrip	10.00	20.00
Parts America Green		
with white number		
arrell Waltrip	10.00	20.00
Parts America Red&White		
arrell Waltrip	10.00	20.00
Parts America Yellow&White		
Michael Waltrip	12.50	25.00
Citgo Top Dog paint scheme		
ichael Waltrip	10.00	25.00
Citgo Pearson white&red		
mmy Spencer	25.00	40.00
Camel		
nie Irvan	12.50	25.00
Havoline Black		
nie Irvan	12.50	25.00
Havoline 10th Anniversary		
white and black		
ff Green	10.00	20.00
Tom & Jerry on hood		
obert Pressley	10.00	20.00
Scooby-Doo		
obert Pressley	10.00	20.00
Flintstones		
remy Mayfield	12.50	25.00
K-Mart RC-Cola		
remy Mayfield	10.00	25.00
K-Mart Kids Against Drugs		
ally Dallenbach	10.00	20.00
Woody Woodpecker		
ck Mast	10.00	20.00
Remington		
ale Jarrett	12.50	25.00
Quality Care		
Mike Wallace	10.00	25.00
Spam		
alifornia 500	10.00	20.00
exas Motor Speedway	10.00	20.00
ff Burton	12.50	25.00
Exide		

1998 Revell Club 1:24

1:24 scale cars were from the same production run as the ction cars. Each car distributed by the club has a serial number on the chassis. The boxes were uniquely colored to match the colors on the car.

1 Dale Earnhardt Jr.	40.00	100.00
Coke Bear/3330		
1 Steve Park	40.00	100.00
Pennzoil Black Roof/1002		
1 Steve Park	40.00	100.00
Pennzoil Yellow Roof		
2 Rusty Wallace	50.00	120.00
Miller Lite/1002		
2 Rusty Wallace	60.00	150.00
Adventures of Rusty/1002		
2 Rusty Wallace	50.00	120.00
Miller Lite Elvis1596		
3 Dale Earnhardt	60.00	150.00
Coke/3333		
3 Dale Earnhardt	75.00	150.00
Goodwrench Plus/1596		
3 Dale Earnhardt	60.00	120.00
Goodwrench Plus Bass Pro/1002		
3 Dale Earnhardt	75.00	150.00
Goodwrench Plus		
Daytona Win/1596		
3 Dale Earnhardt Jr.	75.00	150.00
AC Delco		
4 Bobby Hamilton	20.00	50.00
Kodak Max/1596		
4 Bobby Hamilton	20.00	50.00
Kodak Gold/1596		
5 Terry Labonte	40.00	100.00
Blasted Fruit Loops/2004		
5 Terry Labonte	30.00	80.00
Kellogg's/1596		
5 Terry Labonte	40.00	100.00
Kellogg's Corny		
5 Terry Labonte	50.00	120.00
Kellogg's Ironman/2004		
12 Jeremy Mayfield	30.00	80.00
Mobil 1		
18 Bobby Labonte	40.00	100.00
Interstate Batteries Hot Rod		
18 Bobby Labonte	30.00	80.00
Interstate Batteries		
Small Soldiers/2004		
21 Michael Waltrip	25.00	60.00
Citgo/1002		
23 Jimmy Spencer	125.00	200.00
No Bull		
24 Jeff Gordon	40.00	100.00
DuPont/1596		
24 Jeff Gordon	60.00	120.00
DuPont Chromalusion/2424		
25 John Andretti	30.00	80.00
Bud/1002		
28 Kenny Irwin	40.00	100.00
Havoline		
28 Kenny Irwin	40.00	100.00
Havoline Joker/1002		
31 Mike Skinner	30.00	80.00
Lowe's		
31 Mike Skinner	30.00	80.00
Lowe's Special Olympics		
33 Ken Schrader	40.00	100.00
Skoal		
33 Ken Schrader	40.00	100.00
Skoal Bud Shootout		
35 Todd Bodine	25.00	60.00
Tabasco		
36 Ernie Irvan	30.00	80.00
M&M's/1002		
36 Ernie Irvan	40.00	100.00
Wildberry Skittles		
40 Sterling Marlin	40.00	100.00
Coors Light/804		
41 Steve Grissom	20.00	50.00
Kodiak/1002		
42 Joe Nemechek	20.00	50.00
BellSouth		
44 Tony Stewart	75.00	150.00
Shell/1002		
44 Tony Stewart	70.00	120.00
Shell Small Soldiers		
46 Wally Dallenbach	25.00	60.00
First Union		
46 Jeff Green	25.00	60.00
First Union Devil Rays		
50 Ricky Craven	50.00	120.00
Budweiser		
50 No Driver Association	40.00	100.00
Bud Louie		
74 Randy LaJoie	25.00	60.00
Fina		
75 Rick Mast	20.00	50.00
Remington		
81 Kenny Wallace	20.00	50.00
Square D Lightning		
88 Dale Jarrett	40.00	100.00
Batman		
88 Dale Jarrett	40.00	100.00
Quality Care		
90 Dick Trickle	25.00	60.00
Heilig-Meyers		
96 David Green	20.00	50.00
Caterpillar/1002		
98 Greg Sacks	20.00	50.00
Thorn Apple Valley		

1998 Revell Collection 1:24

This series was produced for and distributed in hobby outlets.

	EX	NM-MT
1 Dale Earnhardt Jr.	50.00	100.00
Coke Bear Bank		
1 Dale Earnhardt Jr.	35.00	75.00
Coke Bear/18,000		
1 Steve Park	25.00	60.00
Pennzoil Black Roof/5598		
1 Steve Park	25.00	60.00
Pennzoil Yellow Roof/5598		
2 Rusty Wallace	25.00	60.00
Adventures of Rusty		
2 Rusty Wallace	20.00	50.00
Miller Lite/5598		
2 Rusty Wallace	25.00	60.00
Miller Lite Elvis		
2 Rusty Wallace	25.00	60.00
Miller Lite TCB Elvis		
2 Rusty Wallace	50.00	100.00
Miller Lite TCB Elvis		
Bank/1002		
3 Dale Earnhardt	40.00	80.00
Coke/18,000		
3 Dale Earnhardt	60.00	120.00
Coke Bank set		
with 1:64 car/2502		
3 Dale Earnhardt	40.00	100.00
Goodwrench Plus		
Daytona Win/7512		
3 Dale Earnhardt	40.00	100.00
Goodwrench Plus		
Bass Pro/14,994		
3 Dale Earnhardt	50.00	100.00
Goodwrench Plus		
Brickyard Win/10,008		
3 Dale Earnhardt Jr.	75.00	125.00
AC Delco Dealer Issued/3500		
3 Dale Earnhardt Jr.	75.00	125.00
AC Delco Trackside Issued		
4 Bobby Hamilton	25.00	40.00
Kodak Gold		
5 Terry Labonte	25.00	60.00
Blasted Fruit Loops/5598		
5 Terry Labonte	20.00	50.00
Kellogg's/5598		
5 Terry Labonte	30.00	80.00
Kellogg's Bank set		
with 1:64 car/1002		
5 Terry Labonte	30.00	80.00
Kellogg's Corny/5598		
5 Terry Labonte	30.00	80.00
Kellogg's Corny Bank set		
with 1:64 car/1002		
5 Terry Labonte	20.00	50.00
Kellogg's Ironman		
5 Terry Labonte	25.00	60.00
Kellogg's Ironman		
Bank set with 1:64 car		
8 Hut Stricklin	15.00	40.00
Circuit City/3120		
9 Lake Speed	20.00	40.00
Birthday Cake		
9 Lake Speed	20.00	40.00
Huckleberry Hound		
9 Lake Speed	40.00	80.00
Huckleberry Hound Bank		
12 Jeremy Mayfield	15.00	40.00
Mobil 1/5598		
18 Bobby Labonte	20.00	50.00
Interstate Batteries/5598		
18 Bobby Labonte	20.00	50.00
Interstate Batteries Hot Rod/5598		
18 Bobby Labonte	25.00	60.00
Interstate Batteries		
Small Soldiers/5598		
21 Michael Waltrip	15.00	40.00
Citgo		
23 Jimmy Spencer	20.00	40.00
No Bull/5598		
24 Jeff Gordon	30.00	70.00
DuPont/6000		
24 Jeff Gordon	25.00	60.00
DuPont Brickyard Win/10,008		
24 Jeff Gordon	40.00	100.00
DuPont Chromalusion/14,400		
25 John Andretti	20.00	40.00
Bud/3120		
28 Kenny Irwin	20.00	50.00
Havoline/5598		
28 Kenny Irwin	25.00	60.00
Havoline Joker/6000		
31 Dale Earnhardt Jr.	75.00	150.00
Wrangler		
1997 Monte Carlo/5004		
31 Dale Earnhardt Jr.	75.00	150.00
Wrangler Bank		
1997 Monte Carlo/2504		
31 Mike Skinner	20.00	40.00
Lowe's/5598		
31 Mike Skinner	20.00	50.00
Lowe's Special Olympics		
33 Ken Schrader	25.00	50.00
Skoal/6600		
33 Ken Schrader	15.00	40.00
Skoal Bud Shootout/5598		
35 Todd Bodine	20.00	40.00
Tabasco		
36 Ernie Irvan	20.00	50.00
M&M's/5598		
36 Ernie Irvan	15.00	40.00
Wildberry Skittles/5598		
40 Sterling Marlin	20.00	50.00
Coors Light/3120		
41 Steve Grissom	20.00	40.00
Kodiak/5598		
42 Joe Nemechek	15.00	40.00
BellSouth/3120		
44 Tony Stewart	35.00	70.00
Shell		
44 Tony Stewart	25.00	50.00
Shell Small Soldiers		
46 Wally Dallenbach	15.00	40.00
First Union/3120		
46 Jeff Green	15.00	40.00
First Union Devil Rays/5598		
50 Ricky Craven	30.00	60.00
Bud/6600		
50 No Driver Association	25.00	50.00
Bud Louie/6000		
74 Randy LaJoie	15.00	40.00
Fina/3120		
75 Rick Mast	15.00	40.00
Remington/3120		
81 Kenny Wallace	20.00	50.00
Square D Lightning		
88 Dale Jarrett	40.00	80.00
Batman/6000		
88 Dale Jarrett	40.00	100.00
Batman Bank		
88 Dale Jarrett	30.00	60.00
Quality Care		
90 Dick Trickle	15.00	40.00
Heilig-Meyers/3120		
96 David Green	15.00	40.00
Caterpillar/5598		
98 Greg Sacks	15.00	40.00
Thorn Apple Valley/3120		

1998 Revell Select 1:24

The Revell Select series returned in 1998 with an upgraded production die-cast car without the upgrade price. The cars themselves appear to have similar production qualities as the Collection cars and some are mounted to a Revell Collection base. However, were issued at a lower initial price point and are packaged in Revell Select window boxes in the color of the sponsor's paint scheme.

	EX	NM-MT
1 Steve Park	25.00	45.00
Pennzoil Black Roof		
2 Rusty Wallace	20.00	35.00
Adventures of Rusty		
2 Rusty Wallace	20.00	35.00
Miller Lite		
2 Rusty Wallace	20.00	35.00
Miller Lite Elvis		
3 Dale Earnhardt	40.00	80.00
Goodwrench Plus		
3 Dale Earnhardt	40.00	80.00
Goodwrench Plus Bass Pro		
3 Dale Earnhardt Jr.	20.00	50.00
AC Delco		
4 Bobby Hamilton	15.00	30.00
Kodak		
5 Terry Labonte	15.00	30.00
Blasted Fruit Loops		
5 Terry Labonte	15.00	30.00
Kellogg's		
5 Terry Labonte	15.00	30.00
Kellogg's Corny		
8 Hut Stricklin	12.50	30.00
Circuit City		
9 Lake Speed	15.00	30.00
Birthday Cake		
9 Lake Speed	15.00	30.00
Huckleberry Hound		
18 Bobby Labonte	15.00	30.00
Interstate Batteries		
18 Bobby Labonte	15.00	30.00
Interstate Batteries Hot Rod		
21 Michael Waltrip	15.00	30.00
Citgo		
23 Jimmy Spencer	12.50	30.00
No Bull		
24 Jeff Gordon	25.00	40.00
DuPont		
28 Kenny Irwin	15.00	30.00
Havoline		
31 Mike Skinner	15.00	30.00
Lowe's		
33 Ken Schrader	15.00	30.00
Skoal Bud Shootout		
35 Todd Bodine	15.00	30.00
Tabasco		
36 Ernie Irvan	12.50	30.00
M&M's		
36 Ernie Irvan	12.50	30.00
Wildberry Skittles		
44 Tony Stewart	15.00	30.00
Shell		
50 Ricky Craven	15.00	30.00
Budweiser		
50 NDA	15.00	30.00
Bud Louie		
77 Robert Pressley	15.00	30.00
Jasper		
81 Kenny Wallace	15.00	30.00
Square D Lightning		
88 Dale Jarrett	20.00	35.00
Quality Care		

1999 Revell Club 1:24

These 1:24 scale cars were produced in very small numbers and were only available through the club.

	EX	NM-MT
2 Rusty Wallace	50.00	100.00
Miller Lite/504		
2 Rusty Wallace	30.00	80.00
Miller Lite Harley/1002		
3 Dale Earnhardt	50.00	120.00
Goodwrench/2004		
3 Dale Earnhardt	50.00	100.00
Goodwrench 25th/1002		
3 Dale Earnhardt	100.00	200.00
GM Goodwrench Sign		
3 Dale Earnhardt	60.00	150.00
Wrangler/3333		
3 Dale Earnhardt Jr.	40.00	100.00
AC Delco/2004		
3 Dale Earnhardt Jr.	60.00	150.00
AC Delco Superman/1500		
4 Bobby Hamilton	40.00	100.00
Advantix		
5 Terry Labonte	25.00	60.00
K-Sentials/1002		
5 Terry Labonte	40.00	100.00
Rice Krispy		
8 Dale Earnhardt Jr.	90.00	150.00
Bud/1002		
9 Jerry Nadeau	25.00	60.00
Dextor's Lab/1002		
9 Jerry Nadeau	30.00	80.00
Jetsons		
10 Ricky Rudd	40.00	100.00
Tide		
11 Dale Jarrett	75.00	150.00
Green Bay Packers/1002		
12 Jeremy Mayfield	25.00	60.00
Mobil 1		
12 Jeremy Mayfield	25.00	60.00
Kentucky Derby		
17 Matt Kenseth	40.00	80.00
DeWalt/3508		
18 Bobby Labonte	50.00	120.00
Interstate Batteries		
20 Tony Stewart	150.00	250.00
Home Depot/1002		
20 Tony Stewart	40.00	100.00
Home Depot Habitat for Humanity		
23 Jimmy Spencer	30.00	80.00
No Bull/1002		
23 Jimmy Spencer	30.00	80.00
Winston Lights/2004		
24 Jeff Gordon	30.00	80.00
DuPont/2424		
24 Jeff Gordon	90.00	150.00
DuPont Daytona		
24 Jeff Gordon	50.00	120.00
DuPont Superman/3500		
24 Jeff Gordon	40.00	100.00
Pepsi/2004		
24 Jeff Gordon	40.00	100.00
Pepsi Star Wars		
27 Casey Atwood	30.00	80.00
Castrol		
28 Kenny Irwin	50.00	100.00
Havoline		
31 Dale Earnhardt Jr.	50.00	100.00
Gargoyles 1997 Monte Carlo/2004		
31 Dale Earnhardt Jr.	50.00	100.00
Mom 'N' Pop's		
1996 Monte Carlo/2004		
31 Dale Earnhardt Jr.	60.00	100.00
Sikkens Blue		
1997 Monte Carlo/1002		
31 Dale Earnhardt Jr.	50.00	100.00
Sikkens White		
1997 Monte Carlo/2004		
33 Ken Schrader	60.00	150.00
Skoal Blue/1002		
36 Ernie Irvan	30.00	80.00
M&M's/1002		
36 Ernie Irvan	25.00	60.00
M&M's Countdown/1002		
36 Ernie Irvan	40.00	100.00
Crispy M&M's/1002		
36 Ernie Irvan	30.00	80.00
Pedigree/504		
40 Kerry Earnhardt	25.00	60.00
Channelock/1002		
40 Sterling Marlin	30.00	80.00
Coors Light Brooks & Dunn		
40 Sterling Marlin	30.00	80.00
Coors Light John Wayne		
55 Kenny Wallace	25.00	60.00
Square D		
66 Darrell Waltrip	25.00	60.00
Big K Route 66/1002		
88 Dale Jarrett	40.00	100.00
Quality Care		
88 Dale Jarrett	40.00	80.00
Quality Care White/1002		

1999 Revell Collection 1:24

This series was produced for and distributed in hobby outlets.

	EX	NM-MT
1 Steve Park	40.00	70.00
Pennzoil		
1 Steve Park	25.00	60.00
Pennzoil Shark/2508		
2 Rusty Wallace	20.00	50.00
Miller Lite/5004		
2 Rusty Wallace	30.00	60.00
Miller Lite Harley/5004		
2 Rusty Wallace	40.00	75.00
Miller Lite Harley		
Matco Tools promo		
3 Dale Earnhardt	60.00	150.00
Goodwrench/7992		
3 Dale Earnhardt	90.00	150.00
Goodwrench 25th		
3 Dale Earnhardt	50.00	120.00
Goodwrench Sign		
3 Dale Earnhardt	40.00	100.00
Wrangler/14,400		
3 Dale Earnhardt Jr.	25.00	60.00
AC Delco/10,530		
3 Dale Earnhardt Jr.	30.00	60.00
AC Delco Superman/10,530		
3 Dale Earnhardt Jr.	30.00	80.00
AC Del.Superman		
Bank set w/1:64 car/2004		
4 Bobby Hamilton	20.00	50.00
Advantix		
5 Terry Labonte	20.00	50.00
Kellogg's/4008		
5 Terry Labonte	20.00	50.00
K-Sentials/4008		
5 Terry Labonte	20.00	50.00
Rice Krispies/3120		
8 Dale Earnhardt Jr.	45.00	80.00
Bud/12,024		
8 Dale Earnhardt Jr.	50.00	100.00
Bud Bank		
set w/1:64 car/2508		
9 Jerry Nadeau	20.00	50.00
Dexter's Laboratory/3120		
9 Jerry Nadeau	20.00	50.00
Jetsons/4128		
9 Jerry Nadeau	40.00	100.00
Dexter's Lab Bank		
10 Ricky Rudd	20.00	50.00
Tide/3120		
10 Ricky Rudd	20.00	50.00
Tide Kids Bank set		
w/1:64 car/3504		
11 Dale Jarrett	25.00	60.00
Rayovac/2508		
11 Dale Jarrett	40.00	70.00
Green Bay Packers		

	EX	NM-MT
12 Jeremy Mayfield Mobil 1	20.00	50.00
12 Jeremy Mayfield Mobil 1 Bank set w/1:64 car	20.00	50.00
12 Jeremy Mayfield Mobil 1 Kentucky Derby/5004	20.00	50.00
18 Bobby Labonte Interstate Batteries/4000	25.00	60.00
20 Tony Stewart Home Depot/3120	100.00	175.00
20 Tony Stewart Home Depot Habitat for Humanity	50.00	100.00
20 Tony Stewart Home Depot Habitat Bank set w/1:64 car/4008	40.00	100.00
22 Ward Burton Caterpillar/2508	25.00	60.00
23 Jimmy Spencer No Bull/4212	20.00	50.00
23 Jimmy Spencer Winston Lights	20.00	50.00
24 Jeff Gordon DuPont/7512	25.00	60.00
24 Jeff Gordon DuPont Daytona/4008	60.00	120.00
24 Jeff Gordon DuPont Superman/16,872	40.00	100.00
24 Jeff Gordon Pepsi/10,008	25.00	60.00
24 Jeff Gordon Pepsi/3504 set with 1:64 car	25.00	60.00
24 Jeff Gordon Pepsi Star Wars/5004	30.00	80.00
25 Wally Dallenbach Budweiser	20.00	50.00
27 Casey Atwood Castrol/4008	20.00	50.00
27 Casey Atwood Castrol Last Lap Mac Tools/5004	15.00	40.00
28 Kenny Irwin Havoline/4000	20.00	50.00
30 Derrike Cope Jimmy Dean/3120	15.00	40.00
31 Dale Earnhardt Jr. Gargoyles 1997 Monte Carlo/5004	50.00	100.00
31 Dale Earnhardt Jr. Mom 'N' Pop's 1996 Monte Carlo/3120	40.00	100.00
31 Dale Earnhardt Jr. Sikkens Blue 1997 Monte Carlo/8500	30.00	70.00
31 Dale Earnhardt Jr. Sikkens White 1997 Monte Carlo	30.00	70.00
31 Mike Skinner Lowe's	20.00	50.00
33 Ken Schrader Skoal Blue/3120	50.00	75.00
36 Ernie Irvan M&M's/3120	20.00	50.00
36 Ernie Irvan M&M's Countdown/5004	20.00	50.00
36 Ernie Irvan Crispy M&M's/3120	20.00	50.00
36 Ernie Irvan Pedigree	20.00	50.00
40 Kerry Earnhardt Channelock	20.00	50.00
40 Sterling Marlin Coors Light Brooks & Dunn	30.00	80.00
40 Sterling Marlin Coors Light John Wayne	30.00	80.00
55 Kenny Wallace Square D/3120	15.00	40.00
66 Darrell Waltrip Big K Route 66/2508	20.00	50.00
88 Dale Jarrett Quality Care	30.00	70.00
88 Dale Jarrett QC White	30.00	70.00
88 Dale Jarrett Quality Care Last Lap Mac Tools/5004	25.00	60.00
99 Kevin Lepage Red Man	15.00	40.00
00 Buckshot Jones Crown Fiber/3120	15.00	40.00
00 Larry Pearson Cheez-it/3120	15.00	40.00

1999 Revell Select 1:24

The Revell Select series was issued again in 1999 with an upgraded production die-cast car without the upgrade price. The cars themselves appear to have similar production qualities as the Collection cars and some are mounted to a Revell Collection base. However, were issued at a lower initial price point and are packaged in black window boxes.

	EX	NM-MT
2 Rusty Wallace Miller Lite Last Lap	12.50	25.00
3 Dale Earnhardt Goodwrench 25th Anniv.	20.00	40.00
3 Dale Earnhardt Goodwrench Sign	20.00	40.00
24 Jeff Gordon Pepsi	12.50	30.00
24 Jeff Gordon Pepsi Star Wars	12.50	30.00
36 Ernie Irvan M&M's Millennium	10.00	25.00
88 Dale Jarrett Quality Care Last Lap	10.00	25.00

2000 Revell Club 1:24

	EX	NM-MT
3 Dale Earnhardt Goodwrench/2004	40.00	100.00
3 Dale Earnhardt Goodwrench Peter Max/2004	75.00	150.00
3 Dale Earnhardt Goodwrench Taz/3333	50.00	120.00
4 Bobby Hamilton Kodak Navy/1002	15.00	40.00
8 Dale Earnhardt Jr. Bud/2004	70.00	120.00
18 Bobby Labonte Interstate Batteries/1002	30.00	80.00
18 Bobby Labonte Interstate Batteries All Star Game	75.00	150.00
20 Tony Stewart Home Depot/2004	40.00	100.00
20 Tony Stewart Home Depot Rookie of the Year/2508	30.00	80.00
24 Jeff Gordon DuPont Millennium	75.00	150.00
24 Jeff Gordon DuPont Peanuts	75.00	125.00
24 Jeff Gordon Pepsi/2508	40.00	100.00
25 Jerry Nadeau Holigan Coast Guard/1002	15.00	40.00
27 Casey Atwood Castrol	15.00	40.00
28 Ricky Rudd Havoline/1002	15.00	40.00
28 Ricky Rudd Havoline Marines/1002	15.00	40.00
31 Mike Skinner Lowe's Army/1002	25.00	60.00
36 Ken Schrader M&M's July 4th/1002	25.00	60.00
37 Kevin Grubb Timber Wolf/1002	20.00	50.00
66 Darrell Waltrip Big K Route 66 Flames/1002	15.00	40.00
88 Dale Jarrett Quality Care/1500	25.00	60.00
88 Dale Jarrett Quality Care Air Force	25.00	60.00
94 Bill Elliott McDonald's Drive Thru/1002	15.00	40.00
94 Bill Elliott McDonald's 25th/1002	15.00	40.00

2000 Revell Collection 1:24

These cars are mounted on a display base with a clear plastic cover.

	EX	NM-MT
2 Rusty Wallace Miller Lite/3120	15.00	40.00
2 Rusty Wallace Miller Lite Harley	25.00	60.00
3 Dale Earnhardt Goodwrench/5004	50.00	120.00
3 Dale Earnhardt Goodwrench Peter Max/5508	150.00	300.00
3 Dale Earnhardt Goodwrench Peter Max Bank set with 1:64 car/1008	125.00	200.00
3 Dale Earnhardt Goodwrench Taz Bank set with 1:64 car/14,400	60.00	120.00
3 Dale Earnhardt Goodwrench Test/1500	75.00	150.00
3 Ron Hornaday NAPA Monsters/2508	20.00	50.00
4 Bobby Hamilton Kodak Navy/3120	20.00	50.00
4 Bobby Hamilton Kodak Navy Bank set with 1:64 car	20.00	50.00
5 Terry Labonte Kellogg's	20.00	50.00
8 Dale Earnhardt Jr. Bud/5004	50.00	100.00
8 Dale Earnhardt Jr. Bud Bank set with 1:64 car	60.00	120.00
8 Dale Earnhardt Jr. Bud Olympic/3120	50.00	100.00
8 Dale Earnhardt Jr. Bud Test/1500	90.00	175.00
12 Jeremy Mayfield Mobil 1	20.00	50.00
12 Jeremy Mayfield Mobil 1 World Series/2004	20.00	50.00
15 Derrick Gilchrist Hot Tamales/2508	15.00	40.00
18 Bobby Labonte Interstate Batteries	40.00	90.00
18 Bobby Labonte Interstate Batteries All Star Game w/baseball/3120	25.00	60.00
18 Bobby Labonte Interstate Batteries Frankenstein/2508	25.00	60.00
19 Dodge Show Car/2508	25.00	50.00
20 Tony Stewart Home Depot/5504	25.00	60.00
20 Tony Stewart Home Depot Kids/2004	25.00	60.00
20 Tony Stewart Home Depot 1999 Rookie of the Year/7500	40.00	70.00
20 Tony Stewart Home Depot 1999 Rookie of the Year Bank set w/1:64 car	35.00	70.00
21 Elliott Sadler Citgo MDA/3120	20.00	50.00
21 Elliott Sadler Citgo MDA Jerry Lewis Telethon Promo	12.50	25.00
21 Elliott Sadler Citgo '60's Red and White/3120	20.00	50.00
24 Jeff Gordon DuPont/10,080	30.00	80.00
24 Jeff Gordon DuPont Millennium	50.00	100.00
24 Jeff Gordon DuPont Millennium Bank set with 1:64 car	80.00	120.00
24 Jeff Gordon DuPont Peanuts	50.00	100.00
24 Jeff Gordon DuPont Test/1500	75.00	150.00
24 Jeff Gordon DuPont Winston/3120	40.00	100.00
24 Jeff Gordon DuPont Winston Bank set with 1:64 car/2508	40.00	100.00
24 Jeff Gordon Pepsi	30.00	80.00
24 Jeff Gordon Pepsi Bank set with 1:64 car	20.00	50.00
25 Jerry Nadeau Holigan Coast Guard/3120	20.00	50.00
25 Jerry Nadeau Holigan Coast Guard Bank set with 1:64 car	20.00	50.00
26 Jimmy Spencer Big K	40.00	80.00
27 Casey Atwood Castrol	20.00	50.00
28 Ricky Rudd Havoline/5004	20.00	50.00
28 Ricky Rudd Havoline Marines/3120	20.00	50.00
28 Ricky Rudd Havoline Marines Bank set with 1:64 car/1008	20.00	50.00
31 Mike Skinner Lowe's Army/3120	20.00	50.00
31 Mike Skinner Lowe's Army Bank set with 1:64 car/1008	20.00	50.00
36 Ken Schrader M&M's Green/3120	20.00	50.00
36 Ken Schrader M&M's Green Bank set with 1:64 car/504	20.00	50.00
36 Ken Schrader M&M's Halloween/2508	25.00	60.00
36 Ken Schrader M&M's July 4th/3120	20.00	50.00
36 Ken Schrader M&M's Keep Back/5004	20.00	50.00
36 Ken Schrader M&M's Keep Back Bank set with 1:64 car	20.00	50.00
36 Ken Schrader Pedigree	20.00	50.00
37 Kevin Grubb Timber Wolf/3120	20.00	50.00
66 Darrell Waltrip Big K-Mart Flames	20.00	50.00
71 Dave Marcis Realtree Camo/2508	20.00	50.00
75 Wally Dallenbach Powerpuff Girls/2508	20.00	50.00
77 Robert Pressley Jasper Cat	20.00	50.00
88 Dale Jarrett Quality Care	20.00	50.00
88 Dale Jarrett Quality Care Air Force/3120	20.00	50.00
88 Dale Jarrett Quality Care Air Force Bank set with 1:64 car	20.00	50.00
94 Bill Elliott McDonald's Drive Thru/3120	20.00	50.00
94 Bill Elliott McDonald's Drive Thru Bank set with 1:64 car	20.00	50.00
94 Bill Elliott McDonald's 25th Anniversary/8120	20.00	50.00
94 Bill Elliott McDonald's 25th Ann.Bank set with 1:64 car	25.00	60.00

2000 Revell Select 1:24

	EX	NM-MT
3 D.Earnhardt/Goodwrench Taz	30.00	50.00
5 Terry Labonte Kellogg's Grinch	12.50	25.00
36 K.Schrader/M&M's Halloween	12.50	25.00

2001 Revell Club 1:24

	EX	NM-MT
3 Dale Earnhardt Goodwrench with Sonic decal/10,000	80.00	175.00
3 Dale Earnhardt Goodwrench Oreo/9996	100.00	200.00
8 Dale Earnhardt Jr. Bud/2508	80.00	175.00
24 Jeff Gordon Pepsi/1200	60.00	120.00
29 Kevin Harvick Goodwrench/1500	60.00	120.00
88 Dale Jarrett UPS	50.00	100.00

2001 Revell Collection 1:24

	EX	NM-MT
1 Steve Park Pennzoil	20.00	50.00
1 Steve Park Pennzoil Rockingham Win/12,996	20.00	50.00
1 Steve Park Pennzoil Looney Toons with figure	20.00	50.00
2 Rusty Wallace Miller Lite California Win	25.00	60.00
3 Dale Earnhardt Goodwrench No Bull	75.00	150.00
3 Dale Earnhardt Goodwrench Oreo	150.00	300.00
3 Dale Earnhardt Goodwrench Test	250.00	400.00
3 Dale Earnhardt Goodwrench with Sonic decal/10,000	50.00	120.00
5 Terry Labonte Kellogg's	30.00	60.00
5 Terry Labonte Kellogg's Bank	60.00	125.00
5 Terry Labonte Kellogg's Looney Toons with figure	20.00	50.00
8 Dale Earnhardt Jr. Bud/22,764	50.00	100.00
8 Dale Earnhardt Jr. Bud All-Star	100.00	175.00
8 Dale Earnhardt Jr. Bud All-Star Game Raced version Daytona Win/40,008	75.00	150.00
8 Dale Earnhardt Jr. Bud No Bull Win	60.00	120.00
8 Dale Earnhardt Jr. Bud Test gray/2508	50.00	120.00
15 Michael Waltrip NAPA Daytona Win/21,016	25.00	60.00
18 Bobby Labonte Interstate Batteries Jurassic Park 3	25.00	60.00
20 Tony Stewart Home Depot Jurassic Park 3/3120	30.00	60.00
24 Jeff Gordon DuPont Bugs with figure	50.00	100.00
24 Jeff Gordon DuPont No Bull Las Vegas Raced/25,020	40.00	100.00
24 Jeff Gordon DuPont Test black/2508	50.00	120.00
24 Jeff Gordon Pepsi/15,016	25.00	60.00
27 Jamie McMurray Williams/3054	30.00	60.00
29 Kevin Harvick Goodwrench Atlanta Win/17,000	25.00	60.00
29 Kevin Harvick Goodwrench Chicago Win	25.00	60.00
29 Kevin Harvick Goodwrench Taz with figure/10,044	25.00	60.00
29 Kevin Harvick Goodwrench Taz Bank/3504	75.00	150.00
30 Jeff Green AOL Daffy Duck with figure/3000	25.00	60.00
31 Mike Skinner Lowe's Yosemite Sam with Figure	30.00	80.00
55 Bobby Hamilton Square D Looney Toons w\figure	30.00	60.00
88 Dale Jarrett UPS/1500	25.00	60.00
88 Dale Jarrett UPS Color Chrome/1500	25.00	60.00
88 Dale Jarrett UPS Darlington Win/14,372	25.00	60.00
88 Dale Jarrett UPS Test/2508	75.00	150.00
K2 Kerry Earnhardt Kannapolis Intimidators/9000	20.00	50.00

2001 Revell Select 1:24

	EX	NM-MT
3 Dale Earnhardt Goodwrench	20.00	40.00
3 Dale Earnhardt Goodwrench Oreo	20.00	40.00
8 Dale Earnhardt Jr. Bud All-Star	90.00	150.00
24 Jeff Gordon DuPont Flames	15.00	30.00

2002 Revell Collection 1:24

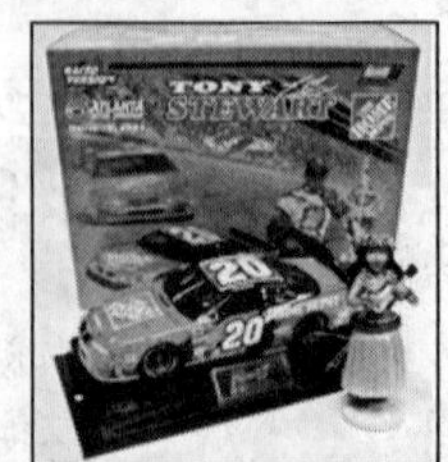

	EX	NM-MT
2 Rusty Wallace Miller Lite Test w/flames/5502	25.00	60.00
3 Dale Earnhardt Jr. Oreo Daytona Win w/CD ROM/48,236	20.00	50.00
3 Dale Earnhardt Jr. Oreo Test Gray/7776	25.00	60.00
8 Dale Earnhardt Jr. Bud/14,952	25.00	60.00
8 Dale Earnhardt Jr. Bud Dover Win with Wilson Volleyball/38,792	40.00	80
8 Dale Earnhardt Jr. Bud Talladega Win raced version/18,908	30.00	60
8 Dale Earnhardt Jr. Bud Test Red/7620	30.00	60
8 Dale Earnhardt Jr. Looney Tunes raced version	30.00	60
9 Bill Elliott Dodge Brickyard Win raced version	20.00	50
19 Jeremy Mayfield Dodge Test/3504	35.00	80
20 Tony Stewart Home Depot Atlanta Win w/hula dancer/8358	30.00	60
24 Jeff Gordon DuPont Color Chrome 2001 Champion/42,024	40.00	80
24 Jeff Gordon DuPont Test/8058	25.00	60
29 Kevin Harvick Goodwrench Test/7584	20.00	50
40 Sterling Marlin Coors Light Darlington Win raced version/5082	25.00	50
40 Jamie McMurray Coors Light raced Charlotte Win/4032	25.00	50
48 Jimmie Johnson Lowe's raced California Win/10,844	25.00	50
83 Kerry Earnhardt racing.usa.com	25.00	60
02 Tropicana 400	25.00	50

2002 Revell Select 1:24

	EX	NM-
3 D.Earnhardt Jr./Nilla Wafer	15.00	30
8 D.Earnhardt Jr./Bud All-Star	15.00	30
29 K.Harvick/Goodwrench	12.50	25
29 K.Harvick/Goodwrench ET	12.50	25
29 K.Harvick/Goodwrench Taz	12.50	25

2003 Revell Collection 1:2

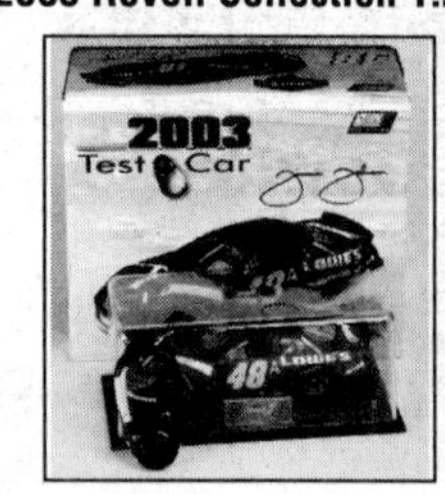

	EX	NM-
8 Dale Earnhardt Jr. Bud Test/5622	35.00	60
8 Dale Earnhardt Jr. Bud Test Red/5622	35.00	60
8 Dale Earnhardt Jr. E Concert Talladega Raced/4872	35.00	60
8 Dale Earnhardt Jr. Oreo Ritz Raced/3888	35.00	50
8 Dale Earnhardt Jr. Test White/4902	30.00	50
15 Michael Waltrip NAPA Raced/4824	35.00	50
20 Tony Stewart Home Depot Pocono Win Raced/1888	35.00	50
20 Tony Stewart Home Depot Test Gray	30.00	50
24 Jeff Gordon DuPont Flames Martinsville Raced/3168	35.00	60
40 Sterling Marlin Coors Light Test/2856	25.00	50
48 Jimmie Johnson Lowe's Test Black	30.00	50

2003 Revell Select 1:24

	EX	NM-
3 Dale Earnhardt Oreo '01 Monte Carlo	25.00	40
8 Dale Earnhardt Jr. Dirty Mo Posse	20.00	35
8 Tony Stewart 3 Doors Down	20.00	35

2004 Revell Collection 1:2

	EX	NM-
8 Dale Earnhardt Jr. Bud Test Brown/3570	35.00	60
15 Michael Waltrip NAPA Test/1278 with Stopwatch	35.00	60
20 Tony Stewart Home Depot Test/3504	35.00	60
24 Jeff Gordon DuPont Test/1848	40.00	70

2004 Revell Select 1:24

	EX	NM-
8 Dale Earnhardt Jr. Bud Born On Feb.15	25.00	50

2005 Revell Collection 1:2

	EX	NM-
8 Dale Earnhardt Jr. Bud Born On Feb.20/1500	40.00	65
8 Dale Earnhardt Jr. Bud Test/1752	45.00	75
18 Bobby Labonte Interstate Batteries Test/732	40.00	65
20 Tony Stewart	40.00	70

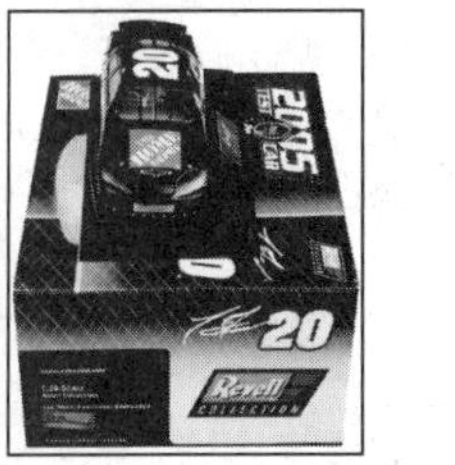

ne Depot Test/972		
Gordon	45.00	75.00
Pont Test/1284		
n Harvick	40.00	65.00
odwrench Test/816		
nie Johnson	40.00	70.00
ve's Test/744		
Elliott	40.00	65.00
o Value		

97 Revell Collection 1:43

ies marks Revell's first attempt to produce a 1:43 scale was distributed to hobby dealers as part of the Revell on line. Each piece was packaged in a hard plastic case with a cardboard box overwrap. Most featured a roduction run number on the top of the outer box.

	EX	NM-MT
Cola 600/7512	10.00	25.00
Wallace	15.00	30.00
ler Lite		
Labonte	15.00	30.00
logg's/5772		
Labonte	12.50	30.00
logg's Tony/10,016		
Labonte	12.50	30.00
ooky Loops/10,520		
Martin	18.00	30.00
voline		
hael Waltrip	10.00	25.00
go		
hael Waltrip	10.00	25.00
go Top Dog paint scheme		
ny Spencer	25.00	40.00
mel/7512		
y Craven	18.00	30.00
dweiser		
e Irvan	18.00	30.00
voline black		
e Irvan	20.00	35.00
voline 10th Anniversary		
te and black/5004		
e Grissom	10.00	25.00
ntstones/5004		
Green	10.00	25.00
n & Jerry		
ert Pressley	10.00	25.00
ntstones		
ert Pressley	10.00	25.00
ooby-Doo		
nny Benson	10.00	25.00
nnzoil		
Schrader	12.00	30.00
mal/7512		
ike Cope	10.00	25.00
ittles		
ny Mayfield	10.00	25.00
Mart Kids Against Drugs		
e Grissom	10.00	25.00
diak/7508		
by Hamilton	10.00	25.00
P Goody's/5004		
y Dallenbach	10.00	25.00
ody Woodpecker/8012		
Jarrett	12.50	30.00
ality Care/10,584		
Elliott	20.00	35.00
c Tonight/7512		
Elliott	10.00	25.00
Donald's/5772		
id Green	10.00	25.00
erpillar		
d Little	12.50	30.00
n Deere		
d Little	12.50	30.00
n Deere		
th Anniversary AUTO/4008		
Burton	10.00	25.00
de/7512		

98 Revell Collection 1:43

ies marks Revell's second attempt to produce a 1:43 r. It was distributed to hobby dealers as part of Revell's on line.

	EX	NM-MT
Earnhardt Jr.	15.00	30.00
ke Bear/7512		
1 Steve Park	8.00	20.00
Pennzoil Black Roof		
1 Steve Park	8.00	20.00
Pennzoil Yellow Roof		
2 Rusty Wallace	10.00	25.00
Adventures of Rusty/5004		
2 Rusty Wallace	10.00	25.00
Miller Lite Elvis/7512		
2 Rusty Wallace	10.00	25.00
Miller Lite TCB Elvis/5004		
3 Dale Earnhardt	15.00	40.00
Coke		
3 Dale Earnhardt	20.00	50.00
Goodwrench Plus		
Daytona Win/5004		
3 Dale Earnhardt	30.00	80.00
Goodwrench Plus Bass Pro		
5 Terry Labonte	10.00	25.00
Blasted Fruit Loops/5004		
5 Terry Labonte	10.00	25.00
Kellogg's		
5 Terry Labonte	10.00	25.00
Kellogg's Corny		
5 Terry Labonte	10.00	25.00
Kellogg's Ironman/4008		
12 Jeremy Mayfield	8.00	20.00
Mobil 1/5004		
18 Bobby Labonte	10.00	25.00
Interstate Batteries		
18 Bobby Labonte	10.00	25.00
Interstate Batteries		
Hot Rod/5004		
18 Bobby Labonte	10.00	25.00
Interstate Batteries		
Small Soldiers/5004		
23 Jimmy Spencer	15.00	40.00
No Bull		
24 Jeff Gordon	20.00	40.00
DuPont/5004		
24 Jeff Gordon	20.00	40.00
DuPont Brickyard Win/5024		
24 Jeff Gordon	25.00	50.00
DuPont Chromalusion		
28 Kenny Irwin	12.50	30.00
Havoline/5004		
28 Kenny Irwin	12.50	30.00
Havoline Joker		
31 Dale Earnhardt Jr.	20.00	50.00
Wrangler 1997 Monte Carlo		
31 Mike Skinner	8.00	20.00
Lowe's		
31 Mike Skinner	8.00	20.00
Lowe's Special Olympics		
33 Ken Schrader	15.00	30.00
Skoal Bud Shootout		
36 Ernie Irvan	10.00	25.00
M&M's		
36 Ernie Irvan	10.00	25.00
Wildberry Skittles/5004		
41 Steve Grissom	8.00	20.00
Kodiak/5004		
44 Tony Stewart	15.00	30.00
Shell Small Soldiers/5004		
50 Ricky Craven	8.00	20.00
Bud/5004		
50 No Driver Association	8.00	20.00
Bud Louie/5004		
81 Kenny Wallace	8.00	20.00
Square D		
81 Kenny Wallace	8.00	20.00
Square D Lightning/5004		
88 Dale Jarrett	10.00	25.00
Quality Care/5004		
88 Dale Jarrett	12.50	30.00
Batman/4008		

1999 Revell Collection 1:43

This series was produced for and distributed in hobby outlets.

	EX	NM-MT
2 Rusty Wallace	12.50	30.00
Miller Lite Harley/3000		
3 Dale Earnhardt	25.00	50.00
Goodwrench		
3 Dale Earnhardt	20.00	40.00
Wrangler/5004		
3 Dale Earnhardt Jr.	15.00	30.00
AC Delco/4008		
3 Dale Earnhardt Jr.	12.50	30.00
AC Delco Superman/5508		
8 Dale Earnhardt Jr.	15.00	30.00
Bud		
12 Jeremy Mayfield	12.50	30.00
Mobil 1 Kentucky Derby/4008		
20 Tony Stewart	15.00	30.00
Home Depot Habitat/3000		
23 Jimmy Spencer	12.50	25.00
No Bull/3508		
23 Jimmy Spencer	12.50	25.00
Winston Lights/3508		
24 Jeff Gordon	15.00	30.00
DuPont/4008		
24 Jeff Gordon	20.00	35.00
DuPont Superman		
24 Jeff Gordon	18.00	30.00
Pepsi		
24 Jeff Gordon	12.50	30.00
Pepsi Star Wars/5508		
40 Coca-Cola 600	10.00	20.00

2000 Revell Collection 1:43

These cars come in a plastic display with the car mounted to the base.

	EX	NM-MT
3 Dale Earnhardt	25.00	50.00
Goodwrench Taz/4000		
3 Dale Earnhardt	30.00	60.00
Goodwrench Peter Max/3000		
20 Tony Stewart	12.50	25.00
Home Depot/3000		
20 Tony Stewart	12.50	20.00
Home Depot		
Rookie of the Year/3000		
24 Jeff Gordon	12.50	25.00
DuPont Millennium		
28 Ricky Rudd	10.00	20.00
Havoline/3504		
94 Bill Elliott	10.00	20.00
McDonald's Drive Thru/3000		

2001 Revell Collection 1:43

	EX	NM-MT
3 Dale Earnhardt	12.50	30.00
Goodwrench Oreo/48,084		
3 Dale Earnhardt	30.00	60.00
Goodwrench Oreo Daytona		

1993-95 Revell Promos 1:64

	EX	NM-MT
5 Ricky Rudd	5.00	12.00
Tide box 1993		
9 Lake Speed	7.50	20.00
Spam blister 1995		
32 Dale Jarrett	15.00	30.00
Mac Tools blister 1995		
43 Richard Petty	7.50	20.00
STP blue		
Wisk promo blister		
43 Richard Petty	7.50	20.00
STP red&blue '72 Charger		
Wisk promo blister		
43 Richard Petty	7.50	20.00
STP red&blue Pontiac		
Wisk promo blister		
52 Ken Schrader	12.50	25.00
Eastman Chemical 1994		
62 Sons of Confederate Veterans	10.00	20.00
1994 box/10,080		
71 Dave Marcis	10.00	20.00
Olive Garden 1995		

1996 Revell Retail 1:64

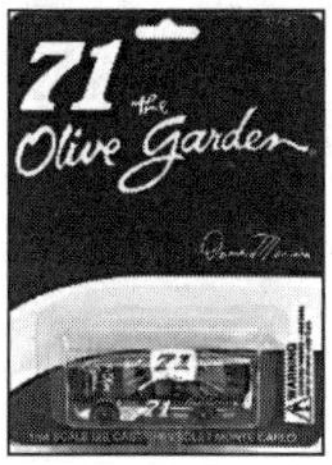

This series was distributed in retail outlets. These cars were packaged in Revell blister packs.

	EX	NM-MT
2 Rusty Wallace	4.00	8.00
Miller Genuine Draft		
Silver 25th Anniversary		
2 Rusty Wallace	5.00	10.00
Miller Genuine Draft		
Silver 25th Anniversary		
Race Day blister		
2 Rusty Wallace	4.00	8.00
Penske Racing		
3 Dale Earnhardt	7.50	20.00
Goodwrench		
3 Dale Earnhardt	6.00	15.00
Olympic blister		
3 Dale Earnhardt	6.00	15.00
Olympic Small Box		
4 Sterling Marlin	3.00	6.00
Kodak		
5 Terry Labonte	3.00	6.00
Kellogg's		
6 Mark Martin	3.00	6.00
Valvoline		
9 Lake Speed	3.00	6.00
SPAM		
10 Ricky Rudd	3.00	6.00
Tide		
11 Brett Bodine	3.00	6.00
Lowe's		
16 Ron Hornaday	3.00	6.00
Smith and Wesson		
16 Ted Musgrave	3.00	6.00
Family Channel Primestar		
17 Darrell Waltrip	3.00	6.00
Parts America		
18 Bobby Labonte	3.00	6.00
Interstate Batteries		
21 Michael Waltrip	3.00	6.00
Citgo		
21 Michael Waltrip	5.00	10.00
Citgo with Eagle on deck lid		
24 Jeff Gordon	4.00	8.00
DuPont		
24 Jack Sprague	3.00	6.00
Quaker State		
28 Ernie Irvan	3.00	6.00
Havoline		
37 Jeremy Mayfield	3.00	6.00
K-Mart Little Caesars		
43 Bobby Hamilton	10.00	20.00
STP Anniversary		
Promo in blister		
71 Dave Marcis	6.00	15.00
Olive Garden Promo		
75 Morgan Shepherd	3.00	6.00
Remington		
75 Morgan Shepherd	3.00	6.00
Remington Camouflage		
77 Bobby Hillin Jr.	3.00	6.00
Jasper Engines		
87 Joe Nemechek	3.00	6.00
Bell South		
87 Joe Nemechek	3.00	6.00
Burger King		
99 Jeff Burton	3.00	6.00
Exide		

1996 Revell Collection 1:64

This series was produced for and distributed through hobby outlets. These cars have significant upgrades in comparison to the standard 1996 Revell 1:64 pieces. Each car is packaged in a box which has the same color scheme as the car. Many include the production run number on the outside of the box.

	EX	NM-MT
2 Rusty Wallace	6.00	15.00
Miller Genuine Draft/14,400		
2 Rusty Wallace	7.50	20.00
Miller Genuine Draft		
Silver 25th Anniversary/14,400		
3 Dale Earnhardt	15.00	30.00
Olympic		
4 Sterling Marlin	4.00	10.00
Kodak		
5 Terry Labonte	30.00	50.00
Honey Crunch/10,080		
5 Terry Labonte	10.00	25.00
Kellogg's/10,080		
6 Mark Martin	4.00	10.00
Valvoline/6912		
6 Mark Martin	5.00	10.00
Valvoline Dura Blend		
10 Ricky Rudd	4.00	8.00
Tide/10,080		
11 Brett Bodine	4.00	8.00
Lowe's Gold		
16 Ted Musgrave	4.00	8.00
Family Channel Primestar		
17 Darrell Waltrip	4.00	8.00
Parts America		
18 Bobby Labonte	5.00	10.00
Interstate Batteries		
23 Chad Little	4.00	10.00
John Deere/10,080		
25 Ken Schrader	4.00	10.00
Bud/10,080		
25 Ken Schrader	4.00	10.00
Bud Olympic/10,080		
28 Ernie Irvan	4.00	8.00
Havoline		
30 Johnny Benson	4.00	8.00
Pennzoil		
37 Jeremy Mayfield	4.00	8.00
K-Mart Little Caesars		
75 Morgan Shepherd	4.00	8.00
Remington		
75 Morgan Shepherd	4.00	8.00
Remington Camouflage		
75 Morgan Shepherd	4.00	8.00
Stren		
76 David Green	4.00	8.00
Smith and Wesson SuperTruck		
87 Joe Nemechek	4.00	8.00
Burger King		
88 Dale Jarrett	4.00	8.00
Quality Care/10,574		
99 Jeff Burton	4.00	8.00
Exide		

1997 Revell Collection 1:64

This series is the continuation of the 1996 series. It signals Revell's expansion into the die cast market by its sheer number of cars in the series.

	EX	NM-MT
1 Coca-Cola 600	5.00	10.00
2 Rusty Wallace	6.00	12.00
Miller Lite/30,000		
2 Rusty Wallace	6.00	12.00
Miller Lite Texas/10,080		
5 Terry Labonte	6.00	12.00
Kellogg's		
5 Terry Labonte	8.00	20.00
Kellogg's 1996 Champion/10,080		
5 Terry Labonte	7.50	15.00
Kellogg's Tony/10,080		
5 Terry Labonte	6.00	15.00
Spooky Loops/10,080		
5/18 Bobby and Terry Labonte	20.00	35.00
Interstate Batteries and Kellogg's		
2-car Tin Set		
6/60 Mark Martin	20.00	35.00
Valvoline/Winn Dixie		
2 car set		
16 Ted Musgrave	5.00	10.00
Primestar		
23 Jimmy Spencer	10.00	20.00
Camel/10,080		
23/97 Chad Little	20.00	30.00
John Deere 2 car set		
Autographed tin		
28 Ernie Irvan	7.50	15.00
Havoline 10th Anniversary		
white and black/10,008		
28 Ernie Irvan	20.00	30.00
Havoline 2-car tin		
30 Johnny Benson	5.00	10.00
Pennzoil		
33 Ken Schrader	6.00	15.00
Skoal		
36 Derrike Cope	4.00	10.00
Skittles		
37 Jeremy Mayfield	5.00	10.00
K-Mart RC Cola		
40 Robby Gordon	5.00	10.00
Coors Light		
41 Steve Grissom	6.00	15.00
Kodiak/10,080		
43 Bobby Hamilton	7.50	15.00
STP Goody's		
91 Mike Wallace	5.00	10.00
Spam		
97 Chad Little	5.00	12.00
John Deere		
97 Chad Little	15.00	30.00
John Deere 2-car tin		
97 California 500	4.00	10.00

1997 Revell Select Hobby 1:64

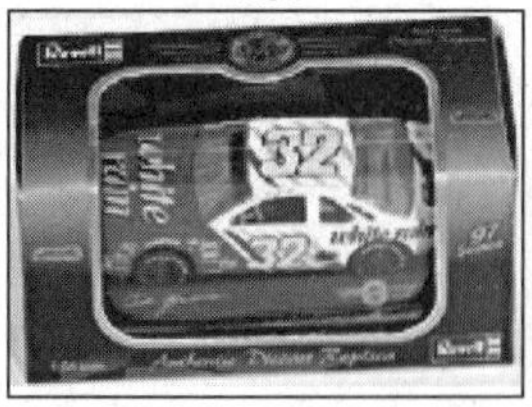

This series, Revell Select, was produced to appease those collectors who wanted an upgraded production die cast without the upgrade price. They were distributed primarily to hobby outlets. The cars themselves appear to have similar production qualities as the Collection cars, but were intially lower in price. Each was packaged in the typical Revell hard plastic clear box with an outer cardboard black window box with gold trim. There is a basic red, white, blue and yellow Revell logo on the box as well.

	EX	NM-MT
1 Coca-Cola 600	4.00	8.00
2 Rusty Wallace	5.00	10.00
Miller Lite		
4 Sterling Marlin	4.00	10.00
Kodak		
5 Terry Labonte	4.00	8.00
Kellogg's		
5 Terry Labonte	5.00	10.00
Spooky Loops		
5 Terry Labonte	5.00	10.00
Tony the Tiger		
6 Mark Martin	4.00	8.00
Valvoline		
7 Geoff Bodine	4.00	8.00
QVC		
17 Darrell Waltrip	4.00	8.00
Parts America blue&white		
17 Darrell Waltrip	5.00	12.00
Parts America Chrome		
17 Darrell Waltrip	4.00	8.00
Parts America Green		
with green number		
17 Darrell Waltrip	4.00	8.00
Parts America Green		
with white number		
17 Darrell Waltrip	4.00	8.00
Parts America Orange		
17 Darrell Waltrip	4.00	8.00
Parts America Red&White		
17 Darrell Waltrip	4.00	8.00
Parts America Yellow&White		
18 Mike Dokken	4.00	8.00
Dana SuperTruck		
18 Bobby Labonte	4.00	8.00
Interstate Batteries		
18 Bobby Labonte	4.00	8.00
Interstate Batteries Texas		
21 Michael Waltrip	4.00	8.00
Citgo Top Dog paint scheme		
25 Ricky Craven	5.00	10.00
Bud Lizard		
28 Ernie Irvan	4.00	8.00
Havoline black		
28 Ernie Irvan	4.00	8.00
Havoline 10th Anniversary		
white and black		
29 Jeff Green	4.00	8.00
Tom & Jerry		
29 Steve Grissom	4.00	8.00
Flintstones		
29 Bob Keselowski	4.00	8.00
Mopar		
29 Robert Pressley	4.00	8.00
Scooby-Doo		
32 Dale Jarrett	4.00	8.00
White Rain		
33 Ken Schrader	4.00	8.00
Skoal		
35 Todd Bodine	4.00	8.00
Tabasco		
36 Derrike Cope	4.00	8.00
Skittles		
37 Jeremy Mayfield	4.00	8.00
K-Mart Kids Against Drugs		
40 Robby Gordon	4.00	8.00
Coors Silver Bullet		
41 Steve Grissom	4.00	8.00
Kodiak		
42 Joe Nemechek	4.00	8.00
Bell South		
43 Bobby Hamilton	4.00	8.00
STP Goody's		
43 Jimmy Hensley	4.00	8.00
Cummins SuperTruck		

75 Rick Mast Remington	4.00	8.00
94 Bill Elliott McDonald's	4.00	8.00
94 Bill Elliott Mac Tonight	4.00	8.00
97 California 500	4.00	8.00
97 Chad Little John Deere 160th Anniversary	4.00	8.00
97 Texas Motor Speedway	4.00	8.00

1997 Revell Retail 1:64

This series was produced for and distributed primarily to mass-market retailers. Each piece is packaged in a blister pack with many printed to match the team colors or sponsor theme.

	EX	NM-MT
1 Coca-Cola 600	3.00	6.00
2 Rusty Wallace Penske	3.00	6.00
5 Terry Labonte Kellogg's Texas	3.00	6.00
5 Terry Labonte Spooky Loops	3.00	6.00
6 Mark Martin Valvoline	3.00	6.00
16 Ted Musgrave Primestar	3.00	6.00
18 Bobby Labonte Interstate Batteries Texas	3.00	6.00
18 Bobby Labonte Interstate Batteries	3.00	6.00
21 Michael Waltrip Citgo Top Dog paint scheme	3.00	6.00
28 Ernie Irvan Havoline Black	3.00	6.00
29 Robert Pressley Cartoon Network	3.00	6.00
29 Robert Pressley Tom & Jerry	3.00	6.00
30 Johnny Benson Pennzoil	3.00	6.00
35 Todd Bodine, Tabasco Promo box	4.00	10.00
37 Jeremy Mayfield K-Mart Kids Against Drugs	3.00	6.00
37 Jeremy Mayfield K-Mart RC Cola	3.00	6.00
42 Joe Nemechek BellSouth	3.00	6.00
91 Mike Wallace Spam	3.00	6.00
97 California 500	3.00	6.00
97 Texas Motor Speedway	3.00	6.00

1998 Revell Collection 1:64

These cars come in a driver detailed box. Cars are mounted to a base and have a clear plastic cover.

	EX	NM-MT
1 Dale Earnhardt Jr. Coke Bear/27,000	10.00	20.00
1 Steve Park Pennzoil Black Roof/10,080	6.00	15.00
1 Steve Park Pennzoil Yellow Roof/12,024	6.00	15.00
2 Rusty Wallace Adventures of Rusty	6.00	12.00
2 Rusty Wallace Miller Lite	6.00	12.00
2 Rusty Wallace Miller Lite Elvis	6.00	12.00
2 Rusty Wallace Miller Lite TCB Elvis	6.00	12.00
3 Dale Earnhardt Coke/27,000	15.00	30.00
3 Dale Earnhardt Goodwrench Plus Daytona Win/14,400	10.00	25.00
3 Dale Earnhardt Goodwrench Plus Bass Pro	20.00	40.00
3 Dale Earnhardt Goodwrench Plus Brickyard Win/20,016	12.50	25.00
3 Dale Earnhardt Jr. AC Delco	15.00	30.00
4 Bobby Hamilton Kodak Max/10,080	4.00	10.00
5 Terry Labonte Blasted Fruit Loops/10,080	6.00	15.00
5 Terry Labonte Kellogg's/10,080	5.00	12.00
5 Terry Labonte Kellogg's Corny/10,080	6.00	15.00
5 Terry Labonte Kellogg's Ironman/10,080	6.00	15.00
9 Lake Speed Birthday Cake	4.00	10.00
9 Lake Speed Huckleberry Hound	4.00	10.00
12 Jeremy Mayfield Mobil 1/10,080	5.00	12.00
18 Bobby Labonte Interstate Batteries	7.50	15.00
18 Bobby Labonte Interstate Batteries Hot Rod	6.00	15.00
18 Bobby Labonte Interstate Batteries Small Soldiers	6.00	15.00
21 Michael Waltrip Citgo	5.00	12.00
23 Jimmy Spencer No Bull	7.50	15.00
24 Jeff Gordon DuPont/10,080	6.00	15.00
24 Jeff Gordon DuPont Brickyard Win	6.00	15.00
24 Jeff Gordon DuPont Chromalusion/24,984	15.00	40.00
25 John Andretti Budweiser	5.00	12.00
28 Kenny Irwin Havoline	6.00	12.00
28 Kenny Irwin Havoline Joker	6.00	12.00
31 Mike Skinner Lowe's/10,080	3.00	8.00
31 Mike Skinner Lowe's Special Olympics	4.00	10.00
33 Ken Schrader Skoal	5.00	12.00
33 Ken Schrader Skoal Bud Shootout	6.00	12.00
36 Ernie Irvan M&M's	6.00	15.00
36 Ernie Irvan Wildberry Skittles	6.00	12.00
40 Sterling Marlin Coors Light	5.00	12.00
41 Steve Grissom Kodiak/10,080	3.00	8.00
42 Joe Nemechek Bell South/10,080	3.00	8.00
44 Tony Stewart Shell/10,080	6.00	12.00
44 Tony Stewart Shell Small Soldiers/10,080	7.50	15.00
46 Wally Dallenbach First Union/10,080	3.00	8.00
46 Jeff Green First union Devil Rays/10,080	3.00	8.00
50 Ricky Craven Bud/10,080	3.00	8.00
50 No Driver Association Bud Louie/10,080	6.00	12.00
75 Rick Mast Remington/10,080	3.00	8.00
81 Kenny Wallace Square D Lightning/10,080	3.00	8.00
88 Dale Jarrett Batman	6.00	15.00
88 Dale Jarrett Quality Care/10,080	6.00	15.00

1998 Revell Select Hobby 1:64

This series, Revell Select, was produced to appease those collectors who wanted an upgraded production die cast without the upgrade price. The cars themselves appear to have similar production qualities as the Collection cars, but were initially offered at a lower price point and were packaged in black window boxes.

	EX	NM-MT
1 Steve Park Pennzoil Black Roof	5.00	10.00
2 Rusty Wallace Miller Lite	4.00	8.00
3 Dale Earnhardt Goodwrench Plus	5.00	12.00
3 Dale Earnhardt Goodwrench Plus Bass Pro	6.00	12.00
3 Dale Earnhardt Jr. AC Delco	7.50	20.00
4 Bobby Hamilton Kodak Max	3.00	8.00
5 Terry Labonte Kellogg's	3.00	8.00
5 Terry Labonte Kellogg's Corny	4.00	10.00
8 Hut Stricklin Circuit City	3.00	8.00
9 Lake Speed Huckleberry Hound	3.00	8.00
18 Bobby Labonte Interstate Batteries	4.00	8.00
18 Bobby Labonte Interstate Batteries Hot Rod	4.00	8.00
21 Michael Waltrip Citgo	3.00	8.00
23 Jimmy Spencer No Bull	6.00	12.00
24 Jeff Gordon DuPont	5.00	10.00
31 Mike Skinner Lowe's	3.00	8.00
33 Ken Schrader Skoal	4.00	10.00
35 Todd Bodine Tabasco Green/Black Promo blister	3.00	8.00
35 Todd Bodine Tabasco Orange/White Promo blister	3.00	8.00
35 Todd Bodine Tabasco Red/Black Promo blister	3.00	8.00
36 Ernie Irvan M&M's	4.00	10.00
44 Tony Stewart Shell	6.00	12.00
44 Tony Stewart Shell Small Soldiers	6.00	12.00
50 No Driver Association Bud Louie	3.00	8.00
77 Robert Pressley Jasper	3.00	8.00
81 Kenny Wallace Square D Lightning	3.00	8.00

1999 Revell Collection 1:64

This series was produced for and distributed through hobby outlets. Each piece was issued in a Revell Collection clear plastic box.

	EX	NM-MT
1 Steve Park Pennzoil/7992	6.00	15.00
2 Rusty Wallace Miller Lite	7.50	15.00
2 Rusty Wallace Miller Lite Harley	5.00	12.00
3 Dale Earnhardt Goodwrench/14,400	12.50	30.00
3 Dale Earnhardt Goodwrench 25th	15.00	30.00
3 Dale Earnhardt Goodwrench Sign	15.00	30.00
3 Dale Earnhardt Wrangler/18,000	12.50	30.00
3 Dale Earnhardt Jr. AC Delco/13,104	6.00	15.00
3 Dale Earnhardt Jr. AC Delco Superman/20,016	7.50	20.00
4 Bobby Hamilton Advantix	4.00	10.00
5 Terry Labonte Kellogg's	5.00	12.00
5 Terry Labonte K-Sentials	5.00	12.00
5 Terry Labonte Rice Krispies	5.00	12.00
8 Dale Earnhardt Jr. Bud	10.00	18.00
9 Jerry Nadeau Dexter's Lab/10,080	4.00	10.00
9 Jerry Nadeau Jetsons	4.00	10.00
11 Dale Jarrett Green Bay Packers/7992	12.50	25.00
12 Jeremy Mayfield Mobil 1	4.00	10.00
12 Jeremy Mayfield Mobil 1 Kentucky Derby/10,080	4.00	10.00
18 Bobby Labonte Interstate Batteries	7.50	15.00
20 Tony Stewart Home Depot/7992	25.00	40.00
20 Tony Stewart Home Depot Habitat for Humanity/10,080	12.50	30.00
21 Elliott Sadler Citgo	4.00	10.00
23 Jimmy Spencer No Bull	6.00	15.00
23 Jimmy Spencer Winston Lights	6.00	15.00
24 Jeff Gordon DuPont	7.50	15.00
24 Jeff Gordon DuPont Superman/23,472	8.00	18.00
24 Jeff Gordon DuPont Daytona 500	10.00	20.00
24 Jeff Gordon Pepsi	7.50	15.00
24 Jeff Gordon Pepsi Star Wars	8.00	18.00
27 Casey Atwood Castrol	4.00	10.00
28 Kenny Irwin Havoline/10,080	5.00	12.00
31 Dale Earnhardt Jr. Gargoyles 1997 Monte Carlo	10.00	20.00
31 Dale Earnhardt Jr. Mom 'N' Pop's 1996 Monte Carlo	6.00	15.00
31 Dale Earnhardt Jr. Sikkens Blue 1997 Monte Carlo/10,080	7.50	15.00
31 Dale Earnhardt Jr. Sikkens White 1997 Monte Carlo	7.50	15.00
31 Mike Skinner Lowe's	4.00	10.00
36 Ernie Irvan M&M's/10,080	7.50	15.00
36 Ernie Irvan M&M's Countdown/10,080	4.00	10.00
36 Ernie Irvan M&M's Millennium/10,080	4.00	10.00
36 Ernie Irvan Crispy M&M's	4.00	10.00
36 Ernie Irvan Pedigree/10,080	4.00	10.00
40 Sterling Marlin Coors Light John Wayne/10,080	7.50	20.00
40 Sterling Marlin Coors Light Brooks & Dunn/10,080	7.50	20.00
40 Kerry Earnhardt Channellock/10,080	4.00	10.00
88 Dale Jarrett Quality Care/10,080	5.00	12.00

2000 Revell Collection 1:64

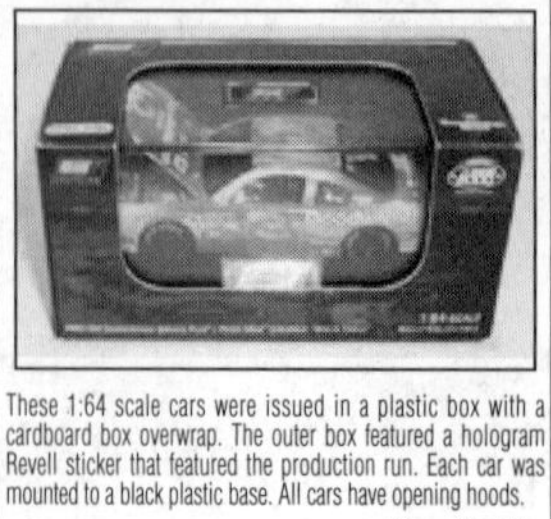

These 1:64 scale cars were issued in a plastic box with a cardboard box overwrap. The outer box featured a hologram Revell sticker that featured the production run. Each car was mounted to a black plastic base. All cars have opening hoods.

	EX	NM-MT
2 Rusty Wallace Miller Lite	6.00	15.00
2 Rusty Wallace Miller Lite Harley/7992	5.00	12.00
3 Dale Earnhardt Goodwrench/12,024	20.00	40.00
3 Dale Earnhardt Goodwrench Peter Max/1008	20.00	40.00
3 Dale Earnhardt Goodwrench Taz No Bull/30,384	15.00	40.00
4 Bobby Hamilton Kodak Navy/10,088	5.00	12.00
8 Dale Earnhardt Jr. Bud/7992	10.00	20.00
8 Dale Earnhardt Jr. Bud Olympic/9000	12.50	25.00
12 Jeremy Mayfield Mobil 1 World Series/5040	5.00	12.00
18 Bobby Labonte Interstate Batteries/7992	6.00	15.00
20 Tony Stewart Home Depot/13,176	10.00	20.00
20 Tony Stewart Home Depot Rookie of the Year/12,080	10.00	20.00
20 Tony Stewart Home Depot Kids	10.00	20.00
21 Elliott Sadler Citgo MDA Promo blister	4.00	10.00
24 Jeff Gordon DuPont/10,080	5.00	12.00
24 Jeff Gordon DuPont Millennium	10.00	20.00
24 Jeff Gordon DuPont Peanuts	10.00	20.00
24 Jeff Gordon DuPont Winston	5.00	12.00
24 Jeff Gordon Pepsi	6.00	15.00
25 Jerry Nadeau Holigan Coast Guard	5.00	12.00
27 Casey Atwood Castrol	5.00	12.00
28 Ricky Rudd Havoline	6.00	15.00
28 Ricky Rudd Havoline Marines/11,088	5.00	12.00
31 Mike Skinner Lowe's Army/11,088	5.00	12.00
36 Ken Schrader M&M's	5.00	12.00
36 Ken Schrader M&M's Green/8496	5.00	12.00
36 Ken Schrader M&M's July 4th/8496	5.00	12.00
36 Ken Schrader M&M's Keep Back/9000	6.00	15.00
88 Dale Jarrett Quality Care	5.00	12.00
88 Dale Jarrett Quality Care Air Force/11,088	5.00	12.00
94 Bill Elliott McDonald's Drive Thru	5.00	12.00
94 Bill Elliott McDonald's 25th/9000	5.00	12.00

2001 Revell Collection 1:64

	EX	NM-MT
3 Dale Earnhardt Goodwrench Oreo Tin	20.00	50.00
8 Dale Earnhardt Jr. Bud	12.50	25.00
8 Dale Earnhardt Jr. Bud All-Star Raced/20,016	20.00	40.00
8/15 Dale Earnhardt Jr. Michael Waltrip Bud MLB All-Star Game NAPA Stars and Stripes 2-car set in tin/12,000	20.00	40.00
18 Bobby Labonte Interstate Batteries 2000 Winston Cup Champ 2-car set in tin/6432	15.00	30.00
18/20 Bobby Labonte Tony Stewart Jurassic Park 3 in tin/7992	12.50	25.00
24 Jeff Gordon DuPont Flames/24,984	7.50	20.00
24 Jeff Gordon Pepsi/17,280	7.50	20.00
88 Dale Jarrett UPS	6.00	15.00

2002 Revell Collection 1:64

	EX	NM-MT
3 Dale Earnhardt Jr. Nilla Wafers in cookie box/28,608	7.50	20.00
3 Dale Earnhardt Jr. Oreo in Cookie tin/20,016	12.50	25.00
3/8/8 Ralph Earnhardt 1969 Camaro Dale Earnhardt 2000 Goodwrench MC Dale Earnhardt Jr. 2000 Budweiser MC 3-car tin/27,597	25.00	50.00
8 Dale Earnhardt Jr. Bud/15,336	10.00	
8 Dale Earnhardt Jr. Bud Talladega Win	10.00	

2002 Revell Collection Tr Sets 1:64

	EX	N
3 Dale Earnhardt 9-car train set/19,504 1995 Goodwrench Silver car 1997 Wheaties car 1998 Goodwrench Bass Pro car 1998 Goodwrench Daytona car 1998 Coca-Cola car 1999 Wrangler car 2000 Goodwrench Taz car 2000 Goodwrench Peter Max car 2001 Goodwrench Oreo car	125.00	2
8 Dale Earnhardt Jr. Looney Tunes 3-car train set/600	30.00	

2003 Revell Collection Tr Sets 1:64

	EX	N
3 Dale Earnhardt Earnhardt Foundation/7560	20.00	
8 Dale Earnhardt Jr. Dirty Mo Posse/5328	15.00	
8 Dale Earnhardt Jr. E Concert/5688	18.00	
8 Dale Earnhardt Jr. Oreo Ritz/5160	15.00	
NNO Dale Earnhardt Earnhardt Legacy/5292	18.00	

2004 Revell Collection Tr Sets 1:64

7 Dale Earnhardt Jr. Church Brothers 1997 Monte Carlo/2556	25.00	
8 Dale Earnhardt Jr. Oreo/2862	25.00	

1992 Road Champs 1:4

Road Champs released this series of 1:43 die-cast (each packaged in a window box that included a ca backer. The driver's photo and car image also appeare package.

	EX	N
2 Rusty Wallace Pontiac	5.00	
4 Ernie Irvan Kodak	4.00	
6 Mark Martin Valvoline	5.00	
21 Morgan Shepherd Citgo	4.00	
43 Richard Petty STP	4.00	

1992 Road Champs Pull B Action 1:43

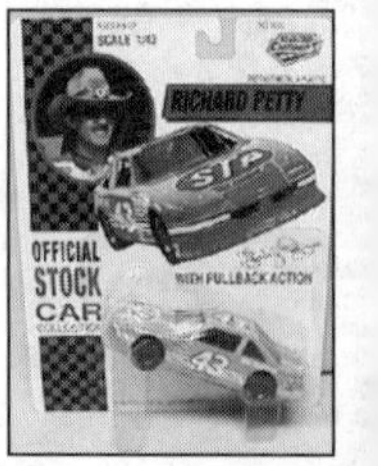

	EX	N
4 Ernie Irvan Kodak	4.00	
21 Morgan Shepherd Citgo	4.00	
43 Richard Petty STP	5.00	

1992 Road Champs Sound Power 1:43

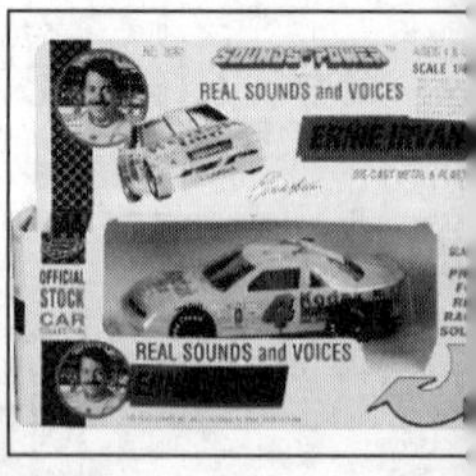

Each die-cast car in this release was produced by Road and packaged in a window box that included a ca backer. The driver's photo and car image also appeare package. The die-cast car itself could play real racing when one of the wheels were pushed.

	EX	N
2 Rusty Wallace Pontiac	3.00	
4 Ernie Irvan Kodak	3.00	
43 Richard Petty STP	5.00	

1992 Road Champs 1:6

	EX	N
1 Jeff Gordon Baby Ruth	5.00	

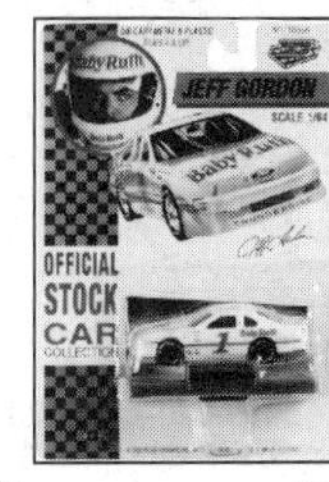

y Wallace 4.00 10.00
ontiac
e Irvan 3.00 8.00
odak
k Martin 4.00 10.00
alvoline
rgan Shepherd 3.00 8.00
itgo
hard Petty 4.00 10.00
TP
Nemechek 6.00 15.00
exas Pete Promo
bag/15,000
stributed by The Source International
ith a card set in a white box

004 Team Caliber Pit Stop 1:18

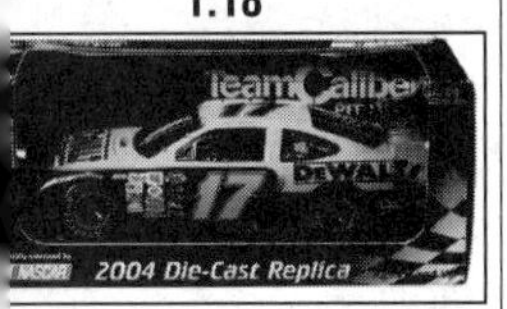

EX NM-MT
k Martin 20.00 35.00
iagra
an Newman 20.00 35.00
ltel
att Kenseth 20.00 35.00
eWalt
rt Busch 15.00 30.00
harpie

2004 Team aliber/Motorworks Model Kits 1:18

EX NM-MT
y Labonte 15.00 25.00
ellogg's
g Biffle 15.00 25.00
ational Guard
att Kenseth 25.00 40.00
eWalt '03 Champ. w/hat
an Vickers 15.00 25.00
tech.com
Nemechek 15.00 25.00
rmy

1999 Team Caliber 1:24

marks Team Calibers inaugural year in the Die-Cast

EX NM-MT
dy LaJoie 25.00 60.00
ob Evan's/3120
by Hamilton 20.00 50.00
odak/3120
y Labonte 40.00 80.00
ellogg's Corny
y Labonte 40.00 80.00
ellogg's K-Sentials/5004
y Labonte 40.00 80.00
ice Krispies/5004
Trickle 25.00 60.00
chneider/3120
k Martin 40.00 80.00
alvoline/5004
k Martin 60.00 120.00
Eagle One
hael Waltrip 25.00 60.00
Phillips
ky Rudd 25.00 60.00
Tide/3120
ky Rudd 20.00 50.00
de Peroxide/3120
emy Mayfield 40.00 80.00
Mobil 1/5004
emy Mayfield 80.00 150.00
obil 25th Anniversary
emy Mayfield 150.00 250.00
obil 1 Chrome
mmy Spencer 30.00 80.00
ppo/3120
mmy Spencer 30.00 80.00
Chips Ahoy/3120
n Schrader 25.00 60.00
akwood Homes/3120
att Kenseth 75.00 150.00
eWalt/5004
att Kenseth 100.00 175.00
eWalt Roush/3120
mmy Spencer 40.00 80.00
inston No Bull
mmy Spencer 50.00 100.00
inston Lights Gold
ally Dallenbach 25.00 60.00
udweiser/3120
ally Dallenbach 40.00 80.00
ud World Series/3120
rike Cope 20.00 50.00
Jimmy Dean/3120
rrike Cope 25.00 60.00
tate Fair/3120
rling Marlin 30.00 80.00
oors Light/3120
rling Marlin 50.00 120.00
oors John Wayne/3120

42 Joe Nemechek 30.00 60.00
BellSouth/5004
43 John Andretti 30.00 80.00
STP/5004
44 Terry Labonte 20.00 50.00
Slim Jim/3120
44 Kyle Petty 40.00 80.00
Hot Wheels/2340
45 Adam Petty 50.00 100.00
Sprint/3120
55 Kenny Wallace 25.00 60.00
Square D/3120
60 Geoffery Bodine 25.00 60.00
Power Team/3120
75 Ted Musgrave 25.00 60.00
Polaris/3120
98 Rick Mast 30.00 60.00
Woody Woodpecker/3120
99 Jeff Burton 45.00 90.00
Exide
99 Jeff Burton 45.00 90.00
Exide No Bull

1999 Team Caliber Banks 1:24

This marks Team Caliber's inaugural year in the die-cast market. Each 1:24 scale bank was packaged in a black Team Caliber solid box along with a certificate of authenticity. The production run for each bank was 1008.

EX NM-MT
1 Randy LaJoie 30.00 80.00
Bob Evan's/1008
5 Terry Labonte 30.00 80.00
Kellogg's K-Sentials
5 Terry Labonte 30.00 80.00
Rice Krispies
10 Ricky Rudd 40.00 100.00
Tide
12 Jeremy Mayfield 30.00 80.00
Mobil 1
12 Jeremy Mayfield 30.00 80.00
Mobil 1 25th Anniversary
23 Jimmy Spencer 40.00 100.00
No Bull
23 Jimmy Spencer 40.00 100.00
Winston Lights
25 Wally Dallenbach 30.00 80.00
Budweiser
40 Sterling Marlin 30.00 80.00
Coors Light
40 Sterling Marlin 40.00 100.00
Coors Light John Wayne
43 John Andretti 40.00 100.00
STP
44 Terry Labonte 30.00 80.00
Slim Jim
45 Adam Petty 60.00 120.00
Sprint
55 Kenny Wallace 30.00 80.00
Square D

2000 Team Caliber Owners Series 1:24

EX NM-MT
4 Bobby Hamilton 25.00 60.00
Kodak/2340
5 Terry Labonte 30.00 80.00
Kellogg's/2340
5 Terry Labonte 30.00 80.00
CherryBerry/3120
5 Terry Labonte 30.00 80.00
Kellogg's Grinch
5 Terry Labonte 30.00 80.00
Kellogg's Frosted Flakes
6 Mark Martin 60.00 100.00
Valvoline/5004
6 Mark Martin 75.00 125.00
Valvoline Eagle One/5004
6 Mark Martin 40.00 100.00
Valvoline Max Life/5004
6 Mark Martin 40.00 100.00
Valvoline Flag/5004
6 Mark Martin 40.00 100.00
Valvoline Zerex/5004
7 Michael Waltrip 30.00 80.00
Nations Rent/2340
8 Shawna Robinson 50.00 100.00
Kids RAD/2340
9 Jeff Burton 50.00 100.00
Northern Light/2340
10 Johnny Benson 40.00 80.00
Lycos/2340
10 Jeff Green 35.00 70.00
Nesquik
11 Brett Bodine 30.00 60.00
Ralph's/2340
12 Jeremy Mayfield 30.00 80.00
Mobil 1/3120
13 Robby Gordon 25.00 60.00
Burger King Flintsones/3120
14 Rick Mast 20.00 50.00
Conseco/2340
16 Kevin Lepage 30.00 60.00
Clemson 2340
16 Kevin Lepage 20.00 50.00
Familyclick.com/2340
16 Kevin Lepage 20.00 50.00
Mac Tools/2340
17 Matt Kenseth 60.00 120.00
DeWalt/5004
17 Matt Kenseth 70.00 110.00
DeWalt 24 Volt/5004
17 Matt Kenseth 60.00 100.00
DeWalt Emazing.com/5004
17 Matt Kenseth 45.00 90.00
Visine/2340
21 Elliott Sadler 20.00 50.00
Citgo/2340
21 Elliott Sadler 35.00 70.00
Citgo VT/2340
24 Ricky Hendrick 20.00 50.00
GMAC/2340
25 Jerry Nadeau 20.00 50.00
Holigan/2340
26 Jimmy Spencer 25.00 60.00
Big K/2340
27 Ryan Newman 90.00 150.00
Alltel/3500

40 Sterling Marlin 25.00 60.00
Coors Light/2340
40 Sterling Marlin 25.00 60.00
Coors Light John Wayne/3120
40 Sterling Marlin 25.00 60.00
Coors Light Brooks & Dunn/3120
42 Kenny Irwin 25.00 60.00
BellSouth/3120
42 Kenny Irwin 25.00 60.00
BellSouth Busch/3120
43 John Andretti 35.00 70.00
Cheerios/2340
43 John Andretti 35.00 70.00
STP/2340
44 Justin Labonte 20.00 50.00
Slim Jim/2340
44 Kyle Petty 35.00 70.00
Hot Wheels
45 Adam Petty 100.00 200.00
Sprint PCS/3120
55 Kenny Wallace 40.00 80.00
Square D/2340
57 Jason Keller 20.00 50.00
Excedrin/2340
60 Geoffery Bodine 25.00 60.00
Power Team/2340
60 Mark Martin 75.00 125.00
Winn Dixie/3120
60 Mark Martin 80.00 150.00
Winn Dixie Flames/3120
60 Mark Martin 80.00 135.00
Winn Dixie Flag/3120
63 Mark Green 20.00 50.00
SuperFlo/2340
66 Darrell Waltrip 25.00 60.00
Big K/2340
66 Darrell Waltrip 50.00 100.00
Big K Flames/2340
77 Robert Pressley 40.00 80.00
Jasper Panther/2340
97 Chad Little 35.00 70.00
John Deere 2340
99 Jeff Burton 30.00 60.00
Citgo Mac Tools/3000
99 Jeff Burton 40.00 100.00
Citgo Steel/3120
99 Jeff Burton 45.00 90.00
Exide/3120
01 Tim Steele 25.00 60.00
Friends of the NRA/2340

2000 Team Caliber Owners Series Gold 1:24

EX NM-MT
6 Mark Martin 75.00 150.00
Valvoline/1200
6 Mark Martin 75.00 150.00
Valvoline Eagle One/1200
17 Matt Kenseth 90.00 150.00
DeWalt/1200
99 Jeff Burton 60.00 125.00
Exide/1200

2000 Team Caliber Preferred 1:24

EX NM-MT
4 Bobby Hamilton 15.00 40.00
Kodak/5508
5 Terry Labonte 20.00 50.00
Cherry Berry/5508
5 Terry Labonte 20.00 50.00
Froot Loops/5508
5 Terry Labonte 20.00 50.00
Kelloggs/5508
6 Mark Martin 25.00 60.00
Valvoline/20,004
6 Mark Martin 25.00 60.00
Valvoline Eagle One/20,004
6 Mark Martin 25.00 50.00
Valvoline Flag/20,004
6 Mark Martin 30.00 60.00
Valvoline Max Life/20,004
6 Mark Martin 20.00 50.00
Zerex/5004
7 Michael Waltrip 25.00 60.00
Nations Rent/5508
8 Shawna Robinson 25.00 50.00
Kids RAD/5508
9 Jeff Burton 25.00 50.00
Northern Light
10 Johnny Benson 20.00 50.00
Lycos/5508
11 Brett Bodine 20.00 50.00
Ralph's/5508
12 Jeremy Mayfield 15.00 40.00
Mobil 1/10,008
14 Rick Mast 15.00 40.00
Conseco/5508
16 Kevin Lepage 20.00 50.00
Clemson/5508
16 Kevin Lepage 15.00 40.00
familyclick.com/7560
16 Kevin Lepage 15.00 40.00
Mac Tools/5508
17 Matt Kenseth 50.00 100.00
DeWalt/20,004
17 Matt Kenseth 60.00 100.00
DeWalt 24 Volt/20,004
17 Matt Kenseth 40.00 80.00
Visine/5508
21 Elliott Sadler 15.00 40.00
Citgo/5508
21 Elliott Sadler 25.00 50.00
Citgo Virginia Tech/5508
24 Ricky Hendrick 15.00 40.00
GMAC/1836
25 Jerry Nadeau 15.00 40.00
Holigan/5508
26 Jimmy Spencer 15.00 40.00
Big K/5508
40 Sterling Marlin 20.00 50.00
Coors Light/5508
40 Sterling Marlin 20.00 50.00
Coors Light
Brooks & Dunn/5508
42 Kenny Irwin 25.00 60.00
BellSouth/5508
44 Justin Labonte 15.00 40.00

Slim Jim/5508
45 Adam Petty 75.00 150.00
Sprint PCS/5508
55 Kenny Wallace 20.00 40.00
Square D/5508
57 Jason Keller 20.00 40.00
Excedrin/5508
60 Geoff Bodine 15.00 40.00
Power Team/5508
60 Mark Martin 30.00 80.00
Winn Dixie/20,008
60 Mark Martin 70.00 120.00
Winn Dixie Flames/5508
60 Mark Martin 70.00 110.00
Winn Dixie Flag/5508
63 Mark Green 20.00 40.00
Super Flo/2340
66 Darrell Waltrip 20.00 50.00
Route 66/5508
66 Darrell Waltrip 20.00 50.00
Route 66 Flames/5508
77 Robert Pressley 25.00 60.00
Jasper Cat/2340
97 Chad Little 25.00 60.00
John Deere/10,008
99 Jeff Burton 20.00 50.00
Exide/10,008
01 Tim Steele 15.00 40.00
Friends of NRA/5580

2000 Team Caliber Preferred Banks 1:24

EX NM-MT
5 Terry Labonte 20.00 50.00
Froot Loops/504
5 Terry Labonte 25.00 50.00
Kellogg's/504
6 Mark Martin 30.00 80.00
Eagle One/756
6 Mark Martin 30.00 80.00
Valvoline/756
6 Mark Martin 25.00 60.00
Valvoline Max Life/756
6 Mark Martin 25.00 50.00
Zerex/504
9 Jeff Burton 20.00 50.00
Northern Light/504
10 Johnny Benson 25.00 50.00
Lycos/504
11 Brett Bodine 25.00 50.00
Ralphs
12 Jeremy Mayfield 25.00 60.00
Mobil 1/504
14 Rick Mast 25.00 50.00
Conseco/504
16 Kevin Lepage 25.00 50.00
Clemson/504
16 Kevin Lepage 25.00 50.00
Familyclick.com/504
16 Kevin Lepage 25.00 50.00
Mac Tools/504
17 Matt Kenseth 50.00 100.00
DeWalt/756
17 Matt Kenseth 50.00 100.00
DeWalt 24 Volt/756
17 Matt Kenseth 50.00 100.00
Visine/504
21 Elliott Sadler 20.00 50.00
Citgo/504
21 Elliott Sadler 25.00 50.00
Citgo Virginia Tech/756
24 Ricky Hendrick 30.00 60.00
GMAC/504
25 Jerry Nadeau 20.00 50.00
Holigan/504
26 Jimmy Spencer 20.00 50.00
Big K-Mart/504
40 Sterling Marlin 30.00 60.00
Coors Light/504
40 Sterling Marlin 30.00 60.00
Coors Light
Brooks & Dunn/504
42 Kenny Irwin 40.00 80.00
BellSouth/504
43 John Andretti 20.00 50.00
Cheerios/504
44 Justin Labonte 30.00 60.00
Slim Jim/504
44 Kyle Petty 30.00 60.00
Hot Wheels/504
45 Adam Petty 75.00 150.00
Sprint PCS/732
57 Jason Keller 20.00 50.00
Excedrin/504
60 Mark Martin 60.00 100.00
Winn Dixie/504
60 Mark Martin 60.00 100.00
Winn Dixie Flag/504
66 Darrell Waltrip 25.00 50.00
Route 66/504
66 Darrell Waltrip 25.00 50.00
Route 66 Flames/504
97 Chad Little 30.00 80.00
John Deere/504
99 Jeff Burton 30.00 80.00
Exide/504

2000 Team Caliber White Knuckle Racing 1:24

These cars are massed produced and come in exclusive packaging. The 1:24 scale cars have an opening hood and are packaged in a clear window box.

EX NM-MT
6 Mark Martin 8.00 20.00
Valvoline
6 Mark Martin 8.00 20.00
Eagle One
17 Matt Kenseth 8.00 20.00
DeWalt
17 Matt Kenseth 12.50 25.00
Visine HO
97 Chad Little 8.00 20.00
John Deere
99 Jeff Burton 8.00 20.00
Exide

2001 Team Caliber Owners Series 1:24

EX NM-MT
1 Jimmy Spencer 125.00 250.00
Flight 93/1200
5 Terry Labonte 30.00 60.00
Kellogg's/2844
5 Terry Labonte 35.00 65.00
Kellogg's Mini Wheats/2340
5 Terry Labonte 25.00 60.00
Kellogg's Monsters Inc./1638
6 Mark Martin 50.00 100.00
JR's Garage/3120
6 Mark Martin 90.00 175.00
JR's Garage Promo/200
6 Mark Martin 30.00 80.00
Pfizer/7494
6 Mark Martin 40.00 80.00
Stroh's Light
1989 Thunderbird/7998
6 Mark Martin 25.00 60.00
Viagra/7494
6 Mark Martin 40.00 80.00
Viagra Metal Flake/4824
9 Jeff Burton 25.00 50.00
Gain/1500
10 Johnny Benson 20.00 40.00
Eagle One/1596
10 Johnny Benson 20.00 50.00
Valvoline/3120
10 Johnny Benson 20.00 50.00
Valvoline Employees/1800
10 Jeff Green 30.00 60.00
Nesquik/1200
12 Jeremy Mayfield 25.00 60.00
Mobil 1 Sony Wega/1008
17 Matt Kenseth 40.00 80.00
DeWalt/5004
17 Matt Kenseth 30.00 80.00
DeWalt AT&T/2058
17 Matt Kenseth 400.00 550.00
DeWalt Flag/804
17 Matt Kenseth 100.00 175.00
DeWalt Rookie of the Year
Yellow Hood/2840
17 Matt Kenseth 50.00 100.00
DeWalt Saw/1200
17 Matt Kenseth 30.00 60.00
Visine-A/2532
21 Elliott Sadler 30.00 60.00
Air Force/2400
21 Elliott Sadler 25.00 60.00
Motorcraft/2340
22 Ward Burton 25.00 50.00
Caterpillar/4050
22 Ward Burton 40.00 80.00
Caterpillar Flag
24 Ricky Hendrick 20.00 50.00
GMAC/1008
25 Jerry Nadeau 20.00 50.00
UAW Delphi/1800
32 Ricky Craven 35.00 75.00
Tide/1230
33 Joe Nemechek 30.00 60.00
Oakwood Homes
Charlie Daniels/1200
40 Sterling Marlin 30.00 60.00
Coors Light/2400
40 Sterling Marlin 35.00 60.00
Coors Light Brooks & Dunn/2406
40 Sterling Marlin 30.00 60.00
Coors Light John Wayne/2400
40 Sterling Marlin 50.00 90.00
Flag/2586
43 John Andretti 25.00 60.00
Cheerios/3396
43 John Andretti 25.00 60.00
Cheerios Mac Tools/3000
43 Dodge by Petty/3120 50.00 100.00
44 Buckshot Jones 30.00 60.00
Four Generations Petty/1896
44 Buckshot Jones 20.00 50.00
Georgia-Pacific
44 Buckshot Jones 20.00 50.00
Georgia Pacific Mac Tools/3000
45 Kyle Petty 30.00 60.00
Sprint PCS/4050
45 Kyle Petty 30.00 60.00
Sprint PCS Mac Tools/3000
45 Kyle Petty 30.00 60.00
Sprint PCS Charity Ride/2100
60 Greg Biffle 30.00 80.00
Grainger/1960
77 Robert Pressley 45.00 80.00
Forever in our
Hearts Flag/978
96 Andy Houston 20.00 50.00
McDonalds/1200
97 Kurt Busch 90.00 150.00
Sharpie/2310
97 Kurt Busch 150.00 300.00
Rubbermaid Flag/904
97 Kurt Busch 60.00 120.00
100 Years Ford/1800
99 Jeff Burton 25.00 60.00
Citgo/2250
99 Jeff Burton 25.00 60.00
Citgo MDA/2250
99 Jeff Burton 75.00 135.00
Citgo Stars&Stripes/1068
100 Hendrick Motor Sports 100 Wins 40.00 80.00
with 8-pewter driver figures/504
01 Kansas Protection One/1380 30.00 60.00
01 NDA 25.00 50.00
Friends of the NRA
02 Ryan Newman 125.00 250.00
Alltel/1200

2001 Team Caliber Owners Series Banks 1:24

EX NM-MT
5 Terry Labonte 20.00 50.00
Kellogg's/504
5 Terry Labonte 35.00 70.00
Kellogg's Mini Wheats/504
5 Terry Labonte 30.00 60.00
Monster's Inc/168
6 Mark Martin 50.00 90.00

JR's Garage/754		
6 Mark Martin Pfizer/1008	40.00	80.00
6 Mark Martin Viagra/1008	40.00	80.00
9 Jeff Burton Gain/504	20.00	50.00
10 Johnny Benson Eagle One/258	25.00	60.00
10 Johnny Benson Valvoline/504	30.00	60.00
10 Jeff Green Nesquik/258	20.00	50.00
12 Jeremy Mayfield Mobil 1/504	20.00	50.00
17 Matt Kenseth DeWalt/1008	45.00	80.00
17 Matt Kenseth DeWalt AT&T/426	25.00	60.00
17 Matt Kenseth DeWalt Saw/504	35.00	60.00
17 Matt Kenseth DeWalt Rookie of the Year/756	50.00	100.00
17 Matt Kenseth Visine-A/504	30.00	60.00
21 Elliott Sadler Motorcraft/756	25.00	60.00
22 Ward Burton Caterpillar	30.00	60.00
24 Ricky Hendrick GMAC/300	20.00	50.00
25 Jerry Nadeau UAW-Delphi/504	20.00	50.00
32 Ricky Craven Tide/258	35.00	70.00
33 Joe Nemechek Oakwood Homes Charlie Daniels Band/258	20.00	50.00
43 John Andretti Cheerios/756	30.00	60.00
44 Buckshot Jones Georgia-Pacific/756	20.00	50.00
44 Buckshot Jones Four Generations of Petty/756	25.00	60.00
45 Kyle Petty Sprint PCS	40.00	80.00
45 Kyle Petty Sprint PCS Charity Ride/504	20.00	50.00
60 Greg Biffle Grainger/756	50.00	90.00
97 Kurt Busch Sharpie/504	60.00	100.00
97 Kurt Busch 100 Years of Ford/258	50.00	100.00
99 Jeff Burton Citgo/426	25.00	60.00
02 Ryan Newman Alltel/258	150.00	225.00

2001 Team Caliber Owners Series Gold 1:24

	EX	NM-MT
5 Terry Labonte Monster's Inc/180	60.00	100.00
5 Terry Labonte Kellogg's	40.00	80.00
5 Terry Labonte Kellogg's Mini Wheats/504	25.00	60.00
6 Mark Martin JR's Garage	45.00	80.00
6 Mark Martin Pfizer/1008	40.00	80.00
6 Mark Martin Stroh's Light 1989 Thunderbird Mac Tools/5004	40.00	80.00
6 Mark Martin Viagra/1008	75.00	150.00
9 Jeff Burton Gain/504	30.00	60.00
10 Johnny Benson Valvoline Employees/258	25.00	50.00
10 Johnny Benson Eagle One/258	30.00	60.00
10 Jeff Green Nesquik/258	25.00	50.00
12 Jeremy Mayfield Mobil 1	30.00	60.00
12 Jeremy Mayfield Sony Wega/258	30.00	60.00
17 Matt Kenseth DeWalt/1008	75.00	150.00
17 Matt Kenseth Visine-A/504	50.00	100.00
21 Elliott Sadler Air Force/258	35.00	75.00
21 Elliott Sadler Motorcraft/504	30.00	60.00
22 Ward Burton Caterpillar/756	30.00	60.00
24 Ricky Hendrick GMAC/300	30.00	60.00
25 Jerry Nadeau UAW-Delphi/504	30.00	60.00
32 Ricky Craven Tide/258	25.00	50.00
33 Joe Nemechek Oakwood Homes Charlie Daniels Band/258	30.00	60.00
40 Sterling Marlin Coors Light/504	45.00	80.00
43 John Andretti Cheerios/756	30.00	70.00
44 Buckshot Jones Georgia-Pacific	25.00	60.00
44 Buckshot Jones Four Generations Petty/756		
45 Kyle Petty Sprint PCS/756	30.00	60.00
45 Kyle Petty Sprint PCS Charity Ride/504	30.00	60.00
60 Greg Biffle Grainger/756	50.00	100.00
96 Andy Houston McDonalds/258	20.00	50.00
97 Kurt Busch Sharpie/504	75.00	150.00
97 Kurt Busch 100 Years of Ford/258	75.00	150.00
99 Jeff Burton Citgo/1008	25.00	60.00

02 Ryan Newman Alltel/258	250.00	400.00

2001 Team Caliber Owners Series Steel 1:24

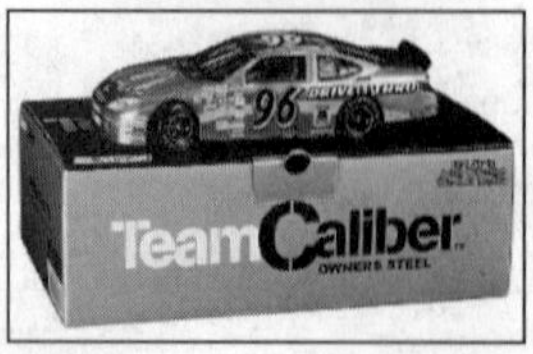

	EX	NM-MT
5 Terry Labonte Kellogg's/504	30.00	80.00
5 Terry Labonte Kellogg's Mini Wheats/504	25.00	50.00
5 Terry Labonte Kellogg's Monster's Inc/138	60.00	100.00
6 Mark Martin JR's Garage	45.00	80.00
6 Mark Martin Pfizer/1008	40.00	80.00
6 Mark Martin Viagra/1008	50.00	100.00
9 Jeff Burton Gain/504	30.00	60.00
10 Johnny Benson Eagle One/258	30.00	60.00
12 Jeremy Mayfield Sony Wega/258	25.00	50.00
17 Matt Kenseth DeWalt/1008	75.00	150.00
17 Matt Kenseth Visine-A/504	50.00	100.00
21 Elliott Sadler Motorcraft/504	25.00	50.00
22 Ward Burton Caterpillar/756	35.00	75.00
24 Ricky Hendrick GMAC/300	25.00	50.00
25 Jerry Nadeau UAW-Delphi/504	30.00	60.00
32 Ricky Craven Tide/258	30.00	60.00
33 Joe Nemechek Oakwood Homes Charlie Daniels/258	25.00	50.00
43 John Andretti Cheerios/756	25.00	50.00
44 Buckshot Jones Four Generations Petty/756	30.00	60.00
44 Buckshot Jones Georgia-Pacific/756	25.00	50.00
45 Kyle Petty Sprint PCS	50.00	75.00
45 Kyle Petty Sprint PCS Charity Ride/504	30.00	60.00
60 Greg Biffle Grainger/756	50.00	100.00
96 Andy Houston McDonalds/258	25.00	60.00
97 Kurt Busch Sharpie/504	75.00	125.00
97 Kurt Busch 100 Years of Ford/258	75.00	125.00
99 Jeff Burton Citgo/1008	35.00	75.00
99 Jeff Burton Citgo MDA/426	30.00	60.00
02 Ryan Newman Alltel/258	200.00	350.00

2001 Team Caliber Pit Stop 1:24

	EX	NM-MT
6 Mark Martin Pfizer	15.00	30.00
6 Mark Martin Viagra/3120	20.00	40.00
17 Matt Kenseth DeWalt/3120	10.00	20.00
17 Matt Kenseth DeWalt Saw/3120	10.00	20.00
22 Ward Burton Caterpillar/2400	10.00	20.00
40 Sterling Marlin Coors Light John Wayne	20.00	40.00
99 Jeff Burton Citgo	10.00	20.00

2001 Team Caliber Preferred 1:24

	EX	NM-MT
5 Terry Labonte Kellogg's	20.00	50.00
5 Terry Labonte Kellogg's Mini Wheats/2106	20.00	50.00
5 Terry Labonte Kellogg's Monster's Inc/4608	20.00	50.00
6 Mark Martin Pfizer/10080	20.00	50.00
6 Mark Martin Viagra/4996	20.00	50.00
6 Mark Martin Viagra Dark Chrome Mac Tools/5004	40.00	80.00
6 Mark Martin Viagra Metal Flake/10,080	20.00	50.00
9 Jeff Burton Gain/1008	25.00	50.00
10 Johnny Benson Eagle One/3624	20.00	40.00
10 Johnny Benson Valvoline/4920	20.00	40.00
10 Johnny Benson Valvoline Employees/5220	15.00	40.00
12 Jeremy Mayfield Sony Wega/900	25.00	50.00
17 Matt Kenseth DeWalt/2760	20.00	40.00
17 Matt Kenseth DeWalt AT&T/1896	20.00	40.00
17 Matt Kenseth DeWalt Saw/1896	20.00	40.00
17 Matt Kenseth Visine-A/5136	20.00	40.00
17 Matt Kenseth Visine-A Mac Tools/3000	15.00	30.00
21 Elliott Sadler Motorcraft/1500	25.00	50.00
22 Ward Burton Caterpillar/10080	20.00	40.00
24 Ricky Hendrick GMAC/900	20.00	40.00
25 Jerry Nadeau UAW-Delphi/1200	20.00	40.00
26 Jimmy Spencer The Mummy/4920	20.00	40.00
32 Ricky Craven Tide/3624	25.00	50.00
33 Joe Nemechek Oakwood Homes Charlie Daniels Band/900	25.00	50.00
36 Ken Schrader Stars&Stripes/10,700	125.00	250.00
40 Sterling Marlin Coors Light/1104	30.00	50.00
40 Sterling Marlin Coors Light Brook&Dunn/2802	25.00	60.00
40 Sterling Marlin Coors Light John Wayne/2940	20.00	40.00
43 John Andretti Cheerios/1980	20.00	40.00
44 Buckshot Jones Four Generations Petty/1800	20.00	40.00
44 Buckshot Jones Georgia-Pacific/4320	20.00	40.00
45 Kyle Petty Sprint PCS/5640	20.00	40.00
45 Kyle Petty Sprint PCS Charity Ride/1224	25.00	50.00
60 Greg Biffle Grainger/5004	20.00	40.00
60 Greg Biffle Grainger Mac Tools/3000	30.00	50.00
96 Andy Houston McDonald's/900	20.00	40.00
97 Kurt Busch Sharpie/5220	45.00	80.00
97 Kurt Busch 100 Years of Ford/4020	45.00	80.00
99 Jeff Burton Citgo MDA/5004	20.00	40.00
99 Jeff Burton Citgo MDA Mac Tools/3000	20.00	40.00
02 Ryan Newman Alltel/3876	70.00	120.00
02 Ryan Newman Alltel Promo/756	30.00	60.00

2001 Team Caliber Promos 1:24

	EX	NM-MT
10 Scott Riggs Nesquik/2400	12.50	25.00
26 Jimmy Spencer Mummy Returns	12.50	25.00
32 Dan Pardus Outdoor Channel	15.00	30.00
71 Kevin Lepage Mini Corn Dogs	15.00	30.00
71 Kevin Lepage State Fair Corn Dogs	12.50	25.00

2002 Team Caliber Owners Series 1:24

	EX	NM-MT
1 Jimmy Spencer Yellow Freight/1200	40.00	70.00
5 Ricky Hendrick GMAC/1200	30.00	60.00
5 Terry Labonte Cheez-It/2340	30.00	60.00
5 Terry Labonte Got Milk/2400	30.00	60.00
5 Terry Labonte Kellogg's/2400	30.00	60.00
6 Mark Martin Kraft/10008	40.00	80.00
6 Mark Martin Pfizer/5004	45.00	80.00
6 Mark Martin Viagra/10008	45.00	80.00
6 Mark Martin Viagra No Bull/6504	50.00	100.00
9 Jeff Burton Gain/1200	40.00	75.00
10 Johnny Benson Valvoline/3120	35.00	70.00
10 Johnny Benson Zerex/1200	40.00	75.00
12 Ryan Newman Alltel/5004	75.00	125.00
12 Ryan Newman Alltel Blue Chrome Rookie of the Year/2400	70.00	120.00
12 Ryan Newman Alltel Sony WEGA/3120	70.00	120.00
12 Ryan Newman Mobil 1/3120	70.00	120.00
17 Matt Kenseth DeWalt/3120	50.00	100.00
17 Matt Kenseth AT&T/2400	50.00	100.00
17 Matt Kenseth DeWalt Flames/3120	50.00	100.00
17 Matt Kenseth DeWalt Million $ Challenge/2400	50.00	100.00
21 Elliott Sadler Air Force/2400	40.00	70.00
21 Elliott Sadler Motorcraft/1800	30.00	60.00
24 Jack Sprague NetZero/1200	30.00	60.00
25 Bobby Hamilton Jr. Marines/1200	40.00	70.00
25 Jerry Nadeau UAW-Delphi/2400	25.00	60.00
27 Jamie McMurray USPS Heroes of 9-11/1500	75.00	150.00
32 Ricky Craven Tide/1200	40.00	70.00
36 Ken Schrader M&Ms/2400	40.00	80.00
36 Ken Schrader M&Ms Halloween/2400	40.00	80.00
36 Ken Schrader M&Ms July 4th/2400	40.00	80.00
36 Ken Schrader M&Ms Vote/3120	40.00	80.00
36 Ken Schrader M&Ms Vote Purple/2438	50.00	90.00
43 John Andretti Cheerios/2400	35.00	80.00
43 John Andretti StarWars/2400	40.00	80.00
43 Richard Petty Garfield/3120	40.00	75.00
45 Kyle Petty Sprint PCS/2400	40.00	80.00
45 Kyle Petty Sprint Charity Ride/1800	50.00	80.00
48 Jimmie Johnson Lowe's/3120	50.00	100.00
48 Jimmie Johnson Lowe's Power of Pride/5004	40.00	80.00
60 Greg Biffle Grainger Red Chrome BGN Champ/1200	60.00	120.00
60 Greg Biffle Grainger/3120	50.00	90.00
60 Jack Sprague HAAS/1200	30.00	60.00
97 Kurt Busch Rubbermaid/2400	40.00	75.00
97 Kurt Busch Rubbermaid Commercial/2400	40.00	70.00
97 Kurt Busch Rubbermaid Little Tikes/1800	45.00	80.00
97 Kurt Busch Sharpie 500/3120	45.00	80.00
97 Kurt Busch Sharpie Million $/2400	40.00	70.00
99 Jeff Burton Citgo/3120	30.00	60.00
99 Jeff Burton Citgo Bass Masters/1800	40.00	75.00
99 Jeff Burton Citgo Peel Out, Reel In & Win/2400	40.00	75.00
02 Daytona 500/1560	25.00	50.00
NNO NDA NBC/1008	50.00	80.00
NNO NDA TNT/1008	50.00	80.00

2002 Team Caliber Owners Series Banks 1:24

	EX	NM-MT
1 Jimmy Spencer Yellow Freight/60	40.00	70.00
2 NDA Daytona/1560	25.00	50.00
5 Ricky Hendrick GMAC/180	30.00	60.00
5 Terry Labonte Cheez-It/108	30.00	60.00
5 Terry Labonte Got Milk/180	30.00	60.00
5 Terry Labonte Kellogg's/264	30.00	60.00
6 Mark Martin Kraft/642	30.00	60.00
6 Mark Martin Pfizer/372	30.00	60.00
6 Mark Martin Viagra/576	35.00	60.00
6 Mark Martin Viagra No Bull/372	35.00	60.00
9 Jeff Burton Gain/180	40.00	75.00
10 Johnny Benson Valvoline/180	30.00	60.00
12 Ryan Newman Alltel/324	75.00	125.00
12 Ryan Newman Alltel Sony WEGA/198	70.00	120.00
12 Ryan Newman Mobil 1/192	70.00	120.00
17 Matt Kenseth DeWalt/270	60.00	100.00
17 Matt Kenseth DeWalt Flames/204	60.00	100.00
17 Matt Kenseth DeWalt Million $ Challenge/198	50.00	90.00
21 Elliott Sadler Air Force/180	30.00	60.00
21 Elliott Sadler Motorcraft/222	25.00	50.00
24 Jack Sprague NetZero/60	30.00	60.00
25 J.Nadeau UAW-Delphi/294	40.00	70.00
36 Ken Schrader M&Ms/180	30.00	70.00
36 Ken Schrader M&Ms July 4th/180	40.00	70.00
36 Ken Schrader M&Ms Vote/180	40.00	70.00
36 Ken Schrader M&Ms Vote Purple/180	40.00	80.00
43 John Andretti Cheerios/1134	25.00	50.00
43 Richard Petty Garfield/180	30.00	60.00
43 John Andretti StarWars/180	40.00	75.00
45 Kyle Petty Sprint PCS/180	30.00	60.00
48 Jimmie Johnson Lowe's/504	40.00	80.00
48 Jimmie Johnson Lowe's Power of Pride/390	40.00	80.00
60 Greg Biffle Grainger/228	40.00	75.00
60 Jack Sprague HAAS/180	30.00	60.00
97 Kurt Busch Rubbermaid/252	30.00	60.00
97 Kurt Busch Rubbermaid Commercial/180	30.00	60.00
97 Kurt Busch Rubbermaid Little Tikes/180	40.00	7
97 Kurt Busch Sharpie 500/180	40.00	7
97 Kurt Busch Sharpie Million $ Challenge/180	30.00	6
99 Jeff Burton Citgo/288	40.00	7
99 Jeff Burton Citgo Bass Masters/180	40.00	7
99 Jeff Burton Citgo Peel Reel Win/180	50.00	8

2002 Team Caliber Owne Series Dark Chrome 1:24

	EX	NM
1 Jimmy Spencer Yellow Freight/96	40.00	7
5 Ricky Hendrick GMAC/180	45.00	7
5 Terry Labonte Cheez-It/180	40.00	7
5 Terry Labonte Got Milk/504	40.00	7
5 Terry Labonte Kellogg's/264	40.00	7
6 Mark Martin Kraft/1296	40.00	7
6 Mark Martin Pfizer/426	50.00	9
6 Mark Martin Viagra/1026	60.00	10
6 Mark Martin Viagra No Bull/942	60.00	10
9 Jeff Burton Gain/504	50.00	9
10 Johnny Benson Valvoline/216	40.00	7
10 Johnny Benson Zerex/252	40.00	7
12 Ryan Newman Alltel/558	125.00	22
12 Ryan Newman Alltel Sony WEGA/1008	70.00	12
12 Ryan Newman Alltel The Winston/1212	90.00	15
12 Ryan Newman Mobil 1/378	60.00	10
17 Matt Kenseth DeWalt/354	125.00	25
17 Matt Kenseth AT&T/504	75.00	12
17 Matt Kenseth DeWalt Flames/930	70.00	12
17 Matt Kenseth DeWalt Million Dollar Challenge/588	50.00	10
21 Elliott Sadler Air Force/336	50.00	10
21 Elliott Sadler Motorcraft/180	40.00	7
24 Jack Sprague NetZero/174	40.00	7
25 Bobby Hamilton Jr. Marines/180	50.00	9
25 Jerry Nadeau UAW-Delphi/180	30.00	6
32 Ricky Craven Tide/180	40.00	7
36 Ken Schrader M&Ms/432	50.00	9
36 Ken Schrader M&Ms Halloween/540	50.00	9
36 Ken Schrader M&Ms July 4th/504	50.00	9
36 Ken Schrader M&Ms Vote/288	60.00	10
36 Ken Schrader M&Ms Vote Purple/900	60.00	10
43 John Andretti Cheerios/180	40.00	7
43 John Andretti StarWars/342	50.00	9
43 Richard Petty Garfield/396	50.00	9
45 Kyle Petty Sprint PCS/180	40.00	7
45 Kyle Petty Sprint Charity Ride/336	45.00	8
48 Jimmie Johnson Lowe's/1002	75.00	15
48 Jimmie Johnson Lowe's Power of Pride/1002	50.00	10
60 Greg Biffle Grainger/354	60.00	10
60 Jack Sprague HAAS/180	30.00	6
97 Kurt Busch Rubbermaid/288	40.00	8
97 Kurt Busch Rubbermaid Commercial/330	40.00	8
97 Kurt Busch Rubbermaid Little Tikes	40.00	8
97 Kurt Busch Sharpie Million $ Challenge/540	40.00	8
97 Kurt Busch Sharpie 500/600	40.00	8
99 Jeff Burton Citgo/384	30.00	6
99 Jeff Burton Citgo Bass Masters/426	40.00	8
99 Jeff Burton Citgo Peel Out, Reel In & Win/504	40.00	7
02 Santa Claus Holiday/3504	50.00	10

2002 Team Caliber Owne Series Vintage 1:24

	EX	NM
6 Mark Martin Folgers 1989 Thunderbird/7770	100.00	17
6 Mark Martin Stroh's Light 1991 ThunderBird	45.00	8
6 Mark Martin Stroh's Light '91 T-Bird	40.00	8

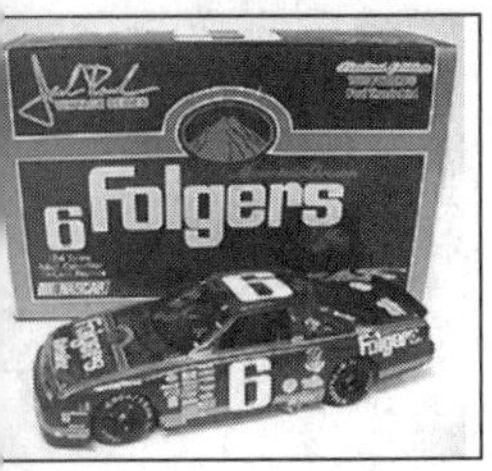

	EX	NM-MT
ark Chrome/5004		
il Bonnett	40.00	100.00
itgo 1989 Thunderbird/3120		

002 Team Caliber Pit Stop 1:24

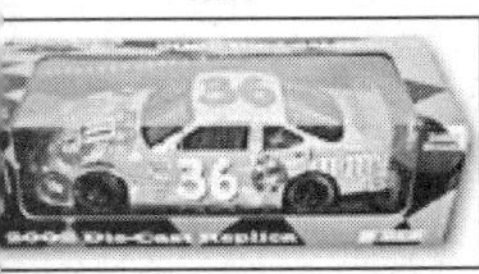

cars were released in 2002 and packaged in a gray and cardboard box with a clear window to view the car inside. rs are hood open models.

	EX	NM-MT
my Spencer ellow Freight	12.50	25.00
y Labonte ot Milk/2400	12.50	25.00
y Labonte ellogg's/2400	12.50	25.00
k Martin raft/5532	15.00	30.00
k Martin fizer/3810	12.50	25.00
k Martin iagra/7494	20.00	35.00
hnny Benson erex/900	15.00	30.00
an Newman ltel/2724	15.00	30.00
an Newman ltel Sony WEGA/2400	20.00	35.00
tt Kenseth eWalt/5520	15.00	30.00
tt Kenseth T&T/1800	15.00	30.00
tt Kenseth eWalt Million $ Challenge/3120	15.00	30.00
ry Nadeau AW-Delphi/2400	12.50	25.00
cky Craven ide Promo/2400	12.50	25.00
n Schrader /&Ms/2400	12.50	25.00
n Schrader M&Ms Halloween/2400	12.50	25.00
n Schrader /&Ms July 4th/2400	15.00	30.00
n Schrader /&Ms Vote/3120	12.50	25.00
n Schrader /&M's Vote Purple/3120	15.00	30.00
chard Petty arfield/2400	15.00	30.00
hn Andretti tarWars/3456	15.00	30.00
le Petty print PCS/708	12.50	25.00
le Petty print Charity Ride/2400	15.00	30.00
mmie Johnson owe's	20.00	35.00
mmie Johnson owe's Power of Pride	20.00	35.00
bby Hamilton quare D Promo	15.00	30.00
eg Biffle rainger/2400	12.50	25.00
rt Busch ubbermaid/2532	15.00	30.00
rt Busch ubbermaid Commercial/2400	15.00	30.00
rt Busch harpie Million $ Challenge/2400	15.00	30.00
rt Busch harpie 500/2400	15.00	30.00
f Burton itgo/3120	12.50	25.00
f Burton itgo Peel Out, Reel In & Win/2400	12.50	25.00
ytona 2002	12.50	25.00

02 Team Caliber Preferred 1:24

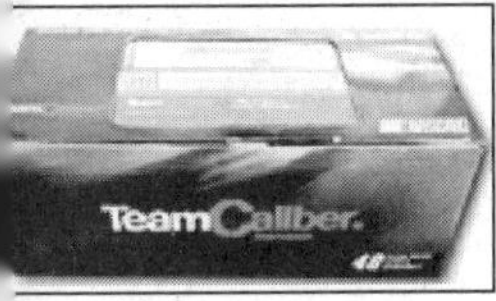

	EX	NM-MT
my Spencer ellow Freight/480	25.00	50.00
y Hendrick MAC/672	20.00	50.00
y Labonte heez-It/924	25.00	50.00
y Labonte ot Milk/1428	25.00	50.00
y Labonte ellogg's/2028	20.00	50.00
k Martin Kraft/6196	30.00	60.00
6 Mark Martin Kraft Mac Tools/2400	30.00	60.00
6 Mark Martin Pfizer/2550	30.00	60.00
6 Mark Martin Viagra/8196	30.00	60.00
6 Mark Martin Viagra Mac Tools/2400	30.00	60.00
6 Mark Martin Viagra No Bull/1480	30.00	60.00
9 Jeff Burton Gain/4020	25.00	50.00
10 Johnny Benson Valvoline/2448	20.00	50.00
10 Johnny Benson Zerex/3876	25.00	50.00
12 Ryan Newman Alltel/2820	30.00	60.00
12 Ryan Newman Alltel Sony WEGA/5004	40.00	75.00
12 Ryan Newman Mobil 1/1536	35.00	60.00
17 Matt Kenseth DeWalt/2448	40.00	80.00
17 Matt Kenseth DeWalt Mac Tools/2400	40.00	80.00
17 Matt Kenseth AT&T/4128	30.00	60.00
17 Matt Kenseth DeWalt Flames/1200	40.00	80.00
17 Matt Kenseth DeWalt Million $ Challenge/1392	40.00	80.00
21 Neil Bonnett Citgo 1989 Thunderbird Mac Tools/1500	75.00	125.00
21 Elliott Sadler Air Force/4260	30.00	60.00
21 Elliott Sadler Motorcraft/1176	20.00	50.00
24 Jack Sprague NetZero/612	25.00	50.00
25 Bobby Hamilton Jr. Marines/900	30.00	50.00
25 Jerry Nadeau UAW-Delphi/1608	20.00	50.00
32 Ricky Craven Tide/600	30.00	60.00
36 Ken Schrader M&Ms/2676	35.00	60.00
36 Ken Schrader M&Ms Halloween/4344	25.00	50.00
36 Ken Schrader M&Ms July 4th/1380	35.00	60.00
36 Ken Schrader M&M's Vote Purple/4008	35.00	60.00
36 Ken Schrader M&Ms Vote/5544	35.00	60.00
43 John Andretti Cheerios/180	20.00	50.00
43 Richard Petty Garfield/4428	35.00	60.00
43 John Andretti StarWars/4572	35.00	60.00
45 Adam Petty 2000 Sprint PCS Mac Tools/1506	75.00	125.00
45 Kyle Petty Sprint PCS/1152	20.00	50.00
45 Kyle Petty Sprint Charity Ride/900	25.00	50.00
48 Jimmie Johnson Lowe's/10,080	45.00	80.00
48 Jimmie Johnson Lowe's Power of Pride	45.00	80.00
60 Greg Biffle Grainger/2340	25.00	50.00
60 Jack Sprague HAAS/900	30.00	60.00
97 Kurt Busch Rubbermaid/2340	30.00	60.00
97 Kurt Busch Rubbermaid Commercial/4116	30.00	60.00
97 Kurt Busch Rubbermaid Little Tikes/4320	40.00	70.00
97 Kurt Busch Sharpie 500/2400	35.00	60.00
97 Kurt Busch Sharpie Million $ Challenge/4668	30.00	60.00
99 Jeff Burton Citgo/2340	20.00	50.00
99 Jeff Burton Citgo Bass Masters/4020	25.00	50.00
99 Jeff Burton Citgo Peel Out, Reel In and Win/4128	25.00	50.00

2002 Team Caliber Promos 1:24

	EX	NM-MT
2 Winston No Bull 5	10.00	20.00
27 Jamie McMurray USPS Heroes	15.00	25.00
60 Greg Biffle Grainger/1960	25.00	50.00
02 AT&T Daytona 500	15.00	30.00

2003 Team Caliber First Choice 1:24

	EX	NM-MT
5 Terry Labonte Kellogg's/250	50.00	100.00
6 Mark Martin Viagra/756	50.00	100.00
12 Ryan Newman Alltel/756	50.00	100.00
17 Matt Kenseth DeWalt/756	150.00	225.00
17 Matt Kenseth DeWalt '03 Champion Employee Promo/2000	200.00	350.00
17 Matt Kenseth DeWalt Victory Lap/717	100.00	200.00
17 Matt Kenseth Smirnoff Champ/717	150.00	225.00
48 Jimmie Johnson Lowe's/756	60.00	120.00

2003 Team Caliber Owners Series 1:24

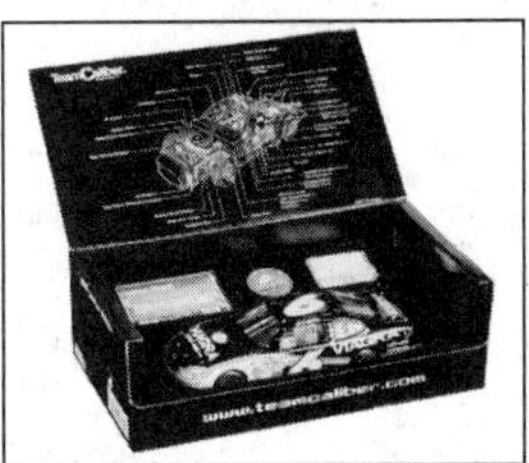

	EX	NM-MT
5 Terry Labonte Kellogg's/1200	45.00	75.00
5 Terry Labonte Kellogg's Cheez-It/1500	45.00	75.00
5 Terry Labonte Finding Nemo/1800	50.00	80.00
5 Terry Labonte Got Milk/1500	45.00	75.00
5 Terry Labonte Power of Cheese/1800	45.00	75.00
6 Mark Martin Kraft/1200	45.00	75.00
6 Mark Martin Pfizer/1200	45.00	75.00
6 Mark Martin Viagra/10,080	45.00	80.00
6 Mark Martin Viagra Blue Chrome/10,080	50.00	80.00
6 Mark Martin Viagra Blue Daytona/1800	50.00	80.00
6 Mark Martin Viagra White/1800	45.00	80.00
6 Mark Martin Viagra 500 Starts/1800	175.00	300.00
9 Greg Biffle Oreo/1200	45.00	75.00
10 Johnny Benson Eagle One/1500	40.00	70.00
10 Johnny Benson Valvoline/2400	40.00	70.00
12 Ryan Newman Alltel/7560	50.00	80.00
12 Ryan Newman Alltel 50th Win/1200	100.00	200.00
12 Ryan Newman Mobil 1/2400	50.00	80.00
12 Ryan Newman Sony Wega/2400	50.00	80.00
16 Greg Biffle Grainger/5004	45.00	80.00
17 Matt Kenseth Alka-Seltzer Plus/1008	50.00	80.00
17 Matt Kenseth Alka-Seltzer Morning Relief/1008	50.00	80.00
17 Matt Kenseth Bayer/1008	50.00	80.00
17 Matt Kenseth Bayer Aleve/1008	50.00	80.00
17 Matt Kenseth DeWalt/7560	90.00	175.00
17 Matt Kenseth DeWalt 2003 Champion/6504	60.00	100.00
17 Matt Kenseth DeWalt Million $ Challenge/2400	50.00	80.00
17 Matt Kenseth DeWalt Pearl Gold 2003 Champ/1008	100.00	200.00
17 Matt Kenseth Smirnoff Ice 2003 Champion/7500	60.00	100.00
17 Matt Kenseth DeWalt Victory Lap/5004	60.00	120.00
21 Ricky Rudd Air Force/2400	40.00	70.00
21 Ricky Rudd AF Cross Into Blue/2400	45.00	75.00
21 Ricky Rudd Ford 100 Years/1200	45.00	75.00
21 Ricky Rudd Motorcraft/7560	50.00	80.00
21 Ricky Rudd Motorcraft 700 Starts/1800	45.00	75.00
23 Kenny Wallace Stacker 2/1200	40.00	70.00
25 Bobby Hamilton Jr. Marines/1800	40.00	70.00
25 Bobby Hamilton Jr. Marines Flag/1212	75.00	150.00
25 Joe Nemechek UAW Delphi/1200	40.00	70.00
32 Ricky Craven Tide/1200	40.00	70.00
43 John Andretti Cheerios/1200	40.00	65.00
43 John Andretti Cheerios Berry Burst/1008	40.00	70.00
43 John Andretti Pillsbury/1500	40.00	65.00
45 Kyle Petty Brawny/1800	45.00	75.00
45 Kyle Petty Georgia Pacific/1600	45.00	75.00
45 Kyle Petty Georgia Pacific Charity Ride/1800	45.00	75.00
45 Kyle Petty GP Garfield/2400	40.00	70.00
48 Jimmie Johnson Lowe's/7560	45.00	75.00
48 Jimmie Johnson Lowe's Blue Chrome/2400	60.00	100.00
48 Jimmie Johnson Lowe's Power of Pride/2400	45.00	75.00
60 Brian Vickers HAAS/1200	40.00	65.00
87 Kyle Busch Ditech.com/1800	40.00	70.00
97 Kurt Busch Rubbermaid/5004	50.00	80.00
97 Kurt Busch Blue Ice	50.00	80.00
97 Kurt Busch Rubbermaid Commercial Products/2400	50.00	80.00
97 Kurt Busch Irwin Tools/2400	45.00	75.00
97 Kurt Busch Sharpie/2400	50.00	80.00
99 Jeff Burton Citgo/7560	40.00	70.00
99 Jeff Burton Velveeta/1200	40.00	70.00
99 Kenny Wallace Cardinals/1200	40.00	70.00
01 Jerry Nadeau Army/1200	40.00	70.00
01 Jerry Nadeau Army Camouflage/1800	40.00	70.00
01 Jerry Nadeau USG Sheet Rock/1500	40.00	70.00

2003 Team Caliber Owners Series Banks 1:24

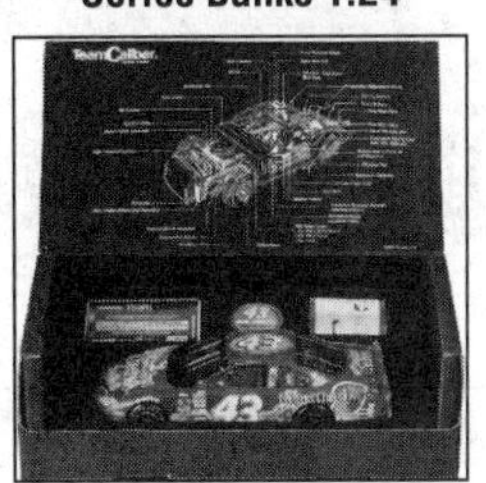

	EX	NM-MT
5 Terry Labonte Kellogg's/180	45.00	75.00
5 Terry Labonte Kellogg's Power of Cheese/180	40.00	75.00
6 Mark Martin Kraft/300	60.00	100.00
6 Mark Martin Pfizer/180	50.00	90.00
6 Mark Martin Viagra/2400	50.00	90.00
6 Mark Martin Viagra Blue Daytona/180	50.00	80.00
6 Mark Martin Viagra White/180	50.00	90.00
6 Mark Martin Viagra 500 Starts/180	100.00	150.00
9 Greg Biffle Oreo/180	40.00	75.00
10 Johnny Benson Valvoline/180	45.00	75.00
12 Ryan Newman Alltel/180	70.00	120.00
12 Ryan Newman Alltel 50th Win/180	100.00	175.00
12 Ryan Newman Mobil 1/180	75.00	125.00
12 Ryan Newman Sony Wega/180	75.00	125.00
16 Greg Biffle Grainger/300	50.00	90.00
17 Matt Kenseth DeWalt/300	90.00	150.00
17 Matt Kenseth DeWalt Million $ Challenge/180	50.00	100.00
21 Ricky Rudd Air Force/180	40.00	75.00
21 Ricky Rudd Ford 100 Years/180	40.00	75.00
21 Ricky Rudd Motorcraft/300	40.00	75.00
21 Ricky Rudd Motorcraft 700 Starts/180	40.00	75.00
23 Kenny Wallace Stacker 2/180	45.00	75.00
25 Bobby Hamilton Jr. Marines/180	40.00	75.00
25 Joe Nemechek UAW Delphi/180	45.00	75.00
32 Ricky Craven Tide/180	45.00	75.00
43 John Andretti Cheerios/120	45.00	75.00
43 John Andretti Cheerios Berry Burst/180	45.00	75.00
45 Kyle Petty Georgia Pacific/180	40.00	80.00
48 Jimmie Johnson Lowe's/180	50.00	90.00
87 Kyle Busch Ditech.com/180	40.00	70.00
97 Kurt Busch Blue Ice/180	50.00	90.00
97 Kurt Busch Rubbermaid/300	50.00	90.00
97 Kurt Busch Rubbermaid Commercial Products/180	50.00	80.00
97 Kurt Busch Irwin Tools/180	50.00	80.00
97 Kurt Busch Sharpie/180	50.00	80.00
99 Jeff Burton Citgo/300	50.00	90.00
99 Jeff Burton Velveeta/180	50.00	80.00
01 Jerry Nadeau Army/180	45.00	75.00
01 Jerry Nadeau Army Camoflauge/180	45.00	75.00
03 Daytona 500/180	45.00	75.00

2003 Team Caliber Owners Series Dark Chrome 1:24

	EX	NM-MT
5 Terry Labonte Kellogg's/250	50.00	90.00
5 Terry Labonte Kellogg's Cheez-It/180	50.00	80.00
5 Terry Labonte Finding Nemo/252	60.00	100.00

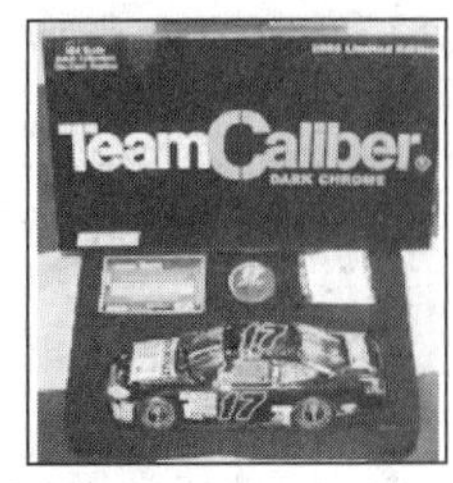

	EX	NM-MT
5 Terry Labonte Kellogg's Got Milk/180	50.00	90.00
5 Terry Labonte Power of Cheese/180	50.00	90.00
6 Mark Martin Kraft/300	60.00	100.00
6 Mark Martin Pfizer/402	60.00	100.00
6 Mark Martin Viagra/1002	60.00	100.00
6 Mark Martin Viagra Blue Daytona/324	50.00	100.00
6 Mark Martin Viagra 500 Starts/300	100.00	175.00
6 Mark Martin Viagra White/360	60.00	100.00
9 Greg Biffle Oreo/180	50.00	80.00
10 Johnny Benson Eagle One/180	50.00	80.00
10 Johnny Benson Valvoline/180	50.00	80.00
12 Ryan Newman Alltel/1008	75.00	125.00
12 Ryan Newman Alltel 50th Win/180	125.00	250.00
12 Ryan Newman Mobil 1/324	100.00	175.00
12 Ryan Newman Alltel 2003 Driver of the Year Silver Chrome/1200	60.00	100.00
12 Ryan Newman Sony Wega/220	125.00	250.00
16 Greg Biffle Grainger/756	60.00	100.00
17 Matt Kenseth Bayer/234	60.00	100.00
17 Matt Kenseth DeWalt/840	90.00	150.00
17 Matt Kenseth DeWalt Million $ Challenge/402	60.00	120.00
17 Matt Kenseth Smirnoff Ice 2003 Champion Pearl Chrome/1008	75.00	125.00
17 Matt Kenseth Victory Lap/600	100.00	175.00
21 Ricky Rudd Air Force/360	50.00	90.00
21 Ricky Rudd AF Cross Into Blue/240	50.00	90.00
21 Ricky Rudd Ford 100 Years/282	50.00	90.00
21 Ricky Rudd Motorcraft/1008	50.00	90.00
21 Ricky Rudd Motorcraft 700 Starts/180	50.00	90.00
23 Kenny Wallace Stacker 2/240	50.00	80.00
25 Bobby Hamilton Jr. Marines/180	50.00	80.00
25 Bobby Hamilton Jr. Marines Flag Blue Chrome/180	100.00	200.00
25 Joe Nemechek UAW Delphi/180	50.00	80.00
32 Ricky Craven Tide/180	50.00	80.00
43 John Andretti Cheerios/180	45.00	75.00
43 John Andretti Cheerios Berry Burst/324	60.00	100.00
43 John Andretti Pillsbury/180	45.00	75.00
45 Kyle Petty Brawny/300	50.00	90.00
45 Kyle Petty Georgia Pacific/225	50.00	90.00
45 Kyle Petty Georgia Pacific Charity Ride/180	50.00	90.00
45 Kyle Petty GP Garfield/180	50.00	90.00
48 Jimmie Johnson Lowe's/684	60.00	100.00
48 Jimmie Johnson Lowe's Power of Pride Winston/180	60.00	120.00
66 Chad Blount Miller High Life/180	60.00	90.00
87 Kyle Busch Ditech.com/180	50.00	75.00
97 Kurt Busch Blue Ice/360	50.00	100.00
97 Kurt Busch Rubbermaid/504	50.00	100.00
97 Kurt Busch Rubbermaid Commercial Products/300	50.00	100.00
97 Kurt Busch Irwin Tools/240	50.00	100.00
97 Kurt Busch Sharpie/360	50.00	100.00
99 Jeff Burton Citgo/756	45.00	80.00
99 Jeff Burton Velveeta/180	50.00	90.00
99 Kenny Wallace Cardinals/180	45.00	80.00
01 Jerry Nadeau Army/402	50.00	80.00
03 Daytona 500/200	50.00	90.00
03 Santa Claus Holiday Blue Chrome/3120	50.00	80.00

2003 Team Caliber Owners Series Vintage 1:24

	EX	NM-MT
11 Darrell Waltrip 1985 Budweiser/1800	50.00	80.00
11 Darrell Waltrip 1987 Pepsi/1800	50.00	80.00
17 Darrell Waltrip 1995 Parts America/1200	45.00	80.00
17 Darrell Waltrip 1992 Western Auto/1200	45.00	80.00
28 Davey Allison 1990 Texaco Thunderbird/2400	40.00	70.00
28 Davey Allison 1990 Texaco Dark Chrome Mac Tools/1506	60.00	100.00

2003 Team Caliber Pit Stop 1:24

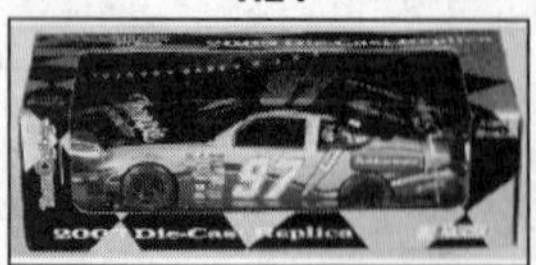

	EX	NM-MT
1 Jamie McMurray Yellow Freight	10.00	20.00
5 Terry Labonte Kellogg's	10.00	20.00
5 Terry Labonte Finding Nemo	10.00	20.00
5 Terry Labonte Got Milk	10.00	20.00
5 Terry Labonte Power of Cheese	10.00	20.00
5 Brian Vickers Carquest	12.50	25.00
5 Brian Vickers GMAC	15.00	30.00
6 Mark Martin Kraft/2400	12.50	25.00
6 Mark Martin Pfizer	12.50	25.00
6 Mark Martin Viagra	12.50	25.00
6 Mark Martin Viagra Blue Daytona	12.50	25.00
6 Mark Martin Viagra White	12.50	25.00
6 Mark Martin Viagra 500 Starts	15.00	30.00
10 Johnny Benson Valvoline	10.00	20.00
12 Ryan Newman Alltel/3120	12.50	25.00
12 Ryan Newman Mobil 1	12.50	25.00
12 Ryan Newman Sony Wega	12.50	25.00
16 Greg Biffle Grainger/3120	12.50	25.00
16 Greg Biffle Grainger 1st Win	12.50	25.00
17 Matt Kenseth Bayer	12.50	25.00
17 Matt Kenseth DeWalt/1200	12.50	25.00
17 Matt Kenseth DeWalt 2003 Champion	15.00	25.00
17 Matt Kenseth DeWalt Million $ Challenge	12.50	25.00
17 Matt Kenseth Victory Lap	12.50	25.00
21 Ricky Rudd Air Force	10.00	20.00
21 Ricky Rudd AF Cross Into Blue	10.00	20.00
21 Ricky Rudd Ford 100 Years	10.00	20.00
21 Ricky Rudd Motorcraft/3120	10.00	20.00
21 Ricky Rudd Motorcraft 700 Starts	10.00	20.00
23 Kenny Wallace Stacker 2	10.00	20.00
23 Kenny Wallace Stacker 2 YJ Stinger	10.00	20.00
25 Bobby Hamilton Jr. Marines	10.00	20.00
25 Joe Nemechek UAW Delphi	10.00	20.00
32 Ricky Craven Tide	10.00	20.00
43 John Andretti Cheerios	10.00	20.00
43 John Andretti Cheerios Berry Burst	10.00	20.00
45 Kyle Petty Brawny	10.00	20.00
45 Kyle Petty Georgia Pacific	10.00	20.00
45 Kyle Petty Georgia Pacific Charity Ride	10.00	20.00
45 Kyle Petty GP Garfield	10.00	20.00
45 Kyle Petty Victory Junction Hands	10.00	20.00
48 Jimmie Johnson Lowe's	12.50	30.00
48 Jimmie Johnson Lowe's Power of Pride	12.50	25.00
66 Chad Blount Miller High Life	15.00	30.00
77 Dave Blaney Jasper Panther	10.00	20.00
87 Kyle Busch Ditech.com	12.50	25.00
97 Kurt Busch Rubbermaid Blue Ice	10.00	20.00
97 Kurt Busch Rubbermaid/3120	10.00	20.00
97 Kurt Busch Rubbermaid Commercial Products	10.00	20.00
97 Kurt Busch Irwin Tools	10.00	20.00
97 Kurt Busch Sharpie	10.00	20.00
99 Jeff Burton Citgo	10.00	20.00
99 Jeff Burton Velveeta	10.00	20.00
99 Kenny Wallace Cardinals	10.00	20.00
01 Jerry Nadeau Army	10.00	20.00
01 Jerry Nadeau Army Camouflage	10.00	20.00
01 Jerry Nadeau USG Sheet Rock	10.00	20.00
03 Daytona 500	12.50	25.00

2003 Team Caliber Preferred 1:24

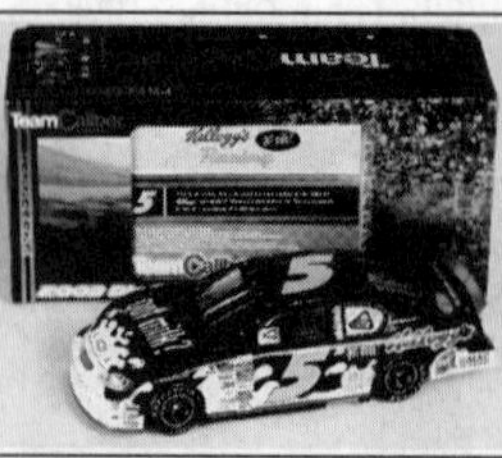

	EX	NM-MT
5 Terry Labonte Kellogg's/900	30.00	60.00
5 Terry Labonte Kellogg's Cheez-It	35.00	60.00
5 Terry Labonte Finding Nemo/5004	40.00	70.00
5 Terry Labonte Got Milk/1500	35.00	60.00
5 Terry Labonte Power of Cheese/4020	35.00	60.00
6 Mark Martin Kraft/10,080	35.00	60.00
6 Mark Martin Pfizer/900	35.00	60.00
6 Mark Martin Viagra/5004	25.00	60.00
6 Mark Martin Viagra Blue Daytona/10,080	35.00	60.00
6 Mark Martin Viagra White/2004	35.00	60.00
6 Mark Martin Viagra 500 Starts	60.00	100.00
9 Greg Biffle Oreo/4020	35.00	60.00
10 Johnny Benson Eagle One/4020	35.00	60.00
10 Johnny Benson Valvoline/4020	35.00	60.00
12 Ryan Newman Alltel/20,008	35.00	60.00
12 Ryan Newman Alltel 50th Win/4090	75.00	150.00
12 Ryan Newman Mobil 1/1200	35.00	60.00
12 Ryan Newman Sony Wega/4320	35.00	60.00
16 Greg Biffle Grainger/10,008	30.00	60.00
17 Matt Kenseth Bayer/4020	40.00	70.00
17 Matt Kenseth DeWalt/2400	40.00	70.00
17 Matt Kenseth DeWalt 2003 Champion/10,080	45.00	70.00
17 Matt Kenseth DeWalt 2003 Champ Gold/504	100.00	175.00
17 Matt Kenseth DeWalt Million $ Challenge/4128	40.00	70.00
17 Matt Kenseth Smirnoff Ice 2003 Champion	40.00	70.00
17 Matt Kenseth DeWalt Victory Lap/10,080	45.00	70.00
17 Matt Kenseth DeWalt Victory Lap Gold/205	150.00	250.00
21 Ricky Rudd Air Force/1200	30.00	60.00
21 Ricky Rudd AF Cross Into Blue/4320	35.00	60.00
21 Ricky Rudd Ford 100 Years/900	35.00	60.00
21 Ricky Rudd Motorcraft/3120	35.00	60.00
21 Ricky Rudd Motorcraft 700 Starts/4020	35.00	60.00
23 Kenny Wallace Stacker 2/600	35.00	60.00
25 Bobby Hamilton Jr. Marines/4020	35.00	60.00
25 Joe Nemechek UAW Delphi/4116	30.00	60.00
32 Ricky Craven Tide/900	35.00	60.00
43 John Andretti Cheerios/900	35.00	60.00
43 John Andretti Cheerios Berry Burst/1008	25.00	60.00
43 John Andretti Pillsbury/4020	30.00	60.00
45 Kyle Petty Brawny/4020	35.00	60.00
45 Kyle Petty Georgia Pacific/900	35.00	60.00
45 Kyle Petty Georgia Pacific Charity Ride/1008	40.00	70.00
45 Kyle Petty GP Garfield	40.00	70.00
48 Jimmie Johnson Lowe's/1200	30.00	60.00
48 Jimmie Johnson Lowe's Power of Pride/4320	30.00	60.00
87 Kyle Busch Ditech.com/4020	30.00	60.00
97 Kurt Busch Rubbermaid/10,080	30.00	60.00
97 Kurt Busch Blue Ice/2004	35.00	60.00
97 Kurt Busch Rubbermaid Commercial Products/4128	30.00	60.00
97 Kurt Busch Irwin Tools/6708	35.00	60.00
97 Kurt Busch Sharpie/4320	35.00	60.00
99 Jeff Burton Citgo/10,152	30.00	60.00
99 Jeff Burton Velveeta/4020	25.00	60.00
99 Kenny Wallace Cardinals/4320	35.00	60.00
01 Jerry Nadeau Army/4128	40.00	65.00
01 Jerry Nadeau Army Camouflage/4020	35.00	60.00
01 Jerry Nadeau USG Sheet Rock/5004	35.00	60.00
03 Daytona 500/1500	25.00	50.00

2003 Team Caliber Promos 1:24

	EX	NM-MT
4 Mike Wallace Geico Promo	20.00	40.00
5 Brian Vickers Carquest Promo	18.00	30.00
17 Matt Kenseth Bayer Blue/400	300.00	400.00
17 Matt Kenseth Bayer Yellow	20.00	35.00
21 Ricky Rudd Rent-A-Center	25.00	40.00

2003 Team Caliber/Motorworks 1:24

	EX	NM-MT
17 Matt Kenseth DeWalt Victory Lap	18.00	30.00
25 Brian Vickers ditech.com	15.00	25.00

2003 Team Caliber/Motorworks Model Kits 1:24

	EX	NM-MT
6 Mark Martin Viagra	12.50	25.00
12 Ryan Newman Alltel	12.50	25.00
16 Greg Biffle Grainger	12.50	25.00
17 Matt Kenseth DeWalt	12.50	25.00
21 Ricky Rudd Motorcraft	12.50	25.00
97 Kurt Busch Irwin Tools	12.50	25.00
97 Kurt Busch Rubbermaid	12.50	25.00

2004 Team Caliber First Choice 1:24

	EX	NM-MT
5 Terry Labonte Spiderman/250	50.00	100.00
6 Mark Martin Batman/250	90.00	150.00
6 Mark Martin Viagra White night race/504	90.00	150.00
12 Ryan Newman Justice League/250	90.00	150.00
12 Ryan Newman Mobil 1 30th Anniversary/250	75.00	125.00
16 Greg Biffle National Guard/250	60.00	120.00
17 Matt Kenseth DeWalt/504	90.00	150.00
17 Matt Kenseth Martian Manhunter/250	60.00	120.00
17 Matt Kenseth Smirnoff/504	60.00	120.00
97 Kurt Busch Irwin Tools/250	50.00	100.00
97 Kurt Busch Sharpie/250	50.00	100.00
97 Kurt Busch Sharpie '04 Champion Employee w/Trophy	125.00	250.00
97 Kurt Busch Superman/250	60.00	120.00
99 Carl Edwards World Financial Group/250	175.00	300.00
01 Joe Nemechek Army/250	50.00	100.00
04 Disney Event Mickey Mouse/250	40.00	80.00

2004 Team Caliber Owners Series 1:24

	EX	NM-MT
5 Kyle Busch Lowe's	40.00	70.00
5 Terry Labonte Delphi	40.00	70.00
5 Terry Labonte Kellogg's/2400	40.00	70.00
5 Terry Labonte Kellogg's Olympics/2340	40.00	70.00
5 Terry Labonte Spiderman/1200	40.00	70.00
6 Mark Martin Batman/7560	60.00	100.00
6 Mark Martin Oscar Mayer/3120	40.00	70.00
6 Mark Martin Pfizer/3120	40.00	80.00
6 Mark Martin Viagra/5004	40.00	80.00
6 Mark Martin Viagra White night race/3120	60.00	100.00
9 Jeff Burton Pennzoil/1200	40.00	70.00
9 Matt Kenseth Pennzoil/1200	40.00	70.00
9 Mark Martin Pennzoil/1200	40.00	70.00
9 Mark Martin Batman/3120	60.00	100.00
10 Scott Riggs Valvoline/1800	40.00	70.00
12 Ryan Newman Alltel/5004	50.00	80.00
12 Ryan Newman Justice League/7560	50.00	80.00
12 Ryan Newman Mobil 1/5004	50.00	80.00
12 Ryan Newman Mobil 1 30th Anniversary/5004	50.00	80.00
12 Ryan Newman Sony Wega/3120	50.00	80.00
16 Greg Biffle Coke C2/2400	40.00	70.00
16 Greg Biffle Flash/3120	25.00	50.00
16 Greg Biffle National Guard/3200	40.00	70.00
17 Matt Kenseth Carhartt/5004	60.00	100.00
17 Matt Kenseth DeWalt/6240	60.00	100.00
17 Matt Kenseth Martian Manhunter/5004	60.00	100.00
17 Matt Kenseth Smirnoff/7560	40.00	70.00
21 Ricky Rudd Air Force/3120	40.00	70.00
21 Ricky Rudd Coke C2/2400	40.00	70.00
21 Ricky Rudd Motorcraft/3120	40.00	70.00
21 Ricky Rudd Rent A Center/2400	40.00	70.00
21 Ricky Rudd Wonder Woman/3120	40.00	70.00
22 Scott Wimmer Caterpillar/1200	40.00	70.00
25 Bobby Hamilton Jr. Marines Flames/2400	40.00	70.00
25 Brian Vickers Ditech.com/1200	40.00	70.00
43 Jeff Green Cheerios/2400	40.00	70.00
45 Kyle Petty Brawny/2400	40.00	70.00
45 Kyle Petty Georgia Pacific/2400	40.00	70.00
48 Jimmie Johnson Lowe's/2400	50.00	80.00
60 Greg Biffle Charter/2400	40.00	70.00
60 Greg Biffle Flash/2400	25.00	50.00
84 Kyle Busch Car Quest/2400	40.00	70.00
97 Kurt Busch Coke C2/2400	30.00	60.00
97 Kurt Busch Irwin Tools/2400	30.00	60.00
97 Kurt Busch Irwin Tools '04 Champion/2400	40.00	70.00
97 Kurt Busch Sharpie/2400	40.00	70.00
97 Kurt Busch Sharpie '04 Champion/2400	40.00	70.00
97 Kurt Busch Sharpie 40th Anniversary/3120	30.00	60.00
97 Kurt Busch Superman/5004	40.00	70.00
99 Jeff Burton Coke C2/2400	40.00	70.00
99 Jeff Burton Green Lantern/3120	40.00	70.00
99 Jeff Burton SKF/2400	40.00	70.00
01 Jerry Nadeau Army	40.00	70.00
NNO Disney Event Car Donald Duck/3120	40.00	70.00
NNO Disney Event Car Goofy/3120	40.00	70.00
NNO Disney Event Car Mickey Mouse/3120	40.00	70.00
NNO Disney Event Car Minnie Mouse/3120	40.00	70.00
NNO Disney Event Car PegLeg/3120	40.00	70.00
NNO Justice League Event Car/3120	40.00	70.00
NNO Justice League Villain Event Car/3120	40.00	70.00

2004 Team Caliber Owners Series Pearl Chrome 1:24

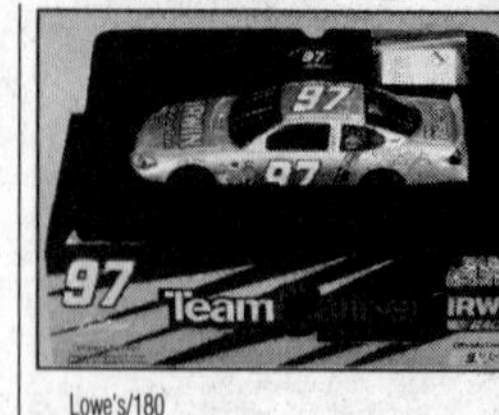

	EX	NM-MT
5 Kyle Busch Lowe's/180	50.00	75.00
5 Kyle Busch Lowe's SpongeBob/250	50.00	7
5 Terry Labonte Kellogg's/504	60.00	10
5 Terry Labonte Delphi/504	50.00	8
5 Terry Labonte Kellogg's Olympics/240	50.00	8
5 Terry Labonte Spiderman/756	60.00	10
6 Mark Martin Batman/1008	75.00	12
6 Mark Martin Oscar Mayer/300	60.00	10
6 Mark Martin Pfizer/402	60.00	10
6 Mark Martin Viagra/504	60.00	10
6 Mark Martin Viagra White night race/504	60.00	10
9 Matt Kenseth Pennzoil/300	60.00	10
9 Mark Martin Pennzoil/252	60.00	10
9 Mark Martin Batman/504	75.00	12
10 Scott Riggs Valvoline/180	60.00	10
12 Ryan Newman Alltel/504	90.00	15
12 Ryan Newman Justice League/1008	75.00	12
12 Ryan Newman Mobil 1/600	75.00	12
12 Ryan Newman Mobil 1 30th Ann./504	75.00	12
12 Ryan Newman Sony Wega/756	60.00	10
16 Greg Biffle Coke C2 Red Chrome/250	50.00	8
16 Greg Biffle Flash/504	40.00	8
16 Greg Biffle National Guard/300	40.00	8
17 Matt Kenseth Carhartt/756	60.00	10
17 Matt Kenseth DeWalt/600	60.00	10
17 Matt Kenseth DeWalt All Star Yellow Chrome AU/1717	125.00	20
17 Matt Kenseth Martian Manhunter	50.00	8
17 Matt Kenseth Smirnoff/1008	60.00	10
21 Ricky Rudd Air Force/600	50.00	8
21 Ricky Rudd Coke C2 Red Chrome/250	50.00	8
21 Ricky Rudd Motorcraft/276	50.00	8
21 Ricky Rudd Rent A Center/180	50.00	8
21 Ricky Rudd Wonder Woman	50.00	8
22 Scott Wimmer Caterpillar/300	50.00	8
25 Bobby Hamilton Jr. Marines Flames	60.00	10
25 Brian Vickers Ditech.com/300	75.00	12
45 Kyle Petty Brawny/180	60.00	10
45 Kyle Petty Georgia Pacific/180	60.00	10
48 Jimmie Johnson Lowe's/222	75.00	12
48 Jimmie Johnson Lowe's SpongeBob/354	60.00	10
60 Greg Biffle Charter/180	60.00	10
60 Greg Biffle Flash	50.00	8
84 Kyle Busch Car Quest/222	50.00	7
97 Kurt Busch Irwin Tools/300	30.00	6
97 Kurt Busch Sharpie/504	40.00	8
97 Kurt Busch Sharpie 40th Anniversary/504	30.00	8
97 Kurt Busch Superman/756	40.00	8
99 Jeff Burton Coke C2 Red Chrome	50.00	8
99 Jeff Burton Green Lantern/504	60.00	10
99 Jeff Burton SKF/180	45.00	7
01 Joe Nemechek Army/300	50.00	8
04 Justice League Event Car/504	45.00	7
04 Justice League Villain Event Car/504	45.00	7
NNO Disney Event Car Donald Duck/504	50.00	8
NNO Disney Event Car Goofy/504	50.00	8
NNO Disney Event Car Mickey Mouse/504	50.00	8
NNO Disney Event Car Minnie Mouse/504	50.00	8
NNO Disney Event Car PegLeg/504	50.00	8

2004 Team Caliber Owne Series Vintage 1:24

	EX	NM
28 Davey Allison Texaco '87 t-bird/1500	50.00	8

4 Team Caliber Pit Stop 1:24

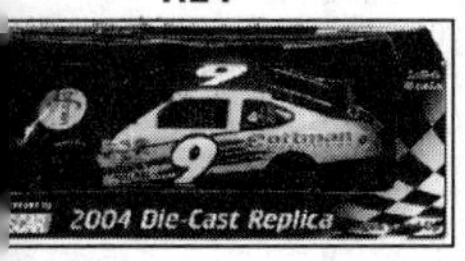

	EX	NM-MT
usch 's	15.00	25.00
sch 's SpongeBob	10.00	20.00
abonte hi	10.00	20.00
abonte gg's	10.00	20.00
abonte gg's Olympics	10.00	20.00
abonte erman	10.00	20.00
Martin an	15.00	25.00
Martin r Mayer	10.00	20.00
Martin r	12.50	25.00
Martin a	12.50	25.00
artin a White	12.50	25.00
rton nan	10.00	20.00
rton zoil	10.00	20.00
enseth zoil	10.00	20.00
Martin zoil	10.00	20.00
Martin an	15.00	25.00
Riggs m Globetrotters	10.00	20.00
Riggs line	10.00	20.00
Newman	12.50	25.00
Newman ce League	15.00	25.00
Newman l 1	12.50	25.00
Newman l 1 30th Anniversary	12.50	25.00
Newman Wega	12.50	25.00
Atwood	10.00	20.00
Biffle C2	10.00	20.00
Biffle	10.00	20.00
Biffle son-Hewitt	10.00	20.00
Biffle nal Guard	12.50	25.00
Biffle vay	12.50	25.00
Biffle lodge	10.00	20.00
Kenseth r	12.50	25.00
Kenseth artt	12.50	25.00
enseth alt	12.50	25.00
Kenseth ss Personnel	10.00	20.00
Kenseth an Manhunter	12.50	25.00
Rudd orce	10.00	20.00
Rudd C2	10.00	20.00
Rudd rcraft	10.00	20.00
Rudd A Center	10.00	20.00
Rudd der Woman	10.00	20.00
Wimmer pillar	10.00	20.00
Vickers h.com	10.00	20.00
Hamilton Jr. nes Flames	10.00	20.00
reen rios	10.00	20.00
reen y Charms	10.00	20.00
etty ny	10.00	20.00
Petty gia Pacific	10.00	20.00
e Johnson 's	12.50	25.00
e Johnson 's SpongeBob	10.00	20.00
Biffle er	10.00	20.00
Biffle	10.00	20.00
Busch Quest	12.50	25.00
Busch C2	10.00	20.00
Busch Tools	10.00	20.00
Busch pie 40th Anniversary	10.00	20.00
Busch rman	12.50	25.00
urton C2	10.00	20.00
urton n Lantern	10.00	20.00
urton zoil	10.00	20.00

	EX	NM-MT
99 Jeff Burton SKF	10.00	20.00
99 Jeff Burton TNT NBA All Star Game	10.00	20.00
01 Jerry Nadeau Army	10.00	20.00
04 Justice League Event Car	10.00	20.00
04 Justice League Villain Event Car	10.00	20.00
NNO Disney Event Car Donald Duck	10.00	20.00
NNO Disney Event Car Goofy	10.00	20.00
NNO Disney Event Car Mickey Mouse	10.00	20.00
NNO Disney Event Car Minnie Mouse	10.00	20.00
NNO Disney Event Car PegLeg	10.00	20.00

2004 Team Caliber Preferred 1:24

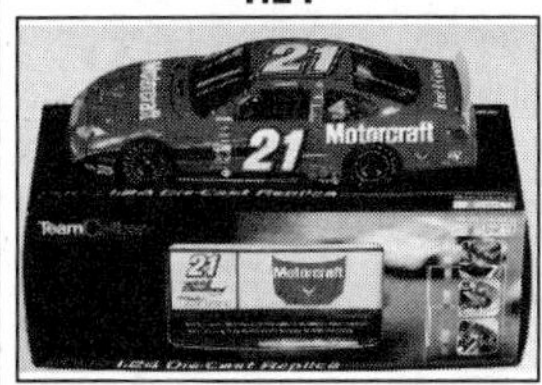

	EX	NM-MT
5 Kyle Busch Lowe's/10,080	45.00	75.00
5 Kyle Busch Lowe's SpongeBob/3120	40.00	70.00
5 Terry Labonte Delphi/10,080	40.00	70.00
5 Terry Labonte Kellogg's/10,080	40.00	70.00
5 Terry Labonte Kellogg's Olympics/10,080	40.00	70.00
5 Terry Labonte Spiderman/5004	40.00	70.00
6 Mark Martin Batman/7560	45.00	75.00
6 Mark Martin Batman Gold/504	75.00	125.00
6 Mark Martin Batman Yellow Chrome/504	75.00	125.00
6 Mark Martin Oscar Mayer/10,008	40.00	70.00
6 Mark Martin Pfizer/10,008	45.00	75.00
6 Mark Martin Viagra	45.00	75.00
6 Mark Martin Viagra Chase/1600	50.00	80.00
6 Mark Martin Viagra White/10,008	40.00	70.00
9 Jeff Burton Pennzoil/5004	35.00	60.00
9 Matt Kenseth Pennzoil/5004	40.00	70.00
9 Mark Martin Batman/5004	45.00	75.00
9 Mark Martin Batman Gold/504	75.00	125.00
9 Mark Martin Pennzoil/5004	40.00	70.00
10 Scott Riggs Valvoline/10,008	35.00	60.00
12 Ryan Newman Alltel/20,080	45.00	75.00
12 Ryan Newman Alltel Chase/1100	50.00	80.00
12 Ryan Newman Justice League	45.00	75.00
12 Ryan Newman Justice League Gold/504	75.00	125.00
12 Ryan Newman Justice League Red Chrome/504	100.00	150.00
12 Ryan Newman Mobil 1/10,080	45.00	75.00
12 Ryan Newman Mobil 1 30th Anniversary/10,080	45.00	75.00
12 Ryan Newman Sony Wega/5004	45.00	75.00
16 Greg Biffle Coke C2/10,080	40.00	70.00
16 Greg Biffle Flash/3120	40.00	70.00
16 Greg Biffle National Guard/10,080	40.00	70.00
17 Matt Kenseth Bayer/4020	35.00	60.00
17 Matt Kenseth Carhartt/7560	40.00	70.00
17 Matt Kenseth DeWalt/20,080	35.00	60.00
17 Matt Kenseth DeWalt Chase/1300	45.00	75.00
17 Matt Kenseth Martian Manhunter/7560	40.00	70.00
17 Matt Kenseth Martian Manhunter Gold/250	75.00	125.00
17 Matt Kenseth Martian Manhunter Green Chrome/504	75.00	125.00
17 Matt Kenseth Smirnoff/20,080	40.00	70.00
17 Matt Kenseth Smirnoff Chase/750	50.00	80.00
21 Ricky Rudd Air Force/10,080	40.00	70.00
21 Ricky Rudd Coke C2/10,080	40.00	60.00
21 Ricky Rudd Motorcraft/10,080	35.00	60.00
21 Ricky Rudd Rent-A-Center/10,008	40.00	70.00
21 Ricky Rudd Wonder Woman/5004	40.00	70.00
22 Scott Wimmer Caterpillar	35.00	60.00
25 Bobby Hamilton Jr. Marines Flames/10,080	40.00	70.00
25 Brian Vickers Ditech.com/10,008	40.00	70.00
36 Boris Said Centrix/1250	40.00	70.00
43 Jeff Green Cheerios/10,080	35.00	60.00
44 Justin Labonte Cosat Guard/288	35.00	60.00
44 Justin Labonte Cosat Guard Promo box/2000	35.00	60.00
45 Kyle Petty Brawny/10,080	40.00	70.00
45 Kyle Petty Georgia Pacific/10,080	40.00	70.00
48 Jimmie Johnson Lowe's/10,080	40.00	70.00
48 Jimmie Johnson Lowe's Chase/500	50.00	80.00
48 Jimmie Johnson Lowe's SpongeBob/3120	40.00	60.00
60 Greg Biffle Charter/10,080	40.00	70.00
60 Greg Biffle Flash/3120	40.00	70.00
84 Kyle Busch Car Quest/10,080	40.00	70.00
97 Kurt Busch Coke C2/10,080	35.00	60.00
97 Kurt Busch Irwin Tools	35.00	60.00
97 Kurt Busch Irwin Tools Chase/900	50.00	100.00
97 Kurt Busch Irwin Tools '04 Champion/2400	40.00	80.00
97 Kurt Busch Sharpie/10,080	35.00	60.00
97 Kurt Busch Sharpie Chase/1000	50.00	100.00
97 Kurt Busch Sharpie '04 Champion/10,080	40.00	80.00
97 Kurt Busch Sharpie 40th Anniversary/5004	35.00	60.00
97 Kurt Busch Superman/7560	40.00	70.00
97 Kurt Busch Superman Gold Chrome/250	75.00	125.00
99 Jeff Burton Coke C2/10,080	35.00	60.00
99 Jeff Burton Green Lantern/5004	40.00	70.00
99 Jeff Burton SKF/5004	35.00	60.00
01 Jerry Nemechek Army	35.00	60.00
04 Justice League Event Car/5004	35.00	60.00
04 Justice League Villain Event Car/5004	35.00	60.00
NNO Disney Event Car Donald Duck/10,008	40.00	70.00
NNO Disney Event Car Goofy/10,008	40.00	70.00
NNO Disney Event Car Mickey Mouse/20,080	40.00	70.00
NNO Disney Event Car Minnie Mouse/10,008	40.00	70.00
NNO Disney Event Car PegLeg/10,008	40.00	70.00

2004 Team Caliber/Motorworks 1:24

	EX	NM-MT
5 Terry Labonte Kellogg's	10.00	20.00
14 Casey Atwood Navy	10.00	20.00
22 Scott Wimmer CAT	10.00	20.00
25 Bobby Hamilton Jr. Marines Flames	10.00	20.00
25 Brian Vickers ditech.com	12.50	25.00
01 Joe Nemechek Army	10.00	20.00
NNO Disney Event Car Donald Duck	10.00	20.00
NNO Disney Event Car Minnie Mouse	10.00	20.00

2004 Team Caliber/Motorworks Model Kits 1:24

	EX	NM-MT
5 Terry Labonte Kellogg's	10.00	20.00

2005 Team Caliber Owners Series 1:24

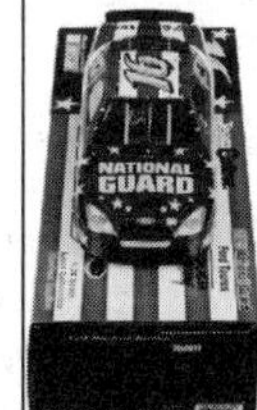

PRINT RUNS LISTED BELOW ARE FIRST RUN ONLY
FINAL PRODUCTION NUMBERS MAY END UP DIFFERENT
PRINT RUNS LISTED WITH * ARE SECOND RUN

	EX	NM-MT
5 Kyle Busch Kellogg's/900	60.00	100.00
6 Mark Martin Batman/756	75.00	125.00
6 Mark Martin Kraft/600	75.00	125.00
6 Mark Martin Viagra/1200	100.00	150.00
6 Mark Martin Viagra/600*	100.00	150.00
6 Mark Martin Viagra Blue Retro Stroh's Light/900	75.00	125.00
6 Mark Martin Viagra Orange AU/1800	75.00	125.00
6 Mark Martin Viagra Red Retro Folgers/900	100.00	175.00
6 Mark Martin Viagra Red, White & Blue Retro Valvoline/900	75.00	150.00
6 Mark Martin Viagra Red, White & Blue Retro Valvoline All Star AU/737	75.00	150.00
6 Mark Martin Viagra Salute to You/1500	75.00	125.00
10 Scott Riggs Valvoline/600	50.00	75.00
12 Ryan Newman Alltel/1200	60.00	100.00
12 Ryan Newman Mobil 1/600	60.00	100.00
12 Ryan Newman Mobil 1 Gold/600	60.00	100.00
16 Greg Biffle National Guard/600	60.00	100.00
17 Matt Kenseth Carhartt/600	60.00	100.00
17 Matt Kenseth DeWalt/1200	60.00	100.00
17 Matt Kenseth Trex/600	60.00	100.00
17 Matt Kenseth USG/600	60.00	100.00
21 Ricky Rudd Motorcraft/600	60.00	100.00
22 Scott Wimmer Cat/600	50.00	75.00
25 Brian Vickers GMAC/1200	60.00	100.00
44 Terry Labonte Kellogg's/600	60.00	100.00
48 Jimmie Johnson Lowe's/600	60.00	100.00
60 Carl Edwards Charter AU/600	100.00	150.00
97 Kurt Busch Crown Royal/756	60.00	100.00
97 Kurt Busch Crown Royal/600*	60.00	100.00
97 Kurt Busch Irwin Tools/600	50.00	100.00
97 Kurt Busch Sharpie/804	50.00	100.00
97 Kurt Busch Sharpie Autographs for Education/600	50.00	100.00
97 Kurt Busch Smirnoff/600	60.00	100.00
99 Carl Edwards AAA/600	75.00	125.00
99 Carl Edwards Office Depot/600	75.00	125.00
99 Carl Edwards Scotts 1st Win AU/999	175.00	250.00
99 Carl Edwards Stonebridge Life Pocono Raced/600	75.00	125.00
01 Joe Nemechek Army/600	50.00	75.00

2005 Team Caliber Pit Stop 1:24

	EX	NM-MT
5 Kyle Busch CarQuest	12.50	25.00
5 Kyle Busch Kellogg's	15.00	25.00
5 Kyle Busch Kellogg's Johnny Bravo	12.50	25.00
6 Mark Martin Batman	15.00	25.00
6 Mark Martin Kraft	10.00	20.00
6 Mark Martin Viagra	15.00	25.00
6 Mark Martin Viagra Blue Retro Stroh's Light	15.00	25.00
6 Mark Martin Viagra Orange	10.00	20.00
6 Mark Martin Viagra Red Retro Folgers	15.00	25.00
6 Mark Martin Viagra Red, White & Blue Retro Valvoline	15.00	25.00
9 Matt Kenseth Pennzoil	10.00	20.00
9 Mark Martin Pennzoil	10.00	20.00
10 Scott Riggs Checker's Promo	15.00	30.00
10 Scott Riggs Valvoline	10.00	20.00
12 Ryan Newman Alltel	12.50	25.00
12 Ryan Newman Mobil 1	12.50	25.00
12 Ryan Newman Mobil 1 Gold	12.50	25.00
16 Greg Biffle National Guard	10.00	20.00
16 Greg Biffle Post-It	12.50	25.00
16 Greg Biffle Subway	12.50	25.00
17 Matt Kenseth Carhartt	10.00	20.00
17 Matt Kenseth DeWalt	10.00	20.00
17 Matt Kenseth Trex	10.00	20.00
17 Matt Kenseth USG	12.50	25.00
17 Matt Kenseth Waste Management	12.50	25.00
21 Ricky Rudd Motorcraft	10.00	20.00
22 Scott Wimmer Cat	12.50	25.00
25 Brian Vickers GMAC	12.50	25.00
25 Brian Vickers GMAC Scooby Doo	12.50	25.00
36 Boris Said Centrix	12.50	25.00
43 Jeff Green Cheerios	12.50	25.00
43 Jeff Green Wheaties	12.50	25.00
44 Justin Labonte Coast Guard	12.50	25.00
44 Terry Labonte Kellogg's	12.50	25.00
45 Kyle Petty Georgia Pacific	12.50	25.00
45 Kyle Petty Quilted Northern	12.50	25.00
48 Jimmie Johnson Lowe's	15.00	25.00
60 Carl Edwards Charter	12.50	25.00
66 Greg Biffle USPS promo in window box	12.50	25.00
76 Jerrick Johnson American Legion Promo	30.00	60.00
97 Kurt Busch Irwin Tools	10.00	20.00
97 Kurt Busch Sharpie	10.00	20.00
97 Kurt Busch Sharpie Autographs For Education	10.00	20.00
99 Carl Edwards AAA	15.00	25.00
99 Carl Edwards Round Up	15.00	25.00
99 Carl Edwards Office Depot	15.00	25.00
99 Carl Edwards Office Depot Promo in window box	15.00	25.00
99 Carl Edwards Office Depot Back To School Promo in window box	20.00	35.00
99 Carl Edwards Stonebridge Life Pocono Raced	12.50	25.00
01 Joe Nemechek Army	12.50	25.00
05 Batman Begins Event	10.00	20.00
05 Daytona Disney Big Bad Wolf	10.00	20.00
05 Daytona Disney Daisy	10.00	20.00
05 Daytona Disney Donald Duck	10.00	20.00
05 Daytona Disney Goofy	10.00	20.00
05 Daytona Disney Mickey Mouse	10.00	20.00
05 Daytona Disney Minnie Mouse	10.00	20.00

2005 Team Caliber Preferred 1:24

	EX	NM-MT
5 Kyle Busch Kellogg's/1200	60.00	100.00
5 Kyle Busch Kellogg's California Win/1800	60.00	100.00
5 Kyle Busch Kellogg's Johnny Bravo/1500	50.00	75.00
6 Mark Martin Batman	50.00	75.00
6 Mark Martin Kraft/2400	50.00	75.00
6 Mark Martin Viagra/5004	50.00	75.00
6 Mark Martin Viagra Blue Retro Stroh's Light/3120	50.00	75.00
6 Mark Martin Viagra Orange AU/5004	75.00	125.00
6 Mark Martin Viagra Red Retro Folgers/2400	50.00	75.00
6 Mark Martin Viagra Red Retro Folgers Color Chrome/Chrome AU/600 2-car set	100.00	200.00
6 Mark Martin Viagra Red, White & Blue Retro Valvoline/7560	50.00	75.00
6 Mark Martin Viagra Red, White & Blue All Star Win/7560	50.00	75.00
6 Mark Martin Viagra Salute to You	50.00	75.00
7 Robby Gordon Fruit of the Loom/1800	50.00	75.00
7 Robby Gordon Harrah's	50.00	75.00
7 Robby Gordon Jim Beam	50.00	75.00
7 Robby Gordon Jim Beam Black	50.00	75.00
7 Robby Gordon Menard's	50.00	75.00
9 Matt Kenseth Pennzoil/600	50.00	75.00
9 Mark Martin Pennzoil/1200	50.00	75.00
10 Scott Riggs	40.00	65.00

Valvoline/1800		
12 Ryan Newman Alltel/7560	50.00	75.00
12 Ryan Newman Alltel Gold/624	60.00	100.00
12 Ryan Newman Mobil 1/2400	50.00	75.00
12 Ryan Newman Mobil 1 Gold/2400	50.00	75.00
12 Ryan Newman Sony HDTV/1200	50.00	75.00
16 Greg Biffle Charter Michigan Win/1800	40.00	65.00
16 Greg Biffle National Guard/1800	40.00	65.00
16 Greg Biffle Post-It/3120	40.00	65.00
17 Matt Kenseth Carhartt/1800	45.00	70.00
17 Matt Kenseth DeWalt/5004	50.00	75.00
17 Matt Kenseth Trex/1800	45.00	70.00
17 Matt Kenseth USG/1200	45.00	70.00
17 Matt Kenseth Waste Management/3120	50.00	75.00
21 Ricky Rudd Motorcraft/3120	40.00	65.00
22 Scott Wimmer Cat/5004	40.00	65.00
25 Brian Vickers GMAC/3120	40.00	65.00
25 Brian Vickers GMAC Scooby Doo/1200	40.00	65.00
39 Ryan Newman Alltel/1800	100.00	150.00
44 Justin Labonte Coast Guard/3204	40.00	65.00
44 Terry Labonte GMAC/1200	40.00	65.00
44 Terry Labonte Kellogg's/1200	50.00	75.00
44 Terry Labonte Kellogg's Iron Man	40.00	65.00
44 Terry Labonte Pizza Hut	40.00	65.00
48 Jimmie Johnson Lowe's/3120	50.00	75.00
60 Carl Edwards Charter/1500	50.00	75.00
66 Greg Biffle USPS/1800	40.00	65.00
97 Kurt Busch Crown Royal/3120	50.00	75.00
97 Kurt Busch Crown Royal Color Chrome AU/1008	75.00	125.00
97 Kurt Busch Irwin Tools/3120	50.00	75.00
97 Kurt Busch Sharpie/3120	50.00	75.00
97 Kurt Busch Sharpie Autographs for Education/2400	50.00	75.00
97 Kurt Busch Smirnoff/3120	50.00	75.00
99 Carl Edwards AAA/2400	50.00	75.00
99 Carl Edwards Office Depot/5004	60.00	100.00
99 Carl Edwards Ortho/600	50.00	75.00
99 Carl Edwards Round Up/1800	50.00	75.00
99 Carl Edwards Scotts 1st Win/10,008	60.00	100.00
99 Carl Edwards Scotts 1st Win AU	125.00	175.00
99 Carl Edwards Scotts 1st Win Color Chrome AU/1008	125.00	200.00
99 Carl Edwards Stonebridge Life Pocono Win/3120	40.00	65.00
99 Carl Edwards World Financial Color Chrome AU/600	100.00	150.00
01 Joe Nemechek Army/1800	40.00	65.00
05 Daytona Disney Minnie Mouse/5004	40.00	60.00

2005 Team Caliber Preferred Nickel 1:24

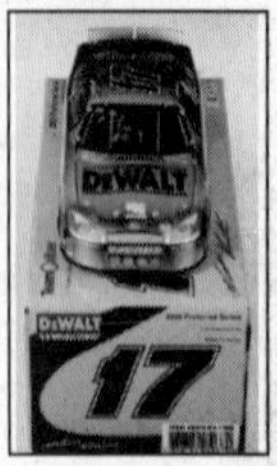

	EX	NM-MT
5 Kyle Busch Kellogg's/504	75.00	125.00
5 Kyle Busch Kellogg's Johnny Bravo/180	50.00	75.00
6 Mark Martin Batman/402	50.00	75.00
6 Mark Martin Kraft/300	50.00	75.00
6 Mark Martin Viagra/756	60.00	100.00
6 Mark Martin Viagra Orange AU/756	75.00	125.00
7 Robby Gordon Fruit of the Loom/180	40.00	60.00
7 Robby Gordon Harrah's	40.00	60.00
7 Robby Gordon Jim Beam	50.00	75.00
7 Robby Gordon Menard's	40.00	60.00
9 Mark Martin Pennzoil/504	50.00	75.00
10 Scott Riggs Valvoline/180	40.00	60.00
12 Ryan Newman Alltel/504	50.00	75.00
12 Ryan Newman Mobil 1/180	60.00	100.00
16 Greg Biffle National Guard/180	60.00	100.00
17 Matt Kenseth Carhartt/300	50.00	75.00
17 Matt Kenseth DeWalt/1008	60.00	100.00
17 Matt Kenseth Trex/180	50.00	75.00
17 Matt Kenseth USG/180	50.00	75.00
17 Matt Kenseth Waste Management/180	50.00	75.00
21 Ricky Rudd Motorcraft/180	50.00	75.00
22 Scott Wimmer Cat/180	40.00	60.00
25 Brian Vickers GMAC/300	40.00	60.00
44 Terry Labonte GMAC/180	40.00	60.00
44 Terry Labonte Kellogg's/180	40.00	60.00
44 Terry Labonte Pizza Hut	50.00	75.00
48 Jimmie Johnson Lowe's/180	75.00	150.00
60 Carl Edwards Charter/180	50.00	75.00
97 Kurt Busch Crown Royal/756	50.00	75.00
97 Kurt Busch Irwin Tools/504	45.00	70.00
97 Kurt Busch Sharpie/504	45.00	70.00
97 Kurt Busch Sharpie Autographs For Education/180	45.00	70.00
97 Kurt Busch Smirnoff/300	45.00	70.00
99 Carl Edwards AAA/180	50.00	75.00
99 Carl Edwards Office Depot/504	75.00	125.00
99 Carl Edwards Ortho/180	45.00	70.00
99 Carl Edwards Scotts 1st Win	60.00	100.00
99 Carl Edwards Stonebridge Life Pocono Win/180	45.00	70.00
01 Joe Nemechek Army/180	40.00	60.00
05 Daytona Disney Big Bad Wolf/504	25.00	50.00
05 Daytona Disney Daisy Duck/504	25.00	50.00
05 Daytona Disney Donald Duck/504	25.00	50.00
05 Daytona Disney Goofy/504	25.00	50.00
05 Daytona Disney Mickey Mouse/1008	25.00	50.00
05 Daytona Disney Minnie Mouse/576	25.00	50.00

2005 Team Caliber Preferred sets 1:24 and 1:64

	EX	NM-MT
05 Daytona Disney Big Bad Wolf/504	35.00	60.00
05 Daytona Disney Daisy/504	35.00	60.00
05 Daytona Disney Donald Duck/750	35.00	60.00
05 Daytona Disney Goofy/1200	35.00	60.00
05 Daytona Disney Mickey Mouse/2700	35.00	60.00
05 Daytona Disney Minnie Mouse/1500	35.00	60.00

2005 Team Caliber/Motorworks Model Kits 1:24

	EX	NM-MT
6 Mark Martin Viagra	12.50	25.00
17 Matt Kenseth DeWalt	10.00	20.00
97 Kurt Busch Sharpie	10.00	20.00

2006 Team Caliber Owner's Series 1:24

	EX	NM-MT
2 Kurt Busch Miller Lite/2400	75.00	125.00
6 Mark Martin AAA/5004	75.00	125.00
6 Mark Martin AAA Insurance/2808	75.00	125.00
6 Mark Martin AAA Last Ride/1080	100.00	150.00
6 Mark Martin Ameriquest Soaring Dreams/1800	75.00	125.00
6 Mark Martin Ford The Road Home AU/2400	100.00	150.00
12 Ryan Newman Alltel/2400	75.00	125.00
12 Ryan Newman Mobil/1500	60.00	100.00
16 Greg Biffle National Guard/2400	60.00	100.00
17 Matt Kenseth DeWalt/2400	60.00	100.00
26 Jamie McMurray Crown Royal Day Purple/1800	60.00	100.00
26 Jamie McMurray Crown Royal Night White	60.00	100.00
55 Michael Waltrip Napa/2400	60.00	100.00
99 Carl Edwards Office Depot/2400	60.00	100.00
00 Bill Elliott Burger King/1800	75.00	125.00

2006 Team Caliber Pit Stop 1:24

	EX	NM-MT
2 Kurt Busch Miller Lite	12.50	25.00
6 Mark Martin AAA	15.00	30.00
6 Mark Martin AAA Insurance	15.00	25.00
6 Mark Martin Ameriquest	12.50	25.00
6 Mark Martin Pennzoil	12.50	25.00
6 Mark Martin Scott's SuperTruck	15.00	30.00
7 Robby Gordon Harrah's	12.50	25.00
7 Robby Gordon Menard's	12.50	25.00
12 Ryan Newman Alltel	12.50	25.00
12 Ryan Newman Alltel Black Brickyard	12.50	25.00
12 Ryan Newman Mobil 1	12.50	25.00
12 Ryan Newman Sony HDTV	12.50	25.00
14 Sterling Marlin Waste Management	15.00	25.00
16 Greg Biffle Ameriquest	12.50	25.00
16 Greg Biffle Jackson Hewitt	12.50	25.00
16 Greg Biffle National Guard	12.50	25.00
16 Greg Biffle Subway	12.50	25.00
17 Matt Kenseth Ameriquest	12.50	25.00
17 Matt Kenseth Ameriquest Soaring Dreams	12.50	25.00
17 Matt Kenseth Carhartt	12.50	25.00
17 Matt Kenseth DeWalt	12.50	25.00
17 Matt Kenseth Pennzoil	12.50	25.00
17 Matt Kenseth Post	12.50	25.00
17 Matt Kenseth R&L Carriers	12.50	25.00
21 Ken Schrader Air Force	12.50	25.00
21 Ken Schrader Little Debbie Promo	20.00	40.00
21 Ken Schrader Motorcraft	12.50	25.00
22 Dave Blaney CAT	12.50	25.00
23 Bill Lester Waste Management	15.00	30.00
26 Jamie McMurray Irwin Tools	12.50	25.00
26 Jamie McMurray Lenox	12.50	25.00
26 Jamie McMurray Sharpie	12.50	25.00
39 Kurt Busch Penske	12.50	25.00
43 Bobby Labonte Cheerios	12.50	25.00
55 Michael Waltrip Domino's	12.50	25.00
55 Michael Waltrip Napa	12.50	25.00
55 Michael Waltrip Napa Stars & Stripes	12.50	25.00
60 Carl Edwards Ameriquest	12.50	25.00
99 Carl Edwards Office Depot	12.50	25.00
99 Michael Waltrip Aaron's	12.50	25.00
99 Michael Waltrip Aaron's UT Longhorns	12.50	25.00
99 Michael Waltrip Best Western	12.50	25.00
00 Bill Elliott Burger King	15.00	25.00
00 Johnny Sauter Fleet Pride Promo	15.00	30.00
01 Joe Nemechek Army	12.50	25.00
06 Todd Kluever 3M	15.00	30.00
06 Daytona Disney Buzz Lightyear	10.00	20.00
06 Daytona Disney Kermit	10.00	20.00
06 Daytona Disney Mickey Mouse	10.00	20.00
06 Daytona Disney Princess	10.00	20.00
06 Daytona Disney Tigger	10.00	20.00

2006 Team Caliber Preferred 1:24

	EX	NM-MT
2 Kurt Busch Miller Lite	50.00	75.00
6 Mark Martin AAA/20,004	50.00	75.00
6 Mark Martin AAA Insurance/5004	50.00	75.00
6 Mark Martin Ameriquest/2400	50.00	75.00
6 Mark Martin Ameriquest Soaring Dreams/3500	50.00	75.00
6 Mark Martin Folger's '89 t-bird Red Chrome AU/1056	100.00	175.00
6 Mark Martin Pennzoil/3000	50.00	75.00
7 Robby Gordon Harrah's/1800	50.00	75.00
7 Robby Gordon Jim Beam/2100	50.00	75.00
7 Robby Gordon Jim Beam Black/1800	50.00	75.00
12 Ryan Newman Alltel	50.00	75.00
12 Ryan Newman Alltel Black Brickyard/1800	50.00	75.00
12 Ryan Newman Mobil 1	50.00	75.00
12 Ryan Newman My Circle/1200	60.00	100.00
12 Ryan Newman Sony HDTV/1800	50.00	75.00
14 Sterling Marlin Waste Management	50.00	75.00
16 Greg Biffle Ameriquest	50.00	75.00
16 Greg Biffle Ameriquest Soaring Dreams/3000	50.00	75.00
16 Greg Biffle Jackson Hewitt/2700	50.00	75.00
16 Greg Biffle National Guard	50.00	75.00
16 Greg Biffle Subway/2508	50.00	75.00
17 Matt Kenseth Ameriquest/1800	50.00	75.00
17 Matt Kenseth Ameriquest Soaring Dreams/3000	50.00	75.00
17 Matt Kenseth Carhartt/2016	50.00	75.00
17 Matt Kenseth DeWalt/5004	50.00	75.00
17 Matt Kenseth Pennzoil/2700	50.00	75.00
17 Matt Kenseth Post/1800	50.00	75.00
17 Matt Kenseth R&L Carriers/1800	50.00	75.00
17 Matt Kenseth USG Promo/3210	60.00	100.00
21 Ken Schrader Air Force/1800	50.00	75.00
21 Ken Schrader Motorcraft/1800	50.00	75.00
22 Dave Blaney CAT	50.00	75.00
23 Bill Lester Waste Management	50.00	75.00
26 Jamie McMurray Crown Royal Day Purple/5004	50.00	75.00
26 Jamie McMurray Crown Royal Day Purple Clear Window Bank AU/300	100.00	150.00
26 Jamie McMurray Crown Royal Night White/3120	50.00	75.00
26 Jamie McMurray Irwin Tools/3120	50.00	75.00
26 Jamie McMurray Lenox/3000	50.00	75.00
26 Jamie McMurray Sharpie	50.00	75.00
39 Kurt Busch Penske/2400	50.00	75.00
43 Bobby Labonte Cheerios/2400	50.00	75.00
43 Richard Petty '69 Torino AU/5035	100.00	175.00
43 Richard Petty '69 Torino 100th Win Wix Filters	60.00	100.00
55 Michael Waltrip Domino's/3000	50.00	75.00
55 Michael Waltrip Napa/5004	50.00	75.00
55 Michael Waltrip Napa Stars & Stripes/2700	50.00	75.00
60 Carl Edwards Ameriquest/2400	50.00	75.00
60 Carl Edwards Ameriquest Soaring Dreams/3300	50.00	75.00
60 Carl Edwards iLevel Weyerhaeuser/2700	50.00	75.00
99 Carl Edwards Office Depot/7500	50.00	75.00
99 Carl Edwards Office Depot Back To School/1800	50.00	75.00
99 Darrell Waltrip Aaron's	50.00	75.00
99 Michael Waltrip Aaron's/6504	50.00	75.00
99 Michael Waltrip Best Western/1800	50.00	75.00
00 Bill Elliott Burger King/2400	60.00	100.00
06 Todd Kluever 3M	50.00	75.00
06 Daytona Disney Buzz Lightyear/756	25.00	50.00
06 Daytona Disney Kermit	25.00	50.00
06 Daytona Disney Mickey Mouse/1800	25.00	50.00
06 Daytona Disney Princess/1200	25.00	50.00
06 Daytona Disney Tigger/1200	25.00	50.00

2006 Team Caliber Preferred Copper 1:24

	EX	NM-MT
6 Mark Martin AAA	60.00	100.00
6 Mark Martin AAA Insurance	50.00	75.00
6 Mark Martin Ameriquest/360	50.00	75.00
6 Mark Martin Pennziol/540	50.00	75.00
12 Ryan Newman Alltel/756	50.00	75.00
12 Ryan Newman Mobil 1	50.00	75.00
12 Ryan Newman Sony HDTV/180	50.00	75.00
14 Sterling Marlin Waste Management/360	50.00	75.00
16 Greg Biffle National Guard	50.00	75.00
16 Greg Biffle Subway/360	50.00	75.00
17 Matt Kenseth Pennzoil/360	50.00	75.00
17 Matt Kenseth Post	50.00	75.00
17 Matt Kenseth R&L Carriers	50.00	75.00
22 Dave Blaney CAT	50.00	75.00
23 Bill Lester Waste Management	50.00	
26 Jamie McMurray Crown Royal Day Purple	50.00	
26 Jamie McMurray Crown Royal Night White	50.00	
26 Jamie McMurray Irwin Tools/432	50.00	
26 Jamie McMurray Lenox	50.00	
26 Jamie McMurray Sharpie/504	50.00	
26 Jamie McMurray Smirnoff Ice/504	50.00	
43 Bobby Labonte Cheerios/432	50.00	
43 Richard Petty '69 Torino AU/180	75.00	
55 Michael Waltrip Napa	50.00	
55 Michael Waltrip Napa Stars & Stripes/180	50.00	
60 Carl Edwards iLevel Weyerhaeuser/360	50.00	
99 Carl Edwards Office Depot	50.00	
99 Darrell Waltrip Aaron's	50.00	
99 Michael Waltrip Aaron's	50.00	
99 Michael Waltrip Best Western/180	50.00	

2006 Team Caliber Prefe Trackside 1:24

	EX
1 Martin Truex Jr. Bass Pro/144	125.00
5 Kyle Busch Kellogg's/48	125.00
11 Paul Menard Menard's/48	75.00
64 Steve Wallace Top Flite/48	75.00

2003 Team Caliber Pit S 1:43

	EX
NNO Centennial of Speed 3-car set 1 300A. Tim Flock/1956 Chrysler 10. Bill France Sr./1935 Ford 300. Lee Petty/1956 Chrysler	40.00
NNO Centennial of Speed 3-car set 2 6. Marshall Teague/1952 Hudson 10. Bill France/1935 Ford 301.Buck Baker/Outboard Chrysler	40.00

2003 Team Caliber Prefe 1:43

	EX
16A Buck Baker Florida Hurricanes 1940 Ford/3120	20.00

1999 Team Caliber 1:

This marks Team Caliber's inaugural year in th market.

	EX
5 Terry Labonte Kellogg's Corny/7560	6.00
5 Terry Labonte Kellogg's K-Sentials/10,080	6.00
5 Terry Labonte Rice Krispies/10,080	8.00
6 Mark Martin Valvoline/7560	8.00
6 Mark Martin Eagle One	8.00
7 Michael Waltrip Phillips	6.00
10 Ricky Rudd Tide/8208	8.00
12 Jeremy Mayfield Mobil 1	8.00
12 Jeremy Mayfield Mobil 25th Anniversary	8.00
12 Jeremy Mayfield Mobil 1 Promo without Speedpass on trunk lid	10.00
12 Jeremy Mayfield Mobil 25th Anniversary Promo	12.50
12 Jimmy Spencer Chips Ahoy	20.00
17 Matt Kenseth DeWalt	12.50
23 Jimmy Spencer No Bull	8.00
23 Jimmy Spencer Winston Lights	15.00
40 Sterling Marlin Coors Light John Wayne/7560	12.00
40 Sterling Marlin Coors Light Brooks & Dunn	12.00
43 John Andretti STP	10.00
45 Adam Petty Sprint/7560	20.00
55 Kenny Wallace Square D/7560	6.00
75 Ted Musgrave Polaris/8208	6.00
97 Chad Little John Deere	6.00
99 Jeff Burton Exide	6.00

2000 Team Caliber Ow Series 1:64

The set of die-cast pieces was issued in its own plastic box with a colorful cardboard box overwrap. issue and the name "Team Caliber Owner's Series" a

on the cardboard box along with the announced 'on run. Each piece features an opening hood and was vith a credit card type certificate of authenticity.

	EX	NM-MT
Labonte logg's/7560	8.00	20.00
Labonte erryBerry	8.00	20.00
Martin jle One/10,080	10.00	25.00
Martin voline/10,080	10.00	25.00
Martin voline Max Life	8.00	20.00
Martin voline Stars & Stripes/7560	10.00	25.00
Martin ex/7560	8.00	20.00
ael Waltrip tions Rent	8.00	20.00
urton rthern Light/7560	8.00	20.00
my Mayfield bil 1	8.00	20.00
Mast nseco	8.00	20.00
n Lepage ilyclick.com	8.00	20.00
Kenseth Walt/10,080	12.50	25.00
Kenseth Walt 24 Volt/10,080	12.50	25.00
Kenseth Walt Emazing.com/7560	10.00	20.00
Kenseth sine/7560	8.00	20.00
tt Sadler go/7560	8.00	20.00
Nadeau ligan	8.00	20.00
my Spencer K	8.00	20.00
ing Marlin ors Light oks & Dunn/7560	6.00	15.00
ny Irwin lSouth/7560	8.00	20.00
n Petty rint PCS Busch	40.00	100.00
fery Bodine wer Team/7560	6.00	15.00
Martin nn Dixie/7560	10.00	25.00
Martin nn Dixie Flames/7560	10.00	25.00
Martin nn Dixie rs & Stripes/7560	8.00	20.00
ell Waltrip K Route 66/7560	8.00	20.00
ert Pressley sper Cat	10.00	25.00
d Little nn Deere/7560	8.00	20.00
Burton de/7560	8.00	20.00

00 Team Caliber Promos 1:64

	EX	NM-MT
tt Sadler go in bag	3.00	8.00
Green perFlo	2.00	5.00

000 Team Caliber White Knuckle Racing 1:64

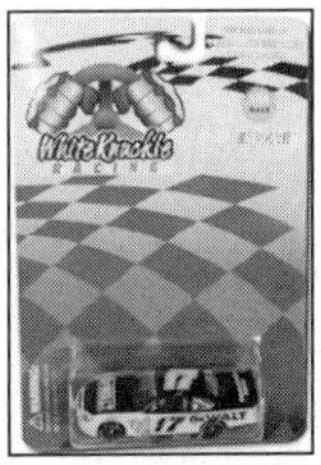

ars are packaged in a cardboard and plastic blister pack ith the name "White Knuckle Racing" and year of issue p. The 1:64 blister pack promo pieces were printed with of the driver and the car on the back board but do not "White Knuckle Racing." The cars in this series do not ening hoods.

	EX	NM-MT
Martin gle One Promo	3.00	8.00
Martin voline	3.00	8.00
my Mayfield bil 1	4.00	8.00
Kenseth Walt	5.00	10.00
Kenseth sine Promo	10.00	20.00
tt Sadler go Promo	10.00	20.00
d Little nn Deere	3.00	8.00
Burton de	3.00	8.00
Burton de Promo	5.00	12.00

2001 Team Caliber Owners Series 1:64

These 1:64 pieces were issued in a hard clear plastic case inside a cardboard box. The box was printed in gray with a picture of a typical race grandstands. The prodcution run total and the year are given on the outside of the box as well.

	EX	NM-MT
6 Mark Martin Pfizer/7560	8.00	20.00
6 Mark Martin Viagra/7560	10.00	25.00
6 Mark Martin Viagra Metal Flake/6264	8.00	20.00
17 Matt Kenseth DeWalt/7560	12.50	25.00
17 Matt Kenseth DeWalt ROY	10.00	20.00
40 Sterling Marlin Coors Light	10.00	25.00
97 Kurt Busch Sharpie/5544	10.00	25.00
99 Jeff Burton Citgo	8.00	20.00

2001 Team Caliber Pit Stop 1:64

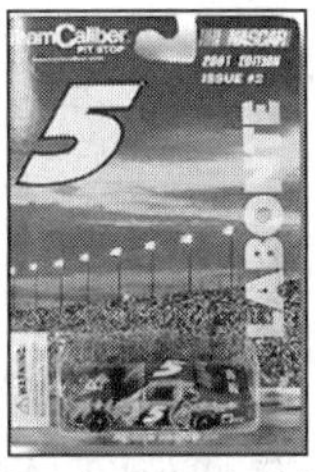

The 2001 Pit Stop series cars were packaged with a cardboard and clear plastic blister pack. The set name and year are clearly printed on the cardboard backing. The regular issue die cast have a night racing photo of the grandstands in the background, while the Ryan Newman promo piece was issued in a box with the team's colors and a photo of the car.

	EX	NM-MT
5 Terry Labonte Kellogg's	5.00	10.00
6 Mark Martin Pfizer	5.00	10.00
10 Johnny Benson Valvoline	5.00	10.00
12 Jeremy Mayfield Mobil 1	3.00	6.00
17 Matt Kenseth DeWalt Yellow	5.00	10.00
17 Matt Kenseth DeWalt Yellow and Black/21168	5.00	10.00
17 Matt Kenseth DeWalt Saw/3120	5.00	10.00
21 Elliott Sadler Motorcraft	3.00	6.00
22 Ward Burton Caterpillar	4.00	10.00
25 Jerry Nadeau UAW-Delphi	4.00	8.00
43 John Andretti Cheerios	3.00	6.00
44 Buckshot Jones Georgia-Pacific	2.50	6.00
45 Kyle Petty Sprint PCS	4.00	8.00
60 Greg Biffle Grainger	3.00	8.00
96 Andy Houston McDonalds	3.00	6.00
97 Kurt Busch Sharpie	7.50	15.00
99 Jeff Burton Citgo	5.00	10.00

2001 Team Caliber Promos 1:64

	EX	NM-MT
10 Jeff Green Nestea	7.50	20.00
12 Jeremy Mayfield Mobil 1 25th Anniversary	2.00	5.00
17 Matt Kenseth AT&T in PVC box	35.00	60.00
33 No Driver Association Aleve	2.00	4.00
33 No Driver Association Alka-Seltzer	2.00	4.00
33 No Driver Association Bayer	2.00	4.00
33 Tony Raines Aleve	2.00	4.00
50 Jon Wood Auto Concierge	12.50	25.00
71 Kevin Lepage Mini Corn Dogs	5.00	12.00
71 Kevin Lepage State Fair Dogs	5.00	12.00
01 Tropicana 400 blister	3.00	8.00
02 Ryan Newman Alltel	5.00	12.00

2002 Team Caliber Owners Series 1:64

	EX	NM-MT
6 Mark Martin Kraft/7560	10.00	20.00
6 Mark Martin Pfizer/5004	10.00	20.00
6 Mark Martin Viagra/10080	10.00	20.00
12 Ryan Newman Alltel/8136	10.00	20.00
12 Ryan Newman Alltel Blue Chrome Rookie of the Year/7560	15.00	30.00
17 Matt Kenseth DeWalt/5004	10.00	20.00
36 Ken Schrader M&Ms/5004	7.50	15.00
36 Ken Schrader M&Ms Vote/5004	7.50	15.00
43 John Andretti StarWars/5004	10.00	20.00
48 Jimmie Johnson Lowes/5004	12.50	25.00
48 Jimmie Johnson Lowe's Power of Pride/5004	12.50	25.00
60 Greg Biffle Grainger/5004	12.50	25.00
97 Kurt Busch Rubbermaid/5004	12.50	25.00
97 Kurt Busch Rubbermaid Commercial/5004	10.00	20.00
97 Kurt Busch Sharpie Million $ Challenge/5004	10.00	20.00
99 Jeff Burton Citgo/5004	7.50	15.00
99 Jeff Burton Citgo Peel Out, Reel In & Win/5004	7.50	15.00

2002 Team Caliber Pit Stop 1:64

The Pit Stop release was issued in a clear plastic clamshell type packaging. Each piece has the year of issue and set name printed on the colorful cardboard insert. We've included the announced production runs below when known. The packaging itself does not include production run information.

	EX	NM-MT
1 Jimmy Spencer Yellow Freight	5.00	10.00
5 Terry Labonte Got Milk/7560	4.00	10.00
5 Terry Labonte Kellogg's/7560	4.00	8.00
6 Mark Martin Kraft/10,368	5.00	10.00
6 Mark Martin Pfizer/8076	5.00	10.00
6 Mark Martin Viagra/25,604	5.00	10.00
12 Ryan Newman Alltel/17,592	5.00	10.00
12 Ryan Newman Alltel Sony WEGA/7992	5.00	10.00
12 Ryan Newman Mobil 1/7560	5.00	10.00
17 Matt Kenseth AT&T	5.00	10.00
17 Matt Kenseth DeWalt/7560	4.00	8.00
17 Matt Kenseth DeWalt Million $ Challenge/7560	4.00	8.00
21 Elliott Sadler Air Force/5004	5.00	10.00
25 Jerry Nadeau UAW-Delphi/7560	3.00	6.00
36 Ken Schrader M&Ms/7560	4.00	8.00
36 Ken Schrader M&Ms Halloween/7560	5.00	10.00
36 Ken Schrader M&Ms July 4th	5.00	10.00
36 Ken Schrader M&Ms Vote/7560	5.00	10.00
36 Ken Schrader M&Ms Vote Purple/900	6.00	12.00
43 Richard Petty Garfield/7560	5.00	12.00
43 John Andretti StarWars/10,080	5.00	10.00
45 Kyle Petty Sprint PCS/7560	4.00	8.00
45 Kyle Petty Sprint Charity Ride/7560	5.00	10.00
48 Jimmie Johnson Lowe's/1002	6.00	12.00
48 Jimmie Johnson Lowe's Power of Pride	6.00	12.00
60 Greg Biffle Grainger/7560	3.00	6.00
97 Kurt Busch Rubbermaid/14,120	4.00	8.00
97 Kurt Busch Rubbermaid Commercial/7560	4.00	8.00
97 Kurt Busch Rubbermaid Little Tikes	5.00	10.00
97 Kurt Busch Sharpie Million $ Challenge/7560	4.00	8.00
97 Kurt Busch Sharpie 500/7572	6.00	12.00
99 Jeff Burton Citgo/10,080	3.00	6.00
99 Jeff Burton Citgo Bass Masters/7560	4.00	8.00
99 Jeff Burton Citgo Peel Out, Reel In and Win/4128	4.00	8.00
02 Santa Claus Holiday/3504	5.00	10.00
02 Daytona 2002/10,584	5.00	10.00

2002 Team Caliber Promos 1:64

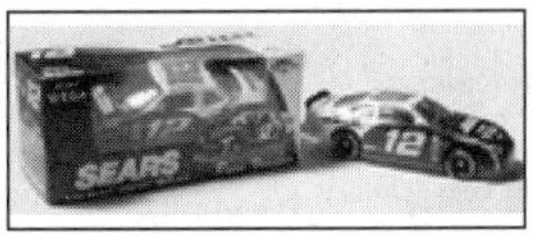

	EX	NM-MT
9 Jeff Burton Gain	7.50	20.00
12 Ryan Newman Alltel Sony WEGA in Sears window box	5.00	10.00
21 Elliott Sadler Air Force Charlotte Race Air Force Recruiters in box	10.00	20.00
33 Tony Raines Alka Seltzer issued in a box	7.50	15.00
97 Kurt Busch Sharpie	2.00	5.00
99 Jeff Burton Citgo	2.00	5.00
02 Lowe's UAW GM 500 issued in clear box	15.00	30.00
02 Ryan Newman Alltel with cellular phone face plate	7.50	15.00

2003 Team Caliber Model Kits 1:64

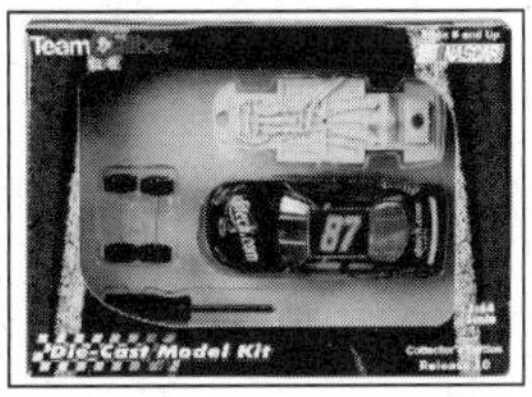

	EX	NM-MT
5 Terry Labonte Finding Nemo	7.50	15.00
6 Mark Martin Viagra	7.50	15.00
6 Mark Martin Viagra White	7.50	15.00
12 Ryan Newman Alltel	7.50	15.00
17 Matt Kenseth DeWalt	7.50	15.00
17 Matt Kenseth DeWalt Million $ Challenge/2400	7.50	15.00
21 Ricky Rudd Motorcraft	7.50	15.00
87 Kyle Busch Ditech.com	7.50	15.00
97 Kurt Busch Blue Ice	7.50	15.00
01 Jerry Nadeau Army	7.50	15.00

2003 Team Caliber Owners Series 1:64

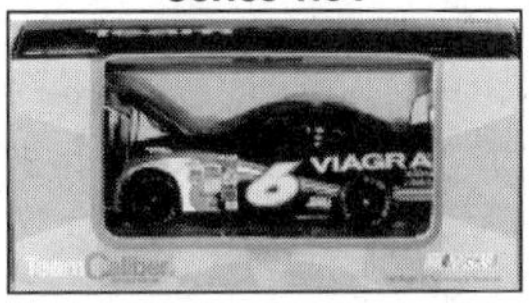

	EX	NM-MT
6 Mark Martin Kraft/5004	8.00	20.00
6 Mark Martin Pfizer/5004	8.00	20.00
6 Mark Martin Viagra/10,080	10.00	20.00
6 Mark Martin Viagra Blue Chrome/10,080	12.50	25.00
6 Mark Martin Viagra White	10.00	20.00
10 Johnny Benson Valvoline	10.00	20.00
12 Ryan Newman Alltel/10,080	10.00	20.00
12 Ryan Newman Mobil 1	10.00	20.00
16 Greg Biffle Grainger/5004	10.00	20.00
17 Matt Kenseth DeWalt/5004	12.50	25.00
21 Ricky Rudd Air Force	7.50	15.00
21 Ricky Rudd Motorcraft/10,080	7.50	15.00
23 Kenny Wallace Stacker 2	7.50	15.00
25 Joe Nemechek UAW Delphi	7.50	15.00
43 John Andretti Cheerios	7.50	15.00
45 Kyle Petty Georgia Pacific	7.50	15.00
48 Jimmie Johnson Lowe's	8.00	20.00
48 Jimmie Johnson Lowe's Blue Chrome/7560	15.00	30.00
97 Kurt Busch Rubbermaid/5004	10.00	20.00
99 Jeff Burton Citgo/5004	7.50	15.00
01 Jerry Nadeau Army	10.00	20.00

2003 Team Caliber Pit Stop 1:64

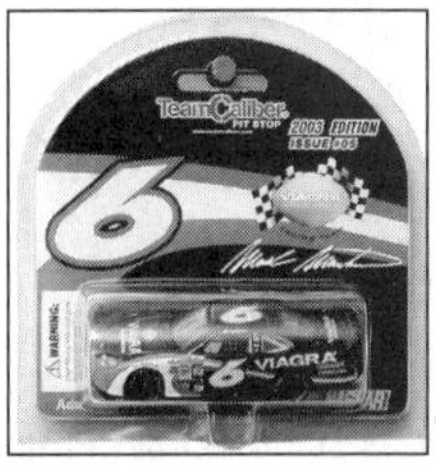

	EX	NM-MT
1 Jamie McMurray Yellow Freight	4.00	8.00
5 Terry Labonte Kellogg's	4.00	8.00
5 Terry Labonte Kellogg's Cheez-It	4.00	8.00
5 Terry Labonte Finding Nemo	5.00	10.00
5 Terry Labonte Got Milk	4.00	8.00
5 Terry Labonte Power of Cheese	4.00	8.00
5 Brian Vickers Carquest	5.00	10.00
5 Brian Vickers GMAC	5.00	10.00
6 Mark Martin Kraft	4.00	8.00
6 Mark Martin Pfizer	4.00	8.00
6 Mark Martin Viagra	4.00	8.00
6 Mark Martin Viagra Blue Daytona	5.00	10.00
6 Mark Martin Viagra White	4.00	8.00
6 Mark Martin Viagra 500 Starts	5.00	10.00
9 Greg Biffle Oreo	5.00	10.00
10 Johnny Benson Eagle One	4.00	8.00
10 Johnny Benson Valvoline	4.00	8.00
12 Ryan Newman Alltel	4.00	8.00
12 Ryan Newman Mobil 1	4.00	8.00
12 Ryan Newman Sony Wega	4.00	8.00
16 Greg Biffle Grainger	4.00	8.00
16 Greg Biffle Grainger 1st Win	5.00	10.00
17 Matt Kenseth DeWalt	5.00	10.00
17 Matt Kenseth DeWalt 2003 Champion	5.00	10.00
17 Matt Kenseth DeWalt Million $ Challenge	4.00	8.00
17 Matt Kenseth Victory Lap	5.00	10.00
21 Ricky Rudd Air Force	4.00	8.00
21 Ricky Rudd AF Cross Into Blue	4.00	8.00
21 Centennial of Speed 3-car set Ricky Rudd/Air Force Ricky Rudd/Ford 100 Years 10.Bill France Sr./1935 Ford	18.00	30.00
21 R.Rudd/Ford 100 Years	4.00	8.00
21 Ricky Rudd Motorcraft/15,060	4.00	8.00
21 Ricky Rudd Motorcraft 700 Starts	4.00	8.00
23 Kenny Wallace Stacker 2	4.00	8.00
25 Bobby Hamilton Jr. Marines	4.00	8.00
25 Joe Nemechek UAW Delphi	4.00	8.00
32 Ricky Craven Tide	4.00	8.00
32/97 Ricky Craven Tide Kurt Busch Rubbermaid Darlington finish 2-car set	12.50	25.00
38 K.Kahne/Great Clips	7.50	15.00
43 John Andretti Cheerios	4.00	8.00
43 John Andretti Cheerios Berry Burst	4.00	8.00
43 John Andretti Pillsbury	4.00	8.00
45 Kyle Petty Brawny	4.00	8.00
45 Kyle Petty Georgia Pacific	4.00	8.00

45 Kyle Petty Georgia Pacific Charity	4.00	8.00
45 Kyle Petty Victory Junction Hands	4.00	8.00
48 Jimmie Johnson Lowe's	4.00	8.00
48 Jimmie Johnson Lowe's Power of Pride	4.00	8.00
77 Dave Blaney Jasper Panther	4.00	8.00
87 Kyle Busch Ditech.com	4.00	8.00
97 Kurt Busch Blue Ice	4.00	8.00
97 Kurt Busch Rubbermaid	4.00	8.00
97 Kurt Busch Rubbermaid Commercial Products	4.00	8.00
97 Kurt Busch Irwin Tools	4.00	8.00
97 Kurt Busch Sharpie	4.00	8.00
99 Jeff Burton Citgo	4.00	8.00
99 Jeff Burton Velveeta	4.00	8.00
99 Kenny Wallace Cardinals	4.00	8.00
0 University of Oregon Ducks	7.50	15.00
01 Jerry Nadeau Army	5.00	10.00
01 Jerry Nadeau Army Camouflage	5.00	10.00
01 Jerry Nadeau USG Sheet Rock	4.00	8.00
03 Daytona 500	4.00	8.00
03 Santa Claus Holiday Blue Chrome	5.00	10.00

2003 Team Caliber Promos 1:64

	EX	NM-MT
12 Ryan Newman Alltel	6.00	12.00
17 Matt Kenseth Aleve	6.00	15.00
17 Matt Kenseth Alka-Seltzer Morning	6.00	15.00
17 Matt Kenseth Alka-Seltzer Plus	6.00	15.00
17 Matt Kenseth Bayer	6.00	15.00
17 Matt Kenseth 4-car set Alka-Seltzer Morning, Alka-Seltzer Plus, Aleve and Bayer cars	20.00	40.00
21 Ricky Rudd Rent-A-Center	10.00	20.00
300 Centennial of Speed Chrysler	5.00	10.00
03 Centennial of Speed 1936 Ford Coupe	5.00	10.00
03 Centennial of Speed Hudson Hornet	5.00	10.00

2003 Team Caliber/Motorworks 1:64

	EX	NM-MT
5 Terry Labonte Finding Nemo	3.00	8.00
12 Ryan Newman Alltel	4.00	10.00
17 Matt Kenseth DeWalt Victory Lap	4.00	10.00
87 Kyle Busch ditech.com	3.00	8.00
03 Christmas Blue Snowman	3.00	6.00
03 Christmas Red Elf	3.00	6.00
03 Christmas Yellow Reindeer	3.00	6.00

2004 Team Caliber Owners Series 1:64

	EX	NM-MT
17 Matt Kenseth DeWalt/5004	10.00	20.00
97 Kurt Busch Irwin Tools	10.00	20.00

2004 Team Caliber Pit Stop 1:64

	EX	NM-MT
5 Kyle Busch Lowe's	4.00	8.00
5 Kyle Busch Lowe's SpongeBob	4.00	8.00
5 Terry Labonte Delphi	4.00	8.00
5 Terry Labonte Kellogg's	4.00	8.00
5 Terry Labonte Kellogg's Olympics	4.00	8.00
5 Terry Labonte Spiderman	4.00	8.00
6 Mark Martin Batman	4.00	8.00
6 Mark Martin Oscar Mayer	4.00	8.00
6 Mark Martin Pfizer	4.00	8.00
6 Mark Martin Viagra	4.00	8.00
6 Mark Martin Viagra White	4.00	8.00
9 Jeff Burton Cottman	3.00	6.00
9 Jeff Burton Pennzoil	3.00	6.00
9 Matt Kenseth Pennzoil	3.00	6.00
9 Mark Martin Pennzoil	3.00	6.00
9 Mark Martin Batman	4.00	8.00
10 Scott Riggs Harlem Globetrotters	4.00	8.00
10 Scott Riggs Valvoline	4.00	8.00
12 Ryan Newman Alltel	5.00	10.00
12 Ryan Newman Justice League	4.00	8.00
12 Ryan Newman Mobil 1	5.00	10.00
12 Ryan Newman Mobil 1 30th Anniversary	5.00	10.00
12 Ryan Newman Sony Wega	5.00	10.00
14 Casey Atwood Navy	3.00	6.00
16 Greg Biffle Coke C2	4.00	8.00
16 Greg Biffle Flash	4.00	8.00
16 Greg Biffle Jackson-Hewitt	3.00	6.00
16 Greg Biffle National Guard	4.00	8.00
16 Greg Biffle Subway	4.00	8.00
16 Greg Biffle Travelodge	3.00	6.00
17 Matt Kenseth Bayer	4.00	8.00
17 Matt Kenseth Carhartt	4.00	8.00
17 Matt Kenseth DeWalt	4.00	8.00
17 Matt Kenseth Express Personnel	4.00	8.00
17 Matt Kenseth Martian Manhunter	4.00	8.00
21 Ricky Rudd Air Force	4.00	8.00
21 Ricky Rudd Coke C2	4.00	8.00
21 Ricky Rudd Motorcraft	4.00	8.00
21 Ricky Rudd Rent A Center	4.00	8.00
21 Ricky Rudd Wonder Woman	4.00	8.00
22 Scott Wimmer Caterpillar	3.00	6.00
25 Bobby Hamilton Jr. Marines Flames	4.00	8.00
25 Brian Vickers Ditech.com	4.00	8.00
43 Jeff Green Cheerios	3.00	6.00
43 Jeff Green Lucky Charms	3.00	6.00
45 Kyle Petty Brawny	3.00	6.00
45 Kyle Petty Georgia Pacific	3.00	6.00
48 Jimmie Johnson Lowe's	4.00	8.00
48 Jimmie Johnson Lowe's SpongeBob	3.00	6.00
60 Greg Biffle Charter	4.00	8.00
60 Greg Biffle Flash	4.00	8.00
84 Kyle Busch Car Quest	4.00	8.00
97 Kurt Busch Coke C2	4.00	8.00
97 Kurt Busch Irwin Tools	4.00	8.00
97 Kurt Busch Irwin Tools '04 Champion	4.00	8.00
97 Kurt Busch Sharpie	4.00	8.00
97 Kurt Busch Sharpie '04 Champion	4.00	8.00
97 Kurt Busch Sharpie 40th Anniversary	4.00	8.00
97 Kurt Busch Superman	4.00	8.00
99 Jeff Burton Coke C2	3.00	6.00
99 Jeff Burton Green Lantern	4.00	8.00
99 Jeff Burton Pennzoil	3.00	6.00
99 Jeff Burton SKF	3.00	6.00
99 Jeff Burton TNT NBA All Star Game	3.00	6.00
01 Jerry Nadeau Army	3.00	6.00
04 Holiday Event Car	3.00	6.00
04 Justice League Event Car	4.00	8.00
04 Justice League Villain Event Car	4.00	8.00
NNO Disney Event Car Donald Duck	3.00	6.00
NNO Disney Event Car Goofy	3.00	6.00
NNO Disney Event Car Mickey Mouse	3.00	6.00
NNO Disney Event Car Minnie Mouse	3.00	6.00
NNO Disney Event Car PegLeg	3.00	6.00

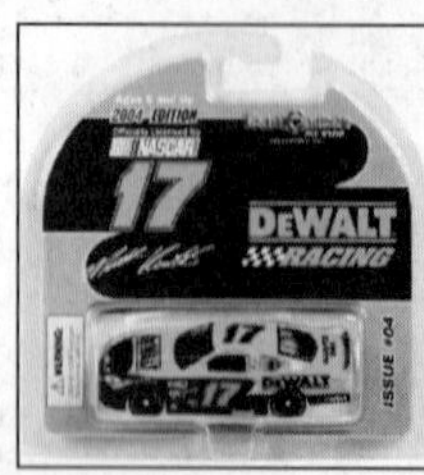

2004 Team Caliber Promos 1:64

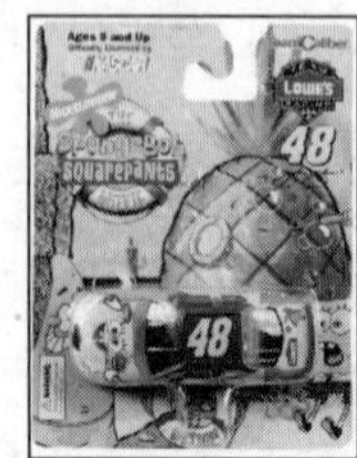

	EX	NM-MT
5 Kyle Busch Lowe's SpongeBob	6.00	12.00
16 Greg Biffle Jackson Hewitt	10.00	20.00
17 Matt Kenseth Carhartt in window box	10.00	20.00
32 David Stremme TrimSpa	20.00	40.00
32 David Stremme TrimSpa Promo in window box	60.00	100.00
48 Jimmie Johnson Lowe's SpongeBob	6.00	12.00

2004 Team Caliber/Motorworks 1:64

	EX	NM-MT
5 Terry Labonte Kellogg's	3.00	6.00
10 Scott Riggs Valvoline	3.00	6.00
14 Casey Atwood Navy	3.00	6.00
22 Scott Wimmer CAT	3.00	6.00
25 Brian Vickers Ditect.com	3.00	6.00
01 Joe Nemechek Army	3.00	6.00
NNO Disney Event Car Donald Duck	3.00	6.00
NNO Disney Event Car Goofy	3.00	6.00
NNO Disney Event Car Mickey Mouse	3.00	6.00
NNO Disney Event Car Minnie Mouse	3.00	6.00

2005 Team Caliber Pit Stop 1:64

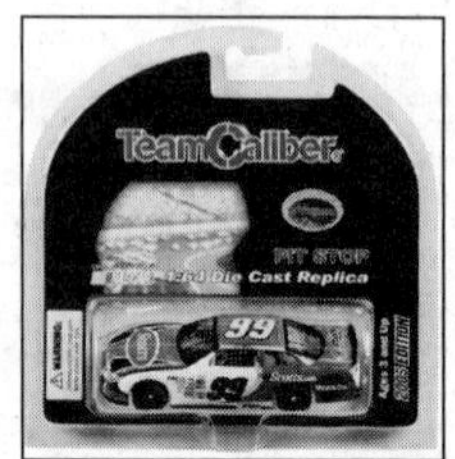

	EX	NM-MT
5 Kyle Busch Kellogg's	4.00	8.00
6 Mark Martin Batman	5.00	10.00
6 Mark Martin Kraft	4.00	8.00
6 Mark Martin Viagra	4.00	8.00
6 Mark Martin Viagra Blue Retro Stroh's Light	5.00	10.00
6 Mark Martin Viagra Orange	5.00	10.00
6 Mark Martin Viagra Red Retro Folgers	5.00	10.00
6 Mark Martin Red, White & Blue Viagra Retro Valvoline	5.00	10.00
6 Mark Martin Viagra Salute to You	5.00	10.00
9 Matt Kenseth Pennzoil	3.00	6.00
9 Mark Martin Pennzoil	3.00	6.00
10 Scott Riggs Valvoline	3.00	6.00
12 Ryan Newman Alltel	4.00	8.00
12 Ryan Newman Mobil 1	4.00	8.00
12 Ryan Newman Mobil 1 Gold	4.00	8.00
12 Ryan Newman Sony HDTV	4.00	8.00
16 Greg Biffle National Guard	3.00	6.00
16 Greg Biffle Post-It	3.00	6.00
16 Greg Biffle Subway	3.00	6.00
17 Matt Kenseth Carhartt	4.00	8.00
17 Matt Kenseth DeWalt	4.00	8.00
17 Matt Kenseth Trex	4.00	8.00
17 Matt Kenseth USG	4.00	8.00
17 Matt Kenseth Waste Management	4.00	8.00
21 Ricky Rudd Air Force	3.00	6.00
21 Ricky Rudd Motorcraft	3.00	6.00
22 Scott Wimmer Cat	3.00	6.00
22 Scott Wimmer CAT Dealers	3.00	6.00
25 Brian Vickers GMAC	3.00	6.00
36 Boris Said Centrix Financial	5.00	10.00
43 Jeff Green Cheerios	3.00	6.00
44 Terry Labonte Kellogg's	3.00	6.00
45 Kyle Petty Georgia Pacific	3.00	6.00
48 Jimmie Johnson Lowe's	4.00	8.00
60 Carl Edwards Charter	5.00	10.00
97 Kurt Busch Irwin Tools	3.00	6.00
97 Kurt Busch Sharpie	3.00	6.00
97 Kurt Busch Sharpie Autographs for Education	3.00	6.00
99 Carl Edwards AAA	6.00	12.00
99 Carl Edwards Office Depot	6.00	12.00
99 Carl Edwards Scotts 1st Win	10.00	20.00
01 Joe Nemechek Army	3.00	6.00
05 Batman Begins Event	4.00	8.00
05 Daytona 500 Event Car	4.00	8.00
05 Christmas Event Car	4.00	8.00
NNO Daytona Disney Big Bad Wolf	3.00	6.00
NNO Daytona Disney Daisy	3.00	6.00
NNO Daytona Disney Donald Duck	3.00	6.00
NNO Daytona Disney Goofy	3.00	6.00
NNO Daytona Disney Mickey Mouse	3.00	6.00
NNO Daytona Disney Minnie Mouse	3.00	6.00

2005 Team Caliber Promos 1:64

	EX	NM-MT
16 Greg Biffle National Guard in window box	15.00	30.00
17 Matt Kenseth USG in window box	7.50	15.00
17 Matt Kenseth Waste Management in window box	15.00	30.00
66 Greg Biffle USPS in window box	20.00	40.00
77 Travis Kvapil Jasper Engines in window box	12.50	25.00

2006 Team Caliber Pit Stop 1:64

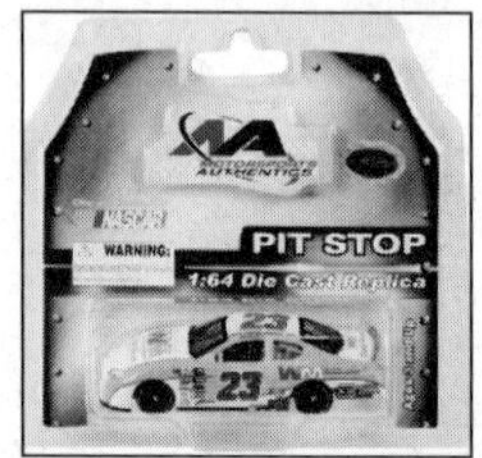

	EX	NM-MT
2 Kurt Busch Kurt	5.00	10.00
2 Kurt Busch Miller Lite in window box	6.00	12.00
6 Mark Martin AAA	7.50	15.00
6 Mark Martin AAA Insurance	6.00	12.00
6 Mark Martin Ameriquest	6.00	12.00
6 Mark Martin Pennzoil	6.00	12.00
7 Robby Gordon Menard's	6.00	12.00
10 Scott Riggs Valvoline	6.00	12.00
12 Ryan Newman Alltel	6.00	12.00
12 Ryan Newman Alltel Black Brickyard	6.00	12.00
12 Ryan Newman Mobil 1	6.00	12.00
12 Ryan Newman Sony HDTV	6.00	12.00
14 Sterling Marlin Waste Management	6.00	12.00
16 Greg Biffle Ameriquest	6.00	12.00
16 Greg Biffle Jackson Hewitt	6.00	12.00
16 Greg Biffle iLevel Weyerhaeuser	6.00	12.00
16 Greg Biffle National Guard	6.00	12.00
17 Matt Kenseth Ameriquest	6.00	12.00
17 Matt Kenseth Ameriquest Soaring Dreams	6.00	
17 Matt Kenseth Carhartt	6.00	
17 Matt Kenseth DeWalt	6.00	
17 Matt Kenseth Pennzoil	6.00	
17 Matt Kenseth Post	6.00	
17 Matt Kenseth R&L Carriers	6.00	
21 Ken Schrader Air Force	6.00	
21 Ken Schrader Motorcraft	6.00	
22 Dave Blaney CAT	6.00	
22 Dave Blaney CAT Engines	6.00	
22 Dave Blaney CAT Financial	6.00	
22 Dave Blaney CAT Rental	6.00	
23 Bill Lester Waste Management	7.50	
26 Jamie McMurray Irwin Tools	6.00	
26 Jamie McMurray Lenox	6.00	
26 Jamie McMurray Sharpie	6.00	
39 Kurt Busch Penske	6.00	
43 Bobby Labonte Cheerios	6.00	
55 Michael Waltrip Domino's	6.00	
55 Michael Waltrip Napa	6.00	
55 Michael Waltrip Napa Stars & Stripes	6.00	
60 Carl Edwards Ameriquest	6.00	
60 Carl Edwards Ameriquest Soaring Dreams	6.00	
60 Carl Edwards iLevel Weyerhaeuser	6.00	
99 Carl Edwards Office Depot	7.50	
99 Darrell Waltrip Aaron's	6.00	
99 Michael Waltrip Aaron's	6.00	
99 Michael Waltrip Best Western	6.00	
00 Bill Elliott Burger King	7.50	
01 Joe Nemechek Army	6.00	
06 Todd Kluever 3M	7.50	
06 Disney Event Car Buzz Lightyear	6.00	
06 Disney Event Car Kermit	6.00	
06 Disney Event Car Mickey Mouse	6.00	
06 Disney Event Car Princess	6.00	
06 Disney Event Car Tigger	6.00	

2006 Team Caliber Pron 1:64

	EX	N
9 Kasey Kahne Ragu in window box	10.00	
9 Kasey Kahne Ultimate Chargers in window box	7.50	
14 Sterling Marlin Waste Management in window box	10.00	
17 Matt Kenseth USG Sheetrock in window box	7.50	
21 Ken Schrader Little Debbie/Air Force/Motorcraft 3-car set in window box	20.00	
27 David Green Kleenex in window box	6.00	
32 Jason Leffler ABF U-Pack in window box	6.00	
66 Greg Biffle Cub Cadet in window box	7.50	
00 Johnny Sauter Yellow Freight in window box	6.00	
06 Atlanta Bass Pro Shops 500 in window box	5.00	
06 Atlanta Nicorette 300 in window box	5.00	
06 Bristol Sharpie 500 in window box	5.00	
06 California Speedway Auto Club 500 in window box	5.00	
06 California Sony HD 500 in window box	5.00	
06 Chicagoland USG Sheetrock 400 in window box	5.00	
06 Daytona 500 in window box	5.00	
06 Daytona Pepsi 400 in window box	5.00	
06 Infineon Save Mart 350 in window box	5.00	
06 Kansas Banquet 400 in window box	5.00	
06 Kentucky Speedway Meijer 300 in window box	5.00	
06 Las Vegas UAW Daimler-Chrysler 400 in window box	5.00	
06 Lowe's Motor Speedway Bank of America 500 in window box	5.00	
06 Lowe's Motor Speedway Coca-Cola 600 in window box	5.00	
06 Martinsville Directv 500 in window box	5.00	
06 Miami-Homestead Ford 400 in window box	5.00	
06 Michigan GFS Marketplace 400 in window box	5.00	
06 Michigan 3M Performance 400 in window box	5.00	
06 Phoenix Checker Auto Parts 500 in window box	5.00	

	EX	NM-MT
enix Subway Fresh 500 window box	5.00	10.00
mond Chevy Rock & Roll 400 window box	5.00	10.00
mond Crown Royal 400 window box	5.00	10.00
adega Aaron's 499 window box	5.00	10.00
adega UAW Ford 500 window box	5.00	10.00
as Dickies 500 window box	5.00	10.00
as Samsung Radio Shack 500 window box	5.00	10.00
kins Glen AMD at The Glen window box	5.00	10.00

2 Team Caliber Pull Backs 1:87

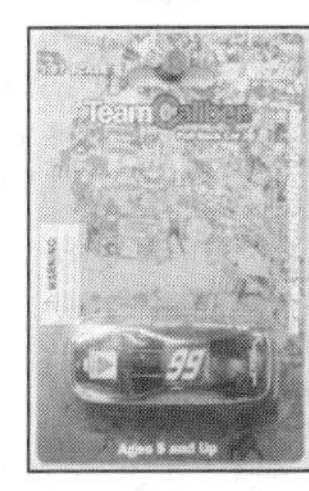

1:87 scale cars were issued on Team Caliber blister es. Each car features black windows and was produced otorized when pulled back across a smooth surface. The t schemes are far less detailed then on the larger scale .

	EX	NM-MT
Martin zer	3.00	8.00
g Biffle ainger	3.00	6.00
t Kenseth Walt	3.00	8.00
y Rudd otorcraft	3.00	6.00
Burton go	3.00	6.00

2003 Team liber/Motorworks 4-Packs 1:87

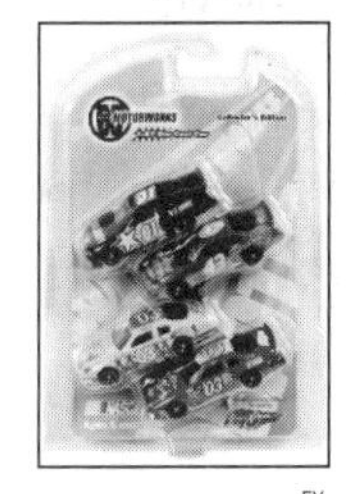

	EX	NM-MT
1 Jerry Nadeau/Army Johnny Benson/Valvoline Red Santa Blue Snowman	7.50	15.00
1 Jerry Nadeau/Army John Andertti/Berry Burst Yellow Reindeer Red Elf	7.50	15.00
Terry Labonte/Kellogg's Ryan Newman/Alltel Red Santa Yellow Reindeer	7.50	15.00
Terry Labonte/Kellogg's Kyle Petty/Brawny Red Elf Blue Snowman	7.50	15.00
0 Johnny Benson/Valvoline Ryan Newman/Alltel Blue Snowman Yellow Reindeer	7.50	15.00
0 Johnny Benson/Valvoline Kyle Petty/Brawny Red Elf Yellow Reindeer	7.50	15.00

002 Winner's Circle 1:18

	EX	NM-MT
Earnhardt odwrench	25.00	50.00
Earnhardt odwrench Oreo	25.00	50.00
Earnhardt odwrench Peter Max	35.00	60.00
Earnhardt odwrench Plus Bull	25.00	50.00
Earnhardt Jr. le Jr.	25.00	50.00
Gordon Pont Flames	25.00	50.00
in Harvick odwrench	20.00	40.00
Jarrett S	25.00	40.00

2003 Winner's Circle 1:18

	EX	NM-MT
3 Dale Earnhardt Foundation	25.00	40.00
3 Dale Earnhardt Goodwrench No Bull '00	25.00	40.00
3 Dale Earnhardt Goodwrench Peter Max '00	30.00	50.00
3 Dale Earnhardt Goodwrench Service Plus '00	25.00	40.00
3 Dale Earnhardt Goodwrench Oreo '01	25.00	40.00
8 Dale Earnhardt Jr. Dale Jr.	25.00	40.00
8 Dale Earnhardt Jr. Earnhardt Tribute Concert in '02 package	25.00	40.00
8 Dale Earnhardt Jr. MLB All Star '03	25.00	40.00
8 Dale Earnhardt Jr. Looney Tunes 2002	20.00	35.00
9 Bill Elliott Dodge	25.00	50.00
24 Jeff Gordon DuPont Flames	25.00	40.00
24 Jeff Gordon Pepsi Talladega '01	25.00	40.00
24 Jeff Gordon Pepsi Billion $	25.00	40.00
29 Kevin Harvick Goodwrench	25.00	40.00
38 Elliott Sadler M&M's	25.00	40.00
48 Jimmie Johnson Lowe's Sylvester & Tweety	25.00	40.00

2004 Winner's Circle 1:18

	EX	NM-MT
3 Dale Earnhardt Goodwrench Service Plus 2001 Monte Carlo	20.00	35.00
8 Dale Earnhardt Jr JR	20.00	35.00
8 Dale Earnhardt Jr. Oreo	20.00	35.00
9 Kasey Kahne Dodge	25.00	60.00
9 Kasey Kahne Dodge refresh	25.00	40.00
20 Tony Stewart Coke C2	15.00	30.00
20 Tony Stewart Home Depot	20.00	35.00
20 Tony Stewart Home Depot Black Reverse Paint	15.00	30.00
20 Tony Stewart Home Depot Declaration of Independence '03	15.00	30.00
21 Kevin Harvick Hershey's Kisses	15.00	30.00
24 Jeff Gordon DuPont Flames	25.00	40.00
24 Jeff Gordon DuPont Rainbow	20.00	35.00
24 Jeff Gordon Pepsi Shards	20.00	35.00
29 Kevin Harvick Coke C2	15.00	30.00
29 Kevin Harvick Goodwrench	15.00	30.00
38 Elliott Sadler M&M's	15.00	30.00
81 Tony Stewart Bass Pro Shops	20.00	35.00
99 Michael Waltrip Aaron's Cat in the Hat	15.00	30.00

2005 Winner's Circle 1:18

	EX	NM-MT
3 Dale Earnhardt Goodwrench '00	25.00	40.00
20 Tony Stewart Home Depot	25.00	40.00

2007 Winner's Circle 1:18

	EX	NM-MT
8 Dale Earnhardt Jr. DEI	25.00	40.00
9 Kasey Kahne Dodge Dealers	20.00	35.00
11 Denny Hamlin Fed Ex Express	20.00	35.00
20 Tony Stewart Home Depot	20.00	35.00
24 Jeff Gordon DuPont Flames	25.00	40.00
48 Jimmie Johnson Lowe's	25.00	40.00
99 Carl Edwards Office Depot	20.00	35.00
01 Mark Martin U.S. Army	20.00	35.00

1996 Winner's Circle 1:24

This first series of die-cast cars by Winner's Circle were issued in a blue and red cardboard double window box that included the "Winner's Circle" name and year of issue. A small picture of the driver was also included on the box in the lower right hand corner.

	EX	NM-MT
3 Dale Earnhardt Goodwrench	15.00	40.00
24 Jeff Gordon DuPont	12.50	25.00

1997 Winner's Circle 1:24

This series marks the teaming of Action Performance and Hasbro. This line of cars was produced for and distributed in the mass-market. It is highlighted by the Jeff Gordon Lifetime Series and the Dale Earnhardt lifetime Series.

	EX	NM-MT
3 Dale Earnhardt AC Delco 1996 Monte Carlo	25.00	60.00
3 Dale Earnhardt Goodwrench	40.00	100.00
3 Dale Earnhardt Goodwrench Plus	20.00	50.00
3 Dale Earnhardt Wheaties gray interior	45.00	100.00
3 Dale Earnhardt Wheaties orange interior	40.00	80.00
3 Jay Sauter Goodwrench SuperTruck	10.00	25.00
16 Ron Hornaday NAPA SuperTruck	8.00	20.00
17 Darrell Waltrip Parts America	8.00	20.00
18 Bobby Labonte Interstate Batteries	10.00	25.00
22 Ward Burton MBNA Gold	8.00	20.00
24 Jeff Gordon DuPont	20.00	50.00
24 Jeff Gordon DuPont Million Dollar Date	20.00	50.00
24 Jeff Gordon DuPont ChromaPremier	25.00	60.00
24 Jeff Gordon Lost World	25.00	60.00
27 Kenny Irwin Tonka	10.00	25.00
31 Mike Skinner Lowe's	10.00	25.00
81 Kenny Wallace Square D	10.00	25.00
88 Dale Jarrett Quality Care Ford Credit on fender	10.00	25.00
88 Dale Jarrett Quality Care Red Carpet Lease on fender	10.00	25.00

1998 Winner's Circle 1:24

	EX	NM-MT
1 Dale Earnhardt Jr. Coke	15.00	30.00
1 Steve Park Pennzoil	12.50	30.00
2 Rusty Wallace Rusty	10.00	20.00
2 Rusty Wallace Rusty Elvis	15.00	30.00
3 Dale Earnhardt Coke	35.00	75.00
3 Dale Earnhardt Goodwrench Plus	30.00	60.00
3 Dale Earnhardt Goodwrench Bass Pro	30.00	80.00
3 Dale Earnhardt Goodwrench Daytona	35.00	80.00
3 Dale Earnhardt Goodwrench Silver	30.00	80.00
3 Dale Earnhardt Jr. AC Delco	30.00	75.00
12 Jeremy Mayfield Mobil 1	8.00	20.00
18 Bobby Labonte Interstate Batteries	10.00	25.00
18 Bobby Labonte Interstate Batteries Small Soldiers	10.00	25.00
22 Ward Burton MBNA	8.00	20.00
24 Jeff Gordon DuPont	20.00	50.00
24 Jeff Gordon DuPont Million Dollar win	25.00	60.00
24 Jeff Gordon DuPont Walmart	20.00	50.00
28 Kenny Irwin Havoline	10.00	25.00
28 Kenny Irwin Havoline Joker	15.00	40.00
31 Mike Skinner Lowe's	10.00	25.00
44 Tony Stewart Shell	15.00	30.00
44 Tony Stewart Shell Small Soldiers	15.00	30.00
88 Dale Jarrett Quality Care	10.00	25.00
88 Dale Jarrett Quality Care Batman	10.00	25.00

1998 Winner's Circle with Figure 1:24

	EX	NM-MT
1 Dale Earnhardt Jr Coke	10.00	25.00
3 Dale Earnhardt Coke	12.50	30.00
3 Dale Earnhardt Jr AC Delco	12.50	25.00
24 Jeff Gordon DuPont No Bull	10.00	25.00
24 Jeff Gordon Pepsi	10.00	25.00

1999 Winner's Circle 1:24

This line is the result of an alliance between Action and Hasbro to bring exclusive license such as Gordon and Earnhardt to the mass market.

	EX	NM-MT
1 Steve Park Pennzoil	12.50	30.00
2 Rusty Wallace Rusty	10.00	25.00
3 Dale Earnhardt Goodwrench	30.00	80.00
3 Dale Earnhardt Goodwrench 25th Anniversary Silver Trunk	30.00	80.00
3 Dale Earnhardt Wrangler	30.00	75.00
3 Dale Earnhardt Jr. AC Delco	20.00	50.00
3 Dale Earnhardt Jr. AC Delco Superman	30.00	75.00
8 Dale Earnhardt Jr. Dale Jr.	20.00	40.00
12 Jeremy Mayfield Mobil 1 Kentucky Derby	10.00	25.00
18 Bobby Labonte Interstate Batteries	12.00	30.00
20 Tony Stewart Home Depot	20.00	50.00
22 Ward Burton Caterpillar	12.00	30.00
24 Jeff Gordon DuPont Daytona 500	20.00	50.00
24 Jeff Gordon DuPont No Bull	20.00	50.00
24 Jeff Gordon DuPont Superman	20.00	50.00
24 Jeff Gordon Pepsi	15.00	40.00
24 Jeff Gordon Pepsi with figure	15.00	40.00
24 Jeff Gordon Star Wars	15.00	40.00
28 Kenny Irwin Havoline	15.00	40.00
31 Mike Skinner Lowe's	8.00	20.00
88 Dale Jarrett Quality Care	8.00	20.00

2000 Winner's Circle Preview 1:24

Winner's Circle takes on a new look for 2000.

	EX	NM-MT
3 Dale Earnhardt GM Goodwrench Sign	30.00	75.00
3 Dale Earnhardt Goodwrench Taz No Bull	40.00	100.00
18 Bobby Labonte Interstate Batteries	10.00	25.00
20 Tony Stewart Home Depot	10.00	25.00
24 Jeff Gordon DuPont	15.00	30.00

2000 Winner's Circle 1:24

	EX	NM-MT
3 Dale Earnhardt Goodwrench	40.00	80.00
3 Dale Earnhardt Goodwrench Peter Max	60.00	100.00
3 Dale Earnhardt Goodwrench Sign	30.00	80.00
3 Dale Earnhardt Goodwrench Taz No Bull	40.00	80.00
9 Bill Elliott Dodge Limited Edition	12.50	25.00
18 Bobby Labonte Interstate Batteries	12.50	25.00
20 Tony Stewart Home Depot Rookie of the Year	15.00	40.00
24 Jeff Gordon DuPont	15.00	40.00
24 Jeff Gordon DuPont Peanuts 2000	30.00	60.00
24 Jeff Gordon DuPont Millennium	20.00	50.00
24 Jeff Gordon Pepsi	15.00	40.00
27 Casey Atwood Castrol	12.50	30.00
28 Ricky Rudd Havoline	12.00	30.00
36 Ken Schrader M&M's	15.00	30.00
88 Dale Jarrett Quality Care	12.00	30.00
88 Dale Jarrett Quality Care Air Force	12.50	25.00
88 Dale Jarrett Quality 1999 Winston Cup Champion	12.00	30.00

2001 Winner's Circle 1:24

	EX	NM-MT
1 Steve Park Pennzoil Tweety	15.00	30.00
2 Rusty Wallace Rusty Harley	12.50	25.00
3 Dale Earnhardt Goodwrench	30.00	60.00
3 Dale Earnhardt Goodwrench Oreo	40.00	75.00
8 Dale Earnhardt Jr. Dale Jr.	20.00	40.00
9 Bill Elliott Dodge	25.00	50.00
9 Bill Elliott Dodge Spiderman	15.00	40.00
15 Michael Waltrip NAPA	12.50	25.00
18 Bobby Labonte Interstate Batteries	15.00	30.00
18 Bobby Labonte Interstate Batteries Jurassic Park 3	12.50	25.00
19 Casey Atwood Mountain Dew	10.00	25.00
19 Casey Atwood Dodge	15.00	40.00
20 Tony Stewart Home Depot Kids 2000	20.00	40.00
24 Jeff Gordon DuPont Flames Quaker State Decal on rear fender	20.00	40.00
28 Ricky Rudd Havoline	12.50	25.00
29 Kevin Harvick Goodwrench Taz	12.50	30.00
29 Kevin Harvick Goodwrench White	12.50	25.00
88 Dale Jarrett UPS	20.00	35.00
88 Dale Jarrett UPS Flames	12.50	25.00
NNO Dodge Test Car	15.00	30.00

2001 Winner's Circle Lifetime Series 1:24

	EX	NM-MT
3 Dale Earnhardt AC Delco	20.00	40.00
3 Dale Earnhardt Goodwrench Olympic	20.00	40.00
8 Dale Earnhardt Jr. Dale Jr.	20.00	40.00
31 Dale Earnhardt Jr. Mom 'N' Pop's	20.00	40.00
44 Tony Stewart Shell	20.00	40.00

2002 Winner's Circle 1:24

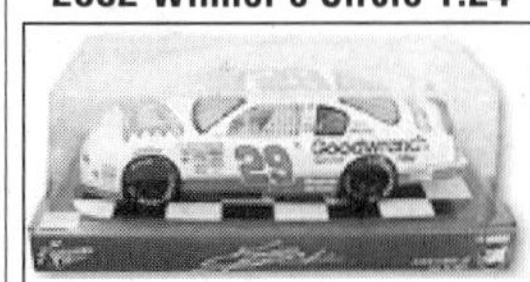

	EX	NM-MT
1 Steve Park Pennzoil	12.50	25.00
2 Rusty Wallace Rusty	15.00	30.00
3 Dale Earnhardt Goodwrench Oreo	15.00	30.00
3 Dale Earnhardt Jr. Nilla Wafers	15.00	30.00
3 Dale Earnhardt Jr. Oreo	15.00	30.00
4 Mike Skinner Kodak Max Yosemite Sam	12.50	25.00
5 Terry Labonte Kellogg's Road Runner&Coyote	15.00	30.00
7 Casey Atwood Sirius Muppets	12.50	25.00
8 Dale Earnhardt Jr. 2002 All-Star Game	15.00	30.00
8 Dale Earnhardt Jr. Looney Tunes	20.00	40.00
9 Bill Elliott Dodge Muppets	15.00	30.00
12 Kerry Earnhardt Jani-King Yosemite Sam	12.50	25.00
12 Kerry Earnhardt Super Cuts	12.50	25.00
18 Bobby Labonte Interstate Batteries	12.50	25.00
18 Bobby Labonte Interstate Batteries Coke	12.50	25.00
18 Bobby Labonte Interstate Batteries Jurassic Park 3	12.50	25.00
18 Bobby Labonte Interstate Batteries Muppets	12.50	25.00
19 Jeremy Mayfield Dodge Muppets	12.50	25.00
20 Tony Stewart Home Depot Coke	15.00	25.00
20 Tony Stewart Home Depot Peanuts Black	20.00	35.00
24 Jeff Gordon DuPont Flames Lowe's Decal on rear fender	15.00	30.00
24 Jeff Gordon DuPont 200th Anniversary	15.00	30.00
24 Jeff Gordon DuPont Bugs 2001	15.00	25.00
24 Jeff Gordon DuPont Bugs Rematch	15.00	25.00
24 Jeff Gordon Pepsi Daytona	15.00	30.00
25 Joe Nemechek UAW Speedy Gonzalez	12.50	25.00
28 Ricky Rudd Havoline	12.50	25.00
28 Ricky Rudd Havoline Iron Man	12.50	25.00
28 Ricky Rudd Havoline Muppets	12.50	25.00
29 Kevin Harvick Action ET	15.00	30.00
29 Kevin Harvick Goodwrench	15.00	25.00
29 Kevin Harvick Goodwrench ET	12.50	25.00
29 Kevin Harvick Goodwrench Taz	12.50	25.00
29 Kevin Harvick Reese's Fast Break	12.50	25.00
30 Jeff Green AOL Daffy Duck	12.50	25.00
31 Robby Gordon Cingular	12.50	25.00
31 Robby Gordon Cingular Pepe le Pew	12.50	25.00

37 Jeremy Mayfield Kmart RC Cola	12.50	25.00
40 Sterling Marlin Sterling Marlin	15.00	30.00
41 Jimmy Spencer Target	12.50	25.00
41 Jimmy Spencer Target Muppets	12.50	25.00
55 Bobby Hamilton Square D Marvin the Martian	12.50	25.00
88 Dale Jarrett UPS	12.50	25.00
88 Dale Jarrett UPS Muppets	12.50	25.00

2002 Winner's Circle Die-Cast Kits 1:24

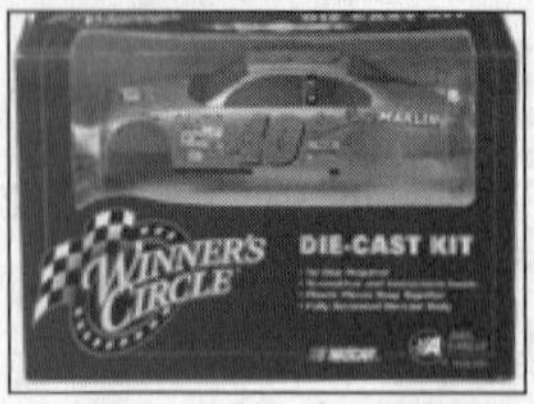

	EX	NM-MT
2 Rusty Wallace Rusty	20.00	35.00
3 Dale Earnhardt Jr. Nilla Wafer	25.00	40.00
8 Dale Earnhardt Jr. Dale Jr.	25.00	40.00
8 Dale Earnhardt Jr. Looney Tunes	25.00	40.00
9 Bill Elliott Dodge	20.00	35.00
24 Jeff Gordon DuPont Bugs Rematch	25.00	40.00
24 Jeff Gordon DuPont Flames	25.00	40.00
29 Kevin Harvick Goodwrench	20.00	35.00
40 Sterling Marlin Sterling	20.00	35.00
41 Jimmy Spencer Target	18.00	30.00
88 Dale Jarrett UPS	20.00	35.00

2003 Winner's Circle 1:24

	EX	NM-MT
2 Rusty Wallace Rusty	12.50	25.00
3 Dale Earnhardt Foundation	20.00	35.00
3 Dale Earnhardt 2000 Goodwrench No Bull	18.00	30.00
3 Dale Earnhardt 2000 Goodwrench Peter Max	30.00	50.00
8 Dale Earnhardt Jr. JR	18.00	30.00
8 Dale Earnhardt Jr. JR thin base	18.00	30.00
8 Dale Earnhardt Jr. Earnhardt Tribute Concert	20.00	35.00
8 Dale Earnhardt Jr. Looney Tunes 2002	18.00	30.00
8 Dale Earnhardt Jr. MLB All Star 2003 paint	18.00	30.00
8 Dale Earnhardt Jr. Oreo Ritz	18.00	30.00
9 Bill Elliott Dodge	15.00	25.00
20 Tony Stewart Home Depot	18.00	30.00
20 Tony Stewart Home Depot thin base	18.00	30.00
20 Tony Stewart Home Depot Peanuts Black	18.00	30.00
20 Tony Stewart Home Depot Peanuts Orange 2002 Champion Sticker	20.00	40.00
24 Jeff Gordon DuPont Flames	20.00	40.00
24 Jeff Gordon DuPont Bugs Rematch '02	18.00	30.00
24 Jeff Gordon 2002 Elmo	20.00	35.00
24 Jeff Gordon 2001 Pepsi Stars&Stripes	18.00	30.00
24 Jeff Gordon Pepsi Billion $	18.00	30.00
29 Kevin Harvick Goodwrench Taz	15.00	25.00
31 Robby Gordon Cingular	15.00	25.00
38 Elliott Sadler M&M's	15.00	25.00
38 Elliott Sadler M&M's Groovy	15.00	25.00
40 Sterling Marlin Sterling	15.00	25.00
45 Kyle Petty Hands to Victory	15.00	30.00
48 Jimmie Johnson Lowe's Distributor Exclusive Sticker	12.50	25.00
48 Jimmie Johnson Lowe's Sylvester.&Tweety	18.00	30.00
88 Dale Jarrett UPS	12.50	25.00
NNO Dale Earnhardt Legacy	25.00	40.00

2003 Winner's Circle Die-Cast Kits 1:24

	EX	NM-MT
3 Dale Earnhardt Jr. Oreo 2002	15.00	30.00
9 Bill Elliott Dodge	12.50	25.00
24 Jeff Gordon Dupont Bugs Rematch 2002	15.00	30.00

2003 Winner's Circle Victory Lap 1:24

	EX	NM-MT
2 Rusty Wallace Miller Lite Victory Lap	15.00	30.00
3 Dale Earnhardt Goodwrench Victory Lap	20.00	40.00
20 Tony Stewart Home Depot Victory Lap	15.00	30.00
24 Jeff Gordon DuPont Victory Lap	20.00	40.00
43 Richard Petty STP Victory Lap	18.00	30.00
88 Dale Jarrett UPS Victory Lap	15.00	30.00

2004 Winner's Circle 1:24

	EX	NM-MT
2 Rusty Wallace Kodak	15.00	25.00
2 Rusty Wallace Rusty	15.00	25.00
3 Dale Earnhardt Coke '98 Monte Carlo	18.00	30.00
3 Dale Earnhardt Goodwrench Olympic 1996 Monte Carlo	18.00	30.00
8 Dale Earnhardt Jr. JR	18.00	30.00
8 Dale Earnhardt Jr. Oreo	18.00	30.00
9 Kasey Kahne Dodge Refresh	25.00	50.00
9 Kasey Kahne Dodge Popeye	25.00	40.00
15 Michael Waltrip NAPA	15.00	25.00
18 Bobby Labonte Interstate Batteries	15.00	25.00
18 Bobby Labonte Interstate Batteries D-Day	15.00	25.00
18 Bobby Labonte Interstate Batteries Shrek 2	15.00	25.00
19 Jeremy Mayfield Dodge NHL All Star	15.00	25.00
19 Jeremy Mayfield Dodge Popeye	15.00	25.00
20 Tony Stewart Coke C2	15.00	25.00
20 Tony Stewart Home Depot	15.00	25.00
20 Tony Stewart Home Depot Black	15.00	25.00
20 Tony Stewart Home Depot Shrek 2	15.00	25.00
20 Tony Stewart Home Depot 25th Anniversary	15.00	25.00
21 Kevin Harvick Hershey's Kisses	15.00	25.00
21 Kevin Harvick Reese's	15.00	25.00
24 Jeff Gordon DuPont Flames	18.00	30.00
24 Jeff Gordon DuPont Flames HMS 20th Anniversary	20.00	35.00
24 Jeff Gordon DuPont Rainbow	20.00	35.00
24 Jeff Gordon DuPont Wizard of Oz	20.00	35.00
24 Jeff Gordon Pepsi	20.00	35.00
24 Jeff Gordon Pepsi Billion	20.00	35.00
29 Kevin Harvick Coke C2	15.00	25.00
29 Kevin Harvick Goodwrench	15.00	25.00
29 Kevin Harvick Goodwrench KISS	18.00	30.00
29 Kevin Harvick Goodwrench Realtree	15.00	25.00
29 Kevin Harvick Goodwrench RCR 35th Anniversary	18.00	30.00
29 Kevin Harvick Powerade	15.00	25.00
29 Bobby Labonte	15.00	25.00
ESGR Army		
38 Kasey Kahne Great Clips	20.00	35.00
38 Kasey Kahne Great Clips Shark Tale	18.00	30.00
38 Elliott Sadler M&M's	15.00	25.00
38 Elliott Sadler M&M's black&white	20.00	35.00
38 Elliott Sadler M&M's July 4	15.00	25.00
38 Elliott Sadler Pedigree Wizard of Oz	15.00	25.00
42 Jamie McMurray Havoline	15.00	25.00
77 Brendan Gaughan Kodak Punisher	15.00	25.00
81 Tony Stewart Bass Pro Shops	15.00	25.00
81 Dale Earnhardt Jr./KFC	15.00	25.00
81 Dale Earnhardt Jr. Taco Bell	15.00	25.00
88 Dale Jarrett UPS	18.00	30.00
92 Tony Stewart McDonald's	15.00	25.00
98 Bill Elliott Coke C2	15.00	25.00
01 Joe Nemechek Army Time Man of the Year	18.00	30.00

2004 Winner's Circle Die-Cast Kits 1:24

	EX	NM-MT
8 Dale Earnhardt Jr JR	20.00	35.00
9 Kasey Kahne Dodge Popeye	20.00	35.00
20 Tony Stewart Home Depot	20.00	35.00
24 Jeff Gordon DuPont Rainbow	20.00	35.00
38 Elliott Sadler M&M's	15.00	30.00
38 Elliott Sadler M&M's July 4	15.00	30.00

2005 Winner's Circle 1:24

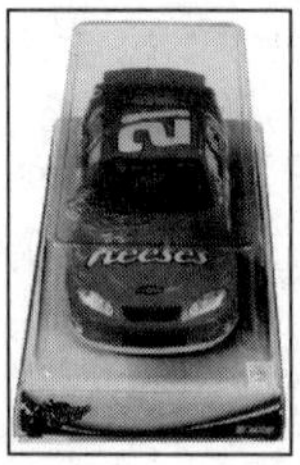

	EX	NM-MT
2 Clint Bowyer Timberland	15.00	30.00
2 Clint Bowyer AC Delco	15.00	30.00
2 Rusty Wallace Rusty	15.00	25.00
3 Dale Earnhardt Foundation '03	15.00	25.00
8 Dale Earnhardt Jr. DEI	15.00	30.00
8 Dale Earnhardt Jr. JR	15.00	30.00
8 Martin Truex Jr. Bass Pro	15.00	25.00
9 Bill Elliott Milestones	15.00	30.00
9 Kasey Kahne Dodge Longest Yard	15.00	30.00
9 Kasey Kahne Dodge Retro Daytona Shootout	15.00	30.00
9 Kasey Kahne Dodge	15.00	30.00
9 Kasey Kahne Dodge 2004 Rookie of the Year	20.00	35.00
9 Kasey Kahne Dodge Mopar '04	20.00	35.00
19 Jeremy Mayfield Dodge	12.50	25.00
19 Jeremy Mayfield Dodge Retro Daytona Shootout	15.00	25.00
20 Tony Stewart Home Depot	20.00	35.00
21 Kevin Harvick Reese's	15.00	25.00
24 Jeff Gordon DuPont Flames	15.00	30.00
29 Kevin Harvick Goodwrench	15.00	25.00
29 Kevin Harvick Goodwrench Atlanta	15.00	25.00
29 Kevin Harvick Goodwrench Daytona	15.00	25.00
29 Kevin Harvick Goodwrench Brickyard	15.00	25.00
29 Kevin Harvick Goodwrench Gretchen Wilson	15.00	25.00
29 Kevin Harvick Goodwrench Quicksilver	15.00	25.00
33 Tony Stewart Mr. Clean AutoDry	15.00	30.00
33 Tony Stewart Old Spice	15.00	30.00
38 Kasey Kahne Great Clips	15.00	30.00
38 Elliott Sadler Pedigree	15.00	25.00
38 Elliott Sadler M&M's	15.00	25.00
41 Reed Sorenson Discount Tire Coats	15.00	30.00
'05 Nashville Raced		
42 Jamie McMurray Havoline	15.00	25.00
42 Jamie McMurray Havoline Shine On '05 Charlotte	15.00	25.00
42 Jamie McMurray Havoline Shine On '05 Sonoma	15.00	25.00
42 Jamie McMurray Havoline Shine On '05 Talladega	15.00	25.00
81 Dale Earnhardt Jr. Oreo Ritz	15.00	30.00
88 Dale Jarrett UPS	15.00	25.00
99 Michael Waltrip Domino's Pizza	15.00	25.00
NNO Dale Earnhardt Legacy '02	10.00	20.00

2006 Winner's Circle 1:24

	EX	NM-MT
1 Martin Truex Jr. Bass Pro 3 Days of Dale Tribute split window box	15.00	25.00
5 Kyle Busch Kellogg's	15.00	25.00
6 Mark Martin AAA	20.00	35.00
8 Dale Earnhardt Jr. Bud 3 Days of Dale Tribute split window box	15.00	30.00
8 Dale Earnhardt Jr. 250 Starts	15.00	25.00
8 Martin Truex Jr. Bass Pro	15.00	25.00
8 Martin Truex Jr. Bass Pro 3 Days of Dale Tribute Talladega Raced split window box	15.00	25.00
9 Kasey Kahne Dodge	15.00	25.00
9 Kasey Kahne Dodge Raced	15.00	25.00
9 Kasey Kahne Dodge SRT		
11 Paul Menard Menard's 3 Days of Dale Tribute split window box	15.00	25.00
12 Ryan Newman Alltel	15.00	25.00
16 Greg Biffle National Guard	15.00	25.00
17 Matt Kenseth DeWalt	15.00	30.00
19 Jeremy Mayfield Dodge	15.00	25.00
19 Jeremy Mayfield Mountain Dew Pitch Black	12.50	25.00
20 Tony Stewart Home Depot	15.00	25.00
24 Jeff Gordon DuPont Flames	15.00	30.00
24 Jeff Gordon DuPont Hot Hues Foose Design		
24 Jeff Gordon Holiday JG Foundation		
26 Jamie McMurray Sharpie	15.00	25.00
29 Kevin Harvick Goodwrench		
31 Jeff Burton Cingular	15.00	30.00
33 Tony Stewart Old Spice		
38 Elliott Sadler M&M's	15.00	25.00
48 Jimmie Johnson Lowe's	15.00	30.00
48 Jimmie Johnson Lowe's Sea World		
64 Rusty Wallace Bell Helicopter '05	15.00	25.00
88 Dale Jarrett UPS	15.00	25.00
99 Carl Edwards Office Depot	15.00	30.00
01 Joe Nemechek Army Camo Call to Duty	15.00	25.00
NNO Dale Earnhardt Hall of Fame Dale Tribute split window box	15.00	30.00

2007 Winner's Circle 1:24

	EX	NM-MT
1 Martin Truex Jr. Bass Pro Shops	15.00	25.00
2 Kurt Busch Kurt	15.00	25.00
8 Dale Earnhardt Jr. DEI	15.00	30.00
9 Kasey Kahne Dodge Dealers	15.00	25.00
11 Denny Hamlin Fed Ex Express	15.00	25.00
12 Ryan Newman Alltel	15.00	25.00
16 Greg Biffle Ameriquest	15.00	25.00
17 Matt Kenseth DeWalt	15.00	25.00
20 Tony Stewart Home Depot	15.00	30.00
20 Tony Stewart Home Depot Daytona Shootout Raced	15.00	30.00
24 Jeff Gordon DuPont Flames	15.00	30.00
24 Jeff Gordon Nicorette	15.00	30.00
24 Jeff Gordon Pepsi	15.00	30.00
26 Jamie McMurray Irwin Tools	15.00	25.00
29 Kevin Harvick Shell Pennzoil Daytona Raced	20.00	40.00
29 Kevin Harvick Shell Pennzoil	20.00	40.00
38 David Gilliland M&M's	15.00	
42 Juan Pablo Montoya Texaco Havoline	15.00	
44 Dale Jarrett UPS	15.00	
48 Jimmie Johnson Lowe's	15.00	
55 Michael Waltrip NAPA	15.00	
88 Ricky Rudd Snickers	15.00	
99 Carl Edwards Office Depot	15.00	
2007 NEXTEL Schedule Car	12.50	
00 David Reutimann Burger King	15.00	
01 Mark Martin U.S. Army	20.00	
07 Clint Bowyer Directv	15.00	

2007 Winner's Circle American Heroes 1:24

	EX	N
8 Dale Earnhardt Jr. Bud Camo American Heroes logo	20.00	
8 Dale Earnhardt Jr. DEI Camo American Hero logo	15.00	
11 Denny Hamlin Fed Ex Freight Marines American Heroes	15.00	
24 Jeff Gordon DuPont Department of Defense American Hero logo	15.00	
48 Jimmie Johnson Lowe's Power of Pride American Heroes	15.00	
01 Mark Martin Army American Hero logo	15.00	

2007 Winner's Circle Lim Edition 1:24

	EX	N
8 Dale Earnhardt Jr. Bud	20.00	
8 Dale Earnhardt Jr. Bud Stars & Stripes	20.00	
8 Dale Earnhardt Jr. Bud Test	20.00	
8 Dale Earnhardt Jr. DEI Stars & Stripes	15.00	
8 Dale Earnhardt Jr. Sharpie	15.00	

2008 Winner's Circle 1:

	EX	N
1 Martin Truex Jr. Bass Pro Shops	15.00	
2 Kurt Busch Kurt	15.00	
5 Casey Mears Carquest	15.00	
5 Casey Mears Kellogg's	15.00	
8 Mark Martin U.S. Army	15.00	
9 Kasey Kahne KK	15.00	
11 Denny Hamlin Fed Ex Express	15.00	
12 Ryan Newman Alltel	15.00	
17 Matt Kenseth DeWalt	15.00	
18 Kyle Busch M&M's	25.00	
20 Tony Stewart Home Depot	15.00	
24 Jeff Gordon DuPont Flames	20.00	
24 Jeff Gordon Nicorette	20.00	
24 Jeff Gordon Pepsi	20.00	
29 Kevin Harvick Shell	15.00	
31 Jeff Burton AT&T	15.00	
42 Juan Pablo Montoya Big Red	15.00	
42 Juan Pablo Montoya Texaco Havoline	15.00	
44 Dale Jarrett UPS	15.00	
48 Jimmie Johnson Lowe's	15.00	
55 Michael Waltrip Napa	15.00	
88 Dale Earnhardt Jr. AMP	20.00	
88 Dale Earnhardt Jr. National Guard	20.00	
99 Carl Edwards Office Depot	15.00	

2008 Winner's Circle Day 500 1:24

	EX	N
1 Martin Truex Jr. Bass Pro Shops	25.00	
9 Kasey Kahne Bud	35.00	
9 Kasey Kahne KK	25.00	
17 Matt Kenseth DeWalt	25.00	
20 Tony Stewart Home Depot	25.00	
24 Jeff Gordon DuPont Flames	25.00	
29 Kevin Harvick Shell Pennzoil	25.00	
42 Juan Pablo Montoya Texaco	25.00	
48 Jimmie Johnson	25.00	

e's		
Earnhardt Jr.	25.00	40.00
Earnhardt Jr. onal Guard	25.00	40.00
Edwards ce Depot	25.00	40.00

8 Winner's Circle Limited Edition 1:24

	EX	NM-MT
Earnhardt Jr.	25.00	40.00

98 Winner's Circle 1:43

ies marks the teaming of Action Performance and This line of cars was produced for and distributed in -market.

	EX	NM-MT
Earnhardt Jr. e	8.00	20.00
Wallace ty	6.00	15.00
Wallace ty Elvis	6.00	15.00
arnhardt e	20.00	40.00
arnhardt dwrench Bass Pro	20.00	40.00
arnhardt dwrench Plus	20.00	40.00
arnhardt Jr. Delco	8.00	20.00
ny Mayfield oil 1	6.00	15.00
Gordon Pont	6.00	15.00
Gordon Pont Million Dollar Win	6.00	15.00
Gordon Pont Winston Cup mpion Walmart special	8.00	20.00
y Irwin oline	6.00	15.00
Earnhardt Jr. kens Blue	6.00	15.00
Schrader rader	5.00	12.00
Jarrett lity Care	6.00	15.00
Jarrett lity Care Batman	5.00	12.00

8 Winner's Circle For Kids 1:43

in this series is close to the scale of 1:43 but not exact. cast piece was issued with a rip cord that could be used the car across the ground. Both the cord and car were d in a Winner's Circle blister.

arnhardt dwrench	10.00	20.00
Gordon Pont	7.50	15.00

8 Winner's Circle Victory Celebration 1:43

	EX	NM-MT
arnhardt kyard 400 8/5/95	20.00	40.00
arnhardt tona 500 2/15/98	10.00	20.00
arnhardt Jr. ch Champion	8.00	20.00
Gordon rlotte Win	8.00	20.00
Gordon Pont Million Dollar 8/31/97	8.00	20.00

99 Winner's Circle 1:43

is the result of an alliance between Action and Hasbro exclusive licenses such as Gordon and Earnhardt to the rket.

	EX	NM-MT
Park nzoil	6.00	15.00
Wallace ty	5.00	12.00
arnhardt dwrench 25th Anniv. on package	12.50	25.00
arnhardt dwrench 25th Anniv. e on package	12.50	30.00
arnhardt Jr. Delco	8.00	20.00
arnhardt Jr. Delco Superman	12.00	30.00
ny Mayfield oil 1	6.00	15.00
ny Mayfield oil 1 Kentucky Derby	6.00	15.00
y Labonte rstate Batteries	8.00	20.00
Stewart ne Depot	12.00	30.00
Burton erpillar	8.00	20.00
Gordon Pont	10.00	25.00
Gordon Pont Daytona 500	10.00	25.00
Gordon Pont Superman	12.00	30.00
Gordon si	8.00	20.00
Gordon si Star Wars	10.00	25.00
y Irwin oline	8.00	20.00
Skinner e's	6.00	15.00
Jarrett lity Care 1999 Winston Cup Champ.	6.00	15.00

88 Dale Jarrett Quality Care No Bull 5 Win	12.00	20.00

1999 Winner's Circle Select 1:43

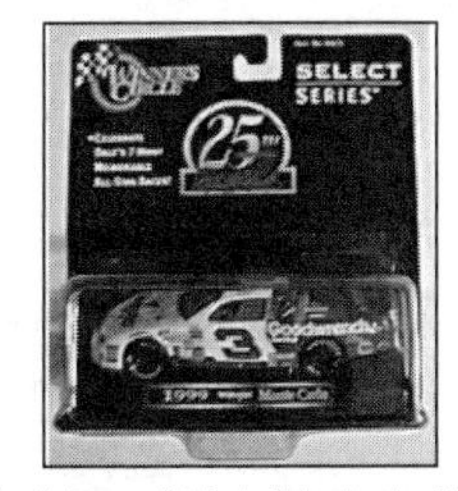

This set features cars Dale Earnhardt drove in various Winston Select races.

	EX	NM-MT
3 Dale Earnhardt Goowrench Silver '95	20.00	40.00
3 Dale Earnhardt Goodwrench Olympic '96	25.00	50.00
3 Dale Earnhardt Goodwrench Bass Pro '98	15.00	30.00
3 Dale Earnhardt Goodwrench Wrangler '99	15.00	30.00

1999 Winner's Circle Speedweeks 1:43

These cars are preview cars for the 1999 Daytona 500.

	EX	NM-MT
3 Dale Earnhardt Goodwrench	15.00	30.00
3 Dale Earnhardt Jr. AC Delco	6.00	12.00
18 Bobby Labonte Interstate Batteries	6.00	12.00
24 Jeff Gordon DuPont	6.00	12.00

1999 Winner's Circle Victory Celebration 1:43

	EX	NM-MT
3 Dale Earnhardt Jr. Coca-Cola 300 4/4/98	10.00	25.00
3 Dale Earnhardt Jr. Richmond 6/5/98	10.00	25.00
12 Jeremy Mayfield Pocono 500 6/21/98	8.00	20.00
24 Jeff Gordon Daytona 500	10.00	25.00
24 Jeff Gordon Daytona 500 2/16/97	10.00	25.00
88 Dale Jarrett Quality Care No Bull 5-win 11/11/98	8.00	20.00

2000 Winner's Circle Preview 1:43

Winner's Circle takes on a new look for 2000.

	EX	NM-MT
3 Dale Earnhardt Jr. AC Delco Superman '99	8.00	20.00
8 Dale Earnhardt Jr. Dale Jr.	8.00	20.00
18 Bobby Labonte Interstate Batteries	6.00	15.00
20 Tony Stewart Home Depot	6.00	15.00
24 Jeff Gordon DuPont	6.00	15.00

2000 Winner's Circle 1:43

	EX	NM-MT
3 Dale Earnhardt Goodwrench	15.00	30.00
18 Bobby Labonte Interstate Batteries	6.00	15.00
24 Jeff Gordon Pepsi	6.00	15.00
36 Ernie Irvan M&M's	6.00	15.00

2000 Winner's Circle Double Platinum 1:43

	EX	NM-MT
3 Dale Earnhardt Richard Childress Goodwrench	35.00	75.00
8 Dale Earnhardt Jr. Dale Earnhardt Dale Jr.	40.00	80.00
18 Bobby Labonte Joe Gibbs Interstate Batteries	10.00	20.00
19 Casey Atwood Ray Evernham Dodge	6.00	15.00
36 Ken Schrader M&M's	10.00	20.00

2000 Winner's Circle Garage Scene 1:43

	EX	NM-MT
3 Dale Earnhardt Goodwrench	25.00	50.00
20 Tony Stewart Home Depot	8.00	20.00
24 Jeff Gordon DuPont	8.00	20.00

2000 Winner's Circle Sam Bass 1:43

Each car in this series was mounted to a black plastic base that included the driver's name, the title of the art work, and the NASCAR and Sam Bass signature logos. They were packaged in a blister that also included a large (roughly 3 1/2" by 5") card created from a Sam Bass illustration.

	EX	NM-MT
3 Dale Earnhardt Goodwrench	20.00	50.00
3 Dale Earnhardt Goodwrench 7-time Champ	25.00	40.00
3 Dale Earnhardt Goodwrench 2001 Oreo	15.00	40.00
3 Dale Earnhardt Goodwrench Peter Max	25.00	50.00
3 Dale Earnhardt Goodwrench Taz No Bull	30.00	60.00
3 Dale Earnhardt Wrangler 1987 Monte Carlo	25.00	40.00
8 Dale Earnhardt Jr. Dale Jr.	15.00	40.00
20 Tony Stewart Home Depot	6.00	15.00
24 Jeff Gordon DuPont	6.00	15.00
88 Dale Jarrett Quality Care	5.00	12.00

2000 Winner's Circle VIP Pass 1:43

	EX	NM-MT
3 Dale Earnhardt Goodwrench Plus	12.50	25.00
20 Tony Stewart Home Depot	10.00	20.00

2001 Winner's Circle Double Platinum 1:43

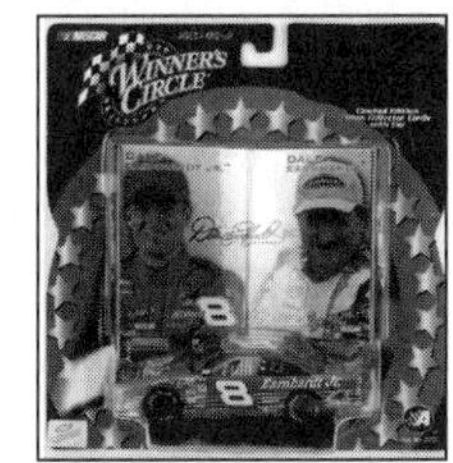

These cars were produced by Action Performance for their Winner's Circle line. Each was packaged in a clear blister pack along with a double-fold holofoil card.

	EX	NM-MT
1 Steve Park Pennzoil Tweety	7.50	15.00
2 Rusty Wallace Robin Pemberton Rusty	7.50	15.00
3 Dale Earnhardt Richard Childress Goodwrench	10.00	20.00
8 Dale Earnhardt Jr Dale with Dale Earnhardt Sr. on card	10.00	20.00
9 Bill Elliott Ray Evernham Dodge	10.00	20.00
24 Jeff Gordon DuPont	10.00	20.00
24 Jeff Gordon DuPont Bugs	10.00	20.00
29 Kevin Harvick Goodwrench Taz	7.50	20.00
88 Dale Jarrett UPS Flames	10.00	20.00

2002 Winner's Circle Double Platinum 1:43

	EX	NM-MT
3 Dale Earnhardt Jr. Nilla Wafer	10.00	20.00
3 Dale Earnhardt Jr. Oreo	10.00	20.00
8 Dale Earnhardt Jr. Dale Jr.	10.00	20.00
8 Dale Earnhardt Jr. Looney Tunes	10.00	20.00

8 Dale Earnhardt Jr 2002 MLB All-Star Game	10.00	20.00
20 Tony Stewart Home Depot	10.00	20.00
24 Jeff Gordon DuPont Bugs 2001	10.00	20.00
24 Jeff Gordon DuPont Flames	10.00	20.00
24 Jeff Gordon DuPont Bugs Rematch 2002	10.00	20.00
24 Jeff Gordon DuPont 200th Anniversary	10.00	20.00
29 Kevin Harvick Reese's Fast Break	10.00	20.00
29 Kevin Harvick Goodwrench	10.00	20.00
29 Kevin Harvick Goodwrench Taz	10.00	20.00

2002 Winner's Circle Race Hood 1:43

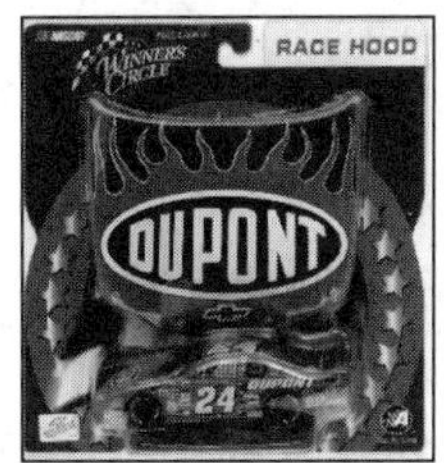

This series was produced by Winner's Circle and packaged in the typical blue blister with the title "Race Hood" printed in the upper right hand corner. Each car was a 1:43 scale die-cast with the hood being roughly 1:12 scale. The year of issue is noted on the back within the copyright information.

	EX	NM-MT
2 Rusty Wallace Rusty	10.00	20.00
3 Dale Earnhardt Jr. Nilla Wafers	12.50	25.00
3 Dale Earnhardt Jr. Oreo	12.50	25.00
4 Mike Skinner Kodak Yosemite Sam	10.00	20.00
7 Casey Atwood Sirius Muppets	10.00	20.00
8 Dale Earnhardt Jr. 2002 All-Star Game	12.50	25.00
8 Dale Earnhardt Jr. Looney Tunes	12.50	25.00
9 Bill Elliott Dodge Muppets	10.00	20.00
12 Kerry Earnhardt Jani-King Yosemite Sam	10.00	20.00
15 Michael Waltrip NAPA	10.00	20.00
18 Bobby Labonte Interstate Batteries Muppets	10.00	20.00
19 Jeremy Mayfield Dodge Muppets	10.00	20.00
24 Jeff Gordon DuPont Bugs 2002	12.50	25.00
24 Jeff Gordon DuPont Flames	12.50	25.00
24 Jeff Gordon DuPont 200th Anniversary	12.50	25.00
29 Kevin Harvick Reese's Fast Break	10.00	20.00
29 Kevin Harvick Goodwrench	10.00	20.00
29 Kevin Harvick Goodwrench Taz	10.00	20.00
55 Bobby Hamilton Square D Marvin Martian	10.00	20.00
88 Dale Jarrett UPS Muppets	10.00	20.00

2003 Winner's Circle Double Platinum 1:43

	EX	NM-MT
8 Dale Earnhardt Jr. Looney Tunes	10.00	20.00
20 Tony Stewart Home Depot Peanuts Black	10.00	20.00
20 Tony Stewart Home Depot Peanuts Orange	10.00	20.00
21 Kevin Harvick Payday	7.50	15.00
25 Joe Nemechek UAW Speedy Gonzalez	7.50	15.00
29 Kevin Harvick Goodwrench Taz	8.00	20.00
30 Jeff Green AOL Daffy	7.50	15.00
48 Jimmie Johnson Lowe's Sylvester	8.00	20.00

2003 Winner's Circle Race Hood 1:43

	EX	NM-MT
8 Dale Earnhardt Jr. Earnhardt Tribute Concert	10.00	20.00
8 Dale Earnhardt Jr. Looney Tunes 2002	10.00	20.00
8 Dale Earnhardt Jr. Oreo Ritz	10.00	20.00
9 Bill Elliott Dodge	7.50	15.00
20 Tony Stewart Home Depot Declaration of Independence	7.50	15.00
20 Tony Stewart Home Depot Peanuts Black	7.50	15.00
20 Tony Stewart Home Depot Peanuts Orange	7.50	15.00
24 Jeff Gordon DuPont Flames Yosemite Sam	7.50	15.00
24 Jeff Gordon Pepsi	7.50	15.00
25 Joe Nemechek UAW-Delphi Speedy Gonzalez	7.50	15.00
29 Kevin Harvick Goodwrench Taz	7.50	15.00
30 Jeff Green AOL Daffy	7.50	15.00
38 Elliott Sadler M&M's	7.50	15.00
48 Jimmie Johnson Lowe's Sylvester&Tweety	7.50	15.00
88 Dale Jarrett UPS brown logo	7.50	15.00
NNO Dale Earnhardt Legacy	10.00	20.00

2004 Winner's Circle Race Hood 1:43

	EX	NM-MT
8 Dale Earnhardt Jr. JR	10.00	20.00
9 Bill Elliott Dodge Lion King	10.00	20.00

1996 Winner's Circle 1:64

	EX	NM-MT
2 Mike Bliss ASE SuperTruck	4.00	8.00
3 Dale Earnhardt Goodwrench	15.00	30.00
16 Ron Hornaday NAPA SuperTruck	4.00	8.00
24 Jeff Gordon DuPont	6.00	15.00
31 Mike Skinner Lowe's	4.00	8.00
88 Dale Jarrett Quality Care	5.00	12.00

1997 Winner's Circle 1:64

This series marks the teaming of Action Performance and Hasbro. This line of cars was produced for and distributed to mass-market retailers. Some 1996 pieces were re-released in early 1997 with only the addition of a sticker that read "1997 Stock Car Series" over the 1996 year on the front of the package. On those, the copyright line still reads 1996 on the back.

	EX	NM-MT
2 Mike Bliss Team ASE SuperTruck	2.00	6.00
3 Dale Earnhardt Goodwrench	15.00	30.00
3 Jay Sauter Goodwrench SuperTruck	2.00	6.00
16 Ron Hornaday NAPA	3.00	8.00
18 Bobby Labonte Interstate Batteries	2.00	6.00
22 Ward Burton MBNA	2.00	6.00
22 Ward Burton MBNA Gold	2.00	6.00
24 Jeff Gordon DuPont	5.00	10.00
24 Jeff Gordon DuPont Million $ Date	5.00	10.00
27 Kenny Irwin G.I. Joe	4.00	8.00
27 Kenny Irwin Tonka	4.00	8.00
31 Mike Skinner Lowe's	2.00	6.00
81 Kenny Wallace Square D	2.00	6.00
88 Dale Jarrett Quality Care	2.00	6.00

1996-97 Winner's Circle Lifetime Dale Earnhardt 1:64

	EX	NM-MT
2 Dale Earnhardt Curb 1980 Olds 4/12 LTS Logo on package	12.50	30.00
2 Dale Earnhardt Curb 1980 Olds 4/12 no LTS Logo on backer	12.50	30.00
2 Dale Earnhardt Wrangler 1981 Pontiac 8/12	10.00	25.00
3 Dale Earnhardt Wrangler 1984 Monte Carlo 9/12	10.00	25.00
3 Dale Earnhardt Wrangler 1986 Monte Carlo 10/12	10.00	25.00
3 Dale Earnhardt Goodwrench 1988 Camaro 7/12 LTS logo on package	15.00	30.00

	EX	NM-MT
3 Dale Earnhardt Goodwrench 1988 Camaro 7/12 no LTS logo on backer	15.00	30.00
3 Dale Earnhardt Lowes 1989 Pontiac 11/12	10.00	20.00
3 Dale Earnhardt Goodwrench 1990 Lumina 12/12	10.00	25.00
3 Dale Earnhardt Goodwrench Silver 1995 Monte Carlo 3/12 1996 package	10.00	25.00
3 Dale Earnhardt Goodwrench Silver 1995 Monte Carlo 3/12 1997 Package	10.00	25.00
3 D.Earnhardt/GW Silver '95 MC 3/12 LTS logo on package with red number and lettering	10.00	25.00
3 Dale Earnhardt Goodwrench Silver 1995 Monte Carlo 3/12 LTS logo on package with orange number and lettering	10.00	25.00
3 Dale Earnhardt AC Delco 1996 Monte Carlo 2/12	25.00	60.00
3 Dale Earnhardt Goodwrench 1997 Monte Carlo 1/12 1997 package	10.00	25.00
3 Dale Earnhardt Goodwrench 1997 Monte Carlo 1/12 LTS logo on package	10.00	25.00
3 Dale Earnhardt Wheaties 1997 Monte Carlo 5/12 no LTS Logo on package	15.00	30.00
3 Dale Earnhardt Wheaties 1997 Monte Carlo 5/12 with LTS Logo on package and gray interior	15.00	30.00
3 Dale Earnhardt Wheaties 1997 Monte Carlo 5/12 with LTS Logo on package and orange interior	15.00	30.00
3 Dale Earnhardt Wheaties 1997 Monte Carlo 5/12 with LTS Logo on package and gray interior with Wheaties trading card	50.00	100.00
8 Dale Earnhardt RPM 1975 Dodge Charger Bonus	12.50	30.00
98 Dale Earnhardt 1978 Monte Carlo 6/12 LTS logo on package	15.00	40.00
98 Dale Earnhardt 1978 Monte Carlo 6/12 no LTS logo on package	15.00	40.00

1996-97 Winner's Circle Lifetime Jeff Gordon 1:64

	EX	NM-MT
1 Jeff Gordon Baby Ruth 1992 Thunderbird 4/6	5.00	12.00
1 Jeff Gordon Carolina 1991 Thunderbird 5/6	6.00	15.00
24 Jeff Gordon DuPont 1993 Lumina 6/6 with car card	8.00	20.00
24 Jeff Gordon DuPont 1993 Lumina 6/6 with Gordon card and LTS logo on package	8.00	20.00
24 Jeff Gordon DuPont 1993 Lumina 6/6 with Gordon card and no LTS logo on package	8.00	20.00
24 Jeff Gordon DuPont 1997 MC 1/6 1996 Package	8.00	20.00
24 Jeff Gordon DuPont 1997 Monte Carlo 1/6 1997 Package	8.00	20.00
24 Jeff Gordon DuPont 1997 Monte Carlo 1/6 LTS logo on package	8.00	20.00
24 Jeff Gordon DuPont 1997 Million Dollar Date LTS Bonus	6.00	12.50
24 Jeff Gordon DuPont ChromaPremiere 1997 Monte Carlo 2/6 1996 Package	10.00	25.00
24 Jeff Gordon DuPont ChromaPremiere 1997 Monte Carlo 2/6 1997 Package	10.00	25.00
24 Jeff Gordon Lost World 1997 Monte Carlo 3/6 LTS logo on package	10.00	20.00
24 Jeff Gordon Lost World 1997 Monte Carlo 3/6 no LTS logo on package	10.00	20.00
40 Jeff Gordon 1987 Sprint bonus LTS logo on left edge	12.00	30.00
40 Jeff Gordon 1987 Sprint bonus LTS logo in upper right	12.00	30.00

1997 Winner's Circle Lifetime Darrell Waltrip 1:64

	EX	NM-MT
17 Darrell Waltrip Parts America 1975-1980 Paint 1/6	6.00	12.00
17 Darrell Waltrip Parts America 1981-1982 Paint 4/6	6.00	12.00
17 Darrell Waltrip Parts America 1983 Paint 6/6	6.00	12.00
17 Darrell Waltrip Parts America 1984-1986 Paint 5/6	6.00	12.00
17 Darrell Waltrip Parts America 1990-1997 Paint 3/6	6.00	12.00
17 Darrell Waltrip Parts America Chroma 1997 Paint 2/6	6.00	12.00

1998 Winner's Circle 1:64

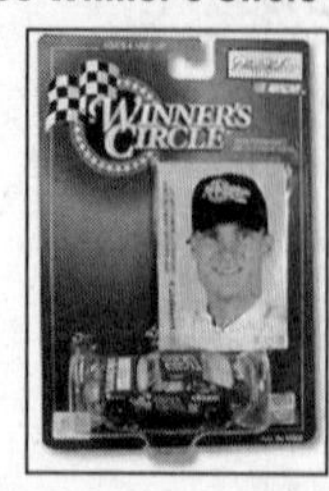

These blister packs include one 1:64 die-cast car and a red bordered card of the featured driver. The NASCAR 50th Anniversary logo is also featured on the packaging.

	EX	NM-MT
1 Dale Earnhardt Jr. Coke	7.50	15.00
1 Steve Park Pennzoil	4.00	10.00
2 Rusty Wallace Adventures of Rusty	6.00	15.00
2 Rusty Wallace Elvis	6.00	15.00
2 Rusty Wallace Rusty	5.00	12.00
3 Dale Earnhardt Coke	12.50	25.00
3 Dale Earnhardt Goodwrench	25.00	50.00
3 Dale Earnhardt Goodwrench with 25th Anniversary sticker	25.00	50.00
3 Dale Earnhardt Goodwrench Plus 1998 Preview blister	15.00	30.00
3 Dale Earnhardt Goodwrench Plus Daytona 500 blister	25.00	50.00
3 Dale Earnhardt Goodwrench Plus Toy's R Us blister	20.00	40.00
3 Dale Earnhardt Jr. AC Delco	10.00	25.00
3 Dale Earnhardt Jr. AC Delco Busch Champion	10.00	25.00
3/3 Dale Earnhardt Goodwrench 25th Wrangler 2-car set	25.00	50.00
12 Jeremy Mayfield Mobil 1	4.00	10.00
16 Ron Hornaday NAPA SuperTruck	4.00	10.00
18 Bobby Labonte Interstate Batteries	6.00	15.00
18 Bobby Labonte Interstate Batteries Hot Rod	12.50	25.00
18 Bobby Labonte Interstate Batteries Small Soldiers	8.00	20.00
22 Ward Burton MBNA	4.00	10.00
24 Jeff Gordon DuPont Champion 11/16/97 with figure	12.50	30.00
24 Jeff Gordon DuPont 1998 Preview blister	8.00	20.00
24 Jeff Gordon DuPont 1998 Winston Cup Champion	8.00	20.00
24 Jeff Gordon DuPont Daytona 500 blister	8.00	20.00
24 Jeff Gordon DuPont Million Dollar win card	8.00	20.00
24 Jeff Gordon DuPont Walmart blister	6.00	15.00
28 Kenny Irwin Havoline	5.00	12.00
28 Kenny Irwin Havoline 1998 Rookie of the Year	5.00	12.00
28 Kenny Irwin Havoline Joker	6.00	15.00
28 Kenny Irwin Havoline Speedweek Special card	5.00	12.00
31 Dale Earnhardt Jr. Sikkens Blue	6.00	15.00
31 Mike Skinner Lowe's Japan Win	4.00	10.00
31 Mike Skinner Lowe's Rookie of the Year	4.00	10.00
32 Dale Jarrett White Rain	6.00	15.00
33 Ken Schrader Schrader	4.00	10.00
40 Coca-Cola Racing	4.00	10.00
44 Tony Stewart Shell	8.00	20.00
44 Tony Stewart Shell Small Soldiers	8.00	20.00
81 Kenny Wallace Square D	4.00	10.00
88 Dale Jarrett Quality Care	6.00	15.00
88 Dale Jarrett Quality Care Batman	6.00	15.00
88 Dale Jarrett Quality Care Million Dollar Win	6.00	15.00
88 Dale Jarrett Quality Care Speedweek Special card	6.00	15.00

1998 Winner's Circle Lifetime Dale Earnhardt 1:64

	EX	NM-MT
K2 Dale Earnhardt Pink 1956 Ford 6/11	15.00	30.00
3 Dale Earnhardt Goodwrench 1991 Champ 1/11 Stock Car Series card	20.00	40.00
3 Dale Earnhardt Goodwrench 1991 Champ 1/11 High Performance Collectibles card	20.00	40.00
3 Dale Earnhardt Goodwrench 1998 Monte Carlo 2/11	10.00	20.00
3 Dale Earnhardt Goodwrench 1994 Champ 4/11	12.50	25.00
3 Dale Earnhardt Wrangler 1985 Monte Carlo 5/11	20.00	40.00
3 Dale Earnhardt Goodwrench 1998 Bass Pro 7/11	12.50	25.00
3 Dale Earnhardt Goodwrench 1993 Champ. 8/11	20.00	40.00
3 Dale Earnhardt Wrangler 1987 Champion 9/11	20.00	40.00
3 Dale Earnhardt Goodwrench 1996 Olympic 10/11	10.00	20.00
3 Dale Earnhardt Goodwrench 1988 Monte Carlo fastback 11/11	15.00	30.00
15 Dale Earnhardt Wrangler 1982 Thunderbird 3/11	12.50	25.00

1998 Winner's Circle Lifetime Jeff Gordon 1:64

	EX	NM-MT
16 Jeff Gordon 1985 Sprint car	15.00	30.00
24 Jeff Gordon DuPont 1994 First Win	8.00	20.00
24 Jeff Gordon DuPont 1998 Monte Carlo Stock Car Series card	5.00	12.00
24 Jeff Gordon DuPont 1998 Monte Carlo High Performance Collectibles card	5.00	12.00

1999 Winner's Circle Lifetime Alan Kulwicki 1:64

	EX	NM-MT
7 Alan Kulwicki Hooters 1992 Thunderbird 1/3	4.00	10.00
7 Alan Kulwicki Army 1991 Thunderbird 3/3	5.00	10.00
7 Alan Kulwicki Zerex 1990 Thunderbird 2/3	4.00	10.00

1998 Winner's Circle Pit Row 1:64

Cars in this set are displayed on pit road being serviced by the crew. Some were issued with variations in the position of the car and/or the crew members as noted below. Others were issued in blister packaging that did or did not include a Fanscan logo.

	EX	NM-MT
1 Dale Earnhardt Jr. Coke	7.50	15.00
1 Steve Park Pennzoil left side raised	7.50	15.00
2 Rusty Wallace Rusty offical behind car	7.50	15.00
2 Rusty Wallace Rusty no offical	7.50	15.00
2 Rusty Wallace Elvis Fanscan package	7.50	15.00
3 Dale Earnhardt Coke	15.00	30.00
3 Dale Earnhardt Goodwrench 25th Anniversary	20.00	35.00
3 Dale Earnhardt Goodwrench Bass Pro	25.00	50.00
3 Dale Earnhardt Goodwrench Plus jumping over wall	12.50	30.00
3 Dale Earnhardt Goodwrench Plus changing tires with gray interior	12.50	30.00
3 Dale Earnhardt Goodwrench Plus changing tires with red interior	12.50	30.00
3 Dale Earnhardt Goodwrench Plus Daytona Pit Road Celebration	6.00	15.00
3 Dale Earnhardt Goodwrench Plus Daytona Victory Donuts	6.00	15.00
3 Dale Earnhardt Jr. AC Delco tires off	7.50	15.00
3 Dale Earnhardt Jr. AC Delco Fanscan package	7.50	15.00
12 Jeremy Mayfield Mobil 1 tires on ground	7.50	15.00
18 Bobby Labonte Interstate Batteries left side raised	7.50	15.00
18 Bobby Labonte Interstate Batteries Small Soldiers	7.50	15.00
22 Ward Burton MBNA	7.50	15.00
24 Jeff Gordon DuPont Fanscan package left side raised	7.50	15.00
24 Jeff Gordon DuPont Fanscan package four tires on ground	7.50	15.00
24 Jeff Gordon DuPont approaching to change right rear tire	7.50	15.00
24 Jeff Gordon DuPont right rear tire already changed	7.50	15.00
24 Jeff Gordon Pepsi	7.50	15.00
28 Kenny Irwin Havoline in pit stall	7.50	15.00
28 Kenny Irwin Havoline Joker	7.50	15.00
31 Mike Skinner Lowe's in pit stall	7.50	15.00
33 Ken Schrader Schrader	7.50	15.00
81 Kenny Wallace Square D	6.00	15.00
88 Dale Jarrett Quality Care right side raised	7.50	15.00
88 Dale Jarrett Quality Care Batman	10.00	25.00

1998 Winner's Circle Tech Series 1:64

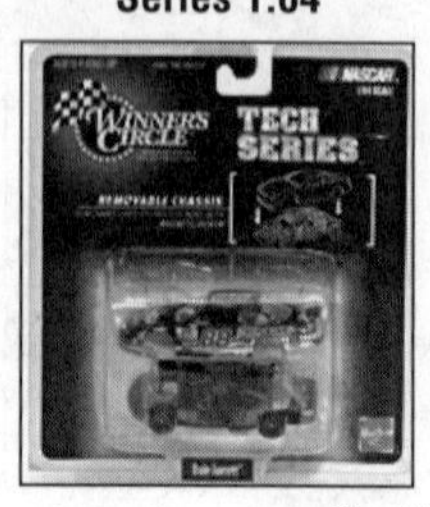

	EX	NM-MT
3 Dale Earnhardt Goodwrench	12.50	30.00
12 Jeremy Mayfield Mobil 1	4.00	8.00
24 Jeff Gordon DuPont	7.50	20.00
28 Kenny Irwin Havoline	4.00	8.00
88 Dale Jarrett Quality Care	4.00	8.00

1998-99 Winner's Circle Championship with Figure 1:64

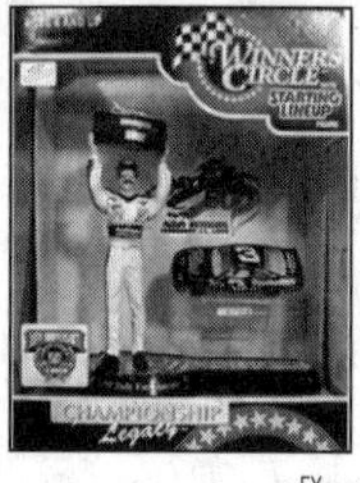

	EX	NM-MT
2 Dale Earnhardt 1980 Championship	7.50	15.00
3 Dale Earnhardt Goodwrench 1993 Champion	7.50	15.00
3 Dale Earnhardt Goodwrench 1994 Champion	7.50	15.00
3 Dale Earnhardt Goodwrench Plus 1998 Daytona 500	7.50	15.00
3 Dale Earnhardt Wrangler 1986 Championship	7.50	15.00
3 Dale Earnhardt Wrangler 1987 Championship	7.50	15.00
3 Dale Earnhardt Jr. AC Delco 1998 BGN Champion	6.00	12.00
7 Alan Kulwicki Hooters 1999	5.00	10.00
24 Jeff Gordon DuPont 1995 Championship	5.00	10.00
24 Jeff Gordon DuPont 1997 Championship	5.00	10.00
24 Jeff Gordon DuPont 1998 Championship	5.00	10.00
24 Jeff Gordon DuPont 1999 Daytona 500	5.00	10.00

1998-99 Winner's Circle Cool Customs 1:64

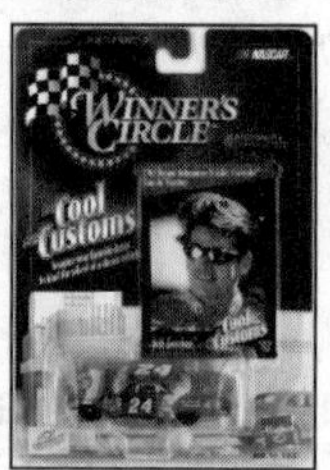

Cool Customs includes a 1:64 scale vintage stock car painted in the color scheme of the featured driver's current stock car. Each piece was packaged in a blister pack along with a trading card of the driver unless noted below. The cars were produced by Hasbro.

	EX	NM-MT
1/3 Dale Earnhardt Jr. Dale Earnhardt Coke 2-car set no card included	12.50	25.00
2 Rusty Wallace Rusty 1965 Ford Galaxie	5.00	12.00
2 Rusty Wallace Rusty/Adventures of Rusty 2-car set	6.00	15.00
3 Dale Earnhardt Goodwrench 1957 Chevy hardtop	12.50	25.00
3 Dale Earnhardt Goodwrench 1957 Chevy Convertible	12.50	25.00
3 Dale Earnhardt Goodwrench Silver 1957 Chevy hardtop	15.00	30.00
3 Dale Earnhardt Jr. AC Delco 1957 Chevy hardtop	6.00	15.00
12 Jeremy Mayfield Mobil 1 1956 Fairlane	4.00	10.00
24 Jeff Gordon DuPont 1957 Chevy Convertible	6.00	15.00
24 Jeff Gordon DuPont 1963 Chevy Impala	6.00	
24 Jeff Gordon Pepsi 1957 Chevy 1999	6.00	
24 Jeff Gordon Pepsi Superman 1957 Chevy 1999	6.00	
28 Kenny Irwin Havoline 1956 Ford Crown Victoria	5.00	
88 Dale Jarrett Quality Care 1956 Ford Crown Victoria	5.00	
88 Dale Jarrett Quality Care 1965 Ford Galaxie	5.00	

1998-99 Winner's Circ Fantasy Pack 1:64

This set includes a plane, a boat, and a car all in same

	EX
3 Dale Earnhardt Goodwrench Plus 1998	10.00
3 Dale Earnhardt Goodwrench 1999	10.00
3 Dale Earnhardt Wrangler	10.00
3 Dale Earnhardt Jr. AC Delco	6.00
24 Jeff Gordon DuPont	6.00
24 Jeff Gordon DuPont 1999	6.00
24 Jeff Gordon DuPont Superman 1999	6.00
24 Jeff Gordon Pepsi	6.00

1999 Winner's Circle 1:

This line is the result of an alliance between Action a to bring exclusive licenses such as Gordon and Earnh mass market.

	EX
1 Steve Park Pennzoil	2.50
2 Rusty Wallace Rusty	2.50
2 Rusty Wallace Rusty True to Texas	8.00
3 Dale Earnhardt Goodwrench Plus	12.50
3 Dale Earnhardt Jr. AC Delco	4.00
3 Dale Earnhardt Jr. AC Delco Superman	5.00
8 Dale Earnhardt Jr. Dale	6.00
12 Jeremy Mayfield Mobil 1	2.50
12 Jeremy Mayfield Mobil 1 Kentucky Derby	2.50
16 Ron Hornaday NAPA '98 Champ	2.50
18 Bobby Labonte Interstate Batteries	3.00
19 Mike Skinner Yellow Freight	5.00
20 Tony Stewart Home Depot	10.00
20 Tony Stewart Home Depot with rookie stripe	8.00
22 Ward Burton Caterpillar	2.50
24 Jeff Gordon DuPont	5.00
24 Jeff Gordon DuPont LTS package	6.00
24 Jeff Gordon Pepsi Star Wars	6.00
28 Kenny Irwin Havoline	3.00
31 Dale Earnhardt Jr. Gargoyles	5.00
31 Dale Earnhardt Jr. Wrangler	5.00
31 Mike Skinner Kolbalt	6.00
31 Mike Skinner Lowe's	2.50
33 Ken Schrader APR	2.50
55 Kenny Wallace Square D	2.50
88 Dale Jarrett Quality Care	2.50
88 Dale Jarrett Quality Care No Bull 5 win	2.50
88 Dale Jarrett Quality Care White	2.50

1999 Winner's Circle 2 Gold 1:64

These cars are gold plated on a gold plated base.

	EX
3 Dale Earnhardt Goodwrench	25.00
3 Dale Earnhardt Jr. AC Delco	12.00
24 Jeff Gordon DuPont	12.00
24 Jeff Gordon Pepsi	12.00

1999 Winner's Circle Life Dale Earnhardt 1:64

	EX
2 Dale Earnhardt 1979 Rookie of the Year 1/13	12.50
2 Dale Earnhardt Wrangler 1980 7/13	15.00
3 Dale Earnhardt Wrangler 1984 11/13	15.00
3 Dale Earnhardt Wrangler 1987 5/13	15.00
3 Dale Earnhardt Goodwrench 1989 Lumina 6/13	12.50

	EX	NM-MT
Earnhardt odwrench 1995 Brickyard Win 2/13	12.50	25.00
Earnhardt odwrench 1996 Monte Carlo 10/13	12.50	25.00
Earnhardt odwrench Wrangler 1999 8/13	12.50	25.00
Earnhardt odwrench 1988 Daytona 4/13	12.50	25.00
e Earnhardt ny 1976 Malibu 12/13	15.00	30.00
e Earnhardt -Gain 1976 13/13	15.00	30.00

9 Winner's Circle Lifetime Jeff Gordon 1:64

	EX	NM-MT
Gordon psi 1990 Midget 8/8	7.50	15.00
Gordon Pont 1992 Lumina 7/8	5.00	12.50
Gordon Pont 1995 Cup Champ 4/8	5.00	12.50
Gordon Pont 1999 Monte Carlo 1/8	5.00	12.50
Gordon Pont 1999 Test 6/8	10.00	20.00
Gordon Pont Superman 5/8	6.00	15.00
Gordon psi 1999 Monte Carlo 2/8	6.00	12.00
Gordon tback 1990 Grand Prix 3/8	10.00	20.00

9 Winner's Circle Pit Row 1:64

	EX	NM-MT
e Park nnzoil tires off	7.50	15.00
Earnhardt odwrench	10.00	25.00
Earnhardt odwrench 25th Anniv.	15.00	30.00
Earnhardt angler	15.00	30.00
Earnhardt angler tires off	15.00	30.00
Earnhardt Jr. Delco t side raised	7.50	15.00
Earnhardt Jr. Delco Superman	7.50	15.00
emy Mayfield obil 1 tires off	7.50	15.00
by Labonte erstate Batteries ht side raised	6.00	15.00
y Stewart me Depot	15.00	30.00
rd Burton terpillar	6.00	15.00
Gordon pont tires off	7.50	15.00
Gordon pont tires off llogg's package	7.50	15.00
Gordon perman pulling in	8.00	20.00
Gordon perman pulling out	8.00	20.00
ey Atwood strol	12.50	25.00
ny Irwin voline pulling out	7.50	15.00
e Skinner we's Union 76 package	7.50	15.00
e Jarrett ality Care es on ground	7.50	15.00

99 Winner's Circle Silver Series 1:64

	EX	NM-MT
Earnhardt 80 Champ 1/7	15.00	45.00
Earnhardt 86 Champ 2/7	15.00	45.00
Earnhardt 87 Champ 3/7	15.00	45.00
Earnhardt 90 Champ 4/7	15.00	45.00
Earnhardt 91 Champ 5/7	15.00	45.00
Earnhardt 93 Champ 6/7	15.00	45.00
Earnhardt 94 Champ 7/7	15.00	45.00

1999 Winner's Circle Speedweeks 1:64

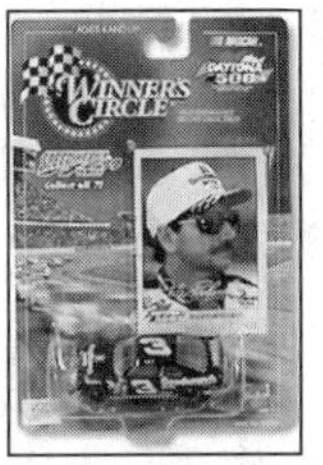

7-cars were released at Speedweeks as a preview to the Daytona 500. Each is packaged in a blister with the a 500 and Speedweeks 1999 logos on the front. A gold ed card was also packaged with each car.

	EX	NM-MT
y Wallace sty	4.00	8.00
Earnhardt odwrench	15.00	30.00
emy Mayfield	4.00	8.00

Mobil 1		
18 Bobby Labonte Interstate Batteries	4.00	8.00
24 Jeff Gordon DuPont	5.00	10.00
28 Kenny Irwin Havoline	4.00	8.00
88 Dale Jarrett Quality Care	4.00	8.00

1999 Winner's Circle Stats and Standings 1:64

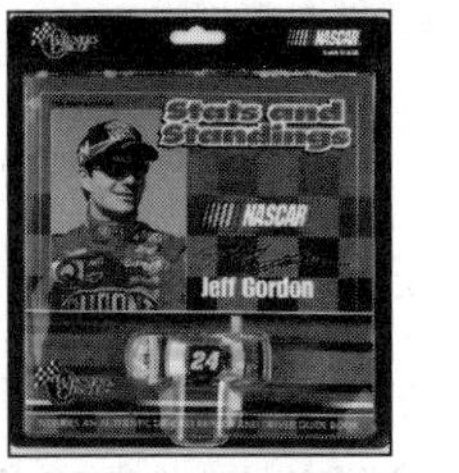

This set was issued with a 1:64 car and a large "Stats and Standings" driver guide book. Both pieces were packaged in a large blister pack.

	EX	NM-MT
2 Rusty Wallace Rusty	4.00	10.00
3 Dale Earnhardt Goodwrench	6.00	15.00
24 Jeff Gordon DuPont	5.00	12.00
88 Dale Jarrett Quality Care	4.00	10.00

1999 Winner's Circle Tech Series 1:64

These 1:64 scale cars feature bodies that are removable from the chassis.

	EX	NM-MT
2 Rusty Wallace Penske	4.00	8.00
3 Dale Earnhardt Jr. AC Delco	7.50	15.00
18 Bobby Labonte Interstate Batteries	7.50	20.00
24 Jeff Gordon DuPont Superman	7.50	20.00
31 Mike Skinner Lowe's	3.00	8.00

1999 Winner's Circle Track Support Crew 1:64

This set features Support vehicles in the drivers colors.

	EX	NM-MT
3 Dale Earnhardt Goodwrench	15.00	30.00
3 Dale Earnhardt Jr. AC Delco	10.00	20.00
24 Jeff Gordon DuPont	12.50	25.00
24 Jeff Gordon Pepsi	10.00	20.00

1999 Winner's Circle Victory Lane 1:64

	EX	NM-MT
3 Dale Earnhardt Goodwrench Daytona Win 2/15/98	25.00	50.00
24 Jeff Gordon DuPont Daytona 2/14/99	8.00	16.00

2000 Winner's Circle Sneak Previews 1:64

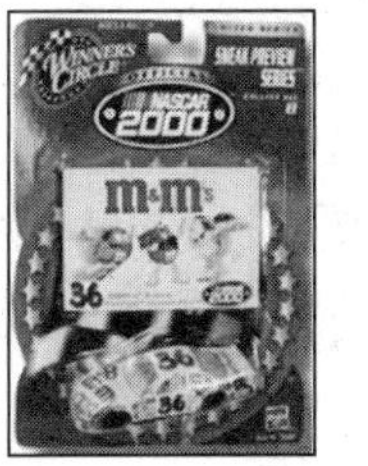

Winner's Circle took on a new look for 2000 by packaging the car at an angle on the blister pack. Each car and card combo package also included the NASCAR 2000 logo and the "Sneak Preview Series" set name.

	EX	NM-MT
2 Rusty Wallace Rusty	3.00	8.00
3 Dale Earnhardt GM Goodwrench Sign	12.50	25.00
18 Bobby Labonte Interstate Batteries	3.00	8.00
20 Tony Stewart Home Depot First Win	4.00	8.00
24 Jeff Gordon DuPont	5.00	10.00
27 Casey Atwood Castrol New Stars of NASCAR	3.00	8.00
31 Mike Skinner Lowe's	3.00	8.00
36 Ken Schrader M&M's with M&M's card	3.00	8.00
88 Dale Jarrett Quality Care	3.00	8.00

2000 Winner's Circle 1:64

	EX	NM-MT
3 Dale Earnhardt GM Goodwrench Sign	12.50	25.00
3 Dale Earnhardt Goodwrench	15.00	30.00
5 Terry Labonte Kellogg's NASCAR Racers	10.00	20.00
8 Dale Earnhardt Jr. New Stars Black Roof	5.00	12.00
8 Dale Earnhardt Jr. New Stars Red Roof	5.00	12.00
18 Bobby Labonte Interstate Batteries	4.00	10.00
18 Bobby Labonte Interstate Batteries NASCAR Racers	7.50	15.00
20 Tony Stewart Home Depot First Win	4.00	10.00
20 Tony Stewart Home Depot Three Win Rookie	4.00	10.00
24 Jeff Gordon DuPont NASCAR Racers	10.00	20.00
27 Casey Atwood Castrol	4.00	10.00
27 Casey Atwood Castrol New Stars	4.00	10.00
28 Ricky Rudd Havoline	4.00	10.00
31 Mike Skinner Lowe's	4.00	10.00
36 Ernie Irvan M&M's	4.00	10.00
55 Kenny Wallace Square D NASCAR Racers	5.00	12.00
88 Dale Jarrett Quality Care 1999 Winston Cup Champion	4.00	10.00

2000 Winner's Circle Cool Customs 1:64

	EX	NM-MT
24 Jeff Gordon Pepsi 1957 Convertible	4.00	8.00
24 Jeff Gordon Superman 1957 Chevy Hard Top	4.00	8.00

2000 Winner's Circle Deluxe Race Hood 1:64

These 1:64 scale cars were packaged with a larger replica hood painted in the sponsor's colors. Both were issued in a blue blister pack with many also featuring the NASCAR 2000 and Hasbro logos. Some packages read "Deluxe Collection" only as a set name while others include the name "Deluxe Race Hood Series."

	EX	NM-MT
3 Dale Earnhardt Goodwrench	25.00	40.00
3 Dale Earnhardt Goodwrench Sign	20.00	40.00
3 Dale Earnhardt Goodwrench Peter Max	40.00	80.00
3 Dale Earnhardt Taz No Bull	12.50	30.00
8 Dale Earnhardt Jr. Dale Jr. black roof no remington	15.00	30.00
8 Dale Earnhardt Jr. Dale Jr. black roof Remington on deck lid	30.00	60.00
8 Dale Earnhardt Jr. Dale Jr. red roof no Remington	20.00	35.00
8 Dale Earnhardt Jr. Dale Jr. red roof Remington on deck lid	50.00	100.00
18 Bobby Labonte Interstate Batteries	4.00	10.00
20 Tony Stewart Home Depot	6.00	15.00
20 Tony Stewart Home Depot Habitat	6.00	15.00
20 Tony Stewart Home Depot Kids	15.00	30.00
24 Jeff Gordon DuPont Corian deck lid	10.00	20.00
24 Jeff Gordon DuPont Tyvek deck lid	10.00	20.00
24 Jeff Gordon DuPont Silver	15.00	25.00
24 Jeff Gordon Pepsi	5.00	12.00
27 Casey Atwood Castrol	4.00	10.00
28 Ricky Rudd Havoline	4.00	10.00
31 Mike Skinner Lowe's	12.50	25.00
36 Ken Schrader M&M's	10.00	20.00
88 Dale Jarrett Quality Care	4.00	10.00
94 Bill Elliott McDonald's	12.50	25.00

2000 Winner's Circle Deluxe Driver Sticker 1:64

These die-cast pieces entitiled "Deluxe Driver Sticker Series" were packaged in a blue blister with a red stars and stripes design around the car. Each package also included an oversized driver sponsor sticker with the Hasbro logo at the bottom of the package. Some were issued in a blister package that read "Deluxe Collection" only at the top right hand corner.

	EX	NM-MT
4 Bobby Hamilton Kodak Navy	3.00	6.00
24 Jeff Gordon DuPont	5.00	10.00
24 Jeff Gordon DuPont Peanuts	6.00	15.00
25 Jerry Nadeau Holigan Homes Coast Guard	3.00	6.00
28 Ricky Rudd Havoline Marines	3.00	6.00
31 Mike Skinner Lowe's Army	3.00	6.00
88 Dale Jarrett Quality Care Air Force	3.00	6.00

2000-01 Winner's Circle Driver Hood 1:64

	EX	NM-MT
3 Dale Earnhardt Goodwrench 2000 car is horizontal in package	12.50	30.00
3 Dale Earnhardt Goodwrench 2001 car is slanted inside package	12.50	30.00
8 Dale Earnhardt Jr. Dale Jr.	10.00	20.00
9 Bill Elliott Dodge	6.00	15.00
18 Bobby Labonte Interstate Batteries	6.00	12.00
20 Tony Stewart Home Depot	12.50	25.00
NNO Dodge Test Gray	5.00	10.00

2000 Winner's Circle Deluxe Winston Cup Scene 1:64

These 1:64 scale cars were packaged with a miniature replica Winston Cup Scene magazine featuring a headline for that driver. Both were issued in a blue blister pack with many also featuring the NASCAR 2000 logo and all including the Hasbro manufacturer logo. Some packages read "Deluxe Collection" only as a set name while others include the name "Deluxe Winston Cup Scene Series."

	EX	NM-MT
2 Rusty Wallace Rusty 50th Win	3.00	8.00
3 Dale Earnhardt Goodwrench Richmond Win	15.00	30.00
8 Dale Earnhardt Jr. Dale Texas Win	5.00	12.00
88 Dale Jarrett Quality Care 1999 Winston Cup Champion	4.00	10.00

2000 Winner's Circle Lifetime Dale Earnhardt 1:64

	EX	NM-MT
3 Dale Earnhardt Goodwrench 1992 Chevy Lumina 5/6	15.00	30.00
3 Dale Earnhardt Goodwrench 1999 Chevy Monte Carlo Notchback 2/6	15.00	30.00
3 Dale Earnhardt Goodwrench 1999 Brickyard 1/6	15.00	30.00
3 Dale Earnhardt Goodwrench 2000 Chevy Monte Carlo 3/6	15.00	30.00
15 Dale Earnhardt Wrangler 1983 Thunderbird 4/6	15.00	30.00

2000 Winner's Circle Lifetime Jeff Gordon 1:64

	EX	NM-MT
4 Jeff Gordon Beast 1990 Sprint Car 2/6	15.00	30.00
24 Jeff Gordon DuPont 1992 Lumina 4/6	4.00	10.00
24 Jeff Gordon DuPont 1993 Lumina 5/6	5.00	10.00
24 Jeff Gordon DuPont 1996 Monte Carlo 6/6	4.00	10.00
24 Jeff Gordon DuPont 2000 Monte Carlo 3/6	4.00	10.00
24 Jeff Gordon Pepsi 2000 Monte Carlo 1/6	4.00	10.00

2000 Winner's Circle New Stars 1:64

	EX	NM-MT
8 Dale Earnhardt Jr. Dale Jr.	5.00	10.00
20 Tony Stewart Home Depot	4.00	10.00
27 Casey Atwood Castrol	3.00	8.00

2001 Winner's Circle Classic Hood 1:64

	EX	NM-MT
3 Dale Earnhardt Goodwrench Silver Select 1995	10.00	20.00
24 Jeff Gordon ChromaPremier	10.00	20.00

2001 Winner's Circle Driver Sticker 1:64

These die-cast pieces entitiled "Driver Sticker Collection" were packaged in a blue blister with a red stars and stripes design around the car. Each package also included an oversized driver sponsor sticker with the Hasbro logo at the bottom of the package.The oval sticker was produced slightly slanted in 2001 versus the traditional oval shaped sticker for 2002.

	EX	NM-MT
3 Dale Earnhardt Goodwrench	12.50	25.00
8 Dale Earnhardt Jr. Dale Jr. July 4th	5.00	10.00
8 Dale Earnhardt Jr. 2001 MLB All-Star Game	5.00	12.00

9 Bill Elliott Dodge	4.00	8.00
19 Casey Atwood Dodge	4.00	10.00
20 Tony Stewart Home Depot	5.00	10.00
24 Jeff Gordon DuPont Flames	6.00	15.00
24 Jeff Gordon DuPont Peanuts	6.00	15.00
28 Ricky Rudd Havoline	4.00	10.00
36 Ken Schrader M&M's	3.00	8.00
88 Dale Jarrett UPS	4.00	10.00

2001 Winner's Circle Gallery 1:64

This series of 1:64 die-cast pieces was issued in the typical blue with red stars Winner's Circle blister packaging. Each car was accompanied by a large framed work of art featuring the subject of the car or team sponsorship. The set title "Gallery Series" is clearly labeled in the upper right hand corner of the blister pack.

	EX	NM-MT
1 Steve Park Pennzoil Sylvester & Tweety	7.50	15.00
5 Terry Labonte Kellogg's Road Runner and Wile E. Coyote	7.50	15.00
24 Jeff Gordon DuPont Bugs Bunny	7.50	15.00
29 Kevin Harvick Goodwrench Taz	7.50	15.00
30 Jeff Green AOL Daffy Duck	7.50	15.00
31 Mike Skinner Lowe's Yosemite Sam	7.50	15.00
55 Bobby Hamilton Square D Marvin the Martian	7.50	15.00

2001 Winner's Circle License Plate Series 1:64

	EX	NM-MT
3 Dale Earnhardt Goodwrench	15.00	40.00
8 Dale Earnhardt Jr. Dale Jr.	6.00	15.00
9 Bill Elliott Dodge	5.00	12.00
18 Bobby Labonte Interstate Batteries	5.00	12.00
20 Tony Stewart Home Depot	6.00	12.00
28 Ricky Rudd Havoline	4.00	10.00
36 Ken Schrader M&M's	4.00	10.00

2001-02 Winner's Circle Lifetime Dale Earnhardt 1:64

Winner's Circle used its typical blue blister pack with the 1:64 scale Lifetime Series. The series takes a look at the various rides of five top drivers on the Winston Cup circuit with each piece including a series number. A card commemorating the historical ride or an event in the life of the featured driver was also included with each piece. The series started in 2001 and was continued with some pieces being released in 2002.

	EX	NM-MT
2 Dale Earnhardt Hodgdon 1979 5/8	5.00	12.00
3 Dale Earnhardt Goodwrench 1993 6/8	5.00	12.00
3 Dale Earnhardt Goodwrench 1992 3/8	5.00	12.00
3 Dale Earnhardt Goodwrench 1994 1/8	5.00	12.00
3 Dale Earnhardt AC Delco 1997 4/8	5.00	12.00
3 Dale Earnhardt Goodwrench 2001 8/8	5.00	12.00
8 D.Earnhardt Goodwrench '86 7/8	5.00	12.00

2001-02 Winner's Circle Lifetime Dale Jr. 1:64

	EX	NM-MT
3 Dale Earnhardt Jr. Goodwrench 1996 4/5	5.00	12.00
8 Dale Earnhardt Jr.	10.00	20.00

	EX	NM-MT
Dale Jr. 1999 1/5		
8 Dale Earnhardt Jr. Dale 2001 5/5	5.00	12.00
31 Dale Earnhardt Jr. Mom 'N' Pops 1996 3/5	5.00	12.00
31 Dale Earnhardt Jr. Sikkens White 1997 2/5	5.00	12.00

2001-02 Winner's Circle Lifetime Jeff Gordon 1:64

	EX	NM-MT
6 Jeff Gordon Sprint Car 1989 4/6	5.00	12.00
24 Jeff Gordon DuPont Brickyard 1994 3/6	5.00	12.00
24 Jeff Gordon DuPont Chromalusion 1998 6/6	5.00	12.00
24 Jeff Gordon DuPont 50th Win 1/6	5.00	12.00
24 Jeff Gordon DuPont 2000 2/6	5.00	12.00
24 Jeff Gordon DuPont Flames 2001 5/6	5.00	12.00

2001-02 Winner's Circle Lifetime Dale Jarrett 1:64

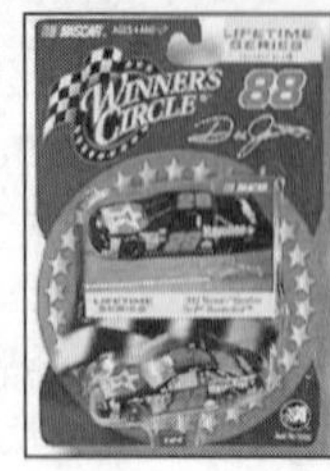

	EX	NM-MT
28 Dale Jarrett Havoline 1995 1/4	4.00	10.00
88 Dale Jarrett Quality Care 1996 3/4	4.00	10.00

2001-02 Winner's Circle Lifetime Tony Stewart 1:64

	EX	NM-MT
9 Tony Stewart Beast '95 1/5	10.00	25.00
15 Tony Stewart Vision 3 '96 3/5	5.00	12.00
20 Tony Stewart Home Depot 2001 4/5	5.00	12.00
44 Tony Stewart Shell 1998 2/5	5.00	12.00

2001-02 Winner's Circle Race Hood 1:64

These 1:64 cars were packaged with a plastic replica race hood. The packaging is a blister pack printed in blue with a white box in the upper right containing the set name of "Race Hood Series."

	EX	NM-MT
1 Steve Park Pennzoil	5.00	12.00
2 Kevin Harvick AC Delco	6.00	15.00
2 Rusty Wallace Rusty	10.00	20.00
2 Rusty Wallace Rusty Harley	10.00	20.00
3 Dale Earnhardt Goodwrench	7.50	20.00
3 Dale Earnhardt Goodwrench Oreo	15.00	40.00
3 Dale Earnhardt Goodwrench Silver	12.50	25.00
3 Dale Earnhardt Jr. Oreo	6.00	15.00
8 Dale Earnhardt Jr. Dale Jr.	6.00	12.00
9 Bill Elliott Dodge	5.00	12.00
15 Michael Waltrip NAPA	5.00	12.00
18 Bobby Labonte Interstate Batteries	5.00	12.00
18 Bobby Labonte Interstate Batteries Coke Bear	5.00	12.00
19 Casey Atwood Dodge	5.00	12.00
20 Tony Stewart Home Depot	6.00	12.00
20 Tony Stewart Home Depot Coke Bear	5.00	12.00
24 Jeff Gordon DuPont ChromaPremier	6.00	12.00
24 Jeff Gordon DuPont Flames	6.00	15.00
24 Jeff Gordon DuPont 200th Anniversary	6.00	12.00
24 Jeff Gordon Pepsi 2002	5.00	12.00
29 Kevin Harvick AOL	5.00	12.00
29 Kevin Harvick Goodwrench White	5.00	12.00
88 Dale Jarrett UPS	5.00	12.00
88 Dale Jarrett UPS Flames 2002	5.00	12.00
NNO Dodge Test Team	4.00	10.00

2001 Winner's Circle Sam Bass Gallery 1:64

This Sam Bass version of the Gallery Series includes a series of 1:64 die-cast pieces accompanied by a large framed work of art by noted racing artist Sam Bass. Each was issued in the typical blue with red stars Winner's Circle blister packaging with the set title "Sam Bass Gallery Series" clearly labeled on the front of the blister pack.

	EX	NM-MT
3 Dale Earnhardt AC Delco with Dale Jr. on artwork	10.00	20.00
3 Dale Earnhardt Goodwrench	7.50	15.00
3 Dale Earnhardt Goodwrench Bass Pro	7.50	15.00
3 Dale Earnhardt Goodwrench Plus	7.50	15.00
3 Dale Earnhardt Wrangler	7.50	15.00
7 Alan Kulwicki Hooters	6.00	15.00

2001 Winner's Circle Team Authentics 1:64

	EX	NM-MT
2 Rusty Wallace Rusty Firesuit	25.00	60.00
2 Rusty Wallace Rusty Sheetmetal	25.00	60.00
3 Dale Earnhardt Goodwrench Firesuit	100.00	200.00
3 Dale Earnhardt Goodwrench Taz Sheetmetal	75.00	150.00
8 Dale Earnhardt Jr. Dale Jr. Firesuit	50.00	100.00
8 Dale Earnhardt Jr. Dale Jr. Sheetmetal	50.00	100.00
18 Bobby Labonte Interstate Batteries Firesuit	30.00	60.00
18 Bobby Labonte Interstate Batteries Sheetmetal	30.00	60.00
20 Tony Stewart Home Depot Firesuit	50.00	120.00
20 Tony Stewart Home Depot Sheetmetal	50.00	120.00
24 Jeff Gordon DuPont Firesuit	50.00	120.00
24 Jeff Gordon DuPont Sheetmetal	50.00	120.00
28 Ricky Rudd Havoline Firesuit	25.00	50.00
28 Ricky Rudd Havoline Sheetmetal	25.00	50.00
31 Mike Skinner Lowe's Firesuit	15.00	30.00
31 Mike Skinner Lowe's Sheetmetal	15.00	40.00

2001 Winner's Circle Winston Cup Scene 1:64

	EX	NM-MT
18 Bobby Labonte Interstate Batteries No Recount	4.00	8.00

2002 Winner's Circle Autographed Hood 1:64

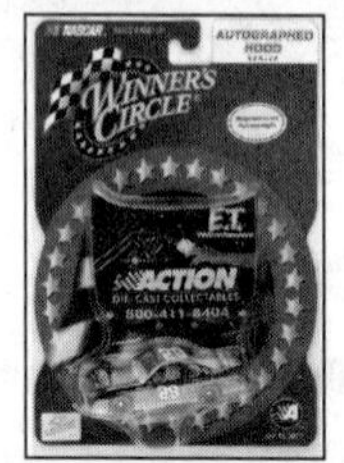

The Autographed Hood Series is a 1:64 car packaged with a plastic replica hood featuring a facsimile driver autograph. Each is sealed in a blue and red blister pack.

	EX	NM-MT
3 Dale Earnhardt Jr. Oreo	5.00	12.00
3 Dale Earnhardt Jr. Nilla Wafers	5.00	12.00
9 Bill Elliott Dodge Muppets	6.00	15.00
12 Kerry Earnhardt Super Cuts	6.00	15.00
24 Jeff Gordon DuPont 200th Anniversary	5.00	12.00
24 Jeff Gordon Pepsi Daytona	6.00	15.00
29 Kevin Harvick Action ET	5.00	12.00
29 Kevin Harvick Goodwrench ET	6.00	15.00
29 Kevin Harvick Reese's Fast Break	5.00	12.00

2002 Winner's Circle Die-Cast Kits 1:64

These 1:64 pieces were issued in a large blue window box with the date printed on the back within a copyright line. Each piece is a die-cast model kit that was to be assembled by the collector. The cars came complete with a small screwdriver to help assemble the model.

	EX	NM-MT
2 Rusty Wallace Rusty	6.00	12.00
8 Dale Earnhardt Jr. Dale Jr.	6.00	12.00
8 Dale Earnhardt Jr. Looney Tunes	6.00	12.00
24 Jeff Gordon DuPont Flames	6.00	12.00
24 Jeff Gordon DuPont Bugs Rematch	6.00	12.00
29 Kevin Harvick Goodwrench	6.00	10.00
40 Sterling Marlin Sterling	5.00	10.00
41 Jimmy Spencer Target	6.00	10.00
88 Dale Jarrett UPS	6.00	10.00
88 Dale Jarrett UPS Flames	6.00	10.00

2002 Winner's Circle Driver Sticker 1:64

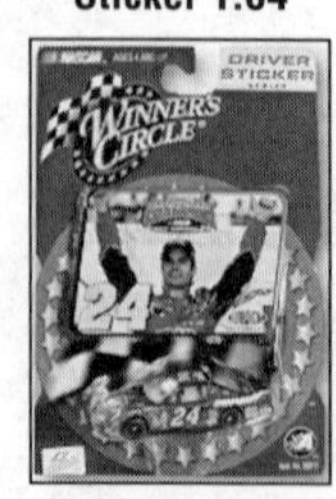

The 2002 Drivers Sticker Series was packaged in the same blue and red blister pack design as 2001. Some 2001 pieces were re-issued in 2002 with only a slight difference in the packaging. However most of the stickers for 2002 are a slanted rectangular card with a photo of the driver, his car, or the sponsor logo on them. The year of issue can be found on the copyright line on the back of the blister.

	EX	NM-MT
2 Kerry Earnhardt K Intimidator	6.00	12.00
2 Kevin Harvick AC Delco '01 BGN Champ	6.00	12.00
8 Dale Earnhardt Jr. Looney Tunes	6.00	12.00
8 Dale Earnhardt Jr. 2001 MLB All-Star Game	6.00	12.00
8 Dale Earnhardt Jr. 2002 MLB All Star Game	6.00	12.00
20 Tony Stewart Home Depot Jurassic	5.00	12.00
24 Jeff Gordon DuPont Bugs Rematch 2002	6.00	12.00
24 Jeff Gordon DuPont Flames	5.00	10.00
24 Jeff Gordon DuPont Flames 2001 WC Champ	5.00	10.00
29 Kevin Harvick Goodwrench Taz	5.00	10.00
29 Kevin Harvick Goodwrench White 2001 Rookie of the Year	6.00	12.00
48 Jimmie Johnson Lowe's Sylvester	6.00	12.00

2002 Winner's Circle Fast Pack 1:64

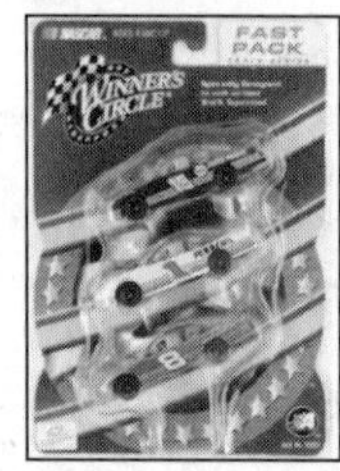

	EX	NM-MT
15/1/8 Micheal Waltrip NAPA Steve Park Pennzoil Dale Earnhardt Jr. Dale Jr.	7.50	15.00
19/9/7 Jeremy Mayfield Dodge Bill Elliott Dodge Casey Atwood Sirius	7.50	15.00
29/30/31 Kevin Harvick Goodwrench Silver Jeff Green AOL Robby Gordon Cingular	7.50	15.00

2002 Winner's Circle Gallery 1:64

The 2002 Gallery Series is nearly identical to the 2001 release but can be distinguished by the copyright line on the back of the package. Each die-cast piece was issued in the typical blue with red stars Winner's Circle blister packaging and included a large framed work of art featuring the subject of the car or team sponsorship. The set title "Gallery Series" is clearly labeled in the upper right hand corner of the blister pack.

	EX	NM-MT
20 Tony Stewart Home Depot Coke Bear	7.50	15.00
24 Jeff Gordon DuPont Flames 2001 WC Champ	7.50	15.00
29 Kevin Harvick Goodwrench	7.50	15.00

2002 Winner's Circle Gift Pack 1:64

	EX	NM-MT
2 Rusty Wallace Rusty Rusty Harley Mobil 25th Anniversary	10.00	20.00
8 Dale Earnhardt Jr. Dale Oreo Nilla Wafers	15.00	30.00
20 Tony Stewart Home Depot/Coke Home Depot w/black trim	10.00	25.00
24 Jeff Gordon Pepsi DuPont Flames DuPont 200th Anniversary	15.00	30.00
29 Kevin Harvick Goodwrench White/Taz Goodwrench Silver	10.00	25.00
88 Dale Jarrett UPS '01/UPS '02 UPS Flames	10.00	20.00

2002 Winner's Circle Gift Pack With Photo 1:64

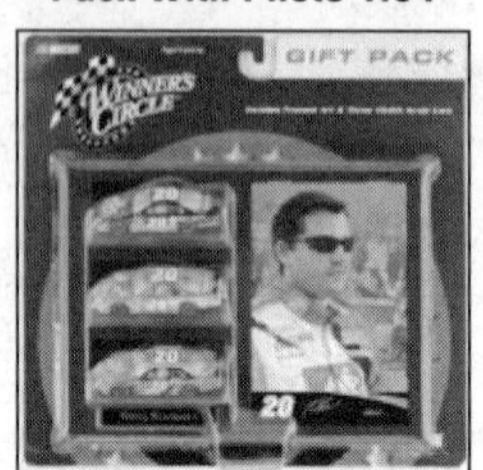

	EX	NM-MT
8 Dale Earnhardt Jr. 2001 All-Star Game 2002 All-Star Game Dale Jr.	20.00	35.00
18 Bobby Labonte Interstate Batteries Interstate Batteries Muppets Interstate Batteries Coke	18.00	30.00
20 Tony Stewart Black Peanuts Orange Peanuts Home Depot	18.00	30.00
24 Jeff Gordon DuPont Bugs DuPont 200th Anniversary DuPont Flames	20.00	35.00

2002 Winner's Circle Pit Pass Preview 1:64

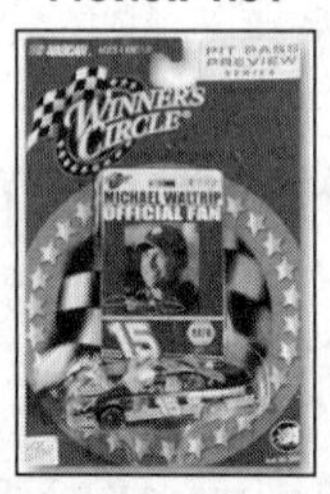

These 1:64 cars were packaged with a plastic card that resembles a race day pit pass. The card includes a photo of the featured driver and the packaging is the usual Winner's Circle blue blister.

	EX	NM-MT
2 Rusty Wallace Rusty	5.00	10.00
8 Dale Earnhardt Jr. Dale Jr.	6.00	12.00
9 Bill Elliott Dodge	5.00	10.00
15 Michael Waltrip NAPA	5.00	10.00
18 Bobby Labonte Interstate Batteries	5.00	10.00
19 Casey Atwood Dodge	5.00	10.00
19 Jeremy Mayfield Dodge	5.00	10.00
20 Tony Stewart Home Depot	5.00	10.00
24 Jeff Gordon DuPont Flames	5.00	10.00
28 Ricky Rudd Havoline	5.00	10.00
29 Kevin Harvick Goodwrench Silver	5.00	10.00
30 Jeff Green AOL	5.00	10.00
31 Robby Gordon Cingular	5.00	10.00
88 Dale Jarrett UPS	5.00	10.00

2003 Winner's Circle Autographed Hood 1:64

This series is a continuation of the Winner's Circle Race Hoods. However each car and oversized hood was packaged in the new 2003 blister pack with the black printed portion at the top. Please note that no mention of "Race Hood" appears on the package unlike previous years. The early pieces were released in late 2002, but are considered part of the 2003 set.

	EX	N
1 Dale Earnhardt Jr. Coke Japan 1998	6.00	
2 Rusty Wallace Rusty	4.00	
3 Dale Earnhardt Coke Japan 1998	6.00	
8 Dale Earnhardt Jr. Dirty Mo Posse	6.00	
8 Dale Earnhardt Jr. Earnhardt Tribute Concert	6.00	
8 Dale Earnhardt Jr. Oreo Ritz Dale Earnhardt Jr. Hood	5.00	
8 Dale Earnhardt Jr. Oreo Ritz Dale Jr. Hood	5.00	
18 Bobby Labonte Interstate Batteries	4.00	
20 Tony Stewart Home Depot Declaration of Independence	5.00	
20 Tony Stewart Home Depot Peanuts Orange	4.00	
21 Kevin Harvick Payday	6.00	
24 Jeff Gordon DuPont Flames	5.00	
24 Jeff Gordon DuPont Flames in small package	5.00	
24 Jeff Gordon Pepsi Billion $	6.00	
24 Jeff Gordon Pepsi Daytona	5.00	
38 Elliott Sadler M&M's Groovy	4.00	
40 Sterling Marlin Sterling	4.00	

2003 Winner's Circle Dec of Champions 1:64

	EX	N
3 Dale Earnhardt Goodwrench 1993	5.00	
3 Dale Earnhardt Goodwrench 1994	5.00	
5 Terry Labonte Kellogg's 1996	5.00	
18 Bobby Labonte Interstate Batteries 2000	5.00	
20 Tony Stewart Home Depot 2002	6.00	
24 Jeff Gordon DuPont 1995	5.00	
24 Jeff Gordon DuPont 1997	5.00	
24 Jeff Gordon DuPont 1998	5.00	
24 Jeff Gordon DuPont Flames 2001	5.00	
88 Dale Jarrett Quality Care 1999	5.00	

2003 Winner's Circle Di Cast Kits 1:64

	EX	N
3 Dale Earnhardt Goodwrench No Bull 2000	8.00	
8 Dale Earnhardt Jr. Looney Tunes 2002	8.00	
9 Bill Elliott Dodge	7.50	
20 Tony Stewart Home Depot 2002	6.00	
24 Jeff Gordon Dupont Bugs Rematch 2002	6.00	
24 Jeff Gordon DuPont Flames	6.00	

2003 Winner's Circle Dri Sticker 1:64

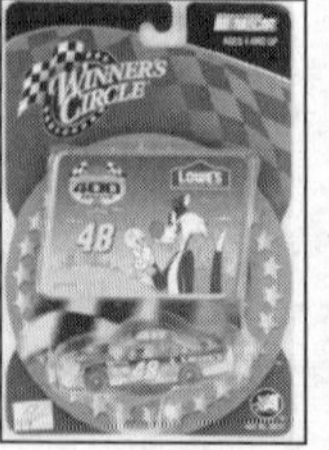

...03 Driver Sticker series was initially released in late 2002. ...pieces feature a 2002 copyright date on the backs but ...ssued in the newly designed 2003 style Winner's Circle ...packaging. Note that a specific product or "set" name is ...luded but each die-cast piece was packaged with a driver

	EX	NM-MT
e Earnhardt rue Value 2000 IROC	7.50	15.00
e Earnhardt rue Value 2001 IROC	7.50	15.00
by Labonte rue Value 2001 IROC	6.00	12.00
rk Martin rue Value 1998 IROC	6.00	12.00
ve Park ennzoil	5.00	10.00
ty Wallace usty Flames	6.00	12.00
e Earnhardt oundation	6.00	12.00
e Earnhardt oundation short package	6.00	12.00
e Earnhardt oodwrench Plus Sign 1999	6.00	12.00
e Earnhardt oodwrench No Bull 6th Win 2000	6.00	12.00
e Earnhardt oodwrench Peter Max 2000	6.00	15.00
ke Skinner odak Yosemite Sam	4.00	8.00
y Labonte ellogg's Coyote and oad Runner	5.00	10.00
Gordon rue Value 1998 IROC	7.50	15.00
e Earnhardt PM 1975	7.50	15.00
e Earnhardt Jr. R	7.50	15.00
e Earnhardt Jr. R short package	7.50	15.00
e Earnhardt Jr. ale Jr.	7.50	15.00
e Earnhardt Jr. MP	6.00	12.00
e Earnhardt Jr. ooney Tunes	6.00	12.00
Elliott odge	5.00	10.00
le Earnhardt Jr. rue Value 1999 IROC	8.00	20.00
ny Stewart rue Value 2001 IROC	6.00	15.00
ny Stewart rue Value '01 IROC 2 Champ. Sticker	6.00	15.00
erry Earnhardt aniKing Yosemite Sam	4.00	8.00
ichael Waltrip APA	5.00	10.00
remy Mayfield odge	5.00	10.00
ony Stewart ome Depot	6.00	12.00
ny Stewart ome Depot short package	6.00	12.00
ny Stewart ome Depot eanuts black	5.00	10.00
ny Stewart ome Depot eanuts Orange	5.00	10.00
ff Gordon ookie Monster	5.00	12.00
ff Gordon upont Bugs Rematch 2002	5.00	10.00
ff Gordon lmo 2002	8.00	20.00
ff Gordon epsi Talladega	5.00	12.00
e Nemechek AW-Delphi Speedy Gonzalez	4.00	8.00
evin Harvick oodwrench Taz	6.00	12.00
le Earnhardt rmy 1976	6.00	12.00
eff Green OL Daffy Duck	4.00	8.00
obby Gordon ingular Pepe Le Pew	4.00	8.00
mmie Johnson owe's Distributor Exclusive	5.00	10.00
mmie Johnson owe's Sylvester&Tweety	5.00	10.00
obby Hamilton quare D Marvin Martian	5.00	10.00
ale Earnhardt y-Gain 1976	7.50	15.00
le Jarrett PS	5.00	10.00
le Jarrett PS Flames	5.00	10.00
ale Earnhardt ayvault's 1956 Ford	6.00	12.00
Dale Earnhardt egacy	7.50	15.00
Dale Earnhardt egacy short package	7.50	15.00

2003 Winner's Circle Fast Pack 1:64

	EX	NM-MT
5 Steve Park ennzoil	7.50	15.00
ale Earnhardt Jr. ale Jr.		
ichael Waltrip APA		
9 Casey Atwood irius	6.00	12.00
ill Elliott odge		
eremy Mayfield Dodge		
/31 Kevin Harvick oodwrench	6.00	12.00
eff Green		

AOL
Robby Gordon
Cingular

2003 Winner's Circle Pit Pass Preview 1:64

Winner's Circle released these die-cast blisters in late 2002 and early 2003. Each includes the newly designed 2003 packaging with the black strip across the top and no specific product release name included. A gold foil sticker was attached in the upper right hand corner that notes "2003 Preview," otherwise the release might be considered a 2002 issue since that is the copyright line date on the backs.

	EX	NM-MT
1 Steve Park Pennzoil	4.00	8.00
1 Steve Park Pennzoil '03 Preview sticker	4.00	8.00
2 Rusty Wallace Rusty	4.00	8.00
2 Rusty Wallace Rusty '03 Preview sticker	4.00	8.00
7 Casey Atwood Sirius	4.00	8.00
8 Dale Earnhardt Jr. JR	6.00	12.00
8 Dale Earnhardt Jr. JR '03 Preview sticker	6.00	12.00
9 Bill Elliott Dodge	4.00	8.00
15 Michael Waltrip NAPA	4.00	8.00
15 Michael Waltrip NAPA '03 Preview sticker	4.00	8.00
19 Jeremy Mayfield Dodge	4.00	8.00
29 Kevin Harvick Goodwrench	6.00	12.00
31 Robby Gordon Cingular	4.00	8.00
88 Dale Jarrett UPS	4.00	8.00

2003 Winner's Circle Pit Scene 1:64

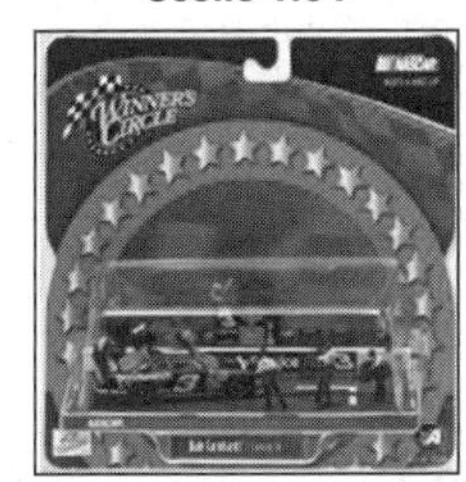

This series was produced by Winner's Circle in 2002. However each piece was packaged in the slightly re-designed 2003 packaging style with the black striped area at the top of the package. A 1:64 scale car is included mounted on a pit road scene base complete with plastic crew members, pit wall, gas cans and cart, and a pit wagon.

	EX	NM-MT
2 Rusty Wallace Rusty Level	10.00	20.00
3 Dale Earnhardt Goodwrench Coming In	12.50	25.00
20 Tony Stewart Home Depot Pulling out	10.00	20.00
24 Jeff Gordon Pepsi Coming In	10.00	20.00
24 Jeff Gordon DuPont Tires Off	10.00	20.00

2003 Winner's Circle Race Hood 1:64

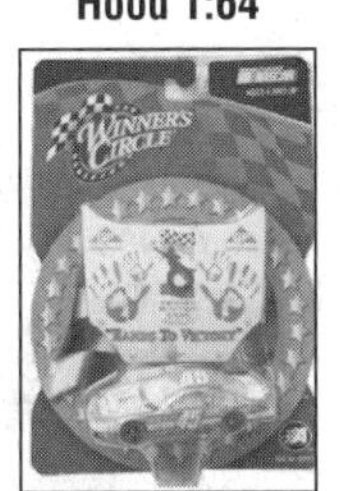

	EX	NM-MT
2 Rusty Wallace Rusty	5.00	12.00
8 Dale Earnhardt Jr. MLB All Star 2003	5.00	12.00
20 Tony Stewart Home Depot 2002 Champion	5.00	12.00
20 Tony Stewart Home Depot Declaration of Independence	5.00	12.00
20 Tony Stewart Home Depot Peanuts Orange	6.00	12.00
24 Jeff Gordon DuPont Flames	6.00	12.00
38 Elliott Sadler M&M's	6.00	12.00
40 Sterling Marlin Sterling	5.00	10.00
45 Kyle Petty Hands to Victory	6.00	12.00

2003 Winner's Circle Victory Lap 1:64

	EX	NM-MT
2 Rusty Wallace Miller Lite Victory Lap	5.00	10.00
3 Dale Earnhardt Goodwrench Victory Lap	6.00	15.00
20 Tony Stewart Home Depot Victory Lap	5.00	10.00
24 Jeff Gordon DuPont Victory Lap	5.00	12.00
43 Richard Petty STP Victory Lap	5.00	10.00
88 Dale Jarrett UPS Victory Lap	5.00	10.00

2004 Winner's Circle 1:64

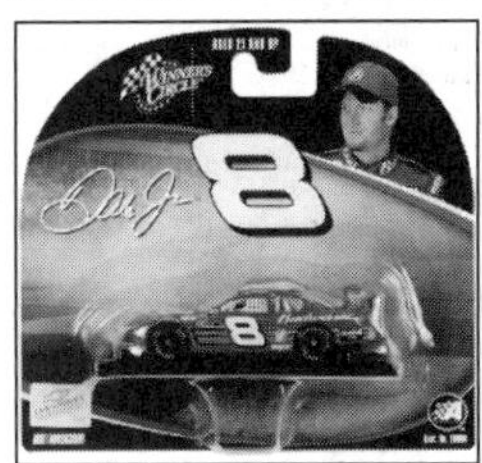

	EX	NM-MT
2 Rusty Wallace Miller Lite	7.50	15.00
2 Rusty Wallace Miller Lite Last Call	7.50	15.00
2 Rusty Wallace Miller Lite President of Beers	7.50	15.00
2 Rusty Wallace Miller Lite Puddle of Mudd	6.00	12.00
8 Dale Earnhardt Jr. Bud	10.00	20.00
8 Dale Earnhardt Jr. Bud Born On Feb.7	10.00	20.00
8 Dale Earnhardt Jr. Bud Born On Feb.15 Raced	10.00	20.00
40 Sterling Marlin Coors Light	6.00	12.00
40 Sterling Marlin Coors Light Kentucky Derby	5.00	10.00

2004 Winner's Circle Autographed Hood 1:64

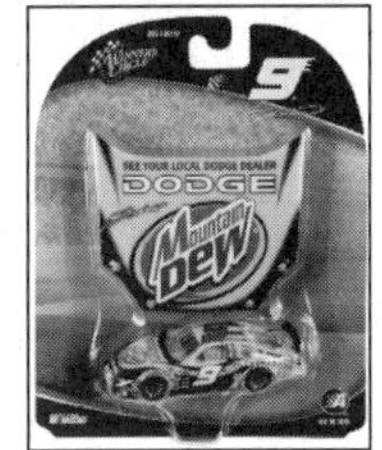

	EX	NM-MT
2 Rusty Wallace Kodak	5.00	12.00
3 Dale Earnhardt Coke	6.00	15.00
3 Dale Earnhardt Goodwrench Olympic 1996 Monte Carlo	6.00	15.00
8 Dale Earnhardt Jr. Dave Matthews Band	5.00	12.00
8 Dale Earnhardt Jr. JR	6.00	15.00
8 Dale Earnhardt Jr. JR short package	6.00	15.00
8 Dale Earnhardt Jr. Oreo	5.00	12.00
8 Dale Earnhardt Jr. StainD	5.00	12.00
9 Bill Elliott Dodge Lion King	4.00	10.00
9 Kasey Kahne Dodge	10.00	20.00
9 Kasey Kahne Dodge Mad Magazine	10.00	20.00
9 Kasey Kahne Dodge Popeye	10.00	20.00
9 Kasey Kahne Mountain Dew short package	12.50	25.00
10 Scott Riggs Valvoline Wizard of Oz	4.00	10.00
18 Bobby Labonte Interstate Batteries short package	5.00	12.00
18 Bobby Labonte Interstate Batteries D-Day short package	5.00	12.00
18 Bobby Labonte Interstate Batteries Shrek 2	4.00	10.00
18 Bobby Labonte Interstate Batteries Shrek 2 small package	4.00	10.00
19 Jeremy Mayfield Dodge Mad Magazine	4.00	10.00
19 Jeremy Mayfield Dodge NHL All Star	4.00	10.00
19 Jeremy Mayfield	6.00	12.00

Dodge Popeye

	EX	NM-MT
20 Tony Stewart Home Depot	5.00	12.00
20 Tony Stewart Home Depot Black Reverse Paint	5.00	12.00
20 Tony Stewart Home Depot Shrek 2	5.00	12.00
20 Tony Stewart Home Depot Shrek 2 small package	5.00	12.00
20 Tony Stewart Home Depot 25th Anniversary	5.00	12.00
21 Kevin Harvick Hershey's Kisses	4.00	10.00
21 Kevin Harvick Reese's	4.00	10.00
21 Kevin Harvick Reese's 35th Anniversary RCR	5.00	12.00
24 Jeff Gordon DuPont Flames HMS 20th Anniversary	6.00	15.00
24 Jeff Gordon DuPont Flames Wizard of Oz	5.00	12.00
24 Jeff Gordon DuPont Flames '03 Yose.Sam	5.00	12.00
24 Jeff Gordon DuPont Rainbow	5.00	12.00
24 Jeff Gordon Pepsi	5.00	12.00
24 Jeff Gordon Pepsi Billion	4.00	10.00
24 Jeff Gordon Pepsi Billion short package	4.00	10.00
29 Kevin Harvick Coke C2	4.00	10.00
29 Kevin Harvick ESGR Coast Guard short package	10.00	20.00
29 Kevin Harvick Goodwrench	5.00	12.00
29 Kevin Harvick Goodwrench KISS	6.00	15.00
29 Kevin Harvick Goodwrench Realtree	4.00	10.00
29 Kevin Harvick Goodwrench RCR 35th Anniversary	6.00	15.00
29 Kevin Harvick Powerade	4.00	10.00
29 Bobby Labonte ESGR Army	4.00	10.00
38 Kasey Kahne Great Clips	6.00	15.00
38 Kasey Kahne Great Clips Shark Tales	6.00	15.00
38 Elliott Sadler M&M's	4.00	10.00
38 Elliott Sadler M&M's short package	4.00	10.00
38 Elliott Sadler M&M's black&white	5.00	12.00
38 Elliott Sadler M&M's July 4	5.00	12.00
38 Elliott Sadler Pedigree Wizard of Oz	4.00	10.00
40 Sterling Marlin Sterling	5.00	12.00
41 Casey Mears Target	4.00	10.00
42 Jamie McMurray Havoline	5.00	12.00
77 Brendan Gaughan Kodak Punisher	4.00	10.00
77 Brendan Gaughan Kodak Wizard of Oz	4.00	10.00
81 Dale Earnhardt Jr. KFC	5.00	12.00
81 Dale Earnhardt Jr. KFC short package	5.00	12.00
81 Dale Earnhardt Jr. Taco Bell	5.00	12.00
81 Tony Stewart Bass Pro Shops	5.00	12.00
88 Dale Jarrett UPS Arnold Palmer	7.50	15.00
92 Tony Stewart McDonald's	5.00	12.00
99 Michael Waltrip Aaron's Cat in the Hat	4.00	10.00
01 Joe Nemechek Army G.I. Joe	5.00	12.00
01 Joe Nemechek Army Time Magazine	5.00	12.00

2004 Winner's Circle Driver Sticker 1:64

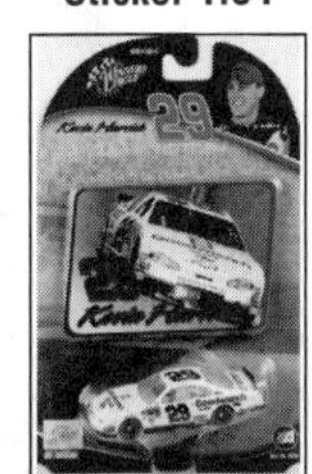

	EX	NM-MT
8 Dale Earnhardt Jr. JR sparkle	6.00	12.00
9 Kasey Kahne Dodge sparkle	12.50	25.00
9 Kasey Kahne Dodge Refresh sparkle	7.50	15.00
20 Tony Stewart Home Depot sparkle short package	5.00	10.00
24 Jeff Gordon DuPont Flames sparkle short package	6.00	12.00
24 Jeff Gordon DuPont Flames Fontana Raced sparkle	7.50	15.00
24 J.Gordon/Pepsi Shards	7.50	15.00

Talladega Raced sparkle

	EX	NM-MT
29 Kevin Harvick Goodwrench '01 black number	7.50	15.00
29 Tony Stewart Kid Rock short package	5.00	10.00
38 Elliott Sadler M&M's Texas Raced sparkle	5.00	10.00
38 Elliott Sadler M&M's July 4 sparkle	5.00	10.00

2004 Winner's Circle Driver Sticker RCR Museum Series 1 1:64

	EX	NM-MT
3 Dale Earnhardt/AC Delco 1996 Monte Carlo	6.00	12.00
3 Dale Earnhardt Coke Japan 1998 Monte Carlo	6.00	12.00
3 Dale Earnhardt Goodwrench 1996 Monte Carlo	6.00	12.00
3 Dale Earnhardt Goodwrench Olympic '96 Monte Carlo	6.00	12.00
3 Dale Earnhardt Goodwrench '97 Monte Carlo Crash Daytona Raced	10.00	20.00
3 Dale Earnhardt Goodwrench Sign '99 Monte Carlo	6.00	12.00
3 Dale Earnhardt Goodwrench 2000 Monte Carlo Talladega	6.00	12.00
3 Dale Earnhardt Goodwrench Peter Max '00 Monte Carlo	6.00	12.00
3 Dale Earnhardt Wrangler 1999 Monte Carlo	6.00	12.00

2004 Winner's Circle Pit Pass Preview 1:64

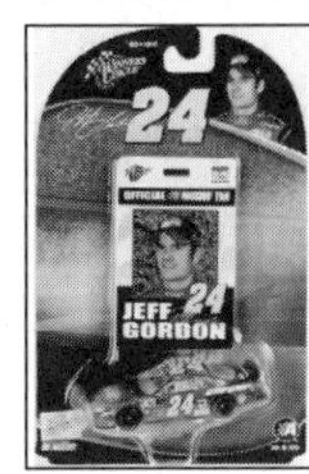

	EX	NM-MT
2 Rusty Wallace Rusty	4.00	8.00
8 Dale Earnhardt Jr. JR	5.00	10.00
15 Michael Waltrip NAPA	4.00	8.00
18 Bobby Labonte Interstate Batteries	4.00	8.00
20 Tony Stewart Home Depot	4.00	8.00
24 Jeff Gordon DuPont Flames	5.00	10.00
29 Kevin Harvick Goodwrench	4.00	8.00
42 Jamie McMurray Havoline	4.00	8.00
88 Dale Jarrett UPS	4.00	8.00

2004 Winner's Circle Race Hood 1:64

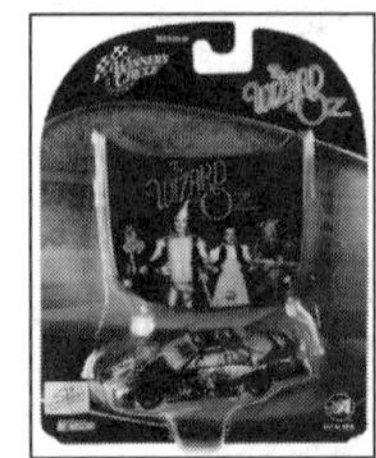

	EX	NM-MT
8 Dale Earnhardt Jr. JR	6.00	12.00
9 Bill Elliott Lion King	5.00	10.00
99 Michael Waltrip Cat in the Hat	4.00	8.00
04 Wizard of Oz Event Car	5.00	10.00

2005 Winner's Circle 1:64

	EX	NM-MT
2 Rusty Wallace Miller Genuine Draft	7.50	15.00
2 Rusty Wallace Miller Lite	6.00	12.00

2 Rusty Wallace Miller Lite Last Call	5.00	10.00
2 Rusty Wallace Miller Lite Last Call Daytona Shootout	5.00	10.00
8 Dale Earnhardt Jr. Bud Test	7.50	15.00
8 Dale Earnhardt Jr. Bud World Series '04	6.00	12.00
39 Bill Elliott Coors Retro	6.00	12.00

2005 Winner's Circle Autographed Hood 1:64

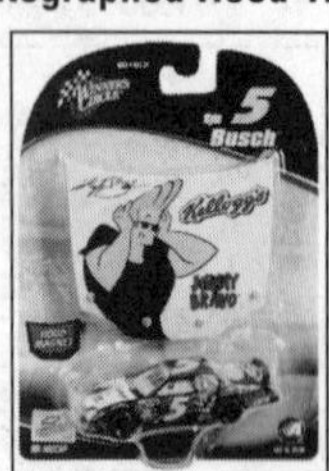

	EX	NM-MT
2 Clint Bowyer AC Delco Chris Cagle	7.50	15.00
2 Clint Bowyer Timberland	7.50	15.00
5 Kyle Busch Kellogg's Johnny Bravo	7.50	15.00
6 Bill Elliott Hellman's Charlie Brown	10.00	20.00
8 Dale Earnhardt Jr. DEI	10.00	20.00
8 Martin Truex Jr. Chance 2 Test '04 Champion	7.50	15.00
9 Bill Elliott Dodge	7.50	15.00
9 Kasey Kahne Dodge Ram Mega Cab	10.00	20.00
9 Kasey Kahne Dodge	7.50	15.00
9 Kasey Kahne Dodge '04 Rookie of the Year	10.00	20.00
9 Kasey Kahne Dodge Longest Yard	10.00	20.00
9 Kasey Kahne Dodge Mopar '04	10.00	20.00
9 Kasey Kahne Dodge Mopar	7.50	15.00
9 Kasey Kahne Mountain Dew	10.00	20.00
10 Scott Riggs Valvoline Herbie	7.50	15.00
10 Scott Riggs Valvoline Nickelback	6.00	12.00
15 Michael Waltrip Napa Stars & Stripes	7.50	15.00
18 Bobby Labonte Boniva	7.50	15.00
18 Bobby Labonte Interstate Batteries	7.50	15.00
18 Bobby Labonte Interstate Batteries Madagascar	7.50	15.00
19 Jeremy Mayfield Dodge	7.50	15.00
19 Jeremy Mayfield Dodge Retro Daytona Shootout	5.00	10.00
19 Jeremy Mayfield Mountain Dew Pitch Black	6.00	12.00
20 Tony Stewart Home Depot	7.50	15.00
20 Tony Stewart Home Depot Madagascar	7.50	15.00
21 Kevin Harvick Hershey's Take 5	7.50	15.00
21 Kevin Harvick Pelon Pelo Rico	7.50	15.00
25 Brian Vickers GMAC Green Day	6.00	12.00
25 Brian Vickers GMAC Scooby Doo	7.50	15.00
29 Kevin Harvick Goodwrench	7.50	15.00
29 Kevin Harvick Goodwrench Brickyard	7.50	15.00
29 Kevin Harvick Goodwrench Gretchen Wilson	7.50	15.00
29 Kevin Harvick Reese's Big Cup	6.00	12.00
31 Jeff Burton Cingular Big & Rich	6.00	12.00
33 Tony Stewart James Dean 50th Anniversary	7.50	15.00
33 Tony Stewart Mr.Clean AutoDry	7.50	15.00
38 Kasey Kahne Great Clips	7.50	15.00
38 Elliott Sadler M&M's	7.50	15.00
38 Elliott Sadler M&M's Halloween	7.50	15.00
38 Elliott Sadler M&M's July 4	7.50	15.00
38 Elliott Sadler M&M's July 4 Green M&M	7.50	15.00
38 Elliott Sadler Pedigree	6.00	12.00
41 Reed Sorenson Discount Tire	12.50	25.00
41 Reed Sorenson Home 123	10.00	20.00
42 Jamie McMurray Havoline	10.00	20.00
42 Jamie McMurray Havoline Shine On Charlotte	7.50	15.00
42 Jamie McMurray Havoline Shine On Sonoma	7.50	15.00
42 Jamie McMurray Havoline Shine On Talladega	7.50	15.00
64 Jamie McMurray Top Flite	7.50	15.00
77 Travis Kvapil Mobil	6.00	12.00
81 Dale Earnhardt Jr. Chance 2 Test '98,'99 Champion	7.50	15.00
88 Dale Jarrett UPS	7.50	15.00
88 Dale Jarrett UPS Toys for Tots	7.50	15.00
91 Bill Elliott Stanley Tools	10.00	20.00
99 Michael Waltrip Aaron's	10.00	20.00
99 Michael Waltrip Domino's Pizza	10.00	20.00

2005 Winner's Circle Driver Photo Hood 1:64

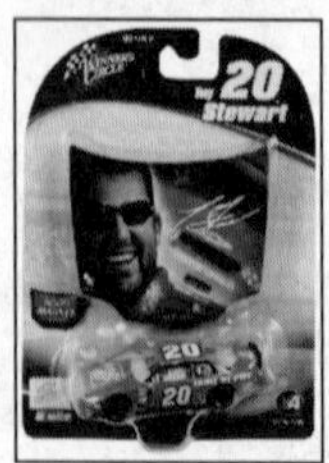

	EX	NM-MT
2 Clint Bowyer AC Delco	10.00	20.00
2 Rusty Wallace Rusty	10.00	20.00
5 Kyle Busch Kellogg's	10.00	20.00
8 Dale Earnhardt Jr. DEI	10.00	20.00
9 Kasey Kahne Dodge Retro Daytona Shootout	10.00	20.00
19 Jeremy Mayfield Dodge Retro Daytona Shootout	6.00	12.00
20 Tony Stewart Home Depot	10.00	20.00
24 Jeff Gordon DuPont Flames	10.00	20.00
24 Jeff Gordon DuPont Flames Reverse Performance Alliance	10.00	20.00
25 Brian Vickers GMAC	7.50	15.00
31 Jeff Burton Cingular	7.50	15.00
41 Reed Sorenson Discount Tire Coats Nashville Raced	10.00	20.00
64 Rusty Wallace Bell Helicopter	7.50	15.00

2005 Winner's Circle Driver Sticker 1:64

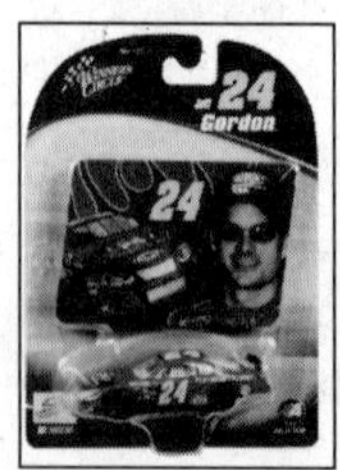

	EX	NM-MT
9 Kasey Kahne Dodge Richmond Raced	10.00	20.00
18 Bobby Labonte Interstate Batteries	6.00	12.00
24 Jeff Gordon DuPont Flames Performance Alliance Reverse	7.50	15.00
24 Jeff Gordon DuPont Flames Daytona Raced	7.50	15.00
38 Elliott Sadler M&M's	6.00	12.00
43 Richard Petty STP '75 Charger	7.50	15.00
43 Richard Petty STP '84 Grand Prix	6.00	12.00

2005 Winner's Circle Driver Sticker RCR Museum Series 2 1:64

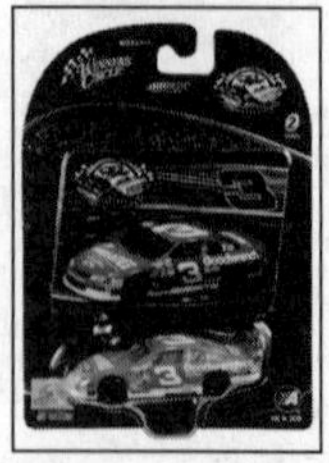

	EX	NM-MT
3 Dale Earnhardt Goodwrench Silver '95 Monte Carlo	10.00	20.00
3 Dale Earnhardt Goodwrench 25th Anniversary	6.00	12.00
3 Dale Earnhardt Goodwrench Plus '98 MC Daytona Win	6.00	12.00
3 Dale Earnhardt Goodwrench Taz '00 Monte Carlo	6.00	12.00
3 Dale Earnhardt Wheaties '97 Monte Carlo	12.50	25.00

2005 Winner's Circle Event Series 1:64

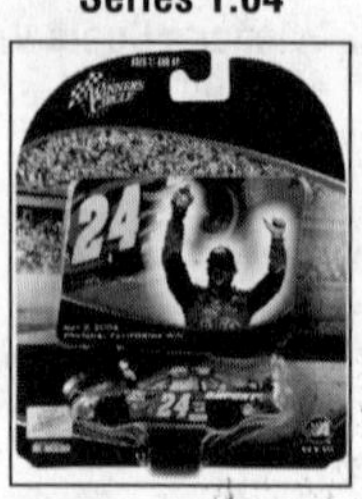

	EX	NM-MT
2 Rusty Wallace Miller Lite '04 Martinsville Win	7.50	15.00
8 Dale Earnhardt Jr. Bud '04 Atlanta Win	7.50	15.00
8 Dale Earnhardt Jr. Bud '04 Richmond Win	7.50	15.00
8 Dale Earnhardt Jr. Bud Born On Feb.15 '04 Daytona Win Feb.7 car	7.50	15.00
24 Jeff Gordon DuPont Flames '04 California Win	7.50	15.00
24 Jeff Gordon Pepsi Shards '04 Talladega Win	7.50	15.00
38 Elliott Sadler M&M's '04 Texas Win	7.50	15.00

2005 Winner's Circle Schedule Hood 1:64

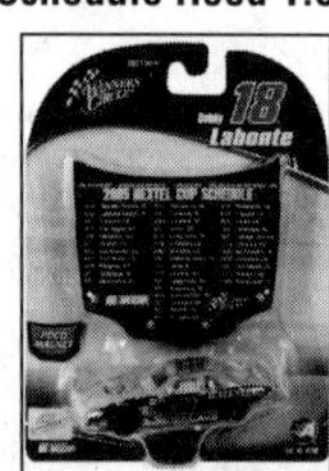

	EX	NM-MT
8 Dale Earnhardt Jr. JR	6.00	12.00
15 Michael Waltrip Napa	6.00	12.00
18 Bobby Labonte Interstate Batteries	5.00	10.00
20 Tony Stewart Home Depot	5.00	10.00
21 Kevin Harvick Hershey's Take 5	5.00	10.00
21 Kevin Harvick Reese's	5.00	10.00
24 Jeff Gordon DuPont Flames	6.00	12.00
38 Elliott Sadler M&M's	5.00	10.00
81 Dale Earnhardt Jr. Oreo Ritz	6.00	12.00
88 Dale Jarrett UPS	6.00	12.00

2005 Winner's Circle Test Hood 1:64

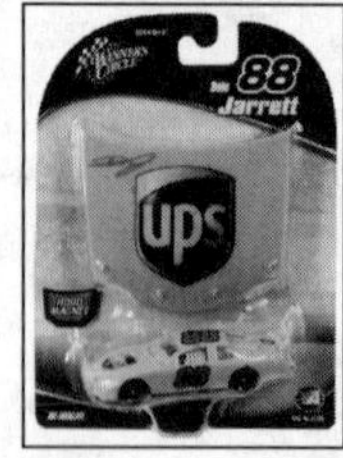

	EX	NM-MT
9 Kasey Kahne Dodge	15.00	30.00
18 Bobby Labonte Interstate Batteries	6.00	12.00
20 Tony Stewart Home Depot	6.00	12.00
24 Jeff Gordon DuPont	20.00	40.00
29 Kevin Harvick Goodwrench	7.50	15.00
38 Elliott Sadler M&M's	10.00	20.00
88 Dale Jarrett UPS	12.50	25.00

2006 Winner's Circle 1:64

	EX	NM-MT
1/8/11 Dale Tribute 5-car set 1.Martin Truex Jr. Bass Pro Dale Tribute 8.Dale Earnhardt Jr. Bud Dale Tribute 8.Martin Truex Jr. Bass Pro Dale Tribute Talladega Raced 11.Paul Menard Menard's Dale Tribute NNO.Dale Earnhardt Hall of Fame Dale Tribute	20.00	35.00
2 Rusty Wallace Miller Lite Bristol '05	4.00	8.00
2 Rusty Wallace Miller Lite 700 Starts '05	4.00	8.00
8 Dale Earnhardt Jr. Bud	5.00	10.00
8 Dale Earnhardt Jr. Bud MLB All Star '05	5.00	10.00
8 Dale Earnhardt Jr. Bud Test	5.00	10.00
8 Dale Earnhardt Jr. Bud 3 Doors Down '05	5.00	10.00

2006 Winner's Circle Autographed Hood 1:64

	EX	NM-MT
1 Martin Truex Jr. Bass Pro Shops	5.00	10.00
1 Martin Truex Jr. Bass Pro 3 Days of Dale Tribute split window box	5.00	10.00
1 Martin Truex Jr. Bass Pro Shops Test	5.00	10.00
2 Rusty Wallace Rusty Bristol Flames	6.00	12.00
6 Mark Martin AAA	10.00	20.00
8 Dale Earnhardt Jr. Bud 3 Days of Dale Tribute split window box	7.50	15.00
8 Dale Earnhardt Jr. DEI	7.50	15.00
8 Dale Earnhardt Jr. Oreo	7.50	15.00
8 Martin Truex Jr. Bass Pro 3 Days of Dale Tribute Talladega Raced split window box	6.00	12.00
9 Kasey Kahne Dodge Test	7.50	15.00
11 Denny Hamlin Fed Ex Express	10.00	20.00
11 Paul Menard Menard's Dale Tribute	5.00	10.00
12 Ryan Newman Alltel	6.00	12.00
16 Greg Biffle National Guard	5.00	10.00
17 Matt Kenseth DeWalt	6.00	12.00
19 Jeremy Mayfield Dodge	5.00	10.00
20 Tony Stewart Home Depot Test	7.50	15.00
24 Jeff Gordon DuPont Flames	7.50	15.00
24 Jeff Gordon DuPont Flames Test	7.50	15.00
24 Jeff Gordon DuPont Hot Hues	10.00	20.00
24 Jeff Gordon Sam Foose Nicorette	7.50	15.00
26 Ricky Bobby Laughing Clown Malt Liquor	6.00	12.00
26 Jamie McMurray Sharpie	6.00	12.00
43 Jeff Green Cheerios Narnia	6.00	12.00
45 Kyle Petty GP Narnia	6.00	12.00
47 Cal Naughton Jr. Old Spice	5.00	10.00
48 Jimmie Johnson Lowe's	7.50	15.00
48 Jimmie Johnson Lowe's Flames Test	7.50	15.00
55 Jean Girard Perrier	5.00	10.00
99 Carl Edwards Office Depot	7.50	15.00
01 Joe Nemechek Army Camo Call to Duty	6.00	12.00
NNO Dale Earnhardt Hall of Fame Dale Tribute split window box	6.00	12.00

2006 Winner's Circle Award Winners 1:64

	EX	NM-MT
11 Denny Hamlin Fed Ex Express Rookie of the Year	10.00	20.00
21 Kevin Harvick Coast Guard 2006 Busch Series Champion	15.00	30.00
48 Jimmie Johnson Lowe's 2006 Nextel Cup Champion	12.50	25.00

2006 Winner's Circle Pit Sign 1:64

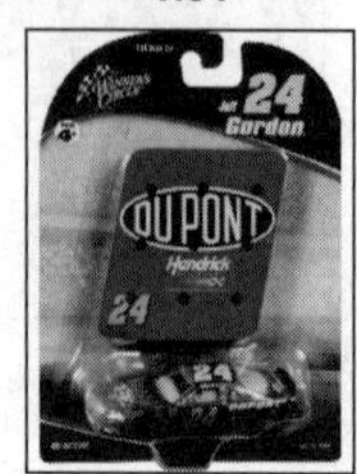

	EX	NM-MT
8 Dale Earnhardt Jr. DEI	5.00	10.00
9 Kasey Kahne Dodge	4.00	8.00
20 Tony Stewart Home Depot	4.00	
24 Jeff Gordon DuPont Flames	5.00	
48 Jimmie Johnson Lowe's	4.00	

2006 Winner's Circle Schedule Hood 1:64

	EX	NM
5 Kyle Busch Kellogg's	6.00	
9 Kasey Kahne Dodge	7.50	
18 Bobby Labonte Interstate Batteries	6.00	
19 Jeremy Mayfield Dodge	5.00	
20 Tony Stewart Home Depot	7.50	
24 Jeff Gordon DuPont Flames	7.50	
33 Tony Stewart Old Spice	7.50	
38 Elliott Sadler M&M's	6.00	
48 Jimmie Johnson Lowe's	7.50	
88 Dale Jarrett UPS	6.00	

2006 Winner's Circle Stic 1:64

	EX	NM
8 Dale Earnhardt Jr. DEI	7.50	
9 Kasey Kahne Dodge	6.00	
20 Tony Stewart Home Depot	6.00	
24 Jeff Gordon DuPont Flames	7.50	
29 Kevin Harvick Goodwrench	6.00	
48 Jimmie Johnson Lowe's	6.00	

2007 Winner's Circle American Heroes Hood 1:

	EX	NM
4 Ward Burton Air Force American Heroes	5.00	
8 Dale Earnhardt Jr. Bud Camo American Heroes	7.50	
8 Dale Earnhardt Jr. DEI Camo AH	6.00	
11 Denny Hamlin Fed Ex Freight Marines American Heroes	6.00	
16 Greg Biffle 3M Coast Guard American Heroes	5.00	
21 Jon Wood Air Force American Heroes	5.00	
24 Jeff Gordon DuPont Department of Defense American Heroes	6.00	
48 Jimmie Johnson Lowe's Power of Pride American Heroes	6.00	
88 Shane Huffman Navy	5.00	
01 Mark Martin U.S. Army American Heroes	6.00	

2007 Winner's Circle Dale Movie Hoods 1:64

	EX	NM
2 Dale Earnhardt Curb '80 Olds	6.00	
2 Dale Earnhardt Wrangler '81 Pontiac	6.00	
3 Dale Earnhardt Wrangler '86 Monte Carlo	6.00	
3 Dale Earnhardt Wrangler '87 Monte Carlo	6.00	
3 Dale Earnhardt Goodwrench '88 Monte Carlo	5.00	
3 Dale Earnhardt Goodwrench '90 Lumina	5.00	
3 Dale Earnhardt Goodwrench '94 Monte Carlo	5.00	
3 Dale Earnhardt Goodwrench '94 Monte Carlo Clinch	5.00	
3 Dale Earnhardt Goodwrench Silver Select '95 Monte Carlo	5.00	
3 Dale Earnhardt Goodwrench '95 Monte Carlo	5.00	
3 Dale Earnhardt Goodwrench '96 Monte Carlo	5.00	
3 Dale Earnhardt Goodwrench Plus '98 Monte Carlo	5.00	

2007 Winner's Circle Helm 1:64

	EX	NM
1 Martin Truex Jr. Bass Pro Shops	4.00	
8 Dale Earnhardt Jr. DEI	5.00	
9 Kasey Kahne Dodge Dealers	4.00	
10 Scott Riggs Valvoline	4.00	
11 Denny Hamlin Fed Ex Express	4.00	
20 Tony Stewart Home Depot	4.00	
24 Jeff Gordon DuPont Flames	5.00	
48 Jimmie Johnson Lowe's	4.00	
88 Ricky Rudd Snickers	4.00	

07 Winner's Circle Hoods 1:64

	EX	NM-MT
Earnhardt Jr.	5.00	10.00
Kahne dge Dealers Test	4.00	8.00
tt Sadler dge Dealers	4.00	8.00
Stewart me Depot Test	5.00	10.00
Gordon Pont Flames	5.00	10.00
Gordon psi	5.00	10.00
d Gilliland M's Shrek	4.00	8.00
nie Johnson ve's	4.00	8.00

7 Winner's Circle License Plate 1:64

	EX	NM-MT
Earnhardt Jr.	5.00	10.00
Kahne dge Dealers	4.00	8.00
t Riggs voline	4.00	8.00
y Hamlin Ex Express	4.00	8.00
Newman el	4.00	8.00
Menard Menards	4.00	8.00
Kenseth Walt	4.00	8.00
Stewart me Depot	4.00	8.00
Gordon Pont Flames	5.00	10.00
n Harvick se's	4.00	8.00
nie Johnson we's	4.00	8.00
Raines P	4.00	8.00
Edwards ice Depot	4.00	8.00

7 Winner's Circle Limited Edition 1:64

	EX	NM-MT
Busch ler Lite	5.00	10.00
Earnhardt Jr.	6.00	12.00
Earnhardt Jr. Test	6.00	12.00
Earnhardt Jr. arpie	6.00	12.00

7 Winner's Circle Limited Edition Hoods 1:64

	EX	NM-MT
Earnhardt Jr. Stars & Stripes	7.50	15.00
Earnhardt Jr. Stars & Stripes	6.00	12.00

2007 Winner's Circle Medallion 1:64

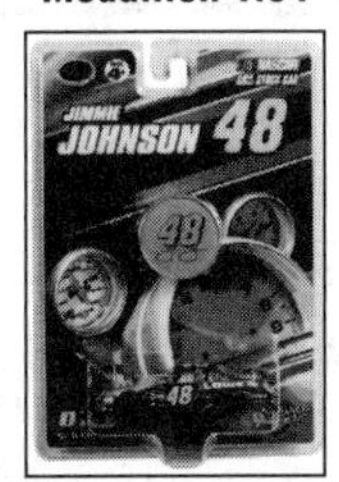

	EX	NM-MT
Earnhardt Jr.	5.00	10.00
Kahne dge Dealers	4.00	8.00
tt Sadler dge Dealers	4.00	8.00
Stewart me Depot	5.00	10.00
Gordon Pont Flames	5.00	10.00
ey Mears tional Guard	4.00	8.00
ie McMurray in Tools	4.00	8.00
n Harvick ell Pennzoil	5.00	10.00
d Gilliland M's	4.00	8.00
nie Johnson we's	4.00	8.00
k Martin S. Army	5.00	10.00

07 Winner's Circle Photo Hoods 1:64

	EX	NM-MT
Busch logg's	4.00	8.00
Burton losec	4.00	8.00
d Gilliland M's Pink	5.00	10.00
ne Huffman vy SEALS	4.00	8.00

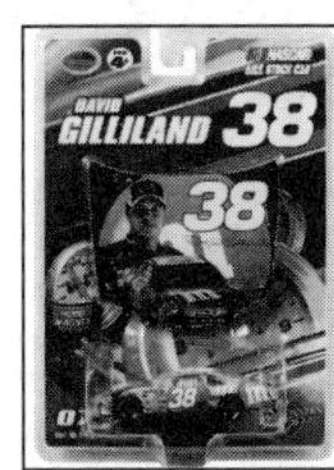

2007 Winner's Circle Photo Hood Spiderman LE 1:64

	EX	NM-MT
43 Bobby Labonte Cheerios Spiderman	5.00	10.00

2007 Winner's Circle Pit Pass 1:64

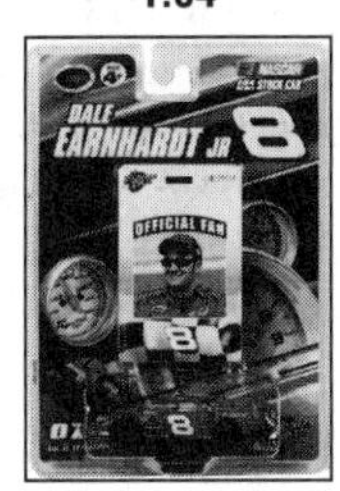

	EX	NM-MT
8 Dale Earnhardt Jr. DEI	5.00	10.00
9 Kasey Kahne Dodge	4.00	8.00
11 Denny Hamlin Fed Ex Express	4.00	8.00
16 Greg Biffle Ameriquest	4.00	8.00
19 Elliott Sadler Dodge Dealers	4.00	8.00
20 Tony Stewart Home Depot	4.00	8.00
22 Dave Blaney CAT	4.00	8.00
24 Jeff Gordon DuPont Flames	5.00	10.00
24 Jeff Gordon Nicorette	5.00	10.00
48 Jimmie Johnson Lowe's	4.00	8.00
01 Mark Martin U.S. Army	5.00	10.00

2007 Winner's Circle Pit Sign 1:64

	EX	NM-MT
6 David Ragan AAA	6.00	12.00
8 Dale Earnhardt Jr. DEI	5.00	10.00
9 Kasey Kahne Dodge Dealers	4.00	8.00
17 Matt Kenseth DeWalt	4.00	8.00
20 Tony Stewart Home Depot	4.00	8.00
24 Jeff Gordon DuPont Flames Test	6.00	12.00
24 Jeff Gordon Pepsi	5.00	10.00
29 Kevin Harvick Shell Pennzoil Test	6.00	12.00
42 Juan Pablo Montoya Texaco Havoline Test	5.00	10.00
44 Dale Jarrett UPS	4.00	8.00
48 Jimmie Johnson Lowe's Test	6.00	12.00

2007 Winner's Circle Sam Bass Hoods 1:64

	EX	NM-MT
9 Kasey Kahne Dodge Dealers Holiday	4.00	8.00
11 Denny Hamlin Fed Ex Express Holiday	4.00	8.00
17 Matt Kenseth DeWalt Holiday	4.00	8.00
20 Tony Stewart Home Depot Holiday	4.00	8.00
24 Jeff Gordon DuPont Flames Holiday	5.00	10.00
29 Kevin Harvick Shell Pennzoil Holiday	4.00	8.00
38 David Gilliland M&M's Holiday	4.00	8.00
42 Juan Pablo Montoya Texaco Havoline Holiday	5.00	10.00
48 Jimmie Johnson Lowe's Holiday	5.00	10.00
99 Carl Edwards Office Depot Holiday	4.00	8.00
01 Mark Martin U.S. Army Holiday	4.00	8.00

2007 Winner's Circle Schedule Hood 1:64

	EX	NM-MT
2 Kurt Busch Kurt	5.00	10.00
5 Kyle Busch Kellogg's	5.00	10.00
8 Dale Earnhardt Jr. DEI	6.00	12.00
9 Kasey Kahne Dodge Dealers	5.00	10.00
11 Denny Hamlin Fed Ex Express	5.00	10.00
12 Ryan Newman Alltel	5.00	10.00
16 Greg Biffle Ameriquest	5.00	10.00
17 Matt Kenseth DeWalt	5.00	10.00
20 Tony Stewart Home Depot	6.00	12.00
24 Jeff Gordon DuPont Flames	6.00	12.00
25 Casey Mears National Guard	5.00	10.00
26 Jamie McMurray Irwin Tools	5.00	10.00
31 Jeff Burton Cingular	5.00	10.00
42 Juan Pablo Montoya Texaco Havoline	6.00	12.00
48 Jimmie Johnson Lowe's	5.00	10.00
55 Michael Waltrip NAPA	5.00	10.00
99 Carl Edwards Office Depot	5.00	10.00
2007 NEXTEL Event Car	5.00	10.00

2007 Winner's Circle Victory Lane Hoods 1:64

	EX	NM-MT
1 Martin Truex Jr. Bass Pro Shops COT Dover Raced	6.00	12.00
2 Kurt Busch Miller Lite Michigan Raced	7.50	15.00
2 Kurt Busch Miller Lite Pocono Raced	7.50	15.00
5 Kyle Busch Carquest COT Bristol Raced	6.00	12.00
11 Denny Hamlin Fed Ex Express COT New Hampshire Raced	6.00	12.00
16 Greg Biffle Aflac Kansas Raced	7.50	15.00
17 Matt Kenseth Carhartt California Raced	10.00	20.00
17 Matt Kenseth DeWalt Homestead-Miami Raced	10.00	20.00
20 Tony Stewart Home Depot Brickyard Raced	7.50	15.00
20 Tony Stewart Home Depot Chicagoland Raced	7.50	15.00
20 Tony Stewart Home Depot Daytona Shootout Raced	7.50	15.00
20 Tony Stewart Home Depot COT Watkins Glen Raced	10.00	15.00
24 Jeff Gordon DuPont Flames Charlotte Raced	7.50	15.00
24 Jeff Gordon DuPont Flames Pocono Raced	7.50	15.00
24 Jeff Gordon DuPont Flames Talladega Raced	7.50	15.00
24 Jeff Gordon DuPont Flames COT Darlington Raced	10.00	20.00
24 Jeff Gordon DuPont Flames COT Phoenix Raced	10.00	20.00
24 Jeff Gordon DuPont Flames COT Talladega Raced	10.00	20.00
25 Casey Mears National Guard Camo Charlotte Raced	6.00	12.00
26 Jamie McMurray Irwin Tools Daytona Raced	6.00	12.00
29 Kevin Harvick Pennzoil Platinum Charlotte Raced	6.00	12.00
29 Kevin Harvick Shell Pennzoil Daytona Raced	10.00	20.00
31 Jeff Burton Prilosec Texas Raced	6.00	12.00
42 Juan Pablo Montoya Texaco Havoline Infineon Raced	10.00	20.00
48 Jimmie Johnson Lowe's Fall Atlanta Raced	10.00	20.00
48 Jimmie Johnson Lowe's California Raced	10.00	20.00
48 Jimmie Johnson Lowe's Las Vegas Raced	10.00	20.00
48 Jimmie Johnson Lowe's Texas Raced	10.00	20.00
48 Jimmie Johnson Lowe's COT Martinsville Raced	12.50	25.00
48 Jimmie Johnson Lowe's COT Fall Martinsville Raced	12.50	25.00
48 Jimmie Johnson Lowe's COT Fall Phoenix Raced	12.50	25.00
48 Jimmie Johnson Lowe's COT Richmond Raced	12.50	25.00
48 Jimmie Johnson Lowe's COT Fall Richmond Raced	12.50	25.00
48 Jimmie Johnson Lowe's Kobalt Atlanta Raced	10.00	20.00
99 Carl Edwards Office Depot Michigan Raced	6.00	12.00
99 Carl Edwards Office Depot COT Bristol Raced	6.00	12.00
99 Carl Edwards Office Depot COT Dover Raced	6.00	12.00

2008 Winner's Circle Autographed Hoods 1:64

	EX	NM-MT
1 Martin Truex Jr. Bass Pro	5.00	10.00
2 Kurt Busch Kurt	5.00	10.00
17 Matt Kenseth DeWalt	5.00	10.00
18 Kyle Busch M&M'S	7.50	15.00
20 Tony Stewart Home Depot	6.00	12.00
24 Jeff Gordon DuPont Flames	6.00	12.00
26 Jamie McMurray Irwin	5.00	10.00
42 Juan Pablo Montoya Texaco	5.00	10.00
43 Bobby Labonte Cheerios	5.00	10.00
88 Dale Earnhardt Jr. AMP	6.00	12.00
88 Dale Earnhardt Jr. National Guard	6.00	12.00

2008 Winner's Circle Daytona 500 1:64

	EX	NM-MT
1 Martin Truex Jr. Bass Pro Shops	7.50	15.00
9 Kasey Kahne KK	10.00	20.00
17 Matt Kenseth DeWalt	10.00	20.00
20 Tony Stewart Home Depot	12.50	25.00
24 Jeff Gordon DuPont Flames	12.50	25.00
48 Jimmie Johnson Lowe's	10.00	20.00
88 Dale Earnhardt Jr. AMP	12.50	25.00
88 Dale Earnhardt Jr. National Guard	12.50	25.00

2008 Winner's Circle Daytona 500 Hoods 1:64

	EX	NM-MT
1 Martin Truex Jr. Bass Pro Shops	5.00	10.00
9 Kasey Kahne Bud	10.00	20.00
9 Kasey Kahne KK	6.00	12.00
17 Matt Kenseth DeWalt	6.00	12.00
20 Tony Stewart Home Depot	7.50	15.00
24 Jeff Gordon DuPont Flames	7.50	15.00
29 Kevin Harvick Shell Pennzoil	6.00	12.00
42 Juan Pablo Montoya Texaco Havoline	6.00	12.00
48 Jimmie Johnson Lowe's	7.50	15.00
88 Dale Earnhardt Jr. AMP	7.50	15.00
88 Dale Earnhardt Jr. National Guard	7.50	15.00
99 Carl Edwards Office Depot	6.00	12.00

2008 Winner's Circle Daytona 500 2-car sets 1:64

	EX	NM-MT
20/88 Tony Stewart Home Depot Daytona 500 Event Car	10.00	20.00
24/08 Jeff Gordon DuPont Flames Daytona 500 Event Car	12.50	25.00
29/08 Kevin Harvick Shell Pennzoil Daytona 500 Event Car	10.00	20.00
48/08 Jimmie Johnson Lowe's Daytona 500 Event Car	10.00	20.00
88/08 Dale Earnhardt Jr. AMP Daytona 500 Event Car	12.50	25.00
88/08 Dale Earnhardt Jr. National Guard Daytona 500 Event Car	12.50	25.00

2008 Winner's Circle Hoods 1:64

	EX	NM-MT
88 Dale Earnhardt Jr./AMP	10.00	20.00

2008 Winner's Circle Number Magnet 1:64

	EX	NM-MT
1 Martin Truex Jr. Bass Pro	5.00	10.00
5 Casey Mears Car Quest	5.00	10.00
5 Casey Mears Kellogg's	5.00	10.00
6 David Ragan AAA Insurance	5.00	10.00
8 Mark Martin U.S. Army	5.00	10.00
9 Kasey Kahne KK	5.00	10.00
11 Denny Hamlin FedEx Express	5.00	10.00
12 Ryan Newman Alltel	5.00	10.00
16 Greg Biffle 3M	5.00	10.00
17 Matt Kenseth DeWalt	5.00	10.00
18 Kyle Busch M&M's	7.50	15.00
20 Tony Stewart Home Depot	6.00	12.00
24 Jeff Gordon DuPont Flames	6.00	12.00
29 Kevin Harvick Shell	5.00	10.00
42 Juan Pablo Montoya Big Red	5.00	10.00
48 Jimmie Johnson Lowe's	6.00	12.00
55 Michael Waltrip NAPA	5.00	10.00
88 Dale Earnhardt Jr. Amp	6.00	12.00
88 Dale Earnhardt Jr. National Guard	6.00	12.00
99 Carl Edwards Office Depot	5.00	10.00

2008 Winner's Circle Pit Board 1:64

	EX	NM-MT
88 Dale Earnhardt Jr. AMP	5.00	10.00

2008 Winner's Circle Sam Bass 1:64

	EX	NM-MT
9 Kasey Kahne KK	6.00	12.00
19 Elliott Sadler Best Buy	6.00	12.00
20 Tony Stewart Home Depot	7.50	15.00
24 Jeff Gordon Foundation Test	7.50	15.00
31 Jeff Burton AT&T	6.00	12.00
44 David Reutimann UPS	6.00	12.00
48 Jimmie Johnson Lowe's	7.50	15.00
60 NASCAR 60th Anniversary	7.50	15.00
88 Dale Earnhardt Jr. Amp	7.50	15.00
88 Dale Earnhardt Jr. National Guard	7.50	15.00
88 Brad Keselowski Navy	6.00	12.00

2008 Winner's Circle Schedule Hoods 1:64

	EX	NM-MT
1 Martin Truex Jr. Bass Pro Shops	4.00	8.00
2 Kurt Busch Kurt	4.00	8.00
9 Kasey Kahne KK	4.00	8.00
17 Matt Kenseth DeWalt	4.00	8.00
18 Kyle Busch M&M's	4.00	8.00
20 Tony Stewart Home Depot	5.00	10.00
24 Jeff Gordon DuPont Flames	5.00	10.00
29 Kevin Harvick Shell Pennzoil	4.00	8.00
42 Juan Pablo Montoya Texaco Havoline	4.00	8.00
48 Jimmie Johnson Lowe's	4.00	8.00
88 Dale Earnhardt Jr. AMP	5.00	10.00
88 Dale Earnhardt Jr. National Guard	5.00	10.00
99 Carl Edwards Office Depot	4.00	8.00

2008 Winner's Circle Stickers 1:64

	EX	NM-MT
1 Martin Truex Jr. Bass Pro	5.00	10.00
5 Dale Earnhardt Jr. All Star Test Car	7.50	15.00
5 Casey Mears Car Quest	5.00	10.00
5 Casey Mears Kellogg's	5.00	10.00
8 Mark Martin U.S. Army	5.00	10.00
9 Kasey Kahne KK	5.00	10.00
11 Denny Hamlin FedEx Express	5.00	10.00
12 Ryan Newman Alltel	5.00	10.00
17 Matt Kenseth Carhartt	5.00	10.00
18 Kyle Busch M&M'S	7.50	15.00
20 Tony Stewart Home Depot	6.00	12.00
24 Jeff Gordon Pepsi	6.00	12.00
29 Kevin Harvick Shell	5.00	10.00
42 Juan Pablo Montoya Texaco	5.00	10.00
43 Bobby Labonte Cheerios	5.00	10.00
48 Jimmie Johnson Lowe's 2007 Champ	6.00	12.00
55 Michael Waltrip NAPA	5.00	10.00
88 Dale Earnhardt Jr. National Guard	6.00	12.00
99 Carl Edwards Office Depot	5.00	10.00

2008 Winner's Circle 2-Car Set w/Hood 1:64

	EX	NM-MT
20 Tony Stewart Home Depot Home Depot Color Chrome	10.00	20.00
24 Jeff Gordon DuPont Flames Nicorette	12.50	25.00
88 Dale Earnhardt Jr. AMP National Guard	12.50	25.00

2008 Winner's Circle 2-Car Set w/Pit Board 1:64

	EX	NM-MT
9 Kasey Kahne Bud Bud Color Chrome	10.00	20.00

2006 Winner's Circle 1:87

	EX	NM-MT
6 Mark Martin AAA	3.00	6.00
8 Dale Earnhardt Jr. DEI	3.00	6.00
8 Dale Earnhardt Jr. 250 Starts		
9 Kasey Kahne Dodge	3.00	6.00
9 Kasey Kahne Dodge SRT		
12 Ryan Newman Alltel	3.00	6.00
16 Greg Biffle National Guard	2.50	5.00
17 Matt Kenseth DeWalt	2.50	5.00
19 Jeremy Mayfield Dodge	2.50	5.00
20 Tony Stewart Home Depot		
24 Jeff Gordon DuPont Flames	3.00	6.00
24 Jeff Gordon DuPont Hot Hues Foose Design		
26 Jamie McMurray Sharpie	2.50	5.00
38 Elliott Sadler M&M's	2.50	5.00
48 Jimmie Johnson Lowe's	3.00	6.00
48 Jimmie Johnson Lowe's Sea World		
99 Carl Edwards Office Depot	3.00	6.00

2007 Winner's Circle 1:87

	EX	NM-MT
1 Martin Truex Jr. Bass Pro Shops	2.50	5.00
2 Kurt Busch Kurt	2.50	5.00
5 Kyle Busch Kellogg's	2.50	5.00
6 David Ragan AAA	3.00	6.00
8 Dale Earnhardt Jr. DEI	4.00	8.00
8 Dale Earnhardt Jr. DEI Stars & Stripes	4.00	8.00
9 Kasey Kahne Dodge Dealers	3.00	6.00
11 Denny Hamlin Fed Ex Express	2.50	5.00
12 Ryan Newman Alltel	2.50	5.00
16 Greg Biffle Ameriquest	2.50	5.00
19 Elliott Sadler Dodge Dealers	2.50	5.00
20 Tony Stewart Home Depot	3.00	6.00
24 Jeff Gordon DuPont Flames	4.00	8.00
24 Jeff Gordon Nicorette	3.00	6.00
24 Jeff Gordon Pepsi	3.00	6.00
25 Casey Mears National Guard	2.50	5.00
26 Jamie McMurray Irwin Tools	2.50	5.00
29 Kevin Harvick Shell Pennzoil	3.00	6.00
38 David Gilliland M&M's	2.50	5.00
38 David Gilliland M&M's Shrek	2.50	5.00
42 Juan Pablo Montoya Texaco Havoline	4.00	8.00
44 Dale Jarrett UPS	2.50	5.00
48 Jimmie Johnson Lowe's	3.00	6.00
55 Michael Waltrip NAPA	2.50	5.00
88 Ricky Rudd Snickers	2.50	5.00
99 Carl Edwards Office Depot	2.50	5.00
00 David Reutimann Burger King	2.50	5.00
01 Mark Martin U.S. Army	3.00	6.00

2007 Winner's Circle American Heroes 1:87

	EX	NM-MT
4 Ward Burton Air Force American Heroes	2.50	5.00
8 Dale Earnhardt Jr. Bud Camo American Heroes	4.00	8.00
11 Denny Hamlin Fed Ex Freight Marines American Heroes	3.00	6.00
16 Greg Biffle 3M Coast Guard American Heroes	3.00	6.00
21 Jon Wood Air Force American Heroes	2.50	5.00
24 Jeff Gordon DuPont Department of Defense American Heroes	4.00	8.00
48 Jimmie Johnson Lowe's Power of Pride American Heroes	3.00	6.00
88 Shane Huffman Navy American Heroes	2.50	5.00
01 Mark Martin U.S. Army American Heroes	3.00	6.00
NNO 4. Ward Burton Air Force American Heroes 24. Jeff Gordon DuPont Department of Defense American Heroes 48. Jimmie Johnson Lowe's Power of Pride American Heroes 3-car set	6.00	12.00
NNO 8. Dale Earnhardt Jr. Bud Camo American Heroes 16. Greg Biffle 3M Coast Guard American Heroes Shane Huffman Navy American Heroes 3-car set	6.00	12.00
NNO 11. Denny Hamlin Fed Ex Freight Marines American Heroes 21. Jon Wood Air Force American Heroes 01. Mark Martin U.S. Army American Heroes 3-car set	5.00	10.00
NNO American Heroes 9-car set 4. Ward Burton Air Force American Heroes 8. Dale Earnhardt Jr. Bud Camo American Heroes 11. Denny Hamlin Fed Ex Freight Marines American Heroes 16. Greg Biffle 3M Coast Guard American Heroes 21. Jon Wood Air Force American Heroes 24. Jeff Gordon DuPont Department of Defense American Heroes 48. Jimmie Johnson Lowe's Power of Pride American Heroes 88. Shane Huffman Navy American Heroes 01. Mark Martin U.S. Army American Heroes	20.00	35.00

2007 Winner's Circle Limited Edition 1:87

	EX	NM-MT
8 Dale Earnhardt Jr. Bud Stars & Stripes	5.00	10.00

2008 Winner's Circle 1:87

	EX	NM-MT
1 Martin Truex Jr. Bass Pro Shops	2.50	5.00
8 Mark Martin U.S. Army	2.50	5.00
9 Kasey Kahne KK	2.50	5.00
11 Denny Hamlin Fed Ex Express	2.50	5.00
17 Matt Kenseth DeWalt	2.50	5.00
18 Kyle Busch M&M's	4.00	8.00
20 Tony Stewart Home Depot	3.00	6.00
24 Jeff Gordon DuPont Flames	3.00	6.00
24 Jeff Gordon Nicorette	3.00	6.00
29 Kevin Harvick Shell Pennzoil	2.50	5.00
42 Juan Pablo Montoya Big Red	2.50	5.00
42 Juan Pablo Montoya Texaco	2.50	5.00
44 Dale Jarrett UPS	2.50	5.00
48 Jimmie Johnson Lowe's	3.00	6.00
55 Michael Waltrip Napa	2.50	5.00
88 Dale Earnhardt Jr. AMP	3.00	6.00
88 Dale Earnhardt Jr. National Guard	3.00	6.00
99 Carl Edwards Office Depot	2.50	5.00

2008 Winner's Circle Daytona 500 1:87

	EX	NM-MT
1 Martin Truex Jr. Bass Pro Shops	2.50	5.00
17 Matt Kenseth DeWalt	2.50	5.00
20 Tony Stewart Home Depot	3.00	6.00
24 Jeff Gordon DuPont Flames	3.00	6.00
29 Kevin Harvick Shell Pennzoil	2.50	5.00
48 Jimmie Johnson Lowe's	3.00	6.00
88 Dale Earnhardt Jr. AMP	3.00	6.00
88 Dale Earnhardt Jr. National Guard	3.00	6.00
99 Carl Edwards Office Depot	2.50	5.00

1999 Winner's Circle Micro Machines 1:144

	EX	NM-MT
1/3 Steve Park Pennzoil Dale Earnhardt Goodwrench (Dueling Drivers)	6.00	15.00
2/24 Rusty Wallace Rusty Jeff Gordon Pepsi (Dueling Drivers)	6.00	15.00
2/18/24 Rusty Wallace Rusty Bobby Labonte Interstate Batteries Jeff Gordon Pepsi (Yellow Flag Series)	6.00	15.00
3 Dale Earnhardt Goodwrench Car and Transporter (Race Hauler Series)	6.00	15.00
3 Dale Earnhardt Goodwrench 3 Cars, Transporter, helicopter & pit wagon (Racing World series)	10.00	20.00
3 Dale Earnhardt Jr. AC Delco Car and Transporter (Race Hauler Series)	6.00	15.00
3/3 Dale Earnhardt Goodwrench Dale Earnhardt Jr. AC Delco (Thunder Blaster)	10.00	20.00
24 Jeff Gordon DuPont 3 Cars, Transporter, tow truck & pit wagon (Racing World series)	6.00	15.00
24 Jeff Gordon Pepsi Car and Transporter (Race Hauler Series)	7.50	15.00
24/28/88 eff Gordon DuPont Kenny Irwin Havoline Dale Jarrett Quality Care (Green Flag Series)	6.00	15.00
NNO 7-car Draft Pack 2. Rusty Wallace/Rusty 18. Bobby Labonte/Inter.Batteries 20. Tony Stewart/Home Depot 24. Jeff Gordon/DuPont 28. Kenny Irwin/Havoline 31. Mike Skinner/Lowe's 88.Dale Jarrett/Quality Care	7.50	15.00

2000 Winner's Circle Micro Machines 1:144

	EX	NM-MT
18/24 Bobby Labonte Interstate Batteries Jeff Gordon DuPont (Dueling Drivers)	6.00	15.00
31/88 Mike Skinner Lowe's Dale Jarrett Quality Care (Dueling Drivers)	5.00	12.00

Transporters

1994 Action/RCCA Dually Trucks 1:2

The majority of these 1:24 scale die cast replicas are banks. Some were issued with a Chaparral type show trailer while others were simply released as single trucks. A dually truck is a pick-up truck with four rear wheels, two on each side. They were distributed through both Action's dealer network and the Racing Collectibles Club of America.

	EX	NM-MT
3 Dale Earnhardt Goodwrench PLS Bank/5016	40.00	100.00
5 Terry Labonte Kellogg's Bank PLS/2508	30.00	60.00
11 Bill Elliott Budweiser Bank/2500	30.00	80.00
16 Ted Musgrave Family Channel PLS Bank/2508	25.00	40.00
18 Dale Jarrett Interstate Batteries PLS Bank/4248	25.00	40.00
21 Morgan Shepherd Cheerwine Bank	25.00	40.00
22 Bobby Labonte Maxwell House PLS Bank/2508	40.00	80.00
24 Jeff Gordon DuPont Coke Bank	80.00	120.00
28 Davey Allison Havoline Bank RCCA/2800	60.00	120.00
59 Dennis Setzer Alliance Bank PLS/2500	25.00	40.00
98 Derrike Cope Fingerhut Bank PLS/2508	20.00	40.00

1995 Action/RCCA Dually Trucks 1:24

	EX	NM-MT
2 Rusty Wallace Miller Genuine Draft Bank in plastic case	40.00	75.00
3 Dale Earnhardt Goodwrench PLS Bank/5016	40.00	100.00
3 Dale Earnhardt Goodwrench Bank 7-Time Champion	75.00	200.00
24 Jeff Gordon DuPont PLS Bank/2508	30.00	80.00
24 Jeff Gordon DuPont RCCA/2008	20.00	50.00
28 Dale Jarrett Havoline PLS Bank/4248	25.00	60.00
51 Neil Bonnett Country Time PLS Bank/5216	25.00	60.00

1996 Action/RCCA Dually Trucks 1:24

	EX	NM-MT
2 Rusty Wallace Miller Splash Bank/5000	20.00	50.00
2 Rusty Wallace Miller Genuine Draft Silver 25th Anniversary Bank/2500	40.00	75.00
3 Dale Earnhardt Goodwrench RCCA Bank/3504	60.00	150.00
5 Terry Labonte Kellogg's RCCA Bank/2500	25.00	60.00
6 Mark Martin Valvoline PLS Bank/4512	35.00	70.00
18 Bobby Labonte Interstate Batteries RCCA Bank/2500	40.00	75.00
24 Jeff Gordon DuPont RCCA Bank/5000	30.00	60.00
28 Ernie Irvan Havoline RCCA Bank/3500	20.00	50.00
42 Kyle Petty Coors Light RCCA Bank/2500	20.00	50.00
88 Dale Jarrett Quality Care PLS Bank/3500	20.00	50.00
94 Bill Elliott McDonald's PLS Bank/4500	20.00	50.00

1997 Action/RCCA Dually Trucks 1:24

	EX	NM-MT
2 Rusty Wallace Miller Lite Bank/2500	30.00	75.00
3 Dale Earnhardt Wheaties Bank/5000	60.00	120.00
17 Darrell Waltrip Parts America Chrome RCCA Bank/2500	25.00	60.00
94 Bill Elliott Mac Tonight Bank	50.00	80.00

1998-00 Action/RCCA Dually Trucks 1:24

	EX	NM-MT
24 Jeff Gordon DuPont PLS Bank/3000 1998	30.00	60.00
24 Jeff Gordon DuPont Millennium Silver Bank/3000 2000	40.00	80.00

1994 Action/RCCA Dually Trucks with Trailer 1:64

This series of 1:64 scale dually Trucks was issued with a Chaparral show trailer. The entire package of the dually and show trailer is a replica of what most teams use to carry their show cars from event to event. Most were issued by t club with many featuring a production run total on the b

	EX
3 Dale Earnhardt Goodwrench PLS/2748	50.00
3/8/3 Earnhardt Kids Mom-n-Pop's/3750 with 3-cars 3. Dale Earnhardt Jr. 8. Kerry Earnhardt 38. Kelley Earnhardt	175.00
7 Geoff Bodine Exide	20.00
11 Bill Elliott Budweiser	30.00
18 Dale Jarrett Interstate Batteries	25.00
21 Morgan Shepherd Cheerwine	25.00
23 Jimmy Spencer Smokin' Joe's in plastic case/2508	60.00
24 Jeff Gordon DuPont	60.00
28 Ernie Irvan Mac Tools	25.00
28 Dale Jarrett Havoline	25.00
42 Kyle Petty Coors Light	30.00

1995 Action/RCCA Dual Trucks with Trailer 1:6

	EX
2 Rusty Wallace Miller Genuine Draft	30.00
3 Dale Earnhardt Goodwrench PLS/3492	50.00
7 Geoff Bodine Exide/4008	15.00
24 Jeff Gordon DuPont RCCA/2508	30.00
42 Kyle Petty Coors Light PLS in plastic case/4008	15.00
94 Bill Elliott McDonald's PLS/2508	25.00

1996 Action/RCCA Dual Trucks with Trailer 1:6

	EX
2 Rusty Wallace Miller in plastic case/2500	30.00
3 Dale Earnhardt Goodwrench RCCA/2500	50.00
3 Dale Earnhardt Goodwrench Silver	50.00
24 Jeff Gordon DuPont/2500	40.00

1997 Action/RCCA Dual Trucks with Trailer 1:6

	EX
2 Rusty Wallace Miller Lite/3000	35.00
3 Dale Earnhardt Wheaties/5000	75.00
17 Darrell Waltrip Parts America Chrome/4000	25.00
94 Bill Elliott Mac Tonight/3500	25.00

1998 Action/RCCA Dual Trucks with Trailer 1:6

	EX
3 Dale Earnhardt Goodwrench Bass Pro/5004	50.00
5 Terry Labonte Kellogg's Corny/3500	25.00
24 Jeff Gordon DuPont PLS/3500	40.00
24 Jeff Gordon DuPont Chromalusion/4500	40.00
88 Dale Jarrett Batman PLS/3500	50.00

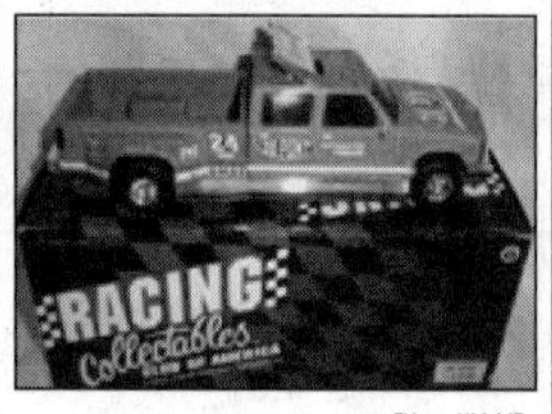

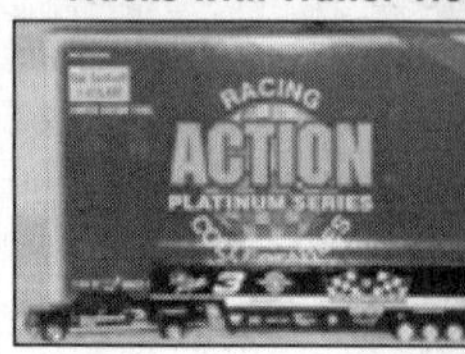

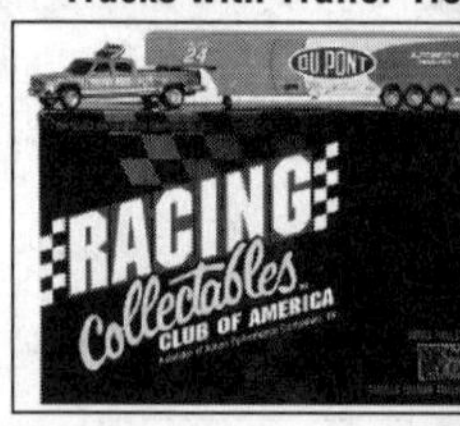

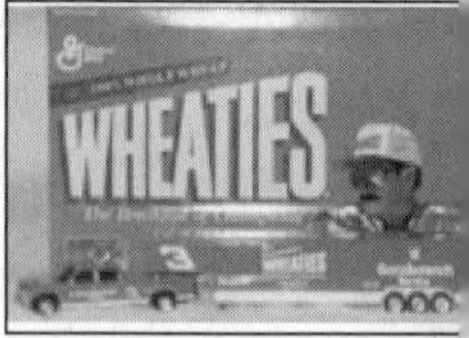

1999 Action/RCCA Dually Trucks with Trailer 1:64

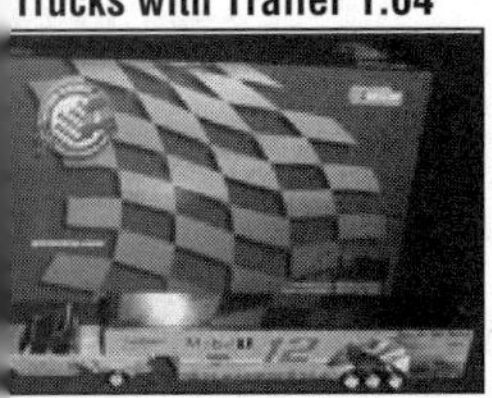

	EX	NM-MT
Earnhardt Goodwrench 5th Anniversary/3000	60.00	150.00
Earnhardt Goodwrench Sign/2508	50.00	100.00
Earnhardt Wrangler/3504	50.00	120.00
Earnhardt Jr. AC Delco Superman/3504	30.00	60.00
emy Mayfield Mobil 1 Kentucky Derby	20.00	40.00

2000 Action/RCCA Dually Trucks with Trailer 1:64

	EX	NM-MT
y Wallace Miller Lite in plastic case	40.00	100.00
Earnhardt Goodwrench Taz/2508	60.00	120.00
Earnhardt Goodwrench Peter Max/2508	90.00	175.00

2001 Action/RCCA Dually Trucks with Trailer 1:64

	EX	NM-MT
e Park Pennzoil Sylvester and Tweety/2508	20.00	50.00
y Labonte Kellogg's Coyote Road Runner/2508	20.00	50.00
y Labonte Kellogg's Coyote and Road Runner RCCA/738	30.00	60.00
Earnhardt Jr. Bud All-Star/2640	60.00	100.00
f Gordon DuPont Bugs/3000	40.00	75.00
vin Harvick Goodwrench Taz/2508	25.00	50.00

2003 Action/RCCA Dually Trucks with Trailer 1:64

	EX	NM-MT
vin Harvick Snap-On/8904	40.00	70.00

94-97 Action/RCCA Dually Trucks 1:64

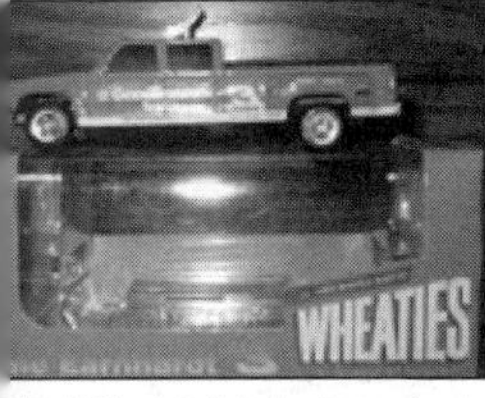

eries of 1:64 scale dually Truck replicas were issued as dual trucks without trailers. Most were issued by the club or in a basic issue Platinum Series (PLS) box with eaturing a production run total on the box.

	EX	NM-MT
y Wallace Miller/10,000 1996	12.50	25.00
Earnhardt Goodwrench PLS blister pack 1994	20.00	50.00
Earnhardt Goodwrench PLS/15,000 1995	20.00	50.00
Earnhardt Goodwrench/15,000 1996	25.00	60.00
Earnhardt Wheaties 1997	30.00	60.00
e Jarrett Interstate Batteries RCCA/7875 1994	12.50	30.00
f Gordon DuPont PLS/15,000 1995	12.50	30.00
f Gordon DuPont RCCA/2000 1995	12.50	30.00
f Gordon DuPont/5000 1996	15.00	30.00
e Jarrett Havoline 1994	12.50	25.00
chael Waltrip Pennzoil RCCA/7572 1994	10.00	20.00

1992 Action/RCCA Transporters 1:64

	EX	NM-MT
Earnhardt Goodwrench DEI	150.00	250.00
vey Allison Havoline	50.00	80.00
chard Petty STP RCCA	45.00	75.00
bby Labonte Penrose Sausage RCCA/5000	40.00	75.00
59 Robert Pressley Alliance	45.00	75.00
66 Cale Yarborough Trop Artic RCCA/7500	25.00	50.00

1993 Action/RCCA Transporters 1:64

	EX	NM-MT
2 Rusty Wallace Delco Remy PLS/1000	50.00	80.00
3 Dale Earnhardt Goodwrench RCCA in box with 2-cars	75.00	150.00
3 Dale Earnhardt Goodwrench RCCA in wooden box with 2-cars/500	100.00	200.00
3 Dale Earnhardt Goodwrench RCCA with 1:64 car in black case/10,000	100.00	200.00
4 Ernie Irvan Delco Remy Platinum Series	45.00	75.00
6 Mark Martin Valvoline RCCA with car/2500	40.00	80.00
7 Harry Gant Morema	50.00	80.00
9 Bill Elliott Melling RCCA with 1:64 car	60.00	90.00
11 Bill Elliott Budweiser	60.00	90.00
17 Darrell Waltrip Delco Remy Platinum Series	35.00	75.00
17 Darrell Waltrip Western Auto RCCA/1392	25.00	60.00
24 Jeff Gordon DuPont GMP in case/2800	70.00	130.00
25 Rob Moroso Swisher RCCA	30.00	60.00
25 Ken Schrader Kodiak	50.00	80.00
28 Davey Allison Havoline RCCA/7500	60.00	120.00
28 Davey Allison Havoline Mac Tools RCCA/5004	50.00	100.00
35 Shawna Robinson Polaroid	40.00	100.00
59 Robert Pressley Alliance Fan Club	60.00	90.00

1994 Action/RCCA Transporters 1:64

This series of 1:64 scale transporters were distributed through both the club and Action's dealer network. Action was also contracted to produce many of the haulers distributed by Peachstate and GMP. Those pieces are listed within the Peachstate set.

	EX	NM-MT
2 Rusty Wallace Miller	40.00	90.00
3 Dale Earnhardt Goodwrench RCCA/2508	60.00	120.00
3 Dale Earnhardt 7-Time Champ 1994 Awards Banquet Promo in plastic case	100.00	200.00
3 Dale Earnhardt 1985 Wrangler blue RCCA/5016	50.00	120.00
3 Dale Earnhardt 1987 Wrangler yellow RCCA/5016	50.00	120.00
11 Bill Elliott Budwesier	60.00	90.00
21 David Pearson Chattanooga Chew	30.00	75.00
21 Morgan Shepherd Cheerwine/5000	25.00	60.00
23 Jimmy Spencer Smokin' Joe's	75.00	125.00
24 Jeff Gordon DuPont RCCA/5016	40.00	80.00
27 Tim Richmond Old Milwaukee/2500	20.00	50.00
28 Dale Jarrett Havoline	30.00	60.00
41 Joe Nemechek Meineke Platinum Series	30.00	60.00
42 Kyle Petty Coors Light	50.00	90.00
51 Neil Bonnett Country Time PLS/5216	30.00	60.00
51 Neil Bonnett Country Time RCCA	60.00	100.00
79 Dave Rezendes KPR Racing	35.00	60.00

1995 Action/RCCA Transporters 1:64

Action issued both Platinum Series and RCCA transporters again in 1995. Each club piece was issued in a large black RCCA box with the tractor and trailer packaged inside a styrofoam shell. Most of the regular (PLS) transporter releases were issued in a blue Platinum Series box that included an oversized SkyBox card.

	EX	NM-MT
1 Rick Mast Skoal/5004	15.00	30.00
2 Rusty Wallace Miller Genuine Draft Platinum Series	30.00	80.00
2 Rusty Wallace Miller Geniune Draft RCCA/3000	25.00	50.00
3 Dale Earnhardt Goodwrench RCCA/5004	50.00	100.00
3 Dale Earnhardt Goodwrench Service RCCA/5000	50.00	100.00
3/43 Dale Earnhardt Richard Petty 7 and 7 Champion special RCCA/3000	30.00	80.00
6 Mark Martin Valvoline	40.00	80.00
7 Alan Kulwicki Zerex/2508	50.00	100.00
11 Brett Bodine Lowe's/2508	15.00	40.00
23 Jimmy Spencer Smokin' Joe's RCCA in plastic case/2508	40.00	75.00
24 Jeff Gordon DuPont/4008	25.00	50.00
25 Ken Schrader Bud RCCA/2508	25.00	60.00
26 Brett Bodine Lowe's RCCA/2508	15.00	40.00
28 Dale Jarrett Havoline RCCA/4500	15.00	40.00
42 Kyle Petty Coors Light PLS/4008	15.00	40.00
42 Kyle Petty Coors Light RCCA/3000	15.00	40.00
94 Bill Elliott McDonald's/2508	15.00	40.00
94 Bill Elliott McDonald's RCCA/3504	20.00	50.00

1996-97 Action/RCCA Transporters 1:64

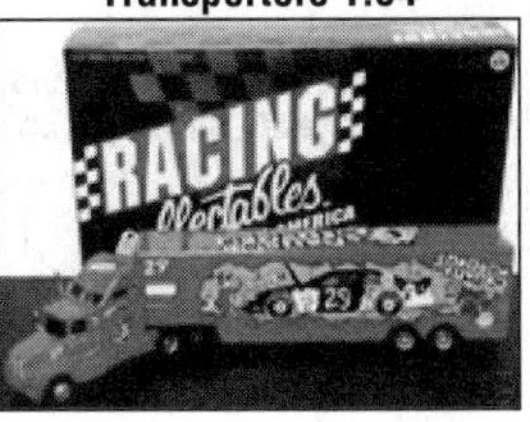

	EX	NM-MT
3 Dale Earnhardt Goodwrench 1996	50.00	100.00
29 Steve Grissom Cartoon Network RCCA/2500 1996	15.00	40.00
42 Joe Nemechek BellSouth Matco Tools/1765 '97	15.00	40.00

2001 Action Racing Collectables Transporters 1:64

	EX	NM-MT
3 Dale Earnhardt Goodwrench/6004	30.00	80.00
3 Dale Earnhardt Oreo/2508	75.00	135.00
18 Bobby Labonte Interstate Batteries Jurassic Park 3	25.00	50.00
18/20 Bobby Labonte Tony Stewart Coke Bears/4008	30.00	60.00
20 Tony Stewart Home Depot Jurassic Park 3/2052	30.00	60.00
20 Tony Stewart Home Depot Jurassic Park 3 RCCA/456	35.00	70.00
24 Jeff Gordon DuPont Bugs/2508	40.00	80.00
24 Jeff Gordon DuPont Flames/2520	75.00	135.00
29 Kevin Harvick Goodwrench/7500	25.00	50.00
88 Dale Jarrett UPS/2004	30.00	80.00

2001 Action/RCCA Transporters 1:64

	EX	NM-MT
18 Bobby Labonte Interstate Batteries Color Chrome Jurassic Park 3 RCCA/456	35.00	70.00
24 Jeff Gordon DuPont Bugs Color Chrome RCCA	70.00	125.00
24 Jeff Gordon DuPont Flames Color Chrome RCCA/204	175.00	300.00
88 Dale Jarrett UPS Color Chrome RCCA/504	70.00	120.00

2002 Action Racing Collectables Transporters 1:64

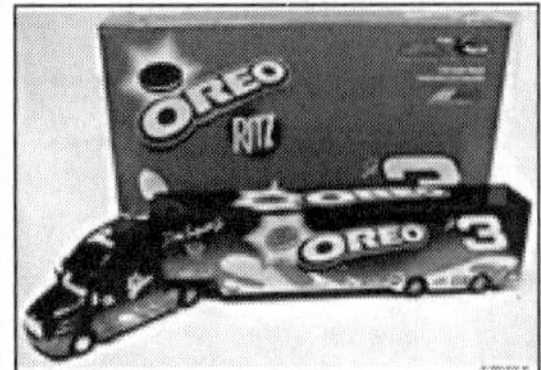

	EX	NM-MT
2 Rusty Wallace Miller Lite/2676	40.00	70.00
3 Dale Earnhardt Forever the Man/28,672	20.00	50.00
3 Dale Earnhardt Goodwrench Legacy with signatures/50,094	20.00	50.00
3 Dale Earnhardt Jr. Oreo/5016	35.00	70.00
8 Dale Earnhardt Jr. Bud/9876	25.00	60.00
20 Tony Stewart Home Depot/3000	30.00	60.00
24 Jeff Gordon DuPont 4-Time Champ/7404	25.00	50.00
24 Jeff Gordon Pepsi Daytona/3132	25.00	50.00
29 Kevin Harvick Goodwrench/6000	25.00	50.00
29 Kevin Harvick Goodwrench ET/4608	25.00	60.00
NNO Looney Tunes Rematch/3888	25.00	50.00
NNO Muppets/2808	25.00	50.00

2002 Action/RCCA Transporters 1:64

	EX	NM-MT
2 Rusty Wallace Miller Lite/336	40.00	75.00
3 Dale Earnhardt Forever the Man/5004	30.00	60.00
3 Dale Earnhardt Jr. Nilla Wafers/2508	40.00	75.00
3 Dale Earnhardt Jr. Oreo Color Chrome/504	45.00	80.00
8 Dale Earnhardt Jr. Bud/2508	30.00	60.00
8 Dale Earnhardt Jr. Bud Color Chrome/504	45.00	80.00
20 Tony Stewart Home Depot/504	40.00	75.00
24 Jeff Gordon DuPont 200th Anniversary/1500	45.00	80.00
24 Jeff Gordon Pepsi Daytona	35.00	70.00
NNO Looney Tunes Rematch/996	20.00	50.00

2003 Action Racing Collectables Transporters 1:64

	EX	NM-MT
2 Rusty Wallace Miller Lite/2448	25.00	60.00
2 Rusty Wallace Miller Lite Route/2628	25.00	60.00
8 Dale Earnhardt Jr./Bud/9876	35.00	70.00
8 Dale Earnhardt Jr. DMP Chance 2/5560	25.00	60.00
20 Tony Stewart Home Depot/2848	25.00	60.00
29 Kevin Harvick Snap-On/12,504	35.00	60.00
40 Sterling Marlin Coors Light/2532	25.00	60.00
48 Jimmie Johnson Lowe's/2952	30.00	60.00
88 Dale Jarrett UPS	40.00	75.00
88 Dale Jarrett UPS Promo in window box	20.00	35.00
NNO Realtree Racing/2712 Dale Earnhardt pictured Dave Marcis pictured	30.00	60.00
NNO Victory Lap Event/2508	35.00	70.00

2003 Action/RCCA Transporters 1:64

	EX	NM-MT
2 Rusty Wallace Miller Lite Route Color Chrome/1008	30.00	60.00
8 Dale Earnhardt Jr. Bud/2508	40.00	70.00

2004 Action Racing Collectables Transporters 1:64

	EX	NM-MT
8 D.Earnhardt Jr. Bud/2352	35.00	60.00
88 Dale Jarrett UPS	35.00	60.00
NNO Dale Earnhardt Foundation Feed the Children/1764	35.00	60.00

2005 Action Racing Collectables Transporters 1:64

	EX	NM-MT
2 Rusty Wallace Miller Lite 1980's Tribute/1500	40.00	65.00
2 Rusty Wallace Miller Lite 1980's Tribute QVC/504	40.00	65.00
2 Rusty Wallace Miller Lite 1990's Tribute/1500	40.00	65.00
2 Rusty Wallace Miller Lite 1990's Tribute QVC/504	40.00	65.00
2 Rusty Wallace Miller Lite 2000's Tribute/1500	40.00	65.00
2 Rusty Wallace Miller Lite 2000's Tribute QVC/504	40.00	65.00
9 Kasey Kahne Dodge/1716	40.00	65.00
9 Kasey Kahne Dodge QVC/288	40.00	65.00
41 Reed Sorenson Discount Tire	40.00	65.00

1994-96 Action/RCCA Transporters 1:96

This series of 1:96 scale transporters features some of the best drivers in Winston Cup over the last 20 years. This is the smallest size piece that Action makes.

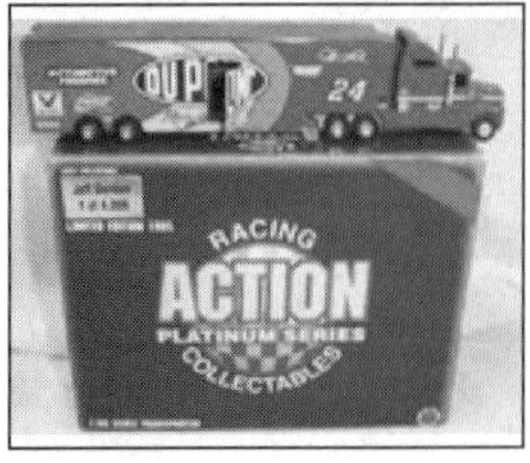

	EX	NM-MT
2 Rusty Wallace MGD/3000 1995	15.00	40.00
3 Dale Earnhardt Goodwrench/3000 '94	75.00	150.00
3 Dale Earnhardt Goodwrench/5000 '95	30.00	60.00
3 Dale Earnhardt Goodwrench/3000 1996	30.00	60.00
3 Dale Earnhardt 1985 Wrangler Blue/2508 1994	60.00	150.00
3 Dale Earnhardt 1987 Wrangler Yellow	75.00	125.00
23 Jimmy Spencer Smokin' Joe's RCCA in plastic case/2508 1995	50.00	80.00
24 Jeff Gordon DuPont PLS/4008 '95	25.00	60.00
25 Ken Schrader Bud/4008 1994	15.00	40.00
27 Tim Richmond Old Milwaukee RCCA/2500 1994	20.00	40.00
28 Dale Jarrett Havoline PLS/4008	15.00	40.00
42 Kyle Petty Coors Light Platinum Series/4008 1995	15.00	40.00
94 Bill Elliott McDonald's RCCA/2508	15.00	40.00

1993-95 Brookfield Dually with Car and Show Trailer 1:25

	EX	NM-MT
3 Dale Earnhardt Goodwrench/40,000 1993	75.00	150.00
3 Dale Earnhardt Goodwrench without car/5000 '94	60.00	120.00
3 Dale Earnhardt Goodwrench Plus/5000 1995	60.00	120.00
3/43 Dale Earnhardt Goodwrench 7&7/5000 Richard Petty STP 7&7 1995	75.00	150.00
5 Terry Labonte Kellogg's/5000 1994	40.00	80.00
24 Jeff Gordon DuPont without car/10,000 1995	75.00	150.00
25 Ken Schrader Bud without car/5000 1995	40.00	80.00
25 Ken Schrader Bud Silver without car/400 1995	60.00	120.00
30 Michael Waltrip Pennzoil without car/5000 1995	40.00	80.00
30 Michael Waltrip Pennzoil w/o car Silver/250 1995	60.00	120.00
NNO Brickyard 400 without car 1994	40.00	80.00
NNO Brickyard 400 without car 1995	40.00	80.00

1997 Brookfield Dually with Car and Show Trailer 1:25

	EX	NM-MT
3 Dale Earnhardt Wheaties/10,000 1997	100.00	200.00
24 Jeff Gordon DuPont Lost World without car/7500 1997	75.00	150.00
24 Jeff Gordon DuPont Lost World Silver without car/400 1997	125.00	225.00

1998 Brookfield Dually with Car and Show Trailer 1:25

	EX	NM-MT
1 Dale Earnhardt Jr. Coke Bear/2500	75.00	150.00
3 Dale Earnhardt Coke/2500	100.00	200.00
3 Dale Earnhardt Goodwrench Plus Bass Pro/5000	150.00	250.00
24 Jeff Gordon DuPont 2-Time Champ/5000	100.00	200.00
24 Jeff Gordon DuPont ChromaPremier/5000	75.00	150.00

1999 Brookfield Dually with Car and Show Trailer 1:25

	EX	NM-MT
3 Dale Earnhardt Goodwrench Plus Silver/2584	100.00	200.00
3 Dale Earnhardt Wrangler/3992	175.00	300.00
3 Dale Earnhardt Jr. AC Delco/4224	75.00	150.00

	EX	NM-MT
3 Dale Earnhardt Jr. AC Delco Superman/4244	75.00	150.00
8 Dale Earnhardt Jr. Bud/2616	90.00	180.00
9 Jerry Nadeau Jetsons/1500	40.00	80.00
20 Tony Stewart Home Depot/3716	100.00	175.00
20 Tony Stewart Home Depot Silver/799	175.00	300.00
20 Tony Stewart Home Depot Habitat for Humanity/2832	100.00	175.00
20 Tony Stewart/Home Depot Habitat Silver/650	200.00	300.00
24 Jeff Gordon Superman/3168	125.00	225.00
36 Ernie Irvan M&M's/1320	60.00	120.00
36 Ernie Irvan M&M's Countdown to Millenium/1316	60.00	120.00
36 Ernie Irvan M&M's Countdown to Millenium Silver/314	75.00	150.00
36 Ernie Irvan M&M's Millennium/1316	60.00	120.00
36 Ernie Irvan M&M's Millennium Silver/313	75.00	150.00
94 Bill Elliott McDonald's Silver/1196	60.00	120.00

2000 Brookfield Dually with Car and Show Trailer 1:25

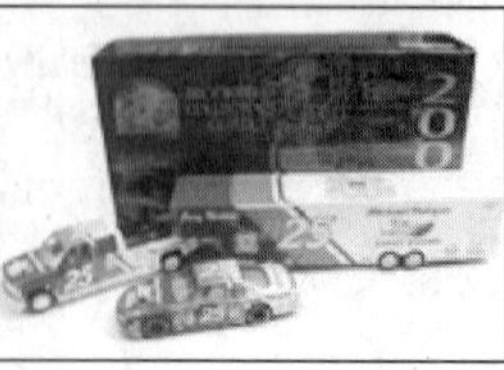

	EX	NM-MT
3 Dale Earnhardt Goodwrench Taz/2164	175.00	300.00
3 Dale Earnhardt Goodwrench Taz Silver/516	350.00	500.00
3 Dale Earnhardt Goodwrench Peter Max/2508	200.00	350.00
8 Dale Earnhardt Jr. Bud/2048	90.00	180.00
8 Dale Earnhardt Jr. Bud Olympics/1648	100.00	200.00
8 Dale Earnhardt Jr. Bud Olympic Silver Incentive/380	125.00	250.00
20 Tony Stewart Home Depot Kids Workshop/1212	60.00	120.00
24 Jeff Gordon DuPont Peanuts/2140	100.00	180.00
25 Jerry Nadeau Coast Guard/736	40.00	80.00
28 Ricky Rudd Havoline Marines/1880	40.00	80.00
28 Ricky Rudd Havoline Marines Silver/628	50.00	100.00
88 Dale Jarrett Quality Care/2008	50.00	100.00
88 Dale Jarrett Quality Care Silver/500	60.00	120.00
88 Dale Jarrett Quality Care Air Force/1880	50.00	100.00
88 Dale Jarrett Quality Care Air Force Silver/628	60.00	120.00
94 Bill Elliott McDonald's Drive Thru 25th Anniversary/1196	40.00	80.00
94 Bill Elliott McDonald's Drive Thru 25th Anniv.Silver/304	60.00	120.00

2001 Brookfield Dually with Car and Show Trailer 1:25

	EX	NM-MT
3 Dale Earnhardt Goodwrench Plus/10,000	60.00	150.00
3 Dale Earnhardt Goodwrench Silver/5004	50.00	100.00
3 Dale Earnhardt Oreo 2-Axle/6504	75.00	150.00
3 Dale Earnhardt Oreo 2-Axle Silver/1004	125.00	200.00
3 Dale Earnhardt Oreo 3-Axle/12,198	75.00	150.00
3 Dale Earnhardt Oreo 3-Axle Silver/2892	125.00	250.00
9 Bill Elliott Dodge Muhammad Ali without car/2028	50.00	100.00
9 Bill Elliott Dodge Muhammad Ali Silver without car/496	60.00	120.00
9 Bill Elliott Casey Atwood Dodge Spiderman 4-piece set/2328	90.00	150.00
9 Bill Elliott Casey Atwood Dodge Spiderman Silver 4-piece set/504	125.00	250.00
18 Bobby Labonte Interstate Batteries Jurassic Park 3 without car/2004	40.00	100.00
18 Bobby Labonte Interstate Batteries Jurassic Park 3 Silver without car/504	50.00	100.00
20 Tony Stewart Home Depot Jurassic Park 3 without car/2004	60.00	120.00
24 Jeff Gordon DuPont Flames/1788	100.00	200.00
88 Dale Jarrett UPS/1308		
88 Dale Jarrett UPS Silver/1200	100.00	175.00

2002 Brookfield Dually with Car and Show Trailer 1:25

	EX	NM-MT
3 Dale Earnhardt Jr. Nilla Wafers/3000	50.00	120.00
3 Dale Earnhardt Jr. Nilla Wafers Silver/660	90.00	180.00
3 Dale Earnhardt Jr. Oreo/3608	75.00	150.00
3 Dale Earnhardt Jr. Oreo Silver/872	90.00	180.00
8 Dale Earnhardt Jr. Bud without car/4480	75.00	150.00
8 Dale Earnhardt Jr. Bud Silver without car/1052	90.00	180.00
8 Dale Earnhardt Jr. Bud Color Chrome	90.00	180.00
24 Jeff Gordon DuPont Flames without car/3492	50.00	100.00
24 Jeff Gordon DuPont Flames Silver without car/784	60.00	150.00
24 Jeff Gordon Pepsi Daytona without car/2172	50.00	100.00
24 Jeff Gordon Pepsi Silver without car/536	75.00	150.00
29 Kevin Harvick Goodwrench/4924	50.00	100.00
29 Kevin Harvick Goodwrench Silver/1192	50.00	120.00

2003 Brookfield Dually and Show Trailer 1:25

	EX	NM-MT
8 Dale Earnhardt Jr. Bud All-Star Game 3-axle/2682	60.00	120.00
8 Dale Earnhardt Jr. Dirty Mo Posse 3-axle/2046	50.00	100.00
8 Dale Earnhardt Jr. DMP Silver 3-axle/929	60.00	120.00
8 Dale Earnhardt Jr. Oreo Ritz/2804	40.00	80.00
8 Dale Earnhardt Jr. Oreo Ritz Silver/572	60.00	120.00
24 Jeff Gordon Pepsi Billion $/2368	50.00	100.00
24 Jeff Gordon Pepsi Billion $ Silver/333	60.00	120.00

2005 Brookfield Dually and Show Trailer 1:24

	EX	NM-MT
24 Jeff Gordon DuPont Flames/1668	40.00	60.00
24 Jeff Gordon DuPont Flames GM Dealers/36	40.00	60.00
24 Jeff Gordon DuPont Flames QVC/400	40.00	60.00

1992-93 Brookfield Suburbans, Blazers, and Tahoes 1:25

Brookfield Collectors Guild began this series in 1992. The 1:25 scale SUVs include primarily Suburbans (with most being banks) and a few Blazers and Tahoes. Each is decorated in team or special event colors and was distributed either through direct sales or hobby outlets. Each was packaged in a clear window cardboard box and most included the year of issue and production run printed on the box.

	EX	NM-MT
3 Dale Earnhardt Goodwrench Bank/5000 1992	40.00	80.00
24 Jeff Gordon DuPont Rookie of the Year Bank/25,000	25.00	60.00
NNO Indianapolis 500 1993	10.00	25.00

1994 Brookfield Suburbans, Blazers, and Tahoes 1:25

	EX	NM-MT
30 Michael Waltrip Pennzoil/10,000	15.00	40.00
42 Kyle Petty Mello Yello Sabco Brickyard/5000	10.00	25.00
42 Kyle Petty Mello Yello Thanks Fans Brickyard/10,000	10.00	25.00
NNO Brickyard 400 Bank White paint/25,000	10.00	25.00
NNO Brickyard 400 Bank Yellow paint scheme	100.00	175.00
NNO Don Prudhomme Snake Final Strike Tour	25.00	50.00

1995 Brookfield Suburbans, Blazers, and Tahoes 1:25

	EX	NM-MT
3 Dale Earnhardt Brickyard/5000	25.00	50.00
3 Dale Earnhardt Goodwrench Tahoe Bank/10,000	25.00	50.00
3 Dale Earnhardt Goodwrench Silver Tahoe Bank/10,000	30.00	80.00
3 Dale Earnhardt Goodwrench Bank 7-Time Champ/30,000	30.00	80.00
3 Dale Earnhardt Goodwrench Bank 7-Time Champ Silver/1500	50.00	100.00
3/43 Dale Earnhardt Richard Petty 7-Time Champion 2-Suburban set/25,000	25.00	60.00
3/43 Dale Earnhardt Richard Petty 7-Time Champion Bank split paint scheme/30,000	20.00	40.00
3/43 Dale Earnhardt Richard Petty 7-Time Champion Bank split paint scheme tampos are reversed/30,000	20.00	40.00
5 Terry Labonte Kellogg's/10,000	15.00	40.00
24 Jeff Gordon DuPont Blue Bank/10,000	30.00	60.00
24 Jeff Gordon DuPont Silver Bank/10,000	30.00	60.00
24 Jeff Gordon DuPont White Bank/15,000	25.00	50.00
42 Kyle Petty Mello Yello Bank/10,000	15.00	40.00
NNO Brickyard 400 Silver Bank/5000	25.00	50.00
NNO Brickyard 400 White Bank/15,000	25.00	50.00
NNO John Force Castrol GTX	40.00	80.00

1996 Brookfield Suburbans, Blazers, and Tahoes 1:25

	EX	NM-MT
3 Dale Earnhardt Olympic Tahoe/10,000	40.00	80.00
3 Dale Earnhardt Olympic Tahoe Silver/832	50.00	120.00
5 Terry Labonte Kellogg's Silver	100.00	175.00
24 Jeff Gordon DuPont Blazer	20.00	50.00
24 Jeff Gordon DuPont Blazer Silver/150	75.00	150.00
24 Jeff Gordon DuPont Tahoe Bank/5000	20.00	50.00
25 Ken Schrader Bud Red	20.00	50.00
25 Ken Schrader Bud White	25.00	50.00
30 Johnny Benson Pennzoil	25.00	50.00

1997 Brookfield Suburbans, Blazers, and Tahoes 1:25

	EX	NM-MT
3 Dale Earnhardt Goodwrench Plus/5000	25.00	60.00
24 Jeff Gordon DuPont Gold 3-time Champ/5000	30.00	60.00
NNO California Inaugural	10.00	25.00

1998 Brookfield Suburbans, Blazers, and Tahoes 1:25

	EX	NM-MT
3 Dale Earnhardt Goodwrench Bass Pro Tahoe/5000	30.00	60.00
24 Jeff Gordon DuPont Chromalusion Tahoe/5000	20.00	50.00
24 Jeff Gordon DuPont Chromalusion Silver Tahoe/250	30.00	60.00

1999 Brookfield Suburbans, Blazers, and Tahoes 1:25

	EX	NM-MT
3 Dale Earnhardt AC-Delco Bank/5000	20.00	50.00
3 Dale Earnhardt Goodwrench 25th Anniversary Blazer/2508	25.00	60.00
3 Dale Earnhardt Goodwrench 25th Anniv. Tahoe/2508	25.00	60.00
3 Dale Earnhardt Wrangler/2508	20.00	50.00
8 Dale Earnhardt Jr. Bud/2508	30.00	60.00
24 Jeff Gordon DuPont Superman/2508	40.00	80.00
24 Jeff Gordon Pepsi Blazer/5004	25.00	60.00

2001 Brookfield Suburbans, Blazers, and Tahoes 1:25

	EX	NM-MT
8 Dale Earnhardt Jr. Bud/2464	30.00	60.00
8 Dale Earnhardt Jr. Bud Silver/620	40.00	80.00
8 Dale Earnhardt Jr. Bud All Star/2876	35.00	60.00
8 Dale Earnhardt Jr. Bud All Star Silver/658	40.00	80.00
29 Kevin Harvick Goodwrench Taz/4008	25.00	50.00

2002 Brookfield Suburbans, Blazers, and Tahoes 1:25

	EX	NM-MT
3 Dale Earnhardt Jr. Oreo Bank/2508	30.00	60.00
29 Kevin Harvick Goodwrench/4428	20.00	50.00
29 Kevin Harvick Goodwrench Incentive/386	25.00	50.00

2003 Brookfield Suburbans, Blazers, and Tahoes 1:25

	EX	NM-MT
3 Dale Earnhardt Goodwrench Bass Pro Suburban/3711	25.00	50.00
3 Dale Earnhardt Goodwrench Silver Select Suburban/2646	25.00	50.00

1995 Brookfield Trackside 1:25

These 3-piece sets are complete with a 1:24 scale car and a flatbed trailer. In some cases a Suburban or other truck type was substituted for the standard dually pick-up.

	EX	NM-MT
3 Dale Earnhardt AC Delco Silver/800	60.00	120.00
3 Dale Earnhardt Goodwrench/10,000	50.00	120.00
3 Dale Earnhardt Goodwrench Silver/10,000	50.00	120.00
24 Jeff Gordon DuPont/10,000	60.00	120.00

1996 Brookfield Trackside 1:25

	EX	NM-MT
3 Dale Earnhardt AC Delco/10,000	50.00	120.00
3 Dale Earnhardt Goodwrench Olympic/10,000	75.00	150.00
5 Terry Labonte Kellogg's Bank/5000	30.00	80.00
25 Wally Dallenbach Budweiser	30.00	60.00

1997 Brookfield Trackside 1:25

	EX	NM-MT
3 Dale Earnhardt Goodwrench Plus Suburban/5000	50.00	100.00
3 Dale Earnhardt Wheaties/10,000	75.00	150.00
3 Dale Earnhardt Wheaties Suburban/10,000	75.00	150.00

1998 Brookfield Trackside 1:25

	EX	NM-MT
1 Dale Earnhardt Jr. Coke Bear Suburban/4086	75.00	150.00
3 Dale Earnhardt Coke/2500	75.00	150.00
3 Dale Earnhardt Coke Suburban/3792	100.00	[illegible]
3 Dale Earnhardt Goodwrench Plus Bass Pro/10,000	60.00	[illegible]
3 Dale Earnhardt Jr. AC Delco	60.00	[illegible]
3 Dale Earnhardt Jr. AC Delco Silver/420	75.00	[illegible]
24 Jeff Gordon DuPont Chromapremier/10,000	60.00	[illegible]

1999 Brookfield Trackside 1:25

	EX	NM-MT
1 Dale Earnhardt Jr. Coke Suburban/1500	40.00	[illegible]
3 Dale Earnhardt Goodwrench Silver/5004	50.00	[illegible]
3 Dale Earnhardt Goodwrench 25th Anniversary Suburban/2748	100.00	[illegible]
3 Dale Earnhardt Goodwrench Plus/2508	50.00	[illegible]
3 Dale Earnhardt Wrangler/2508	50.00	[illegible]
3 Dale Earnhardt Wrangler Suburban/10,002	50.00	[illegible]
3 Dale Earnhardt Jr. AC Delco Suburban/2928	40.00	[illegible]
5 Terry Labonte K-Sentials Suburban/2202	40.00	[illegible]
8 Dale Earnhardt Jr. Bud/3072	75.00	[illegible]
12 Jeremy Mayfield Mobil 1 Kentucky Derby/1800	30.00	[illegible]
24 Jeff Gordon DuPont/2508	70.00	[illegible]
24 Jeff Gordon DuPont 24K Gold/3504	100.00	[illegible]
24 Jeff Gordon Pepsi/3504	60.00	[illegible]
24 Jeff Gordon Pepsi Suburban/2406	50.00	[illegible]
24 Jeff Gordon Superman/2508	100.00	[illegible]
31 Dale Earnhardt Jr. Gargoyles/2508	75.00	[illegible]
31 Dale Earnhardt Jr. Sikkens White/3000	50.00	[illegible]
36 Ernie Irvin M&M's/2508	70.00	[illegible]
40 Sterling Marlin Coors Light Brooks&Dunn/1086	50.00	[illegible]
88 Dale Jarrett Quality Care White/1932	75.00	[illegible]

2000 Brookfield Trackside 1:25

	EX	NM-MT
3 Dale Earnhardt Goodwrench Taz/2508	75.00	[illegible]
8 Dale Earnhardt Jr. Bud/3072	75.00	[illegible]

2001 Brookfield Trackside 1:25

	EX	NM-MT
2 Rusty Wallace Milelr Lite/1788	50.00	[illegible]
2 Rusty Wallace Miller Lite Silver/720	70.00	[illegible]
3 Dale Earnhardt Goodwrench/3504	50.00	[illegible]
3 Dale Earnhardt Goodwrench Silver/960	75.00	[illegible]
3 Dale Earnhardt Goodwrench Plus/5004	75.00	[illegible]
8 Dale Earnhardt Jr. Bud/2508	60.00	[illegible]
24 Jeff Gordon DuPont Flames/1788	50.00	[illegible]
24 Jeff Gordon DuPont Flames Silver/960	60.00	[illegible]
24 Jeff Gordon DuPont Flames 2001 Champ with Suburban and 24K Gold car/2508	125.00	[illegible]
29 Kevin Harvick Goodwrench Taz/2508	40.00	[illegible]

2002 Brookfield Trackside 1:25

	EX	NM-MT
3 Dale Earnhardt Jr. Oreo/2508	60.00	[illegible]
3 Dale Earnhardt Jr. Nilla Wafers/2508	60.00	[illegible]
8 Dale Earnhardt Jr. Bud Color Chrome/800	100.00	[illegible]
24 Jeff Gordon DuPont Flames/2172	50.00	[illegible]
24 Jeff Gordon DuPont Flames Color Chrome/960	60.00	[illegible]
29 Kevin Harvick Goodwrench Color Chrome/1708	50.00	[illegible]

2004 Brookfield Trackside 1:25

	EX	NM-MT
29 Kevin Harvick Snap On RCR 35th Ann./2508	100.00	[illegible]

000 Brookfield Dually with Car and Show Trailer 1:64

	EX	NM-MT
le Earnhardt Goodwrench Taz/2508	50.00	100.00

2004 Brookfield Trackside 1:64

e were released in Skybox packaging.

	EX	NM-MT
ale Earnhardt Jr. Bud/7624 on a base	15.00	30.00
ale Earnhardt Jr. Bud Born On February 15/6384	15.00	30.00
ale Earnhardt Jr. Oreo Ritz/4704	12.50	25.00
artin Truex Jr. Bass Pro Shops/2400	15.00	30.00
asey Kahne Dodge refresh/4224	15.00	30.00
'ony Stewart Home Depot/4944	12.50	25.00
'ony Stewart Home Depot Black Reverse Paint/3000	12.50	25.00
Kevin Harvick Goodwrench/3924	12.50	25.00

2005 Brookfield Trackside 1:64

	EX	NM-MT
usty Wallace Miller Lite/2136	15.00	30.00
ale Earnhardt Jr. Bud Born On Feb.20/4008	15.00	30.00
asey Kahne Dodge Retro Bud Shootout/2760	15.00	30.00

1993-95 Corgi Race Image Transporters 1:64

Transporter in this series was produced by Corgi and buted by Race Image. Each was packaged in a blue and window box.

	EX	NM-MT
ark Martin Valvoline 1993	15.00	40.00
obby Labonte Maxwell House	15.00	30.00
rett Bodine Quaker State	15.00	30.00
avey Allison Havoline 1993	15.00	40.00

1992 Ertl Founding Fathers Transporters 1:43

of these vintage transporters were issued in a red and checkered box with a picture of the featured driver's car on utside. The trailer itself also included a picture of the car.

	EX	NM-MT
rtis Crider 1948 Chevy	35.00	60.00
iny Lund 1950 Chevy	35.00	60.00
Fireball Roberts 1937 Ford	35.00	60.00

990 Ertl Transporters 1:64

e Transporters were issued by Ertl and packaged in a white kered flag designed blister with a large NASCAR logo s the top.

	EX	NM-MT
A/Kodak (Rick Wilson's Car)	6.00	15.00
DA/Citgo Wood Brothers (Dale Jarrett's Car)	12.50	25.00
DA/Country Time (Michael Waltrip's Car)	12.50	25.00
ichard Petty STP	10.00	25.00

1992-94 Ertl White Rose Transporters Promos 1:64

series features many of the BGN drivers from the early and other special NASCAR promo pieces that were racted. The pieces were made by Ertl and distributed gh White Rose Collectibles.

	EX	NM-MT
ff Burton Baby Ruth 1993	30.00	50.00
ff Gordon Baby Ruth	50.00	90.00
cky Craven DuPont	30.00	50.00
an Kulwicki 1992 Winston Cup Champion	100.00	160.00
Bill Elliott Budweiser in Wooden case	75.00	125.00
Hut Stricklin Smokin' Joe's in pastic case	35.00	60.00
Phil Parsons White Rose	25.00	45.00
Harry Gant Manheim	30.00	50.00
Kenny Wallace Dirt Devil	25.00	45.00
41 Stanley Smith White House Apple Juice	25.00	45.00
43 Richard Petty Petty 35th Anniversary Tour	100.00	175.00
52 Ken Schrader AC Delco	25.00	45.00
75 Jack Sprague Staff America	25.00	45.00
87 Joe Nemechek Dentyne	25.00	45.00
87 Joe Nemechek 1992 BGN Champion	45.00	75.00

1992-94 Ertl White Rose Transporters Past and Present 1:64

This series produced by Ertl and distributed by White Rose features many of the greats from Past and Present. The 1:64 scale replicas features greats like Davey Allison, Dale Earnhardt and Richard Petty.

	EX	NM-MT
3 Dale Earnhardt Goodwrench 1993	50.00	120.00
3 Dale Earnhardt 1986 Wrangler 1992	60.00	150.00
7 Geoff Bodine Exide	30.00	60.00
7 Alan Kulwicki Hooters 1992	30.00	80.00
7 Alan Kulwicki Zerex 1994	30.00	80.00
7 Kyle Petty 7-Eleven 1993	25.00	50.00
11 Darrell Waltrip Mountain Dew	30.00	60.00
12 Jimmy Spencer Meineke	20.00	40.00
14 Terry Labonte Kellogg's	30.00	50.00
15 Lake Speed Quality Care	20.00	40.00
16 Ted Musgrave Family Channel	20.00	40.00
17 Darrell Waltrip Western Auto 1994	20.00	40.00
18 Dale Jarrett Interstate Batteries 1992	20.00	50.00
21 Neil Bonnett Warner Hodgdon 1992	35.00	70.00
21 Morgan Shepherd Citgo	25.00	45.00
24 Jeff Gordon DuPont 1993	40.00	100.00
27 Junior Johnson Mountain Dew	30.00	50.00
28 Davey Allison Havoline black&white	50.00	120.00
28 Cale Yarborough Hardee's	20.00	50.00
41 Phil Parsons Manheim	25.00	45.00
42/43 Kyle Petty Richard Petty STP Combo 1992	40.00	100.00
44 Sterling Marlin Piedmont	30.00	50.00
98 Derrike Cope Bojangles	20.00	40.00
NNO Past and Present Promo	25.00	50.00

1997-99 Hartoy American Racing Scene Transporters 1:64

Each Transporter in this series was manufactured by Hartoy and issued in an "American Racing Scene Series II" box. It was a continuation of the Winross American Racing Scene Series Transporters.

	EX	NM-MT
4 Sterling Marlin Kodak 1997	45.00	80.00
16 Ted Musgrave Family Channel	35.00	70.00

1998 Hot Wheels Transporters 1:64

These 1:64 scale transporters were primarily distributed through retail outlets with each being packaged in a black Hot Wheels Racing window box. The 1998 box features the NASCAR 50th Anniversary logo.

	EX	NM-MT
6 Mark Martin Valvoline	7.50	15.00
12 Jeremy Mayfield Mobil 1	7.50	15.00
35 Todd Bodine Tabasco	7.50	15.00

1999 Hot Wheels Transporters 1:64

These 1:64 scale transporters were primarily distributed through retail outlets with each being packaged in a black Hot Wheels Racing window box. The box is similar to the 1998 release without the 50th Anniversary logo.

	EX	NM-MT
6 Mark Martin Valvoline	7.50	20.00
10 Ricky Rudd Tide	7.50	15.00
12 Jeremy Mayfield Mobil 1	7.50	15.00
36 Ken Schrader M&M's	10.00	20.00
43 John Andretti STP	7.50	15.00
44 Kyle Petty Hot Wheels	7.50	15.00
66 Darrell Waltrip Big K	7.50	15.00
97 Chad Little John Deere	7.50	15.00

2000 Hot Wheels Deluxe Transporters 1:64

	EX	NM-MT
43 John Andretti STP	10.00	20.00
44 Kyle Petty Hot Wheels	10.00	20.00
45 Adam Petty Sprint PCS	25.00	60.00
55 Kenny Wallace Square D	7.50	15.00
94 Bill Elliott McDonald's	7.50	20.00

2001 Hot Wheels Racing Transporters 1:64

These Transporters were issued by Hot Wheels in an orange and blue box with a display window. Each piece is identified specifically as 2001 on the front of the package and entitled either Team Transporter or Transporter Tribute.

	EX	NM-MT
5 Terry Labonte Kellogg's Tony		
6 Mark Martin Pfizer	10.00	20.00
10 Johnny Benson Valvoline	10.00	20.00
10 Jeff Green Nesquik	10.00	20.00
11 Davey Allison Davey Tribute	12.50	25.00
11 Darrell Waltrip Darrell Waltrip Tribute	12.50	25.00
12 Jeremy Mayfield Mobil 1	10.00	20.00
17 Matt Kenseth DeWalt	12.50	25.00
36 Ken Schrader M&M's	10.00	20.00
42 Kyle Petty STP Tribute	12.00	20.00
43 Richard Petty STP Tribute	12.00	20.00
45 Kyle Petty Sprint	10.00	20.00
55 Bobby Hamilton Square D	10.00	20.00
96 Andy Houston McDonald's	10.00	20.00
99 Jeff Burton Citgo	10.00	20.00

2002 Hot Wheels Transporters 1:64

These Transporters were issued by Hot Wheels in the same orange and blue boxes with a display window that were used in 2001. However, each piece is identified specifically as 2002 on the package itself and entitled either Team Transporter or Transporter Tribute.

	EX	NM-MT
5 Terry Labonte Kellogg's	10.00	20.00
10 Johnny Benson Valvoline	10.00	20.00
10 Scott Riggs Nesquik	10.00	20.00
11 Cale Yarborough Tribute	10.00	20.00
12 Ryan Newman Alltel	12.50	25.00
14 Larry Foyt Harrah's	10.00	20.00
17 Matt Kenseth DeWalt	12.50	25.00
21 Buddy Baker Valvoline Tribute	10.00	20.00
21 Elliott Sadler Motorcraft	10.00	20.00
22 Ward Burton Caterpillar	10.00	20.00
25 Jerry Nadeau UAW	10.00	20.00
25 Randy Tolsma Marines Red/Black	10.00	20.00
32 Ricky Craven Tide	10.00	20.00
36 Ken Schrader M&M's	10.00	20.00
43 John Andretti Cheerios	10.00	20.00
45 Kyle Petty Sprint	10.00	20.00
60 Greg Biffle Grainger	12.50	25.00
NNO Hendrick 100-Victories Tribute Rick Hendrick, Jeff Gordon, Ken Schrader, Geoff Bodine, and Jerry Nadeau	12.00	20.00
NNO Petty Family Tribute Lee Petty, Richard Petty, Kyle Petty, and Adam Petty	12.50	25.00

2003 Hot Wheels Transporters 1:64

The 2003 Transporters are a re-package of a few die-cast pieces from 2002 and 2001 with a few new paint schemes included. The same orange and blue window box design from 2001 and 2002 was used except that a specific year of issue was omitted from the front of the box for 2003. The Kenseth Championship

	EX	NM-MT
6 Mark Martin Pfizer	12.00	20.00
10 Scott Riggs Nesquik	12.00	20.00
12 Ryan Newman Alltel	12.50	25.00
17 Matt Kenseth DeWalt	15.00	25.00
21 Ricky Rudd Motorcraft	15.00	25.00
25 Bobby Hamilton Jr. Marines	12.50	25.00
32 Ricky Craven Tide	12.00	20.00
36 Ken Schrader M&M's	12.00	20.00
43 John Andretti Cheerios	12.00	20.00
45 Kyle Petty Georgia Pacific	12.50	25.00
97 Kurt Busch Rubbermaid	12.50	25.00
99 Jeff Burton Citgo	12.00	20.00
M2 Fireball Roberts Tribute	12.00	20.00
NNO Ned Jarrett Tribute	12.00	20.00

2003 Hot Wheels Racing Matt Kenseth Championship Transporters 1:64

	EX	NM-MT
17 Matt Kenseth DeWalt	15.00	30.00

2004 Hot Wheels Team Transporters 1:64

	EX	NM-MT
12 Ryan Newman Alltel	12.50	25.00
16 Greg Biffle National Guard	12.50	25.00
04 Justice League Event	15.00	25.00
04 Justice League Villains	15.00	25.00

2004 Hot Wheels Victory Lane Transporters 1:64

	EX	NM-MT
12 Ryan Newman Alltel	15.00	25.00
12B Ryan Newman Alltel	15.00	25.00
16 Greg Biffle Grainger	15.00	25.00
17 Matt Kenseth DeWalt	15.00	25.00
97 Kurt Busch Rubbermaid	15.00	25.00
97B Kurt Busch Rubbermaid	15.00	25.00

2005 Hot Wheels Batman Begins Transporters 1:64

	EX	NM-MT
6 Mark Martin Batman	20.00	35.00

1990-93 Matchbox White Rose Team Convoys 1:64

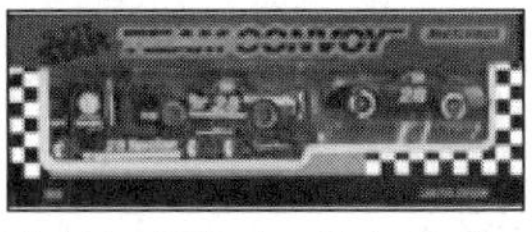

Each set of die-cast in this series consists of one Team Convoy flatbed truck and 2-1:64 scale cars or 1-car and 1-truck or van. They were produced by Matchbox for White Rose and packaged in a cardboard window box. The year of issue was printed on the backs of the early pieces and on the fronts of the newer releases.

	EX	NM-MT
3 Dale Earnhardt Goodwrench with Van 1991	20.00	40.00
3 Dale Earnhardt Goodwrench 1991 Champ w/Van '92	20.00	35.00
3 Dale Earnhardt Goodwrench 1993	15.00	30.00
4 Ernie Irvan Kodak w/van 1991	10.00	20.00
7 Harry Gant Manheim Auctions 1994	10.00	20.00
7 Alan Kulwicki Hooters 1993	10.00	20.00
10 Derrike Cope Purolator w/van 1991	10.00	20.00
11 Bill Elliott Amoco with truck 1992	10.00	20.00
15 Lake Speed Quality Care with truck 1993	10.00	20.00
24 Jeff Gordon DuPont Rookie of the Year 1993	20.00	35.00
25 Ken Schrader Hendrick w/van 1993	10.00	20.00
28 Davey Allison Havoline 1993	12.50	25.00
30 Michael Waltrip Pennzoil w/Van 1991	10.00	20.00
42 Kyle Petty Mello Yello w/van 1992	7.50	20.00
43 Richard Petty STP w/van 1992	10.00	25.00
68 Bobby Hamilton Country Time Daytona 500 1993	10.00	20.00

1993-94 Matchbox White Rose Transporters Promos 1:64

	EX	NM-MT
3 Dale Earnhardt Goodwrench 6-Time Champ in plastic case/5000 '93	100.00	200.00
3 Dale Earnhardt Goodwrench 7-Time Champ in plastic case/4000 '94	100.00	200.00

1997 Matchbox White Rose Transporters 1:64

This series of replica transporters represents the first year White Rose switched to the 1:64 scale size. The transporters were produced by Matchbox and distributed by White Rose Collectibles with each in its own acrylic case. The stated production run was 5000.

	EX	NM-MT
2 Rusty Wallace Miller Lite	45.00	70.00
5 Terry Labonte Kellogg's	30.00	60.00
25 Ricky Craven Budweiser	35.00	60.00
33 Ken Schrader Skoal	30.00	60.00
94 Bill Elliott McDonald's	35.00	60.00
94 Bill Elliott Mac Tonight	35.00	60.00

1994 Matchbox White Rose Transporters Super Star Series 1:80

This series of 1:80 scale replicas represents the first year White Rose switched to the 1:80 scale size. The transporters were produced by Matchbox and distributed by White Rose Collectibles.

	EX	NM-MT
2 Ricky Craven DuPont	5.00	10.00
3 Dale Earnhardt Goodwrench Snap-on	10.00	20.00
4 Sterling Marlin Kodak	5.00	12.00
5 Terry Labonte Kellogg's	5.00	10.00
7 Geoff Bodine Exide	5.00	10.00
7 Harry Gant Manheim Auctions	5.00	10.00
15 Lake Speed Quality Care	5.00	10.00
16 Ted Musgrave Family Channel	5.00	10.00
17 Darrell Waltrip Western Auto	5.00	10.00
19 Loy Allen Hooters	5.00	10.00
24 Jeff Gordon DuPont	10.00	20.00
29 Phil Parsons White Rose	5.00	10.00
32 Dale Jarrett Pic-N-Pay Shoes	5.00	10.00
40 Bobby Hamilton Kendall	5.00	10.00
41 Stanley Smith White House Apple Juice	5.00	10.00
41 Stanley Smith White House Apple Juice Gold box	12.00	18.00
43 Harry Gant Black Flag French's	5.00	10.00
46 Shawna Robinson Polaroid	5.00	10.00
52 Ken Schrader AC Delco	5.00	10.00
75 Todd Bodine Factory Stores of America	5.00	10.00
94 No Driver Association White Rose Promo	5.00	10.00
98 Derrike Cope Fingerhut	5.00	10.00

1995 Matchbox White Rose Transporters Super Star Series 1:80

This series of 1:80 scale transporters features drivers from the Winston Cup, Busch and SuperTruck circuits. The series includes special Ken Schrader Budweiser and Kyle Petty Coors Light pieces issued in a acrylic cases.

	EX	NM-MT
1 P.J. Jones Diehard	5.00	10.00
1 Hermie Sadler DeWalt	5.00	10.00
2 Ricky Craven DuPont	5.00	10.00
3 Dale Earnhardt Goodwrench	10.00	20.00
3 Dale Earnhardt Snap On	10.00	20.00
3 Mike Skinner Goodwrench	5.00	10.00
4 Sterling Marlin Kodak	5.00	10.00
6 Rick Carelli Total Petroleum	5.00	10.00
6 Mark Martin Valvoline	5.00	10.00
8 Jeff Burton Raybestos	5.00	10.00
11 Brett Bodine Lowe's	5.00	10.00
12 Derrike Cope Straight Arrow	5.00	10.00
23 Jimmy Spencer Smokin' Joe's	7.50	15.00

	EX	NM-MT
24 Jeff Gordon DuPont	7.50	15.00
24 Scott Lagasse DuPont	5.00	10.00
25 Ken Schrader Budweiser in acrylic case	12.50	25.00
26 Steve Kinser Quaker State	5.00	10.00
28 Dale Jarrett Havoline	5.00	10.00
40 Patty Moise Dial Purex	5.00	10.00
42 Kyle Petty Coors Light in acrylic case	12.50	25.00
57 Jason Keller Budget Gourmet	5.00	10.00
60 Mark Martin Winn Dixie	6.00	12.00
71 Kevin Lepage Vermont Teddy Bear	5.00	10.00
72 Tracy Leslie Detroit Gasket	5.00	10.00
74 Johnny Benson Lipton Tea	5.00	10.00
87 Joe Nemechek Burger King	5.00	10.00
90 Mike Wallace Heilig-Meyers	5.00	10.00
94 Bill Elliott McDonald's	8.00	12.00
95 John Tanner Caterpillar	5.00	10.00
99 Phil Parsons Luxaire	5.00	10.00
08 Bobby Dotter Hyde Tools	5.00	10.00

1996 Matchbox White Rose Transporters Super Star Series 1:80

These 1:80 scale transporters featured many of the new driver and color changes for 1996. The pieces are distributed through White Rose Collectibles and are produced by Matchbox.

	EX	NM-MT
2 Mike Bliss ASE	6.00	12.00
9 Lake Speed SPAM	6.00	12.00
10 Phil Parsons Channellock	6.00	12.00
21 Michael Waltrip Citgo	6.00	12.00
22 Ward Burton MBNA	6.00	12.00
24 Jack Sprague Quaker State	6.00	12.00
24 Jeff Gordon DuPont	7.50	15.00
34 Mike McLaughlin Royal Oak	6.00	12.00
37 John Andretti K-Mart Little Caesars	6.00	12.00
40 Tim Fedewa Kleenex	6.00	12.00
41 Ricky Craven Kodiak in acrylic case	12.00	20.00
43 Rodney Combs Lance	6.00	12.00
77 Bobby Hillin Jr. Jasper Engines	6.00	12.00
88 Dale Jarrett Quality Care	6.00	12.00
94 Bill Elliott McDonald's	6.00	12.00
95 David Green Caterpillar	6.00	12.00

1997 Matchbox White Rose Transporters Super Star Series 1:80

These 1:80 scale transporters featured many of the new driver and color changes for 1997. The pieces are distributed through White Rose Collectibles and are produced by Matchbox. Most transporters were packaged with a car.

	EX	NM-MT
8 Hut Stricklin Circuit City/3000	5.00	12.00
36 Derrike Cope Skittles	5.00	12.00
37 Mark Green Timber Wolf	5.00	12.00
74 Randy LaJoie Fina	5.00	12.00
96 David Green Caterpillar	5.00	12.00

1989 Matchbox White Rose Transporters Super Star Series 1:87

	EX	NM-MT
3 Dale Earnhardt Goodwrench	100.00	200.00
21 Neil Bonnett Citgo	100.00	160.00
28 Cale Yarborough Hardee's	90.00	150.00
43 Richard Petty STP	250.00	350.00

1990 Matchbox White Rose Transporters Super Star Series 1:87

This series of pieces represents some of the most valuable 1:87 scale die cast transporters available. The series features many greats from Winston Cup racing.

	EX	NM-MT
3 Dale Earnhardt Goodwrench	40.00	100.00
6 Mark Martin Folgers	90.00	150.00
9 Bill Elliott Melling	60.00	90.00
20 Rob Moroso Crown	40.00	75.00
43 Richard Petty STP	75.00	125.00
66 Dick Trickle TropArtic	35.00	60.00
94 Sterling Marlin Sunoco name on cab	125.00	225.00
94 Sterling Marlin Sunoco no name on cab	125.00	225.00
NNO Goodyear Racing	12.50	25.00

1991 Matchbox White Rose Transporters Super Star Series 1:87

This series of 1:87 scale transporters features the top names in Winston Cup racing from '91. The pieces are packaged in a red and black box and the year of the release is on the end of each box. The pieces were distributed by White Rose Collectibles.

	EX	NM-MT
3 Dale Earnhardt Goodwrench	15.00	40.00
4 Ernie Irvan Kodak	10.00	18.00
6 Mark Martin Folgers with Ford cab	10.00	20.00
6 Mark Martin Folgers with Mack cab	15.00	30.00
9 Bill Elliott Melling with Ford cab	10.00	20.00
9 Bill Elliott Melling with Mack cab	20.00	40.00
10 Derrike Cope Purolator Pink car	8.00	20.00
10 Derrike Cope Purolator Red car	15.00	30.00
10 Ernie Irvan Mac Tools	12.50	25.00
17 Darrell Waltrip Western Auto	10.00	20.00
22 Sterling Marlin Maxwell House	7.50	15.00
25 Ken Schrader No sponsor	7.50	15.00
28 Davey Allison Havoline black&gold	15.00	40.00
42 Kyle Petty Mello Yello	7.50	15.00
43 Richard Petty STP 20th Anniversary	15.00	30.00
66 Lake Speed TropArtic	7.50	15.00
68 Bobby Hamilton Country Time	7.50	15.00

1992 Matchbox White Rose Transporters Super Star Series 1:87

These pieces are a continuation in the Super Star Series produced by Matchbox and distributed by White Rose Collectibles. Each piece is packaged in a red and checkered flag designed box and has the year of release stamped on the end of the box.

	EX	NM-MT
1 Jeff Gordon Baby Ruth	20.00	50.00
2 Rusty Wallace Penske	6.00	12.00
3 Dale Earnhardt Goodwrench	12.50	25.00
7 Harry Gant Mac Tools	12.50	25.00
7 Alan Kulwicki Hooters	15.00	40.00
8 Dick Trickle Snickers	5.00	10.00
9 Bill Elliott Melling	7.50	15.00
12 Hut Stricklin Raybestos	5.00	10.00
15 Morgan Shepherd Motorcraft	5.00	10.00
18 Dale Jarrett Interstate Batteries	6.00	12.00
26 Brett Bodine Quaker State	5.00	10.00
28 Davey Allison Havoline black&orange	12.50	30.00
30 Michael Waltrip Pennzoil	5.00	10.00
31 Bobby Hillin Jr. Team Ireland	5.00	10.00
43 Richard Petty STP	7.50	15.00
44 Bobby Labonte Slim Jim	6.00	12.00
49 Ed Ferree Fergaed Racing	5.00	10.00
55 Ted Musgrave Jasper Engines	5.00	10.00
59 Robert Pressley Alliance	10.00	20.00
72 Ken Bouchard ADAP	5.00	10.00
89 Jim Sauter Evinrude	5.00	10.00
92 Hut Stricklin Stanley Tools	5.00	10.00

1993 Matchbox White Rose Transporters Super Star Series 1:87

This is the last series of 1:87 scale size transporters done by Matchbox White Rose Collectibles. The pieces were distributed through White Rose Collectibles.

	EX	NM-MT
6 Mark Martin Valvoline	6.00	12.00
8 Jeff Burton TIC Financial	5.00	10.00
8 Jeff Burton Baby Ruth	5.00	10.00
8 Sterling Marlin Raybestos	5.00	10.00
12 Jimmy Spencer Meineke	5.00	10.00
14 Terry Labonte MW Windows	6.00	12.00
21 Morgan Shepherd Citgo	5.00	10.00
22 Bobby Labonte Maxwell House	6.00	12.00
24 Jeff Gordon DuPont	7.50	15.00
25 Hermie Sadler Virginia is for Lovers	5.00	10.00
28 Davey Allison Havoline Mac Tools	12.50	25.00
29 Phil Parsons Matchbox White Rose Collectibles	5.00	10.00
32 Jimmy Horton Active Racing	5.00	10.00
34 Todd Bodine Fiddle Faddle	5.00	10.00
40 Kenny Wallace Dirt Devil	7.50	15.00
41 Phil Parsons Manheim Auctions	5.00	10.00
48 Sterling Marlin Cappio	5.00	10.00
59 Robert Pressley Alliance	12.50	25.00
75 Jack Sprague Staff America	5.00	10.00
83 Lake Speed Purex	5.00	10.00
87 Joe Nemechek Dentyne	5.00	10.00
94 Terry Labonte Sunoco	6.00	12.00
98 Derrike Cope Bojangles	5.00	10.00
98 Jimmy Spencer Moly Black Gold	5.00	10.00
99 Ricky Craven DuPont	5.00	10.00
08 Bobby Dotter DeWalt	5.00	10.00

2007 Motorsports Authentics/RCCA Transporters Bank 1:24

	EX	NM-MT
9 Kasey Kahne Dodge Dealers/708*	35.00	60.00
11 Denny Hamlin Fed Ex Express/708*	40.00	70.00
20 Tony Stewart Home Depot/Home Depot/708*	40.00	70.00
24 Jeff Gordon DuPont Flames/708*	50.00	75.00
29 Kevin Harvick Shell Pennzoil/708*	40.00	70.00
44 Dale Jarrett UPS/708*	40.00	70.00
48 Jimmie Johnson Lowe's/708*	40.00	70.00
00 David Reutimann Domino's/708*	35.00	60.00
01 Mark Martin U.S. Army/708*	35.00	60.00

1996-01 Peachstate/GMP Transporters 1:64

These transporters were produced by GMP and distributed by Peachstate.

	EX	NM-MT
1 Jeff Gordon Baby Ruth RCCA/5000	100.00	150.00
1 Jeff Gordon Baby Ruth/2800	45.00	75.00
3 Dale Earnhardt Goodwrench/2500 1996	75.00	150.00
4 Ernie Irvan Kodak RCCA/3500 1993	40.00	75.00
5 Terry Labonte Kellogg's RCCA	40.00	75.00
6 Mark Martin Valvoline 1996	40.00	60.00
7 Harry Gant Mac Tools with Buick Logo/7500	50.00	80.00
7 Harry Gant Mac Tools w/o Buick Logo/2500	60.00	100.00
8 Sterling Marlin Raybestos RCCA/3500	30.00	60.00
10 Ricky Rudd Tide/2004 1996	25.00	60.00
11 Steve Kinser Quaker State 1996/2800	30.00	60.00
12 Jeremy Mayfield Mobil 1 2001	35.00	60.00
16 Ted Musgrave Family Channel RCCA	40.00	75.00
18 Bobby Labonte Interstate Batteries 1996	40.00	60.00
20 Tony Stewart Home Depot/2400 1999 Rookie of the Year 2000	45.00	75.00
22 Bobby Labonte Maxwell House RCCA/2500	50.00	100.00
26 Johnny Benson Cheerios 2001	35.00	60.00
35 Todd Bodine Tabasco	35.00	60.00
36 Kenny Wallace Dirt Devil RCCA/5000	30.00	60.00
42 Kyle Petty Mello Yello RCCA/3500	25.00	60.00
60 Mark Martin Winn Dixie RCCA/3500	40.00	80.00
75 Rick Mast Remington	30.00	50.00
87 Joe Nemechek Burger King/2500 1996	25.00	60.00
87 Joe Nemechek Dentyne RCCA	35.00	60.00
92 Larry Pearson Stanley RCCA	30.00	55.00
94 Bill Elliott McDonald's/2004 1996	30.00	60.00
97 Chad Little John Deere/2004 1997	40.00	70.00
99 Jeff Burton Citgo SuperGard/1308 '01	35.00	60.00
99 Jeff Burton Exide/1440	35.00	60.00

2002 Peachstate/GMP Transporters 1:64

	EX	NM-MT
17 Matt Kenseth DeWalt/1200	30.00	60.00
20 Tony Stewart Home Depot/1500	30.00	60.00
21 Elliott Sadler Motorcraft/1400	30.00	60.00

2003 Peachstate/GMP Transporters 1:64

	EX	NM-MT
12 Ryan Newman Alltel/1200	30.00	60.00

1993 Racing Champions Transporters 1:43

	EX	NM-MT
3 Dale Earnhardt Goodwrench	20.00	40.00
7 Alan Kulwicki Hooters	30.00	50.00
8 Sterling Marlin Raybestos	12.50	25.00
24 Jeff Gordon DuPont	20.00	40.00
27 Hut Stricklin McDonald's	10.00	25.00
28 Davey Allison Havoline	12.50	25.00

1994 Racing Champions Transporters 1:43

	EX	NM-MT
10 Ricky Rudd Tide	10.00	25.00
19 Loy Allen Hooters	8.00	20.00

1991 Racing Champions Transporters 1:64

This small series was the first group of transporters done by Racing Champions. They were packaged in a black box and distributed through retail and hobby outlets.

	EX	NM-MT
2 Rusty Wallace Penske Racing	18.00	30.00
9 Bill Elliott Melling with Red paint scheme	60.00	100.00
11 Geoff Bodine	10.00	20.00
28 Davey Allison Havoline	30.00	50.00

1992 Racing Champions Transporters 1:64

This series of 1:64 scale transporters features many of the top names from both Winston Cup and Busch in 1992. The pieces were packaged in a black box and were distributed through hobby and retail outlets.

	EX	NM-MT
1 Jeff Gordon Baby Ruth	50.00	75.00
1 Rick Mast Majik Market	10.00	20.00
2 Rusty Wallace Penske	10.00	20.00
3 Dale Earnhardt Goodwrench	20.00	40.00
4 Ernie Irvan Kodak	8.00	16.00
5 Jay Fogleman Inn Keeper	6.00	12.00
5 Ricky Rudd Tide	7.50	15.00
6 Mark Martin Valvoline	8.00	16.00
7 Alan Kulwicki Hooters	30.00	60.00
9 Bill Elliott Melling with Blue paint scheme	12.50	25.00
9 Chad Little Melling	10.00	25.00
9 Joe Bessey Auto Palace	6.00	12
10 Derrike Cope Purolator	6.00	12
11 Bill Elliott Amoco	8.00	16
12 Bobby Allison Allison Motorsports	7.50	15
12 Hut Stricklin Raybestos	6.00	12
14 A.J. Foyt	10.00	20
15 Geoff Bodine Motorcraft	6.00	12
16 Wally Dallenbach Jr. Roush Racing	10.00	20
17 Darrell Waltrip Western Auto	6.00	12
17 Darrell Waltrip Western Auto Promo	7.50	15
18 Dale Jarrett Interstate Batteries	6.00	12
20 Joe Ruttman Fina	12.50	25
21 Morgan Shepherd Citgo	6.00	12
22 Sterling Marlin Maxwell House	6.00	12
25 Ken Schrader No Sponsor	7.50	15
25 Bill Venturini Rain X	25.00	50
26 Brett Bodine Quaker State	6.00	12
28 Davey Allison Havoline	15.00	30
30 Michael Waltrip Pennzoil	6.00	12
33 Harry Gant Food Lion	10.00	20
36 Kenny Wallace Dirt Devil	12.50	25
42 Kyle Petty Mello Yello	6.00	12
43 Richard Petty STP	7.50	15
43 Richard Petty STP Fan Appreciation Tour	10.00	20
49 Stanley Smith Ameritron Batteries	15.00	30
59 Andy Belmont FDP Brakes	15.00	30
59 Robert Pressley Alliance	25.00	50
60 Mark Martin Winn Dixie	15.00	30
66 Cale Yarborough TropArtic	6.00	12
68 Bobby Hamilton Country Time	6.00	12
70 J.D. McDuffie Son's Auto	15.00	30
71 Dave Marcis Big Apple Market	10.00	20
72 Ken Bouchard ADAP	6.00	12
90 Wally Dallenbach Jr. Ford Motorsports	15.00	30
97 Terry Labonte Sunoco	15.00	30

1993 Racing Champions Transporters 1:64

This series of 1:64 transporters was issued in red boxes with a 1:64 scale car. The pieces feature the top nar racing. The Ricky Rudd piece in the series comes wi different paint schemes. Promo pieces were made o Earnhardt, Darrell Waltrip and Hut Stricklin.

	EX	NM
1 Jeff Gordon Baby Ruth	40.00	7
1 Rick Mast Majik Market	7.50	1
2 Rusty Wallace Penske	8.00	2
3 Dale Earnhardt Goodwrench	30.00	6
3 Dale Earnhardt Goodwrench Bank/10,000	35.00	6
3 Dale Earnhardt Goodwrench Promo	50.00	10
3 Dale Earnhardt Winston Win	40.00	7
4 Ernie Irvan Kodak	7.50	1
4 Ernie Irvan Kodak Bank	8.00	2
5 Ricky Rudd Tide with Orange paint scheme	7.50	1
5 Ricky Rudd Tide with White paint scheme	8.00	2
6 Mark Martin Valvoline	8.00	2
7 Alan Kulwicki Hooters	20.00	4
7 Alan Kulwicki Hooters Bank	20.00	4
8 Sterling Marlin Raybestos	6.00	1
11 Bill Elliott Amoco	8.00	2
11 Bill Elliott Amoco Bank/5000	8.00	2
12 Jimmy Spencer Meineke	6.00	1
14 Terry Labonte Kellogg's	15.00	3
15 Geoff Bodine Motorcraft	6.00	1
17 Darrell Waltrip Western Auto	6.00	1
17 Darrell Waltrip	7.50	1

estern Auto Promo		
e Jarrett Iterstate Batteries	6.00	12.00
organ Shepherd itgo	6.00	12.00
bby Labonte axwell House	25.00	50.00
Gordon uPont	25.00	50.00
f Gordon uPont Bank/10,000	25.00	50.00
ett Bodine uaker State	6.00	12.00
Stricklin cDonald's	6.00	12.00
Stricklin cDonald's Bank/7500	12.50	25.00
t Stricklin cDonald's Promo	8.00	16.00
vey Allison avoline	12.50	25.00
vey Allison avoline Bank	20.00	40.00
chael Waltrip ennzoil	6.00	12.00
rry Gant ood Lion	6.00	12.00
le Petty ello Yello	6.00	12.00
k Wilson TP	6.00	12.00
dy Belmont DP Brakes	12.50	25.00
rk Martin inn Dixie	10.00	20.00
dd Bodine actory Stores of America	6.00	12.00
Nemechek entyne	6.00	12.00
rrike Cope ojangles	6.00	12.00
Dodge IROC	10.00	20.00

1993 Racing Champions remier Transporters 1:64

vas the first year Racing Champions did 1:64 scale r series pieces. The pieces come in a black shadow box. ox has a gold stamped quantity of production on the

	EX	NM-MT
y Wallace ord Motorsports	20.00	35.00
Earnhardt oodwrench/7500	40.00	100.00
e Irvan odak	20.00	35.00
ky Rudd de	20.00	35.00
Kulwicki ooters/7500	40.00	80.00
ling Marlin aybestos	18.00	30.00
Elliott udweiser/5000	20.00	35.00
Gordon uPont/7500	30.00	50.00
tt Bodine uaker State Bank/2500	18.00	30.00
t Stricklin cDonald's	18.00	30.00
vey Allison avoline/5028	25.00	50.00
ie Irvan ac Tools	25.00	45.00
ry Gant hevrolet/3000	18.00	30.00
ry Gant hevrolet Food Lion ank/2500	18.00	30.00
le Petty ello Yello	18.00	30.00
Driver Association imer Ford cab	18.00	30.00
Driver Association imer paint scheme Kenworth	15.00	25.00
Driver Association ickyard 400 special	30.00	50.00
Dodge IROC Bank/5000	15.00	30.00

1994 Racing Champions Transporters Hobby 1:64

eries of Transporters was issued directly to hobby shops. as packaged in a Racing Champions yellow box.

	EX	NM-MT
y Wallace enske	10.00	20.00
ing Marlin odak	7.50	20.00
Labonte ellogg's	10.00	20.00
e Jarrett terstate Batteries	10.00	20.00
chael Waltrip ennzoil	6.00	15.00
ry Gant eo Jackson	6.00	15.00
e Petty ello Yello	6.00	15.00

1994 Racing Champions Transporters Retail 1:64

eries features NASCAR racing transporters issued through outlets and packaged in a red clear window box. Some so issued in a yellow box hobby version and solid red nk versions. All packages include the hauler as well as a e cast car. The year of issue is featured on the front of the d a driver checklist on the back. Some drivers on the list ot produced for this set.

	EX	NM-MT
1 Rick Mast Majik Market	6.00	15.00
1 Rick Mast Precision Products	6.00	15.00
2 Ricky Craven DuPont	6.00	15.00
2 Rusty Wallace Penske	8.00	20.00
3 Dale Earnhardt Goodwrench Promo	40.00	80.00
4 Sterling Marlin Kodak	6.00	15.00
4 Sterling Marlin Kodak Bank/1500	8.00	20.00
5 Terry Labonte Kellogg's	8.00	20.00
6 Mark Martin Valvoline	8.00	20.00
7 Geoff Bodine Exide Batteries	6.00	15.00
7 Harry Gant Manheim Auctions	6.00	15.00
8 Jeff Burton Raybestos	6.00	15.00
10 Ricky Rudd Tide	6.00	15.00
11 Bill Elliott Amoco	6.00	15.00
15 Lake Speed Quality Care	6.00	15.00
16 Ted Musgrave Family Channel	6.00	15.00
17 Darrell Waltrip Western Auto	6.00	15.00
18 Dale Jarrett Interstate Batteries	6.00	15.00
19 Loy Allen Hooters	6.00	15.00
22 Bobby Labonte Maxwell House	6.00	15.00
24 Jeff Gordon DuPont	10.00	20.00
24 Jeff Gordon DuPont Bank	25.00	50.00
26 Brett Bodine Quaker State	6.00	15.00
27 Jimmy Spencer McDonald's	6.00	15.00
28 Ernie Irvan Havoline	6.00	15.00
30 Michael Waltrip Pennzoil	6.00	15.00
33 Harry Gant Leo Jackson	6.00	15.00
33 Bobby Labonte Dentyne	30.00	50.00
40 Bobby Hamilton Kendall	6.00	15.00
41 Joe Nemechek Meineke	6.00	15.00
42 Kyle Petty Mello Yello	6.00	15.00
52 Ken Schrader AC Delco	6.00	15.00
54 Robert Pressley Manheim Auctions	6.00	15.00
60 Mark Martin Winn Dixie	8.00	20.00
75 Todd Bodine Factory Stores of America	6.00	15.00
98 Derrike Cope Fingerhut	6.00	15.00

1994 Racing Champions Premier Transporters 1:64

This is a small series of 1:64 scale Premier transporters. It does however feature four of the best and most popular drivers in racing. The Jeff Gordon piece was a special made for the Winston Select.

	EX	NM-MT
3 Dale Earnhardt Goodwrench	75.00	150.00
4 Sterling Marlin Kodak FunSaver/3000	18.00	40.00
24 Jeff Gordon DuPont Winston Select special	20.00	35.00
33 Harry Gant Farewell Tour	20.00	35.00

1995 Racing Champions Preview Transporters 1:64

This series of 1:64 scale transporters was the first time Racing Champions produced preview pieces for transporters. The series features drivers from both the Winston Cup and Busch circuits.

	EX	NM-MT
2 Rusty Wallace Penske	8.00	20.00
7 Geoff Bodine Exide	7.50	15.00
10 Ricky Rudd Tide	7.50	15.00
14 Terry Labonte MW Windows	7.50	15.00
16 Ted Musgrave Family Channel	7.50	15.00
24 Jeff Gordon DuPont	10.00	20.00
27 Loy Allen Hooters	7.50	15.00
38 Elton Sawyer Red Carpet	7.50	15.00
40 Bobby Hamilton Kendall	7.50	15.00
57 Jason Keller Budget Gourmet	7.50	15.00

1995 Racing Champions Transporters 1:64

Many of the top names in Winston Cup and Busch are featured in this series. The pieces were distributed through both hobby and retail outlets. A special series of Jeff Gordon Signature Series die cast was issued in '95 and included a 1:64 transporter.

	EX	NM-MT
2 Rusty Wallace Penske	7.50	15.00
5 Terry Labonte Kellogg's	7.50	15.00
6 Tommy Houston Red Devil	6.00	12.00
6 Mark Martin Valvoline	7.50	15.00
7 Geoff Bodine Exide	6.00	12.00
8 Jeff Burton Raybestos	6.00	12.00
8 Kenny Wallace Red Dog	6.00	12.00
10 Ricky Rudd Tide	6.00	12.00
12 Derrike Cope Straight Arrow	6.00	12.00
18 Bobby Labonte Interstate Batteries	6.00	12.00
23 Chad Little Bayer	6.00	12.00
24 Jeff Gordon DuPont	10.00	18.00
24 Jeff Gordon DuPont Signature Series 1995 WC Champion	20.00	35.00
26 Steve Kinser Quaker State	6.00	12.00
27 Loy Allen Hooter's	6.00	12.00
28 Dale Jarrett Ernie Irvan Havoline both signatures on trailer	6.00	12.00
34 Mike McLaughlin French's	6.00	12.00
40 Patty Moise Dial	6.00	12.00
44 David Green Slim Jim	6.00	12.00
47 Jeff Fuller Sunoco	6.00	12.00
60 Mark Martin Winn Dixie	7.50	15.00
90 Mike Wallace Heilig-Meyers	6.00	12.00
94 Bill Elliott McDonald's	7.50	15.00
94 Bill Elliott McDonald's Thunderbat	10.00	20.00
95 Brickyard 400 Bank/2500	6.00	12.00
99 Phil Parsons Luxaire	6.00	12.00

1995 Racing Champions Premier Transporters 1:64

This series of 1:64 scale transporters was higlighted by two beer special transporters. The Rusty Wallace Miller Genuine Draft transporter and the Kyle Petty Coors Light transporters both came in acrylic cases.

	EX	NM-MT
2 Rusty Wallace Miller Genuine Draft in acrylic case	30.00	45.00
2 Rusty Wallace Penske Bank	30.00	40.00
8 Jeff Burton Raybestos/1000	10.00	20.00
12 Derrike Cope Straight Arrow	10.00	20.00
26 Steve Kinser Quaker State	12.00	20.00
26 Steve Kinser Quaker State Bank	25.00	40.00
27 Loy Allen Hooters	10.00	20.00
32 Dale Jarrett Mac Tools/3000	25.00	40.00
40 Bobby Hamilton Kendall	10.00	20.00
40 Patty Moise Dial	10.00	20.00
42 Kyle Petty Coors Light in acrylic case	30.00	50.00
90 Mike Wallace Heilig-Meyers	10.00	20.00
94 Bill Elliott McDonald's	10.00	20.00
95 Brickyard 400/10,000	10.00	20.00

1996 Racing Champions Preview Transporters 1:64

This series of transporters was issued in a red box and has the word preview below the year of release. The pieces feature both Winston Cup and Busch series drivers.

	EX	NM-MT
4 Sterling Marlin Kodak	6.00	15.00
5 Terry Labonte Kellogg's	7.00	14.00
6 Mark Martin Valvoline	7.00	14.00
11 Brett Bodine Lowe's	6.00	12.00
12 Derrike Cope Mane N' Tail	6.00	12.00
16 Ted Musgrave Family Channel	6.00	12.00
17 Darrell Waltrip Western Auto	7.00	14.00
47 Jeff Fuller Sunoco	6.00	12.00
57 Jason Keller Slim Jim	6.00	12.00
90 Mike Wallace Heilig-Meyers	6.00	12.00

1996 Racing Champions Transporters 1:64

These pieces were issued in three different variations. Transporters were issued with no cars, one car, and with two cars. Transporters with one or two cars carry a slight premium over those issued without cars. The Chad Little transporters were issued in standard Racing Champion packaging and in John Deere promotional boxes. The Ken Schrader transporters were issued as part of a special Budweiser program. The Ricky Craven transporter was produced for and distributed by his fan club. The Mark Martin Winn Dixie transporter was distributed in Winn Dixie stores primarily in the Southeast.

	EX	NM-MT
1 Rick Mast Hooter's	10.00	20.00
1 Hermie Sadler DeWalt	10.00	20.00
2 Rusty Wallace Miller Genuine Draft	15.00	30.00
2 Rusty Wallace Penske	10.00	20.00
2 Rusty Wallace Penske with one car or two cars	12.50	25.00
3 Mike Skinner Goodwrench 1995 Champ with truck(s)	10.00	20.00
4 Sterling Marlin Kodak with one or two cars	12.50	25.00
5 Terry Labonte Kellogg's with one car or two cars	15.00	30.00
7 Geoff Bodine QVC	10.00	20.00
8 Hut Stricklin Circuit City	10.00	20.00
10 Ricky Rudd Tide with one car or two cars	12.50	25.00
11 Brett Bodine Lowe's	10.00	20.00
11 Brett Bodine Lowe's with one car or two cars	12.50	25.00
14 Patty Moise Dial Purex with one car or two cars	12.50	25.00
15 Wally Dallenbach Hayes	10.00	20.00
17 Darrell Waltrip Parts America	10.00	20.00
21 Michael Waltrip Citgo with one car or two cars	12.50	25.00
22 Ward Burton MBNA	10.00	20.00
23 Chad Little John Deere	10.00	20.00
23 Chad Little John Deere with one car or two cars	12.50	25.00
23 Chad Little John Deere Promo	10.00	25.00
23 Chad Little John Deere with one car Promo	15.00	35.00
24 Jeff Gordon DuPont with one car or two cars	15.00	30.00
25 Ken Schrader Budweiser	20.00	40.00
25 Ken Schrader Budweiser Chrome	150.00	300.00
28 Ernie Irvan Havoline	10.00	20.00
28 Ernie Irvan Havoline with one car or two cars	12.50	25.00
29 Steve Grissom Cartoon Network	10.00	20.00
29 Steve Grissom Cartoon Network with one car or two cars	12.50	25.00
29 Steve Grissom WCW	10.00	20.00
29 Steve Grissom WCW with one car or two cars	12.50	25.00
29 No Driver Association Scooby-Doo woth one car or two	10.00	20.00
30 Johnny Benson Pennzoil	10.00	20.00
32 Dale Jarrett Band-Aid with one car or two cars	25.00	40.00
37 John Andretti K-Mart Promo	15.00	25.00
41 Ricky Craven Kodiak Fan Club	20.00	40.00
43 Rodney Combs Lance	10.00	20.00
43 Bobby Hamilton STP	10.00	20.00
43 Bobby Hamilton STP with one car or two cars	12.50	25.00
44 Bobby Labonte Shell	15.00	25.00
47 Jeff Fuller Sunoco	10.00	20.00
60 Mark Martin Winn Dixie	15.00	25.00
60 Mark Martin Winn Dixie with one car or two cars	20.00	35.00
74 Johnny Benson Lipton Tea with one car or two cars	10.00	20.00
74 Randy LaJoie Fina	10.00	20.00
87 Joe Nemechek Bell South	10.00	20.00
87 Joe Nemechek Burger King	10.00	20.00
88 Dale Jarrett Quality Care	30.00	50.00
88 Dale Jarrett Quality Care with one car or two cars	30.00	50.00
94 Bill Elliott McDonald's	10.00	20.00
94 Bill Elliott McDonald's with one car or two cars	12.50	25.00
94 Bill Elliott McDonald's Monopoly	10.00	20.00
94 Bill Elliott McDonald's Monopoly with one or two cars	12.50	25.00

1996 Racing Champions Premier Transporters 1:64

These pieces were issued with a premier car and distributed through both hobby and retail outlets.

	EX	NM-MT
2 Rusty Wallace Penske	15.00	30.00
6 Mark Martin Valvoline	15.00	30.00
11 Brett Bodine Lowe's	12.50	25.00
24 Jeff Gordon DuPont	15.00	30.00
29 Steve Grissom Cartoon Network	12.50	25.00
29 Steve Grissom WCW	12.50	25.00
43 Bobby Hamilton STP Silver	12.50	25.00
88 Dale Jarrett Quality Care	15.00	30.00
94 Bill Elliott McDonald's	15.00	30.00

1997 Racing Champions Preview Transporters 1:64

Many of the top drivers from the Winston Cup circuit are featured in this series. The pieces were distributed through both hobby and retail outlets.

	EX	NM-MT
4 Sterling Marlin Kodak	12.00	25.00
5 Terry Labonte Kellogg's	12.00	20.00
6 Mark Martin Valvoline	12.00	20.00
7 Geoff Bodine QVC	10.00	20.00
8 Hut Stricklin Circuit City	10.00	20.00
24 Jeff Gordon DuPont	12.50	25.00
29 Robert Pressley Scooby-Doo	10.00	20.00
75 Rick Mast Remington	10.00	20.00

1997 Racing Champions Transporters 1:64

Like 1996, Racing Champions has distributed standard transporters in three different variations. These transporters come with one car, two cars, or no car. This series features drivers from both the Winston Cup and Busch circuits.

	EX	NM-MT
1 Hermie Sadler DeWalt	10.00	20.00
1 Hermie Sadler DeWalt with one car or two cars	12.50	25.00
2 Ricky Craven Raybestos	10.00	20.00
2 Rusty Wallace Penske	10.00	20.00
4 Sterling Marlin Kodak	10.00	20.00
4 Sterling Marlin Kodak with one car or two	12.50	25.00
5 Terry Labonte Kellogg's	10.00	20.00
5 Terry Labonte Kellogg's 1996 Winston Cup Champion	12.50	25.00
6 Mark Martin Valvoline	10.00	20.00
6 Mark Martin Valvoline with one car or two cars	12.50	25.00
7 Geoff Bodine QVC	10.00	20.00
8 Hut Stricklin Circuit City	10.00	20.00
9 Jeff Burton Track Gear	10.00	20.00
10 Phil Parsons Channellock	10.00	20.00
10 Ricky Rudd Tide	10.00	20.00
10 Ricky Rudd Tide with one car or two cars	12.50	25.00
11 Brett Bodine Close Call	10.00	20.00
11 Brett Bodine Close Call with one car or two cars	12.50	25.00
11 Jimmy Foster Speedvision	10.00	20.00
11 Jimmy Foster Speedvision with one car or two cars	12.50	25.00
16 Ted Musgrave Primestar	10.00	20.00
17 Darrell Waltrip Parts America	10.00	20.00
17 Darrell Waltrip Parts America with one or two cars	12.50	25.00
19 Gary Bradberry CSR	10.00	20.00
19 Gary Bradberry CSR with one car or two cars	12.50	25.00
21 Michael Waltrip Citgo	10.00	20.00
24 Jeff Gordon DuPont	12.50	25.00
25 Ricky Craven Bud Lizard with one car	20.00	35.00
28 Ernie Irvan Havoline 10th Anniversary paint scheme	10.00	20.00
28 Ernie Irvan Havoline with one or two cars 10th Anniversary paint scheme	12.50	25.00
29 No Driver Association Tom & Jerry	10.00	20.00
29 Jeff Green Tom and Jerry with one or two cars	12.50	25.00
29 Robert Pressley Cartoon Network	10.00	20.00
30 Johnny Benson Pennzoil	10.00	20.00
32 Dale Jarrett Gillette	10.00	20.00
32 Dale Jarrett Gillette with one or two cars	12.50	25.00
32 Dale Jarrett White Rain	10.00	20.00
33 Tim Fedewa	10.00	20.00

Kleenex

	EX	NM-MT
34 Mike McLaughlin Royal Oak	10.00	20.00
34 Mike McLaughlin Royal Oak with one or two cars	12.50	25.00
36 Todd Bodine Stanley	10.00	20.00
36 Derrike Cope Skittles	10.00	20.00
38 Elton Sawyer Barbasol	10.00	20.00
38 Elton Sawyer Barbasol with one or two cars	12.50	25.00
40 Robby Gordon Sabco Racing	10.00	20.00
43 Dennis Setzer Lance	10.00	20.00
43 Rodney Combs Lance	10.00	20.00
46 Wally Dallenbach First Union	10.00	20.00
57 Jason Keller Slim Jim	10.00	20.00
60 Mark Martin Winn Dixie	10.00	20.00
60 Mark Martin Winn Dixie Promo	18.00	30.00
63 Tracy Leslie Lysol	10.00	20.00
72 Mike Dillon Detroit Gasket	10.00	20.00
74 Randy LaJoie Fina	10.00	20.00
74 Randy LaJoie Fina with one or two cars	12.50	25.00
75 Rick Mast Remington	10.00	20.00
75 Rick Mast Remington with one or two cars	12.50	25.00
88 Kevin Lepage Hype	10.00	20.00
88 Kevin Lepage Hype with one or two cars	12.50	25.00
90 Dick Trickle Heilig-Meyers	10.00	20.00
94 Ron Barfield New Holland	10.00	20.00
94 Ron Barfield New Holland with one or two cars	12.50	25.00
94 Bill Elliott McDonald's	10.00	20.00
96 David Green Caterpillar	10.00	20.00
96 David Green Caterpillar Promo	10.00	25.00
97 No Driver Association Brickyard 400	10.00	20.00
97 Chad Little John Deere	8.00	20.00
97 Chad Little John Deere Promo with one car	10.00	20.00
99 Jeff Burton Exide	10.00	20.00
00 Buckshot Jones Aqua Fresh	10.00	20.00
00 Buckshot Jones Aqua Fresh with one or two cars	12.50	25.00

1997 Racing Champions Premier Transporters 1:64

This is the second year that Racing Champions has produced premier transporters that are packaged with a premier car. This series is highlighted by the special 1996 Winston Cup Champion Terry Labonte Kellogg's transporter.

	EX	NM-MT
5 Terry Labonte Kellogg's	20.00	35.00
29 Robert Pressley Cartoon Network	15.00	30.00
60 Mark Martin Winn Dixie	20.00	35.00

1998 Racing Champions Transporters 1:64

The 1:64 scale transporters that appear in this series are replicas of many of the cars that ran in the 1997 season, but also many replicas are of the cars slated to appear in the 1998 season. The transporters in this series are packaged in special boxes that display the NASCAR 50th anniversary logo.

	EX	NM-MT
4 Bobby Hamilton Kodak	8.00	20.00
4 Bobby Hamilton Kodak with Car	10.00	25.00
4 Jeff Purvis Lance	8.00	20.00
4 Jeff Purvis Lance with car	10.00	25.00
5 Terry Labonte Kellogg's	10.00	25.00
5 Terry Labonte Kellogg's with car	12.00	30.00
5 Terry Labonte Kellogg's Corny	10.00	25.00
5 Terry Labonte Kellogg's Corny with car	12.00	30.00
6 Joe Bessey Power Team	8.00	20.00
6 Joe Bessey Power Team with car	10.00	25.00
6 Mark Martin Eagle One	10.00	20.00
6 Mark Martin Eagle One with car	10.00	25.00
8 Hut Stricklin Circuit City	8.00	20.00
8 Hut Stricklin Circuit City with car	10.00	25.00
9 Lake Speed Birthday Cake	8.00	20.00
9 Lake Speed Birthday Cake with car	10.00	25.00
9 Lake Speed Huckleberry Hound	8.00	20.00
9 Lake Speed Huckleberry Hound with car	10.00	25.00
10 Ricky Rudd Tide	10.00	20.00
10 Ricky Rudd Tide with car	10.00	25.00
11 Brett Bodine Paychex	8.00	20.00
13 Jerry Nadeau First Plus	8.00	20.00
13 Jerry Nadeau First Plus with car	10.00	25.00
21 Michael Waltrip Citgo	8.00	20.00
21 Michael Waltrip Citgo with car	10.00	25.00
21 Michael Waltrip Goodwill Games	8.00	20.00
21 Michael Waltrip Goodwill Games with car	10.00	25.00
30 Mike Cope Slim Jim	8.00	20.00
33 Ken Schrader Petree	8.00	20.00
35 Todd Bodine Tabasco	8.00	20.00
35 Todd Bodine Tabasco with car	10.00	25.00
36 Ernie Irvan M&M's	15.00	30.00
36 Ernie Irvan M&M's with car	15.00	35.00
36 Ernie Irvan Skittles	10.00	20.00
36 Ernie Irvan Skittles with car	10.00	25.00
40 Kevin Lepage Channellock	8.00	20.00
40 Sterling Marlin Sabco	10.00	20.00
40 Sterling Marlin Sabco with car	10.00	25.00
42 Joe Nemechek BellSouth	8.00	20.00
46 Wally Dallenbach First Union	8.00	20.00
50 Ricky Craven Hendrick	8.00	20.00
50 Ricky Craven Hendrick with car	10.00	25.00
59 Robert Pressley Kingsford	8.00	20.00
59 Robert Pressley Kingsford with car	10.00	25.00
60 Mark Martin Winn Dixie	10.00	20.00
60 Mark Martin Winn Dixie with car	10.00	25.00
60 Mark Martin Winn Dixie Promo with car	20.00	40.00
66 Elliott Sadler Phillips 66	8.00	20.00
66 Elliott Sadler Phillips 66 with car	10.00	25.00
75 Rick Mast Remington	8.00	20.00
94 Bill Elliott Happy Meal with car	10.00	25.00
94 Bill Elliott McDonald's Service Merchandise Promo with Gold car	10.00	25.00
96 David Green Caterpillar Promo with car	10.00	25.00
97 Chad Little John Deere	8.00	20.00
99 Jeff Burton Exide	10.00	20.00
99 Jeff Burton Exide with car	10.00	25.00
00 Buckshot Jones Aqua Fresh	8.00	20.00
00 Buckshot Jones Aqua Fresh with car	10.00	25.00

1998 Racing Champions Transporters Gold 1:64

This was a special series produced by Racing Champions to celebrate NASCAR's 50th anniversary. Each car was packaged in a gold window box and was produced in a limited edition of 1500. Each transporter and 1:64 car was plated in gold chrome and featured a serial number on its chassis.

	EX	NM-MT
4 Bobby Hamilton Kodak	12.50	30.00
4 Jeff Purvis Lance	12.50	30.00
5 Terry Labonte Kellogg's	20.00	50.00
5 Terry Labonte Kellogg's Corny	15.00	40.00
6 Joe Bessey Power Team	12.50	30.00
6 Mark Martin Eagle One	20.00	50.00
6 Mark Martin Valvoline	20.00	50.00
8 Hut Stricklin Circuit City	12.50	30.00
9 Jerry Nadeau Zombie Island	12.50	30.00
9 Lake Speed Birthday Cake	12.50	30.00
9 Lake Speed Huckleberry Hound	12.50	30.00
10 Ricky Rudd Tide	12.50	30.00
11 Brett Bodine Paychex	12.50	30.00
13 Jerry Nadeau First Plus	12.50	30.00
16 Ted Musgrave Primestar	12.50	30.00
19 Tony Raines Yellow Freight	12.50	30.00
21 Michael Waltrip Citgo	12.50	30.00
23 Jimmy Spencer Winston/1998 in solid box	15.00	40.00
29 Hermie Sadler Phillips 66 DeWalt	12.50	30.00
30 Mike Cope Slim Jim	12.50	30.00
33 Tim Fedewa Kleenex	12.50	30.00
33 Ken Schrader Petree	12.50	30.00
35 Todd Bodine Tabasco	12.50	30.00
36 Ernie Irvan Skittles	15.00	40.00
36 Ernie Irvan M&M's	20.00	50.00
40 Rick Fuller Channellock	12.50	30.00
40 Sterling Marlin Sabco	30.00	50.00
42 Joe Nemechek BellSouth	12.50	30.00
46 Wally Dallenbach First Union	12.50	30.00
50 Ricky Craven Bud/1998 in solid box	12.50	30.00
50 Ricky Craven Hendrick	12.50	30.00
59 Robert Pressley Kingsford	12.50	30.00
66 Elliott Sadler Phillips 66	12.50	30.00
74 Randy LaJoie Fina	12.50	30.00
75 Rick Mast Remington	12.50	30.00
78 Gary Bradberry Pilot	12.50	30.00
88 Kevin Schwantz Ryder	12.50	30.00
90 Dick Trickle Heilig-Meyers	12.50	30.00
94 Bill Elliott Happy Meal	20.00	50.00
94 Bill Elliott McDonald's	20.00	50.00
94 Bill Elliott Mac Tonight	20.00	50.00
94 Bill Elliott McDonald's w/5-cars	20.00	40.00
97 Chad Little John Deere Promo	20.00	50.00
00 Buckshot Jones Aqua Fresh	25.00	50.00

1998 Racing Champions Transporters Signature Series 1:64

This is a special series produced by Racing Champions to celebrate NASCAR's 50th anniversary. It parallels the regular 1998 series. Each car is packaged in a decorative box with the driver's facsimile autograph on the front.

	EX	NM-MT
4 Bobby Hamilton Kodak	6.00	15.00
5 Terry Labonte Kellogg's	10.00	20.00
6 Mark Martin Valvoline	10.00	20.00
8 Hut Stricklin Circuit City	6.00	15.00
9 Lake Speed Huckleberry Hound	6.00	15.00
10 Ricky Rudd Tide	10.00	20.00
11 Brett Bodine Paychex	6.00	15.00
13 Jerry Nadeau First Plus	6.00	15.00
21 Michael Waltrip Citgo	6.00	15.00
33 Ken Schrader Petree	6.00	15.00
35 Todd Bodine Tabasco	6.00	15.00
42 Joe Nemechek Bell South	6.00	15.00
59 Robert Pressley Kingsford	6.00	15.00
94 Bill Elliott Happy Meal	10.00	20.00

1999 Racing Champions Transporters 1:64

The 1:64 scale transporters that appear in this series are replicas of many of the cars that ran in the 1998 season, but also some slated to appear in 1999. The die-cast in this series were packaged in special boxes that display the Racing Champions "The Originals" 10th anniversary logo.

	EX	NM-MT
4 Bobby Hamilton Kodak	8.00	20.00
5 Terry Labonte Kellogg's	10.00	20.00
6 Joe Bessey Power Team	8.00	20.00
6 Mark Martin Valvoline	10.00	20.00
6 Mark Martin Valvoline Chrome/1499	15.00	30.00
9 Jerry Nadeau Dexter's Laboratory	8.00	20.00
10 Ricky Rudd Tide	8.00	20.00
11 Brett Bodine Paychex	8.00	20.00
11 Brett Bodine Paychex Chrome	12.50	25.00
15 Ken Schrader Oakwood Homes	8.00	20.00
16 Kevin Lepage Primestar	8.00	20.00
17 Matt Kenseth DeWalt	25.00	40.00
18 Butch Miller Dana SuperTruck Promo	30.00	50.00
23 Jimmy Spencer TCE Lights	8.00	20.00
25 Wally Dallenbach Hendrick	8.00	20.00
26 Johnny Benson Cheerios	8.00	20.00
30 Derrike Cope Bahari Racing set w/4-cars	15.00	30.00
36 Ken Schrader M&M's	10.00	20.00
36 Ken Schrader M&M's with 3-cars	12.50	25.00
38 Glen Allen Barbasol	8.00	20.00
43 Richard Petty STP w/7 championship cars	20.00	40.00
50 Mark Green Dr. Pepper	8.00	20.00
55 Kenny Wallace Square D	8.00	20.00
94 Bill Elliott Drive Thru	10.00	20.00
97 Chad Little John Deere	8.00	20.00
99 Jeff Burton Exide	8.00	20.00

1999 Racing Champions Transporters 24K Gold 1:64

These transporter and car sets were issued in a gold checkered flag designed "Reflections in Gold" window box. Each transporter and 1:64 scale car was produced with a complete gold chrome finish. The stated production run was 1499 for each piece.

	EX	NM-MT
4 Bobby Hamilton Kodak	15.00	40.00
5 Terry Labonte Kellogg's	30.00	60.00
6 Mark Martin Valvoline	30.00	60.00
6 Joe Bessey Power Team	15.00	40.00
10 Ricky Rudd Tide	20.00	40.00
11 Brett Bodine Paychex	15.00	40.00
16 Kevin Lepage Primestar	15.00	40.00
25 Wally Dallenbach Hendrick	15.00	40.00
32 Jeff Green Kleenex	15.00	40.00
36 Ernie Irvan M&M's	20.00	40.00
55 Kenny Wallace Square D	15.00	40.00
77 Robert Pressley Jasper	15.00	40.00
94 Bill Elliott Drive Thru	25.00	50.00
97 Chad Little John Deere	20.00	50.00
99 Jeff Burton Exide	15.00	40.00

1999 Racing Champions Transporters Gold 1:64

These transporter and car sets were issued in a gold checkered flag designed window box. Each transporter tractor and 1:64 scale car were produced using gold chrome paint. The stated production run was 2499 for each piece.

	EX	NM-MT
4 Bobby Hamilton Kodak	12.50	30.00
5 Terry Labonte Kellogg's	20.00	50.00
6 Mark Martin Valvoline	20.00	50.00
9 Jerry Nadeau Cartoon Network	12.50	30.00
10 Ricky Rudd Tide	12.50	30.00
11 Brett Bodine Paychex	12.50	30.00
15 Ken Schrader Oakwood Homes	12.50	30.00
16 Kevin Lepage Primestar	12.50	30.00
17 Matt Kenseth DeWalt	40.00	80.00
23 Jimmy Spencer TCE	12.50	30.00
25 Wally Dallenbach Hendrick	12.50	30.00
26 Johnny Benson Cheerios	12.50	30.00
33 Ken Schrader Petree	12.50	30.00
42 Joe Nemechek BellSouth	12.50	30.00
43 John Andretti STP	12.50	30.00
55 Kenny Wallace Square D	12.50	30.00
66 Darrell Waltrip Big K	12.50	30.00
77 Robert Pressley Jasper	12.50	30.00
78 Gary Bradberry Pilot	12.50	30.00
94 Bill Elliott Drive Thru	25.00	50.00
97 Chad Little John Deere	15.00	40.00
99 Jeff Burton Exide	20.00	40.00

1999 Racing Champions Transporters Platinum 1:64

These transporter and car sets were issued in a silver checkered flag "Reflections in Platinum" window box. Each transporter and 1:64 scale car were produced in a solid platinum chrome finish. The stated production run was 1499 for each piece.

	EX	NM-MT
4 Bobby Hamilton Kodak	20.00	40.00
5 Terry Labonte Kellogg's	30.00	60.00
6 Mark Martin Valvoline	30.00	60.00
6 Joe Bessey Power Team	12.50	30.00
9 Jerry Nadeau Dexter's Lab	12.50	
10 Ricky Rudd Tide	20.00	
11 Brett Bodine Paychex	12.50	
15 Ken Schrader Oakwood Homes	12.50	
16 Kevin Lepage Primestar	12.50	
25 Wally Dallenbach Hendrick	12.50	
32 Jeff Green Kleenex	12.50	
40 Sterling Marlin Sabco	15.00	
50 Mark Green Dr.Pepper	15.00	
55 Kenny Wallace Square D	12.50	
77 Robert Pressley Jasper	12.50	
97 Chad Little John Deere	20.00	
99 Jeff Burton Exide	20.00	

1999 Racing Champion Transporters Signature Se 1:64

This is a special series produced by Racing Champ celebrate their 10th anniversary. It parallels the regu series. Each car is a packaged in a decorative box w driver's facsimile autograph on the front.

	EX	NM
4 Bobby Hamilton Kodak	8.00	
5 Terry Labonte Kellogg's	10.00	
6 Mark Martin Valvoline	10.00	
6 Joe Bessey Power Team	8.00	
9 Jerry Nadeau Dexter's Laboratory	8.00	
10 Ricky Rudd Tide	10.00	
16 Kevin Lepage Primestar	8.00	
25 Wally Dallenbach Hendrick	8.00	
26 Johnny Benson Cheerios	8.00	
30 Derrike Cope Bryan Foods	8.00	
40 Sterling Marlin John Wayne	10.00	
55 Kenny Wallace Square D	8.00	
77 Robert Pressley Jasper	8.00	
94 Bill Elliott Drive Thru	10.00	
99 Jeff Burton Exide	8.00	

1999 Racing Champion Transporters Under the Li 1:64

	EX	NM
4 Bobby Hamilton Kodak	12.50	
5 Terry Labonte Kellogg's	15.00	
6 Mark Martin Valvoline	15.00	
94 Bill Elliott Drive Thru	15.00	
99 Jeff Burton Exide	15.00	

2000 Racing Champion Preview Transporters 1:

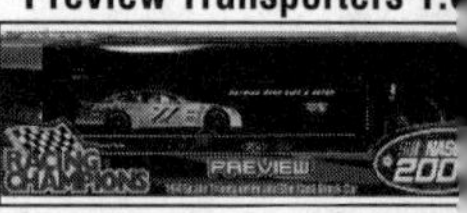

These Transporters were issued in a red and black clear display box with the NASCAR 2000 logo clearly printe front. Each came with a 1:64 scale car as well.

	EX	NM
6 Mark Martin Valvoline	8.00	
33 Joe Nemecheck Oakwood Homes	7.50	
36 Ernie Irvan M&M's '99	8.00	
66 Darrell Waltrip Big K	7.50	
97 Chad Little John Deere	6.00	
99 Jeff Burton Exide	7.50	

2000 Racing Champion Premier Preview Transpo 1:64

	EX	NM
6 Mark Martin Valvoline	8.00	
99 Jeff Burton Exide	10.00	
99 Jeff Burton Exide Chrome/999	15.00	

2000 Racing Champion Transporters 1:64

	EX	NM
4 Bobby Hamilton	6.00	

odak		
y Labonte ellogg's	7.50	15.00
k Martin alvoline	7.50	15.00
k Martin alvoline Chrome/999	25.00	50.00
chael Waltrip ation's Rent	6.00	12.00
remy Mayfield obil 1	6.00	12.00
ike Bliss onseco	6.00	12.00
att Kenseth eWalt	20.00	35.00
att Kenseth isine Promo	20.00	40.00
ard Burton at Dealers	6.00	12.00
ard Burton aterpillar Chrome/999	25.00	50.00
e Nemechek akwood Bud Shoot Out	6.00	12.00
nie Irvan &M's	10.00	20.00
erling Marlin eam Sabco	6.00	15.00
arrell Waltrip ig K	6.00	12.00
odd Bodine hillips 66	6.00	12.00
obert Pressley asper	6.00	12.00
bert Pressley asper Chrome/999	10.00	20.00
e Nemechek ellular One	6.00	12.00
ave Blaney moco	6.00	12.00
ave Blaney moco Chrome/999	10.00	25.00
nad Little ohn Deere	6.00	12.00
ff Burton xide	6.00	12.00
ff Burton xide Chrome/999	20.00	40.00

2000 Racing Champions remier Transporters 1:64

	EX	NM-MT
by Hamilton odak	10.00	20.00
k Martin alvoline	15.00	30.00
att Kenseth eWalt	20.00	35.00
dd Bodine hillips 66	10.00	20.00
ff Burton xide	12.50	25.00
f Burton xide Chrome/999	20.00	40.00
DA ord Taurus 2000	8.00	20.00

2000 Racing Champions ansporters Time Trial 1:64

	EX	NM-MT
by Hamilton odak	10.00	20.00
k Martin alvoline	12.50	25.00
ard Burton aterpillar	12.50	25.00

2000 Racing Champions ansporters War Paint 1:64

	EX	NM-MT
k Martin alvoline	10.00	20.00
Burton xide	10.00	20.00

2001 Racing Champions review Transporters 1:64

	EX	NM-MT
hnny Benson alvoline	10.00	18.00
hnny Benson alvoline Chrome	20.00	30.00
emy Mayfield obil 1	10.00	18.00
emy Mayfield obil 1 Chrome	20.00	40.00
emy Mayfield obil 1 Layin' Rubber	15.00	40.00
emy Mayfield obil 1 Race Rubber	20.00	40.00
ard Burton aterpillar	10.00	18.00
ard Burton aterpillar Autographed	30.00	60.00
ard Burton aterpillar Chrome	15.00	40.00
ard Burton aterpillar Layin' Rubber/500	15.00	40.00
ard Burton aterpillar Race Rubber	20.00	40.00
bby Hamilton quare D	7.50	15.00
bby Hamilton quare D AUTO	25.00	50.00
bby Hamilton quare D Chrome	20.00	40.00
bby Hamilton quare D Race Rubber	15.00	40.00
acy Compton elling	7.50	15.00
acy Compton elling Autographed	30.00	60.00
Dodge Test Car	7.50	15.00

2001 Racing Champions Transporters 1:64

	EX	NM-MT
5 Terry Labonte Kellogg's	12.50	25.00
5 Terry Labonte Kellogg's Chrome/1500	15.00	40.00
5 Terry Labonte Kellogg's Layin' Rubber/500	15.00	40.00
5 Terry Labonte Monster's Inc.	15.00	30.00
10 Johnny Benson Valvoline	10.00	20.00
10 Johnny Benson Valvoline Chrome/1500	15.00	30.00
12 Jeremy Mayfield Mobil 1 Chrome/1500	15.00	30.00
12 Jeremy Mayfield Mobil 1 Layin' Rubber	15.00	40.00
22 Ward Burton Caterpillar	10.00	20.00
22 Ward Burton Caterpillar Layin' Rubber	15.00	40.00
25 Jerry Nadeau UAW	10.00	20.00
25 Jerry Nadeau UAW Chrome/1500	15.00	30.00
25 Jerry Nadeau UAW Layin' Rubber/500	15.00	40.00
25 Jerry Nadeau UAW Race Rubber	20.00	40.00
36 Hank Parker Jr. GNC	10.00	20.00
36 Ken Schrader M&M's	10.00	20.00
36 Ken Schrader M&M's Layin' Rubber	15.00	40.00
36 Ken Schrader M&M's Race Rubber	20.00	40.00
55 Bobby Hamilton Square D	10.00	20.00
55 Bobby Hamilton Square D AUTO	25.00	50.00
55 Bobby Hamilton Square D Race Rubber	15.00	30.00
66 Todd Bodine K-Mart	10.00	20.00
93 Dave Blaney Amoco	10.00	20.00
93 Dave Blaney Amoco Layin' Rubber/500	15.00	40.00
93 Dave Blaney Amoco Race Rubber	15.00	40.00

2001 Racing Champions American Muscle Body Shop Transporters 1:64

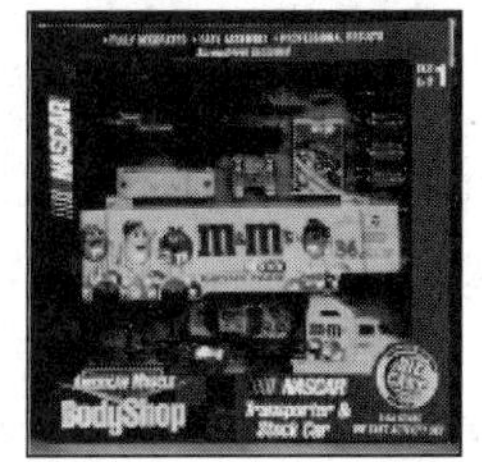

This 1:64 Transporter and car set was produced by Racing Champions for their American Muscle Body Shop series. Each set was issued in a box and blister combination package and both the transporter and car had to be assembled by the collector similar to the line of Racing Champions Model Kits.

	EX	NM-MT
4 Mike Skinner Kodak	6.00	15.00
10 Johnny Benson Valvoline with Maxlife car	6.00	15.00
22 Ward Burton Caterpillar	6.00	15.00
25 Jerry Nadeau UAW	6.00	15.00
36 Ken Schrader M&M's with Stars&Stripes car	6.00	15.00
40 Sterling Marlin Sterling	6.00	15.00
55 Bobby Hamilton Square D	6.00	15.00
92 Stacy Compton Melling	6.00	15.00
93 Dave Blaney Amoco Ultimate	6.00	15.00

2002 Racing Champions Preview Transporters 1:64

	EX	NM-MT
4 Mike Skinner Kodak	10.00	18.00
5 Terry Labonte Kellogg's	10.00	18.00
10 Johnny Benson Valvoline	10.00	18.00
22 Ward Burton Caterpillar	10.00	18.00
25 Jerry Nadeau UAW	10.00	18.00
26 Jimmy Spencer K-Mart with Shrek car	10.00	18.00
36 Ken Schrader M&M's	10.00	18.00

2002 Racing Champions Transporters 1:64

	EX	NM-MT
1 Jimmy Spencer Yellow Freight	10.00	18.00
5 Terry Labonte Kellogg's with Got Milk 1:64 car	10.00	20.00
10 Johnny Benson Valvoline with Eagle One car	10.00	20.00
11 Brett Bodine Hooter's	15.00	30.00
22 Ward Burton Caterpillar Promo	12.50	25.00
22 Ward Burton Caterpillar Daytona Win	12.00	20.00
22 Ward Burton Cat Dealers '03 packaging	15.00	25.00
32 Ricky Craven Tide	10.00	20.00
32 Ricky Craven Tide with Give Kids 1:64 car	10.00	20.00
36 Ken Schrader M&M's w/Halloween car in 2003 packaging	15.00	25.00
36 Ken Schrader M&M's with July 4th 1:64 car	12.50	25.00
48 Jimmie Johnson Lowe's	10.00	25.00
48 Jimmie Johnson Lowe's w/Power of Pride car	15.00	30.00
48 Jimmie Johnson Lowe's with 3-cars	20.00	35.00
55 Bobby Hamilton Schneider	10.00	18.00

2003 Racing Champions Preview Transporters 1:64

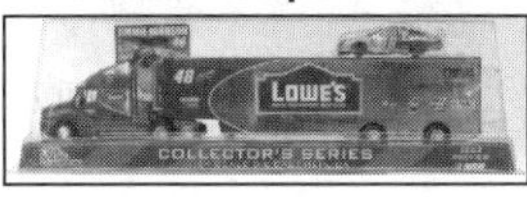

Racing Champions created a more narrow clamshell package for its 2003 transporters. This series features the title "2003 Preview" in the lower right corner of the package. Each transporter included a die-cast car and was packaged with a mini (roughly 2 /14" by 3") sized Racing Champions or Press Pass card.

	EX	NM-MT
22 Ward Burton Caterpillar	10.00	20.00
22 Ward Burton Cat Rental	10.00	20.00
48 Jimmie Johnson Lowe's 2002 Season to Remember	12.50	25.00

2003 Racing Champions Transporters 1:64

	EX	NM-MT
1 Jamie McMurray Yellow Freight	12.50	25.00
5 Terry Labonte Kellogg's	12.50	25.00
10 Johnny Benson Valvoline	10.00	20.00
25 Joe Nemechek UAW Delphi	10.00	20.00
32 Ricky Craven Tide	10.00	20.00
48 Jimmie Johnson Lowe's 2002 Season to Remember	10.00	25.00
48 Jimmie Johnson Lowe's 2003	10.00	20.00
77 Dave Blaney Jasper	12.50	25.00
01 Jerry Nadeau Army	12.50	30.00

2004 Racing Champions Ultra Transporters 1:64

	EX	NM-MT
5 Terry Labonte Kellogg's	10.00	20.00
22 Scott Wimmer Caterpillar	10.00	20.00
25 Brian Vickers Ditech.com	10.00	20.00
48 Jimmie Johnson Lowe's	10.00	20.00
0 Ward Burton NetZero	15.00	30.00
01 Joe Nemechek Army	10.00	20.00

1993-94 Racing Champions Transporters Retail 1:87

This is one of the first series Racing Champions made of 1:87 scale transporters. They were issued primarily to retail outlets with each being packaged in a Racing Champions blister.

	EX	NM-MT
2 Rusty Wallace Penske	4.00	8.00
3 Dale Earnhardt Goodwrench	6.00	12.00
4 Ernie Irvan Kodak	3.00	6.00
5 Ricky Rudd Tide	3.00	6.00
6 Mark Martin Valvoline	3.00	6.00
7 Harry Gant Manheim Auctions	5.00	10.00
7 Harry Gant Morema	3.00	6.00
7 Alan Kulwicki Hooters	10.00	20.00
8 Sterling Marlin Raybestos	4.00	8.00
9 Chad Little IOF Hotline	3.00	6.00
11 Bill Elliott Amoco	3.00	6.00
12 Jimmy Spencer Meineke	3.00	6.00
14 Terry Labonte Kellogg's	3.00	8.00
15 Geoff Bodine Motorcraft	3.00	6.00
17 Darrell Waltrip Western Auto	3.00	6.00
18 Dale Jarrett Interstate Batteries	3.00	6.00
21 Morgan Shepherd Citgo	3.00	6.00
22 Bobby Labonte Maxwell House	4.00	8.00
24 Jeff Gordon DuPont 1993	7.50	15.00
25 Ken Schrader No sponsor	3.00	6.00
26 Brett Bodine Quaker State	3.00	6.00
27 Hut Stricklin McDonald's	3.00	6.00
28 Davey Allison Havoline	6.00	12.00
28 Davey Allison Havoline with Black and White paint scheme	7.50	15.00
30 Michael Waltrip Pennzoil	3.00	6.00
33 Harry Gant Food Lion	4.00	8.00
33 Harry Gant Morema	6.00	12.00
35 Bill Venturini Amoco	10.00	20.00
42 Kyle Petty Mello Yello	3.00	6.00
44 Rick Wilson STP	3.00	6.00
52 Ken Schrader AC Delco	3.00	6.00
52 Ken Schrader Morema	5.00	10.00
66 Cale Yarborough TropArtic	6.00	12.00
87 Joe Nemechek Dentyne	3.00	6.00
98 Derrike Cope Bojangles	3.00	6.00

1993 Racing Champions Premier Transporters 1:87

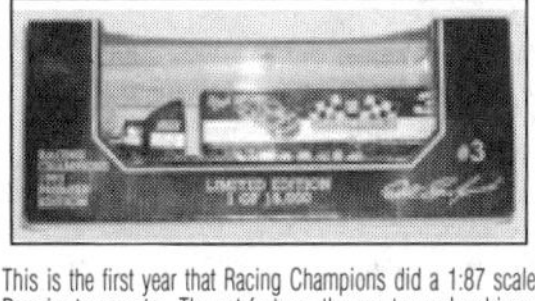

This is the first year that Racing Champions did a 1:87 scale Premier transporter. The set features the most popular drivers from Winston Cup racing. Each piece comes in a black shadow box and has the number produced stamped on the front of that box.

	EX	NM-MT
2 Ward Burton Hardee's/7500	10.00	20.00
2 Rusty Wallace Penske	15.00	30.00
3 Dale Earnhardt Goodwrench/15,000	15.00	30.00
3 Dale Earnhardt Goodwrench DEI/5000	20.00	50.00
4 Ernie Irvan Kodak/5000	10.00	20.00
5 Ricky Rudd Tide/15,000	10.00	20.00
6 Mark Martin Valvoline	10.00	20.00
7 Alan Kulwicki Hooters	40.00	75.00
8 Sterling Marlin Raybestos/2500	10.00	20.00
11 Bill Elliott Amoco/15,000	10.00	20.00
11 Bill Elliott Budweiser	18.00	35.00
12 Jimmy Spencer Meineke/10,000	10.00	20.00
14 Terry Labonte Kellogg's	10.00	20.00
15 Geoff Bodine Motorcraft/5000	10.00	20.00
18 Dale Jarrett Interstate Batteries	10.00	20.00
21 Morgan Shepherd Citgo/10,000	10.00	20.00
22 Bobby Labonte Maxwell House	10.00	25.00
24 Jeff Gordon DuPont/15,000	15.00	25.00
27 Hut Stricklin McDonald's/15,000	10.00	20.00
28 Davey Allison Havoline Black paint scheme	18.00	35.00
28 Davey Allison Havoline with Black and White paint scheme	18.00	35.00
28 Ernie Irvan Havoline/5000	15.00	25.00
33 Harry Gant Food Lion	10.00	20.00
42 Kyle Petty Mello Yello/3000	10.00	20.00
44 David Green Slim Jim/5000	10.00	20.00
44 Rick Wilson STP/5000	10.00	20.00
51 No Driver Association Chevy Prototype/7500	10.00	20.00
51 No Driver Association Ford Prototype/7500	10.00	20.00
51 No Driver Association Kenworth Prototype/7500	10.00	20.00
59 Robert Pressley Alliance/5000	10.00	20.00
60 Mark Martin Winn Dixie/5000	20.00	40.00
87 Joe Nemechek Dentyne	10.00	20.00
NNO NDA/Dodge IROC/7500	10.00	20.00

1994 Racing Champions Transporters Hobby 1:87

This series of Transporters was issued directly to hobby shops. Each was packaged in a Racing Champions yellow box.

	EX	NM-MT
1 Rick Mast Precision Products	6.00	10.00
2 Rusty Wallace Penske	6.00	10.00
4 Sterling Marlin Kodak	6.00	15.00
5 Terry Labonte Kellogg's	6.00	10.00
6 Mark Martin Valvoline	6.00	10.00
8 Jeff Burton Raybestos	6.00	10.00
18 Dale Jarrett Interstate Batteries	6.00	10.00
24 Jeff Gordon DuPont	10.00	20.00
26 Brett Bodine Quaker State	6.00	10.00
30 Michael Waltrip Pennzoil	6.00	10.00
33 Harry Gant Leo Jackson	6.00	10.00
42 Kyle Petty Mello Yello	6.00	10.00
75 Todd Bodine Factory Stores of America	6.00	10.00

1994 Racing Champions Premier Transporters 1:87

Racing Champions continued their line of 1:87 Premier transporters in 1994. The pieces were again packaged in a black shadow box and carry the number produced on the front of that box.

	EX	NM-MT
2 Ward Burton Hardee's	10.00	20.00
2 Rusty Wallace Penske Mac Tools/7500	25.00	40.00
3 Dale Earnhardt Goodwrench	15.00	25.00
4 Sterling Marlin Kodak	12.00	25.00
4 Sterling Marlin Kodak FunSaver	12.00	25.00
5 Terry Labonte Kellogg's	10.00	20.00
7 Geoff Bodine Exide	10.00	20.00
7 Harry Gant Manheim Auctions	15.00	25.00
8 Kenny Wallace TIC Financial	10.00	20.00
15 Lake Speed Quality Care	10.00	20.00
16 Ted Musgrave Family Channel	10.00	20.00
17 Darrell Waltrip Western Auto	10.00	20.00
19 Loy Allen Hooters	10.00	20.00
21 Morgan Shepherd Cheerwine/7500	10.00	20.00
28 Ernie Irvan Havoline	15.00	25.00
28 Ernie Irvan Mac Tools Promo/15,028	12.50	25.00
32 Dale Jarrett Shoe World/2500	25.00	40.00
40 Bobby Hamilton Kendall	10.00	20.00
52 Ken Schrader AC Delco	10.00	20.00
60 Mark Martin Winn Dixie/7500	15.00	25.00
94 Brickyard 400 special	15.00	30.00
98 Derrike Cope Fingerhut	10.00	20.00

1995 Racing Champions Transporters 1:87

These 1:87 scale pieces were produced by Racing Champions. They were distributed through both hobby and retail outlets. This series is highlighted by the Rusty Wallace transporter which was released in an acrylic case.

	EX	NM-MT
2 Rusty Wallace Miller Genuine Draft in acrylic case	10.00	20.00
7 Geoff Bodine Exide	3.00	6.00
24 Jeff Gordon DuPont	7.50	15.00
26 Steve Kinser Quaker State	3.00	6.00
27 Loy Allen Hooters	3.00	6.00
28 Dale Jarrett Ernie Irvan Havoline both signatures on trailer	3.00	6.00
99 Phil Parsons Luxaire	3.00	6.00

1995 Racing Champions Premier Transporters 1:87

	EX	NM-MT
8 Jeff Burton Raybestos	10.00	20.00
12 Derrike Cope Straight Arrow	10.00	20.00
25 Ken Schrader Budweiser	10.00	20.00
26 Steve Kinser Quaker State	10.00	20.00
40 Patty Moise Dial Purex	10.00	20.00
90 Mike Wallace	10.00	20.00

	EX	NM-MT
Heilig-Meyers		
94 Bill Elliott McDonald's/5000	12.50	25.00
95 Brickyard 500/20,000	10.00	20.00

1996 Racing Champions Transporters 1:87

This series was produced by Racing Champions. It is highlighted by the Kyle Petty transporter which was released in an acrylic case.

	EX	NM-MT
1 Rick Mast Hooter's	3.00	6.00
1 Hermie Sadler DeWalt	3.00	6.00
2 Rusty Wallace Penske	3.00	6.00
4 Sterling Marlin Kodak	3.00	6.00
5 Terry Labonte Kellogg's	3.00	6.00
6 Mark Martin Valvoline	3.00	6.00
7 Geoff Bodine QVC	3.00	6.00
8 Hut Stricklin Circuit City	3.00	6.00
10 Ricky Rudd Tide	3.00	6.00
11 Brett Bodine Lowe's	3.00	6.00
12 Michael Waltrip MW Windows	3.00	6.00
15 Wally Dallenbach Hayes	3.00	6.00
16 Ted Musgrave Family Channel	3.00	6.00
17 Darrell Waltrip Parts America	3.00	6.00
18 Bobby Labonte Interstate Batteries	3.00	6.00
21 Michael Waltrip Citgo	3.00	6.00
22 Ward Burton MBNA	3.00	6.00
23 Chad Little John Deere	3.00	6.00
24 Jeff Gordon DuPont Premier	15.00	25.00
29 No Driver Association Scooby-Doo	3.00	6.00
30 Johnny Benson Pennzoil	3.00	6.00
34 Mike McLaughlin Royal Oak	3.00	6.00
37 John Andretti K-Mart	3.00	6.00
40 Tim Fedewa Kleenex	3.00	6.00
40 Patty Moise Dial Purex	3.00	6.00
42 Kyle Petty Coors Light in acrylic case	10.00	20.00
43 Rodney Combs Lance	3.00	6.00
44 David Green Slim Jim	3.00	6.00
44 Bobby Labonte Shell	4.00	8.00
47 Jeff Fuller Sunoco	3.00	6.00
74 Randy LaJoie Fina	3.00	6.00
81 Kenny Wallace TIC Financial	3.00	6.00
87 Joe Nemechek Bell South	3.00	6.00
87 Joe Nemechek Burger King	3.00	6.00
90 Mike Wallace Heilig-Meyers	3.00	6.00
99 Glenn Allen Jr. Luxaire	3.00	6.00

1997 Racing Champions Preview Transporters 1:87

The set features the most popular drivers from Winston Cup racing.

	EX	NM-MT
5 Terry Labonte Kellogg's	4.00	8.00
6 Mark Martin Valvoline	3.00	6.00
7 Geoff Bodine QVC	2.50	6.00
8 Hut Stricklin Circuit City	2.50	6.00
24 Jeff Gordon DuPont	4.00	8.00
29 Robert Pressley Cartoon Network	2.50	6.00

1997 Racing Champions Transporters 1:87

These 1:87 pieces were produced by Racing Champions. They were distributed through both hobby and retail outlets. This series features drivers from the Winston Cup and Busch circuits.

	EX	NM-MT
1 Hermie Sadler DeWalt	3.00	6.00
2 Ricky Craven Raybestos	3.00	6.00
2 Rusty Wallace Penske	3.00	6.00
4 Sterling Marlin Kodak	3.00	6.00
5 Terry Labonte Kellogg's	3.00	6.00
6 Mark Martin Valvoline	3.00	6.00
7 Geoff Bodine QVC	3.00	6.00
8 Hut Stricklin Circuit City	3.00	6.00
9 Jeff Burton Track Gear	3.00	6.00
10 Phil Parsons Channellock	3.00	6.00
10 Ricky Rudd Tide	3.00	6.00
11 Brett Bodine Close Call	3.00	6.00
11 Jimmy Foster Speedvision	3.00	6.00
16 Ted Musgrave Primestar	3.00	6.00
17 Darrell Waltrip Parts America	3.00	6.00
18 Bobby Labonte Interstate Batteries	3.00	6.00
19 Gary Bradberry CSR	3.00	6.00
21 Michael Waltrip Citgo	3.00	6.00
24 Jeff Gordon DuPont	4.00	8.00
28 Ernie Irvan Havoline 10th Anniversary paint scheme	3.00	6.00
29 Jeff Green Tom & Jerry	3.00	6.00
29 Robert Pressley Cartoon Network	3.00	6.00
30 Johnny Benson Pennzoil	3.00	6.00
32 Dale Jarrett Gillette	3.00	6.00
32 Dale Jarrett White Rain	3.00	6.00
34 Mike McLaughlin Royal Oak	3.00	6.00
36 Todd Bodine Stanley Tools	3.00	6.00
36 Derrike Cope Skittles	3.00	6.00
37 Jeremy Mayfield K-Mart	3.00	6.00
38 Elton Sawyer Barbasol	3.00	6.00
40 Robby Gordon Sabco Racing	3.00	6.00
43 Rodney Combs Lance	3.00	6.00
46 Wally Dallenbach First Union	3.00	6.00
57 Jason Keller Slim Jim	3.00	6.00
60 Mark Martin Winn Dixie	3.00	6.00
75 Rick Mast Remington	3.00	6.00
90 Dick Trickle Heilig-Meyers	3.00	6.00
94 Ron Barfield New Holland	3.00	6.00
94 Bill Elliott McDonald's	3.00	6.00
96 David Green Caterpillar	3.00	6.00
97 Chad Little John Deere	3.00	6.00
99 Jeff Burton Exide	3.00	6.00

1998 Racing Champions Transporters 1:87

These 1:87 pieces were produced by Racing Champions. They were distributed through both hobby and retail outlets. This series features drivers from the Winston Cup and Busch circuits.

	EX	NM-MT
4 Bobby Hamilton Kodak	3.00	6.00
4 Jeff Purvis Lance	3.00	6.00
5 Terry Labonte Kellogg's	3.00	6.00
6 Joe Bessey Power Team	3.00	6.00
6 Mark Martin Valvoline	3.00	6.00
8 Hut Stricklin Circuit City	3.00	6.00
9 Lake Speed Birthday Cake	3.00	6.00
9 Lake Speed Huckleberry Hound	3.00	6.00
10 Ricky Rudd Tide	3.00	6.00
11 Brett Bodine Paychex	3.00	6.00
13 Jerry Nadeau First Plus	3.00	6.00
21 Michael Waltrip Citgo	3.00	6.00
21 Michael Waltrip Goodwill Games	3.00	6.00
33 Ken Schrader Petree	3.00	6.00
35 Todd Bodine Tabasco	3.00	6.00
36 Ernie Irvan M&M's	3.00	6.00
36 Ernie Irvan Skittles	3.00	6.00
40 Sterling Marlin Sabco	3.00	6.00
42 Joe Nemechek BellSouth	3.00	6.00
46 Wally Dallenbach First Union	3.00	6.00
50 Ricky Craven Hendrick	3.00	6.00
59 Robert Pressley Kingsford	3.00	6.00
66 Elliott Sadler Phillips 66	3.00	6.00
75 Rick Mast Remington	3.00	6.00
00 Buckshot Jones Aqua Fresh	3.00	6.00

2002 Racing Champions Preview Transporters 1:87

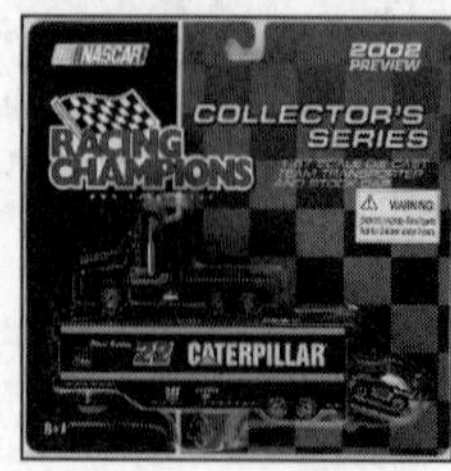

These 1:87 haulers and cars were packaged in a red and black Racing Champions blister. The copyright date on the back is 2001, but they are considered an early 2002 release.

	EX	NM-MT
4 Mike Skinner Kodak	3.00	6.00
5 Terry Labonte Kellogg's	3.00	6.00
10 Johnny Benson Valvoline	3.00	6.00
22 Ward Burton Caterpillar	3.00	6.00
25 Jerry Nadeau UAW	3.00	6.00

2002 Racing Champions Transporters 1:87

	EX	NM-MT
5 Terry Labonte Kellogg's	3.00	6.00
10 Johnny Benson Valvoline	3.00	6.00
22 Ward Burton Caterpillar	3.00	6.00
25 Jerry Nadeau UAW	3.00	6.00
48 Jimmie Johnson Lowe's	5.00	10.00
55 Bobby Hamilton Scneider	3.00	6.00

1991-92 Racing Champions Transporters 1:144

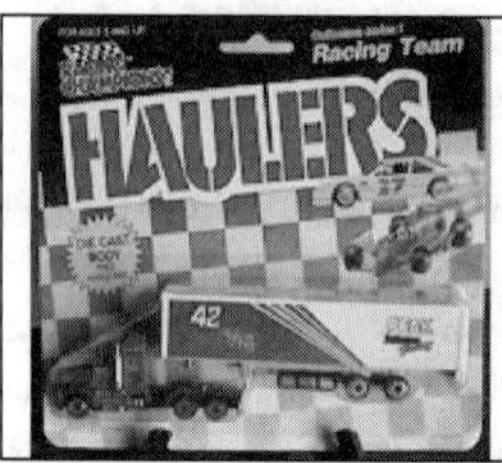

This series of Transporters was issued by Racing Champions in the early 1990s. Several different blister packaging styles were used. The first of which features a black and checkered flag design with title "Racing Champions Haulers" and a notation of "Collectors Series 1 Racing Team" at the top. The second is entitled "Racing Champions Racing Team" and makes no mention of a series number. Unless noted each piece below was issued in this second packaging type. This second type can also be found with or without a mini car included.

	EX	NM-MT
1 Rick Mast Majik Market	3.00	8.00
4 Ernie Irvan Kodak	3.00	8.00
5 Jay Fogleman Innkeeper	3.00	8.00
6 Mark Martin Valvoline	4.00	10.00
8 Sterling Marlin Raybestos	4.00	10.00
9 Bill Elliott Melling Blue	4.00	10.00
9 Bill Elliott Melling Red	4.00	10.00
10 Derrike Cope Purolator with mini car	3.00	8.00
11 Bill Elliott Amoco	4.00	10.00
12 Bobby Allison No sponsor with mini car	4.00	10.00
12 Hut Stricklin Raybestos	3.00	8.00
14 A.J. Foyt No Sponsor	4.00	10.00
15 Geoff Bodine Motorcraft	3.00	8.00
15 Lake Speed Quality Care	3.00	8.00
17 Darrell Waltrip Western Auto	3.00	8.00
18 Dale Jarrett Interstate Batteries	4.00	10.00
21 Morgan Shepherd Citgo	3.00	8.00
22 Sterling Marlin Maxwell House	3.00	8.00
25 Ken Schrader No Sponsor	3.00	8.00
28 Davey Allison Havoline black&gold	6.00	15.00
30 Michael Waltrip Pennzoil with mini car	3.00	8.00
42 Kyle Petty Mello Yello	3.00	8.00
42 Kyle Petty Peak series 1 package	4.00	10.00
42 Kyle Petty Peak Racing Team package	3.00	8.00
42 Kyle Petty Peak Racing Team package with mini car	3.00	8.00
43 Richard Petty STP	5.00	12.00
66 Cale Yarborough Phillips 66 with mini car	3.00	8.00
68 Bobby Hamilton Country Time	3.00	8.00
71 Dave Marcis Big Apple	3.00	8.00
72 Ken Bouchard ADAP	3.00	8.00
94 Terry Labonte Sunoco	4.00	10.00

1994 Racing Champions Transporters 1:144

This series of Transporters was issued by Racing Champions in 1994. The blister packaging reads "Racing Team Transporter" on the front and is the same packaging used for 1995, except that there is no year designation on the 1994 release. Unless noted below each was also packaged with a mini car.

	EX	NM-MT
2 Rusty Wallace Penske	3.00	8.00
2 Ricky Craven DuPont	3.00	6.00
7 Geoff Bodine Exide	3.00	6.00
10 Ricky Rudd Tide	3.00	6.00
28 Ernie Irvan Havoline	3.00	8.00
41 Joe Nemechek Meineke	3.00	6.00

1995 Racing Champions Transporters 1:144

This series of Transporters was issued by Racing Champions in 1995. The blister packaging reads "Racing Team Transporter" on the front of most. A few pieces were released in a slightly different blister design without a "set name" with the scale being incorrectly identified as 1:87. Regardless, the year of issue is clearly printed on the front of both blister types. Unless noted below each was also packaged with a mini car.

	EX	NM-MT
7 Geoff Bodine Exide	3.00	6.00
24 Jeff Gordon DuPont	5.00	12.00
26 Steve Kinser Quaker State	3.00	6.00
28 Dale Jarrett Havoline	5.00	12.00
30 Michael Waltrip Pennzoil	3.00	6.00
37 John Andretti K-Mart	3.00	6.00
52 Ken Schrader AC Delco	4.00	8.00
94 Bill Elliott McDonald's	4.00	8.00

1996 Racing Champions Transporters 1:144

This series of Transporters was issued by Racing Champions in a red blister pack in 1996. The blister packaging reads "1996 Edition" on the front. Unless noted below each was also packaged with a mini car.

	EX	NM-MT
2 Rusty Wallace Penske	4.00	8.00
14 Patty Moise Dial Purex	3.00	6.00
16 Ted Musgrave Family Channel	3.00	6.00
24 Jeff Gordon DuPont	5.00	12.00

1997 Racing Champions Preview Transporters 1:144

These 1:144 scale mini Transporters were issued in a red and black Racing Champions blister package. The blister reads "1997 Preview Edition" on the front. Each was also packaged with a yellow bordered trading card and a 1:144 scale mini car.

	EX	NM-MT
5 Terry Labonte Kellogg's	3.00	8.00
7 Geoff Bodine QVC	3.00	6.00
8 Hut Stricklin Circuit City	3.00	6.00
29 Robert Pressley Cartoon Network	3.00	6.00

1997 Racing Champions Transporters 1:144

These 1:144 scale mini Transporters were issued in a red and black Racing Champions blister package. The blister reads "1997 Edition" on the front. Each was also packaged with a yellow bordered trading card and a 1:144 scale mini car.

	EX	NM-MT
00 Buckshot Jones Aquafresh	3.00	6.00
1 Hermie Sadler DeWalt	3.00	6.00
2 Ricky Craven DuPont	3.00	6.00
2 Rusty Wallace Penske	3.00	8.00
4 Sterling Marlin Kodak	3.00	8.00
5 Terry Labonte Bayer	3.00	8.00
5 Terry Labonte Kellogg's	3.00	8.00
5 Terry Labonte Kellogg's Tony	3.00	8.00
6 Mark Martin Valvoline	3.00	
7 Geoff Bodine QVC	3.00	
9 Joe Bessey Power Team	3.00	
10 Phil Parsons Channellock	3.00	
11 Brett Bodine Close Call	3.00	
11 Jimmy Foster Speedvision	3.00	
16 Ted Musgrave Family Channel	3.00	
17 Darrell Waltrip Western Auto	3.00	
17 Darrell Waltrip Western Auto Chrome	3.00	
18 Bobby Labonte Interstate Batteries	3.00	
19 Gary Bradberry Child Support	3.00	
21 Michael Waltrip Citgo	3.00	
24 Jeff Gordon DuPont	6.00	
28 Ernie Irvan Havoline w/black&orange car	3.00	
28 Ernie Irvan Havoline w/black&white car	3.00	
29 Jeff Green Tom&Jerry	3.00	
29 Robert Pressley Cartoon Network	3.00	
30 Johnny Benson Pennzoil	3.00	
32 Dale Jarrett White Rain	3.00	
34 Mike McLaughlin Royal Oak	3.00	
36 Todd Bodine Stanley Tools	3.00	
36 Derrike Cope Skittles	3.00	
37 Jeremy Mayfield K-Mart	3.00	
40 Robby Gordon Sabco	3.00	
42 Joe Nemechek BellSouth	3.00	
43 Rodney Combs Lance	3.00	
46 Wally Dallenbach First Union	3.00	
57 Jason Keller Slim Jim	3.00	
60 Mark Martin Winn Dixie	4.00	
63 Tracy Leslie Lysol	3.00	
72 Mike Dillon Detroit Gasket	3.00	
74 Randy LaJoie Fina	3.00	
75 Rick Mast Remington	3.00	
88 Kevin Lepage Hype	3.00	
90 Dick Trickle Heilig-Meyers	3.00	
91 Mike Wallace Spam	3.00	
94 Ron Barfield New Holland	3.00	
94 Bill Elliott McDonald's	3.00	
94 Bill Elliott Mac Tonight	3.00	
96 David Green Caterpillar	3.00	
97 Chad Little John Deere	3.00	

1998 Racing Champions Transporters 1:144

These mini Transporters were issued in a red Champions blister package that reads "1998 Edition" front. Each transporter was also packaged with a tradi and a 1:144 scale mini car.

	EX	NM
4 Bobby Hamilton Kodak	3.00	
4 Jeff Purvis Lance	3.00	
5 Terry Labonte Kellogg's	3.00	
9 Lake Speed Cartoon Network Red	3.00	
9 Lake Speed Cartoon Network White	3.00	
13 Jerry Nadeau First Plus	3.00	
35 Todd Bodine Tabasco	3.00	
36 Ernie Irvan M&M's	3.00	
36 Ernie Irvan Skittles	3.00	
50 Ricky Craven Hendrick	3.00	
00 Buckshot Jones Aqua Fresh	3.00	

1997 Revell Transporte 1:64

	EX	N
97 Chad Little John Deere AUTO/756 GMP produced issued with 1:64 car	40.00	

1998 Revell Select Hobb Transporters 1:64

These die-cast pieces are packaged in a Revell Select b one 1:64 hauler and one 1:64 Revell Select car. The r blister wrap that protects the die-cast inside the box.

	EX	NM-MT
ale Earnhardt Goodwrench	20.00	35.00
eff Gordon DuPont	15.00	30.00
Robert Pressley Jasper	15.00	30.00

1992 Road Champs Transporters 1:64

e 1:64 scale transporters were issued with two 1:64 scale in a large oversized Road Champs window box.

	EX	NM-MT
nie Irvan Kodak	7.50	20.00
ark Martin Valvoline	10.00	25.00
Richard Petty STP	10.00	25.00

1992 Road Champs Transporters 1:87

of these 1:87 Transporters was issued in a Road Champs er that features both a small photo of the driver and his car.

	EX	NM-MT
ff Gordon Baby Ruth	10.00	25.00
usty Wallace Pontiac	6.00	15.00
nie Irvan Kodak	5.00	12.00
ark Martin Valvoline	6.00	15.00
Morgan Shepherd Citgo	5.00	12.00
Richard Petty STP	6.00	15.00

1996-98 Scaleworks Transporters 1:24

	EX	NM-MT
erry Labonte Kellogg's 1998	75.00	150.00
erry Labonte Kellogg's Corny/1000	75.00	150.00
ark Martin Valvoline/2000 1997	90.00	150.00
Ernie Irvan Havoline/2000 1996	75.00	150.00
Ernie Irvan M&M's	90.00	150.00
Ernie Irvan Skittles	75.00	150.00
Richard Petty STP 25th Anniversary/1025 1997	125.00	225.00
Dale Jarrett Quality Care/2000 1996	90.00	150.00
Bill Elliott McDonald's/1000 1996	80.00	150.00
Bill Elliott Mac Tonight/1000 1998	80.00	150.00

2003 Team Caliber Owners Series Transporters 1:64

	EX	NM-MT
Mark Martin Viagra/1800	35.00	70.00
Ryan Newman Alltel/1200	35.00	70.00
Greg Biffle Grainger/1200	25.00	50.00
Matt Kenseth DeWalt/1200	40.00	80.00
Ricky Rudd Motorcraft/1200	25.00	50.00
Jimmie Johnson Lowe's/800	30.00	60.00
Jerry Nadeau Army/600	30.00	60.00

2003 Team Caliber Pit Stop Transporters 1:64

	EX	NM-MT
erry Labonte Kellogg's	12.50	25.00
ark Martin Viagra	15.00	30.00
Johnny Benson Valvoline	12.50	25.00
Ryan Newman Alltel	15.00	30.00
Greg Biffle Grainger	12.50	25.00
Matt Kenseth DeWalt	15.00	30.00
Kenny Wallace Stacker 2	12.50	25.00
John Andretti Cheerios	12.50	25.00
Kyle Petty Georgia Pacific	12.50	25.00
Jimmie Johnson Lowe's	12.50	25.00
Kurt Busch Rubbermaid	12.50	25.00
Jeff Burton Citgo	12.50	25.00
Jerry Nadeau Army	15.00	30.00

2004 Team Caliber Owners Series Transporters 1:64

	EX	NM-MT
Matt Kenseth DeWalt/600	40.00	60.00

2004 Team Caliber Pit Stop Transporters 1:64

	EX	NM-MT
Mark Martin Viagra	18.00	30.00
12 Ryan Newman Alltel	18.00	30.00
17 Matt Kenseth DeWalt	18.00	30.00
22 Scott Wimmer Caterpillar	18.00	30.00
97 Kurt Busch Sharpie	18.00	30.00
NNO Disney Event Car Mickey Mouse	12.50	25.00

1998 Winner's Circle Race 'N' Play Transporters 1:64

This series of Transporters was issued by Winner's Circle and packaged in the standard blue Winner's Circle window box. Each transporter when opened folded out into a larger pit scene racing set.

	EX	NM-MT
3 Dale Earnhardt Goodwrench	15.00	30.00
24 Jeff Gordon DuPont	15.00	25.00

2000 Winner's Circle Transporters 1:64

Transporters in this release were issued in a blue Winner's Circle box that featured a photo of the driver on the bottom right corner of the front of the box. Some pieces may have been released in 2001 as well, but have been included as a 2000 piece for ease in cataloging.

	EX	NM-MT
2 Rusty Wallace Rusty	10.00	20.00
3 Dale Earnhardt Goodwrench Earnhardt photo with hat no 2000 NASCAR logo	15.00	30.00
3 Dale Earnhardt Goodwrench Earnhardt photo with hat with 2000 NASCAR logo	15.00	30.00
3 Dale Earnhardt Goodwrench Earnhardt photo w/o hat	15.00	30.00
8 Dale Earnhardt Jr. Dale Jr.	20.00	40.00
18 Bobby Labonte Interstate Batteries light green trailer	10.00	20.00
18 Bobby Labonte Interstate Batteries dark green trailer	10.00	20.00
20 Tony Stewart Home Depot with small Home Depot logo on side of trailer	12.50	25.00
20 Tony Stewart Home Depot without small Home Depot logo on side of trailer	12.50	25.00
24 Jeff Gordon DuPont without NASCAR 2000 logo on box	15.00	30.00
24 Jeff Gordon DuPont with NASCAR 2000 logo on box	15.00	30.00
88 Dale Jarrett Quality Care	12.50	25.00
NNO Everham Motorsports Dodge Test Team	15.00	30.00

2001 Winner's Circle Transporters 1:64

Each Transporter in this release came in a blue Winner's Circle box that included a photo of a group of transporters on the bottom right corner. Please note that the 2001 box looks nearly identical to the 2002 year box. However, the 2001 does not included the words "Trailer Rig" on the front lower center of the box.

	EX	NM-MT
1 Steve Park Pennzoil	12.50	25.00
3 Dale Earnhardt Goodwrench	20.00	40.00
8 Dale Earnhardt Jr. Dale Jr.	20.00	40.00
9 Bill Elliott Dodge	15.00	30.00
24 Jeff Gordon DuPont Flames	25.00	50.00
29 Kevin Harvick Goodwrench White	12.50	25.00
29 Kevin Harvick Goodwrench Taz	12.50	30.00
88 Dale Jarrett UPS	25.00	50.00
88 Dale Jarrett UPS Flames Truck	40.00	70.00

2002 Winner's Circle Transporters 1:64

These Transporters were issued in a blue Winner's Circle box that included an orange oval with the words "Trailer Rig" across the front. It also included a photo of a group of transporters on the bottom right corner just like the 2001 box.

	EX	NM-MT
2 Rusty Wallace Rusty	12.50	25.00
3 Dale Earnhardt Jr. Nilla Wafers	15.00	30.00
3 Dale Earnhardt Jr. Oreo	15.00	30.00
7 Casey Atwood Sirius Muppets	12.50	25.00
8 Dale Earnhardt Jr. Dale Jr.	15.00	30.00
8 Dale Earnhardt Jr. 2001 MLB All-Star Game	25.00	40.00
8 Dale Earnhardt Jr. 2002 MLB All-Star Game	15.00	30.00
9 Bill Elliott Dodge Muppets	12.50	25.00
12 Kerry Earnhardt Jani-King Yoseemitie Sam	12.50	25.00
15 Michael Waltrip NAPA	12.50	25.00
15 Michael Waltrip NAPA Star&Stripes	12.50	25.00
18 Bobby Labonte Interstate Batteries	12.50	25.00
18 Bobby Labonte Interstate Batteries Jurassic	12.50	25.00
18 Bobby Labonte Interstate Batteries Muppets	12.50	25.00
19 Jeremy Mayfield Dodge Muppets	12.50	25.00
19 Jeremy Mayfield Mountain Dew	12.50	25.00
20 Tony Stewart Home Depot	12.50	25.00
20 Tony Stewart Jurassic Park III	12.50	25.00
20 Tony Stewart Home Depot Coca Cola	12.50	25.00
24 Jeff Gordon DuPont Bugs Bunny	12.50	25.00
24 Jeff Gordon DuPont Flames	12.50	30.00
24 Jeff Gordon DuPont 200th Anniversary	12.50	25.00
24 Jeff Gordon Pepsi Daytona	15.00	30.00
28 Ricky Rudd Havoline Muppets	12.50	25.00
29 Kevin Harvick Goodwrench Taz	12.50	25.00
31 Robby Gordon Cingular Pepe le Pew	12.50	25.00
40 Sterling Marlin Sterling	15.00	30.00
48 Jimmie Johnson Lowe's Sylvester	15.00	30.00
88 Dale Jarrett UPS Muppets	12.50	25.00

2003 Winner's Circle Transporters 1:64

These Transporters were issued in a blue Winner's Circle window box that closely resembles the 2001 and 2002 boxes. The difference can be found in the oval "Trailer Rig" logo across the front. The background of that logo for 2003 features a blue checkered flag pattern instead of solid orange for 2002. It also included a photo of a group of transporters on the bottom right corner just like the 2001 and 2002 boxes. Many of these transporters are simply a re-issue of a previous piece in the new box.

	EX	NM-MT
3 Dale Earnhardt Forever the Man	15.00	30.00
4 Mike Skinner Kodak Yosemite Sam	12.50	25.00
5 Terry Labonte Kellogg's Road Runner and Wile E.Coyote	12.50	25.00
8 Dale Earnhardt Jr. 2002 MLB All-Star Game	15.00	30.00
8 Dale Earnhardt Jr. 2003 All-Star	15.00	30.00
8 Dale Earnhardt Jr. DMP Chance 2	15.00	30.00
8 Dale Earnhardt Jr. E Tribute Concert	18.00	30.00
8 Dale Earnhardt Jr. Looney Tunes	15.00	30.00
8 Dale Earnhardt Jr. Oreo Ritz	15.00	30.00
8 Tony Stewart Chance 2 3 Doors Down	18.00	30.00
12 Kerry Earnhardt JaniKing Yosemite Sam	12.50	25.00
19 Jeremy Mayfield Mountain Dew	12.50	25.00
20 Tony Stewart Home Depot Peanuts Black 2002	15.00	30.00
20 Tony Stewart Home Depot Peanuts Orange 2002	15.00	30.00
24 Jeff Gordon DuPont 4-Time Champ	15.00	30.00
24 Jeff Gordon DuPont Bugs 2001	12.50	25.00
24 Jeff Gordon DuPont Bugs Rematch	12.50	25.00
24 Jeff Gordon Elmo 2002	20.00	40.00
24 Jeff Gordon Pepsi Billion $	15.00	30.00
25 Joe Nemechek 2002 UAW Delphi Speedy Gonzales	12.50	25.00
29 Kevin Harvick Goodwrench	12.50	25.00
29 Kevin Harvick Goodwrench Taz	12.50	25.00
30 Jeff Green AOL Daffy Duck	12.50	25.00
31 Robby Gordon Cingular Pepe le Pew	12.50	25.00
38 Elliott Sadler M&M's Groovy	12.50	25.00
48 Jimmie Johnson Lowe's Sylvester and Tweety	12.50	25.00
55 Bobby Hamilton Square D Marvin the Martian '02	12.50	25.00

2004 Winner's Circle Transporters 1:64

	EX	NM-MT
8 Dale Earnhardt Jr. JR	20.00	35.00
8 Dale Earnhardt Jr. JR Souvenir	15.00	30.00

	EX	NM-MT
8 Dale Earnhardt Jr. MLB All Star '03	15.00	30.00
8 Dale Earnhardt Jr. Oreo	15.00	30.00
8 Dale Earnhardt Jr. StainD	15.00	30.00
9 Kasey Kahne Dodge Souvenir	15.00	30.00
9 Kasey Kahne Dodge Mad Magazine	20.00	35.00
18 Bobby Labonte Interstate Batteries	15.00	25.00
20 Tony Stewart Home Depot	15.00	30.00
20 Tony Stewart Home Depot Shrek 2	15.00	25.00
20 Tony Stewart Home Depot Souvenir	15.00	25.00
21 Kevin Harvick Hershey's Kisses	15.00	30.00
24 Jeff Gordon DuPont Flames	20.00	35.00
24 Jeff Gordon DuPont Flames HMS 20th Anniversary	15.00	30.00
24 Jeff Gordon DuPont Flames Wizard of Oz	15.00	30.00
24 Jeff Gordon DuPont Rainbow	15.00	30.00
24 Jeff Gordon Pepsi Billion	15.00	30.00
24 Jeff Gordon Pepsi Shards	15.00	30.00
29 Kevin Harvick Goodwrench	15.00	25.00
38 Elliott Sadler M&M's	15.00	30.00
38 Elliott Sadler M&M's July 4	15.00	30.00
38 Elliott Sadler Pedigree Wizard of Oz	15.00	30.00
77 Brendan Gaughan Kodak Wizard of Oz	15.00	30.00
88 Dale Jarrett UPS	15.00	30.00
99 Michael Waltrip Aaron's Cat in the Hat	15.00	30.00

2005 Winner's Circle Transporters 1:64

	EX	NM-MT
6 Bill Elliott Hellman's Charlie Brown	15.00	30.00
8 Dale Earnhardt Jr. JR	15.00	30.00
9 Bill Elliott Milestones	15.00	25.00
9 Kasey Kahne Dodge Longest Yard	15.00	25.00
9 Kasey Kahne Mopar	15.00	30.00
9 Kasey Kahne Dodge	15.00	30.00
9 Kasey Kahne Mountain Dew	15.00	30.00
9 Kasey Kahne Dodge Pit Cap White	15.00	30.00
19 Jeremy Mayfield Dodge	12.50	25.00
19 Jeremy Mayfield Mountain Dew Pitch Black	15.00	25.00
20 Tony Stewart Home Depot	15.00	30.00
21 Kevin Harvick Reese's	15.00	25.00
21 Kevin Harvick Take 5	15.00	30.00
24 Jeff Gordon DuPont Flames	15.00	30.00
29 Kevin Harvick Goodwrench	15.00	25.00
33 Tony Stewart Mr. Clean AutoDry	15.00	25.00
38 Kasey Kahne Great Clips	15.00	30.00
38 Elliott Sadler M&M's	15.00	25.00
38 Elliott Sadler M&M's Halloween	15.00	25.00
38 Elliott Sadler M&M's July 4	15.00	25.00
38 Elliott Sadler M&M's	15.00	25.00
42 Jamie McMurray Havoline	15.00	25.00
81 Dale Earnhardt Jr. Oreo Ritz	15.00	30.00
88 Dale Jarrett UPS	15.00	25.00
01 Joe Nemechek Army	15.00	25.00
NNO James Dean 50th Anniversary Event	15.00	25.00

2006 Winner's Circle Transporters 1:64

	EX	NM-MT
19 Jeremy Mayfield Dodge	12.50	25.00
20 Tony Stewart Home Depot	15.00	30.00
29 Kevin Harvick Hershey's	15.00	25.00
88 Dale Jarrett UPS	15.00	25.00
NNO Dale Earnhardt Hall of Fame Dale Tribute split window box	15.00	25.00

2007 Winner's Circle Transporters 1:64

	EX	NM-MT
1 Martin Truex Jr. Bass Pro Shops	10.00	20.00
2 Kurt Busch Kurt	10.00	20.00
8 Dale Earnhardt Jr. DEI	12.50	25.00
8 Dale Earnhardt Jr. DEI Camo American Heroes	12.50	25.00
8 Dale Earnhardt Jr. DEI Stars & Stripes	12.50	25.00
9 Kasey Kahne Dodge Dealers	10.00	20.00
9 Kasey Kahne McDonald's	10.00	20.00
11 Denny Hamlin Fed Ex Express	10.00	20.00
11 Denny Hamlin Fed Ex Freight Marines American Heroes	10.00	20.00
12 Ryan Newman Alltel	10.00	20.00
17 Matt Kenseth DeWalt	12.50	25.00
19 Elliott Sadler Dodge Dealers Fantastic 4	15.00	30.00
20 Tony Stewart Home Depot	10.00	20.00
24 Jeff Gordon DuPont Department of Defense American Heroes	10.00	20.00
24 Jeff Gordon DuPont Flames	12.50	25.00
24 Jeff Gordon Pepsi	10.00	20.00
29 Kevin Harvick Shell Pennzoil	10.00	20.00
38 David Gilliland M&M's	10.00	20.00
43 Bobby Labonte Spiderman	10.00	20.00
43 Bobby Labonte STP	10.00	20.00
44 Dale Jarrett UPS	12.50	25.00
48 Jimmie Johnson Lowe's	10.00	20.00
48 Jimmie Johnson Lowe's Power of Pride American Heroes	10.00	20.00
55 Michael Waltrip NAPA	10.00	20.00
00 David Reutimann Burger King	10.00	20.00
01 Mark Martin U.S. Army American Heroes	10.00	20.00

2008 Winner's Circle Daytona 500 Transporters 1:64

	EX	NM-MT
29 Kevin Harvick Shell Pennzoil	12.50	25.00
42 Juan Pablo Montoya Texaco Havoline	12.50	25.00
48 Jimmie Johnson Lowe's	15.00	30.00
88 Dale Earnhardt Jr. AMP	15.00	30.00

2008 Winner's Circle Dually w/Car on Trackside Trailer 1:64

	EX	NM-MT
1 Martin Truex Jr. Bass Pro Shops	10.00	20.00
9 Kasey Kahne KK	10.00	20.00
24 Jeff Gordon DuPont Flames	12.50	25.00
29 Kevin Harvick Shell	10.00	20.00
42 Juan Pablo Montoya Texaco	10.00	20.00
42 Juan Pablo Montoya Big Red	10.00	20.00
48 Jimmie Johnson Lowe's	12.50	25.00
88 Dale Earnhardt Jr. AMP	15.00	30.00
88 Dale Earnhardt Jr. National Guard	15.00	30.00

2008 Winner's Circle Transporters 1:64

	EX	NM-MT
9 Kasey Kahne KK	15.00	25.00
12 Ryan Newman Daytona 500 Win	15.00	25.00
18 Kyle Busch M&M's	25.00	40.00
20 Tony Stewart Home Depot	20.00	35.00
24 Jeff Gordon DuPont Flames	20.00	35.00
24 Jeff Gordon Pepsi	20.00	35.00

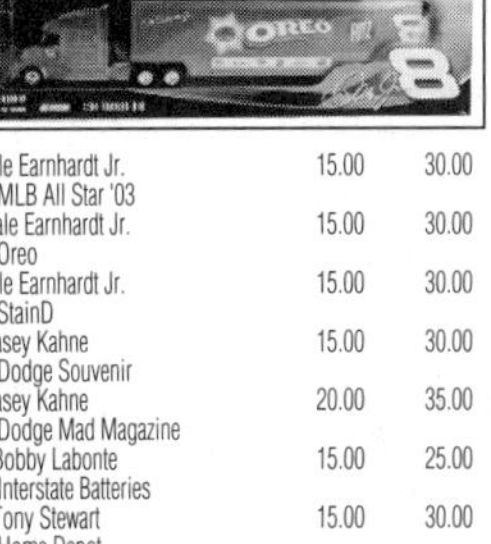

	EX	NM-MT
29 Kevin Harvick Shell	15.00	25.00
42 Juan Pablo Montoya Texaco	15.00	25.00
48 Jimmie Johnson Lowe's	20.00	35.00
88 Dale Earnhardt Jr. 3 Doors Down	20.00	35.00
88 Dale Earnhardt Jr. AMP	20.00	35.00
88 Dale Earnhardt Jr. Go Daddy	20.00	35.00
88 Dale Earnhardt Jr. National Guard	20.00	35.00

1987-90 Winross Transporters 1:64

Winross entered the transporter market in 1987. The pieces originally had a cost higher than the mass marketed pieces and were produced in short quantities. This makes these pieces some of the most valuable transporters available on the market.

	EX	NM-MT
NNO Bill Elliott Coors '90	100.00	200.00
NNO Bobby Gerhart ARCA '88	175.00	300.00
NNO Sterling Marlin Sunoco '90	60.00	100.00
NNO Stanley Smith Hamilton Trucking '88	90.00	150.00
NNO Rick Wilson Kodak Ford 1987	200.00	350.00
NNO Rick Wilson Kodak Mack 1987	300.00	500.00

1991 Winross Transporters 1:64

Winross continued their series of 1:64 transporters in 1991. They issued three different Bill Elliott transporters that year along with their first Richard Petty piece.

	EX	NM-MT
NNO Ken Bouchard ADAP	40.00	75.00
NNO Bill Elliott Coors Light	75.00	125.00
NNO Bill Elliott Fan Club	50.00	100.00
NNO Bill Elliott Museum with Blue Paint scheme	30.00	80.00
NNO Tommy Ellis Polaroid	100.00	175.00
NNO Terry Labonte Sunoco	90.00	160.00
NNO Richard Petty STP	100.00	175.00
NNO Ken Schrader Kodiak	50.00	90.00

1992 Winross Transporters 1:64

Winross produced several special issue transporters in their 1992 series. Dale Earnhardt was the focus of two of these specials having one produced for White Rose Collectibles and another one produced and packaged in a wooden box.

	EX	NM-MT
NNO Junie Donlavey Truxmore	50.00	90.00
NNO Bill Elliott Fan Club	50.00	90.00
NNO Bill Elliott Museum with red paint scheme	50.00	90.00
NNO Dale Earnhardt Goodwrench produced for White Rose Collectibles	90.00	150.00
NNO Dale Earnhardt Goodwrench in Wooden box	175.00	300.00
NNO Bobby Hamilton Country Time	30.00	60.00
NNO Tommy Ellis Polaroid	50.00	90.00
NNO Terry Labonte Sunoco	30.00	60.00
NNO Tiny Lund	20.00	40.00
NNO Jeff McClure Superior Performance	50.00	90.00
NNO J.D. McDuffie Pontiac Rumple	40.00	75.00
NNO Phil Parsons	50.00	90.00
NNO Kyle Petty Mello Yello	20.00	50.00
NNO Robert Pressley Alliance	90.00	150.00
NNO Richard Petty STP Fan Appreciation Tour	25.00	60.00
NNO Fireball (Glenn) Roberts	40.00	75.00
NNO Darrell Waltrip Western Auto Black,White&Red	30.00	80.00
NNO Darrell Waltrip Western Auto with Red paint scheme	75.00	125.00

1993 Winross Transporters 1:64

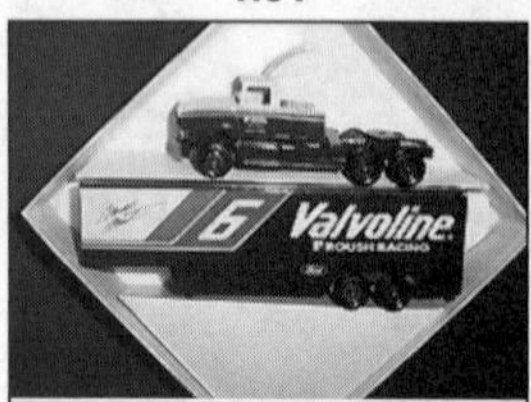

This series of Winross transporters is highlighted by a die cast for the late Alan Kulwicki. The series also includes the third year in a row that Winross produced a piece for the Bill Elliott Fan Club.

	EX	NM-MT
NNO Joe Bessey AC Delco	25.00	50.00
NNO Bill Elliott Fan Club	40.00	75.00
NNO Doyle Ford NASCAR Flags	20.00	40.00
NNO Jeff Gordon DuPont	30.00	80.00
NNO Steve Grissom Channellock	25.00	50.00
NNO Dale Jarrett Interstate Batteries	30.00	60.00
NNO Alan Kulwicki Hooters	40.00	80.00
NNO Sterling Marlin Maxwell House	30.00	60.00
NNO Mark Martin Valvoline	25.00	60.00
NNO Robert Pressley Alliance	50.00	90.00
NNO Mike Stefanik Auto Palace	25.00	50.00
NNO No Driver Association McClure Racing Kodak	75.00	125.00

1994 Winross Transporters 1:64

This series features a variation on the Davey Allison piece. The sponsors name was misspelled on the original pieces produced.

	EX	NM-MT
NNO Davey Allison Havoline misspelled Error	75.00	125.00
NNO Davey Allison Havoline Corrected	50.00	100.00
NNO Bill Elliott Budweiser	35.00	70.00
NNO Harry Gant Farewell Tour	50.00	90.00
NNO Goodyear Racing	25.00	50.00
NNO Terry Labonte Kellogg's	35.00	70.00
NNO Mac Tools Racing/4800	25.00	50.00
NNO Sterling Marlin Kodak	25.00	60.00
NNO Michael Waltrip Pennzoil	30.00	60.00

1995 Winross Transporters 1:64

This was the first series of transporters released under Winross' new price structure. The series features Bill Elliott's new McDonald's colors and Dale Jarrett sporting the colors of Mac Tools, his Busch ride at the time.

	EX	NM-MT
NNO Geoff Bodine Exide	25.00	60.00
NNO Bill Elliott McDonald's	35.00	70.00
NNO Dale Jarrett Mac Tools/2600	35.00	60.00
NNO Kevin Lepage Vermont Teddy Bear	35.00	60.00
NNO Dick Trickle Quality Care	35.00	60.00
NNO Mike Wallace Heilig-Meyers	35.00	60.00

1996 Winross Transporters 1:64

	EX	NM-MT
NNO Ward Burton MBNA	30.00	45.00
NNO Bill Elliott Mac Tonight	40.00	75.00
NNO David Green Caterpillar	20.00	45.00
NNO Ernie Irvan Havoline	45.00	60.00
NNO Sterling Marlin Kodak	35.00	60.00
NNO Michael Waltrip Citgo	35.00	50.00

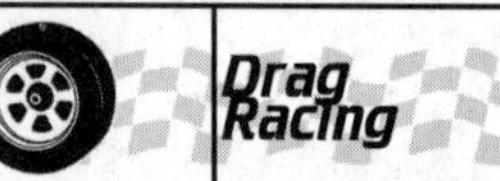

1995 Action/RCCA Dragsters 1:24

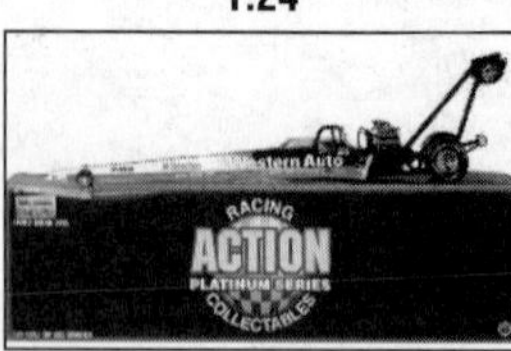

This series of dragsters started with the Mac Tools releases at the beginning of 1995. The first pieces all featured a Mac Tools logo and are the most difficult of all the dragsters to find. The 1997 and 1998 RCCA upgrade pieces contain serial numbers on the chassis of each car. Most were issued in the typical Action Racing Collectibles box for that era of release, with many also featuring a production run number on the box itself.

	EX	NM-MT
NNO Joe Amato Valvoline/5640	30.00	80.00
NNO Joe Amato Valvoline Mac Tools	50.00	120.00
NNO Shelly Anderson Western Auto/5520	25.00	60.00
NNO Pat Austin Castrol Syntex	30.00	60.00
NNO Kenny Bernstein Budweiser King/6492	30.00	80.00
NNO Kenny Bernstein Budweiser King Mac Tools	50.00	120.00
NNO Larry Dixon Miller Genuine Draft/6000	125.00	250.00
NNO Mike Dunn La Victoria Mac Tools	250.00	400.00
NNO Gatornationals Mac Tools	60.00	150.00
NNO Darrell Gwynn Extra Gold/Kendall	75.00	150.00
NNO Darrell Gwynn Extra Gold Quaker State/7000	40.00	80.00
NNO Darrell Gwynn Mopar Mac Tools	50.00	100.00
NNO Frank Hawley Coors Light	40.00	80.00
NNO Jim Head Smokin' Joe's/5004 (in plastic case)	200.00	400.00
NNO Eddie Hill 1988 Pennzoil Super Shops/3500	90.00	150.00
NNO Eddie Hill Pennzoil/6000	40.00	80.00
NNO Tommy Johnson Jr. Mopar	30.00	60.00
NNO Connie Kalitta American	25.00	50.00
NNO Shirley Muldowney Action/5004	50.00	100.00
NNO Gary Ormsby 1989 Castrol GTX RCCA/5712	30.00	80.00
NNO Don Prudhomme Skoal Bandit	100.00	200.00
NNO Don Prudhomme Skoal Bandit RCCA/5004	100.00	200.00
NNO Don Prudhomme Snake Final Strike	125.00	200.00
NNO Don Prudhomme Snake Final Strike Mac Tools	150.00	250.00
NNO Bill Reichert Bars Leak	25.00	60.00

1996 Action/RCCA Dragsters 1:24

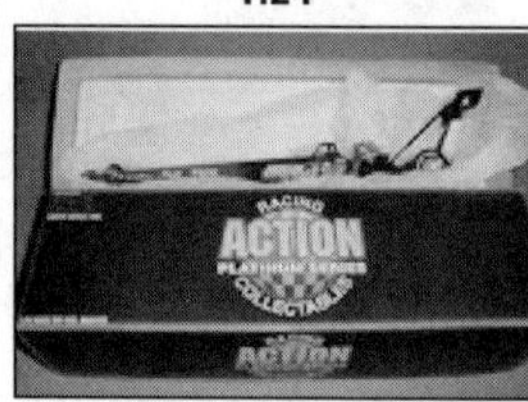

	EX	NM-MT
NNO Joe Amato Keystone	30.00	60.00
NNO Shelly Anderson Parts America RCCA/6000	30.00	80.00
NNO Mike Austin Red Wing Shoes/3500	25.00	60.00
NNO Kenny Bernstein Budweiser/2544	25.00	60.00
NNO Kenny Bernstein Budweiser Mac Tools Champion	40.00	100.00
NNO Larry Dixon Miller Splash/7500	30.00	80.00
NNO Larry Dixon Miller Splash Silver/10,000	30.00	80.00
NNO Mike Dunn Mopar/9000	25.00	60.00
NNO Don Garlits 1992 Kendall Supershops RCCA/3000	100.00	175.00
NNO Gatornationals Mac Tools	15.00	40.00
NNO Darrell Gwynn 1988 Budweiser RCCA	25.00	60.00
NNO Blaine Johnson Travers Blue/Yellow/7500	60.00	120.00
NNO Scott Kalitta American/7500	25.00	50.00
NNO Scott Kalitta American Mac Tools	40.00	80.00
NNO Chris Karamesines The Greek	25.00	50.00
NNO Cory McClenathan 1992 MacAttack	40.00	80.00
NNO Cory McClenathan McDonald's	25.00	60.00
NNO Cory McClenathan McDonald's Olympic/9000	25.00	60.00
NNO Tom McEwen Mobil RCCA/5500	25.00	60.00
NNO Shirley Muldowney Action RCCA	40.00	100.00
NNO Al Segrini Spies Hecker/5000	25.00	60.00
NNO Bob Vandergriff Jerzees	25.00	60.00
NNO Winston Eagle Red/7500	15.00	40.00
NNO Winston Select/5000	15.00	40.00

1997 Action/RCCA Dragsters 1:24

	EX	NM-MT
NNO Joe Amato Action White/1500	25.00	60.00
NNO Joe Amato Keystone	25.00	60.00
NNO Joe Amato Keystone Mac Tools	40.00	80.00
NNO Kenny Bernstein Budweiser/9008	25.00	60.00
NNO Kenny Bernstein Budweiser Mac Tools	50.00	100.00
NNO Kenny Bernstein Budweiser RCCA/3500	40.00	100.00
NNO Larry Dixon Miller Lite/10,000	30.00	60.00
NNO Gatornationals Mac Tools/8500	20.00	50.00
NNO Darrell Gwynn 1991 Coors Light/5004	40.00	80.00
NNO Jim Head Close Call	25.00	50.00
NNO Jim Head Close Call RCCA	30.00	60.00
NNO Doug Herbert Snap-On	25.00	60.00
NNO Eddie Hill Pennzoil/5700	40.00	80.00
NNO Blaine Johnson Travers Red and White/5000	50.00	100.00
NNO Scott Kalitta American RCCA/7500	25.00	60.00
NNO Cory McClenathan McDonald's	30.00	60.00
NNO Matco Supernationals	20.00	50.00
NNO Shirley Muldowney Action/5004	25.00	60.00
NNO Shirley Muldowney Action Mac Tools	50.00	100.00
NNO Shirley Muldowney Action RCCA	30.00	80.00
NNO Shirley Muldowney 1991 Otter Pops/5000	25.00	60.00
NNO Cristen Powell Royal Purple/4704	25.00	60.00
NNO Cristen Powell Royal Purple RCCA/2500	30.00	60.00
NNO Race Rock Cafe/1500	30.00	80.00
NNO Bruce Sarver CarQuest	20.00	50.00
NNO Gary Scelzi Winston	50.00	100.00
NNO Gary Scelzi Winston Matco Tools	50.00	100.00
NNO Gary Scelzi Winston RCCA/3000	50.00	100.00
NNO Bob Vandergriff Jerzees	25.00	60.00
NNO Bob Vandergriff Jerzees Mac Tools	30.00	80.00

1998 Action/RCCA Dragsters 1:24

	EX	NM-MT
NNO Joe Amato Tenneco/4008	25.00	60.00
NNO Joe Amato Tenneco Mac Tools/4500	30.00	60.00
NNO Joe Amato Tenneco RCCA	40.00	80.00
NNO Kenny Bernstein 1992 Budweiser 300 MPH/5000	50.00	100.00
NNO Kenny Bernstein 1992 Budweiser 300 MPH Mac Tools/4500	50.00	100.00
NNO Kenny Bernstein Budweiser/5000	40.00	80.00
NNO Kenny Bernstein Budweiser Mac Tools/4500	40.00	80.00
NNO Kenny Bernstein Budweiser RCCA/1200	50.00	100.00
NNO Kenny Bernstein Bud Lizard/5000	40.00	100.00
NNO Kenny Bernstein Bud Lizard Mac Tools	50.00	120.00
NNO Larry Dixon Miller Lite/4008	60.00	120.00
NNO Gatornationals Mac Tools/8000	15.00	40.00
NNO Eddie Hill Pennzoil/3500	30.00	60.00
NNO Cory McClenathan McDonald's	30.00	60.00
NNO Cory McClenathan McDonald's RCCA	40.00	75.00
NNO Cristen Powell Reebok White/3500	25.00	60.00
NNO Cristen Powell Reebok Orange	25.00	60.00
NNO Cristen Powell Reebok Orange RCCA	30.00	80.00
NNO Gary Scelzi Winston	40.00	80.00
NNO Gary Scelzi Winston RCCA/1500	40.00	100.00

1999 Action/RCCA Dragsters 1:24

	EX	NM-MT
NNO Joe Amato Dynomax Superman/7008	40.00	80.00
NNO Joe Amato Tenneco/3500	25.00	60.00
NNO Kenny Bernstein Bud 20th Ann/5508	30.00	80.00
NNO Larry Dixon Miller Lite Harley/5724	40.00	75.00
NNO Mike Dunn Mac Tools/5004	20.00	50.00
NNO Gatornationals Mac Tools/7500	20.00	50.00
NNO Gary Scelzi Winston/5004	25.00	60.00
NNO Gary Scelzi Winston Matco Tools/3000	30.00	60.00

2000 Action/RCCA Dragsters 1:24

	EX	NM-MT
NNO Joe Amato Dynomax/3708	30.00	80.00
NNO Joe Amato Dynomax Monsters/3816	40.00	80.00
NNO Kenny Bernstein Bud King/5004	25.00	60.00
NNO Kenny Bernstein Budweiser King Mac Tools/3000	25.00	60.00
NNO Kenny Bernstein Bud Olympic/7452	30.00	80.00
NNO Kenny Bernstein Budweiser Olympic Mac Tools/3000	30.00	80.00
NNO Larry Dixon Miller Lite Mac Tools/3300	30.00	80.00
NNO Mike Dunn Yankees Mac Tools/2498	40.00	100.00
NNO Mike Dunn Yankees DG Racing/1008	50.00	100.00
NNO Gatornationals Mac Tools/7000	20.00	5
NNO Doug Kalitta MGM Grand Mac Tools/3000	20.00	5
NNO Cory McClenathan MBNA	20.00	5
NNO Shirley Muldowney goracing.com RCCA/1500	20.00	5
NNO Tony Schumacher Exide/3504	25.00	5

2001 Action/RCCA Dragste 1:24

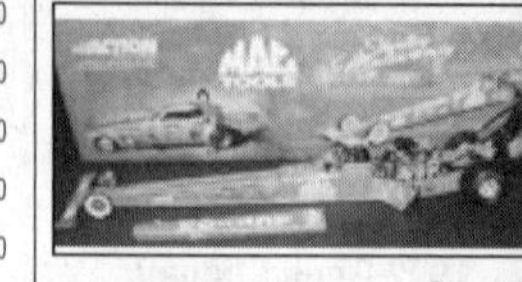

	EX	NM-
NNO Kenny Bernstein Budweiser/2772	50.00	8
NNO Larry Dixon Miller Lite Color/2396	30.00	6
NNO Larry Dixon Miller Lite Color Chrome/1300	40.00	8
NNO Mike Dunn Yankees/4428	40.00	8
NNO Mike Dunn Yankees Mac Tools/3000	40.00	8
NNO Mike Dunn Yankees Blue Chrome RCCA/504	60.00	12
NNO Gatornationals Mac Tools Gold/6000	20.00	5
NNO Doug Kalitta KISS Mac Tools/6000	40.00	8
NNO Mac Tools Thunder Valley/5004	25.00	5
NNO Mac Tools U.S Nationals/5004	30.00	6
NNO Shirley Muldowney Cha Cha Mac Tools/5004	25.00	6
NNO Shirley Muldowney goosehead.com/2100	20.00	5
NNO Shirley Muldowney goosehead.com Color Chrome/900	40.00	8
NNO Darrell Russell Valvoline James Dean/3720	25.00	6
NNO Gary Scelzi Winston/4236	35.00	7
NNO Tony Schumacher Army Color Chrome/900	40.00	8

2002 Action/RCCA Dragste 1:24

	EX	NM-
NNO Kenny Bernstein Budweiser Forever Red/9516	50.00	10
NNO Kenny Bernstein Budweiser Forever Red Mac Tools/1008	60.00	12
NNO Andrew Cowin Yankees/5796	30.00	6
NNO Andrew Cowin New York Yankees Muppets/4596	25.00	6
NNO Larry Dixon Miller Lite/3672	40.00	7
NNO Larry Dixon Miller Lite Mac Tools/1608	40.00	7
NNO Larry Dixon Miller Lite Elvis/5132	40.00	7
NNO Larry Dixon Miller Lite Elvis Mac Tools	40.00	8
NNO Larry Dixon Miller Lite Snake/1440	75.00	13
NNO Larry Dixon Miller Lite Snake Mac Tools/1296	90.00	15
NNO Don Garlits Matco Tools/5004	60.00	10
NNO Gatornationals Mac Tools/3504	25.00	6
NNO Doug Kalitta Mac Tools/3504	30.00	6
NNO Doug Kalitta Mac Tools KISS/3432	50.00	9
NNO Cory McClenathan Mac Tools U.S. Nationals/2500	30.00	6
NNO Shirley Muldowney Mac Tools Blue Angels/4104	30.00	7
NNO Shirley Muldowney Mac Tools Heart/6708	40.00	7
NNO Shirley Muldowney Mac Tools Muppet/7128	25.00	6
NNO Shirley Muldowney Mac Tools Peanuts/3676	25.00	6
NNO Darrell Russell Bilstein Engine Flush/3000	20.00	5
NNO Tony Schumacher Army/2346	30.00	6

2003 Action/RCCA Dragste 1:24

	EX	NM-
NNO Brandon Bernstein Budweiser/3804	35.00	7
NNO Larry Dixon Miller Lite/2712	35.00	7
NNO Don Garlits Summit 35th Anniversary/3504	50.00	9
NNO Gatornationals Mac Tools/1200	45.00	7
NNO Doug Herbert Snap-On Hulk/14,224	35.00	7
NNO Doug Kalitta	35.00	7

	EX	NM-MT
id Rock/3388		
Doug Kalitta lac Tools/2532	35.00	70.00
Doug Kalitta lac Tools KISS/1002	40.00	75.00
Doug Kalitta Vright Bros./2728	35.00	70.00
Mac Tools U.S Nationals/1200	40.00	75.00
Cory McClenathan 'ankees 100th Anniversary/2538	30.00	60.00
Cory McClenathan 'ankees 100th Anniversary Mac Tools/288	40.00	75.00
Shirley Muldowney Mac Tools Grease/2400	30.00	60.00
Shirley Muldowney Mac Tools Grease Mac Tools/2000	30.00	60.00
Shirley Muldowney Mac Tools Last Pass/4628	30.00	70.00
Shirley Muldowney Mac Tools Terminator 3/4408	35.00	60.00
Shirley Muldowney ink Flames/2100	35.00	60.00
Shirley Muldowney ink Flames Mac Tools/2000	35.00	60.00
Tony Schumacher rmy/2304	35.00	60.00

04 Action/RCCA Dragsters 1:24

	EX	NM-MT
Brandon Bernstein udweiser/2484	45.00	70.00
Brandon Bernstein udweiser Born On pril 4/3984	45.00	70.00
Larry Dixon Miller Lite/1512	40.00	60.00
Larry Dixon Miller Lite Can Promotion/1728	40.00	60.00
Larry Dixon Miller Lite Miller for President of Beers/1944	40.00	60.00
Larry Dixon Miller Lite President of Beers Mac Tools/408	40.00	60.00
Gatornationals Mac Tools	45.00	70.00
Doug Herbert ougzilla Brainerd/540	40.00	60.00
Doug Herbert ougzilla Chicago/696	40.00	60.00
Doug Herbert ougzilla Denver/684	40.00	60.00
D.Herbert/Dougzilla Gainesville	40.00	60.00
Doug Herbert ougzilla Indianapolis/1536	40.00	60.00
Doug Herbert ougzilla Pomona/1728	40.00	60.00
Doug Herbert ougzilla Reading/504	40.00	60.00
Doug Herbert ougzilla Saint Louis/684	40.00	60.00
Doug Herbert ougzilla Sonoma/528	40.00	60.00
Doug Herbert nap-On/3552	45.00	75.00
Tony Schumacher .S. Army Time MOTY/2004	45.00	70.00

05 Action/RCCA Dragsters 1:24

	EX	NM-MT
Brandon Bernstein ud AU/1716	60.00	100.00
Bradon Bernstein ud AU GM Dealers/278	60.00	100.00
Larry Dixon Miller Lite/1632	40.00	65.00
Doug Kalitta Mac Tools ames Dean 50th Anniversary/684	40.00	65.00
Tony Schumacher rmy/1478	40.00	65.00

06 Action/RCCA Dragsters 1:24

	EX	NM-MT
Doug Kalitta Mac Tools/1080*	50.00	75.00
Doug Kalitta Mac Tools GM Dealers*	50.00	75.00

1994 Action/RCCA Drag Racing Legends 1:64

	EX	NM-MT
Arnie Beswick Mr. B's	5.00	10.00
Bill Golden op Stock Eliminator	5.00	10.00

96 Action/RCCA Dragsters 1:64

eries started in 1996 and is highlight by two Blaine on issues. Each piece was packaged in a clear blister pack (Action Racing) or cardboard window box (RCCA). Most pieces featured a production run total on the package itself.

	EX	NM-MT
NNO Blaine Johnson Travers Blue and Yellow/22,128	7.50	15.00
NNO Blaine Johnson Travers Blue/Yellow RCCA/3500	10.00	20.00
NNO Cristen Powell Reebok White/5976	5.00	10.00

1997 Action/RCCA Dragsters 1:64

	EX	NM-MT
NNO Joe Amato Keystone/9000	5.00	12.00
NNO Joe Amato Keystone RCCA/3500	5.00	12.00
NNO Kenny Bernstein 1992 Budweiser 300 MPH RCCA	15.00	25.00
NNO Kenny Bernstein Bud King	6.00	15.00
NNO Larry Dixon Miller Lite/9000 in acrylic case	10.00	25.00
NNO Gatornationals Mac Tools/10,000	5.00	12.00
NNO Jim Head Close Call/10,080	6.00	12.00
NNO Eddie Hill Pennzoil/9432	6.00	12.00
NNO Blaine Johnson Travers Red and White	6.00	12.00
NNO Blaine Johnson Travers Red and White RCCA	15.00	25.00
NNO Cory McClenathan McDonald's	5.00	12.00
NNO Cory McClenathan McDonald's RCCA	6.00	15.00
NNO Shirley Muldowney Action	6.00	12.00
NNO Shirley Muldowney 1991 Otter Pops/10,080	6.00	12.00
NNO Cristen Powell Royal Purple	5.00	12.00
NNO Gary Scelzi Winston/12,000	6.00	12.00
NNO Gary Scelzi Winston RCCA/2500	6.00	12.00

1998 Action/RCCA Dragsters 1:64

	EX	NM-MT
NNO Joe Amato Tenneco/9000	5.00	12.00
NNO Kenny Bernstein Budweiser/7272	6.00	15.00
NNO Kenny Bernstein Budweiser RCCA/9772	7.50	15.00
NNO Kenny Bernstein Bud Lizard	5.00	12.00
NNO Kenny Bernstein Bud Lizard RCCA	6.00	15.00
NNO Larry Dixon Miller Lite/7056 in acrylic case	7.50	15.00
NNO Gatornationals Mac Tools	4.00	10.00
NNO Cory McClenathan McDonald's/7056	5.00	12.00
NNO Cory McClenathan McDonald's RCCA/2500	7.50	15.00
NNO Cristen Powell Reebok White/5976	6.00	12.00
NNO Cristen Powell Reebok White RCCA	6.00	15.00
NNO Gary Scelzi Winston	5.00	12.00
NNO Gary Scelzi Winston RCCA	6.00	15.00

1999 Action/RCCA Dragsters 1:64

	EX	NM-MT
NNO Joe Amato Dynomax Superman/7008	5.00	12.00
NNO Kenny Bernstein Bud 20th Ann/9000	7.50	15.00
NNO Larry Dixon Miller Lite Harley/7056 in acrylic case	15.00	25.00
NNO Mike Dunn Mopar/6048	5.00	12.00
NNO Gary Scelzi Winston/7560	5.00	12.00

2000 Action/RCCA Dragsters 1:64

	EX	NM-MT
NO Kenny Bernstein Bud Olympic	6.00	12.00

2002 Action/RCCA Funny Car 1:16

	EX	NM-MT
NNO John Force Castrol GTX 11-Time Champ/4248	50.00	90.00
NNO John Force Castrol GTX 100th Win/4132	60.00	100.00
NNO John Force Castrol GTX Norwalk Experience/4200	60.00	100.00

2003 Action/RCCA Funny Car 1:16

	EX	NM-MT
NNO John Force Castrol GTX High Mileage Halloween/300	250.00	400.00
NNO John Force Castrol GTX High Mileage Space Shuttle/4350	50.00	90.00
NNO John Force Castrol GTX High Mileage Three Stooges/3642	50.00	90.00
NNO Tony Pedregon Castrol Syntec/1000	50.00	90.00

2004 Action/RCCA Funny Car 1:16

	EX	NM-MT
NNO John Force Castrol High Mileage/1178	60.00	100.00
NNO John Force Castrol Mustang 40th Anniversary/714	100.00	200.00
NNO John Force Castrol GTX Start-Up Freedom's Flight/300	200.00	400.00

2005 Action/RCCA Funny Car 1:16

	EX	NM-MT
NNO John Force GTX Start Up James Dean 50th Anniversary/786	75.00	125.00
NNO John Force Castrol GTX 13X Champ/1266	100.00	150.00

1996 Action/RCCA Funny Car 1:24

This series of Funny Cars is highlighted by the first John Force issues. The 1997 RCCA upgrade pieces contain serial numbers on the chassis of each car. Most were issued in the typical Action Racing Collectibles Platinum Series box with many also featuring a production run number on the box itself.

	EX	NM-MT
NNO Pat Austin Red Wing Shoes/7500	20.00	50.00
NNO Whit Bazemore Smokin' Joe's RCCA/7500	60.00	100.00
NNO Kenny Bernstein 1988 Bud King RCCA/10,000	60.00	120.00
NNO Gary Densham NEC/5004	20.00	50.00
NNO Jim Epler 1994 Rug Doctor/7500	20.00	50.00
NNO John Force 1993 Castrol GTX RCCA/7500	50.00	100.00
NNO John Force 1994 Castrol GTX Flames RCCA/15,000	50.00	120.00
NNO John Force Castrol GTX	40.00	100.00
NNO John Force Castrol GTX Black	150.00	250.00
NNO John Force Castrol GTX Mac Tools	90.00	150.00
NNO John Force Castrol GTX Mac Tools Champion	100.00	150.00
NNO Gatornationals Mac Tools	15.00	40.00
NNO Al Hofmann Parts America/7500	20.00	50.00
NNO Kenji Okazaki Mooneyes	25.00	60.00
NNO Cruz Pedregon McDonald's	30.00	80.00
NNO Cruz Pedregon McDonald's RCCA/5000	30.00	80.00
NNO Winston Select RCCA/3500	30.00	60.00

1997 Action/RCCA Funny Car 1:24

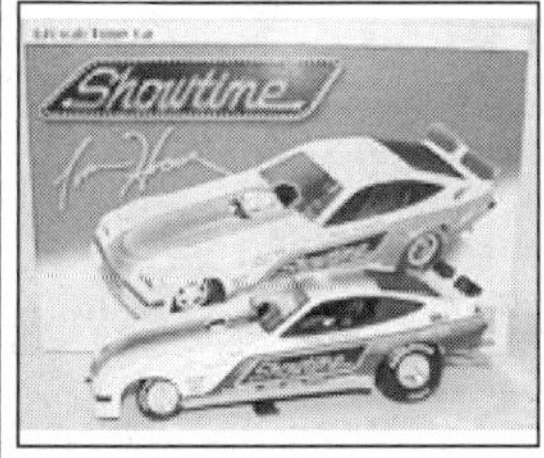

	EX	NM-MT
NNO Randy Anderson Parts America RCCA	30.00	60.00
NNO Whit Bazemore 1995 Fast Orange/6000	20.00	50.00
NNO Whit Bazemore 1995 Mobil 1/5508	20.00	50.00
NNO Whit Bazemore 1995 Mobil 1 RCCA/3500	20.00	50.00
NNO Whit Bazemore Winston/5748	40.00	80.00
NNO Whit Bazemore Winston RCCA/3500	50.00	100.00
NNO Raymond Beadle 1979 Blue Max/3500	25.00	60.00
NNO Kenny Bernstein 1979 Budweiser	40.00	80.00
NNO Kenny Bernstein '79 Chelsea King/6000	25.00	60.00
NNO Kenny Bernstein 1979 Chelsea King RCCA/3500	60.00	100.00
NNO Kenny Bernstein 1989 Budweiser Mac Tools	60.00	100.00
NNO Ron Capps Copenhagen/5468	40.00	100.00
NNO Ron Capps Copenhagen Mac Tools/4000	40.00	100.00
NNO Mike Dunn 1992 Pisano	30.00	60.00
NNO Chuck Etchells Kendall	30.00	60.00
NNO John Force 1977 Brute Force blue	40.00	80.00
NNO John Force 1978 Brute Force orange/9000	40.00	80.00
NNO John Force 1978 Brute Force orange RCCA/5000	40.00	80.00
NNO John Force Castrol GTX 6X Champ	125.00	200.00
NNO John Force Castrol GTX Mac Tools Mustang	60.00	100.00
NNO John Force Castrol GTX RCCA/3500 Mustang	50.00	120.00
NNO John Force Castrol GTX/15,000 Pontiac	30.00	80.00
NNO John Force Castrol GTX RCCA Pontiac/3500	50.00	100.00
NNO John Force Castrol GTX Driver of the Year	40.00	80.00
NNO John Force Castrol GTX Driver of the Year Mac Tools	60.00	100.00
NNO John Force Castrol GTX Driver of the Year RCCA	60.00	100.00
NNO John Force Castrol GTX Mustang	30.00	80.00
NNO Gatornationals Mac Tools/10,000	20.00	50.00
NNO Tom Hoover 1975 Showtime/5000	25.00	60.00
NNO Tom Hoover Pioneer/6000	25.00	60.00
NNO Bruce Larson 1989 Sentry/6000	20.00	50.00
NNO Bruce Larson USA-1 1975 Monza RCCA/3500	30.00	80.00
NNO Ed McCulloch 1988 Miller RCCA	40.00	100.00
NNO Ed McCulloch 1991 Otter Pops RCCA/3500	20.00	50.00
NNO Matco Supernationals	40.00	80.00
NNO Kenji Okazaki Mooneyes	30.00	60.00
NNO Cruz Pedregon McDonald's/5000	25.00	60.00
NNO Cruz Pedregon McDonald's RCCA	35.00	70.00
NNO Tony Pedregon Castrol GTX/5004	25.00	60.00
NNO Tony Pedregon Castrol GTX RCCA	30.00	80.00
NNO Don Prudhomme Army 1975 Monza RCCA/3500	40.00	80.00
NNO Don Prudhomme 1978 Army/4008	50.00	100.00
NNO Don Prudhomme 1978 Army RCCA/800	75.00	125.00
NNO Dean Skuza Matco	30.00	80.00

1998 Action/RCCA Funny Car 1:24

	EX	NM-MT
NNO Whit Bazemore 1996 Smokin' Joe's Mustang/4008	75.00	150.00
NNO Whit Bazemore 1996 Smokin' Joe's Pontiac RCCA/1000	125.00	225.00
NNO Whit Bazemore Winston Camaro/2508	40.00	80.00
NNO Whit Bazemore Winston Mustang/5004	40.00	80.00
NNO Whit Bazemore Winston Mac Tools	75.00	150.00
NNO Whit Bazemore Winston No Bull RCCA/2508	70.00	120.00
NNO Ron Capps Copenhagen Mac Tools/4500	40.00	100.00
NNO John Force Castrol GTX/9504	40.00	80.00
NNO John Force Castrol GTX Mac Tools	50.00	100.00
NNO John Force Castrol GTX RCCA/2500	60.00	120.00
NNO John Force Castrol GTX 7-Time Champ	75.00	150.00
NNO John Force Castrol GTX 7X Champ Mac Tools	75.00	150.00
NNO John Force Castrol GTX 7X Champ RCCA/2000	90.00	150.00
NNO John Force Castrol GTX Elvis/15,000	30.00	80.00
NNO John Force Castrol GTX Elvis Mac Tools/5000	40.00	80.00
NNO John Force Castrol GTX Elvis RCCA	50.00	100.00
NNO Gatornationals Mac Tools	20.00	50.00
NNO Al Hofmann Goodwrench	40.00	75.00
NNO Tom Hoover Pioneer	30.00	60.00
NNO Mac Tools 60th Anniversary	20.00	50.00
NNO Matco Supernationals/3000	25.00	60.00
NNO Cruz Pedregon Interstate Batteries	40.00	80.00
NNO Cruz Pedregon Interstate Batteries Hot Rod RCCA/1000	40.00	80.00
NNO Cruz Pedregon Interstate Batteries Small Soldiers	40.00	80.00
NNO Cruz Pedregon Interstate Batteries Small Soldiers Mac Tools	50.00	100.00
NNO Cruz Pedregon Interstate Batteries Small Soldiers RCCA	45.00	90.00
NNO Tony Pedregon Castrol Selena/7500	35.00	70.00
NNO Don Prudhomme 1983 Pepsi Challenge/4008	30.00	80.00
NNO Don Prudhomme 1983 Pepsi Challenge Mac Tools	35.00	70.00
NNO Dean Skuza Matco/3000	30.00	80.00
NNO Dean Skuza Matco Texas	40.00	80.00
NNO Jerry Toliver Mad	50.00	100.00
NNO Jerry Toliver Mad RCCA/1200	50.00	100.00
NNO Jerry Toliver Spy vs. Spy/3504	50.00	100.00
NNO Jerry Toliver Spy vs. Spy RCCA/1100	50.00	100.00

1999 Action/RCCA Funny Car 1:24

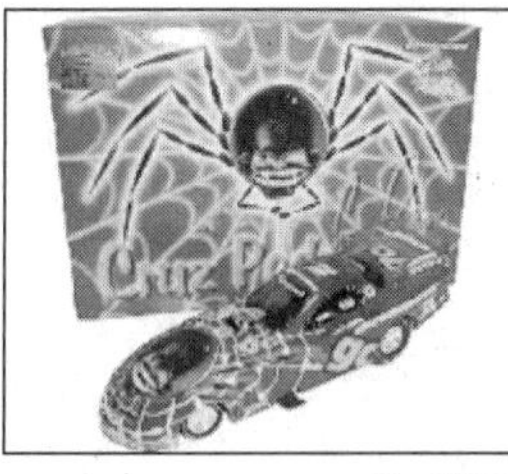

	EX	NM-MT
NNO Phil Burkhart Nitro Fish Mac Tools/5004	30.00	60.00
NNO Scotty Cannon Oakley Yellow/7500	40.00	80.00
NNO Ron Capps Copenhagen	125.00	250.00
NNO Ron Capps Copenhagen Gold/4008	75.00	150.00
NNO John Force Castrol GTX	50.00	100.00
NNO John Force Castrol GTX Mac Tools/5004	50.00	100.00
NNO John Force Castrol GTX 8-Time Champ	30.00	80.00
NNO John Force Castrol GTX Superman/15,944	75.00	150.00
NNO John Force Castrol GTX Superman Mac Tools	75.00	150.00
NNO Gatornationals Mac Tools	20.00	50.00
NNO Cruz Pedregon goracing.com/3504	30.00	60.00
NNO Frank Pedregon Penthouse/4008	25.00	60.00
NNO Don Prudhomme 1989 Skoal Red/2508	125.00	200.00
NNO Jerry Toliver WWF Smack Down Mac Tools/4500	40.00	80.00

2000 Action/RCCA Funny Car 1:24

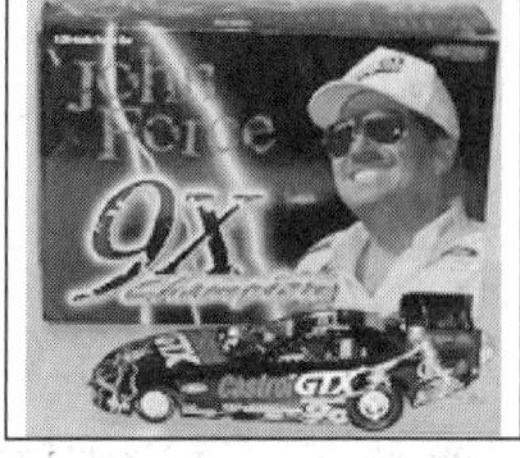

	EX	NM-MT
NNO Scotty Cannon Oakley Silver/5004	40.00	80.00
NNO Scotty Cannon Oakley Red/5004	40.00	80.00
NNO Ron Capps U.S.Tobacco/4692	25.00	60.00
NNO Dale Creasy Jr. Mad Ugly/3504	30.00	60.00
NNO Dale Creasy Jr. Mad Vote/4402	30.00	60.00
NNO Jim Epler WWF Kane/8424	30.00	60.00
NNO Jim Epler WWF Undertaker/7500	30.00	60.00
NNO John Force Castrol GTX/8292	30.00	80.00
NNO John Force Castrol GTX 9-Time Champ/20,016	30.00	80.00
NNO John Force Castrol GTX 9X Champ QVC Gold/2000	150.00	250.00
NNO John Force Cast.GTX Grinch/10,008	75.00	150.00
NNO John Force Castrol GTX Monsters/14,184	50.00	100.00
NNO Gatornationals Mac Tools/7000	20.00	50.00
NNO Al Hofmann Mooneyes Yellow	30.00	80.00
NNO Al Hofmann Mooneyes Yellow Mac Tools/3000	40.00	80.00
NNO Al Hofmann Mooneyes 50th/4008	30.00	60.00
NNO Al Hofmann Mooneyes 50th Mac Tools/3000	30.00	60.00
NNO Cruz Pedregon	25.00	60.00

	EX	NM-MT
Mac Tools Chili Pepper/4008		
NNO Tony Pedregon Castrol Syntec/3504	25.00	60.00
NNO Tony Pedregon Castrol Syntec Mac Tools/7000	30.00	60.00
NNO Tony Pedregon Castrol Syntec Monsters/5448	30.00	80.00
NNO Jerry Toliver WWF The Rock/14,400	25.00	60.00
NNO Jerry Toliver Stone Cold/7296	40.00	80.00

2001 Action/RCCA Funny Car 1:24

	EX	NM-MT
NNO Ron Capps Skoal Blue Mac Tools/3000	25.00	60.00
NNO Ron Capps Skoal Green Mac Tools/3000	25.00	60.00
NNO Gary Densham Mac Tools/3646	25.00	60.00
NNO Chuck Etchells Sunoco/3504	25.00	60.00
NNO John Force Castrol GTX/10,968	25.00	60.00
NNO John Force Castrol GTX Color Chrome/6504	30.00	60.00
NNO John Force Castrol GTX 10-Time Champ/20,016	20.00	50.00
NNO John Force Castrol GTX 10X Champ Mac Tools/3000	25.00	60.00
NNO John Force Castrol GTX 10X Champ RCCA/5004	30.00	80.00
NNO Gatornationals Mac Tools Gold/3000	20.00	50.00
NNO Mac Tools Thunder Valley/5004	25.00	50.00
NNO Mac Tools U.S Nationals/5004	25.00	50.00
NNO Matco Supernationals/3500	30.00	60.00
NNO Cruz Pedregon Flamin' Frank/2508	25.00	60.00
NNO Frank Pedregon 3A Racing/3504	30.00	60.00
NNO Frank Pedregon CSK/3504	30.00	60.00
NNO Frank Pedregon CSK Jurassic Park 3/6000	25.00	60.00
NNO Frank Pedregon Fram/3504	30.00	60.00
NNO Frank Pedregon Havoline/3504	30.00	60.00
NNO Tony Pedregon Castrol Syntec/3888	25.00	60.00
NNO Tony Pedregon Castrol Syntec Mac Tools/1608	30.00	60.00
NNO Tony Pedregon Castrol Syntec RCCA	40.00	80.00
NNO Tony Pedregon Castrol Syntec KISS/4008	50.00	100.00
NNO Tony Pedregon Castrol Syntec KISS Mac Tools/3000	50.00	100.00
NNO Cristen Powell Nitro Fish	25.00	60.00
NNO Dean Skuza Mopar Spider-Man/4008	40.00	80.00
NNO Jerry Toliver WWF Smackdown Mac Tools/3000	30.00	60.00
NNO Jerry Toliver XFL/5508	20.00	50.00
NNO Jerry Toliver XFL Mac Tools/3000	30.00	60.00
NNO Del Worsham Autolite/3504	50.00	100.00
NNO Del Worsham Checker/3504	40.00	80.00
NNO Del Worsham Checker Jurassic Park 3/6000	30.00	60.00
NNO Del Worsham Mountain Dew/3504	60.00	120.00

2002 Action/RCCA Funny Car 1:24

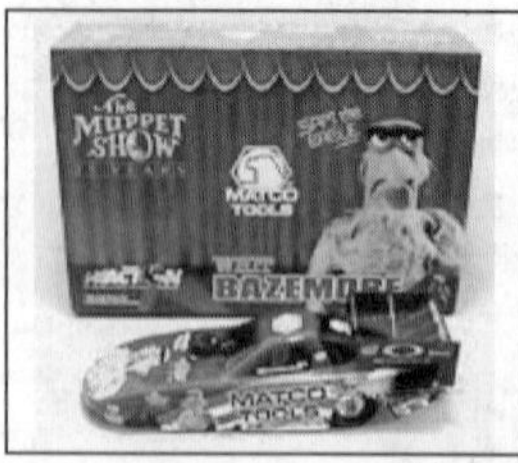

	EX	NM-MT
NNO Whit Bazemore Matco Tools Muppets/6288	25.00	60.00
NNO Ron Capps Skoal/3504	40.00	80.00
NNO Ron Capps Skoal Mac Tools/1704	50.00	80.00
NNO Gary Densham AAA of Southern California/4938	25.00	60.00
NNO Gary Densham AAA Mac Tools/1608	25.00	60.00
NNO John Force Castrol GTX/12,780	25.00	60.00
NNO John Force Castrol GTX Mac Tools/1800	30.00	80.00
NNO John Force Castrol GTX Clear/6396	20.00	50.00
NNO John Force Castrol GTX Color Chrome/1008	75.00	150.00
NNO John Force Castrol GTX 100th Win/4132	40.00	80.00
NNO John Force Castrol GTX 11-Time Champ/10,800	35.00	70.00
NNO John Force Castrol GTX 11-Time Champ Mac Tools/1800	45.00	80.00
NNO John Force Castrol GTX 11-Time Champ RCCA/480	75.00	125.00
NNO John Force Castrol GTX 11-Time Champ Mac Tools Platinum/504	300.00	500.00
NNO John Force Castrol GTX Elvis Chrome/2508	35.00	70.00
NNO John Force Castrol GTX Elvis Clear/5376	25.00	60.00
NNO John Force Castrol GTX Elvis Silver/18,036	25.00	60.00
NNO John Force Castrol GTX Norwalk Experience/5004	75.00	135.00
NNO John Force Castrol GTX Tasca unsigned	250.00	350.00
NNO John Force Castrol GTX Tasca Bob Tasca Signed/204	200.00	325.00
NNO John Force Castrol GTX Tasca Mac Tools/1299	150.00	250.00
NNO Gatornationals Mac Tools/3504	45.00	70.00
NNO Tommy Johnson Jr. Skoal/3504	50.00	100.00
NNO Tommy Johnson Jr. Skoal Mac Tools/1704	50.00	100.00
NNO Tommy Johnson Jr. Wildberry Skoal/2000	90.00	150.00
NNO Todd Paton Nitro Fish/2046	30.00	60.00
NNO Todd Paton Nitro Fish Mac Tools/1296	30.00	60.00
NNO Tony Pedregon Castrol Syntec/2754	30.00	60.00
NNO Tony Pedregon Castrol Syntec Mac Tools/1608	30.00	60.00
NNO Tony Pedregon Castrol Syntec KISS/3036	50.00	90.00
NNO Tony Pedregon Castrol Syntec Muppet/5124	30.00	60.00
NNO Tony Pedregon Castrol Syntec Muppet Mac Tools/1608	30.00	60.00
NNO Tim Wilkerson Mac Tools US Nationals/2508	30.00	60.00

2003 Action/RCCA Funny Car 1:24

	EX	NM-MT
NNO Gary Densham AAA/1776	35.00	60.00
NNO John Force Castrol GTX High Mileage/9756	35.00	60.00
NNO John Force Castrol GTX High Mileage Mac Tools/1464	40.00	75.00
NNO John Force Castrol GTX High Mileage 12X Champ Boxcars/9518	35.00	60.00
NNO John Force Castrol GTX High Mileage Halloween/2004	100.00	175.00
NNO John Force Castrol GTX High Mileage Three Stooges/9308	35.00	60.00
NNO John Force Castrol GTX King of the Hill/7800	35.00	60.00
NNO John Force Castrol King of Hill Mac Tools/1754	40.00	70.00
NNO John Force Castrol King of Hill Clear/2625	25.00	50.00
NNO Gatornationals Mac Tools/1200	45.00	70.00
NNO Mac Tools U.S Nationals	45.00	80.00
NNO Cruz Pedregon Advance Auto Parts/2028	35.00	60.00
NNO Cruz Pedregon Advance Auto Hulk/2354	35.00	60.00
NNO Tony Pedregon Castrol Syntec/2754	35.00	60.00
NNO Tony Pedregon Castrol Syntec Mac Tools/456	40.00	70.00
NNO Tony Pedregon Castrol Syntec KISS Green/3906	40.00	75.00
NNO Tony Pedregon Castrol Syntec X-Men/2754	35.00	60.00
NNO Dean Skuza Cornwell Tools Meatloaf/3378	35.00	70.00

2004 Action/RCCA Funny Car 1:24

	EX	NM-MT
NNO Gary Densham AAA of So.Cal/1500	40.00	60.00
NNO Gary Densham AAA of Southern California Popeye/1506	40.00	60.00
NNO John Force Castrol GTX High Mileage/4458	45.00	75.00
NNO John Force Castrol GTX Start Up/2418	45.00	75.00
NNO John Force Castrol GTX Start Up Mac Tools/408	45.00	75.00
NNO John Force Castrol GTX Start Up Freedom's Flight/1500	125.00	250.00
NNO John Force Castrol GTX Start-Up Mustang 40th Ann/2616	50.00	80.00
NNO John Force Castrol GTX Start-Up Mustang 40th Anniversary Color Chrome/444	150.00	250.00
NNO Gatornationals Mac Tools	45.00	70.00
NNO Eric Medlen Castrol Syntec/1992	100.00	200.00
NNO Cruz Pedregon Advanced Auto Supply Santana/996	50.00	80.00
NNO Tony Pedregon Quaker State/2340	45.00	70.00
NNO Tony Pedregon Quaker State Santana/1104	45.00	70.00
NNO Tony Pedregon Quaker State Shrek 2/2268	45.00	70.00
NNO Tony Pedregon Quaker State Shrek 2 RCCA/408	45.00	70.00
NNO Gary Scelzi Oakley HEMI/2082	60.00	100.00

2005 Action/RCCA Funny Car 1:24

	EX	NM-MT
NNO Whit Bazemore Matco Tools Vegas Centennial Liquid Metal/708	50.00	75.00
NNO Ron Capps Brut/1104	50.00	75.00
NNO Ron Capps Brut Hero Card/260	50.00	75.00
NNO John Force Castrol GTX Start Up Norwalk Bill Bader/2508	50.00	75.00
NNO John Force Castrol GTX Start Up Mustang Liquid Color/108	100.00	175.00
NNO John Force Castrol GTX Start Up James Dean 50th Ann Liquid Color/108	125.00	200.00
NNO John Force Castrol GTX 13X Champion/3600	50.00	75.00
NNO John Force Castrol GTX 13X Champ Hero Card/168	50.00	75.00
NNO John Force Castrol GTX 13X Champ Black Pearl/240	100.00	175.00
NNO John Force Milestones 30 Years of Racing/2364	50.00	75.00
NNO John Force Milestones 30 Years of Racing Mac Tools/300	50.00	75.00
NNO John Force Milestones 30 Years of Racing Maingate/150	50.00	75.00
NNO John Force Milestones 30 Years of Racing RCCA/444	50.00	75.00
NNO Eric Medlen Castrol Syntec/1650	75.00	150.00
NNO Eric Medlen Castrol Syntec Mac Tools/96	100.00	200.00
NNO Eric Medlen Castrol Syntec RCCA Liquid Color/78	125.00	250.00
NNO Eric Medlen Castrol Syntec '04 Pomona Raced Liquid Color/200	150.00	300.00
NNO Cruz Pedregon Advanced Auto/1096	40.00	65.00
NNO Gary Scelzi Oakley Mopar '05 Champion Chrome/444	60.00	100.00

2006 Action/RCCA Funny Car 1:24

	EX	NM-MT
NNO Whit Bazemore Matco Tools/1920	50.00	75.00
NNO Whit Bazemore Matco Tools Matco	50.00	75.00
NNO Ron Capps Brut/402	50.00	75.00
NNO Ron Capps Brut Matco	50.00	75.00
NNO John Force Castrol GTX/1668*	50.00	75.00
NNO John Force Castrol GTX Mac Tools*	50.00	75.00
NNO John Force Castrol GTX Matco*	50.00	75.00
NNO John Force Castrol GTX Carbon Fiber/2004	50.00	75.00
NNO John Force Castrol GTX Norwalk Raceway Soldier Tribute Color Chrome/2004	175.00	300.00
NNO John Force Castrol GTX Norwalk Soldier Tribute Liquid Color/2004	175.00	300.00
NNO John Force Castrol GTX Test/1500	50.00	75.00
NNO Robert Hight AAA So. Cal/780	50.00	75.00
NNO Robert Hight AAA Color Chrome/100	75.00	125.00
NNO Robert Hight AAA So. Cal. Mac Tools	50.00	75.00
NNO Robert Hight AAA White Gold/25	250.00	400.00
NNO Scott Kalitta Air Color Chrome/240	75.00	125.00
NNO Eric Medlen Castrol Syntec/672	75.00	150.00
NNO Eric Medlen Castrol Syntec Color Chrome/150	125.00	250.00
NNO Eric Medlen Castrol Syntec Mac Tools/692	75.00	150.00
NNO Eric Medlen Castrol Syntec White Gold/25	400.00	600.00
NNO Eric Medlen Castrol Syntec Fast & Furious Tokyo Drift/474	75.00	150.00
NNO Eric Medlen Castrol Syntec Fast & Furious Tokyo Drift Color Chrome/200	100.00	200.00
NNO Eric Medlen Castrol Syntec Fast & Furious Tokyo Drift White Gold/25	350.00	500.00
NNO Eric Medlen Ford Test/1200	75.00	150.00
NNO Eric Medlen Ford Test Color Chrome/240	100.00	175.00
NNO Cruz Pedregon Advance Auto Parts Color Chrome/300	75.00	125.00
NNO Tony Pedregon Quaker State Color Chrome/150	75.00	125.00

2006 Action/RCCA Funny Car Historical 1:24

	EX	NM-MT
6 John Force Castrol GTX '90 Champion/3072*	50.00	75.00
6 John Force Castrol GTX '90 Champion Mac Tools *	50.00	75.00
6 John Force Castrol GTX '90 Champion Matco *	50.00	75.00
6 John Force Castrol GTX '90 Champion Chrome/390	75.00	125.00
6 John Force Castrol GTX '90 Champion White Gold/25	600.00	800.00
NNO John Force Castrol GTX '91 Champion/3072*	50.00	75.00
NNO John Force Castrol GTX '91 Champion Mac Tools *	50.00	75.00
NNO John Force Castrol GTX '91 Champion Matco *	50.00	75.00
NNO John Force Castrol GTX '91 Champion Chrome/391	75.00	125.00
NNO John Force Castrol GTX '91 Champion White Gold/25	600.00	800.00
NNO John Force Castrol GTX '95 Champion/3072*	50.00	75.00
NNO John Force Castrol GTX '95 Champion Mac Tools *	50.00	75.00
NNO John Force Castrol GTX '95 Champion Matco *	50.00	75.00
NNO John Force Castrol GTX '95 Champion Chrome/395	75.00	125.00

1997-99 Action/RCCA Funny Car 1:32

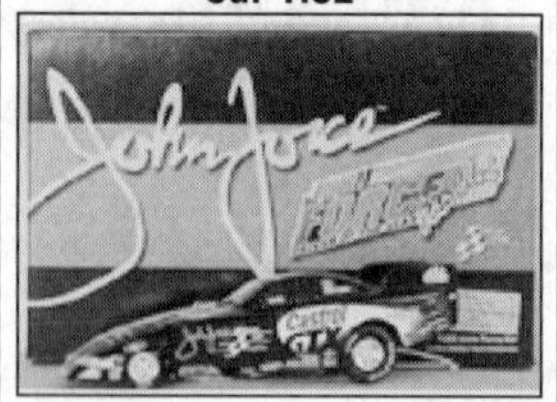

	EX	NM-MT
NNO John Force Castrol GTX 6-Time Champ/5000 1997	25.00	50.00
NNO John Force Castrol GTX DOY '97	15.00	40.00
NNO John Force Castrol GTX '98	15.00	40.00
NNO John Force Castrol GTX Superman/3500 '99	30.00	60.00
NNO John Force Castrol GTX 8X Champ/3500 '99	15.00	40.00
NNO John Force Tony Pedregon Elvis/Selena 2-car set '98	25.00	50.00
NNO Cruz Pedregon Inter.Batt.Hot Rod/2000 '99	15.00	30.00
NNO Frank Pedregon Penthouse/2500 '99	15.00	30.00
NNO Tony Pedregon Castrol Syntec RCCA/1500 '99	15.00	30.00

	EX
NNO Gary Scelzi Winston Mac Tools set with dragster 1998	35.00

1996 Action/RCCA Funny 1:64

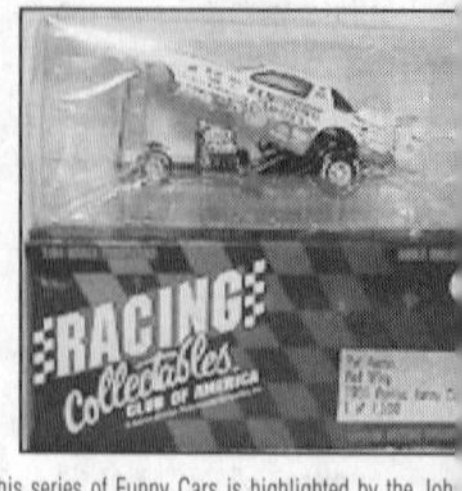

This series of Funny Cars is highlighted by the Joh issues and the Whit Bazemore Smokin' Joe's piece.

	EX	NM
NNO Pat Austin Red Wing Shoes/7500	5.00	
NNO Gary Densham NEC 1996/13,580	5.00	
NNO Jim Epler Rug Doctor	5.00	
NNO John Force Castrol GTX	7.50	
NNO John Force Castrol GTX black	15.00	
NNO John Force Castrol GTX black Mac Tools	15.00	
NNO John Force Castrol GTX black 6-time Champ Promo	3.00	
NNO John Force Castrol GTX black 6-time Champ/20,000	10.00	
NNO John Force Castrol GTX black 6-time Champ Fan Club	7.50	
NNO Al Hofmann Parts America	6.00	
NNO Kenji Okazaki Mooneyes	5.00	

1997 Action/RCCA Funny 1:64

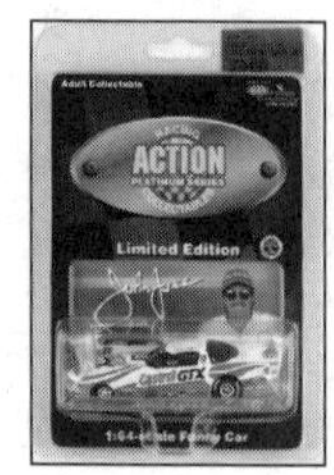

	EX	N
NNO Randy Anderson Parts America/9000	4.00	
NNO Randy Anderson Parts America RCCA/3500	5.00	
NNO Whit Bazemore 1995 Fast Orange	5.00	
NNO Whit Bazemore 1995 Mobil 1	5.00	
NNO Whit Bazemore 1995 Mobil 1 RCCA/9000	6.00	
NNO Whit Bazemore Winston/9000	7.50	
NNO Whit Bazemore Winston RCCA	15.00	
NNO Raymond Beadle 1979 Blue Max/12,000	5.00	
NNO Kenny Bernstein 1988 Budweiser RCCA/5000	12.50	
NNO Kenny Bernstein 1979 Budweiser/10,728	10.00	
NNO Kenny Bernstein 1979 Bud RCCA/2500	10.00	
NNO Kenny Bernstein 1979 Chelsea King	7.50	
NNO Kenny Bernstein 1979 Chelsea King RCCA/2000	7.50	
NNO Mike Dunn 1992 Pisano	4.00	
NNO Chuck Etchells Kendall	4.00	
NNO John Force 1977 Brute Force blue/16,056	7.50	
NNO John Force 1977 Brute Force blue RCCA/3500	8.00	
NNO John Force 1978 Brute Force orange	6.00	
NNO John Force 1993 Castrol GTX Jolly Rancher	6.00	
NNO John Force 1994 Castrol GTX RCCA/5000	6.00	
NNO John Force Castrol GTX Driver of the Year	6.00	
NNO John Force Castrol GTX Driver of Year RCCA/10,000	6.00	
NNO John Force Castrol GTX Mustang	6.00	
NNO John Force Castrol GTX Pontiac	6.00	
NNO John Force 1994 Castrol GTX Flames RCCA/5000	7.50	
NNO Gatornationals Mac Tools/10,000	6.00	
NNO Tom Hoover	5.00	

Pioneer RCCA/10,080

Bruce Larson Sentry	5.00	12.00
Bruce Larson USA-1 1975 Monza	5.00	12.00
Bruce Larson USA-1 1975 Monza RCCA	6.00	12.00
Ed McCulloch Miller Acrylic	6.00	15.00
Ed McCulloch 1991 Otter Pops	5.00	12.00
Cruz Pedregon McDonald's/10,080	5.00	12.00
Cruz Pedregon McDonald's RCCA/3500	5.00	12.00
Tony Pedregon Castrol GTX	5.00	12.00
Don Prudhomme Army 1975 Monza RCCA/3500	6.00	15.00
Don Prudhomme 1978 Army	6.00	15.00

998 Action/RCCA Funny Car 1:64

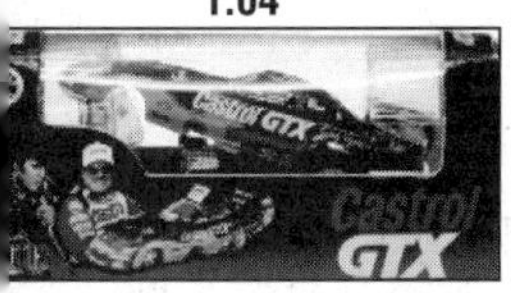

	EX	NM-MT
Whit Bazemore Winston/11,500	6.00	15.00
Whit Bazemore Winston RCCA/2500	10.00	20.00
Ron Capps Copenhagen	6.00	15.00
John Force Castrol GTX	7.50	15.00
John Force Castrol GTX RCCA	10.00	20.00
John Force Castrol GTX 7-Time Champ	6.00	15.00
John Force Castrol GTX Elvis	6.00	15.00
John Force Castrol GTX Elvis Mac Tools	7.50	15.00
John Force Castrol GTX Elvis RCCA	7.50	15.00
Gatornationals Mac Tools/10,080	5.00	12.00
Al Hofmann Goodwrench	6.00	15.00
Tom Hoover Pioneer	5.00	12.00
Cruz Pedregon Interstate Batteries	6.00	12.00
Cruz Pedregon Interstate Batteries Small Soldiers/12,000	5.00	12.00
Cruz Pedregon Interstate Batteries Small Soldiers RCCA/3500	6.00	15.00
Tony Pedregon Castrol Selena	5.00	12.00
Tony Pedregon Castrol Selena RCCA/5000	6.00	15.00
Tony Pedregon Castrol Syntec/8004	5.00	12.00
Tony Pedregon Castrol Syntec RCCA/2500	6.00	15.00
Don Prudhomme 1983 Pepsi Challenge/7056	5.00	12.00
Jerry Toliver Mad/7056	5.00	12.00
Jerry Toliver Mad RCCA/2500	6.00	15.00
Jerry Toliver Spy vs. Spy/7056	5.00	12.00
Jerry Toliver Spy vs. Spy RCCA/2500	6.00	15.00

999 Action/RCCA Funny Car 1:64

	EX	NM-MT
John Force Castrol GTX 8-Time Champ	6.00	15.00
John Force Castrol GTX Superman	6.00	15.00
Cruz Pedregon goracing.com/7500	5.00	12.00

000 Action/RCCA Funny Car 1:64

	EX	NM-MT
Dale Creasy Jr. Mad Ugly	5.00	12.00
Jim Epler WWF Undertaker/7992	5.00	12.00
John Force Castrol GTX/7560	7.50	15.00
John Force Castrol GTX Monsters	6.00	15.00
John Force Castrol GTX 9-Time Champ/19,008	10.00	20.00
Tony Pedregon Castrol Syntec Monsters/4392	6.00	15.00
Jerry Toliver The Rock/9000	5.00	12.00
Jerry Toliver Stone Cold/7992	5.00	12.00

001 Action/RCCA Funny Car 1:64

	EX	NM-MT
John Force Castrol GTX/12,000	7.50	15.00
John Force Castrol GTX RCCA/1104	10.00	20.00
John Force	10.00	20.00

Castrol GTX in oil can

NNO John Force Castrol GTX 10-Time Champ	7.50	15.00
NNO John Force Castrol GTX 10-Time Champ RCCA/504	10.00	20.00
NNO Tony Pedregon Castrol Syntec KISS	20.00	40.00

2002 Action/RCCA Funny Car 1:64

	EX	NM-MT
NNO John Force Castrol GTX/8856	10.00	20.00
NNO John Force Castrol GTX 11-Time Champ/7752	10.00	20.00
NNO John Force Castrol GTX 4-car set/7500	40.00	80.00
NNO John Force Castrol GTX Elvis Silver in tin/17,280	7.50	20.00

2003 Action/RCCA Funny Car 1:64

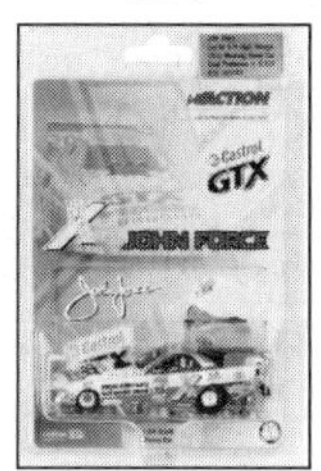

	EX	NM-MT
NNO John Force Castrol GTX High Mileage/6124	10.00	20.00
NNO John Force Castrol GTX King of the Hill/5796	10.00	20.00

2004 Action/RCCA Funny Car 1:64

	EX	NM-MT
NNO John Force Castrol GTX High Mileage w/tire/5136	10.00	20.00

1996 Action/RCCA Pro Stock 1:24

	EX	NM-MT
NNO Jerry Eckman Pennzoil/5004	25.00	60.00
NNO Jerry Eckman Pennzoil RCCA/1500	40.00	100.00

1997 Action/RCCA Pro Stock 1:24

This series of cars marks the entry of Action into the Pro Stock division of the NHRA. The series is highlighted by the RCCA pieces in which each chassis is serial numbered. The RCCA pieces also contain more detail than their Action counterparts.

	EX	NM-MT
NNO Darrell Alderman Mopar white roof	30.00	60.00
NNO Darrell Alderman Mopar black roof Mac Tools	40.00	80.00
NNO Darrell Alderman Mopar black roof RCCA/3500	30.00	60.00
NNO Darrell Alderman Mopar white roof RCCA/3500	40.00	80.00
NNO Bruce Allen Slick 50	20.00	50.00
NNO Bruce Allen Slick 50 RCCA	40.00	80.00
NNO Gatornationals Mac Tools/8000	20.00	50.00
NNO Scott Geoffrion Mopar black roof/5504	20.00	50.00
NNO Scott Geoffrion Mopar black roof Mac Tools	40.00	80.00
NNO Scott Geoffrion Mopar black roof RCCA	25.00	60.00
NNO Scott Geoffrion Mopar white roof/9504	20.00	50.00
NNO Scott Geoffrion Mopar white roof RCCA	25.00	60.00
NNO Bob Glidden 1996 Quality Care/6000	30.00	60.00
NNO Bob Glidden 1996 Quality Care RCCA	40.00	80.00
NNO Roy Hill Castrol Hill's Racing School/6000	25.00	60.00
NNO Roy Hill Castrol Hill's Racing School RCCA	40.00	80.00
NNO Allen Johnson Amoco/6000	20.00	50.00
NNO Allen Johnson Amoco RCCA/1500	40.00	80.00
NNO Kurt Johnson AC Delco/7008	20.00	50.00
NNO Kurt Johnson AC Delco GM Dealer/3000	30.00	60.00
NNO Warren Johnson 1995 Performance Parts/3508	35.00	70.00
NNO Warren Johnson 1995 Performance Parts RCCA	40.00	80.00
NNO Warren Johnson Performance Parts/7008	25.00	60.00
NNO Warren Johnson Performance Parts RCCA/3508	40.00	80.00
NNO Warren Johnson Goodwrench Plus/9024	30.00	60.00
NNO Warren Johnson Goodwrench Plus RCCA	40.00	80.00
NNO Tom Martino Six Flags	30.00	60.00
NNO Larry Morgan Raybestos	25.00	60.00
NNO Larry Morgan Raybestos RCCA	30.00	80.00
NNO Mark Pawuk Summit Racing/6000	15.00	40.00
NNO Mark Pawuk Summit Racing RCCA/1200	25.00	60.00
NNO Rickie Smith Carrier	20.00	50.00
NNO Rickie Smith Carrier RCCA	40.00	80.00
NNO Jim Yates McDonald's	25.00	60.00
NNO Jim Yates McDonald's RCCA	40.00	80.00

1998 Action/RCCA Pro Stock 1:24

	EX	NM-MT
NNO Darrell Alderman Mopar	35.00	70.00
NNO Mike Edwards JK Racing	20.00	50.00
NNO Gatornationals Mac Tools/8000	15.00	40.00
NNO Warren Johnson GM Performance 1995 Olds RCCA/1500	30.00	60.00
NNO Scott Geoffion Mopar	30.00	60.00
NNO Tom Martino Six Flags	30.00	60.00

1999 Action/RCCA Pro Stock 1:24

	EX	NM-MT
NNO Jeg Coughlin Jeg's Mac Tools/4000	15.00	40.00
NNO Jeg Coughlin Jeg's ROY Mac Tools/4000	15.00	40.00
NNO Troy Coughlin Jeg's Mac Tools/4000	15.00	40.00
NNO Gatornationals Mac Tools/7000	20.00	50.00
NNO Kurt Johnson AC Delco/3000	20.00	50.00
NNO Warren Johnson Goodwrench/3000	90.00	150.00
NNO Warren Johnson Goodwrench Superman	60.00	100.00
NNO Pat Musi NEC/2500	20.00	50.00
NNO Mark Pawuk Summit Racing	25.00	50.00

2000 Action/RCCA Pro Stock 1:24

	EX	NM-MT
NNO Kurt Johnson AC Delco/1500	25.00	50.00
NNO Warren Johnson Goodwrench Plus/3684	45.00	80.00
NNO Gatornationals Mac Tools/6000	20.00	50.00

2001 Action/RCCA Pro Stock 1:24

	EX	NM-MT
NNO Gatornationals Mac Tools Gold/3000	20.00	50.00
NNO Mac Tools U.S Nationals/5004	25.00	50.00
NNO Matco Supernationals/5000	20.00	50.00

2002 Action/RCCA Pro Stock 1:24

	EX	NM-MT
NNO Jeg Coughlin Jeg's/4456	25.00	60.00
NNO M Edwards Mac Tools US Nationals/2508	25.00	50.00
NNO Gatornationals Mac Tools/3504	25.00	50.00
NNO Kurt Johnson AC Delco/3612	30.00	60.00
NNO Kurt Johnson AC Delco KISS/3760	40.00	80.00
NNO Mac Tools Thunder Valley/3504	20.00	50.00

2003 Action/RCCA Pro Stock 1:24

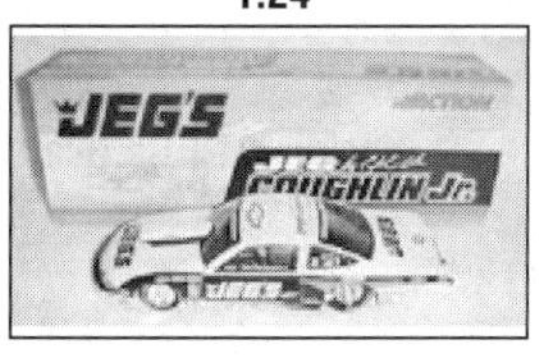

	EX	NM-MT
NNO Jeg Coughlin Jeg's Mail Order/2988	30.00	60.00
NNO Troy Coughlin Jeg's Mail Order/1896	30.00	60.00
NNO Gatornationals Mac Tools/1200	45.00	70.00
NNO Kurt Johnson AC Delco KISS/3124	35.00	60.00
NNO Kurt Johnson AC Delco KISS RCCA/340		
NNO Mac Tools U.S Nationals/1200	45.00	70.00

2004 Action/RCCA Pro Stock 1:24

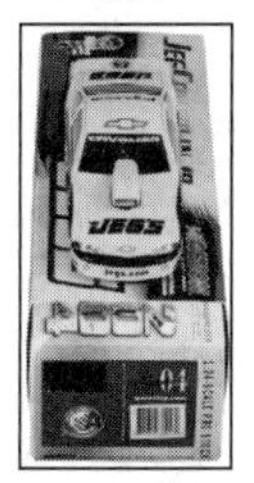

	EX	NM-MT
NNO Jeg Coughlin Jr. Jeg's Mail Order/2008	45.00	70.00
NNO Jeg Coughlin Jr. Jeg's Mail Order Spy vs. Spy/888	45.00	70.00
NNO Troy Coughlin Jeg's Mail Order/1656	45.00	70.00
NNO Gatornationals Mac Tools/1400	40.00	70.00
NNO Kurt Johnson AC Delco/2712	45.00	70.00

1997 Action/RCCA Pro Stock 1:64

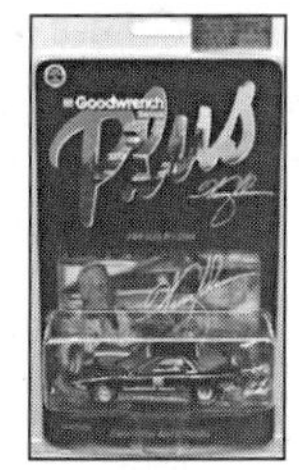

This series of cars marked the entry of Action into the Pro Stock division of the NHRA. The Action Racing pieces were issued in blister packages while the RCCA pieces were packaged in typical RCCA boxes. Most cars were serial numbered on the package itself. The RCCA pieces feature a serial numbered chassis as well.

	EX	NM-MT
NNO Darrell Alderman Mopar black roof/16,244	5.00	12.00
NNO Darrell Alderman Mopar black roof RCCA	6.00	15.00
NNO Darrell Alderman Mopar white roof/9000	5.00	12.00
NNO Darrell Alderman Mopar white roof RCCA	6.00	15.00
NNO Bruce Allen Slick 50/10,080	5.00	12.00
NNO Bruce Allen Slick 50 RCCA	6.00	15.00
NNO Jerry Eckman Pennzoil/10,080	5.00	12.00
NNO Gatornationals Mac Tools	4.00	10.00
NNO Scott Geoffrion Mopar black roof/9000	5.00	12.00
NNO Scott Geoffrion Mopar black roof RCCA	6.00	15.00
NNO Scott Geoffrion Mopar white roof/10,000	5.00	12.00
NNO Scott Geoffrion Mopar white roof RCCA/3500	6.00	15.00
NNO Bob Glidden 1996 Quality Care	5.00	12.00
NNO Bob Glidden 1996 Quality Care RCCA/1500	10.00	20.00
NNO Allen Johnson Amoco/9000	5.00	12.00
NNO Kurt Johnson AC Delco/12,000	5.00	12.00
NNO Kurt Johnson AC Delco RCCA/1500	10.00	18.00
NNO Warren Johnson Performance Parts/12,024	6.00	12.00
NNO Warren Johnson Performance Parts RCCA	7.50	15.00
NNO Warren Johnson Goodwrench Plus/15,000	6.00	12.00
NNO Warren Johnson	10.00	20.00

Goodwrench Plus RCCA/3500

NNO George Marnell Marnell Red&White		
NNO Larry Morgan Raybestos	6.00	12.00
NNO Don Nicholson Nalley&Nicholson 1963 Chevy/10,080	6.00	12.00
NNO Mark Pawuk Summit Racing	5.00	12.00
NNO Rickie Smith Carrier	5.00	12.00
NNO Rickie Smith Carrier RCCA	6.00	15.00
NNO Dave Strickler Old Reliable 1963 Chevy/10,080	6.00	12.00
NNO Jim Yates McDonald's/10,000	5.00	12.00
NNO Jim Yates McDonald's RCCA/3500	6.00	15.00

1998 Action/RCCA Pro Stock 1:64

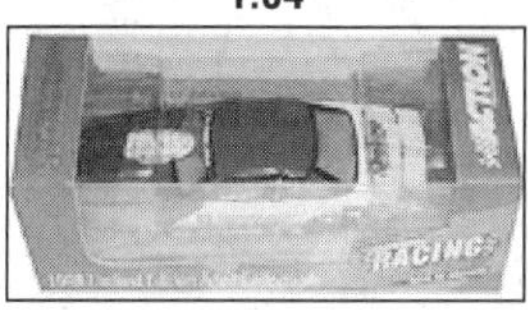

	EX	NM-MT
NNO Gatornationals Mac Tools	4.00	10.00
NNO Warren Johnson 1995 Performance Parts RCCA/3500	6.00	15.00

1999 Action/RCCA Pro Stock 1:64

	EX	NM-MT
NNO Warren Johnson Goodwrench Superman	10.00	20.00

1995-02 Action/RCCA NHRA Transporters 1:64

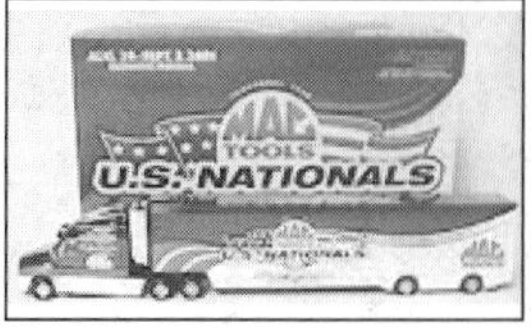

This series of die-cast pieces features the trucks and transporters that haul the cars from race to race. The first piece released in this series was the Gator Nationals promotional piece.

	EX	NM-MT
NNO Joe Amato Valvoline Mac Tools	50.00	90.00
NNO Mike Dunn Yankees/2934 '01	25.00	50.00
NNO John Force Castrol GTX Bus	40.00	70.00
NNO John Force Castrol GTX Mac Tools 1996	125.00	200.00
NNO John Force Castrol GTX Mac Tools/4000 1997	60.00	100.00
NNO John Force Castrol GTX/3012 '02	30.00	60.00
NNO John Force Cast.GTX RCCA/120 '02		
NNO John Force Castrol GTX Color Chrome/504 '02	30.00	80.00
NNO Gatornationals Mac Tools '95	250.00	350.00
NNO Gatornationals Mac Tools '96	25.00	60.00
NNO Gatornationals Mac Tools '97/5000	25.00	60.00
NNO Gatornationals Mac Tools '98/7500	20.00	50.00
NNO Gatornationals Mac Tools '99/5000	20.00	50.00
NNO Gatornationals Mac Tools '00/4000	20.00	40.00
NNO Gatornationals Mac Tools '02/2508	20.00	40.00
NNO Bob Glidden Quality Care Mac Tools	60.00	100.00
NNO Mac Tools U.S Nationals '01/5016	20.00	50.00
NNO Matco Supernationals '97	50.00	100.00

1999 Action/RCCA Pro Stock Bikes 1:9

These bikes were only available thru the club.

	EX	NM-MT
NNO Ron Ayers Mac Tools/5000	75.00	150.00
NNO Antron Brown Troy Vincent's/5000	75.00	150.00
NNO Gatornationals Mac Tools/7000	60.00	100.00
NNO Matt Hines Superman/4440	175.00	300.00
NNO Matt Hines Vance&Hines/5000	75.00	150.00
NNO Angelle Seeling Winston/6000	125.00	250.00

2000 Action/RCCA Pro Stock Bikes 1:9

	EX	NM-MT
NNO Brian Ayers Mac Tools/5004	30.00	60.00
NNO Ron Ayers Mac Tools/3504	30.00	80.00

	EX	NM-MT
NNO Ron Ayers Mac Tools Club/3000	30.00	80.00
NNO Gatornationals Mac Tools/5208	30.00	80.00
NNO Matt Hines Eagle One	30.00	60.00
NNO Matt Hines Eagle One Mac Tools/3000	45.00	80.00
NNO Steve Johnson Snap-on/4866	25.00	60.00
NNO John Myers 1996 Snap-on Torco/3066	50.00	100.00
NNO Tony Mullen mall.com/3156	30.00	80.00
NNO Angelle Seeling Close Call/3906	50.00	100.00

2001 Action/RCCA Pro Stock Bikes 1:9

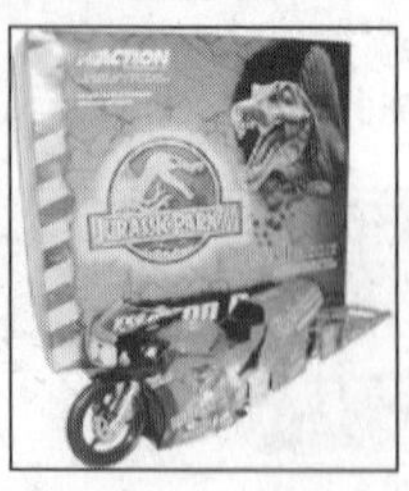

	EX	NM-MT
NNO Ron Ayers Mac Tools/2508	30.00	80.00
NNO Antron Brown Jurassic Park III/5010	30.00	80.00
NNO Antron Brown Mac Tools/2508	40.00	80.00
NNO Scotty Cannon Oakley	60.00	100.00
NNO Gatornationals Mac Tools/6000	25.00	50.00
NNO Matt Hines Eagle One James Dean/2676	40.00	80.00
NNO Steve Johnson Snap-on/2850	40.00	80.00
NNO Mac Tools U.S.Nationals/5004	40.00	80.00
NNO Dave Schultz Sunoco/4200	50.00	100.00
NNO Dave Schultz Sunoco Dealer/1200	60.00	100.00
NNO Angelle Seeling Winston/6196	60.00	100.00
NNO Angelle Seeling Winston Dealer/3208	60.00	100.00
NNO Angelle Seeling Winston Silver/3504	60.00	100.00
NNO Angelle Seeling Winston Silver RCCA/504	60.00	120.00

2002 Action/RCCA Pro Stock Bikes 1:9

	EX	NM-MT
NNO Antron Brown Mac Tools/2000	90.00	150.00
NNO Gatornationals Mac Tools/2508	25.00	60.00
NNO Craig Treble Matco Tools Muppet/4014	40.00	80.00

2003 Action/RCCA Pro Stock Bikes 1:9

	EX	NM-MT
NNO Gatornationals Mac Tools/1200	75.00	125.00
NNO Mac Tools Thunder Valley/1200	90.00	150.00
NNO Mac Tools U.S.Nationals	75.00	150.00

2005 Action/RCCA Pro Stock Bikes 1:9

	EX	NM-MT
NNO Craig Treble Matco Tools Las Vegas 100th Anniversary/228	50.00	75.00
NNO Craig Treble Matco Tools Las Vegas 100th Anniversary Matco/750	50.00	75.00

2000 Action/RCCA Pro Stock Bikes 1:24

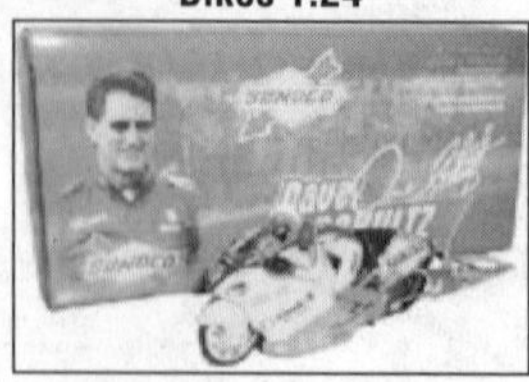

	EX	NM-MT
NNO Dave Schultz Sunoco/4200	15.00	30.00
NNO Dave Schultz Sunoco Mac Tools/3000	25.00	50.00

2000 Action/RCCA Pro Stock Bikes 1:43

	EX	NM-MT
NNO Matt Hines Eagle One/5400	15.00	30.00

2000 Action QVC For Race Fans Only Funny Car 1:24

	EX	NM-MT
NNO John Force Castrol GTX 9X Champ. Gold/2000	125.00	200.00

1999 Brookfield NHRA Dually with Trailer 1:24

	EX	NM-MT
NNO John Force Castrol GTX Superman Mac Tools	100.00	175.00

2002 Brookfield NHRA Dually with Trailer 1:24

	EX	NM-MT
NNO John Force Castrol GTX/1768	50.00	100.00
NNO John Force Castrol GTX Silver/456	75.00	135.00

2004 Classic Garage/Ertl Vintage Pro Stock 1:18

	EX	NM-MT
NNO Dick Brannan 1964 Ford Thunderbolt/4000	60.00	100.00

2002 Ertl American Muscle Arnie Beswick 1:18

	EX	NM-MT
NNO Arnie Beswick 1962 Catalina	20.00	40.00
NNO Arnie Beswick 1968 GTO	20.00	40.00
NNO Arnie Beswick 1969 GTO	20.00	40.00
NNO Arnie Beswick 1973 Trans Am	20.00	40.00

1999 Ertl Proshop Funny Car 1:24

	EX	NM-MT
NNO Cory Lee Pioneer/2499	20.00	40.00
NNO Frank Manzo Kendall/2499	20.00	40.00
NNO Bob Newberry Valvoline	15.00	40.00

1992-95 Ertl/Race Image NHRA Transporters 1:64

	EX	NM-MT
NNO Joe Amato Valvoline 1992	15.00	40.00
NNO Pat Austin Castrol GTX '93	15.00	40.00
NNO Mike Dunn La Victoria '94	15.00	40.00
NNO Chuck Etchells Wiz '93	15.00	40.00
NNO John Force Castrol GTX 1993	15.00	40.00
NNO Bob Glidden Quality Care '94	12.50	30.00
NNO Darrell Gwynn Wiltel '92	15.00	40.00
NNO Al Hanna Eastern Rider '92	15.00	40.00
NNO Eddie Hill Pennzoil '93	12.50	30.00
NNO Warren Johnson AC Delco '92	15.00	40.00
NNO Cruz Pedregon McDonald's '93	15.00	40.00
NNO Rick Smith Slick 50 '94	15.00	40.00

2002-03 GMP Vintage Dragsters 1:18

	EX	NM-MT
NNO Don Garlits Swamp Rat 1/5004	75.00	135.00
NNO Don Garlits Swamp Rat 1B/5904	75.00	125.00
NNO Don Garlits Swamp Rat III	75.00	125.00
NNO Don Garlits Swamp Rat VI	75.00	125.00
NNO Connie Kalitta Bounty Hunter	75.00	125.00
NNO Don Prudhomme Greer&Black	60.00	120.00

2002-03 GMP Vintage Dragsters 1:43

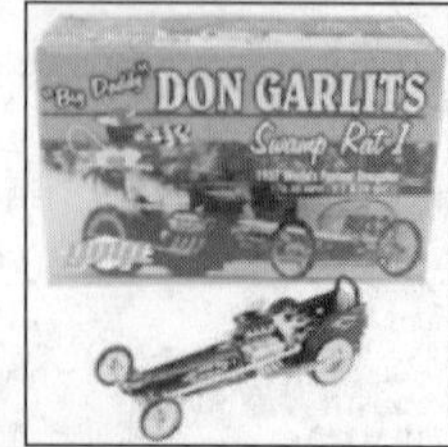

	EX	NM-MT
NNO Don Garlits Swamp Rat 1	18.00	30.00
NNO Don Garlits Swamp Rat 1B	18.00	30.00
NNO Don Garlits Swamp Rat III	18.00	30.00
NNO Don Garlits Swamp Rat VI	18.00	30.00
NNO Don Prudhomme Greer&Black	18.00	30.00

2002-03 GMP Vintage Pro Stock 1:18

	EX	NM-MT
NNO Mark Donohue Roger Penske Chevrolet 1967 Camaro	50.00	90.00
NNO Dick Harrell Fred Gibb Chevrolet 1968 Nova	50.00	90.00
NNO Bill Jenkins Grumpy's Toy/4400 1968 Chevy Nova	75.00	125.00

2002-03 GMP Vintage Pro Stock 1:43

	EX	NM-MT
NNO Dick Harrell Fred Gibb Chevrolet 1968 Nova	18.00	30.00
NNO Bill Jenkins Grumpy's Toy V 1968 Nova/2502	20.00	35.00

2004 Hot Wheels Dragsters Promos 1:64

	EX	NM-MT
NNO Ashley Force Mattel Toy Store Irvine Convention	20.00	40.00

1996 Johnny Lightning Top Fuel Legends Dragsters 1:64

	EX	NM-MT
NNO Jeb Allen Praying Mantis	2.00	5.00
NNO Jim Annin Annin Racing	2.00	5.00
NNO Sarge Arciero Jade Grenade	2.00	5.00
NNO Ron Attebury Jungle Jim	2.00	5.00
NNO Tim Beebe Beebe&Mullican	2.00	5.00
NNO Steve Carbone Carbone Racing	2.00	5.00
NNO Steve Carbone Creitz&Donavan	2.00	5.00
NNO Steve Carbone Soapy Sales	2.00	5.00
NNO Don Garlits Swamp Rat	2.00	5.00
NNO Don Garlits Swamp Rat 10	2.00	5.00
NNO Don Garlits Swamp Rat 22	2.00	5.00
NNO Don Garlits Swamp Rat 24	2.00	5.00
NNO Don Garlits Wynn's Charger	2.00	5.00
NNO Leroy Goldstein Ramchargers	2.00	5.00
NNO Tommy Ivo Nationwise	2.00	5.00
NNO Tommy Ivo Valvoline	2.00	5.00
NNO Don Moody Walton Cerny&Moody	2.00	5.00
NNO Tony Nancy Nancy Racing	2.00	5.00
NNO Bennie Osborn Osborn Racing	2.00	5.00
NNO Rick Ramsey Keeling&Clayton	2.00	5.00
NNO Jerry Ruth Ruth Racing	2.00	5.00
NNO Mike Snively Hawaiian	2.00	5.00
NNO Warren&Coburn/Rain for Rent	2.00	5.00
NNO John Weibe Weibe Racing	2.00	5.00

1998 Johnny Lightning Super Magmas Funny Cars 1:24

	EX	NM-MT
NNO Jim Liberman Jungle Jim Vega	60.00	120.00
NNO Barry Setzer Chevy Vega	25.00	50.00
NNO Gene Snow Snowman Charger	40.00	75.00

1997 Johnny Lightning Dragsters USA Funny Cars and Pro Stock 1:64

This series was issued in 1997 by Johnny Lightning in "Dragsters USA" blister packages. Each die-cast piece featured a famous funny car ride from the 1990s and was packaged with a collectible coin that featured a picture of the car and an issue number. Each driver was issued more than once with a different color paint scheme and different issue number as noted below. We've included the issue number after each car description below. The stated production run was 15,000 of each piece.

	EX	NM-MT
NNO Whit Bazemore 1994 Fast Orange White&Blue 1	4.00	8.00
NNO Whit Bazemore 1994 Fast Orange White&Yellow 13	4.00	8.00
NNO Jim Epler 1994 Rug Doctor Red 15	4.00	8.00
NNO Jim Epler 1994 Rug Doctor Black 24	4.00	8.00
NNO Chuck Etchells 1995 Kendall Black 14	4.00	8.00
NNO Chuck Etchells 1995 Kendall Red 21	4.00	8.00
NNO Al Hofmann 1995 Western Auto Green&Black 25	4.00	8.00
NNO Al Hofmann 1995 Western Auto Orange&Black	4.00	8.00
NNO Tom Hoover 1994 Pioneer Green 11	4.00	8.00
NNO Tom Hoover 1994 Pioneer Blue 19	4.00	8.00
NNO Bruce Larson 1990 Sentry Red 4	4.00	8.00
NNO Bruce Larson 1990 Sentry Green 12	4.00	8.00
NNO Bruce Larson 1990 Sentry Red 23	4.00	8.00
NNO Ed McCulloch 1991 Otter Pops Purple 27	4.00	8.00
NNO Kenji Okazaki 1995 Mooneyes Orange	4.00	8.00
NNO Kenji Okazaki 1995 Mooneyes Orange	4.00	8.00
NNO K.C. Spurlock 1995 King of the Burnouts Blue 5	4.00	8.00
NNO K.C. Spurlock 1995 King of the Burnouts Purple 18	4.00	8.00
NNO K.C. Spurlock 1995 King of the Burnouts Purple 26	4.00	8.00

1999 Johnny Lightning Racing Dreams Funny Cars 1:64

	EX	NM-MT
NNO Frosted Frakes Promo	1.50	4.00

1999 Johnny Lightning Racing Machines 1:64

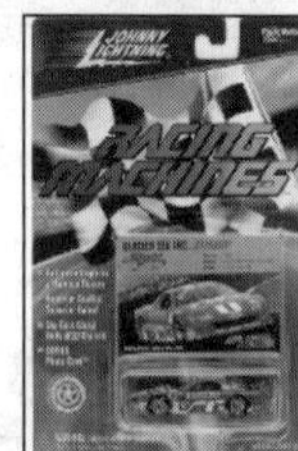

This series of 1:64 die-casts was issued by Johnny Lightning in their Racing Machines blister packs. Each package included a trading card along with the car. As noted below, drivers from a number of different non-NASCAR racing series are included in this set.

	EX	NM-MT
1 Olivier Beretta Oreca Viper GTS GT2 Racing Series	3.00	6.00
1 Paul Gentilozzi HomeLink Trans-Am Series	3.00	6.00
2 Greg Ray Glidden Menard Indy Racing League	3.00	6.00
8 Tom Coleman TWC Trans-Am Series	3.00	6.00
13 Tom Hoover Pioneer NHRA	3.00	6.00
14 Kenny Brack Power Team IRL	3.00	6.00
64 Johnny Miller Automation Trans-Am Series	3.00	6.00
296 Bunny Burkett Dodge Daytona NHRA	3.00	6.00

2000 Johnny Lightning Racing Machines 1:64

This series of 1:64 die-casts was issued by Johnny Lightning in their "Racing Machines" blister packs. Each package included a trading card along with the car. As noted below, drivers from a number of different non-NASCAR racing series are included in this set.

	EX	NM-MT
NNO Tim Wilkinson 1996 NAPA NHRA	3.00	8.00
NNO Frank Pedregon 1998 Johnny Lightning NHRA	3.00	8.00
NNO Ray Higley 1996 Red Line Oil	3.00	8.00

2003 Lane/Ertl Vintage Pro Stock 1:18

	EX	NM-MT
NNO Herb Fox Fred Gibb Chevrolet 1967 Camaro/2000	50.00	90.00

	EX	NM-MT
NNO Bill Hielscher Mr.Bardahl Camaro/2500	50.00	9(
NNO Bill Jenkins Grumpy's Toy 1967 Camaro/5094	100.00	17
NNO Bill Knafel Tin Indian 1967 Firebird	50.00	10(
NNO Dave Strickler Old Reliable 1968 Camaro/3996	50.00	9(

2003 Ertl Chevy Legends P Stock 1:18

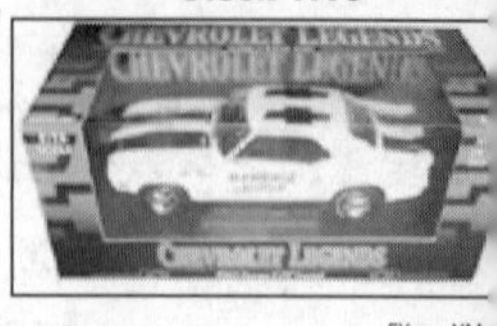

	EX	NM-
NO Bill Jenkins Grumpy's Toy 1966 Nova	45.00	7
NNO Dave Strickler Old Reliable 1969 Camaro/2004	45.00	7

2003 Ertl Ford Racing Pr Stock 1:18

	EX	NM-
NNO Butch Leal 1964 Ford Thunderbolt/2004 black painted wheels	60.00	9(

2003 Ertl Mopar 50 Years Hemi Pro Stock 1:18

	EX	NM-
NNO Don Carlton Motown Missile 1971 Dodge Challenger	45.00	7
NNO Don Carlton Motown Missile 1972 Plymouth Barracuda/2500	45.00	7
NNO Dick Landy 1968 Dodge Challenger	45.00	7
NNO Dick Landy 1971 Dodge Challenger	45.00	7
NNO Butch Leal California Flash 1971 Plymouth Duster	45.00	7
NNO Ronnie Sox Sox&Martin 1971 Plymouth Barracuda	45.00	7
NNO Arlen Vanke 1971 Plymouth Duster	45.00	7

2003 Milestone Developme Dragsters 1:16

	EX	NM-
NNO Kenny Bernstein Budweiser/1500	135.00	20(
NNO Clay Millican Werner/1250	135.00	20(

2004 Milestone Developme Dragsters 1:16

	EX	NM-
NNO Larry Dixon Miller Lite/1250	135.00	20(

2002 Milestone Developme Funny Car 1:16

	EX	NM-
NNO Whit Bazemore Matco Tools/1250	125.00	20(
NNO Whit Bazemore Matco Tools Speed Racer/1250	125.00	20(
NNO Scotty Cannon Oakley Idea/1500	125.00	20(
NNO Scotty Cannon Oakley Time Bomb/3500	125.00	20(

2003 Milestone Developme Funny Car 1:16

	EX	NM
NNO Whit Bazemore Matco Tools/1250	135.00	20(
NNO Whit Bazemore Matco Tools Speed Racer/1250	150.00	22
NNO Whit Bazemore Mopar/1500	125.00	20(
NNO Scotty Cannon Oakley Elite Forces/1250	135.00	20(
NNO Scotty Cannon Oakley Sleep Tight/1250	135.00	20(
NNO Gary Scelzi Dodge Grab Life/2600	135.00	20(
NNO Gary Scelzi Oakley Time Bomb/1250	200.00	32

2004 Milestone Developme Funny Car 1:16

	EX	NM-
NNO Whit Bazemore Matco Tools Rat Fink/1250	100.00	15(
NNO Whit Bazemore Matco Tools 25th Anniversary	100.00	15(
NNO Tony Pedregon Quaker State	100.00	15(
NNO Gary Scelzi HEMI	100.00	15(

2003 PMC Dragsters 1:24

	EX	NM-
NNO Brandon Bernstein Budweiser/1008	40.00	7

2003 PMC Funny Car 1:24

	EX	NM-MT
Del Worsham Checker/1008	40.00	70.00

2004 PMC Funny Car 1:24

	EX	NM-MT
Gary Scelzi Oakley HEMI/1008	50.00	75.00

2003 PMC Pro Stock 1:24

	EX	NM-MT
Warren Johnson GM Performance Parts/1008	75.00	125.00

2000 Racing Champions Authentics NHRA 1:24

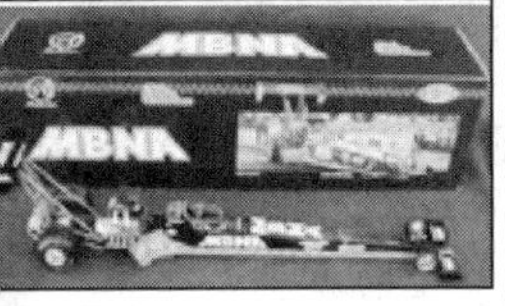

	EX	NM-MT
Joe Amato Valvoline	40.00	75.00
Whit Bazemore Matco Tools Kendall/3100	25.00	60.00
Kenny Bernstein Bud King	25.00	60.00
Ron Capps U.S. Tobacco	30.00	60.00
Dale Creasy MAD Magazine	25.00	60.00
Gary Densham NEC	20.00	50.00
Larry Dixon Miller Lite	40.00	80.00
Al Hofmann Redline Mooneyes	25.00	60.00
Doug Kalitta MGM Grand	30.00	60.00
Don Lampus Express.com	40.00	75.00
Cory Lee ProMotorsports Rat Fink/5000	35.00	70.00
Frank Manzo Kendall Oil	30.00	60.00
Matco Spring Supernationals/3100	30.00	60.00
Cory McClenathan MBNA	20.00	50.00
Frank Pedregon CSK Texaco	40.00	80.00
Tony Schumacher Exide	40.00	80.00
Dean Skuza Matco Tools/3100	25.00	60.00
Dean Skuza Matco Tools Platinum	40.00	80.00
Del Worsham CSK Texaco	30.00	60.00

2001 Racing Champions Authentics NHRA 1:24

	EX	NM-MT
Joe Amato Dynomax/2500	15.00	40.00
Whit Bazemore Matco Tools Black/3500	30.00	60.00
Whit Bazemore Matco Tools Fire Red/3500	30.00	60.00
Whit Bazemore Matco Tools Iron Eagle/3500	35.00	60.00
Kenny Bernstein Bud/2500	30.00	60.00
Kenny Bernstein Bud King Mac Tools/3000	20.00	50.00
Ron Capps Skoal Mac Tools/3000	30.00	60.00
Jeg Coughlin Jr. Jeg's/3000	20.00	40.00
Larry Dixon Miller Lite Mac Tools/3000	15.00	40.00
Jim Dunn Mooneyes Gold Chrome/416	50.00	90.00
Mike Dunn Yankees Gold Mac Tools/1500	60.00	100.00
NNO Chuck Etchells Sunoco Matco Tools/3500	30.00	60.00
NNO Chuck Etchells Kendall Matco Tools/3500	30.00	60.00
NNO Jim Epler Bass Pro/3500	20.00	50.00
NNO Jim Epler Cabela's/3000	40.00	75.00
NNO Jim Epler Motley Crue/3000	50.00	90.00
NNO Jim Epler NAPA/3500	35.00	60.00
NNO Jim Epler Rug Doctor	25.00	60.00
NNO Jim Epler Toys'R'Us/3500	30.00	60.00
NNO Don Garlits Matco Tools/3011	20.00	50.00
NNO Don Garlits Matco Tools Stars&Stripes	60.00	100.00
NNO Al Hofmann Mooneyes Mac Tools/3000	15.00	40.00
NNO Tommy Johnson Skoal Mac Tools/3000	20.00	50.00
NNO Doug Kalitta Mac Tools/6000	20.00	50.00
NNO Doug Kalitta Mac Tools Gold/1500	35.00	60.00
NNO Matco Tools SuperNationals Englishtown/3500	25.00	50.00
NNO Mark Pawuk Summit/3500	20.00	50.00
NNO Frank Pedregon Checker	20.00	50.00
NNO Cristen Powell Nitro Fish/2500	20.00	40.00
NNO Cristen Powell Nitro Fish Gold/416	30.00	60.00
NNO Darrell Russell Matco Tools/3000	25.00	50.00
NNO Gary Scelzi Winston Matco Tools/3500	30.00	60.00
NNO Tony Schumacher Army/5000	15.00	40.00
NNO Tony Schumacher Army Gold/416	30.00	60.00
NNO Dean Skuza Mopar/2500	15.00	40.00
NNO Dean Skuza Mopar Gold/416	30.00	60.00

2002 Racing Champions Authentics NHRA 1:24

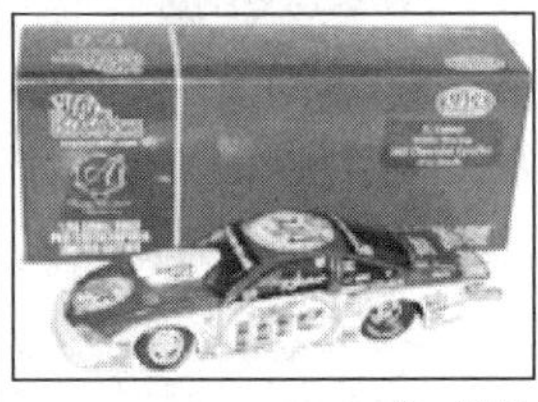

	EX	NM-MT
NNO Darrell Alderman Mopar	45.00	80.00
NNO Whit Bazemore Speed Racer Matco Tools/2400	60.00	100.00
NNO Kenny Bernstein Budweiser King Color Chrome	50.00	100.00
NNO Kenny Bernstein Bud Gold/199	75.00	150.00
NNO Jeg Coughlin Jr. Jeg's/999	25.00	50.00
NNO Jeg Coughlin Jeg's Gold/199	40.00	80.00
NNO Larry Dixon Miller Lite/999	30.00	60.00
NNO Vern Gaines Miller Lite/250	50.00	90.00
NNO Vern Gaines Miller Lite Chrome/250	50.00	100.00
NNO Johnny Gray Checker/1656	25.00	50.00
NNO Al Hofmann K&N Filters/999	35.00	70.00
NNO Al Hofmann K&N Filters Gold/199	75.00	150.00
NNO Clay Millican Werner Matco Tools/2000	30.00	50.00
NNO Clay Millican Werner Matco Tools Gold/199	40.00	80.00
NNO Mark Pawuk Summit/999	25.00	50.00
NNO Mark Pawuk Summit Gold/199	40.00	80.00
NNO Darrell Russell Bilstein/999	25.00	50.00
NNO Darrell Russell Joe Amato Racing	20.00	40.00
NNO Bruce Sarver White Cap/2000	60.00	120.00
NNO Tony Schumacher Army/999	30.00	60.00
NNO Tony Schumacher Army Gold/199	75.00	150.00
NNO Tony Schumacher Matco Tools/2750	25.00	50.00
NNO Dean Skuza Team Mopar/1000	35.00	60.00
NNO Del Worsham Checker/1656	30.00	50.00

2003 Racing Champions Authentics NHRA 1:24

	EX	NM-MT
NNO Greg Anderson Vegas General Mac Tools/1250	40.00	75.00
NNO Whit Bazemore Matco Animal House/2500	50.00	90.00
NNO Whit Bazemore Matco Distributor/2000	40.00	75.00
NNO Whit Bazemore Matco Fast&Furious/2150	40.00	75.00
NNO Whit Bazemore Matco Iron Eagle/2000	40.00	75.00
NNO Whit Bazemore Mopar Matco Tools/2000	45.00	80.00
NNO Scott Kalitta Mac Tools Jesse James/2500	45.00	80.00
NNO George Marnell Fast&Furious/2000	35.00	60.00
NNO Clay Millican Werner Matco Tools 104+ Octane		
NNO Darrell Russell Bilstein Matco Tools/2000	30.00	60.00
NNO Darrell Russell Matco Fast&Furious/2000	30.00	60.00
NNO Gary Scelzi Dodge Matco Tools/2150	60.00	100.00
NNO Gary Scelzi Dodge Matco Tools Chrome/250	70.00	120.00
NNO Tony Schumacher Army Matco Tools/2000	30.00	60.00
NNO Tony Schumacher Army Camo Matco Tools/2000	45.00	80.00

2004 Racing Champions Authentics NHRA 1:24

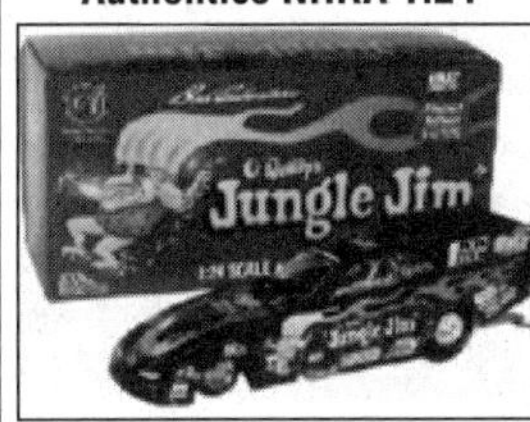

	EX	NM-MT
NNO Bob Gilbertson Jungle Jim/500	45.00	80.00
NNO Bob Gilbertson Jungle Jim Chrome/500	45.00	80.00
NNO Warren Johnson GM Performance Parts/1002	50.00	80.00
NNO Warren Johnson GM Performance Parts Chrome/252	125.00	200.00
NNO Dean Skuza Black Label Society/512	40.00	75.00

2003 Racing Champions Authentics Pro Stock Bikes 1:9

	EX	NM-MT
NNO Antron Brown Army/670	50.00	90.00
NNO Andrew Hines Vance&Hines Harley/2500	50.00	90.00
NNO Angelle Savoie Army/1066	50.00	90.00
NNO G.T. Tonglet Vance&Hines Harley	50.00	90.00
NNO Craig Treble Matco Fast&Furious/2000	60.00	100.00
NNO Craig Treble Matco Iron Eagle/2000	60.00	100.00

2005 Racing Champions Authentics Pro Stock Bikes 1:9

	EX	NM-MT
NNO Antron Brown Army/2004	35.00	60.00
NNO Angelle Sampey Army/2004	35.00	60.00
NNO GT Tonglett Harley Eagle/2202	35.00	60.00

1995 Racing Champions Dragsters 1:24

This was Racing Champions first 1:24 Dragster issue. Former Winston NHRA Top Fuel Champions Joe Amato and Eddie Hill are a couple of the featured drivers.

	EX	NM-MT
NNO Joe Amato Valvoline	20.00	40.00
NNO Shelly Anderson Western Auto	25.00	40.00
NNO Eddie Hill Pennzoil	25.00	40.00
NNO Doug Herbert Snap On	25.00	40.00
NNO Tommy Johnson Jr. Mopar	25.00	40.00
NNO Cory McClenathan McDonald's	25.00	40.00

1996 Racing Champions Dragsters 1:24

This was the second year that Racing Champions released 1:24 scale Dragsters. The most expensive and desired piece in the series is that of Blaine Johnson.

	EX	NM-MT
NNO Joe Amato Valvoline	15.00	30.00
NNO Shelly Anderson Parts America	15.00	30.00
NNO Bill Blair Fugowie! Lost Tribe	15.00	30.00
NNO Ron Capps RPR	15.00	30.00
NNO Chuck Etchells Kendall	15.00	30.00
NNO Rick Fuller Montana Express	15.00	30.00
NNO Gatornationals Mac Tools	15.00	30.00
NNO Spike Gorr Greer Motorsports	15.00	30.00
NNO Rhonda Hartman Hartman Enterprises	15.00	30.00
NNO Doug Herbert Snap On	15.00	30.00
NNO Eddie Hill Pennzoil	15.00	30.00
NNO Blaine Johnson Travers	20.00	40.00
NNO Lawren Jones Matco	20.00	40.00
NNO Connie Kalitta American	20.00	30.00
NNO Scott Kalitta American	15.00	30.00
NNO Cory McClenathan McDonald's	15.00	30.00
NNO Cory McClenathan McDonald's Olympic	15.00	30.00
NNO Rance McDaniel La Bac Systems	15.00	30.00
NNO Jack Ostrander Vista Food	15.00	30.00
NNO Bruce Sarver Carquest	15.00	30.00
NNO Bob Vandergriff Jerzees	15.00	30.00
NNO Winter Nationals	15.00	30.00

1997 Racing Champions Dragsters 1:24

This was the third year that Racing Champions released 1:24 scale Dragsters. The most expensive and desired piece in the series is that of Blaine Johnson.

	EX	NM-MT
NNO Joe Amato Keystone	15.00	30.00
NNO Shelly Anderson Parts America	25.00	50.00
NNO Tony Bartone Bartone Bros.	15.00	30.00
NNO Jim Epler Rug Doctor	15.00	30.00
NNO Doug Foxworth Havoc	15.00	30.00
NNO Spike Gorr Greer Motorsports	15.00	30.00
NNO Doug Grubnic Geronimo	12.00	30.00
NNO Rhonda Hartman Hartman Racing	15.00	30.00
NNO Jim Head Close Call	15.00	30.00
NNO Doug Herbert Snap On	20.00	40.00
NNO Eddie Hill Pennzoil	15.00	30.00
NNO Eddie Hill Pennzoil Matco	20.00	40.00
NNO Blaine Johnson Travers	40.00	80.00
NNO Connie Kalitta American	15.00	30.00
NNO Scott Kalitta American	15.00	30.00
NNO Cory McClenathan McDonald's	15.00	30.00
NNO Randy Parks Fluke	35.00	50.00
NNO Cristen Powell CP Racing	15.00	40.00
NNO Cristen Powell Royal Purple	20.00	45.00
NNO Bruce Sarver Carquest	15.00	30.00
NNO Tony Schumacher Peek Brothers	15.00	30.00
NNO John Shoemaker American Eagle	15.00	30.00
NNO Paul Smith Smith Racing School	15.00	30.00
NNO Bobby Taylor Turner Racing	15.00	30.00
NNO Marshall Topping Montana Express	15.00	30.00
NNO Bob Vandergriff Jerzees	15.00	30.00

1998 Racing Champions Dragsters 1:24

This was the fourth year that Racing Champions released 1:24 scale Dragsters.

	EX	NM-MT
NNO Jim Head Close Call	12.00	30.00
NNO Doug Herbert Snap On	12.00	30.00
NNO Larry Meirsch Powermate	12.00	30.00
NNO Cristen Powell Reebok	12.00	30.00
NNO Paul Romaine CarQuest	12.00	30.00
NNO Bob Vandergriff Jerzees	12.00	30.00

1999 Racing Champions Dragsters 1:24

	EX	NM-MT
NO Gary Scelzi Winston Matco Tools	20.00	35.00

2001 Racing Champions Dragsters 1:24

	EX	NM-MT
NNO Joe Amato Dynomax	12.50	25.00
NNO Kenny Bernstein King Kenny	15.00	30.00
NNO Kenny Bernstein King Kenny AUTO	50.00	100.00
NNO Kenny Bernstein King Kenny Gold	20.00	50.00
NNO Larry Dixon The Snake	12.50	25.00
NNO Larry Dixon The Snake Gold	20.00	40.00
NNO Rhonda Hartman-Smith FRAM	10.00	25.00
NNO Doug Kalitta MGM Grand	12.50	25.00
NNO Doug Kalitta MGM Grand AUTO	30.00	60.00
NNO Mac Tools Thunder Valley/5000	12.50	25.00
NNO Gary Scelzi Matco Tools	12.50	25.00
NNO Gary Scelzi Matco Tools Gold/1000	12.50	30.00

2002 Racing Champions Dragsters 1:24

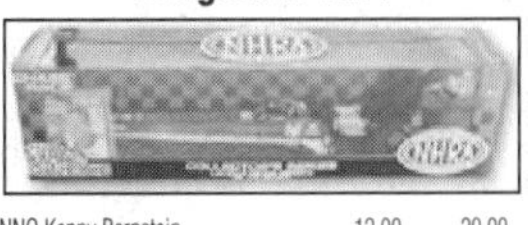

	EX	NM-MT
NNO Kenny Bernstein Bernstein	12.00	20.00
NNO Kenny Bernstein Bernstein Gold/1000	15.00	30.00
NNO Mike Dunn N.Y.Yankees	12.00	20.00
NNO Mike Dunn N.Y.Yankees Gold/1000	15.00	25.00
NNO Don Garlits Matco Tools	12.00	20.00
NNO Rhonda Hartman-Smith FRAM	12.00	20.00
NNO Rhonda Hartman-Smith FRAM Gold/1000	15.00	25.00
NNO Tony Schumacher Army with Army Card	12.00	20.00
NNO Tony Schumacher Army with Schumacher card	12.00	20.00

2005 Racing Champions Authentics Dragsters 1:24

	EX	NM-MT
NNO Morgan Lucas Lucas Oil/1200	40.00	65.00
NNO Cory McLenathan Fram/1254	40.00	65.00
NNO Clay Millican Werner/1002	40.00	65.00
NNO Tony Schumacher Army Camo Call to Duty/1002	40.00	65.00
NNO Melanie Troxell Skull Gear/1002	40.00	65.00

2006 Racing Champions Authentics Dragsters 1:24

	EX	NM-MT
NNO Cory McClenathan Jeg's Mail Order/1248	50.00	75.00

1989 Racing Champions Dragsters 1:64

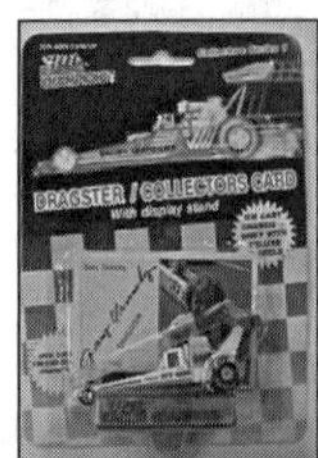

	EX	NM-MT
NNO Joe Amato TRW	5.00	12.00
NNO Frank Bradley	5.00	12.00
NNO Don Garlits	6.00	12.00
NNO Darrell Gwynn	5.00	12.00
NNO Eddie Hill Super Shops	5.00	12.00
NNO Lori Johns Jolly Rancher	4.00	10.00
NNO Shirley Muldowney Otter Pops Blue	5.00	12.00
NNO Shirley Muldowney Pink	5.00	12.00
NNO Gary Ormsby	4.00	10.00

Castrol GTX		
NNO Don Prudhomme	5.00	12.00

1996 Racing Champions Dragsters 1:64

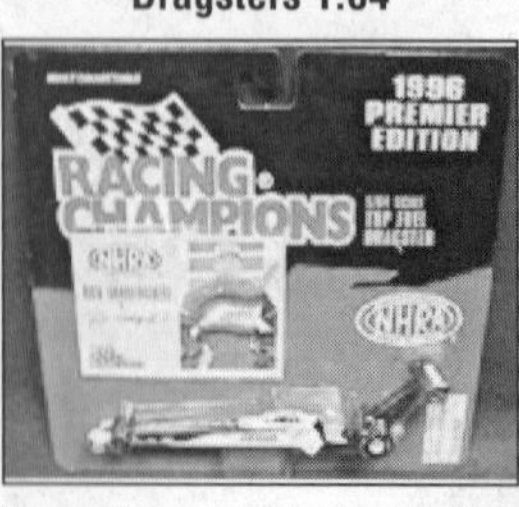

This was the first isssue of a Racing Champions 1:64 scale Dragster. The series is lead by the Blaine Johnson Travers piece. There was also a four pack available. There are many different combinations of Dragsters that could be found in those four packs.

	EX	NM-MT
NNO Joe Amato Keystone	4.00	10.00
NNO Shelly Anderson Parts America	4.00	10.00
NNO Bill Blair Fugowie! Lost Tribe	4.00	10.00
NNO Ron Capps RPR	4.00	10.00
NNO Rick Fuller Montana Express	4.00	10.00
NNO Spike Gorr Greer Motorsports	4.00	10.00
NNO Rhonda Hartman Hartman Enterprises	4.00	10.00
NNO Doug Herbert Snap On	4.00	10.00
NNO Eddie Hill Pennzoil	4.00	10.00
NNO Blaine Johnson Travers	7.50	15.00
NNO Lawren Jones Matco	6.00	12.00
NNO Connie Kalitta American	4.00	10.00
NNO Scott Kalitta American	4.00	10.00
NNO Cory McClenathan McDonald's	4.00	10.00
NNO Cory McClenathan McDonald's Olympic	4.00	10.00
NNO Rance McDaniel La Bac Systems	4.00	10.00
NNO Jack Ostrander Vista Food	4.00	10.00
NNO Bruce Sarver CarQuest	4.00	10.00
NNO Mac Tools U.S.Nationals	4.00	10.00
NNO Bob Vandergriff Jerzees	4.00	10.00
NNO 4 Car Drag Set (any of them)	18.00	25.00

1997 Racing Champions Dragsters 1:64

Racing Champions returned their 1:64 Dragster line in 1997. The series features former Winston NHRA Champions Joe Amato and Scott Kalitta.

	EX	NM-MT
NNO Joe Amato Keystone	4.00	10.00
NNO Shelly Anderson Parts America	4.00	10.00
NNO Jim Epler Rug Doctor	4.00	10.00
NNO Spike Gorr Greer Motorsports	4.00	10.00
NNO Doug Grubnic Geronimo	3.00	10.00
NNO Rhonda Hartman Hartman Racing	4.00	10.00
NNO Jim Head Close Call	4.00	10.00
NNO Doug Herbert Snap On	4.00	10.00
NNO Eddie Hill Pennzoil Matco	6.00	12.00
NNO Connie Kalita American	4.00	10.00
NNO Scott Kalitta American	4.00	10.00
NNO Randy Parks Fluke	4.00	10.00
NNO Cristen Powell Powell Racing	4.00	10.00
NNO Bruce Sarver Carquest	4.00	10.00
NNO Tony Schumacher Peek Brothers	4.00	10.00
NNO John Shoemaker American Eagle	4.00	10.00
NNO Paul Smith Roy Smith Racing School	4.00	10.00
NNO Bobby Taylor Turner Racing	4.00	10.00
NNO Marshall Topping Montana Express	4.00	10.00
NNO Bob Vandergriff Jerzees	4.00	10.00

2001 Racing Champions Preview Dragsters 1:64

	EX	NM-MT
NNO Gary Scelzi Matco Tools	3.00	6.00
NNO Tony Schumacher Army	3.00	6.00

2001 Racing Champions Dragsters 1:64

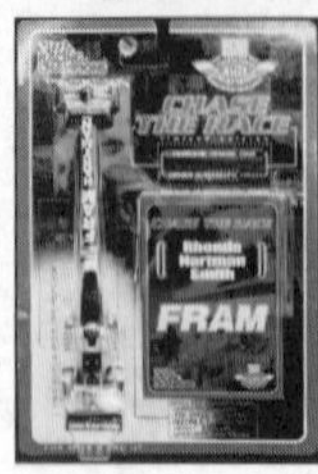

	EX	NM-MT
NNO Joe Amato Dynomax	3.00	6.00
NNO Kenny Bernstein King Kenny	3.00	8.00
NNO Kenny Bernstein King Kenny Gold	6.00	15.00
NNO Rhonda Hartman-Smith FRAM	2.00	5.00
NNO Doug Kalitta MGM Grand	3.00	6.00
NNO Clay Millican Werner Promo	6.00	15.00
NNO Tony Schumacher Exide	2.00	5.00
NNO Tony Schumacher Exide Gold	6.00	12.00

2002 Racing Champions Preview Dragsters 1:64

Each car in this series was packaged in a typical red and black Racing Champions Previews blister along with a card. Many of the cards feature the team and sponsor logos and not the driver himself. The packaging carries a 2001 copyright date on the back, but is considered a 2002 release. The various NHRA sanctioned racing series are represented. Some cars were also issued with either Chrome or Autographed card numbered "chase" versions.

	EX	NM-MT
NNO Kenny Bernstein Bernstein	3.00	6.00
NNO Kenny Bernstein Bernstein Chrome/1000	6.00	15.00
NNO Mike Dunn N.Y.Yankees	3.00	6.00
NNO Don Garlits Matco Tools	4.00	10.00
NNO Tony Schumacher Army w/Army Card	3.00	6.00

2002 Racing Champions Dragsters 1:64

Similar to the Preview series, each car in this series was packaged in a typical red and black Racing Champions blister along with a card. The packaging carries a 2002 copyright date on the back and the various NHRA sanctioned racing series are represented. Some cars were also issued with either Chrome or Autographed card numbered "chase" versions.

	EX	NM-MT
NNO Mike Dunn N.Y.Yankees	3.00	6.00
NNO Tony Schumacher Army with Schumacher card	3.00	6.00

2006 Racing Champions Dragsters 1:64

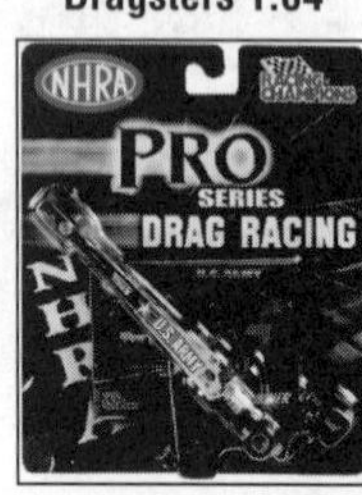

	EX	NM-MT
NNO Tony Schumacher U.S. Army	5.00	10.00

1997 Racing Champions Dragsters 1:144

These 1:144 scale mini dragsters were issued in a red and black Racing Champions blister package. The blister reads "1997 Edition" on the front. Each was also packaged with a yellow bordered trading card.

	EX	NM-MT
NNO Joe Amato Keystone	2.00	5.00
NNO Doug Herbert Snap On	2.00	5.00
NNO Blaine Johnson Travers	2.00	5.00
NNO Scott Kalitta American	2.00	5.00
NNO Bob Vandergriff Jerzees	2.00	5.00

1995-96 Racing Champions Funny Car 1:24

This is the first 1:24 scale Funny Car series to hit the market. Racing Champions distributed the pieces through both hobby and retail outlets. The cars come in a red and black box.

	EX	NM-MT
NNO Randy Anderson Parts America 1996	12.50	30.00
NNO Whit Bazemore	15.00	30.00
Mobil 1		
NNO Gary Bolger Creasy 1996	12.50	30.00
NNO Jerry Caminito Blue Thunder	15.00	30.00
NNO Gary Clapshaw Fuelish Pleasure 1996	10.00	25.00
NNO Gary Densham NEC 1996	10.00	25.00
NNO Jim Epler Rug Doctor 1996	10.00	25.00
NNO Gatornationals Mac Tools	15.00	30.00
NNO Al Hofmann Parts America	15.00	30.00
NNO Tom Hoover Pioneer	15.00	30.00
NNO Kenji Okazaki Mooneyes	15.00	30.00
NNO Cruz Pedregon McDonald's 1996	12.50	30.00
NNO Tony Pedregon Geronimo	15.00	30.00
NNO Wyatt Radke Nitro Bandit 1996	15.00	30.00
NNO Tim Simpson Simpson Racing	15.00	30.00
NNO Dean Skuza Matco Promo 1996	20.00	40.00
NNO Mac Tools U.S.Nationals 1996	10.00	25.00
NNO Tim Wilkerson NAPA	15.00	30.00
NNO Winter Nationals	15.00	30.00
NNO Del Worsham Worsham Fink 1996	10.00	25.00

1997 Racing Champions Funny Car 1:24

This was the third year for Racing Champions to release the 1:24 scale Funny Car series. A couple of regulars on the Alcohol Funny Car circuit Randy Anderson and Tony Bartone are in the set. 1997 saw Randy Anderson move up to Top Fuel.

	EX	NM-MT
NNO Randy Anderson Parts America	15.00	30.00
NNO Tony Bartone Bartone Racing	15.00	30.00
NNO Tony Bartone Quaker State	15.00	30.00
NNO Bunny Burkett Mopar	15.00	30.00
NNO Gary Bolger Creasy	15.00	30.00
NNO Jim Dunn Moon Eyes	15.00	30.00
NNO Chuck Etchells Kendall	15.00	30.00
NNO Rhonda Hartman Geronimo	15.00	30.00
NNO Ray Higley Red Line Oil	15.00	30.00
NNO Tom Hoover Pioneer	15.00	30.00
NNO Frank Manzo Kendall	15.00	30.00
NNO Vern Moats Mopar	15.00	30.00
NNO Todd Payton Optima Batteries	15.00	30.00
NNO Cruz Pedregon McDonald's	15.00	30.00
NNO Jimmy Penland Penland Racing	15.00	30.00
NNO John Powell Etterman Racing	15.00	30.00
NNO Von Smith Atomic City Tools	15.00	30.00
NNO Dean Skuza Matco 1994	20.00	40.00
NNO Dean Skuza Matco 1994 Gold	125.00	250.00
NNO Dean Skuza Matco 1997	20.00	40.00
NNO Tim Wilkerson NAPA	15.00	30.00
NNO Del Worsham CSK	15.00	30.00

1999-00 Racing Champions Funny Car 1:24

	EX	NM-MT
NNO Matco Supernationals 1999	10.00	20.00
NNO Nitro Fish Promo 2000	10.00	20.00

1998 Racing Champions Funny Car 1:24

This was the fourth year for Racing Champions to release the 1:24 scale Funny Car series.

	EX	NM-MT
NO Randy Anderson Parts America	12.00	30.00
NNO Bunny Burkett Burkett-Mopar	12.00	30.00
NNO Jim Epler East Care	12.00	30.00
NNO Brent Fanning Udder Nonsense	15.00	40.00
NNO Al Hofmann Hoffman Racing	15.00	30.00
NNO Tom Hoover Pioneer	12.00	30.00
NNO Frank Manzo Kendall	12.00	30.00
NNO Cruz Pedregon Interstate Batteries	15.00	30.00

2001 Racing Champions Funny Car 1:24

	EX	NM-MT
NNO Whit Bazemore Matco Tools	12.50	25.00
NNO Dale Creasy Jr. Mad Ugly	15.00	30.00
NNO Dale Creasy Jr. Nitromaniac	10.00	25.00
NNO Jim Epler	12.50	30.00

Bass Pro Promo		
NNO Jim Epler Matco Tools	10.00	25.00
NNO Jim Epler Matco Tools Gold/1000	12.50	30.00
NNO Al Hofmann Mooneyes	12.50	25.00
NNO Al Hofmann Mooneyes Gold/1000	20.00	40.00
NNO Mac Tools Thunder Valley/5000	12.50	25.00
NNO Matco Supernationals/3500	12.50	25.00
NNO Dean Skuza Matco Tools	12.50	25.00
NNO Dean Skuza Matco Tools Gold/1000	15.00	30.00

2005 Racing Champions Authentics Funny Cars 1:24

	EX	NM-MT
NNO Tony Bartone Lucas Oil Got CMKX/1254	40.00	65.00
NNO Tony Bartone Lucas Oil Got CMKX Johnny Lightning/1266	40.00	65.00
NNO Phil Burkart Jr. CSK/1002	40.00	65.00
NNO Tim Wilkerson LRS/1002	40.00	65.00
NNO Del Worsham CSK/1500	40.00	65.00

2006 Racing Champions Funny Cars 1:24

	EX	NM-MT
NNO Del Worsham Checker Schuck's Kragen	10.00	20.00

1989 Racing Champions Funny Car 1:64

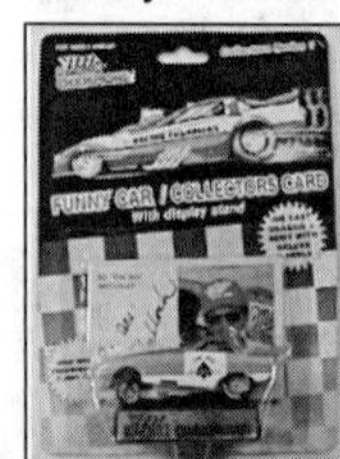

	EX	NM-MT
NNO Pat Austin Castrol GTX	4.00	10.00
NNO Raymond Beadle Blue Max	4.00	10.00
NNO Kenny Bernstein King Kenny	5.00	12.00
NNO Kenny Bernstein Quaker State	5.00	12.00
NNO Tom Hoover Showtime	4.00	10.00
NNO Bruce Larson Sentry	4.00	10.00
NNO Ed McCulloch The Ace	4.00	10.00
NNO Mark Oswald Motorcraft	4.00	10.00
NNO Don Prudhomme	5.00	10.00

1994-95 Racing Champions Funny Car 1:64

	EX	NM-MT
NNO Al Hofmann Western Auto Promo 1995	4.00	8.00
NNO Kenny Koretsky Sunoco Promo 1994	4.00	8.00

1996 Racing Champions Funny Car 1:64

This was the first year that Racing Champions did a 1:64 scale Funny Car. The only Winston Nitro Funny Car champion in 90's beside John Force, Cruz Pedregon (1992) is in the series.

	EX	NM-MT
NNO Randy Anderson Parts America	4.00	10.00
NNO Gary Bolger Creasy	4.00	10.00
NNO Gary Clapshaw Fuelish Pleasure	4.00	10.00
NNO Gary Densham NEC	4.00	10.00
NNO Chuck Etchells Kendall	4.00	10.00
NNO Al Hofmann Parts America	5.00	10
NNO Tom Hoover Pioneer	4.00	10
NNO Vern Moates Mopar	4.00	10
NNO Kenji Okazaki Mooneyes	4.00	10
NNO Cruz Pedregon McDonald's	5.00	10
NNO Jimmy Penland Penland Racing	4.00	10
NNO Wyatt Radke Nitro Bandit	4.00	10
NNO Dean Skuza Matco	4.00	10
NNO Tim Wilkerson NAPA	4.00	10
NNO Dle Worsham Worsham Fink	4.00	10
NNO 4 piece Funny Car set There are numerous combinations	18.00	25

1997 Racing Champions Funny Car 1:64

Long time Funny Car driver Bunny Burkett is one of the d to highlight this series. The cars feature drivers from bo Alcohol and Nitro Funny Car circuits.

	EX	NM-
NNO Randy Anderson Parts America	4.00	10
NNO Anthony Bartone Bartone Racing	4.00	10
NNO Anthony Bartone Quaker State	4.00	10
NNO Gary Bolger Creasy	4.00	10
NNO Bunny Burkett Burkett Racing	4.00	10
NNO Jim Dunn Moon Eyes	4.00	10
NNO Chuck Etchells Kendall	4.00	10
NNO Rhonda Hartman Geronimo	4.00	10
NNO Ray Higley Red Line Oil	6.00	15
NNO Tom Hoover Pioneer	4.00	10
NNO Frank Manzo Kendall	4.00	10
NNO Vern Moats Mopar	4.00	10
NNO Bob Newberry Keystone	10.00	20
NNO Cruz Pedregon McDonald's	4.00	10
NNO Jimmy Penland Penland Racing	6.00	15
NNO John Powell Etterman Racing	4.00	10
NNO Von Smith Atomic City Tools	4.00	10
NNO Dean Skuza Matco 1994	6.00	12
NNO Dean Skuza Matco 1994 Gold	25.00	50
NNO Dean Skuza Matco Four Pack	20.00	40
NNO Tim Wilkerson NAPA	4.00	10
NNO Del Worsham CSK	4.00	10

2000 Racing Champions Funny Car 1:64

	EX	NM-
NNO Nitro Fish Promo in box	3.00	6

2001 Racing Champions Funny Car 1:64

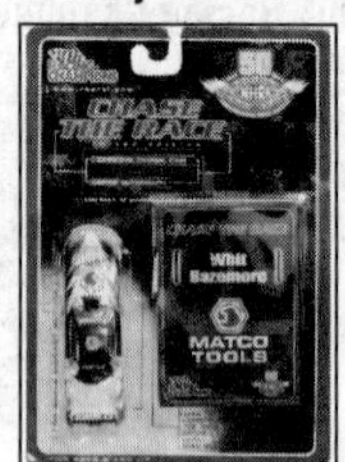

	EX	NM-
NNO Whit Bazemore Matco Tools	2.00	5
NNO Dale Creasy Jr. Mad	3.00	6
NNO Jim Epler Bass Pro Promo	3.00	6
NNO Jim Epler Matco Tools Flames	2.00	5
NNO Al Hofmann Mooneyes	3.00	6
NNO Al Hofmann Mooneyes AUTO		
NNO Al Hofmann Mooneyes Chrome	5.00	12
NNO Nitro Fish	3.00	6
NNO Bruce Sarver e-moola.com	2.00	5
NNO Bruce Sarver e-moola.com Chrome/1000	5.00	12
NNO Del Worsham Checker	2.00	5

2002 Racing Champions Preview Funny Car 1:64

	EX	NM-
NNO Whit Bazemore	3.00	6

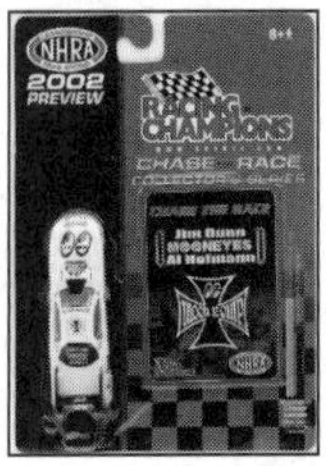

	EX	NM-MT
atco Tools		
im Dunn ooneyes	3.00	6.00
im Dunn ooneyes Chrome/1000	6.00	15.00
Varren Johnson oodwrench	3.00	6.00

2002 Racing Champions Funny Car 1:64

	EX	NM-MT
el Worsham ecker	3.00	6.00

2006 Racing Champions Funny Cars 1:64

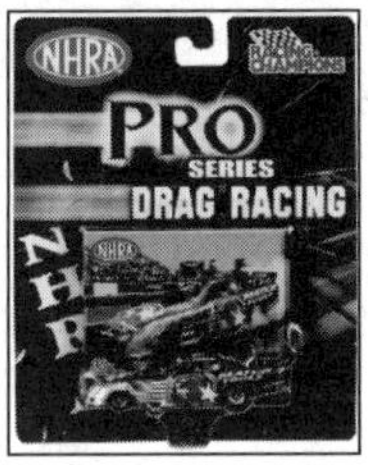

	EX	NM-MT
Vhit Bazemore atco Tools	5.00	10.00

1997 Racing Champions Funny Car 1:144

	EX	NM-MT
ary Bolger easy	2.00	5.00
im Epler innebago	2.00	5.00
honda Hartman eronimo	2.00	5.00
om Hoover oneer	2.00	5.00
ruz Pedregon cDonald's	2.00	5.00
immy Penland nland Racing	2.00	5.00

97 Racing Champions Pro Stock 1:24

Champions expanded its drag racing line to Pro s with this release. The series features former Pro Stock ions Warren Johnson and Jim Yates.

	EX	NM-MT
roy Coughlin g's	15.00	30.00
erry Eckman ecker	15.00	30.00
like Edwards innebago	15.00	30.00
ay Franks anks-Haas	15.00	30.00
ern Gaines estern Racing	15.00	30.00
ommy Hammonds mmonds Racing	15.00	30.00
huck Harris Racing.com	15.00	30.00
urt Johnson Delco	20.00	40.00
Varren Johnson Performance	15.00	30.00
eorge Marnell arnell Black	15.00	30.00
ony Martino artino Racing	15.00	30.00
arry Morgan ybestos	15.00	30.00
lark Osborne aMa Rosa	15.00	30.00
lark Pawuk mmit Racing	15.00	30.00
teve Schmidt nagear	15.00	30.00
like Thomas mout	15.00	30.00
im Yates cDonald's	15.00	30.00

98 Racing Champions Pro Stock 1:24

s the second year for Racing Champions to release the ale Pro Stock series.

	EX	NM-MT
raig Eaton SCO Autographed/2502	12.50	25.00
eorge Marnell nneco	12.00	30.00
om Martino Flags	12.00	30.00
lark Pawuk mmit Racing	12.00	30.00
like Thomas	12.00	30.00

	EX	NM-MT
Gumout		
NNO Jim Yates Peak-Split Fire	12.00	30.00

2005 Racing Champions Authentics Pro Stock 1:24

	EX	NM-MT
NNO Jeg Coughlin Jr. Jeg's Mail Order Cancer Research/1002	40.00	65.00
NNO Mike Edwards Young Life Racing/1002	40.00	65.00
NNO Vieri Gaines Kendall Dodge/1002	40.00	65.00
NNO Kurt Johnson AC Delco/1254	40.00	65.00
NNO Kenny Koretsky Nitro Fish/1002	40.00	65.00
NNO Jason Line KB Framers/1002	40.00	65.00

2006 Racing Champions Pro Stock 1:24

	EX	NM-MT
NNO Kurt Johnson AC Delco	10.00	20.00

1989 Racing Champions Pro Stock 1:64

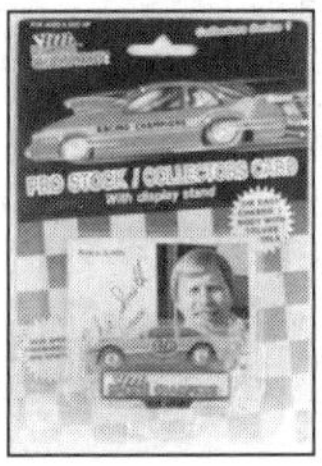

	EX	NM-MT
NNO Darrell Alderman	4.00	10.00
NNO Bruce Allen	4.00	10.00
NNO Don Beverley Crown	4.00	10.00
NNO Jerry Eckman Pennzoil	4.00	10.00
NNO Warren Johnson AC Delco	5.00	10.00
NNO Joe Lepone Jr.	4.00	10.00
NNO Larry Morgan Castrol	4.00	10.00
NNO David Nickens Castrol	4.00	10.00
NNO Rick Smith STP	4.00	10.00

1997 Racing Champions Pro Stock 1:64

This was the first year Racing Champions released 1:64 scale series Pro Stock cars. The series is highlighted by the appearance of Warren Johnson and Jim Yates.

	EX	NM-MT
NNO Troy Coughlin Jeg's	5.00	10.00
NNO Jerry Eckman CSK	5.00	10.00
NNO Marty Edwards Winnebago	5.00	10.00
NNO Ray Franks Franks-Haas	5.00	10.00
NNO Vern Gaines Western Racing	5.00	10.00
NNO Tommy Hammonds Hammonds Racing	5.00	10.00
NNO Chuck Harris Go Racing.com	5.00	10.00
NNO Kurt Johnson AC Delco	5.00	10.00
NNO Warren Johnson Performance Parts	5.00	10.00
NNO George Marnell Marnell Black	5.00	10.00
NNO George Marnell Marnell Red&White	4.00	10.00
NNO Tony Martino Martino Racing	5.00	10.00
NNO Larry Morgan Raybestos	5.00	10.00
NNO John Nobile Nobile Trucking	5.00	10.00
NNO Mark Osborne MaMa Rosa	5.00	10.00
NNO Mark Pawuk Summit Racing	5.00	10.00
NNO S.Schmidt/Dynagear	5.00	10.00
NNO Mike Thomas Gumout	5.00	10.00
NNO Pete Williams Williams Racing	5.00	10.00
NNO Jim Yates McDonald's	5.00	10.00

2002 Racing Champions Pro Stock 1:64

	EX	NM-MT
NNO Allen Johnson Amoco Ultimate Promo in box	3.00	6.00

2006 Racing Champions Pro Stock 1:64

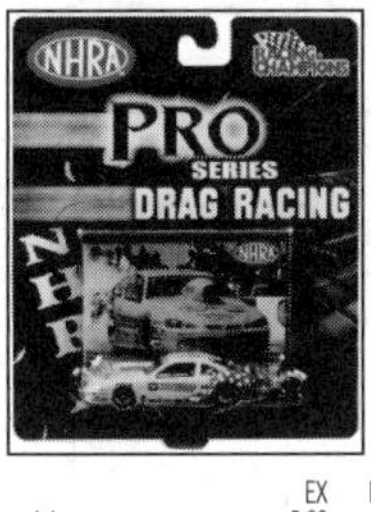

	EX	NM-MT
NNO Warren Johnson GM Performance Parts School's Out	5.00	10.00

1997 Racing Champions Pro Stock 1:144

	EX	NM-MT
NNO George Marnell Marnell Red&White	2.00	5.00
NNO Jim Yates McDonald's	2.00	5.00
NNO Mike Edwards Winnebago	2.00	5.00
NNO Mark Osborne MaMa Rosa	2.00	5.00
NNO Mark Pawuk Summit Racing	2.00	5.00
NNO Mike Thomas Gumout	2.00	5.00
NNO Vern Gaines Western Racing	2.00	5.00
NNO Steve Schmidt Dynagear	2.00	5.00
NNO Troy Coughlin Jeg's	2.00	5.00
NNO Warren Johnson Performance Parts	2.00	5.00

2002 Racing Champions Drivers of All Time NHRA 1:18

	EX	NM-MT
NNO John Force 1970 Mustang/1042	20.00	40.00
NNO John Force 1970 Mustang Chrome/208	35.00	60.00
NNO Don Garlits 1969 Charger/1042	50.00	90.00
NNO Don Garlits 1969 Charger Chrome/208	40.00	75.00
NNO Don Prudhomme 1969 Camaro/1042	25.00	50.00
NNO Don Prudhomme 1969 Camaro Chrome/208	40.00	75.00

2001 Racing Champions Force Field 1:64

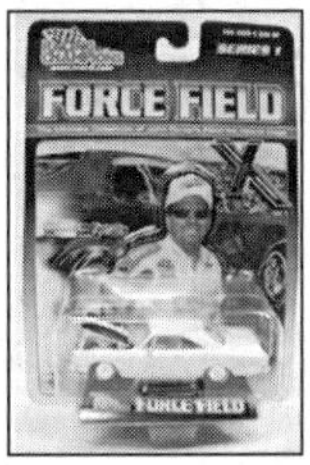

	EX	NM-MT
NNO John Force 1953 Corvette	2.50	5.00
NNO John Force 1958 Edsel	2.50	5.00
NNO John Force 1957 Plymouth Fury	2.50	5.00
NNO John Force 1964 Mustang	2.50	5.00
NNO John Force 1968 Firebird	2.50	5.00
NNO John Force 1968 Plymouth	2.50	5.00
NNO John Force 1969 GTO	2.50	5.00
NNO John Force 1969 Olds	2.50	5.00
NNO John Force 1971 Cuda	2.50	5.00

2001 Racing Champions Wheels of Fame NHRA 1:64

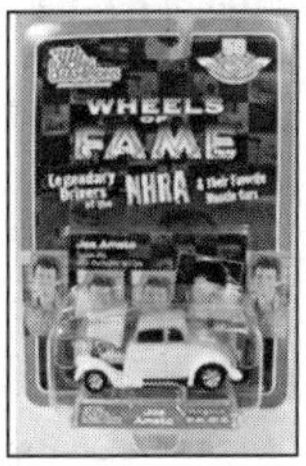

	EX	NM-MT
NNO Joe Amato 1933 Willys	3.00	6.00
NNO Joe Amato 1939 Chevy Coupe	3.00	6.00
NNO Joe Amato 1957 Chevy Bel Air	3.00	6.00
NNO Kenny Bernstein 1966 Camaro	3.00	6.00
NNO Kenny Bernstein 1970 Buick GSX 2	3.00	6.00
NNO Kenny Bernstein 1971 Barracuda 12	3.00	6.00
NNO Kenny Bernstein 1996 Camaro	3.00	6.00
NNO Eddie Hill 1934 Ford Coupe	3.00	6.00
NNO Eddie Hill 1969 Olds	3.00	6.00
NNO Tom McEwen 1956 Chevy Nomade	3.00	6.00
NNO Tom McEwen 1967 Chevelle	3.00	6.00
NNO Don Prudhomme 1934 Ford Highboy	3.00	6.00
NNO Don Prudhomme 1969 Camaro	3.00	6.00

2001 Racing Champions NHRA Transporters 1:64

	EX	NM-MT
NNO Doug Kalitta Mac Tools/3500	12.50	25.00
NNO Mac Tools Thunder Valley/5000	10.00	25.00

1998 Revell Dragsters 1:24

This series is the debut of the production of NHRA pieces by Revell.

	EX	NM-MT
NNO Joe Amato Tenneco	20.00	50.00
NNO Eddie Hill Pennzoil Matco/3000	30.00	60.00

1998-99 Revell Pro Stock 1:24

This series is the debut of the production of NHRA pieces by Revell.

	EX	NM-MT
NNO Kurt Johnson AC Delco/2502 1998	25.00	60.00
NNO Warren Johnson 1997 GM Performance Parts/2502	25.00	60.00
NNO Warren Johnson Goodwrench Superman/3000 1999	40.00	80.00
NNO Mac Tools 50th Anniversary '98	15.00	40.00

1998-00 Revell Club Dragsters 1:24

	EX	NM-MT
NNO Joe Amato Superman/2502 1999	40.00	80.00
NNO Kenny Bernstein Bud Lizard/1500 1999	50.00	100.00
NNO Kenny Bernstein Bud King/2000 2000	30.00	80.00
NNO Doug Kalitta MGM Grand/1500 2000	20.00	50.00
NNO Cory McClenathan MBNA/1500 1998	20.00	50.00
NNO Gary Scelzi Winston/1500 1999	40.00	80.00

2001 Revell Funny Car 1:24

	EX	NM-MT
NNO Tony Pedregon Castrol Test/3504	25.00	60.00
NNO John Force Aero Force Test/2508	100.00	175.00

2003 RSC Collectibles Vintage Pro Stock 1:24

	EX	NM-MT
NNN Bill Jenkins Grumpy's Toys 1968 Camaro	50.00	90.00

1999-03 Supercar/Ertl Vintage Pro Stock 1:18

	EX	NM-MT
NNO Wally Booth Rat Pack 1971 Camaro	40.00	70.00
NNO Don Grotheer 1970 Plymouth Barracuda/2000	40.00	70.00
NNO Bill Jenkins Grumpy's Toy 1969 Camaro/2500 1999	175.00	300.00
NNO Bill Jenkins Grumpy's Toy 1970 Camaro	70.00	110.00
NNO Don Nicholson	40.00	70.00

	EX	NM-MT
Cobra Jet 1968 Mustang		
NNO Gas Ronda Russ Davis Ford/2500 1964 Thunderbolt with 1:64 car	50.00	90.00
NNO Shirley Shahan Drag-On-Lady 1969 AMX	50.00	80.00
NNO Ronnie Sox Sox&Martin 1969 Plymouth GTX/5000 2000	60.00	100.00
NNO Ronnie Sox Sox&Martin '70 Barracuda/3500	60.00	100.00

2002 Team Caliber Dragsters 1:24

	EX	NM-MT
NNO Brandon Bernstein Budweiser/1200	45.00	70.00
NNO Kenny Bernstein Budweiser King/1200	40.00	70.00
NNO Larry Dixon Miller Lite/1200	35.00	70.00

2003 Team Caliber Owner's Series Dragsters 1:24

	EX	NM-MT
NNO Brandon Bernstein Budweiser/1200	45.00	80.00
NNO Kenny Bernstein Budweiser Mac Tools Color Chrome	60.00	100.00

2004 Team Caliber Owner's Series Dragsters 1:24

	EX	NM-MT
NNO Scott Kalitta Mac Tools Jesse James WCC Mac Tools/200	60.00	100.00
NNO Tony Schumacher Army Camo/1200	40.00	60.00

2001 Thirteen-Twenty Fuelers Dragsters 1:24

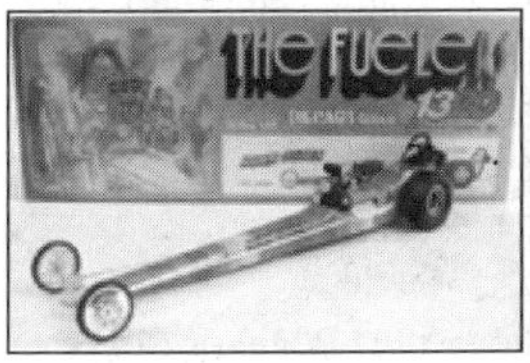

	EX	NM-MT
NNO Jim Dunn Rainbow/3500	35.00	60.00
NNO Don Garlits Swamp Rat XII/5000	90.00	150.00
NNO Dick Kalivoda The Joker/3500	35.00	60.00
NNO John Mulligan Fighting Irish/3500	40.00	75.00
NNO Tony Nancy Superior Sizzler/5000	35.00	60.00
NNO Bruce Wheeler Wheeler Dealer/5000	40.00	75.00

2002 Thirteen-Twenty Fuelers Dragsters 1:24

	EX	NM-MT
NNO Kenny Bernstein Forever Red Budweiser/5000	35.00	60.00
NNO Gary Cochran Mr.C/3500	35.00	60.00
NNO Tommy Ivo Valvoline Deist/5000	35.00	60.00
NNO Chris Karamesines Captain of the Greek Fleet/3500	35.00	60.00
NNO Tom McEwen Mongoose/5000	35.00	60.00
NNO Rick Ramsey Keeling&Clayton California Charger/5000	35.00	60.00
NNO Pete Robinson Tinker Toy V/5000	40.00	75.00

2003 Thirteen-Twenty Fuelers Dragsters 1:24

	EX	NM-MT
NNO Steve Carbone Black		
NNO Larry Dixon Sr. Rattler/2500	35.00	60.00
NNO Don Garlits Swamp Rat X/5000	35.00	60.00
NNO Connie Kalitta Bounty Hunter/3500	35.00	60.00
NNO Don Prudhomme Wynn's Winder/3500	35.00	60.00
NNO Kenny Safford Gotelli Speed Shop/2500	35.00	60.00

2004 Thirteen-Twenty Fuelers/Diggers Dragsters 1:24

	EX	NM-MT
NNO Steve Carbone Crietz&Donovan/2500	35.00	60.00
NNO Don Garlits	40.00	70.00

	EX	NM-MT
Swamp Rat VI/5000		
NNO Roland Leong Hawaiian/5000	45.00	75.00
NNO Bennie Osborn The Wizard/2000	35.00	60.00
NNO Tom McEwen Yeakel Plymouth	35.00	60.00
NNO Don Prudhomme Greer, Black&Prud/5000	35.00	60.00

2002 Thirteen-Twenty Floppers Funny Cars 1:24

	EX	NM-MT
NNO Don Cook Damn Yankee/3500	50.00	80.00
NNO Jim Dunn Dunn&Reath/5000	50.00	80.00
NNO Don Schumacher Stardust/5000	50.00	80.00

2003 Thirteen-Twenty Floppers Funny Cars 1:24

	EX	NM-MT
NNO Leroy Goldstein Candies&Hughes/2000	45.00	80.00
NNO Ed McCulloch Wipple&McCulloch/2500	45.00	80.00
NNO Ron O'Donnell Big Noise/2000	45.00	80.00
NNO Don Prudhomme 40th Anniversary/3500	45.00	80.00
NNO Don Prudhomme Army/5000	45.00	80.00
NNO Don Schumacher Wonder Wagon/2500	45.00	80.00

2004 Thirteen-Twenty Floppers Funny Cars 1:24

	EX	NM-MT
NNO Braskett&Burgin	40.00	60.00
NNO Jim Green Green Elephant/1500	45.00	70.00
NNO Jim Liberman Jungle Jim	40.00	60.00
NNO Mike Mitchell Hippie	45.00	80.00
NNO Pisano&Matsubara/1500	50.00	75.00

1997 Winner's Circle Dragsters 1:24

This series marks the teaming of Action Performance and Hasbro. This line of cars was produced for and distributed in the mass-market.

	EX	NM-MT
NNO Kenny Bernstein King of Speed	10.00	25.00
NNO Kenny Bernstein Quaker State	10.00	25.00
NNO Larry Dixon Don Prudhomme	10.00	25.00
NNO Mike Dunn Mopar	10.00	25.00
NNO Shirley Muldowney Action	10.00	25.00
NNO Don Prudhomme MBNA	10.00	25.00

1996 Winner's Circle Dragsters 1:64

NNO Shirley Muldowney Action	5.00	10.00

1997 Winner's Circle Dragsters 1:64

This series marks the teaming of Action Performance and Hasbro. This line of cars was produced for and distributed in the mass-market.

	EX	NM-MT
NNO Kenny Bernstein King of Speed	7.50	15.00
NNO Larry Dixon Don Prudhomme Black	3.00	8.00
NNO Larry Dixon Don Prudhomme White	6.00	12.00
NNO M.Dunn/Mopar	3.00	8.00
NNO Eddie Hill Pennzoil	7.50	15.00
NNO Shirley Muldowney Action	6.00	12.00

1997 Winner's Circle Funny Car 1:24

This series marks the teaming of Action Performance and Hasbro. This line of cars was produced for and distributed in the mass-market. It is highlighted by the John Force Lifetime Series.

	EX	NM-MT
NNO Pat Austin Red Wing Shoes	10.00	25.00
NNO Chuck Etchells Kendell	12.50	25.00
NNO John Force Castrol GTX	15.00	30.00
NNO John Force Castrol GTX Black Flames	15.00	30.00
NNO Tom Hoover Pioneer	12.50	25.00

1998 Winner's Circle Funny Car 1:24

	EX	NM-MT
NNO John Force Castrol GTX	15.00	30.00
NNO John Force Castrol GTX Elvis	15.00	30.00

2000 Winner's Circle Funny Car 1:24

NNO John Force Castrol GTX Superman	20.00	35.00

2001 Winner's Circle Funny Car 1:24

	EX	NM-MT
NNO Tony Pedregon Castrol Syntec	10.00	25.00

2002 Winner's Circle Funny Car 1:24

	EX	NM-MT
NNO John Force Castrol GTX	10.00	25.00
NNO John Force Castrol GTX Elvis	10.00	25.00
NNO John Force Castrol GTX 11-Time Champ	15.00	30.00
NNO John Force Castrol GTX Tasca Red	15.00	30.00
NNO Tony Pedregon Castrol Muppets	15.00	30.00

2003 Winner's Circle Funny Car 1:24

	EX	NM-MT
NNO John Force Castrol GTX 11X Champ	15.00	30.00
NNO John Force Castrol King of Hill	12.50	25.00
NNO Tony Pedregon Castrol KISS	15.00	30.00

1997 Winner's Circle Funny Car 1:64

This series marks the teaming of Action Performance and Hasbro. This line of cars was produced for and distributed in the mass-market. It is highlighted by the John Force Lifetime Series.

	EX	NM-MT
NNO Pat Austin Red Wing	3.00	8.00
NNO Chuck Etchells Kendell	4.00	10.00
NNO John Force Castrol GTX	4.00	10.00
NNO John Force Castrol GTX Black	4.00	10.00
NNO Tom Hoover Pioneer	4.00	10.00

1998 Winner's Circle Funny Car 1:64

	EX	NM-MT
NNO John Force Castrol GTX Gold 7-Time Champ	4.00	10.00
NNO John Force Castrol GTX Elvis	4.00	10.00
NNO John Force Castrol GTX Superman	5.00	12.00
NNO Cruz Pedregon Interstate Batteries Small Soldiers	3.00	8.00

2002 Winner's Circle Driver Sticker Funny Car 1:64

	EX	NM-MT
NNO John Force Castrol GTX 11-Time Champ	5.00	10.00
NNO Tony Pedregon Castrol Muppets	5.00	10.00

2003 Winner's Circle Driver Sticker Funny Car 1:64

	EX	NM-MT
NNO John Force Castrol GTX King of the Hill	4.00	8.00

1998 Winner's Circle Lifetime Series John Force 1:64

	EX	NM-MT
1 John Force Castrol GTX 1997	3.00	6.00
2 John Force Castrol GTX Flames 1996	3.00	6.00
3 John Force Castrol GTX 1993	3.00	6.00
4 John Force Brute Force blue 1977	3.00	6.00
5 John Force Castrol GTX 1994 Champ	3.00	6.00
6 John Force Brute Force orange 1978	3.00	6.00
7 John Force Castrol GTX Black 1997	3.00	6.00
8 John Force Castrol GTX 1998	3.00	6.00

2002 Winner's Circle NHRA Transporters 1:64

	EX	NM-MT
NNO John Force Castrol GTX 11-Time Champ	12.50	25.00
NNO Tony Pedregon Castrol Muppets	12.50	25.00

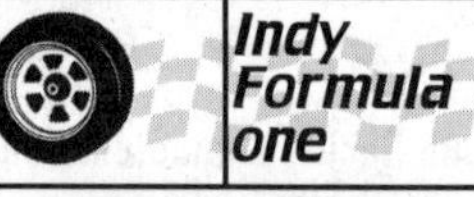

1999 Action Indy Cars 1:18

	EX	NM-MT
4 Juan Montoya Target Renard/5000	75.00	125.00
6 Michael Andretti K-Mart Swift/5000	60.00	120.00
7 Max Papis Miller Lite Renard/3500	30.00	60.00
7 Max Papis Miller Harley-Davidson Renard/4008	60.00	120.00
8 Brian Herta Shell Renard/3500	35.00	70.00
10 Richie Hearn Budweiser/3500	45.00	80.00
12 Jimmy Vasser Target Renard/3500	40.00	80.00
12 Jimmy Vasser Target Superman/5784	125.00	250.00
17 Mauricio Gugelmin Pac West Renard/3500	20.00	50.00
33 Patrick Carpentier Forsythe Renard/3500	50.00	100.00
40 Adrian Fernandez Tecate	90.00	150.00
97 Cristiano Da Matta Pioneer Renard	60.00	100.00
99 Greg Moore Forsythe Renard/3500	125.00	200.00

2000 Action Indy Cars 1:18

	EX	NM-MT
1 Greg Ray Conseco Menards/2304	25.00	60.00
3 Al Unser Jr. Tickets.com G-Force/3504	30.00	60.00
3 Al Unser Jr. Tickets.com AP Box	20.00	35.00
3 Al Unser Jr. Tickets.com Dracula/1416	40.00	80.00
4 Scott Goodyear Pennzoil Dallara/2304	35.00	80.00
8 Kenny Brack Shell Renard/2502	30.00	60.00
9 Juan Montoya Target/2304	75.00	125.00
27 Dario Franchitti Team Green Reynard/3500	40.00	80.00
40 Adrian Frenandez Quaker State Tecate	60.00	100.00
97 Cristiano DaMatta Pioneer MCI/3504	50.00	100.00

2001 Action Indy Cars 1:18

	EX	NM-MT
1 NDA Indy 500 Event Car G-Force	40.00	80.00
8 Kenny Brack Shell Renard/3800	35.00	70.00
33 Tony Stewart Target Indy 500/7704	50.00	100.00
51 Eddie Cheever Excite@Home Infiniti/990	40.00	70.00
91 Buddy Lazier TaeBo/666	40.00	80.00

2002 Action Indy Cars 1:18

	EX	NM-MT
4 Sam Hornish Jr. Pennzoil/2004 in AP Box	60.00	90.00
5 Rick Treadway Meijer/3000 in an AP box	20.00	40.00
02 Indianapolis 500/108	40.00	75.00

2003 Action Indy Cars 1:18

	EX	NM-MT
3 Paul Tracy Forsythe Norick/1284 in window box	50.00	80.00
3 Paul Tracy It's Your World/1560	75.00	125.00
4 Sam Hornish Pennzoil/958	40.00	75.00
4 Sam Hornish Jr. Pennzoil T3/1196	40.00	75.00
5 Adrian Fernandez Tecate/144	90.00	150.00
5 Adrian Fernandez Tecate AP window box	40.00	75.00
7 Michael Andretti 7-11/2326	40.00	75.00
8 Scott Sharp Delphi/1328	40.00	70.00
10 Thomas Scheckter Target/1232	40.00	70.00
11 Tony Kanaan 7-11 Hulk/1272	40.00	75.00
31 Al Unser Jr. Corteco/1410	40.00	70.00
32 Patrick Carpentier It's Your World	60.00	100.00
51 Eddie Cheever Red Bull/1196	40.00	70.00

2004 Action Indy Cars 1:18

	EX	NM-MT
2 Sebastien Bourdais McDonald's/1008	75.00	125.00
3 Paul Tracy Forsythe Last Lap 2003 Champion/1596	90.00	150.00

1999 Action Indy Cars 1:43

	EX	NM-MT
1 Max Papis Miller Lite Renard/5000	12.50	25.00
4 Juan Montoya Target Renard/6000	20.00	40.00
6 Michael Andretti K-Mart Havoline/6000	15.00	30.00
12 Jimmy Vasser Target Renard	15.00	25.00
33 Patrick Carpentier Forsythe Renard/5000	12.50	25.00
40 Adrian Fernandez Tecate	20.00	40.00
99 Greg Moore Forsythe Renard/5000	40.00	80.00

2000 Action Indy Cars 1:43

	EX	NM-MT
26 Paul Tracy Kool Green/3816	15.00	40.00
NNO Team Ganassi Target 4 for 4 Champs Four car set in tin/2800 Jimmy Vasser Alex Zanardi Juan Montoya	30.00	50.00

2000 Action Indy Cars 1:64

	EX	NM-MT
3 Al Unser Jr. Tickets.com Dracula	3.00	8.00
4 Juan Montoya Target Renard Indy 500 Win	3.00	8.00

1998-04 Carousel 1 Vintage Indy 1:18

Carousel 1 produces this line of former Indy 500 racers. Each was manufactured in great detail and produced in limited quantities. The series began in 1998 with the A.J. Foyt 1961 Bowes Seal Fast car.

	EX	NM-MT
1 A.J. Foyt Bowes Seal Fast 1961	200.00	350.00
1 A.J. Foyt Sheraton Thompson 1964	75.00	135.00
2 Johnny Rutherford Gatorade 1975	75.00	125.00
2 Bill Vukovich Jr. Sugaripe Prunes 1973	60.00	120.00
3 Johnny Rutherford McLaren 1974	60.00	120.00
3 Rodger Ward Leader Card 1962	75.00	125.00
4 Jim Rathmann Ken-Paul 1960	75.00	125.00
4 Bill Vukovich Hopkins 1955	70.00	110.00
6 Bob Sweikert John Zink 1955	70.00	110.00
6 Bobby Unser Olsonite Eagle 1972	75.00	125.00
8 Pat Flaherty John Zink 1956	70.00	110.00
10 Tony Bettenhausen Chapman 1955	75.00	
11 Pancho Carter Firestone 1974	60.00	
12 Don Freeland Bob Estes Special 1955	70.00	
12 Eddie Sachs Dean Van Lines 1961	70.00	
14 A.J. Foyt Sheraton Thompson 1967	80.00	
14 Bill Vukovich Fuel Injection 1953	70.00	
16 Johnnie Parsons Trio Brass	70.00	
19 Rodger Ward Filter Queen 1956	75.00	
20 Gordon Johncock STP 1973	75.00	
26 Norm Hall Nothing Special 1964	70.00	
36 Dan Gurney Eagle-Gurney 1967	75.00	
44 Jim Rathmann Simoniz Vista 1962	70.00	
48 Jerry Grant Mystery 1972	75.00	
48 Bobby Unser Jergensen 1975	75.00	
56 Jim Hurtubise Travelon Trailer 1960	60.00	
66 Mark Donohue Sunoco '73	75.00	
73 David Hobbs Carling 1974	75.00	
73 Mike Nazaruk McNamara 1954	75.00	
82 Jim Clark Lotus 1965	75.00	
86 Johnny Rutherford Bardahl 1964	75.00	
98 Parnelli Jones Agajanian 1962	60.00	
98 Lloyd Ruby Agajanian 1960	60.00	

2002 Carousel 1 Hobby H Vintage Indy 1:43

	EX	N
1 A.J. Foyt Bowes Seal Fast 1961	40.00	
3 Rodger Ward Leader Card 1962	20.00	
4 Jim Rathmann Ken-Paul 1960	20.00	
32 Ray Harroun Marmom Wasp 1911	20.00	

1996 EPI Indy 1:24

	EX	N
28 Bryan Herta Shell/20,000	7.50	

1998 Ertl Indy CART 1:1

	EX	N
4 Alex Zanardi Target	25.00	
5 Gil DeFerran Valvoline	15.00	
7 Bobby Rahal Miller Lite	15.00	
12 Jimmy Vasser Target	20.00	

1999 Ertl Indy CART 1:1

	EX	N
2 Target Coca-Cola	20.00	
6 Michael Andretti Newman-Haas	25.00	
11 Christian Fittipaldi K-Mart Coca-Cola	20.00	

1985 Ertl Motorized Pullb Indy Cars 1:43

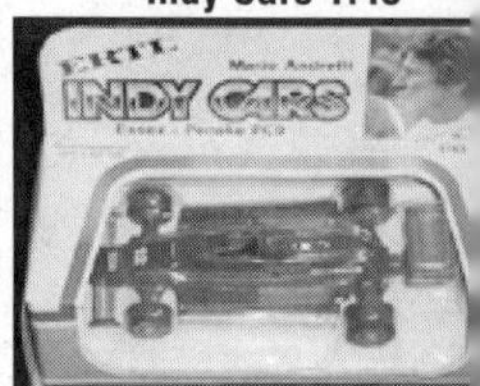

	EX	N
1 Rick Mears Gould	30.00	
11 Bobby Unser Gould Norton Spirit	12.50	
12 Bill Alsup A.B. Dick Pacemaker	10.00	
12 Mario Andretti Essex	20.00	

1998 Ertl Indy CART 1:4

	EX	N
3 Robbie Buhl Glidden	10.00	
5 Arie Luyendyk Nortel	150.00	2

2004 GreenLight IRL 1:1

	EX	N
2 Mark Taylor Johns Mansville/1500	30.00	
3 Helio Castroneves Penske Mobil 1/2502	35.00	
4 Thomas Schecter Pennzoil/2502	30.00	
5 Adrian Fernandez Quaker State Tecate	30.00	
6 Sam Hornish Jr.	35.00	

	EX	NM-MT
Penske Mobil 1/3504		
ott Sharp	35.00	50.00
Delphi/2502		
ony Kanaan	35.00	50.00
7-11 Big Gulp/2004		
J. Foyt IV	35.00	50.00
Conseco/1002		
an Wheldon	30.00	50.00
Klein Tools/2004		
ario Franchitti	30.00	50.00
Arca Ex/1500		
arah Fisher	35.00	50.00
Bryant/2502		
obby Gordon	35.00	50.00
Meijer/1080		
ndy 500 Event Car	30.00	50.00

2005 GreenLight IRL 1:18

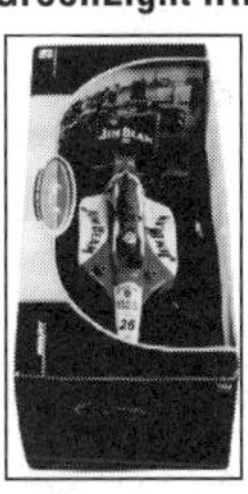

	EX	NM-MT
anica Patrick	100.00	200.00
Argent white number/1500		
anica Patrick	50.00	100.00
Argent yellow number/10,000		

007 GreenLight IRL Garage Series 1:18

	EX	NM-MT
io Castroneves	40.00	70.00
Team Penske/1200		
or Meira	40.00	70.00
Delphi		
n Hornish Jr.	40.00	70.00
Team Penske/1800		
nica Patrick	60.00	100.00
Motorola/7500		
ott Sharp	40.00	70.00
Patron Tequilla/996		
ott Dixon	40.00	70.00
Target/750		
an Wheldon	40.00	70.00
Target/1002		
ony Kanaan	40.00	70.00
7-Eleven/2400		
arren Manning	40.00	70.00
ABC Supply/3500		
ff Simmons	40.00	70.00
Ethanol/1800		
arco Andretti	40.00	70.00
New York Stock Exchange/3000		
ichael Andretti	40.00	70.00
New York Stock Exchange/1500		
ario Franchitti	40.00	70.00
Canadian Club/996		

002 GreenLight Indy Cars 1:64

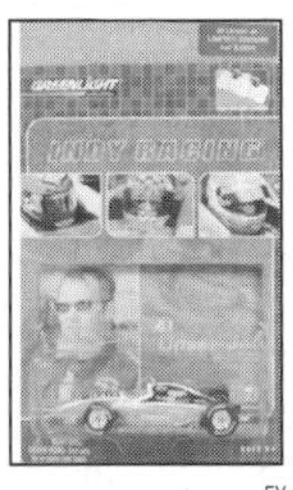

	EX	NM-MT
ues Lazier	6.00	10.00
Team Menard/1600		
io Castroneves	6.00	10.00
Penske Chrome		
2002 Indy 500 Champ/5000		
n Hornish Jr.	6.00	10.00
Pennzoil 2002 IRL		
Champ/1600		
Unser Jr.	6.00	10.00
Corteco/2000		
Ward	6.00	10.00
Target/1200		
arah Fisher	6.00	12.00
SmartBlade/2400		
ndy Racing Trophy/1600	7.50	15.00

003 GreenLight Indy Cars 1:64

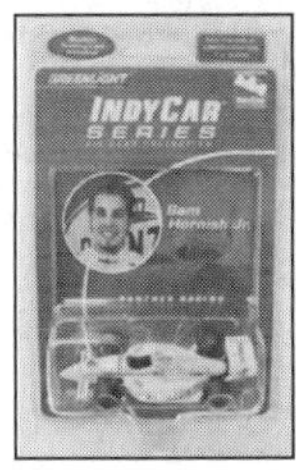

	EX	NM-MT
n Hornish	7.50	15.00
Pennzoil/5000		

	EX	NM-MT
7 Michael Andretti	7.50	15.00
7-11/3000		
9 Scott Dixon	7.50	20.00
Target Fuji/1200		
10 Thomas Scheckter	7.50	15.00
Target Fuji/3000		
14 A.J. Foyt IV	7.50	15.00
Conseco/3500		
21 Filipe Giaffone	7.50	15.00
MoNunn/3000		
23 Sarah Fisher	7.50	20.00
Purex/5000		
24 Robbie Buhl	7.50	15.00
Purex Dial/3000		
31 Al Unser Jr.	7.50	15.00
Corteco/3500		
51 Eddie Cheever Jr.	7.50	15.00
Red Bull/3500		
03 Indianapolis 500/2003	7.50	15.00
03 IRL Art in Motion in box	6.00	12.00
03 IRL Art in Motion in box	7.50	15.00
500 Festival hood/750		
NNO Indy Japan 300 Promo/3700	7.50	15.00
NNO Sam Schmidt	7.50	15.00
Sprint PCS Paralysis		
Foundation Promo/5000		

2004 GreenLight IRL 1:64

	EX	NM-MT
1 Scott Dixon	6.00	12.00
Target Ganassi/4032		
2 Mark Taylor	6.00	12.00
Johns Manville/3204		
3 Helio Castroneves	6.00	12.00
Penske Mobil 1/5040		
4 Thomas Scheckter	6.00	12.00
Pennzoil/4032		
6 Sam Hornish Jr.	6.00	12.00
Penske Mobil 1/7536		
8 Scott Sharp	6.00	12.00
Delphi/3800		
11 Tony Kanaan	6.00	12.00
7-11 Big Gulp/4512		
14 A.J. Foyt IV	6.00	12.00
Conseco/7008		
26 Dan Wheldon	6.00	12.00
Klein Tools/3024		
27 Dario Franchitti	6.00	12.00
Arca Ex/3024		
39 Sarah Fisher	6.00	12.00
Bryant/4512		
04 Indy 500 Corvette Pace Car/2000	5.00	10.00
04 Indy 500 Event Car/2004	5.00	10.00

2005 GreenLight IRL 1:64

	EX	NM-MT
3 Helio Castroneves	7.50	15.00
Penske Mobil		
4 Tomas Scheckter	7.50	15.00
Pennzoil		
6 Sam Hornish Jr.	7.50	15.00
Penske Mobil		
7 Brian Herta	7.50	15.00
XM Satellite Radio		
9 Scott Dixon	7.50	15.00
Target		
10 Darren Manning	7.50	15.00
Target		
11 Tony Kanaan	10.00	20.00
7-Eleven		
15 Buddy Rice	7.50	15.00
Argent		
16 Danica Patrick	15.00	30.00
Argent white number		
16 Danica Patrick	12.50	25.00
Argent yellow number		
26 Dan Wheldon	10.00	20.00
Klein Tools		
27 Dario Franchitti	7.50	15.00
Arca Ex		

2006 GreenLight IRL 1:64

	EX	NM-MT
1 Michael Andretti	7.50	15.00
Vonage		

2003 GreenLight Indy Transporters 1:64

	EX	NM-MT
4 Sam Hornish Jr.	10.00	18.00
Pennzoil/1500		
51 Eddie Cheever Jr.	10.00	18.00
Red Bull/1500		
NNO IndyCar Series/1500	10.00	18.00

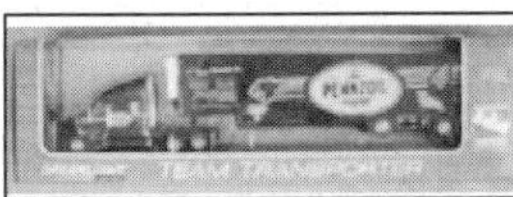

1993 Hot Wheels Pro Circuit Indy 1:64

	EX	NM-MT
1 Michael Andretti	2.50	6.00
Texaco		
2 Mario Andretti	2.50	6.00
Texaco		
3 Al Unser Jr.	2.00	5.00
Valvoline		
4 Rick Mears	2.00	5.00
Penske		

1998 Hot Wheels First Edition Indy 1:64

	EX	NM-MT
4 Alex Zanardi	4.00	10.00
Target		
5 Gil DeFerran	3.00	8.00
Walker		
6 Michael Andretti	3.00	8.00
Havoline		
16 Patrick Carpentier	4.00	10.00
Alumax		
25 Max Papis	3.00	8.00
MCI		

1998 Hot Wheels Pro Racing 1 Indy 1:64

This was Hot Wheels basic issue CART IndyCar brand for 1998. Each car was issued in a blue and red blister package in the shape of the #1.

	EX	NM-MT
5 Gil DeFerran	2.00	4.00
Walker		
8 Bryan Herta	2.00	4.00
Team Rahal		
21 Richie Hearn	2.00	4.00
Della Penna		
31 Andre Ribeiro	2.00	4.00
Tasman		

1970 Johnny Lightning Indy 500 1:64

	EX	NM-MT
NNO Al Unser		
NNO A.J. Foyt		

1996 Johnny Lightning Indy 500 Champs and Pace Cars 1:64

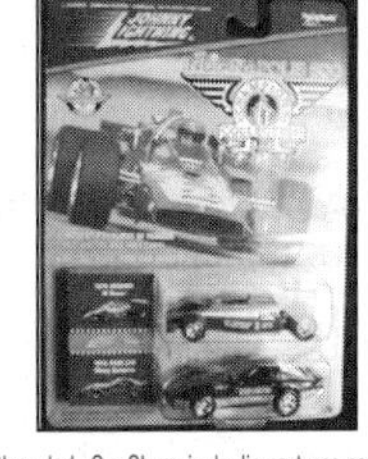

Each of these Indy Car Champion's die-cast was packaged with a die-cast replica of that year's Indy 500 pace car. There were six different packaging types used for each of the two-car packs. Five of the packaging types featured a series number (from 1-5) at the lower right hand corner. The sixth included no series number. The top half of the blister pack for series 1-5 featured a different race scene as follows: series 1-aerial view of track, 2-pit road action, 3-view down straight away, 4-car in a pit stall, and 5-cars crossing the finish line. The final unnumbered package included a large art image of an Indy car.

	EX	NM-MT
2 Mario Andretti	2.00	5.00
1969 Winner		
2 Al Unser	2.00	5.00
1970 Winner		
2 Al Unser	2.00	5.00
1978 Winner		
3 Johnny Rutherford	2.00	5.00
1974 Winner		
3 Al Unser Jr.	2.00	5.00
1992 Winner		
9 Rick Mears	2.00	5.00
1979 Winner		
14 A.J. Foyt	2.00	5.00
1977 Winner		
48 Bobby Unser	2.00	5.00
1975 Winner		

1999 Johnny Lightning Indy 1:64

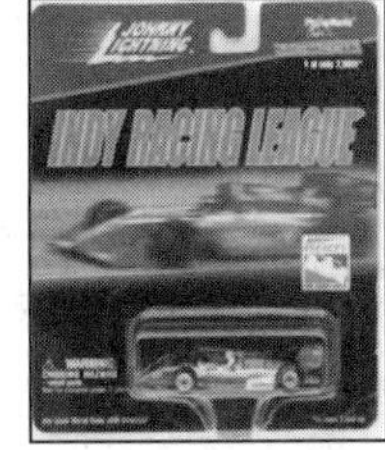

Johnny Lightning issued these Indy Car die-cast in 1999 in traditional blister packaging. Most were part of their regular series of "Indy Racing League" as noted on the blisters in red lettering. Each of those also included a production run number of 7500. The others in this checklist are various promos issued through their club or at racing events throughout the season.

	EX	NM-MT
1 Al Unser	10.00	20.00
1971 Indy Winner		
Club Promo/1000		
2 Glidden/7500	2.00	5.00
4 Scott Goodyear	2.50	6.00
Pennzoil/7500		
5 Arie Luyendyk	2.00	5.00
Sprint Meijer/7500		
8 Scott Sharp	2.50	6.00
Delphi/7500		
11 Billy Boat	2.00	5.00
Conseco/7500		
14 Kenny Brack	3.00	6.00
Pep Boys		
14 Kenny Brack	4.00	8.00
Power Team Indy 500 Win		
28 Mark Dismore	3.00	6.00
MCIWorldcom/7500		
99 Indy 500 Promo/12,000	2.50	6.00

2000 Johnny Lightning Indy 1:64

This series of Johnny Lightning die-cast pieces were issued in "IRL" blister packs as noted by the IRL logo in the center of the packaging. A few others listed below were issued in promo style blister packages.

	EX	NM-MT
4 S.Goodyear/Pennzoil	2.50	6.00
11 Greg Ray	2.50	6.00
Conseco		
24 Robbie Buhl	2.50	6.00
Purex		
28 Mark Dismore	2.50	6.00
Delphi/5000		
91 Buddy Lazier	2.50	6.00
Tae Bo		
0 Indy 500 Promo/15,000	2.50	6.00

2001 Johnny Lightning Indy 1:64

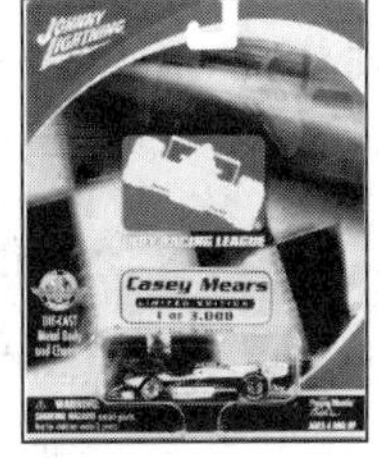

This series of Johnny Lightning die-cast pieces were issued in "IRL" blister packs as noted by the IRL logo in the center of the packaging. The packaging is virtually identical to the 2000 release except for the addition of a large silver sticker featuring the driver's name and the production total. The 2001 IRL season schedule is included on the back of the blisters.

	EX	NM-MT
15 Sarah Fisher	10.00	25.00
IRL/5000		
31 Casey Mears	3.00	8.00
Sportsline.com/3000		

1998 Maisto Indy Racing 1:18

	EX	NM-MT
1 Tony Stewart	70.00	120.00
Glidden		
40 Jack Miller	15.00	40.00
Crest		
91 Buddy Lazier	15.00	40.00
Delta Faucet		
98 American Red Cross	20.00	40.00

1999 Maisto Indy Racing 1:18

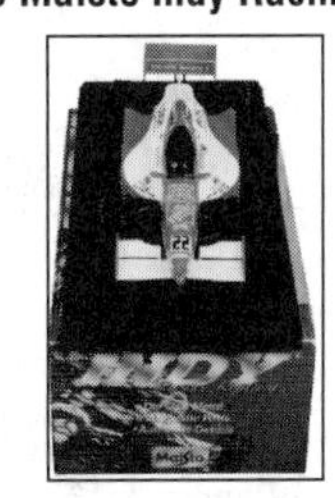

	EX	NM-MT
5 Arie Luyendyk	30.00	60.00
Meijer/5000		
22 Tony Stewart	75.00	150.00
Home Depot		

1999 Maisto Indy Racing 1:64

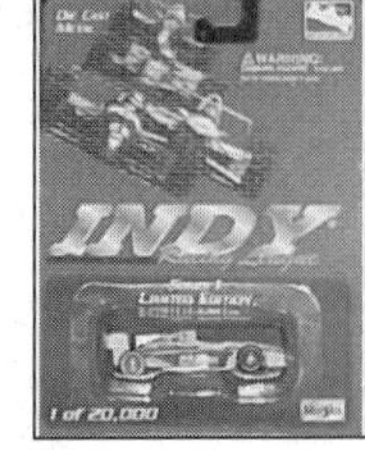

	EX	NM-MT
1 Tony Stewart	6.00	15.00
Glidden/20,000		
3 Robbie Buhl	2.00	5.00
Johns Manville		
4 Scott Goodyear	2.00	5.00
Pennzoil		
5 Arie Luyendyk	2.00	5.00
Sprint Meijer		
11 Billy Boat	2.00	5.00
Conseco		
40 Jack Miller	2.00	5.00
Crest		
91 Buddy Lazier	2.00	5.00
Delta Faucet		

1991 Matchbox Indy 500 Coins/Die-Cast 1:55

This series was released in 1991 by Matchbox. Each yellow, red and black blister package included one Indy 500 collector coin featuring a car and/or driver of a race winning Indy 500 event or other event such as fastest lap. The coin was packaged with a random die-cast Indy car or other Indy related piece such as a fuel truck. Many of the plastic Indy cars were produced to resemble actual cars driven during the event while others are generic in nature. There are many different combinations of die-cast and coins packaged together at random so we've cataloged each blister package below only by the identification of the coin and in order of the year of the Indy event featured on the coin. Note also that the backs of the blisters sometimes feature a copyright year of 1990, but all were issued for the 75th running of the Indy 500 in 1991 as noted on the logo included on the blister.

	EX	NM-MT
1911 Ray Harroun	2.50	6.00
1956 Graham Hill	2.50	6.00
1965 Jim Clark	2.50	6.00
1966 Graham Hill	2.50	6.00
1977 A.J. Foyt	2.50	6.00
1987 Al Unser	2.50	6.00
1989 Rick Mears	2.50	6.00
1990 Emerson Fittipaldi	2.50	6.00

1992 Matchbox Indy 500 Coins/Die-Cast 1:55

This series was released in 1992 by Matchbox. Each yellow, red and black blister package included one die-cast Indy 500 collector coin featuring a car and/or driver of a race winning Indy 500 event or other event such as fastest lap. The coin was packaged with a random plastic Indy car or other Indy related piece such as a fuel truck. Many of the cars were produced to resemble actual Indy cars driven during the event while others are generic in nature. There are many different combinations of die-cast and coins packaged together at random so we've cataloged each blister package below only by the identification of the coin and in order of the year of the Indy event featured on the coin. Note also that the backs of the blisters sometimes feature a copyright year of 1990 or 1991, but all were issued for the 76th running of the Indy 500 in 1992 as noted on the logo included on the blister.

	EX	NM-MT
1911 Ray Harroun	2.50	6.00
1937 Wilbur Shaw	2.50	6.00
1956 Graham Hill	2.50	6.00
1965 Jim Clark	2.50	6.00
1977 A.J. Foyt	2.50	6.00
1977 Tom Sneva Fast Lap	2.50	6.00
1987 Al Unser	2.50	6.00
1990 Arie Luyendyk Fast Lap	2.50	6.00
1991 Rick Mears	5.00	10.00

1993 Matchbox Indy 500 Closest Finish 1:55

This series of die-cast cars was produced by Matchbox and issued on a blister card carrying the title "Indy 500 Closest Finish Ever." Each blister contained two Indy car die-casts positioned as if they were crossing the finish line at the race. Note that the copyright line on the back reads "1992" but is considered a 1993 issued since it was predominantly issued that year.

	EX	NM-MT
3/15 A.Unser Jr.	6.00	15.00
Valvoline		
Scott Goodyear		
MacKenzie		

1993 Matchbox Indy 500 Coins/Die-Cast 1:55

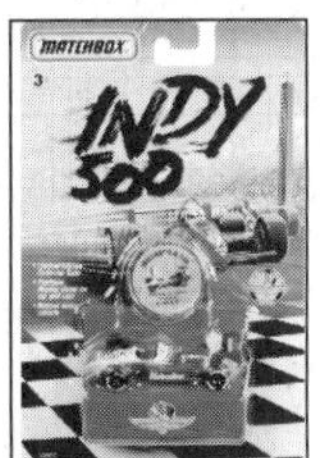

This series was released in 1993 by Matchbox. Each yellow, red and blue blister package included one plastic Indy 500 collector coin featuring a car and/or driver of a race winning Indy 500 event or other event such as fastest lap. The coin was packaged with either a die-cast Indy car, a fuel truck, or a wrecker. There were six different die-cast cars produced to resemble actual Indy cars driven during the event, one generic Indy car die-cast (black, green and pink paint scheme), and the fuel truck and wrecker which were all randomly packaged with one of the coins. We've cataloged and priced each blister package below only by the identification of the coin and in order of the year of the Indy event featured on the coin since this is how they are normally sold. Slight premiums are often paid on combinations that include one of the more popular coins and a popular paint scheme of die-cast. Note also that the backs of the blisters feature a copyright year of 1992, but all were issued during 1993. This series is a continuation of the 1991 and 1992 sets and can be identified by the simple Indianapolis Motor Speedway logo on the front instead of the logos which indicate the year of issue used in 1991 and 1992. Also, the die-cast piece rests on top of a red cardboard display within the blister package.

	EX	NM-MT
1936 Louis Meyer	2.50	6.00
1980 Johnny Rutherford	2.50	6.00
1985 Danny Sullivan	2.50	6.00
1989 Emerson Fittipaldi	2.50	6.00
1992 Al Unser Jr.	2.50	6.00

1991 Matchbox Indy 500 Transporters 1:87

This series of was produced by Matchbox and issued in a yellow window box carrying the title "Indy 500" along with the logo for the 75th Indy 500. Each package contained an Indy car die-cast with a flat bed transporter or a tractor trailer rig with or without die-cast cars.

	EX	NM-MT
2 Rick Mears Pennzoil Trailer Rig	5.00	12.00
2 Rick Mears Pennzoil Flat Bed w/car	6.00	15.00
3 Al Unser Jr. Valvoline Kraco	6.00	15.00
5 Emerson Fittipaldi Valvoline Flat Bed	6.00	15.00
22 Scott Brayton Amway	6.00	15.00
NNO Team Matchbox Rig	5.00	12.00
NNO 75th Indy 500 black&pink Tractor Trailer Rig with 2-cars	10.00	20.00
NNO Team Valvoline Rig	5.00	12.00

1992 Matchbox Indy 500 Transporters 1:87

This series of was produced by Matchbox and issued in a yellow window box carrying the title "Indy 500" along with the logo for the 76th Indy 500. Each package contained a tractor trailer rig without a car or a flat bed truck with a car.

	EX	NM-MT
6 Michael Andretti Havoline Flat Bed	6.00	15.00
NNO Pennzoil Rig	5.00	12.00
NNO K-Mart Havoline Rig	5.00	12.00
NNO Panasonic Rig	5.00	12.00

1993 Matchbox Indy 500 Transporters 1:87

This series of was produced by Matchbox and issued in a yellow window box carrying the title "Indy 500" along with a generic Indianapolis Motor Speedway logo instead of the year specific logos found in the 1991 and 1992 releases. Similar to 1991 and 1992, each package contained a tractor trailer rig without a car or a flat bed truck with a car. Additionally, a 1:55 scale Indy 500 event trailer was also released along with 2-Indy cars.

	EX	NM-MT
3 Al Unser Jr. Valvoline Flat Bed	6.00	15.00
11 Raul Boesel Panasonic Flat Bed	6.00	15.00
15 Scott Goodyear Mackenzie Flat Bed	6.00	15.00
NNO Indy 500 1:55 scale Rig with 2-cars	10.00	20.00
NNO Team Mackenzie Rig	5.00	12.00
NNO Team Valvoline Rig	5.00	12.00

1993 MiniChamps Indy Road Course 1:18

	EX	NM-MT
3 Al Unser Jr. Valvoline	150.00	250.00
4 Emerson Fittipaldi Marlboro	75.00	125.00
5 Nigel Mansell Kmart	75.00	125.00
6 Michael Andretti K-Mart	60.00	100.00
9 Raul Boesel Duracell	40.00	75.00
12 Paul Tracy Marlboro/3333	150.00	250.00
12 Paul Tracy Penske	60.00	100.00

1993 MiniChamps Indy Speedway 1:18

	EX	NM-MT
3 Al Unser Jr. Valvoline	90.00	150.00
4 Emerson Fittipaldi Marlboro	75.00	125.00
4 Emerson Fittipaldi Penske	35.00	60.00
5 Nigel Mansell Kmart	40.00	75.00
6 Michael Andretti K-Mart	60.00	100.00
9 Raul Boesel Duracell	40.00	75.00
12 Paul Tracy Marlboro	125.00	200.00
12 Paul Tracy Penske	60.00	100.00

1994 MiniChamps Indy Road Course 1:18

	EX	NM-MT
6 Michael Andretti K-Mart	40.00	75.00
19 Alessandro Zampedri Mi-Jack	40.00	60.00
23 Buddy Lazier Owens	40.00	60.00
24 Willy T. Ribbs Service Merchandise	40.00	75.00
31 Al Unser Jr. Marlboro	125.00	200.00
31 Al Unser Jr. Penske	90.00	150.00
55 John Andretti Gillette	40.00	60.00

1994 MiniChamps Indy Speedway 1:18

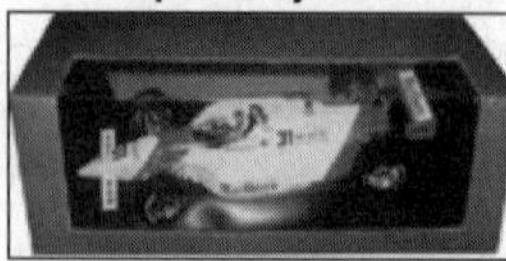

	EX	NM-MT
2 Emerson Fittipaldi Marlboro	125.00	200.00
2 Emerson Fittipaldi Penske	40.00	75.00
3 Paul Tracy Marlboro	125.00	200.00
19 Alessandro Zampedri Mi-Jack	35.00	60.00
31 Al Unser Jr. Marlboro	150.00	250.00
31 Al Unser Jr. Penske	60.00	100.00

1995 MiniChamps Indy 1:18

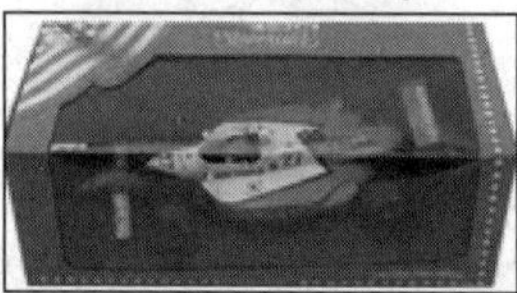

	EX	NM-MT
3 Pual Tracy Budweiser Kmart	100.00	175.00
5 Robby Gordon Valvoline	40.00	75.00
6 Michael Andretti K-Mart Texaco	75.00	125.00
9 Bobby Rahal Miller Genuine Draft/3333	75.00	150.00
27 Jacques Villeneuve Klein Tools Players/3333	250.00	400.00

1996 MiniChamps Indy IRL 1:18

	EX	NM-MT
4 Richie Hearn Food For Less	35.00	50.00
12 Buzz Calkins Bradley	35.00	50.00
36 Juan Fangio Toyota-Castrol	30.00	50.00
91 Buddy Lazier Delta	35.00	50.00
98 P.J. Jones Toyota-Castrol	35.00	50.00

1997 MiniChamps Indy 1:18

	EX	NM-MT
31 Al Unser Jr. Penske	40.00	75.00

1999 MiniChamps Indy 1:18

	EX	NM-MT
26 Paul Tracy Klein Tools Green	75.00	135.00

1993 MiniChamps Indy 1:43

Each piece comes in both a road course and speedway version. This was the first year for Paul's Model Art to do 1:43 scale Indy cars.

	EX	NM-MT
3 Al Unser Jr. Valvoline	15.00	30.00
4 Emerson Fittipaldi Penske	12.50	25.00
5 Nigel Mansell K-Mart	12.00	20.00
6 Mario Andretti K-Mart	15.00	25.00
9 Raul Boesel Duracell	12.00	20.00
12 Paul Tracy Penske	12.00	20.00

1994 MiniChamps Indy Road Course 1:43

	EX	NM-MT
12 Jacques Villeneuve Players/4444	200.00	350.00
19 Alessandro Zampedri Mi-Jack	10.00	25.00
28 Arie Luyendyk Regency IBM/4444	12.50	25.00
31 Al Unser Jr. Penske	18.00	30.00

1994 MiniChamps Indy Speedway 1:43

	EX	NM-MT
2 Emerson Fittipaldi Penske/5555	20.00	35.00
3 Paul Tracy Penske/3333	15.00	25.00
5 Nigel Mansell Kmart	30.00	50.00
6 Mario Andretti K-Mart	15.00	25.00
7 Adrian Fernandez Tecate/4444	15.00	25.00
8 Michael Andretti Target	25.00	40.00
16 Stefan Johansson Alumax	12.00	20.00
19 Alessandro Zampedri Mi-Jack	12.00	20.00
22 Hiro Matsushita Panasonic	12.00	20.00
31 Al Unser Jr. Penske	18.00	30.00

1995 MiniChamps Indy Road Course 1:43

	EX	NM-MT
15 Christian Fittipaldi Walker Racing/4444	15.00	25.00
27 Jacques Villeneuve Klein Tools/4444	40.00	75.00
31 Andre Ribeiro LCI	15.00	25.00

1995 MiniChamps Indy Speedway 1:43

	EX	NM-MT
27 Jacques Villeneuve Klein Tools/4444	40.00	75.00

1996 MiniChamps Indy IRL 1:43

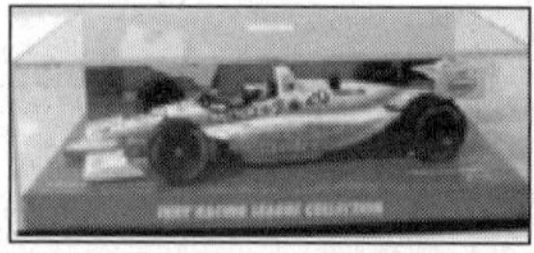

Only three drivers and four Indy cars were released from Paul's Model Art in 1995. Each car features a Road Course set up.

	EX	NM-MT
4 Richie Hearn Food 4 Less	10.00	22.00
12 Buzz Calkins Bradley	10.00	22.00
20 Tony Stewart Menards Glidden/4444	25.00	40.00
20 Tony Stewart Quaker State/4444	15.00	30.00

1996 MiniChamps Indy Road Course 1:43

	EX	NM-MT
1 Nigel Mansell K-Mart	12.00	20.00
4 Bobby Rahal Miller Genuine Draft	12.00	20.00
6 Mario Andretti K-Mart	15.00	25.00
9 Robby Gordon Valvoline	15.00	25.00
17 Mauricio Gugelmin Hollywood	10.00	20.00
19 Alessandro Zampedri Mi-Jack	12.00	20.00
23 Buddy Lazier Randy Owens	12.00	20.00
24 Willy T. Ribbs Walker Racing	12.00	20.00
28 Arie Luyendyk Eurosports	12.00	20.00
31 Al Unser Jr. Penske	15.00	30.00
55 John Andretti Gillette	12.00	20.00

1993 Onyx Indy 1:24

This was the first year die-cast manufacturer Onyx began producing 1:24 scale indy cars. There were four cars featured.

	EX	NM-MT
2 Scott Goodyear Mackenzie Financial	20.00	35.00
3 Al Unser Jr. Valvoline	15.00	40.00
5 Nigel Mansell K-Mart	20.00	35.00
6 Mario Andretti K-Mart	20.00	35.00

1994 Onyx Indy 1:24

The late Scott Brayton highlights the two 1:24 Indy cars released by Onyx in 1994.

	EX	NM-MT
9 Raul Boesel Duracell	20.00	40.00
23 Scott Brayton Amway	25.00	50.00

1995 Onyx Indy 1:24

	EX	NM-MT
60 Scott Brayton Quaker State Menards Indy 500 Pole Win	60.00	100.00

1996 Onyx Indy 1:24

	EX	NM-MT
6 Arie Luyendyk Target	20.00	35.00
20 Tony Stewart Quaker State Menards Indy 500 Pole Win	75.00	150.00
NNO Scott Pruett Firestone	18.00	30.00

1990 Onyx Indy 1:43

This was the first year Onyx began producing 1:43 scale Indy cars. The series is highlighted by Rick Mears and variations of the Emerson Fittipaldi and Danny Sullivan cars.

	EX	NM-MT
1 Emerson Fittipaldi Marlboro w/black wheels	50.00	80.00
1 Emerson Fittipaldi Marlboro w/ silver wheels	20.00	40.00
2 Rick Mears Pennzoil	50.00	100.00
3 Michael Andretti K-Mart	20.00	35.00
4 Teo Fabi Quaker State	15.00	25.00
5 Al Unser Jr. Valvoline	35.00	70.00
6 Mario Andretti K-Mart	25.00	40.00
7 Danny Sullivan Marlboro with decals	30.00	60.00
7 Danny Sullivan Marlboro w/o decals	20.00	40.00
9 Tom Sneva RCA	12.50	25.00
11 Kevin Cogan Tuneup Masters	12.50	25.00
12 Randy Lewis AMP Oracle	12.50	25.00
14 A.J. Foyt Copenhagen	25.00	50.00
15 Jim Crawford Glidden	15.00	25.00
18 Bobby Rahal Kraco	18.00	30.00
19 Raul Boesel Budweiser	18.00	30.00
20 Roberto Guerrero Miller Genuine Draft	15.00	25.00
22 Scott Brayton Amway	25.00	40.00
25 Eddie Cheever Target	15.00	25.00
28 Scott Goodyear Mackenzie Financial	15.00	25.00
29 Pancho Carter Hardee's	12.50	25.00
30 Arie Luyendyk Domino's	30.00	50.00
40 Al Unser Sr. Miller	15.00	30.00
41 John Andretti Foster's Quaker State	15.00	25.00
70 Didier Theys Tuneup Masters RCA	12.50	25.00
86 Dominic Dobson Texaco	12.50	25.00

1991 Onyx Indy 1:43

Three members of the Andretti family had cars in this series, Mario, Michael and John. The Kevin Cogan/Glidden car is one of the most difficult of all the Onyx Indy die-cast to find.

	EX	NM-MT
2 Al Unser Jr. Valvoline	15.00	40.00
4 John Andretti Pennzoil	15.00	25.00
6 Mario Andretti K-Mart	15.00	25.00
9 Kevin Cogan Glidden	60.00	100.00
10 Michael Andretti K-Mart	25.00	40.00
51 Gary Bettenhausen Glidden	15.00	25.00

1992 Onyx Indy 1:43

This set is highlighted by the A.J.Foyt Copenhagen car. The series also has two beer sponsors Bud and Miller.

	EX	NM-MT
10 Scott Pruett Budweiser	12.00	20.00
12 Bobby Rahal Miller Genuine Draft	12.00	20.00
14 A.J. Foyt Copenhagen	25.00	50.00
15 Scott Goodyear Mackenzie Financial	10.00	20.00
23 Scott Brayton Amway	15.00	30.00
27 Al Unser Sr. Conseco	15.00	3
36 Roberto Guerrero Quaker State	10.00	2

1993 Onyx Indy 1:43

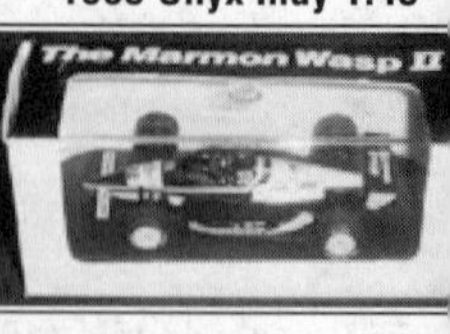

This series marks the first appearance by Nigel Mansell Indy car die-cast.

	EX	NM
5 Nigel Mansell K-Mart	12.50	2
6 Arie Luyendyk Target	12.50	2
7 Danny Sullivan Molson	12.00	2
9 Raul Boesel Duracell	10.00	2
19 Robbie Buhl Mi-Jack	20.00	3
27 Geoff Brabham Glidden	20.00	4
29 Olivier Grouillard Eurosport	10.00	2
32 Eric Bachelart Marmon Wasp II	40.00	7
36 Roberto Guerrero Quaker State	10.00	2
39 Ross Bentley Rain-X	10.00	2

1994 Onyx Indy 1:43

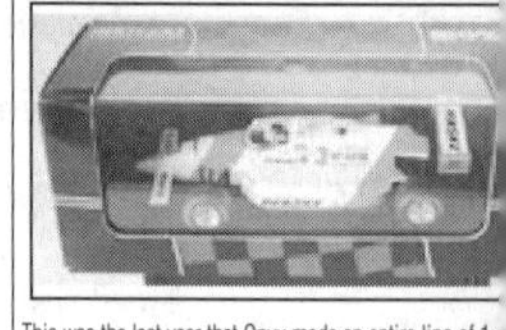

This was the last year that Onyx made an entire line of 1: cars.

	EX	NM
1 Nigel Mansell K-Mart	10.00	2
3 Paul Tracy Penske	15.00	3
5 Raul Boesel Duracell	10.00	2
6 Mario Andretti K-Mart	10.00	2
7 Adrian Fernandez Tecate	10.00	2
8 Michael Andretti Target	12.50	2
9 Robby Gordon Valvoline	10.00	2
11 Teo Fabi Pennzoil	10.00	2
18 Jimmy Vasser Conseco	10.00	2
21 Roberto Guerrero Interstate Batteries	10.00	2
27 Eddie Cheever Quaker State	10.00	2
88 Mauricio Gugelmin Hollywood	10.00	2

1995 Onyx Indy 1:43

	EX	NM
3 Paul Tracy Budweiser	12.50	2
60 Scott Brayton Quaker State Promo	15.00	4

1996 Onyx Indy 1:43

	EX	NM
5 Arie Luyendyk Bryant	12.50	2
5 Arie Luyendyk Wavephore	12.50	2

1997 Onyx Indy 1:43

	EX	NM
17 Mauricio Gugelmin Hollywood Pac West	10.00	2

1994-95 Racing Champio Indy Banks 1:24

	EX	NM
6 Mario Andretti K-Mart Texaco Bank 1994	12.50	3
6 Mario Andretti K-Mart Texaco Bank 1995	12.50	3
9 Robby Gordon Valvoline	12.50	3

1994-95 Racing Champio Indy Series 1 1:24

Racing Champions issued their 1995 Indy cars in two The red, white and blue boxes the pieces come in th which serie they are from.

	EX	NM
1 Nigel Mansell Texaco 1994	12.50	2
2 Emerson Fittipaldi Penske Racing	10.00	2
3 Paul Tracy Penske	10.00	2
4 Bobby Rahal Rahal-Hogan	10.00	2

ul Boesel	10.00	20.00
Duracell		
gel Mansell	10.00	20.00
Texaco		
rio Andretti	10.00	20.00
Texaco		
rian Fernandez	10.00	20.00
Tecate		
chael Andretti	10.00	20.00
Target 1994		
de Farran	10.00	20.00
Pennzoil		
bby Gordon	10.00	20.00
Valvoline		
ike Groff	10.00	20.00
Motorola		
eo Fabi	10.00	20.00
Pennzoil		
immy Vasser	10.00	20.00
Conseco		
iro Matsushita	10.00	20.00
Panasonic		
Villy T. Ribbs	10.00	20.00
Service Merchandise		
tefan Johansson	10.00	20.00
Eurosports		
l Unser Jr.	15.00	30.00
Penske Racing		
ynn St. James	12.00	22.00
JC Penny's		

995 Racing Champions Indy Series 2 1:24

is the second series of Indy cars from Racing Champions 95. The boxes state what series the cars are from.

	EX	NM-MT
Unser Jr.	10.00	30.00
Penske		
erson Fittipaldi	10.00	20.00
Penske		
ul Tracy	10.00	20.00
K-Mart		
yan Herta	10.00	20.00
Target		
bby Gordon	12.50	25.00
Valvoline		
chael Andretti	10.00	20.00
K-Mart		
ex Salazar	10.00	20.00
Crystal		
l de Ferran	10.00	20.00
Pennzoil		
bby Rahal	10.00	20.00
Honda		
drian Fernandez	10.00	20.00
Tecate		
aul Boesel	10.00	20.00
Duracell		
immy Vasser	10.00	20.00
Target		
hristian Fittipaldi	10.00	20.00
Telesena		
anny Sullivan	10.00	20.00
VISA		
tefan Johansson	10.00	20.00
Alumax		
cott Pruett	10.00	20.00
Firestone		
oberto Guerrero	10.00	20.00
iro Matsushita	10.00	20.00
Panasonic		
lberto Ribeiro	10.00	20.00
LCI		
lex Sampadri	10.00	20.00
ndy 500 Promo/20,000	7.50	20.00
avid Hall	10.00	20.00
Subway		

996 Racing Champions Indy Cart 1:24

1:24 scale Indy car series was highlighted by the arance of Michael Andretti and Robby Gordon. There is an ex-Formula 1 driver Marc Blundell in the series.

	EX	NM-MT
ex Zanardi	12.50	25.00
Target		
bby Gordon	12.50	25.00
Valvoline		
chael Andretti	10.00	20.00
Texaco		
l de Ferran	10.00	20.00
Pennzoil		
mmy Vasser	10.00	20.00
Target		
cott Goodyear	10.00	20.00
Firestone		
tefan Johansson	10.00	20.00
Alumax		
lauricio Gugelmin	10.00	20.00
Hollywood Pac West		
iro Matsushita	10.00	20.00
Panasonic		
cott Pruett	10.00	20.00
Firestone		
ark Blundell	10.00	20.00
VISA		
lichel Jourdain	10.00	20.00
Herdez		
lberto Ribeiro	10.00	20.00
LCI		
arker Johnstone	10.00	20.00
Motorola		
Disney 200 Promo	10.00	20.00

996 Racing Champions Indy Racing League 1:24

was Racing Champions first year to make Indy Racing ue cars.

	EX	NM-MT
e Luyendyk	12.00	22.00
Bryant		
uzz Calkins	12.00	22.00
Bradley		
ony Stewart	30.00	60.00
Quaker State		
yn St. James	12.00	22.00

San Antonio		
70 Davy Jones	12.00	22.00
AC Delco		
91 Buddy Lazier	12.50	25.00
Delta Faucets		

1997 Racing Champions Indy Racing League 1:24

Tony Stewart and Buddy Lazier are among the two most popular drivers in the Indy Racing League featured in this series.

	EX	NM-MT
1 Scott Sharp	12.00	22.00
Conseco		
4 Davy Jones	12.00	22.00
Monsoon		
10 Mike Groff	12.00	22.00
Byrd's Cafeteria		
20 Tony Stewart	50.00	100.00
Glidden Menards		
21 Roberto Guerrero	12.00	22.00
Pennzoil		
91 Buddy Lazier	12.00	22.00
Delco		

1998 Racing Champions Indy Cart 1:24

	EX	NM-MT
16 Helio Castroneves	10.00	20.00
Alumax Promo		

1994 Racing Champions Indy Premier 1:43

	EX	NM-MT
15 Jim Crawford	12.00	20.00
Mac Tools/7500		

1995 Racing Champions Indy Premier 1:43

This series of 1:43 scale Indy Cars come in a red, white and blue Premier series box. The pieces do have a serial number on the back but unlike most Premier issues the number of quantity produced is not stated anywhere on the box.

	EX	NM-MT
1 Nigel Mansell	7.00	12.00
Texaco		
2 Emerson Fittipaldi	7.00	12.00
Penske Racing		
3 Paul Tracy	7.00	12.00
Penske		
4 Bobby Rahal	7.00	12.00
Rahal-Hogan		
5 Raul Boesel	7.00	12.00
Duracell		
5 Nigel Mansell	7.00	12.00
Texaco		
6 Mario Andretti	7.00	12.00
Texaco		
7 Adrian Fernandez	7.00	12.00
Tecate		
8 Michael Andretti	7.00	12.00
K-Mart		
9 Robby Gordon	7.50	15.00
Valvoline		
11 Teo Fabi	7.00	12.00
Pennzoil		
18 Jimmy Vasser	7.00	12.00
Conseco		
31 Al Unser Jr.	7.50	15.00
Penske Racing		

1996 Racing Champions Indy Premier 1:43

	EX	NM-MT
91 Buddy Lazier	15.00	25.00
Delta Hemelgarn		
Indy 500 Win/5091		

1989-94 Racing Champions Indy Series 1 1:64

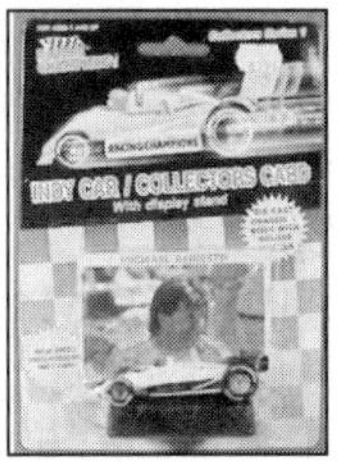

	EX	NM-MT
1 Emerson Fittipaldi	2.50	6.00
black helmet 1990		
1 Al Unser Jr.	5.00	12.00
Valvoline		
2 Rick Mears	3.00	8.00
Pennzoil 1989		
3 Mario Andretti	2.00	5.00
Havoline		
3 Rick Mears	2.00	5.00
Mobil 1 Promo 1991		
4 John Andretti	2.00	4.00
Pennzoil		
4 Rick Mears	2.00	5.00
Pennzoil		
4 Rick Mears	2.00	5.00
Pennzoil yellow helmet '89		
4 Bobby Rahal	2.00	5.00
Rahal-Hogan		
5 Mario Andretti	2.00	5.00
Havoline with Black Helmet 1989		
5 Mario Andretti	2.00	5.00
Havoline with		
White Helmet 1989		
5 Mario Andretti	2.00	5.00
No Sponsor White Helmet 1989		
5 Al Unser Jr.	6.00	12.00
Valvoline 1989		
6 Michael Andretti	3.00	8.00
Havoline black helmet 1989		
6 Michael Andretti	3.00	8.00
Havoline white helmet 1989		
8 John Andretti	2.00	4.00
Pennzoil		
8 Scott Pruett	2.00	4.00
Red Roof Inn 1989		
10 Derek Daly	2.00	4.00
Black helmet with no		
driver name 1989		
10 Derek Daly	2.00	4.00
Black helmet with		
driver signature 1989		
10 Derek Daly	2.00	4.00
Red helmet 1989		
14 A.J. Foyt 1991	4.00	8.00
16 Tony Bettenhausen	2.00	4.00
Amax		
18 Bobby Rahal	3.00	6.00
Kraco 1991		
21 Geoff Brabham	2.00	4.00
Mac Tools		
25 Al Unser Sr.	6.00	12.00
Black helmet 1989		
25 Al Unser Sr.	6.00	12.00
Mobil 1 White helmet 1989		
25 Al Unser Sr.	6.00	12.00
White helmet 1989		
86 Barry Dodson	2.00	4.00
Havoline		

1990 Racing Champions Indy 3-Car Sets 1:64

	EX	NM-MT
NNO Geoff Brabham	12.50	25.00
A.J. Foyt		
Scott Pruett		
NNO Dominic Dobson	10.00	20.00
Rick Mears		
Al Unser		
NNO Emerson Fittipaldi	10.00	20.00
A.J. Foyt		
Bobby Rahal		

1994 Racing Champions Indy Premier 1:64

	EX	NM-MT
1 Nigell Mansel	3.00	6.00
Texaco		
2 Emerson Fittipaldi	3.00	6.00
Penske Racing		
4 Bobby Rahal	3.00	6.00
Rahal-Hogan		
5 Nigell Mansel	4.00	8.00
Texaco		
7 A Fernandez	3.00	6.00
Tecate		
8 Michael Andretti	3.00	8.00
Target		
10 M Groff	3.00	6.00
Motorola		
11 Teo Fabi	3.00	6.00
Pennzoil		
18 Jimmy Vasser	3.00	6.00
Conseco		
22 Hito Matsushita	3.00	6.00
Panasonic		
78 Indy 500 Promo/5000	3.00	8.00

1995-96 Racing Champions Indy Series 2 Premier 1:64

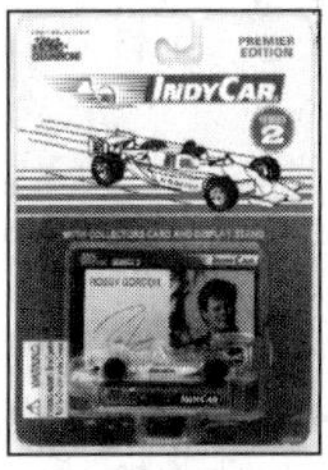

This was the series two release of Racing Champions Premier Edition Indy 1:64 scale cars. The cars were released in late 1995 and early 1996 in typical Racing Champions style blister packs. Each was also packaged with a Racing Champions standard-sized card that includes the "series 2" set name.

	EX	NM-MT
1 Al Unser Jr.	2.00	5.00
Penske		
2 Emerson Fittipaldi	2.00	5.00
Penske		
3 Paul Tracy	2.50	5.00
Penske		
4 Bryan Herta	2.00	4.00
Target		
4 Alex Zanardi	2.00	5.00
Target		
5 Robby Gordon	4.00	10.00
Valvoline		
6 Michael Andretti	2.00	5.00
K-Mart		
7 Eliseo Salazar	2.00	4.00
Crystal		
8 Gil de Ferran	2.00	4.00
Pennzoil		
9 Emerson Fittipaldi	2.00	5.00
Mobil 1		
9 Bobby Rahal	2.00	4.00
Honda		
10 Adrian Fernandez	2.00	4.00
Tecate		
11 Raul Boesel	2.00	4.00
Duracell		
12 Jimmy Vasser	2.00	4.00
Target		
15 Christian Fittipaldi	2.00	4.00
Telesena		
17 Danny Sullivan	2.50	5.00
VISA		
18 Stefan Johansson	2.00	4.00
Alumax		
20 Scott Pruett	2.00	4.00
Firestone		
22 Roberto Guerrero	2.00	4.00
25 Hiro Matsushita	2.00	4.00
Panasonic		
31 Al Unser Jr.	3.00	8.00
Penske		
31 Alberto Ribeiro	2.00	4.00
LCI		
34 Alessandro Zampedri	2.00	4.00
99 David Hall	2.00	4.00
Subway		

1996 Racing Champions Indy Cart 1:64

This series was the regular release in 1996 of 1:64 scale Indy cars. The series includes Michael Andretti and Jeff Krosnoff.

	EX	NM-MT
2 Al Unser Jr.	3.00	6.00
Penske		
3 Paul Tracy	2.00	5.00
Penske		
4 Alex Zanardi	2.50	6.00
Target		
4 Richie Hearn	2.00	5.00
Ralph's Foods		
5 Robby Gordon	4.00	10.00
Valvoline		
6 Michael Andretti	2.50	6.00
Texaco		
8 Gil de Ferran	2.00	5.00
Pennzoil		
9 Emerson Fittipaldi	2.00	5.00
Hogan-Penske		
10 Eddie Lawson	2.00	5.00
Delco		
12 Jimmy Vasser	2.00	5.00
Target		
15 Scott Goodyear	2.00	5.00
Firestone		
16 Stefan Johansson	2.00	5.00
Alumax		
17 Mauricio Gugelmin	2.00	5.00
Hollywood		
19 Hiro Matsushita	2.00	5.00
Panazonic		
20 Scott Pruett	2.00	5.00
Firestone		
21 Mark Blundell	2.00	5.00
VISA		
22 Michel Jourdain	2.00	5.00
Herdez		
25 Jeff Krosnoff	2.00	5.00
Arciero Wines		
28 Bryan Herta	2.00	5.00
Shell Promo		
31 Alberto Ribeiro	2.00	5.00
LCI		
49 Parker Johnstone	2.00	5.00
Motorola		

1995 Racing Champions Premier Matched Serial Numbers Indy 1:64

	EX	NM-MT
1 Al Unser Jr.	2.00	5.00
Penske		
5 Robby Gordon	3.00	8.00
Valvoline		
6 Michael Andretti	2.50	6.00
Havoline		
11 Raul Boesel	2.00	5.00
Duracell		
12 Jimmy Vasser	2.00	5.00
Target		
20 Scott Pruett	2.00	5.00
Firestone		

1996 Racing Champions Indy Racing League 1:64

This series includes popular drivers Tony Stewart and Lyn St. James. The cars came in a red white and blue blister package and were sold through mass market retailers.

	EX	NM-MT
2 Scott Brayton	2.00	5.00
Glidden		
3 Eddie Cheever	2.00	5.00
Quaker State		
4 Richie Hearn	2.00	5.00
Food 4 Less		
5 Arie Luyendyk	2.00	5.00
Bryant		
7 Eliseo Salazar	2.00	5.00
Crystal		
11 Scott Sharp	2.00	5.00
Conseco		
12 Buzz Calkins	2.00	5.00
Bradley		
20 Tony Stewart	5.00	12.00
Quaker State		
21 Roberto Guerrero	2.00	5.00
Pennzoil		
60 Mike Groff	2.00	5.00
Valvoline		
70 Davy Jones	2.00	5.00
AC Delco		
90 Lyn St. James	2.00	5.00
Lifetime Channel		
91 Buddy Lazier	2.00	5.00
Delta Faucets		

1997 Racing Champions Indy Cart 1:64

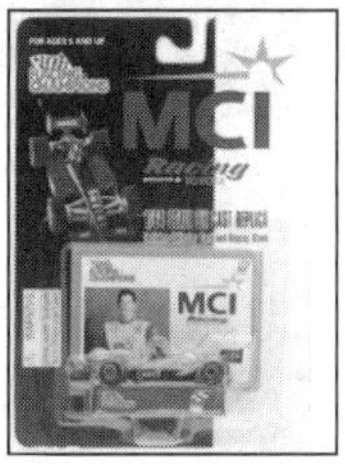

	EX	NM-MT
1 Jimmy Vasser	2.00	5.00
Target		
4 Anthony Lazzaro	4.00	10.00
Per4mer Promo		
(Atlantic Championship Series)		
4 Alex Zanardi	2.00	5.00
Target		
6 Micheal Andretti	2.00	5.00
K-Mart		
11 Christian Fittipaldi	2.00	5.00
K-Mart		
17 Mauricio Gugelmin	2.00	5.00
Hollywood Pacwest		
18 Mark Blundell	2.00	5.00
Motorola		
24 Hiro Matsushita	2.00	5.00
Panasonic		
25 Max Papis	2.00	5.00
MCI Promo		
36 Juan Manuel Fangio	2.00	5.00
Castrol		

1997 Racing Champions Indy Racing League 1:64

This was the first series of 1:64 Indy Racing League cars issued by Racing Champions. The 1996 Indy 500 winner Buddy Lazier and NASCAR Champion Tony Stewart are key parts of the set.

	EX	NM-MT
1 Scott Sharp	2.00	5.00
Conseco		
4 Mike Groff	2.50	6.00
Byrd's Cafeteria		
4 Davy Jones	2.50	6.00
Monsoon		
5 Arie Luyendyk	3.00	6.00
Bryant		
10 Jack Miller	2.50	6.00
Crest		
20 Tony Stewart	6.00	15.00
Glidden		
21 Roberto Guerrero	2.50	6.00
Pennzoil		
91 Buddy Lazier	3.00	6.00
Delco		

1998 Racing Champions Indy Cart 1:64

	EX	NM-MT
1 Alex Zanardi	4.00	10.00
Target 1998 Champion		

1999 Racing Champions Indy Racing League 1:64

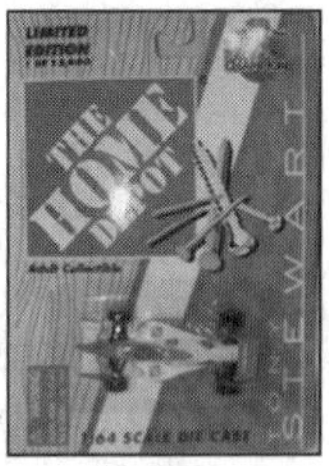

	EX	NM-MT
22 Tony Stewart	6.00	15.00
Home Depot Promo/12,000		

2002 Racing Champions IRL 1:64

	EX	NM-MT
39 Michael Andretti Motorola Promo in wind. Box	5.00	10.00

1994 Racing Champions Indy Transporters 1:64

	EX	NM-MT
NNO Scott Goodyear Budweiser/7500	10.00	20.00

1997 UT Models Indy 1:18

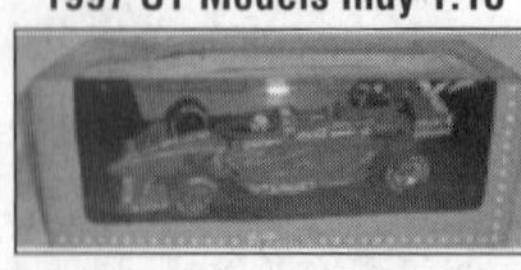

Each car in this series was issued in a UT Models blue window box. The car itself was mounted to a cardboard base.

1 Alex Zanardi Target

1997 UT Models Indy 1:43

Each car in this series was issued in a UT Models hard plastic case. The car itself was mounted on a blue cardboard base.

	EX	NM-MT
4 Alex Zanardi Target	20.00	35.00

1998 UT Models Indy 1:43

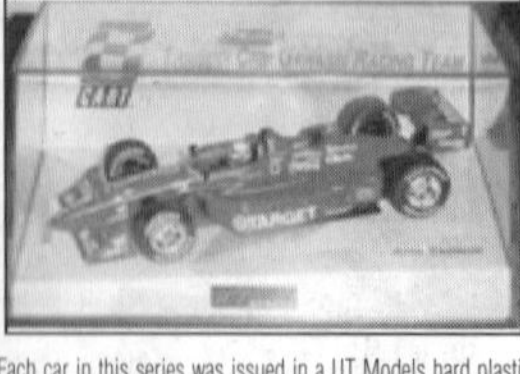

Each car in this series was issued in a UT Models hard plastic case. The car itself was mounted to a white cardboard base.

	EX	NM-MT
1 Alex Zanardi Target	18.00	30.00
7 Bobby Rahal Miller Lite	12.50	30.00
8 Bryan Herta Shell	15.00	30.00
9 J.J. Lehto Hogan	12.50	30.00
12 Jimmy Vasser Target	12.50	30.00
18 Mark Blundell Motorola	12.50	30.00
27 Dario Franchitti KOOL Green	20.00	35.00
40 Adrian Fernandez Tecate	18.00	30.00

1998 Hot Wheels Racing F1 1:18

	EX	NM-MT
3 Michael Schumacher Shell	30.00	60.00

1999 Hot Wheels Racing F1 1:18

Cars in this series were issued in a colorful Hot Wheels Racing window box. Each piece was mounted on a base that resembled a section of track.

	EX	NM-MT
3 Michael Schumacher Shell	30.00	60.00
7 Damon Hill Buzzin Hornets	30.00	60.00
8 Heinz-Harold Frentzen Buzzin Hornets	30.00	60.00
16 Rubens Barrichello HSBC	40.00	80.00
NNO Eddie Irvine Shell	30.00	60.00
NNO Alex Zanardi Williams	30.00	60.00

2000 Hot Wheels Racing F1 1:18

This series of 1:18 scale cars was produced by Hot Wheels. Each car was mounted to a black plastic base and packaged in a "2000 Hot Wheels Racing" black window box.

	EX	NM-MT
1 Mika Hakkinen Mobil 1	30.00	60.00
2 David Coulthard Mobil 1	30.00	60.00
3 Michael Schumacher Shell Launch	30.00	60.00
4 Jarno Trulli Buzzin Hornets	30.00	60.00
5 Heinz-Harold Frentzen Buzzin Hornets	30.00	60.00
7 Eddie Irvine HSBC	30.00	60.00
8 Johnny Herbert HSBC	25.00	50.00
9 Ralf Schumacher Compaq Allianz	30.00	60.00
9 Ralf Schumacher Compaq Allianz Launch	30.00	60.00
10 Jenson Button Compaq Allianz Launch	30.00	60.00
NNO Rubens Barrichello Shell	30.00	60.00

2001 Hot Wheels Racing F1 1:18

	EX	NM-MT
1 Rubens Barrichello Shell Launch Edition	25.00	60.00
1 Michael Schumacher Shell Race Edition	40.00	75.00
1 Michael Schumacher Shell King of Rain/14,999	40.00	75.00
3 Mika Hakkinen Mobil 1 Launch Edition	35.00	60.00
3 Michael Schumacher Shell 2000 World Champ in plastic case	40.00	75.00
4 David Coulthard Siemens Mobil 1	25.00	60.00
4 Jarno Trulli Buzzin Hornets	30.00	60.00
5 Heinz-Harold Frentzen Buzzin Hornets Launch Edition	35.00	60.00
5 Juan Montoya Compaq Allianz Race Edition	35.00	60.00
5 Ralf Schumacher Compaq Allianz Launch Edition	35.00	60.00
18 Eddie Irvine HSBC Launch Edition	25.00	60.00
18 Eddie Irvine HSBC Race Edition	30.00	50.00

2002 Hot Wheels Racing F1 1:18

	EX	NM-MT
1 Michael Schumacher Shell 2001 World Champ/25,000 in plastic case	35.00	60.00
1 Michael Schumacher Shell/20,000	35.00	60.00
1 Michael Schumacher Shell 5-Time Champ/25,000	40.00	75.00
1 Michael Schumacher Shell 52 Wins	40.00	75.00
2 Rubens Barrichello Shell	30.00	50.00
4 Kimi Raikkonen Kimi Mobil 1	30.00	50.00
5 Ralf Schumacher HP Allianz	30.00	50.00
6 Juan Montoya HP Allianz	30.00	50.00
10 Takuma Sato DHL/1000	30.00	50.00
16 Eddie Irvine HSBC	25.00	50.00

2003 Hot Wheels Racing F1 1:18

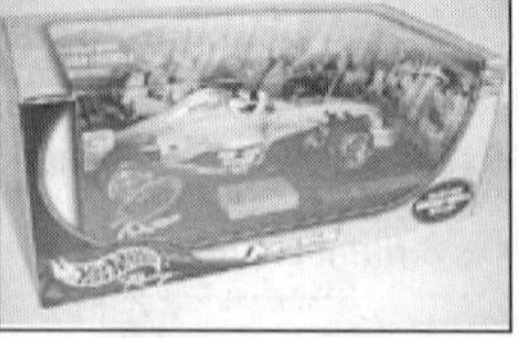

	EX	NM-MT
1 Michael Schumacher Ferrari 9-11 Tribute/500	100.00	175.00
1 Michael Schumacher Canadian Grand Prix/20,000	40.00	75.00
1 Michael Schumacher Shell	60.00	100.00
1 Michael Schumacher Shell Champ	40.00	75.00
3 Juan Montoya Castrol HP	35.00	50.00
4 Ralf Schumacher Castrol HP	35.00	50.00
6 Kimi Raikkonen Kimi Mobil 1	35.00	60.00
6 Kimi Raikkonen Kimi First Win/5000	40.00	75.00
7 Jarno Trulli Elf	35.00	50.00
7 Jarno Trulli Elf Mild Seven	50.00	80.00
8 Fernando Alonso Elf	35.00	50.00
11 Giancarlo Fisichella Be on Edge	35.00	50.00
11 Giancarlo Fisichella Be on Edge First Win/5000	35.00	60.00
14 Mark Webber HSBC	35.00	50.00
0 Rubens Barrichello Shell	35.00	50.00

2004 Hot Wheels Racing F1 1:18

	EX	NM-MT
1 Michael Schumacher Ferrari Sakhir Bahrain Raced/15,000	40.00	65.00
1 Michael Schumacher Ferrari 75 Wins w/figure and firesuit	200.00	300.00
2 Juan Montoya Allianz	40.00	65.00
3 Nick Heidfeld Jordon Ford	40.00	65.00
4 Ralf Schumacher Allianz	40.00	65.00
7 Jarno Trulli Elf	40.00	65.00
8 Fernando Alonso Elf	40.00	65.00
14 Mark Webber Jaguar	40.00	65.00

2000 Hot Wheels Racing F1 1:24

	EX	NM-MT
1 Mika Hakkinen Mobil 1 Launch	12.50	25.00

2002 Hot Wheels Racing F1 1:24

	EX	NM-MT
1 Michael Schumacher Shell	15.00	30.00
6 Juan Montoya HP	12.50	25.00

1999 Hot Wheels Racing F1 1:43

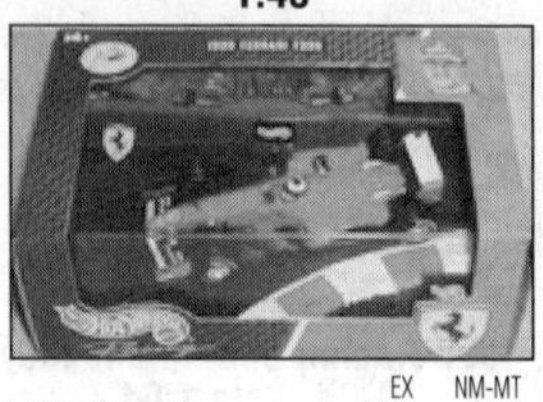

	EX	NM-MT
3 Michael Schumacher Shell	10.00	20.00
16 Rubens Barrichello Stewart	10.00	20.00
NNO Johnny Herbert Stewart	10.00	20.00
NNO Ralf Schumacher Williams	10.00	20.00
NNO Alex Zanardi Williams	10.00	20.00

2000 Hot Wheels Racing F1 1:43

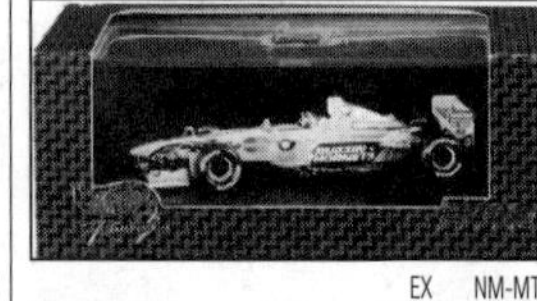

	EX	NM-MT
2 David Coulthard Mobil 1	10.00	20.00
3 Mika Hakkinen Mobil 1	10.00	20.00
5 Heinz-Harold Frentzen Buzzin Hornets	7.50	20.00
8 Johnny Herbert HSBC	10.00	20.00
0 Jenson Button Compaq Allianz	7.50	20.00
NNO Eddie Irvine	7.50	20.00
NNO Ralf Schumacher Williams	10.00	20.00
NNO Jarno Trulli Jordan Hart	10.00	20.00

2001 Hot Wheels Racing F1 1:43

	EX	NM-MT
1 Michael Schumacher Shell	7.50	20.00
2 Rubens Barrichello Shell	6.00	15.00
3 Mika Hakkinen Mobil 1	7.50	20.00
4 David Coulthard Mobil 1	6.00	15.00
5 Heinz-Harold Frentzen Buzzin Hornets	7.50	20.00

2002 Hot Wheels Racing F1 1:43

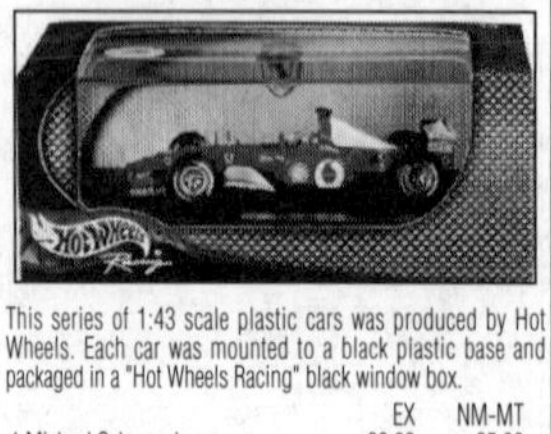

This series of 1:43 scale plastic cars was produced by Hot Wheels. Each car was mounted to a black plastic base and packaged in a "Hot Wheels Racing" black window box.

	EX	NM-MT
1 Michael Schumacher Shell	20.00	35.00
2 Rubens Barrichello Shell	20.00	35.00
18 Rubens Barrichello HSBC Ford/9998	12.50	25.00

2003 Hot Wheels Racing F1 1:43

	EX	NM-MT
1 Michael Schumacher Shell 3-car set	30.00	50.00
NNO Rubens Barrichello Ferrari	10.00	20.00

1999 Hot Wheels Racing F1 1:64

	EX	NM-MT
1/2 avid Coulthard Mika Hakkinen Mobil 1 2-car set	6.00	15.00

2001 Hot Wheels Racing F1 1:64

	EX	NM-MT
3 Mika Hakkinen Mobil 1	3.00	6.00
18 Eddie Irvine HSBC	3.00	6.00

2002 Hot Wheels Racing F1 1:64

	EX	NM-MT
3 David Coulthard Mobil 1	3.00	6.00
16 Eddie Irvine HSBC	3.00	6.00

2003 Hot Wheels Racing F1 1:64

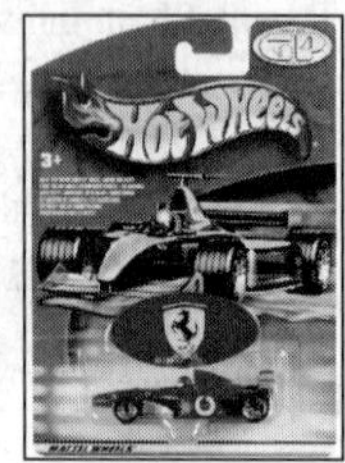

	EX	NM-MT
1 Michael Schumacher Shell	5.00	10.00
3 Juan Montoya Castrol HP	4.00	8.00
5 David Coulthard David Mobil 1	4.00	8.00
7 Jarno Trulli Elf	4.00	8.00
11 Giancarlo Fisichella Be on Edge	4.00	8.00
14 Mark Webber HSBC	4.00	8.00

1988-92 MiniChamps F1 1:18

	EX	NM-MT
2 Gerhard Berger Marlboro '91	50.00	80.00
2 Alan Prost Marlboro '89	50.00	80.00
2 Gerhard Berger Marlboro '92	50.00	80.00
11 Alan Prost Marlboro WC '88	50.00	80.00
12 Ayrton Senna Shell '88	50.00	100.00
19 Michael Schumacher Camel '92	150.00	250.00
28 Gerhard Berger Marlboro '90	30.00	60.00
NNO Saturo Nakajima Lotus '87	40.00	80.00

1993 MiniChamps F1 1:18

	EX	NM-MT
0 Damon Hill Canon	50.00	80.00
2 Alain Prost Canon	50.00	80.00
5 Michael Schumacher Camel Nordica	175.00	300.00
6 Riccardo Patrese Camel	40.00	80.00
7 Mario Andretti Marlboro	60.00	100.00
8 Ayrton Senna Marlboro	60.00	100.00
27 Jean Alesi Ferrari	60.00	100.00
28 Gerhard Berger Ferrari	50.00	80.00
29 K.Wendlinger Broker/Sauber	40.00	80.00
30 Heinz-Harold Frentzen Broker Sauber	40.00	80.00
30 J.J.Lehto Broker/Sauber	40.00	80.00

1994 MiniChamps F1 1:18

	EX	NM-MT
0 Damon Hill Rothmans Presentation	40.00	75.00
0 Damon Hill Rothmans	40.00	75.00
2 Ayrton Senna Rothmans	50.00	100.00
2 Ayrton Senna Rothmans Presentation	50.00	100.00
5 Michael Schumacher Mild Seven B194	125.00	200.00
5 Michael Schumacher Mild Seven German GP	125.00	200.00
5 Michael Schumacher Mild Seven BB(Bitburger)	125.00	200.00
5 Michael Schumacher Mild Seven B193B	125.00	200.00
6 J.J.Lehto Mild Seven	40.00	75.00
6 Jos Verstappen Mild Seven	40.00	75.00
6 Jos Verstappen Mild Seven German GP	40.00	7
7 Mika Hakkinen Marlboro	40.00	7
8 Martin Brundle Marlboro	40.00	7
27 Jean Alesi Ferrari	60.00	10
27 Nicola Larini Ferrari	40.00	7
28 Gerhard Berger Ferrari	40.00	7
29 Andrea deCesaris Broker/Sauber	40.00	7
29 K.Wendlinger Tissot/Sauber	40.00	7
30 Heinz-Harold Frentzen Tissot Sauber	40.00	7

1995 MiniChamps F1 1:1

	EX	NM
1 Alesi/Schumacher/MS Alesi 1st Win	150.00	25
1 Michael Schumacher MS Europe GP	125.00	20
1 Michael Schumacher MS French GP	250.00	40
1 Michael Schumacher MS German GP	125.00	20
1 Michael Schumacher MS Showcar	125.00	20
2 Jonny Herbert Mild Seven British GP	35.00	5
2 Jonny Herbert Mild Seven Showcar	35.00	5
5 Damon Hill Rothmans	40.00	7
5 Damon Hill Rothmans Test Car	40.00	7
6 David Coulthard Rothmans	40.00	10
6 David Coulthard Rothmans Test Car	40.00	10
7 Martin Brundle Marlboro	35.00	5
7 Nigel Mansell Marlboro	35.00	6
8 Mika Hakkinen Marlboro	35.00	7
14 Rubens Barrichello Peugeot/Jordan	35.00	5
15 Eddie Irvine/Peugeot/Jordan	35.00	5
25 Aguri Suzuki Gitanes/Ligier	35.00	5
26 O.Panis Gitanes/Ligier	35.00	5
27 Jean Alesi Ferrari	60.00	10
28 Gerhard Berger Ferrari	35.00	5
29 Karl Wendlinger Red Bull/Sauber	35.00	5
30 Heinz-Harold Frentzen Red Bull Sauber	35.00	5

1996 MiniChamps F1 1:1

	EX	NM
1 Michael Schumacher Benetton 1995 Champ	150.00	25
1 Michael Schumacher Ferrari	125.00	20
1 Michael Schumacher Ferrari Italian GP	125.00	20
1 Michael Schumacher Ferrari Launch	125.00	20
1 Michael Schumacher Ferrari Spanish GP/9662	175.00	30
2 Eddie Irvine Shell Ferrari	35.00	5
2 Eddie Irvine Shell Ferrari Launch	40.00	6
3 Jean Alesi Mild Seven	40.00	7
4 Gerhard Berger Mild Seven	35.00	5
5 Damon Hill Rothmans	35.00	6
6 Jacques Villenueve Rothmans	60.00	10
7 Mika Hakkinen Marlboro	35.00	7
8 David Coulthard Marlboro	30.00	8
11 Rubens Barrichello Benson & Hedges	35.00	5
11 Rubens Barrichello BH Launch	35.00	6
12 Martin Brundle Benson & Hedges	35.00	5
12 Martin Brundle BH Launch	35.00	6
14 Jonny Herbert Petronas	35.00	5
15 Heinz-Harold Frentzen Petronas	35.00	5

1997 MiniChamps F1 1:1

	EX	NM
5 Michael Schumacher Shell Ferrari	100.00	17
22 Rubens Barrichello HSBC	35.00	6
23 J Magnussen HSBC	40.00	7

1998 MiniChamps F1 1:1

	EX	NM
1 Jacques Villeneuve Williams	35.00	7
3 Jacques Villeneuve Castrol 1997 Champ/4444	75.00	12
4 Eddie Irvine Shell	45.00	8
5 Giancarlo Fisichella Korean Air Benetton	40.00	8
9 Damon Hill Buzzin Hornets	35.00	7

lichael Schumacher	100.00	175.00
rrari Black Testcar/6500		

999 MiniChamps F1 1:18

	EX	NM-MT
Hakkinen	30.00	75.00
obil 1 Mika		
Prost	30.00	60.00
ayStation Peugeot		
l Coulthard	30.00	60.00
obil 1		
Schumacher	35.00	70.00
illiams		
Schumacher	35.00	70.00
illiams Showcar/3333		
xander Wurz	20.00	50.00
netton		
ques Villeneuve	30.00	60.00
pertec		
anoskne Takagi	30.00	60.00
VR		
ro Diniz	30.00	60.00
d Bull Petronas		
ier Panis	25.00	60.00
aystation Showcar/2222		
ardo Zonta	30.00	60.00
pertec		

000 MiniChamps F1 1:18

	EX	NM-MT
Schumacher	30.00	60.00
lianz Compaq Williams		
son Button	30.00	60.00
lianz Compaq Williams		
ncarlo Fisichella	30.00	60.00
netton		
xander Wurz	30.00	60.00
netton		
ardo Zonta	30.00	60.00
R Honda		
.S. Grand Prix Gold	25.00	50.00

001 MiniChamps F1 1:18

	EX	NM-MT
Hakkinen	35.00	70.00
emens Mobil 1		
Schumacher	25.00	50.00
lianz Compaq		
Schumacher	25.00	50.00
lianz Compaq first win		
Montoya	35.00	70.00
astrol Compaq Showcar		
ques Villeneuve	35.00	70.00
owcar/3000		
i Raikkonen	75.00	125.00
tronas Showcar/800		
son Button	25.00	50.00
arconi Korean Air		

002 MiniChamps F1 1:18

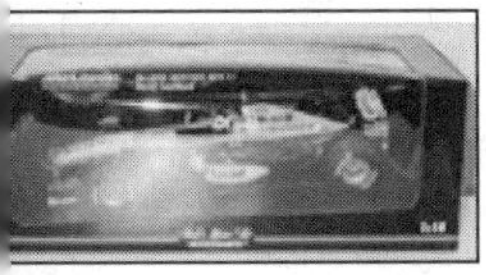

	EX	NM-MT
l Coulthard	40.00	75.00
obil 1		
Raikkonen	40.00	75.00
obil 1		
Schumacher	30.00	60.00
astrol Compaq Launch		
Schumacher	40.00	75.00
astrol Compaq Race		
Montoya	30.00	60.00
astrol Compaq Race		
Heidfeld	40.00	75.00
tronas		
e Massa	25.00	50.00
tronas Race		
e Massa	25.00	50.00
tronas Showcar/1002		
nz-Harold Frentzen	30.00	60.00
ange		
ka Salo	30.00	60.00
nasonic		
a Salo	30.00	60.00
nasonic Showcar/1200		
n McNish	30.00	60.00
nasonic Race		
n McNish	30.00	60.00
nasonic Showcar/750		
adian Grand Prix/2002	30.00	50.00
anasonic Showcar/5002	35.00	60.00
solid box		

003 MiniChamps F1 1:18

	EX	NM-MT
ques Villeneuve	35.00	60.00
R Honda/1206		
k Webber	40.00	70.00
guar Cosworth HSBC DuPont		

004 MiniChamps F1 1:18

	EX	NM-MT
on Button	40.00	70.00
r Honda		
9 Jenson Button	50.00	75.00
Bar Honda Lucky Strike/1002		
10 Takuma Sato	40.00	70.00
Bar Honda		
10 Takuma Sato	50.00	75.00
Bar Honda Lucky Strike/1002		
14 Mark Webber	40.00	70.00
Jaguar HSBC DuPont		
14 Mark Webber	50.00	75.00
Jaguar Showcar		
HSBC DuPont		

2004 MiniChamps Ayrton Senna Collection 1:18

	EX	NM-MT
2 Ayrton Senna	75.00	125.00
Williams Renault '94		

2005 MiniChamps F1 1:18

	EX	NM-MT
11 Jacques Villenuve	50.00	80.00
Sauber Petronas/1602		

2006 MiniChamps F1 1:18

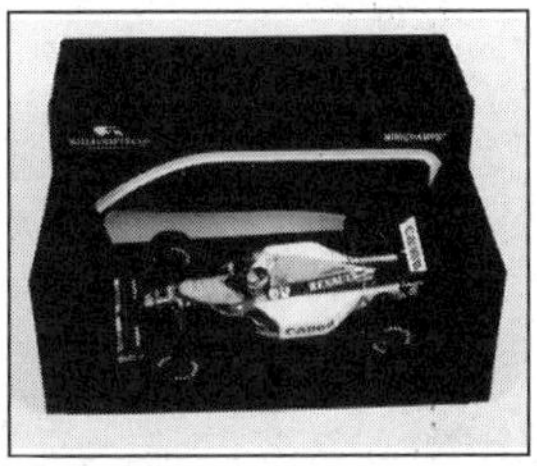

	EX	NM-MT
5 Nigel Mansell		
Canon Renault '91		

1992 MiniChamps F1 1:43

This was the first year for Paul's Model Art to produce 1:43 scale Formula 1 die-cast. Three teams were represented.

	EX	NM-MT
5 Nigel Mansell	30.00	60.00
Canon Williams		
6 Riccardo Patrese	30.00	60.00
Canon Williams		
19 Michael Schumacher	125.00	200.00
Benetton		
20 Marc Brundle	15.00	25.00
Benetton		
27 Jean Alesi	18.00	30.00
Ferrari		
28 Ivan Capelli	18.00	30.00
Ferrari		

1993 MiniChamps F1 1:43

Damon Hill and Aryton Senna make their first Paul's Model Art 1:43 scale appearance in this series.

	EX	NM-MT
0 Damon Hill	18.00	30.00
Canon Williams		
2 Alain Prost	15.00	25.00
Canon Williams		
5 Michael Schumacher	125.00	200.00
Benetton		
6 Riccardo Patrese	15.00	25.00
Benetton		
7 Michael Andretti	35.00	60.00
McLaren		
7 Mika Hakkinen	25.00	50.00
McLaren		
8 Ayrton Senna	25.00	40.00
McLaren		
27 Jean Alesi	15.00	25.00
Ferrari		
28 Gerhard Berger	15.00	25.00
Ferrari		
29 Karl Wendlinger	15.00	25.00
Broker/Sauber		
30 Heinz-Harold Frentzen	15.00	25.00
Liquid Moly/Sauber		
30 J.J.Lehto	15.00	25.00
Liqui Moly Sauber		

1994 MiniChamps F1 1:43

This was the first year that Paul's Model Art did special edition 1:43 cars. Michael Schumacher's F1 Championship car and Nigel Mansell's French Grand Prix car are among the most popular.

	EX	NM-MT
0 Damon Hill	15.00	25.00
Rothmans Williams FW15		
0 Damon Hill	15.00	25.00
Rothmans Williams FW16		
0 Damon Hill	15.00	25.00
Rothmans Williams FW16		
British Grand Prix		
2 Nigel Mansell	15.00	25.00
Rothmans FW16		
French Grand Prix/11,111		
2 David Coulthard	20.00	50.00
Rothmans Williams/3333		
2 Ayrton Senna	25.00	50.00
Rothmans		
3 Ukyo Katayama	15.00	35.00
Calbee Tyrell		
4 Mark Blundell	15.00	25.00
Calbee Tyrell		
5 Michael Schumacher	90.00	150.00
Benetton		
5 Michael Schumacher	90.00	150.00
Benetton German Grand Prix		
5 Michael Schumacher	90.00	150.00
Benetton Formula 1 Champion		
6 Johnny Herbert	15.00	25.00
Bitburger		
6 J.J. Lehto	15.00	25.00
Mild Seven		
6 Jos Verstappen	15.00	25.00
Mild Seven		
6 Jos Verstappen	15.00	25.00
Mild Seven German Grand Prix		
7 Mika Hakkinen	15.00	40.00
McLaren		
8 Martin Brundle	15.00	25.00
McLaren		
27 Jean Alesi	15.00	25.00
Ferrari		
27 Nicola Larini	15.00	25.00
Ferrari		
28 Gerhard Berger	15.00	25.00
Ferrari		
29 Andrea deCesaris	15.00	25.00
Broker		
200th Grand Prix		
29 Andrea deCesaris	15.00	25.00
Broker		
German Grand Prix		
29 Karl Wendlinger	15.00	25.00
Broker Sauber		
30 Heinz-Harold Frentzen	15.00	25.00
Broker Sauber		
31 David Brabham	15.00	25.00
MTV Ford		
32 Roland Ratzenberger	25.00	50.00
MTV Ford		

1995 MiniChamps F1 1:43

Ayrton Senna is noticeably absent from this set. The show car of Damon Hill and the Test car of David Coulthard are the special editions in this series.

	EX	NM-MT
1 Michael Schumacher	125.00	200.00
Jean Alesi		
Alesi 1st Win/11,695		
1 Michael Schumacher	75.00	125.00
Mild Seven B195		
2 Johnny Herbert	15.00	25.00
Mild Seven B195		
3 Ukyo Katayama	15.00	25.00
Calbee Tyrell		
4 Mika Salo	15.00	25.00
Calbee Tyrell		
5 Damon Hill	15.00	25.00
Rothmans FW16 Showcar/4444		
5 Damon Hill	15.00	25.00
Rothmans Williams FW17		
6 David Coulthard	20.00	50.00
Rothmans FW17		
6 David Coulthard	12.00	30.00
Rothmans FW 16 Test car		
7 Mark Blundell	15.00	25.00
McLaren		
7 Nigel Mansell	15.00	25.00
McLaren		
8 Mika Hakkinen	15.00	40.00
McLaren		
11 Mimmo Schiattarella	15.00	25.00
MTV Simtek Ford NI		
12 Jos Verstappen	15.00	25.00
MTV Simtek Ford		
14 Rubens Barrichello	15.00	25.00
Peugeot Jordan		
15 Eddie Irvine	15.00	25.00
Peugeot Jordan		
25 Martin Brundle	15.00	25.00
Gitanes Ligier		
25 Aguri Suzuki	15.00	25.00
Gitanes Ligier		
26 Olivier Panis	15.00	25.00
Gitanes Ligier		
27 Jean Alesi	15.00	25.00
Ferrari		
28 Gerhard Berger	15.00	25.00
Ferrari		
29 Jean-Christophe Bouillion	15.00	25.00
Red Bull Sauber		
29 Karl Wendlinger	15.00	25.00
Red Bull Sauber		
30 Heinz-Harold Frentzen	15.00	25.00
Red Bull Sauber		

1996 MiniChamps F1 1:43

Michael Schumacher has four different versions in this series. His first win in a Ferrari is commemorated as one of the special pieces.

	EX	NM-MT
1 Michael Schumacher	75.00	125.00
Ferrari		
1 Michael Schumacher	150.00	250.00
Ferrari 1st Win/962		
1 Michael Schumacher	75.00	125.00
Ferrari High Nose		
1 Michael Schumacher	75.00	125.00
Ferrari Launch car		
2 Eddie Irvine	25.00	40.00
Ferrari		
2 Eddie Irvine	25.00	40.00
Ferrari Launch car		
3 Jean Alesi	15.00	25.00
Benetton Mild Seven		
4 Gerhard Berger	15.00	25.00
Benetton Mild Seven		
5 Heinz-Harold Frentzen	15.00	25.00
Rothmans Test car		
5 Damon Hill	15.00	25.00
Rothmans Williams FW18		
6 Jacques Villeneuve	18.00	30.00
Rothmans		
6 Jacques Villeneuve	18.00	30.00
Rothmans Test car		
7 Mika Hakkinen	15.00	40.00
McLaren		
8 David Coulthard	12.00	30.00
McLaren		
9 Olivier Panis	15.00	25.00
Parmalat Ligier		
9 Olivier Panis	40.00	80.00
Parmalat Ligier		
Monaco Grand Prix Win/6000		
10 Pedro Diniz	15.00	25.00
Parmalat Ligier		
11 Rubens Barrichello	15.00	25.00
Peugeot Launch car		
11 Rubens Barrichello	15.00	25.00
Peugeot		
12 Martin Brundle	15.00	25.00
Peugeot Launch car		
12 Martin Brundle	15.00	25.00
Peugeot		
14 Johnny Herbert	15.00	25.00
Petronas Sauber		
15 Heinz-Harold Frentzen	15.00	25.00
Petronas Sauber		
18 Ukyo Katayama	15.00	25.00
Korean Air Tyrrell		
19 Mika Salo	15.00	25.00
Korean Air Tyrrell		

1997 MiniChamps F1 1:43

	EX	NM-MT
1 Damon Hill	50.00	100.00
Zepler Danka		
6 Eddie Irvine	25.00	40.00
Shell		
NNO Michael Schumacher	12.50	25.00
Shell/9999		

1998 MiniChamps F1 1:43

	EX	NM-MT
1 Jacques Villeneuve	12.50	25.00
Veltins		
3 Jacques Villeneuve	35.00	60.00
Castrol 1997 Champ/6666		
4 Eddie Irvine	35.00	60.00
Shell/3333		
8 Mika Hakkinen	12.50	25.00
Mobil 1		
11 Olivier Panis	12.50	25.00
Playstation		

1999 MiniChamps F1 1:43

	EX	NM-MT
11 Jean Alesi	18.00	30.00
Red Bull		
NNO Olivier Panis	20.00	35.00
Playstation		
NNO Jacques Villeneuve	20.00	35.00
Supertec Test		

1999-02 MiniChamps Ayrton Senna Collection 1:43

CARS ARE LISTED BY MODEL NUMBER
STATED PRODUCTION RUN 600

	EX	NM-MT
1 Ayrton Senna	40.00	75.00
1988 Honda Turbo		
2 Ayrton Senna	40.00	75.00
1989 Honda V10		
3 Ayrton Senna	35.00	60.00
1990 Honda V10		
4 Ayrton Senna	35.00	60.00
1993 Penske Chevrolet		
5 Ayrton Senna	35.00	60.00
1991 Honda V12		
6 Ayrton Senna	35.00	60.00
1992 Honda V12		
7 Ayrton Senna	35.00	60.00
1994 Renault V12		
8 Ayrton Senna	30.00	50.00
1993 Ford V8		
9 Ayrton Senna	30.00	50.00
1985 Renault Turbo		
10 Ayrton Senna	30.00	50.00
1984 Hart Turbo		
11 Ayrton Senna	30.00	50.00
1984 Mercedes Benz		
12 Ayrton Senna	30.00	50.00
1986 Renault Turbo		
13 Ayrton Senna	30.00	50.00
1984 Hart Turbo		
14 Ayrton Senna	15.00	40.00
1980&1993 Kart Models		
15 Ayrton Senna	30.00	50.00
1987 Honda Turbo		
16 Ayrton Senna	30.00	50.00
1983 Williams Ford		
17 Ayrton Senna	30.00	50.00
1984 Porsche 956		

2000 MiniChamps F1 1:43

	EX	NM-MT
11 Giancarlo Fisichella	18.00	30.00
Benetton		
12 Alexander Wurz	18.00	30.00
Benetton		
0 Jenson Button	15.00	30.00
Marconi Korean Air		
First Test Drive/2999		

2001 MiniChamps F1 1:43

	EX	NM-MT
3 Mika Hakkinen	20.00	35.00
Siemens Mobil 1		
3 Kimi Raikkonen	25.00	40.00
Petronas		
3 Kimi Raikkonen	35.00	60.00
Petronas Malaysian GP/2222		
4 David Coulthard	20.00	35.00
Siemens Mobil 1		
5 Ralf Schumacher	20.00	35.00
Castrol Compaq		
5 Ralf Schumacher	20.00	35.00
Castrol Compaq		
Keep Your Distance/5701		
5 Ralf Schumacher	20.00	35.00
Castrol Compaq		
First Grand Prix Win/7001		
6 Juan Montoya	20.00	35.00
Castrol Compaq		
6 Juan Montoya	20.00	35.00
Castrol Compaq		
First Grand Prix Win		
6 Juan Montoya	20.00	35.00
Castrol Compaq		
Malaysian Grand Prix/3024		
8 Jenson Button	10.00	25.00
Marconi Korean Air		
Showcar/4500		
17 Kimi Raikkonen	25.00	40.00
Petronas		
17 Kimi Raikkonen	25.00	50.00
Petronas 1st Point		
17 Kimi Raikkonen	35.00	60.00
Petronas Showcar/1400		
0 Jenson Button	15.00	30.00
Marconi Korean Air		
0 Jenson Button	15.00	30.00
Marconi Korean Air		
US Grand Prix/2811		
01 U.S. Grand Prix	10.00	20.00

2002 MiniChamps F1 1:43

	EX	NM-MT
4 Kimi Raikkonen	25.00	40.00
Mobil 1		
5 Ralf Schumacher	20.00	35.00
Castrol Compaq		
5 Ralf Schumacher	20.00	35.00
Castrol HP		
5/6 R.Schumacher	50.00	80.00
Juan Montoya		
Castrol Compaq		
Malaysian Grand Prix		
Finish 2-car set		
6 Juan Montoya	20.00	35.00
Castrol Compaq		
6 Juan Montoya	20.00	35.00
Castrol HP		
6 Juan Montoya	20.00	35.00
Castrol Compaq Showcar		
7 Nick Heidfeld	20.00	35.00
Petronas US GP/3024		
8 Heinz-Harold Frentzen	20.00	35.00
Petronas US Grand Prix/3744		
15 Jenson Button	15.00	30.00
Barcelona Test/3144		
15 Jenson Button	15.00	30.00
Blue World Renault		
15 Jenson Button	15.00	30.00
Launch Renault/2201		
21 Anthony Davidson	20.00	35.00
KL Hungarian GP/1872		
23 Mark Webber	20.00	35.00
KL		
23 Mark Webber	20.00	35.00
KL Australian GP/3096		
24 Mika Salo	20.00	35.00
Panasonic Raced		
24 Mika Salo	20.00	35.00
Panasonic Showcar		
25 Alan McNish	20.00	35.00
Panasonic Raced		
25 Alan McNish	20.00	35.00
Panasonic Showcar		
NNO Canadian Grand Prix/2002	25.00	40.00
NNO Panasonic Toyota Showcar/2002	25.00	40.00

2003 MiniChamps F1 1:43

	EX	NM-MT
3 Juan Montoya	20.00	35.00
Castrol HP		
3 Juan Montoya	20.00	35.00

	EX	NM-MT
Castrol HP Showcar/2404		
4 Ralf Schumacher Castrol HP	20.00	35.00
4 Ralf Schumacher Castrol HP Showcar/2160	20.00	35.00
5 David Coulthard Siemens Mobil 1	20.00	35.00
6 Kimi Raikkonen Siemens Mobil 1	30.00	50.00
9 Jenson Button Bar Honda	20.00	35.00
14 Mark Webber HSBC	20.00	35.00
16 Jacques Villeneuve Honda Showcar/2448	20.00	35.00
17 Jenson Button Honda Showcar/2016	20.00	35.00
18 Jos Verstappen European Showcar/2160	20.00	35.00
19 John Wilson European Trust/2808	20.00	35.00
19 John Wilson European Showcar/1224	20.00	35.00
20 Olivier Panis Panasonic/2303	20.00	35.00
21 Cristiano DaMatta Panasonic	20.00	35.00
21 Cristiano DaMatta Panasonic Showcar/2303	20.00	35.00
NNO Heinz-Harold Frentzen Petronas/2448	20.00	35.00
NNO Nick Heidfeld Petronas/2304	20.00	35.00
NNO Panasonic Showcar/2503	25.00	40.00
NNO USA Grand Prix	25.00	40.00

2003 MiniChamps F1 Michelin Promos 1:43

	EX	NM-MT
4 Ralf Schumacher Castrol HP	60.00	100.00
5 David Coulthard Siemens Mobil 1/504	60.00	100.00

2003 MiniChamps F1 Vintage 1:43

	EX	NM-MT
1 Eric Van de Poele 1992 Brabham Judd	25.00	40.00
2 Keke Rosberg 1986 McClaren Tag Turbo	25.00	40.00
3 Ronnie Peterson 1977 Tyrrell Ford	25.00	40.00
4 Patrick Depailler 1976 Tyrrell Ford	25.00	40.00
5 Emerson Fittipaldi 1974 McLaren Ford	25.00	40.00
7 Denis Hulme 1973 McLaren Ford	25.00	40.00
8 Damon Hill 1992 Brabham Judd	25.00	40.00
8 Peter Revson 1973 McLaren Ford	25.00	40.00
15 Eddie Irvine 1993 Barclay Jordan Hart/2808	25.00	40.00
22 Piers Courage 1970 DeTomaso Ford	25.00	40.00
34 Hans Stuck 1976 March Ford/3744	25.00	40.00

2004 MiniChamps F1 1:43

	EX	NM-MT
9 Jenson Button Bar Honda	20.00	40.00
9 Jenson Button Bar Honda 1st Pole San Marino/8784	20.00	40.00
9 Jenson Button Bar Honda Lucky Strike 1st Pole San Marino/8784	30.00	60.00
14 Mark Webber Jaguar HSBC DuPont	20.00	40.00

2005 MiniChamps F1 1:43

	EX	NM-MT
10 Takuma Sato Bar Honda Michelin	75.00	125.00
10 Takuma Sato Bar Honda '04 Japanese GP/15,408	25.00	40.00
11 Jacques Villenueve Sauber Petronas/2016	25.00	40.00

1995 Onyx F1 1:18

This was the first year for Onyx to produce 1:18 scale Formula 1 cars. The two teams represented were the Williams team and the Ferrari team. The Williams cars were issued with an umbrella with variations on the sponsor featured.

	EX	NM-MT
5 Damon Hill Rothmans with Renault Umbrella	30.00	50.00
5 Damon Hill Rothmans with Rothmans Umbrella	30.00	50.00
6 David Coulthard Rothmans with Renault Umbrella	40.00	100.00
6 David Coulthard Rothmans with Rothmans Umbrella	40.00	100.00
27 Jean Alesi Ferrari	30.00	50.00
28 Gerhard Berger Ferrari	30.00	50.00

1996 Onyx F1 1:18

Onyx cut back in its 1996 1:18 line to only include the Williams team. The Jacques Villeneuve is one of his first Formula 1 die-cast pieces.

	EX	NM-MT
5 Damon Hill Rothmans	30.00	50.00
6 Jacques Villeneuve Rothmans	30.00	50.00

1992 Onyx F1 1:24

This was the first year for Onyx to make 1:24 scale Formula 1 cars. Williams, Ligier and Ferrari were the three teams represented in the set.

	EX	NM-MT
5 Nigel Mansell Canon	16.00	28.00
6 Riccardo Patrese Canon	15.00	25.00
25 Thierry Boutsen Gitanes	15.00	25.00
26 Erik Comas Gitanes	15.00	25.00
27 Jean Alesi Ferrari	15.00	25.00
28 Ivan Capelli Ferrari	15.00	25.00

1993 Onyx F1 1:24

This series of Formula 1 cars was cut down to just two teams Williams-Renault and Benetton-Ford.

	EX	NM-MT
0 Damon Hill Canon	15.00	25.00
2 Alain Prost Canon	15.00	25.00
5 Michael Schumacher Benetton	25.00	50.00
6 Riccardo Patrese Benetton	15.00	25.00

1994 Onyx F1 1:24

This series of 1:24 scale Formula 1 cars includes test cars for the Benetton-Ford team. The cars are done in the Mild Seven paint scheme. For the second year in a row only the Williams-Renault and Benetton-Ford teams were represented.

	EX	NM-MT
0 Damon Hill Rothmans	15.00	25.00
2 David Coulthard Rothmans	20.00	50.00
2 Nigel Mansell Rothmans	16.00	28.00
2 Ayrton Senna Rothmans	20.00	35.00
5 Michael Schumacher Benetton Bitburger	25.00	50.00
5 Michael Schumacher Benetton Mild Seven	25.00	50.00
5 Michael Schumacher Benetton Mild Seven Test car	25.00	50.00
6 Jos Verstappen Benetton Mild Seven Test car	15.00	25.00
6 Jos Verstappen Benetton Mild Seven	15.00	25.00
6 J.J. Lehto Benetton Mild Seven Test car	15.00	25.00
6 J.J. Lehto Benetton Mild Seven	15.00	25.00

1988 Onyx F1 1:43

This was the first year Onyx starting making 1:43 scale Formula 1 replicas. The key pieces in the set are Ayrton Senna and Alain Prost. Both of the pieces carry the popular Marlboro sponsorship.

	EX	NM-MT
1 Nelson Piquet Camel	30.00	50.00
1 Nelson Piquet Coultaulds	25.00	40.00
2 Saturo Nakajima Camel	25.00	40.00
2 Saturo Nakajima Coultaulds	20.00	35.00
11 Alain Prost Marlboro	70.00	120.00
12 Ayrton Senna Marlboro	50.00	100.00
19 Alessandro Nannini Benetton	25.00	40.00
20 Thierry Boutsen Benetton	25.00	40.00
27 Michele Alboreto Ferrari	25.00	40.00
28 Gerhard Berger Ferrari	25.00	40.00

1989 Onyx F1 1:43

Nine different Formula 1 teams were represented in this series. The most popular cars for the second year in a row are the Ayrton Senna and Alain Prost with the Marlboro sponsorship. The Nelson Piquet and Saturo Nakajima cars carried another tobacco sponsor, Camel.

	EX	NM-MT
1 Ayrton Senna Marlboro	70.00	100.00
2 Alain Prost Marlboro	45.00	75.00
5 Thierry Boutsen Canon	15.00	30.00
6 Riccardo Patrese Canon	15.00	30.00
11 Nelson Piquet Camel	25.00	45.00
12 Saturo Nakajima Camel	15.00	30.00
15 Mauricio Gugelmin Leyton House	12.50	30.00
16 Ivan Capelli Leyton House	18.00	30.00
19 Alessandro Nannini Benetton	25.00	40.00
20 Emanuele Pirro Benetton 7Up	15.00	30.00
21 Alex Caffi Marlboro Scuderi Itallia	15.00	30.00
22 Andrea deCesaris Marlboro Scuderi Itallia	15.00	30.00
23 Pierluigi Martini SCM	15.00	30.00
24 Luis Perez-Sala SCM	12.50	30.00
27 Nigel Mansell Ferrari	25.00	40.00
28 Gerhard Berger Ferrari	18.00	30.00
29 Michele Alboreto Camel BP Larrousse	18.00	30.00
30 Philippe Alliott Camel BP Larrousse	18.00	30.00

1990 Onyx F1 1:43

Seven different Formula 1 teams were represented in this series. The Ayrton Senna is the most difficult to find but unlike previous years the car doesn't carry the Marlboro sponsorship.

	EX	NM-MT
1 Alain Prost Ferrari	25.00	50.00
2 Nigel Mansell Ferrari	15.00	25.00
3 Saturo Nakajima Epson	12.00	20.00
4 Jean Alesi Epson	12.00	20.00
5 Thierry Boutsen Canon	18.00	30.00
6 Riccardo Patrese Canon	12.00	20.00
11 Derek Warwick Camel	15.00	25.00
12 Martin Donnelly Camel	15.00	25.00
15 Mauricio Gugelmin Leyton House	12.00	20.00
16 Ivan Capelli Leyton House	12.00	20.00
19 Roberto Moreno Riello	12.00	20.00
19 Alessandro Nannini Riello	18.00	30.00
20 Nelson Piquet Riello	12.00	20.00
23 Pierluigi Martini SCM	12.00	20.00
24 Barilla Vittirio SCM	12.00	20.00
27 Ayrton Senna Honda Shell	25.00	35.00
28 Gerhard Berger Honda Shell	12.00	20.00
29 Eric Bernard Toshiba ESPO	12.00	20.00
30 Aguri Suzuki Toshiba ESPO	12.00	20.00

1991 Onyx F1 1:43

The Michael Schumacher and Nelson Piquet cars in this series actually have multiple logos of a Camel on the car and not the printed word Camel. The Ayrton Senna and Gerhard Berger pieces are painted in the Marlboro colors but do not carry that actual sponsorship. It is also Michael Schumacher's first appearance in the Onyx 1:43 scale F1 cars.

	EX	NM-MT
1 Ayrton Senna McLaren Honda	20.00	40.00
2 Gerhard Berger	15.00	25.00
3 Saturo Nakajima Braun Epson	10.00	20.00
4 Stefano Modena Braun Epson	10.00	20.00
5 Nigel Mansell Canon	20.00	30.00
6 Riccardo Patrese Canon	15.00	25.00
11 Mika Hakkinen Yellow Hat	18.00	30.00
12 Johnny Herbert Yellow Hat	12.00	20.00
19 Michael Schumacher Camel Mobil1	30.00	50.00
20 Nelson Piquet Camel Mobil1	12.00	20.00
27 Gianni Morbidelli Ferrari	12.00	20.00
27 Alain Prost Ferrari	12.00	20.00
28 Jean Alesi Ferrari	15.00	25.00
29 Eric Bernard Toshiba Larrousse	10.00	20.00
30 Aguri Suzuki Toshiba Larrousse	10.00	20.00
32 Bertrand Gachot 7Up	15.00	25.00
32 Roberto Moreno Pepsi	15.00	25.00
32 Alex Zanardi Pepsi	12.00	20.00
33 Andrea deCesaris 7Up	12.00	20.00

1992 Onyx F1 1:43

Noticeably absent from this series is Ayrton Senna. The series represents eight different Formula 1 teams.

	EX	NM-MT
3 Olivier Grouillard Calbee Tyrell	12.00	20.00
4 Andrea deCesaris Calbee Tyrell	12.00	20.00
5 Nigel Mansell Canon	15.00	25.00
6 Riccardo Patrese Canon	12.00	20.00
9 Michele Alboreto Footwork	12.00	20.00
10 Aguri Suzuki Footwork	12.00	20.00
11 Mika Hakkinen Hitachi	25.00	40.00
12 Johnny Herbert Hitachi	12.00	20.00
19 Michael Schumacher Benetton	25.00	50.00
20 Martin Brundle Benetton	12.00	20.00
25 Thierry Boutsen ELF Renault	12.00	20.00
26 Erik Comas ELF Renault	12.00	20.00
27 Jean Alesi Ferrari	12.00	20.00
28 Ivan Capelli Ferrari	12.00	20.00
32 Stefano Modena Sasol	18.00	30.00
33 Mauricio Gugelmin Sasol	12.00	20.00

1993 Onyx F1 1:43

Michael Andretti stayed in Formula 1 just long enough to get a die-cast made by Onyx in 1993. He left Fl early in 1993 to return to the Indy Car circuit. The car is in the Marlboro team colors but doesn't carry the sponsor's name.

	EX	NM-MT
0 Damon Hill Canon	15.00	25.00
2 Alain Prost Canon	12.00	20.00
3 Ukyo Katayama Calbee Tyrell	12.00	20.00
4 Andrea deCesaris Calbee Tyrell	12.00	20.00
5 Nigel Mansell K-Mart Benetton Back to Back Two car set	35.00	50.00
5 Michael Schumacher Benetton Camel Paint scheme	25.00	50.00
5 Michael Schumacher Benetton Mild Seven paint scheme	25.00	50.00
5 Michael Schumacher Kastle	25.00	50.00
5 Michael Schumacher Killer Loop	25.00	50.00
5 Michael Schumacher Nordica	25.00	50.00
5 Michael Schumacher Prince	25.00	50.00
5 Michael Schumacher Rollerblade	25.00	50.00
6 J.J. Lehto Benetton	12.00	20.00
6 Riccardo Patrese Benetton	12.00	20.00
6 Riccardo Patrese Prince	12.00	20.00
6 Riccardo Patrese Rollerblade	12.00	20.00
7 Michael Andretti Shell	15.00	25.00
8 Ayrton Senna Shell	18.00	30.00
11 Pedro Lamy Castrol	12.00	20.00
11 Alex Zanardi Castrol	12.00	20.00
12 Johnny Herbert Castrol	12.00	20.00
14 Rubens Barrichello Sasol	12.00	20.00
15 Thierry Boutsen Sasol	12.00	20.00
27 Jean Alesi Ferrari	12.00	20.00
28 Gerhard Berger Ferrari	12.00	20.00
29 Karl Wendlinger Liqui Moly	12.00	20.00
30 J.J. Lehto Liqui Moly	12.00	20.00

1994 Onyx F1 1:43

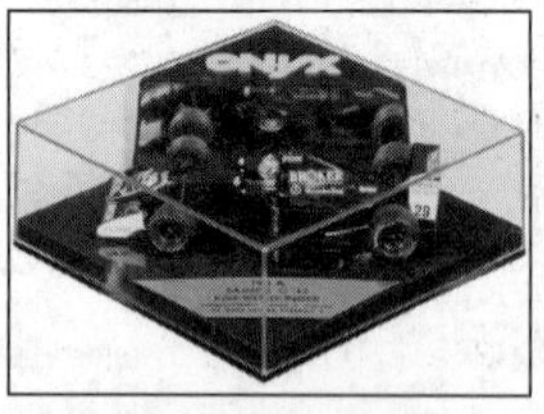

This series marks the first appearance of special race cars. There are three different Australian Grand Prix cars with seven different teams represented in this series.

	EX	NM-MT
0 Damon Hill Rothmans	15.00	25.00
0 Damon Hill Rothmans Australian Grand Prix	15.00	25.00
0 Damon Hill Rothmans Test car	15.00	25.00
2 David Coulthard Rothmans	20.00	50.00
2 Nigel Mansell Rothmans	15.00	25.00
2 Ayrton Senna Rothmans	25.00	40.00
2 Ayrton Senna Rothmans Test car	20.00	35.00
3 Ukyo Katayama Calbee	12.00	20.00
4 Mark Blundell Calbee	12.00	20.00
5 Damon Hill Rothmans	15.00	25.00
5 Michael Schumacher Benetton Mild Seven	25.00	50.00
5 Michael Schumacher Benetton Mild Seven Australian Grand Prix	25.00	50.00
6 David Coulthard Rothmans	20.00	50.00
6 Johnny Herbert Benetton Bitburger Mild Seven Australian Grand Prix	12.00	
6 J.J. Lehto Benetton Mild Seven	12.00	
6 Jos Verstappen Benetton Mild Seven	12.00	
11 Pedro Lamy Loctite	12.00	
12 Johnny Herbert Loctite	12.00	
14 Rubens Barrichello Sasol	12.00	
15 Andrea deCesaris Sasol	12.00	
15 Eddie Irvine Sasol	12.00	
25 Eric Bernard ELF Renault	12.00	
25 Martin Brundle Hugo Pratt Art	12.00	
26 Olivier Panis ELF Renault	12.00	
27 Nicola Larini Ferrari	12.00	
27 Jean Alesi Ferrari 412 T1	12.00	
27 Jean Alesi Ferrari 412 T1b	12.00	
28 Gerhard Berger Ferrari	12.00	
28 Gerhard Berger Ferrari 412 T1b	12.00	
29 Andrea deCesaris Broker 200th Grand Prix	12.00	
29 Andrea deCesaris Tissot	12.00	
29 Karl Wendlinger Broker/Sauber	12.00	
30 Heinz-Harold Frentzen Broker	12.00	
30 Heinz-Harold Frentzen Tissot	12.00	
33 Paul Belmondo Ursus	12.00	
34 Gachot Bernard Ursus	12.00	

1995 Onyx F1 1:43

Both Damon Hill and David Coulthard were represente regular and a Portugal Grand Prix car in this series. I last year that the Ferrari team was part of the set.

	EX	N
3 Ukyo Katayama Nokia	12.00	
3 Gabriele Tarquini Nokia	12.00	
4 Mika Salo Nokia	12.00	
5 Damon Hill Rothmans Portugal Grand Prix	15.00	
5 Damon Hill Rothmans	15.00	
6 David Coulthard Rothmans	15.00	
6 David Coulthard Rothmans Protugal Grand Prix	20.00	
9 Gianni Morbidelli Hype	12.00	
9 Max Papis Hype	12.00	
10 Taki Inoue Hype	12.00	
16 Jean-Denis Deletraz Ursus	12.00	
16 Giovanni Lavaggi Ursus	12.00	
16 Bertrand Gachot Ursus	12.00	
17 Andrea Montermini Ursus	12.00	
23 Pierluigi Martini Lucchini	12.00	
24 Luca Badoer Lucchini	12.00	
27 Jean Alesi Ferrari	12.00	
28 Gerhard Berger Ferrari	12.00	

1996 Onyx F1 1:43

Onyx retained only the Williams license and a few of marker teams for the 1996 series. Five teams were rep in this set.

	EX	N
5 Damon Hill Rothmans French Grand Prix	15.00	
5 Jacques Villeneuve Rothmans French Grand Prix	12.00	
16 Ricardo Rosset Power Horse	12.00	
17 Ricardo Rosset Phillips	12.00	
17 Jos Verstappen Phillips	12.00	
17 Jos Verstappen Power Horse	12.00	
18 Ukyo Katayama Korean Air	12.00	
19 Mika Salo Korean Air	12.00	
20 Pedro Lamy Doimo	12.00	
21 Giancarlo Fisichella Doimo	12.00	
21 Tarso Marques Doimo	12.00	
22 Luca Badoer Forti Yellow Paint scheme	12.00	
22 Luca Badoer Shannon Green and White paint	12.00	
23 Andre Montermini Forti Yellow Paint scheme	12.00	
23 Andre Montermini Shannon Green and White paint	12.00	

1997 Onyx F1 1:43

	EX	NM-MT
rentzen/Castrol	10.00	20.00
hnny Herbert ed Bull	10.00	20.00

1998 Onyx F3 1:43

	EX	NM-MT
io Haberfeld opimax	10.00	20.00
er Dumbreck om's	10.00	20.00
id Saelens ina	10.00	20.00

2005 Quartzo F1 1:18

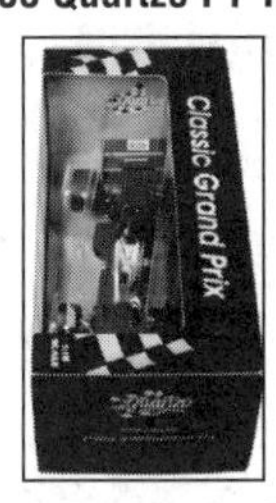

	EX	NM-MT
Clark otus '68 Grand Prix outh Africa	60.00	100.00
el Mansell lf Renault Canon 32 Grand Prix South Africa/5000	75.00	125.00
erson Fittipaldi otus 70 Grand Prix USA/2500	75.00	125.00

1992-93 Tamiya F1 Collector's Club 1:20

	EX	NM-MT
el Mansell anon 1992	120.00	175.00
chael Schumacher enetton 1993	100.00	200.00
ika Hakkinen astrol 1992	100.00	175.00
hnny Herbert astrol 1993	100.00	160.00
ean Alesi errari 1993	75.00	150.00

Dirt Sprint Modified

994 Action/RCCA Dirt Cars 1:24

	EX	NM-MT
ney Combs ull & Hannah	25.00	40.00
ly Moyer	25.00	40.00
eddy Smith azooka/5004	20.00	40.00

995 Action/RCCA Dirt Cars 1:24

	EX	NM-MT
ney Combs enson/5004	20.00	40.00
ck Boggs awkeye Trucking/4500	30.00	60.00
nie Johnson ction	25.00	40.00
eve Francis ussell Baker/5520	20.00	40.00
ott Bloomquist/5004	35.00	60.00
n Schrader udweiser/5004	30.00	60.00
ck Simmons ne Stop/5568	25.00	40.00
hn Gill astersplit/5004	25.00	40.00

996 Action/RCCA Dirt Cars 1:24

	EX	NM-MT
art Hartman ro Stocks	30.00	45.00
ott Bloomquist ction RCCA/4000	35.00	60.00
ck Eckert aye-Vest/4008	30.00	50.00
vey Allison avoline RCCA	40.00	75.00
nnie Moran ig Johnson/4008	30.00	45.00
eddy Smith hristenberry/5000	30.00	45.00
evin Weaver ayburn Pizza Hut	30.00	45.00

1997 Action/RCCA Dirt Cars 1:24

	EX	NM-MT
E1 Mike Balzano J.D. Cals/3504	25.00	45.00
3 Randy Sellars	25.00	40.00
5 Rodney Combs Lance/2500	25.00	40.00
6M Wendall Wallace Rebco	25.00	40.00
21 Billy Moyer Bazooka/4008	30.00	45.00
28 Jimmy Mars Parker Store/4000	30.00	45.00
30 Steve Shaver Simonton/3500	25.00	40.00
66 Bob Frey GRT	20.00	40.00
75 Terry Phillips/3348	25.00	40.00
89 Steve Barnett Rayburn	25.00	40.00

1998 Action/RCCA Dirt Cars 1:24

	EX	NM-MT
5 Ronnie Johnson	30.00	45.00
12 Rick Auckland EZ-Crusher/2508	60.00	100.00
21 Billy Moyer Bazooka/3500	60.00	100.00
75 Bart Hartman Pennzoil/2508	60.00	100.00
99 Donnie Moran/2508	25.00	50.00
0 Scott Bloomquist/4008	100.00	175.00

1999 Action/RCCA Dirt Cars 1:24

	EX	NM-MT
1 Jimmy Mars Parker Stores/3168	50.00	80.00
5 Ronnie Johnson AFCO/2508	50.00	80.00
21 Billy Moyer Petroff Towing/3300	40.00	75.00
98 Tony Stewart 1998 J.D. Byrider/3000	175.00	300.00
00 Freddy Smith Christenberry/3504	35.00	60.00

2000 Action/RCCA Dirt Cars 1:24

	EX	NM-MT
12 Ray Guss Jr. PB Body Shop/2712	40.00	75.00
17M Dale McDowell Dover Cylinder Heads/2856	40.00	80.00
20 Tony Stewart J.D.Byrider/9000	60.00	120.00
99 Donnie Moran McCullough/2508	40.00	75.00

2001 Action/RCCA Dirt Cars 1:24

	EX	NM-MT
0 Scott Bloomquist No Weak Links	40.00	75.00
15 Steve Francis Valvoline/3504	30.00	50.00
18 Scott Bloomquist Lane Automotive/4944	40.00	75.00
24 Rick Eckert Raye-Vest/3504	40.00	75.00
53 Ray Cook Youngblood/3504	30.00	60.00
56 Gary Webb Moring Disposal/3612	30.00	60.00

2002 Action/RCCA Dirt Cars 1:24

	EX	NM-MT
1 Steve Francis Valvoline Mopar/3504	30.00	50.00
21 Billy Moyer Petroff Towing/4008	30.00	50.00
99 Ken Schrader Federated/4560	35.00	60.00
201 Billy Ogle Calhoun's/2892	30.00	50.00

2003 Action/RCCA Dirt Cars 1:24

	EX	NM-MT
99 Donnie Moran QPI Tools/3168	30.00	50.00
99 Donnie Moran QPI Tools Silver/192	175.00	300.00

1994 Action/RCCA Dirt Cars 1:64

These 1:64 dirt cars were produced and distributed by Action Performance. The cars were available through both the dealer network and Action's Racing Collectibles Club of America.

	EX	NM-MT
F1 Mike Duvall	5.00	10.00
1 C.J. Rayburn	5.00	10.00
1J Davey Johnson	5.00	12.00
5 Rodney Combs Bull & Hannah	5.00	10.00
15 Jeff Purvis	10.00	20.00
18 Scott Bloomquist	15.00	40.00
21 Jack Hewitt blister package	30.00	45.00
21 Jack Hewitt box package	6.00	12.00
21 Billy Moyer	60.00	90.00
28 Davey Allison Havoline RCCA/15,000	10.00	18.00
32 Bob Pierce Tall Cool One	10.00	20.00
52 Ken Schrader AC Delco	6.00	10.00
52 Ken Schrader Bud	6.00	10.00
75 Bart Hartman Pennzoil	6.00	12.00
00 Freddy Smith Bazooka with Orange paint scheme	6.00	15.00

1995 Action/RCCA Dirt Cars 1:64

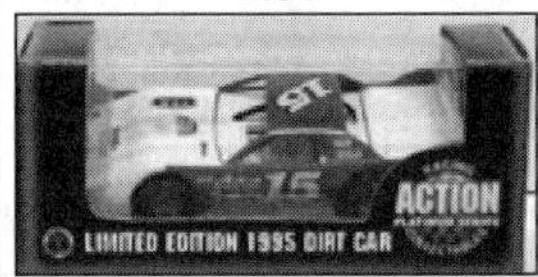

Each of these Late Model Dirt 1:64 cars were issued in an Action Platinum Series window box. The year "1995" is clearly labeled on the outside of the box.

	EX	NM-MT
1 Rodney Combs Benson/20,880	5.00	12.00
1 Charlie Swartz Malcuit Racing/16,128	6.00	15.00
B4 Jack Boggs Hawkeye Trucking/18,000	5.00	10.00
5 Ronnie Johnson Action/16,128	5.00	10.00
15 Steve Francis in window box/21,888	5.00	10.00
18 Scott Bloomquist Action Ford Motorsports Promo/16,128	10.00	20.00
18 Scott Bloomquist Action/30,000	5.00	12.00
25 Ken Schrader Budweiser	6.00	15.00
41 Buck Simmons One Stop/24,912	5.00	10.00
75 John Gill Mastersplit/18,000	5.00	10.00
00 Freddy Smith Bazooka Blue	5.00	10.00

1996 Action/RCCA Dirt Cars 1:64

This series of 1:64 cars were issued in an Action Platinum Series clam-shell style blister pack. An Action card of the featured driver was also included.

	EX	NM-MT
5 Ronnie Johnson Hawkeye Trucking	6.00	12.00
11 Bart Hartman Pro-Shocks	5.00	10.00
18 Scott Bloomquist RCCA box/10,080	10.00	20.00
21 Billy Moyer Bullet Baker	5.00	10.00
24 Rick Eckert Raye-Vest	5.00	10.00
99 Donnie Moran Big Johnson	6.00	12.00
00 Freddy Smith Christenberry	5.00	10.00
B12 Kevin Weaver Rayburn Pizza Hut	5.00	10.00

1997 Action/RCCA Dirt Cars 1:64

	EX	NM-MT
E1 Mike Balzano J.D. Cals/10,080	5.00	10.00
5 Rodney Combs/Lance	60.00	90.00
6M Wendall Wallace Rebco/10,080	5.00	10.00
21 Billy Moyer Bazooka/10,080	10.00	20.00
28 Jimmy Mars Parker Store	5.00	10.00
30 Steve Shaver Simonton/10,080	5.00	10.00
56 Gary Webb/9000	6.00	12.00
66 Bob Frey GRT/10,080	6.00	10.00
89 Steve Barnett Rayburn/10,080	5.00	10.00

1998 Action/RCCA Dirt Cars 1:64

	EX	NM-MT
0 Scott Bloomquist Miller Bros.Coal/9000	15.00	30.00
12 Rick Auckland EZ-Crusher	5.00	10.00
21 Billy Moyer Bazooka	10.00	20.00
75 Bart Hartman BHR/7560	6.00	12.00

1999-00 Action/RCCA Dirt Cars 1:64

	EX	NM-MT
20 Tony Stewart J.D.Byrider/9072 2000	20.00	40.00
98 Tony Stewart 1998 J.D. Byrider/7992 released in 1999	35.00	60.00

2003 ADC Dirt Late Model Cars 1:24

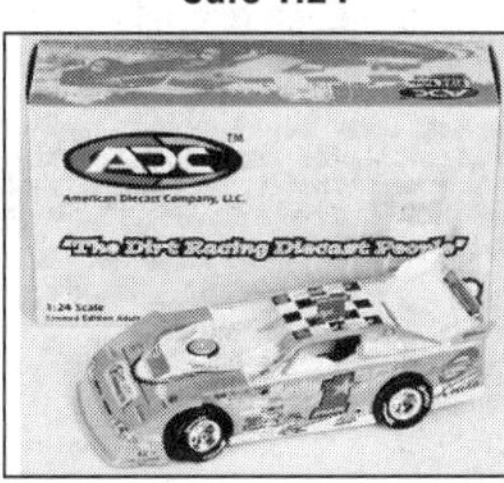

	EX	NM-MT
1 ADC Promo	40.00	75.00
1 Eddie Carrier Jr. Hawkeye Trucking		
1 Chub Frank Corry Laser/2504	40.00	70.00
1 O'Reilly Mars Promo	40.00	70.00
1 Earl Pearson Lucas Oil/1008	40.00	70.00
5 Rodney Combs ADC Superman/2504	40.00	70.00
9 Dan Schlieper MBC/1008	50.00	80.00
11 Batesville Topless Promo/250	60.00	120.00
15B Brian Birkhofer/1008	50.00	75.00
17M Dale McDowell/2504	40.00	70.00
21 Billy Moyer Hawkeye/2504	40.00	70.00
31 Skip Arp/500	50.00	75.00
32 Bob Pierce Clawson's/1008	50.00	75.00
37 Chuck LaSalle NAPA	40.00	70.00
38 Jerry Pridal D&K RV Sales	40.00	70.00
44 Clint Smith CSR	50.00	75.00
71 Don O'Neal Petroff/2504	40.00	70.00
88 Wendell Wallace Craft/1008	40.00	70.00
89 Steve Barnett J.D. Byrider/1008	40.00	70.00
89 Marshall Green Hatfield	50.00	75.00
90 Gary Stuhler Nininger/1008	40.00	70.00
96 Terry English AAA Fence/500	50.00	75.00
99 Donnie Moran McCullough Club/2504	50.00	75.00
00 Freddy Smith White Oaks/2504	40.00	70.00
B12 Kevin Weaver/500	50.00	75.00
E1 Mike Balzano Baker/1008	40.00	70.00

2003 ADC Dirt Modified Cars 1:24

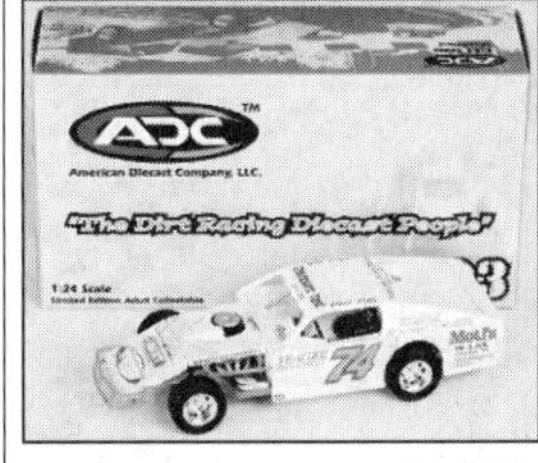

	EX	NM-MT
3 Batesville Topless Promo/50	60.00	120.00
4G Gary Clark	40.00	70.00
4X Kevin Larkins JET/1008	40.00	70.00
7 Ron Jones/1008	40.00	70.00
11C Chris Prussman	50.00	90.00
12 Jason Hughes Hughes Racing/1008	40.00	70.00
20 Jimmy Owens Hovis Racing/2504	40.00	70.00
69 John Logue Pat Clemons/2504	40.00	70.00
74 Mark Noble Yeager/2504	40.00	70.00
96 Johnny Saathoff JET/2504	40.00	70.00
A1 George Handley Handleys Auto Salvage		

2004 ADC Dirt Late Model Cars 1:24

	EX	NM-MT
1 Frank Chubb 25th Anniversary/1008	35.00	60.00
1 Charlie Schwartz 1008	35.00	60.00
3 Kelly Shryock Shryock Racing/1008	35.00	60.00
9 Bill Elliott 5004	50.00	80.00
15 Steve Francis 3500	35.00	60.00
19 Davey Johnson 1008	35.00	60.00
24 Rick Eckert Rayevest/1500	35.00	60.00
41 Buck Simmons 1008	35.00	60.00
44 Chris Madden 1008	35.00	60.00
50 Ed Dixon 1008	35.00	60.00
50B Larry McDaniels		
53 Ray Cook 1008	35.00	60.00
66 Bill Frye 1008	35.00	60.00
71C R.J. Conley 1008	35.00	60.00
75 Bart Hartman 1008	35.00	60.00
75 John Gill Helena/1008	35.00	60.00
75 Terry Phillips 1008	35.00	60.00
99 Ken Schrader 1008	40.00	70.00
114 Randall Chupp 1008	35.00	60.00
W11 Rob Blair 1008	35.00	60.00

2004 ADC Dirt Modified Cars 1:24

	EX	NM-MT
3L Jeff Leka 1008	35.00	60.00
17S M.Spaulding/Puggley's/1008	35.00	60.00
21S Denny Schwartz 1008	35.00	60.00
75 John Thompson 1008	35.00	60.00
97M Dave Murray 1008	35.00	60.00
99 Ken Schrader 1008	35.00	60.00
701 Henry Wilt 1008	35.00	60.00

2005 ADC Dirt Late Model Cars 1:24

	EX	NM-MT
00 Randy Korte 500	40.00	65.00

2003 ADC Dirt Late Model Cars 1:64

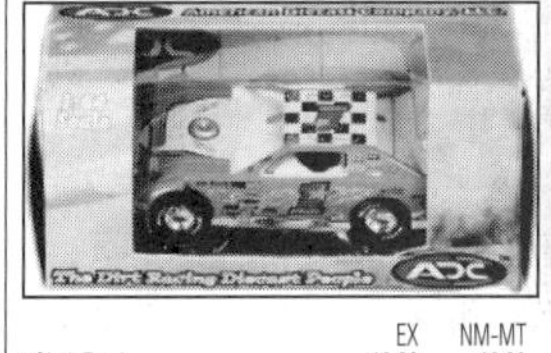

	EX	NM-MT
1 Chub Frank Corry Laser/5004	10.00	18.00
5 Rodney Combs ADC Superman/5004	10.00	18.00
17M Dale McDowell/5004	10.00	18.00
21 Billy Moyer Petroff/5004	10.00	18.00
24 Rick Eckert Rayevest/5004	10.00	18.00
32 Bob Pierce Clawson's/5004	10.00	18.00
71 Don O'Neal Petroff/5004	10.00	18.00
88 Wendall Wallace Craft	10.00	18.00
99 Donnie Moran McCullough Club/5004	15.00	25.00
99 Donnie Moran QPI/5004	10.00	18.00
00 Freddy Smith White Oaks/5004	10.00	18.00
E Steve Francis Mopar	10.00	18.00

2003 ADC Dirt Modified Cars 1:64

	EX	NM-MT
20 Jimmy Owens	10.00	18.00
69 John Logue Pat Clemons	10.00	18.00
74 Mark Noble Yeager	10.00	18.00
96 Johnny Saathoff JET	10.00	18.00

2004 ADC Dirt Late Model Cars 1:64

	EX	NM-MT
1 Frank Chubb 25th Anniversary/3500	7.50	15.00

	EX	NM-MT
3 Kelly Shryock Shyrock Racing	7.50	15.00
9 Bill Elliott 5000	10.00	20.00
15 Steve Francis 4000	7.50	15.00
15B Brian Birkhofer 3500	7.50	15.00
20 Darrell Lanigan 3500	7.50	15.00
21 Billy Moyer 2504	7.50	15.00
75 John Gill 5004	7.50	15.00
75 Bart Hartman 3500	7.50	15.00
92 Dick Potts 3500	7.50	15.00
99 Ken Schrader 3500	7.50	15.00
E1 Mike Balzano 3500	7.50	15.00

2004 ADC Dirt Modified Cars 1:64

	EX	NM-MT
12B Johnny Bone Jr. 3500	7.50	15.00

1993 Ertl/Nutmeg Modified Legends 1:64

Ertl produced a series of 1:64 scale Modified Legends cars for Nutmeg Collectibles. Each piece in the 1993 release was issued in a small blue window display box that featured the Ertl notation on the top and the Nutmeg name on the front side. The driver's name, car number, and issue number (included below) of the series was also included. Each car was produced in quantities of 5000 and feature the Coupe body style unless noted below.

	EX	NM-MT
0 Bud Olsen #22	6.00	12.00
1 Charlie Jarzombek Coupe #12	6.00	12.00
2 Frank Schneider Frankie's Salvage #10	6.00	12.00
2X Ed Flemke #5	6.00	12.00
4 Ted Harfield Adams Heating #23	6.00	12.00
4 Lou Lazzaro Fonda Express #24	8.00	20.00
11 Ray Hendrick #21	6.00	12.00
12 Ken Bouchard Sherwood Vega #20	6.00	12.00
12A Jack Johnson Johnson's Garage #6	6.00	12.00
15 Bugsy Stevens #3	6.00	15.00
17 Ron Bouchard Pinto #13	6.00	12.00
24 Will Cagle Coupe #4	8.00	20.00
24 Will Cagle Pinto #16	6.00	12.00
29 Ernie Gahan #11	6.00	12.00
33 Bill Wimble #26	10.00	25.00
38 Jerry Cook B&M Speed #2	8.00	20.00
39 Al Tasnady Piscopo's Auto #25	15.00	25.00
43 Bill Greco Greco Auto Parts Pinto #15	6.00	12.00
61 Richie Evans B&M Speed Yellow #1	15.00	25.00
61 Richie Evans B&M Speed Orange #7	10.00	20.00
93 Gold Christmas Coupe/2000	7.50	15.00
93 Green Christmas Coupe/5000	3.00	6.00
93 Red Christmas Coupe/3000	5.00	10.00
93 Brian Ross #9	6.00	12.00
711 Bob Polverari Perry Auto Vega #17	6.00	12.00
01 Ray Miller Chamberlian Vega #18	6.00	12.00
V8 Bill Slater Conn Valley #8	6.00	12.00
X3 Jim Hendrickson Vega #19	6.00	12.00
X90 Fred Harbach Flying Dutchman Pinto #14	6.00	12.00

1994 Ertl/Nutmeg Modified Legends 1:64

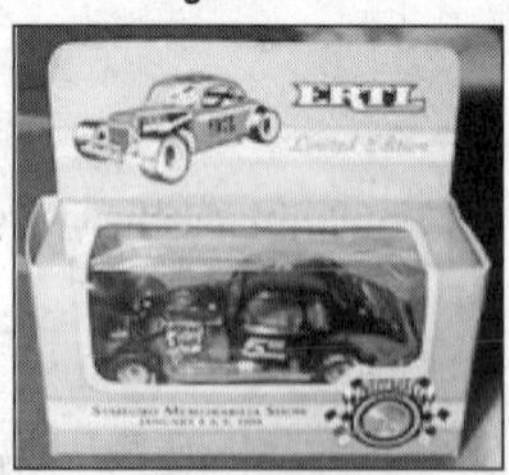

	EX	NM-MT
5 Stafford Speedway Show Promo	3.00	8.00

1996 Ertl/Nutmeg Modified Legends 1:64

Ertl produced this series of 1:64 scale Legends cars for Nutmeg Collectibles. Each was issued in a small window display box that featured a blue marbelized design. The driver's name, car number, and/or issue number of the series was included on the box. Each car was produced in quantities of 5000 and feature the Coupe body style unless noted below.

	EX	NM-MT
3 Fred DeSarro Boehler's #31	6.00	12.00
7 Dutch Hoag Genesee Beer #28	15.00	30.00
8 Jim Shampine Village Collision #32	6.00	12.00
9J Don MacTavish #30	6.00	12.00
58 Merv Treichler #29	6.00	12.00
74 Rog Treichler Jenny Power Vega #33	6.00	12.00
00 Buzzie Ruetimann Dover Brake #27	12.50	25.00

1998 Ertl/Nutmeg Modified Legends 1:64

Ertl produced this series for Nutmeg Collectibles. Each was issued in a small window display box that featured the Ertl notation on the top and the Nutmeg name on the front side. The driver's name, car number, and issue number (noted below) of the series was also included. Each car was produced in quantities of 5000 and feature the Coupe body style unless noted below.

	EX	NM-MT
1 Charlie Jarzombek Vega #37	6.00	12.00
3 Pete Corey #42	6.00	12.00
4 Leo Cleary #39	6.00	12.00
6 Richie Evans N.Y. #40	6.00	12.00
8 Jim Shampine Village Collision Pinto #43	6.00	12.00
13 Joe Kelly #46	6.00	12.00
17 Dick Tobias Tobias Speed #45	6.00	12.00
18 Dutch Hoag #38	6.00	12.00
43 Billy Greco Tasmanian Devil #36	6.00	12.00
44 Jim Tasnady #44	6.00	15.00
61 Richie Evans B.R.DeWitt Pinto #35	6.00	12.00
77 Jackie Evans #34	6.00	12.00
99 Bobby Malzahn #47	6.00	12.00
XL1 Tommie Elliott #41	6.00	12.00

1990 Matchbox Modifieds Series 1 1:64

	EX	NM-MT
1 Tony Hirschman Clark Concrete	6.00	12.00
15 Mike Stefanik Koszela Speed Shop Red	6.00	12.00
44 Reggie Ruggiero Magnum Oil Yellow	6.00	12.00
U2 Jamie Tomaino Danny's Market	6.00	12.00

1991 Matchbox Modifieds Series 2 1:64

	EX	NM-MT
12 Mike McLaughlin Sherri Cup	6.00	12.00
15 Mike Stefanik Auto Palace ADAP	6.00	12.00
36 Mike Ewanitsko Mutual Engraving	6.00	12.00
41 Jay Hedgecock C&C	6.00	12.00

1992 Matchbox Modifieds Series 3 1:64

	EX	NM-MT
3 Doug Heveron	5.00	10.00
4 Satch Worley Mystic River Marina	5.00	10.00
21 George Kent	5.00	10.00
U2 Jamie Tomaino	5.00	10.00

1992 Matchbox Modifieds Series 4 1:64

	EX	NM-MT
7NW Tom Baldwin	4.00	8.00
25 Jan Leaty	4.00	8.00
44 Rick Fuller	4.00	8.00
69 Reggie Ruggiero	4.00	8.00

1993 Matchbox Modifieds Series 5 1:64

STATED PRODUCTION RUN 5000 SETS

	EX	NM-MT
2X Jerry Marquis	4.00	8.00
5 Charlie Pasteryak	4.00	8.00
11 Ed Flemke	4.00	8.00
77 Rick Fuller	4.00	8.00

1994 Matchbox Modifieds Series 6 1:64

STATED PRODUCTION RUN 5000 SETS

	EX	NM-MT
15 Wayne Anderson	4.00	8.00
27 Jan Leaty	4.00	8.00
31 Tony Ferrante	4.00	8.00
56 Tim Arre	4.00	8.00

1994 Matchbox Modifieds Series 7 1:64

STATED PRODUCTION RUN 5000 SETS

	EX	NM-MT
0 Ed Kennedy	4.00	8.00
17 Jamie Tomaino	4.00	8.00
21 Mike McLaughlin	4.00	8.00
39 Bruce D'Alessandro	4.00	8.00

1992 Matchbox Modified Legends Series 1 1:64

STATED PRODUCTION RUN 10,000 SETS

	EX	NM-MT
3 Ron Bouchard	6.00	12.00
4 Carl Stevens	6.00	12.00
6 Maynard Troyer	6.00	12.00
38 Jerry Cook	6.00	12.00

1993 Matchbox Modified Legends Series 2 1:64

	EX	NM-MT
12 Brett Bodine Sherri Cup	6.00	12.00
24 Jimmy Spencer	6.00	12.00
61 Richie Evans B.R.DeWitt Orange	6.00	12.00
99 Geoff Bodine	6.00	12.00

1994 Matchbox Modified Legends Series 3 1:64

STATED PRODUCTION RUN 5000 SETS

	EX	NM-MT
1 Charlie Jarzombek	6.00	12.00
8 Mike McLaughlin	6.00	12.00
37 Mike Stefanik	6.00	12.00
73 B Roth	6.00	12.00

1992 Matchbox White Rose DIRT Super Stars 1:64

	EX	NM-MT
1 Doug Hoffman Phelps Cement	7.50	15.00
6 Danny Johnson Freightliner Trucks	7.50	15.00
7X Steve Paine Turbo Blue	7.50	15.00
9 Bob McCreadie Syracuse Frame	7.50	15.00
72 Brett Hearn Kenyon	10.00	20.00
91 Billy Decker Wheels Auto Supply	10.00	20.00

1993 Matchbox White Rose DIRT Super Stars 1:64

	EX	NM-MT
1 Joe Plazek Steak Out Restaurant	6.00	12.00
12 Jack Johnson B.R.DeWitt	6.00	12.00
14J Alan Johnson R.P. LaFrois	6.00	12.00
21J Jeff Trombley Hutter Altair Audio	6.00	12.00
35 Toby Tobias Tobias Speed	6.00	12.00
44 Frank Cozze Carquest	6.00	12.00
74 Rick Elliott Smith Bros. Concrete	6.00	12.00
115 Kenny Tremont Fane Doherty Bros.	6.00	12.00

2003 Nutmeg Modified Legends 1:25

	EX	NM-MT
2 Frankie Schneider Frankie's Sausage 2	30.00	50.00
7 Dutch Hoag Genesee 4	30.00	50.00
00 Buzzie Ruetimann Dover Brake 1	30.00	50.00

1998-01 Action/RCCA Sprint 1:18

These 1:18 scale cars are part of the Action Racing Collectables Xtreme Series.

	EX	NM-MT
1BK Johnny Herrera Burger King/2004 1999	30.00	80.00
7 Kevin Huntley Peterbilt/4008 1998	20.00	50.00
11 Steve Kinser Quaker State/2500 1998	50.00	100.00
11 Steve Kinser Quaker State/2508 1999	40.00	80.00
11 Steve Kinser Quaker State Superman/8004 1999	125.00	250.00
11 Steve Kinser Quaker State/3000 2000	30.00	60.00
12 Greg Hodnett Wirtgen/1500 2000	25.00	50.00
12 Greg Hodnett Apple Chevrolet/2508 1999	40.00	80.00
17 Joey Saldana Mox Motorsport/2508 1999	25.00	60.00
19 Stevie Smith Ingersoll-Rand 1998	50.00	80.00
20 Johnny Herrera NetWorks/2004 2000	30.00	80.00
22 Jac Haudenschild Pennzoil 1998	50.00	80.00
23S Frankie Kerr Shoff/4008 1998	20.00	50.00
83 Danny Lasoski Beef Packers/2508 1998	50.00	80.00

1994 Action/RCCA Sprint 1:24

	EX	NM-MT
11 Steve Kinser Valvoline/3516	50.00	80.00
21 Fred Rahmer Budweiser/2508	50.00	100.00
22 Jac Haudenschild Pennzoil/1728	50.00	100.00
28D Brad Doty Bower's/2508	45.00	80.00
38 Ken Schrader Crawford/2508	45.00	80.00
55 Tim Richmond Elder Cadillac/3516	30.00	50.00
63 Jack Hewitt Murphy's IGA/3500	40.00	65.00

1995 Action/RCCA Sprint 1:24

	EX	NM-MT
1 Sammy Swindell Hooters/2712	75.00	135.00
1 Sammy Swindell Old Milwaukee/5004	30.00	50.00
1 Sammy Swindell TMC/4800	35.00	60.00
5 Johnny Herrera Jackpot Junction/3516	20.00	40.00
7TW Jeff Swindell Gold Eagle/5004	30.00	60.00
10 Dave Blaney Vivarin/2508	150.00	250.00
18 Brad Doty Coors Light Silver Bullet Red and Silver RCCA/5004	30.00	60.00
18 Brad Doty Coors Light Silver Bullet Blue and Silver/2508	30.00	60.00
18 Brad Doty Coors Light blue&silver Platinum Series/5004	30.00	60.00
19 Tony Stewart Triple Crown/3500	75.00	125.00
20 Jeff Gordon Hap's RCCA/7500	150.00	250.00
33 Danny Drinan IWX/2500	35.00	60.00

1996 Action/RCCA Sprint 1:24

	EX	NM-MT
1 Billy Pauch Zemco/4500	12.50	30.00
1 Sammy Swindell Channellock/5004	30.00	50.00
2 Andy Hillenburg STP/4500	20.00	50.00
10 Dave Blaney Vivarin/4500	40.00	80.00
11 Steve Kinser Quaker State/5000	50.00	100.00
20 Tony Stewart 1995 Triple Crown/5004	75.00	135.00
21 Lance Blevins Citgo/4008	20.00	40.00
22 Jac Haudenschild Pennzoil	35.00	60.00
40 Jeff Gordon 1987 Stanton RCCA/4008	150.00	300.00
47 Johnny Herrera Strange King's Royal/4008	25.00	50.00
71M Stevie Smith Ecowater/6000	15.00	40.00
75 Joey Saldana Mopar/4704	20.00	50.00

1997 Action/RCCA Sprint 1:24

	EX	NM-MT
1 Sammy Swindell Channellock Silver/4008	35.00	60.00
4 J.J. Yeley Action blue/2508	25.00	50.00
4 J.J. Yeley Action red/2508	25.00	50.00
5M Mark Kinser Wirtgen/4008	30.00	50.00
7TW Jeff Swindell Gold Eagle Flames/4008	15.00	40.00
10 Dave Blaney Vivarin/4560	25.00	50.00
11 Steve Kinser Quaker State/6000	30.00	60.00
11 Steve Kinser Quaker State Mac Tools	100.00	150.00
11H Greg Hodnett Selma Shell/4500	15.00	
15 Donny Schatz Schatz Crossroads/4008	12.50	
19 Stevie Smith Jr. Mac Tools/3804	15.00	
69 Brent Kaeding Pioneer Concrete	15.00	
77 Fred Rahmer Manheim Auctions/4224	20.00	

1998 Action/RCCA Sprint 1

	EX	NM
19 Stevie Smith Jr. Ingersoll-Rand/4008	25.00	
69K Donny Kreitz Kreitzer Excavating	30.00	

1999 Action/RCCA Sprint 1

	EX	NM
4 Jeff Gordon 1990 Diet Pepsi/7500	125.00	
39 Ryan Newman Gearheads Lewis Racing/2508	100.00	
83 Danny Lasoski Beef Packers Matco Tools	45.00	

2000 Action/RCCA Sprint 1

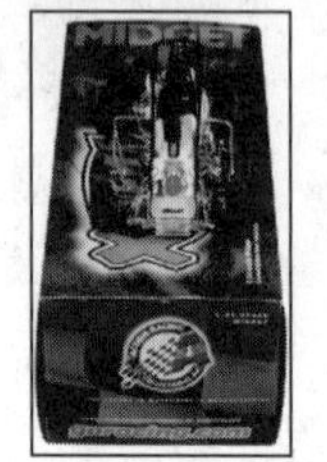

	EX	NM
8 Wally Pankratz Sta-Rite/2004	35.00	
19 Tony Stewart Turkey Night/4800	60.00	
58 Sarah McCune GTE A-1/2508	20.00	
77 Dane Carter Wabash National Pedigo Chevrolet City/2004	20.00	

2001 Action/RCCA Sprint 1

	EX	NM
1 Sammy Swindell Channellock/4104	20.00	
4 Kenny Irwin 1994 Wynn's/2808	25.00	
4 Kenny Irwin 1994 Wynn's Silver/504	40.00	
5M Mark Kinser Mopar Spider-Man/4212	30.00	
11 Steve Kinser Napa/5004	25.00	
11 Steve Kinser Quaker State/5004	20.00	
19 Stevie Smith Ingersoll-Rand	15.00	
19 Tony Stewart Performance/8004	25.00	
20 Danny Lasoski J.D.Byrider/4536	30.00	
20 Danny Lasoski J.D.Byrider Jurassic Park 3/5340	25.00	
91 Kasey Kahne Wingless Midget/2004	75.00	

2002 Action/RCCA Sprint 1

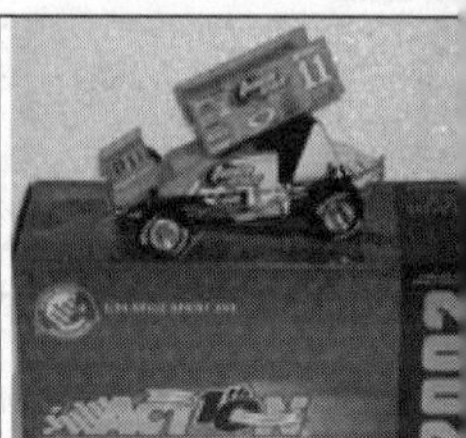

	EX	NM
11 Steve Kinser Quaker State/3600	25.00	
11H Stevie Smith Jr. Vivarin/2856	25.00	
15 Donny Schatz Parker/2220	20.00	
20 Danny Lasoski J.D.Byrider/3504	30.00	
20 Danny Lasoski J.D.Byrider Muppet/3648	25.00	
20 Danny Lasoski	30.00	

	EX	NM-MT
J.D.Byrider Muppet RCCA/180		
anny Lasoski Beef Packers/2508	40.00	80.00

03 Action/RCCA Sprint 1:24

	EX	NM-MT
mmy Swindell Ore-Cal Beef Packers/2184	30.00	60.00
Yeley Beast '03 Champion/1908	35.00	60.00
teve Kinser Quaker State 2002 Champ. Color Chrome/3684	35.00	60.00
teve Kinser Quaker State 2002 Champ. Color Chrome RCCA/360		
teve Kinser Quaker State Hulk/4468	35.00	60.00
anny Lasoski J.D. Byrider/3496	30.00	60.00
anny Lasoski J.D. Byrider Cat in the Hat/2392	35.00	60.00

04 Action/RCCA Sprint 1:24

	EX	NM-MT
sey Kahne Dodge Curb Records/5004	60.00	100.00
teve Kinser Quaker State 500th Win Raced/3168	40.00	60.00
teve Kinser Quaker State Popeye/2438	40.00	60.00
onny Schatz Parker Stores/2004	35.00	60.00
Danny Lasoski J.D. Byrider/2928	35.00	60.00
Danny Lasoski J.D. Byrider Mad Magazine/1908	35.00	60.00
Danny Lasoski J.D. Byrider Michael Ross Memorial Foundation/3000	35.00	60.00
Danny Lasoski J.D. Byrider Shrek 2/2496	35.00	60.00
ony Stewart American Compressed Steel Michael Ross Foundation/4776	40.00	60.00

05 Action/RCCA Sprint 1:24

	EX	NM-MT
sey Kahne Valvoline/4116	40.00	65.00
sey Kahne Valvoline Color Chrome/504	50.00	75.00
Steve Kinser Quaker State James Dean 50th Anniversary/2304	40.00	65.00
teve Kinser Quaker State '05 Champion/2100	40.00	65.00
teve Kinser Quaker State '05 Champion Brushed Metal/408		
teve Kinser Quaker State '05 Champion Color Chrome/2100	50.00	75.00
J. Yeley Old Spice/1800	40.00	65.00
J. Yeley Old Spice Color Chrome/300	50.00	75.00
yler Walker Dodge Curb Records AU/2508	50.00	75.00
Danny Lasoski Bass Pro/1872	40.00	65.00
anny Lasoski Bass Pro Shops GM Dealers/36	40.00	65.00
Danny Lasoski Bass Pro Madagascar/1428	40.00	65.00

	EX	NM-MT
20 Danny Lasoski Bass Pro Michael Ross Foundation/1272	50.00	75.00
20 Danny Lasoski Mopar/2220	50.00	75.00
20 Tony Stewart Artic Cat Michael Ross Foundation/2148	50.00	75.00
20 Tony Stewart Bass Pro Shops/3276	50.00	75.00
20 Tony Stewart Bass Pro Shops Color Chrome/504	60.00	100.00
20 Tony Stewart Bass Pro Shops GM Dealers/60	50.00	75.00
20 Tony Stewart Bass Pro Shops QVC/120	50.00	75.00
20 Tony Stewart Bass Pro Shops Madagascar/4752	50.00	75.00
20 Tony Stewart Bass Pro Shops Madagascar Mac Tools/300	50.00	75.00
20 Tony Stewart Bass Pro Shops Madagascar Matco/144	50.00	75.00
20 Tony Stewart Bass Pro Shops Madagascar QVC/504	50.00	75.00
83 Kasey Kahne Beef Packers '03 QVC/120	50.00	80.00

2006 Action/RCCA Sprint 1:24

	EX	NM-MT
9 Kasey Kahne Sage Fruit/852	60.00	100.00

1998-99 Action/RCCA Sprint 1:50

	EX	NM-MT
1 Sammy Swindell Channellock/9000 1998	6.00	15.00
5M Mark Kinser Wirtgen	6.00	12.00
5M Mark Kinser Mopar/6120 1999	7.50	20.00
7 Kevin Huntley Peterbilt/9000 1998	6.00	12.00
11 Steve Kinser Quaker State/5040 1998	15.00	40.00
11 Steve Kinser Quaker State Superman/17,496 1999	15.00	40.00
23 Frankie Kerr Shoff Motrosports	6.00	12.00
47 Johnny Herrera Strange	6.00	12.00
69K Donnie Kreitz Kreitzer Excavating	6.00	12.00

1995 Action/RCCA Sprint 1:64

	EX	NM-MT
1 Sammy Swindell TMC/10,080	5.00	12.00
7TW Jeff Swindell Gold Eagle	5.00	10.00

1996 Action/RCCA Sprint 1:64

	EX	NM-MT
1 Billy Pauch Zemco/10,080	5.00	10.00
22 Jac Haudenschild Pennzoil	5.00	10.00
40 Jeff Gordon 1987 Stanton/10,080	20.00	35.00

1997 Action/RCCA Sprint 1:64

	EX	NM-MT
1 Sammy Swindell Channellock/10,080	5.00	12.00
1 Sammy Swindell Channellock Silver/10,080	5.00	12.00
2 Andy Hillenburg STP/10,080	6.00	12.00
5 Steve Kinser Maxim	5.00	10.00
10 Dale Blaney Vivarin/10,080	4.00	10.00
11 Steve Kinser Quaker State/12,024	6.00	10.00
15 Donny Schatz Blue Beacon/10,000	3.00	8.00
19 Stevie Smith/8352	5.00	10.00
77 Fred Rahmer Manheim Auctions/10,080	5.00	10.00

1998 Action/RCCA Sprint 1:64

	EX	NM-MT
19 Stevie Smith Jr. Ingersoll-Rand	5.00	10.00
69K Donny Kreitz Kreitzer Excavating	5.00	10.00

1995 Ertl/Nutmeg Sprint Cars 1:55

Ertl produced this series of 1:55 scale sprint cars for Nutmeg. Each was issued in a clear window display box that featured a cardboard tab to attach the box to a retail rack display.

	EX	NM-MT
1 Sammy Swindell/7500	4.00	8.00
5 Mark Kinser/7500	4.00	10.00
23S Frankie Kerr Shoff/5000	4.00	8.00
77 Stevie Smith/7500	4.00	8.00

1992-94 Ertl Sprint Transporters 1:64

	EX	NM-MT
1 Billy Pauch Zemco	30.00	60.00
1 Sammy Swindell	50.00	100.00

	EX	NM-MT
TMC Racing		
1A Bobby Allen Allen Racing	45.00	80.00
1W Keith Kauffman LEW Racing	30.00	60.00
7TW Joe Gaerte Gaerte Engines	50.00	100.00
17 Chris Esch E&G Classics	40.00	80.00
19 Steve Smith Sr. Leiby's Mobile Homes	40.00	80.00
25 Dan Dietrich Cooper Motors	30.00	60.00
28 Brad Doty Bowers Coal 1993	45.00	80.00
69 Donnie Kreitz Jr.	50.00	100.00
99 Fred Rahmer Busch	50.00	100.00
NNO Fletcher's Racing	30.00	60.00

2002 GMP Vintage Sprint Cars 1:12

	EX	NM-MT
1 A.J.Foyt Bowes Seal/1500	175.00	350.00
1 Bobby Unser Bardahl	150.00	300.00
2 Mario Andretti Castrol Viceroy/900	175.00	350.00
2 Al Unser Johnny Lightning	300.00	500.00
4 Don Branson Wynn's/896	175.00	350.00

1996-01 GMP Sprint Cars 1:18

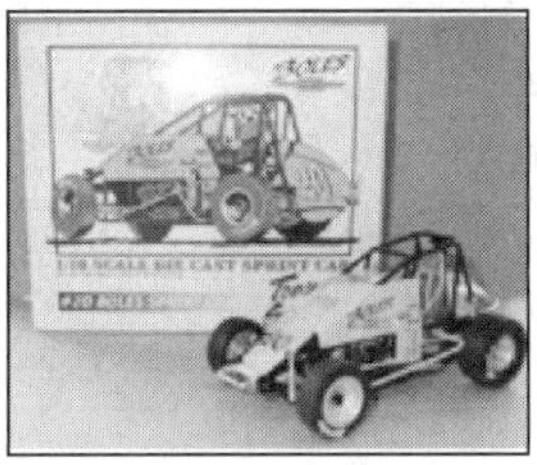

The first spring car piece released by GMP was the Steve Kinser. Upon release it was quickly one of the most popular pieces on the market. The Jeff Gordon and Jac Haudenschild pieces have also done well.

	EX	NM-MT
1 GMP Platinum/1200 '99	45.00	80.00
1 Steve Kinser Aristocrat/3504 1998	40.00	80.00
1 Billy Pauch Zemco/3504 1997	30.00	80.00
1 Jimmy Sills Sills/2808 1997	40.00	80.00
1 Sammy Swindell Channellock 1997	80.00	140.00
1 Sammy Swindell Channellock 25th Anniversary/3504 1997	150.00	250.00
1 Sammy Swindell Channellock/3792 1998	50.00	100.00
1 Sammy Swindell Old Milwaukee/3072 1998	60.00	120.00
1 Sammy Swindell TMC/3576 1997	70.00	120.00
1A Bobby Allen Shark/2400 1999	50.00	100.00
1N Sammy Swindell Nance/2508 2001	50.00	100.00
2 Andy Hillenburg Luxaire/1500 2001	50.00	90.00
2 Andy Hillenburg STP/3504 1997	30.00	80.00
2 Rich Volger Seibert Olds/1200	45.00	80.00
4X Jan Opperman Speedway Motors/3504 1998	75.00	135.00
5 Danny Lasoski Ethanol Jackpot Junction/3504 1997	65.00	90.00
5M Mark Kinser Wirtgen/3504 1997	50.00	100.00
5M Mark Kinser Mopar/2496 2000	70.00	110.00
6 Jeff Gordon Molds Unlimited/3672 1997	200.00	400.00
7TW Jeff Swindell Gold Eagle/3504	50.00	100.00
10 Dave Blaney Vivarin/3504 1997	50.00	100.00
10 Bobby Davis Jr. Casey Luma/1500 2000	45.00	80.00
10 Tyler Walker Ratbag/1404	60.00	100.00
11 Steve Kinser Aristocrat/3504	45.00	80.00
11 Steve Kinser Quaker State 1997	200.00	350.00
11H Greg Hodnett Vivarin/3192 1998	50.00	80.00
15 Donny Schatz Petro Blue Beacon/2504 1997	60.00	120.00
18 Brad Doty Coors Light/3504 1997	150.00	250.00
20 Tony Stewart Boles/3204 1994	100.00	200.00
20 Tony Stewart Boles 1995 Sprint Champ/3504 2000	150.00	250.00
22 Jac Haudenschild Pennzoil/3504 1997	70.00	120.00
22 Jac Haudenschild Pennzoil Black/2208 1998	75.00	125.00
22 Jac Haudenschild Radioactive Wild Child 1999	50.00	100.00
22 Jac Haudenschild Radioactive Krypton 1999	125.00	250.00
22 Jac Haudenschild Wild Child TNT/2068 2000	75.00	135.00
23 Kasey Kahne Speed Racer/2004 2001	75.00	125.00
29 Doug Wolfgang Weikert's Livestock 1999	90.00	150.00
40 Amoco Knoxville 40th Anniversary/1200 2000	50.00	90.00
40 Northern Auto Racing Club 40th Anniversary Budweiser/2292 1999	40.00	80.00
47 Johnny Herrera Strange/3000 Casey's General Store 1997	60.00	110.00
63 Jack Hewitt Hampshire Racing/2400 '99	50.00	90.00
69 Brent Kaeding Pioneer Concrete/2904 1997	40.00	100.00
75 Brad Doty Stanton/2004 2000	40.00	80.00
93 Dale Blaney Amoco/1788 2000	50.00	120.00
96 Eldora Speedway 1997	90.00	150.00
97 Knoxville Raceway/3276 1997	50.00	100.00
98 Devil's Bowl Speedway Texas 1998	60.00	120.00
104 Jeff Swindell 104+ Octane/3204 1998	50.00	120.00
NNO Devil's Bowl 25th Anniv/2508	50.00	90.00

2002 GMP Sprint Cars 1:18

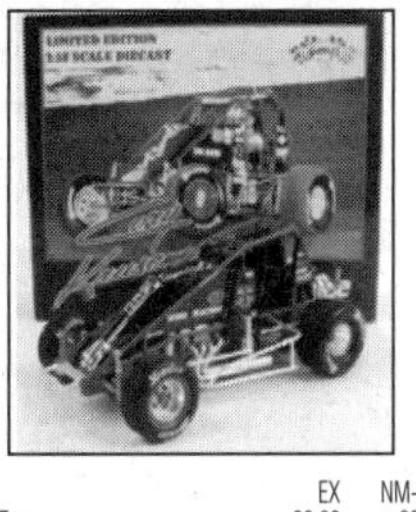

	EX	NM-MT
2 Brad Furr Sanmina green/2004	30.00	80.00
2 Brad Furr Sanmina red/2004	30.00	80.00
11 Steve Kinser Quaker State Black Chrome/2508	50.00	90.00
45 Cory Kruseman Willis Machine/1260	45.00	80.00
50 Richard Griffin Arizona Race Mart/1260	45.00	80.00

2003 GMP Sprint Cars 1:18

	EX	NM-MT
3 Dave Darland Arctic Cat/1400	50.00	80.00
7 Craig Dollansky VMAC/1200	50.00	80.00
28D Brad Doty Bowers Coal/1200	50.00	80.00

2004 GMP Sprint Cars 1:18

	EX	NM-MT
2 Brad Furr Sanmina/2004	30.00	60.00

1998-03 GMP Vintage Sprint Cars 1:18

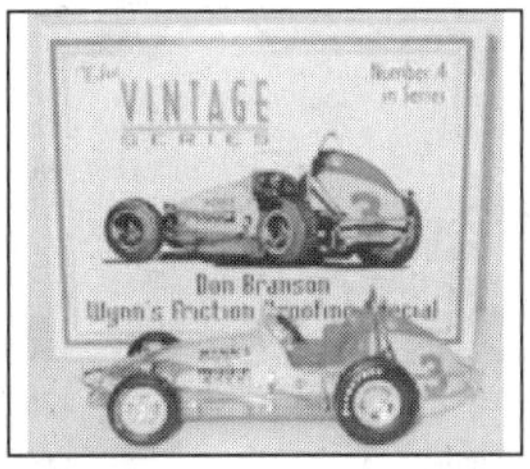

	EX	NM-MT
1 A.J. Foyt Bowes Seal/3504	200.00	300.00
1 A.J.Foyt Bowes Seal Black Chrome/2508 2002	50.00	90.00
1 A.J.Foyt Sheraton Thompson/3000	40.00	80.00
1 Parnelli Jones Fike Plumbing/3504	100.00	175.00
1 Ralph Pratt Jum White	40.00	80.00
1 Sprint Car Hall of Fame Black/950 2002	125.00	225.00
1 Sprint Car Hall of Fame Red/1999 '99	100.00	175.00
1 Sprint Car Hall of Fame White/1998 '98	125.00	225.00
1 Shorty Templeman Bardahl/2004	40.00	80.00
1 Al Unser Johnny Lightning/3504	70.00	120.00
1 Rodger Ward Kaiser Aluminum/3900 1999	50.00	80.00
2 A.J.Foyt Dart Kart/3996	60.00	100.00
2 Mario Andretti STP/4200	60.00	120.00
2 Jud Larson Watson Special/4104 2001	40.00	80.00
2 Roger McCluskey Konstant Hot/3624 1999	90.00	150.00
3 Don Branson Wynn's/3552 1998	100.00	175.00
3 Bobby Unser Key Special/3660 2000	60.00	100.00
5 Lloyd Axel Foster's Auto Supply/2196	40.00	80.00
5 Bobby Marshman Econo-Car/3192	40.00	80.00
6 A.J. Foyt Sheraton Thompson/4260 2000	80.00	135.00
6 Eddie Sachs Dean Van Lines/2592 2002	40.00	80.00
9 Johnny Rutherford 3504 1998	100.00	175.00
12 Rodger Ward Edelbrock V8/3900	50.00	100.00
22 Henry Banks Hopkins Special	40.00	80.00
27 Rodger Ward Edelbrock	45.00	80.00
44 Duke Nalon Bowes Seal/2508	40.00	80.00
56 Jim Hurtubise Sterling Plumbing/3552 1998	125.00	200.00
56 Jim Hurtubise Sterling Plumbing/2598 2002	40.00	80.00
83 Mario Andretti Gapco Special/4200	75.00	125.00
98 Parnelli Jones Willard Battery/2880	45.00	90.00
98 Bill Vukovich Rev 500	75.00	125.00
154 Freddie Agabashian Burgermeister	40.00	80.00

2000-02 GMP Sprint Car Sets 1:18/1:50

	EX	NM-MT
5 Jac Haudenschild Wirtgen 2002	50.00	90.00
11 Steve Kinser Quaker State/3000 2000	50.00	100.00
11 Steve Kinser Quaker State/2508 2002	60.00	120.00
15 Donny Schatz Parker Store/1500 2002	40.00	80.00
83 Sammy Swindell Ore-Cal Beef Packers/2508 2002	60.00	100.00

1996-02 GMP Sprint Cars 1:25

With the release of the Dale Blaney piece in early 1997, GMP started a whole new scale size for Sprint Cars.

	EX	NM-MT
1 Lincoln Speedway/200 2002	30.00	60.00
1 Fred Rahmer O'Brien Stars&Stripes/2196	50.00	100.00
1 Sammy Swindell Channellock Raced/2004 2001	30.00	60.00
1F Dean Jacobs Frigidare/4404 1997	20.00	50.00
1W Danny Lasoski ConnWest/3480 1997	15.00	40.00
2 Andy Hillenburg Luxaire/2004 2001	50.00	90.00
2 Lincoln Speedway 50 Years/200	60.00	100.00
2A Bobby Adamson Johnny Lightning/3972 1997	40.00	70.00
2M Brent Kaeding Pioneer Concrete DuPont/2998	25.00	50.00
7TW Jeff Swindell Gold Eagle/3972 1997	35.00	60.00
8H Joe Gaerte Holbrook Motorsports/2196	25.00	50.00
10 Dale Blaney MBNA raced/1500 2001	20.00	40.00
11 Steve Kinser Quaker State/4404	30.00	80.00
11 Steve Kinser Quaker State/9804 1997	30.00	60.00
11 Steve Kinser Quaker St.Raced/2496 2001	50.00	100.00
15 Donny Schatz Parker Store/2004	25.00	50.00
19 Stevie Smith Jr. Ingersoll-Rand/3792	25.00	50.00
22 Jac Haudenschild Pennzoil/3972	25.00	60.00
23S Frankie Kerr Shoff Motrosports	25.00	50.00
35 Tyler Walker Air Sep/2504	25.00	50.00
69 Brent Kaeding Pioneer Concrete 1997	30.00	60.00
75 Joey Saldana Mopar/4404 1997	25.00	60.00
77 Fred Rahmer Manheim Auctions/2496 1997	20.00	50.00
83 Danny Lasoski Beef Packers/2196 1998	25.00	60.00
94 Dale Blaney Hughes Axel/4404 1996	25.00	60.00
97 Eldora Speedway/2508 1997	30.00	80.00
U2 Keith Kauffman United/2196	25.00	50.00

2002 GMP Vintage Sprint Cars 1:43

	EX	NM-MT
1 Grimm Grant Piston Ring	15.00	25.00
15 Faulkner	15.00	25.00
27 Rodger Ward Edelbrock V8	15.00	25.00
45 Bill Vukovich	15.00	25.00
65 Oaks	15.00	25.00

2001-02 GMP Vintage Sprint Car Sets 1:43

	EX	NM-MT
NNO A.J.Foyt Bowes Seal/3504 2001	50.00	90.00
NNO Parnelli Jones Fike Plumbing Willard Batteries/2004 2002	40.00	75.00
NNO Roger McCluskey Konstant Hot/1500 2002	40.00	75.00

1998-01 GMP Sprint Cars 1:50

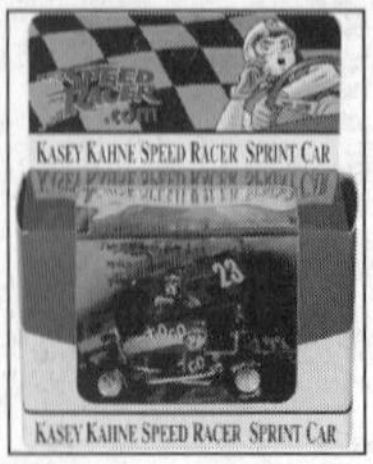

1 Sammy Swindell Channellock/3476	12.50	25.00
1A Bobby Allen Shark/4032 1999	10.00	20.00
2 Andy Hillenburg Luxaire/2448 2001	10.00	20.00
5 Jac Haudenschild Wirtgen/1728	12.50	25.00
10 Bobby Davis Jr. Casey Luma	15.00	25.00
11 Steve Kinser Quaker State/14,976 1998	10.00	20.00
11 Steve Kinser Quaker State/2592 2001	10.00	20.00
11H Greg Hodnett Vivarin 1998	7.50	15.00
15 Donny Schatz Petro Blue Beacon	7.50	15.00
19 Stevie Smith Jr. Ingersoll-Rand 1999	15.00	30.00
22 Jac Haudenschild Pennzoil black	10.00	20.00
22 Jac Haudenschild Radioactive Wild Child	12.50	25.00
23 Kasey Kahne Speed Racer/3600 2001	15.00	30.00
29 Doug Wolfgang Weikerts Livestock/5004 1999	7.50	15.00
35 Tyler Walker Air Sep 1999	7.50	15.00
40 Amoco Knoxville 40th Anniversary	10.00	20.00
63 Jack Hewitt Hampshire Motorsports/5004	7.50	15.00
77 Fred Rahmer Hamilton	7.50	15.00
83 Danny Lasoski Beef Packers 1999	10.00	20.00
93 Kevin Gobrecht Amoco/2016 2000	7.50	15.00

2002 GMP Sprint Cars 1:50

	EX	NM-MT
2 Brad Furr Sanmina/2160	7.50	15.00
10 Dale Blaney MBNA/2160	10.00	20.00
15 Donny Schatz Parker Store/1728	7.50	15.00
45 Cory Kruseman Willis Machine/1584	7.50	15.00
50 Richard Griffin Arizona Race Mart/1584	7.50	15.00
50 Lincoln Speedway/700	20.00	40.00

1991 Matchbox Sprint Cars 1:55

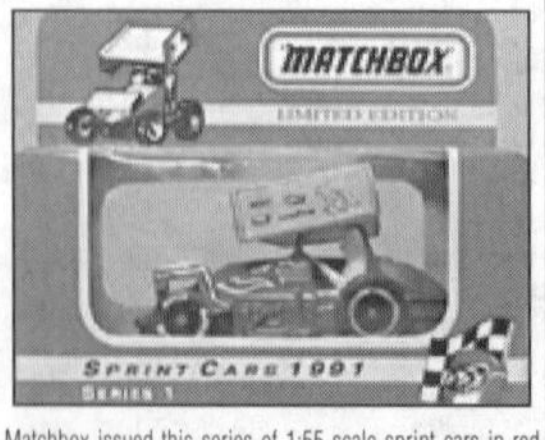

Matchbox issued this series of 1:55 scale sprint cars in red window display boxes. Each box included the year on the front as well as the "Series 1" notation. The packaging also featured a cardboard tab to attach the box to a retail rack display.

	EX	NM-MT
1 Sammy Swindell TMC	7.50	15.00
1A Bobby Allen Blue	4.00	10.00
5M Mark Kinser Williams	7.50	15.00
8D Doug Wolfgang White	4.00	10.00
11 Steve Kinser White	10.00	20.00
33X Steve Siegel Yellow	4.00	10.00

1992 Matchbox Sprint Cars 1:55

This series was produced in 1992 by Matchbox. Each 1:55 scale sprint car was packaged in a blue window display box. Each box included the year on the front as well as the "Series 2" notation. The packaging also featured a cardboard tab to attach the box to a retail rack display.

	EX	NM-MT
4 Bobby Davis Jr. Gambler	2.00	5.00
7C Dave Blaney Vivarin	2.50	6.00
7TW Joe Gaerte Red	2.00	5.00
17E Cris Eash E&S Classics	2.00	5.00
49 Doug Wolfgang/Olsen	2.00	5.00
69K Donnie Kreitz Jr. Light Blue	2.00	5.00

1993 Matchbox Sprint Cars 1:55

This series of 1:55 scale sprint cars was issued by Matchbox in small window red display boxes. Each box included the year on the front as well as the "Series 3" or "Series 4" notation. The packaging also featured a cardboard tab to attach the box to a retail rack display.

	EX	NM-MT
1 Sammy Swindell TMC	2.00	5.00
1W Keith Kauffman	2.50	6.00
5M Mark Kinser Orange	2.00	5.00
10 Jac Haudenschild	3.00	8.00
11 Steve Kinser Valvoline	4.00	10.00
14 Tim Green	2.50	6.00
69 Brent Kaeding Black	2.00	5.00
69 Howard Kaeding White	2.00	5.00

1993-94 Racing Champions Sprint Cars 1:24

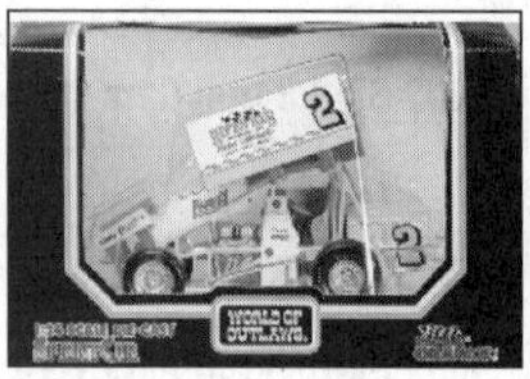

This series of 1:24 Racing Champions sprint cars is a good cross section of all the different drivers that raced World of Outlaws sprints at the time. Each piece is housed in a large black shadow box type box with a yellow interior. The year of issue is printed on the back of the box along with a driver checklist. Not all drivers on the list were produced for this set.

	EX	NM-MT
0 Rick Ferkel Kears	10.00	20.00
0 Randy Smith Mesquaki Bingo	12.50	25.00
1 Garry Brazier O'Brien	8.00	22.00
1 Sammy Swindell Bull and Hannah	30.00	50.00
1 Sammy Swindell TMC	45.00	70.00
1A Bobby Allen Kriners	30.00	60.00
2 Frankie Herr Family Ford	10.00	20.00
2 Frankie Herr Rifes RV	10.00	20.00
2 Andy Hillenburg STP with Dark Blue paint scheme	12.50	25.00
2 Andy Hillenburg STP with Light Blue paint scheme	15.00	40.00
2 Andy Hillenburg STP Signature Series	20.00	40.00
2 Garry Rush Castrol	10.00	20.00
2L Ed Lynch	12.50	25.00
U2 Rocky Hodges United Express	10.00	20.00
4A Greg Hodnett Mid So Forklift	10.00	20.00
4 Bobby Davis Jr. Pro Shocks	10.00	20.00
5 Max Dumesny Valvoline	60.00	90.00
5 Dennis Lasoski	30.00	50.00
7 Richard Griffin Sanders	8.00	20.00
7 Jimmy Sills Berry B Racing	8.00	20.00
7TW Jeff Swindell Gold Eagle	10.00	20.00
8TW Greg Hodnett Kele	8.00	20.00
9TW Joe Gaerte Gaerte Engines	8.00	20.00
10 Dave Blaney Vivarin	15.00	30.00
11 Steve Kinser Valvoline	20.00	50.00
11 Ron Shuman CH Enginering	8.00	20.00
12 Fred Rahmer Apple Chevrolet	15.00	30.00
12X Danny Smith Beaver Drill	12.50	25.00
14 Tim Green Swift Met Finish	12.50	25.00
14P Kevin Pylant Taco Bravo	10.00	20.00
18 Brad Doty Shaver Racing	15.00	30.00
21 Steve Beitler Brownfield	12.50	25.00
21 Lance Blevins Citgo	8.00	20.00
22 Jac Haudenschild Pennzoil with Red numbers	12.50	25.00
22 Jac Haudenschild Pennzoil with Yellow numbers	10.00	20.00
23S Frankie Kerr Shoff Motorsports	12.50	25.00
24 Jerry Stone Aeroweld Racing	8.00	20.00
27 Terry McCarl Westside Radiator	8.00	20.00
29 Keith Kauffman Weckert's Livestock	8.00	20.00
45 Doug Wolfgang Snap On	15.00	30.00
45X Johnny Herrera Herrera Motorsports	15.00	25.00
47 Danny Lasoski Casey's	15.00	25.00
49 Doug Wolfgang Bob Olsen	15.00	40.00
55 Max Dumesny Halletts Mats	12.50	25.00
65 Jim Carr Maxim	12.50	25.00
66 Mike Peters TropArtic	12.50	25.00
69 Brent Kaeding JW Hunt	10.00	20.00
69 Brent Kaeding High-Five Pizza	8.00	20.00
69K Donnie Kreitz Jr. Vollmer Patterns	12.50	25.00
71M Kenny Jacobs Beltline	15.00	25.00
71M Kenny Jacobs Eco Water	8.00	20.00
77 J.Shepard Mac Tools	18.00	30.00
77 Stevie Smith Jr. Hamilton	10.00	20.00
77 Stevie Smith Jr. Mac Tools	20.00	35.00
97B Aaron Berryhill Berryhill Racing	10.00	20.00
00 Jason Statler Rios	8.00	20.00
07 Smokey Snellbaker Rifes RV	12.50	25.00

1995 Racing Champions Sprint Cars 1:24

This was the second year that Racing Champions produced a 1:24 sprint car series. The series again included many of the big names from the World of Outlaw circuit. Each was packaged in a black window box with "Series 2" clearly marked on the outside.

	EX	NM-MT
0 Danny Smith	7.50	15.00
0 Randy Smith Bingo Casino	7.50	15.00
1 Billy Pauch Zemco	8.00	20.00
1 Sammy Swindell Bull and Hannah	12.50	25.00
1 Sammy Swindell Hooters Series 2	12.50	25.00
2 Andy Hillenburg STP	10.00	20.00
2 Andy Hillenburg STP Oil	10.00	20.00
2J J.J. Yeley Bull&Hannah	12.50	25.00
4S Tommy Scott Scott Performance	7.50	15.00
5 Terry McCarl CS Enterprises	10.00	20.00
5M Mark Kinser Wirtgen	30.00	50.00
7TW Jeff Swindell Gold Eagle	10.00	20.00
8TW Greg Hodnett Kele with red numbers	8.00	20.00
8TW Greg Hodnett Kele with yellow numbers	15.00	25.00
9W Joe Gaerte Two Winners	10.00	20.00
9TW Gary Wright Action Rent	7.50	15.00
10 Dave Blaney Vivarin	12.50	25.00
11 Steve Kinser Valvoline	10.00	20.00
11 Ron Shuman CH Enginering	12.50	25.00
12 Fred Rahmer Apple Chevrolet	10.00	20.00
14P Kevin Pylant Unicopy	10.00	20.00
16 Jeff Gordon JG Motorsports/5000	125.00	225.00
17E Cris Eash Miller Brothers	7.50	15.00
21 Steve Beitler Brownfield	7.50	15.00
21 Lance Blevins Citgo	7.50	15.00
21K Lou Kennedy CT Fleet	7.50	15.00
21K Lou Kennedy Shamrock Carpet	7.50	15.00
22 Jac Haudenschild Pennzoil	10.00	20.00
23S Frankie Kerr	10.00	20.00
31 Sid Blandford Avenger	7.50	15.00
47 Danny Lasoski Housby Trucking	8.00	20.00
65 Jim Carr Maxim	7.50	15.00
66 Mike Peters TropArtic	7.50	15.00
69 Brent Kaeding Motorola	7.50	15.00
71M Kenny Jacobs EcoWater	7.50	15.00
71M Stevie Smith Jr. EcoWater	10.00	20.00
77 Joe Gaerte Cornwell	15.00	30.00
97B Aaron Berryhill	7.50	15.00

1996 Racing Champions Sprint Cars 1:24

For the thrid consecutive year Racing Champions produced 1:24 scale Sprint cars. The cars were primarily distributed through mass market retailiers. 1996 World of Outlaw Champion Mark Kinser is one of the highlights of the series.

	EX	NM-MT
1X Randy Hannagan Carrera	12.50	25.00
5 Danny Lasoski Jackpot Junction	8.00	20.00
5M Mark Kinser Wirtgen	8.00	20.00
7M Jim Carr American Fire Exting.	15.00	30.00
7TW Jeff Swindell Gold Eagle	10.00	20.00
9W Gary Wright	7.50	15.00
10 Dave Blaney Vivarin	7.50	20.00
11 Steve Kinser Quaker State	20.00	40.00
22 Jac Haudenschild Pennzoil	8.00	20.00
47 Johnny Herrera	8.00	20.00
69 Brent Kaeding Motorola	7.50	15.00
71M Stevie Smith EcoWater	8.00	20.00
83 Joey Saldana Southwest Hide	7.50	15.00
461 Lance Dewease Dyer Masonary	7.50	15.00

1997 Racing Champions Sprint Cars 1:24

This was the fourth year of production of 1:24 scale Sprint cars by Racing Champions.

	EX	NM-MT
1 Billy Pauch Zemco	12.00	20.00
1F Dean Jacobs Frigidaire	12.50	25.00
1J Marlon Jones Energy Release	12.00	20.00
1X Randy Hannagan TRW	12.50	25.00
2 Andy Hillenburg STP	15.00	30.00
2 Ron Shuman Havoline	12.00	20.00
2M Brent Kaeding Pioneer	12.00	20.00
3G Joe Gaerte Gaerte Engines	12.00	20.00
7TW Jeff Swindell Gold Eagle	12.50	25.00
8 Terry McCarl Holbrook	12.00	20.00
8R Stevie Reeves D&B Racing	12.00	20.00
9W Gary Wright Action	12.00	20.00
11H Greg Hodnett Selma Shell	12.00	20.00
12 Keith Kauffman Apple Chevrolet	12.50	25.00
15 Donny Schatz Blue Beacon	12.00	20.00
17E Cris Eash Miller Brothers	12.00	20.00
21L Lance Blevins Citgo	12.00	20.00
22 Jac Haudenschild Pennzoil	12.00	20.00
23S Frankie Kerr Shoff Motorsports	12.00	20.00
28 Brian Paulus P&P Racing	12.00	20.00
29 Brent Kaeding BK Racing	12.00	20.00
29 Tommie Estes Jr. F&J Construction	12.00	20.00
47 Johnny Herrera Casey's	12.00	20.00
69K Donnie Kreitz Stockdale	12.00	20.00
83 Paul McMahan Beef Packers	12.00	20.00
88 Todd Shaffer Turnbaugh	12.00	20.00
92 Kenny Jacobs Imperial	12.00	20.00
94 Dale Blaney Hughes	8.00	20.00
461 Lance Dewease Dyer Masonary	12.00	20.00

1998 Racing Champions Sprint Cars 1:24

This series of 1:24 Sprint cars by Racing Champions was primarily issued through mass market retailers.

	EX	NM-
0 Jason Statler Rios Construction	12.00	2
1J Marlon Jones Energy Release	12.00	2
1W Craig Dollansky Conn West	12.00	2
2M Brent Kaeding Pioneer	12.00	2
3G Joe Gaerte Gaerte	12.00	2
7 Kevin Huntley Peterbilt	12.00	2
9S Shane Stewart RC Cola	12.00	2
11H Greg Hodnet Selma Shell	12.00	2
11H Greg Hodnett Vivarin	12.00	2
12S Shane Carson Helms Motorsports	12.00	2
15 Donny Schatz Blue Beacon	12.00	2
23S Frankie Kerr Shoff Motorsports	12.00	2
28 B.Paulus P&P Racing Not In	12.00	2
29 Brent Kaeding BK Motorsports	12.00	2
35 Tyler Walker Air Sep	12.00	2
47 Johnny Herrera Strange	12.00	2
55 Skip Jackson Jensen Construction	12.00	2
69K Donnie Kreitz Stockdale	12.00	2
83 Bob Auld Matco Tools Promo/5000	25.00	4
88 Tania Schafer Turnbaugh Oil	12.00	2
461 Lance Dewease Dyer	12.00	2
01 Paul McMahan Mt.Impact	12.00	2
U2 Keith Kauffman United Express	12.00	2

2003 Racing Champions Midwest Sprint Cars 1:24

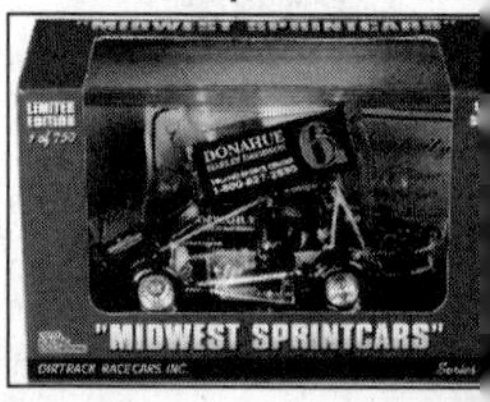

	EX	NM
1W Rob Tvedte Subway Shell/750	25.00	4
6R Roger Rager Donahue Harley/750	25.00	4
57X Jake Peters Folkens/750	25.00	4
75 Gordy Vogelaar Bob's Fleet/750	25.00	4

2004 Racing Champions Knoxville Sprint Cars 1:2

	EX	NM
2 Skip Jackson Mid Land Equiptment/956	20.00	3
5J Jeff Mitrisin Cahill Racing/956	20.00	3
6 Brian Brown Casey's/956	20.00	3
6 Brian Brown Casey's Mopar/960	20.00	3
14 Randy Martin Diamond Pet Foods/956	20.00	3
17G Ricky Logan Lucas Oil/956	20.00	3
20 Bob Trostle B&B Performance/956	20.00	3
20 Doug Wolfgang Bob Trostle Racing/960	20.00	3
22 Billy Alley Ray Lipsey/956	20.00	3
24 Terry McCarl Big Game Hunting/956	20.00	3
71M Doug Wolfgang Beltline Body Shop/960	20.00	3

1993 Racing Champions Sprint Cars 1:64

This was the first release of World of Outlaws sprint c Racing Champions. Each car was packaged in a black-bo blister with one driver card. The print on the packaging and features an artist's rendering of a racing scene. Each was packaged in one or more blister varieties: "Trac featuring only the #51 car at the top, or regular R Champions packaging with the #1, #11, and #22 cars #51, #93, and #00 cars at the top.

	EX	NM-MT
ny Swindell C 1/11/22 package	5.00	12.00
Hillenburg P black 1/22 package	3.00	6.00
Hillenburg P black Trackside	3.00	6.00
Hillenburg P dark blue '93/00 package	3.00	6.00
Hillenburg P light blue	3.00	6.00
ie Kerr s RV 51/92/00 package	3.00	6.00
y Davis Shocks 1/11/22 package	3.00	6.00
y Davis Shocks 51/93/00 package	3.00	8.00
y Davis Shocks Trackside package	3.00	6.00
y Lasoski Enterprises	3.00	8.00
rd Griffin nders 51/93/00 package	3.00	6.00
e Blaney ns 51/93/00 package	12.50	25.00
e Blaney arin 51/93/00 package	15.00	25.00
e Kinser voline 1/11/22 package	4.00	10.00
e Kinser voline Trackside package	5.00	12.00
Shuman Engineering '93/00 package	7.50	15.00
Green ift Met Finish '93/00 package	3.00	6.00
vin Pylant Racing Fuels '93/00 package	3.00	6.00
Doty aver 51/93/00 package	3.00	6.00
e Beitler ownfield	4.00	10.00
Haudenschild nnzoil '93/00 package	3.00	8.00
Haudenschild nnzoil Trackside package	3.00	8.00
y Stone roweld	3.00	6.00
y Stone roweld Trackside package	3.00	6.00
y McCarl estside 1/11/22 package	4.00	10.00
y McCarl estside Trackside	3.00	8.00
nny Herrera W Trucking 1/11/22 package	3.00	8.00
nny Herrera W Trucking '93/00 package	3.00	6.00
nny Herrera W Trucking Trackside package	3.00	8.00
h Kaufman ikert's Livestock '93/00 package	3.00	6.00
g Wolfgang ap On white eedway Piece	4.00	10.00
g Wolfgang sen black	3.00	8.00
ing Champions Prototype y car in clear box/10,000	2.50	6.00
x Dumesny nsen Construction	3.00	6.00
Carr xim 1/11/22 package	3.00	6.00
e Peters opArtic 1/11/22 package	3.00	6.00
e Peters opArtic Trackside	3.00	6.00
onnie Kreitz llmer Patterns	3.00	6.00
ie Smith Jr. milton 1/11/22 package	4.00	8.00
ie Smith Jr. milton 51/93/00 package	4.00	8.00
ron Berryhill rryhill Racing 1/22 package	3.00	6.00
on Statler atler Racing	3.00	6.00
key Snellbaker es RV's '93/00 package	3.00	6.00

994 Racing Champions Sprint Cars 1:64

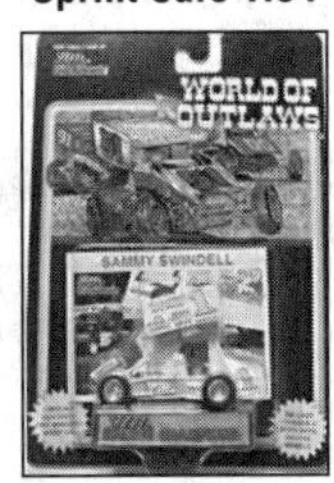

ster packages for the 1994 and 1995 1:64 releases the #51, 93, and 00 sprint cars at the top. All of the 1995 clude the words "series 2" at the top while a few of the r 1994 cars do also.

	EX	NM-MT
y Brazier Brien	7.50	15.00
ny Swindell ll&Hannah White	10.00	20.00
ny Swindell MC black '93/00 package	6.00	12.00
2 Andy Hillenburg STP dark blue Series 2 package	4.00	8.00
2 Garry Rush Castrol	7.50	15.00
2L Ed Lynch Jr. Black	7.50	15.00
4 Bobby Davis Pro Shocks 51/93/00 package	3.00	6.00
4A Greg Hodnett Kele 51/93/00 package	3.00	6.00
7 Richard Griffin Sanders 51/93/00 package	4.00	8.00
7 Jimmy Sills Berry Brothers 51/93/00 package	3.00	6.00
7C Joe Gaerte Gaerte Engines	3.00	6.00
7TW Jeff Swindell Gold Eagle	3.00	8.00
8TW Greg Hodnett Kele	3.00	6.00
11 Steve Kinser Valvoline 51/93/00 package	3.00	8.00
12 Fred Rahmer Apple Series 2 package	4.00	10.00
12X Danny Smith Beaver 51/93/00 package	3.00	6.00
21 Lance Blevins Citgo 51/93/00 package	3.00	6.00
22 Jac Haudenschild Pennzoil with Red numbers Series 2 package	5.00	10.00
23 Frankie Kerr Shoff Motrosports 51/93/00 package	3.00	6.00
24 Jerry Stone Aeroweld Racing	3.00	6.00
45X Johnny Herrera Herrera Motorsports	3.00	6.00
47 Danny Lasoski Casey's	3.00	8.00
49 Doug Wolfgang Olsen 51/93/00 package	3.00	6.00
65 Jim Carr Maxim 51/93/00 package	3.00	6.00
69 Brent Kaeding Motorola Series 2 package	3.00	6.00
69K Donnie Kreitz Vollmer Pattern	3.00	6.00
71M Kenny Jacobs Ecowater 51/93/00 package	3.00	6.00
71M Kenny Jacobs Ecowater Series 2	3.00	6.00
77 Joe Gaerte Hamilton Series 2	3.00	6.00
97B Aaron Berryhill Berryhill Racing 51/93/00 package	3.00	6.00
0 Rick Ferkel Kears	4.00	10.00
U2 Rocky Hodges United Express 51/93/00 package	3.00	6.00

1994 Racing Champions Sprint Transporters 1:64

	EX	NM-MT
7TW Jeff Swindell Gold Eagle	12.50	25.00
8TW Greg Hodnett Kele	10.00	20.00
22 Jac Haudenschild Pennzoil	12.50	25.00
23 Frankie Kerr Shoff Motorsports	15.00	30.00
45X Johnny Herrera Herrera Motorsports	12.50	25.00
77 Jeff Shepard Mac Tools	10.00	20.00

1995 Racing Champions Sprint Cars 1:64

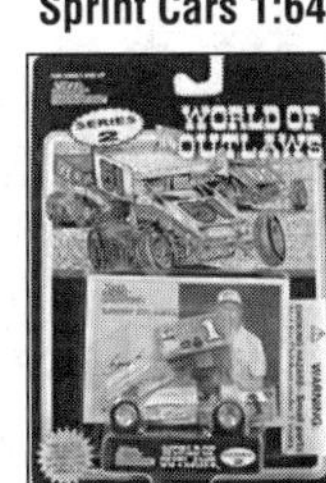

The blister packages for the 1994 and 1995 1:64 releases feature the #51, 93, and 00 sprint cars at the top. The 1995 issue includes the words "series 2" at the top as well.

	EX	NM-MT
1 Garry Brazier O'Brien	12.00	20.00
1 Sammy Swindell Hooters Series 2 package	18.00	30.00
1W Keith Kauffman Wahlie	15.00	25.00
2J J.J. Yeley Bul&Hannah	10.00	20.00
4S Tommy Scott Scott Performance	3.00	6.00
5 Terry McCarl Jackpot Junction	3.00	6.00
7TW Jeff Swindell Gold Eagle	4.00	10.00
8TW Greg Hodnett Kele	4.00	8.00
8TW Greg Hodnett Kele yellow numbers	4.00	8.00
9 Gary Wright TKW	3.00	6.00
11 Steve Kinser Valvoline Series 2 package	4.00	10.00
11 Ron Shuman CH Engineering	3.00	8.00
12S Shane Carson Helms	3.00	6.00
14P Kevin Pylant Unicopy	3.00	6.00
16 Jeff Gordon JG Motorsports Promo/10,000	10.00	20.00
21K Lou Kennedy Superior Custom Series 2 package	3.00	6.00
23 Frankie Kerr Shoff Motrosports	3.00	6.00
31 Sid Blandford Avenger Series 2 package	3.00	6.00
47 Danny Lasoski Casey's	5.00	10.00
65 Jim Carr Maxim Red&Blue	3.00	6.00
66 Mike Peters TropArtic	3.00	6.00
97B Aaron Berryhill Berryhill Racing	3.00	6.00

1996 Racing Champions Sprint Cars 1:64

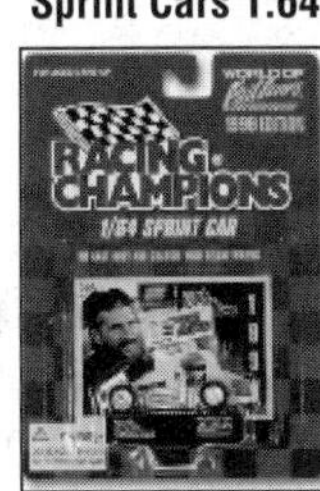

This series of 1:64 scale Sprint cars features some of the most talented drivers in the World of Outlaws series. 14-time Champion Steve Kinser and Winston Cup star Jeff Gordon are a couple of the highlights in the series.

	EX	NM-MT
1 Sammy Swindell Channellock	10.00	20.00
1W Jeff Shepard Conn West	7.50	15.00
1X Randy Hannagan Carrera	3.00	6.00
2 Andy Hillenburg STP	3.00	8.00
4S Tommy Scott Scott Performance/5000	6.00	15.00
5 Danny Lasoski Jackpot Junction	5.00	10.00
5M Mark Kinser Wirtgen	3.00	6.00
7M Jim Carr American Fire Extinguisher	15.00	25.00
7TW Jeff Swindell Gold Eagle	2.00	5.00
9 Gary Wright TRW	3.00	6.00
10 Dave Blaney Vivarin	6.00	12.00
11 Steve Kinser Quaker State	7.50	15.00
11H Greg Hodnett Selma Shell	3.00	6.00
16 Jeff Gordon JG Motorsports	75.00	125.00
21 Lance Blevins Citgo	3.00	6.00
22 Jac Haudenschild Pennzoil New number 22	3.00	8.00
22 Jac Haudenschild Pennzoil Old number 22	3.00	8.00
28D Brad Doty Bower's Coal numbered of 5,000	10.00	18.00
28D Brad Doty Bower's Coal unnumbered version	3.00	6.00
47 Johnny Herrera Housby Trucks	3.00	6.00
51 Terry McCarl McCroskey Chevrolet	4.00	10.00
69 Brent Kaeding Motorola	3.00	6.00
69 Brent Kaeding Pioneer Concrete	4.00	8.00
71M Stevie Smith EcoWater No red stripe	3.00	8.00
71M Stevie Smith EcoWater with Red stripe	3.00	8.00
83 Joey Saldana Beef Packers	3.00	6.00
88 Todd Shaffer Leiby's Mobile Home	3.00	6.00
94 Dale Blaney Hughes Motorsports	3.00	6.00
461 Lance Dewease Dyer Masonry	6.00	12.00

1997 Racing Champions Sprint Cars 1:64

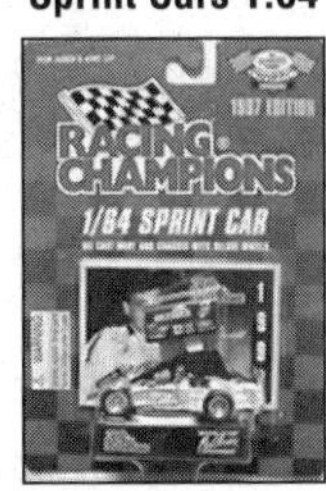

This series of 1:64 Sprint cars by Racing Champions was primarily issued through mass market retailers. Two slightly different blister packages were used: one with a Pennzoil logo in the upper right hand corner and the other with "1997 Edition" printed in the upper right corner.

	EX	NM-MT
1 Billy Pauch Zemco Pennzoil	3.00	6.00
1F Dean Jacobs Frigidaire Pennzoil	3.00	6.00
1J Marlon Jones Energy Release	3.00	6.00
1X Randy Hannagan TRW 1997 Edition	3.00	6.00
2 Andy Hillenburg STP	3.00	8.00
2 Ron Shuman Havoline	3.00	6.00
2M Brent Kaeding Pioneer 1997 Edition	3.00	6.00
3G Joe Gaerte Gaerte Engines	3.00	6.00
4S Tommy Scott On Broadway/5000	4.00	8.00
7TW Jeff Swindell Gold Eagle	5.00	10.00
8 Terry McCarl Holbrook	3.00	6.00
8R Stevie Reeves D&B Racing	3.00	6.00
9W Gary Wright Action	3.00	6.00
11H Greg Hodnett Selma Shell 1997 Edition	3.00	6.00
12 Keith Kauffman Apple Chevrolet 1997 Edition	5.00	10.00
15 Donny Schatz Blue Beacon	6.00	12.00
17E Cris Eash Miller Brothers	3.00	6.00
21L Lance Blevins Citgo 1997 Edition	3.00	6.00
22 Jac Haudenschild Pennzoil	3.00	6.00
23S Frankie Kerr Shoff Motorsports	3.00	6.00
28 Brian Paulus P&P Racing Pennzoil	4.00	8.00
29 Tommie Estes Jr. F&J Construction Pennzoil	3.00	6.00
29 Brent Kaeding BK Racing Pennzoil	3.00	6.00
36 Joe Gaerte Gaerte Engines	3.00	6.00
47 Johnny Herrera Casey's Pennzoil	3.00	6.00
69K Donnie Kreitz Stockdale Pennzoil	3.00	6.00
83 Paul McMahan Beef Packers maroon 1997 Edition	3.00	6.00
83 Paul McMahan Beef Packers maroon&white	3.00	6.00
88 Todd Shaffer Turnbaugh 1997 Edition	3.00	6.00
92 Kenny Jacobs Imperial 1997 Edition	3.00	6.00
94 Dale Blaney Hughes Pennzoil	3.00	6.00
461 Lance Dewease Dyer Masonry	3.00	6.00
U2 Keith Kauffman United Express	7.50	15.00

1998 Racing Champions Sprint Cars 1:64

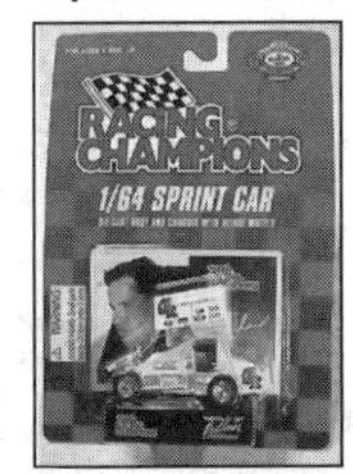

This series of 1:64 Sprint cars by Racing Champions was primarily issued through mass market retailers.

	EX	NM-MT
1 Billy Pauch Zemco	3.00	6.00
1J Marlon Jones Energy Release Pennzoil blister	3.00	6.00
1W Craig Dollansky Conn West	3.00	6.00
1X Randy Hannagan TIR	6.00	12.00
2M Brent Kaeding Al's Roofing	7.50	15.00
2M Brent Kaeding Pioneer	3.00	6.00
3G Joe Gaerte Gaerte	3.00	6.00
4J Jeff Shepard York Excavating	15.00	30.00
7 Kevin Huntley Peterbilt Pennzoil blister	3.00	6.00
9S Shane Stewart RC Cola	3.00	6.00
9S Shane Stewart RC Cola Pennzoil blister	4.00	8.00
11H Greg Hodnet Selma Shell	3.00	6.00
11H Greg Hodnett Vivarin	3.00	6.00
12S Shane Carson Helms Motorsports	3.00	6.00
15 Donny Schatz Blue Beacon	3.00	6.00
18 Dion Hindi Albuquerque	15.00	30.00
23S Frankie Kerr Shoff Motorsports	3.00	6.00
24 Terry McCarl McCroskey	4.00	10.00
28 Brian Paulus Paulus Power Pennzoil blister	3.00	8.00
28 Brian Paulus P&P Racing Pennzoil blister	3.00	8.00
29 Tommie Estes Jr. F&J Construction	3.00	6.00
29 Brent Kaeding BK Motorsports	3.00	6.00
29 Brent Kaeding BK Motorsports Pennzoil blister	4.00	8.00
35 Tyler Walker Air Sep	5.00	12.00
47 Johnny Herrera Strange	3.00	8.00
55 Skip Jackson Jensen Construction	3.00	6.00
69K Donny Kreitz Jr. Stockdale	3.00	6.00
88 Tania Schafer Turnbaugh Oil	6.00	12.00
94 Kenny Jacobs Hughes Pennzoil blister	3.00	8.00
104 Sammy Swindell 104+ Octane	20.00	35.00
461 Lance Dewease Dyer Pennzoil blister	3.00	6.00
00 Jason Statler Rios Construction maroon and white	3.00	6.00
01 Paul McMahan Mt.Impact	6.00	12.00
U2 Keith Kauffman United Express	3.00	6.00

2000 Racing Champions Sprint Cars 1:64

	EX	NM-MT
93 Dale Blaney Amoco Promo box	3.00	8.00

2003 Racing Champions Midwest Sprint Cars 1:64

	EX	NM-MT
1W Loren Woodke Woodke Racing	7.50	15.00
9 Matt Spies Steve Evans Equipment	7.50	15.00
16 Marv DeWall Randy's Towing/4000	7.50	15.00
98A Jack McCorkell Woodke Racing	7.50	15.00

2004 Racing Champions Knoxville Sprint Cars 1:64

	EX	NM-MT
2 Skip Jackson Mid Land Equipment/5000	7.50	15.00
5J Jeff Mitrisin Cahill Racing/5000	7.50	15.00
6 Brian Brown Casey's/2000	7.50	15.00
6 Casey's General Stores/3000	7.50	15.00
14 Randy Martin Diamond Pet Foods/5000	7.50	15.00
17G Ricky Logan Lucas Oil/5000	7.50	15.00
20 Doug Wolfgang Beltline Body Shop/5000	7.50	15.00
22 Billy Alley Ray Lipsey/5000	7.50	15.00
24 Terry McCarl Big Game Hunting/5000	7.50	15.00

1993 Racing Champions Sprint Transporters 1:87

	EX	NM-MT
23 Frankie Kerr Shoff Motorsports	5.00	10.00
45X Johnny Herrera Herrera Motorsports	5.00	10.00
47 Danny Lasoski Casey's	5.00	10.00
71M Kenny Jacobs Ecowater	5.00	10.00

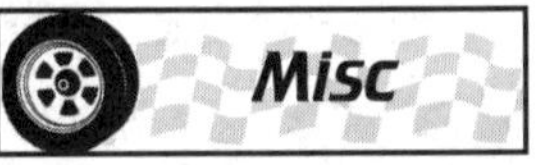

2005 Action/Funline Muscle Machines 1:18

	EX	NM-MT
3 Dale Earnhardt Goodwrench '69 Chevelle/728	25.00	40.00
9 Kasey Kahne Dodge '68 Dart/692	30.00	50.00
9 Kasey Kahne Dodge '68 Dart RCCA/120	30.00	50.00
9 Kasey Kahne Dodge '68 Dart QVC/400	30.00	50.00
9 Kasey Kahne Dodge Pit Cap White '68 Dart/504	25.00	40.00
9 Kasey Kahne Dodge Pit Cap White '68 Dart RCCA/80	25.00	40.00
9 Kasey Kahne Dodge Pit Cap White	25.00	40.00

	EX	NM-MT
'68 Dart QVC/504		
9 Kasey Kahne Dodge Pit Cap White '69 Charger/540	25.00	40.00
9 Kasey Kahne Dodge Pit Cap White '69 Charger RCCA/144	25.00	40.00
9 Kasey Kahne Dodge Pit Cap White '69 Charger QVC/504	25.00	40.00
9 Kasey Kahne Mopar '68 Dart/516	25.00	40.00
9 Kasey Kahne Mopar '68 Dart RCCA/60	25.00	40.00
9 Kasey Kahne Mopar '68 Dart QVC/504	25.00	40.00
9 Kasey Kahne Mopar '69 Charger/616	25.00	40.00
9 Kasey Kahne Mopar '69 Charger RCCA/120	25.00	40.00
9 Kasey Kahne Mopar '69 Charger QVC/504	25.00	40.00
20 Tony Stewart Home Depot '69 Camaro/512	25.00	40.00
43 Richard Petty STP '69 Charger/316	30.00	50.00
43 Richard Petty STP '69 Charger RCCA/300	30.00	50.00
43 Richard Petty STP '69 Charger QVC/180	30.00	50.00
48 Jimmie Johnson Lowe's '69 Camaro/368	25.00	40.00
NNO John Force Castrol GTX '66 Shelby/716	25.00	40.00

2004 Action/Funline Muscle Machines 1:64

	EX	NM-MT
8 Dale Earnhardt Jr. Earnhardt Jr. '69 Chevelle	7.50	15.00
20 Tony Stewart Home Depot '69 Chevelle	7.50	15.00
24 Jeff Gordon DuPont Flames '69 Chevelle	7.50	15.00

2004 Action/Funline Monster Truck 1:43

	EX	NM-MT
8 Dale Earnhardt Jr. DMP	10.00	20.00
8 Dale Earnhardt Jr. JR	10.00	20.00
18 Bobby Labonte Interstate Batteries	10.00	20.00
20 Tony Stewart Home Depot	10.00	20.00
20 Tony Stewart Smoke	10.00	20.00
24 Jeff Gordon DuPont Flames	10.00	20.00
29 Kevin Harvick Kid Rock	10.00	20.00
29 Kevin Harvick KISS	10.00	20.00
01 Joe Nemechek Army GI Joe	10.00	20.00
NNO John Force Castrol GTX Start-Up	10.00	20.00

2005 Brookfield Dually and Tailgate Set 1:24

	EX	NM-MT
24 Jeff Gordon DuPont Flames/1440	20.00	40.00
24 Jeff Gordon DuPont Flames QVC/504	20.00	40.00

2005 GreenLight Pace Cars 1:24

	EX	NM-MT
NNO Indianapolis 500 Corvette	15.00	30.00
NNO Daytona 500 Corvette	15.00	30.00

2005 GreenLight Pace Cars 1:64

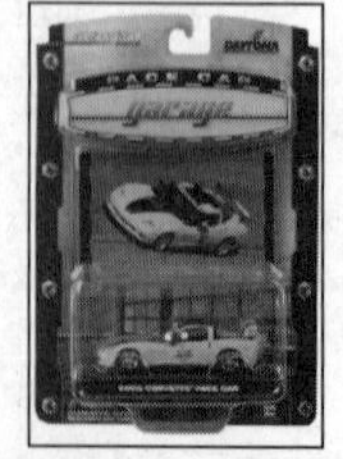

	EX	NM-MT
NNO Daytona 500 Corvette	4.00	8.00
NNO Indianapolis 500 Corvette	4.00	8.00

2003 Action Racing Collectables MLB 1:24

	EX	NM-MT
NNO New York Yankees/1061	30.00	60.00

2004 Action Performance MLB 1:24

	EX	NM-MT
NNO Boston Red Sox/1512	35.00	60.00
NNO Boston Red Sox Promo/288	25.00	50.00

2005 Ertl Collectibles World Series Champions MLB 1:18

	EX	NM-MT
NNO Boston Red Sox '04 Corvette	40.00	70.00
NNO New York Mets '69 Mustang	35.00	60.00
NNO Pittsburgh Pirates '71 Mustang		
NNO St. Louis Cardinals '64 Mustang	35.00	60.00

2005 Ertl Collectibles Cruzin' Series MLB 1:25

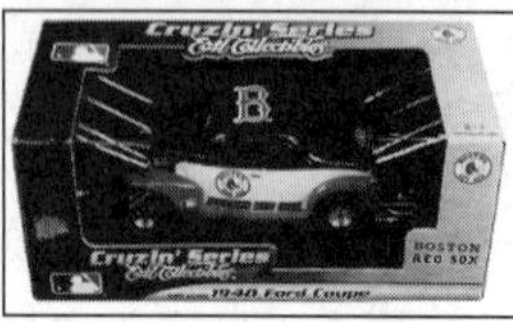

	EX	NM-MT
NNO Boston Red Sox '40 Ford Coupe	20.00	40.00
NNO Boston Red Sox '50 Olds Rocket 88	20.00	40.00
NNO Chicago Cubs '40 Ford Coupe	15.00	30.00
NNO New York Mets '40 Ford Coupe	12.50	25.00
NNO New York Yankees '40 Ford Coupe	20.00	40.00
NNO New York Yankees '50 Olds Rocket 88	20.00	40.00
NNO New York Yankees '57 Chevy Hardtop	20.00	40.00

2005 Ertl Collectibles Delivery Series MLB 1:25

	EX	NM-MT
NNO Boston Red Sox '36 Ford Panel Van	20.00	40.00
NNO Chicago Cubs '59 El Camino	15.00	30.00
NNO Los Angeles Dodgers '59 El Camino	15.00	30.00
NNO New York Yankees '57 Chevy Suburban	20.00	40.00
NNO St. Louis Cardinals '36 Ford Panel Van	15.00	30.00
NNO Washington Nationals '57 Chevy Suburban	12.50	25.00

2006 Ertl Collectibles Delivery Series Sports Truck MLB 1:25

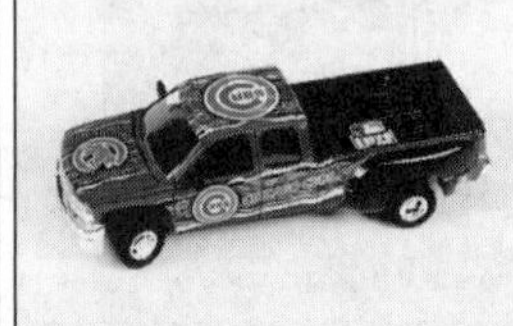

	EX	NM-MT
NNO Boston Red Sox Silverado	20.00	40.00
NNO Chicago Cubs Silverado	15.00	30.00
NNO Cleveland Indians Durango	12.50	25.00
NNO New York Yankees Durango	20.00	40.00
NNO Philadelphia Phillies Durango	12.50	25.00
NNO St. Louis Cardinals Silverado	15.00	30.00
NNO Washington Nationals Silverado	12.50	25.00

2005 Ertl Collectibles Classic Rides MLB 1:64

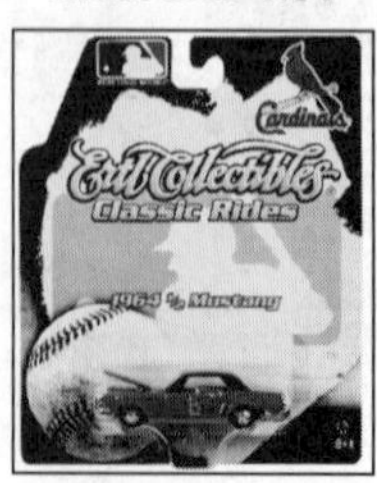

	EX	NM-MT
NNO Boston Red Sox '64 Mustang	5.00	10.00
NNO Chicago Cubs '64 Mustang	4.00	8.00
NNO New York Mets '64 Mustang	4.00	8.00
NNO New York Yankees '64 Mustang	5.00	10.00
NNO St. Louis Cardinals '64 Mustang	4.00	8.00
NNO Washington Nationals '64 Mustang	4.00	8.00

2006 Ertl Collectibles Delivery Series Sports Truck MLB 1:64

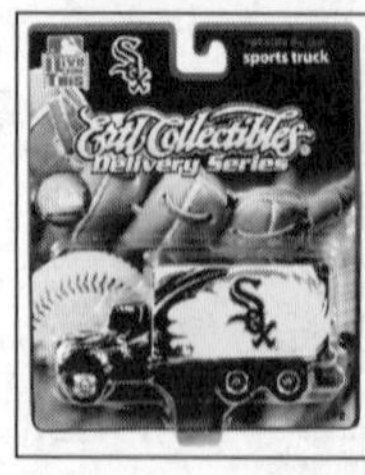

	EX	NM-MT
NNO Atlanta Braves	6.00	12.00
NNO Baltimore Orioles	5.00	10.00
NNO Boston Red Sox	10.00	20.00
NNO Chicago Cubs	7.50	15.00
NNO Chicago White Sox	6.00	12.00
NNO Cleveland Indians	6.00	12.00
NNO New York Mets	6.00	12.00
NNO New York Yankees	10.00	20.00
NNO Philadelphia Phillies	6.00	12.00
NNO St. Louis Cardinals	7.50	15.00

2005 Ertl Collectibles Chopper Series MLB 1:10

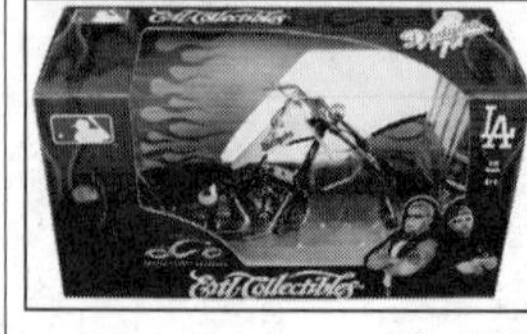

	EX	NM-MT
NNO Boston Red Sox OCC	20.00	40.00
NNO Chicago Cubs OCC	15.00	30.00
NNO New York Yankees OCC 1	20.00	40.00
NNO New York Yankees OCC 2	20.00	40.00
NNO Los Angeles Dodgers OCC	15.00	30.00

2005 Ertl Collectibles Chopper Series MLB 1:18

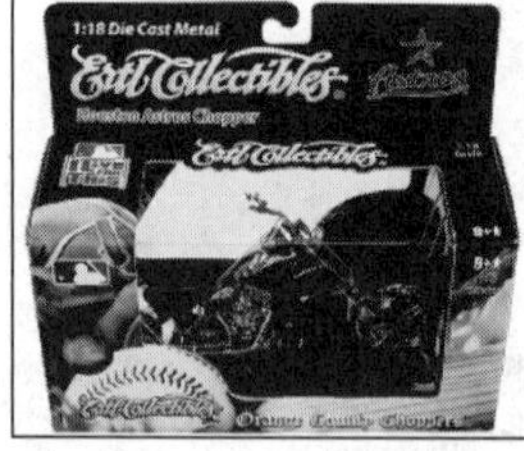

	EX	NM-MT
NNO Boston Red Sox OCC	10.00	20.00
NNO Chicago Cubs OCC	7.50	15.00
NNO Houston Astros OCC		
NNO New York Mets OCC	6.00	12.00
NNO New York Yankees OCC	10.00	20.00

2005 Ertl Collectibles Snowmobile Series MLB 1:18

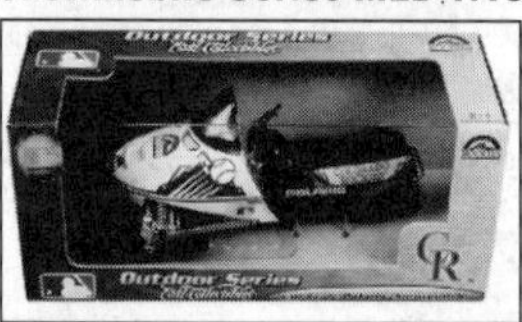

	EX	NM-MT
NNO Boston Red Sox	15.00	30.00
NNO Colorado Rockies	10.00	20.00
NNO New York Yankess	15.00	30.00
NNO Chicago Cubs	12.50	25.00

2006 Ertl Collectibles Transporters Throwback Series MLB 1:64

	EX	NM-MT
NNO Boston Red Sox	12.50	25.00
NNO Chicago Cubs	10.00	20.00
NNO New York Yankees	12.50	25.00
NNO Pittsburgh Pirates	7.50	15.00

2005 Ertl Collectibles Transporters MLB 1:87

	EX	NM-MT
NNO Arizona Diamondbacks	5.00	10.00
NNO Atlanta Braves	6.00	12.00
NNO Baltimore Orioles	5.00	10.00

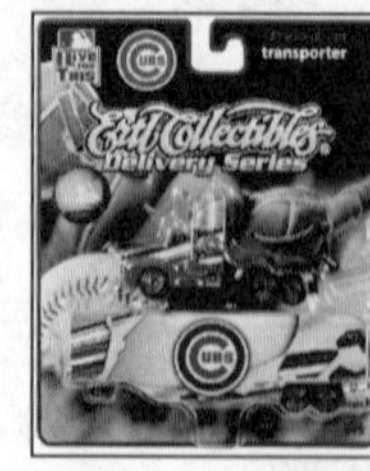

	EX	NM-MT
NNO Boston Red Sox	10.00	20.00
NNO Chicago White Sox	6.00	12.00
NNO Chicago Cubs	7.50	15.00
NNO Cincinnati Reds	5.00	10.00
NNO Cleveland Indians	5.00	10.00
NNO Colorado Rockies	5.00	10.00
NNO Detroit Tigers	5.00	10.00
NNO Florida Marlins	5.00	10.00
NNO Houston Astros	6.00	12.00
NNO Kansas City Royals	5.00	10.00
NNO Los Angeles Angels	5.00	10.00
NNO Los Angeles Dodgers	7.50	15.00
NNO Milwaukee Brewers	5.00	10.00
NNO Minnesota Twins	5.00	10.00
NNO New York Mets	6.00	12.00
NNO New York Yankees	10.00	20.00
NNO Oakland A's	5.00	10.00
NNO Philadelphia Phillies	5.00	10.00
NNO Pittsburgh Pirates	5.00	10.00
NNO San Diego Padres	5.00	10.00
NNO San Fransisco Giants	6.00	12.00
NNO Seattle Mariners	5.00	10.00
NNO St. Louis Cardinals	7.50	15.00
NNO Tampa Bay Devil Rays	5.00	10.00
NNO Toronto Blue Jays	5.00	10.00
NNO Texas Rangers	5.00	10.00
NNO Washington Nationals	6.00	12.00

2002 Fleer Collectibles BMW X-5 MLB 1:24

	EX	NM-MT
NNO Atlanta Braves/1000	10.00	20.00
NNO Baltimore Orioles/2000	10.00	20.00
NNO Boston Red Sox/1000	15.00	30.00
NNO Chicago Cubs/1000	12.50	25.00
NNO Cleveland Indians/1000	10.00	20.00
NNO New York Mets/1500	10.00	20.00
NNO New York Yankees/4000	15.00	30.00
NNO Philadelphia Phillies/1500	10.00	20.00
NNO Seattle Mariners/1000	10.00	20.00
NNO St. Louis Cardinals/1000	12.50	25.00

2002 Fleer Collectibles Greats of the Game MLB 1:24

	EX	NM-MT
8 New York Yankees Yogi Berra '57 Chevy	20.00	40.00
21 Pittsburgh Pirates Roberto Clemente '69 GTO	20.00	40.00
41 New York Mets Tom Seaver '69 GTO	15.00	30.00

2003 Fleer Collectibles All Stars of Today MLB 1:24

	EX	NM-MT
2 New York Yankees w/Derek Jeter Porsche Boxter/2000	20.00	40.00
3 Texas Rangers w/Alex Rodriguez Mercedes 500 SL/2000	20.00	40.00
5 Boston Red Sox w/Nomar Garciaparra Jaguar XK180/2000	15.00	30.00
21 Chicago Cubs w/Sammy Sosa Lamborghini Diablo/2000	15.00	30.00
25 New York Yankees w/Jason Giambi Jaguar XK180/2000	12.50	25.00
25 San Francisco Giants w/Barry Bonds Mercedes 500 SL/2000	20.00	40.00
31 New York Mets w/Mike Piazza Porsche Boxter	15.00	30.00
51 Seattle Mariners w/Ichiro Lamborghini Diablo	20.00	40.00

2003 Fleer Collectibles 1959 Corvettes MLB 1:24

	EX	NM-MT
NNO Atlanta Braves/1000	15.00	30.00
NNO Baltimore Orioles/1000	15.00	30.00
NNO Boston Red Sox/1000	20.00	40.00
NNO New York Mets/1000	15.00	30.00
NNO New York Yankees/1000	20.00	40.00
NNO San Francisco Giants/1000	15.00	30.00

2003 Fleer Collectibles Monster Trucks MLB 1:32

	EX	NM-MT
NNO Atlanta Braves/680	7.50	15.00
NNO Baltimore Orioles/500	7.50	15.00
NNO Boston Red Sox/700	7.50	15.00
NNO Cleveland Indians/700	7.50	15.00
NNO New York Mets/1000	7.50	15.00
NNO New York Yankees/3000	7.50	15.00

2002 Fleer Collectibles Prowler w/Ultra Card MLB 1:64

	EX	NM-MT
NNO Seattle Mariners w/Ichiro Suzuki	10.00	20.00
NNO New York Mets w/Mike Piazza	5.00	10.00
NNO New York Yankees w/Derek Jeter	7.50	15.00

2002 Fleer Collectibles Team Bus MLB 1:64

	EX	NM-MT
NNO Seattle Mariners	5.00	10.00
NNO New York Mets	5.00	10.00
NNO Baltimore Orioles	5.00	10.00
NNO New York Yankees	7.50	15.00

2003 Fleer Collectible Bullpen Cars 1:64

	EX	N
NNO Atlanta Braves	4.00	
NNO Baltimore Orioles	4.00	
NNO Boston Red Sox	5.00	
NNO Cleveland Indians	4.00	
NNO New York Mets	4.00	
NNO New York Yankees	5.00	

2003 Fleer Collectible Monster Trucks MLB 1:

	EX	N
NNO Atlanta Braves	4.00	
NNO Anaheim Angels	4.00	
NNO Baltimore Orioles	4.00	
NNO Boston Red Sox	5.00	
NNO Chicago Cubs	5.00	
NNO Cleveland Indians	4.00	
NNO Los Angeles Dodgers	5.00	
NNO New York Mets	4.00	
NNO New York Yankees	5.00	
NNO Oakland A's	4.00	
NNO San Francisco Giants	4.00	
NNO St. Louis Cardinals	5.00	

2003 Fleer Collectible Mustang w/Ultra Card M 1:64

	EX	N
NNO New York Mets w/Tom Glavine	4.00	
NNO New York Mets w/Mike Piazza	4.00	
NNO New York Yankees w/Jason Giambi	4.00	
NNO New York Yankees w/Derek Jeter	6.00	

2003 Fleer Collectible Transporters MLB 1:8

	EX	N
NNO Atlanta Braves	7.50	
NNO Anaheim Angels '02 Champions	10.00	
NNO Baltimore Orioles	7.50	
NNO New York Mets	7.50	
NNO New York Yankees	10.00	
NNO San Francisco Giants	7.50	

2005-06 Ertl Collectible Choppers Series NBA 1:

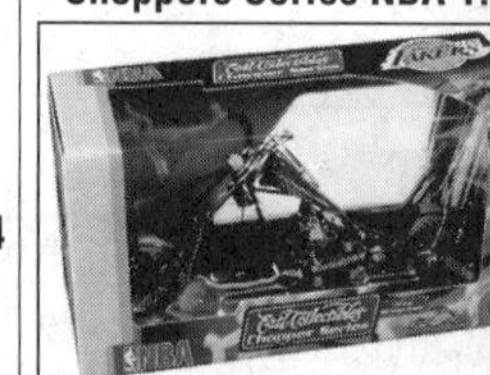

	EX	N
NNO Cleveland Cavaliers	15.00	
NNO Los Angeles Lakers	15.00	
NNO Miami Heat	15.00	
NNO New York Knicks	12.50	

2005-06 Ertl Collectible Choppers Series NBA 1:

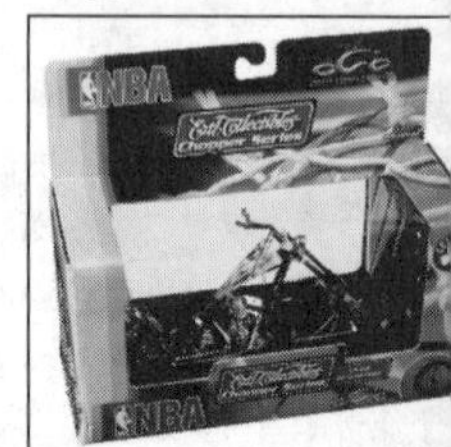

	EX	N
NNO Boston Celtics	7.50	
NNO Chicago Bulls	7.50	
NNO Detroit Pistons	7.50	
NNO Los Angeles Lakers	10.00	
NNO Miami Heat	7.50	
NNO Philadelphia 76ers	7.50	

2005-06 Ertl Collectible Cruzin' Series NBA 1:2

	EX	N
NNO Boston Celtics	12.50	
NNO Chicago Bulls	12.50	
NNO Los Angeles Lakers	15.00	
NNO Philadelphia 76ers	12.50	

2005-06 Ertl Collectible Slammed F150 NBA 1:6

	EX	N
NNO Boston Celtics		
NNO Chicago Bulls	4.00	
NNO Cleveland Cavaliers	5.00	

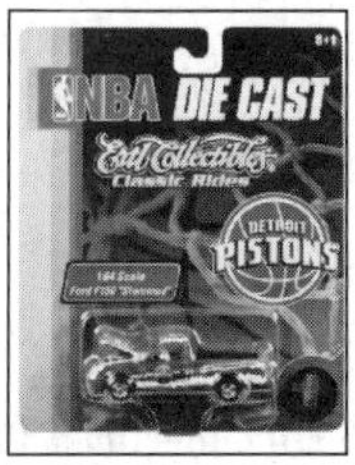

allas Mavericks	5.00	10.00
enver Nuggets	4.00	8.00
etroit Pistons	4.00	8.00
ouston Rockets	4.00	8.00
os Angeles Lakers	6.00	12.00
iami Heat	5.00	10.00
innesota Timberwolves	4.00	8.00
ew Jersey Nets	4.00	8.00
ew York Knicks	4.00	8.00
hiladelphia 76ers	4.00	8.00
hoenix Suns	4.00	8.00
an Antonio Spurs	5.00	10.00
eattle Supersonics	4.00	8.00

003-04 Fleer H2 w/Ultra card NBA 1:64

	EX	NM-MT
leveland Cavaliers w/LeBron James	15.00	30.00
enver Nuggets w/Carmelo Anthony	10.00	20.00
oronto Raptors w/Chris Bosh	6.00	12.00

004-05 Fleer H2 NBA 1:43

	EX	NM-MT
oston Celtics	7.50	15.00
hicago Bulls	7.50	15.00
leveland Cavaliers	7.50	15.00
allas Mavericks	7.50	15.00
etroit Pistons	7.50	15.00
ouston Rockets	7.50	15.00
os Angeles Lakers	10.00	20.00
ew Jersey Nets	7.50	15.00
ew York Knicks	7.50	15.00
hiladelphia 76ers	7.50	15.00
acramento Kings	7.50	15.00
an Antonio Spurs	7.50	15.00

004-05 Fleer H2 w/Ultra card NBA 1:64

	EX	NM-MT
oston Celtics w/Paul Pierce	6.00	12.00
harlotte Bobcats w/Emeka Okafor	7.50	15.00
hicago Bulls w/Ben Gordon	7.50	15.00
leveland Cavaliers w/LeBron James	7.50	15.00
allas Mavericks w/Devon Harris	6.00	12.00
allas Mavericks w/Dirk Nowitzki	7.50	15.00
enver Nuggets w/Carmelo Anthony	7.50	15.00
etroit Pistons w/Ben Wallace	6.00	12.00
ouston Rockets w/Yao Ming	7.50	15.00
os Angeles Clippers w/Shaun Livingston	6.00	12.00
os Angeles Lakers w/Kobe Bryant	7.50	15.00
iami Heat w/Dwyane Wade	7.50	15.00
iami Heat w/Shaquille O'Neal	7.50	15.00
innesota Timberwolves w/Kevin Garnett	7.50	15.00
ew York Knicks w/Stephon Marbury	6.00	12.00
rlando Magic w/Dwight Howard	7.50	15.00
hiladelphia 76ers w/Allen Iverson	6.00	12.00
ortland Trailblazers w/Sebastian Telfair	6.00	12.00
acramento Kings w/Peja Stojakovic	6.00	12.00
tah Jazz w/Carlos Arroyo	6.00	12.00

004-05 Fleer Collectibles Transporters NBA 1:80

	EX	NM-MT
oston Celtics	7.50	15.00
leveland Cavaliers	7.50	15.00
allas Mavericks	7.50	15.00
enver Nuggets	7.50	15.00
etroit Pistons	7.50	15.00
ouston Rockets	7.50	15.00
os Angeles Lakers	7.50	15.00
innesota Timberwolves	10.00	20.00
ew Jersey Nets	7.50	15.00
ew York Knicks	7.50	15.00
hiladelphia 76ers	7.50	15.00
acramento Kings	7.50	15.00
oronto Raptors	7.50	15.00

05-06 Upper Deck Cadillac calade w/UD card NBA 1:64

	EX	NM-MT
oston Celtics w/Paul Pierce	5.00	10.00
hicago Bulls w/Kurt Hinrich	6.00	12.00
leveland Cavaliers w/LeBron James	7.50	15.00
enver Nuggets w/Carmelo Anthony	6.00	12.00
etroit Pistons w/Ben Wallace	5.00	10.00
ouston Rockets w/Tracy McGrady	5.00	10.00
os Angeles Lakers w/Kobe Bryant	7.50	15.00
iami Heat w/Dwyane Wade	7.50	15.00
iami Heat w/Shaquille O'Neal	7.50	15.00
innesota Timberwolves w/Kevin Garnett	6.00	12.00
ew York Knicks w/Stephon Marbury	5.00	10.00
an Antonio Spurs w/Manu Ginobili	5.00	10.00

03 Action Performance NFL 1:24

	EX	NM-MT
arolina Panthers	12.50	25.00
allas Cowboys	20.00	40.00
reen Bay Packers	20.00	40.00
akland Raiders	20.00	40.00
hiladelphia Eagles	15.00	30.00
ittsburgh Steelers	20.00	40.00

NNO San Francisco 49ers	20.00	40.00
NNO Tampa Bay Buccaneers	12.50	25.00
NNO Washington Redskins	15.00	30.00
NNO Super Bowl XXXVII	12.50	25.00

2003 Action Racing Collectables NFL 1:24

	EX	NM-MT
NNO Dallas Cowboys/1500	30.00	60.00
NNO Green Bay Packers/1500	30.00	60.00
NNO Pittsburgh Steelers/1397	30.00	60.00
NNO San Francisco 49ers/2327	30.00	60.00
NNO Washington Redskins/1307	25.00	50.00

2004 Action Performance NFL 1:24

	EX	NM-MT
NNO Chicago Bears	15.00	30.00
NNO Dallas Cowboys	20.00	40.00
NNO Denver Broncos	15.00	30.00
NNO Green Bay Packers	20.00	40.00
NNO Houston Texans	12.50	25.00
NNO Kansas City Chiefs	15.00	30.00
NNO Miami Dolphins	20.00	40.00
NNO Minnesota Vikings	15.00	30.00
NNO New England Patriots	12.50	25.00
NNO New York Giants	15.00	30.00
NNO New York Jets	12.50	25.00
NNO Oakland Raiders	20.00	40.00
NNO Philadelphia Eagles	15.00	30.00
NNO Pittsburgh Steelers	20.00	40.00
NNO San Francisco 49ers	20.00	40.00
NNO St. Louis Rams	12.50	25.00
NNO Tampa Bay Buccaneers	12.50	25.00
NNO Tennessee Titans	12.50	25.00
NNO Washington Redskins	15.00	30.00

2004 Action Racing Collectables NFL 1:24

	EX	NM-MT
NNO Chicago Bears/1464	30.00	60.00
NNO Dallas Cowboys/2004	40.00	80.00
NNO Denver Broncos/2004	30.00	60.00
NNO Green Bay Packers/3360	40.00	80.00
NNO Houston Texans/2000	25.00	50.00
NNO Kansas City Chiefs/1344	30.00	60.00
NNO Miami Dolphins/1440	40.00	80.00
NNO Minnesota Vikings/1536	30.00	60.00
NNO New York Giants/1584	30.00	60.00
NNO New York Jets/1644	25.00	50.00
NNO Oakland Raiders/1584	40.00	80.00
NNO Philadelphia Eagles/1392	30.00	60.00
NNO Pittsburgh Steelers/1248	40.00	80.00
NNO San Francisco 49ers/2004	40.00	80.00
NNO St. Louis Rams/1548	25.00	50.00
NNO Tampa Bay Buccaneers/1632	25.00	50.00
NNO Tennessee Titans/1380	25.00	50.00
NNO Washington Redskins/1272	30.00	60.00

2005 Ertl Collectibles Chopper Series NFL 1:10

	EX	NM-MT
NNO Dallas Cowboys	30.00	60.00
NNO Kansas City Chiefs	25.00	50.00
NNO New England Patriots	20.00	40.00
NNO New York Giants	25.00	50.00
NNO New York Jets	20.00	40.00
NNO Oakland Raiders	30.00	60.00
NNO Philadelphia Eagles	25.00	50.00

2005 Ertl Collectibles Chopper Series NFL 1:18

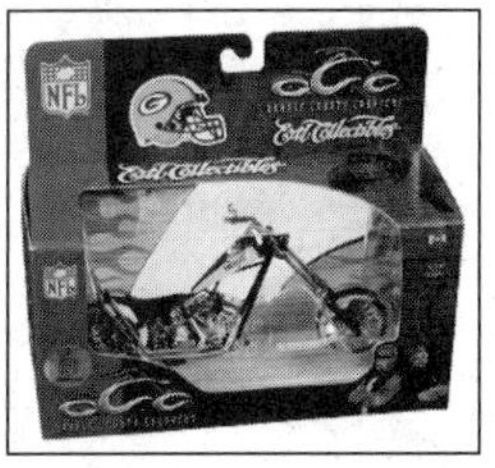

	EX	NM-MT
NNO Baltimore Ravens	7.50	15.00
NNO Green Bay Packers	12.50	25.00
NNO Kansas City Chiefs	10.00	20.00
NNO New York Jets	7.50	15.00
NNO Oakland Raiders	12.50	25.00
NNO Philadelphia Eagles	10.00	20.00
NNO Washington Redskins	10.00	20.00

2005 Ertl Collectibles Snowmobile Series NFL 1:18

	EX	NM-MT
NNO Buffalo Bills	12.50	25.00
NNO Chicago Bears	15.00	30.00
NNO Denver Broncos	15.00	30.00
NNO Detroit Lions	12.50	25.00
NNO Green Bay Packers	20.00	40.00
NNO Indianapolis Colts	12.50	25.00

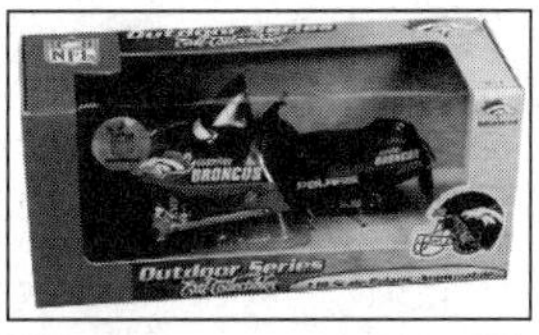

NNO Minnesota Vikings	15.00	30.00
NNO New England Patriots	12.50	25.00

2005 Ertl Collectibles Super Bowl Series NFL 1:18

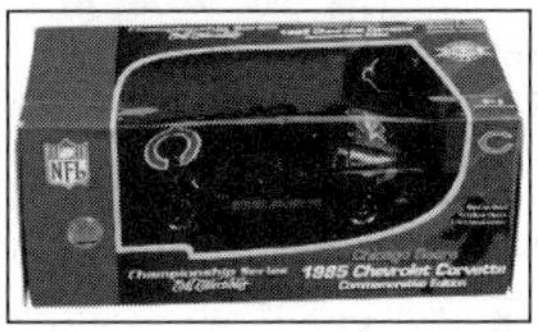

	EX	NM-MT
NNO New York Jets '68	30.00	60.00
NNO Miami Dolphins '72 Challenger	40.00	80.00
NNO Oakland Raiders '76 Gran Torino	40.00	80.00
NNO Dallas Cowboys '77 Firebird	40.00	80.00
NNO Chicago Bears '85 Corvette	40.00	80.00
NNO Green Bay Packers '96 Trans Am	40.00	80.00
NNO Pittsburgh Steelers '78 Warlock	40.00	80.00

2007 Ertl Collectibles Chopper Series NFL 1:18

	EX	NM-MT
NNO Green Bay Packers	12.50	25.00
NNO Indianapolis Colts	10.00	20.00
NNO New York Giants	10.00	20.00
NNO Oakland Raiders	10.00	20.00

2005 Ertl Collectibles Cruzin' Series NFL 1:25

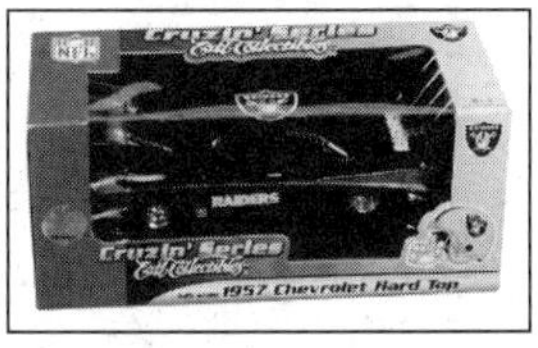

	EX	NM-MT
NNO Atlanta Falcons '50 Olds Rocket	15.00	30.00
NNO Dallas Cowboys '40 Ford Coupe	20.00	40.00
NNO Dallas Cowboys '50 Olds Rocket	20.00	40.00
NNO Denver Broncos '57 Chevy	15.00	30.00
NNO Minnesota Vikings '57 Chevy	15.00	30.00
NNO New England Patriots '50 Olds Rocket	15.00	30.00
NNO New York Giants '50 Olds Rocket	15.00	30.00
NNO Oakland Raiders '40 Ford Coupe	20.00	40.00
NNO Oakland Raiders '57 Chevy	20.00	40.00
NNO Philadelphia Eagles '40 Ford Coupe	15.00	30.00
NNO Philadelphia Eagles '50 Olds Rocket	15.00	30.00
NNO Washington Redskins '40 Ford Coupe	15.00	30.00

2005 Ertl Collectibles Delivery Series NFL 1:25

	EX	NM-MT
NNO Dallas Cowboys '57 Suburban	20.00	40.00
NNO Indianapolis Colts '36 Ford Van	15.00	30.00
NNO Kansas City Chiefs '57 Suburban	15.00	30.00
NNO Kansas City Chiefs '59 El Camino	15.00	30.00
NNO New York Jets '57 Suburban	15.00	30.00
NNO Oakland Raiders '59 El Camino	20.00	40.00
NNO Philadelphia Eagles '57 Suburban	15.00	30.00
NNO Washington Redskins '36 Ford Van	15.00	30.00

2006 Ertl Collectibles Cruzin' Series NFL 1:25

NNO Carolina Panthers Cadillac Escalade
NNO Chicago Bears Toyota Supra
NNO Dallas Cowboys Toyota Supra
NNO Indianapolis Colts Cadillac Escalade
NNO New England Patriots Cadillac Escalade
NNO Philadelphia Eagles Toyota Supra
NNO Pittsburgh Steelers Toyota Supra
NNO Seattle Seahawks Cadillac Escalade
NNO Tampa Bay Buccaneers Cadillac Escalade
NNO Washington Redskins Toyota Supra

2006 Ertl Collectibles Delivery Series NFL 1:25

	EX	NM-MT
NNO Green Bay Packers Durango		
NNO Kansas City Chiefs Silverado		
NNO Miami Dolphins Silverado		
NNO Minnesota Vikings Silverado		
NNO New York Giants Durango		
NNO Oakland Raiders Durango		
NNO Pittsburgh Steelers Durango		
NNO San Diego Chargers Silverado		

2003 Fleer Collectibles Monster Trucks NFL 1:32

	EX	NM-MT
NNO Arizona Cardinals	15.00	30.00
NNO Atlanta Falcons	15.00	30.00
NNO Baltimore Ravens	15.00	30.00
NNO Buffalo Bills	15.00	30.00
NNO Carolina Panthers	15.00	30.00
NNO Chicago Bears	15.00	30.00
NNO Cincinnati Bengals	15.00	30.00
NNO Cleveland Browns	15.00	30.00
NNO Dallas Cowboys	20.00	40.00
NNO Denver Broncos	15.00	30.00
NNO Detroit Lions	15.00	30.00
NNO Green Bay Packers	20.00	40.00
NNO Indianapolis Colts	15.00	30.00
NNO Jacksonville Jaguars	15.00	30.00
NNO Kansas City Chiefs	15.00	30.00
NNO Miami Dolphins	15.00	30.00
NNO Minnesota Vikings	15.00	30.00
NNO New England Patriots	15.00	30.00
NNO New York Giants	15.00	30.00
NNO New York Jets	15.00	30.00
NNO Oakland Raiders	15.00	30.00
NNO Philadelphia Eagles	15.00	30.00
NNO Pittsburgh Steelers	20.00	40.00
NNO San Diego Chargers	15.00	30.00
NNO San Francisco 49ers	15.00	30.00
NNO Seattle Seahawks	15.00	30.00
NNO St. Louis Rams	15.00	30.00
NNO Tampa Bay Buccaneers	15.00	30.00
NNO Tennessee Titans	15.00	30.00
NNO Washington Redskins	15.00	30.00

2004 Fleer Collectibles Monster Trucks NFL 1:32

	EX	NM-MT
NNO Arizona Cardinals	15.00	30.00
NNO Atlanta Falcons	15.00	30.00
NNO Baltimore Ravens	15.00	30.00
NNO Buffalo Bills	15.00	30.00
NNO Carolina Panthers	15.00	30.00
NNO Chicago Bears	15.00	30.00
NNO Cincinnati Bengals	15.00	30.00
NNO Cleveland Browns	15.00	30.00
NNO Dallas Cowboys	20.00	40.00
NNO Denver Broncos	15.00	30.00
NNO Detroit Lions	15.00	30.00
NNO Green Bay Packers	20.00	40.00
NNO Indianapolis Colts	15.00	30.00
NNO Jacksonville Jaguars	15.00	30.00
NNO Kansas City Chiefs	15.00	30.00
NNO Miami Dolphins	15.00	30.00
NNO Minnesota Vikings	15.00	30.00
NNO New England Patriots	15.00	30.00
NNO New York Giants	15.00	30.00
NNO New York Jets	15.00	30.00
NNO Oakland Raiders	15.00	30.00
NNO Philadelphia Eagles	15.00	30.00
NNO San Francisco 49ers	15.00	30.00
NNO Seattle Seahawks	15.00	30.00
NNO St. Louis Rams	15.00	30.00
NNO Tampa Bay Buccaneers	15.00	30.00
NNO Tennessee Titans	15.00	30.00
NNO Washington Redskins	15.00	30.00

2003 Action Performance NFL 1:64

	EX	NM-MT
NNO Chicago Bears	7.50	15.00
NNO Dallas Cowboys	10.00	20.00
NNO Dallas Cowboys Promo	12.50	25.00
NNO Denver Broncos	7.50	15.00
NNO Green Bay Packers	10.00	20.00
NNO Miami Dolphins	10.00	20.00
NNO New York Giants	6.00	12.00
NNO Oakland Raiders	10.00	20.00
NNO Oakland Raiders Promo	12.50	25.00
NNO Philadelphia Eagles	7.50	15.00
NNO Pittsburgh Steelers	10.00	20.00
NNO San Francisco 49ers	10.00	20.00
NNO Washington Redskins	7.50	15.00

2005 Ertl Collectibles Classic Rides NFL 1:64

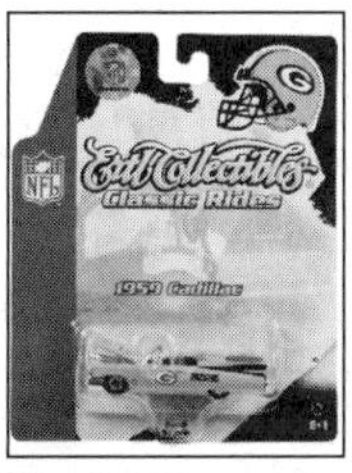

NNO Atlanta Falcons '40 Ford Coupe	6.00	12.00
NNO Chicago Bears '40 Ford Coupe	7.50	15.00
NNO Dallas Cowboys '64 Mustang	10.00	20.00
NNO Dallas Cowboys '70 Chevelle	10.00	20.00
NNO Detroit Lions '64 Mustang	6.00	12.00
NNO Green Bay Packers '40 Ford Coupe	10.00	20.00
NNO Green Bay Packers '59 Cadillac	10.00	20.00
NNO Kansas City Chiefs '64 Mustang	7.50	15.00
NNO Minnesota Vikings '70 Chevelle	7.50	15.00
NNO New York Giants '59 Cadillac	7.50	15.00
NNO New York Jets '70 Chevelle	6.00	12.00
NNO Oakland Raiders '64 Mustang	10.00	20.00
NNO Philadelphia Eagles '59 Cadillac	7.50	15.00
NNO Philadelphia Eagles '64 Mustang	7.50	15.00
NNO St. Louis Rams '70 Chevelle	6.00	12.00
NNO Washington Redskins '40 Ford Coupe	7.50	15.00

2001 Fleer Collectibles PT Cruiser w/Ultra Card NFL 1:64

	EX	NM-MT
NNO Arizona Cardinals Jake Plummer	6.00	12.00
NNO Baltimore Ravens Jamal Lewis	6.00	12.00
NNO Buffalo Bills Eric Moulds	6.00	12.00
NNO Carolina Panthers Chris Weinke	6.00	12.00
NNO Cincinnati Bengals Peter Warrick	6.00	12.00
NNO Cleveland Browns Tim Couch	6.00	12.00
NNO Dallas Cowboys Emmitt Smith	10.00	20.00
NNO Denver Broncos Terrell Davis	6.00	12.00
NNO Detroit Lions Charlie Batch	6.00	12.00
NNO Green Bay Packers w/Brett Favre	10.00	20.00
NNO Indianapolis Colts Edgerrin James	10.00	20.00
NNO Indianapolis Colts Peyton Manning	10.00	20.00
NNO Jacksonville Jaguars Fred Taylor	6.00	12.00
NNO Kansas City Chiefs Tony Gonzalez	6.00	12.00
NNO Miami Dolphins Zach Thomas	6.00	12.00
NNO Minnesota Vikings Daunte Culpepper	7.50	15.00
NNO Minnesota Vikings Randy Moss	7.50	15.00
NNO New England Patriots Drew Bledsoe	6.00	12.00
NNO New Orleans Saints Ricky Williams	6.00	12.00
NNO New York Giants Ron Dayne	6.00	12.00
NNO New York Jets Santana Moss	6.00	12.00
NNO Oakland Raiders Tim Brown	6.00	12.00
NNO Oakland Raiders Rich Gannon	6.00	12.00
NNO Philadelphia Eagles Donovan McNabb	7.50	15.00
NNO San Francisco 49ers Jeff Garcia	6.00	12.00
NNO Seattle Seahawks Koren Robinson	6.00	12.00
NNO St. Louis Rams Marshall Faulk	6.00	12.00
NNO St. Louis Rams Kurt Warner	6.00	12.00
NNO Tampa Bay Buccaneers Keyshawn Johnson	6.00	12.00
NNO Washington Redskins Stephen Davis	6.00	12.00
NNO Washington Redskins Rod Gardner	6.00	12.00

2001 Fleer Collectibles Transporters NFL 1:80

	EX	NM-MT
NNO Arizona Cardinals	10.00	20.00
NNO Atlanta Falcons	10.00	20.00
NNO Baltimore Ravens	10.00	20.00
NNO Buffalo Bills	10.00	20.00
NNO Chicago Bears	10.00	20.00
NNO Cincinnati Bengals	10.00	20.00
NNO Cleveland Browns	10.00	20.00
NNO Dallas Cowboys	15.00	30.00
NNO Denver Broncos	10.00	20.00
NNO Detroit Lions	10.00	20.00
NNO Green Bay Packers	15.00	30.00
NNO Indianapolis Colts	10.00	20.00
NNO Jacksonville Jaguars	10.00	20.00
NNO Kansas City Chiefs	10.00	20.00
NNO Miami Dolphins	10.00	20.00
NNO Minnesota Vikings	10.00	20.00
NNO New Orleans Saints	10.00	20.00
NNO New York Giants	10.00	20.00
NNO New York Jets	10.00	20.00
NNO Oakland Raiders	10.00	20.00
NNO Philadelphia Eagles	10.00	20.00
NNO San Diego Chargers	10.00	20.00
NNO San Francisco 49ers	10.00	20.00
NNO Seattle Seahawks	10.00	20.00
NNO St. Louis Rams	10.00	20.00
NNO Tampa Bay Buccaneers	10.00	20.00
NNO Tennessee Titans	10.00	20.00
NNO Washington Redskins	10.00	20.00

2002 Fleer Collectibles Transporters NFL 1:80

	EX	NM-MT
NNO Arizona Cardinals	10.00	20.00
NNO Atlanta Falcons	10.00	20.00
NNO Baltimore Ravens	10.00	20.00
NNO Buffalo Bills	10.00	20.00
NNO Chicago Bears	10.00	20.00
NNO Cincinnati Bengals	10.00	20.00
NNO Cleveland Browns	10.00	20.00
NNO Dallas Cowboys	15.00	30.00
NNO Denver Broncos	10.00	20.00
NNO Detroit Lions	10.00	20.00
NNO Green Bay Packers	15.00	30.00
NNO Houston Texans	10.00	20.00
NNO Indianapolis Colts	10.00	20.00
NNO Jacksonville Jaguars	10.00	20.00
NNO Kansas City Chiefs	10.00	20.00
NNO Miami Dolphins	10.00	20.00
NNO Minnesota Vikings	10.00	20.00
NNO New England Patriots	10.00	20.00
NNO New York Jets	10.00	20.00
NNO Pittsburgh Steelers	15.00	30.00
NNO San Francisco 49ers	10.00	20.00
NNO Seattle Seahawks	10.00	20.00
NNO St. Louis Rams	10.00	20.00
NNO Tampa Bay Buccaneers	10.00	20.00
NNO Tennessee Titans	10.00	20.00
NNO Washington Redskins	10.00	20.00

2003 Fleer Collectibles Transporters NFL 1:80

	EX	NM-MT
NNO Arizona Cardinals	10.00	20.00
NNO Atlanta Falcons	10.00	20.00
NNO Baltimore Ravens	10.00	20.00
NNO Buffalo Bills	10.00	20.00
NNO Carolina Panthers	10.00	20.00
NNO Chicago Bears	10.00	20.00

NNO Cincinnati Bengals	10.00	20.00
NNO Cleveland Browns	10.00	20.00
NNO Dallas Cowboys	15.00	30.00
NNO Denver Broncos	10.00	20.00
NNO Detroit Lions	10.00	20.00
NNO Green Bay Packers	15.00	30.00
NNO Houston Texans	10.00	20.00
NNO Indianapolis Colts	10.00	20.00
NNO Jacksonville Jaguars	10.00	20.00
NNO Kansas City Chiefs	10.00	20.00
NNO Miami Dolphins	10.00	20.00
NNO Minnesota Vikings	10.00	20.00
NNO New England Patriots	10.00	20.00
NNO New Orleans Saints	10.00	20.00
NNO New York Giants	10.00	20.00
NNO New York Jets	10.00	20.00
NNO Oakland Raiders	10.00	20.00
NNO Pittsburgh Steelers	15.00	30.00
NNO San Diego Chargers	10.00	20.00
NNO San Francisco 49ers	10.00	20.00
NNO Seattle Seahawks	10.00	20.00
NNO St. Louis Rams	10.00	20.00
NNO Tampa Bay Buccaneers	10.00	20.00
NNO Tennessee Titans	10.00	20.00
NNO Washington Redskins	10.00	20.00

2004 Fleer Collectibles Transporters NFL 1:80

	EX	NM-MT
NNO Arizona Cardinals	10.00	20.00
NNO Atlanta Falcons	10.00	20.00
NNO Baltimore Ravens	10.00	20.00
NNO Buffalo Bills	10.00	20.00
NNO Carolina Panthers	10.00	20.00
NNO Chicago Bears	10.00	20.00
NNO Cincinnati Bengals	10.00	20.00
NNO Cleveland Browns	10.00	20.00
NNO Dallas Cowboys	15.00	30.00
NNO Denver Broncos	10.00	20.00
NNO Detroit Lions	10.00	20.00
NNO Green Bay Packers	15.00	30.00
NNO Houston Texans	10.00	20.00
NNO Indianapolis Colts	10.00	20.00
NNO Jacksonville Jaguars	10.00	20.00
NNO Kansas City Chiefs	10.00	20.00
NNO Miami Dolphins	10.00	20.00
NNO Minnesota Vikings	10.00	20.00
NNO New England Patriots	10.00	20.00
NNO New England Patriots Super Bowl Champs	10.00	20.00
NNO New Orleans Saints	10.00	20.00
NNO New York Giants	10.00	20.00
NNO New York Jets	10.00	20.00
NNO Oakland Raiders	10.00	20.00
NNO Philadelphia Eagles	10.00	20.00
NNO Pittsburgh Steelers	15.00	30.00
NNO San Diego Chargers	10.00	20.00
NNO San Francisco 49ers	10.00	20.00
NNO Seattle Seahawks	10.00	20.00
NNO St. Louis Rams	10.00	20.00
NNO Tampa Bay Buccaneers	10.00	20.00
NNO Tennessee Titans	10.00	20.00
NNO Washington Redskins	10.00	20.00

2005 Fleer Collectibles Transporters NFL 1:80

	EX	NM-MT
NNO Arizona Cardinals	10.00	20.00
NNO Atlanta Falcons	10.00	20.00
NNO Baltimore Ravens	10.00	20.00
NNO Buffalo Bills	10.00	20.00
NNO Carolina Panthers	10.00	20.00
NNO Chicago Bears	10.00	20.00
NNO Cincinnati Bengals	10.00	20.00
NNO Cleveland Browns	10.00	20.00
NNO Dallas Cowboys	15.00	30.00
NNO Denver Broncos	10.00	20.00
NNO Detroit Lions	10.00	20.00
NNO Green Bay Packers	15.00	30.00
NNO Houston Texans	10.00	20.00
NNO Indianapolis Colts	10.00	20.00
NNO Jacksonville Jaguars	10.00	20.00
NNO Kansas City Chiefs	10.00	20.00
NNO Miami Dolphins	10.00	20.00
NNO Minnesota Vikings	10.00	20.00
NNO New England Patriots	10.00	20.00
NNO New Orleans Saints	10.00	20.00
NNO New York Giants	10.00	20.00
NNO New York Jets	10.00	20.00
NNO Oakland Raiders	10.00	20.00
NNO Philadelphia Eagles	10.00	20.00
NNO Pittsburgh Steelers	15.00	30.00
NNO San Diego Chargers	10.00	20.00
NNO San Francisco 49ers	10.00	20.00
NNO Seattle Seahawks	10.00	20.00
NNO St. Louis Rams	10.00	20.00
NNO Tampa Bay Buccaneers	10.00	20.00
NNO Tennessee Titans	10.00	20.00
NNO Washington Redskins	10.00	20.00

1993 White Rose Transporters NFL 1:80

	EX	NM-MT
NNO Arizona Cardinals	10.00	20.00
NNO Atlanta Falcons	15.00	30.00
NNO Buffalo Bills	20.00	40.00
NNO Chicago Bears	20.00	40.00
NNO Cincinnati Bengals	10.00	20.00
NNO Cleveland Browns	15.00	30.00
NNO Dallas Cowboys	50.00	100.00
NNO Denver Broncos	20.00	40.00
NNO Detroit Lions	15.00	30.00
NNO Green Bay Packers	30.00	60.00
NNO Houston Oilers	20.00	40.00
NNO Indianapolis Colts	15.00	30.00
NNO Kansas City Chiefs	15.00	30.00
NNO Los Angeles Raiders	60.00	120.00
NNO Los Angeles Rams	15.00	30.00
NNO New England Patriots	20.00	40.00
NNO New Orleans Saints	15.00	30.00
NNO New York Giants	15.00	30.00
NNO New York Jets	15.00	30.00
NNO Philadelphia Eagles	15.00	30.00
NNO San Diego Chargers	15.00	30.00
NNO San Francisco 49ers	15.00	30.00
NNO Seattle Seahawks	15.00	30.00
NNO Tampa Bay Buccaneers	15.00	30.00
NNO Washington Redskins	15.00	30.00

1994 White Rose Transporters NFL 1:80

	EX	NM-MT
NNO Arizona Cardinals	10.00	20.00
NNO Atlanta Falcons	15.00	30.00
NNO Buffalo Bills	20.00	40.00
NNO Chicago Bears	20.00	40.00
NNO Cleveland Browns	15.00	30.00
NNO Dallas Cowboys	25.00	50.00
NNO Denver Broncos	50.00	100.00
NNO Detroit Lions	25.00	50.00
NNO Green Bay Packers	200.00	300.00
NNO Houston Oilers	30.00	60.00
NNO Indianapolis Colts	25.00	50.00
NNO Kansas City Chiefs	20.00	40.00
NNO Miami Dolphins	75.00	150.00
NNO Minnesota Vikings	50.00	100.00
NNO Los Angeles Raiders	50.00	100.00
NNO New England Patriots	30.00	60.00
NNO New Orleans Saints	20.00	40.00
NNO New York Giants	30.00	60.00
NNO New York Jets	40.00	80.00
NNO Philadelphia Eagles	50.00	100.00
NNO San Diego Chargers	15.00	30.00
NNO Seattle Seahawks	20.00	40.00
NNO St. Louis Rams	20.00	40.00
NNO Tampa Bay Buccaneers	20.00	40.00
NNO Washington Redskins	40.00	80.00

1995 White Rose Transporters NFL 1:80

	EX	NM-MT
NNO Arizona Cardinals	10.00	20.00
NNO Atlanta Falcons	15.00	30.00
NNO Baltimore Ravens	20.00	40.00
NNO Buffalo Bills	20.00	40.00
NNO Carolina Panthers	30.00	60.00
NNO Chicago Bears	20.00	40.00
NNO Cincinnati Bengals	10.00	20.00
NNO Cleveland Browns	15.00	30.00
NNO Dallas Cowboys	125.00	200.00
NNO Denver Broncos	40.00	80.00
NNO Detroit Lions	15.00	30.00
NNO Green Bay Packers	100.00	175.00
NNO Houston Oilers	20.00	40.00
NNO Indianapolis Colts	20.00	40.00
NNO Jacksonville Jaguars	25.00	50.00
NNO Kansas City Chiefs	40.00	80.00
NNO Miami Dolphins	60.00	120.00
NNO Minnesota Vikings	40.00	80.00
NNO New England Patriots	75.00	150.00
NNO New Orleans Saints	10.00	20.00
NNO New York Giants	30.00	60.00
NNO New York Jets	50.00	100.00
NNO Oakland Raiders	60.00	120.00
NNO Philadelphia Eagles	15.00	30.00
NNO Pittsburgh Steelers	60.00	120.00
NNO San Diego Chargers	15.00	30.00
NNO Seattle Seahawks	30.00	60.00
NNO St. Louis Rams	40.00	80.00
NNO Tampa Bay Buccaneers	30.00	60.00
NNO Washington Redskins	50.00	100.00

1996 White Rose Transporters NFL 1:80

	EX	NM-MT
NNO Miami Dolphins	15.00	30.00

1997 White Rose Transporters NFL 1:80

	EX	NM-MT
NNO Arizona Cardinals	15.00	30.00
NNO Atlanta Falcons	15.00	30.00
NNO Cincinnati Bengals	15.00	30.00
NNO Denver Broncos	15.00	30.00
NNO Detroit Lions	15.00	30.00
NNO Green Bay Packers	20.00	40.00
NNO Jacksonville Jaguars	15.00	30.00
NNO New England Patriots	15.00	30.00
NNO New Orleans Saints	15.00	30.00
NNO Philadelphia Eagles	15.00	30.00
NNO San Diego Chargers	15.00	30.00
NNO San Francisco 49ers	15.00	30.00
NNO Seattle Seahawks	15.00	30.00
NNO Tampa Bay Buccaneers	15.00	30.00
NNO Tennessee Oilers	15.00	30.00
NNO Washington Redskins	15.00	30.00

1998 White Rose Transporters NFL 1:80

	EX	NM-MT
NNO Arizona Cardinals	15.00	30.00
NNO Baltimore Ravens	15.00	30.00
NNO Buffalo Bills	15.00	30.00
NNO Carolina Panthers	15.00	30.00
NNO Detroit Lions	15.00	30.00
NNO Green Bay Packers	20.00	40.00
NNO Indianapolis Colts	15.00	30.00
NNO Jacksonville Jaguars	15.00	30.00
NNO Kansas City Chiefs	15.00	30.00
NNO Miami Dolphins	15.00	30.00
NNO New England Patriots	15.00	30.00
NNO New Orleans Saints	15.00	30.00
NNO New York Giants	15.00	30.00
NNO New York Jets	15.00	30.00
NNO Philadelphia Eagles	15.00	30.00
NNO Pittsburgh Steelers	20.00	40.00
NNO San Diego Chargers	15.00	30.00
NNO Seattle Seahawks	15.00	30.00
NNO St. Louis Rams	15.00	30.00
NNO Washington Redskins	15.00	30.00

1999 White Rose Transporters NFL 1:80

	EX	NM-MT
NNO Arizona Cardinals	10.00	20.00
NNO Buffalo Bills	15.00	30.00
NNO Carolina Panthers	15.00	30.00
NNO Chicago Bears	15.00	30.00
NNO Cincinnati Bengals	15.00	30.00
NNO Cleveland Browns	15.00	30.00
NNO Dallas Cowboys	20.00	40.00
NNO Denver Broncos	15.00	30.00
NNO Detroit Lions	15.00	30.00
NNO Green Bay Packers	20.00	40.00
NNO Indianapolis Colts	15.00	30.00
NNO Jacksonville Jaguars	15.00	30.00
NNO Kansas City Chiefs	15.00	30.00
NNO Miami Dolphins	15.00	30.00
NNO Minnesota Vikings	15.00	30.00
NNO New England Patriots	15.00	30.00
NNO New Orleans Saints	15.00	30.00
NNO New York Giants	15.00	30.00
NNO New York Jets	15.00	30.00
NNO Oakland Raiders	15.00	30.00
NNO Philadelphia Eagles	15.00	30.00
NNO Pittsburgh Steelers	20.00	40.00
NNO San Diego Chargers	15.00	30.00
NNO San Francisco 49ers	15.00	30.00
NNO Seattle Seahawks	15.00	30.00
NNO St. Louis Rams	15.00	30.00
NNO Tampa Bay Buccaneers	15.00	30.00
NNO Tennessee Titans	15.00	30.00
NNO Washington Redskins	15.00	30.00

2000 White Rose Transporters NFL 1:80

	EX	NM-MT
NNO Arizona Cardinals	10.00	20.00
NNO Buffalo Bills	15.00	30.00
NNO Chicago Bears	15.00	30.00
NNO Cincinnati Bengals	15.00	30.00
NNO Cleveland Browns	15.00	30.00
NNO Dallas Cowboys	20.00	40.00
NNO Denver Broncos	15.00	30.00
NNO Detroit Lions	15.00	30.00
NNO Green Bay Packers	20.00	40.00
NNO Indianapolis Colts	15.00	30.00
NNO Jacksonville Jaguars	15.00	30.00
NNO Kansas City Chiefs	15.00	30.00
NNO Miami Dolphins	15.00	30.00
NNO Minnesota Vikings	15.00	30.00
NNO New Orleans Saints	15.00	30.00
NNO New York Giants	15.00	30.00
NNO New York Jets	15.00	30.00
NNO San Diego Chargers	15.00	30.00
NNO San Francisco 49ers	15.00	30.00
NNO St. Louis Rams	15.00	30.00
NNO Tampa Bay Buccaneers	15.00	30.00
NNO Tennessee Titans	15.00	30.00
NNO Washington Redskins	15.00	30.00

2007 Ertl Collectibles Transporters NFL 1:87

	EX	NM-MT
NNO Chicago Bears	10.00	20.00
NNO Cinncinnati Bengals	10.00	20.00
NNO Denver Broncos	10.00	20.00
NNO Indianapolis Colts	10.00	20.00
NNO Minnesota Vikings	10.00	20.00
NNO New York Jets	10.00	20.00
NNO Pittsburgh Steelers	12.50	25.00
NNO Washington Redskins	10.00	20.00

2004 Action Performance Blisters Zamboni NHL 1:50

	EX	NM-MT
NNO Chicago Blackhawks/348	10.00	20.00
NNO Dallas Stars/300	10.00	20.00
NNO St. Louis Blues/300	10.00	20.00

2004 Action Performance Zamboni NHL 1:50

	EX	NM-MT
NNO Boston Bruins	6.00	12.00
NNO Chicago Blackhawks	6.00	12.00
NNO Dallas Stars	6.00	12.00
NNO Detroit Red Wings	6.00	12.00
NNO Minnesota Wild	5.00	10.00
NNO New Jersey Devils '03 Champs	7.50	15.00
NNO New York Rangers	6.00	12.00
NNO Pittsburgh Penguins	6.00	12.00
NNO St. Louis Blues	6.00	12.00

2005 Ertl Collectibles Choppers Series NHL 1:18

NNO Boston Bruins	7.50	15.00
NNO Calgary Flames	7.50	15.00
NNO Chicago Blackhawks	6.00	12.00
NNO Detroit Red Wings	10.00	20.00
NNO Edmonton Oilers	6.00	12.00

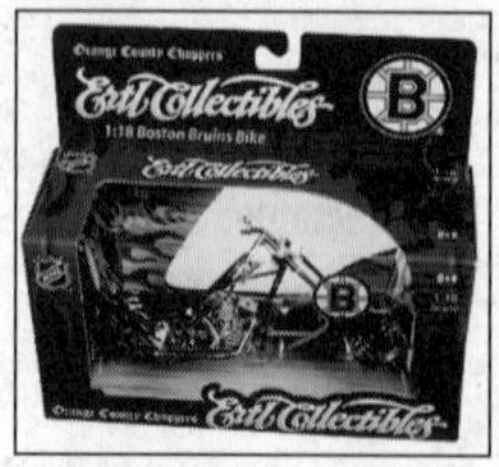

NNO Montreal Canadiens	7.50	15.00
NNO New York Rangers	6.00	12.00
NNO Ottawa Senators	6.00	12.00
NNO Philadelphia Flyers	6.00	12.00
NNO Toronto Maple Leafs	10.00	20.00
NNO Vancouver Canucks	7.50	15.00

2007 Ertl Collectibles Chopper Series NHL 1:18

	EX	NM-MT
NNO Calgary Flames	10.00	20.00
NNO Edmonton Oilers	10.00	20.00
NNO Montreal Canadiens	12.50	25.00
NNO New York Rangers	12.50	25.00
NNO Ottawa Senators	10.00	20.00
NNO Philadelphia Flyers	10.00	20.00
NNO Toronto Maple Leafs	12.50	25.00
NNO Vancouver Canucks	10.00	20.00

2005 Ertl Collectibles Snowmobile Series NHL 1:32

	EX	NM-MT
AVAILABLE IN CANADA ONLY		
NNO Calgary Flames	7.50	15.00
NNO Detroit Red Wings	10.00	20.00
NNO Edmonton Oilers	6.00	12.00
NNO Montreal Canadiens	7.50	15.00
NNO Ottawa Senators	6.00	12.00
NNO Toronto Maple Leafs	10.00	20.00
NNO Vancouver Canucks	7.50	15.00

2005 Ertl Collectibles Zamboni NHL 1:50

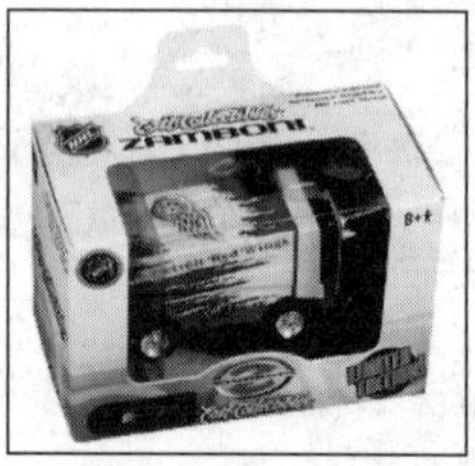

	EX	NM-MT
NNO Anaheim Mighty Ducks	5.00	10.00
NNO Atlanta Thrashers	4.00	8.00
NNO Boston Bruins	5.00	10.00
NNO Buffalo Sabres	4.00	8.00
NNO Calgary Flames	5.00	10.00
NNO Carolina Hurricanes	4.00	8.00
NNO Chicago Blackhawks	5.00	10.00
NNO Colorado Avalanche	6.00	12.00
NNO Columbus Blue Jackets	4.00	8.00
NNO Dallas Stars	5.00	10.00
NNO Detroit Red Wings	6.00	12.00
NNO Edmonton Oilers	4.00	8.00
NNO Florida Panthers	4.00	8.00
NNO Los Angeles Kings	5.00	10.00
NNO Minnesota Wild	4.00	8.00
NNO Montreal Canadiens	5.00	10.00
NNO Nashville Predators	4.00	8.00
NNO New Jersey Devils	5.00	10.00
NNO New York Islanders	5.00	10.00
NNO New York Rangers	5.00	10.00
NNO Ottawa Senators	4.00	8.00
NNO Philadelphia Flyers	4.00	8.00
NNO Phoenix Coyotes	4.00	8.00
NNO Pittsburgh Penguins	5.00	10.00
NNO San Jose Sharks	4.00	8.00
NNO St Louis Blues	5.00	10.00
NNO Tampa Bay Lightning	5.00	10.00
NNO Toronto Maple Leafs	6.00	12.00
NNO Vancouver Canucks	5.00	10.00
NNO Washington Capitals	4.00	8.00

2007 Ertl Collectibles Zamboni NHL 1:50

	EX	NM-MT
NNO Anaheim Ducks	3.00	6.00
NNO Atlanta Thrashers	3.00	6.00
NNO Boston Bruins	5.00	10.00
NNO Buffalo Sabres	4.00	8.00
NNO Colorado Avalanche	5.00	
NNO Columbus Bluejackets	3.00	
NNO Dallas Stars	4.00	
NNO Detroit Red Wings	5.00	
NNO Los Angeles Kings	4.00	
NNO Minnesota Wild	3.00	
NNO Nashville Predators	3.00	
NNO New York Rangers	5.00	
NNO Pittsburgh Penguins	5.00	
NNO St. Louis Blues	4.00	
NNO Toronto Maple Leafs	5.00	
NNO Washington Capitals	4.00	

2005 Ertl Collectibles Cla Rides NHL 1:64

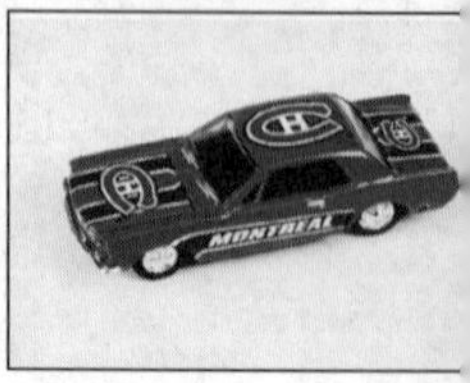

	EX
NNO Calgary Flames	5.00
NNO Detroit Red Wings	6.00
NNO Edmonton Oilers	5.00
NNO Montreal Canadiens	5.00
NNO Ottawa Senators	4.00
NNO Toronto Maple Leafs	6.00
NNO Vancouver Canucks	5.00

2002 Fleer Collectibles Zamboni NHL 1:50

	EX
NNO Detroit Red Wings Stanley Cup	10.00

2003 Fleer Collectibles Zamboni NHL 1:50

	EX
NNO All-Star Game Florida/2500	12.50
NNO Anaheim Mighty Ducks	3.00
NNO Atlanta Thrashers	3.00
NNO Boston Bruins	3.00
NNO Buffalo Sabres	3.00
NNO Calgary Flames	3.00
NNO Carolina Hurricanes	3.00
NNO Chicago Blackhawks	3.00
NNO Colorado Avalanche	4.00
NNO Columbus Blue Jackets	3.00
NNO Dallas Stars	3.00
NNO Detroit Red Wings	4.00
NNO Edminton Oilers	3.00
NNO Florida Panthers	3.00
NNO Los Angeles Kings	3.00
NNO Minnesota Wild	3.00
NNO Montreal Canadiens	3.00
NNO Nashville Predators	3.00
NNO New Jersey Devils	3.00
NNO New Jersey Devils Stanley Cup	5.00
NNO New York Islanders	3.00
NNO New York Rangers	3.00
NNO Ottawa Senators	3.00
NNO Philadelphia Flyers	3.00
NNO Phoenix Coyotes	3.00
NNO Pittsburgh Penguins	3.00
NNO San Jose Sharks	3.00
NNO St. Louis Blues	3.00
NNO Tampa Bay Lightning	3.00
NNO Toronto Maple Leafs	3.00
NNO Vancouver Canucks	3.00
NNO Washington Capitals	3.00

2004 Fleer Collectibles Zamboni NHL 1:50

	EX
NNO All-Star Game Minnesota	10.00
NNO Atlanta Thrashers	3.00
NNO Boston Bruins	3.00
NNO Carolina Hurricanes	3.00
NNO Columbus Blue Jackets	3.00
NNO Detroit Red Wings	4.00
NNO Los Angeles Kings	3.00
NNO Montreal Canadiens	3.00
NNO Nashville Predators	3.00
NNO New Jersey Devils	3.00
NNO New York Islanders	3.00
NNO New York Rangers	3.00
NNO Philadelphia Flyers	3.00
NNO Pittsburgh Penguins	3.00
NNO Washington Capitals	3.00

2002 Fleer Collectibles Transporter NHL 1:80

	EX
NNO Detroit Red Wings Stanley Cup	12.50

2006 Upper Deck Zambo w/card NHL 1:50

	EX
NNO Calgary Flames w/Jarome Iginla	5.00
NNO Detroit Red Wings w/Steve Yzerman	6.00
NNO Edmonton Oilers w/Chris Pronger	5.00
NNO Montreal Canadiens w/Jose Theodore	5.00
NNO New Jersey Devils w/Martin Brodeur	5.00
NNO New York Islanders w/Alexei Yashin	5.00
NNO New York Rangers w/Jaromir Jagr	5.00
NNO Ottawa Senators w/Dany Heatley	5.00
NNO Philadelphia Flyers w/Peter Forsberg	5.00
NNO Pittsburgh Penguins w/Sidney Crosby	7.50
NNO Toronto Maple Leafs w/Eric Lindros	6.00
NNO Vancouver Canucks w/Markus Naslund	5.00

Alphabetical Card Checklist

Ambrose, Marcos

Press Pass
2008 #39 Marcos Ambrose NBS
2008 #87 Marcos Ambrose RR
Press Pass Autographs
2008 #3 Marcos Ambrose NBS P/E
Press Pass Autographs Press Plates Black
2008 #3 Marcos Ambrose NBS P
Press Pass Autographs Press Plates Cyan
2008 #3 Marcos Ambrose NBS E
Press Pass Autographs Press Plates Magenta
2008 #3 Marcos Ambrose NBS P
Press Pass Autographs Press Plates Yellow
2008 #3 Marcos Ambrose NBS E
Press Pass Blue
2008 #B39 Marcos Ambrose NBS
2008 #B87 Marcos Ambrose RR
Press Pass Gold
2008 #G39 Marcos Ambrose NBS
2008 #G87 Marcos Ambrose RR
Press Pass Platinum
2008 #P39 Marcos Ambrose NBS
2008 #P87 Marcos Ambrose RR
Press Pass Signings
2007 #5 Marcos Ambrose NBS
Press Pass Signings Gold
2007 #3 Marcos Ambrose NBS
Press Pass Signings Silver
2007 #2 Marcos Ambrose NBS
Press Pass Speedway
2008 #44 Marcos Ambrose NNS
Press Pass Speedway Gold
2008 #G44 Marcos Ambrose NNS
Press Pass Speedway Holofoil
2008 #H44 Marcos Ambrose NNS
Press Pass Speedway Previews
2008 #EB44 Marcos Ambrose NNS
Press Pass Speedway Red
2008 #R44 Marcos Ambrose NNS
Press Pass Stealth
2007 #37 Marcos Ambrose NBS RC
Press Pass Stealth Chrome
2007 #37 Marcos Ambrose NBS RC
Press Pass Stealth Chrome Exclusives
2007 #X37 Marcos Ambrose NBS
Press Pass Stealth Chrome Platinum
2007 #P37 Marcos Ambrose NBS
Press Pass Stealth Previews
2007 #EB37 Marcos Ambrose NBS
Press Pass Top Prospects Gloves
2007 #MA-G Marcos Ambrose
Press Pass Top Prospects Sheet Metal
2007 #MA-SM Marcos Ambrose
Press Pass Top Prospects Sheet Metal-Tire
2007 #MA-ST Marcos Ambrose
Press Pass Top Prospects Shoes
2007 #MA-S Marcos Ambrose
Press Pass Top Prospects Tire Autographs
2007 #MA-A Marcos Ambrose
Press Pass Top Prospects Tires Gold
2007 #MA-T Marcos Ambrose
Press Pass Top Prospects Tires Silver
2007 #MA-T Marcos Ambrose
Traks
2007 #38 Marcos Ambrose NBS RC
Traks Gold
2007 #G38 Marcos Ambrose NBS
Traks Holofoil
2007 #H38 Marcos Ambrose NBS
Traks Previews
2007 #EB38 Marcos Ambrose NBS
Traks Red
2007 #R38 Marcos Ambrose NBS
Wheels American Thunder Thunder Strokes
2007 #2 Marcos Ambrose
Wheels American Thunder Thunder Strokes Press Plates Black
2007 #2 Marcos Ambrose
Wheels American Thunder Thunder Strokes Press Plates Cyan
2007 #2 Marcos Ambrose
Wheels American Thunder Thunder Strokes Press Plates Magenta
2007 #2 Marcos Ambrose
Wheels American Thunder Thunder Strokes Press Plates Yellow
2007 #2 Marcos Ambrose
Wheels Autographs
2008 #2 Marcos Ambrose NBS HG
Wheels Autographs Press Plates Black
2008 #2 Marcos Ambrose NBS HG
Wheels Autographs Press Plates Cyan
2008 #2 Marcos Ambrose NBS HG
Wheels Autographs Press Plates Magenta
2008 #2 Marcos Ambrose NBS HG
Wheels Autographs Press Plates Yellow
2008 #2 Marcos Ambrose NBS HG
Wheels High Gear
2008 #28 Marcos Ambrose NBS
Wheels High Gear MPH
2008 #M28 Marcos Ambrose NBS

Biffle, Greg

eTopps
2003 #19 Greg Biffle/2802
Maxx
2000 #71 Greg Biffle RF
Post Cereal
2004 #1 Greg Biffle
Press Pass
2001 #73 Greg Biffle
2002 #37 Greg Biffle NBS
2003 #34 Greg Biffle NBS
2004 #1 Greg Biffle
2004 #80 The Drive for Five WCS
2004 #90 Greg Biffle RR
2005 #11 Greg Biffle
2005 #48 Greg Biffle
2006 #12 Greg Biffle
2006 #78 Greg Biffle's Car OTW
2006 #86 Greg Biffle NS
2006 #92 Greg Biffle NS
2006 #110 Greg Biffle TT
2007 #12 Greg Biffle
2007 #85 Greg Biffle NS
2007 #102 Greg Biffle U
2008 #15 Greg Biffle
Press Pass Autographs
2001 #2 Greg Biffle
2002 #6 Greg Biffle
2003 #4 Greg Biffle E/P
2004 #3 Greg Biffle P
2005 #2 Greg Biffle BGN E/P
2005 #3 Greg Biffle NCS E/P
2007 #1 Greg Biffle NC P
2008 #5 Greg Biffle NC P/E
Press Pass Autographs Press Plates Black
2008 #4 Greg Biffle NC P
Press Pass Autographs Press Plates Cyan
2008 #4 Greg Biffle NC P
Press Pass Autographs Press Plates Magenta
2008 #4 Greg Biffle NC E
Press Pass Autographs Press Plates Yellow
2007 #1 Greg Biffle NC
2008 #4 Greg Biffle NC E
Press Pass Blue
2006 #B12 Greg Biffle
2006 #B78 Greg Biffle's car OTW
2006 #B86 Greg Biffle NS
2006 #B92 Greg Biffle NS
2006 #B110 Greg Biffle TT
2007 #B12 Greg Biffle
2007 #B85 Greg Biffle NS
2007 #B102 Greg Biffle U
2008 #B15 Greg Biffle
Press Pass Burning Rubber Drivers
2007 #BRD8 Greg Biffle Darlington 5-13
Press Pass Burning Rubber Drivers Gold
2007 #BRD8 Greg Biffle Darlington 5-13
Press Pass Burning Rubber Team
2007 #BRT8 Greg Biffle Darlington 5-13
Press Pass Coca Cola AutoZone
2006 #GB Greg Biffle
Press Pass Collectors Series Making the Show
2006 #MS15 Greg Biffle
Press Pass Cup Chase
2004 #CCR17 Greg Biffle
2005 #CCR11 Greg Biffle Winner
2006 #CCR2 Greg Biffle
2007 #CCR9 Greg Biffle
2008 #CC17 Greg Biffle
Press Pass Cup Chase Prizes
2004 #CCR17 Greg Biffle
2005 #CCP11 Greg Biffle
Press Pass Eclipse
2004 #19 Greg Biffle
2004 #68 Greg Biffle WCS
2005 #17 Greg Biffle
2005 #74 Greg Biffle LL
2006 #2 Greg Biffle
2006 #46 Greg Biffle P
2006 #61 Greg Biffle TN
2006 #65 NCS Top-10 BA
2006 #69 Tony Stewart BA
2007 #13 Greg Biffle
2008 #13 Greg Biffle
2008 #48 Greg Biffle NS
Press Pass Eclipse Destination WIN
2004 #18 Greg Biffle
2005 #20 Greg Biffle
2005 #27 Greg Biffle
Press Pass Eclipse Gold
2007 #G13 Greg Biffle
2008 #G13 Greg Biffle
2008 #G48 Greg Biffle NS
Press Pass Eclipse Hyperdrive
2007 #HD3 Greg Biffle
Press Pass Eclipse Maxim
2004 #MX11 Greg Biffle
Press Pass Eclipse Previews
2004 #19 Greg Biffle
2005 #EB17 Greg Biffle
2005 #EB74 Greg Biffle LL/1
2006 #E2 Greg Biffle
2006 #EB61 Greg Biffle TN
2007 #EB13 Greg Biffle
2008 #EB13 Greg Biffle
Press Pass Eclipse Racing Champions
2006 #RC2 Greg Biffle
2007 #RC6 Greg Biffle
2007 #RC22 Greg Biffle
Press Pass Eclipse Red
2007 #R13 Greg Biffle
2008 #R13 Greg Biffle
2008 #R48 Greg Biffle NS
Press Pass Eclipse Samples
2004 #19 Greg Biffle
2004 #68 Greg Biffle WCS
2005 #17 Greg Biffle
2005 #74 Greg Biffle LL
Press Pass Eclipse Skidmarks
2004 #SM12 Greg Biffle
2006 #SM13 Greg Biffle
2007 #SM15 Greg Biffle
Press Pass Eclipse Skidmarks Holofoil
2004 #SM12 Greg Biffle
2006 #SM13 Greg Biffle
2007 #SM15 Greg Biffle
Press Pass Eclipse Stellar
2008 #ST12 Greg Biffle
Press Pass Eclipse Teammates Autographs
2004 #3 G.Biffle/M.Martin
2006 #1 G.Biffle/M.Kenseth
2007 #6 Biffle/Edwards/Kenseth
Press Pass Eclipse Under Cover Autographs
2006 #GB Greg Biffle/16
2007 #UC-GB Greg Biffle/16
Press Pass Eclipse Under Cover Cars
2006 #UCT14 Greg Biffle
Press Pass Eclipse Under Cover Double Cover
2006 #DC3 M.Martin/G.Biffle
2006 #DC9 G.Biffle/C.Edwards
Press Pass Eclipse Under Cover Double Cover Holofoil
2006 #DC3 M.Martin/G.Biffle
2006 #DC9 G.Biffle/C.Edwards
Press Pass Eclipse Under Cover Double Cover Name
2007 #DC1 Edwards/Biffle
Press Pass Eclipse Under Cover Double Cover NASCAR
2007 #DC1 Edwards/Biffle
Press Pass Eclipse Under Cover Drivers
2007 #UCD6 Greg Biffle
Press Pass Eclipse Under Cover Drivers Eclipse
2007 #UCD6 Greg Biffle
Press Pass Eclipse Under Cover Drivers Gold
2006 #UCD14 Greg Biffle
Press Pass Eclipse Under Cover Drivers Holofoil
2006 #UCD14 Greg Biffle
Press Pass Eclipse Under Cover Drivers Name
2007 #UCD6 Greg Biffle
Press Pass Eclipse Under Cover Drivers NASCAR
2007 #UCD6 Greg Biffle
Press Pass Eclipse Under Cover Drivers Silver
2006 #UCD14 Greg Biffle
Press Pass Eclipse Under Cover Teams
2007 #UCT6 Greg Biffle
Press Pass Eclipse Under Cover Teams NASCAR
2007 #UCT6 Greg Biffle
Press Pass Gold
2006 #G12 Greg Biffle
2006 #G78 Greg Biffle's car OTW
2006 #G86 Greg Biffle NS
2006 #G92 Greg Biffle NS
2006 #G110 Greg Biffle TT
2007 #G12 Greg Biffle
2007 #G85 Greg Biffle NS
2007 #G102 Greg Biffle U
2008 #G15 Greg Biffle
Press Pass Gold Holofoil
2003 #P34 Greg Biffle
Press Pass Hot Treads
2004 #HTR8 Greg Biffle
Press Pass Hot Treads Holofoil
2004 #HTR8 Greg Biffle
Press Pass Legends Autographs Blue
2006 #4 Greg Biffle/50
Press Pass Making the Show Collector's Series
2004 #MS10 Greg Biffle
Press Pass Millennium
2001 #73 Greg Biffle
Press Pass Optima
2002 #31 Greg Biffle
2003 #1 Greg Biffle CRC
2004 #1 Greg Biffle
2004 #98 Greg Biffle NP
2005 #2 Greg Biffle
2005 #2B Greg Biffle Cup Chase
2005 #68 Greg Biffle DP
2005 #94 Greg Biffle's Car RTV
2006 #14 Greg Biffle
Press Pass Optima Corporate Cuts Cars
2005 #CCT5 Greg Biffle
Press Pass Optima Corporate Cuts Drivers
2005 #CCD5 Greg Biffle
Press Pass Optima Fan Favorite
2003 #FF17 Greg Biffle
2004 #FF1 Greg Biffle
2005 #FF2 Greg Biffle
Press Pass Optima Gold
2002 #31 Greg Biffle
2003 #G1 Greg Biffle
2004 #G1 Greg Biffle
2004 #G98 Greg Biffle NP
2005 #G2 Greg Biffle
2005 #G68 Greg Biffle DP
2005 #G94 Greg Biffle's Car RTV
2006 #G14 Greg Biffle
Press Pass Optima Pole Position
2006 #PP3 Greg Biffle
Press Pass Optima Previews
2003 #1 Greg Biffle
2004 #EB1 Greg Biffle
2005 #2 Greg Biffle
2006 #EB14 Greg Biffle
Press Pass Optima Promos
2002 #31 Greg Biffle
Press Pass Optima Q and A
2003 #QA5 Greg Biffle
Press Pass Optima Samples
2002 #31 Greg Biffle
2003 #1 Greg Biffle
2004 #1 Greg Biffle
2004 #98 Greg Biffle NP
2005 #2 Greg Biffle
2005 #68 Greg Biffle DP
2005 #94 Greg Biffle RTV
Press Pass Platinum
2002 #37 Greg Biffle NBS
2004 #P1 Greg Biffle
2004 #P80 The Drive for Five WCS
2004 #P90 Greg Biffle RR
2005 #P11 Greg Biffle
2005 #P48 Greg Biffle
2006 #P12 Greg Biffle
2006 #P78 Greg Biffle's car OTW
2006 #P86 Greg Biffle NS
2006 #P92 Greg Biffle NS
2006 #P110 Greg Biffle TT
2007 #P12 Greg Biffle
2007 #P85 Greg Biffle NS
2007 #P102 Greg Biffle U
2008 #P15 Greg Biffle
Press Pass Premium
2003 #31 Greg Biffle CRC
2003 #45 Greg Biffle's Car
2004 #11 Greg Biffle
2004 #49 Greg Biffle NS
2004 #58 Greg Biffle CC
2005 #2 Greg Biffle
2006 #1 Greg Biffle
2006 #40 Greg Biffle's Car M
2006 #64 Greg Biffle C
2007 #14 Greg Biffle
2007 #60 Greg Biffle RTTC
2008 #13 Greg Biffle
2008 #61 Greg Biffle F
Press Pass Premium Previews
2003 #31 Greg Biffle
2004 #11 Greg Biffle
2008 #EB13 Greg Biffle
Press Pass Premium Red
2007 #R14 Greg Biffle
2007 #R60 Greg Biffle RTTC
2008 #13 Greg Biffle
2008 #61 Greg Biffle F
Press Pass Premium Red Reflectors
2003 #31 Greg Biffle
2003 #45 Greg Biffle's Car
Press Pass Premium Samples
2003 #31 Greg Biffle
2003 #45 Greg Biffle's Car
2004 #11 Greg Biffle
2004 #49 Greg Biffle NS
2005 #2 Greg Biffle
Press Pass Previews
2004 #1 Greg Biffle
2006 #EB12 Greg Biffle
2007 #EB12 Greg Biffle
2008 #EB15 Greg Biffle
Press Pass Previews Green
2005 #EB11 Greg Biffle
Press Pass Samples
2003 #34 Greg Biffle NBS
2004 #1 Greg Biffle
2004 #80 The Drive for Five WCS
2004 #90 Greg Biffle RR
2005 #11 Greg Biffle
2005 #48 Greg Biffle
Press Pass Signings
2001 #3 Greg Biffle V/S
2002 #4 Greg Biffle O/S/V
2003 #5 Greg Biffle O/P/S/T/V
2004 #2 Greg Biffle BGN T/V
2004 #3 Greg Biffle NC O/S/T/V
2006 #4 Greg Biffle NC S
2007 #7 Greg Biffle NC
Press Pass Signings Gold
2002 #5 Greg Biffle O/S/V
2003 #5 Greg Biffle O/P/S/T/V
2004 #2 Greg Biffle BGN S/T/V
2004 #3 Greg Biffle NC O/S/T/V
2006 #4 Greg Biffle NC S
2007 #4 Greg Biffle NC
Press Pass Signings Press Plates Black
2007 #4 Greg Biffle
Press Pass Signings Silver
2006 #4 Greg Biffle NC S
2007 #3 Greg Biffle NC
Press Pass Snapshots
2004 #SN1 Greg Biffle
2005 #SN1 Greg Biffle
2007 #SN1 Greg Biffle
Press Pass Speedway
2008 #21 Greg Biffle
Press Pass Speedway Gold
2008 #G21 Greg Biffle
Press Pass Speedway Holofoil
2008 #H21 Greg Biffle
Press Pass Speedway Previews
2008 #EB21 Greg Biffle
Press Pass Speedway Red
2008 #R21 Greg Biffle
Press Pass Stealth
2001 #46 Greg Biffle BGN
2002 #46 Greg Biffle
2004 #43 Greg Biffle
2004 #44 Greg Biffle's Car
2004 #45 Greg Biffle
2004 #79 Greg Biffle WW
2005 #28 Greg Biffle
2005 #31 Greg Biffle's Car
2005 #34 Greg Biffle
2006 #1 Greg Biffle
2006 #37 Greg Biffle NBS
2006 #48 17/6/16/26/99 TM
2006 #81 Greg Biffle DD
2007 #1 Greg Biffle
2007 #58 Greg Biffle's Crew GC
2007 #69 Edwards/Biffle/Kenseth/McMurray/Ragan
2007 #80 Greg Biffle DD
2008 #1 Greg Biffle
2008 #58 Greg Biffle's Car GC
2008 #70 Greg Biffle Jamie McMurray Carl Edwards Matt Kenseth David Ragan
2008 #73 Greg Biffle DD
Press Pass Stealth Autographed Hat Entry
2006 #PPH1 Greg Biffle
Press Pass Stealth Battle Armor Drivers
2007 #BAD2 Greg Biffle
Press Pass Stealth Battle Armor Teams
2007 #BAT2 Greg Biffle
Press Pass Stealth Chrome
2007 #1 Greg Biffle
2007 #58 Greg Biffle's Crew GC
2007 #69 Edwards/Biffle/Kenseth/McMurray/Ragan
2007 #80 Greg Biffle DD
2008 #1 Greg Biffle
2008 #58 Greg Biffle's Car GC
2008 #70 Greg Biffle Jamie McMurray Carl Edwards Matt Kenseth David Ragan
2008 #73 Greg Biffle DD
Press Pass Stealth Chrome Exclusives
2007 #X58 Greg Biffle's Crew GC
2007 #X69 Edwards/Biffle/Kenseth/McMurray/Ragan
2007 #X80 Greg Biffle DD
2007 #X1 Greg Biffle
2008 #1 Greg Biffle
2008 #58 Greg Biffle's Car GC
2008 #70 Greg Biffle Jamie McMurray Carl Edwards Matt Kenseth David Ragan
2008 #73 Greg Biffle DD
Press Pass Stealth Chrome Exclusives Gold
2008 #1 Greg Biffle
2008 #58 Greg Biffle's Car GC
2008 #70 Greg Biffle Jamie McMurray Carl Edwards Matt Kenseth David Ragan
2008 #73 Greg Biffle DD
Press Pass Stealth Chrome Platinum
2007 #P58 Greg Biffle's Crew GC
2007 #P69 Edwards/Biffle/Kenseth/McMurray/Ragan
2007 #P80 Greg Biffle DD
2007 #P1 Greg Biffle
Press Pass Stealth Corporate Cuts
2006 #CCD1 Greg Biffle
Press Pass Stealth EFX
2003 #FX2 Greg Biffle
2006 #EFX10 Greg Biffle 1:14
Press Pass Stealth Gear Grippers Cars
2005 #GGT17 Greg Biffle
Press Pass Stealth Gear Grippers Drivers
2004 #GGD18 Greg Biffle
2005 #GGD17 Greg Biffle
Press Pass Stealth Gear Grippers Drivers Retail
2004 #GGT18 Greg Biffle
Press Pass Stealth Gold
2002 #46 Greg Biffle
Press Pass Stealth Holofoils
2001 #46 Greg Biffle BGN
Press Pass Stealth Hot Pass
2006 #HP1 Greg Biffle
Press Pass Stealth Maximum Access
2007 #MA2 Greg Biffle
2008 #MA2 Greg Biffle
Press Pass Stealth Maximum Access Autographs
2007 #MA2 Greg Biffle
2008 #MA2 Greg Biffle
Press Pass Stealth No Boundaries
2003 #NB9 Greg Biffle
Press Pass Stealth Previews
2005 #28 Greg Biffle
2005 #31 Greg Biffle's Car
2005 #34 Greg Biffle
2006 #1 Greg Biffle
2007 #EB1 Greg Biffle
2008 #1 Greg Biffle
Press Pass Stealth Profile
2004 #P9 Greg Biffle 1:14
Press Pass Stealth Retail
2006 #1 Greg Biffle
2006 #37 Greg Biffle NBS
2006 #48 17/6/16/26/99 TM
2006 #81 Greg Biffle DD
Press Pass Stealth Samples
2002 #46 Greg Biffle
2004 #X43 Greg Biffle
2004 #X44 Greg Biffle's Car
2004 #X45 Greg Biffle
2004 #X79 Greg Biffle WW
2005 #28 Greg Biffle
2005 #31 Greg Biffle's Car
2005 #34 Greg Biffle
Press Pass Stealth X-Ray
2004 #43 Greg Biffle
2004 #44 Greg Biffle's Car
2004 #45 Greg Biffle
2004 #79 Greg Biffle WW
2005 #X28 Greg Biffle
2005 #X31 Greg Biffle's Car
2005 #X34 Greg Biffle
2006 #X1 Greg Biffle
2006 #X37 Greg Biffle NBS
2006 #X48 17/6/16/26/99 TM
2006 #X81 Greg Biffle DD
Press Pass Top 25 Drivers & Rides
2006 #C10 Greg Biffle's Car
2006 #D10 Greg Biffle
Press Pass Trackside
2001 #57 Greg Biffle
2003 #1 Greg Biffle CRC
2003 #66 Greg Biffle in Pits
2003 #78 Mart/J.Bur/Bif/Kens/Bus TM
2004 #12 Greg Biffle
2004 #57 Greg Biffle's Car HS
2004 #68 Burt/Kens/Mart/Busch/Bif. TM
2004 #101 Greg Biffle TT
2005 #26 Greg Biffle
Press Pass Trackside Die Cuts
2001 #57 Greg Biffle
Press Pass Trackside Gold Holofoil
2003 #P1 Greg Biffle
2003 #P66 Greg Biffle's Crew
2003 #P78 Martin/J.Burton/Biffle/Kenseth/Busch
Press Pass Trackside Golden
2001 #57 Greg Biffle
2003 #G1 Greg Biffle
2004 #G12 Greg Biffle
2004 #G57 Greg Biffle's Car HS
2004 #G68 Burt/Kens/Mart/Busch/Biffle TM
2004 #G101 Greg Biffle TT
2005 #G26 Greg Biffle
Press Pass Trackside Hat Giveaway
2003 #PPH2 Greg Biffle
2004 #PPH1 Greg Biffle
2005 #PPH44 Greg Biffle
Press Pass Trackside Hot Pass
2004 #HP1 Greg Biffle
2004 #HP20 Greg Biffle BGN
Press Pass Trackside Hot Pass National
2004 #HP1 Greg Biffle
2004 #HP20 Greg Biffle BGN
Press Pass Trackside License to Drive
2003 #LD1 Greg Biffle
Press Pass Trackside Previews
2003 #1 Greg Biffle
2004 #EB12 Greg Biffle
2005 #26 Greg Biffle
Press Pass Trackside Runnin n' Gunnin
2004 #RG8 Greg Biffle
Press Pass Trackside Samples
2003 #1 Greg Biffle
2003 #66 Greg Biffle in Pits
2003 #78 Mart/J.Bur/Bif/Kens/Bus TM
2004 #12 Greg Biffle
2004 #57 Greg Biffle's Car HS
2004 #68 Burt/Kens/Mart/Busch/Biffle TM
2004 #101 Greg Biffle TT
2005 #26 Greg Biffle
Press Pass UMI Cup Chase
2005 #1 Cup Chase Drivers CL
2005 #3 Greg Biffle
SP Authentic Sign of the Times
2000 #BI Greg Biffle
SP Authentic Sign of the Times Gold
2000 #BI Greg Biffle
TRAKS
2006 #1 Greg Biffle
2006 #44 Greg Biffle's Car
2006 #103 Greg Biffle's Car PS
2007 #1 Greg Biffle
TRAKS Autographs
2006 #1 Greg Biffle NC
TRAKS Autographs 100
2006 #1 Greg Biffle NC
TRAKS Autographs 25
2006 #1 Greg Biffle NC
Traks Corporate Cuts Driver
2007 #CCD11 Greg Biffle
Traks Corporate Cuts Patch
2007 #CCD11 Greg Biffle/15
Traks Corporate Cuts Team
2007 #CCT11 Greg Biffle
Traks Driver's Seat
2007 #DS16 Greg Biffle
2007 #DS16B Greg Biffle VAR
Traks Driver's Seat National
2007 #DS16 Greg Biffle
Traks Gold
2007 #G1 Greg Biffle
Traks Holofoil
2007 #H1 Greg Biffle
Traks Previews
2007 #EB1 Greg Biffle
Traks Red
2007 #R1 Greg Biffle
TRAKS Stickers
2006 #16 Greg Biffle
VIP
2004 #19 Greg Biffle
2005 #1 Greg Biffle
2005 #44 Greg Biffle SG
2005 #49 Greg Biffle SG
2005 #52 Greg Biffle SG
2006 #1 Greg Biffle
2006 #50 Greg Biffle SG
2006 #63 Greg Biffle BTN
2006 #68 Greg Biffle RF
2007 #2 Greg Biffle
VIP Making the Show
2003 #MS7 Greg Biffle
2004 #MS10 Greg Biffle
2005 #10 Greg Biffle
2006 #MS15 Greg Biffle
VIP Previews
2004 #EB19 Greg Biffle
2005 #EB1 Greg Biffle
2007 #EB2 Greg Biffle
VIP Samples
2004 #19 Greg Biffle
2005 #1 Greg Biffle
2005 #44 Greg Biffle SG
2005 #49 Greg Biffle SG
2005 #52 Greg Biffle SG
Wheels
1999 #91 Greg Biffle CTS RC
Wheels American Thunder
2005 #2 Greg Biffle
2006 #1 Greg Biffle
2006 #64 Greg Biffle SS
2006 #84 Greg Biffle NN
2007 #2 Greg Biffle
2007 #42 Greg Biffle's Car DT
2007 #67 Greg Biffle BP
Wheels American Thunder American Eagle
2004 #AE7 Greg Biffle
2005 #AE12 Greg Biffle
Wheels American Thunder American Muscle
2005 #AM7 Greg Biffle
Wheels American Thunder Autographed Hat Instant Winner
2007 #AH2 Greg Biffle
Wheels American Thunder Double Hat
2006 #DH1 Greg Biffle
Wheels American Thunder Golden Eagle
2004 #AE7 Greg Biffle
2005 #GE12 Greg Biffle
Wheels American Thunder Head to Toe

2005 #HT2 Greg Biffle
Wheels American Thunder Heads Up Manufacturer
2003 #HUM24 Greg Biffle
Wheels American Thunder Heads Up Team
2003 #HUT22 Greg Biffle/90
Wheels American Thunder Heads Up Winston
2003 #HUW24 Greg Biffle
Wheels American Thunder Post Mark
2004 #PM10 Greg Biffle
Wheels American Thunder Previews
2005 #2 Greg Biffle
2006 #EB1 Greg Biffle
2007 #EB2 Greg Biffle
Wheels American Thunder Pushin Pedal
2004 #PP1 Greg Biffle
2005 #PP1 Greg Biffle
Wheels American Thunder Rookie Class
2003 #RC2 Greg Biffle WIN
Wheels American Thunder Rookie Class Prizes
2003 #RC2 Greg Biffle
Wheels American Thunder Rookie Thunder
2003 #RT2 Greg Biffle
Wheels American Thunder Samples
2005 #2 Greg Biffle
Wheels American Thunder Thunder Strokes
2007 #3 Greg Biffle
Wheels American Thunder Thunder Strokes Press Plates Black
2007 #3 Greg Biffle
Wheels American Thunder Thunder Strokes Press Plates Cyan
2007 #3 Greg Biffle
Wheels American Thunder Thunder Strokes Press Plates Magenta
2007 #3 Greg Biffle
Wheels American Thunder Thunder Strokes Press Plates Yellow
2007 #3 Greg Biffle
Wheels American Thunder Triple Hat
2003 #TH14 Greg Biffle
2004 #TH26 Greg Biffle
2005 #TH1 Greg Biffle
2007 #TH1 Greg Biffle
Wheels Autographs
2003 #3 Greg Biffle Blue BGN HG
2003 #4 Greg Biffle Red WC AT
2004 #2 Greg Biffle HG
2005 #2 Greg Biffle BGN
2005 #3 Greg Biffle NC
2006 #4 Greg Biffle
2007 #1 Greg Biffle NC HG
2008 #3 Greg Biffle NC HG
Wheels Autographs Press Plates Black
2007 #1 Greg Biffle NC
2008 #3 Greg Biffle NC HG
Wheels Autographs Press Plates Cyan
2007 #1 Greg Biffle NC
2008 #3 Greg Biffle NC HG
Wheels Autographs Press Plates Magenta
2007 #1 Greg Biffle NC
2008 #3 Greg Biffle NC HG
Wheels Autographs Press Plates Yellow
2007 #1 Greg Biffle NC
2008 #3 Greg Biffle NC HG
Wheels Golden
1999 #91 Greg Biffle
Wheels High Gear
2003 #41 Greg Biffle CRC
2003 #69 Greg Biffle NA
2004 #1 Greg Biffle
2005 #9 Greg Biffle
2005 #31 Greg Biffle
2006 #2 Greg Biffle
2007 #12 Greg Biffle
2007 #84 Greg Biffle's Car C
2008 #14 Greg Biffle
Wheels High Gear Autographs
2002 #4 Greg Biffle
Wheels High Gear Blue Hawaii SCDA Promos
2003 #41 Greg Biffle
2003 #69 Greg Biffle BSC
Wheels High Gear Driven
2007 #DR10 Greg Biffle
2008 #DR14 Greg Biffle
Wheels High Gear Final Standings
2008 #F14 Greg Biffle/14
Wheels High Gear Final Standings Gold
2007 #FS12 Greg Biffle/13
Wheels High Gear First Gear
2003 #F41 Greg Biffle
2003 #F69 Greg Biffle BSC
Wheels High Gear Flag to Flag
2005 #FF1 Greg Biffle
2006 #FF1 Greg Biffle
Wheels High Gear High Groove
2004 #HG1 Greg Biffle
Wheels High Gear MPH
2003 #M41 Greg Biffle
2003 #M69 Greg Biffle BSC
2004 #M1 Greg Biffle
2005 #M9 Greg Biffle
2005 #M31 Greg Biffle
2006 #M2 Greg Biffle
2007 #M12 Greg Biffle
2007 #M84 Greg Biffle's Car C
2008 #M14 Greg Biffle
Wheels High Gear Previews
2003 #41 Greg Biffle
2004 #1 Greg Biffle
2007 #EB12 Greg Biffle
2008 #EB14 Greg Biffle
Wheels High Gear Previews Green
2005 #EB9 Greg Biffle
2005 #EB31 Greg Biffle
2006 #EB2 Greg Biffle
Wheels High Gear Samples
2003 #41 Greg Biffle
2003 #69 Greg Biffle BSC
2004 #1 Greg Biffle
2005 #9 Greg Biffle
2005 #31 Greg Biffle
2005 #44 Greg Biffle's Car C
Wheels High Gear Top Tier
2006 #TT2 Greg Biffle

Wheels Solos
1999 #91 Greg Biffle

Bowyer, Clint

Press Pass
2006 #32 Clint Bowyer NBS
2007 #16 Clint Bowyer
2007 #37 Clint Bowyer NBS
2007 #64 Clint Bowyer RR
2008 #9 Clint Bowyer
2008 #118 Clint Bowyer Top 12
2008 #0 Cup Chase Matt Kenseth Tony Stewart Jeff Gordon Jimmie Johnson Denny Hamlin Kurt Busch Kevin Harvick Carl Edwards Kyle Busch Martin Truex Jr. Jeff Burton Clint Bowyer
Press Pass Autographs
2005 #5 Clint Bowyer E/P
2006 #5 Clint Bowyer NBS
2007 #3 Clint Bowyer NC P
2008 #8 Clint Bowyer NC P/E
Press Pass Autographs Press Plates Black
2007 #1 Clint Bowyer NC
2008 #7 Clint Bowyer NC E
Press Pass Autographs Press Plates Cyan
2007 #1 Clint Bowyer NC
2008 #7 Clint Bowyer NC P
Press Pass Autographs Press Plates Magenta
2007 #1 Clint Bowyer NC
2008 #7 Clint Bowyer NC E
Press Pass Autographs Press Plates Yellow
2007 #2 Clint Bowyer NC
2008 #7 Clint Bowyer NC P
Press Pass Blue
2006 #B32 Clint Bowyer NBS
2007 #B16 Clint Bowyer
2007 #B37 Clint Bowyer NBS
2007 #B64 Clint Bowyer RR
2008 #B9 Clint Bowyer
2008 #B118 Clint Bowyer Top 12
Press Pass Burnouts
2006 #HT8 Clint Bowyer
Press Pass Burnouts Holofoil
2006 #HT8 Clint Bowyer
Press Pass Collector's Series Box Set
2007 #SB1 Clint Bowyer
Press Pass Collectors Series Sunday Best
2007 #CB1 Clint Bowyer
Press Pass Cup Chase
2008 #CC7 Clint Bowyer
Press Pass Cup Chase Prizes
2007 #CC12 Clint Bowyer
Press Pass Eclipse
2006 #29 Clint Bowyer NBS
2007 #16 Clint Bowyer
2008 #3 Clint Bowyer
2008 #31 Clint Bowyer RM
2008 #44 Clint Bowyer TO
2008 #46 Clint Bowyer NS
2008 #75 Top 10 Drivers SO
Press Pass Eclipse Gold
2007 #G16 Clint Bowyer
2008 #G3 Clint Bowyer
2008 #G31 Clint Bowyer RM
2008 #G44 Clint Bowyer TO
2008 #G46 Clint Bowyer NS
2008 #G75 Top 10 Drivers SO
Press Pass Eclipse Previews
2006 #EB29 Clint Bowyer NBS
2007 #EB16 Clint Bowyer
2008 #EB3 Clint Bowyer
2008 #EB31 Clint Bowyer RM
2008 #EB75 Top 10 Drivers SO
Press Pass Eclipse Racing Champions
2006 #RC23 Clint Bowyer NBS
2007 #RC21 Clint Bowyer
Press Pass Eclipse Red
2007 #R16 Clint Bowyer
2008 #R3 Clint Bowyer
2008 #R31 Clint Bowyer RM
2008 #R44 Clint Bowyer TO
2008 #R46 Clint Bowyer NS
2008 #R75 Top 10 Drivers SO
Press Pass Eclipse Skidmarks
2007 #SM14 Clint Bowyer
Press Pass Eclipse Skidmarks Holofoil
2007 #SM14 Clint Bowyer
Press Pass Eclipse Stellar
2008 #ST7 Clint Bowyer
2008 #ST19 Clint Bowyer
Press Pass Eclipse Teammates Autographs
2007 #8 K.Harvick/C.Bowyer/J.Burton
2008 #BBH Clint Bowyer Jeff Burton Kevin Harvick
Press Pass Gold
2006 #G32 Clint Bowyer NBS
2007 #G16 Clint Bowyer
2007 #G37 Clint Bowyer NBS
2007 #G64 Clint Bowyer RR
2008 #G9 Clint Bowyer
2008 #G118 Clint Bowyer Top 12
Press Pass Optima
2004 #30 Clint Bowyer RC
2005 #31 Clint Bowyer BGN
2005 #53 Clint Bowyer YG
2006 #2 Clint Bowyer CRC
2006 #35 Clint Bowyer NBS
2006 #73 Clint Bowyer YG
Press Pass Optima Fan Favorite
2006 #FF1 Clint Bowyer
Press Pass Optima Gold
2004 #G30 Clint Bowyer
2005 #G31 Clint Bowyer BGN
2005 #G53 Clint Bowyer YG
2006 #G2 Clint Bowyer
2006 #G35 Clint Bowyer NBS
2006 #G73 Clint Bowyer YG
Press Pass Optima Previews
2004 #EB30 Clint Bowyer
2005 #31 Clint Bowyer BGN
2005 #53 Clint Bowyer YG/1
2006 #EB2 Clint Bowyer
2006 #EB73 Clint Bowyer YG
Press Pass Optima Rookie Relics Cars
2006 #RRT1 Clint Bowyer
Press Pass Optima Rookie Relics Drivers
2006 #RRD1 Clint Bowyer
Press Pass Optima Samples

2004 #30 Clint Bowyer
2005 #31 Clint Bowyer BGN
2005 #53 Clint Bowyer YG
Press Pass Panorama
2005 #PPP68 Clint Bowyer
Press Pass Platinum
2006 #P32 Clint Bowyer NBS
2007 #P16 Clint Bowyer
2007 #P37 Clint Bowyer NBS
2007 #P64 Clint Bowyer RR
2008 #P9 Clint Bowyer
2008 #P118 Clint Bowyer Top 12
Press Pass Premium
2006 #30 Clint Bowyer CRC
2006 #52 M.Truex/C.Bowyer/R.Sorenson CL
2007 #3 Clint Bowyer
2008 #3 Clint Bowyer
2008 #76 Clint Bowyer F
Press Pass Premium Previews
2008 #EB3 Clint Bowyer
Press Pass Premium Red
2007 #R3 Clint Bowyer
2008 #3 Clint Bowyer
2008 #76 Clint Bowyer F
Press Pass Previews
2006 #EB32 Clint Bowyer NBS
2007 #EB16 Clint Bowyer
2007 #EB37 Clint Bowyer NBS
2008 #EB9 Clint Bowyer
2008 #EB118 Clint Bowyer Top 12
Press Pass Signings
2004 #6 Clint Bowyer S/T/V
2005 #4 Clint Bowyer
2006 #6 Clint Bowyer NC S
2007 #10 Clint Bowyer NC
2008 #7 Clint Bowyer
Press Pass Signings Blue
2007 #2 Clint Bowyer NC
2008 #4 Clint Bowyer
Press Pass Signings Gold
2004 #6 Clint Bowyer S/T/V
2005 #3 Clint Bowyer
2006 #5 Clint Bowyer NC S
2007 #7 Clint Bowyer NC
2008 #5 Clint Bowyer
Press Pass Signings Press Plates Black
2007 #6 Clint Bowyer
2008 #6 Clint Bowyer
Press Pass Signings Press Plates Cyan
2007 #5 Clint Bowyer
2008 #6 Clint Bowyer
Press Pass Signings Press Plates Magenta
2007 #5 Clint Bowyer
2008 #6 Clint Bowyer
Press Pass Signings Press Plates Yellow
2007 #5 Clint Bowyer
2008 #6 Clint Bowyer
Press Pass Signings Red Ink
2006 #2 Clint Bowyer
Press Pass Signings Silver
2006 #5 Clint Bowyer NC S
2007 #6 Clint Bowyer NC
2008 #4 Clint Bowyer
Press Pass Speedway
2008 #2 Clint Bowyer
2008 #37 Clint Bowyer NNS
2008 #96 Jeff Burton's Car Kevin Harvick's Car Clint Bowyer's Car H
Press Pass Speedway Blur
2008 #B7 Clint Bowyer
Press Pass Speedway Cockpit
2008 #CP2 Clint Bowyer
Press Pass Speedway Gold
2008 #G2 Clint Bowyer
2008 #G37 Clint Bowyer NNS
2008 #G96 Jeff Burton's Car Kevin Harvick's Car Clint Bowyer's Car H
Press Pass Speedway Holofoil
2008 #H2 Clint Bowyer
2008 #H37 Clint Bowyer NNS
2008 #H96 Jeff Burton's Car Kevin Harvick's Car Clint Bowyer's Car H
Press Pass Speedway Previews
2008 #EB2 Clint Bowyer
2008 #EB37 Clint Bowyer NNS
2008 #EB96 Jeff Burton's Car Kevin Harvick's Car Clint Bowyer's Car H
Press Pass Speedway Red
2008 #R2 Clint Bowyer
2008 #R37 Clint Bowyer NNS
2008 #R96 Jeff Burton's Car Kevin Harvick's Car Clint Bowyer's Car H
Press Pass Stealth
2005 #65 Clint Bowyer
2006 #36 Clint Bowyer NBS
2006 #50 Harvick/Burton/Bowyer TM
2006 #76 Clint Bowyer DD
2006 #91 Clint Bowyer CRC
2007 #2 Clint Bowyer
2007 #38 Clint Bowyer NBS
2007 #64 Bowyer/Harvick/Burton
2008 #3 Clint Bowyer
2008 #37 Clint Bowyer NNS
2008 #69 Jeff Burton Clint Bowyer Kevin Harvick
2008 #74 Clint Bowyer DO
2008 #82 Clint Bowyer PM
Press Pass Stealth Autographed Hat Entry
2006 #PPH2 Clint Bowyer
Press Pass Stealth Chrome
2007 #2 Clint Bowyer
2007 #38 Clint Bowyer NBS
2007 #64 Bowyer/Harvick/Burton
2008 #3 Clint Bowyer
2008 #37 Clint Bowyer NNS
2008 #69 Jeff Burton Clint Bowyer Kevin Harvick
2008 #74 Clint Bowyer DO
2008 #82 Clint Bowyer PM
2008 #69B Jeff Burton Kevin Harvick Clint Bowyer VAR
Press Pass Stealth Chrome Exclusives
2007 #X2 Clint Bowyer
2007 #X38 Clint Bowyer NBS
2007 #X64 Bowyer/Harvick/Burton
2008 #3 Clint Bowyer
2008 #37 Clint Bowyer NNS
2008 #69 Jeff Burton Clint Bowyer Kevin Harvick
2008 #74 Clint Bowyer DO
2008 #82 Clint Bowyer PM

Press Pass Stealth Chrome Exclusives Gold
2008 #3 Clint Bowyer
2008 #37 Clint Bowyer NNS
2008 #69 Jeff Burton Clint Bowyer Kevin Harvick
2008 #74 Clint Bowyer DO
2008 #82 Clint Bowyer PM
Press Pass Stealth Chrome Platinum
2007 #P2 Clint Bowyer
2007 #P38 Clint Bowyer NBS
2007 #P64 Bowyer/Harvick/Burton
Press Pass Stealth Corporate Cuts
2006 #CCD12 Clint Bowyer
Press Pass Stealth Gear Grippers Autographs
2006 #CB Clint Bowyer/7
Press Pass Stealth Gear Grippers Drivers
2006 #GGD14 Clint Bowyer
Press Pass Stealth Hot Pass
2006 #HP3 Clint Bowyer
Press Pass Stealth Maximum Access
2007 #MA3 Clint Bowyer
2008 #MA4 Clint Bowyer
Press Pass Stealth Maximum Access Autographs
2007 #MA3 Clint Bowyer
2008 #MA4 Clint Bowyer
Press Pass Stealth No Boundaries
2004 #NB1 Clint Bowyer
2005 #NB27 Clint Bowyer
Press Pass Stealth Previews
2005 #65 Clint Bowyer
2006 #91 Clint Bowyer
2007 #EB2 Clint Bowyer
2007 #EB38 Clint Bowyer NBS
2008 #3 Clint Bowyer
2008 #37 Clint Bowyer NNS
2008 #82 Clint Bowyer PM
Press Pass Stealth Retail
2006 #36 Clint Bowyer NBS
2006 #50 Harvick/Burton/Bowyer TM
2006 #76 Clint Bowyer DD
2006 #91 Clint Bowyer CRC
Press Pass Stealth Retail Gear Grippers Cars
2006 #GGT14 Clint Bowyer
Press Pass Stealth Samples
2005 #65 Clint Bowyer
Press Pass Stealth Synthesis
2008 #S2 Clint Bowyer
Press Pass Stealth X-Ray
2005 #X65 Clint Bowyer
2006 #X36 Clint Bowyer NBS
2006 #X50 Harvick/Burton/Bowyer TM
2006 #X76 Clint Bowyer DD
2006 #X91 Clint Bowyer
Press Pass Top 25 Drivers & Rides
2006 #C5 Clint Bowyer's Car
2006 #D5 Clint Bowyer
Press Pass Top Prospects Memorabilia
2004 #CBT Clint Bowyer Tire
2004 #CBSM Clint Bowyer Metal
Press Pass Trackside
2004 #42 Clint Bowyer RC
2005 #34 Clint Bowyer
Press Pass Trackside Golden
2004 #G42 Clint Bowyer
2005 #G34 Clint Bowyer
Press Pass Trackside Previews
2004 #EB42 Clint Bowyer
2005 #34 Clint Bowyer
Press Pass Trackside Samples
2004 #42 Clint Bowyer
2005 #34 Clint Bowyer
TRAKS
2006 #3 Clint Bowyer CRC
TRAKS Autographs
2006 #3 Clint Bowyer NC
TRAKS Autographs 100
2006 #3 Clint Bowyer NC
TRAKS Autographs 25
2006 #3 Clint Bowyer NC
TRAKS Stickers
2006 #7 Clint Bowyer
VIP
2006 #90 Clint Bowyer CRC
2007 #3 Clint Bowyer
VIP Get A Grip Drivers
2007 #GGD21 Clint Bowyer
VIP Get A Grip Teams
2007 #GGT21 Clint Bowyer
VIP Previews
2007 #EB3 Clint Bowyer
VIP Rookie Stripes
2006 #RS1 Clint Bowyer
VIP Rookie Stripes Autographs
2006 #RS-CB Clint Bowyer
VIP Sunday Best
2007 #SB1 Clint Bowyer
VIP Tradin' Paint Cars Bronze
2006 #TPT1 Clint Bowyer
VIP Tradin' Paint Drivers Gold
2006 #TPD1 Clint Bowyer
VIP Tradin' Paint Drivers Silver
2006 #TPD1 Clint Bowyer
Wheels American Thunder
2006 #90 Clint Bowyer RT AU CRC
2007 #4 Clint Bowyer
Wheels American Thunder Autographed Hat Instant Winner
2007 #AH4 Clint Bowyer
Wheels American Thunder Double Hat
2006 #DH2 Clint Bowyer
Wheels American Thunder License to Drive
2005 #7 Clint Bowyer
Wheels American Thunder Previews
2007 #EB4 Clint Bowyer
Wheels American Thunder Thunder Strokes
2006 #1 Clint Bowyer
2007 #6 Clint Bowyer
Wheels American Thunder Thunder Strokes Press Plates Black
2007 #6 Clint Bowyer
Wheels American Thunder Thunder Strokes Press Plates Cyan
2007 #6 Clint Bowyer
Wheels American Thunder Thunder Strokes

Press Plates Magenta
2007 #6 Clint Bowyer
Wheels American Thunder Thunder Strokes Press Plates Yellow
2007 #6 Clint Bowyer
Wheels American Thunder Triple Hat
2007 #TH3 Clint Bowyer
Wheels Autographs
2004 #7 Clint Bowyer AT
2005 #5 Clint Bowyer
2006 #6 Clint Bowyer NBS
2007 #3 Clint Bowyer NC HG
2008 #6 Clint Bowyer NC HG
Wheels Autographs Chase Edition
2008 #1 Clint Bowyer NC
Wheels Autographs Press Plates Black
2007 #3 Clint Bowyer NC
2008 #6 Clint Bowyer NC HG
Wheels Autographs Press Plates Cyan
2007 #3 Clint Bowyer NC
2008 #6 Clint Bowyer NC HG
Wheels Autographs Press Plates Magenta
2007 #3 Clint Bowyer NC
2008 #6 Clint Bowyer NC HG
Wheels Autographs Press Plates Yellow
2007 #3 Clint Bowyer NC
2008 #6 Clint Bowyer NC HG
Wheels High Gear
2006 #29 Clint Bowyer NBS
2007 #16 Clint Bowyer
2007 #78 Clint Bowyer's Car C
2008 #3 Clint Bowyer
2008 #30 Clint Bowyer NBS
2008 #48 Clint Bowyer's Car C
2008 #77 Clint Bowyer NI
Wheels High Gear Driven
2007 #DR13 Clint Bowyer
2008 #DR4 Clint Bowyer
Wheels High Gear Final Standings
2008 #F3 Clint Bowyer/3
Wheels High Gear Final Standings Gold
2007 #FS16 Clint Bowyer/17
Wheels High Gear Last Lap
2008 #LL7 Clint Bowyer
Wheels High Gear Last Lap Holofoil
2008 #LL7 Clint Bowyer
Wheels High Gear MPH
2006 #M29 Clint Bowyer NBS
2007 #M16 Clint Bowyer
2007 #M78 Clint Bowyer's Car C
2008 #M3 Clint Bowyer
2008 #M30 Clint Bowyer NBS
2008 #M48 Clint Bowyer's Car C
2008 #M77 Clint Bowyer NI
Wheels High Gear Previews
2007 #EB16 Clint Bowyer
2008 #EB3 Clint Bowyer
Wheels High Gear Previews Green
2006 #EB29 Clint Bowyer NBS
Wheels High Gear The Chase
2008 #TC3 Clint Bowyer

Burton, Jeff

Action Packed
1994 #55 Jeff Burton R
1994 #125 Jeff Burton's Car
1994 #142 Jeff Burton
Action Packed Country
1995 #83 Jeff Burton
Action Packed Country Silver Speed
1995 #83 Jeff Burton
Action Packed Credentials
1996 #51 Jeff Burton
Action Packed Credentials Fan Scan
1996 #9 Jeff Burton
Action Packed Credentials Silver Speed
1996 #51 Jeff Burton
Action Packed Mint
1994 #55 Jeff Burton R
1994 #125 Jeff Burton's Car
1994 #142 Jeff Burton
Action Packed Preview
1995 #5 Jeff Burton
Action Packed Stars
1995 #5 Jeff Burton OC
Action Packed Stars Silver Speed
1995 #5 Jeff Burton OC
Assets
1995 #15 Jeff Burton
Assets Gold Signature
1995 #15 Jeff Burton
Assets Racing
1996 #34 Jeff Burton
Assets Racing $100 Cup Champion Interactive Phone Cards
1996 #3 Jeff Burton
Assets Racing $1000 Cup Champion Interactive Phone Cards
1996 #8 Jeff Burton
Assets Racing $5 Phone Cards
1996 #2 Jeff Burton
Assets Racing Competitor's License
1996 #CL19 Jeff Burton
Autographed Racing
1996 #27 Jeff Burton
1997 #13 Jeff Burton
1997 #43 J.Burton/R.Craven
Autographed Racing Autographs
1996 #8 Jeff Burton
1997 #6 Jeff Burton
Autographed Racing Autographs Certified Golds
1996 #8 Jeff Burton
Autographed Racing Front Runners
1996 #5 J.Burton/J.Burton's Car
1996 #6 J.Burton/W.Burton
1996 #7 J.Burton/M.Martin with hat
1996 #8 J.Burton/M.Martin no hat
1996 #9 J.Burton's Car/M.Martin's Car
1996 #10 J.Burton/T.Musgrave
1996 #11 J.Burton/J.Roush
1996 #12 J.Burton's Car/J.Roush
Autographed Racing Mayne Street
1997 #KM13 Jeff Burton
Classic Five Sport

1995 #172 Jeff Burton
Classic Five Sport Printer's Proofs
1995 #172 Jeff Burton
Classic Five Sport Red Die Cuts
1995 #172 Jeff Burton
Classic Five Sport Signings Freshly Inked
1995-96 #FS30 Jeff Burton
Classic Five Sport Silver Die Cuts
1995 #172 Jeff Burton
Classic Five Sport Strive For Five
1995 #RC11 Jeff Burton
Classic Five-Sport *
1995 #172 Jeff Burton
Classic Five-Sport Autographs *
1995 #172 Jeff Burton/225--Not Confirmed
Classic Five-Sport Printer's Proofs *
1995 #172 Jeff Burton
Classic Five-Sport Red Die Cuts *
1995 #172 Jeff Burton
Classic Five-Sport Silver Die Cuts *
1995 #172 Jeff Burton
Classic Five-Sport Strive For Five *
1995 #RC11 Jeff Burton
Classic Signings Freshly Inked *
1996 #FS30 Jeff Burton
Coca-Cola Racing Family
1999 #1 Jeff Burton
2000 #1 Jeff Burton
2000 #2 Jeff Burton '99 Win
2000 #16 Coca-Cola Racing Family
Collector's Choice
1997 #34 Jeff Burton
1997 #84 Jeff Burton's Car MM
1997 #142 Jeff Burton T3
1997 #143 Jeff Burton T3
1997 #144 Jeff Burton's Car T3
1998 #34 Jeff Burton
1998 #70 Jeff Burton's Car
1998 #73 Jeff Burton FS
1998 #102 Jeff Burton TD
Collector's Choice CC600
1998 #CC37 Jeff Burton
1998 #CC70 Jeff Burton's Car
Collector's Choice Speedecals
1997 #S27 Jeff Burton's Car
1997 #S28 Jeff Burton's Helmet
Collector's Choice Star Quest
1998 #SQ33 Jeff Burton
Collector's Choice Triple Force
1997 #B2 Jeff Burton
Collector's Choice Upper Deck 500
1997 #UD71 Jeff Burton
1997 #UD72 Jeff Burton's Car
Crown Jewels Elite
1996 #17 Jeff Burton
Crown Jewels Elite Diamond Tribute
1996 #17 Jeff Burton
Crown Jewels Elite Diamond Tribute Citrine
1996 #17 Jeff Burton
Crown Jewels Elite Diamonds in the Rough Citrine
1996 #DR1 Jeff Burton
Crown Jewels Elite Diamonds in the Rough Ruby
1996 #DR1 Jeff Burton
Crown Jewels Elite Diamonds in the Rough Sapphire
1996 #DR1 Jeff Burton
Crown Jewels Elite Dual Jewels Amethyst
1996 #DJ8 W.Burton/J.Burton
Crown Jewels Elite Dual Jewels Amethyst Diamond Tribute
1996 #DJ8 W.Burton/J.Burton
Crown Jewels Elite Dual Jewels Amethyst Treasure Chest
1996 #DJ8 W.Burton/J.Burton
Crown Jewels Elite Dual Jewels Garnet
1996 #DJ8 W.Burton/J.Burton
Crown Jewels Elite Dual Jewels Garnet Diamond Tribute
1996 #DJ8 W.Burton/J.Burton
Crown Jewels Elite Dual Jewels Garnet Treasure Chest
1996 #DJ8 W.Burton/J.Burton
Crown Jewels Elite Dual Jewels Sapphire
1996 #DJ8 W.Burton/J.Burton
Crown Jewels Elite Dual Jewels Sapphire Treasure Chest
1996 #DJ8 W.Burton/J.Burton
Crown Jewels Elite Emerald
1996 #17 Jeff Burton
Crown Jewels Elite Emerald Treasure Chest
1996 #17 Jeff Burton
Crown Jewels Elite Sapphire
1996 #17 Jeff Burton
Crown Jewels Elite Sapphire Treasure Chest
1996 #17 Jeff Burton
Crown Jewels Elite Treasure Chest
1996 #17 Jeff Burton
Dayco Series 3
1994 #30 Jeff Burton
eTopps
2003 #12 Jeff Burton/1682
Finish Line
1993 #29 Jeff Burton
1994 #45 Jeff Burton's Car
1994 #113 Jeff Burton
1995 #8 Jeff Burton
1995 #93 Jeff Burton
1996 #12 Jeff Burton
1996 #64 Jeff Burton
Finish Line Busch Grand National
1994 #BGN2 Jeff Burton
Finish Line Coca-Cola 600
1995 #15 Jeff Burton
Finish Line Commemorative Sheets
1993 #1 Daytona
Finish Line New Stars on the Horizon
1994 #4 Jeff Burton
Finish Line Phone Pak
1996 #5 Jeff Burton
Finish Line Phone Pak $2 Signature
1996 #5 Jeff Burton

Finish Line Phone Pak $5
1996 #4 Jeff Burton
Finish Line Printer's Proof
1995 #8 Jeff Burton
1995 #93 Jeff Burton
1996 #12 Jeff Burton
1996 #64 Jeff Burton
Finish Line Silver
1993 #29 Jeff Burton
1994 #45 Jeff Burton's Car
1994 #113 Jeff Burton
1995 #8 Jeff Burton
1995 #93 Jeff Burton
1996 #12 Jeff Burton
1996 #64 Jeff Burton
Flair
1996 #5 Jeff Burton
1996 #61 Jeff Burton's Car
Hi-Tech Brickyard 400
1995 #36 Jeff Burton's Car
1995 #51 Jeff Burton
Images
1995 #8 Jeff Burton
1995 #78 Jeff Burton
Images Gold
1995 #8 Jeff Burton
1995 #78 Jeff Burton
Jurassic Park
1997 #8 Jeff Burton
Jurassic Park Thunder Lizard
1997 #TL6 Jeff Burton
Jurassic Park Triceratops
1997 #8 Jeff Burton
Maxx
1991 #201 Jeff Burton RC
1993 #45 Jeff Burton
1994 #66 Jeff Burton's Car
1994 #175 Jeff Burton
1995 #8 Jeff Burton
1995 #160 Jeff Burton
1996 #8 Jeff Burton
1996 #59 Jeff Burton's Car
1997 #34 Jeff Burton
1997 #79 Jeff Burton's Car
1997 #104 Jeff Burton PS
1998 #9 Jeff Burton
1998 #39 Jeff Burton's Car
1998 #67 Jeff Burton's Car HC
1998 #85 Jeff Burton's Car LTD
1998 #94 Jeff Burton's Car FR
1999 #4 Jeff Burton
1999 #5 Jeff Burton's Car
1999 #6 Jeff Burton RR
2000 #29 Jeff Burton
2000 #55 Jeff Burton's Car
Maxx 10th Anniversary
1998 #13 Jeff Burton
1998 #58 Jeff Burton's Car
Maxx 10th Anniversary Maxximum Preview
1998 #P9 Jeff Burton
Maxx 1997 Year In Review
1998 #26 Jeff Burton
1998 #43 Jeff Burton's Car
1998 #54 Jeff Burton's Car
1998 #58 Jeff Burton's Car
1998 #81 Jeff Burton
1998 #105 Jeff Burton's Car
1998 #115 Jeff Burton's Car
1998 #131 Jeff Burton
1998 #P04 Jeff Burton
Maxx Autographs
1994 #175 Jeff Burton
Maxx Baby Ruth Jeff Burton
1993 #1 Jeff Burton
1993 #2 Jeff Burton's Car
1993 #3 Jeff Burton in Pits
1993 #4 Jeff Burton/Gil Martin
Maxx Black
1992 #57 Jeff Burton
Maxx Black Update
1992 #U3 Jeff Burton
Maxx Chase the Champion
1997 #C5 Jeff Burton
Maxx Chase the Champion Gold Die Cuts
1997 #C5 Jeff Burton
Maxx Drive Time
2000 #DT4 Jeff Burton
Maxx Family Ties
1996 #FT2 J.Burton/W.Burton
Maxx FANtastic Finishes
1999 #F12 Jeff Burton's Car
2000 #FF6 Jeff Burton
Maxx Flag Firsts
1997 #FF21 Jeff Burton
Maxx Focus on a Champion
1998 #FC5 Jeff Burton
1999 #FC9 Jeff Burton
2000 #FC4 Jeff Burton
Maxx Focus on a Champion Cel
1998 #FC5 Jeff Burton
Maxx Focus on a Champion Gold
1999 #FC9 Jeff Burton
Maxx Made in America
1996 #15 Jeff Burton's Car
1996 #99 Jeff Burton
Maxx Medallion
1994 #18 Jeff Burton
1994 #58 Jeff Burton's Car
1995 #7 Jeff Burton
1995 #37 Jeff Burton's Car
Maxx Medallion Blue
1995 #7 Jeff Burton
1995 #37 Jeff Burton's Car
Maxx Medallion On the Road Again
1995 #OTR6 Jeff Burton's Transporter
Maxx Motorsport
1994 #10 Jeff Burton
Maxx Odyssey
1996 #15 Jeff Burton's Car
1996 #99 Jeff Burton
Maxx Over the Wall
1996 #OTW3 Jeff Burton's Car
Maxx Premier Plus
1993 #45 Jeff Burton
1994 #66 Jeff Burton's Car
1994 #162 Jeff Burton
1995 #8 Jeff Burton
1995 #65 Jeff Burton's Car
1995 #181 Jeff Burton ROY
Maxx Premier Plus Crown Chrome
1995 #8 Jeff Burton
1995 #65 Jeff Burton's Car
1995 #181 Jeff Burton ROY
Maxx Premier Plus Retail Jumbos
1995 #2 Jeff Burton
Maxx Premier Series
1993 #45 Jeff Burton
1994 #66 Jeff Burton's Car
1994 #175 Jeff Burton
1995 #8 Jeff Burton
1995 #65 Jeff Burton's Car
1995 #232 J.Burton/W.Burton MM
1995 #259 Jeff Burton Winston Cup ROY
1995 #P1G Jeff Burton Gold Promo
1995 #P1R Jeff Burton Red Promo
1996 #8 Jeff Burton
Maxx Race Ticket
1999 #RT2 Jeff Burton's Car
Maxx Racer's Ink
2000 #JB Jeff Burton
Maxx Racing Images
1999 #RI5 Jeff Burton
Maxx Red
1992 #57 Jeff Burton
Maxx Red Update
1992 #U3 Jeff Burton
Maxx Rookie Class of '94
1994 #1 Jeff Burton
Maxx Rookies of the Year
1997 #MR7 Jeff Burton
Maxx Sam Bass
1996 #3 Jeff Burton
1996 #4 Jeff Burton's Car
Maxx Signed, Sealed, and Delivered
1999 #S5 Jeff Burton/250
Maxx Speedway Boogie
2000 #SB8 Jeff Burton
Maxx Stand Ups
1995 #3 Jeff Burton ROY
Maxx Swappin' Paint
1998 #SW9 Jeff Burton's Car
Maxx Teamwork
1998 #TW5 Jeff Burton's Car
Maxximum
1998 #9 Jeff Burton
1998 #34 Jeff Burton's Car
1998 #59 Jeff Burton
1998 #84 Jeff Burton's Car
2000 #5 Jeff Burton
Maxximum Battle Proven
1998 #B15 Jeff Burton
Maxximum Dialed In
2000 #DI7 Jeff Burton
Maxximum Die Cuts
2000 #5 Jeff Burton
Maxximum Field Generals Four Star Autographs
1998 #7 Jeff Burton
Maxximum Field Generals One Star
1998 #7 Jeff Burton
Maxximum Field Generals Three Star Autographs
1998 #7 Jeff Burton
Maxximum Field Generals Two Star
1998 #7 Jeff Burton
Maxximum First Class
1998 #F12 Jeff Burton
Maxximum MPH
2000 #5 Jeff Burton/99
Maxximum Pure Adrenaline
2000 #PA8 Jeff Burton
Maxximum Signatures
2000 #WJ2 W.Burton/J.Burton
2000 #ROU4 Mart/Litt/J.Brtn/Kens
M-Force
1996 #38 Jeff Burton
Pinnacle Certified
1997 #43 Jeff Burton's Car
Pinnacle Certified Mirror Blue
1997 #43 Jeff Burton's Car
Pinnacle Certified Mirror Gold
1997 #43 Jeff Burton's Car
Pinnacle Certified Mirror Red
1997 #43 Jeff Burton's Car
Pinnacle Certified Red
1997 #43 Jeff Burton's Car
Pinnacle Pole Position
1996 #15 Jeff Burton
1996 #49 Jeff Burton's Car
Pinnacle Pole Position Lightning Fast
1996 #15 Jeff Burton
1996 #49 Jeff Burton's Car
Pinnacle Pole Position No Limit
1996 #13 Jeff Burton
Pinnacle Pole Position No Limit Gold
1996 #13 Jeff Burton
Post Cereal
2004 #2 Jeff Burton
Power
1994 #35 Jeff Burton PP
1994 #130 Jeff Burton
Power Gold
1994 #35 Jeff Burton PP
1994 #130 Jeff Burton
Predator
1997 #9 Jeff Burton
Predator Black Wolf First Strike
1997 #9 Jeff Burton
Predator First Slash
1997 #9 Jeff Burton
Predator Grizzly
1997 #9 Jeff Burton
Predator Grizzly First Slash
1997 #9 Jeff Burton
Predator Red Wolf
1997 #9 Jeff Burton
Predator Red Wolf First Slash
1997 #9 Jeff Burton
Press Pass
1995 #6 Jeff Burton
1995 #109 Jeff Burton AW
1996 #5 Jeff Burton
1997 #13 Jeff Burton
1998 #13 Jeff Burton
1999 #7 Jeff Burton
1999 #34 Jeff Burton's Car
1999 #50 Jeff Burton
1999 #107 Jeff Burton RET
2000 #5 Jeff Burton
2000 #38 Jeff Burton REP
2000 #69 Jeff Burton
2001 #3 Jeff Burton
2001 #50 Jeff Burton's Car
2001 #61 Jeff Burton REP
2001 #93 Jeff Burton SO
2001 #97 Jeff Burton PV
2002 #6 Jeff Burton
2002 #67 Jeff Burton REP
2002 #88 Jeff Burton's Car
2003 #5 Jeff Burton
2003 #70 Bouncing Back WCS
2004 #5 Jeff Burton
2004 #80 The Drive for Five WCS
2005 #22 Jeff Burton
2006 #21 Jeff Burton
2006 #80 Jeff Burton's Car OTW
2007 #8 Jeff Burton
2007 #107 Jeff Burton U
2007 #115 Jeff Burton TT
2008 #7 Jeff Burton
2008 #67 Jeff Burton's Car BFS
2008 #93 Jeff Burton's Car U
2008 #116 Jeff Burton Top 12
2008 #0 Cup Chase Matt Kenseth Tony Stewart Jeff Gordon Jimmie Johnson Denny Hamlin Kurt Busch Kevin Harvick Carl Edwards Kyle Busch Martin Truex Jr. Jeff Burton Clint Bowyer
Press Pass Autographs
1997 #12 Jeff Burton VIP/ACTN
1998 #7 Jeff Burton
1999 #2 Jeff Burton/250
2001 #8 Jeff Burton
2002 #10 Jeff Burton
2003 #7 Jeff Burton Citgo E
2003 #8 Jeff Burton Gain E
2004 #8 Jeff Burton P
2005 #6 Jeff Burton E
2006 #6 Jeff Burton NCS
2007 #6 Jeff Burton NC P
Press Pass Blue
2006 #B21 Jeff Burton
2006 #B80 Jeff Burton's Car OTW
2007 #B8 Jeff Burton
2007 #B107 Jeff Burton U
2007 #B115 Jeff Burton TT
2008 #B7 Jeff Burton
2008 #B67 Jeff Burton's Car BFS
2008 #B93 Jeff Burton's Car U
2008 #B116 Jeff Burton Top 12
Press Pass Bosch
2002 #2 Jeff Burton
Press Pass Burning Rubber
1999 #BR4 Jeff Burton's Car
Press Pass Burning Rubber Drivers
2007 #BRD18 Jeff Burton Dover 9-24
2008 #BRD7 Jeff Burton Texas
Press Pass Burning Rubber Drivers Gold
2007 #BRD18 Jeff Burton Dover 9-24
2008 #BRD7 Jeff Burton Texas
Press Pass Burning Rubber Drivers Prime Cuts
2008 #BRD7 Jeff Burton Texas
Press Pass Burning Rubber Team
2007 #BRT18 Jeff Burton Dover 9-24
Press Pass Burning Rubber Teams
2008 #BRT7 Jeff Burton Texas
Press Pass Chase Cars
1999 #8B Jeff Burton's Car
Press Pass Coca-Cola Racing Family
2003 #2 Jeff Burton
Press Pass Collector's Series Box Set
2007 #SB2 Jeff Burton
Press Pass Collectors Series Making the Show
2006 #MS18 Jeff Burton
Press Pass Collectors Series Sunday Best
2007 #CB2 Jeff Burton
Press Pass Cup Chase
1995 #6 Jeff Burton
1996 #5 Jeff Burton
1997 #CC2 Jeff Burton WIN
1998 #CC2 Jeff Burton Win 2
1999 #3 Jeff Burton WIN 2
2000 #CC3 Jeff Burton WIN
2001 #CC8 Jeff Burton WIN
2002 #CC1 Jeff Burton
2003 #CCR1 Jeff Burton
2004 #CCR14 Jeff Burton
2006 #CCR17 Jeff Burton Winner
2007 #CCR10 Jeff Burton Winner
2008 #CC12 Jeff Burton
Press Pass Cup Chase Blue Die Cut Prizes
1997 #CC2 Jeff Burton
Press Pass Cup Chase Die Cut Prizes
1998 #CC2 Jeff Burton
1999 #3 Jeff Burton
2000 #CC3 Jeff Burton
2001 #CC8 Jeff Burton
Press Pass Cup Chase Foil Prizes
1996 #5 Jeff Burton
Press Pass Cup Chase Gold Die Cuts
1997 #CC2 Jeff Burton
Press Pass Cup Chase Prizes
2002 #CC1 Jeff Burton
2003 #CCR1 Jeff Burton
2004 #CCR14 Jeff Burton
2006 #CC7 Jeff Burton
2007 #CC10 Jeff Burton
Press Pass Eclipse
2002 #10 Jeff Burton
2003 #12 Jeff Burton
2004 #11 Jeff Burton
2006 #17 Jeff Burton
2007 #7 Jeff Burton
2007 #43 Jeff Burton P
2007 #64 Martin/Kahne/Burton NS
2007 #66 Jeff Burton NS
2007 #0 Cup Chase 10
2008 #7 Jeff Burton
2008 #45 Jeff Burton TO
2008 #62 Jeff Burton's Car LP
2008 #80 Jeff Burton SO
Press Pass Eclipse Double Hot Treads
2003 #DT7 J.Burton/K.Busch
Press Pass Eclipse Escape Velocity
2008 #EV10 Jeff Burton
Press Pass Eclipse Gold
2007 #G7 Jeff Burton
2007 #G43 Jeff Burton P
2007 #G64 Martin/Kahne/Burton NS
2007 #G66 Jeff Burton NS
2008 #G7 Jeff Burton
2008 #G45 Jeff Burton TO
2008 #G62 Jeff Burton's Car LP
2008 #G80 Jeff Burton SO
Press Pass Eclipse Hyperdrive
2007 #HD8 Jeff Burton
2008 #HP9 Jeff Burton
Press Pass Eclipse Previews
2003 #12 Jeff Burton
2004 #11 Jeff Burton
2006 #EB17 Jeff Burton
2007 #EB7 Jeff Burton
2008 #EB7 Jeff Burton
2008 #EB80 Jeff Burton SO
Press Pass Eclipse Racing Champions
2002 #RC12 Jeff Burton
2002 #RC32 Jeff Burton
2007 #RC9 Jeff Burton
2007 #RC16 Jeff Burton
Press Pass Eclipse Red
2007 #R7 Jeff Burton
2007 #R43 Jeff Burton P
2007 #R64 Martin/Kahne/Burton NS
2007 #R66 Jeff Burton NS
2008 #R7 Jeff Burton
2008 #R45 Jeff Burton TO
2008 #R62 Jeff Burton's Car LP
2008 #R80 Jeff Burton SO
Press Pass Eclipse Samples
2002 #10 Jeff Burton
2003 #12 Jeff Burton
2004 #11 Jeff Burton
Press Pass Eclipse Skidmarks
2003 #SM18 Jeff Burton
2006 #SM18 Jeff Burton
2007 #SM9 Jeff Burton
Press Pass Eclipse Skidmarks Holofoil
2006 #SM18 Jeff Burton
2007 #SM9 Jeff Burton
Press Pass Eclipse Solar Eclipse
2002 #S10 Jeff Burton
2003 #P12 Jeff Burton
Press Pass Eclipse Star Tracks
2008 #ST11 Jeff Burton
Press Pass Eclipse Star Tracks Holofoil
2008 #ST11 Jeff Burton
Press Pass Eclipse Stellar
2008 #ST8 Jeff Burton
2008 #ST16 Jeff Burton
Press Pass Eclipse Supernova
2002 #SN1 Jeff Burton
2006 #SU9 Jeff Burton
Press Pass Eclipse Supernova Numbered
2002 #SN1 Jeff Burton
Press Pass Eclipse Teammates Autographs
2003 #JBKB J.Burton/K.Busch
2006 #8 K.Harvick/J.Burton
2007 #8 K.Harvick/C.Bowyer/J.Burton
2008 #BBH Clint Bowyer Jeff Burton Kevin Harvick
Press Pass Eclipse Under Cover Cars
2003 #UCT8 Jeff Burton
2004 #UCD15 Jeff Burton
Press Pass Eclipse Under Cover Double Cover
2004 #DC9 M.Kenseth/J.Burton
2004 #DC14 M.Martin/J.Burton
2004 #DC15 J.Burton/K.Busch
Press Pass Eclipse Under Cover Double Cover Name
2008 #DC2 Kevin Harvick Jeff Burton
Press Pass Eclipse Under Cover Double Cover NASCAR
2008 #DC2 Kevin Harvick Jeff Burton
Press Pass Eclipse Under Cover Driver Gold
2003 #UCD8 Jeff Burton
2004 #UCD15 Jeff Burton
Press Pass Eclipse Under Cover Driver Red
2003 #UCD8 Jeff Burton
2004 #UCD15 Jeff Burton
Press Pass Eclipse Under Cover Driver Silver
2003 #UCD8 Jeff Burton
2004 #UCD15 Jeff Burton
Press Pass Eclipse Under Cover Drivers
2008 #UCD11 Jeff Burton
Press Pass Eclipse Under Cover Drivers Eclipse
2008 #UCD11 Jeff Burton
Press Pass Eclipse Under Cover Drivers Name
2008 #UCD11 Jeff Burton
Press Pass Eclipse Under Cover Drivers NASCAR
2008 #UCD11 Jeff Burton
Press Pass Eclipse Under Cover Teams
2008 #UCT11 Jeff Burton
Press Pass Eclipse Under Cover Teams NASCAR
2008 #UCT11 Jeff Burton
Press Pass Eclipse Warp Speed
2002 #WS7 Jeff Burton
Press Pass Game Face
2006 #GF9 Jeff Burton
Press Pass Gatorade Front Runner Award
2000 #1 Jeff Burton
2001 #4 Jeff Burton
Press Pass Gold
2006 #G21 Jeff Burton
2006 #G80 Jeff Burton's Car OTW
2007 #G8 Jeff Burton
2007 #G107 Jeff Burton U
2007 #G115 Jeff Burton TT
2008 #G7 Jeff Burton
2008 #G67 Jeff Burton's Car BFS
2008 #G93 Jeff Burton's Car U
2008 #G116 Jeff Burton Top 12
Press Pass Gold Holofoil
2003 #P5 Jeff Burton
2003 #P70 Bouncing Back WCS
Press Pass Hot Treads
2001 #HT14 Jeff Burton/1660
2002 #HT15 Jeff Burton's Car/1555
2002 #HT42 Jeff Burton's Car/900
Press Pass Lasers
1997 #13 Jeff Burton
Press Pass Legends
2007 #38 Jeff Burton
Press Pass Legends Autographs Black
2006 #19 Jeff Burton
Press Pass Legends Blue
2007 #B38 Jeff Burton
Press Pass Legends Bronze
2007 #Z38 Jeff Burton
Press Pass Legends Gold
2007 #G38 Jeff Burton
Press Pass Legends Holofoil
2007 #H38 Jeff Burton
Press Pass Legends Press Plates Black
2007 #PP38 Jeff Burton
Press Pass Legends Press Plates Black Backs
2007 #PP38 Jeff Burton
Press Pass Legends Press Plates Cyan
2007 #PP38 Jeff Burton
Press Pass Legends Press Plates Cyan Backs
2007 #PP38 Jeff Burton
Press Pass Legends Press Plates Magenta
2007 #PP38 Jeff Burton
Press Pass Legends Press Plates Magenta Backs
2007 #PP38 Jeff Burton
Press Pass Legends Press Plates Yellow
2007 #PP38 Jeff Burton
Press Pass Legends Press Plates Yellow Backs
2007 #PP38 Jeff Burton
Press Pass Legends Previews
2007 #EB38 Jeff Burton
Press Pass Legends Solo
2007 #S38 Jeff Burton
Press Pass Making the Show Collector's Series
2004 #MS27 Jeff Burton CL
Press Pass Millennium
2000 #5 Jeff Burton
2000 #38 Jeff Burton
2000 #69 Jeff Burton
2001 #3 Jeff Burton
2001 #61 Jeff Burton REP
2001 #93 Jeff Burton SO
2001 #97 Jeff Burton PV
Press Pass Oil Cans
1998 #OC1 Jeff Burton
1999 #2 Jeff Burton
2000 #OC5 Jeff Burton
Press Pass Oil Slicks
1997 #13 Jeff Burton
1998 #13 Jeff Burton
Press Pass Optima
2000 #3 Jeff Burton
2000 #40 Jeff Burton WCL
2001 #2 Jeff Burton
2001 #40 Jeff Burton WCL
2002 #3 Jeff Burton
2003 #3 Jeff Burton
2005 #5 Jeff Burton
2005 #86 Jeff Burton DT
2006 #23 Jeff Burton
2006 #58 Jeff Burton's Car HS
2006 #23B Jeff Burton Chase
Press Pass Optima Cool Persistence
2001 #CP1 Jeff Burton
2002 #CP1 Jeff Burton
2005 #CP10 Jeff Burton
Press Pass Optima Fan Favorite
2002 #FF2 Jeff Burton
2003 #FF2 Jeff Burton
2005 #FF4 Jeff Burton
2006 #FF2 Jeff Burton
Press Pass Optima G Force
2000 #GF2 Jeff Burton
2001 #GF1 Jeff Burton
Press Pass Optima Gold
2001 #2 Jeff Burton
2001 #40 Jeff Burton WCL
2002 #3 Jeff Burton
2003 #G3 Jeff Burton
2005 #G5 Jeff Burton
2005 #G86 Jeff Burton DT
2006 #G23 Jeff Burton
2006 #G58 Jeff Burton's Car HS
Press Pass Optima Overdrive
2000 #OD1 Jeff Burton
Press Pass Optima Overdrive Square Cut
2000 #OD1 Jeff Burton
Press Pass Optima Platinum
2000 #3 Jeff Burton
2000 #40 Jeff Burton WCL
Press Pass Optima Pole Position
2006 #PP1 Jeff Burton
Press Pass Optima Previews
2003 #3 Jeff Burton
2005 #5 Jeff Burton
2006 #EB23 Jeff Burton
Press Pass Optima Promos
2002 #3 Jeff Burton
Press Pass Optima Q & A
2006 #QA4 Jeff Burton
Press Pass Optima Race Used Lugnuts Cars
2000 #LC2 Jeff Burton's Car
2001 #LNC1 Jeff Burton's Car
2002 #LNC1 Jeff Burton's Car
Press Pass Optima Race Used Lugnuts Drivers
2000 #LD2 Jeff Burton
2001 #LND1 Jeff Burton
2002 #LND1 Jeff Burton
Press Pass Optima Rookie Relics Cars
2006 #RRT14 Jeff Burton
Press Pass Optima Rookie Relics Drivers
2006 #RRD14 Jeff Burton
Press Pass Optima Samples
2002 #3 Jeff Burton
2003 #3 Jeff Burton
2005 #5 Jeff Burton
2005 #86 Jeff Burton DT
Press Pass Optima Thunder Bolts Cars
2003 #TBT12 Jeff Burton's Car
Press Pass Optima Thunder Bolts Drivers
2003 #TBD12 Jeff Burton/65
Press Pass Optima XL
1994 #3 Jeff Burton
1994 #55 Steve Grissom/Jeff Burton WCS
Press Pass Optima XL Prototypes
1995 #XL1 Jeff Burton
Press Pass Optima XL Red Hot
1994 #3 Jeff Burton
1994 #55 S.Grissom/J.Burton WCS
Press Pass Panorama
2005 #PPP2 Jeff Burton
2005 #PPP19 Jeff Burton
Press Pass Pit Stop
1998 #PS18 Jeff Burton's Car
1999 #18 Jeff Burton's Car
Press Pass Pitstop
2000 #PS18 Jeff Burton's Car
Press Pass Platinum
2002 #6 Jeff Burton
2002 #67 Jeff Burton REP
2002 #88 Jeff Burton's Car
2004 #P5 Jeff Burton
2004 #P80 The Drive for Five WCS
2005 #P22 Jeff Burton
2006 #P21 Jeff Burton
2006 #P80 Jeff Burton's Car OTW
2007 #P8 Jeff Burton
2007 #P107 Jeff Burton U
2007 #P115 Jeff Burton TT
2008 #P7 Jeff Burton
2008 #P67 Jeff Burton's Car BFS
2008 #P93 Jeff Burton's Car U
2008 #P116 Jeff Burton Top 12
Press Pass Premium
1996 #28 Jeff Burton
1997 #13 Jeff Burton
1998 #6 Jeff Burton
1998 #27 Jeff Burton's Car
1998 #31 Jeff Burton
1999 #4 Jeff Burton
1999 #32 Jeff Burton's Car
2000 #27 Jeff Burton
2000 #39 Jeff Burton's Car
2000 #63 Jeff Burton
2000 #71 Jeff Burton
2001 #2 Jeff Burton
2001 #57 Jeff Burton CC
2002 #3 Jeff Burton
2002 #37 Jeff Burton's Car
2002 #56 Jeff Burton CH
2002 #70 Jeff Burton PC
2003 #3 Jeff Burton
2003 #34 Jeff Burton's Car
2003 #57 Jeff Burton CC
2003 #81 Jeff Burton PC
2004 #28 Jeff Burton
2004 #62 Jeff Burton CC
2005 #3 Jeff Burton
2005 #69 Jeff Burton CC
2005 #70 Jeff Burton PC
2006 #3 Jeff Burton
2006 #38 Jeff Burton's Car M
2006 #51 Jeff Burton NS
2006 #66 Jeff Burton C
2006 #83 Jeff Burton PC
2007 #24 Jeff Burton
2008 #23 Jeff Burton
Press Pass Premium Badge of Honor
1999 #BH16 Jeff Burton
1999 #BH27 Jeff Burton's Car
Press Pass Premium Badge of Honor Reflectors
1999 #BH16 Jeff Burton
1999 #BH27 Jeff Burton's Car
Press Pass Premium Burning Desire
1999 #FD4B Jeff Burton 1:72
Press Pass Premium Clean Air
2008 #CA9 Jeff Burton
Press Pass Premium Emerald Proofs
1996 #28 Jeff Burton
1997 #13 Jeff Burton
Press Pass Premium Flag Chasers
1998 #FC5 Jeff Burton
1998 #FC27 Jeff Burton's Car
Press Pass Premium Flag Chasers Reflectors
1998 #FC5 Jeff Burton
1998 #FC27 Jeff Burton's Car
Press Pass Premium Gold
2001 #2 Jeff Burton
2001 #57 Jeff Burton CC
Press Pass Premium Holofoil
1996 #28 Jeff Burton
Press Pass Premium In The Zone
2000 #IZ6 Jeff Burton
2001 #IZ1 Jeff Burton
2002 #IZ1 Jeff Burton
2005 #IZ5 Jeff Burton
Press Pass Premium In the Zone Elite Edition
2005 #IZ5 Jeff Burton
Press Pass Premium Mirrors
1997 #13 Jeff Burton
Press Pass Premium Oil Slicks
1997 #13 Jeff Burton
Press Pass Premium Performance Driven
2005 #PD7 Jeff Burton
Press Pass Premium Previews
2003 #3 Jeff Burton
2004 #28 Jeff Burton
2008 #EB23 Jeff Burton
Press Pass Premium Race Used Firesuit
1999 #F9 Jeff Burton
2000 #F9 Jeff Burton
Press Pass Premium Red
2007 #R24 Jeff Burton
2008 #23 Jeff Burton
Press Pass Premium Red Reflectors
2002 #3 Jeff Burton
2002 #37 Jeff Burton's Car
2002 #56 Jeff Burton CH
2002 #70 Jeff Burton PC
2003 #3 Jeff Burton
2003 #34 Jeff Burton's Car
2003 #57 Jeff Burton CC

2003 #81 Jeff Burton PC
Press Pass Premium Reflectors
1998 #6 Jeff Burton
1998 #27 Jeff Burton's Car
1998 #31 Jeff Burton
1999 #R4 Jeff Burton
1999 #R32 Jeff Burton's Car
2000 #27 Jeff Burton
2000 #39 Jeff Burton
2000 #63 Jeff Burton
2000 #71 Jeff Burton
Press Pass Premium Rivalries
1998 #1A Jeff Burton
Press Pass Premium Samples
2002 #3 Jeff Burton
2002 #37 Jeff Burton's Car
2003 #3 Jeff Burton
2003 #34 Jeff Burton's Car
2004 #28 Jeff Burton
2005 #3 Jeff Burton
Press Pass Premium Steel Horses
1998 #SH12 Jeff Burton's Car
1999 #SH12 Jeff Burton's Car
Press Pass Premium Triple Gear Firesuit
1998 #TGF9 Jeff Burton
Press Pass Previews
2003 #5 Jeff Burton
2004 #5 Jeff Burton
2006 #EB21 Jeff Burton
2007 #EB8 Jeff Burton
2007 #EB115 Jeff Burton TT
2008 #EB7 Jeff Burton
2008 #EB116 Jeff Burton Top 12
Press Pass Previews Green
2005 #EB22 Jeff Burton
Press Pass R and N China
1996 #5 Jeff Burton
Press Pass Race Day
2007 #RD8 Jeff Burton
2008 #RD6 Jeff Burton
Press Pass Red Hot
1995 #6 Jeff Burton
1995 #109 Jeff Burton AW
Press Pass Samples
2003 #5 Jeff Burton
2003 #70 Bouncing Back WCS
2004 #5 Jeff Burton
2004 #80 The Drive for Five WCS
2005 #22 Jeff Burton
Press Pass Scorchers
1996 #5 Jeff Burton
Press Pass Shockers
1998 #ST11A Jeff Burton
Press Pass Showcar
2003 #S1B Jeff Burton
2004 #S1B Jeff Burton's Car
Press Pass Showcar Die Cuts
2000 #SC6 Jeff Burton's Car
Press Pass Showman
1999 #8A Jeff Burton
2000 #SM6 Jeff Burton
2003 #S1A Jeff Burton
2004 #S1A Jeff Burton's Car
Press Pass Showman Die Cuts
2000 #SM6 Jeff Burton
Press Pass Signings
1998 #12 Jeff Burton PPP/VIP
1999 #9A Jeff Burton/250
1999 #9B Jeff Burton/500
2000 #8 Jeff Burton
2001 #7 Jeff Burton P/T/V
2002 #8 Jeff Burton O/S/T/V
2003 #10 Jeff Burton O/S/V
2004 #8 Jeff Burton O/T/V
2006 #7 Jeff Burton NC S
2007 #11 Jeff Burton NC
Press Pass Signings Blue
2007 #3 Jeff Burton NC
Press Pass Signings Gold
1998 #12 Jeff Burton PPP/VIP
2000 #6 Jeff Burton
2001 #6 Jeff Burton T/V/S
2002 #9 Jeff Burton O/S/T/V
2003 #10 Jeff Burton O/S/V
2004 #8 Jeff Burton O/T/V
2006 #6 Jeff Burton NC S
2007 #8 Jeff Burton NC
Press Pass Signings Press Plates Black
2007 #7 Jeff Burton
Press Pass Signings Press Plates Cyan
2007 #6 Jeff Burton
Press Pass Signings Press Plates Magenta
2007 #6 Jeff Burton
Press Pass Signings Press Plates Yellow
2007 #6 Jeff Burton
Press Pass Signings Silver
2006 #6 Jeff Burton NC S
2007 #7 Jeff Burton NC
Press Pass Signings Transparent
2001 #1 Jeff Burton V/S
Press Pass Skidmarks
1999 #7 Jeff Burton
1999 #34 Jeff Burton's Car
1999 #50 Jeff Burton
Press Pass Slideshow
2008 #SS3 Jeff Burton
Press Pass Snapshots
2003 #SN3 Jeff Burton
2004 #SN2 Jeff Burton
2005 #SN3 Jeff Burton
2006 #SN3 Jeff Burton
2006 #SN29 Jeff Burton
2007 #SN3 Jeff Burton
Press Pass Speedway
2008 #3 Jeff Burton
2008 #70 Jeff Burton UTH
2008 #87 Jeff Burton's Car WS
2008 #96 Jeff Burton's Car Kevin Harvick's Car Clint Bowyer's Car H
2008 #100 Jeff Burton CL
Press Pass Speedway Cockpit
2008 #CP3 Jeff Burton
Press Pass Speedway Gold
2008 #G3 Jeff Burton
2008 #G70 Jeff Burton UTH
2008 #G87 Jeff Burton's Car WS
2008 #G96 Jeff Burton's Car Kevin Harvick's Car Clint Bowyer's Car H
2008 #G100 Jeff Burton CL
Press Pass Speedway Holofoil
2008 #H3 Jeff Burton
2008 #H70 Jeff Burton UTH
2008 #H87 Jeff Burton's Car WS
2008 #H96 Jeff Burton's Car Kevin Harvick's Car Clint Bowyer's Car H
2008 #H100 Jeff Burton CL
Press Pass Speedway Previews
2008 #EB3 Jeff Burton
2008 #EB96 Jeff Burton's Car Kevin Harvick's Car Clint Bowyer's Car H
Press Pass Speedway Red
2008 #R3 Jeff Burton
2008 #R70 Jeff Burton UTH
2008 #R87 Jeff Burton's Car WS
2008 #R96 Jeff Burton's Car Kevin Harvick's Car Clint Bowyer's Car H
2008 #R100 Jeff Burton CL
Press Pass Speedway Test Drive
2008 #TD8 Jeff Burton
Press Pass Stealth
1998 #4 Jeff Burton
1998 #5 Jeff Burton's Car
1998 #51 Jeff Burton TM
1999 #1 Jeff Burton
1999 #2 Jeff Burton's Car
1999 #51 Exide Car Jack TT
2000 #52 Jeff Burton
2000 #53 Jeff Burton's Car
2001 #43 Jeff Burton
2001 #44 Jeff Burton's Car
2001 #45 Jeff Burton
2002 #43 Jeff Burton
2002 #44 Jeff Burton's Car
2002 #45 Jeff Burton
2002 #57 Jeff Burton's Car SST
2003 #43 Jeff Burton
2003 #44 Jeff Burton's Car
2003 #45 Jeff Burton
2004 #73 Jeff Burton WW
2005 #37 Jeff Burton
2005 #40 Jeff Burton's Car
2005 #43 Jeff Burton
2006 #3 Jeff Burton
2006 #42 Jeff Burton's Rig
2006 #50 Harvick/Burton/Bowyer TM
2007 #3 Jeff Burton
2007 #61 Jeff Burton's Crew GC
2007 #64 Bowyer/Harvick/Burton
2007 #88 Jeff Burton PO
2008 #4 Jeff Burton
2008 #52 Jeff Burton's Rig C
2008 #61 Jeff Burton's Car GC
2008 #69 Jeff Burton Clint Bowyer Kevin Harvick
Press Pass Stealth Autographed Hat Entry
2006 #PPH3 Jeff Burton
Press Pass Stealth Awards
1998 #2 Jeff Burton 1:68
Press Pass Stealth Battle Armor Drivers
2007 #BAD9 Jeff Burton
2008 #BAD21 Jeff Burton
Press Pass Stealth Battle Armor Teams
2007 #BAT9 Jeff Burton
2008 #BAT21 Jeff Burton
Press Pass Stealth Big Numbers
1999 #BN2 Jeff Burton
Press Pass Stealth Big Numbers Die Cuts
1999 #BN2 Jeff Burton
Press Pass Stealth Chrome
2007 #3 Jeff Burton
2007 #61 Jeff Burton's Crew GC
2007 #64 Bowyer/Harvick/Burton
2007 #88 Jeff Burton PO
2008 #4 Jeff Burton
2008 #52 Jeff Burton's Rig C
2008 #61 Jeff Burton's Car GC
2008 #69 Jeff Burton Clint Bowyer Kevin Harvick
2008 #69B Jeff Burton Kevin Harvick Clint Bowyer VAR
Press Pass Stealth Chrome Exclusives
2007 #X3 Jeff Burton
2007 #X61 Jeff Burton's Crew GC
2007 #X64 Bowyer/Harvick/Burton
2007 #X88 Jeff Burton PO
2008 #4 Jeff Burton
2008 #52 Jeff Burton's Rig C
2008 #61 Jeff Burton's Car GC
2008 #69 Jeff Burton Clint Bowyer Kevin Harvick
Press Pass Stealth Chrome Exclusives Gold
2008 #4 Jeff Burton
2008 #52 Jeff Burton's Rig C
2008 #61 Jeff Burton's Car GC
2008 #69 Jeff Burton Clint Bowyer Kevin Harvick
Press Pass Stealth Chrome Platinum
2007 #P3 Jeff Burton
2007 #P61 Jeff Burton's Crew GC
2007 #P64 Bowyer/Harvick/Burton
2007 #P88 Jeff Burton PO
Press Pass Stealth Corporate Cuts
2006 #CCD14 Jeff Burton
Press Pass Stealth EFX
2002 #FX9 Jeff Burton
2003 #FX1 Jeff Burton
2005 #EFX10 Jeff Burton
Press Pass Stealth Fusion
1998 #4 Jeff Burton
1998 #5 Jeff Burton's Car
1998 #51 Jeff Burton TM
1999 #F1 Jeff Burton
1999 #F2 Jeff Burton's Car
1999 #F51 Exide Car Jack TT
2000 #FS25 Jeff Burton
2000 #FS26 Jeff Burton's Car
2000 #FS27 Jeff Burton
2002 #F1 Jeff Burton
2003 #FU1 Jeff Burton
2005 #FU11 Jeff Burton 1:14
Press Pass Stealth Fusion Green
2000 #FS25 Jeff Burton
2000 #FS26 Jeff Burton
2000 #FS27 Jeff Burton
Press Pass Stealth Fusion Red
2000 #FS25 Jeff Burton
2000 #FS26 Jeff Burton
2000 #FS27 Jeff Burton
Press Pass Stealth Gear Grippers Cars
2003 #GGT13 Jeff Burton
2005 #GGT10 Jeff Burton
Press Pass Stealth Gear Grippers Drivers
2003 #GGD13 Jeff Burton
2004 #GGD11 Jeff Burton
2005 #GGD10 Jeff Burton
2006 #GGD18 Jeff Burton
Press Pass Stealth Gear Grippers Drivers Retail
2004 #GGT11 Jeff Burton
Press Pass Stealth Gold
2002 #43 Jeff Burton
2002 #44 Jeff Burton's Car
2002 #45 Jeff Burton
2002 #57 Jeff Burton's Car SST
Press Pass Stealth Holofoils
2001 #43 Jeff Burton
2001 #44 Jeff Burton
2001 #45 Jeff Burton
Press Pass Stealth Hot Pass
2006 #HP4 Jeff Burton
Press Pass Stealth Lap Leaders
2001 #LL18 Jeff Burton
2001 #LL36 Jeff Burton's Car
2002 #LL3 Jeff Burton
Press Pass Stealth Lap Leaders Clear Cars
2001 #LL36 Jeff Burton's Car
Press Pass Stealth Lap Leaders Clear Drivers
2001 #LL18 Jeff Burton
Press Pass Stealth Mach 07
2007 #M7-10 Jeff Burton
Press Pass Stealth Mach 08
2008 #M8-10 Jeff Burton
Press Pass Stealth Maximum Access
2007 #MA4 Jeff Burton
2008 #MA5 Jeff Burton
Press Pass Stealth Maximum Access Autographs
2007 #MA4 Jeff Burton
2008 #MA5 Jeff Burton
Press Pass Stealth No Boundaries
2003 #NB10 Jeff Burton
2005 #NB17 Jeff Burton
Press Pass Stealth Octane
1998 #5 Jeff Burton
1998 #6 Jeff Burton's Car
Press Pass Stealth Octane Die Cuts
1998 #5 Jeff Burton
1998 #6 Jeff Burton's Car
Press Pass Stealth Octane SLX
1999 #O3 Jeff Burton
1999 #O27 Jeff Burton's Car
Press Pass Stealth Octane SLX Die Cuts
1999 #O3 Jeff Burton
1999 #O27 Jeff Burton's Car
Press Pass Stealth Previews
2003 #43 Jeff Burton
2003 #44 Jeff Burton's Car
2003 #45 Jeff Burton
2005 #37 Jeff Burton
2005 #40 Jeff Burton's Car
2005 #43 Jeff Burton
2006 #3 Jeff Burton
2007 #EB3 Jeff Burton
2007 #EB88 Jeff Burton PO
2008 #4 Jeff Burton
Press Pass Stealth Profile
2005 #PR4 Jeff Burton
Press Pass Stealth Race Used Glove Cars
2001 #RGC9 Jeff Burton/170
2002 #GLC8 Jeff Burton's Car
Press Pass Stealth Race Used Glove Drivers
2001 #RGD9 Jeff Burton/170
2002 #GLD8 Jeff Burton
Press Pass Stealth Race Used Gloves
1998 #G2 Jeff Burton
1999 #G1 Jeff Burton/150
2000 #G4 Jeff Burton/100
Press Pass Stealth Red
2003 #P43 Jeff Burton
2003 #P44 Jeff Burton's Car
2003 #P45 Jeff Burton
Press Pass Stealth Retail
2006 #3 Jeff Burton
2006 #42 Jeff Burton's Rig
2006 #50 Harvick/Burton/Bowyer TM
Press Pass Stealth Retail Gear Grippers Cars
2006 #GGT18 Jeff Burton
Press Pass Stealth Samples
2002 #43 Jeff Burton
2002 #44 Jeff Burton's Car
2002 #45 Jeff Burton
2002 #57 Jeff Burton's Car SST
2003 #43 Jeff Burton
2003 #44 Jeff Burton's Car
2003 #45 Jeff Burton
2004 #X73 Jeff Burton WW
2005 #37 Jeff Burton
2005 #40 Jeff Burton's Car
2005 #43 Jeff Burton
Press Pass Stealth SST
2000 #SST6 Jeff Burton
Press Pass Stealth Stars
1998 #2 Jeff Burton
Press Pass Stealth Stars Die Cuts
1998 #2 Jeff Burton
Press Pass Stealth Synthesis
2008 #S3 Jeff Burton
Press Pass Stealth X-Ray
2004 #73 Jeff Burton WW
2005 #X37 Jeff Burton
2005 #X40 Jeff Burton's Car
2005 #X43 Jeff Burton
2006 #X3 Jeff Burton
2006 #X42 Jeff Burton's Rig
2006 #X50 Harvick/Burton/Bowyer TM
Press Pass Techno-Retro
2000 #TR3 Jeff Burton
Press Pass Top 25 Drivers & Rides
2006 #C16 Jeff Burton's Car
2006 #D16 Jeff Burton
Press Pass Torpedoes
1998 #ST11B Jeff Burton's Car
Press Pass Torquers
1996 #5 Jeff Burton
1997 #13 Jeff Burton
Press Pass Trackside
2000 #27 Jeff Burton
2000 #28 Jeff Burton's Car
2000 #NNO Jeff Burton Power Pick
2001 #17 Jeff Burton
2001 #50 Jeff Burton's Car
2002 #18 Jeff Burton
2002 #79 Jeff Burton TM
2003 #2 Jeff Burton
2003 #57 J.Burton/W.Burton FA
2003 #72 Jeff Burton in Pits
2003 #78 Mart/J.Bur/Bif/Kens/Bus TM
2004 #14 Jeff Burton
2004 #68 Burt/Kens/Mart/Busch/Bif. TM
2005 #1 Jeff Burton
2005 #63 Jeff Burton's Car HS
2005 #72 Blaney/J.Burton/Harvick TM
2005 #84 Jeff Burton GP
Press Pass Trackside Dialed In
2000 #DI6 Jeff Burton
2001 #D10 Jeff Burton
2002 #DI1 Jeff Burton
Press Pass Trackside Die Cuts
2000 #27 Jeff Burton
2000 #28 Jeff Burton
2001 #17 Jeff Burton
2001 #50 Jeff Burton's Car
Press Pass Trackside Gold Holofoil
2003 #P2 Jeff Burton
2003 #P57 J.Burton/W.Burton
2003 #P72 Jeff Burton's Crew
2003 #P78 Martin/J.Burton/Biffle/Kenseth/Busch
Press Pass Trackside Golden
2000 #27 Jeff Burton
2000 #28 Jeff Burton
2001 #17 Jeff Burton
2001 #50 Jeff Burton's Car
2002 #G18 Jeff Burton
2003 #G2 Jeff Burton
2004 #G14 Jeff Burton
2004 #G68 Burt/Kens/Mart/Busch/Biffle TM
2005 #G1 Jeff Burton
2005 #G63 Jeff Burton's Car HS
2005 #G72 Blaney/J.Burton/Harvick TM
2005 #G84 Jeff Burton GP
Press Pass Trackside Hat Giveaway
2003 #PPH4 Jeff Burton
2004 #PPH3 Jeff Burton
2005 #PPH3 Jeff Burton
Press Pass Trackside Hot Pass
2004 #HP2 Jeff Burton
2005 #2 Jeff Burton
Press Pass Trackside Hot Pass National
2004 #HP2 Jeff Burton
2005 #2 Jeff Burton
Press Pass Trackside License to Drive
2002 #4 Jeff Burton
2003 #LD10 Jeff Burton
Press Pass Trackside License to Drive Die Cuts
2002 #4 Jeff Burton
Press Pass Trackside Panorama
2000 #P29 Jeff Burton
Press Pass Trackside Pit Stoppers
2000 #PS12 Jeff Burton
Press Pass Trackside Pit Stoppers Cars
2004 #PST11 Jeff Burton
Press Pass Trackside Pit Stoppers Drivers
2004 #PSD11 Jeff Burton
Press Pass Trackside Previews
2003 #2 Jeff Burton
2004 #EB14 Jeff Burton
2005 #1 Jeff Burton
2005 #84 Jeff Burton GP
Press Pass Trackside Runnin N' Gunnin
2000 #RG7 Jeff Burton
2005 #RG12 Jeff Burton
Press Pass Trackside Samples
2002 #18 Jeff Burton
2002 #79 Jeff Burton TM
2003 #2 Jeff Burton
2003 #57 J.Burton/W.Burton FA
2003 #72 Jeff Burton in Pits
2003 #78 Mart/J.Bur/Bif/Kens/Bus TM
2004 #14 Jeff Burton
2004 #68 Burt/Kens/Mart/Busch/Biffle TM
2005 #1 Jeff Burton
2005 #63 Jeff Burton's Car HS
2005 #72 Blaney/J.Burton/Harvick TM
2005 #84 Jeff Burton GP
Press Pass Triple Gear 3 in 1
1998 #STG9 Jeff Burton
1999 #TG7 Jeff Burton
Press Pass Triple Gear Burning Rubber
1998 #TG9 Jeff Burton
Press Pass Velocity
2001 #VL7 Jeff Burton
2002 #VL1 Jeff Burton
Press Pass Vintage
2001 #VN3 Jeff Burton
2002 #VN3 Jeff Burton
Press Pass Weekend Warriors
2008 #WW6 Jeff Burton
Pro Set
1992 #135 Jeff Burton
Race Sharks
1997 #18 Jeff Burton
Race Sharks First Bite
1997 #18 Jeff Burton
Race Sharks Great White
1997 #18 Jeff Burton
Race Sharks Hammerhead
1997 #18 Jeff Burton
Race Sharks Hammerhead First Bite
1997 #18 Jeff Burton
Race Sharks Shark Attack
1997 #SA10 Jeff Burton
Race Sharks Shark Attack First Bite
1997 #SA10 Jeff Burton
Race Sharks Shark Attack First Bite Previews
1997 #10 Jeff Burton
Race Sharks Shark Tooth Signatures
1997 #ST9 Jeff Burton
Race Sharks Shark Tooth Signatures First Bite
1997 #ST9 Jeff Burton
Race Sharks Tiger Shark
1997 #18 Jeff Burton
Race Sharks Tiger Shark First Bite
1997 #18 Jeff Burton
Redline Standups
1992 #14 Jeff Burton
SB Motorsports
1997 #17 Jeff Burton
SB Motorsports Winston Cup Rewind
1997 #WC21 Jeff Burton
Score Board IQ
1997 #13 Jeff Burton
Select
1995 #6 Jeff Burton
1995 #117 Jeff Burton/Ward Burton IB
1995 #119 Jeff Burton YS
Select Flat Out
1995 #6 Jeff Burton
1995 #117 Jeff Burton/Ward Burton IB
1995 #119 Jeff Burton YS
SP
1995 #7 Jeff Burton CC
1995 #40 Jeff Burton
1995 #82 Jeff Burton's Car
1996 #34 Jeff Burton
1996 #72 Jeff Burton CC
1997 #34 Jeff Burton
1997 #76 Jeff Burton's Car
1997 #109 Jeff Burton
SP Authentic
1998 #9 Jeff Burton
1998 #43 Jeff Burton's Car
1999 #15 Jeff Burton
1999 #39 Jeff Burton's Car
1999 #70 Jeff Burton CLASS
1999 #78 Jeff Burton SP
2000 #4 Jeff Burton
2000 #79 Jeff Burton SUP
SP Authentic Behind the Wheel
1998 #BW4 Jeff Burton
SP Authentic Behind the Wheel Die Cuts
1998 #BW4 Jeff Burton
SP Authentic Behind the Wheel Gold
1998 #BW4 Jeff Burton
SP Authentic Cup Challengers
1999 #CC3 Jeff Burton
SP Authentic Dominance
2000 #D6 Jeff Burton
SP Authentic Driver's Seat
2000 #DS5 Jeff Burton
SP Authentic Driving Force
1999 #DF6 Jeff Burton
SP Authentic In the Driver's Seat
1999 #DS9 Jeff Burton
SP Authentic Overdrive
1999 #15 Jeff Burton
1999 #39 Jeff Burton CAR
1999 #70 Jeff Burton CLASS
1999 #78 Jeff Burton SP/99
SP Authentic Overdrive Gold
2000 #4 Jeff Burton/99
2000 #79 Jeff Burton SUP/99
SP Authentic Overdrive Silver
2000 #4 Jeff Burton
2000 #79 Jeff Burton SUP
SP Authentic Race for the Cup
2000 #R4 Jeff Burton
SP Authentic Sign of the Times
1999 #JB Jeff Burton
2000 #JB Jeff Burton
SP Authentic Sign of the Times Gold
2000 #JB Jeff Burton
SP Authentic Sign of the Times Red
1998 #ST8 Jeff Burton's Car
SP Die Cuts
1995 #7 Jeff Burton
1995 #40 Jeff Burton
1995 #82 Jeff Burton's Car
SP Driving Force
1996 #DF5 Jeff Burton
SP Holoview Maximum Effects
1996 #ME25 Jeff Burton
SP Holoview Maximum Effects Die Cuts
1996 #ME25 Jeff Burton
SP Speed Merchants
1995 #SM8 Jeff Burton
SP Speed Merchants Die Cuts
1995 #SM8 Jeff Burton
SP Super Series
1997 #34 Jeff Burton
1997 #76 Jeff Burton's Car
1997 #109 Jeff Burton
Speedflix
1996 #29 Jeff Burton
Speedflix Artist Proof's
1996 #29 Jeff Burton
SportsCom FanScan
1997 #1 Jeff Burton
SPx
1996 #7 Jeff Burton
1997 #15 Jeff Burton
SPx Blue
1997 #15 Jeff Burton
SPx Gold
1996 #7 Jeff Burton
1997 #15 Jeff Burton
SPx Silver
1997 #15 Jeff Burton
SPx Tag Team
1997 #TT3 M.Martin/J.Burton
SPx Tag Team Autographs
1997 #TA3 M.Martin/J.Burton
Traks
1992 #99 Jeff Burton
1993 #37 Jeff Burton
1993 #153 Jeff Burton
1994 #8 Jeff Burton
1994 #161 Jeff Burton
1995 #39 Jeff Burton
1995 #56 Jeff Burton
2006 #4 Jeff Burton
2006 #49 Jeff Burton's Car
2006 #106 Jeff Burton's Car PS
2007 #2 Jeff Burton
2007 #91 Jeff Burton FT
Traks 5th Anniversary
1995 #30 Jeff Burton
1995 #61 Jeff Burton's Car
Traks 5th Anniversary Gold
1995 #30 Jeff Burton
1995 #61 Jeff Burton's Car
Traks Auto Value
1994 #19 Jeff Burton
1995 #5 Jeff Burton
Traks Autographs
1994 #A2 Jeff/Ward Burton
2006 #4 Jeff Burton NC
TRAKS Autographs 25
2006 #4 Jeff Burton NC
Traks Driver's Seat
2007 #DS20 Jeff Burton
2007 #DS20B Jeff Burton VAR
Traks Driver's Seat National
2007 #DS20 Jeff Burton
Traks First Run
1993 #37 Jeff Burton
1993 #153 Jeff Burton
1994 #8 Jeff Burton
1994 #161 Jeff Burton
1995 #39 Jeff Burton
1995 #56 Jeff Burton
Traks Gold
2007 #G2 Jeff Burton
2007 #G91 Jeff Burton FT
Traks Goody's
1992 #10 Jeff Burton
Traks Holofoil
2007 #H2 Jeff Burton
2007 #H91 Jeff Burton FT
Traks On The Rise
1995 #OTR14 Jeff Burton
1995 #P1 Jeff Burton Prototype
Traks On The Rise First Run
1995 #OTR14 Jeff Burton
Traks Previews
2007 #EB2 Jeff Burton
Traks Racing Machines
1995 #RM19 Jeff Burton's Car
Traks Racing Machines Bonus
1992 #18B Jeff Burton/Ward Burton
Traks Racing Machines First Run
1995 #RM19 Jeff Burton's Car
Traks Red
2007 #R2 Jeff Burton
2007 #R91 Jeff Burton FT
Traks Review and Preview
1996 #20 Jeff Burton
1996 #49 Checklist III
Traks Review and Preview First Run
1996 #20 Jeff Burton
1996 #49 Checklist III
Traks Review and Preview Liquid Gold
1996 #LG4 Jeff Burton
Traks Review and Preview Magnets
1996 #20 Jeff Burton
TRAKS Stickers
2006 #31 Jeff Burton
Ultra
1996 #102 Jeff Burton
1996 #103 Jeff Burton
1996 #104 Jeff Burton's Car
1997 #5 Jeff Burton
1997 #56 Jeff Burton's Car
Ultra Update
1996 #5 Jeff Burton
1996 #51 Jeff Burton's Car
1996 #85 J.Burton/B.Parrott
Ultra Update Rising Star
1996 #3 Jeff Burton
Ultra Winn Dixie
1997 #WD10 Jeff Burton
Upper Deck
1995 #26 Jeff Burton
1995 #94 Jeff Burton's Car
1995 #131 Jeff Burton
1995 #168 Jeff Burton DYK
1995 #190 Jeff Burton
1995 #234 Jeff Burton SD
1995 #274 Jeff Burton's Car
1996 #7 Jeff Burton
1996 #47 Jeff Burton SB
1996 #87 Jeff Burton PP
1996 #143 Jeff Burton HB
Upper Deck Autographs
1995 #190 Jeff Burton
Upper Deck Diamond Vision
1998 #11 Jeff Burton
Upper Deck Diamond Vision Signature Moves
1998 #11 Jeff Burton
Upper Deck Gold Signature/Electric Gold
1995 #26 Jeff Burton
1995 #94 Jeff Burton's Car
1995 #131 Jeff Burton
1995 #168 Jeff Burton DYK
1995 #190 Jeff Burton
1995 #234 Jeff Burton SD
1995 #274 Jeff Burton's Car
Upper Deck MVP
2000 #29 Jeff Burton
2000 #64 Jeff Burton's Car
Upper Deck MVP Cup Quest 2000
2000 #CQ6 Jeff Burton
Upper Deck MVP Gold Script
2000 #29 Jeff Burton
2000 #64 Jeff Burton
Upper Deck MVP Legends in the Making
2000 #LM8 Jeff Burton
Upper Deck MVP NASCAR Gallery
2000 #NG4 Jeff Burton
Upper Deck MVP NASCAR Stars
2000 #NS4 Jeff Burton
Upper Deck MVP ProSign
2000 #PSJB Jeff Burton
Upper Deck MVP Silver Script
2000 #29 Jeff Burton
2000 #64 Jeff Burton
Upper Deck MVP Super Script
2000 #29 Jeff Burton/99
2000 #64 Jeff Burton's Car/99
Upper Deck Pop Weaver
1998 #PW4 Jeff Burton
Upper Deck Racing

2000 #5 Jeff Burton
Upper Deck Racing High Groove
2000 #HG1 Jeff Burton
Upper Deck Racing Record Pace
2000 #RP1 Jeff Burton
Upper Deck Racing Road Signs
2000 #RSJB Jeff Burton
Upper Deck Racing Trophy Dash
2000 #TD5 Jeff Burton
Upper Deck Road To The Cup
1996 #RC30 Jeff Burton
1996 #RC79 Jeff Burton's Car
1996 #RC112 Jeff Burton
1996 #RC147 Jeff Burton
1997 #15 Jeff Burton
1997 #57 Jeff Burton's Car
1997 #99 Jeff Burton
1997 #109 Jeff Burton's Trans.
1998 #9 Jeff Burton's Car
1998 #60 Jeff Burton's Car
1998 #89 Jeff Burton
1998 #108 Jeff Burton
1999 #16 Jeff Burton
1999 #46 Jeff Burton's Car
Upper Deck Road To The Cup Autographs
1996 #H30 Jeff Burton
Upper Deck Road To The Cup Cup Quest Turn 1
1998 #CQ9 Jeff Burton's Car
Upper Deck Road To The Cup Cup Quest Turn 2
1998 #CQ9 Jeff Burton's Car
Upper Deck Road To The Cup Cup Quest Turn 3
1998 #CQ9 Jeff Burton's Car
Upper Deck Road To The Cup Cup Quest Turn 4
1998 #CQ9 Jeff Burton's Car
Upper Deck Road To The Cup Cup Quest Victory Lane
1998 #CQ9 Jeff Burton's Car
Upper Deck Road to the Cup NASCAR Chronicles
1999 #NC7 Jeff Burton
Upper Deck Road To The Cup Predictor Plus
1997 #21 Jeff Burton
Upper Deck Road To The Cup Predictor Plus Cel Die Cuts
1997 #21 Jeff Burton
Upper Deck Road To The Cup Predictor Plus Cels
1997 #21 Jeff Burton
Upper Deck Road To The Cup Premiere Position
1997 #PP23 Jeff Burton
1997 #PP48 Jeff Burton
Upper Deck Road to the Cup Road to the Cup Bronze Level 1
1999 #RTTC7Jeff Burton
Upper Deck Road to the Cup Road to the Cup Gold Level 3
1999 #RTTC7Jeff Burton
Upper Deck Road to the Cup Road to the Cup Silver Level 2
1999 #RTTC7Jeff Burton
Upper Deck Road to the Cup Signature Collection
1999 #JB Jeff Burton
Upper Deck Road to the Cup Signature Collection Checkered Flag
1999 #JB Jeff Burton
Upper Deck Road to the Cup Tires of Daytona
1999 #T5 Jeff Burton
Upper Deck Road to the Cup Upper Deck Profiles
1999 #P14 Jeff Burton
Upper Deck Road To The Cup Winning Materials
1998 #W5 Jeff Burton
Upper Deck Silver Signature/Electric Silver
1995 #26 Jeff Burton
1995 #94 Jeff Burton's Car
1995 #131 Jeff Burton
1995 #168 Jeff Burton DYK
1995 #190 Jeff Burton
1995 #234 Jeff Burton SD
1995 #274 Jeff Burton's Car
Upper Deck Victory Circle
1997 #34 Jeff Burton
1997 #84 Jeff Burton's Car
1998 #34 Jeff Burton
1998 #79 Jeff Burton's Car
1998 #96 Jeff Burton
1998 #143 Jeff Burton
1999 #23 Jeff Burton
1999 #54 Jeff Burton's Car
2000 #15 Jeff Burton
2000 #58 Jeff Burton's Car
2000 #74 Jeff Burton's Car
Upper Deck Victory Circle 32 Days of Speed
1998 #D6 Jeff Burton
Upper Deck Victory Circle 32 Days of Speed Gold
1998 #D6 Jeff Burton
Upper Deck Victory Circle Autographs
1998 #AG2 Jeff Burton
Upper Deck Victory Circle Exclusives Level 1 Silver
2000 #15 Jeff Burton
2000 #58 Jeff Burton's Car
2000 #74 Jeff Burton's Car
Upper Deck Victory Circle Exclusives Level 2 Gold
2000 #15 Jeff Burton/99
2000 #58 Jeff Burton's Car/99
2000 #74 Jeff Burton's Car/99
Upper Deck Victory Circle Income Statement
1999 #IS5 Jeff Burton
2000 #IS2 Jeff Burton
Upper Deck Victory Circle Income Statement LTD
2000 #IS2 Jeff Burton
Upper Deck Victory Circle Point Leaders
1998 #PL4 Jeff Burton
Upper Deck Victory Circle Predictor Plus
1998 #14 Jeff Burton
Upper Deck Victory Circle Predictor Plus Cel Redemption
1998 #14 Jeff Burton
Upper Deck Victory Circle Signature Collection
1999 #JB Jeff Burton

2000 #JB Jeff Burton
Upper Deck Victory Circle Sparks of Brilliance
1998 #SB10 Jeff Burton
Upper Deck Victory Circle Speed Zone
1999 #SZ7 Jeff Burton
Upper Deck Victory Circle Track Masters
1999 #TM7 Jeff Burton
Upper Deck Victory Circle UD Exclusives
1999 #23 Jeff Burton
1999 #54 Jeff Burton
Upper Deck Victory Circle Victory Circle
1999 #V4 Jeff Burton
2000 #V4 Jeff Burton
Upper Deck Victory Circle Victory Circle LTD
2000 #V4 Jeff Burton
Upper Deck Victory Circle Winning Material Autographed Victory Hat
2000 #HJB Jeff Burton
Velveeta Jeff Burton
2002 #1 Jeff Burton
2002 #2 Jeff Burton
2002 #3 Jeff Burton
VIP
1994 #6 Jeff Burton
1995 #5 Jeff Burton
1996 #4 Jeff Burton
1997 #3 Jeff Burton
1997 #46 Jeff Burton
1998 #4 Jeff Burton
1998 #37 Jeff Burton's Car
1999 #4 Jeff Burton
1999 #40 Jeff Burton's Car
1999 #50 J.Burton/M.Martin CL
2000 #6 Jeff Burton
2000 #21 Jeff Burton V
2000 #30 Jeff Burton NB
2000 #33 Jeff Burton DF
2001 #6 Jeff Burton
2001 #34 Jeff Burton RT
2002 #18 Jeff Burton
2002 #35 Jeff Burton AS
2003 #1 Jeff Burton
2004 #1 Jeff Burton
2004 #42 Jeff Burton's Car R
2005 #2 Jeff Burton
2005 #41 Jeff Burton's Car R
2005 #82 Jeff Burton BN
2005 #88 Jeff Burton ATML
2006 #2 Jeff Burton
2006 #38 Jeff Burton's Car R
2006 #57 Jeff Burton BTN
2007 #4 Jeff Burton
2007 #62 Jeff Burton Red C
2007 #75 Jeff Burton Texas AP
VIP Autographs
1996 #4 Jeff Burton
VIP Cool Blue
1995 #5 Jeff Burton
VIP Driving Force
1998 #DF3 Jeff Burton's Car
VIP Driving Force Die Cuts
1998 #DF3 Jeff Burton's Car
VIP Emerald Proofs
1995 #5 Jeff Burton
1996 #4 Jeff Burton
VIP Explosives
1997 #3 Jeff Burton
1997 #46 Jeff Burton
1998 #4 Jeff Burton
1998 #37 Jeff Burton's Car
1999 #X4 Jeff Burton
1999 #X40 Jeff Burton's Car
1999 #X50 Burton/Martin CL
2000 #X6 Jeff Burton
2000 #X21 Jeff Burton V
2000 #X30 Jeff Burton NB
2000 #X33 Jeff Burton DF
2001 #6 Jeff Burton
2001 #34 Jeff Burton RT
2002 #X18 Jeff Burton
2002 #X35 Jeff Burton AS
2003 #X1 Jeff Burton
VIP Explosives Lasers
1999 #4 Jeff Burton
1999 #40 Jeff Burton's Car
1999 #50 Burton/Martin CL
2000 #LX6 Jeff Burton
2000 #LX21 Jeff Burton V
2000 #LX30 Jeff Burton NB
2000 #LX33 Jeff Burton DF
2001 #LX6 Jeff Burton
2001 #LX34 Jeff Burton RT
2002 #LX18 Jeff Burton
2002 #LX35 Jeff Burton AS
VIP Get A Grip Drivers
2007 #GGD25 Jeff Burton
VIP Get A Grip Teams
2007 #GGT25 Jeff Burton
VIP Head Gear
1998 #HG1 Jeff Burton
1999 #HG9 Jeff Burton
2005 #1 Jeff Burton
2006 #HG12 Jeff Burton
VIP Head Gear Die Cuts
1998 #HG1 Jeff Burton
VIP Head Gear Plastic
1999 #HG9 Jeff Burton
VIP Head Gear Transparent
2005 #1 Jeff Burton
2006 #HG12 Jeff Burton
VIP Helmets
1995 #H2 Jeff Burton
VIP Helmets Gold
1995 #H2 Jeff Burton
VIP Lap Leader
2006 #LL9 Jeff Burton
VIP Lap Leader Transparent
2006 #LL9 Jeff Burton
VIP Lap Leaders
1998 #LL1 Jeff Burton's Car
1999 #LL9 Jeff Burton
2000 #LL4 Jeff Burton
VIP Lap Leaders Acetate
1998 #LL1 Jeff Burton's Car
VIP Lap Leaders Explosives
2000 #LL4 Jeff Burton
VIP Lap Leaders Explosives Lasers

2000 #LL4 Jeff Burton
VIP Laser Explosive
2003 #LX1 Jeff Burton
VIP Making the Show
2000 #MS6 Jeff Burton
2001 #24 Jeff Burton CL
2002 #MS23 Jeff Burton
2003 #MS24 Jeff Burton CL
2004 #MS27 Jeff Burton CL
2005 #27 Jeff Burton
2006 #MS18 Jeff Burton
VIP Mile Masters
2001 #MM10Jeff Burton
2002 #MM10Jeff Burton
VIP Mile Masters Precious Metal
2001 #MM10Jeff Burton
VIP Mile Masters Transparent
2001 #MM10Jeff Burton
2002 #MM10Jeff Burton
VIP Mile Masters Transparent LTD
2002 #MM10Jeff Burton
VIP Oil Slicks
1997 #3 Jeff Burton
1997 #46 Jeff Burton
VIP Out of the Box
1999 #OB9 Jeff Burton
VIP Previews
2003 #1 Jeff Burton
2004 #EB1 Jeff Burton
2004 #EB42 Jeff Burton's Car R
2005 #EB2 Jeff Burton
2005 #EB41 Jeff Burton's Car R
2007 #EB4 Jeff Burton
VIP Rear View Mirror
1999 #RM5 Jeff Burton
VIP Red Hot
1995 #5 Jeff Burton
VIP Samples
2002 #18 Jeff Burton
2002 #35 Jeff Burton AS
2003 #1 Jeff Burton
2004 #1 Jeff Burton
2004 #42 Jeff Burton's Car R
2005 #2 Jeff Burton
2005 #41 Jeff Burton's Car R
2005 #82 Jeff Burton BN
2005 #88 Jeff Burton ATML
VIP Sheet Metal
2000 #SM2 Jeff Burton
VIP Solos
1998 #4 Jeff Burton
1998 #37 Jeff Burton's Car
VIP Sunday Best
2007 #SB2 Jeff Burton
VIP Tin
2003 #CT1 Jeff Burton
VIP Torquers
1996 #4 Jeff Burton
VIP Tradin' Paint Bronze
2004 #TPT14Jeff Burton
VIP Tradin' Paint Cars
2003 #TPT11Jeff Burton's Car
VIP Tradin' Paint Cars Bronze
2006 #TPT14Jeff Burton
VIP Tradin' Paint Drivers
2003 #TPD11 Jeff Burton
VIP Tradin' Paint Drivers Gold
2006 #TPD14 Jeff Burton
VIP Tradin' Paint Drivers Silver
2006 #TPD14 Jeff Burton
VIP Tradin' Paint Gold
2004 #TPD14 Jeff Burton
VIP Tradin' Paint Silver
2004 #TPD14 Jeff Burton
VIP Triple Gear Sheet Metal
1998 #TGS9 Jeff Burton
VIP Trophy Club
2007 #TC5 Jeff Burton
VIP Trophy Club Transparent
2007 #TC5 Jeff Burton
VIP Vintage Performance
1999 #5 Jeff Burton
Viper
1996 #18 Jeff Burton
1997 #8 Jeff Burton
1997 #38 Jeff Burton
1997 #54 Jeff Burton
Viper Anaconda Jumbos
1997 #A11 Jeff Burton
Viper Black Mamba
1996 #18 Jeff Burton
Viper Black Mamba First Strike
1996 #18 Jeff Burton
Viper Black Racer
1997 #8 Jeff Burton
1997 #38 Jeff Burton
1997 #54 Jeff Burton
Viper Black Racer First Strike
1997 #8 Jeff Burton
1997 #38 Jeff Burton
1997 #54 Jeff Burton
Viper Copperhead Die Cuts
1996 #18 Jeff Burton
Viper Copperhead Die Cuts First Strike
1996 #18 Jeff Burton
Viper Diamondback
1997 #DB6 Jeff Burton
Viper Diamondback Authentic
1997 #DBA6 Jeff Burton
Viper Diamondback Authentic Eastern
1997 #DBA6 Jeff Burton
Viper Diamondback Authentic Eastern First Strike
1997 #DBA6 Jeff Burton
Viper Diamondback Authentic First Strike
1997 #DBA6 Jeff Burton
Viper Diamondback First Strike
1997 #DB6 Jeff Burton
Viper First Strike
1996 #18 Jeff Burton
1997 #8 Jeff Burton
1997 #38 Jeff Burton
1997 #54 Jeff Burton
Viper Green Mamba
1996 #18 Jeff Burton

Viper Red Cobra
1996 #18 Jeff Burton
Viper Snake Eyes
1997 #SE9 Jeff Burton
Viper Snake Eyes First Strike
1997 #SE9 Jeff Burton
Wheels
1998 #5 Jeff Burton
1998 #33 Jeff Burton's Car
1998 #46 Jeff Burton
1999 #4 Jeff Burton
1999 #63 Jeff Burton's Car
Wheels 50th Anniversary
1998 #A2 Jeff Burton
1998 #A17 Jeff Burton's Car
Wheels American Thunder
2003 #2 Jeff Burton
2003 #35 Jeff Burton DT
2004 #1 Jeff Burton
2004 #82 Jeff Burton CC
2005 #3 Jeff Burton
2005 #33 Jeff Burton's Rig Rt. 66
2005 #71 Jeff Burton RR
2006 #3 Jeff Burton
2006 #41 Jeff Burton DT
2006 #46 Jeff Burton's Car HR
2006 #65 Jeff Burton SS
2007 #3 Jeff Burton
2007 #47 Jeff Burton's Car DT
2007 #71 Jeff Burton BP
2007 #81 Jeff Burton HC
Wheels American Thunder American Dreams
2007 #AD5 Jeff Burton
Wheels American Thunder American Dreams Gold
2007 #ADG5 Jeff Burton
Wheels American Thunder American Eagle
2004 #AE1 Jeff Burton
2005 #AE1 Jeff Burton
Wheels American Thunder American Muscle
2006 #AM6 Jeff Burton
Wheels American Thunder American Racing Idol
2006 #RI4 Jeff Burton
Wheels American Thunder American Racing Idol Golden
2006 #RI4 Jeff Burton
Wheels American Thunder Autographed Hat Instant Winner
2007 #AH5 Jeff Burton
Wheels American Thunder Born On
2003 #BO2 Jeff Burton
2003 #BO35 Jeff Burton DT
Wheels American Thunder Cool Threads
2003 #CT1 Jeff Burton
2004 #CT1 Jeff Burton
Wheels American Thunder Cup Quest
2004 #CQ11 Jeff Burton
Wheels American Thunder Double Hat
2006 #DH3 Jeff Burton
2007 #DH6 Jeff Burton
Wheels American Thunder Golden Eagle
2004 #AE1 Jeff Burton
2005 #GE1 Jeff Burton
Wheels American Thunder Grandstand
2006 #GS1 Jeff Burton
Wheels American Thunder Head to Toe
2003 #HT1 Jeff Burton
2004 #HT1 Jeff Burton/50
Wheels American Thunder Heads Up Goodyear
2003 #HUG1 Jeff Burton
Wheels American Thunder Heads Up Manufacturer
2003 #HUM3Jeff Burton
Wheels American Thunder Heads Up Team
2003 #HUT2 Jeff Burton/90
Wheels American Thunder Heads Up Winston
2003 #HUW3Jeff Burton
Wheels American Thunder Holofoil
2003 #P2 Jeff Burton
2003 #P35 Jeff Burton DT
Wheels American Thunder Medallion
2005 #MD22 Jeff Burton
Wheels American Thunder Post Mark
2003 #PM1 Jeff Burton
2004 #PM26 Jeff Burton
Wheels American Thunder Previews
2003 #2 Jeff Burton
2003 #35 Jeff Burton DT
2004 #EB1 Jeff Burton
2005 #3 Jeff Burton
2006 #EB3 Jeff Burton
2007 #EB3 Jeff Burton
Wheels American Thunder Pushin Pedal
2003 #PP1 Jeff Burton
2004 #PP2 Jeff Burton/200
Wheels American Thunder Rookie Thunder
2003 #RT4 Jeff Burton
Wheels American Thunder Samples
2003 #P2 Jeff Burton
2003 #P35 Jeff Burton DT
2004 #1 Jeff Burton
2004 #82 Jeff Burton CC
2005 #3 Jeff Burton
2005 #33 Jeff Burton's Rig Rt. 66
2005 #71 Jeff Burton RR
Wheels American Thunder Single Hat
2005 #SH1 Jeff Burton
Wheels American Thunder Starting Grid
2007 #SG1 Jeff Burton
Wheels American Thunder Thunder Road
2003 #TR18 Jeff Burton
2004 #TR18 Jeff Burton
2005 #TR18 Jeff Burton
2006 #TR15 Jeff Burton
2007 #TR12 Jeff Burton
Wheels American Thunder Triple Hat
2003 #TH3 Jeff Burton
2004 #TH27 Jeff Burton
Wheels Autographs
1998 #7 Jeff Burton/200
1999 #4 Jeff Burton/150
2003 #8 Jeff Burton Citgo AT
2003 #9 Jeff Burton Gain AT
2004 #8 Jeff Burton HG

2006 #7 Jeff Burton NC
2007 #4 Jeff Burton NC HG
Wheels Autographs Press Plates Black
2007 #4 Jeff Burton NC
Wheels Autographs Press Plates Cyan
2007 #4 Jeff Burton NC
Wheels Autographs Press Plates Magenta
2007 #4 Jeff Burton NC
Wheels Autographs Press Plates Yellow
2007 #4 Jeff Burton NC
Wheels Dialed In
1999 #DI9 Jeff Burton
Wheels Double Take
1998 #E1 Jeff Burton
Wheels Golden
1998 #5 Jeff Burton
1998 #33 Jeff Burton's Car
1998 #46 Jeff Burton
1999 #4 Jeff Burton
1999 #63 Jeff Burton's Car
Wheels Green Flags
1998 #GF3 Jeff Burton's Car
Wheels High Gear
1994 #65 Jeff Burton
1994 #108 Jeff Burton
1995 #23 Jeff Burton
1995 #99 Jeff Burton ROY
1998 #4 Jeff Burton
1998 #36 Jeff Burton's Car
1998 #51 Jeff Burton
1999 #5 Jeff Burton
1999 #36 Jeff Burton's Car
1999 #51 Jeff Burton
2000 #6 Jeff Burton
2000 #36 Jeff Burton's Car
2000 #50 Jeff Burton
2001 #4 Jeff Burton
2001 #60 Jeff Burton CA
2001 #67 Jeff Burton WCP
2002 #2 Jeff Burton
2003 #4 Jeff Burton
2003 #58 The Fab Four
2004 #3 Jeff Burton
2006 #17 Jeff Burton
2006 #54 Jeff Burton's Car C
2006 #69 Jeff Burton CM
2007 #7 Jeff Burton
2008 #8 Jeff Burton
2008 #31 Jeff Burton NBS
2008 #49 Jeff Burton's Car C
2008 #69 Jeff Burton's Car EL
2008 #79 Jeff Burton NI
Wheels High Gear Autographs
1998 #2 Jeff Burton/250
1999 #5 Jeff Burton/350
2000 #8 Jeff Burton
2001 #5 Jeff Burton
2002 #8 Jeff Burton
Wheels High Gear Blue Hawaii SCDA Promos
2003 #4 Jeff Burton
2003 #58 The Fab Four
Wheels High Gear Day One
1994 #108 Jeff Burton
1995 #23 Jeff Burton
1995 #99 Jeff Burton ROY
Wheels High Gear Day One Gold
1994 #108 Jeff Burton
1995 #23 Jeff Burton
1995 #99 Jeff Burton ROY
Wheels High Gear Driven
2007 #DR2 Jeff Burton
2008 #DR20 Jeff Burton
Wheels High Gear Final Standings
2008 #F8 Jeff Burton/8
Wheels High Gear Final Standings Gold
2007 #FS7 Jeff Burton/7
Wheels High Gear First Gear
1998 #13 Jeff Burton
1998 #36 Jeff Burton's Car
1998 #51 Jeff Burton
1999 #36 Jeff Burton's Car
1999 #51 Jeff Burton
2000 #6 Jeff Burton
2000 #36 Jeff Burton
2000 #50 Jeff Burton
2001 #4 Jeff Burton
2001 #60 Jeff Burton CA
2001 #67 Jeff Burton WCP
2002 #2 Jeff Burton
2003 #F4 Jeff Burton
2003 #F58 The Fab Four
Wheels High Gear Flag to Flag
2006 #FF2 Jeff Burton
Wheels High Gear Full Throttle
2008 #FT6 Jeff Burton
Wheels High Gear Gear Jammers
1998 #GJ17 Jeff Burton
Wheels High Gear Gear Shifters
1999 #GS7 Jeremy Mayfield
2000 #GS5 Jeff Burton
2001 #GS4 Jeff Burton
Wheels High Gear Gold
1994 #65 Jeff Burton
1994 #108 Jeff Burton
1995 #23 Jeff Burton
1995 #99 Jeff Burton ROY
Wheels High Gear High Groove
1998 #HG9 Jeff Burton's Car
2002 #HG2 Jeff Burton
2003 #HG2 Jeff Burton
2004 #HG2 Jeff Burton
Wheels High Gear Hot Streaks
2001 #HS9 Jeff Burton
2002 #HS1 Jeff Burton
Wheels High Gear Hot Treads
2003 #HT2 Jeff Burton
Wheels High Gear Man & Machine (Machine)
2006 #MMB8 Jeff Burton
Wheels High Gear Man & Machine (Man)
2006 #MMA8 Jeff Burton
Wheels High Gear Man and Machine Cars
1998 #4 Jeff Burton's Car
1999 #MM4B Jeff Burton's Car
2000 #MM7B Jeff Burton's Car
2001 #MM6B Jeff Burton's Car
Wheels High Gear Man and Machine Drivers
1998 #MM4 Jeff Burton

1999 #MM4A Jeff Burton
1999 #MM7A Jeremy Mayfield
2000 #MM7A Jeff Burton
2001 #MM8A Jeff Burton
Wheels High Gear MPH
1998 #13 Jeff Burton
1998 #36 Jeff Burton's Car
1998 #51 Jeff Burton
1999 #7 Jeff Burton
1999 #36 Jeff Burton's Car
1999 #51 Jeff Burton
2000 #6 Jeff Burton
2000 #36 Jeff Burton
2000 #50 Jeff Burton
2001 #4 Jeff Burton
2001 #60 Jeff Burton CA
2001 #67 Jeff Burton WCP
2002 #2 Jeff Burton
2003 #M4 Jeff Burton
2003 #M58 The Fab Four
2004 #M3 Jeff Burton
2006 #M17 Jeff Burton
2006 #M54 Jeff Burton's Car C
2006 #M69 Jeff Burton CM
2007 #M7 Jeff Burton
2008 #M8 Jeff Burton
2008 #M31 Jeff Burton NBS
2008 #M49 Jeff Burton's Car C
2008 #M69 Jeff Burton's Car EL
2008 #M79 Jeff Burton NI
Wheels High Gear Previews
2003 #4 Jeff Burton
2004 #3 Jeff Burton
2007 #EB7 Jeff Burton
2008 #EB8 Jeff Burton
Wheels High Gear Previews Green
2006 #EB17 Jeff Burton
Wheels High Gear Rookie Shootout Autographs
1994 #RS3 Jeff Burton AUTO/1500
Wheels High Gear Samples
2003 #4 Jeff Burton
2003 #58 The Fab Four
2004 #3 Jeff Burton
Wheels High Gear Sunday Sensation
2000 #OC5 Jeff Burton
2001 #SS9 Jeff Burton
2002 #SS2 Jeff Burton
Wheels High Gear The Chase
2008 #TC8 Jeff Burton
Wheels High Gear Top Tier
1998 #TT4 Jeff Burton 1:60
1999 #TT7 Jeremy Mayfield 1:20
2000 #TT6 Jeff Burton
2001 #TT3 Jeff Burton
2007 #TT7 Jeff Burton
Wheels High Gear Top Tier Holofoils
2001 #TT3 Jeff Burton
Wheels Runnin and Gunnin
1999 #RG11 Jeff Burton
Wheels Runnin and Gunnin Foils
1999 #RG11 Jeff Burton
Wheels Solos
1999 #4 Jeff Burton
1999 #63 Jeff Burton
Winner's Choice Busch
1992 #78 Jeff Burton
1992 #79 Jeff Burton's Car
Zenith
1995 #8 Jeff Burton HG
1995 #55 Jeff Burton's Transporter
1996 #20 Jeff Burton
Zenith Artist Proofs
1996 #20 Jeff Burton RP

Busch, Kurt

Coca-Cola Racing Family AutoZone
2005 #1 Kurt Busch
eTopps
2003 #33 Kurt Busch/3000
Maxx
2000 #75 Kurt Busch RF RC
Post Cereal
2004 #3 Kurt Busch
Press Pass
2002 #7 Kurt Busch
2003 #7 Kurt Busch
2003 #58 Kurt Busch DS
2003 #63 Jr./JJ/New/Sad/Ken/Bus DS
2003 #75 Kurt-ain Call WCS
2004 #7 Kurt Busch
2004 #75 Kurt Busch's Car OTW
2004 #75B Kurt Busch's Car OTW SP
2004 #78 One For The Ages WCS
2004 #80 The Drive for Five WCS
2004 #82 Growing Up Fast WCS
2004 #94 Kurt Busch DS
2005 #36 Kurt Busch
2005 #69 Kurt Busch's Car OTW
2005 #77 Kurt Busch NS
2005 #97 Ky.Busch/K.Busch Y
2005 #117 Kurt Busch's Car
2006 #29 Kurt Busch
2006 #82 Kurt Busch's Car OTW
2006 #108 Kurt Busch U
2006 #114 Kurt Busch TT
2007 #14 Kurt Busch
2007 #81 Kurt Busch's Car OT
2007 #87 Kurt Busch NS
2007 #99 Kurt Busch U
2008 #12 Kurt Busch
2008 #111 Kurt Busch Top 12
2008 #0 Cup Chase Matt Kenseth Tony Stewart Jeff Gordon Jimmie Johnson Denny Hamlin Kurt Busch Kevin Harvick Carl Edwards Kyle Busch Martin Truex Jr. Jeff Burton Clint Bowyer
Press Pass Autographs
2002 #12 Kurt Busch
2003 #9 Kurt Busch E/P
2004 #9 Kurt Busch P
2005 #7 Kurt Busch E/P
2006 #7 Kurt Busch NC
2007 #4 Kurt Busch NC P
2008 #9 Kurt Busch NC E
Press Pass Blue
2006 #B29 Kurt Busch
2006 #B82 Kurt Busch's Car OTW
2006 #B108 Kurt Busch U

2006 #B114 Kurt Busch TT
2007 #B14 Kurt Busch
2007 #B81 Kurt Busch's Car OT
2007 #B87 Kurt Busch NS
2007 #B99 Kurt Busch U
2008 #B12 Kurt Busch
2008 #B111 Kurt Busch Top 12

Press Pass Burning Rubber Autographs
2004 #BRKB Kurt Busch/97
2007 #BRS-KB Kurt Busch/2

Press Pass Burning Rubber Cars
2004 #BRT5 Kurt Busch's Car
2005 #BRT17 Kurt Busch's Car
2006 #BRT1 Kurt Busch

Press Pass Burning Rubber Drivers
2004 #BRD5 Kurt Busch
2005 #BRD17 Kurt Busch
2006 #BRD1 Kurt Busch
2008 #BRD20 Kurt Busch Pocono
2008 #BRD22 Kurt Busch Mich.

Press Pass Burning Rubber Drivers Gold
2005 #BRD17 Kurt Busch
2006 #BRD1 Kurt Busch
2008 #BRD20 Kurt Busch Pocono
2008 #BRD22 Kurt Busch Mich.

Press Pass Burning Rubber Drivers Prime Cuts
2008 #BRD20 Kurt Busch Pocono
2008 #BRD22 Kurt Busch Mich.

Press Pass Burning Rubber Teams
2008 #BRT20 Kurt Busch Pocono
2008 #BRT22 Kurt Busch Mich.

Press Pass Coca-Cola Racing Family
2003 #3 Kurt Busch

Press Pass Coca-Cola Racing Family Scratch-off
2003 #2 Kurt Busch

Press Pass Collector's Series Box Set
2007 #SB3 Kurt Busch

Press Pass Collectors Series Making the Show
2006 #MS24 Kurt Busch

Press Pass Collectors Series Sunday Best
2007 #CB3 Kurt Busch

Press Pass Cup Chase
2004 #CCR6 Kurt Busch
2005 #CCR1 Kurt Busch Winner
2006 #CCR4 Kurt Busch
2007 #CCR13 Kurt Busch Winner
2008 #CC16 Kurt Busch

Press Pass Cup Chase Prizes
2004 #CCR6 Kurt Busch
2005 #CCP1 Kurt Busch
2005 #CCP18 Kurt Busch '04 Champ
2007 #CC5 Kurt Busch

Press Pass Double Burner
2005 #DB11 Kurt Busch

Press Pass Double Burner Exchange
2005 #DB11 Kurt Busch

Press Pass Double Burner Firesuit-Glove
2007 #DB8 Kurt Busch

Press Pass Double Burner Firesuit-Glove Exchange
2007 #DB8 Kurt Busch

Press Pass Eclipse
2002 #21 Kurt Busch
2002 #49 Kurt Busch SO
2003 #3 Kurt Busch
2003 #42 The Spin Doctor WCS
2004 #10 Kurt Busch
2004 #36 Kurt Busch's Car
2004 #67 Kurt Busch WCS
2005 #1 Kurt Busch
2005 #52 Kurt Busch Z
2005 #54 Kurt Busch Z
2005 #67 Kurt Busch NS
2005 #88 Kurt Busch SM
2005 #0 Kurt Busch Gold/200
2005 #0 Kurt Busch Holofoil/50
2006 #65 NCS Top-10 BA
2007 #15 Kurt Busch
2007 #34 Kurt Busch TO
2008 #6 Kurt Busch
2008 #33 Kurt Busch RM
2008 #40 Kurt Busch TO
2008 #65 Kurt Busch BTF
2008 #75 Top 10 Drivers SO

Press Pass Eclipse Destination WIN
2004 #8 Kurt Busch
2004 #12 Kurt Busch
2005 #5 Kurt Busch
2005 #17 Kurt Busch

Press Pass Eclipse Double Hot Treads
2003 #DT7 J.Burton/K.Busch

Press Pass Eclipse Gold
2007 #G15 Kurt Busch
2007 #G34 Kurt Busch TO
2008 #G6 Kurt Busch
2008 #G33 Kurt Busch RM
2008 #G40 Kurt Busch TO
2008 #G65 Kurt Busch BTF
2008 #G75 Top 10 Drivers SO

Press Pass Eclipse Hyperdrive
2005 #HD9 Kurt Busch

Press Pass Eclipse Maxim
2004 #MX8 Kurt Busch

Press Pass Eclipse Previews
2003 #3 Kurt Busch
2004 #10 Kurt Busch
2005 #EB1 Kurt Busch
2005 #EB52 Kurt Busch Z
2005 #EB54 Kurt Busch Z
2005 #EB67 Kurt Busch NS
2005 #EB88 Kurt Busch SM
2007 #EB15 Kurt Busch
2007 #EB34 Kurt Busch TO
2008 #EB6 Kurt Busch
2008 #EB33 Kurt Busch RM
2008 #EB75 Top 10 Drivers SO

Press Pass Eclipse Racing Champions
2003 #RC8 Kurt Busch
2003 #RC33 Kurt Busch
2003 #RC34 Kurt Busch
2003 #RC36 Kurt Busch
2007 #RC10 Kurt Busch
2007 #RC17 Kurt Busch

Press Pass Eclipse Red
2007 #R15 Kurt Busch
2007 #R34 Kurt Busch TO
2008 #R6 Kurt Busch
2008 #R33 Kurt Busch RM
2008 #R40 Kurt Busch TO
2008 #R65 Kurt Busch BTF
2008 #R75 Top 10 Drivers SO

Press Pass Eclipse Samples
2002 #21 Kurt Busch
2002 #49 Kurt Busch SO
2003 #3 Kurt Busch
2003 #42 The Spin Doctor WCS
2004 #10 Kurt Busch
2004 #36 Kurt Busch's Car
2004 #67 Kurt Busch WCS
2005 #1 Kurt Busch
2005 #52 Kurt Busch Z
2005 #54 Kurt Busch Z
2005 #67 Kurt Busch NS
2005 #88 Kurt Busch SM

Press Pass Eclipse Skidmarks
2003 #SM6 Kurt Busch
2004 #SM2 Kurt Busch
2005 #SM2 Kurt Busch

Press Pass Eclipse Skidmarks Holofoil
2004 #SM2 Kurt Busch
2005 #SM2 Kurt Busch

Press Pass Eclipse Solar Eclipse
2002 #S21 Kurt Busch
2002 #S49 Kurt Busch SO
2003 #P3 Kurt Busch
2003 #P42 The Spin Doctor WCS

Press Pass Eclipse Star Tracks
2008 #ST9 Kurt Busch

Press Pass Eclipse Star Tracks Holofoil
2008 #ST9 Kurt Busch

Press Pass Eclipse Stellar
2008 #ST5 Kurt Busch

Press Pass Eclipse Teammates Autographs
2003 #JBKB J.Burton/K.Busch
2005 #2 Busch/Martin/Kenseth
2005 #8 K.Busch/C.Edwards
2007 #5 Busch/Newman
2008 #BN Kurt Busch Ryan Newman/35

Press Pass Eclipse Under Cover Autographs
2008 #UC-KB Kurt Busch/2

Press Pass Eclipse Under Cover Cars
2004 #UCD5 Kurt Busch
2005 #UCT5 Kurt Busch

Press Pass Eclipse Under Cover Double Cover
2004 #DC12 K.Busch/M.Kenseth
2004 #DC15 J.Burton/K.Busch
2005 #DC4 K.Busch/M.Martin
2005 #DC6 K.Busch/M.Kenseth

Press Pass Eclipse Under Cover Double Cover Name
2007 #DC4 Newman/Busch
2008 #DC5 Kurt Busch Ryan Newman

Press Pass Eclipse Under Cover Double Cover NASCAR
2007 #DC4 Newman/Busch
2008 #DC5 Kurt Busch Ryan Newman

Press Pass Eclipse Under Cover Driver Gold
2004 #UCD5 Kurt Busch

Press Pass Eclipse Under Cover Driver Red
2004 #UCD5 Kurt Busch
2005 #UCD5 Kurt Busch

Press Pass Eclipse Under Cover Driver Silver
2004 #UCD5 Kurt Busch

Press Pass Eclipse Under Cover Drivers
2007 #UCD14 Kurt Busch
2008 #UCD4 Kurt Busch

Press Pass Eclipse Under Cover Drivers Eclipse
2007 #UCD14 Kurt Busch
2008 #UCD4 Kurt Busch

Press Pass Eclipse Under Cover Drivers Holofoil
2005 #UCD5 Kurt Busch

Press Pass Eclipse Under Cover Drivers Name
2007 #UCD14 Kurt Busch
2008 #UCD4 Kurt Busch

Press Pass Eclipse Under Cover Drivers NASCAR
2007 #UCD14 Kurt Busch
2008 #UCD4 Kurt Busch

Press Pass Eclipse Under Cover Drivers Silver
2005 #UCD5 Kurt Busch

Press Pass Eclipse Under Cover Teams
2007 #UCT14 Kurt Busch
2008 #UCT4 Kurt Busch

Press Pass Eclipse Under Cover Teams NASCAR
2007 #UCT14 Kurt Busch
2008 #UCT4 Kurt Busch

Press Pass Four Wide
2008 #FW-KB Kurt Busch

Press Pass Four Wide Checkered
2008 #FW-KB Kurt Busch

Press Pass Gold
2006 #G29 Kurt Busch
2006 #G82 Kurt Busch's Car OTW
2006 #G108 Kurt Busch U
2006 #G114 Kurt Busch TT
2007 #G14 Kurt Busch
2007 #G81 Kurt Busch's Car OT
2007 #G87 Kurt Busch NS
2007 #G99 Kurt Busch U
2008 #G12 Kurt Busch
2008 #G111 Kurt Busch Top 12

Press Pass Gold Holofoil
2003 #P7 Kurt Busch
2003 #P58 Kurt Busch DS
2003 #P63 Jr./Johnson/Newman Sadler/Kenseth/Busch DS
2003 #P75 Kurt-ain Call WCS

Press Pass Hot Treads
2002 #HT16 Kurt Busch's Car/1555
2004 #HTR14 Kurt Busch
2005 #HTR5 Kurt Busch

Press Pass Hot Treads Holofoil
2004 #HTR14 Kurt Busch
2005 #HTR5 Kurt Busch

Press Pass Hot Treads Rookie Rubber
2001 #RR2 Kurt Busch

Press Pass Legends
2005 #46 Kurt Busch C
2006 #39 Kurt Busch
2007 #47 Kurt Busch

Press Pass Legends Autographs Black
2005 #13 Kurt Busch
2006 #20 Kurt Busch

Press Pass Legends Autographs Blue
2007 #4 Kurt Busch/70

Press Pass Legends Blue
2005 #46B Kurt Busch C
2006 #B39 Kurt Busch
2007 #B47 Kurt Busch

Press Pass Legends Bronze
2006 #Z39 Kurt Busch
2007 #Z47 Kurt Busch

Press Pass Legends Champion Threads & Treads Bronze
2006 #CTT-KB Kurt Busch

Press Pass Legends Champion Threads & Treads Gold
2006 #CTT-KB Kurt Busch

Press Pass Legends Champion Threads & Treads Silver
2006 #CTT-KB Kurt Busch

Press Pass Legends Champion Threads Bronze
2006 #CT-KB Kurt Busch

Press Pass Legends Champion Threads Gold
2006 #CT-KB Kurt Busch

Press Pass Legends Champion Threads Patch
2006 #CT-KB Kurt Busch

Press Pass Legends Champion Threads Silver
2006 #CT-KB Kurt Busch

Press Pass Legends Double Threads Bronze
2005 #DT-BK K.Busch/M.Kenseth
2005 #DT-MB M.Martin/K.Busch

Press Pass Legends Double Threads Gold
2005 #DT-BK K.Busch/M.Kenseth
2005 #DT-MB M.Martin/K.Busch

Press Pass Legends Double Threads Silver
2005 #DT-BK K.Busch/M.Kenseth
2005 #DT-MB M.Martin/K.Busch

Press Pass Legends Gold
2005 #46G Kurt Busch C
2006 #G39 Kurt Busch
2007 #G47 Kurt Busch

Press Pass Legends Greatest Moments
2005 #GM18 R.Craven/K.Busch

Press Pass Legends Holofoil
2005 #46H Kurt Busch C
2006 #H39 Kurt Busch
2007 #H47 Kurt Busch

Press Pass Legends Press Plates Black
2005 #46 Kurt Busch C
2006 #PPB39 Kurt Busch
2007 #PP47 Kurt Busch

Press Pass Legends Press Plates Black Backs
2006 #PPB39B Kurt Busch
2007 #PP47 Kurt Busch

Press Pass Legends Press Plates Cyan
2005 #46 Kurt Busch C
2006 #PPC39 Kurt Busch
2007 #PP47 Kurt Busch

Press Pass Legends Press Plates Cyan Backs
2006 #PPC39B Kurt Busch
2007 #PP47 Kurt Busch

Press Pass Legends Press Plates Magenta
2005 #46 Kurt Busch C
2006 #PPM39 Kurt Busch
2007 #PP47 Kurt Busch

Press Pass Legends Press Plates Magenta Backs
2006 #PPM39B Kurt Busch
2007 #PP47 Kurt Busch

Press Pass Legends Press Plates Yellow
2005 #46 Kurt Busch C
2006 #PPY39 Kurt Busch
2007 #PP47 Kurt Busch

Press Pass Legends Press Plates Yellow Backs
2006 #PPY39B Kurt Busch
2007 #PP47 Kurt Busch

Press Pass Legends Previews
2005 #46 Kurt Busch C
2006 #EB39 Kurt Busch
2007 #EB47 Kurt Busch

Press Pass Legends Signature Series
2007 #KB Kurt Busch

Press Pass Legends Solo
2005 #46S Kurt Busch C
2006 #S39 Kurt Busch
2007 #S47 Kurt Busch

Press Pass Optima
2001 #4 Kurt Busch CRC
2002 #5 Kurt Busch
2002 #49 Kurt Busch YG
2003 #5 Kurt Busch
2003 #45 Kurt Busch UC
2004 #3 Kurt Busch
2004 #63 Kurt Busch's Car RV
2004 #96 Kurt Busch NP
2005 #6 Kurt Busch
2005 #6B Kurt Busch Cup Chase
2005 #63 Kurt Busch RR
2005 #81 Kurt Busch CP
2006 #4 Kurt Busch
2006 #56 Kurt Busch's Car HS

Press Pass Optima Corporate Cuts Cars
2005 #CCT7 Kurt Busch

Press Pass Optima Corporate Cuts Drivers
2005 #CCD7 Kurt Busch

Press Pass Optima Fan Favorite
2002 #FF4 Kurt Busch
2003 #FF13 Kurt Busch
2004 #FF3 Kurt Busch
2005 #FF5 Kurt Busch
2006 #FF3 Kurt Busch

Press Pass Optima G Force
2001 #GF3 Kurt Busch

Press Pass Optima Gold
2001 #4 Kurt Busch
2002 #5 Kurt Busch
2002 #49 Kurt Busch YG
2003 #G5 Kurt Busch
2003 #G45 Kurt Busch UC
2004 #G3 Kurt Busch
2004 #G63 Kurt Busch's Car RV
2004 #G96 Kurt Busch NP
2005 #G6 Kurt Busch
2005 #G63 Kurt Busch RR
2005 #G81 Kurt Busch CP
2006 #G4 Kurt Busch
2006 #G56 Kurt Busch's Car HS

Press Pass Optima Pole Position
2006 #PP2 Kurt Busch

Press Pass Optima Previews
2003 #5 Kurt Busch
2004 #EB3 Kurt Busch
2005 #6 Kurt Busch
2006 #EB4 Kurt Busch

Press Pass Optima Promos
2002 #5 Kurt Busch
2002 #49 Kurt Busch YG

Press Pass Optima Q & A
2006 #QA6 Kurt Busch

Press Pass Optima Q and A
2002 #QA1 Kurt Busch
2003 #QA8 Kurt Busch

Press Pass Optima Q&A
2004 #QA7 Kurt Busch

Press Pass Optima Race Used Lugnuts Cars
2002 #LNC3 Kurt Busch's Car

Press Pass Optima Race Used Lugnuts Drivers
2002 #LND3 Kurt Busch

Press Pass Optima Samples
2002 #5 Kurt Busch
2002 #49 Kurt Busch YG
2003 #5 Kurt Busch
2003 #45 Kurt Busch UC
2004 #3 Kurt Busch
2004 #63 Kurt Busch's Car RV
2004 #96 Kurt Busch NP
2005 #6 Kurt Busch
2005 #63 Kurt Busch RR
2005 #81 Kurt Busch CP

Press Pass Optima Thunder Bolts Autographs
2005 #TB-KB Kurt Busch/97

Press Pass Optima Thunder Bolts Cars
2003 #TBT14 Kurt Busch's Car
2004 #TBT16 Kurt Busch's Car

Press Pass Optima Thunder Bolts Drivers
2003 #TBD14 Kurt Busch/65
2004 #TBD16 Kurt Busch

Press Pass Optima Young Guns
2003 #YG6 Kurt Busch

Press Pass Platinum
2002 #7 Kurt Busch
2004 #P7 Kurt Busch
2004 #P75 Kurt Busch's Car OTW
2004 #P78 One For The Ages WCS
2004 #P80 The Drive for Five WCS
2004 #P82 Growing Up Fast WCS
2004 #P94 Kurt Busch DS
2005 #P36 Kurt Busch
2005 #P69 Kurt Busch's Car OTW
2005 #P77 Kurt Busch NS
2005 #P97 Ky.Busch/K.Busch Y
2005 #P117 Kurt Busch's Car
2006 #P29 Kurt Busch
2006 #P82 Kurt Busch's Car OTW
2006 #P108 Kurt Busch U
2006 #P114 Kurt Busch TT
2007 #P14 Kurt Busch
2007 #P81 Kurt Busch's Car OT
2007 #P87 Kurt Busch NS
2007 #P99 Kurt Busch U
2008 #P12 Kurt Busch
2008 #P111 Kurt Busch Top 12

Press Pass Premium
2001 #46 Kurt Busch CRC
2002 #5 Kurt Busch
2002 #58 Kurt Busch CH
2003 #5 Kurt Busch
2003 #35 Kurt Busch's Car
2003 #58 Kurt Busch CC
2003 #69 Kurt Busch PC
2004 #13 Kurt Busch
2004 #45 Kurt Busch's Car
2004 #81 Kurt Busch PC
2005 #4 Kurt Busch
2005 #37 Kurt Busch's Car M
2005 #58 Kurt Busch CC
2005 #81 Kurt Busch PC
2006 #4 Kurt Busch
2006 #56 Kurt Busch CC
2007 #5 Kurt Busch
2007 #38 Kurt Busch's Car M
2008 #5 Kurt Busch
2008 #54 Kurt Busch EOP

Press Pass Premium Gold
2001 #46 Kurt Busch

Press Pass Premium Hot Threads Autographs
2007 #HT-KB Kurt Busch/2

Press Pass Premium Hot Threads Cars
2005 #HTT1 Kurt Busch

Press Pass Premium Hot Threads Drivers
2005 #HTD1 Kurt Busch
2007 #HTD7 Kurt Busch
2008 #HTD12 Kurt Busch

Press Pass Premium Hot Threads Drivers Bronze
2004 #HTD5 Kurt Busch

Press Pass Premium Hot Threads Drivers Bronze Retail
2004 #HTT5 Kurt Busch

Press Pass Premium Hot Threads Drivers Gold
2004 #HTD5 Kurt Busch
2005 #HTD1 Kurt Busch
2007 #HTD7 Kurt Busch
2008 #HTD12 Kurt Busch

Press Pass Premium Hot Threads Drivers Silver
2004 #HTD5 Kurt Busch

Press Pass Premium Hot Threads Patch
2007 #HTP15 Kurt Busch Penske Racing/10

Press Pass Premium Hot Threads Patches
2008 #HTP1 Kurt Busch U.S. Flag

Press Pass Premium Hot Threads Team
2007 #HTT7 Kurt Busch
2008 #HTT12 Kurt Busch

Press Pass Premium In the Zone
2006 #IZ6 Kurt Busch

Press Pass Premium In the Zone Red
2006 #IZ6 Kurt Busch

Press Pass Premium Performance Driven
2003 #PD5 Kurt Busch
2004 #PD5 Kurt Busch
2007 #PD7 Kurt Busch

Press Pass Premium Performance Driven Red
2007 #PD7 Kurt Busch

Press Pass Premium Previews
2003 #5 Kurt Busch
2004 #13 Kurt Busch
2008 #EB5 Kurt Busch
2008 #EB54 Kurt Busch EOP

Press Pass Premium Red
2007 #R5 Kurt Busch
2007 #R38 Kurt Busch's Car M
2008 #5 Kurt Busch
2008 #54 Kurt Busch EOP

Press Pass Premium Red Reflectors
2002 #5 Kurt Busch
2002 #58 Kurt Busch CH
2003 #5 Kurt Busch
2003 #35 Kurt Busch's Car
2003 #58 Kurt Busch CC
2003 #69 Kurt Busch PC

Press Pass Premium Samples
2002 #5 Kurt Busch
2003 #5 Kurt Busch
2003 #35 Kurt Busch's Car
2004 #13 Kurt Busch
2004 #45 Kurt Busch's Car
2005 #4 Kurt Busch
2005 #37 Kurt Busch's Car M

Press Pass Previews
2003 #7 Kurt Busch
2004 #7 Kurt Busch
2006 #EB29 Kurt Busch
2006 #EB108 Kurt Busch U
2007 #EB14 Kurt Busch
2008 #EB12 Kurt Busch
2008 #EB111 Kurt Busch Top 12

Press Pass Previews Green
2005 #EB36 Kurt Busch

Press Pass Samples
2003 #7 Kurt Busch
2003 #58 Kurt Busch DS
2003 #63 Jr./JJ/New/Sad/Ken/Bus DS
2003 #75 Kurt-ain Call WCS
2004 #7 Kurt Busch
2004 #75 Kurt Busch's Car OTW
2004 #78 One For The Ages WCS
2004 #80 The Drive for Five WCS
2004 #82 Growing Up Fast WCS
2004 #94 Kurt Busch DS
2005 #36 Kurt Busch
2005 #69 Kurt Busch's Car OTW
2005 #77 Kurt Busch NS
2005 #97 Ky.Busch/K.Busch Y
2005 #117 Kurt Busch's Car

Press Pass Showcar
2004 #S2B Kurt Busch's Car
2005 #SC2 Kurt Busch

Press Pass Showman
2004 #S2A Kurt Busch
2005 #SM2 Kurt Busch

Press Pass Signings
2001 #9 Kurt Busch P/T/V/S
2002 #10 Kurt Busch O/P/S/T/V
2003 #12 Kurt Busch O/S/T/V
2004 #9 Kurt Busch S/T/V
2005 #5 Kurt Busch P/S
2006 #8 Kurt Busch NC S
2007 #12 Kurt Busch NC
2008 #9 Kurt Busch

Press Pass Signings Blue
2007 #4 Kurt Busch NC
2008 #5 Kurt Busch

Press Pass Signings Gold
2001 #8 Kurt Busch P/T/V/S
2002 #11 Kurt Busch O/P/S/T/V
2003 #12 Kurt Busch O/S/T/V
2004 #9 Kurt Busch O/S/T/V
2005 #4 Kurt Busch P/S
2006 #7 Kurt Busch NC S
2007 #9 Kurt Busch NC
2008 #6 Kurt Busch

Press Pass Signings Platinum
2005 #4 Kurt Busch P/S

Press Pass Signings Press Plates Black
2008 #7 Kurt Busch

Press Pass Signings Press Plates Cyan
2008 #7 Kurt Busch

Press Pass Signings Press Plates Magenta
2008 #7 Kurt Busch

Press Pass Signings Press Plates Yellow
2008 #7 Kurt Busch

Press Pass Signings Silver
2006 #7 Kurt Busch NC S
2007 #8 Kurt Busch NC
2008 #6 Kurt Busch

Press Pass Signings Transparent
2003 #1 Kurt Busch O/S/T/V

Press Pass Snapshots
2003 #SN18 Kurt Busch
2004 #SN4 Kurt Busch
2005 #SN4 Kurt Busch
2007 #SN4 Kurt Busch

Press Pass Speedway
2008 #12 Kurt Busch
2008 #93 Ryan Newman's Car Kurt Busch's Car H

Press Pass Speedway Cockpit
2008 #CP4 Kurt Busch

Press Pass Speedway Corporate Cuts Drivers
2008 #CD-KuB Kurt Busch

Press Pass Speedway Corporate Cuts Drivers Patches
2008 #CD-KuB Kurt Busch

Press Pass Speedway Corporate Cuts Team
2008 #CT-KuB Kurt Busch

Press Pass Speedway Gold
2008 #G12 Kurt Busch
2008 #G93 Ryan Newman's Car Kurt Busch's Car H

Press Pass Speedway Holofoil
2008 #H12 Kurt Busch
2008 #H93 Ryan Newman's Car Kurt Busch's Car H

Press Pass Speedway Previews
2008 #EB12 Kurt Busch
2008 #EB93 Ryan Newman's Car Kurt Busch's Car H

Press Pass Speedway Red
2008 #R12 Kurt Busch
2008 #R93 Ryan Newman's Car Kurt Busch's Car H

Press Pass Speedway Test Drive
2008 #TD2 Kurt Busch

Press Pass Stealth
2003 #40 Kurt Busch
2003 #41 Kurt Busch's Car
2003 #42 Kurt Busch
2004 #1 Kurt Busch
2004 #2 Kurt Busch's Car
2004 #3 Kurt Busch
2004 #90 Kurt Busch SST
2004 #95 Kurt Busch SF
2005 #29 Kurt Busch
2005 #32 Kurt Busch's Car
2005 #35 Kurt Busch
2005 #90 Kurt Busch H
2006 #4 Kurt Busch
2006 #55 Busch/Newman TM
2007 #4 Kurt Busch
2007 #56 Kurt Busch's Crew GC
2007 #67 R.Newman/K.Busch
2008 #5 Kurt Busch

Press Pass Stealth Autographed Hat Entry
2006 #PPH4 Kurt Busch

Press Pass Stealth Battle Armor Drivers
2007 #BAD11 Kurt Busch
2008 #BAD12 Kurt Busch

Press Pass Stealth Battle Armor Teams
2007 #BAT11 Kurt Busch
2008 #BAT12 Kurt Busch

Press Pass Stealth Chrome
2007 #4 Kurt Busch
2007 #56 Kurt Busch's Crew GC
2007 #67 R.Newman/K.Busch
2008 #5 Kurt Busch

Press Pass Stealth Chrome Exclusives
2007 #X4 Kurt Busch
2007 #X56 Kurt Busch's Crew GC
2007 #X67 R.Newman/K.Busch
2008 #5 Kurt Busch

Press Pass Stealth Chrome Exclusives Gold
2008 #5 Kurt Busch

Press Pass Stealth Chrome Platinum
2007 #P4 Kurt Busch
2007 #P56 Kurt Busch's Crew GC
2007 #P67 R.Newman/K.Busch

Press Pass Stealth Corporate Cuts
2006 #CCD11 Kurt Busch

Press Pass Stealth EFX
2004 #EF6 Kurt Busch

Press Pass Stealth Fusion
2004 #FU7 Kurt Busch

Press Pass Stealth Gear Grippers Cars
2005 #GGT5 Kurt Busch

Press Pass Stealth Gear Grippers Drivers
2004 #GGD5 Kurt Busch
2005 #GGD5 Kurt Busch

Press Pass Stealth Gear Grippers Drivers Retail
2004 #GGT5 Kurt Busch

Press Pass Stealth Hot Pass
2006 #HP5 Kurt Busch

Press Pass Stealth Lap Leaders
2002 #LL5 Kurt Busch

Press Pass Stealth Maximum Access
2008 #MA6 Kurt Busch

Press Pass Stealth Maximum Access Autographs
2008 #MA6 Kurt Busch

Press Pass Stealth No Boundaries
2005 #NB16 Kurt Busch

Press Pass Stealth Previews
2003 #40 Kurt Busch
2003 #41 Kurt Busch's Car
2003 #42 Kurt Busch
2004 #EB1 Kurt Busch
2004 #EB2 Kurt Busch's Car
2004 #EB3 Kurt Busch
2005 #29 Kurt Busch
2005 #32 Kurt Busch's Car
2005 #35 Kurt Busch
2006 #4 Kurt Busch
2007 #EB4 Kurt Busch
2008 #5 Kurt Busch

Press Pass Stealth Profile
2004 #P4 Kurt Busch 1:112

Press Pass Stealth Red
2003 #P40 Kurt Busch
2003 #P41 Kurt Busch's Car
2003 #P42 Kurt Busch

Press Pass Stealth Retail
2006 #4 Kurt Busch
2006 #55 Busch/Newman TM

Press Pass Stealth Samples
2003 #40 Kurt Busch
2003 #41 Kurt Busch's Car
2003 #42 Kurt Busch
2004 #X1 Kurt Busch
2004 #X2 Kurt Busch's Car
2004 #X3 Kurt Busch
2004 #X90 Kurt Busch SST
2004 #X95 Kurt Busch SF
2005 #29 Kurt Busch
2005 #32 Kurt Busch's Car
2005 #35 Kurt Busch
2005 #90 Kurt Busch H

Press Pass Stealth X-Ray
2004 #1 Kurt Busch
2004 #2 Kurt Busch's Car
2004 #3 Kurt Busch
2004 #90 Kurt Busch SST
2004 #95 Kurt Busch SF
2005 #X29 Kurt Busch
2005 #X32 Kurt Busch's Car
2005 #X35 Kurt Busch
2005 #X90 Kurt Busch H
2006 #X4 Kurt Busch
2006 #X55 Busch/Newman TM

Press Pass Top 25 Drivers & Rides
2006 #C2 Kurt Busch's Car
2006 #D2 Kurt Busch

Press Pass Top Shelf
2004 #TS10 Kurt Busch

Press Pass Top Ten
2005 #TT7 Kurt Busch

Press Pass Total Memorabilia Power Pick

2005 #TM12 Kurt Busch
Press Pass Trackside
2001 #18 Kurt Busch CRC
2002 #19 Kurt Busch
2002 #76 Kurt Busch TM
2003 #3 Kurt Busch
2003 #78 Mart/J.Bur/Bif/Kens/Bus TM
2004 #13 Kurt Busch
2004 #68 Burt/Kens/Mart/Busch/Bif. TM
2004 #96 Kurt Busch LD
2005 #27 Kurt Busch
2005 #76 K.Busch/K.Busch FA
Press Pass Trackside Dialed In
2004 #DI9 Kurt Busch
Press Pass Trackside Die Cuts
2001 #18 Kurt Busch
Press Pass Trackside Generation Now
2002 #GN7 Kurt Busch
Press Pass Trackside Gold Holofoil
2003 #P3 Kurt Busch
2003 #P78 Martin/J.Burton/Biffle/Kenseth/Busch
Press Pass Trackside Golden
2001 #18 Kurt Busch
2002 #G19 Kurt Busch
2003 #G3 Kurt Busch
2004 #G13 Kurt Busch
2004 #G68 Burt/Kens/Mart/Busch/Biffle TM
2004 #G96 Kurt Busch LD
2005 #G27 Kurt Busch
2005 #G76 K.Busch/K.Busch FA
Press Pass Trackside Hat Giveaway
2003 #PPH5 Kurt Busch
2004 #PPH5 Kurt Busch
2005 #PPH4 Kurt Busch
Press Pass Trackside License to Drive
2002 #6 Kurt Busch
Press Pass Trackside License to Drive Die Cuts
2002 #6 Kurt Busch
Press Pass Trackside Previews
2003 #3 Kurt Busch
2004 #EB13 Kurt Busch
2005 #27 Kurt Busch
Press Pass Trackside Samples
2002 #19 Kurt Busch
2002 #76 Kurt Busch TM
2003 #3 Kurt Busch
2003 #78 Mart/J.Bur/Bif/Kens/Bus TM
2004 #13 Kurt Busch
2004 #68 Burt/Kens/Mart/Busch/Biffle TM
2004 #96 Kurt Busch LD
2005 #27 Kurt Busch
2005 #76 K.Busch/K.Busch FA
Press Pass Triple Burner
2005 #TB11 Kurt Busch
Press Pass Triple Burner Exchange
2005 #TB11 Kurt Busch
Press Pass UMI Cup Chase
2005 #1 Cup Chase Drivers CL
2005 #6 Kurt Busch
Press Pass Velocity
2004 #VC9 Kurt Busch
SP Authentic
2000 #40 Kurt Busch RC
SP Authentic Overdrive Gold
2000 #40 Kurt Busch/99
SP Authentic Overdrive Silver
2000 #40 Kurt Busch
SP Authentic Sign of the Times
2000 #KB Kurt Busch
SP Authentic Sign of the Times Gold
2000 #KB Kurt Busch
Sports Illustrated for Kids
2005 #459 Kurt Busch NASCAR
Sports Illustrated for Kids *
2005 #459 Kurt Busch
TRAKS
2006 #5 Kurt Busch
2006 #38 Kurt Busch's Car
2007 #4 Kurt Busch
2007 #67 Kurt Busch MG
2007 #92 Kurt Busch FT
TRAKS Autographs
2006 #5 Kurt Busch NC
TRAKS Autographs 100
2006 #4 Kurt Busch NC
TRAKS Autographs 25
2006 #5 Kurt Busch NC
Traks Corporate Cuts Driver
2007 #CCD8 Kurt Busch
Traks Corporate Cuts Patch
2007 #CCD8 Kurt Busch/6
Traks Corporate Cuts Team
2007 #CCT8 Kurt Busch
Traks Driver's Seat
2007 #DS18 Kurt Busch
2007 #DS18B Kurt Busch VAR
Traks Driver's Seat National
2007 #DS18 Kurt Busch
Traks Gold
2007 #G4 Kurt Busch
2007 #G67 Kurt Busch MG
2007 #G92 Kurt Busch FT
Traks Holofoil
2007 #H4 Kurt Busch
2007 #H67 Kurt Busch MG
2007 #H92 Kurt Busch FT
Traks Previews
2007 #EB4 Kurt Busch
Traks Red
2007 #R4 Kurt Busch
2007 #R67 Kurt Busch MG
2007 #R92 Kurt Busch FT
TRAKS Stickers
2006 #2 Kurt Busch
VIP
2003 #3 Kurt Busch
2003 #24 Kurt Busch SG
2004 #3 Kurt Busch
2004 #48 Kurt Busch SG
2005 #3 Kurt Busch
2005 #36 Kurt Busch's Car R
2005 #50 Kurt Busch SG
2006 #3 Kurt Busch
2006 #29 Kurt Busch's Car R
2006 #44 Kurt Busch SG
2006 #64 Kurt Busch BTN
2006 #69 Kurt Busch RF
2006 #89 Kurt Busch IF
2007 #5 Kurt Busch
2007 #42 Kurt Busch's Car R
VIP Explosives
2003 #X3 Kurt Busch
2003 #X24 Kurt Busch SG
VIP Head Gear
2006 #HG9 Kurt Busch
VIP Head Gear Transparent
2006 #HG9 Kurt Busch
VIP Lap Leader
2006 #LL8 Kurt Busch
VIP Lap Leader Transparent
2006 #LL8 Kurt Busch
VIP Laser Explosive
2003 #LX3 Kurt Busch
2003 #LX24 Kurt Busch SG
VIP Making the Show
2006 #MS24 Kurt Busch
VIP Previews
2003 #3 Kurt Busch
2003 #24 Kurt Busch SG
2004 #EB3 Kurt Busch
2004 #EB48 Kurt Busch SG
2005 #EB3 Kurt Busch
2005 #EB36 Kurt Busch's Car R
2007 #EB5 Kurt Busch
VIP Samples
2003 #3 Kurt Busch
2003 #24 Kurt Busch SG
2004 #3 Kurt Busch
2004 #48 Kurt Busch SG
2005 #3 Kurt Busch
2005 #36 Kurt Busch's Car R
2005 #50 Kurt Busch SG
VIP Sunday Best
2007 #SB3 Kurt Busch
VIP Tin
2003 #CT3 Kurt Busch
2003 #CT24 Kurt Busch SG
VIP Tradin' Paint Bronze
2004 #TPT10 Kurt Busch
VIP Tradin' Paint Cars
2003 #TPT12 Kurt Busch's Car
2005 #TPT10 Kurt Busch
VIP Tradin' Paint Cars Bronze
2006 #TPT2 Kurt Busch
VIP Tradin' Paint Drivers
2003 #TPD12 Kurt Busch
2005 #TPD10 Kurt Busch
VIP Tradin' Paint Drivers Gold
2006 #TPD2 Kurt Busch
VIP Tradin' Paint Drivers Silver
2006 #TPD2 Kurt Busch
VIP Tradin' Paint Gold
2004 #TPD10 Kurt Busch
VIP Tradin' Paint Silver
2004 #TPD10 Kurt Busch
VIP Trophy Club
2007 #TC6 Kurt Busch
VIP Trophy Club Transparent
2007 #TC6 Kurt Busch
Wheels American Thunder
2003 #4 Kurt Busch
2004 #2 Kurt Busch
2004 #63 Kurt Busch DT
2004 #90 Kahne/Busch/McMurray CL
2005 #4 Kurt Busch
2006 #4 Kurt Busch
2007 #5 Kurt Busch
2007 #77 Kurt Busch HC
Wheels American Thunder American Eagle
2003 #AE8 Kurt Busch
Wheels American Thunder American Muscle
2004 #AM9 Kurt Busch
2005 #AM9 Kurt Busch
Wheels American Thunder Autographed Hat Instant Winner
2007 #AH6 Kurt Busch
Wheels American Thunder Born On
2003 #B04 Kurt Busch
Wheels American Thunder Cool Threads
2005 #CT9 Kurt Busch
2006 #CT6 Kurt Busch
2007 #CT12 Kurt Busch
Wheels American Thunder Double Hat
2006 #DH4 Kurt Busch
Wheels American Thunder Golden Eagle
2003 #AEG8 Kurt Busch
Wheels American Thunder Grandstand
2006 #GS2 Kurt Busch
Wheels American Thunder Head to Toe
2005 #HT3 Kurt Busch
Wheels American Thunder Heads Up Goodyear
2003 #HUG14 Kurt Busch
Wheels American Thunder Heads Up Manufacturer
2003 #HUM30 Kurt Busch
Wheels American Thunder Heads Up Team
2003 #HUT28 Kurt Busch/60
Wheels American Thunder Heads Up Winston
2003 #HUW30 Kurt Busch
Wheels American Thunder Holofoil
2003 #P4 Kurt Busch
Wheels American Thunder Post Mark
2003 #PM3 Kurt Busch
Wheels American Thunder Previews
2003 #4 Kurt Busch
2004 #EB2 Kurt Busch
2005 #4 Kurt Busch
2006 #EB4 Kurt Busch
2007 #EB5 Kurt Busch
Wheels American Thunder Pushin Pedal
2004 #PP4 Kurt Busch
2005 #PP2 Kurt Busch
Wheels American Thunder Rookie Thunder
2003 #RT6 Kurt Busch
Wheels American Thunder Samples
2003 #P4 Kurt Busch
2004 #2 Kurt Busch
2004 #63 Kurt Busch DT
2004 #90 Kahne/Busch/McMurray CL
2005 #4 Kurt Busch
Wheels American Thunder Thunder Road
2003 #TR6 Kurt Busch
2005 #TR5 Kurt Busch
2006 #TR16 Kurt Busch
Wheels American Thunder Thunder Strokes
2006 #2 Kurt Busch
2007 #7 Kurt Busch
Wheels American Thunder Thunder Strokes Press Plates Black
2007 #7 Kurt Busch
Wheels American Thunder Thunder Strokes Press Plates Cyan
2007 #7 Kurt Busch
Wheels American Thunder Thunder Strokes Press Plates Magenta
2007 #7 Kurt Busch
Wheels American Thunder Thunder Strokes Press Plates Yellow
2007 #7 Kurt Busch
Wheels American Thunder Triple Hat
2004 #TH1 Kurt Busch
2005 #TH2 Kurt Busch
2007 #TH4 Kurt Busch
Wheels Autographs
2003 #11 Kurt Busch AT/HG
2004 #10 Kurt Busch HG
2005 #6 Kurt Busch
2006 #8 Kurt Busch NC
2007 #5 Kurt Busch NC HG
2008 #7 Kurt Busch NC HG
Wheels Autographs Chase Edition
2008 #2 Kurt Busch NC
Wheels Autographs Press Plates Black
2007 #5 Kurt Busch NC
2008 #7 Kurt Busch NC HG
Wheels Autographs Press Plates Cyan
2007 #5 Kurt Busch NC
2008 #7 Kurt Busch NC HG
Wheels Autographs Press Plates Magenta
2007 #5 Kurt Busch NC
2008 #7 Kurt Busch NC HG
Wheels Autographs Press Plates Yellow
2007 #5 Kurt Busch NC
2008 #7 Kurt Busch NC HG
Wheels High Gear
2002 #4 Kurt Busch
2003 #6 Kurt Busch
2003 #58 The Fab Four
2004 #4 Kurt Busch
2004 #30 Kurt Busch's Car C
2004 #64 Kurt Busch HL
2004 #68 Kurt Busch's Car PREV
2005 #27 Kurt Busch
2005 #46 Kurt Busch A
2005 #90 Kenseth/Busch/Martin CL
2005 #0 Kurt Busch '04 Champion
2007 #15 Kurt Busch
2008 #7 Kurt Busch
2008 #65 Kurt Busch's Car EL
Wheels High Gear Autographs
2002 #10 Kurt Busch
Wheels High Gear Blue Hawaii SCDA Promos
2003 #6 Kurt Busch
2003 #58 The Fab Four
Wheels High Gear Driven
2007 #DR17 Kurt Busch
2008 #DR3 Kurt Busch
Wheels High Gear Final Standings
2008 #F7 Kurt Busch/7
Wheels High Gear Final Standings Gold
2007 #FS15 Kurt Busch/16
Wheels High Gear First Gear
2002 #4 Kurt Busch
2003 #F6 Kurt Busch
2003 #F58 The Fab Four
Wheels High Gear Flag Chasers Black
2003 #FC8 Kurt Busch
Wheels High Gear Flag Chasers Blue-Yellow
2003 #FC8 Kurt Busch
Wheels High Gear Flag Chasers Checkered
2003 #FC8 Kurt Busch
Wheels High Gear Flag Chasers Green
2003 #FC8 Kurt Busch
Wheels High Gear Flag Chasers Red
2003 #FC8 Kurt Busch
Wheels High Gear Flag Chasers White
2003 #FC8 Kurt Busch
Wheels High Gear Flag Chasers Yellow
2003 #FC8 Kurt Busch
Wheels High Gear High Groove
2002 #HG4 Kurt Busch
2003 #HG4 Kurt Busch
2004 #HG3 Kurt Busch
Wheels High Gear Hot Treads
2003 #HT4 Kurt Busch
Wheels High Gear Last Lap
2008 #LL12 Kurt Busch
Wheels High Gear Last Lap Holofoil
2008 #LL12 Kurt Busch
Wheels High Gear Machine
2004 #MM2B Kurt Busch
Wheels High Gear Man
2004 #MM2A Kurt Busch
Wheels High Gear MPH
2002 #4 Kurt Busch
2003 #M6 Kurt Busch
2003 #M58 The Fab Four
2004 #M4 Kurt Busch
2004 #M30 Kurt Busch C
2004 #M64 Kurt Busch HL
2004 #M68 Kurt Busch's Car PREV
2005 #M27 Kurt Busch
2005 #M46 Kurt Busch A
2005 #M90 Kenseth/Busch/Martin CL
2007 #M15 Kurt Busch
2008 #M7 Kurt Busch
2008 #M65 Kurt Busch's Car EL
Wheels High Gear Previews
2003 #6 Kurt Busch
2004 #4 Kurt Busch
2004 #30 Kurt Busch C
2007 #EB15 Kurt Busch
2008 #EB7 Kurt Busch
Wheels High Gear Previews Green
2005 #EB27 Kurt Busch
Wheels High Gear Samples
2003 #6 Kurt Busch
2003 #58 The Fab Four
2004 #4 Kurt Busch
2004 #30 Kurt Busch C
2004 #64 Kurt Busch HL
2004 #68 Kurt Busch's Car PREV
2005 #27 Kurt Busch
2005 #46 Kurt Busch A
2005 #90 Kenseth/Busch/Martin CL
Wheels High Gear The Chase
2008 #TC7 Kurt Busch
Wheels High Gear Top Tier
2003 #TT3 Kurt Busch
2005 #TT1 Kurt Busch

Busch, Kyle

Choice Rising Stars
2002 #18 Kyle Busch
Kellogg's Racing
2006 #1 Kyle Busch
Press Pass
2004 #38 Kyle Busch RC
2004 #38B Kyle Busch infield
2005 #39 Kyle Busch
2005 #97 Ky.Busch/K.Busch Y
2006 #5 Kyle Busch
2006 #67 Kyle Busch RR
2006 #96 Kyle Busch NS
2007 #4 Kyle Busch
2007 #92 Kyle Busch NS
2007 #104 Kyle Busch U
2007 #111 Kyle Busch TT
2008 #8 Kyle Busch
2008 #94 Kyle Busch's Car U
2008 #115 Kyle Busch Top 12
2008 #0 Cup Chase Matt Kenseth Tony Stewart Jeff Gordon Jimmie Johnson Denny Hamlin Kurt Busch Kevin Harvick Carl Edwards Kyle Busch Martin Truex Jr. Jeff Burton Clint Bowyer
Press Pass Autographs
2004 #10 Kyle Busch P
2005 #8 Kyle Busch BGN E/P
2005 #9 Kyle Busch NCS E/P
2006 #8 Kyle Busch NC
2007 #5 Kyle Busch BK; MG; PL Kyle Busch
2008 #10 Kyle Busch NC P/E
Press Pass Autographs Press Plates Black
2008 #8 Kyle Busch NC E
Press Pass Autographs Press Plates Cyan
2008 #8 Kyle Busch NC P
Press Pass Autographs Press Plates Magenta
2008 #8 Kyle Busch NC P
Press Pass Autographs Press Plates Yellow
2008 #8 Kyle Busch NC E
Press Pass Blue
2006 #B5 Kyle Busch
2006 #B67 Kyle Busch RR
2006 #B96 Kyle Busch NS
2007 #B4 Kyle Busch
2007 #B92 Kyle Busch NS
2007 #B104 Kyle Busch U
2007 #B111 Kyle Busch TT
2008 #B8 Kyle Busch
2008 #B94 Kyle Busch's Car U
2008 #B115 Kyle Busch Top 12
Press Pass Burning Rubber Autographs
2006 #BR-KBKyle Busch/5
2008 #BR-KBKyle Busch/5
Press Pass Burning Rubber Cars
2006 #BRT2 Kyle Busch
Press Pass Burning Rubber Drivers
2006 #BRD2 Kyle Busch
2007 #BRD14 Kyle Busch New Hampshire 7-16
2008 #BRD5 Kyle Busch Bristol
Press Pass Burning Rubber Drivers Gold
2006 #BRD2 Kyle Busch
2007 #BRD14 Kyle Busch New Hampshire 7-16
2008 #BRD5 Kyle Busch Bristol
Press Pass Burning Rubber Drivers Prime Cuts
2008 #BRD5 Kyle Busch Bristol
Press Pass Burning Rubber Team
2007 #BRT14Kyle Busch New Hampshire 7-16
Press Pass Burning Rubber Teams
2008 #BRT5 Kyle Busch Bristol
Press Pass Burnouts
2006 #HT1 Kyle Busch
Press Pass Burnouts Holofoil
2006 #HT1 Kyle Busch
Press Pass Collector's Series Box Set
2007 #SB4 Kyle Busch
Press Pass Collectors Series Making the Show
2006 #MS19 Kyle Busch
Press Pass Collectors Series Sunday Best
2007 #CB4 Kyle Busch
Press Pass Cup Chase
2006 #CCR5 Kyle Busch Winner
2007 #CCR15 Kyle Busch Winner
Press Pass Cup Chase Prizes
2006 #CC10 Kyle Busch
2007 #CC9 Kyle Busch
Press Pass Eclipse
2005 #38 Kyle Busch
2006 #19 Kyle Busch
2006 #38 Kyle Busch WS
2006 #83 Kyle Busch LL
2006 #87 Kyle Busch SM
2006 #87B Kyle Busch SM d
2007 #10 Kyle Busch
2007 #45 Kyle Busch P
2007 #0 Cup Chase 10
2008 #75 Top 10 Drivers SO
2008 #88 Kyle Busch PREV
Press Pass Eclipse Gold
2007 #G10 Kyle Busch
2007 #G45 Kyle Busch P
2008 #G75 Top 10 Drivers SO
2008 #G88 Kyle Busch PREV
Press Pass Eclipse Previews
2005 #EB38 Kyle Busch
2006 #EB19 Kyle Busch
2007 #EB10 Kyle Busch
2008 #EB75 Top 10 Drivers SO
Press Pass Eclipse Racing Champions
2006 #RC11 Kyle Busch
2006 #RC27 Kyle Busch NBS
2007 #RC11 Kyle Busch
2007 #RC23 Kyle Busch
Press Pass Eclipse Red
2007 #R10 Kyle Busch
2007 #R45 Kyle Busch P
2008 #R75 Top 10 Drivers SO
2008 #R88 Kyle Busch PREV
Press Pass Eclipse Samples
2005 #38 Kyle Busch
Press Pass Eclipse Skidmarks
2006 #SM1 Kyle Busch
2007 #SM7 Kyle Busch
Press Pass Eclipse Skidmarks Holofoil
2006 #SM1 Kyle Busch
2007 #SM7 Kyle Busch
Press Pass Eclipse Teammates Autographs
2006 #2 Ky.Busch/B.Vickers
2007 #7 J.Gordon/J.Johnson/Ky.Busch
2008 #BHS Kyle Busch Denny Hamlin Tony Stewart/35
Press Pass Gold
2006 #G5 Kyle Busch
2006 #G67 Kyle Busch RR
2006 #G96 Kyle Busch NS
2007 #G4 Kyle Busch
2007 #G92 Kyle Busch NS
2007 #G104 Kyle Busch U
2007 #G111 Kyle Busch TT
2008 #G8 Kyle Busch
2008 #G94 Kyle Busch's Car U
2008 #G115 Kyle Busch Top 12
Press Pass Legends
2005 #33 Kyle Busch CRC
Press Pass Legends Blue
2005 #33B Kyle Busch
Press Pass Legends Gold
2005 #33G Kyle Busch
Press Pass Legends Holofoil
2005 #33H Kyle Busch
Press Pass Legends Press Plates Black
2005 #33 Kyle Busch
Press Pass Legends Press Plates Cyan
2005 #33 Kyle Busch
Press Pass Legends Press Plates Magenta
2005 #33 Kyle Busch
Press Pass Legends Press Plates Yellow
2005 #33 Kyle Busch
Press Pass Legends Previews
2005 #33 Kyle Busch
Press Pass Legends Solo
2005 #33S Kyle Busch
Press Pass Optima
2004 #54 Kyle Busch YG RC
2005 #7 Kyle Busch CRC
2005 #54 Kyle Busch YG
2006 #5 Kyle Busch
2006 #85 Kyle Busch RTV New Hamp.
2006 #4B Kyle Busch Chase
Press Pass Optima Fan Favorite
2005 #FF6 Kyle Busch
Press Pass Optima Gold
2004 #G54 Kyle Busch YG
2005 #G7 Kyle Busch
2005 #G54 Kyle Busch YG
2006 #G5 Kyle Busch
2006 #G85 Kyle Busch RTV New Hamp.
Press Pass Optima Pole Position
2006 #PP6 Kyle Busch
Press Pass Optima Previews
2005 #7 Kyle Busch
2005 #54 Kyle Busch YG/1
2006 #EB5 Kyle Busch
Press Pass Optima Q & A
2005 #QA2 Kyle Busch
Press Pass Optima Rookie Relics Cars
2006 #RRT7 Kyle Busch
Press Pass Optima Rookie Relics Drivers
2006 #RRD7 Kyle Busch
Press Pass Optima Samples
2004 #54 Kyle Busch YG
2005 #7 Kyle Busch
2005 #54 Kyle Busch YG
Press Pass Platinum
2004 #P38 Kyle Busch
2005 #P39 Kyle Busch
2005 #P97 Ky.Busch/K.Busch Y
2006 #P5 Kyle Busch
2006 #P67 Kyle Busch RR
2006 #P96 Kyle Busch NS
2007 #P4 Kyle Busch
2007 #P92 Kyle Busch NS
2007 #P104 Kyle Busch U
2007 #P111 Kyle Busch TT
2008 #P8 Kyle Busch
2008 #P94 Kyle Busch's Car U
2008 #P115 Kyle Busch Top 12
Press Pass Premium
2005 #35 Kyle Busch CRC
2006 #5 Kyle Busch
2006 #67 Kyle Busch C
2007 #6 Kyle Busch
2008 #15 Kyle Busch
2008 #44 Kyle Busch's Car M
2008 #63 Kyle Busch EOP
2008 #80 Kyle Busch F
Press Pass Premium Hot Threads Autographs
2007 #HT-KBKyle Busch/5
Press Pass Premium Hot Threads Cars
2006 #HTT14Kyle Busch
Press Pass Premium Hot Threads Drivers
2006 #HTD14 Kyle Busch
2007 #HTD13 Kyle Busch
Press Pass Premium Hot Threads Drivers Gold
2006 #HTD14 Kyle Busch
2007 #HTD13 Kyle Busch
Press Pass Premium Hot Threads Patch
2007 #HTP7 Kyle Busch Tucan Sam/20
Press Pass Premium Hot Threads Team
2007 #HTT13Kyle Busch
Press Pass Premium Previews
2008 #EB15 Kyle Busch
2008 #EB63 Kyle Busch EOP
Press Pass Premium Red
2007 #R6 Kyle Busch
2008 #15 Kyle Busch
2008 #44 Kyle Busch's Car M
2008 #63 Kyle Busch EOP
2008 #80 Kyle Busch F
Press Pass Premium Samples
2005 #35 Kyle Busch
Press Pass Premium Team Signed Baseballs
2008 #GIB Kyle Busch Denny Hamlin Tony Stewart
2008 #E-GIB Kyle Busch Denny Hamlin Tony Stewart Entry Card
Press Pass Previews
2004 #38 Kyle Busch
2006 #EB5 Kyle Busch
2007 #EB4 Kyle Busch
2007 #EB111 Kyle Busch TT
2008 #EB8 Kyle Busch
2008 #EB115Kyle Busch Top 12
Press Pass Previews Green
2005 #EB39 Kyle Busch
Press Pass Samples
2004 #38 Kyle Busch
2005 #39 Kyle Busch
2005 #97 Ky.Busch/K.Busch Y
Press Pass Signings
2004 #10 Kyle Busch O/P/S/T/V
2005 #6 Kyle Busch
2006 #9 Kyle Busch NC S
2007 #13 Kyle Busch NC
2008 #10 Kyle Busch
Press Pass Signings Blue
2007 #5 Kyle Busch NC
2008 #6 Kyle Busch
Press Pass Signings Gold
2004 #10 Kyle Busch O/P/S/T/V
2005 #5 Kyle Busch NC
2006 #8 Kyle Busch NC S
2007 #10 Kyle Busch NC
2008 #7 Kyle Busch
Press Pass Signings Platinum
2005 #5 Kyle Busch
Press Pass Signings Press Plates Black
2007 #8 Kyle Busch
Press Pass Signings Press Plates Cyan
2007 #7 Kyle Busch
Press Pass Signings Press Plates Magenta
2007 #7 Kyle Busch
Press Pass Signings Press Plates Yellow
2007 #7 Kyle Busch
Press Pass Signings Silver
2006 #8 Kyle Busch NC S
2007 #9 Kyle Busch NC
2008 #7 Kyle Busch
Press Pass Speedway
2008 #29 Kyle Busch
2008 #47 Kyle Busch NNS
2008 #83 Kyle Busch's Car WS
2008 #94 Kyle Busch H
2008 #99 Kyle Busch H
Press Pass Speedway Cockpit
2008 #CP5 Kyle Busch
Press Pass Speedway Corporate Cuts Drivers
2008 #CD-KyB Kyle Busch
Press Pass Speedway Corporate Cuts Drivers Patches
2008 #CD-KyB Kyle Busch
Press Pass Speedway Corporate Cuts Team
2008 #CT-KyB Kyle Busch
Press Pass Speedway Gold
2008 #G29 Kyle Busch
2008 #G47 Kyle Busch NNS
2008 #G83 Kyle Busch's Car WS
2008 #G94 Kyle Busch H
2008 #G99 Kyle Busch H
Press Pass Speedway Holofoil
2008 #H29 Kyle Busch
2008 #H47 Kyle Busch NNS
2008 #H83 Kyle Busch's Car WS
2008 #H94 Kyle Busch H
2008 #H99 Kyle Busch H
Press Pass Speedway Previews
2008 #EB29 Kyle Busch
2008 #EB47 Kyle Busch NNS
2008 #EB94 Kyle Busch H
2008 #EB99 Kyle Busch H
Press Pass Speedway Red
2008 #R29 Kyle Busch
2008 #R47 Kyle Busch NNS
2008 #R83 Kyle Busch's Car WS
2008 #R94 Kyle Busch H
2008 #R99 Kyle Busch H
Press Pass Stealth
2004 #65 Kyle Busch RC
2006 #5 Kyle Busch
2006 #54 24/44/48/25/5 TM
2006 #80 Kyle Busch DD
2007 #5 Kyle Busch
2007 #72 Mears/Ky.Busch/JJ/Gordon
2008 #68 Denny Hamlin Tony Stewart Kyle Busch
2008 #75 Kyle Busch DO
Press Pass Stealth Battle Armor Drivers
2007 #BAD14 Kyle Busch
2008 #BAD16 Kyle Busch
Press Pass Stealth Battle Armor Teams
2007 #BAT14Kyle Busch
2007 #BAS-KB Kyle Busch
2008 #BAT16Kyle Busch
Press Pass Stealth Chrome
2007 #5 Kyle Busch
2007 #72 Mears/Ky.Busch/JJ/Gordon
2008 #68 Denny Hamlin Tony Stewart Kyle Busch
2008 #75 Kyle Busch DO
Press Pass Stealth Chrome Exclusives
2007 #X5 Kyle Busch
2007 #X72 Mears/Ky.Busch/JJ/Gordon
2008 #68 Denny Hamlin Tony Stewart Kyle Busch
2008 #75 Kyle Busch DO
Press Pass Stealth Chrome Exclusives Gold
2008 #68 Denny Hamlin Tony Stewart Kyle Busch
2008 #75 Kyle Busch DO
Press Pass Stealth Chrome Platinum
2007 #P5 Kyle Busch
2007 #P72 Mears/Ky.Busch/JJ/Gordon
Press Pass Stealth EFX
2006 #EFX12Kyle Busch 1:14
Press Pass Stealth Hot Pass
2006 #HP6 Kyle Busch
Press Pass Stealth Maximum Access
2007 #MA5 Kyle Busch
2008 #MA7 Kyle Busch
Press Pass Stealth Maximum Access

Autographs
2007 #MA5 Kyle Busch
2008 #MA7 Kyle Busch
Press Pass Stealth No Boundaries
2004 #NB2 Kyle Busch
Press Pass Stealth Previews
2006 #5 Kyle Busch
2007 #EB5 Kyle Busch
Press Pass Stealth Retail
2006 #5 Kyle Busch
2006 #54 24/44/48/25/5 TM
2006 #80 Kyle Busch DD
Press Pass Stealth Samples
2004 #X65 Kyle Busch
Press Pass Stealth X-Ray
2004 #65 Kyle Busch
2006 #X5 Kyle Busch
2006 #X54 24/44/48/25/5 TM
2006 #X80 Kyle Busch DD
Press Pass Top 25 Drivers & Rides
2006 #C3 Kyle Busch's Car
2006 #D3 Kyle Busch
Press Pass Top Prospects Memorabilia
2004 #KBG Kyle Busch Glove
2004 #KBT Kyle Busch Tire
2004 #KBSM Kyle Busch Metal
Press Pass Trackside
2004 #31 Kyle Busch RC
2004 #84 R.Hendrick/Ky.Busch H
2004 #92 Kyle Busch LD
2005 #12 Kyle Busch CRC
2005 #75 T.Labonte/Vickers/Ky.Busch TM
2005 #76 K.Busch/K.Busch FA
Press Pass Trackside Golden
2004 #G31 Kyle Busch
2004 #G84 R.Hendrick/Ky.Busch H
2004 #G92 Kyle Busch LD
2005 #G12 Kyle Busch
2005 #G75 T.Labonte/Vickers/Ky.Busch TM
2005 #G76 K.Busch/K.Busch FA
Press Pass Trackside Hat Giveaway
2005 #PPH5 Kyle Busch
Press Pass Trackside Previews
2004 #EB31 Kyle Busch
2005 #12 Kyle Busch
Press Pass Trackside Samples
2004 #31 Kyle Busch
2004 #84 R.Hendrick/Ky.Busch H
2004 #92 Kyle Busch LD
2005 #12 Kyle Busch
2005 #75 T.Labonte/Vickers/Ky.Busch TM
2005 #76 K.Busch/K.Busch FA
TRAKS
2006 #6 Kyle Busch
2007 #3 Kyle Busch
2007 #72 Kyle Busch MG
TRAKS Autographs
2006 #6 Kyle Busch NC SP
TRAKS Autographs 25
2006 #6 Kyle Busch NC
Traks Gold
2007 #G3 Kyle Busch
2007 #G72 Kyle Busch MG
Traks Holofoil
2007 #H3 Kyle Busch
2007 #H72 Kyle Busch MG
Traks Hot Pursuit
2007 #HP2 Kyle Busch
Traks Previews
2007 #EB3 Kyle Busch
Traks Red
2007 #R3 Kyle Busch
2007 #R72 Kyle Busch MG
TRAKS Stickers
2006 #5 Kyle Busch
VIP
2005 #4 Kyle Busch CRC
2006 #4 Kyle Busch
2006 #77 Kyle Busch AS
2007 #6 Kyle Busch
2007 #73 Kyle Busch Bristol AP
VIP Gear Gallery
2007 #GG12 Kyle Busch
VIP Gear Gallery Transparent
2007 #GG12 Kyle Busch
VIP Get A Grip Drivers
2007 #GGD23 Kyle Busch
VIP Get A Grip Teams
2007 #GGT23 Kyle Busch
VIP Making the Show
2006 #MS19 Kyle Busch
VIP Previews
2005 #EB4 Kyle Busch
2007 #EB6 Kyle Busch
VIP Samples
2005 #4 Kyle Busch
VIP Sunday Best
2007 #SB4 Kyle Busch
VIP Tradin' Paint Cars Bronze
2006 #TPT3 Kyle Busch
VIP Tradin' Paint Drivers Gold
2006 #TPD3 Kyle Busch
VIP Tradin' Paint Drivers Silver
2006 #TPD3 Kyle Busch
Wheels American Thunder
2005 #5 Kyle Busch CRC
2005 #61 Kyle Busch DT
2005 #74 Kyle Busch RR
2005 #85 Kyle Busch RT
2005 #90 C.Edwards/Ky.Busch CL
2006 #5 Kyle Busch
2006 #38 Kyle Busch DT
2007 #6 Kyle Busch
2007 #83 Kyle Busch HC
Wheels American Thunder American Dreams
2007 #AD4 Kyle Busch
Wheels American Thunder American Dreams Gold
2007 #ADG4 Kyle Busch
Wheels American Thunder American Muscle
2007 #AM5 Kyle Busch
Wheels American Thunder Autographed Hat Instant Winner
2007 #AH7 Kyle Busch
Wheels American Thunder Grandstand
2006 #GS3 Kyle Busch
Wheels American Thunder Medallion
2005 #MD2 Kyle Busch
Wheels American Thunder Previews
2005 #5 Kyle Busch
2005 #85 Kyle Busch RT/1
2006 #EB5 Kyle Busch
2007 #EB6 Kyle Busch
Wheels American Thunder Samples
2005 #5 Kyle Busch
2005 #61 Kyle Busch DT
2005 #74 Kyle Busch RR
2005 #85 Kyle Busch RT
2005 #90 C.Edwards/Ky.Busch CL
Wheels American Thunder Thunder Road
2005 #TR7 Kyle Busch
Wheels American Thunder Thunder Strokes
2007 #8 Kyle Busch
Wheels American Thunder Thunder Strokes Press Plates Black
2007 #6 Kyle Busch
Wheels American Thunder Thunder Strokes Press Plates Cyan
2007 #8 Kyle Busch
Wheels American Thunder Thunder Strokes Press Plates Magenta
2007 #8 Kyle Busch
Wheels American Thunder Thunder Strokes Press Plates Yellow
2007 #8 Kyle Busch
Wheels American Thunder Triple Hat
2005 #TH3 Kyle Busch
2007 #TH5 Kyle Busch
Wheels Autographs
2004 #11 Kyle Busch HG
2005 #7 Kyle Busch BGN
2005 #8 Kyle Busch NC
2006 #9 Kyle Busch NC
2007 #6 Kyle Busch NC HG
Wheels Autographs Press Plates Black
2007 #6 Kyle Busch NC
Wheels Autographs Press Plates Cyan
2007 #6 Kyle Busch NC
Wheels Autographs Press Plates Magenta
2007 #6 Kyle Busch NC
Wheels Autographs Press Plates Yellow
2007 #6 Kyle Busch NC
Wheels High Gear
2004 #45 Kyle Busch RC
2005 #29 Kyle Busch
2005 #86 Kyle Busch P
2006 #19 Kyle Busch
2006 #56 Kyle Busch NA
2007 #10 Kyle Busch
2007 #85 Kyle Busch's Car C
2008 #5 Kyle Busch
2008 #89 Kyle Busch's Car P
Wheels High Gear Final Standings
2008 #F5 Kyle Busch/5
Wheels High Gear Final Standings Gold
2007 #FS10 Kyle Busch/10
Wheels High Gear Flag to Flag
2006 #FF4 Kyle Busch
Wheels High Gear MPH
2004 #M45 Kyle Busch
2005 #M29 Kyle Busch
2005 #M86 Kyle Busch P
2006 #M19 Kyle Busch
2006 #M56 Kyle Busch NA
2007 #M10 Kyle Busch
2007 #M85 Kyle Busch's Car C
2008 #M5 Kyle Busch
2008 #M89 Kyle Busch's Car P
Wheels High Gear Previews
2004 #45 Kyle Busch
2007 #EB10 Kyle Busch
2008 #EB5 Kyle Busch
2008 #EB89 Kyle Busch's Car P
Wheels High Gear Previews Green
2005 #EB29 Kyle Busch
2006 #EB19 Kyle Busch
Wheels High Gear Samples
2004 #45 Kyle Busch
2005 #29 Kyle Busch
2005 #86 Kyle Busch P
Wheels High Gear The Chase
2008 #TC5 Kyle Busch
Wheels High Gear Top Tier
2007 #TT10 Kyle Busch

Carpentier, Patrick

Press Pass Eclipse
2008 #89 Patrick Carpentier PREV RC
Press Pass Eclipse Gold
2008 #G89 Patrick Carpentier PREV
Press Pass Eclipse Red
2008 #R89 Patrick Carpentier PREV
Press Pass Premium
2008 #87 Patrick Carpentier RD RC
Press Pass Premium Going Global
2008 #GG2 Patrick Carpentier
Press Pass Premium Going Global Red
2008 #GG2 Patrick Carpentier
Press Pass Premium Red
2008 #87 Patrick Carpentier RD
Press Pass Speedway
2008 #13 Patrick Carpentier RC
Press Pass Speedway Gold
2008 #G13 Patrick Carpentier
Press Pass Speedway Holofoil
2008 #H13 Patrick Carpentier
Press Pass Speedway Previews
2008 #EB13 Patrick Carpentier
Press Pass Speedway Red
2008 #R13 Patrick Carpentier
Press Pass Stealth
2008 #7 Patrick Carpentier RC
2008 #66 Kasey Kahne Elliott Sadler Patrick Carpentier
Press Pass Stealth Battle Armor Drivers
2008 #BAD4 Patrick Carpentier
Press Pass Stealth Battle Armor Teams
2008 #BAT4 Patrick Carpentier
Press Pass Stealth Chrome
2008 #7 Patrick Carpentier RC
2008 #66 Kasey Kahne Elliott Sadler Patrick Carpentier
Press Pass Stealth Chrome Exclusives
2008 #7 Patrick Carpentier
2008 #66 Kasey Kahne Elliott Sadler Patrick Carpentier
Press Pass Stealth Chrome Exclusives Gold
2008 #7 Patrick Carpentier
2008 #66 Kasey Kahne Elliott Sadler Patrick Carpentier
Press Pass Stealth Previews
2008 #7 Patrick Carpentier
Wheels High Gear
2008 #88 Patrick Carpentier's Car P
Wheels High Gear MPH
2008 #M88 Patrick Carpentier's Car P
Wheels High Gear Previews
2008 #EB88 Patrick Carpentier's Car P

Cassill, Landon

Press Pass Signings
2008 #11 Landon Cassill
Press Pass Signings Gold
2008 #8 Landon Cassill
Press Pass Signings Silver
2008 #8 Landon Cassill
Press Pass Top Prospects Gloves
2008 #LC-G Landon Cassill
Press Pass Top Prospects Metal-Tire
2008 #LC-ST Landon Cassill
Press Pass Top Prospects Sheet Metal
2008 #LC-SM Landon Cassill
Press Pass Top Prospects Shoes
2008 #LC-S Landon Cassill
Press Pass Top Prospects Tires
2008 #LCT Landon Cassill
Press Pass Top Prospects Tires Autographs
2008 #LC-AT Landon Cassill
Press Pass Top Prospects Tires Gold
2008 #LCT Landon Cassill

Earnhardt, Dale

AC Racing
1991 #1 Dale Earnhardt
AC Racing Foldouts
1993 #3 Dale Earnhardt
AC Racing Postcards
1992 #1 Dale Earnhardt
AC Racing Proven Winners
1990 #3 Dale Earnhardt
Action Packed
1993 #88 Dale Earnhardt
1993 #89 Dale Earnhardt's Car
1993 #94 Dale Earnhardt D93
1993 #95 Dale Earnhardt D93
1993 #120 Dale Earnhardt BB
1993 #121 Dale Earnhardt BB
1993 #122 Dale Earnhardt BB
1993 #123 Dale Earnhardt BB
1993 #124 Dale Earnhardt BR
1993 #125 Dale Earnhardt BR
1993 #126 Dale Earnhardt BR
1993 #127 Dale Earnhardt BR
1993 #138 Dale Earnhardt PW
1993 #139 D.Earnhardt WIN/Jr./Kerry
1993 #171 Dale Earnhardt
1993 #198 Dale Earnhardt WIN
1993 #202 Dale Earnhardt WIN
1993 #207 Dale Earnhardt WIN
1994 #1 Dale Earnhardt
1994 #8 Dale Earnhardt WC Champ
1994 #32 Dale Earnhardt WIN
1994 #41 Dale Earnhardt's Car
1994 #68 Dale Earnhardt
1994 #99 Dale Earnhardt/Bonnett
1994 #104 Dale Earnhardt DR
1994 #126 Dale Earnhardt's Car
1994 #179 Dale Earnhardt WIN
1994 #180 Dale Earnhardt WIN
1994 #187 Dale Earnhardt WIN
1997 #3 Dale Earnhardt
1997 #45 Dale Earnhardt's Car
1997 #84 Dale Earnhardt's Car
Action Packed 24K Gold
1993 #18G Dale Earnhardt BB
1993 #19G Dale Earnhardt BB
1993 #20G Dale Earnhardt BB
1993 #21G Dale Earnhardt BB
1993 #22G Dale Earnhardt BB Braille
1993 #23G Dale Earnhardt BB Braille
1993 #24G Dale Earnhardt BB Braille
1993 #25G Dale Earnhardt BB Braille
1993 #37G Dale Earnhardt D93
1993 #38G Dale Earnhardt D93
1993 #53G Dale Earnhardt
1994 #2G Dale Earnhardt
1994 #11G Dale Earnhardt's Car
1994 #22G Dale Earnhardt
1994 #179G Dale Earnhardt WIN
1994 #180G Dale Earnhardt WIN
1994 #187G Dale Earnhardt WIN
1997 #2 Dale Earnhardt
Action Packed Champ and Challenger
1994 #21 Dale Earnhardt
1994 #22 Dale Earnhardt
1994 #23 Dale Earnhardt
1994 #24 Dale Earnhardt
1994 #25 Dale Earnhardt
1994 #26 Dale Earnhardt
1994 #27 Dale Earnhardt
1994 #28 Dale Earnhardt
1994 #29 Dale Earnhardt
1994 #30 Dale Earnhardt
1994 #31 Dale Earnhardt/Neil Bonnett
1994 #32 Dale Earnhardt's Car
1994 #33 Dale Earnhardt's Car
1994 #34 Dale Earnhardt/Alan Kulwicki Cars
1994 #35 Dale Earnhardt's Car
1994 #36 Dale Earnhardt's Car
1994 #37 Dale Earnhardt/Rusty Wallace Cars
1994 #38 Dale Earnhardt
1994 #39 Dale Earnhardt
1994 #40 Dale Earnhardt
1994 #41 Dale Earnhardt/Jeff Gordon Cars
1994 #42 Dale Earnhardt/Jeff Gordon
Action Packed Champ and Challenger 24K Gold
1994 #22G Dale Earnhardt
1994 #28G Dale Earnhardt
1994 #30G Dale Earnhardt
1994 #32G Dale Earnhardt's Car
1994 #39G Dale Earnhardt
1994 #41G D.Earnhardt/J.Gordon Cars
1994 #42G D.Earnhardt/J.Gordon
Action Packed Chevy Madness
1997 #1 Dale Earnhardt's Car
Action Packed Coastars
1994 #2 Dale Earnhardt
Action Packed Country
1995 #11 Dale Earnhardt S
1995 #17 D.Earnhardt/Tay.Earn
1995 #25 D.Earn/Teresa/Helton
1995 #26 Dale Earnhardt NT
1995 #27 Dale Earnhardt NT
1995 #28 Dale Earnhardt NT
1995 #29 Dale Earnhardt NT
1995 #30 Dale Earnhardt NT
1995 #31 Dale Earnhardt NT
1995 #45 D.Earnhardt/Teresa WIN
1995 #54 Dale Earnhardt WIN
1995 #62 Dale Earnhardt
1995 #5 Dale Earnhardt RS
Action Packed Country 24K Team
1995 #5 Dale Earnhardt
1995 #6 Dale Earnhardt
1995 #7 Dale Earnhardt
Action Packed Country 2nd Career Choice
1995 #6 Dale Earnhardt
Action Packed Country Silver Speed
1995 #5 Dale Earnhardt RS
1995 #11 Dale Earnhardt S
1995 #17 D.Earnhardt/T.N.Earnhardt S
1995 #25 D.Earnhardt/T.Earnhardt
1995 #26 Dale Earnhardt NT
1995 #27 Dale Earnhardt NT
1995 #28 Dale Earnhardt NT
1995 #29 Dale Earnhardt NT
1995 #30 Dale Earnhardt NT
1995 #31 Dale Earnhardt NT
1995 #45 D.Earnhardt/Teresa WIN
1995 #54 Dale Earnhardt WIN
1995 #62 Dale Earnhardt
Action Packed Credentials
1996 #6 Dale Earnhardt STC
1996 #7 Dale Earnhardt STC
1996 #8 Dale Earnhardt STC
1996 #9 Dale Earnhardt STC
1996 #10 Dale Earnhardt STC
1996 #17 Dale Earnhardt DW
1996 #21 Dale Earnhardt
1996 #104 Dale Earnhardt CL
1996 #57 Dale Earnhardt SM
Action Packed Credentials Fan Scan
1996 #1 Dale Earnhardt
1996 #2 Dale Earnhardt's Car
Action Packed Credentials Jumbos
1996 #1 Dale Earnhardt
Action Packed Credentials Leaders of the Pack
1996 #1 Dale Earnhardt
1996 #2 Dale Earnhardt
1996 #3 Dale Earnhardt
1996 #4 Dale Earnhardt
Action Packed Credentials Silver Speed
1996 #6 Dale Earnhardt STC
1996 #7 Dale Earnhardt STC
1996 #8 Dale Earnhardt STC
1996 #9 Dale Earnhardt STC
1996 #10 Dale Earnhardt STC
1996 #17 Dale Earnhardt DW
1996 #21 Dale Earnhardt
Action Packed Fifth Anniversary
1997 #6 Dale Earnhardt
Action Packed First Impressions
1997 #45 Dale Earnhardt's Car
1997 #84 Dale Earnhardt's Car
1997 #3 Dale Earnhardt
Action Packed Mammoth
1995 #MM1 Dale Earnhardt
1995 #MM6 Dale Earnhardt
Action Packed McDonald's
1996 #2 Dale Earnhardt
1996 #12 Dale Earnhardt's Car
Action Packed Mint
1994 #1 Dale Earnhardt
1994 #8 Dale Earnhardt WC Champ
1994 #32 Dale Earnhardt WIN
1994 #41 Dale Earnhardt's Car
1994 #68 Dale Earnhardt
1994 #99 Dale Earnhardt/Bonnett
1994 #104 Dale Earnhardt DR
1994 #126 Dale Earnhardt's Car
1994 #179 Dale Earnhardt WIN
1994 #180 Dale Earnhardt WIN
1994 #187 Dale Earnhardt WIN
Action Packed Preview
1995 #7 Dale Earnhardt
1995 #33 Dale Earnhardt PW
1995 #48 Dale Earnhardt WIN
1995 #59 Dale Earnhardt WC Champ
1995 #BP1 Dale Earnhardt
Action Packed Prototypes
1993 #DE1 Dale Earnhardt
1994 #2R941 Dale Earnhardt
Action Packed Richard Childress Racing
1994 #RCR2 Dale Earnhardt's Car
1994 #RCR3 Dale Earnhardt
1994 #RCR4 Dale Earnhardt
1994 #RCR5 Dale Earnhardt's Car
1994 #RCR6 Dale Earnhardt's Car
Action Packed Rolling Thunder
1997 #2 Dale Earnhardt
Action Packed Select 24K Gold
1994 #W3 Dale Earnhardt
1994 #W6 Dale Earnhardt
1994 #W9 Dale Earnhardt
Action Packed Stars
1995 #23 Dale Earnhardt OC
1995 #31 Dale Earnhardt's Car
1995 #52 Dale Earnhardt RW
1995 #NNO Dale Earnhardt Brick. 400
Action Packed Stars 24K Gold
1995 #7G Dale Earnhardt
1995 #9G Dale Earnhardt
1995 #10G Dale Earnhardt
1995 #11G Dale Earnhardt
1995 #12G Dale Earnhardt
1995 #13G Dale Earnhardt
1995 #14G Dale Earnhardt
1995 #15G Dale Earnhardt
1995 #16G Dale Earnhardt
Action Packed Stars Dale Earnhardt Race for Eight
1995 #DE4 Dale Earnhardt
1995 #DE5 Dale Earnhardt w/Teresa
1995 #DE6 Dale Earnhardt
1995 #DE7 Dale Earnhardt
1995 #DE8 Dale Earnhardt's Car
1995 #DE3 Dale Earnhardt
1995 #DE2 Dale Earnhardt
1995 #DE1 Dale Earnhardt
Action Packed Stars Dale Earnhardt Silver Salute
1995 #1 Dale Earnhardt w/Silver Car
1995 #2 Dale Earnhardt/Richard Childress
1995 #3 Dale Earnhardt's Silver Car
1995 #4 Dale/Teresa Earnhardt
Action Packed Stars Silver Speed
1995 #23 Dale Earnhardt OC
1995 #31 Dale Earnhardt's Car
1995 #52 Dale Earnhardt RW
Action Packed Sundrop Dale Earnhardt
1995 #SD1 Dale Earnhardt
1995 #SD2 Dale Earnhardt
1995 #SD3 D.Earnhardt/Dale Jr.
ActionVision
1997 #3 Dale Earnhardt Qualifying
1997 #8 Dale Earnhardt Pit Stop
ActionVision Precious Metal
1997 #6 Dale Earnhardt
Assets
1995 #1 Dale Earnhardt
1995 #29 Dale Earnhardt
1995 #44 Dale Earnhardt
1995 #46 Dale Earnhardt's Car
1995 #P1 Dale Earnhardt Promo
1996 #9 Dale Earnhardt
1994-95 #5 Dale Earnhardt
1994-95 #30 Dale Earnhardt
Assets $100 Phone Cards
1995 #P1 Dale Earnhardt Promo
1995 #2 Dale Earnhardt
Assets $1000 Phone Cards
1995 #2 Dale Earnhardt
Assets $2 Phone Cards
1995 #4 Dale Earnhardt
Assets $2 Phone Cards Gold Signature
1995 #4 Dale Earnhardt
Assets $25 Phone Cards
1995 #2 Dale Earnhardt
Assets $5 Phone Cards
1995 #2 Dale Earnhardt
Assets *
1996 #9 Dale Earnhardt
1994-95 #5 Dale Earnhardt
1994-95 #30 Dale Earnhardt
Assets 1-Minute Phone Cards
1995 #4 Dale Earnhardt
Assets 1-Minute Phone Cards Gold Signature
1995 #4 Dale Earnhardt
Assets A Cut Above Phone Cards
1996 #1 Dale Earnhardt
Assets A Cut Above Phone Cards *
1996 #1 Dale Earnhardt
Assets Coca-Cola 600 Die Cut Phone Cards
1995 #1 Dale Earnhardt
Assets Crystal Phone Cards
1996 #3 Dale Earnhardt
Assets Crystal Phone Cards $20
1996 #3 Dale Earnhardt
Assets Crystal Phone Cards $20 *
1996 #3 Dale Earnhardt
Assets Crystal Phone Cards *
1996 #3 Dale Earnhardt
Assets Die Cuts
1994-95 #DC5Dale Earnhardt
Assets Die Cuts *
1994-95 #DC5Dale Earnhardt
Assets Gold
1995 #1 Dale Earnhardt SP
Assets Gold *
1995 #1 Dale Earnhardt SP
Assets Gold Die Cuts Gold
1995 #SDC10 Dale Earnhardt
Assets Gold Die Cuts Gold *
1995 #SDC10 Dale Earnhardt
Assets Gold Die Cuts Silver
1995 #SDC10 Dale Earnhardt
Assets Gold Die Cuts Silver *
1995 #SDC10 Dale Earnhardt
Assets Gold Phone Cards $1000
1995 #2 Dale Earnhardt
Assets Gold Phone Cards $1000 *
1995 #2 Dale Earnhardt
Assets Gold Phone Cards $2
1995 #1 Dale Earnhardt
Assets Gold Phone Cards $2 *
1995 #1 Dale Earnhardt
Assets Gold Phone Cards $5
1995 #12 Dale Earnhardt
Assets Gold Phone Cards $5 *
1995 #12 Dale Earnhardt
Assets Gold Phone Cards $5 Microlined
1995 #12 Dale Earnhardt
Assets Gold Phone Cards $5 Microlined *
1995 #12 Dale Earnhardt
Assets Gold Printer's Proofs
1995 #1 Dale Earnhardt SP
Assets Gold Printer's Proofs *
1995 #1 Dale Earnhardt SP
Assets Gold Signature
1995 #1 Dale Earnhardt
1995 #29 Dale Earnhardt
1995 #44 Dale Earnhardt
1995 #46 Dale Earnhardt's Car
Assets Gold Silver Signatures
1995 #1 Dale Earnhardt SP
Assets Gold Silver Signatures *
1995 #1 Dale Earnhardt SP
Assets Hot Prints
1996 #9 Dale Earnhardt
Assets Hot Prints *
1996 #9 Dale Earnhardt
Assets Images Previews
1995 #RI1 Dale Earnhardt
Assets Phone Cards $1
1996 #6 Dale Earnhardt
Assets Phone Cards $1 *
1996 #6 Dale Earnhardt
Assets Phone Cards $10
1996 #3 Dale Earnhardt
Assets Phone Cards $10 *
1996 #3 Dale Earnhardt
Assets Phone Cards $100
1996 #1 Dale Earnhardt
Assets Phone Cards $100 *
1996 #1 Dale Earnhardt
Assets Phone Cards $1000
1996 #1 Dale Earnhardt
1994-95 #1 Dale Earnhardt
Assets Phone Cards $1000 *
1994-95 #1 Dale Earnhardt
Assets Phone Cards $2
1996 #6 Dale Earnhardt
1994-95 #5 Dale Earnhardt
Assets Phone Cards $2 *
1996 #6 Dale Earnhardt
1994-95 #5 Dale Earnhardt
Assets Phone Cards $2 Hot Prints
1996 #6 Dale Earnhardt
Assets Phone Cards $2 Hot Prints *
1996 #6 Dale Earnhardt
Assets Phone Cards $20
1996 #1 Dale Earnhardt
Assets Phone Cards $20 *
1996 #1 Dale Earnhardt
Assets Phone Cards $25
1994-95 #1 Dale Earnhardt
Assets Phone Cards $25 *
1994-95 #1 Dale Earnhardt
Assets Phone Cards $5
1996 #6 Dale Earnhardt
Assets Phone Cards $5 *
1996 #6 Dale Earnhardt
Assets Phone Cards One Minute
1994-95 #5 Dale Earnhardt
Assets Phone Cards One Minute/$2 *
1994-95 #5 Dale Earnhardt
Assets Racing
1996 #1 Dale Earnhardt
1996 #38 Dale Earnhardt
1996 #44 Dale Earnhardt
1996 #P1 Dale Earnhardt Promo
1996 #P2 Dale Earnhardt PC Promo
Assets Racing $10 Phone Cards
1996 #4 Dale Earnhardt
1996 #9 Dale Earnhardt's Car
Assets Racing $100 Cup Champion Interactive Phone Cards
1996 #1 Dale Earnhardt
Assets Racing $1000 Cup Champion Interactive Phone Cards
1996 #1 Dale Earnhardt
Assets Racing $2 Phone Cards
1996 #1 Dale Earnhardt
1996 #10 Dale Earnhardt's Car
Assets Racing $5 Phone Cards
1996 #6 Dale Earnhardt
1996 #11 Dale Earnhardt's Car
Assets Racing Competitor's License
1996 #CL4 Dale Earnhardt
Assets Racing Race Day
1996 #RD3 Dale Earnhardt's Car
Assets Silksations
1996 #3 Dale Earnhardt
Assets Silksations *
1996 #3 Dale Earnhardt
Assets Silver Signature
1994-95 #5 Dale Earnhardt
Assets Silver Signature *
1994-95 #5 Dale Earnhardt
Autographed Racing
1996 #1 Dale Earnhardt
1996 #25 Dale Earnhardt's Car
1997 #1 Dale Earnhardt
1997 #36 Dale Earnhardt's Car
1997 #47 D.Earnhardt/D.Jarrett
1997 #49 D.Earnhardt/R.Wall.Cars
Autographed Racing Autographs
1996 #13 Dale Earnhardt
1997 #12 Dale Earnhardt
Autographed Racing Autographs Certified Golds
1996 #13 Dale Earnhardt's Car
Autographed Racing Front Runners
1996 #13 R.Childress/Dale Earnhardt
1996 #14 R.Childress/D.Earnhardt's Car
1996 #19 D.Earnhardt/D.Earnhardt
1996 #20 D.Earnhardt/D.Earnhardt's Car
1996 #21 D.Earn.w/Olympic car
1996 #22 D.Earnhardt/R.Petty
Autographed Racing High Performance
1996 #HP1 Dale Earnhardt
Autographed Racing Kings of the Circuit $5 Phone Cards
1996 #KC6 Dale Earnhardt
1996 #KC8 Dale Earnhardt's Car
1996 #KC10 Dale Earnhardt
Autographed Racing Mayne Street
1997 #KM1 Dale Earnhardt
Big League Cards Creative Images
1998 #29 Dale Earnhardt
Bleachers NASCAR
1994-96 #2 Dale Earnhardt (#1)
1994 Classic 10,000
1994-96 #3 Dale Earnhardt (Triple Image)
1995 Classic 10,000
1994-96 #4 Dale Earnhardt (#3)
1996 Classic 10,000
1994-96 #5 Dale Earnhardt (#4)
1996 Classic 10,000
1994-96 #6 Dale Earnhardt (Diamond Star)
1996 Classic 10,000
1994-96 #7 Dale Earnhardt/Richard Petty
1995 Finish Line 10,
Burger King Dale Earnhardt
1998 #1 Dale Earnhardt's Car
1998 #2 Dale Earnhardt
1998 #3 Dale Earnhardt's Car

1998 #4 Dale Earnhardt
Card Dynamics Black Top Busch Series
1994 #1 Dale Earnhardt
Card Dynamics Double Eagle Dale Earnhardt
1994 #1 Dale Earnhardt 1979 Rookie of the Year
1994 #2 Dale Earnhardt 1980 Winston Cup Champion
1994 #3 Dale Earnhardt 1986 Winston Cup Champion
1994 #4 Dale Earnhardt 1987 Winston Cup Champion
1994 #5 Dale Earnhardt 1990 Winston Cup Champion
1994 #6 Dale Earnhardt 1991 Winston Cup Champion
Card Dynamics Double Eagle Postcards
1993-95 #3 Dale Earnhardt
Card Dynamics Gant Oil
1993 #8 Dale Earnhardt
Card Dynamics North State Chevrolet
1993-95 #2 Dale Earnhardt
Card Dynamics Quik Chek
1993 #8 Dale Earnhardt/7000
Classic
1996 #HP96 Dale Earnhardt Promo
1996 #RP96 Dale Earnhardt Promo
1996 #32 Dale Earnhardt's Car
1996 #53 Dale Earnhardt SP
Classic Dale Earnhardt 23K Gold
1994 #1 Dale Earnhardt/10000
Classic Five Sport
1995 #161 Dale Earnhardt
Classic Five Sport Autographs Numbered
1995 #161 Dale Earnhardt
Classic Five Sport Classic Standouts
1995 #CS3 Dale Earnhardt
Classic Five Sport Hot Box Autographs
1995 #3 Dale Earnhardt/635
Classic Five Sport On Fire
1995 #H3 Dale Earnhardt
Classic Five Sport Phone Cards $3
1995 #1 Dale Earnhardt
Classic Five Sport Phone Cards $4
1995 #1 Dale Earnhardt
Classic Five Sport Previews
1995 #SP1 Dale Earnhardt
Classic Five Sport Printer's Proofs
1995 #161 Dale Earnhardt
Classic Five Sport Record Setters
1995 #RS4 Dale Earnhardt
Classic Five Sport Red Die Cuts
1995 #161 Dale Earnhardt
Classic Five Sport Signings
1995-96 #79 Dale Earnhardt
Classic Five Sport Signings Blue Signature
1995-96 #79 Dale Earnhardt
Classic Five Sport Signings Die Cuts
1995-96 #79 Dale Earnhardt
Classic Five Sport Signings Red Signature
1995-96 #79 Dale Earnhardt
Classic Five Sport Silver Die Cuts
1995 #161 Dale Earnhardt
Classic Five-Sport *
1995 #161 Dale Earnhardt
Classic Five-Sport Autographs *
1995 #161A Dale Earnhardt/635
1995 #161B Dale Earnhardt/225
Classic Five-Sport Classic Standouts *
1995 #CS3 Dale Earnhardt
Classic Five-Sport Hot Box Autographs *
1995 #3 Dale Earnhardt/635
Classic Five-Sport On Fire *
1995 #H3 Dale Earnhardt
Classic Five-Sport Phone Cards $3 *
1995 #1 Dale Earnhardt
Classic Five-Sport Phone Cards $4 *
1995 #1 Dale Earnhardt
Classic Five-Sport Previews *
1995 #SP1 Dale Earnhardt
Classic Five-Sport Printer's Proofs *
1995 #161 Dale Earnhardt
Classic Five-Sport Record Setters *
1995 #RS4 Dale Earnhardt
Classic Five-Sport Red Die Cuts *
1995 #161 Dale Earnhardt
Classic Five-Sport Silver Die Cuts *
1995 #161 Dale Earnhardt
Classic Images Preview
1996 #RP5 Dale Earnhardt's Car/R.Child.
Classic Innerview
1996 #IV3 Dale Earnhardt
1996 #IV7 Dale Earnhardt
Classic Mark Martin's Challengers
1996 #MC3 Dale Earnhardt's Car
Classic National *
1995 #NC4 Dale Earnhardt
Classic Printer's Proof
1996 #32 Dale Earnhardt's Car
Classic Race Chase
1996 #RC3 Dale Earnhardt's Car
1996 #RC13 Dale Earnhardt's Car
Classic Signings *
1996 #S79 Dale Earnhardt
Classic Signings Blue Signature *
1996 #79 Dale Earnhardt
Classic Signings Die Cuts *
1996 #79 Dale Earnhardt
Classic Signings Red Signature *
1996 #79 Dale Earnhardt
Classic Silver
1996 #32 Dale Earnhardt's Car
Clear Assets
1996 #64 Dale Earnhardt
Clear Assets *
1996 #64 Dale Earnhardt
Clear Assets Phone Cards $1
1996 #19 Dale Earnhardt
Clear Assets Phone Cards $1 *
1996 #19 Dale Earnhardt
Clear Assets Phone Cards $10
1996 #3 Dale Earnhardt
Clear Assets Phone Cards $10 *
1996 #3 Dale Earnhardt
Clear Assets Phone Cards $2
1996 #19 Dale Earnhardt
Clear Assets Phone Cards $2 *
1996 #19 Dale Earnhardt
Clear Assets Phone Cards $5
1996 #4 Dale Earnhardt

Clear Assets Phone Cards $5 *
1996 #4 Dale Earnhardt
Coca-Cola Racing Family
1999 #2 Dale Earnhardt
2000 #3 Dale Earnhardt
2000 #4 Dale Earnhardt 7T Champ
2000 #16 Coca-Cola Racing Family
Collector's Choice
1997 #3 Dale Earnhardt
1998 #3 Dale Earnhardt
1998 #39 Dale Earnhardt's Car
1998 #103 Dale Earnhardt TD
Collector's Choice Star Quest
1998 #SQ26 Dale Earnhardt
Collector's Choice Upper Deck 500
1997 #UD1 Dale Earnhardt
Collector's Choice Victory Circle
1997 #VC2 Dale Earnhardt
Crown Jewels
1995 #64 D.Earn/Waltrip Cars CJT
1995 #1 Dale Earnhardt
Crown Jewels Diamond
1995 #1 Dale Earnhardt
1995 #64 Dale Earnhardt Darrell Waltrip CJT
Crown Jewels Dual Jewels
1995 #DJ6 D.Earnhardt/Dave Marcis
1995 #DJ1 D.Earnhardt/J.Gordon
Crown Jewels Dual Jewels Diamond
1995 #DJ1 Dale Earnhardt/Jeff Gordon
1995 #DJ6 Dale Earnhardt/Dave Marcis
Crown Jewels Dual Jewels Emerald
1995 #DJ1 Dale Earnhardt/Jeff Gordon
1995 #DJ6 Dale Earnhardt/Dave Marcis
Crown Jewels Elite
1996 #1 Dale Earnhardt
1996 #27 Dale Earnhardt
1996 #56 D.Earnhardt/D.Smith
1996 #57 Dale Earnhardt's Trans.
1996 #SD1 D.Earnhardt 7 Diam/300
1996 #SG1 D.Earnhardt 7 Gems/1500
1996 #SGTC1 Earnh.7 Gems TC/1500
Crown Jewels Elite Birthstones of the Champions
1996 #BC1 Dale Earnhardt
Crown Jewels Elite Birthstones of the Champions Diamond Tribute
1996 #BC1 Dale Earnhardt
Crown Jewels Elite Birthstones of the Champions Treasure Chest
1996 #BC1 Dale Earnhardt
Crown Jewels Elite Crown Signature Amethyst
1996 #CS1 Dale Earnhardt
Crown Jewels Elite Crown Signature Garnet
1996 #CS1 Dale Earnhardt
Crown Jewels Elite Crown Signature Peridot
1996 #CS1 Dale Earnhardt
Crown Jewels Elite Diamond Tribute
1996 #1 Dale Earnhardt
1996 #27 Dale Earnhardt
1996 #56 D.Smith/D.Earnhardt
1996 #57 Dale Earnhardt's Trans.
Crown Jewels Elite Diamond Tribute Citrine
1996 #1 Dale Earnhardt
1996 #27 Dale Earnhardt
1996 #56 D.Smith/D.Earnhardt
1996 #57 Dale Earnhardt's Trans.
Crown Jewels Elite Dual Jewels Amethyst
1996 #DJ1 D.Earnhardt/J.Gordon
Crown Jewels Elite Dual Jewels Amethyst Diamond Tribute
1996 #DJ1 D.Earnhardt/J.Gordon
Crown Jewels Elite Dual Jewels Amethyst Treasure Chest
1996 #DJ1 D.Earnhardt/J.Gordon
Crown Jewels Elite Dual Jewels Garnet
1996 #DJ1 D.Earnhardt/J.Gordon
Crown Jewels Elite Dual Jewels Garnet Diamond Tribute
1996 #DJ1 D.Earnhardt/J.Gordon
Crown Jewels Elite Dual Jewels Garnet Treasure Chest
1996 #DJ1 D.Earnhardt/J.Gordon
Crown Jewels Elite Dual Jewels Sapphire
1996 #DJ1 D.Earnhardt/J.Gordon
Crown Jewels Elite Dual Jewels Sapphire Treasure Chest
1996 #DJ1 D.Earnhardt/J.Gordon
Crown Jewels Elite Emerald
1996 #1 Dale Earnhardt
1996 #27 Dale Earnhardt
1996 #56 D.Smith/D.Earnhardt
1996 #57 Dale Earnhardt's Trans.
Crown Jewels Elite Emerald Treasure Chest
1996 #1 Dale Earnhardt
1996 #27 Dale Earnhardt
1996 #56 D.Smith/D.Earnhardt
1996 #57 Dale Earnhardt's Trans.
Crown Jewels Elite Sapphire
1996 #1 Dale Earnhardt
1996 #27 Dale Earnhardt
1996 #56 D.Smith/D.Earnhardt
1996 #57 Dale Earnhardt's Trans.
Crown Jewels Elite Sapphire Treasure Chest
1996 #1 Dale Earnhardt
1996 #27 Dale Earnhardt
1996 #56 D.Smith/D.Earnhardt
1996 #57 Dale Earnhardt's Trans.
Crown Jewels Elite Treasure Chest
1996 #1 Dale Earnhardt
1996 #27 Dale Earnhardt
1996 #56 D.Smith/D.Earnhardt
1996 #57 Dale Earnhardt's Trans.
Crown Jewels Emerald
1995 #1 Dale Earnhardt
1995 #64 Dale Earnhardt CJT Darrell Waltip
Crown Jewels Sapphire
1995 #1 Dale Earnhardt
1995 #64 Dale Earnhardt CJT Darrell Waltrip's Cars
Crown Jewels Signature Gems
1995 #SG3 Dale Earnhardt
Dayco Series 2 Rusty Wallace
1993 #12 Rusty Wallace/Earnhardt Cars
Finish Line
1995 #1 Dale Earnhardt
1995 #89 Dale Earnhardt

1995 #111 Dale Earnhardt
1995 #HP1 Dale Earnhardt Promo (hobby version)
1995 #RP1 Dale Earnhardt Promo (retail version)
1995 #89AUH D.Earn. AU/250 Red
1995 #89AUR D.Earn. AU/250 Blue
1995 #111AU D.Earn. AU/250
1995 #CE1 Dale Earnhardt Club Promo
Finish Line Coca-Cola 600
1995 #1 Dale Earnhardt
1995 #29 Dale Earnhardt
1995 #44 Dale Earnhardt
1995 #46 Dale Earnhardt's Car
Finish Line Coca-Cola 600 Die Cuts
1995 #C1 Dale Earnhardt
Finish Line Coca-Cola 600 Winners
1995 #CC2 Dale Earnhardt
1995 #CC8 Dale Earnhardt
1995 #CC9 Dale Earnhardt
Finish Line Dale Earnhardt
1995 #DE1 Dale Earnhardt
1995 #DE2 Dale Earnhardt
1995 #DE3 Dale Earnhardt
1995 #DE4 Dale Earnhardt
1995 #DE5 Dale Earnhardt
1995 #DE6 Dale Earnhardt
1995 #DE7 Dale Earnhardt
1995 #DE8 Dale Earnhardt
1995 #DE9 Dale Earnhardt
1995 #DE10 Dale Earnhardt
Finish Line Gold Signature
1995 #GS3 Dale Earnhardt
Finish Line Printer's Proof
1995 #1 Dale Earnhardt
1995 #89 Dale Earnhardt
1995 #111 Dale Earnhardt
Finish Line Silver
1995 #1 Dale Earnhardt
1995 #89 Dale Earnhardt
1995 #111 Dale Earnhardt
Finish Line Standout Cars
1995 #SC1 Dale Earnhardt's Car
Finish Line Standout Drivers
1995 #SD1 Dale Earnhardt
Flair
1996 #10 Dale Earnhardt
1996 #66 Dale Earnhardt's Car
Flair Autographs
1996 #2 Dale Earnhardt
Flair Center Spotlight
1996 #2 Dale Earnhardt
Flair Hot Numbers
1996 #1 Dale Earnhardt
Flair Power Performance
1996 #2 Dale Earnhardt
Gold Collectibles Dale Earnhardt
2001 #1 Dale Earnhardt
2001 #2 Dale Earnhardt
2001 #3 Dale Earnhardt's Car
2001 #4 Dale Earnhardt
Hasbro/Winner's Circle
1999 #NNO Dale Earnhardt '99 GWSP
Hickory Motor Speedway
1991 #6 Earnhardt/Gant/T.Houston/Shepherd/D.Jarrett
1991 #10 D.Earnhardt/J.Nemechek Cars
Highland Mint/VIP
1994-95 #1B Dale Earnhardt/5000
1994-95 #1G Dale Earnhardt/500
1994-95 #1S Dale Earnhardt/1000
Hi-Tech Brickyard 400
1994 #9 Dale Earnhardt's Car
1994 #38 Dale Earnhardt
1995 #2 Dale Earnhardt's Car
1995 #41 Dale Earnhardt
1995 #56 Dale Earnhardt
1995 #77 Dale Earnhardt's Car
1995 #87 Dale Earnhardt
Hi-Tech Brickyard 400 Artist Proofs
1994 #9 Dale Earnhardt's Car
1994 #38 Dale Earnhardt
Hi-Tech Brickyard 400 Prototypes
1995 #P3 Dale Earnhardt
Hi-Tech Brickyard 400 Top Ten
1995 #BY5 Dale Earnhardt
Hi-Tech Tire Test
1993 #1 Dale Earnhardt's Car
Images
1995 #3 Dale Earnhardt
1995 #50 Dale Earnhardt
1995 #97 Dale Earnhardt
1995 #99 Dale Earnhardt CL
Images Circuit Champions
1995 #8 Dale Earnhardt
Images Driven
1995 #D1 Dale Earnhardt
Images Gold
1995 #3 Dale Earnhardt
1995 #50 Dale Earnhardt
1995 #97 Dale Earnhardt
1995 #100 Dale Earnhardt CL
Images Hard Chargers
1995 #HC9 Dale Earnhardt
Images Owner's Pride
1995 #OP13 Dale Earnhardt
Images Race Reflections Dale Earnhardt
1995 #DE1 Dale Earnhardt
1995 #DE2 Dale Earnhardt
1995 #DE3 Dale Earnhardt
1995 #DE4 Dale Earnhardt
1995 #DE5 Dale Earnhardt
1995 #DE6 Dale Earnhardt
1995 #DE7 Dale Earnhardt
1995 #DE8 Dale Earnhardt
1995 #DE9 Dale Earnhardt
1995 #DE10 Dale Earnhardt
Images Race Reflections Dale Earnhardt Facsimile Signature
1995 #DE1 Dale Earnhardt
1995 #DE2 Dale Earnhardt
1995 #DE3 Dale Earnhardt
1995 #DE4 Dale Earnhardt
1995 #DE5 Dale Earnhardt
1995 #DE6 Dale Earnhardt
1995 #DE7 Dale Earnhardt
1995 #DE8 Dale Earnhardt
1995 #DE9 Dale Earnhardt
1995 #DE10 Dale Earnhardt

IROC
1991 #12 Dale Earnhardt
Jurassic Park Carnivore
1997 #C1 Dale Earnhardt
Jurassic Park Pteranodon
1997 #P1 Dale Earnhardt
Jurassic Park Thunder Lizard
1997 #TL8 Dale Earnhardt
Jurassic Park T-Rex
1997 #TR5 Dale Earnhardt
Kenner 12-Inch Specials *
1997 #2 D.Earnhardt (WalMart)
1998 #5 Earnhardt./Earn.Jr.(Sam's)
KnightQuest
1996 #1 Dale Earnhardt K
1996 #22 Dale Earnhardt C
1996 #25 Dale Earnhardt C
KnightQuest Black Knights
1996 #1 Dale Earnhardt K
1996 #22 Dale Earnhardt C
1996 #25 Dale Earnhardt C
KnightQuest First Knights
1996 #FK1 Dale Earnhardt
KnightQuest Knights of the Round Table
1996 #KT2 Dale Earnhardt
KnightQuest Protectors of the Crown
1996 #PC2 Dale Earnhardt
KnightQuest Red Knight Preview
1996 #1 Dale Earnhardt K
1996 #22 Dale Earnhardt C
1996 #25 Dale Earnhardt C
KnightQuest Royalty
1996 #1 Dale Earnhardt K
1996 #22 Dale Earnhardt C
1996 #25 Dale Earnhardt C
KnightQuest Santa Claus
1996 #SC1 Dale Earnhardt
KnightQuest Santa Claus Green
1996 #SC1 Dale Earnhardt
KnightQuest White Knights
1996 #1 Dale Earnhardt K
1996 #22 Dale Earnhardt C
1996 #25 Dale Earnhardt C
Matchbook Winston Cup Champions
1995 #10 1980 Champion Dale Earnhardt
1995 #16 1986 Champion Dale Earnhardt
1995 #17 1987 Champion Dale Earnhardt
1995 #20 1990 Champion Dale Earnhardt
1995 #21 1991 Champion Dale Earnhardt
1995 #23 1993 Champion Dale Earnhardt
1995 #24 1994 Champion Dale Earnhardt
Maxx
1989 #60 D.Earnhardt Pit Champs
1989 #102 D.Earn./Bonnett Cars YR
1989 #108 Dale Earnhardt's Car YR
1989 #121 Dale Earnhardt's Car YR
1989 #144 D.Earnhardt w/Crew VL
1989 #148 D.Earnhardt/Teresa VL
1989 #160 Dale Earnhardt VL
1989 #3 Dale Earnhardt RC
1990 #3 Dale Earnhardt
1990 #116 Dale Earnhardt AP
1990 #179 D.Earnhardt/Teresa YR
1990 #191 Dale Earnhardt's Car YR
1990 #195 D.Earnhardt/M.Martin Cars YR
1990 #183 Earnhardt/R.Wilson/Shepherd/Schrader Cars
1991 #173 Dale Earnhardt YR
1991 #174 Dale Earnhardt YR
1991 #178 Dale Earnhardt YR
1991 #179 Dale Earnhardt YR
1991 #184 Dale Earnhardt YR
1991 #185 Dale Earnhardt YR
1991 #187 Dale Earnhardt YR
1991 #191 Dale Earnhardt/Teresa YR
1991 #192 Dale Earnhardt/Teresa YR
1991 #198 Dale Earnhardt YR
1991 #200 Dale Earnhardt/Teresa YR
1991 #220 Dale Earnhardt AP
1991 #3 Dale Earnhardt
1993 #3 Dale Earnhardt
1993 #56 Dale Earnhardt's Car
1993 #274 Dale Earnhardt YR/Jr./Kerry
1994 #3 Dale Earnhardt
1994 #23 Dale Earnhardt's Car
1994 #211 Dale Earnhardt YR
1994 #218 Dale Earnhardt YR
1994 #219 Dale Earnhardt YR
1994 #222 Dale Earnhardt YR
1994 #224 Dale Earnhardt YR
1994 #225 Dale Earnhardt YR
1994 #238 Dale Earnhardt WC Champ
1994 #334 Irvan/D.Earnhardt/W.Burton Cars
1994 #335 Gordon/R.Wall/Earn.Cars
1996 #3 Dale Earnhardt
1997 #3 Dale Earnhardt
1997 #48 Dale Earnhardt's Car
1997 #NNO D.Earnhardt/50 '88 AU
1998 #3 Dale Earnhardt
1998 #33 Dale Earnhardt's Car
1998 #95 Dale Earnhardt's Car FR
1999 #88 Dale Earnhardt
1999 #89 Dale Earnhardt's Car
2000 #3 Dale Earnhardt
2000 #43 Dale Earnhardt's Car
Maxx 10th Anniversary
1998 #96 Dale Earnhardt
1998 #119 Dale Earnhardt
Maxx 10th Anniversary Champions Past
1998 #CP3 Dale Earnhardt
Maxx 10th Anniversary Champions Past Die Cuts
1998 #CP3 Dale Earnhardt
Maxx 1997 Year In Review
1998 #9 Dale Earnhardt's Car
1998 #33 Dale Earnhardt's Car
1998 #53 Dale Earnhardt's Car
1998 #128 Dale Earnhardt's Car
1998 #PO5 Dale Earnhardt
Maxx All-Pro Team
1992 #1 Dale Earnhardt
Maxx Black
1992 #3 Dale Earnhardt
1992 #203 Dale Earnhardt's Car MM
1992 #231 Dale Earnhardt AP
1992 #265 Dale Earnhardt/Teresa YR
1992 #271 Dale Earnhardt/Teresa YR
1992 #281 Dale Earnhardt/Teresa YR

1992 #289 Dale Earnhardt YR
1992 #294 Dale Earnhardt YR
Maxx Charlotte
1988 #9 Dale Earnhardt's Car
1988 #13 Dale Earnhardt's Car
1988 #17 Dale Earnhardt's Car
1988 #38 Dale Earnhardt's Car
1988 #45 Tire Wars/Earnhardt's Trailer
1988 #49 D.Earnhardt/D.Allison Cars
1988 #54 Dale Earnhardt's Car
1988 #99P Dale Earnhardt Promo
1988 #87 D.Earnhardt WC Champ
1988 #84 D.Earnhardt/R.Petty Cars
Maxx Chase the Champion
1995 #3 Dale Earnhardt
1995 #4 Dale Earnhardt's Car
1995 #5 Dale Earnhardt
1995 #6 Dale Earnhardt
1995 #7 D.Earnhardt/T.Earnhardt
1995 #8 Dale Earnhardt
1995 #9 D.Earn/Childress/Teresa
1995 #10 Dale Earnhardt
1995 #1 Dale Earnhardt
1995 #2 Dale Earnhardt
Maxx Crisco
1989 #6 Dale Earnhardt
Maxx FANtastic Finishes
1999 #F10 Dale Earnhardt's Car
2000 #FF1 Dale Earnhardt
Maxx Flag Firsts
1997 #FF14 Dale Earnhardt
Maxx Focus on a Champion
1998 #FC3 Dale Earnhardt
1999 #FC2 Dale Earnhardt
Maxx Focus on a Champion Cel
1998 #FC3 Dale Earnhardt
Maxx Focus on a Champion Gold
1999 #FC2 Dale Earnhardt
Maxx Glossy
1990 #3 Dale Earnhardt
1990 #116 Dale Earnhardt AP
1990 #179 D.Earnhardt/Teresa YR
1990 #183 Earnhardt/R.Wilson/Shepherd/Schrader Cars
1990 #191 Dale Earnhardt's Car YR
1990 #195 D.Earnhardt/M.Martin Cars YR
Maxx Holly Farms
1990 #HF1 Dale Earnhardt
Maxx Larger than Life Dale Earnhardt
1995 #1 Dale Earnhardt
1995 #2 Dale Earnhardt
1995 #3 Dale Earnhardt
1995 #4 Dale Earnhardt
1995 #5 Dale Earnhardt
1995 #6 Dale Earnhardt
1995 #7 Dale Earnhardt
Maxx McDonald's
1991 #1A Dale Earnhardt ERR
1991 #1B Dale Earnhardt COR
1991 #30 D.Earnhardt/Martin/Elliott
1992 #1 D.Earnhardt/D.Allison/Elliott
1992 #2 Dale Earnhardt
Maxx Medallion
1994 #46 J.Gordon/Earnhardt Cars
1994 #99SP D.Earnhardt 1988/999
Maxx Odyssey Millennium
1996 #MM1 Dale Earnhardt's Car
Maxx Oval Office
2000 #OO2 Dale Earnhardt
Maxx Premier Plus
1993 #3 Dale Earnhardt
1993 #56 Dale Earnhardt's Car
1993 #189 Dale Earnhardt YR/Jr./Kerry
1994 #3 Dale Earnhardt
1994 #23 Dale Earnhardt's Car
1994 #165 Dale Earnhardt w/Crew
1994 #170 Dale Earnhardt YR
1994 #177 Dale Earnhardt YR
1994 #178 Dale Earnhardt w/Crew YR
1994 #181 Dale Earnhardt w/Crew YR
1994 #183 Dale Earnhardt/Childress YR
1994 #184 Dale Earnhardt YR
1995 #SS1 D.Earnhardt Sil.Select/750
Maxx Premier Plus Jumbos
1993 #2 Dale Earnhardt
Maxx Premier Series
1993 #3 Dale Earnhardt
1993 #56 Dale Earnhardt's Car
1993 #274 Dale Earnhardt YR/Jr./Kerry
1994 #3 Dale Earnhardt
1994 #23 Dale Earnhardt's Car
1994 #270 Dale Earnhardt YR
1994 #277 Dale Earnhardt YR
1994 #278 Dale Earnhardt YR
1994 #281 Dale Earnhardt YR
1994 #283 Dale Earnhardt YR
1994 #284 Dale Earnhardt YR
1994 #297 D.Earnhardt WC Champ
1996 #3 Dale Earnhardt
1996 #73 Dale Earnhardt's Car
1996 #262 Dale Earnhardt
Maxx Racer's Ink
2000 #DE Dale Earnhardt
Maxx Racing for Kids
1991 #1 Sheet 1
Maxx Red
1992 #3 Dale Earnhardt
1992 #203 Dale Earnhardt's Car MM
1992 #231 Dale Earnhardt AP
1992 #265 Dale Earnhardt/Teresa YR
1992 #271 Dale Earnhardt/Teresa YR
1992 #281 Dale Earnhardt/Teresa YR
1992 #289 Dale Earnhardt YR
1992 #294 Dale Earnhardt YR
Maxx Rookies of the Year
1994 #3 Dale Earnhardt
Maxx Texaco Davey Allison
1992 #12 Dav.Allison/Earnhardt Cars
Maxx The Select 25
1994 #1 Dale Earnhardt
Maxx The Winston
1992 #14 Dale Earnhardt
1992 #34 Dale Earnhardt's Car
1993 #1 Dale Earnhardt
1993 #21 Dale Earnhardt's Car
1993 #49 Dale Earnhardt's Car Win
1993 #50 Dale Earnhardt VL
1993 #51 Dale Earnhardt Chromium

Maxx The Winston Acrylics
1991 #5 Dale Earnhardt
Maxx Update
1991 #200 Dale Earnhardt/Teresa YR
1991 #220 Dale Earnhardt AP
1991 #3 Dale Earnhardt
Maxx Winston 20th Anniversary Foils
1991 #20 Dale Earnhardt 1990 Car
1991 #10 Dale Earnhardt 1980 Car
1991 #16 Dale Earnhardt 1986 Car
1991 #17 Dale Earnhardt 1987 Car
Maxximum
1998 #3 Dale Earnhardt
1998 #28 Dale Earnhardt's Car
2000 #7 Dale Earnhardt
Maxximum Battle Proven
1998 #B2 Dale Earnhardt
Maxximum Die Cuts
2000 #7 Dale Earnhardt
Maxximum Field Generals Four Star Autographs
1998 #10 Dale Earnhardt
Maxximum Field Generals One Star
1998 #10 Dale Earnhardt
Maxximum Field Generals Three Star Autographs
1998 #10 Dale Earnhardt
Maxximum Field Generals Two Star
1998 #10 Dale Earnhardt
Maxximum MPH
2000 #7 Dale Earnhardt/3
Maxximum Roots of Racing
2000 #R1 Dale Earnhardt
Maxximum Signatures
2000 #DE2 D.Earn/D.Earnhardt Jr.
2000 #DE Dale Earnhardt
McFarlane NASCAR Dale Earnhardt Deluxe Boxed Set
2004 #10 Dale Earnhardt
McFarlane NASCAR Series 1
2003 #NNO D.Earnhardt R Blk Hat
2003 #NNO Dale Earnhardt R Black Hat w/Glasses
2003 #NNO D.Earnhardt H Red Hat
McFarlane NASCAR Series 2
2004 #15 Dale Earnhardt H Coke
2004 #20 Dale Earnhardt Jr. R
Red w/o Hat w/o Glasses
2004 #21 Dale Earnhardt Jr. R Red with Hat
2004 #22 Dale Earnhardt Jr. R
Red with Hat and Glasses
2004 #25 Dale Earnhardt Jr. H
Oreo w/o Hat and Glasses
2004 #26 Dale Earnhardt Jr. H
Oreo with Hat and Glasses
2004 #16 Dale Earnhardt H Coke with Glasses
2004 #10 Dale Earnhardt R Delco
2004 #11 Dale Earnhardt R Delco with Glasses
Metallic Impressions 25th Anniversary Winston Cup Champions
1996 #16 Dale Earnhardt
1996 #17 Dale Earnhardt
1996 #20 Dale Earnhardt
1996 #21 Dale Earnhardt
1996 #23 Dale Earnhardt
1996 #24 Dale Earnhardt
1996 #10 Dale Earnhardt
Metallic Impressions Avon All-Time Racing Greatest
1996 #1 Dale Earnhardt
Metallic Impressions Classic Dale Earnhardt 10-Card Tin
1995 #1 Dale Earnhardt
1995 #2 Dale Earnhardt
1995 #3 Dale Earnhardt
1995 #4 Dale Earnhardt
1995 #5 Dale Earnhardt
1995 #6 Dale Earnhardt
1995 #7 Dale Earnhardt
1995 #8 Dale Earnhardt
1995 #9 Dale Earnhardt
1995 #10 Dale Earnhardt
Metallic Impressions Classic Dale Earnhardt 21-Card Tin
1995 #1 Dale Earnhardt
1995 #2 Dale Earnhardt
1995 #3 Dale Earnhardt
1995 #4 Dale Earnhardt
1995 #5 Dale Earnhardt/Teresa Earnhardt
1995 #6 Dale Earnhardt
1995 #7 Dale Earnhardt's Car
1995 #8 Dale Earnhardt in Pits
1995 #9 Dale Earnhardt
1995 #10 Dale Earnhardt's Car
1995 #11 Dale Earnhardt w/Car
1995 #12 Dale Earnhardt
1995 #13 Dale Earnhardt's Car
1995 #14 Dale Earnhardt
1995 #15 Dale Earnhardt's Car
1995 #16 Dale Earnhardt's Car
1995 #17 Dale Earnhardt's Car
1995 #18 Dale Earnhardt's Car
1995 #19 Dale Earnhardt's Car
1995 #20 Dale Earnhardt
1995 #E1 Dale Earnhardt/Richard Childress
Metallic Impressions Classic Dale Earnhardt 5-Card Tin
1995 #1 Dale Earnhardt
1995 #2 Dale Earnhardt
1995 #3 Dale Earnhardt
1995 #4 Dale Earnhardt
1995 #5 Dale Earnhardt
Metallic Impressions Dale Earnhardt Burger King
1996 #1 Dale Earnhardt's Car 1987
1996 #2 Dale Earnhardt 1990
1996 #3 Dale Earnhardt's Car 1995
Metallic Impressions Winston Cup Champions 10-Card Tin
1995 #4 Dale Earnhardt
Metallic Impressions Winston Cup Top Five
1996 #4 Dale Earnhardt
M-Force
1996 #45 Dale Earnhardt's Car CL
1996 #3 Dale Earnhardt
1996 #4 Dale Earnhardt's Car
M-Force Black

1996 #B3 Dale Earnhardt
1996 #B4 Dale Earnhardt's Car

M-Force Sheet Metal
1996 #M2 Dale Earnhardt

M-Force Silvers
1996 #S2 Dale Earnhardt
1996 #S3 Dale Earnhardt's Car

Pinnacle
1996 #3 Dale Earnhardt
1996 #91 Dale Earnhardt's Transporter
1996 #38 Dale Earnhardt's Car
1997 #3 Dale Earnhardt
1997 #32 Dale Earnhardt's Car
1997 #68 Dale Earnhardt's Car RR
1997 #69 Dale Earnhardt RR
1997 #70 Dale Earnhardt's Car RR
1997 #82 Dale Earnhardt TT
1997 #84 Dale Earnhardt TT
1997 #91 Dale Earnhardt's Car T4
1997 #95 Dale Earnhardt's Car T4
1997 #66 Dale Earnhardt's Car RR

Pinnacle Artist Proofs
1996 #3 Dale Earnhardt
1996 #38 Dale Earnhardt's Car
1996 #91 Dale Earnhardt's Transporter
1997 #3 Dale Earnhardt P
1997 #32 Dale Earnhardt's Car B
1997 #66 Dale Earnhardt's Car RR R
1997 #68 Dale Earnhardt's Car RR R
1997 #69 Dale Earnhardt RR R
1997 #70 Dale Earnhardt's Car RR R
1997 #82 Dale Earnhardt TT R
1997 #84 Dale Earnhardt TT R
1997 #91 Dale Earnhardt's Car T4 R
1997 #95 Dale Earnhardt's Car T4 R

Pinnacle Certified
1997 #3 Dale Earnhardt
1997 #37 Dale Earnhardt's Car
1997 #76 Dale Earnhardt's Car WP
1997 #93 Dale Earnhardt BD

Pinnacle Certified Certified Team
1997 #1 Dale Earnhardt

Pinnacle Certified Certified Team Gold
1997 #1 Dale Earnhardt

Pinnacle Certified Epix
1997 #E1 Dale Earnhardt

Pinnacle Certified Epix Emerald
1997 #E1 Dale Earnhardt

Pinnacle Certified Epix Purple
1997 #E1 Dale Earnhardt

Pinnacle Certified Mirror Blue
1997 #3 Dale Earnhardt
1997 #37 Dale Earnhardt's Car
1997 #76 Dale Earnhardt's Car WP
1997 #93 Dale Earnhardt BD

Pinnacle Certified Mirror Gold
1997 #3 Dale Earnhardt
1997 #37 Dale Earnhardt's Car
1997 #76 Dale Earnhardt's Car WP
1997 #93 Dale Earnhardt BD

Pinnacle Certified Mirror Red
1997 #3 Dale Earnhardt
1997 #37 Dale Earnhardt's Car
1997 #76 Dale Earnhardt's Car WP
1997 #93 Dale Earnhardt BD

Pinnacle Certified Red
1997 #3 Dale Earnhardt
1997 #37 Dale Earnhardt's Car
1997 #76 Dale Earnhardt's Car WP
1997 #93 Dale Earnhardt BD

Pinnacle Checkered Flag
1996 #3 Dale Earnhardt

Pinnacle Chevy Madness
1997 #13 Dale Earnhardt's Car

Pinnacle Foil
1997 #66 Dale Earnhardt's Car RR
1997 #68 Dale Earnhardt's Car RR
1997 #69 Dale Earnhardt RR
1997 #70 Dale Earnhardt's Car RR
1997 #82 Dale Earnhardt TT
1997 #84 Dale Earnhardt TT
1997 #91 Dale Earnhardt's Car T4
1997 #95 Dale Earnhardt's Car T4
1997 #32 Dale Earnhardt's Car
1997 #3 Dale Earnhardt

Pinnacle Mint
1997 #21 Dale Earnhardt's Car
1998 #3 Dale Earnhardt
1998 #17 Dale Earnhardt's Car

Pinnacle Mint Bronze
1997 #21 Dale Earnhardt's Car

Pinnacle Mint Coins
1997 #21 Dale Earnhardt's Car
1998 #3 Dale Earnhardt
1998 #17 Dale Earnhardt's Car

Pinnacle Mint Coins 24K Gold Plated
1997 #21 Dale Earnhardt's Car

Pinnacle Mint Coins Bronze Proof
1998 #3 Dale Earnhardt
1998 #17 Dale Earnhardt's Car

Pinnacle Mint Coins Gold Plated
1998 #3 Dale Earnhardt
1998 #17 Dale Earnhardt's Car

Pinnacle Mint Coins Gold Plated Proofs
1998 #3 Dale Earnhardt
1998 #17 Dale Earnhardt's Car

Pinnacle Mint Coins Nickel-Silver
1997 #21 Dale Earnhardt's Car
1998 #3 Dale Earnhardt
1998 #17 Dale Earnhardt's Car

Pinnacle Mint Coins Silver Plated Proofs
1998 #3 Dale Earnhardt
1998 #17 Dale Earnhardt's Car

Pinnacle Mint Coins Solid Gold
1998 #3 Dale Earnhardt
1998 #17 Dale Earnhardt's Car

Pinnacle Mint Coins Solid Silver
1998 #3 Dale Earnhardt
1998 #17 Dale Earnhardt's Car

Pinnacle Mint Die Cuts
1998 #3 Dale Earnhardt
1998 #17 Dale Earnhardt's Car

Pinnacle Mint Gold
1997 #21 Dale Earnhardt's Car

Pinnacle Mint Gold Team
1998 #3 Dale Earnhardt
1998 #17 Dale Earnhardt's Car

Pinnacle Mint Silver
1997 #21 Dale Earnhardt's Car

Pinnacle Mint Silver Team
1998 #3 Dale Earnhardt
1998 #17 Dale Earnhardt's Car

Pinnacle Pole Position
1996 #3 Dale Earnhardt
1996 #27 Dale Earnhardt's Car
1996 #56 Dale Earnhardt SE
1996 #57 Dale Earnhardt SE
1996 #58 Dale Earnhardt SE
1996 #59 Dale Earnhardt SE
1996 #60 Dale Earnhardt SE
1996 #72 Dale Earnhardt EY

Pinnacle Pole Position Certified Strong
1996 #3 Dale Earnhardt

Pinnacle Pole Position Lightning Fast
1996 #3 Dale Earnhardt
1996 #27 Dale Earnhardt's Car
1996 #56 Dale Earnhardt
1996 #57 Dale Earnhardt
1996 #58 Dale Earnhardt
1996 #59 Dale Earnhardt
1996 #60 Dale Earnhardt
1996 #72 Dale Earnhardt

Pinnacle Pole Position No Limit
1996 #3 Dale Earnhardt

Pinnacle Pole Position No Limit Gold
1996 #3 Dale Earnhardt

Pinnacle Portraits
1997 #23 Dale Earnhardt's Car
1997 #3 Dale Earnhardt

Pinnacle Portraits 8x10
1997 #DE2 Dale Earnhardt
1997 #DE3 Dale Earnhardt
1997 #DE4 Dale Earnhardt
1997 #DE1 Dale Earnhardt

Pinnacle Portraits 8x10 Dufex
1997 #DE1 Dale Earnhardt
1997 #DE2 Dale Earnhardt
1997 #DE3 Dale Earnhardt
1997 #DE4 Dale Earnhardt

Pinnacle Precision
1997 #15 Dale Earnhardt
1997 #18 Dale Earnhardt

Pinnacle Precision Bronze
1997 #12 Dale Earnhardt's Transporter
1997 #13 Dale Earnhardt Pit Action
1997 #14 Dale Earnhardt's Car
1997 #15 Dale Earnhardt
1997 #17 Dale Earnhardt's Car
1997 #18 Dale Earnhardt

Pinnacle Precision Gold
1997 #12 Dale Earnhardt's Transporter
1997 #13 Dale Earnhardt Pit Action
1997 #14 Dale Earnhardt's Car
1997 #15 Dale Earnhardt
1997 #17 Dale Earnhardt's Car
1997 #18 Dale Earnhardt

Pinnacle Precision Silver
1997 #12 Dale Earnhardt's Transporter
1997 #13 Dale Earnhardt Pit Action
1997 #14 Dale Earnhardt's Car
1997 #15 Dale Earnhardt
1997 #17 Dale Earnhardt's Car
1997 #18 Dale Earnhardt

Pinnacle Press Plates
1997 #3 Dale Earnhardt
1997 #69 Dale Earnhardt RR
1997 #70 Dale Earnhardt's Car RR
1997 #82 Dale Earnhardt TT
1997 #84 Dale Earnhardt TT
1997 #91 Dale Earnhardt's Car T4
1997 #95 Dale Earnhardt's Car T4
1997 #32 Dale Earnhardt's Car
1997 #66 Dale Earnhardt's Car RR
1997 #68 Dale Earnhardt's Car RR
1997 #S3-S Dale Earnhardt
1997 #CM13 Dale Earnhardt
1997 #TP3A Dale Earnhardt

Pinnacle Spellbound
1997 #3S Dale Earnhardt

Pinnacle Spellbound Autographs
1997 #3S Dale Earnhardt

Pinnacle Spellbound Promos
1997 #3S Dale Earnhardt

Pinnacle Team Pinnacle
1996 #3 Dale Earnhardt
1996 #11 Dale Earnhardt
1997 #3 Dale Earnhardt

Pinnacle Team Pinnacle Red
1997 #3 Dale Earnhardt

Pinnacle Totally Certified Platinum Blue
1997 #3 Dale Earnhardt
1997 #37 Dale Earnhardt's Car
1997 #76 Dale Earnhardt WP
1997 #93 Dale Earnhardt BD

Pinnacle Totally Certified Platinum Gold
1997 #3 Dale Earnhardt
1997 #37 Dale Earnhardt's Car
1997 #76 Dale Earnhardt WP
1997 #93 Dale Earnhardt BD

Pinnacle Totally Certified Platinum Red
1997 #37 Dale Earnhardt's Car
1997 #76 Dale Earnhardt WP
1997 #93 Dale Earnhardt BD
1997 #3 Dale Earnhardt

Pinnacle Trophy Collection
1997 #32 Dale Earnhardt's Car
1997 #3 Dale Earnhardt
1997 #66 Dale Earnhardt's Car RR
1997 #82 Dale Earnhardt TT
1997 #84 Dale Earnhardt TT
1997 #91 Dale Earnhardt's Car T4
1997 #95 Dale Earnhardt's Car T4
1997 #68 Dale Earnhardt's Car RR
1997 #69 Dale Earnhardt RR
1997 #70 Dale Earnhardt's Car RR

Pinnacle Winston Cup Collection
1996 #3 Dale Earnhardt
1996 #38 Dale Earnhardt's Car
1996 #91 Dale Earnhardt's Transporter

Power
1994 #2 Dale Earnhardt DB
1994 #16 Dale Earnhardt PW
1994 #38 Dale Earnhardt SL
1994 #59 Dale Earnhardt's Trans. PR
1994 #DB1 Dale Earnhardt Promo
1994 #NNO D.Earnhardt HOLO/3500

Power Gold
1994 #2 Dale Earnhardt DB
1994 #16 Dale Earnhardt PW
1994 #38 Dale Earnhardt SL
1994 #59 Dale Earnhardt's Trans. PR

Power Preview
1994 #31 Dale Earnhardt WC Champ

Predator
1997 #3 Dale Earnhardt

Predator American Eagle
1997 #AE1 Dale Earnhardt

Predator American Eagle First Slash
1997 #AE1 Dale Earnhardt

Predator Black Wolf First Strike
1997 #3 Dale Earnhardt

Predator Eye of the Tiger
1997 #ET1 Dale Earnhardt

Predator Eye of the Tiger First Slash
1997 #ET1 Dale Earnhardt

Predator First Slash
1997 #3 Dale Earnhardt

Predator Gatorback
1997 #GB1 Dale Earnhardt

Predator Gatorback Authentic
1997 #GBA1 Dale Earnhardt

Predator Gatorback Authentic First Slash
1997 #GBA1 Dale Earnhardt

Predator Gatorback First Slash
1997 #GB1 Dale Earnhardt

Predator Golden Eagle
1997 #GE1 Dale Earnhardt

Predator Golden Eagle First Slash
1997 #GE1 Dale Earnhardt

Predator Grizzly
1997 #3 Dale Earnhardt

Predator Grizzly First Slash
1997 #3 Dale Earnhardt

Predator Red Wolf
1997 #3 Dale Earnhardt

Predator Red Wolf First Slash
1997 #3 Dale Earnhardt

Press Pass
1994 #5 Dale Earnhardt
1995 #9 Dale Earnhardt
1995 #41 Dale Earnhardt's Car
1995 #115 Dale Earnhardt's Car AW
1996 #9 Dale Earnhardt
1996 #40 Dale Earnhardt's Car
1997 #4 Dale Earnhardt
1997 #32 Dale Earnhardt's Car
1997 #56 Dale Earnhardt's Car
1997 #95 Dale Earnhardt's Car
1998 #4 Dale Earnhardt
1998 #29 Dale Earnhardt's Car
1998 #104 Dale Earnhardt RET
1999 #8 Dale Earnhardt
1999 #35 Dale Earnhardt's Car
2000 #7 Dale Earnhardt
2001 #2 Dale Earnhardt
2001 #49 Dale Earnhardt's Car
2001 #67 Dale Earnhardt REP
2008 #61 Dale Earnhardt

Press Pass 10th Anniversary Earnhardt
2003-04 #TA1 Dale Earnhardt
2003-04 #TA2 Dale Earnhardt
2003-04 #TA3 Dale Earnhardt
2003-04 #TA4 Dale Earnhardt
2003-04 #TA5 Dale Earnhardt
2003-04 #TA6 Dale Earnhardt
2003-04 #TA7 Dale Earnhardt
2003-04 #TA8 Dale Earnhardt
2003-04 #TA9 Dale Earnhardt
2003-04 #TA10 Dale Earnhardt
2003-04 #TA11 Dale Earnhardt
2003-04 #TA12 Dale Earnhardt
2003-04 #TA13 Dale Earnhardt
2003-04 #TA14 Dale Earnhardt
2003-04 #TA15 Dale Earnhardt
2003-04 #TA16 Dale Earnhardt
2003-04 #TA17 Dale Earnhardt
2003-04 #TA18 Dale Earnhardt
2003-04 #TA19 Dale Earnhardt
2003-04 #TA20 Dale Earnhardt
2003-04 #TA21 Dale Earnhardt
2003-04 #TA22 Dale Earnhardt
2003-04 #TA23 Dale Earnhardt
2003-04 #TA24 Dale Earnhardt
2003-04 #TA25 Dale Earnhardt
2003-04 #TA26 Dale Earnhardt
2003-04 #TA27 Dale Earnhardt
2003-04 #TA28 Dale Earnhardt
2003-04 #TA29 Dale Earnhardt
2003-04 #TA30 Dale Earnhardt
2003-04 #TA31 Dale Earnhardt
2003-04 #TA32 Dale Earnhardt
2003-04 #TA33 Dale Earnhardt
2003-04 #TA34 Dale Earnhardt
2003-04 #TA35 Dale Earnhardt
2003-04 #TA36 Dale Earnhardt
2003-04 #TA37 Dale Earnhardt
2003-04 #TA38 Dale Earnhardt
2003-04 #TA39 Dale Earnhardt
2003-04 #TA40 Dale Earnhardt
2003-04 #TA41 Dale Earnhardt
2003-04 #TA42 Dale Earnhardt
2003-04 #TA43 Dale Earnhardt
2003-04 #TA44 Dale Earnhardt
2003-04 #TA45 Dale Earnhardt
2003-04 #TA46 Dale Earnhardt
2003-04 #TA47 Dale Earnhardt
2003-04 #TA48 Dale Earnhardt
2003-04 #TA49 Dale Earnhardt
2003-04 #TA50 Dale Earnhardt
2003-04 #TA51 Dale Earnhardt
2003-04 #TA52 Dale Earnhardt
2003-04 #TA53 Dale Earnhardt
2003-04 #TA54 Dale Earnhardt
2003-04 #TA55 Dale Earnhardt
2003-04 #TA56 Dale Earnhardt
2003-04 #TA57 Dale Earnhardt
2003-04 #TA58 Dale Earnhardt
2003-04 #TA59 Dale Earnhardt
2003-04 #TA60 Dale Earnhardt
2003-04 #TA61 Dale Earnhardt
2003-04 #TA62 Dale Earnhardt
2003-04 #TA63 Dale Earnhardt
2003-04 #TA64 Dale Earnhardt
2003-04 #TA65 Dale Earnhardt
2003-04 #TA66 Dale Earnhardt
2003-04 #TA67 Dale Earnhardt
2003-04 #TA68 Dale Earnhardt
2003-04 #TA69 Dale Earnhardt
2003-04 #TA70 Dale Earnhardt
2003-04 #TA71 Dale Earnhardt
2003-04 #TA72 Dale Earnhardt
2003-04 #TA73 Dale Earnhardt
2003-04 #TA74 Dale Earnhardt
2003-04 #TA75 Dale Earnhardt
2003-04 #TA76 Dale Earnhardt
2003-04 #TA77 Dale Earnhardt
2003-04 #TA78 Dale Earnhardt
2003-04 #TA79 Dale Earnhardt
2003-04 #TA80 Dale Earnhardt
2003-04 #TA81 Dale Earnhardt
2003-04 #TA82 Dale Earnhardt
2003-04 #TA83 Dale Earnhardt
2003-04 #TA84 Dale Earnhardt
2003-04 #TA85 Dale Earnhardt
2003-04 #TA86 Dale Earnhardt
2003-04 #TA87 Dale Earnhardt
2003-04 #TA88 Dale Earnhardt
2003-04 #TA89 Dale Earnhardt
2003-04 #TA90 Dale Earnhardt
2003-04 #TA91 Dale Earnhardt
2003-04 #TA92 Dale Earnhardt
2003-04 #TA93 Dale Earnhardt
2003-04 #TA94 Dale Earnhardt
2003-04 #TA95 Dale Earnhardt
2003-04 #TA96 Dale Earnhardt
2003-04 #TA97 Dale Earnhardt
2003-04 #TA98 Dale Earnhardt
2003-04 #TA99 Dale Earnhardt
2003-04 #TA100 Dale Earnhardt

Press Pass 10th Anniversary Earnhardt Gold
2003-04 #TA1 Dale Earnhardt
2003-04 #TA2 Dale Earnhardt
2003-04 #TA3 Dale Earnhardt
2003-04 #TA4 Dale Earnhardt
2003-04 #TA5 Dale Earnhardt
2003-04 #TA6 Dale Earnhardt
2003-04 #TA7 Dale Earnhardt
2003-04 #TA8 Dale Earnhardt
2003-04 #TA9 Dale Earnhardt
2003-04 #TA10 Dale Earnhardt
2003-04 #TA11 Dale Earnhardt
2003-04 #TA12 Dale Earnhardt
2003-04 #TA13 Dale Earnhardt
2003-04 #TA14 Dale Earnhardt
2003-04 #TA15 Dale Earnhardt
2003-04 #TA16 Dale Earnhardt
2003-04 #TA17 Dale Earnhardt
2003-04 #TA18 Dale Earnhardt
2003-04 #TA19 Dale Earnhardt
2003-04 #TA20 Dale Earnhardt
2003-04 #TA21 Dale Earnhardt
2003-04 #TA22 Dale Earnhardt
2003-04 #TA23 Dale Earnhardt
2003-04 #TA24 Dale Earnhardt
2003-04 #TA25 Dale Earnhardt
2003-04 #TA26 Dale Earnhardt
2003-04 #TA27 Dale Earnhardt
2003-04 #TA28 Dale Earnhardt
2003-04 #TA29 Dale Earnhardt
2003-04 #TA30 Dale Earnhardt
2003-04 #TA31 Dale Earnhardt
2003-04 #TA32 Dale Earnhardt
2003-04 #TA33 Dale Earnhardt
2003-04 #TA34 Dale Earnhardt
2003-04 #TA35 Dale Earnhardt
2003-04 #TA36 Dale Earnhardt
2003-04 #TA37 Dale Earnhardt
2003-04 #TA38 Dale Earnhardt
2003-04 #TA39 Dale Earnhardt
2003-04 #TA40 Dale Earnhardt
2003-04 #TA41 Dale Earnhardt
2003-04 #TA42 Dale Earnhardt
2003-04 #TA43 Dale Earnhardt
2003-04 #TA44 Dale Earnhardt
2003-04 #TA45 Dale Earnhardt
2003-04 #TA46 Dale Earnhardt
2003-04 #TA47 Dale Earnhardt
2003-04 #TA48 Dale Earnhardt
2003-04 #TA49 Dale Earnhardt
2003-04 #TA50 Dale Earnhardt
2003-04 #TA51 Dale Earnhardt
2003-04 #TA52 Dale Earnhardt
2003-04 #TA53 Dale Earnhardt
2003-04 #TA54 Dale Earnhardt
2003-04 #TA55 Dale Earnhardt
2003-04 #TA56 Dale Earnhardt
2003-04 #TA57 Dale Earnhardt
2003-04 #TA58 Dale Earnhardt
2003-04 #TA59 Dale Earnhardt
2003-04 #TA60 Dale Earnhardt
2003-04 #TA61 Dale Earnhardt
2003-04 #TA62 Dale Earnhardt
2003-04 #TA63 Dale Earnhardt
2003-04 #TA64 Dale Earnhardt
2003-04 #TA65 Dale Earnhardt
2003-04 #TA66 Dale Earnhardt
2003-04 #TA67 Dale Earnhardt
2003-04 #TA68 Dale Earnhardt
2003-04 #TA69 Dale Earnhardt
2003-04 #TA70 Dale Earnhardt
2003-04 #TA71 Dale Earnhardt
2003-04 #TA72 Dale Earnhardt
2003-04 #TA73 Dale Earnhardt
2003-04 #TA74 Dale Earnhardt
2003-04 #TA75 Dale Earnhardt
2003-04 #TA76 Dale Earnhardt
2003-04 #TA77 Dale Earnhardt
2003-04 #TA78 Dale Earnhardt
2003-04 #TA79 Dale Earnhardt
2003-04 #TA80 Dale Earnhardt
2003-04 #TA81 Dale Earnhardt
2003-04 #TA82 Dale Earnhardt
2003-04 #TA83 Dale Earnhardt
2003-04 #TA84 Dale Earnhardt
2003-04 #TA85 Dale Earnhardt
2003-04 #TA86 Dale Earnhardt
2003-04 #TA87 Dale Earnhardt
2003-04 #TA88 Dale Earnhardt
2003-04 #TA89 Dale Earnhardt
2003-04 #TA90 Dale Earnhardt
2003-04 #TA91 Dale Earnhardt
2003-04 #TA92 Dale Earnhardt
2003-04 #TA93 Dale Earnhardt
2003-04 #TA94 Dale Earnhardt
2003-04 #TA95 Dale Earnhardt
2003-04 #TA96 Dale Earnhardt
2003-04 #TA97 Dale Earnhardt
2003-04 #TA98 Dale Earnhardt
2003-04 #TA99 Dale Earnhardt
2003-04 #TA100 Dale Earnhardt

Press Pass Autographs
1997 #4 D.Earnhardt PPP/VIP/ACTN
1998 #1 Dale Earnhardt
1999 #3 Dale Earnhardt/75
2001 #11 Dale Earnhardt

Press Pass Banquet Bound
1997 #BB4 Dale Earnhardt

Press Pass Blue
2008 #B61 Dale Earnhardt

Press Pass Burning Rubber
1996 #BR3 Dale Earnhardt's Car
1997 #BR2 Dale Earnhardt
1999 #BR9 Dale Earnhardt's Car
2000 #BR6 Dale Earnhardt's Car

Press Pass Burning Rubber Cars
2001 #BRC3 Dale Earnhardt/105
2002 #BRC3 Dale Earnhardt's Car
2003 #BRT16Dale Earnhardt's Car
2004 #BRT17Dale Earnhardt's Car

Press Pass Burning Rubber Drivers
2001 #BRD3 Dale Earnhardt/90
2002 #BRD3 Dale Earnhardt
2003 #BRD16 Dale Earnhardt
2004 #BRD17 Dale Earnhardt

Press Pass Chase Cars
1999 #7B Dale Earnhardt's Car

Press Pass Checkered Flags
1994 #CF1 Dale Earnhardt
1995 #CF2 Dale Earnhardt

Press Pass Clear Cut
1997 #C1 Dale Earnhardt

Press Pass Cup Chase
1994 #CC5 Dale Earnhardt W1
1994 #SPCL1 Dale Earnhardt Prize
1995 #9 Dale Earnhardt WIN
1996 #9 Dale Earnhardt WIN
1997 #CC5 Dale Earnhardt
1998 #CC5 Dale Earnhardt's Car Win 2
1999 #4 Dale Earnhardt WIN 2
2000 #CC4 Dale Earnhardt
2001 #CC3 Dale Earnhardt

Press Pass Cup Chase Blue Die Cut Prizes
1997 #CC5 Dale Earnhardt

Press Pass Cup Chase Die Cut Prizes
1998 #CC5 Dale Earnhardt's Car
1999 #4 Dale Earnhardt
2000 #CC4 Dale Earnhardt
2001 #CC3 Dale Earnhardt

Press Pass Cup Chase Foil Prizes
1996 #9 Dale Earnhardt

Press Pass Cup Chase Gold Die Cuts
1997 #CC5 Dale Earnhardt

Press Pass Cup Chase Prizes
1995 #CCR2 Dale Earnhardt

Press Pass Dale Earnhardt
2001-03 #DE1 Dale Earnhardt WCC CL
2001-03 #DE2 Dale Earnhardt 1980
2001-03 #DE3 Dale Earnhardt 1986
2001-03 #DE4 Dale Earnhardt 1987
2001-03 #DE5 Dale Earnhardt 1990
2001-03 #DE6 Dale Earnhardt 1991
2001-03 #DE7 Dale Earnhardt 1993
2001-03 #DE8 Dale Earnhardt 1994
2001-03 #DE9 Dale Earnhardt SH CL
2001-03 #DE10Dale Earnhardt 1980
2001-03 #DE11Dale Earnhardt 1986
2001-03 #DE12Dale Earnhardt 1987
2001-03 #DE13Dale Earnhardt 1990
2001-03 #DE14Dale Earnhardt 1991
2001-03 #DE15Dale Earnhardt 1993
2001-03 #DE16Dale Earnhardt 1994
2001-03 #DE17Dale Earnhardt OP CL
2001-03 #DE18Dale Earnhardt 79/90
2001-03 #DE19Dale Earnhardt 1987
2001-03 #DE20Dale Earnhardt 1987
2001-03 #DE21Dale Earnhardt 1994
2001-03 #DE22Dale Earnhardt 2000
2001-03 #DE23Dale Earnhardt 1987
2001-03 #DE24Dale Earnhardt 1987
2001-03 #DE25Dale Earnhardt 2000
2001-03 #DE26Dale Earnhardt PP CL
2001-03 #DE27Dale Earnhardt PP 3
2001-03 #DE28Dale Earnhardt PP 4
2001-03 #DE29Dale Earnhardt PP 6
2001-03 #DE30Dale Earnhardt PP 7
2001-03 #DE31Dale Earnhardt PP 11
2001-03 #DE32Dale Earnhardt PP 27
2001-03 #DE33Dale Earnhardt PP 48
2001-03 #DE34Dale Earnhardt PP 676
2001-03 #DE35Dale Earnhardt CL
2001-03 #DE35BDale Earnhardt CL
2001-03 #DE36Dale Earnhardt 1995
2001-03 #DE36BDale Earnhardt 1988
2001-03 #DE37Dale Earnhardt 1996
2001-03 #DE37BDale Earnhardt 76
2001-03 #DE38Dale Earnhardt 1997
2001-03 #DE38BDale Earnhardt 4
2001-03 #DE39Dale Earnhardt 1998
2001-03 #DE39BDale Earnhardt 17
2001-03 #DE40Dale Earnhardt 1998
2001-03 #DE40BDale Earnhardt 9
2001-03 #DE41Dale Earnhardt 1999
2001-03 #DE41BDale Earnhardt 5
2001-03 #DE42Dale Earnhardt 2000
2001-03 #DE42BDale Earnhardt 10
2001-03 #DE43Dale Earnhardt 2000
2001-03 #DE43BDale Earnhardt 489
2001-03 #DE44Dale Earnhardt
2001-03 #DE45Dale Earnhardt 1979
2001-03 #DE46Dale Earnhardt
2001-03 #DE47Dale Earnhardt
2001-03 #DE48Dale Earnhardt
2001-03 #DE49Dale Earnhardt
2001-03 #DE50Dale Earnhardt
2001-03 #DE51Dale Earnhardt
2001-03 #DE52Dale Earnhardt
2001-03 #DE53Dale Earnhardt
2001-03 #DE54Dale Earnhardt
2001-03 #DE55Dale Earnhardt
2001-03 #DE56Dale Earnhardt
2001-03 #DE57Dale Earnhardt
2001-03 #DE58Dale Earnhardt
2001-03 #DE59Dale Earnhardt
2001-03 #DE60Dale Earnhardt
2001-03 #DE61Dale Earnhardt
2001-03 #DE62Dale Earnhardt TS CL
2001-03 #DE63Dale Earnhardt
2001-03 #DE64Dale Earnhardt
2001-03 #DE65Dale Earnhardt
2001-03 #DE66Dale Earnhardt
2001-03 #DE67Dale Earnhardt
2001-03 #DE68Dale Earnhardt
2001-03 #DE69Dale Earnhardt
2001-03 #DE70Dale Earnhardt VIP CL
2001-03 #DE71Dale Earnhardt
2001-03 #DE72Dale Earnhardt
2001-03 #DE73Dale Earnhardt
2001-03 #DE74Dale Earnhardt
2001-03 #DE75Dale Earnhardt
2001-03 #DE76Dale Earnhardt
2001-03 #DE77Dale Earnhardt
2001-03 #DE78Dale Earnhardt
2001-03 #DE79Dale Earnhardt
2001-03 #DE80Dale Earnhardt
2001-03 #DE81Dale Earnhardt
2001-03 #DE82Dale Earnhardt
2001-03 #DE83Dale Earnhardt
2001-03 #DE84Dale Earnhardt
2001-03 #DE85Dale Earnhardt
2001-03 #DE86Dale Earnhardt
2001-03 #DE87Dale Earnhardt
2001-03 #DE88Dale Earnhardt
2001-03 #DE89Dale Earnhardt
2001-03 #DE90Dale Earnhardt
2001-03 #DE91Dale Earnhardt
2001-03 #DE92Dale Earnhardt
2001-03 #DE93Dale Earnhardt
2001-03 #DE94Dale Earnhardt
2001-03 #DE95Dale Earnhardt
2001-03 #DE96Dale Earnhardt
2001-03 #DE97Dale Earnhardt
2001-03 #DE98Dale Earnhardt
2001-03 #DE99Dale Earnhardt
2001-03 #DE100Dale Earnhardt

Press Pass Dale Earnhardt Celebration Foil
2001-03 #DE1 Dale Earnhardt WCC CL
2001-03 #DE2 Dale Earnhardt 1980
2001-03 #DE3 Dale Earnhardt 1986
2001-03 #DE4 Dale Earnhardt 1987
2001-03 #DE5 Dale Earnhardt 1990
2001-03 #DE6 Dale Earnhardt 1991
2001-03 #DE7 Dale Earnhardt 1993
2001-03 #DE8 Dale Earnhardt 1994
2001-03 #DE9 Dale Earnhardt SH CL
2001-03 #DE10Dale Earnhardt 1980
2001-03 #DE11Dale Earnhardt 1986
2001-03 #DE12Dale Earnhardt 1987
2001-03 #DE13Dale Earnhardt 1990
2001-03 #DE14Dale Earnhardt 1991
2001-03 #DE15Dale Earnhardt 1993
2001-03 #DE16Dale Earnhardt 1994
2001-03 #DE17Dale Earnhardt CL
2001-03 #DE18Dale Earnhardt '79/'90
2001-03 #DE19Dale Earnhardt 1987
2001-03 #DE20Dale Earnhardt 1987
2001-03 #DE21Dale Earnhardt 1994
2001-03 #DE22Dale Earnhardt 2000
2001-03 #DE23Dale Earnhardt 1987
2001-03 #DE24Dale Earnhardt 1987
2001-03 #DE25Dale Earnhardt 2000
2001-03 #DE26Dale Earnhardt PP CL
2001-03 #DE27Dale Earnhardt PP 3
2001-03 #DE28Dale Earnhardt PP 4
2001-03 #DE29Dale Earnhardt PP 6
2001-03 #DE30Dale Earnhardt PP 7
2001-03 #DE31Dale Earnhardt PP 11
2001-03 #DE32Dale Earnhardt PP 27
2001-03 #DE33Dale Earnhardt PP 48
2001-03 #DE34Dale Earnhardt PP 676
2001-03 #DE35Dale Earnhardt CL
2001-03 #DE35BDale Earnhardt CL
2001-03 #DE36Dale Earnhardt 1995
2001-03 #DE36BDale Earnhardt 1988
2001-03 #DE37Dale Earnhardt 1996
2001-03 #DE37BDale Earnhardt 76
2001-03 #DE38Dale Earnhardt 1997
2001-03 #DE38BDale Earnhardt 4
2001-03 #DE39Dale Earnhardt 1998
2001-03 #DE39BDale Earnhardt 17
2001-03 #DE40Dale Earnhardt 1998
2001-03 #DE40BDale Earnhardt 9
2001-03 #DE41Dale Earnhardt 1999
2001-03 #DE41BDale Earnhardt 5
2001-03 #DE42Dale Earnhardt 2000
2001-03 #DE42BDale Earnhardt 10
2001-03 #DE43Dale Earnhardt 2000
2001-03 #DE43BDale Earnhardt 489
2001-03 #DE44Dale Earnhardt
2001-03 #DE45Dale Earnhardt 1979
2001-03 #DE46Dale Earnhardt
2001-03 #DE47Dale Earnhardt
2001-03 #DE48Dale Earnhardt
2001-03 #DE49Dale Earnhardt
2001-03 #DE50Dale Earnhardt
2001-03 #DE51Dale Earnhardt
2001-03 #DE52Dale Earnhardt
2001-03 #DE53Dale Earnhardt
2001-03 #DE54Dale Earnhardt
2001-03 #DE55Dale Earnhardt
2001-03 #DE56Dale Earnhardt
2001-03 #DE57Dale Earnhardt
2001-03 #DE58Dale Earnhardt
2001-03 #DE59Dale Earnhardt
2001-03 #DE60Dale Earnhardt
2001-03 #DE61Dale Earnhardt
2001-03 #DE62Dale Earnhardt
2001-03 #DE63Dale Earnhardt
2001-03 #DE64Dale Earnhardt
2001-03 #DE65Dale Earnhardt
2001-03 #DE66Dale Earnhardt
2001-03 #DE67Dale Earnhardt
2001-03 #DE68Dale Earnhardt
2001-03 #DE69Dale Earnhardt
2001-03 #DE70Dale Earnhardt
2001-03 #DE71Dale Earnhardt
2001-03 #DE72Dale Earnhardt
2001-03 #DE73Dale Earnhardt
2001-03 #DE74Dale Earnhardt
2001-03 #DE75Dale Earnhardt

2001-03 #DE76Dale Earnhardt
2001-03 #DE77Dale Earnhardt
2001-03 #DE78Dale Earnhardt
2001-03 #DE79Dale Earnhardt
2001-03 #DE80Dale Earnhardt
2001-03 #DE81Dale Earnhardt
2001-03 #DE82Dale Earnhardt
2001-03 #DE83Dale Earnhardt
2001-03 #DE84Dale Earnhardt
2001-03 #DE85Dale Earnhardt
2001-03 #DE86Dale Earnhardt
2001-03 #DE87Dale Earnhardt
2001-03 #DE88Dale Earnhardt
2001-03 #DE89Dale Earnhardt
2001-03 #DE90Dale Earnhardt
2001-03 #DE91Dale Earnhardt
2001-03 #DE92Dale Earnhardt
2001-03 #DE93Dale Earnhardt
2001-03 #DE94Dale Earnhardt
2001-03 #DE95Dale Earnhardt
2001-03 #DE96Dale Earnhardt
2001-03 #DE97Dale Earnhardt
2001-03 #DE98Dale Earnhardt
2001-03 #DE99Dale Earnhardt
2001-03 #DE100Dale Earnhardt

Press Pass Dale Earnhardt Gallery
2004 #DEG1Dale Earnhardt
2004 #DEG2Dale Earnhardt
2004 #DEG3Dale Earnhardt
2004 #DEG4Dale Earnhardt
2004 #DEG5Dale Earnhardt
2004 #DEG6Dale Earnhardt
2004 #DEG7Dale Earnhardt
2004 #DEG8Dale Earnhardt
2004 #DEG9Dale Earnhardt
2004 #DEG10Dale Earnhardt
2004 #DEG11Dale Earnhardt
2004 #DEG12Dale Earnhardt
2004 #DEG13Dale Earnhardt
2004 #DEG14Dale Earnhardt
2004 #DEG15Dale Earnhardt
2004 #DEG16Dale Earnhardt
2004 #DEG17Dale Earnhardt
2004 #DEG18Dale Earnhardt
2004 #DEG19Dale Earnhardt
2004 #DEG20Dale Earnhardt
2004 #DEG21Dale Earnhardt
2004 #DEG22Dale Earnhardt
2004 #DEG23Dale Earnhardt
2004 #DEG24Dale Earnhardt
2004 #DEG25Dale Earnhardt
2004 #DEG26Dale Earnhardt
2004 #DEG27Dale Earnhardt
2004 #DEG28Dale Earnhardt
2004 #DEG29Dale Earnhardt
2004 #DEG30Dale Earnhardt
2004 #DEG31Dale Earnhardt
2004 #DEG32Dale Earnhardt
2004 #DEG33Dale Earnhardt
2004 #DEG34Dale Earnhardt
2004 #DEG35Dale Earnhardt
2004 #DEG36Dale Earnhardt
2004 #DEG37Dale Earnhardt
2004 #DEG38Dale Earnhardt
2004 #DEG39Dale Earnhardt
2004 #DEG40Dale Earnhardt
2004 #DEG41Dale Earnhardt
2004 #DEG42Dale Earnhardt
2004 #DEG43Dale Earnhardt
2004 #DEG44Dale Earnhardt
2004 #DEG45Dale Earnhardt
2004 #DEG54Dale Earnhardt
2004 #DEG50Dale Earnhardt
2004 #DEG46Dale Earnhardt
2004 #DEG49Dale Earnhardt
2004 #DEG51Dale Earnhardt
2004 #DEG47Dale Earnhardt
2004 #DEG53Dale Earnhardt
2004 #DEG48Dale Earnhardt
2004 #DEG52Dale Earnhardt

Press Pass Dale Earnhardt Gallery Gold
2004 #DEG1 Dale Earnhardt
2004 #DEG2 Dale Earnhardt
2004 #DEG3 Dale Earnhardt
2004 #DEG4 Dale Earnhardt
2004 #DEG5 Dale Earnhardt
2004 #DEG6 Dale Earnhardt
2004 #DEG7 Dale Earnhardt
2004 #DEG8 Dale Earnhardt
2004 #DEG9 Dale Earnhardt
2004 #DEG10Dale Earnhardt
2004 #DEG11Dale Earnhardt
2004 #DEG12Dale Earnhardt
2004 #DEG13Dale Earnhardt
2004 #DEG14Dale Earnhardt
2004 #DEG15Dale Earnhardt
2004 #DEG16Dale Earnhardt
2004 #DEG17Dale Earnhardt
2004 #DEG18Dale Earnhardt
2004 #DEG19Dale Earnhardt
2004 #DEG20Dale Earnhardt
2004 #DEG21Dale Earnhardt
2004 #DEG22Dale Earnhardt
2004 #DEG23Dale Earnhardt
2004 #DEG24Dale Earnhardt
2004 #DEG25Dale Earnhardt
2004 #DEG26Dale Earnhardt
2004 #DEG27Dale Earnhardt
2004 #DEG28Dale Earnhardt
2004 #DEG29Dale Earnhardt
2004 #DEG30Dale Earnhardt
2004 #DEG31Dale Earnhardt
2004 #DEG32Dale Earnhardt
2004 #DEG33Dale Earnhardt
2004 #DEG34Dale Earnhardt
2004 #DEG35Dale Earnhardt
2004 #DEG36Dale Earnhardt
2004 #DEG37Dale Earnhardt
2004 #DEG38Dale Earnhardt
2004 #DEG39Dale Earnhardt
2004 #DEG40Dale Earnhardt
2004 #DEG41Dale Earnhardt
2004 #DEG42Dale Earnhardt
2004 #DEG43Dale Earnhardt
2004 #DEG44Dale Earnhardt
2004 #DEG45Dale Earnhardt
2004 #DEG46Dale Earnhardt
2004 #DEG47Dale Earnhardt
2004 #DEG48Dale Earnhardt
2004 #DEG49Dale Earnhardt
2004 #DEG50Dale Earnhardt
2004 #DEG51Dale Earnhardt
2004 #DEG52Dale Earnhardt
2004 #DEG53Dale Earnhardt
2004 #DEG54Dale Earnhardt

Press Pass Dale Earnhardt Jr.
2004 #10 Dale Jr./Dale Sr. FS
2004 #14 Dale Jr./Dale Sr. FS
2004 #15 Dale Jr./Dale Sr. FS
2004 #16 Dale Jr./Dale Sr. FS
2004 #17 Dale Jr./Dale Sr. FS
2004 #18 Dale Jr./Dale Sr. FS
2004 #11 Dale Jr./Dale Sr. FS
2004 #12 Dale Jr./Dale Sr. FS
2004 #13 Dale Jr./Dale Sr. FS

Press Pass Dale Earnhardt Jr. Gallery
2004 #G2 Dale Jr./Dale Sr. FS

Press Pass Dale Earnhardt The Legacy Victories
2004 #1 Dale Earnhardt
2004 #2 Dale Earnhardt
2004 #3 Dale Earnhardt
2004 #4 Dale Earnhardt
2004 #5 Dale Earnhardt
2004 #6 Dale Earnhardt
2004 #7 Dale Earnhardt
2004 #8 Dale Earnhardt
2004 #9 Dale Earnhardt
2004 #10 Dale Earnhardt
2004 #11 Dale Earnhardt
2004 #12 Dale Earnhardt
2004 #13 Dale Earnhardt
2004 #14 Dale Earnhardt
2004 #15 Dale Earnhardt
2004 #16 Dale Earnhardt
2004 #17 Dale Earnhardt
2004 #18 Dale Earnhardt
2004 #19 Dale Earnhardt
2004 #20 Dale Earnhardt
2004 #21 Dale Earnhardt
2004 #22 Dale Earnhardt
2004 #23 Dale Earnhardt
2004 #24 Dale Earnhardt
2004 #25 Dale Earnhardt
2004 #26 Dale Earnhardt
2004 #27 Dale Earnhardt
2004 #28 Dale Earnhardt
2004 #29 Dale Earnhardt
2004 #30 Dale Earnhardt
2004 #31 Dale Earnhardt
2004 #32 Dale Earnhardt
2004 #33 Dale Earnhardt
2004 #34 Dale Earnhardt
2004 #35 Dale Earnhardt
2004 #36 Dale Earnhardt
2004 #37 Dale Earnhardt
2004 #38 Dale Earnhardt
2004 #39 Dale Earnhardt
2004 #40 Dale Earnhardt
2004 #41 Dale Earnhardt
2004 #42 Dale Earnhardt
2004 #43 Dale Earnhardt
2004 #44 Dale Earnhardt
2004 #45 Dale Earnhardt
2004 #46 Dale Earnhardt
2004 #47 Dale Earnhardt
2004 #48 Dale Earnhardt
2004 #49 Dale Earnhardt
2004 #50 Dale Earnhardt
2004 #51 Dale Earnhardt
2004 #52 Dale Earnhardt
2004 #53 Dale Earnhardt
2004 #54 Dale Earnhardt
2004 #55 Dale Earnhardt
2004 #56 Dale Earnhardt
2004 #57 Dale Earnhardt
2004 #58 Dale Earnhardt
2004 #59 Dale Earnhardt
2004 #60 Dale Earnhardt
2004 #61 Dale Earnhardt
2004 #62 Dale Earnhardt
2004 #63 Dale Earnhardt
2004 #64 Dale Earnhardt
2004 #65 Dale Earnhardt
2004 #66 Dale Earnhardt
2004 #67 Dale Earnhardt
2004 #68 Dale Earnhardt
2004 #69 Dale Earnhardt
2004 #70 Dale Earnhardt
2004 #71 Dale Earnhardt
2004 #72 Dale Earnhardt
2004 #73 Dale Earnhardt
2004 #74 Dale Earnhardt
2004 #75 Dale Earnhardt
2004 #76 Dale Earnhardt

Press Pass Dale Earnhardt The Legacy Victories Tin
2004 #NNO Dale Earnhardt

Press Pass Dale Earnhardt Victories
2005 #1 Dale Earnhardt
2005 #2 Dale Earnhardt
2005 #3 Dale Earnhardt
2005 #4 Dale Earnhardt
2005 #5 Dale Earnhardt
2005 #6 Dale Earnhardt
2005 #7 Dale Earnhardt
2005 #8 Dale Earnhardt
2005 #9 Dale Earnhardt
2005 #10 Dale Earnhardt
2005 #11 Dale Earnhardt
2005 #12 Dale Earnhardt
2005 #13 Dale Earnhardt
2005 #14 Dale Earnhardt
2005 #15 Dale Earnhardt
2005 #16 Dale Earnhardt
2005 #17 Dale Earnhardt
2005 #18 Dale Earnhardt
2005 #19 Dale Earnhardt
2005 #20 Dale Earnhardt
2005 #21 Dale Earnhardt
2005 #22 Dale Earnhardt
2005 #23 Dale Earnhardt
2005 #24 Dale Earnhardt
2005 #25 Dale Earnhardt
2005 #26 Dale Earnhardt
2005 #27 Dale Earnhardt
2005 #28 Dale Earnhardt
2005 #29 Dale Earnhardt
2005 #30 Dale Earnhardt
2005 #31 Dale Earnhardt
2005 #32 Dale Earnhardt
2005 #33 Dale Earnhardt
2005 #34 Dale Earnhardt
2005 #35 Dale Earnhardt
2005 #36 Dale Earnhardt
2005 #37 Dale Earnhardt
2005 #38 Dale Earnhardt
2005 #39 Dale Earnhardt
2005 #40 Dale Earnhardt
2005 #41 Dale Earnhardt
2005 #42 Dale Earnhardt
2005 #43 Dale Earnhardt
2005 #44 Dale Earnhardt
2005 #45 Dale Earnhardt
2005 #46 Dale Earnhardt
2005 #47 Dale Earnhardt
2005 #48 Dale Earnhardt
2005 #49 Dale Earnhardt
2005 #50 Dale Earnhardt
2005 #51 Dale Earnhardt
2005 #52 Dale Earnhardt
2005 #53 Dale Earnhardt
2005 #54 Dale Earnhardt
2005 #55 Dale Earnhardt
2005 #56 Dale Earnhardt
2005 #57 Dale Earnhardt
2005 #58 Dale Earnhardt
2005 #59 Dale Earnhardt
2005 #60 Dale Earnhardt
2005 #61 Dale Earnhardt
2005 #62 Dale Earnhardt
2005 #63 Dale Earnhardt
2005 #64 Dale Earnhardt
2005 #65 Dale Earnhardt
2005 #66 Dale Earnhardt
2005 #67 Dale Earnhardt
2005 #68 Dale Earnhardt
2005 #69 Dale Earnhardt
2005 #70 Dale Earnhardt
2005 #71 Dale Earnhardt
2005 #72 Dale Earnhardt
2005 #73 Dale Earnhardt
2005 #74 Dale Earnhardt
2005 #75 Dale Earnhardt
2005 #76 Dale Earnhardt

Press Pass Dale The Movie
2007 #50 Dale Earnhardt Statue CL
2007 #49 Dale Earnhardt Career Milestones
2007 #48 Dale Earnhardt Honored Hero
2007 #47 Dale Earnhardt American Dream
2007 #45 Dale Earnhardt's Car Bobby Labonte's Car Kevin Harvick's Car Jeff Gordon's Car
2007 #43 Mourning A Legend
2007 #42 Dale Earnhardt Reflections
2007 #41 Dale Earnhardt 1998 Daytona 500 Celebration
2007 #40 Dale Earnhardt's Car 1998 Daytona 500 Victory Lane
2007 #39 Dale Earnhardt's Car 1998 Daytona 500 Burnout
2007 #38 Dale Earnhardt's Car 1998 Daytona 500 Congratulations
2007 #37 Dale Earnhardt's Car 1998 Daytona 500 Final Pit Stop
2007 #36 Dale Earnhardt Girl with Penny
2007 #35 Dale Earnhardt's Car Jeff Gordon's Car 1997 Daytona 500
2007 #34 Dale Earnhardt's Car 1990 Daytona 500
2007 #33 Dale Earnhardt's Car 1986 Daytona 500
2007 #32 Dale Earnhardt Hands On Racer
2007 #31 Dale Earnhardt Dale Earnhardt Jr.
2007 #30 Dale Earnhardt Taylor Nicole Earnhardt
2007 #29 Dale Earnhardt Darrell Waltrip DEI
2007 #28 Dale Earnhardt's Car Final Victory Talladega
2007 #27 Dale Earnhardt Working on the Farm
2007 #26 Dale Earnhardt's Car Brian Williams
2007 #25 Dale Earnhardt Teresa Earnhardt Four Championships
2007 #24 Dale Earnhardt Intimidator
2007 #23 Dale Earnhardt's Car Goodwrench Era Begins
2007 #22 Dale Earnhardt Darrell Waltrip Rivalry
2007 #21 Dale Earnhardt's Car Pass in the Grass
2007 #20 Dale Earnhardt Steve Byrnes
2007 #16 Dale Earnhardt Wild Side
2007 #15 Dale Earnhardt 16 Wins in 2 Years
2007 #14 Dale Earnhardt Richard Childress
2007 #13 Dale Earnhardt One Tough Customer
2007 #12 Dale Earnhardt Great American Cowboy
2007 #11 Dale Earnhardt Wrangler Sponsorship
2007 #10 Dale Earnhardt First Championship
2007 #9 Dale Earnhardt First Cup Win
2007 #8 Dale Earnhardt Early Cup Racing
2007 #7 Dale Earnhardt Darrell Waltrip
2007 #6 Dale Earnhardt Picks Up Where His Father Left Off
2007 #4 Dale Earnhardt Son of a Legend
2007 #3 Dale Earnhardt Legendary Racer
2007 #2 Dale Earnhardt Daytona Dominance
2007 #1 Dale Earnhardt Racer's Perspective

Press Pass Daytona 500 50th Anniversary
2008 #35 Dale Earnhardt '98
2008 #48 Dale Earnhardt FF

Press Pass Dominator Dale Earnhardt
2006 #1 Dale Earnhardt '76 The Earnly Years
2006 #2 Dale Earnhardt '79 ROY
2006 #3 Dale Earnhardt '79 Bristol Win
2006 #4 Dale Earnhardt '80 Atlanta Win
2006 #5 Dale Earnhardt '80 Champion
2006 #6 Dale Earnhardt '81 Year in Review
2006 #7 Dale Earnhardt '82 Year in Review
2006 #8 Dale Earnhardt's Car '83 Year in Review
2006 #9 Dale Earnhardt '84 Year in Review
2006 #10 Dale Earnhardt '85 Year in Review
2006 #11 Dale Earnhardt '86 Champion
2006 #12 Dale Earnhardt '86 Atlanta Win
2006 #13 Dale Earnhardt '87 Champion
2006 #14 Dale Earnhardt's Car '87 Charlotte Win
2006 #15 Dale Earnhardt's Car '88 Year in Review
2006 #16 Dale Earnhardt '89 Year in Review
2006 #17 Dale Earnhardt '90 Champion
2006 #18 Dale Earnhardt '91 Champion
2006 #19 Dale Earnhardt '92 Year in Review
2006 #20 Dale Earnhardt '93 Champion
2006 #21 Dale Earnhardt '93 Charlotte Win
2006 #22 Dale Earnhardt '94 Champion
2006 #23 Dale Earnhardt '94 Talladega Win
2006 #24 Dale Earnhardt '96 Year in Review UER
2006 #25 Dale Earnhardt '95 Year in Review UER
2006 #26 Dale Earnhardt '97 Year in Review
2006 #27 Dale Earnhardt '98 Year in Review
2006 #28 Dale Earnhardt '98 Daytona 500 Win
2006 #29 Dale Earnhardt '99 Year in Review
2006 #30 Dale Earnhardt's Car '99 Bristol Win
2006 #31 Dale Earnhardt '00 Year in Review
2006 #32 Dale Earnhardt's Car '00 Atlanta Win
2006 #33 Dale Earnhardt '00 Talladega Win

Press Pass Dominator Dale Earnhardt Jumbo
2006 #SR1 Dale Earnhardt Appeal
2006 #SR2 Dale Earnhardt
2006 #SR3 Dale Earnhardt

Press Pass Dominator Tins
2006 #DE Dale Earnhardt

Press Pass Double Burner
2001 #DB3 Dale Earnhardt

Press Pass F.Q.S.
1996 #FQS1A Dale Earnhardt
1996 #FQS1B Dale Earnhardt's Car

Press Pass Focused
1996 #F1 Dale Earnhardt

Press Pass Gatorade Front Runner Award
2000 #12 Dale Earnhardt

Press Pass Gold
2008 #G61 Dale Earnhardt

Press Pass Ground Zero
2001 #GZ3 Dale Earnhardt

Press Pass Holofoils
1994 #H1 Dale Earnhardt

Press Pass Hot Treads
2001 #HT6 Dale Earnhardt/1000

Press Pass Lasers
1997 #4 Dale Earnhardt
1997 #32 Dale Earnhardt's Car
1997 #56 Dale Earnhardt's Car
1997 #95 Dale Earnhardt's Car

Press Pass Legends
2005 #19 Dale Earnhardt
2005 #40 Dale Earnhardt C
2006 #24 Dale Earnhardt
2006 #47 Dale Sr./Dale Jr. REC
2007 #29 Dale Earnhardt
2007 #51 Dale Earnhardt N
2007 #65 Darrell Waltrip Dale Earnhardt R
2007 #68 Dale Earnhardt Jeff Gordon R

Press Pass Legends Blue
2005 #19B Dale Earnhardt
2005 #40B Dale Earnhardt C
2006 #B24 Dale Earnhardt
2006 #B47 Dale Sr./Dale Jr. REC
2007 #B29 Dale Earnhardt
2007 #B51 Dale Earnhardt N
2007 #B65 Darrell Waltrip Dale Earnhardt R
2007 #B68 Dale Earnhardt Jeff Gordon R

Press Pass Legends Bronze
2006 #Z24 Dale Earnhardt
2006 #Z47 Dale Sr./Dale Jr. REC
2007 #Z29 Dale Earnhardt
2007 #Z51 Dale Earnhardt N
2007 #Z65 Darrell Waltrip Dale Earnhardt R
2007 #Z68 Dale Earnhardt Jeff Gordon R

Press Pass Legends Cut Signatures
2007 #DE Dale Earnhardt/2

Press Pass Legends Dale Earnhardt Gold
2007 #DE1 Dale Earnhardt
2007 #DE2 Dale Earnhardt
2007 #DE3 Dale Earnhardt
2007 #DE4 Dale Earnhardt
2007 #DE5 Dale Earnhardt
2007 #DE6 Dale Earnhardt
2007 #DE7 Dale Earnhardt
2007 #DE8 Dale Earnhardt
2007 #DE9 Dale Earnhardt

Press Pass Legends Dale Earnhardt Silver
2007 #DE1 Dale Earnhardt
2007 #DE2 Dale Earnhardt
2007 #DE3 Dale Earnhardt
2007 #DE4 Dale Earnhardt
2007 #DE5 Dale Earnhardt
2007 #DE6 Dale Earnhardt
2007 #DE7 Dale Earnhardt
2007 #DE8 Dale Earnhardt
2007 #DE9 Dale Earnhardt

Press Pass Legends Gold
2005 #19G Dale Earnhardt
2005 #40G Dale Earnhardt C
2006 #G24 Dale Earnhardt
2006 #G47 Dale Sr./Dale Jr. REC
2007 #G29 Dale Earnhardt
2007 #G51 Dale Earnhardt N
2007 #G65 Darrell Waltrip Dale Earnhardt R
2007 #G68 Dale Earnhardt Jeff Gordon R

Press Pass Legends Greatest Moments
2005 #GM7 Dale Earnhardt Winst.'87
2005 #GM14 Dale Earnhardt Daytona
2005 #GM15 Dale Earnhardt Winst.'00

Press Pass Legends Heritage Gold
2006 #HE6 Dale Earnhardt
2006 #HE15 Dale Sr./Dale Jr.

Press Pass Legends Heritage Silver
2006 #HE15 Dale Sr./Dale Jr.
2006 #HE6 Dale Earnhardt

Press Pass Legends Holofoil
2005 #19H Dale Earnhardt
2005 #40H Dale Earnhardt C
2006 #H24 Dale Earnhardt
2006 #H47 Dale Sr./Dale Jr. REC
2007 #H29 Dale Earnhardt
2007 #H51 Dale Earnhardt N
2007 #H65 Darrell Waltrip Dale Earnhardt R
2007 #H68 Dale Earnhardt Jeff Gordon R

Press Pass Legends Legends Gallery Gold
2007 #LG5 Dale Earnhardt

Press Pass Legends Legends Gallery Silver
2007 #LG5 Dale Earnhardt

Press Pass Legends Memorable Moments Gold
2006 #MM7 Dale Earnhardt
2007 #MM4 Dale Earnhardt B
2007 #MM8 Dale Earnhardt D
2007 #MM13Dale Earnhardt T
2007 #MM15Dale Earnhardt Jr. T

Press Pass Legends Memorable Moments Silver
2006 #MM7 Dale Earnhardt
2007 #MM4 Dale Earnhardt B
2007 #MM8 Dale Earnhardt D
2007 #MM13Dale Earnhardt T
2007 #MM15Dale Earnhardt Jr. T

Press Pass Legends Press Plates Black
2005 #19 Dale Earnhardt
2005 #40 Dale Earnhardt C
2006 #PPB24 Dale Earnhardt
2006 #PPB47 Dale Sr./Dale Jr. REC
2007 #PP29 Dale Earnhardt
2007 #PP51 Dale Earnhardt N
2007 #PP65 Darrell Waltrip Dale Earnhardt R
2007 #PP68 Dale Earnhardt Jeff Gordon R

Press Pass Legends Press Plates Black Backs
2006 #PPB24B Dale Earnhardt
2006 #PPB47B Dale Sr./Dale Jr. REC
2007 #PP29 Dale Earnhardt
2007 #PP51 Dale Earnhardt N
2007 #PP65 Darrell Waltrip Dale Earnhardt R
2007 #PP68 Dale Earnhardt Jeff Gordon R

Press Pass Legends Press Plates Cyan
2005 #19 Dale Earnhardt
2005 #40 Dale Earnhardt C
2006 #PPC24 Dale Earnhardt
2006 #PPC47 Dale Sr./Dale Jr. REC
2007 #PP29 Dale Earnhardt
2007 #PP51 Dale Earnhardt N
2007 #PP65 Darrell Waltrip Dale Earnhardt R
2007 #PP68 Dale Earnhardt Jeff Gordon R

Press Pass Legends Press Plates Cyan Backs
2006 #PPC24B Dale Earnhardt
2006 #PPC47B Dale Sr./Dale Jr. REC
2007 #PP29 Dale Earnhardt
2007 #PP51 Dale Earnhardt N
2007 #PP65 Darrell Waltrip Dale Earnhardt R
2007 #PP68 Dale Earnhardt Jeff Gordon R

Press Pass Legends Press Plates Magenta
2005 #19 Dale Earnhardt
2005 #40 Dale Earnhardt C
2006 #PPM24 Dale Earnhardt
2006 #PPM47 Dale Sr./Dale Jr. REC
2007 #PP29 Dale Earnhardt
2007 #PP51 Dale Earnhardt N
2007 #PP65 Darrell Waltrip Dale Earnhardt R
2007 #PP68 Dale Earnhardt Jeff Gordon R

Press Pass Legends Press Plates Magenta Backs
2006 #PPM24B Dale Earnhardt
2006 #PPM47B Dale Sr./Dale Jr. REC
2007 #PP29 Dale Earnhardt
2007 #PP51 Dale Earnhardt N
2007 #PP65 Darrell Waltrip Dale Earnhardt R
2007 #PP68 Dale Earnhardt Jeff Gordon R

Press Pass Legends Press Plates Yellow
2005 #19 Dale Earnhardt
2005 #40 Dale Earnhardt C
2006 #PPY24 Dale Earnhardt
2006 #PPY47 Dale Sr./Dale Jr. REC
2007 #PP29 Dale Earnhardt
2007 #PP51 Dale Earnhardt N
2007 #PP65 Darrell Waltrip Dale Earnhardt R
2007 #PP68 Dale Earnhardt Jeff Gordon R

Press Pass Legends Press Plates Yellow Backs
2006 #PPY24B Dale Earnhardt
2006 #PPY47B Dale Sr./Dale Jr. REC
2007 #PP29 Dale Earnhardt
2007 #PP51 Dale Earnhardt N
2007 #PP65 Darrell Waltrip Dale Earnhardt R
2007 #PP68 Dale Earnhardt Jeff Gordon R

Press Pass Legends Previews
2005 #19 Dale Earnhardt
2005 #40 Dale Earnhardt C
2006 #EB24 Dale Earnhardt
2006 #EB47 Dale Sr./Dale Jr. REC
2007 #EB29 Dale Earnhardt
2007 #EB65 Darrell Waltrip Dale Earnhardt R
2007 #EB68 Dale Earnhardt Jeff Gordon R

Press Pass Legends Racing Artifacts Firesuit Bronze
2006 #DE-F Dale Earnhardt
2007 #DE-F Dale Earnhardt

Press Pass Legends Racing Artifacts Firesuit Gold
2006 #DE-F Dale Earnhardt
2007 #DE-F Dale Earnhardt

Press Pass Legends Racing Artifacts Firesuit Patch
2006 #DE-F Dale Earnhardt
2007 #DE-F Dale Earnhardt

Press Pass Legends Racing Artifacts Firesuit Silver
2006 #DE-F Dale Earnhardt
2007 #DE-F Dale Earnhardt

Press Pass Legends Racing Artifacts Tire Bronze
2006 #DE-T Dale Earnhardt
2007 #DE-T Dale Earnhardt

Press Pass Legends Racing Artifacts Tire Gold
2006 #DE-T Dale Earnhardt Jr.
2007 #DE-T Dale Earnhardt

Press Pass Legends Racing Artifacts Tire Silver
2006 #DE-T Dale Earnhardt
2007 #DE-T Dale Earnhardt

Press Pass Legends Racing Cuts
2006 #DE Dale Earnhardt Sr./3

Press Pass Legends Solo
2005 #19S Dale Earnhardt
2005 #40S Dale Earnhardt C
2006 #S24 Dale Earnhardt
2006 #S47 Dale Sr./Dale Jr. REC
2007 #S29 Dale Earnhardt
2007 #S51 Dale Earnhardt N
2007 #S65 Darrell Waltrip Dale Earnhardt R
2007 #S68 Dale Earnhardt Jeff Gordon R

Press Pass Legends Threads & Treads Bronze
2005 #TTDE Dale Earnhardt

Press Pass Legends Threads & Treads Gold
2005 #TTDE Dale Earnhardt

Press Pass Legends Threads & Treads Silver
2005 #TTDE Dale Earnhardt

Press Pass Millennium
2000 #7 Dale Earnhardt
2001 #2 Dale Earnhardt
2001 #49 Dale Earnhardt's Car
2001 #67 Dale Earnhardt REP

Press Pass Oil Cans
1998 #OC2 Dale Earnhardt's Car
2000 #OC7 Dale Earnhardt's Car

Press Pass Oil Slicks
1997 #4 Dale Earnhardt
1997 #32 Dale Earnhardt's Car
1997 #56 Dale Earnhardt's Car
1997 #95 Dale Earnhardt's Car
1998 #4 Dale Earnhardt
1998 #29 Dale Earnhardt's Car

Press Pass Optima
2000 #5 Dale Earnhardt

Press Pass Optima Encore
2000 #EN6 Dale Earnhardt's Car

Press Pass Optima G Force
2000 #GF5 Dale Earnhardt's Car

Press Pass Optima On the Edge
2000 #OE1 Dale Earnhardt's Car

Press Pass Optima Platinum
2000 #5 Dale Earnhardt

Press Pass Optima Race Used Lugnuts Cars
2000 #LC15 Dale Earnhardt's Car
2001 #LNC3 Dale Earnhardt's Car
2002 #LNC4 Dale Earnhardt's Car/10

Press Pass Optima Race Used Lugnuts Drivers
2000 #LD15 Dale Earnhardt/55
2001 #LNDO Dale Earnhardt/45
2002 #LND4 Dale Earnhardt/10

Press Pass Optima Thunder Bolts Cars
2003 #TBT11 Dale Earnhardt's Car/3
2004 #TBT18 Dale Earnhardt's Car/3

Press Pass Optima Thunder Bolts Drivers
2003 #TBD11 Dale Earnhardt/3
2004 #TBD18 Dale Earnhardt/3

Press Pass Optima XL
1994 #4 Dale Earnhardt
1994 #41 Dale Earnhardt's Car TC
1994 #43B T.Earnhardt w/Dale
1995 #51 Dale Earnhardt's Car
1995 #6 Dale Earnhardt

Press Pass Optima XL Cool Blue
1995 #6 Dale Earnhardt
1995 #51 Dale Earnhardt's Car

Press Pass Optima XL Die Cut
1995 #6 Dale Earnhardt
1995 #51 Dale Earnhardt's Car

Press Pass Optima XL Double Clutch
1994 #DC1 Dale Earnhardt

Press Pass Optima XL Red Hot
1994 #4 Dale Earnhardt
1994 #41 Dale Earnhardt's Car TC
1994 #43B Teresa Earnhardt w/Dale
1995 #6 Dale Earnhardt
1995 #51 Dale Earnhardt's Car

Press Pass Optima XL Stealth
1995 #XLS2 Dale Earnhardt

Press Pass Pit Stop
1998 #PS2 Dale Earnhardt's Car
1999 #3 Dale Earnhardt's Car

Press Pass Pitstop
2000 #PS3 Dale Earnhardt's Car

Press Pass Platinum
2008 #P61 Dale Earnhardt

Press Pass Premium
1995 #1 Dale Earnhardt
1996 #2 Dale Earnhardt
1996 #35 Dale Earnhardt's Car
1997 #4 Dale Earnhardt
1997 #29 Dale Earnhardt's Car
1998 #15 Dale Earnhardt's Car
1998 #32 Dale Earnhardt
1998 #0 Dale Earnhardt Daytona
1999 #6 Dale Earnhardt
1999 #35 Dale Earnhardt's Car
2000 #49 Dale Earnhardt
2000 #64 Dale Earnhardt
2001 #3 Dale Earnhardt
2001 #30 Dale Earnhardt
2001 #51 Dale Earnhardt CC
2001 #77 Dale Earnhardt PC

Press Pass Premium Badge of Honor
1999 #BH19 Dale Earnhardt's Car

Press Pass Premium Badge of Honor Reflectors
1999 #BH19 Dale Earnhardt's Car

Press Pass Premium Burning Rubber II
1996 #BR5 Dale Earnhardt's Car

Press Pass Premium Crystal Ball
1996 #CB3 Dale Earnhardt
1997 #CB2 Dale Earnhardt's Car

Press Pass Premium Crystal Ball Die Cut
1997 #CB2 Dale Earnhardt's Car

Press Pass Premium Double Burners
1997 #DB1 Dale Earnhardt

Press Pass Premium Emerald Proofs
1996 #2 Dale Earnhardt
1996 #35 Dale Earnhardt's Car
1997 #4 Dale Earnhardt
1997 #29 Dale Earnhardt's Car

Press Pass Premium Extreme Fire
1999 #FD2A Dale Earnhardt 1:192

Press Pass Premium Flag Chasers
1998 #FC20 Dale Earnhardt's Car

Press Pass Premium Flag Chasers Reflectors
1998 #FC20 Dale Earnhardt's Car

Press Pass Premium Gold
2001 #3 Dale Earnhardt
2001 #30 Dale Earnhardt
2001 #51 Dale Earnhardt CC
2001 #77 Dale Earnhardt PC

Press Pass Premium Holofoil
1995 #1 Dale Earnhardt
1996 #2 Dale Earnhardt
1996 #35 Dale Earnhardt's Car

Press Pass Premium Hot Pursuit
1995 #HP2 Dale Earnhardt
1996 #HP1 Dale Earnhardt UER

Press Pass Premium Hot Threads Cars
2003 #HTT0 Dale Earnhardt

Press Pass Premium Hot Threads Drivers
2003 #HTD0 Dale Earnhardt

Press Pass Premium Hot Threads Drivers Bronze
2004 #HTD16 Dale Earnhardt

Press Pass Premium Hot Threads Drivers Bronze Retail
2004 #HTT16Dale Earnhardt

Press Pass Premium Hot Threads Drivers Gold
2004 #HTD16 Dale Earnhardt

Press Pass Premium Hot Threads Drivers Silver

2004 #HTD16 Dale Earnhardt
Press Pass Premium Hot Threads Patch
2007 #HTP1 Dale Earnhardt Coke/10
Press Pass Premium In The Zone
2001 #IZ3 Dale Earnhardt
Press Pass Premium Lap Leaders
1997 #LL1 Dale Earnhardt
Press Pass Premium Mirrors
1997 #4 Dale Earnhardt
1997 #29 Dale Earnhardt's Car
Press Pass Premium Oil Slicks
1997 #4 Dale Earnhardt
1997 #29 Dale Earnhardt's Car
Press Pass Premium Performance Driven
2000 #PD6 Dale Earnhardt
2001 #PD3 Dale Earnhardt
Press Pass Premium Race Used Firesuit
1999 #F3 Dale Earnhardt
2000 #F3 Dale Earnhardt
Press Pass Premium Race Used Firesuit Cars
2001 #FC3 Dale Earnhardt
2002 #FC11 Dale Earnhardt
Press Pass Premium Race Used Firesuit Drivers
2001 #FD3 Dale Earnhardt
2002 #FD11 Dale Earnhardt
Press Pass Premium Red Hot
1995 #1 Dale Earnhardt
Press Pass Premium Reflectors
1998 #15 Dale Earnhardt's Car
1998 #32 Dale Earnhardt
1999 #R6 Dale Earnhardt
1999 #R35 Dale Earnhardt's Car
2000 #49 Dale Earnhardt
2000 #64 Dale Earnhardt
Press Pass Premium Rivalries
1998 #3A Dale Earnhardt
1998 #6B Dale Earnhardt's Car
Press Pass Premium Steel Horses
1998 #SH2 Dale Earnhardt's Car
1999 #SH22 Dale Earnhardt's Car
Press Pass Premium Triple Gear Firesuit
1998 #TGF2 Dale Earnhardt
Press Pass R and N China
1996 #9 Dale Earnhardt
Press Pass Race Day
1994 #RD10 Dale Earnhardt
1995 #RD3 Dale Earnhardt
Press Pass Red Hot
1995 #9 Dale Earnhardt
1995 #41 Dale Earnhardt's Car
1995 #115 Dale Earnhardt's Car AW
Press Pass Scorchers
1996 #9 Dale Earnhardt
1996 #40 Dale Earnhardt's Car
Press Pass Shockers
1998 #ST3A Dale Earnhardt
Press Pass Showcar Die Cuts
2000 #SC5 Dale Earnhardt's Car
Press Pass Showman/Showcar
2001 #S7A Dale Earnhardt
2001 #S7B Dale Earnhardt's Car
Press Pass Signings
1998 #3 Dale Earnhardt PPP/VIP/S
1999 #14 Dale Earnhardt/400
2000 #14 Dale Earnhardt
Press Pass Signings Gold
1998 #3 Dale Earnhardt PPP/VIP
1999 #3 Dale Earnhardt/100
2000 #9 Dale Earnhardt
Press Pass Skidmarks
1999 #8 Dale Earnhardt
1999 #35 Dale Earnhardt's Car
2000 #SK6 Dale Earnhardt
Press Pass Snapshots
2003 #SN6 Dale Earnhardt Jr.
Press Pass Stealth
1998 #1 Dale Earnhardt's Car
1998 #2 Dale Earnhardt's Car
1998 #59 Dale Earnhardt's Car TM
1999 #7 Dale Earnhardt
1999 #8 Dale Earnhardt's Car
1999 #53 Goodwrench Tool Cart TT
2000 #7 Dale Earnhardt
2000 #8 Dale Earnhardt's Car
2003 #0 Dale Earnhardt Sunday Money
2006 #82 Dale Earnhardt '79 RS
2006 #83 Dale Earnhardt '79 RS
2006 #84 Dale Earnhardt '79 RS
2006 #85 Dale Earnhardt '79 RS
2006 #86 Dale Earnhardt '79 RS
2006 #87 Dale Earnhardt '79 RS
2006 #88 Dale Earnhardt '79 RS
2006 #89 Dale Earnhardt '79 RS
Press Pass Stealth Big Numbers
1999 #BN3 Dale Earnhardt
Press Pass Stealth Big Numbers Die Cuts
1999 #BN3 Dale Earnhardt
Press Pass Stealth Fan Talk
1998 #1 Dale Earnhardt
Press Pass Stealth Fan Talk Die Cuts
1998 #1 Dale Earnhardt
Press Pass Stealth Fusion
1998 #1 Dale Earnhardt's Car
1998 #2 Dale Earnhardt's Car
1998 #59 Dale Earnhardt's Car TM
1999 #F7 Dale Earnhardt
1999 #F8 Dale Earnhardt's Car
1999 #F53 Goodwrench Tool Cart TT
Press Pass Stealth Gear Grippers Cars
2003 #GGT11 Dale Earnhardt/3
Press Pass Stealth Gear Grippers Drivers
2003 #GGD11 Dale Earnhardt/3
Press Pass Stealth Headlines
1999 #SH2 Dale Earnhardt
Press Pass Stealth Intensity
2000 #IN6 Dale Earnhardt's Car
Press Pass Stealth Octane
1998 #9 Dale Earnhardt's Car
1998 #10 Dale Earnhardt's Car
Press Pass Stealth Octane Die Cuts
1998 #9 Dale Earnhardt's Car
1998 #10 Dale Earnhardt's Car
Press Pass Stealth Octane SLX
1999 #028 Dale Earnhardt's Car
Press Pass Stealth Octane SLX Die Cuts
1999 #028 Dale Earnhardt's Car
Press Pass Stealth Profile
2000 #PR10 Dale Earnhardt
Press Pass Stealth Race Used Glove Cars
2002 #GLC16 Dale Earnhardt's Car/10
Press Pass Stealth Race Used Glove Drivers
2002 #GLD16 Dale Earnhardt/10
Press Pass Stealth Race Used Gloves
1998 #G8 Dale Earnhardt
1999 #G3 Dale Earnhardt's Car/30
2000 #G3 Dale Earnhardt/100
Press Pass Stealth Retail
2006 #82 Dale Earnhardt '79 RS
2006 #83 Dale Earnhardt '79 RS
2006 #84 Dale Earnhardt '79 RS
2006 #85 Dale Earnhardt '79 RS
2006 #86 Dale Earnhardt '79 RS
2006 #87 Dale Earnhardt '79 RS
2006 #88 Dale Earnhardt '79 RS
2006 #89 Dale Earnhardt '79 RS
Press Pass Stealth SST Cars
1999 #SS2 Dale Earnhardt's Car
Press Pass Stealth SST Drivers
1999 #SS2 Dale Earnhardt's Car
Press Pass Stealth X-Ray
2006 #X82 Dale Earnhardt '79 RS
2006 #X83 Dale Earnhardt '79 RS
2006 #X84 Dale Earnhardt '79 RS
2006 #X85 Dale Earnhardt '79 RS
2006 #X86 Dale Earnhardt '79 RS
2006 #X87 Dale Earnhardt '79 RS
2006 #X88 Dale Earnhardt '79 RS
2006 #X89 Dale Earnhardt '79 RS
Press Pass Techno-Retro
2000 #TR6 Dale Earnhardt's Car
Press Pass Torpedoes
1998 #ST3B Dale Earnhardt's Car
Press Pass Torquers
1996 #9 Dale Earnhardt
1996 #40 Dale Earnhardt's Car
1997 #4 Dale Earnhardt
1997 #32 Dale Earnhardt's Car
1997 #56 Dale Earnhardt's Car
1997 #95 Dale Earnhardt's Car
Press Pass Total Memorabilia
2001 #TM3 Dale Earnhardt
Press Pass Total Memorabilia Power Pick
2002 #TM0 Dale Earnhardt
Press Pass Trackside
2000 #2 Dale Earnhardt
2000 #36 Dale Earnhardt's Car
2001 #3 Dale Earnhardt
Press Pass Trackside Dialed In
2000 #DI9 Dale Earnhardt
2001 #D3 Dale Earnhardt
2003 #DI2 Dale Earnhardt Jr.
Press Pass Trackside Die Cuts
2000 #2 Dale Earnhardt
2000 #36 Dale Earnhardt
2001 #3 Dale Earnhardt
Press Pass Trackside Golden
2000 #2 Dale Earnhardt
2000 #36 Dale Earnhardt
2001 #3 Dale Earnhardt
Press Pass Trackside License to Drive
2003 #LD4 Dale Earnhardt Jr.
Press Pass Trackside Mirror Image
2001 #MI3 Dale Earnhardt
Press Pass Trackside Panorama
2000 #P28 Dale Earnhardt
Press Pass Trackside Pit Stoppers
2000 #PS3 Dale Earnhardt
Press Pass Trackside Pit Stoppers Cars
2001 #PSC3 Dale Earnhardt's Car
2002 #PSC15 Dale Earnhardt's Car/20
2003 #PST9 Dale Earnhardt/3
2004 #PST9 Dale Earnhardt
Press Pass Trackside Pit Stoppers Drivers
2001 #PSD3 Dale Earnhardt/10
2002 #PSD15 Dale Earnhardt/20
2003 #PSD9 Dale Earnhardt/3
2004 #PSD9 Dale Earnhardt
Press Pass Trackside Too Tough To Tame
2000 #TT6 Dale Earnhardt
Press Pass Triple Burner
2001 #TB3A Dale Earnhardt lug nut
2001 #TB3B Dale Earnhardt pit board
Press Pass Triple Gear 3 in 1
1998 #TG2 Dale Earnhardt
1999 #TG9 Dale Earnhardt
Press Pass Triple Gear Burning Rubber
1998 #TG2 Dale Earnhardt
Press Pass Velocity
2001 #VL9 Dale Earnhardt
2003 #VC1 Dale Earnhardt Jr.
Press Pass Victory Lane
1997 #VL1A Dale Earnhardt
1997 #VL1B Dale Earnhardt's Car
Press Pass Victory Lap
2003 #5 Dale Earnhardt
Press Pass Vintage
2001 #VN2 Dale Earnhardt
Pro Set
1992 #1 Dale Earnhardt
1992 #59 Dale Earnhardt's Car
1992 #161 Dale Earnhardt
1992 #172 Dale Earnhardt's Transporter
1992 #182 Dale Earnhardt
1992 #224 Dale Earnhardt w/Crew
1992 #NNO Earnhardt HOLO/5000 WHI
1992 #NNO Earnhardt HOLO/5000 BLK
Pro Set Prototypes
1992 #P1 Dale Earnhardt
Race Call Phone Cards
1995 #3 D.Earnhardt Chev./2200 $10
1995 #4 D.Earnhardt Chev./3000 20-Units
1995 #5 Dale Earnhardt Silver/2500 $25 #1
1995 #6 Dale Earnhardt Silver/2500 $25 #2
1995 #7 Dale Earnhardt Silver/2500 $25 #3
1995 #8 The Earnhardts 20-Units
Race Sharks
1997 #1 Dale Earnhardt
Race Sharks First Bite
1997 #1 Dale Earnhardt
Race Sharks Great White
1997 #1 Dale Earnhardt
Race Sharks Great White Shark's Teeth
1997 #GW1 Dale Earnhardt
Race Sharks Great White Shark's Teeth First Bite
1997 #GW1 Dale Earnhardt
Race Sharks Hammerhead
1997 #1 Dale Earnhardt
Race Sharks Hammerhead First Bite
1997 #1 Dale Earnhardt
Race Sharks Shark Attack
1997 #SA1 Dale Earnhardt
Race Sharks Shark Attack First Bite
1997 #SA1 Dale Earnhardt
Race Sharks Shark Attack First Bite Previews
1997 #1 Dale Earnhardt
Race Sharks Shark Tooth Signatures
1997 #ST1 Dale Earnhardt/300
Race Sharks Shark Tooth Signatures First Bite
1997 #ST1 Dale Earnhardt
Race Sharks Tiger Shark
1997 #1 Dale Earnhardt
Race Sharks Tiger Shark First Bite
1997 #1 Dale Earnhardt
Racer's Choice
1996 #3 Dale Earnhardt
1996 #27 Dale Earnhardt's Car
1996 #57 Dale Earnhardt I
1996 #58 Dale Earnhardt I
1996 #59 Dale Earnhardt I
1996 #60 Dale Earnhardt I
1996 #84 Dale Earnhardt RW
1996 #89 Dale Earnhardt RW
1996 #92 Dale Earnhardt BC
1996 #56 Dale Earnhardt I
1997 #3 Dale Earnhardt
1997 #38 Dale Earnhardt's Car
1997 #62 Dale Earnhardt's Car
1997 #90 Dale Earnhardt TR
1997 #104 Dale Earnhardt TR
1997 #106 Dale Earnhardt CL
1997 #27 Dale Earnhardt
Racer's Choice Artist's Proofs
1996 #3 Dale Earnhardt
1996 #27 Dale Earnhardt's Car
1996 #56 Dale Earnhardt I
1996 #57 Dale Earnhardt I
1996 #58 Dale Earnhardt I
1996 #59 Dale Earnhardt I
1996 #60 Dale Earnhardt I
1996 #84 Dale Earnhardt RW
1996 #89 Dale Earnhardt RW
1996 #92 Dale Earnhardt BC
Racer's Choice Busch Clash
1997 #1 Dale Earnhardt
1997 #11 Dale Earnhardt
Racer's Choice Chevy Madness
1997 #8 Dale Earnhardt
Racer's Choice High Octane
1997 #2 Dale Earnhardt
1997 #15 Dale Earnhardt
Racer's Choice High Octane Glow in the Dark
1997 #2 Dale Earnhardt
1997 #15 Dale Earnhardt
Racer's Choice Showcase Series
1997 #3 Dale Earnhardt
1997 #27 Dale Earnhardt
1997 #38 Dale Earnhardt's Car
1997 #62 Dale Earnhardt's Car
1997 #90 Dale Earnhardt TR
1997 #104 Dale Earnhardt TR
1997 #106 Dale Earnhardt CL
Racer's Choice Speedway Collection
1996 #3 Dale Earnhardt
1996 #27 Dale Earnhardt's Car
1996 #56 Dale Earnhardt I
1996 #57 Dale Earnhardt I
1996 #58 Dale Earnhardt I
1996 #59 Dale Earnhardt I
1996 #60 Dale Earnhardt I
1996 #84 Dale Earnhardt RW
1996 #89 Dale Earnhardt RW
1996 #92 Dale Earnhardt BC
Racer's Choice Sundrop
1996 #SD1 Dale Earnhardt
1996 #SD2 Dale Earnhardt
1996 #SD3 Dale Earnhardt
Racer's Choice Top Ten
1996 #P2 Dale Earnhardt Promo
1996 #2 Dale Earnhardt
Racer's Choice Up Close with Dale Earnhardt
1996 #1 Dale Earnhardt
1996 #2 Dale Earnhardt
1996 #3 Dale Earnhardt
1996 #4 Dale Earnhardt
1996 #5 Dale Earnhardt
1996 #6 Dale Earnhardt
1996 #7 Dale Earnhardt
SB Motorsports
1997 #1 Dale Earnhardt
1997 #47 Dale Earnhardt's Car
1997 #50 Dale Earnhardt's Car CL
1997 #92 Dale Earnhardt
1997 #93 Dale Earnhardt
SB Motorsports Autographs
1997 #1 Dale Earnhardt/500
SB Motorsports Race Chat
1997 #RC1 Dale Earnhardt
SB Motorsports Winston Cup Rewind
1997 #WC2 Dale Earnhardt's Car
1997 #WC20 Dale Earnhardt's Car
Score Board Dale Earnhardt
1996 #1 Dale Earnhardt
1996 #2 Dale Earnhardt
1996 #3 Dale Earnhardt
1996 #4 Dale Earnhardt
1996 #5 Dale Earnhardt
1996 #6 Dale Earnhardt
1996 #7 Dale Earnhardt
1996 #8 Dale Earnhardt
1996 #9 Dale Earnhardt
1996 #10 Dale Earnhardt
Score Board IQ
1997 #1 Dale Earnhardt
1997 #27 Dale Earnhardt
1997 #38 Dale Earnhardt
1997 #40 Dale Earnhardt's Car
Score Board IQ $10 Phone Cards
1997 #PC1 Dale Earnhardt
1997 #PC4 Dale Earnhardt's Car
Score Board IQ Remarques
1997 #SB1 Dale Earnhardt
Score Board IQ Remarques Sam Bass Finished
1997 #SB1 Dale Earnhardt
Score Board National Promos *
1994 #14 Dale Earnhardt
1994 #15 Dale Earnhardt
1994 #16 Dale Earnhardt
1994 #17 D.Earnhardt/Teresa
1994 #18 Dale Earnhardt
1994 #20B Dale Earnhardt CL
Score Board Seven-Eleven Phone Cards
1997 #1 Dale Earnhardt
Select
1995 #41 Dale Earnhardt's Car
1995 #151S Dale Earnhardt
Select Flat Out
1995 #41 Dale Earnhardt's Car
1995 #151FO Dale Earnhardt
SkyBox
1994 #1 Dale Earnhardt
SkyBox Profile
1997 #63 Dale Earnhardt's Car
1997 #5 Dale Earnhardt
SkyBox Profile Autographs
1997 #5 Dale Earnhardt
SkyBox Profile Pace Setters
1997 #E1 Dale Earnhardt
SkyBox Profile Team
1997 #T4 Dale Earnhardt
SLU Racing Winner's Circle
1997 #2A D.Earnhardt w/o BK
1997 #2B D.Earnhardt w/BK
1998 #2A D.Earnhardt '97 uni
1998 #2B D.Earnhardt '98 uni
1999 #10 D.Earnhardt Coca Cola
1999 #11 D.Earnhardt GM
2000 #10 Dale Earnhardt
SLU Racing Winner's Circle 12-inch Figures
1999 #1 Dale Earnhardt
2000 #10 Dale Earnhardt
SP
1996 #3 Dale Earnhardt
1996 #KR1 D.Earnhardt/J.Gordon Aces
1997 #3 Dale Earnhardt 3F
1997 #45 Dale Earnhardt's Car 3F
SP Authentic
1998 #3 Dale Earnhardt
1998 #37 Dale Earnhardt's Car
1999 #2 Dale Earnhardt
1999 #53 Dale Earnhardt's Car
1999 #79 Dale Earnhardt SP
2000 #5 Dale Earnhardt
2000 #80 Dale Earnhardt SUP
SP Authentic Driving Force
1999 #DF7 Dale Earnhardt
SP Authentic In the Driver's Seat
1999 #DS1 Dale Earnhardt
SP Authentic Overdrive
1999 #2 Dale Earnhardt
1999 #53 Dale Earnhardt CAR
1999 #79 Dale Earnhardt SP/3
SP Authentic Overdrive Gold
2000 #5 Dale Earnhardt/3
2000 #80 Dale Earnhardt SUP/3
SP Authentic Overdrive Silver
2000 #5 Dale Earnhardt
2000 #80 Dale Earnhardt SUP
SP Authentic Power Surge
2000 #PS1 Dale Earnhardt
SP Authentic Sign of the Times
1999 #DE Dale Earnhardt
2000 #DE Dale Earnhardt
SP Authentic Sign of the Times Gold
2000 #DE Dale Earnhardt
SP Authentic Sign of the Times Red
1998 #ST3 Dale Earnhardt's Car
SP Authentic Traditions
1998 #T1 R.Petty/D.Earnhardt
SP Holoview Maximum Effects
1996 #ME3 Dale Earnhardt
SP Holoview Maximum Effects Die Cuts
1996 #ME3 Dale Earnhardt
SP Race Film
1997 #RD3 Dale Earnhardt
SP Super Series
1997 #3 Dale Earnhardt 3F
1997 #45 Dale Earnhardt's Car 3F
Speedflix
1996 #17 Dale Earnhardt
1996 #51 Dale Earnhardt BL
1996 #52 Dale Earnhardt BL
1996 #53 Dale Earnhardt BL
1996 #54 Dale Earnhardt BL
1996 #83 Dale Earnhardt W
1996 #85 Dale Earnhardt W
1996 #37 Dale Earnhardt's Car in pits
Speedflix Artist Proof's
1996 #17 Dale Earnhardt
1996 #37 Dale Earnhardt in Pits
1996 #51 Dale Earnhardt
1996 #52 Dale Earnhardt
1996 #53 Dale Earnhardt
1996 #54 Dale Earnhardt
1996 #83 Dale Earnhardt W
1996 #85 Dale Earnhardt W
Speedflix Clear Shots
1996 #1 Dale Earnhardt
Speedflix In Motion
1996 #1 Dale Earnhardt's Helmet
Speedflix ProMotion
1996 #1 Dale Earnhardt
Sports Legends Alan Kulwicki
1992 #AK11 Alan Kulwicki/M.Martin/Earnhardt Cars
Sports Legends Phil Parsons
1991 #PP18 Phil Parsons/Earnhardt Cars
SportsCom FanScan
1997 #2 Dale Earnhardt
1998 #1 Dale Earnhardt
1999 #1 Dale Earnhardt
SportStars Photo-Graphics
1986 #4 Dale Earnhardt SP
SPx
1996 #3 Dale Earnhardt
1997 #3 Dale Earnhardt
SPx Blue
1997 #3 Dale Earnhardt
SPx Gold
1996 #3 Dale Earnhardt
1997 #3 Dale Earnhardt
SPx Silver
1997 #3 Dale Earnhardt
Sunbelt Racing Legends
1991 #3 Dale Earnhardt
Traks
1991 #103A Dale Earnhardt ERR
1991 #103B Dale Earnhardt COR
1991 #190A Dale Earnhardt ERR
1991 #190B Dale Earnhardt COR
1991 #3B Dale Earnhardt COR
1991 #3A Dale Earnhardt ERR
1992 #3 Dale Earnhardt
1992 #60 Dale Earnhardt in Pits
1992 #103 Dale Earnhardt
1992 #175 Dale Earnhardt w/Crew
1992 #190 Dale Earnhardt
1992 #193 Dale Earnhardt's Car CL
1995 #27 Dale Earnhardt
2006 #74 Dale Earnhardt
Traks 5th Anniversary
1995 #3 Dale Earnhardt
Traks 5th Anniversary Clear Contenders
1995 #C1 Dale Earnhardt
Traks 5th Anniversary Gold
1995 #3 Dale Earnhardt
Traks 5th Anniversary Jumbos
1995 #E6 Dale Earnhardt
Traks 5th Anniversary Jumbos Gold
1995 #E6 Dale Earnhardt
Traks 5th Anniversary Retrospective
1995 #R2 Dale Earnhardt
Traks Autographs
1992 #A1 Dale Earnhardt/R.Petty
Traks First Run
1995 #27 Dale Earnhardt
Traks Goody's
1992 #19 Dale Earnhardt
Traks Mom-n-Pop's Biscuits Dale Earnhardt
1991 #2 Dale Earnhardt
1991 #3 Dale Earnhardt's Car
1991 #4 Dale Earnhardt
1991 #5 Dale Earnhardt's Car
1991 #6 Dale Earnhardt in Pits
1991 #1 Dale Earnhardt/R.Childress
Traks Mom-n-Pop's Ham Dale Earnhardt
1991 #1 Dale Earnhardt/R.Childress
1991 #2 Dale Earnhardt w/Crew
1991 #3 Dale Earnhardt
1991 #4 Dale Earnhardt
1991 #5 Dale Earnhardt
1991 #6 Dale Earnhardt's Car
1992 #1 Dale Earnhardt w/Crew
1992 #2 Dale Earnhardt's Car
1992 #3 Dale Earnhardt/R.Childress
1992 #4 Dale Earnhardt in Pits
1992 #5 Dale Earnhardt
1992 #6 Dale Earnhardt
1992 #NNO Dale Earnhardt w/Pig
Traks Racing Machines
1992 #1 Dale Earnhardt's Transp.
1992 #3 Dale Earnhardt's Car
1992 #9 D.Earn/Rudd/Gant Cars
1992 #34 D.Earnhardt/D.Allison Cars
1992 #44 Dale Earnhardt Race Action
1992 #54 Dale Earnhardt in Pits
1992 #84 Dale Earnhardt Race Action
1992 #89 Dale Earnhardt in Pits
1992 #91 D.Earnhardt/Houston Cars
1992 #100 D.Earnhardt/R.Petty Cars CL
1992 #P1 D.Earnhardt's Trans. Promo
Traks Racing Machines Bonus
1992 #3B Dale Earnhardt's Car
Traks Review and Preview
1996 #37 Dale Earnhardt
Traks Review and Preview First Run
1996 #37 Dale Earnhardt
Traks Review and Preview Magnets
1996 #37 Dale Earnhardt
Traks Richard Petty
1991 #22 Richard Petty/Earn/D.Waltrip Cars
Traks Series Stars
1995 #SS19 Dale Earnhardt
Traks Series Stars First Run
1995 #SS19 Dale Earnhardt
Traks Team Sets
1992 #1 Dale Earnhardt's Car
1992 #2 Dale Earnhardt
1992 #3 D.Earnhardt/Dav.Allison Cars
1992 #4 Dale Earnhardt's Car
1992 #13 Dale Earnhardt/Childress
1992 #15 Dale Earnhardt w/crew
1992 #16 Dale Earnhardt's Cars
1992 #17 Dale Earnhardt
1992 #18 Dale Earnhardt
1992 #19 Dale Earnhardt's Car
1992 #20 Dale Earnhardt's Car
1992 #21 Dale Earnhardt
1992 #22 Dale Earnhardt's Planes
1992 #23 Dale Earnhardt
1992 #24 Dale Earnhardt's Cars
1992 #25 Dale Earnhardt's Car CL
1992 #101 Earnhardt/D.Allison/Irvan/B.Lab/K.Petty Cars
Ultra
1996 #6 Dale Earnhardt
1996 #7 Dale Earnhardt's Car
1996 #175 Dale Earnhardt's Car RW
1996 #176 D.Earnhardt/M.Martin's Car
1996 #185 Dale Earnhardt/Teresa
1996 #187 Dale Earnhart's Car RW
1996 #192 Dale Earnhardt RW
1996 #197 Dale Earnhardt in Pits RW
1996 #200 D.Earn/Gordon/R.Wall.Race Act.
1996 #5 Dale Earnhardt
1996 #173 Dale Earnhardt RW
1997 #10 Dale Earnhardt
1997 #43 Dale Earnhardt's Car
Ultra AKA
1997 #A1 Dale Earnhardt
Ultra Autographs
1996 #9 Dale Earnhardt
Ultra Boxed Set
1996 #2 Dale Earnhardt
Ultra Champions Club
1996 #2 Dale Earnhardt
Ultra Flair Preview
1996 #2 Dale Earnhardt
Ultra Golden Memories
1996 #4 Dale Earnhardt
Ultra Inside Out
1997 #DC1 Dale Earnhardt
Ultra Season Crowns
1996 #3 Dale Earnhardt
1996 #5 Dale Earnhardt
1996 #9 Dale Earnhardt
1996 #12 D.Earnhardt/J.Gordon Cars
1996 #15 Dale Earnhardt
Ultra Shoney's
1997 #3 Dale Earnhardt
Ultra Thunder and Lightning
1996 #5 Dale Earnhardt's Car
1996 #6 Dale Earnhardt's Car
Ultra Update
1996 #10 Dale Earnhardt
1996 #45 Dale Earnhardt HS
1996 #56 Dale Earnhardt's Car
1996 #96 D.Earnhardt/D.Smith
1997 #2 Dale Earnhardt
1997 #77 Dale Earnhardt's Car
Ultra Update Autographs
1996 #2 Dale Earnhardt
1997 #2 Dale Earnhardt
Ultra Update Driver View
1997 #D6 Dale Earnhardt
Ultra Update Elite Seats
1997 #E2 Dale Earnhardt
Ultra Update Proven Power
1996 #2 Dale Earnhardt
Ultra Update Winner
1996 #7 Dale Earnhardt
1996 #16 Dale Earnhardt
Ultra Winn Dixie
1997 #WD3 Dale Earnhardt
UNO Racing
1983 #27 Dale Earnhardt
Upper Deck Diamond Vision
1998 #3 Dale Earnhardt
Upper Deck Diamond Vision Signature Moves
1998 #3 Dale Earnhardt
Upper Deck Diamond Vision Vision of a Champion
1998 #VC2 Dale Earnhardt
Upper Deck MVP
2000 #3 Dale Earnhardt
2000 #87 Dale Earnhardt's Car
Upper Deck MVP Cup Quest 2000
2000 #CQ1 Dale Earnhardt
Upper Deck MVP Gold Script
2000 #3 Dale Earnhardt
2000 #87 Dale Earnhardt's Car
Upper Deck MVP NASCAR Stars
2000 #NS3 Dale Earnhardt
Upper Deck MVP Silver Script
2000 #3 Dale Earnhardt
2000 #87 Dale Earnhardt's Car
Upper Deck MVP Super Script
2000 #3 Dale Earnhardt/3
2000 #87 Dale Earnhardt's Car/3
Upper Deck Pop Weaver
1998 #PW2 Dale Earnhardt
Upper Deck Racing
2000 #7 Dale Earnhardt
Upper Deck Racing High Groove
2000 #HG5 Dale Earnhardt
Upper Deck Racing Record Pace
2000 #RP3 Dale Earnhardt
Upper Deck Racing Road Signs
2000 #RSDE Dale Earnhardt
Upper Deck Racing Speeding Ticket
2000 #ST5 Dale Earnhardt
Upper Deck Racing Trophy Dash
2000 #TD6 Dale Earnhardt
Upper Deck Racing Winning Formula
2000 #WF3 Dale Earnhardt
Upper Deck Road To The Cup
1996 #RC42 Dale Earnhardt
1996 #301 Dale Earnhardt
1996 #DE1 Dale Earnhardt
1997 #4 Dale Earnhardt
1997 #121 Dale Earnhardt's Trans.
1998 #3 Dale Earnhardt
1998 #75 Dale Earnhardt
1999 #26 Dale Earnhardt
1999 #60 Dale Earnhardt's Car
Upper Deck Road To The Cup 50th Anniversary
1998 #AN49 Dale Earnhardt
Upper Deck Road To The Cup 50th Anniversary Autographs
1998 #AN49 Dale Earnhardt
Upper Deck Road To The Cup Cover Story
1998 #CS10 Dale Earnhardt
Upper Deck Road To The Cup Cup Quest
1997 #CQ3 Dale Earnhardt
Upper Deck Road To The Cup Cup Quest Checkered
1997 #CQ3 Dale Earnhardt
Upper Deck Road To The Cup Cup Quest White
1997 #CQ3 Dale Earnhardt
Upper Deck Road to the Cup NASCAR Chronicles
1999 #NC11 Dale Earnhardt
Upper Deck Road To The Cup Predictor Points Prizes
1996 #PR10 Dale Earnhardt
Upper Deck Road To The Cup Premiere Position
1997 #PP4 Dale Earnhardt
Upper Deck Road to the Cup Signature Collection
1999 #DE Dale Earnhardt
Upper Deck Road to the Cup Signature Collection Checkered Flag
1999 #DE Dale Earnhardt
Upper Deck Road to the Cup Upper Deck Profiles
1999 #P3 Dale Earnhardt
Upper Deck Victory Circle
1997 #3 Dale Earnhardt

1998 #3 Dale Earnhardt
1998 #48 Dale Earnhardt's Car
1999 #83 Dale Earnhardt
2000 #9 Dale Earnhardt
2000 #55 Dale Earnhardt's Car
2000 #70 Dale Earnhardt's Car

Upper Deck Victory Circle Championship Reflections
1997 #CR4 Dale Earnhardt

Upper Deck Victory Circle Driver's Seat
1997 #DS1 Dale Earnhardt

Upper Deck Victory Circle Exclusives Level 1 Silver
2000 #9 Dale Earnhardt
2000 #55 Dale Earnhardt's Car
2000 #70 Dale Earnhardt's Car

Upper Deck Victory Circle Exclusives Level 2 Gold
2000 #9 Dale Earnhardt/3
2000 #55 Dale Earnhardt's Car/3
2000 #70 Dale Earnhardt's Car/3

Upper Deck Victory Circle Point Leaders
1998 #PL5 Dale Earnhardt

Upper Deck Victory Circle PowerDeck
2000 #PD1 Dale Earnhardt

Upper Deck Victory Circle Signature Collection
1999 #DE Dale Earnhardt

Upper Deck Victory Circle Sparks of Brilliance
1998 #SB3 Dale Earnhardt

Upper Deck Victory Circle UD Exclusives
1999 #83 Dale Earnhardt

Upper Deck Victory Circle Victory Circle
1999 #V1 Dale Earnhardt

Upper Deck Victory Circle Victory Lap
1997 #VL1 Dale Earnhardt

Upper Deck Victory Circle Winning Material Tire
2000 #TDE Dale Earnhardt

VIP
1994 #10 Dale Earnhardt
1994 #42 Dale Earnhardt w/Car
1995 #9 Dale Earnhardt
1996 #8 Dale Earnhardt
1996 #38 Dale Earnhardt's Car
1997 #6 Dale Earnhardt
1998 #6 Dale Earnhardt
1998 #38 Dale Earnhardt's Car
1999 #7 Dale Earnhardt
1999 #41 Dale Earnhardt's Car
2000 #4 Dale Earnhardt
2000 #41 Dale Earnhardt's Car 50 W
2000 #48 Dale Earnhardt's Car DT
2004 #87 Dale Earnhardt ATW
2004 #0 Dale Earnhardt SM

VIP Autographs
1996 #6 Dale Earnhardt

VIP Cool Blue
1995 #9 Dale Earnhardt

VIP Dale Earnhardt Firesuit
1996 #DE1B Dale Earnhardt B
1996 #DE1S Dale Earnhardt S
1996 #DE1GL Dale Earnhardt GLD
1996 #DE1GR Dale Earnhardt GRN
1996 #DE2B Dale Earnhardt B
1996 #DE2S Dale Earnhardt S
1996 #DE2GL Dale Earnhardt GLD
1996 #DE2GR Dale Earnhardt GRN

VIP Driver's Choice
1994 #DC1 Dale Earnhardt

VIP Driving Force
1998 #DF5 Dale Earnhardt's Car

VIP Driving Force Die Cuts
1998 #DF5 Dale Earnhardt's Car

VIP Emerald Proofs
1995 #9 Dale Earnhardt
1996 #8 Dale Earnhardt
1996 #38 Dale Earnhardt's Car

VIP Explosives
1997 #6 Dale Earnhardt
1998 #6 Dale Earnhardt
1998 #38 Dale Earnhardt's Car
1999 #X7 Dale Earnhardt
1999 #X41 Dale Earnhardt's Car
2000 #X4 Dale Earnhardt
2000 #X41 Dale Earnhardt's Car 50 W
2000 #X48 Dale Earnhardt's Car DT

VIP Explosives Lasers
1999 #7 Dale Earnhardt
1999 #41 Dale Earnhardt's Car
2000 #LX4 Dale Earnhardt
2000 #LX41 Dale Earnhardt's Car 50 W
2000 #LX48 Dale Earnhardt's Car DT

VIP Fan's Choice
1995 #FC1 Dale Earnhardt

VIP Fan's Choice Gold
1995 #FC1 Dale Earnhardt

VIP Gold Signature
1994 #EC1 Dale Earnhardt

VIP Head Gear
1996 #HG2 Dale Earnhardt
1997 #HG1 Dale Earnhardt
1998 #HG2 Dale Earnhardt

VIP Head Gear Die Cuts
1996 #HG2 Dale Earnhardt
1997 #HG1 Dale Earnhardt
1998 #HG2 Dale Earnhardt

VIP Knights of Thunder
1997 #KT1 Dale Earnhardt

VIP Knights of Thunder Gold
1997 #KT1 Dale Earnhardt

VIP Lap Leaders
1998 #LL2 Dale Earnhardt's Car
1999 #LL3 Dale Earnhardt

VIP Lap Leaders Acetate
1998 #LL2 Dale Earnhardt's Car

VIP NASCAR Country
1998 #NC1 Dale Earnhardt

VIP NASCAR Country Die Cuts
1998 #NC1 Dale Earnhardt

VIP Oil Slicks
1997 #6 Dale Earnhardt

VIP Out of the Box
1999 #OB3 Dale Earnhardt's Car

VIP Race Used Sheet Metal Cars
2002 #SC16 Dale Earnhardt's Car

VIP Race Used Sheet Metal Drivers
2002 #SD16 Dale Earnhardt/50

VIP Rear View Mirror
1999 #RM3 Dale Earnhardt
2000 #RM3 Dale Earnhardt

VIP Rear View Mirror Explosives
2000 #RM3 Dale Earnhardt

VIP Rear View Mirror Explosives Laser Die Cuts
2000 #RM3 Dale Earnhardt

VIP Red Hot
1995 #9 Dale Earnhardt

VIP Ring of Honor
1997 #RH2 Dale Earnhardt's Car

VIP Ring of Honor Die Cuts
1997 #RH2 Dale Earnhardt's Car

VIP Sam Bass Top Flight
1996 #SB1 Dale Earnhardt

VIP Sam Bass Top Flight Gold
1996 #SB1 Dale Earnhardt

VIP Samples
2004 #87 Dale Earnhardt ATW

VIP Sheet Metal
1999 #SM2 Dale Earnhardt's Car
2000 #SM3 Dale Earnhardt

VIP Sheet Metal Cars
2001 #SC3 Dale Earnhardt's Car

VIP Sheet Metal Drivers
2001 #SD3 Dale Earnhardt

VIP Solos
1998 #6 Dale Earnhardt
1998 #38 Dale Earnhardt's Car

VIP Torquers
1996 #8 Dale Earnhardt
1996 #38 Dale Earnhardt's Car

VIP Tradin' Paint Cars
2003 #TPT13 Dale Earnhardt's Car/3

VIP Tradin' Paint Drivers
2003 #TPD13 Dale Earnhardt

VIP Triple Gear Sheet Metal
1998 #TGS2 Dale Earnhardt

VIP Vintage Performance
1999 #8 Dale Earnhardt's Car

VIP War Paint
1996 #WP2 Dale Earnhardt's Car

VIP War Paint Gold
1996 #WP2 Dale Earnhardt's Car

Viper
1996 #1 Dale Earnhardt
1996 #43 Dale Earnhardt
1996 #R3 Dale Earnhardt Promo
1996 #R3FS Dale Earnhardt FS Promo
1997 #68 Dale Earnhardt's Car

Viper Anaconda Jumbos
1997 #A5 Dale Earnhardt

Viper Black Mamba
1996 #1 Dale Earnhardt
1996 #43 Dale Earnhardt
1996 #R3B Dale Earnhardt Black

Viper Black Mamba First Strike
1996 #1 Dale Earnhardt
1996 #43 Dale Earnhardt

Viper Black Racer
1997 #68 Dale Earnhardt's Car

Viper Black Racer First Strike
1997 #68 Dale Earnhardt's Car

Viper Busch Clash
1996 #B14 Dale Earnhardt

Viper Busch Clash First Strike
1996 #B14 Dale Earnhardt

Viper Cobra
1996 #C1 Dale Earnhardt
1997 #C1 Dale Earnhardt

Viper Cobra First Strike
1996 #C1 Dale Earnhardt
1997 #C1 Dale Earnhardt

Viper Copperhead Die Cuts
1996 #1 Dale Earnhardt
1996 #43 Dale Earnhardt

Viper Copperhead Die Cuts First Strike
1996 #1 Dale Earnhardt
1996 #43 Dale Earnhardt

Viper Dale Earnhardt
1996 #1 Dale Earnhardt
1996 #2 Dale Earnhardt
1996 #3 Dale Earnhardt

Viper Dale Earnhardt Cobra Mom-n-Pop's
1996 #3 Dale Earnhardt
1996 #2 Dale Earnhardt
1996 #1 Dale Earnhardt

Viper Diamondback
1996 #D2 Dale Earnhardt
1997 #DB8 Dale Earnhardt

Viper Diamondback Authentic
1996 #DA2 Dale Earnhardt
1997 #DBA8 Dale Earnhardt

Viper Diamondback Authentic California
1996 #DA2 Dale Earnhardt

Viper Diamondback Authentic Eastern
1996 #DA2 Dale Earnhardt
1997 #DBA8 Dale Earnhardt

Viper Diamondback Authentic Eastern First Strike
1997 #DBA8 Dale Earnhardt

Viper Diamondback Authentic First Strike
1996 #DA2 Dale Earnhardt
1997 #DBA8 Dale Earnhardt

Viper Diamondback First Strike
1996 #D2 Dale Earnhardt
1997 #DB8 Dale Earnhardt

Viper First Strike
1996 #1 Dale Earnhardt
1996 #43 Dale Earnhardt
1997 #68 Dale Earnhardt's Car

Viper Green Mamba
1996 #1 Dale Earnhardt
1996 #43 Dale Earnhardt
1996 #R3G Dale Earnhardt Green

Viper King Cobra
1996 #KC1 Dale Earnhardt
1997 #KC1 Dale Earnhardt

Viper King Cobra First Strike
1996 #KC1 Dale Earnhardt

Viper Red Cobra
1996 #1 Dale Earnhardt
1996 #43 Dale Earnhardt

Viper Snake Eyes
1997 #SE1 Dale Earnhardt

Viper Snake Eyes First Strike
1997 #SE1 Dale Earnhardt

Visions
1996 #108 Dale Earnhardt's Car
1996 #124 Dale Earnhardt

Visions *
1996 #108 Dale Earnhardt's Car
1996 #124 Dale Earnhardt

Visions Signings
1996 #100 Dale Earnhardt's Car

Visions Signings *
1996 #100 Dale Earnhardt's Car

Visions Signings Artistry
1996 #3 Dale Earnhardt

Western Steer Earnhardt Next Generation
1995 #1 D.Earnhardt/Kerry Earnhardt
1995 #2 D.Earnhardt/Kelley Earnhardt
1995 #3 D.Earnhardt/D.Earnhardt Jr.
1995 #JUM Earnhardt Family

Wheels
1998 #9 Dale Earnhardt
1998 #34 Dale Earnhardt's Car
1998 #83 Dale Earnhardt
1998 #99 Dale Earnhardt's Car
1999 #9 Dale Earnhardt
1999 #56 Dale Earnhardt's Car

Wheels 50th Anniversary
1998 #A3 Dale Earnhardt
1998 #A18 Dale Earnhardt's Car

Wheels American Thunder Dale Earnhardt Retrospective
2003 #AT1 Dale Earnhardt
2003 #AT2 Dale Earnhardt
2003 #AT3 Dale Earnhardt
2003 #AT4 Dale Earnhardt
2003 #AT5 Dale Earnhardt
2003 #AT6 Dale Earnhardt
2003 #AT7 Dale Earnhardt
2003 #AT8 Dale Earnhardt
2003 #AT9 Dale Earnhardt

Wheels American Thunder Dale Earnhardt Retrospective Foil
2003 #AT1 Dale Earnhardt
2003 #AT2 Dale Earnhardt
2003 #AT3 Dale Earnhardt
2003 #AT4 Dale Earnhardt
2003 #AT5 Dale Earnhardt
2003 #AT6 Dale Earnhardt
2003 #AT7 Dale Earnhardt
2003 #AT8 Dale Earnhardt
2003 #AT9 Dale Earnhardt

Wheels Autographs
1998 #1 Dale Earnhardt

Wheels Circuit Breaker
1999 #CB3 Dale Earnhardt

Wheels Dale Earnhardt Mom-n-Pop's
1996 #MPC1 Dale Earnhardt
1996 #MPC2 Dale Earnhardt
1996 #MPC3 Dale Earnhardt

Wheels Dale Earnhardt Tribute Hologram
1992 #1A Dale Earnhardt Facsimile Signature
1992 #1G Dale Earnhardt Gold
1992 #1P Dale Earnhardt Platinum
1992 #1S Dale Earnhardt Silver

Wheels Dialed In
1999 #DI3 Dale Earnhardt's Car

Wheels Double Take
1998 #E2 Dale Earnhardt

Wheels Flag Chasers Daytona Seven
1999 #DS2 Dale Earnhardt

Wheels Flag Chasers Daytona Seven Blue-Yellow
1999 #DS2 Dale Earnhardt

Wheels Flag Chasers Daytona Seven Checkered
1999 #DS2 Dale Earnhardt

Wheels Flag Chasers Daytona Seven Green
1999 #DS2 Dale Earnhardt

Wheels Flag Chasers Daytona Seven Red
1999 #DS2 Dale Earnhardt

Wheels Flag Chasers Daytona Seven White
1999 #DS2 Dale Earnhardt

Wheels Flag Chasers Daytona Seven Yellow
1999 #DS2 Dale Earnhardt

Wheels Golden
1998 #9 Dale Earnhardt
1998 #34 Dale Earnhardt's Car
1998 #83 Dale Earnhardt
1998 #99 Dale Earnhardt's Car
1999 #9 Dale Earnhardt
1999 #56 GM Goodwrench

Wheels Green Flags
1998 #GF4 Dale Earnhardt's Car

Wheels High Gear
1994 #1 Dale Earnhardt
1994 #79 Dale Earnhardt WIN
1994 #85 Dale Earnhardt WIN
1994 #92 Dale Earnhardt BC
1994 #186 Dale Earnhardt WIN
1994 #188 Dale Earnhardt WIN
1995 #1 Dale Earnhardt
1995 #71 Dale Earnhardt's Car
1995 #86 Dale Earnhardt RW
1998 #5 Dale Earnhardt
1998 #29 Dale Earnhardt's Car
1998 #48 Dale Earnhardt's Car
1998 #64 Dale Earnhardt's Car
1999 #8 Dale Earnhardt
1999 #29 Dale Earnhardt's Car
1999 #48 Dale Earnhardt's Car
1999 #64 Dale Earnhardt's Car
2000 #7 Dale Earnhardt
2001 #2 Dale Earnhardt
2001 #61 Dale Earnhardt CA

Wheels High Gear Autographs
1998 #6 Dale Earnhardt/50
1999 #6 Dale Earnhardt/55
2000 #9 Dale Earnhardt
2001 #8 Dale Earnhardt

Wheels High Gear Busch Clash
1995 #BC8 Dale Earnhardt

Wheels High Gear Busch Clash Gold
1995 #BC8 Dale Earnhardt

Wheels High Gear Custom Shop
1998 #CS1 Dale Earnhardt EXCH
1999 #CSDE Dale Earnhardt EXCH

Wheels High Gear Custom Shop Prizes
1999 #DEA1 Dale Earnhardt
1999 #DEA2 Dale Earnhardt
1999 #DEA3 Dale Earnhardt
1999 #DEB1 Dale Earnhardt
1999 #DEB2 Dale Earnhardt
1999 #DEB3 Dale Earnhardt
1999 #39783 Dale Earnhardt
1999 #39784 Dale Earnhardt
1999 #39785 Dale Earnhardt

Wheels High Gear Dale Earnhardt Retrospective
2003 #RT1 Dale Earnhardt
2003 #RT2 Dale Earnhardt
2003 #RT3 Dale Earnhardt
2003 #RT4 Dale Earnhardt
2003 #RT5 Dale Earnhardt
2003 #RT6 Dale Earnhardt
2003 #RT7 Dale Earnhardt
2003 #RT8 Dale Earnhardt
2003 #RT9 Dale Earnhardt

Wheels High Gear Dale Earnhardt Retrospective Foil
2003 #RT1 Dale Earnhardt
2003 #RT2 Dale Earnhardt
2003 #RT3 Dale Earnhardt
2003 #RT4 Dale Earnhardt
2003 #RT5 Dale Earnhardt
2003 #RT6 Dale Earnhardt
2003 #RT7 Dale Earnhardt
2003 #RT8 Dale Earnhardt
2003 #RT9 Dale Earnhardt

Wheels High Gear Day One
1994 #186 Dale Earnhardt WIN
1994 #188 Dale Earnhardt WIN
1995 #1 Dale Earnhardt
1995 #71 Dale Earnhardt's Car
1995 #86 Dale Earnhardt RW

Wheels High Gear Day One Gold
1994 #186 Dale Earnhardt WIN
1994 #188 Dale Earnhardt WIN
1995 #1 Dale Earnhardt
1995 #71 Dale Earnhardt's Car
1995 #86 Dale Earnhardt RW

Wheels High Gear Dominators
1994 #D3 Dale Earnhardt/3000
1995 #D3 Dale Earnhardt/1750

Wheels High Gear Dominators Jumbos
1995 #D3 Dale Earnhardt/1750

Wheels High Gear First Gear
1998 #4 Dale Earnhardt
1998 #29 Dale Earnhardt's Car
1998 #48 Dale Earnhardt's Car
1998 #64 Dale Earnhardt's Car
1999 #8 Dale Earnhardt
1999 #29 Dale Earnhardt's Car
1999 #48 Dale Earnhardt's Car
1999 #64 Dale Earnhardt's Car
2000 #7 Dale Earnhardt
2001 #2 Dale Earnhardt
2001 #61 Dale Earnhardt CA

Wheels High Gear Flag Chasers
1999 #FC5 Dale Earnhardt
2000 #FC3 Dale Earnhardt
2001 #FC3 Dale Earnhardt

Wheels High Gear Flag Chasers Blue-Yellow
1999 #FC5 Dale Earnhardt
2000 #FC3 Dale Earnhardt
2001 #FC3 Dale Earnhardt

Wheels High Gear Flag Chasers Checkered
1999 #FC5 Dale Earnhardt
2000 #FC3 Dale Earnhardt
2001 #FC3 Dale Earnhardt

Wheels High Gear Flag Chasers Checkered Blue/Orange
2000 #FC3 Dale Earnhardt
2001 #FC3 Dale Earnhardt

Wheels High Gear Flag Chasers Green
1999 #FC5 Dale Earnhardt
2000 #FC3 Dale Earnhardt
2001 #FC3 Dale Earnhardt

Wheels High Gear Flag Chasers Power Pick
2001 #FCPP Dale Earnhardt

Wheels High Gear Flag Chasers Red
1999 #FC5 Dale Earnhardt
2000 #FC3 Dale Earnhardt
2001 #FC3 Dale Earnhardt

Wheels High Gear Flag Chasers White
1999 #FC5 Dale Earnhardt
2000 #FC3 Dale Earnhardt
2001 #FC3 Dale Earnhardt

Wheels High Gear Flag Chasers Yellow
1999 #FC5 Dale Earnhardt
2000 #FC3 Dale Earnhardt
2001 #FC3 Dale Earnhardt

Wheels High Gear Gear Jammers
1998 #GJ2 Dale Earnhardt's Car

Wheels High Gear Gear Shifters
1999 #GS8 Dale Earnhardt
2000 #GS7 Dale Earnhardt
2001 #GS2 Dale Earnhardt

Wheels High Gear Gold
1994 #188 Dale Earnhardt WIN
1994 #79 Dale Earnhardt WIN
1994 #85 Dale Earnhardt WIN
1994 #92 Dale Earnhardt BC
1994 #1 Dale Earnhardt SP
1994 #186 Dale Earnhardt WIN
1995 #1 Dale Earnhardt
1995 #71 Dale Earnhardt's Car
1995 #86 Dale Earnhardt RW

Wheels High Gear High Groove
1998 #HG2 Dale Earnhardt's Car

Wheels High Gear Hot Streaks
1999 #HS3 Dale Earnhardt's Car
2001 #HS3 Dale Earnhardt

Wheels High Gear Man and Machine Cars
1998 #7 Dale Earnhardt's Car
2001 #MM6B Dale Earnhardt's Car

Wheels High Gear Man and Machine Drivers
1998 #MM7 Dale Earnhardt
2001 #MM6A Dale Earnhardt

Wheels High Gear Mega Gold
1994 #MG1 Dale Earnhardt
1994 #MG1S Dale Earnhardt 7T Champ

Wheels High Gear MPH
1998 #4 Dale Earnhardt
1998 #29 Dale Earnhardt's Car
1998 #48 Dale Earnhardt's Car
1998 #64 Dale Earnhardt's Car
1999 #8 Dale Earnhardt
1999 #29 Dale Earnhardt's Car
1999 #48 Dale Earnhardt's Car
1999 #64 Dale Earnhardt's Car
2000 #7 Dale Earnhardt
2001 #2 Dale Earnhardt
2001 #61 Dale Earnhardt CA

Wheels High Gear Power Pak Teams
1994 #E3 Dale Earnhardt
1994 #E4 Dale Earnhardt/Richard Childress
1994 #E5 Dale Earnhardt/Andy Petree
1994 #E18 Dale Earnhardt in Pits
1994 #E19 Dale Earnhardt w/Crew
1994 #E20 Dale Earnhardt's Car
1994 #E21 Dale Earnhardt's Car CL

Wheels High Gear Power Pak Teams Gold
1994 #3E Dale Earnhardt
1994 #4E Dale Earnhardt/Richard Childress
1994 #5E Dale Earnhardt/Andy Petree
1994 #18E Dale Earnhardt in Pits
1994 #19E Dale Earnhardt w/Crew
1994 #20E Dale Earnhardt 's Car

Wheels High Gear Pure Gold
1998 #PG1 Dale Earnhardt

Wheels High Gear Rookie Thunder Update
1994 #104 Dale Earnhardt

Wheels High Gear Rookie Thunder Update Platinum
1994 #104 Dale Earnhardt

Wheels High Gear Sunday Sensation
2000 #OC7 Dale Earnhardt's Car
2001 #SS6 Dale Earnhardt

Wheels High Gear Top Tier
1998 #TT5 Dale Earnhardt 1:40
1999 #TT8 Dale Earnhardt's Car 1:20
2000 #TT7 Dale Earnhardt
2001 #TT2 Dale Earnhardt

Wheels High Gear Top Tier Holofoils
2001 #TT2 Dale Earnhardt

Wheels High Gear Winning Edge
2000 #WE6 Dale Earnhardt

Wheels High Gear Winston Victory Lap Tribute
2004 #WVL4 Dale Earnhardt

Wheels High Gear Winston Victory Lap Tribute Gold
2004 #WVL4 Dale Earnhardt

Wheels High Groove
1999 #HG4 Dale Earnhardt's Car

Wheels Jackpot
1998 #J1 Dale Earnhardt

Wheels Mom-n-Pop's Dale Earnhardt
1993 #1 Dale Earnhardt Daytona
1993 #2 Dale Earnhardt Daytona
1993 #3 Dale Earnhardt Darlington
1993 #4 Dale Earnhardt Charlotte
1993 #5 Dale Earnhardt Charlotte
1993 #6 Dale Earnhardt Dover

Wheels Runnin and Gunnin
1999 #RG3 Dale Earnhardt's Car

Wheels Runnin and Gunnin Foils
1999 #RG3 Dale Earnhardt's Car

Wheels Solos
1999 #9 Dale Earnhardt
1999 #56 Dale Earnhardt's Car

Zenith
1995 #3 Dale Earnhardt HG
1995 #36 Dale Earnhardt's Transporter
1995 #76 Dale Earnhardt CL
1995 #P3 Dale Earnhardt HG Promo
1996 #1 Dale Earnhardt
1996 #65 Dale Earnhardt BD
1996 #66 Dale Earnhardt BD
1996 #67 Dale Earnhardt BD
1996 #68 Dale Earnhardt BD
1996 #69 Dale Earnhardt T
1996 #WC1 Dale Earnhardt 7W/94
1996 #35 Dale Earnhardt's Car HV
1996 #50 Dale Earnhardt S

Zenith Artist Proofs
1996 #1 Dale Earnhardt RP
1996 #35 Dale Earnhardt's Car HV
1996 #50 Dale Earnhardt S
1996 #65 Dale Earnhardt BD
1996 #66 Dale Earnhardt BD
1996 #67 Dale Earnhardt BD
1996 #68 Dale Earnhardt BD
1996 #69 Dale Earnhardt T

Zenith Champion Salute
1996 #3 Dale Earnhardt
1996 #5 Dale Earnhardt
1996 #6 Dale Earnhardt
1996 #9 Dale Earnhardt
1996 #10 Dale Earnhardt
1996 #16 Dale Earnhardt
1996 #2 Dale Earnhardt

Zenith Helmets
1995 #1 Dale Earnhardt

Zenith Highlights
1996 #1 Dale Earnhardt

Zenith Tribute
1995 #1 Dale Earnhardt

Zenith Winston Winners
1995 #7 Dale Earnhardt
1995 #10 Dale Earnhardt/T.Earnhardt
1995 #19 Dale Earnhardt
1995 #24 Dale Earnhardt

Zenith Z-Team
1995 #1 Dale Earnhardt

Earnhardt, Dale Jr.

Action Packed
1993 #139 D.Earnhardt WIN/Jr./Kerry

Action Packed Sundrop Dale Earnhardt
1995 #SD3 D.Earnhardt/Dale Jr.

Bass Pro Shops Racing
2004 #1 Dale Earnhardt Jr.
2004 #3 D.Earnhardt Jr./M.Truex Jr.

Bud All-Star Promos
2001 #DEJ Dale Earnhardt Jr.

Go Daddy Promos
2008 #DEJ Dale Earnhardt Jr.

Gold Collectibles Dale Earnhardt Jr.
2001 #1 Dale Earnhardt Jr.
2001 #2 Dale Earnhardt Jr.
2001 #3 Dale Earnhardt Jr.'s Car
2001 #4 Dale Earnhardt Jr.

Kenner 12-inch Specials *
1998 #5 Earnhardt./Earn.Jr.(Sam's)

Maxx
1993 #274 Dale Earnhardt YR/Jr./Kerry
1999 #19 Dale Earnhardt Jr.
1999 #20 Dale Earnhardt Jr.'s Car
1999 #21 D.Earnhardt Jr.'s Car RR
2000 #6 Dale Earnhardt Jr. CRC
2000 #48 Dale Earnhardt Jr.'s Car

Maxx 10th Anniversary
1998 #34 Dale Earnhardt Jr.
1998 #79 Dale Earnhardt Jr.'s Car
1998 #97 Dale Earnhardt Jr.

Maxx FANtastic Finishes
1999 #F15 Dale Earnhardt Jr.'s Car
2000 #FF2 Dale Earnhardt Jr.

Maxx Focus on a Champion
1999 #FC3 Dale Earnhardt Jr.

Maxx Focus on a Champion Gold
1999 #FC3 Dale Earnhardt Jr.

Maxx Premier Plus
1993 #189 Dale Earnhardt YR/Jr./Kerry

Maxx Premier Series
1993 #274 Dale Earnhardt YR/Jr./Kerry

Maxx Race Ticket
1999 #RT4 Dale Earnhardt Jr.'s Car

Maxx Racer's Ink
1999 #DE Dale Earnhardt Jr.
2000 #JR Dale Earnhardt Jr.

Maxx Racing Images
1999 #RI28 Dale Earnhardt Jr.

Maxx Speedway Boogie
2000 #SB5 Dale Earnhardt Jr.

Maxximum
1998 #53 Dale Earnhardt Jr.
1998 #78 Dale Earnhardt Jr.
2000 #31 Dale Earnhardt Jr. CRC

Maxximum Cruise Control
2000 #CC5 Dale Earnhardt Jr.

Maxximum Die Cuts
2000 #31 Dale Earnhardt Jr.

Maxximum MPH
2000 #31 Dale Earnhardt Jr./8

Maxximum Signatures
2000 #DE2 D.Earn/D.Earnhardt Jr.

McFarlane NASCAR Series 1
2003 #NNO Dale Earnhardt Jr. R
Red and Black Suit w/Glasses
2003 #NNO Dale Earnhardt Jr. R
Orange Gossamer Suit
2003 #NNO Dale Earnhardt Jr. H Red and Black Suit
2003 #NNO Dale Earnhardt Jr. H
Red/Black Suit w/Glasses
2003 #NNO D.Earnhardt Jr. Talladega Tribute w/Glasses
2003 #NNO D.Earnhardt Jr. Talladega
Tribute w/o Glasses

McFarlane NASCAR Series 3
2005 #10 Dale Earnhardt Jr. R
2005 #15 Dale Earnhardt Jr. H

McFarlane NASCAR Series 4
2005 #20 Dale Earnhardt Jr. R Daytona
2005 #21 Dale Earnhardt Jr. R Daytona Blk Hat
2005 #25 Dale Earnhardt Jr. H Daytona

McFarlane NASCAR Series 6
2005 #40 Dale Earnhardt Jr. Oreo Ritz

NAPA
2005 #NNO Dale Earnhardt Jr.

National Trading Card Day
2004 #PP4 Dale Earnhardt Jr.

National Trading Card Day *
2004 #PP4 Dale Earnhardt Jr.

Nilla Wafers Team Nabisco
2003 #1 Dale Earnhardt Jr. Oreo
2003 #2 Dale Earnhardt Jr. Nilla Waf
2003 #4 Earn.Jr./Green/Harvick/M.Walt

Post Cereal
2004 #4 Dale Earnhardt Jr.

Press Pass
1998 #46 Dale Earnhardt Jr.
1999 #37 Dale Earnhardt Jr.
1999 #58 Dale Earnhardt Jr. YG
1999 #73 Dale Earnhardt Jr. Champ
2000 #39 Dale Earnhardt Jr. REP CRC
2000 #46 Dale Earnhardt Jr.'s Car DD
2000 #62 Dale Earnhardt Jr.
2000 #70 Dale Earnhardt Jr.
2000 #85 Dale Earnhardt Jr. GN
2000 #93 Dale Earnhardt Jr. 00P
2001 #15 Dale Earnhardt Jr.
2001 #64 Dale Earnhardt Jr. REP
2001 #89 Dale Earnhardt Jr. SO
2002 #10 Dale Earnhardt Jr.
2002 #75 Dale Earnhardt Jr. REP
2002 #100 Dale Earnhardt Jr. CL
2003 #9 Dale Earnhardt Jr.
2003 #55 Dale Earnhardt Jr. DS
2003 #63 Jr./JJ/New/Sad/Ken/Bus DS
2003 #99 Dale Earnhardt Jr.'s Car OTW
2004 #9 Dale Earnhardt Jr.
2004 #9B Dale Earnhardt Jr. grand.
2004 #66 Dale Earnhardt Jr.'s Car OTW
2004 #91 Dale Earnhardt Jr. DS
2005 #6 Dale Earnhardt Jr.
2005 #65 Dale Earnhardt Jr's Car OTW
2005 #73 Dale Earnhardt Jr. NS
2005 #75 Dale Earnhardt Jr. NS
2005 #78 Dale Earnhardt Jr. NS
2005 #94 Dale Earnhardt Jr. Y
2005 #102 Dale Earnhardt Jr. P
2005 #109 Dale Earnhardt Jr's Car
2005 #113 Dale Earnhardt Jr's Car
2005 #120 Dale Jr/JJ/Gordon CL
2006 #9 Dale Earnhardt Jr.
2006 #76 Dale Earnhardt Jr's Car OTW
2006 #97 Dale Earnhardt Jr. U
2007 #6 Dale Earnhardt Jr.
2007 #86 Dale Earnhardt Jr. NS
2007 #106 Dale Earnhardt Jr. U
2007 #113 Dale Earnhardt Jr. TT
2008 #13 Dale Earnhardt Jr.
2008 #96 Dale Earnhardt Jr. First Cup Start

2008 #97 Dale Earnhardt Jr. Rookie All-Star
2008 #98 Dale Earnhardt Jr. First Cup Win
2008 #99 Dale Earnhardt Jr. Best Finish
2008 #100 Dale Earnhardt Jr. Most Wins
2008 #101 Dale Earnhardt Jr. Daytona Win
2008 #102 Dale Earnhardt Jr. Talladega
2008 #103 Dale Earnhardt Jr. Daytona
2008 #104 Dale Earnhardt Jr. AMP
2008 #105 Dale Earnhardt Jr. National Guard
2008 #106 Dale Earnhardt Jr. HMS

Press Pass Autographs
1999 #4 Dale Earnhardt Jr./250
2001 #12 Dale Earnhardt Jr.
2002 #17 Dale Earnhardt Jr.
2004 #16 Dale Earnhardt Jr. E
2005 #14 Dale Earnhardt Jr. E
2007 #11 Dale Earnhardt Jr.
2008 #14 Dale Earnhardt Jr. NC P/E

Press Pass Autographs Press Plates Black
2008 #10 Dale Earnhardt Jr. NC E

Press Pass Autographs Press Plates Cyan
2008 #10 Dale Earnhardt Jr. NC P

Press Pass Autographs Press Plates Magenta
2008 #10 Dale Earnhardt Jr. NC E

Press Pass Autographs Press Plates Yellow
2008 #10 Dale Earnhardt Jr. NC P

Press Pass Blaster Kmart
2006 #DEC Dale Earnhardt Jr.

Press Pass Blaster Target
2006 #DEB Dale Earnhardt Jr.

Press Pass Blaster Wal-Mart
2006 #DEA Dale Earnhardt Jr.

Press Pass Blue
2006 #B9 Dale Earnhardt Jr.
2006 #B76 Dale Earnhardt Jr.'s Car OTW
2006 #B97 Dale Earnhardt Jr. U
2007 #B6 Dale Earnhardt Jr.
2007 #B86 Dale Earnhardt Jr. NS
2007 #B106 Dale Earnhardt Jr. U
2007 #B113 Dale Earnhardt Jr. TT
2008 #B13 Dale Earnhardt Jr.
2008 #B96 Dale Earnhardt Jr. First Cup Start
2008 #B97 Dale Earnhardt Jr. Rookie All-Star
2008 #B98 Dale Earnhardt Jr. First Cup Win
2008 #B99 Dale Earnhardt Jr. Best Finish
2008 #B100 Dale Earnhardt Jr. Most Wins
2008 #B101 Dale Earnhardt Jr. Daytona Win
2008 #B102 Dale Earnhardt Jr. Talladega
2008 #B103 Dale Earnhardt Jr. Daytona
2008 #B104 Dale Earnhardt Jr. AMP
2008 #B105 Dale Earnhardt Jr. National Guard
2008 #B106 Dale Earnhardt Jr. HMS

Press Pass Burning Rubber
2000 #BR9 Dale Earnhardt Jr.

Press Pass Burning Rubber Autographs
2005 #BR-DEDale Earnhardt Jr./8
2008 #BR-DEDale Earnhardt Jr./8

Press Pass Burning Rubber Cars
2001 #BRC8 Dale Earnhardt Jr./105
2002 #BRC9 Dale Earnhardt Jr.'s Car
2003 #BRT10Dale Earnhardt Jr.'s Car
2004 #BRT10Dale Earnhardt Jr.'s Car
2005 #BRT7 Dale Earnhardt Jr.'s Car
2006 #BRT3 Dale Earnhardt Jr.'s Car

Press Pass Burning Rubber Drivers
2001 #BRD8 Dale Earnhardt Jr./90
2002 #BRD9 Dale Earnhardt Jr.
2003 #BRD10 Dale Earnhardt Jr.
2004 #BRD10 Dale Earnhardt Jr.
2005 #BRD7 Dale Earnhardt Jr.
2006 #BRD3 Dale Earnhardt Jr.
2007 #BRD7 Dale Earnhardt Jr. Richmond 5-6

Press Pass Burning Rubber Drivers Gold
2005 #BRD7 Dale Earnhardt Jr.
2006 #BRD3 Dale Earnhardt Jr.
2007 #BRD7 Dale Earnhardt Jr. Richmond 5-6

Press Pass Burning Rubber Team
2007 #BRT7 Dale Earnhardt Jr. Richmond 5-6

Press Pass Burnouts
2006 #HT11 Dale Earnhardt Jr.
2007 #B02 Dale Earnhardt Jr.

Press Pass Burnouts Blue
2007 #B02 Dale Earnhardt Jr.

Press Pass Burnouts Gold
2007 #B02 Dale Earnhardt Jr.

Press Pass Burnouts Holofoil
2006 #HT11 Dale Earnhardt Jr.

Press Pass Collector's Series Box Set
2007 #SB5 Dale Earnhardt Jr.

Press Pass Collectors Series Making the Show
2006 #MS23 Dale Earnhardt Jr.

Press Pass Collectors Series Sunday Best
2007 #CB5 Dale Earnhardt Jr.

Press Pass Cup Chase
2000 #CC5 Dale Earnhardt Jr. WIN
2001 #CC7 Dale Earnhardt Jr.
2002 #CC3 Dale Earnhardt Jr. WIN
2003 #CCR3 Dale Earnhardt Jr.
2004 #CCR3 Dale Earnhardt Jr. WIN
2005 #CCR15 Dale Earnhardt Jr.
2006 #CCR12 Dale Earnhardt Jr. Winner
2007 #CCR14 Dale Earnhardt Jr.
2008 #CC4 Dale Earnhardt Jr.

Press Pass Cup Chase Die Cut Prizes
2000 #CC5 Dale Earnhardt Jr.
2001 #CC7 Dale Earnhardt Jr.

Press Pass Cup Chase Prizes
2002 #CC3 Dale Earnhardt Jr.
2003 #CCR3 Dale Earnhardt Jr.
2004 #CCR3 Dale Earnhardt Jr.
2005 #CCP15 Dale Earnhardt Jr.
2006 #CC5 Dale Earnhardt Jr.

Press Pass Dale Earnhardt Jr.
2004 #1 Dale Earnhardt Jr. RR
2004 #2 Dale Earnhardt Jr. RR
2004 #3 Dale Earnhardt Jr. RR
2004 #4 Dale Earnhardt Jr. RR
2004 #5 Dale Earnhardt Jr. RR
2004 #6 Dale Earnhardt Jr. RR
2004 #7 Dale Earnhardt Jr. RR
2004 #8 Dale Earnhardt Jr. RR
2004 #9 Dale Earnhardt Jr. RR
2004 #10 Dale Jr./Dale Sr. FS
2004 #11 Dale Jr./Dale Sr. FS
2004 #12 Dale Jr./Dale Sr. FS
2004 #13 Dale Jr./Dale Sr. FS
2004 #14 Dale Jr./Dale Sr. FS
2004 #15 Dale Jr./Dale Sr. FS
2004 #16 Dale Jr./Dale Sr. FS
2004 #17 Dale Jr./Dale Sr. FS
2004 #18 Dale Jr./Dale Sr. FS
2004 #19 Dale Jr. V Texas '00
2004 #20 Dale Jr. V Richmond '00
2004 #21 Dale Jr. V Daytona '01
2004 #22 Dale Jr.'s Car V Dover '01
2004 #23 Dale Jr. V Talladega '01
2004 #24 Dale Jr. V Talladega Apr. '02
2004 #25 Dale Jr. V Talladega Oct. '02
2004 #26 Dale Jr. V Talladega '03
2004 #27 Dale Jr. V Phoenix '03
2004 #28 Dale Jr. V Daytona '04
2004 #29 Dale Jr. V Atlanta '04
2004 #30 Dale Jr. V Richmond '04
2004 #31 Dale Earnhardt Jr. M
2004 #32 Dale Earnhardt Jr. M
2004 #33 Dale Earnhardt Jr. M
2004 #34 Dale Earnhardt Jr. M
2004 #35 Dale Earnhardt Jr. M
2004 #36 Dale Earnhardt Jr. M
2004 #37 Dale Earnhardt Jr. T
2004 #38 Dale Earnhardt Jr. T
2004 #39 Dale Earnhardt Jr. T
2004 #40 Dale Earnhardt Jr. T
2004 #41 Dale Earnhardt Jr. T
2004 #42 Dale Jr./M.Waltrip T
2004 #43 Dale Earnhardt Jr. T
2004 #44 Dale Jr./M.Truex Jr. T
2004 #45 Dale Jr.'s Car/M.Truex Jr.'s Car T
2004 #46 Dale Earnhardt Jr. P
2004 #47 Dale Earnhardt Jr. P
2004 #48 Dale Earnhardt Jr. P
2004 #49 Dale Earnhardt Jr. P
2004 #50 Dale Earnhardt Jr. P
2004 #51 Dale Earnhardt Jr. P
2004 #52 Dale Earnhardt Jr. P
2004 #53 Dale Earnhardt Jr. P
2004 #54 Dale Earnhardt Jr. P
2004 #55 Dale Earnhardt Jr. TO
2004 #56 Dale Earnhardt Jr. TO
2004 #57 Dale Earnhardt Jr. TO
2004 #58 Dale Earnhardt Jr. TO
2004 #61 Dale Jr./M.Truex Jr. TO
2004 #62 Dale Earnhardt Jr. TO
2004 #63 Dale Earnhardt Jr. TO
2004 #64 Dale Earnhardt Jr. C
2004 #65 Dale Earnhardt Jr. C
2004 #66 Dale Earnhardt Jr. C
2004 #67 Dale Earnhardt Jr. C
2004 #68 Dale Earnhardt Jr. C
2004 #69 Dale Earnhardt Jr. C
2004 #70 Dale Earnhardt Jr. C
2004 #71 Dale Earnhardt Jr. C
2004 #72 Dale Earnhardt Jr. C

Press Pass Dale Earnhardt Jr. Firesuit
2002 #NNO Dale Earnhardt Jr.

Press Pass Dale Earnhardt Jr. Gallery
2004 #G1 Dale Earnhardt Jr. RR
2004 #G2 Dale Jr./Dale Sr. FS
2004 #G3 Dale Earnhardt Jr. V
2004 #G4 Dale Earnhardt Jr. M
2004 #G5 Dale Earnhardt Jr. T
2004 #G6 Dale Earnhardt Jr. P
2004 #G7 Dale Earnhardt Jr. TO
2004 #G8 Dale Earnhardt Jr. C

Press Pass Dale Earnhardt Jr. Tins
2004 #NNO Dale Earnhardt Celebrity Blue
2004 #NNO Dale Earnhardt Victory Blue
2004 #NNO Dale Earnhardt Profile Red
2004 #NNO Dale Earnhardt Owner Orange

Press Pass Dale The Movie
2007 #46 Dale Earnhardt Jr.'s Car Kevin Harvick's Car Michael Waltrip's Car Jimmie Johnson's Car
2007 #31 Kelley Earnhardt Dale Earnhardt Jr.
2007 #18 Kelley Earnhardt Dale Earnhardt Jr.

Press Pass Daytona 500 50th Anniversary
2008 #41 Dale Earnhardt Jr. '04

Press Pass Dominator Dale Earnhardt Jr.
2006 #1 Dale Jr. '98 BGN Champ
2006 #2 Dale Jr. '99 BGN Champ
2006 #3 Dale Jr. '00 Directv 500 Win
2006 #4 Dale Jr. '00 Pontiac 400 Win
2006 #5 Dale Jr. '00 The Winston Win
2006 #6 Dale Jr. '00 Rookie Recap
2006 #7 Dale Jr. '01 MBNA 400 Win
2006 #8 Dale Jr. '01 EA Sports 500 Win
2006 #9 Dale Jr. '01 Pepsi 400 Win
2006 #10 Dale Jr. '02 Aaron's 499 Win
2006 #11 Dale Jr. '02 EA Sports 500 Win
2006 #12 Dale Jr. '03 Aaron's 499 Win
2006 #13 Dale Jr.'s Car '03 Checker 500 Win
2006 #14 Dale Jr. '03 Breakout Season
2006 #15 Dale Jr. '03 Most Popular Driver
2006 #16 Dale Jr. '04 Daytona 500 Win
2006 #17 Dale Jr.'s Car '04 Golden Corral 500 Win
2006 #18 Dale Jr. '04 Chevy 400 Win
2006 #19 Dale Jr.'s Car '04 Sharpie 500 Win
2006 #20 Dale Jr. '04 EA Sports 500 Win
2006 #21 Dale Jr. '04 Checker 500 Win
2006 #22 Dale Jr. '04 Inaugural Chase
2006 #23 Dale Jr. '04 Most Popular Driver
2006 #24 Dale Jr./Truex Jr. '04 Owner BGN Champ.
2006 #25 Dale Jr.'s Car '05 USG 400 Win
2006 #26 Dale Jr. '05 Most Popular Driver
2006 #27 Dale Jr./Truex Jr. '05 Owner BGN Champ.
2006 #28 Dale Jr. '06 Winn-Dixie 250 Win
2006 #29 Dale Jr. '06 Ties Dale Sr. BGN Wins
2006 #30 Dale Jr. '06 Pontiac 400 Win
2006 #31 Dale Jr. '06 Chase
2006 #32 Dale Jr. '06 Cars Movie Premiere
2006 #33 Dale Jr. '06 Fan Favorite

Press Pass Dominator Dale Earnhardt Jr. Jumbo
2006 #JR1 Dale Jr.
2006 #JR2 Dale Jr.
2006 #JR3 Dale Jr. Competitor

Press Pass Dominator Tins
2006 #JR Dale Earnhardt Jr.

Press Pass Double Burner
2001 #DB8 Dale Earnhardt Jr.
2002 #DB1 Dale Earnhardt Jr.
2003 #DB10 Dale Earnhardt Jr.
2004 #DB10 Dale Earnhardt Jr.
2005 #DB10 Dale Earnhardt Jr.

Press Pass Double Burner Exchange
2003 #DB10 Dale Earnhardt Jr. EXCH
2004 #DB10 Dale Earnhardt Jr.
2005 #DB10 Dale Earnhardt Jr.

Press Pass Double Burner Firesuit-Glove
2006 #DB2 Dale Earnhardt Jr.
2007 #DB2 Dale Earnhardt Jr.

Press Pass Double Burner Firesuit-Glove Exchange
2007 #DB2 Dale Earnhardt Jr.

Press Pass Double Burner Metal-Tire
2006 #DB2 Dale Earnhardt Jr.
2007 #DB-DE Dale Earnhardt Jr.
2008 #DB-DE Dale Earnhardt Jr.

Press Pass Double Burner Metal-Tire Exchange
2007 #DB-DE Dale Earnhardt Jr.

Press Pass Eclipse
2002 #8 Dale Earnhardt Jr.
2002 #40 Dale Earnhardt Jr. SO
2003 #11 Dale Earnhardt Jr.
2003 #30 Dale Earnhardt Jr. ACC
2003 #40 Any Given Sunday WCS
2003 #49 Dale Earnhardt Jr. HS
2004 #3 Dale Earnhardt Jr.
2004 #30 Dale Earnhardt Jr.'s Car
2004 #47 Dale Earnhardt Jr. Z
2004 #47B Dale Earnhardt Jr. Z SP
2004 #52 Dale Earnhardt Jr. Z
2004 #56 Dale Earnhardt Jr. P
2004 #73 Dale Earnhardt Jr. LL
2004 #78 Earnhardt Jr./Johnson LL
2005 #5 Dale Earnhardt Jr.
2005 #30 Dale Earnhardt Jr's Car S
2005 #53 Dale Earnhardt Jr. Z
2005 #56 Dale Earnhardt Jr. P
2005 #71 Dale Earnhardt Jr. NS
2005 #73 Dale Earnhardt Jr. LL
2006 #18 Dale Earnhardt Jr.
2006 #63 Dale Earnhardt Jr. TN
2006 #73 Dale Earnhardt Jr. LL
2006 #90 Dale Earnhardt Jr. CL
2007 #5B Dale Earnhardt Jr. missing Target logo
2007 #5 Dale Earnhardt Jr.
2007 #41 Dale Earnhardt Jr. P
2007 #77 Dale Earnhardt Jr. NYC
2007 #CL Dale Earnhardt Jr. CL
2007 #0 Cup Chase 10
2008 #67B Dale Earnhardt Jr. BTF go-kart
2008 #67 Dale Earnhardt Jr. BTF
2008 #86 Dale Earnhardt Jr. PREV
2008 #90 Dale Earnhardt Jr. CL

Press Pass Eclipse Destination WIN
2004 #1 Dale Earnhardt Jr.
2004 #2 Dale Earnhardt Jr.
2004 #10 Dale Earnhardt Jr.
2004 #27 Dale Earnhardt Jr.
2005 #1 Dale Earnhardt Jr.
2005 #3 Dale Earnhardt Jr.
2005 #10 Dale Earnhardt Jr.
2005 #21 Dale Earnhardt Jr.
2005 #23 Dale Earnhardt Jr.
2005 #26 Dale Earnhardt Jr.

Press Pass Eclipse Double Hot Treads
2003 #DT10 D.Earnhardt Jr./M.Waltrip

Press Pass Eclipse Ecliptic
2007 #EC8 Dale Earnhardt Jr.

Press Pass Eclipse Gold
2007 #G5 Dale Earnhardt Jr.
2007 #G41 Dale Earnhardt Jr. P
2007 #G77 Dale Earnhardt Jr. NYC
2007 #GCL Dale Earnhardt Jr. CL
2008 #G67 Dale Earnhardt Jr. BTF
2008 #G86 Dale Earnhardt Jr. PREV
2008 #G90 Dale Earnhardt Jr. CL

Press Pass Eclipse Hyperdrive
2004 #HP5 Dale Earnhardt Jr.
2005 #HD5 Dale Earnhardt Jr.
2006 #HP3 Dale Earnhardt Jr.
2007 #HD9 Dale Earnhardt Jr.

Press Pass Eclipse Maxim
2004 #MX3 Dale Earnhardt Jr.
2005 #MX3 Dale Earnhardt Jr.

Press Pass Eclipse Previews
2003 #11 Dale Earnhardt Jr.
2003 #30 Dale Earnhardt Jr. ACC
2004 #3 Dale Earnhardt Jr.
2005 #E5 Dale Earnhardt Jr.
2005 #EB30 Dale Earnhardt Jr.'s Car S
2005 #EB53 Dale Earnhardt Jr. Z
2005 #EB56 Dale Earnhardt Jr. P
2005 #EB71 Dale Earnhardt Jr. NS
2005 #EB73 Dale Earnhardt Jr. LL/1
2006 #EB18 Dale Earnhardt Jr.
2006 #EB63 Dale Earnhardt Jr. TN
2007 #EB5 Dale Earnhardt Jr.

Press Pass Eclipse Racing Champions
2002 #RC17 Dale Earnhardt Jr.
2002 #RC27 Dale Earnhardt Jr.
2002 #RC31 Dale Earnhardt Jr.
2003 #RC11 Dale Earnhardt Jr.
2003 #RC31 Dale Earnhardt Jr.
2006 #RC8 Dale Earnhardt Jr.
2007 #RC12 Dale Earnhardt Jr.
2007 #RC18 Dale Earnhardt Jr.

Press Pass Eclipse Red
2007 #R5 Dale Earnhardt Jr.
2007 #R41 Dale Earnhardt Jr. P
2007 #R77 Dale Earnhardt Jr. NYC
2007 #RCL Dale Earnhardt Jr. CL
2008 #R67 Dale Earnhardt Jr. BTF
2008 #R86 Dale Earnhardt Jr. PREV
2008 #R90 Dale Earnhardt Jr. CL

Press Pass Eclipse Samples
2002 #8 Dale Earnhardt Jr.
2002 #40 Dale Earnhardt Jr. SO
2003 #11 Dale Earnhardt Jr.
2003 #30 Dale Earnhardt Jr. ACC
2003 #40 Any Given Sunday WCS
2003 #49 Dale Earnhardt Jr. HS
2004 #3 Dale Earnhardt Jr.
2004 #30 Dale Earnhardt Jr.'s Car
2004 #47 Dale Earnhardt Jr. Z
2004 #52 Dale Earnhardt Jr. Z
2004 #56 Dale Earnhardt Jr. P
2004 #73 Dale Earnhardt Jr. LL
2004 #78 Earnhardt Jr./Johnson LL
2005 #5 Dale Earnhardt Jr.
2005 #30 Dale Earnhardt Jr's Car S
2005 #53 Dale Earnhardt Jr. Z
2005 #56 Dale Earnhardt Jr. P
2005 #71 Dale Earnhardt Jr. NS
2005 #73 Dale Earnhardt Jr. LL

Press Pass Eclipse Skidmarks
2002 #SK2 Dale Earnhardt Jr.
2004 #SM7 Dale Earnhardt Jr.
2005 #SM7 Dale Earnhardt Jr.
2006 #SM2 Dale Earnhardt Jr.
2007 #SM1 Dale Earnhardt Jr.

Press Pass Eclipse Skidmarks Holofoil
2004 #SM7 Dale Earnhardt Jr.
2005 #SM7 Dale Earnhardt Jr.
2006 #SM2 Dale Earnhardt Jr.
2007 #SM1 Dale Earnhardt Jr.

Press Pass Eclipse Solar Eclipse
2002 #S8 Dale Earnhardt Jr.
2002 #S40 Dale Earnhardt Jr. SO
2003 #P11 Dale Earnhardt Jr.
2003 #P30 Dale Earnhardt Jr. ACC
2003 #P40 Any Given Sunday WCS
2003 #P49 Dale Earnhardt Jr. HS

Press Pass Eclipse Star Tracks
2008 #ST15 Dale Earnhardt Jr.

Press Pass Eclipse Star Tracks Holofoil
2008 #ST15 Dale Earnhardt Jr.

Press Pass Eclipse Supernova
2002 #SN2 Dale Earnhardt Jr.
2003 #SN2 Dale Earnhardt Jr.
2006 #SU10 Dale Earnhardt Jr.

Press Pass Eclipse Supernova Numbered
2002 #SN2 Dale Earnhardt Jr.

Press Pass Eclipse Teammates Autographs
2007 #1 Dale Jr./Truex Jr./Menard
2008 #EGJM Dale Earnhardt Jr. Jeff Gordon Jimmie Johnson Casey Mears
2008 #EJ Dale Earnhardt Jr. Jimmie Johnson
2008 #EM Dale Earnhardt Jr. Casey Mears
2008 #EG Dale Earnhardt Jr. Jeff Gordon

Press Pass Eclipse Under Cover Autographs
2004 #UCDE Dale Earnhardt Jr./8
2005 #UCDE Dale Earnhardt Jr./8
2007 #UC-DE Dale Earnhardt Jr./8
2008 #UC-DE Dale Earnhardt Jr./8

Press Pass Eclipse Under Cover Cars
2003 #UCT7 Dale Earnhardt Jr.
2004 #UCT12 Dale Earnhardt Jr.
2005 #UCT11 Dale Earnhardt Jr.
2006 #UCT3 Dale Earnhardt Jr.

Press Pass Eclipse Under Cover Double Cover
2002 #DC8 D.Earn.Jr./M.Waltrip
2004 #DC1 D.Earnhardt Jr./M.Waltrip
2005 #DC1 D.Earnhardt Jr./M.Waltrip

Press Pass Eclipse Under Cover Double Cover Name
2007 #DC6 Dale Jr./Truex Jr.

Press Pass Eclipse Under Cover Double Cover NASCAR
2007 #DC6 Dale Jr./Truex Jr.

Press Pass Eclipse Under Cover Driver Gold
2003 #UCD7 Dale Earnhardt Jr.
2004 #UCD12 Dale Earnhardt Jr.

Press Pass Eclipse Under Cover Driver Red
2003 #UCD7 Dale Earnhardt Jr.
2004 #UCD12 Dale Earnhardt Jr.
2005 #UCD11 Dale Earnhardt Jr.

Press Pass Eclipse Under Cover Driver Silver
2003 #UCD7 Dale Earnhardt Jr.
2004 #UCD12 Dale Earnhardt Jr.

Press Pass Eclipse Under Cover Drivers
2002 #CD12 Dale Earnhardt Jr.
2007 #UCD1 Dale Earnhardt Jr.

Press Pass Eclipse Under Cover Drivers Eclipse
2007 #UCD1 Dale Earnhardt Jr.

Press Pass Eclipse Under Cover Drivers Gold
2006 #UCD3 Dale Earnhardt Jr.

Press Pass Eclipse Under Cover Drivers Holofoil
2005 #UCD11 Dale Earnhardt Jr.
2006 #UCD3 Dale Earnhardt Jr.

Press Pass Eclipse Under Cover Drivers Name
2007 #UCD1 Dale Earnhardt Jr.

Press Pass Eclipse Under Cover Drivers NASCAR
2007 #UCD1 Dale Earnhardt Jr.

Press Pass Eclipse Under Cover Drivers Silver
2005 #UCD11 Dale Earnhardt Jr.
2006 #UCD3 Dale Earnhardt Jr.

Press Pass Eclipse Under Cover Gold Cars
2002 #CD12 Dale Earnhardt Jr.

Press Pass Eclipse Under Cover Gold Drivers
2002 #CD12 Dale Earnhardt Jr.

Press Pass Eclipse Under Cover Holofoil Drivers
2002 #CD12 Dale Earnhardt Jr.

Press Pass Eclipse Under Cover Teams
2007 #UCT1 Dale Earnhardt Jr.

Press Pass Eclipse Under Cover Teams NASCAR
2007 #UCT1 Dale Earnhardt Jr.

Press Pass Eclipse Warp Speed
2002 #WS2 Dale Earnhardt Jr.
2003 #WS2 Dale Earnhardt Jr.

Press Pass Four Wide
2006 #FW-DE Dale Earnhardt Jr.
2007 #FW-DE Dale Earnhardt Jr.
2008 #FW-DE1 Dale Earnhardt Jr. Bud
2008 #FW-DE3 Dale Earnhardt Jr. NG
2008 #FW-DE2 Dale Earnhardt Jr. AMP

Press Pass Four Wide Checkered
2007 #FW-DE Dale Earnhardt Jr.
2008 #FW-DE Dale Earnhardt Jr.

Press Pass Four Wide Checkered Exchange
2007 #FW-DE Dale Earnhardt Jr.

Press Pass Four Wide Checkered Flag
2006 #FW-DE Dale Earnhardt Jr.

Press Pass Four Wide Exchange
2007 #FW-DE Dale Earnhardt Jr.

Press Pass Game Face
2005 #GF3 Dale Earnhardt Jr.
2006 #GF4 Dale Earnhardt Jr.

Press Pass Gold
2006 #G9 Dale Earnhardt Jr.
2006 #G76 Dale Earnhardt Jr's Car OTW
2006 #G97 Dale Earnhardt Jr. U
2007 #G6 Dale Earnhardt Jr.
2007 #G86 Dale Earnhardt Jr. NS
2007 #G106 Dale Earnhardt Jr. U
2007 #G113 Dale Earnhardt Jr. TT
2008 #G13 Dale Earnhardt Jr.
2008 #G96 Dale Earnhardt Jr. First Cup Start
2008 #G97 Dale Earnhardt Jr. Rookie All-Star
2008 #G98 Dale Earnhardt Jr. First Cup Win
2008 #G99 Dale Earnhardt Jr. Best Finish
2008 #G100 Dale Earnhardt Jr. Most Wins
2008 #G101 Dale Earnhardt Jr. Daytona Win
2008 #G102 Dale Earnhardt Jr. Talladega
2008 #G103 Dale Earnhardt Jr. Daytona
2008 #G104 Dale Earnhardt Jr. AMP
2008 #G105 Dale Earnhardt Jr. National Guard
2008 #G106 Dale Earnhardt Jr. HMS

Press Pass Gold Holofoil
2003 #P9 Dale Earnhardt Jr.
2003 #P55 Dale Earnhardt Jr. DS
2003 #P63 Jr./Johnson/Newman Sadler/Kenseth/Busch DS
2003 #P99 Dale Earnhardt Jr.'s Car OTW

Press Pass Ground Zero
2001 #GZ8 Dale Earnhardt Jr.

Press Pass Hot Treads
2001 #HT16 Dale Earnhardt Jr./2405
2002 #HT25 Dale Jr.'s Car/2375
2004 #HTR2 Dale Earnhardt Jr.
2005 #HTR1 Dale Earnhardt Jr.
2007 #HT5 Dale Earnhardt Jr.

Press Pass Hot Treads Blue
2007 #HT5 Dale Earnhardt Jr.

Press Pass Hot Treads Gold
2007 #HT5 Dale Earnhardt Jr.

Press Pass Hot Treads Holofoil
2004 #HTR2 Dale Earnhardt Jr.
2005 #HTR1 Dale Earnhardt Jr.

Press Pass K-Mart
2007 #DE-C Dale Earnhardt Jr.

Press Pass Legends
2005 #30 Dale Earnhardt Jr.
2006 #37 Dale Earnhardt Jr.
2006 #47 Dale Sr./Dale Jr. REC
2007 #42 Dale Earnhardt Jr.

Press Pass Legends Autographs Black
2005 #14 Dale Earnhardt Jr.
2006 #21 Dale Earnhardt Jr.

Press Pass Legends Autographs Blue
2007 #5 Dale Earnhardt Jr./59

Press Pass Legends Autographs Inscriptions Blue
2007 #4 Dale Jr. 07/1
2007 #3 Dale Jr. 8/7

Press Pass Legends Blue
2005 #30B Dale Earnhardt Jr.
2006 #B37 Dale Earnhardt Jr.
2006 #B47 Dale Sr./Dale Jr. REC
2007 #B42 Dale Earnhardt Jr.

Press Pass Legends Bronze
2006 #Z37 Dale Earnhardt Jr.
2006 #Z47 Dale Sr./Dale Jr. REC
2007 #Z42 Dale Earnhardt Jr.

Press Pass Legends Double Threads Bronze
2005 #DT-EW D.Earnhardt Jr./M.Waltrip

Press Pass Legends Double Threads Gold
2005 #DT-EW D.Earnhardt Jr./M.Waltrip

Press Pass Legends Double Threads Silver
2005 #DT-EW D.Earnhardt Jr./M.Waltrip

Press Pass Legends Gold
2005 #30G Dale Earnhardt Jr.
2006 #G37 Dale Earnhardt Jr.
2006 #G47 Dale Sr./Dale Jr. REC
2007 #G42 Dale Earnhardt Jr.

Press Pass Legends Greatest Moments
2005 #GM17 Dale Earnhardt Jr.

Press Pass Legends Heritage Gold
2006 #HE12 Dale Earnhardt Jr.
2006 #HE15 Dale Sr./Dale Jr.

Press Pass Legends Heritage Silver
2006 #HE12 Dale Earnhardt Jr.
2006 #HE15 Dale Sr./Dale Jr.

Press Pass Legends Holofoil
2005 #30H Dale Earnhardt Jr.
2006 #H37 Dale Earnhardt Jr.
2006 #H47 Dale Sr./Dale Jr. REC
2007 #H42 Dale Earnhardt Jr.

Press Pass Legends Press Plates Black
2005 #30 Dale Earnhardt Jr.
2006 #PPB37 Dale Earnhardt Jr.
2006 #PPB47 Dale Sr./Dale Jr. REC
2007 #PP42 Dale Earnhardt Jr.

Press Pass Legends Press Plates Black Backs
2006 #PPB37B Dale Earnhardt Jr.
2006 #PPB47B Dale Sr./Dale Jr. REC
2007 #PP42 Dale Earnhardt Jr.

Press Pass Legends Press Plates Cyan
2005 #30 Dale Earnhardt Jr.
2006 #PPC37 Dale Earnhardt Jr.
2006 #PPC47 Dale Sr./Dale Jr. REC
2007 #PP42 Dale Earnhardt Jr.

Press Pass Legends Press Plates Cyan Backs
2006 #PPC37B Dale Earnhardt Jr.
2006 #PPC47B Dale Sr./Dale Jr. REC
2007 #PP42 Dale Earnhardt Jr.

Press Pass Legends Press Plates Magenta
2005 #30 Dale Earnhardt Jr.
2006 #PPM37 Dale Earnhardt Jr.
2006 #PPM47 Dale Sr./Dale Jr. REC
2007 #PP42 Dale Earnhardt Jr.

Press Pass Legends Press Plates Magenta Backs
2006 #PPM37B Dale Earnhardt Jr.
2006 #PPM47B Dale Sr./Dale Jr. REC
2007 #PP42 Dale Earnhardt Jr.

Press Pass Legends Press Plates Yellow
2005 #30 Dale Earnhardt Jr.
2006 #PPY37 Dale Earnhardt Jr.
2006 #PPY47 Dale Sr./Dale Jr. REC
2007 #PP42 Dale Earnhardt Jr.

Press Pass Legends Press Plates Yellow Backs
2006 #PPY37B Dale Earnhardt Jr.
2006 #PPY47B Dale Sr./Dale Jr. REC
2007 #PP42 Dale Earnhardt Jr.

Press Pass Legends Previews
2005 #30 Dale Earnhardt Jr.
2006 #EB37 Dale Earnhardt Jr.
2006 #EB47 Dale Sr./Dale Jr. REC
2007 #EB42 Dale Earnhardt Jr.

Press Pass Legends Solo
2005 #30S Dale Earnhardt Jr.
2006 #S37 Dale Earnhardt Jr.
2006 #S47 Dale Sr./Dale Jr. REC
2007 #S42 Dale Earnhardt Jr.

Press Pass Legends Sunday Swatches Bronze
2007 #DE-SSDale Earnhardt Jr.

Press Pass Legends Sunday Swatches Gold
2007 #DE-SSDale Earnhardt Jr.

Press Pass Legends Sunday Swatches Silver
2007 #DE-SSDale Earnhardt Jr.

Press Pass Legends Threads & Treads Bronze
2005 #TTJR Dale Earnhardt Jr.

Press Pass Legends Threads & Treads Gold
2005 #TTJR Dale Earnhardt Jr.

Press Pass Legends Threads & Treads Silver
2005 #TTJR Dale Earnhardt Jr.

Press Pass Legends Triple Threads
2006 #TT-DE Dale Earnhardt Jr.

Press Pass Legends Victory Lane Bronze
2007 #VL1 Dale Earnhardt Jr.

Press Pass Legends Victory Lane Gold
2007 #VL1 Dale Earnhardt Jr.

Press Pass Legends Victory Lane Silver
2007 #VL1 Dale Earnhardt Jr.

Press Pass Making the Show Collector's Series
2004 #MS5 Dale Earnhardt Jr.

Press Pass Making the Show Collector's Series Tins
2004 #NNO Dale Jr./Stewart/J.Gordon

Press Pass Millennium
2000 #39 Dale Earnhardt Jr.
2000 #46 Dale Earnhardt Jr.
2000 #62 Dale Earnhardt Jr.
2000 #70 Dale Earnhardt Jr.
2000 #85 Dale Earnhardt Jr.
2000 #93 Dale Earnhardt Jr.
2001 #15 Dale Earnhardt Jr.
2001 #64 Dale Earnhardt Jr. REP
2001 #89 Dale Earnhardt Jr. SO

Press Pass Nabisco Albertsons
2002 #1 Dale Earnhardt Jr.
2003 #1 Dale Earnhardt Jr.

Press Pass Nilla Wafers
2004 #1 Dale Earnhardt Jr.
2004 #2 Dale Earnhardt Jr. w/car
2004 #3 Dale Earnhardt Jr.'s Oreo Car

Press Pass Oil Slicks
1998 #46 Dale Earnhardt Jr.

Press Pass Optima
2000 #6 Dale Earnhardt Jr. CRC
2000 #43 Dale Earnhardt Jr. WCL
2001 #5 Dale Earnhardt Jr.
2001 #41 Dale Earnhardt Jr. WCL
2002 #7 Dale Earnhardt Jr.
2002 #45 Dale Earnhardt Jr. YG
2003 #6 Dale Earnhardt Jr.
2003 #40 Dale Earnhardt Jr. UC
2003 #46 Dale Earnhardt Jr. TV
2003 #47 Dale Earnhardt Jr. Music
2003 #48 Dale Earnhardt Jr. Magazines
2003 #49 Dale Earnhardt Jr. Talk Shows
2004 #4 Dale Earnhardt Jr.
2004 #55 Dale Earnhardt Jr.'s Car RV
2004 #73 Dale Earnhardt Jr. CP
2004 #83 Dale Earnhardt Jr. RR
2004 #88 Dale Earnhardt Jr. SS
2004 #NNO Signings Entry Dale Jr.
2005 #8 Dale Earnhardt Jr.
2005 #56 Dale Earnhardt Jr. RR
2005 #74 Dale Earnhardt Jr. CP
2005 #93 Dale Earnhardt Jr's Car RTV
2006 #8 Dale Earnhardt Jr.
2006 #60 Dale Earnhardt Jr.'s Car HS
2006 #68 Dale Earnhardt Jr. CP
2006 #8B Dale Earnhardt Jr. Chase

Press Pass Optima Cool Persistence
2000 #CP1 Dale Earnhardt Jr.
2001 #CP3 Dale Earnhardt Jr.
2002 #CP2 Dale Earnhardt Jr.
2003 #CP1 Dale Earnhardt Jr.
2004 #CP3 Dale Earnhardt Jr.

Press Pass Optima Encore
2000 #EN4 Dale Earnhardt Jr.

Press Pass Optima Fan Favorite
2002 #FF6 Dale Earnhardt Jr.
2003 #FF6 Dale Earnhardt Jr.
2004 #FF4 Dale Earnhardt Jr.
2006 #FF4 Dale Earnhardt Jr.

Press Pass Optima G Force
2000 #GF6 Dale Earnhardt Jr.
2001 #GF4 Dale Earnhardt Jr.
2004 #GF1 Dale Earnhardt Jr.

Press Pass Optima Gold
2001 #5 Dale Earnhardt Jr.
2001 #41 Dale Earnhardt Jr. WCL
2002 #7 Dale Earnhardt Jr.
2002 #45 Dale Earnhardt Jr. YG
2003 #G6 Dale Earnhardt Jr.
2003 #G40 Dale Earnhardt Jr. UC
2003 #G46 Dale Earnhardt Jr.
2003 #G47 Dale Earnhardt Jr.
2003 #G48 Dale Earnhardt Jr.
2003 #G49 Dale Earnhardt Jr.
2004 #G4 Dale Earnhardt Jr.
2004 #G55 Dale Earnhardt Jr.'s Car RV
2004 #G73 Dale Earnhardt Jr. CP
2004 #G83 Dale Earnhardt Jr. RR
2004 #G88 Dale Earnhardt Jr. SS
2005 #G8 Dale Earnhardt Jr.
2005 #G56 Dale Earnhardt Jr. RR
2005 #G74 Dale Earnhardt Jr. CP
2005 #G93 Dale Earnhardt Jr's Car RTV
2006 #G8 Dale Earnhardt Jr.
2006 #G60 Dale Earnhardt Jr.'s Car HS
2006 #G68 Dale Earnhardt Jr. CP

Press Pass Optima On the Edge
2000 #OE2 Dale Earnhardt Jr.
2001 #OE1 Dale Earnhardt Jr.

Press Pass Optima Platinum
2000 #6 Dale Earnhardt Jr.
2000 #43 Dale Earnhardt Jr. WCL

Press Pass Optima Previews
2003 #6 Dale Earnhardt Jr.
2004 #EB4 Dale Earnhardt Jr.
2005 #8 Dale Earnhardt Jr.

2006 #EB8 Dale Earnhardt Jr.
Press Pass Optima Promos
2002 #7 Dale Earnhardt Jr.
2002 #45 Dale Earnhardt Jr. YG
Press Pass Optima Q & A
2005 #QA6 Dale Earnhardt Jr.
2006 #QA7 Dale Earnhardt Jr.
Press Pass Optima Q and A
2002 #QA2 Dale Earnhardt Jr.
Press Pass Optima Q&A
2004 #QA9 Dale Earnhardt Jr.
Press Pass Optima Race Used Lugnuts Cars
2000 #LC16 Dale Earnhardt Jr.'s Car/50
2001 #LNC4 Dale Earnhardt Jr.'s Car
2002 #LNC5 Dale Earnhardt Jr.'s Car
Press Pass Optima Race Used Lugnuts Drivers
2000 #LD16 Dale Earnhardt Jr./55
2001 #LND3 Dale Earnhardt Jr.
2002 #LND5 Dale Earnhardt Jr.
Press Pass Optima Samples
2002 #7 Dale Earnhardt Jr.
2002 #45 Dale Earnhardt Jr. YG
2003 #6 Dale Earnhardt Jr.
2003 #40 Dale Earnhardt Jr. UC
2003 #46 Dale Earnhardt Jr.
2003 #47 Dale Earnhardt Jr.
2003 #48 Dale Earnhardt Jr.
2003 #49 Dale Earnhardt Jr.
2004 #4 Dale Earnhardt Jr.
2004 #55 Dale Earnhardt Jr.'s Car RV
2004 #73 Dale Earnhardt Jr. CP
2004 #83 Dale Earnhardt Jr. RR
2004 #88 Dale Earnhardt Jr. SS
2005 #8 Dale Earnhardt Jr.
2005 #56 Dale Earnhardt Jr. RR
2005 #74 Dale Earnhardt Jr. CP
2005 #93 Dale Earnhardt Jr. RTV
Press Pass Optima Thunder Bolts Autographs
2004 #TBDE Dale Earnhardt Jr./8
2005 #TB-DE Dale Earnhardt Jr./8
Press Pass Optima Thunder Bolts Cars
2003 #TBT10 Dale Earnhardt Jr.'s Car
2004 #TBT1 Dale Earnhardt Jr.'s Car
Press Pass Optima Thunder Bolts Drivers
2003 #TBD10 Dale Earnhardt Jr./65
2004 #TBD1 Dale Earnhardt Jr.
Press Pass Optima Up Close
2001 #UC1 Dale Earnhardt Jr.
2002 #UC6 Dale Earnhardt Jr.
Press Pass Optima XL
1994 #46 Dale Earnhardt Jr. RC
Press Pass Optima XL Red Hot
1994 #46 Dale Earnhardt Jr.
Press Pass Optima Young Guns
2003 #YG1 Dale Earnhardt Jr.
Press Pass Panorama
2005 #PPP33 Dale Earnhardt Jr.
Press Pass Pitstop
2000 #PS17 Dale Earnhardt Jr.'s Car
Press Pass Platinum
2002 #10 Dale Earnhardt Jr.
2002 #75 Dale Earnhardt Jr. REP
2002 #100 Dale Earnhardt Jr. CL
2004 #P9 Dale Earnhardt Jr.
2004 #P66 Dale Earnhardt Jr.'s Car OTW
2004 #P91 Dale Earnhardt Jr. DS
2005 #P6 Dale Earnhardt Jr.
2005 #P65 Dale Earnhardt's Car OTW
2005 #P73 Dale Earnhardt Jr. NS
2005 #P75 Dale Earnhardt Jr. NS
2005 #P78 Dale Earnhardt Jr. NS
2005 #P94 Dale Earnhardt Jr. Y
2005 #P102 Dale Earnhardt Jr. P
2005 #P109 Dale Earnhardt Jr.'s Car
2005 #P113 Dale Earnhardt Jr's Car
2005 #P120 Dale Jr/JJ/Gordon CL
2006 #P9 Dale Earnhardt Jr.
2006 #P76 Dale Earnhardt Jr's Car OTW
2006 #P97 Dale Earnhardt Jr. U
2007 #P6 Dale Earnhardt Jr.
2007 #P86 Dale Earnhardt Jr. NS
2007 #P106 Dale Earnhardt Jr. U
2007 #P113 Dale Earnhardt Jr. TT
2008 #P13 Dale Earnhardt Jr.
2008 #P96 Dale Earnhardt Jr. First Cup Start
2008 #P97 Dale Earnhardt Jr. Rookie All-Star
2008 #P98 Dale Earnhardt Jr. First Cup Win
2008 #P99 Dale Earnhardt Jr. Best Finish
2008 #P100 Dale Earnhardt Jr. Most Wins
2008 #P101 Dale Earnhardt Jr. Daytona Win
2008 #P102 Dale Earnhardt Jr. Talladega
2008 #P103 Dale Earnhardt Jr. Daytona
2008 #P104 Dale Earnhardt Jr. AMP
2008 #P105 Dale Earnhardt Jr. National Guard
2008 #P106 Dale Earnhardt Jr. HMS
Press Pass Premium
1998 #12 Dale Earnhardt Jr.
1999 #41 Dale Earnhardt Jr.
1999 #P1 Dale Earnhardt Jr. Promo
2000 #43 Dale Earnhardt Jr. CRC
2000 #53 Dale Earnhardt Jr.
2000 #66 Dale Earnhardt Jr.
2001 #5 Dale Earnhardt Jr.
2001 #32 Dale Earnhardt Jr.
2001 #59 Dale Earnhardt Jr. CC
2001 #72 Dale Earnhardt Jr. PC
2002 #7 Dale Earnhardt Jr.
2002 #36 Dale Earnhardt Jr.'s Car
2002 #60 Dale Earnhardt Jr. CH
2002 #71 Dale Earnhardt Jr. PC
2003 #7 Dale Earnhardt Jr.
2003 #36 Dale Earnhardt Jr.'s Car
2003 #46 Dale Earnhardt Jr.
2003 #48 Dale Earnhardt Jr.
2003 #50 Dale Jr/Park/Waltrip CL
2003 #59 Dale Earnhardt Jr. CC
2003 #70 Dale Earnhardt Jr.PC
2004 #1 Dale Earnhardt Jr.
2004 #39 Dale Earnhardt Jr.'s Car
2004 #46 Dale Earnhardt Jr. NS
2004 #59 Dale Earnhardt Jr. CC
2004 #80 Dale Earnhardt Jr. PC
2004 #0 Dale Earnhardt Jr. Daytona
2005 #5 Dale Earnhardt Jr.
2005 #61 Dale Earnhardt Jr. CC
2005 #71 Dale Earnhardt Jr. PC
2006 #6 Dale Earnhardt Jr.
2006 #63 Dale Earnhardt Jr. C
2006 #80 Dale Earnhardt Jr. PC
2007 #7 Dale Earnhardt Jr.
2007 #52 Dale Earnhardt Jr. RTTC
2007 #65 Dale Earnhardt Jr. MD
2007 #73 Dale Earnhardt Jr. DD
2007 #77 Dale Earnhardt Jr. FF
2008 #34 Dale Earnhardt Jr.
2008 #84 Dale Earnhardt Jr. OD
2008 #75 Dale Earnhardt Jr. F
2008 #71 Dale Earnhardt Jr. MD
2008 #57 Dale Earnhardt Jr. EOP
2008 #51 Dale Earnhardt Jr. SW Gatorade Duel
2008 #49 Dale Earnhardt Jr. SW Shootout
2008 #37 Dale Earnhardt Jr.'s Car M
2008 #1 Dale Earnhardt Jr. CL
Press Pass Premium Asphalt Jungle
2004 #A5 Dale Earnhardt Jr.
2006 #AJ1 Dale Earnhardt Jr.
Press Pass Premium Badge of Honor
1999 #BH2 Dale Earnhardt Jr.
1999 #BH26 Dale Earnhardt Jr.'s Car
Press Pass Premium Badge of Honor Reflectors
1999 #BH2 Dale Earnhardt Jr.
1999 #BH26 Dale Earnhardt Jr.'s Car
Press Pass Premium Burning Desire
1999 #FD2B Dale Earnhardt Jr. 1:192
Press Pass Premium Clean Air
2008 #CA4 Dale Earnhardt Jr.
Press Pass Premium Concrete Chaos
2007 #CC2 Dale Earnhardt Jr.
Press Pass Premium Going Global
2008 #GG1 Dale Earnhardt Jr.
Press Pass Premium Going Global Red
2008 #GG1 Dale Earnhardt Jr.
Press Pass Premium Gold
2001 #5 Dale Earnhardt Jr.
2001 #32 Dale Earnhardt Jr.
2001 #59 Dale Earnhardt Jr. CC
2001 #72 Dale Earnhardt Jr. PC
Press Pass Premium Hot Threads Autographs
2004 #HT-DE Dale Earnhardt Jr./8
2005 #HT-DE Dale Earnhardt Jr./8
2007 #HT-DE Dale Earnhardt Jr./8
Press Pass Premium Hot Threads Cars
2003 #HTT10 Dale Earnhardt Jr.
2005 #HTT4 Dale Earnhardt Jr.
2006 #HTT3 Dale Earnhardt Jr.
Press Pass Premium Hot Threads Drivers
2003 #HTD10 Dale Earnhardt Jr.
2005 #HTD4 Dale Earnhardt Jr.
2006 #HTD3 Dale Earnhardt Jr.
2007 #HTD11 Dale Earnhardt Jr.
2008 #HTD18 Dale Earnhardt Jr. AMP
2008 #HTD19 Dale Earnhardt Jr. NG
Press Pass Premium Hot Threads Drivers Bronze
2004 #HTD11 Dale Earnhardt Jr.
Press Pass Premium Hot Threads Drivers Bronze Retail
2004 #HTT11 Dale Earnhardt Jr.
Press Pass Premium Hot Threads Drivers Gold
2004 #HTD11 Dale Earnhardt Jr.
2005 #HTD4 Dale Earnhardt Jr.
2006 #HTD3 Dale Earnhardt Jr.
2007 #HTD11 Dale Earnhardt Jr.
2008 #HTD18 Dale Earnhardt Jr. AMP
2008 #HTD19 Dale Earnhardt Jr. NG
Press Pass Premium Hot Threads Drivers Silver
2004 #HTD11 Dale Earnhardt Jr.
Press Pass Premium Hot Threads Patch
2007 #HTP14 Dale Earnhardt Jr. Wrangler/8
2007 #HTP13 Dale Earnhardt Jr. DEI/10
Press Pass Premium Hot Threads Team
2007 #HTT11 Dale Earnhardt Jr.
2008 #HTT18 Dale Earnhardt Jr. AMP
2008 #HTT19 Dale Earnhardt Jr. NG
Press Pass Premium In The Zone
2000 #IZ9 Dale Earnhardt Jr.
2001 #IZ2 Dale Earnhardt Jr.
2002 #IZ3 Dale Earnhardt Jr.
2003 #IZ1 Dale Earnhardt Jr.
2004 #IZ2 Dale Earnhardt Jr.
2005 #IZ10 Dale Earnhardt Jr.
2006 #IZ1 Dale Earnhardt Jr.
Press Pass Premium In the Zone Elite Edition
2004 #IZ2 Dale Earnhardt Jr.
2005 #IZ10 Dale Earnhardt Jr.
Press Pass Premium In the Zone Red
2006 #IZ1 Dale Earnhardt Jr.
Press Pass Premium Performance Driven
2000 #PD4 Dale Earnhardt Jr.
2001 #PD2 Dale Earnhardt Jr.
2002 #PD1 Dale Earnhardt Jr.
2003 #PD1 Dale Earnhardt Jr.
2004 #PD9 Dale Earnhardt Jr.
2005 #PD1 Dale Earnhardt Jr.
2007 #PD3 Dale Earnhardt Jr.
Press Pass Premium Performance Driven Red
2007 #PD3 Dale Earnhardt Jr.
Press Pass Premium Previews
2003 #7 Dale Earnhardt Jr.
2004 #1 Dale Earnhardt Jr.
2008 #EB1 Dale Earnhardt Jr. CL
2008 #EB34 Dale Earnhardt Jr.
2008 #EB57 Dale Earnhardt Jr. EOP
Press Pass Premium Race Used Firesuit
2000 #F1 Dale Earnhardt Jr./130
Press Pass Premium Race Used Firesuit Cars
2001 #FC0 Dale Earnhardt Jr.
2002 #FC12 Dale Earnhardt Jr.
Press Pass Premium Race Used Firesuit Drivers
2001 #FD0 Dale Earnhardt Jr.
2002 #FD12 Dale Earnhardt Jr.
Press Pass Premium Red
2007 #R7 Dale Earnhardt Jr.
2007 #R52 Dale Earnhardt Jr. RTTC
2007 #R65 Dale Earnhardt Jr. MD
2007 #R73 Dale Earnhardt Jr. DD
2007 #R77 Dale Earnhardt Jr. FF
2008 #1 Dale Earnhardt Jr. CL
2008 #34 Dale Earnhardt Jr.
2008 #37 Dale Earnhardt Jr.'s Car M
2008 #49 Dale Earnhardt Jr. SW Shootout
2008 #51 Dale Earnhardt Jr. SW Duel
2008 #57 Dale Earnhardt Jr. EOP
2008 #71 Dale Earnhardt Jr. MD
2008 #75 Dale Earnhardt Jr. F
2008 #84 Dale Earnhardt Jr. OD
Press Pass Premium Red Reflectors
2002 #7 Dale Earnhardt, Jr.
2002 #36 Dale Earnhardt Jr.'s Car
2002 #60 Dale Earnhardt Jr. CH
2002 #71 Dale Earnhardt Jr. PC
2003 #7 Dale Earnhardt Jr.
2003 #36 Dale Earnhardt Jr.'s Car
2003 #46 Dale Earnhardt Jr.
2003 #48 Dale Earnhardt Jr.
2003 #50 Dale Jr./Park/Waltrip CL
2003 #59 Dale Earnhardt Jr. CC
2003 #70 Dale Earnhardt Jr.PC
Press Pass Premium Reflectors
1998 #12 Dale Earnhardt Jr.
1999 #R41 Dale Earnhardt Jr.
2000 #43 Dale Earnhardt Jr.
2000 #53 Dale Earnhardt Jr.
2000 #66 Dale Earnhardt Jr.
Press Pass Premium Samples
2002 #7 Dale Earnhardt, Jr.
2002 #36 Dale Earnhardt Jr.'s Car
2003 #7 Dale Earnhardt Jr.
2003 #36 Dale Earnhardt Jr.'s Car
2003 #46 Dale Earnhardt Jr.
2003 #48 Dale Earnhardt Jr.
2003 #50 Dale Jr./Park/Waltrip CL
2004 #1 Dale Earnhardt Jr.
2004 #39 Dale Earnhardt Jr.'s Car
2004 #46 Dale Earnhardt Jr. NS
2005 #5 Dale Earnhardt Jr.
Press Pass Premium Steel Horses
1999 #SH6 Dale Earnhardt Jr.'s Car
Press Pass Premium Target
2008 #TA5 Dale Earnhardt Jr.
Press Pass Premium Team Signed Baseballs
2008 #E-HMS Dale Earnhardt Jr. Jeff Gordon Jimmie Johnson Casey Mears Entry Card
2008 #HMS Dale Earnhardt Jr. Jeff Gordon Jimmie Johnson Casey Mears
Press Pass Premium Wal-Mart
2008 #WM1 Dale Earnhardt Jr.
Press Pass Previews
2003 #9 Dale Earnhardt Jr.
2004 #9 Dale Earnhardt Jr.
2006 #EB9 Dale Earnhardt Jr.
2006 #EB97 Dale Earnhardt Jr. U
2007 #EB6 Dale Earnhardt Jr.
2007 #EB113 Dale Earnhardt Jr. TT
2008 #EB13 Dale Earnhardt Jr.
2008 #EB96 Dale Earnhardt Jr. First Cup Start
2008 #EB97 Dale Earnhardt Jr. Rookie All-Star
2008 #EB98 Dale Earnhardt Jr. First Cup Win
2008 #EB99 Dale Earnhardt Jr. Best Finish
2008 #EB100 Dale Earnhardt Jr. Most Wins
2008 #EB101 Dale Earnhardt Jr. Daytona Win
2008 #EB102 Dale Earnhardt Jr. Talladega
2008 #EB103 Dale Earnhardt Jr. Daytona
Press Pass Previews Green
2005 #EB6 Dale Earnhardt Jr.
Press Pass Previews Silver
2005 #EB102 Dale Earnhardt Jr.
Press Pass Race Day
2007 #RD6 Dale Earnhardt Jr.
2008 #RD8 Dale Earnhardt Jr.
Press Pass Race Exclusives
2003 #1 Dale Earnhardt Jr.
Press Pass Samples
2003 #9 Dale Earnhardt Jr.
2003 #55 Dale Earnhardt Jr. DS
2003 #63 Jr./JJ/New/Sad/Ken/Bus DS
2003 #99 Dale Earnhardt Jr.'s Car OTW
2004 #9 Dale Earnhardt Jr.
2004 #66 Dale Earnhardt Jr.'s Car OTW
2004 #91 Dale Earnhardt Jr. DS
2005 #6 Dale Earnhardt Jr.
2005 #65 Dale Earnhardt's Car OTW
2005 #73 Dale Earnhardt Jr. NS
2005 #75 Dale Earnhardt Jr. NS
2005 #78 Dale Earnhardt Jr. NS
2005 #94 Dale Earnhardt Jr. Y
2005 #102 Dale Earnhardt Jr. P
2005 #109 Dale Earnhardt Jr.'s Car
2005 #113 Dale Earnhardt Jr's Car
2005 #120 Dale Jr/JJ/Gordon CL
Press Pass Schedule
2004 #3 Dale Earnhardt Jr.
Press Pass Showcar
2002 #S2A Dale Earnhardt Jr.'s Car
2004 #S4B Dale Earnhardt Jr.'s Car
2005 #SC4 Dale Earnhardt Jr.
Press Pass Showcar Die Cuts
2000 #SC4 Dale Earnhardt Jr.'s Car
Press Pass Showman
1999 #7A Dale Earnhardt Jr.
1999 #P1 Dale Earnhardt Jr. Promo
2000 #SM4 Dale Earnhardt Jr.
2000 #SM5 Dale Earnhardt Jr.
2002 #S2A Dale Earnhardt Jr.
2004 #S4A Dale Earnhardt Jr.
2005 #SM4 Dale Earnhardt Jr.
Press Pass Showman Die Cuts
2000 #SM4 Dale Earnhardt Jr.
2000 #SM5 Dale Earnhardt Jr.
Press Pass Showman/Showcar
2001 #S8A Dale Earnhardt Jr.
2001 #S8B Dale Earnhardt Jr.'s Car
Press Pass Signings
1998 #3 D.Earnhardt Jr. PPP/VIP/S
1999 #15A Dale Earnhardt Jr./875
2000 #15 Dale Earnhardt Jr.
2001 #12 Dale Earnhardt Jr. P/S/T/V
2002 #14 Dale Earnhardt Jr. P/T
2003 #17 Dale Jr. O/S/V/04PP
2004 #17 Dale Earnhardt Jr. O/T/V
2005 #13 Dale Earnhardt Jr.
2006 #14 Dale Earnhardt Jr. NC S
2006 #NNO Entry Card
2007 #17 Dale Earnhardt Jr. NC
2008 #15 Dale Earnhardt Jr. AMP
2008 #16 Dale Earnhardt Jr. NG
Press Pass Signings Blue
2007 #6 Dale Earnhardt Jr. NC
2008 #7 Dale Earnhardt Jr./8
Press Pass Signings Gold
1999 #4A D.Earnhardt Jr. Gold/85
1999 #4B D.Earnhardt Jr. Blue/125
2000 #10 Dale Earnhardt Jr.
2001 #11 Dale Earnhardt Jr.
2002 #14 Dale Earnhardt Jr.
2003 #17 Dale Jr. O/S/V/04PP
2004 #16 Dale Jr. O/P/S/T/V
2006 #12 Dale Earnhardt Jr. NC S
2007 #14 Dale Earnhardt Jr. NC
2008 #11 Dale Earnhardt Jr. AMP/25
2008 #12 Dale Earnhardt Jr. NG/25
Press Pass Signings Platinum
2005 #11 Dale Earnhardt Jr.
Press Pass Signings Press Plates Black
2007 #11 Dale Earnhardt Jr.
2008 #10 Dale Earnhardt Jr. AMP
2008 #11 Dale Earnhardt Jr. NG
Press Pass Signings Press Plates Cyan
2007 #10 Dale Earnhardt Jr.
2008 #10 Dale Earnhardt Jr. AMP
2008 #11 Dale Earnhardt Jr. NG
Press Pass Signings Press Plates Magenta
2007 #10 Dale Earnhardt Jr.
2008 #10 Dale Earnhardt Jr. AMP
2008 #11 Dale Earnhardt Jr. NG
Press Pass Signings Press Plates Yellow
2007 #10 Dale Earnhardt Jr.
2008 #10 Dale Earnhardt Jr. AMP
2008 #11 Dale Earnhardt Jr. NG
Press Pass Signings Red Ink
2006 #4 Dale Earnhardt Jr.
Press Pass Signings Silver
2006 #13 Dale Earnhardt Jr. NC S
2007 #13 Dale Earnhardt Jr. NC
2008 #12 Dale Earnhardt Jr. AMP/50
2008 #13 Dale Earnhardt Jr. NG/50
Press Pass Signings Transparent
2001 #3 Dale Earnhardt Jr.
2002 #1 Dale Earnhardt Jr.
Press Pass Skidmarks
1999 #37 Dale Earnhardt Jr.
1999 #58 Dale Earnhardt Jr. YR
1999 #73 Dale Earnhardt Jr. Champ
2000 #SK9 Dale Earnhardt Jr.
Press Pass Slideshow
2008 #SS12 Dale Earnhardt Jr.
2008 #SS36 Dale Earnhardt Jr.
Press Pass Snapshots
2004 #SN6 Dale Earnhardt Jr.
2005 #SN5 Dale Earnhardt Jr.
2006 #SN11 Dale Earnhardt Jr.
2007 #SN5 Dale Earnhardt Jr.
Press Pass Snapshots Extra
2005 #SS1 Dale Earnhardt Jr.
Press Pass Speedway
2008 #4 Dale Earnhardt Jr.
2008 #62 Dale Earnhardt Jr. SH
2008 #68 Dale Earnhardt Jr. UTH
2008 #77 Dale Earnhardt Jr.'s Car RSG
2008 #91 Dale Earnhardt Jr.'s Car H
Press Pass Speedway Blur
2008 #B3 Dale Earnhardt Jr.
Press Pass Speedway Garage Graphs Duals
2008 #EE Dale Earnhardt Jr. Tony Eury Jr.
Press Pass Speedway Gold
2008 #G4 Dale Earnhardt Jr.
2008 #G62 Dale Earnhardt Jr. SH
2008 #G68 Dale Earnhardt Jr. UTH
2008 #G77 Dale Earnhardt Jr.'s Car RSG
2008 #G91 Dale Earnhardt Jr.'s Car H
Press Pass Speedway Holofoil
2008 #H4 Dale Earnhardt Jr.
2008 #H62 Dale Earnhardt Jr. SH
2008 #H68 Dale Earnhardt Jr. UTH
2008 #H77 Dale Earnhardt Jr.'s Car RSG
2008 #H91 Dale Earnhardt Jr.'s Car H
Press Pass Speedway Previews
2008 #EB4 Dale Earnhardt Jr.
2008 #EB91 Dale Earnhardt Jr.'s Car H
Press Pass Speedway Red
2008 #R4 Dale Earnhardt Jr.
2008 #R62 Dale Earnhardt Jr. SH
2008 #R68 Dale Earnhardt Jr. UTH
2008 #R77 Dale Earnhardt Jr.'s Car RSG
2008 #R91 Dale Earnhardt Jr.'s Car H
Press Pass Speedway Test Drive
2008 #TD7 Dale Earnhardt Jr.
Press Pass Stealth
1998 #37 Dale Earnhardt Jr.
1998 #60 Dale Earnhardt Jr. CL
1999 #39 Dale Earnhardt Jr.
2000 #16 Dale Earnhardt Jr. CRC
2000 #17 Dale Earnhardt Jr.'s Car
2000 #70 Dale Earnhardt Jr. FF
2001 #13 Dale Earnhardt Jr.
2001 #14 Dale Earnhardt Jr.'s Car
2001 #15 Dale Earnhardt Jr.
2001 #66 Dale Earnhardt Jr. SST
2002 #10 Dale Earnhardt Jr.
2002 #11 Dale Earnhardt Jr.'s Car
2002 #12 Dale Earnhardt Jr.
2002 #55 Dale Earnhardt Jr.'s Car SST
2002 #64 Dale Earnhardt Jr. WW
2003 #10 Dale Earnhardt Jr.
2003 #11 Dale Earnhardt Jr.'s Car
2003 #12 Dale Earnhardt Jr.
2003 #57 Dale Earnhardt Jr. SST
2003 #72 Dale Jr./M.Kenseth CL
2004 #52 Dale Earnhardt Jr.
2004 #53 Dale Earnhardt Jr.'s Car
2004 #54 Dale Earnhardt Jr.
2004 #83 Dale Earnhardt Jr. SST
2004 #99 Dale Earnhardt Jr. SF
2005 #38 Dale Earnhardt Jr.
2005 #41 Dale Earnhardt Jr.'s Car
2005 #44 Dale Earnhardt Jr.
2005 #83 Dale Earnhardt Jr. H
2006 #6 Dale Earnhardt Jr.
2006 #47 Dale Earnhardt Jr.'s Rig
2006 #52 Truex Jr./Dale Jr. TM
2006 #57 Dale Earnhardt Jr. F
2006 #71 Dale Earnhardt Jr. DD
2007 #6 Dale Earnhardt Jr.
2007 #47 Dale Jr.'s Rig
2007 #57 Dale Jr.'s Crew PC
2007 #71 Truex/Dale Jr./Menard
2007 #82 Dale Earnhardt Jr. PO
2007 #90 Dale Earnhardt Jr. CL
2008 #8 Dale Earnhardt Jr.
2008 #53 Dale Earnhardt Jr.'s Rig C
2008 #67 Jimmie Johnson Jeff Gordon Dale Earnhardt Jr. Casey Mears
2008 #83 Dale Earnhardt Jr. PM
Press Pass Stealth Autographed Hat Entry
2006 #PPH5 Dale Earnhardt Jr.
Press Pass Stealth Battle Armor Autographs
2007 #BAS-DE Dale Earnhardt Jr./8
Press Pass Stealth Battle Armor Drivers
2007 #BAD6 Dale Earnhardt Jr.
2008 #BAD23 Dale Earnhardt Jr.
Press Pass Stealth Battle Armor Teams
2007 #BAT6 Dale Earnhardt Jr.
2008 #BAT23 Dale Earnhardt Jr.
Press Pass Stealth Behind the Numbers
2000 #BN2 Dale Earnhardt Jr.
Press Pass Stealth Big Numbers
1999 #BN4 Dale Earnhardt Jr.
1999 #BN5 Dale Earnhardt Jr.
Press Pass Stealth Big Numbers Die Cuts
1999 #BN4 Dale Earnhardt Jr.
1999 #BN5 Dale Earnhardt Jr.
Press Pass Stealth Chrome
2007 #6 Dale Earnhardt Jr.
2007 #47 Dale Jr.'s Rig
2007 #57 Dale Jr.'s Crew PC
2007 #71 Truex/Dale Jr./Menard
2007 #82 Dale Earnhardt Jr. PO
2007 #90 Dale Earnhardt Jr. CL
2007 #6A Dale Earnhardt Jr. L1 2-white dots
2007 #6B Dale Earnhardt Jr. L2 2-white dots w/line
2008 #8 Dale Earnhardt Jr.
2008 #53 Dale Earnhardt Jr.'s Rig C
2008 #67 Jimmie Johnson Jeff Gordon Dale Earnhardt Jr. Casey Mears
2008 #83 Dale Earnhardt Jr. PM
2008 #83B Dale Earnhardt Jr. PM VAR
Press Pass Stealth Chrome Exclusives
2007 #X6 Dale Earnhardt Jr.
2007 #X47 Dale Jr.'s Rig
2007 #X57 Dale Jr.'s Crew PC
2007 #X71 Truex/Dale Jr./Menard
2007 #X82 Dale Earnhardt Jr. PO
2007 #X90 Dale Earnhardt Jr. CL
2008 #8 Dale Earnhardt Jr.
2008 #53 Dale Earnhardt Jr.'s Rig C
2008 #67 Jimmie Johnson Jeff Gordon Dale Earnhardt Jr. Casey Mears
2008 #83 Dale Earnhardt Jr. PM
Press Pass Stealth Chrome Exclusives Gold
2008 #8 Dale Earnhardt Jr.
2008 #53 Dale Earnhardt Jr.'s Rig C
2008 #67 Jimmie Johnson Jeff Gordon Dale Earnhardt Jr. Casey Mears
2008 #83 Dale Earnhardt Jr. PM
Press Pass Stealth Chrome Platinum
2007 #P6 Dale Earnhardt Jr.
2007 #P47 Dale Jr.'s Rig
2007 #P57 Dale Jr.'s Crew PC
2007 #P71 Truex/Dale Jr./Menard
2007 #P82 Dale Earnhardt Jr. PO
2007 #P90 Dale Earnhardt Jr. CL
Press Pass Stealth Corporate Cuts
2006 #CCD3 Dale Earnhardt Jr.
Press Pass Stealth EFX
2002 #FX4 Dale Earnhardt Jr.
2003 #FX3 Dale Earnhardt Jr.
2004 #EF1 Dale Earnhardt Jr.
2006 #EFX2 Dale Earnhardt Jr. 1:112
Press Pass Stealth Fusion
1998 #37 Dale Earnhardt Jr.
1998 #60 Dale Earnhardt Jr. CL
1999 #F39 Dale Earnhardt Jr.
2000 #FS16 Dale Earnhardt Jr.
2000 #FS17 Dale Earnhardt Jr.'s Car
2000 #FS18 Dale Earnhardt Jr.
2001 #F1 Dale Earnhardt Jr.
2002 #F2 Dale Earnhardt Jr.
2003 #FU3 Dale Earnhardt Jr.
2004 #FU3 Dale Earnhardt Jr.
2007 #F7 Dale Earnhardt Jr.
Press Pass Stealth Fusion Green
2000 #FS16 Dale Earnhardt Jr.
2000 #FS17 Dale Earnhardt Jr.
2000 #FS18 Dale Earnhardt Jr.
Press Pass Stealth Fusion Red
2000 #FS16 Dale Earnhardt Jr.
2000 #FS17 Dale Earnhardt Jr.
2000 #FS18 Dale Earnhardt Jr.
Press Pass Stealth Gear Grippers Autographs
2004 #HT-DE Dale Earnhardt Jr./8
2005 #GG-DE Dale Earnhardt Jr./8
2006 #DE Dale Earnhardt Jr./8
Press Pass Stealth Gear Grippers Cars
2003 #GGT10 Dale Earnhardt Jr.
2005 #GGT18 Dale Earnhardt Jr.
Press Pass Stealth Gear Grippers Drivers
2003 #GGD10 Dale Earnhardt Jr.
2004 #GGD9 Dale Earnhardt Jr.
2005 #GGD18 Dale Earnhardt Jr.
2006 #GGD6 Dale Earnhardt Jr.
Press Pass Stealth Gear Grippers Drivers Retail
2004 #GGT9 Dale Earnhardt Jr.
Press Pass Stealth Gold
2002 #10 Dale Earnhardt Jr.
2002 #11 Dale Earnhardt Jr.'s Car
2002 #12 Dale Earnhardt Jr.
2002 #55 Dale Earnhardt Jr.'s Car SST
2002 #64 Dale Earnhardt Jr. WW
Press Pass Stealth Headlines
1999 #SH3 Dale Earnhardt Jr.
1999 #SH7 Dale Earnhardt Jr.
Press Pass Stealth Holofoils
2001 #13 Dale Earnhardt Jr.
2001 #14 Dale Earnhardt Jr.'s Car
2001 #15 Dale Earnhardt Jr.
2001 #66 Dale Earnhardt Jr. SST
Press Pass Stealth Hot Pass
2006 #HP7 Dale Earnhardt Jr.
Press Pass Stealth Intensity
2000 #IN9 Dale Earnhardt Jr.
Press Pass Stealth Lap Leaders
2001 #LL4 Dale Earnhardt Jr.
2001 #LL22 Dale Earnhardt Jr.'s Car
2002 #LL6 Dale Earnhardt Jr.
Press Pass Stealth Lap Leaders Clear Cars
2001 #LL22 Dale Earnhardt Jr.'s Car
Press Pass Stealth Lap Leaders Clear Drivers
2001 #LL4 Dale Earnhardt Jr.
Press Pass Stealth Mach 07
2007 #M7-1 Dale Earnhardt Jr.
Press Pass Stealth Mach 08
2008 #M8-2 Dale Earnhardt Jr.
Press Pass Stealth Maximum Access
2007 #MA6 Dale Earnhardt Jr.
2008 #MA8 Dale Earnhardt Jr.
Press Pass Stealth Maximum Access Autographs
2007 #MA6 Dale Earnhardt Jr.
2008 #MA8 Dale Earnhardt Jr.
Press Pass Stealth No Boundaries
2003 #NB11 Dale Earnhardt Jr.
2004 #NB11 Dale Earnhardt Jr.
2005 #NB15 Dale Earnhardt Jr.
Press Pass Stealth Octane SLX
1999 #O4 Dale Earnhardt Jr.
1999 #O5 Dale Earnhardt Jr.
1999 #O24 Dale Earnhardt Jr.'s Car
1999 #O25 Dale Earnhardt Jr.'s Car
Press Pass Stealth Octane SLX Die Cuts
1999 #O4 Dale Earnhardt Jr.
1999 #O5 Dale Earnhardt Jr.
1999 #O24 Dale Earnhardt Jr.'s Car
1999 #O25 Dale Earnhardt Jr.'s Car
Press Pass Stealth Previews
2003 #10 Dale Earnhardt Jr.
2003 #11 Dale Earnhardt Jr.'s Car
2003 #12 Dale Earnhardt Jr.
2005 #38 Dale Earnhardt Jr.
2005 #41 Dale Earnhardt Jr.'s Car
2005 #44 Dale Earnhardt Jr.
2006 #6 Dale Earnhardt Jr.
2007 #EB90 Dale Earnhardt Jr. CL
2007 #EB82 Dale Earnhardt Jr. PO
2007 #EB6 Dale Earnhardt Jr.
2008 #8 Dale Earnhardt Jr.
2008 #83 Dale Earnhardt Jr. PM
Press Pass Stealth Profile
2000 #PR8 Dale Earnhardt Jr.
2001 #SP6 Dale Earnhardt Jr.
2003 #PR1 Dale Earnhardt Jr.
2004 #P3 Dale Earnhardt Jr. 1:112
2005 #PR3 Dale Earnhardt Jr.
2006 #P1 Dale Earnhardt Jr.
Press Pass Stealth Race Used Glove Cars
2001 #RGC8 Dale Earnhardt Jr./50
2002 #GLC7 Dale Earnhardt Jr.'s Car
Press Pass Stealth Race Used Glove Drivers
2001 #RGD8 Dale Earnhardt Jr./50
2002 #GLD7 Dale Earnhardt Jr.
Press Pass Stealth Race Used Gloves
2000 #G8 Dale Earnhardt Jr./50
Press Pass Stealth Red
2003 #P10 Dale Earnhardt Jr.
2003 #P11 Dale Earnhardt Jr.'s Car
2003 #P12 Dale Earnhardt Jr.
2003 #P57 Dale Earnhardt Jr. SST
2003 #P72 Dale Jr./M.Kenseth CL
Press Pass Stealth Retail
2006 #6 Dale Earnhardt Jr.
2006 #47 Dale Earnhardt Jr.'s Rig
2006 #52 Truex Jr./Dale Jr. TM
2006 #57 Dale Earnhardt Jr. F
2006 #71 Dale Earnhardt Jr. DD
Press Pass Stealth Retail Gear Grippers Cars
2006 #GGT6 Dale Earnhardt Jr.
Press Pass Stealth Samples
2002 #10 Dale Earnhardt Jr.
2002 #11 Dale Earnhardt Jr.'s Car
2002 #12 Dale Earnhardt Jr.
2002 #55 Dale Earnhardt Jr.'s Car SST
2002 #64 Dale Earnhardt Jr. WW
2003 #10 Dale Earnhardt Jr.
2003 #11 Dale Earnhardt Jr.'s Car
2003 #12 Dale Earnhardt Jr.
2003 #57 Dale Earnhardt Jr. SST
2003 #72 Dale Jr./M.Kenseth CL
2004 #X52 Dale Earnhardt Jr.
2004 #X54 Dale Earnhardt Jr.
2004 #X53 Dale Earnhardt Jr.'s Car
2004 #X83 Dale Earnhardt Jr. SST
2004 #X99 Dale Earnhardt Jr. SF
2005 #38 Dale Earnhardt Jr.
2005 #41 Dale Earnhardt Jr.'s Car
2005 #44 Dale Earnhardt Jr.
2005 #83 Dale Earnhardt Jr. H
Press Pass Stealth SST
2000 #SST12 Dale Earnhardt Jr.
Press Pass Stealth SST Cars
1999 #SS1 Dale Earnhardt Jr.'s Car
Press Pass Stealth SST Drivers
1999 #SS1 Dale Earnhardt Jr.
Press Pass Stealth Stars
1998 #3 Dale Earnhardt Jr.
Press Pass Stealth Stars Die Cuts
1998 #3 Dale Earnhardt Jr.
Press Pass Stealth Supercharged
2003 #SC3 Dale Earnhardt Jr.
Press Pass Stealth Synthesis
2008 #S7 Dale Earnhardt Jr.
Press Pass Stealth X-Ray
2004 #52 Dale Earnhardt Jr.
2004 #53 Dale Earnhardt Jr.'s Car
2004 #54 Dale Earnhardt Jr.
2004 #83 Dale Earnhardt Jr. SST
2004 #99 Dale Earnhardt Jr. SF
2005 #X38 Dale Earnhardt Jr.
2005 #X41 Dale Earnhardt Jr.'s Car
2005 #X44 Dale Earnhardt Jr.
2005 #X83 Dale Earnhardt Jr. H
2006 #X6 Dale Earnhardt Jr.
2006 #X47 Dale Earnhardt Jr.'s Rig
2006 #X52 Truex Jr./Dale Jr. TM
2006 #X57 Dale Earnhardt Jr. F
2006 #X71 Dale Earnhardt Jr. DD
Press Pass Target
2007 #DE-B Dale Earnhardt Jr.
2008 #DE-B Dale Earnhardt Jr.
Press Pass Target Race Win Tires
2007 #RW3 Dale Earnhardt Jr. Richmond 5-6
Press Pass Techno-Retro

2000 #TR7 Dale Earnhardt Jr.
Press Pass Top 25 Drivers & Rides
2006 #C6 Dale Earnhardt Jr.'s Car
2006 #D6 Dale Earnhardt Jr.
Press Pass Top Shelf
2002 #TS1 Dale Earnhardt Jr.
2003 #TS1 Dale Earnhardt Jr.
2004 #TS3 Dale Earnhardt Jr.
Press Pass Top Ten
2005 #TT3 Dale Earnhardt Jr.
Press Pass Total Memorabilia
2001 #TM8 Dale Earnhardt Jr.
Press Pass Total Memorabilia Power Pick
2002 #TM1 Dale Earnhardt Jr.
2003 #TM10 Dale Earnhardt Jr.
2004 #TM10 Dale Earnhardt Jr.
2005 #TM10 Dale Earnhardt Jr.
Press Pass Trackside
2000 #6 Dale Earnhardt Jr. CRC
2000 #29 Dale Earnhardt Jr.'s Car
2001 #1 Dale Earnhardt Jr.
2001 #43 Dale Earnhardt Jr.'s Car
2002 #1 Dale Earnhardt Jr.
2002 #52 Dale Earnhardt Jr. RD
2002 #67 Dale Earnhardt Jr.'s Car
2002 #73 Dale Earnhardt Jr. TM
2002 #90 Dale Jr./K.Earnhardt CL
2003 #19 Dale Earnhardt Jr.
2003 #62 Dale Earnhardt Jr. in Pits
2004 #19 Dale Earnhardt Jr.
2004 #53 Dale Earnhardt Jr.'s Car HS
2004 #72 Dale Jr./M.Waltrip TM
2004 #100 Dale Earnhardt Jr. TT
2004 #109 Dale Earnhardt Jr. F
2005 #2 Dale Earnhardt Jr.
2005 #28 Dale Earnhardt Jr. no car
2005 #82 Dale Earnhardt Jr. GP
2005 #94 Dale Earnhardt Jr. F
2005 #100 Dale Earnhardt Jr. CL
Press Pass Trackside Dialed In
2000 #DI12 Dale Earnhardt Jr.
2001 #D8 Dale Earnhardt Jr.
2002 #DI2 Dale Earnhardt, Jr.
2004 #DI2 Dale Earnhardt Jr.
Press Pass Trackside Die Cuts
2000 #6 Dale Earnhardt Jr.
2000 #29 Dale Earnhardt Jr.
2001 #1 Dale Earnhardt Jr.
2001 #43 Dale Earnhardt Jr.'s Car
Press Pass Trackside Generation Now
2002 #GN3 Dale Earnhardt Jr.
Press Pass Trackside Generation.now
2000 #GN2 Dale Earnhardt Jr.
Press Pass Trackside Gold Holofoil
2003 #P19 Dale Earnhardt Jr.
2003 #P62 Dale Jr.'s Crew
Press Pass Trackside Golden
2000 #6 Dale Earnhardt Jr.
2000 #29 Dale Earnhardt Jr.
2001 #1 Dale Earnhardt Jr.
2001 #43 Dale Earnhardt Jr.'s Car
2002 #G1 Dale Earnhardt Jr.
2003 #G19 Dale Earnhardt Jr.
2004 #G19 Dale Earnhardt Jr.
2004 #G53 Dale Earnhardt Jr.'s Car HS
2004 #G72 D.Earnhardt Jr./M.Waltrip TM
2004 #G100 Dale Earnhardt Jr. TT
2004 #G109 Dale Earnhardt Jr. F
2005 #G2 Dale Earnhardt Jr.
2005 #G82 Dale Earnhardt Jr. GP
2005 #G94 Dale Earnhardt Jr. F
2005 #G100 Dale Earnhardt Jr. CL
Press Pass Trackside Hat Giveaway
2004 #PPH6 Dale Earnhardt Jr.
2005 #PPH6 Dale Earnhardt Jr.
Press Pass Trackside Hot Pass
2004 #HP5 Dale Earnhardt Jr.
2005 #3 Dale Earnhardt Jr.
Press Pass Trackside Hot Pass National
2004 #HP5 Dale Earnhardt Jr.
2005 #3 Dale Earnhardt Jr.
Press Pass Trackside Hot Pursuit
2003 #HP2 Dale Earnhardt Jr.
2004 #HP1 Dale Earnhardt Jr.
Press Pass Trackside License to Drive
2002 #8 Dale Earnhardt Jr.
Press Pass Trackside License to Drive Die Cuts
2002 #8 Dale Earnhardt Jr.
Press Pass Trackside Mirror Image
2001 #MI8 Dale Earnhardt Jr.
2002 #MI1 Dale Earnhardt Jr.
2003 #MI2 Dale Earnhardt Jr.
Press Pass Trackside Pit Stoppers
2000 #PS13 Dale Earnhardt Jr.
Press Pass Trackside Pit Stoppers Autographs
2004 #PS-DE Dale Earnhardt Jr./8
2005 #PSDE Dale Earnhardt Jr./8
Press Pass Trackside Pit Stoppers Cars
2001 #PSC1 D.Earnhardt Jr.'s Car/250
2002 #PSC4 D.Earnhardt Jr.'s Car/50
2003 #PST18 Dale Earnhardt Jr.
2004 #PST15 Dale Earnhardt Jr.
2005 #PST14 Dale Earnhardt Jr.
Press Pass Trackside Pit Stoppers Drivers
2001 #PSD1 Dale Earnhardt Jr./100
2002 #PSD4 Dale Earnhardt Jr./50
2003 #PSD18 Dale Earnhardt Jr.
2004 #PSD15 Dale Earnhardt Jr.
2005 #PSD14 Dale Earnhardt Jr.
Press Pass Trackside Previews
2003 #19 Dale Earnhardt Jr.
2004 #EB19 Dale Earnhardt Jr.
2005 #2 Dale Earnhardt Jr.
2005 #82 Dale Earnhardt Jr. GP
Press Pass Trackside Runnin N' Gunnin
2000 #RG2 Dale Earnhardt Jr.
2001 #RG2 Dale Earnhardt Jr.
2002 #RG1 Dale Earnhardt, Jr.
2003 #RG2 Dale Earnhardt Jr.
2004 #RG1 Dale Earnhardt Jr.
2005 #RG1 Dale Earnhardt Jr.
Press Pass Trackside Samples
2002 #1 Dale Earnhardt Jr.
2002 #52 Dale Earnhardt Jr. RD
2002 #67 Dale Earnhardt Jr.'s Car
2002 #73 Dale Earnhardt Jr. TM
2002 #90 Dale Jr./K.Earnhardt CL
2003 #19 Dale Earnhardt Jr.
2003 #62 Dale Earnhardt Jr. in Pits
2004 #19 Dale Earnhardt Jr.
2004 #53 Dale Earnhardt Jr.'s Car HS
2004 #72 D.Earnhardt Jr./M.Waltrip TM
2004 #100 Dale Earnhardt Jr. TT
2004 #109 Dale Earnhardt Jr. F
2005 #2 Dale Earnhardt Jr.
2005 #82 Dale Earnhardt Jr. GP
2005 #94 Dale Earnhardt Jr. F
2005 #100 Dale Earnhardt Jr. CL
Press Pass Trackside Too Tough To Tame
2000 #TT9 Dale Earnhardt Jr.
Press Pass Triple Burner
2001 #TB8 Dale Earnhardt Jr.
2002 #TB1 Dale Earnhardt Jr.
2003 #TB10 Dale Earnhardt Jr.
2004 #TB10 Dale Earnhardt Jr.
2005 #TB10 Dale Earnhardt Jr.
Press Pass Triple Burner Exchange
2003 #TB10 Dale Earnhardt Jr. EXCH
2004 #TB10 Dale Earnhardt Jr.
2005 #TB10 Dale Earnhardt Jr.
Press Pass Velocity
2001 #VL8 Dale Earnhardt Jr.
2002 #VL2 Dale Earnhardt Jr.
2004 #VC8 Dale Earnhardt Jr.
2005 #V7 Dale Earnhardt Jr.
2006 #VE1 Dale Earnhardt Jr.
2007 #V4 Dale Earnhardt Jr.
Press Pass Vintage
2001 #VN15 Dale Earnhardt Jr.
2002 #VN6 Dale Earnhardt Jr.
Press Pass Wal-Mart
2007 #DE-A Dale Earnhardt Jr.
2008 #DE-A Dale Earnhardt Jr.
Press Pass Wal-Mart Autographs
2008 #1 Dale Earnhardt Jr.
Press Pass Weekend Warriors
2008 #WW5 Dale Earnhardt Jr.
SLU Racing Winner's Circle
1999 #12 D.Earnhardt Jr. Coca Cola
1999 #13 D.Earnhardt Jr. AC Delco
SLU Racing Winner's Circle 12-inch Figures
2000 #20 Dale Earnhardt Jr.
SP Authentic
1999 #30 Dale Earnhardt Jr.
1999 #37 Dale Earnhardt Jr.'s Car
1999 #66 Dale Earnhardt Jr. CLASS
1999 #72 Dale Earnhardt Jr. CL
1999 #83 D.Earnhardt Jr. SP AU/500
2000 #19 Dale Earnhardt Jr. CRC
2000 #89 Dale Earnhardt Jr. SUP
SP Authentic Dominance
2000 #D2 Dale Earnhardt Jr.
SP Authentic Driving Force
1999 #DF9 Dale Earnhardt Jr.
SP Authentic In the Driver's Seat
1999 #DS7 Dale Earnhardt Jr.
SP Authentic Overdrive
1999 #30 Dale Earnhardt Jr.
1999 #37 Dale Earnhardt Jr. CAR
1999 #66 Dale Earnhardt Jr. CLASS
1999 #72 Dale Earnhardt Jr. CL
1999 #83 D.Earnhardt Jr. SP AU/3
SP Authentic Overdrive Gold
2000 #19 Dale Earnhardt Jr./8
2000 #89 Dale Earnhardt Jr. SUP/8
SP Authentic Overdrive Silver
2000 #19 Dale Earnhardt Jr.
2000 #89 Dale Earnhardt Jr. SUP
SP Authentic Power Surge
2000 #PS4 Dale Earnhardt Jr.
SP Authentic Sign of the Times
1999 #DEJ Dale Earnhardt Jr.
2000 #JR Dale Earnhardt Jr.
SP Authentic Sign of the Times Gold
2000 #JR Dale Earnhardt Jr.
Sports Illustrated for Kids
2002 #126 Dale Earnhardt Jr. Nascar
Sports Illustrated for Kids *
2001-02 #126 Dale Earnhardt Jr.
TRAKS
2006 #7 Dale Earnhardt Jr.
2006 #40 Dale Earnhardt Jr.'s Car
2007 #5 Dale Earnhardt Jr.
2007 #73 Dale Earnhardt Jr. MG
2007 #79 Dale Earnhardt Jr. GP
2007 #83 Dale Jr.'s Car NFS
2007 #93 Dale Earnhardt Jr. FT
TRAKS Autographs
2006 #8 Dale Earnhardt Jr. NC SP
TRAKS Autographs 25
2006 #8 Dale Earnhardt Jr. NC
Traks Corporate Cuts Driver
2007 #CCD12 Dale Earnhardt Jr.
Traks Corporate Cuts Patch
2007 #CCD12 Dale Earnhardt Jr./8
Traks Corporate Cuts Team
2007 #CCT12 Dale Earnhardt Jr.
Traks Driver's Seat
2007 #DS14B Dale Earnhardt Jr. VAR
2007 #DS14 Dale Earnhardt Jr.
Traks Driver's Seat National
2007 #DS14 Dale Earnhardt Jr.
Traks Gold
2007 #G5 Dale Earnhardt Jr.
2007 #G73 Dale Earnhardt Jr. MG
2007 #G79 Dale Earnhardt Jr. GP
2007 #G83 Dale Jr.'s Car NFS
2007 #G93 Dale Earnhardt Jr. FT
Traks Holofoil
2007 #H5 Dale Earnhardt Jr.
2007 #H73 Dale Earnhardt Jr. MG
2007 #H79 Dale Earnhardt Jr. GP
2007 #H83 Dale Jr.'s Car NFS
2007 #H93 Dale Earnhardt Jr. FT
Traks Hot Pursuit
2007 #HP10 Dale Earnhardt Jr.
Traks Previews
2007 #EB5 Dale Earnhardt Jr.
2007 #EB79 Dale Earnhardt Jr. GP
Traks Red
2007 #R5 Dale Earnhardt Jr.
2007 #R73 Dale Earnhardt Jr. MG
2007 #R79 Dale Earnhardt Jr. GP
2007 #R83 Dale Jr.'s Car NFS
2007 #R93 Dale Earnhardt Jr. FT
TRAKS Stickers
2006 #8 Dale Earnhardt Jr.
Traks Target Exclusives
2007 #DE-A Dale Earnhardt Jr.
Traks Track Time
2007 #TT1 Dale Earnhardt Jr.
Traks Wal-Mart Exclusives
2007 #DE-B Dale Earnhardt Jr.
Upper Deck MVP
2000 #93 Dale Earnhardt Jr.
2000 #98 Dale Earnhardt Jr.'s Car
Upper Deck MVP Cup Quest 2000
2000 #CQ2 Dale Earnhardt Jr.
Upper Deck MVP Gold Script
2000 #93 Dale Earnhardt Jr.
2000 #98 Dale Earnhardt Jr.
Upper Deck MVP Legends in the Making
2000 #LM5 Dale Earnhardt Jr.
Upper Deck MVP NASCAR Gallery
2000 #NG5 Dale Earnhardt Jr.
Upper Deck MVP NASCAR Stars
2000 #NS11 Dale Earnhardt Jr.
Upper Deck MVP ProSign
1999 #JR Dale Earnhardt Jr.
2000 #PSJR Dale Earnhardt Jr.
Upper Deck MVP Silver Script
2000 #93 Dale Earnhardt Jr.
2000 #98 Dale Earnhardt Jr.
Upper Deck MVP Super Script
2000 #93 Dale Earnhardt Jr./3
2000 #98 Dale Earnhardt Jr.'s Car/8
Upper Deck Racing
2000 #31 Dale Earnhardt Jr. CRC
Upper Deck Racing High Groove
2000 #HG2 Dale Earnhardt Jr.
Upper Deck Racing Record Pace
2000 #RP6 Dale Earnhardt Jr.
Upper Deck Racing Road Signs
2000 #RSJR Dale Earnhardt Jr.
Upper Deck Racing Speeding Ticket
2000 #ST3 Dale Earnhardt Jr.
Upper Deck Racing Trophy Dash
2000 #TD2 Dale Earnhardt Jr.
Upper Deck Road To The Cup
1998 #83 Dale Earnhardt Jr.'s Car
1998 #94 Dale Earnhardt Jr.'s Car
1999 #30 Dale Earnhardt Jr.
1999 #37 Dale Earnhardt Jr.'s Car
1999 #67 Dale Earnhardt Jr. FF
1999 #90 Dale Earnhardt Jr. CL
Upper Deck Road to the Cup NASCAR Chronicles
1999 #NC14 Dale Earnhardt Jr.
Upper Deck Road to the Cup Road to the Cup Bronze Level 1
1999 #RTTC10 Dale Earnhardt Jr.
Upper Deck Road to the Cup Road to the Cup Gold Level 3
1999 #RTTC10 Dale Earnhardt Jr.
Upper Deck Road to the Cup Road to the Cup Silver Level 2
1999 #RTTC10 Dale Earnhardt Jr.
Upper Deck Road to the Cup Signature Collection
1999 #DEJR Dale Earnhardt Jr.
Upper Deck Road to the Cup Signature Collection Checkered Flag
1999 #DEJR Dale Earnhardt Jr.
Upper Deck Road to the Cup Upper Deck Profiles
1999 #P10 Dale Earnhardt Jr.
Upper Deck Victory Circle
1999 #14 Dale Earnhardt Jr.
1999 #50 Dale Earnhardt Jr.'s Car
1999 #85 Dale Earnhardt Jr.
2000 #37 Dale Earnhardt Jr. CRC
2000 #56 Dale Earnhardt Jr.'s Car
2000 #78 Dale Earnhardt Jr.'s Car
Upper Deck Victory Circle A Day in the Life
2000 #JR1 Dale Earnhardt Jr.
2000 #JR2 Dale Earnhardt Jr.
2000 #JR3 Dale Earnhardt Jr.
2000 #JR4 Dale Earnhardt Jr.
2000 #JR5 Dale Earnhardt Jr.
2000 #JR6 Dale Earnhardt Jr.
Upper Deck Victory Circle A Day in the Life LTD
2000 #JR1 Dale Earnhardt Jr.
2000 #JR2 Dale Earnhardt Jr.
2000 #JR3 Dale Earnhardt Jr.
2000 #JR4 Dale Earnhardt Jr.
2000 #JR5 Dale Earnhardt Jr.
2000 #JR6 Dale Earnhardt Jr.
Upper Deck Victory Circle Exclusives Level 1 Silver
2000 #37 Dale Earnhardt Jr.
2000 #56 Dale Earnhardt Jr.'s Car
2000 #78 Dale Earnhardt Jr.'s Car
Upper Deck Victory Circle Exclusives Level 2 Gold
2000 #37 Dale Earnhardt Jr./8
2000 #56 Dale Earnhardt Jr.'s Car/8
2000 #78 Dale Earnhardt Jr.'s Car/8
Upper Deck Victory Circle Income Statement
1999 #IS15 Dale Earnhardt Jr.
Upper Deck Victory Circle PowerDeck
2000 #PD2 Dale Earnhardt Jr.
2000 #PD6 Dale Earnhardt Jr.
Upper Deck Victory Circle Signature Collection
1999 #DEJ Dale Earnhardt Jr.
Upper Deck Victory Circle Speed Zone
1999 #SZ10 Dale Earnhardt Jr.
Upper Deck Victory Circle Track Masters
1999 #TM15 Dale Earnhardt Jr.
Upper Deck Victory Circle UD Exclusives
1999 #14 Dale Earnhardt Jr.
1999 #50 Dale Earnhardt Jr.
1999 #85 Dale Earnhardt Jr.
Upper Deck Victory Circle Victory Circle
2000 #V9 Dale Earnhardt Jr.
Upper Deck Victory Circle Victory Circle LTD
2000 #V9 Dale Earnhardt Jr.
Upper Deck Victory Circle Winning Material Tire
2000 #TJR Dale Earnhardt Jr.
VIP
1998 #28 Dale Earnhardt Jr.
1999 #30 Dale Earnhardt Jr.
2000 #17 Dale Earnhardt Jr. CRC
2000 #24 Dale Earnhardt Jr. V
2000 #P1 Dale Earnhardt Jr. Promo
2001 #17 Dale Earnhardt Jr.
2001 #45 Dale Earnhardt Jr. AS
2002 #5 Dale Earnhardt Jr.
2002 #26 Dale Earnhardt Jr. SG
2002 #33 Dale Earnhardt Jr. AS
2003 #4 Dale Earnhardt Jr.
2003 #26 Dale Earnhardt Jr. SG
2003 #31 Dale Earnhardt Jr. AS
2004 #4 Dale Earnhardt Jr.
2004 #28 Dale Earnhardt Jr.'s Car R
2004 #43 Dale Earnhardt Jr. SG
2004 #46 Dale Earnhardt Jr. SG
2004 #53 Dale Earnhardt Jr. SG
2004 #55 Dale Earnhardt Jr. HR
2004 #77 Dale Earnhardt Jr. BTN
2004 #90 Dale Earnhardt Jr. CL
2005 #5 Dale Earnhardt Jr.
2005 #33 Dale Earnhardt Jr.'s Car R
2005 #73 Dale Earnhardt Jr. BN
2006 #5 Dale Earnhardt Jr.
2006 #49 Dale Earnhardt Jr. SG
2006 #54 Dale Earnhardt Jr. BTN
2006 #83 Dale Earnhardt Jr. IF
2007 #7 Dale Earnhardt Jr.
2007 #50 Dale Earnhardt Jr.'s Car SV
2007 #67 Dale Earnhardt Jr. Red C
VIP Double Take
1999 #DT4 Dale Earnhardt Jr.
VIP Driver's Choice
2001 #DC4 Dale Earnhardt Jr.
2002 #DC4 Dale Earnhardt Jr.
2003 #DC2 Dale Earnhardt Jr.
2004 #DC2 Dale Earnhardt Jr.
2005 #DC2 Dale Earnhardt Jr.
VIP Driver's Choice Die Cuts
2003 #DC2 Dale Earnhardt Jr.
2004 #DC2 Dale Earnhardt Jr.
2005 #DC2 Dale Earnhardt Jr.
VIP Driver's Choice National
2003 #DC2 Dale Earnhardt Jr.
VIP Driver's Choice Precious Metal
2001 #DC4 Dale Earnhardt Jr.
VIP Driver's Choice Transparent
2001 #DC4 Dale Earnhardt Jr.
2002 #DC4 Dale Earnhardt Jr.
VIP Driver's Choice Transparent LTD
2002 #DC4 Dale Earnhardt Jr.
VIP Explosives
1998 #28 Dale Earnhardt Jr.
1999 #X30 Dale Earnhardt Jr.
2000 #X17 Dale Earnhardt Jr.
2000 #X24 Dale Earnhardt Jr. V
2001 #17 Dale Earnhardt Jr.
2001 #45 Dale Earnhardt Jr. AS
2002 #X5 Dale Earnhardt Jr.
2002 #X26 Dale Earnhardt Jr. SG
2002 #X33 Dale Earnhardt Jr. AS
2003 #X4 Dale Earnhardt Jr.
2003 #X26 Dale Earnhardt Jr. SG
2003 #X31 Dale Earnhardt Jr. AS
VIP Explosives Lasers
1999 #30 Dale Earnhardt Jr.
2000 #LX17 Dale Earnhardt Jr.
2000 #LX24 Dale Earnhardt Jr. V
2001 #LX17 Dale Earnhardt Jr.
2001 #LX45 Dale Earnhardt Jr. AS
2002 #LX5 Dale Earnhardt Jr.
2002 #LX26 Dale Earnhardt Jr. SG
2002 #LX33 Dale Earnhardt Jr. AS
VIP Get A Grip Autographs
2007 #GG-DE Dale Earnhardt Jr./8
VIP Get A Grip Drivers
2007 #GGD27 Dale Earnhardt Jr.
VIP Get A Grip Teams
2007 #GGT27 Dale Earnhardt Jr.
VIP Head Gear
1999 #HG4 Dale Earnhardt Jr.
2000 #HG4 Dale Earnhardt Jr.
2001 #HG4 Dale Earnhardt Jr.
2002 #HG4 Dale Earnhardt Jr.
2003 #HG4 Dale Earnhardt Jr.
2004 #HG1 Dale Earnhardt Jr.
VIP Head Gear Die Cuts
2001 #HG4 Dale Earnhardt Jr.
2002 #HG4 Dale Earnhardt Jr.
2003 #HG4 Dale Earnhardt Jr.
VIP Head Gear Explosives
2000 #HG4 Dale Earnhardt Jr.
VIP Head Gear Explosives Laser Die Cuts
2000 #HG4 Dale Earnhardt Jr.
VIP Head Gear National
2003 #HG2 Dale Earnhardt Jr.
VIP Head Gear Plastic
1999 #HG4 Dale Earnhardt Jr.
1999 #HG10 Dale Earnhardt Jr.
VIP Head Gear Transparent
2004 #HG1 Dale Earnhardt Jr.
VIP Lap Leader
2006 #LL3 Dale Earnhardt Jr.
VIP Lap Leader Transparent
2006 #LL3 Dale Earnhardt Jr.
VIP Lap Leaders
1999 #LL4 Dale Earnhardt Jr.
2003 #LL2 Dale Earnhardt Jr.
2004 #LL2 Dale Earnhardt Jr.
2005 #2 Dale Earnhardt Jr.
VIP Lap Leaders National
2003 #LL2 Dale Earnhardt Jr.
VIP Lap Leaders Transparent
2003 #LL2 Dale Earnhardt Jr.
2004 #LL2 Dale Earnhardt Jr.
2005 #2 Dale Earnhardt Jr.
VIP Lap Leaders Transparent LTD
2003 #LL2 Dale Earnhardt Jr.
VIP Laser Explosive
2003 #LX4 Dale Earnhardt Jr.
2003 #LX26 Dale Earnhardt Jr. SG
2003 #LX31 Dale Earnhardt Jr. AS
VIP Making the Show
2000 #MS4 Dale Earnhardt Jr.
2001 #5 Dale Earnhardt Jr.
2002 #MS6 Dale Earnhardt Jr.
2003 #MS4 Dale Earnhardt Jr.
2004 #MS5 Dale Earnhardt Jr.
2005 #5 Dale Earnhardt Jr.
2006 #MS23 Dale Earnhardt Jr.
VIP Mile Masters
2001 #MM4 Dale Earnhardt Jr.
2002 #MM4 Dale Earnhardt Jr.
2003 #MM2 Dale Earnhardt Jr.
VIP Mile Masters National
2003 #MM2 Dale Earnhardt Jr.
VIP Mile Masters Precious Metal
2001 #MM4 Dale Earnhardt Jr.
VIP Mile Masters Transparent
2001 #MM4 Dale Earnhardt Jr.
2002 #MM4 Dale Earnhardt Jr.
2003 #MM2 Dale Earnhardt Jr.
VIP Mile Masters Transparent LTD
2002 #MM4 Dale Earnhardt Jr.
2003 #MM2 Dale Earnhardt Jr.
VIP Out of the Box
1999 #OB4 Dale Earnhardt Jr.
VIP Pedal To The Metal
2007 #PM3 Dale Earnhardt Jr.
VIP Previews
2003 #4 Dale Earnhardt Jr.
2003 #26 Dale Earnhardt Jr. SG
2003 #31 Dale Earnhardt Jr. AS
2004 #EB4 Dale Earnhardt Jr.
2004 #EB43 Dale Earnhardt Jr. SG
2004 #EB46 Dale Earnhardt Jr. SG
2004 #EB28 Dale Earnhardt Jr.'s Car R
2004 #EB53 Dale Earnhardt Jr. SG
2005 #EB5 Dale Earnhardt Jr.
2005 #EB33 Dale Earnhardt Jr.'s Car R
2007 #EB7 Dale Earnhardt Jr.
VIP Race Used Sheet Metal Cars
2002 #SC15 Dale Earnhardt Jr.'s Car
VIP Race Used Sheet Metal Drivers
2002 #SD15 Dale Earnhardt Jr.
VIP Rear View Mirror
1999 #RM4 Dale Earnhardt Jr.
2000 #RM4 Dale Earnhardt Jr.
2001 #RV4 Dale Earnhardt Jr.
VIP Rear View Mirror Die Cuts
2001 #RV4 Dale Earnhardt Jr.
VIP Rear View Mirror Explosives
2000 #RM4 Dale Earnhardt Jr.
VIP Rear View Mirror Explosives Laser Die Cuts
2000 #RM4 Dale Earnhardt Jr.
VIP Samples
2002 #5 Dale Earnhardt Jr.
2002 #26 Dale Earnhardt Jr. SG
2002 #33 Dale Earnhardt Jr. AS
2003 #4 Dale Earnhardt Jr.
2003 #26 Dale Earnhardt Jr. SG
2003 #31 Dale Earnhardt Jr. AS
2004 #4 Dale Earnhardt Jr.
2004 #28 Dale Earnhardt Jr.'s Car R
2004 #53 Dale Earnhardt Jr. SG
2004 #77 Dale Earnhardt Jr. BTN
2004 #46 Dale Earnhardt Jr. SG
2004 #90 Dale Earnhardt Jr. CL
2004 #43 Dale Earnhardt Jr. SG
2004 #55 Dale Earnhardt Jr. HR
2005 #5 Dale Earnhardt Jr.
2005 #33 Dale Earnhardt Jr.'s Car R
2005 #73 Dale Earnhardt Jr. BN
VIP Sheet Metal
2000 #SM7 Dale Earnhardt Jr.
2000 #SM10 Dale Earnhardt Jr.
VIP Sheet Metal Cars
2001 #SC8 Dale Earnhardt Jr.'s Car
VIP Sheet Metal Drivers
2001 #SD8 Dale Earnhardt Jr.
VIP Solos
1998 #28 Dale Earnhardt Jr.
VIP Sunday Best
2007 #SB5 Dale Earnhardt Jr.
VIP Tin
2003 #CT4 Dale Earnhardt Jr.
2003 #CT26 Dale Earnhardt Jr. SG
2003 #CT31 Dale Earnhardt Jr. AS
VIP Tradin' Paint Autographs
2004 #TP-DE Dale Earnhardt Jr./8
2005 #DE Dale Earnhardt Jr./8
2006 #TP-DE Dale Earnhardt Jr./8
VIP Tradin' Paint Bronze
2004 #TPT1 Dale Earnhardt Jr.
VIP Tradin' Paint Cars
2003 #TPT10 Dale Earnhardt Jr.'s Car
2005 #TPT1 Dale Earnhardt Jr.
VIP Tradin' Paint Cars Bronze
2006 #TPT4 Dale Earnhardt Jr.
VIP Tradin' Paint Drivers
2003 #TPD10 Dale Earnhardt Jr.
2005 #TPD1 Dale Earnhardt Jr.
VIP Tradin' Paint Drivers Gold
2006 #TPD4 Dale Earnhardt Jr.
VIP Tradin' Paint Drivers Silver
2006 #TPD4 Dale Earnhardt Jr.
VIP Tradin' Paint Gold
2004 #TPD1 Dale Earnhardt Jr.
VIP Tradin' Paint Silver
2004 #TPD1 Dale Earnhardt Jr.
VIP Trophy Club
2007 #TC4 Dale Earnhardt Jr.
VIP Trophy Club Transparent
2007 #TC4 Dale Earnhardt Jr.
VIP Under the Lights
2000 #UL4 Dale Earnhardt Jr.
VIP Under the Lights Explosives
2000 #UL4 Dale Earnhardt Jr.
VIP Under the Lights Explosives Lasers
2000 #UL4 Dale Earnhardt Jr.
Western Steer Earnhardt Next Generation
1995 #3 D.Earnhardt/D.Earnhardt Jr.
1995 #JUM Earnhardt Family
Wheels
1998 #47 Dale Earnhardt Jr.
1998 #60 Dale Earnhardt Jr.'s Car
1999 #39 Dale Earnhardt Jr. BGN
1999 #65 Dale Earnhardt Jr.'s Car
1999 #96 Dale Earnhardt Jr. TP
Wheels American Thunder
2003 #5 Dale Earnhardt Jr.
2003 #37 Dale Earnhardt Jr. CC
2003 #46 Dale Jr.'s Transporter
2004 #4 Dale Earnhardt Jr.
2004 #33 Dale Earnhardt Jr.'s Rig Rt. 66
2004 #41 Dale Earnhardt Jr. AS
2004 #47 Dale Earnhardt's Car HR
2004 #62 Dale Earnhardt Jr. DT
2004 #69 Dale Earnhardt Jr. RR
2004 #77 Dale Earnhardt Jr. CC
2005 #6 Dale Earnhardt Jr.
2005 #36 Dale Earnhardt Jr.'s Rig Rt. 66
2005 #38 Dale Earnhardt Jr. AS
2005 #57 Dale Earnhardt Jr. DT
2005 #69 Dale Earnhardt Jr. RR
2005 #77 Dale Earnhardt Jr. CC
2006 #6 Dale Earnhardt Jr.
2006 #32 Dale Earnhardt Jr. DT
2006 #47 Dale Earnhardt Jr.'s Car HR
2006 #74 Dale Earnhardt Jr. MIA
2006 #85 Dale Earnhardt Jr. NN
2007 #7 Dale Earnhardt Jr.
2007 #39 Dale Earnhardt Jr.'s Car DT
2007 #57 Dale Earnhardt Jr.'s Car HR
2007 #80 Dale Earnhardt Jr. HC
Wheels American Thunder American Dreams
2007 #AD10 Dale Earnhardt Jr.
Wheels American Thunder American Dreams Gold
2007 #ADG10 Dale Earnhardt Jr.
Wheels American Thunder American Eagle
2005 #AE2 Dale Earnhardt Jr.
Wheels American Thunder American Muscle
2003 #AM1 Dale Earnhardt Jr.
2004 #AM1 Dale Earnhardt Jr.
2005 #AM6 Dale Earnhardt Jr.
2006 #AM7 Dale Earnhardt Jr.
Wheels American Thunder American Racing Idol
2006 #RI3 Dale Earnhardt Jr.
Wheels American Thunder American Racing Idol Golden
2006 #RI3 Dale Earnhardt Jr.
Wheels American Thunder Autographed Hat Instant Winner
2007 #AH8 Dale Earnhardt Jr.
Wheels American Thunder Born On
2003 #BO5 Dale Earnhardt Jr.
2003 #BO37 Dale Earnhardt Jr. CC
2003 #BO46 Dale Jr. Transporter
Wheels American Thunder Cool Threads
2004 #CT2 Dale Earnhardt Jr.
2005 #CT4 Dale Earnhardt Jr.
2006 #CT4 Dale Earnhardt Jr.
2007 #CT6 Dale Earnhardt Jr.
Wheels American Thunder Cup Quest
2004 #CQ2 Dale Earnhardt Jr.
Wheels American Thunder Double Hat
2006 #DH5 Dale Earnhardt Jr.
Wheels American Thunder Golden Eagle
2005 #GE2 Dale Earnhardt Jr.
Wheels American Thunder Grandstand
2006 #GS4 Dale Earnhardt Jr.
Wheels American Thunder Head to Toe
2004 #HT3 Dale Earnhardt Jr.
2005 #HT4 Dale Earnhardt Jr.
2006 #HT9 Dale Earnhardt Jr.
2007 #HT5 Dale Earnhardt Jr.
Wheels American Thunder Heads Up Team
2003 #HUT26 Dale Earnhardt Jr./60
Wheels American Thunder Holofoil
2003 #P5 Dale Earnhardt Jr.
2003 #P37 Dale Earnhardt Jr. CC
2003 #P46 Dale Jr.Transporter
Wheels American Thunder Post Mark
2003 #PM4 Dale Earnhardt Jr.
2004 #PM6 Dale Earnhardt Jr.
Wheels American Thunder Previews
2003 #5 Dale Earnhardt Jr.
2004 #EB4 Dale Earnhardt Jr.
2004 #EB33 Dale Earnhardt Jr. Rt. 66
2004 #EB41 Dale Earnhardt Jr. AS
2005 #6 Dale Earnhardt Jr.
2005 #77 Dale Earnhardt Jr. CC
2006 #EB6 Dale Earnhardt Jr.
2006 #EB74 Dale Earnhardt Jr. MIA
2007 #EB7 Dale Earnhardt Jr.
2007 #EB57 Dale Earnhardt Jr.'s Car HR
Wheels American Thunder Pushin Pedal
2004 #PP5 Dale Earnhardt Jr.
2005 #PP3 Dale Earnhardt Jr.
Wheels American Thunder Pushin' Pedal
2006 #PP1 Dale Earnhardt Jr.
2007 #PP1 Dale Earnhardt Jr.
Wheels American Thunder Rookie Thunder
2003 #RT8 Dale Earnhardt Jr.
Wheels American Thunder Samples
2003 #P5 Dale Earnhardt Jr.
2003 #P37 Dale Earnhardt Jr. CC
2003 #P46 Dale Jr.Transporter
2004 #4 Dale Earnhardt Jr.
2004 #33 Dale Earnhardt Jr.'s Rig Rt. 66
2004 #41 Dale Earnhardt Jr. AS
2004 #47 Dale Earnhardt's Car HR
2004 #62 Dale Earnhardt Jr. DT
2004 #69 Dale Earnhardt Jr. RR
2004 #77 Dale Earnhardt Jr. CC
2005 #6 Dale Earnhardt Jr.
2005 #36 Dale Earnhardt Jr's Rig Rt. 66
2005 #38 Dale Earnhardt Jr. AS
2005 #57 Dale Earnhardt Jr. DT
2005 #69 Dale Earnhardt Jr. RR
2005 #77 Dale Earnhardt Jr. CC
Wheels American Thunder Starting Grid
2007 #SG2 Dale Earnhardt Jr.
Wheels American Thunder Thunder Road
2003 #TR1 Dale Earnhardt Jr.
2004 #TR4 Dale Earnhardt Jr.
2005 #TR4 Dale Earnhardt Jr.
2006 #TR2 Dale Earnhardt Jr.
2007 #TR10 Dale Earnhardt Jr.
Wheels American Thunder Thunder Strokes
2006 #3 Dale Earnhardt Jr.
2007 #12 Dale Earnhardt Jr.
Wheels American Thunder Thunder Strokes Press Plates Black

2007 #12 Dale Earnhardt Jr.
Wheels American Thunder Thunder Strokes Press Plates Cyan
2007 #12 Dale Earnhardt Jr.
Wheels American Thunder Thunder Strokes Press Plates Magenta
2007 #12 Dale Earnhardt Jr.
Wheels American Thunder Thunder Strokes Press Plates Yellow
2007 #12 Dale Earnhardt Jr.
Wheels American Thunder Triple Hat
2004 #TH33 Dale Earnhardt Jr.
2005 #TH4 Dale Earnhardt Jr.
2007 #TH6 Dale Earnhardt Jr.
Wheels Autographs
1999 #6 Dale Earnhardt Jr./75
2004 #17 Dale Earnhardt Jr. AT
2005 #13 Dale Earnhardt Jr.
2007 #10 Dale Earnhardt Jr. NC HG
2008 #10 Dale Earnhardt Jr. NC HG
Wheels Autographs Press Plates Black
2007 #9 Dale Earnhardt Jr. NC
2008 #10 Dale Earnhardt Jr. NC HG
Wheels Autographs Press Plates Cyan
2007 #9 Dale Earnhardt Jr. NC
2008 #10 Dale Earnhardt Jr. NC HG
Wheels Autographs Press Plates Magenta
2007 #9 Dale Earnhardt Jr. NC
2008 #10 Dale Earnhardt Jr. NC HG
Wheels Autographs Press Plates Yellow
2007 #10 Dale Earnhardt Jr. NC
2008 #10 Dale Earnhardt Jr. NC HG
Wheels Custom Shop
1999 #CS3 Dale Earnhardt Jr.
Wheels Custom Shop Prizes
1999 #DEA1 Dale Earnhardt Jr.
1999 #DEA2 Dale Earnhardt Jr.
1999 #DEA3 Dale Earnhardt Jr.
1999 #DEB1 Dale Earnhardt Jr.
1999 #DEB2 Dale Earnhardt Jr.
1999 #DEB3 Dale Earnhardt Jr.
1999 #39783 Dale Earnhardt Jr.
1999 #39784 Dale Earnhardt Jr.
1999 #39785 Dale Earnhardt Jr.
Wheels Dialed In
1999 #DI4 Dale Earnhardt Jr.
Wheels Golden
1998 #47 Dale Earnhardt Jr.
1998 #60 Dale Earnhardt Jr.'s Car
1999 #39 Dale Earnhardt Jr.
1999 #65 Dale Earnhardt Jr.
1999 #96 Dale Earnhardt Jr.
Wheels High Gear
1994 #180 Earnhardt Kids/Dale Jr.
1994 #183 Dale Earnhardt Jr. RC
1999 #37 Dale Earnhardt Jr.
2000 #37 Dale Earnhardt Jr.
2000 #65 Dale Earnhardt Jr.
2001 #13 Dale Earnhardt Jr.
2001 #56 Dale Earnhardt Jr. HL
2002 #6 Dale Earnhardt Jr.
2002 #46 Dale Earnhardt Jr.'s Car
2002 #55 Dale Earnhardt Jr. HL
2003 #8 Dale Earnhardt Jr.
2003 #52 Dale Earnhardt Jr.'s Car CM
2004 #6 Dale Earnhardt Jr.
2004 #29 Dale Earnhardt Jr.'s Car C
2004 #50 Dale Earnhardt Jr. NA
2004 #61 Dale Earnhardt Jr. HL
2005 #4 Dale Earnhardt Jr.
2005 #52 Dale Earnhardt Jr. A
2005 #61 Dale Earnhardt Jr.'s Car
2005 #65 Dale Earnhardt Jr. NI
2005 #67 Dale Earnhardt Jr. NI
2005 #72 Dale Earnhardt Jr. NI
2005 #75 Dale Earnhardt Jr. IF
2005 #84 Dale Earnhardt Jr. RS
2006 #18 Dale Earnhardt Jr.
2006 #18B Dale Earnhardt Jr. Daytona
2006 #47 Dale Earnhardt Jr.'s Car C
2006 #79 Dale Earnhardt Jr. FF
2007 #5 Dale Earnhardt Jr. blue
2007 #5B Dale Earnhardt Jr. red
2008 #80 Dale Earnhardt Jr. P
2008 #81 Dale Earnhardt Jr. P
2008 #82 Dale Earnhardt Jr. P
2008 #83 Dale Earnhardt Jr. P
2008 #84 Dale Earnhardt Jr. P
2008 #85 Dale Earnhardt Jr. P
2008 #90 Dale Earnhardt Jr. CL
2008 #82B Dale Earnhardt Jr. P w/o helicopter
2008 #85B Dale Earnhardt Jr. P w/o can
Wheels High Gear Autographs
1999 #7 Dale Earnhardt Jr./350
2000 #10 Dale Earnhardt Jr.
2001 #9 Dale Earnhardt Jr.
2002 #14 Dale Earnhardt Jr.
Wheels High Gear Blue Hawaii SCDA Promos
2003 #8 Dale Earnhardt Jr.
2003 #52 Dale Earnhardt Jr.'s Car CM
Wheels High Gear Custom Shop
1999 #CSJR Dale Earnhardt Jr. EXCH
2000 #CSDE Dale Earnhardt Jr. EXCH
2001 #CSDEJ Dale Earnhardt Jr. EXCH
2003 #CSDE Dale Earnhardt Jr. EXCH
2004 #CSDE Dale Earnhardt Jr.
Wheels High Gear Custom Shop Autograph Redemption
2003 #CSDE Dale Earnhardt Jr. EXCH
Wheels High Gear Custom Shop Prizes
1999 #JRA1 Dale Earnhardt Jr.
1999 #JRA2 Dale Earnhardt Jr.
1999 #JRA2 Dale Earnhardt Jr.
1999 #JRB1 Dale Earnhardt Jr.
1999 #JRB2 Dale Earnhardt Jr.
1999 #JRB3 Dale Earnhardt Jr.
1999 #JRC1 Dale Earnhardt Jr.
1999 #JRC2 Dale Earnhardt Jr.
1999 #JRC3 Dale Earnhardt Jr.
2000 #DEA1 Dale Earnhardt Jr.
2000 #DEA2 Dale Earnhardt Jr.
2000 #DEA3 Dale Earnhardt Jr.
2000 #DEB1 Dale Earnhardt Jr.
2000 #DEB2 Dale Earnhardt Jr.
2000 #DEB3 Dale Earnhardt Jr.
2000 #39783 Dale Earnhardt Jr.
2000 #39784 Dale Earnhardt Jr.
2000 #39785 Dale Earnhardt Jr.
2001 #DEJA1 Dale Earnhardt Jr.
2001 #DEJA2 Dale Earnhardt Jr.
2001 #DEJA3 Dale Earnhardt Jr.
2001 #DEJB1 Dale Earnhardt Jr.
2001 #DEJB2 Dale Earnhardt Jr.
2001 #DEJB3 Dale Earnhardt Jr.
2001 #DEJC1 Dale Earnhardt Jr.
2001 #DEJC2 Dale Earnhardt Jr.
2001 #DEJC3 Dale Earnhardt Jr.
2003 #DEA1 Dale Earnhardt Jr.
2003 #DEA2 Dale Earnhardt Jr.
2003 #DEA3 Dale Earnhardt Jr.
2003 #DEB1 Dale Earnhardt Jr.
2003 #DEB2 Dale Earnhardt Jr.
2003 #DEB3 Dale Earnhardt Jr.
2003 #39783 Dale Earnhardt Jr.
2003 #39784 Dale Earnhardt Jr.
2003 #39785 Dale Earnhardt Jr.
Wheels High Gear Dale Earnhardt Jr.
2004 #DJR1 Dale Earnhardt Jr.
2004 #DJR2 Dale Earnhardt Jr.
2004 #DJR3 Dale Earnhardt Jr.
2004 #DJR4 Dale Earnhardt Jr.
2004 #DJR5 Dale Earnhardt Jr.
2004 #DJR6 Dale Earnhardt Jr.
Wheels High Gear Day One
1994 #183 Dale Earnhardt Jr.
1994 #180 Earnhardt Kids/Dale Jr.
Wheels High Gear Day One Gold
1994 #180 Earnhardt Kids/Dale Jr.
1994 #183 Dale Earnhardt Jr.
Wheels High Gear Driven
2007 #DR18 Dale Earnhardt Jr.
Wheels High Gear Final Standings Gold
2007 #FS5 Dale Earnhardt Jr./5
Wheels High Gear First Gear
1999 #37 Dale Earnhardt Jr.
2000 #37 Dale Earnhardt Jr.
2000 #65 Dale Earnhardt Jr.
2001 #13 Dale Earnhardt Jr.
2001 #56 Dale Earnhardt Jr. HL
2002 #6 Dale Earnhardt Jr.
2002 #46 Dale Earnhardt Jr.'s Car
2002 #55 Dale Earnhardt Jr. HL
2003 #8 Dale Earnhardt Jr.
2003 #52 Dale Earnhardt Jr.'s Car CM
Wheels High Gear Flag Chasers
2001 #FC5 Dale Earnhardt Jr.
2002 #FC1 Dale Earnhardt Jr.
Wheels High Gear Flag Chasers Black
2002 #FC1 Dale Earnhardt Jr.
2003 #FC1 Dale Earnhardt Jr.
2004 #FC7 Dale Earnhardt Jr.
2005 #FC7 Dale Earnhardt Jr.
2006 #FC3 Dale Earnhardt Jr.
2007 #FC1 Dale Earnhardt Jr.
Wheels High Gear Flag Chasers Blue
2004 #FC7 Dale Earnhardt Jr.
Wheels High Gear Flag Chasers Blue-Yellow
2001 #FC5 Dale Earnhardt Jr.
2002 #FC1 Dale Earnhardt Jr.
2003 #FC1 Dale Earnhardt Jr.
2005 #FC7 Dale Earnhardt Jr.
2006 #FC3 Dale Earnhardt Jr.
2007 #FC1 Dale Earnhardt Jr.
Wheels High Gear Flag Chasers Checkered
2001 #FC5 Dale Earnhardt Jr.
2002 #FC1 Dale Earnhardt Jr.
2003 #FC1 Dale Earnhardt Jr.
2004 #FC7 Dale Earnhardt Jr.
2005 #FC7 Dale Earnhardt Jr.
2006 #FC3 Dale Earnhardt Jr.
2007 #FC1 Dale Earnhardt Jr.
Wheels High Gear Flag Chasers Checkered Blue/Orange
2001 #FC5 Dale Earnhardt Jr.
2002 #FC1 Dale Earnhardt Jr.
Wheels High Gear Flag Chasers Green
2001 #FC5 Dale Earnhardt Jr.
2002 #FC1 Dale Earnhardt Jr.
2003 #FC1 Dale Earnhardt Jr.
2004 #FC7 Dale Earnhardt Jr.
2005 #FC7 Dale Earnhardt Jr.
2006 #FC3 Dale Earnhardt Jr.
2007 #FC1 Dale Earnhardt Jr.
Wheels High Gear Flag Chasers Power Pick
2001 #FCPP Dale Earnhardt Jr.
Wheels High Gear Flag Chasers Red
2001 #FC5 Dale Earnhardt Jr.
2002 #FC1 Dale Earnhardt Jr.
2003 #FC1 Dale Earnhardt Jr.
2004 #FC7 Dale Earnhardt Jr.
2005 #FC7 Dale Earnhardt Jr.
2006 #FC3 Dale Earnhardt Jr.
2007 #FC1 Dale Earnhardt Jr.
Wheels High Gear Flag Chasers White
2001 #FC5 Dale Earnhardt Jr.
2003 #FC1 Dale Earnhardt Jr.
2004 #FC7 Dale Earnhardt Jr.
2005 #FC7 Dale Earnhardt Jr.
2006 #FC3 Dale Earnhardt Jr.
2007 #FC1 Dale Earnhardt Jr.
Wheels High Gear Flag Chasers Yellow
2001 #FC5 Dale Earnhardt Jr.
2002 #FC1 Dale Earnhardt Jr.
2003 #FC1 Dale Earnhardt Jr.
2004 #FC7 Dale Earnhardt Jr.
2005 #FC7 Dale Earnhardt Jr.
2006 #FC3 Dale Earnhardt Jr.
2007 #FC1 Dale Earnhardt Jr.
Wheels High Gear Flag to Flag
2005 #FF3 Dale Earnhardt Jr.
2006 #FF5 Dale Earnhardt Jr.
Wheels High Gear Full Throttle
2003 #FT7 Dale Earnhardt Jr.
2005 #FT1 Dale Earnhardt Jr.
2006 #FT4 Dale Earnhardt Jr.
2007 #FT4 Dale Earnhardt Jr.
Wheels High Gear Gear Shifters
2000 #GS23 Dale Earnhardt Jr.
2001 #GS14 Dale Earnhardt Jr.
Wheels High Gear Gold
1994 #180 Earnhardt Kids/Dale Jr.
1994 #183 Dale Earnhardt Jr.
Wheels High Gear High Groove
2002 #HG6 Dale Earnhardt Jr.
2003 #HG6 Dale Earnhardt Jr.
2004 #HG5 Dale Earnhardt Jr.
Wheels High Gear Hot Streaks
2001 #HS8 Dale Earnhardt Jr.
2002 #HS2 Dale Earnhardt Jr.
Wheels High Gear Hot Treads
2003 #HT18 Dale Earnhardt Jr.
Wheels High Gear Last Lap
2007 #LL8 Dale Earnhardt Jr.
Wheels High Gear Machine
2003 #MM6B Dale Earnhardt Jr.
2004 #MM9B Dale Earnhardt Jr.
2005 #MMB4 Dale Earnhardt Jr.
Wheels High Gear Man
2003 #MM6A Dale Earnhardt Jr.
2004 #MM9A Dale Earnhardt Jr.
2005 #MMA4 Dale Earnhardt Jr.
Wheels High Gear Man & Machine (Machine)
2006 #MMB4 Dale Earnhardt Jr.
Wheels High Gear Man & Machine (Man)
2006 #MMA4 Dale Earnhardt Jr.
Wheels High Gear Man and Machine Cars
2000 #MM2B Dale Earnhardt Jr.'s Car
2001 #MM7B Dale Earnhardt Jr.'s Car
2002 #MM1B Dale Earnhardt Jr.
Wheels High Gear Man and Machine Drivers
2000 #MM2A Dale Earnhardt Jr.
2001 #MM7A Dale Earnhardt Jr.
2002 #MM1A Dale Earnhardt Jr.
Wheels High Gear MPH
1999 #37 Dale Earnhardt Jr.
2000 #37 Dale Earnhardt Jr.
2000 #65 Dale Earnhardt Jr.
2001 #13 Dale Earnhardt Jr.
2001 #56 Dale Earnhardt Jr. HL
2002 #6 Dale Earnhardt Jr.
2002 #46 Dale Earnhardt Jr.'s Car
2002 #55 Dale Earnhardt Jr. HL
2003 #M8 Dale Earnhardt Jr.
2003 #M52 Dale Earnhardt Jr.'s Car CM
2004 #M6 Dale Earnhardt Jr.
2004 #M29 Dale Earnhardt Jr. C
2004 #M50 Dale Earnhardt Jr. NA
2004 #M61 Dale Earnhardt Jr. HL
2005 #M4 Dale Earnhardt Jr.
2005 #M52 Dale Earnhardt Jr. A
2005 #M61 Dale Earnhardt Jr.'s Car
2005 #M65 Dale Earnhardt Jr. NI
2005 #M67 Dale Earnhardt Jr. NI
2005 #M72 Dale Earnhardt Jr. NI
2005 #M75 Dale Earnhardt Jr. IF
2005 #M84 Dale Earnhardt Jr. RS
2006 #M18 Dale Earnhardt Jr.
2006 #M47 Dale Earnhardt Jr.'s Car C
2006 #M79 Dale Earnhardt Jr. FF
2007 #M5 Dale Earnhardt Jr.
2008 #M80 Dale Earnhardt Jr. P
2008 #M81 Dale Earnhardt Jr. P
2008 #M82 Dale Earnhardt Jr. P
2008 #M83 Dale Earnhardt Jr. P
2008 #M84 Dale Earnhardt Jr. P
2008 #M85 Dale Earnhardt Jr. P
2008 #M90 Dale Earnhardt Jr. CL
Wheels High Gear Previews
2003 #8 Dale Earnhardt Jr.
2004 #6 Dale Earnhardt Jr.
2004 #29 Dale Earnhardt Jr. C
2004 #50 Dale Earnhardt Jr. NA
2007 #EB5 Dale Earnhardt Jr.
2008 #EB80 Dale Earnhardt Jr. P
2008 #EB81 Dale Earnhardt Jr. P
2008 #EB82 Dale Earnhardt Jr. P
2008 #EB83 Dale Earnhardt Jr. P
2008 #EB84 Dale Earnhardt Jr. P
2008 #EB85 Dale Earnhardt Jr. P
Wheels High Gear Previews Green
2005 #EB4 Dale Earnhardt Jr.
2006 #EB18 Dale Earnhardt Jr.
Wheels High Gear Previews Silver
2005 #EB75 Dale Earnhardt Jr. IF
2006 #EB79 Dale Earnhardt Jr. FF
Wheels High Gear Samples
2003 #8 Dale Earnhardt Jr.
2003 #52 Dale Earnhardt Jr.'s Car CM
2004 #6 Dale Earnhardt Jr.
2004 #29 Dale Earnhardt Jr. C
2004 #50 Dale Earnhardt Jr. NA
2004 #61 Dale Earnhardt Jr. HL
2005 #4 Dale Earnhardt Jr.
2005 #52 Dale Earnhardt Jr. A
2005 #61 Dale Earnhardt Jr.'s Car
2005 #65 Dale Earnhardt Jr. NI
2005 #67 Dale Earnhardt Jr. NI
2005 #72 Dale Earnhardt Jr. NI
2005 #75 Dale Earnhardt Jr. IF
2005 #84 Dale Earnhardt Jr. RS
Wheels High Gear Sunday Sensation
2003 #SS9 Dale Earnhardt Jr.
2004 #SS3 Dale Earnhardt Jr.
Wheels High Gear Top Ten
2004 #TT3 Dale Earnhardt Jr.
Wheels High Gear Top Tier
2005 #TT5 Dale Earnhardt Jr.
2007 #TT5 Dale Earnhardt Jr.
Wheels High Gear Winning Edge
2000 #WE9 Dale Earnhardt Jr.
Wheels Runnin and Gunnin
1999 #RG13 Dale Earnhardt Jr.
Wheels Runnin and Gunnin Foils
1999 #RG13 Dale Earnhardt Jr.
Wheels Solos
1999 #39 Dale Earnhardt Jr.
1999 #65 Dale Earnhardt Jr.
1999 #96 Dale Earnhardt Jr.

Edwards, Carl

Press Pass
2004 #51 Carl Edwards
2005 #57 Carl Edwards
2006 #30 Carl Edwards
2006 #42 Carl Edwards NBS
2006 #69 Carl Edwards RR
2006 #83 Carl Edwards' Car OTW
2006 #87 Carl Edwards NS
2006 #101 Carl Edwards U
2006 #116 Carl Edwards TT
2007 #13 Carl Edwards
2007 #35 Carl Edwards NBS
2007 #82 Carl Edwards' Car OT
2007 #88 Carl Edwards NS
2008 #5 Carl Edwards
2008 #37 Carl Edwards NBS
2008 #110 Carl Edwards Top 12
2008 #0 Cup Chase Matt Kenseth Tony Stewart Jeff Gordon Jimmie Johnson Denny Hamlin Kurt Busch Kevin Harvick Carl Edwards Kyle Busch Martin Truex Jr. Jeff Burton Clint Bowyer
Press Pass Autographs
2004 #18 Carl Edwards P
2005 #16 Carl Edwards E/P
2006 #13 Carl Edwards NBS
2006 #14 Carl Edwards NCS
2007 #12 Carl Edwards NC P
Press Pass Autographs Press Plates Magenta
2007 #3 Carl Edwards NC
Press Pass Autographs Press Plates Yellow
2007 #40 Carl Edwards
Press Pass Blaster Kmart
2006 #CEC Carl Edwards
Press Pass Blaster Target
2006 #CEB Carl Edwards
Press Pass Blaster Wal-Mart
2006 #CEA Carl Edwards
Press Pass Blue
2006 #B30 Carl Edwards
2006 #B42 Carl Edwards NBS
2006 #B69 Carl Edwards RR
2006 #B83 Carl Edwards' Car OTW
2006 #B87 Carl Edwards NS
2006 #B101 Carl Edwards U
2006 #B116 Carl Edwards TT
2007 #B13 Carl Edwards
2007 #B35 Carl Edwards NBS
2007 #B82 Carl Edwards' Car OT
2007 #B88 Carl Edwards NS
2008 #B5 Carl Edwards
2008 #B37 Carl Edwards NBS
2008 #B110 Carl Edwards Top 12
Press Pass Burning Rubber Autographs
2006 #BR-CE Carl Edwards/99
Press Pass Burning Rubber Cars
2006 #BRT4 Carl Edwards
Press Pass Burning Rubber Drivers
2006 #BRD4 Carl Edwards
2008 #BRD14 Carl Edwards Michigan
2008 #BRD23 Carl Edwards Bristol
Press Pass Burning Rubber Drivers Gold
2006 #BRD4 Carl Edwards
2008 #BRD14 Carl Edwards Michigan
2008 #BRD23 Carl Edwards Bristol
Press Pass Burning Rubber Drivers Prime Cuts
2008 #BRD14 Carl Edwards Michigan
2008 #BRD23 Carl Edwards Bristol
Press Pass Burning Rubber Teams
2008 #BRT14 Carl Edwards Michigan
2008 #BRT23 Carl Edwards Bristol
Press Pass Burnouts
2006 #HT7 Carl Edwards
2008 #BO2 Carl Edwards
Press Pass Burnouts Blue
2008 #BO2 Carl Edwards
Press Pass Burnouts Gold
2008 #BO2 Carl Edwards
Press Pass Burnouts Holofoil
2006 #HT7 Carl Edwards
Press Pass Collector's Series Box Set
2007 #SB6 Carl Edwards
Press Pass Collectors Series Making the Show
2006 #MS11 Carl Edwards
Press Pass Collectors Series Sunday Best
2007 #CB6 Carl Edwards
Press Pass Cup Chase
2006 #CCR6 Carl Edwards
2007 #CCR17 Carl Edwards Winner
2008 #CC15 Carl Edwards
Press Pass Cup Chase Prizes
2007 #CC4 Carl Edwards
Press Pass Double Burner Firesuit-Glove
2006 #DB7 Carl Edwards
2007 #DB9 Carl Edwards
2008 #DBCE Carl Edwards
Press Pass Double Burner Firesuit-Glove Exchange
2007 #DB9 Carl Edwards
Press Pass Double Burner Metal-Tire
2006 #DB1 Carl Edwards
2007 #DB-CE Carl Edwards
2008 #DB-CE Carl Edwards
Press Pass Double Burner Metal-Tire Exchange
2007 #DB-CE Carl Edwards
Press Pass Eclipse
2006 #3 Carl Edwards
2006 #30 Carl Edwards NBS
2006 #57 Carl Edwards NS
2006 #64 Carl Edwards BA
2006 #65 NCS Top-10 BA
2006 #69 Tony Stewart BA
2006 #76 Carl Edwards LL
2006 #88 Carl Edwards SM
2006 #57B Carl Edwards NS -cameraman
2007 #12 Carl Edwards
2008 #8 Carl Edwards
2008 #47 Carl Edwards NS
2008 #58 Carl Edwards' Car LP
2008 #75 Top 10 Drivers SO
2008 #76 Carl Edwards SO
Press Pass Eclipse Ecliptic
2007 #EC12 Carl Edwards
Press Pass Eclipse Gold
2007 #G12 Carl Edwards
2008 #G8 Carl Edwards
2008 #G47 Carl Edwards NS
2008 #G58 Carl Edwards' Car LP
2008 #G75 Top 10 Drivers SO
2008 #G76 Carl Edwards SO
Press Pass Eclipse Hyperdrive
2006 #HP1 Carl Edwards
Press Pass Eclipse Previews
2006 #EB3 Carl Edwards
2006 #EB30 Carl Edwards NBS
2007 #EB12 Carl Edwards
2008 #EB8 Carl Edwards
2008 #EB75 Top 10 Drivers SO
2008 #EB76 Carl Edwards SO
Press Pass Eclipse Racing Champions
2006 #RC4 Carl Edwards
2006 #RC18 Carl Edwards NBS
2007 #RC14 Carl Edwards
Press Pass Eclipse Red
2007 #R12 Carl Edwards
2008 #R8 Carl Edwards
2008 #R47 Carl Edwards NS
2008 #R58 Carl Edwards' Car LP
2008 #R75 Top 10 Drivers SO
2008 #R76 Carl Edwards SO
Press Pass Eclipse Skidmarks
2006 #SM15 Carl Edwards
2007 #SM13 Carl Edwards
Press Pass Eclipse Skidmarks Holofoil
2006 #SM15 Carl Edwards
2007 #SM13 Carl Edwards
Press Pass Eclipse Star Tracks
2008 #ST14 Carl Edwards
Press Pass Eclipse Star Tracks Holofoil
2008 #ST14 Carl Edwards
Press Pass Eclipse Stellar
2008 #ST3 Carl Edwards
2008 #ST17 Carl Edwards
Press Pass Eclipse Supernova
2006 #SU7 Carl Edwards
Press Pass Eclipse Teammates Autographs
2005 #8 K.Busch/C.Edwards
2006 #3 C.Edwards/M.Martin
2007 #6 Biffle/Edwards/Kenseth
Press Pass Eclipse Under Cover Cars
2006 #UCT10 Carl Edwards
Press Pass Eclipse Under Cover Double Cover
2006 #DC6 M.Kenseth/C.Edwards
2006 #DC7 C.Edwards/M.Martin
2006 #DC9 G.Biffle/C.Edwards
Press Pass Eclipse Under Cover Double Cover Holofoil
2006 #DC6 M.Kenseth/C.Edwards
2006 #DC7 C.Edwards/M.Martin
2006 #DC9 G.Biffle/C.Edwards
Press Pass Eclipse Under Cover Double Cover Name
2007 #DC1 Edwards/Biffle
2007 #DC5 Kenseth/Edwards
2008 #DC3 Carl Edwards Matt Kenseth
2008 #DC7 Carl Edwards David Ragan
Press Pass Eclipse Under Cover Double Cover NASCAR
2007 #DC1 Edwards/Biffle
2007 #DC5 Kenseth/Edwards
2008 #DC3 Carl Edwards Matt Kenseth
2008 #DC7 Carl Edwards David Ragan
Press Pass Eclipse Under Cover Drivers
2007 #UCD11 Carl Edwards
2008 #UCD5 Carl Edwards
Press Pass Eclipse Under Cover Drivers Eclipse
2007 #UCD11 Carl Edwards
2008 #UCD5 Carl Edwards
Press Pass Eclipse Under Cover Drivers Gold
2006 #UCD10 Carl Edwards
Press Pass Eclipse Under Cover Drivers Holofoil
2006 #UCD10 Carl Edwards
Press Pass Eclipse Under Cover Drivers Name
2007 #UCD11 Carl Edwards
2008 #UCD5 Carl Edwards
Press Pass Eclipse Under Cover Drivers NASCAR
2007 #UCD11 Carl Edwards
2008 #UCD5 Carl Edwards
Press Pass Eclipse Under Cover Drivers Silver
2006 #UCD10 Carl Edwards
Press Pass Eclipse Under Cover Teams
2007 #UCT11 Carl Edwards
2008 #UCT5 Carl Edwards
Press Pass Eclipse Under Cover Teams NASCAR
2007 #UCT11 Carl Edwards
2008 #UCT5 Carl Edwards
Press Pass Four Wide
2008 #FW-CE Carl Edwards
Press Pass Four Wide Checkered
2008 #FW-CE Carl Edwards
Press Pass Gold
2006 #G30 Carl Edwards
2006 #G42 Carl Edwards NBS
2006 #G69 Carl Edwards RR
2006 #G83 Carl Edwards' Car OTW
2006 #G87 Carl Edwards NS
2006 #G101 Carl Edwards U
2006 #G116 Carl Edwards TT
2007 #G13 Carl Edwards
2007 #G35 Carl Edwards NBS
2007 #G82 Carl Edwards' Car OT
2007 #G88 Carl Edwards NS
2008 #G5 Carl Edwards
2008 #G37 Carl Edwards NBS
2008 #G110 Carl Edwards Top 12
Press Pass Hot Treads
2008 #HT6 Carl Edwards
Press Pass Hot Treads Blue
2008 #HT6 Carl Edwards
Press Pass Hot Treads Gold
2008 #HT6 Carl Edwards
Press Pass Legends
2006 #44 Carl Edwards
2007 #48 Carl Edwards
Press Pass Legends Autographs Black
2006 #22 Carl Edwards
Press Pass Legends Autographs Blue
2007 #6 Carl Edwards/71
Press Pass Legends Blue
2006 #B44 Carl Edwards
2007 #B48 Carl Edwards
Press Pass Legends Bronze
2006 #Z44 Carl Edwards
2007 #Z48 Carl Edwards
Press Pass Legends Gold
2006 #G44 Carl Edwards
2007 #G48 Carl Edwards
Press Pass Legends Holofoil
2006 #H44 Carl Edwards
2007 #H48 Carl Edwards
Press Pass Legends Press Plates Black
2006 #PPB44 Carl Edwards
2007 #PP48 Carl Edwards
Press Pass Legends Press Plates Black Backs
2006 #PPB44B Carl Edwards
2007 #PP48 Carl Edwards
Press Pass Legends Press Plates Cyan
2006 #PPC44 Carl Edwards
2007 #PP48 Carl Edwards
Press Pass Legends Press Plates Cyan Backs
2006 #PPC44B Carl Edwards
2007 #PP48 Carl Edwards
Press Pass Legends Press Plates Magenta
2006 #PPM44 Carl Edwards
2007 #PP48 Carl Edwards
Press Pass Legends Press Plates Magenta Backs
2006 #PPM44B Carl Edwards
2007 #PP48 Carl Edwards
Press Pass Legends Press Plates Yellow
2006 #PPY44 Carl Edwards
2007 #PP48 Carl Edwards
Press Pass Legends Press Plates Yellow Backs
2006 #PPY44B Carl Edwards
2007 #PP48 Carl Edwards
Press Pass Legends Previews
2006 #EB44 Carl Edwards
2007 #EB48 Carl Edwards
Press Pass Legends Signature Series
2007 #CE Carl Edwards
Press Pass Legends Solo
2006 #S44 Carl Edwards
2007 #S48 Carl Edwards
Press Pass Legends Triple Threads
2006 #TT-CE Carl Edwards
Press Pass Optima
2004 #42 Carl Edwards
2005 #9 Carl Edwards CRC
2005 #9B Carl Edwards Cup Chase
2005 #32 Carl Edwards BGN
2005 #50 Carl Edwards YG
2005 #61 Carl Edwards RR
2005 #84 Carl Edwards DT
2005 #NNO Carl Edwards Signings Entry
2006 #33 Carl Edwards
2006 #43 Carl Edwards NBS
Press Pass Optima Cool Persistence
2005 #CP6 Carl Edwards
Press Pass Optima Fan Favorite
2005 #FF7 Carl Edwards
2006 #FF5 Carl Edwards
Press Pass Optima Gold
2004 #G42 Carl Edwards
2005 #G9 Carl Edwards
2005 #G32 Carl Edwards BGN
2005 #G50 Carl Edwards YG
2005 #G61 Carl Edwards RR
2005 #G84 Carl Edwards DT
2006 #G33 Carl Edwards
2006 #G43 Carl Edwards NBS
Press Pass Optima Previews
2004 #EB42 Carl Edwards
2005 #9 Carl Edwards
2005 #32 Carl Edwards BGN
2005 #50 Carl Edwards YG/1
2006 #EB33 Carl Edwards
Press Pass Optima Q & A
2005 #QA4 Carl Edwards
Press Pass Optima Samples
2004 #42 Carl Edwards
2005 #9 Carl Edwards
2005 #32 Carl Edwards BGN
2005 #50 Carl Edwards YG
2005 #61 Carl Edwards RR
2005 #84 Carl Edwards DT
Press Pass Platinum
2004 #P51 Carl Edwards
2005 #P57 Carl Edwards
2006 #P30 Carl Edwards
2006 #P42 Carl Edwards NBS
2006 #P69 Carl Edwards RR
2006 #P83 Carl Edwards' Car OTW
2006 #P87 Carl Edwards NS
2006 #P101 Carl Edwards U
2006 #P116 Carl Edwards TT
2007 #P13 Carl Edwards
2007 #P35 Carl Edwards NBS
2007 #P82 Carl Edwards' Car OT
2007 #P88 Carl Edwards NS
2008 #P5 Carl Edwards
2008 #P37 Carl Edwards NBS
2008 #P110 Carl Edwards Top 12
Press Pass Premium
2005 #6 Carl Edwards CRC
2006 #7 Carl Edwards
2006 #41 Carl Edwards' Car M
2006 #60 Carl Edwards C
2006 #79 Carl Edwards PC
2007 #33 Carl Edwards
2007 #44 Carl Edwards' Car M
2007 #55 Carl Edwards RTTC
2008 #36 Carl Edwards
2008 #56 Carl Edwards EOP
2008 #70 Carl Edwards MD
2008 #78 Carl Edwards F
2008 #86 Carl Edwards OD
Press Pass Premium Hot Threads Cars
2006 #HTT4 Carl Edwards
Press Pass Premium Hot Threads Drivers
2006 #HTD4 Carl Edwards
2007 #HTD14 Carl Edwards
2008 #HTD8 Carl Edwards
Press Pass Premium Hot Threads Drivers Gold
2006 #HTD4 Carl Edwards
2007 #HTD14 Carl Edwards
2008 #HTD8 Carl Edwards
Press Pass Premium Hot Threads Patch
2007 #HTP20 Carl Edwards Coke/8
2007 #HTP21 Carl Edwards Gillette Young Guns/8
Press Pass Premium Hot Threads Patches
2008 #HTP2 Carl Edwards CE Signature
2008 #HTP3 Carl Edwards Ford Racing/6
2008 #HTP4 Carl Edwards NASCAR bar
Press Pass Premium Hot Threads Team
2007 #HTT14 Carl Edwards
2008 #HTT8 Carl Edwards
Press Pass Premium In the Zone

2006 #IZ2 Carl Edwards
Press Pass Premium In the Zone Red
2006 #IZ2 Carl Edwards
Press Pass Premium Previews
2008 #EB36 Carl Edwards
2008 #EB56 Carl Edwards EOP
Press Pass Premium Red
2007 #R33 Carl Edwards
2007 #R44 Carl Edwards' Car M
2007 #R55 Carl Edwards RTTC
2008 #36 Carl Edwards
2008 #56 Carl Edwards EOP
2008 #70 Carl Edwards MD
2008 #78 Carl Edwards F
2008 #86 Carl Edwards DD
Press Pass Premium Samples
2005 #6 Carl Edwards
Press Pass Premium Team Signed Baseballs
2008 #ROU Carl Edwards Matt Kenseth Jamie McMurray#David Ragan
2008 #E-ROU Carl Edwards Matt Kenseth Jamie McMurray#David Ragan Entry Card
Press Pass Premium Wal-Mart
2008 #WM4 Carl Edwards
Press Pass Previews
2006 #EB30 Carl Edwards
2006 #EB42 Carl Edwards NBS
2006 #EB101 Carl Edwards U
2007 #EB13 Carl Edwards
2007 #EB35 Carl Edwards NBS
2008 #EB5 Carl Edwards
2008 #EB110 Carl Edwards Top 12
Press Pass Race Day
2008 #RD11 Carl Edwards
Press Pass Samples
2004 #51 Carl Edwards
2005 #57 Carl Edwards
Press Pass Signings
2003 #19 Carl Edwards O/S/V
2004 #18 Carl Edwards O/P/S/T/V
2005 #14 Carl Edwards BGN
2005 #15 Carl Edwards NC
2006 #15 Carl Edwards
2007 #18 Carl Edwards NC
2008 #17 Carl Edwards
Press Pass Signings Gold
2003 #19 Carl Edwards O/S/V
2004 #17 Carl Edwards O/P/S/T/V
2005 #13 Carl Edwards BGN
2005 #14 Carl Edwards NC
2007 #15 Carl Edwards NC
2008 #13 Carl Edwards
Press Pass Signings Platinum
2005 #13 Carl Edwards BGN
2005 #14 Carl Edwards NC
Press Pass Signings Press Plates Black
2008 #12 Carl Edwards
Press Pass Signings Press Plates Cyan
2008 #12 Carl Edwards
Press Pass Signings Press Plates Magenta
2008 #12 Carl Edwards
Press Pass Signings Press Plates Yellow
2008 #12 Carl Edwards
Press Pass Signings Red Ink
2006 #5 Carl Edwards
Press Pass Signings Silver
2006 #14 Carl Edwards
2007 #14 Carl Edwards NC
2008 #14 Carl Edwards
Press Pass Snapshots
2005 #SN6 Carl Edwards
2007 #SN6 Carl Edwards
Press Pass Speedway
2008 #22 Carl Edwards
2008 #45 Carl Edwards NNS
2008 #79 Carl Edwards's Car RSG
2008 #90 Carl Edwards' Car WS
2008 #95 Carl Edwards H
Press Pass Speedway Corporate Cuts Drivers
2008 #CD-CE Carl Edwards
Press Pass Speedway Corporate Cuts Drivers Patches
2008 #CD-CE Carl Edwards/13
Press Pass Speedway Corporate Cuts Team
2008 #CT-CE Carl Edwards
Press Pass Speedway Gold
2008 #G22 Carl Edwards
2008 #G45 Carl Edwards NNS
2008 #G79 Carl Edwards's Car RSG
2008 #G90 Carl Edwards' Car WS
2008 #G95 Carl Edwards H
Press Pass Speedway Holofoil
2008 #H22 Carl Edwards
2008 #H45 Carl Edwards NNS
2008 #H79 Carl Edwards's Car RSG
2008 #H90 Carl Edwards' Car WS
2008 #H95 Carl Edwards H
Press Pass Speedway Previews
2008 #EB22 Carl Edwards
2008 #EB45 Carl Edwards NNS
2008 #EB95 Carl Edwards H
Press Pass Speedway Red
2008 #R22 Carl Edwards
2008 #R45 Carl Edwards NNS
2008 #R79 Carl Edwards's Car RSG
2008 #R90 Carl Edwards' Car WS
2008 #R95 Carl Edwards H
Press Pass Speedway Test Drive
2008 #TD10 Carl Edwards
Press Pass Stealth
2006 #7 Carl Edwards
2006 #46 Carl Edwards' Rig
2006 #48 17/6/16/26/99 TM
2006 #62 Carl Edwards F
2006 #72 Carl Edwards DD
2007 #7 Carl Edwards
2007 #39 Carl Edwards NBS
2007 #69 Edwards/Biffle/Kenseth/McMurray/Ragan
2007 #79 Carl Edwards DD
2008 #9 Carl Edwards
2008 #39 Carl Edwards NNS
2008 #54 Carl Edwards' Rig C
2008 #70 Greg Biffle Jamie McMurray Carl Edwards Matt Kenseth David Ragan
2008 #76 Carl Edwards DD
Press Pass Stealth Autographed Hat Entry
2006 #PPH6 Carl Edwards
Press Pass Stealth Battle Armor Drivers
2007 #BAD7 Carl Edwards
2008 #BAD5 Carl Edwards
Press Pass Stealth Battle Armor Teams
2007 #BAT7 Carl Edwards
2008 #BAT5 Carl Edwards
Press Pass Stealth Chrome
2007 #7 Carl Edwards
2007 #39 Carl Edwards NBS
2007 #69 Edwards/Biffle/Kenseth/McMurray/Ragan
2007 #79 Carl Edwards DD
2008 #9 Carl Edwards
2008 #39 Carl Edwards NNS
2008 #54 Carl Edwards' Rig C
2008 #70 Greg Biffle Jamie McMurray Carl Edwards Matt Kenseth David Ragan
2008 #76 Carl Edwards DD
Press Pass Stealth Chrome Exclusives
2007 #X7 Carl Edwards
2007 #X39 Carl Edwards NBS
2007 #X69 Edwards/Biffle/Kenseth/McMurray/Ragan
2007 #X79 Carl Edwards DD
2008 #9 Carl Edwards
2008 #39 Carl Edwards NNS
2008 #54 Carl Edwards' Rig C
2008 #70 Greg Biffle Jamie McMurray Carl Edwards Matt Kenseth David Ragan
2008 #76 Carl Edwards DD
Press Pass Stealth Chrome Exclusives Gold
2008 #9 Carl Edwards
2008 #39 Carl Edwards NNS
2008 #54 Carl Edwards' Rig C
2008 #70 Greg Biffle Jamie McMurray Carl Edwards Matt Kenseth David Ragan
2008 #76 Carl Edwards DD
Press Pass Stealth Chrome Platinum
2007 #P7 Carl Edwards
2007 #P39 Carl Edwards NBS
2007 #P69 Edwards/Biffle/Kenseth/McMurray/Ragan
2007 #P79 Carl Edwards DD
Press Pass Stealth Corporate Cuts
2006 #CCD4 Carl Edwards
Press Pass Stealth EFX
2006 #EFX8 Carl Edwards 1:48
Press Pass Stealth Gear Grippers Drivers
2006 #GGD17 Carl Edwards
Press Pass Stealth Hot Pass
2006 #HP8 Carl Edwards
Press Pass Stealth Maximum Access
2007 #MA7 Carl Edwards
2008 #MA9 Carl Edwards
Press Pass Stealth Maximum Access Autographs
2007 #MA7 Carl Edwards
2008 #MA9 Carl Edwards
Press Pass Stealth Previews
2006 #7 Carl Edwards
2007 #EB7 Carl Edwards
2007 #EB39 Carl Edwards NBS
2008 #9 Carl Edwards
2008 #39 Carl Edwards NNS
Press Pass Stealth Retail
2006 #7 Carl Edwards
2006 #46 Carl Edwards' Rig
2006 #48 17/6/16/26/99 TM
2006 #62 Carl Edwards F
2006 #72 Carl Edwards DD
Press Pass Stealth Retail Gear Grippers Cars
2006 #GGT17 Carl Edwards
Press Pass Stealth X-Ray
2006 #X7 Carl Edwards
2006 #X46 Carl Edwards' Rig
2006 #X48 17/6/16/26/99 TM
2006 #X62 Carl Edwards F
2006 #X72 Carl Edwards DD
Press Pass Target Victory Tires
2008 #TT-CE Carl Edwards Bristol
Press Pass Top 25 Drivers & Rides
2006 #C25 Carl Edwards' Car
2006 #D25 Carl Edwards
Press Pass Top Prospects Memorabilia
2005 #CE-G Carl Edwards Glove
2005 #CE-S Carl Edwards Shoe
2005 #CE-SM Carl Edwards Metal
2005 #CE-T Carl Edwards Tire
Press Pass Trackside
2003 #48 Carl Edwards CTS RC
2005 #28 Carl Edwards CRC
2005 #28B Carl Edwards no wire
Press Pass Trackside Gold Holofoil
2003 #P48 Carl Edwards CTS
Press Pass Trackside Golden
2005 #G28 Carl Edwards
Press Pass Trackside Hat Giveaway
2005 #PPH7 Carl Edwards
Press Pass Trackside Previews
2005 #28 Carl Edwards
Press Pass Trackside Samples
2003 #48 Carl Edwards CTS
2005 #28 Carl Edwards
Press Pass UMI Cup Chase
2005 #1 Cup Chase Drivers CL
2005 #10 Carl Edwards
Press Pass Velocity
2006 #VE3 Carl Edwards
Press Pass Wal-Mart Autographs
2007 #CE Carl Edwards
2008 #2 Carl Edwards EXCH
TRAKS
2006 #8 Carl Edwards
2006 #54 Carl Edwards' Car
2006 #109 Carl Edwards' Car PS
2007 #6 Carl Edwards
2007 #56 Carl Edwards' Car CTG
TRAKS Autographs
2006 #9 Carl Edwards
Traks Corporate Cuts Driver
2007 #CCD10 Carl Edwards
Traks Corporate Cuts Patch
2007 #CCD10 Carl Edwards/12
Traks Corporate Cuts Team
2007 #CCT10 Carl Edwards
Traks Driver's Seat
2007 #DS24 Carl Edwards
2007 #DS24B Carl Edwards VAR
Traks Driver's Seat National
2007 #DS24 Carl Edwards
Traks Gold
2007 #G6 Carl Edwards
2007 #G56 Carl Edwards' Car CTG
Traks Holofoil
2007 #H6 Carl Edwards
2007 #H56 Carl Edwards' Car CTG
Traks Hot Pursuit
2007 #HP6 Carl Edwards
Traks Previews
2007 #EB6 Carl Edwards
Traks Red
2007 #R6 Carl Edwards
2007 #R56 Carl Edwards' Car CTG
TRAKS Stickers
2006 #99 Carl Edwards
VIP
2005 #6 Carl Edwards CRC
2005 #46 Carl Edwards SG
2006 #6 Carl Edwards
2006 #36 Carl Edwards' Car R
2006 #56 Carl Edwards BTN
2006 #85 Carl Edwards IF
2007 #8 Carl Edwards
2007 #83 Carl Edwards Michigan AP
VIP Get A Grip Drivers
2007 #GGD2 Carl Edwards
VIP Get A Grip Teams
2007 #GGT2 Carl Edwards
VIP Head Gear
2005 #8 Carl Edwards
VIP Head Gear Transparent
2005 #8 Carl Edwards
VIP Making the Show
2006 #MS11 Carl Edwards
VIP Pedal To The Metal
2007 #PM6 Carl Edwards
VIP Previews
2005 #EB6 Carl Edwards
2007 #EB8 Carl Edwards
VIP Samples
2005 #6 Carl Edwards
2005 #46 Carl Edwards SG
VIP Sunday Best
2007 #SB6 Carl Edwards
VIP Tradin' Paint Cars Bronze
2006 #TPT5 Carl Edwards
VIP Tradin' Paint Drivers Gold
2006 #TPD5 Carl Edwards
VIP Tradin' Paint Drivers Silver
2006 #TPD5 Carl Edwards
Wheels American Thunder
2005 #7 Carl Edwards CRC
2005 #55 Carl Edwards DT
2005 #64 Carl Edwards RR
2005 #87 Carl Edwards RT
2005 #90 C.Edwards/Ky.Busch CL
2006 #7 Carl Edwards
2006 #36 Carl Edwards DT
2006 #58 Carl Edwards' Car HR
2006 #78 Carl Edwards MIA
2007 #8 Carl Edwards
2007 #49 Carl Edwards' Car HR
2007 #64 Carl Edwards RW
Wheels American Thunder American Dreams
2007 #AD9 Carl Edwards
Wheels American Thunder American Dreams Gold
2007 #ADG9 Carl Edwards
Wheels American Thunder American Muscle
2005 #AM5 Carl Edwards
Wheels American Thunder Autographed Hat Instant Winner
2007 #AH9 Carl Edwards
Wheels American Thunder Cool Threads
2007 #CT10 Carl Edwards
Wheels American Thunder Double Hat
2005 #DH3 Carl Edwards
2006 #DH6 Carl Edwards
Wheels American Thunder Grandstand
2006 #GS5 Carl Edwards
Wheels American Thunder Head to Toe
2005 #HT1 Carl Edwards
2006 #HT15 Carl Edwards
Wheels American Thunder License to Drive
2005 #1 Carl Edwards
Wheels American Thunder Previews
2005 #7 Carl Edwards
2005 #87 Carl Edwards RT/1
2006 #EB7 Carl Edwards
2006 #EB78 Carl Edwards MIA
2007 #EB8 Carl Edwards
2007 #EB49 Carl Edwards' Car HR
Wheels American Thunder Pushin Pedal
2005 #PP9 Carl Edwards
Wheels American Thunder Pushin' Pedal
2006 #PP12 Carl Edwards
2007 #PP8 Carl Edwards
Wheels American Thunder Samples
2005 #7 Carl Edwards
2005 #55 Carl Edwards DT
2005 #64 Carl Edwards RR
2005 #87 Carl Edwards RT
2005 #90 C.Edwards/Ky.Busch CL
Wheels American Thunder Thunder Road
2005 #TR13 Carl Edwards
2006 #TR18 Carl Edwards
Wheels American Thunder Thunder Strokes
2007 #13 Carl Edwards
Wheels American Thunder Thunder Strokes Press Plates Black
2007 #13 Carl Edwards
Wheels American Thunder Thunder Strokes Press Plates Cyan
2007 #13 Carl Edwards
Wheels American Thunder Thunder Strokes Press Plates Magenta
2007 #13 Carl Edwards
Wheels American Thunder Thunder Strokes Press Plates Yellow
2007 #13 Carl Edwards
Wheels American Thunder Triple Hat
2007 #TH7 Carl Edwards
Wheels Autographs
2004 #19 Carl Edwards HG
2006 #14 Carl Edwards NBS
2006 #15 Carl Edwards NC
2007 #11 Carl Edwards NC HG
Wheels Autographs Press Plates Black
2007 #10 Carl Edwards NC
Wheels Autographs Press Plates Cyan
2007 #10 Carl Edwards NC
Wheels Autographs Press Plates Magenta
2007 #10 Carl Edwards NC
Wheels Autographs Press Plates Yellow
2007 #11 Carl Edwards NC
Wheels High Gear
2006 #3 Carl Edwards
2006 #31 Carl Edwards NBS
2006 #50 Carl Edwards' Car C
2006 #58 Carl Edwards NA
2006 #64 Carl Edwards CM
2007 #13 Carl Edwards
2007 #33 Carl Edwards NBS
2007 #74 Carl Edwards NI
2008 #9 Carl Edwards
2008 #32 Carl Edwards NBS
2008 #54 Carl Edwards' Car C
2008 #72 Carl Edwards' Car EL
2008 #72B Carl Edwards' Car EL -car on track
Wheels High Gear Driven
2007 #DR20 Carl Edwards
2008 #DR25 Carl Edwards
Wheels High Gear Final Standings
2008 #F9 Carl Edwards/9
Wheels High Gear Final Standings Gold
2007 #FS13 Carl Edwards/12
Wheels High Gear Flag Chasers Black
2006 #FC1 Carl Edwards
2007 #FC2 Carl Edwards
2008 #FC7 Carl Edwards
Wheels High Gear Flag Chasers Blue-Yellow
2006 #FC1 Carl Edwards
2007 #FC2 Carl Edwards
2008 #FC7 Carl Edwards
Wheels High Gear Flag Chasers Checkered
2006 #FC1 Carl Edwards
2007 #FC2 Carl Edwards
2008 #FC7 Carl Edwards
Wheels High Gear Flag Chasers Green
2006 #FC1 Carl Edwards
2007 #FC2 Carl Edwards
2008 #FC7 Carl Edwards
Wheels High Gear Flag Chasers Red
2006 #FC1 Carl Edwards
2007 #FC2 Carl Edwards
2008 #FC7 Carl Edwards
Wheels High Gear Flag Chasers White
2006 #FC1 Carl Edwards
2007 #FC2 Carl Edwards
2008 #FC7 Carl Edwards
Wheels High Gear Flag Chasers Yellow
2006 #FC1 Carl Edwards
2007 #FC2 Carl Edwards
2008 #FC7 Carl Edwards
Wheels High Gear Flag to Flag
2006 #FF6 Carl Edwards
Wheels High Gear Full Throttle
2008 #FT5 Carl Edwards
Wheels High Gear Last Lap
2008 #LL3 Carl Edwards
Wheels High Gear Last Lap Holofoil
2008 #LL3 Carl Edwards
Wheels High Gear MPH
2006 #M3 Carl Edwards
2006 #M31 Carl Edwards NBS
2006 #M50 Carl Edwards' Car C
2006 #M58 Carl Edwards NA
2006 #M64 Carl Edwards CM
2007 #M13 Carl Edwards
2007 #M33 Carl Edwards NBS
2007 #M74 Carl Edwards NI
2008 #M9 Carl Edwards
2008 #M32 Carl Edwards NBS
2008 #M54 Carl Edwards' Car C
2008 #M72 Carl Edwards' Car EL
Wheels High Gear Previews
2007 #EB13 Carl Edwards
2007 #EB33 Carl Edwards NBS
2008 #EB9 Carl Edwards
Wheels High Gear Previews Green
2006 #EB3 Carl Edwards
2006 #EB31 Carl Edwards NBS
Wheels High Gear The Chase
2008 #TC9 Carl Edwards
Wheels High Gear Top Tier
2006 #TT3 Carl Edwards

Gordon, Jeff

AC Racing Foldouts
1993 #24 Jeff Gordon
Action Packed
1993 #32 Jeff Gordon
1993 #61 Jeff Gordon YG
1993 #63 J.Gordon/Wallace/Lab.YG
1993 #86 Jeff Gordon CRC
1993 #87 Jeff Gordon's Car
1993 #93 Jeff Gordon D93
1993 #150 Jeff Gordon YG
1993 #153 Jeff Gordon YG
1993 #156 J.Gordon/Wallace/Lab.YG
1993 #173 Jeff Gordon
1993 #205 Jeff Gordon PS
1994 #14 Jeff Gordon
1994 #30 Jeff Gordon ROY
1994 #73 Jeff Gordon
1994 #103 Jeff Gordon DR
1994 #131 Jeff Gordon's Car
1994 #146 Jeff Gordon
1994 #189 Jeff Gordon WIN
1994 #209 Jeff Gordon WS
1997 #8 Jeff Gordon
1997 #29 Jeff Gordon's Car
1997 #P8 Jeff Gordon Promo
Action Packed 24K Gold
1993 #10G Jeff Gordon
1993 #12G J.Gordon/Wall./Lab.YG
1993 #26G Jeff Gordon YG
1993 #29G Jeff Gordon YG
1993 #32G J.Gordon/Wall./Lab.YG
1993 #36G Jeff Gordon D93
1993 #55G Jeff Gordon
1994 #27G Jeff Gordon
1994 #189G Jeff Gordon WIN AUTO
1997 #3 Jeff Gordon
Action Packed Badge of Honor Pins
1994 #1 Jeff Gordon
1995 #2 Jeff Gordon
Action Packed Champ and Challenger
1994 #1 Jeff Gordon
1994 #3 Jeff Gordon
1994 #4 Jeff Gordon
1994 #5 Jeff Gordon
1994 #6 Jeff Gordon
1994 #7 Jeff Gordon in Pits
1994 #8 Jeff Gordon in Pits
1994 #9 Jeff Gordon
1994 #10 Jeff Gordon
1994 #11 Jeff Gordon
1994 #13 Jeff Gordon
1994 #14 Jeff Gordon
1994 #15 Jeff Gordon
1994 #16 Jeff Gordon's Car
1994 #17 Jeff Gordon's Car
1994 #18 Jeff Gordon
1994 #19 Jeff Gordon
1994 #20 Jeff Gordon
1994 #41 Dale Earnhardt/Jeff Gordon Cars
1994 #42 Dale Earnhardt/Jeff Gordon
Action Packed Champ and Challenger 24K Gold
1994 #1G Jeff Gordon
1994 #5G Jeff Gordon
1994 #9G Jeff Gordon
1994 #17G Jeff Gordon's Car
1994 #20G Jeff Gordon
1994 #41G D.Earnhardt/J.Gordon Cars
1994 #42G D.Earnhardt/J.Gordon
Action Packed Chevy Madness
1997 #4 Jeff Gordon's Car
Action Packed Coastars
1994 #5 Jeff Gordon
Action Packed Country
1995 #6 Jeff Gordon RS
1995 #14 Jeff Gordon S
1995 #22 J.Gordon/Brooke MRO
1995 #50 Jeff Gordon WIN
1995 #51 Jeff Gordon WIN
1995 #63 Jeff Gordon
1995 #99 J.Gordon/R.Hendrick STO
1995 #P1 Jeff Gordon Promo
Action Packed Country 24K Team
1995 #1 Jeff Gordon
1995 #2 Jeff Gordon
1995 #3 Jeff Gordon
Action Packed Country Silver Speed
1995 #6 Jeff Gordon RS
1995 #14 Jeff Gordon S
1995 #22 B.Gordon/J.Gordon MRO
1995 #50 Jeff Gordon WIN
1995 #51 Jeff Gordon WIN
1995 #63 Jeff Gordon
Action Packed Country Team Rainbow
1995 #1 Jeff Gordon/Brooke Gordon
1995 #2 Jeff Gordon's Car
1995 #3 Jeff Gordon w/Crew
1995 #5 Jeff Gordon/Brooke Gordon
1995 #6 Pit Stop
1995 #7 Jeff Gordon's Car
1995 #8 Gordon/Evernham/Hendrick
1995 #9 Jeff Gordon's Helmet
1995 #10 Victory Shout
1995 #11 Interview
1995 #12 Jeff Gordon/Ray Evernham
1995 #P1 Jeff Gordon Promo #1
Action Packed Credentials
1996 #1 Jeff Gordon DC
1996 #2 Jeff Gordon DC
1996 #3 Jeff Gordon DC
1996 #4 Jeff Gordon DC
1996 #5 Jeff Gordon DC
1996 #20 Jeff Gordon
1996 #99 Jeff Gordon WCA
1996 #105 Jeff Gordon CL
Action Packed Credentials Fan Scan
1996 #4 Jeff Gordon
Action Packed Credentials Jumbos
1996 #2 Jeff Gordon
Action Packed Credentials Leaders of the Pack
1996 #5 Jeff Gordon
1996 #6 Jeff Gordon
1996 #7 Jeff Gordon
1996 #8 Jeff Gordon
Action Packed Credentials Promos
1996 #5 Jeff Gordon/Leader of the Pack
Action Packed Credentials Silver Speed
1996 #1 Jeff Gordon DC
1996 #2 Jeff Gordon DC
1996 #3 Jeff Gordon DC
1996 #4 Jeff Gordon DC
1996 #5 Jeff Gordon DC
1996 #20 Jeff Gordon
Action Packed Fifth Anniversary
1997 #8 Jeff Gordon
Action Packed First Impressions
1997 #8 Jeff Gordon
1997 #29 Jeff Gordon's Car
Action Packed Hendrick Motorsports
1995 #1 Jeff Gordon
Action Packed Mammoth
1994 #14 Jeff Gordon
1995 #MM4 Jeff Gordon
Action Packed McDonald's
1996 #3 Jeff Gordon
1996 #13 Jeff Gordon's Car
Action Packed Mint
1994 #14 Jeff Gordon
1994 #30 Jeff Gordon ROY
1994 #73 Jeff Gordon
1994 #103 Jeff Gordon DR
1994 #131 Jeff Gordon's Car
1994 #146 Jeff Gordon
1994 #189 Jeff Gordon WIN
1994 #209 Jeff Gordon WS
Action Packed Mint Collection Jeff Gordon
1994 #11 Jeff Gordon Gold Leaf
1994 #11 Jeff Gordon
1994 #19 Jeff Gordon Gold Leaf
1994 #19 Jeff Gordon
Action Packed Preview
1995 #9 Jeff Gordon
1995 #36 Jeff Gordon PW
1995 #50 Jeff Gordon WIN
1995 #66 Jeff Gordon T10
1995 #70 Jeff Gordon DD
Action Packed Preview 24K Gold
1995 #2G Jeff Gordon
Action Packed Prototypes
1993 #JG1 Jeff Gordon
1994 #2R942 Jeff Gordon
1994 #2R942G Jeff Gordon 24K Gold
1994 #3R94S Jeff Gordon
Action Packed Rolling Thunder
1997 #3 Jeff Gordon
Action Packed Stars
1995 #24 Jeff Gordon OC
1995 #40 Jeff Gordon's Car
1995 #47 Jeff Gordon RW
1995 #49 Jeff Gordon RW
1995 #51 Jeff Gordon RW
1995 #60 Jeff Gordon PP
1995 #61 Jeff Gordon PP
1995 #62 Jeff Gordon PP
1995 #63 Jeff Gordon PP
1995 #64 Jeff Gordon PP
1995 #65 Jeff Gordon PP
1995 #86 J.Gordon/B.Labonte/T.Lab.
Action Packed Stars 24K Gold
1995 #6G Jeff Gordon
1995 #19G Jeff Gordon
1995 #20G Jeff Gordon
1995 #2G Jeff Gordon
1995 #4G Jeff Gordon
Action Packed Stars Silver Speed
1995 #24 Jeff Gordon OC
1995 #40 Jeff Gordon's Car
1995 #47 Jeff Gordon RW
1995 #49 Jeff Gordon RW
1995 #51 Jeff Gordon RW
1995 #60 Jeff Gordon PP
1995 #61 Jeff Gordon PP
1995 #62 Jeff Gordon PP
1995 #63 Jeff Gordon PP
1995 #64 Jeff Gordon PP
1995 #65 Jeff Gordon PP
1995 #86 J.Gordon/B.Labonte/T.Labonte
Action Packed Stars Trucks That Haul
1995 #1 J.Gordon/Hend.Truck
ActionVision
1997 #2 J.Gordon Victory Lane
1997 #5 J.Gordon/R.Wall/T.Labonte
1997 #6 J.Gordon/T.Labonte/R.Craven
1997 #10 Jeff Gordon Pit Stop
Assets
1995 #3 Jeff Gordon
1995 #31 Jeff Gordon
1995 #49 Jeff Gordon's Car
1994-95 #68 Jeff Gordon
1994-95 #93 Jeff Gordon
Assets $100 Phone Cards
1995 #3 Jeff Gordon
Assets $1000 Phone Cards
1995 #3 Jeff Gordon
Assets $2 Phone Cards
1995 #9 Jeff Gordon
Assets $2 Phone Cards Gold Signature
1995 #9 Jeff Gordon
Assets $25 Phone Cards
1995 #4 Jeff Gordon
Assets $5 Phone Cards
1995 #4 Jeff Gordon
Assets *
1994-95 #68 Jeff Gordon
1994-95 #93 Jeff Gordon
Assets 1-Minute Phone Cards
1995 #9 Jeff Gordon
Assets 1-Minute Phone Cards Gold Signature
1995 #9 Jeff Gordon
Assets Coca-Cola 600 Die Cut Phone Cards
1995 #3 Jeff Gordon
Assets Die Cuts
1994-95 #DC19 Jeff Gordon's Car
Assets Die Cuts *
1994-95 #DC19 Jeff Gordon's Car
Assets Gold Signature
1995 #3 Jeff Gordon
1995 #31 Jeff Gordon
1995 #49 Jeff Gordon's Car
Assets Images Previews
1995 #RI4 Jeff Gordon
Assets Phone Cards $2
1994-95 #30 Jeff Gordon
Assets Phone Cards $2 *
1994-95 #30 Jeff Gordon
Assets Phone Cards $5
1994-95 #9 Jeff Gordon
Assets Phone Cards $5 *
1994-95 #9 Jeff Gordon
Assets Phone Cards One Minute
1994-95 #30 Jeff Gordon
Assets Phone Cards One Minute/$2 *
1994-95 #30 Jeff Gordon
Assets Racing
1996 #2 Jeff Gordon
Assets Racing $100 Cup Champion Interactive Phone Cards
1996 #2 Jeff Gordon
Assets Silver Signature
1994-95 #68 Jeff Gordon
Assets Silver Signature *
1994-95 #68 Jeff Gordon
Autographed Racing
1996 #2 Jeff Gordon
1997 #4 Jeff Gordon
Autographed Racing Autographs
1996 #16 Jeff Gordon
1997 #16 Jeff Gordon
Autographed Racing Autographs Certified Golds
1996 #16 Jeff Gordon
Autographed Racing Mayne Street
1997 #KM4 Jeff Gordon
Autographed Racing Take the Checkered Flag
1997 #TF1 Jeff Gordon/325
Big League Cards Creative Images

1998 #30 Jeff Gordon
Bleachers NASCAR
1994-96 #8 Jeff Gordon (#1) 1995 Upper Deck 10,000
1994-96 #9 Jeff Gordon (#2) 1996 10,000
1994-96 #10 Jeff Gordon (#3) 1995 Classic 2,500
Card Dynamics Black Top Busch Series
1994 #3 Jeff Gordon
Card Dynamics Double Eagle Postcards
1993-95 #1 Jeff Gordon Baby Ruth
1993-95 #7 Jeff Gordon DuPont
Card Dynamics Gant Oil
1993 #6 Jeff Gordon
1994 #4 Jeff Gordon
Card Dynamics Jeff Gordon Fan Club
1994 #1 Jeff Gordon
1994 #2 Jeff Gordon
1994 #3 Jeff Gordon
Card Dynamics Quik Chek
1993 #9 Jeff Gordon/7000
Classic Winston Cup Champion
1996 #J1 Jeff Gordon
1996 #J2 Jeff Gordon
1996 #J3 Jeff Gordon
1996 #J4 Jeff Gordon
1996 #J5 Jeff Gordon
Collector's Choice
1997 #24 Jeff Gordon
1997 #101 Jeff Gordon SC
1997 #127 Jeff Gordon T3
1997 #128 Jeff Gordon T3
1997 #129 Jeff Gordon's Car T3
1997 #154 Jeff Gordon CL
1997 #NNO Jeff Gordon 5X7 DD
1997 #NNO Jeff Gordon 5X7 MM
1997 #74 Jeff Gordon's Car MM
1998 #24 Jeff Gordon
1998 #60 Jeff Gordon's Car
1998 #88 Jeff Gordon PP
1998 #98 Jeff Gordon TD
Collector's Choice Speedecals
1997 #S47 Jeff Gordon's Car
1997 #S48 Jeff Gordon's Helmet
Collector's Choice Star Quest
1998 #SQ36 Jeff Gordon
1998 #SQ41 Jeff Gordon AUTO
Collector's Choice Triple Force
1997 #F1 Jeff Gordon
1997 #G2 Jeff Gordon
1997 #G3 Jeff Gordon
Collector's Choice Upper Deck 500
1997 #UD48 Jeff Gordon
1997 #UD49 Jeff Gordon's Car
Collector's Choice Victory Circle
1997 #VC9 Jeff Gordon
Crown Jewels
1995 #2 Jeff Gordon
1995 #68 J.Gordon/T.Labonte CJT
1995 #73 J.Gordon/T.Lab.Car CJT
1995 #75 Jeff Gordon RW
1995 #77 Jeff Gordon RW
1995 #DT1 J.Gordon/T.Labonte DT
Crown Jewels Diamond
1995 #2 Jeff Gordon
1995 #68 Jeff Gordon Terry Labonte CJT
1995 #73 Jeff Gordon Terry Labonte CJT
1995 #75 Jeff Gordon RW
1995 #77 Jeff Gordon RW
Crown Jewels Dual Jewels
1995 #DJ1 D.Earnhardt/J.Gordon
Crown Jewels Dual Jewels Diamond
1995 #DJ1 Dale Earnhardt/Jeff Gordon
Crown Jewels Dual Jewels Emerald
1995 #DJ1 Dale Earnhardt/Jeff Gordon
Crown Jewels Elite
1996 #2 Jeff Gordon
1996 #28 Jeff Gordon
1996 #29 Jeff Gordon
1996 #30 Jeff Gordon
Crown Jewels Elite Birthstones of the Champions
1996 #BC2 Jeff Gordon
Crown Jewels Elite Birthstones of the Champions Diamond Tribute
1996 #BC2 Jeff Gordon
Crown Jewels Elite Birthstones of the Champions Treasure Chest
1996 #BC2 Jeff Gordon
Crown Jewels Elite Crown Signature Amethyst
1996 #CS2 Jeff Gordon
Crown Jewels Elite Crown Signature Garnet
1996 #CS2 Jeff Gordon
Crown Jewels Elite Crown Signature Peridot
1996 #CS2 Jeff Gordon
Crown Jewels Elite Diamond Tribute
1996 #2 Jeff Gordon
1996 #28 Jeff Gordon
1996 #29 Jeff Gordon
1996 #30 Jeff Gordon
Crown Jewels Elite Diamond Tribute Citrine
1996 #2 Jeff Gordon
1996 #28 Jeff Gordon
1996 #29 Jeff Gordon
1996 #30 Jeff Gordon
Crown Jewels Elite Dual Jewels Amethyst
1996 #DJ1 D.Earnhardt/J.Gordon
Crown Jewels Elite Dual Jewels Amethyst Diamond Tribute
1996 #DJ1 D.Earnhardt/J.Gordon
Crown Jewels Elite Dual Jewels Amethyst Treasure Chest
1996 #DJ1 D.Earnhardt/J.Gordon
Crown Jewels Elite Dual Jewels Garnet
1996 #DJ1 D.Earnhardt/J.Gordon
Crown Jewels Elite Dual Jewels Garnet Diamond Tribute
1996 #DJ1 D.Earnhardt/J.Gordon
Crown Jewels Elite Dual Jewels Garnet Treasure Chest
1996 #DJ1 D.Earnhardt/J.Gordon
Crown Jewels Elite Dual Jewels Sapphire
1996 #DJ1 D.Earnhardt/J.Gordon
Crown Jewels Elite Dual Jewels Sapphire Treasure Chest
1996 #DJ1 D.Earnhardt/J.Gordon
Crown Jewels Elite Emerald
1996 #2 Jeff Gordon
1996 #28 Jeff Gordon
1996 #29 Jeff Gordon
1996 #30 Jeff Gordon
Crown Jewels Elite Emerald Treasure Chest
1996 #2 Jeff Gordon
1996 #28 Jeff Gordon
1996 #29 Jeff Gordon
1996 #30 Jeff Gordon
Crown Jewels Elite Sapphire
1996 #2 Jeff Gordon
1996 #28 Jeff Gordon
1996 #29 Jeff Gordon
1996 #30 Jeff Gordon
Crown Jewels Elite Sapphire Treasure Chest
1996 #2 Jeff Gordon
1996 #28 Jeff Gordon
1996 #29 Jeff Gordon
1996 #30 Jeff Gordon
Crown Jewels Elite Treasure Chest
1996 #2 Jeff Gordon
1996 #28 Jeff Gordon
1996 #29 Jeff Gordon
1996 #30 Jeff Gordon
Crown Jewels Emerald
1995 #2 Jeff Gordon
1995 #68 J. Gordon CJT/T.Labonte CJT
1995 #73 Jeff Gordon CJT Terry Labonte
1995 #75 Jeff Gordon RW
1995 #77 Jeff Gordon RW
Crown Jewels Promos
1995 #PD1 Jeff Gordon Diamond/3000
1995 #PE1 Jeff Gordon Emerald/6000
1995 #PR1 Jeff Gordon Ruby/12,000
Crown Jewels Sapphire
1995 #2 Jeff Gordon
1995 #68 Jeff Gordon/T.Labonte CJT
1995 #73 Jeff Gordon/T.Labonte's Car CJT
1995 #75 Jeff Gordon RW
1995 #77 Jeff Gordon RW
Crown Jewels Signature Gems
1995 #SG1 Jeff Gordon
eTopps
2003 #4 Jeff Gordon/6000
Finish Line
1993 #14 Jeff Gordon's Car
1993 #83 Jeff Gordon CRC
1993 #110 Jeff Gordon
1994 #36 Jeff Gordon
1994 #75 Jeff Gordon
1994 #123 Jeff Gordon's Car
1994 #NNO Jeff Gordon ROY
1995 #24 Jeff Gordon
1995 #53 Jeff Gordon
1995 #67 Jeff Gordon w/Crew
1995 #105 Jeff Gordon
1996 #1 Jeff Gordon
1996 #87 Jeff Gordon
1996 #95 Jeff Gordon's Car
Finish Line Black Gold
1996 #C1 Jeff Gordon's Car
1996 #D1 Jeff Gordon
1996 #SG1 Jeff Gordon Special Gold
1996 #JPC2 Jeff Gordon
Finish Line Coca-Cola 600
1995 #3 Jeff Gordon
1995 #31 Jeff Gordon
1995 #49 Jeff Gordon's Car
Finish Line Coca-Cola 600 Die Cuts
1995 #C3 Jeff Gordon
Finish Line Coca-Cola 600 Winners
1995 #CC10 Jeff Gordon
Finish Line Commemorative Sheets
1993 #10 Sonoma
1993 #11 Charlotte
1993 #23 Richmond
Finish Line Diamond Collection $5 Phone Cards
1996 #1 Jeff Gordon
Finish Line Gold
1994 #11 Jeff Gordon
1994 #28 Jeff Gordon
1994 #60 Jeff Gordon
1994 #65 Jeff Gordon's Car
1994 #88 Jeff Gordon
Finish Line Gold Phone Cards
1994 #2 Jeff Gordon/3000
Finish Line Gold Promos
1994 #P1 Jeff Gordon's Car Promo
Finish Line Gold Signature
1995 #GS1 Jeff Gordon
1996 #GS1 Jeff Gordon
Finish Line Gold Teamwork
1994 #TG6 Jeff Gordon/R.Evernham
Finish Line Man and Machine
1996 #MM1 Jeff Gordon
Finish Line Mega-Phone XL Phone Cards
1996 #2 Jeff Gordon
Finish Line Phone Card of the Month
1995 #1 Jeff Gordon/1500
Finish Line Phone Cards
1994 #2 Jeff Gordon
1994 #8 Jeff Gordon
Finish Line Phone Pak
1996 #11 Jeff Gordon
1996 #12 Jeff Gordon's Car
Finish Line Phone Pak $10
1996 #3 Jeff Gordon
Finish Line Phone Pak $100
1996 #2 Jeff Gordon
Finish Line Phone Pak $1000
1996 #K1 Jeff Gordon
Finish Line Phone Pak $2 Signature
1996 #11 Jeff Gordon
1996 #12 Jeff Gordon's Car
Finish Line Phone Pak $5
1996 #9 Jeff Gordon
Finish Line Phone Pak $50
1996 #2 Jeff Gordon
Finish Line Phone Pak II
1997 #1 Jeff Gordon
1997 #80 Jeff Gordon's Car $10
1997 #87 Jeff Gordon $50
1997 #95 Jeff Gordon $100
1997 #P1 Jeff Gordon Promo
1997 #39 Jeff Gordon $5
Finish Line Platinum 5-Unit Phone Cards
1995 #1 Jeff Gordon
Finish Line Printer's Proof
1995 #24 Jeff Gordon
1995 #53 Jeff Gordon
1995 #67 Jeff Gordon w/Crew
1995 #105 Jeff Gordon
1996 #1 Jeff Gordon
1996 #87 Jeff Gordon
1996 #95 Jeff Gordon's Car
Finish Line Promos
1993 #P2 Jeff Gordon
Finish Line Rise To The Top Jeff Gordon
1996 #JG1 Jeff Gordon
1996 #JG2 Jeff Gordon
1996 #JG3 Jeff Gordon
1996 #JG4 Jeff Gordon
1996 #JG5 Jeff Gordon
1996 #JG6 Jeff Gordon
1996 #JG7 Jeff Gordon
1996 #JG8 Jeff Gordon
1996 #JG9 Jeff Gordon
1996 #JG10 Jeff Gordon
Finish Line Silver
1993 #14 Jeff Gordon's Car
1993 #83 Jeff Gordon
1993 #110 Jeff Gordon
1994 #36 Jeff Gordon
1994 #75 Jeff Gordon
1994 #123 Jeff Gordon's Car
1995 #24 Jeff Gordon/Brooke Sealy
1995 #53 Jeff Gordon
1995 #67 Jeff Gordon/Ray Evernham
1995 #105 Jeff Gordon
1996 #1 Jeff Gordon
1996 #87 Jeff Gordon
1996 #95 Jeff Gordon's Car
Finish Line Standout Cars
1995 #SC7 Jeff Gordon's Car
Finish Line Standout Drivers
1995 #SD7 Jeff Gordon
Finish Line SuperTrucks
1995 #17 Jeff Gordon
Finish Line SuperTrucks Rainbow Foil
1995 #17 Jeff Gordon
Finish Line SuperTrucks Super Signature
1995 #SS1 Jeff Gordon
Flair
1996 #12 Jeff Gordon
1996 #68 Jeff Gordon's Car
1996 #99 Jeff Gordon CL
1996 #P1 Jeff Gordon Promo
Flair Autographs
1996 #4 Jeff Gordon
Flair Center Spotlight
1996 #4 Jeff Gordon
Flair Hot Numbers
1996 #3 Jeff Gordon
Flair Power Performance
1996 #4 Jeff Gordon
High Gear Promos
1994 #P1 Jeff Gordon Silver
1995 #P2 Jeff Gordon
High Gear Promos Gold
1994 #P1 Jeff Gordon Gold
Highland Mint/VIP
1994-95 #3B Jeff Gordon/5000
1994-95 #3S Jeff Gordon/1000
Hi-Tech Brickyard 400
1994 #20 Jeff Gordon's Car
1994 #52 Jeff Gordon
1994 #69 Jeff Gordon
1995 #P1 Jeff Gordon Club Promo
1995 #3 Jeff Gordon's Car UER 00
1995 #40 Jeff Gordon Race Action
1995 #53 Gordon/G.Bod/Schr.Cars
1995 #88 Jeff Gordon
1995 #89 Jeff Gordon's Car
1995 #NNO J.Gordon Silver/1000
1995 #NNO Jeff Gordon Gold/10000
Hi-Tech Brickyard 400 Artist Proofs
1994 #20 Jeff Gordon's Car
1994 #52 Jeff Gordon
1994 #69 Jeff Gordon
Hi-Tech Brickyard 400 Prototypes
1994 #2 Jeff Gordon's Car
Hi-Tech Brickyard 400 Top Ten
1995 #BY1 Jeff Gordon
Images
1995 #24 Jeff Gordon
1995 #48 Jeff Gordon
1995 #72 Jeff Gordon
1995 #100 Jeff Gordon CL
1995 #P1 Jeff Gordon Promo
Images Driven
1995 #D2 Jeff Gordon
Images Gold
1995 #24 Jeff Gordon
1995 #48 Jeff Gordon
1995 #72 Jeff Gordon
1995 #99 Jeff Gordon CL
Images Hard Chargers
1995 #HC8 Jeff Gordon
Images Owner's Pride
1995 #OP5 Jeff Gordon
Images Race Reflections Jeff Gordon
1995 #JG1 Jeff Gordon
1995 #JG2 Jeff Gordon
1995 #JG3 Jeff Gordon
1995 #JG4 Jeff Gordon
1995 #JG5 Jeff Gordon
1995 #JG6 Jeff Gordon
1995 #JG7 Jeff Gordon
1995 #JG8 Jeff Gordon
1995 #JG9 Jeff Gordon
1995 #JG10 Jeff Gordon
Images Race Reflections Jeff Gordon Facsimile Signature
1995 #JG1 Jeff Gordon
1995 #JG2 Jeff Gordon
1995 #JG3 Jeff Gordon
1995 #JG4 Jeff Gordon
1995 #JG5 Jeff Gordon
1995 #JG6 Jeff Gordon
1995 #JG7 Jeff Gordon
1995 #JG8 Jeff Gordon
1995 #JG9 Jeff Gordon
1995 #JG10 Jeff Gordon
Jurassic Park
1997 #1 Jeff Gordon
1997 #48 Jeff Gordon
1997 #51 Jeff Gordon
Jurassic Park Carnivore
1997 #C2 Jeff Gordon
Jurassic Park Pteranodon
1997 #P2 Jeff Gordon
Jurassic Park Raptors
1997 #R2 Jeff Gordon
Jurassic Park The Ride Jeff Gordon
1997 #1 Jeff Gordon
1997 #2 Jeff Gordon
1997 #3 Jeff Gordon
1997 #4 Jeff Gordon
1997 #5 Jeff Gordon
Jurassic Park Thunder Lizard
1997 #TL1 Jeff Gordon
Jurassic Park T-Rex
1997 #TR2 Jeff Gordon
Jurassic Park Triceratops
1997 #1 Jeff Gordon
1997 #48 Jeff Gordon
1997 #51 Jeff Gordon
Kenner 12-inch Specials *
1998 #4 Jeff Gordon (Hills)
KnightQuest
1996 #2 Jeff Gordon K
1996 #21 Jeff Gordon C
1996 #30 Jeff Gordon C
1996 #31 Jeff Gordon C
KnightQuest Black Knights
1996 #2 Jeff Gordon K
1996 #21 Jeff Gordon C
1996 #30 Jeff Gordon C
1996 #31 Jeff Gordon C
KnightQuest First Knights
1996 #FK3 Jeff Gordon
KnightQuest Knights of the Round Table
1996 #KT1 Jeff Gordon
KnightQuest Protectors of the Crown
1996 #PC6 Jeff Gordon
KnightQuest Red Knight Preview
1996 #2 Jeff Gordon K
1996 #21 Jeff Gordon C
1996 #30 Jeff Gordon C
1996 #31 Jeff Gordon C
KnightQuest Royalty
1996 #2 Jeff Gordon K
1996 #21 Jeff Gordon C
1996 #30 Jeff Gordon C
1996 #31 Jeff Gordon C
KnightQuest White Knights
1996 #2 Jeff Gordon K
1996 #21 Jeff Gordon C
1996 #30 Jeff Gordon C
1996 #31 Jeff Gordon C
Limited Editions Jeff Gordon
1992 #3 Jeff Gordon's Car
1992 #4 Jeff Gordon
1992 #5 Jeff Gordon
1992 #6 Jeff Gordon
1992 #7 Jeff Gordon's Car
1992 #8 Jeff Gordon
1992 #9 Jeff Gordon
1992 #10 Jeff Gordon Race Action
1992 #11 Jeff Gordon
1992 #12 Jeff Gordon
1992 #2 Jeff Gordon
1992 #AU2 Jeff Gordon AU/300
Limited Editions Promos
1992 #4 Jeff Gordon
Maxwell House
1993 #24 Jeff Gordon/K.Wall/B.Labonte
1993 #25 Jeff Gordon
Maxx
1993 #24 Jeff Gordon CRC
1993 #168 Jeff Gordon's Car
1994 #13 Jeff Gordon MM
1994 #24 Jeff Gordon
1994 #65 Jeff Gordon's Car
1994 #201 Jeff Gordon WC ROY
1994 #327 Jeff Gordon's Car WS
1994 #328 Jeff Gordon WS
1994 #335 Gordon/R.Wall/Earn.Cars
1994 #S24 Jeff Gordon Sample
1995 #80 Jeff Gordon VL
1995 #105 Jeff Gordon VL
1995 #139 Gord/DW/T.Lab/Sch.Cars VL
1995 #169 Jeff Gordon's Car
1995 #3 Jeff Gordon's Car MM
1995 #237 Jeff Gordon's Car
1995 #P1G Jeff Gordon in Pits Promo
1995 #P1R Jeff Gordon in Pits Promo Red Foil
1995 #24 Jeff Gordon
1995 #72 Jeff Gordon VL
1995 #236 Jeff Gordon
1996 #24 Jeff Gordon
1996 #88 Jeff Gordon's Car
1997 #24 Jeff Gordon
1997 #69 Jeff Gordon's Car
1998 #24 Jeff Gordon
1998 #54 Jeff Gordon's Car
1998 #64 Jeff Gordon's Car HC
1998 #91 Jeff Gordon's Car FR
1999 #1 Jeff Gordon
1999 #2 Jeff Gordon's Car
1999 #3 Jeff Gordon's Car RR
1999 #90 Jeff Gordon CL
2000 #24 Jeff Gordon
2000 #59 Jeff Gordon's Car
2000 #77 Jeff Gordon's Car FRF
Maxx 10th Anniversary
1998 #24 Jeff Gordon
1998 #69 Jeff Gordon's Car
1998 #124 Jeff Gordon
1998 #125 Jeff Gordon
1998 #126 Jeff Gordon
Maxx 10th Anniversary Buy Back Autographs
1998 #21 Jeff Gordon '92 #29
1998 #22 Jeff Gordon '92 #50 ROY/10
1998 #23 Jeff Gordon '93 #24/10
1998 #24 Jeff Gordon '94 #13/10
1998 #25 Jeff Gordon '94 #16
Maxx 10th Anniversary Card of the Year
1998 #CY5 Jeff Gordon
1998 #CY10 Jeff Gordon
Maxx 10th Anniversary Champions Past
1998 #CP1 Jeff Gordon
Maxx 10th Anniversary Champions Past Die Cuts
1998 #CP1 Jeff Gordon
Maxx 10th Anniversary Maxximum Preview
1998 #P24 Jeff Gordon
Maxx 1997 Year In Review
1998 #1 Jeff Gordon
1998 #5 Hendrick Sweep
1998 #6 Jeff Gordon's Car
1998 #29 Jeff Gordon's Car
1998 #31 Jeff Gordon's Car
1998 #36 Jeff Gordon's Car
1998 #51 Jeff Gordon's Car
1998 #52 Jeff Gordon
1998 #61 Jeff Gordon
1998 #71 Jeff Gordon
1998 #96 Jeff Gordon's Car
1998 #111 Jeff Gordon
1998 #121 Jeff Gordon
1998 #130 Jeff Gordon's Car
1998 #AW1 Jeff Gordon
1998 #P01 Jeff Gordon
Maxx Autographs
1994 #24 Jeff Gordon
1995 #24 Jeff Gordon
1996 #24 Jeff Gordon
Maxx Black
1992 #29 Jeff Gordon
1992 #50 Jeff Gordon ROY
Maxx Black Update
1992 #U6 Jeff Gordon
Maxx Chase the Champion
1996 #1 Jeff Gordon
1996 #2 Jeff Gordon
1996 #3 Jeff Gordon
1996 #4 Jeff Gordon
1996 #5 Jeff Gordon
1996 #6 Jeff Gordon
1996 #7 Jeff Gordon
1996 #8 Jeff Gordon
1996 #9 Jeff Gordon
1996 #10 Jeff Gordon
1996 #11 Jeff Gordon
1996 #12 Jeff Gordon
1996 #13 Jeff Gordon
1996 #14 Jeff Gordon
1997 #C1 Jeff Gordon
Maxx Chase the Champion Gold Die Cuts
1997 #C1 Jeff Gordon
Maxx Club Sam Bass Chromium
1993 #7 Jeff Gordon
1993 #10 Jeff Gordon
Maxx Drive Time
2000 #DT2 Jeff Gordon
Maxx FANtastic Finishes
1999 #F1 Jeff Gordon's Car
2000 #FF9 Jeff Gordon
Maxx Flag Firsts
1997 #FF24 Jeff Gordon
Maxx Focus on a Champion
1998 #FC1 Jeff Gordon
1999 #FC1 Jeff Gordon
2000 #FC5 Jeff Gordon
Maxx Focus on a Champion Cel
1998 #FC1 Jeff Gordon
Maxx Focus on a Champion Gold
1999 #FC1 Jeff Gordon
Maxx Jeff Gordon
1993 #1 Jeff Gordon Youth
1993 #2 Jeff Gordon Youth
1993 #3 Jeff Gordon Youth
1993 #4 Jeff Gordon Youth
1993 #5 Jeff Gordon Youth
1993 #6 Jeff Gordon Youth
1993 #7 Jeff Gordon Youth
1993 #8 Jeff Gordon 1986
1993 #9 Jeff Gordon 1989
1993 #10 Jeff Gordon BGN ROY
1993 #11 Jeff Gordon
1993 #12 Jeff Gordon
1993 #13 Jeff Gordon w/Crew
1993 #14 Jeff Gordon w/Crew
1993 #15 Jeff Gordon's Car
1993 #16 Jeff Gordon w/Mom
1993 #17 Jeff Gordon's Car
1993 #18 Jeff Gordon
1993 #19 Jeff Gordon
1993 #20 Jeff Gordon
1993 #NNO Jeff Gordon AU
Maxx Lowes Foods Stickers
1993 #2 B.Elliott/D.Waltrip/J.Gordon
Maxx Made in America
1996 #24 Jeff Gordon
Maxx Medallion
1994 #1 Jeff Gordon's Car
1994 #46 J.Gordon/Earnhardt Cars
1994 #47 Gordon's Car YL
1994 #48 Coming Off Turn One/Gordon's Car
1994 #49 Jeff Gordon/G.Bodine Cars
1994 #50 Jeff Gordon's Car JR
1994 #52 Jeff Gordon/Irvan Cars
1994 #53 Jeff Gordon BY
1994 #56 Jeff Gordon
1995 #17 Jeff Gordon
1995 #47 Jeff Gordon's Car
Maxx Medallion Blue
1995 #17 Jeff Gordon
1995 #47 Jeff Gordon's Car
Maxx Medallion Jeff Gordon Puzzle
1995 #3 Jeff Gordon
1995 #4 Jeff Gordon SP
1995 #5 Jeff Gordon
1995 #6 Jeff Gordon
1995 #7 Jeff Gordon
1995 #8 Jeff Gordon
1995 #9 Jeff Gordon
1995 #NNO Jeff Gordon AUTO/999
1995 #2 Jeff Gordon
1995 #1 Jeff Gordon
Maxx Medallion On the Road Again
1995 #OTR2 Jeff Gordon's Transporter
Maxx Odyssey
1996 #24 Jeff Gordon
Maxx Odyssey Millennium
1996 #MM6 Jeff Gordon
Maxx Oval Office
2000 #OO3 Jeff Gordon
Maxx Over the Wall
1995 #1 Jeff Gordon in Pits
Maxx Premier Plus
1993 #24 Jeff Gordon CRC
1993 #39 Jeff Gordon's Car
1993 #NNO J.Gordon/B.Lab/K.Wall
1994 #13 Jeff Gordon MM
1994 #24 Jeff Gordon
1994 #46 Jeff Gordon WC ROY
1994 #65 Jeff Gordon's Car
1995 #24 Jeff Gordon
1995 #64 Jeff Gordon's Car
1995 #158 Jeff Gordon VL
1995 #160 Jeff Gordon VL
1995 #168 Jeff Gordon VL
1995 #147 Jeff Gordon VL
Maxx Premier Plus Crown Chrome
1995 #24 Jeff Gordon
1995 #64 Jeff Gordon's Car
1995 #147 Jeff Gordon VL
1995 #158 Jeff Gordon VL
1995 #160 Jeff Gordon VL
1995 #168 Jeff Gordon VL
Maxx Premier Plus PaceSetters
1995 #PS7 Jeff Gordon
Maxx Premier Plus PaceSetters Crown Chrome
1995 #PS7 Jeff Gordon
Maxx Premier Series
1993 #24 Jeff Gordon CRC
1993 #168 Jeff Gordon's Car
1994 #13 Jeff Gordon MM
1994 #24 Jeff Gordon
1994 #65 Jeff Gordon's Car
1994 #260 Jeff Gordon WC ROY
1995 #64 Jeff Gordon's Car
1995 #3 Jeff Gordon's Car MM
1995 #24 Jeff Gordon
1995 #257 Jeff Gordon w/ Crew
1995 #283 Jeff Gordon YR
1995 #273 Jeff Gordon YR
1995 #275 Jeff Gordon YR
1995 #262 Jeff Gordon YR
1996 #24 Jeff Gordon
1996 #296 Jeff Gordon WC Champ
Maxx Premier Series Jumbos
1994 #8 Jeff Gordon
Maxx Race Ticket
1999 #RT22 Jeff Gordon's Car
Maxx Racer's Ink
1999 #JG Jeff Gordon
Maxx Racing Champions
1994 #1 Jeff Gordon
Maxx Racing Images
1999 #RI24 Jeff Gordon
Maxx Red
1992 #29 Jeff Gordon
1992 #50 Jeff Gordon ROY
Maxx Red Update
1992 #U6 Jeff Gordon
Maxx Rookies of the Year
1994 #16 Jeff Gordon
1997 #MR6 Jeff Gordon
Maxx Sam Bass
1996 #1 Jeff Gordon
1996 #2 Jeff Gordon's Car
Maxx Signed, Sealed, and Delivered
1999 #S3 Jeff Gordon/250
Maxx Speedway Boogie
2000 #SB1 Jeff Gordon
Maxx Teamwork
1996 #TW1 Jeff Gordon's Car
Maxx The Select 25
1994 #14 Jeff Gordon
Maxx Winnebago Motorsports
1993 #2 J.Gordon/B.Lab/Bickle/K.Wall.
Maxximum
1998 #24 Jeff Gordon
1998 #49 Jeff Gordon's Car
1998 #74 Jeff Gordon
1998 #99 Jeff Gordon's Car
1998 #S24 Jeff Gordon Sample
2000 #6 Jeff Gordon
2000 #44 Jeff Gordon CL
Maxximum Battle Proven
1998 #B5 Jeff Gordon
Maxximum Cruise Control
2000 #CC9 Jeff Gordon
Maxximum Dialed In
2000 #DI3 Jeff Gordon
Maxximum Die Cuts
2000 #6 Jeff Gordon
2000 #44 Jeff Gordon CL
Maxximum Field Generals Four Star Autographs
1998 #3 Jeff Gordon
Maxximum Field Generals One Star
1998 #3 Jeff Gordon
Maxximum Field Generals Three Star Autographs
1998 #3 Jeff Gordon
Maxximum Field Generals Two Star
1998 #3 Jeff Gordon
Maxximum First Class
1998 #F1 Jeff Gordon
Maxximum MPH
2000 #6 Jeff Gordon/24
2000 #44 Jeff Gordon CL/24
Maxximum Roots of Racing
2000 #R5 Jeff Gordon
McFarlane NASCAR 12-Inch Figures Series 1
2005 #10 Jeff Gordon
McFarlane NASCAR 3-Inch Series 1
2005 #20 Jeff Gordon
McFarlane NASCAR Series 1
2003 #NNO Jeff Gordon R w/o Hat
2003 #NNO Jeff Gordon R w/Hat
2003 #NNO Jeff Gordon H w/o Hat
2003 #NNO Jeff Gordon H w/Hat and Glasses
McFarlane NASCAR Series 2
2004 #30 Jeff Gordon R DuPont with Hat
2004 #31 Jeff Gordon R DuPont with Hat and Glasses
2004 #35 Jeff Gordon H Pepsi without Hat

2004 #36 Jeff Gordon H Pepsi with Hat

McFarlane NASCAR Series 4

2005 #40 Jeff Gordon R
2005 #41 Jeff Gordon R Glasses
2005 #45 Jeff Gordon H Pepsi

McFarlane NASCAR Series 6

2005 #80 Jeff Gordon

Metallic Impressions 25th Anniversary Winston Cup Champions

1996 #25 Jeff Gordon

Metallic Impressions Jeff Gordon Winston Cup Champ 10-Card Tin

1996 #1 Jeff Gordon
1996 #2 Jeff Gordon
1996 #3 Jeff Gordon
1996 #4 Jeff Gordon
1996 #5 Jeff Gordon
1996 #6 Jeff Gordon
1996 #7 Jeff Gordon
1996 #8 Jeff Gordon
1996 #9 Jeff Gordon
1996 #10 Jeff Gordon

Metallic Impressions Jeff Gordon Winston Cup Champ 5-Card Tin

1996 #1 Jeff Gordon
1996 #2 Jeff Gordon
1996 #3 Jeff Gordon
1996 #4 Jeff Gordon
1996 #5 Jeff Gordon

Metallic Impressions Winston Cup Top Five

1996 #2 Jeff Gordon

M-Force

1996 #19 Jeff Gordon
1996 #20 Jeff Gordon's Car
1996 #40 Jeff Gordon
1996 #P1 Jeff Gordon Blue Promo
1996 #P2 Jeff Gordon Green Promo
1996 #P3 Jeff Gordon Silver Promo

M-Force Black

1996 #B7 Jeff Gordon
1996 #B8 Jeff Gordon's Car
1996 #B12 Jeff Gordon

M-Force Sheet Metal

1996 #M5 Jeff Gordon

M-Force Silvers

1996 #S10 Jeff Gordon's Car
1996 #S14 Jeff Gordon

MW Windows

1994 #1 Jeff Gordon
1994 #5 Gordon/B.Labonte/T.Labonte/Schrader

National Trading Card Day

2004 #PP2 Jeff Gordon

National Trading Card Day *

2004 #PP2 Jeff Gordon

Pinnacle

1996 #24 Jeff Gordon
1996 #51 Jeff Gordon's Car
1996 #66 Jeff Gordon PER
1996 #67 Jeff Gordon PER
1996 #68 Jeff Gordon PER
1996 #69 Jeff Gordon PER
1996 #70 Jeff Gordon PER
1996 #71 Jeff Gordon PER
1996 #72 Jeff Gordon PER
1996 #73 Jeff Gordon PER
1996 #85 Jeff Gordon W
1996 #92 Jeff Gordon's Transporter
1996 #95 Jeff Gordon CL
1997 #24 Jeff Gordon
1997 #53 Jeff Gordon's Car

Pinnacle Artist Proofs

1996 #24 Jeff Gordon
1996 #51 Jeff Gordon's Car
1996 #66 Jeff Gordon PER
1996 #67 Jeff Gordon PER
1996 #68 Jeff Gordon PER
1996 #69 Jeff Gordon PER
1996 #70 Jeff Gordon PER
1996 #71 Jeff Gordon PER
1996 #72 Jeff Gordon PER
1996 #73 Jeff Gordon PER
1996 #85 Jeff Gordon W
1996 #92 Jeff Gordon's Transporter
1996 #95 Jeff Gordon CL
1997 #24 Jeff Gordon P
1997 #53 Jeff Gordon's Car B

Pinnacle Certified

1997 #89 Jeff Gordon BD
1997 #74 Jeff Gordon's Car WP
1997 #58 Jeff Gordon's Car
1997 #24 Jeff Gordon

Pinnacle Certified Certified Team

1997 #2 Jeff Gordon

Pinnacle Certified Certified Team Gold

1997 #2 Jeff Gordon

Pinnacle Certified Epix

1997 #E2 Jeff Gordon

Pinnacle Certified Epix Emerald

1997 #E2 Jeff Gordon

Pinnacle Certified Epix Purple

1997 #E2 Jeff Gordon

Pinnacle Certified Mirror Blue

1997 #24 Jeff Gordon
1997 #58 Jeff Gordon's Car
1997 #74 Jeff Gordon's Car WP
1997 #89 Jeff Gordon BD

Pinnacle Certified Mirror Gold

1997 #24 Jeff Gordon
1997 #58 Jeff Gordon's Car
1997 #74 Jeff Gordon's Car WP
1997 #89 Jeff Gordon BD

Pinnacle Certified Mirror Red

1997 #24 Jeff Gordon
1997 #58 Jeff Gordon's Car
1997 #74 Jeff Gordon's Car WP
1997 #89 Jeff Gordon BD

Pinnacle Certified Red

1997 #24 Jeff Gordon
1997 #58 Jeff Gordon's Car
1997 #74 Jeff Gordon's Car WP
1997 #89 Jeff Gordon BD

Pinnacle Checkered Flag

1996 #1 Jeff Gordon

Pinnacle Chevy Madness

1997 #15 Jeff Gordon's Car

Pinnacle Collector's Club

1997 #RC4 Jeff Gordon

Pinnacle Cut Above

1996 #1 Jeff Gordon

Pinnacle Foil

1997 #24 Jeff Gordon
1997 #53 Jeff Gordon's Car

Pinnacle Mint

1997 #2 Jeff Gordon
1997 #24 Jeff Gordon's Car
1998 #1 Jeff Gordon
1998 #13 Jeff Gordon's Car
1998 #27 Jeff Gordon MM

Pinnacle Mint Bronze

1997 #2 Jeff Gordon
1997 #24 Jeff Gordon's Car

Pinnacle Mint Championship Mint

1998 #1 Jeff Gordon
1998 #2 Jeff Gordon's Car

Pinnacle Mint Championship Mint Coins

1998 #1A Jeff Gordon's Car
1998 #1B Jeff Gordon's Car Jumbo
1998 #2A Jeff Gordon
1998 #2B Jeff Gordon Jumbo

Pinnacle Mint Coins

1997 #2 Jeff Gordon
1997 #24 Jeff Gordon's Car
1998 #1 Jeff Gordon
1998 #13 Jeff Gordon's Car
1998 #3 Jeff Gordon MM

Pinnacle Mint Coins 24K Gold Plated

1997 #2 Jeff Gordon
1997 #24 Jeff Gordon's Car

Pinnacle Mint Coins Bronze Proof

1998 #1 Jeff Gordon
1998 #13 Jeff Gordon's Car
1998 #3 Jeff Gordon MM

Pinnacle Mint Coins Gold Plated

1998 #1 Jeff Gordon
1998 #13 Jeff Gordon's Car
1998 #27 Jeff Gordon MM

Pinnacle Mint Coins Gold Plated Proofs

1998 #1 Jeff Gordon
1998 #13 Jeff Gordon's Car
1998 #27 Jeff Gordon MM

Pinnacle Mint Coins Nickel-Silver

1997 #2 Jeff Gordon
1997 #24 Jeff Gordon's Car
1998 #1 Jeff Gordon
1998 #13 Jeff Gordon's Car
1998 #27 Jeff Gordon MM

Pinnacle Mint Coins Silver Plated Proofs

1998 #1 Jeff Gordon
1998 #13 Jeff Gordon's Car
1998 #27 Jeff Gordon MM

Pinnacle Mint Coins Solid Gold

1998 #1 Jeff Gordon
1998 #13 Jeff Gordon's Car
1998 #27 Jeff Gordon MM

Pinnacle Mint Coins Solid Silver

1998 #1 Jeff Gordon
1998 #13 Jeff Gordon's Car
1998 #27 Jeff Gordon MM

Pinnacle Mint Die Cuts

1998 #1 Jeff Gordon
1998 #13 Jeff Gordon's Car
1998 #27 Jeff Gordon MM

Pinnacle Mint Gold

1997 #2 Jeff Gordon
1997 #24 Jeff Gordon's Car

Pinnacle Mint Gold Team

1998 #1 Jeff Gordon
1998 #13 Jeff Gordon's Car
1998 #27 Jeff Gordon MM

Pinnacle Mint Silver

1997 #2 Jeff Gordon
1997 #24 Jeff Gordon's Car

Pinnacle Mint Silver Team

1998 #1 Jeff Gordon
1998 #13 Jeff Gordon's Car
1998 #27 Jeff Gordon MM

Pinnacle Pepsi Jeff Gordon

1997 #1 Jeff Gordon
1997 #2 Jeff Gordon's Car
1997 #3 Jeff Gordon

Pinnacle Pole Position

1996 #24 Jeff Gordon
1996 #40 Jeff Gordon's Car
1996 #51 Jeff Gordon 95C
1996 #52 Jeff Gordon 95C
1996 #53 Jeff Gordon 95C
1996 #54 Jeff Gordon 95C
1996 #55 Jeff Gordon 95C
1996 #68 Jeff Gordon WIN
1996 #69 Jeff Gordon WIN
1996 #73 Jeff Gordon EY

Pinnacle Pole Position Certified Strong

1996 #1 Jeff Gordon

Pinnacle Pole Position Lightning Fast

1996 #24 Jeff Gordon
1996 #40 Jeff Gordon's Car
1996 #51 Jeff Gordon
1996 #52 Jeff Gordon
1996 #53 Jeff Gordon
1996 #54 Jeff Gordon
1996 #55 Jeff Gordon
1996 #68 Jeff Gordon
1996 #69 Jeff Gordon
1996 #73 Jeff Gordon

Pinnacle Pole Position No Limit

1996 #1 Jeff Gordon

Pinnacle Pole Position No Limit Gold

1996 #1 Jeff Gordon

Pinnacle Portraits

1997 #1 Jeff Gordon
1997 #21 Jeff Gordon's Car

Pinnacle Portraits 8x10

1997 #JG1 Jeff Gordon
1997 #JG2 Jeff Gordon
1997 #JG3 Jeff Gordon
1997 #JG4 Jeff Gordon

Pinnacle Portraits 8x10 Dufex

1997 #JG1 Jeff Gordon
1997 #JG2 Jeff Gordon
1997 #JG3 Jeff Gordon
1997 #JG4 Jeff Gordon

Pinnacle Precision

1997 #3 Jeff Gordon
1997 #4 Jeff Gordon Pit Action
1997 #5 Jeff Gordon's Car
1997 #6 Jeff Gordon
1997 #8 Jeff Gordon's Car
1997 #9 Jeff Gordon

Pinnacle Precision Bronze

1997 #3 Jeff Gordon
1997 #4 Jeff Gordon Pit Action
1997 #5 Jeff Gordon's Car
1997 #6 Jeff Gordon
1997 #8 Jeff Gordon's Car
1997 #9 Jeff Gordon

Pinnacle Precision Gold

1997 #3 Jeff Gordon
1997 #4 Jeff Gordon Pit Action
1997 #5 Jeff Gordon's Car
1997 #6 Jeff Gordon
1997 #8 Jeff Gordon's Car
1997 #9 Jeff Gordon

Pinnacle Precision Silver

1997 #3 Jeff Gordon
1997 #4 Jeff Gordon Pit Action
1997 #5 Jeff Gordon's Car
1997 #6 Jeff Gordon
1997 #8 Jeff Gordon's Car
1997 #9 Jeff Gordon

Pinnacle Press Plates

1997 #24 Jeff Gordon
1997 #53 Jeff Gordon's Car
1997 #S6-R Jeff Gordon
1997 #CM15 Jeff Gordon
1997 #TP1A Jeff Gordon

Pinnacle Spellbound

1997 #6R Jeff Gordon

Pinnacle Spellbound Autographs

1997 #6R Jeff Gordon EXCH
1997 #6RAU Jeff Gordon AUTO

Pinnacle Spellbound Promos

1997 #6R Jeff Gordon

Pinnacle Team Pinnacle

1996 #1 Jeff Gordon
1996 #10 Jeff Gordon
1997 #1 Jeff Gordon

Pinnacle Team Pinnacle Red

1997 #1 Jeff Gordon

Pinnacle Totally Certified Platinum Blue

1997 #24 Jeff Gordon
1997 #58 Jeff Gordon's Car
1997 #74 Jeff Gordon WP
1997 #89 Jeff Gordon BD

Pinnacle Totally Certified Platinum Gold

1997 #24 Jeff Gordon
1997 #58 Jeff Gordon's Car
1997 #74 Jeff Gordon WP
1997 #89 Jeff Gordon BD

Pinnacle Totally Certified Platinum Red

1997 #24 Jeff Gordon
1997 #58 Jeff Gordon's Car
1997 #74 Jeff Gordon WP
1997 #89 Jeff Gordon BD

Pinnacle Trophy Collection

1997 #24 Jeff Gordon
1997 #53 Jeff Gordon's Car

Pinnacle Winston Cup Collection

1996 #24 Jeff Gordon
1996 #51 Jeff Gordon's Car
1996 #66 Jeff Gordon PER
1996 #67 Jeff Gordon PER
1996 #68 Jeff Gordon PER
1996 #69 Jeff Gordon PER
1996 #70 Jeff Gordon PER
1996 #71 Jeff Gordon PER
1996 #72 Jeff Gordon PER
1996 #73 Jeff Gordon PER
1996 #85 Jeff Gordon W
1996 #92 Jeff Gordon's Transporter
1996 #95 Jeff Gordon CL

Power

1994 #5 Jeff Gordon DB
1994 #89 Jeff Gordon
1994 #90 Jeff Gordon
1994 #132 Jeff Gordon's Car
1994 #P1 Jeff Gordon Promo

Power Gold

1994 #5 Jeff Gordon DB
1994 #89 Jeff Gordon
1994 #90 Jeff Gordon
1994 #132 Jeff Gordon's Car

Power Preview

1994 #12 Jeff Gordon
1994 #22 Jeff Gordon's Car FOIL

Predator

1997 #1 Jeff Gordon
1997 #44 Jeff Gordon

Predator American Eagle

1997 #AE2 Jeff Gordon

Predator American Eagle First Slash

1997 #AE2 Jeff Gordon

Predator Black Wolf First Strike

1997 #1 Jeff Gordon
1997 #44 Jeff Gordon

Predator Eye of the Tiger

1997 #ET2 Jeff Gordon

Predator Eye of the Tiger First Slash

1997 #ET2 Jeff Gordon

Predator First Slash

1997 #1 Jeff Gordon
1997 #44 Jeff Gordon

Predator Gatorback

1997 #GB2 Jeff Gordon

Predator Gatorback Authentic

1997 #GBA2 Jeff Gordon

Predator Gatorback Authentic First Slash

1997 #GBA2 Jeff Gordon

Predator Gatorback First Slash

1997 #GB2 Jeff Gordon

Predator Golden Eagle

1997 #GE2 Jeff Gordon

Predator Golden Eagle First Slash

1997 #GE2 Jeff Gordon

Predator Grizzly

1997 #1 Jeff Gordon
1997 #44 Jeff Gordon

Predator Grizzly First Slash

1997 #1 Jeff Gordon
1997 #44 Jeff Gordon

Predator Promos

1997 #P1 Jeff Gordon Predator
1997 #P1 Jeff Gordon Pred.1st Slash
1997 #P2 Jeff Gordon Red Wolf
1997 #P2 Jeff Gordon Red Wolf 1st
1997 #P3 Jeff Gordon Black Wolf
1997 #P3 Jeff Gordon Black Wolf 1st Slash

Predator Red Wolf

1997 #1 Jeff Gordon
1997 #44 Jeff Gordon

Predator Red Wolf First Slash

1997 #1 Jeff Gordon
1997 #44 Jeff Gordon

Press Pass

1994 #7 Jeff Gordon
1994 #40 Jeff Gordon's Car
1994 #124 Jeff Gordon ROY
1995 #10 Jeff Gordon
1995 #38 Jeff Gordon's Car
1995 #102 Jeff Gordon ST
1995 #129 Jeff Gordon PR
1995 #136 Jeff Gordon BT
1996 #11 Jeff Gordon
1996 #38 Jeff Gordon's Car
1996 #78 J.Gordon/Hend/Evern.TW
1996 #93 Jeff Gordon S
1996 #100 J.Gordon/B.Gordon WCC
1996 #111 J.Gordon/J.Benson WC
1996 #0 Jeff Gordon Championship
1997 #2 Jeff Gordon
1997 #39 Jeff Gordon's Car
1997 #57 Jeff Gordon's Car
1997 #96 J.Gordon/D.Jarrett's Cars
1997 #104 Jeff Gordon's Car
1997 #105 Jeff Gordon's Car
1997 #134 Jeff Gordon W
1997 #135 Jeff Gordon W
1997 #136 Jeff Gordon W
1997 #137 Jeff Gordon W
1997 #138 Jeff Gordon W
1997 #SB1 Jeff Gordon Sam Bass
1998 #1 Jeff Gordon
1998 #34 Jeff Gordon's Car
1998 #101 Jeff Gordon RET
1998 #P1 Jeff Gordon Promo
1998 #0 Jeff Gordon 1997 Champion
1999 #1 Jeff Gordon
1999 #28 Jeff Gordon's Car
1999 #79 Jeff Gordon OTP
1999 #99 Jeff Gordon PRE
1999 #101 Jeff Gordon RET
1999 #P1 Jeff Gordon Promo
1999 #0 Jeff Gordon '98 Champ/800
2000 #6 Jeff Gordon
2000 #37 Jeff Gordon's Car REP
2000 #53 Jeff Gordon DD
2000 #63 Jeff Gordon
2001 #9 Jeff Gordon
2001 #35 Jeff Gordon
2001 #56 Jeff Gordon's Car
2001 #88 Jeff Gordon SO
2002 #11 Jeff Gordon
2002 #66 Jeff Gordon REP
2002 #83 Jeff Gordon's Car
2002 #99 Jeff Gordon WC Champ
2002 #0 Jeff Gordon 2001 WC Champ
2003 #10 Jeff Gordon
2003 #60 Jeff Gordon DS
2003 #78 The California Kid WCS
2003 #98 Jeff Gordon's Car OTW
2003 #100 Jeff Gordon Header
2004 #10 Jeff Gordon
2004 #10B Jeff Gordon infield
2004 #93 Jeff Gordon DS
2005 #19 Jeff Gordon
2005 #80 Jeff Gordon NS
2005 #84 Jeff Gordon NS
2005 #92 J.Hend./Gordon/JJ/T.Lab/B.Vick Y
2005 #95 Jeff Gordon Y
2005 #105 Jeff Gordon P
2005 #112 Jeff Gordon's Car
2005 #120 Dale Jr/JJ/Gordon CL
2006 #18 Jeff Gordon
2006 #77 Jeff Gordon's Car OTW
2006 #85 Jeff Gordon NS
2006 #104 Jeff Gordon U
2007 #9 Jeff Gordon
2007 #73 Jeff Gordon's Car OT
2007 #100 Jeff Gordon U
2007 #116 Jeff Gordon TT
2008 #1 Jeff Gordon
2008 #64 Jeff Gordon's Car BFS
2008 #92 Jeff Gordon's Car U
2008 #108 Jeff Gordon Top 12
2008 #0 Cup Chase Matt Kenseth Tony Stewart Jeff Gordon Jimmie Johnson Denny Hamlin Kurt Busch Kevin Harvick Carl Edwards Kyle Busch Martin Truex Jr. Jeff Burton Clint Bowyer

Press Pass Authentics

1994 #1 Jeff Gordon

Press Pass Authentics Autographs

1994 #1 Jeff Gordon AUTO

Press Pass Autographs

1997 #2 J.Gordon PPP/VIP/ACTN
1998 #2 Jeff Gordon/60
1999 #7 Jeff Gordon/75
2001 #14 Jeff Gordon
2002 #22 Jeff Gordon
2003 #16 Jeff Gordon E/P
2004 #21 Jeff Gordon P
2005 #19 Jeff Gordon E/P
2006 #16 Jeff Gordon NC
2007 #13 Jeff Gordon
2008 #15 Jeff Gordon NC P/E

Press Pass Autographs Press Plates Black

2008 #11 Jeff Gordon NC E

Press Pass Autographs Press Plates Cyan

2008 #11 Jeff Gordon NC E

Press Pass Autographs Press Plates Magenta

2008 #11 Jeff Gordon NC E

Press Pass Autographs Press Plates Yellow

2008 #11 Jeff Gordon NC E

Press Pass Banquet Bound

1997 #BB2 Jeff Gordon

Press Pass Blaster Kmart

2006 #JGC Jeff Gordon

Press Pass Blaster Target

2006 #JGB Jeff Gordon

Press Pass Blaster Wal-Mart

2006 #JGA Jeff Gordon

Press Pass Blue

2006 #B18 Jeff Gordon
2006 #B77 Jeff Gordon's car OTW
2006 #B85 Jeff Gordon NS
2006 #B104 Jeff Gordon U
2007 #B9 Jeff Gordon
2007 #B73 Jeff Gordon's Car OT
2007 #B100 Jeff Gordon U
2007 #B116 Jeff Gordon TT
2008 #B1 Jeff Gordon
2008 #B64 Jeff Gordon's Car BFS
2008 #B92 Jeff Gordon's Car U
2008 #B108 Jeff Gordon Top 12

Press Pass Burning Rubber

1996 #BR2 Jeff Gordon's Car
1997 #BR5 Jeff Gordon
1999 #BR7 Jeff Gordon's Car
2000 #BR5 Jeff Gordon

Press Pass Burning Rubber Autographs

2004 #BRJG Jeff Gordon/24
2006 #BR-JG Jeff Gordon/24

Press Pass Burning Rubber Cars

2001 #BRC1 Jeff Gordon/105
2002 #BRC1 Jeff Gordon's Car
2003 #BRT1 Jeff Gordon's Car
2004 #BRT4 Jeff Gordon's Car
2005 #BRT4 Jeff Gordon's Car
2006 #BRT5 Jeff Gordon

Press Pass Burning Rubber Cars Autographs

2003 #BRT-JG Jeff Gordon/24

Press Pass Burning Rubber Drivers

2001 #BRD1 Jeff Gordon/90
2002 #BRD1 Jeff Gordon
2003 #BRD1 Jeff Gordon
2004 #BRD4 Jeff Gordon
2005 #BRD4 Jeff Gordon
2006 #BRD5 Jeff Gordon
2007 #BRD11 Jeff Gordon Sonoma 6-26
2007 #BRD13 Jeff Gordon Chicago 7-9
2008 #BRD8 Jeff Gordon Phoenix
2008 #BRD9 Jeff Gordon Talladega
2008 #BRD13 Jeff Gordon Pocono

Press Pass Burning Rubber Drivers Autographs

2003 #BRD-JG Jeff Gordon/24

Press Pass Burning Rubber Drivers Gold

2005 #BRD4 Jeff Gordon
2006 #BRD5 Jeff Gordon
2007 #BRD11 Jeff Gordon Sonoma 6-26
2007 #BRD13 Jeff Gordon Chicago 7-9
2008 #BRD8 Jeff Gordon Phoenix
2008 #BRD9 Jeff Gordon Talladega
2008 #BRD13 Jeff Gordon Pocono

Press Pass Burning Rubber Drivers Prime Cuts

2008 #BRD8 Jeff Gordon Phoenix
2008 #BRD9 Jeff Gordon Talladega
2008 #BRD13 Jeff Gordon Pocono

Press Pass Burning Rubber Team

2007 #BRT11Jeff Gordon Sonoma 6-26
2007 #BRT13Jeff Gordon Chicago 7-9

Press Pass Burning Rubber Teams

2008 #BRT8 Jeff Gordon Phoenix
2008 #BRT9 Jeff Gordon Talladega
2008 #BRT13Jeff Gordon Pocono

Press Pass Burnouts

2006 #HT2 Jeff Gordon
2007 #BO6 Jeff Gordon
2008 #BO1 Jeff Gordon

Press Pass Burnouts Blue

2007 #BO6 Jeff Gordon
2008 #BO1 Jeff Gordon

Press Pass Burnouts Gold

2007 #BO6 Jeff Gordon
2008 #BO1 Jeff Gordon

Press Pass Burnouts Holofoil

2006 #HT2 Jeff Gordon

Press Pass Chase Cars

1999 #11B Jeff Gordon's Car

Press Pass Checkered Flags

1995 #CF3 Jeff Gordon
1996 #CF1 Jeff Gordon

Press Pass Clear Cut

1997 #C2 Jeff Gordon

Press Pass Collector's Series Box Set

2007 #SB7 Jeff Gordon

Press Pass Collectors Series Making the Show

2006 #MS2 Jeff Gordon

Press Pass Collectors Series Sunday Best

2007 #CB7 Jeff Gordon

Press Pass Cup Chase

1994 #CC7 Jeff Gordon
1995 #10 Jeff Gordon WIN
1996 #11 Jeff Gordon WIN
1997 #CC7 Jeff Gordon WIN
1998 #CC7 Jeff Gordon Win 2 Champ
1999 #6 Jeff Gordon WIN 2
2000 #CC6 Jeff Gordon WIN
2001 #CC4 Jeff Gordon WIN
2002 #CC4 Jeff Gordon WIN
2003 #CCR4 Jeff Gordon
2004 #CCR2 Jeff Gordon WIN
2005 #CCR7 Jeff Gordon Winner
2006 #CCR10 Jeff Gordon Winner
2007 #CCR1 Jeff Gordon Winner
2008 #CC3 Jeff Gordon

Press Pass Cup Chase Blue Die Cut Prizes

1997 #CC7 Jeff Gordon

Press Pass Cup Chase Die Cut Prizes

1998 #CC7 Jeff Gordon
1999 #6 Jeff Gordon
1999 #20 Jeff Gordon WC Champ
2000 #CC6 Jeff Gordon
2001 #CC4 Jeff Gordon
2001 #CCC1 Jeff Gordon Tire/400

Press Pass Cup Chase Foil Prizes

1996 #11 Jeff Gordon

Press Pass Cup Chase Gold Die Cuts

1997 #CC7 Jeff Gordon

Press Pass Cup Chase Prizes

1995 #CCR3 Jeff Gordon
1995 #CCR4 Jeff Gordon
2002 #CC4 Jeff Gordon
2002 #CC18 Jeff Gordon WC Champ
2003 #CCR4 Jeff Gordon
2004 #CCR2 Jeff Gordon
2005 #CCP7 Jeff Gordon
2006 #CC6 Jeff Gordon
2007 #CC2 Jeff Gordon

Press Pass Dale The Movie

2007 #45 Dale Earnhardt's Car Bobby Labonte's Car Kevin Harvick's Car Jeff Gordon's Car
2007 #35 Dale Earnhardt's Car Jeff Gordon's Car 1997 Daytona 500

Press Pass Daytona 500 50th Anniversary

2008 #34 Jeff Gordon '97
2008 #36 Jeff Gordon '99
2008 #42 Jeff Gordon '05

Press Pass Delphi

2002 #D2 Jeff Gordon

Press Pass Dominator Jeff Gordon

2006 #1 Jeff Gordon '92 BGN Pole Record
2006 #2 Jeff Gordon '93 125 Qualifying Win
2006 #3 Jeff Gordon '93 ROY
2006 #4 Jeff Gordon '93 Year in Review
2006 #5 Jeff Gordon '94 Brickyard 400 Win
2006 #6 Jeff Gordon '94 Year in Review
2006 #7 Jeff Gordon '95 Champion
2006 #8 Jeff Gordon '95 Year in Review
2006 #9 Jeff Gordon '96 Year in Review
2006 #10 Jeff Gordon '97 Daytona 500 Win
2006 #11 Jeff Gordon '97 Winston Win
2006 #12 Jeff Gordon '97 Champion
2006 #13 Jeff Gordon '97 Year in Review
2006 #14 Jeff Gordon '98 Brickyard 400 Win
2006 #15 Jeff Gordon '98 Champion
2006 #16 Jeff Gordon '98 Year in Review
2006 #17 Jeff Gordon '99 Daytona 500 Win
2006 #18 Jeff Gordon '99 Year in Review
2006 #19 Jeff Gordon '00 50 Career Wins
2006 #20 Jeff Gordon's Car '00 King of the Road
2006 #21 Jeff Gordon '00 Year in Review
2006 #22 Jeff Gordon '01 Champion
2006 #23 Jeff Gordon '01 Year in Review
2006 #24 Jeff Gordon '02 Year in Review
2006 #25 Jeff Gordon '03 Year in Review
2006 #26 Jeff Gordon '04 Year in Review
2006 #27 Jeff Gordon '05 Daytona 500 Win
2006 #28 Jeff Gordon '05 Year in Review
2006 #29 Jeff Gordon '06 Eye on the Prize
2006 #30 Jeff Gordon '06 75 Career Wins
2006 #31 Jeff Gordon '06 Fan Favorite
2006 #32 Jeff Gordon '06 Jeff Gordon Foundation
2006 #33 Jeff Gordon '06 Chase

Press Pass Dominator Jeff Gordon Jumbo

2006 #JG1 Jeff Gordon
2006 #JG2 Jeff Gordon Performance
2006 #JG3 Jeff Gordon

Press Pass Dominator Tins

2006 #JG Jeff Gordon

Press Pass Double Burner

2001 #DB1 Jeff Gordon
2002 #DB2 Jeff Gordon
2003 #DB1 Jeff Gordon
2004 #DB1 Jeff Gordon
2005 #DB1 Jeff Gordon

Press Pass Double Burner Exchange

2003 #DB1 Jeff Gordon EXCH
2004 #DB1 Jeff Gordon
2005 #DB1 Jeff Gordon

Press Pass Double Burner Firesuit-Glove

2006 #DB1 Jeff Gordon
2007 #DB6 Jeff Gordon
2008 #DBJG Jeff Gordon

Press Pass Double Burner Firesuit-Glove Exchange

2007 #DB6 Jeff Gordon

Press Pass Double Burner Metal-Tire

2006 #DB3 Jeff Gordon
2007 #DB-JGJeff Gordon
2008 #DB-JGJeff Gordon

Press Pass Double Burner Metal-Tire Exchange

2007 #DB-JGJeff Gordon

Press Pass Eclipse

2002 #1 Jeff Gordon
2002 #29 Jeff Gordon ACC
2002 #30 Jeff Gordon ACC
2002 #31 Jeff Gordon ACC
2002 #32 Jeff Gordon ACC
2002 #33 Jeff Gordon ACC
2002 #35 Jeff Gordon ACC
2002 #36 Jeff Gordon ACC
2002 #38 Jeff Gordon SO
2002 #P1 Jeff Gordon Promo
2003 #4 Jeff Gordon
2003 #35 Jeff Gordon ACC
2003 #38 Kansas City Chiefs WCS
2003 #42 The Spin Doctor WCS
2003 #46 Jeff Gordon HS
2004 #4 Jeff Gordon
2004 #53 Jeff Gordon Z
2004 #57 Jeff Gordon P
2004 #75 Jeff Gordon LL
2005 #3 Jeff Gordon
2005 #48 Jeff Gordon Z
2005 #57 Jeff Gordon P
2005 #65 J.Gordon/J.Johnson NS
2005 #70 Jeff Gordon NS
2005 #72 J.Gordon/J.Johnson NS
2005 #75 Jeff Gordon LL
2006 #10 Jeff Gordon
2006 #42 Jeff Gordon WS
2006 #56 Jeff Gordon NS
2006 #74 Jeff Gordon LL
2007 #6B Jeff Gordon crew missing shirt logo
2007 #6 Jeff Gordon
2007 #33 Jeff Gordon TO
2007 #47 Jeff Gordon P
2007 #55 Jeff Gordon FP
2007 #0 Cup Chase 10
2008 #2 Jeff Gordon
2008 #28 Jeff Gordon RM
2008 #38 Jeff Gordon TO
2008 #49 Jeff Gordon NS
2008 #50 Jeff Gordon NS
2008 #79 Jeff Gordon SO
2008 #28B Jeff Gordon RM blank red background
2008 #55 Jeff Gordon's Car LP
2008 #75 Top 10 Drivers SO

Press Pass Eclipse Destination WIN

2004 #11 Jeff Gordon
2004 #26 Jeff Gordon
2005 #8 Jeff Gordon
2005 #9 Jeff Gordon
2005 #15 Jeff Gordon
2005 #18 Jeff Gordon

Press Pass Eclipse Double Hot Treads
2003 #DT8 J.Gordon/J.Johnson
Press Pass Eclipse Ecliptic
2007 #EC5 Jeff Gordon
Press Pass Eclipse Escape Velocity
2008 #EV1 Jeff Gordon
Press Pass Eclipse Gold
2007 #G6 Jeff Gordon
2007 #G33 Jeff Gordon TO
2007 #G47 Jeff Gordon P
2007 #G55 Jeff Gordon FP
2008 #G2 Jeff Gordon
2008 #G28 Jeff Gordon RM
2008 #G38 Jeff Gordon TO
2008 #G49 Jeff Gordon NS
2008 #G50 Jeff Gordon NS
2008 #G55 Jeff Gordon's Car LP
2008 #G75 Top 10 Drivers SO
2008 #G79 Jeff Gordon SO
Press Pass Eclipse Hyperdrive
2004 #HP7 Jeff Gordon
2005 #HD7 Jeff Gordon
2006 #HP7 Jeff Gordon
2007 #HD7 Jeff Gordon
2008 #HP3 Jeff Gordon
Press Pass Eclipse Maxim
2004 #MX4 Jeff Gordon
2005 #MX4 Jeff Gordon
Press Pass Eclipse Previews
2003 #4 Jeff Gordon
2003 #35 Jeff Gordon ACC
2004 #4 Jeff Gordon
2005 #EB3 Jeff Gordon
2005 #EB48 Jeff Gordon Z
2005 #EB57 Jeff Gordon P
2005 #EB65 J.Gordon/J.Johnson NS
2005 #EB70 Jeff Gordon NS
2005 #EB72 J.Gordon/J.Johnson NS
2005 #EB75 Jeff Gordon LL/1
2006 #EB10 Jeff Gordon
2007 #EB6 Jeff Gordon
2007 #EB33 Jeff Gordon TO
2008 #EB2 Jeff Gordon
2008 #EB28 Jeff Gordon RM
2008 #EB75 Top 10 Drivers SO
2008 #EB79 Jeff Gordon SO
Press Pass Eclipse Racing Champions
2002 #RC3 Jeff Gordon
2002 #RC13 Jeff Gordon
2002 #RC14 Jeff Gordon
2002 #RC21 Jeff Gordon
2002 #RC22 Jeff Gordon
2002 #RC28 Jeff Gordon
2003 #RC25 Jeff Gordon
2003 #RC26 Jeff Gordon
2003 #RC30 Jeff Gordon
2006 #RC1 Jeff Gordon
2007 #RC7 Jeff Gordon
Press Pass Eclipse Red
2007 #R6 Jeff Gordon
2007 #R33 Jeff Gordon TO
2007 #R47 Jeff Gordon P
2007 #R55 Jeff Gordon FP
2008 #R2 Jeff Gordon
2008 #R28 Jeff Gordon RM
2008 #R38 Jeff Gordon TO
2008 #R49 Jeff Gordon NS
2008 #R50 Jeff Gordon NS
2008 #R55 Jeff Gordon's Car LP
2008 #R75 Top 10 Drivers SO
2008 #R79 Jeff Gordon SO
Press Pass Eclipse Samples
2002 #1 Jeff Gordon
2002 #29 Jeff Gordon ACC
2002 #30 Jeff Gordon ACC
2002 #31 Jeff Gordon ACC
2002 #32 Jeff Gordon ACC
2002 #33 Jeff Gordon ACC
2002 #35 Jeff Gordon ACC
2002 #36 Jeff Gordon ACC
2002 #38 Jeff Gordon SO
2003 #4 Jeff Gordon
2003 #35 Jeff Gordon ACC
2003 #38 Kansas City Chiefs WCS
2003 #42 The Spin Doctor WCS
2003 #46 Jeff Gordon HS
2004 #4 Jeff Gordon
2004 #53 Jeff Gordon Z
2004 #57 Jeff Gordon P
2004 #75 Jeff Gordon LL
2005 #3 Jeff Gordon
2005 #48 Jeff Gordon Z
2005 #57 Jeff Gordon P
2005 #65 J.Gordon/J.Johnson NS
2005 #70 Jeff Gordon NS
2005 #72 J.Gordon/J.Johnson NS
2005 #75 Jeff Gordon LL
Press Pass Eclipse Skidmarks
2002 #SK4 Jeff Gordon
2003 #SM2 Jeff Gordon
2004 #SM1 Jeff Gordon
2005 #SM1 Jeff Gordon
2006 #SM14 Jeff Gordon
2007 #SM16 Jeff Gordon
Press Pass Eclipse Skidmarks Holofoil
2004 #SM1 Jeff Gordon
2005 #SM1 Jeff Gordon
2006 #SM14 Jeff Gordon
2007 #SM16 Jeff Gordon
Press Pass Eclipse Solar Eclipse
2002 #S1 Jeff Gordon
2002 #S29 Jeff Gordon ACC
2002 #S30 Jeff Gordon ACC
2002 #S31 Jeff Gordon ACC
2002 #S32 Jeff Gordon ACC
2002 #S33 Jeff Gordon ACC
2002 #S35 Jeff Gordon ACC
2002 #S36 Jeff Gordon ACC
2002 #S38 Jeff Gordon SO
2003 #P4 Jeff Gordon
2003 #P35 Jeff Gordon ACC
2003 #P38 Kansas City Chiefs WCS
2003 #P42 The Spin Doctor WCS
2003 #P46 Jeff Gordon HS
Press Pass Eclipse Star Tracks
2008 #ST4 Jeff Gordon
Press Pass Eclipse Star Tracks Holofoil
2008 #ST4 Jeff Gordon
Press Pass Eclipse Stellar
2008 #ST2 Jeff Gordon
Press Pass Eclipse Supernova
2002 #SN5 Jeff Gordon
2003 #SN3 Jeff Gordon
2006 #SU2 Jeff Gordon
Press Pass Eclipse Supernova Numbered
2002 #SN5 Jeff Gordon
Press Pass Eclipse Teammates Autographs
2003 #JGJJ J.Gordon/J.Johnson
2004 #2 J.Johnson/J.Gordon
2005 #6 J.Gordon/J.Johnson
2006 #5 J.Johnson/J.Gordon
2007 #7 J.Gordon/J.Johnson/Ky.Busch
2008 #EGJM Dale Earnhardt Jr. Jeff Gordon Jimmie Johnson Casey /Mears
2008 #EG Dale Earnhardt Jr. Jeff Gordon
Press Pass Eclipse Under Cover Autographs
2004 #UCJG Jeff Gordon/24
2005 #UCJG Jeff Gordon/24
2006 #JG Jeff Gordon/24
2007 #UC-JG Jeff Gordon/24
2008 #UC-JG Jeff Gordon/24
Press Pass Eclipse Under Cover Cars
2003 #UCT1 Jeff Gordon
2004 #UCD4 Jeff Gordon
2005 #UCT4 Jeff Gordon
2006 #UCT11 Jeff Gordon
Press Pass Eclipse Under Cover Cars Autographs
2003 #UCTJG Jeff Gordon/24
Press Pass Eclipse Under Cover Double Cover
2002 #DC1 J.Nadeau/J.Gordon
2002 #DC2 J.Johnson/J.Gordon
2002 #DC3 J.Gordon/T.Labonte
2003 #DC1 J.Nemechek/J.Gordon
2003 #DC2 J.Johnson/J.Gordon
2003 #DC3 T.Labonte/J.Gordon
2004 #DC3 J.Johnson/J.Gordon
2004 #DC4 T.Labonte/J.Gordon
2004 #DC7 J.Nemechek/J.Gordon
2005 #DC3 J.Johnson/J.Gordon
2005 #DC9 J.Gordon/T.Labonte
2006 #DC1 J.Johnson/J.Gordon
2006 #DC5 J.Gordon/T.Labonte
Press Pass Eclipse Under Cover Double Cover Holofoil
2006 #DC1 J.Johnson/J.Gordon
2006 #DC5 J.Gordon/T.Labonte
Press Pass Eclipse Under Cover Double Cover Name
2007 #DC3 Gordon/Johnson
2008 #DC6 Jeff Gordon Jimme Johnson
Press Pass Eclipse Under Cover Double Cover NASCAR
2007 #DC3 Gordon/Johnson
2008 #DC6 Jeff Gordon Jimme Johnson
Press Pass Eclipse Under Cover Driver Autographs
2003 #UCD-JG Jeff Gordon/24
Press Pass Eclipse Under Cover Driver Gold
2003 #UCD1 Jeff Gordon
2004 #UCD4 Jeff Gordon
Press Pass Eclipse Under Cover Driver Red
2003 #UCD1 Jeff Gordon
2004 #UCD4 Jeff Gordon
2005 #UCD4 Jeff Gordon
Press Pass Eclipse Under Cover Driver Silver
2003 #UCD1 Jeff Gordon
2004 #UCD4 Jeff Gordon
Press Pass Eclipse Under Cover Drivers
2002 #CD3 Jeff Gordon
2007 #UCD13 Jeff Gordon
2008 #UCD15 Jeff Gordon
Press Pass Eclipse Under Cover Drivers Eclipse
2007 #UCD13 Jeff Gordon
2008 #UCD15 Jeff Gordon
Press Pass Eclipse Under Cover Drivers Gold
2006 #UCD11 Jeff Gordon
Press Pass Eclipse Under Cover Drivers Holofoil
2005 #UCD4 Jeff Gordon
2006 #UCD11 Jeff Gordon
Press Pass Eclipse Under Cover Drivers Name
2007 #UCD13 Jeff Gordon
2008 #UCD15 Jeff Gordon
Press Pass Eclipse Under Cover Drivers NASCAR
2007 #UCD13 Jeff Gordon
2008 #UCD15 Jeff Gordon
Press Pass Eclipse Under Cover Drivers Silver
2005 #UCD4 Jeff Gordon
2006 #UCD11 Jeff Gordon
Press Pass Eclipse Under Cover Gold Cars
2002 #CD3 Jeff Gordon
Press Pass Eclipse Under Cover Gold Drivers
2002 #CD3 Jeff Gordon
Press Pass Eclipse Under Cover Holofoil Drivers
2002 #CD3 Jeff Gordon
Press Pass Eclipse Under Cover Teams
2007 #UCT13 Jeff Gordon
2008 #UCT15 Jeff Gordon
Press Pass Eclipse Under Cover Teams NASCAR
2007 #UCT13 Jeff Gordon
2008 #UCT15 Jeff Gordon
Press Pass Eclipse Warp Speed
2002 #WS1 Jeff Gordon
2003 #WS1 Jeff Gordon
Press Pass F.Q.S.
1996 #FQS3A Jeff Gordon
1996 #FQS3B Jeff Gordon's Car
Press Pass Focused
1996 #F3 Jeff Gordon
1996 #P1 Jeff Gordon Promo
Press Pass Four Wide
2006 #FW-JG Jeff Gordon
2007 #FW-JG Jeff Gordon
2008 #FW-JG Jeff Gordon
Press Pass Four Wide Checkered
2007 #FW-JG Jeff Gordon
2008 #FW-JG Jeff Gordon
Press Pass Four Wide Checkered Exchange
2007 #FW-JG Jeff Gordon
Press Pass Four Wide Checkered Flag
2006 #FW-JG Jeff Gordon
Press Pass Four Wide Exchange
2007 #FW-JG Jeff Gordon
Press Pass Game Face
2005 #GF6 Jeff Gordon
2006 #GF1 Jeff Gordon
Press Pass Gatorade Front Runner Award
2000 #8 Jeff Gordon
2001 #3 Jeff Gordon
Press Pass Gold
2006 #G18 Jeff Gordon
2006 #G77 Jeff Gordon's car OTW
2006 #G85 Jeff Gordon NS
2006 #G104 Jeff Gordon U
2007 #G9 Jeff Gordon
2007 #G73 Jeff Gordon's Car OT
2007 #G100 Jeff Gordon U
2007 #G116 Jeff Gordon TT
2008 #G1 Jeff Gordon
2008 #G64 Jeff Gordon's Car BFS
2008 #G92 Jeff Gordon's Car U
2008 #G108 Jeff Gordon Top 12
Press Pass Gold Holofoil
2003 #P10 Jeff Gordon
2003 #P60 Jeff Gordon DS
2003 #P78 The California Kid WCS
2003 #P98 Jeff Gordon's Car OTW
2003 #P100 Jeff Gordon Set Header
Press Pass Ground Zero
2001 #GZ4 Jeff Gordon
Press Pass Holofoils
1994 #H2 Jeff Gordon
Press Pass Hot Treads
2001 #HT11 Jeff Gordon/1665
2002 #HT17 Jeff Gordon's Car/2425
2004 #HTR11 Jeff Gordon
2005 #HTR10 Jeff Gordon
2007 #HT3 Jeff Gordon
2008 #HT5 Jeff Gordon
Press Pass Hot Treads Blue
2007 #HT3 Jeff Gordon
2008 #HT5 Jeff Gordon
Press Pass Hot Treads Gold
2007 #HT3 Jeff Gordon
2008 #HT5 Jeff Gordon
Press Pass Hot Treads Holofoil
2004 #HTR11 Jeff Gordon
2005 #HTR10 Jeff Gordon
Press Pass Jeff Gordon Fan Club
1999 #JG Jeff Gordon
Press Pass K-Mart
2007 #JG-C Jeff Gordon
Press Pass Lasers
1997 #2 Jeff Gordon
1997 #39 Jeff Gordon's Car
1997 #57 Jeff Gordon's Car
1997 #96 J.Gordon/D.Jarrett's Cars
1997 #104 Jeff Gordon's Car
1997 #105 Jeff Gordon's Car
1997 #134 Jeff Gordon W
1997 #135 Jeff Gordon W
1997 #136 Jeff Gordon W
1997 #137 Jeff Gordon W
1997 #138 Jeff Gordon W
Press Pass Legends
2005 #28 Jeff Gordon
2005 #43 Jeff Gordon C
2005 #50 D.Allison/Gordon/Petty CL
2006 #35 Jeff Gordon
2006 #46 R.Petty/J.Gordon REC Poles
2006 #48 R.Petty/J.Gordon REC Champs
2006 #49 R.Petty/J.Gordon REC Top 10s
2007 #40 Jeff Gordon
2007 #68 Dale Earnhardt Jeff Gordon R
Press Pass Legends Autographs Black
2005 #15 Jeff Gordon
2006 #23 Jeff Gordon
Press Pass Legends Autographs Blue
2007 #8 Jeff Gordon/48
Press Pass Legends Autographs Inscriptions Black
2007 #4 Jeff Gordon 24/9
Press Pass Legends Blue
2005 #28B Jeff Gordon
2005 #43B Jeff Gordon C
2005 #50B D.Allison/Gordon/Petty CL
2006 #B35 Jeff Gordon
2006 #B46 R.Petty/J.Gordon REC Poles
2006 #B48 R.Petty/J.Gordon REC Champs
2006 #B49 R.Petty/J.Gordon REC Top 10s
2007 #B40 Jeff Gordon
2007 #B68 Dale Earnhardt Jeff Gordon R
Press Pass Legends Bronze
2006 #Z35 Jeff Gordon
2006 #Z46 R.Petty/J.Gordon REC Poles
2006 #Z48 R.Petty/J.Gordon REC Champs
2006 #Z49 R.Petty/J.Gordon REC Top 10s
2007 #Z40 Jeff Gordon
2007 #Z68 Dale Earnhardt Jeff Gordon R
Press Pass Legends Champion Threads & Treads Bronze
2006 #CTT-JG Jeff Gordon
Press Pass Legends Champion Threads & Treads Gold
2006 #CTT-JG Jeff Gordon
Press Pass Legends Champion Threads & Treads Silver
2006 #CTT-JG Jeff Gordon
Press Pass Legends Champion Threads Bronze
2006 #CT-JG Jeff Gordon
Press Pass Legends Champion Threads Gold
2006 #CT-JG Jeff Gordon
Press Pass Legends Champion Threads Patch
2006 #CT-JG Jeff Gordon
Press Pass Legends Champion Threads Silver
2006 #CT-JG Jeff Gordon
Press Pass Legends Double Threads Bronze
2005 #DT-GJ J.Gordon/J.Johnson
2005 #DT-LG T.Labonte/J.Gordon
Press Pass Legends Double Threads Gold
2005 #DT-GJ J.Gordon/J.Johnson
2005 #DT-LG T.Labonte/J.Gordon
Press Pass Legends Double Threads Silver
2005 #DT-GJ J.Gordon/J.Johnson
2005 #DT-LG T.Labonte/J.Gordon
Press Pass Legends Gold
2005 #28G Jeff Gordon
2005 #43G Jeff Gordon C
2005 #50G D.Allison/Gordon/Petty CL
2006 #G35 Jeff Gordon
2006 #G46 R.Petty/J.Gordon REC Poles
2006 #G48 R.Petty/J.Gordon REC Champs
2006 #G49 R.Petty/J.Gordon REC Top 10s
2007 #G40 Jeff Gordon
2007 #G68 Dale Earnhardt Jeff Gordon R
Press Pass Legends Greatest Moments
2005 #GM12 Jeff Gordon
Press Pass Legends Heritage
2005 #HE2 Jeff Gordon
Press Pass Legends Heritage Gold
2006 #HE7 Jeff Gordon
Press Pass Legends Heritage Silver
2006 #HE7 Jeff Gordon
Press Pass Legends Holofoil
2005 #28H Jeff Gordon
2005 #43H Jeff Gordon C
2005 #50H D.Allison/Gordon/Petty CL
2006 #H35 Jeff Gordon
2006 #H46 R.Petty/J.Gordon REC Poles
2006 #H48 R.Petty/J.Gordon REC Champs
2006 #H49 R.Petty/J.Gordon REC Top 10s
2007 #H40 Jeff Gordon
2007 #H68 Dale Earnhardt Jeff Gordon R
Press Pass Legends Memorable Moments Gold
2006 #MM3 Jeff Gordon Charlotte
2006 #MM6 Jeff Gordon Darlington
2006 #MM8 Jeff Gordon Darlington '97
2006 #MM11 Jeff Gordon N.Wilkesboro
2007 #MM3 Jeff Gordon B
Press Pass Legends Memorable Moments Silver
2006 #MM3 Jeff Gordon Charlotte
2006 #MM6 Jeff Gordon Darlington
2006 #MM8 Jeff Gordon Darlington '97
2006 #MM11 Jeff Gordon N.Wilkesboro
2007 #MM3 Jeff Gordon B
Press Pass Legends Press Plates Black
2005 #28 Jeff Gordon
2005 #43 Jeff Gordon C
2005 #50 D.Allison/Gordon/Petty CL
2006 #PPB35 Jeff Gordon
2006 #PPB46 R.Petty/J.Gordon REC Poles
2006 #PPB48 R.Petty/J.Gordon REC Champs
2006 #PPB49 R.Petty/J.Gordon REC Top 10s
2007 #PP40 Jeff Gordon
2007 #PP68 Dale Earnhardt Jeff Gordon R
Press Pass Legends Press Plates Black Backs
2006 #PPB35B Jeff Gordon
2006 #PPB46B R.Petty/J.Gordon REC Poles
2006 #PPB48B R.Petty/J.Gordon REC Champs
2006 #PPB49B R.Petty/J.Gordon REC Top 10s
2007 #PP40 Jeff Gordon
2007 #PP68 Dale Earnhardt Jeff Gordon R
Press Pass Legends Press Plates Cyan
2005 #28 Jeff Gordon
2005 #43 Jeff Gordon C
2005 #50 D.Allison/Gordon/Petty CL
2006 #PPC35 Jeff Gordon
2006 #PPC46 R.Petty/J.Gordon REC Poles
2006 #PPC48 R.Petty/J.Gordon REC Champs
2006 #PPC49 R.Petty/J.Gordon REC Top 10s
2007 #PP40 Jeff Gordon
2007 #PP68 Dale Earnhardt Jeff Gordon R
Press Pass Legends Press Plates Cyan Backs
2006 #PPC35B Jeff Gordon
2006 #PPC46B R.Petty/J.Gordon REC Poles
2006 #PPC48B R.Petty/J.Gordon REC Champs
2006 #PPC49B R.Petty/J.Gordon REC Top 10s
2007 #PP40 Jeff Gordon
2007 #PP68 Dale Earnhardt Jeff Gordon R
Press Pass Legends Press Plates Magenta
2005 #28 Jeff Gordon
2005 #43 Jeff Gordon C
2005 #50 D.Allison/Gordon/Petty CL
2006 #PPM35 Jeff Gordon
2006 #PPM46 R.Petty/J.Gordon REC Poles
2006 #PPM48 R.Petty/J.Gordon REC Champs
2006 #PPM49 R.Petty/J.Gordon REC Top 10s
2007 #PP40 Jeff Gordon
2007 #PP68 Dale Earnhardt Jeff Gordon R
Press Pass Legends Press Plates Magenta Backs
2006 #PPM35B Jeff Gordon
2006 #PPM46B R.Petty/J.Gordon REC Poles
2006 #PPM48B R.Petty/J.Gordon REC Champs
2006 #PPM49B R.Petty/J.Gordon REC Top 10s
2007 #PP40 Jeff Gordon
2007 #PP68 Dale Earnhardt Jeff Gordon R
Press Pass Legends Press Plates Yellow
2005 #28 Jeff Gordon
2005 #43 Jeff Gordon C
2005 #50 D.Allison/Gordon/Petty CL
2006 #PPY35 Jeff Gordon
2006 #PPY46 R.Petty/J.Gordon REC Poles
2006 #PPY48 R.Petty/J.Gordon REC Champs
2006 #PPY49 R.Petty/J.Gordon REC Top 10s
2007 #PP40 Jeff Gordon
2007 #PP68 Dale Earnhardt Jeff Gordon R
Press Pass Legends Press Plates Yellow Backs
2006 #PPY35B Jeff Gordon
2006 #PPY46B R.Petty/J.Gordon REC Poles
2006 #PPY48B R.Petty/J.Gordon REC Champs
2006 #PPY49B R.Petty/J.Gordon REC Top 10s
2007 #PP40 Jeff Gordon
2007 #PP68 Dale Earnhardt Jeff Gordon R
Press Pass Legends Previews
2005 #28 Jeff Gordon
2005 #43 Jeff Gordon C
2005 #50 D.Allison/Gordon/Petty CL
2006 #EB35 Jeff Gordon
2006 #EB46 R.Petty/J.Gordon REC Poles
2006 #EB48 R.Petty/J.Gordon REC Champs
2006 #EB49 R.Petty/J.Gordon REC Top 10s
2007 #EB40 Jeff Gordon
2007 #EB68 Dale Earnhardt Jeff Gordon R
Press Pass Legends Signature Series
2007 #JG Jeff Gordon
Press Pass Legends Solo
2005 #28S Jeff Gordon
2005 #43S Jeff Gordon C
2005 #50S D.Allison/Gordon/Petty CL
2006 #S35 Jeff Gordon
2006 #S46 R.Petty/J.Gordon REC Poles
2006 #S48 R.Petty/J.Gordon REC Champs
2006 #S49 R.Petty/J.Gordon REC Top 10s
2007 #S40 Jeff Gordon
2007 #S68 Dale Earnhardt Jeff Gordon R
Press Pass Legends Sunday Swatches Bronze
2007 #JG-SS Jeff Gordon
Press Pass Legends Sunday Swatches Gold
2007 #JG-SS Jeff Gordon
Press Pass Legends Sunday Swatches Silver
2007 #JG-SS Jeff Gordon
Press Pass Legends Threads & Treads Bronze
2005 #TTJG Jeff Gordon
Press Pass Legends Threads & Treads Gold
2005 #TTJG Jeff Gordon
Press Pass Legends Threads & Treads Silver
2005 #TTJG Jeff Gordon
Press Pass Legends Triple Threads
2006 #TT-JG Jeff Gordon
Press Pass Legends Victory Lane Bronze
2007 #VL2 Jeff Gordon
2007 #VL3 Jeff Gordon
Press Pass Legends Victory Lane Gold
2007 #VL2 Jeff Gordon
2007 #VL3 Jeff Gordon
Press Pass Legends Victory Lane Silver
2007 #VL2 Jeff Gordon
2007 #VL3 Jeff Gordon
Press Pass Making the Show Collector's Series
2004 #MS16 Jeff Gordon
Press Pass Making the Show Collector's Series Tins
2004 #NNO Dale Jr/Stewart/J.Gordon
Press Pass Millennium
2000 #6 Jeff Gordon
2000 #37 Jeff Gordon
2000 #53 Jeff Gordon
2000 #63 Jeff Gordon
2001 #9 Jeff Gordon
2001 #35 Jeff Gordon
2001 #56 Jeff Gordon's Car
2001 #88 Jeff Gordon SO
Press Pass Oil Cans
1998 #OC3 Jeff Gordon
1999 #6 Jeff Gordon
2000 #OC6 Jeff Gordon
Press Pass Oil Slicks
1997 #2 Jeff Gordon
1997 #39 Jeff Gordon's Car
1997 #57 Jeff Gordon's Car
1997 #96 J.Gordon/D.Jarrett's Cars
1997 #104 Jeff Gordon's Car
1997 #105 Jeff Gordon's Car
1997 #134 Jeff Gordon W
1997 #135 Jeff Gordon W
1997 #136 Jeff Gordon W
1997 #137 Jeff Gordon W
1997 #138 Jeff Gordon W
1998 #1 Jeff Gordon
1998 #34 Jeff Gordon's Car
Press Pass Optima
2000 #7 Jeff Gordon
2001 #6 Jeff Gordon
2001 #42 Jeff Gordon WCL
2002 #8 Jeff Gordon
2002 #0 J.Gordon/J.Johnson
2003 #7 Jeff Gordon
2004 #6 Jeff Gordon
2004 #62 Jeff Gordon's Car RV
2004 #68 Jeff Gordon CS
2004 #76 Jeff Gordon CP
2004 #94 Jeff Gordon SS
2004 #100 Jeff Gordon CL
2005 #10 Jeff Gordon
2005 #58 Jeff Gordon RR
2005 #88 Jeff Gordon's Car RTV
2006 #19 Jeff Gordon
2006 #53 Jeff Gordon's Car HS
2006 #64 Jeff Gordon CP
2006 #82 Jeff Gordon RTV Sonoma
2006 #84 Jeff Gordon RTV Chicago
2006 #19B Jeff Gordon Chase
Press Pass Optima Cool Persistence
2000 #CP2 Jeff Gordon
2001 #CP4 Jeff Gordon
2002 #CP3 Jeff Gordon
2003 #CP8 Jeff Gordon
2004 #CP1 Jeff Gordon
2005 #CP1 Jeff Gordon
Press Pass Optima Encore
2000 #EN5 Jeff Gordon
Press Pass Optima Fan Favorite
2002 #FF7 Jeff Gordon
2003 #FF7 Jeff Gordon
2004 #FF6 Jeff Gordon
2005 #FF8 Jeff Gordon
2006 #FF6 Jeff Gordon
Press Pass Optima G Force
2000 #GF7 Jeff Gordon
2001 #GF5 Jeff Gordon
2004 #GF2 Jeff Gordon
2005 #GF5 Jeff Gordon
Press Pass Optima Gold
2001 #6 Jeff Gordon
2001 #42 Jeff Gordon WCL
2002 #8 Jeff Gordon
2003 #G7 Jeff Gordon
2004 #G6 Jeff Gordon
2004 #G62 Jeff Gordon's Car RV
2004 #G68 Jeff Gordon CS
2004 #G76 Jeff Gordon CP
2004 #G94 Jeff Gordon SS
2004 #G100 Jeff Gordon CL
2005 #G10 Jeff Gordon
2005 #G58 Jeff Gordon RR
2005 #G88 Jeff Gordon's Car RTV
2006 #G19 Jeff Gordon
2006 #G53 Jeff Gordon's Car HS
2006 #G64 Jeff Gordon CP
2006 #G82 Jeff Gordon RTV Sonoma
2006 #G84 Jeff Gordon RTV Chicago
Press Pass Optima On the Edge
2000 #OE3 Jeff Gordon
2001 #OE2 Jeff Gordon
Press Pass Optima Overdrive
2000 #OD4 Jeff Gordon
Press Pass Optima Overdrive Square Cut
2000 #OD4 Jeff Gordon
Press Pass Optima Platinum
2000 #7 Jeff Gordon
Press Pass Optima Previews
2003 #7 Jeff Gordon
2004 #EB6 Jeff Gordon
2005 #10 Jeff Gordon
2006 #EB19 Jeff Gordon
Press Pass Optima Promos
2002 #8 Jeff Gordon
Press Pass Optima Q & A
2005 #QA5 Jeff Gordon
2006 #QA11 Jeff Gordon
Press Pass Optima Q and A
2003 #QA3 Jeff Gordon
Press Pass Optima Q&A
2004 #QA1 Jeff Gordon
Press Pass Optima Race Used Lugnuts Autographs
2002 #LNDA6 Jeff Gordon/24
Press Pass Optima Race Used Lugnuts Cars
2000 #LC17 Jeff Gordon's Car/50
2001 #LNC5 Jeff Gordon's Car
2002 #LNC6 Jeff Gordon's Car
Press Pass Optima Race Used Lugnuts Drivers
2000 #LD17 Jeff Gordon/55
2001 #LND4 Jeff Gordon
2002 #LND6 Jeff Gordon
Press Pass Optima Rookie Relics Cars
2006 #RRT15 Jeff Gordon
Press Pass Optima Rookie Relics Drivers
2006 #RRD15 Jeff Gordon
Press Pass Optima Samples
2002 #8 Jeff Gordon
2003 #7 Jeff Gordon
2004 #6 Jeff Gordon
2004 #62 Jeff Gordon's Car RV
2004 #68 Jeff Gordon CS
2004 #76 Jeff Gordon CP
2004 #94 Jeff Gordon SS
2004 #100 Jeff Gordon CL
2005 #10 Jeff Gordon
2005 #58 Jeff Gordon RR
2005 #88 Jeff Gordon RTV
Press Pass Optima Thunder Bolts Autographs
2004 #TBJG Jeff Gordon/24
2005 #TB-JG Jeff Gordon/24
Press Pass Optima Thunder Bolts Cars
2003 #TBT1 Jeff Gordon's Car
2004 #TBT13 Jeff Gordon's Car
Press Pass Optima Thunder Bolts Cars Autographs
2003 #TBT-JG Jeff Gordon/24
Press Pass Optima Thunder Bolts Drivers
2003 #TBD1 Jeff Gordon/60
2004 #TBD13 Jeff Gordon
Press Pass Optima Thunder Bolts Drivers Autographs
2003 #TBD-JG Jeff Gordon/24
Press Pass Optima Up Close
2001 #UC2 Jeff Gordon
2002 #UC2 Jeff Gordon
Press Pass Optima XL
1994 #6 Jeff Gordon
1994 #26 Jeff Gordon
1994 #38 Jeff Gordon TC
1994 #56 Jeff Gordon WCS
1994 #62 Jeff Gordon NM
1994 #CC1 Jeff Gordon Chrome
1995 #8 Jeff Gordon
1995 #31 Jeff Gordon TC
1995 #50 Jeff Gordon's Car
1995 #56 Jeff Gordon OR
Press Pass Optima XL Cool Blue
1995 #8 Jeff Gordon
1995 #31 Jeff Gordon TC
1995 #50 Jeff Gordon's Car
1995 #56 Jeff Gordon
Press Pass Optima XL Die Cut
1995 #8 Jeff Gordon
1995 #31 Jeff Gordon TC
1995 #50 Jeff Gordon's Car
1995 #56 Jeff Gordon
Press Pass Optima XL JG/XL
1995 #1 Jeff Gordon (1:36)
1995 #2 Jeff Gordon (1:72)
1995 #3 Jeff Gordon (1:216)
1995 #4 Jeff Gordon (1:864)
Press Pass Optima XL Prototypes
1994 #3 Jeff Gordon
Press Pass Optima XL Red Hot
1994 #6 Jeff Gordon
1994 #26 Jeff Gordon
1994 #38 Jeff Gordon TC
1994 #56 Jeff Gordon WCS
1994 #62 Jeff Gordon NM
1995 #8 Jeff Gordon
1995 #31 Jeff Gordon TC
1995 #50 Jeff Gordon's Car
1995 #56 Jeff Gordon
Press Pass Optima XL Stealth
1995 #XLS4 Jeff Gordon
Press Pass Panorama
2005 #PPP3 Jeff Gordon
2005 #PPP20 Jeff Gordon
2005 #PPP27 Jeff Gordon
2005 #PPP30 Jeff Gordon
2005 #PPP37 Jeff Gordon
2005 #PPP38 Jeff Gordon
2005 #PPP39 Jeff Gordon
Press Pass Pit Stop
1998 #PS12 Jeff Gordon's Car
1999 #12 Jeff Gordon's Car
Press Pass Pitstop
2000 #PS12 Jeff Gordon's Car
Press Pass Platinum
2002 #11 Jeff Gordon
2002 #66 Jeff Gordon REP
2002 #83 Jeff Gordon's Car
2002 #99 Jeff Gordon NWC Champ
2004 #P10 Jeff Gordon
2004 #P93 Jeff Gordon DS
2005 #P19 Jeff Gordon
2005 #P80 Jeff Gordon NS
2005 #P84 Jeff Gordon NS
2005 #P92 J.Hendrick/Gordon/JJ/T.Lab/Vickers Y

2005 #P95 Jeff Gordon Y
2005 #P105 Jeff Gordon P
2005 #P112 Jeff Gordon's Car
2005 #P120 Dale Jr/JJ/Gordon CL
2006 #P18 Jeff Gordon
2006 #P77 Jeff Gordon's car OTW
2006 #P85 Jeff Gordon NS
2006 #P104 Jeff Gordon U
2007 #P9 Jeff Gordon
2007 #P73 Jeff Gordon's Car OT
2007 #P100 Jeff Gordon U
2007 #P116 Jeff Gordon TT
2008 #P1 Jeff Gordon
2008 #P64 Jeff Gordon's Car BFS
2008 #P92 Jeff Gordon's Car U
2008 #P108 Jeff Gordon Top 12

Press Pass Premium
1995 #8 Jeff Gordon
1995 #33 Jeff Gordon
1996 #1 Jeff Gordon
1996 #34 Jeff Gordon's Car
1997 #2 Jeff Gordon
1997 #33 Jeff Gordon's Car
1997 #38 Jeff Gordon
1997 #P1 Jeff Gordon Promo
1998 #21 Jeff Gordon's Car
1998 #28 Jeff Gordon
1998 #P1 Jeff Gordon Promo
1999 #8 Jeff Gordon
1999 #28 Jeff Gordon's Car
1999 #43 Jeff Gordon
1999 #0 Jeff Gordon Daytona
2000 #13 Jeff Gordon
2000 #36 Jeff Gordon's Car
2000 #47 Jeff Gordon
2000 #65 Jeff Gordon
2001 #6 Jeff Gordon
2001 #36 Jeff Gordon
2001 #52 Jeff Gordon CC
2001 #73 Jeff Gordon PC
2001 #0 Jeff Gordon No Bull 5
2002 #8 Jeff Gordon
2002 #38 Jeff Gordon's Car
2002 #46 Jeff Gordon SW
2002 #51 Jeff Gordon CH
2002 #72 Jeff Gordon PC
2003 #8 Jeff Gordon
2003 #37 Jeff Gordon's Car
2003 #53 Jeff Gordon CC
2003 #71 Jeff Gordon PC
2004 #7 Jeff Gordon
2004 #42 Jeff Gordon's Car
2004 #53 Jeff Gordon CC
2004 #79 Jeff Gordon PC
2005 #7 Jeff Gordon
2005 #40 Jeff Gordon's Car M
2005 #53 Jeff Gordon CC
2005 #72 Jeff Gordon PC
2005 #0 Jeff Gordon Daytona
2006 #8 Jeff Gordon
2006 #37 Jeff Gordon's Car M
2006 #48 Jeff Gordon NS
2006 #57 Jeff Gordon CC
2006 #76 Jeff Gordon PC
2007 #21 Jeff Gordon
2007 #35 Jeff Gordon's Car M
2007 #49 Jeff Gordon SW
2007 #57 Jeff Gordon RTTC
2007 #69 Jeff Gordon MD
2007 #72 Jeff Gordon DD
2007 #78 Jeff Gordon FF
2008 #82 Jeff Gordon D
2008 #79 Jeff Gordon F
2008 #59 Jeff Gordon EOP
2008 #19 Jeff Gordon
2008 #43 Jeff Gordon's Car M

Press Pass Premium Asphalt Jungle
2004 #A2 Jeff Gordon
2005 #AJ3 Jeff Gordon
2006 #AJ3 Jeff Gordon

Press Pass Premium Badge of Honor
1999 #BH10 Jeff Gordon
1999 #BH24 Jeff Gordon's Car

Press Pass Premium Badge of Honor Reflectors
1999 #BH10 Jeff Gordon
1999 #BH24 Jeff Gordon's Car

Press Pass Premium Burning Desire
1999 #FD1B Jeff Gordon 1:240

Press Pass Premium Burning Rubber II
1996 #BR1 Jeff Gordon's Car

Press Pass Premium Clean Air
2008 #CA1 Jeff Gordon

Press Pass Premium Concrete Chaos
2007 #CC1 Jeff Gordon

Press Pass Premium Crystal Ball
1996 #CB5 Jeff Gordon
1997 #CB4 Jeff Gordon

Press Pass Premium Crystal Ball Die Cut
1997 #CB4 Jeff Gordon

Press Pass Premium Double Burners
1997 #DB2 Jeff Gordon

Press Pass Premium Emerald Proofs
1996 #1 Jeff Gordon
1996 #34 Jeff Gordon's Car
1997 #2 Jeff Gordon
1997 #33 Jeff Gordon's Car
1997 #38 Jeff Gordon

Press Pass Premium Extreme Fire
1999 #FD1A Jeff Gordon 1:240

Press Pass Premium Flag Chasers
1998 #FC1 Jeff Gordon
1998 #FC24 Jeff Gordon's Car

Press Pass Premium Flag Chasers Reflectors
1998 #FC1 Jeff Gordon
1998 #FC24 Jeff Gordon's Car

Press Pass Premium Going Global
2008 #GG5 Jeff Gordon

Press Pass Premium Going Global Red
2008 #GG5 Jeff Gordon

Press Pass Premium Gold
2001 #6 Jeff Gordon
2001 #36 Jeff Gordon
2001 #52 Jeff Gordon CC
2001 #73 Jeff Gordon PC

Press Pass Premium Holofoil
1995 #8 Jeff Gordon
1995 #33 Jeff Gordon
1996 #1 Jeff Gordon
1996 #34 Jeff Gordon's Car

Press Pass Premium Hot Pursuit
1995 #HP3 Jeff Gordon
1996 #HP3 Jeff Gordon

Press Pass Premium Hot Threads Autographs
2004 #HT-JG Jeff Gordon/24
2005 #HT-JG Jeff Gordon/24
2007 #HT-JG Jeff Gordon/24
2008 #HTJG Jeff Gordon/24

Press Pass Premium Hot Threads Cars
2003 #HTT1 Jeff Gordon
2005 #HTT3 Jeff Gordon
2006 #HTT11 Jeff Gordon

Press Pass Premium Hot Threads Cars Autographs
2003 #HTD-JG Jeff Gordon/24

Press Pass Premium Hot Threads Drivers
2003 #HTD1 Jeff Gordon
2005 #HTD3 Jeff Gordon
2006 #HTD11 Jeff Gordon
2007 #HTD8 Jeff Gordon
2008 #HTD9 Jeff Gordon

Press Pass Premium Hot Threads Drivers Autographs
2003 #HTT-JG Jeff Gordon/24

Press Pass Premium Hot Threads Drivers Bronze
2004 #HTD4 Jeff Gordon

Press Pass Premium Hot Threads Drivers Bronze Retail
2004 #HTT4 Jeff Gordon

Press Pass Premium Hot Threads Drivers Gold
2004 #HTD4 Jeff Gordon
2005 #HTD3 Jeff Gordon
2006 #HTD11 Jeff Gordon
2007 #HTD8 Jeff Gordon
2008 #HTD9 Jeff Gordon

Press Pass Premium Hot Threads Drivers Silver
2004 #HTD4 Jeff Gordon

Press Pass Premium Hot Threads Patch
2007 #HTP3 Jeff Gordon DuPont/8
2007 #HTP2 Jeff Gordon Pepsi/15

Press Pass Premium Hot Threads Patches
2008 #HTP5 Jeff Gordon Bosch Spark Plugs/8
2008 #HTP6 Jeff Gordon Goodyear
2008 #HTP7 Jeff Gordon NASCAR bar

Press Pass Premium Hot Threads Team
2007 #HTT8 Jeff Gordon
2008 #HTT9 Jeff Gordon

Press Pass Premium In The Zone
2000 #IZ4 Jeff Gordon
2001 #IZ5 Jeff Gordon
2002 #IZ4 Jeff Gordon
2003 #IZ2 Jeff Gordon
2004 #IZ4 Jeff Gordon
2005 #IZ9 Jeff Gordon
2006 #IZ10 Jeff Gordon

Press Pass Premium In the Zone Elite Edition
2004 #IZ4 Jeff Gordon
2005 #IZ9 Jeff Gordon

Press Pass Premium In the Zone Red
2006 #IZ10 Jeff Gordon

Press Pass Premium Lap Leaders
1997 #LL3 Jeff Gordon

Press Pass Premium Mirrors
1997 #2 Jeff Gordon
1997 #33 Jeff Gordon's Car
1997 #38 Jeff Gordon

Press Pass Premium Oil Slicks
1997 #2 Jeff Gordon
1997 #27 Mike Skinner/Robby Gordon/David Green
1997 #33 Jeff Gordon's Car
1997 #38 Jeff Gordon

Press Pass Premium Performance Driven
2000 #PD2 Jeff Gordon
2001 #PD4 Jeff Gordon
2002 #PD2 Jeff Gordon
2003 #PD2 Jeff Gordon
2004 #PD7 Jeff Gordon
2005 #PD4 Jeff Gordon
2007 #PD10 Jeff Gordon

Press Pass Premium Performance Driven Red
2007 #PD10 Jeff Gordon

Press Pass Premium Phone Cards $5
1995 #2 Jeff Gordon
1995 #10 Jeff Gordon $1995 AUTO

Press Pass Premium Phone Cards $50
1995 #2 Jeff Gordon

Press Pass Premium Previews
2003 #8 Jeff Gordon
2004 #7 Jeff Gordon
2008 #EB19 Jeff Gordon
2008 #EB59 Jeff Gordon EOP

Press Pass Premium Race Used Firesuit
1999 #F1 Jeff Gordon
2000 #F4 Jeff Gordon

Press Pass Premium Race Used Firesuit Cars
2001 #FC1 Jeff Gordon
2002 #FC1 Jeff Gordon

Press Pass Premium Race Used Firesuit Drivers
2001 #FD1 Jeff Gordon
2002 #FD1 Jeff Gordon

Press Pass Premium Red
2007 #R21 Jeff Gordon
2007 #R35 Jeff Gordon's Car M
2007 #R49 Jeff Gordon SW
2007 #R57 Jeff Gordon RTTC
2007 #R69 Jeff Gordon MD
2007 #R72 Jeff Gordon DD
2007 #R78 Jeff Gordon FF
2008 #19 Jeff Gordon
2008 #43 Jeff Gordon's Car M
2008 #59 Jeff Gordon EOP
2008 #79 Jeff Gordon F
2008 #82 Jeff Gordon DD

Press Pass Premium Red Hot
1995 #8 Jeff Gordon
1995 #33 Jeff Gordon

Press Pass Premium Red Reflectors
2002 #8 Jeff Gordon
2002 #38 Jeff Gordon's Car
2002 #46 Jeff Gordon SW
2002 #51 Jeff Gordon CC
2002 #72 Jeff Gordon PC
2003 #8 Jeff Gordon
2003 #37 Jeff Gordon's Car
2003 #53 Jeff Gordon CC
2003 #71 Jeff Gordon PC

Press Pass Premium Reflectors
1998 #21 Jeff Gordon's Car
1998 #28 Jeff Gordon
1999 #R8 Jeff Gordon
1999 #R28 Jeff Gordon's Car
1999 #R43 Jeff Gordon
2000 #13 Jeff Gordon
2000 #36 Jeff Gordon's Car
2000 #47 Jeff Gordon
2000 #65 Jeff Gordon

Press Pass Premium Rivalries
1998 #1B Jeff Gordon
1998 #6A Jeff Gordon's Car

Press Pass Premium Samples
2002 #8 Jeff Gordon
2002 #38 Jeff Gordon's Car
2002 #46 Jeff Gordon SW
2003 #8 Jeff Gordon
2003 #37 Jeff Gordon's Car
2004 #7 Jeff Gordon
2004 #42 Jeff Gordon's Car
2005 #7 Jeff Gordon
2005 #40 Jeff Gordon's Car M

Press Pass Premium Steel Horses
1998 #SH7 Jeff Gordon's Car
1999 #SH9 Jeff Gordon's Car

Press Pass Premium Team Signed Baseballs
2008 #E-HMS Dale Earnhardt Jr. Jeff Gordon Jimmie Johnson Casey Mears Entry Card
2008 #HMS Dale Earnhardt Jr. Jeff Gordon Jimmie Johnson Casey Mears

Press Pass Premium Triple Gear Firesuit
1998 #TGF6 Jeff Gordon

Press Pass Premium Wal-Mart
2008 #WM5 Jeff Gordon

Press Pass Previews
1993 #17 J.Gordon/K.Wall./B.Lab.
1993 #18A J.Gordon Redemp. Expired
1993 #18B Jeff Gordon Foil
1993 #26 Jeff Gordon's Car
2003 #10 Jeff Gordon
2004 #10 Jeff Gordon
2006 #EB18 Jeff Gordon
2006 #EB104 Jeff Gordon U
2007 #EB9 Jeff Gordon
2007 #EB116 Jeff Gordon TT
2008 #EB1 Jeff Gordon
2008 #EB108 Jeff Gordon Top 12

Press Pass Previews Green
2005 #EB19 Jeff Gordon

Press Pass Previews Silver
2005 #EB105 Jeff Gordon

Press Pass Prototypes
1995 #3 Jeff Gordon

Press Pass R and N China
1996 #11 Jeff Gordon
1996 #38 Jeff Gordon's Car

Press Pass Race Day
1994 #RD7 Jeff Gordon
1995 #RD4 Jeff Gordon
2007 #RD1 Jeff Gordon
2008 #RD4 Jeff Gordon

Press Pass Red Hot
1995 #10 Jeff Gordon
1995 #38 Jeff Gordon's Car
1995 #102 Jeff Gordon ST
1995 #129 Jeff Gordon PR
1995 #136 Jeff Gordon BT

Press Pass Samples
2003 #10 Jeff Gordon
2003 #60 Jeff Gordon DS
2003 #78 The California Kid WCS
2003 #98 Jeff Gordon's Car OTW
2003 #100 Jeff Gordon Header
2004 #10 Jeff Gordon
2004 #93 Jeff Gordon DS
2005 #19 Jeff Gordon
2005 #80 Jeff Gordon NS
2005 #84 Jeff Gordon NS
2005 #92 J.Hend./Gordon/JJ/T.Lab/B.Vick Y
2005 #95 Jeff Gordon Y
2005 #105 Jeff Gordon P
2005 #112 Jeff Gordon's Car
2005 #120 Dale Jr/JJ/Gordon CL

Press Pass Schedule
2004 #1 Jeff Gordon

Press Pass Scorchers
1996 #11 Jeff Gordon
1996 #38 Jeff Gordon's Car
1996 #78 R.Hendrick/Evernham/Gordon TW
1996 #93 Jeff Gordon S
1996 #100 J.Gordon/B.Gordon WCC
1996 #111 Jeff Gordon/J.Benson WC

Press Pass Shockers
1998 #ST2A Jeff Gordon

Press Pass Showcar
2002 #S3A Jeff Gordon's Car
2003 #S3B Jeff Gordon
2004 #S5B Jeff Gordon's Car
2005 #SC5 Jeff Gordon

Press Pass Showcar Die Cuts
2000 #SC7 Jeff Gordon's Car

Press Pass Showman
1999 #11A Jeff Gordon
2000 #SM7 Jeff Gordon
2002 #S3A Jeff Gordon
2003 #S3A Jeff Gordon
2004 #S5A Jeff Gordon
2005 #SM5 Jeff Gordon

Press Pass Showman Die Cuts
2000 #SM7 Jeff Gordon

Press Pass Showman/Showcar
2001 #S4A Jeff Gordon
2001 #S4B Jeff Gordon's Car

Press Pass Signings
1998 #1 Jeff Gordon PPP/VIP/S
1999 #19 Jeff Gordon/400
2000 #20 Jeff Gordon
2001 #15 Jeff Gordon T/V/S
2002 #18 Jeff Gordon O/P/S/T/V
2003 #23 Jeff Gordon O/P/S/T/V
2004 #21 Jeff Gordon O/P/S/T/V
2005 #18 Jeff Gordon P/S
2006 #17 Jeff Gordon NC P/S
2007 #22 Jeff Gordon NC
2008 #21 Jeff Gordon

Press Pass Signings Blue
2007 #8 Jeff Gordon NC
2008 #8 Jeff Gordon

Press Pass Signings Gold
1998 #1 Jeff Gordon PPP/VIP
1999 #5 Jeff Gordon/100
2000 #12 Jeff Gordon
2001 #13 Jeff Gordon S
2002 #18 Jeff Gordon O/P/S/T/V
2003 #23 Jeff Gordon O/P/S/T/V
2004 #20 Jeff Gordon O/P/S/T/V
2005 #17 Jeff Gordon P/S
2006 #14 Jeff Gordon NC P/S
2007 #18 Jeff Gordon NC
2008 #17 Jeff Gordon

Press Pass Signings Platinum
2005 #17 Jeff Gordon P/S

Press Pass Signings Press Plates Black
2007 #15 Jeff Gordon
2008 #14 Jeff Gordon

Press Pass Signings Press Plates Cyan
2007 #14 Jeff Gordon
2008 #14 Jeff Gordon

Press Pass Signings Press Plates Magenta
2007 #14 Jeff Gordon
2008 #14 Jeff Gordon

Press Pass Signings Press Plates Yellow
2007 #14 Jeff Gordon
2008 #14 Jeff Gordon

Press Pass Signings Silver
2006 #16 Jeff Gordon/50 P/S
2007 #17 Jeff Gordon NC

Press Pass Signings Transparent
2002 #2 Jeff Gordon O/P/S/T/V
2003 #2 Jeff Gordon O/P/S/T/V
2004 #1 Jeff Gordon O/P/S/T

Press Pass Skidmarks
1999 #1 Jeff Gordon
1999 #28 Jeff Gordon's Car
1999 #79 Jeff Gordon OTP
1999 #99 Jeff Gordon PRE
2000 #SK5 Jeff Gordon

Press Pass Snapshots
2003 #SN7 Jeff Gordon
2004 #SN7 Jeff Gordon
2005 #SN8 Jeff Gordon
2006 #SN30 Jeff Gordon
2007 #SN7 Jeff Gordon

Press Pass Snapshots Extra
2005 #SS2 Jeff Gordon

Press Pass Speedway
2008 #5 Jeff Gordon
2008 #61 Jeff Gordon SH
2008 #73 Jeff Gordon UTH
2008 #78 Jeff Gordon's Car RSG
2008 #85 Jeff Gordon's Car WS

Press Pass Speedway Blur
2008 #B5 Jeff Gordon

Press Pass Speedway Cockpit
2008 #CP7 Jeff Gordon

Press Pass Speedway Garage Graphs Duals
2008 #GL Jeff Gordon Steve Letarte

Press Pass Speedway Gold
2008 #G5 Jeff Gordon
2008 #G61 Jeff Gordon SH
2008 #G73 Jeff Gordon UTH
2008 #G78 Jeff Gordon's Car RSG
2008 #G85 Jeff Gordon's Car WS

Press Pass Speedway Holofoil
2008 #H5 Jeff Gordon
2008 #H61 Jeff Gordon SH
2008 #H73 Jeff Gordon UTH
2008 #H78 Jeff Gordon's Car RSG
2008 #H85 Jeff Gordon's Car WS

Press Pass Speedway Previews
2008 #EB5 Jeff Gordon

Press Pass Speedway Red
2008 #R5 Jeff Gordon
2008 #R61 Jeff Gordon SH
2008 #R73 Jeff Gordon UTH
2008 #R78 Jeff Gordon's Car RSG
2008 #R85 Jeff Gordon's Car WS

Press Pass Speedway Test Drive
2008 #TD1 Jeff Gordon

Press Pass Stealth
1998 #10 Jeff Gordon
1998 #11 Jeff Gordon's Car
1998 #47 Jeff Gordon TM
1998 #P1 Jeff Gordon Promo
1998 #0 J.Gordon Champ Bnz 1:110
1998 #0 J.Gordon Champ Slv 1:220
1998 #0 J.Gordon Champ Gld 1:440
1999 #10 Jeff Gordon
1999 #11 Jeff Gordon's Car
1999 #40 Jeff Gordon
1999 #50 Dupont Air Gun TT
2000 #34 Jeff Gordon
2000 #35 Jeff Gordon's Car
2000 #65 Jeff Gordon FF
2001 #28 Jeff Gordon
2001 #29 Jeff Gordon's Car
2001 #30 Jeff Gordon
2001 #55 Jeff Gordon WIN
2001 #56 Jeff Gordon WIN
2001 #57 Jeff Gordon WIN
2001 #58 Jeff Gordon WIN
2001 #59 Jeff Gordon WIN
2001 #60 Jeff Gordon WIN
2001 #61 Jeff Gordon WIN
2001 #62 Jeff Gordon WIN
2001 #63 Jeff Gordon WIN
2001 #65 Jeff Gordon SST
2002 #28 Jeff Gordon
2002 #29 Jeff Gordon's Car
2002 #30 Jeff Gordon
2002 #60 Jeff Gordon's Car SST
2002 #71 Jeff Gordon WW
2003 #31 Jeff Gordon
2003 #32 Jeff Gordon's Car
2003 #33 Jeff Gordon
2003 #62 Jeff Gordon SST
2003 #64 Jeff Gordon SF
2004 #25 Jeff Gordon
2004 #26 Jeff Gordon's Car
2004 #27 Jeff Gordon
2004 #86 Jeff Gordon SST
2005 #48 Jeff Gordon
2005 #51 Jeff Gordon's Car
2005 #54 Jeff Gordon
2005 #87 Jeff Gordon H
2005 #97 Jeff Gordon SF
2005 #100 Jeff Gordon CL
2006 #8 Jeff Gordon
2006 #45 Jeff Gordon's Rig
2006 #54 24/44/48/25/5 TM
2006 #58 Jeff Gordon F
2006 #90 Johnson/Gordon CL
2007 #8 Jeff Gordon
2007 #52 Jeff Gordon's Rig
2007 #60 Jeff Gordon's Crew GC
2007 #72 Mears/Ky.Busch/JJ/Gordon
2007 #89 Jeff Gordon PO
2008 #11 Jeff Gordon
2008 #60 Jeff Gordon's Car GC
2008 #67 Jimmie Johnson Jeff Gordon Dale Earnhardt Jr. Casey Mears
2008 #84 Jeff Gordon PM

Press Pass Stealth Autographed Hat Entry
2006 #PPH7 Jeff Gordon

Press Pass Stealth Awards
1998 #5 Jeff Gordon 1:200
1998 #7 Jeff Gordon 1:420

Press Pass Stealth Battle Armor Autographs
2007 #BAS-JG Jeff Gordon/24

Press Pass Stealth Battle Armor Drivers
2007 #BAD1 Jeff Gordon
2008 #BAD3 Jeff Gordon

Press Pass Stealth Battle Armor Teams
2007 #BAT1 Jeff Gordon
2008 #BAT3 Jeff Gordon

Press Pass Stealth Behind the Numbers
2000 #BN7 Jeff Gordon
2002 #BN9 Jeff Gordon

Press Pass Stealth Big Numbers
1999 #BN7 Jeff Gordon
1999 #BN8 Jeff Gordon

Press Pass Stealth Big Numbers Die Cuts
1999 #BN7 Jeff Gordon
1999 #BN8 Jeff Gordon

Press Pass Stealth Chrome
2007 #8 Jeff Gordon
2007 #52 Jeff Gordon's Rig
2007 #60 Jeff Gordon's Crew GC
2007 #72 Mears/Ky.Busch/JJ/Gordon
2007 #89 Jeff Gordon PO
2007 #8A Jeff Gordon L1 -white dot in corners
2007 #8B Jeff Gordon L2 -white dot -background text
2008 #11 Jeff Gordon
2008 #11B Jeff Gordon VAR
2008 #60 Jeff Gordon's Car GC
2008 #67 Jimmie Johnson Jeff Gordon Dale Earnhardt Jr. Casey Mears
2008 #84 Jeff Gordon PM

Press Pass Stealth Chrome Exclusives
2007 #X8 Jeff Gordon
2007 #X52 Jeff Gordon's Rig
2007 #X60 Jeff Gordon's Crew GC
2007 #X72 Mears/Ky.Busch/JJ/Gordon
2007 #X89 Jeff Gordon PO
2008 #11 Jeff Gordon
2008 #60 Jeff Gordon's Car GC
2008 #67 Jimmie Johnson Jeff Gordon Dale Earnhardt Jr. Casey Mears
2008 #84 Jeff Gordon PM

Press Pass Stealth Chrome Exclusives Gold
2008 #11 Jeff Gordon
2008 #60 Jeff Gordon's Car GC
2008 #67 Jimmie Johnson Jeff Gordon Dale Earnhardt Jr. Casey Mears
2008 #84 Jeff Gordon PM

Press Pass Stealth Chrome Platinum
2007 #P8 Jeff Gordon
2007 #P52 Jeff Gordon's Rig
2007 #P60 Jeff Gordon's Crew GC
2007 #P72 Mears/Ky.Busch/JJ/Gordon
2007 #P89 Jeff Gordon PO

Press Pass Stealth EFX
2002 #FX5 Jeff Gordon
2003 #FX4 Jeff Gordon
2004 #EF2 Jeff Gordon
2005 #EFX1 Jeff Gordon
2006 #EFX3 Jeff Gordon 1:112

Press Pass Stealth Fan Talk
1998 #3 Jeff Gordon

Press Pass Stealth Fan Talk Die Cuts
1998 #3 Jeff Gordon

Press Pass Stealth Fusion
1998 #10 Jeff Gordon
1998 #11 Jeff Gordon's Car
1998 #47 Jeff Gordon TM
1999 #F10 Jeff Gordon
1999 #F11 Jeff Gordon's Car
1999 #F40 Jeff Gordon
1999 #F50 Dupont Air Gun TT
2000 #FS13 Jeff Gordon
2000 #FS14 Jeff Gordon's Car
2000 #FS15 Jeff Gordon
2001 #F2 Jeff Gordon
2002 #F3 Jeff Gordon
2003 #FU4 Jeff Gordon
2004 #FU1 Jeff Gordon
2005 #FU1 Jeff Gordon 1:112
2007 #F2 Jeff Gordon

Press Pass Stealth Fusion Green
2000 #FS13 Jeff Gordon
2000 #FS14 Jeff Gordon
2000 #FS15 Jeff Gordon

Press Pass Stealth Fusion Red
2000 #FS13 Jeff Gordon
2000 #FS14 Jeff Gordon
2000 #FS15 Jeff Gordon

Press Pass Stealth Gear Grippers Autographs
2004 #HT-JG Jeff Gordon/24
2005 #GG-JG Jeff Gordon/24
2006 #JG Jeff Gordon/24

Press Pass Stealth Gear Grippers Cars
2003 #GGT1 Jeff Gordon
2005 #GGT4 Jeff Gordon

Press Pass Stealth Gear Grippers Cars Autographs
2003 #JG Jeff Gordon/24

Press Pass Stealth Gear Grippers Drivers
2003 #GGD1 Jeff Gordon
2004 #GGD4 Jeff Gordon
2005 #GGD4 Jeff Gordon
2006 #GGD1 Jeff Gordon

Press Pass Stealth Gear Grippers Drivers Autographs
2003 #JG Jeff Gordon/24

Press Pass Stealth Gear Grippers Drivers Retail
2004 #GGT4 Jeff Gordon

Press Pass Stealth Gold
2002 #28 Jeff Gordon
2002 #29 Jeff Gordon's Car
2002 #30 Jeff Gordon
2002 #60 Jeff Gordon's Car SST
2002 #71 Jeff Gordon WW

Press Pass Stealth Headlines
1999 #SH1 Jeff Gordon

Press Pass Stealth Holofoils
2001 #28 Jeff Gordon
2001 #29 Jeff Gordon's Car
2001 #30 Jeff Gordon
2001 #55 Jeff Gordon WIN
2001 #56 Jeff Gordon WIN
2001 #57 Jeff Gordon WIN
2001 #58 Jeff Gordon WIN
2001 #59 Jeff Gordon WIN
2001 #60 Jeff Gordon WIN
2001 #61 Jeff Gordon WIN
2001 #62 Jeff Gordon WIN
2001 #63 Jeff Gordon WIN
2001 #65 Jeff Gordon SST

Press Pass Stealth Hot Pass
2006 #HP9 Jeff Gordon

Press Pass Stealth Intensity
2000 #IN5 Jeff Gordon

Press Pass Stealth Lap Leaders
2001 #LL10 Jeff Gordon
2001 #LL28 Jeff Gordon's Car
2002 #LL7 Jeff Gordon

Press Pass Stealth Lap Leaders Clear Cars
2001 #LL28 Jeff Gordon's Car

Press Pass Stealth Lap Leaders Clear Drivers
2001 #LL10 Jeff Gordon

Press Pass Stealth Mach 07
2007 #M7-2 Jeff Gordon

Press Pass Stealth Mach 08
2008 #M8-1 Jeff Gordon

Press Pass Stealth Maximum Access
2007 #MA8 Jeff Gordon
2008 #MA10 Jeff Gordon

Press Pass Stealth Maximum Access Autographs
2007 #MA8 Jeff Gordon
2008 #MA10 Jeff Gordon

Press Pass Stealth No Boundaries
2003 #NB12 Jeff Gordon
2004 #NB12 Jeff Gordon
2005 #NB14 Jeff Gordon

Press Pass Stealth Octane
1998 #13 Jeff Gordon
1998 #14 Jeff Gordon's Car

Press Pass Stealth Octane Die Cuts
1998 #13 Jeff Gordon
1998 #14 Jeff Gordon's Car

Press Pass Stealth Octane SLX
1999 #O6 Jeff Gordon
1999 #O7 Jeff Gordon
1999 #O26 Jeff Gordon's Car
1999 #O34 Jeff Gordon's Car

Press Pass Stealth Octane SLX Die Cuts
1999 #O6 Jeff Gordon
1999 #O7 Jeff Gordon
1999 #O26 Jeff Gordon's Car
1999 #O34 Jeff Gordon's Car

Press Pass Stealth Previews
2003 #31 Jeff Gordon
2003 #32 Jeff Gordon's Car
2003 #33 Jeff Gordon
2004 #EB25 Jeff Gordon
2004 #EB26 Jeff Gordon's Car
2004 #EB27 Jeff Gordon
2005 #48 Jeff Gordon
2005 #51 Jeff Gordon's Car
2005 #54 Jeff Gordon
2005 #97 Jeff Gordon SF
2006 #8 Jeff Gordon
2007 #EB89 Jeff Gordon PO
2007 #EB8 Jeff Gordon
2008 #11 Jeff Gordon
2008 #84 Jeff Gordon PM

Press Pass Stealth Profile
2000 #PR9 Jeff Gordon
2001 #SP5 Jeff Gordon
2002 #P1 Jeff Gordon
2003 #PR2 Jeff Gordon
2004 #P1 Jeff Gordon 1:112
2005 #PR1 Jeff Gordon
2006 #P3 Jeff Gordon

Press Pass Stealth Race Used Glove Cars
2001 #RGC1 Jeff Gordon/50
2002 #GLC1 Jeff Gordon's Car

Press Pass Stealth Race Used Glove Drivers
2001 #RGD1 Jeff Gordon/50
2002 #GLD1 Jeff Gordon

Press Pass Stealth Race Used Gloves
1998 #G6 Jeff Gordon
1999 #G2 Jeff Gordon/24
2000 #G7 Jeff Gordon/100

Press Pass Stealth Red
2003 #P31 Jeff Gordon
2003 #P32 Jeff Gordon's Car
2003 #P33 Jeff Gordon
2003 #P62 Jeff Gordon SST
2003 #P64 Jeff Gordon SF

Press Pass Stealth Retail
2006 #8 Jeff Gordon
2006 #45 Jeff Gordon's Rig
2006 #58 Jeff Gordon F
2006 #90 J.Johnson/J.Gordon CL
2006 #54 24/44/48/25/5 TM

Press Pass Stealth Retail Gear Grippers Cars
2006 #GGT1 Jeff Gordon

Press Pass Stealth Samples
2002 #28 Jeff Gordon
2002 #29 Jeff Gordon's Car
2002 #30 Jeff Gordon

2002 #60 Jeff Gordon's Car SST
2002 #71 Jeff Gordon WW
2003 #31 Jeff Gordon
2003 #32 Jeff Gordon's Car
2003 #33 Jeff Gordon
2003 #62 Jeff Gordon SST
2003 #64 Jeff Gordon SF
2004 #X26 Jeff Gordon's Car
2004 #X25 Jeff Gordon
2004 #X27 Jeff Gordon
2004 #X86 Jeff Gordon SST
2005 #48 Jeff Gordon
2005 #51 Jeff Gordon's Car
2005 #54 Jeff Gordon
2005 #87 Jeff Gordon H
2005 #97 Jeff Gordon SF
2005 #100 Jeff Gordon CL

Press Pass Stealth SST
2000 #SST4 Jeff Gordon

Press Pass Stealth SST Cars
1999 #SS3 Jeff Gordon's Car

Press Pass Stealth SST Drivers
1999 #SS3 Jeff Gordon

Press Pass Stealth Stars
1998 #5 Jeff Gordon

Press Pass Stealth Stars Die Cuts
1998 #5 Jeff Gordon

Press Pass Stealth Supercharged
2003 #SC1 Jeff Gordon

Press Pass Stealth Synthesis
2008 #S9 Jeff Gordon

Press Pass Stealth X-Ray
2004 #25 Jeff Gordon
2004 #26 Jeff Gordon's Car
2004 #27 Jeff Gordon
2004 #86 Jeff Gordon SST
2005 #X48 Jeff Gordon
2005 #X51 Jeff Gordon's Car
2005 #X54 Jeff Gordon
2005 #X87 Jeff Gordon H
2005 #X97 Jeff Gordon SF
2005 #X100 Jeff Gordon CL
2006 #X8 Jeff Gordon
2006 #X45 Jeff Gordon's Rig
2006 #X54 24/44/48/25/5 TM
2006 #X58 Jeff Gordon F
2006 #X90 J.Johnson/J.Gordon CL

Press Pass Target
2007 #JG-B Jeff Gordon
2008 #JG-B Jeff Gordon

Press Pass Target Race Win Tires
2007 #RW6 Jeff Gordon Sonoma 6-26
2007 #RW8 Jeff Gordon Chicago 7-9

Press Pass Target Victory Tires
2008 #TT-JG Jeff Gordon Talladega

Press Pass Techno-Retro
2000 #TR8 Jeff Gordon

Press Pass Top 25 Drivers & Rides
2006 #C14 Jeff Gordon's Car
2006 #D14 Jeff Gordon

Press Pass Top Shelf
2002 #TS2 Jeff Gordon
2003 #TS2 Jeff Gordon
2004 #TS6 Jeff Gordon

Press Pass Top Ten
2005 #TT1 Jeff Gordon

Press Pass Torpedoes
1998 #ST2B Jeff Gordon's Car

Press Pass Torquers
1996 #11 Jeff Gordon
1996 #38 Jeff Gordon's Car
1996 #78 Hendrick/Evern/Gordon TW
1996 #93 Jeff Gordon S
1996 #100 J.Gordon/B.Gordon WCC
1996 #111 J.Gordon/J.Benson WC
1997 #2 Jeff Gordon
1997 #39 Jeff Gordon's Car
1997 #57 Jeff Gordon's Car
1997 #96 J.Gordon/D.Jarrett's Cars
1997 #104 Jeff Gordon's Car
1997 #105 Jeff Gordon's Car
1997 #134 Jeff Gordon W
1997 #135 Jeff Gordon W
1997 #136 Jeff Gordon W
1997 #137 Jeff Gordon W
1997 #138 Jeff Gordon W

Press Pass Total Memorabilia
2001 #TM1 Jeff Gordon

Press Pass Total Memorabilia Power Pick
2002 #TM2 Jeff Gordon
2003 #TM1 Jeff Gordon
2004 #TM1 Jeff Gordon
2005 #TM1 Jeff Gordon

Press Pass Trackside
2000 #7 Jeff Gordon
2000 #30 Jeff Gordon's Car
2001 #2 Jeff Gordon
2001 #48 Jeff Gordon's Car
2001 #85 Jeff Gordon CS
2002 #2 Jeff Gordon
2002 #53 Jeff Gordon RD
2002 #72 Jeff Gordon's Car
2002 #82 Jeff Gordon TM
2003 #20 Jeff Gordon
2003 #79 J.Johnson/J.Gordon TM
2004 #20 Jeff Gordon
2004 #20B J.Gordon dark background
2004 #69 J.Johnson/J.Gordon TM
2004 #89 Jeff Gordon H
2004 #108 J.Gordon/J.J./Vickers TT
2004 #111 Jeff Gordon F
2004 #120 J.Gordon/J.Johnson CL
2005 #3 Jeff Gordon
2005 #61 Jeff Gordon's Car HS
2005 #61B Jeff Gordon's Car HS -orange spots
2005 #70 J.Gordon/J.Johnson TM
2005 #83 Jeff Gordon GP
2005 #95 Jeff Gordon F

Press Pass Trackside Dialed In
2000 #DI4 Jeff Gordon
2001 #D4 Jeff Gordon
2002 #DI3 Jeff Gordon
2003 #DI3 Jeff Gordon
2004 #DI3 Jeff Gordon
2005 #DI3 Jeff Gordon

Press Pass Trackside Die Cuts
2000 #7 Jeff Gordon
2000 #30 Jeff Gordon

2001 #2 Jeff Gordon
2001 #48 Jeff Gordon's Car
2001 #85 Jeff Gordon CS

Press Pass Trackside Generation.now
2000 #GN6 Jeff Gordon

Press Pass Trackside Gold Holofoil
2003 #P20 Jeff Gordon
2003 #P79 J.Johnson/J.Gordon

Press Pass Trackside Golden
2000 #7 Jeff Gordon
2000 #30 Jeff Gordon
2001 #2 Jeff Gordon
2001 #48 Jeff Gordon's Car
2001 #85 Jeff Gordon CS
2002 #G2 Jeff Gordon
2003 #G20 Jeff Gordon
2004 #G20 Jeff Gordon
2004 #G69 J.Johnson/J.Gordon TM
2004 #G89 Jeff Gordon H
2004 #G108 J.Gordon/Johnson/Vickers TT
2004 #G111 Jeff Gordon F
2004 #G120 J.Gordon/J.Johnson CL
2005 #G3 Jeff Gordon
2005 #G61 Jeff Gordon's Car HS
2005 #G70 J.Gordon/J.Johnson TM
2005 #G83 Jeff Gordon GP
2005 #G95 Jeff Gordon F

Press Pass Trackside Hat Giveaway
2003 #PPH7 Jeff Gordon
2004 #PPH8 Jeff Gordon
2005 #PPH8 Jeff Gordon

Press Pass Trackside Hot Pass
2004 #HP7 Jeff Gordon
2005 #4 Jeff Gordon

Press Pass Trackside Hot Pass National
2004 #HP7 Jeff Gordon
2005 #4 Jeff Gordon

Press Pass Trackside Hot Pursuit
2004 #HP4 Jeff Gordon
2005 #HP4 Jeff Gordon

Press Pass Trackside License to Drive
2002 #9 Jeff Gordon
2003 #LD5 Jeff Gordon

Press Pass Trackside License to Drive Die Cuts
2002 #9 Jeff Gordon

Press Pass Trackside Mirror Image
2001 #MI5 Jeff Gordon
2002 #MI2 Jeff Gordon
2003 #MI3 Jeff Gordon

Press Pass Trackside Panorama
2000 #P31 Jeff Gordon

Press Pass Trackside Pit Stoppers Autographs
2005 #PSJG Jeff Gordon/24

Press Pass Trackside Pit Stoppers Cars
2003 #PST1 Jeff Gordon
2004 #PST1 Jeff Gordon
2005 #PST1 Jeff Gordon

Press Pass Trackside Pit Stoppers Drivers
2003 #PSD1 Jeff Gordon
2004 #PSD1 Jeff Gordon
2005 #PSD1 Jeff Gordon

Press Pass Trackside Previews
2003 #20 Jeff Gordon
2004 #EB20 Jeff Gordon
2005 #3 Jeff Gordon
2005 #83 Jeff Gordon GP

Press Pass Trackside Runnin N' Gunnin
2000 #RG6 Jeff Gordon
2001 #RG6 Jeff Gordon
2002 #RG2 Jeff Gordon
2003 #RG3 Jeff Gordon
2004 #RG2 Jeff Gordon
2005 #RG2 Jeff Gordon

Press Pass Trackside Samples
2002 #2 Jeff Gordon
2002 #53 Jeff Gordon RD
2002 #72 Jeff Gordon's Car
2002 #82 Jeff Gordon TM
2003 #20 Jeff Gordon
2003 #79 J.Johnson/J.Gordon TM
2004 #20 Jeff Gordon
2004 #69 J.Johnson/J.Gordon TM
2004 #89 Jeff Gordon H
2004 #108 J.Gordon/Johnson/Vickers TT
2004 #111 Jeff Gordon F
2004 #120 J.Gordon/J.Johnson CL
2005 #3 Jeff Gordon
2005 #61 Jeff Gordon's Car HS
2005 #70 J.Gordon/J.Johnson TM
2005 #83 Jeff Gordon GP
2005 #95 Jeff Gordon F

Press Pass Trackside Too Tough To Tame
2000 #TT5 Jeff Gordon

Press Pass Triple Burner
2001 #TB1 Jeff Gordon
2002 #TB2 Jeff Gordon
2003 #TB1 Jeff Gordon
2004 #TB1 Jeff Gordon
2005 #TB1 Jeff Gordon

Press Pass Triple Burner Exchange
2003 #TB1 Jeff Gordon EXCH
2004 #TB1 Jeff Gordon
2005 #TB1 Jeff Gordon

Press Pass Triple Gear 3 in 1
1998 #STG6 Jeff Gordon
1999 #TG3 Jeff Gordon

Press Pass Triple Gear Burning Rubber
1998 #TG6 Jeff Gordon

Press Pass Velocity
2001 #VL1 Jeff Gordon
2002 #VL3 Jeff Gordon
2003 #VC2 Jeff Gordon
2004 #VC7 Jeff Gordon
2005 #V3 Jeff Gordon
2006 #VE4 Jeff Gordon
2007 #V5 Jeff Gordon

Press Pass Victory Lane
1997 #VL2A Jeff Gordon
1997 #VL2B Jeff Gordon's Car

Press Pass Victory Lap
2003 #11 Jeff Gordon

Press Pass Vintage
2001 #VN9 Jeff Gordon
2002 #VN7 Jeff Gordon

Press Pass Wal-Mart
2007 #JG-A Jeff Gordon
2008 #JG-A Jeff Gordon

Press Pass Wal-Mart Autographs
2008 #3 Jeff Gordon

Press Pass Weekend Warriors
2008 #WW1 Jeff Gordon

Pro Set
1992 #128 Jeff Gordon

Race Sharks
1997 #2 Jeff Gordon
1997 #35 Jeff Gordon
1997 #36 Jeff Gordon
1997 #40 Jeff Gordon
1997 #43 Jeff Gordon
1997 #P1 Jeff Gordon Promo

Race Sharks First Bite
1997 #2 Jeff Gordon
1997 #35 Jeff Gordon
1997 #36 Jeff Gordon
1997 #40 Jeff Gordon
1997 #43 Jeff Gordon

Race Sharks Great White
1997 #2 Jeff Gordon
1997 #35 Jeff Gordon
1997 #36 Jeff Gordon
1997 #40 Jeff Gordon
1997 #43 Jeff Gordon

Race Sharks Great White Shark's Teeth
1997 #GW2 Jeff Gordon

Race Sharks Great White Shark's Teeth First Bite
1997 #GW2 Jeff Gordon

Race Sharks Hammerhead
1997 #2 Jeff Gordon
1997 #35 Jeff Gordon
1997 #36 Jeff Gordon
1997 #40 Jeff Gordon
1997 #43 Jeff Gordon

Race Sharks Hammerhead First Bite
1997 #2 Jeff Gordon
1997 #35 Jeff Gordon
1997 #36 Jeff Gordon
1997 #40 Jeff Gordon
1997 #43 Jeff Gordon

Race Sharks Shark Attack
1997 #SA2 Jeff Gordon

Race Sharks Shark Attack First Bite
1997 #SA2 Jeff Gordon

Race Sharks Shark Attack First Bite Previews
1997 #2 Jeff Gordon

Race Sharks Shark Tooth Signatures
1997 #ST2 Jeff Gordon/400

Race Sharks Shark Tooth Signatures First Bite
1997 #ST2 Jeff Gordon

Race Sharks Tiger Shark
1997 #2 Jeff Gordon
1997 #35 Jeff Gordon
1997 #36 Jeff Gordon
1997 #40 Jeff Gordon
1997 #43 Jeff Gordon

Race Sharks Tiger Shark First Bite
1997 #2 Jeff Gordon
1997 #35 Jeff Gordon
1997 #36 Jeff Gordon
1997 #40 Jeff Gordon
1997 #43 Jeff Gordon

Racer's Choice
1996 #9 Jeff Gordon
1996 #40 Jeff Gordon's Car
1996 #51 Jeff Gordon WCC
1996 #52 Jeff Gordon WCC
1996 #53 Jeff Gordon WCC
1996 #54 Jeff Gordon WCC
1996 #55 Jeff Gordon WCC
1996 #83 Jeff Gordon RW
1996 #90 Jeff Gordon BC
1996 #110 Jeff Gordon CL
1996 #J52 Jeff Gordon 5x7
1996 #P9 Jeff Gordon Promo
1997 #24 Jeff Gordon

Racer's Choice Artist's Proofs
1996 #9 Jeff Gordon
1996 #40 Jeff Gordon's Car
1996 #51 Jeff Gordon WCC
1996 #52 Jeff Gordon WCC
1996 #53 Jeff Gordon WCC
1996 #54 Jeff Gordon WCC
1996 #55 Jeff Gordon WCC
1996 #83 Jeff Gordon RW
1996 #90 Jeff Gordon BC
1996 #110 Jeff Gordon CL

Racer's Choice Busch Clash
1997 #8 Jeff Gordon

Racer's Choice Chevy Madness
1997 #7 Jeff Gordon

Racer's Choice High Octane
1997 #3 Jeff Gordon

Racer's Choice High Octane Glow in the Dark
1997 #3 Jeff Gordon

Racer's Choice Showcase Series
1997 #24 Jeff Gordon

Racer's Choice Speedway Collection
1996 #9 Jeff Gordon
1996 #40 Jeff Gordon's Car
1996 #51 Jeff Gordon WCC
1996 #52 Jeff Gordon WCC
1996 #53 Jeff Gordon WCC
1996 #54 Jeff Gordon WCC
1996 #55 Jeff Gordon WCC
1996 #83 Jeff Gordon RW
1996 #90 Jeff Gordon BC
1996 #110 Jeff Gordon CL

Racer's Choice Top Ten
1996 #1 Jeff Gordon

Racer's Choice Up Close with Jeff Gordon
1996 #1 Jeff Gordon
1996 #2 Jeff Gordon
1996 #3 Jeff Gordon
1996 #4 Jeff Gordon
1996 #5 Jeff Gordon
1996 #6 Jeff Gordon
1996 #7 Jeff Gordon

SB Motorsports
1997 #2 Jeff Gordon
1997 #63 The Rainbow Warriors

SB Motorsports Autographs
1997 #2 Jeff Gordon/250

Score Board IQ
1997 #2 Jeff Gordon
1997 #26 Jeff Gordon
1997 #37 Jeff Gordon
1997 #45 Jeff Gordon's Car
1997 #50 T.Lab/J.Gordon/Craven

Score Board IQ Remarques
1997 #SB2 Jeff Gordon

Score Board IQ Remarques Sam Bass Finished
1997 #SB2 Jeff Gordon

Select
1995 #12 Jeff Gordon
1995 #38 Jeff Gordon's Car
1995 #118 Jeff Gordon YS
1995 #141 Jeff Gordon PS
1995 #NNO Jeff Gordon YS Jumbo

Select Dream Machines
1995 #DM8 Jeff Gordon's Car

Select Flat Out
1995 #12 Jeff Gordon
1995 #38 Jeff Gordon's Car
1995 #118 Jeff Gordon YS
1995 #141 Jeff Gordon PS

Select Promos
1995 #12 Jeff Gordon
1995 #DM8 Jeff Gordon's Car Dream Machine

Select Skills
1995 #SS3 Jeff Gordon

SkyBox
1994 #4 Jeff Gordon's Car
1994 #NNO Brickyard Exch/Jeff Gordon

SkyBox Profile
1997 #7 Jeff Gordon
1997 #70 Jeff Gordon's Car
1997 #D1 Jeff Gordon Daytona
1997 #P1 Jeff Gordon Promo

SkyBox Profile Autographs
1997 #7 Jeff Gordon

SkyBox Profile Break Out
1997 #B1 Jeff Gordon

SkyBox Profile Pace Setters
1997 #E5 Jeff Gordon

SkyBox Profile Team
1997 #T2 Jeff Gordon

SLU Racing Winner's Circle
1997 #4A J.Gordon w/o Pepsi
1997 #4B J.Gordon w/Pepsi
1998 #4A Jeff Gordon
1998 #4B Jeff Gordon JP
1999 #20 Jeff Gordon Dupont '98
1999 #21 Jeff Gordon Pepsi
1999 #22 Jeff Gordon Dupont '99
1999 #23 Gordon Superman Wal.
1999 #24 J.Gordon Chroma Boscov
2000 #20 Jeff Gordon

SLU Racing Winner's Circle 12-inch Figures
1999 #2 Jeff Gordon
2000 #30 Jeff Gordon

SP
1995 #18 Jeff Gordon CC
1995 #100 Jeff Gordon's Car
1995 #JG1 Jeff Gordon Promo
1995 #97 Jeff Gordon's Car
1995 #56 Jeff Gordon
1995 #55 Jeff Gordon
1996 #24 Jeff Gordon
1996 #43 Jeff Gordon CC
1996 #80 Jeff Gordon RPM
1996 #KR1 D.Earnhardt/J.Gordon Aces
1997 #24 Jeff Gordon 3F
1997 #66 Jeff Gordon's Car
1997 #102 Jeff Gordon 2F
1997 #122 Jeff Gordon 3F
1997 #S24 Jeff Gordon Sample

SP Authentic
1998 #24 Jeff Gordon
1998 #58 Jeff Gordon's Car
1998 #72 Jeff Gordon VL
1999 #1 Jeff Gordon
1999 #51 Jeff Gordon's Car
1999 #65 Jeff Gordon CLASS
1999 #82 Jeff Gordon SP
2000 #12 Jeff Gordon
2000 #87 Jeff Gordon SUP

SP Authentic Behind the Wheel
1998 #BW1 Jeff Gordon

SP Authentic Behind the Wheel Die Cuts
1998 #BW1 Jeff Gordon

SP Authentic Behind the Wheel Gold
1998 #BW1 Jeff Gordon

SP Authentic Cup Challengers
1999 #CC1 Jeff Gordon

SP Authentic Driver's Seat
2000 #DS6 Jeff Gordon

SP Authentic Driving Force
1999 #DF8 Jeff Gordon

SP Authentic In the Driver's Seat
1999 #DS10 Jeff Gordon

SP Authentic Overdrive
1999 #1 Jeff Gordon
1999 #51 Jeff Gordon CAR
1999 #65 Jeff Gordon CLASS
1999 #82 Jeff Gordon SP/24

SP Authentic Overdrive Gold
2000 #12 Jeff Gordon/24
2000 #87 Jeff Gordon SUP/24

SP Authentic Overdrive Silver
2000 #12 Jeff Gordon
2000 #87 Jeff Gordon SUP

SP Authentic Power Surge
2000 #PS2 Jeff Gordon

SP Authentic Race for the Cup
2000 #R1 Jeff Gordon

SP Authentic Sign of the Times
1999 #JG Jeff Gordon
2000 #JG Jeff Gordon

SP Authentic Sign of the Times Gold
2000 #JG Jeff Gordon

SP Authentic Sign of the Times Red
1998 #ST1 Jeff Gordon's Car/45

SP Authentic Traditions
1998 #T2 D.Pearson/J.Gordon

SP Die Cuts
1995 #18 Jeff Gordon
1995 #55 Jeff Gordon
1995 #56 Jeff Gordon
1995 #97 Jeff Gordon's Car
1995 #100 Jeff Gordon's Car

SP Holoview Maximum Effects
1996 #ME1 Jeff Gordon

SP Holoview Maximum Effects Die Cuts
1996 #ME1 Jeff Gordon

SP Race Film
1997 #RD1 Jeff Gordon

SP Racing Legends
1996 #RL24 Jeff Gordon

SP Speed Merchants
1995 #SM24 Jeff Gordon

SP Speed Merchants Die Cuts
1995 #SM24 Jeff Gordon

SP SPx Force Autographs
1997 #SF1 Jeff Gordon

SP Super Series
1997 #24 Jeff Gordon 3F
1997 #66 Jeff Gordon's Car
1997 #102 Jeff Gordon 2F
1997 #122 Jeff Gordon 3F

Speedflix
1996 #9 Jeff Gordon
1996 #16 Jeff Gordon
1996 #44 Jeff Gordon's Car in pits
1996 #55 Jeff Gordon CM
1996 #56 Jeff Gordon CM
1996 #57 Jeff Gordon CM
1996 #58 Jeff Gordon CM
1996 #59 Jeff Gordon CM
1996 #60 Jeff Gordon CM
1996 #61 Jeff Gordon CM
1996 #62 Jeff Gordon CM
1996 #84 Jeff Gordon W
1996 #86 Jeff Gordon CL

Speedflix Artist Proof's
1996 #9 Jeff Gordon
1996 #16 Jeff Gordon
1996 #44 Jeff Gordon in Pits
1996 #55 Jeff Gordon
1996 #56 Jeff Gordon
1996 #57 Jeff Gordon
1996 #58 Jeff Gordon
1996 #59 Jeff Gordon
1996 #60 Jeff Gordon
1996 #61 Jeff Gordon
1996 #62 Jeff Gordon
1996 #84 Jeff Gordon W
1996 #86 Jeff Gordon CL

Speedflix Clear Shots
1996 #2 Jeff Gordon

Speedflix In Motion
1996 #2 Jeff Gordon's Helmet

Speedflix ProMotion
1996 #2 Jeff Gordon

Sports Illustrated for Kids
2002 #160 Jeff Gordon Racing
2005 #495 Jeff Gordon NASCAR

Sports Illustrated for Kids *
2005 #495 Jeff Gordon
1992-00 #602 Jeff Gordon
1992-00 #735 Jeff Gordon
2001-02 #160 Jeff Gordon

Sports Illustrated for Kids II
1997 #602 Jeff Gordon Auto Racing
1998 #735 Jeff Gordon Auto Racing

SportsCom FanScan
1997 #3 Jeff Gordon
1998 #2 Jeff Gordon
1999 #2 Jeff Gordon

SPx
1996 #1 Jeff Gordon
1996 #T1 Jeff Gordon Tribute
1996 #T1A Jeff Gordon AU
1996 #S1 Jeff Gordon Sample
1997 #24 Jeff Gordon

SPx Blue
1997 #24 Jeff Gordon

SPx Elite
1996 #E1 Jeff Gordon

SPx Gold
1996 #1 Jeff Gordon
1997 #24 Jeff Gordon

SPx Silver
1997 #24 Jeff Gordon

SPx SpeedView Autographs
1997 #SV1 Jeff Gordon

SPx Tag Team
1997 #TT1 T.Labonte/J.Gordon
1997 #TT4 J.Gordon/R.Craven

SPx Tag Team Autographs
1997 #TA1 T.Labonte/J.Gordon
1997 #TA4 J.Gordon/R.Craven

Stove Top
1993 #1 Jeff Gordon

Super Shots CHP Sonoma
2004 #1 Jeff Gordon

Super Shots Hendrick Motorsports
2001 #H8 Jeff Gordon
2001 #H9 Jeff Gordon
2001 #H10 Jeff Gordon
2001 #H11 Jeff Gordon
2001 #H14 T.Labonte/J.Gordon/Craven
2001 #H15 Jeff Gordon
2001 #H17 Jeff Gordon
2001 #H19 Jeff Gordon
2001 #HR22 Race Team Jumbo
2001 #NNO Jeff Gordon Tire

Super Shots Hendrick Motorsports Autographs
2001 #HSA1 Jeff Gordon/71

Super Shots Hendrick Motorsports Gold
2001 #HG8 Jeff Gordon
2001 #HG9 Jeff Gordon
2001 #HG10 Jeff Gordon
2001 #HG11 Jeff Gordon
2001 #HG14 T.Labonte/J.Gordon/Craven
2001 #HG15 Jeff Gordon
2001 #HG17 Jeff Gordon
2001 #HG19 Jeff Gordon

Super Shots Hendrick Motorsports Silver
2001 #HS8 Jeff Gordon
2001 #HS9 Jeff Gordon
2001 #HS10 Jeff Gordon
2001 #HS11 Jeff Gordon
2001 #HS14 T.Labonte/J.Gordon/Craven
2001 #HS15 Jeff Gordon
2001 #HS17 Jeff Gordon
2001 #HS19 Jeff Gordon

Super Shots Hendrick Motorsports Victory

Banners
2001 #HRB2 Jeff Gordon
2001 #HSB1 J.Gordon/T.Labonte/500
2001 #HSB2 Hendrick Race Team/500

Super Shots Race-Used Tire Jumbos
2001 #JGG1 Jeff Gordon Gold/2001
2001 #JGS1 Jeff Gordon's Car Silver/2001

Super Shots Sears Point CHP
2001 #SP4 Jeff Gordon's Car

Traks
1991 #1 Jeff Gordon RC
1992 #101 Jeff Gordon
1993 #24 Jeff Gordon's Car
1993 #39 Jeff Gordon CRC
1993 #151 Jeff Gordon
1993 #P1 Jeff Gordon Promo
1994 #10 Jeff Gordon's Car
1994 #24 Jeff Gordon
1994 #36 Jeff Gordon
1994 #86 Jeff Gordon
1994 #106 Jeff Gordon
1994 #171 Jeff Gordon
1994 #200 Jeff Gordon in Pits CL
1995 #4 Jeff Gordon
1995 #26 Jeff Gordon
1995 #52 Jeff Gordon
1995 #58 Jeff Gordon
1995 #68 Jeff Gordon
1995 #P26 J.Gordon Proto.First Run
2006 #9 Jeff Gordon
2006 #47 Jeff Gordon's Car
2007 #8 Jeff Gordon
2007 #58 Jeff Gordon's Car CTG
2007 #74 Jeff Gordon MG
2007 #87 Jeff Gordon's Car NFS
2007 #94 Jeff Gordon FT

Traks 5th Anniversary
1995 #4 Jeff Gordon
1995 #38 Jeff Gordon
1995 #49 Jeff Gordon's Car

Traks 5th Anniversary Clear Contenders
1995 #C3 Jeff Gordon

Traks 5th Anniversary Gold
1995 #4 Jeff Gordon
1995 #38 Jeff Gordon
1995 #49 Jeff Gordon's Car

Traks 5th Anniversary Jumbos
1995 #E1 Jeff Gordon

Traks 5th Anniversary Jumbos Gold
1995 #E1 Jeff Gordon

Traks 5th Anniversary Retrospective
1995 #R3 Jeff Gordon

Traks Auto Value
1994 #25 Jeff Gordon
1995 #1 Jeff Gordon

Traks Autographs
1992 #A7 Jeff Gordon
1994 #A4 Jeff Gordon
2006 #10 Jeff Gordon NC SP

TRAKS Autographs 25
2006 #9 Jeff Gordon NC

Traks Baby Ruth Jeff Gordon
1992 #1 Jeff Gordon
1992 #2 Jeff Gordon
1992 #3 Jeff Gordon's Car
1992 #4 Jeff Gordon's Crew

Traks Cartoons
1994 #C5 Jeff Gordon

Traks Challengers
1995 #C1 Jeff Gordon WIN

Traks Challengers First Run
1995 #C1 Jeff Gordon

Traks Driver's Seat
2007 #DS2B Jeff Gordon VAR
2007 #DS2 Jeff Gordon

Traks Driver's Seat National
2007 #DS2 Jeff Gordon

Traks First Run
1993 #24 Jeff Gordon's Car
1993 #39 Jeff Gordon
1993 #151 Jeff Gordon
1994 #10 Jeff Gordon's Car
1994 #24 Jeff Gordon
1994 #36 Jeff Gordon
1994 #86 Jeff Gordon
1994 #106 Jeff Gordon
1994 #171 Jeff Gordon
1994 #200 Jeff Gordon in Pits CL
1995 #4 Jeff Gordon
1995 #26 Jeff Gordon
1995 #52 Jeff Gordon
1995 #58 Jeff Gordon
1995 #68 Jeff Gordon

Traks Gold
2007 #G8 Jeff Gordon
2007 #G58 Jeff Gordon's Car CTG
2007 #G74 Jeff Gordon MG
2007 #G87 Jeff Gordon's Car NFS
2007 #G94 Jeff Gordon FT

Traks Goody's
1992 #9 Jeff Gordon

Traks Holofoil
2007 #H8 Jeff Gordon
2007 #H58 Jeff Gordon's Car CTG
2007 #H74 Jeff Gordon MG
2007 #H87 Jeff Gordon's Car NFS
2007 #H94 Jeff Gordon FT

Traks Hot Pursuit
2007 #HP1 Jeff Gordon

Traks Preferred Collector
1994 #33 Jeff Gordon

Traks Previews
2007 #EB8 Jeff Gordon

Traks Racing Machines
1992 #40 J.Gordon/D.Allison Cars
1995 #RM7 Jeff Gordon's Car

Traks Racing Machines Bonus
1992 #20B Jeff Gordon Baby Boomer

Traks Racing Machines First Run
1995 #RM7 Jeff Gordon's Car

Traks Red
2007 #R8 Jeff Gordon
2007 #R58 Jeff Gordon's Car CTG
2007 #R74 Jeff Gordon MG
2007 #R87 Jeff Gordon's Car NFS
2007 #R94 Jeff Gordon FT

Traks Review and Preview

1996 #15 Jeff Gordon
Traks Review and Preview First Run
1996 #15 Jeff Gordon
Traks Review and Preview Liquid Gold
1996 #LG18 Jeff Gordon
Traks Review and Preview Magnets
1996 #15 Jeff Gordon
Traks Series Stars
1995 #SS8 Jeff Gordon
Traks Series Stars First Run
1995 #SS8 Jeff Gordon
TRAKS Stickers
2006 #24 Jeff Gordon
Traks Target Exclusives
2007 #JG-A Jeff Gordon
Traks Track Time
2007 #TT6 Jeff Gordon
Traks Trivia
1993 #2 Jeff Gordon
1993 #24 Jeff Gordon
1993 #36 Jeff Gordon
1993 #38 Jeff Gordon's Car
1993 #45 Jeff Gordon
Traks Valvoline
1995 #100 Jeff Gordon's Car
Traks Wal-Mart Exclusives
2007 #JG-B Jeff Gordon
Traks Winners
1994 #W8 Jeff Gordon
1994 #W21 Jeff Gordon
1994 #W22 Jeff Gordon
UDA Jeff Gordon Commemorative Cards
1997 #NNO 19?? Career/???
1997 #NNO 1997 First Championship/???
1997 #NNO 1995 Coming Home a Winner/2400
1997 #NNO 1995 Mid-Season Points Leader/2373
1997 #NNO 1996 Points Champ/2500
Ultra
1996 #1 Jeff Gordon
1996 #2 Jeff Gordon
1996 #3 Jeff Gordon's Car
1996 #152 Jeff Gordon A
1996 #157 Jeff Gordon's Helmet
1996 #168 Jeff Gordon's Car RW
1996 #170 J.Gordon/B.Lab/T.Lab.RW
1996 #172 J.Gordon/Brooke RW
1996 #181 Jeff Gordon's Car/Race Act.
1996 #182 Jeff Gordon's Car/Race Act.
1996 #191 Jeff Gordon in Pits RW
1996 #200 D.Earn/Gordon/R.Wall.Race Act.
1996 #P1 Jeff Gordon Promo Sheet
1997 #12 Jeff Gordon
1997 #41 Jeff Gordon's Car
Ultra AKA
1997 #A2 Jeff Gordon
Ultra Autographs
1996 #11 Jeff Gordon
Ultra Boxed Set
1996 #1 Jeff Gordon
Ultra Champions Club
1996 #5 Jeff Gordon
Ultra Flair Preview
1996 #1 Jeff Gordon
Ultra Inside Out
1997 #DC2 Jeff Gordon
Ultra Season Crowns
1996 #2 Jeff Gordon
1996 #4 Jeff Gordon
1996 #7 Jeff Gordon
1996 #10 Jeff Gordon
1996 #11 Jeff Gordon
1996 #12 D.Earnhardt/J.Gordon Cars
Ultra Shoney's
1997 #4 Jeff Gordon
Ultra Thunder and Lightning
1996 #3 Jeff Gordon's Car
1996 #4 Jeff Gordon's Car
Ultra Update
1996 #12 Jeff Gordon
1996 #46 Jeff Gordon HS
1996 #58 Jeff Gordon's Car
1997 #1 Jeff Gordon
1997 #86 Jeff Gordon's Car
Ultra Update Autographs
1996 #4 Jeff Gordon
1997 #1 Jeff Gordon
Ultra Update Driver View
1997 #D1 Jeff Gordon
Ultra Update Elite Seats
1997 #E1 Jeff Gordon
Ultra Update Proven Power
1996 #4 Jeff Gordon
Ultra Update Winner
1996 #1 Jeff Gordon
1996 #4 Jeff Gordon
1996 #10 Jeff Gordon
Ultra Winn Dixie
1997 #WD4 Jeff Gordon
Upper Deck
1995 #2 Jeff Gordon
1995 #45 Jeff Gordon w/Car
1995 #70 Jeff Gordon's Car
1995 #138 Jeff Gordon's Car
1995 #163 Jeff Gordon DYK
1995 #202 Jeff Gordon
1995 #246 Jeff Gordon SD
1995 #281 Jeff Gordon's Car
1995 #UD2 Jeff Gordon Salute
1996 #22 Jeff Gordon
1996 #72 Jeff Gordon SB
1996 #73 Jeff Gordon SB
1996 #98 Jeff Gordon PP
1996 #102 Jeff Gordon PP
1996 #138 Jeff Gordon HB
1996 #150 Jeff Gordon HB
1996 #C1 Jeff Gordon Tribute
1996 #C2 Jeff Gordon Tribute
1996 #JG1 Jeff Gordon Promo
Upper Deck All-Pro
1996 #AP1 Jeff Gordon
Upper Deck Autographs
1995 #202 Jeff Gordon
Upper Deck Diamond Vision
1998 #1 Jeff Gordon
1998 #RT1 Jeff Gordon RT
Upper Deck Diamond Vision Signature Moves
1998 #RT1 Jeff Gordon
1998 #1 Jeff Gordon
Upper Deck Diamond Vision Vision of a Champion
1998 #VC3 Jeff Gordon
Upper Deck Gold Signature/Electric Gold
1995 #2 Jeff Gordon
1995 #45 Jeff Gordon w/Car
1995 #70 Jeff Gordon's Car
1995 #138 Jeff Gordon's Car
1995 #163 Jeff Gordon DYK
1995 #202 Jeff Gordon
1995 #246 Jeff Gordon SD
1995 #281 Jeff Gordon's Car
Upper Deck Illustrations
1995 #I9 Jeff Gordon
Upper Deck Jeff Gordon Phone Cards
1995 #1 Jeff Gordon
1995 #2 Jeff Gordon
1995 #3 Jeff Gordon
1995 #4 Jeff Gordon
1995 #5 Jeff Gordon
Upper Deck Jeff Gordon Profiles
1996 #1 Jeff Gordon
1996 #2 Jeff Gordon
1996 #3 Jeff Gordon
1996 #4 Jeff Gordon
1996 #5 Jeff Gordon
1996 #6 Jeff Gordon
1996 #7 Jeff Gordon
1996 #8 Jeff Gordon
1996 #9 Jeff Gordon
1996 #10 Jeff Gordon
1996 #11 Jeff Gordon
1996 #12 Jeff Gordon
1996 #13 Jeff Gordon
1996 #14 Jeff Gordon
1996 #15 Jeff Gordon
1996 #16 Jeff Gordon
1996 #17 Jeff Gordon
1996 #18 Jeff Gordon
1996 #19 Jeff Gordon
1996 #20 Jeff Gordon
Upper Deck Jumbos
1995 #OS3 Jeff Gordon
Upper Deck MVP
2000 #24 Jeff Gordon
2000 #65 Jeff Gordon's Car
2000 #102 Jeff Gordon CL
Upper Deck MVP Cup Quest 2000
2000 #CQ9 Jeff Gordon
Upper Deck MVP Gold Script
2000 #24 Jeff Gordon
2000 #65 Jeff Gordon
2000 #102 Jeff Gordon CL
Upper Deck MVP Legends in the Making
2000 #LM1 Jeff Gordon
Upper Deck MVP NASCAR Gallery
2000 #NG9 Jeff Gordon
Upper Deck MVP NASCAR Stars
2000 #NS2 Jeff Gordon
Upper Deck MVP ProSign
1999 #JGH Jeff Gordon Gold
1999 #JGR Jeff Gordon Silver
2000 #PSJG Jeff Gordon
Upper Deck MVP Silver Script
2000 #24 Jeff Gordon
2000 #65 Jeff Gordon
2000 #102 Jeff Gordon CL
Upper Deck MVP Super Script
2000 #24 Jeff Gordon/24
2000 #65 Jeff Gordon's Car/24
2000 #102 Jeff Gordon CL/24
Upper Deck Pop Weaver
1998 #PW1 Jeff Gordon
Upper Deck Predictor Poles
1996 #RP1 Jeff Gordon WIN
Upper Deck Predictor Poles Prizes
1996 #RP1 Jeff Gordon
Upper Deck Predictor Race Winners
1995 #P4 Jeff Gordon WIN
Upper Deck Predictor Race Winners Coca-Cola 600
1995 #P4 Jeff Gordon
Upper Deck Predictor Race Winners Daytona 500
1995 #P4 Jeff Gordon
Upper Deck Predictor Race Winners Prizes
1995 #P4 Jeff Gordon
Upper Deck Predictor Series Points
1995 #PP6 Jeff Gordon WIN
Upper Deck Predictor Series Points Prizes
1995 #PP6 Jeff Gordon WIN
Upper Deck Predictor Wins
1996 #HP1 Jeff Gordon WIN
Upper Deck Predictor Wins Prizes
1996 #HP1 Jeff Gordon
Upper Deck Racing
2000 #6 Jeff Gordon
Upper Deck Racing Brickyard's Best
2000 #B86 Jeff Gordon
Upper Deck Racing High Groove
2000 #HG6 Jeff Gordon
Upper Deck Racing Record Pace
2000 #RP5 Jeff Gordon
Upper Deck Racing Road Signs
2000 #RSJG Jeff Gordon
Upper Deck Racing Speeding Ticket
2000 #ST1 Jeff Gordon
Upper Deck Racing Thunder Road
2000 #TR5 Jeff Gordon
Upper Deck Racing Trophy Dash
2000 #TD7 Jeff Gordon
Upper Deck Racing Winning Formula
2000 #WF6 Jeff Gordon
Upper Deck Road To The Cup
1996 #RC1 Jeff Gordon
1996 #RC51 Jeff Gordon's Car
1996 #RC121 Jeff Gordon
1996 #RC124 Jeff Gordon
1996 #RC148 Jeff Gordon
1996 #JG1 Jeff Gordon 2-D
1997 #2 Jeff Gordon
1997 #45 Jeff Gordon's Car
1997 #87 Jeff Gordon
1997 #107 Jeff Gordon's Trans.
1998 #24 Jeff Gordon
1998 #66 Jeff Gordon
1998 #88 Jeff Gordon's Car
1999 #24 Jeff Gordon
1999 #43 Jeff Gordon's Car
1999 #61 Jeff Gordon FF
1999 #77 Jeff Gordon HH
Upper Deck Road To The Cup 50th Anniversary
1998 #AN43 Jeff Gordon
1998 #AN47 Jeff Gordon
Upper Deck Road To The Cup 50th Anniversary Autographs
1998 #AN47 Jeff Gordon
Upper Deck Road to the Cup A Day in the Life
1999 #JG1 Jeff Gordon
1999 #JG2 Jeff Gordon
1999 #JG3 Jeff Gordon
1999 #JG4 Jeff Gordon
1999 #JG5 Jeff Gordon
1999 #JG6 Jeff Gordon
1999 #JG7 Jeff Gordon
1999 #JG8 Jeff Gordon
1999 #JG9 Jeff Gordon
1999 #JG10 Jeff Gordon
Upper Deck Road To The Cup Autographs
1996 #H1 Jeff Gordon
Upper Deck Road To The Cup Cover Story
1998 #CS8 Jeff Gordon
1998 #CS13 Jeff Gordon
1998 #CS15 Gordon/Labonte/Craven
1998 #CS16 J.Gordon/D.Waltrip
Upper Deck Road To The Cup Cup Quest
1997 #CQ2 Jeff Gordon
Upper Deck Road To The Cup Cup Quest Checkered
1997 #CQ2 Jeff Gordon
Upper Deck Road To The Cup Cup Quest Turn 1
1998 #CQ1 Jeff Gordon's Car
Upper Deck Road To The Cup Cup Quest Turn 2
1998 #CQ1 Jeff Gordon's Car
Upper Deck Road To The Cup Cup Quest Turn 3
1998 #CQ1 Jeff Gordon's Car
Upper Deck Road To The Cup Cup Quest Turn 4
1998 #CQ1 Jeff Gordon's Car
Upper Deck Road To The Cup Cup Quest Victory Lane
1998 #CQ1 Jeff Gordon's Car
Upper Deck Road To The Cup Cup Quest White
1997 #CQ2 Jeff Gordon
Upper Deck Road To The Cup Diary of a Champion
1996 #DC1 Jeff Gordon
1996 #DC2 Jeff Gordon
1996 #DC3 Jeff Gordon
1996 #DC4 Jeff Gordon
1996 #DC5 Jeff Gordon
1996 #DC6 Jeff Gordon
1996 #DC7 Jeff Gordon
1996 #DC8 Jeff Gordon
1996 #DC9 Jeff Gordon
1996 #DC10 Jeff Gordon
Upper Deck Road To The Cup Game Face
1996 #GF1 Jeff Gordon
Upper Deck Road To The Cup Jumbos
1996 #WC1 Jeff Gordon
Upper Deck Road To The Cup Leaders of the Pack
1996 #LP1 Jeff Gordon
Upper Deck Road To The Cup Million Dollar Memoirs
1997 #MM5 Jeff Gordon
1997 #MM6 Jeff Gordon
1997 #MM7 Jeff Gordon
1997 #MM8 Jeff Gordon
Upper Deck Road To The Cup Million Dollar Memoirs Autographs
1997 #MM5 Jeff Gordon
1997 #MM6 Jeff Gordon
1997 #MM7 Jeff Gordon
1997 #MM8 Jeff Gordon
Upper Deck Road to the Cup NASCAR Chronicles
1999 #NC2 Jeff Gordon
Upper Deck Road To The Cup Piece of the Action
1997 #1 Jeff Gordon Seat Cover
1997 #2 Jeff Gordon Should.Harness
1997 #3 Jeff Gordon Window Net
Upper Deck Road To The Cup Predictor Plus
1997 #2 Jeff Gordon
1997 #11 Jeff Gordon WIN
1997 #28 Jeff Gordon
Upper Deck Road To The Cup Predictor Plus Cel Die Cuts
1997 #2 Jeff Gordon
1997 #11 Jeff Gordon
1997 #28 Jeff Gordon
Upper Deck Road To The Cup Predictor Plus Cels
1997 #2 Jeff Gordon
1997 #11 Jeff Gordon
1997 #28 Jeff Gordon
Upper Deck Road To The Cup Predictor Points
1996 #PP1 Jeff Gordon
Upper Deck Road To The Cup Predictor Points Prizes
1996 #PR1 Jeff Gordon
Upper Deck Road To The Cup Predictor Top 3
1996 #T1 J.Gordon/R.Wallace/T.Labonte
1996 #T3 Gordon/Irvan/Long.WIN
1996 #T6 Marlin/Gordon/LS WIN
1996 #T7 J.Gordon/M.Martin/J.Benson
Upper Deck Road To The Cup Predictor Top 3 Prizes
1996 #R1 Jeff Gordon
Upper Deck Road To The Cup Premiere Position
1997 #PP2 Jeff Gordon
1997 #PP11 Jeff Gordon
1997 #PP12 Jeff Gordon
1997 #PP20 Jeff Gordon
1997 #PP21 Jeff Gordon
1997 #PP28 Jeff Gordon
1997 #PP32 Jeff Gordon
1997 #PP42 Jeff Gordon
Upper Deck Road to the Cup Road to the Cup Bronze Level 1
1999 #RTTC1 Jeff Gordon
Upper Deck Road to the Cup Road to the Cup Gold Level 3
1999 #RTTC1 Jeff Gordon
Upper Deck Road to the Cup Road to the Cup Silver Level 2
1999 #RTTC1 Jeff Gordon
Upper Deck Road to the Cup Signature Collection
1999 #JG Jeff Gordon
Upper Deck Road to the Cup Signature Collection Checkered Flag
1999 #JG Jeff Gordon
Upper Deck Road to the Cup Tires of Daytona
1999 #T1 Jeff Gordon
Upper Deck Road to the Cup Tires of Daytona Autographed
1999 #TS1 Jeff Gordon/24
Upper Deck Road to the Cup Upper Deck Profiles
1999 #P15 Jeff Gordon
Upper Deck Silver Signature/Electric Silver
1995 #2 Jeff Gordon
1995 #45 Jeff Gordon w/Car
1995 #70 Jeff Gordon's Car
1995 #138 Jeff Gordon's Car
1995 #163 Jeff Gordon DYK
1995 #202 Jeff Gordon
1995 #246 Jeff Gordon SD
1995 #281 Jeff Gordon's Car
Upper Deck Victory Circle
1997 #24 Jeff Gordon
1997 #74 Jeff Gordon's Car
1997 #111 Jeff Gordon
1998 #24 Jeff Gordon
1998 #69 Jeff Gordon's Car
1998 #92 J.Gordon/T.Labonte/Craven
1998 #93 Jeff Gordon
1998 #100 Jeff Gordon
1998 #105 Jeff Gordon
1998 #119 Jeff Gordon
1998 #120 Jeff Gordon
1999 #3 Jeff Gordon
1999 #41 Jeff Gordon's Car
1999 #76 Jeff Gordon
1999 #80 Jeff Gordon
1999 #84 Jeff Gordon
2000 #16 Jeff Gordon
2000 #59 Jeff Gordon's Car
2000 #65 Jeff Gordon's Car
2000 #66 Jeff Gordon's Car
2000 #73 Jeff Gordon's Car
Upper Deck Victory Circle 32 Days of Speed
1998 #D2 Jeff Gordon
1998 #D11 Jeff Gordon
1998 #D32 Jeff Gordon
Upper Deck Victory Circle 32 Days of Speed Gold
1998 #D2 Jeff Gordon
1998 #D11 Jeff Gordon
1998 #D32 Jeff Gordon
Upper Deck Victory Circle Autographs
1998 #AG1 Jeff Gordon
Upper Deck Victory Circle Championship Reflections
1997 #CR2 Jeff Gordon
Upper Deck Victory Circle Driver's Seat
1997 #DS2 Jeff Gordon
Upper Deck Victory Circle Exclusives Level 1 Silver
2000 #16 Jeff Gordon
2000 #59 Jeff Gordon's Car
2000 #65 Jeff Gordon's Car
2000 #66 Jeff Gordon's Car
2000 #73 Jeff Gordon's Car
Upper Deck Victory Circle Exclusives Level 2 Gold
2000 #16 Jeff Gordon/24
2000 #59 Jeff Gordon's Car/24
2000 #65 Jeff Gordon's Car/24
2000 #66 Jeff Gordon's Car/24
2000 #73 Jeff Gordon's Car/24
Upper Deck Victory Circle Generation Excitement
1997 #GE1 Jeff Gordon
Upper Deck Victory Circle Income Statement
1999 #IS1 Jeff Gordon
2000 #IS1 Jeff Gordon
Upper Deck Victory Circle Income Statement LTD
2000 #IS1 Jeff Gordon
Upper Deck Victory Circle Piece of the Action
1997 #FS1 Jeff Gordon Firesuit
1997 #FS2 Jeff Gordon Glove
1997 #FS3 Jeff Gordon Shoe
Upper Deck Victory Circle Point Leaders
1998 #PL1 Jeff Gordon
Upper Deck Victory Circle PowerDeck
2000 #PD5 Jeff Gordon
Upper Deck Victory Circle Predictor
1997 #PE1 Jeff Gordon WIN
Upper Deck Victory Circle Predictor Winner Cels
1997 #PH1 Jeff Gordon
Upper Deck Victory Circle Signature Collection
1999 #JG Jeff Gordon
2000 #JG Jeff Gordon
Upper Deck Victory Circle Signature Collection Gold
2000 #3 Jeff Gordon/24
Upper Deck Victory Circle Sparks of Brilliance
1998 #SB1 Jeff Gordon
Upper Deck Victory Circle Speed Zone
1999 #SZ3 Jeff Gordon
Upper Deck Victory Circle Track Masters
1999 #TM1 Jeff Gordon
Upper Deck Victory Circle UD Exclusives
1999 #3 Jeff Gordon
1999 #41 Jeff Gordon
1999 #76 Jeff Gordon
1999 #80 Jeff Gordon
1999 #84 Jeff Gordon
Upper Deck Victory Circle Victory Circle
1999 #V8 Jeff Gordon
Upper Deck Victory Circle Victory Lap
1997 #VL2 Jeff Gordon
Upper Deck Victory Circle Winning Material Tire
2000 #TJG Jeff Gordon
Upper Deck Virtual Velocity
1996 #VV1 Jeff Gordon
Upper Deck Virtual Velocity Gold
1996 #VV1 Jeff Gordon
VIP
1994 #12 Jeff Gordon
1994 #38 Jeff Gordon w/Car
1994 #74 Jeff Gordon ART
1994 #P1 Jeff Gordon's Car Prototype
1995 #11 Jeff Gordon
1995 #31 Jeff Gordon
1995 #61 Jeff Gordon's Truck
1996 #10 Jeff Gordon
1996 #30 Jeff Gordon
1996 #37 Jeff Gordon's Car
1997 #8 Jeff Gordon
1998 #8 Jeff Gordon
1998 #40 Jeff Gordon's Car
1999 #8 Jeff Gordon
1999 #31 Jeff Gordon BGN
1999 #42 Jeff Gordon's Car
2000 #12 Jeff Gordon
2000 #26 Jeff Gordon V
2000 #29 Jeff Gordon NB
2000 #32 Jeff Gordon DF
2000 #34 Jeff Gordon DF
2000 #45 Jeff Gordon 50 W
2000 #49 Jeff Gordon DT
2001 #12 Jeff Gordon
2001 #21 Jeff Gordon SM
2001 #33 Jeff Gordon RT
2001 #43 Jeff Gordon AS
2001 #50 Jeff Gordon CL
2002 #11 Jeff Gordon
2002 #28 Jeff Gordon AS
2002 #48 Jeff Gordon PP
2002 #50 J.Gordon/J.Johnson CL
2003 #5 Jeff Gordon
2003 #27 Jeff Gordon SG
2003 #30 Jeff Gordon AS '01
2003 #34 Jeff Gordon AS '97
2003 #36 Jeff Gordon AS '95
2004 #5 Jeff Gordon
2004 #38 Jeff Gordon's Car R
2004 #51 Jeff Gordon SG
2004 #52 Jeff Gordon SG
2004 #56 Jeff Gordon HR
2004 #74 Jeff Gordon BTN
2004 #88 Jeff Gordon ATW
2005 #7 Jeff Gordon
2005 #43 Jeff Gordon SG
2005 #48 Jeff Gordon SG
2005 #51 Jeff Gordon SG
2005 #63 Jeff Gordon HR
2005 #74 Jeff Gordon BN
2005 #85 Jeff Gordon ATML
2006 #7 Jeff Gordon
2006 #28 Jeff Gordon's Car R
2006 #60 Jeff Gordon BTN
2006 #67 Jeff Gordon RF
2006 #88 Jeff Gordon IF
2006 #C Jeff Gordon CL
2007 #9 Jeff Gordon
2007 #43 Jeff Gordon's Car R
2007 #53 Jeff Gordon's Car SV
2007 #76 Jeff Gordon Phoenix AP
2007 #77 Jeff Gordon Talladega AP
2007 #79 Jeff Gordon Darlington AP
2007 #82 Jeff Gordon Pocono AP
VIP Autographs
1995 #11 Jeff Gordon
1996 #8 Jeff Gordon
VIP Cool Blue
1995 #11 Jeff Gordon
1995 #31 Jeff Gordon
1995 #61 Jeff Gordon's Truck
VIP Double Take
1999 #DT1 Jeff Gordon
VIP Driver's Choice
2001 #DC1 Jeff Gordon
2002 #DC1 Jeff Gordon
2003 #DC3 Jeff Gordon
2004 #DC3 Jeff Gordon
2005 #DC3 Jeff Gordon
VIP Driver's Choice Die Cuts
2003 #DC3 Jeff Gordon
2004 #DC3 Jeff Gordon
2005 #DC3 Jeff Gordon
VIP Driver's Choice National
2003 #DC3 Jeff Gordon
VIP Driver's Choice Precious Metal
2001 #DC1 Jeff Gordon
VIP Driver's Choice Transparent
2001 #DC1 Jeff Gordon
2002 #DC1 Jeff Gordon
VIP Driver's Choice Transparent LTD
2002 #DC1 Jeff Gordon
VIP Driving Force
1998 #DF7 Jeff Gordon's Car
VIP Driving Force Die Cuts
1998 #DF7 Jeff Gordon's Car
VIP Emerald Proofs
1995 #11 Jeff Gordon
1995 #31 Jeff Gordon
1995 #61 Jeff Gordon's Truck
1996 #10 Jeff Gordon
1996 #30 Jeff Gordon
1996 #37 Jeff Gordon's Car
VIP Explosives
1997 #8 Jeff Gordon
1998 #8 Jeff Gordon
1998 #40 Jeff Gordon's Car
1999 #X8 Jeff Gordon
1999 #X31 Jeff Gordon
1999 #X42 Jeff Gordon's Car
2000 #X12 Jeff Gordon
2000 #X26 Jeff Gordon V
2000 #X29 Jeff Gordon NB
2000 #X32 Jeff Gordon DF
2000 #X34 Jeff Gordon DF
2000 #X45 Jeff Gordon 50 W
2000 #X49 Jeff Gordon DT
2001 #12 Jeff Gordon
2001 #21 Jeff Gordon SM
2001 #33 Jeff Gordon RT
2001 #43 Jeff Gordon AS
2001 #50 Jeff Gordon CL
2002 #X11 Jeff Gordon
2002 #X28 Jeff Gordon AS
2002 #X48 Jeff Gordon PP
2002 #X50 J.Gordon/J.Johnson CL
2003 #X5 Jeff Gordon
2003 #X27 Jeff Gordon SG
2003 #X30 Jeff Gordon AS '01
2003 #X34 Jeff Gordon AS '97
2003 #X36 Jeff Gordon AS '95
VIP Explosives Lasers
1999 #8 Jeff Gordon
1999 #31 Jeff Gordon
1999 #42 Jeff Gordon's Car
2000 #LX12 Jeff Gordon
2000 #LX26 Jeff Gordon V
2000 #LX29 Jeff Gordon NB
2000 #LX32 Jeff Gordon DF
2000 #LX34 Jeff Gordon DF
2000 #LX45 Jeff Gordon 50 W
2000 #LX49 Jeff Gordon DT
2001 #LX12 Jeff Gordon
2001 #LX21 Jeff Gordon SM
2001 #LX33 Jeff Gordon RT
2001 #LX43 Jeff Gordon AS
2001 #LX50 Jeff Gordon CL
2002 #LX11 Jeff Gordon
2002 #LX28 Jeff Gordon AS
2002 #LX48 Jeff Gordon PP
2002 #LX50 J.Gordon/J.Johnson CL
VIP Fan's Choice
1995 #FC3 Jeff Gordon
VIP Fan's Choice Gold
1995 #FC3 Jeff Gordon
VIP Gear Gallery
2007 #GG4 Jeff Gordon
VIP Gear Gallery Transparent
2007 #GG4 Jeff Gordon
VIP Get A Grip Drivers
2007 #GGD13 Jeff Gordon
VIP Get A Grip Teams
2007 #GGT13 Jeff Gordon
VIP Gold Signature
1994 #EC3 Jeff Gordon
VIP Head Gear
1996 #HG3 Jeff Gordon
1997 #HG3 Jeff Gordon
1998 #HG4 Jeff Gordon
1999 #HG1 Jeff Gordon
2000 #HG1 Jeff Gordon
2001 #HG1 Jeff Gordon
2002 #HG1 Jeff Gordon
2003 #HG3 Jeff Gordon
2004 #HG2 Jeff Gordon
2005 #2 Jeff Gordon
2006 #HG7 Jeff Gordon
VIP Head Gear Die Cuts
1996 #HG3 Jeff Gordon
1997 #HG3 Jeff Gordon
1998 #HG4 Jeff Gordon
2001 #HG1 Jeff Gordon
2002 #HG1 Jeff Gordon
2003 #HG3 Jeff Gordon
VIP Head Gear Explosives
2000 #HG1 Jeff Gordon
VIP Head Gear Explosives Laser Die Cuts
2000 #HG1 Jeff Gordon
VIP Head Gear National
2003 #HG3 Jeff Gordon
VIP Head Gear Plastic
1999 #HG1 Jeff Gordon
VIP Head Gear Transparent
2004 #HG2 Jeff Gordon
2005 #2 Jeff Gordon
2006 #HG7 Jeff Gordon
VIP Helmets
1995 #H4 Jeff Gordon
VIP Helmets Gold
1995 #H4 Jeff Gordon
VIP Knights of Thunder
1997 #KT2 Jeff Gordon
VIP Knights of Thunder Gold
1997 #KT2 Jeff Gordon
VIP Lap Leader
2006 #LL7 Jeff Gordon
VIP Lap Leader Transparent
2006 #LL7 Jeff Gordon
VIP Lap Leaders
1998 #LL3 Jeff Gordon's Car
1999 #LL1 Jeff Gordon
2000 #LL1 Jeff Gordon
2003 #LL1 Jeff Gordon
2004 #LL7 Jeff Gordon
2005 #7 Jeff Gordon
VIP Lap Leaders Acetate
1998 #LL3 Jeff Gordon's Car
VIP Lap Leaders Explosives
2000 #LL1 Jeff Gordon
VIP Lap Leaders Explosives Lasers
2000 #LL1 Jeff Gordon
VIP Lap Leaders National
2003 #LL1 Jeff Gordon
VIP Lap Leaders Transparent
2003 #LL1 Jeff Gordon
2004 #LL7 Jeff Gordon
2005 #7 Jeff Gordon
VIP Lap Leaders Transparent LTD
2003 #LL1 Jeff Gordon
VIP Laser Explosive
2003 #LX5 Jeff Gordon
2003 #LX27 Jeff Gordon SG
2003 #LX30 Jeff Gordon AS '01
2003 #LX34 Jeff Gordon AS '97
2003 #LX36 Jeff Gordon AS '95
VIP Making the Show
2000 #MS7 Jeff Gordon
2001 #12 Jeff Gordon
2002 #MS13 Jeff Gordon
2003 #MS14 Jeff Gordon
2004 #MS16 Jeff Gordon
2005 #16 Jeff Gordon
2006 #MS2 Jeff Gordon
VIP Mile Masters
2001 #MM1 Jeff Gordon
2002 #MM1 Jeff Gordon
2003 #MM3 Jeff Gordon

VIP Mile Masters National
2003 #MM3 Jeff Gordon
VIP Mile Masters Precious Metal
2001 #MM1 Jeff Gordon
VIP Mile Masters Transparent
2001 #MM1 Jeff Gordon
2002 #MM1 Jeff Gordon
2003 #MM3 Jeff Gordon
VIP Mile Masters Transparent LTD
2002 #MM1 Jeff Gordon
2003 #MM3 Jeff Gordon
VIP NASCAR Country
1998 #NC3 Jeff Gordon
VIP NASCAR Country Die Cuts
1998 #NC3 Jeff Gordon
VIP Oil Slicks
1997 #8 Jeff Gordon
VIP Out of the Box
1999 #OB1 Jeff Gordon
VIP Pedal To The Metal
2007 #PM8 Jeff Gordon
VIP Precious Metal
1997 #SM1 Jeff Gordon
VIP Previews
2003 #5 Jeff Gordon
2003 #27 Jeff Gordon SG
2003 #30 Jeff Gordon AS
2003 #34 Jeff Gordon AS
2003 #36 Jeff Gordon AS
2004 #EB38 Jeff Gordon's Car R
2004 #EB51 Jeff Gordon SG
2004 #EB52 Jeff Gordon SG
2004 #EB5 Jeff Gordon
2005 #EB7 Jeff Gordon
2007 #EB9 Jeff Gordon
VIP Race Used Sheet Metal Cars
2002 #SC1 Jeff Gordon's Car
VIP Race Used Sheet Metal Drivers
2002 #SD1 Jeff Gordon
VIP Rear View Mirror
1999 #RM1 Jeff Gordon
2002 #RM5 Jeff Gordon
VIP Rear View Mirror Die Cuts
2002 #RM5 Jeff Gordon
VIP Red Hot
1995 #11 Jeff Gordon
1995 #31 Jeff Gordon
1995 #61 Jeff Gordon's Truck
VIP Reflections
1995 #R2 Jeff Gordon
VIP Reflections Gold
1995 #R2 Jeff Gordon
VIP Ring of Honor
1997 #RH8 Jeff Gordon's Car
VIP Ring of Honor Die Cuts
1997 #RH8 Jeff Gordon's Car
VIP Samples
2002 #11 Jeff Gordon
2002 #28 Jeff Gordon AS
2002 #48 Jeff Gordon PP
2002 #50 J.Gordon/J.Johnson CL
2003 #5 Jeff Gordon
2003 #27 Jeff Gordon SG
2003 #30 Jeff Gordon AS
2003 #34 Jeff Gordon AS
2003 #36 Jeff Gordon AS
2004 #5 Jeff Gordon
2004 #52 Jeff Gordon SG
2004 #56 Jeff Gordon HR
2004 #38 Jeff Gordon's Car R
2004 #88 Jeff Gordon ATW
2004 #74 Jeff Gordon BTN
2004 #51 Jeff Gordon SG
2005 #7 Jeff Gordon
2005 #43 Jeff Gordon SG
2005 #48 Jeff Gordon SG
2005 #51 Jeff Gordon SG
2005 #63 Jeff Gordon HR
2005 #74 Jeff Gordon BN
2005 #85 Jeff Gordon ATML
VIP Sheet Metal
1999 #SM3 Jeff Gordon
2000 #SM9 Jeff Gordon
VIP Sheet Metal Cars
2001 #SC9 Jeff Gordon's Car
VIP Sheet Metal Drivers
2001 #SD9 Jeff Gordon
VIP Solos
1998 #8 Jeff Gordon
1998 #40 Jeff Gordon's Car
VIP Sunday Best
2007 #SB7 Jeff Gordon
VIP Tin
2003 #CT5 Jeff Gordon
2003 #CT27 Jeff Gordon SG
2003 #CT30 Jeff Gordon AS '01
2003 #CT34 Jeff Gordon AS '97
2003 #CT36 Jeff Gordon AS '95
VIP Torquers
1996 #10 Jeff Gordon
1996 #30 Jeff Gordon
1996 #37 Jeff Gordon's Car
VIP Tradin' Paint Autographs
2004 #TP-JG Jeff Gordon/24
2006 #TP-JG Jeff Gordon/24
VIP Tradin' Paint Bronze
2004 #TPT2 Jeff Gordon
VIP Tradin' Paint Cars
2003 #TPT1 Jeff Gordon's Car
2005 #TPT2 Jeff Gordon
VIP Tradin' Paint Cars Bronze
2006 #TPT6 Jeff Gordon
VIP Tradin' Paint Drivers
2003 #TPD1 Jeff Gordon
2005 #TPD2 Jeff Gordon
VIP Tradin' Paint Drivers Gold
2006 #TPD6 Jeff Gordon
VIP Tradin' Paint Drivers Silver
2006 #TPD6 Jeff Gordon
VIP Tradin' Paint Gold
2004 #TPD2 Jeff Gordon
VIP Tradin' Paint Silver
2004 #TPD2 Jeff Gordon
VIP Triple Gear Sheet Metal
1998 #TGS6 Jeff Gordon
VIP Trophy Club
2007 #TC9 Jeff Gordon
VIP Trophy Club Transparent
2007 #TC9 Jeff Gordon
VIP Under the Lights
2000 #UL1 Jeff Gordon
VIP Under the Lights Explosives
2000 #UL1 Jeff Gordon
VIP Under the Lights Explosives Lasers
2000 #UL1 Jeff Gordon
VIP Vintage Performance
1999 #4 Jeff Gordon
VIP War Paint
1996 #WP12 Jeff Gordon's Car
VIP War Paint Gold
1996 #WP12 Jeff Gordon's Car
Viper
1996 #2 Jeff Gordon
1996 #40 Jeff Gordon
1996 #42 Jeff Gordon
1997 #1 Jeff Gordon
1997 #51 Jeff Gordon
1997 #74 Jeff Gordon's Car
1997 #P2 Jeff Gordon Promo
Viper Anaconda Jumbos
1997 #A2 Jeff Gordon
Viper Black Mamba
1996 #2 Jeff Gordon
1996 #40 Jeff Gordon
1996 #42 Jeff Gordon
Viper Black Mamba First Strike
1996 #2 Jeff Gordon
1996 #40 Jeff Gordon
1996 #42 Jeff Gordon
Viper Black Racer
1997 #1 Jeff Gordon
1997 #51 Jeff Gordon
1997 #74 Jeff Gordon's Car
Viper Black Racer First Strike
1997 #1 Jeff Gordon
1997 #51 Jeff Gordon
1997 #74 Jeff Gordon's Car
Viper Busch Clash
1996 #B5 Jeff Gordon
Viper Busch Clash First Strike
1996 #B5 Jeff Gordon
Viper Cobra
1996 #C2 Jeff Gordon
1997 #C2 Jeff Gordon
Viper Cobra First Strike
1996 #C2 Jeff Gordon
1997 #C2 Jeff Gordon
Viper Copperhead Die Cuts
1996 #2 Jeff Gordon
1996 #40 Jeff Gordon
1996 #42 Jeff Gordon
Viper Copperhead Die Cuts First Strike
1996 #2 Jeff Gordon
1996 #40 Jeff Gordon
1996 #42 Jeff Gordon
Viper Diamondback
1996 #D1 Jeff Gordon
1997 #DB1 Jeff Gordon
Viper Diamondback Authentic
1996 #DA1 Jeff Gordon
1997 #DBA1 Jeff Gordon
Viper Diamondback Authentic California
1996 #DA1 Jeff Gordon
Viper Diamondback Authentic Eastern
1997 #DBA1 Jeff Gordon
Viper Diamondback Authentic Eastern First Strike
1997 #DBA1 Jeff Gordon
Viper Diamondback Authentic First Strike
1996 #DA1 Jeff Gordon
1997 #DBA1 Jeff Gordon
Viper Diamondback First Strike
1996 #D1 Jeff Gordon
1997 #DB1 Jeff Gordon
Viper First Strike
1996 #2 Jeff Gordon
1996 #40 Jeff Gordon
1996 #42 Jeff Gordon
1997 #1 Jeff Gordon
1997 #51 Jeff Gordon
1997 #74 Jeff Gordon's Car
Viper Green Mamba
1996 #2 Jeff Gordon
1996 #40 Jeff Gordon
1996 #42 Jeff Gordon
Viper King Cobra
1996 #KC2 Jeff Gordon
1997 #KC2 Jeff Gordon
Viper King Cobra First Strike
1996 #KC2 Jeff Gordon
Viper Promos
1996 #P3 Jeff Gordon
Viper Red Cobra
1996 #2 Jeff Gordon
1996 #40 Jeff Gordon
1996 #42 Jeff Gordon
Viper Sidewinder
1997 #S2 Jeff Gordon
Viper Sidewinder First Strike
1997 #S2 Jeff Gordon
Viper Snake Eyes
1997 #SE2 Jeff Gordon
Viper Snake Eyes First Strike
1997 #SE2 Jeff Gordon
Wheels
1998 #11 Jeff Gordon
1998 #36 Jeff Gordon's Car
1998 #65 Jeff Gordon
1999 #12 Jeff Gordon
1999 #42 Jeff Gordon BGN
1999 #60 Jeff Gordon's Car
1999 #72 Jeff Gordon's Car
1999 #P2 Jeff Gordon Promo
Wheels 50th Anniversary
1998 #A5 Jeff Gordon
1998 #A20 Jeff Gordon's Car
Wheels American Thunder
2003 #6 Jeff Gordon
2003 #22 Jeff Gordon SS
2003 #43 Jeff Gordon CC
2003 #P1 Jeff Gordon Promo
2004 #5 Jeff Gordon
2004 #34 Jeff Gordon's Rig Rt. 66
2004 #42 Jeff Gordon AS
2004 #52 Jeff Gordon's Car HR
2004 #65 Jeff Gordon RR
2004 #76 Jeff Gordon CC
2005 #8 Jeff Gordon
2005 #34 Jeff Gordon's Rig Rt. 66
2005 #40 Jeff Gordon AS
2005 #52 Jeff Gordon's Car HR
2005 #63 Jeff Gordon DT
2005 #65 Jeff Gordon RR
2006 #8 Jeff Gordon
2006 #37 Jeff Gordon DT
2006 #43 Jeff Gordon's Car HR
2006 #70 Jeff Gordon SS
2006 #73 Jeff Gordon MIA
2006 #CL Jeff Gordon CL
2007 #1 Jeff Gordon CL
2007 #9 Jeff Gordon
2007 #45 Jeff Gordon's Car DT
2007 #50 Jeff Gordon's Car HR
2007 #60 Jeff Gordon RW
2007 #70 Jeff Gordon BP
2007 #76 Jeff Gordon HC
Wheels American Thunder American Dreams
2007 #AD6 Jeff Gordon
Wheels American Thunder American Dreams Gold
2007 #ADG6 Jeff Gordon
Wheels American Thunder American Eagle
2003 #AE5 Jeff Gordon
2004 #AE2 Jeff Gordon
2005 #AE7 Jeff Gordon
Wheels American Thunder American Muscle
2003 #AM2 Jeff Gordon
2004 #AM4 Jeff Gordon
2005 #AM4 Jeff Gordon
2006 #AM2 Jeff Gordon
2007 #AM9 Jeff Gordon
Wheels American Thunder American Racing Idol
2006 #RI6 Jeff Gordon
Wheels American Thunder American Racing Idol Golden
2006 #RI6 Jeff Gordon
Wheels American Thunder Autographed Hat Instant Winner
2007 #AH10 Jeff Gordon
Wheels American Thunder Born On
2003 #BO6 Jeff Gordon
2003 #BO22 Jeff Gordon SS
2003 #BO43 Jeff Gordon CC
Wheels American Thunder Cool Threads
2003 #CT6 Jeff Gordon
2004 #CT3 Jeff Gordon
2005 #CT1 Jeff Gordon
2006 #CT7 Jeff Gordon
2007 #CT13 Jeff Gordon
Wheels American Thunder Cup Quest
2004 #CQ3 Jeff Gordon
Wheels American Thunder Double Hat
2006 #DH7 Jeff Gordon
Wheels American Thunder Golden Eagle
2003 #AEG5 Jeff Gordon
2004 #AE2 Jeff Gordon
2005 #GE7 Jeff Gordon
Wheels American Thunder Grandstand
2006 #GS6 Jeff Gordon
Wheels American Thunder Head to Toe
2004 #HT4 Jeff Gordon/50
2005 #HT10 Jeff Gordon
2006 #HT14 Jeff Gordon
2007 #HT14 Jeff Gordon
Wheels American Thunder Heads Up Manufacturer
2003 #HUM4 Jeff Gordon
Wheels American Thunder Heads Up Team
2003 #HUT3 Jeff Gordon/60
Wheels American Thunder Heads Up Winston
2003 #HUW4 Jeff Gordon
Wheels American Thunder Holofoil
2003 #P6 Jeff Gordon
2003 #P22 Jeff Gordon SS
2003 #P43 Jeff Gordon CC
Wheels American Thunder Medallion
2005 #MD14 Jeff Gordon
Wheels American Thunder Post Mark
2003 #PM5 Jeff Gordon
2004 #PM16 Jeff Gordon
Wheels American Thunder Previews
2003 #6 Jeff Gordon
2003 #22 Jeff Gordon SS
2004 #EB5 Jeff Gordon
2004 #EB34 Jeff Gordon Rt. 66
2004 #EB42 Jeff Gordon AS
2005 #8 Jeff Gordon
2006 #EB8 Jeff Gordon
2006 #EB73 Jeff Gordon MIA
2007 #EB1 Jeff Gordon CL
2007 #EB9 Jeff Gordon
2007 #EB50 Jeff Gordon's Car HR
Wheels American Thunder Pushin Pedal
2003 #PP2 Jeff Gordon
2004 #PP6 Jeff Gordon/200
2005 #PP12 Jeff Gordon
Wheels American Thunder Pushin' Pedal
2006 #PP13 Jeff Gordon
2007 #PP16 Jeff Gordon
Wheels American Thunder Rookie Thunder
2003 #RT9 Jeff Gordon
Wheels American Thunder Samples
2003 #P6 Jeff Gordon
2003 #P22 Jeff Gordon SS
2003 #P43 Jeff Gordon CC
2004 #5 Jeff Gordon
2004 #34 Jeff Gordon's Rig Rt. 66
2004 #42 Jeff Gordon AS
2004 #52 Jeff Gordon's Car HR
2004 #65 Jeff Gordon RR
2004 #76 Jeff Gordon CC
2005 #8 Jeff Gordon
2005 #34 Jeff Gordon's Rig Rt. 66
2005 #40 Jeff Gordon AS
2005 #52 Jeff Gordon's Car HR
2005 #63 Jeff Gordon DT
2005 #65 Jeff Gordon RR
Wheels American Thunder Starting Grid
2007 #SG3 Jeff Gordon
Wheels American Thunder Thunder Road
2003 #TR2 Jeff Gordon
2003 #TR17 Jeff Green
2004 #TR12 Jeff Gordon
2005 #TR12 Jeff Gordon
2006 #TR10 Jeff Gordon
2007 #TR7 Jeff Gordon
Wheels American Thunder Thunder Strokes
2007 #14 Jeff Gordon
Wheels American Thunder Thunder Strokes Press Plates Black
2007 #14 Jeff Gordon
Wheels American Thunder Thunder Strokes Press Plates Cyan
2007 #14 Jeff Gordon
Wheels American Thunder Thunder Strokes Press Plates Magenta
2007 #14 Jeff Gordon
Wheels American Thunder Thunder Strokes Press Plates Yellow
2007 #14 Jeff Gordon
Wheels American Thunder Triple Hat
2003 #TH7 Jeff Gordon
2004 #TH3 Jeff Gordon
2005 #TH5 Jeff Gordon
2007 #TH8 Jeff Gordon
Wheels Autographs
1998 #2 Jeff Gordon/200
1999 #8 Jeff Gordon/75
2003 #16 Jeff Gordon AT/HG
2004 #24 Jeff Gordon HG
2005 #17 Jeff Gordon
2006 #17 Jeff Gordon NC
2008 #11 Jeff Gordon NC HG EXCH
Wheels Autographs Chase Edition
2008 #3 Jeff Gordon NC
Wheels Autographs Press Plates Black
2008 #11 Jeff Gordon NC
Wheels Autographs Press Plates Cyan
2008 #11 Jeff Gordon NC
Wheels Autographs Press Plates Magenta
2008 #11 Jeff Gordon NC
Wheels Autographs Press Plates Yellow
2008 #11 Jeff Gordon NC
Wheels Circuit Breaker
1999 #CB5 Jeff Gordon
Wheels Custom Shop
1998 #CSJG Jeff Gordon
1999 #CS2 Jeff Gordon
Wheels Custom Shop Prizes
1998 #JGA1 Jeff Gordon
1998 #JGA2 Jeff Gordon
1998 #JGA3 Jeff Gordon
1998 #JGB1 Jeff Gordon
1998 #JGB2 Jeff Gordon
1998 #JGB3 Jeff Gordon
1998 #JGC1 Jeff Gordon
1998 #JGC2 Jeff Gordon
1998 #JGC3 Jeff Gordon
1999 #JGA1 Jeff Gordon
1999 #JGA2 Jeff Gordon
1999 #JGA3 Jeff Gordon
1999 #JGB1 Jeff Gordon
1999 #JGB2 Jeff Gordon
1999 #JGB3 Jeff Gordon
1999 #JGC1 Jeff Gordon
1999 #JGC2 Jeff Gordon
1999 #JGC3 Jeff Gordon
Wheels Dialed In
1999 #DI1 Jeff Gordon
Wheels Double Take
1998 #E4 Jeff Gordon
Wheels Flag Chasers Daytona Seven
1999 #DS1 Jeff Gordon
Wheels Flag Chasers Daytona Seven Blue-Yellow
1999 #DS1 Jeff Gordon
Wheels Flag Chasers Daytona Seven Checkered
1999 #DS1 Jeff Gordon
Wheels Flag Chasers Daytona Seven Green
1999 #DS1 Jeff Gordon
Wheels Flag Chasers Daytona Seven Red
1999 #DS1 Jeff Gordon
Wheels Flag Chasers Daytona Seven White
1999 #DS1 Jeff Gordon
Wheels Flag Chasers Daytona Seven Yellow
1999 #DS1 Jeff Gordon
Wheels Golden
1998 #11 Jeff Gordon
1998 #36 Jeff Gordon's Car
1998 #65 Jeff Gordon
1999 #12 Jeff Gordon
1999 #42 Jeff Gordon
1999 #60 Jeff Gordon
1999 #72 Jeff Gordon
Wheels Green Flags
1998 #GF6 Jeff Gordon's Car
Wheels Harry Gant
1994 #66 Jeff Gordon
1994 #1994 J.Gordon Harry Gant set
Wheels Harry Gant Gold
1994 #66 Jeff Gordon
Wheels High Gear
1994 #73 Jeff Gordon WC ROY
1994 #97 Jeff Gordon BC
1994 #101 Jeff Gordon
1994 #NNO Jeff Gordon BC AU/1500
1995 #6 Jeff Gordon
1995 #78 Jeff Gordon's Car
1995 #91 Jeff Gordon RW
1995 #98 Jeff Gordon in Pits
1998 #1 Jeff Gordon
1998 #33 Jeff Gordon's Car
1998 #50 Jeff Gordon
1998 #69 Jeff Gordon's Car
1999 #1 Jeff Gordon
1999 #33 Jeff Gordon's Car
1999 #46 Jeff Gordon
1999 #54 Jeff Gordon
1999 #58 Jeff Gordon
1999 #69 Jeff Gordon's Car
1999 #72 Jeff Gordon CL
1999 #P1 Jeff Gordon Promo
2000 #4 Jeff Gordon
2000 #33 Jeff Gordon's Car
2000 #41 Jeff Gordon
2000 #46 Jeff Gordon
2000 #48 Jeff Gordon
2000 #59 Jeff Gordon's Car
2002 #7 Jeff Gordon
2002 #28 Jeff Gordon's Car
2002 #47 Jeff Gordon's Car
2002 #56 Jeff Gordon HL
2002 #61 Jeff Gordon CA
2002 #62 Jeff Gordon CA
2002 #65 Jeff Gordon WC Champ
2002 #71 Jeff Gordon WC Sched.
2003 #10 Jeff Gordon
2003 #49 Jeff Gordon's Car CM
2003 #61 Contenders and Pretenders WCS
2003 #62 Southern Comfort WCS
2004 #8 Jeff Gordon
2004 #34 Jeff Gordon's Car C
2004 #52 Jeff Gordon NA
2004 #59 Jeff Gordon's Car
2005 #16 Jeff Gordon
2005 #53 Jeff Gordon A
2005 #59 Jeff Gordon's Car
2005 #66 Jeff Gordon NI
2005 #77 Jeff Gordon IF
2005 #80 Jeff Gordon RS
2006 #10 Jeff Gordon
2006 #16B Jeff Gordon Daytona
2006 #67 Jeff Gordon CM
2006 #80 Jeff Gordon FF
2006 #90 Jeff Gordon CL
2007 #6 Jeff Gordon
2007 #77 Jeff Gordon NI
2007 #82 Jeff Gordon's Car C
2007 #CL Jeff Gordon CL
2007 #6B Jeff Gordon -yellow 24
2008 #2 Jeff Gordon
2008 #52 Jeff Gordon's Car C
2008 #56 Jeff Gordon NA
2008 #58 Jeff Gordon NA
2008 #60 Jeff Gordon NA
2008 #60B Jeff Gordon CA with hat
2008 #62 Jeff Gordon NA
2008 #67 Jeff Gordon's Car EL
Wheels High Gear Autographs
1998 #8 Jeff Gordon/50
1999 #9 Jeff Gordon/100
2001 #10 Jeff Gordon
2002 #17 Jeff Gordon
Wheels High Gear Blue Hawaii SCDA Promos
2003 #10 Jeff Gordon
2003 #49 Jeff Gordon's Car CM
2003 #61 Contenders and Pretenders
2003 #62 Southern Comfort
Wheels High Gear Busch Clash
1995 #BC7 Jeff Gordon
Wheels High Gear Busch Clash Gold
1995 #BC7 Jeff Gordon
Wheels High Gear Custom Shop
1998 #CS2 Jeff Gordon EXCH
1999 #CSJG Jeff Gordon EXCH
2000 #CSJG Jeff Gordon EXCH
2001 #CSJG Jeff Gordon EXCH
2002 #CSJG Jeff Gordon EXCH
2003 #CSJG Jeff Gordon EXCH
2004 #CSJG Jeff Gordon
Wheels High Gear Custom Shop Autograph Redemption
2003 #CSJG Jeff Gordon EXCH
Wheels High Gear Custom Shop Autographs
2003 #JGB2 Jeff Gordon/10
Wheels High Gear Custom Shop Prizes
1998 #JGA1 Jeff Gordon
1998 #JGA2 Jeff Gordon
1998 #JGA3 Jeff Gordon
1998 #JGB1 Jeff Gordon
1998 #JGB2 Jeff Gordon
1998 #JGB3 Jeff Gordon
1998 #JGC1 Jeff Gordon
1998 #JGC2 Jeff Gordon
1998 #JGC3 Jeff Gordon
1999 #JGA1 Jeff Gordon
1999 #JGA2 Jeff Gordon
1999 #JGA3 Jeff Gordon
1999 #JGB1 Jeff Gordon
1999 #JGB2 Jeff Gordon
1999 #JGB3 Jeff Gordon
1999 #JGC1 Jeff Gordon
1999 #JGC2 Jeff Gordon
1999 #JGC3 Jeff Gordon
2000 #JGA1 Jeff Gordon
2000 #JGA2 Jeff Gordon
2000 #JGA3 Jeff Gordon
2000 #JGB1 Jeff Gordon
2000 #JGB2 Jeff Gordon
2000 #JGB3 Jeff Gordon
2000 #JGC1 Jeff Gordon
2000 #JGC2 Jeff Gordon
2000 #JGC3 Jeff Gordon
2001 #JGA1 Jeff Gordon
2001 #JGA2 Jeff Gordon
2001 #JGA3 Jeff Gordon
2001 #JGB1 Jeff Gordon
2001 #JGB2 Jeff Gordon
2001 #JGB3 Jeff Gordon
2001 #JGC1 Jeff Gordon
2001 #JGC2 Jeff Gordon
2001 #JGC3 Jeff Gordon
2002 #JGA1 Jeff Gordon
2002 #JGA2 Jeff Gordon
2002 #JGA3 Jeff Gordon
2002 #JGB1 Jeff Gordon
2002 #JGB2 Jeff Gordon
2002 #JGB3 Jeff Gordon
2002 #JGC1 Jeff Gordon
2002 #JGC2 Jeff Gordon
2002 #JGC3 Jeff Gordon
2003 #JGA1 Jeff Gordon
2003 #JGA2 Jeff Gordon
2003 #JGA3 Jeff Gordon
2003 #JGB1 Jeff Gordon
2003 #JGB2 Jeff Gordon
2003 #JGB3 Jeff Gordon
2003 #JGC1 Jeff Gordon
2003 #JGC2 Jeff Gordon
2003 #JGC3 Jeff Gordon
Wheels High Gear Day One
1994 #101 Jeff Gordon
1995 #6 Jeff Gordon
1995 #78 Jeff Gordon's Car
1995 #91 Jeff Gordon RW
1995 #98 Jeff Gordon in Pits
Wheels High Gear Day One Gold
1994 #101 Jeff Gordon
1995 #6 Jeff Gordon
1995 #78 Jeff Gordon's Car
1995 #91 Jeff Gordon RW
1995 #98 Jeff Gordon in Pits
Wheels High Gear Dominators
1994 #D5 Jeff Gordon/1750
Wheels High Gear Driven
2007 #DR14 Jeff Gordon
2008 #DR22 Jeff Gordon
Wheels High Gear Final Standings
2008 #F2 Jeff Gordon/2
Wheels High Gear Final Standings Gold
2007 #FS6 Jeff Gordon/6
Wheels High Gear First Gear
1998 #1 Jeff Gordon
1998 #33 Jeff Gordon's Car
1998 #50 Jeff Gordon
1998 #69 Jeff Gordon's Car
1999 #1 Jeff Gordon
1999 #33 Jeff Gordon's Car
1999 #46 Jeff Gordon
1999 #54 Jeff Gordon
1999 #58 Jeff Gordon
1999 #69 Jeff Gordon's Car
1999 #72 Jeff Gordon CL
2000 #4 Jeff Gordon
2000 #33 Jeff Gordon
2000 #41 Jeff Gordon
2000 #46 Jeff Gordon
2000 #48 Jeff Gordon
2000 #59 Jeff Gordon
2002 #7 Jeff Gordon
2002 #28 Jeff Gordon's Car
2002 #47 Jeff Gordon's Car
2002 #56 Jeff Gordon HL
2002 #61 Jeff Gordon CA
2002 #62 Jeff Gordon CA
2002 #65 Jeff Gordon WC Champ
2002 #71 Jeff Gordon 2002 WC Sched.
2003 #F10 Jeff Gordon
2003 #F49 Jeff Gordon's Car CM
2003 #F61 Contenders and Pretenders
2003 #F62 Southern Comfort
Wheels High Gear Flag Chasers
1999 #FC1 Jeff Gordon
2000 #FC2 Jeff Gordon
2002 #FC2 Jeff Gordon
Wheels High Gear Flag Chasers Black
2002 #FC2 Jeff Gordon
2003 #FC2 Jeff Gordon
2004 #FC6 Jeff Gordon
2005 #FC8 Jeff Gordon
2006 #FC2 Jeff Gordon
2007 #FC8 Jeff Gordon
2008 #FC3 Jeff Gordon
Wheels High Gear Flag Chasers Blue
2004 #FC6 Jeff Gordon
Wheels High Gear Flag Chasers Blue-Yellow
1999 #FC1 Jeff Gordon
2000 #FC2 Jeff Gordon
2002 #FC2 Jeff Gordon
2003 #FC2 Jeff Gordon
2005 #FC8 Jeff Gordon
2006 #FC2 Jeff Gordon
2007 #FC8 Jeff Gordon
2008 #FC3 Jeff Gordon
Wheels High Gear Flag Chasers Checkered
1999 #FC1 Jeff Gordon
2000 #FC2 Jeff Gordon
2002 #FC2 Jeff Gordon
2003 #FC2 Jeff Gordon
2004 #FC6 Jeff Gordon
2005 #FC8 Jeff Gordon
2006 #FC2 Jeff Gordon
2007 #FC8 Jeff Gordon
2008 #FC3 Jeff Gordon
Wheels High Gear Flag Chasers Checkered Blue/Orange
2000 #FC2 Jeff Gordon
2002 #FC2 Jeff Gordon
Wheels High Gear Flag Chasers Green
1999 #FC1 Jeff Gordon
2000 #FC2 Jeff Gordon
2002 #FC2 Jeff Gordon
2003 #FC2 Jeff Gordon
2004 #FC6 Jeff Gordon
2005 #FC8 Jeff Gordon
2006 #FC2 Jeff Gordon
2007 #FC8 Jeff Gordon
2008 #FC3 Jeff Gordon
Wheels High Gear Flag Chasers Red
1999 #FC1 Jeff Gordon
2000 #FC2 Jeff Gordon
2002 #FC2 Jeff Gordon
2003 #FC2 Jeff Gordon
2004 #FC6 Jeff Gordon
2005 #FC8 Jeff Gordon
2006 #FC2 Jeff Gordon
2007 #FC8 Jeff Gordon
2008 #FC3 Jeff Gordon
Wheels High Gear Flag Chasers White
1999 #FC1 Jeff Gordon
2000 #FC2 Jeff Gordon
2003 #FC2 Jeff Gordon
2004 #FC6 Jeff Gordon
2005 #FC8 Jeff Gordon
2006 #FC2 Jeff Gordon
2007 #FC8 Jeff Gordon
2008 #FC3 Jeff Gordon
Wheels High Gear Flag Chasers Yellow
1999 #FC1 Jeff Gordon
2000 #FC2 Jeff Gordon
2002 #FC2 Jeff Gordon
2003 #FC2 Jeff Gordon
2004 #FC6 Jeff Gordon
2005 #FC8 Jeff Gordon
2006 #FC2 Jeff Gordon
2007 #FC8 Jeff Gordon
2008 #FC3 Jeff Gordon
Wheels High Gear Flag to Flag
2005 #FF5 Jeff Gordon
2006 #FF7 Jeff Gordon
Wheels High Gear Full Throttle

2003 #FT2 Jeff Gordon
2004 #FT2 Jeff Gordon
2005 #FT4 Jeff Gordon
2006 #FT3 Jeff Gordon
2007 #FT1 Jeff Gordon
2008 #FT1 Jeff Gordon
Wheels High Gear Gear Jammers
1998 #GJ12 Jeff Gordon
Wheels High Gear Gear Shifters
1999 #GS1 Jeff Gordon
2000 #GS6 Jeff Gordon
Wheels High Gear Gold
1994 #73 Jeff Gordon WC ROY
1994 #97 Jeff Gordon BC
1994 #101 Jeff Gordon
1995 #6 Jeff Gordon
1995 #78 Jeff Gordon's Car
1995 #91 Jeff Gordon RW
1995 #98 Jeff Gordon in Pits
Wheels High Gear High Groove
1998 #HG5 Jeff Gordon's Car
2002 #HG7 Jeff Gordon
2003 #HG7 Jeff Gordon
2004 #HG6 Jeff Gordon
Wheels High Gear Hot Streaks
1999 #HS1 Jeff Gordon
2002 #HS3 Jeff Gordon
Wheels High Gear Hot Treads
2003 #HT5 Jeff Gordon
Wheels High Gear Last Lap
2007 #LL6 Jeff Gordon
2008 #LL2 Jeff Gordon
Wheels High Gear Last Lap Holofoil
2008 #LL2 Jeff Gordon
Wheels High Gear Machine
2003 #MM9B Jeff Gordon
2004 #MM3B Jeff Gordon
2005 #MM7B Jeff Gordon
Wheels High Gear Man
2003 #MM9A Jeff Gordon
2004 #MM3A Jeff Gordon
2005 #MM7A Jeff Gordon
Wheels High Gear Man & Machine (Machine)
2006 #MMB2 Jeff Gordon
Wheels High Gear Man & Machine (Man)
2006 #MMA2 Jeff Gordon
Wheels High Gear Man and Machine Cars
1998 #1 Jeff Gordon's Car
1999 #MM1B Jeff Gordon's Car
2000 #MM6B Jeff Gordon's Car
2002 #MM2B Jeff Gordon
Wheels High Gear Man and Machine Drivers
1998 #MM1 Jeff Gordon
1999 #MM1A Jeff Gordon
2000 #MM6A Jeff Gordon
2002 #MM2A Jeff Gordon
Wheels High Gear Mega Gold
1994 #MG5 Jeff Gordon
Wheels High Gear MPH
1996 #1 Jeff Gordon
1998 #33 Jeff Gordon's Car
1998 #50 Jeff Gordon
1998 #69 Jeff Gordon's Car
1999 #1 Jeff Gordon
1999 #33 Jeff Gordon's Car
1999 #46 Jeff Gordon
1999 #54 Jeff Gordon
1999 #58 Jeff Gordon
1999 #69 Jeff Gordon's Car
1999 #72 Jeff Gordon CL
2000 #4 Jeff Gordon
2000 #33 Jeff Gordon
2000 #41 Jeff Gordon
2000 #46 Jeff Gordon
2000 #48 Jeff Gordon
2000 #59 Jeff Gordon
2002 #7 Jeff Gordon
2002 #28 Jeff Gordon's Car
2002 #47 Jeff Gordon's Car
2002 #56 Jeff Gordon HL
2002 #61 Jeff Gordon CA
2002 #62 Jeff Gordon CA
2002 #65 Jeff Gordon WC Champ
2002 #71 Jeff Gordon 2002 WC Sched.
2003 #M10 Jeff Gordon
2003 #M49 Jeff Gordon's Car CM
2003 #M61 Contenders and Pretenders
2003 #M62 Southern Comfort
2004 #M8 Jeff Gordon
2004 #M34 Jeff Gordon C
2004 #M52 Jeff Gordon NA
2004 #M59 Jeff Gordon's Car
2005 #M16 Jeff Gordon
2005 #M53 Jeff Gordon A
2005 #M59 Jeff Gordon's Car
2005 #M66 Jeff Gordon NI
2005 #M77 Jeff Gordon IF
2005 #M80 Jeff Gordon RS
2006 #M10 Jeff Gordon
2006 #M67 Jeff Gordon CM
2006 #M80 Jeff Gordon FF
2006 #M90 Jeff Gordon CL
2007 #M6 Jeff Gordon
2007 #M77 Jeff Gordon NI
2007 #M82 Jeff Gordon's Car C
2007 #MCL Jeff Gordon CL
2008 #M2 Jeff Gordon
2008 #M52 Jeff Gordon's Car C
2008 #M56 Jeff Gordon NA
2008 #M58 Jeff Gordon NA
2008 #M60 Jeff Gordon NA
2008 #M62 Jeff Gordon NA
2008 #M67 Jeff Gordon's Car EL
Wheels High Gear Previews
2003 #10 Jeff Gordon
2004 #8 Jeff Gordon
2004 #34 Jeff Gordon C
2004 #52 Jeff Gordon NA
2004 #59 Jeff Gordon's Car
2007 #EB6 Jeff Gordon
2008 #EB2 Jeff Gordon
Wheels High Gear Previews Green
2005 #EB16 Jeff Gordon
2006 #EB10 Jeff Gordon
Wheels High Gear Previews Silver
2005 #EB77 Jeff Gordon IF
2006 #EB80 Jeff Gordon FF
Wheels High Gear Pure Gold
1998 #PG3 Jeff Gordon
Wheels High Gear Rookie Thunder Update
1994 #102 Jeff Gordon
Wheels High Gear Rookie Thunder Update Platinum
1994 #102 Jeff Gordon
Wheels High Gear Samples
2003 #10 Jeff Gordon
2003 #49 Jeff Gordon's Car CM
2003 #61 Contenders and Pretenders
2003 #62 Southern Comfort
2004 #8 Jeff Gordon
2004 #34 Jeff Gordon C
2004 #52 Jeff Gordon NA
2004 #59 Jeff Gordon's Car
2005 #16 Jeff Gordon
2005 #53 Jeff Gordon A
2005 #59 Jeff Gordon's Car
2005 #66 Jeff Gordon NI
2005 #77 Jeff Gordon IF
2005 #80 Jeff Gordon RS
Wheels High Gear Sunday Sensation
2000 #OC6 Jeff Gordon
2002 #SS4 Jeff Gordon
2003 #SS4 Jeff Gordon
2004 #SS9 Jeff Gordon
Wheels High Gear The Chase
2008 #TC2 Jeff Gordon
Wheels High Gear Top Ten
2004 #TT4 Jeff Gordon
Wheels High Gear Top Tier
1998 #TT1 Jeff Gordon 1:384
1999 #TT1 Jeff Gordon 1:400
2000 #TT4 Jeff Gordon
2002 #TT1 Jeff Gordon
2003 #TT4 Jeff Gordon
2005 #TT3 Jeff Gordon
2007 #TT6 Jeff Gordon
Wheels High Gear Top Tier Numbered
2002 #TT1 Jeff Gordon
Wheels High Gear Winning Edge
2000 #WE5 Jeff Gordon
Wheels High Gear Winston Victory Lap Tribute
2004 #WVL1 Jeff Gordon
Wheels High Gear Winston Victory Lap Tribute Gold
2004 #WVL1 Jeff Gordon
Wheels High Groove
1999 #HG3 Jeff Gordon
1999 #HG7 Jeff Gordon
Wheels Jackpot
1998 #J3 Jeff Gordon
Wheels Rookie Thunder
1993 #32 Jeff Gordon CRC
1993 #37 Jeff Gordon
1993 #50 Jeff Gordon
1993 #51 Jeff Gordon
1993 #62 Jeff Gordon w/Car
1993 #70 Jeff Gordon
1993 #71 Jeff Gordon
1993 #82 Jeff Gordon
1993 #93 Jeff Gordon's Car
1993 #97 Jeff Gordon
1993 #98 Jeff Gordon/K.Schrader
Wheels Rookie Thunder Platinum
1993 #32 Jeff Gordon
1993 #37 Jeff Gordon
1993 #50 Jeff Gordon
1993 #51 Jeff Gordon
1993 #62 Jeff Gordon and Car
1993 #70 Jeff Gordon
1993 #71 Jeff Gordon
1993 #82 Jeff Gordon
1993 #93 Jeff Gordon's Car
1993 #97 Jeff Gordon
1993 #98 Jeff Gordon/Ken Schrader
Wheels Rookie Thunder Promos
1993 #P2 Jeff Gordon
Wheels Runnin and Gunnin
1999 #RG9 Jeff Gordon
1999 #RG29 Jeff Gordon
Wheels Runnin and Gunnin Foils
1999 #RG9 Jeff Gordon
1999 #RG29 Jeff Gordon
Wheels Solos
1999 #12 Jeff Gordon
1999 #42 Jeff Gordon
1999 #60 Jeff Gordon
1999 #72 Jeff Gordon
Winner's Choice Busch
1992 #76 Jeff Gordon
1992 #77 Jeff Gordon's Car
World of Outlaws
1987 #52 Jeff Gordon XRC
1988 #54 Jeff Gordon
Zenith
1995 #23 Jeff Gordon HG
1995 #51 Jeff Gordon's Transporter
1995 #64 Jeff Gordon EOD
1995 #77 Jeff Gordon CL
1995 #78 Jeff Gordon CQ
1995 #79 Jeff Gordon CQ
1995 #80 Jeff Gordon CQ
1995 #81 Jeff Gordon CQ
1995 #82 Jeff Gordon CQ
1995 #83 Jeff Gordon CQ
1996 #2 Jeff Gordon
1996 #36 Jeff Gordon's Car HV
1996 #51 Jeff Gordon S
1996 #73 Jeff Gordon CS
1996 #74 Jeff Gordon CS
1996 #75 Jeff Gordon CS
1996 #76 Jeff Gordon CS
1996 #77 Jeff Gordon CS
1996 #78 Jeff Gordon CS
1996 #79 Jeff Gordon CS
1996 #80 Jeff Gordon CS
1996 #91 Jeff Gordon W
1996 #92 Jeff Gordon W
1996 #98 Jeff Gordon/Brooke W
1996 #99 Jeff Gordon CL
Zenith Artist Proofs
1996 #2 Jeff Gordon RP
1996 #36 Jeff Gordon's Car HV
1996 #51 Jeff Gordon S
1996 #73 Jeff Gordon CS
1996 #74 Jeff Gordon CS
1996 #75 Jeff Gordon CS
1996 #76 Jeff Gordon CS
1996 #77 Jeff Gordon CS
1996 #78 Jeff Gordon CS
1996 #79 Jeff Gordon CS
1996 #80 Jeff Gordon CS
1996 #91 Jeff Gordon W
1996 #92 Jeff Gordon W
1996 #98 Jeff/Brooke Gordon W
1996 #99 Jeff Gordon CL
Zenith Champion Salute
1996 #1 Jeff Gordon
Zenith Helmets
1995 #3 Jeff Gordon
Zenith Highlights
1996 #2 Jeff Gordon
Zenith Tribute
1995 #2 Jeff Gordon
Zenith Winston Winners
1995 #2 Jeff Gordon
1995 #4 Jeff Gordon/Evernham
1995 #6 Jeff Gordon
1995 #15 Jeff Gordon
1995 #16 Jeff Gordon
1995 #23 Jeff Gordon
1995 #25 Jeff Gordon
Zenith Z-Team
1995 #2 Jeff Gordon

Hamlin, Denny

Press Pass
2006 #35 Denny Hamlin NBS
2006 #70 Denny Hamlin RR
2007 #5 Denny Hamlin
2007 #36 Denny Hamlin NBS
2007 #65 Denny Hamlin RR
2007 #80 Denny Hamlin's Car OT
2007 #90 Denny Hamlin NS
2007 #98 Denny Hamlin U
2007 #112 Denny Hamlin TT
2008 #3 Denny Hamlin
2008 #112 Denny Hamlin Top 12
2008 #0 Cup Chase Matt Kenseth Tony Stewart Jeff Gordon Jimmie Johnson Denny Hamlin Kurt Busch Kevin Harvick Carl Edwards Kyle Busch Martin Truex Jr. Jeff Burton Clint Bowyer
Press Pass Autographs
2006 #20 Denny Hamlin NBS
2007 #16 Denny Hamlin NC P
2008 #16 Denny Hamlin NC P/E
Press Pass Autographs Press Plates Black
2007 #4 Denny Hamlin NC
2008 #12 Denny Hamlin NC E
Press Pass Autographs Press Plates Cyan
2007 #4 Denny Hamlin NC
2008 #12 Denny Hamlin NC P
Press Pass Autographs Press Plates Magenta
2007 #5 Denny Hamlin NC
2008 #12 Denny Hamlin NC E
Press Pass Autographs Press Plates Yellow
2007 #5 Denny Hamlin NC
2008 #12 Denny Hamlin NC P
Press Pass Blue
2006 #B35 Denny Hamlin NBS
2006 #B70 Denny Hamlin RR
2007 #B5 Denny Hamlin
2007 #B36 Denny Hamlin NBS
2007 #B65 Denny Hamlin RR
2007 #B80 Denny Hamlin's Car OT
2007 #B90 Denny Hamlin NS
2007 #B98 Denny Hamlin U
2007 #B112 Denny Hamlin TT
2008 #B3 Denny Hamlin
2008 #B112 Denny Hamlin Top 12
Press Pass Burning Rubber Autographs
2008 #BR-DH Denny Hamlin/11
Press Pass Burning Rubber Drivers
2007 #BRD10 Denny Hamlin Pocono 6-11
2007 #BRD15 Denny Hamlin Pocono 7-23
2008 #BRD16 Denny Hamlin New Hampshire
Press Pass Burning Rubber Drivers Gold
2007 #BRD10 Denny Hamlin Pocono 6-11
2007 #BRD15 Denny Hamlin Pocono 7-23
2008 #BRD16 Denny Hamlin New Hampshire
Press Pass Burning Rubber Drivers Prime Cuts
2008 #BRD16 Denny Hamlin New Hampshire
Press Pass Burning Rubber Team
2007 #BRT10Denny Hamlin Pocono 6-11
2007 #BRT15Denny Hamlin Pocono 7-23
Press Pass Burning Rubber Teams
2008 #BRT16Denny Hamlin New Hampshire
Press Pass Burnouts
2006 #HT5 Denny Hamlin
2008 #BO4 Denny Hamlin
Press Pass Burnouts Blue
2008 #BO4 Denny Hamlin
Press Pass Burnouts Gold
2008 #BO4 Denny Hamlin
Press Pass Burnouts Holofoil
2006 #HT5 Denny Hamlin
Press Pass Collector's Series Box Set
2007 #SB8 Denny Hamlin
Press Pass Collectors Series Making the Show
2006 #MS5 Denny Hamlin
Press Pass Collectors Series Sunday Best
2007 #CB8 Denny Hamlin
Press Pass Cup Chase
2007 #CCR12 Denny Hamlin Winner
2008 #CC5 Denny Hamlin
Press Pass Cup Chase Prizes
2006 #CC3 Denny Hamlin
2007 #CC6 Denny Hamlin
Press Pass Double Burner Firesuit-Glove
2007 #DB3 Denny Hamlin
Press Pass Double Burner Firesuit-Glove Exchange
2007 #DB3 Denny hamlin
Press Pass Double Burner Metal-Tire
2007 #DB-DH Denny Hamlin
2008 #DB-DH Denny Hamlin
Press Pass Double Burner Metal-Tire Exchange
2007 #DB-DH Denny Hamlin
Press Pass Eclipse
2006 #32 Denny Hamlin NBS
2007 #3 Denny Hamlin
2007 #38 Denny Hamlin TO
2007 #57 Denny Hamlin NT
2007 #75 Denny Hamlin NYC
2007 #80 Denny Hamlin SM
2007 #0 Cup Chase 10
2008 #11 Denny Hamlin
2008 #34 Denny Hamlin RM
2008 #39 Denny Hamlin TO
Press Pass Eclipse Ecliptic
2007 #EC9 Denny Hamlin
Press Pass Eclipse Gold
2007 #G3 Denny Hamlin
2007 #G38 Denny Hamlin TO
2007 #G57 Denny Hamlin NT
2007 #G75 Denny Hamlin NYC
2007 #G80 Denny Hamlin SM
2008 #G11 Denny Hamlin
2008 #G34 Denny Hamlin RM
2008 #G39 Denny Hamlin TO
Press Pass Eclipse Previews
2006 #EB32 Denny Hamlin NBS
2007 #EB3 Denny Hamlin
2007 #EB38 Denny Hamlin TO
2008 #EB11 Denny Hamlin
2008 #EB34 Denny Hamlin RM
Press Pass Eclipse Racing Champions
2007 #RC8 Denny Hamlin
2007 #RC19 Denny Hamlin
Press Pass Eclipse Red
2007 #R3 Denny Hamlin
2007 #R38 Denny Hamlin TO
2007 #R57 Denny Hamlin NT
2007 #R75 Denny Hamlin NYC
2007 #R80 Denny Hamlin SM
2008 #R11 Denny Hamlin
2008 #R34 Denny Hamlin RM
2008 #R39 Denny Hamlin TO
Press Pass Eclipse Skidmarks
2007 #SM5 Denny Hamlin
Press Pass Eclipse Skidmarks Holofoil
2007 #SM5 Denny Hamlin
Press Pass Eclipse Stellar
2008 #ST10 Denny Hamlin
2008 #ST18 Denny Hamlin
Press Pass Eclipse Teammates Autographs
2007 #4 Hamlin/Stewart/Yeley
2008 #BHS Kyle Busch Denny Hamlin Tony Stewart/35
Press Pass Four Wide
2007 #FW-DH Denny Hamlin
2008 #FW-DH Denny Hamlin
Press Pass Four Wide Checkered
2007 #FW-DH Denny Hamlin
2008 #FW-DH Denny Hamlin
Press Pass Four Wide Checkered Exchange
2007 #FW-DH Denny Hamlin
Press Pass Four Wide Exchange
2007 #FW-DH Denny Hamlin
Press Pass Gold
2006 #G35 Denny Hamlin NBS
2006 #G70 Denny Hamlin RR
2007 #G5 Denny Hamlin
2007 #G36 Denny Hamlin NBS
2007 #G65 Denny Hamlin RR
2007 #G80 Denny Hamlin's Car OT
2007 #G90 Denny Hamlin NS
2007 #G98 Denny Hamlin U
2007 #G112 Denny Hamlin TT
2008 #G3 Denny Hamlin
2008 #G112 Denny Hamlin Top 12
Press Pass Hot Treads
2008 #HT8 Denny Hamlin
Press Pass Hot Treads Blue
2008 #HT8 Denny Hamlin
Press Pass Hot Treads Gold
2008 #HT8 Denny Hamlin
Press Pass Legends
2006 #45 Denny Hamlin CRC
2007 #50 Denny Hamlin
Press Pass Legends Autographs Blue
2007 #10 Denny Hamlin/59
Press Pass Legends Autographs Inscriptions Blue
2007 #7 Denny Hamlin 11/9
Press Pass Legends Blue
2006 #B45 Denny Hamlin
2007 #B50 Denny Hamlin
Press Pass Legends Bronze
2006 #Z45 Denny Hamlin
2007 #Z50 Denny Hamlin
Press Pass Legends Gold
2006 #G45 Denny Hamlin
2007 #G50 Denny Hamlin
Press Pass Legends Holofoil
2006 #H45 Denny Hamlin
2007 #H50 Denny Hamlin
Press Pass Legends Press Plates Black
2006 #PPB45 Denny Hamlin
2007 #PP50 Denny Hamlin
Press Pass Legends Press Plates Black Backs
2006 #PPB45B Denny Hamlin
2007 #PP50 Denny Hamlin
Press Pass Legends Press Plates Cyan
2006 #PPC45 Denny Hamlin
2007 #PP50 Denny Hamlin
Press Pass Legends Press Plates Cyan Backs
2006 #PPC45B Denny Hamlin
2007 #PP50 Denny Hamlin
Press Pass Legends Press Plates Magenta
2006 #PPM45 Denny Hamlin
2007 #PP50 Denny Hamlin
Press Pass Legends Press Plates Magenta Backs
2006 #PPM45B Denny Hamlin
2007 #PP50 Denny Hamlin
Press Pass Legends Press Plates Yellow
2006 #PPY45 Denny Hamlin
2007 #PP50 Denny Hamlin
Press Pass Legends Press Plates Yellow Backs
2006 #PPY45B Denny Hamlin
2007 #PP50 Denny Hamlin
Press Pass Legends Previews
2006 #EB45 Denny Hamlin
2007 #EB50 Denny Hamlin
Press Pass Legends Signature Series
2007 #DH Denny Hamlin
Press Pass Legends Solo
2006 #S45 Denny Hamlin
2007 #S50 Denny Hamlin
Press Pass Legends Sunday Swatches Bronze
2007 #DH-SS Denny Hamlin
Press Pass Legends Sunday Swatches Gold
2007 #DH-SS Denny Hamlin
Press Pass Legends Sunday Swatches Silver
2007 #DH-SS Denny Hamlin
Press Pass Legends Victory Lane Bronze
2007 #VL4 Denny Hamlin
Press Pass Legends Victory Lane Gold
2007 #VL4 Denny Hamlin
Press Pass Legends Victory Lane Silver
2007 #VL4 Denny Hamlin
Press Pass Optima
2005 #34 Denny Hamlin BGN RC
2006 #11 Denny Hamlin CRC
2006 #37 Denny Hamlin NBS
2006 #74 Denny Hamlin YG
2006 #80 Denny Hamlin RTV Pocono
2006 #86 Denny Hamlin RTV Pocono
2006 #11B Denny Hamlin Chase
Press Pass Optima Fan Favorite
2006 #FF7 Denny Hamlin
Press Pass Optima Gold
2005 #G34 Denny Hamlin BGN
2006 #G11 Denny Hamlin
2006 #G37 Denny Hamlin NBS
2006 #G74 Denny Hamlin YG
2006 #G80 Denny Hamlin RTV Pocono
2006 #G86 Denny Hamlin RTV Pocono
Press Pass Optima Pole Position
2006 #PP8 Denny Hamlin
Press Pass Optima Previews
2005 #34 Denny Hamlin BGN
2006 #EB11 Denny Hamlin
2006 #EB74 Denny Hamlin YG
Press Pass Optima Rookie Relics Cars
2006 #RRT2 Denny Hamlin
Press Pass Optima Rookie Relics Drivers
2006 #RRD2 Denny Hamlin/40
Press Pass Optima Samples
2005 #34 Denny Hamlin BGN
Press Pass Panorama
2005 #PPP4 Denny Hamlin
2005 #PPP76 Denny Hamlin
Press Pass Platinum
2006 #P35 Denny Hamlin NBS
2006 #P70 Denny Hamlin RR
2007 #P5 Denny Hamlin
2007 #P36 Denny Hamlin NBS
2007 #P65 Denny Hamlin RR
2007 #P80 Denny Hamlin's Car OT
2007 #P90 Denny Hamlin NS
2007 #P98 Denny Hamlin U
2007 #P112 Denny Hamlin TT
2008 #P3 Denny Hamlin
2008 #P112 Denny Hamlin Top 12
Press Pass Premium
2006 #31 Denny Hamlin CRC
2006 #50 Denny Hamlin NS
2007 #10 Denny Hamlin
2007 #39 Denny Hamlin's Car M
2007 #53 Denny Hamlin RTTC
2008 #10 Denny Hamlin
2008 #42 Denny Hamlin's Car M
2008 #52 Denny Hamlin SW Gatorade Duel
2008 #65 Denny Hamlin EOP
Press Pass Premium Hot Threads Autographs
2008 #HTDH Denny Hamlin/11
Press Pass Premium Hot Threads Cars
2006 #HTT12Denny Hamlin
Press Pass Premium Hot Threads Drivers
2006 #HTD12 Denny Hamlin
2007 #HTD6 Denny Hamlin
2008 #HTD5 Denny Hamlin
Press Pass Premium Hot Threads Drivers Gold
2006 #HTD12 Denny Hamlin
2007 #HTD6 Denny Hamlin
2008 #HTD5 Denny Hamlin
Press Pass Premium Hot Threads Patch
2007 #HTP5 Denny Hamlin Fed Ex/15
2007 #HTP6 Denny Hamlin Flag/8
Press Pass Premium Hot Threads Patches
2008 #HTP8 Denny Hamlin Fed Ex/4
Press Pass Premium Hot Threads Team
2007 #HTT6 Denny Hamlin
2008 #HTT5 Denny Hamlin
Press Pass Premium Performance Driven
2007 #PD4 Denny Hamlin
Press Pass Premium Performance Driven Red
2007 #PD4 Denny Hamlin
Press Pass Premium Previews
2008 #EB10 Denny Hamlin
2008 #EB65 Denny Hamlin EOP
Press Pass Premium Red
2007 #R10 Denny Hamlin
2007 #R39 Denny Hamlin's Car M
2007 #R53 Denny Hamlin RTTC
2008 #10 Denny Hamlin
2008 #42 Denny Hamlin's Car M
2008 #52 Denny Hamlin SW
2008 #65 Denny Hamlin EOP
Press Pass Premium Target
2008 #TA2 Denny Hamlin
Press Pass Premium Team Signed Baseballs
2008 #GIB Kyle Busch Denny Hamlin Tony Stewart
2008 #E-GIB Kyle Busch Denny Hamlin Tony Stewart Entry Card
Press Pass Previews
2006 #EB35 Denny Hamlin NBS
2007 #EB5 Denny Hamlin
2007 #EB36 Denny Hamlin NBS
2007 #EB112 Denny Hamlin TT
2008 #EB3 Denny Hamlin
2008 #EB112Denny Hamlin Top 12
Press Pass Race Day
2007 #RD7 Denny Hamlin
Press Pass Signings
2005 #21 Denny Hamlin
2006 #20 Denny Hamlin V
2007 #25 Denny Hamlin NC
2008 #23 Denny Hamlin
Press Pass Signings Blue
2007 #10 Denny Hamlin NC
2008 #9 Denny Hamlin
Press Pass Signings Gold
2005 #20 Denny Hamlin
2006 #17 Denny Hamlin V
2007 #20 Denny Hamlin NC
2008 #18 Denny Hamlin
Press Pass Signings Platinum
2005 #20 Denny Hamlin
2008 #18 Denny Hamlin
Press Pass Signings Press Plates Black
2007 #18 Denny Hamlin
2008 #16 Denny Hamlin
Press Pass Signings Press Plates Cyan
2007 #17 Denny Hamlin
2008 #16 Denny Hamlin
Press Pass Signings Press Plates Magenta
2007 #17 Denny Hamlin
2008 #16 Denny Hamlin
Press Pass Signings Press Plates Yellow
2007 #17 Denny Hamlin
2008 #16 Denny Hamlin
Press Pass Signings Silver
2006 #20 Denny Hamlin V
2007 #19 Denny Hamlin NC
2008 #16 Denny Hamlin
Press Pass Snapshots
2007 #SN10 Denny Hamlin
Press Pass Speedway
2008 #30 Denny Hamlin
2008 #76 Denny Hamlin's Car RSG
Press Pass Speedway Corporate Cuts Drivers
2008 #CD -DH Denny Hamlin
Press Pass Speedway Corporate Cuts Drivers Patches
2008 #CD -DH Denny Hamlin
Press Pass Speedway Corporate Cuts Team
2008 #CT -DH Denny Hamlin
Press Pass Speedway Gold
2008 #G30 Denny Hamlin
2008 #G76 Denny Hamlin's Car RSG
Press Pass Speedway Holofoil
2008 #H30 Denny Hamlin
2008 #H76 Denny Hamlin's Car RSG
Press Pass Speedway Previews
2008 #EB30 Denny Hamlin
Press Pass Speedway Red
2008 #R30 Denny Hamlin
2008 #R76 Denny Hamlin's Car RSG
Press Pass Stealth
2006 #49 Stewart/Hamlin/Yeley TM
2006 #73 Denny Hamlin DD
2006 #92 Denny Hamlin CRC
2007 #9 Denny Hamlin
2007 #49 Denny Hamlin's Rig
2007 #65 Hamlin/Stewart/Yeley
2007 #75 Denny Hamlin DD
2008 #12 Denny Hamlin
2008 #57 Denny Hamlin's Car GC
2008 #68 Denny Hamlin Tony Stewart Kyle Busch
2008 #85 Denny Hamlin PM
Press Pass Stealth Autographed Hat Entry
2006 #PPH9 Denny Hamlin
Press Pass Stealth Battle Armor Autographs
2008 #BASDH Denny Hamlin/11
Press Pass Stealth Battle Armor Drivers
2007 #BAD3 Denny Hamlin
2008 #BAD18 Denny Hamlin
Press Pass Stealth Battle Armor Teams
2007 #BAT3 Denny Hamlin
2008 #BAT18Denny Hamlin
Press Pass Stealth Chrome
2007 #9 Denny Hamlin
2007 #49 Denny Hamlin's Rig
2007 #65 Hamlin/Stewart/Yeley
2007 #75 Denny Hamlin DD
2008 #12 Denny Hamlin
2008 #57 Denny Hamlin's Car GC
2008 #68 Denny Hamlin Tony Stewart Kyle Busch
2008 #85 Denny Hamlin PM
Press Pass Stealth Chrome Exclusives
2007 #X9 Denny Hamlin
2007 #X49 Denny Hamlin's Rig
2007 #X65 Hamlin/Stewart/Yeley
2007 #X75 Denny Hamlin DD
2008 #12 Denny Hamlin
2008 #57 Denny Hamlin's Car GC
2008 #68 Denny Hamlin Tony Stewart Kyle Busch
2008 #85 Denny Hamlin PM
Press Pass Stealth Chrome Exclusives Gold
2008 #12 Denny Hamlin
2008 #57 Denny Hamlin's Car GC
2008 #68 Denny Hamlin Tony Stewart Kyle Busch
2008 #85 Denny Hamlin PM
Press Pass Stealth Chrome Platinum
2007 #P9 Denny Hamlin
2007 #P49 Denny Hamlin's Rig
2007 #P65 Hamlin/Stewart/Yeley
2007 #P75 Denny Hamlin DD
Press Pass Stealth Fusion
2007 #F6 Denny Hamlin
Press Pass Stealth Gear Grippers Autographs
2006 #DH Denny Hamlin/11
Press Pass Stealth Gear Grippers Drivers
2006 #GGD9 Denny Hamlin
Press Pass Stealth Hot Pass
2006 #HP11 Denny Hamlin
Press Pass Stealth Mach 07
2007 #M7-8 Denny Hamlin
Press Pass Stealth Maximum Access
2007 #MA10 Denny Hamlin
2008 #MA11 Denny Hamlin
Press Pass Stealth Maximum Access Autographs
2007 #MA10 Denny Hamlin
2008 #MA11 Denny Hamlin
Press Pass Stealth No Boundaries
2005 #NB24 Denny Hamlin
Press Pass Stealth Previews
2006 #92 Denny Hamlin
2007 #EB9 Denny Hamlin
2008 #12 Denny Hamlin
2008 #85 Denny Hamlin PM
Press Pass Stealth Retail
2006 #49 Stewart/Hamlin/Yeley TM
2006 #73 Denny Hamlin DD
2006 #92 Denny Hamlin CRC
Press Pass Stealth Retail Gear Grippers Cars

2006 #GGT9 Denny Hamlin
Press Pass Stealth X-Ray
2006 #X49 Stewart/Hamlin/Yeley TM
2006 #X73 Denny Hamlin DD
2006 #X92 Denny Hamlin
Press Pass Target Race Win Tires
2007 #RW4 Denny Hamlin Pocono 6-11
Press Pass Target Victory Tires
2008 #TT-DH Denny Hamlin New Hampshire
Press Pass Top 25 Drivers & Rides
2006 #C8 Denny Hamlin's Car
2006 #D8 Denny Hamlin
Press Pass Top Prospects Memorabilia
2005 #DH-S Denny Hamlin Shoe
2005 #DH-SM Denny Hamlin Metal
2005 #DH-T Denny Hamlin Tire
Press Pass Trackside
2005 #37 Denny Hamlin RC
Press Pass Trackside Golden
2005 #G37 Denny Hamlin
Press Pass Trackside Hot Pass
2005 #19 Denny Hamlin
Press Pass Trackside Hot Pass National
2005 #19 Denny Hamlin
Press Pass Trackside Previews
2005 #37 Denny Hamlin
Press Pass Trackside Samples
2005 #37 Denny Hamlin
Press Pass Velocity
2007 #V9 Denny Hamlin
Press Pass Wal-Mart Autographs
2008 #4 Denny Hamlin
Sports Illustrated for Kids
2007 #153 Denny Hamlin NASCAR
TRAKS
2006 #12 Denny Hamlin CRC
2006 #42 Denny Hamlin's Car
2007 #9 Denny Hamlin
2007 #95 Denny Hamlin FT
TRAKS Autographs
2006 #13 Denny Hamlin
Traks Corporate Cuts Driver
2007 #CCD6 Denny Hamlin
Traks Corporate Cuts Patch
2007 #CCD6 Denny Hamlin/10
Traks Corporate Cuts Team
2007 #CCT6 Denny Hamlin
Traks Gold
2007 #G9 Denny Hamlin
2007 #G95 Denny Hamlin FT
Traks Holofoil
2007 #H9 Denny Hamlin
2007 #H95 Denny Hamlin FT
Traks Previews
2007 #EB9 Denny Hamlin
Traks Red
2007 #R9 Denny Hamlin
2007 #R95 Denny Hamlin FT
TRAKS Stickers
2006 #11 Denny Hamlin
VIP
2006 #91 Denny Hamlin CRC
2007 #11 Denny Hamlin
VIP Get A Grip Drivers
2007 #GGD17 Denny Hamlin
VIP Get A Grip Teams
2007 #GGT17 Denny Hamlin
VIP Head Gear
2006 #HG5 Denny Hamlin
VIP Head Gear Transparent
2006 #HG5 Denny Hamlin
VIP Making the Show
2006 #MS5 Denny Hamlin
VIP Previews
2007 #EB11 Denny Hamlin
VIP Rookie Stripes
2006 #RS2 Denny Hamlin
VIP Rookie Stripes Autographs
2006 #RS-DH Denny Hamlin
VIP Sunday Best
2007 #SB8 Denny Hamlin
VIP Tradin' Paint Cars Bronze
2006 #TPT8 Denny Hamlin
VIP Tradin' Paint Drivers Gold
2006 #TPD8 Denny Hamlin
VIP Tradin' Paint Drivers Silver
2006 #TPD8 Denny Hamlin
VIP Trophy Club
2007 #TC7 Denny Hamlin
VIP Trophy Club Transparent
2007 #TC7 Denny Hamlin
Wheels American Thunder
2005 #89 Denny Hamlin RT RC
2006 #91 Denny Hamlin RT AU CRC
2007 #11 Denny Hamlin
2007 #56 Denny Hamlin's Car HR
Wheels American Thunder Autographed Hat Instant Winner
2007 #AH12 Denny Hamlin
Wheels American Thunder Double Hat
2006 #DH8 Denny Hamlin
Wheels American Thunder Grandstand
2006 #GS7 Denny Hamlin
Wheels American Thunder License to Drive
2005 #8 Denny Hamlin
Wheels American Thunder Previews
2005 #89 Denny Hamlin RT/1
2007 #EB11 Denny Hamlin
2007 #EB56 Denny Hamlin's Car HR
Wheels American Thunder Pushin' Pedal
2007 #PP4 Denny Hamlin
Wheels American Thunder Samples
2005 #89 Denny Hamlin RT
Wheels American Thunder Thunder Road
2007 #TR11 Denny Hamlin
Wheels American Thunder Thunder Strokes
2007 #17 Denny Hamlin
Wheels American Thunder Thunder Strokes Press Plates Black
2007 #17 Denny Hamlin
Wheels American Thunder Thunder Strokes Press Plates Cyan
2007 #17 Denny Hamlin
Wheels American Thunder Thunder Strokes Press Plates Magenta
2007 #17 Denny Hamlin
Wheels American Thunder Thunder Strokes Press Plates Yellow
2007 #17 Denny Hamlin
Wheels American Thunder Triple Hat
2007 #TH10 Denny Hamlin
Wheels Autographs
2006 #21 Denny Hamlin NBS
2007 #14 Denny Hamlin NC HG
2008 #12 Denny Hamlin NC HG
Wheels Autographs Chase Edition
2008 #4 Denny Hamlin NC
Wheels Autographs Press Plates Black
2007 #13 Denny Hamlin NC
2008 #12 Denny Hamlin NC HG
Wheels Autographs Press Plates Cyan
2007 #13 Denny Hamlin NC
2008 #12 Denny Hamlin NC HG
Wheels Autographs Press Plates Magenta
2007 #13 Denny Hamlin NC
2008 #12 Denny Hamlin NC HG
Wheels Autographs Press Plates Yellow
2007 #14 Denny Hamlin NC
2008 #12 Denny Hamlin NC HG
Wheels High Gear
2006 #32 Denny Hamlin NBS
2007 #3 Denny Hamlin
2007 #34 Denny Hamlin NBS
2007 #60 Denny Hamlin NA
2007 #65 Denny Hamlin NA
2007 #66 Denny Hamlin CM
2007 #3B Denny Hamlin blurred
2008 #12 Denny Hamlin
2008 #33 Denny Hamlin NBS
2008 #63 Denny Hamlin NA
Wheels High Gear Driven
2007 #DR9 Denny Hamlin
2008 #DR18 Denny Hamlin
Wheels High Gear Final Standings
2008 #F12 Denny Hamlin/12
Wheels High Gear Final Standings Gold
2007 #FS3 Denny Hamlin/3
Wheels High Gear Flag Chasers Black
2007 #FC6 Denny Hamlin
Wheels High Gear Flag Chasers Blue-Yellow
2007 #FC6 Denny Hamlin
Wheels High Gear Flag Chasers Checkered
2007 #FC6 Denny Hamlin
Wheels High Gear Flag Chasers Green
2007 #FC6 Denny Hamlin
Wheels High Gear Flag Chasers Red
2007 #FC6 Denny Hamlin
Wheels High Gear Flag Chasers White
2007 #FC6 Denny Hamlin
Wheels High Gear Flag Chasers Yellow
2007 #FC6 Denny Hamlin
Wheels High Gear Last Lap
2007 #LL7 Denny Hamlin
2008 #LL10 Denny Hamlin
Wheels High Gear Last Lap Holofoil
2008 #LL10 Denny Hamlin
Wheels High Gear MPH
2006 #M32 Denny Hamlin NBS
2007 #M3 Denny Hamlin
2007 #M34 Denny Hamlin NBS
2007 #M60 Denny Hamlin NA
2007 #M65 Denny Hamlin NA
2007 #M66 Denny Hamlin CM
2008 #M12 Denny Hamlin
2008 #M33 Denny Hamlin NBS
2008 #M63 Denny Hamlin NA
Wheels High Gear Previews
2007 #EB3 Denny Hamlin
2007 #EB34 Denny Hamlin NBS
2007 #EB60 Denny Hamlin NA
2007 #EB65 Denny Hamlin NA
2008 #EB12 Denny Hamlin
Wheels High Gear Previews Green
2006 #EB32 Denny Hamlin NBS
Wheels High Gear The Chase
2008 #TC12 Denny Hamlin
Wheels High Gear Top Tier
2007 #TT3 Denny Hamlin

Harvick, Kevin

Authentic Images Gold Signature
2002 #S9 K.Harvick White Car/5029
2002 #S13 Kevin Harvick Silver Car/5029
2002 #S16 Kevin Harvick First Win/5029
Authentic Images Gold Signature Metal Set
2002 #NAS13 Kevin Harvick Silver Car/2902
Coca-Cola Racing Family AutoZone
2005 #4 Kevin Harvick
eTopps
2003 #21 Kevin Harvick/4000
Maxx
2000 #63 Kevin Harvick RF
Maxximum
2000 #39 Kevin Harvick
Maxximum Die Cuts
2000 #39 Kevin Harvick
Maxximum MPH
2000 #39 Kevin Harvick/2
Maxximum Signatures
2000 #KH Kevin Harvick
Maxximum Young Lions
2000 #YL10 Kevin Harvick
McFarlane NASCAR Series 3
2005 #50 Kevin Harvick R
2005 #51 Kevin Harvick R Glasses
2005 #55 Kevin Harvick H Realtree
2005 #56 Kevin Harvick H Realtree with Glasses
McFarlane NASCAR Series 5
2005 #40 Kevin Harvick Reese's
2005 #50 Kevin Harvick Goodwrench
Nilla Wafers Team Nabisco
2003 #4 Earn.Jr./Green/Harvick/M.Walt
Press Pass
1999 #76 Kevin Harvick Champ RC
2001 #37 Kevin Harvick
2002 #13 Kevin Harvick
2002 #43 Kevin Harvick NBS
2002 #65 Kevin Harvick REP
2002 #85 Kevin Harvick's Car
2002 #98 Kevin Harvick BGN Champ
2003 #14 Kevin Harvick
2003 #56 Kevin Harvick DS
2003 #83 Defending his Turf WCS
2003 #93 Kevin Harvick's Car OTW
2004 #12 Kevin Harvick
2004 #70 Kevin Harvick's Car OTW
2004 #99 Kevin Harvick DS
2005 #21 Kevin Harvick
2005 #70 Kevin Harvick's Car OTW
2005 #93 Kevin Harvick Y
2006 #20 Kevin Harvick
2006 #79 Kevin Harvick's Car OTW
2006 #88 Kevin Harvick NS
2006 #107 Kevin Harvick U
2007 #3 Kevin Harvick
2007 #34 Kevin Harvick NBS
2007 #76 Kevin Harvick's car OT
2007 #93 K.Harvick/D.Harvick NS
2007 #97 Kevin Harvick U
2007 #110 Kevin Harvick TT
2008 #10 Kevin Harvick
2008 #75 Kevin Harvick's Car Mark Martin's Car NS
2008 #76 Kevin Harvick NS
2008 #80 Juan Pablo Montoya Kevin Harvick NS
2008 #88 Kevin Harvick's Car U
2008 #117 Kevin Harvick Top 12
2008 #0 Cup Chase Matt Kenseth Tony Stewart Jeff Gordon Jimmie Johnson Denny Hamlin Kurt Busch Kevin Harvick Carl Edwards Kyle Busch Martin Truex Jr. Jeff Burton Clint Bowyer
Press Pass Autographs
2001 #20 Kevin Harvick
2002 #26 Kevin Harvick
2003 #22 Kevin Harvick E/P
2004 #25 Kevin Harvick P
2005 #23 Kevin Harvick E/P
2006 #21 Kevin Harvick NC
2007 #17 Kevin Harvick NC P
2008 #17 Kevin Harvick NC P/E
Press Pass Autographs Press Plates Black
2007 #5 Kevin Harvick NC
2008 #13 Kevin Harvick NC E
Press Pass Autographs Press Plates Cyan
2007 #5 Kevin Harvick NC
2008 #13 Kevin Harvick NC P
Press Pass Autographs Press Plates Magenta
2007 #6 Kevin Harvick NC
2008 #13 Kevin Harvick NC E
Press Pass Autographs Press Plates Yellow
2007 #6 Kevin Harvick NC
2008 #13 Kevin Harvick NC P
Press Pass Blaster Kmart
2006 #KHC Kevin Harvick
Press Pass Blaster Target
2006 #KHB Kevin Harvick
Press Pass Blaster Wal-Mart
2006 #KHA Kevin Harvick
Press Pass Blue
2006 #B20 Kevin Harvick
2006 #B79 Kevin Harvick's Car OTW
2006 #B88 Kevin Harvick NS
2006 #B107 Kevin Harvick U
2007 #B3 Kevin Harvick
2007 #B34 Kevin Harvick NBS
2007 #B76 Kevin Harvick's car OT
2007 #B93 K.Harvick/D.Harvick NS
2007 #B97 Kevin Harvick U
2007 #B110 Kevin Harvick TT
2008 #B10 Kevin Harvick
2008 #B75 Kevin Harvick's Car Mark Martin's Car NS
2008 #B76 Kevin Harvick NS
2008 #B80 Juan Pablo Montoya Kevin Harvick NS
2008 #B88 Kevin Harvick's Car U
2008 #B117 Kevin Harvick Top 12
Press Pass Burning Rubber Autographs
2004 #BRKH Kevin Harvick/29
2005 #BR-KH Kevin Harvick/29
2006 #BR-KH Kevin Harvick/29
2007 #BRS-KH Kevin Harvick/29
2008 #BR-KH Kevin Harvick/29
Press Pass Burning Rubber Cars
2002 #BRC4 Kevin Harvick's Car
2003 #BRT3 Kevin Harvick's Car
2004 #BRT3 Kevin Harvick's Car
2005 #BRT3 Kevin Harvick's Car
2006 #BRT6 Kevin Harvick
Press Pass Burning Rubber Cars Autographs
2003 #BRT-KH Kevin Harvick/29
Press Pass Burning Rubber Drivers
2002 #BRD4 Kevin Harvick
2003 #BRD3 Kevin Harvick
2004 #BRD3 Kevin Harvick
2005 #BRD3 Kevin Harvick
2006 #BRD6 Kevin Harvick
2007 #BRD5 Kevin Harvick Phoenix 4-22
2007 #BRD17 Kevin Harvick Watkins Glen 8-13
2008 #BRD1 Kevin Harvick Daytona
Press Pass Burning Rubber Drivers Autographs
2003 #BRD-KH Kevin Harvick/29
Press Pass Burning Rubber Drivers Gold
2005 #BRD3 Kevin Harvick
2006 #BRD6 Kevin Harvick
2007 #BRD5 Kevin Harvick Phoenix 4-22
2007 #BRD17 Kevin Harvick Watkins Glen 8-13
2008 #BRD1 Kevin Harvick Daytona
Press Pass Burning Rubber Drivers Prime Cuts
2008 #BRD1 Kevin Harvick Daytona
Press Pass Burning Rubber Team
2007 #BRT5 Kevin Harvick Phoenix 4-22
2007 #BRT17 Kevin Harvick Watkins Glen 8-13
Press Pass Burning Rubber Teams
2008 #BRT1 Kevin Harvick Daytona
Press Pass Burnouts
2006 #HT4 Kevin Harvick
2007 #B03 Kevin Harvick
2008 #B03 Kevin Harvick
Press Pass Burnouts Blue
2007 #B03 Kevin Harvick
2008 #B03 Kevin Harvick
Press Pass Burnouts Gold
2007 #B03 Kevin Harvick
2008 #B03 Kevin Harvick
Press Pass Burnouts Holofoil
2006 #HT4 Kevin Harvick
Press Pass Coca-Cola Racing Family
2003 #5 Kevin Harvick
Press Pass Coca-Cola Racing Family Regional
2003 #4 Kevin Harvick
Press Pass Collector's Series Box Set
2007 #SB9 Kevin Harvick
Press Pass Collectors Series Making the Show
2006 #MS16 Kevin Harvick
Press Pass Collectors Series Sunday Best
2007 #CB9 Kevin Harvick
Press Pass Cup Chase
2002 #CC5 Kevin Harvick WIN
2003 #CCR5 Kevin Harvick WIN
2004 #CCR9 Kevin Harvick
2005 #CCR6 Kevin Harvick Winner
2006 #CCR14 Kevin Harvick Winner
2007 #CCR16 Kevin Harvick Winner
2008 #CC6 Kevin Harvick
Press Pass Cup Chase Prizes
2002 #CC5 Kevin Harvick
2003 #CCR5 Kevin Harvick
2004 #CCR9 Kevin Harvick
2005 #CCP6 Kevin Harvick
2006 #CC4 Kevin Harvick
2007 #CC11 Kevin Harvick
Press Pass Dale The Movie
2007 #45 Dale Earnhardt's Car Bobby Labonte's Car Kevin Harvick's Car Jeff Gordon's Car
2007 #46 Dale Earnhardt Jr.'s Car Kevin Harvick's Car Michael Waltrip's Car Jimmie Johnson's Car
Press Pass Daytona 500 50th Anniversary
2008 #44 Kevin Harvick '07
2008 #49 Kevin Harvick FF
Press Pass Double Burner
2002 #DB3 Kevin Harvick
2003 #DB3 Kevin Harvick
2004 #DB3 Kevin Harvick
2005 #DB3 Kevin Harvick
Press Pass Double Burner Exchange
2003 #DB3 Kevin Harvick EXCH
2004 #DB3 Kevin Harvick
2005 #DB3 Kevin Harvick
Press Pass Double Burner Firesuit-Glove
2006 #DB5 Kevin Harvick
Press Pass Double Burner Metal-Tire
2007 #DB-KH Kevin Harvick
Press Pass Double Burner Metal-Tire Exchange
2007 #DB-KH Kevin Harvick
Press Pass Eclipse
2002 #9 Kevin Harvick
2003 #20 Kevin Harvick
2004 #5 Kevin Harvick
2004 #35 Kevin Harvick's Car
2004 #59 Kevin Harvick P
2004 #71 Kevin Harvick WCS
2004 #74 Kevin Harvick LL
2004 #82 R.Gordon/K.Harvick LL
2005 #14 Kevin Harvick
2005 #59 Kevin Harvick P
2006 #13 Kevin Harvick
2006 #43 Kevin Harvick WS
2006 #84 Kevin Harvick LL
2007 #4 Kevin Harvick
2007 #39 Kevin Harvick TO
2007 #44 Kevin Harvick P
2007 #51 Kevin Harvick FP
2007 #65 Kevin Harvick NS
2007 #76 Kevin Harvick NYC
2007 #81 Kevin Harvick SM
2007 #0 Cup Chase 10
2007 #44B Kevin Harvick -official
2008 #9 Kevin Harvick
2008 #75 Top 10 Drivers SO
2008 #77 Kevin Harvick SO
Press Pass Eclipse Destination WIN
2004 #21 Kevin Harvick
Press Pass Eclipse Double Hot Treads
2003 #DT2 R.Gordon/K.Harvick
Press Pass Eclipse Ecliptic
2007 #EC11 Kevin Harvick
Press Pass Eclipse Escape Velocity
2008 #EV9 Kevin Harvick
Press Pass Eclipse Gold
2007 #G4 Kevin Harvick
2007 #G39 Kevin Harvick TO
2007 #G44 Kevin Harvick P
2007 #G51 Kevin Harvick FP
2007 #G65 Kevin Harvick NS
2007 #G76 Kevin Harvick NYC
2007 #G81 Kevin Harvick SM
2008 #G9 Kevin Harvick
2008 #G75 Top 10 Drivers SO
2008 #G77 Kevin Harvick SO
Press Pass Eclipse Hyperdrive
2005 #HD4 Kevin Harvick
2007 #HD4 Kevin Harvick
2008 #HP5 Kevin Harvick
Press Pass Eclipse Maxim
2004 #MX5 Kevin Harvick
Press Pass Eclipse Previews
2003 #20 Kevin Harvick
2004 #5 Kevin Harvick
2005 #EB14 Kevin Harvick
2005 #EB59 Kevin Harvick P
2006 #EB13 Kevin Harvick
2007 #EB4 Kevin Harvick
2007 #EB39 Kevin Harvick TO
2008 #EB9 Kevin Harvick
2008 #EB75 Top 10 Drivers SO
2008 #EB77 Kevin Harvick SO
Press Pass Eclipse Racing Champions
2002 #RC4 Kevin Harvick
2002 #RC18 Kevin Harvick
2003 #RC21 Kevin Harvick
2006 #RC5 Kevin Harvick
2006 #RC19 Kevin Harvick NBS
2007 #RC2 Kevin Harvick
2007 #RC13 Kevin Harvick
Press Pass Eclipse Red
2007 #R4 Kevin Harvick
2007 #R39 Kevin Harvick TO
2007 #R44 Kevin Harvick P
2007 #R51 Kevin Harvick FP
2007 #R65 Kevin Harvick NS
2007 #R76 Kevin Harvick NYC
2007 #R81 Kevin Harvick SM
2008 #R9 Kevin Harvick
2008 #R75 Top 10 Drivers SO
2008 #R77 Kevin Harvick SO
Press Pass Eclipse Samples
2002 #9 Kevin Harvick
2003 #20 Kevin Harvick
2004 #5 Kevin Harvick
2004 #35 Kevin Harvick's Car
2004 #59 Kevin Harvick P
2004 #71 Kevin Harvick WCS
2004 #74 Kevin Harvick LL
2004 #82 R.Gordon/K.Harvick LL
2005 #14 Kevin Harvick
2005 #59 Kevin Harvick P
Press Pass Eclipse Skidmarks
2002 #SK3 Kevin Harvick
2003 #SM13 Kevin Harvick
2004 #SM9 Kevin Harvick
2005 #SM9 Kevin Harvick
2006 #SM17 Kevin Harvick
2007 #SM3 Kevin Harvick
Press Pass Eclipse Skidmarks Holofoil
2004 #SM9 Kevin Harvick
2005 #SM9 Kevin Harvick
2006 #SM17 Kevin Harvick
2007 #SM3 Kevin Harvick
Press Pass Eclipse Solar Eclipse
2002 #S9 Kevin Harvick
2003 #P20 Kevin Harvick
Press Pass Eclipse Star Tracks
2008 #ST7 Kevin Harvick
Press Pass Eclipse Star Tracks Holofoil
2008 #ST7 Kevin Harvick
Press Pass Eclipse Stellar
2008 #ST9 Kevin Harvick
2008 #ST15 Kevin Harvick
Press Pass Eclipse Supernova
2002 #SN3 Kevin Harvick
2003 #SN4 Kevin Harvick
Press Pass Eclipse Supernova Numbered
2002 #SN3 Kevin Harvick
Press Pass Eclipse Teammates Autographs
2003 #KHRG K.Harvick/R.Gordon
2004 #1 R.Gordon/K.Harvick
2006 #8 K.Harvick/J.Burton
2007 #8 K.Harvick/C.Bowyer/J.Burton
2008 #BBH Clint Bowyer Jeff Burton Kevin Harvick
Press Pass Eclipse Under Cover Autographs
2004 #UCKH Kevin Harvick/29
2005 #UCKH Kevin Harvick/29
2006 #KH Kevin Harvick/29
Press Pass Eclipse Under Cover Cars
2003 #UCT3 Kevin Harvick
2004 #UCD3 Kevin Harvick
2005 #UCT3 Kevin Harvick
2006 #UCT12 Kevin Harvick
Press Pass Eclipse Under Cover Double Cover
2003 #DC8 K.Harvick/R.Gordon
2003 #DC9 K.Harvick/J.Green
2004 #DC11 K.Harvick/R.Gordon
Press Pass Eclipse Under Cover Double Cover Name
2008 #DC2 Kevin Harvick Jeff Burton
Press Pass Eclipse Under Cover Double Cover NASCAR
2008 #DC2 Kevin Harvick Jeff Burton
Press Pass Eclipse Under Cover Driver Gold
2003 #UCD3 Kevin Harvick
2004 #UCD3 Kevin Harvick
Press Pass Eclipse Under Cover Driver Red
2003 #UCD3 Kevin Harvick
2004 #UCD3 Kevin Harvick
2005 #UCD3 Kevin Harvick
Press Pass Eclipse Under Cover Driver Silver
2003 #UCD3 Kevin Harvick
2004 #UCD3 Kevin Harvick
Press Pass Eclipse Under Cover Drivers
2007 #UCD5 Kevin Harvick
2008 #UCD3 Kevin Harvick
Press Pass Eclipse Under Cover Drivers Eclipse
2007 #UCD5 Kevin Harvick
2008 #UCD3 Kevin Harvick
Press Pass Eclipse Under Cover Drivers Gold
2006 #UCD12 Kevin Harvick
Press Pass Eclipse Under Cover Drivers Holofoil
2005 #UCD3 Kevin Harvick
2006 #UCD12 Kevin Harvick
Press Pass Eclipse Under Cover Drivers Name
2007 #UCD5 Kevin Harvick
2008 #UCD3 Kevin Harvick
Press Pass Eclipse Under Cover Drivers NASCAR
2007 #UCD5 Kevin Harvick
2008 #UCD3 Kevin Harvick
Press Pass Eclipse Under Cover Drivers Silver
2005 #UCD3 Kevin Harvick
2006 #UCD12 Kevin Harvick
Press Pass Eclipse Under Cover Teams
2007 #UCT5 Kevin Harvick
2008 #UCT3 Kevin Harvick
Press Pass Eclipse Under Cover Teams NASCAR
2007 #UCT5 Kevin Harvick
2008 #UCT3 Kevin Harvick
Press Pass Eclipse Warp Speed
2002 #WS6 Kevin Harvick
Press Pass Four Wide
2006 #FW-KH Kevin Harvick
2007 #FW-KH Kevin Harvick
2008 #FW-KH Kevin Harvick
Press Pass Four Wide Checkered
2007 #FW-KH Kevin Harvick
2008 #FW-KH Kevin Harvick
Press Pass Four Wide Checkered Exchange
2007 #FW-KH Kevin Harvick
Press Pass Four Wide Checkered Flag
2006 #FW-KH Kevin Harvick
Press Pass Four Wide Exchange
2007 #FW-KH Kevin Harvick
Press Pass Game Face
2005 #GF4 Kevin Harvick
Press Pass Gold
2006 #G20 Kevin Harvick
2006 #G79 Kevin Harvick's Car OTW
2006 #G88 Kevin Harvick NS
2006 #G107 Kevin Harvick U
2007 #G3 Kevin Harvick
2007 #G34 Kevin Harvick NBS
2007 #G76 Kevin Harvick's car OT
2007 #G93 K.Harvick/D.Harvick NS
2007 #G97 Kevin Harvick U
2007 #G110 Kevin Harvick TT
2008 #G10 Kevin Harvick
2008 #G75 Kevin Harvick's Car Mark Martin's Car NS
2008 #G76 Kevin Harvick NS
2008 #G80 Juan Pablo Montoya Kevin Harvick NS
2008 #G88 Kevin Harvick's Car U
2008 #G117 Kevin Harvick Top 12
Press Pass Gold Holofoil
2003 #P14 Kevin Harvick
2003 #P56 Kevin Harvick DS
2003 #P83 Defending his Turf WCS
2003 #P93 Kevin Harvick's Car OTW
Press Pass Hot Treads
2002 #HT9 Kevin Harvick's Car/1555
2002 #HT38 Kevin Harvick's Car/900
2004 #HTR6 Kevin Harvick
2005 #HTR8 Kevin Harvick
2007 #HT6 Kevin Harvick
2008 #HT7 Kevin Harvick
Press Pass Hot Treads Blue
2007 #HT6 Kevin Harvick
2008 #HT7 Kevin Harvick
Press Pass Hot Treads Gold
2007 #HT6 Kevin Harvick
2008 #HT7 Kevin Harvick
Press Pass Hot Treads Holofoil
2004 #HTR6 Kevin Harvick
2005 #HTR8 Kevin Harvick
Press Pass Hot Treads Rookie Rubber
2001 #RR5 Kevin Harvick
Press Pass K-Mart
2007 #KH-C Kevin Harvick
Press Pass Legends
2006 #40 Kevin Harvick
2007 #45 Kevin Harvick
2007 #59 Kevin Harvick N
Press Pass Legends Autographs Black
2005 #16 Kevin Harvick
Press Pass Legends Autographs Blue
2006 #7 Kevin Harvick/50
2007 #11 Kevin Harvick/71
Press Pass Legends Blue
2006 #B40 Kevin Harvick
2007 #B45 Kevin Harvick
2007 #B59 Kevin Harvick N
Press Pass Legends Bronze
2006 #Z40 Kevin Harvick
2007 #Z45 Kevin Harvick
2007 #Z59 Kevin Harvick N
Press Pass Legends Gold
2006 #G40 Kevin Harvick
2007 #G45 Kevin Harvick
2007 #G59 Kevin Harvick N
Press Pass Legends Greatest Moments
2005 #GM16 Kevin Harvick
Press Pass Legends Holofoil
2006 #H40 Kevin Harvick
2007 #H45 Kevin Harvick
2007 #H59 Kevin Harvick N
Press Pass Legends Press Plates Black
2006 #PPB40 Kevin Harvick
2007 #PP45 Kevin Harvick
2007 #PP59 Kevin Harvick N
Press Pass Legends Press Plates Black Backs
2006 #PPB40B Kevin Harvick
2007 #PP45 Kevin Harvick
2007 #PP59 Kevin Harvick N
Press Pass Legends Press Plates Cyan
2006 #PPC40 Kevin Harvick
2007 #PP45 Kevin Harvick
2007 #PP59 Kevin Harvick N
Press Pass Legends Press Plates Cyan Backs
2006 #PPC40B Kevin Harvick
2007 #PP45 Kevin Harvick
2007 #PP59 Kevin Harvick N
Press Pass Legends Press Plates Magenta
2006 #PPM40 Kevin Harvick
2007 #PP45 Kevin Harvick
2007 #PP59 Kevin Harvick N
Press Pass Legends Press Plates Magenta Backs
2006 #PPM40B Kevin Harvick
2007 #PP45 Kevin Harvick
2007 #PP59 Kevin Harvick N
Press Pass Legends Press Plates Yellow
2006 #PPY40 Kevin Harvick
2007 #PP45 Kevin Harvick
2007 #PP59 Kevin Harvick N
Press Pass Legends Press Plates Yellow Backs
2006 #PPY40B Kevin Harvick
2007 #PP45 Kevin Harvick
2007 #PP59 Kevin Harvick N
Press Pass Legends Previews
2006 #EB40 Kevin Harvick
2007 #EB45 Kevin Harvick
Press Pass Legends Signature Series
2007 #KH Kevin Harvick
Press Pass Legends Solo
2006 #S40 Kevin Harvick
2007 #S45 Kevin Harvick
2007 #S59 Kevin Harvick N
Press Pass Legends Sunday Swatches Bronze
2007 #KH-SS Kevin Harvick
Press Pass Legends Sunday Swatches Gold
2007 #KH-SS Kevin Harvick
Press Pass Legends Sunday Swatches Silver
2007 #KH-SS Kevin Harvick
Press Pass Legends Triple Threads
2006 #TT-KH Kevin Harvick
Press Pass Legends Victory Lane Bronze
2007 #VL5 Kevin Harvick
Press Pass Legends Victory Lane Gold
2007 #VL5 Kevin Harvick
Press Pass Legends Victory Lane Silver
2007 #VL5 Kevin Harvick
Press Pass Making the Show Collector's Series
2004 #MS18 Kevin Harvick

Press Pass Millennium
2001 #37 Kevin Harvick
Press Pass Nabisco Albertsons
2002 #2 Kevin Harvick
Press Pass Optima
2000 #32 Kevin Harvick BGN
2001 #8 Kevin Harvick CRC
2001 #31 Kevin Harvick BGN
2001 #43 Kevin Harvick WCL
2001 #0 Kevin Harvick DD/550
2002 #12 Kevin Harvick
2002 #48 Kevin Harvick YG
2003 #9 Kevin Harvick
2003 #43 Kevin Harvick UC
2004 #8 Kevin Harvick
2004 #85 Kevin Harvick RR
2004 #89 Kevin Harvick SS
2005 #11 Kevin Harvick
2005 #91 Kevin Harvick's Car RTV
2006 #22 Kevin Harvick
2006 #38 Kevin Harvick NBS
2006 #88 Kevin Harvick RTV Wat. Glen
2006 #22B Kevin Harvick Chase
Press Pass Optima Cool Persistence
2001 #CP5 Kevin Harvick
2002 #CP4 Kevin Harvick
2003 #CP12 Kevin Harvick
2005 #CP9 Kevin Harvick
Press Pass Optima Fan Favorite
2002 #FF9 Kevin Harvick
2003 #FF9 Kevin Harvick
2004 #FF8 Kevin Harvick
2005 #FF10 Kevin Harvick
2006 #FF8 Kevin Harvick
Press Pass Optima G Force
2001 #GF7 Kevin Harvick
Press Pass Optima Gold
2001 #8 Kevin Harvick
2001 #31 Kevin Harvick BGN
2001 #43 Kevin Harvick WCL
2002 #12 Kevin Harvick
2002 #48 Kevin Harvick YG
2003 #G9 Kevin Harvick
2003 #G43 Kevin Harvick UC
2004 #G8 Kevin Harvick
2004 #G85 Kevin Harvick RR
2004 #G89 Kevin Harvick SS
2005 #G11 Kevin Harvick
2005 #G91 Kevin Harvick's Car RTV
2006 #G22 Kevin Harvick
2006 #G38 Kevin Harvick NBS
2006 #G88 Kevin Harvick RTV Wat. Glen
Press Pass Optima On the Edge
2001 #OE3 Kevin Harvick
Press Pass Optima Platinum
2000 #32 Kevin Harvick BGN
Press Pass Optima Previews
2003 #9 Kevin Harvick
2004 #EB8 Kevin Harvick
2005 #11 Kevin Harvick
2006 #EB22 Kevin Harvick
Press Pass Optima Promos
2002 #12 Kevin Harvick
2002 #48 Kevin Harvick YG
Press Pass Optima Q & A
2006 #QA5 Kevin Harvick
Press Pass Optima Race Used Lugnuts Autographs
2002 #LNDA7 Kevin Harvick/29
Press Pass Optima Race Used Lugnuts Cars
2001 #LNC6 Kevin Harvick's Car
2002 #LNC7 Kevin Harvick's Car
Press Pass Optima Race Used Lugnuts Drivers
2001 #LND5 Kevin Harvick
2002 #LND7 Kevin Harvick
Press Pass Optima Rookie Relics Cars
2006 #RRT11 Kevin Harvick
Press Pass Optima Rookie Relics Drivers
2006 #RRD11 Kevin Harvick
Press Pass Optima Samples
2002 #12 Kevin Harvick
2002 #48 Kevin Harvick YG
2003 #9 Kevin Harvick
2003 #43 Kevin Harvick UC
2004 #8 Kevin Harvick
2004 #85 Kevin Harvick RR
2004 #89 Kevin Harvick SS
2005 #11 Kevin Harvick
2005 #91 Kevin Harvick RTV
Press Pass Optima Thunder Bolts Cars
2003 #TBT3 Kevin Harvick's Car/20
2004 #TBT6 Kevin Harvick's Car
Press Pass Optima Thunder Bolts Cars Autographs
2003 #TBT-KH Kevin Harvick/29
Press Pass Optima Thunder Bolts Drivers
2003 #TBD3 Kevin Harvick/15
2004 #TBD6 Kevin Harvick
Press Pass Optima Thunder Bolts Drivers Autographs
2003 #TBD-KH Kevin Harvick/29
Press Pass Optima Up Close
2001 #UC3 Kevin Harvick
Press Pass Optima Young Guns
2003 #YG4 Kevin Harvick
Press Pass Panorama
2005 #PPP11 Kevin Harvick
2005 #PPP28 Kevin Harvick
Press Pass Platinum
2002 #13 Kevin Harvick
2002 #43 Kevin Harvick NBS
2002 #65 Kevin Harvick REP
2002 #85 Kevin Harvick's Car
2002 #98 Kevin Harvick NBS Champ
2004 #P12 Kevin Harvick
2004 #P70 Kevin Harvick's Car OTW
2004 #P99 Kevin Harvick DS
2005 #P21 Kevin Harvick
2005 #P70 Kevin Harvick's Car OTW
2005 #P93 Kevin Harvick Y
2006 #P20 Kevin Harvick
2006 #P79 Kevin Harvick's Car OTW
2006 #P88 Kevin Harvick NS
2006 #P107 Kevin Harvick U
2007 #P3 Kevin Harvick
2007 #P34 Kevin Harvick NBS
2007 #P76 Kevin Harvick's car OT
2007 #P93 K.Harvick/D.Harvick NS
2007 #P97 Kevin Harvick U
2007 #P110 Kevin Harvick TT
2008 #P10 Kevin Harvick
2008 #P75 Kevin Harvick's Car Mark Martin's Car NS
2008 #P76 Kevin Harvick NS
2008 #P80 Juan Pablo Montoya Kevin Harvick NS
2008 #P88 Kevin Harvick's Car U
2008 #P117 Kevin Harvick Top 12
Press Pass Premium
2001 #43 Kevin Harvick CRC
2001 #49 Kevin Harvick
2002 #11 Kevin Harvick
2002 #39 Kevin Harvick's Car
2002 #61 Kevin Harvick CH
2002 #73 Kevin Harvick PC
2003 #11 Kevin Harvick
2003 #38 Kevin Harvick's Car
2003 #60 Kevin Harvick CC
2004 #3 Kevin Harvick
2004 #43 Kevin Harvick's Car
2004 #60 Kevin Harvick CC
2004 #77 Kevin Harvick PC
2005 #9 Kevin Harvick
2005 #43 Kevin Harvick's Car M
2005 #66 Kevin Harvick CC
2005 #78 Kevin Harvick PC
2006 #10 Kevin Harvick
2006 #44 Kevin Harvick's Car M
2006 #68 Kevin Harvick C
2007 #23 Kevin Harvick
2007 #36 Kevin Harvick's Car M
2007 #51 Kevin Harvick SW
2007 #0 Kevin Harvick Daytona
2008 #22 Kevin Harvick
2008 #38 Kevin Harvick's Car M
2008 #66 Kevin Harvick EOP
Press Pass Premium Asphalt Jungle
2004 #A6 Kevin Harvick
Press Pass Premium Clean Air
2008 #CA6 Kevin Harvick
Press Pass Premium Gold
2001 #43 Kevin Harvick
2001 #49 Kevin Harvick
Press Pass Premium Hot Threads Autographs
2004 #HT-KH Kevin Harvick/29
2006 #HT-KH Kevin Harvick/29
2008 #HTKH Kevin Harvick/29
Press Pass Premium Hot Threads Cars
2003 #HTT3 Kevin Harvick
2005 #HTT8 Kevin Harvick
2006 #HTT6 Kevin Harvick
Press Pass Premium Hot Threads Cars Autographs
2003 #HTD-KH Kevin Harvick/29
Press Pass Premium Hot Threads Drivers
2003 #HTD3 Kevin Harvick
2005 #HTD8 Kevin Harvick
2006 #HTD6 Kevin Harvick
2008 #HTD1 Kevin Harvick
Press Pass Premium Hot Threads Drivers Autographs
2003 #HTT-KH Kevin Harvick/29
Press Pass Premium Hot Threads Drivers Bronze
2004 #HTD3 Kevin Harvick
Press Pass Premium Hot Threads Drivers Bronze Retail
2004 #HTT3 Kevin Harvick
Press Pass Premium Hot Threads Drivers Gold
2004 #HTD3 Kevin Harvick
2005 #HTD8 Kevin Harvick
2006 #HTD6 Kevin Harvick
2008 #HTD1 Kevin Harvick
Press Pass Premium Hot Threads Drivers Silver
2004 #HTD3 Kevin Harvick
Press Pass Premium Hot Threads Patches
2008 #HTP9 Kevin Harvick Pennzoil
2008 #HTP10 Kevin Harvick Saftey Kleen/6
2008 #HTP11 Kevin Harvick U.S. Flag/6
Press Pass Premium Hot Threads Team
2008 #HTT1 Kevin Harvick
Press Pass Premium In The Zone
2002 #IZ5 Kevin Harvick
2005 #IZ6 Kevin Harvick
2006 #IZ8 Kevin Harvick
Press Pass Premium In the Zone Elite Edition
2005 #IZ6 Kevin Harvick
Press Pass Premium In the Zone Red
2006 #IZ8 Kevin Harvick
Press Pass Premium Performance Driven
2002 #PD3 Kevin Harvick
2005 #PD3 Kevin Harvick
Press Pass Premium Previews
2003 #11 Kevin Harvick
2004 #3 Kevin Harvick
2008 #EB22 Kevin Harvick
2008 #EB66 Kevin Harvick EOP
Press Pass Premium Red
2007 #R23 Kevin Harvick
2007 #R36 Kevin Harvick's Car M
2007 #R51 Kevin Harvick SW
2008 #22 Kevin Harvick
2008 #38 Kevin Harvick's Car M
2008 #66 Kevin Harvick EOP
Press Pass Premium Red Reflectors
2002 #11 Kevin Harvick
2002 #39 Kevin Harvick's Car
2002 #61 Kevin Harvick CH
2002 #73 Kevin Harvick PC
2003 #11 Kevin Harvick
2003 #38 Kevin Harvick's Car
2003 #60 Kevin Harvick CC
Press Pass Premium Samples
2002 #11 Kevin Harvick
2002 #39 Kevin Harvick's Car
2003 #11 Kevin Harvick
2003 #38 Kevin Harvick's Car
2004 #3 Kevin Harvick
2004 #43 Kevin Harvick's Car
2005 #9 Kevin Harvick
2005 #43 Kevin Harvick's Car M
Press Pass Premium Target
2008 #TA3 Kevin Harvick
Press Pass Previews
2003 #14 Kevin Harvick
2004 #12 Kevin Harvick
2006 #EB20 Kevin Harvick
2006 #EB107 Kevin Harvick U
2007 #EB3 Kevin Harvick
2007 #EB34 Kevin Harvick NBS
2007 #EB110 Kevin Harvick TT
2008 #EB10 Kevin Harvick
2008 #EB117 Kevin Harvick Top 12
Press Pass Previews Green
2005 #EB21 Kevin Harvick
Press Pass Race Day
2007 #RD4 Kevin Harvick
Press Pass Samples
2003 #14 Kevin Harvick
2003 #56 Kevin Harvick DS
2003 #83 Defending his Turf WCS
2003 #93 Kevin Harvick's Car OTW
2004 #12 Kevin Harvick
2004 #70 Kevin Harvick's Car OTW
2004 #99 Kevin Harvick DS
2005 #21 Kevin Harvick
2005 #70 Kevin Harvick's Car OTW
2005 #93 Kevin Harvick Y
Press Pass Showcar
2002 #S4A Kevin Harvick's Car
2003 #S4B Kevin Harvick
2005 #SC8 Kevin Harvick
Press Pass Showman
2002 #S4A Kevin Harvick
2003 #S4A Kevin Harvick
2005 #SM8 Kevin Harvick
Press Pass Signings
2001 #21 Kevin Harvick BGN P/V/S
2001 #22 Kevin Harvick WC V/S
2002 #26 Kevin Harvick O/P/S/T/V
2003 #29 Kevin Harvick O/P/S/T/V
2004 #26 Kevin Harvick O/P/S/T/V
2005 #22 Kevin Harvick P/S
2006 #21 Kevin Harvick NC P/S
2007 #26 Kevin Harvick NC
2008 #24 Kevin Harvick
Press Pass Signings Blue
2007 #11 Kevin Harvick NC
2008 #10 Kevin Harvick
Press Pass Signings Gold
2001 #14 Kevin Harvick WC V/S
2002 #24 Kevin Harvick O/P/S/T/V
2003 #29 Kevin Harvick O/P/S/T/V
2004 #24 Kevin Harvick O/P/S/T/V
2005 #21 Kevin Harvick P/S
2006 #18 Kevin Harvick NC P/S
2007 #21 Kevin Harvick NC
2008 #19 Kevin Harvick
Press Pass Signings Platinum
2005 #21 Kevin Harvick P/S
Press Pass Signings Press Plates Black
2007 #19 Kevin Harvick
2008 #17 Kevin Harvick
Press Pass Signings Press Plates Cyan
2007 #18 Kevin Harvick
2008 #17 Kevin Harvick
Press Pass Signings Press Plates Magenta
2007 #18 Kevin Harvick
2008 #17 Kevin Harvick
Press Pass Signings Press Plates Yellow
2007 #18 Kevin Harvick
2008 #17 Kevin Harvick
Press Pass Signings Red Ink
2006 #7 Kevin Harvick
Press Pass Signings Silver
2006 #21 Kevin Harvick NC P/S
2007 #20 Kevin Harvick NC
2008 #17 Kevin Harvick
Press Pass Signings Transparent
2002 #3 Kevin Harvick O/P/S/T/V
2003 #3 Kevin Harvick O/P/S/T/V
2004 #2 Kevin Harvick O/P/S/T
Press Pass Skidmarks
1999 #76 Kevin Harvick Champ
Press Pass Snapshots
2003 #SN9 Kevin Harvick
2004 #SN9 Kevin Harvick
2005 #SN10 Kevin Harvick
2007 #SN11 Kevin Harvick
Press Pass Speedway
2008 #6 Kevin Harvick
2008 #59 Kevin Harvick SH
2008 #67 Kevin Harvick UTH
2008 #96 Jeff Burton's Car Kevin Harvick's Car Clint Bowyer's Car H
Press Pass Speedway Blur
2008 #B9 Kevin Harvick
Press Pass Speedway Cockpit
2008 #CP8 Kevin Harvick
Press Pass Speedway Corporate Cuts Drivers
2008 #CD-KH Kevin Harvick
Press Pass Speedway Corporate Cuts Drivers Patches
2008 #CD-KH Kevin Harvick
Press Pass Speedway Corporate Cuts Team
2008 #CT-KH Kevin Harvick
Press Pass Speedway Gold
2008 #G6 Kevin Harvick
2008 #G59 Kevin Harvick SH
2008 #G67 Kevin Harvick UTH
2008 #G96 Jeff Burton's Car Kevin Harvick's Car Clint Bowyer's Car H
Press Pass Speedway Holofoil
2008 #H6 Kevin Harvick
2008 #H59 Kevin Harvick SH
2008 #H67 Kevin Harvick UTH
2008 #H96 Jeff Burton's Car Kevin Harvick's Car Clint Bowyer's Car H
Press Pass Speedway Previews
2008 #EB6 Kevin Harvick
2008 #EB96 Jeff Burton's Car Kevin Harvick's Car Clint Bowyer's Car H
Press Pass Speedway Red
2008 #R6 Kevin Harvick
2008 #R59 Kevin Harvick SH
2008 #R67 Kevin Harvick UTH
2008 #R96 Jeff Burton's Car Kevin Harvick's Car Clint Bowyer's Car H
Press Pass Stealth
2000 #62 Kevin Harvick BGN
2001 #34 Kevin Harvick CRC
2001 #35 Kevin Harvick's Car
2001 #36 Kevin Harvick
2001 #50 Kevin Harvick BGN
2001 #68 Kevin Harvick SST
2002 #31 Kevin Harvick
2002 #32 Kevin Harvick's Car
2002 #33 Kevin Harvick
2002 #53 Kevin Harvick's Car SST
2002 #65 Kevin Harvick WW
2004 #19 Kevin Harvick
2004 #20 Kevin Harvick's Car
2004 #21 Kevin Harvick
2004 #76 Kevin Harvick WW
2004 #87 Kevin Harvick SST
2004 #93 Kevin Harvick SF
2004 #100 Kevin Harvick CL
2005 #47 Kevin Harvick
2005 #50 Kevin Harvick's Car
2005 #53 Kevin Harvick
2005 #88 Kevin Harvick H
2005 #99 Kevin Harvick SF
2006 #11 Kevin Harvick
2006 #39 Kevin Harvick's Rig
2006 #50 Harvick/Burton/Bowyer TM
2006 #66 Kevin Harvick F
2006 #69 Kevin Harvick DD
2007 #10 Kevin Harvick
2007 #40 Kevin Harvick NBS
2007 #64 Bowyer/Harvick/Burton
2007 #77 Kevin Harvick DD
2007 #86 Kevin Harvick PO
2008 #13 Kevin Harvick
2008 #42 Kevin Harvick NNS
2008 #51 Kevin Harvick's Rig C
2008 #69 Jeff Burton Clint Bowyer Kevin Harvick
2008 #78 Kevin Harvick DO
2008 #86 Kevin Harvick PM
Press Pass Stealth Autographed Hat Entry
2006 #PPH8 Kevin Harvick
Press Pass Stealth Battle Armor Autographs
2008 #BASKH Kevin Harvick/29
Press Pass Stealth Battle Armor Drivers
2008 #BAD17 Kevin Harvick
Press Pass Stealth Battle Armor Teams
2008 #BAT17 Kevin Harvick
Press Pass Stealth Behind The Numbers
2001 #BN1 Kevin Harvick
2002 #BN1 Kevin Harvick
Press Pass Stealth Chrome
2007 #10 Kevin Harvick
2007 #40 Kevin Harvick NBS
2007 #64 Bowyer/Harvick/Burton
2007 #77 Kevin Harvick DD w/w/sil stripes
2007 #86 Kevin Harvick PO
2007 #77A Kevin Harvick DD L1 w/sil/w stripes
2008 #13 Kevin Harvick
2008 #42 Kevin Harvick NNS
2008 #51 Kevin Harvick's Rig C
2008 #69 Jeff Burton Clint Bowyer Kevin Harvick
2008 #78 Kevin Harvick DO
2008 #86 Kevin Harvick PM
2008 #69B Jeff Burton Kevin Harvick Clint Bowyer VAR
Press Pass Stealth Chrome Exclusives
2007 #X10 Kevin Harvick
2007 #X40 Kevin Harvick NBS
2007 #X64 Bowyer/Harvick/Burton
2007 #X77 Kevin Harvick DD
2007 #X86 Kevin Harvick PO
2008 #13 Kevin Harvick
2008 #42 Kevin Harvick NNS
2008 #51 Kevin Harvick's Rig C
2008 #69 Jeff Burton Clint Bowyer Kevin Harvick
2008 #78 Kevin Harvick DO
2008 #86 Kevin Harvick PM
Press Pass Stealth Chrome Exclusives Gold
2008 #13 Kevin Harvick
2008 #42 Kevin Harvick NNS
2008 #51 Kevin Harvick's Rig C
2008 #69 Jeff Burton Clint Bowyer Kevin Harvick
2008 #78 Kevin Harvick DO
2008 #86 Kevin Harvick PM
Press Pass Stealth Chrome Platinum
2007 #P10 Kevin Harvick
2007 #P40 Kevin Harvick NBS
2007 #P64 Bowyer/Harvick/Burton
2007 #P77 Kevin Harvick DD
2007 #P86 Kevin Harvick PO
Press Pass Stealth EFX
2002 #FX6 Kevin Harvick
2005 #EFX9 Kevin Harvick
Press Pass Stealth Fusion
2002 #F4 Kevin Harvick
2003 #FU5 Kevin Harvick
2005 #FU10 Kevin Harvick 1:14
2007 #F9 Kevin Harvick
Press Pass Stealth Gear Grippers Autographs
2004 #HT-KH Kevin Harvick/29
2005 #GG-KH Kevin Harvick/29
2006 #KH Kevin Harvick/29
Press Pass Stealth Gear Grippers Cars
2003 #GGT3 Kevin Harvick
2005 #GGT3 Kevin Harvick
Press Pass Stealth Gear Grippers Cars Autographs
2003 #KH Kevin Harvick/29
Press Pass Stealth Gear Grippers Drivers
2003 #GGD3 Kevin Harvick
2004 #GGD3 Kevin Harvick
2005 #GGD3 Kevin Harvick
2006 #GGD8 Kevin Harvick
Press Pass Stealth Gear Grippers Drivers Autographs
2003 #KH Kevin Harvick/29
Press Pass Stealth Gear Grippers Drivers Retail
2004 #GGT3 Kevin Harvick
Press Pass Stealth Gold
2002 #31 Kevin Harvick
2002 #32 Kevin Harvick's Car
2002 #33 Kevin Harvick
2002 #53 Kevin Harvick's Car SST
2002 #65 Kevin Harvick WW
Press Pass Stealth Holofoils
2001 #34 Kevin Harvick
2001 #35 Kevin Harvick
2001 #36 Kevin Harvick
2001 #50 Kevin Harvick BGN
2001 #68 Kevin Harvick SST
Press Pass Stealth Hot Pass
2006 #HP12 Kevin Harvick
Press Pass Stealth Lap Leaders
2001 #LL12 Kevin Harvick
2001 #LL30 Kevin Harvick's Car
2002 #LL11 Kevin Harvick
Press Pass Stealth Lap Leaders Clear Cars
2001 #LL30 Kevin Harvick's Car
Press Pass Stealth Lap Leaders Clear Drivers
2001 #LL12 Kevin Harvick
Press Pass Stealth Mach 07
2007 #M7-7 Kevin Harvick
Press Pass Stealth Mach 08
2008 #M8-7 Kevin Harvick
Press Pass Stealth Maximum Access
2007 #MA11 Kevin Harvick
2008 #MA12 Kevin Harvick
Press Pass Stealth Maximum Access Autographs
2007 #MA11 Kevin Harvick
2008 #MA12 Kevin Harvick
Press Pass Stealth No Boundaries
2003 #NB13 Kevin Harvick
2004 #NB13 Kevin Harvick
2005 #NB13 Kevin Harvick
Press Pass Stealth Previews
2004 #EB19 Kevin Harvick
2004 #EB20 Kevin Harvick's Car
2004 #EB21 Kevin Harvick
2005 #47 Kevin Harvick
2005 #50 Kevin Harvick's Car
2005 #53 Kevin Harvick
2006 #11 Kevin Harvick
2007 #EB10 Kevin Harvick
2007 #EB40 Kevin Harvick NBS
2007 #EB86 Kevin Harvick PO
2008 #13 Kevin Harvick
2008 #42 Kevin Harvick NNS
2008 #86 Kevin Harvick PM
Press Pass Stealth Profile
2001 #SP2 Kevin Harvick
2002 #P4 Kevin Harvick
2005 #PR7 Kevin Harvick
2006 #P9 Kevin Harvick
Press Pass Stealth Race Used Glove Cars
2001 #RGC11 Kevin Harvick/120
2002 #GLC10 Kevin Harvick's Car
Press Pass Stealth Race Used Glove Drivers
2001 #RGD11 Kevin Harvick/120
2002 #GLD10 Kevin Harvick
Press Pass Stealth Retail
2006 #11 Kevin Harvick
2006 #39 Kevin Harvick's Rig
2006 #50 Harvick/Burton/Bowyer TM
2006 #66 Kevin Harvick F
2006 #69 Kevin Harvick DD
Press Pass Stealth Retail Gear Grippers Cars
2006 #GGT8 Kevin Harvick
Press Pass Stealth Samples
2002 #31 Kevin Harvick
2002 #32 Kevin Harvick's Car
2002 #33 Kevin Harvick
2002 #53 Kevin Harvick's Car SST
2002 #65 Kevin Harvick WW
2004 #X19 Kevin Harvick
2004 #X20 Kevin Harvick's Car
2004 #X21 Kevin Harvick
2004 #X76 Kevin Harvick WW
2004 #X87 Kevin Harvick SST
2004 #X93 Kevin Harvick SF
2004 #X100 Kevin Harvick CL
2005 #47 Kevin Harvick
2005 #50 Kevin Harvick's Car
2005 #53 Kevin Harvick
2005 #88 Kevin Harvick H
2005 #99 Kevin Harvick SF
Press Pass Stealth X-Ray
2004 #19 Kevin Harvick
2004 #20 Kevin Harvick's Car
2004 #21 Kevin Harvick
2004 #76 Kevin Harvick WW
2004 #87 Kevin Harvick SST
2004 #93 Kevin Harvick SF
2004 #100 Kevin Harvick CL
2005 #X47 Kevin Harvick
2005 #X50 Kevin Harvick's Car
2005 #X53 Kevin Harvick
2005 #X88 Kevin Harvick H
2005 #X99 Kevin Harvick SF
2006 #X11 Kevin Harvick
2006 #X39 Kevin Harvick's Rig
2006 #X50 Harvick/Burton/Bowyer TM
2006 #X66 Kevin Harvick F
2006 #X69 Kevin Harvick DD
Press Pass Target
2007 #KH-B Kevin Harvick
Press Pass Target Race Win Tires
2007 #RW2 Kevin Harvick Phoenix 4-22
Press Pass Target Victory Tires
2008 #TT-KH Kevin Harvick Daytona
Press Pass Top 25 Drivers & Rides
2006 #C15 Kevin Harvick's Car
2006 #D15 Kevin Harvick
Press Pass Top Shelf
2002 #TS3 Kevin Harvick
2003 #TS10 Kevin Harvick
2004 #TS2 Kevin Harvick
Press Pass Total Memorabilia Power Pick
2002 #TM3 Kevin Harvick
2003 #TM3 Kevin Harvick
2004 #TM3 Kevin Harvick
2005 #TM3 Kevin Harvick
Press Pass Trackside
2001 #5 Kevin Harvick CRC
2001 #53 Kevin Harvick
2001 #64 Kevin Harvick TM
2002 #6 Kevin Harvick
2002 #54 Kevin Harvick RD
2003 #23 Kevin Harvick
2003 #68 Kevin Harvick in Pits
2004 #22 Kevin Harvick
2004 #59 Kevin Harvick's Car HS
2004 #71 R.Gord/K.Harv/Jo.Sauter TM
2004 #102 Kevin Harvick TT
2004 #115 Kevin Harvick F
2004 #115B Kevin Harvick F blue sky
2005 #4 Kevin Harvick
2005 #62 Kevin Harvick's Car HS
2005 #72 Blaney/J.Burton/Harvick TM
2005 #85 Kevin Harvick GP
Press Pass Trackside Dialed In
2002 #DI4 Kevin Harvick
2005 #DI2 Kevin Harvick
Press Pass Trackside Die Cuts
2001 #5 Kevin Harvick
2001 #53 Kevin Harvick
2001 #64 Kevin Harvick TM
Press Pass Trackside Generation Now
2002 #GN1 Kevin Harvick
Press Pass Trackside Gold Holofoil
2003 #P23 Kevin Harvick
2003 #P68 Kevin Harvick's Crew
Press Pass Trackside Golden
2001 #5 Kevin Harvick
2001 #53 Kevin Harvick
2001 #64 Kevin Harvick TM
2002 #G6 Kevin Harvick
2003 #G23 Kevin Harvick
2004 #G22 Kevin Harvick
2004 #G59 Kevin Harvick's Car HS
2004 #G71 R.Gordon/Harvick/Jo.Sauter TM
2004 #G102 Kevin Harvick TT
2004 #G115 Kevin Harvick F
2005 #G4 Kevin Harvick
2005 #G62 Kevin Harvick's Car HS
2005 #G72 Blaney/J.Burton/Harvick TM
2005 #G85 Kevin Harvick GP
Press Pass Trackside Hat Giveaway
2003 #PPH10 Kevin Harvick
2004 #PPH10 Kevin Harvick
2005 #PPH10 Kevin Harvick
Press Pass Trackside Hot Pass
2004 #HP21 Kevin Harvick BGN
2005 #6 Kevin Harvick
Press Pass Trackside Hot Pass National
2004 #HP21 Kevin Harvick BGN
2005 #6 Kevin Harvick
Press Pass Trackside Hot Pursuit
2003 #HP4 Kevin Harvick
2004 #HP9 Kevin Harvick
2005 #HP1 Kevin Harvick
Press Pass Trackside License to Drive
2002 #13 Kevin Harvick
Press Pass Trackside License to Drive Die Cuts
2002 #13 Kevin Harvick
Press Pass Trackside Mirror Image
2002 #MI3 Kevin Harvick
Press Pass Trackside Pit Stoppers Autographs
2004 #PS-KH Kevin Harvick/29
Press Pass Trackside Pit Stoppers Cars
2002 #PSC5 Kevin Harvick's Car/200
2003 #PST3 Kevin Harvick
2004 #PST3 Kevin Harvick
Press Pass Trackside Pit Stoppers Cars Autographs
2003 #KH Kevin Harvick/29
Press Pass Trackside Pit Stoppers Drivers
2002 #PSD5 Kevin Harvick/100
2003 #PSD3 Kevin Harvick
2004 #PSD3 Kevin Harvick/40
Press Pass Trackside Pit Stoppers Drivers Autographs
2003 #PSD-KH Kevin Harvick/29
Press Pass Trackside Previews
2003 #23 Kevin Harvick
2004 #EB22 Kevin Harvick
2005 #4 Kevin Harvick
2005 #85 Kevin Harvick GP
Press Pass Trackside Runnin N' Gunnin
2001 #RG8 Kevin Harvick
2002 #RG3 Kevin Harvick
2003 #RG11 Kevin Harvick
2005 #RG11 Kevin Harvick
Press Pass Trackside Samples
2002 #6 Kevin Harvick
2002 #54 Kevin Harvick RD
2003 #23 Kevin Harvick
2003 #68 Kevin Harvick in Pits
2004 #22 Kevin Harvick
2004 #59 Kevin Harvick's Car HS
2004 #71 R.Gordon/Harvick/Jo.Sauter TM
2004 #102 Kevin Harvick TT
2004 #115 Kevin Harvick F
2005 #4 Kevin Harvick
2005 #62 Kevin Harvick's Car HS
2005 #72 Blaney/J.Burton/Harvick TM
2005 #85 Kevin Harvick GP
Press Pass Triple Burner
2002 #TB3 Kevin Harvick
2003 #TB3 Kevin Harvick
2004 #TB3 Kevin Harvick
2005 #TB3 Kevin Harvick
Press Pass Triple Burner Exchange
2003 #TB3 Kevin Harvick EXCH
2004 #TB3 Kevin Harvick
2005 #TB3 Kevin Harvick
Press Pass Velocity
2002 #VL4 Kevin Harvick
2004 #VC3 Kevin Harvick
Press Pass Vintage
2002 #VN9 Kevin Harvick
Press Pass Wal-Mart
2007 #KH-A Kevin Harvick
Press Pass Wal-Mart Autographs
2007 #KH Kevin Harvick
2008 #5 Kevin Harvick
Press Pass Weekend Warriors
2008 #WW4 Kevin Harvick
SP Authentic
2000 #44 Kevin Harvick
2000 #74 Kevin Harvick PER
SP Authentic Overdrive Gold
2000 #44 Kevin Harvick/2
2000 #74 Kevin Harvick PER/2
SP Authentic Overdrive Silver
2000 #44 Kevin Harvick
2000 #74 Kevin Harvick PER
SP Authentic Sign of the Times
2000 #KH Kevin Harvick
SP Authentic Sign of the Times Gold
2000 #KH Kevin Harvick
Super Shots California Speedway
2002 #CS1 Kevin Harvick's Car
Super Shots Sears Point CHP

2001 #SP5 Kevin Harvick's Car
TRAKS
2006 #13 Kevin Harvick
2006 #48 Kevin Harvick's Car
2006 #105 Kevin Harvick's Car PS
2007 #10 Kevin Harvick
2007 #78 Kevin Harvick GP
2007 #88 Kevin Harvick's Car NFS
TRAKS Autographs
2006 #14 Kevin Harvick NC SP
TRAKS Autographs 100
2006 #8 Kevin Harvick NC
TRAKS Autographs 25
2006 #12 Kevin Harvick NC
Traks Driver's Seat
2007 #DS12 Kevin Harvick
2007 #DS12B Kevin Harvick VAR
Traks Driver's Seat National
2007 #DS12 Kevin Harvick
Traks Gold
2007 #G10 Kevin Harvick
2007 #G78 Kevin Harvick GP
2007 #G88 Kevin Harvick's Car NFS
Traks Holofoil
2007 #H10 Kevin Harvick
2007 #H78 Kevin Harvick GP
2007 #H88 Kevin Harvick's Car NFS
Traks Hot Pursuit
2007 #HP12 Kevin Harvick
Traks Previews
2007 #EB10 Kevin Harvick
2007 #EB78 Kevin Harvick GP
Traks Red
2007 #R10 Kevin Harvick
2007 #R78 Kevin Harvick GP
2007 #R88 Kevin Harvick's Car NFS
TRAKS Stickers
2006 #29 Kevin Harvick
Traks Target Exclusives
2007 #KH-A Kevin Harvick
Traks Track Time
2007 #TT3 Kevin Harvick
Traks Wal-Mart Exclusives
2007 #KH-B Kevin Harvick
Upper Deck Racing
2000 #39 Kevin Harvick
Upper Deck Racing Road Signs
2000 #RSKH Kevin Harvick
Upper Deck Twizzlers
2002 #9 Kevin Harvick
2002 #10 Kevin Harvick
VIP
2001 #10 Kevin Harvick CRC
2001 #22 Kevin Harvick SM
2002 #13 Kevin Harvick
2002 #29 Kevin Harvick AS
2003 #6 Kevin Harvick
2004 #6 Kevin Harvick
2004 #30 Kevin Harvick's Car R
2005 #9 Kevin Harvick
2005 #47 Kevin Harvick SG
2006 #9 Kevin Harvick
2006 #31 Kevin Harvick's Car R
2006 #47 Kevin Harvick SG
2006 #78 Kevin Harvick AS
2006 #87 Kevin Harvick IF
2007 #12 Kevin Harvick
2007 #59 Kevin Harvick Red C
2007 #69 Kevin Harvick Daytona AP
VIP Driver's Choice
2001 #DC7 Kevin Harvick
2002 #DC7 Kevin Harvick
VIP Driver's Choice Precious Metal
2001 #DC7 Kevin Harvick
VIP Driver's Choice Transparent
2001 #DC7 Kevin Harvick
2002 #DC7 Kevin Harvick
VIP Driver's Choice Transparent LTD
2002 #DC7 Kevin Harvick
VIP Explosives
2001 #10 Kevin Harvick
2001 #22 Kevin Harvick SM
2002 #X13 Kevin Harvick
2002 #X29 Kevin Harvick AS
2003 #X6 Kevin Harvick
VIP Explosives Lasers
2001 #LX10 Kevin Harvick
2001 #LX22 Kevin Harvick SM
2002 #LX13 Kevin Harvick
2002 #LX29 Kevin Harvick AS
VIP Gear Gallery
2007 #GG2 Kevin Harvick
VIP Gear Gallery Transparent
2007 #GG2 Kevin Harvick
VIP Get A Grip Autographs
2007 #GG-KH Kevin Harvick/29
VIP Get A Grip Drivers
2007 #GGD18 Kevin Harvick
VIP Get A Grip Teams
2007 #GGT18 Kevin Harvick
VIP Head Gear
2001 #HG3 Kevin Harvick
2002 #HG3 Kevin Harvick
2004 #HG3 Kevin Harvick
2005 #3 Kevin Harvick
2006 #HG10 Kevin Harvick
VIP Head Gear Die Cuts
2001 #HG3 Kevin Harvick
2002 #HG3 Kevin Harvick
VIP Head Gear Transparent
2004 #HG3 Kevin Harvick
2005 #3 Kevin Harvick
2006 #HG10 Kevin Harvick
VIP Laser Explosive
2003 #LX6 Kevin Harvick
VIP Making the Show
2001 #15 Kevin Harvick
2002 #MS15 Kevin Harvick
2003 #MS15 Kevin Harvick
2004 #MS18 Kevin Harvick
2005 #18 Kevin Harvick
2006 #MS16 Kevin Harvick
VIP Mile Masters
2001 #MM12 Kevin Harvick
2002 #MM12 Kevin Harvick
VIP Mile Masters Precious Metal
2001 #MM12 Kevin Harvick
VIP Mile Masters Transparent
2001 #MM12 Kevin Harvick
2002 #MM12 Kevin Harvick
VIP Mile Masters Transparent LTD
2002 #MM12 Kevin Harvick
VIP Pedal To The Metal
2007 #PM9 Kevin Harvick
VIP Previews
2003 #6 Kevin Harvick
2004 #EB6 Kevin Harvick
2004 #EB30 Kevin Harvick's Car R
2005 #EB9 Kevin Harvick
2007 #EB12 Kevin Harvick
VIP Race Used Sheet Metal Cars
2002 #SC2 Kevin Harvick's Car
VIP Race Used Sheet Metal Drivers
2002 #SD2 Kevin Harvick
VIP Rear View Mirror
2001 #RV3 Kevin Harvick
2002 #RM3 Kevin Harvick
VIP Rear View Mirror Die Cuts
2001 #RV3 Kevin Harvick
2002 #RM3 Kevin Harvick
VIP Samples
2002 #13 Kevin Harvick
2002 #29 Kevin Harvick AS
2003 #6 Kevin Harvick
2004 #6 Kevin Harvick
2004 #30 Kevin Harvick's Car R
2005 #9 Kevin Harvick
2005 #47 Kevin Harvick SG
VIP Sheet Metal Cars
2001 #SC11 Kevin Harvick's Car
VIP Sheet Metal Drivers
2001 #SD11 Kevin Harvick
VIP Sunday Best
2007 #SB9 Kevin Harvick
VIP Tin
2003 #CT6 Kevin Harvick
VIP Tradin' Paint Autographs
2004 #TP-KH Kevin Harvick/29
2005 #KH Kevin Harvick/29
VIP Tradin' Paint Bronze
2004 #TPT6 Kevin Harvick
VIP Tradin' Paint Car Autographs
2003 #KH Kevin Harvick/29
VIP Tradin' Paint Cars
2003 #TPT3 Kevin Harvick's Car
2005 #TPT6 Kevin Harvick
VIP Tradin' Paint Cars Bronze
2006 #TPT7 Kevin Harvick
VIP Tradin' Paint Driver Autographs
2003 #KH Kevin Harvick/29
VIP Tradin' Paint Drivers
2003 #TPD3 Kevin Harvick
2005 #TPD6 Kevin Harvick
VIP Tradin' Paint Drivers Gold
2006 #TPD7 Kevin Harvick
VIP Tradin' Paint Drivers Silver
2006 #TPD7 Kevin Harvick
VIP Tradin' Paint Gold
2004 #TPD6 Kevin Harvick
VIP Tradin' Paint Silver
2004 #TPD6 Kevin Harvick
Wheels
1999 #88 Kevin Harvick CTS RC
Wheels American Thunder
2003 #8 Kevin Harvick
2004 #8 Kevin Harvick
2004 #61 Kevin Harvick DT
2004 #75 Kevin Harvick RR
2005 #10 Kevin Harvick
2005 #35 Kevin Harvick's Rig Rt. 66
2005 #46 Kevin Harvick's Car HR
2006 #11 Kevin Harvick
2006 #54 Kevin Harvick's Car HR
2006 #68 Kevin Harvick SS
2006 #89 Kevin Harvick NN
2007 #12 Kevin Harvick
2007 #53 Kevin Harvick's Car HR
2007 #66 Kevin Harvick RW
Wheels American Thunder American Dreams
2007 #AD1 Kevin Harvick
Wheels American Thunder American Dreams Gold
2007 #ADG1 Kevin Harvick
Wheels American Thunder American Muscle
2003 #AM3 Kevin Harvick
2004 #AM2 Kevin Harvick
2005 #AM2 Kevin Harvick
2007 #AM7 Kevin Harvick
Wheels American Thunder American Racing Idol
2006 #RI8 Kevin Harvick
Wheels American Thunder American Racing Idol Golden
2006 #RI8 Kevin Harvick
Wheels American Thunder Autographed Hat Instant Winner
2007 #AH13 Kevin Harvick
Wheels American Thunder Born On
2003 #B08 Kevin Harvick
Wheels American Thunder Cool Threads
2003 #CT2 Kevin Harvick
2004 #CT4 Kevin Harvick
2005 #CT11 Kevin Harvick
2006 #CT12 Kevin Harvick
Wheels American Thunder Double Hat
2006 #DH9 Kevin Harvick
Wheels American Thunder Grandstand
2006 #GS8 Kevin Harvick
Wheels American Thunder Head to Toe
2006 #HT10 Kevin Harvick
Wheels American Thunder Heads Up Goodyear
2003 #HUG3 Kevin Harvick
Wheels American Thunder Heads Up Manufacturer
2003 #HUM7 Kevin Harvick
Wheels American Thunder Heads Up Team
2003 #HUT6 Kevin Harvick/60
Wheels American Thunder Heads Up Winston
2003 #HUW7 Kevin Harvick
Wheels American Thunder Holofoil
2003 #P8 Kevin Harvick
Wheels American Thunder Medallion
2005 #MD15 Kevin Harvick
Wheels American Thunder Post Mark
2003 #PM7 Kevin Harvick
2004 #PM18 Kevin Harvick
Wheels American Thunder Previews
2003 #8 Kevin Harvick
2004 #EB8 Kevin Harvick
2005 #10 Kevin Harvick
2006 #EB11 Kevin Harvick
2007 #EB12 Kevin Harvick
2007 #EB53 Kevin Harvick's Car HR
Wheels American Thunder Pushin Pedal
2004 #PP8 Kevin Harvick
2005 #PP5 Kevin Harvick
Wheels American Thunder Pushin' Pedal
2006 #PP7 Kevin Harvick
Wheels American Thunder Rookie Thunder
2003 #RT12 Kevin Harvick
Wheels American Thunder Samples
2003 #P8 Kevin Harvick
2004 #8 Kevin Harvick
2004 #61 Kevin Harvick DT
2004 #75 Kevin Harvick RR
2005 #10 Kevin Harvick
2005 #35 Kevin Harvick's Rig Rt. 66
2005 #46 Kevin Harvick's Car HR
Wheels American Thunder Thunder Road
2003 #TR13 Kevin Harvick
2006 #TR5 Kevin Harvick
2007 #TR8 Kevin Harvick
Wheels American Thunder Thunder Strokes
2007 #18 Kevin Harvick
Wheels American Thunder Thunder Strokes Press Plates Black
2007 #18 Kevin Harvick
Wheels American Thunder Thunder Strokes Press Plates Cyan
2007 #18 Kevin Harvick
Wheels American Thunder Thunder Strokes Press Plates Magenta
2007 #18 Kevin Harvick
Wheels American Thunder Thunder Strokes Press Plates Yellow
2007 #18 Kevin Harvick
Wheels American Thunder Triple Hat
2003 #TH8 Kevin Harvick
2005 #TH7 Kevin Harvick
2007 #TH11 Kevin Harvick
Wheels Autographs
2003 #22 Kevin Harvick AT/HG
2004 #29 Kevin Harvick HG
2005 #22 Kevin Harvick
2006 #22 Kevin Harvick NC
2007 #15 Kevin Harvick NC HG
2008 #13 Kevin Harvick NC HG
Wheels Autographs Chase Edition
2008 #5 Kevin Harvick NC
Wheels Autographs Press Plates Black
2007 #14 Kevin Harvick NC
2008 #13 Kevin Harvick NC HG
Wheels Autographs Press Plates Cyan
2007 #14 Kevin Harvick NC
2008 #13 Kevin Harvick NC HG
Wheels Autographs Press Plates Magenta
2007 #14 Kevin Harvick NC
2008 #13 Kevin Harvick NC HG
Wheels Autographs Press Plates Yellow
2007 #15 Kevin Harvick NC
2008 #13 Kevin Harvick NC HG
Wheels Golden
1999 #88 Kevin Harvick
Wheels High Gear
2001 #38 Kevin Harvick BGN
2002 #9 Kevin Harvick
2002 #29 Kevin Harvick's Car
2002 #37 Kevin Harvick BGN
2002 #48 Kevin Harvick's Car
2002 #57 Kevin Harvick HL
2002 #64 Kevin Harvick CA
2002 #66 Kevin Harvick BGN Champ
2002 #72 Kevin Harvick CL
2003 #12 Kevin Harvick
2003 #56 Kevin Harvick's Car CM
2003 #71 Kevin Harvick PREV
2004 #9 Kevin Harvick
2004 #58 Kevin Harvick's Car
2005 #18 Kevin Harvick
2005 #41 Kevin Harvick's Car C
2006 #13 Kevin Harvick
2006 #52 Kevin Harvick's Car C
2007 #4 Kevin Harvick
2007 #32 Kevin Harvick NBS
2007 #59 Kevin Harvick NA
2007 #64 Kevin Harvick NA
2007 #71 Kevin Harvick CM
2007 #76 Kevin Harvick NI
2007 #83 Kevin Harvick's Car C
2007 #71B Kevin Harvick CM mixed signs
2008 #10 Kevin Harvick
2008 #34 Kevin Harvick NBS
2008 #43 Kevin Harvick DD
2008 #44 Kevin Harvick DD
2008 #51 Kevin Harvick's Car C
2008 #68 Kevin Harvick's Car EL
Wheels High Gear Autographs
2001 #15 Kevin Harvick
2002 #21 Kevin Harvick
Wheels High Gear Blue Hawaii SCDA Promos
2003 #12 Kevin Harvick
2003 #56 Kevin Harvick's Car CM
2003 #71 Kevin Harvick's Car '03 Pre.
Wheels High Gear Custom Shop
2002 #CSKH Kevin Harvick EXCH
2004 #CSKH Kevin Harvick
Wheels High Gear Custom Shop Prizes
2002 #KHA1 Kevin Harvick
2002 #KHA2 Kevin Harvick
2002 #KHA3 Kevin Harvick
2002 #KHB1 Kevin Harvick
2002 #KHB2 Kevin Harvick
2002 #KHB3 Kevin Harvick
2002 #KHC1 Kevin Harvick
2002 #KHC2 Kevin Harvick
2002 #KHC3 Kevin Harvick
Wheels High Gear Driven
2007 #DR7 Kevin Harvick
2008 #DR9 Kevin Harvick
Wheels High Gear Final Standings
2008 #F10 Kevin Harvick/10
Wheels High Gear Final Standings Gold
2007 #FS4 Kevin Harvick/4
Wheels High Gear First Gear
2001 #38 Kevin Harvick BGN
2002 #9 Kevin Harvick
2002 #29 Kevin Harvick's Car
2002 #37 Kevin Harvick BGN
2002 #48 Kevin Harvick's Car
2002 #57 Kevin Harvick HL
2002 #64 Kevin Harvick CA
2002 #66 Kevin Harvick BGN Champ
2002 #72 Kevin Harvick CL
2003 #F12 Kevin Harvick
2003 #F56 Kevin Harvick's Car CM
2003 #F71 Kevin Harvick's Car '03 Preview
Wheels High Gear Flag Chasers
2002 #FC3 Kevin Harvick
Wheels High Gear Flag Chasers Black
2002 #FC3 Kevin Harvick
2004 #FC2 Kevin Harvick
2005 #FC6 Kevin Harvick
2006 #FC7 Kevin Harvick
2007 #FC3 Kevin Harvick
2008 #FC4 Kevin Harvick
Wheels High Gear Flag Chasers Blue
2004 #FC2 Kevin Harvick
Wheels High Gear Flag Chasers Blue-Yellow
2002 #FC3 Kevin Harvick
2005 #FC6 Kevin Harvick
2006 #FC7 Kevin Harvick
2007 #FC3 Kevin Harvick
2008 #FC4 Kevin Harvick
Wheels High Gear Flag Chasers Checkered
2002 #FC3 Kevin Harvick
2004 #FC2 Kevin Harvick
2005 #FC6 Kevin Harvick
2006 #FC7 Kevin Harvick
2007 #FC3 Kevin Harvick
2008 #FC4 Kevin Harvick
Wheels High Gear Flag Chasers Checkered Blue/Orange
2002 #FC3 Kevin Harvick
Wheels High Gear Flag Chasers Green
2002 #FC3 Kevin Harvick
2004 #FC2 Kevin Harvick
2005 #FC6 Kevin Harvick
2006 #FC7 Kevin Harvick
2007 #FC3 Kevin Harvick
2008 #FC4 Kevin Harvick
Wheels High Gear Flag Chasers Red
2002 #FC3 Kevin Harvick
2004 #FC2 Kevin Harvick
2005 #FC6 Kevin Harvick
2006 #FC7 Kevin Harvick
2007 #FC3 Kevin Harvick
2008 #FC4 Kevin Harvick
Wheels High Gear Flag Chasers White
2004 #FC2 Kevin Harvick
2005 #FC6 Kevin Harvick
2006 #FC7 Kevin Harvick
2007 #FC3 Kevin Harvick
2008 #FC4 Kevin Harvick
Wheels High Gear Flag Chasers Yellow
2002 #FC3 Kevin Harvick
2004 #FC2 Kevin Harvick
2005 #FC6 Kevin Harvick
2006 #FC7 Kevin Harvick
2007 #FC3 Kevin Harvick
2008 #FC4 Kevin Harvick
Wheels High Gear Flag to Flag
2005 #FF7 Kevin Harvick
2006 #FF9 Kevin Harvick
Wheels High Gear Full Throttle
2003 #FT1 Kevin Harvick
2004 #FT6 Kevin Harvick
2005 #FT3 Kevin Harvick
2007 #FT3 Kevin Harvick
2008 #FT3 Kevin Harvick
Wheels High Gear High Groove
2002 #HG9 Kevin Harvick
2003 #HG10 Kevin Harvick
2004 #HG8 Kevin Harvick
Wheels High Gear Hot Streaks
2002 #HS4 Kevin Harvick
Wheels High Gear Hot Treads
2003 #HT6 Kevin Harvick
Wheels High Gear Last Lap
2007 #LL4 Kevin Harvick
2008 #LL6 Kevin Harvick
Wheels High Gear Last Lap Holofoil
2008 #LL6 Kevin Harvick
Wheels High Gear Machine
2003 #MM2B Kevin Harvick
2004 #MM5B Kevin Harvick
Wheels High Gear Man
2003 #MM2A Kevin Harvick
2004 #MM5A Kevin Harvick
Wheels High Gear Man and Machine Cars
2002 #MM3B Kevin Harvick
Wheels High Gear Man and Machine Drivers
2002 #MM3A Kevin Harvick
Wheels High Gear MPH
2001 #38 Kevin Harvick BGN
2002 #9 Kevin Harvick
2002 #29 Kevin Harvick's Car
2002 #37 Kevin Harvick BGN
2002 #48 Kevin Harvick's Car
2002 #57 Kevin Harvick HL
2002 #64 Kevin Harvick CA
2002 #66 Kevin Harvick BGN Champ
2002 #72 Kevin Harvick CL
2003 #M12 Kevin Harvick
2003 #M56 Kevin Harvick's Car CM
2003 #M71 Kevin Harvick's Car '03 Preview
2004 #M9 Kevin Harvick
2004 #M58 Kevin Harvick's Car
2005 #M18 Kevin Harvick
2005 #M41 Kevin Harvick's Car C
2006 #M13 Kevin Harvick
2006 #M52 Kevin Harvick's Car C
2007 #M4 Kevin Harvick
2007 #M32 Kevin Harvick NBS
2007 #M59 Kevin Harvick NA
2007 #M64 Kevin Harvick NA
2007 #M71 Kevin Harvick CM
2007 #M76 Kevin Harvick NI
2007 #M83 Kevin Harvick's Car C
2008 #M10 Kevin Harvick
2008 #M34 Kevin Harvick NBS
2008 #M43 Kevin Harvick DD
2008 #M44 Kevin Harvick DD
2008 #M51 Kevin Harvick's Car C
2008 #M68 Kevin Harvick's Car EL
Wheels High Gear Previews
2003 #12 Kevin Harvick
2004 #9 Kevin Harvick
2004 #58 Kevin Harvick's Car
2007 #EB4 Kevin Harvick
2007 #EB32 Kevin Harvick NBS
2007 #EB59 Kevin Harvick NA
2007 #EB64 Kevin Harvick NA
2008 #EB10 Kevin Harvick
Wheels High Gear Previews Green
2005 #EB18 Kevin Harvick
2006 #EB13 Kevin Harvick
Wheels High Gear Samples
2003 #12 Kevin Harvick
2003 #56 Kevin Harvick's Car CM
2003 #71 Kevin Harvick's Car '03 Pre.
2004 #9 Kevin Harvick
2004 #58 Kevin Harvick's Car
2005 #18 Kevin Harvick
2005 #41 Kevin Harvick's Car C
Wheels High Gear Sunday Sensation
2002 #SS5 Kevin Harvick
2004 #SS7 Kevin Harvick
Wheels High Gear The Chase
2008 #TC10 Kevin Harvick
Wheels High Gear Top Ten
2004 #TT5 Kevin Harvick
Wheels High Gear Top Tier
2007 #TT4 Kevin Harvick
Wheels Solos
1999 #88 Kevin Harvick

Jarrett, Dale

Action Packed
1993 #15 Dale Jarrett
1993 #90 Dale Jarrett D93
1993 #115 Dale Jarrett
1993 #165 Ned Jarrett/ Dale Jarrett
1993 #183 Dale Jarrett
1994 #4 Dale Jarrett
1994 #35 Dale Jarrett WIN
1994 #44 D.Jarrett/K.Petty w/Car
1994 #71 Dale Jarrett
1994 #128 Dale Jarrett's Car
1994 #149 Dale Jarrett
1997 #13 Dale Jarrett
1997 #34 Dale Jarrett's Car
1997 #54 Dale Jarrett
1997 #63 Dale Jarrett
1997 #72 Dale Jarrett
1997 #78 Dale Jarrett's Car
Action Packed 24K Gold
1993 #33G Dale Jarrett D93
1993 #65G Dale Jarrett
1994 #5G Dale Jarrett WIN
1994 #14G D.Jarrett/K.Petty
1994 #25G Dale Jarrett
1997 #8 Dale Jarrett
Action Packed Badge of Honor Pins
1995 #3 Dale Jarrett
Action Packed Coastars
1994 #7 Dale Jarrett
Action Packed Country
1995 #13 Dale Jarrett S
1995 #52 Dale Jarrett WIN
1995 #65 Dale Jarrett
Action Packed Country 2nd Career Choice
1995 #4 Dale Jarrett
Action Packed Country Silver Speed
1995 #13 Dale Jarrett S
1995 #52 Dale Jarrett WIN
1995 #65 Dale Jarrett
Action Packed Credentials
1996 #16 Dale Jarrett DW
1996 #19 Dale Jarrett DW
1996 #32 Dale Jarrett
Action Packed Credentials Fan Scan
1996 #8 Dale Jarrett
Action Packed Credentials Jumbos
1996 #3 Dale Jarrett
Action Packed Credentials Silver Speed
1996 #16 Dale Jarrett DW
1996 #19 Dale Jarrett DW
1996 #32 Dale Jarrett
Action Packed Fifth Anniversary
1997 #10 Dale Jarrett
Action Packed First Impressions
1997 #13 Dale Jarrett
1997 #34 Dale Jarrett's Car
1997 #54 Dale Jarrett
1997 #63 Dale Jarrett
1997 #72 Dale Jarrett
1997 #78 Dale Jarrett's Car
Action Packed McDonald's
1996 #10 Dale Jarrett
1996 #20 Dale Jarrett's Car
Action Packed Mint
1994 #4 Dale Jarrett
1994 #35 Dale Jarrett WIN
1994 #44 D.Jarrett/K.Petty w/Car
1994 #71 Dale Jarrett
1994 #128 Dale Jarrett's Car
1994 #149 Dale Jarrett
Action Packed Preview
1995 #11 Dale Jarrett
1995 #52 Dale Jarrett WIN
Action Packed Prototypes
1993 #DJ1 Dale Jarrett
1994 #2R944 Dale Jarrett
Action Packed Rolling Thunder
1997 #10 Dale Jarrett
Action Packed Stars
1995 #15 Dale Jarrett OC
1995 #43 Dale Jarrett's Car
Action Packed Stars Silver Speed
1995 #15 Dale Jarrett OC
1995 #43 Dale Jarrett's Car
ActionVision
1997 #4 Dale Jarrett Victory Lane
1997 #11 Dale Jarrett Pit Stop
ActionVision Precious Metal
1997 #7 Dale Jarrett
Arena Joe Gibbs Racing
1992 #2 Dale Jarrett
1992 #4 Dale Jarrett's Crew
1992 #5 Dale Jarrett's Car
1992 #6 Dale Jarrett's Car
1992 #7 Dale Jarrett/Jimmy Makar
1992 #8 Dale Jarrett
1992 #10 Dale Jarrett's Transporter
1992 #NNO Dale Jarrett's Car HOLO
Assets
1995 #13 Dale Jarrett
1995 #36 Dale Jarrett
Assets $2 Phone Cards
1995 #5 Dale Jarrett
Assets $2 Phone Cards Gold Signature
1995 #5 Dale Jarrett
Assets 1-Minute Phone Cards
1995 #5 Dale Jarrett
Assets 1-Minute Phone Cards Gold Signature
1995 #5 Dale Jarrett
Assets Coca-Cola 600 Die Cut Phone Cards
1995 #7 Dale Jarrett
Assets Gold Signature
1995 #13 Dale Jarrett
1995 #36 Dale Jarrett
Assets Racing
1996 #9 Dale Jarrett
1996 #42 Dale Jarrett
Assets Racing $100 Cup Champion Interactive Phone Cards
1996 #4 Dale Jarrett
Assets Racing $1000 Cup Champion Interactive Phone Cards
1996 #6 Dale Jarrett
Assets Racing $2 Phone Cards
1996 #5 Dale Jarrett
1996 #22 Dale Jarrett's Car
Assets Racing Competitor's License
1996 #CL12 Dale Jarrett
Assets Racing Race Day
1996 #RD8 Dale Jarrett's Car
Autographed Racing
1996 #15 Dale Jarrett
1997 #6 Dale Jarrett
1997 #34 Dale Jarrett's Car
1997 #42 D.Jarrett/E.Irvan
1997 #47 D.Earnhardt/D.Jarrett
Autographed Racing Autographs
1996 #22 Dale Jarrett
1997 #25 Dale Jarrett
Autographed Racing Autographs Certified Golds
1996 #22 Dale Jarrett
Autographed Racing Front Runners
1996 #36 E.Irvan/D.Jarrett VL
1996 #37 E.Irvan/D.Jarrett shades
1996 #38 Irvan facing front/Jarr.shades
1996 #39 E.Irvan facing front/D.Jarrett VL
1996 #40 E.Irvan's Car/D.Jarrett's Car
1996 #46 D.Jarrett/D.Jarrett
1996 #47 D.Jarrett VL/D.Jarrett's Car
1996 #48 D.Jarrett shades/D.Jarrett's Car
1996 #49 D.Jarrett VL/N.Jarrett
1996 #50 D.Jarrett VL/T.Parrott
1996 #51 D.Jarrett VL/R.Yates
1996 #52 D.Jarrett shades/R.Yates
1996 #53 D.Jarrett's Car/R.Yates
Autographed Racing High Performance
1996 #HP13 Dale Jarrett
Autographed Racing Kings of the Circuit $5 Phone Cards
1996 #KC1 Dale Jarrett
Autographed Racing Mayne Street
1997 #KM6 Dale Jarrett
Big League Cards Creative Images
1998 #10 Dale Jarrett
Card Dynamics Gant Oil
1993 #9 Dale Jarrett
Classic
1996 #33 Dale Jarrett's Car
1996 #49 Dale Jarrett
1996 #57 Dale Jarrett SP
Classic Five Sport
1995 #175 Dale Jarrett
Classic Five Sport Autographs Numbered
1995 #175 Dale Jarrett
Classic Five Sport Printer's Proofs
1995 #175 Dale Jarrett
Classic Five Sport Red Die Cuts
1995 #175 Dale Jarrett
Classic Five Sport Silver Die Cuts
1995 #175 Dale Jarrett
Classic Five Sport Strive For Five
1995 #RC7 Dale Jarrett
Classic Five-Sport *
1995 #175 Dale Jarrett
Classic Five-Sport Autographs *
1995 #175 Dale Jarrett/225
Classic Five-Sport Printer's Proofs *
1995 #175 Dale Jarrett
Classic Five-Sport Red Die Cuts *
1995 #175 Dale Jarrett
Classic Five-Sport Silver Die Cuts *
1995 #175 Dale Jarrett
Classic Five-Sport Strive For Five *
1995 #RC7 Dale Jarrett
Classic Mark Martin's Challengers
1996 #MC4 Dale Jarrett
Classic Printer's Proof
1996 #33 Dale Jarrett's Car
1996 #49 Dale Jarrett
Classic Silver
1996 #33 Dale Jarrett's Car
1996 #49 Dale Jarrett
Clear Assets
1996 #62 Dale Jarrett
Clear Assets *
1996 #62 Dale Jarrett
Coca-Cola Econo Lodge
2001 #2 Dale Jarrett
2001 #4 Andretti/Jarrett/Petty

Coca-Cola Racing Family
1999 #4 Dale Jarrett
2000 #6 Dale Jarrett
2000 #7 Dale Jarrett '99 Champ
2000 #16 Coca-Cola Racing Family
Collector's Choice
1997 #36 Dale Jarrett
1997 #86 Dale Jarrett's Car MM
1997 #109 Dale Jarrett SC
1998 #12 Dale Jarrett
1998 #48 Dale Jarrett's Car
1998 #92 Dale Jarrett PP
1998 #101 Dale Jarrett TD
Collector's Choice CC600
1998 #CC16 Dale Jarrett
1998 #CC49 Dale Jarrett's Car
1998 #CC82 Dale Jarrett
Collector's Choice Speedecals
1997 #S37 Dale Jarrett's Car
1997 #S38 Dale Jarrett's Helmet
Collector's Choice Star Quest
1998 #SQ39 Dale Jarrett
1998 #SQ43 Dale Jarrett AUTO
Collector's Choice Triple Force
1997 #A1 Dale Jarrett
1997 #A3 Dale Jarrett
1997 #E2 Dale Jarrett
1997 #I3 Dale Jarrett
Collector's Choice Upper Deck 500
1997 #UD75 Dale Jarrett
1997 #UD76 Dale Jarrett's Car
Crown Jewels
1995 #13 Dale Jarrett
1995 #70 Dale Jarrett CJT
Crown Jewels Diamond
1995 #13 Dale Jarrett
1995 #70 Dale Jarrett CJT
Crown Jewels Dual Jewels
1995 #DJ2 R.Wallace/Dale Jarrett
Crown Jewels Dual Jewels Diamond
1995 #DJ2 Rusty Wallace/Dale Jarrett
Crown Jewels Dual Jewels Emerald
1995 #DJ2 Rusty Wallace/Dale Jarrett
Crown Jewels Elite
1996 #9 Dale Jarrett
1996 #26 Dale Jarrett
1996 #52 T.Parrott/D.Jarrett
1996 #62 Dale Jarrett's Trans.
Crown Jewels Elite Crown Signature Amethyst
1996 #CS9 Dale Jarrett
Crown Jewels Elite Crown Signature Garnet
1996 #CS9 Dale Jarrett
Crown Jewels Elite Crown Signature Peridot
1996 #CS9 Dale Jarrett
Crown Jewels Elite Diamond Tribute
1996 #9 Dale Jarrett
1996 #26 Dale Jarrett
1996 #52 T.Parrott/D.Jarrett
1996 #62 Dale Jarrett's Trans.
Crown Jewels Elite Diamond Tribute Citrine
1996 #9 Dale Jarrett
1996 #26 Dale Jarrett
1996 #52 T.Parrott/D.Jarrett
1996 #62 Dale Jarrett's Trans.
Crown Jewels Elite Dual Jewels Amethyst
1996 #DJ2 D.Jarrett/S.Marlin
Crown Jewels Elite Dual Jewels Amethyst Diamond Tribute
1996 #DJ2 D.Jarrett/S.Marlin
Crown Jewels Elite Dual Jewels Amethyst Treasure Chest
1996 #DJ2 D.Jarrett/S.Marlin
Crown Jewels Elite Dual Jewels Garnet
1996 #DJ2 D.Jarrett/S.Marlin
Crown Jewels Elite Dual Jewels Garnet Diamond Tribute
1996 #DJ2 D.Jarrett/S.Marlin
Crown Jewels Elite Dual Jewels Garnet Treasure Chest
1996 #DJ2 D.Jarrett/S.Marlin
Crown Jewels Elite Dual Jewels Sapphire
1996 #DJ2 D.Jarrett/S.Marlin
Crown Jewels Elite Dual Jewels Sapphire Treasure Chest
1996 #DJ2 D.Jarrett/S.Marlin
Crown Jewels Elite Emerald
1996 #9 Dale Jarrett
1996 #26 Dale Jarrett
1996 #52 T.Parrott/D.Jarrett
1996 #62 Dale Jarrett's Trans.
Crown Jewels Elite Emerald Treasure Chest
1996 #9 Dale Jarrett
1996 #26 Dale Jarrett
1996 #52 T.Parrott/D.Jarrett
1996 #62 Dale Jarrett's Trans.
Crown Jewels Elite Sapphire
1996 #9 Dale Jarrett
1996 #26 Dale Jarrett
1996 #52 T.Parrott/D.Jarrett
1996 #62 Dale Jarrett's Trans.
Crown Jewels Elite Sapphire Treasure Chest
1996 #9 Dale Jarrett
1996 #26 Dale Jarrett
1996 #52 T.Parrott/D.Jarrett
1996 #62 Dale Jarrett's Trans.
Crown Jewels Elite Treasure Chest
1996 #9 Dale Jarrett
1996 #26 Dale Jarrett
1996 #52 T.Parrott/D.Jarrett
1996 #62 Dale Jarrett's Trans.
Crown Jewels Emerald
1995 #13 Dale Jarrett
1995 #70 Dale Jarrett CJT
Crown Jewels Sapphire
1995 #13 Dale Jarrett
1995 #70 Dale Jarrett CJT
Dayco Series 1
1992 #5 Dale Jarrett
Finish Line
1993 #42 Dale Jarrett
1993 #111 Dale Jarrett's Car
1993 #169 Dale Jarrett
1993 #173 Dale Jarrett/J.Gibbs
1994 #20 Dale Jarrett
1994 #67 Dale Jarrett
1994 #78 Dale Jarrett
1994 #109 Dale Jarrett's Car
1995 #18 Dale Jarrett
1995 #37 Dale Jarrett
1995 #110 Dale Jarrett
1996 #43 Dale Jarrett
1996 #90 Dale Jarrett's Car
1996 #100 Dale Jarrett
Finish Line Black Gold
1996 #C11 Dale Jarrett's Car
1996 #D14 Dale Jarrett
Finish Line Coca-Cola 600
1995 #13 Dale Jarrett
1995 #36 Dale Jarrett
Finish Line Coca-Cola 600 Die Cuts
1995 #C4 Dale Jarrett
Finish Line Commemorative Sheets
1993 #1 Daytona
1993 #13 Pocono
1993 #28 Rockingham
Finish Line Diamond Collection $5 Phone Cards
1996 #3 Dale Jarrett
Finish Line Down Home
1994 #3 Dale Jarrett
Finish Line Gold
1994 #9 Dale Jarrett
1994 #38 Dale Jarrett
1994 #75 Dale Jarrett
1994 #89 Dale Jarrett
1994 #95 Dale Jarrett's Car
Finish Line Gold Autographs
1994 #38 Dale Jarrett
Finish Line Gold Phone Cards
1994 #4 Dale Jarrett/3000
Finish Line Gold Signature
1994 #2 Dale Jarrett
1995 #GS13 Dale Jarrett
1996 #GS14 Dale Jarrett
Finish Line Gold Teamwork
1994 #TG4 Dale Jarrett/Jimmy Makar
Finish Line Phone Cards
1994 #10 Dale Jarrett
Finish Line Phone Pak
1996 #17 Dale Jarrett
Finish Line Phone Pak $2 Signature
1996 #17 Dale Jarrett
Finish Line Phone Pak $5
1996 #12 Dale Jarrett
Finish Line Phone Pak II
1997 #12 Dale Jarrett
1997 #50 Dale Jarrett $5
1997 #85 Dale Jarrett's Car $10
Finish Line Printer's Proof
1995 #18 Dale Jarrett
1995 #37 Dale Jarrett
1995 #110 Dale Jarrett
1996 #43 Dale Jarrett
1996 #90 Dale Jarrett's Car
1996 #100 Dale Jarrett
Finish Line Silver
1993 #42 Dale Jarrett
1993 #111 Dale Jarrett's Car
1993 #169 Dale Jarrett
1993 #173 Joe Gibbs/Dale Jarrett
1994 #20 Dale Jarrett
1994 #67 Dale Jarrett
1994 #78 Dale Jarrett
1994 #109 Dale Jarrett's Car
1995 #18 Dale Jarrett
1995 #37 Dale Jarrett
1995 #110 Dale Jarrett
1996 #43 Dale Jarrett
1996 #90 Dale Jarrett's Car
1996 #100 Dale Jarrett
Finish Line Victory Lane
1994 #VL4 Dale Jarrett
1994 #VL15 Dale Jarrett
Flair
1996 #16 Dale Jarrett
1996 #72 Dale Jarrett's Car
1996 #93 D.Jarrett/E.Irvin
1996 #94 Dale Jarrett
Flair Autographs
1996 #6 Dale Jarrett
Flair Hot Numbers
1996 #5 Dale Jarrett
Flair Power Performance
1996 #5 Dale Jarrett
Hickory Motor Speedway
1991 #6 Earnhardt/Gant/T.Houston/Shepherd/D.Jarrett
Hi-Tech Brickyard 400
1994 #49 Dale Jarrett
1995 #13 Dale Jarrett's Car
1995 #75 Dale Jarrett
Hi-Tech Brickyard 400 Artist Proofs
1994 #49 Dale Jarrett
Images
1995 #28 Dale Jarrett
1995 #77 Dale Jarrett
Images Gold
1995 #28 Dale Jarrett
1995 #77 Dale Jarrett
Jurassic Park
1997 #2 Dale Jarrett
1997 #37 Dale Jarrett
Jurassic Park Carnivore
1997 #C3 Dale Jarrett
Jurassic Park Pteranodon
1997 #P9 Dale Jarrett
Jurassic Park Raptors
1997 #R9 Dale Jarrett
Jurassic Park Thunder Lizard
1997 #TL2 Dale Jarrett
Jurassic Park T-Rex
1997 #TR3 Dale Jarrett
Jurassic Park Triceratops
1997 #2 Dale Jarrett
1997 #37 Dale Jarrett
KnightQuest
1996 #15 Dale Jarrett K
1996 #32 Dale Jarrett C
KnightQuest Black Knights
1996 #15 Dale Jarrett K
1996 #32 Dale Jarrett C
KnightQuest First Knights
1996 #FK2 Dale Jarrett
KnightQuest Red Knight Preview
1996 #15 Dale Jarrett K
1996 #32 Dale Jarrett C
KnightQuest Royalty
1996 #15 Dale Jarrett K
1996 #32 Dale Jarrett C
KnightQuest White Knights
1996 #15 Dale Jarrett K
1996 #32 Dale Jarrett C
Maxwell House
1993 #14 Dale Jarrett
1993 #22 Dale Jarrett/Ned Jarrett
Maxx
1989 #29 Dale Jarrett
1990 #29 Dale Jarrett
1990 #185 D.Waltrip/T.Labonte/Martin/Jarrett Cars YR
1991 #21 Dale Jarrett
1993 #18 Dale Jarrett
1994 #18 Dale Jarrett
1994 #36 Dale Jarrett's Car
1994 #38 Dale Jarrett's Car MM
1994 #205 Dale Jarrett/Kyle Petty Cars MM
1994 #207 Dale Jarrett/Gibbs YR
1994 #252 Dale Jarrett
1994 #253 Dale Jarrett's Car
1995 #18 Dale Jarrett
1995 #136 Dale Jarrett VL
1995 #175 Dale Jarrett's Car
1995 #216 Dale Jarrett
1996 #28 Dale Jarrett
1996 #48 Dale Jarrett's Car
1996 #98 D.Jarrett/E.Irvan Cars MM
1996 #P3 D.Jarrett Promo Sheet
1997 #12 Dale Jarrett
1997 #57 Dale Jarrett's Car
1997 #117 Dale Jarrett MO
1998 #12 Dale Jarrett
1998 #42 Dale Jarrett's Car
1998 #70 Dale Jarrett's Car HC
1998 #92 Dale Jarrett's Car FR
1999 #7 Dale Jarrett
1999 #8 Dale Jarrett's Car
1999 #9 Dale Jarrett's Car RR
2000 #1 Dale Jarrett
2000 #41 Dale Jarrett's Car
Maxx 10th Anniversary
1998 #23 Dale Jarrett
1998 #68 Dale Jarrett's Car
Maxx 10th Anniversary Buy Back Autographs
1998 #27 Dale Jarrett '88 #61
Maxx 10th Anniversary Card of the Year
1998 #CY8 Dale Jarrett
Maxx 10th Anniversary Maxximum Preview
1998 #P11 Dale Jarrett
Maxx 1997 Year In Review
1998 #16 Dale Jarrett
1998 #21 Dale Jarrett
1998 #22 Dale Jarrett's Car
1998 #27 Dale Jarrett's Car
1998 #45 Dale Jarrett's Car
1998 #67 Dale Jarrett
1998 #85 Dale Jarrett
1998 #86 Dale Jarrett's Car
1998 #106 Dale Jarrett
1998 #116 Dale Jarrett
1998 #136 Dale Jarrett
1998 #151 Dale Jarrett
1998 #154 Dale Jarrett's Car
1998 #AW3 Dale Jarrett
1998 #PO2 Dale Jarrett
Maxx Autographs
1994 #18 Dale Jarrett
Maxx Band-Aid Dale Jarrett
1996 #1 Dale Jarrett
1996 #2 Dale Jarrett
1996 #3 Dale Jarrett's Car
1996 #4 D.Jarrett/Zachary Jarrett
Maxx Black
1992 #18 Dale Jarrett
1992 #198 Davey Allison/Dale Jarrett Cars MM
1992 #283 Dale Jarrett YR
Maxx Black Update
1992 #U9 Dale Jarrett
Maxx Charlotte
1988 #61 Dale Jarrett RC
Maxx Chase the Champion
1997 #C4 Dale Jarrett
Maxx Chase the Champion Gold Die Cuts
1997 #C4 Dale Jarrett
Maxx Club Sam Bass Chromium
1993 #5 Dale Jarrett's Car
Maxx Collectible Covers
2000 #CCDJ Dale Jarrett
Maxx Crisco
1989 #22 Dale Jarrett
Maxx Drive Time
2000 #DT5 Dale Jarrett
Maxx FANtastic Finishes
1999 #F9 Dale Jarrett's Car
2000 #FF7 Dale Jarrett
Maxx Flag Firsts
1997 #FF3 Dale Jarrett
Maxx Focus on a Champion
1998 #FC2 Dale Jarrett
1999 #FC5 Dale Jarrett
2000 #FC1 Dale Jarrett
Maxx Focus on a Champion Cel
1998 #FC2 Dale Jarrett
Maxx Focus on a Champion Gold
1999 #FC5 Dale Jarrett
Maxx Glossy
1990 #29 Dale Jarrett
1990 #185 D.Walt/T.Lab/Mart/Jarrett Cars YR
Maxx Holly Farms
1990 #HF20 Dale Jarrett
Maxx Made in America
1996 #40 Dale Jarrett's Car
1996 #88 Dale Jarrett
1996 #96 Dale Jarrett
1996 #97 Dale Jarrett's Car
Maxx McDonald's
1991 #25 Dale Jarrett
1992 #24 Dale Jarrett
Maxx Medallion
1994 #37 Dale Jarrett
1995 #20 Dale Jarrett
1995 #50 Dale Jarrett's Car
Maxx Medallion Blue
1995 #20 Dale Jarrett
1995 #50 Dale Jarrett's Car
Maxx Motorsport
1991 #8 Dale Jarrett
1991 #36 Dale Jarrett's Car
Maxx Odyssey
1996 #40 Dale Jarrett's Car
1996 #88 Dale Jarrett
1996 #96 Dale Jarrett
1996 #97 Dale Jarrett's Car
Maxx Oval Office
2000 #OO1 Dale Jarrett
Maxx Premier Plus
1993 #18 Dale Jarrett
1994 #18 Dale Jarrett
1994 #19 Dale Jarrett's Car MM
1994 #36 Dale Jarrett's Car
1994 #79 Dale Jarrett/Kyle Petty Cars MM
1994 #166 Dale Jarrett YR
1995 #18 Dale Jarrett
1995 #48 Dale Jarrett's Car
1995 #177 Dale Jarrett VL
Maxx Premier Plus Crown Chrome
1995 #18 Dale Jarrett
1995 #48 Dale Jarrett's Car
1995 #177 Dale Jarrett VL
Maxx Premier Plus Series Two Previews
1995 #PRE4 Dale Jarrett
Maxx Premier Plus Series Two Previews Crown Chrome
1995 #PRE4 Dale Jarrett
Maxx Premier Series
1993 #18 Dale Jarrett
1994 #18 Dale Jarrett
1994 #36 Dale Jarrett's Car
1994 #38 Dale Jarrett's Car MM
1994 #263 Dale Jarrett/Kyle Petty Cars MM
1994 #266 Dale Jarrett YR
1995 #18 Dale Jarrett
1995 #48 Dale Jarrett's Car
1995 #292 Dale Jarrett YR
1996 #28 Dale Jarrett
1996 #89 Dale Jarrett's Car
Maxx Premier Series Jumbos
1994 #3 Dale Jarrett's Car
Maxx Race Ticket
1999 #RT8 Dale Jarrett's Car
Maxx Racer's Ink
2000 #DJ Dale Jarrett
Maxx Racing Images
1999 #RI9 Dale Jarrett
Maxx Red
1992 #18 Dale Jarrett
1992 #198 Davey Allison Dale Jarrett Cars MM
1992 #283 Dale Jarrett YR
Maxx Red Update
1992 #U9 Dale Jarrett
Maxx Retail Jumbos
1993 #6 Dale Jarrett
Maxx Speedway Boogie
2000 #SB6 Dale Jarrett
Maxx Teamwork
1998 #TW9 Dale Jarrett's Car
Maxx The Select 25
1994 #4 Dale Jarrett
Maxx The Winston
1992 #18 Dale Jarrett
1992 #38 Dale Jarrett's Car
1993 #19 Dale Jarrett
1993 #39 Dale Jarrett's Car
Maxximum
1998 #11 Dale Jarrett
1998 #36 Dale Jarrett's Car
1998 #61 Dale Jarrett
1998 #86 Dale Jarrett's Car
2000 #1 Dale Jarrett
Maxximum Battle Proven
1998 #B11 Dale Jarrett
Maxximum Dialed In
2000 #DI1 Dale Jarrett
Maxximum Die Cuts
2000 #1 Dale Jarrett
Maxximum Field Generals Four Star Autographs
1998 #5 Dale Jarrett
Maxximum Field Generals One Star
1998 #5 Dale Jarrett
Maxximum Field Generals Three Star Autographs
1998 #5 Dale Jarrett
Maxximum Field Generals Two Star
1998 #5 Dale Jarrett
Maxximum First Class
1998 #F10 Dale Jarrett
Maxximum MPH
2000 #1 Dale Jarrett/88
Maxximum Roots of Racing
2000 #R4 Dale Jarrett
Maxximum Signatures
2000 #DN2 D.Jarrett/N.Jarrett
2000 #DR2 D.Jarrett/R.Rudd
2000 #NDJ3 Ned/D.Jarrett/J.Jarrett
2000 #DJ2 D.Jarrett/J.Jarrett
McFarlane NASCAR 3-Inch Series 1
2005 #40 Dale Jarrett
McFarlane NASCAR Series 3
2005 #60 Dale Jarrett R
2005 #61 Dale Jarrett R Glasses
2005 #65 Dale Jarrett H A.Palmer
McFarlane NASCAR Series 5
2005 #70 Dale Jarrett
Metallic Impressions Winston Cup Top Five
1996 #3 Dale Jarrett
M-Force
1996 #33 Dale Jarrett
1996 #34 Dale Jarrett's Car
M-Force Black
1996 #B10 Dale Jarrett
MW Windows
1995 #2 Dale Jarrett
1995 #5 T.Labonte/M.Waltrip/D.Jarrett/D.Green
Pinnacle
1996 #13 Dale Jarrett
1996 #64 Dale Jarrett's Car
1997 #27 Dale Jarrett
1997 #56 Dale Jarrett's Car
1997 #60 Dale Jarrett RR
1997 #74 Dale Jarrett TT
1997 #89 Dale Jarrett's Car T4
Pinnacle Artist Proofs
1996 #13 Dale Jarrett
1996 #64 Dale Jarrett's Car
1997 #27 Dale Jarrett P
1997 #56 Dale Jarrett's Car B
1997 #60 Dale Jarrett RR R
1997 #74 Dale Jarrett TT R
1997 #89 Dale Jarrett's Car T4 R
Pinnacle Certified
1997 #15 Dale Jarrett
1997 #49 Dale Jarrett's Car
1997 #92 Dale Jarrett BD
Pinnacle Certified Certified Team
1997 #9 Dale Jarrett
Pinnacle Certified Certified Team Gold
1997 #9 Dale Jarrett
Pinnacle Certified Epix
1997 #E9 Dale Jarrett
Pinnacle Certified Epix Emerald
1997 #E9 Dale Jarrett
Pinnacle Certified Epix Purple
1997 #E9 Dale Jarrett
Pinnacle Certified Mirror Blue
1997 #15 Dale Jarrett
1997 #49 Dale Jarrett's Car
1997 #92 Dale Jarrett BD
Pinnacle Certified Mirror Gold
1997 #15 Dale Jarrett
1997 #49 Dale Jarrett's Car
1997 #92 Dale Jarrett BD
Pinnacle Certified Mirror Red
1997 #15 Dale Jarrett
1997 #49 Dale Jarrett's Car
1997 #92 Dale Jarrett BD
Pinnacle Certified Red
1997 #15 Dale Jarrett
1997 #49 Dale Jarrett's Car
1997 #92 Dale Jarrett BD
Pinnacle Checkered Flag
1996 #8 Dale Jarrett
Pinnacle Cut Above
1996 #7 Dale Jarrett
Pinnacle Foil
1997 #27 Dale Jarrett
1997 #56 Dale Jarrett's Car
1997 #60 Dale Jarrett RR
1997 #74 Dale Jarrett TT
1997 #89 Dale Jarrett's Car T4
Pinnacle Mint
1997 #3 Dale Jarrett
1997 #23 Dale Jarrett's Car
1997 #P1 Dale Jarrett Promo
1998 #5 Dale Jarrett
1998 #15 Dale Jarrett's Car
1998 #28 Dale Jarrett MM
Pinnacle Mint Bronze
1997 #3 Dale Jarrett
1997 #23 Dale Jarrett's Car
Pinnacle Mint Coins
1997 #3 Dale Jarrett
1997 #23 Dale Jarrett's Car
1998 #5 Dale Jarrett
1998 #15 Dale Jarrett's Car
1998 #4 Dale Jarrett MM
Pinnacle Mint Coins 24K Gold Plated
1997 #3 Dale Jarrett
1997 #23 Dale Jarrett's Car
Pinnacle Mint Coins Bronze Proof
1998 #5 Dale Jarrett
1998 #15 Dale Jarrett's Car
1998 #4 Dale Jarrett MM
Pinnacle Mint Coins Gold Plated
1998 #5 Dale Jarrett
1998 #15 Dale Jarrett's Car
1998 #28 Dale Jarrett MM
Pinnacle Mint Coins Gold Plated Proofs
1998 #5 Dale Jarrett
1998 #15 Dale Jarrett's Car
1998 #28 Dale Jarrett MM
Pinnacle Mint Coins Nickel-Silver
1997 #3 Dale Jarrett
1997 #23 Dale Jarrett's Car
1998 #5 Dale Jarrett
1998 #15 Dale Jarrett's Car
1998 #28 Dale Jarrett MM
Pinnacle Mint Coins Silver Plated Proofs
1998 #5 Dale Jarrett
1998 #15 Dale Jarrett's Car
1998 #28 Dale Jarrett MM
Pinnacle Mint Coins Solid Gold
1998 #5 Dale Jarrett
1998 #15 Dale Jarrett's Car
1998 #28 Dale Jarrett MM
Pinnacle Mint Coins Solid Silver
1998 #5 Dale Jarrett
1998 #15 Dale Jarrett's Car
1998 #28 Dale Jarrett MM
Pinnacle Mint Die Cuts
1998 #5 Dale Jarrett
1998 #15 Dale Jarrett's Car
1998 #28 Dale Jarrett MM
Pinnacle Mint Gold
1997 #3 Dale Jarrett
1997 #23 Dale Jarrett's Car
Pinnacle Mint Gold Team
1998 #5 Dale Jarrett
1998 #15 Dale Jarrett's Car
1998 #28 Dale Jarrett MM
Pinnacle Mint Silver
1997 #3 Dale Jarrett
1997 #23 Dale Jarrett's Car
Pinnacle Mint Silver Team
1998 #5 Dale Jarrett
1998 #15 Dale Jarrett's Car
1998 #28 Dale Jarrett MM
Pinnacle Pole Position
1996 #13 Dale Jarrett
1996 #44 Dale Jarrett's Car
1996 #67 Dale Jarrett WIN
Pinnacle Pole Position Certified Strong
1996 #8 Dale Jarrett
Pinnacle Pole Position Lightning Fast
1996 #13 Dale Jarrett
1996 #44 Dale Jarrett's Car
1996 #67 Dale Jarrett
Pinnacle Pole Position No Limit
1996 #9 Dale Jarrett
Pinnacle Pole Position No Limit Gold
1996 #9 Dale Jarrett
Pinnacle Portraits
1997 #8 Dale Jarrett
1997 #28 Dale Jarrett's Car
1997 #44 Dale Jarrett SS
Pinnacle Portraits 8x10
1997 #DJ1 Dale Jarrett
1997 #DJ2 Dale Jarrett
1997 #DJ3 Dale Jarrett
1997 #DJ4 Dale Jarrett
Pinnacle Portraits 8x10 Dufex
1997 #DJ1 Dale Jarrett
1997 #DJ2 Dale Jarrett
1997 #DJ3 Dale Jarrett
1997 #DJ4 Dale Jarrett
Pinnacle Precision
1997 #28 Dale Jarrett's Transporter
1997 #30 Dale Jarrett
1997 #31 Dale Jarrett Pit Action
1997 #33 Dale Jarrett
1997 #36 Dale Jarrett
Pinnacle Precision Bronze
1997 #28 Dale Jarrett's Transporter
1997 #30 Dale Jarrett
1997 #31 Dale Jarrett Pit Action
1997 #32 Dale Jarrett's Car
1997 #33 Dale Jarrett
1997 #35 Dale Jarrett's Car
1997 #36 Dale Jarrett
Pinnacle Precision Gold
1997 #28 Dale Jarrett's Transporter
1997 #30 Dale Jarrett
1997 #31 Dale Jarrett Pit Action
1997 #32 Dale Jarrett's Car
1997 #33 Dale Jarrett
1997 #35 Dale Jarrett's Car
1997 #36 Dale Jarrett
Pinnacle Precision Silver
1997 #28 Dale Jarrett's Transporter
1997 #30 Dale Jarrett
1997 #31 Dale Jarrett Pit Action
1997 #32 Dale Jarrett's Car
1997 #33 Dale Jarrett
1997 #35 Dale Jarrett's Car
1997 #36 Dale Jarrett
Pinnacle Press Plates
1997 #27 Dale Jarrett
1997 #56 Dale Jarrett's Car
1997 #60 Dale Jarrett RR
1997 #74 Dale Jarrett TT
1997 #89 Dale Jarrett's Car T4
1997 #S2-A Dale Jarrett
1997 #TP9A Dale Jarrett
Pinnacle Spellbound
1997 #2A Dale Jarrett
Pinnacle Spellbound Autographs
1997 #2A Dale Jarrett
Pinnacle Spellbound Promos
1997 #2A Dale Jarrett
Pinnacle Team Pinnacle
1996 #4 Dale Jarrett
1996 #12 Dale Jarrett
1997 #9 Dale Jarrett
Pinnacle Team Pinnacle Red
1997 #9 Dale Jarrett
Pinnacle Totally Certified Platinum Blue
1997 #15 Dale Jarrett
1997 #49 Dale Jarrett's Car
1997 #92 Dale Jarrett BD
Pinnacle Totally Certified Platinum Gold
1997 #15 Dale Jarrett
1997 #49 Dale Jarrett's Car
1997 #92 Dale Jarrett BD
Pinnacle Totally Certified Platinum Red
1997 #15 Dale Jarrett
1997 #49 Dale Jarrett's Car
1997 #92 Dale Jarrett BD
Pinnacle Trophy Collection
1997 #27 Dale Jarrett
1997 #56 Dale Jarrett's Car
1997 #60 Dale Jarrett RR
1997 #74 Dale Jarrett TT
1997 #89 Dale Jarrett's Car T4
Pinnacle Winston Cup Collection
1996 #13 Dale Jarrett
1996 #64 Dale Jarrett's Car
Power
1994 #19 Dale Jarrett PW
Power Gold
1994 #19 Dale Jarrett PW
Power Preview
1994 #10 Dale Jarrett
1994 #29 Dale Jarrett's Car FOIL
Predator
1997 #4 Dale Jarrett
1997 #39 Dale Jarrett
Predator American Eagle
1997 #AE5 Dale Jarrett
Predator American Eagle First Slash
1997 #AE5 Dale Jarrett
Predator Black Wolf First Strike
1997 #4 Dale Jarrett
1997 #39 Dale Jarrett
Predator Eye of the Tiger
1997 #ET5 Dale Jarrett
Predator Eye of the Tiger First Slash
1997 #ET5 Dale Jarrett
Predator First Slash
1997 #4 Dale Jarrett
1997 #39 Dale Jarrett
Predator Gatorback
1997 #GB4 Dale Jarrett
Predator Gatorback Authentic
1997 #GBA4 Dale Jarrett
Predator Gatorback Authentic First Slash
1997 #GBA4 Dale Jarrett
Predator Gatorback First Slash
1997 #GB4 Dale Jarrett
Predator Golden Eagle
1997 #GE5 Dale Jarrett

Predator Golden Eagle First Slash
1997 #GE5 Dale Jarrett
Predator Grizzly
1997 #4 Dale Jarrett
1997 #39 Dale Jarrett
Predator Grizzly First Slash
1997 #4 Dale Jarrett
1997 #39 Dale Jarrett
Predator Red Wolf
1997 #4 Dale Jarrett
1997 #39 Dale Jarrett
Predator Red Wolf First Slash
1997 #4 Dale Jarrett
1997 #39 Dale Jarrett
Press Pass
1994 #12 Dale Jarrett
1994 #34 Dale Jarrett/Joe Gibbs
1994 #42 Dale Jarrett's Car
1994 #122 Dale Jarrett TT
1994 #140 Dale Jarrett Art
1995 #14 Dale Jarrett
1995 #42 Dale Jarrett's Car
1996 #15 Dale Jarrett
1996 #50 Dale Jarrett's Car
1996 #79 Yates/McReynolds/D.Jarrett
1996 #87 Dale Jarrett DW
1996 #115 Dale Jarrett PRE
1997 #3 Dale Jarrett
1997 #44 Dale Jarrett's Car
1997 #59 Dale Jarrett's Car
1997 #70 Dale Jarrett
1997 #80 Dale Jarrett
1997 #94 Dale Jarrett
1997 #96 J.Gordon/D.Jarrett's Cars
1997 #102 Dale Jarrett
1997 #124 Dale Jarrett
1997 #P1 Dale Jarrett Promo
1998 #3 Dale Jarrett
1998 #35 Dale Jarrett's Car
1998 #45 Dale Jarrett
1998 #103 Dale Jarrett RET
1999 #3 Dale Jarrett
1999 #30 Dale Jarrett's Car
1999 #48 Dale Jarrett
1999 #87 Dale Jarrett OTP
1999 #103 Dale Jarrett RET
2000 #1 Dale Jarrett
2000 #41 Dale Jarrett REP
2000 #0 D.Jarrett 1999 Champ/800
2000 #P1 Dale Jarrett Promo
2001 #4 Dale Jarrett
2001 #51 Dale Jarrett's Car
2001 #66 Dale Jarrett REP
2001 #82 Dale Jarrett SO
2001 #99 Dale Jarrett PV
2002 #15 Dale Jarrett
2002 #87 Dale Jarrett's Car
2003 #15 Dale Jarrett
2003 #60 Ups and Downs WCS
2004 #13 Dale Jarrett
2004 #74 Dale Jarrett's Car OTW
2005 #35 Dale Jarrett
2005 #71 Dale Jarrett's Car OTW
2005 #108 Dale Jarrett P
2006 #28 Dale Jarrett
2006 #74 Dale Jarrett's Car OTW
2006 #106 Dale Jarrett U
2007 #23 Dale Jarrett
2007 #78 Dale Jarrett's Car OT
2008 #34 Dale Jarrett
2008 #66 Dale Jarrett's Car BFS
Press Pass Autographs
1997 #3 Dale Jarrett VIP/ACTN
1998 #3 Dale Jarrett
1999 #12 Dale Jarrett/250
2001 #22 Dale Jarrett
2002 #29 Dale Jarrett
2003 #25 Dale Jarrett E/P
2004 #27 Dale Jarrett P
2005 #26 Dale Jarrett E/P
2006 #23 Dale Jarrett NC
2007 #19 Dale Jarrett
2008 #19 Dale Jarrett NC P/E
Press Pass Autographs Press Plates Black
2008 #15 Dale Jarrett NC E
Press Pass Autographs Press Plates Cyan
2008 #15 Dale Jarrett NC P
Press Pass Autographs Press Plates Magenta
2008 #15 Dale Jarrett NC P
Press Pass Autographs Press Plates Yellow
2008 #15 Dale Jarrett NC E
Press Pass Banquet Bound
1997 #BB3 Dale Jarrett
Press Pass Blue
2006 #B28 Dale Jarrett
2006 #B74 Dale Jarrett's Car OTW
2006 #B106 Dale Jarrett U
2007 #B23 Dale Jarrett
2007 #B78 Dale Jarrett's Car OT
2008 #B34 Dale Jarrett
2008 #B66 Dale Jarrett's Car BFS
Press Pass Bryan
1999 #6 Dale Jarrett
Press Pass Burning Rubber
1997 #BR7 Dale Jarrett
1999 #BR5 Dale Jarrett's Car
2000 #BR1 Dale Jarrett
Press Pass Burning Rubber Cars
2001 #BRC4 Dale Jarrett/105
2002 #BRC5 Dale Jarrett's Car
2003 #BRT17 Dale Jarrett's Car
2004 #BRT16 Dale Jarrett's Car
2005 #BRT13 Dale Jarrett's Car
2006 #BRT7 Dale Jarrett
Press Pass Burning Rubber Drivers
2001 #BRD4 Dale Jarrett/90
2002 #BRD5 Dale Jarrett
2003 #BRD17 Dale Jarrett
2004 #BRD16 Dale Jarrett
2005 #BRD13 Dale Jarrett
2006 #BRD7 Dale Jarrett
Press Pass Burning Rubber Drivers Gold
2005 #BRD13 Dale Jarrett
2006 #BRD7 Dale Jarrett
Press Pass Chase Cars
1999 #1B Dale Jarrett's Car
Press Pass Clear Cut
1997 #C4 Dale Jarrett
Press Pass Coca Cola AutoZone
2006 #DJ Dale Jarrett
Press Pass Coca-Cola Racing Family
2001 #1 D.Jarrett/R.Rudd
2003 #6 Dale Jarrett
Press Pass Coca-Cola Racing Family Regional
2003 #2 Dale Jarrett
Press Pass Collector's Series Box Set
2007 #SB10 Dale Jarrett
Press Pass Collectors Series Making the Show
2006 #MS12 Dale Jarrett
Press Pass Collectors Series Sunday Best
2007 #CB10 Dale Jarrett
Press Pass Cup Chase
1994 #CC12 Dale Jarrett
1995 #14 Dale Jarrett
1996 #15 Dale Jarrett WIN
1997 #CC10 Dale Jarrett WIN
1998 #CC10 Dale Jarrett Win 2
1999 #10 Dale Jarrett WIN 2
2000 #CC7 Dale Jarrett WIN
2001 #CC14 Dale Jarrett
2002 #CC6 Dale Jarrett
2003 #CCR6 Dale Jarrett
2005 #CCR2 Dale Jarrett
2006 #CCR13 Dale Jarrett
Press Pass Cup Chase Blue Die Cut Prizes
1997 #CC10 Dale Jarrett
Press Pass Cup Chase Die Cut Prizes
1998 #CC10 Dale Jarrett
1999 #10 Dale Jarrett
2000 #CC7 Dale Jarrett
2000 #CC17 Dale Jarrett 2000 Champ
2001 #CC14 Dale Jarrett
Press Pass Cup Chase Foil Prizes
1996 #15 Dale Jarrett
Press Pass Cup Chase Gold Die Cuts
1997 #CC10 Dale Jarrett
Press Pass Cup Chase Prizes
2002 #CC6 Dale Jarrett
2003 #CCR6 Dale Jarrett
2005 #CCP2 Dale Jarrett
Press Pass Dale Jarrett Fan Club
2003 #DJ Dale Jarrett
Press Pass Daytona 500 50th Anniversary
2008 #30 Dale Jarrett '93
2008 #33 Dale Jarrett '96
2008 #37 Dale Jarrett '00
Press Pass Double Burner
2001 #DB4 Dale Jarrett
2002 #DB4 Dale Jarrett
Press Pass Double Burner Firesuit-Glove
2006 #DB2 Dale Jarrett
2008 #DBDJ Dale Jarrett
Press Pass Double Burner Metal-Tire
2006 #DB4 Dale Jarrett
Press Pass Eclipse
2002 #5 Dale Jarrett
2002 #39 Dale Jarrett SO
2003 #9 Dale Jarrett
2004 #22 Dale Jarrett
2005 #15 Dale Jarrett
2005 #83 Dale Jarrett LL
2006 #14 Dale Jarrett
2006 #37 Dale Jarrett WS
2006 #53 Dale Jarrett NS
2006 #75 Dale Jarrett LL
2006 #75B Dale Jarrett LL -pic in book
2007 #58 Dale Jarrett NT
2007 #89 Dale Jarrett
2008 #26 Dale Jarrett
Press Pass Eclipse Destination WIN
2004 #4 Dale Jarrett
Press Pass Eclipse Escape Velocity
2008 #EV12 Dale Jarrett
Press Pass Eclipse Father and Son Autographs
2002 #FS3 Ned/Dale Jarrett
Press Pass Eclipse Gold
2007 #G58 Dale Jarrett NT
2007 #G89 Dale Jarrett
2008 #G26 Dale Jarrett
Press Pass Eclipse Hyperdrive
2005 #HD3 Dale Jarrett
Press Pass Eclipse Maxim
2004 #MX12 Dale Jarrett
2005 #MX8 Dale Jarrett
Press Pass Eclipse Previews
2003 #9 Dale Jarrett
2004 #22 Dale Jarrett
2005 #EB15 Dale Jarrett
2005 #EB83 Dale Jarrett LL/1
2006 #EB14 Dale Jarrett
2007 #EB89 Dale Jarrett
2008 #EB26 Dale Jarrett
Press Pass Eclipse Racing Champions
2002 #RC5 Dale Jarrett
2002 #RC7 Dale Jarrett
2002 #RC8 Dale Jarrett
2002 #RC19 Dale Jarrett
2003 #RC17 Dale Jarrett
2003 #RC24 Dale Jarrett
2006 #RC13 Dale Jarrett
Press Pass Eclipse Red
2007 #R58 Dale Jarrett NT
2007 #R89 Dale Jarrett
2008 #R26 Dale Jarrett
Press Pass Eclipse Samples
2002 #5 Dale Jarrett
2002 #39 Dale Jarrett SO
2003 #9 Dale Jarrett
2004 #22 Dale Jarrett
2005 #15 Dale Jarrett
2005 #83 Dale Jarrett LL
Press Pass Eclipse Skidmarks
2002 #SK7 Dale Jarrett
2003 #SM12 Dale Jarrett
2004 #SM10 Dale Jarrett
2005 #SM10 Dale Jarrett
2006 #SM9 Dale Jarrett
Press Pass Eclipse Skidmarks Holofoil
2004 #SM10 Dale Jarrett
2005 #SM10 Dale Jarrett
2006 #SM9 Dale Jarrett
Press Pass Eclipse Solar Eclipse
2002 #S5 Dale Jarrett
2002 #S39 Dale Jarrett SO
2003 #P9 Dale Jarrett
Press Pass Eclipse Star Tracks
2008 #ST1 Dale Jarrett
Press Pass Eclipse Star Tracks Holofoil
2008 #ST1 Dale Jarrett
Press Pass Eclipse Supernova
2002 #SN6 Dale Jarrett
2003 #SN5 Dale Jarrett
2006 #SU3 Dale Jarrett
Press Pass Eclipse Supernova Numbered
2002 #SN6 Dale Jarrett
Press Pass Eclipse Teammates Autographs
2004 #5 D.Jarrett/E.Sadler
2005 #5 D.Jarrett/E.Sadler
2006 #4 D.Jarrett/E.Sadler
Press Pass Eclipse Under Cover Drivers
2008 #UCD12 Dale Jarrett
Press Pass Eclipse Under Cover Drivers Eclipse
2008 #UCD12 Dale Jarrett
Press Pass Eclipse Under Cover Drivers Name
2008 #UCD12 Dale Jarrett
Press Pass Eclipse Under Cover Drivers NASCAR
2008 #UCD12 Dale Jarrett
Press Pass Eclipse Under Cover Teams
2008 #UCT12 Dale Jarrett
Press Pass Eclipse Under Cover Teams NASCAR
2008 #UCT12 Dale Jarrett
Press Pass Eclipse Warp Speed
2002 #WS4 Dale Jarrett
Press Pass E.Q.S.
1996 #FQS4A Dale Jarrett
1996 #FQS4B Dale Jarrett's Car
Press Pass Game Face
2005 #GF1 Dale Jarrett
2006 #GF5 Dale Jarrett
Press Pass Gatorade Front Runner Award
2000 #5 Dale Jarrett
Press Pass Gold
2006 #G28 Dale Jarrett
2006 #G74 Dale Jarrett's Car OTW
2006 #G106 Dale Jarrett U
2007 #G23 Dale Jarrett
2007 #G78 Dale Jarrett's Car OT
2008 #G34 Dale Jarrett
2008 #G66 Dale Jarrett's Car BFS
Press Pass Gold Holofoil
2003 #P15 Dale Jarrett
2003 #P80 Ups and Downs WCS
Press Pass Ground Zero
2001 #GZ7 Dale Jarrett
Press Pass Hot Treads
2001 #HT9 Dale Jarrett/1000
2002 #HT22 Dale Jarrett's Car/2425
2002 #HT41 Dale Jarrett's Car/900
2004 #HTR18 Dale Jarrett
2005 #HTR7 Dale Jarrett
Press Pass Hot Treads Holofoil
2004 #HTR18 Dale Jarrett
2005 #HTR7 Dale Jarrett
Press Pass Lasers
1997 #3 Dale Jarrett
1997 #44 Dale Jarrett's Car
1997 #59 Dale Jarrett's Car
1997 #70 Dale Jarrett
1997 #80 Dale Jarrett
1997 #94 Dale Jarrett
1997 #96 J.Gordon/D.Jarrett's Cars
1997 #102 Dale Jarrett
1997 #124 Dale Jarrett
Press Pass Legends
2005 #25 Dale Jarrett
2006 #31 Dale Jarrett
2007 #34 Dale Jarrett
Press Pass Legends Autographs Black
2005 #17 Dale Jarrett
Press Pass Legends Autographs Blue
2007 #13 Dale Jarrett/61
Press Pass Legends Autographs Inscriptions Blue
2007 #8 Dale Jarrett #44/9
Press Pass Legends Blue
2005 #25B Dale Jarrett
2006 #B31 Dale Jarrett
2007 #B34 Dale Jarrett
Press Pass Legends Bronze
2006 #Z31 Dale Jarrett
2007 #Z34 Dale Jarrett
Press Pass Legends Champion Threads & Treads Bronze
2006 #CTT-DJ Dale Jarrett
Press Pass Legends Champion Threads & Treads Gold
2006 #CTT-DJ Dale Jarrett
Press Pass Legends Champion Threads & Treads Silver
2006 #CTT-DJ Dale Jarrett
Press Pass Legends Champion Threads Bronze
2006 #CT-DJ Dale Jarrett
Press Pass Legends Champion Threads Gold
2006 #CT-DJ Dale Jarrett
Press Pass Legends Champion Threads Patch
2006 #CT-DJ Dale Jarrett
Press Pass Legends Champion Threads Silver
2006 #CT-DJ Dale Jarrett
Press Pass Legends Gold
2005 #25G Dale Jarrett
2006 #G31 Dale Jarrett
2007 #G34 Dale Jarrett
Press Pass Legends Heritage
2005 #HE3 Dale Jarrett
Press Pass Legends Holofoil
2005 #25H Dale Jarrett
2006 #H31 Dale Jarrett
2007 #H34 Dale Jarrett
Press Pass Legends Press Plates Black
2005 #25 Dale Jarrett
2006 #PPB31 Dale Jarrett
2007 #PP34 Dale Jarrett
Press Pass Legends Press Plates Black Backs
2006 #PPB31B Dale Jarrett
2007 #PP34 Dale Jarrett
Press Pass Legends Press Plates Cyan
2005 #25 Dale Jarrett
2006 #PPC31 Dale Jarrett
2007 #PP34 Dale Jarrett
Press Pass Legends Press Plates Cyan Backs
2006 #PPC31B Dale Jarrett
2007 #PP34 Dale Jarrett
Press Pass Legends Press Plates Magenta
2005 #25 Dale Jarrett
2006 #PPM31 Dale Jarrett
2007 #PP34 Dale Jarrett
Press Pass Legends Press Plates Magenta Backs
2006 #PPM31B Dale Jarrett
2007 #PP34 Dale Jarrett
Press Pass Legends Press Plates Yellow
2005 #25 Dale Jarrett
2006 #PPY31 Dale Jarrett
2007 #PP34 Dale Jarrett
Press Pass Legends Press Plates Yellow Backs
2006 #PPY31B Dale Jarrett
2007 #PP34 Dale Jarrett
Press Pass Legends Previews
2005 #25 Dale Jarrett
2006 #EB31 Dale Jarrett
2007 #EB34 Dale Jarrett
Press Pass Legends Signature Series
2007 #DJ Dale Jarrett
Press Pass Legends Solo
2005 #25S Dale Jarrett
2006 #S31 Dale Jarrett
2007 #S34 Dale Jarrett
Press Pass Legends Sunday Swatches Bronze
2007 #DJ-SS Dale Jarrett
Press Pass Legends Sunday Swatches Gold
2007 #DJ-SS Dale Jarrett
Press Pass Legends Sunday Swatches Silver
2007 #DJ-SS Dale Jarrett
Press Pass Legends Threads & Treads Bronze
2005 #TTDJ Dale Jarrett
Press Pass Legends Threads & Treads Gold
2005 #TTDJ Dale Jarrett
Press Pass Legends Threads & Treads Silver
2005 #TTDJ Dale Jarrett
Press Pass Millennium
2000 #1 Dale Jarrett
2000 #41 Dale Jarrett
2001 #4 Dale Jarrett
2001 #51 Dale Jarrett's Car
2001 #66 Dale Jarrett REP
2001 #82 Dale Jarrett SO
2001 #99 Dale Jarrett PV
Press Pass Oil Cans
1998 #OC4 Dale Jarrett
1999 #4 Dale Jarrett
2000 #OC8 Dale Jarrett
Press Pass Oil Slicks
1997 #3 Dale Jarrett
1997 #44 Dale Jarrett's Car
1997 #59 Dale Jarrett's Car
1997 #70 Dale Jarrett
1997 #80 Dale Jarrett
1997 #94 Dale Jarrett
1997 #96 J.Gordon/D.Jarrett's Cars
1997 #102 Dale Jarrett
1997 #124 Dale Jarrett
1998 #3 Dale Jarrett
1998 #35 Dale Jarrett's Car
1998 #45 Dale Jarrett
Press Pass Optima
2000 #9 Dale Jarrett
2000 #45 Dale Jarrett WCL
2001 #9 Dale Jarrett
2001 #44 Dale Jarrett WCL
2002 #13 Dale Jarrett
2003 #10 Dale Jarrett
2004 #9 Dale Jarrett
2004 #69 Dale Jarrett CS
2005 #12 Dale Jarrett
2005 #55 Dale Jarrett RR
2005 #79 Dale Jarrett CP
2005 #87 Dale Jarrett DT
2005 #98 Dale Jarrett R&R
2006 #31 Dale Jarrett
2006 #52 Dale Jarrett's Car HS
2006 #CL Dale Jarrett CL
Press Pass Optima Cool Persistence
2000 #CP3 Dale Jarrett
2001 #CP6 Dale Jarrett
2002 #CP5 Dale Jarrett
2003 #CP6 Dale Jarrett
2004 #CP11 Dale Jarrett
2005 #CP7 Dale Jarrett
Press Pass Optima Corporate Cuts Cars
2005 #CCT6 Dale Jarrett
Press Pass Optima Corporate Cuts Drivers
2005 #CCD6 Dale Jarrett
Press Pass Optima Encore
2000 #EN1 Dale Jarrett
Press Pass Optima Fan Favorite
2002 #FF10 Dale Jarrett
2003 #FF10 Dale Jarrett
2004 #FF9 Dale Jarrett
2005 #FF11 Dale Jarrett
2006 #FF9 Dale Jarrett
Press Pass Optima G Force
2000 #GF9 Dale Jarrett
2001 #GF8 Dale Jarrett
2005 #GF6 Dale Jarrett
Press Pass Optima Gold
2001 #9 Dale Jarrett
2001 #44 Dale Jarrett WCL
2002 #13 Dale Jarrett
2003 #G10 Dale Jarrett
2004 #G9 Dale Jarrett
2004 #G69 Dale Jarrett CS
2005 #G12 Dale Jarrett
2005 #G55 Dale Jarrett RR
2005 #G79 Dale Jarrett CP
2005 #G87 Dale Jarrett DT
2005 #G98 Dale Jarrett R&R
2006 #G31 Dale Jarrett
2006 #G52 Dale Jarrett's Car HS
2006 #GCL Dale Jarrett CL
Press Pass Optima On the Edge
2001 #OE4 Dale Jarrett
Press Pass Optima Overdrive
2000 #OD5 Dale Jarrett
Press Pass Optima Overdrive Square Cut
2000 #OD5 Dale Jarrett
Press Pass Optima Platinum
2000 #9 Dale Jarrett
2000 #45 Dale Jarrett WCL
Press Pass Optima Previews
2003 #10 Dale Jarrett
2004 #EB9 Dale Jarrett
2005 #12 Dale Jarrett
2006 #EB31 Dale Jarrett
Press Pass Optima Promos
2002 #13 Dale Jarrett
Press Pass Optima Q & A
2006 #QA10 Dale Jarrett
Press Pass Optima Q and A
2003 #QA4 Dale Jarrett
Press Pass Optima Race Used Lugnuts Cars
2000 #LC4 Dale Jarrett's Car
2001 #LNC7 Dale Jarrett's Car
2002 #LNC8 Dale Jarrett's Car
Press Pass Optima Race Used Lugnuts Drivers
2000 #LD4 Dale Jarrett
2001 #LND6 Dale Jarrett
2002 #LND8 Dale Jarrett
Press Pass Optima Samples
2002 #13 Dale Jarrett
2003 #10 Dale Jarrett
2004 #9 Dale Jarrett
2004 #69 Dale Jarrett CS
2005 #12 Dale Jarrett
2005 #55 Dale Jarrett RR
2005 #79 Dale Jarrett CP
2005 #87 Dale Jarrett DT
2005 #98 Dale Jarrett R&R
Press Pass Optima Thunder Bolts Cars
2003 #TBT15 Dale Jarrett's Car
2004 #TBT12 Dale Jarrett's Car
Press Pass Optima Thunder Bolts Drivers
2003 #TBD15 Dale Jarrett/65
2004 #TBD12 Dale Jarrett
Press Pass Optima Up Close
2001 #UC4 Dale Jarrett
2002 #UC1 Dale Jarrett
Press Pass Optima XL
1994 #9 Dale Jarrett
1995 #10 Dale Jarrett
1995 #46 Dale Jarrett's Car
Press Pass Optima XL Cool Blue
1995 #10 Dale Jarrett
1995 #46 Dale Jarrett's Car
Press Pass Optima XL Die Cut
1995 #10 Dale Jarrett
1995 #46 Dale Jarrett's Car
Press Pass Optima XL Red Hot
1994 #9 Dale Jarrett
1995 #10 Dale Jarrett
1995 #46 Dale Jarrett's Car
Press Pass Panorama
2005 #PPP5 Dale Jarrett
2005 #PPP26 Dale Jarrett
2005 #PPP40 Dale Jarrett
2005 #PPP41 Dale Jarrett
2005 #PPP42 Dale Jarrett
2005 #PPP58 Dale Jarrett
Press Pass Pit Stop
1998 #PS16 Dale Jarrett's Car
1999 #16 Dale Jarrett's Car
Press Pass Pitstop
2000 #PS1 Dale Jarrett's Car
Press Pass Platinum
2002 #15 Dale Jarrett
2002 #87 Dale Jarrett's Car
2004 #P13 Dale Jarrett
2004 #P74 Dale Jarrett's Car OTW
2005 #P35 Dale Jarrett
2005 #P71 Dale Jarrett's Car OTW
2005 #P108 Dale Jarrett P
2006 #P28 Dale Jarrett
2006 #P74 Dale Jarrett's Car OTW
2006 #P106 Dale Jarrett U
2007 #P23 Dale Jarrett
2007 #P78 Dale Jarrett's Car OT
2008 #P34 Dale Jarrett
2008 #P66 Dale Jarrett's Car BFS
Press Pass Premium
1995 #14 Dale Jarrett
1996 #13 Dale Jarrett
1996 #41 Dale Jarrett's Car
1997 #3 Dale Jarrett
1997 #35 Dale Jarrett's Car
1997 #40 Dale Jarrett
1997 #P2 Dale Jarrett MO Promo
1998 #8 Dale Jarrett
1998 #25 Dale Jarrett's Car
1998 #29 Dale Jarrett
1999 #12 Dale Jarrett
1999 #30 Dale Jarrett's Car
2000 #25 Dale Jarrett
2000 #46 Dale Jarrett
2000 #68 Dale Jarrett
2000 #0 Dale Jarrett Daytona Win
2001 #8 Dale Jarrett
2001 #44 Dale Jarrett
2001 #53 Dale Jarrett CC
2001 #74 Dale Jarrett PC
2002 #12 Dale Jarrett
2002 #40 Dale Jarrett's Car
2002 #52 Dale Jarrett CH
2002 #74 Dale Jarrett PC
2003 #12 Dale Jarrett
2003 #39 Dale Jarrett's Car
2003 #54 Dale Jarrett CC
2003 #72 Dale Jarrett PC
2004 #9 Dale Jarrett
2004 #48 Dale Jarrett NS
2004 #54 Dale Jarrett CC
2004 #76 Dale Jarrett PC
2005 #10 Dale Jarrett
2005 #44 Dale Jarrett's Car M
2005 #49 Dale Jarrett S
2005 #54 Dale Jarrett CC
2006 #11 Dale Jarrett
2006 #42 Dale Jarrett's Car M
2006 #54 Dale Jarrett CC
2006 #77 Dale Jarrett PC
2007 #28 Dale Jarrett
2007 #41 Dale Jarrett's Car M
2007 #74 Dale Jarrett DD
2008 #48 Dale Jarrett's Car M
2008 #28 Dale Jarrett
Press Pass Premium $10 Phone Cards
1996 #4 Dale Jarrett
Press Pass Premium $20 Phone Cards
1996 #4 Dale Jarrett
Press Pass Premium $5 Phone Cards
1996 #4 Dale Jarrett
Press Pass Premium Asphalt Jungle
2006 #AJ6 Dale Jarrett
Press Pass Premium Badge of Honor
1999 #BH14 Dale Jarrett
1999 #BH25 Dale Jarrett's Car
Press Pass Premium Badge of Honor Reflectors
1999 #BH14 Dale Jarrett
1999 #BH25 Dale Jarrett's Car
Press Pass Premium Burning Desire
1999 #FD5B Dale Jarrett 1:36
Press Pass Premium Burning Rubber II
1996 #BR3 Dale Jarrett's Car
Press Pass Premium Concrete Chaos
2007 #CC5 Dale Jarrett
Press Pass Premium Crystal Ball
1996 #CB7 Dale Jarrett
1997 #CB6 Dale Jarrett
Press Pass Premium Crystal Ball Die Cut
1997 #CB6 Dale Jarrett
Press Pass Premium Emerald Proofs
1996 #13 Dale Jarrett
1996 #41 Dale Jarrett's Car
1997 #3 Dale Jarrett
1997 #35 Dale Jarrett's Car
1997 #40 Dale Jarrett
Press Pass Premium Flag Chasers
1998 #FC3 Dale Jarrett
1998 #FC25 Dale Jarrett's Car
Press Pass Premium Flag Chasers Reflectors
1998 #FC3 Dale Jarrett
1998 #FC25 Dale Jarrett's Car
Press Pass Premium Gold
2001 #8 Dale Jarrett
2001 #44 Dale Jarrett
2001 #53 Dale Jarrett CC
2001 #74 Dale Jarrett PC
Press Pass Premium Holofoil
1995 #14 Dale Jarrett
1996 #13 Dale Jarrett
1996 #41 Dale Jarrett's Car
Press Pass Premium Hot Pursuit
1995 #HP4 Dale Jarrett
Press Pass Premium Hot Threads Cars
2003 #HTT11 Dale Jarrett
2005 #HTT11 Dale Jarrett
2006 #HTT7 Dale Jarrett
Press Pass Premium Hot Threads Drivers
2003 #HTD11 Dale Jarrett
2005 #HTD11 Dale Jarrett
2006 #HTD7 Dale Jarrett
2008 #HTD7 Dale Jarrett
Press Pass Premium Hot Threads Drivers Bronze
2004 #HTD12 Dale Jarrett
Press Pass Premium Hot Threads Drivers Bronze Retail
2004 #HTT12 Dale Jarrett
Press Pass Premium Hot Threads Drivers Gold
2004 #HTD12 Dale Jarrett
2005 #HTD11 Dale Jarrett
2006 #HTD7 Dale Jarrett
2008 #HTD7 Dale Jarrett
Press Pass Premium Hot Threads Drivers Silver
2004 #HTD12 Dale Jarrett
Press Pass Premium Hot Threads Patches
2008 #HTP12 Dale Jarrett Coca Cola/8
2008 #HTP13 Dale Jarrett UPS/12
2008 #HTP14 Dale Jarrett NASCAR bar
Press Pass Premium Hot Threads Team
2008 #HTT7 Dale Jarrett
Press Pass Premium In The Zone
2000 #IZ8 Dale Jarrett
2001 #IZ6 Dale Jarrett
2002 #IZ6 Dale Jarrett
2003 #IZ3 Dale Jarrett
2004 #IZ3 Dale Jarrett
2005 #IZ8 Dale Jarrett
2006 #IZ3 Dale Jarrett
Press Pass Premium In the Zone Elite Edition
2004 #IZ3 Dale Jarrett
2005 #IZ8 Dale Jarrett
Press Pass Premium In the Zone Red
2006 #IZ3 Dale Jarrett
Press Pass Premium Lap Leaders
1997 #LL5 Dale Jarrett
Press Pass Premium Mirrors
1997 #3 Dale Jarrett
1997 #35 Dale Jarrett's Car
1997 #40 Dale Jarrett
Press Pass Premium Oil Slicks
1997 #3 Dale Jarrett
1997 #35 Dale Jarrett's Car
1997 #40 Dale Jarrett
Press Pass Premium Performance Driven
2000 #PD1 Dale Jarrett
2002 #PD4 Dale Jarrett
2004 #PD8 Dale Jarrett
2005 #PD2 Dale Jarrett
2007 #PD9 Dale Jarrett
Press Pass Premium Performance Driven Red
2007 #PD9 Dale Jarrett
Press Pass Premium Phone Cards $5
1995 #3 Dale Jarrett
Press Pass Premium Phone Cards $50
1995 #3 Dale Jarrett
Press Pass Premium Previews
2003 #12 Dale Jarrett
2004 #9 Dale Jarrett
2008 #EB28 Dale Jarrett
Press Pass Premium Race Used Firesuit
1999 #F8 Dale Jarrett
2000 #F8 Dale Jarrett
Press Pass Premium Race Used Firesuit Cars
2002 #FC5 Dale Jarrett
Press Pass Premium Race Used Firesuit Drivers

2002 #FD5 Dale Jarrett
Press Pass Premium Red
2007 #R28 Dale Jarrett
2007 #R41 Dale Jarrett's Car M
2007 #R74 Dale Jarrett DD
2008 #28 Dale Jarrett
2008 #48 Dale Jarrett's Car M
Press Pass Premium Red Hot
1995 #14 Dale Jarrett
Press Pass Premium Red Reflectors
2002 #12 Dale Jarrett
2002 #40 Dale Jarrett's Car
2002 #52 Dale Jarrett CC
2002 #74 Dale Jarrett PC
2003 #12 Dale Jarrett
2003 #39 Dale Jarrett's Car
2003 #54 Dale Jarrett CC
2003 #72 Dale Jarrett PC
Press Pass Premium Reflectors
1998 #8 Dale Jarrett
1998 #25 Dale Jarrett's Car
1998 #29 Dale Jarrett
1999 #R12 Dale Jarrett
1999 #R30 Dale Jarrett's Car
2000 #25 Dale Jarrett
2000 #46 Dale Jarrett
2000 #68 Dale Jarrett
Press Pass Premium Rivalries
1998 #5B Dale Jarrett
Press Pass Premium Samples
2002 #12 Dale Jarrett
2002 #40 Dale Jarrett's Car
2003 #12 Dale Jarrett
2003 #39 Dale Jarrett's Car
2004 #9 Dale Jarrett
2004 #48 Dale Jarrett NS
2005 #10 Dale Jarrett
2005 #44 Dale Jarrett's Car M
2005 #49 Dale Jarrett S
Press Pass Premium Steel Horses
1998 #SH10 Dale Jarrett's Car
1999 #SH10 Dale Jarrett's Car
Press Pass Premium Triple Gear Firesuit
1998 #TGF8 Dale Jarrett
Press Pass Previews
1993 #7 Dale Jarrett
1993 #27 Dale Jarrett's Car
2003 #15 Dale Jarrett
2004 #13 Dale Jarrett
2006 #EB28 Dale Jarrett
2006 #EB106 Dale Jarrett U
2007 #EB23 Dale Jarrett
2008 #EB34 Dale Jarrett
Press Pass Previews Green
2005 #EB35 Dale Jarrett
Press Pass Previews Silver
2005 #EB108 Dale Jarrett
Press Pass R and N China
1996 #15 Dale Jarrett
1996 #50 Dale Jarrett's Car
Press Pass Race Day
1994 #RD4 Dale Jarrett
1995 #RD6 Dale Jarrett
2007 #RD2 Dale Jarrett
2008 #RD5 Dale Jarrett
Press Pass Red Hot
1995 #14 Dale Jarrett
1995 #42 Dale Jarrett's Car
Press Pass Samples
2003 #15 Dale Jarrett
2003 #80 Ups and Downs WCS
2004 #13 Dale Jarrett
2004 #74 Dale Jarrett's Car OTW
2005 #35 Dale Jarrett
2005 #71 Dale Jarrett's Car OTW
2005 #108 Dale Jarrett P
Press Pass Scorchers
1996 #15 Dale Jarrett
1996 #50 Dale Jarrett's Car
1996 #79 Yates/McReynolds/D.Jarrett
1996 #87 Dale Jarrett DW
1996 #115 Dale Jarrett PRE
Press Pass Shockers
1998 #ST4A Dale Jarrett
1998 #P2 Dale Jarrett Promo
Press Pass Showcar
2002 #S5A Dale Jarrett's Car
2003 #S5B Dale Jarrett
2004 #S6B Dale Jarrett's Car
2005 #SC6 Dale Jarrett
Press Pass Showcar Die Cuts
2000 #SC3 Dale Jarrett's Car
Press Pass Showman
1999 #1A Dale Jarrett
2000 #SM3 Dale Jarrett
2002 #S5A Dale Jarrett
2003 #S5A Dale Jarrett
2004 #S6A Dale Jarrett
2005 #SM6 Dale Jarrett
Press Pass Showman Die Cuts
2000 #SM3 Dale Jarrett
Press Pass Showman/Showcar
2001 #S11A Dale Jarrett
2001 #S11B Dale Jarrett's Car
Press Pass Signings
1998 #2 Dale Jarrett PPP/VIP/S
1999 #25A Dale Jarrett Blue/600
1999 #25B Dale Jarrett Black/60
2000 #27 Dale Jarrett
2001 #24 Dale Jarrett P/T/N/S
2002 #27 Dale Jarrett O/P/S/T/V
2003 #33 Dale Jarrett O/P/S/T/V
2004 #29 Dale Jarrett O/P/S/T/V
2005 #24 Dale Jarrett P/S
2006 #24 Dale Jarrett NC P/S
2007 #31 Dale Jarrett NC
2008 #28 Dale Jarrett
Press Pass Signings Blue
2007 #12 Dale Jarrett NC
2008 #12 Dale Jarrett
Press Pass Signings Gold
1998 #2 Dale Jarrett PPP/VIP
1999 #9 Dale Jarrett/100
2000 #14 Dale Jarrett
2001 #16 Dale Jarrett P/T/N/S
2002 #25 Dale Jarrett O/P/S/T/V
2003 #33 Dale Jarrett O/P/S/T/V
2004 #27 Dale Jarrett O/P/S/T/V
2005 #23 Dale Jarrett P/S
2006 #21 Dale Jarrett NC P/S
2007 #24 Dale Jarrett NC
2008 #22 Dale Jarrett
Press Pass Signings Platinum
2005 #23 Dale Jarrett P/S
Press Pass Signings Press Plates Magenta
2007 #22 Dale Jarrett
Press Pass Signings Red Ink
2006 #8 Dale Jarrett
Press Pass Signings Silver
2006 #24 Dale Jarrett NC P/S
2007 #23 Dale Jarrett NC
2008 #20 Dale Jarrett
Press Pass Signings Transparent
2001 #4 Dale Jarrett P/T/N/S
2002 #4 Dale Jarrett O/P/S/T/V
2003 #4 Dale Jarrett O/P/S/T/V
Press Pass Skidmarks
1999 #3 Dale Jarrett
1999 #30 Dale Jarrett's Car
1999 #48 Dale Jarrett
1999 #87 Dale Jarrett OTP
2000 #SK1 Dale Jarrett
Press Pass Snapshots
2003 #SN10 Dale Jarrett
2004 #SN10 Dale Jarrett
2005 #SN11 Dale Jarrett
2006 #SN15 Dale Jarrett
2006 #SN31 Dale Jarrett
2007 #SN12 Dale Jarrett
Press Pass Snapshots Extra
2005 #SS4 Dale Jarrett
Press Pass Speedway
2008 #31 Dale Jarrett
2008 #97 Dale Jarrett Fans H
Press Pass Speedway Cockpit
2008 #CP9 Dale Jarrett
Press Pass Speedway Corporate Cuts Drivers
2008 #CD-DJ Dale Jarrett
Press Pass Speedway Corporate Cuts Drivers Patches
2008 #CD-DJ Dale Jarrett
Press Pass Speedway Corporate Cuts Team
2008 #CT-DJ Dale Jarrett
Press Pass Speedway Gold
2008 #G31 Dale Jarrett
2008 #G97 Dale Jarrett Fans H
Press Pass Speedway Holofoil
2008 #H31 Dale Jarrett
2008 #H97 Dale Jarrett Fans H
Press Pass Speedway Previews
2008 #EB31 Dale Jarrett
2008 #EB97 Dale Jarrett Fans H
Press Pass Speedway Red
2008 #R31 Dale Jarrett
2008 #R97 Dale Jarrett Fans H
Press Pass Stealth
1998 #16 Dale Jarrett
1998 #17 Dale Jarrett's Car
1998 #45 Dale Jarrett TM
1999 #13 Dale Jarrett
1999 #14 Dale Jarrett's Car
1999 #52 Quality Care Gas Can TT
2000 #46 Dale Jarrett
2000 #47 Dale Jarrett's Car
2000 #68 Dale Jarrett FF
2001 #40 Dale Jarrett
2001 #41 Dale Jarrett's Car
2001 #42 Dale Jarrett
2001 #69 Dale Jarrett SST
2002 #40 Dale Jarrett
2002 #41 Dale Jarrett's Car
2002 #42 Dale Jarrett
2002 #54 Dale Jarrett's Car SST
2003 #37 Dale Jarrett
2003 #38 Dale Jarrett's Car
2003 #39 Dale Jarrett
2003 #66 Dale Jarrett SF
2004 #4 Dale Jarrett
2004 #5 Dale Jarrett's Car
2004 #6 Dale Jarrett
2004 #89 Dale Jarrett SST
2005 #19 Dale Jarrett
2005 #22 Dale Jarrett's Car
2005 #25 Dale Jarrett
2006 #12 Dale Jarrett
2006 #44 Dale Jarrett's Rig
2006 #56 Jarrett/Sadler TM
2006 #59 Dale Jarrett F
2007 #11 Dale Jarrett
2007 #53 Dale Jarrett's Rig
2008 #15 Dale Jarrett
Press Pass Stealth Autographed Hat Entry
2006 #PPH10 Dale Jarrett
Press Pass Stealth Battle Armor Drivers
2007 #BAD16 Dale Jarrett
2008 #BAD19 Dale Jarrett
Press Pass Stealth Battle Armor Teams
2007 #BAT16 Dale Jarrett
2008 #BAT19 Dale Jarrett
Press Pass Stealth Behind the Numbers
2000 #BN5 Dale Jarrett
2001 #BN3 Dale Jarrett
2002 #BN3 Dale Jarrett
Press Pass Stealth Big Numbers
1999 #BN10 Dale Jarrett
Press Pass Stealth Big Numbers Die Cuts
1999 #BN10 Dale Jarrett
Press Pass Stealth Chrome
2007 #11 Dale Jarrett
2007 #53 Dale Jarrett's Rig
2008 #15 Dale Jarrett
Press Pass Stealth Chrome Exclusives
2007 #X11 Dale Jarrett
2007 #X53 Dale Jarrett's Rig
2008 #15 Dale Jarrett
Press Pass Stealth Chrome Exclusives Gold
2008 #15 Dale Jarrett
Press Pass Stealth Chrome Platinum
2007 #P11 Dale Jarrett
2007 #P53 Dale Jarrett's Rig
Press Pass Stealth Corporate Cuts
2006 #CCD6 Dale Jarrett
Press Pass Stealth EFX
2002 #FX8 Dale Jarrett
2005 #EFX3 Dale Jarrett
2006 #EFX7 Dale Jarrett 1:48
Press Pass Stealth Fan Talk
1998 #4 Dale Jarrett
Press Pass Stealth Fan Talk Die Cuts
1998 #4 Dale Jarrett
Press Pass Stealth Fusion
1998 #16 Dale Jarrett
1998 #17 Dale Jarrett's Car
1998 #45 Dale Jarrett TM
1999 #F13 Dale Jarrett
1999 #F14 Dale Jarrett's Car
1999 #F52 Quality Care Gas Can TT
2000 #FS1 Dale Jarrett
2000 #FS2 Dale Jarrett's Car
2000 #FS3 Dale Jarrett
2001 #F3 Dale Jarrett
2002 #F5 Dale Jarrett
2005 #FU9 Dale Jarrett 1:14
2007 #F1 Dale Jarrett
Press Pass Stealth Fusion Green
2000 #FS1 Dale Jarrett
2000 #FS2 Dale Jarrett
2000 #FS3 Dale Jarrett
Press Pass Stealth Fusion Red
2000 #FS1 Dale Jarrett
2000 #FS2 Dale Jarrett
2000 #FS3 Dale Jarrett
Press Pass Stealth Gear Grippers Cars
2003 #GGT14 Dale Jarrett
2005 #GGT11 Dale Jarrett
Press Pass Stealth Gear Grippers Drivers
2003 #GGD14 Dale Jarrett
2004 #GGD12 Dale Jarrett
2005 #GGD11 Dale Jarrett
2006 #GGD3 Dale Jarrett
Press Pass Stealth Gear Grippers Drivers Retail
2004 #GGT12 Dale Jarrett
Press Pass Stealth Gold
2002 #40 Dale Jarrett
2002 #41 Dale Jarrett's Car
2002 #42 Dale Jarrett
2002 #54 Dale Jarrett's Car SST
Press Pass Stealth Headlines
1999 #SH8 Dale Jarrett
Press Pass Stealth Holofoils
2001 #40 Dale Jarrett
2001 #41 Dale Jarrett
2001 #42 Dale Jarrett
2001 #69 Dale Jarrett SST
Press Pass Stealth Hot Pass
2006 #HP13 Dale Jarrett
Press Pass Stealth Intensity
2000 #IN1 Dale Jarrett
Press Pass Stealth Lap Leaders
2001 #LL17 Dale Jarrett
2001 #LL35 Dale Jarrett's Car
2002 #LL12 Dale Jarrett
Press Pass Stealth Lap Leaders Clear Cars
2001 #LL35 Dale Jarrett's Car
Press Pass Stealth Lap Leaders Clear Drivers
2001 #LL17 Dale Jarrett
Press Pass Stealth Mach 07
2007 #M7-12 Dale Jarrett
Press Pass Stealth Mach 08
2008 #M8-12 Dale Jarrett
Press Pass Stealth Maximum Access
2007 #MA12 Dale Jarrett
2008 #MA13 Dale Jarrett
Press Pass Stealth Maximum Access Autographs
2007 #MA12 Dale Jarrett
2008 #MA13 Dale Jarrett
Press Pass Stealth No Boundaries
2003 #NB14 Dale Jarrett
2004 #NB14 Dale Jarrett
2005 #NB12 Dale Jarrett
Press Pass Stealth Octane
1998 #17 Dale Jarrett
1998 #18 Dale Jarrett's Car
Press Pass Stealth Octane Die Cuts
1998 #17 Dale Jarrett
1998 #18 Dale Jarrett's Car
Press Pass Stealth Octane SLX
1999 #O10 Dale Jarrett
1999 #O35 Dale Jarrett's Car
Press Pass Stealth Octane SLX Die Cuts
1999 #O10 Dale Jarrett
1999 #O35 Dale Jarrett's Car
Press Pass Stealth Previews
2003 #37 Dale Jarrett
2003 #38 Dale Jarrett's Car
2003 #39 Dale Jarrett
2004 #EB4 Dale Jarrett
2004 #EB5 Dale Jarrett's Car
2004 #EB6 Dale Jarrett
2005 #19 Dale Jarrett
2005 #22 Dale Jarrett's Car
2005 #25 Dale Jarrett
2006 #12 Dale Jarrett
2007 #EB11 Dale Jarrett
2008 #15 Dale Jarrett
Press Pass Stealth Profile
2000 #PR1 Dale Jarrett
2002 #P8 Dale Jarrett
2003 #PR3 Dale Jarrett
2004 #P12 Dale Jarrett 1:14
2006 #P5 Dale Jarrett
Press Pass Stealth Race Used Glove Cars
2002 #GLC14 Dale Jarrett's Car/10
Press Pass Stealth Race Used Glove Drivers
2002 #GLD14 Dale Jarrett/10
Press Pass Stealth Race Used Gloves
1998 #G7 Dale Jarrett
1999 #G4 Dale Jarrett/25
2000 #G11 Dale Jarrett/50
Press Pass Stealth Red
2003 #P37 Dale Jarrett
2003 #P38 Dale Jarrett's Car
2003 #P39 Dale Jarrett
2003 #P66 Dale Jarrett SF
Press Pass Stealth Retail
2006 #12 Dale Jarrett
2006 #44 Dale Jarrett's Rig
2006 #56 Jarrett/Sadler TM
2006 #59 Dale Jarrett F
Press Pass Stealth Retail Gear Grippers Cars
2006 #GGT3 Dale Jarrett
Press Pass Stealth Samples
2002 #40 Dale Jarrett
2002 #41 Dale Jarrett's Car
2002 #42 Dale Jarrett
2002 #54 Dale Jarrett's Car SST
2003 #37 Dale Jarrett
2003 #38 Dale Jarrett's Car
2003 #39 Dale Jarrett
2003 #66 Dale Jarrett SF
2004 #X4 Dale Jarrett
2004 #X6 Dale Jarrett
2004 #X5 Dale Jarrett's Car
2004 #X89 Dale Jarrett SST
2005 #19 Dale Jarrett
2005 #22 Dale Jarrett's Car
2005 #25 Dale Jarrett
Press Pass Stealth SST
2000 #SST1 Dale Jarrett
Press Pass Stealth SST Cars
1999 #SS4 Dale Jarrett's Car
Press Pass Stealth SST Drivers
1999 #SS4 Dale Jarrett
Press Pass Stealth Stars
1998 #8 Dale Jarrett
Press Pass Stealth Stars Die Cuts
1998 #8 Dale Jarrett
Press Pass Stealth X-Ray
2004 #4 Dale Jarrett
2004 #5 Dale Jarrett's Car
2004 #6 Dale Jarrett
2004 #89 Dale Jarrett SST
2005 #X19 Dale Jarrett
2005 #X22 Dale Jarrett's Car
2005 #X25 Dale Jarrett
2006 #X12 Dale Jarrett
2006 #X44 Dale Jarrett's Rig
2006 #X56 Jarrett/Sadler TM
2006 #X59 Dale Jarrett F
Press Pass Techno-Retro
2000 #TR11 Dale Jarrett
Press Pass Top 25 Drivers & Rides
2006 #C24 Dale Jarrett's Car
2006 #D24 Dale Jarrett
Press Pass Top Shelf
2002 #TS4 Dale Jarrett
2003 #TS3 Dale Jarrett
Press Pass Torpedoes
1998 #ST4B Dale Jarrett's Car
Press Pass Torquers
1996 #15 Dale Jarrett
1996 #50 Dale Jarrett's Car
1996 #79 Yates/McReynolds/D.Jarrett
1996 #87 Dale Jarrett DW
1996 #115 Dale Jarrett PRE
1997 #3 Dale Jarrett
1997 #44 Dale Jarrett's Car
1997 #59 Dale Jarrett's Car
1997 #70 Dale Jarrett
1997 #80 Dale Jarrett
1997 #94 Dale Jarrett
1997 #96 J.Gordon/D.Jarrett's Cars
1997 #102 Dale Jarrett
1997 #124 Dale Jarrett
Press Pass Total Memorabilia
2001 #TM4 Dale Jarrett
Press Pass Total Memorabilia Power Pick
2002 #TM4 Dale Jarrett
Press Pass Trackside
2000 #26 Dale Jarrett
2000 #34 Dale Jarrett's Car
2000 #61 Dale Jarrett WBM
2001 #21 Dale Jarrett
2001 #49 Dale Jarrett's Car
2001 #69 Dale Jarrett TM
2001 #86 Dale Jarrett CS
2002 #21 Dale Jarrett
2002 #55 Dale Jarrett RD
2002 #86 Dale Jarrett TM
2003 #4 Dale Jarrett
2003 #59 D.Jarrett/N.Jarrett FA
2003 #71 Dale Jarrett in Pits
2003 #75 E.Sadler/D.Jarrett TM
2004 #15 Dale Jarrett
2004 #62 Dale Jarrett's Car HS
2004 #66 D.Jarrett/E.Sadler TM
2005 #29 Dale Jarrett
2005 #66 Dale Jarrett's Car HS
2005 #69 D.Jarrett/E.Sadler/ TM
2005 #90 Dale Jarrett GP
2005 #99 Dale Jarrett F
Press Pass Trackside Dialed In
2000 #DI1 Dale Jarrett
2001 #DI1 Dale Jarrett
2002 #DI5 Dale Jarrett
2003 #DI4 Dale Jarrett
2005 #DI8 Dale Jarrett
Press Pass Trackside Die Cuts
2000 #26 Dale Jarrett
2000 #34 Dale Jarrett
2001 #21 Dale Jarrett
2001 #49 Dale Jarrett's Car
2001 #69 Dale Jarrett TM
2001 #86 Dale Jarrett CS
Press Pass Trackside Gold Holofoil
2003 #P4 Dale Jarrett
2003 #P59 D.Jarrett/N.Jarrett
2003 #P71 Dale Jarrett's Crew
2003 #P75 E.Sadler/D.Jarrett
Press Pass Trackside Golden
2000 #26 Dale Jarrett
2000 #34 Dale Jarrett
2001 #21 Dale Jarrett
2001 #49 Dale Jarrett's Car
2001 #69 Dale Jarrett TM
2001 #86 Dale Jarrett CS
2002 #G21 Dale Jarrett
2003 #G4 Dale Jarrett
2004 #G15 Dale Jarrett
2004 #G62 Dale Jarrett's Car HS
2004 #G66 D.Jarrett/E.Sadler TM
2005 #G29 Dale Jarrett
2005 #G66 Dale Jarrett's Car HS
2005 #G69 D.Jarrett/E.Sadler/ TM
2005 #G90 Dale Jarrett GP
2005 #G99 Dale Jarrett F
Press Pass Trackside Hat Giveaway
2003 #PPH11 Dale Jarrett
2004 #PPH12 Dale Jarrett
2005 #PPH11 Dale Jarrett
Press Pass Trackside Hot Pass
2005 #7 Dale Jarrett
Press Pass Trackside Hot Pass National
2005 #7 Dale Jarrett
Press Pass Trackside Hot Pursuit
2004 #HP8 Dale Jarrett
Press Pass Trackside License to Drive
2002 #14 Dale Jarrett
Press Pass Trackside License to Drive Die Cuts
2002 #14 Dale Jarrett
Press Pass Trackside Mirror Image
2001 #MI1 Dale Jarrett
2002 #MI4 Dale Jarrett
Press Pass Trackside Panorama
2000 #P32 Dale Jarrett
Press Pass Trackside Previews
2003 #4 Dale Jarrett
2004 #EB15 Dale Jarrett
2005 #29 Dale Jarrett
2005 #90 Dale Jarrett GP
Press Pass Trackside Runnin N' Gunnin
2000 #RG8 Dale Jarrett
2002 #RG6 Dale Jarrett
2003 #RG4 Dale Jarrett
2005 #RG8 Dale Jarrett
Press Pass Trackside Samples
2002 #21 Dale Jarrett
2002 #55 Dale Jarrett RD
2002 #86 Dale Jarrett TM
2003 #4 Dale Jarrett
2003 #59 D.Jarrett/N.Jarrett FA
2003 #71 Dale Jarrett in Pits
2003 #75 E.Sadler/D.Jarrett TM
2004 #15 Dale Jarrett
2004 #62 Dale Jarrett's Car HS
2004 #66 D.Jarrett/E.Sadler TM
2005 #29 Dale Jarrett
2005 #66 Dale Jarrett's Car HS
2005 #69 D.Jarrett/E.Sadler/ TM
2005 #90 Dale Jarrett GP
2005 #99 Dale Jarrett F
Press Pass Trackside Too Tough To Tame
2000 #TT1 Dale Jarrett
Press Pass Triple Burner
2001 #TB4 Dale Jarrett
2002 #TB4 Dale Jarrett
Press Pass Triple Gear 3 in 1
1998 #STG8 Dale Jarrett
1999 #TG6 Dale Jarrett
Press Pass Triple Gear Burning Rubber
1998 #TG8 Dale Jarrett
Press Pass Velocity
2001 #VL3 Dale Jarrett
2002 #VL5 Dale Jarrett
2003 #VC3 Dale Jarrett
2005 #V1 Dale Jarrett
2006 #VE9 Dale Jarrett
2007 #V6 Dale Jarrett
Press Pass Victory Lane
1997 #VL4A Dale Jarrett
1997 #VL4B Dale Jarrett's Car
Press Pass Victory Lap
2003 #12 Dale Jarrett
Press Pass Vintage
2001 #VN4 Dale Jarrett
2002 #VN10 Dale Jarrett
Pro Set
1991 #43 Dale Jarrett
1991 #44 Dale Jarrett's Car
1991 #55 Ned Jarrett/Dale Jarrett
1992 #24 Dale Jarrett
1992 #105 Dale Jarrett
Pro Set Maxwell House
1992 #22 Dale Jarrett
Proline Portraits Collectibles Autographs *
1992 #NNO Dale Jarrett
Race Sharks
1997 #3 Dale Jarrett
1997 #30 Dale Jarrett
1997 #34 Dale Jarrett
1997 #41 Dale Jarrett
Race Sharks First Bite
1997 #3 Dale Jarrett
1997 #30 Dale Jarrett
1997 #34 Dale Jarrett
1997 #41 Dale Jarrett
Race Sharks Great White
1997 #3 Dale Jarrett
1997 #30 Dale Jarrett
1997 #34 Dale Jarrett
1997 #41 Dale Jarrett
Race Sharks Great White Shark's Teeth
1997 #GW4 Dale Jarrett
Race Sharks Great White Shark's Teeth First Bite
1997 #GW4 Dale Jarrett
Race Sharks Hammerhead
1997 #3 Dale Jarrett
1997 #30 Dale Jarrett
1997 #34 Dale Jarrett
1997 #41 Dale Jarrett
Race Sharks Hammerhead First Bite
1997 #3 Dale Jarrett
1997 #30 Dale Jarrett
1997 #34 Dale Jarrett
1997 #41 Dale Jarrett
Race Sharks Shark Attack
1997 #SA3 Dale Jarrett
Race Sharks Shark Attack First Bite
1997 #SA3 Dale Jarrett
Race Sharks Shark Attack First Bite Previews
1997 #3 Dale Jarrett
Race Sharks Shark Tooth Signatures
1997 #ST3 Dale Jarrett
Race Sharks Shark Tooth Signatures First Bite
1997 #ST3 Dale Jarrett
Race Sharks Tiger Shark
1997 #3 Dale Jarrett
1997 #30 Dale Jarrett
1997 #34 Dale Jarrett
1997 #41 Dale Jarrett
Race Sharks Tiger Shark First Bite
1997 #3 Dale Jarrett
1997 #30 Dale Jarrett
1997 #34 Dale Jarrett
1997 #41 Dale Jarrett
Racer's Choice
1996 #16 Dale Jarrett
1996 #32 Dale Jarrett's Car
1996 #91 Dale Jarrett BC
1997 #32 Dale Jarrett
1997 #67 Dale Jarrett's Car
1997 #105 Dale Jarrett TR
Racer's Choice Artist's Proofs
1996 #16 Dale Jarrett
1996 #32 Dale Jarrett's Car
1996 #91 Dale Jarrett BC
Racer's Choice Busch Clash
1997 #12 Dale Jarrett
Racer's Choice High Octane
1997 #4 Dale Jarrett
Racer's Choice High Octane Glow in the Dark
1997 #4 Dale Jarrett
Racer's Choice Showcase Series
1997 #32 Dale Jarrett
1997 #67 Dale Jarrett's Car
1997 #105 Dale Jarrett TR
Racer's Choice Speedway Collection
1996 #16 Dale Jarrett
1996 #32 Dale Jarrett's Car
1996 #91 Dale Jarrett BC
Redline Standups
1992 #21 Dale Jarrett
SB Motorsports
1997 #4 Dale Jarrett
1997 #40 Dale Jarrett
1997 #55 Dale Jarrett's Car
1997 #93 Dale Jarrett
SB Motorsports Autographs
1997 #4 Dale Jarrett
SB Motorsports Race Chat
1997 #RC4 Dale Jarrett
SB Motorsports Winston Cup Rewind
1997 #WC1 Dale Jarrett
1997 #WC11 Dale Jarrett
1997 #WC19 Dale Jarrett
Score Board IQ
1997 #4 Dale Jarrett
1997 #7 Dale Jarrett
1997 #28 Dale Jarrett
1997 #49 Dale Jarrett's Car
1997 #P1 Dale Jarrett Promo
Score Board IQ $10 Phone Cards
1997 #PC8 Dale Jarrett
Score Board Seven-Eleven Phone Cards
1997 #3 Dale Jarrett
Select
1995 #16 Dale Jarrett
1995 #42 Dale Jarrett's Car
1995 #115 Dale Jarrett/Ned Jarrett IB
Select Flat Out
1995 #16 Dale Jarrett
1995 #42 Dale Jarrett's Car
1995 #115 Dale Jarrett/Ned Jarrett IB
SkyBox Profile
1997 #14 Dale Jarrett
1997 #77 Dale Jarrett's Car
SkyBox Profile Autographs
1997 #14 Dale Jarrett
SkyBox Profile Pace Setters
1997 #E6 Dale Jarrett
SkyBox Profile Team
1997 #T3 Dale Jarrett
SLU Racing Winner's Circle
1997 #5 Dale Jarrett
1998 #6 Dale Jarrett
1999 #30 Dale Jarrett
2000 #30 Dale Jarrett
SP
1995 #21 Dale Jarrett CC
1995 #60 Dale Jarrett
1995 #101 Dale Jarrett's Car
1996 #36 Dale Jarrett
1996 #54 Dale Jarrett CC
1996 #76 Dale Jarrett RPM
1997 #12 Dale Jarrett
1997 #54 Dale Jarrett's Car
1997 #92 Dale Jarrett 2F
1997 #118 Dale Jarrett 3F
SP Authentic
1998 #12 Dale Jarrett
1998 #46 Dale Jarrett's Car
1998 #78 Dale Jarrett VL
1999 #4 Dale Jarrett
1999 #52 Dale Jarrett's Car
1999 #71 Dale Jarrett CLASS
1999 #80 Dale Jarrett SP
2000 #7 Dale Jarrett
2000 #82 Dale Jarrett SUP
2000 #P88 Dale Jarrett Promo
SP Authentic Behind the Wheel
1998 #BW2 Dale Jarrett
SP Authentic Behind the Wheel Die Cuts
1998 #BW2 Dale Jarrett
SP Authentic Behind the Wheel Gold
1998 #BW2 Dale Jarrett
SP Authentic Cup Challengers
1999 #CC2 Dale Jarrett
SP Authentic Driver's Seat
2000 #DS1 Dale Jarrett
SP Authentic Overdrive
1999 #4 Dale Jarrett
1999 #52 Dale Jarrett CAR
1999 #71 Dale Jarrett CLASS
1999 #80 Dale Jarrett SP/88
SP Authentic Overdrive Gold
2000 #7 Dale Jarrett/88
2000 #82 Dale Jarrett SUP/88
SP Authentic Overdrive Silver
2000 #7 Dale Jarrett
2000 #82 Dale Jarrett SUP
SP Authentic Power Surge
2000 #PS7 Dale Jarrett
SP Authentic Race for the Cup
2000 #R2 Dale Jarrett
SP Authentic Sign of the Times
1999 #DJ Dale Jarrett
2000 #DJ Dale Jarrett

SP Authentic Sign of the Times Gold
2000 #DJ Dale Jarrett
SP Authentic Sign of the Times Red
1998 #ST7 Dale Jarrett's Car/239
SP Authentic Traditions
1998 #T4 N.Jarrett/D.Jarrett
SP Die Cuts
1995 #21 Dale Jarrett
1995 #60 Dale Jarrett
1995 #101 Dale Jarrett's Car
SP Holoview Maximum Effects
1996 #ME22 Dale Jarrett
SP Holoview Maximum Effects Die Cuts
1996 #ME22 Dale Jarrett
SP Race Film
1997 #RD7 Dale Jarrett
SP Speed Merchants
1995 #SM28 Dale Jarrett
SP Speed Merchants Die Cuts
1995 #SM28 Dale Jarrett
SP Super Series
1997 #12 Dale Jarrett
1997 #54 Dale Jarrett's Car
1997 #92 Dale Jarrett 2F
1997 #118 Dale Jarrett 3F
Speedflix
1996 #10 Dale Jarrett
1996 #24 Dale Jarrett
1996 #47 Dale Jarrett DT
1996 #P1 Dale Jarrett Promo
Speedflix Artist Proof's
1996 #10 Dale Jarrett
1996 #24 Dale Jarrett
1996 #47 Dale Jarrett DT
Speedflix Clear Shots
1996 #7 Dale Jarrett
Speedflix ProMotion
1996 #7 Dale Jarrett
Sports Illustrated for Kids
2001 #78 Dale Jarrett Nascar
Sports Illustrated for Kids *
1992-00 #480 Dale Jarrett
2001-02 #78 Dale Jarrett
Sports Illustrated for Kids II
1996 #480 Dale Jarrett Auto Racing
Sports Legends Dale Jarrett
1991 #DJ1 Dale Jarrett
1991 #DJ2 Dale Jarrett/N.Jarrett
1991 #DJ3 Dale Jarrett's Car
1991 #DJ4 Dale Jarrett w/Car
1991 #DJ5 Dale Jarrett/N.Jarrett
1991 #DJ6 Dale Jarrett w/Crew
1991 #DJ7 Dale Jarrett w/Car
1991 #DJ8 Dale Jarrett/Dav.Allison Cars
1991 #DJ9 Dale Jarrett w/Crew
1991 #DJ10 Dale Jarrett/N.Jarrett
1991 #DJ11 Dale Jarrett
1991 #DJ12 Dale Jarrett w/Car
1991 #DJ13 Dale Jarrett
1991 #DJ14 Dale Jarrett
1991 #DJ15 Dale Jarrett
1991 #DJ16 Dale Jarrett's Car
1991 #DJ17 Dale Jarrett/C.Yarborough
1991 #DJ18 Dale Jarrett w/Car
1991 #DJ19 Dale Jarrett's Car
1991 #DJ20 Dale Jarrett's Car
1991 #DJ21 Dale Jarrett
1991 #DJ22 Dale Jarrett
1991 #DJ23 Dale Jarrett
1991 #DJ24 Dale Jarrett w/Car
1991 #DJ25 Dale Jarrett Crash
1991 #DJ26 Dale Jarrett/A.Petree
1991 #DJ27 Dale Jarrett's Car
1991 #DJ28 Dale Jarrett
1991 #DJ29 Dale Jarrett w/Car
1991 #DJ30 Dale Jarrett
1991 #P1 Dale Jarrett Prototype
Sports Legends Ned Jarrett
1991 #NJ3 Ned Jarrett/Glenn/Dale
1991 #NJ4 Ned Jarrett/Dale Jarrett
SportsCom FanScan
1997 #6 Dale Jarrett
1998 #4 Dale Jarrett
1999 #4 Dale Jarrett
SPx
1996 #23 Dale Jarrett
1997 #8 Dale Jarrett
SPx Blue
1997 #8 Dale Jarrett
SPx Elite
1996 #E2 Dale Jarrett
SPx Gold
1996 #23 Dale Jarrett
1997 #8 Dale Jarrett
SPx Silver
1997 #8 Dale Jarrett
SPx SpeedView Autographs
1997 #SV7 Dale Jarrett
SPx Tag Team Autographs
1997 #TA2 D.Jarrett/E.Irvan
Super Shots Sears Point CHP
2001 #SP6 Dale Jarrett's Car
Traks
1991 #21 Dale Jarrett
1991 #32 Dale Jarrett
1992 #18 Dale Jarrett
1992 #32 Dale Jarrett
1993 #18 Dale Jarrett's Car
1994 #13 Dale Jarrett
1994 #65 Dale Jarrett
1994 #103 Dale Jarrett
1994 #108 Dale Jarrett's Car
1994 #146 Dale Jarrett
1995 #18 Dale Jarrett
1995 #43 Dale Jarrett
1995 #60 Dale Jarrett
2006 #14 Dale Jarrett
2006 #53 Dale Jarrett's Car
2006 #108 Dale Jarrett's Car PS
2007 #11 Dale Jarrett
2007 #57 Dale Jarrett's Car CTG
2007 #76 Dale Jarrett GP
2007 #100 Dale Jarrett CL
Traks 5th Anniversary
1995 #20 Dale Jarrett
1995 #41 Dale Jarrett
1995 #54 Dale Jarrett's Car
Traks 5th Anniversary Gold
1995 #20 Dale Jarrett
1995 #41 Dale Jarrett
1995 #54 Dale Jarrett's Car
Traks 5th Anniversary Retrospective
1995 #R7 Dale Jarrett
Traks Auto Value
1994 #9 Dale Jarrett
1995 #24 Dale Jarrett
TRAKS Autographs
2006 #16 Dale Jarrett NC SP
TRAKS Autographs 100
2006 #10 Dale Jarrett NC
TRAKS Autographs 25
2006 #14 Dale Jarrett NC
Traks Challengers
1995 #C7 Dale Jarrett
Traks Challengers First Run
1995 #C7 Dale Jarrett
Traks Corporate Cuts Driver
2007 #CCD4 Dale Jarrett
Traks Corporate Cuts Patch
2007 #CCD4 Dale Jarrett/10
Traks Corporate Cuts Team
2007 #CCT4 Dale Jarrett
Traks Driver's Seat
2007 #DS22B Dale Jarrett VAR
2007 #DS22 Dale Jarrett
Traks Driver's Seat National
2007 #DS22 Dale Jarrett
Traks First Run
1993 #18 Dale Jarrett's Car
1994 #13 Dale Jarrett
1994 #65 Dale Jarrett
1994 #103 Dale Jarrett
1994 #108 Dale Jarrett's Car
1994 #146 Dale Jarrett
1995 #18 Dale Jarrett
1995 #43 Dale Jarrett
1995 #60 Dale Jarrett
Traks Gold
2007 #G11 Dale Jarrett
2007 #G57 Dale Jarrett's Car CTG
2007 #G76 Dale Jarrett GP
2007 #G100 Dale Jarrett CL
Traks Goody's
1992 #18 Dale Jarrett
Traks Holofoil
2007 #H11 Dale Jarrett
2007 #H57 Dale Jarrett's Car CTG
2007 #H76 Dale Jarrett GP
2007 #H100 Dale Jarrett CL
Traks Preferred Collector
1993 #13 Dale Jarrett
Traks Previews
2007 #EB11 Dale Jarrett
2007 #EB76 Dale Jarrett GP
Traks Racing Machines
1995 #RM12 Dale Jarrett's Car
Traks Racing Machines First Run
1995 #RM12 Dale Jarrett's Car
Traks Red
2007 #R11 Dale Jarrett
2007 #R57 Dale Jarrett's Car CTG
2007 #R76 Dale Jarrett GP
2007 #R100 Dale Jarrett FT CL
Traks Review and Preview
1996 #6 Dale Jarrett
1996 #22 Dale Jarrett
1996 #39 Dale Jarrett
1996 #47 Checklist I
Traks Review and Preview First Run
1996 #6 Dale Jarrett
1996 #22 Dale Jarrett
1996 #39 Dale Jarrett
1996 #47 Checklist I
Traks Review and Preview Liquid Gold
1996 #LG1 Dale Jarrett
Traks Review and Preview Magnets
1996 #6 Dale Jarrett
1996 #22 Dale Jarrett
1996 #39 Dale Jarrett
Traks Review and Preview Triple-Chase
1996 #TC6 Dale Jarrett
1996 #TC20 Dale Jarrett's Car
Traks Review and Preview Triple-Chase Gold
1996 #TC6 Dale Jarrett
1996 #TC20 Quality Care Racing
Traks Review and Preview Triple-Chase Holofoil
1996 #TC6 Dale Jarrett
1996 #TC20 Quality Care Racing
Traks Series Stars
1995 #SS20 Dale Jarrett
Traks Series Stars First Run
1995 #SS20 Dale Jarrett
TRAKS Stickers
2006 #B8 Dale Jarrett
Traks Track Time
2007 #TT5 Dale Jarrett
Ultra
1996 #47 Dale Jarrett
1996 #48 Dale Jarrett
1996 #49 Dale Jarrett's Car
1996 #183 Dale Jarrett RW
1997 #16 Dale Jarrett
1997 #40 Dale Jarrett's Car
Ultra AKA
1997 #A4 Dale Jarrett
Ultra Autographs
1996 #13 Dale Jarrett
Ultra Boxed Set
1996 #13 Dale Jarrett
Ultra Inside Out
1997 #DC4 Dale Jarrett
Ultra Shoney's
1997 #6 Dale Jarrett
Ultra Update
1996 #16 Dale Jarrett
1996 #44 Dale Jarrett HS
1996 #62 Dale Jarrett's Car
1996 #86 D.Jarrett/T.Parrott
1997 #3 Dale Jarrett
1997 #94 Dale Jarrett's Car
Ultra Update Autographs
1996 #6 Dale Jarrett
1997 #3 Dale Jarrett
Ultra Update Double Trouble
1997 #DT6 Dale Jarrett
Ultra Update Driver View
1997 #D2 Dale Jarrett
Ultra Update Elite Seats
1997 #E6 Dale Jarrett
Ultra Update Proven Power
1996 #6 Dale Jarrett
Ultra Update Winner
1996 #13 Dale Jarrett
Ultra Winn Dixie
1997 #WD7 Dale Jarrett
Upper Deck
1995 #7 Dale Jarrett
1995 #50 Dale Jarrett with Car
1995 #75 Dale Jarrett's Car
1995 #143 Dale Jarrett's Car
1995 #165 Dale Jarrett DYK
1995 #206 Dale Jarrett
1995 #250 Dale Jarrett SD
1995 #285 Dale Jarrett's Car
1996 #26 Dale Jarrett
1996 #66 Dale Jarrett SB
1996 #106 Dale Jarrett PP
Upper Deck Autographs
1995 #206 Dale Jarrett
Upper Deck Diamond Vision
1998 #7 Dale Jarrett
Upper Deck Diamond Vision Signature Moves
1998 #7 Dale Jarrett
Upper Deck Gold Signature/Electric Gold
1995 #7 Dale Jarrett
1995 #50 Dale Jarrett with Car
1995 #75 Dale Jarrett's Car
1995 #143 Dale Jarrett's Car
1995 #165 Dale Jarrett DYK
1995 #206 Dale Jarrett
1995 #250 Dale Jarrett SD
1995 #285 Dale Jarrett's Car
Upper Deck MVP
2000 #1 Dale Jarrett
2000 #62 Dale Jarrett's Car
2000 #85 D.Jarrett/N.Jarrett
2000 #92 Dale Jarrett
Upper Deck MVP Cup Quest 2000
2000 #CQ7 Dale Jarrett
Upper Deck MVP Gold Script
2000 #1 Dale Jarrett
2000 #62 Dale Jarrett
2000 #85 Dale Jarrett/Ned Jarrett
2000 #92 Dale Jarrett
Upper Deck MVP Legends in the Making
2000 #LM6 Dale Jarrett
Upper Deck MVP Magic Numbers
2000 #MDJ Dale Jarrett's Car
Upper Deck MVP Magic Numbers Autographs
2000 #MADJ Dale Jarrett's Car/88
Upper Deck MVP NASCAR Gallery
2000 #NG7 Dale Jarrett
Upper Deck MVP NASCAR Stars
2000 #NS5 Dale Jarrett
Upper Deck MVP ProSign
1999 #DJR Dale Jarrett Silver
2000 #PSDJ Dale Jarrett
Upper Deck MVP Silver Script
2000 #1 Dale Jarrett
2000 #62 Dale Jarrett
2000 #85 Dale Jarrett/Ned Jarrett
2000 #92 Dale Jarrett
Upper Deck MVP Super Script
2000 #1 Dale Jarrett/88
2000 #62 Dale Jarrett's Car/88
2000 #85 D.Jarrett's/N.Jarrett/88
2000 #92 Dale Jarrett/88
Upper Deck Predictor Race Winners
1995 #P7 Dale Jarrett WIN
Upper Deck Predictor Race Winners Coca-Cola 600
1995 #P7 Dale Jarrett
Upper Deck Predictor Race Winners Daytona 500
1995 #P7 Dale Jarrett
Upper Deck Predictor Race Winners Prizes
1995 #P7 Dale Jarrett
Upper Deck Predictor Series Points
1995 #PP7 Dale Jarrett
Upper Deck Predictor Series Points Prizes
1995 #PP7 Dale Jarrett
Upper Deck Predictor Wins
1996 #HP9 Dale Jarrett WIN
Upper Deck Predictor Wins Prizes
1996 #HP9 Dale Jarrett
Upper Deck Racing
2000 #1 Dale Jarrett
Upper Deck Racing Brickyard's Best
2000 #BB5 Dale Jarrett
Upper Deck Racing Record Pace
2000 #RP7 Dale Jarrett
Upper Deck Racing Road Signs
2000 #RSDJ Dale Jarrett
Upper Deck Racing Speeding Ticket
2000 #ST6 Dale Jarrett
Upper Deck Racing Tear Aways
2000 #TADJ Dale Jarrett
Upper Deck Racing Trophy Dash
2000 #TD8 Dale Jarrett
Upper Deck Racing Winning Formula
2000 #WF4 Dale Jarrett
Upper Deck Road To The Cup
1996 #RC12 Dale Jarrett
1996 #RC61 Dale Jarrett's Car
1996 #RC97 Dale Jarrett
1997 #3 Dale Jarrett
1997 #46 Dale Jarrett's Car
1997 #88 Dale Jarrett
1997 #108 Dale Jarrett's Trans.
1998 #20 Dale Jarrett
1998 #58 Dale Jarrett's Car
1998 #90 Dale Jarrett's Car
1998 #102 Dale Jarrett
1999 #2 Dale Jarrett
1999 #48 Dale Jarrett's Car
1999 #63 Dale Jarrett FF
1999 #81 Dale Jarrett HH
Upper Deck Road To The Cup Autographs
1996 #H12 Dale Jarrett
Upper Deck Road To The Cup Cup Quest
1997 #CQ4 Dale Jarrett
Upper Deck Road To The Cup Cup Quest Checkered
1997 #CQ4 Dale Jarrett
Upper Deck Road To The Cup Cup Quest Turn 1
1998 #CQ8 Dale Jarrett's Car
Upper Deck Road To The Cup Cup Quest Turn 2
1998 #CQ8 Dale Jarrett's Car
Upper Deck Road To The Cup Cup Quest Turn 3
1998 #CQ8 Dale Jarrett's Car
Upper Deck Road To The Cup Cup Quest Turn 4
1998 #CQ8 Dale Jarrett's Car
Upper Deck Road To The Cup Cup Quest Victory Lane
1998 #CQ8 Dale Jarrett's Car
Upper Deck Road To The Cup Cup Quest White
1997 #CQ4 Dale Jarrett
Upper Deck Road To The Cup Game Face
1996 #GF4 Dale Jarrett
Upper Deck Road To The Cup Jumbos
1996 #WC4 Dale Jarrett
Upper Deck Road To The Cup Leaders of the Pack
1996 #LP4 Dale Jarrett
Upper Deck Road To The Cup Million Dollar Memoirs
1997 #MM13 Dale Jarrett
1997 #MM14 Dale Jarrett
1997 #MM15 Dale Jarrett
1997 #MM16 Dale Jarrett
Upper Deck Road To The Cup Million Dollar Memoirs Autographs
1997 #MM13 Dale Jarrett
1997 #MM14 Dale Jarrett
1997 #MM15 Dale Jarrett
1997 #MM16 Dale Jarrett
Upper Deck Road to the Cup NASCAR Chronicles
1999 #NC17 Dale Jarrett
Upper Deck Road To The Cup Piece of the Action
1997 #4 Dale Jarrett Seat Cover
1997 #5 Dale Jarrett Should.Harness
1997 #6 Dale Jarrett Window Net
Upper Deck Road To The Cup Predictor Plus
1997 #3 Dale Jarrett
1997 #13 Dale Jarrett WIN
Upper Deck Road To The Cup Predictor Plus Cel Die Cuts
1997 #3 Dale Jarrett
1997 #13 Dale Jarrett
Upper Deck Road To The Cup Predictor Plus Cels
1997 #3 Dale Jarrett
1997 #13 Dale Jarrett
Upper Deck Road To The Cup Predictor Points
1996 #PP8 Dale Jarrett
Upper Deck Road To The Cup Predictor Points Prizes
1996 #PR8 Dale Jarrett
Upper Deck Road To The Cup Predictor Top 3
1996 #T2 T.Labonte/D.Jarrett/S.Marlin
Upper Deck Road To The Cup Predictor Top 3 Prizes
1996 #R9 Dale Jarrett
Upper Deck Road To The Cup Premiere Position
1997 #PP22 Dale Jarrett
1997 #PP24 Dale Jarrett
1997 #PP27 Dale Jarrett
1997 #PP35 Dale Jarrett
1997 #PP45 Dale Jarrett
1997 #PP46 Dale Jarrett
1997 #PP47 Dale Jarrett
Upper Deck Road To The Cup Racing Legends
1996 #RL15 Dale Jarrett
Upper Deck Road to the Cup Road to the Cup Bronze Level 1
1999 #RTTC8 Dale Jarrett
Upper Deck Road to the Cup Road to the Cup Gold Level 3
1999 #RTTC8 Dale Jarrett
Upper Deck Road to the Cup Road to the Cup Silver Level 2
1999 #RTTC8 Dale Jarrett
Upper Deck Road to the Cup Signature Collection
1999 #DJ Dale Jarrett
Upper Deck Road to the Cup Upper Deck Profiles
1999 #P5 Dale Jarrett
Upper Deck Road To The Cup Winning Materials
1998 #W3 Dale Jarrett
Upper Deck Silver Signature/Electric Silver
1995 #7 Dale Jarrett
1995 #50 Dale Jarrett with Car
1995 #75 Dale Jarrett's Car
1995 #143 Dale Jarrett's Car
1995 #165 Dale Jarrett DYK
1995 #206 Dale Jarrett
1995 #250 Dale Jarrett SD
1995 #285 Dale Jarrett's Car
Upper Deck Victory Circle
1997 #36 Dale Jarrett
1997 #86 Dale Jarrett's Car
1997 #101 Dale Jarrett
1998 #12 Dale Jarrett
1998 #57 Dale Jarrett's Car
1998 #95 Dale Jarrett
1998 #116 Dale Jarrett
1998 #149 Dale Jarrett
1999 #1 Dale Jarrett
1999 #52 Dale Jarrett's Car
2000 #34 Dale Jarrett
2000 #57 Dale Jarrett's Car
2000 #69 Dale Jarrett's Car
Upper Deck Victory Circle 32 Days of Speed
1998 #D5 Dale Jarrett
1998 #D18 Dale Jarrett
Upper Deck Victory Circle 32 Days of Speed Gold
1998 #D5 Dale Jarrett
1998 #D18 Dale Jarrett
Upper Deck Victory Circle Autographs
1998 #AG3 Dale Jarrett
Upper Deck Victory Circle Championship Reflections
1997 #CR3 Dale Jarrett
Upper Deck Victory Circle Driver's Seat
1997 #DS10 Dale Jarrett
Upper Deck Victory Circle Exclusives Level 1 Silver
2000 #34 Dale Jarrett
2000 #57 Dale Jarrett's Car
2000 #69 Dale Jarrett's Car
Upper Deck Victory Circle Exclusives Level 2 Gold
2000 #34 Dale Jarrett/38
2000 #57 Dale Jarrett's Car/88
2000 #69 Dale Jarrett's Car/88
Upper Deck Victory Circle Income Statement
1999 #IS8 Dale Jarrett
2000 #IS4 Dale Jarrett
Upper Deck Victory Circle Income Statement LTD
2000 #IS4 Dale Jarrett
Upper Deck Victory Circle Magic Numbers
1999 #M3 Dale Jarrett
Upper Deck Victory Circle Magic Numbers Autographs
1999 #M3 Dale Jarrett/88
Upper Deck Victory Circle Piece of the Action
1997 #FS7 Dale Jarrett Firesuit
1997 #FS8 Dale Jarrett Glove
1997 #FS9 Dale Jarrett Shoe
Upper Deck Victory Circle Piece of the Engine
1998 #PE3 Dale Jarrett
1998 #PE8 Dale Jarrett
Upper Deck Victory Circle Point Leaders
1998 #PL2 Dale Jarrett
Upper Deck Victory Circle Predictor
1997 #PE3 Dale Jarrett WIN
Upper Deck Victory Circle Predictor Plus
1998 #3 Dale Jarrett
Upper Deck Victory Circle Predictor Plus Cel Redemption
1998 #3 Dale Jarrett
Upper Deck Victory Circle Predictor Winner Cels
1997 #PH3 Dale Jarrett
Upper Deck Victory Circle Signature Collection
1999 #DJ Dale Jarrett
2000 #DJ Dale Jarrett
Upper Deck Victory Circle Signature Collection Gold
2000 #4 Dale Jarrett/88
Upper Deck Victory Circle Sparks of Brilliance
1998 #SB9 Dale Jarrett
Upper Deck Victory Circle Speed Zone
1999 #SZ8 Dale Jarrett
Upper Deck Victory Circle Track Masters
1999 #TM2 Dale Jarrett
Upper Deck Victory Circle UD Exclusives
1999 #1 Dale Jarrett
1999 #52 Dale Jarrett
Upper Deck Victory Circle Victory Circle
1999 #V6 Dale Jarrett
2000 #V6 Dale Jarrett
Upper Deck Victory Circle Victory Circle LTD
2000 #V6 Dale Jarrett
Upper Deck Victory Circle Victory Lap
1997 #VL4 Dale Jarrett
Upper Deck Victory Circle Winning Material Combination
2000 #CDJ Dale Jarrett
Upper Deck Victory Circle Winning Material Firesuit
2000 #FSDJ Dale Jarrett
Upper Deck Victory Circle Winning Material Tire
2000 #TDJ Dale Jarrett
Upper Deck Virtual Velocity Gold
1996 #VV7 Bill Elliott
VIP
1994 #17 Dale Jarrett
1994 #43 Dale Jarrett w/Car
1994 #76 Dale Jarrett ART
1995 #14 Dale Jarrett
1996 #13 Dale Jarrett
1996 #41 Dale Jarrett's Car
1997 #12 Dale Jarrett
1997 #47 Dale Jarrett
1997 #P1 Dale Jarrett Promo
1998 #12 Dale Jarrett
1998 #41 Dale Jarrett's Car
1998 #48 Dale Jarrett
1999 #12 Dale Jarrett
1999 #43 Dale Jarrett's Car
2000 #8 Dale Jarrett
2000 #19 Dale Jarrett V
2000 #28 Dale Jarrett NB
2001 #8 Dale Jarrett
2001 #23 Dale Jarrett SM
2002 #17 Dale Jarrett
2002 #46 Dale Jarrett PP
2003 #7 Dale Jarrett
2003 #20 Dale Jarrett SG
2003 #50 Dale Jarrett HR
2004 #7 Dale Jarrett
2004 #62 Dale Jarrett HR
2005 #10 Dale Jarrett
2005 #81 Dale Jarrett BN
2005 #89 Dale Jarrett ATML
2006 #10 Dale Jarrett
2006 #30 Dale Jarrett's Car R
2006 #53 Dale Jarrett BTN
2006 #70 Dale Jarrett RF
2006 #80 Dale Jarrett IF
2007 #13 Dale Jarrett
2007 #58 Dale Jarrett's Car SV
VIP Cool Blue
1995 #14 Dale Jarrett
VIP Driver's Choice
1994 #DC3 Dale Jarrett
2001 #DC2 Dale Jarrett
2002 #DC2 Dale Jarrett
2003 #DC4 Dale Jarrett
VIP Driver's Choice Die Cuts
2003 #DC4 Dale Jarrett
VIP Driver's Choice National
2003 #DC4 Dale Jarrett
VIP Driver's Choice Precious Metal
2001 #DC2 Dale Jarrett
VIP Driver's Choice Transparent
2001 #DC2 Dale Jarrett
2002 #DC2 Dale Jarrett
VIP Driver's Choice Transparent LTD
2002 #DC2 Dale Jarrett
VIP Driving Force
1998 #DF10 Dale Jarrett's Car
VIP Driving Force Die Cuts
1998 #DF10 Dale Jarrett's Car
VIP Emerald Proofs
1995 #14 Dale Jarrett
1996 #13 Dale Jarrett
1996 #41 Dale Jarrett's Car
VIP Explosives
1997 #12 Dale Jarrett
1997 #47 Dale Jarrett
1997 #P1 Dale Jarrett Promo
1998 #12 Dale Jarrett
1998 #41 Dale Jarrett's Car
1998 #48 Dale Jarrett
1999 #X12 Dale Jarrett
1999 #X43 Dale Jarrett's Car
2000 #X8 Dale Jarrett
2000 #X19 Dale Jarrett V
2000 #X28 Dale Jarrett NB
2001 #8 Dale Jarrett
2001 #23 Dale Jarrett SM
2002 #X17 Dale Jarrett
2002 #X46 Dale Jarrett PP
2003 #X7 Dale Jarrett
2003 #X20 Dale Jarrett SG
2003 #X50 Dale Jarrett HR
VIP Explosives Lasers
1999 #12 Dale Jarrett
1999 #43 Dale Jarrett's Car
2000 #LX8 Dale Jarrett
2000 #LX19 Dale Jarrett V
2000 #LX28 Dale Jarrett NB
2001 #LX8 Dale Jarrett
2001 #LX23 Dale Jarrett SM
2002 #LX17 Dale Jarrett
2002 #LX46 Dale Jarrett PP
VIP Gear Gallery
2007 #GG3 Dale Jarrett
VIP Gear Gallery Transparent
2007 #GG3 Dale Jarrett
VIP Get A Grip Drivers
2007 #GGD11 Dale Jarrett
VIP Get A Grip Teams
2007 #GGT11 Dale Jarrett
VIP Head Gear
1998 #HG5 Dale Jarrett
1999 #HG8 Dale Jarrett
2000 #HG6 Dale Jarrett
2001 #HG6 Dale Jarrett
2002 #HG6 Dale Jarrett
2003 #HG4 Dale Jarrett
2005 #12 Dale Jarrett
2006 #HG4 Dale Jarrett
VIP Head Gear Die Cuts
1998 #HG5 Dale Jarrett
2001 #HG6 Dale Jarrett
2002 #HG6 Dale Jarrett
2003 #HG4 Dale Jarrett
VIP Head Gear Explosives
2000 #HG6 Dale Jarrett
VIP Head Gear Explosives Laser Die Cuts
2000 #HG6 Dale Jarrett
VIP Head Gear National
2003 #HG4 Dale Jarrett
VIP Head Gear Plastic
1999 #HG8 Dale Jarrett
VIP Head Gear Transparent
2005 #12 Dale Jarrett
2006 #HG4 Dale Jarrett
VIP Knights of Thunder
1997 #KT3 Dale Jarrett
VIP Knights of Thunder Gold
1997 #KT3 Dale Jarrett
VIP Lap Leader
2006 #LL6 Dale Jarrett
VIP Lap Leader Transparent
2006 #LL6 Dale Jarrett
VIP Lap Leaders
1998 #LL4 Dale Jarrett's Car
1999 #LL8 Dale Jarrett
2000 #LL5 Dale Jarrett
2003 #LL8 Dale Jarrett
VIP Lap Leaders Acetate
1998 #LL4 Dale Jarrett's Car
VIP Lap Leaders Explosives
2000 #LL5 Dale Jarrett
VIP Lap Leaders Explosives Lasers
2000 #LL5 Dale Jarrett
VIP Lap Leaders National
2003 #LL8 Dale Jarrett
VIP Lap Leaders Transparent
2003 #LL8 Dale Jarrett
VIP Lap Leaders Transparent LTD
2003 #LL8 Dale Jarrett
VIP Laser Explosive
2003 #LX7 Dale Jarrett
2003 #LX20 Dale Jarrett SG
2003 #LX50 Dale Jarrett HR
VIP Making the Show
2000 #MS5 Dale Jarrett
2001 #23 Dale Jarrett
2002 #MS22 Dale Jarrett
2003 #MS23 Dale Jarrett
2006 #MS12 Dale Jarrett
VIP Mile Masters
2001 #MM5 Dale Jarrett
2002 #MM5 Dale Jarrett
2003 #MM4 Dale Jarrett
VIP Mile Masters National
2003 #MM4 Dale Jarrett
VIP Mile Masters Precious Metal
2001 #MM5 Dale Jarrett
VIP Mile Masters Transparent
2001 #MM5 Dale Jarrett
2002 #MM5 Dale Jarrett

2003 #MM4 Dale Jarrett
VIP Mile Masters Transparent LTD
2002 #MM5 Dale Jarrett
2003 #MM4 Dale Jarrett
VIP NASCAR Country
1998 #NC4 Dale Jarrett
VIP NASCAR Country Die Cuts
1998 #NC4 Dale Jarrett
VIP Oil Slicks
1997 #12 Dale Jarrett
1997 #47 Dale Jarrett
VIP Out of the Box
1999 #OB8 Dale Jarrett
VIP Previews
2003 #7 Dale Jarrett
2003 #20 Dale Jarrett SG
2004 #EB7 Dale Jarrett
2005 #EB10 Dale Jarrett
2007 #EB13 Dale Jarrett
VIP Promos
1995 #1R Dale Jarrett Red
1995 #1G Dale Jarrett Gold
VIP Race Used Sheet Metal Cars
2002 #SC14 Dale Jarrett's Car
VIP Race Used Sheet Metal Drivers
2002 #SD14 Dale Jarrett
VIP Rear View Mirror
1999 #RM2 Dale Jarrett
VIP Red Hot
1995 #14 Dale Jarrett
VIP Ring of Honor
1997 #RH11 Dale Jarrett's Car
VIP Ring of Honor Die Cuts
1997 #RH11 Dale Jarrett's Car
VIP Samples
2002 #17 Dale Jarrett
2002 #46 Dale Jarrett PP
2003 #7 Dale Jarrett
2003 #20 Dale Jarrett SG
2003 #50 Dale Jarrett HR
2004 #62 Dale Jarrett HR
2004 #7 Dale Jarrett
2005 #10 Dale Jarrett
2005 #81 Dale Jarrett BN
2005 #89 Dale Jarrett ATML
VIP Sheet Metal
1999 #SM7 Dale Jarrett
VIP Sheet Metal Cars
2001 #SC6 Dale Jarrett's Car
VIP Sheet Metal Drivers
2001 #SD6 Dale Jarrett
VIP Solos
1998 #12 Dale Jarrett
1998 #41 Dale Jarrett's Car
1998 #48 Dale Jarrett
VIP Sunday Best
2007 #SB10 Dale Jarrett
VIP Tin
2003 #CT7 Dale Jarrett
2003 #CT20 Dale Jarrett SG
2003 #CT50 Dale Jarrett HR
VIP Torquers
1996 #13 Dale Jarrett
1996 #41 Dale Jarrett's Car
VIP Tradin' Paint Bronze
2004 #TPT12 Dale Jarrett
VIP Tradin' Paint Cars
2003 #TPT5 Dale Jarrett's Car
2005 #TPT12 Dale Jarrett
VIP Tradin' Paint Cars Bronze
2006 #TPT9 Dale Jarrett's Car
VIP Tradin' Paint Drivers
2003 #TPD5 Dale Jarrett
2005 #TPD12 Dale Jarrett
VIP Tradin' Paint Drivers Gold
2006 #TPD9 Dale Jarrett
VIP Tradin' Paint Drivers Silver
2006 #TPD9 Dale Jarrett
VIP Tradin' Paint Gold
2004 #TPD12 Dale Jarrett
VIP Tradin' Paint Silver
2004 #TPD12 Dale Jarrett
VIP Triple Gear Sheet Metal
1998 #TGS8 Dale Jarrett
VIP Trophy Club
2007 #TC2 Dale Jarrett
VIP Trophy Club Transparent
2007 #TC2 Dale Jarrett
VIP Under the Lights
2000 #UL2 Dale Jarrett
VIP Under the Lights Explosives
2000 #UL2 Dale Jarrett
VIP Under the Lights Explosives Lasers
2000 #UL2 Dale Jarrett
VIP Vintage Performance
1999 #1 Dale Jarrett
VIP War Paint
1996 #WP17 Dale Jarrett's Car
VIP War Paint Gold
1996 #WP17 Dale Jarrett's Car
Viper
1996 #11 Dale Jarrett
1996 #58 Dale Jarrett
1997 #2 Dale Jarrett
1997 #40 Dale Jarrett
1997 #53 Dale Jarrett
1997 #55 Dale Jarrett
1997 #79 Dale Jarrett's Car
1997 #P1 Dale Jarrett Promo
Viper Anaconda Jumbos
1997 #A3 Dale Jarrett
Viper Black Mamba
1996 #11 Dale Jarrett
1996 #58 Dale Jarrett
Viper Black Mamba First Strike
1996 #11 Dale Jarrett
1996 #58 Dale Jarrett
Viper Black Racer
1997 #2 Dale Jarrett
1997 #40 Dale Jarrett
1997 #53 Dale Jarrett
1997 #55 Dale Jarrett
1997 #79 Dale Jarrett's Car
Viper Black Racer First Strike
1997 #2 Dale Jarrett
1997 #40 Dale Jarrett
1997 #53 Dale Jarrett
1997 #55 Dale Jarrett
1997 #79 Dale Jarrett's Car
Viper Busch Clash
1996 #B7 Dale Jarrett
Viper Busch Clash First Strike
1996 #B7 Dale Jarrett
Viper Cobra
1996 #C10 Dale Jarrett
1997 #C9 Dale Jarrett
Viper Cobra First Strike
1996 #C10 Dale Jarrett
1997 #C9 Dale Jarrett
Viper Copperhead Die Cuts
1996 #11 Dale Jarrett
1996 #58 Dale Jarrett
Viper Copperhead Die Cuts First Strike
1996 #11 Dale Jarrett
1996 #58 Dale Jarrett
Viper Diamondback
1997 #DB2 Dale Jarrett
Viper Diamondback Authentic
1997 #DBA2 Dale Jarrett
Viper Diamondback Authentic Eastern
1997 #DBA2 Dale Jarrett
Viper Diamondback Authentic Eastern First Strike
1997 #DBA2 Dale Jarrett
Viper Diamondback Authentic First Strike
1997 #DBA2 Dale Jarrett
Viper Diamondback First Strike
1997 #DB2 Dale Jarrett
Viper First Strike
1996 #11 Dale Jarrett
1996 #58 Dale Jarrett
1997 #2 Dale Jarrett
1997 #40 Dale Jarrett
1997 #53 Dale Jarrett
1997 #55 Dale Jarrett
1997 #79 Dale Jarrett's Car
Viper Green Mamba
1996 #11 Dale Jarrett
1996 #58 Dale Jarrett
Viper King Cobra
1996 #KC3 Dale Jarrett
1997 #KC9 Dale Jarrett
Viper King Cobra First Strike
1996 #KC3 Dale Jarrett
Viper Red Cobra
1996 #11 Dale Jarrett
1996 #58 Dale Jarrett
Viper Sidewinder
1997 #S9 Dale Jarrett
Viper Sidewinder First Strike
1997 #S9 Dale Jarrett
Viper Snake Eyes
1997 #SE3 Dale Jarrett
Viper Snake Eyes First Strike
1997 #SE3 Dale Jarrett
Visions
1996 #109 Dale Jarrett
Visions *
1996 #109 Dale Jarrett
Visions Signings
1996 #88 Dale Jarrett
Visions Signings *
1996 #88 Dale Jarrett
Wheels
1998 #16 Dale Jarrett
1998 #38 Dale Jarrett's Car
1998 #49 Dale Jarrett
1998 #87 Dale Jarrett
1999 #16 Dale Jarrett
1999 #61 Dale Jarrett's Car
1999 #80 Dale Jarrett TC
Wheels 50th Anniversary
1998 #A7 Dale Jarrett
1998 #A22 Dale Jarrett's Car
Wheels American Thunder
2003 #9 Dale Jarrett
2003 #23 Dale Jarrett SS
2003 #31 Dale Jarrett DT
2003 #50 D.Jarrett's Transporter CL
2004 #9 Dale Jarrett
2004 #83 Dale Jarrett CC
2005 #11 Dale Jarrett
2005 #42 Dale Jarrett AS
2005 #51 Dale Jarrett's Car HR
2005 #72 Dale Jarrett RR
2006 #12 Dale Jarrett
2006 #45 Dale Jarrett's Car HR
2006 #77 Dale Jarrett MIA
2007 #13 Dale Jarrett
Wheels American Thunder American Eagle
2004 #AE3 Dale Jarrett
2005 #AE3 Dale Jarrett
Wheels American Thunder American Muscle
2006 #AM4 Dale Jarrett
Wheels American Thunder American Racing Idol
2006 #RI9 Dale Jarrett
Wheels American Thunder American Racing Idol Golden
2006 #RI9 Dale Jarrett
Wheels American Thunder Autographed Hat Instant Winner
2007 #AH14 Dale Jarrett
Wheels American Thunder Born On
2003 #BO9 Dale Jarrett
2003 #BO23 Dale Jarrett SS
2003 #BO31 Dale Jarrett DT
2003 #BO50 UPS Transporter CL
Wheels American Thunder Cool Threads
2003 #CT7 Dale Jarrett
2004 #CT5 Dale Jarrett
2005 #CT12 Dale Jarrett
2006 #CT15 Dale Jarrett
2007 #CT5 Dale Jarrett
Wheels American Thunder Cup Quest
2004 #CQ7 Dale Jarrett
Wheels American Thunder Double Hat
2006 #DH10 Dale Jarrett
Wheels American Thunder Golden Eagle
2004 #AE3 Dale Jarrett
2005 #GE3 Dale Jarrett
Wheels American Thunder Grandstand
2006 #GS9 Dale Jarrett
Wheels American Thunder Head to Toe
2007 #HT6 Dale Jarrett
Wheels American Thunder Heads Up Goodyear
2003 #HUG4 Dale Jarrett
Wheels American Thunder Heads Up Manufacturer
2003 #HUM8 Dale Jarrett
Wheels American Thunder Heads Up Team
2003 #HUT7 Dale Jarrett/90
Wheels American Thunder Heads Up Winston
2003 #HUW8 Dale Jarrett
Wheels American Thunder Holofoil
2003 #P9 Dale Jarrett
2003 #P23 Dale Jarrett SS
2003 #P31 Dale Jarrett DT
2003 #P50 UPS Transporter CL
Wheels American Thunder Medallion
2005 #MD9 Dale Jarrett
Wheels American Thunder Post Mark
2003 #PM8 Dale Jarrett
Wheels American Thunder Previews
2003 #9 Dale Jarrett
2003 #23 Dale Jarrett SS
2003 #31 Dale Jarrett DT
2004 #EB9 Dale Jarrett
2005 #11 Dale Jarrett
2006 #EB12 Dale Jarrett
2006 #EB77 Dale Jarrett MIA
2007 #EB13 Dale Jarrett
Wheels American Thunder Pushin' Pedal
2007 #PP3 Dale Jarrett
Wheels American Thunder Rookie Thunder
2003 #RT13 Dale Jarrett
Wheels American Thunder Samples
2003 #P9 Dale Jarrett
2003 #P23 Dale Jarrett SS
2003 #P31 Dale Jarrett DT
2003 #P50 UPS Transporter CL
2004 #9 Dale Jarrett
2004 #83 Dale Jarrett CC
2005 #11 Dale Jarrett
2005 #42 Dale Jarrett AS
2005 #51 Dale Jarrett's Car HR
2005 #72 Dale Jarrett RR
Wheels American Thunder Starting Grid
2007 #SG4 Dale Jarrett
Wheels American Thunder Thunder Road
2004 #TR17 Dale Jarrett
2005 #TR17 Dale Jarrett
2006 #TR9 Dale Jarrett
2007 #TR6 Dale Jarrett
Wheels American Thunder Thunder Strokes
2007 #20 Dale Jarrett
Wheels American Thunder Thunder Strokes Press Plates Black
2007 #20 Dale Jarrett
Wheels American Thunder Thunder Strokes Press Plates Cyan
2007 #20 Dale Jarrett
Wheels American Thunder Thunder Strokes Press Plates Magenta
2007 #20 Dale Jarrett
Wheels American Thunder Thunder Strokes Press Plates Yellow
2007 #20 Dale Jarrett
Wheels American Thunder Triple Hat
2003 #TH10 Dale Jarrett
2004 #TH5 Dale Jarrett
2005 #TH8 Dale Jarrett
2007 #TH12 Dale Jarrett
Wheels Autographs
1998 #3 Dale Jarrett/200
1999 #9 Dale Jarrett/100
2003 #25 Dale Jarrett AT/HG
2004 #31 Dale Jarrett HG
2005 #25 Dale Jarrett
2006 #25 Dale Jarrett NC
2008 #15 Dale Jarrett NC HG
Wheels Autographs Press Plates Black
2008 #15 Dale Jarrett NC
Wheels Autographs Press Plates Cyan
2008 #15 Dale Jarrett NC
Wheels Autographs Press Plates Magenta
2008 #15 Dale Jarrett NC
Wheels Autographs Press Plates Yellow
2008 #15 Dale Jarrett NC
Wheels Circuit Breaker
1999 #CB8 Dale Jarrett
Wheels Custom Shop
1998 #CSDJ Dale Jarrett
Wheels Custom Shop Prizes
1998 #DJA1 Dale Jarrett
1998 #DJA2 Dale Jarrett
1998 #DJA3 Dale Jarrett
1998 #DJB1 Dale Jarrett
1998 #DJB2 Dale Jarrett
1998 #DJB3 Dale Jarrett
1998 #DJC1 Dale Jarrett
1998 #DJC2 Dale Jarrett
1998 #DJC3 Dale Jarrett
Wheels Dialed In
1999 #DI8 Dale Jarrett
Wheels Double Take
1998 #E5 Dale Jarrett
Wheels Golden
1998 #16 Dale Jarrett
1998 #38 Dale Jarrett's Car
1998 #87 Dale Jarrett
1999 #16 Dale Jarrett
1999 #61 Dale Jarrett
1999 #80 Dale Jarrett
Wheels Green Flags
1998 #GF9 Dale Jarrett's Car
Wheels High Gear
1994 #75 Dale Jarrett WIN
1994 #118 Dale Jarrett
1995 #19 Dale Jarrett
1995 #95 Dale Jarrett RW
1998 #2 Dale Jarrett
1998 #34 Dale Jarrett's Car
1998 #54 Dale Jarrett
1999 #3 Dale Jarrett
1999 #34 Dale Jarrett's Car
1999 #70 Dale Jarrett's Car
2000 #1 Dale Jarrett
2000 #35 Dale Jarrett's Car
2000 #63 Dale Jarrett's Car
2001 #3 Dale Jarrett
2001 #31 Dale Jarrett WCM
2001 #70 Dale Jarrett WCP
2002 #10 Dale Jarrett
2002 #30 Dale Jarrett's Car
2002 #49 Dale Jarrett's Car
2003 #13 Dale Jarrett
2003 #36 Dale Jarrett's Car
2003 #50 Dale Jarrett's Car CM
2004 #10 Dale Jarrett
2005 #26 Dale Jarrett
2005 #42 Dale Jarrett's Car C
2005 #88 Dale Jarrett P
2006 #14 Dale Jarrett
2006 #14B Dale Jarrett Daytona
2006 #53 Dale Jarrett's Car C
2006 #66 Dale Jarrett CM
2006 #77 Dale Jarrett FF
2008 #26 Dale Jarrett
2008 #53 Dale Jarrett's Car C
Wheels High Gear Autographs
1998 #11 Dale Jarrett/200
1999 #13 Dale Jarrett/350
2000 #14 Dale Jarrett
2001 #16 Dale Jarrett
2002 #24 Dale Jarrett
Wheels High Gear Blue Hawaii SCDA Promos
2003 #13 Dale Jarrett
2003 #36 Dale Jarrett's Car
2003 #50 Dale Jarrett's Car CM
Wheels High Gear Custom Shop
1998 #CS5 Dale Jarrett EXCH
2000 #CSDJ Dale Jarrett EXCH
2002 #CSDJ Dale Jarrett EXCH
Wheels High Gear Custom Shop Prizes
1998 #DJA1 Dale Jarrett
1998 #DJA2 Dale Jarrett
1998 #DJA3 Dale Jarrett
1998 #DJB1 Dale Jarrett
1998 #DJB2 Dale Jarrett
1998 #DJB3 Dale Jarrett
1998 #DJC1 Dale Jarrett
1998 #DJC2 Dale Jarrett
1998 #DJC3 Dale Jarrett
2000 #DJA1 Dale Jarrett
2000 #DJA2 Dale Jarrett
2000 #DJA3 Dale Jarrett
2000 #DJB1 Dale Jarrett
2000 #DJB2 Dale Jarrett
2000 #DJB3 Dale Jarrett
2000 #DJC1 Dale Jarrett
2000 #DJC2 Dale Jarrett
2000 #DJC3 Dale Jarrett
2002 #DJA1 Dale Jarrett
2002 #DJA2 Dale Jarrett
2002 #DJA3 Dale Jarrett
2002 #DJB1 Dale Jarrett
2002 #DJB2 Dale Jarrett
2002 #DJB3 Dale Jarrett
2002 #DJC1 Dale Jarrett
2002 #DJC2 Dale Jarrett
2002 #DJC3 Dale Jarrett
Wheels High Gear Day One
1994 #118 Dale Jarrett
1995 #19 Dale Jarrett
1995 #95 Dale Jarrett RW
Wheels High Gear Day One Gold
1994 #118 Dale Jarrett
1995 #19 Dale Jarrett
1995 #95 Dale Jarrett RW
Wheels High Gear Driven
2008 #DR11 Dale Jarrett
Wheels High Gear Final Standings
2008 #F26 Dale Jarrett/41
Wheels High Gear First Gear
1998 #3 Dale Jarrett
1998 #34 Dale Jarrett's Car
1998 #54 Dale Jarrett
1999 #3 Dale Jarrett
1999 #34 Dale Jarrett's Car
1999 #70 Dale Jarrett's Car
2000 #1 Dale Jarrett
2000 #35 Dale Jarrett
2000 #63 Dale Jarrett
2001 #3 Dale Jarrett
2001 #31 Dale Jarrett WCM
2001 #70 Dale Jarrett WCP
2002 #10 Dale Jarrett
2002 #30 Dale Jarrett's Car
2002 #49 Dale Jarrett's Car
2003 #F13 Dale Jarrett
2003 #F36 Dale Jarrett's Car
2003 #F50 Dale Jarrett's Car CM
Wheels High Gear Flag Chasers
2000 #FC1 Dale Jarrett
2002 #FC4 Dale Jarrett
Wheels High Gear Flag Chasers Black
2002 #FC4 Dale Jarrett
2006 #FC8 Dale Jarrett
Wheels High Gear Flag Chasers Blue-Yellow
2000 #FC1 Dale Jarrett
2002 #FC4 Dale Jarrett
2006 #FC8 Dale Jarrett
Wheels High Gear Flag Chasers Checkered
2000 #FC1 Dale Jarrett
2002 #FC4 Dale Jarrett
2006 #FC8 Dale Jarrett
Wheels High Gear Flag Chasers Checkered Blue/Orange
2000 #FC1 Dale Jarrett
2002 #FC4 Dale Jarrett
Wheels High Gear Flag Chasers Green
2000 #FC1 Dale Jarrett
2002 #FC4 Dale Jarrett
2006 #FC8 Dale Jarrett
Wheels High Gear Flag Chasers Red
2000 #FC1 Dale Jarrett
2002 #FC4 Dale Jarrett
2006 #FC8 Dale Jarrett
Wheels High Gear Flag Chasers White
2000 #FC1 Dale Jarrett
2006 #FC8 Dale Jarrett
Wheels High Gear Flag Chasers Yellow
2000 #FC1 Dale Jarrett
2002 #FC4 Dale Jarrett
2006 #FC8 Dale Jarrett
Wheels High Gear Flag to Flag
2005 #FF8 Dale Jarrett
2006 #FF10 Dale Jarrett
Wheels High Gear Full Throttle
2003 #FT5 Dale Jarrett
2005 #FT5 Dale Jarrett
Wheels High Gear Gear Jammers
1998 #GJ15 Dale Jarrett
Wheels High Gear Gear Shifters
1999 #GS3 Dale Jarrett
2000 #GS1 Dale Jarrett
2001 #GS3 Dale Jarrett
Wheels High Gear Gold
1994 #75 Dale Jarrett WIN
1994 #118 Dale Jarrett
1995 #19 Dale Jarrett
1995 #95 Dale Jarrett RW
Wheels High Gear High Groove
1998 #HG7 Dale Jarrett's Car
2002 #HG10 Dale Jarrett
2003 #HG11 Dale Jarrett
2004 #HG9 Dale Jarrett
Wheels High Gear Hot Streaks
1999 #HS6 Dale Jarrett
2001 #HS5 Dale Jarrett
2002 #HS5 Dale Jarrett
Wheels High Gear Machine
2003 #MM7B Dale Jarrett
2004 #MM8B Dale Jarrett
Wheels High Gear Man
2003 #MM7A Dale Jarrett
2004 #MM8A Dale Jarrett
Wheels High Gear Man & Machine (Machine)
2006 #MMB6 Dale Jarrett
Wheels High Gear Man & Machine (Man)
2006 #MMA6 Dale Jarrett
Wheels High Gear Man and Machine Cars
1998 #3 Dale Jarrett's Car
1999 #MM3B Dale Jarrett's Car
2000 #MM8B Dale Jarrett's Car
2001 #MM5B Dale Jarrett's Car
2002 #MM4B Dale Jarrett
Wheels High Gear Man and Machine Drivers
1998 #MM3 Dale Jarrett
1999 #MM5A Terry Labonte
2000 #MM8A Dale Jarrett
2001 #MM5A Dale Jarrett
2002 #MM4A Dale Jarrett
Wheels High Gear MPH
1998 #3 Dale Jarrett
1998 #34 Dale Jarrett's Car
1998 #54 Dale Jarrett
1999 #3 Dale Jarrett
1999 #34 Dale Jarrett's Car
1999 #70 Dale Jarrett's Car
2000 #1 Dale Jarrett
2000 #35 Dale Jarrett
2000 #63 Dale Jarrett
2001 #3 Dale Jarrett
2001 #31 Dale Jarrett WCM
2001 #70 Dale Jarrett WCP
2002 #10 Dale Jarrett
2002 #30 Dale Jarrett's Car
2002 #49 Dale Jarrett's Car
2003 #M13 Dale Jarrett
2003 #M36 Dale Jarrett's Car
2003 #M50 Dale Jarrett's Car CM
2004 #M10 Dale Jarrett
2005 #M26 Dale Jarrett
2005 #M42 Dale Jarrett's Car C
2005 #M88 Dale Jarrett P
2006 #M14 Dale Jarrett
2006 #M53 Dale Jarrett's Car C
2006 #M66 Dale Jarrett CM
2006 #M77 Dale Jarrett FF
2008 #M26 Dale Jarrett
2008 #M53 Dale Jarrett's Car C
Wheels High Gear Previews
2003 #13 Dale Jarrett
2004 #10 Dale Jarrett
2008 #EB26 Dale Jarrett
Wheels High Gear Previews Green
2005 #EB26 Dale Jarrett
2006 #EB14 Dale Jarrett
Wheels High Gear Previews Silver
2006 #EB77 Dale Jarrett FF
Wheels High Gear Samples
2003 #13 Dale Jarrett
2003 #36 Dale Jarrett's Car
2003 #50 Dale Jarrett's Car CM
2004 #10 Dale Jarrett
2005 #26 Dale Jarrett
2005 #42 Dale Jarrett's Car C
2005 #88 Dale Jarrett P
Wheels High Gear Sunday Sensation
2000 #OC8 Dale Jarrett
2001 #SS1 Dale Jarrett
2002 #SS6 Dale Jarrett
Wheels High Gear Top Tier
1998 #TT2 Dale Jarrett 1:192
1999 #TT3 Dale Jarrett 1:100
2000 #TT1 Dale Jarrett
2001 #TT4 Dale Jarrett
2002 #TT5 Dale Jarrett
Wheels High Gear Top Tier Holofoils
2001 #TT4 Dale Jarrett
Wheels High Gear Top Tier Numbered
2002 #TT5 Dale Jarrett
Wheels High Gear Vintage
2000 #V1 Dale Jarrett
Wheels High Gear Winning Edge
2000 #WE1 Dale Jarrett
Wheels High Groove
1999 #HG8 Dale Jarrett
Wheels Jackpot
1998 #J4 Dale Jarrett
Wheels Runnin and Gunnin
1999 #RG5 Dale Jarrett
Wheels Runnin and Gunnin Foils
1999 #RG5 Dale Jarrett
Wheels Solos
1999 #16 Dale Jarrett
1999 #61 Dale Jarrett
1999 #80 Dale Jarrett
Zenith
1995 #27 Dale Jarrett HG
1995 #53 Dale Jarrett's Transporter
1996 #10 Dale Jarrett
1996 #43 Dale Jarrett's Car HV
1996 #60 Dale Jarrett S
1996 #89 Dale Jarrett RYR
1996 #97 Dale Jarrett W
Zenith Artist Proofs
1996 #10 Dale Jarrett RP
1996 #43 Dale Jarrett's Car HV
1996 #60 Dale Jarrett S
1996 #89 Dale Jarrett RYR
1996 #97 Dale Jarrett W
Zenith Winston Winners
1995 #17 Dale Jarrett

Johnson, Jimmie

eTopps
2003 #5 Jimmie Johnson/2945
Maxx
2000 #60 Jimmie Johnson RF RC
Maxximum
2000 #38 Jimmie Johnson RC
Maxximum Die Cuts
2000 #38 Jimmie Johnson
Maxximum MPH
2000 #38 Jimmie Johnson/92
Maxximum Signatures
2000 #JO Jimmie Johnson
Maxximum Young Lions
2000 #YL9 Jimmie Johnson
McFarlane NASCAR 3-Inch Series 1
2005 #60 Jimmie Johnson
McFarlane NASCAR Series 2
2004 #40 Jimmie Johnson FP R Lowes without Glasses Photo
2004 #41 Jimmie Johnson R Lowes with Glasses Photo
2004 #45 Jimmie Johnson H Lowes
McFarlane NASCAR Series 4
2005 #70 Jimmie Johnson R Glasses
2005 #72 Jimmie Johnson R w/o Glasses
2005 #75 Jimmie Johnson H
McFarlane NASCAR Series 6
2005 #100 Jimmie Johnson
2005 #105 Jimmie Johnson No Glasses
National Trading Card Day
2004 #PP3 Jimmie Johnson
National Trading Card Day *
2004 #PP3 Jimmie Johnson
Press Pass
2002 #44 Jimmie Johnson NBS
2003 #16 Jimmie Johnson
2003 #59 Jimmie Johnson DS
2003 #63 Jr./JJ/New/Sad/Ken/Bus DS
2003 #64 J.Johnson Feb.17 RR
2003 #65 J.Johnson Apr.28 RR
2003 #66 J.Johnson Dover June RR
2003 #67 J.Johnson Dover Sept RR
2003 #78 The California Kid WCS
2003 #79 Two of a Kind WCS
2004 #14 Jimmie Johnson
2004 #83 Spring Reign WCS
2004 #84 Million-dollar Magic WCS
2004 #86 In the Groove WCS
2004 #95 Jimmie Johnson DS
2004 #95B Jimmie Johnson DS red
2005 #32 Jimmie Johnson
2005 #76 Jimmie Johnson NS
2005 #82 Jimmie Johnson NS
2005 #92 J.Hend./Gordon/JJ/T.Lab/B.Vick Y
2005 #106 Jimmie Johnson P
2005 #114 Jimmie Johnson's Car
2005 #118 Jimmie Johnson's Car
2005 #120 Dale Jr/JJ/Gordon CL
2006 #27 Jimmie Johnson
2006 #73 Jimmie Johnson's Car OTW
2006 #91 Jimmie Johnson NS
2006 #103 Jimmie Johnson U
2006 #111 Jimmie Johnson TT
2007 #2 Jimmie Johnson
2007 #77 Jimmie Johnson's Car OT
2007 #94 Jimmie Johnson NS
2007 #96 Jimmie Johnson U
2007 #109 Jimmie Johnson TT
2007 #CL Jimmie Johnson CL
2008 #6 Jimmie Johnson
2008 #68 Jimmie Johnson's Car BFS
2008 #81 Jimmie Johnson NS
2008 #107 Jimmie Johnson Top 12
2008 #0 Cup Chase Matt Kenseth Tony Stewart Jeff Gordon Jimmie Johnson Denny Hamlin Kurt Busch Kevin Harvick Carl Edwards Kyle Busch Martin Truex Jr. Jeff Burton Clint Bowyer
Press Pass Autographs
2002 #31 Jimmie Johnson
2003 #27 Jimmie Johnson E/P
2004 #29 Jimmie Johnson P
2005 #27 Jimmie Johnson E/P
2006 #24 Jimmie Johnson NC
2007 #20 Jimmie Johnson
2008 #20 Jimmie Johnson NC EXCH P
Press Pass Autographs Press Plates Black
2008 #16 Jimmie Johnson NC E
Press Pass Autographs Press Plates Cyan
2008 #16 Jimmie Johnson NC E
Press Pass Autographs Press Plates Magenta
2008 #16 Jimmie Johnson NC E
Press Pass Autographs Press Plates Yellow
2008 #16 Jimmie Johnson NC E
Press Pass Blue
2006 #B27 Jimmie Johnson
2006 #B73 Jimmie Johnson's Car OTW
2006 #B91 Jimmie Johnson NS
2006 #B103 Jimmie Johnson U
2006 #B111 Jimmie Johnson TT
2007 #B2 Jimmie Johnson
2007 #B77 Jimmie Johnson's Car OT
2007 #B94 Jimmie Johnson NS
2007 #B96 Jimmie Johnson U
2007 #B109 Jimmie Johnson TT
2007 #BCL Jimmie Johnson CL
2008 #B6 Jimmie Johnson
2008 #B68 Jimmie Johnson's Car BFS
2008 #B81 Jimmie Johnson NS
2008 #B107 Jimmie Johnson Top 12
Press Pass Burning Rubber Autographs

2004 #BRJJ Jimmie Johnson/48
2005 #BR-JJ Jimmie Johnson/48
2006 #BR-JJ Jimmie Johnson/48
2007 #BRS-JJ Jimmie Johnson/48

Press Pass Burning Rubber Cars
2003 #BRT4 Jimmie Johnson's Car
2004 #BRT1 Jimmie Johnson's Car
2005 #BRT1 Jimmie Johnson's Car
2006 #BRT8 Jimmie Johnson

Press Pass Burning Rubber Cars Autographs
2003 #BRT-JJ Jimmie Johnson/48

Press Pass Burning Rubber Drivers
2003 #BRD4 Jimmie Johnson
2004 #BRD1 Jimmie Johnson
2005 #BRD1 Jimmie Johnson
2006 #BRD8 Jimmie Johnson
2007 #BRD1 Jimmie Johnson Daytona 2-19
2007 #BRD6 Jimmie Johnson Talladega 5-1
2007 #BRD16 Jimmie Johnson Indianapolis 8-6
2008 #BRD3 Jimmie Johnson Las Vegas
2008 #BRD4 Jimmie Johnson Atlanta
2008 #BRD6 Jimmie Johnson Martinsville
2008 #BRD10 Jimmie Johnson Richmond May
2008 #BRD24 Jimmie Johnson Cal.
2008 #BRD25 Jimmie Johnson Richmond September

Press Pass Burning Rubber Drivers Autographs
2003 #BRD-JJ Jimmie Johnson/48

Press Pass Burning Rubber Drivers Gold
2005 #BRD1 Jimmie Johnson
2006 #BRD8 Jimmie Johnson
2007 #BRD1 Jimmie Johnson Daytona 2-19
2007 #BRD6 Jimmie Johnson Talladega 5-1
2007 #BRD16 Jimmie Johnson Indianapolis 8-6
2008 #BRD3 Jimmie Johnson Las Vegas
2008 #BRD4 Jimmie Johnson Atlanta
2008 #BRD6 Jimmie Johnson Martinsville
2008 #BRD10 Jimmie Johnson Richmond May
2008 #BRD24 Jimmie Johnson Cal.
2008 #BRD25 Jimmie Johnson Richmond September

Press Pass Burning Rubber Drivers Prime Cuts
2008 #BRD3 Jimmie Johnson Las Vegas
2008 #BRD4 Jimmie Johnson Atlanta
2008 #BRD6 Jimmie Johnson Martinsville
2008 #BRD10 Jimmie Johnson Richmond May
2008 #BRD24 Jimmie Johnson Cal.
2008 #BRD25 Jimmie Johnson Richmond September

Press Pass Burning Rubber Team
2007 #BRT1 Jimmie Johnson Daytona 2-19
2007 #BRT6 Jimmie Johnson Talladega 5-1
2007 #BRT16 Jimmie Johnson Indianapolis 8-6

Press Pass Burning Rubber Teams
2008 #BRT3 Jimmie Johnson Las Vegas
2008 #BRT4 Jimmie Johnson Atlanta
2008 #BRT6 Jimmie Johnson Martinsville
2008 #BRT10 Jimmie Johnson Richmond May
2008 #BRT24 Jimmie Johnson Cal.
2008 #BRT25 Jimmie Johnson Richmond September

Press Pass Burnouts
2006 #HT10 Jimmie Johnson
2007 #B01 Jimmie Johnson
2008 #B07 Jimmie Johnson

Press Pass Burnouts Blue
2007 #B01 Jimmie Johnson
2008 #B07 Jimmie Johnson

Press Pass Burnouts Gold
2007 #B01 Jimmie Johnson
2008 #B07 Jimmie Johnson

Press Pass Burnouts Holofoil
2006 #HT10 Jimmie Johnson

Press Pass Collector's Series Box Set
2007 #SB11 Jimmie Johnson

Press Pass Collectors Series Making the Show
2006 #MS7 Jimmie Johnson

Press Pass Collectors Series Sunday Best
2007 #CB11 Jimmie Johnson

Press Pass Cup Chase
2003 #CCR7 Jimmie Johnson WIN
2004 #CCR7 Jimmie Johnson WIN
2005 #CCR3 Jimmie Johnson Winner
2006 #CCR3 Jimmie Johnson Winner
2007 #CCR8 J.Johnson Winner Champ
2008 #CC14 Jimmie Johnson

Press Pass Cup Chase Prizes
2003 #CCR7 Jimmie Johnson
2004 #CCR7 Jimmie Johnson
2005 #CCP3 Jimmie Johnson
2006 #CC1 Jimmie Johnson
2006 #CCP1 Jimmie Johnson Firesuit/475
2007 #CC1 Jimmie Johnson
2007 #CCP1 Jimmie Johnson TIRE

Press Pass Dale The Movie
2007 #46 Dale Earnhardt Jr.'s Car Kevin Harvick's Car Michael Waltrip's Car Jimmie Johnson's Car

Press Pass Daytona 500 50th Anniversary
2008 #43 Jimmie Johnson '06

Press Pass Delphi
2002 #D4 Jimmie Johnson

Press Pass Double Burner
2003 #DB4 Jimmie Johnson
2004 #DB4 Jimmie Johnson
2005 #DB4 Jimmie Johnson

Press Pass Double Burner Exchange
2003 #DB4 Jimmie Johnson EXCH
2004 #DB4 Jimmie Johnson
2005 #DB4 Jimmie Johnson

Press Pass Double Burner Firesuit-Glove
2006 #DB4 Jimmie Johnson
2007 #DB4 Jimmie Johnson
2008 #DBJJ Jimmie Johnson

Press Pass Double Burner Firesuit-Glove Exchange
2007 #DB4 Jimmie Johnson

Press Pass Double Burner Metal-Tire
2006 #DB5 Jimmie Johnson
2007 #DB-JJ Jimmie Johnson
2008 #DB-JJ Jimmie Johnson

Press Pass Double Burner Metal-Tire Exchange
2007 #DB-JJ Jimmie Johnson

Press Pass Eclipse
2003 #5 Jimmie Johnson
2003 #37 All-American Kid WCS
2003 #43 Born to Run WCS
2003 #48 Jimmie Johnson HS
2004 #2 Jimmie Johnson
2004 #2B Jimmie Johnson -official
2004 #48 Jimmie Johnson Z
2004 #58 Jimmie Johnson P
2004 #78 Earnhardt Jr./Johnson LL
2004 #85 Jimmie Johnson LL
2005 #2 Jimmie Johnson
2005 #46 Jimmie Johnson Z
2005 #49 Jimmie Johnson Z
2005 #50 Jimmie Johnson Z
2005 #58 Jimmie Johnson P
2005 #65 J.Gordon/J.Johnson NS
2005 #68 Jimmie Johnson's Car NS
2005 #72 J.Gordon/J.Johnson NS
2005 #85 Jimmie Johnson LL
2005 #90 Jimmie Johnson SM CL
2006 #5 Jimmie Johnson
2006 #40 Jimmie Johnson WS
2006 #55 Jimmie Johnson NS
2006 #65 NCS Top-10 BA
2006 #69 Tony Stewart BA
2006 #81 Jimmie Johnson LL
2007 #1 Jimmie Johnson
2007 #35 Jimmie Johnson TO
2007 #50 Jimmie Johnson FP
2007 #69 Jimmie Johnson NS
2007 #71 Jimmie Johnson NS
2007 #72 Jimmie Johnson NS
2007 #73 Jimmie Johnson NYC
2007 #79 Jimmie Johnson SM
2007 #73B Jimmie Johnson signs reversed
2008 #1 Jimmie Johnson
2008 #30 Jimmie Johnson RM
2008 #37B Jimmie Johnson TO
2008 #51 Jimmie Johnson NS
2008 #52 Jimmie Johnson NS
2008 #53 Jimmie Johnson NS
2008 #64 Jimmie Johnson's Car LP
2008 #73 Jimmie Johnson SO
2008 #75 Top 10 Drivers SO
2008 #81 Jimmie Johnson SO
2008 #37 Jimmie Johnson Track background

Press Pass Eclipse Destination WIN
2004 #14 Jimmie Johnson
2004 #19 Jimmie Johnson
2005 #4 Jimmie Johnson
2005 #11 Jimmie Johnson
2005 #13 Jimmie Johnson
2005 #25 Jimmie Johnson

Press Pass Eclipse Double Hot Treads
2003 #DT8 J.Gordon/J.Johnson

Press Pass Eclipse Ecliptic
2007 #EC1 Jimmie Johnson

Press Pass Eclipse Escape Velocity
2008 #EV7 Jimmie Johnson

Press Pass Eclipse Gold
2007 #G1 Jimmie Johnson
2007 #G35 Jimmie Johnson TO
2007 #G50 Jimmie Johnson FP
2007 #G69 Jimmie Johnson NS
2007 #G71 Jimmie Johnson NS
2007 #G72 Jimmie Johnson NS
2007 #G73 Jimmie Johnson NYC
2007 #G79 Jimmie Johnson SM
2008 #G1 Jimmie Johnson
2008 #G30 Jimmie Johnson RM
2008 #G37 Jimmie Johnson TO
2008 #G51 Jimmie Johnson NS
2008 #G52 Jimmie Johnson NS
2008 #G53 Jimmie Johnson NS
2008 #G64 Jimmie Johnson's Car LP
2008 #G73 Jimmie Johnson SO
2008 #G75 Top 10 Drivers SO
2008 #G81 Jimmie Johnson SO

Press Pass Eclipse Hyperdrive
2004 #HP8 Jimmie Johnson
2005 #HD8 Jimmie Johnson
2006 #HP4 Jimmie Johnson
2007 #HD5 Jimmie Johnson
2008 #HP8 Jimmie Johnson

Press Pass Eclipse Maxim
2004 #MX2 Jimmie Johnson
2005 #MX2 Jimmie Johnson

Press Pass Eclipse Previews
2003 #5 Jimmie Johnson
2004 #2 Jimmie Johnson
2005 #EB2 Jimmie Johnson
2005 #EB46 Jimmie Johnson Z
2005 #EB49 Jimmie Johnson Z
2005 #EB50 Jimmie Johnson Z
2005 #EB58 Jimmie Johnson P
2005 #EB65 J.Gordon/J.Johnson NS
2005 #EB68 Jimmie Johnson's Car NS
2005 #EB72 J.Gordon/J.Johnson NS
2005 #EB85 Jimmie Johnson LL/1
2005 #EB90 Jimmie Johnson SM CL
2006 #EB5 Jimmie Johnson
2007 #EB1 Jimmie Johnson
2007 #EB35 Jimmie Johnson TO
2008 #EB1 Jimmie Johnson
2008 #EB30 Jimmie Johnson RM
2008 #EB73 Jimmie Johnson SO
2008 #EB75 Top 10 Drivers SO
2008 #EB81 Jimmie Johnson SO

Press Pass Eclipse Racing Champions
2003 #RC2 Jimmie Johnson
2003 #RC12 Jimmie Johnson
2003 #RC16 Jimmie Johnson
2003 #RC29 Jimmie Johnson
2006 #RC3 Jimmie Johnson
2007 #RC3 Jimmie Johnson

Press Pass Eclipse Red
2007 #R1 Jimmie Johnson
2007 #R35 Jimmie Johnson TO
2007 #R50 Jimmie Johnson FP
2007 #R69 Jimmie Johnson NS
2007 #R71 Jimmie Johnson NS
2007 #R72 Jimmie Johnson NS
2007 #R73 Jimmie Johnson NYC
2007 #R79 Jimmie Johnson SM
2008 #R1 Jimmie Johnson
2008 #R30 Jimmie Johnson RM
2008 #R37 Jimmie Johnson TO
2008 #R51 Jimmie Johnson NS
2008 #R52 Jimmie Johnson NS
2008 #R53 Jimmie Johnson NS
2008 #R64 Jimmie Johnson's Car LP
2008 #R73 Jimmie Johnson SO
2008 #R75 Top 10 Drivers SO
2008 #R81 Jimmie Johnson SO

Press Pass Eclipse Samples
2003 #5 Jimmie Johnson
2003 #37 All-American Kid WCS
2003 #43 Born to Run WCS
2003 #48 Jimmie Johnson HS
2004 #2 Jimmie Johnson
2004 #48 Jimmie Johnson Z
2004 #58 Jimmie Johnson P
2004 #78 Earnhardt Jr./Johnson LL
2004 #85 Jimmie Johnson LL
2005 #2 Jimmie Johnson
2005 #46 Jimmie Johnson Z
2005 #49 Jimmie Johnson Z
2005 #50 Jimmie Johnson Z
2005 #58 Jimmie Johnson P
2005 #65 J.Gordon/J.Johnson NS
2005 #68 Jimmie Johnson's Car NS
2005 #72 J.Gordon/J.Johnson NS
2005 #85 Jimmie Johnson LL
2005 #90 Jimmie Johnson SM CL

Press Pass Eclipse Skidmarks
2003 #SM8 Jimmie Johnson
2004 #SM3 Jimmie Johnson
2005 #SM3 Jimmie Johnson
2006 #SM7 Jimmie Johnson
2007 #SM6 Jimmie Johnson

Press Pass Eclipse Skidmarks Holofoil
2004 #SM3 Jimmie Johnson
2005 #SM3 Jimmie Johnson
2006 #SM7 Jimmie Johnson
2007 #SM6 Jimmie Johnson

Press Pass Eclipse Solar Eclipse
2003 #P5 Jimmie Johnson
2003 #P37 All-American Kid WCS
2003 #P43 Born to Run WCS
2003 #P48 Jimmie Johnson HS

Press Pass Eclipse Star Tracks
2008 #ST10 Jimmie Johnson

Press Pass Eclipse Star Tracks Holofoil
2008 #ST10 Jimmie Johnson

Press Pass Eclipse Stellar
2008 #ST1 Jimmie Johnson

Press Pass Eclipse Supernova
2003 #SN8 Jimmie Johnson
2006 #SU12 Jimmie Johnson

Press Pass Eclipse Teammates Autographs
2003 #JGJJ J.Gordon/J.Johnson
2004 #2 J.Johnson/J.Gordon
2005 #6 J.Gordon/J.Johnson
2006 #5 J.Johnson/J.Gordon
2007 #7 J.Gordon/J.Johnson/Ky.Busch
2008 #EJ Dale Earnhardt Jr. Jimmie Johnson
2008 #EGJM Dale Earnhardt Jr. Jeff Gordon Jimmie Johnson Casey /Mears

Press Pass Eclipse Under Cover Autographs
2004 #UCJJ Jimmie Johnson/48
2005 #UCJJ Jimmie Johnson/48
2006 #JJ Jimmie Johnson/48
2007 #UC-JJ Jimmie Johnson/48
2008 #UC-JJ Jimmie Johnson/48

Press Pass Eclipse Under Cover Cars
2003 #UCT4 Jimmie Johnson
2004 #UCD1 Jimmie Johnson
2005 #UCT1 Jimmie Johnson
2006 #UCT7 Jimmie Johnson

Press Pass Eclipse Under Cover Cars Autographs
2003 #UCTJJ Jimmie Johnson/48

Press Pass Eclipse Under Cover Double Cover
2002 #DC2 J.Gordon/J.Johnson
2002 #DC4 J.Nadeau/J.Johnson
2002 #DC5 T.Labonte/J.Johnson
2003 #DC2 J.Johnson/J.Gordon
2003 #DC4 J.Nemechek/J.Johnson
2003 #DC5 T.Labonte/J.Johnson
2004 #DC3 J.Johnson/J.Gordon
2004 #DC5 T.Labonte/J.Johnson
2004 #DC8 J.Johnson/J.Nemechek
2005 #DC3 J.Johnson/J.Gordon
2005 #DC8 J.Johnson/T.Labonte
2006 #DC1 J.Johnson/J.Gordon
2006 #DC8 T.Labonte/J.Johnson

Press Pass Eclipse Under Cover Double Cover Holofoil
2006 #DC1 J.Johnson/J.Gordon
2006 #DC8 T.Labonte/J.Johnson

Press Pass Eclipse Under Cover Double Cover Name
2007 #DC3 Gordon/Johnson
2008 #DC6 Jeff Gordon Jimme Johnson

Press Pass Eclipse Under Cover Double Cover NASCAR
2007 #DC3 Gordon/Johnson
2008 #DC6 Jeff Gordon Jimme Johnson

Press Pass Eclipse Under Cover Driver Autographs
2003 #UCD-JJ Jimmie Johnson/48

Press Pass Eclipse Under Cover Driver Gold
2003 #UCD4 Jimmie Johnson
2004 #UCD1 Jimmie Johnson

Press Pass Eclipse Under Cover Driver Red
2003 #UCD4 Jimmie Johnson
2004 #UCD1 Jimmie Johnson
2005 #UCD1 Jimmie Johnson

Press Pass Eclipse Under Cover Driver Silver
2003 #UCD4 Jimmie Johnson
2004 #UCD1 Jimmie Johnson

Press Pass Eclipse Under Cover Drivers
2002 #CD1 Jimmie Johnson
2007 #UCD7 Jimmie Johnson
2008 #UCD14 Jimmie Johnson

Press Pass Eclipse Under Cover Drivers Eclipse
2007 #UCD7 Jimmie Johnson
2008 #UCD14 Jimmie Johnson

Press Pass Eclipse Under Cover Drivers Gold
2006 #UCD7 Jimmie Johnson

Press Pass Eclipse Under Cover Drivers Holofoil
2005 #UCD1 Jimmie Johnson
2006 #UCD7 Jimmie Johnson

Press Pass Eclipse Under Cover Drivers Name
2007 #UCD7 Jimmie Johnson
2008 #UCD14 Jimmie Johnson

Press Pass Eclipse Under Cover Drivers NASCAR
2007 #UCD7 Jimmie Johnson
2008 #UCD14 Jimmie Johnson

Press Pass Eclipse Under Cover Drivers Silver
2005 #UCD1 Jimmie Johnson
2006 #UCD7 Jimmie Johnson

Press Pass Eclipse Under Cover Gold Cars
2002 #CD1 Jimmie Johnson

Press Pass Eclipse Under Cover Gold Drivers
2002 #CD1 Jimmie Johnson

Press Pass Eclipse Under Cover Holofoil Drivers
2002 #CD1 Jimmie Johnson

Press Pass Eclipse Under Cover Teams
2007 #UCT7 Jimmie Johnson
2008 #UCT14 Jimmie Johnson

Press Pass Eclipse Under Cover Teams NASCAR
2007 #UCT7 Jimmie Johnson
2008 #UCT14 Jimmie Johnson

Press Pass Eclipse Warp Speed
2003 #WS6 Jimmie Johnson

Press Pass Four Wide
2006 #FW-JJ Jimmie Johnson
2007 #FW-JJ Jimmie Johnson
2008 #FW-JJ Jimmie Johnson

Press Pass Four Wide Checkered
2007 #FW-JJ Jimmie Johnson
2008 #FW-JJ Jimmie Johnson

Press Pass Four Wide Checkered Exchange
2007 #FW-JJ Jimmie Johnson

Press Pass Four Wide Checkered Flag
2006 #FW-JJ Jimmie Johnson

Press Pass Four Wide Exchange
2007 #FW-JJ Jimmie Johnson

Press Pass Game Face
2005 #GF2 Jimmie Johnson
2006 #GF2 Jimmie Johnson

Press Pass Gatorade Jumbos
2003 #1 Jimmie Johnson

Press Pass Gold
2006 #G27 Jimmie Johnson
2006 #G73 Jimmie Johnson's Car OTW
2006 #G91 Jimmie Johnson NS
2006 #G103 Jimmie Johnson U
2006 #G111 Jimmie Johnson TT
2007 #G2 Jimmie Johnson
2007 #G77 Jimmie Johnson's Car OT
2007 #G94 Jimmie Johnson NS
2007 #G96 Jimmie Johnson U
2007 #G109 Jimmie Johnson TT
2007 #G120 Jimmie Johnson CL
2008 #G6 Jimmie Johnson
2008 #G68 Jimmie Johnson's Car BFS
2008 #G81 Jimmie Johnson NS
2008 #G107 Jimmie Johnson Top 12

Press Pass Gold Holofoil
2003 #P16 Jimmie Johnson
2003 #P59 Jimmie Johnson DS
2003 #P63 Jr./Johnson/Newman Sadler/Kenseth/Busch DS
2003 #P64 J.Johnson Daytona RR
2003 #P65 J.Johnson California RR
2003 #P66 J.Johnson Dover June RR
2003 #P67 J.Johnson Dover Sept RR
2003 #P78 The California Kid WCS
2003 #P79 Two of a Kind WCS

Press Pass Hot Treads
2002 #HT14 Jim Johnson's Car/1555
2002 #HT30 Ji.Johnson's Car/2375
2004 #HTR3 Jimmie Johnson
2005 #HTR18 Jimmie Johnson
2007 #HT4 Jimmie Johnson
2008 #HT3 Jimmie Johnson

Press Pass Hot Treads Blue
2007 #HT4 Jimmie Johnson
2008 #HT3 Jimmie Johnson

Press Pass Hot Treads Gold
2007 #HT4 Jimmie Johnson
2008 #HT3 Jimmie Johnson

Press Pass Hot Treads Holofoil
2004 #HTR3 Jimmie Johnson
2005 #HTR18 Jimmie Johnson

Press Pass K-Mart
2007 #JJ-C Jimmie Johnson

Press Pass Legends
2005 #31 Jimmie Johnson
2006 #41 Jimmie Johnson
2007 #43 Jimmie Johnson

Press Pass Legends Autographs Black
2005 #18 Jimmie Johnson
2006 #25 Jimmie Johnson

Press Pass Legends Autographs Blue
2007 #15 Jimmie Johnson/71

Press Pass Legends Blue
2005 #31B Jimmie Johnson
2006 #B41 Jimmie Johnson
2007 #B43 Jimmie Johnson

Press Pass Legends Bronze
2006 #Z41 Jimmie Johnson
2007 #Z43 Jimmie Johnson

Press Pass Legends Double Threads Bronze
2005 #DT-GJ J.Gordon/J.Johnson

Press Pass Legends Double Threads Gold
2005 #DT-GJ J.Gordon/J.Johnson

Press Pass Legends Double Threads Silver
2005 #DT-GJ J.Gordon/J.Johnson

Press Pass Legends Gold
2005 #31G Jimmie Johnson
2006 #G41 Jimmie Johnson
2007 #G43 Jimmie Johnson

Press Pass Legends Heritage Gold
2006 #HE11 Jimmie Johnson

Press Pass Legends Heritage Silver
2006 #HE11 Jimmie Johnson

Press Pass Legends Holofoil
2005 #31H Jimmie Johnson
2006 #H41 Jimmie Johnson
2007 #H43 Jimmie Johnson

Press Pass Legends Memorable Moments Gold
2006 #MM4 Jimmie Johnson

Press Pass Legends Memorable Moments Silver
2006 #MM4 Jimmie Johnson

Press Pass Legends Press Plates Black
2005 #31 Jimmie Johnson
2006 #PPB41 Jimmie Johnson
2007 #PP43 Jimmie Johnson

Press Pass Legends Press Plates Black Backs
2006 #PPB41B Jimmie Johnson
2007 #PP43 Jimmie Johnson

Press Pass Legends Press Plates Cyan
2005 #31 Jimmie Johnson
2006 #PPC41 Jimmie Johnson
2007 #PP43 Jimmie Johnson

Press Pass Legends Press Plates Cyan Backs
2006 #PPC41B Jimmie Johnson
2007 #PP43 Jimmie Johnson

Press Pass Legends Press Plates Magenta
2005 #31 Jimmie Johnson
2006 #PPM41 Jimmie Johnson
2007 #PP43 Jimmie Johnson

Press Pass Legends Press Plates Magenta Backs
2006 #PPM41B Jimmie Johnson
2007 #PP43 Jimmie Johnson

Press Pass Legends Press Plates Yellow
2005 #31 Jimmie Johnson
2006 #PPY41 Jimmie Johnson
2007 #PP43 Jimmie Johnson

Press Pass Legends Press Plates Yellow Backs
2006 #PPY41B Jimmie Johnson
2007 #PP43 Jimmie Johnson

Press Pass Legends Previews
2005 #31 Jimmie Johnson
2006 #EB41 Jimmie Johnson
2007 #EB43 Jimmie Johnson

Press Pass Legends Signature Series
2007 #JJ Jimmie Johnson

Press Pass Legends Solo
2005 #31S Jimmie Johnson
2006 #S41 Jimmie Johnson
2007 #S43 Jimmie Johnson

Press Pass Legends Sunday Swatches Bronze
2007 #JJ-SS Jimmie Johnson

Press Pass Legends Sunday Swatches Gold
2007 #JJ-SS Jimmie Johnson

Press Pass Legends Sunday Swatches Silver
2007 #JJ-SS Jimmie Johnson

Press Pass Legends Threads & Treads Bronze
2005 #TTJJ Jimmie Johnson

Press Pass Legends Threads & Treads Gold
2005 #TTJJ Jimmie Johnson

Press Pass Legends Threads & Treads Silver
2005 #TTJJ Jimmie Johnson

Press Pass Legends Triple Threads
2006 #TT-JJ Jimmie Johnson

Press Pass Legends Victory Lane Bronze
2007 #VL6 Jimmie Johnson

Press Pass Legends Victory Lane Gold
2007 #VL6 Jimmie Johnson

Press Pass Legends Victory Lane Silver
2007 #VL6 Jimmie Johnson

Press Pass Making the Show Collector's Series
2004 #MS23 Jimmie Johnson

Press Pass Optima
2001 #32 Jimmie Johnson BGN
2002 #14 Jimmie Johnson CRC
2002 #47 Jimmie Johnson YG
2002 #0 J.Gordon/J.Johnson
2003 #11 Jimmie Johnson
2004 #10 Jimmie Johnson
2004 #58 Jimmie Johnson's Car RV
2004 #77 Jimmie Johnson CP
2004 #90 Jimmie Johnson SS
2005 #13 Jimmie Johnson
2005 #13B Jimmie Johnson Cup Chase
2005 #62 Jimmie Johnson RR
2005 #67 Jimmie Johnson DP
2005 #85 Jimmie Johnson DT
2005 #92 Jimmie Johnson's Car RTV
2005 #95 Jimmie Johnson R&R
2006 #30 Jimmie Johnson
2006 #61 Jimmie Johnson's Car HS
2006 #66 Jimmie Johnson CP
2006 #87 Jimmie Johnson RTV Indy
2006 #98 Jimmie Johnson VOTC
2006 #30B Jimmie Johnson Chase

Press Pass Optima Cool Persistence
2002 #CP6 Jimmie Johnson
2003 #CP2 Jimmie Johnson
2004 #CP6 Jimmie Johnson
2005 #CP4 Jimmie Johnson

Press Pass Optima Fan Favorite
2002 #FF11 Jimmie Johnson
2003 #FF1 Jimmie Johnson
2004 #FF10 Jimmie Johnson
2005 #FF12 Jimmie Johnson
2006 #FF10 Jimmie Johnson

Press Pass Optima G Force
2004 #GF5 Jimmie Johnson
2005 #GF2 Jimmie Johnson

Press Pass Optima Gold
2001 #32 Jimmie Johnson BGN
2002 #14 Jimmie Johnson CRC
2002 #47 Jimmie Johnson YG
2003 #G11 Jimmie Johnson
2004 #G10 Jimmie Johnson
2004 #G58 Jimmie Johnson's Car RV
2004 #G77 Jimmie Johnson CP
2004 #G90 Jimmie Johnson SS
2005 #G13 Jimmie Johnson
2005 #G62 Jimmie Johnson RR
2005 #G67 Jimmie Johnson DP
2005 #G85 Jimmie Johnson DT
2005 #G92 Jimmie Johnson's Car RTV
2005 #G95 Jimmie Johnson R&R
2006 #G30 Jimmie Johnson
2006 #G61 Jimmie Johnson's Car HS
2006 #G66 Jimmie Johnson CP
2006 #G87 Jimmie Johnson RTV Indy
2006 #G98 Jimmie Johnson VOTC

Press Pass Optima Pole Position
2006 #PP5 Jimmie Johnson

Press Pass Optima Previews
2003 #11 Jimmie Johnson
2004 #EB10 Jimmie Johnson
2005 #13 Jimmie Johnson
2006 #EB30 Jimmie Johnson

Press Pass Optima Promos
2002 #14 Jimmie Johnson
2002 #47 Jimmie Johnson YG

Press Pass Optima Q & A
2006 #QA1 Jimmie Johnson

Press Pass Optima Q and A
2002 #QA3 Jimmie Johnson

Press Pass Optima Q&A
2004 #QA6 Jimmie Johnson

Press Pass Optima Race Used Lugnuts Autographs
2002 #LNDA9 Jimmie Johnson/48

Press Pass Optima Race Used Lugnuts Cars
2002 #LNC9 Jimmie Johnson's Car

Press Pass Optima Race Used Lugnuts Drivers
2002 #LND9 Jimmie Johnson

Press Pass Optima Samples
2002 #14 Jimmie Johnson
2002 #47 Jimmie Johnson YG
2003 #11 Jimmie Johnson
2004 #10 Jimmie Johnson
2004 #58 Jimmie Johnson's Car RV
2004 #77 Jimmie Johnson CP
2004 #90 Jimmie Johnson SS
2005 #13 Jimmie Johnson
2005 #62 Jimmie Johnson RR
2005 #67 Jimmie Johnson DP
2005 #85 Jimmie Johnson DT
2005 #92 Jimmie Johnson RTV
2005 #95 Jimmie Johnson R&R

Press Pass Optima Thunder Bolts Autographs
2005 #TB-JJ Jimmie Johnson/48

Press Pass Optima Thunder Bolts Cars
2003 #TBT4 Jimmie Johnson's Car
2004 #TBT9 Jimmie Johnson's Car

Press Pass Optima Thunder Bolts Cars Autographs
2003 #TBT-JJ Jimmie Johnson/48

Press Pass Optima Thunder Bolts Drivers
2003 #TBD4 Jimmie Johnson/50
2004 #TBD9 Jimmie Johnson

Press Pass Optima Thunder Bolts Drivers Autographs
2003 #TBD-JJ Jimmie Johnson/48

Press Pass Optima Up Close
2002 #UC4 Jimmie Johnson

Press Pass Optima Young Guns
2003 #YG5 Jimmie Johnson

Press Pass Panorama
2005 #PPP12 Jimmie Johnson
2005 #PPP21 Jimmie Johnson
2005 #PPP25 Jimmie Johnson
2005 #PPP36 Jimmie Johnson
2005 #PPP43 Jimmie Johnson
2005 #PPP44 Jimmie Johnson
2005 #PPP59 Jimmie Johnson

Press Pass Platinum
2002 #44 Jimmie Johnson NBS
2004 #P14 Jimmie Johnson
2004 #P83 Spring Reign WCS
2004 #P84 Million-dollar Magic WCS
2004 #P86 In the Groove WCS
2004 #P95 Jimmie Johnson DS
2005 #P32 Jimmie Johnson
2005 #P76 Jimmie Johnson NS
2005 #P82 Jimmie Johnson NS
2005 #P92 J.Hendrick/Gordon/JJ/T.Lab/Vickers Y
2005 #P106 Jimmie Johnson P
2005 #P114 Jimmie Johnson's Car
2005 #P118 Jimmie Johnson's Car
2005 #P120 Dale Jr/JJ/Gordon CL
2006 #P27 Jimmie Johnson
2006 #P73 Jimmie Johnson's Car OTW
2006 #P91 Jimmie Johnson NS
2006 #P103 Jimmie Johnson U
2006 #P111 Jimmie Johnson TT
2007 #P2 Jimmie Johnson
2007 #P77 Jimmie Johnson's Car OT
2007 #P94 Jimmie Johnson NS
2007 #P96 Jimmie Johnson U
2007 #P109 Jimmie Johnson TT
2007 #PCL Jimmie Johnson CL
2008 #P6 Jimmie Johnson
2008 #P68 Jimmie Johnson's Car BFS
2008 #P81 Jimmie Johnson NS
2008 #P107 Jimmie Johnson Top 12

Press Pass Premium
2002 #13 Jimmie Johnson CRC
2002 #34 Jimmie Johnson's Car
2002 #49 Jimmie Johnson SW
2002 #62 Jimmie Johnson CH
2002 #75 Jimmie Johnson PC
2003 #13 Jimmie Johnson
2003 #40 Jimmie Johnson's Car
2003 #61 Jimmie Johnson CC
2003 #73 Jimmie Johnson PC
2004 #4 Jimmie Johnson
2004 #44 Jimmie Johnson's Car
2004 #58 Jimmie Johnson CC
2004 #75 Jimmie Johnson PC
2005 #11 Jimmie Johnson
2005 #38 Jimmie Johnson's Car M
2005 #48 Jimmie Johnson S
2005 #59 Jimmie Johnson CC
2005 #74 Jimmie Johnson PC
2006 #12 Jimmie Johnson
2006 #45 Jimmie Johnson's Car M
2006 #61 Jimmie Johnson C
2006 #73 Jimmie Johnson PC
2006 #0 Jimmie Johnson Daytona
2007 #1 Jimmie Johnson CL
2007 #30 Jimmie Johnson
2007 #45 Jimmie Johnson's Car M
2007 #59 Jimmie Johnson RTTC
2007 #62 Jimmie Johnson MD
2007 #71 Jimmie Johnson DD
2007 #82 Jimmie Johnson FF
2008 #29 Jimmie Johnson
2008 #41 Jimmie Johnson's Car M
2008 #50 Jimmie Johnson SW Daytona Pole
2008 #55 Jimmie Johnson EOP
2008 #69 Jimmie Johnson MD
2008 #74 Jimmie Johnson F
2008 #83 Jimmie Johnson OD

Press Pass Premium Asphalt Jungle
2004 #A4 Jimmie Johnson
2005 #AJ1 Jimmie Johnson
2006 #AJ5 Jimmie Johnson

Press Pass Premium Clean Air
2008 #CA10 Jimmie Johnson

Press Pass Premium Concrete Chaos
2007 #CC3 Jimmie Johnson

Press Pass Premium Hot Threads Autographs

2004 #HT-JJ Jimmie Johnson/48
2005 #HT-JJ Jimmie Johnson/48
2006 #HT-JJ Jimmie Johnson/48
2007 #HT-JJ Jimmie Johnson/48

Press Pass Premium Hot Threads Cars
2003 #HTT4 Jimmie Johnson
2005 #HTT2 Jimmie Johnson
2006 #HTT5 Jimmie Johnson

Press Pass Premium Hot Threads Cars Autographs
2003 #HTD-JJ Jimmie Johnson/48

Press Pass Premium Hot Threads Drivers
2003 #HTD4 Jimmie Johnson
2005 #HTD2 Jimmie Johnson
2006 #HTD5 Jimmie Johnson
2007 #HTD15 Jimmie Johnson
2008 #HTD4 Jimmie Johnson

Press Pass Premium Hot Threads Drivers Autographs
2003 #HTT-JJ Jimmie Johnson/48

Press Pass Premium Hot Threads Drivers Bronze
2004 #HTD1 Jimmie Johnson

Press Pass Premium Hot Threads Drivers Bronze Retail
2004 #HTT1 Jimmie Johnson

Press Pass Premium Hot Threads Drivers Gold
2004 #HTD1 Jimmie Johnson
2005 #HTD2 Jimmie Johnson
2006 #HTD5 Jimmie Johnson
2007 #HTD15 Jimmie Johnson
2008 #HTD4 Jimmie Johnson

Press Pass Premium Hot Threads Drivers Silver
2004 #HTD1 Jimmie Johnson

Press Pass Premium Hot Threads Patch
2007 #HTP11 Jimmie Johnson Lowe's/15
2007 #HTP12 Jimmie Johnson Nextel Cup/10

Press Pass Premium Hot Threads Patches
2008 #HTP15 Jimmie Johnson Delphi/8
2008 #HTP16 Jimmie Johnson Hendrick Motorsports/6
2008 #HTP17 Jimmie Johnson NASCAR bar/6

Press Pass Premium Hot Threads Team
2007 #HTT15 Jimmie Johnson
2008 #HTT4 Jimmie Johnson

Press Pass Premium In the Zone
2003 #IZ4 Jimmie Johnson
2004 #IZ5 Jimmie Johnson
2005 #IZ7 Jimmie Johnson
2006 #IZ7 Jimmie Johnson

Press Pass Premium In the Zone Elite Edition
2004 #IZ5 Jimmie Johnson
2005 #IZ7 Jimmie Johnson

Press Pass Premium In the Zone Red
2006 #IZ7 Jimmie Johnson

Press Pass Premium Performance Driven
2003 #PD3 Jimmie Johnson
2004 #PD6 Jimmie Johnson
2005 #PD5 Jimmie Johnson
2007 #PD6 Jimmie Johnson

Press Pass Premium Performance Driven Red
2007 #PD6 Jimmie Johnson

Press Pass Premium Previews
2003 #13 Jimmie Johnson
2004 #4 Jimmie Johnson
2008 #EB29 Jimmie Johnson
2008 #EB55 Jimmie Johnson EOP

Press Pass Premium Red
2007 #R1 Jimmie Johnson CL
2007 #R30 Jimmie Johnson
2007 #R45 Jimmie Johnson's Car M
2007 #R59 Jimmie Johnson RTTC
2007 #R62 Jimmie Johnson MD
2007 #R71 Jimmie Johnson DD
2007 #R82 Jimmie Johnson FF
2008 #29 Jimmie Johnson
2008 #41 Jimmie Johnson's Car M
2008 #50 Jimmie Johnson SW
2008 #55 Jimmie Johnson EOP
2008 #69 Jimmie Johnson MD
2008 #74 Jimmie Johnson F
2008 #83 Jimmie Johnson OD

Press Pass Premium Red Reflectors
2002 #13 Jimmie Johnson
2002 #34 Jimmie Johnson's Car
2002 #49 Jimmie Johnson SW
2002 #62 Jimmie Johnson CH
2002 #75 Jimmie Johnson PC
2003 #13 Jimmie Johnson
2003 #40 Jimmie Johnson's Car
2003 #61 Jimmie Johnson CC
2003 #73 Jimmie Johnson PC

Press Pass Premium Samples
2002 #13 Jimmie Johnson
2002 #34 Jimmie Johnson's Car
2002 #49 Jimmie Johnson SW
2003 #13 Jimmie Johnson
2003 #40 Jimmie Johnson's Car
2004 #4 Jimmie Johnson
2004 #44 Jimmie Johnson's Car
2005 #11 Jimmie Johnson
2005 #38 Jimmie Johnson's Car M
2005 #48 Jimmie Johnson S

Press Pass Premium Team Signed Baseballs
2008 #HMS Dale Earnhardt Jr. Jeff Gordon Jimmie Johnson Casey Mears
2008 #E-HMS Dale Earnhardt Jr. Jeff Gordon Jimmie Johnson Casey Mears Entry Card

Press Pass Premium Wal-Mart
2008 #WM2 Jimmie Johnson

Press Pass Previews
2003 #16 Jimmie Johnson
2004 #14 Jimmie Johnson
2006 #EB27 Jimmie Johnson
2006 #EB103 Jimmie Johnson U
2007 #EB2 Jimmie Johnson
2007 #EB109 Jimmie Johnson TT
2008 #EB6 Jimmie Johnson
2008 #EB107 Jimmie Johnson Top 12

Press Pass Previews Green
2005 #EB32 Jimmie Johnson

Press Pass Previews Silver
2005 #EB106 Jimmie Johnson

Press Pass Race Day
2007 #RD5 Jimmie Johnson

Press Pass Samples
2003 #16 Jimmie Johnson
2003 #59 Jimmie Johnson DS
2003 #63 Jr./JJ/New/Sad/Ken/Bus DS
2003 #64 J.Johnson Feb.17 RR
2003 #65 J.Johnson Apr.28 RR
2003 #66 J.Johnson Dover June RR
2003 #67 J.Johnson Dover Sept RR
2003 #78 The California Kid WCS
2003 #79 Two of a Kind WCS
2004 #14 Jimmie Johnson
2004 #83 Spring Reign WCS
2004 #84 Million-dollar Magic WCS
2004 #86 In the Groove WCS
2004 #95 Jimmie Johnson DS
2005 #32 Jimmie Johnson
2005 #76 Jimmie Johnson NS
2005 #82 Jimmie Johnson NS
2005 #92 J.Hend./Gordon/JJ/T.Lab/B.Vick Y
2005 #106 Jimmie Johnson P
2005 #114 Jimmie Johnson's Car
2005 #118 Jimmie Johnson's Car
2005 #120 Dale Jr/JJ/Gordon CL

Press Pass Schedule
2004 #2 Jimmie Johnson

Press Pass Showcar
2003 #S6B Jimmie Johnson
2003 #S7B Jimmie Johnson's Car
2005 #SC3 Jimmie Johnson

Press Pass Showman
2003 #S6A Jimmie Johnson
2004 #S7A Jimmie Johnson
2005 #SM3 Jimmie Johnson

Press Pass Signings
2002 #29 Jimmie Johnson O/P/S/T/V
2003 #35 J.Johnson O/P/S/T/V
2004 #32 Jimmie Johnson O/P/S/T/V
2005 #26 Jimmie Johnson P/S
2006 #25 Jimmie Johnson NC P/S
2007 #32 Jimmie Johnson NC
2008 #29 Jimmie Johnson

Press Pass Signings Blue
2007 #13 Jimmie Johnson NC
2008 #13 Jimmie Johnson

Press Pass Signings Gold
2002 #27 Jimmie Johnson O/P/S/T/V
2003 #35 J.Johnson O/P/S/T/V
2004 #29 Jimmie Johnson O/P/S/T/V
2005 #25 Jimmie Johnson P/S
2006 #22 Jimmie Johnson NC P/S
2007 #25 Jimmie Johnson NC
2008 #23 Jimmie Johnson

Press Pass Signings Platinum
2005 #25 Jimmie Johnson P/S

Press Pass Signings Press Plates Black
2007 #22 Jimmie Johnson
2008 #21 Jimmie Johnson

Press Pass Signings Press Plates Cyan
2007 #21 Jimmie Johnson
2008 #21 Jimmie Johnson

Press Pass Signings Press Plates Magenta
2007 #23 Jimmie Johnson
2008 #21 Jimmie Johnson

Press Pass Signings Press Plates Yellow
2007 #21 Jimmie Johnson
2008 #21 Jimmie Johnson

Press Pass Signings Silver
2006 #25 Jimmie Johnson NC P/S
2007 #24 Jimmie Johnson NC

Press Pass Signings Transparent
2003 #5 Jimmie Johnson O/P/S/T/V
2004 #3 Jimmie Johnson O/P/S/T

Press Pass Slideshow
2008 #SS6 Jimmie Johnson

Press Pass Snapshots
2003 #SN11 Jimmie Johnson
2004 #SN11 Jimmie Johnson
2005 #SN12 Jimmie Johnson
2006 #SN7 Jimmie Johnson
2006 #SN17 Jimmie Johnson
2007 #SN13 Jimmie Johnson

Press Pass Snapshots Extra
2005 #SS3 Jimmie Johnson

Press Pass Speedway
2008 #7 Jimmie Johnson
2008 #71 Jimmie Johnson UTH
2008 #88 Jimmie Johnson's Car WS

Press Pass Speedway Blur
2008 #B1 Jimmie Johnson

Press Pass Speedway Cockpit
2008 #CP10 Jimmie Johnson

Press Pass Speedway Garage Graphs Duals
2008 #JK Jimmie Johnson Chad Knaus

Press Pass Speedway Gold
2008 #G7 Jimmie Johnson
2008 #G71 Jimmie Johnson UTH
2008 #G88 Jimmie Johnson's Car WS

Press Pass Speedway Holofoil
2008 #H7 Jimmie Johnson
2008 #H71 Jimmie Johnson UTH
2008 #H88 Jimmie Johnson's Car WS

Press Pass Speedway Previews
2008 #EB7 Jimmie Johnson

Press Pass Speedway Red
2008 #R7 Jimmie Johnson
2008 #R71 Jimmie Johnson UTH
2008 #R88 Jimmie Johnson's Car WS

Press Pass Speedway Test Drive
2008 #TD11 Jimmie Johnson

Press Pass Stealth
2002 #37 Jimmie Johnson CRC
2002 #38 Jimmie Johnson's Car
2002 #39 Jimmie Johnson
2002 #52 Jimmie Johnson's Car SST
2002 #69 Jimmie Johnson WW
2003 #34 Jimmie Johnson
2003 #35 Jimmie Johnson's Car
2003 #36 Jimmie Johnson
2003 #63 Jimmie Johnson SST
2003 #67 Jimmie Johnson SF
2004 #7 Jimmie Johnson
2004 #8 Jimmie Johnson's Car
2004 #9 Jimmie Johnson
2004 #88 Jimmie Johnson SST
2004 #94 Jimmie Johnson SF
2005 #39 Jimmie Johnson
2005 #42 Jimmie Johnson's Car
2005 #45 Jimmie Johnson
2005 #89 Jimmie Johnson H
2005 #96 Jimmie Johnson SF
2006 #13 Jimmie Johnson
2006 #40 Jimmie Johnson's Rig
2006 #54 24/44/48/25/5 TM
2006 #65 Jimmie Johnson F
2006 #90 Johnson/Gordon CL
2007 #12 Jimmie Johnson
2007 #54 Jimmie Johnson's Rig
2007 #63 Jimmie Johnson's Crew GC
2007 #72 Mears/Ky.Busch/JJ/Gordon
2007 #83 Jimmie Johnson PO
2008 #16 Jimmie Johnson
2008 #63 Jimmie Johnson's Car GC
2008 #67 Jimmie Johnson Jeff Gordon Dale Earnhardt Jr. Casey Mears
2008 #90 Jimmie Johnson PM

Press Pass Stealth Autographed Hat Entry
2006 #PPH11 Jimmie Johnson

Press Pass Stealth Battle Armor Autographs
2007 #BAS-JJ Jimmie Johnson/48

Press Pass Stealth Battle Armor Drivers
2007 #BAD8 Jimmie Johnson
2008 #BAD1 Jimmie Johnson

Press Pass Stealth Battle Armor Teams
2007 #BAT8 Jimmie Johnson
2008 #BAT1 Jimmie Johnson

Press Pass Stealth Behind the Numbers
2002 #BN7 Jimmie Johnson

Press Pass Stealth Chrome
2007 #12 Jimmie Johnson
2007 #54 Jimmie Johnson's Rig
2007 #63 Jimmie Johnson's Crew GC
2007 #72 Mears/Ky.Busch/JJ/Gordon
2007 #83 Jimmie Johnson PO
2007 #63A Jimmie Johnson's Car GC L1 yellow hose
2008 #16 Jimmie Johnson
2008 #63 Jimmie Johnson's Car GC
2008 #67 Jimmie Johnson Jeff Gordon Dale Earnhardt Jr. Casey Mears
2008 #90 Jimmie Johnson PM
2008 #63B Jimmie Johnson's Car GC VAR

Press Pass Stealth Chrome Exclusives
2007 #X12 Jimmie Johnson
2007 #X54 Jimmie Johnson's Rig
2007 #X63 Jimmie Johnson's Crew GC
2007 #X72 Mears/Ky.Busch/JJ/Gordon
2007 #X83 Jimmie Johnson PO
2008 #16 Jimmie Johnson
2008 #63 Jimmie Johnson's Car GC
2008 #67 Jimmie Johnson Jeff Gordon Dale Earnhardt Jr. Casey Mears
2008 #90 Jimmie Johnson PM

Press Pass Stealth Chrome Exclusives Gold
2008 #16 Jimmie Johnson
2008 #63 Jimmie Johnson's Car GC
2008 #67 Jimmie Johnson Jeff Gordon Dale Earnhardt Jr. Casey Mears
2008 #90 Jimmie Johnson PM

Press Pass Stealth Chrome Platinum
2007 #P12 Jimmie Johnson
2007 #P54 Jimmie Johnson's Rig
2007 #P63 Jimmie Johnson's Crew GC
2007 #P72 Mears/Ky.Busch/JJ/Gordon
2007 #P83 Jimmie Johnson PO

Press Pass Stealth EFX
2002 #FX11 Jimmie Johnson
2003 #FX6 Jimmie Johnson
2004 #EF3 Jimmie Johnson
2005 #EFX2 Jimmie Johnson
2006 #EFX4 Jimmie Johnson 1:112

Press Pass Stealth Fusion
2002 #F6 Jimmie Johnson
2003 #FU7 Jimmie Johnson
2005 #FU2 Jimmie Johnson 1:112
2007 #F5 Jimmie Johnson

Press Pass Stealth Gear Grippers Autographs
2004 #HT-JJ Jimmie Johnson/48

Press Pass Stealth Gear Grippers Cars
2003 #GGT4 Jimmie Johnson

Press Pass Stealth Gear Grippers Cars Autographs
2003 #JJ Jimmie Johnson/48

Press Pass Stealth Gear Grippers Drivers
2003 #GGD4 Jimmie Johnson
2004 #GGD1 Jimmie Johnson
2006 #GGD13 Jimmie Johnson

Press Pass Stealth Gear Grippers Drivers Autographs
2003 #JJ Jimmie Johnson/48

Press Pass Stealth Gear Grippers Drivers Retail
2004 #GGT1 Jimmie Johnson

Press Pass Stealth Gold
2002 #37 Jimmie Johnson
2002 #38 Jimmie Johnson's Car
2002 #39 Jimmie Johnson
2002 #52 Jimmie Johnson's Car SST
2002 #69 Jimmie Johnson WW

Press Pass Stealth Hot Pass
2006 #HP14 Jimmie Johnson

Press Pass Stealth Lap Leaders
2002 #LL13 Jimmie Johnson

Press Pass Stealth Mach 07
2007 #M7-6 Jimmie Johnson

Press Pass Stealth Mach 08
2008 #M8-4 Jimmie Johnson

Press Pass Stealth Maximum Access
2007 #MA13 Jimmie Johnson
2008 #MA14 Jimmie Johnson

Press Pass Stealth Maximum Access Autographs
2007 #MA13 Jimmie Johnson
2008 #MA14 Jimmie Johnson

Press Pass Stealth No Boundaries
2003 #NB16 Jimmie Johnson
2004 #NB15 Jimmie Johnson
2005 #NB11 Jimmie Johnson

Press Pass Stealth Previews
2003 #34 Jimmie Johnson
2003 #35 Jimmie Johnson's Car
2003 #36 Jimmie Johnson
2004 #EB7 Jimmie Johnson
2004 #EB8 Jimmie Johnson's Car
2004 #EB9 Jimmie Johnson
2005 #39 Jimmie Johnson
2005 #42 Jimmie Johnson's Car
2005 #45 Jimmie Johnson
2006 #13 Jimmie Johnson
2007 #EB12 Jimmie Johnson
2007 #EB83 Jimmie Johnson PO
2008 #16 Jimmie Johnson
2008 #90 Jimmie Johnson PM

Press Pass Stealth Profile
2002 #P6 Jimmie Johnson
2003 #PR4 Jimmie Johnson
2004 #P2 Jimmie Johnson 1:112
2005 #PR2 Jimmie Johnson
2006 #P6 Jimmie Johnson

Press Pass Stealth Race Used Glove Cars
2002 #GLC13 Jimmie Johnson's Car

Press Pass Stealth Race Used Glove Drivers
2002 #GLD13 Jimmie Johnson

Press Pass Stealth Red
2003 #P34 Jimmie Johnson
2003 #P35 Jimmie Johnson's Car
2003 #P36 Jimmie Johnson
2003 #P63 Jimmie Johnson SST
2003 #P67 Jimmie Johnson SF

Press Pass Stealth Retail
2006 #13 Jimmie Johnson
2006 #40 Jimmie Johnson's Rig
2006 #54 24/44/48/25/5 TM
2006 #65 Jimmie Johnson F
2006 #90 J.Johnson/J.Gordon CL

Press Pass Stealth Retail Gear Grippers Cars
2006 #GGT13 Jimmie Johnson

Press Pass Stealth Samples
2002 #37 Jimmie Johnson
2002 #38 Jimmie Johnson's Car
2002 #39 Jimmie Johnson
2002 #52 Jimmie Johnson's Car SST
2002 #69 Jimmie Johnson WW
2003 #34 Jimmie Johnson
2003 #35 Jimmie Johnson's Car
2003 #36 Jimmie Johnson
2003 #63 Jimmie Johnson SST
2003 #67 Jimmie Johnson SF
2004 #X7 Jimmie Johnson
2004 #X8 Jimmie Johnson's Car
2004 #X9 Jimmie Johnson
2004 #X88 Jimmie Johnson SST
2004 #X94 Jimmie Johnson SF
2005 #39 Jimmie Johnson
2005 #42 Jimmie Johnson's Car
2005 #45 Jimmie Johnson
2005 #89 Jimmie Johnson H
2005 #96 Jimmie Johnson SF

Press Pass Stealth Supercharged
2003 #SC2 Jimmie Johnson

Press Pass Stealth Synthesis
2008 #S1 Jimmie Johnson

Press Pass Stealth X-Ray
2004 #7 Jimmie Johnson
2004 #8 Jimmie Johnson's Car
2004 #9 Jimmie Johnson
2004 #88 Jimmie Johnson SST
2004 #94 Jimmie Johnson SF
2005 #X39 Jimmie Johnson
2005 #X42 Jimmie Johnson's Car
2005 #X45 Jimmie Johnson
2005 #X89 Jimmie Johnson H
2005 #X96 Jimmie Johnson SF
2006 #X13 Jimmie Johnson
2006 #X40 Jimmie Johnson's Rig
2006 #X54 24/44/48/25/5 TM
2006 #X65 Jimmie Johnson F
2006 #X90 J.Johnson/J.Gordon CL

Press Pass Target
2007 #JJ-B Jimmie Johnson
2008 #JJ-B Jimmie Johnson

Press Pass Target Race Win Tires
2007 #RW1 Jimmie Johnson Daytona 2-19

Press Pass Target Victory Tires
2008 #TT-JJ Jimmie Johnson Las Vegas

Press Pass Top 25 Drivers & Rides
2006 #C22 Jimmie Johnson's Car
2006 #D22 Jimmie Johnson

Press Pass Top Shelf
2003 #TS4 Jimmie Johnson
2004 #TS5 Jimmie Johnson

Press Pass Top Ten
2005 #TT2 Jimmie Johnson

Press Pass Total Memorabilia Power Pick
2003 #TM4 Jimmie Johnson
2004 #TM4 Jimmie Johnson
2005 #TM4 Jimmie Johnson

Press Pass Trackside
2002 #7 Jimmie Johnson CRC
2002 #56 Jimmie Johnson RD
2002 #83 Jimmie Johnson TM
2003 #24 Jimmie Johnson
2003 #79 J.Johnson/J.Gordon TM
2004 #23 Jimmie Johnson
2004 #63 Jimmie Johnson's Car HS
2004 #69 J.Johnson/J.Gordon TM
2004 #85 Jimmie Johnson H
2004 #108 J.Gordon/J.J./Vickers TT
2004 #112 Jimmie Johnson F
2004 #120 J.Gordon/J.Johnson CL
2005 #5 Jimmie Johnson
2005 #65 Jimmie Johnson's Car HS
2005 #70 J.Gordon/J.Johnson TM
2005 #86 Jimmie Johnson GP
2005 #86B Jimmie Johnson GP -Chevy logo
2005 #96 Jimmie Johnson F

Press Pass Trackside Dialed In
2002 #DI6 Jimmie Johnson
2003 #DI5 Jimmie Johnson
2004 #DI1 Jimmie Johnson
2005 #DI1 Jimmie Johnson

Press Pass Trackside Generation Now
2002 #GN4 Jimmie Johnson

Press Pass Trackside Gold Holofoil
2003 #P24 Jimmie Johnson
2003 #P79 J.Johnson/J.Gordon

Press Pass Trackside Golden
2002 #G7 Jimmie Johnson
2003 #G24 Jimmie Johnson
2004 #G23 Jimmie Johnson
2004 #G63 Jimmie Johnson's Car HS
2004 #G69 J.Johnson/J.Gordon TM
2004 #G85 Jimmie Johnson H
2004 #G108 J.Gordon/Johnson/Vickers TT
2004 #G112 Jimmie Johnson F
2004 #G120 J.Gordon/J.Johnson CL
2005 #G5 Jimmie Johnson
2005 #G65 Jimmie Johnson's Car HS
2005 #G70 J.Gordon/J.Johnson TM
2005 #G86 Jimmie Johnson GP
2005 #G96 Jimmie Johnson F

Press Pass Trackside Hat Giveaway
2003 #PPH12 Jimmie Johnson
2004 #PPH13 Jimmie Johnson
2005 #PPH12 Jimmie Johnson

Press Pass Trackside Hot Pass
2004 #HP9 Jimmie Johnson
2005 #8 Jimmie Johnson

Press Pass Trackside Hot Pass National
2004 #HP9 Jimmie Johnson
2005 #8 Jimmie Johnson

Press Pass Trackside Hot Pursuit
2003 #HP3 Jimmie Johnson
2004 #HP2 Jimmie Johnson
2005 #HP2 Jimmie Johnson

Press Pass Trackside License to Drive
2002 #15 Jimmie Johnson

Press Pass Trackside License to Drive Die Cuts
2002 #15 Jimmie Johnson

Press Pass Trackside Pit Stoppers Autographs
2005 #PSJJ Jimmie Johnson/48

Press Pass Trackside Pit Stoppers Cars
2003 #PST4 Jimmie Johnson
2004 #PST4 Jimmie Johnson
2005 #PST3 Jimmie Johnson

Press Pass Trackside Pit Stoppers Cars Autographs
2003 #JJ Jimmie Johnson/48

Press Pass Trackside Pit Stoppers Drivers
2003 #PSD4 Jimmie Johnson
2004 #PSD4 Jimmie Johnson
2005 #PSD3 Jimmie Johnson

Press Pass Trackside Pit Stoppers Drivers Autographs
2003 #PSD-JJ Jimmie Johnson/48

Press Pass Trackside Previews
2003 #24 Jimmie Johnson
2004 #EB23 Jimmie Johnson
2005 #5 Jimmie Johnson
2005 #86 Jimmie Johnson GP

Press Pass Trackside Runnin n' Gunnin
2003 #RG6 Jimmie Johnson
2004 #RG3 Jimmie Johnson
2005 #RG3 Jimmie Johnson

Press Pass Trackside Samples
2002 #7 Jimmie Johnson
2002 #56 Jimmie Johnson RD
2002 #83 Jimmie Johnson TM
2003 #24 Jimmie Johnson
2003 #79 J.Johnson/J.Gordon TM
2004 #23 Jimmie Johnson
2004 #63 Jimmie Johnson's Car HS
2004 #69 J.Johnson/J.Gordon TM
2004 #85 Jimmie Johnson H
2004 #108 J.Gordon/Johnson/Vickers TT
2004 #112 Jimmie Johnson F
2004 #120 J.Gordon/J.Johnson CL
2005 #5 Jimmie Johnson
2005 #65 Jimmie Johnson's Car HS
2005 #70 J.Gordon/J.Johnson TM
2005 #86 Jimmie Johnson GP
2005 #96 Jimmie Johnson F

Press Pass Triple Burner
2003 #TB4 Jimmie Johnson
2004 #TB4 Jimmie Johnson
2005 #TB4 Jimmie Johnson

Press Pass Triple Burner Exchange
2003 #TB4 Jimmie Johnson EXCH
2004 #TB4 Jimmie Johnson
2005 #TB4 Jimmie Johnson

Press Pass UMI Cup Chase
2005 #1 Cup Chase Drivers CL
2005 #5 Jimmie Johnson

Press Pass Velocity
2003 #VC4 Jimmie Johnson
2004 #VC6 Jimmie Johnson
2005 #V2 Jimmie Johnson
2006 #VE8 Jimmie Johnson
2007 #V2 Jimmie Johnson

Press Pass Wal-Mart
2007 #JJ-A Jimmie Johnson
2008 #JJ-A Jimmie Johnson

Press Pass Wal-Mart Autographs
2008 #6 Jimmie Johnson

Press Pass Weekend Warriors
2008 #WW8 Jimmie Johnson

SP Authentic
2000 #39 Jimmie Johnson RC
2000 #67 Jimmie Johnson PER

SP Authentic Overdrive Gold
2000 #39 Jimmie Johnson/92
2000 #67 Jimmie Johnson PER/92

SP Authentic Overdrive Silver
2000 #39 Jimmie Johnson
2000 #67 Jimmie Johnson PER

SP Authentic Sign of the Times
2000 #JI Jimmie Johnson

SP Authentic Sign of the Times Gold
2000 #JI Jimmie Johnson

Sports Illustrated for Kids *
2003 #243 Jimmie Johnson's Car

Sunoco OCC Postcards
2007 #JJ Jimmie Johnson

Super Shots CHP Sonoma
2004 #2 Jimmie Johnson

TRAKS
2006 #15 Jimmie Johnson
2006 #52 Jimmie Johnson's Car
2007 #12 Jimmie Johnson
2007 #62 Jimmie Johnson CTG
2007 #71 Jimmie Johnson MG
2007 #81 Jimmie Johnson GP
2007 #89 Jimmie Johnson's Car NFS
2007 #96 Jimmie Johnson FT

TRAKS Autographs
2006 #17 Jimmie Johnson NC SP

TRAKS Autographs 25
2006 #15 Jimmie Johnson NC

Traks Driver's Seat
2007 #DS8 Jimmie Johnson
2007 #DS8B Jimmie Johnson VAR

Traks Driver's Seat National
2007 #DS8 Jimmie Johnson

Traks Gold
2007 #G12 Jimmie Johnson
2007 #G62 Jimmie Johnson CTG
2007 #G71 Jimmie Johnson MG
2007 #G81 Jimmie Johnson GP
2007 #G89 Jimmie Johnson's Car NFS
2007 #G96 Jimmie Johnson FT

Traks Holofoil
2007 #H12 Jimmie Johnson
2007 #H62 Jimmie Johnson CTG
2007 #H71 Jimmie Johnson MG
2007 #H81 Jimmie Johnson GP
2007 #H89 Jimmie Johnson's Car NFS
2007 #H96 Jimmie Johnson FT

Traks Hot Pursuit
2007 #HP7 Jimmie Johnson

Traks Previews
2007 #EB12 Jimmie Johnson
2007 #EB81 Jimmie Johnson GP

Traks Red
2007 #R12 Jimmie Johnson
2007 #R62 Jimmie Johnson CTG
2007 #R71 Jimmie Johnson MG
2007 #R81 Jimmie Johnson GP
2007 #R89 Jimmie Johnson's Car NFS
2007 #R96 Jimmie Johnson FT

TRAKS Stickers
2006 #48 Jimmie Johnson

Traks Target Exclusives
2007 #JJ-A Jimmie Johnson

Traks Track Time
2007 #TT4 Jimmie Johnson

Traks Wal-Mart Exclusives
2007 #JJ-B Jimmie Johnson

Upper Deck Racing
2000 #38 Jimmie Johnson RC

VIP
2002 #16 Jimmie Johnson CRC
2002 #23 Jimmie Johnson SG
2002 #34 Jimmie Johnson AS
2002 #50 J.Gordon/J.Johnson CL
2003 #8 Jimmie Johnson
2003 #28 Jimmie Johnson AS
2003 #48 Jimmie Johnson HR
2004 #6 Jimmie Johnson
2004 #39 Jimmie Johnson's Car R
2004 #47 Jimmie Johnson SG
2004 #57 Jimmie Johnson HR
2004 #80 Jimmie Johnson BTN
2005 #11 Jimmie Johnson
2005 #42 Jimmie Johnson's Car R
2005 #45 Jimmie Johnson SG
2005 #54 Jimmie Johnson SG
2005 #76 Jimmie Johnson BN
2006 #11 Jimmie Johnson
2006 #35 Jimmie Johnson's Car R
2006 #40 Jimmie Johnson SG
2006 #42 Jimmie Johnson SG
2006 #48 Jimmie Johnson SG
2006 #52 Jimmie Johnson BTN
2006 #71 Jimmie Johnson RF
2006 #79 Jimmie Johnson AS
2006 #84 Jimmie Johnson IF
2007 #14 Jimmie Johnson
2007 #55 Jimmie Johnson's Car SV
2007 #60 Jimmie Johnson Red C
2007 #71 Jimmie Johnson Las Vegas AP
2007 #72 Jimmie Johnson Atlanta AP
2007 #74 Jimmie Johnson Martinsville AP
2007 #78 Jimmie Johnson Richmond AP

VIP Driver's Choice
2002 #DC9 Jimmie Johnson
2003 #DC1 Jimmie Johnson
2004 #DC1 Jimmie Johnson
2005 #DC1 Jimmie Johnson

VIP Driver's Choice Die Cuts
2003 #DC1 Jimmie Johnson
2004 #DC1 Jimmie Johnson
2005 #DC1 Jimmie Johnson

VIP Driver's Choice National
2003 #DC1 Jimmie Johnson

VIP Driver's Choice Transparent
2002 #DC9 Jimmie Johnson

VIP Driver's Choice Transparent LTD
2002 #DC9 Jimmie Johnson

VIP Explosives
2002 #X16 Jimmie Johnson
2002 #X23 Jimmie Johnson SG
2002 #X34 Jimmie Johnson AS
2002 #X50 J.Gordon/J.Johnson CL
2003 #X8 Jimmie Johnson
2003 #X28 Jimmie Johnson AS
2003 #X48 Jimmie Johnson HR

VIP Explosives Lasers
2002 #LX16 Jimmie Johnson
2002 #LX23 Jimmie Johnson SG
2002 #LX34 Jimmie Johnson AS
2002 #LX50 J.Gordon/J.Johnson CL

VIP Gear Gallery
2007 #GG10 Jimmie Johnson

VIP Gear Gallery Transparent
2007 #GG10 Jimmie Johnson

VIP Get A Grip Drivers
2007 #GGD29 Jimmie Johnson

VIP Get A Grip Teams
2007 #GGT29 Jimmie Johnson

VIP Head Gear
2003 #HG1 Jimmie Johnson
2004 #HG4 Jimmie Johnson
2005 #4 Jimmie Johnson
2006 #HG2 Jimmie Johnson

VIP Head Gear Die Cuts
2003 #HG1 Jimmie Johnson

VIP Head Gear National
2003 #HG1 Jimmie Johnson

VIP Head Gear Transparent
2004 #HG4 Jimmie Johnson
2005 #4 Jimmie Johnson
2006 #HG2 Jimmie Johnson

VIP Lap Leader
2006 #LL5 Jimmie Johnson

VIP Lap Leader Transparent
2006 #LL5 Jimmie Johnson

VIP Lap Leaders
2003 #LL5 Jimmie Johnson

VIP Lap Leaders National
2003 #LL5 Jimmie Johnson
VIP Lap Leaders Transparent
2003 #LL5 Jimmie Johnson
VIP Lap Leaders Transparent LTD
2003 #LL5 Jimmie Johnson
VIP Laser Explosive
2003 #LX8 Jimmie Johnson
2003 #LX28 Jimmie Johnson AS
2003 #LX48 Jimmie Johnson HR
VIP Making the Show
2002 #MS21 Jimmie Johnson
2003 #MS20 Jimmie Johnson
2004 #MS23 Jimmie Johnson
2005 #23 Jimmie Johnson
2006 #MS7 Jimmie Johnson
VIP Mile Masters
2002 #MM3 Jimmie Johnson
2003 #MM5 Jimmie Johnson
VIP Mile Masters National
2003 #MM5 Jimmie Johnson
VIP Mile Masters Transparent
2002 #MM3 Jimmie Johnson
2003 #MM5 Jimmie Johnson
VIP Mile Masters Transparent LTD
2002 #MM3 Jimmie Johnson
2003 #MM5 Jimmie Johnson
VIP Previews
2003 #8 Jimmie Johnson
2003 #28 Jimmie Johnson AS
2004 #EB8 Jimmie Johnson
2004 #EB39 Jimmie Johnson's Car R
2004 #EB47 Jimmie Johnson SG
2005 #EB11 Jimmie Johnson
2005 #EB42 Jimmie Johnson's Car R
2007 #EB14 Jimmie Johnson
VIP Race Used Sheet Metal Cars
2002 #SC12 Jimmie Johnson's Car
VIP Race Used Sheet Metal Drivers
2002 #SD12 Jimmie Johnson
VIP Samples
2002 #16 Jimmie Johnson
2002 #23 Jimmie Johnson SG
2002 #34 Jimmie Johnson AS
2002 #50 J.Gordon/J.Johnson CL
2003 #8 Jimmie Johnson
2003 #28 Jimmie Johnson AS
2003 #48 Jimmie Johnson HR
2004 #8 Jimmie Johnson
2004 #39 Jimmie Johnson's Car R
2004 #47 Jimmie Johnson SG
2004 #57 Jimmie Johnson HR
2004 #80 Jimmie Johnson BTN
2005 #11 Jimmie Johnson
2005 #42 Jimmie Johnson's Car R
2005 #45 Jimmie Johnson SG
2005 #54 Jimmie Johnson SG
2005 #76 Jimmie Johnson BN
VIP Sunday Best
2007 #SB11 Jimmie Johnson
VIP Tin
2003 #CT8 Jimmie Johnson
2003 #CT28 Jimmie Johnson AS
2003 #CT48 Jimmie Johnson HR
VIP Tradin' Paint Autographs
2004 #TP-JJ Jimmie Johnson/48
2005 #JJ Jimmie Johnson/48
2006 #TP-JJ Jimmie Johnson/48
VIP Tradin' Paint Bronze
2004 #TPT3 Jimmie Johnson
VIP Tradin' Paint Car Autographs
2003 #JJ Jimmie Johnson/48
VIP Tradin' Paint Cars
2003 #TPT4 Jimmie Johnson's Car
2005 #TPT3 Jimmie Johnson
VIP Tradin' Paint Cars Bronze
2006 #TPT10 Jimmie Johnson
VIP Tradin' Paint Driver Autographs
2003 #JJ Jimmie Johnson/48
VIP Tradin' Paint Drivers
2003 #TPD4 Jimmie Johnson
2005 #TPD3 Jimmie Johnson
VIP Tradin' Paint Drivers Gold
2006 #TPD10 Jimmie Johnson
VIP Tradin' Paint Drivers Silver
2006 #TPD10 Jimmie Johnson
VIP Tradin' Paint Gold
2004 #TPD3 Jimmie Johnson
VIP Tradin' Paint Silver
2004 #TPD3 Jimmie Johnson
VIP Trophy Club
2007 #TC3 Jimmie Johnson
VIP Trophy Club Transparent
2007 #TC3 Jimmie Johnson
Wheels American Thunder
2003 #10 Jimmie Johnson
2003 #34 Jimmie Johnson DT
2003 #48 J.Johnson's Transporter
2004 #10 Jimmie Johnson
2004 #31 Jimmie Johnson's Rig Rt. 66
2004 #54 Jimmie Johnson's Car HR
2004 #72 Jimmie Johnson RR
2004 #84 Jimmie Johnson CC
2005 #12 Jimmie Johnson
2005 #31 Jimmie Johnson's Rig Rt. 66
2005 #53 Jimmie Johnson's Car HR
2005 #60 Jimmie Johnson DT
2005 #67 Jimmie Johnson RR
2005 #84 Jimmie Johnson CC
2006 #13 Jimmie Johnson
2006 #34 Jimmie Johnson DT
2006 #48 Jimmie Johnson's Car HR
2006 #66 Jimmie Johnson SS
2006 #72 Jimmie Johnson MIA
2006 #83 Jimmie Johnson NN
2007 #14 Jimmie Johnson
2007 #48 Jimmie Johnson's Car DT
2007 #54 Jimmie Johnson's Car HR
Wheels American Thunder American Dreams
2007 #AD3 Jimmie Johnson
Wheels American Thunder American Dreams Gold
2007 #ADG3 Jimmie Johnson
Wheels American Thunder American Eagle
2003 #AE6 Jimmie Johnson
2004 #AE4 Jimmie Johnson
2005 #AE11 Jimmie Johnson
Wheels American Thunder American Muscle
2003 #AM4 Jimmie Johnson
2004 #AM3 Jimmie Johnson
2005 #AM3 Jimmie Johnson
2006 #AM9 Jimmie Johnson
2007 #AM4 Jimmie Johnson
Wheels American Thunder American Racing Idol
2006 #RI1 Jimmie Johnson
Wheels American Thunder American Racing Idol Golden
2006 #RI1 Jimmie Johnson
Wheels American Thunder Autographed Hat Instant Winner
2007 #AH15 Jimmie Johnson
Wheels American Thunder Born On
2003 #BO10 Jimmie Johnson
2003 #BO34 Jimmie Johnson DT
2003 #BO48 Lowe's Transporter
Wheels American Thunder Cool Threads
2007 #CT16 Jimmie Johnson
Wheels American Thunder Cup Quest
2004 #CQ1 Jimmie Johnson
Wheels American Thunder Double Hat
2006 #DH11 Jimmie Johnson
Wheels American Thunder Golden Eagle
2003 #AEG6 Jimmie Johnson
2004 #AE4 Jimmie Johnson
2005 #GE11 Jimmie Johnson
Wheels American Thunder Grandstand
2006 #GS10 Jimmie Johnson
Wheels American Thunder Head to Toe
2005 #HT13 Jimmie Johnson/60
2006 #HT12 Jimmie Johnson/35
Wheels American Thunder Heads Up Manufacturer
2003 #HUM9 Jimmie Johnson
Wheels American Thunder Heads Up Team
2003 #HUT8 Jimmie Johnson/90
Wheels American Thunder Heads Up Winston
2003 #HUW9 Jimmie Johnson
Wheels American Thunder Holofoil
2003 #P10 Jimmie Johnson
2003 #P34 Jimmie Johnson DT
2003 #P48 Lowe's Transporter
Wheels American Thunder Medallion
2005 #MD20 Jimmie Johnson
Wheels American Thunder Post Mark
2003 #PM9 Jimmie Johnson
2004 #PM24 Jimmie Johnson
Wheels American Thunder Previews
2003 #10 Jimmie Johnson
2003 #34 Jimmie Johnson DT
2004 #EB10 Jimmie Johnson
2004 #EB31 Jimmie Johnson Rt. 66
2005 #12 Jimmie Johnson
2005 #84 Jimmie Johnson CC
2006 #EB13 Jimmie Johnson
2006 #EB72 Jimmie Johnson MIA
2007 #EB14 Jimmie Johnson
2007 #EB54 Jimmie Johnson's Car HR
Wheels American Thunder Pushin Pedal
2003 #PP11 Jimmie Johnson
2004 #PP9 Jimmie Johnson
2005 #PP13 Jimmie Johnson/60
Wheels American Thunder Pushin' Pedal
2006 #PP14 Jimmie Johnson/35
2007 #PP14 Jimmie Johnson
Wheels American Thunder Rookie Thunder
2003 #RT14 Jimmie Johnson
Wheels American Thunder Samples
2003 #P10 Jimmie Johnson
2003 #P34 Jimmie Johnson DT
2003 #P48 Lowe's Transporter
2004 #10 Jimmie Johnson
2004 #31 Jimmie Johnson's Rig Rt. 66
2004 #54 Jimmie Johnson's Car HR
2004 #72 Jimmie Johnson RR
2004 #84 Jimmie Johnson CC
2005 #12 Jimmie Johnson
2005 #31 Jimmie Johnson's Rig Rt. 66
2005 #53 Jimmie Johnson's Car HR
2005 #60 Jimmie Johnson DT
2005 #67 Jimmie Johnson RR
2005 #84 Jimmie Johnson CC
Wheels American Thunder Starting Grid
2007 #SG5 Jimmie Johnson
Wheels American Thunder Thunder Road
2003 #TR8 Jimmie Johnson
2004 #TR16 Jimmie Johnson
2005 #TR16 Jimmie Johnson
2006 #TR4 Jimmie Johnson
2007 #TR1 Jimmie Johnson
Wheels American Thunder Thunder Strokes
2007 #21 Jimmie Johnson
Wheels American Thunder Thunder Strokes Press Plates Black
2007 #21 Jimmie Johnson
Wheels American Thunder Thunder Strokes Press Plates Cyan
2007 #21 Jimmie Johnson
Wheels American Thunder Thunder Strokes Press Plates Magenta
2007 #21 Jimmie Johnson
Wheels American Thunder Thunder Strokes Press Plates Yellow
2007 #21 Jimmie Johnson
Wheels American Thunder Triple Hat
2003 #TH9 Jimmie Johnson
2004 #TH6 Jimmie Johnson
2005 #TH9 Jimmie Johnson
2007 #TH13 Jimmie Johnson
Wheels Autographs
2003 #26 Jimmie Johnson AT/HG
2004 #33 Jimmie Johnson HG
2005 #26 Jimmie Johnson
2006 #26 Jimmie Johnson NC
2007 #17 Jimmie Johnson NC HG
2008 #16 Jimmie Johnson NC HG EXCH
Wheels Autographs Chase Edition
2008 #6 Jimmie Johnson NC EXCH
Wheels Autographs Press Plates Black
2007 #16 Jimmie Johnson NC
2008 #16 Jimmie Johnson NC
Wheels Autographs Press Plates Cyan
2007 #16 Jimmie Johnson NC
2008 #16 Jimmie Johnson NC
Wheels Autographs Press Plates Magenta
2007 #16 Jimmie Johnson NC
2008 #16 Jimmie Johnson NC
Wheels Autographs Press Plates Yellow
2007 #17 Jimmie Johnson NC
2008 #16 Jimmie Johnson NC
Wheels High Gear
2002 #38 Jimmie Johnson BGN
2002 #70 Jimmie Johnson PRE
2003 #14 Jimmie Johnson
2003 #33 Jimmie Johnson's Car
2003 #61 Contenders and Pretenders WCS
2004 #11 Jimmie Johnson
2004 #36 Jimmie Johnson's Car C
2004 #51 Jimmie Johnson NA
2004 #57 Jimmie Johnson's Car
2004 #72 Jimmie Johnson CL
2005 #23 Jimmie Johnson
2005 #54 Jimmie Johnson A
2005 #55 Jimmie Johnson's Car
2005 #70 Jimmie Johnson NI
2005 #73 Jimmie Johnson IF
2005 #83 Jimmie Johnson RS
2006 #5 Jimmie Johnson
2006 #68 Jimmie Johnson CM
2006 #78 Jimmie Johnson FF
2007 #1 Jimmie Johnson
2007 #56 Jimmie Johnson NA
2007 #73 Jimmie Johnson NI red take
2007 #0 Jimmie Johnson Champion
2007 #73B Jimmie Johnson NI yellow take
2008 #1 Jimmie Johnson
2008 #55 Jimmie Johnson NA
2008 #61 Jimmie Johnson NA
2008 #71 Jimmie Johnson's Car EL
2008 #78 Jimmie Johnson NI
2008 #0 Jimmie Johnson Champ
2008 #1B Jimmie Johnson Yellow 48
Wheels High Gear Autographs
2002 #26 Jimmie Johnson
Wheels High Gear Blue Hawaii SCDA Promos
2003 #14 Jimmie Johnson
2003 #33 Jimmie Johnson's Car
2003 #61 Contenders and Pretenders
Wheels High Gear Custom Shop
2003 #CSJJ Jimmie Johnson EXCH
2004 #CSJJ Jimmie Johnson
Wheels High Gear Custom Shop Autograph Redemption
2003 #CSJJ Jimmie Johnson EXCH
Wheels High Gear Custom Shop Autographs
2003 #JJB2 Jimmie Johnson/10
Wheels High Gear Custom Shop Prizes
2003 #JJA1 Jimmie Johnson
2003 #JJA2 Jimmie Johnson
2003 #JJA3 Jimmie Johnson
2003 #JJB1 Jimmie Johnson
2003 #JJB2 Jimmie Johnson
2003 #JJB3 Jimmie Johnson
2003 #JJC1 Jimmie Johnson
2003 #JJC2 Jimmie Johnson
2003 #JJC3 Jimmie Johnson
Wheels High Gear Driven
2007 #DR4 Jimmie Johnson
2008 #DR1 Jimmie Johnson
Wheels High Gear Final Standings
2008 #F1 Jimmie Johnson/1
Wheels High Gear Final Standings Gold
2007 #FS1 Jimmie Johnson/1
Wheels High Gear First Gear
2002 #38 Jimmie Johnson BGN
2002 #70 Jimmie Johnson PRE
2003 #F14 Jimmie Johnson
2003 #F33 Jimmie Johnson's Car
2003 #F61 Contenders and Pretenders
Wheels High Gear Flag Chasers Black
2003 #FC3 Jimmie Johnson
2004 #FC1 Jimmie Johnson
2005 #FC4 Jimmie Johnson
2006 #FC9 Jimmie Johnson
2007 #FC5 Jimmie Johnson
2008 #FC6 Jimmie Johnson
Wheels High Gear Flag Chasers Blue
2004 #FC1 Jimmie Johnson
Wheels High Gear Flag Chasers Blue-Yellow
2003 #FC3 Jimmie Johnson
2005 #FC4 Jimmie Johnson
2006 #FC9 Jimmie Johnson
2007 #FC5 Jimmie Johnson
2008 #FC6 Jimmie Johnson
Wheels High Gear Flag Chasers Checkered
2003 #FC3 Jimmie Johnson
2004 #FC1 Jimmie Johnson
2005 #FC4 Jimmie Johnson
2006 #FC9 Jimmie Johnson
2007 #FC5 Jimmie Johnson
2008 #FC6 Jimmie Johnson
Wheels High Gear Flag Chasers Green
2003 #FC3 Jimmie Johnson
2004 #FC1 Jimmie Johnson
2005 #FC4 Jimmie Johnson
2006 #FC9 Jimmie Johnson
2007 #FC5 Jimmie Johnson
2008 #FC6 Jimmie Johnson
Wheels High Gear Flag Chasers Red
2003 #FC3 Jimmie Johnson
2004 #FC1 Jimmie Johnson
2005 #FC4 Jimmie Johnson
2006 #FC9 Jimmie Johnson
2007 #FC5 Jimmie Johnson
2008 #FC6 Jimmie Johnson
Wheels High Gear Flag Chasers White
2003 #FC3 Jimmie Johnson
2004 #FC1 Jimmie Johnson
2005 #FC4 Jimmie Johnson
2006 #FC9 Jimmie Johnson
2007 #FC5 Jimmie Johnson
2008 #FC6 Jimmie Johnson
Wheels High Gear Flag Chasers Yellow
2003 #FC3 Jimmie Johnson
2004 #FC1 Jimmie Johnson
2005 #FC4 Jimmie Johnson
2006 #FC9 Jimmie Johnson
2007 #FC5 Jimmie Johnson
2008 #FC6 Jimmie Johnson
Wheels High Gear Flag to Flag
2005 #FF9 Jimmie Johnson
2006 #FF11 Jimmie Johnson
Wheels High Gear Full Throttle
2003 #FT4 Jimmie Johnson
2004 #FT1 Jimmie Johnson
2005 #FT6 Jimmie Johnson
2006 #FT2 Jimmie Johnson
2007 #FT6 Jimmie Johnson
2008 #FT7 Jimmie Johnson
Wheels High Gear High Groove
2003 #HG12 Jimmie Johnson
2004 #HG10 Jimmie Johnson
Wheels High Gear Hot Treads
2003 #HT7 Jimmie Johnson
Wheels High Gear Last Lap
2007 #LL3 Jimmie Johnson
2008 #LL4 Jimmie Johnson
Wheels High Gear Last Lap Holofoil
2008 #LL4 Jimmie Johnson
Wheels High Gear Machine
2003 #MM1B Jimmie Johnson
2004 #MM6B Jimmie Johnson
2005 #MMB5 Jimmie Johnson
Wheels High Gear Man
2003 #MM1A Jimmie Johnson
2004 #MM6A Jimmie Johnson
2005 #MMA5 Jimmie Johnson
Wheels High Gear Man & Machine (Machine)
2006 #MMB3 Jimmie Johnson
Wheels High Gear Man & Machine (Man)
2006 #MMA3 Jimmie Johnson
Wheels High Gear MPH
2002 #38 Jimmie Johnson BGN
2002 #70 Jimmie Johnson PRE
2003 #M14 Jimmie Johnson
2003 #M33 Jimmie Johnson's Car
2003 #M61 Contenders and Pretenders
2004 #M11 Jimmie Johnson
2004 #M36 Jimmie Johnson C
2004 #M51 Jimmie Johnson NA
2004 #M57 Jimmie Johnson's Car
2004 #M72 Jimmie Johnson CL
2005 #M23 Jimmie Johnson
2005 #M54 Jimmie Johnson A
2005 #M55 Jimmie Johnson's Car
2005 #M70 Jimmie Johnson NI
2005 #M73 Jimmie Johnson IF
2005 #M83 Jimmie Johnson RS
2006 #M5 Jimmie Johnson
2006 #M68 Jimmie Johnson CM
2006 #M78 Jimmie Johnson FF
2007 #M1 Jimmie Johnson
2007 #M56 Jimmie Johnson NA
2007 #M73 Jimmie Johnson NI
2008 #M1 Jimmie Johnson
2008 #M55 Jimmie Johnson NA
2008 #M61 Jimmie Johnson NA
2008 #M71 Jimmie Johnson's Car EL
2008 #M78 Jimmie Johnson NI
Wheels High Gear Previews
2003 #14 Jimmie Johnson
2004 #11 Jimmie Johnson
2004 #36 Jimmie Johnson C
2004 #51 Jimmie Johnson NA
2004 #57 Jimmie Johnson's Car
2007 #EB1 Jimmie Johnson
2007 #EB56 Jimmie Johnson NA
2008 #EB1 Jimmie Johnson
Wheels High Gear Previews Green
2005 #EB23 Jimmie Johnson
2006 #EB5 Jimmie Johnson
Wheels High Gear Previews Silver
2005 #EB73 Jimmie Johnson IF
2006 #EB78 Jimmie Johnson FF
Wheels High Gear Samples
2003 #14 Jimmie Johnson
2003 #33 Jimmie Johnson's Car
2003 #61 Contenders and Pretenders
2004 #11 Jimmie Johnson
2004 #36 Jimmie Johnson C
2004 #51 Jimmie Johnson NA
2004 #57 Jimmie Johnson's Car
2004 #72 Jimmie Johnson CL
2005 #23 Jimmie Johnson
2005 #54 Jimmie Johnson A
2005 #55 Jimmie Johnson's Car
2005 #70 Jimmie Johnson NI
2005 #73 Jimmie Johnson IF
2005 #83 Jimmie Johnson RS
Wheels High Gear Sunday Sensation
2003 #SS5 Jimmie Johnson
2004 #SS4 Jimmie Johnson
Wheels High Gear The Chase
2008 #TC1 Jimmie Johnson
Wheels High Gear Top Ten
2004 #TT2 Jimmie Johnson
Wheels High Gear Top Tier
2003 #TT5 Jimmie Johnson
2005 #TT2 Jimmie Johnson
2006 #TT5 Jimmie Johnson
2007 #TT1 Jimmie Johnson

Kahne, Kasey

McFarlane NASCAR 12-Inch Figures Series 1
2005 #20 Kasey Kahne
McFarlane NASCAR Series 4
2005 #80 Kasey Kahne H
2005 #85 Kasey Kahne R FP
Press Pass
2004 #42 Kasey Kahne
2005 #7 Kasey Kahne
2005 #46 Kasey Kahne
2005 #85 Kasey Kahne RR
2006 #10 Kasey Kahne
2006 #40 Kasey Kahne NBS
2006 #89 Kasey Kahne NS
2006 #98 Kasey Kahne U
2007 #10 Kasey Kahne
2007 #64 Kasey Kahne's Car OT
2007 #89 Kasey Kahne NS
2007 #101 Kasey Kahne U
2007 #117 Kasey Kahne TT
2008 #22 Kasey Kahne
Press Pass Autographs
2004 #30 Kasey Kahne BGN P
2004 #31 Kasey Kahne NCS
2005 #28 Kasey Kahne BGN E/P
2005 #29 Kasey Kahne NCS E/P
2006 #25 Kasey Kahne NBS
2006 #26 Kasey Kahne NC
2007 #21 Kasey Kahne BK; MG; PL Kasey Kahne
2008 #21 Kasey Kahne NC P/E
Press Pass Autographs Press Plates Black
2008 #17 Kasey Kahne NC E
Press Pass Autographs Press Plates Cyan
2008 #17 Kasey Kahne NC P
Press Pass Autographs Press Plates Magenta
2007 #8 Kasey Kahne
2008 #17 Kasey Kahne NC P
Press Pass Autographs Press Plates Yellow
2008 #17 Kasey Kahne NC E
Press Pass Blaster Kmart
2006 #KKC Kasey Kahne
Press Pass Blaster Target
2006 #KKB Kasey Kahne
Press Pass Blaster Wal-Mart
2006 #KKA Kasey Kahne
Press Pass Blue
2006 #B10 Kasey Kahne
2006 #B40 Kasey Kahne NBS
2006 #B89 Kasey Kahne NS
2006 #B98 Kasey Kahne U
2007 #B10 Kasey Kahne
2007 #B84 Kasey Kahne's Car OT
2007 #B89 Kasey Kahne NS
2007 #B101 Kasey Kahne U
2007 #B117 Kasey Kahne TT
2008 #B22 Kasey Kahne
Press Pass Burning Rubber Autographs
2006 #BR-KK Kasey Kahne/9
Press Pass Burning Rubber Cars
2006 #BRT9 Kasey Kahne
Press Pass Burning Rubber Drivers
2006 #BRD9 Kasey Kahne
2007 #BRD4 Kasey Kahne Texas 4-9
2007 #BRD9 Kasey Kahne Charlotte 5-28
Press Pass Burning Rubber Drivers Gold
2006 #BRD9 Kasey Kahne
2007 #BRD4 Kasey Kahne Texas 4-9
2007 #BRD9 Kasey Kahne Charlotte 5-28
Press Pass Burning Rubber Team
2007 #BRT4 Kasey Kahne Texas 4-9
2007 #BRT9 Kasey Kahne Charlotte 5-28
Press Pass Burnouts
2006 #HT12 Kasey Kahne
2007 #BO4 Kasey Kahne
Press Pass Burnouts Blue
2007 #BO4 Kasey Kahne
Press Pass Burnouts Gold
2007 #BO4 Kasey Kahne
Press Pass Burnouts Holofoil
2006 #HT12 Kasey Kahne
Press Pass Collector's Series Box Set
2007 #SB12 Kasey Kahne
Press Pass Collectors Series Making the Show
2006 #MS13 Kasey Kahne
Press Pass Collectors Series Sunday Best
2007 #CB12 Kasey Kahne
Press Pass Cup Chase
2005 #CCR14 Kasey Kahne
2007 #CCR3 Kasey Kahne
2008 #CC13 Kasey Kahne
Press Pass Cup Chase Prizes
2005 #CCP14 Kasey Kahne
2006 #CC8 Kasey Kahne
Press Pass Double Burner Firesuit-Glove
2007 #DB7 Kasey Kahne
Press Pass Double Burner Firesuit-Glove Exchange
2007 #DB7 Kasey Kahne
Press Pass Double Burner Metal-Tire
2007 #DB-KK Kasey Kahne
2008 #DB-KK Kasey Kahne
Press Pass Double Burner Metal-Tire Exchange
2007 #DB-KK Kasey Kahne
Press Pass Eclipse
2004 #40 Kasey Kahne
2005 #13 Kasey Kahne
2005 #51 Kasey Kahne Z
2005 #78 Kasey Kahne LL
2006 #22 Kasey Kahne
2006 #36 Kasey Kahne NBS
2006 #44 Kasey Kahne WS
2006 #60 Kasey Kahne TN
2006 #60B Kasey Kahne TN -license
2007 #8 Kasey Kahne
2007 #37 Kasey Kahne TO
2007 #40 Kasey Kahne P
2007 #64 Martin/Kahne/Burton NS
2007 #68 Kasey Kahne NS
2007 #0 Cup Chase 10
2008 #16 Kasey Kahne
2008 #32 Kasey Kahne RM
2008 #42 Kasey Kahne TO
2008 #87 Kasey Kahne PREV
Press Pass Eclipse Ecliptic
2007 #EC3 Kasey Kahne
Press Pass Eclipse Gold
2007 #G8 Kasey Kahne
2007 #G37 Kasey Kahne TO
2007 #G40 Kasey Kahne P
2007 #G64 Martin/Kahne/Burton NS
2007 #G68 Kasey Kahne NS
2008 #G16 Kasey Kahne
2008 #G32 Kasey Kahne RM
2008 #G42 Kasey Kahne TO
2008 #G87 Kasey Kahne PREV
Press Pass Eclipse Hyperdrive
2006 #HP6 Kasey Kahne
2007 #HD6 Kasey Kahne
2008 #HP6 Kasey Kahne
Press Pass Eclipse Maxim
2005 #MX11 Kasey Kahne
Press Pass Eclipse Previews
2005 #EB13 Kasey Kahne
2005 #EB51 Kasey Kahne Z
2005 #EB78 Kasey Kahne LL/1
2006 #EB22 Kasey Kahne
2006 #EB36 Kasey Kahne NBS
2006 #EB60 Kasey Kahne TN
2007 #EB8 Kasey Kahne
2007 #EB37 Kasey Kahne TO
2008 #EB16 Kasey Kahne
2008 #EB32 Kasey Kahne RM
Press Pass Eclipse Racing Champions
2006 #RC6 Kasey Kahne
2006 #RC21 Kasey Kahne NBS
2007 #RC1 Kasey Kahne
2007 #RC20 Kasey Kahne
Press Pass Eclipse Red
2007 #R8 Kasey Kahne
2007 #R37 Kasey Kahne TO
2007 #R40 Kasey Kahne P
2007 #R64 Martin/Kahne/Burton NS
2007 #R68 Kasey Kahne NS
2008 #R16 Kasey Kahne
2008 #R32 Kasey Kahne RM
2008 #R42 Kasey Kahne TO
2008 #R87 Kasey Kahne PREV
Press Pass Eclipse Samples
2004 #40 Kasey Kahne
2005 #13 Kasey Kahne
2005 #51 Kasey Kahne Z
2005 #78 Kasey Kahne LL
Press Pass Eclipse Skidmarks
2005 #SM12 Kasey Kahne
2006 #SM12 Kasey Kahne
2007 #SM8 Kasey Kahne
Press Pass Eclipse Skidmarks Holofoil
2005 #SM12 Kasey Kahne
2006 #SM12 Kasey Kahne
2007 #SM8 Kasey Kahne
Press Pass Eclipse Star Tracks
2008 #ST8 Kasey Kahne
Press Pass Eclipse Star Tracks Holofoil
2008 #ST8 Kasey Kahne
Press Pass Eclipse Stellar
2008 #ST20 Kasey Kahne
Press Pass Eclipse Teammates Autographs
2005 #4 K.Kahne/J.Mayfield
2006 #6 K.Kahne/J.Mayfield
2007 #2 Kahne/Riggs/Sadler
2008 #KS Kasey Kahne Elliott Sadler/35
Press Pass Eclipse Under Cover Autographs
2007 #UC-KK Kasey Kahne/9
2008 #UC-KK Kasey Kahne/9
Press Pass Eclipse Under Cover Cars
2006 #UCT5 Kasey Kahne
Press Pass Eclipse Under Cover Drivers
2007 #UCD12 Kasey Kahne
Press Pass Eclipse Under Cover Drivers Eclipse
2007 #UCD12 Kasey Kahne
Press Pass Eclipse Under Cover Drivers Gold
2006 #UCD5 Kasey Kahne
Press Pass Eclipse Under Cover Drivers Holofoil
2006 #UCD5 Kasey Kahne
Press Pass Eclipse Under Cover Drivers Name
2007 #UCD12 Kasey Kahne
Press Pass Eclipse Under Cover Drivers NASCAR
2007 #UCD12 Kasey Kahne
Press Pass Eclipse Under Cover Drivers Silver
2006 #UCD5 Kasey Kahne
Press Pass Eclipse Under Cover Teams
2007 #UCT12 Kasey Kahne
Press Pass Eclipse Under Cover Teams NASCAR
2007 #UCT12 Kasey Kahne
Press Pass Four Wide
2007 #FW-KK Kasey Kahne
2008 #FW-KK Kasey Kahne
Press Pass Four Wide Checkered
2007 #FW-KK Kasey Kahne
2008 #FW-KK Kasey Kahne
Press Pass Four Wide Checkered Exchange
2007 #FW-KK Kasey Kahne
Press Pass Four Wide Exchange
2007 #FW-KK Kasey Kahne
Press Pass Gold
2006 #G10 Kasey Kahne
2006 #G40 Kasey Kahne NBS
2006 #G89 Kasey Kahne NS
2006 #G98 Kasey Kahne U
2007 #G10 Kasey Kahne
2007 #G84 Kasey Kahne's Car OT
2007 #G89 Kasey Kahne NS
2007 #G101 Kasey Kahne U
2007 #G117 Kasey Kahne TT
2008 #G22 Kasey Kahne
Press Pass Hot Treads
2005 #HTR6 Kasey Kahne
2007 #HT1 Kasey Kahne
Press Pass Hot Treads Blue
2007 #HT1 Kasey Kahne
Press Pass Hot Treads Gold
2007 #HT1 Kasey Kahne
Press Pass Hot Treads Holofoil
2005 #HTR6 Kasey Kahne
Press Pass K-Mart
2007 #KK-C Kasey Kahne
Press Pass Legends
2005 #32 Kasey Kahne
2006 #43 Kasey Kahne
2007 #49 Kasey Kahne
Press Pass Legends Autographs Black
2005 #19 Kasey Kahne
2006 #26 Kasey Kahne
Press Pass Legends Blue
2005 #32B Kasey Kahne
2006 #B43 Kasey Kahne
2007 #B49 Kasey Kahne
Press Pass Legends Bronze
2006 #Z43 Kasey Kahne
2007 #Z49 Kasey Kahne
Press Pass Legends Double Threads Bronze
2005 #DT-KVK K.Kahne/B.Vickers
Press Pass Legends Double Threads Gold
2005 #DT-KVK K.Kahne/B.Vickers
Press Pass Legends Double Threads Silver
2005 #DT-KVK K.Kahne/B.Vickers
Press Pass Legends Gold
2005 #32G Kasey Kahne
2006 #G43 Kasey Kahne
2007 #G49 Kasey Kahne
Press Pass Legends Holofoil

2005 #32H Kasey Kahne
2006 #H43 Kasey Kahne
2007 #H49 Kasey Kahne
Press Pass Legends Press Plates Black
2005 #32 Kasey Kahne
2006 #PPB43 Kasey Kahne
2007 #PP49 Kasey Kahne
Press Pass Legends Press Plates Black Backs
2006 #PPB43B Kasey Kahne
2007 #PP49 Kasey Kahne
Press Pass Legends Press Plates Cyan
2005 #32 Kasey Kahne
2006 #PPC43 Kasey Kahne
2007 #PP49 Kasey Kahne
Press Pass Legends Press Plates Cyan Backs
2006 #PPC43B Kasey Kahne
2007 #PP49 Kasey Kahne
Press Pass Legends Press Plates Magenta
2005 #32 Kasey Kahne
2006 #PPM43 Kasey Kahne
2007 #PP49 Kasey Kahne
Press Pass Legends Press Plates Magenta Backs
2006 #PPM43B Kasey Kahne
2007 #PP49 Kasey Kahne
Press Pass Legends Press Plates Yellow
2005 #32 Kasey Kahne
2006 #PPY43 Kasey Kahne
2007 #PP49 Kasey Kahne
Press Pass Legends Press Plates Yellow Backs
2006 #PPY43B Kasey Kahne
2007 #PP49 Kasey Kahne
Press Pass Legends Previews
2005 #32 Kasey Kahne
2006 #EB43 Kasey Kahne
2007 #EB49 Kasey Kahne
Press Pass Legends Solo
2005 #32S Kasey Kahne
2006 #S43 Kasey Kahne
2007 #S49 Kasey Kahne
Press Pass Legends Sunday Swatches Bronze
2007 #KK-SSKasey Kahne
Press Pass Legends Sunday Swatches Gold
2007 #KK-SSKasey Kahne
Press Pass Legends Sunday Swatches Silver
2007 #KK-SSKasey Kahne
Press Pass Legends Threads & Treads Bronze
2005 #TTKK Kasey Kahne
Press Pass Legends Threads & Treads Gold
2005 #TTKK Kasey Kahne
Press Pass Legends Threads & Treads Silver
2005 #TTKK Kasey Kahne
Press Pass Making the Show Collector's Series
2004 #MS6 Kasey Kahne
Press Pass Optima
2003 #31 Kasey Kahne RC
2004 #11 Kasey Kahne CRC
2004 #49 Kasey Kahne YG
2004 #78 Kasey Kahne CP
2004 #87 Kasey Kahne RR
2005 #14 Kasey Kahne
2005 #35 Kasey Kahne BGN
2005 #51 Kasey Kahne YG
2006 #9 Kasey Kahne
2006 #71 Kasey Kahne CP
2006 #81 Kasey Kahne RTV Michigan
2006 #9B Kasey Kahne Chase
Press Pass Optima Cool Persistence
2004 #CP12 Kasey Kahne
Press Pass Optima Corporate Cuts Cars
2005 #CCT3 Kasey Kahne
Press Pass Optima Corporate Cuts Drivers
2005 #CCD3 Kasey Kahne
Press Pass Optima Fan Favorite
2004 #FF11 Kasey Kahne
2005 #FF13 Kasey Kahne
2006 #FF11 Kasey Kahne
Press Pass Optima Gold
2003 #G31 Kasey Kahne
2004 #G11 Kasey Kahne
2004 #G49 Kasey Kahne YG
2004 #G78 Kasey Kahne CP
2004 #G87 Kasey Kahne RR
2005 #G14 Kasey Kahne
2005 #G35 Kasey Kahne BGN
2005 #G51 Kasey Kahne YG
2006 #G9 Kasey Kahne
2006 #G71 Kasey Kahne CP
2006 #G81 Kasey Kahne RTV Michigan
Press Pass Optima Pole Position
2006 #PP4 Kasey Kahne
Press Pass Optima Previews
2003 #31 Kasey Kahne
2004 #EB11 Kasey Kahne
2005 #14 Kasey Kahne
2005 #35 Kasey Kahne BGN
2005 #51 Kasey Kahne YG/1
2006 #EB9 Kasey Kahne
Press Pass Optima Q & A
2005 #QA8 Kasey Kahne
2006 #QA3 Kasey Kahne
Press Pass Optima Rookie Relics Cars
2006 #RRT8 Kasey Kahne
Press Pass Optima Rookie Relics Drivers
2006 #RRD8 Kasey Kahne
Press Pass Optima Samples
2003 #31 Kasey Kahne
2004 #11 Kasey Kahne
2004 #49 Kasey Kahne YG
2004 #78 Kasey Kahne CP
2004 #87 Kasey Kahne RR
2005 #14 Kasey Kahne
2005 #35 Kasey Kahne BGN
2005 #51 Kasey Kahne YG
Press Pass Optima Thunder Bolts Autographs
2004 #TBKK Kasey Kahne/9
2005 #TB-KK Kasey Kahne/9
Press Pass Optima Thunder Bolts Cars
2004 #TBT2 Kasey Kahne's Car
Press Pass Optima Thunder Bolts Drivers
2004 #TBD2 Kasey Kahne
Press Pass Panorama
2005 #PPP60 Kasey Kahne
Press Pass Platinum
2004 #P42 Kasey Kahne
2005 #P7 Kasey Kahne
2005 #P46 Kasey Kahne
2005 #P85 Kasey Kahne RR
2006 #P10 Kasey Kahne
2006 #P40 Kasey Kahne NBS
2006 #P89 Kasey Kahne NS
2006 #P98 Kasey Kahne U
2007 #P10 Kasey Kahne
2007 #P84 Kasey Kahne's Car OT
2007 #P89 Kasey Kahne NS
2007 #P101 Kasey Kahne U
2007 #P117 Kasey Kahne TT
2008 #P22 Kasey Kahne
Press Pass Premium
2004 #32 Kasey Kahne CRC
2005 #12 Kasey Kahne
2005 #65 Kasey Kahne CC
2006 #13 Kasey Kahne
2006 #62 Kasey Kahne C
2006 #82 Kasey Kahne PC
2007 #8 Kasey Kahne
2007 #34 Kasey Kahne's Car M
2007 #58 Kasey Kahne RTTC
2007 #79 Kasey Kahne FF
2008 #9 Kasey Kahne
2008 #60 Kasey Kahne EOP
Press Pass Premium Clean Air
2008 #CA8 Kasey Kahne
Press Pass Premium Hot Threads Autographs
2005 #HT-KKKasey Kahne/9
2006 #HT-KKKasey Kahne/9
Press Pass Premium Hot Threads Cars
2006 #HTT8 Kasey Kahne
Press Pass Premium Hot Threads Drivers
2006 #HTD8 Kasey Kahne
2007 #HTD1 Kasey Kahne
Press Pass Premium Hot Threads Drivers Gold
2006 #HTD8 Kasey Kahne
2007 #HTD1 Kasey Kahne
Press Pass Premium Hot Threads Patch
2007 #HTP8 Kasey Kahne Stanley/10
2007 #HTP9 Kasey Kahne Valvoline/15
Press Pass Premium Hot Threads Team
2007 #HTT1 Kasey Kahne
Press Pass Premium Performance Driven
2007 #PD2 Kasey Kahne
Press Pass Premium Performance Driven Red
2007 #PD2 Kasey Kahne
Press Pass Premium Previews
2004 #32 Kasey Kahne
2008 #EB9 Kasey Kahne
2008 #EB60 Kasey Kahne EOP
Press Pass Premium Red
2007 #R8 Kasey Kahne
2007 #R34 Kasey Kahne's Car M
2007 #R58 Kasey Kahne RTTC
2007 #R79 Kasey Kahne FF
2008 #9 Kasey Kahne
2008 #60 Kasey Kahne EOP
Press Pass Premium Samples
2004 #32 Kasey Kahne
2005 #12 Kasey Kahne
Press Pass Premium Wal-Mart
2008 #WM3 Kasey Kahne
Press Pass Previews
2004 #42 Kasey Kahne
2006 #EB10 Kasey Kahne
2006 #EB40 Kasey Kahne NBS
2006 #EB98 Kasey Kahne U
2007 #EB10 Kasey Kahne
2007 #EB117Kasey Kahne TT
2008 #EB22 Kasey Kahne
Press Pass Previews Green
2005 #EB7 Kasey Kahne
Press Pass Race Day
2007 #RD10 Kasey Kahne
Press Pass Rookie Class
2004 #RC1 Kasey Kahne
Press Pass Samples
2004 #42 Kasey Kahne
2005 #7 Kasey Kahne
2005 #46 Kasey Kahne
2005 #85 Kasey Kahne RR
Press Pass Signings
2003 #36 Kasey Kahne O
2004 #33 Kasey Kahne BGN O/S/T/V
2004 #34 Kasey Kahne NCS O/S/T/V
2005 #27 Kasey Kahne BGN S
2005 #28 Kasey Kahne NC P/S
2006 #26 Kasey Kahne NC P/S
2007 #33 Kasey Kahne NC
2008 #30 Kasey Kahne
Press Pass Signings Blue
2007 #14 Kasey Kahne NC
2008 #14 Kasey Kahne
Press Pass Signings Gold
2003 #36 Kasey Kahne O
2004 #30 Kasey Kahne BGN O/S/T/V
2004 #31 Kasey Kahne NC O/S/T/V
2005 #26 Kasey Kahne BGN S
2005 #27 Kasey Kahne NC P/S
2006 #23 Kasey Kahne NC P/S
2007 #26 Kasey Kahne NC/20
2008 #24 Kasey Kahne
Press Pass Signings Platinum
2005 #26 Kasey Kahne BGN S
2005 #27 Kasey Kahne NC P/S
Press Pass Signings Press Plates Black
2007 #23 Kasey Kahne
2008 #22 Kasey Kahne
Press Pass Signings Press Plates Cyan
2007 #22 Kasey Kahne
2008 #22 Kasey Kahne
Press Pass Signings Press Plates Magenta
2007 #24 Kasey Kahne
2008 #22 Kasey Kahne
Press Pass Signings Press Plates Yellow
2007 #22 Kasey Kahne
2008 #22 Kasey Kahne
Press Pass Signings Red Ink
2006 #9 Kasey Kahne
Press Pass Signings Silver
2006 #26 Kasey Kahne NC P/S
2007 #25 Kasey Kahne NC/45 P/S/T
2008 #21 Kasey Kahne
Press Pass Snapshots
2005 #SN13 Kasey Kahne
2006 #SN5 Kasey Kahne
2007 #SN14 Kasey Kahne
Press Pass Speedway
2008 #16 Kasey Kahne
Press Pass Speedway Gold
2008 #G16 Kasey Kahne
Press Pass Speedway Holofoil
2008 #H16 Kasey Kahne
Press Pass Speedway Previews
2008 #EB16 Kasey Kahne
Press Pass Speedway Red
2008 #R16 Kasey Kahne
Press Pass Speedway Test Drive
2008 #TD12 Kasey Kahne
Press Pass Stealth
2004 #78 Kasey Kahne WW CRC
2005 #2 Kasey Kahne
2005 #5 Kasey Kahne's Car
2005 #8 Kasey Kahne
2005 #67 Kasey Kahne
2006 #14 Kasey Kahne
2006 #51 Kahne/Mayfield/Riggs TM
2006 #64 Kasey Kahne F
2006 #70 Kasey Kahne DD
2007 #13 Kasey Kahne
2007 #48 Kasey Kahne's Rig
2007 #84 Kasey Kahne PO
2008 #17 Kasey Kahne
2008 #66 Kasey Kahne Elliott Sadler Patrick Carpentier
Press Pass Stealth Autographed Hat Entry
2006 #PPH12 Kasey Kahne
Press Pass Stealth Battle Armor Autographs
2008 #BASKK Kasey Kahne/9
Press Pass Stealth Battle Armor Drivers
2007 #BAD15 Kasey Kahne SP/8
2008 #BAD6 Kasey Kahne
Press Pass Stealth Battle Armor Teams
2007 #BAT15Kasey Kahne SP
2008 #BAT6 Kasey Kahne
Press Pass Stealth Chrome
2007 #13 Kasey Kahne
2007 #48 Kasey Kahne's Rig
2007 #84 Kasey Kahne PO
2007 #84A Kasey Kahne PO L1 -logo-squares
2008 #17 Kasey Kahne
2008 #66 Kasey Kahne Elliott Sadler Patrick Carpentier
2008 #17B Kasey Kahne VAR
Press Pass Stealth Chrome Exclusives
2007 #X13 Kasey Kahne
2007 #X48 Kasey Kahne's Rig
2007 #X84 Kasey Kahne PO
2008 #17 Kasey Kahne
2008 #66 Kasey Kahne Elliott Sadler Patrick Carpentier
Press Pass Stealth Chrome Exclusives Gold
2008 #17 Kasey Kahne
2008 #66 Kasey Kahne Elliott Sadler Patrick Carpentier
Press Pass Stealth Chrome Platinum
2007 #P13 Kasey Kahne
2007 #P48 Kasey Kahne's Rig
2007 #P84 Kasey Kahne PO
Press Pass Stealth Corporate Cuts
2006 #CCD8 Kasey Kahne
Press Pass Stealth Gear Grippers Drivers
2006 #GGD10 Kasey Kahne
Press Pass Stealth Hot Pass
2006 #HP15 Kasey Kahne
Press Pass Stealth Mach 07
2007 #M7-5 Kasey Kahne
Press Pass Stealth Maximum Access
2007 #MA14 Kasey Kahne
Press Pass Stealth Maximum Access Autographs
2007 #MA14 Kasey Kahne
Press Pass Stealth Previews
2005 #2 Kasey Kahne
2005 #5 Kasey Kahne's Car
2005 #8 Kasey Kahne
2005 #67 Kasey Kahne
2006 #14 Kasey Kahne
2007 #EB13 Kasey Kahne
2007 #EB84 Kasey Kahne PO
2008 #17 Kasey Kahne
Press Pass Stealth Profile
2006 #P4 Kasey Kahne
Press Pass Stealth Retail
2006 #14 Kasey Kahne
2006 #51 Kahne/Mayfield/Riggs TM
2006 #64 Kasey Kahne F
2006 #70 Kasey Kahne DD
Press Pass Stealth Retail Gear Grippers Cars
2006 #GGT10 Kasey Kahne
Press Pass Stealth Samples
2004 #X78 Kasey Kahne WW
2005 #2 Kasey Kahne
2005 #5 Kasey Kahne's Car
2005 #8 Kasey Kahne
2005 #67 Kasey Kahne
Press Pass Stealth X-Ray
2004 #78 Kasey Kahne WW
2005 #X2 Kasey Kahne
2005 #X5 Kasey Kahne's Car
2005 #X8 Kasey Kahne
2005 #X67 Kasey Kahne
2006 #X14 Kasey Kahne
2006 #X51 Kahne/Mayfield/Riggs TM
2006 #X64 Kasey Kahne F
2006 #X70 Kasey Kahne DD
Press Pass Target
2007 #KK-B Kasey Kahne
2008 #KK-B Kasey Kahne
Press Pass Target Race Win Tires
2007 #RW5 Kasey Kahne Michigan 6-18
Press Pass Top 25 Drivers & Rides
2006 #C7 Kasey Kahne's Car
2006 #D7 Kasey Kahne
Press Pass Top Prospects Memorabilia
2004 #KKG Kasey Kahne Glove
2004 #KKS Kasey Kahne Shoe
2004 #KKT Kasey Kahne Tire
2004 #KKSM Kasey Kahne Metal
Press Pass Trackside
2004 #2 Kasey Kahne CRC
2004 #54 Kasey Kahne's Car HS
2004 #75 J.Mayfield/K.Kahne TM
2004 #93 Kasey Kahne LD
2005 #14 Kasey Kahne
2005 #14B Kasey Kahne -white t-shirt
2005 #56 Kasey Kahne's Car HS
2005 #74 K.Kahne/J.Mayfield TM
Press Pass Trackside Golden
2004 #G2 Kasey Kahne
2004 #G54 Kasey Kahne's Car HS
2004 #G75 J.Mayfield/K.Kahne TM
2004 #G93 Kasey Kahne LD
2005 #G14 Kasey Kahne
2005 #G56 Kasey Kahne's Car HS
2005 #G74 K.Kahne/J.Mayfield TM
Press Pass Trackside Hat Giveaway
2004 #PPH14 Kasey Kahne
2005 #PPH13 Kasey Kahne
Press Pass Trackside Hot Pass
2004 #HP22 Kasey Kahne BGN
2005 #20 Kasey Kahne
Press Pass Trackside Hot Pass National
2004 #HP22 Kasey Kahne BGN
2005 #20 Kasey Kahne
Press Pass Trackside Previews
2004 #EB2 Kasey Kahne
2005 #14 Kasey Kahne
Press Pass Trackside Samples
2004 #2 Kasey Kahne
2004 #54 Kasey Kahne's Car HS
2004 #75 J.Mayfield/K.Kahne TM
2004 #93 Kasey Kahne LD
2005 #14 Kasey Kahne
2005 #56 Kasey Kahne's Car HS
2005 #74 K.Kahne/J.Mayfield TM
Press Pass Velocity
2007 #V1 Kasey Kahne
Press Pass Wal-Mart
2007 #KK-A Kasey Kahne
2008 #KK-A Kasey Kahne
Sports Illustrated for Kids
2006 #69 Kasey Kahne's Car NASCAR
Stanley Tools Promo
2006 #2 Kasey Kahne
2006 #5 Kasey Kahne First Win
Sunoco OCC Postcards
2007 #KK Kasey Kahne
Super Shots CHP Sonoma
2004 #3 Kasey Kahne
TRAKS
2006 #16 Kasey Kahne
2006 #41 Kasey Kahne's Car
2007 #13 Kasey Kahne
2007 #59 Kasey Kahne's Car CTG
2007 #66 Kasey Kahne MG
2007 #84 Kasey Kahne's Car NFS
2007 #97 Kasey Kahne FT
TRAKS Autographs
2006 #18 Kasey Kahne NC
TRAKS Autographs 25
2006 #16 Kasey Kahne NC
Traks Corporate Cuts Driver
2007 #CCD2 Kasey Kahne
Traks Corporate Cuts Patch
2007 #CCD2 Kasey Kahne/12
Traks Corporate Cuts Team
2007 #CCT2 Kasey Kahne
Traks Driver's Seat
2007 #DS9 Kasey Kahne
2007 #DS9B Kasey Kahne VAR
Traks Driver's Seat National
2007 #DS9 Kasey Kahne
Traks Gold
2007 #G13 Kasey Kahne
2007 #G59 Kasey Kahne's Car CTG
2007 #G66 Kasey Kahne MG
2007 #G84 Kasey Kahne's Car NFS
2007 #G97 Kasey Kahne FT
Traks Holofoil
2007 #H13 Kasey Kahne
2007 #H59 Kasey Kahne's Car CTG
2007 #H66 Kasey Kahne MG
2007 #H84 Kasey Kahne's Car NFS
2007 #H97 Kasey Kahne FT
Traks Hot Pursuit
2007 #HP8 Kasey Kahne
Traks Previews
2007 #EB13 Kasey Kahne
Traks Red
2007 #R13 Kasey Kahne
2007 #R59 Kasey Kahne's Car CTG
2007 #R66 Kasey Kahne MG
2007 #R84 Kasey Kahne's Car NFS
2007 #R97 Kasey Kahne FT
TRAKS Stickers
2006 #9 Kasey Kahne
Traks Target Exclusives
2007 #KK-A Kasey Kahne
Traks Wal-Mart Exclusives
2007 #KK-B Kasey Kahne
Valvoline Racing
2007 #NNO Kasey Kahne
VIP
2004 #20 Kasey Kahne CRC
2004 #41 Kasey Kahne's Car R
2005 #12 Kasey Kahne
2005 #53 Kasey Kahne SG
2005 #55 Kasey Kahne HR
2006 #12 Kasey Kahne
2006 #37 Kasey Kahne's Car R
2006 #43 Kasey Kahne SG
2006 #46 Kasey Kahne SG
2006 #51 Kasey Kahne SG
2006 #62 Kasey Kahne BTN
2006 #66 Kasey Kahne RF
2006 #74 Kasey Kahne AS
2007 #15 Kasey Kahne
VIP Get A Grip Autographs
2007 #GG-KK Kasey Kahne/9
VIP Get A Grip Drivers
2007 #GGD8 Kasey Kahne
VIP Get A Grip Teams
2007 #GGT8 Kasey Kahne
VIP Head Gear
2004 #HG5 Kasey Kahne
2005 #5 Kasey Kahne
2006 #HG3 Kasey Kahne
VIP Head Gear Transparent
2004 #HG5 Kasey Kahne
2005 #5 Kasey Kahne
2006 #HG3 Kasey Kahne
VIP Lap Leader
2006 #LL4 Kasey Kahne
VIP Lap Leader Transparent
2006 #LL4 Kasey Kahne
VIP Lap Leaders
2004 #LL3 Kasey Kahne
2005 #3 Kasey Kahne
VIP Lap Leaders Transparent
2004 #LL3 Kasey Kahne
2005 #3 Kasey Kahne
VIP Making the Show
2004 #MS6 Kasey Kahne
2005 #6 Kasey Kahne
2006 #MS13 Kasey Kahne
VIP Pedal To The Metal
2007 #PM5 Kasey Kahne
VIP Previews
2004 #EB20 Kasey Kahne
2004 #EB41 Kasey Kahne's Car R
2005 #EB12 Kasey Kahne
2007 #EB15 Kasey Kahne
VIP Samples
2004 #20 Kasey Kahne
2004 #41 Kasey Kahne's Car R
2005 #12 Kasey Kahne
2005 #53 Kasey Kahne SG
2005 #55 Kasey Kahne HR
VIP Sunday Best
2007 #SB12 Kasey Kahne
VIP Tradin' Paint Autographs
2005 #KK Kasey Kahne/9
2006 #TP-KKKasey Kahne/9
VIP Tradin' Paint Cars
2005 #TPT11Kasey Kahne
VIP Tradin' Paint Cars Bronze
2006 #TPT11Kasey Kahne
VIP Tradin' Paint Drivers
2005 #TPD11 Kasey Kahne
VIP Tradin' Paint Drivers Gold
2006 #TPD11 Kasey Kahne
VIP Tradin' Paint Drivers Silver
2006 #TPD11 Kasey Kahne
Wheels American Thunder
2004 #11 Kasey Kahne CRC
2004 #43 Kasey Kahne AS
2004 #64 Kasey Kahne RR
2004 #85 Kasey Kahne RT
2004 #90 Kahne/Busch/McMurray CL
2005 #13 Kasey Kahne
2005 #54 Kasey Kahne DT
2005 #78 Kasey Kahne CC
2006 #14 Kasey Kahne
2006 #52 Kasey Kahne's Car HR
2006 #60 Kasey Kahne GR
2006 #79 Kasey Kahne MIA
2006 #87 Kasey Kahne NN
2007 #15 Kasey Kahne
Wheels American Thunder American Muscle
2004 #AM7 Kasey Kahne
Wheels American Thunder American Racing Idol
2006 #RI7 Kasey Kahne
Wheels American Thunder American Racing Idol Golden
2006 #RI7 Kasey Kahne
Wheels American Thunder Autographed Hat Instant Winner
2007 #AH16 Kasey Kahne
Wheels American Thunder Cool Threads
2006 #CT8 Kasey Kahne
Wheels American Thunder Double Hat
2006 #DH12 Kasey Kahne
Wheels American Thunder Grandstand
2006 #GS11 Kasey Kahne
Wheels American Thunder Head to Toe
2007 #HT4 Kasey Kahne
Wheels American Thunder Medallion
2005 #MD26 Kasey Kahne
Wheels American Thunder Post Mark
2004 #PM27 Kasey Kahne CL
Wheels American Thunder Previews
2004 #EB11 Kasey Kahne
2004 #EB43 Kasey Kahne AS
2005 #13 Kasey Kahne
2005 #78 Kasey Kahne CC
2006 #EB14 Kasey Kahne
2006 #EB79 Kasey Kahne MIA
2007 #EB15 Kasey Kahne
Wheels American Thunder Samples
2004 #11 Kasey Kahne
2004 #43 Kasey Kahne AS
2004 #64 Kasey Kahne RR
2004 #85 Kasey Kahne RT
2004 #90 Kahne/Busch/McMurray CL
2005 #13 Kasey Kahne
2005 #54 Kasey Kahne DT
2005 #78 Kasey Kahne CC
Wheels American Thunder Thunder Road
2005 #TR6 Kasey Kahne
2006 #TR14 Kasey Kahne
2007 #TR15 Kasey Kahne
Wheels American Thunder Triple Hat
2004 #TH7 Kasey Kahne
2005 #TH10 Kasey Kahne
2007 #TH14 Kasey Kahne
Wheels Autographs
2004 #34 Kasey Kahne HG
2005 #27 Kasey Kahne BGN
2005 #28 Kasey Kahne NC
2006 #27 Kasey Kahne NBS
2006 #28 Kasey Kahne NC
2007 #18 Kasey Kahne NC HG
2008 #17 Kasey Kahne NC HG
Wheels Autographs Press Plates Black
2007 #17 Kasey Kahne NC
2008 #17 Kasey Kahne NC HG
Wheels Autographs Press Plates Cyan
2007 #17 Kasey Kahne NC
2008 #17 Kasey Kahne NC HG
Wheels Autographs Press Plates Magenta
2007 #17 Kasey Kahne NC
2008 #17 Kasey Kahne NC HG
Wheels Autographs Press Plates Yellow
2007 #18 Kasey Kahne NC
2008 #17 Kasey Kahne NC HG
Wheels High Gear
2004 #40 Kasey Kahne
2005 #5 Kasey Kahne
2005 #36 Kasey Kahne
2005 #40 Kasey Kahne's Car C
2005 #49 Kasey Kahne A
2005 #74 Kasey Kahne IF
2006 #22 Kasey Kahne
2006 #48 Kasey Kahne's Car C
2006 #81 Kasey Kahne FF
2006 #85 Kasey Kahne NI
2007 #8 Kasey Kahne
2007 #55 Kasey Kahne NA
2007 #57 Kasey Kahne NA
2007 #61 Kasey Kahne NA
2007 #67 Kasey Kahne CM
2007 #75 Kasey Kahne NI
2007 #79 Kasey Kahne's Car C
2008 #17 Kasey Kahne
2008 #74 Kasey Kahne NI
Wheels High Gear Driven
2007 #DR21 Kasey Kahne
2008 #DR12 Kasey Kahne
Wheels High Gear Final Standings
2008 #F17 Kasey Kahne/19
Wheels High Gear Final Standings Gold
2007 #FS8 Kasey Kahne/8
Wheels High Gear Flag Chasers Black
2005 #FC1 Kasey Kahne
2006 #FC5 Kasey Kahne
2007 #FC9 Kasey Kahne
2008 #FC8 Kasey Kahne
Wheels High Gear Flag Chasers Blue-Yellow
2005 #FC1 Kasey Kahne
2006 #FC5 Kasey Kahne
2007 #FC9 Kasey Kahne
2008 #FC8 Kasey Kahne
Wheels High Gear Flag Chasers Checkered
2005 #FC1 Kasey Kahne
2006 #FC5 Kasey Kahne
2007 #FC9 Kasey Kahne
2008 #FC8 Kasey Kahne
Wheels High Gear Flag Chasers Green
2005 #FC1 Kasey Kahne
2006 #FC5 Kasey Kahne
2007 #FC9 Kasey Kahne
2008 #FC8 Kasey Kahne
Wheels High Gear Flag Chasers Red
2005 #FC1 Kasey Kahne
2006 #FC5 Kasey Kahne
2007 #FC9 Kasey Kahne
2008 #FC8 Kasey Kahne
Wheels High Gear Flag Chasers White
2005 #FC1 Kasey Kahne
2006 #FC5 Kasey Kahne
2007 #FC9 Kasey Kahne
2008 #FC8 Kasey Kahne
Wheels High Gear Flag Chasers Yellow
2005 #FC1 Kasey Kahne
2006 #FC5 Kasey Kahne
2007 #FC9 Kasey Kahne
2008 #FC8 Kasey Kahne
Wheels High Gear Flag to Flag
2005 #FF10 Kasey Kahne
2006 #FF12 Kasey Kahne
Wheels High Gear Full Throttle
2007 #FT5 Kasey Kahne
Wheels High Gear Last Lap
2007 #LL1 Kasey Kahne
Wheels High Gear Man
2005 #MMA6 Kasey Kahne
Wheels High Gear MPH
2004 #M40 Kasey Kahne
2005 #M5 Kasey Kahne
2005 #M36 Kasey Kahne
2005 #M40 Kasey Kahne's Car C
2005 #M49 Kasey Kahne A
2005 #M74 Kasey Kahne IF
2006 #M22 Kasey Kahne
2006 #M48 Kasey Kahne's Car C
2006 #M81 Kasey Kahne FF
2006 #M85 Kasey Kahne NI
2007 #M8 Kasey Kahne
2007 #M55 Kasey Kahne NA
2007 #M57 Kasey Kahne NA
2007 #M61 Kasey Kahne NA
2007 #M67 Kasey Kahne CM
2007 #M75 Kasey Kahne NI
2007 #M79 Kasey Kahne's Car C
2008 #M17 Kasey Kahne
2008 #M74 Kasey Kahne NI
Wheels High Gear Previews
2004 #40 Kasey Kahne
2007 #EB8 Kasey Kahne
2007 #EB55 Kasey Kahne NA
2007 #EB57 Kasey Kahne NA
2007 #EB61 Kasey Kahne NA
2008 #EB17 Kasey Kahne
Wheels High Gear Previews Green
2005 #EB5 Kasey Kahne
2005 #EB36 Kasey Kahne
2006 #EB22 Kasey Kahne
Wheels High Gear Previews Silver
2005 #EB74 Kasey Kahne IF
2006 #EB81 Kasey Kahne FF
Wheels High Gear Samples
2004 #40 Kasey Kahne
2005 #5 Kasey Kahne
2005 #36 Kasey Kahne
2005 #40 Kasey Kahne's Car C
2005 #49 Kasey Kahne A
2005 #74 Kasey Kahne IF
Wheels High Gear Top Tier
2007 #TT8 Kasey Kahne

Kenseth, Matt

eTopps
2003 #11 Matt Kenseth/5000
Langenberg ARTGO
1991 #1 Matt Kenseth XRC
Maxx
2000 #17 Matt Kenseth CRC
2000 #47 Matt Kenseth's Car
Maxx Collectible Covers
2000 #CCMK Matt Kenseth
Maxx Drive Time

2000 #DT9 Matt Kenseth
Maxx Fantastic Finishes
2000 #FF4 Matt Kenseth
Maxx Speedway Boogie
2000 #SB2 Matt Kenseth
Maxximum
2000 #32 Matt Kenseth CRC
Maxximum Cruise Control
2000 #CC6 Matt Kenseth
Maxximum Die Cuts
2000 #32 Matt Kenseth
Maxximum MPH
2000 #32 Matt Kenseth/17
Maxximum Signatures
2000 #MK Matt Kenseth
2000 #MK2 M.Martin/M.Kenseth
2000 #ROU4 Mart/Litt/J.Brtn/Kens
Maxximum Young Lions
2000 #YL2 Matt Kenseth
Post Cereal
2004 #5 Matt Kenseth
Press Pass
1999 #38 Matt Kenseth RC
1999 #62 Matt Kenseth YG
2000 #47 Matt Kenseth's Car DD
2000 #64 Matt Kenseth
2000 #72 Matt Kenseth SO
2000 #94 Matt Kenseth 00P
2001 #13 Matt Kenseth
2001 #45 Matt Kenseth
2001 #59 Matt Kenseth's Car
2001 #62 Matt Kenseth REP
2002 #17 Matt Kenseth
2002 #79 Matt Kenseth's Car
2003 #17 Matt Kenseth
2003 #63 Jr./JJ/New/Sad/Ken/Bus DS
2003 #74 Rock Steady WCS
2003 #76 Texas Tornado WCS
2003 #81 Pit Bulls WCS
2003 #95 Matt Kenseth's Car OTW
2004 #9C Matt Kenseth blue sky
2004 #15 Matt Kenseth
2004 #80 The Drive for Five WCS
2004 #85 Quiet Confidence WCS
2004 #97 Matt Kenseth DS
2004 #100 Matt Kenseth Schedule
2005 #12 Matt Kenseth
2005 #74 Matt Kenseth NS
2006 #13 Matt Kenseth
2006 #95 Matt Kenseth NS
2006 #105 Matt Kenseth U
2006 #117 Matt Kenseth TT
2007 #1 Matt Kenseth
2007 #75 Matt Kenseth's Car OT
2007 #95 Matt Kenseth NS
2007 #105 Matt Kenseth U
2007 #108 Matt Kenseth TT
2008 #4 Matt Kenseth
2008 #114 Matt Kenseth Top 12
2008 #0 Cup Chase Matt Kenseth Tony Stewart Jeff Gordon Jimmie Johnson Denny Hamlin Kurt Busch Kevin Harvick Carl Edwards Kyle Busch Martin Truex Jr. Jeff Burton Clint Bowyer
Press Pass Autographs
2001 #24 Matt Kenseth
2002 #34 Matt Kenseth
2003 #30 Matt Kenseth E/P
2004 #33 Matt Kenseth P
2005 #31 Matt Kenseth BGN E/P
2005 #32 Matt Kenseth NCS E/P
2006 #28 Matt Kenseth NC
2007 #22 Matt Kenseth NC P
2008 #22 Matt Kenseth NC P/E
Press Pass Autographs Press Plates Black
2007 #7 Matt Kenseth NC
2008 #18 Matt Kenseth NC E
Press Pass Autographs Press Plates Cyan
2007 #7 Matt Kenseth NC
2008 #18 Matt Kenseth NC P
Press Pass Autographs Press Plates Magenta
2007 #9 Matt Kenseth NC
2008 #18 Matt Kenseth NC E
Press Pass Autographs Press Plates Yellow
2007 #8 Matt Kenseth NC
2008 #18 Matt Kenseth NC P
Press Pass Blue
2006 #B13 Matt Kenseth
2006 #B95 Matt Kenseth NS
2006 #B105 Matt Kenseth U
2006 #B117 Matt Kenseth TT
2007 #B1 Matt Kenseth
2007 #B75 Matt Kenseth's Car OT
2007 #B95 Matt Kenseth NS
2007 #B105 Matt Kenseth U
2007 #B108 Matt Kenseth TT
2008 #B4 Matt Kenseth
2008 #B114 Matt Kenseth Top 12
Press Pass Burning Rubber Autographs
2004 #BRMK Matt Kenseth/17
2005 #BR-MK Matt Kenseth/17
2006 #BR-MK Matt Kenseth/17
2007 #BRS-MK Matt Kenseth/17
Press Pass Burning Rubber Cars
2002 #BRC11 Matt Kenseth's Car
2003 #BRT7 Matt Kenseth's Car
2004 #BRT2 Matt Kenseth's Car
2005 #BRT2 Matt Kenseth's Car
2006 #BRT10 Matt Kenseth
Press Pass Burning Rubber Cars Autographs
2003 #BRT-MK Matt Kenseth/17
Press Pass Burning Rubber Drivers
2002 #BRD11 Matt Kenseth
2003 #BRD7 Matt Kenseth
2004 #BRD2 Matt Kenseth
2005 #BRD2 Matt Kenseth
2006 #BRD10 Matt Kenseth
2007 #BRD2 Matt Kenseth California 2-19
2008 #BRD2 Matt Kenseth California
Press Pass Burning Rubber Drivers Autographs
2003 #BRD-MK Matt Kenseth/17
Press Pass Burning Rubber Drivers Gold
2005 #BRD2 Matt Kenseth
2006 #BRD10 Matt Kenseth
2007 #BRD2 Matt Kenseth California 2-19
2008 #BRD2 Matt Kenseth California
Press Pass Burning Rubber Drivers Prime Cuts
2008 #BRD2 Matt Kenseth California
Press Pass Burning Rubber Team
2007 #BRT2 Matt Kenseth California 2-19
Press Pass Burning Rubber Teams
2008 #BRT2 Matt Kenseth California
Press Pass Burnouts
2006 #HT17 Matt Kenseth
Press Pass Burnouts Holofoil
2006 #HT17 Matt Kenseth
Press Pass Collector's Series Box Set
2007 #SB13 Matt Kenseth
Press Pass Collectors Series Making the Show
2006 #MS3 Matt Kenseth
Press Pass Collectors Series Sunday Best
2007 #CB13 Matt Kenseth
Press Pass Cup Chase
2000 #CC8 Matt Kenseth
2001 #CC15 Matt Kenseth
2002 #CC7 Matt Kenseth WIN
2003 #CCR8 Matt Kenseth
2004 #CCR1 Matt Kenseth
2005 #CCR10 Matt Kenseth
2006 #CCR7 Matt Kenseth Winner
2007 #CCR4 Matt Kenseth Winner
2008 #CC2 Matt Kenseth
Press Pass Cup Chase Die Cut Prizes
2000 #CC8 Matt Kenseth
2001 #CC15 Matt Kenseth
Press Pass Cup Chase Prizes
2002 #CC7 Matt Kenseth
2003 #CCR8 Matt Kenseth
2004 #CCR1 Matt Kenseth
2004 #CCR18 Matt Kenseth Champion
2005 #CCP10 Matt Kenseth
2006 #CC2 Matt Kenseth
2007 #CC8 Matt Kenseth
Press Pass Double Burner
2001 #DB7 Matt Kenseth
2003 #DB7 Matt Kenseth
2004 #DB7 Matt Kenseth
2005 #DB7 Matt Kenseth
Press Pass Double Burner Exchange
2003 #DB7 Matt Kenseth EXCH
2004 #DB7 Matt Kenseth
2005 #DB7 Matt Kenseth
Press Pass Double Burner Firesuit-Glove
2006 #DB3 Matt Kenseth
2007 #DB1 Matt Kenseth
2008 #DBMK Matt Kenseth
Press Pass Double Burner Firesuit-Glove Exchange
2007 #DB1 Matt Kenseth
Press Pass Double Burner Metal-Tire
2007 #DB-MK Matt Kenseth
Press Pass Double Burner Metal-Tire Exchange
2007 #DB-MK Matt Kenseth
Press Pass Eclipse
2002 #12 Matt Kenseth
2002 #37 Matt Kenseth ACC
2003 #8 Matt Kenseth
2003 #29 Matt Kenseth ACC
2003 #44 High Five WCS
2004 #1 Matt Kenseth
2004 #32 Matt Kenseth's Car
2004 #49 Matt Kenseth Z
2004 #51 Matt Kenseth Z
2004 #60 Matt Kenseth P
2004 #77 Matt Kenseth LL
2004 #88 Matt Kenseth SM
2005 #8 Matt Kenseth
2005 #34 Matt Kenseth's Car S
2005 #60 Matt Kenseth P
2006 #7 Matt Kenseth
2006 #65 NCS Top-10 BA
2007 #2 Matt Kenseth
2007 #48 Matt Kenseth P
2007 #49 Matt Kenseth FP
2007 #74 Matt Kenseth NYC
2007 #0 Cup Chase 10
2008 #4 Matt Kenseth
2008 #61 Matt Kenseth's Car LP
2008 #75 Top 10 Drivers SO
Press Pass Eclipse Destination WIN
2004 #5 Matt Kenseth
2005 #2 Matt Kenseth
Press Pass Eclipse Double Hot Treads
2003 #DT6 M.Kenseth/M.Martin
Press Pass Eclipse Ecliptic
2007 #EC4 Matt Kenseth
Press Pass Eclipse Gold
2007 #G2 Matt Kenseth
2007 #G48 Matt Kenseth P
2007 #G49 Matt Kenseth FP
2007 #G74 Matt Kenseth NYC
2008 #G4 Matt Kenseth
2008 #G61 Matt Kenseth's Car LP
2008 #G75 Top 10 Drivers SO
Press Pass Eclipse Hyperdrive
2004 #HP9 Matt Kenseth
2007 #HD2 Matt Kenseth
2008 #HP7 Matt Kenseth
Press Pass Eclipse Maxim
2004 #MX1 Matt Kenseth
Press Pass Eclipse Previews
2003 #8 Matt Kenseth
2003 #29 Matt Kenseth ACC
2004 #1 Matt Kenseth
2005 #EB8 Matt Kenseth
2005 #EB34 Matt Kenseth's Car S
2005 #EB60 Matt Kenseth P
2006 #EB7 Matt Kenseth
2007 #EB2 Matt Kenseth
2008 #EB4 Matt Kenseth
2008 #EB75 Top 10 Drivers SO
Press Pass Eclipse Racing Champions
2003 #RC4 Matt Kenseth
2003 #RC9 Matt Kenseth
2003 #RC18 Matt Kenseth
2003 #RC27 Matt Kenseth
2003 #RC35 Matt Kenseth
2006 #RC10 Matt Kenseth
2006 #RC22 Matt Kenseth NBS
2007 #RC5 Matt Kenseth
2007 #RC15 Matt Kenseth
Press Pass Eclipse Red
2007 #R2 Matt Kenseth
2007 #R48 Matt Kenseth P
2007 #R49 Matt Kenseth FP
2007 #R74 Matt Kenseth NYC
2008 #R4 Matt Kenseth
2008 #R61 Matt Kenseth's Car LP
2008 #R75 Top 10 Drivers SO
Press Pass Eclipse Samples
2002 #12 Matt Kenseth
2002 #37 Matt Kenseth ACC
2003 #8 Matt Kenseth
2003 #29 Matt Kenseth ACC
2003 #44 High Five WCS
2004 #1 Matt Kenseth
2004 #32 Matt Kenseth's Car
2004 #49 Matt Kenseth Z
2004 #51 Matt Kenseth Z
2004 #60 Matt Kenseth P
2004 #77 Matt Kenseth LL
2004 #88 Matt Kenseth SM
2005 #8 Matt Kenseth
2005 #34 Matt Kenseth's Car S
2005 #60 Matt Kenseth P
Press Pass Eclipse Skidmarks
2003 #SM9 Matt Kenseth
2004 #SM4 Matt Kenseth
2005 #SM4 Matt Kenseth
2006 #SM4 Matt Kenseth
2007 #SM4 Matt Kenseth
Press Pass Eclipse Skidmarks Holofoil
2004 #SM4 Matt Kenseth
2005 #SM4 Matt Kenseth
2006 #SM4 Matt Kenseth
2007 #SM4 Matt Kenseth
Press Pass Eclipse Solar Eclipse
2002 #S12 Matt Kenseth
2002 #S37 Matt Kenseth ACC
2003 #P8 Matt Kenseth
2003 #P29 Matt Kenseth ACC
2003 #P44 High Five WCS
Press Pass Eclipse Star Tracks
2008 #ST13 Matt Kenseth
Press Pass Eclipse Star Tracks Holofoil
2008 #ST13 Matt Kenseth
Press Pass Eclipse Stellar
2008 #ST6 Matt Kenseth
2008 #ST21 Matt Kenseth
Press Pass Eclipse Supernova
2002 #SN7 Matt Kenseth
2003 #SN6 Matt Kenseth
2006 #SU8 Matt Kenseth
Press Pass Eclipse Supernova Numbered
2002 #SN7 Matt Kenseth
Press Pass Eclipse Teammates Autographs
2003 #MMMK M.Martin/M.Kenseth
2005 #2 Busch/Martin/Kenseth
2005 #9 M.Kenseth/M.Martin
2006 #1 G.Biffle/M.Kenseth
2007 #6 Biffle/Edwards/Kenseth
Press Pass Eclipse Under Cover Autographs
2005 #UCMK Matt Kenseth/17
2006 #MK Matt Kenseth/17
2007 #UC-MK Matt Kenseth/17
2008 #UC-MK Matt Kenseth/17
Press Pass Eclipse Under Cover Cars
2003 #UCT16 Matt Kenseth
2004 #UCD2 Matt Kenseth
2005 #UCT2 Matt Kenseth
2006 #UCT1 Matt Kenseth
Press Pass Eclipse Under Cover Double Cover
2004 #DC9 M.Kenseth/J.Burton
2004 #DC12 K.Busch/M.Kenseth
2004 #DC13 M.Kenseth/M.Martin
2005 #DC6 K.Busch/M.Kenseth
2005 #DC7 M.Kenseth/M.Martin
2006 #DC2 M.Martin/M.Kenseth
2006 #DC6 M.Kenseth/C.Edwards
Press Pass Eclipse Under Cover Double Cover Holofoil
2006 #DC2 M.Martin/M.Kenseth
2006 #DC6 M.Kenseth/C.Edwards
Press Pass Eclipse Under Cover Double Cover Name
2007 #DC5 Kenseth/Edwards
2008 #DC3 Carl Edwards Matt Kenseth
2008 #DC4 Matt Kenseth David Ragan
Press Pass Eclipse Under Cover Double Cover NASCAR
2007 #DC5 Kenseth/Edwards
2008 #DC3 Carl Edwards Matt Kenseth
2008 #DC4 Matt Kenseth David Ragan
Press Pass Eclipse Under Cover Driver Gold
2003 #UCD16 Matt Kenseth
2004 #UCD2 Matt Kenseth
Press Pass Eclipse Under Cover Driver Red
2003 #UCD16 Matt Kenseth
2004 #UCD2 Matt Kenseth
2005 #UCD2 Matt Kenseth
Press Pass Eclipse Under Cover Driver Silver
2003 #UCD16 Matt Kenseth
2004 #UCD2 Matt Kenseth
Press Pass Eclipse Under Cover Drivers
2007 #UCD4 Matt Kenseth
2008 #UCD9 Matt Kenseth
Press Pass Eclipse Under Cover Drivers Eclipse
2007 #UCD4 Matt Kenseth
2008 #UCD9 Matt Kenseth
Press Pass Eclipse Under Cover Drivers Gold
2006 #UCD1 Matt Kenseth
Press Pass Eclipse Under Cover Drivers Holofoil
2005 #UCD2 Matt Kenseth
2006 #UCD1 Matt Kenseth
Press Pass Eclipse Under Cover Drivers Name
2007 #UCD4 Matt Kenseth
2008 #UCD9 Matt Kenseth
Press Pass Eclipse Under Cover Drivers NASCAR
2007 #UCD4 Matt Kenseth
2008 #UCD9 Matt Kenseth
Press Pass Eclipse Under Cover Drivers Silver
2005 #UCD2 Matt Kenseth
2006 #UCD1 Matt Kenseth
Press Pass Eclipse Under Cover Teams
2007 #UCT4 Matt Kenseth
2008 #UCT9 Matt Kenseth
Press Pass Eclipse Under Cover Teams NASCAR
2007 #UCT4 Matt Kenseth
2008 #UCT9 Matt Kenseth
Press Pass Four Wide
2006 #FW-MK Matt Kenseth
2008 #FW-MK Matt Kenseth
Press Pass Four Wide Checkered
2008 #FW-MK Matt Kenseth
Press Pass Four Wide Checkered Flag
2006 #FW-MK Matt Kenseth
Press Pass Gatorade Front Runner Award
2001 #2 Matt Kenseth
Press Pass Gatorade Jumbos
2003 #2 Matt Kenseth
Press Pass Gold
2006 #G13 Matt Kenseth
2006 #G95 Matt Kenseth NS
2006 #G105 Matt Kenseth U
2006 #G117 Matt Kenseth TT
2007 #G1 Matt Kenseth
2007 #G75 Matt Kenseth's Car OT
2007 #G95 Matt Kenseth NS
2007 #G105 Matt Kenseth U
2007 #G108 Matt Kenseth TT
2008 #G4 Matt Kenseth
2008 #G114 Matt Kenseth Top 12
Press Pass Gold Holofoil
2003 #P17 Matt Kenseth
2003 #P63 Jr./Johnson/Newman Sadler/Kenseth/Busch DS
2003 #P74 Rock Steady WCS
2003 #P76 Texas Tornado WCS
2003 #P81 Pit Bulls WCS
2003 #P95 Matt Kenseth's Car OTW
Press Pass Ground Zero
2001 #GZ1 Matt Kenseth
Press Pass Hot Treads
2001 #HT18 Matt Kenseth/2405
2002 #HT21 Matt Kenseth's Car/2425
2004 #HTR4 Matt Kenseth
2005 #HTR4 Matt Kenseth
Press Pass Hot Treads Holofoil
2004 #HTR4 Matt Kenseth
2005 #HTR4 Matt Kenseth
Press Pass Legends
2005 #45 Matt Kenseth C
2006 #38 Matt Kenseth
2007 #41 Matt Kenseth
Press Pass Legends Autographs Black
2005 #20 Matt Kenseth
2006 #27 Matt Kenseth
Press Pass Legends Autographs Blue
2007 #16 Matt Kenseth/60
Press Pass Legends Autographs Inscriptions Blue
2007 #10 Matt Kenseth 03 Cup Champion/9
Press Pass Legends Blue
2005 #45B Matt Kenseth C
2006 #B38 Matt Kenseth
2007 #B41 Matt Kenseth
Press Pass Legends Bronze
2006 #Z38 Matt Kenseth
2007 #Z41 Matt Kenseth
Press Pass Legends Champion Threads & Treads Bronze
2006 #CTT-MK Matt Kenseth
Press Pass Legends Champion Threads & Treads Gold
2006 #CTT-MK Matt Kenseth
Press Pass Legends Champion Threads & Treads Silver
2006 #CTT-MK Matt Kenseth
Press Pass Legends Champion Threads Bronze
2006 #CT-MK Matt Kenseth
Press Pass Legends Champion Threads Gold
2006 #CT-MK Matt Kenseth
Press Pass Legends Champion Threads Patch
2006 #CT-MK Matt Kenseth
Press Pass Legends Champion Threads Silver
2006 #CT-MK Matt Kenseth
Press Pass Legends Double Threads Bronze
2005 #DT-BKK.Busch/M.Kenseth
2005 #DT-MK M.Martin/M.Kenseth
Press Pass Legends Double Threads Gold
2005 #DT-BKK.Busch/M.Kenseth
2005 #DT-MK M.Martin/M.Kenseth
Press Pass Legends Double Threads Silver
2005 #DT-BKK.Busch/M.Kenseth
2005 #DT-MK M.Martin/M.Kenseth
Press Pass Legends Gold
2005 #45G Matt Kenseth C
2006 #G38 Matt Kenseth
2007 #G41 Matt Kenseth
Press Pass Legends Holofoil
2005 #45H Matt Kenseth C
2006 #H38 Matt Kenseth
2007 #H41 Matt Kenseth
Press Pass Legends Memorable Moments Gold
2006 #MM14 Matt Kenseth
Press Pass Legends Memorable Moments Silver
2006 #MM14 Matt Kenseth
Press Pass Legends Press Plates Black
2005 #45 Matt Kenseth C
2006 #PPB38 Matt Kenseth
2007 #PP41 Matt Kenseth
Press Pass Legends Press Plates Black Backs
2006 #PPB38B Matt Kenseth
2007 #PP41 Matt Kenseth
Press Pass Legends Press Plates Cyan
2005 #45 Matt Kenseth C
2006 #PPC38 Matt Kenseth
2007 #PP41 Matt Kenseth
Press Pass Legends Press Plates Cyan Backs
2006 #PPC38B Matt Kenseth
2007 #PP41 Matt Kenseth
Press Pass Legends Press Plates Magenta
2005 #45 Matt Kenseth C
2006 #PPM38 Matt Kenseth
2007 #PP41 Matt Kenseth
Press Pass Legends Press Plates Magenta Backs
2006 #PPM38B Matt Kenseth
2007 #PP41 Matt Kenseth
Press Pass Legends Press Plates Yellow
2005 #45 Matt Kenseth C
2006 #PPY38 Matt Kenseth
2007 #PP41 Matt Kenseth
Press Pass Legends Press Plates Yellow Backs
2006 #PPY38B Matt Kenseth
2007 #PP41 Matt Kenseth
Press Pass Legends Previews
2005 #45 Matt Kenseth C
2006 #EB38 Matt Kenseth
2007 #EB41 Matt Kenseth
Press Pass Legends Signature Series
2007 #MK Matt Kenseth
Press Pass Legends Solo
2005 #45S Matt Kenseth C
2006 #S38 Matt Kenseth
2007 #S41 Matt Kenseth
Press Pass Legends Triple Threads
2006 #TT-MK Matt Kenseth
Press Pass Making the Show Collector's Series
2004 #MS11 Matt Kenseth
Press Pass Millennium
2000 #47 Matt Kenseth
2000 #64 Matt Kenseth
2000 #72 Matt Kenseth
2000 #94 Matt Kenseth
2001 #13 Matt Kenseth
2001 #45 Matt Kenseth
2001 #59 Matt Kenseth's Car
2001 #62 Matt Kenseth REP
Press Pass Optima
2000 #10 Matt Kenseth CRC
2000 #36 Matt Kenseth BGN
2000 #46 Matt Kenseth WCL
2000 #P1 Matt Kenseth Promo
2001 #10 Matt Kenseth
2002 #15 Matt Kenseth
2002 #50 Matt Kenseth YG
2003 #12 Matt Kenseth
2004 #12 Matt Kenseth
2004 #39 Matt Kenseth
2004 #56 Matt Kenseth's Car RV
2004 #80 Matt Kenseth CP w/Pres.Bush
2004 #95 Matt Kenseth NP
2005 #15 Matt Kenseth
2005 #15B Matt Kenseth Cup Chase
2006 #15 Matt Kenseth
2006 #63 Matt Kenseth's Car HS
2006 #79 Matt Kenseth RTV Dover
2006 #89 Matt Kenseth RTV Michigan
2006 #90 Matt Kenseth RTV Bristol
2006 #99 Matt Kenseth VOTC
2006 #15B Matt Kenseth Chase
Press Pass Optima Cool Persistence
2002 #CP7 Matt Kenseth
2003 #CP11 Matt Kenseth
2004 #CP9 Matt Kenseth
Press Pass Optima Corporate Cuts Cars
2005 #CCT9 Matt Kenseth
Press Pass Optima Corporate Cuts Drivers
2005 #CCD9 Matt Kenseth
Press Pass Optima Fan Favorite
2002 #FF12 Matt Kenseth
2003 #FF3 Matt Kenseth
2004 #FF12 Matt Kenseth
2005 #FF14 Matt Kenseth
Press Pass Optima G Force
2000 #GF10 Matt Kenseth
2001 #GF9 Matt Kenseth
Press Pass Optima Gold
2001 #10 Matt Kenseth
2002 #15 Matt Kenseth
2002 #50 Matt Kenseth YG
2003 #G12 Matt Kenseth
2004 #G12 Matt Kenseth
2004 #G39 Matt Kenseth
2004 #G56 Matt Kenseth's Car RV
2004 #G80 Matt Kenseth CP w/Pres.G.W.Bush
2004 #G95 Matt Kenseth NP
2005 #G15 Matt Kenseth
2006 #G15 Matt Kenseth
2006 #G63 Matt Kenseth's Car HS
2006 #G79 Matt Kenseth RTV Dover
2006 #G89 Matt Kenseth RTV Michigan
2006 #G90 Matt Kenseth RTV Bristol
2006 #G99 Matt Kenseth VOTC
Press Pass Optima On the Edge
2000 #OE5 Matt Kenseth
Press Pass Optima Overdrive
2000 #OD10 Matt Kenseth
Press Pass Optima Overdrive Square Cut
2000 #OD10 Matt Kenseth
Press Pass Optima Platinum
2000 #10 Matt Kenseth
2000 #36 Matt Kenseth BGN
2000 #46 Matt Kenseth WCL
Press Pass Optima Previews
2003 #12 Matt Kenseth
2004 #EB12 Matt Kenseth
2004 #EB39 Matt Kenseth
2005 #15 Matt Kenseth
2006 #EB15 Matt Kenseth
Press Pass Optima Promos
2002 #15 Matt Kenseth
2002 #50 Matt Kenseth YG
Press Pass Optima Q and A
2002 #QA4 Matt Kenseth
Press Pass Optima Q&A
2004 #QA3 Matt Kenseth
Press Pass Optima Race Used Lugnuts Autographs
2002 #LNDA10 Matt Kenseth/17
Press Pass Optima Race Used Lugnuts Cars
2000 #LC18 Matt Kenseth's Car/50
2001 #LNC8 Matt Kenseth's Car
2002 #LNC10 Matt Kenseth's Car
Press Pass Optima Race Used Lugnuts Drivers
2000 #LD18 Matt Kenseth/55
2001 #LND7 Matt Kenseth
2002 #LND10 Matt Kenseth
Press Pass Optima Rookie Relics Cars
2006 #RRT12 Matt Kenseth
Press Pass Optima Rookie Relics Drivers
2006 #RRD12 Matt Kenseth
Press Pass Optima Samples
2002 #15 Matt Kenseth
2002 #50 Matt Kenseth YG
2003 #12 Matt Kenseth
2004 #12 Matt Kenseth
2004 #39 Matt Kenseth
2004 #56 Matt Kenseth's Car RV
2004 #80 Matt Kenseth CP w/Pres.G.W.Bush
2004 #95 Matt Kenseth NP
2005 #15 Matt Kenseth
Press Pass Optima Thunder Bolts Autographs
2004 #TBMK Matt Kenseth/17
Press Pass Optima Thunder Bolts Cars
2003 #TBT7 Matt Kenseth's Car
2004 #TBT8 Matt Kenseth's Car
Press Pass Optima Thunder Bolts Cars Autographs
2003 #TBT-MK Matt Kenseth/17
Press Pass Optima Thunder Bolts Drivers
2003 #TBD7 Matt Kenseth/60
2004 #TBD8 Matt Kenseth
Press Pass Optima Thunder Bolts Drivers Autographs
2003 #TBD-MK Matt Kenseth/17
Press Pass Panorama
2005 #PPP6 Matt Kenseth
Press Pass Pitstop
2000 #PS16 Matt Kenseth's Car
Press Pass Platinum
2002 #17 Matt Kenseth
2002 #79 Matt Kenseth's Car
2004 #P15 Matt Kenseth
2004 #P80 The Drive for Five WCS
2004 #P85 Quiet Confidence WCS
2004 #P97 Matt Kenseth DS
2004 #P100 Matt Kenseth Schedule
2005 #P12 Matt Kenseth
2005 #P74 Matt Kenseth NS
2006 #P13 Matt Kenseth
2006 #P95 Matt Kenseth NS
2006 #P105 Matt Kenseth U
2006 #P117 Matt Kenseth TT
2007 #P1 Matt Kenseth
2007 #P75 Matt Kenseth's Car OT
2007 #P95 Matt Kenseth NS
2007 #P105 Matt Kenseth U
2007 #P108 Matt Kenseth TT
2008 #P4 Matt Kenseth
2008 #P114 Matt Kenseth Top 12
Press Pass Premium
1999 #46 Matt Kenseth RC
2000 #33 Matt Kenseth CRC
2000 #44 Matt Kenseth
2000 #55 Matt Kenseth
2001 #10 Matt Kenseth
2001 #61 Matt Kenseth CC
2002 #15 Matt Kenseth
2002 #41 Matt Kenseth's Car
2002 #63 Matt Kenseth CH
2003 #14 Matt Kenseth
2003 #42 Matt Kenseth's Car
2003 #62 Matt Kenseth CC
2004 #8 Matt Kenseth
2004 #41 Matt Kenseth's Car
2004 #57 Matt Kenseth CC
2004 #74 Matt Kenseth PC
2005 #13 Matt Kenseth
2005 #57 Matt Kenseth CC
2006 #14 Matt Kenseth
2006 #39 Matt Kenseth's Car M
2006 #58 Matt Kenseth CC
2006 #81 Matt Kenseth PC
2007 #15 Matt Kenseth
2007 #42 Matt Kenseth's Car M
2007 #56 Matt Kenseth RTTC
2008 #14 Matt Kenseth
2008 #58 Matt Kenseth EOP
Press Pass Premium Clean Air
2008 #CA7 Matt Kenseth
Press Pass Premium Gold
2001 #10 Matt Kenseth
2001 #61 Matt Kenseth CC
Press Pass Premium Hot Threads Autographs
2004 #HT-MK Matt Kenseth/17
2005 #HT-MK Matt Kenseth/17
2007 #HT-MK Matt Kenseth/17
2008 #HTMK Matt Kenseth/17
Press Pass Premium Hot Threads Cars
2003 #HTT7 Matt Kenseth
2005 #HTT7 Matt Kenseth
2006 #HTT2 Matt Kenseth
Press Pass Premium Hot Threads Cars Autographs
2003 #HTD-MK Matt Kenseth/17
Press Pass Premium Hot Threads Drivers
2003 #HTD7 Matt Kenseth
2005 #HTD7 Matt Kenseth
2006 #HTD2 Matt Kenseth
2007 #HTD12 Matt Kenseth
2008 #HTD16 Matt Kenseth
Press Pass Premium Hot Threads Drivers Autographs
2003 #HTT-MK Matt Kenseth/17
Press Pass Premium Hot Threads Drivers Bronze
2004 #HTD2 Matt Kenseth
Press Pass Premium Hot Threads Drivers Bronze Retail
2004 #HTT2 Matt Kenseth
Press Pass Premium Hot Threads Drivers Gold
2004 #HTD2 Matt Kenseth
2005 #HTD7 Matt Kenseth
2006 #HTD2 Matt Kenseth
2007 #HTD12 Matt Kenseth
2008 #HTD16 Matt Kenseth
Press Pass Premium Hot Threads Drivers Silver
2004 #HTD2 Matt Kenseth
Press Pass Premium Hot Threads Patch
2007 #HTP22 Matt Kenseth Carhartt/10
2007 #HTP23 Matt Kenseth RL Carriers/6
Press Pass Premium Hot Threads Patches
2008 #HTP18 Matt Kenseth #17/4
2008 #HTP19 Matt Kenseth Kraft Singles
Press Pass Premium Hot Threads Team
2007 #HTT12 Matt Kenseth
2008 #HTT16 Matt Kenseth
Press Pass Premium In The Zone
2000 #IZ5 Matt Kenseth

2001 #IZ7 Matt Kenseth
2002 #IZ7 Matt Kenseth
2003 #IZ5 Matt Kenseth
2004 #IZ7 Matt Kenseth
2005 #IZ11 Matt Kenseth
2006 #IZ5 Matt Kenseth
Press Pass Premium In the Zone Elite Edition
2004 #IZ7 Matt Kenseth
2005 #IZ11 Matt Kenseth
Press Pass Premium In the Zone Red
2006 #IZ5 Matt Kenseth
Press Pass Premium Previews
2003 #14 Matt Kenseth
2004 #8 Matt Kenseth
2008 #EB14 Matt Kenseth
2008 #EB58 Matt Kenseth EOP
Press Pass Premium Race Used Firesuit Cars
2001 #FC4 Matt Kenseth
2002 #FC3 Matt Kenseth
Press Pass Premium Race Used Firesuit Drivers
2001 #FD4 Matt Kenseth
2002 #FD3 Matt Kenseth
Press Pass Premium Red
2007 #R15 Matt Kenseth
2007 #R42 Matt Kenseth's Car M
2007 #R56 Matt Kenseth RTTC
2008 #14 Matt Kenseth
2008 #58 Matt Kenseth EOP
Press Pass Premium Red Reflectors
2002 #15 Matt Kenseth
2002 #41 Matt Kenseth's Car
2002 #63 Matt Kenseth CH
2003 #14 Matt Kenseth
2003 #42 Matt Kenseth's Car
2003 #62 Matt Kenseth CC
Press Pass Premium Reflectors
1999 #R46 Matt Kenseth
2000 #33 Matt Kenseth
2000 #44 Matt Kenseth
2000 #55 Matt Kenseth
Press Pass Premium Samples
2002 #15 Matt Kenseth
2002 #41 Matt Kenseth's Car
2003 #14 Matt Kenseth
2003 #42 Matt Kenseth's Car
2004 #8 Matt Kenseth
2004 #41 Matt Kenseth's Car
2005 #13 Matt Kenseth
Press Pass Premium Target
2008 #TA1 Matt Kenseth
Press Pass Premium Team Signed Baseballs
2008 #ROU Carl Edwards Matt Kenseth Jamie McMurray#David Ragan
2008 #E-ROU Carl Edwards Matt Kenseth Jamie McMurray#David Ragan Entry Card
Press Pass Previews
2003 #17 Matt Kenseth
2004 #15 Matt Kenseth
2006 #EB13 Matt Kenseth
2006 #EB105 Matt Kenseth U
2007 #EB1 Matt Kenseth
2007 #EB108 Matt Kenseth TT
2008 #EB4 Matt Kenseth
2008 #EB114 Matt Kenseth Top 12
Press Pass Previews Green
2005 #EB12 Matt Kenseth
Press Pass Race Day
2008 #RD9 Matt Kenseth
Press Pass Samples
2003 #17 Matt Kenseth
2003 #63 Jr./JJ/New/Sad/Ken/Bus DS
2003 #74 Rock Steady WCS
2003 #76 Texas Tornado WCS
2003 #81 Pit Bulls WCS
2003 #95 Matt Kenseth's Car OTW
2004 #15 Matt Kenseth
2004 #80 The Drive for Five WCS
2004 #86 Quiet Confidence WCS
2004 #97 Matt Kenseth DS
2004 #100 Matt Kenseth Schedule
2005 #12 Matt Kenseth
2005 #74 Matt Kenseth NS
Press Pass Showcar
2004 #S3B Matt Kenseth's Car
Press Pass Showman
2004 #S3A Matt Kenseth
Press Pass Showman/Showcar
2001 #S3A Matt Kenseth
2001 #S3B Matt Kenseth's Car
Press Pass Signings
1999 #29A Matt Kenseth Blue/500
1999 #29B Matt Kenseth Black/155
2000 #30 Matt Kenseth
2001 #27 Matt Kenseth P/T/N/S
2002 #33 Matt Kenseth O/P/S/T/V
2003 #38 Matt Kenseth O/P/S/T/V
2004 #36 Matt Kenseth BGN O/V
2004 #37 M.Kenseth NCS O/P/S/T/V
2005 #29 Matt Kenseth BGN
2005 #30 Matt Kenseth NC P/S
2006 #27 Matt Kenseth NC P/S
2007 #34 Matt Kenseth NC
2008 #31 Matt Kenseth
Press Pass Signings Blue
2007 #15 Matt Kenseth NC
2008 #15 Matt Kenseth
Press Pass Signings Gold
1999 #11 Matt Kenseth/100
2000 #16 Matt Kenseth
2001 #18 Matt Kenseth P/T/N/S
2002 #31 Matt Kenseth O/P/S/T/V
2003 #38 Matt Kenseth O/P/S/T/V
2004 #33 Matt Kenseth BGN O/V
2004 #34 M.Kenseth NCS O/P/S/T/V
2005 #28 Matt Kenseth P/S
2006 #24 Matt Kenseth NC P/S
2007 #27 Matt Kenseth NC
2008 #25 Matt Kenseth
Press Pass Signings Platinum
2005 #28 Matt Kenseth NC P/S
Press Pass Signings Press Plates Black
2007 #24 Matt Kenseth
2008 #23 Matt Kenseth
Press Pass Signings Press Plates Cyan
2007 #23 Matt Kenseth
2008 #23 Matt Kenseth
Press Pass Signings Press Plates Magenta
2007 #25 Matt Kenseth
2008 #23 Matt Kenseth
Press Pass Signings Press Plates Yellow
2007 #23 Matt Kenseth
2008 #23 Matt Kenseth
Press Pass Signings Silver
2006 #27 Matt Kenseth NC P/S
2007 #26 Matt Kenseth NC
2008 #22 Matt Kenseth
Press Pass Signings Transparent
2001 #5 Matt Kenseth P/T/N/S
2002 #5 Matt Kenseth O
2004 #4 Matt Kenseth O/P/S/T
Press Pass Skidmarks
1999 #38 Matt Kenseth
1999 #62 Matt Kenseth YR
Press Pass Snapshots
2003 #SN12 Matt Kenseth
2004 #SN12 Matt Kenseth
2005 #SN14 Matt Kenseth
2007 #SN15 Matt Kenseth
Press Pass Speedway
2008 #24 Matt Kenseth
Press Pass Speedway Blur
2008 #B2 Matt Kenseth
Press Pass Speedway Cockpit
2008 #CP11 Matt Kenseth
Press Pass Speedway Corporate Cuts Drivers
2008 #CD-MK Matt Kenseth
Press Pass Speedway Corporate Cuts Drivers Patches
2008 #CD-MK Matt Kenseth/12
Press Pass Speedway Corporate Cuts Team
2008 #CT-MK Matt Kenseth
Press Pass Speedway Gold
2008 #G24 Matt Kenseth
Press Pass Speedway Holofoil
2008 #H24 Matt Kenseth
Press Pass Speedway Previews
2008 #EB24 Matt Kenseth
Press Pass Speedway Red
2008 #R24 Matt Kenseth
Press Pass Stealth
1999 #43 Matt Kenseth RC
2000 #22 Matt Kenseth CRC
2000 #23 Matt Kenseth's Car
2000 #57 Matt Kenseth BGN
2002 #16 Matt Kenseth
2002 #17 Matt Kenseth's Car
2002 #18 Matt Kenseth
2002 #56 Matt Kenseth's Car SST
2003 #16 Matt Kenseth
2003 #17 Matt Kenseth's Car
2003 #18 Matt Kenseth
2004 #37 Matt Kenseth
2004 #38 Matt Kenseth's Car
2004 #39 Matt Kenseth
2004 #85 Matt Kenseth SST
2004 #97 Matt Kenseth SF
2005 #21 Matt Kenseth
2005 #24 Matt Kenseth's Car
2005 #27 Matt Kenseth
2005 #94 Matt Kenseth SF
2006 #15 Matt Kenseth
2006 #41 Matt Kenseth's Rig
2006 #48 17/6/16/26/99 TM
2006 #74 Matt Kenseth DD
2007 #14 Matt Kenseth
2007 #50 Matt Kenseth's Rig
2007 #69 Edwards/Biffle/Kenseth/McMurray/Ragan
2007 #85 Matt Kenseth PO
2008 #18 Matt Kenseth
2008 #49 Matt Kenseth's Rig C
2008 #70 Greg Biffle Jamie McMurray Carl Edwards Matt Kenseth David Ragan
2008 #79 Matt Kenseth DO
Press Pass Stealth Autographed Hat Entry
2006 #PPH13 Matt Kenseth
Press Pass Stealth Battle Armor Autographs
2007 #BAS-MK Matt Kenseth/17
2007 #BASMK Matt Kenseth/17
Press Pass Stealth Battle Armor Drivers
2007 #BAD13 Matt Kenseth
2008 #BAD14 Matt Kenseth
Press Pass Stealth Battle Armor Teams
2007 #BAT13 Matt Kenseth
2008 #BAT14 Matt Kenseth
Press Pass Stealth Behind the Numbers
2000 #BN1 Matt Kenseth
Press Pass Stealth Chrome
2007 #14 Matt Kenseth
2007 #50 Matt Kenseth's Rig
2007 #69 Edwards/Biffle/Kenseth/McMurray/Ragan
2007 #85 Matt Kenseth PO
2008 #18 Matt Kenseth
2008 #49 Matt Kenseth's Rig C
2008 #70 Greg Biffle Jamie McMurray Carl Edwards Matt Kenseth David Ragan
2008 #79 Matt Kenseth DO
Press Pass Stealth Chrome Exclusives
2007 #X14 Matt Kenseth
2007 #X50 Matt Kenseth's Rig
2007 #X69 Edwards/Biffle/Kenseth/McMurray/Ragan
2007 #X85 Matt Kenseth PO
2008 #18 Matt Kenseth
2008 #49 Matt Kenseth's Rig C
2008 #70 Greg Biffle Jamie McMurray Carl Edwards Matt Kenseth David Ragan
2008 #79 Matt Kenseth DO
Press Pass Stealth Chrome Exclusives Gold
2008 #18 Matt Kenseth
2008 #49 Matt Kenseth's Rig C
2008 #70 Greg Biffle Jamie McMurray Carl Edwards Matt Kenseth David Ragan
2008 #79 Matt Kenseth DO
Press Pass Stealth Chrome Platinum
2007 #P14 Matt Kenseth
2007 #P50 Matt Kenseth's Rig
2007 #P69 Edwards/Biffle/Kenseth/McMurray/Ragan
2007 #P85 Matt Kenseth PO
Press Pass Stealth Corporate Cuts
2006 #CCD9 Matt Kenseth
Press Pass Stealth EFX
2004 #EF12 Matt Kenseth
2005 #EFX12 Matt Kenseth
2006 #EFX11 Matt Kenseth 1:14
Press Pass Stealth Fusion
1999 #F43 Matt Kenseth
2000 #FS19 Matt Kenseth
2000 #FS20 Matt Kenseth's Car
2000 #FS21 Matt Kenseth
2005 #FU8 Matt Kenseth 1:48
Press Pass Stealth Fusion Green
2000 #FS19 Matt Kenseth
2000 #FS20 Matt Kenseth
2000 #FS21 Matt Kenseth
Press Pass Stealth Fusion Red
2000 #FS19 Matt Kenseth
2000 #FS20 Matt Kenseth
2000 #FS21 Matt Kenseth
Press Pass Stealth Gear Grippers Autographs
2004 #HT-MK Matt Kenseth/17
2006 #MK Matt Kenseth/17
Press Pass Stealth Gear Grippers Cars
2005 #GGT2 Matt Kenseth
Press Pass Stealth Gear Grippers Cars Autographs
2003 #MK Matt Kenseth/17
Press Pass Stealth Gear Grippers Drivers
2004 #GGD2 Matt Kenseth
2005 #GGD2 Matt Kenseth
2006 #GGD7 Matt Kenseth
Press Pass Stealth Gear Grippers Drivers Autographs
2003 #MK Matt Kenseth/17
Press Pass Stealth Gear Grippers Drivers Retail
2004 #GGT2 Matt Kenseth
Press Pass Stealth Gold
2002 #16 Matt Kenseth
2002 #17 Matt Kenseth's Car
2002 #18 Matt Kenseth
2002 #56 Matt Kenseth's Car SST
Press Pass Stealth Hot Pass
2006 #HP16 Matt Kenseth
Press Pass Stealth Lap Leaders
2001 #LL6 Matt Kenseth
2001 #LL24 Matt Kenseth's Car
2002 #LL14 Matt Kenseth
Press Pass Stealth Lap Leaders Clear Cars
2001 #LL24 Matt Kenseth's Car
Press Pass Stealth Lap Leaders Clear Drivers
2001 #LL6 Matt Kenseth
Press Pass Stealth Maximum Access
2007 #MA15 Matt Kenseth
2008 #MA15 Matt Kenseth
Press Pass Stealth Maximum Access Autographs
2007 #MA15 Matt Kenseth
2008 #MA15 Matt Kenseth
Press Pass Stealth No Boundaries
2003 #NB15 Matt Kenseth
2004 #NB16 Matt Kenseth
2005 #NB10 Matt Kenseth
Press Pass Stealth Previews
2003 #16 Matt Kenseth
2003 #17 Matt Kenseth's Car
2003 #18 Matt Kenseth
2005 #21 Matt Kenseth
2005 #24 Matt Kenseth's Car
2005 #27 Matt Kenseth
2006 #15 Matt Kenseth
2007 #EB14 Matt Kenseth
2007 #EB85 Matt Kenseth PO
2008 #18 Matt Kenseth
Press Pass Stealth Profile
2000 #PR7 Matt Kenseth
2002 #P5 Matt Kenseth
2004 #P5 Matt Kenseth 1:48
Press Pass Stealth Race Used Glove Cars
2001 #RGC7 Matt Kenseth/120
2002 #GLC6 Matt Kenseth's Car
Press Pass Stealth Race Used Glove Drivers
2001 #RGD7 Matt Kenseth/120
2002 #GLD6 Matt Kenseth
Press Pass Stealth Race Used Gloves
2000 #G9 Matt Kenseth/100
Press Pass Stealth Red
2003 #P16 Matt Kenseth
2003 #P17 Matt Kenseth's Car
2003 #P18 Matt Kenseth
Press Pass Stealth Retail
2006 #15 Matt Kenseth
2006 #41 Matt Kenseth's Rig
2006 #48 17/6/16/26/99 TM
2006 #74 Matt Kenseth DD
Press Pass Stealth Retail Gear Grippers Cars
2006 #GGT7 Matt Kenseth
Press Pass Stealth Samples
2002 #16 Matt Kenseth
2002 #17 Matt Kenseth's Car
2002 #18 Matt Kenseth
2002 #56 Matt Kenseth's Car SST
2003 #16 Matt Kenseth
2003 #17 Matt Kenseth's Car
2003 #18 Matt Kenseth
2004 #X37 Matt Kenseth
2004 #X38 Matt Kenseth's Car
2004 #X39 Matt Kenseth
2004 #X85 Matt Kenseth SST
2004 #X97 Matt Kenseth SF
2005 #21 Matt Kenseth
2005 #24 Matt Kenseth's Car
2005 #27 Matt Kenseth
2005 #94 Matt Kenseth SF
Press Pass Stealth SST
2000 #SST7 Matt Kenseth
Press Pass Stealth Synthesis
2008 #S5 Matt Kenseth
Press Pass Stealth X-Ray
2004 #37 Matt Kenseth
2004 #38 Matt Kenseth's Car
2004 #39 Matt Kenseth
2004 #85 Matt Kenseth SST
2004 #97 Matt Kenseth SF
2005 #X21 Matt Kenseth
2005 #X24 Matt Kenseth's Car
2005 #X27 Matt Kenseth
2005 #X94 Matt Kenseth SF
2006 #X15 Matt Kenseth
2006 #X41 Matt Kenseth's Rig
2006 #X48 17/6/16/26/99 TM
2006 #X74 Matt Kenseth DD
Press Pass Target Race Win Tires
2007 #RW9 Matt Kenseth Bristol 8-26
Press Pass Target Victory Tires
2008 #TT-MK Matt Kenseth California
Press Pass Top 25 Drivers & Rides
2006 #C11 Matt Kenseth's Car
2006 #D11 Matt Kenseth
Press Pass Top Shelf
2004 #TS1 Matt Kenseth
Press Pass Top Ten
2005 #TT5 Matt Kenseth
Press Pass Total Memorabilia
2001 #TM7 Matt Kenseth
Press Pass Total Memorabilia Power Pick
2003 #TM7 Matt Kenseth
2004 #TM7 Matt Kenseth
2005 #TM7 Matt Kenseth
Press Pass Trackside
2000 #22 Matt Kenseth CRC
2001 #22 Matt Kenseth
2001 #45 Matt Kenseth's Car
2002 #22 Matt Kenseth
2002 #69 Matt Kenseth's Car
2002 #77 Matt Kenseth TM
2003 #5 Matt Kenseth
2003 #78 Mart/J.Bur/Bif/Kens/Bus TM
2004 #16 Matt Kenseth
2004 #68 Burt/Kens/Mart/Busch/Bif. TM
2004 #117 Matt Kenseth F
2005 #30 Matt Kenseth
2005 #93 Matt Kenseth GP
Press Pass Trackside Dialed In
2000 #DI7 Matt Kenseth
2005 #DI7 Matt Kenseth
Press Pass Trackside Die Cuts
2000 #22 Matt Kenseth
2001 #22 Matt Kenseth
2001 #45 Matt Kenseth's Car
Press Pass Trackside Generation Now
2002 #GN6 Matt Kenseth
Press Pass Trackside Generation.now
2000 #GN1 Matt Kenseth
Press Pass Trackside Gold Holofoil
2003 #P5 Matt Kenseth
2003 #P78 Martin/J.Burton/Biffle/Kenseth/Busch
Press Pass Trackside Golden
2000 #22 Matt Kenseth
2001 #22 Matt Kenseth
2001 #45 Matt Kenseth's Car
2002 #G22 Matt Kenseth
2003 #G5 Matt Kenseth
2004 #G16 Matt Kenseth
2004 #G68 Burt/Kens/Mart/Busch/Biffle TM
2004 #G117 Matt Kenseth F
2005 #G30 Matt Kenseth
2005 #G93 Matt Kenseth GP
Press Pass Trackside Hat Giveaway
2003 #PPH13 Matt Kenseth
2004 #PPH38 Matt Kenseth
2005 #PPH14 Matt Kenseth
Press Pass Trackside Hot Pass
2005 #9 Matt Kenseth
Press Pass Trackside Hot Pass National
2005 #9 Matt Kenseth
Press Pass Trackside Hot Pursuit
2004 #HP6 Matt Kenseth
2005 #HP3 Matt Kenseth
Press Pass Trackside License to Drive
2002 #17 Matt Kenseth
Press Pass Trackside License to Drive Die Cuts
2002 #17 Matt Kenseth
Press Pass Trackside Panorama
2000 #P33 Matt Kenseth
Press Pass Trackside Pit Stoppers
2000 #PS11 Matt Kenseth
Press Pass Trackside Pit Stoppers Autographs
2004 #PS-MK Matt Kenseth/17
Press Pass Trackside Pit Stoppers Cars
2001 #PSC9 Matt Kenseth's Car/250
2002 #PSC13 Matt Kenseth's Car/60
2003 #PST16 Matt Kenseth/10
2004 #PST14 Matt Kenseth/20
2005 #PST10 Matt Kenseth
Press Pass Trackside Pit Stoppers Cars Autographs
2003 #MK Matt Kenseth/17
Press Pass Trackside Pit Stoppers Drivers
2001 #PSD9 Matt Kenseth/100
2002 #PSD13 Matt Kenseth/60
2003 #PSD16 Matt Kenseth/10
2004 #PSD14 Matt Kenseth/20
2005 #PSD10 Matt Kenseth
Press Pass Trackside Pit Stoppers Drivers Autographs
2003 #PSD-MK Matt Kenseth/17
Press Pass Trackside Previews
2003 #5 Matt Kenseth
2004 #EB16 Matt Kenseth
2005 #30 Matt Kenseth
2005 #93 Matt Kenseth GP
Press Pass Trackside Runnin N' Gunnin
2002 #RG5 Matt Kenseth
2003 #RG12 Matt Kenseth
2004 #RG12 Matt Kenseth
2005 #RG7 Matt Kenseth
Press Pass Trackside Samples
2002 #22 Matt Kenseth
2002 #69 Matt Kenseth's Car
2002 #77 Matt Kenseth TM
2003 #5 Matt Kenseth
2003 #78 Mart/J.Bur/Bif/Kens/Bus TM
2004 #16 Matt Kenseth
2004 #68 Burt/Kens/Mart/Busch/Biffle TM
2004 #117 Matt Kenseth F
2005 #30 Matt Kenseth
2005 #93 Matt Kenseth GP
Press Pass Triple Burner
2001 #TB7 Matt Kenseth
2003 #TB7 Matt Kenseth
2004 #TB7 Matt Kenseth
2005 #TB7 Matt Kenseth
Press Pass Triple Burner Exchange
2003 #TB7 Matt Kenseth EXCH
2004 #TB7 Matt Kenseth
2005 #TB7 Matt Kenseth
Press Pass UMI Cup Chase
2005 #1 Cup Chase Drivers CL
2005 #9 Matt Kenseth
Press Pass Velocity
2001 #VL4 Matt Kenseth
2004 #VC5 Matt Kenseth
2005 #V5 Matt Kenseth
2007 #V3 Matt Kenseth
Press Pass Victory Lap
2003 #15 Matt Kenseth
Press Pass Vintage
2001 #VN13 Matt Kenseth
2002 #VN11 Matt Kenseth
Press Pass Wal-Mart Autographs
2007 #MK Matt Kenseth
2008 #7 Matt Kenseth
SP Authentic
2000 #21 Matt Kenseth CRC
2000 #90 Matt Kenseth SUP
SP Authentic Dominance
2000 #D3 Matt Kenseth
SP Authentic Driver's Seat
2000 #DS7 Matt Kenseth
SP Authentic Overdrive Gold
2000 #21 Matt Kenseth/17
2000 #90 Matt Kenseth SUP/17
SP Authentic Overdrive Silver
2000 #21 Matt Kenseth
2000 #90 Matt Kenseth SUP
SP Authentic Power Surge
2000 #PS5 Matt Kenseth
SP Authentic Sign of the Times
2000 #MK Matt Kenseth
SP Authentic Sign of the Times Gold
2000 #MK Matt Kenseth
Sports Illustrated for Kids
2003 #324 Matt Kenseth Racing
Sports Illustrated for Kids *
2003 #324 Matt Kenseth
TRAKS
2006 #17 Matt Kenseth
2006 #45 Matt Kenseth's Car
2006 #104 Matt Kenseth's Car PS
2007 #14 Matt Kenseth
2007 #85 Matt Kenseth's Car NFS
2007 #98 Matt Kenseth FT
TRAKS Autographs
2006 #19 Matt Kenseth NC SP
TRAKS Autographs 25
2006 #17 Matt Kenseth NC
Traks Corporate Cuts Driver
2007 #CCD5 Matt Kenseth
Traks Corporate Cuts Patch
2007 #CCD5 Matt Kenseth/12
Traks Corporate Cuts Team
2007 #CCT5 Matt Kenseth
Traks Driver's Seat
2007 #DS11 Matt Kenseth
2007 #DS11B Matt Kenseth VAR
Traks Driver's Seat National
2007 #DS11 Matt Kenseth
Traks Gold
2007 #G14 Matt Kenseth
2007 #G85 Matt Kenseth's Car NFS
2007 #G98 Matt Kenseth FT
Traks Holofoil
2007 #H14 Matt Kenseth
2007 #H85 Matt Kenseth's Car NFS
2007 #H98 Matt Kenseth FT
Traks Hot Pursuit
2007 #HP11 Matt Kenseth
Traks Previews
2007 #EB14 Matt Kenseth
Traks Red
2007 #R14 Matt Kenseth
2007 #R85 Matt Kenseth's Car NFS
2007 #R98 Matt Kenseth FT
TRAKS Stickers
2006 #17 Matt Kenseth
Upper Deck MVP
2000 #34 Matt Kenseth CRC
2000 #76 Matt Kenseth's Car
2000 #99 Matt Kenseth
Upper Deck MVP Gold Script
2000 #34 Matt Kenseth
2000 #76 Matt Kenseth
2000 #99 Matt Kenseth
Upper Deck MVP Legends in the Making
2000 #LM2 Matt Kenseth
Upper Deck MVP Magic Numbers
2000 #MMK Matt Kenseth's Car
Upper Deck MVP Magic Numbers Autographs
2000 #MAMK M.Kenseth's Car/17
Upper Deck MVP NASCAR Gallery
2000 #NG6 Matt Kenseth
Upper Deck MVP NASCAR Stars
2000 #NS9 Matt Kenseth
Upper Deck MVP ProSign
1999 #MKH Matt Kenseth Gold
1999 #MKR Matt Kenseth Silver
2000 #PSMK Matt Kenseth
Upper Deck MVP Silver Script
2000 #34 Matt Kenseth
2000 #76 Matt Kenseth
2000 #99 Matt Kenseth
Upper Deck MVP Super Script
2000 #34 Matt Kenseth/17
2000 #76 Matt Kenseth's Car/17
2000 #99 Matt Kenseth/17
Upper Deck Racing
2000 #32 Matt Kenseth CRC
Upper Deck Racing High Groove
2000 #HG3 Matt Kenseth
Upper Deck Racing Record Pace
2000 #RP8 Matt Kenseth
Upper Deck Racing Road Signs
2000 #RSMK Matt Kenseth
Upper Deck Racing Tear Aways
2000 #TAMK Matt Kenseth
Upper Deck Racing Trophy Dash
2000 #TD4 Matt Kenseth
Upper Deck Victory Circle
2000 #31 Matt Kenseth CRC
2000 #61 Matt Kenseth's Car
2000 #83 Matt Kenseth
Upper Deck Victory Circle Exclusives Level 1 Silver
2000 #31 Matt Kenseth
2000 #61 Matt Kenseth's Car
2000 #83 Matt Kenseth
Upper Deck Victory Circle Exclusives Level 2 Gold
2000 #31 Matt Kenseth/17
2000 #61 Matt Kenseth's Car/17
2000 #83 Matt Kenseth/17
Upper Deck Victory Circle Income Statement
2000 #IS9 Matt Kenseth
Upper Deck Victory Circle Income Statement LTD
2000 #IS9 Matt Kenseth
Upper Deck Victory Circle Signature Collection
2000 #MK Matt Kenseth
Upper Deck Victory Circle Victory Circle
2000 #V2 Matt Kenseth
Upper Deck Victory Circle Victory Circle LTD
2000 #V2 Matt Kenseth
Upper Deck Victory Circle Winning Material Combination
2000 #CMK Matt Kenseth
Upper Deck Victory Circle Winning Material Firesuit
2000 #FSMK Matt Kenseth
Upper Deck Victory Circle Winning Material Tire
2000 #TMK Matt Kenseth
VIP
1999 #33 Matt Kenseth RC
2000 #18 Matt Kenseth CRC
2001 #38 Matt Kenseth RT
2002 #7 Matt Kenseth
2002 #20 Matt Kenseth SG
2002 #24 Matt Kenseth SG
2003 #9 Matt Kenseth
2003 #21 Matt Kenseth SG
2004 #9 Matt Kenseth
2004 #44 Matt Kenseth SG
2004 #45 Matt Kenseth SG
2005 #13 Matt Kenseth
2005 #34 Matt Kenseth's Car R
2006 #13 Matt Kenseth
2006 #34 Matt Kenseth's Car R
2006 #41 Matt Kenseth SG
2007 #16 Matt Kenseth
2007 #65 Matt Kenseth Red C
2007 #70 Matt Kenseth California AP
VIP Explosives
1999 #X33 Matt Kenseth
2000 #X18 Matt Kenseth
2001 #38 Matt Kenseth RT
2002 #X7 Matt Kenseth
2002 #X20 Matt Kenseth SG
2002 #X24 Matt Kenseth SG
2003 #X9 Matt Kenseth
2003 #X21 Matt Kenseth SG
VIP Explosives Lasers
1999 #33 Matt Kenseth
2000 #LX18 Matt Kenseth
2001 #LX38 Matt Kenseth RT
2002 #LX7 Matt Kenseth
2002 #LX20 Matt Kenseth SG
2002 #LX24 Matt Kenseth SG
VIP Get A Grip Autographs
2007 #GG-MK Matt Kenseth/17
VIP Get A Grip Drivers
2007 #GGD10 Matt Kenseth
VIP Get A Grip Teams
2007 #GGT10 Matt Kenseth
VIP Head Gear
2004 #HG6 Matt Kenseth
2005 #6 Matt Kenseth
VIP Head Gear Transparent
2004 #HG6 Matt Kenseth
2005 #6 Matt Kenseth
VIP Lap Leaders
2005 #5 Matt Kenseth
VIP Lap Leaders Transparent
2005 #5 Matt Kenseth
VIP Laser Explosive
2003 #LX9 Matt Kenseth
2003 #LX21 Matt Kenseth SG
VIP Making the Show
2000 #MS13 Matt Kenseth
2001 #8 Matt Kenseth
2002 #MS8 Matt Kenseth
2004 #MS11 Matt Kenseth
2005 #9 Matt Kenseth
2006 #MS3 Matt Kenseth
VIP Previews
2003 #9 Matt Kenseth
2003 #21 Matt Kenseth SG
2004 #EB9 Matt Kenseth
2004 #EB44 Matt Kenseth SG
2004 #EB45 Matt Kenseth SG
2005 #EB13 Matt Kenseth
2005 #EB34 Matt Kenseth's Car R
2007 #EB16 Matt Kenseth
VIP Race Used Sheet Metal Cars
2002 #SC10 Matt Kenseth's Car
VIP Race Used Sheet Metal Drivers
2002 #SD10 Matt Kenseth
VIP Samples
2002 #7 Matt Kenseth
2002 #20 Matt Kenseth SG
2002 #24 Matt Kenseth SG
2003 #9 Matt Kenseth
2003 #21 Matt Kenseth SG
2004 #9 Matt Kenseth
2004 #44 Matt Kenseth SG
2004 #45 Matt Kenseth SG
2005 #13 Matt Kenseth
2005 #34 Matt Kenseth's Car R
VIP Sheet Metal Cars
2001 #SC12 Matt Kenseth's Car
VIP Sheet Metal Drivers
2001 #SD12 Matt Kenseth
VIP Sunday Best
2007 #SB13 Matt Kenseth
VIP Tin
2003 #CT9 Matt Kenseth
2003 #CT21 Matt Kenseth SG
VIP Tradin' Paint Autographs

2005 #MK Matt Kenseth/17
VIP Tradin' Paint Bronze
2004 #TPT7 Matt Kenseth
VIP Tradin' Paint Car Autographs
2003 #MK Matt Kenseth/17
VIP Tradin' Paint Cars
2003 #TPT7 Matt Kenseth's Car
2005 #TPT7 Matt Kenseth
VIP Tradin' Paint Driver Autographs
2003 #MK Matt Kenseth/17
VIP Tradin' Paint Drivers
2003 #TPD7 Matt Kenseth
2005 #TPD7 Matt Kenseth
VIP Tradin' Paint Gold
2004 #TPD7 Matt Kenseth
VIP Tradin' Paint Silver
2004 #TPD7 Matt Kenseth
Wheels
1999 #46 Matt Kenseth BGN RC
1999 #98 Matt Kenseth TP
Wheels American Thunder
2003 #11 Matt Kenseth
2003 #40 Matt Kenseth CC
2004 #12 Matt Kenseth
2004 #37 Matt Kenseth AS
2004 #60 Matt Kenseth DT
2005 #14 Matt Kenseth
2005 #39 Matt Kenseth AS
2006 #15 Matt Kenseth
2006 #31 Matt Kenseth DT
2006 #82 Matt Kenseth NN
2007 #16 Matt Kenseth
2007 #43 Matt Kenseth's Car DT
Wheels American Thunder American Dreams
2007 #AD2 Matt Kenseth
Wheels American Thunder American Dreams Gold
2007 #ADG2 Matt Kenseth
Wheels American Thunder American Eagle
2003 #AE4 Matt Kenseth
Wheels American Thunder American Muscle
2007 #AM3 Matt Kenseth
Wheels American Thunder American Racing Idol
2006 #RI11 Matt Kenseth
Wheels American Thunder American Racing Idol Golden
2006 #RI11 Matt Kenseth
Wheels American Thunder Autographed Hat Instant Winner
2007 #AH17 Matt Kenseth
Wheels American Thunder Born On
2003 #BO11 Matt Kenseth
2003 #BO40 Matt Kenseth CC
Wheels American Thunder Cool Threads
2004 #CT6 Matt Kenseth
2005 #CT5 Matt Kenseth
2006 #CT14 Matt Kenseth
2007 #CT15 Matt Kenseth
Wheels American Thunder Double Hat
2006 #DH13 Matt Kenseth
Wheels American Thunder Golden Eagle
2003 #AEG4 Matt Kenseth
Wheels American Thunder Grandstand
2006 #GS12 Matt Kenseth
Wheels American Thunder Head to Toe
2003 #HT3 Matt Kenseth
2004 #HT5 Matt Kenseth
2005 #HT11 Matt Kenseth
2006 #HT11 Matt Kenseth
2007 #HT13 Matt Kenseth
Wheels American Thunder Heads Up Goodyear
2003 #HUG5 Matt Kenseth
Wheels American Thunder Heads Up Manufacturer
2003 #HUM10 Matt Kenseth
Wheels American Thunder Heads Up Team
2003 #HUT9 Matt Kenseth/90
Wheels American Thunder Heads Up Winston
2003 #HUW10 Matt Kenseth
Wheels American Thunder Holofoil
2003 #P11 Matt Kenseth
2003 #P40 Matt Kenseth CC
Wheels American Thunder Post Mark
2003 #PM10 Matt Kenseth
2004 #PM11 Matt Kenseth
Wheels American Thunder Previews
2003 #11 Matt Kenseth
2004 #EB12 Matt Kenseth
2004 #EB37 Matt Kenseth AS
2005 #14 Matt Kenseth
2006 #EB15 Matt Kenseth
2007 #EB16 Matt Kenseth
Wheels American Thunder Pushin Pedal
2003 #PP4 Matt Kenseth
2004 #PP10 Matt Kenseth
2005 #PP14 Matt Kenseth
Wheels American Thunder Rookie Thunder
2003 #RT15 Matt Kenseth
Wheels American Thunder Samples
2003 #P11 Matt Kenseth
2003 #P40 Matt Kenseth CC
2004 #12 Matt Kenseth
2004 #37 Matt Kenseth AS
2004 #60 Matt Kenseth DT
2005 #14 Matt Kenseth
2005 #39 Matt Kenseth AS
Wheels American Thunder Thunder Road
2003 #TR9 Matt Kenseth
2004 #TR8 Matt Kenseth
2006 #TR17 Matt Kenseth
2007 #TR14 Matt Kenseth
Wheels American Thunder Thunder Strokes
2007 #22 Matt Kenseth
Wheels American Thunder Thunder Strokes Press Plates Black
2007 #22 Matt Kenseth
Wheels American Thunder Thunder Strokes Press Plates Cyan
2007 #22 Matt Kenseth
Wheels American Thunder Thunder Strokes Press Plates Magenta
2007 #22 Matt Kenseth
Wheels American Thunder Thunder Strokes Press Plates Yellow
2007 #22 Matt Kenseth
Wheels American Thunder Triple Hat
2004 #TH8 Matt Kenseth
2005 #TH11 Matt Kenseth
2007 #TH15 Matt Kenseth
Wheels Autographs
2003 #28 Matt Kenseth AT/HG
2004 #36 Matt Kenseth HG
2005 #30 Matt Kenseth BGN
2005 #31 Matt Kenseth NC
2006 #30 Matt Kenseth NBS
2006 #31 Matt Kenseth NC
2007 #19 Matt Kenseth NC HG
2008 #18 Matt Kenseth NC HG
Wheels Autographs Chase Edition
2008 #7 Matt Kenseth NC
Wheels Autographs Press Plates Black
2007 #18 Matt Kenseth NC
2008 #18 Matt Kenseth NC HG
Wheels Autographs Press Plates Cyan
2007 #18 Matt Kenseth NC
2008 #18 Matt Kenseth NC HG
Wheels Autographs Press Plates Magenta
2007 #18 Matt Kenseth NC
2008 #18 Matt Kenseth NC HG
Wheels Autographs Press Plates Yellow
2007 #19 Matt Kenseth NC
2008 #18 Matt Kenseth NC HG
Wheels Golden
1999 #46 Matt Kenseth
1999 #98 Matt Kenseth
Wheels High Gear
1999 #38 Matt Kenseth RC
2000 #38 Matt Kenseth
2000 #66 Matt Kenseth
2001 #11 Matt Kenseth
2001 #29 Matt Kenseth WCM
2001 #40 Matt Kenseth BGN
2001 #55 Matt Kenseth HL
2001 #59 Matt Kenseth CA
2002 #11 Matt Kenseth
2003 #15 Matt Kenseth
2003 #35 Matt Kenseth's Car
2003 #58 The Fab Four
2004 #12 Matt Kenseth
2004 #46 Matt Kenseth NA
2004 #49 Matt Kenseth NA
2004 #60 Matt Kenseth's Car
2004 #0 Matt Kenseth Champ
2005 #10 Matt Kenseth
2005 #51 Matt Kenseth A
2005 #56 Matt Kenseth's Car
2005 #64 Matt Kenseth NI
2005 #90 Kenseth/Busch/Martin CL
2006 #7 Matt Kenseth
2006 #49 Matt Kenseth's Car C
2007 #2 Matt Kenseth
2007 #58 Matt Kenseth NA
2007 #70 Matt Kenseth CM
2008 #4 Matt Kenseth
2008 #46 Matt Kenseth's Car C
2008 #59 Matt Kenseth NA
2008 #66 Matt Kenseth's Car EL
Wheels High Gear Autographs
2000 #16 Matt Kenseth
2001 #18 Matt Kenseth
2002 #28 Matt Kenseth
Wheels High Gear Blue Hawaii SCDA Promos
2003 #15 Matt Kenseth
2003 #35 Matt Kenseth's Car
2003 #58 The Fab Four
Wheels High Gear Custom Shop
2001 #CSMK Matt Kenseth EXCH
Wheels High Gear Custom Shop Prizes
2001 #MKA1 Matt Kenseth
2001 #MKA2 Matt Kenseth
2001 #MKA3 Matt Kenseth
2001 #MKB1 Matt Kenseth
2001 #MKB2 Matt Kenseth
2001 #MKB3 Matt Kenseth
2001 #MKC1 Matt Kenseth
2001 #MKC2 Matt Kenseth
2001 #MKC3 Matt Kenseth
Wheels High Gear Driven
2007 #DR8 Matt Kenseth
2008 #DR19 Matt Kenseth
Wheels High Gear Final Standings
2008 #F4 Matt Kenseth/4
Wheels High Gear Final Standings Gold
2007 #FS2 Matt Kenseth/2
Wheels High Gear First Gear
1999 #38 Matt Kenseth
2000 #38 Matt Kenseth
2000 #66 Matt Kenseth
2001 #11 Matt Kenseth
2001 #29 Matt Kenseth WCM
2001 #40 Matt Kenseth BGN
2001 #55 Matt Kenseth HL
2001 #59 Matt Kenseth CA
2002 #11 Matt Kenseth
2003 #15 Matt Kenseth
2003 #F35 Matt Kenseth's Car
2003 #F58 The Fab Four
Wheels High Gear Flag Chasers
2001 #FC4 Matt Kenseth
Wheels High Gear Flag Chasers Black
2003 #FC6 Matt Kenseth
2004 #FC9 Matt Kenseth
2007 #FC10 Matt Kenseth
2008 #FC9 Matt Kenseth
Wheels High Gear Flag Chasers Blue
2004 #FC9 Matt Kenseth
Wheels High Gear Flag Chasers Blue-Yellow
2001 #FC4 Matt Kenseth
2003 #FC6 Matt Kenseth
2007 #FC10 Matt Kenseth
2008 #FC9 Matt Kenseth
Wheels High Gear Flag Chasers Checkered
2001 #FC4 Matt Kenseth
2003 #FC6 Matt Kenseth
2004 #FC9 Matt Kenseth
2007 #FC10 Matt Kenseth
2008 #FC9 Matt Kenseth
Wheels High Gear Flag Chasers Checkered Blue/Orange
2001 #FC4 Matt Kenseth
Wheels High Gear Flag Chasers Green
2001 #FC4 Matt Kenseth
2003 #FC6 Matt Kenseth
2004 #FC9 Matt Kenseth
2007 #FC10 Matt Kenseth
2008 #FC9 Matt Kenseth
Wheels High Gear Flag Chasers Power Pick
2001 #FCPP Matt Kenseth
Wheels High Gear Flag Chasers Red
2001 #FC4 Matt Kenseth
2003 #FC6 Matt Kenseth
2004 #FC9 Matt Kenseth
2007 #FC10 Matt Kenseth
2008 #FC9 Matt Kenseth
Wheels High Gear Flag Chasers White
2001 #FC4 Matt Kenseth
2003 #FC6 Matt Kenseth
2004 #FC9 Matt Kenseth
2007 #FC10 Matt Kenseth
2008 #FC9 Matt Kenseth
Wheels High Gear Flag Chasers Yellow
2001 #FC4 Matt Kenseth
2003 #FC6 Matt Kenseth
2004 #FC9 Matt Kenseth
2007 #FC10 Matt Kenseth
2008 #FC9 Matt Kenseth
Wheels High Gear Flag to Flag
2005 #FF11 Matt Kenseth
2006 #FF13 Matt Kenseth
Wheels High Gear Full Throttle
2003 #FT9 Matt Kenseth
2004 #FT5 Matt Kenseth
Wheels High Gear Gear Shifters
2000 #GS13 Matt Kenseth
2001 #GS12 Matt Kenseth
Wheels High Gear High Groove
2002 #HG11 Matt Kenseth
2003 #HG13 Matt Kenseth
2004 #HG11 Matt Kenseth
Wheels High Gear Hot Streaks
2001 #HS7 Matt Kenseth
Wheels High Gear Hot Treads
2003 #HT8 Matt Kenseth
Wheels High Gear Last Lap
2007 #LL2 Matt Kenseth
2008 #LL9 Matt Kenseth
Wheels High Gear Last Lap Holofoil
2008 #LL9 Matt Kenseth
Wheels High Gear Machine
2004 #MM7B Matt Kenseth
Wheels High Gear Man
2004 #MM7A Matt Kenseth
Wheels High Gear MPH
1999 #38 Matt Kenseth
2000 #38 Matt Kenseth
2000 #66 Matt Kenseth
2001 #11 Matt Kenseth
2001 #29 Matt Kenseth WCM
2001 #40 Matt Kenseth BGN
2001 #55 Matt Kenseth HL
2001 #59 Matt Kenseth CA
2002 #11 Matt Kenseth
2003 #M15 Matt Kenseth
2003 #M35 Matt Kenseth's Car
2003 #M58 The Fab Four
2004 #M12 Matt Kenseth
2004 #M46 Matt Kenseth NA
2004 #M49 Matt Kenseth NA
2004 #M60 Matt Kenseth's Car
2005 #M10 Matt Kenseth
2005 #M51 Matt Kenseth A
2005 #M56 Matt Kenseth's Car
2005 #M64 Matt Kenseth NI
2005 #M90 Kenseth/Busch/Martin CL
2006 #M7 Matt Kenseth
2006 #M49 Matt Kenseth's Car C
2007 #M2 Matt Kenseth
2007 #M58 Matt Kenseth NA
2007 #M70 Matt Kenseth CM
2008 #M4 Matt Kenseth
2008 #M46 Matt Kenseth's Car C
2008 #M59 Matt Kenseth NA
2008 #M66 Matt Kenseth's Car EL
Wheels High Gear Previews
2003 #15 Matt Kenseth
2004 #12 Matt Kenseth
2004 #46 Matt Kenseth NA
2004 #49 Matt Kenseth NA
2004 #60 Matt Kenseth's Car
2007 #EB2 Matt Kenseth
2007 #EB58 Matt Kenseth NA
2008 #EB4 Matt Kenseth
Wheels High Gear Previews Green
2005 #EB10 Matt Kenseth
2006 #EB7 Matt Kenseth
Wheels High Gear Samples
2003 #15 Matt Kenseth
2003 #35 Matt Kenseth's Car
2003 #58 The Fab Four
2004 #12 Matt Kenseth
2004 #46 Matt Kenseth NA
2004 #49 Matt Kenseth NA
2004 #60 Matt Kenseth's Car
2005 #10 Matt Kenseth
2005 #51 Matt Kenseth A
2005 #56 Matt Kenseth's Car
2005 #64 Matt Kenseth NI
2005 #90 Kenseth/Busch/Martin CL
Wheels High Gear Sunday Sensation
2001 #SS3 Matt Kenseth
2003 #SS1 Matt Kenseth
2004 #SS2 Matt Kenseth
Wheels High Gear The Chase
2008 #TC4 Matt Kenseth
Wheels High Gear Top Ten
2004 #TT1 Matt Kenseth
Wheels High Gear Top Tier
2005 #TT8 Matt Kenseth
2006 #TT7 Matt Kenseth
2007 #TT2 Matt Kenseth
Wheels Runnin and Gunnin
1999 #RG23 Matt Kenseth
Wheels Runnin and Gunnin Foils
1999 #RG23 Matt Kenseth
Wheels Soles
1999 #46 Matt Kenseth
1999 #98 Matt Kenseth
Press Pass Signings Gold
2008 #26 Brad Keselowski
Press Pass Speedway
2008 #39 Brad Keselowski NNS RC
Press Pass Speedway Gold
2008 #G39 Brad Keselowski NNS
Press Pass Speedway Holofoil
2008 #H39 Brad Keselowski NNS
Press Pass Speedway Previews
2008 #EB39 Brad Keselowski NNS
Press Pass Speedway Red
2008 #R39 Brad Keselowski NNS
Press Pass Stealth
2008 #43 Brad Keselowski NNS RC
Press Pass Stealth Chrome
2008 #43 Brad Keselowski NNS RC
Press Pass Stealth Chrome Exclusives
2008 #43 Brad Keselowski NNS
Press Pass Stealth Chrome Exclusives Gold
2008 #43 Brad Keselowski NNS
Press Pass Stealth Previews
2008 #43 Brad Keselowski NNS
Press Pass Top Prospects Gloves
2008 #BK-G Brad Keselowski
Press Pass Top Prospects Metal-Tire
2008 #BK-ST Brad Keselowski
Press Pass Top Prospects Sheet Metal
2008 #BK-SM Brad Keselowski
Press Pass Top Prospects Shoes
2008 #BK-S Brad Keselowski
Press Pass Top Prospects Tires
2008 #BKT Brad Keselowski
Press Pass Top Prospects Tires Autographs
2008 #BK-AT Brad Keselowski
Press Pass Top Prospects Tires Gold
2008 #BKT Brad Keselowski

Labonte, Bobby

Action Packed
1993 #12 Bobby Labonte
1993 #62 Bobby Labonte YG
1993 #63 J.Gordon/Wallace/Lab.YG
1993 #152 Bobby Labonte YG
1993 #155 Bobby Labonte YG
1993 #156 J.Gordon/Wallace/Lab.YG
1993 #162 T.Labonte/B.Labonte B
1993 #166 Bobby Labonte
1993 #184 Bobby Labonte
1994 #19 Bobby Labonte
1994 #85 Bobby Labonte
1994 #130 Bobby Labonte's Car
1994 #150 Bobby Labonte
1997 #18 Bobby Labonte
1997 #39 Bobby Labonte's Car
Action Packed 24K Gold
1993 #11G Bobby Labonte YG
1993 #12G J.Gordon/Wall./Lab.YG
1993 #28G Bobby Labonte YG
1993 #31G Bobby Labonte YG
1993 #32G J.Gordon/Wall./Lab.YG
1993 #66G Bobby Labonte
1994 #39G Bobby Labonte
Action Packed Coastars
1994 #8 Bobby Labonte
Action Packed Country
1995 #1 Bobby Labonte RS
1995 #46 Bobby Labonte WIN
1995 #49 Bobby Labonte WIN
1995 #56 B.Labonte/Gibbs WIN
1995 #68 Bobby Labonte
1995 #P46 Bobby Labonte Promo
Action Packed Country 24K Team
1995 #10 Bobby Labonte
Action Packed Country 2nd Career Choice
1995 #7 Bobby Labonte
Action Packed Country Silver Speed
1995 #1 Bobby Labonte RS
1995 #46 Bobby Labonte WIN
1995 #49 Bobby Labonte WIN
1995 #56 Bobby Labonte/Gibbs WIN
1995 #68 Bobby Labonte
Action Packed Credentials
1996 #29 Bobby Labonte
1996 #60 Bobby Labonte SM
1996 #98 Bobby Labonte WCA
Action Packed Credentials Silver Speed
1996 #29 Bobby Labonte
Action Packed First Impressions
1997 #18 Bobby Labonte
1997 #39 Bobby Labonte's Car
Action Packed Ironman Champion
1997 #2 T.Labonte/B.Labonte
Action Packed McDonald's
1996 #6 Bobby Labonte
1996 #16 Bobby Labonte's Car
Action Packed Mint
1994 #19 Bobby Labonte
1994 #85 Bobby Labonte
1994 #130 Bobby Labonte's Car
1994 #150 Bobby Labonte
Action Packed Preview
1995 #13 Bobby Labonte
Action Packed Stars
1995 #11 Bobby Labonte OC
1995 #86 J.Gordon/B.Labonte/T.Lab.
Action Packed Stars Silver Speed
1995 #11 Bobby Labonte OC
1995 #86 J.Gordon/B.Labonte/T.Labonte
ActionVision
1997 #P1 Bobby Labonte Promo
Assets
1995 #12 Bobby Labonte
Assets $2 Phone Cards
1995 #2 Bobby Labonte
Assets $2 Phone Cards Gold Signature
1995 #2 Bobby Labonte
Assets 1-Minute Phone Cards
1995 #2 Bobby Labonte
Assets 1-Minute Phone Cards Gold Signature
1995 #2 Bobby Labonte
Assets Coca-Cola 600 Die Cut Phone Cards
1995 #4 Bobby Labonte WIN
Assets Gold Signature
1995 #12 Bobby Labonte
Assets Racing
1996 #20 Bobby Labonte
Assets Racing $100 Cup Champion Interactive Phone Cards
1996 #16 Bobby Labonte
Assets Racing $1000 Cup Champion Interactive Phone Cards
1996 #18 Bobby Labonte
Assets Racing Competitor's License
1996 #CL17 Bobby Labonte
Assets Racing Race Day
1996 #RD5 Bobby Labonte's Car
Autographed Racing
1996 #43 Bobby Labonte
1997 #8 Bobby Labonte
1997 #39 Bobby Labonte's Car
1997 #45 M.Waltrip/B.Labonte
1997 #50 B.Labonte/T.Labonte
Autographed Racing Autographs
1996 #25 Bobby Labonte
1997 #28 Bobby Labonte
Autographed Racing Autographs Certified Golds
1996 #25 Bobby Labonte
Autographed Racing Front Runners
1996 #23 J.Gibbs/B.Labonte shades
1996 #24 J.Gibbs/B.Labonte w/o shades
1996 #25 J.Gibbs/B.Labonte's Car
1996 #54 B.Labonte shades/B.Labonte
1996 #55 B.Lab.shades/B.Lab.Car
1996 #56 B.Lab.no shades/B.Lab.Car
1996 #57 B.Labonte shades/J.Makar
1996 #58 B.Labonte no shades/J.Makar
Autographed Racing High Performance
1996 #HP7 Bobby Labonte
Autographed Racing Mayne Street
1997 #KM8 Bobby Labonte
Blue Bonnet Bobby Labonte
2004 #1 Bobby Labonte 21 wins
2004 #2 Bobby Labonte '00 Champion
2004 #3 Bobby Labonte 26 Top 10s
2004 #4 Bobby Labonte career winnings
Card Dynamics Black Top Busch Series
1994 #7 Bobby Labonte
Card Dynamics Gant Oil
1994 #9 Bobby Labonte
Classic
1996 #43 Bobby Labonte
1996 #58 Bobby Labonte SP
Classic Five Sport
1995 #166 Bobby Labonte
Classic Five Sport Autographs Numbered
1995 #166 Bobby Labonte
Classic Five Sport Printer's Proofs
1995 #166 Bobby Labonte
Classic Five Sport Red Die Cuts
1995 #166 Bobby Labonte
Classic Five Sport Signings
1995-96 #82 Bobby Labonte
Classic Five Sport Signings Blue Signature
1995-96 #82 Bobby Labonte
Classic Five Sport Signings Die Cuts
1995-96 #82 Bobby Labonte
Classic Five Sport Signings Red Signature
1995-96 #82 Bobby Labonte
Classic Five Sport Silver Die Cuts
1995 #166 Bobby Labonte
Classic Five Sport Strive For Five
1995 #RC4 Bobby Labonte
Classic Five-Sport *
1995 #166 Bobby Labonte
Classic Five-Sport Autographs *
1995 #166 Bobby Labonte/225
Classic Five-Sport Printer's Proofs *
1995 #166 Bobby Labonte
Classic Five-Sport Red Die Cuts *
1995 #166 Bobby Labonte
Classic Five-Sport Silver Die Cuts *
1995 #166 Bobby Labonte
Classic Five-Sport Strive For Five *
1995 #RC4 Bobby Labonte
Classic Images Preview
1996 #RP3 Bobby Labonte
Classic Innerview
1996 #IV12 Bobby Labonte
Classic Mark Martin's Challengers
1996 #MC9 Bobby Labonte
Classic Printer's Proof
1996 #43 Bobby Labonte
Classic Race Chase
1996 #RC7 Bobby Labonte's Car
1996 #RC17 Bobby Labonte's Car
Classic Signings *
1996 #S82 Bobby Labonte
Classic Signings Blue Signature *
1996 #82 Bobby Labonte
Classic Signings Die Cuts *
1996 #82 Bobby Labonte
Classic Signings Red Signature *
1996 #82 Bobby Labonte
Classic Silver
1996 #43 Bobby Labonte
Clear Assets
1996 #68 Bobby Labonte
Clear Assets *
1996 #68 Bobby Labonte
Coca-Cola Racing Family
2000 #8 Bobby Labonte
2000 #9 Bobby Labonte '99 Win
2000 #16 Coca-Cola Racing Family
Collector's Choice
1997 #18 Bobby Labonte
1997 #68 Bobby Labonte's Car MM
1997 #113 Bobby Labonte SC
1998 #18 Bobby Labonte
1998 #54 Bobby Labonte's Car
1998 #83 Bobby Labonte FS
1998 #95 Bobby Labonte PP
Collector's Choice CC600
1998 #CC22 Bobby Labonte
1998 #CC55 Bobby Labonte's Car
1998 #CC88 Bobby Labonte's Car
Collector's Choice Speedecals
1997 #S35 Bobby Labonte's Car
1997 #S36 Bobby Labonte's Helmet
Collector's Choice Star Quest
1998 #SQ4 Bobby Labonte
1998 #SQ45 Bobby Labonte AUTO
Collector's Choice Upper Deck 500
1997 #UD36 Bobby Labonte
1997 #UD37 Bobby Labonte's Car
Crown Jewels
1995 #7 Bobby Labonte
1995 #42 Bobby Labonte's Car
1995 #71 Bobby Labonte CJT
Crown Jewels Diamond
1995 #7 Bobby Labonte
1995 #42 Bobby Labonte's Car
1995 #71 Bobby Labonte CJT
Crown Jewels Elite
1996 #8 Bobby Labonte
1996 #55 B.Labonte/J.Makar
1996 #64 Bobby Labonte's Trans.
1996 #76 Bobby Labonte BGN
Crown Jewels Elite Crown Signature Amethyst
1996 #CS6 Bobby Labonte
Crown Jewels Elite Crown Signature Garnet
1996 #CS6 Bobby Labonte
Crown Jewels Elite Crown Signature Peridot
1996 #CS6 Bobby Labonte
Crown Jewels Elite Diamond Tribute
1996 #8 Bobby Labonte
1996 #55 B.Labonte/J.Makar
1996 #64 Bobby Labonte's Trans.
1996 #76 Bobby Labonte
Crown Jewels Elite Diamond Tribute Citrine
1996 #8 Bobby Labonte
1996 #55 B.Labonte/J.Makar
1996 #64 Bobby Labonte's Trans.
1996 #76 Bobby Labonte
Crown Jewels Elite Dual Jewels Amethyst
1996 #DJ3 T.Labonte/B.Labonte
Crown Jewels Elite Dual Jewels Amethyst Diamond Tribute
1996 #DJ3 T.Labonte/B.Labonte
Crown Jewels Elite Dual Jewels Amethyst Treasure Chest
1996 #DJ3 T.Labonte/B.Labonte
Crown Jewels Elite Dual Jewels Garnet
1996 #DJ3 T.Labonte/B.Labonte
Crown Jewels Elite Dual Jewels Garnet Diamond Tribute
1996 #DJ3 T.Labonte/B.Labonte
Crown Jewels Elite Dual Jewels Garnet Treasure Chest
1996 #DJ3 T.Labonte/B.Labonte
Crown Jewels Elite Dual Jewels Sapphire
1996 #DJ3 T.Labonte/B.Labonte
Crown Jewels Elite Dual Jewels Sapphire Treasure Chest
1996 #DJ3 T.Labonte/B.Labonte
Crown Jewels Elite Emerald
1996 #8 Bobby Labonte
1996 #55 B.Labonte/J.Makar
1996 #64 Bobby Labonte's Trans.
1996 #76 Bobby Labonte
Crown Jewels Elite Emerald Treasure Chest
1996 #8 Bobby Labonte
1996 #55 B.Labonte/J.Makar
1996 #64 Bobby Labonte's Trans.
1996 #76 Bobby Labonte
Crown Jewels Elite Promos
1996 #PC1 Bobby Labonte Citrine
1996 #PD1 Bobby Labonte Diamond
1996 #PE1 Bobby Labonte Emerald
1996 #PS1 Bobby Labonte Sapphire
Crown Jewels Elite Sapphire
1996 #8 Bobby Labonte
1996 #55 B.Labonte/J.Makar
1996 #64 Bobby Labonte's Trans.
1996 #76 Bobby Labonte
Crown Jewels Elite Sapphire Treasure Chest
1996 #8 Bobby Labonte
1996 #55 B.Labonte/J.Makar
1996 #64 Bobby Labonte's Trans.
1996 #76 Bobby Labonte
Crown Jewels Elite Treasure Chest
1996 #8 Bobby Labonte
1996 #55 B.Labonte/J.Makar
1996 #64 Bobby Labonte's Trans.
1996 #76 Bobby Labonte
Crown Jewels Emerald
1995 #7 Bobby Labonte
1995 #42 Bobby Labonte's Car
1995 #71 Bobby Labonte CJT
Crown Jewels Sapphire
1995 #7 Bobby Labonte
1995 #42 Bobby Labonte's Car
1995 #71 Bobby Labonte CJT
Dayco Series 3
1994 #34 Bobby Labonte
eTopps
2003 #16 Bobby Labonte/2249
Finish Line
1993 #27 T.Labonte/B.Labonte
1993 #117 Bobby Labonte
1993 #135 Bobby Labonte
1993 #165 Bobby Labonte's Car
1994 #26 Bobby Labonte
1994 #63 Bobby Labonte's Car
1994 #128 Bobby Labonte
1995 #91 Bobby Labonte
1995 #103 Bobby Labonte
1996 #26 Bobby Labonte
1996 #69 Bobby Labonte
1996 #85 Bobby Labonte's Car
Finish Line Black Gold
1996 #C7 Bobby Labonte's Car
1996 #D8 Bobby Labonte
Finish Line Coca-Cola 600
1995 #12 Bobby Labonte
Finish Line Commemorative Sheets
1993 #16 New Hampshire
1993 #19 Watkins Glen
1993 #28 Rockingham
Finish Line Gold
1994 #32 Bobby Labonte's Car
Finish Line Gold Signature
1996 #GS7 Bobby Labonte
Finish Line Man and Machine
1996 #MM7 Bobby Labonte

Finish Line Phone Cards
1994 #3 Bobby Labonte
Finish Line Phone Pak
1996 #18 Bobby Labonte
1996 #19 Bobby Labonte's Car
Finish Line Phone Pak $10
1996 #5 Bobby Labonte
Finish Line Phone Pak $2 Signature
1996 #18 Bobby Labonte
1996 #19 Bobby Labonte's Car
Finish Line Phone Pak $5
1996 #13 Bobby Labonte
Finish Line Phone Pak $50
1996 #4 Bobby Labonte
Finish Line Phone Pak II
1997 #8 Bobby Labonte
1997 #46 Bobby Labonte $5
1997 #76 Bobby Labonte's Car $10
1997 #94 Bobby Labonte $50
Finish Line Printer's Proof
1995 #91 Bobby Labonte
1995 #103 Bobby Labonte
1996 #26 Bobby Labonte
1996 #69 Bobby Labonte
1996 #85 Bobby Labonte's Car
Finish Line Promos
1993 #P3 Terry Labonte/Bobby Labonte
Finish Line Silver
1993 #27 Terry Labonte/Bobby Labonte
1993 #117 Bobby Labonte
1993 #135 Bobby Labonte
1993 #165 Bobby Labonte's Car
1994 #26 Bobby Labonte
1994 #63 Bobby Labonte's Car
1994 #128 Bobby Labonte
1995 #91 Bobby Labonte
1995 #103 Bobby Labonte
1996 #26 Bobby Labonte
1996 #69 Bobby Labonte
1996 #85 Bobby Labonte's Car
Flair
1996 #17 Bobby Labonte
1996 #73 Bobby Labonte's Car
1996 #95 Bobby Labonte
Flair Autographs
1996 #7 Bobby Labonte
Flair Center Spotlight
1996 #6 Bobby Labonte
Flair Hot Numbers
1996 #6 Bobby Labonte
Hi-Tech Brickyard 400
1994 #12 Bobby Labonte's Car
1994 #51 Bobby Labonte
1995 #5 Bobby Labonte's Car
1995 #61 Bobby Labonte
Hi-Tech Brickyard 400 Artist Proofs
1994 #12 Bobby Labonte's Car
1994 #51 Bobby Labonte
Images
1995 #18 Bobby Labonte
1995 #46 Bobby Labonte
1995 #81 Bobby Labonte
Images Driven
1995 #D3 Bobby Labonte
Images Gold
1995 #18 Bobby Labonte
1995 #46 Bobby Labonte
1995 #81 Bobby Labonte
Images Hard Chargers
1995 #HC1 Bobby Labonte
Jurassic Park
1997 #6 Bobby Labonte
Jurassic Park Carnivore
1997 #C4 Bobby Labonte
Jurassic Park Pteranodon
1997 #P3 Bobby Labonte
Jurassic Park Raptors
1997 #R8 Bobby Labonte
Jurassic Park Thunder Lizard
1997 #TL3 Bobby Labonte
Jurassic Park T-Rex
1997 #TR4 Bobby Labonte
Jurassic Park Triceratops
1997 #6 Bobby Labonte
KnightQuest
1996 #9 Bobby Labonte K
1996 #26 Bobby Labonte C
1996 #29 Bobby Labonte C
KnightQuest Black Knights
1996 #9 Bobby Labonte K
1996 #26 Bobby Labonte C
1996 #29 Bobby Labonte C
KnightQuest First Knights
1996 #FK5 Bobby Labonte
KnightQuest Red Knight Preview
1996 #9 Bobby Labonte K
1996 #26 Bobby Labonte C
1996 #29 Bobby Labonte C
KnightQuest Royalty
1996 #9 Bobby Labonte K
1996 #26 Bobby Labonte C
1996 #29 Bobby Labonte C
KnightQuest Santa Claus
1996 #SC2 Bobby Labonte
KnightQuest Santa Claus Green
1996 #SC2 Bobby Labonte
KnightQuest White Knights
1996 #9 Bobby Labonte K
1996 #26 Bobby Labonte C
1996 #29 Bobby Labonte C
Mac Tools Winner's Cup
1992 #14 Bobby Labonte
Maxwell House
1993 #1 Bobby Labonte
1993 #16 Bobby Labonte/Terry Labonte
1993 #24 Jeff Gordon/K.Wall/B.Labonte
Maxx
1991 #53 Bobby Labonte RC
1993 #22 Bobby Labonte
1993 #113 Bobby Labonte's Car
1993 #199 Da.All./R.Petty/Mart.Cars MM
1994 #22 Bobby Labonte
1994 #74 Bobby Labonte's Car
1994 #254 Bobby Labonte
1994 #255 Bobby Labonte's Car
1995 #22 Bobby Labonte
1995 #148 Bobby Labonte Crash MM
1995 #240 Bobby Labonte
1995 #241 Bobby Labonte's Car
1995 #243 Bobby Labonte
1996 #18 Bobby Labonte
1996 #22 Bobby Labonte's Car
1997 #18 Bobby Labonte
1997 #63 Bobby Labonte's Car
1997 #93 Bobby Labonte PS
1998 #18 Bobby Labonte
1998 #48 Bobby Labonte's Car
1998 #71 Bobby Labonte's Car HC
1998 #90 Bobby Labonte's Car LTD
1998 #97 Bobby Labonte's Car FR
1999 #28 Bobby Labonte
1999 #29 Bobby Labonte's Car
1999 #30 Bobby Labonte RR
2000 #18 Bobby Labonte
2000 #58 Bobby Labonte's Car
2000 #76 Bobby Labonte's Car FRF
Maxx 10th Anniversary
1998 #17 Bobby Labonte
1998 #62 Bobby Labonte's Car
1998 #107 Bobby Labonte
Maxx 10th Anniversary Maxximum Preview
1998 #P18 Bobby Labonte
Maxx 1997 Year In Review
1998 #57 Bobby Labonte
1998 #59 Bobby Labonte's Car
1998 #112 Bobby Labonte
1998 #139 Bobby Labonte's Car
1998 #147 Bobby Labonte
1998 #156 Bobby Labonte
1998 #PO7 Bobby Labonte
Maxx Autographs
1994 #22 Bobby Labonte
1995 #22 Bobby Labonte
Maxx Black
1992 #44 Bobby Labonte
1992 #91 Bobby Labonte BGN Champ
Maxx Chase the Champion
1997 #C6 Bobby Labonte
Maxx Chase the Champion Gold Die Cuts
1997 #C6 Bobby Labonte
Maxx Collectible Covers
2000 #CCBL Bobby Labonte
Maxx Drive Time
2000 #DT7 Bobby Labonte
Maxx Family Ties
1996 #FT3 T.Labonte/B.Labonte
Maxx FANtastic Finishes
1999 #F29 Bobby Labonte's Car
2000 #FF8 Bobby Labonte
Maxx Flag Firsts
1997 #FF18 Bobby Labonte
Maxx Focus on a Champion
1998 #FC8 Bobby Labonte
1999 #FC12 Bobby Labonte
2000 #FC3 Bobby Labonte
Maxx Focus on a Champion Cel
1998 #FC8 Bobby Labonte
Maxx Focus on a Champion Gold
1999 #FC12 Bobby Labonte
Maxx Lowes Foods Stickers
1993 #4 T.Labonte/S.Marlin/B.Labonte
Maxx Made in America
1996 #18 Bobby Labonte
1996 #29 Bobby Labonte
1996 #34 Bobby Labonte's Car
1996 #90 Bobby Labonte's Car
Maxx Made in America Blue Ribbon
1996 #BR7 Bobby Labonte's Car
Maxx Medallion
1994 #15 Bobby Labonte
1994 #57 Bobby Labonte
1995 #14 Bobby Labonte
1995 #44 Bobby Labonte's Car
Maxx Medallion Blue
1995 #14 Bobby Labonte
1995 #44 Bobby Labonte's Car
Maxx Medallion On the Road Again
1995 #OTR7 Bobby Labonte's Trans.
Maxx Motorsport
1993 #11 Bobby Labonte
1993 #31 Bobby Labonte's Car
Maxx Odyssey
1996 #18 Bobby Labonte
1996 #34 Bobby Labonte's Car
1996 #P1 Bobby Labonte Promo
Maxx Odyssey Radio Active
1996 #RA7 Bobby Labonte's Car
Maxx Over the Wall
1996 #OTW7 Bobby Labonte's Car
Maxx Premier Plus
1993 #22 Bobby Labonte
1993 #51 Bobby Labonte's Car
1993 #57 Da.All/R.Pet/Mart/B.Lab.Cars MM
1993 #NNO J.Gordon/B.Lab/K.Wall
1994 #22 Bobby Labonte
1994 #74 Bobby Labonte's Car
1995 #22 Bobby Labonte
1995 #36 Bobby Labonte's Car
Maxx Premier Plus Crown Chrome
1995 #22 Bobby Labonte
1995 #36 Bobby Labonte's Car
Maxx Premier Series
1993 #22 Bobby Labonte
1993 #113 Bobby Labonte's Car
1993 #199 Allison/Petty/Martin/Lab.Cars MM
1994 #22 Bobby Labonte
1994 #74 Bobby Labonte's Car
1995 #22 Bobby Labonte
1995 #36 Bobby Labonte's Car
1995 #213 B.Labonte/B.Hamilton/Mast Cars MM
1995 #296 Bobby Labonte Crash MM
1996 #18 Bobby Labonte
1996 #36 Bobby Labonte's Car
Maxx Premier Series Superlatives
1996 #SL3 Bobby Labonte
Maxx Race Ticket
1999 #RT27 Bobby Labonte's Car
Maxx Racer's Ink
2000 #BL Bobby Labonte
Maxx Racing Images
1999 #RI3 Bobby Labonte
Maxx Red
1992 #44 Bobby Labonte
1992 #91 Bobby Labonte BGN Champ
Maxx Rookies of the Year
1994 #15 Bobby Labonte
Maxx Speedway Boogie
2000 #SB3 Bobby Labonte
Maxx The Select 25
1994 #19 Bobby Labonte
Maxx Top 5 of 2005
1995 #TOP2 Bobby Labonte
Maxx Update
1991 #53 Bobby Labonte RC
Maxx Winnebago Motorsports
1993 #2 J.Gordon/B.Lab/Bickle/K.Wall.
Maxximum
1998 #18 Bobby Labonte
1998 #43 Bobby Labonte's Car
1998 #68 Bobby Labonte
1998 #93 Bobby Labonte's Car
2000 #2 Bobby Labonte
Maxximum Battle Proven
1998 #B14 Bobby Labonte
Maxximum Cruise Control
2000 #CC2 Bobby Labonte
Maxximum Dialed In
2000 #DI4 Bobby Labonte
Maxximum Die Cuts
2000 #2 Bobby Labonte
Maxximum Field Generals Four Star Autographs
1998 #12 Bobby Labonte
Maxximum Field Generals One Star
1998 #12 Bobby Labonte
Maxximum Field Generals Three Star Autographs
1998 #12 Bobby Labonte
Maxximum Field Generals Two Star
1998 #12 Bobby Labonte
Maxximum First Class
1998 #F6 Bobby Labonte
Maxximum MPH
2000 #2 Bobby Labonte/18
Maxximum Pure Adrenaline
2000 #PA3 Bobby Labonte
Maxximum Signatures
2000 #SL2 T.Stewart/B.Labonte EXCH
2000 #TB2 T.Labonte/B.Labonte
2000 #BTJ3 B.Labon/Stewart/Gibbs
2000 #TBJ3 Terry/Bobby/J.Labonte
2000 #GIB4 Stew/Leffir/B.Labn/Gibbs
McFarlane NASCAR 3-Inch Series 1
2005 #80 Bobby Labonte
McFarlane NASCAR Series 2
2004 #50 B.Labonte R Interstate Batteries with Trophy
2004 #55 B.Labonte H Shrek without Trophy
McFarlane NASCAR Shrek 2 Boxed Sets
2004 #10 B.Labonte w/Shrek
M-Force
1996 #17 Bobby Labonte
M-Force Silvers
1996 #S9 Bobby Labonte
MW Windows
1994 #2 Bobby Labonte
1994 #5 Gordon/B.Labonte/T.Labonte/Schrader
Pinnacle
1996 #18 Bobby Labonte
1996 #47 Bobby Labonte's Car
1996 #79 Bobby Labonte HOF
1996 #81 Bobby Labonte's Car HOF
1996 #90 Bobby Labonte's Transporter
1997 #18 Bobby Labonte
1997 #47 Bobby Labonte's Car
1997 #64 Bobby Labonte RR
1997 #77 Bobby Labonte TT
Pinnacle Artist Proofs
1996 #18 Bobby Labonte
1996 #47 Bobby Labonte's Car
1996 #79 Bobby Labonte HOF
1996 #81 Bobby Labonte's Car HOF
1996 #90 Bobby Labonte's Transporter
1997 #18 Bobby Labonte P
1997 #47 Bobby Labonte's Car B
1997 #64 Bobby Labonte RR R
1997 #77 Bobby Labonte TT R
Pinnacle Bobby Labonte Helmets
1997 #1 Bobby Labonte
1997 #2 Bobby Labonte
1997 #3 Bobby Labonte
1997 #4 Bobby Labonte
1997 #5 Bobby Labonte
1997 #6 Bobby Labonte
1997 #7 Bobby Labonte
1997 #8 Bobby Labonte
1997 #9 Bobby Labonte
1997 #10 Bobby Labonte
Pinnacle Certified
1997 #18 Bobby Labonte
1997 #52 Bobby Labonte's Car
1997 #77 Bobby Labonte's Car WP
1997 #97 Bobby Labonte BD
Pinnacle Certified Certified Team
1997 #4 Bobby Labonte
Pinnacle Certified Certified Team Gold
1997 #4 Bobby Labonte
Pinnacle Certified Epix
1997 #E4 Bobby Labonte
Pinnacle Certified Epix Emerald
1997 #E4 Bobby Labonte
Pinnacle Certified Epix Purple
1997 #E4 Bobby Labonte
Pinnacle Certified Mirror Blue
1997 #18 Bobby Labonte
1997 #52 Bobby Labonte's Car
1997 #77 Bobby Labonte's Car WP
1997 #97 Bobby Labonte BD
Pinnacle Certified Mirror Gold
1997 #18 Bobby Labonte
1997 #52 Bobby Labonte's Car
1997 #77 Bobby Labonte's Car WP
1997 #97 Bobby Labonte BD
Pinnacle Certified Mirror Red
1997 #18 Bobby Labonte
1997 #52 Bobby Labonte's Car
1997 #77 Bobby Labonte's Car WP
1997 #97 Bobby Labonte BD
Pinnacle Certified Red
1997 #18 Bobby Labonte
1997 #52 Bobby Labonte's Car
1997 #77 Bobby Labonte's Car WP
1997 #97 Bobby Labonte BD
Pinnacle Checkered Flag
1996 #7 Bobby Labonte
Pinnacle Cut Above
1996 #9 Bobby Labonte
Pinnacle Foil
1997 #18 Bobby Labonte
1997 #47 Bobby Labonte's Car
1997 #64 Bobby Labonte RR
1997 #77 Bobby Labonte TT
Pinnacle Mint
1997 #11 Bobby Labonte
1997 #27 Bobby Labonte's Car
1998 #6 Bobby Labonte
1998 #18 Bobby Labonte's Car
Pinnacle Mint Bronze
1997 #11 Bobby Labonte
1997 #27 Bobby Labonte's Car
Pinnacle Mint Coins
1997 #11 Bobby Labonte
1997 #27 Bobby Labonte's Car
1998 #6 Bobby Labonte
1998 #18 Bobby Labonte's Car
Pinnacle Mint Coins 24K Gold Plated
1997 #11 Bobby Labonte
1997 #27 Bobby Labonte's Car
Pinnacle Mint Coins Bronze Proof
1998 #6 Bobby Labonte
1998 #18 Bobby Labonte's Car
Pinnacle Mint Coins Gold Plated
1998 #6 Bobby Labonte
1998 #18 Bobby Labonte's Car
Pinnacle Mint Coins Gold Plated Proofs
1998 #6 Bobby Labonte
1998 #18 Bobby Labonte's Car
Pinnacle Mint Coins Nickel-Silver
1997 #11 Bobby Labonte
1997 #27 Bobby Labonte's Car
1998 #6 Bobby Labonte
1998 #18 Bobby Labonte's Car
Pinnacle Mint Coins Silver Plated Proofs
1998 #6 Bobby Labonte
1998 #18 Bobby Labonte's Car
Pinnacle Mint Coins Solid Gold
1998 #6 Bobby Labonte
1998 #18 Bobby Labonte's Car
Pinnacle Mint Coins Solid Silver
1998 #6 Bobby Labonte
1998 #18 Bobby Labonte's Car
Pinnacle Mint Die Cuts
1998 #6 Bobby Labonte
1998 #18 Bobby Labonte's Car
Pinnacle Mint Gold
1997 #11 Bobby Labonte
1997 #27 Bobby Labonte's Car
Pinnacle Mint Gold Team
1998 #6 Bobby Labonte
1998 #18 Bobby Labonte's Car
Pinnacle Mint Silver
1997 #11 Bobby Labonte
1997 #27 Bobby Labonte's Car
Pinnacle Mint Silver Team
1998 #6 Bobby Labonte
1998 #18 Bobby Labonte's Car
Pinnacle Pole Position
1996 #18 Bobby Labonte
1996 #36 Bobby Labonte's Car
1996 #75 Bobby Labonte EY
Pinnacle Pole Position Certified Strong
1996 #11 Bobby Labonte
Pinnacle Pole Position Lightning Fast
1996 #18 Bobby Labonte
1996 #36 Bobby Labonte's Car
1996 #75 Bobby Labonte
Pinnacle Pole Position No Limit
1996 #15 Bobby Labonte
Pinnacle Pole Position No Limit Gold
1996 #15 Bobby Labonte
Pinnacle Portraits
1997 #5 Bobby Labonte
1997 #25 Bobby Labonte's Car
Pinnacle Precision
1997 #73 Bobby Labonte
Pinnacle Precision Bronze
1997 #73 Bobby Labonte
Pinnacle Precision Gold
1997 #73 Bobby Labonte
Pinnacle Precision Silver
1997 #73 Bobby Labonte
Pinnacle Press Plates
1997 #18 Bobby Labonte
1997 #47 Bobby Labonte's Car
1997 #64 Bobby Labonte RR
1997 #77 Bobby Labonte TT
1997 #H1 Bobby Labonte/Carolina Panthers
1997 #H2 Bobby Labonte/Jacsonville Jaguars
1997 #H3 Bobby Labonte/Dallas Cowboys
1997 #H4 Bobby Labonte/Miami Dolphins
1997 #H5 Bobby Labonte/New York Giants
1997 #H6 Bobby Labonte/Detroit Lions
1997 #H7 Bobby Labonte/San Francisco 49ers
1997 #H8 Bobby Labonte/Atlanta Falcons
1997 #H9 Bobby Labonte/Pittsburgh Steelers
1997 #H10 Bobby Labonte/Arizona Panthers
1997 #S12-G Bobby Labonte
1997 #TP7A Bobby Labonte
Pinnacle Spellbound
1997 #12G Bobby Labonte
Pinnacle Spellbound Promos
1997 #12G Bobby Labonte
Pinnacle Team Pinnacle
1997 #7 Bobby Labonte
Pinnacle Team Pinnacle Red
1997 #7 Bobby Labonte
Pinnacle Totally Certified Platinum Blue
1997 #18 Bobby Labonte
1997 #52 Bobby Labonte's Car
1997 #77 Bobby Labonte WP
1997 #97 Bobby Labonte BD
Pinnacle Totally Certified Platinum Gold
1997 #18 Bobby Labonte
1997 #52 Bobby Labonte's Car
1997 #77 Bobby Labonte WP
1997 #97 Bobby Labonte BD
Pinnacle Totally Certified Platinum Red
1997 #18 Bobby Labonte
1997 #52 Bobby Labonte's Car
1997 #77 Bobby Labonte WP
1997 #97 Bobby Labonte BD
Pinnacle Trophy Collection
1997 #18 Bobby Labonte
1997 #47 Bobby Labonte's Car
1997 #64 Bobby Labonte RR
1997 #77 Bobby Labonte TT
Pinnacle Winston Cup Collection
1996 #18 Bobby Labonte
1996 #47 Bobby Labonte's Car
1996 #79 Bobby Labonte HOF
1996 #81 Bobby Labonte's Car HOF
1996 #90 Bobby Labonte's Transporter
Power
1994 #98 Bobby Labonte
Power Gold
1994 #98 Bobby Labonte
Predator
1997 #12 Bobby Labonte
1997 #38 Bobby Labonte
1997 #47 Bobby Labonte
Predator American Eagle
1997 #AE8 Bobby Labonte
Predator American Eagle First Slash
1997 #AE8 Bobby Labonte
Predator Black Wolf First Strike
1997 #12 Bobby Labonte
1997 #38 Bobby Labonte
1997 #47 Bobby Labonte
Predator Eye of the Tiger
1997 #ET7 Bobby Labonte
Predator Eye of the Tiger First Slash
1997 #ET7 Bobby Labonte
Predator First Slash
1997 #12 Bobby Labonte
1997 #38 Bobby Labonte
1997 #47 Bobby Labonte
Predator Gatorback
1997 #GB6 Bobby Labonte
Predator Gatorback Authentic
1997 #GBA6 Bobby Labonte
Predator Gatorback Authentic First Slash
1997 #GBA6 Bobby Labonte
Predator Gatorback First Slash
1997 #GB6 Bobby Labonte
Predator Golden Eagle
1997 #GE8 Bobby Labonte
Predator Golden Eagle First Slash
1997 #GE8 Bobby Labonte
Predator Grizzly
1997 #12 Bobby Labonte
1997 #38 Bobby Labonte
1997 #47 Bobby Labonte
Predator Grizzly First Slash
1997 #12 Bobby Labonte
1997 #38 Bobby Labonte
1997 #47 Bobby Labonte
Predator Red Wolf
1997 #12 Bobby Labonte
1997 #38 Bobby Labonte
1997 #47 Bobby Labonte
Predator Red Wolf First Slash
1997 #12 Bobby Labonte
1997 #38 Bobby Labonte
1997 #47 Bobby Labonte
Press Pass
1994 #13 Bobby Labonte
1994 #44 Bobby Labonte's Car
1995 #15 Bobby Labonte
1996 #16 Bobby Labonte
1996 #41 Bobby Labonte's Car
1996 #77 Gibbs/Makar/B.Labonte TW
1996 #94 Bobby Labonte S
1996 #PN1 Bobby Labonte Gold Promo
1996 #PN2 Bobby Labonte Red Promo
1997 #11 Bobby Labonte
1997 #37 Bobby Labonte's Car
1997 #81 Bobby Labonte
1997 #109 Bobby Labonte
1997 #P2 Bobby Labonte National Promo
1997 #P3 Bobby Labonte's Car Natl.Promo
1998 #11 Bobby Labonte
1998 #33 Bobby Labonte's Car
1999 #5 Bobby Labonte
1999 #17 Bobby Labonte
1999 #32 Bobby Labonte's Car
1999 #83 Bobby Labonte OTP
1999 #105 Bobby Labonte RET
2000 #2 Bobby Labonte
2000 #40 Bobby Labonte REP
2000 #52 Bobby Labonte DD
2001 #1 Bobby Labonte
2001 #48 Bobby Labonte's Car
2001 #63 Bobby Labonte REP
2001 #71 Bobby Labonte REP
2001 #91 Bobby Labonte SO
2001 #P1 Bobby Labonte Promo
2001 #0 Bobby Labonte WC Champ
2002 #18 Bobby Labonte
2002 #80 Bobby Labonte's Car
2003 #18 Bobby Labonte
2003 #77 Screeching Halt WCS
2004 #16 Bobby Labonte
2004 #68 Bobby Labonte's Car OTW
2004 #68B B.Labonte's Car OTW SP
2004 #77 Figuring It Out WCS
2004 #79 Duking'-ing It Out WCS
2005 #13 Bobby Labonte
2005 #67 Bobby Labonte's Car OTW
2005 #104 Bobby Labonte P
2006 #14 Bobby Labonte
2007 #24 Bobby Labonte
2008 #17 Bobby Labonte
Press Pass Autographs
1997 #10 Bobby Labonte PPP/VIP
1998 #6 Bobby Labonte
2001 #25 Bobby Labonte
2002 #36 Bobby Labonte
2003 #32 Bobby Labonte E/P
2004 #35 Bobby Labonte P
2005 #33 Bobby Labonte E/P
2006 #31 Bobby Labonte NC
2007 #24 Bobby Labonte NC P
2008 #25 Bobby Labonte NC P/E
Press Pass Autographs Press Plates Black
2007 #9 Bobby Labonte NC
2008 #20 Bobby Labonte NC E
Press Pass Autographs Press Plates Cyan
2007 #9 Bobby Labonte NC
2008 #20 Bobby Labonte NC P
Press Pass Autographs Press Plates Magenta
2007 #11 Bobby Labonte NC
2008 #20 Bobby Labonte NC P
Press Pass Autographs Press Plates Yellow
2007 #10 Bobby Labonte NC
2008 #20 Bobby Labonte NC E
Press Pass Blue
2006 #B14 Bobby Labonte
2007 #B24 Bobby Labonte
2008 #B17 Bobby Labonte
Press Pass Burning Rubber
1999 #BR3 Bobby Labonte's Car
2000 #BR3 Bobby Labonte
Press Pass Burning Rubber Cars
2001 #BRC7 Bobby Labonte/105
2002 #BRC8 Bobby Labonte's Car
2003 #BRT8 Bobby Labonte's Car
2004 #BRT8 Bobby Labonte's Car
2005 #BRT5 Bobby Labonte's Car
2006 #BRT11 Bobby Labonte
Press Pass Burning Rubber Die Cast Inserts
1996 #1 Bobby Labonte's Car/1008
Press Pass Burning Rubber Drivers
2001 #BRD7 Bobby Labonte/90
2002 #BRD8 Bobby Labonte
2003 #BRD8 Bobby Labonte
2004 #BRD8 Bobby Labonte
2005 #BRD5 Bobby Labonte
2006 #BRD11 Bobby Labonte
Press Pass Burning Rubber Drivers Gold
2005 #BRD5 Bobby Labonte
2006 #BRD11 Bobby Labonte
Press Pass Chase Cars
1999 #2B Bobby Labonte's Car
Press Pass Checkered Flags
1996 #CF2 Bobby Labonte
Press Pass Chef Boyardee
2000 #1 Bobby Labonte
2000 #3 Bobby Labonte
2000 #6 B.Labonte/T.Stewart
Press Pass Clear Cut
1997 #C5 Bobby Labonte
Press Pass Coca-Cola Racing Family
2001 #2 B.Labonte/T.Stewart
2003 #7 Bobby Labonte
Press Pass Coca-Cola Racing Family Regional
2003 #1 Bobby Labonte
Press Pass Collector's Series Box Set
2007 #SB14 Bobby Labonte
Press Pass Collectors Series Making the Show
2006 #MS22 Bobby Labonte
Press Pass Collectors Series Sunday Best
2007 #CB14 Bobby Labonte
Press Pass Cup Chase
1994 #CC13 Bobby Labonte
1995 #15 Bobby Labonte WIN
1996 #16 Bobby Labonte
1997 #CC11 Bobby Labonte WIN
1998 #CC11 Bobby Labonte Win 2
1999 #11 Bobby Labonte WIN 2
2000 #CC9 Bobby Labonte WIN
2001 #CC16 Bobby Labonte
2002 #CC8 Bobby Labonte
2003 #CCR9 Bobby Labonte
2004 #CCR4 Bobby Labonte
2005 #CCR9 Bobby Labonte
2006 #CCR15 Bobby Labonte
2007 #CCR2 Bobby Labonte
Press Pass Cup Chase Blue Die Cut Prizes
1997 #CC11 Bobby Labonte
Press Pass Cup Chase Die Cut Prizes
1998 #CC11 Bobby Labonte
1999 #11 Bobby Labonte
2000 #CC9 Bobby Labonte
2000 #CCC1 Bobby Labonte Tire/650
2001 #CC16 Bobby Labonte
2001 #CC17 Bobby Labonte Champ
Press Pass Cup Chase Foil Prizes
1996 #16 Bobby Labonte
Press Pass Cup Chase Gold Die Cuts
1997 #CC11 Bobby Labonte
Press Pass Cup Chase Prizes
2002 #CC8 Bobby Labonte
2003 #CCR9 Bobby Labonte
2004 #CCR4 Bobby Labonte
2005 #CCP9 Bobby Labonte
Press Pass Dale The Movie
2007 #45 Dale Earnhardt's Car Bobby Labonte's Car Kevin Harvick's Car Jeff Gordon's Car
Press Pass Double Burner
2001 #DB9 Bobby Labonte
2002 #DB5 Bobby Labonte
2003 #DB8 Bobby Labonte
2004 #DB8 Bobby Labonte
2005 #DB8 Bobby Labonte
Press Pass Double Burner Exchange
2003 #DB8 Bobby Labonte EXCH
2004 #DB8 Bobby Labonte
2005 #DB8 Bobby Labonte
Press Pass Double Burner Metal-Tire
2006 #DB7 Bobby Labonte
Press Pass Eclipse
2002 #6 Bobby Labonte
2002 #34 Bobby Labonte ACC
2002 #42 Bobby Labonte SO
2003 #15 Bobby Labonte
2004 #8 Bobby Labonte
2004 #33 Bobby Labonte's Car
2004 #55 Bobby Labonte P
2004 #55B Bobby Labonte P SP
2004 #66 Bobby Labonte WCS
2004 #87 Bobby Labonte LL
2005 #12 Bobby Labonte
2005 #55 Bobby Labonte P
2005 #87 Bobby Labonte LL
2006 #23 Bobby Labonte
2006 #58 Bobby Labonte TN
2007 #20 Bobby Labonte
2008 #15 Bobby Labonte
Press Pass Eclipse Destination WIN

2004 #6 Bobby Labonte
Press Pass Eclipse Double Hot Treads
2003 #DT1 B.Labonte/T.Stewart
Press Pass Eclipse Escape Velocity
2008 #EV11 Bobby Labonte
Press Pass Eclipse Gold
2007 #G20 Bobby Labonte
2008 #G15 Bobby Labonte
Press Pass Eclipse Hyperdrive
2005 #HD2 Bobby Labonte
Press Pass Eclipse Maxim
2004 #MX7 Bobby Labonte
Press Pass Eclipse Previews
2003 #15 Bobby Labonte
2004 #8 Bobby Labonte
2005 #EB12 Bobby Labonte
2005 #EB55 Bobby Labonte P
2005 #EB87 Bobby Labonte LL/1
2006 #EB23 Bobby Labonte
2006 #EB58 Bobby Labonte TN
2007 #EB20 Bobby Labonte
2008 #EB15 Bobby Labonte
Press Pass Eclipse Racing Champions
2002 #RC20 Bobby Labonte
2002 #RC34 Bobby Labonte
2003 #RC10 Bobby Labonte
Press Pass Eclipse Red
2007 #R20 Bobby Labonte
2008 #R15 Bobby Labonte
Press Pass Eclipse Samples
2002 #6 Bobby Labonte
2002 #34 Bobby Labonte ACC
2002 #42 Bobby Labonte SO
2003 #15 Bobby Labonte
2004 #8 Bobby Labonte
2004 #33 Bobby Labonte's Car
2004 #55 Bobby Labonte P
2004 #66 Bobby Labonte WCS
2004 #87 Bobby Labonte LL
2005 #12 Bobby Labonte
2005 #55 Bobby Labonte P
2005 #87 Bobby Labonte LL
Press Pass Eclipse Skidmarks
2002 #SK5 Bobby Labonte
2003 #SM14 Bobby Labonte
2004 #SM14 Bobby Labonte
2005 #SM14 Bobby Labonte
2006 #SM3 Bobby Labonte
2006 #SM5 Bobby Labonte
Press Pass Eclipse Skidmarks Holofoil
2004 #SM14 Bobby Labonte
2005 #SM14 Bobby Labonte
2006 #SM3 Bobby Labonte
2006 #SM5 Bobby Labonte
Press Pass Eclipse Solar Eclipse
2002 #S6 Bobby Labonte
2002 #S34 Bobby Labonte ACC
2002 #S42 Bobby Labonte SO
2003 #P15 Bobby Labonte
Press Pass Eclipse Stellar
2008 #ST22 Bobby Labonte
Press Pass Eclipse Supernova
2002 #SN8 Bobby Labonte
2003 #SN7 Bobby Labonte
Press Pass Eclipse Supernova Numbered
2002 #SN8 Bobby Labonte
Press Pass Eclipse Teammates Autographs
2004 #4 B.Labonte/T.Stewart
2005 #1 Stewart/Leffler/Labonte
Press Pass Eclipse Under Cover Autographs
2004 #UCBL Bobby Labonte/18
2005 #UCBL Bobby Labonte/18
Press Pass Eclipse Under Cover Cars
2003 #UCT6 Bobby Labonte
2004 #UCD8 Bobby Labonte
2005 #UCT8 Bobby Labonte
2006 #UCT6 Bobby Labonte
Press Pass Eclipse Under Cover Cars Autographs
2003 #UCTBL Bobby Labonte/18
Press Pass Eclipse Under Cover Double Cover
2002 #DC7 B.Labonte/T.Stewart
2003 #DC7 B.Labonte/T.Stewart
2004 #DC10 B.Labonte/T.Stewart
2005 #DC5 B.Labonte/T.Stewart
Press Pass Eclipse Under Cover Driver Autographs
2003 #UCD-BL Bobby Labonte/18
Press Pass Eclipse Under Cover Driver Gold
2003 #UCD6 Bobby Labonte
2004 #UCD8 Bobby Labonte
Press Pass Eclipse Under Cover Driver Red
2003 #UCD6 Bobby Labonte
2004 #UCD8 Bobby Labonte
2005 #UCD8 Bobby Labonte
Press Pass Eclipse Under Cover Driver Silver
2003 #UCD6 Bobby Labonte
2004 #UCD8 Bobby Labonte
Press Pass Eclipse Under Cover Drivers
2002 #CD5 Bobby Labonte
Press Pass Eclipse Under Cover Drivers Gold
2006 #UCD6 Bobby Labonte
Press Pass Eclipse Under Cover Drivers Holofoil
2005 #UCD8 Bobby Labonte
2006 #UCD6 Bobby Labonte
Press Pass Eclipse Under Cover Drivers Silver
2005 #UCD8 Bobby Labonte
2006 #UCD6 Bobby Labonte
Press Pass Eclipse Under Cover Gold Cars
2002 #CD5 Bobby Labonte
Press Pass Eclipse Under Cover Gold Drivers
2002 #CD5 Bobby Labonte
Press Pass Eclipse Under Cover Holofoil Drivers
2002 #CD5 Bobby Labonte
Press Pass F.Q.S.
1996 #FQS5A Bobby Labonte
1996 #FQS5B Bobby Labonte's Car
Press Pass Four Wide
2006 #FW-BL Bobby Labonte
Press Pass Four Wide Checkered Flag
2006 #FW-BL Bobby Labonte
Press Pass Game Face
2005 #GF5 Bobby Labonte
2006 #GF7 Bobby Labonte
Press Pass Gatorade Front Runner Award
2000 #10 Bobby Labonte
Press Pass Gold
2006 #G14 Bobby Labonte
2007 #G24 Bobby Labonte
2008 #G17 Bobby Labonte
Press Pass Gold Holofoil
2003 #P18 Bobby Labonte
2003 #P77 Screeching Halt WCS
Press Pass Hot Treads
2001 #HT1 Bobby Labonte/2405
2002 #HT23 B.Labonte's Car/2425
2002 #HT35 Bobby Labonte's Car/900
2004 #HTR7 Bobby Labonte
2005 #HTR16 Bobby Labonte
Press Pass Hot Treads Holofoil
2004 #HTR7 Bobby Labonte
2005 #HTR16 Bobby Labonte
Press Pass Lasers
1997 #11 Bobby Labonte
1997 #37 Bobby Labonte's Car
1997 #81 Bobby Labonte
1997 #109 Bobby Labonte
Press Pass Legends
2005 #42 Bobby Labonte C
2005 #49 T.Labonte/B.Labonte/J.Labonte FT
2006 #34 Bobby Labonte
2007 #37 Bobby Labonte
Press Pass Legends Autographs Black
2005 #21 Bobby Labonte
2006 #28 Bobby Labonte
Press Pass Legends Blue
2005 #42B Bobby Labonte C
2005 #49B T.Labonte/B.Labonte/J.Labonte FT
2006 #B34 Bobby Labonte
2007 #B37 Bobby Labonte
Press Pass Legends Bronze
2006 #Z34 Bobby Labonte
2007 #Z37 Bobby Labonte
Press Pass Legends Champion Threads & Treads Bronze
2006 #CTT-BL Bobby Labonte
Press Pass Legends Champion Threads & Treads Gold
2006 #CTT-BL Bobby Labonte
Press Pass Legends Champion Threads & Treads Silver
2006 #CTT-BL Bobby Labonte
Press Pass Legends Champion Threads Bronze
2006 #CT-BL Bobby Labonte
Press Pass Legends Champion Threads Gold
2006 #CT-BL Bobby Labonte
Press Pass Legends Champion Threads Patch
2006 #CT-BL Bobby Labonte
Press Pass Legends Champion Threads Silver
2006 #CT-BL Bobby Labonte
Press Pass Legends Double Threads Bronze
2005 #DT-LL B.Labonte/T.Labonte
Press Pass Legends Double Threads Gold
2005 #DT-LL B.Labonte/T.Labonte
Press Pass Legends Double Threads Silver
2005 #DT-LL B.Labonte/T.Labonte
Press Pass Legends Gold
2005 #42G Bobby Labonte C
2005 #49G T.Labonte/B.Labonte/J.Labonte FT
2006 #G34 Bobby Labonte
2007 #G37 Bobby Labonte
Press Pass Legends Holofoil
2005 #42H Bobby Labonte C
2005 #49H T.Labonte/B.Labonte/J.Labonte FT
2006 #H34 Bobby Labonte
2007 #H37 Bobby Labonte
Press Pass Legends Press Plates Black
2005 #42 Bobby Labonte C
2005 #49 T.Labonte/B.Labonte/J.Labonte FT
2006 #PPB34 Bobby Labonte
2007 #PP37 Bobby Labonte
Press Pass Legends Press Plates Black Backs
2006 #PPB34B Bobby Labonte
2007 #PP37 Bobby Labonte
Press Pass Legends Press Plates Cyan
2005 #42 Bobby Labonte C
2005 #49 T.Labonte/B.Labonte/J.Labonte FT
2006 #PPC34 Bobby Labonte
2007 #PP37 Bobby Labonte
Press Pass Legends Press Plates Cyan Backs
2006 #PPC34B Bobby Labonte
2007 #PP37 Bobby Labonte
Press Pass Legends Press Plates Magenta
2005 #42 Bobby Labonte C
2005 #49 T.Labonte/B.Labonte/J.Labonte FT
2006 #PPM34 Bobby Labonte
2007 #PP37 Bobby Labonte
Press Pass Legends Press Plates Magenta Backs
2006 #PPM34B Bobby Labonte
2007 #PP37 Bobby Labonte
Press Pass Legends Press Plates Yellow
2005 #42 Bobby Labonte C
2005 #49 T.Labonte/B.Labonte/J.Labonte FT
2006 #PPY34 Bobby Labonte
2007 #PP37 Bobby Labonte
Press Pass Legends Press Plates Yellow Backs
2006 #PPY34B Bobby Labonte
2007 #PP37 Bobby Labonte
Press Pass Legends Previews
2005 #42 Bobby Labonte C
2005 #49 T.Labonte/B.Labonte/J.Labonte FT/1
2006 #EB34 Bobby Labonte
2007 #EB37 Bobby Labonte
Press Pass Legends Signature Series
2007 #BL Bobby Labonte
Press Pass Legends Solo
2005 #42S Bobby Labonte C
2005 #49S T.Labonte/B.Labonte/J.Labonte FT
2006 #S34 Bobby Labonte
2007 #S37 Bobby Labonte
Press Pass Making the Show Collector's Series
2004 #MS12 Bobby Labonte
Press Pass Millennium
2000 #2 Bobby Labonte
2000 #40 Bobby Labonte
2000 #52 Bobby Labonte
2001 #1 Bobby Labonte
2001 #48 Bobby Labonte's Car
2001 #63 Bobby Labonte REP
2001 #71 Bobby Labonte REP
2001 #91 Bobby Labonte SO
Press Pass Moon Pie
1998 #3 Bobby Labonte
Press Pass Oil Cans
1998 #OC5 Bobby Labonte
1999 #7 Bobby Labonte
2000 #OC9 Bobby Labonte
Press Pass Oil Slicks
1997 #11 Bobby Labonte
1997 #37 Bobby Labonte's Car
1997 #81 Bobby Labonte
1997 #109 Bobby Labonte
1998 #11 Bobby Labonte
1998 #33 Bobby Labonte's Car
Press Pass Optima
2000 #11 Bobby Labonte
2000 #47 Bobby Labonte WCL
2001 #11 Bobby Labonte
2001 #50 Bobby Labonte WCL CL
2002 #16 Bobby Labonte
2003 #13 Bobby Labonte
2003 #41 Bobby Labonte UC
2004 #13 Bobby Labonte
2005 #16 Bobby Labonte
2005 #59 Bobby Labonte RR
2005 #96 Bobby Labonte R&R
2006 #27 Bobby Labonte
2006 #62 Bobby Labonte's Car HS
Press Pass Optima Cool Persistence
2000 #CP4 Bobby Labonte
2001 #CP7 Bobby Labonte
2003 #CP7 Bobby Labonte
2004 #CP10 Bobby Labonte
2005 #CP11 Bobby Labonte
Press Pass Optima Corporate Cuts Cars
2005 #CCT2 Bobby Labonte
Press Pass Optima Corporate Cuts Drivers
2005 #CCD2 Bobby Labonte
Press Pass Optima Encore
2000 #EN2 Bobby Labonte
Press Pass Optima Fan Favorite
2002 #FF13 Bobby Labonte
2003 #FF19 Bobby Labonte
2004 #FF13 Bobby Labonte
2005 #FF15 Bobby Labonte
Press Pass Optima G Force
2000 #GF11 Bobby Labonte
2001 #GF10 Bobby Labonte
Press Pass Optima Gold
2001 #11 Bobby Labonte
2001 #50 Bobby Labonte WCL CL
2002 #16 Bobby Labonte
2003 #G13 Bobby Labonte
2003 #G41 Bobby Labonte UC
2004 #G13 Bobby Labonte
2005 #G16 Bobby Labonte
2005 #G59 Bobby Labonte RR
2005 #G96 Bobby Labonte R&R
2006 #G27 Bobby Labonte
2006 #G62 Bobby Labonte's Car HS
Press Pass Optima On the Edge
2000 #OE4 Bobby Labonte
Press Pass Optima Overdrive
2000 #OD6 Bobby Labonte
Press Pass Optima Overdrive Square Cut
2000 #OD6 Bobby Labonte
Press Pass Optima Platinum
2000 #11 Bobby Labonte
2000 #47 Bobby Labonte WCL
Press Pass Optima Previews
2003 #13 Bobby Labonte
2004 #EB13 Bobby Labonte
2005 #16 Bobby Labonte
2006 #EB27 Bobby Labonte
Press Pass Optima Promos
2002 #16 Bobby Labonte
Press Pass Optima Q and A
2002 #QA5 Bobby Labonte
2003 #QA9 Bobby Labonte
Press Pass Optima Race Used Lugnuts Autographs
2002 #LNDA11 Bobby Labonte/18
Press Pass Optima Race Used Lugnuts Cars
2000 #LC19 Bobby Labonte's Car/50
2001 #LNC10 Bobby Labonte's Car
2002 #LNC11 Bobby Labonte's Car
Press Pass Optima Race Used Lugnuts Drivers
2000 #LD19 Bobby Labonte/55
2001 #LND9 Bobby Labonte
2002 #LND11 Bobby Labonte
Press Pass Optima Samples
2002 #16 Bobby Labonte
2003 #13 Bobby Labonte
2003 #41 Bobby Labonte UC
2004 #13 Bobby Labonte
2005 #16 Bobby Labonte
2005 #59 Bobby Labonte RR
2005 #96 Bobby Labonte R&R
Press Pass Optima Thunder Bolts Autographs
2004 #TBBL Bobby Labonte/18
Press Pass Optima Thunder Bolts Cars
2003 #TBT8 Bobby Labonte's Car
2004 #TBT11 Bobby Labonte's Car
Press Pass Optima Thunder Bolts Cars Autographs
2003 #TBT-BL Bobby Labonte/18
Press Pass Optima Thunder Bolts Drivers
2003 #TBD8 Bobby Labonte/60
2004 #TBD11 Bobby Labonte
Press Pass Optima Thunder Bolts Drivers Autographs
2003 #TBD-BL Bobby Labonte/18
Press Pass Optima XL
1995 #11 Bobby Labonte
1995 #32 Bobby Labonte TC
1995 #52 Bobby Labonte's Car
Press Pass Optima XL Cool Blue
1995 #11 Bobby Labonte
1995 #32 Bobby Labonte TC
1995 #52 Bobby Labonte's Car
Press Pass Optima XL Die Cut
1995 #11 Bobby Labonte
1995 #32 Bobby Labonte TC
1995 #52 Bobby Labonte's Car
Press Pass Optima XL Red Hot
1995 #11 Bobby Labonte
1995 #32 Bobby Labonte TC
1995 #52 Bobby Labonte's Car
Press Pass Optima XL Stealth
1995 #XLS6 Bobby Labonte
Press Pass Panorama
2005 #PPP7 Bobby Labonte
2005 #PPP29 Bobby Labonte
2005 #PPP48 Bobby Labonte
2005 #PPP49 Bobby Labonte
2005 #PPP63 Bobby Labonte
Press Pass Pit Stop
1998 #PS9 Bobby Labonte's Car
1999 #10 Bobby Labonte's Car
Press Pass Pitstop
2000 #PS9 Bobby Labonte's Car
Press Pass Platinum
2002 #18 Bobby Labonte
2002 #80 Bobby Labonte's Car
2004 #P16 Bobby Labonte
2004 #P68 Bobby Labonte's Car OTW
2004 #P77 Figuring It Out WCS
2004 #P79 Duking'-ing It Out WCS
2005 #P13 Bobby Labonte
2005 #P67 Bobby Labonte's Car OTW
2005 #P104 Bobby Labonte P
2006 #P14 Bobby Labonte
2007 #P24 Bobby Labonte
2008 #P17 Bobby Labonte
Press Pass Premium
1995 #18 Bobby Labonte
1996 #10 Bobby Labonte
1996 #36 Bobby Labonte's Car
1996 #P1 Bobby Labonte Promo
1997 #11 Bobby Labonte
1997 #41 Bobby Labonte
1998 #20 Bobby Labonte's Car
1998 #34 Bobby Labonte
1999 #13 Bobby Labonte
1999 #33 Bobby Labonte's Car
2000 #9 Bobby Labonte
2000 #34 Bobby Labonte's Car
2000 #56 Bobby Labonte
2000 #70 Bobby Labonte
2000 #P1 Bobby Labonte Promo
2001 #11 Bobby Labonte
2001 #34 Bobby Labonte
2001 #54 Bobby Labonte CC
2001 #76 Bobby Labonte PC
2002 #16 Bobby Labonte
2002 #53 Bobby Labonte CH
2002 #76 Bobby Labonte PC
2003 #15 Bobby Labonte
2003 #55 Bobby Labonte CC
2003 #74 Bobby Labonte PC
2004 #10 Bobby Labonte
2004 #55 Bobby Labonte CC
2004 #73 Bobby Labonte PC
2005 #14 Bobby Labonte
2005 #55 Bobby Labonte CC
2005 #76 Bobby Labonte PC
2006 #15 Bobby Labonte
2006 #53 Bobby Labonte CC
2007 #27 Bobby Labonte
2008 #27 Bobby Labonte
Press Pass Premium $10 Phone Cards
1996 #5 Bobby Labonte
Press Pass Premium $20 Phone Cards
1996 #5 Bobby Labonte
Press Pass Premium $5 Phone Cards
1996 #5 Bobby Labonte
Press Pass Premium Asphalt Jungle
2005 #AJ4 Bobby Labonte
Press Pass Premium Badge of Honor
1999 #BH9 Bobby Labonte
1999 #BH23 Bobby Labonte's Car
Press Pass Premium Badge of Honor Reflectors
1999 #BH9 Bobby Labonte
1999 #BH23 Bobby Labonte's Car
Press Pass Premium Clean Air
2008 #CA11 Bobby Labonte
Press Pass Premium Crystal Ball
1996 #CB8 Bobby Labonte
1997 #CB7 Bobby Labonte
Press Pass Premium Crystal Ball Die Cut
1997 #CB7 Bobby Labonte
Press Pass Premium Emerald Proofs
1996 #10 Bobby Labonte
1996 #36 Bobby Labonte's Car
1997 #11 Bobby Labonte
1997 #41 Bobby Labonte
Press Pass Premium Extreme Fire
1999 #FD6A Bobby Labonte 1:18
Press Pass Premium Flag Chasers
1998 #FC9 Bobby Labonte
1998 #FC23 Bobby Labonte's Car
Press Pass Premium Flag Chasers Reflectors
1998 #FC9 Bobby Labonte
1998 #FC23 Bobby Labonte's Car
Press Pass Premium Gold
2001 #11 Bobby Labonte
2001 #34 Bobby Labonte
2001 #54 Bobby Labonte CC
2001 #76 Bobby Labonte PC
Press Pass Premium Holofoil
1995 #18 Bobby Labonte
1996 #10 Bobby Labonte
1996 #36 Bobby Labonte's Car
Press Pass Premium Hot Pursuit
1996 #HP5 Bobby Labonte
Press Pass Premium Hot Threads Autographs
2005 #HT-BL Bobby Labonte/18
2007 #HT-BL Bobby Labonte/43
Press Pass Premium Hot Threads Cars
2003 #HTT8 Bobby Labonte
2005 #HTT9 Bobby Labonte
Press Pass Premium Hot Threads Cars Autographs
2003 #HTD-BL Bobby Labonte/18
Press Pass Premium Hot Threads Drivers
2003 #HTD8 Bobby Labonte
2005 #HTD9 Bobby Labonte
2007 #HTD9 Bobby Labonte
Press Pass Premium Hot Threads Drivers Autographs
2003 #HTT-BL Bobby Labonte/18
Press Pass Premium Hot Threads Drivers Bronze
2004 #HTD8 Bobby Labonte
Press Pass Premium Hot Threads Drivers Bronze Retail
2004 #HTT8 Bobby Labonte
Press Pass Premium Hot Threads Drivers Gold
2004 #HTD8 Bobby Labonte
2005 #HTD9 Bobby Labonte
2007 #HTD9 Bobby Labonte
Press Pass Premium Hot Threads Drivers Silver
2004 #HTD8 Bobby Labonte
Press Pass Premium Hot Threads Patch
2007 #HTP18 Bobby Labonte Pop Secret/10
2007 #HTP19 Bobby Labonte Victory Junction Gang/10
Press Pass Premium Hot Threads Patches
2008 #HTP20 Bobby Labonte Hamburger Helper/8
2008 #HTP21 Bobby Labonte Pillsbury/6
2008 #HTP22 Bobby Labonte U.S. Flag/6
Press Pass Premium Hot Threads Team
2007 #HTT9 Bobby Labonte
Press Pass Premium In The Zone
2000 #IZ2 Bobby Labonte
2001 #IZ8 Bobby Labonte
2002 #IZ8 Bobby Labonte
2004 #IZ1 Bobby Labonte
2005 #IZ12 Bobby Labonte
2006 #IZ12 Bobby Labonte
Press Pass Premium In the Zone Elite Edition
2004 #IZ1 Bobby Labonte
2005 #IZ12 Bobby Labonte
Press Pass Premium In the Zone Red
2006 #IZ12 Bobby Labonte
Press Pass Premium Lap Leaders
1997 #LL6 Bobby Labonte
Press Pass Premium Mirrors
1997 #11 Bobby Labonte
1997 #41 Bobby Labonte
Press Pass Premium Oil Slicks
1997 #11 Bobby Labonte
1997 #41 Bobby Labonte
Press Pass Premium Performance Driven
2001 #PD5 Bobby Labonte
2002 #PD5 Bobby Labonte
2005 #PD6 Bobby Labonte
2007 #PD1 Bobby Labonte
Press Pass Premium Performance Driven Red
2007 #PD1 Bobby Labonte
Press Pass Premium Previews
2003 #15 Bobby Labonte
2004 #10 Bobby Labonte
2008 #EB27 Bobby Labonte
Press Pass Premium Race Used Firesuit
1999 #F4 Bobby Labonte
2000 #F6 Bobby Labonte
Press Pass Premium Race Used Firesuit Cars
2001 #FC5 Bobby Labonte
2002 #FC4 Bobby Labonte
Press Pass Premium Race Used Firesuit Drivers
2001 #FD5 Bobby Labonte
2002 #FD4 Bobby Labonte
Press Pass Premium Red
2007 #R27 Bobby Labonte
2008 #27 Bobby Labonte
Press Pass Premium Red Hot
1995 #18 Bobby Labonte
Press Pass Premium Red Reflectors
2002 #16 Bobby Labonte
2002 #53 Bobby Labonte CC
2002 #76 Bobby Labonte PC
2003 #15 Bobby Labonte
2003 #55 Bobby Labonte CC
2003 #74 Bobby Labonte PC
Press Pass Premium Reflectors
1998 #20 Bobby Labonte's Car
1998 #34 Bobby Labonte
1999 #R13 Bobby Labonte
1999 #R33 Bobby Labonte's Car
2000 #9 Bobby Labonte
2000 #34 Bobby Labonte
2000 #56 Bobby Labonte
2000 #70 Bobby Labonte
Press Pass Premium Samples
2002 #16 Bobby Labonte
2003 #15 Bobby Labonte
2004 #10 Bobby Labonte
2005 #14 Bobby Labonte
Press Pass Premium Steel Horses
1998 #SH6 Bobby Labonte's Car
1999 #SH8 Bobby Labonte's Car
Press Pass Premium Triple Gear Firesuit
1998 #TGF5 Bobby Labonte
Press Pass Previews
1993 #17 J.Gordon/K.Wall./B.Lab.
1993 #19 Bobby Labonte
1993 #28 Bobby Labonte's Car
2003 #18 Bobby Labonte
2004 #16 Bobby Labonte
2006 #EB14 Bobby Labonte
2007 #EB24 Bobby Labonte
2008 #EB17 Bobby Labonte
Press Pass Previews Green
2005 #EB13 Bobby Labonte
Press Pass Previews Silver
2005 #EB104 Bobby Labonte
Press Pass R and N China
1996 #16 Bobby Labonte
Press Pass Race Day
2007 #RD12 Bobby Labonte
Press Pass Red Hot
1995 #15 Bobby Labonte
Press Pass Samples
2003 #18 Bobby Labonte
2003 #77 Screeching Halt WCS
2004 #16 Bobby Labonte
2004 #68 Bobby Labonte's Car OTW
2004 #77 Figuring It Out WCS
2004 #79 Duking'-ing It Out WCS
2005 #13 Bobby Labonte
2005 #67 Bobby Labonte's Car OTW
2005 #104 Bobby Labonte P
Press Pass Scorchers
1996 #16 Bobby Labonte
1996 #41 Bobby Labonte's Car
1996 #77 Gibbs/Makar/B.Labonte TW
1996 #94 Bobby Labonte S
Press Pass Shockers
1998 #ST9A Bobby Labonte
Press Pass Showcar
2002 #S7A Bobby Labonte's Car
2003 #S7B Bobby Labonte
2004 #S8B Bobby Labonte's Car
2005 #SC11 Bobby Labonte
Press Pass Showcar Die Cuts
2000 #SC2 Bobby Labonte's Car
Press Pass Showman
1999 #2A Bobby Labonte
2000 #SM2 Bobby Labonte
2002 #S7A Bobby Labonte
2003 #S7A Bobby Labonte
2004 #S8A Bobby Labonte
2005 #SM11 Bobby Labonte
Press Pass Showman Die Cuts
2000 #SM2 Bobby Labonte
Press Pass Showman/Showcar
2001 #S9A Bobby Labonte
2001 #S9B Bobby Labonte's Car
Press Pass Signings
1998 #10 Bobby Labonte VIP/S
1999 #30 Bobby Labonte/500
2001 #28 Bobby Labonte P/T/N/S
2002 #35 Bobby Labonte O/P/S/T/N
2003 #40 Bobby Labonte O/P/S/T/N
2004 #38 Bobby Labonte O/P/S/T/N
2005 #32 Bobby Labonte
2006 #29 Bobby Labonte NC S
2007 #38 Bobby Labonte NC
2008 #33 Bobby Labonte
Press Pass Signings Blue
2007 #16 Bobby Labonte NC
2008 #16 Bobby Labonte
Press Pass Signings Gold
1998 #10 Bobby Labonte VIP
1999 #12 Bobby Labonte/100
2000 #17 Bobby Labonte
2001 #19 Bobby Labonte S
2002 #33 Bobby Labonte O/P/S/T/N
2003 #40 Bobby Labonte O/P/S/T/N
2004 #35 Bobby Labonte O/P/S/T/N
2005 #30 Bobby Labonte
2006 #26 Bobby Labonte NC S
2007 #31 Bobby Labonte NC
2008 #28 Bobby Labonte
Press Pass Signings Platinum
2005 #29 Bobby Labonte
Press Pass Signings Press Plates Black
2007 #26 Bobby Labonte
2008 #24 Bobby Labonte
Press Pass Signings Press Plates Cyan
2007 #25 Bobby Labonte
2008 #24 Bobby Labonte
Press Pass Signings Press Plates Magenta
2007 #27 Bobby Labonte
2008 #24 Bobby Labonte
Press Pass Signings Press Plates Yellow
2007 #25 Bobby Labonte
2008 #24 Bobby Labonte
Press Pass Signings Silver
2007 #30 Bobby Labonte NC
2008 #24 Bobby Labonte
Press Pass Signings Transparent
2001 #6 Bobby Labonte S
2002 #6 Bobby Labonte O/P/S/T/N
2003 #6 Bobby Labonte O/P/S/T/N
2004 #5 Bobby Labonte O/P/S/T
Press Pass Skidmarks
1999 #5 Bobby Labonte
1999 #17 Bobby Labonte
1999 #32 Bobby Labonte's Car
1999 #83 Bobby Labonte OTP
2000 #SK3 Bobby Labonte
Press Pass Snapshots
2003 #SN13 Bobby Labonte
2004 #SN13 Bobby Labonte
2005 #SN15 Bobby Labonte
2006 #SN4 Bobby Labonte
2006 #SN23 Bobby Labonte
2007 #SN16 Bobby Labonte
Press Pass Speedway
2008 #17 Bobby Labonte
2008 #69 Bobby Labonte UTH
Press Pass Speedway Cockpit
2008 #CP12 Bobby Labonte
Press Pass Speedway Gold
2008 #G17 Bobby Labonte
2008 #G69 Bobby Labonte UTH
Press Pass Speedway Holofoil
2008 #H17 Bobby Labonte
2008 #H69 Bobby Labonte UTH
Press Pass Speedway Previews
2008 #EB17 Bobby Labonte
Press Pass Speedway Red
2008 #R17 Bobby Labonte
2008 #R69 Bobby Labonte UTH
Press Pass Stealth
1998 #19 Bobby Labonte
1998 #20 Bobby Labonte's Car
1999 #16 Bobby Labonte
1999 #17 Bobby Labonte's Car
1999 #55 Interstate Generator TT
2000 #25 Bobby Labonte
2000 #26 Bobby Labonte's Car
2000 #64 Bobby Labonte FF
2001 #19 Bobby Labonte
2001 #20 Bobby Labonte's Car
2001 #21 Bobby Labonte
2002 #19 Bobby Labonte
2002 #20 Bobby Labonte's Car
2002 #21 Bobby Labonte
2002 #62 Bobby Labonte's Car SST
2002 #66 Bobby Labonte WW
2003 #19 Bobby Labonte
2003 #20 Bobby Labonte's Car
2003 #21 Bobby Labonte
2003 #60 Bobby Labonte SST
2004 #40 Bobby Labonte
2004 #41 Bobby Labonte's Car
2004 #42 Bobby Labonte
2005 #57 Bobby Labonte

2005 #60 Bobby Labonte's Car
2005 #63 Bobby Labonte
2005 #85 Bobby Labonte H
2005 #92 Bobby Labonte SF
2006 #17 Bobby Labonte
2006 #67 Bobby Labonte F
2007 #15 Bobby Labonte
2007 #62 Bobby Labonte's Crew GC
2008 #20 Bobby Labonte

Press Pass Stealth Autographed Hat Entry
2006 #PPH14 Bobby Labonte

Press Pass Stealth Battle Armor Drivers
2007 #BAD23 Bobby Labonte

Press Pass Stealth Battle Armor Teams
2007 #BAT23 Bobby Labonte

Press Pass Stealth Behind the Numbers
2000 #BN9 Bobby Labonte
2002 #BN8 Bobby Labonte

Press Pass Stealth Big Numbers
1999 #BN11 Bobby Labonte

Press Pass Stealth Big Numbers Die Cuts
1999 #BN11 Bobby Labonte

Press Pass Stealth Chrome
2007 #15 Bobby Labonte
2007 #62 Bobby Labonte's Crew GC
2008 #20 Bobby Labonte

Press Pass Stealth Chrome Exclusives
2007 #X15 Bobby Labonte
2007 #X62 Bobby Labonte's Crew GC
2008 #20 Bobby Labonte

Press Pass Stealth Chrome Exclusives Gold
2008 #20 Bobby Labonte

Press Pass Stealth Chrome Platinum
2007 #P15 Bobby Labonte
2007 #P62 Bobby Labonte's Crew GC

Press Pass Stealth EFX
2003 #FX7 Bobby Labonte
2005 #EFX8 Bobby Labonte

Press Pass Stealth Fan Talk
1998 #5 Bobby Labonte

Press Pass Stealth Fan Talk Die Cuts
1998 #5 Bobby Labonte

Press Pass Stealth Fusion
1998 #19 Bobby Labonte
1998 #20 Bobby Labonte's Car
1999 #F16 Bobby Labonte
1999 #F17 Bobby Labonte's Car
1999 #F55 Interstate Generator TT
2000 #FS4 Bobby Labonte
2000 #FS5 Bobby Labonte's Car
2000 #FS6 Bobby Labonte
2001 #F4 Bobby Labonte
2002 #F7 Bobby Labonte
2003 #FU8 Bobby Labonte
2004 #FU9 Bobby Labonte
2005 #FU12 Bobby Labonte 1:14

Press Pass Stealth Fusion Green
2000 #FS4 Bobby Labonte
2000 #FS5 Bobby Labonte
2000 #FS6 Bobby Labonte

Press Pass Stealth Fusion Red
2000 #FS4 Bobby Labonte
2000 #FS5 Bobby Labonte
2000 #FS6 Bobby Labonte

Press Pass Stealth Gear Grippers Autographs
2004 #HT-BL Bobby Labonte/18

Press Pass Stealth Gear Grippers Cars
2003 #GGT18 Bobby Labonte
2005 #GGT7 Bobby Labonte

Press Pass Stealth Gear Grippers Drivers
2003 #GGD18 Bobby Labonte
2004 #GGD7 Bobby Labonte
2005 #GGD7 Bobby Labonte

Press Pass Stealth Gear Grippers Drivers Retail
2004 #GGT7 Bobby Labonte

Press Pass Stealth Gold
2002 #19 Bobby Labonte
2002 #20 Bobby Labonte's Car
2002 #21 Bobby Labonte
2002 #62 Bobby Labonte's Car SST
2002 #66 Bobby Labonte WW

Press Pass Stealth Holofoils
2001 #19 Bobby Labonte
2001 #20 Bobby Labonte
2001 #21 Bobby Labonte

Press Pass Stealth Hot Pass
2006 #HP17 Bobby Labonte

Press Pass Stealth Intensity
2000 #IN3 Bobby Labonte

Press Pass Stealth Lap Leaders
2001 #LL7 Bobby Labonte
2001 #LL25 Bobby Labonte's Car
2002 #LL15 Bobby Labonte

Press Pass Stealth Lap Leaders Clear Cars
2001 #LL25 Bobby Labonte's Car

Press Pass Stealth Lap Leaders Clear Drivers
2001 #LL7 Bobby Labonte

Press Pass Stealth Mach 07
2007 #M7-11 Bobby Labonte

Press Pass Stealth Maximum Access
2007 #MA16 Bobby Labonte
2008 #MA16 Bobby Labonte

Press Pass Stealth Maximum Access Autographs
2007 #MA16 Bobby Labonte
2008 #MA16 Bobby Labonte

Press Pass Stealth No Boundaries
2003 #NB17 Bobby Labonte
2004 #NB17 Bobby Labonte
2005 #NB9 Bobby Labonte

Press Pass Stealth Octane
1998 #19 Bobby Labonte
1998 #20 Bobby Labonte's Car

Press Pass Stealth Octane Die Cuts
1998 #19 Bobby Labonte
1998 #20 Bobby Labonte's Car

Press Pass Stealth Octane SLX
1999 #O12 Bobby Labonte
1999 #O30 Bobby Labonte's Car

Press Pass Stealth Octane SLX Die Cuts
1999 #O12 Bobby Labonte
1999 #O30 Bobby Labonte's Car

Press Pass Stealth Previews
2003 #19 Bobby Labonte
2003 #20 Bobby Labonte's Car

2003 #21 Bobby Labonte
2005 #57 Bobby Labonte
2005 #60 Bobby Labonte's Car
2005 #63 Bobby Labonte
2006 #17 Bobby Labonte
2007 #EB15 Bobby Labonte
2008 #20 Bobby Labonte

Press Pass Stealth Profile
2000 #PR4 Bobby Labonte
2002 #P9 Bobby Labonte
2003 #PR5 Bobby Labonte
2004 #P10 Bobby Labonte 1:14
2005 #PR8 Bobby Labonte

Press Pass Stealth Race Used Glove Cars
2001 #RGC10 Bobby Labonte/120
2002 #GLC9 Bobby Labonte's Car

Press Pass Stealth Race Used Glove Drivers
2001 #RGD10 Bobby Labonte/120
2002 #GLD9 Bobby Labonte

Press Pass Stealth Race Used Gloves
1998 #G5 Bobby Labonte
1999 #G5 Bobby Labonte/150
2000 #G1 Bobby Labonte/100

Press Pass Stealth Red
2003 #P19 Bobby Labonte
2003 #P20 Bobby Labonte's Car
2003 #P21 Bobby Labonte
2003 #P60 Bobby Labonte SST

Press Pass Stealth Retail
2006 #17 Bobby Labonte
2006 #67 Bobby Labonte F

Press Pass Stealth Samples
2002 #19 Bobby Labonte
2002 #20 Bobby Labonte's Car
2002 #21 Bobby Labonte
2002 #62 Bobby Labonte's Car SST
2002 #66 Bobby Labonte WW
2003 #19 Bobby Labonte
2003 #20 Bobby Labonte's Car
2003 #21 Bobby Labonte
2003 #60 Bobby Labonte SST
2004 #X40 Bobby Labonte
2004 #X41 Bobby Labonte's Car
2004 #X42 Bobby Labonte
2005 #57 Bobby Labonte
2005 #60 Bobby Labonte's Car
2005 #63 Bobby Labonte
2005 #85 Bobby Labonte H
2005 #92 Bobby Labonte SF

Press Pass Stealth SST
2000 #SST2 Bobby Labonte

Press Pass Stealth SST Cars
1999 #SS5 Bobby Labonte's Car

Press Pass Stealth SST Drivers
1999 #SS5 Bobby Labonte

Press Pass Stealth Stars
1998 #9 Bobby Labonte

Press Pass Stealth Stars Die Cuts
1998 #9 Bobby Labonte

Press Pass Stealth Synthesis
2008 #S6 Bobby Labonte

Press Pass Stealth X-Ray
2004 #40 Bobby Labonte
2004 #41 Bobby Labonte's Car
2004 #42 Bobby Labonte
2005 #X57 Bobby Labonte
2005 #X60 Bobby Labonte's Car
2005 #X63 Bobby Labonte
2005 #X85 Bobby Labonte H
2005 #X92 Bobby Labonte SF
2006 #X17 Bobby Labonte
2006 #X67 Bobby Labonte F

Press Pass Techno-Retro
2000 #TR12 Bobby Labonte

Press Pass Top 25 Drivers & Rides
2006 #C21 Bobby Labonte's Car
2006 #D21 Bobby Labonte

Press Pass Top Shelf
2002 #TS5 Bobby Labonte
2003 #TS5 Bobby Labonte
2004 #TS8 Bobby Labonte

Press Pass Torpedoes
1998 #ST9B Bobby Labonte's Car

Press Pass Torquers
1996 #16 Bobby Labonte
1996 #41 Bobby Labonte's Car
1996 #77 Gibbs/Makar/B.Labonte TW
1996 #94 Bobby Labonte S
1997 #11 Bobby Labonte
1997 #37 Bobby Labonte's Car
1997 #81 Bobby Labonte
1997 #109 Bobby Labonte

Press Pass Total Memorabilia
2001 #TM9 Bobby Labonte

Press Pass Total Memorabilia Power Pick
2002 #TM5 Bobby Labonte
2003 #TM8 Bobby Labonte
2004 #TM8 Bobby Labonte
2005 #TM8 Bobby Labonte

Press Pass Trackside
2000 #13 Bobby Labonte
2000 #33 Bobby Labonte's Car
2001 #13 Bobby Labonte
2001 #46 Bobby Labonte's Car
2001 #66 Bobby Labonte TM
2002 #13 Bobby Labonte
2002 #62 Bobby Labonte RD
2002 #70 Bobby Labonte's Car
2002 #81 Bobby Labonte TM
2003 #25 Bobby Labonte
2003 #67 Bobby Labonte in Pits
2003 #74 T.Stewart/B.Labonte TM
2004 #24 Bobby Labonte
2004 #58 Bobby Labonte's Car HS
2004 #65 T.Stewart/B.Labonte TM
2004 #106 Bobby Labonte TT
2004 #119 Bobby Labonte F
2005 #6 Bobby Labonte
2005 #59 Bobby Labonte's Car HS
2005 #68 Stewart/Leffler/B.Labonte TM
2005 #80 B.Labonte/T.Labonte FA
2005 #87 Bobby Labonte GP

Press Pass Trackside Dialed In
2000 #DI2 Bobby Labonte
2001 #D7 Bobby Labonte
2002 #DI7 Bobby Labonte
2003 #DI6 Bobby Labonte
2004 #DI8 Bobby Labonte

2005 #DI6 Bobby Labonte

Press Pass Trackside Die Cuts
2000 #13 Bobby Labonte
2000 #33 Bobby Labonte
2001 #13 Bobby Labonte
2001 #46 Bobby Labonte's Car
2001 #66 Bobby Labonte TM

Press Pass Trackside Gold Holofoil
2003 #P25 Bobby Labonte
2003 #P67 Bobby Labonte's Crew
2003 #P74 T.Stewart/B.Labonte

Press Pass Trackside Golden
2000 #13 Bobby Labonte
2000 #33 Bobby Labonte
2001 #13 Bobby Labonte
2001 #46 Bobby Labonte's Car
2001 #66 Bobby Labonte TM
2002 #G13 Bobby Labonte
2003 #G25 Bobby Labonte
2004 #G24 Bobby Labonte
2004 #G58 Bobby Labonte's Car HS
2004 #G65 T.Stewart/B.Labonte TM
2004 #G106 Bobby Labonte TT
2004 #G119 Bobby Labonte F
2005 #G6 Bobby Labonte
2005 #G59 Bobby Labonte's Car HS
2005 #G68 Stewart/Leffler/B.Labonte TM
2005 #G80 B.Labonte/T.Labonte FA
2005 #G87 Bobby Labonte GP

Press Pass Trackside Hat Giveaway
2003 #PPH14 Bobby Labonte
2004 #PPH15 Bobby Labonte
2005 #PPH17 Bobby Labonte

Press Pass Trackside Hot Pass
2004 #HP10 Bobby Labonte
2005 #10 Bobby Labonte

Press Pass Trackside Hot Pass National
2004 #HP10 Bobby Labonte
2005 #10 Bobby Labonte

Press Pass Trackside Hot Pursuit
2005 #HP9 Bobby Labonte

Press Pass Trackside License to Drive
2002 #18 Bobby Labonte
2003 #LD8 Bobby Labonte

Press Pass Trackside License to Drive Die Cuts
2002 #18 Bobby Labonte

Press Pass Trackside Mirror Image
2002 #MI5 Bobby Labonte
2003 #MI5 Bobby Labonte

Press Pass Trackside Panorama
2000 #P34 Bobby Labonte

Press Pass Trackside Pit Stoppers
2000 #PS4 Bobby Labonte

Press Pass Trackside Pit Stoppers Autographs
2004 #PS-BL Bobby Labonte/18

Press Pass Trackside Pit Stoppers Cars
2001 #PSC7 Bobby Labonte's Car
2002 #PSC1 Bobby Labonte's Car/350
2003 #PST6 Bobby Labonte
2004 #PST6 Bobby Labonte
2005 #PST13 Bobby Labonte

Press Pass Trackside Pit Stoppers Cars Autographs
2003 #BL Bobby Labonte/18

Press Pass Trackside Pit Stoppers Drivers
2001 #PSD7 Bobby Labonte
2002 #PSD1 Bobby Labonte/150
2003 #PSD6 Bobby Labonte
2004 #PSD6 Bobby Labonte
2005 #PSD13 Bobby Labonte

Press Pass Trackside Pit Stoppers Drivers Autographs
2003 #PSD-BL Bobby Labonte/18

Press Pass Trackside Previews
2003 #25 Bobby Labonte
2004 #EB24 Bobby Labonte
2005 #6 Bobby Labonte
2005 #87 Bobby Labonte GP

Press Pass Trackside Runnin N' Gunnin
2000 #RG9 Bobby Labonte
2001 #RG9 Bobby Labonte
2002 #RG4 Bobby Labonte
2003 #RG5 Bobby Labonte
2004 #RG5 Bobby Labonte
2005 #RG5 Bobby Labonte

Press Pass Trackside Samples
2002 #13 Bobby Labonte
2002 #62 Bobby Labonte RD
2002 #70 Bobby Labonte's Car
2002 #81 Bobby Labonte TM
2003 #25 Bobby Labonte
2003 #67 Bobby Labonte in Pits
2003 #74 T.Stewart/B.Labonte TM
2004 #24 Bobby Labonte
2004 #58 Bobby Labonte's Car HS
2004 #65 T.Stewart/B.Labonte TM
2004 #106 Bobby Labonte TT
2004 #119 Bobby Labonte F
2005 #6 Bobby Labonte
2005 #59 Bobby Labonte's Car HS
2005 #68 Stewart/Leffler/B.Labonte TM
2005 #80 B.Labonte/T.Labonte FA
2005 #87 Bobby Labonte GP

Press Pass Trackside Too Tough To Tame
2000 #TT3 Bobby Labonte

Press Pass Triple Burner
2001 #TB9 Bobby Labonte
2002 #TB5 Bobby Labonte
2003 #TB8 Bobby Labonte
2004 #TB8 Bobby Labonte
2005 #TB8 Bobby Labonte

Press Pass Triple Burner Exchange
2003 #TB8 Bobby Labonte EXCH
2004 #TB8 Bobby Labonte
2005 #TB8 Bobby Labonte

Press Pass Triple Gear 3 in 1
1998 #STG5 Bobby Labonte
1999 #TG4 Bobby Labonte

Press Pass Triple Gear Burning Rubber
1998 #TG5 Bobby Labonte

Press Pass Velocity
2002 #VL6 Bobby Labonte

Press Pass Victory Lap
2003 #13 Bobby Labonte

Press Pass Vintage
2001 #VN1 Bobby Labonte
2002 #VN12 Bobby Labonte

Pro Set
1992 #6 Bobby Labonte

Race Sharks
1997 #9 Bobby Labonte
1997 #25 Bobby Labonte

Race Sharks First Bite
1997 #9 Bobby Labonte
1997 #25 Bobby Labonte

Race Sharks Great White
1997 #9 Bobby Labonte
1997 #25 Bobby Labonte

Race Sharks Great White Shark's Teeth
1997 #GW7 Bobby Labonte

Race Sharks Great White Shark's Teeth First Bite
1997 #GW7 Bobby Labonte

Race Sharks Hammerhead
1997 #9 Bobby Labonte
1997 #25 Bobby Labonte

Race Sharks Hammerhead First Bite
1997 #9 Bobby Labonte
1997 #25 Bobby Labonte

Race Sharks Shark Tooth Signatures
1997 #ST11 Bobby Labonte/800

Race Sharks Shark Tooth Signatures First Bite
1997 #ST11 Bobby Labonte

Race Sharks Tiger Shark
1997 #9 Bobby Labonte
1997 #25 Bobby Labonte

Race Sharks Tiger Shark First Bite
1997 #9 Bobby Labonte
1997 #25 Bobby Labonte

Racer's Choice
1996 #14 Bobby Labonte
1996 #38 Bobby Labonte's Car
1996 #66 Bobby Labonte OF
1996 #67 Bobby Labonte OF
1996 #68 Bobby Labonte OF
1996 #69 Bobby Labonte OF
1996 #70 Bobby Labonte OF
1996 #94 Bobby Labonte BC
1997 #18 Bobby Labonte
1997 #53 Bobby Labonte's Car
1997 #98 Bobby Labonte TR

Racer's Choice Artist's Proofs
1996 #14 Bobby Labonte
1996 #38 Bobby Labonte's Car
1996 #66 Bobby Labonte OF
1996 #67 Bobby Labonte OF
1996 #68 Bobby Labonte OF
1996 #69 Bobby Labonte OF
1996 #70 Bobby Labonte OF
1996 #94 Bobby Labonte BC

Racer's Choice Busch Clash
1997 #13 Bobby Labonte

Racer's Choice High Octane
1997 #8 Bobby Labonte

Racer's Choice High Octane Glow in the Dark
1997 #8 Bobby Labonte

Racer's Choice Showcase Series
1997 #18 Bobby Labonte
1997 #53 Bobby Labonte's Car
1997 #98 Bobby Labonte TR

Racer's Choice Speedway Collection
1996 #14 Bobby Labonte
1996 #38 Bobby Labonte's Car
1996 #66 Bobby Labonte OF
1996 #67 Bobby Labonte OF
1996 #68 Bobby Labonte OF
1996 #69 Bobby Labonte OF
1996 #70 Bobby Labonte OF
1996 #94 Bobby Labonte BC

Racer's Choice Top Ten
1996 #10 Bobby Labonte

Redline Standups
1992 #4 Bobby Labonte
1992 #35 Bobby Labonte

SB Motorsports
1997 #12 Bobby Labonte
1997 #51 Bobby Labonte's Car
1997 #87 Bobby Labonte

SB Motorsports Race Chat
1997 #RC9 Bobby Labonte

SB Motorsports Winston Cup Rewind
1997 #WC12 Bobby Labonte
1997 #WC25 Bobby Labonte

Score Board IQ
1997 #8 Bobby Labonte
1997 #43 Bobby Labonte's Car

Score Board IQ $10 Phone Cards
1997 #PC3 Bobby Labonte

Score Board IQ Remarques
1997 #SB8 Bobby Labonte

Score Board IQ Remarques Sam Bass Finished
1997 #SB8 Bobby Labonte

Select
1995 #17 Bobby Labonte
1995 #114 B.Labonte/T.Labonte IB
1995 #125 Bobby Labonte YS

Select Flat Out
1995 #17 Bobby Labonte
1995 #114 B.Labonte/T.Labonte IB
1995 #125 Bobby Labonte YS

SkyBox Profile
1997 #15 Bobby Labonte
1997 #68 Bobby Labonte's Car

SkyBox Profile Autographs
1997 #15 Bobby Labonte

SkyBox Profile Break Out
1997 #B7 Bobby Labonte

Slim Jim Bobby Labonte
1992 #2 Bobby Labonte's Car
1992 #3 Bobby Labonte
1992 #4 Bobby Labonte's Car
1992 #5 Bobby Labonte's Car
1992 #6 Bobby Labonte
1992 #7 Bobby Labonte/Terry Labonte
1992 #8 Bobby Labonte
1992 #9 Bobby Labonte in Pits
1992 #10 Bobby Labonte's Car
1992 #11 Bobby Labonte
1992 #12 Bobby Labonte's Car
1992 #13 Bobby Labonte Autograph Card
1992 #14 Bobby Labonte in Pits
1992 #15 Bobby Labonte
1992 #16 Bobby Labonte/S.Grissom/D.Earnhardt Cars
1992 #17 Bobby Labonte

1992 #18 Bobby Labonte in Pits
1992 #19 Bobby Labonte's Car
1992 #20 Bobby Labonte/Chad Little Cars
1992 #21 Bobby Labonte
1992 #22 Bobby Labonte's Car
1992 #23 Bobby Labonte/Donna Labonte
1992 #24 Bobby Labonte/Bob Labonte Sr.
1992 #25 Bobby Labonte
1992 #26 Bobby Labonte's Car
1992 #27 Bobby Labonte's Car
1992 #28 Bobby Labonte w/Car
1992 #29 Bobby Labonte w/Car

SLU Racing Winner's Circle
1997 #6 Bobby Labonte
1998 #7A Bobby Labonte
1998 #7B B.Labonte Small Soldiers
1999 #40 Bobby Labonte

SP
1995 #15 Bobby Labonte CC
1995 #49 Bobby Labonte
1995 #91 Bobby Labonte's Car
1996 #18 Bobby Labonte
1996 #51 Bobby Labonte CC
1997 #18 Bobby Labonte
1997 #60 Bobby Labonte's Car
1997 #98 Bobby Labonte 2F
1997 #120 Bobby Labonte 2F

SP Authentic
1998 #18 Bobby Labonte
1998 #52 Bobby Labonte's Car
1998 #82 Bobby Labonte VL
1999 #5 Bobby Labonte
1999 #55 Bobby Labonte's Car
1999 #67 Bobby Labonte CLASS
1999 #73 Bobby Labonte SP
2000 #1 Bobby Labonte
2000 #76 Bobby Labonte SUP

SP Authentic Behind the Wheel
1998 #BW6 Bobby Labonte

SP Authentic Behind the Wheel Die Cuts
1998 #BW6 Bobby Labonte

SP Authentic Behind the Wheel Gold
1998 #BW6 Bobby Labonte

SP Authentic Cup Challengers
1999 #CC8 Bobby Labonte

SP Authentic Driver's Seat
2000 #DS2 Bobby Labonte

SP Authentic Driving Force
1999 #DF1 Bobby Labonte

SP Authentic In the Driver's Seat
1999 #DS5 Bobby Labonte

SP Authentic Overdrive
1999 #5 Bobby Labonte
1999 #55 Bobby Labonte CAR
1999 #67 Bobby Labonte CLASS
1999 #73 Bobby Labonte SP/18

SP Authentic Overdrive Gold
2000 #1 Bobby Labonte/18
2000 #76 Bobby Labonte SUP/18

SP Authentic Overdrive Silver
2000 #1 Bobby Labonte
2000 #76 Bobby Labonte SUP

SP Authentic Race for the Cup
2000 #R6 Bobby Labonte

SP Authentic Sign of the Times
1999 #BL Bobby Labonte
2000 #BL Bobby Labonte EXCH

SP Authentic Sign of the Times Red
1998 #ST9 Bobby Labonte's Car

SP Die Cuts
1995 #15 Bobby Labonte
1995 #49 Bobby Labonte
1995 #91 Bobby Labonte's Car

SP Driving Force
1996 #DF8 Bobby Labonte

SP Holoview Maximum Effects
1996 #ME18 Bobby Labonte

SP Holoview Maximum Effects Die Cuts
1996 #ME18 Bobby Labonte

SP Speed Merchants
1995 #SM18 Bobby Labonte

SP Speed Merchants Die Cuts
1995 #SM18 Bobby Labonte

SP Super Series
1997 #18 Bobby Labonte
1997 #60 Bobby Labonte's Car
1997 #98 Bobby Labonte 2F
1997 #120 Bobby Labonte 2F

Speedflix
1996 #23 Bobby Labonte
1996 #45 Bobby Labonte's Car in pits

Speedflix Artist Proof's
1996 #23 Bobby Labonte
1996 #45 Bobby Labonte in Pits

Speedflix Clear Shots
1996 #5 Bobby Labonte

SPx
1996 #18 Bobby Labonte
1997 #18 Bobby Labonte

SPx Blue
1997 #18 Bobby Labonte

SPx Gold
1996 #18 Bobby Labonte
1997 #18 Bobby Labonte

SPx Silver
1997 #18 Bobby Labonte

SPx SpeedView Autographs
1997 #SV9 Bobby Labonte

Stove Top
1993 #3 Bobby Labonte

Super Shots California Speedway
2002 #CS2 Bobby Labonte's Car

Super Shots Sears Point CHP
2001 #SP2 Bobby Labonte's Car

Traks
1992 #11 Bobby Labonte
1992 #44 Bobby Labonte
1993 #22 Bobby Labonte
1993 #176 Bobby Labonte
1994 #22 Bobby Labonte
1994 #48 Bobby Labonte
1994 #59 Bobby Labonte's Car
1994 #123 Bobby Labonte
1995 #5 Bobby Labonte
2006 #18 Bobby Labonte
2006 #51 Bobby Labonte's Car

2007 #15 Bobby Labonte
2007 #80 Bobby Labonte GP

Traks 5th Anniversary
1995 #33 Bobby Labonte

Traks 5th Anniversary Clear Contenders
1995 #C7 Bobby Labonte

Traks 5th Anniversary Gold
1995 #33 Bobby Labonte
1995 #62 Bobby Labonte

Traks 5th Anniversary Jumbos
1995 #E9 Bobby Labonte

Traks 5th Anniversary Jumbos Gold
1995 #E9 Bobby Labonte

Traks Auto Value
1994 #27 Bobby Labonte
1995 #25 Bobby Labonte

Traks Autographs
1992 #A8 Bobby Labonte
2006 #21 Bobby Labonte NC

TRAKS Autographs 100
2006 #12 Bobby Labonte NC

TRAKS Autographs 25
2006 #19 Bobby Labonte NC

Traks Driver's Seat
2007 #DS7 Bobby Labonte
2007 #DS7B Bobby Labonte VAR

Traks Driver's Seat National
2007 #DS7 Bobby Labonte

Traks First Run
1993 #22 Bobby Labonte
1993 #176 Bobby Labonte
1994 #22 Bobby Labonte
1994 #48 Bobby Labonte
1994 #59 Bobby Labonte's Car
1994 #123 Bobby Labonte
1995 #5 Bobby Labonte

Traks Gold
2007 #G15 Bobby Labonte
2007 #G80 Bobby Labonte GP

Traks Goody's
1992 #1 Bobby Labonte

Traks Holofoil
2007 #H15 Bobby Labonte
2007 #H80 Bobby Labonte GP

Traks On The Rise
1995 #OTR20 Bobby Labonte

Traks On The Rise First Run
1995 #OTR20 Bobby Labonte

Traks Preferred Collector
1994 #35 Bobby Labonte

Traks Previews
2007 #EB15 Bobby Labonte
2007 #EB80 Bobby Labonte GP

Traks Racing Machines
1992 #57 Bobby Labonte in Pits
1992 #60 H.Gant/B.Labonte Cars
1992 #98 B.Lab/T.Lab/R.Wil/Irv Cars CL
1995 #RM20 Bobby Labonte's Car

Traks Racing Machines First Run
1995 #RM20 Bobby Labonte's Car

Traks Red
2007 #R15 Bobby Labonte
2007 #R80 Bobby Labonte GP

TRAKS Stickers
2006 #43 Bobby Labonte

Traks Team Sets
1992 #101 Earnhardt/D.Allison/Irvan/B.Lab/K.Petty Cars

Traks Trivia
1993 #22 Bobby Labonte
1993 #31 Bobby Labonte

Ultra
1996 #29 Bobby Labonte
1996 #30 Bobby Labonte
1996 #31 Bobby Labonte's Car
1996 #166 Bobby Labonte's Helmet
1996 #170 J.Gordon/B.Lab/T.Lab RW
1996 #171 Bobby Labonte's Car RW
1996 #177 Bobby Labonte's Car RW
1996 #180 Bobby Labonte RW
1997 #17 Bobby Labonte
1997 #49 Bobby Labonte's Car

Ultra AKA
1997 #A7 Bobby Labonte

Ultra Autographs
1996 #15 Bobby Labonte

Ultra Boxed Set
1996 #10 Bobby Labonte

Ultra Flair Preview
1996 #10 Bobby Labonte

Ultra Golden Memories
1996 #7 Bobby Labonte

Ultra Inside Out
1997 #DC12 Bobby Labonte

Ultra Shoney's
1997 #7 Bobby Labonte

Ultra Thunder and Lightning
1996 #9 Bobby Labonte's Car
1996 #10 Bobby Labonte's Car

Ultra Update
1996 #17 Bobby Labonte
1996 #63 Bobby Labonte's Car
1997 #11 Bobby Labonte
1997 #84 Bobby Labonte's Car

Ultra Update Autographs
1996 #7 Bobby Labonte
1997 #11 Bobby Labonte

Ultra Update Double Trouble
1997 #DT3 Bobby Labonte

Ultra Update Driver View
1997 #D4 Bobby Labonte

Ultra Update Proven Power
1996 #7 Bobby Labonte

Ultra Update Winner
1996 #3 Bobby Labonte
1996 #9 Bobby Labonte

Ultra Winn Dixie
1997 #WD6 Bobby Labonte

Upper Deck
1995 #18 Bobby Labonte
1995 #61 Bobby Labonte with Car
1995 #86 Bobby Labonte's Car
1995 #114 Bobby Labonte's Car NIL
1995 #171 Bobby Labonte DYK
1995 #198 Bobby Labonte
1995 #242 Bobby Labonte SD

1995 #279 Bobby Labonte's Car
1996 #16 Bobby Labonte
1996 #56 Bobby Labonte SB
1996 #96 Bobby Labonte PP
Upper Deck Diamond Vision
1998 #13 Bobby Labonte
Upper Deck Diamond Vision Signature Moves
1998 #13 Bobby Labonte
Upper Deck Gold Signature/Electric Gold
1995 #18 Bobby Labonte
1995 #61 Bobby Labonte with Car
1995 #86 Bobby Labonte's Car
1995 #114 Bobby Labonte's Car
1995 #171 Bobby Labonte DYK
1995 #198 Bobby Labonte
1995 #242 Bobby Labonte SD
1995 #279 Bobby Labonte's Car
Upper Deck MVP
2000 #18 Bobby Labonte
2000 #75 Bobby Labonte's Car
Upper Deck MVP Cup Quest 2000
2000 #CQ8 Bobby Labonte
Upper Deck MVP Gold Script
2000 #18 Bobby Labonte
2000 #75 Bobby Labonte
Upper Deck MVP Legends in the Making
2000 #LM3 Bobby Labonte
Upper Deck MVP Magic Numbers
2000 #MBL Bobby Labonte's Car
Upper Deck MVP Magic Numbers Autographs
2000 #MABL B.Labonte's Car/18
Upper Deck MVP NASCAR Gallery
2000 #NG1 Terry Labonte
2000 #NG10 Bobby Labonte
Upper Deck MVP NASCAR Stars
2000 #NS7 Bobby Labonte
Upper Deck MVP ProSign
2000 #PSBL Bobby Labonte EXCH
Upper Deck MVP Silver Script
2000 #18 Bobby Labonte
2000 #75 Bobby Labonte
Upper Deck MVP Super Script
2000 #18 Bobby Labonte/18
2000 #75 Bobby Labonte's Car/18
Upper Deck Predictor Poles
1996 #RP5 Bobby Labonte
Upper Deck Predictor Poles Prizes
1996 #RP5 Bobby Labonte
Upper Deck Predictor Series Points
1995 #PP5 Bobby Labonte
Upper Deck Predictor Series Points Prizes
1995 #PP5 Bobby Labonte
Upper Deck Predictor Wins
1996 #HP4 Bobby Labonte
Upper Deck Predictor Wins Prizes
1996 #HP4 Bobby Labonte
Upper Deck Racing
2000 #2 Bobby Labonte
Upper Deck Racing Record Pace
2000 #RP2 Bobby Labonte
Upper Deck Racing Road Signs
2000 #RSBL Bobby Labonte
Upper Deck Racing Speeding Ticket
2000 #ST2 Bobby Labonte
Upper Deck Racing Trophy Dash
2000 #TD3 Bobby Labonte
Upper Deck Racing Winning Formula
2000 #WF1 Bobby Labonte
Upper Deck Road To The Cup
1996 #RC9 Bobby Labonte
1996 #RC58 Bobby Labonte's Car
1996 #RC94 Bobby Labonte
1996 #RC132 Bobby Labonte
1997 #11 Bobby Labonte
1997 #53 Bobby Labonte's Car
1997 #95 Bobby Labonte
1997 #118 Bobby Labonte's Trans.
1997 #128 Bobby Labonte
1998 #18 Bobby Labonte's Car
1998 #68 Bobby/Terry Labonte
1998 #70 Bobby Labonte's Car
1999 #11 Bobby Labonte
1999 #38 Bobby Labonte's Car
1999 #70 Bobby Labonte FF
1999 #82 Bobby Labonte HH
Upper Deck Road To The Cup Autographs
1996 #H9 Bobby Labonte
Upper Deck Road To The Cup Cup Quest Turn 1
1998 #CQ7 Bobby Labonte's Car
Upper Deck Road To The Cup Cup Quest Turn 2
1998 #CQ7 Bobby Labonte's Car
Upper Deck Road To The Cup Cup Quest Turn 3
1998 #CQ7 Bobby Labonte's Car
Upper Deck Road To The Cup Cup Quest Turn 4
1998 #CQ7 Bobby Labonte's Car
Upper Deck Road To The Cup Cup Quest Victory Lane
1998 #CQ7 Bobby Labonte's Car
Upper Deck Road To The Cup Game Face
1996 #GF8 Bobby Labonte
Upper Deck Road to the Cup NASCAR Chronicles
1999 #NC1 Bobby Labonte
Upper Deck Road To The Cup Predictor Plus
1997 #29 Bobby Labonte WIN 2
Upper Deck Road To The Cup Predictor Plus Cel Die Cuts
1997 #29 Bobby Labonte
Upper Deck Road To The Cup Predictor Plus Cels
1997 #29 Bobby Labonte
Upper Deck Road To The Cup Predictor Points
1996 #PP9 Bobby Labonte
Upper Deck Road To The Cup Predictor Points Prizes
1996 #PR9 Bobby Labonte
Upper Deck Road To The Cup Predictor Top 3
1996 #T5 Martin/R.Wallace/B.Labonte
Upper Deck Road To The Cup Predictor Top 3 Prizes
1996 #R8 Bobby Labonte
Upper Deck Road To The Cup Premiere Position
1997 #PP33 Bobby Labonte
1997 #PP37 Bobby Labonte
1997 #PP39 Bobby Labonte
1997 #PP40 Bobby Labonte
Upper Deck Road To The Cup Racing Legends
1996 #RL12 Bobby Labonte
Upper Deck Road to the Cup Road to the Cup Bronze Level 1
1999 #RTTC5Bobby Labonte
Upper Deck Road to the Cup Road to the Cup Gold Level 3
1999 #RTTC5Bobby Labonte
Upper Deck Road to the Cup Road to the Cup Silver Level 2
1999 #RTTC5Bobby Labonte
Upper Deck Road to the Cup Signature Collection Checkered Flag
1999 #BL Bobby Labonte
Upper Deck Road to the Cup Upper Deck Profiles
1999 #P8 Bobby Labonte
Upper Deck Road To The Cup Winning Materials
1998 #W4 Bobby Labonte
Upper Deck Silver Signature/Electric Silver
1995 #18 Bobby Labonte
1995 #61 Bobby Labonte with Car
1995 #86 Bobby Labonte's Car
1995 #114 Bobby Labonte's Car NIL
1995 #171 Bobby Labonte DYK
1995 #198 Bobby Labonte
1995 #242 Bobby Labonte SD
1995 #279 Bobby Labonte's Car
Upper Deck Victory Circle
1997 #18 Bobby Labonte
1997 #68 Bobby Labonte's Car
1997 #118 Bobby Labonte
1998 #18 Bobby Labonte
1998 #63 Bobby Labonte's Car
1998 #112 Bobby Labonte
1998 #147 Bobby Labonte
1999 #5 Bobby Labonte
1999 #68 Bobby Labonte's Car
2000 #18 Bobby Labonte
2000 #53 Bobby Labonte's Car
2000 #72 Bobby Labonte's Car
Upper Deck Victory Circle 32 Days of Speed
1998 #D23 Bobby Labonte
1998 #D28 Bobby Labonte
Upper Deck Victory Circle 32 Days of Speed Gold
1998 #D23 Bobby Labonte
1998 #D28 Bobby Labonte
Upper Deck Victory Circle Driver's Seat
1997 #DS8 Bobby Labonte
Upper Deck Victory Circle Exclusives Level 1 Silver
2000 #18 Bobby Labonte
2000 #53 Bobby Labonte's Car
2000 #72 Bobby Labonte's Car
Upper Deck Victory Circle Exclusives Level 2 Gold
2000 #18 Bobby Labonte/18
2000 #53 Bobby Labonte's Car/18
2000 #72 Bobby Labonte/18
Upper Deck Victory Circle Generation Excitement
1997 #GE5 Bobby Labonte
Upper Deck Victory Circle Income Statement
1999 #IS2 Bobby Labonte
2000 #IS3 Bobby Labonte
Upper Deck Victory Circle Income Statement LTD
2000 #IS3 Bobby Labonte
Upper Deck Victory Circle Magic Numbers
1999 #M2 Bobby Labonte
Upper Deck Victory Circle Magic Numbers Autographs
1999 #M2 Bobby Labonte/18
Upper Deck Victory Circle Piece of the Engine
1998 #PE5 Bobby Labonte
1998 #PE10 Bobby Labonte
Upper Deck Victory Circle Point Leaders
1998 #PL7 Bobby Labonte
Upper Deck Victory Circle Predictor
1997 #PE7 Bobby Labonte WIN
Upper Deck Victory Circle Predictor Plus
1998 #18 Bobby Labonte
Upper Deck Victory Circle Predictor Plus Cel Redemption
1998 #18 Bobby Labonte
Upper Deck Victory Circle Predictor Winner Cels
1997 #PH7 Bobby Labonte
Upper Deck Victory Circle Signature Collection
1999 #BL Bobby Labonte
Upper Deck Victory Circle Sparks of Brilliance
1998 #SB7 Bobby Labonte
Upper Deck Victory Circle Speed Zone
1999 #SZ1 Bobby Labonte
Upper Deck Victory Circle Track Masters
1999 #TM11 Bobby Labonte
Upper Deck Victory Circle UD Exclusives
1999 #5 Bobby Labonte
1999 #68 Bobby Labonte
Upper Deck Victory Circle Victory Circle
1999 #V2 Bobby Labonte
2000 #V1 Bobby Labonte
Upper Deck Victory Circle Victory Circle LTD
2000 #V1 Bobby Labonte
Upper Deck Victory Circle Victory Lap
1997 #VL3 Bobby Labonte
Upper Deck Victory Circle Winning Material Autographed Victory Hat
2000 #HBL Bobby Labonte
Upper Deck Victory Circle Winning Material Tire
2000 #TBL Bobby Labonte
Upper Deck Virtual Velocity
1996 #VV13 Bobby Labonte
Upper Deck Virtual Velocity Gold
1996 #VV13 Bobby Labonte
VIP
1994 #18 Bobby Labonte
1994 #46 Bobby Labonte w/Car
1995 #15 Bobby Labonte
1996 #14 Bobby Labonte
1997 #13 Bobby Labonte
1998 #13 Bobby Labonte
1998 #42 Bobby Labonte's Car
1999 #13 Bobby Labonte
1999 #44 Bobby Labonte's Car
2000 #1 Bobby Labonte
2000 #20 Bobby Labonte V
2001 #1 Bobby Labonte
2002 #8 Bobby Labonte
2002 #25 Bobby Labonte SG
2003 #10 Bobby Labonte
2003 #22 Bobby Labonte SG
2003 #47 Bobby Labonte HR
2004 #10 Bobby Labonte
2004 #37 Bobby Labonte's Car R
2004 #81 Bobby Labonte BTN
2005 #15 Bobby Labonte
2005 #35 Bobby Labonte's Car R
2005 #80 Bobby Labonte BN
2005 #83 Bobby Labonte ATML
2006 #14 Bobby Labonte
2006 #81 Bobby Labonte IF
2007 #17 Bobby Labonte
VIP Autographs
1996 #14 Bobby Labonte
VIP Cool Blue
1995 #15 Bobby Labonte
VIP Driver's Choice
2001 #DC3 Bobby Labonte
2002 #DC3 Bobby Labonte
VIP Driver's Choice Precious Metal
2001 #DC3 Bobby Labonte
VIP Driver's Choice Transparent
2001 #DC3 Bobby Labonte
2002 #DC3 Bobby Labonte
VIP Driver's Choice Transparent LTD
2002 #DC3 Bobby Labonte
VIP Driving Force
1998 #DF11 Bobby Labonte's Car
VIP Driving Force Die Cuts
1998 #DF11 Bobby Labonte's Car
VIP Emerald Proofs
1995 #15 Bobby Labonte
1996 #14 Bobby Labonte
VIP Explosives
1997 #13 Bobby Labonte
1998 #13 Bobby Labonte
1998 #42 Bobby Labonte's Car
1999 #X13 Bobby Labonte
1999 #X44 Bobby Labonte's Car
2000 #X1 Bobby Labonte
2000 #X20 Bobby Labonte V
2001 #1 Bobby Labonte
2002 #X8 Bobby Labonte
2002 #X25 Bobby Labonte SG
2003 #X10 Bobby Labonte
2003 #X22 Bobby Labonte SG
2003 #X47 Bobby Labonte HR
VIP Explosives Lasers
1999 #13 Bobby Labonte
1999 #44 Bobby Labonte's Car
2000 #LX1 Bobby Labonte
2000 #LX20 Bobby Labonte V
2001 #LX1 Bobby Labonte
2002 #LX8 Bobby Labonte
2002 #LX25 Bobby Labonte SG
VIP Head Gear
1998 #HG6 Bobby Labonte
1999 #HG7 Bobby Labonte
2006 #HG11 Bobby Labonte
VIP Head Gear Die Cuts
1998 #HG6 Bobby Labonte
VIP Head Gear Plastic
1999 #HG7 Bobby Labonte
VIP Head Gear Transparent
2006 #HG11 Bobby Labonte
VIP Knights of Thunder
1997 #KT4 Bobby Labonte
VIP Knights of Thunder Gold
1997 #KT4 Bobby Labonte
VIP Lap Leaders
1998 #LL5 Bobby Labonte's Car
1999 #LL7 Bobby Labonte
2000 #LL3 Bobby Labonte
2003 #LL3 Bobby Labonte
2004 #LL8 Bobby Labonte
2005 #8 Bobby Labonte
VIP Lap Leaders Acetate
1998 #LL5 Bobby Labonte's Car
VIP Lap Leaders Explosives
2000 #LL3 Bobby Labonte
VIP Lap Leaders Explosives Lasers
2000 #LL3 Bobby Labonte
VIP Lap Leaders National
2003 #LL3 Bobby Labonte
VIP Lap Leaders Transparent
2003 #LL3 Bobby Labonte
2004 #LL8 Bobby Labonte
2005 #8 Bobby Labonte
VIP Lap Leaders Transparent LTD
2003 #LL3 Bobby Labonte
VIP Laser Explosive
2003 #LX10 Bobby Labonte
2003 #LX22 Bobby Labonte SG
2003 #LX47 Bobby Labonte HR
VIP Making the Show
2000 #MS1 Bobby Labonte
2001 #9 Bobby Labonte
2002 #MS9 Bobby Labonte
2003 #MS8 Bobby Labonte
2004 #MS12 Bobby Labonte
2005 #12 Bobby Labonte
2006 #MS22 Bobby Labonte
VIP Mile Masters
2003 #MM6 Bobby Labonte
VIP Mile Masters National
2003 #MM6 Bobby Labonte
VIP Mile Masters Transparent
2003 #MM6 Bobby Labonte
VIP Mile Masters Transparent LTD
2003 #MM6 Bobby Labonte
VIP NASCAR Country
1998 #NC5 Bobby Labonte
VIP NASCAR Country Die Cuts
1998 #NC5 Bobby Labonte
VIP Oil Slicks
1997 #13 Bobby Labonte
VIP Out of the Box
1999 #OB7 Bobby Labonte
VIP Precious Metal
1997 #SM2 Bobby Labonte
VIP Previews
2003 #10 Bobby Labonte
2003 #22 Bobby Labonte SG
2004 #EB10 Bobby Labonte
2004 #EB37 Bobby Labonte's Car R
2005 #EB15 Bobby Labonte
2005 #EB35 Bobby Labonte's Car R
2007 #EB17 Bobby Labonte
VIP Promos
1995 #2G Bobby Labonte Gold
1995 #2R Bobby Labonte Red
VIP Race Used Sheet Metal Cars
2002 #SC3 Bobby Labonte's Car
VIP Race Used Sheet Metal Drivers
2002 #SD3 Bobby Labonte
VIP Rear View Mirror
2000 #RM1 Bobby Labonte
2001 #RV1 Bobby Labonte
2002 #RM1 Bobby Labonte
VIP Rear View Mirror Die Cuts
2001 #RV1 Bobby Labonte
2002 #RM1 Bobby Labonte
VIP Rear View Mirror Explosives
2000 #RM1 Bobby Labonte
VIP Rear View Mirror Explosives Laser Die Cuts
2000 #RM1 Bobby Labonte
VIP Red Hot
1995 #15 Bobby Labonte
VIP Ring of Honor
1997 #RH7 Bobby Labonte's Car
VIP Ring of Honor Die Cuts
1997 #RH7 Bobby Labonte's Car
VIP Samples
2002 #8 Bobby Labonte
2002 #25 Bobby Labonte SG
2003 #10 Bobby Labonte
2003 #22 Bobby Labonte SG
2003 #47 Bobby Labonte HR
2004 #10 Bobby Labonte
2004 #37 Bobby Labonte's Car R
2004 #81 Bobby Labonte BTN
2005 #15 Bobby Labonte
2005 #35 Bobby Labonte's Car R
2005 #80 Bobby Labonte BN
2005 #83 Bobby Labonte ATML
VIP Sheet Metal
1999 #SM8 Bobby Labonte
2000 #SM8 Bobby Labonte
VIP Sheet Metal Cars
2001 #SC7 Bobby Labonte's Car
VIP Sheet Metal Drivers
2001 #SD7 Bobby Labonte
VIP Solos
1998 #13 Bobby Labonte
1998 #42 Bobby Labonte's Car
VIP Sunday Best
2007 #SB14 Bobby Labonte
VIP Tin
2003 #CT10 Bobby Labonte
2003 #CT22 Bobby Labonte SG
2003 #CT47 Bobby Labonte HR
VIP Torquers
1996 #14 Bobby Labonte
VIP Tradin' Paint Bronze
2004 #TPT8 Bobby Labonte
VIP Tradin' Paint Car Autographs
2003 #BL Bobby Labonte/18
VIP Tradin' Paint Cars
2003 #TPT8 Bobby Labonte's Car
2005 #TPT8 Bobby Labonte
VIP Tradin' Paint Cars Bronze
2006 #TPT13Bobby Labonte
VIP Tradin' Paint Driver Autographs
2003 #BL Bobby Labonte/18
VIP Tradin' Paint Drivers
2003 #TPD8 Bobby Labonte
2005 #TPD8 Bobby Labonte
VIP Tradin' Paint Drivers Gold
2006 #TPD13 Bobby Labonte
VIP Tradin' Paint Drivers Silver
2006 #TPD13 Bobby Labonte
VIP Tradin' Paint Gold
2004 #TPD8 Bobby Labonte
VIP Tradin' Paint Silver
2004 #TPD8 Bobby Labonte
VIP Triple Gear Sheet Metal
1998 #TGS5 Bobby Labonte
VIP Under the Lights
2000 #UL3 Bobby Labonte
VIP Under the Lights Explosives
2000 #UL3 Bobby Labonte
VIP Under the Lights Explosives Lasers
2000 #UL3 Bobby Labonte
VIP Vintage Performance
1999 #6 Bobby Labonte
VIP War Paint
1996 #WP9 Bobby Labonte's Car
VIP War Paint Gold
1996 #WP9 Bobby Labonte's Car
Viper
1996 #8 Bobby Labonte
1996 #38 Bobby Labonte
1997 #6 Bobby Labonte
1997 #43 Bobby Labonte
1997 #72 Bobby Labonte's Car
Viper Anaconda Jumbos
1997 #A4 Bobby Labonte
Viper Black Mamba
1996 #8 Bobby Labonte
1996 #38 Bobby Labonte
Viper Black Mamba First Strike
1996 #8 Bobby Labonte
1996 #38 Bobby Labonte
Viper Black Racer
1997 #6 Bobby Labonte
1997 #43 Bobby Labonte
1997 #72 Bobby Labonte's Car
Viper Black Racer First Strike
1997 #6 Bobby Labonte
1997 #43 Bobby Labonte
1997 #72 Bobby Labonte's Car
Viper Busch Clash
1996 #B15 Bobby Labonte
Viper Busch Clash First Strike
1996 #B15 Bobby Labonte
Viper Cobra
1996 #C3 Bobby Labonte
1997 #C3 Bobby Labonte
Viper Cobra First Strike
1996 #C3 Bobby Labonte
1997 #C3 Bobby Labonte
Viper Copperhead Die Cuts
1996 #8 Bobby Labonte
1996 #38 Bobby Labonte
Viper Copperhead Die Cuts First Strike
1996 #8 Bobby Labonte
1996 #38 Bobby Labonte
Viper Diamondback
1996 #D3 Bobby Labonte
1997 #DB3 Bobby Labonte
Viper Diamondback Authentic
1996 #DA4 Bobby Labonte
1997 #DBA3 Bobby Labonte
Viper Diamondback Authentic California
1996 #DA4 Bobby Labonte
Viper Diamondback Authentic Eastern
1997 #DBA3 Bobby Labonte
Viper Diamondback Authentic Eastern First Strike
1997 #DBA3 Bobby Labonte
Viper Diamondback Authentic First Strike
1996 #DA4 Bobby Labonte
1997 #DBA3 Bobby Labonte
Viper Diamondback First Strike
1996 #D3 Bobby Labonte
1997 #DB3 Bobby Labonte
Viper First Strike
1996 #8 Bobby Labonte
1996 #38 Bobby Labonte
1997 #6 Bobby Labonte
1997 #43 Bobby Labonte
1997 #72 Bobby Labonte's Car
Viper Green Mamba
1996 #8 Bobby Labonte
1996 #38 Bobby Labonte
Viper King Cobra
1996 #KC9 Bobby Labonte
1997 #KC3 Bobby Labonte
Viper King Cobra First Strike
1996 #KC9 Bobby Labonte
Viper Promos
1996 #P1 Bobby Labonte
Viper Red Cobra
1996 #8 Bobby Labonte
1996 #38 Bobby Labonte
Viper Sidewinder
1997 #S8 Bobby Labonte
Viper Sidewinder First Strike
1997 #S8 Bobby Labonte
Viper Snake Eyes
1997 #SE4 Bobby Labonte
Viper Snake Eyes First Strike
1997 #SE4 Bobby Labonte
Visions
1996 #113 Bobby Labonte
Visions *
1996 #113 Bobby Labonte
Visions Signings
1996 #92 Bobby Labonte
Visions Signings *
1996 #92 Bobby Labonte
Wheels
1998 #17 Bobby Labonte
1998 #39 Bobby Labonte's Car
1999 #17 Bobby Labonte
1999 #59 Bobby Labonte's Car
1999 #77 Bobby Labonte TC
1999 #P1 Bobby Labonte Promo
Wheels 50th Anniversary
1998 #A8 Bobby Labonte
1998 #A23 Bobby Labonte's Car
Wheels American Thunder
2003 #12 Bobby Labonte
2003 #24 Bobby Labonte SS
2003 #28 Bobby Labonte DT
2003 #41 Bobby Labonte CC
2004 #13 Bobby Labonte
2004 #50 Bobby Labonte's Car HR
2004 #59 Bobby Labonte DT
2004 #68 Bobby Labonte RR
2005 #16 Bobby Labonte
2005 #44 Bobby Labonte AS
2005 #59 Bobby Labonte DT
2005 #68 Bobby Labonte RR
2006 #16 Bobby Labonte
2006 #42 Bobby Labonte DT
2006 #51 Bobby Labonte's Car HR
2006 #57 Bobby Labonte's Car HR
2006 #81 Bobby Labonte MIA
2007 #17 Bobby Labonte
2007 #59 Bobby Labonte's Car HR
2007 #79 Bobby Labonte HC
Wheels American Thunder American Eagle
2003 #AE7 Bobby Labonte
2004 #AE5 Bobby Labonte
2005 #AE5 Bobby Labonte
Wheels American Thunder American Muscle
2003 #AM5 Bobby Labonte
2004 #AM8 Bobby Labonte
Wheels American Thunder Autographed Hat Instant Winner
2007 #AH18 Bobby Labonte
Wheels American Thunder Born On
2003 #BO12 Bobby Labonte
2003 #BO24 Bobby Labonte SS
2003 #BO28 Bobby Labonte DT
2003 #BO41 Bobby Labonte CC
Wheels American Thunder Cup Quest
2004 #CQ5 Bobby Labonte
Wheels American Thunder Double Hat
2005 #DH4 Bobby Labonte
Wheels American Thunder Golden Eagle
2003 #AEG7 Bobby Labonte
2004 #AE5 Bobby Labonte
2005 #GE5 Bobby Labonte
Wheels American Thunder Grandstand
2006 #GS14 Bobby Labonte
Wheels American Thunder Head to Toe
2005 #HT7 Bobby Labonte
Wheels American Thunder Heads Up Manufacturer
2003 #HUM11 Bobby Labonte
Wheels American Thunder Heads Up Team
2003 #HUT10 Bobby Labonte/60
Wheels American Thunder Heads Up Winston
2003 #HUW11 Bobby Labonte
Wheels American Thunder Holofoil
2003 #P12 Bobby Labonte
2003 #P24 Bobby Labonte SS
2003 #P28 Bobby Labonte DT
2003 #P41 Bobby Labonte CC
Wheels American Thunder Medallion
2005 #MD10 Bobby Labonte
Wheels American Thunder Post Mark
2003 #PM11 Bobby Labonte
2004 #PM12 Bobby Labonte
Wheels American Thunder Previews
2003 #12 Bobby Labonte
2003 #24 Bobby Labonte SS
2003 #28 Bobby Labonte DT
2004 #EB13 Bobby Labonte
2005 #16 Bobby Labonte
2006 #EB16 Bobby Labonte
2006 #EB81 Bobby Labonte MIA
2007 #EB17 Bobby Labonte
2007 #EB59 Bobby Labonte's Car HR
Wheels American Thunder Pushin Pedal
2005 #PP10 Bobby Labonte
Wheels American Thunder Pushin' Pedal
2006 #PP15 Bobby Labonte
2007 #PP12 Bobby Labonte
Wheels American Thunder Rookie Thunder
2003 #RT16 Bobby Labonte
Wheels American Thunder Samples
2003 #12 Bobby Labonte
2003 #24 Bobby Labonte SS
2003 #28 Bobby Labonte DT
2003 #41 Bobby Labonte CC
2004 #13 Bobby Labonte
2004 #50 Bobby Labonte's Car HR
2004 #59 Bobby Labonte DT
2004 #68 Bobby Labonte RR
2005 #16 Bobby Labonte
2005 #44 Bobby Labonte AS
2005 #59 Bobby Labonte DT
2005 #68 Bobby Labonte RR
Wheels American Thunder Single Hat
2006 #SH3 Bobby Labonte
Wheels American Thunder Thunder Road
2003 #TR14 Bobby Labonte
2004 #TR9 Bobby Labonte
2005 #TR9 Bobby Labonte
2006 #TR3 Bobby Labonte
2007 #TR9 Bobby Labonte
Wheels American Thunder Thunder Strokes
2006 #4 Bobby Labonte
2007 #25 Bobby Labonte
Wheels American Thunder Thunder Strokes Press Plates Black
2007 #25 Bobby Labonte
Wheels American Thunder Thunder Strokes Press Plates Cyan
2007 #25 Bobby Labonte
Wheels American Thunder Thunder Strokes Press Plates Magenta
2007 #25 Bobby Labonte
Wheels American Thunder Thunder Strokes Press Plates Yellow
2007 #25 Bobby Labonte
Wheels American Thunder Triple Hat
2003 #TH6 Bobby Labonte
2004 #TH9 Bobby Labonte
2007 #TH16 Bobby Labonte
Wheels Autographs
1998 #5 Bobby Labonte/200
1999 #10 Bobby Labonte/250
2003 #30 Bobby Labonte AT/HG
2004 #38 Bobby Labonte HG
2005 #32 Bobby Labonte
2006 #34 Bobby Labonte NC
2007 #21 Bobby Labonte NC HG
2008 #20 Bobby Labonte NC HG
Wheels Autographs Press Plates Black
2007 #20 Bobby Labonte NC
2008 #20 Bobby Labonte NC HG
Wheels Autographs Press Plates Cyan
2007 #20 Bobby Labonte NC
2008 #20 Bobby Labonte NC HG
Wheels Autographs Press Plates Magenta
2007 #20 Bobby Labonte NC
2008 #20 Bobby Labonte NC HG
Wheels Autographs Press Plates Yellow
2007 #21 Bobby Labonte NC
2008 #20 Bobby Labonte NC HG
Wheels Circuit Breaker
1999 #CB2 Bobby Labonte
Wheels Custom Shop
1999 #CS1 Bobby Labonte
Wheels Custom Shop Prizes
1999 #BLA1 Bobby Labonte
1999 #BLA2 Bobby Labonte
1999 #BLA3 Bobby Labonte
1999 #BLB1 Bobby Labonte
1999 #BLB2 Bobby Labonte
1999 #BLB3 Bobby Labonte
1999 #BLC1 Bobby Labonte
1999 #BLC2 Bobby Labonte
1999 #BLC3 Bobby Labonte
Wheels Dialed In
1999 #DI7 Bobby Labonte
Wheels Double Take
1998 #E6 Bobby Labonte
Wheels Golden
1998 #17 Bobby Labonte
1998 #39 Bobby Labonte's Car
1999 #17 Bobby Labonte
1999 #59 Bobby Labonte
1999 #77 Bobby Labonte
Wheels Green Flags
1998 #GF10 Bobby Labonte's Car
Wheels Harry Gant
1994 #70 Bobby Labonte
Wheels Harry Gant Gold

1994 #70 Bobby Labonte
Wheels High Gear
1994 #13 Bobby Labonte
1994 #96 Bobby Labonte BC
1994 #177 Bobby Labonte
1995 #21 Bobby Labonte
1995 #66 Bobby Labonte SS
1998 #7 Bobby Labonte
1998 #32 Bobby Labonte's Car
1998 #67 Bobby Labonte's Car
1998 #P1 Bobby Labonte Promo
1999 #6 Bobby Labonte
1999 #32 Bobby Labonte's Car
1999 #66 Bobby Labonte's Car
2000 #2 Bobby Labonte
2000 #31 Bobby Labonte's Car
2000 #49 Bobby Labonte
2000 #51 Bobby Labonte
2000 #52 Bobby Labonte
2000 #60 Bobby Labonte's Car
2001 #1 Bobby Labonte
2001 #48 Bobby Labonte's Car
2001 #57 Bobby Labonte HL
2002 #12 Bobby Labonte
2002 #50 Bobby Labonte's Car
2003 #16 Bobby Labonte
2003 #57 Bobby Labonte's Car CM
2003 #61 Contenders and Pretenders WCS
2004 #13 Bobby Labonte
2004 #31 Bobby Labonte's Car C
2004 #56 Bobby Labonte's Car
2004 #65 Bobby Labonte HL
2005 #11 Bobby Labonte
2005 #43 Bobby Labonte's Car C
2006 #23 Bobby Labonte
2006 #72 Bobby Labonte PREV
2007 #20 Bobby Labonte
2008 #16 Bobby Labonte
Wheels High Gear Autographs
1998 #12 Bobby Labonte/250
1999 #14 Bobby Labonte/250
2000 #17 Bobby Labonte
2002 #30 Bobby Labonte
Wheels High Gear Blue Hawaii SCDA Promos
2003 #16 Bobby Labonte
2003 #57 Bobby Labonte's Car CM
2003 #61 Contenders and Pretenders
Wheels High Gear Custom Shop
2001 #CSBL Bobby Labonte EXCH
Wheels High Gear Custom Shop Prizes
2001 #BLA1 Bobby Labonte
2001 #BLA2 Bobby Labonte
2001 #BLA3 Bobby Labonte
2001 #BLB1 Bobby Labonte
2001 #BLB2 Bobby Labonte
2001 #BLB3 Bobby Labonte
2001 #BLC1 Bobby Labonte
2001 #BLC2 Bobby Labonte
2001 #BLC3 Bobby Labonte
Wheels High Gear Day One
1994 #177 Bobby Labonte
1995 #21 Bobby Labonte
1995 #66 Bobby Labonte SS
Wheels High Gear Day One Gold
1994 #177 Bobby Labonte
1995 #21 Bobby Labonte
1995 #66 Bobby Labonte SS
Wheels High Gear Driven
2007 #DR16 Bobby Labonte
2008 #DR8 Bobby Labonte
Wheels High Gear Final Standings
2008 #F16 Bobby Labonte/18
Wheels High Gear Final Standings Gold
2007 #FS20 Bobby Labonte/21
Wheels High Gear First Gear
1998 #11 Bobby Labonte
1998 #32 Bobby Labonte's Car
1998 #67 Bobby Labonte's Car
1999 #6 Bobby Labonte
1999 #32 Bobby Labonte's Car
1999 #66 Bobby Labonte's Car
2000 #2 Bobby Labonte
2000 #31 Bobby Labonte
2000 #49 Bobby Labonte
2000 #51 Bobby Labonte
2000 #52 Bobby Labonte
2000 #60 Bobby Labonte
2001 #1 Bobby Labonte
2001 #48 Bobby Labonte's CAR
2001 #57 Bobby Labonte HL
2002 #12 Bobby Labonte
2002 #50 Bobby Labonte's Car
2003 #F16 Bobby Labonte
2003 #F57 Bobby Labonte's Car CM
2003 #F61 Contenders and Pretenders
Wheels High Gear Flag Chasers
2001 #FC1 Bobby Labonte
Wheels High Gear Flag Chasers Black
2004 #FC3 Bobby Labonte
Wheels High Gear Flag Chasers Blue
2004 #FC3 Bobby Labonte
Wheels High Gear Flag Chasers Blue-Yellow
2001 #FC1 Bobby Labonte
Wheels High Gear Flag Chasers Checkered
2001 #FC1 Bobby Labonte
2004 #FC3 Bobby Labonte
Wheels High Gear Flag Chasers Checkered Blue/Orange
2001 #FC1 Bobby Labonte
Wheels High Gear Flag Chasers Green
2001 #FC1 Bobby Labonte
2004 #FC3 Bobby Labonte
Wheels High Gear Flag Chasers Power Pick
2001 #FCPP Bobby Labonte
Wheels High Gear Flag Chasers Red
2001 #FC1 Bobby Labonte
2004 #FC3 Bobby Labonte
Wheels High Gear Flag Chasers White
2001 #FC1 Bobby Labonte
2004 #FC3 Bobby Labonte
Wheels High Gear Flag Chasers Yellow
2001 #FC1 Bobby Labonte
2004 #FC3 Bobby Labonte
Wheels High Gear Flag to Flag
2005 #FF12 Bobby Labonte
2006 #FF14 Bobby Labonte
Wheels High Gear Gear Jammers
1998 #GJ9 Bobby Labonte
Wheels High Gear Gear Shifters
1999 #GS5 Jeff Burton
2000 #GS3 Bobby Labonte
2001 #GS1 Bobby Labonte
2001 #GS27 Bobby Labonte
Wheels High Gear Gold
1994 #13 Bobby Labonte
1994 #96 Bobby Labonte BC
1994 #177 Bobby Labonte
1995 #21 Bobby Labonte
1995 #66 Bobby Labonte SS
Wheels High Gear High Groove
1998 #HG6 Bobby Labonte's Car
2002 #HG12 Bobby Labonte
2003 #HG14 Bobby Labonte
2004 #HG12 Bobby Labonte
Wheels High Gear Hot Streaks
2001 #HS2 Bobby Labonte
Wheels High Gear Hot Treads
2003 #HT9 Bobby Labonte
Wheels High Gear Machine
2003 #MM8B Bobby Labonte
Wheels High Gear Man
2003 #MM8A Bobby Labonte
Wheels High Gear Man and Machine Cars
1998 #6 Bobby Labonte's Car
1999 #MM6B Bobby Labonte's Car
2000 #MM9B Bobby Labonte's Car
2001 #MM2B Bobby Labonte's Car
2002 #MM5B Bobby Labonte
Wheels High Gear Man and Machine Drivers
1998 #MM6 Bobby Labonte
1999 #MM6A Bobby Labonte
2000 #MM9A Bobby Labonte
2001 #MM2A Bobby Labonte
2002 #MM5A Bobby Labonte
Wheels High Gear MPH
1998 #11 Bobby Labonte
1998 #32 Bobby Labonte's Car
1998 #67 Bobby Labonte's Car
1999 #5 Bobby Labonte
1999 #32 Bobby Labonte's Car
1999 #66 Bobby Labonte's Car
2000 #2 Bobby Labonte
2000 #31 Bobby Labonte
2000 #49 Bobby Labonte
2000 #51 Bobby Labonte
2000 #52 Bobby Labonte
2000 #60 Bobby Labonte
2001 #1 Bobby Labonte
2001 #48 Bobby Labonte's CAR
2001 #57 Bobby Labonte HL
2002 #12 Bobby Labonte
2002 #50 Bobby Labonte's Car
2003 #M16 Bobby Labonte
2003 #M57 Bobby Labonte's Car CM
2003 #M61 Contenders and Pretenders
2004 #M13 Bobby Labonte
2004 #M31 Bobby Labonte C
2004 #M56 Bobby Labonte's Car
2004 #M65 Bobby Labonte HL
2005 #M11 Bobby Labonte
2005 #M43 Bobby Labonte's Car C
2006 #M23 Bobby Labonte
2006 #M72 Bobby Labonte PREV
2007 #M20 Bobby Labonte
2008 #M16 Bobby Labonte
Wheels High Gear Previews
2003 #16 Bobby Labonte
2004 #13 Bobby Labonte
2004 #31 Bobby Labonte C
2004 #56 Bobby Labonte's Car
2007 #EB20 Bobby Labonte
2008 #EB16 Bobby Labonte
Wheels High Gear Previews Green
2005 #EB11 Bobby Labonte
2006 #EB23 Bobby Labonte
Wheels High Gear Samples
2003 #16 Bobby Labonte
2003 #57 Bobby Labonte's Car CM
2003 #61 Contenders and Pretenders
2004 #13 Bobby Labonte
2004 #31 Bobby Labonte C
2004 #56 Bobby Labonte's Car
2004 #65 Bobby Labonte HL
2005 #11 Bobby Labonte
2005 #43 Bobby Labonte's Car C
Wheels High Gear Sunday Sensation
2000 #OC9 Bobby Labonte
2001 #SS7 Bobby Labonte
Wheels High Gear Top Ten
2004 #TT8 Bobby Labonte
Wheels High Gear Top Tier
1998 #TT7 Bobby Labonte 1:20
1999 #TT5 Jeff Burton 1:40
2000 #TT2 Bobby Labonte
2001 #TT1 Bobby Labonte
2002 #TT6 Bobby Labonte
Wheels High Gear Top Tier Holofoils
2001 #TT1 Bobby Labonte
Wheels High Gear Top Tier Numbered
2002 #TT6 Bobby Labonte
Wheels High Gear Winning Edge
2000 #WE3 Bobby Labonte
Wheels High Groove
1999 #HG1 Bobby Labonte
Wheels Jackpot
1998 #J5 Bobby Labonte
Wheels Rookie Thunder
1993 #33 Bobby Labonte
1993 #52 Bobby Labonte
1993 #64 Bobby Labonte
1993 #72 Bobby Labonte
1993 #73 Bobby Labonte
1993 #78 Bobby Labonte
1993 #81 Bobby Labonte
1993 #92 Bobby Labonte
1993 #94 Bobby Labonte in Pits
Wheels Rookie Thunder Platinum
1993 #33 Bobby Labonte
1993 #52 Bobby Labonte
1993 #64 Bobby Labonte
1993 #72 Bobby Labonte
1993 #73 Bobby Labonte
1993 #78 Bobby Labonte
1993 #81 Bobby Labonte
1993 #92 Bobby Labonte
1993 #94 Bobby Labonte in Pits
Wheels Rookie Thunder Promos
1993 #P4 Bobby Labonte
Wheels Runnin and Gunnin
1999 #RG8 Bobby Labonte
Wheels Runnin and Gunnin Foils
1999 #RG8 Bobby Labonte
Wheels Solos
1999 #17 Bobby Labonte
1999 #59 Bobby Labonte
1999 #77 Bobby Labonte
Zenith
1995 #18 Bobby Labonte HG
1995 #48 Bobby Labonte's Transporter
1995 #63 Bobby Labonte EOD
1995 #75 Bobby Labonte JG
1996 #19 Bobby Labonte
1996 #40 Bobby Labonte's Car HV
1996 #63 Bobby Labonte S
Zenith Artist Proofs
1996 #19 Bobby Labonte RP
1996 #40 Bobby Labonte's Car HV
1996 #63 Bobby Labonte S
Zenith Helmets
1995 #6 Bobby Labonte
Zenith Highlights
1996 #8 Bobby Labonte
Zenith Winston Winners
1995 #11 Bobby Labonte
1995 #14 Bobby Labonte
1995 #21 Bobby Labonte
Zenith Z-Team
1995 #3 Bobby Labonte

Logano, Joey

Press Pass Signings
2008 #34 Joey Logano
Press Pass Signings Gold
2008 #29 Joey Logano
Press Pass Signings Silver
2008 #25 Joey Logano

Martin, Mark

Action Packed
1993 #9 Mark Martin WIN
1993 #22 Mark Martin PW
1993 #44 Mark Martin T10
1993 #77 Mark Martin
1993 #78 Mark Martin's Car
1993 #109 Mark Martin
1993 #110 Mark Martin's Car
1993 #176 Mark Martin
1994 #3 Mark Martin
1994 #33 Mark Martin WIN
1994 #43 Mark Martin's Car
1994 #69 Mark Martin
1994 #115 Mark Martin's Car
1994 #153 Mark Martin
1994 #199 Mark Martin
1994 #200 Mark Martin
1994 #201 Mark Martin
1994 #202 Mark Martin
1994 #203 Mark Martin
1997 #6 Mark Martin
1997 #27 Mark Martin's Car
Action Packed 24K Gold
1993 #5G Mark Martin T10
1993 #58G Mark Martin
1994 #3G Mark Martin
1994 #13G Mark Martin's Car
1994 #23G Mark Martin
1997 #11 Mark Martin
Action Packed Badge of Honor Pins
1995 #6 Mark Martin
Action Packed Coastars
1994 #11 Mark Martin
Action Packed Country
1995 #44 Mark Martin WIN
1995 #55 Mark Martin WIN
Action Packed Country 24K Team
1995 #4 Mark Martin
Action Packed Country Silver Speed
1995 #44 Mark Martin WIN
1995 #55 Mark Martin WIN
Action Packed Credentials
1996 #11 Mark Martin OTM
1996 #12 Mark Martin OTM
1996 #13 Mark Martin OTM
1996 #14 Mark Martin OTM
1996 #15 Mark Martin OTM
1996 #23 Mark Martin
1996 #62 Mark Martin SM
Action Packed Credentials Fan Scan
1996 #3 Mark Martin
Action Packed Credentials Promos
1996 #23 Mark Martin
Action Packed Credentials Silver Speed
1996 #11 Mark Martin OTM
1996 #12 Mark Martin OTM
1996 #13 Mark Martin OTM
1996 #14 Mark Martin OTM
1996 #15 Mark Martin OTM
1996 #23 Mark Martin
Action Packed Fifth Anniversary
1997 #11 Mark Martin
Action Packed First Impressions
1997 #6 Mark Martin
1997 #27 Mark Martin's Car
Action Packed Mammoth
1994 #3 Mark Martin
1995 #MM5 Mark Martin
Action Packed McDonald's
1996 #5 Mark Martin
1996 #15 Mark Martin's Car
Action Packed Mint
1994 #3 Mark Martin
1994 #33 Mark Martin WIN
1994 #43 Mark Martin's Car
1994 #69 Mark Martin
1994 #115 Mark Martin's Car
1994 #153 Mark Martin
1994 #199 Mark Martin
1994 #200 Mark Martin
1994 #201 Mark Martin
1994 #202 Mark Martin
1994 #203 Mark Martin
Action Packed Preview
1995 #15 Mark Martin
1995 #40 Mark Martin PW
1995 #55 Mark Martin WIN
1995 #60 Mark Martin T10
1995 #72 Mark Martin DD
Action Packed Preview 24K Gold
1995 #4G Mark Martin
Action Packed Prototypes
1994 #3R944 Mark Martin
Action Packed Rolling Thunder
1997 #1 Mark Martin
Action Packed Stars
1995 #3 Mark Martin OC
1995 #35 Mark Martin's Car
Action Packed Stars Silver Speed
1995 #3 Mark Martin OC
1995 #35 Mark Martin's Car
ActionVision Precious Metal
1997 #9 Mark Martin
Assets
1995 #27 Mark Martin
1995 #41 Mark Martin
1995 #48 Mark Martin's Car
1996 #22 Mark Martin
Assets $2 Phone Cards
1995 #14 Mark Martin
Assets $2 Phone Cards Gold Signature
1995 #13 Mark Martin
Assets $25 Phone Cards
1995 #7 Mark Martin
Assets $5 Phone Cards
1995 #7 Mark Martin
Assets *
1996 #22 Mark Martin
Assets 1-Minute Phone Cards
1995 #13 Mark Martin
Assets 1-Minute Phone Cards Gold Signature
1995 #13 Mark Martin
Assets A Cut Above
1996 #CA6 Mark Martin
Assets A Cut Above *
1996 #CA6 Mark Martin
Assets Coca-Cola 600 Die Cut Phone Cards
1995 #8 Mark Martin
Assets Gold Signature
1995 #27 Mark Martin
1995 #41 Mark Martin
1995 #48 Mark Martin's Car
Assets Hot Prints
1996 #22 Mark Martin
Assets Hot Prints *
1996 #22 Mark Martin
Assets Phone Cards $1
1996 #13 Mark Martin
Assets Phone Cards $1 *
1996 #13 Mark Martin
Assets Phone Cards $2
1996 #13 Mark Martin
Assets Phone Cards $2 *
1996 #13 Mark Martin
Assets Phone Cards $2 Hot Prints
1996 #13 Mark Martin
Assets Phone Cards $2 Hot Prints *
1996 #13 Mark Martin
Assets Phone Cards $5
1996 #10 Mark Martin
Assets Phone Cards $5 *
1996 #10 Mark Martin
Assets Racing
1996 #18 Mark Martin
1996 #29 Mark Martin
1996 #49 Mark Martin
Assets Racing $10 Phone Cards
1996 #8 Mark Martin
Assets Racing $100 Cup Champion Interactive Phone Cards
1996 #11 Mark Martin
Assets Racing $1000 Cup Champion Interactive Phone Cards
1996 #10 Mark Martin
Assets Racing $2 Phone Cards
1996 #9 Mark Martin
Assets Racing $5 Phone Cards
1996 #3 Mark Martin
Assets Racing Competitor's License
1996 #CL3 Mark Martin
Assets Racing Race Day
1996 #RD6 Mark Martin's Car
Autographed Racing
1996 #20 Mark Martin's Car
1996 #24 Mark Martin
1997 #17 Mark Martin
1997 #38 Mark Martin's Car
1997 #44 M.Martin/S.Marlin
Autographed Racing Autographs
1996 #31 Mark Martin
1997 #33 Mark Martin
Autographed Racing Autographs Certified Golds
1996 #31 Mark Martin
Autographed Racing Front Runners
1996 #7 J.Burton/M.Martin with hat
1996 #8 J.Burton/M.Martin no hat
1996 #9 J.Burton's Car/M.Martin's Car
1996 #31 S.Hmiel/M.Martin with hat
1996 #32 S.Hmiel/M.Martin no hat
1996 #67 Martin with hat/Martin no hat
1996 #68 Martin with hat/Martin's Car
1996 #69 Martin no hat/Martin's Car
1996 #70 M.Martin with hat/T.Musgrave
1996 #71 M.Martin no hat/T.Musgrave
1996 #72 M.Martin with hat/J.Roush
1996 #73 M.Martin no hat/J.Roush
1996 #74 M.Martin's Car/J.Roush
Autographed Racing High Performance
1996 #HP6 Mark Martin
Autographed Racing Kings of the Circuit $5 Phone Cards
1996 #KC2 Mark Martin
Autographed Racing Mayne Street
1997 #KM17 Mark Martin
Autographed Racing Take the Checkered Flag
1997 #TF2 Mark Martin
Big League Cards Creative Images
1998 #9 Mark Martin
Card Dynamics Black Top Busch Series
1994 #9 Mark Martin
Card Dynamics Double Eagle Postcards
1993-95 #8 Mark Martin
Card Dynamics Gant Oil
1992 #6 Mark Martin/4000
1994 #8 Mark Martin
Card Dynamics Montgomery Motors
1994 #2 Mark Martin
Card Dynamics Quik Chek
1993 #10 Mark Martin/5000
Classic
1996 #14 Mark Martin
1996 #30 Mark Martin's Car
1996 #51 Mark Martin SP
Classic Five Sport Signings Etched in Stone
1995-96 #9 Mark Martin
Classic Images Preview
1996 #RP2 Mark Martin
Classic Innerview
1996 #IV1 Mark Martin
1996 #IV6 Mark Martin
Classic Mark Martin's Challengers
1996 #MC10 Mark Martin
Classic Printer's Proof
1996 #14 Mark Martin
1996 #30 Mark Martin's Car
Classic Race Chase
1996 #RC6 Mark Martin's Car
1996 #RC16 Mark Martin's Car
Classic Signings Etched in Stone *
1996 #9 Mark Martin
Classic Silver
1996 #14 Mark Martin
1996 #30 Mark Martin's Car
Clear Assets
1996 #66 Mark Martin
Clear Assets *
1996 #66 Mark Martin
Clear Assets 3X
1996 #X1 Mark Martin
Clear Assets 3X *
1996 #X1 Mark Martin
Clear Assets Phone Cards $1
1996 #4 Mark Martin
Clear Assets Phone Cards $1 *
1996 #4 Mark Martin
Clear Assets Phone Cards $10
1996 #8 Mark Martin
Clear Assets Phone Cards $10 *
1996 #8 Mark Martin
Clear Assets Phone Cards $2
1996 #4 Mark Martin
Clear Assets Phone Cards $2 *
1996 #4 Mark Martin
Collector's Choice
1997 #6 Mark Martin
1997 #56 Mark Martin's Car MM
1997 #105 Mark Martin SC
1997 #136 Mark Martin T3
1997 #137 Mark Martin T3
1997 #138 Mark Martin's Car T3
1998 #6 Mark Martin
1998 #42 Mark Martin's Car
1998 #97 Mark Martin PP
1998 #99 Mark Martin TD
Collector's Choice CC600
1998 #CC10 Mark Martin
1998 #CC43 Mark Martin
1998 #CC76 Mark Martin
Collector's Choice Speedecals
1997 #S11 Mark Martin's Car
1997 #S12 Mark Martin's Helmet
Collector's Choice Star Quest
1998 #SQ29 Mark Martin's Car
1998 #SQ46 Mark Martin AUTO
Collector's Choice Triple Force
1997 #B3 Mark Martin
1997 #J1 Mark Martin
Collector's Choice Upper Deck 500
1997 #UD9 Mark Martin
1997 #UD10 Mark Martin's Car
Collector's Choice Victory Circle
1997 #VC5 Mark Martin
Crown Jewels
1995 #3 Mark Martin
Crown Jewels Diamond
1995 #3 Mark Martin
Crown Jewels Dual Jewels
1995 #DJ4 Mark Martin/Ernie Irvan
Crown Jewels Dual Jewels Diamond
1995 #DJ4 Mark Martin/Ernie Irvan
Crown Jewels Dual Jewels Emerald
1995 #DJ4 Mark Martin/Ernie Irvan
Crown Jewels Elite
1996 #4 Mark Martin
1996 #53 M.Martin/S.Hmiel
1996 #74 Mark Martin BGN
Crown Jewels Elite Crown Signature Amethyst
1996 #CS10 Mark Martin
Crown Jewels Elite Crown Signature Garnet
1996 #CS10 Mark Martin
Crown Jewels Elite Crown Signature Peridot
1996 #CS10 Mark Martin
Crown Jewels Elite Diamond Tribute
1996 #4 Mark Martin
1996 #53 S.Hmiel/M.Martin
1996 #74 Mark Martin
Crown Jewels Elite Diamond Tribute Citrine
1996 #4 Mark Martin
1996 #53 S.Hmiel/M.Martin
1996 #74 Mark Martin
Crown Jewels Elite Dual Jewels Amethyst
1996 #DJ4 B.Elliott/M.Martin
Crown Jewels Elite Dual Jewels Amethyst Diamond Tribute
1996 #DJ4 B.Elliott/M.Martin
Crown Jewels Elite Dual Jewels Amethyst Treasure Chest
1996 #DJ4 B.Elliott/M.Martin
Crown Jewels Elite Dual Jewels Garnet
1996 #DJ4 B.Elliott/M.Martin
Crown Jewels Elite Dual Jewels Garnet Diamond Tribute
1996 #DJ4 B.Elliott/M.Martin
Crown Jewels Elite Dual Jewels Garnet Treasure Chest
1996 #DJ4 B.Elliott/M.Martin
Crown Jewels Elite Dual Jewels Sapphire
1996 #DJ4 B.Elliott/M.Martin
Crown Jewels Elite Dual Jewels Sapphire Treasure Chest
1996 #DJ4 B.Elliott/M.Martin
Crown Jewels Elite Emerald
1996 #4 Mark Martin
1996 #53 S.Hmiel/M.Martin
1996 #74 Mark Martin
Crown Jewels Elite Emerald Treasure Chest
1996 #4 Mark Martin
1996 #53 S.Hmiel/M.Martin
1996 #74 Mark Martin
Crown Jewels Elite Sapphire
1996 #4 Mark Martin
1996 #53 S.Hmiel/M.Martin
1996 #74 Mark Martin
Crown Jewels Elite Sapphire Treasure Chest
1996 #4 Mark Martin
1996 #53 S.Hmiel/M.Martin
1996 #74 Mark Martin
Crown Jewels Elite Treasure Chest
1996 #4 Mark Martin
1996 #53 S.Hmiel/M.Martin
1996 #74 Mark Martin
Crown Jewels Emerald
1995 #3 Mark Martin
Crown Jewels Sapphire
1995 #3 Mark Martin
Crown Jewels Signature Gems
1995 #SG6 Mark Martin
eTopps
2003 #2 Mark Martin/3403
2003 #2B Mark Martin AU/100
eTopps Autographs
2005 #MM1 Mark Martin 2003 eTopps/100
Finish Line
1993 #12 Mark Martin's Car
1993 #133 Mark Martin
1993 #164 Mark Martin
1994 #7 Mark Martin
1994 #85 Mark Martin
1994 #99 Mark Martin's Car
1994 #126 Mark Martin
1995 #6 Mark Martin
1995 #54 Mark Martin
1995 #79 Mark Martin
1996 #8 Mark Martin
1996 #9 Mark Martin's Car
1996 #60 Mark Martin
Finish Line Black Gold
1996 #C5 Mark Martin's Car
1996 #D6 Mark Martin
Finish Line Coca-Cola 600
1995 #27 Mark Martin
1995 #41 Mark Martin
1995 #48 Mark Martin's Car
Finish Line Coca-Cola 600 Die Cuts
1995 #C5 Mark Martin
Finish Line Commemorative Sheets
1993 #5 Darlington
1993 #11 Charlotte
1993 #27 Charlotte
Finish Line Diamond Collection $5 Phone Cards
1996 #5 Mark Martin
Finish Line Down Home
1994 #4 Mark Martin
Finish Line Gold
1994 #14 Mark Martin
1994 #48 Mark Martin
1994 #72 Mark Martin
1994 #79 Mark Martin's Car
1994 #81 Mark Martin
Finish Line Gold Autographs
1994 #81 Mark Martin
Finish Line Gold Phone Cards
1994 #5 Mark Martin/3000
Finish Line Gold Signature
1994 #3 Mark Martin
1995 #GS6 Mark Martin
1996 #GS3 Mark Martin
Finish Line Gold Teamwork
1994 #TG2 Mark Martin/S.Hmiel
Finish Line Man and Machine
1996 #MM2 Mark Martin
Finish Line Mega-Phone XL Phone Cards
1996 #3 Mark Martin
Finish Line Phone Card of the Month
1995 #3 Mark Martin/1500
Finish Line Phone Cards
1994 #11 Mark Martin
Finish Line Phone Pak
1996 #24 Mark Martin
1996 #25 Mark Martin's Car
1996 #P1 Mark Martin Promo
Finish Line Phone Pak $10
1996 #8 Mark Martin
Finish Line Phone Pak $100
1996 #5 Mark Martin
Finish Line Phone Pak $1000
1996 #K3 Mark Martin
Finish Line Phone Pak $2 Signature
1996 #24 Mark Martin
1996 #25 Mark Martin's Car
Finish Line Phone Pak $5
1996 #16 Mark Martin
Finish Line Phone Pak $50
1996 #6 Mark Martin
Finish Line Phone Pak II
1997 #3 Mark Martin
1997 #41 Mark Martin $5
1997 #70 Mark Martin's Car $10
1997 #89 Mark Martin $50
1997 #97 Mark Martin $100
Finish Line Platinum 5-Unit Phone Cards
1995 #2 Mark Martin
Finish Line Printer's Proof
1995 #6 Mark Martin
1995 #54 Mark Martin

1995 #79 Mark Martin
1996 #8 Mark Martin
1996 #9 Mark Martin's Car
1996 #60 Mark Martin
Finish Line Promos
1994 #P2 Mark Martin
Finish Line Silver
1993 #12 Mark Martin's Car
1993 #133 Mark Martin
1993 #164 Mark Martin
1994 #7 Mark Martin
1994 #85 Mark Martin
1994 #99 Mark Martin's Car
1994 #126 Mark Martin
1995 #6 Mark Martin
1995 #54 Mark Martin
1995 #79 Mark Martin
1996 #8 Mark Martin
1996 #9 Mark Martin's Car
1996 #60 Mark Martin
Finish Line Standout Cars
1995 #SC2 Mark Martin's Car
Finish Line Standout Drivers
1995 #SD2 Mark Martin
Finish Line Victory Lane
1994 #VL5 Mark Martin
1994 #VL14 Mark Martin
Flair
1996 #21 Mark Martin
1996 #77 Mark Martin's Car
1996 #97 Mark Martin
Flair Autographs
1996 #10 Mark Martin
Flair Center Spotlight
1996 #8 Mark Martin
Flair Hot Numbers
1996 #8 Mark Martin
Flair Power Performance
1996 #8 Mark Martin
High Gear Promos
1995 #P3 Mark Martin
Highland Mint/VIP
1994-95 #5B Mark Martin/5000
1994-95 #5S Mark Martin/1000
Hi-Tech Brickyard 400
1994 #14 Mark Martin's Car
1994 #19 Mark Martin's Car
1994 #27 M.Martin/J.Spencer Cars
1994 #29 Mark Martin's Car
1994 #31 Mark Martin's Car
1994 #40 Mark Martin
1995 #9 Mark Martin's Car
1995 #70 Mark Martin
Hi-Tech Brickyard 400 Artist Proofs
1994 #14 Mark Martin's Car
1994 #19 Mark Martin's Car
1994 #27 M.Martin/J.Spencer Cars
1994 #29 Mark Martin's Car
1994 #31 Mark Martin's Car
1994 #40 Mark Martin
Hi-Tech Brickyard 400 Prototypes
1995 #P1 Mark Martin's Car
Hi-Tech Tire Test
1993 #6 Mark Martin's Car
Images
1995 #6 Mark Martin
1995 #65 Mark Martin
1995 #88 Mark Martin
Images Driven
1995 #D5 Mark Martin
Images Gold
1995 #6 Mark Martin
1995 #65 Mark Martin
1995 #88 Mark Martin
Images Hard Chargers
1995 #HC3 Mark Martin
IROC
1991 #4 Mark Martin
Jurassic Park
1997 #4 Mark Martin
1997 #44 Mark Martin
1997 #49 Mark Martin
1997 #50 Mark Martin
1997 #P1 Mark Martin Promo
Jurassic Park Carnivore
1997 #C10 Mark Martin
Jurassic Park Pteranodon
1997 #P8 Mark Martin
Jurassic Park Thunder Lizard
1997 #TL7 Mark Martin
Jurassic Park Triceratops
1997 #4 Mark Martin
1997 #44 Mark Martin
1997 #49 Mark Martin
1997 #50 Mark Martin
KnightQuest
1996 #5 Mark Martin K
1996 #24 Mark Martin C
KnightQuest Black Knights
1996 #5 Mark Martin K
1996 #24 Mark Martin C
KnightQuest First Knights
1996 #FK4 Mark Martin
KnightQuest Knights of the Round Table
1996 #KT4 Mark Martin
KnightQuest Red Knight Preview
1996 #5 Mark Martin K
1996 #24 Mark Martin C
KnightQuest Royalty
1996 #5 Mark Martin K
1996 #24 Mark Martin C
KnightQuest Santa Claus
1996 #SC4 Mark Martin
KnightQuest Santa Claus Green
1996 #SC4 Mark Martin
KnightQuest White Knights
1996 #5 Mark Martin K
1996 #24 Mark Martin C
Mac Tools Winner's Cup
1992 #15 Mark Martin
Maxwell House
1993 #6 Mark Martin
Maxx
1989 #127 Kul/Elliott/R.Wall/D.Allis/Martin Cars YR
1989 #6 Mark Martin
1990 #6 Mark Martin
1990 #185 D.Waltrip/T.Labonte/Martin/Jarrett Cars YR
1990 #195 D.Earnhardt/M.Martin Cars YR
1991 #6 Mark Martin
1991 #113 Martin/G.Bodine/Marlin/Irvan Cars MM
1991 #171 Mark Martin YR
1991 #189 Mark Martin YR
1991 #195 Mark Martin YR
1993 #6 Mark Martin
1993 #85 Mark Martin's Car
1993 #199 Da.All./R.Petty/Mart.Cars MM
1993 #271 Mark Martin YR
1993 #290 Mark Martin YR
1994 #6 Mark Martin
1994 #35 Mark Martin's Car
1994 #226 Mark Martin YR
1994 #227 Mark Martin YR
1994 #228 Mark Martin YR
1994 #229 Mark Martin YR
1994 #236 Mark Martin YR
1994 #258 Mark Martin
1994 #259 Mark Martin's Car
1995 #6 Mark Martin
1995 #109 Mark Martin VL
1995 #125 Mark Martin MM
1995 #146 Mark Martin VL
1995 #162 Mark Martin's Car
1995 #215 Mark Martin
1995 #P3 M.Martin/S.Hmiel Promo Sheet
1996 #6 Mark Martin
1996 #54 Mark Martin's Car
1996 #70 Mark Martin's Car
1997 #6 Mark Martin
1997 #51 Mark Martin's Car
1997 #103 Mark Martin PS
1997 #106 Mark Martin MO
1998 #6 Mark Martin
1998 #36 Mark Martin's Car
1998 #93 Mark Martin's Car FR
1999 #52 Mark Martin
1999 #53 Mark Martin's Car
1999 #54 Mark Martin RR
2000 #6 Mark Martin
2000 #46 Mark Martin's Car
2000 #83 Mark Martin's Car FRF
Maxx 10th Anniversary
1998 #5 Mark Martin
1998 #50 Mark Martin's Car
Maxx 10th Anniversary Card of the Year
1998 #CY9 Mark Martin
Maxx 10th Anniversary Maxximum Preview
1998 #P6 Mark Martin
Maxx 1997 Year In Review
1998 #7 Mark Martin's Car
1998 #38 Mark Martin's Car
1998 #41 Mark Martin
1998 #46 Mark Martin
1998 #47 Mark Martin's Car
1998 #101 Mark Martin
1998 #126 Mark Martin
1998 #127 Mark Martin's Car
1998 #144 Mark Martin's Car
1998 #159 Mark Martin's Car
1998 #P03 Mark Martin
Maxx All-Pro Team
1992 #3 Mark Martin
Maxx Autographs
1994 #6 Mark Martin
1994 #227 Mark Martin
Maxx Black
1992 #6 Mark Martin
1992 #200 Mark Martin's Car MM
1992 #233 Mark Martin AP
1992 #293 Mark Martin YR
Maxx Black Update
1992 #U11 Mark Martin
Maxx Charlotte
1988 #48 Mark Martin RC
Maxx Chase the Champion
1997 #C2 Mark Martin
Maxx Chase the Champion Gold Die Cuts
1997 #C2 Mark Martin
Maxx Drive Time
2000 #DT6 Mark Martin
Maxx FANtastic Finishes
1999 #F17 Mark Martin's Car
2000 #FF10 Mark Martin
Maxx Flag Firsts
1997 #FF6 Mark Martin
Maxx Focus on a Champion
1998 #FC4 Mark Martin
1999 #FC4 Mark Martin
Maxx Focus on a Champion Cel
1998 #FC4 Mark Martin
Maxx Focus on a Champion Gold
1999 #FC4 Mark Martin
Maxx Glossy
1990 #6 Mark Martin
1990 #185 D.Walt/T.Lab/Mart/Jarrett Cars YR
1990 #195 D.Earnhardt/M.Martin Cars YR
Maxx Holly Farms
1990 #HF8 Mark Martin
Maxx License to Drive
1995 #7 Mark Martin's Car
Maxx License to Drive Crown Chrome
1995 #7 Mark Martin's Car
Maxx Made in America
1996 #6 Mark Martin
1996 #54 Mark Martin's Car
Maxx McDonald's
1991 #2A Mark Martin ERR
1991 #2B Mark Martin COR
1991 #30 D.Earnhardt/Martin/Elliott
1992 #14 Mark Martin
Maxx Medallion
1994 #33 Mark Martin
1994 #70 Mark Martin
1995 #5 Mark Martin
1995 #35 Mark Martin's Car
Maxx Medallion Blue
1995 #5 Mark Martin
1995 #35 Mark Martin's Car
Maxx Motorsport
1991 #5 Mark Martin
1991 #33 Mark Martin's Car
1992 #5 Mark Martin
1992 #40 Mark Martin w/Crew
1992 #49 Formation Flying cars
1992 #50 Martin/Kulwicki/Allison/Elliott
1993 #13 Mark Martin
1993 #33 Mark Martin's Car
1993 #50 Mark Martin's Car
1994 #3 Mark Martin
Maxx Odyssey
1996 #6 Mark Martin
1996 #54 Mark Martin's Car
Maxx Oval Office
2000 #OO5 Mark Martin
Maxx Premier Plus
1993 #6 Mark Martin
1993 #57 Da.All/R.Pet/Mart/B.Lab.Cars MM
1993 #85 Mark Martin's Car
1993 #186 Mark Martin YR
1993 #205 Mark Martin YR
1994 #6 Mark Martin
1994 #35 Mark Martin's Car
1994 #185 Mark Martin YR
1994 #186 Mark Martin YR
1994 #187 Mark Martin YR
1994 #188 Mark Martin w/Crew YR
1994 #195 Mark Martin/Roush YR
1995 #6 Mark Martin
1995 #35 Mark Martin's Car
1995 #169 Mark Martin VL
1995 #180 Mark Martin VL
Maxx Premier Plus Crown Chrome
1995 #6 Mark Martin
1995 #35 Mark Martin's Car
1995 #169 Mark Martin VL
1995 #180 Mark Martin VL
Maxx Premier Plus PaceSetters
1995 #PS1 Mark Martin
Maxx Premier Plus PaceSetters Crown Chrome
1995 #PS1 Mark Martin
Maxx Premier Plus Retail Jumbos
1995 #3 Mark Martin
Maxx Premier Series
1993 #6 Mark Martin
1993 #85 Mark Martin's Car
1993 #199 Allison/Petty/Martin/Lab.Cars MM
1993 #271 Mark Martin YR
1993 #290 Mark Martin YR
1994 #6 Mark Martin
1994 #35 Mark Martin's Car
1994 #285 Mark Martin YR
1994 #286 Mark Martin YR
1994 #287 Mark Martin YR
1994 #288 Mark Martin YR
1994 #295 Mark Martin YR
1995 #6 Mark Martin
1995 #35 Mark Martin's Car
1995 #261 Mark Martin IROC Champ
1995 #284 Mark Martin/Roush YR
1995 #295 Mark Martin YR
1996 #6 Mark Martin
1996 #35 Mark Martin's Car
Maxx Premier Series Jumbos
1994 #4 Mark Martin
Maxx Premier Series Superlatives
1996 #SL2 Mark Martin
Maxx Previews
1989 #5 Mark Martin
Maxx Race Ticket
1999 #RT19 Mark Martin's Car
Maxx Racer's Ink
1999 #MM Mark Martin
Maxx Racing Champions
1994 #4 Mark Martin
Maxx Racing for Kids
1991 #1 Sheet 1
Maxx Racing Images
1999 #RI30 Mark Martin
Maxx Red
1992 #6 Mark Martin
1992 #200 Mark Martin's Car MM
1992 #233 Mark Martin AP
1992 #293 Mark Martin YR
Maxx Red Update
1992 #U11 Mark Martin
Maxx Retail Jumbos
1993 #5 Mark Martin
Maxx Speedway Boogie
2000 #SB7 Mark Martin
Maxx Swappin' Paint
1998 #SW19 Mark Martin's Car
Maxx Teamwork
1998 #TW4 Mark Martin's Car
Maxx The Select 25
1994 #3 Mark Martin
Maxx The Winston
1992 #17 Mark Martin
1992 #37 Mark Martin's Car
1993 #2 Mark Martin
1993 #22 Mark Martin's Car
Maxx The Winston Acrylics
1991 #11 Mark Martin
Maxx Update
1991 #6 Mark Martin
Maxximum
1998 #6 Mark Martin
1998 #31 Mark Martin's Car
1998 #56 Mark Martin
1998 #81 Mark Martin's Car
2000 #3 Mark Martin
Maxximum Battle Proven
1998 #B6 Mark Martin
Maxximum Dialed In
2000 #DI6 Mark Martin
Maxximum Die Cuts
2000 #3 Mark Martin
Maxximum Field Generals Four Star Autographs
1998 #6 Mark Martin
Maxximum Field Generals One Star
1998 #6 Mark Martin
Maxximum Field Generals Three Star Autographs
1998 #6 Mark Martin
Maxximum Field Generals Two Star
1998 #6 Mark Martin
Maxximum First Class
1998 #F15 Mark Martin
Maxximum MPH
2000 #3 Mark Martin/6
Maxximum Signatures
2000 #MK2 M.Martin/M.Kenseth
2000 #ROU4 Mart/Litt/J.Brtn/Kens
Metallic Impressions Winston Cup Top Five
1996 #5 Mark Martin
M-Force
1996 #9 Mark Martin
1996 #10 Mark Martin's Car
1996 #41 Mark Martin
M-Force Black
1996 #B6 Mark Martin
M-Force Sheet Metal
1996 #M4 Mark Martin
M-Force Silvers
1996 #S15 Mark Martin
Motorcraft Manufacturers Championship
1993 #7 Mark Martin
Pinnacle
1996 #6 Mark Martin
1996 #41 Mark Martin's Car
1996 #96 Mark Martin CL
1997 #6 Mark Martin
1997 #35 Mark Martin's Car
1997 #61 Mark Martin RR
1997 #75 Mark Martin TT
1997 #90 Mark Martin's Car T4
Pinnacle Artist Proofs
1996 #6 Mark Martin
1996 #41 Mark Martin's Car
1996 #96 Mark Martin CL
1997 #6 Mark Martin P
1997 #35 Mark Martin's Car B
1997 #61 Mark Martin RR R
1997 #75 Mark Martin TT R
1997 #90 Mark Martin's Car T4 R
Pinnacle Certified
1997 #6 Mark Martin
1997 #40 Mark Martin's Car
1997 #91 Mark Martin BD
1997 #P6 Mark Martin Promo
Pinnacle Certified Certified Team
1997 #7 Mark Martin
Pinnacle Certified Certified Team Gold
1997 #7 Mark Martin
Pinnacle Certified Epix
1997 #E7 Mark Martin
Pinnacle Certified Epix Emerald
1997 #E7 Mark Martin
Pinnacle Certified Epix Purple
1997 #E7 Mark Martin
Pinnacle Certified Mirror Blue
1997 #6 Mark Martin
1997 #40 Mark Martin's Car
1997 #91 Mark Martin BD
Pinnacle Certified Mirror Gold
1997 #6 Mark Martin
1997 #40 Mark Martin's Car
1997 #91 Mark Martin BD
Pinnacle Certified Mirror Red
1997 #6 Mark Martin
1997 #40 Mark Martin's Car
1997 #91 Mark Martin BD
Pinnacle Certified Red
1997 #6 Mark Martin
1997 #40 Mark Martin's Car
1997 #91 Mark Martin BD
Pinnacle Checkered Flag
1996 #6 Mark Martin
Pinnacle Collector's Club
1997 #RC3 Mark Martin
Pinnacle Cut Above
1996 #10 Mark Martin
Pinnacle Foil
1997 #6 Mark Martin
1997 #35 Mark Martin's Car
1997 #61 Mark Martin RR
1997 #75 Mark Martin TT
1997 #90 Mark Martin's Car T4
Pinnacle Mint
1997 #5 Mark Martin
1997 #26 Mark Martin's Car
1998 #2 Mark Martin
1998 #14 Mark Martin's Car
1998 #25 Mark Martin MM
1998 #P1 Mark Martin Promo
Pinnacle Mint Bronze
1997 #5 Mark Martin
1997 #26 Mark Martin's Car
Pinnacle Mint Coins
1997 #5 Mark Martin
1997 #26 Mark Martin's Car
1998 #2 Mark Martin
1998 #14 Mark Martin's Car
1998 #1 Mark Martin MM
Pinnacle Mint Coins 24K Gold Plated
1997 #5 Mark Martin
1997 #26 Mark Martin's Car
Pinnacle Mint Coins Bronze Proof
1998 #2 Mark Martin
1998 #14 Mark Martin's Car
1998 #1 Mark Martin MM
Pinnacle Mint Coins Gold Plated
1998 #2 Mark Martin
1998 #14 Mark Martin's Car
1998 #25 Mark Martin MM
Pinnacle Mint Coins Gold Plated Proofs
1998 #2 Mark Martin
1998 #14 Mark Martin's Car
1998 #25 Mark Martin MM
Pinnacle Mint Coins Nickel-Silver
1997 #5 Mark Martin
1997 #26 Mark Martin's Car
1998 #2 Mark Martin
1998 #14 Mark Martin's Car
1998 #25 Mark Martin MM
Pinnacle Mint Coins Silver Plated Proofs
1998 #2 Mark Martin
1998 #14 Mark Martin's Car
1998 #25 Mark Martin MM
Pinnacle Mint Coins Solid Gold
1998 #2 Mark Martin
1998 #14 Mark Martin's Car
1998 #25 Mark Martin MM
Pinnacle Mint Coins Solid Silver
1998 #2 Mark Martin
1998 #14 Mark Martin's Car
1998 #25 Mark Martin MM
Pinnacle Mint Die Cuts
1998 #2 Mark Martin
1998 #14 Mark Martin's Car
1998 #25 Mark Martin MM
Pinnacle Mint Gold
1997 #5 Mark Martin
1997 #26 Mark Martin's Car
Pinnacle Mint Gold Team
1998 #2 Mark Martin
1998 #14 Mark Martin's Car
1998 #25 Mark Martin MM
Pinnacle Mint Silver
1997 #5 Mark Martin
1997 #26 Mark Martin's Car
Pinnacle Mint Silver Team
1998 #2 Mark Martin
1998 #14 Mark Martin's Car
1998 #25 Mark Martin MM
Pinnacle Pole Position
1996 #6 Mark Martin
1996 #30 Mark Martin's Car
1996 #77 Mark Martin EY
Pinnacle Pole Position Certified Strong
1996 #6 Mark Martin
Pinnacle Pole Position Lightning Fast
1996 #6 Mark Martin
1996 #30 Mark Martin's Car
1996 #77 Mark Martin
Pinnacle Pole Position No Limit
1996 #6 Mark Martin
Pinnacle Pole Position No Limit Gold
1996 #6 Mark Martin
Pinnacle Portraits
1997 #2 Mark Martin
1997 #22 Mark Martin's Car
1997 #41 Mark Martin SS
Pinnacle Portraits 8x10
1997 #MM1 Mark Martin
1997 #MM2 Mark Martin
1997 #MM3 Mark Martin
1997 #MM4 Mark Martin
Pinnacle Portraits 8x10 Dufex
1997 #MM1 Mark Martin
1997 #MM2 Mark Martin
1997 #MM3 Mark Martin
1997 #MM4 Mark Martin
Pinnacle Press Plates
1997 #6 Mark Martin
1997 #35 Mark Martin's Car
1997 #61 Mark Martin RR
1997 #75 Mark Martin TT
1997 #90 Mark Martin's Car T4
1997 #SS-A Mark Martin
1997 #TP6A Mark Martin
Pinnacle Spellbound
1997 #5A Mark Martin
Pinnacle Spellbound Promos
1997 #5A Mark Martin
Pinnacle Team Pinnacle
1996 #6 Mark Martin
1997 #6 Mark Martin
Pinnacle Team Pinnacle Red
1997 #6 Mark Martin
Pinnacle Totally Certified Platinum Blue
1997 #6 Mark Martin
1997 #40 Mark Martin's Car
1997 #91 Mark Martin BD
Pinnacle Totally Certified Platinum Gold
1997 #6 Mark Martin
1997 #40 Mark Martin's Car
1997 #91 Mark Martin BD
Pinnacle Totally Certified Platinum Red
1997 #6 Mark Martin
1997 #40 Mark Martin's Car
1997 #91 Mark Martin BD
Pinnacle Trophy Collection
1996 #6 Mark Martin
1997 #35 Mark Martin's Car
1997 #61 Mark Martin RR
1997 #75 Mark Martin TT
1997 #90 Mark Martin's Car T4
Pinnacle Winston Cup Collection
1996 #6 Mark Martin
1996 #41 Mark Martin's Car
1996 #96 Mark Martin CL
Post Cereal
2004 #6 Mark Martin
Power
1994 #20 Mark Martin PW
1994 #44 Mark Martin SL
1994 #56 Mark Martin in Pits SL
1994 #62 Mark Martin's Trans. PR
Power Gold
1994 #20 Mark Martin PW
1994 #44 Mark Martin SL
1994 #56 Mark Martin in Pits SL
1994 #62 Mark Martin's Trans. PR
Power Preview
1994 #15 Mark Martin
1994 #19 Mark Martin's Car FOIL
Predator
1997 #5 Mark Martin
1997 #41 Mark Martin
Predator American Eagle
1997 #AE7 Mark Martin
Predator American Eagle First Slash
1997 #AE7 Mark Martin
Predator Black Wolf First Strike
1997 #5 Mark Martin
1997 #41 Mark Martin
Predator Eye of the Tiger
1997 #ET6 Mark Martin
Predator Eye of the Tiger First Slash
1997 #ET6 Mark Martin
Predator First Slash
1997 #5 Mark Martin
1997 #41 Mark Martin
Predator Gatorback
1997 #GB7 Mark Martin
Predator Gatorback Authentic
1997 #GBA7 Mark Martin
Predator Gatorback Authentic First Slash
1997 #GBA7 Mark Martin
Predator Gatorback First Slash
1997 #GB7 Mark Martin
Predator Golden Eagle
1997 #GE7 Mark Martin
Predator Golden Eagle First Slash
1997 #GE7 Mark Martin
Predator Grizzly
1997 #5 Mark Martin
1997 #41 Mark Martin
Predator Grizzly First Slash
1997 #5 Mark Martin
1997 #41 Mark Martin
Predator Red Wolf
1997 #5 Mark Martin
1997 #41 Mark Martin
Predator Red Wolf First Slash
1997 #5 Mark Martin
1997 #41 Mark Martin
Press Pass
1994 #17 Mark Martin
1994 #32 Mark Martin/Jack Roush
1994 #54 Mark Martin's Car
1994 #121 Mark Martin TT
1994 #141 Mark Martin ART
1995 #19 Mark Martin
1995 #53 Mark Martin's Car
1995 #66 Mark Martin
1995 #104 Mark Martin ST
1995 #116 Mark Martin's Car AW
1996 #20 Mark Martin
1996 #53 Mark Martin's Car
1996 #76 M.Martin/Roush/Hmiel TW
1996 #96 Mark Martin S
1997 #5 Mark Martin
1997 #35 Mark Martin's Car
1997 #75 Mark Martin
1997 #89 Mark Martin
1997 #112 Mark Martin
1998 #2 Mark Martin
1998 #31 Mark Martin's Car
1998 #41 Mark Martin
1998 #92 Mark Martin IROC
1998 #102 Mark Martin RET
1998 #P2 Mark Martin Club Promo
1999 #2 Mark Martin
1999 #29 Mark Martin's Car
1999 #49 Mark Martin
1999 #88 Mark Martin OTP
1999 #102 Mark Martin RET
1999 #P2 Mark Martin Promo
2000 #3 Mark Martin
2000 #45 Mark Martin REP
2000 #49 Mark Martin's Car DD
2000 #60 Mark Martin
2001 #8 Mark Martin
2001 #46 Mark Martin
2001 #55 Mark Martin's Car
2001 #98 Mark Martin PV
2002 #22 Mark Martin
2002 #77 Mark Martin's Car
2003 #21 Mark Martin
2003 #92 Mark Martin's Car OTW
2004 #19 Mark Martin
2004 #65 Mark Martin's Car OTW
2004 #80 The Drive for Five WCS
2005 #5 Mark Martin
2005 #72 Mark Martin's Car OTW
2005 #83 Mark Martin/T.Stewart NS
2005 #101 Mark Martin P
2005 #115 Mark Martin's Car
2006 #6 Mark Martin
2006 #81 Mark Martin's Car OTW
2006 #90 Mark Martin NS
2006 #113 Mark Martin TT
2007 #7 Mark Martin
2007 #74 Mark Martin's Car OT
2007 #114 Mark Martin TT
2008 #21 Mark Martin
2008 #70 Mark Martin's Car BFS
2008 #0 Cup Chase Matt Kenseth Tony Stewart Jeff Gordon Jimmie Johnson Denny Hamlin Kurt Busch Kevin Harvick Carl Edwards Kyle Busch Martin Truex Jr. Jeff Burton Clint Bowyer
2008 #75 Kevin Harvick's Car Mark Martin's Car NS
Press Pass Authentics
1994 #3 Mark Martin
Press Pass Authentics Autographs
1994 #3 Mark Martin AUTO
Press Pass Autographs
1998 #5 Mark Martin/101
1999 #15 Mark Martin/235
2001 #31 Mark Martin
2002 #42 Mark Martin
2003 #37 Mark Martin E/P
2004 #39 Mark Martin P
2005 #37 Mark Martin E/P
2006 #36 Mark Martin NC
2007 #29 Mark Martin NC P
2008 #26 Mark Martin NC P/E
Press Pass Autographs Press Plates Black
2007 #14 Mark Martin NC
2008 #21 Mark Martin NC P
Press Pass Autographs Press Plates Cyan
2007 #14 Mark Martin NC
2008 #21 Mark Martin NC E
Press Pass Autographs Press Plates Magenta
2007 #16 Mark Martin NC
2008 #21 Mark Martin NC P
Press Pass Autographs Press Plates Yellow
2007 #15 Mark Martin NC
2008 #21 Mark Martin NC E
Press Pass Banquet Bound
1997 #BB5 Mark Martin
Press Pass Blue
2006 #B6 Mark Martin
2006 #B81 Mark Martin's Car OTW
2006 #B90 Mark Martin NS
2006 #B113 Mark Martin TT
2007 #B7 Mark Martin
2007 #B74 Mark Martin's Car OT
2007 #B114 Mark Martin TT
2008 #B21 Mark Martin
2008 #B70 Mark Martin's Car BFS
2008 #B75 Kevin Harvick's Car Mark Martin's Car NS
Press Pass Burning Rubber
1996 #BR7 Mark Martin's Car
1999 #BR2 Mark Martin's Car
2000 #BR2 Mark Martin
Press Pass Burning Rubber Autographs

2004 #BRMM Mark Martin/6
2005 #BR-MM Mark Martin/6
2006 #BR-MM Mark Martin/6
Press Pass Burning Rubber Cars
2001 #BRC6 Mark Martin/105
2002 #BRC7 Mark Martin's Car
2003 #BRT6 Mark Martin's Car
2004 #BRT6 Mark Martin's Car
2005 #BRT18 Mark Martin's Car
2006 #BRT13 Mark Martin
Press Pass Burning Rubber Cars Autographs
2003 #BRT-MM Mark Martin/6
Press Pass Burning Rubber Drivers
2001 #BRD6 Mark Martin/90
2002 #BRD7 Mark Martin
2003 #BRD6 Mark Martin
2004 #BRD6 Mark Martin
2005 #BRD18 Mark Martin
2006 #BRD13 Mark Martin
Press Pass Burning Rubber Drivers Autographs
2003 #BRD-MM Mark Martin/6
Press Pass Burning Rubber Drivers Gold
2005 #BRD18 Mark Martin
2006 #BRD13 Mark Martin
Press Pass Burnouts
2006 #HT14 Mark Martin
Press Pass Burnouts Holofoil
2006 #HT14 Mark Martin
Press Pass Chase Cars
1999 #3B Mark Martin's Car
Press Pass Checkered Flags
1994 #CF3 Mark Martin
1995 #CF6 Mark Martin
1996 #CF5 Mark Martin
Press Pass Clear Cut
1997 #C7 Mark Martin
Press Pass Coca Cola AutoZone
2006 #MM Mark Martin
Press Pass Collector's Series Box Set
2007 #SB16 Mark Martin
Press Pass Collectors Series Making the Show
2006 #MS1 Mark Martin
Press Pass Collectors Series Sunday Best
2007 #CB16 Mark Martin
Press Pass Cup Chase
1994 #CC17 Mark Martin W2
1995 #19 Mark Martin WIN
1996 #20 Mark Martin WIN
1997 #CC14 Mark Martin WIN
1998 #CC14 Mark Martin Win 2
1999 #14 Mark Martin WIN 2
2000 #CC11 Mark Martin
2002 #CC10 Mark Martin WIN
2003 #CCR11 Mark Martin
2004 #CCR12 Mark Martin
2005 #CCR16 Mark Martin
Press Pass Cup Chase Blue Die Cut Prizes
1997 #CC14 Mark Martin
Press Pass Cup Chase Die Cut Prizes
1998 #CC14 Mark Martin
1999 #14 Mark Martin
2000 #CC11 Mark Martin
Press Pass Cup Chase Foil Prizes
1996 #20 Mark Martin
Press Pass Cup Chase Gold Die Cuts
1997 #CC14 Mark Martin
Press Pass Cup Chase Prizes
2002 #CC10 Mark Martin
2003 #CCR11 Mark Martin
2004 #CCR12 Mark Martin
2005 #CCP16 Mark Martin
2006 #CC9 Mark Martin
Press Pass Double Burner
2001 #DB6 Mark Martin
2002 #DB7 Mark Martin
2003 #DB6 Mark Martin
2004 #DB6 Mark Martin
2005 #DB6 Mark Martin
Press Pass Double Burner Exchange
2003 #DB6 Mark Martin EXCH
2004 #DB6 Mark Martin
2005 #DB6 Mark Martin
Press Pass Double Burner Firesuit-Glove
2008 #DBMM Mark Martin
Press Pass Double Burner Metal-Tire
2006 #DB6 Mark Martin
2008 #DB-MM Mark Martin
Press Pass Eclipse
2003 #2 Mark Martin
2003 #31 Mark Martin ACC
2003 #33 Mark Martin ACC
2004 #16 Mark Martin
2004 #29 Mark Martin's Car
2004 #76 M.Martin/R.Wallace LL
2004 #79 Mark Martin LL
2005 #4 Mark Martin
2005 #29 Mark Martin's Car S
2005 #79 Mark Martin LL
2006 #4 Mark Martin
2006 #54 Mark Martin NS
2006 #65 NCS Top-10 BA
2006 #68 Mark Martin BA
2006 #69 Tony Stewart BA
2006 #82 Mark Martin LL
2007 #9 Mark Martin
2007 #53 Mark Martin FP
2007 #64 Martin/Kahne/Burton NS
2007 #83 Mark Martin SM
2007 #88 Mark Martin
2007 #0 Cup Chase 10
2008 #21 Mark Martin
2008 #63 Mark Martin's Car LP
2008 #21B Mark Martin Army hat
Press Pass Eclipse Destination WIN
2005 #12 Mark Martin
Press Pass Eclipse Double Hot Treads
2003 #DT6 M.Kenseth/M.Martin
Press Pass Eclipse Ecliptic
2007 #EC2 Mark Martin
Press Pass Eclipse Gold
2007 #G9 Mark Martin
2007 #G53 Mark Martin FP
2007 #G64 Martin/Kahne/Burton NS
2007 #G83 Mark Martin SM
2007 #G88 Mark Martin
2008 #G21 Mark Martin
2008 #G63 Mark Martin's Car LP
Press Pass Eclipse Hyperdrive
2004 #HP6 Mark Martin
2005 #HD6 Mark Martin
2006 #HP5 Mark Martin
2008 #HP2 Mark Martin
Press Pass Eclipse Maxim
2004 #MX10 Mark Martin
2005 #MX10 Mark Martin
Press Pass Eclipse Previews
2003 #2 Mark Martin
2003 #31 Mark Martin ACC
2003 #33 Mark Martin ACC
2004 #16 Mark Martin
2005 #EB4 Mark Martin
2005 #EB29 Mark Martin's Car S
2005 #EB79 Mark Martin LL/1
2006 #EB4 Mark Martin
2007 #EB9 Mark Martin
2007 #EB88 Mark Martin
2008 #EB21 Mark Martin
Press Pass Eclipse Racing Champions
2003 #RC15 Mark Martin
2005 #RC14 Mark Martin
2006 #RC16 Mark Martin NBS
Press Pass Eclipse Red
2007 #R9 Mark Martin
2007 #R53 Mark Martin FP
2007 #R64 Martin/Kahne/Burton NS
2007 #R83 Mark Martin SM
2007 #R88 Mark Martin
2008 #R21 Mark Martin
2008 #R63 Mark Martin's Car LP
Press Pass Eclipse Samples
2003 #2 Mark Martin
2003 #31 Mark Martin ACC
2003 #33 Mark Martin ACC
2004 #16 Mark Martin
2004 #29 Mark Martin's Car
2004 #76 M.Martin/R.Wallace LL
2004 #79 Mark Martin LL
2005 #4 Mark Martin
2005 #29 Mark Martin's Car S
2005 #79 Mark Martin LL
Press Pass Eclipse Skidmarks
2003 #SM7 Mark Martin
2004 #SM5 Mark Martin
2005 #SM5 Mark Martin
2006 #SM8 Mark Martin
2008 #SM11 Mark Martin
Press Pass Eclipse Skidmarks Holofoil
2004 #SM5 Mark Martin
2005 #SM5 Mark Martin
2006 #SM8 Mark Martin
2008 #SM11 Mark Martin
Press Pass Eclipse Solar Eclipse
2003 #P2 Mark Martin
2003 #P31 Mark Martin ACC
2003 #P33 Mark Martin ACC
Press Pass Eclipse Star Tracks
2008 #ST5 Mark Martin
Press Pass Eclipse Star Tracks Holofoil
2008 #ST5 Mark Martin
Press Pass Eclipse Supernova
2003 #SN9 Mark Martin
2006 #SU11 Mark Martin
Press Pass Eclipse Teammates Autographs
2003 #MMMK M.Martin/M.Kenseth
2004 #3 G.Biffle/M.Martin
2005 #2 Busch/Martin/Kenseth
2005 #9 M.Kenseth/M.Martin
2006 #3 C.Edwards/M.Martin
Press Pass Eclipse Under Cover Autographs
2004 #UCMM Mark Martin/6
2006 #MM Mark Martin/6
Press Pass Eclipse Under Cover Cars
2003 #UCT17 Mark Martin
2004 #UCD6 Mark Martin
2005 #UCT6 Mark Martin
2006 #UCT4 Mark Martin
Press Pass Eclipse Under Cover Double Cover
2003 #DC13 M.Kenseth/M.Martin
2004 #DC14 M.Martin/J.Burton
2005 #DC4 K.Busch/M.Martin
2005 #DC7 M.Kenseth/M.Martin
2006 #DC2 M.Martin/M.Kenseth
2006 #DC3 M.Martin/G.Biffle
2006 #DC7 C.Edwards/M.Martin
Press Pass Eclipse Under Cover Double Cover Holofoil
2006 #DC2 M.Martin/M.Kenseth
2006 #DC3 M.Martin/G.Biffle
2006 #DC7 C.Edwards/M.Martin
Press Pass Eclipse Under Cover Double Cover Name
2008 #DC1 Mark Martin Martin Truex Jr.
Press Pass Eclipse Under Cover Double Cover NASCAR
2008 #DC1 Mark Martin Martin Truex Jr.
Press Pass Eclipse Under Cover Driver Gold
2003 #UCD17 Mark Martin
2004 #UCD6 Mark Martin
Press Pass Eclipse Under Cover Driver Red
2003 #UCD17 Mark Martin
2004 #UCD6 Mark Martin
2005 #UCD6 Mark Martin
Press Pass Eclipse Under Cover Driver Silver
2003 #UCD17 Mark Martin
2004 #UCD6 Mark Martin
Press Pass Eclipse Under Cover Drivers
2008 #UCD6 Mark Martin
Press Pass Eclipse Under Cover Drivers Eclipse
2008 #UCD6 Mark Martin
Press Pass Eclipse Under Cover Drivers Gold
2006 #UCD4 Mark Martin
Press Pass Eclipse Under Cover Drivers Holofoil
2005 #UCD6 Mark Martin
2006 #UCD4 Mark Martin
Press Pass Eclipse Under Cover Drivers Name
2008 #UCD6 Mark Martin
Press Pass Eclipse Under Cover Drivers NASCAR
2008 #UCD6 Mark Martin
Press Pass Eclipse Under Cover Drivers Silver
2005 #UCD6 Mark Martin
2006 #UCD4 Mark Martin
Press Pass Eclipse Under Cover Teams
2008 #UCT6 Mark Martin
Press Pass Eclipse Under Cover Teams NASCAR
2008 #UCT6 Mark Martin
Press Pass Eclipse Warp Speed
2003 #WS7 Mark Martin
Press Pass F.Q.S.
1996 #FQS8A Mark Martin
1996 #FQS8B Mark Martin's Car
Press Pass Focused
1996 #F7 Mark Martin
Press Pass Four Wide
2006 #FW-MM Mark Martin
Press Pass Four Wide Checkered Flag
2006 #FW-MM Mark Martin
Press Pass Game Face
2005 #GF9 Mark Martin
2006 #GF2 Mark Martin
Press Pass Gatorade Front Runner Award
2000 #2 Mark Martin
2001 #1 Mark Martin
Press Pass Gatorade Jumbos
2003 #3 Mark Martin
Press Pass Gold
2006 #G6 Mark Martin
2006 #G81 Mark Martin's Car OTW
2006 #G90 Mark Martin NS
2006 #G113 Mark Martin TT
2007 #G7 Mark Martin
2007 #G74 Mark Martin's Car OT
2007 #G114 Mark Martin TT
2008 #G21 Mark Martin
2008 #G70 Mark Martin's Car BFS
2008 #G75 Kevin Harvick's Car Mark Martin's Car NS
Press Pass Gold Holofoil
2003 #P21 Mark Martin
2003 #P92 Mark Martin's Car OTW
Press Pass Ground Zero
2001 #GZ6 Mark Martin
Press Pass Holofoils
1994 #H4 Mark Martin
Press Pass Hot Treads
2001 #HT13 Mark Martin/1665
2002 #HT6 Mark Martin's Car/2300
2004 #HTR15 Mark Martin
2005 #HTR2 Mark Martin
Press Pass Hot Treads Holofoil
2004 #HTR15 Mark Martin
2005 #HTR2 Mark Martin
Press Pass Lasers
1997 #5 Mark Martin
1997 #35 Mark Martin's Car
1997 #75 Mark Martin
1997 #89 Mark Martin
1997 #112 Mark Martin
Press Pass Legends
2005 #24 Mark Martin
2006 #30 Mark Martin
2007 #35 Mark Martin
Press Pass Legends Autographs Black
2005 #23 Mark Martin
2006 #30 Mark Martin
Press Pass Legends Autographs Blue
2007 #17 Mark Martin/62
Press Pass Legends Autographs Inscriptions Blue
2007 #11 Mark Martin The Kid/9
Press Pass Legends Blue
2005 #24B Mark Martin
2006 #B30 Mark Martin
2007 #B35 Mark Martin
Press Pass Legends Bronze
2006 #Z30 Mark Martin
2007 #Z35 Mark Martin
Press Pass Legends Double Threads Bronze
2005 #DT-MB M.Martin/K.Busch
2005 #DT-MK M.Martin/M.Kenseth
Press Pass Legends Double Threads Gold
2005 #DT-MB M.Martin/K.Busch
2005 #DT-MK M.Martin/M.Kenseth
Press Pass Legends Double Threads Silver
2005 #DT-MB M.Martin/K.Busch
2005 #DT-MK M.Martin/M.Kenseth
Press Pass Legends Gold
2005 #24G Mark Martin
2006 #G30 Mark Martin
2007 #G35 Mark Martin
Press Pass Legends Heritage
2005 #HE6 Mark Martin
Press Pass Legends Holofoil
2005 #24H Mark Martin
2006 #H30 Mark Martin
2007 #H35 Mark Martin
Press Pass Legends Press Plates Black
2005 #24 Mark Martin
2006 #PPB30 Mark Martin
2007 #PP35 Mark Martin
Press Pass Legends Press Plates Black Backs
2006 #PPB30B Mark Martin
2007 #PP35 Mark Martin
Press Pass Legends Press Plates Cyan
2005 #24 Mark Martin
2006 #PPC30 Mark Martin
2007 #PP35 Mark Martin
Press Pass Legends Press Plates Cyan Backs
2006 #PPC30B Mark Martin
2007 #PP35 Mark Martin
Press Pass Legends Press Plates Magenta
2005 #24 Mark Martin
2006 #PPM30 Mark Martin
2007 #PP35 Mark Martin
Press Pass Legends Press Plates Magenta Backs
2006 #PPM30B Mark Martin
2007 #PP35 Mark Martin
Press Pass Legends Press Plates Yellow
2005 #24 Mark Martin
2006 #PPY30 Mark Martin
2007 #PP35 Mark Martin
Press Pass Legends Press Plates Yellow Backs
2006 #PPY30B Mark Martin
2007 #PP35 Mark Martin
Press Pass Legends Previews
2005 #24 Mark Martin
2006 #EB30 Mark Martin
2007 #EB35 Mark Martin
Press Pass Legends Signature Series
2007 #MM Mark Martin
Press Pass Legends Solo
2005 #24S Mark Martin
2006 #S30 Mark Martin
2007 #S35 Mark Martin
Press Pass Legends Threads & Treads Bronze
2005 #TTMM Mark Martin
Press Pass Legends Threads & Treads Gold
2005 #TTMM Mark Martin
Press Pass Legends Threads & Treads Silver
2005 #TTMM Mark Martin
Press Pass Making the Show Collector's Series
2004 #MS26 Mark Martin
Press Pass Millennium
2000 #3 Mark Martin
2000 #45 Mark Martin
2000 #49 Mark Martin
2000 #60 Mark Martin
2001 #8 Mark Martin
2001 #46 Mark Martin
2001 #55 Mark Martin's Car
2001 #98 Mark Martin PV
Press Pass Oil Cans
1998 #OC7 Mark Martin
1999 #1 Mark Martin
2000 #OC4 Mark Martin
Press Pass Oil Slicks
1997 #5 Mark Martin
1997 #35 Mark Martin's Car
1997 #75 Mark Martin
1997 #89 Mark Martin
1997 #112 Mark Martin
1998 #2 Mark Martin
1998 #31 Mark Martin's Car
1998 #41 Mark Martin
1998 #92 Mark Martin
Press Pass Optima
2000 #16 Mark Martin
2000 #44 Mark Martin WCL
2001 #14 Mark Martin
2001 #45 Mark Martin WCL
2002 #19 Mark Martin
2003 #16 Mark Martin
2004 #15 Mark Martin
2004 #61 Mark Martin's Car RV
2005 #18 Mark Martin
2005 #18B Mark Martin Cup Chase
2005 #57 Mark Martin RR
2005 #72 Mark Martin CP
2005 #75 Mark Martin CP
2005 #80 Mark Martin CP
2005 #82 Mark Martin DT
2005 #99 Mark Martin R&R
2006 #6 Mark Martin
2006 #57 Mark Martin's Car HS
2006 #67 Mark Martin CP
2006 #97 Mark Martin VOTC
2006 #6B Mark Martin Chase
Press Pass Optima Cool Persistence
2002 #CP10 Mark Martin
2003 #CP3 Mark Martin
2004 #CP4 Mark Martin
2005 #CP3 Mark Martin
Press Pass Optima Corporate Cuts Cars
2005 #CCT8 Mark Martin
Press Pass Optima Corporate Cuts Drivers
2005 #CCD8 Mark Martin
Press Pass Optima Encore
2000 #EN3 Mark Martin
Press Pass Optima Fan Favorite
2002 #FF16 Mark Martin
2003 #FF16 Mark Martin
2004 #FF15 Mark Martin
2005 #FF17 Mark Martin
2006 #FF14 Mark Martin
Press Pass Optima G Force
2000 #GF16 Mark Martin
2001 #GF13 Mark Martin
2005 #GF4 Mark Martin
Press Pass Optima Gold
2001 #14 Mark Martin
2001 #45 Mark Martin WCL
2002 #19 Mark Martin
2003 #G16 Mark Martin
2004 #G15 Mark Martin
2004 #G61 Mark Martin's Car RV
2005 #G18 Mark Martin
2005 #G57 Mark Martin RR
2005 #G72 Mark Martin CP
2005 #G75 Mark Martin CP
2005 #G80 Mark Martin CP
2005 #G82 Mark Martin DT
2005 #G99 Mark Martin R&R
2006 #G6 Mark Martin
2006 #G57 Mark Martin's Car HS
2006 #G67 Mark Martin CP
2006 #G97 Mark Martin VOTC
Press Pass Optima On the Edge
2001 #OE5 Mark Martin
Press Pass Optima Overdrive
2000 #OD7 Mark Martin
Press Pass Optima Overdrive Square Cut
2000 #OD7 Mark Martin
Press Pass Optima Platinum
2000 #16 Mark Martin
2000 #44 Mark Martin WCL
Press Pass Optima Previews
2003 #16 Mark Martin
2004 #EB15 Mark Martin
2005 #18 Mark Martin
2006 #EB6 Mark Martin
Press Pass Optima Promos
2002 #19 Mark Martin
Press Pass Optima Q & A
2005 #QA1 Mark Martin
Press Pass Optima Q and A
2002 #QA6 Mark Martin
Press Pass Optima Q&A
2004 #QA2 Mark Martin
Press Pass Optima Race Used Lugnuts Autographs
2002 #LNDA13 Mark Martin/6
Press Pass Optima Race Used Lugnuts Cars
2000 #LC9 Mark Martin's Car
2001 #LNC12 Mark Martin's Car
2002 #LNC13 Mark Martin's Car
Press Pass Optima Race Used Lugnuts Drivers
2000 #LD9 Mark Martin
2001 #LND11 Mark Martin
2002 #LND13 Mark Martin
Press Pass Optima Samples
2002 #19 Mark Martin
2003 #16 Mark Martin
2004 #15 Mark Martin
2004 #61 Mark Martin's Car RV
2005 #18 Mark Martin
2005 #57 Mark Martin RR
2005 #72 Mark Martin CP
2005 #75 Mark Martin CP
2005 #80 Mark Martin CP
2005 #82 Mark Martin DT
2005 #99 Mark Martin R&R
Press Pass Optima Thunder Bolts Autographs
2005 #TB-MM Mark Martin/6
Press Pass Optima Thunder Bolts Cars
2003 #TBT6 Mark Martin's Car
2004 #TBT14 Mark Martin's Car
Press Pass Optima Thunder Bolts Cars Autographs
2003 #TBT-MM Mark Martin/6
Press Pass Optima Thunder Bolts Drivers
2003 #TBD6 Mark Martin/60
2004 #TBD14 Mark Martin
Press Pass Optima Thunder Bolts Drivers Autographs
2003 #TBD-MM Mark Martin/6
Press Pass Optima Up Close
2001 #UC5 Mark Martin
Press Pass Optima XL
1994 #12 Mark Martin
1994 #27 Mark Martin
1994 #52 E.Irvan/R.Wall./Martin WCS
1995 #14 Mark Martin
1995 #35 Mark Martin TC
1995 #48 Mark Martin's Car
1995 #58 Mark Martin OR
Press Pass Optima XL Cool Blue
1995 #14 Mark Martin
1995 #35 Mark Martin TC
1995 #48 Mark Martin's Car
1995 #58 Mark Martin
Press Pass Optima XL Die Cut
1995 #14 Mark Martin
1995 #35 Mark Martin TC
1995 #48 Mark Martin's Car
1995 #58 Mark Martin
Press Pass Optima XL Double Clutch
1994 #DC5 Mark Martin
Press Pass Optima XL Prototypes
1995 #XL3 Mark Martin
Press Pass Optima XL Red Hot
1994 #12 Mark Martin
1994 #27 Mark Martin
1994 #52 R.Wallace/M.Martin/Irvan WCS
1995 #14 Mark Martin
1995 #35 Mark Martin TC
1995 #48 Mark Martin's Car
1995 #58 Mark Martin
Press Pass Optima XL Stealth
1995 #XLS9 Mark Martin
Press Pass Panorama
2005 #PPP13 Mark Martin
Press Pass Pit Stop
1998 #PS5 Mark Martin's Car
1999 #6 Mark Martin's Car
Press Pass Pitstop
2000 #PS6 Mark Martin's Car
Press Pass Platinum
2002 #22 Mark Martin
2002 #77 Mark Martin's Car
2004 #P19 Mark Martin
2004 #P65 Mark Martin's Car OTW
2004 #P80 The Drive for Five WCS
2005 #P5 Mark Martin
2005 #P72 Mark Martin's Car OTW
2005 #P83 Mark Martin/T.Stewart NS
2005 #P101 Mark Martin P
2005 #P115 Mark Martin's Car
2006 #P6 Mark Martin
2006 #P81 Mark Martin's Car OTW
2006 #P90 Mark Martin NS
2006 #P113 Mark Martin TT
2007 #P7 Mark Martin
2007 #P74 Mark Martin's Car OT
2007 #P114 Mark Martin TT
2008 #P21 Mark Martin
2008 #P70 Mark Martin's Car BFS
2008 #P75 Kevin Harvick's Car Mark Martin's Car NS
Press Pass Premium
1995 #2 Mark Martin
1995 #30 Mark Martin
1996 #4 Mark Martin
1996 #45 Mark Martin's Car CL
1997 #5 Mark Martin
1997 #31 Mark Martin's Car
1997 #43 Mark Martin
1998 #9 Mark Martin
1998 #18 Mark Martin's Car
1998 #30 Mark Martin
1999 #17 Mark Martin
1999 #29 Mark Martin's Car
1999 #48 Mark Martin
2000 #5 Mark Martin
2000 #31 Mark Martin's Car
2000 #52 Mark Martin
2000 #69 Mark Martin
2001 #14 Mark Martin
2001 #63 Mark Martin CC
2001 #78 Mark Martin PC
2002 #19 Mark Martin
2002 #43 Mark Martin's Car
2002 #65 Mark Martin CH
2002 #79 Mark Martin PC
2003 #18 Mark Martin
2003 #43 Mark Martin's Car
2003 #64 Mark Martin CC
2003 #75 Mark Martin PC
2004 #29 Mark Martin
2004 #38 Mark Martin's Car
2005 #19 Mark Martin
2005 #60 Mark Martin CC
2005 #77 Mark Martin PC
2006 #18 Mark Martin
2006 #43 Mark Martin's Car M
2006 #46 Mark Martin NS
2006 #65 Mark Martin C
2006 #72 Mark Martin PC
2007 #2 Mark Martin
2007 #68 Mark Martin MD
2007 #81 Mark Martin FF
2008 #73 Mark Martin F
2008 #46 Mark Martin's Car M
2008 #8 Mark Martin
Press Pass Premium $10 Phone Cards
1996 #7 Mark Martin
Press Pass Premium $20 Phone Cards
1996 #7 Mark Martin
Press Pass Premium $5 Phone Cards
1996 #1 Mark Martin
1996 #7 Mark Martin
Press Pass Premium Asphalt Jungle
2005 #AJ2 Mark Martin
2006 #AJ2 Mark Martin
Press Pass Premium Badge of Honor
1999 #BH5 Mark Martin
1999 #BH21 Mark Martin's Car
Press Pass Premium Badge of Honor Reflectors
1999 #BH5 Mark Martin
1999 #BH21 Mark Martin's Car
Press Pass Premium Burning Rubber II
1996 #BR2 Mark Martin's Car
Press Pass Premium Clean Air
2008 #CA5 Mark Martin
Press Pass Premium Concrete Chaos
2007 #CC6 Mark Martin
Press Pass Premium Crystal Ball
1996 #CB11 Mark Martin
1997 #CB10 Mark Martin
Press Pass Premium Crystal Ball Die Cut
1997 #CB10 Mark Martin
Press Pass Premium Emerald Proofs
1996 #4 Mark Martin
1996 #45 Mark Martin's Car Checklist
1997 #5 Mark Martin
1997 #31 Mark Martin's Car
1997 #43 Mark Martin
Press Pass Premium Extreme Fire
1999 #FD4A Mark Martin 1:72
Press Pass Premium Flag Chasers
1998 #FC4 Mark Martin
Press Pass Premium Flag Chasers Reflectors
1998 #FC4 Mark Martin
Press Pass Premium Gold
2001 #14 Mark Martin
2001 #63 Mark Martin CC
2001 #78 Mark Martin PC
Press Pass Premium Holofoil
1995 #2 Mark Martin
1995 #30 Mark Martin
1996 #4 Mark Martin
1996 #45 Mark Martin's Car Checklist
Press Pass Premium Hot Pursuit
1995 #HP5 Mark Martin
1996 #HP6 Mark Martin
Press Pass Premium Hot Threads Autographs
2004 #HT-MM Mark Martin/6
2008 #HTMM Mark Martin/8
Press Pass Premium Hot Threads Cars
2003 #HTT6 Mark Martin
Press Pass Premium Hot Threads Cars Autographs
2003 #HTD-MM Mark Martin/6
Press Pass Premium Hot Threads Drivers
2003 #HTD6 Mark Martin
2008 #HTD13 Mark Martin
Press Pass Premium Hot Threads Drivers Autographs
2003 #HTT-MM Mark Martin/6
Press Pass Premium Hot Threads Drivers Bronze
2004 #HTD6 Mark Martin
Press Pass Premium Hot Threads Drivers Bronze Retail
2004 #HTT6 Mark Martin
Press Pass Premium Hot Threads Drivers Gold
2004 #HTD6 Mark Martin
2008 #HTD13 Mark Martin
Press Pass Premium Hot Threads Drivers Silver
2004 #HTD6 Mark Martin
Press Pass Premium Hot Threads Patches
2008 #HTP25 Mark Martin NASCAR bar/5
2008 #HTP26 Mark Martin U.S. Flag
2008 #HTP23 Mark Martin U.S. Army/27
2008 #HTP24 Mark Martin Mighty/6
Press Pass Premium Hot Threads Team
2008 #HTT13 Mark Martin
Press Pass Premium In The Zone
2000 #IZ7 Mark Martin
2001 #IZ10 Mark Martin
2002 #IZ10 Mark Martin
2003 #IZ6 Mark Martin
2006 #IZ11 Mark Martin
Press Pass Premium In the Zone Red
2006 #IZ11 Mark Martin
Press Pass Premium Lap Leaders
1997 #LL8 Mark Martin
Press Pass Premium Mirrors
1997 #5 Mark Martin
1997 #31 Mark Martin's Car
1997 #43 Mark Martin
Press Pass Premium Oil Slicks
1997 #5 Mark Martin
1997 #31 Mark Martin's Car
1997 #43 Mark Martin
Press Pass Premium Performance Driven
2000 #PD5 Mark Martin
2001 #PD6 Mark Martin
2002 #PD6 Mark Martin
2003 #PD4 Mark Martin
2007 #PD11 Mark Martin
Press Pass Premium Performance Driven Red
2007 #PD11 Mark Martin

Press Pass Premium Phone Cards $5
1995 #6 Mark Martin

Press Pass Premium Phone Cards $50
1995 #6 Mark Martin

Press Pass Premium Previews
2003 #18 Mark Martin
2004 #29 Mark Martin
2008 #EB8 Mark Martin

Press Pass Premium Race Used Firesuit
1999 #F6 Mark Martin

Press Pass Premium Race Used Firesuit Cars
2001 #FC2 Mark Martin
2002 #FC2 Mark Martin

Press Pass Premium Race Used Firesuit Drivers
2001 #FD2 Mark Martin
2002 #FD2 Mark Martin

Press Pass Premium Red
2007 #R2 Mark Martin
2007 #R68 Mark Martin MD
2007 #R81 Mark Martin FF
2008 #8 Mark Martin
2008 #46 Mark Martin's Car M
2008 #73 Mark Martin F

Press Pass Premium Red Hot
1995 #2 Mark Martin
1995 #30 Mark Martin

Press Pass Premium Red Reflectors
2002 #19 Mark Martin
2002 #43 Mark Martin's Car
2002 #65 Mark Martin CH
2002 #79 Mark Martin PC
2003 #18 Mark Martin
2003 #43 Mark Martin's Car
2003 #64 Mark Martin CC
2003 #75 Mark Martin PC

Press Pass Premium Reflectors
1998 #9 Mark Martin
1998 #18 Mark Martin's Car
1998 #30 Mark Martin
1999 #R17 Mark Martin
1999 #R29 Mark Martin's Car
1999 #R48 Mark Martin
2000 #5 Mark Martin
2000 #31 Mark Martin
2000 #52 Mark Martin
2000 #69 Mark Martin

Press Pass Premium Rivalries
1998 #5A Mark Martin

Press Pass Premium Samples
2002 #19 Mark Martin
2002 #43 Mark Martin's Car
2003 #18 Mark Martin
2003 #43 Mark Martin's Car
2004 #29 Mark Martin
2004 #38 Mark Martin's Car
2005 #19 Mark Martin

Press Pass Premium Steel Horses
1998 #SH4 Mark Martin's Car
1999 #SH5 Mark Martin's Car

Press Pass Premium Triple Gear Firesuit
1998 #TGF4 Mark Martin

Press Pass Previews
1993 #10 Mark Martin
1993 #34 Mark Martin's Car
2003 #21 Mark Martin
2004 #19 Mark Martin
2006 #EB6 Mark Martin
2007 #EB7 Mark Martin
2007 #EB114 Mark Martin TT
2008 #EB21 Mark Martin

Press Pass Previews Green
2005 #EB5 Mark Martin

Press Pass Previews Silver
2005 #EB101 Mark Martin

Press Pass R and N China
1996 #20 Mark Martin
1996 #53 Mark Martin's Car

Press Pass Race Day
1994 #RD5 Mark Martin
1995 #RD9 Mark Martin
2007 #RD9 Mark Martin

Press Pass Red Hot
1995 #19 Mark Martin
1995 #53 Mark Martin's Car
1995 #66 Mark Martin
1995 #104 Mark Martin ST
1995 #116 Mark Martin's Car AW

Press Pass Samples
2003 #21 Mark Martin
2003 #92 Mark Martin's Car OTW
2004 #19 Mark Martin
2004 #65 Mark Martin's Car OTW
2004 #80 The Drive for Five WCS
2005 #5 Mark Martin
2005 #72 Mark Martin's Car OTW
2005 #83 Mark Martin/T.Stewart NS
2005 #101 Mark Martin P
2005 #115 Mark Martin's Car

Press Pass Scorchers
1996 #20 Mark Martin
1996 #53 Mark Martin's Car
1996 #76 Roush/S.Hmiel/M.Martin TW
1996 #96 Mark Martin S

Press Pass Shockers
1998 #ST5A Mark Martin

Press Pass Showcar
2003 #S9B Mark Martin
2004 #S10B Mark Martin's Car
2005 #SC1 Mark Martin

Press Pass Showcar Die Cuts
2000 #SC11 Mark Martin's Car

Press Pass Showman
1999 #3A Mark Martin
2000 #SM11 Mark Martin
2003 #S9A Mark Martin
2004 #S10A Mark Martin
2005 #SM1 Mark Martin

Press Pass Showman Die Cuts
2000 #SM11 Mark Martin

Press Pass Showman/Showcar
2001 #S6A Mark Martin
2001 #S6B Mark Martin's Car

Press Pass Signings
1999 #37 Mark Martin/430
2000 #37 Mark Martin
2001 #34 Mark Martin P/T/N/S
2002 #41 Mark Martin O/P/S/T/N
2003 #46 Mark Martin O/P/S/T/N
2004 #41 Mark Martin O/T/N
2005 #38 Mark Martin P/S
2006 #34 Mark Martin NC S
2007 #43 Mark Martin NC
2008 #36 Mark Martin

Press Pass Signings Blue
2007 #18 Mark Martin NC
2008 #17 Mark Martin

Press Pass Signings Gold
1999 #15 Mark Martin/100
2000 #20 Mark Martin
2001 #23 Mark Martin P/T/N/S
2002 #39 Mark Martin O/P/S/T/N
2003 #46 Mark Martin O/P/S/T/N
2004 #38 Mark Martin O/T/N
2005 #36 Mark Martin P/S
2006 #31 Mark Martin NC S
2007 #34 Mark Martin NC
2008 #30 Mark Martin

Press Pass Signings Platinum
2005 #35 Mark Martin P/S

Press Pass Signings Press Plates Black
2007 #29 Mark Martin
2008 #26 Mark Martin

Press Pass Signings Press Plates Cyan
2007 #28 Mark Martin
2008 #26 Mark Martin

Press Pass Signings Press Plates Magenta
2007 #30 Mark Martin
2008 #26 Mark Martin

Press Pass Signings Press Plates Yellow
2007 #28 Mark Martin
2008 #26 Mark Martin

Press Pass Signings Silver
2006 #33 Mark Martin NC S
2007 #33 Mark Martin NC
2008 #26 Mark Martin

Press Pass Signings Transparent
2001 #7 Mark Martin P/T/N/S

Press Pass Skidmarks
1999 #2 Mark Martin
1999 #29 Mark Martin's Car
1999 #49 Mark Martin
1999 #88 Mark Martin OTP
2000 #SK2 Mark Martin

Press Pass Slideshow
2008 #SS14 Mark Martin

Press Pass Snapshots
2003 #SN16 Mark Martin
2004 #SN16 Mark Martin
2005 #SN17 Mark Martin
2006 #SN25 Mark Martin
2006 #SN34 Mark Martin
2007 #SN19 Mark Martin

Press Pass Speedway
2008 #64 Mark Martin SH

Press Pass Speedway Cockpit
2008 #CP13 Mark Martin

Press Pass Speedway Corporate Cuts Drivers
2008 #CD-MM Mark Martin

Press Pass Speedway Corporate Cuts Drivers Patches
2008 #CD-MM Mark Martin/29

Press Pass Speedway Corporate Cuts Team
2008 #CT-MM Mark Martin

Press Pass Speedway Gold
2008 #G64 Mark Martin SH

Press Pass Speedway Holofoil
2008 #H64 Mark Martin SH

Press Pass Speedway Red
2008 #R64 Mark Martin SH

Press Pass Speedway Test Drive
2008 #TD3 Mark Martin

Press Pass Stealth
1998 #25 Mark Martin
1998 #26 Mark Martin's Car
1998 #40 Mark Martin
1998 #55 Mark Martin TM
1999 #22 Mark Martin
1999 #23 Mark Martin's Car
1999 #45 Mark Martin
1999 #60 Valvoline Springs TT CL
2000 #13 Mark Martin
2000 #14 Mark Martin's Car
2001 #10 Mark Martin
2001 #11 Mark Martin's Car
2001 #12 Mark Martin
2001 #67 Mark Martin SST
2002 #7 Mark Martin
2002 #8 Mark Martin's Car
2002 #9 Mark Martin
2002 #58 Mark Martin's Car SST
2002 #68 Mark Martin WW
2003 #7 Mark Martin
2003 #8 Mark Martin's Car
2003 #9 Mark Martin
2003 #69 Mark Martin SF
2004 #55 Mark Martin
2004 #56 Mark Martin's Car
2004 #57 Mark Martin
2004 #74 Mark Martin WW
2006 #19 Mark Martin
2006 #48 17/6/16/26/99 TM
2006 #68 Mark Martin F
2007 #16 Mark Martin
2007 #46 Mark Martin's Rig
2007 #68 Nemechek/Martin/Marlin/Smith
2008 #21 Mark Martin
2008 #47 Mark Martin's Rig C
2008 #55 Mark Martin's Car GC
2008 #65 Aric Almirola Mark Martin Martin Truex Jr. Paul Menard Regan Smith

Press Pass Stealth Autographed Hat Entry
2006 #PPH15 Mark Martin

Press Pass Stealth Awards
1998 #4 Mark Martin 1:120
1998 #6 Mark Martin 1:420

Press Pass Stealth Battle Armor Autographs
2008 #BASMM Mark Martin/8

Press Pass Stealth Battle Armor Drivers
2007 #BAD19 Mark Martin
2008 #BAD10 Mark Martin

Press Pass Stealth Battle Armor Teams
2007 #BAT19 Mark Martin
2008 #BAT10 Mark Martin

Press Pass Stealth Behind the Numbers
2000 #BN3 Mark Martin
2001 #BN2 Mark Martin
2002 #BN2 Mark Martin

Press Pass Stealth Big Numbers
1999 #BN14 Mark Martin

Press Pass Stealth Big Numbers Die Cuts
1999 #BN14 Mark Martin

Press Pass Stealth Chrome
2007 #16 Mark Martin
2007 #46 Mark Martin's Rig
2007 #68 Nemechek/Martin/Marlin/Smith
2008 #21 Mark Martin
2008 #47 Mark Martin's Rig C
2008 #55 Mark Martin's Car GC
2008 #65 Aric Almirola Mark Martin Martin Truex Jr. Paul Menard Regan Smith

Press Pass Stealth Chrome Exclusives
2007 #X16 Mark Martin
2007 #X46 Mark Martin's Rig
2007 #X68 Nemechek/Martin/Marlin/Smith
2008 #21 Mark Martin
2008 #47 Mark Martin's Rig C
2008 #55 Mark Martin's Car GC
2008 #65 Aric Almirola Mark Martin Martin Truex Jr. Paul Menard Regan Smith

Press Pass Stealth Chrome Exclusives Gold
2008 #21 Mark Martin
2008 #47 Mark Martin's Rig C
2008 #55 Mark Martin's Car GC
2008 #65 Aric Almirola Mark Martin Martin Truex Jr. Paul Menard Regan Smith

Press Pass Stealth Chrome Platinum
2007 #P16 Mark Martin
2007 #P46 Mark Martin's Rig
2007 #P68 Nemechek/Martin/Marlin/Smith

Press Pass Stealth EFX
2004 #EF7 Mark Martin
2006 #EFX6 Mark Martin 1:48

Press Pass Stealth Fan Talk
1998 #7 Mark Martin

Press Pass Stealth Fan Talk Die Cuts
1998 #7 Mark Martin

Press Pass Stealth Fusion
1998 #25 Mark Martin
1998 #26 Mark Martin's Car
1998 #40 Mark Martin
1998 #55 Mark Martin TM
1999 #F22 Mark Martin
1999 #F23 Mark Martin's Car
1999 #F45 Mark Martin
1999 #F60 Valvoline Springs TT CL
2000 #FS10 Mark Martin
2000 #FS11 Mark Martin's Car
2000 #FS12 Mark Martin
2001 #F6 Mark Martin
2002 #F9 Mark Martin
2003 #FU9 Mark Martin
2004 #FU8 Mark Martin

Press Pass Stealth Fusion Green
2000 #FS10 Mark Martin
2000 #FS11 Mark Martin
2000 #FS12 Mark Martin

Press Pass Stealth Fusion Red
2000 #FS10 Mark Martin
2000 #FS11 Mark Martin
2000 #FS12 Mark Martin

Press Pass Stealth Gear Grippers Autographs
2004 #HT-MM Mark Martin/6
2005 #GG-MM Mark Martin/6
2006 #MM Mark Martin/6

Press Pass Stealth Gear Grippers Cars
2003 #GGT6 Mark Martin

Press Pass Stealth Gear Grippers Cars Autographs
2003 #MM Mark Martin/6

Press Pass Stealth Gear Grippers Drivers
2003 #GGD6 Mark Martin
2004 #GGD17 Mark Martin
2006 #GGD15 Mark Martin

Press Pass Stealth Gear Grippers Drivers Autographs
2003 #MM Mark Martin/6

Press Pass Stealth Gear Grippers Drivers Retail
2004 #GGT17 Mark Martin

Press Pass Stealth Gold
2002 #7 Mark Martin
2002 #8 Mark Martin's Car
2002 #9 Mark Martin
2002 #58 Mark Martin's Car SST
2002 #68 Mark Martin WW

Press Pass Stealth Headlines
1999 #SH4 Mark Martin

Press Pass Stealth Holofoils
2001 #10 Mark Martin
2001 #11 Mark Martin's Car
2001 #12 Mark Martin
2001 #67 Mark Martin SST

Press Pass Stealth Hot Pass
2006 #HP18 Mark Martin

Press Pass Stealth Intensity
2000 #IN2 Mark Martin

Press Pass Stealth Lap Leaders
2002 #LL18 Mark Martin

Press Pass Stealth Mach 07
2007 #M7-9 Mark Martin

Press Pass Stealth Mach 08
2008 #M8-5 Mark Martin

Press Pass Stealth Maximum Access
2007 #MA17 Mark Martin
2008 #MA17 Mark Martin

Press Pass Stealth Maximum Access Autographs
2007 #MA17 Mark Martin
2008 #MA17 Mark Martin

Press Pass Stealth No Boundaries
2003 #NB19 Mark Martin
2004 #NB19 Mark Martin

Press Pass Stealth Octane
1998 #25 Mark Martin
1998 #26 Mark Martin's Car

Press Pass Stealth Octane Die Cuts
1998 #25 Mark Martin
1998 #26 Mark Martin's Car

Press Pass Stealth Octane SLX
1999 #014 Mark Martin
1999 #036 Mark Martin's Car

Press Pass Stealth Octane SLX Die Cuts
1999 #014 Mark Martin
1999 #036 Mark Martin's Car

Press Pass Stealth Previews
2003 #7 Mark Martin
2003 #8 Mark Martin's Car
2003 #9 Mark Martin
2006 #19 Mark Martin
2007 #EB16 Mark Martin
2008 #21 Mark Martin

Press Pass Stealth Profile
2000 #PR6 Mark Martin
2001 #SP1 Mark Martin
2002 #P2 Mark Martin
2003 #PR6 Mark Martin
2005 #PR5 Mark Martin
2006 #P2 Mark Martin

Press Pass Stealth Race Used Glove Cars
2001 #RGC6 Mark Martin/50
2002 #GLC5 Mark Martin's Car

Press Pass Stealth Race Used Glove Drivers
2001 #RGD6 Mark Martin/50
2002 #GLD5 Mark Martin

Press Pass Stealth Race Used Gloves
1998 #G4 Mark Martin
1999 #G7 Mark Martin/150
2000 #G6 Mark Martin/50

Press Pass Stealth Red
2003 #P7 Mark Martin
2003 #P8 Mark Martin's Car
2003 #P9 Mark Martin
2003 #P69 Mark Martin SF

Press Pass Stealth Retail
2006 #19 Mark Martin
2006 #48 17/6/16/26/99 TM
2006 #68 Mark Martin F

Press Pass Stealth Retail Gear Grippers Cars
2006 #GGT15 Mark Martin

Press Pass Stealth Samples
2002 #7 Mark Martin
2002 #8 Mark Martin's Car
2002 #9 Mark Martin
2002 #58 Mark Martin's Car SST
2002 #68 Mark Martin WW
2003 #7 Mark Martin
2003 #8 Mark Martin's Car
2003 #9 Mark Martin
2003 #69 Mark Martin SF
2004 #X56 Mark Martin's Car
2004 #X74 Mark Martin WW
2004 #X57 Mark Martin
2004 #X55 Mark Martin

Press Pass Stealth SST
2000 #SST3 Mark Martin

Press Pass Stealth SST Cars
1999 #SS7 Mark Martin's Car

Press Pass Stealth SST Drivers
1999 #SS7 Mark Martin

Press Pass Stealth Stars
1998 #12 Mark Martin

Press Pass Stealth Stars Die Cuts
1998 #12 Mark Martin

Press Pass Stealth Supercharged
2003 #SC6 Mark Martin

Press Pass Stealth X-Ray
2004 #55 Mark Martin
2004 #56 Mark Martin's Car
2004 #57 Mark Martin
2004 #74 Mark Martin WW
2006 #X19 Mark Martin
2006 #X48 17/6/16/26/99 TM
2006 #X68 Mark Martin F

Press Pass Techno-Retro
2000 #TR16 Mark Martin

Press Pass Top 25 Drivers & Rides
2006 #C4 Mark Martin's Car
2006 #D4 Mark Martin

Press Pass Top Shelf
2003 #TS6 Mark Martin

Press Pass Top Ten
2005 #TT8 Mark Martin

Press Pass Torpedoes
1998 #ST5B Mark Martin's Car

Press Pass Torquers
1996 #20 Mark Martin
1996 #53 Mark Martin's Car
1996 #76 Roush/Hmiel/M.Martin TW
1996 #96 Mark Martin S
1997 #5 Mark Martin
1997 #35 Mark Martin's Car
1997 #75 Mark Martin
1997 #89 Mark Martin
1997 #112 Mark Martin

Press Pass Total Memorabilia
2001 #TM6 Mark Martin

Press Pass Total Memorabilia Power Pick
2002 #TM7 Mark Martin
2003 #TM6 Mark Martin
2004 #TM6 Mark Martin
2005 #TM6 Mark Martin

Press Pass Trackside
2000 #20 Mark Martin
2000 #32 Mark Martin's Car
2000 #P1 Mark Martin Promo
2000 #NNO Mark Martin Power Pick
2001 #23 Mark Martin
2001 #42 Mark Martin's Car
2002 #23 Mark Martin
2002 #61 Mark Martin RD
2002 #66 Mark Martin's Car
2002 #78 Mark Martin TM
2003 #6 Mark Martin
2003 #78 Mart/J.Bur/Bif/Kens/Bus TM
2004 #17 Mark Martin
2004 #68 Burt/Kens/Mart/Busch/Bif. TM
2004 #113 Mark Martin F
2005 #31 Mark Martin

Press Pass Trackside Dialed In
2000 #DI3 Mark Martin
2001 #D6 Mark Martin
2002 #DI10 Mark Martin

Press Pass Trackside Die Cuts
2000 #20 Mark Martin
2000 #32 Mark Martin's Car
2001 #23 Mark Martin
2001 #42 Mark Martin's Car

Press Pass Trackside Gold Holofoil
2003 #P6 Mark Martin
2003 #P78 Martin/J.Burton/Biffle/Kenseth/Busch

Press Pass Trackside Golden
2000 #20 Mark Martin
2000 #32 Mark Martin
2001 #23 Mark Martin
2001 #42 Mark Martin's Car
2002 #G23 Mark Martin
2003 #G6 Mark Martin
2004 #G17 Mark Martin
2004 #G68 Burt/Kens/Mart/Busch/Biffle TM
2004 #G113 Mark Martin F
2005 #G31 Mark Martin

Press Pass Trackside Hat Giveaway
2003 #PPH16 Mark Martin
2004 #PPH19 Mark Martin
2005 #PPH45 Mark Martin

Press Pass Trackside Hot Pass
2005 #13 Mark Martin

Press Pass Trackside Hot Pass National
2005 #13 Mark Martin

Press Pass Trackside License to Drive
2002 #21 Mark Martin

Press Pass Trackside License to Drive Die Cuts
2002 #21 Mark Martin

Press Pass Trackside Mirror Image
2001 #MI6 Mark Martin
2002 #MI7 Mark Martin
2003 #MI4 Mark Martin

Press Pass Trackside Panorama
2000 #P35 Mark Martin

Press Pass Trackside Pit Stoppers Cars Autographs
2003 #MM Mark Martin/6

Press Pass Trackside Pit Stoppers Drivers Autographs
2003 #PSD-MM Mark Martin/6

Press Pass Trackside Previews
2003 #6 Mark Martin
2004 #EB17 Mark Martin
2005 #31 Mark Martin

Press Pass Trackside Runnin N' Gunnin
2000 #RG4 Mark Martin
2001 #RG4 Mark Martin

Press Pass Trackside Samples
2002 #23 Mark Martin
2002 #61 Mark Martin RD
2002 #66 Mark Martin's Car
2002 #78 Mark Martin TM
2003 #6 Mark Martin
2003 #78 Mart/J.Bur/Bif/Kens/Bus TM
2004 #17 Mark Martin
2004 #68 Burt/Kens/Mart/Busch/Biffle TM
2004 #113 Mark Martin F
2005 #31 Mark Martin

Press Pass Trackside Too Tough To Tame
2000 #TT2 Mark Martin

Press Pass Triple Burner
2001 #TB6 Mark Martin
2002 #TB7 Mark Martin
2003 #TB6 Mark Martin
2004 #TB6 Mark Martin
2005 #TB6 Mark Martin

Press Pass Triple Burner Exchange
2003 #TB6 Mark Martin EXCH
2004 #TB6 Mark Martin
2005 #TB6 Mark Martin

Press Pass Triple Gear 3 in 1
1998 #STG4 Mark Martin
1999 #TG2 Mark Martin

Press Pass Triple Gear Burning Rubber
1998 #TG4 Mark Martin

Press Pass UMI Cup Chase
2005 #1 Cup Chase Drivers CL
2005 #7 Mark Martin

Press Pass Velocity
2001 #VL6 Mark Martin
2002 #VL8 Mark Martin
2003 #VC6 Mark Martin
2004 #VC4 Mark Martin
2005 #V8 Mark Martin
2006 #VE2 Mark Martin

Press Pass Vintage
2001 #VN8 Mark Martin
2002 #VN15 Mark Martin

Press Pass Wal-Mart Autographs
2007 #MM Mark Martin
2008 #8 Mark Martin

Press Pass Weekend Warriors
2008 #WW9 Mark Martin

Pro Set
1991 #21 Mark Martin
1991 #25 Mark Martin's Car
1991 #99 Mark Martin
1992 #61 Mark Martin's Car
1992 #71 Mark Martin
1992 #96 Mark Martin
1992 #184 Mark Martin's Transporter
1992 #242 Mark Martin Busch Pole

Pro Set Maxwell House
1992 #13 Mark Martin

Pro Set Rudy Farms
1992 #5 Mark Martin

Race Call Phone Cards
1995 #15 Mark Martin/10,000 $3
1995 #16 Mark Martin/5000 $10
1995 #17 Mark Martin/5000 20-Units

Race Sharks
1997 #6 Mark Martin
1997 #27 Mark Martin

Race Sharks First Bite
1997 #6 Mark Martin
1997 #27 Mark Martin

Race Sharks Great White
1997 #6 Mark Martin
1997 #27 Mark Martin

Race Sharks Great White Shark's Teeth
1997 #GW6 Mark Martin

Race Sharks Great White Shark's Teeth First Bite
1997 #GW6 Mark Martin

Race Sharks Hammerhead
1997 #6 Mark Martin
1997 #27 Mark Martin

Race Sharks Hammerhead First Bite
1997 #6 Mark Martin
1997 #27 Mark Martin

Race Sharks Tiger Shark
1997 #6 Mark Martin
1997 #27 Mark Martin

Race Sharks Tiger Shark First Bite
1997 #6 Mark Martin
1997 #27 Mark Martin

Racer's Choice
1996 #6 Mark Martin
1996 #30 Mark Martin's Car
1996 #85 Mark Martin RW
1996 #86 Mark Martin RW
1996 #93 Mark Martin BC
1996 #109 Mark Martin CL
1997 #6 Mark Martin
1997 #41 Mark Martin's Car
1997 #94 Mark Martin TR

Racer's Choice Artist's Proofs
1996 #6 Mark Martin
1996 #30 Mark Martin's Car
1996 #85 Mark Martin RW
1996 #86 Mark Martin RW
1996 #93 Mark Martin BC
1996 #109 Mark Martin CL

Racer's Choice Busch Clash
1997 #5 Mark Martin

Racer's Choice High Octane
1997 #5 Mark Martin

Racer's Choice High Octane Glow in the Dark
1997 #5 Mark Martin

Racer's Choice Showcase Series
1997 #6 Mark Martin
1997 #41 Mark Martin's Car
1997 #94 Mark Martin TR

Racer's Choice Speedway Collection
1996 #6 Mark Martin
1996 #30 Mark Martin's Car
1996 #85 Mark Martin RW
1996 #86 Mark Martin RW
1996 #93 Mark Martin BC
1996 #109 Mark Martin CL

Racer's Choice Top Ten
1996 #4 Mark Martin

Redline Standups
1992 #6 Mark Martin

SB Motorsports
1997 #6 Mark Martin
1997 #42 Mark Martin
1997 #49 Mark Martin's Car
1997 #95 Mark Martin

SB Motorsports Race Chat
1997 #RC6 Mark Martin

SB Motorsports Winston Cup Rewind
1997 #WC6 Mark Martin
1997 #WC22 Mark Martin

Score Board IQ
1997 #6 Mark Martin
1997 #42 Mark Martin's Car

Score Board IQ $10 Phone Cards
1997 #PC6 Mark Martin

Select
1995 #20 Mark Martin
1995 #53 Mark Martin's Car
1995 #66 Mark Martin
1995 #129 R.Petty/M.Martin I
1995 #143 Mark Martin PS

Select Dream Machines
1995 #DM3 Mark Martin's Car

Select Flat Out
1995 #20 Mark Martin
1995 #53 Mark Martin's Car
1995 #66 Mark Martin
1995 #129 Richard Petty/Mark Martin I
1995 #143 Mark Martin PS

Select Skills
1995 #SS2 Mark Martin

SkyBox
1994 #9 Mark Martin's Car

SkyBox Profile
1997 #19 Mark Martin
1997 #66 Mark Martin's Car

SkyBox Profile Autographs
1997 #19 Mark Martin

SkyBox Profile Pace Setters
1997 #E9 Mark Martin

SkyBox Profile Team
1997 #T5 Mark Martin

SP
1995 #5 Mark Martin CC
1995 #37 Mark Martin
1995 #38 Mark Martin
1995 #80 Mark Martin's Car
1996 #6 Mark Martin
1996 #45 Mark Martin CC
1996 #83 Mark Martin RPM
1997 #6 Mark Martin 2F
1997 #48 Mark Martin's Car
1997 #88 Mark Martin 2F
1997 #116 Mark Martin 3F

SP Authentic
1998 #6 Mark Martin
1998 #40 Mark Martin's Car
1998 #75 Mark Martin VL
1999 #20 Mark Martin
1999 #61 Mark Martin's Car
1999 #62 Mark Martin CLASS
1999 #76 Mark Martin SP
2000 #2 Mark Martin
2000 #77 Mark Martin SUP

SP Authentic Behind the Wheel
1998 #BW3 Mark Martin

SP Authentic Behind the Wheel Die Cuts
1998 #BW3 Mark Martin

SP Authentic Behind the Wheel Gold
1998 #BW3 Mark Martin

SP Authentic Cup Challengers
1999 #CC5 Mark Martin

SP Authentic Driver's Seat
2000 #DS3 Mark Martin

SP Authentic Driving Force
1999 #DF4 Mark Martin

SP Authentic In the Driver's Seat
1999 #DS8 Mark Martin

SP Authentic Overdrive

1999 #20 Mark Martin
1999 #61 Mark Martin CAR
1999 #62 Mark Martin CLASS
1999 #76 Mark Martin SP/6

SP Authentic Overdrive Gold
2000 #2 Mark Martin/6
2000 #77 Mark Martin SUP/6

SP Authentic Overdrive Silver
2000 #2 Mark Martin
2000 #77 Mark Martin SUP

SP Authentic Power Surge
2000 #PS6 Mark Martin

SP Authentic Race for the Cup
2000 #R5 Mark Martin

SP Authentic Sign of the Times
1999 #MM Mark Martin
2000 #MM Mark Martin

SP Authentic Sign of the Times Gold
2000 #MM Mark Martin

SP Authentic Sign of the Times Red
1998 #ST6 Mark Martin's Car

SP Die Cuts
1995 #5 Mark Martin
1995 #37 Mark Martin
1995 #38 Mark Martin
1995 #80 Mark Martin's Car

SP Holoview Maximum Effects
1996 #ME6 Mark Martin

SP Holoview Maximum Effects Die Cuts
1996 #ME6 Mark Martin

SP Race Film
1997 #RD6 Mark Martin

SP Racing Legends
1996 #RL23 Mark Martin

SP Speed Merchants
1995 #SM6 Mark Martin

SP Speed Merchants Die Cuts
1995 #SM6 Mark Martin

SP Super Series
1997 #6 Mark Martin 2F
1997 #48 Mark Martin's Car
1997 #88 Mark Martin 2F
1997 #116 Mark Martin 3F

Speedflix
1996 #20 Mark Martin
1996 #40 Mark Martin's Car in pits
1996 #50 Mark Martin DT
1996 #67 Mark Martin RO
1996 #68 Mark Martin RO
1996 #69 Mark Martin RO
1996 #70 Mark Martin RO
1996 #87 Mark Martin CL

Speedflix Artist Proof's
1996 #20 Mark Martin
1996 #40 Mark Martin in Pits
1996 #50 Mark Martin DT
1996 #67 Mark Martin
1996 #68 Mark Martin
1996 #69 Mark Martin
1996 #70 Mark Martin
1996 #87 Mark Martin CL

Speedflix Clear Shots
1996 #8 Mark Martin

Speedflix In Motion
1996 #8 Mark Martin's Helmet

Speedflix ProMotion
1996 #8 Mark Martin

Sports Legends Alan Kulwicki
1992 #AK9 Alan Kulwicki/M.Martin Cars
1992 #AK11 Alan Kulwicki/M.Martin/Earnhardt Cars

SportsCom FanScan
1997 #8 Mark Martin
1998 #6 Mark Martin
1999 #6 Mark Martin

SPx
1996 #6 Mark Martin
1997 #6 Mark Martin

SPx Blue
1997 #6 Mark Martin

SPx Gold
1996 #6 Mark Martin
1997 #6 Mark Martin

SPx Silver
1997 #6 Mark Martin

SPx SpeedView Autographs
1997 #SV6 Mark Martin

SPx Tag Team
1997 #TT3 M.Martin/J.Burton

SPx Tag Team Autographs
1997 #TA3 M.Martin/J.Burton

Sunbelt Racing Legends
1991 #6 Mark Martin

Superior Racing Metals
1991 #7 Mark Martin

Traks
1991 #6 Mark Martin
1991 #50 Mark Martin
1992 #6 Mark Martin
1992 #38 Mark Martin
1993 #6 Mark Martin
1993 #32 M.Martin/K.Schrader Cars
1993 #56 Mark Martin's Car
1993 #60 Mark Martin's Busch Car
1993 #67 Mark Martin
1993 #78 Mark Martin's Car
1993 #109 Mark Martin's Car
1993 #161 Mark Martin
1994 #6 Mark Martin
1994 #37 Mark Martin's Car
1994 #60 Mark Martin
1994 #82 Mark Martin
1994 #100 Mark Martin's Car CL
1994 #113 Mark Martin
1994 #144 Mark Martin
1994 #176 Mark Martin
1994 #P2 Mark Martin T10 Prototype
1995 #30 Mark Martin
1995 #48 Mark Martin
1995 #53 Mark Martin
1995 #62 Mark Martin
2006 #21 Mark Martin
2006 #39 Mark Martin's Car
2006 #68 Mark Martin CTS
2006 #101 Mark Martin's Car PS
2007 #65 M.Martin/R.Smith MG

Traks 5th Anniversary
1995 #1 Mark Martin
1995 #40 Mark Martin
1995 #51 Mark Martin's Car
1995 #P3 Mark Martin Promo
1995 #P4 Mark Martin Promo/4000

Traks 5th Anniversary Clear Contenders
1995 #C2 Mark Martin

Traks 5th Anniversary Gold
1995 #1 Mark Martin
1995 #40 Mark Martin
1995 #51 Mark Martin's Car

Traks 5th Anniversary Jumbos
1995 #E10 Mark Martin

Traks 5th Anniversary Jumbos Gold
1995 #E10 Mark Martin

Traks 5th Anniversary Retrospective
1995 #R1 Mark Martin

Traks ASA
1992 #41 Mark Martin

Traks Auto Value
1994 #33 Mark Martin
1995 #29 Mark Martin

Traks Autographs
1994 #A8 Mark Martin
2006 #24 Mark Martin NC SP

TRAKS Autographs 25
2006 #22 Mark Martin NC

Traks Cartoons
1994 #C1 Mark Martin

Traks Challengers
1995 #C8 Mark Martin

Traks Challengers First Run
1995 #C8 Mark Martin

Traks Corporate Cuts Driver
2007 #CCD15 Mark Martin

Traks Corporate Cuts Patch
2007 #CCD15 Mark Martin/15

Traks Corporate Cuts Team
2007 #CCT15 Mark Martin

Traks Driver's Seat
2007 #DS6B Mark Martin VAR
2007 #DS6 Mark Martin

Traks Driver's Seat National
2007 #DS6 Mark Martin

Traks First Run
1993 #6 Mark Martin
1993 #32 M.Martin/K.Schrader Cars
1993 #56 Mark Martin's Car
1993 #60 Mark Martin's Busch Car
1993 #67 Mark Martin
1993 #78 Mark Martin's Car
1993 #109 Mark Martin's Car
1993 #161 Mark Martin
1994 #6 Mark Martin
1994 #37 Mark Martin's Car
1994 #60 Mark Martin
1994 #82 Mark Martin
1994 #100 Mark Martin's Car CL
1994 #113 Mark Martin
1994 #144 Mark Martin
1994 #176 Mark Martin
1995 #30 Mark Martin
1995 #48 Mark Martin
1995 #53 Mark Martin
1995 #62 Mark Martin

Traks Gold
2007 #G65 M.Martin/R.Smith MG

Traks Holofoil
2007 #H65 M.Martin/R.Smith MG

Traks Hot Pursuit
2007 #HP5 Mark Martin

Traks Preferred Collector
1993 #6 Mark Martin
1994 #24 Mark Martin

Traks Promos
1991 #P2 Mark Martin

Traks Racing Machines
1992 #6 Mark Martin's Car
1992 #53 Mark Martin's Transp.
1992 #73 Mark Martin in Pits
1992 #76 Mark Martin in Pits
1992 #P76 M.Martin in Pits Promo
1995 #RM9 Mark Martin's Car

Traks Racing Machines Bonus
1992 #16B M.Martin/Dallenbach Jr. Cars

Traks Racing Machines First Run
1995 #RM9 Mark Martin's Car

Traks Red
2007 #R65 M.Martin/R.Smith MG

Traks Review and Preview
1996 #5 Mark Martin
1996 #11 Mark Martin
1996 #36 Mark Martin
1996 #P2 Mark Martin's Car Promo

Traks Review and Preview First Run
1996 #5 Mark Martin
1996 #11 Mark Martin
1996 #36 Mark Martin

Traks Review and Preview Liquid Gold
1996 #LG3 Mark Martin

Traks Review and Preview Magnets
1996 #5 Mark Martin
1996 #11 Mark Martin
1996 #36 Mark Martin

Traks Review and Preview Triple-Chase
1996 #TC3 Mark Martin
1996 #TC16 Mark Martin's Car

Traks Review and Preview Triple-Chase Gold
1996 #TC3 Mark Martin
1996 #TC16 Valvoline Racing

Traks Review and Preview Triple-Chase Holofoil
1996 #TC3 Mark Martin
1996 #TC16 Valvoline Racing

Traks Series Stars
1995 #SS5 Mark Martin

Traks Series Stars First Run
1995 #SS5 Mark Martin

TRAKS Stickers
2006 #6 Mark Martin

Traks Trivia
1993 #1 Mark Martin
1993 #6 Mark Martin
1993 #19 Mark Martin
1993 #23 Mark Martin
1993 #32 Mark Martin
1993 #37 Mark Martin
1993 #41 Mark Martin

Traks Valvoline
1995 #99 Mark Martin's Car

Traks Winners
1994 #W14 Mark Martin

Ultra
1996 #9 Mark Martin
1996 #10 Mark Martin
1996 #11 Mark Martin's Car
1996 #165 Mark Martin's Helmet
1996 #176 D.Earnhardt/M.Martin's Car
1996 #186 Mark Martin's Car RW
1996 #193 Mark Martin RW
1997 #21 Mark Martin
1997 #42 Mark Martin's Car
1997 #S1 Mark Martin Sample

Ultra AKA
1997 #A6 Mark Martin

Ultra Autographs
1996 #20 Mark Martin

Ultra Boxed Set
1996 #4 Mark Martin

Ultra Flair Preview
1996 #4 Mark Martin

Ultra Inside Out
1997 #DC7 Mark Martin

Ultra Season Crowns
1996 #6 Mark Martin
1996 #8 Mark Martin

Ultra Shoney's
1997 #10 Mark Martin

Ultra Update
1996 #21 Mark Martin
1996 #67 Mark Martin's Car
1997 #4 Mark Martin
1997 #80 Mark Martin's Car

Ultra Update Autographs
1996 #10 Mark Martin
1997 #4 Mark Martin

Ultra Update Double Trouble
1997 #DT1 Mark Martin

Ultra Update Driver View
1997 #D7 Mark Martin

Ultra Update Elite Seats
1997 #E8 Mark Martin

Ultra Update Proven Power
1996 #10 Mark Martin

Ultra Update Winner
1996 #11 Mark Martin
1996 #18 Mark Martin

Ultra Winn Dixie
1997 #WD1 Mark Martin Winn Dixie
1997 #WD2 Mark Martin Valvoline

Upper Deck
1995 #8 Mark Martin
1995 #51 Mark Martin w/Car
1995 #76 Mark Martin's Car
1995 #144 Mark Martin's Car
1995 #164 Mark Martin DYK
1995 #187 Mark Martin
1995 #188 Mark Martin
1995 #232 Mark Martin SD
1996 #5 Mark Martin
1996 #45 Mark Martin SB
1996 #85 Mark Martin PP
1996 #99 Mark Martin PP

Upper Deck All-Pro
1996 #AP7 Mark Martin

Upper Deck Autographs
1995 #187 Mark Martin

Upper Deck Diamond Vision
1998 #6 Mark Martin

Upper Deck Diamond Vision Signature Moves
1998 #6 Mark Martin

Upper Deck Gold Signature/Electric Gold
1995 #8 Mark Martin
1995 #51 Mark Martin w/Car
1995 #76 Mark Martin's Car
1995 #144 Mark Martin's Car
1995 #164 Mark Martin DYK
1995 #187 Mark Martin
1995 #188 Mark Martin
1995 #232 Mark Martin SD

Upper Deck Jumbos
1995 #OS4 Mark Martin

Upper Deck MVP
2000 #6 Mark Martin
2000 #58 Mark Martin's Car

Upper Deck MVP Cup Quest 2000
2000 #CQ10 Mark Martin

Upper Deck MVP Gold Script
2000 #6 Mark Martin
2000 #58 Mark Martin

Upper Deck MVP Legends in the Making
2000 #LM7 Mark Martin

Upper Deck MVP NASCAR Gallery
2000 #NG3 Mark Martin

Upper Deck MVP NASCAR Stars
2000 #NS6 Mark Martin

Upper Deck MVP ProSign
2000 #PSMM Mark Martin

Upper Deck MVP Silver Script
2000 #6 Mark Martin
2000 #58 Mark Martin

Upper Deck MVP Super Script
2000 #6 Mark Martin/6
2000 #58 Mark Martin's Car/6

Upper Deck Predictor Poles
1996 #RP2 Mark Martin WIN

Upper Deck Predictor Poles Prizes
1996 #RP2 Mark Martin

Upper Deck Predictor Race Winners
1995 #P2 Mark Martin WIN

Upper Deck Predictor Race Winners Coca-Cola 600
1995 #P2 Mark Martin

Upper Deck Predictor Race Winners Daytona 500
1995 #P2 Mark Martin

Upper Deck Predictor Race Winners Prizes
1995 #P2 Mark Martin

Upper Deck Predictor Series Points
1995 #PP4 Mark Martin

Upper Deck Predictor Series Points Prizes
1995 #PP4 Mark Martin

Upper Deck Predictor Wins
1996 #HP5 Mark Martin

Upper Deck Predictor Wins Prizes
1996 #HP5 Mark Martin

Upper Deck Racing
2000 #3 Mark Martin

Upper Deck Racing Brickyard's Best
2000 #BB2 Mark Martin

Upper Deck Racing CHP
2000 #3 Mark Martin

Upper Deck Racing Record Pace
2000 #RP4 Mark Martin

Upper Deck Racing Road Signs
2000 #RSMM Mark Martin

Upper Deck Racing Thunder Road
2000 #TR3 Mark Martin

Upper Deck Racing Winning Formula
2000 #WF2 Mark Martin

Upper Deck Road To The Cup
1996 #RC3 Mark Martin
1996 #RC52 Mark Martin's Car
1996 #RC91 Mark Martin
1996 #RC126 Mark Martin
1997 #5 Mark Martin
1997 #47 Mark Martin's Car
1997 #89 Mark Martin
1997 #147 Mark Martin
1998 #6 Mark Martin's Car
1998 #47 Mark Martin's Car
1998 #100 Mark Martin's Car
1998 #101 Mark Martin
1999 #18 Mark Martin
1999 #57 Mark Martin's Car
1999 #74 Mark Martin FF
1999 #78 Mark Martin HH

Upper Deck Road To The Cup Autographs
1996 #H3 Mark Martin

Upper Deck Road To The Cup Cup Quest
1997 #CQ7 Mark Martin

Upper Deck Road To The Cup Cup Quest Checkered
1997 #CQ7 Mark Martin

Upper Deck Road To The Cup Cup Quest Turn 1
1998 #CQ6 Mark Martin's Car

Upper Deck Road To The Cup Cup Quest Turn 2
1998 #CQ6 Mark Martin's Car

Upper Deck Road To The Cup Cup Quest Turn 3
1998 #CQ6 Mark Martin's Car

Upper Deck Road To The Cup Cup Quest Turn 4
1998 #CQ6 Mark Martin's Car

Upper Deck Road To The Cup Cup Quest Victory Lane
1998 #CQ6 Mark Martin's Car

Upper Deck Road To The Cup Cup Quest White
1997 #CQ7 Mark Martin

Upper Deck Road To The Cup Game Face
1996 #GF6 Mark Martin

Upper Deck Road to the Cup NASCAR Chronicles
1999 #NC10 Mark Martin

Upper Deck Road To The Cup Predictor Plus
1997 #8 Mark Martin
1997 #16 Mark Martin

Upper Deck Road To The Cup Predictor Plus Cel Die Cuts
1997 #8 Mark Martin
1997 #16 Mark Martin

Upper Deck Road To The Cup Predictor Plus Cels
1997 #8 Mark Martin
1997 #16 Mark Martin

Upper Deck Road To The Cup Predictor Points
1996 #PP3 Mark Martin

Upper Deck Road To The Cup Predictor Points Prizes
1996 #PR3 Mark Martin

Upper Deck Road To The Cup Predictor Top 3
1996 #T5 Martin/R.Wallace/B.Labonte
1996 #T7 J.Gordon/M.Martin/J.Benson
1996 #T8 R.Rudd/M.Martin/B.Elliott
1996 #T9 Martin/Musgrave/Longshot

Upper Deck Road To The Cup Predictor Top 3 Prizes
1996 #R6 Mark Martin

Upper Deck Road To The Cup Premiere Position
1997 #PP17 Mark Martin
1997 #PP25 Mark Martin
1997 #PP29 Mark Martin
1997 #PP41 Mark Martin

Upper Deck Road to the Cup Road to the Cup Bronze Level 1
1999 #RTTC2Mark Martin's Car

Upper Deck Road to the Cup Road to the Cup Gold Level 3
1999 #RTTC2Mark Martin's Car

Upper Deck Road to the Cup Road to the Cup Silver Level 2
1999 #RTTC2Mark Martin's Car

Upper Deck Road to the Cup Signature Collection
1999 #MM Mark Martin

Upper Deck Road to the Cup Tires of Daytona
1999 #T4 Mark Martin

Upper Deck Road to the Cup Tires of Daytona Autographed
1999 #TS2 Mark Martin/6

Upper Deck Road to the Cup Upper Deck Profiles
1999 #P7 Mark Martin

Upper Deck Silver Signature/Electric Silver
1995 #8 Mark Martin
1995 #51 Mark Martin w/Car
1995 #76 Mark Martin's Car
1995 #144 Mark Martin's Car
1995 #164 Mark Martin DYK
1995 #187 Mark Martin
1995 #188 Mark Martin
1995 #232 Mark Martin SD

Upper Deck Victory Circle
1997 #6 Mark Martin
1997 #56 Mark Martin's Car
1997 #109 Mark Martin
1998 #6 Mark Martin
1998 #51 Mark Martin's Car
1998 #97 Mark Martin
1998 #98 Mark Martin
1998 #106 Mark Martin
1998 #117 Mark Martin
1998 #140 Mark Martin
1999 #6 Mark Martin
1999 #45 Mark Martin's Car
1999 #75 Mark Martin
1999 #79 Mark Martin's Car
2000 #25 Mark Martin
2000 #60 Mark Martin's Car
2000 #75 Mark Martin's Car

Upper Deck Victory Circle 32 Days of Speed
1998 #D9 Mark Martin
1998 #D10 Mark Martin
1998 #D26 Mark Martin

Upper Deck Victory Circle 32 Days of Speed Gold
1998 #D9 Mark Martin
1998 #D10 Mark Martin
1998 #D26 Mark Martin

Upper Deck Victory Circle Autographs
1998 #AG4 Mark Martin

Upper Deck Victory Circle Championship Reflections
1997 #CR5 Mark Martin

Upper Deck Victory Circle Driver's Seat
1997 #DS6 Mark Martin

Upper Deck Victory Circle Exclusives Level 1 Silver
2000 #25 Mark Martin
2000 #60 Mark Martin's Car
2000 #75 Mark Martin's Car

Upper Deck Victory Circle Exclusives Level 2 Gold
2000 #25 Mark Martin/6
2000 #60 Mark Martin's Car/5
2000 #75 Mark Martin's Car/6

Upper Deck Victory Circle Income Statement
1999 #IS10 Mark Martin
2000 #IS6 Mark Martin

Upper Deck Victory Circle Income Statement LTD
2000 #IS6 Mark Martin

Upper Deck Victory Circle Magic Numbers
1999 #M1 Mark Martin

Upper Deck Victory Circle Magic Numbers Autographs
1999 #M1 Mark Martin/6

Upper Deck Victory Circle Point Leaders
1998 #PL3 Mark Martin

Upper Deck Victory Circle Predictor
1997 #PE6 Mark Martin WIN

Upper Deck Victory Circle Predictor Plus
1998 #6 Mark Martin

Upper Deck Victory Circle Predictor Plus Cel Redemption
1998 #6 Mark Martin

Upper Deck Victory Circle Predictor Winner Cels
1997 #PH6 Mark Martin

Upper Deck Victory Circle Signature Collection
1999 #MM Mark Martin

Upper Deck Victory Circle Sparks of Brilliance
1998 #SB6 Mark Martin

Upper Deck Victory Circle Speed Zone
1999 #SZ2 Mark Martin

Upper Deck Victory Circle Track Masters
1999 #TM6 Mark Martin

Upper Deck Victory Circle UD Exclusives
1999 #6 Mark Martin
1999 #45 Mark Martin
1999 #75 Mark Martin
1999 #79 Mark Martin

Upper Deck Victory Circle Victory Circle
1999 #V5 Mark Martin
2000 #V7 Mark Martin

Upper Deck Victory Circle Victory Circle LTD
2000 #V7 Mark Martin

Upper Deck Victory Circle Winning Material Autographed Victory Hat
2000 #HMM Mark Martin

Upper Deck Victory Circle Winning Material Combination
2000 #CMM Mark Martin

Upper Deck Victory Circle Winning Material Firesuit
2000 #FSMM Mark Martin

Upper Deck Victory Circle Winning Material Tire
2000 #TMM Mark Martin

Upper Deck Virtual Velocity
1996 #VV6 Mark Martin

Upper Deck Virtual Velocity Gold
1996 #VV6 Mark Martin

VIP
1994 #21 Mark Martin
1994 #53 Mark Martin w/Car
1994 #78 Mark Martin ART
1995 #19 Mark Martin
1995 #33 Mark Martin
1995 #53 Mark Martin TD
1996 #17 Mark Martin
1996 #31 Mark Martin
1996 #45 Mark Martin's Car
1996 #P1 Mark Martin Promo
1997 #16 Mark Martin
1997 #35 Mark Martin
1997 #48 Mark Martin
1998 #16 Mark Martin
1998 #32 Mark Martin
1998 #45 Mark Martin's Car
1998 #47 Mark Martin
1998 #49 Roush Racing
1999 #16 Mark Martin
1999 #35 Mark Martin BGN
1999 #46 Mark Martin's Car
1999 #50 J.Burton/M.Martin CL
1999 #P1 Mark Martin Promo
2000 #2 Mark Martin
2000 #25 Mark Martin V
2000 #35 Mark Martin DF
2001 #2 Mark Martin
2001 #46 Mark Martin AS
2002 #4 Mark Martin
2002 #36 Mark Martin AS
2002 #40 Mark Martin PP
2003 #12 Mark Martin
2003 #33 Mark Martin AS
2004 #12 Mark Martin
2004 #54 Mark Martin SG
2005 #17 Mark Martin
2005 #58 Mark Martin HR
2005 #60 Mark Martin HR
2005 #67 Mark Martin F
2005 #68 Mark Martin F
2005 #69 Mark Martin F
2005 #77 Mark Martin BN
2005 #87 Mark Martin ATML
2005 #90 Wallace/Martin/T.Labonte CL
2006 #16 Mark Martin
2006 #32 Mark Martin's Car R
2006 #59 Mark Martin BTN
2006 #82 Mark Martin IF
2007 #19 Mark Martin
2007 #61 Mark Martin Red C

VIP Autographs
1995 #19 Mark Martin

VIP Cool Blue
1995 #19 Mark Martin
1995 #33 Mark Martin
1995 #53 Mark Martin TD

VIP Double Take
1999 #DT6 Mark Martin

VIP Driver's Choice
1994 #DC5 Mark Martin
2002 #DC8 Mark Martin
2003 #DC7 Mark Martin

VIP Driver's Choice Die Cuts
2003 #DC7 Mark Martin

VIP Driver's Choice National
2003 #DC7 Mark Martin

VIP Driver's Choice Transparent
2002 #DC8 Mark Martin

VIP Driver's Choice Transparent LTD
2002 #DC8 Mark Martin

VIP Driving Force
1998 #DF14 Mark Martin's Car

VIP Driving Force Die Cuts
1998 #DF14 Mark Martin's Car

VIP Emerald Proofs
1995 #19 Mark Martin
1995 #33 Mark Martin
1995 #53 Mark Martin TD
1996 #17 Mark Martin
1996 #31 Mark Martin
1996 #45 Mark Martin's Car

VIP Explosives
1997 #16 Mark Martin
1997 #35 Mark Martin
1997 #48 Mark Martin
1998 #16 Mark Martin
1998 #32 Mark Martin
1998 #45 Mark Martin's Car
1998 #47 Mark Martin
1998 #49 Roush Racing
1998 #50 Mark Martin CL
1999 #X16 Mark Martin
1999 #X35 Mark Martin
1999 #X46 Mark Martin's Car
1999 #X50 Burton/Martin CL
2000 #X2 Mark Martin
2000 #X25 Mark Martin V
2000 #X35 Mark Martin DF
2001 #2 Mark Martin
2001 #46 Mark Martin AS
2002 #X4 Mark Martin
2002 #X36 Mark Martin AS
2002 #X40 Mark Martin PP
2003 #X12 Mark Martin
2003 #X33 Mark Martin AS

VIP Explosives Lasers
1999 #16 Mark Martin
1999 #35 Mark Martin
1999 #46 Mark Martin's Car
1999 #50 Burton/Martin CL
2000 #LX2 Mark Martin
2000 #LX25 Mark Martin V
2000 #LX35 Mark Martin DF
2001 #LX2 Mark Martin
2001 #LX46 Mark Martin AS
2002 #LX4 Mark Martin
2002 #LX36 Mark Martin AS
2002 #LX40 Mark Martin PP

VIP Fan's Choice
1995 #FC6 Mark Martin

VIP Fan's Choice Gold
1995 #FC6 Mark Martin

VIP Gear Gallery
2007 #GG7 Mark Martin

VIP Gear Gallery Transparent
2007 #GG7 Mark Martin

VIP Get A Grip Drivers
2007 #GGD1 Mark Martin

VIP Get A Grip Teams
2007 #GGT1 Mark Martin

VIP Gold Signature
1994 #EC5 Mark Martin

VIP Head Gear
1996 #HG5 Mark Martin
1997 #HG5 Mark Martin
1998 #HG8 Mark Martin
1999 #HG6 Mark Martin
2002 #HG9 Mark Martin
2003 #HG6 Mark Martin
2006 #HG6 Mark Martin

VIP Head Gear Die Cuts
1996 #HG5 Mark Martin
1997 #HG5 Mark Martin
1998 #HG8 Mark Martin
2002 #HG9 Mark Martin
2003 #HG6 Mark Martin

VIP Head Gear National
2003 #HG6 Mark Martin

VIP Head Gear Plastic
1999 #HG6 Mark Martin

VIP Head Gear Transparent
2006 #HG6 Mark Martin

VIP Lap Leader
2006 #LL2 Mark Martin

VIP Lap Leader Transparent
2006 #LL2 Mark Martin

VIP Lap Leaders
1998 #LL7 Mark Martin's Car
1999 #LL6 Mark Martin
2000 #LL7 Mark Martin
2003 #LL6 Mark Martin
2004 #LL1 Mark Martin
2005 #1 Mark Martin
VIP Lap Leaders Acetate
1998 #LL7 Mark Martin's Car
VIP Lap Leaders Explosives
2000 #LL7 Mark Martin
VIP Lap Leaders Explosives Lasers
2000 #LL7 Mark Martin
VIP Lap Leaders National
2003 #LL6 Mark Martin
VIP Lap Leaders Transparent
2003 #LL6 Mark Martin
2004 #LL1 Mark Martin
2005 #1 Mark Martin
VIP Lap Leaders Transparent LTD
2003 #LL6 Mark Martin
VIP Laser Explosive
2003 #LX12 Mark Martin
2003 #LX33 Mark Martin AS
VIP Making the Show
2000 #MS12 Mark Martin
2001 #4 Mark Martin
2002 #MS5 Mark Martin
2003 #MS3 Mark Martin
2004 #MS26 Mark Martin
2005 #26 Mark Martin
2006 #MS1 Mark Martin
VIP Member's Only
1994 #2 Mark Martin
VIP Mile Masters
2002 #MM8 Mark Martin
2003 #MM8 Mark Martin
VIP Mile Masters National
2003 #MM8 Mark Martin
VIP Mile Masters Transparent
2002 #MM8 Mark Martin
2003 #MM8 Mark Martin
VIP Mile Masters Transparent LTD
2002 #MM8 Mark Martin
2003 #MM8 Mark Martin
VIP NASCAR Country
1998 #NC7 Mark Martin
VIP NASCAR Country Die Cuts
1998 #NC7 Mark Martin
VIP Oil Slicks
1997 #16 Mark Martin
1997 #35 Mark Martin
1997 #48 Mark Martin
VIP Out of the Box
1999 #OB6 Mark Martin
VIP Previews
2003 #12 Mark Martin
2003 #33 Mark Martin AS
2004 #EB12 Mark Martin
2004 #EB54 Mark Martin SG
2005 #EB17 Mark Martin
2005 #EB67 Mark Martin F
2005 #EB68 Mark Martin F
2005 #EB69 Mark Martin F
2007 #EB19 Mark Martin
VIP Race Used Sheet Metal Cars
2002 #SC9 Mark Martin's Car
VIP Race Used Sheet Metal Drivers
2002 #SD9 Mark Martin
VIP Rear View Mirror
1999 #RM6 Mark Martin
2000 #RM5 Mark Martin
2002 #RM4 Mark Martin
VIP Rear View Mirror Die Cuts
2002 #RM4 Mark Martin
VIP Rear View Mirror Explosives
2000 #RM5 Mark Martin
VIP Rear View Mirror Explosives Laser Die Cuts
2000 #RM5 Mark Martin
VIP Red Hot
1995 #19 Mark Martin
1995 #33 Mark Martin
1995 #53 Mark Martin TD
VIP Reflections
1995 #R4 Mark Martin
VIP Reflections Gold
1995 #R4 Mark Martin
VIP Ring of Honor
1997 #RH5 Mark Martin's Car
VIP Ring of Honor Die Cuts
1997 #RH5 Mark Martin's Car
VIP Sam Bass Top Flight
1996 #SB4 Mark Martin
VIP Sam Bass Top Flight Gold
1996 #SB4 Mark Martin
VIP Samples
2002 #4 Mark Martin
2002 #36 Mark Martin AS
2002 #40 Mark Martin PP
2003 #12 Mark Martin
2003 #33 Mark Martin AS
2004 #12 Mark Martin
2004 #54 Mark Martin SG
2005 #17 Mark Martin
2005 #58 Mark Martin HR
2005 #60 Mark Martin HR
2005 #67 Mark Martin F
2005 #68 Mark Martin F
2005 #69 Mark Martin F
2005 #77 Mark Martin BN
2005 #87 Mark Martin ATML
2005 #90 Wallace/Martin/T.Labonte CL
VIP Sheet Metal
1999 #SM5 Mark Martin
2000 #SM6 Mark Martin
VIP Solos
1998 #16 Mark Martin
1998 #32 Mark Martin
1998 #45 Mark Martin's Car
1998 #47 Mark Martin
1998 #49 Roush Racing
VIP Sunday Best
2007 #SB16 Mark Martin
VIP Tin
2003 #CT12 Mark Martin
2003 #CT33 Mark Martin AS
VIP Torquers
1996 #17 Mark Martin
1996 #31 Mark Martin
1996 #45 Mark Martin's Car
VIP Tradin' Paint Autographs
2004 #TP-MM Mark Martin/6
2005 #MM Mark Martin/6
VIP Tradin' Paint Bronze
2004 #TPT17 Mark Martin
VIP Tradin' Paint Car Autographs
2003 #MM Mark Martin/6
VIP Tradin' Paint Cars
2003 #TPT6 Mark Martin's Car
2005 #TPT17 Mark Martin
VIP Tradin' Paint Driver Autographs
2003 #MM Mark Martin/6
VIP Tradin' Paint Drivers
2003 #TPD6 Mark Martin/65
2005 #TPD17 Mark Martin
VIP Tradin' Paint Gold
2004 #TPD17 Mark Martin
VIP Tradin' Paint Silver
2004 #TPD17 Mark Martin
VIP Triple Gear Sheet Metal
1998 #TGS4 Mark Martin
VIP Under the Lights
2000 #UL7 Mark Martin
VIP Under the Lights Explosives
2000 #UL7 Mark Martin
VIP Under the Lights Explosives Lasers
2000 #UL7 Mark Martin
VIP Vintage Performance
1999 #3 Mark Martin
VIP War Paint
1996 #WP5 Mark Martin's Car
VIP War Paint Gold
1996 #WP5 Mark Martin's Car
Viper
1996 #4 Mark Martin
1996 #37 Mark Martin
1996 #44 Mark Martin
1996 #45 Mark Martin
1996 #57 Mark Martin
1997 #4 Mark Martin
1997 #47 Mark Martin
1997 #70 Mark Martin's Car
Viper Anaconda Jumbos
1997 #A12 Mark Martin
Viper Black Mamba
1996 #4 Mark Martin
1996 #37 Mark Martin
1996 #44 Mark Martin
1996 #45 Mark Martin
1996 #57 Mark Martin
Viper Black Mamba First Strike
1996 #4 Mark Martin
1996 #37 Mark Martin
1996 #44 Mark Martin
1996 #45 Mark Martin
1996 #57 Mark Martin
Viper Black Racer
1997 #4 Mark Martin
1997 #47 Mark Martin
1997 #70 Mark Martin's Car
Viper Black Racer First Strike
1997 #4 Mark Martin
1997 #47 Mark Martin
1997 #70 Mark Martin's Car
Viper Busch Clash
1996 #B11 Mark Martin
Viper Busch Clash First Strike
1996 #B11 Mark Martin
Viper Cobra
1996 #C4 Mark Martin
1997 #C8 Mark Martin
Viper Cobra First Strike
1996 #C4 Mark Martin
1997 #C8 Mark Martin
Viper Copperhead Die Cuts
1996 #4 Mark Martin
1996 #37 Mark Martin
1996 #44 Mark Martin
1996 #45 Mark Martin
1996 #57 Mark Martin
Viper Copperhead Die Cuts First Strike
1996 #4 Mark Martin
1996 #37 Mark Martin
1996 #44 Mark Martin
1996 #45 Mark Martin
1996 #57 Mark Martin
Viper Diamondback
1996 #D4 Mark Martin
1997 #DB7 Mark Martin
Viper Diamondback Authentic
1996 #DA7 Mark Martin
1997 #DBA7 Mark Martin
Viper Diamondback Authentic California
1996 #DA7 Mark Martin
Viper Diamondback Authentic Eastern
1997 #DBA7 Mark Martin
Viper Diamondback Authentic Eastern First Strike
1997 #DBA7 Mark Martin
Viper Diamondback Authentic First Strike
1996 #DA7 Mark Martin
1997 #DBA7 Mark Martin
Viper Diamondback First Strike
1996 #D4 Mark Martin
1997 #DB7 Mark Martin
Viper First Strike
1996 #4 Mark Martin
1996 #37 Mark Martin
1996 #44 Mark Martin
1996 #45 Mark Martin
1996 #57 Mark Martin
1997 #4 Mark Martin
1997 #47 Mark Martin
1997 #70 Mark Martin's Car
Viper Green Mamba
1996 #4 Mark Martin
1996 #37 Mark Martin
1996 #44 Mark Martin
1996 #45 Mark Martin
1996 #57 Mark Martin
Viper King Cobra
1996 #KC8 Mark Martin
1997 #KC8 Mark Martin
Viper King Cobra First Strike
1996 #KC8 Mark Martin
Viper Red Cobra
1996 #4 Mark Martin
1996 #37 Mark Martin
1996 #44 Mark Martin
1996 #45 Mark Martin
1996 #57 Mark Martin
Viper Snake Eyes
1997 #SE10 Mark Martin
Viper Snake Eyes First Strike
1997 #SE10 Mark Martin
Visions
1996 #110 Mark Martin
1996 #127 Mark Martin
Visions *
1996 #110 Mark Martin
1996 #127 Mark Martin
Visions Signings
1996 #89 Mark Martin
Visions Signings *
1996 #89 Mark Martin
Visions Signings Artistry
1996 #9 Mark Martin
Visions Signings Autographs Silver
1996 #42 Mark Martin/315
Visions Signings Autographs Silver *
1996 #89A Mark Martin/315
Wheels
1998 #20 Mark Martin
1998 #42 Mark Martin's Car
1998 #53 Mark Martin
1998 #P1 Mark Martin Promo
1998 #0 Mark Martin Las Vegas
1999 #22 Mark Martin
1999 #48 Mark Martin BGN
1999 #58 Mark Martin's Car
Wheels 50th Anniversary
1998 #A11 Mark Martin
1998 #A26 Mark Martin's Car
Wheels American Thunder
2003 #15 Mark Martin
2003 #36 Mark Martin DT
2003 #38 Mark Martin CC
2003 #49 M.Martin's Transporter
2004 #16 Mark Martin
2004 #53 Mark Martin's Car HR
2004 #70 Mark Martin RR
2005 #20 Mark Martin
2005 #32 Mark Martin's Rig RT. 66
2005 #37 Mark Martin AS
2005 #49 Mark Martin's Car HR
2005 #70 Mark Martin RR
2006 #19 Mark Martin
2006 #39 Mark Martin DT
2006 #44 Mark Martin's Car HR
2006 #76 Mark Martin MIA
2006 #86 Mark Martin NN
2007 #19 Mark Martin
2007 #37 Mark Martin's Car DT
Wheels American Thunder American Eagle
2005 #AE10 Mark Martin
Wheels American Thunder American Muscle
2003 #AM6 Mark Martin
2005 #AM1 Mark Martin
2006 #AM1 Mark Martin
2007 #AM1 Mark Martin
Wheels American Thunder American Racing Idol
2006 #RI5 Mark Martin
Wheels American Thunder American Racing Idol Golden
2006 #RI5 Mark Martin
Wheels American Thunder Autographed Hat Instant Winner
2007 #AH20 Mark Martin
Wheels American Thunder Born On
2003 #BO15 Mark Martin
2003 #BO36 Mark Martin DT
2003 #BO38 Mark Martin CC
2003 #BO49 Pfizer Transporter
Wheels American Thunder Cool Threads
2003 #CT5 Mark Martin
2004 #CT8 Mark Martin
2005 #CT6 Mark Martin
2006 #CT13 Mark Martin
2007 #CT3 Mark Martin
Wheels American Thunder Cup Quest
2004 #CQ8 Mark Martin
Wheels American Thunder Double Hat
2006 #DH14 Mark Martin
Wheels American Thunder Golden Eagle
2005 #GE10 Mark Martin
Wheels American Thunder Grandstand
2006 #GS16 Mark Martin
Wheels American Thunder Head to Toe
2003 #HT5 Mark Martin
2004 #HT7 Mark Martin/50
2005 #HT12 Mark Martin
2006 #HT13 Mark Martin
Wheels American Thunder Heads Up Goodyear
2003 #HUG11 Mark Martin
Wheels American Thunder Heads Up Manufacturer
2003 #HUM25 Mark Martin
Wheels American Thunder Heads Up Team
2003 #HUT23 Mark Martin/90
Wheels American Thunder Heads Up Winston
2003 #HUW25 Mark Martin
Wheels American Thunder Holofoil
2003 #P15 Mark Martin
2003 #P36 Mark Martin DT
2003 #P38 Mark Martin CC
2003 #P49 Pfizer Transporter
Wheels American Thunder Medallion
2005 #MD5 Mark Martin
Wheels American Thunder Post Mark
2003 #PM13 Mark Martin
2004 #PM5 Mark Martin
Wheels American Thunder Previews
2003 #15 Mark Martin
2003 #36 Mark Martin DT
2004 #EB16 Mark Martin
2005 #20 Mark Martin
2006 #EB19 Mark Martin
2006 #EB76 Mark Martin MIA
2007 #EB19 Mark Martin
Wheels American Thunder Pushin Pedal
2003 #PP5 Mark Martin
2004 #PP12 Mark Martin/200
2005 #PP11 Mark Martin
Wheels American Thunder Pushin' Pedal
2006 #PP11 Mark Martin
Wheels American Thunder Rookie Thunder
2003 #RT19 Mark Martin
Wheels American Thunder Samples
2003 #P15 Mark Martin
2003 #P36 Mark Martin DT
2003 #P38 Mark Martin CC
2003 #P49 Pfizer Transporter
2004 #16 Mark Martin
2004 #53 Mark Martin's Car HR
2004 #70 Mark Martin RR
2005 #20 Mark Martin
2005 #32 Mark Martin's Rig RT. 66
2005 #37 Mark Martin AS
2005 #49 Mark Martin's Car HR
2005 #70 Mark Martin RR
Wheels American Thunder Starting Grid
2007 #SG11 Mark Martin
Wheels American Thunder Thunder Road
2003 #TR7 Mark Martin
2004 #TR3 Mark Martin
2005 #TR3 Mark Martin
2006 #TR11 Mark Martin
Wheels American Thunder Thunder Strokes
2006 #6 Mark Martin
2007 #28 Mark Martin
Wheels American Thunder Thunder Strokes Press Plates Black
2007 #28 Mark Martin
Wheels American Thunder Thunder Strokes Press Plates Cyan
2007 #28 Mark Martin
Wheels American Thunder Thunder Strokes Press Plates Magenta
2007 #28 Mark Martin
Wheels American Thunder Thunder Strokes Press Plates Yellow
2007 #28 Mark Martin
Wheels American Thunder Triple Hat
2004 #TH12 Mark Martin
2005 #TH14 Mark Martin
2007 #TH17 Mark Martin
Wheels Autographs
1999 #15 Mark Martin/100
2003 #36 Mark Martin AT/HG
2004 #42 Mark Martin HG
2005 #36 Mark Martin
2006 #39 Mark Martin NC
2007 #25 Mark Martin NC HG
2008 #21 Mark Martin NC HG
Wheels Autographs Press Plates Black
2007 #24 Mark Martin NC
2008 #21 Mark Martin NC HG
Wheels Autographs Press Plates Cyan
2007 #24 Mark Martin NC
2008 #21 Mark Martin NC HG
Wheels Autographs Press Plates Magenta
2007 #24 Mark Martin NC
2008 #21 Mark Martin NC HG
Wheels Autographs Press Plates Yellow
2007 #25 Mark Martin NC
2008 #21 Mark Martin NC HG
Wheels Circuit Breaker
1999 #CB4 Mark Martin
1999 #CB9 Mark Martin
Wheels Custom Shop
1999 #CS4 Mark Martin
Wheels Custom Shop Prizes
1999 #MMA1 Mark Martin
1999 #MMA2 Mark Martin
1999 #MMA3 Mark Martin
1999 #MMB1 Mark Martin
1999 #MMB2 Mark Martin
1999 #MMB3 Mark Martin
1999 #MMC1 Mark Martin
1999 #MMC2 Mark Martin
1999 #MMC3 Mark Martin
Wheels Dialed In
1999 #DI6 Mark Martin
Wheels Double Take
1998 #E8 Mark Martin
Wheels Flag Chasers Daytona Seven
1999 #DS4 Mark Martin
Wheels Flag Chasers Daytona Seven Blue-Yellow
1999 #DS4 Mark Martin
Wheels Flag Chasers Daytona Seven Checkered
1999 #DS4 Mark Martin
Wheels Flag Chasers Daytona Seven Green
1999 #DS4 Mark Martin
Wheels Flag Chasers Daytona Seven Red
1999 #DS4 Mark Martin
Wheels Flag Chasers Daytona Seven White
1999 #DS4 Mark Martin
Wheels Flag Chasers Daytona Seven Yellow
1999 #DS4 Mark Martin
Wheels Golden
1998 #20 Mark Martin
1998 #42 Mark Martin's Car
1998 #53 Mark Martin
1999 #22 Mark Martin
1999 #48 Mark Martin
1999 #58 Mark Martin
Wheels Green Flags
1998 #GF13 Mark Martin's Car
Wheels Harry Gant
1994 #74 Mark Martin
Wheels Harry Gant Gold
1994 #74 Mark Martin
Wheels High Gear
1994 #3 Mark Martin
1994 #89 Mark Martin BC
1994 #106 Mark Martin
1994 #175 Mark Martin
1994 #189 Mark Martin WIN
1994 #190 Mark Martin WIN
1994 #191 Mark Martin WIN
1994 #192 Mark Martin WIN
1994 #199 Mark Martin WIN
1994 #MMS1 Mark Martin AU/1000
1995 #3 Mark Martin
1995 #63 Mark Martin SS
1995 #73 Mark Martin's Car
1995 #88 Mark Martin RW
1998 #3 Mark Martin
1998 #31 Mark Martin's Car
1998 #46 Mark Martin
1999 #2 Mark Martin
1999 #31 Mark Martin's Car
1999 #41 Mark Martin
1999 #50 Mark Martin
2000 #3 Mark Martin
2000 #30 Mark Martin's Car
2000 #58 Mark Martin's Car
2001 #8 Mark Martin
2001 #49 Mark Martin's Car
2001 #69 Mark Martin WCP
2002 #15 Mark Martin
2003 #19 Mark Martin
2003 #58 The Fab Four
2003 #60 On The Mark WCS
2004 #16 Mark Martin
2005 #3 Mark Martin
2005 #63 Mark Martin's Car
2005 #90 Kenseth/Busch/Martin CL
2006 #4 Mark Martin
2006 #74 Mark Martin PREV
2006 #76 Mark Martin FF
2006 #89 R. Wallace/M. Martin NI
2007 #9 Mark Martin
2008 #22 Mark Martin
Wheels High Gear Autographs
1998 #14 Mark Martin/100
1999 #18 Mark Martin/200
2001 #23 Mark Martin
2002 #35 Mark Martin
Wheels High Gear Blue Hawaii SCDA Promos
2003 #19 Mark Martin
2003 #58 The Fab Four
2003 #60 On The Mark
Wheels High Gear Busch Clash
1995 #BC10 Mark Martin
Wheels High Gear Busch Clash Gold
1995 #BC10 Mark Martin
Wheels High Gear Custom Shop
1998 #CS3 Mark Martin EXCH
1999 #CSMM Mark Martin EXCH
2000 #CSMK Mark Martin EXCH
Wheels High Gear Custom Shop Prizes
1999 #MMA1 Mark Martin
1999 #MMA2 Mark Martin
1999 #MMA3 Mark Martin
1999 #MMB1 Mark Martin
1999 #MMB2 Mark Martin
1999 #MMB3 Mark Martin
1999 #MMC1 Mark Martin
1999 #MMC2 Mark Martin
1999 #MMC3 Mark Martin
2000 #MKA1 Mark Martin
2000 #MKA2 Mark Martin
2000 #MKA3 Mark Martin
2000 #MKB1 Mark Martin
2000 #MKB2 Mark Martin
2000 #MKB3 Mark Martin
2000 #MKC1 Mark Martin
2000 #MKC2 Mark Martin
2000 #MKC3 Mark Martin
Wheels High Gear Day One
1994 #106 Mark Martin
1994 #175 Mark Martin
1994 #189 Mark Martin WIN
1994 #190 Mark Martin WIN
1994 #191 Mark Martin WIN
1994 #192 Mark Martin WIN
1994 #199 Mark Martin WIN
1995 #3 Mark Martin
1995 #63 Mark Martin SS
1995 #73 Mark Martin's Car
1995 #88 Mark Martin RW
Wheels High Gear Day One Gold
1994 #106 Mark Martin
1994 #175 Mark Martin
1994 #189 Mark Martin WIN
1994 #190 Mark Martin WIN
1994 #191 Mark Martin WIN
1994 #192 Mark Martin WIN
1994 #199 Mark Martin WIN
1995 #3 Mark Martin
1995 #63 Mark Martin SS
1995 #73 Mark Martin's Car
1995 #88 Mark Martin RW
Wheels High Gear Dominators
1994 #D1 Mark Martin/3000
1994 #D6 Mark Martin/1750
Wheels High Gear Driven
2007 #DR1 Mark Martin
2008 #DR10 Mark Martin
Wheels High Gear Final Standings
2008 #F22 Mark Martin/27
Wheels High Gear Final Standings Gold
2007 #FS9 Mark Martin/9
Wheels High Gear First Gear
1998 #2 Mark Martin
1998 #31 Mark Martin's Car
1998 #46 Mark Martin
1999 #2 Mark Martin
1999 #31 Mark Martin's Car
1999 #41 Mark Martin
1999 #50 Mark Martin
2000 #3 Mark Martin
2000 #30 Mark Martin
2000 #58 Mark Martin
2001 #8 Mark Martin
2001 #49 Mark Martin's CAR
2001 #69 Mark Martin WCP
2002 #15 Mark Martin
2003 #F19 Mark Martin
2003 #F58 The Fab Four
2003 #F60 On The Mark
Wheels High Gear Flag Chasers
1999 #FC2 Mark Martin
2000 #FC4 Mark Martin
Wheels High Gear Flag Chasers Black
2003 #FC9 Mark Martin
2005 #FC9 Mark Martin
2007 #FC7 Mark Martin
2008 #FC1 Mark Martin
Wheels High Gear Flag Chasers Blue-Yellow
1999 #FC2 Mark Martin
2000 #FC4 Mark Martin
2003 #FC9 Mark Martin
2005 #FC9 Mark Martin
2007 #FC7 Mark Martin
2008 #FC1 Mark Martin
Wheels High Gear Flag Chasers Checkered
1999 #FC2 Mark Martin
2000 #FC4 Mark Martin
2003 #FC9 Mark Martin
2005 #FC9 Mark Martin
2007 #FC7 Mark Martin
2008 #FC1 Mark Martin
Wheels High Gear Flag Chasers Checkered Blue/Orange
2000 #FC4 Mark Martin
Wheels High Gear Flag Chasers Green
1999 #FC2 Mark Martin
2000 #FC4 Mark Martin
2003 #FC9 Mark Martin
2005 #FC9 Mark Martin
2007 #FC7 Mark Martin
2008 #FC1 Mark Martin
Wheels High Gear Flag Chasers Red
1999 #FC2 Mark Martin
2000 #FC4 Mark Martin
2003 #FC9 Mark Martin
2005 #FC9 Mark Martin
2007 #FC7 Mark Martin
2008 #FC1 Mark Martin
Wheels High Gear Flag Chasers White
1999 #FC2 Mark Martin
2000 #FC4 Mark Martin
2003 #FC9 Mark Martin
2005 #FC9 Mark Martin
2007 #FC7 Mark Martin
2008 #FC1 Mark Martin
Wheels High Gear Flag Chasers Yellow
1999 #FC2 Mark Martin
2000 #FC4 Mark Martin
2003 #FC9 Mark Martin
2005 #FC9 Mark Martin
2007 #FC7 Mark Martin
2008 #FC1 Mark Martin
Wheels High Gear Flag to Flag
2005 #FF14 Mark Martin
2006 #FF16 Mark Martin
Wheels High Gear Full Throttle
2003 #FT7 Mark Martin
2006 #FT5 Mark Martin
2007 #FT7 Mark Martin
2008 #FT2 Mark Martin
Wheels High Gear Gear Jammers
1998 #GJ5 Mark Martin
Wheels High Gear Gear Shifters
1999 #GS2 Mark Martin
2000 #GS2 Mark Martin
2001 #GS8 Mark Martin
Wheels High Gear Gold
1994 #3 Mark Martin
1994 #89 Mark Martin BC
1994 #106 Mark Martin
1994 #175 Mark Martin
1994 #189 Mark Martin WIN
1994 #190 Mark Martin WIN
1994 #191 Mark Martin WIN
1994 #192 Mark Martin WIN
1994 #199 Mark Martin WIN
1995 #3 Mark Martin
1995 #63 Mark Martin SS
1995 #73 Mark Martin's Car
1995 #88 Mark Martin RW
Wheels High Gear High Groove
1998 #HG4 Mark Martin's Car
2002 #HG15 Mark Martin
2003 #HG17 Mark Martin
2004 #HG15 Mark Martin
Wheels High Gear Hot Streaks
1999 #HS5 Mark Martin
2001 #HS4 Mark Martin
Wheels High Gear Hot Treads
2003 #HT11 Mark Martin
Wheels High Gear Machine
2005 #MMB6 Mark Martin
Wheels High Gear Man
2005 #MMA6 Mark Martin
Wheels High Gear Man & Machine (Machine)
2006 #MMB5 Mark Martin
Wheels High Gear Man & Machine (Man)
2006 #MMA5 Mark Martin
Wheels High Gear Man and Machine Cars
1998 #2 Mark Martin's Car
1999 #MM2B Mark Martin's Car
2000 #MM4B Mark Martin's Car
2001 #MM4B Mark Martin's Car
Wheels High Gear Man and Machine Drivers
1998 #MM2 Mark Martin
1999 #MM2A Mark Martin
1999 #MM3A Dale Jarrett
2000 #MM4A Mark Martin
2001 #MM4A Mark Martin
Wheels High Gear Mega Gold
1994 #MG4 Mark Martin
Wheels High Gear MPH
1998 #2 Mark Martin
1998 #31 Mark Martin's Car
1998 #46 Mark Martin
1999 #2 Mark Martin
1999 #31 Mark Martin's Car
1999 #50 Mark Martin
2000 #3 Mark Martin
2000 #30 Mark Martin
2000 #58 Mark Martin
2001 #8 Mark Martin
2001 #49 Mark Martin's CAR
2001 #69 Mark Martin WCP
2002 #15 Mark Martin
2003 #M19 Mark Martin
2003 #M58 The Fab Four
2003 #M60 On The Mark
2004 #M16 Mark Martin
2005 #M3 Mark Martin
2005 #M63 Mark Martin's Car
2005 #M90 Kenseth/Busch/Martin CL
2006 #M4 Mark Martin
2006 #M74 Mark Martin PREV
2006 #M76 Mark Martin FF

2006 #M89 R. Wallace/M. Martin NI
2007 #M9 Mark Martin
2008 #M22 Mark Martin
Wheels High Gear Previews
2003 #19 Mark Martin
2004 #16 Mark Martin
2007 #EB9 Mark Martin
2008 #EB22 Mark Martin
Wheels High Gear Previews Green
2005 #EB3 Mark Martin
2006 #EB4 Mark Martin
Wheels High Gear Previews Silver
2006 #EB76 Mark Martin FF
Wheels High Gear Pure Gold
1998 #PG5 Mark Martin
Wheels High Gear Samples
2003 #19 Mark Martin
2003 #58 The Fab Four
2003 #60 On The Mark
2004 #16 Mark Martin
2005 #3 Mark Martin
2005 #63 Mark Martin's Car
2005 #90 Kenseth/Busch/Martin CL
Wheels High Gear Sunday Sensation
2000 #OC4 Mark Martin
2003 #SS3 Mark Martin
Wheels High Gear Top Tier
1998 #TT3 Mark Martin 1:100
1999 #TT2 Mark Martin 1:200
2000 #TT3 Mark Martin
2003 #TT2 Mark Martin
2005 #TT4 Mark Martin
2006 #TT4 Mark Martin
2007 #TT9 Mark Martin
Wheels High Gear Vintage
2000 #V2 Mark Martin
Wheels High Gear Winning Edge
2000 #WE2 Mark Martin
Wheels High Groove
1999 #HG5 Mark Martin
1999 #HG9 Mark Martin
Wheels Runnin and Gunnin
1999 #RG1 Mark Martin
Wheels Runnin and Gunnin Foils
1999 #RG1 Mark Martin
Wheels Solos
1999 #22 Mark Martin
1999 #48 Mark Martin
1999 #58 Mark Martin
Zenith
1995 #6 Mark Martin HG
1995 #39 Mark Martin's Transporter
1996 #6 Mark Martin
1996 #38 Mark Martin's Car HV
1996 #52 Mark Martin S
Zenith Artist Proofs
1996 #6 Mark Martin RP
1996 #38 Mark Martin's Car HV
1996 #52 Mark Martin S
Zenith Helmets
1995 #4 Mark Martin
Zenith Highlights
1996 #4 Mark Martin
Zenith Winston Winners
1995 #9 Mark Martin
1995 #20 Mark Martin
Zenith Z-Team
1995 #12 Mark Martin

Montoya, Juan Pablo

Press Pass
2007 #119 Juan Pablo Montoya RC
2008 #18 Juan Pablo Montoya
2008 #73 Juan Pablo Montoya NS
2008 #78 Juan Pablo Montoya NS
2008 #80 Juan Pablo Montoya Kevin Harvick NS
2008 #82 Juan Pablo Montoya RR
2008 #89 Juan Pablo Montoya's Car U
Press Pass Blue
2007 #B119 Juan Pablo Montoya
2008 #B18 Juan Pablo Montoya
2008 #B73 Juan Pablo Montoya NS
2008 #B78 Juan Pablo Montoya NS
2008 #B80 Juan Pablo Montoya Kevin Harvick NS
2008 #B82 Juan Pablo Montoya RR
2008 #B89 Juan Pablo Montoya's Car U
Press Pass Burning Rubber Drivers
2008 #BRD15 J.Montoya Infineon
Press Pass Burning Rubber Drivers Gold
2008 #BRD15 J.Montoya Infineon
Press Pass Burning Rubber Drivers Prime Cuts
2008 #BRD15 J.Montoya Infineon
Press Pass Burning Rubber Teams
2008 #BRT15J.Montoya Infineon
Press Pass Burnouts
2008 #B06 Juan Pablo Montoya
Press Pass Burnouts Blue
2008 #B06 Juan Pablo Montoya
Press Pass Burnouts Gold
2008 #B06 Juan Pablo Montoya
Press Pass Collector's Series Box Set
2007 #SB18 Juan Pablo Montoya
Press Pass Collectors Series Sunday Best
2007 #CB18 Juan Pablo Montoya
Press Pass Cup Chase
2008 #CC9 Juan Pablo Montoya
Press Pass Double Burner Firesuit-Glove
2008 #DBJM Juan Pablo Montoya
Press Pass Double Burner Metal-Tire
2008 #DB-JM Juan Pablo Montoya
Press Pass Eclipse
2007 #84 Juan Pablo Montoya RC
2008 #17 Juan Pablo Montoya
2008 #72 Juan Pablo Montoya BTF
2008 #74 Tony Stewart Juan Pablo Montoya SO
Press Pass Eclipse Escape Velocity
2008 #EV3 Juan Pablo Montoya
Press Pass Eclipse Gold
2007 #G84 Juan Pablo Montoya
2008 #G17 Juan Pablo Montoya
2008 #G72 Juan Pablo Montoya BTF
2008 #G74 Tony Stewart Juan Pablo Montoya SO
Press Pass Eclipse Previews
2007 #EB84 Juan Pablo Montoya
2008 #EB17 Juan Pablo Montoya
2008 #EB74 Tony Stewart Juan Pablo Montoya SO
Press Pass Eclipse Red
2007 #R84 Juan Pablo Montoya
2008 #R17 Juan Pablo Montoya
2008 #R72 Juan Pablo Montoya BTF
2008 #R74 Tony Stewart Juan Pablo Montoya SO
Press Pass Eclipse Star Tracks
2008 #ST17 Juan Pablo Montoya
Press Pass Eclipse Star Tracks Holofoil
2008 #ST17 Juan Pablo Montoya
Press Pass Eclipse Stellar
2008 #ST14 Juan Pablo Montoya
2008 #ST23 Juan Pablo Montoya
Press Pass Eclipse Teammates Autographs
2007 #3 Montoya/Sorenson/Stremme
2008 #FMS Dario Franchitti Juan Pablo Montoya Reed Sorenson
Press Pass Four Wide
2008 #FW-JM Juan Pablo Montoya
Press Pass Four Wide Checkered
2008 #FW-JM Juan Pablo Montoya
Press Pass Gold
2007 #G119 Juan Pablo Montoya
2008 #G18 Juan Pablo Montoya
2008 #G73 Juan Pablo Montoya NS
2008 #G78 Juan Pablo Montoya NS
2008 #G80 Juan Pablo Montoya Kevin Harvick NS
2008 #G82 Juan Pablo Montoya RR
2008 #G89 Juan Pablo Montoya's Car U
Press Pass Hot Treads
2008 #HT2 Juan Pablo Montoya
Press Pass Hot Treads Blue
2008 #HT2 Juan Pablo Montoya
Press Pass Hot Treads Gold
2008 #HT2 Juan Pablo Montoya
Press Pass Legends
2007 #44 Juan Pablo Montoya RC
Press Pass Legends Autographs Blue
2007 #18 Juan Pablo Montoya/73
Press Pass Legends Blue
2007 #B44 Juan Pablo Montoya
Press Pass Legends Bronze
2007 #Z44 Juan Pablo Montoya
Press Pass Legends Gold
2007 #G44 Juan Pablo Montoya
Press Pass Legends Holofoil
2007 #H44 Juan Pablo Montoya
Press Pass Legends Press Plates Black
2007 #PP44 Juan Pablo Montoya
Press Pass Legends Press Plates Black Backs
2007 #PP44 Juan Pablo Montoya
Press Pass Legends Press Plates Cyan
2007 #PP44 Juan Pablo Montoya
Press Pass Legends Press Plates Cyan Backs
2007 #PP44 Juan Pablo Montoya
Press Pass Legends Press Plates Magenta
2007 #PP44 Juan Pablo Montoya
Press Pass Legends Press Plates Magenta Backs
2007 #PP44 Juan Pablo Montoya
Press Pass Legends Press Plates Yellow
2007 #PP44 Juan Pablo Montoya
Press Pass Legends Press Plates Yellow Backs
2007 #PP44 Juan Pablo Montoya
Press Pass Legends Previews
2007 #EB44 Juan Pablo Montoya
Press Pass Legends Signature Series
2007 #JM Juan Pablo Montoya
Press Pass Legends Solo
2007 #S44 Juan Pablo Montoya
Press Pass Legends Sunday Swatches Bronze
2007 #JM-SS Juan Pablo Montoya/13
Press Pass Legends Sunday Swatches Gold
2007 #JM-SS Juan Pablo Montoya
Press Pass Legends Sunday Swatches Silver
2007 #JM-SS Juan Pablo Montoya
Press Pass Legends Victory Lane Bronze
2007 #VL7 Juan Pablo Montoya
Press Pass Legends Victory Lane Gold
2007 #VL7 Juan Pablo Montoya
Press Pass Legends Victory Lane Silver
2007 #VL7 Juan Pablo Montoya
Press Pass Platinum
2007 #P119 Juan Pablo Montoya
2008 #P18 Juan Pablo Montoya
2008 #P73 Juan Pablo Montoya NS
2008 #P78 Juan Pablo Montoya NS
2008 #P80 Juan Pablo Montoya Kevin Harvick NS
2008 #P82 Juan Pablo Montoya RR
2008 #P89 Juan Pablo Montoya's Car U
Press Pass Premium
2007 #86 Juan Pablo Montoya RD RC
2007 #P1 Juan Pablo Montoya Stealth
2008 #26 Juan Pablo Montoya
2008 #45 Juan Pablo Montoya's Car M
2008 #64 Juan Pablo Montoya EOP
2008 #72 Juan Pablo Montoya MD
Press Pass Premium Going Global
2008 #GG4 Juan Pablo Montoya
Press Pass Premium Going Global Red
2008 #GG4 Juan Pablo Montoya
Press Pass Premium Hot Threads Drivers
2007 #HTD16 Juan Pablo Montoya
2008 #HTD6 Juan Pablo Montoya
Press Pass Premium Hot Threads Drivers Gold
2007 #HTD16 Juan Pablo Montoya
2008 #HTD6 Juan Pablo Montoya
Press Pass Premium Hot Threads Patch
2007 #HTP24 Juan Pablo Montoya Havoline/5
2007 #HTP25 Juan Pablo Montoya Raybestos/15
Press Pass Premium Hot Threads Patches
2008 #HTP30 Juan Pablo Montoya Big Red
2008 #HTP31 Juan Pablo Montoya Havoline
2008 #HTP32 Juan Pablo Montoya NASCAR bar/5
2008 #HTP33 Juan Pablo Montoya Columbian Flag
Press Pass Premium Hot Threads Team
2007 #HTT16Juan Pablo Montoya
2008 #HT6 Juan Pablo Montoya
Press Pass Premium Performance Driven
2007 #PD12 Juan Pablo Montoya
Press Pass Premium Performance Driven Red
2007 #PD12 Juan Pablo Montoya
Press Pass Premium Previews
2008 #EB26 Juan Pablo Montoya
2008 #EB64 Juan Pablo Montoya EOP
Press Pass Premium Red
2007 #R86 Juan Pablo Montoya RD
2008 #26 Juan Pablo Montoya
2008 #45 Juan Pablo Montoya's Car M
2008 #64 Juan Pablo Montoya EOP
2008 #72 Juan Pablo Montoya MD
Press Pass Premium Target
2008 #TA6 Juan Pablo Montoya
Press Pass Premium Team Signed Baseballs
2008 #GAN Dario Franchitti Juan Pablo Montoya Reed Sorenson
2008 #E-GAN Dario Franchitti Juan Pablo Montoya Reed Sorenson Entry Card
Press Pass Previews
2007 #EB119Juan Pablo Montoya
2008 #EB18 Juan Pablo Montoya
Press Pass Race Day
2008 #RD10 Juan Pablo Montoya
Press Pass Signings
2007 #48 Juan Pablo Montoya NC
2007 #49 Juan Pablo Montoya w/o glasses NC
Press Pass Signings Blue
2007 #21 Juan Pablo Montoya NC
Press Pass Signings Gold
2007 #38 Juan Pablo Montoya NC
2007 #39 Juan Pablo Montoya w/o glasses NC
Press Pass Signings Press Plates Black
2007 #31 Juan Pablo Montoya
Press Pass Signings Press Plates Cyan
2007 #30 Juan Pablo Montoya
Press Pass Signings Press Plates Magenta
2007 #32 Juan Pablo Montoya
Press Pass Signings Press Plates Yellow
2007 #31 Juan Pablo Montoya
Press Pass Signings Silver
2007 #37 Juan Pablo Montoya NC
2007 #38 Juan Pablo Montoya w/o glasses NC
Press Pass Speedway
2008 #18 Juan Pablo Montoya
2008 #92 Dario Franchitti Juan Pablo Montoya H
Press Pass Speedway Corporate Cuts Drivers
2008 #CD-JPM Juan Pablo Montoya
Press Pass Speedway Corporate Cuts Drivers Patches
2008 #CD-JPM Juan Pablo Montoya/7
Press Pass Speedway Corporate Cuts Team
2008 #CT-JPM Juan Pablo Montoya
Press Pass Speedway Gold
2008 #G18 Juan Pablo Montoya
2008 #G92 Dario Franchitti Juan Pablo Montoya H
Press Pass Speedway Holofoil
2008 #H18 Juan Pablo Montoya
2008 #H92 Dario Franchitti Juan Pablo Montoya H
Press Pass Speedway Previews
2008 #EB18 Juan Pablo Montoya
2008 #EB92 Dario Franchitti Juan Pablo Montoya H
Press Pass Speedway Red
2008 #R18 Juan Pablo Montoya
2008 #R92 Dario Franchitti Juan Pablo Montoya H
Press Pass Stealth
2007 #32 Juan Pablo Montoya RC
2007 #70 Sorenson/Montoya/Stremme
2008 #26 Juan Pablo Montoya
2008 #62 Juan Pablo Montoya's Car GC
2008 #64 Juan Pablo Montoya Dario Franchitti Reed Sorenson
Press Pass Stealth Battle Armor Drivers
2007 #BAD18 Juan Pablo Montoya
2008 #BAD7 Juan Pablo Montoya
Press Pass Stealth Battle Armor Teams
2007 #BAT18Juan Pablo Montoya
2008 #BAT7 Juan Pablo Montoya
Press Pass Stealth Chrome
2007 #32 Juan Pablo Montoya RC
2007 #70 Sorenson/Montoya/Stremme
2007 #32A Juan Pablo Montoya L1 2 yellow corners
2007 #32B Juan Pablo Montoya L2 2 yellow corners - NNCS line
2008 #26 Juan Pablo Montoya
2008 #62 Juan Pablo Montoya's Car GC
2008 #64 Juan Pablo Montoya Dario Franchitti Reed Sorenson
Press Pass Stealth Chrome Exclusives
2007 #X32 Juan Pablo Montoya
2007 #X70 Sorenson/Montoya/Stremme
2008 #26 Juan Pablo Montoya
2008 #62 Juan Pablo Montoya's Car GC
2008 #64 Juan Pablo Montoya Dario Franchitti Reed Sorenson
Press Pass Stealth Chrome Exclusives Gold
2008 #26 Juan Pablo Montoya
2008 #62 Juan Pablo Montoya's Car GC
2008 #64 Juan Pablo Montoya Dario Franchitti Reed Sorenson
Press Pass Stealth Chrome Platinum
2007 #P32 Juan Pablo Montoya
2007 #P70 Sorenson/Montoya/Stremme
Press Pass Stealth Fusion
2007 #F8 Juan Pablo Montoya
Press Pass Stealth Mach 07
2007 #M7-4 Juan Pablo Montoya
Press Pass Stealth Mach 08
2008 #M8-8 Juan Pablo Montoya
Press Pass Stealth Maximum Access
2007 #MA20 Juan Pablo Montoya
2008 #MA20 Juan Pablo Montoya
Press Pass Stealth Maximum Access Autographs
2007 #MA20 Juan Pablo Montoya
2008 #MA20 Juan Pablo Montoya
Press Pass Stealth Previews
2007 #EB32 Juan Pablo Montoya
2008 #26 Juan Pablo Montoya
Press Pass Target
2008 #JM-B Juan Pablo Montoya
Press Pass Target Victory Tires
2008 #TT-JMJ.Montoya Infineon
Press Pass Wal-Mart
2008 #JM-A Juan Pablo Montoya
Traks
2007 #34 Juan Pablo Montoya RC
2007 #69 Juan Pablo Montoya MG
Traks Corporate Cuts Driver
2007 #CCD17 Juan Pablo Montoya
Traks Corporate Cuts Patch
2007 #CCD17 Juan Pablo Montoya/5
Traks Corporate Cuts Team
2007 #CCT17 Juan Pablo Montoya
Traks Driver's Seat
2007 #DS21 Juan Pablo Montoya
2007 #DS21B Juan Pablo Montoya VAR
Traks Driver's Seat National
2007 #DS21 Juan Pablo Montoya
Traks Gold
2007 #G34 Juan Pablo Montoya
2007 #G69 Juan Pablo Montoya MG
Traks Holofoil
2007 #H34 Juan Pablo Montoya
2007 #H69 Juan Pablo Montoya MG
Traks Hot Pursuit
2007 #HP9 Juan Pablo Montoya
Traks Previews
2007 #EB34 Juan Pablo Montoya
Traks Red
2007 #R34 Juan Pablo Montoya
2007 #R69 Juan Pablo Montoya MG
Traks Track Time
2007 #TT2 Juan Pablo Montoya
VIP
2007 #87 Juan Pablo Montoya SP RC
VIP Gear Gallery
2007 #GG5 Juan Pablo Montoya
VIP Gear Gallery Transparent
2007 #GG5 Juan Pablo Montoya
VIP Get A Grip Autographs
2007 #GG-JM Juan Pablo Montoya/42
VIP Get A Grip Drivers
2007 #GGD7 Juan Pablo Montoya
VIP Get A Grip Teams
2007 #GGT7 Juan Pablo Montoya
VIP Previews
2007 #EB87 Juan Pablo Montoya
VIP Rookie Stripes
2007 #RS3 Juan Pablo Montoya
VIP Rookie Stripes Autographs
2007 #RS-JM Juan Pablo Montoya
VIP Sunday Best
2007 #SB18 Juan Pablo Montoya
Wheels American Thunder
2007 #87 Juan Pablo Montoya RT AU/300 RC
2007 #87B Juan Pablo Montoya RT AU/50 JPM
Wheels American Thunder American Dreams
2007 #AD11 Juan Pablo Montoya
Wheels American Thunder American Dreams Gold
2007 #ADG11 Juan Pablo Montoya
Wheels American Thunder Autographed Hat Instant Winner
2007 #AH23 Juan Pablo Montoya
Wheels American Thunder Cool Threads
2007 #CT14 Juan Pablo Montoya
Wheels American Thunder Pushin' Pedal
2007 #PP13 Juan Pablo Montoya
Wheels American Thunder Thunder Road
2007 #TR18 Juan Pablo Montoya
Wheels American Thunder Triple Hat
2007 #TH20 Juan Pablo Montoya
Wheels High Gear
2007 #88 Juan Pablo Montoya RC
2007 #88B Juan Pablo Montoya infield
2008 #18 Juan Pablo Montoya
2008 #57 Juan Pablo Montoya NA
2008 #73 Juan Pablo Montoya NI
Wheels High Gear Driven
2008 #DR26 Juan Pablo Montoya
Wheels High Gear Final Standings
2008 #F18 Juan Pablo Montoya/20
Wheels High Gear Flag Chasers Black
2008 #FC5 Juan Pablo Montoya
Wheels High Gear Flag Chasers Blue-Yellow
2008 #FC5 Juan Pablo Montoya
Wheels High Gear Flag Chasers Checkered
2008 #FC5 Juan Pablo Montoya
Wheels High Gear Flag Chasers Green
2008 #FC5 Juan Pablo Montoya
Wheels High Gear Flag Chasers Red
2008 #FC5 Juan Pablo Montoya
Wheels High Gear Flag Chasers White
2008 #FC5 Juan Pablo Montoya
Wheels High Gear Flag Chasers Yellow
2008 #FC5 Juan Pablo Montoya
Wheels High Gear Full Throttle
2008 #FT4 Juan Pablo Montoya
Wheels High Gear Last Lap
2008 #LL8 Juan Pablo Montoya
Wheels High Gear Last Lap Holofoil
2008 #LL8 Juan Pablo Montoya
Wheels High Gear MPH
2007 #M88 Juan Pablo Montoya
2008 #M18 Juan Pablo Montoya
2008 #M57 Juan Pablo Montoya NA
2008 #M73 Juan Pablo Montoya NI
Wheels High Gear Previews
2007 #EB88 Juan Pablo Montoya
2008 #EB18 Juan Pablo Montoya

Newman, Ryan

eTopps
2003 #6 Ryan Newman/4000
McFarlane NASCAR Series 1
2003 #NNO Ryan Newman R Gatorade w/Hat
2003 #NNO Ryan Newman R Gatorade w/o Hat
2003 #NNO Ryan Newman H Champagne w/Hat
2003 #NNO Ryan Newman H Champagne w/o Hat
McFarlane NASCAR Series 4
2005 #100 Ryan Newman R Hat
2005 #103 Ryan Newman R w/o Hat
2005 #105 Ryan Newman H Hat
2005 #107 Ryan Newman H w/o Hat
Press Pass
2001 #96 Ryan Newman PV RC
2002 #26 Ryan Newman CRC
2002 #50 Ryan Newman NBS
2002 #71 Ryan Newman REP
2003 #23 Ryan Newman
2003 #62 Ryan Newman DS
2003 #63 Jr./JJ/New/Sad/Ken/Bus DS
2003 #68 R.Newman Winston RR
2003 #69 R.Newman Loudon RR
2003 #94 Ryan Newman's Car OTW
2004 #24 Ryan Newman
2004 #67 Ryan Newman's Car OTW
2004 #76 Penske Power WCS
2004 #98 Ryan Newman DS
2004 #0 Ryan Newman/600
2005 #9 Ryan Newman
2005 #64 Ryan Newman's Car OTW
2005 #116 Ryan Newman's Car
2006 #11 Ryan Newman
2006 #99 Ryan Newman U
2006 #118 Ryan Newman TT
2007 #17 Ryan Newman
2008 #14 Ryan Newman
2008 #72 Ryan Newman's Car BFS
Press Pass Autographs
2002 #48 Ryan Newman
2003 #42 Ryan Newman E/P
2004 #45 Ryan Newman P
2005 #43 Ryan Newman E/P
2006 #41 Ryan Newman NC
2007 #34 Ryan Newman NC P
2008 #29 Ryan Newman NC P/E
Press Pass Autographs Press Plates Black
2008 #24 Ryan Newman NC P
Press Pass Autographs Press Plates Cyan
2008 #24 Ryan Newman NC E
Press Pass Autographs Press Plates Magenta
2008 #24 Ryan Newman NC P
Press Pass Autographs Press Plates Yellow
2008 #24 Ryan Newman NC E
Press Pass Blue
2006 #B11 Ryan Newman
2006 #B99 Ryan Newman U
2006 #B118 Ryan Newman TT
2007 #B17 Ryan Newman
2008 #B14 Ryan Newman
2008 #B72 Ryan Newman's Car BFS
Press Pass Burning Rubber Autographs
2004 #BRRN Ryan Newman/12
2005 #BR-RN Ryan Newman/12
2006 #BR-RN Ryan Newman/12
Press Pass Burning Rubber Cars
2003 #BRT2 Ryan Newman's Car
2004 #BRT7 Ryan Newman's Car
Press Pass Burning Rubber Cars Autographs
2003 #BRT-RN Ryan Newman/12
Press Pass Burning Rubber Drivers
2003 #BRD2 Ryan Newman
2004 #BRD7 Ryan Newman
Press Pass Burning Rubber Drivers Autographs
2003 #BRD-RN Ryan Newman/12
Press Pass Burnouts
2006 #HT18 Ryan Newman
Press Pass Burnouts Holofoil
2006 #HT18 Ryan Newman
Press Pass Collector's Series Box Set
2007 #SB19 Ryan Newman
Press Pass Collectors Series Making the Show
2006 #MS4 Ryan Newman
Press Pass Collectors Series Sunday Best
2007 #CB19 Ryan Newman
Press Pass Cup Chase
2003 #CCR12 Ryan Newman WIN
2004 #CCR15 Ryan Newman
2005 #CCR13 Ryan Newman
2006 #CCR9 Ryan Newman
2007 #CCR6 Ryan Newman
2008 #CC1 Ryan Newman
Press Pass Cup Chase Prizes
2003 #CCR12 Ryan Newman
2004 #CCR15 Ryan Newman
2005 #CCP13 Ryan Newman
Press Pass Double Burner
2003 #DB2 Ryan Newman
2004 #DB2 Ryan Newman
2005 #DB2 Ryan Newman
Press Pass Double Burner Exchange
2003 #DB2 Ryan Newman EXCH
2004 #DB2 Ryan Newman
2005 #DB2 Ryan Newman
Press Pass Double Burner Firesuit-Glove
2006 #DB8 Ryan Newman
Press Pass Eclipse
2002 #28 Ryan Newman CRC
2002 #43 Ryan Newman SO
2003 #6 Ryan Newman
2003 #28 Ryan Newman ACC
2003 #34 Ryan Newman ACC
2003 #43 Born to Run WCS
2003 #47 Ryan Newman HS
2004 #6 Ryan Newman
2004 #46 Ryan Newman Z
2004 #50 Ryan Newman Z
2004 #54 Ryan Newman Z
2004 #65 Ryan Newman's Car WCS
2004 #69 Ryan Newman WCS
2004 #70 Ryan Newman WCS
2004 #83 Ryan Newman LL
2005 #7 Ryan Newman
2005 #32 Ryan Newman's Car S
2005 #47 Ryan Newman Z
2005 #64 Ryan Newman's Car NS
2006 #6 Ryan Newman
2006 #39 Ryan Newman WS
2006 #52 Ryan Newman NS
2006 #65 NCS Top-10 BA
2006 #67 Ryan Newman BA
2006 #69 Tony Stewart BA
2007 #17 Ryan Newman
2007 #36 Ryan Newman TO
2008 #12 Ryan Newman
2008 #29 Ryan Newman RM
2008 #41 Ryan Newman TO
2008 #57 Ryan Newman's Car LP
2008 #66 Ryan Newman BTF
Press Pass Eclipse Destination WIN
2004 #9 Ryan Newman
2004 #15 Ryan Newman
2004 #20 Ryan Newman
2004 #23 Ryan Newman
2005 #14 Ryan Newman
Press Pass Eclipse Double Hot Treads
2003 #DT9 R.Newman/R.Wallace
Press Pass Eclipse Ecliptic
2007 #EC6 Ryan Newman
Press Pass Eclipse Escape Velocity
2008 #EV8 Ryan Newman
Press Pass Eclipse Gold
2007 #G17 Ryan Newman
2007 #G36 Ryan Newman TO
2008 #G12 Ryan Newman
2008 #G29 Ryan Newman RM
2008 #G41 Ryan Newman TO
2008 #G57 Ryan Newman's Car LP
2008 #G66 Ryan Newman BTF
Press Pass Eclipse Hyperdrive
2004 #HP4 Ryan Newman
Press Pass Eclipse Maxim
2005 #MX1 Ryan Newman
Press Pass Eclipse Previews
2003 #6 Ryan Newman
2003 #28 Ryan Newman ACC
2003 #34 Ryan Newman ACC
2004 #6 Ryan Newman
2005 #EB7 Ryan Newman
2005 #EB32 Ryan Newman's Car S
2005 #EB47 Ryan Newman Z
2005 #EB64 Ryan Newman's Car NS
2006 #EB6 Ryan Newman
2007 #EB17 Ryan Newman
2007 #EB36 Ryan Newman TO
2008 #EB12 Ryan Newman
2008 #EB29 Ryan Newman RM
Press Pass Eclipse Racing Champions
2003 #RC14 Ryan Newman
2003 #RC28 Ryan Newman
2006 #RC12 Ryan Newman
2006 #RC26 Ryan Newman NBS
Press Pass Eclipse Red
2007 #R17 Ryan Newman
2007 #R36 Ryan Newman TO
2008 #R12 Ryan Newman
2008 #R29 Ryan Newman RM
2008 #R41 Ryan Newman TO
2008 #R57 Ryan Newman's Car LP
2008 #R66 Ryan Newman BTF
Press Pass Eclipse Samples
2002 #28 Ryan Newman
2002 #43 Ryan Newman SO
2003 #6 Ryan Newman
2003 #28 Ryan Newman ACC
2003 #34 Ryan Newman ACC
2003 #43 Born to Run WCS
2003 #47 Ryan Newman HS
2004 #6 Ryan Newman
2004 #46 Ryan Newman Z
2004 #50 Ryan Newman Z
2004 #54 Ryan Newman Z
2004 #65 Ryan Newman's Car WCS
2004 #69 Ryan Newman WCS
2004 #70 Ryan Newman WCS
2004 #83 Ryan Newman LL
2005 #7 Ryan Newman
2005 #32 Ryan Newman's Car S
2005 #47 Ryan Newman Z
2005 #64 Ryan Newman's Car NS
Press Pass Eclipse Skidmarks
2003 #SM5 Ryan Newman
2004 #SM11 Ryan Newman
2005 #SM11 Ryan Newman
2006 #SM6 Ryan Newman
2007 #SM17 Ryan Newman
Press Pass Eclipse Skidmarks Holofoil
2004 #SM11 Ryan Newman
2005 #SM11 Ryan Newman
2006 #SM6 Ryan Newman
2007 #SM17 Ryan Newman
Press Pass Eclipse Solar Eclipse
2002 #S28 Ryan Newman
2002 #S43 Ryan Newman SO
2003 #P6 Ryan Newman
2003 #P28 Ryan Newman ACC
2003 #P34 Ryan Newman ACC
2003 #P43 Born to Run WCS
2003 #P47 Ryan Newman HS
Press Pass Eclipse Star Tracks
2008 #ST6 Ryan Newman
Press Pass Eclipse Star Tracks Holofoil
2008 #ST6 Ryan Newman
Press Pass Eclipse Supernova
2006 #SU1 Ryan Newman
Press Pass Eclipse Teammates Autographs
2003 #RNRW R.Newman/R.Wallace
2004 #7 R.Newman/R.Wallace
2005 #3 R.Newman/R.Wallace
2006 #7 R.Wallace/R.Newman
2007 #5 Busch/Newman
2008 #BN Kurt Busch Ryan Newman/35
Press Pass Eclipse Under Cover Autographs
2004 #UCRN Ryan Newman/12
2005 #UCRN Ryan Newman/12
2006 #RN Ryan Newman/12
2007 #UC-RN Ryan Newman/12
2008 #UC-RN Ryan Newman/12
Press Pass Eclipse Under Cover Cars
2003 #UCT2 Ryan Newman
2004 #UCD7 Ryan Newman
2005 #UCT7 Ryan Newman
2006 #UCT2 Ryan Newman
Press Pass Eclipse Under Cover Cars Autographs
2003 #UCTRN Ryan Newman/12
Press Pass Eclipse Under Cover Double Cover
2004 #DC2 R.Wallace/R.Newman
2005 #DC2 R.Wallace/R.Newman
2006 #DC4 R.Newman/R.Wallace
Press Pass Eclipse Under Cover Double Cover Holofoil
2006 #DC4 R.Newman/R.Wallace
Press Pass Eclipse Under Cover Double Cover Name
2007 #DC4 Newman/Busch
2008 #DC5 Kurt Busch Ryan Newman
Press Pass Eclipse Under Cover Double Cover NASCAR
2007 #DC4 Newman/Busch
2008 #DC5 Kurt Busch Ryan Newman
Press Pass Eclipse Under Cover Driver Autographs
2003 #UCD-RN Ryan Newman/12

Press Pass Eclipse Under Cover Driver Gold
2003 #UCD2 Ryan Newman
2004 #UCD7 Ryan Newman
Press Pass Eclipse Under Cover Driver Red
2003 #UCD2 Ryan Newman
2004 #UCD7 Ryan Newman
2005 #UCD7 Ryan Newman
Press Pass Eclipse Under Cover Driver Silver
2003 #UCD2 Ryan Newman
2004 #UCD7 Ryan Newman
Press Pass Eclipse Under Cover Drivers
2002 #CD9 Ryan Newman
2007 #UCD8 Ryan Newman
2008 #UCD7 Ryan Newman
Press Pass Eclipse Under Cover Drivers Eclipse
2007 #UCD8 Ryan Newman
2008 #UCD7 Ryan Newman
Press Pass Eclipse Under Cover Drivers Gold
2006 #UCD2 Ryan Newman
Press Pass Eclipse Under Cover Drivers Holofoil
2005 #UCD7 Ryan Newman
2006 #UCD2 Ryan Newman
Press Pass Eclipse Under Cover Drivers Name
2007 #UCD8 Ryan Newman
2008 #UCD7 Ryan Newman
Press Pass Eclipse Under Cover Drivers NASCAR
2007 #UCD8 Ryan Newman
2008 #UCD7 Ryan Newman
Press Pass Eclipse Under Cover Drivers Silver
2005 #UCD7 Ryan Newman
2006 #UCD2 Ryan Newman
Press Pass Eclipse Under Cover Gold Cars
2002 #CD9 Ryan Newman
Press Pass Eclipse Under Cover Gold Drivers
2002 #CD9 Ryan Newman
Press Pass Eclipse Under Cover Holofoil Drivers
2002 #CD9 Ryan Newman
Press Pass Eclipse Under Cover Teams
2007 #UCT8 Ryan Newman
2008 #UCT7 Ryan Newman
Press Pass Eclipse Under Cover Teams NASCAR
2007 #UCT8 Ryan Newman
2008 #UCT7 Ryan Newman
Press Pass Four Wide
2006 #FW-RN Ryan Newman
2007 #FW-RN Ryan Newman
Press Pass Four Wide Checkered
2007 #FW-RN Ryan Newman
Press Pass Four Wide Checkered Exchange
2007 #FW-RN Ryan Newman
Press Pass Four Wide Checkered Flag
2006 #FW-RN Ryan Newman
Press Pass Four Wide Exchange
2007 #FW-RN Ryan Newman
Press Pass Gatorade Jumbos
2003 #4 Ryan Newman
Press Pass Gold
2006 #G11 Ryan Newman
2006 #G99 Ryan Newman U
2006 #G118 Ryan Newman TT
2007 #G17 Ryan Newman
2008 #G14 Ryan Newman
2008 #G72 Ryan Newman's Car BFS
Press Pass Gold Holofoil
2003 #P23 Ryan Newman
2003 #P62 Ryan Newman DS
2003 #P63 Jr./Johnson/Newman Sadler/Kenseth/Busch DS
2003 #P68 R.Newman Winston RR
2003 #P69 R.Newman Loudon RR
2003 #P94 Ryan Newman's Car OTW
Press Pass Hot Treads
2002 #HT31 R.Newman's Car/2375
2004 #HTR5 Ryan Newman
2005 #HTR3 Ryan Newman
Press Pass Hot Treads Holofoil
2004 #HTR5 Ryan Newman
2005 #HTR3 Ryan Newman
Press Pass Legends
2006 #42 Ryan Newman
2007 #46 Ryan Newman
Press Pass Legends Autographs Black
2005 #24 Ryan Newman
2006 #31 Ryan Newman
Press Pass Legends Blue
2006 #B42 Ryan Newman
2007 #B46 Ryan Newman
Press Pass Legends Bronze
2006 #Z42 Ryan Newman
2007 #Z46 Ryan Newman
Press Pass Legends Double Threads Bronze
2005 #DT-NW R.Newman/R.Wallace
Press Pass Legends Double Threads Gold
2005 #DT-NW R.Newman/R.Wallace
Press Pass Legends Double Threads Silver
2005 #DT-NW R.Newman/R.Wallace
Press Pass Legends Gold
2006 #G42 Ryan Newman
2007 #G46 Ryan Newman
Press Pass Legends Holofoil
2006 #H42 Ryan Newman
2007 #H46 Ryan Newman
Press Pass Legends Press Plates Black
2006 #PPB42 Ryan Newman
2007 #PP46 Ryan Newman
Press Pass Legends Press Plates Black Backs
2006 #PPB42B Ryan Newman
2007 #PP46 Ryan Newman
Press Pass Legends Press Plates Cyan
2006 #PPC42 Ryan Newman
2007 #PP46 Ryan Newman
Press Pass Legends Press Plates Cyan Backs
2006 #PPC42B Ryan Newman
2007 #PP46 Ryan Newman
Press Pass Legends Press Plates Magenta
2006 #PPM42 Ryan Newman
2007 #PP46 Ryan Newman
Press Pass Legends Press Plates Magenta Backs
2006 #PPM42B Ryan Newman
2007 #PP46 Ryan Newman
Press Pass Legends Press Plates Yellow
2006 #PPY42 Ryan Newman
2007 #PP46 Ryan Newman
Press Pass Legends Press Plates Yellow Backs
2006 #PPY42B Ryan Newman
2007 #PP46 Ryan Newman
Press Pass Legends Previews
2006 #EB42 Ryan Newman
2007 #EB46 Ryan Newman
Press Pass Legends Signature Series
2007 #RN Ryan Newman
Press Pass Legends Solo
2006 #S42 Ryan Newman
2007 #S46 Ryan Newman
Press Pass Legends Threads & Treads Bronze
2005 #TTRN Ryan Newman
Press Pass Legends Threads & Treads Gold
2005 #TTRN Ryan Newman
Press Pass Legends Threads & Treads Silver
2005 #TTRN Ryan Newman
Press Pass Legends Triple Threads
2006 #TT-RN Ryan Newman
Press Pass Making the Show Collector's Series
2004 #MS8 Ryan Newman
Press Pass Millennium
2001 #96 Ryan Newman PV
Press Pass Optima
2001 #37 Ryan Newman BGN RC
2002 #21 Ryan Newman CRC
2002 #46 Ryan Newman YG
2003 #19 Ryan Newman
2003 #50 Ryan Newman CL
2004 #19 Ryan Newman
2004 #57 Ryan Newman's Car RV
2005 #23 Ryan Newman
2005 #23B Ryan Newman Cup Chase
2005 #69 Ryan Newman DP
2006 #12 Ryan Newman
Press Pass Optima Cool Persistence
2004 #CP7 Ryan Newman
Press Pass Optima Fan Favorite
2002 #FF18 Ryan Newman
2003 #FF18 Ryan Newman
2004 #FF18 Ryan Newman
2005 #FF18 Ryan Newman
2006 #FF17 Ryan Newman
Press Pass Optima Gold
2001 #37 Ryan Newman BGN
2002 #21 Ryan Newman
2002 #46 Ryan Newman YG
2003 #G19 Ryan Newman
2003 #G50 Ryan Newman CL
2004 #G19 Ryan Newman
2004 #G57 Ryan Newman's Car RV
2005 #G23 Ryan Newman
2005 #G69 Ryan Newman DP
2006 #G12 Ryan Newman
Press Pass Optima Pole Position
2006 #PP7 Ryan Newman
Press Pass Optima Previews
2003 #19 Ryan Newman
2004 #EB19 Ryan Newman
2005 #23 Ryan Newman
2006 #EB12 Ryan Newman
Press Pass Optima Promos
2002 #21 Ryan Newman
2002 #46 Ryan Newman YG
Press Pass Optima Q and A
2003 #QA6 Ryan Newman
Press Pass Optima Race Used Lugnuts Autographs
2002 #LNDA14 Ryan Newman/12
Press Pass Optima Race Used Lugnuts Cars
2002 #LNC14 Ryan Newman's Car
Press Pass Optima Race Used Lugnuts Drivers
2002 #LND14 Ryan Newman
Press Pass Optima Rookie Relics Cars
2006 #RRT10 Ryan Newman
Press Pass Optima Rookie Relics Drivers
2006 #RRD10 Ryan Newman
Press Pass Optima Samples
2002 #21 Ryan Newman
2002 #46 Ryan Newman YG
2003 #19 Ryan Newman
2003 #50 Ryan Newman CL
2004 #19 Ryan Newman
2004 #57 Ryan Newman's Car RV
2005 #23 Ryan Newman
2005 #69 Ryan Newman DP
Press Pass Optima Thunder Bolts Autographs
2004 #TBRN Ryan Newman/12
2005 #TB-RN Ryan Newman/12
Press Pass Optima Thunder Bolts Cars
2003 #TBT2 Ryan Newman's Car
2004 #TBT5 Ryan Newman's Car
Press Pass Optima Thunder Bolts Cars Autographs
2003 #TBT-RN Ryan Newman/12
Press Pass Optima Thunder Bolts Drivers
2003 #TBD2 Ryan Newman/60
2004 #TBD5 Ryan Newman
Press Pass Optima Thunder Bolts Drivers Autographs
2003 #TBD-RN Ryan Newman/12
Press Pass Optima Up Close
2002 #UC3 Ryan Newman
Press Pass Platinum
2002 #26 Ryan Newman
2002 #50 Ryan Newman NBS
2002 #71 Ryan Newman REP
2004 #P24 Ryan Newman
2004 #P67 Ryan Newman's Car OTW
2004 #P76 Penske Power WCS
2004 #P98 Ryan Newman DS
2005 #P9 Ryan Newman
2005 #P64 Ryan Newman's Car OTW
2005 #P116 Ryan Newman's Car
2006 #P11 Ryan Newman
2006 #P99 Ryan Newman U
2006 #P118 Ryan Newman TT
2007 #P17 Ryan Newman
2008 #P14 Ryan Newman
2008 #P72 Ryan Newman's Car BFS
Press Pass Premium
2002 #23 Ryan Newman CRC
2002 #35 Ryan Newman's Car
2002 #66 Ryan Newman CH
2003 #21 Ryan Newman
2003 #65 Ryan Newman CC
2003 #76 Ryan Newman PC
2004 #21 Ryan Newman
2004 #61 Ryan Newman CC
2005 #24 Ryan Newman
2005 #62 Ryan Newman CC
2005 #73 Ryan Newman PC
2006 #22 Ryan Newman
2006 #78 Ryan Newman PC
2007 #11 Ryan Newman
2008 #11 Ryan Newman
2008 #0 Ryan Newman Daytona
Press Pass Premium Asphalt Jungle
2004 #A3 Ryan Newman
Press Pass Premium Hot Threads Autographs
2004 #HT-RN Ryan Newman/12
Press Pass Premium Hot Threads Cars
2003 #HTT2 Ryan Newman
2005 #HTT6 Ryan Newman
2006 #HTT10 Ryan Newman
Press Pass Premium Hot Threads Cars Autographs
2003 #HTD-RN Ryan Newman/12
Press Pass Premium Hot Threads Drivers
2003 #HTD2 Ryan Newman
2005 #HTD6 Ryan Newman
2006 #HTD10 Ryan Newman
2007 #HTD3 Ryan Newman
2008 #HTD10 Ryan Newman
Press Pass Premium Hot Threads Drivers Autographs
2003 #HTT-RN Ryan Newman/12
Press Pass Premium Hot Threads Drivers Bronze
2004 #HTD7 Ryan Newman
Press Pass Premium Hot Threads Drivers Bronze Retail
2004 #HTT7 Ryan Newman
Press Pass Premium Hot Threads Drivers Gold
2004 #HTD7 Ryan Newman
2005 #HTD6 Ryan Newman
2006 #HTD10 Ryan Newman
2007 #HTD3 Ryan Newman
2008 #HTD10 Ryan Newman
Press Pass Premium Hot Threads Drivers Silver
2004 #HTD7 Ryan Newman
Press Pass Premium Hot Threads Patch
2007 #HTP27 Ryan Newman Alltel/10
Press Pass Premium Hot Threads Patches
2008 #HTP34 Ryan Newman Gatorade/5
2008 #HTP35 Ryan Newman Gillette Young Guns/7
2008 #HTP36 Ryan Newman NASCAR bar
2008 #HTP37 Ryan Newman U.S. Flag
Press Pass Premium Hot Threads Team
2007 #HTT3 Ryan Newman
2008 #HTT10 Ryan Newman
Press Pass Premium In the Zone
2003 #IZ7 Ryan Newman
2004 #IZ11 Ryan Newman
2005 #IZ4 Ryan Newman
Press Pass Premium In the Zone Elite Edition
2004 #IZ11 Ryan Newman
2005 #IZ4 Ryan Newman
Press Pass Premium Performance Driven
2004 #PD2 Ryan Newman
Press Pass Premium Previews
2003 #21 Ryan Newman
2004 #21 Ryan Newman
2008 #EB11 Ryan Newman
Press Pass Premium Red
2007 #R11 Ryan Newman
2008 #11 Ryan Newman
Press Pass Premium Red Reflectors
2002 #23 Ryan Newman
2002 #35 Ryan Newman's Car
2002 #66 Ryan Newman CH
2003 #21 Ryan Newman
2003 #65 Ryan Newman CC
2003 #76 Ryan Newman PC
Press Pass Premium Samples
2002 #23 Ryan Newman
2002 #35 Ryan Newman's Car
2003 #21 Ryan Newman
2004 #21 Ryan Newman
2005 #24 Ryan Newman
Press Pass Previews
2003 #23 Ryan Newman
2004 #24 Ryan Newman
2006 #EB11 Ryan Newman
2006 #EB99 Ryan Newman U
2007 #EB17 Ryan Newman
2008 #EB14 Ryan Newman
Press Pass Previews Green
2005 #EB9 Ryan Newman
Press Pass Race Day
2008 #RD2 Ryan Newman
Press Pass Samples
2003 #23 Ryan Newman
2003 #62 Ryan Newman DS
2003 #63 Jr./JJ/New/Sad/Ken/Bus DS
2003 #68 R.Newman Winston RR
2003 #69 R.Newman Loudon RR
2003 #94 Ryan Newman's Car OTW
2004 #24 Ryan Newman
2004 #67 Ryan Newman's Car OTW
2004 #76 Penske Power WCS
2004 #98 Ryan Newman DS
2005 #9 Ryan Newman
2005 #64 Ryan Newman's Car OTW
2005 #116 Ryan Newman's Car
Press Pass Showcar
2003 #S2B Ryan Newman
Press Pass Showman
2003 #S2A Ryan Newman
Press Pass Signings
2001 #39 Ryan Newman P/N/S
2002 #48 Ryan Newman O/P/S/T/V
2003 #53 Ryan Newman O/P/S/T/V
2004 #47 Ryan Newman O/P/S/T/V
2005 #43 Ryan Newman P/S
2006 #41 Ryan Newman NC S
2007 #51 Ryan Newman NC
2008 #42 Ryan Newman
Press Pass Signings Blue
2007 #23 Ryan Newman NC
2008 #22 Ryan Newman
Press Pass Signings Gold
2002 #45 Ryan Newman O/P/S/T/V
2003 #53 Ryan Newman O/P/S/T/V
2004 #43 Ryan Newman/20 O/P/S/T/V
2005 #41 Ryan Newman P/S
2006 #36 Ryan Newman NC S
2007 #41 Ryan Newman NC
2008 #36 Ryan Newman
Press Pass Signings Platinum
2005 #39 Ryan Newman P/S
Press Pass Signings Press Plates Black
2008 #29 Ryan Newman
Press Pass Signings Press Plates Cyan
2008 #29 Ryan Newman
Press Pass Signings Press Plates Magenta
2008 #29 Ryan Newman
Press Pass Signings Press Plates Yellow
2008 #29 Ryan Newman
Press Pass Signings Silver
2006 #39 Ryan Newman NC S
2007 #40 Ryan Newman NC
2008 #32 Ryan Newman
Press Pass Signings Transparent
2002 #7 Ryan Newman O/P/S/T/V
2003 #7 Ryan Newman O/P/S/T/V
2004 #6 Ryan Newman O/S/T
Press Pass Slideshow
2008 #SS25 Ryan Newman
Press Pass Snapshots
2003 #SN17 Ryan Newman
2004 #SN20 Ryan Newman
Press Pass Speedway
2008 #19 Ryan Newman
2008 #60 Ryan Newman SH
2008 #72 Ryan Newman UTH
2008 #93 Ryan Newman's Car Kurt Busch's Car H
2008 #98 Ryan Newman H
Press Pass Speedway Blur
2008 #B4 Ryan Newman
Press Pass Speedway Cockpit
2008 #CP17 Ryan Newman
Press Pass Speedway Corporate Cuts Drivers
2008 #CD-RN Ryan Newman
Press Pass Speedway Corporate Cuts Drivers Patches
2008 #CD-RN Ryan Newman/15
Press Pass Speedway Corporate Cuts Team
2008 #CT-RN Ryan Newman
Press Pass Speedway Gold
2008 #G19 Ryan Newman
2008 #G60 Ryan Newman SH
2008 #G72 Ryan Newman UTH
2008 #G93 Ryan Newman's Car Kurt Busch's Car H
2008 #G98 Ryan Newman H
Press Pass Speedway Holofoil
2008 #H19 Ryan Newman
2008 #H60 Ryan Newman SH
2008 #H72 Ryan Newman UTH
2008 #H93 Ryan Newman's Car Kurt Busch's Car H
2008 #H98 Ryan Newman H
Press Pass Speedway Previews
2008 #EB19 Ryan Newman
2008 #EB93 Ryan Newman's Car Kurt Busch's Car H
2008 #EB98 Ryan Newman H
Press Pass Speedway Red
2008 #R19 Ryan Newman
2008 #R60 Ryan Newman SH
2008 #R72 Ryan Newman UTH
2008 #R93 Ryan Newman's Car Kurt Busch's Car H
2008 #R98 Ryan Newman H
Press Pass Speedway Test Drive
2008 #TD6 Ryan Newman
Press Pass Stealth
2002 #13 Ryan Newman CRC
2002 #14 Ryan Newman's Car
2002 #15 Ryan Newman
2002 #72 R.Wallace/R.Newman CL
2004 #46 Ryan Newman
2004 #47 Ryan Newman's Car
2004 #48 Ryan Newman
2005 #10 Ryan Newman
2005 #13 Ryan Newman's Car
2005 #16 Ryan Newman
2006 #23 Ryan Newman
2006 #55 Busch/Newman TM
2007 #19 Ryan Newman
2007 #67 R.Newman/K.Busch
2008 #27 Ryan Newman
2008 #48 Ryan Newman's Rig C
2008 #87 Ryan Newman PM
Press Pass Stealth Autographed Hat Entry
2006 #PPH19 Ryan Newman
Press Pass Stealth Battle Armor Autographs
2007 #BAS-RN Ryan Newman/12
Press Pass Stealth Battle Armor Drivers
2007 #BAD5 Ryan Newman
2008 #BAD8 Ryan Newman
Press Pass Stealth Battle Armor Teams
2007 #BAT5 Ryan Newman
2008 #BAT8 Ryan Newman
Press Pass Stealth Chrome
2007 #19 Ryan Newman
2007 #67 R.Newman/K.Busch
2008 #27 Ryan Newman
2008 #48 Ryan Newman's Rig C
2008 #87 Ryan Newman PM
Press Pass Stealth Chrome Exclusives
2007 #X19 Ryan Newman
2007 #X67 R.Newman/K.Busch
2008 #27 Ryan Newman
2008 #48 Ryan Newman's Rig C
2008 #87 Ryan Newman PM
Press Pass Stealth Chrome Exclusives Gold
2008 #27 Ryan Newman
2008 #48 Ryan Newman's Rig C
2008 #87 Ryan Newman PM
Press Pass Stealth Chrome Platinum
2007 #P19 Ryan Newman
2007 #P67 R.Newman/K.Busch
Press Pass Stealth Corporate Cuts
2006 #CCD13 Ryan Newman
Press Pass Stealth EFX
2002 #FX10 Ryan Newman
2003 #FX5 Ryan Newman
2004 #EF5 Ryan Newman
Press Pass Stealth Fusion
2002 #F10 Ryan Newman
2004 #FU5 Ryan Newman
2005 #FU3 Ryan Newman 1:112
Press Pass Stealth Gear Grippers Autographs
2004 #HT-RN Ryan Newman/12
2006 #RN Ryan Newman/12
Press Pass Stealth Gear Grippers Cars
2003 #GGT2 Ryan Newman
2005 #GGT6 Ryan Newman
Press Pass Stealth Gear Grippers Cars Autographs
2003 #RN Ryan Newman/12
Press Pass Stealth Gear Grippers Drivers
2003 #GGD2 Ryan Newman
2004 #GGD6 Ryan Newman
2005 #GGD6 Ryan Newman
2006 #GGD2 Ryan Newman
Press Pass Stealth Gear Grippers Drivers Autographs
2003 #RN Ryan Newman/12
Press Pass Stealth Gear Grippers Drivers Retail
2004 #GGT6 Ryan Newman
Press Pass Stealth Gold
2002 #13 Ryan Newman
2002 #14 Ryan Newman's Car
2002 #15 Ryan Newman
2002 #72 R.Wallace/R.Newman CL
Press Pass Stealth Hot Pass
2006 #HP21 Ryan Newman
Press Pass Stealth Lap Leaders
2002 #LL20 Ryan Newman
Press Pass Stealth Mach 08
2008 #M8-9 Ryan Newman
Press Pass Stealth Maximum Access
2007 #MA21 Ryan Newman
2008 #MA21 Ryan Newman
Press Pass Stealth Maximum Access Autographs
2007 #MA21 Ryan Newman
2008 #MA21 Ryan Newman
Press Pass Stealth No Boundaries
2004 #NB22 Ryan Newman
2005 #NB7 Ryan Newman
Press Pass Stealth Previews
2005 #10 Ryan Newman
2005 #13 Ryan Newman's Car
2005 #16 Ryan Newman
2006 #23 Ryan Newman
2007 #EB19 Ryan Newman
2008 #27 Ryan Newman
2008 #87 Ryan Newman PM
Press Pass Stealth Profile
2002 #P7 Ryan Newman
2003 #PR7 Ryan Newman
Press Pass Stealth Race Used Glove Cars
2002 #GLC12 Ryan Newman's Car
Press Pass Stealth Race Used Glove Drivers
2002 #GLD12 Ryan Newman
Press Pass Stealth Retail
2006 #23 Ryan Newman
2006 #55 Busch/Newman TM
Press Pass Stealth Retail Gear Grippers Cars
2006 #GGT2 Ryan Newman
Press Pass Stealth Samples
2002 #13 Ryan Newman
2002 #14 Ryan Newman's Car
2002 #15 Ryan Newman
2002 #72 R.Wallace/R.Newman CL
2004 #X46 Ryan Newman
2004 #X47 Ryan Newman's Car
2004 #X48 Ryan Newman
2005 #10 Ryan Newman
2005 #13 Ryan Newman's Car
2005 #16 Ryan Newman
Press Pass Stealth X-Ray
2004 #46 Ryan Newman
2004 #47 Ryan Newman's Car
2004 #48 Ryan Newman
2005 #X10 Ryan Newman
2005 #X13 Ryan Newman's Car
2005 #X16 Ryan Newman
2006 #X23 Ryan Newman
2006 #X55 Busch/Newman TM
Press Pass Top 25 Drivers & Rides
2006 #C9 Ryan Newman's Car
2006 #D9 Ryan Newman
Press Pass Top Shelf
2003 #TS7 Ryan Newman
2004 #TS4 Ryan Newman
Press Pass Top Ten
2005 #TT10 Ryan Newman
Press Pass Total Memorabilia Power Pick
2003 #TM2 Ryan Newman
2004 #TM2 Ryan Newman
2005 #TM2 Ryan Newman
Press Pass Trackside
2002 #24 Ryan Newman CRC
2002 #57 Ryan Newman RD
2002 #89 Ryan Newman TM
2003 #16 Ryan Newman
2003 #63 Ryan Newman in Pits
2003 #76 R.Wallace/R.Newman TM
2004 #6 Ryan Newman
2004 #55 Ryan Newman's Car HS
2004 #67 Rusty/Gaughan/Newman TM
2004 #103 Ryan Newman TT
2004 #118 Ryan Newman F
2005 #20 Ryan Newman
2005 #57 Ryan Newman's Car HS
Press Pass Trackside Dialed In
2003 #DI9 Ryan Newman
Press Pass Trackside Generation Now
2002 #GN5 Ryan Newman
Press Pass Trackside Gold Holofoil
2003 #P16 Ryan Newman
2003 #P63 Ryan Newman's Crew
2003 #P76 R.Wallace/R.Newman
Press Pass Trackside Golden
2002 #G24 Ryan Newman
2003 #G16 Ryan Newman
2004 #G6 Ryan Newman
2004 #G55 Ryan Newman's Car HS
2004 #G67 Wallace/Gaughan/Newman TM
2004 #G103 Ryan Newman TT
2004 #G118 Ryan Newman F
2005 #G20 Ryan Newman
2005 #G57 Ryan Newman's Car HS
Press Pass Trackside Hat Giveaway
2003 #PPH21 Ryan Newman
2004 #PPH24 Ryan Newman
2005 #PPH24 Ryan Newman
Press Pass Trackside Hot Pass
2004 #HP12 Ryan Newman
2005 #12 Ryan Newman
Press Pass Trackside Hot Pass National
2004 #HP12 Ryan Newman
2005 #12 Ryan Newman
Press Pass Trackside Hot Pursuit
2003 #HP5 Ryan Newman
2005 #HP6 Ryan Newman
Press Pass Trackside License to Drive
2002 #24 Ryan Newman
2003 #LD13 Ryan Newman
Press Pass Trackside License to Drive Die Cuts
2002 #24 Ryan Newman
Press Pass Trackside Pit Stoppers Autographs
2004 #PS-RN Ryan Newman/12
2005 #PSRN Ryan Newman/12
Press Pass Trackside Pit Stoppers Cars
2002 #PSC6 Ryan Newman's Car/350
2003 #PST8 Ryan Newman
2004 #PST8 Ryan Newman
2005 #PST6 Ryan Newman
Press Pass Trackside Pit Stoppers Cars Autographs
2003 #RN Ryan Newman/12
Press Pass Trackside Pit Stoppers Drivers
2002 #PSD6 Ryan Newman/175
2003 #PSD8 Ryan Newman
2004 #PSD8 Ryan Newman
2005 #PSD6 Ryan Newman
Press Pass Trackside Pit Stoppers Drivers Autographs
2003 #PSD-RN Ryan Newman/12
Press Pass Trackside Previews
2003 #16 Ryan Newman
2004 #EB6 Ryan Newman
2005 #20 Ryan Newman
Press Pass Trackside Runnin n' Gunnin
2003 #RG10 Ryan Newman
2005 #RG4 Ryan Newman
Press Pass Trackside Samples
2002 #24 Ryan Newman
2002 #57 Ryan Newman RD
2002 #89 Ryan Newman TM
2003 #16 Ryan Newman
2003 #63 Ryan Newman in Pits
2003 #76 R.Wallace/R.Newman TM
2004 #6 Ryan Newman
2004 #55 Ryan Newman's Car HS
2004 #67 Wallace/Gaughan/Newman TM
2004 #103 Ryan Newman TT
2004 #118 Ryan Newman F
2005 #20 Ryan Newman
2005 #57 Ryan Newman's Car HS
Press Pass Triple Burner
2003 #TB2 Ryan Newman
2004 #TB2 Ryan Newman
2005 #TB2 Ryan Newman
Press Pass Triple Burner Exchange
2003 #TB2 Ryan Newman EXCH
2004 #TB2 Ryan Newman
2005 #TB2 Ryan Newman
Press Pass UMI Cup Chase
2005 #1 Cup Chase Drivers CL
2005 #11 Ryan Newman
TRAKS
2006 #25 Ryan Newman
2006 #43 Ryan Newman's Car
2007 #20 Ryan Newman
2007 #60 Ryan Newman CTG
TRAKS Autographs
2006 #28 Ryan Newman NC SP
TRAKS Autographs 25
2006 #26 Ryan Newman NC
Traks Corporate Cuts Driver
2007 #CCD9 Ryan Newman
Traks Corporate Cuts Patch
2007 #CCD9 Ryan Newman/15
Traks Corporate Cuts Team
2007 #CCT9 Ryan Newman
Traks Driver's Seat
2007 #DS5 Ryan Newman
2007 #DS5B Ryan Newman VAR
Traks Driver's Seat National
2007 #DS5 Ryan Newman
Traks Gold
2007 #G20 Ryan Newman
2007 #G60 Ryan Newman CTG
Traks Holofoil
2007 #H20 Ryan Newman
2007 #H60 Ryan Newman CTG
Traks Previews
2007 #EB20 Ryan Newman
Traks Red
2007 #R20 Ryan Newman
2007 #R60 Ryan Newman CTG
TRAKS Stickers
2006 #12 Ryan Newman
VIP
2002 #6 Ryan Newman CRC
2002 #30 Ryan Newman AS
2003 #14 Ryan Newman
2003 #25 Ryan Newman SG
2003 #29 Ryan Newman AS
2003 #46 Ryan Newman HR
2004 #14 Ryan Newman
2004 #34 Ryan Newman's Car R
2004 #63 Ryan Newman HR
2004 #79 Ryan Newman BTN
2005 #23 Ryan Newman
2005 #56 Ryan Newman HR
2005 #59 Ryan Newman HR
2006 #21 Ryan Newman
2006 #65 Ryan Newman RF
2007 #66 Ryan Newman Red C
VIP Explosives

2002 #X6 Ryan Newman
2002 #X30 Ryan Newman AS
2003 #X14 Ryan Newman
2003 #X25 Ryan Newman SG
2003 #X29 Ryan Newman AS
2003 #X46 Ryan Newman HR
VIP Explosives Lasers
2002 #LX6 Ryan Newman
2002 #LX30 Ryan Newman AS
VIP Gear Gallery
2007 #GG1 Ryan Newman
VIP Gear Gallery Transparent
2007 #GG1 Ryan Newman
VIP Get A Grip Drivers
2007 #GGD6 Ryan Newman
VIP Get A Grip Teams
2007 #GGT6 Ryan Newman
VIP Lap Leaders
2004 #LL4 Ryan Newman
VIP Lap Leaders Transparent
2004 #LL4 Ryan Newman
VIP Laser Explosive
2003 #LX14 Ryan Newman
2003 #LX25 Ryan Newman SG
2003 #LX29 Ryan Newman AS
2003 #LX46 Ryan Newman HR
VIP Making the Show
2002 #MS7 Ryan Newman
2004 #MS8 Ryan Newman
2005 #8 Ryan Newman
2006 #MS4 Ryan Newman
VIP Mile Masters
2002 #MM7 Ryan Newman
VIP Mile Masters Transparent
2002 #MM7 Ryan Newman
VIP Mile Masters Transparent LTD
2002 #MM7 Ryan Newman
VIP Previews
2003 #14 Ryan Newman
2003 #25 Ryan Newman SG
2003 #29 Ryan Newman AS
2004 #EB14 Ryan Newman
2004 #EB34 Ryan Newman's Car R
2005 #EB23 Ryan Newman
VIP Race Used Sheet Metal Cars
2002 #SC5 Ryan Newman's Car
VIP Race Used Sheet Metal Drivers
2002 #SD5 Ryan Newman
VIP Samples
2002 #6 Ryan Newman
2002 #30 Ryan Newman AS
2003 #14 Ryan Newman
2003 #25 Ryan Newman SG
2003 #29 Ryan Newman AS
2003 #46 Ryan Newman HR
2004 #14 Ryan Newman
2004 #34 Ryan Newman's Car R
2004 #63 Ryan Newman HR
2004 #79 Ryan Newman BTN
2005 #23 Ryan Newman
2005 #56 Ryan Newman HR
2005 #59 Ryan Newman HR
VIP Sunday Best
2007 #SB19 Ryan Newman
VIP Tin
2003 #CT14 Ryan Newman
2003 #CT25 Ryan Newman SG
2003 #CT29 Ryan Newman AS
2003 #CT46 Ryan Newman HR
VIP Tradin' Paint Bronze
2004 #TPT5 Ryan Newman
VIP Tradin' Paint Car Autographs
2003 #RN Ryan Newman/12
VIP Tradin' Paint Cars
2003 #TPT2 Ryan Newman's Car
VIP Tradin' Paint Cars Bronze
2006 #TPT15 Ryan Newman
VIP Tradin' Paint Driver Autographs
2003 #RN Ryan Newman/12
VIP Tradin' Paint Drivers
2003 #TPD2 Ryan Newman
VIP Tradin' Paint Drivers Gold
2006 #TPD15 Ryan Newman
VIP Tradin' Paint Drivers Silver
2006 #TPD15 Ryan Newman
VIP Tradin' Paint Gold
2004 #TPD5 Ryan Newman
VIP Tradin' Paint Silver
2004 #TPD5 Ryan Newman
VIP Trophy Club
2007 #TC8 Ryan Newman
VIP Trophy Club Transparent
2007 #TC8 Ryan Newman
Wheels American Thunder
2003 #17 Ryan Newman
2003 #30 Ryan Newman DT
2003 #42 Ryan Newman CC
2004 #21 Ryan Newman
2004 #38 Ryan Newman AS
2006 #24 Ryan Newman
2006 #80 Ryan Newman MIA
2007 #23 Ryan Newman
2007 #40 Ryan Newman's Car DT
2007 #62 Ryan Newman RW
Wheels American Thunder American Eagle
2003 #AE3 Ryan Newman
Wheels American Thunder American Muscle
2003 #AM7 Ryan Newman
Wheels American Thunder Autographed Hat Instant Winner
2007 #AH25 Ryan Newman
Wheels American Thunder Born On
2003 #BO17 Ryan Newman
2003 #BO30 Ryan Newman DT
2003 #BO42 Ryan Newman CC
Wheels American Thunder Cool Threads
2003 #CT3 Ryan Newman
2004 #CT12 Ryan Newman
2005 #CT13 Ryan Newman
2006 #CT10 Ryan Newman
2007 #CT9 Ryan Newman
Wheels American Thunder Cup Quest
2004 #CQ6 Ryan Newman
Wheels American Thunder Double Hat
2005 #DH8 Ryan Newman
2006 #DH18 Ryan Newman
Wheels American Thunder Golden Eagle
2003 #AEG3 Ryan Newman
Wheels American Thunder Grandstand
2006 #GS19 Ryan Newman
Wheels American Thunder Head to Toe
2006 #HT2 Ryan Newman
Wheels American Thunder Heads Up Goodyear
2003 #HUG6 Ryan Newman
Wheels American Thunder Heads Up Manufacturer
2003 #HUM15 Ryan Newman
Wheels American Thunder Heads Up Team
2003 #HUT13 Ryan Newman/90
Wheels American Thunder Heads Up Winston
2003 #HUW15 Ryan Newman
Wheels American Thunder Holofoil
2003 #P17 Ryan Newman
2003 #P30 Ryan Newman DT
2003 #P42 Ryan Newman CC
Wheels American Thunder Post Mark
2003 #PM14 Ryan Newman
2004 #PM8 Ryan Newman
Wheels American Thunder Previews
2003 #17 Ryan Newman
2003 #30 Ryan Newman DT
2004 #EB21 Ryan Newman
2004 #EB38 Ryan Newman AS
2006 #EB24 Ryan Newman
2006 #EB80 Ryan Newman MIA
2007 #EB23 Ryan Newman
Wheels American Thunder Pushin' Pedal
2006 #PP5 Ryan Newman
Wheels American Thunder Rookie Class
2003 #RC1 Ryan Newman WIN
Wheels American Thunder Rookie Class Prizes
2003 #RC1 Ryan Newman
Wheels American Thunder Rookie Thunder
2003 #RT24 Ryan Newman
Wheels American Thunder Samples
2003 #P17 Ryan Newman
2003 #P30 Ryan Newman DT
2003 #P42 Ryan Newman CC
2004 #21 Ryan Newman
2004 #38 Ryan Newman AS
Wheels American Thunder Thunder Road
2003 #TR5 Ryan Newman
2004 #TR5 Ryan Newman
2007 #TR5 Ryan Newman
Wheels American Thunder Thunder Strokes
2007 #31 Ryan Newman
Wheels American Thunder Thunder Strokes Press Plates Black
2007 #31 Ryan Newman
Wheels American Thunder Thunder Strokes Press Plates Cyan
2007 #31 Ryan Newman
Wheels American Thunder Thunder Strokes Press Plates Magenta
2007 #31 Ryan Newman
Wheels American Thunder Thunder Strokes Press Plates Yellow
2007 #31 Ryan Newman
Wheels American Thunder Triple Hat
2004 #TH35 Ryan Newman
2007 #TH21 Ryan Newman
Wheels Autographs
2003 #45 Ryan Newman AT/HG
2004 #48 Ryan Newman HG
2005 #42 Ryan Newman
2006 #44 Ryan Newman NC
2007 #30 Ryan Newman NC HG
2008 #22 Ryan Newman NC HG
Wheels Autographs Press Plates Black
2007 #29 Ryan Newman NC
2008 #22 Ryan Newman NC HG
Wheels Autographs Press Plates Cyan
2007 #29 Ryan Newman NC
2008 #22 Ryan Newman NC HG
Wheels Autographs Press Plates Magenta
2007 #29 Ryan Newman NC
2008 #22 Ryan Newman NC HG
Wheels Autographs Press Plates Yellow
2007 #30 Ryan Newman NC
2008 #22 Ryan Newman NC HG
Wheels High Gear
2001 #66 Ryan Newman WCP RC
2002 #43 Ryan Newman BGN
2002 #67 Ryan Newman PRE
2003 #20 Ryan Newman
2003 #31 Ryan Newman's Car
2003 #59 Man Of Steel
2003 #63 Feeling Like A New Man WCS
2003 #65 Ryan Newman NA
2003 #68 Ryan Newman NA
2004 #20 Ryan Newman
2004 #48 Ryan Newman NA
2004 #63 Ryan Newman HL
2005 #7 Ryan Newman
2005 #44 Ryan Newman's Car C
2005 #50 Ryan Newman A
2005 #57 Ryan Newman's Car
2005 #82 Ryan Newman RS
2006 #6 Ryan Newman
2006 #59 Ryan Newman NA
2006 #63 Ryan Newman NA
2006 #87 Ryan Newman NI
2007 #17 Ryan Newman
2007 #68 Ryan Newman CM
2007 #80 Ryan Newman's Car C
2008 #13 Ryan Newman
Wheels High Gear Autographs
2002 #41 Ryan Newman
Wheels High Gear Blue Hawaii SCDA Promos
2003 #20 Ryan Newman
2003 #31 Ryan Newman's Car
2003 #59 Man Of Steel
2003 #63 Feeling Like A New Man
2003 #65 Ryan Newman BPA
2003 #68 Ryan Newman RRA
Wheels High Gear Custom Shop
2002 #CSRN Ryan Newman EXCH
2003 #CSRN Ryan Newman EXCH
Wheels High Gear Custom Shop Autograph Redemption
2003 #CSRN Ryan Newman EXCH
Wheels High Gear Custom Shop Prizes
2002 #RNA1 Ryan Newman
2002 #RNA2 Ryan Newman
2002 #RNA3 Ryan Newman
2002 #RNB1 Ryan Newman
2002 #RNB2 Ryan Newman
2002 #RNB3 Ryan Newman
2002 #RNC1 Ryan Newman
2002 #RNC2 Ryan Newman
2002 #RNC3 Ryan Newman
2003 #RNA1 Ryan Newman
2003 #RNA2 Ryan Newman
2003 #RNA3 Ryan Newman
2003 #RNB1 Ryan Newman
2003 #RNB2 Ryan Newman
2003 #RNB3 Ryan Newman
2003 #RNC1 Ryan Newman
2003 #RNC2 Ryan Newman
2003 #RNC3 Ryan Newman
Wheels High Gear Driven
2007 #DR11 Ryan Newman
2008 #DR21 Ryan Newman
Wheels High Gear Final Standings
2008 #F13 Ryan Newman/13
Wheels High Gear Final Standings Gold
2007 #FS17 Ryan Newman/18
Wheels High Gear First Gear
2001 #66 Ryan Newman WCP
2002 #43 Ryan Newman BGN
2002 #67 Ryan Newman PRE
2003 #F20 Ryan Newman
2003 #F31 Ryan Newman's Car
2003 #F59 Man Of Steel
2003 #F63 Feeling Like A New Man
2003 #F65 Ryan Newman BPA
2003 #F68 Ryan Newman RRA
Wheels High Gear Flag Chasers Black
2003 #FC4 Ryan Newman
2004 #FC8 Ryan Newman
2005 #FC5 Ryan Newman
2006 #FC6 Ryan Newman
Wheels High Gear Flag Chasers Blue
2004 #FC8 Ryan Newman
Wheels High Gear Flag Chasers Blue-Yellow
2003 #FC4 Ryan Newman
2005 #FC5 Ryan Newman
2006 #FC6 Ryan Newman
Wheels High Gear Flag Chasers Checkered
2003 #FC4 Ryan Newman
2004 #FC8 Ryan Newman
2005 #FC5 Ryan Newman
2006 #FC6 Ryan Newman
Wheels High Gear Flag Chasers Green
2003 #FC4 Ryan Newman
2004 #FC8 Ryan Newman
2005 #FC5 Ryan Newman
2006 #FC6 Ryan Newman
Wheels High Gear Flag Chasers Red
2003 #FC4 Ryan Newman
2004 #FC8 Ryan Newman
2005 #FC5 Ryan Newman
2006 #FC6 Ryan Newman
Wheels High Gear Flag Chasers White
2003 #FC4 Ryan Newman
2004 #FC8 Ryan Newman
2005 #FC5 Ryan Newman
2006 #FC6 Ryan Newman
Wheels High Gear Flag Chasers Yellow
2003 #FC4 Ryan Newman
2004 #FC8 Ryan Newman
2005 #FC5 Ryan Newman
2006 #FC6 Ryan Newman
Wheels High Gear Flag to Flag
2005 #FF19 Ryan Newman
2006 #FF19 Ryan Newman
Wheels High Gear Full Throttle
2003 #FT3 Ryan Newman
2004 #FT3 Ryan Newman
Wheels High Gear High Groove
2003 #HG18 Ryan Newman
2004 #HG19 Ryan Newman
Wheels High Gear Hot Treads
2003 #HT13 Ryan Newman
Wheels High Gear Machine
2003 #MM5B Ryan Newman
Wheels High Gear Man
2003 #MM5A Ryan Newman
Wheels High Gear MPH
2001 #66 Ryan Newman WCP
2002 #43 Ryan Newman BGN
2002 #67 Ryan Newman PRE
2003 #M20 Ryan Newman
2003 #M31 Ryan Newman's Car
2003 #M59 Man Of Steel
2003 #M63 Feeling Like A New Man
2003 #M65 Ryan Newman BPA
2003 #M68 Ryan Newman RRA
2004 #M20 Ryan Newman
2004 #M48 Ryan Newman NA
2004 #M63 Ryan Newman HL
2005 #M7 Ryan Newman
2005 #M44 Ryan Newman's Car C
2005 #M50 Ryan Newman A
2005 #M57 Ryan Newman's Car
2005 #M82 Ryan Newman RS
2006 #M6 Ryan Newman
2006 #M59 Ryan Newman NA
2006 #M63 Ryan Newman NA
2006 #M87 Ryan Newman NI
2007 #M17 Ryan Newman
2007 #M68 Ryan Newman CM
2007 #M80 Ryan Newman's Car C
2008 #M13 Ryan Newman
Wheels High Gear Previews
2003 #20 Ryan Newman
2004 #20 Ryan Newman
2004 #48 Ryan Newman NA
2007 #EB17 Ryan Newman
2008 #EB13 Ryan Newman
Wheels High Gear Previews Green
2005 #EB7 Ryan Newman
2006 #EB6 Ryan Newman
Wheels High Gear Samples
2003 #20 Ryan Newman
2003 #31 Ryan Newman's Car
2003 #59 Man Of Steel
2003 #63 Feeling Like A New Man
2003 #65 Ryan Newman BPA
2003 #68 Ryan Newman RRA
2004 #20 Ryan Newman
2004 #48 Ryan Newman NA
2004 #63 Ryan Newman HL
2005 #7 Ryan Newman
2005 #50 Ryan Newman A
2005 #57 Ryan Newman's Car
2005 #82 Ryan Newman RS
Wheels High Gear Sunday Sensation
2003 #SS6 Ryan Newman
2004 #SS6 Ryan Newman
2004 #SS8 Ryan Newman
Wheels High Gear Top Ten
2004 #TT6 Ryan Newman
Wheels High Gear Top Tier
2003 #TT6 Ryan Newman
2005 #TT7 Ryan Newman
2006 #TT6 Ryan Newman

Petty, Richard

Action Packed
1993 #10 Richard Petty BR
1993 #31 Richard Petty's Car BR
1993 #50 Richard Petty's Car KR
1993 #51 Richard Petty KR
1993 #52 Richard Petty KR
1993 #53 Richard Petty KR
1993 #54 Richard Petty KR
1993 #70 Richard Petty's Car BR
1993 #71 Richard Petty BR
1993 #72 Richard Petty BR
1993 #75 Richard Petty BR
1993 #76 Richard Petty BR
1993 #81 Richard Petty
1993 #82 Richard Petty's Car
1993 #92 Richard Petty D93
1993 #160 R.Petty/Kyle Petty FS
1994 #178 Richard Petty
1997 #67 Richard Petty
Action Packed 24K Gold
1993 #13G Richard Petty KR
1993 #14G Richard Petty KR
1993 #15G Richard Petty KR
1993 #16G Richard Petty KR
1993 #17G Richard Petty KR
1993 #35G Richard Petty D93
Action Packed Alan Kulwicki
1993 #AK3 Alan Kulwicki/Richard Petty
Action Packed Country
1995 #20 Richard Petty S
Action Packed Country Silver Speed
1995 #20 Richard Petty S
Action Packed Credentials
1996 #78 Richard Petty OWN
Action Packed Fifth Anniversary
1997 #1 Richard Petty
Action Packed Fifth Anniversary Autographs
1997 #1 Richard Petty
Action Packed First Impressions
1997 #67 Richard Petty
Action Packed Mint
1994 #178 Richard Petty
Action Packed Preview
1995 #73 Richard Petty DD
Action Packed Preview 24K Gold
1995 #5G Richard Petty
Action Packed Richard Petty
1992 #RP1 Richard Petty/100,000
1992 #RP2 Richard Petty's Car/100,000
1992 #RP3 Richard Petty/50,000
Assets $100 Phone Cards
1995 #4 Mark Martin
Assets $1000 Phone Cards
1995 #4 Mark Martin
Assets $25 Phone Cards
1995 #8 Richard Petty
Assets $5 Phone Cards
1995 #8 Richard Petty
Assets Racing
1996 #47 Richard Petty
Autographed Racing
1996 #10 Richard Petty
Autographed Racing Front Runners
1996 #15 R.Childress/R.Petty
1996 #22 D.Earnhardt/R.Petty
1996 #29 B.Hamilton/R.Petty
1996 #30 B.Hamilton profile/R.Petty
1996 #78 K.Petty/R.Petty
Bikers of the Racing Scene
1992 #1 Richard Petty
Card Dynamics Gant Oil
1993 #1 Richard Petty
Card Dynamics Quik Chek
1993 #3 Richard Petty/5000
Celebrity Cuts *
2008 #73 Richard Petty
Celebrity Cuts Century Gold *
2008 #73 Richard Petty
Celebrity Cuts Century Material *
2008 #73 Richard Petty/100
Celebrity Cuts Century Material Combo *
2008 #73 Richard Petty/50
Celebrity Cuts Century Platinum *
2008 #73 Richard Petty
Celebrity Cuts Century Signature Gold *
2008 #73 Richard Petty/200
Celebrity Cuts Century Signature Material *
2008 #73 Richard Petty/50
Celebrity Cuts Century Signature Material Combo *
2008 #73 Richard Petty/10
Celebrity Cuts Century Signature Platinum *
2008 #73 Richard Petty
Celebrity Cuts Century Silver *
2008 #73 Richard Petty
Classic
1996 #12 Richard Petty
Classic Printer's Proof
1996 #12 Richard Petty
Classic Silver
1996 #12 Richard Petty
Collector's Choice
1997 #126 Richard Petty SC
Collector's Choice Upper Deck 500
1997 #UD29 Richard Petty
Donruss Americana Sports Legends
2007-08 #12 Richard Petty
Donruss Americana Sports Legends Material
2007-08 #2 Richard Petty/100
Donruss Americana Sports Legends Signature
2007-08 #2 Richard Petty/50
Donruss Americana Sports Legends Signature Material
2007-08 #2 Richard Petty/100
eTopps
2003 #25 Richard Petty/3065
Finish Line
1993 #61 Richard Petty
1993 #85 Richard Petty
1993 #114 Richard Petty
1994 #58 Richard Petty OWN
1994 #64 Richard Petty
1995 #43 Richard Petty
1995 #104 Richard Petty
Finish Line Commemorative Sheets
1993 #12 Dover
1993 #27 Charlotte
1993 #29 Phoenix
Finish Line Gold
1994 #63 Richard Petty
Finish Line Printer's Proof
1995 #43 Richard Petty
1995 #104 Richard Petty
Finish Line Silver
1993 #61 Richard Petty
1993 #85 Richard Petty
1993 #114 Richard Petty
1994 #58 Richard Petty OWN
1994 #64 Richard Petty
1995 #43 Richard Petty
1995 #104 Richard Petty
Flair
1996 #51 Richard Petty
Food Lion Richard Petty
1992 #2 Richard Petty 1964
1992 #3 Richard Petty w/Car
1992 #4 Richard Petty 1981
1992 #6 Richard Petty 1971
1992 #7 Richard Petty 1974
1992 #8 Richard Petty's Car
1992 #10 Richard Petty's Car
1992 #11 Richard Petty
1992 #12 Richard Petty
1992 #14 Richard Petty's Car
1992 #15 Richard Petty
1992 #16 Richard Petty's Car
1992 #18 Richard Petty
1992 #19 Richard Petty's Car
1992 #20 Richard Petty's Car
1992 #22 Richard Petty
1992 #23 Richard Petty in Car
1992 #24 Richard Petty w/Car
1992 #26 Richard Petty w/Dad
1992 #27 Richard Petty's Car
1992 #28 Richard Petty's Car
1992 #30 Richard Petty
1992 #31 Richard Petty
1992 #32 Richard Petty
1992 #34 Richard Petty w/Car
1992 #35 Richard Petty's Trailer
1992 #36 Richard Petty 1983
1992 #38 Richard Petty w/Car
1992 #39 Richard Petty on Car
1992 #40 Richard Petty 1977
1992 #42 Richard Petty in Car
1992 #43 Richard Petty
1992 #44 Richard Petty 1984
1992 #46 Richard Petty w/Car
1992 #47 Richard Petty w/Car
1992 #48 Richard Petty w/Car
1992 #50 Richard Petty
1992 #51 Richard Petty
1992 #52 Richard Petty w/Brother
1992 #54 Richard Petty
1992 #55 Richard Petty 1981
1992 #56 Richard Petty w/Car
1992 #58 Richard Petty's Car
1992 #59 Richard Petty 1975
1992 #60 Richard Petty 1984
1992 #62 Richard Petty's Car
1992 #63 Richard Petty
1992 #64 Richard Petty's Car
1992 #66 Richard Petty on Bike
1992 #67 Richard Petty 1984
1992 #68 Richard Petty's Car
1992 #70 Richard Petty w/Car
1992 #71 Richard Petty
1992 #72* Richard Petty
1992 #74 Richard Petty w/Brother
1992 #75 Richard Petty 1974
1992 #76 Richard Petty
1992 #78 Richard Petty's Car
1992 #79 Richard Petty
1992 #80 Richard Petty in Car
1992 #82 Richard Petty's Car
1992 #83 Richard Petty
1992 #84 Richard Petty
1992 #86 Richard Petty 1970
1992 #87 Richard Petty's Car
1992 #88 Richard Petty w/Dodge
1992 #90 Richard Petty
1992 #91 Richard Petty
1992 #92 Richard Petty
1992 #94 Richard Petty 1970
1992 #95 Richard Petty 1969
1992 #96 Richard Petty
1992 #98 Richard Petty w/Brother
1992 #99 Richard Petty
1992 #100 Richard Petty
1992 #102 Richard Petty
1992 #103 Richard Petty w/Car
1992 #104 Richard Petty
1992 #106 Richard Petty's Car
1992 #107 Richard Petty's Car
1992 #108 Richard Petty Pit Stop
1992 #110 Richard Petty
1992 #111 Richard Petty
1992 #112 Richard Petty
1992 #114 Richard Petty's Car
1992 #115 Richard Petty's Transporter
1992 #116 Richard Petty's Car
1992 #NNO Richard Petty HOLO
High Gear Promos
1994 #P3 Kyle Petty Silver
High Gear Promos Gold
1994 #P3 Kyle Petty Gold
Hi-Tech Brickyard 400 Prototypes
1994 #1 Richard Petty w/Car
Hi-Tech Brickyard 400 Richard Petty
1994 #1 Richard Petty w/Car
1994 #2 Richard Petty 's Car
1994 #3 Richard Petty's Car
1994 #4 Richard Petty w/car
1994 #5 Richard Petty w/Car
1994 #6 Richard Petty's Car
John Deere
1994-96 #4 Richard Petty
Mac Tools Winner's Cup
1992 #17 Richard Petty
Matchbook Winston Cup Champions
1995 #1 1971 Champion Richard Petty
1995 #2 1972 Champion Richard Petty
1995 #4 1974 Champion Richard Petty
1995 #5 1975 Champion Richard Petty
1995 #9 1979 Champion Richard Petty
Maxwell House
1993 #15 Richard Petty
1993 #18 Richard Petty/Kyle Petty
Maxx
1989 #43 Richard Petty
1989 #101 Richard Petty's Car YR
1989 #181 Richard Petty's Car C
1989 #193 R.Petty/J.Smith Cars C
1989 #220 R.Petty/Kyle Petty
1990 #43 Richard Petty
1990 #192 Richard Petty/Kyle Petty Cars YR
1991 #43 Richard Petty
1991 #122 Richard Petty/Rob Moroso Crash MM
1993 #43 Richard Petty
1993 #156 Richard Petty MM
1993 #199 Da.All./R.Petty/Mart.Cars MM
1993 #245 Richard Petty w/Car MM
1994 #43 Richard Petty
1995 #43 Richard Petty
1996 #43 Richard Petty
Maxx 10th Anniversary
1998 #39 Richard Petty
1998 #64 Richard Petty's Car
1998 #94 Richard Petty
1998 #108 Richard Petty
Maxx 10th Anniversary Buy Back Autographs
1998 #40 K.Petty/R.Petty '89 #220/12
1998 #41 Richard Petty '88 #43
1998 #42 Richard Petty SSD/250
Maxx 10th Anniversary Card of the Year
1998 #CY2 K.Petty/R.Petty
1998 #CY6 Richard Petty
Maxx 10th Anniversary Champions Past
1998 #CP9 Richard Petty
Maxx 10th Anniversary Champions Past Die Cuts
1998 #CP9 Richard Petty
Maxx Black
1992 #43 Richard Petty
Maxx Charlotte
1988 #2 Richard Petty's Car
1988 #15 Pit Row Action
1988 #31 R.Petty/R.Rudd Cars
1988 #43 Richard Petty RC
1988 #60 Richard Petty's Car
1988 #82 Riverside Int./R.Petty's Car
1988 #84 D.Earnhardt/R.Petty Cars
Maxx Crisco
1989 #17 Richard Petty
Maxx Glossy
1990 #43 Richard Petty
1990 #192 Richard Petty/Kyle Petty Cars YR
Maxx Holly Farms
1990 #HF6 Richard Petty
Maxx IMHOF
1992 #35 Richard Petty's Car
Maxx Made in America
1996 #43 Richard Petty
Maxx McDonald's
1991 #26 Richard Petty
1992 #30 Richard Petty
Maxx Odyssey
1996 #43 Richard Petty
Maxx Premier Plus
1993 #43 Richard Petty
1993 #48 Richard Petty MM
1993 #57 Da.All/R.Pet/Mart/B.Lab.Cars MM
1993 #74 Richard Petty w/Car MM
1994 #43 Richard Petty
1995 #43 Richard Petty
Maxx Premier Plus Crown Chrome
1995 #43 Richard Petty
Maxx Premier Series
1993 #43 Richard Petty
1993 #156 Richard Petty MM
1993 #199 Allison/Petty/Martin/Lab.Cars MM
1993 #245 Richard Petty w/Car MM
1994 #43 Richard Petty
1995 #43 Richard Petty
1996 #43 Richard Petty
1996 #52 Richard Petty's Car
Maxx Premier Series Jumbos
1994 #6 Richard Petty
Maxx Previews
1989 #6 Richard Petty
Maxx Racing for Kids
1991 #3 Sheet 3
Maxx Red
1992 #43 Richard Petty
Maxx Sam Bass
1992 #1 Richard Petty
Maxx Signed, Sealed, and Delivered
1999 #S4 Richard Petty/250
Maxx Stand Ups
1995 #6 Richard Petty
Maxx The Winston
1992 #9 Richard Petty
1992 #29 Richard Petty's Car
Maxx Update
1991 #43 Richard Petty
Maxx Winston 20th Anniversary Foils
1991 #1 Richard Petty 1971 Car
1991 #2 Richard Petty 1972 Car
1991 #4 Richard Petty 1974 Car
1991 #5 Richard Petty 1975 Car

1991 #9 Richard Petty 1979 Car
McFarlane NASCAR 3-Inch Series 1
2005 #100 Richard Petty
McFarlane NASCAR Series 2
2004 #60 Richard Petty FP R
2004 #65 Richard Petty H Yankees
Metallic Impressions 25th Anniversary Winston Cup Champions
1996 #1 Richard Petty
1996 #2 Richard Petty
1996 #4 Richard Petty
1996 #5 Richard Petty
1996 #9 Richard Petty
Metallic Impressions Richard Petty
1995 #1 Richard Petty
1995 #2 Richard Petty
1995 #3 Richard Petty
1995 #4 Richard Petty's Car
1995 #5 Richard Petty's Car
Metallic Impressions Winston Cup Champions 10-Card Tin
1995 #1 Richard Petty
M-Force
1996 #14 Richard Petty
M-Force Silvers
1996 #S8 Richard Petty
Miscellaneous Phone Cards
1993-95 #15 Richard Petty/5000 $10, '94 Ameritech
Pepsi 400 Victory Lane
1994 #1 Donnie Allison
Pepsi Richard Petty
1992 #1 Richard Petty
1992 #2 Richard Petty
1992 #3 Richard Petty
1992 #4 Richard Petty
1992 #5 Richard Petty
Power
1994 #64 Richard Petty PO
1994 #110 Richard Petty
Power Gold
1994 #64 Richard Petty PO
1994 #110 Richard Petty
Press Pass
1995 #86 Richard Petty
1995 #126 Richard Petty S
1995 #132 Richard Petty PR
1996 #80 R.Petty/Loomis/Hamilton
1996 #89 Richard Petty DW
1997 #97 T.Labonte/R.Petty
1997 #108 B.Hamilton/R.Petty
1998 #134 Richard Petty RET
1999 #132 Richard Petty RET
2005 #81 Richard Petty NS
2005 #91 Richard Petty Y
Press Pass Autographs
2002 #54 Richard Petty
2003 #47 Richard Petty E/P
2004 #49 Richard Petty P
2005 #48 Richard Petty E/P
2006 #45 Richard Petty
Press Pass Daytona 500 50th Anniversary
2008 #5 Richard Petty '64
2008 #7 Richard Petty '66
2008 #11 Richard Petty '71
2008 #12 Richard Petty '73
2008 #13 Richard Petty '74
2008 #18 Richard Petty '79
2008 #20 Richard Petty '81
2008 #46 David Pearson Richard Petty FF
Press Pass Eclipse Father and Son Autographs
2002 #FS5 Richard/Kyle Petty
Press Pass Eclipse Racing Champions
2002 #RC36 Richard Petty
Press Pass Goody's
2006 #GCC1 Richard Petty
2006 #GCC2 Richard Petty
2006 #GCC4 Richard Petty
Press Pass Lasers
1997 #97 T.Labonte/R.Petty
1997 #108 B.Hamilton/R.Petty
Press Pass Legends
2005 #10 Richard Petty
2005 #34 Richard Petty C
2005 #47 L.Petty/R.Petty/K.Petty FT
2005 #50 D.Allison/Gordon/Petty CL
2006 #14 Richard Petty
2006 #46 R.Petty/J.Gordon REC Poles
2006 #48 R.Petty/J.Gordon REC Champs
2006 #49 R.Petty/J.Gordon REC Top 10s
2007 #18 Richard Petty
2007 #55 Richard Petty N
2007 #66 Bobby Allison Richard Petty R
2007 #69 David Pearson Richard Petty R
Press Pass Legends Autographs Black
2005 #9 Richard Petty
2006 #12 Richard Petty
2007 #12 Richard Petty/48
Press Pass Legends Autographs Blue
2005 #9 Richard Petty/100
2006 #14 Richard Petty/100
2007 #23 Richard Petty/570
Press Pass Legends Autographs Inscriptions Blue
2007 #14 Richard Petty 43/19
Press Pass Legends Blue
2005 #10B Richard Petty
2005 #34B Richard Petty C
2005 #47B L.Petty/R.Petty/K.Petty FT
2005 #50B D.Allison/Gordon/Petty CL
2006 #B14 Richard Petty
2006 #B46 R.Petty/J.Gordon REC Poles
2006 #B48 R.Petty/J.Gordon REC Champs
2006 #B49 R.Petty/J.Gordon REC Top 10s
2007 #B18 Richard Petty
2007 #B55 Richard Petty N
2007 #B66 Bobby Allison Richard Petty R
2007 #B69 David Pearson Richard Petty R
Press Pass Legends Bronze
2006 #Z14 Richard Petty
2006 #Z46 R.Petty/J.Gordon REC Poles
2006 #Z48 R.Petty/J.Gordon REC Champs
2006 #Z49 R.Petty/J.Gordon REC Top 10s
2007 #Z18 Richard Petty
2007 #Z55 Richard Petty N
2007 #Z66 Bobby Allison Richard Petty R
2007 #Z69 David Pearson Richard Petty R
Press Pass Legends Gold
2005 #10G Richard Petty
2005 #34G Richard Petty C
2005 #47G L.Petty/R.Petty/K.Petty FT
2005 #50G D.Allison/Gordon/Petty CL
2006 #G14 Richard Petty
2006 #G46 R.Petty/J.Gordon REC Poles
2006 #G48 R.Petty/J.Gordon REC Champs
2006 #G49 R.Petty/J.Gordon REC Top 10s
2007 #G18 Richard Petty
2007 #G55 Richard Petty N
2007 #G66 Bobby Allison Richard Petty R
2007 #G69 David Pearson Richard Petty R
Press Pass Legends Greatest Moments
2005 #GM4 Richard Petty Day.500
2005 #GM6 Richard Petty Firecrkr.400
Press Pass Legends Heritage
2005 #HE8 Richard Petty
Press Pass Legends Heritage Gold
2006 #HE1 Richard Petty
2006 #HE13 L.Petty/R.Petty
Press Pass Legends Heritage Silver
2006 #HE1 Richard Petty
2006 #HE13 L.Petty/R.Petty
Press Pass Legends Holofoil
2005 #10H Richard Petty
2005 #34H Richard Petty C
2005 #47H L.Petty/R.Petty/K.Petty FT
2005 #50H D.Allison/Gordon/Petty CL
2006 #H14 Richard Petty
2006 #H46 R.Petty/J.Gordon REC Poles
2006 #H48 R.Petty/J.Gordon REC Champs
2006 #H49 R.Petty/J.Gordon REC Top 10s
2007 #H18 Richard Petty
2007 #H55 Richard Petty N
2007 #H66 Bobby Allison Richard Petty R
2007 #H69 David Pearson Richard Petty R
Press Pass Legends Memorable Moments Gold
2006 #MM9 Richard Petty N.Wilkesboro
2006 #MM10Richard Petty N.Wilkesboro '72
2006 #MM15Richard Petty Rockingham
2007 #MM6 Richard Petty D
2007 #MM11Richard Petty D
Press Pass Legends Memorable Moments Silver
2006 #MM9 Richard Petty N.Wilkesboro
2006 #MM10Richard Petty N.Wilkesboro '72
2006 #MM15Richard Petty Rockingham
2007 #MM6 Richard Petty D
2007 #MM11Richard Petty D
Press Pass Legends Press Plates Black
2005 #10 Richard Petty
2005 #34 Richard Petty C
2005 #47 L.Petty/R.Petty/K.Petty FT
2005 #50 D.Allison/Gordon/Petty CL
2006 #PPB14 Richard Petty
2006 #PPB46 R.Petty/J.Gordon REC Poles
2006 #PPB48 R.Petty/J.Gordon REC Champs
2006 #PPB49 R.Petty/J.Gordon REC Top 10s
2007 #PP18 Richard Petty
2007 #PP55 Richard Petty N
2007 #PP66 Bobby Allison Richard Petty R
2007 #PP69 David Pearson Richard Petty R
Press Pass Legends Press Plates Black Backs
2006 #PPB14B Richard Petty
2006 #PPB46B R.Petty/J.Gordon REC Poles
2006 #PPB48B R.Petty/J.Gordon REC Champs
2006 #PPB49B R.Petty/J.Gordon REC Top 10s
2007 #PP18 Richard Petty
2007 #PP55 Richard Petty N
2007 #PP66 Bobby Allison Richard Petty R
2007 #PP69 David Pearson Richard Petty R
Press Pass Legends Press Plates Cyan
2005 #10 Richard Petty
2005 #34 Richard Petty C
2005 #47 L.Petty/R.Petty/K.Petty FT
2005 #50 D.Allison/Gordon/Petty CL
2006 #PPC14 Richard Petty
2006 #PPC46 R.Petty/J.Gordon REC Poles
2006 #PPC48 R.Petty/J.Gordon REC Champs
2006 #PPC49 R.Petty/J.Gordon REC Top 10s
2007 #PP18 Richard Petty
2007 #PP55 Richard Petty N
2007 #PP66 Bobby Allison Richard Petty R
2007 #PP69 David Pearson Richard Petty R
Press Pass Legends Press Plates Cyan Backs
2006 #PPC14B Richard Petty
2006 #PPC46B R.Petty/J.Gordon REC Poles
2006 #PPC48B R.Petty/J.Gordon REC Champs
2006 #PPC49B R.Petty/J.Gordon REC Top 10s
2007 #PP18 Richard Petty
2007 #PP55 Richard Petty N
2007 #PP66 Bobby Allison Richard Petty R
2007 #PP69 David Pearson Richard Petty R
Press Pass Legends Press Plates Magenta
2005 #10 Richard Petty
2005 #34 Richard Petty C
2005 #47 L.Petty/R.Petty/K.Petty FT
2005 #50 D.Allison/Gordon/Petty CL
2006 #PPM14 Richard Petty
2006 #PPM46 R.Petty/J.Gordon REC Poles
2006 #PPM48 R.Petty/J.Gordon REC Champs
2006 #PPM49 R.Petty/J.Gordon REC Top 10s
2007 #PP18 Richard Petty
2007 #PP55 Richard Petty N
2007 #PP66 Bobby Allison Richard Petty R
2007 #PP69 David Pearson Richard Petty R
Press Pass Legends Press Plates Magenta Backs
2006 #PPM14B Richard Petty
2006 #PPM46B R.Petty/J.Gordon REC Poles
2006 #PPM48B R.Petty/J.Gordon REC Champs
2006 #PPM49B R.Petty/J.Gordon REC Top 10s
2007 #PP18 Richard Petty
2007 #PP55 Richard Petty N
2007 #PP66 Bobby Allison Richard Petty R
2007 #PP69 David Pearson Richard Petty R
Press Pass Legends Press Plates Yellow
2005 #10 Richard Petty
2005 #34 Richard Petty C
2005 #47 L.Petty/R.Petty/K.Petty FT
2005 #50 D.Allison/Gordon/Petty CL
2006 #PPY14 Richard Petty
2006 #PPY46 R.Petty/J.Gordon REC Poles
2006 #PPY48 R.Petty/J.Gordon REC Champs
2006 #PPY49 R.Petty/J.Gordon REC Top 10s
2007 #PP18 Richard Petty
2007 #PP55 Richard Petty N
2007 #PP66 Bobby Allison Richard Petty R
2007 #PP69 David Pearson Richard Petty R
Press Pass Legends Press Plates Yellow Backs
2006 #PPY14B Richard Petty
2006 #PPY46B R.Petty/J.Gordon REC Poles
2006 #PPY48B R.Petty/J.Gordon REC Champs
2006 #PPY49B R.Petty/J.Gordon REC Top 10s
2007 #PP18 Richard Petty
2007 #PP55 Richard Petty N
2007 #PP66 Bobby Allison Richard Petty R
2007 #PP69 David Pearson Richard Petty R
Press Pass Legends Previews
2005 #10 Richard Petty
2005 #34 Richard Petty C
2005 #47 L.Petty/R.Petty/K.Petty FT/1
2005 #50 D.Allison/Gordon/Petty CL
2006 #EB14 Richard Petty
2006 #EB46 R.Petty/J.Gordon REC Poles
2006 #EB48 R.Petty/J.Gordon REC Champs
2006 #EB49 R.Petty/J.Gordon REC Top 10s
2007 #EB18 Richard Petty
2007 #EB66 Bobby Allison Richard Petty R
2007 #EB69 David Pearson Richard Petty R
Press Pass Legends Racing Artifacts Hat
2006 #RP-H Richard Petty
2007 #RP-H Richard Petty
Press Pass Legends Solo
2005 #10S Richard Petty
2005 #34S Richard Petty C
2005 #47S L.Petty/R.Petty/K.Petty FT
2005 #50S D.Allison/Gordon/Petty CL
2006 #S14 Richard Petty
2006 #S46 R.Petty/J.Gordon REC Poles
2006 #S48 R.Petty/J.Gordon REC Champs
2006 #S49 R.Petty/J.Gordon REC Top 10s
2007 #S18 Richard Petty
2007 #S55 Richard Petty N
2007 #S66 Bobby Allison Richard Petty R
2007 #S69 David Pearson Richard Petty R
Press Pass Oil Slicks
1997 #97 T.Labonte/R.Petty
1997 #108 B.Hamilton/R.Petty
Press Pass Optima
2006 #65 Richard Petty CP
Press Pass Optima Gold
2006 #G65 Richard Petty CP
Press Pass Platinum
2005 #P81 Richard Petty NS
2005 #P91 Richard Petty Y
Press Pass Premium
1995 #20 Richard Petty
Press Pass Premium Holofoil
1995 #20 Richard Petty
Press Pass Premium Red Hot
1995 #20 Richard Petty
Press Pass Premium Rivalries
1998 #2B Richard Petty
Press Pass Red Hot
1995 #86 Richard Petty
1995 #126 Richard Petty S
1995 #132 Richard Petty PR
Press Pass Samples
2005 #81 Richard Petty NS
2005 #91 Richard Petty Y
Press Pass Scorchers
1996 #80 R.Petty/Loomis/Hamilton
1996 #89 Richard Petty DW
Press Pass Signings
2001 #43 Richard Petty V/S
2002 #53 Richard Petty O/P/S/T/V
2003 #59 Richard Petty O/S/T/V
2004 #52 Richard Petty O/P/S/T/V
2005 #46 Richard Petty P/S
2006 #46 Richard Petty P/S
2007 #57 Richard Petty
2008 #45 Richard Petty
Press Pass Signings Blue
2008 #24 Richard Petty/100
Press Pass Signings Blue Daytona
2007 #6 Richard Petty
Press Pass Signings Gold
2002 #50 Richard Petty O/P/S/T/V
2003 #59 Richard Petty O/S/T/V
2004 #48 Richard Petty O/P/S/T/V
2005 #44 Richard Petty P/S
2006 #41 Richard Petty P/S
Press Pass Signings Platinum
2005 #42 Richard Petty P/S
Press Pass Signings Press Plates Black
2007 #35 Richard Petty
2008 #32 Richard Petty
Press Pass Signings Press Plates Cyan
2007 #34 Richard Petty
2008 #32 Richard Petty
Press Pass Signings Press Plates Magenta
2007 #36 Richard Petty
2008 #32 Richard Petty
Press Pass Signings Press Plates Yellow
2007 #35 Richard Petty
2008 #32 Richard Petty
Press Pass Signings Silver
2006 #44 Richard Petty P/S
Press Pass Signings Transparent
2004 #7 Richard Petty O/P/T
Press Pass Snapshots
2003 #SN27 Richard Petty
2004 #SN27 Richard Petty
2005 #SN34 Richard Petty
Press Pass Techno-Retro
2000 #TR34 Richard Petty
Press Pass Torquers
1996 #80 R.Petty/Loomis/B.Hamilton
1996 #89 Richard Petty DW
1997 #97 T.Labonte/R.Petty
1997 #108 B.Hamilton/R.Petty
Press Pass Trackside
2003 #60 K.Petty/R.Petty FA
2003 #NNO King for a Day Yellow
2005 #79 R.Petty/K.Petty FA
Press Pass Trackside Gold Holofoil
2003 #P60 K.Petty/R.Petty
Press Pass Trackside Golden
2005 #G79 R.Petty/K.Petty FA
Press Pass Trackside Samples
2003 #60 K.Petty/R.Petty FA
2005 #79 R.Petty/K.Petty FA
Press Pass Victory Lap
2003 #2 Richard Petty
Press Pass Vintage
2002 #VN27 Richard Petty
Pro Set
1991 #65 Richard Petty
1991 #68 Richard Petty's Car
1991 #130 Richard Petty
1992 #43 Richard Petty
1992 #45 Richard Petty
1992 #114 Richard Petty's Car
1992 #124 Richard Petty's Transporter
Pro Set Maxwell House
1992 #25 Richard Petty
Pro Set Petty Family
1991 #1 Maurice Petty Art/R.Petty ART/Lee Petty ART
1991 #2 1949 Reaper Shed
1991 #9 L.Petty/Richard Petty/M.Petty
1991 #13 Richard Petty 1958
1991 #15 L.Petty/Richard Petty/M.Petty
1991 #16 Richard Petty's Car 1961
1991 #17 Richard Petty 1962
1991 #18 Richard Petty/Lee Petty Cars 1963
1991 #19 Richard Petty's Car 1964
1991 #20 Richard Petty's Car 1965
1991 #21 Richard Petty's Car 1966
1991 #22 Richard Petty 1967
1991 #23 Richard Petty's Car 1968
1991 #24 Richard Petty's Car 1969
1991 #27 Richard Petty's Car 1972
1991 #28 Petty Family
1991 #30 Petty Family
1991 #31 Richard Petty's Trans.
1991 #32 Richard Petty's Car 1977
1991 #33 Richard Petty's Car 1978
1991 #34 Richard Petty/Kyle Petty Art
1991 #35 Richard Petty/Kyle Petty Cars
1991 #36 Richard Petty/Kyle Petty Cars
1991 #37 Petty Family
1991 #38 Richard Petty's Car 1983
1991 #41 Richard Petty's Car 1986
1991 #42 Richard Petty's Car 1987
1991 #43 Richard Petty's Car 1989
1991 #44 Petty Enterprises
1991 #47 Richard Petty
1991 #49 Richard Petty/Maurice Petty
1991 #50 Richard Petty Museum
Pro Set Petty Family Prototypes
1991 #P3 Richard Petty's Car
Pro Set Racing Club
1992 #6 Richard Petty's Car
Pro Set Rudy Farms
1992 #15 Richard Petty
Racer's Choice
1997 #86 Richard Petty SS
Racer's Choice Showcase Series
1997 #86 Richard Petty SS
Redline Standups
1992 #3 Richard Petty
SB Motorsports
1997 #8 Richard Petty
1997 #30 Richard Petty
Score Board IQ
1997 #32 Richard Petty
Score Board IQ Remarques
1997 #SB7 Richard Petty
Score Board IQ Remarques Sam Bass Finished
1997 #SB7 Richard Petty
Select
1995 #73 Richard Petty OWN
1995 #109 Richard Petty/K.Petty IB
1995 #129 R.Petty/M.Martin I
Select Flat Out
1995 #73 Richard Petty OWN
1995 #109 Richard Petty/Kyle Petty IB
1995 #129 Richard Petty/Mark Martin I
SkyBox Profile
1997 #33 Richard Petty OWN
SP
1995 #127 Richard Petty OWN
SP Authentic Mark of a Legend
1998 #M1 Richard Petty/220
SP Authentic Traditions
1998 #T1 R.Petty/D.Earnhardt
SP Back-To-Back
1995 #BB1 Richard Petty
SP Die Cuts
1995 #127 Richard Petty
SP Richard Petty/STP 25th Anniversary
1996 #RP1 Richard Petty
1996 #RP2 Richard Petty
1996 #RP3 Richard Petty
1996 #RP4 Richard Petty
1996 #RP5 Richard Petty
1996 #RP6 Richard Petty
1996 #RP7 Richard Petty
1996 #RP8 Richard Petty
1996 #RP9 Richard Petty
Sports Illustrated for Kids *
1992-00 #66 Richard Petty
Sports Illustrated for Kids II
1992 #66 Richard Petty Auto Racing
Sportscasters *
1977 #1115 Richard Petty
SportsCom FanScan
1997 #10 Richard Petty
SportStars Photo-Graphics
1986 #10 Richard Petty
SportStars Photo-Graphics Stickers
1985 #NNO Richard Petty
SPx Tag Team
1997 #TT5 R.Petty/K.Petty
SPx Tag Team Autographs
1997 #TA5 R.Petty/K.Petty
STP
1972 #11 Richard Petty
STP Daytona 500
1992 #1 Richard Petty
1992 #2 Richard Petty in Car
1992 #4 Richard Petty's Car
1992 #5 Richard Petty in Pits
1992 #7 Richard Petty in Pits
1992 #9 Richard Petty
STP Richard Petty
1991 #1 Richard Petty
1991 #2 Richard Petty's Car
1991 #3 Richard Petty
1991 #4 Richard/Kyle Petty in Pits
1991 #5 Richard Petty's Car
1991 #6 Richard Petty
1991 #7 Richard Petty's Car
1991 #8 Richard Petty w/Car
1991 #9 Richard Petty
Sunbelt Racing Legends
1991 #1 Richard Petty
Superior Racing Metals
1991 #10 Richard Petty
Texas World Speedway
1991 #5 Richard Petty
1991 #7 Richard Petty/Bill France
TG Racing David Pearson
1991 #5 David Pearson/Richard Petty
TG Racing Masters of Racing
1989-90 #59 D.Pearson/R.Petty/J.Johnson Cars
1989-90 #237 Jim Paschal w/Car
TG Racing Masters of Racing Update
1991-92 #59 D.Pearson/R.Petty/J.Johnson Cars
Tiger Tom Pistone
1991 #13 Tom Pistone/Richard Petty
Traks
1991 #43 Richard Petty
1991 #85 Richard Petty w/Car
1991 #200 Richard Petty The King
1992 #43 Richard Petty
1992 #85 Richard Petty
1992 #200 Richard Petty w/Lynda
1992 #P3 Richard Petty Prototype
1995 #NNO Richard Petty AUTO
2006 #83 Richard Petty
Traks 5th Anniversary Retrospective
1995 #R15 Richard Petty
Traks Autographs
1992 #A1 Dale Earnhardt/R.Petty
Traks Benny Parsons
1992 #28 Richard Petty/Benny Parsons
1992 #31 Benny Parsons/Richard Petty Cars
1992 #39 Benny Parsons/R.Petty's Cars
Traks Goody's
1992 #25 Richard Petty
Traks Kodak Ernie Irvan
1992 #1A Ernie Irvan/R.Petty
1992 #1B Ernie Irvan/R.Petty Gold
Traks Preferred Collector
1993 #15 Richard Petty/George Bush
1993 #16 Richard Petty
Traks Promos
1991 #P4 Richard Petty The King
1991 #P5 Richard/Lee Petty
1991 #P6 Richard Petty
Traks Racing Machines
1992 #18 Richard Petty's Transp.
1992 #19 Richard Petty in Pits
1992 #43 Richard Petty's Car
1992 #55 Richard Petty's Transp.
1992 #80 Richard Petty Action
1992 #97 Richard Petty in Pits CL
1992 #100 D.Earnhardt/R.Petty Cars CL
Traks Richard Petty
1991 #1 Richard Petty
1991 #2 Richard Petty's Car
1991 #3 Richard Petty's Car
1991 #4 Richard Petty w/Car
1991 #5 Richard Petty's Car
1991 #6 Richard Petty w/Car
1991 #7 Richard Petty's Car
1991 #8 Richard Petty w/Car
1991 #9 Richard Petty
1991 #10 Richard Petty in Pits
1991 #11 Richard Petty w/Car
1991 #12 Richard Petty's Car
1991 #13 Richard Petty's Car
1991 #14 Richard Petty
1991 #15 Richard Petty's Car
1991 #16 Richard Petty's Car
1991 #17 Richard Petty's Car
1991 #18 Richard Petty
1991 #19 Richard Petty
1991 #20 Richard Petty's Car
1991 #21 Richard Petty w/Car
1991 #22 Richard Petty/Earn/D.Waltrip Cars
1991 #23 Richard Petty in Pits
1991 #24 Richard Petty's Car
1991 #25 Richard Petty's Car
1991 #26 Richard Petty's Car
1991 #27 Richard Petty
1991 #28 Richard Petty's Car
1991 #29 Richard Petty
1991 #30 Richard Petty in Pits
1991 #31 Richard Petty's Car
1991 #32 Richard Petty w/Car
1991 #33 Richard Petty in Pits
1991 #34 Richard Petty's Car
1991 #35 Richard Petty's Car
1991 #36 Richard Petty
1991 #37 Richard Petty w/Car
1991 #38 Richard Petty in Pits
1991 #39 Richard Petty
1991 #40 Richard Petty's Car
1991 #41 Richard Petty w/Car
1991 #42 Richard Petty in Pits
1991 #43 Richard Petty
1991 #44 Richard Petty
1991 #45 Richard Petty's Car
1991 #46 Richard Petty
1991 #47 Richard Petty
1991 #48 Richard Petty
1991 #49 Richard Petty w/Car
1991 #50 Richard Petty w/Car
Traks Team Sets
1992 #176 Richard Petty
1992 #184 Richard Petty w/Crew
1992 #185 Richard Petty w/Crew
1992 #195 R.Petty/Louise Loftin
1992 #200 Richard Petty King CL
Traks Valvoline
1995 #73 Richard Petty's Car
1995 #85 Richard Petty's Car
Ultra
1996 #146 Richard Petty
1997 #62 Richard Petty
Ultra Autographs
1996 #28 Richard Petty
Ultra Shoney's
1997 #15 Richard Petty
Ultra Update
1997 #47 Richard Petty
Ultra Winn Dixie
1997 #WD5 Richard Petty
UNO Racing
1983 #23 Richard Petty
Upper Deck
1995 #151 Richard Petty SL
1996 #127 Richard Petty HB
1996 #139 Richard Petty HB
Upper Deck Gold Signature/Electric Gold
1995 #151 Richard Petty SL
Upper Deck Racing Legends
1996 #RLC1 Richard Petty
Upper Deck Road To The Cup 50th Anniversary
1998 #AN10 Richard Petty
1998 #AN14 Richard Petty
1998 #AN17 Richard Petty's Car
1998 #AN21 Richard Petty
1998 #AN27 Richard Petty
1998 #AN36 Richard Petty's Car
1998 #AN41 Richard Petty
Upper Deck Road To The Cup 50th Anniversary Autographs
1998 #AN14 Richard Petty
Upper Deck Silver Signature/Electric Silver
1995 #151 Richard Petty SL
VIP
1995 #49 Richard Petty HR
2002 #49 Richard Petty PP
2003 #42 Richard Petty LEG
2004 #72 Richard Petty L
2004 #82 Richard Petty ATW
VIP Cool Blue
1995 #49 Richard Petty HR
VIP Emerald Proofs
1995 #49 Richard Petty HR
VIP Explosives
2002 #X49 Richard Petty PP
2003 #X42 Richard Petty LEG
VIP Explosives Lasers
2002 #LX49 Richard Petty PP
VIP Helmets
1995 #H7 Richard Petty 1960s
1995 #H8 Richard Petty 1980s
1995 #H9 Richard Petty 1990s
VIP Helmets Gold
1995 #H7 Richard Petty 1960's
1995 #H8 Richard Petty 1980's
1995 #H9 Richard Petty 1990's
VIP Laser Explosive
2003 #LX42 Richard Petty LEG
VIP Previews
2003 #42 Richard Petty LEG
VIP Red Hot
1995 #49 Richard Petty HR
VIP Samples
2002 #49 Richard Petty PP
2003 #42 Richard Petty LEG
2004 #72 Richard Petty L
2004 #82 Richard Petty ATW
VIP Tin
2003 #CT42 Richard Petty LEG
Wheels
1998 #90 Richard Petty
Wheels Autographs
2004 #53 Richard Petty HG
2005 #47 Richard Petty
2006 #48 Richard Petty
Wheels Golden
1998 #90 Richard Petty
Wheels High Gear
1994 #28 Richard Petty
Wheels High Gear Autographs
2002 #45 Richard Petty
Wheels High Gear Gold
1994 #28 Richard Petty
Wheels High Gear Legends
1994 #LS4 Richard Petty
Wheels High Gear Pure Gold
1998 #PG2 Richard Petty
Wheels High Gear Winston Victory Lap Tribute
2004 #WVL3 Richard Petty
Wheels High Gear Winston Victory Lap Tribute Gold
2004 #WVL3 Richard Petty
Wheels Rookie Thunder
1993 #2 Richard Petty
1993 #61 Richard Petty
1993 #79 Richard Petty
1993 #80 Richard Petty
1993 #95 Richard Petty/David Pearson Cars
1993 #96 Richard Petty
1993 #99 Richard Petty
Wheels Rookie Thunder Platinum
1993 #2 Richard Petty
1993 #61 Richard Petty
1993 #79 Richard Petty
1993 #80 Richard Petty
1993 #95 Richard Petty/David Pearson Cars
1993 #96 Richard Petty
1993 #99 Richard Petty
Wheels Rookie Thunder Promos
1993 #P1 Richard Petty
Wheels Rookie Thunder SPs
1993 #SP6 Richard Petty
1993 #SP7 Richard Petty
Winner's Choice Ricky Craven
1991 #17 Richard Petty/R.Craven
Zenith Champion Salute
1996 #17 Richard Petty
1996 #21 Richard Petty
1996 #22 Richard Petty
1996 #24 Richard Petty
1996 #25 Richard Petty

Ragan, David

AAA Limited Edition
2007 #1 David Ragan Daytona 2-10
2007 #2 David Ragan Daytona 2-18
2007 #3 David Ragan California 2-25
2007 #4 David Ragan Las Vegas 3-15
2007 #5 David Ragan Atlanta 3-18
2007 #6 David Ragan Bristol 3-25
2007 #7 David Ragan Martinsville 4-1
2007 #8 David Ragan Texas 4-15

2007 #9 David Ragan Phoenix 4-21
2007 #10 David Ragan Talladega 4-29
2007 #11 David Ragan Richmond 5-6
2007 #12 David Ragan Darlington 5-13
2007 #13 David Ragan Charlotte 5-19
2007 #14 David Ragan Charlotte 5-27
2007 #15 David Ragan Dover 6-3
2007 #16 David Ragan Pocono 6-10
2007 #17 David Ragan Michigan 6-17
2007 #18 David Ragan Infineon 6-24
2007 #19 David Ragan New Hampshire 7-1
2007 #20 David Ragan Daytona 7-7
2007 #21 David Ragan Chicagoland 7-15
2007 #22 David Ragan Brickyard 7-29
2007 #23 David Ragan Pocono 8-5
2007 #24 David Ragan Watkins Glen 8-12
2007 #25 David Ragan Michigan 8-21
2007 #26 David Ragan Bristol 8-25
2007 #27 David Ragan California 9-2
2007 #28 David Ragan Richmond 9-8
2007 #29 David Ragan New Hampshire 9-16
2007 #30 David Ragan Dover 9-23
2007 #31 David Ragan Kansas 9-30
2007 #32 David Ragan Talladega 10-7
2007 #33 David Ragan Charlotte 10-13
2007 #34 David Ragan Martinsville 10-21
2007 #35 David Ragan Atlanta 10-28
2007 #36 David Ragan Texas 11-4
2007 #37 David Ragan Phoenix 11-11
2007 #38 David Ragan Miami-Homestead 11-18

Press Pass
2007 #51 David Regan CTS
2008 #23 David Ragan
2008 #83 David Ragan RR
2008 #86 David Ragan NBS RR

Press Pass Autographs
2007 #36 David Ragan CTS P
2008 #30 David Ragan NC P/E

Press Pass Autographs Press Plates Black
2008 #25 David Ragan NC P

Press Pass Autographs Press Plates Cyan
2008 #25 David Ragan NC P

Press Pass Autographs Press Plates Magenta
2008 #25 David Ragan NC E

Press Pass Autographs Press Plates Yellow
2008 #25 David Ragan NC E

Press Pass Blue
2007 #B51 David Regan CTS
2008 #B23 David Ragan
2008 #B83 David Ragan RR
2008 #B86 David Ragan NBS RR

Press Pass Eclipse
2008 #19 David Ragan
2008 #60 David Ragan's Car LP

Press Pass Eclipse Gold
2008 #G19 David Ragan
2008 #G60 David Ragan's Car LP

Press Pass Eclipse Previews
2008 #EB19 David Ragan

Press Pass Eclipse Red
2008 #R19 David Ragan
2008 #R60 David Ragan's Car LP

Press Pass Eclipse Under Cover Double Cover Name
2008 #DC4 Matt Kenseth David Ragan
2008 #DC7 Carl Edwards David Ragan

Press Pass Eclipse Under Cover Double Cover NASCAR
2008 #DC4 Matt Kenseth David Ragan
2008 #DC7 Carl Edwards David Ragan

Press Pass Eclipse Under Cover Drivers
2008 #UCD10 David Ragan

Press Pass Eclipse Under Cover Drivers Eclipse
2008 #UCD10 David Ragan

Press Pass Eclipse Under Cover Drivers Name
2008 #UCD10 David Ragan

Press Pass Eclipse Under Cover Drivers NASCAR
2008 #UCD10 David Ragan

Press Pass Eclipse Under Cover Teams
2008 #UCT10 David Ragan

Press Pass Eclipse Under Cover Teams NASCAR
2008 #UCT10 David Ragan

Press Pass Gold
2007 #G51 David Regan CTS
2008 #G23 David Ragan
2008 #G83 David Ragan RR
2008 #G86 David Ragan NBS RR

Press Pass Optima
2006 #47 David Ragan CTS RC

Press Pass Optima Fan Favorite
2006 #FF27 David Regan

Press Pass Optima Gold
2006 #G47 David Regan CTS

Press Pass Platinum
2007 #P51 David Regan CTS
2008 #P23 David Ragan
2008 #P83 David Ragan RR
2008 #P86 David Ragan NBS RR

Press Pass Premium
2007 #87 David Ragan RD CRC
2008 #7 David Ragan

Press Pass Premium Previews
2008 #EB7 David Ragan

Press Pass Premium Red
2007 #R87 David Ragan RD
2008 #7 David Ragan

Press Pass Premium Team Signed Baseballs
2008 #ROU Carl Edwards Matt Kenseth Jamie McMurray#David Ragan
2008 #E-ROU Carl Edwards Matt Kenseth Jamie McMurray#David Ragan Entry Card

Press Pass Previews
2008 #EB23 David Ragan

Press Pass Signings
2007 #58 David Ragan NC
2008 #46 David Ragan

Press Pass Signings Blue
2007 #24 David Ragan NC
2008 #25 David Ragan

Press Pass Signings Gold
2007 #44 David Ragan NC
2008 #37 David Ragan

Press Pass Signings Press Plates Black
2007 #36 David Ragan
2008 #33 David Ragan

Press Pass Signings Press Plates Cyan
2007 #35 David Ragan
2008 #33 David Ragan

Press Pass Signings Press Plates Magenta
2007 #37 David Ragan
2008 #33 David Ragan

Press Pass Signings Press Plates Yellow
2007 #36 David Ragan
2008 #33 David Ragan

Press Pass Signings Silver
2007 #42 David Ragan NC
2008 #33 David Ragan

Press Pass Speedway
2008 #27 David Ragan
2008 #46 David Ragan NNS

Press Pass Speedway Corporate Cuts Drivers
2008 #CD-DR David Ragan

Press Pass Speedway Corporate Cuts Drivers Patches
2008 #CD-DR David Ragan

Press Pass Speedway Corporate Cuts Team
2008 #CT-DRDavid Ragan

Press Pass Speedway Gold
2008 #G27 David Ragan
2008 #G46 David Ragan NNS

Press Pass Speedway Holofoil
2008 #H27 David Ragan
2008 #H46 David Ragan NNS

Press Pass Speedway Previews
2008 #EB27 David Ragan
2008 #EB46 David Ragan NNS

Press Pass Speedway Red
2008 #R27 David Ragan
2008 #R46 David Ragan NNS

Press Pass Stealth
2007 #33 David Ragan CRC
2007 #42 David Ragan NBS
2007 #69 Edwards/Biffle/Kenseth/McMurray/Ragan
2007 #74 David Ragan DD
2008 #29 David Ragan
2008 #70 Greg Biffle Jamie McMurray Carl Edwards Matt Kenseth David Ragan
2008 #80 David Ragan DO

Press Pass Stealth Battle Armor Drivers
2007 #BAD4 David Ragan

Press Pass Stealth Battle Armor Teams
2007 #BAT4 David Ragan

Press Pass Stealth Chrome
2007 #33 David Ragan CRC
2007 #42 David Ragan NBS
2007 #69 Edwards/Biffle/Kenseth/McMurray/Ragan
2007 #74 David Ragan DD
2008 #29 David Ragan
2008 #70 Greg Biffle Jamie McMurray Carl Edwards Matt Kenseth David Ragan
2008 #80 David Ragan DO

Press Pass Stealth Chrome Exclusives
2007 #X33 David Ragan
2007 #X42 David Ragan NBS
2007 #X69 Edwards/Biffle/Kenseth/McMurray/Ragan
2007 #X74 David Ragan DD
2008 #29 David Ragan
2008 #70 Greg Biffle Jamie McMurray Carl Edwards Matt Kenseth David Ragan
2008 #80 David Ragan DO

Press Pass Stealth Chrome Exclusives Gold
2008 #29 David Ragan
2008 #70 Greg Biffle Jamie McMurray Carl Edwards Matt Kenseth David Ragan
2008 #80 David Ragan DO

Press Pass Stealth Chrome Platinum
2007 #P33 David Ragan
2007 #P42 David Ragan NBS
2007 #P69 Edwards/Biffle/Kenseth/McMurray/Ragan
2007 #P74 David Ragan DD

Press Pass Stealth Maximum Access
2007 #MA22 David Ragan
2008 #MA22 David Ragan

Press Pass Stealth Maximum Access Autographs
2007 #MA22 David Ragan
2008 #MA22 David Ragan

Press Pass Stealth Previews
2007 #EB33 David Ragan
2007 #EB42 David Ragan NBS
2008 #29 David Ragan

Press Pass Top Prospects Sheet Metal
2007 #DRA-SM David Ragan

Press Pass Top Prospects Sheet Metal-Tire
2007 #DRA-ST David Ragan

Press Pass Top Prospects Shoes
2007 #DRA-S David Ragan

Press Pass Top Prospects Tire Autographs
2007 #DRA-A David Ragan

Press Pass Top Prospects Tires Gold
2007 #DRa-T David Ragan

Press Pass Top Prospects Tires Silver
2007 #DRa-T David Ragan

Traks
2007 #35 David Ragan CRC

Traks Corporate Cuts Driver
2007 #CCD3 David Ragan

Traks Corporate Cuts Patch
2007 #CCD3 David Ragan/15

Traks Corporate Cuts Team
2007 #CCT3 David Ragan

Traks Gold
2007 #G35 David Ragan

Traks Holofoil
2007 #H35 David Ragan

Traks Previews
2007 #EB35 David Ragan

Traks Red
2007 #R35 David Ragan

VIP
2007 #88 David Ragan SP CRC

VIP Get A Grip Drivers
2007 #GGD24 David Ragan

VIP Get A Grip Teams
2007 #GGT24 David Ragan

VIP Previews
2007 #EB88 David Ragan

VIP Rookie Stripes
2007 #RS4 David Ragan

VIP Rookie Stripes Autographs
2007 #RS-DRA David Ragan

Wheels American Thunder
2007 #88 David Ragan RT AU/305 CRC

Wheels American Thunder Autographed Hat Instant Winner
2007 #AH28 David Ragan

Wheels American Thunder Head to Toe
2007 #HT7 David Ragan

Wheels American Thunder Triple Hat
2007 #TH23 David Ragan

Wheels Autographs
2007 #33 David Ragan CTS HG
2008 #23 David Ragan NC HG

Wheels Autographs Press Plates Black
2007 #32 David Ragan CTS
2008 #23 David Ragan NC HG

Wheels Autographs Press Plates Cyan
2007 #32 David Ragan CTS
2008 #23 David Ragan NC HG

Wheels Autographs Press Plates Magenta
2007 #32 David Ragan CTS
2008 #23 David Ragan NC HG

Wheels Autographs Press Plates Yellow
2007 #32 David Ragan CTS
2008 #23 David Ragan NC HG

Wheels High Gear
2007 #45 David Ragan CTS
2008 #20 David Ragan

Wheels High Gear Driven
2008 #DR5 David Ragan

Wheels High Gear Final Standings
2008 #F20 David Ragan/23

Wheels High Gear MPH
2007 #M45 David Ragan CTS
2008 #M20 David Ragan

Wheels High Gear Previews
2008 #EB20 David Ragan

Reutimann, David

Press Pass
2008 #85 David Reutimann RR

Press Pass Blue
2008 #B85 David Reutimann RR

Press Pass Gold
2008 #G85 David Reutimann RR

Press Pass Platinum
2008 #P85 David Reutimann RR

Press Pass Premium
2007 #88 David Reutimann RD RC

Press Pass Premium Red
2007 #R88 David Reutimann RD

Press Pass Signings
2007 #60 David Reutimann NC
2008 #47 David Reutimann

Press Pass Signings Blue
2007 #25 David Reutimann NC
2008 #26 David Reutimann

Press Pass Signings Gold
2007 #45 David Reutimann NC

Press Pass Signings Press Plates Magenta
2007 #38 David Reutimann

Press Pass Signings Silver
2007 #44 David Reutimann NC
2008 #34 David Reutimann

Press Pass Speedway
2008 #32 David Reutimann
2008 #48 David Reutimann NNS

Press Pass Speedway Cockpit
2008 #CP19 David Reutimann

Press Pass Speedway Gold
2008 #G32 David Reutimann
2008 #G48 David Reutimann NNS

Press Pass Speedway Holofoil
2008 #H32 David Reutimann
2008 #H48 David Reutimann NNS

Press Pass Speedway Previews
2008 #EB32 David Reutimann
2008 #EB48 David Reutimann NNS

Press Pass Speedway Red
2008 #R32 David Reutimann
2008 #R48 David Reutimann NNS

Press Pass Stealth
2007 #34 David Reutimann RC
2007 #43 David Reutimann NBS
2007 #76 David Reutimann DD

Press Pass Stealth Battle Armor Drivers
2007 #BAD22 David Reutimann

Press Pass Stealth Battle Armor Teams
2007 #BAT22 David Reutimann

Press Pass Stealth Chrome
2007 #34 David Reutimann RC
2007 #43 David Reutimann NBS
2007 #76 David Reutimann DD

Press Pass Stealth Chrome Exclusives
2007 #X34 David Reutimann
2007 #X43 David Reutimann NBS
2007 #X76 David Reutimann DD

Press Pass Stealth Chrome Platinum
2007 #P34 David Reutimann
2007 #P43 David Reutimann NBS
2007 #P76 David Reutimann DD

Press Pass Stealth Previews
2007 #EB34 David Reutimann
2007 #EB43 David Reutimann NBS

Press Pass Top Prospects Gloves
2007 #DRE-G David Reutimann

Press Pass Top Prospects Sheet Metal
2007 #DRE-SM David Reutimann

Press Pass Top Prospects Sheet Metal-Tire
2007 #DRE-ST David Reutimann

Press Pass Top Prospects Shoes
2007 #DRE-SDavid Reutimann

Press Pass Top Prospects Tire Autographs
2007 #DRE-ADavid Reutimann

Press Pass Top Prospects Tires Gold
2007 #DRe-T David Reutimann

Press Pass Top Prospects Tires Silver
2007 #DRe-T David Reutimann

Traks
2007 #68 David Reutimann MG

Traks Corporate Cuts Driver
2007 #CCD18 David Reutimann

Traks Corporate Cuts Patch
2007 #CCD18 David Reutimann/15

Traks Corporate Cuts Team
2007 #CCT18 David Reutimann

Traks Gold
2007 #G68 David Reutimann MG

Traks Holofoil
2007 #H68 David Reutimann MG

Traks Red
2007 #R68 David Reutimann MG

VIP
2007 #89 David Reutimann SP RC

VIP Previews
2007 #EB89 David Reutimann

VIP Rookie Stripes
2007 #RS5 David Reutimann

VIP Rookie Stripes Autographs
2007 #RS-DRE David Reutimann

Wheels American Thunder
2007 #89 David Reutimann RT AU/310 RC
2007 #89B David Reutimann RT AU/50 Bea K

Wheels American Thunder Autographed Hat Instant Winner
2007 #AH29 David Reutimann

Wheels American Thunder Pushin' Pedal
2007 #PP11 David Reutimann

Wheels American Thunder Triple Hat
2007 #TH24 David Reutimann

Sadler, Elliott

eTopps
2003 #8 Elliott Sadler/2648

Maxx
1997 #45 Elliott Sadler RC
1997 #90 Elliott Sadler's Car
1999 #82 Elliott Sadler
1999 #83 Elliott Sadler
1999 #84 Elliott Sadler
2000 #21 Elliott Sadler

Maxx FANtastic Finishes
1999 #F3 Elliott Sadler's Car

Maxx Race Ticket
1999 #RT21 Elliott Sadler's Car

Maxx Racing Images
1999 #RI27 Elliott Sadler

Maxximum
2000 #23 Elliott Sadler

Maxximum Die Cuts
2000 #23 Elliott Sadler

Maxximum MPH
2000 #23 Elliott Sadler/21

McFarlane NASCAR Series 4
2005 #110 Elliott Sadler R Glasses
2005 #112 Elliott Sadler R w/o Glasses
2005 #115 Elliott Sadler H Blk&Wht

Press Pass
1998 #48 Elliott Sadler
1999 #43 Elliott Sadler
1999 #59 Elliott Sadler YG
1999 #92 Elliott Sadler PRE
2000 #23 Elliott Sadler
2000 #66 Elliott Sadler
2001 #26 Elliott Sadler
2001 #94 Elliott Sadler PV
2002 #30 Elliott Sadler
2002 #68 Elliott Sadler REP
2003 #27 Elliott Sadler
2003 #57 Elliott Sadler DS
2003 #63 Jr./JJ/New/Sad/Ken/Bus DS
2004 #28 Elliott Sadler
2004 #71 Elliott Sadler's Car OTW
2005 #26 Elliott Sadler
2005 #66 Elliott Sadler's Car OTW
2005 #110 Elliott Sadler's Car
2008 #24 Elliott Sadler

Press Pass Autographs
2002 #61 Elliott Sadler
2003 #52 Elliott Sadler E/P
2008 #33 Elliott Sadler NC P/E

Press Pass Autographs Press Plates Black
2008 #28 Elliott Sadler NC P

Press Pass Autographs Press Plates Cyan
2008 #28 Elliott Sadler NC E

Press Pass Autographs Press Plates Magenta
2008 #28 Elliott Sadler NC P

Press Pass Autographs Press Plates Yellow
2008 #28 Elliott Sadler NC E

Press Pass Blue
2008 #B24 Elliott Sadler

Press Pass Burnouts
2006 #HT13 Elliott Sadler

Press Pass Burnouts Holofoil
2006 #HT13 Elliott Sadler

Press Pass Coca-Cola Racing Family Scratch-off
2003 #5 Elliott Sadler

Press Pass Cup Chase
2004 #CCR16 Elliott Sadler
2005 #CCR5 Elliott Sadler
2006 #CCR16 Elliott Sadler

Press Pass Cup Chase Prizes
2004 #CCR16 Elliott Sadler
2005 #CCP5 Elliott Sadler

Press Pass Eclipse
2002 #17 Elliott Sadler
2003 #22 Elliott Sadler
2004 #20 Elliott Sadler
2005 #9 Elliott Sadler
2006 #12 Elliott Sadler
2007 #21 Elliott Sadler
2008 #20 Elliott Sadler

Press Pass Eclipse Destination WIN
2005 #6 Elliott Sadler

Press Pass Eclipse Gold
2007 #G21 Elliott Sadler
2008 #G20 Elliott Sadler

Press Pass Eclipse Previews
2003 #22 Elliott Sadler
2004 #20 Elliott Sadler
2005 #EB9 Elliott Sadler
2006 #EB12 Elliott Sadler
2007 #EB21 Elliott Sadler
2008 #EB20 Elliott Sadler

Press Pass Eclipse Racing Champions
2002 #RC6 Elliott Sadler

Press Pass Eclipse Red
2007 #R21 Elliott Sadler
2008 #R20 Elliott Sadler

Press Pass Eclipse Samples
2002 #17 Elliott Sadler
2003 #22 Elliott Sadler
2004 #20 Elliott Sadler
2005 #9 Elliott Sadler

Press Pass Eclipse Skidmarks
2005 #SM6 Elliott Sadler

Press Pass Eclipse Skidmarks Holofoil
2005 #SM6 Elliott Sadler

Press Pass Eclipse Solar Eclipse
2002 #S17 Elliott Sadler
2003 #P22 Elliott Sadler

Press Pass Eclipse Teammates Autographs
2004 #5 D.Jarrett/E.Sadler
2005 #5 D.Jarrett/E.Sadler
2006 #4 D.Jarrett/E.Sadler
2007 #2 Kahne/Riggs/Sadler
2008 #KS Kasey Kahne Elliott Sadler/35

Press Pass Eclipse Under Cover Cars
2003 #UCT14 Elliott Sadler

Press Pass Eclipse Under Cover Driver Gold
2003 #UCD14 Elliott Sadler

Press Pass Eclipse Under Cover Driver Red
2003 #UCD14 Elliott Sadler

Press Pass Eclipse Under Cover Driver Silver
2003 #UCD14 Elliott Sadler

Press Pass Eclipse Under Cover Drivers
2002 #CD8 Elliott Sadler

Press Pass Eclipse Under Cover Gold Cars
2002 #CD8 Elliott Sadler

Press Pass Eclipse Under Cover Gold Drivers
2002 #CD8 Elliott Sadler

Press Pass Eclipse Under Cover Holofoil Drivers
2002 #CD8 Elliott Sadler

Press Pass Gold
2008 #G24 Elliott Sadler

Press Pass Gold Holofoil
2003 #P27 Elliott Sadler
2003 #P57 Elliott Sadler DS
2003 #P63 Jr./Johnson/Newman Sadler/Kenseth/Busch DS

Press Pass Hot Treads
2002 #HT3 Elliott Sadler's Car/2300
2005 #HTR12 Elliott Sadler

Press Pass Hot Treads Holofoil
2005 #HTR12 Elliott Sadler

Press Pass Millennium
2000 #23 Elliott Sadler
2000 #66 Elliott Sadler
2001 #26 Elliott Sadler
2001 #50 Jeff Burton's Car
2001 #94 Elliott Sadler PV

Press Pass Oil Slicks
1998 #48 Elliott Sadler

Press Pass Optima
2000 #23 Elliott Sadler
2001 #21 Elliott Sadler
2002 #25 Elliott Sadler
2003 #22 Elliott Sadler
2003 #42 Elliott Sadler UC
2004 #22 Elliott Sadler
2004 #59 Elliott Sadler's Car RV
2004 #65 Elliott Sadler CS
2004 #93 Elliott Sadler SS
2005 #25 Elliott Sadler
2005 #64 Elliott Sadler DP
2005 #76 Elliott Sadler CP

Press Pass Optima Fan Favorite
2003 #FF21 Elliott Sadler
2004 #FF21 Elliott Sadler
2005 #FF23 Elliott Sadler

Press Pass Optima G Force
2000 #GF21 Elliott Sadler
2001 #GF21 Elliott Sadler

Press Pass Optima Gold
2001 #21 Elliott Sadler
2002 #25 Elliott Sadler
2003 #G22 Elliott Sadler
2003 #G42 Elliott Sadler UC
2004 #G22 Elliott Sadler
2004 #G59 Elliott Sadler's Car RV
2004 #G65 Elliott Sadler CS
2004 #G93 Elliott Sadler SS
2005 #G25 Elliott Sadler
2005 #G64 Elliott Sadler DP
2005 #G76 Elliott Sadler CP

Press Pass Optima Platinum
2000 #23 Elliott Sadler

Press Pass Optima Previews
2003 #22 Elliott Sadler
2004 #EB22 Elliott Sadler
2005 #25 Elliott Sadler

Press Pass Optima Promos
2002 #25 Elliott Sadler

Press Pass Optima Q & A
2005 #QA3 Elliott Sadler

Press Pass Optima Q&A
2004 #QA5 Elliott Sadler

Press Pass Optima Race Used Lugnuts Cars
2000 #LC13 Elliott Sadler's Car
2002 #LNC16 Elliott Sadler's Car

Press Pass Optima Race Used Lugnuts Drivers
2000 #LD13 Elliott Sadler
2002 #LND16 Elliott Sadler

Press Pass Optima Samples
2002 #25 Elliott Sadler
2003 #22 Elliott Sadler
2003 #42 Elliott Sadler UC
2004 #22 Elliott Sadler
2004 #59 Elliott Sadler's Car RV
2004 #65 Elliott Sadler CS
2004 #93 Elliott Sadler SS
2005 #25 Elliott Sadler
2005 #64 Elliott Sadler DP
2005 #76 Elliott Sadler CP

Press Pass Optima Young Guns
2003 #YG2 Elliott Sadler

Press Pass Pitstop
2000 #PS10 Elliott Sadler's Car

Press Pass Platinum
2002 #30 Elliott Sadler
2002 #68 Elliott Sadler REP
2004 #P28 Elliott Sadler
2004 #P71 Elliott Sadler's Car OTW
2005 #P26 Elliott Sadler
2005 #P66 Elliott Sadler's Car OTW
2005 #P110 Elliott Sadler's Car
2008 #P24 Elliott Sadler

Press Pass Premium
1998 #4 Elliott Sadler
1999 #22 Elliott Sadler
2000 #11 Elliott Sadler
2001 #21 Elliott Sadler
2002 #26 Elliott Sadler
2003 #25 Elliott Sadler
2003 #41 Elliott Sadler's Car
2004 #6 Elliott Sadler
2004 #47 Elliott Sadler NS
2004 #66 Elliott Sadler CC
2005 #28 Elliott Sadler
2006 #26 Elliott Sadler
2006 #49 Elliott Sadler NS
2006 #71 Elliott Sadler C
2007 #17 Elliott Sadler
2007 #61 Elliott Sadler RTTC
2008 #16 Elliott Sadler

Press Pass Premium Gold
2001 #21 Elliott Sadler

Press Pass Premium Previews
2003 #25 Elliott Sadler
2004 #6 Elliott Sadler
2008 #EB16 Elliott Sadler

Press Pass Premium Red
2007 #R17 Elliott Sadler
2007 #R61 Elliott Sadler RTTC
2008 #16 Elliott Sadler

Press Pass Premium Red Reflectors
2002 #26 Elliott Sadler
2003 #25 Elliott Sadler
2003 #41 Elliott Sadler's Car

Press Pass Premium Reflectors
1998 #4 Elliott Sadler
1999 #R22 Elliott Sadler
2000 #11 Elliott Sadler

Press Pass Premium Samples
2002 #26 Elliott Sadler
2003 #25 Elliott Sadler
2003 #41 Elliott Sadler's Car
2004 #6 Elliott Sadler
2004 #47 Elliott Sadler NS
2005 #28 Elliott Sadler

Press Pass Previews
2003 #27 Elliott Sadler
2004 #28 Elliott Sadler
2008 #EB24 Elliott Sadler

Press Pass Previews Green
2005 #EB26 Elliott Sadler

Press Pass Samples
2003 #27 Elliott Sadler
2003 #57 Elliott Sadler DS
2003 #63 Jr./JJ/New/Sad/Ken/Bus DS
2004 #28 Elliott Sadler
2004 #71 Elliott Sadler's Car OTW
2005 #26 Elliott Sadler
2005 #66 Elliott Sadler's Car OTW
2005 #110 Elliott Sadler's Car

Press Pass Signings
1999 #48A Elliott Sadler Blue/650
1999 #48B Elliott Sadler Black/250
2000 #51 Elliott Sadler
2001 #47 Elliott Sadler P/V/S
2002 #57 Elliott Sadler O/S/V
2006 #49 Elliott Sadler NC S
2007 #62 Elliott Sadler NC
2008 #48 Elliott Sadler

Press Pass Signings Blue
2007 #27 Elliott Sadler NC
2008 #27 Elliott Sadler

Press Pass Signings Gold
1999 #23 Elliott Sadler/65
2000 #28 Elliott Sadler
2001 #30 Elliott Sadler T/V/S
2002 #54 Elliott Sadler O/S/V
2003 #63 Elliott Sadler O
2006 #44 Elliott Sadler NC S
2007 #47 Elliott Sadler NC
2008 #39 Elliott Sadler

Press Pass Signings Press Plates Black
2007 #38 Elliott Sadler
2008 #34 Elliott Sadler

Press Pass Signings Press Plates Cyan
2007 #37 Elliott Sadler
2008 #34 Elliott Sadler

Press Pass Signings Press Plates Magenta
2007 #40 Elliott Sadler
2008 #34 Elliott Sadler

Press Pass Signings Press Plates Yellow
2007 #38 Elliott Sadler
2008 #34 Elliott Sadler

Press Pass Signings Silver
2006 #47 Elliott Sadler NC S
2007 #46 Elliott Sadler NC
2008 #35 Elliott Sadler

Press Pass Skidmarks
1999 #43 Elliott Sadler
1999 #59 Elliott Sadler YR
1999 #92 Elliott Sadler PRE

Press Pass Slideshow
2008 #SS28 Elliott Sadler

Press Pass Snapshots
2003 #SN20 Elliott Sadler
2004 #SN22 Elliott Sadler
2005 #SN22 Elliott Sadler

Press Pass Speedway
2008 #20 Elliott Sadler
2008 #65 Elliott Sadler SH

Press Pass Speedway Cockpit
2008 #CP20 Elliott Sadler

Press Pass Speedway Gold
2008 #G20 Elliott Sadler
2008 #G65 Elliott Sadler SH

Press Pass Speedway Holofoil
2008 #H20 Elliott Sadler
2008 #H65 Elliott Sadler SH

Press Pass Speedway Previews
2008 #EB20 Elliott Sadler

Press Pass Speedway Red

2008 #R20 Elliott Sadler
2008 #R65 Elliott Sadler SH
Press Pass Stealth
1998 #42 Elliott Sadler
2006 #27 Elliott Sadler
2006 #56 Jarrett/Sadler TM
2007 #22 Elliott Sadler
2008 #30 Elliott Sadler
2008 #66 Kasey Kahne Elliott Sadler Patrick Carpentier
Press Pass Stealth Autographed Hat Entry
2006 #PPH20 Elliott Sadler
Press Pass Stealth Battle Armor Drivers
2008 #BAD15 Elliott Sadler
Press Pass Stealth Battle Armor Teams
2008 #BAT15 Elliott Sadler
Press Pass Stealth Chrome
2007 #22 Elliott Sadler
2008 #30 Elliott Sadler
2008 #66 Kasey Kahne Elliott Sadler Patrick Carpentier
Press Pass Stealth Chrome Exclusives
2007 #X22 Elliott Sadler
2008 #30 Elliott Sadler
2008 #66 Kasey Kahne Elliott Sadler Patrick Carpentier
Press Pass Stealth Chrome Exclusives Gold
2008 #30 Elliott Sadler
2008 #66 Kasey Kahne Elliott Sadler Patrick Carpentier
Press Pass Stealth Chrome Platinum
2007 #P22 Elliott Sadler
Press Pass Stealth Fusion
1998 #42 Elliott Sadler
Press Pass Stealth No Boundaries
2004 #NB24 Elliott Sadler
Press Pass Stealth Octane SLX
1999 #022 Elliott Sadler
1999 #033 Elliott Sadler's Car
Press Pass Stealth Octane SLX Die Cuts
1999 #022 Elliott Sadler
1999 #033 Elliott Sadler's Car
Press Pass Stealth Previews
2006 #27 Elliott Sadler
2007 #EB22 Elliott Sadler
2008 #30 Elliott Sadler
Press Pass Stealth Retail
2006 #27 Elliott Sadler
2006 #56 Jarrett/Sadler TM
Press Pass Stealth X-Ray
2006 #X27 Elliott Sadler
2006 #X56 Jarrett/Sadler TM
Press Pass Techno-Retro
2000 #TR21 Elliott Sadler
Press Pass Top 25 Drivers & Rides
2006 #C17 Elliott Sadler's Car
2006 #D17 Elliott Sadler
Press Pass Top Ten
2005 #TT6 Elliott Sadler
Press Pass Trackside
2000 #62 Elliott Sadler WBM
2001 #27 Elliott Sadler
2002 #26 Elliott Sadler
2003 #8 Elliott Sadler
2003 #70 Elliott Sadler in Pits
2003 #75 E.Sadler/D.Jarrett TM
2004 #18 Elliott Sadler
2004 #61 Elliott Sadler's Car HS
2004 #66 D.Jarrett/E.Sadler TM
2005 #33 Elliott Sadler
2005 #64 Elliott Sadler's Car HS
2005 #69 D.Jarrett/E.Sadler/TM
Press Pass Trackside Die Cuts
2001 #27 Elliott Sadler
Press Pass Trackside Generation Now
2002 #GN8 Elliott Sadler
Press Pass Trackside Generation.now
2000 #GN4 Elliott Sadler
Press Pass Trackside Gold Holofoil
2003 #P8 Elliott Sadler
2003 #P70 Elliott Sadler's Crew
2003 #P75 E.Sadler/D.Jarrett
Press Pass Trackside Golden
2001 #27 Elliott Sadler
2002 #G26 Elliott Sadler
2003 #G8 Elliott Sadler
2004 #G18 Elliott Sadler
2004 #G61 Elliott Sadler's Car HS
2004 #G66 D.Jarrett/E.Sadler TM
2005 #G33 Elliott Sadler
2005 #G64 Elliott Sadler's Car HS
2005 #G69 D.Jarrett/E.Sadler/TM
Press Pass Trackside Hat Giveaway
2003 #PPH25 Elliott Sadler
2004 #PPH27 Elliott Sadler
2005 #PPH28 Elliott Sadler
Press Pass Trackside Hot Pass
2004 #HP15 Elliott Sadler
Press Pass Trackside Hot Pass National
2004 #HP15 Elliott Sadler
Press Pass Trackside Hot Pursuit
2003 #HP8 Elliott Sadler
Press Pass Trackside License to Drive
2002 #28 Elliott Sadler
2003 #LD11 Elliott Sadler
Press Pass Trackside License to Drive Die Cuts
2002 #28 Elliott Sadler
Press Pass Trackside Panorama
2000 #P10 Elliott Sadler
Press Pass Trackside Pit Stoppers
2000 #PS6 Mark Martin
2000 #PS8 Elliott Sadler
Press Pass Trackside Previews
2003 #8 Elliott Sadler
2004 #EB18 Elliott Sadler
2005 #33 Elliott Sadler
Press Pass Trackside Samples
2002 #26 Elliott Sadler
2003 #8 Elliott Sadler
2003 #70 Elliott Sadler in Pits
2003 #75 E.Sadler/D.Jarrett TM
2004 #18 Elliott Sadler
2004 #61 Elliott Sadler's Car HS
2004 #66 D.Jarrett/E.Sadler TM
2005 #33 Elliott Sadler
2005 #64 Elliott Sadler's Car HS
2005 #69 D.Jarrett/E.Sadler/TM
Press Pass Vintage
2001 #VN26 Elliott Sadler
2002 #VN20 Elliott Sadler

SP Authentic
1999 #18 Elliott Sadler
1999 #45 Elliott Sadler's Car
2000 #29 Elliott Sadler
2000 #56 Elliott Sadler PER
SP Authentic Cup Challengers
1999 #CC10 Elliott Sadler
SP Authentic Driving Force
1999 #DF10 Elliott Sadler
SP Authentic Overdrive
1999 #18 Elliott Sadler
1999 #45 Elliott Sadler CAR
SP Authentic Overdrive Gold
2000 #29 Elliott Sadler/21
2000 #56 Elliott Sadler PER/21
SP Authentic Overdrive Silver
2000 #29 Elliott Sadler
2000 #56 Elliott Sadler PER
SP Authentic Sign of the Times
2000 #ES Elliott Sadler
SP Authentic Sign of the Times Gold
2000 #ES Elliott Sadler
TRAKS
2006 #28 Elliott Sadler
2006 #50 Elliott Sadler's Car
2006 #107 Elliott Sadler's Car PS
2006 #118 Elliott Sadler MG
TRAKS Autographs
2006 #31 Elliott Sadler NC
TRAKS Autographs 25
2006 #29 Elliott Sadler NC
Traks Gold
2007 #G70 Elliott Sadler MG
Traks Holofoil
2007 #H70 Elliott Sadler MG
Traks Red
2007 #R70 Elliott Sadler MG
TRAKS Stickers
2006 #38 Elliott Sadler
Upper Deck MVP
2000 #21 Elliott Sadler
2000 #51 Elliott Sadler's Car
Upper Deck MVP Gold Script
2000 #21 Elliott Sadler
2000 #51 Elliott Sadler
Upper Deck MVP Silver Script
2000 #21 Elliott Sadler
2000 #51 Elliott Sadler
Upper Deck MVP Super Script
2000 #21 Elliott Sadler/21
2000 #51 Elliott Sadler's Car/21
Upper Deck Racing
2000 #23 Elliott Sadler
Upper Deck Racing Road Signs
2000 #RSES Elliott Sadler
Upper Deck Road To The Cup
1998 #113 Elliott Sadler
1999 #17 Elliott Sadler
1999 #51 Elliott Sadler's Car
1999 #88 Elliott Sadler HH
Upper Deck Road to the Cup NASCAR Chronicles
1999 #NC9 Elliott Sadler
Upper Deck Road to the Cup Upper Deck Profiles
1999 #P12 Elliott Sadler
Upper Deck Victory Circle
1999 #86 Elliott Sadler
2000 #36 Elliott Sadler
Upper Deck Victory Circle Exclusives Level 1 Silver
2000 #36 Elliott Sadler
Upper Deck Victory Circle Exclusives Level 2 Gold
2000 #36 Elliott Sadler/21
Upper Deck Victory Circle Signature Collection
1999 #ES Elliott Sadler
Upper Deck Victory Circle UD Exclusives
1999 #86 Elliott Sadler
Valvoline Racing
2007 #NNO Elliott Sadler
VIP
1998 #34 Elliott Sadler
1999 #21 Elliott Sadler
2001 #24 Elliott Sadler SM
2004 #49 Elliott Sadler SG
2004 #73 Elliott Sadler BTN
2005 #26 Elliott Sadler
2005 #40 Elliott Sadler's Car R
2005 #61 Elliott Sadler HR
2006 #24 Elliott Sadler
VIP Explosives
1998 #34 Elliott Sadler
1999 #X21 Elliott Sadler
2001 #24 Elliott Sadler SM
VIP Explosives Lasers
1999 #21 Elliott Sadler
2001 #LX24 Elliott Sadler SM
VIP Get A Grip Drivers
2007 #GGD9 Elliott Sadler
VIP Get A Grip Teams
2007 #GGT9 Elliott Sadler
VIP Head Gear
2004 #HG9 Elliott Sadler
2005 #9 Elliott Sadler
VIP Head Gear Transparent
2004 #HG9 Elliott Sadler
2005 #9 Elliott Sadler
VIP Lap Leaders
2005 #4 Elliott Sadler
VIP Lap Leaders Transparent
2005 #4 Elliott Sadler
VIP Making the Show
2000 #MS3 Elliott Sadler
2003 #MS16 Elliott Sadler
VIP Pedal To The Metal
2007 #PM2 Elliott Sadler
VIP Previews
2004 #EB49 Elliott Sadler SG
2005 #EB26 Elliott Sadler
2005 #EB40 Elliott Sadler's Car R
VIP Samples
2004 #49 Elliott Sadler SG
2004 #73 Elliott Sadler BTN
2005 #26 Elliott Sadler
2005 #40 Elliott Sadler's Car R

2005 #61 Elliott Sadler HR
VIP Solos
1998 #34 Elliott Sadler
Wheels
1998 #56 Elliott Sadler
1998 #62 Elliott Sadler's Car
1999 #29 Elliott Sadler
1999 #97 Elliott Sadler TP
Wheels American Thunder
2004 #23 Elliott Sadler
2004 #44 Elliott Sadler AS
2004 #58 Elliott Sadler DT
2004 #73 Elliott Sadler RR
2005 #26 Elliott Sadler
2005 #48 Elliott Sadler's Car HR
2006 #28 Elliott Sadler
2007 #28 Elliott Sadler
2007 #65 Elliott Sadler RW
Wheels American Thunder American Muscle
2005 #AM8 Elliott Sadler
Wheels American Thunder Autographed Hat Instant Winner
2007 #AH32 Elliott Sadler
Wheels American Thunder Double Hat
2006 #DH21 Elliott Sadler
Wheels American Thunder Head to Toe
2007 #HT8 Elliott Sadler
Wheels American Thunder Heads Up Manufacturer
2003 #HUM18 Elliott Sadler
Wheels American Thunder Heads Up Team
2003 #HUT16 Elliott Sadler/60
Wheels American Thunder Heads Up Winston
2003 #HUW18 Elliott Sadler
Wheels American Thunder Medallion
2005 #MD23 Elliott Sadler
Wheels American Thunder Previews
2004 #EB23 Elliott Sadler
2004 #EB44 Elliott Sadler AS
2005 #26 Elliott Sadler
2006 #EB28 Elliott Sadler
2007 #EB28 Elliott Sadler
Wheels American Thunder Rookie Thunder
2003 #RT28 Elliott Sadler
Wheels American Thunder Samples
2004 #23 Elliott Sadler
2004 #44 Elliott Sadler AS
2004 #58 Elliott Sadler DT
2004 #73 Elliott Sadler RR
2005 #26 Elliott Sadler
2005 #48 Elliott Sadler's Car HR
Wheels American Thunder Triple Hat
2004 #TH19 Elliott Sadler
2005 #TH22 Elliott Sadler
2007 #TH26 Elliott Sadler
Wheels Autographs
2003 #52 Elliott Sadler AT/HG
2004 #57 Elliott Sadler AT
2008 #26 Elliott Sadler NC HG
Wheels Autographs Press Plates Black
2008 #26 Elliott Sadler NC HG
Wheels Autographs Press Plates Cyan
2008 #26 Elliott Sadler NC HG
Wheels Autographs Press Plates Magenta
2008 #26 Elliott Sadler NC HG
Wheels Autographs Press Plates Yellow
2007 #34 Elliott Sadler
2008 #26 Elliott Sadler NC HG
Wheels Golden
1998 #56 Elliott Sadler
1998 #62 Elliott Sadler's Car
1999 #29 Elliott Sadler
1999 #97 Elliott Sadler
Wheels High Gear
1998 #41 Elliott Sadler
1999 #62 Elliott Sadler
2000 #25 Elliott Sadler
2000 #57 Elliott Sadler's Car
2001 #26 Elliott Sadler
2001 #50 Elliott Sadler's Car
2001 #64 Elliott Sadler WCP
2002 #22 Elliott Sadler
2003 #24 Elliott Sadler
2003 #70 Elliott Sadler PREV
2004 #23 Elliott Sadler
2004 #32 Elliott Sadler's Car C
2005 #19 Elliott Sadler
2005 #39 Elliott Sadler's Car C
2005 #81 Elliott Sadler RS
2006 #12 Elliott Sadler
2007 #21 Elliott Sadler
2008 #21 Elliott Sadler
Wheels High Gear Autographs
2000 #24 Elliott Sadler
Wheels High Gear Blue Hawaii SCDA Promos
2003 #24 Elliott Sadler
2003 #70 Elliott Sadler's Car '03 Pre.
Wheels High Gear Driven
2008 #DR7 Elliott Sadler
Wheels High Gear Final Standings
2008 #F21 Elliott Sadler/25
Wheels High Gear Final Standings Gold
2007 #FS21 Elliott Sadler/22
Wheels High Gear First Gear
1998 #41 Elliott Sadler
1999 #62 Elliott Sadler
2000 #25 Elliott Sadler
2000 #57 Elliott Sadler
2001 #26 Elliott Sadler
2001 #50 Elliott Sadler's CAR
2001 #64 Elliott Sadler WCP
2002 #22 Elliott Sadler
2003 #F24 Elliott Sadler
2003 #F70 Elliott Sadler's Car '03 Preview
Wheels High Gear Flag to Flag
2005 #FF22 Elliott Sadler
2006 #FF22 Elliott Sadler
Wheels High Gear Gear Shifters
2000 #GS24 Elliott Sadler
2001 #GS10 Elliott Sadler
Wheels High Gear High Groove
2002 #HG22 Elliott Sadler
2003 #HG22 Elliott Sadler
2004 #HG22 Elliott Sadler
Wheels High Gear MPH
1998 #41 Elliott Sadler

1999 #43 Elliott Sadler
1999 #62 Elliott Sadler
2000 #25 Elliott Sadler
2000 #57 Elliott Sadler
2001 #26 Elliott Sadler
2001 #50 Elliott Sadler's CAR
2001 #64 Elliott Sadler WCP
2002 #22 Elliott Sadler
2003 #M24 Elliott Sadler
2003 #M70 Elliott Sadler's Car '03 Preview
2004 #M23 Elliott Sadler
2004 #M32 Elliott Sadler C
2005 #M19 Elliott Sadler
2005 #M39 Elliott Sadler's Car C
2005 #M81 Elliott Sadler RS
2006 #M12 Elliott Sadler
2007 #M21 Elliott Sadler
2008 #M21 Elliott Sadler
Wheels High Gear Previews
2003 #24 Elliott Sadler
2004 #23 Elliott Sadler
2004 #32 Elliott Sadler C
2007 #EB21 Elliott Sadler
2008 #EB21 Elliott Sadler
Wheels High Gear Previews Green
2005 #EB19 Elliott Sadler
2006 #EB12 Elliott Sadler
Wheels High Gear Samples
2003 #24 Elliott Sadler
2003 #70 Elliott Sadler's Car '03 Pre.
2004 #23 Elliott Sadler
2004 #32 Elliott Sadler C
2005 #19 Elliott Sadler
2005 #39 Elliott Sadler's Car C
2005 #81 Elliott Sadler RS
Wheels High Gear Top Tier
2005 #TT9 Elliott Sadler
Wheels Runnin and Gunnin
1999 #RG34 Elliott Sadler
Wheels Runnin and Gunnin Foils
1999 #RG34 Elliott Sadler
Wheels Solos
1999 #29 Elliott Sadler
1999 #97 Elliott Sadler

Stewart, Tony

Coca-Cola Racing Family
2000 #14 Tony Stewart
2000 #15 Tony Stewart '99 ROY
2000 #16 Coca-Cola Racing Family
Coca-Cola Racing Family AutoZone
2005 #8 Tony Stewart
DK IMCA Dirt Track
1991 #20 Tony Stewart
eTopps
2003 #1 Tony Stewart/3194
Hi-Tech IRL
1997 #9 Tony Stewart XRC
Hi-Tech IRL Disney 200
1997 #D3 T.Stewart/B.Calkins' Cars
Hi-Tech IRL Phoenix
1997 #P7 R.Guerrero/T.Stewart Cars
Maxx
1999 #70 Tony Stewart CRC
1999 #71 Tony Stewart's Car
1999 #72 Tony Stewart RR
2000 #20 Tony Stewart
2000 #40 Tony Stewart's Car
2000 #80 Tony Stewart's Car FRF
Maxx Collectible Covers
2000 #CCTS Tony Stewart
Maxx Drive Time
2000 #DT1 Tony Stewart
Maxx FANtastic Finishes
1999 #F28 Tony Stewart's Car
2000 #FF5 Tony Stewart
Maxx Focus On A Champion
2000 #FC2 Tony Stewart
Maxx Race Ticket
1999 #RT18 Tony Stewart's Car
Maxx Racer's Ink
2000 #TS Tony Stewart
Maxx Racing Images
1999 #RI15 Tony Stewart
Maxx Speedway Boogie
2000 #SB10 Tony Stewart
Maxximum
2000 #4 Tony Stewart
Maxximum Dialed In
2000 #DI2 Tony Stewart
Maxximum Die Cuts
2000 #4 Tony Stewart
Maxximum MPH
2000 #4 Tony Stewart/20
Maxximum Pure Adrenaline
2000 #PA1 Tony Stewart
Maxximum Roots of Racing
2000 #R3 Tony Stewart
Maxximum Signatures
2000 #TS Tony Stewart
2000 #SL2 T.Stewart/B.Labonte EXCH
2000 #BTJ3 B.Labon/Stewart/Gibbs
2000 #GIB4 Stew/Leftlr/B.Labn/Gibbs
McFarlane NASCAR 3-Inch Series 1
2005 #120 Tony Stewart
McFarlane NASCAR Series 1
2003 #NNO Tony Stewart R w/o Hat
2003 #NNO Tony Stewart R w/Hat and Glasses
2003 #NNO T.Stewart H Trophy w/Hat
2003 #NNO T.Stewart H Trophy w/o Hat
McFarlane NASCAR Series 3
2005 #120 Tony Stewart R
2005 #121 Tony Stewart R Glasses
2005 #125 Tony Stewart H Kid Rock with Glasses
McFarlane NASCAR Series 5
2005 #90 Tony Stewart
McFarlane NASCAR Shrek 2 Boxed Sets
2004 #20 T.Stewart w/Donkey
National Trading Card Day
2004 #PP5 Tony Stewart
National Trading Card Day *
2004 #PP5 Tony Stewart
Press Pass
1999 #61 Tony Stewart YG
1999 #94 Tony Stewart PRE

2000 #4 Tony Stewart
2000 #42 Tony Stewart REP
2000 #44 Tony Stewart REP
2000 #55 Tony Stewart
2000 #67 Tony Stewart
2001 #6 Tony Stewart
2001 #53 Tony Stewart's Car
2001 #68 Tony Stewart REP
2001 #92 Tony Stewart SO
2002 #34 Tony Stewart
2002 #70 Tony Stewart REP
2002 #81 Tony Stewart's Car
2003 #31 Tony Stewart
2003 #61 Tony Stewart DS
2003 #72 Double Take WCS
2003 #84 Rags to Riches WCS
2003 #96 Tony Stewart's Car OTW
2004 #31B Tony Stewart skyline
2004 #69 Tony Stewart's Car OTW
2005 #15 Tony Stewart
2005 #83 Mark Martin/T.Stewart NS
2006 #16 Tony Stewart
2006 #93 Tony Stewart NS
2006 #94 Tony Stewart NS
2006 #100 Tony Stewart U
2006 #109 Tony Stewart TT
2006 #120 Tony Stewart Schedule
2007 #11 Tony Stewart
2007 #79 Tony Stewart's Car OT
2007 #91 Tony Stewart NS
2007 #103 Tony Stewart U
2008 #2 Tony Stewart
2008 #95 Tony Stewart's Car U
2008 #109 Tony Stewart Top 12
2008 #0 Cup Chase Matt Kenseth Tony Stewart Jeff Gordon Jimmie Johnson Denny Hamlin Kurt Busch Kevin Harvick Carl Edwards Kyle Busch Martin Truex Jr. Jeff Burton Clint Bowyer
Press Pass Autographs
1999 #19 Tony Stewart/500
2001 #42 Tony Stewart
2002 #66 Tony Stewart
2005 #56 Tony Stewart E/P
2006 #53 Tony Stewart NC
2007 #43 Tony Stewart NC P
2008 #40 Tony Stewart NC EXCH P
Press Pass Autographs Press Plates Black
2007 #23 Tony Stewart NC
2008 #32 Tony Stewart NC E
Press Pass Autographs Press Plates Cyan
2007 #24 Tony Stewart NC
2008 #33 Tony Stewart NC E
Press Pass Autographs Press Plates Magenta
2007 #25 Tony Stewart NC
2008 #33 Tony Stewart NC E
Press Pass Autographs Press Plates Yellow
2007 #24 Tony Stewart NC
2008 #32 Tony Stewart NC E
Press Pass Blaster Kmart
2006 #TSC Tony Stewart
Press Pass Blaster Target
2006 #TSB Tony Stewart
Press Pass Blaster Wal-Mart
2006 #TSA Tony Stewart
Press Pass Blue
2006 #B16 Tony Stewart
2006 #B93 Tony Stewart NS
2006 #B94 Tony Stewart NS
2006 #B100 Tony Stewart U
2006 #B109 Tony Stewart TT
2006 #B120 Tony Stewart Schedule
2007 #B11 Tony Stewart
2007 #B79 Tony Stewart's Car OT
2007 #B91 Tony Stewart NS
2007 #B103 Tony Stewart U
2008 #B2 Tony Stewart
2008 #B95 Tony Stewart's Car U
2008 #B109 Tony Stewart Top 12
Press Pass Burning Rubber
2000 #BR4 Tony Stewart
Press Pass Burning Rubber Autographs
2005 #BR-TS Tony Stewart/20
2006 #BR-TS Tony Stewart/20
2007 #BRS-TS Tony Stewart/20
Press Pass Burning Rubber Cars
2001 #BRC9 Tony Stewart/105
2002 #BRC10 Tony Stewart's Car
2003 #BRT9 Tony Stewart's Car
2004 #BRT13 Tony Stewart's Car
2005 #BRT10 Tony Stewart's Car
2006 #BRT16 Tony Stewart
Press Pass Burning Rubber Drivers
2001 #BRD9 Tony Stewart/90
2002 #BRD10 Tony Stewart
2003 #BRD9 Tony Stewart
2004 #BRD13 Tony Stewart
2005 #BRD10 Tony Stewart
2006 #BRD16 Tony Stewart
2007 #BRD3 Tony Stewart Martinsville 4-2
2007 #BRD12 Tony Stewart Daytona 7-1
2008 #BRD18 Tony Stewart Chicago
2008 #BRD19 Tony Stewart Indianapolis
2008 #BRD21 Tony Stewart Watkins
Press Pass Burning Rubber Drivers Autographs
2003 #BRD-TS Tony Stewart/20
Press Pass Burning Rubber Drivers Gold
2005 #BRD10 Tony Stewart
2006 #BRD16 Tony Stewart
2007 #BRD3 Tony Stewart Martinsville 4-2
2007 #BRD12 Tony Stewart Daytona 7-1
2008 #BRD18 Tony Stewart Chicago
2008 #BRD19 Tony Stewart Indianapolis
2008 #BRD21 Tony Stewart Watkins
Press Pass Burning Rubber Drivers Prime Cuts
2008 #BRD18 Tony Stewart Chicago
2008 #BRD19 Tony Stewart Indianapolis
2008 #BRD21 Tony Stewart Watkins
Press Pass Burning Rubber Team
2007 #BRT3 Tony Stewart Martinsville 4-2
2007 #BRT12 Tony Stewart Daytona 7-1
Press Pass Burning Rubber Teams
2008 #BRT18 Tony Stewart Chicago
2008 #BRT19 Tony Stewart Indianapolis
2008 #BRT21 Tony Stewart Watkins
Press Pass Burnouts

2007 #BO5 Tony Stewart
2008 #BO5 Tony Stewart
Press Pass Burnouts Blue
2007 #BO5 Tony Stewart
2008 #BO5 Tony Stewart
Press Pass Burnouts Gold
2007 #BO5 Tony Stewart
2008 #BO5 Tony Stewart
Press Pass Chef Boyardee
2000 #2 Tony Stewart
2000 #4 Tony Stewart
2000 #6 B.Labonte/T.Stewart
Press Pass Coca Cola AutoZone
2006 #TS Tony Stewart
Press Pass Coca-Cola Racing Family
2001 #2 B.Labonte/T.Stewart
2003 #11 Tony Stewart
Press Pass Coca-Cola Racing Family Regional
2003 #3 Tony Stewart SP
Press Pass Collector's Series Box Set
2007 #SB21 Tony Stewart
Press Pass Collectors Series Making the Show
2006 #MS17 Tony Stewart
Press Pass Collectors Series Sunday Best
2007 #CB21 Tony Stewart
Press Pass Cup Chase
2000 #CC15 Tony Stewart WIN
2001 #CC9 Tony Stewart
2002 #CC15 Tony Stewart
2003 #CCR15 Tony Stewart
2004 #CCR11 Tony Stewart
2005 #CCR8 Tony Stewart Winner
2006 #CCR1 Tony Stewart
2007 #CCR5 Tony Stewart Winner
2008 #CC11 Tony Stewart
Press Pass Cup Chase Die Cut Prizes
2000 #CC15 Tony Stewart
2001 #CC9 Tony Stewart
Press Pass Cup Chase Prizes
2002 #CC15 Tony Stewart
2002 #NNO Tony Stewart Tire
2003 #CCR15 Tony Stewart
2003 #CCR18 Tony Stewart Champion
2004 #CCR11 Tony Stewart
2005 #CCP8 Tony Stewart
2005 #NNO Tony Stewart Firesuit
2007 #CC3 Tony Stewart
Press Pass Double Burner
2001 #DB5 Tony Stewart
2002 #DB8 Tony Stewart
2003 #DB9 Tony Stewart
2004 #DB9 Tony Stewart
2005 #DB9 Tony Stewart
Press Pass Double Burner Exchange
2003 #DB9 Tony Stewart EXCH
2004 #DB9 Tony Stewart
2005 #DB9 Tony Stewart
Press Pass Double Burner Firesuit-Glove
2006 #DB9 Tony Stewart
2008 #DBTS Tony Stewart
Press Pass Double Burner Metal-Tire
2006 #DB8 Tony Stewart
2007 #DB-TS Tony Stewart
Press Pass Double Burner Metal-Tire Exchange
2007 #DB-TS Tony Stewart
Press Pass Eclipse
2002 #2 Tony Stewart
2003 #1 Tony Stewart
2003 #32 Tony Stewart ACC
2003 #41 Speed Demons WCS
2003 #45 CHAMP-agne Celebration WCS
2003 #50 Tony Stewart HS
2004 #7 Tony Stewart
2004 #7B Tony Stewart blue sky
2004 #34 Tony Stewart's Car
2004 #63 Tony Stewart P
2004 #73 Tony Stewart WCS
2004 #84 Tony Stewart LL
2005 #6 Tony Stewart
2005 #63 Tony Stewart P
2005 #66 Tony Stewart NS
2005 #69 Tony Stewart NS
2005 #84 Tony Stewart LL
2006 #1 Tony Stewart
2006 #45 Tony Stewart WS
2006 #50 Tony Stewart P
2006 #62 Tony Stewart TN
2006 #65 NCS Top-10 BA
2006 #69 Tony Stewart BA
2006 #70 Tony Stewart BA
2006 #71 Tony Stewart BA
2006 #72 Tony Stewart BA
2006 #78 Tony Stewart LL
2006 #85 Tony Stewart SM
2006 #0 Tony Stewart Champ
2006 #70 Tony Stewart BA
2007 #11 Tony Stewart
2007 #59 Tony Stewart NT
2007 #67 Tony Stewart NS
2007 #70 Tony Stewart NS
2007 #78 Tony Stewart NYC
2007 #59B Tony Stewart NT missing table
2008 #5 Tony Stewart
2008 #74 Tony Stewart Juan Pablo Montoya SO
2008 #75 Top 10 Drivers SO
2008 #78 Tony Stewart SO
2008 #58 Tony Stewart no background
Press Pass Eclipse Destination WIN
2004 #16 Tony Stewart
2004 #25 Tony Stewart
2005 #16 Tony Stewart
2005 #19 Tony Stewart
Press Pass Eclipse Double Hot Treads
2003 #DT1 B.Labonte/T.Stewart
Press Pass Eclipse Ecliptic
2007 #EC7 Tony Stewart
Press Pass Eclipse Escape Velocity
2008 #EV4 Tony Stewart
Press Pass Eclipse Gold
2007 #G11 Tony Stewart
2007 #G59 Tony Stewart NT
2007 #G67 Tony Stewart NS
2007 #G70 Tony Stewart NS
2007 #G78 Tony Stewart NYC
2008 #G5 Tony Stewart
2008 #G74 Tony Stewart Juan Pablo Montoya SO
2008 #G75 Top 10 Drivers SO
2008 #G78 Tony Stewart SO

Press Pass Eclipse Hyperdrive
2004 #HP3 Tony Stewart
2006 #HP2 Tony Stewart
2007 #HD1 Tony Stewart
2008 #HP1 Tony Stewart
Press Pass Eclipse Maxim
2004 #MX6 Tony Stewart
2005 #MX6 Tony Stewart
Press Pass Eclipse Previews
2003 #1 Tony Stewart
2003 #32 Tony Stewart ACC
2004 #7 Tony Stewart
2005 #EB6 Tony Stewart
2005 #EB63 Tony Stewart P
2005 #EB66 Tony Stewart NS
2005 #EB69 Tony Stewart NS
2005 #EB84 Tony Stewart LL/1
2006 #EB1 Tony Stewart
2006 #EB62 Tony Stewart TN
2007 #EB11 Tony Stewart
2008 #EB5 Tony Stewart
2008 #EB74 Tony Stewart Juan Pablo Montoya SO
2008 #EB75 Top 10 Drivers SO
2008 #EB78 Tony Stewart SO
Press Pass Eclipse Racing Champions
2002 #RC11 Tony Stewart
2002 #RC16 Tony Stewart
2002 #RC24 Tony Stewart
2003 #RC1 Tony Stewart
2003 #RC6 Tony Stewart
2003 #RC13 Tony Stewart
2003 #RC23 Tony Stewart
2006 #RC7 Tony Stewart
2006 #RC15 Tony Stewart NBS
2007 #RC4 Tony Stewart
2007 #RC26 Tony Stewart
Press Pass Eclipse Red
2007 #R11 Tony Stewart
2007 #R59 Tony Stewart NT
2007 #R67 Tony Stewart NS
2007 #R70 Tony Stewart NS
2007 #R78 Tony Stewart NYC
2008 #R5 Tony Stewart
2008 #R74 Tony Stewart Juan Pablo Montoya SO
2008 #R75 Top 10 Drivers SO
2008 #R78 Tony Stewart SO
Press Pass Eclipse Samples
2002 #2 Tony Stewart
2003 #1 Tony Stewart
2003 #32 Tony Stewart ACC
2003 #41 Speed Demons WCS
2003 #45 CHAMP-agne Celebration WCS
2003 #50 Tony Stewart HS
2004 #7 Tony Stewart
2004 #34 Tony Stewart's Car
2004 #63 Tony Stewart P
2004 #64 Tony Stewart WCS
2004 #84 Tony Stewart LL
2005 #6 Tony Stewart
2005 #63 Tony Stewart P
2005 #66 Tony Stewart NS
2005 #69 Tony Stewart NS
2005 #84 Tony Stewart LL
Press Pass Eclipse Skidmarks
2002 #SK8 Tony Stewart
2003 #SM3 Tony Stewart
2004 #SM13 Tony Stewart
2005 #SM13 Tony Stewart
2006 #SM16 Tony Stewart
2007 #SM10 Tony Stewart
Press Pass Eclipse Skidmarks Holofoil
2004 #SM13 Tony Stewart
2005 #SM13 Tony Stewart
2006 #SM16 Tony Stewart
2007 #SM10 Tony Stewart
Press Pass Eclipse Solar Eclipse
2002 #S2 Tony Stewart
2003 #P1 Tony Stewart
2003 #P32 Tony Stewart ACC
2003 #P41 Speed Demons WCS
2003 #P45 CHAMP-agne Celebration WCS
2003 #P50 Tony Stewart HS
Press Pass Eclipse Star Tracks
2008 #ST2 Tony Stewart
Press Pass Eclipse Star Tracks Holofoil
2008 #ST2 Tony Stewart
Press Pass Eclipse Stellar
2008 #ST4 Tony Stewart
Press Pass Eclipse Supernova
2002 #SN9 Tony Stewart
2003 #SN11 Tony Stewart
2006 #SU5 Tony Stewart
Press Pass Eclipse Supernova Numbered
2002 #SN9 Tony Stewart
Press Pass Eclipse Teammates Autographs
2004 #4 B.Labonte/T.Stewart
2005 #1 Stewart/Leffler/Labonte
2007 #4 Hamlin/Stewart/Yeley
2008 #BHS Kyle Busch Denny Hamlin Tony Stewart/35
Press Pass Eclipse Under Cover Autographs
2005 #UCTS Tony Stewart/20
2006 #TS Tony Stewart/20
2007 #UC-TS Tony Stewart/20
Press Pass Eclipse Under Cover Cars
2003 #UCT5 Tony Stewart
2004 #UCD14 Tony Stewart
2005 #UCT13 Tony Stewart
2006 #UCT9 Tony Stewart
Press Pass Eclipse Under Cover Double Cover
2002 #DC7 B.Labonte/T.Stewart
2003 #DC7 B.Labonte/T.Stewart
2004 #DC10 B.Labonte/T.Stewart
2005 #DC5 B.Labonte/T.Stewart
Press Pass Eclipse Under Cover Driver Gold
2003 #UCD5 Tony Stewart
2004 #UCD14 Tony Stewart
Press Pass Eclipse Under Cover Driver Red
2003 #UCD5 Tony Stewart
2004 #UCD14 Tony Stewart
2005 #UCD13 Tony Stewart
Press Pass Eclipse Under Cover Driver Silver
2003 #UCD5 Tony Stewart
2004 #UCD14 Tony Stewart
Press Pass Eclipse Under Cover Drivers
2002 #CD6 Tony Stewart
2007 #UCD9 Tony Stewart
2008 #UCD2 Tony Stewart
Press Pass Eclipse Under Cover Drivers Eclipse
2007 #UCD9 Tony Stewart
2008 #UCD2 Tony Stewart
Press Pass Eclipse Under Cover Drivers Gold
2006 #UCD9 Tony Stewart
Press Pass Eclipse Under Cover Drivers Holofoil
2005 #UCD13 Tony Stewart
2006 #UCD9 Tony Stewart
Press Pass Eclipse Under Cover Drivers Name
2007 #UCD9 Tony Stewart
2008 #UCD2 Tony Stewart
Press Pass Eclipse Under Cover Drivers NASCAR
2007 #UCD9 Tony Stewart
2008 #UCD2 Tony Stewart
Press Pass Eclipse Under Cover Drivers Silver
2005 #UCD13 Tony Stewart
2006 #UCD9 Tony Stewart
Press Pass Eclipse Under Cover Gold Cars
2002 #CD6 Tony Stewart
Press Pass Eclipse Under Cover Gold Drivers
2002 #CD6 Tony Stewart
Press Pass Eclipse Under Cover Holofoil Drivers
2002 #CD6 Tony Stewart
Press Pass Eclipse Under Cover Teams
2007 #UCT9 Tony Stewart
2008 #UCT2 Tony Stewart
Press Pass Eclipse Under Cover Teams NASCAR
2007 #UCT9 Tony Stewart
2008 #UCT2 Tony Stewart
Press Pass Eclipse Warp Speed
2002 #WS5 Tony Stewart
2003 #WS5 Tony Stewart
Press Pass Four Wide
2006 #FW-TS Tony Stewart
2007 #FW-TS Tony Stewart
2008 #FW-TS Tony Stewart
Press Pass Four Wide Checkered
2007 #FW-TS Tony Stewart
2008 #FW-TS Tony Stewart
Press Pass Four Wide Checkered Exchange
2007 #FW-TS Tony Stewart
Press Pass Four Wide Checkered Flag
2006 #FW-TS Tony Stewart
Press Pass Four Wide Exchange
2007 #FW-TS Tony Stewart
Press Pass Game Face
2005 #GF7 Tony Stewart
Press Pass Gatorade Front Runner Award
2000 #4 Tony Stewart
Press Pass Gold
2006 #G16 Tony Stewart
2006 #G93 Tony Stewart NS
2006 #G94 Tony Stewart NS
2006 #G100 Tony Stewart U
2006 #G109 Tony Stewart TT
2006 #G120 Tony Stewart Schedule
2007 #G11 Tony Stewart
2007 #G79 Tony Stewart's Car OT
2007 #G91 Tony Stewart NS
2007 #G103 Tony Stewart U
2008 #G2 Tony Stewart
2008 #G95 Tony Stewart's Car U
2008 #G109 Tony Stewart Top 12
Press Pass Gold Holofoil
2003 #P31 Tony Stewart
2003 #P61 Tony Stewart DS
2003 #P72 Double Take WCS
2003 #P84 Rags to Riches WCS
2003 #P96 Tony Stewart's Car OTW
Press Pass Ground Zero
2001 #GZ5 Tony Stewart
Press Pass Hot Treads
2001 #HT2 Tony Stewart/2405
2002 #HT5 Tony Stewart's Car/2300
2002 #HT36 Tony Stewart's Car/900
2004 #HTR12 Tony Stewart
2005 #HTR11 Tony Stewart
2007 #HT2 Tony Stewart
2008 #HT1 Tony Stewart
Press Pass Hot Treads Blue
2007 #HT2 Tony Stewart
2008 #HT1 Tony Stewart
Press Pass Hot Treads Gold
2007 #HT2 Tony Stewart
2008 #HT1 Tony Stewart
Press Pass Hot Treads Holofoil
2004 #HTR12 Tony Stewart
2005 #HTR11 Tony Stewart
Press Pass K-Mart
2007 #TS-C Tony Stewart
Press Pass Legends
2005 #29 Tony Stewart
2005 #44 Tony Stewart C
2006 #36 Tony Stewart
2007 #39 Tony Stewart
Press Pass Legends Autographs Black
2005 #26 Tony Stewart
2006 #32 Tony Stewart
Press Pass Legends Blue
2005 #29B Tony Stewart
2005 #44B Tony Stewart C
2006 #B36 Tony Stewart
2007 #B39 Tony Stewart
Press Pass Legends Bronze
2006 #Z36 Tony Stewart
2007 #Z39 Tony Stewart
Press Pass Legends Champion Threads & Treads Bronze
2006 #CTT-TS Tony Stewart
Press Pass Legends Champion Threads & Treads Gold
2006 #CTT-TS Tony Stewart
Press Pass Legends Champion Threads & Treads Silver
2006 #CTT-TS Tony Stewart
Press Pass Legends Champion Threads Bronze
2006 #CT-TS Tony Stewart
Press Pass Legends Champion Threads Gold
2006 #CT-TS Tony Stewart
Press Pass Legends Champion Threads Patch
2006 #CT-TS Tony Stewart
Press Pass Legends Champion Threads Silver
2006 #CT-TS Tony Stewart
Press Pass Legends Double Threads Bronze
2005 #DT-SL T.Stewart/T.Labonte
Press Pass Legends Double Threads Gold
2005 #DT-SL T.Stewart/T.Labonte
Press Pass Legends Double Threads Silver
2005 #DT-SL T.Stewart/T.Labonte
Press Pass Legends Gold
2005 #29G Tony Stewart
2005 #44G Tony Stewart C
2006 #G36 Tony Stewart
2007 #G39 Tony Stewart
Press Pass Legends Heritage Gold
2006 #HE10 Tony Stewart
Press Pass Legends Heritage Silver
2006 #HE10 Tony Stewart
Press Pass Legends Holofoil
2005 #29H Tony Stewart
2005 #44H Tony Stewart C
2006 #H36 Tony Stewart
2007 #H39 Tony Stewart
Press Pass Legends Press Plates Black
2005 #29 Tony Stewart
2005 #44 Tony Stewart C
2006 #PPB36 Tony Stewart
2007 #PP39 Tony Stewart
Press Pass Legends Press Plates Black Backs
2006 #PPB36B Tony Stewart
2007 #PP39 Tony Stewart
Press Pass Legends Press Plates Cyan
2005 #29 Tony Stewart
2005 #44 Tony Stewart C
2006 #PPC36 Tony Stewart
2007 #PP39 Tony Stewart
Press Pass Legends Press Plates Cyan Backs
2006 #PPC36B Tony Stewart
2007 #PP39 Tony Stewart
Press Pass Legends Press Plates Magenta
2005 #29 Tony Stewart
2005 #44 Tony Stewart C
2006 #PPM36 Tony Stewart
2007 #PP39 Tony Stewart
Press Pass Legends Press Plates Magenta Backs
2006 #PPM36B Tony Stewart
2007 #PP39 Tony Stewart
Press Pass Legends Press Plates Yellow
2005 #29 Tony Stewart
2005 #44 Tony Stewart C
2006 #PPY36 Tony Stewart
2007 #PP39 Tony Stewart
Press Pass Legends Press Plates Yellow Backs
2006 #PPY36B Tony Stewart
2007 #PP39 Tony Stewart
Press Pass Legends Previews
2005 #29 Tony Stewart
2005 #44 Tony Stewart C
2006 #EB36 Tony Stewart
2007 #EB39 Tony Stewart
Press Pass Legends Signature Series
2007 #TS Tony Stewart
Press Pass Legends Solo
2005 #29S Tony Stewart
2005 #44S Tony Stewart C
2006 #S36 Tony Stewart
2007 #S39 Tony Stewart
Press Pass Legends Sunday Swatches Bronze
2007 #TS-SS Tony Stewart
Press Pass Legends Sunday Swatches Gold
2007 #TS-SS Tony Stewart
Press Pass Legends Sunday Swatches Silver
2007 #TS-SS Tony Stewart
Press Pass Legends Threads & Treads Bronze
2005 #TTTS Tony Stewart
Press Pass Legends Threads & Treads Gold
2005 #TTTS Tony Stewart
Press Pass Legends Threads & Treads Silver
2005 #TTTS Tony Stewart
Press Pass Legends Triple Threads
2006 #TT-TS Tony Stewart
Press Pass Legends Victory Lane Bronze
2007 #VL8 Tony Stewart
Press Pass Legends Victory Lane Gold
2007 #VL8 Tony Stewart
Press Pass Legends Victory Lane Silver
2007 #VL8 Tony Stewart
Press Pass Making the Show Collector's Series
2004 #MS14 Tony Stewart
Press Pass Making the Show Collector's Series Tins
2004 #NNO Dale Jr/Stewart/J.Gordon
Press Pass Millennium
2000 #4 Tony Stewart
2000 #42 Tony Stewart
2000 #44 Tony Stewart
2000 #55 Tony Stewart
2000 #67 Tony Stewart
2001 #6 Tony Stewart
2001 #53 Tony Stewart's Car
2001 #68 Tony Stewart REP
2001 #92 Tony Stewart SO
Press Pass Oil Cans
2000 #OC1 Tony Stewart
Press Pass Optima
2000 #24 Tony Stewart
2000 #48 Tony Stewart WCL
2001 #25 Tony Stewart
2001 #48 Tony Stewart WCL
2002 #28 Tony Stewart
2003 #24 Tony Stewart
2003 #44 Tony Stewart UC
2004 #24 Tony Stewart
2004 #79 Tony Stewart CP
2004 #86 Tony Stewart RR
2005 #27 Tony Stewart
2005 #27B Tony Stewart Cup Chase
2005 #66 Tony Stewart DP
2005 #89 Tony Stewart's Car RTV
2005 #100 Tony Stewart CL
2006 #17 Tony Stewart
2006 #55 Tony Stewart's Car HS
2006 #70 Tony Stewart CP
2006 #83 Tony Stewart RTV Daytona
Press Pass Optima Cool Persistence
2002 #CP11 Tony Stewart
2003 #CP9 Tony Stewart
2004 #CP8 Tony Stewart
2005 #CP12 Tony Stewart
Press Pass Optima Corporate Cuts Cars
2005 #CCT1 Tony Stewart
Press Pass Optima Corporate Cuts Drivers
2005 #CCD1 Tony Stewart
Press Pass Optima Encore
2000 #EN7 Tony Stewart
Press Pass Optima Fan Favorite
2002 #FF25 Tony Stewart
2003 #FF23 Tony Stewart
2004 #FF22 Tony Stewart
2005 #FF24 Tony Stewart
2006 #FF21 Tony Stewart
Press Pass Optima G Force
2000 #GF23 Tony Stewart
2001 #GF25 Tony Stewart
2004 #GF3 Tony Stewart
Press Pass Optima Gold
2001 #25 Tony Stewart
2001 #48 Tony Stewart WCL
2002 #28 Tony Stewart
2003 #G24 Tony Stewart
2003 #G44 Tony Stewart UC
2004 #G24 Tony Stewart
2004 #G79 Tony Stewart CP
2004 #G86 Tony Stewart RR
2005 #G27 Tony Stewart
2005 #G66 Tony Stewart DP
2005 #G89 Tony Stewart's Car RTV
2005 #G100 Tony Stewart CL
2006 #G17 Tony Stewart
2006 #G55 Tony Stewart's Car HS
2006 #G70 Tony Stewart CP
2006 #G83 Tony Stewart RTV Daytona
Press Pass Optima On the Edge
2000 #OE6 Tony Stewart
2001 #OE8 Tony Stewart
Press Pass Optima Overdrive
2000 #OD8 Tony Stewart
Press Pass Optima Overdrive Square Cut
2000 #OD8 Tony Stewart
Press Pass Optima Platinum
2000 #24 Tony Stewart
2000 #48 Tony Stewart WCL
Press Pass Optima Previews
2003 #24 Tony Stewart
2004 #EB24 Tony Stewart
2005 #27 Tony Stewart
2006 #EB17 Tony Stewart
Press Pass Optima Promos
2002 #28 Tony Stewart
Press Pass Optima Q & A
2005 #QA7 Tony Stewart
2006 #QA12 Tony Stewart
Press Pass Optima Q and A
2002 #QA9 Tony Stewart
2003 #QA1 Tony Stewart
Press Pass Optima Q&A
2004 #QA4 Tony Stewart
Press Pass Optima Race Used Lugnuts Autographs
2002 #LNDA17 Tony Stewart/20
Press Pass Optima Race Used Lugnuts Cars
2000 #LC20 Tony Stewart's Car/50
2001 #LNC15 Tony Stewart's Car
2002 #LNC17 Tony Stewart's Car
Press Pass Optima Race Used Lugnuts Drivers
2000 #LD20 Tony Stewart/55
2001 #LND14 Tony Stewart
2002 #LND17 Tony Stewart
Press Pass Optima Rookie Relics Cars
2006 #RRT13 Tony Stewart
Press Pass Optima Rookie Relics Drivers
2006 #RRD13 Tony Stewart
Press Pass Optima Samples
2002 #28 Tony Stewart
2003 #24 Tony Stewart
2003 #44 Tony Stewart UC
2004 #24 Tony Stewart
2004 #79 Tony Stewart CP
2004 #86 Tony Stewart RR
2005 #27 Tony Stewart
2005 #66 Tony Stewart DP
2005 #89 Tony Stewart RTV
2005 #100 Tony Stewart CL
Press Pass Optima Thunder Bolts Autographs
2005 #TB-TS Tony Stewart/20
Press Pass Optima Thunder Bolts Cars
2003 #TBT16 Tony Stewart's Car
2004 #TBT3 Tony Stewart's Car
Press Pass Optima Thunder Bolts Drivers
2003 #TBD16 Tony Stewart/65
2004 #TBD3 Tony Stewart
Press Pass Panorama
2005 #PPP14 Tony Stewart
2005 #PPP32 Tony Stewart
2005 #PPP46 Tony Stewart
2005 #PPP47 Tony Stewart
2005 #PPP62 Tony Stewart
Press Pass Pitstop
2000 #PS13 Tony Stewart's Car
Press Pass Platinum
2002 #34 Tony Stewart
2002 #70 Tony Stewart REP
2002 #81 Tony Stewart's Car
2004 #P31 Tony Stewart
2004 #P69 Tony Stewart's Car OTW
2005 #P15 Tony Stewart
2005 #P83 Mark Martin/T.Stewart NS
2006 #P16 Tony Stewart
2006 #P93 Tony Stewart NS
2006 #P94 Tony Stewart NS
2006 #P100 Tony Stewart U
2006 #P109 Tony Stewart TT
2006 #P120 Tony Stewart Schedule
2007 #P11 Tony Stewart
2007 #P79 Tony Stewart's Car OT
2007 #P91 Tony Stewart NS
2007 #P103 Tony Stewart U
2008 #P2 Tony Stewart
2008 #P95 Tony Stewart's Car U
2008 #P109 Tony Stewart Top 12
Press Pass Premium
1998 #5 Tony Stewart RC
1999 #23 Tony Stewart CRC
2000 #10 Tony Stewart
2000 #35 Tony Stewart's Car
2000 #57 Tony Stewart
2000 #67 Tony Stewart
2001 #25 Tony Stewart
2001 #35 Tony Stewart
2001 #68 Tony Stewart CC
2001 #80 Tony Stewart PC
2002 #30 Tony Stewart
2002 #44 Tony Stewart's Car
2002 #48 Tony Stewart SW
2002 #50 Tony Stewart CL
2002 #68 Tony Stewart CH
2002 #80 Tony Stewart PC
2003 #27 Tony Stewart
2003 #56 Tony Stewart CC
2003 #78 Tony Stewart PC
2004 #2 Tony Stewart
2004 #50 Tony Stewart CL
2004 #56 Tony Stewart CC
2004 #72 Tony Stewart PC
2005 #30 Tony Stewart
2005 #41 Tony Stewart's Car M
2005 #46 Tony Stewart S
2005 #50 Tony Stewart CL
2005 #56 Tony Stewart CC
2005 #79 Tony Stewart PC
2006 #28 Tony Stewart
2006 #47 Tony Stewart NS
2006 #55 Tony Stewart CC
2006 #75 Tony Stewart PC
2007 #18 Tony Stewart
2007 #37 Tony Stewart's Car M
2007 #46 Tony Stewart SW
2007 #48 Tony Stewart SW
2007 #54 Tony Stewart RTTC
2007 #67 Tony Stewart MD
2007 #76 Tony Stewart DD
2007 #80 Tony Stewart FF
2008 #17 Tony Stewart
2008 #47 Tony Stewart's Car M
2008 #53 Tony Stewart SW Camping World 300
2008 #61 Tony Stewart EOP
2008 #68 Tony Stewart MD
2008 #85 Tony Stewart OD
Press Pass Premium Asphalt Jungle
2004 #A1 Tony Stewart
2005 #AJ5 Tony Stewart
2006 #AJ4 Tony Stewart
Press Pass Premium Burning Desire
1999 #FD6B Tony Stewart 1:18
Press Pass Premium Clean Air
2008 #CA12 Tony Stewart
Press Pass Premium Concrete Chaos
2007 #CC4 Tony Stewart
Press Pass Premium Going Global
2008 #GG3 Tony Stewart
Press Pass Premium Going Global Red
2008 #GG3 Tony Stewart
Press Pass Premium Gold
2001 #25 Tony Stewart
2001 #35 Tony Stewart
2001 #68 Tony Stewart CC
2001 #80 Tony Stewart PC
Press Pass Premium Hot Threads Autographs
2004 #HT-TS Tony Stewart/20
2005 #HT-TS Tony Stewart/20
2006 #HT-TS Tony Stewart/20
2007 #HT-TS Tony Stewart/20
Press Pass Premium Hot Threads Cars
2003 #HTT9 Tony Stewart
2005 #HTT5 Tony Stewart
2006 #HTT1 Tony Stewart
Press Pass Premium Hot Threads Drivers
2003 #HTD9 Tony Stewart
2005 #HTD5 Tony Stewart
2006 #HTD1 Tony Stewart
2007 #HTD5 Tony Stewart
2008 #HTD17 Tony Stewart
Press Pass Premium Hot Threads Drivers Bronze
2004 #HTD10 Tony Stewart
Press Pass Premium Hot Threads Drivers Bronze Retail
2004 #HTT10 Tony Stewart
Press Pass Premium Hot Threads Drivers Gold
2004 #HTD10 Tony Stewart
2005 #HTD5 Tony Stewart
2006 #HTD1 Tony Stewart
2007 #HTD5 Tony Stewart
2008 #HTD17 Tony Stewart
Press Pass Premium Hot Threads Drivers Silver
2004 #HTD10 Tony Stewart
Press Pass Premium Hot Threads Patch
2007 #HTP16 Tony Stewart Joe Gibbs Racing/8
2007 #HTP17 Tony Stewart Home Depot/15
Press Pass Premium Hot Threads Patches
2008 #HTP40 Tony Stewart #20
2008 #HTP41 Tony Stewart Smoke
2008 #HTP42 Tony Stewart NASCAR bar
2008 #HTP43 Tony Stewart U.S. Flag/8
Press Pass Premium Hot Threads Team
2007 #HTT5 Tony Stewart
2008 #HTT17 Tony Stewart
Press Pass Premium In The Zone
2000 #IZ1 Tony Stewart
2002 #IZ11 Tony Stewart
2003 #IZ10 Tony Stewart
2004 #IZ12 Tony Stewart
2005 #IZ3 Tony Stewart
2006 #IZ4 Tony Stewart
Press Pass Premium In the Zone Elite Edition
2004 #IZ12 Tony Stewart
2005 #IZ3 Tony Stewart
Press Pass Premium In the Zone Red
2006 #IZ4 Tony Stewart
Press Pass Premium Performance Driven
2000 #PD3 Tony Stewart
2001 #PD8 Tony Stewart
2002 #PD8 Tony Stewart
2003 #PD7 Tony Stewart
2004 #PD1 Tony Stewart
2005 #PD9 Tony Stewart
2007 #PD8 Tony Stewart
Press Pass Premium Performance Driven Red
2007 #PD8 Tony Stewart
Press Pass Premium Previews
2003 #27 Tony Stewart
2004 #2 Tony Stewart
2008 #EB17 Tony Stewart
2008 #EB61 Tony Stewart EOP
Press Pass Premium Race Used Firesuit
2000 #F7 Tony Stewart
Press Pass Premium Race Used Firesuit Cars
2001 #FC7 Tony Stewart
2002 #FC6 Tony Stewart
Press Pass Premium Race Used Firesuit Drivers
2001 #FD7 Tony Stewart
2002 #FD6 Tony Stewart
Press Pass Premium Red
2007 #R18 Tony Stewart
2007 #R37 Tony Stewart's Car M
2007 #R46 Tony Stewart SW
2007 #R48 Tony Stewart SW
2007 #R54 Tony Stewart RTTC
2007 #R67 Tony Stewart MD
2007 #R76 Tony Stewart DD
2007 #R80 Tony Stewart FF
2008 #17 Tony Stewart
2008 #47 Tony Stewart's Car M
2008 #53 Tony Stewart SW
2008 #61 Tony Stewart EOP
2008 #68 Tony Stewart MD
2008 #85 Tony Stewart OD
Press Pass Premium Red Reflectors
2002 #30 Tony Stewart
2002 #44 Tony Stewart's Car
2002 #48 Tony Stewart SW
2002 #50 Tony Stewart CL
2002 #68 Tony Stewart CH
2002 #80 Tony Stewart PC
2003 #27 Tony Stewart
2003 #56 Tony Stewart CC
2003 #78 Tony Stewart PC
Press Pass Premium Reflectors
1998 #5 Tony Stewart
1999 #R23 Tony Stewart
2000 #10 Tony Stewart
2000 #35 Tony Stewart
2000 #57 Tony Stewart
2000 #67 Tony Stewart
Press Pass Premium Samples
2002 #30 Tony Stewart
2002 #44 Tony Stewart's Car
2002 #48 Tony Stewart SW
2002 #50 Tony Stewart CL
2003 #27 Tony Stewart
2004 #2 Tony Stewart
2004 #50 Tony Stewart CL
2005 #30 Tony Stewart
2005 #41 Tony Stewart's Car M
2005 #46 Tony Stewart S
2005 #50 Tony Stewart CL
Press Pass Premium Target
2008 #TA4 Tony Stewart
Press Pass Premium Team Signed Baseballs
2008 #GIB Kyle Busch Denny Hamlin Tony Stewart
2008 #E-GIB Kyle Busch Denny Hamlin Tony Stewart Entry Card
Press Pass Previews
2003 #31 Tony Stewart
2004 #31 Tony Stewart
2006 #EB16 Tony Stewart
2006 #EB100 Tony Stewart U
2007 #EB11 Tony Stewart
2008 #EB2 Tony Stewart
2008 #EB109 Tony Stewart Top 12
Press Pass Previews Green
2005 #EB15 Tony Stewart
Press Pass Race Day
2007 #RD3 Tony Stewart
2008 #RD1 Tony Stewart
Press Pass Samples
2003 #31 Tony Stewart
2003 #61 Tony Stewart DS
2003 #72 Double Take WCS
2003 #84 Rags to Riches WCS
2003 #96 Tony Stewart's Car OTW
2004 #31 Tony Stewart
2004 #69 Tony Stewart's Car OTW
2005 #15 Tony Stewart
2005 #83 Mark Martin/T.Stewart NS
Press Pass Schedule
2004 #4 Tony Stewart
Press Pass Showcar
2002 #S11A Tony Stewart's Car
2003 #S11B Tony Stewart
2004 #S11B Tony Stewart's Car
2005 #SC10 Tony Stewart
Press Pass Showcar Die Cuts
2000 #SC17 Tony Stewart's Car
Press Pass Showman
2000 #SM17 Tony Stewart
2002 #S11A Tony Stewart
2003 #S11A Tony Stewart
2004 #S11A Tony Stewart
2005 #SM10 Tony Stewart
Press Pass Showman Die Cuts
2000 #SM17 Tony Stewart
Press Pass Showman/Showcar
2001 #S10A Tony Stewart
2001 #S10B Tony Stewart's Car
Press Pass Signings
1998 #21 Tony Stewart S
1999 #55 Tony Stewart/500
2000 #57 Tony Stewart
2001 #51 Tony Stewart P/T/V
2002 #65 Tony Stewart O
2003 #70 Tony Stewart O/S/V
2004 #59 Tony Stewart O/P/S/T
2005 #55 Tony Stewart P/S
2006 #57 Tony Stewart NC P/S
2007 #69 Tony Stewart NC
2008 #53 Tony Stewart
Press Pass Signings Blue
2007 #31 Tony Stewart NC
2008 #30 Tony Stewart
Press Pass Signings Gold
1999 #26 Tony Stewart/100
2000 #30 Tony Stewart
2001 #33 Tony Stewart P/T/V/S

2003 #71 Tony Stewart O/S/V
2004 #55 Tony Stewart O/S/T/V
2005 #52 Tony Stewart P/S
2006 #50 Tony Stewart NC P/S
2007 #52 Tony Stewart NC
2008 #43 Tony Stewart
Press Pass Signings Platinum
2005 #50 Tony Stewart P/S
Press Pass Signings Press Plates Black
2007 #40 Tony Stewart
2008 #38 Tony Stewart
Press Pass Signings Press Plates Cyan
2007 #39 Tony Stewart
2008 #38 Tony Stewart
Press Pass Signings Press Plates Magenta
2007 #42 Tony Stewart
2008 #38 Tony Stewart
Press Pass Signings Press Plates Yellow
2007 #40 Tony Stewart
2008 #38 Tony Stewart
Press Pass Signings Red Ink
2006 #14 Tony Stewart
Press Pass Signings Silver
2006 #53 Tony Stewart NC P/S
2007 #51 Tony Stewart NC
2008 #40 Tony Stewart
Press Pass Signings Transparent
2001 #11 Tony Stewart V/S
2002 #9 Tony Stewart O/P/S/T/V
2003 #8 Tony Stewart O/S/V
2004 #9 Tony Stewart O/S/T
Press Pass Skidmarks
1999 #61 Tony Stewart YR
1999 #94 Tony Stewart PRE
2000 #SK4 Tony Stewart
Press Pass Slideshow
2008 #SS17 Tony Stewart
Press Pass Snapshots
2003 #SN24 Tony Stewart
2004 #SN25 Tony Stewart
2005 #SN24 Tony Stewart
2007 #SN26 Tony Stewart
Press Pass Speedway
2008 #33 Tony Stewart
2008 #75 Tony Stewart UTH
2008 #81 Tony Stewart's Car RSG
2008 #84 Tony Stewart's Car WS
Press Pass Speedway Blur
2008 #B8 Tony Stewart
Press Pass Speedway Cockpit
2008 #CP23 Tony Stewart
Press Pass Speedway Corporate Cuts Drivers
2008 #CD-TS Tony Stewart
Press Pass Speedway Corporate Cuts Drivers Patches
2008 #CD-TS Tony Stewart
Press Pass Speedway Corporate Cuts Team
2008 #CT-TS Tony Stewart
Press Pass Speedway Garage Graphs Duals
2008 #SZ Tony Stewart Greg Zipadelli
Press Pass Speedway Gold
2008 #G33 Tony Stewart
2008 #G75 Tony Stewart UTH
2008 #G81 Tony Stewart's Car RSG
2008 #G84 Tony Stewart's Car WS
Press Pass Speedway Holofoil
2008 #H33 Tony Stewart
2008 #H75 Tony Stewart UTH
2008 #H81 Tony Stewart's Car RSG
2008 #H84 Tony Stewart's Car WS
Press Pass Speedway Previews
2008 #EB33 Tony Stewart
Press Pass Speedway Red
2008 #R33 Tony Stewart
2008 #R75 Tony Stewart UTH
2008 #R81 Tony Stewart's Car RSG
2008 #R84 Tony Stewart's Car WS
Press Pass Speedway Test Drive
2008 #TD4 Tony Stewart
Press Pass Stealth
1998 #44 Tony Stewart RC
1999 #31 Tony Stewart CRC
1999 #32 Tony Stewart's Car
1999 #54 Home Depot Ratchet TT
1999 #P1 Tony Stewart Promo
2000 #28 Tony Stewart
2000 #29 Tony Stewart's Car
2000 #66 Tony Stewart FF
2001 #22 Tony Stewart
2001 #23 Tony Stewart's Car
2001 #24 Tony Stewart
2001 #70 Tony Stewart SST
2002 #22 Tony Stewart
2002 #23 Tony Stewart's Car
2002 #24 Tony Stewart
2002 #61 Tony Stewart's Car SST
2002 #70 Tony Stewart WW
2003 #22 Tony Stewart
2003 #23 Tony Stewart's Car
2003 #24 Tony Stewart
2003 #70 Tony Stewart SF
2004 #31 Tony Stewart
2004 #32 Tony Stewart's Car
2004 #33 Tony Stewart
2004 #96 Tony Stewart SF
2005 #55 Tony Stewart
2005 #58 Tony Stewart's Car
2005 #61 Tony Stewart
2005 #86 Tony Stewart H
2005 #91 Tony Stewart SF
2006 #28 Tony Stewart
2006 #49 Stewart/Hamlin/Yeley TM
2006 #60 Tony Stewart F
2006 #79 Tony Stewart DD
2007 #24 Tony Stewart
2007 #51 Tony Stewart's Rig
2007 #59 Tony Stewart's Crew GC
2007 #65 Hamlin/Stewart/Yeley
2007 #87 Tony Stewart PO
2008 #32 Tony Stewart
2008 #44 Tony Stewart NNS
2008 #50 Tony Stewart's Rig C
2008 #59 Tony Stewart's Car GC
2008 #68 Denny Hamlin Tony Stewart Kyle Busch
2008 #81 Tony Stewart DO
2008 #88 Tony Stewart PM
Press Pass Stealth Autographed Hat Entry

2006 #PPH22 Tony Stewart
Press Pass Stealth Battle Armor Autographs
2008 #BASTS Tony Stewart/20
Press Pass Stealth Battle Armor Drivers
2007 #BAD10 Tony Stewart
2008 #BAD20 Tony Stewart
Press Pass Stealth Battle Armor Teams
2007 #BAT10 Tony Stewart
2008 #BAT20 Tony Stewart
Press Pass Stealth Behind the Numbers
2000 #BN6 Tony Stewart
2001 #BN5 Tony Stewart
2002 #BN5 Tony Stewart
Press Pass Stealth Big Numbers
1999 #BN16 Tony Stewart
Press Pass Stealth Big Numbers Die Cuts
1999 #BN16 Tony Stewart
Press Pass Stealth Chrome
2007 #24 Tony Stewart
2007 #51 Tony Stewart's Rig
2007 #59 Tony Stewart's Crew GC
2007 #65 Hamlin/Stewart/Yeley
2007 #87 Tony Stewart PO
2008 #32 Tony Stewart
2008 #44 Tony Stewart NNS
2008 #50 Tony Stewart's Rig C
2008 #59 Tony Stewart's Car GC
2008 #68 Denny Hamlin Tony Stewart Kyle Busch
2008 #81 Tony Stewart DO
2008 #88 Tony Stewart PM
2008 #81B Tony Stewart DO VAR
Press Pass Stealth Chrome Exclusives
2007 #X24 Tony Stewart
2007 #X51 Tony Stewart's Rig
2007 #X59 Tony Stewart's Crew GC
2007 #X65 Hamlin/Stewart/Yeley
2007 #X87 Tony Stewart PO
2008 #32 Tony Stewart
2008 #44 Tony Stewart NNS
2008 #50 Tony Stewart's Rig C
2008 #59 Tony Stewart's Car GC
2008 #68 Denny Hamlin Tony Stewart Kyle Busch
2008 #81 Tony Stewart DO
2008 #88 Tony Stewart PM
Press Pass Stealth Chrome Exclusives Gold
2008 #32 Tony Stewart
2008 #44 Tony Stewart NNS
2008 #50 Tony Stewart's Rig C
2008 #59 Tony Stewart's Car GC
2008 #68 Denny Hamlin Tony Stewart Kyle Busch
2008 #81 Tony Stewart DO
2008 #88 Tony Stewart PM
Press Pass Stealth Chrome Platinum
2007 #P24 Tony Stewart
2007 #P51 Tony Stewart's Rig
2007 #P59 Tony Stewart's Crew GC
2007 #P65 Hamlin/Stewart/Yeley
2007 #P87 Tony Stewart PO
Press Pass Stealth Corporate Cuts
2006 #CCD10 Tony Stewart
Press Pass Stealth EFX
2002 #FX7 Tony Stewart
2003 #FX10 Tony Stewart
2004 #EF4 Tony Stewart
2005 #EFX5 Tony Stewart
2006 #EFX1 Tony Stewart 1:112
Press Pass Stealth Fusion
1998 #44 Tony Stewart
1999 #F31 Tony Stewart
1999 #F32 Tony Stewart's Car
1999 #F54 Home Depot Ratchet TT
2000 #FS22 Tony Stewart
2000 #FS23 Tony Stewart
2000 #FS24 Tony Stewart
2000 #FS34 Tony Stewart
2000 #FS35 Tony Stewart's Car
2000 #FS36 Tony Stewart
2001 #F8 Tony Stewart
2002 #F11 Tony Stewart
2005 #FU7 Tony Stewart 1:48
2007 #F3 Tony Stewart
Press Pass Stealth Fusion Green
2000 #FS22 Tony Stewart
2000 #FS23 Tony Stewart
2000 #FS24 Tony Stewart
2000 #FS34 Tony Stewart
2000 #FS35 Tony Stewart
2000 #FS36 Tony Stewart
Press Pass Stealth Fusion Red
2000 #FS22 Tony Stewart
2000 #FS23 Tony Stewart
2000 #FS24 Tony Stewart
2000 #FS34 Tony Stewart
2000 #FS35 Tony Stewart
2000 #FS36 Tony Stewart
Press Pass Stealth Gear Grippers Autographs
2005 #GG-TS Tony Stewart/20
2006 #TS Tony Stewart/20
Press Pass Stealth Gear Grippers Cars
2003 #GGT8 Tony Stewart
2005 #GGT13 Tony Stewart
Press Pass Stealth Gear Grippers Drivers
2003 #GGD8 Tony Stewart
2004 #GGD16 Tony Stewart
2005 #GGD13 Tony Stewart
2006 #GGD5 Tony Stewart
Press Pass Stealth Gear Grippers Drivers Retail
2004 #GGT16 Tony Stewart
Press Pass Stealth Gold
2002 #22 Tony Stewart
2002 #23 Tony Stewart's Car
2002 #24 Tony Stewart
2002 #61 Tony Stewart's Car SST
2002 #70 Tony Stewart WW
Press Pass Stealth Headlines
1999 #SH6 Tony Stewart
Press Pass Stealth Holofoils
2001 #22 Tony Stewart
2001 #23 Tony Stewart
2001 #24 Tony Stewart
2001 #70 Tony Stewart SST
Press Pass Stealth Hot Pass
2006 #HP25 Tony Stewart
Press Pass Stealth Intensity
2000 #IN4 Tony Stewart
Press Pass Stealth Lap Leaders

2001 #LL8 Tony Stewart
2001 #LL26 Tony Stewart's Car
2002 #LL26 Tony Stewart
Press Pass Stealth Lap Leaders Clear Cars
2001 #LL26 Tony Stewart's Car
Press Pass Stealth Lap Leaders Clear Drivers
2001 #LL8 Tony Stewart
Press Pass Stealth Mach 07
2007 #M7-3 Tony Stewart
Press Pass Stealth Mach 08
2008 #M8-3 Tony Stewart
Press Pass Stealth Maximum Access
2007 #MA25 Tony Stewart
2008 #MA24 Tony Stewart
Press Pass Stealth Maximum Access Autographs
2007 #MA25 Tony Stewart
2008 #MA24 Tony Stewart
Press Pass Stealth No Boundaries
2005 #NB3 Tony Stewart
Press Pass Stealth Octane SLX
1999 #O21 Tony Stewart
1999 #O29 Tony Stewart's Car
Press Pass Stealth Octane SLX Die Cuts
1999 #O21 Tony Stewart
1999 #O29 Tony Stewart's Car
Press Pass Stealth Previews
2003 #22 Tony Stewart
2003 #23 Tony Stewart's Car
2003 #24 Tony Stewart
2004 #EB31 Tony Stewart
2004 #EB32 Tony Stewart's Car
2004 #EB33 Tony Stewart
2005 #55 Tony Stewart
2005 #58 Tony Stewart's Car
2005 #61 Tony Stewart
2006 #28 Tony Stewart
2007 #EB24 Tony Stewart
2007 #EB87 Tony Stewart PO
2008 #32 Tony Stewart
2008 #44 Tony Stewart NNS
2008 #88 Tony Stewart PM
Press Pass Stealth Profile
2000 #PR3 Tony Stewart
2001 #SP3 Tony Stewart
2002 #P3 Tony Stewart
2004 #P7 Tony Stewart 1:48
2005 #PR9 Tony Stewart
2006 #P7 Tony Stewart
Press Pass Stealth Race Used Glove Cars
2001 #RGC4 Tony Stewart/120
2002 #GLC3 Tony Stewart's Car
Press Pass Stealth Race Used Glove Drivers
2001 #RGD4 Tony Stewart/120
2002 #GLD3 Tony Stewart
Press Pass Stealth Race Used Gloves
1999 #G8 Tony Stewart/150
2000 #G12 Tony Stewart/100
Press Pass Stealth Red
2003 #P22 Tony Stewart
2003 #P23 Tony Stewart's Car
2003 #P24 Tony Stewart
2003 #P70 Tony Stewart SF
Press Pass Stealth Retail
2006 #28 Tony Stewart
2006 #49 Stewart/Hamlin/Yeley TM
2006 #60 Tony Stewart F
2006 #79 Tony Stewart DD
Press Pass Stealth Retail Gear Grippers Cars
2006 #GGT5 Tony Stewart
Press Pass Stealth Samples
2002 #22 Tony Stewart
2002 #23 Tony Stewart's Car
2002 #24 Tony Stewart
2002 #61 Tony Stewart's Car SST
2002 #70 Tony Stewart WW
2003 #22 Tony Stewart
2003 #23 Tony Stewart's Car
2003 #24 Tony Stewart
2003 #70 Tony Stewart SF
2004 #X31 Tony Stewart
2004 #X32 Tony Stewart's Car
2004 #X33 Tony Stewart
2004 #X96 Tony Stewart SF
2005 #55 Tony Stewart
2005 #58 Tony Stewart's Car
2005 #61 Tony Stewart
2005 #86 Tony Stewart H
2005 #91 Tony Stewart SF
Press Pass Stealth SST
2000 #SST5 Tony Stewart
Press Pass Stealth SST Cars
1999 #SS8 Tony Stewart's Car
Press Pass Stealth SST Drivers
1999 #SS8 Tony Stewart
Press Pass Stealth Synthesis
2008 #S4 Tony Stewart
Press Pass Stealth X-Ray
2004 #31 Tony Stewart
2004 #32 Tony Stewart's Car
2004 #33 Tony Stewart
2004 #96 Tony Stewart SF
2005 #X55 Tony Stewart
2005 #X58 Tony Stewart's Car
2005 #X61 Tony Stewart
2005 #X86 Tony Stewart H
2005 #X91 Tony Stewart SF
2006 #X28 Tony Stewart
2006 #X49 Stewart/Hamlin/Yeley TM
2006 #X60 Tony Stewart F
2006 #X79 Tony Stewart DD
Press Pass Target
2007 #TS-B Tony Stewart
2008 #TS-B Tony Stewart
Press Pass Target Race Win Tires
2007 #RW7 Tony Stewart Daytona 7-1
Press Pass Target Victory Tires
2008 #TT-TS Tony Stewart Indianapolis
Press Pass Techno-Retro
2000 #TR24 Tony Stewart
Press Pass Tony Stewart Fan Club
1999 #NNO Tony Stewart
2002 #NNO Tony Stewart
Press Pass Top 25 Drivers & Rides
2006 #C13 Tony Stewart's Car
2006 #D13 Tony Stewart
Press Pass Top Shelf

2002 #TS8 Tony Stewart
2003 #TS8 Tony Stewart
2004 #TS7 Tony Stewart
Press Pass Top Ten
2005 #TT4 Tony Stewart
Press Pass Total Memorabilia
2001 #TM5 Tony Stewart
Press Pass Total Memorabilia Power Pick
2002 #TM8 Tony Stewart
2003 #TM9 Tony Stewart
2004 #TM9 Tony Stewart
2005 #TM9 Tony Stewart
Press Pass Trackside
2000 #14 Tony Stewart
2000 #35 Tony Stewart's Car
2001 #15 Tony Stewart
2001 #47 Tony Stewart's Car
2001 #67 Tony Stewart TM
2001 #88 Tony Stewart CS
2002 #15 Tony Stewart
2002 #58 Tony Stewart RD
2002 #71 Tony Stewart's Car
2002 #80 Tony Stewart TM
2003 #29 Tony Stewart
2003 #74 T.Stewart/B.Labonte TM
2004 #28 Tony Stewart
2004 #65 T.Stewart/B.Labonte TM
2004 #105 Tony Stewart TT
2004 #116 Tony Stewart F
2005 #10 Tony Stewart
2005 #60 Tony Stewart's Car HS
2005 #68 Stewart/Leffler/B.Labonte TM
2005 #88 Tony Stewart GP
2005 #97 Tony Stewart F
Press Pass Trackside Dialed In
2000 #DI5 Tony Stewart
2002 #DI11 Tony Stewart
2003 #DI10 Tony Stewart
2004 #DI6 Tony Stewart
2005 #DI5 Tony Stewart
Press Pass Trackside Die Cuts
2000 #14 Tony Stewart
2000 #35 Tony Stewart
2001 #15 Tony Stewart
2001 #47 Tony Stewart's Car
2001 #67 Tony Stewart TM
2001 #88 Tony Stewart CS
Press Pass Trackside Generation Now
2002 #GN2 Tony Stewart
Press Pass Trackside Generation.now
2000 #GN5 Tony Stewart
Press Pass Trackside Gold Holofoil
2003 #P29 Tony Stewart
2003 #P74 T.Stewart/B.Labonte
Press Pass Trackside Golden
2000 #14 Tony Stewart
2000 #35 Tony Stewart
2001 #15 Tony Stewart
2001 #47 Tony Stewart's Car
2001 #67 Tony Stewart TM
2001 #88 Tony Stewart CS
2002 #G15 Tony Stewart
2003 #G29 Tony Stewart
2004 #G28 Tony Stewart
2004 #G65 T.Stewart/B.Labonte TM
2004 #G105 Tony Stewart TT
2004 #G116 Tony Stewart F
2005 #G10 Tony Stewart
2005 #G60 Tony Stewart's Car HS
2005 #G68 Stewart/Leffler/B.Labonte TM
2005 #G88 Tony Stewart GP
2005 #G97 Tony Stewart F
Press Pass Trackside Hat Giveaway
2003 #PPH27 Tony Stewart
2004 #PPH30 Tony Stewart
2005 #PPH31 Tony Stewart
Press Pass Trackside Hot Pass
2004 #HP16 Tony Stewart
2005 #16 Tony Stewart
Press Pass Trackside Hot Pass National
2004 #HP16 Tony Stewart
2005 #16 Tony Stewart
Press Pass Trackside Hot Pursuit
2003 #HP6 Tony Stewart
2005 #HP8 Tony Stewart
Press Pass Trackside License to Drive
2002 #32 Tony Stewart
2003 #LD18 Tony Stewart
Press Pass Trackside License to Drive Die Cuts
2002 #32 Tony Stewart
Press Pass Trackside Mirror Image
2001 #MI4 Tony Stewart
2002 #MI8 Tony Stewart
2003 #MI7 Tony Stewart
Press Pass Trackside Panorama
2000 #P36 Tony Stewart
Press Pass Trackside Pit Stoppers
2000 #PS7 Tony Stewart
Press Pass Trackside Pit Stoppers Autographs
2004 #PS-TS Tony Stewart/20
2005 #PSTS Tony Stewart/20
Press Pass Trackside Pit Stoppers Cars
2001 #PSC2 Tony Stewart's Car/250
2002 #PSC2 Tony Stewart's Car/350
2003 #PST7 Tony Stewart
2004 #PST7 Tony Stewart
2005 #PST5 Tony Stewart
Press Pass Trackside Pit Stoppers Drivers
2001 #PSD2 Tony Stewart/100
2002 #PSD2 Tony Stewart/150
2003 #PSD7 Tony Stewart
2004 #PSD7 Tony Stewart
2005 #PSD5 Tony Stewart
Press Pass Trackside Previews
2003 #29 Tony Stewart
2004 #EB28 Tony Stewart
2005 #10 Tony Stewart
2005 #88 Tony Stewart GP
Press Pass Trackside Runnin N' Gunnin
2000 #RG1 Tony Stewart
2001 #RG7 Tony Stewart
2002 #RG8 Tony Stewart
2004 #RG6 Tony Stewart
2005 #RG6 Tony Stewart
Press Pass Trackside Samples
2002 #15 Tony Stewart
2002 #58 Tony Stewart RD

2002 #71 Tony Stewart's Car
2002 #80 Tony Stewart TM
2003 #29 Tony Stewart
2003 #74 T.Stewart/B.Labonte TM
2004 #28 Tony Stewart
2004 #65 T.Stewart/B.Labonte TM
2004 #105 Tony Stewart TT
2004 #116 Tony Stewart F
2005 #10 Tony Stewart
2005 #60 Tony Stewart's Car HS
2005 #68 Stewart/Leffler/B.Labonte TM
2005 #88 Tony Stewart GP
2005 #97 Tony Stewart F
Press Pass Trackside Too Tough To Tame
2000 #TT4 Tony Stewart
Press Pass Triple Burner
2001 #TB5 Tony Stewart
2002 #TB8 Tony Stewart
2003 #TB9 Tony Stewart
2004 #TB9 Tony Stewart
2005 #TB9 Tony Stewart
Press Pass Triple Burner Exchange
2003 #TB9 Tony Stewart EXCH
2004 #TB9 Tony Stewart
2005 #TB9 Tony Stewart
Press Pass UMI Cup Chase
2005 #1 Cup Chase Drivers CL
2005 #2 Tony Stewart
Press Pass Velocity
2001 #VL5 Tony Stewart
2003 #VC8 Tony Stewart
2006 #VE6 Tony Stewart
2007 #V8 Tony Stewart
Press Pass Victory Lap
2003 #14 Tony Stewart
Press Pass Vintage
2001 #VN6 Tony Stewart
2002 #VN24 Tony Stewart
Press Pass Wal-Mart
2007 #TS-A Tony Stewart
2008 #TS-A Tony Stewart
Press Pass Wal-Mart Autographs
2007 #TS Tony Stewart
2008 #9 Tony Stewart EXCH
Press Pass Weekend Warriors
2008 #WW2 Tony Stewart
SLU Racing Winner's Circle
2000 #40 Tony Stewart FP
SP Authentic
1999 #3 Tony Stewart CRC
1999 #36 Tony Stewart's Car
1999 #81 Tony Stewart SP
2000 #10 Tony Stewart
2000 #85 Tony Stewart SUP
SP Authentic Cup Challengers
1999 #CC9 Tony Stewart
SP Authentic Dominance
2000 #D1 Tony Stewart
SP Authentic Driver's Seat
2000 #DS4 Tony Stewart
SP Authentic Driving Force
1999 #DF11 Tony Stewart
SP Authentic In the Driver's Seat
1999 #DS4 Tony Stewart
SP Authentic Overdrive
1999 #3 Tony Stewart
1999 #36 Tony Stewart CAR
1999 #81 Tony Stewart SP/20
SP Authentic Overdrive Gold
2000 #10 Tony Stewart/20
2000 #85 Tony Stewart SUP/20
SP Authentic Overdrive Silver
2000 #10 Tony Stewart
2000 #85 Tony Stewart SUP
SP Authentic Power Surge
2000 #PS3 Tony Stewart
SP Authentic Race for the Cup
2000 #R7 Tony Stewart
SP Authentic Sign of the Times
1999 #TS Tony Stewart
Sports Illustrated for Kids
2006 #9 Tony Stewart NASCAR
Sunoco OCC Postcards
2007 #TS Tony Stewart
Super Shots California Speedway
2002 #CS4 Tony Stewart's Car
Super Shots Sears Point CHP
2001 #SP3 Tony Stewart's Car
TRAKS
2006 #32 Tony Stewart
2006 #46 Tony Stewart's Car
2007 #28 Tony Stewart
2007 #61 Tony Stewart's Car CTG
2007 #75 Tony Stewart GP
2007 #86 Tony Stewart's Car NFS
2007 #99 Tony Stewart FT
TRAKS Autographs
2006 #36 Tony Stewart NC
TRAKS Autographs 25
2006 #34 Tony Stewart NC
Traks Corporate Cuts Driver
2007 #CCD13 Tony Stewart
Traks Corporate Cuts Patch
2007 #CCD13 Tony Stewart/4
Traks Corporate Cuts Team
2007 #CCT13 Tony Stewart
Traks Driver's Seat
2007 #DS4 Tony Stewart
2007 #DS4B Tony Stewart VAR
Traks Driver's Seat National
2007 #DS4 Tony Stewart
Traks Gold
2007 #G28 Tony Stewart
2007 #G61 Tony Stewart's Car CTG
2007 #G75 Tony Stewart GP
2007 #G86 Tony Stewart's Car NFS
2007 #G99 Tony Stewart FT
Traks Holofoil
2007 #H28 Tony Stewart
2007 #H61 Tony Stewart's Car CTG
2007 #H75 Tony Stewart GP
2007 #H86 Tony Stewart's Car NFS
2007 #H99 Tony Stewart FT
Traks Hot Pursuit
2007 #HP3 Tony Stewart
Traks Previews

2007 #EB28 Tony Stewart
2007 #EB75 Tony Stewart GP
Traks Red
2007 #R28 Tony Stewart
2007 #R61 Tony Stewart's Car CTG
2007 #R75 Tony Stewart GP
2007 #R86 Tony Stewart's Car NFS
2007 #R99 Tony Stewart FT
TRAKS Stickers
2006 #20 Tony Stewart
Traks Target Exclusives
2007 #TS-A Tony Stewart
Traks Track Time
2007 #TT8 Tony Stewart
Traks Wal-Mart Exclusives
2007 #TS-B Tony Stewart
Upper Deck MVP
2000 #20 Tony Stewart
2000 #48 Tony Stewart's Car
2000 #78 Tony Stewart's Car
2000 #101 Tony Stewart CL
Upper Deck MVP Cup Quest 2000
2000 #CQ5 Tony Stewart
Upper Deck MVP Gold Script
2000 #20 Tony Stewart
2000 #48 Tony Stewart
2000 #78 Tony Stewart
2000 #101 Tony Stewart CL
Upper Deck MVP Legends in the Making
2000 #LM10 Tony Stewart
Upper Deck MVP Magic Numbers
2000 #MTS Tony Stewart's Car
Upper Deck MVP Magic Numbers Autographs
2000 #MATS Tony Stewart's Car/20
Upper Deck MVP NASCAR Gallery
2000 #NG2 Tony Stewart
Upper Deck MVP NASCAR Stars
2000 #NS1 Tony Stewart
Upper Deck MVP ProSign
1999 #TSH Tony Stewart Gold
1999 #TSR Tony Stewart Silver
2000 #PSTS Tony Stewart
Upper Deck MVP Silver Script
2000 #20 Tony Stewart
2000 #48 Tony Stewart
2000 #78 Tony Stewart
2000 #101 Tony Stewart CL
Upper Deck MVP Super Script
2000 #20 Tony Stewart/20
2000 #48 Tony Stewart's Car/20
2000 #78 Tony Stewart's Car/20
2000 #101 Tony Stewart CL/20
Upper Deck Racing
2000 #4 Tony Stewart
2000 #45 Tony Stewart CL
Upper Deck Racing High Groove
2000 #HG4 Tony Stewart
Upper Deck Racing Record Pace
2000 #RP9 Tony Stewart
Upper Deck Racing Road Signs
2000 #RSTS Tony Stewart SP
Upper Deck Racing Speeding Ticket
2000 #ST4 Tony Stewart
Upper Deck Racing Thunder Road
2000 #TR6 Tony Stewart
Upper Deck Racing Trophy Dash
2000 #TD9 Tony Stewart
Upper Deck Racing Winning Formula
2000 #WF5 Tony Stewart
Upper Deck Road To The Cup
1998 #115 Tony Stewart RC
1999 #6 Tony Stewart CRC
1999 #58 Tony Stewart's Car
1999 #66 Tony Stewart FF
1999 #84 Tony Stewart HH
Upper Deck Road to the Cup NASCAR Chronicles
1999 #NC19 Tony Stewart
Upper Deck Road to the Cup Signature Collection
1999 #TS Tony Stewart
Upper Deck Road to the Cup Signature Collection Checkered Flag
1999 #TS Tony Stewart
Upper Deck Road to the Cup Upper Deck Profiles
1999 #P11 Tony Stewart
Upper Deck Victory Circle
1999 #88 Tony Stewart
2000 #22 Tony Stewart
2000 #64 Tony Stewart's Car
2000 #67 Tony Stewart's Car
2000 #80 Tony Stewart's Car
2000 #85 Tony Stewart CL
Upper Deck Victory Circle Exclusives Level 1 Silver
2000 #22 Tony Stewart
2000 #64 Tony Stewart's Car
2000 #67 Tony Stewart's Car
2000 #80 Tony Stewart's Car
2000 #85 Tony Stewart CL
Upper Deck Victory Circle Exclusives Level 2 Gold
2000 #22 Tony Stewart/20
2000 #64 Tony Stewart's Car/20
2000 #67 Tony Stewart's Car/20
2000 #80 Tony Stewart's Car/20
2000 #85 Tony Stewart CL/20
Upper Deck Victory Circle Income Statement
2000 #IS5 Tony Stewart
Upper Deck Victory Circle Income Statement LTD
2000 #IS5 Tony Stewart
Upper Deck Victory Circle PowerDeck
2000 #PD4 Tony Stewart
Upper Deck Victory Circle Signature Collection
2000 #TS Tony Stewart
Upper Deck Victory Circle Signature Collection Gold
2000 #5 Tony Stewart/20
Upper Deck Victory Circle UD Exclusives
1999 #88 Tony Stewart
Upper Deck Victory Circle Winning Material Tire
2000 #TTS Tony Stewart

VIP
1998 #36 Tony Stewart RC
1999 #25 Tony Stewart CRC
1999 #48 Tony Stewart's Car
2000 #11 Tony Stewart
2000 #27 Tony Stewart V
2000 #36 Tony Stewart DF
2001 #11 Tony Stewart
2001 #27 Tony Stewart SM
2001 #37 Tony Stewart RT
2001 #48 Tony Stewart AS
2002 #9 Tony Stewart
2002 #21 Tony Stewart SG
2002 #27 Tony Stewart SG
2002 #32 Tony Stewart AS
2003 #16 Tony Stewart
2004 #16 Tony Stewart
2004 #36 Tony Stewart's Car R
2004 #60 Tony Stewart HR
2004 #75 Tony Stewart BTN
2005 #27 Tony Stewart
2005 #39 Tony Stewart's Car R
2005 #78 Tony Stewart BN
2005 #86 Tony Stewart ATML
2006 #26 Tony Stewart
2006 #39 Tony Stewart's Car R
2006 #45 Tony Stewart SG
2006 #55 Tony Stewart BTN
2006 #72 Tony Stewart RF
2007 #27 Tony Stewart
2007 #41 Tony Stewart's Car R
2007 #52 Tony Stewart's Car SV
2007 #63 Tony Stewart Red C
VIP Double Take
1999 #DT3 Tony Stewart
VIP Driver's Choice
2001 #DC5 Tony Stewart
2002 #DC5 Tony Stewart
2005 #DC6 Tony Stewart
VIP Driver's Choice Die Cuts
2005 #DC6 Tony Stewart
VIP Driver's Choice Precious Metal
2001 #DC5 Tony Stewart
VIP Driver's Choice Transparent
2001 #DC5 Tony Stewart
2002 #DC5 Tony Stewart
VIP Driver's Choice Transparent LTD
2002 #DC5 Tony Stewart
VIP Explosives
1998 #36 Tony Stewart
1999 #X25 Tony Stewart
1999 #X48 Tony Stewart's Car
2000 #X11 Tony Stewart
2000 #X27 Tony Stewart V
2000 #X36 Tony Stewart DF
2001 #11 Tony Stewart
2001 #27 Tony Stewart SM
2001 #37 Tony Stewart RT
2001 #48 Tony Stewart AS
2002 #X9 Tony Stewart
2002 #X21 Tony Stewart SG
2002 #X27 Tony Stewart SG
2002 #X32 Tony Stewart AS
2003 #X16 Tony Stewart
VIP Explosives Lasers
1999 #25 Tony Stewart
1999 #48 Tony Stewart's Car
2000 #LX11 Tony Stewart
2000 #LX27 Tony Stewart V
2000 #LX36 Tony Stewart DF
2001 #LX11 Tony Stewart
2001 #LX27 Tony Stewart SM
2001 #LX37 Tony Stewart RT
2001 #LX48 Tony Stewart AS
2002 #LX9 Tony Stewart
2002 #LX21 Tony Stewart SG
2002 #LX27 Tony Stewart SG
2002 #LX32 Tony Stewart AS
VIP Gear Gallery
2007 #GG9 Tony Stewart
VIP Gear Gallery Transparent
2007 #GG9 Tony Stewart
VIP Get A Grip Drivers
2007 #GGD12 Tony Stewart
VIP Get A Grip Teams
2007 #GGT12 Tony Stewart
VIP Head Gear
1999 #HG3 Tony Stewart
2000 #HG3 Tony Stewart
2002 #HG7 Tony Stewart
2004 #HG10 Tony Stewart
2005 #10 Tony Stewart
2006 #HG8 Tony Stewart
VIP Head Gear Die Cuts
2002 #HG7 Tony Stewart
VIP Head Gear Explosives
2000 #HG3 Tony Stewart
VIP Head Gear Explosives Laser Die Cuts
2000 #HG3 Tony Stewart
VIP Head Gear Plastic
1999 #HG3 Tony Stewart
VIP Head Gear Transparent
2004 #HG10 Tony Stewart
2005 #10 Tony Stewart
2006 #HG8 Tony Stewart
VIP Lap Leader
2006 #LL1 Tony Stewart
VIP Lap Leader Transparent
2006 #LL1 Tony Stewart
VIP Lap Leaders
2000 #LL2 Tony Stewart
2004 #LL6 Tony Stewart
2005 #6 Tony Stewart
VIP Lap Leaders Explosives
2000 #LL2 Tony Stewart
VIP Lap Leaders Explosives Lasers
2000 #LL2 Tony Stewart
VIP Lap Leaders Transparent
2004 #LL6 Tony Stewart
2005 #6 Tony Stewart
VIP Laser Explosive
2003 #LX16 Tony Stewart
VIP Making the Show
2000 #MS21 Tony Stewart
2001 #10 Tony Stewart
2002 #MS11 Tony Stewart
2003 #MS10 Tony Stewart
2004 #MS14 Tony Stewart
2005 #14 Tony Stewart
2006 #MS17 Tony Stewart
VIP Mile Masters
2001 #MM2 Tony Stewart
2002 #MM2 Tony Stewart
2003 #MM10Tony Stewart
VIP Mile Masters National
2003 #MM10Tony Stewart
VIP Mile Masters Precious Metal
2001 #MM2 Tony Stewart
VIP Mile Masters Transparent
2001 #MM2 Tony Stewart
2002 #MM2 Tony Stewart
2003 #MM10Tony Stewart
VIP Mile Masters Transparent LTD
2002 #MM2 Tony Stewart
2003 #MM10Tony Stewart
VIP Out of the Box
1999 #OB11 Tony Stewart
VIP Pedal To The Metal
2007 #PM1 Tony Stewart
VIP Previews
2003 #16 Tony Stewart
2004 #EB16 Tony Stewart
2004 #EB36 Tony Stewart's Car R
2005 #EB27 Tony Stewart
2005 #EB39 Tony Stewart's Car R
2007 #EB27 Tony Stewart
VIP Race Used Sheet Metal Cars
2002 #SC8 Tony Stewart's Car
VIP Race Used Sheet Metal Drivers
2002 #SD8 Tony Stewart
VIP Rear View Mirror
1999 #RM9 Tony Stewart
2000 #RM6 Tony Stewart
2001 #RV6 Tony Stewart
2002 #RM6 Tony Stewart
VIP Rear View Mirror Die Cuts
2001 #RV6 Tony Stewart
2002 #RM6 Tony Stewart
VIP Rear View Mirror Explosives
2000 #RM6 Tony Stewart
VIP Rear View Mirror Explosives Laser Die Cuts
2000 #RM6 Tony Stewart
VIP Samples
2002 #9 Tony Stewart
2002 #21 Tony Stewart SG
2002 #27 Tony Stewart SG
2002 #32 Tony Stewart AS
2003 #16 Tony Stewart
2004 #16 Tony Stewart
2004 #36 Tony Stewart's Car R
2004 #60 Tony Stewart HR
2004 #75 Tony Stewart BTN
2005 #27 Tony Stewart
2005 #39 Tony Stewart's Car R
2005 #78 Tony Stewart BN
2005 #86 Tony Stewart ATML
VIP Sheet Metal
1999 #SM6 Tony Stewart
2000 #SM6 Tony Stewart
VIP Sheet Metal Cars
2001 #SC4 Tony Stewart's Car
VIP Sheet Metal Drivers
2001 #SD4 Tony Stewart
VIP Solos
1998 #36 Tony Stewart RC
VIP Sunday Best
2007 #SB21 Tony Stewart
VIP Tin
2003 #CT16 Tony Stewart
VIP Tradin' Paint Autographs
2004 #TP-TS Tony Stewart/20
2005 #TS Tony Stewart/20
2006 #TP-TS Tony Stewart/20
VIP Tradin' Paint Bronze
2004 #TPT4 Tony Stewart
VIP Tradin' Paint Cars
2003 #TPT9 Tony Stewart's Car
2005 #TPT4 Tony Stewart
VIP Tradin' Paint Cars Bronze
2006 #TPT17 Tony Stewart
VIP Tradin' Paint Drivers
2003 #TPD9 Tony Stewart
2005 #TPD4 Tony Stewart
VIP Tradin' Paint Drivers Gold
2006 #TPD17 Tony Stewart
VIP Tradin' Paint Drivers Silver
2006 #TPD17 Tony Stewart
VIP Tradin' Paint Gold
2004 #TPD4 Tony Stewart
VIP Tradin' Paint Silver
2004 #TPD4 Tony Stewart
VIP Trophy Club
2007 #TC1 Tony Stewart
VIP Trophy Club Transparent
2007 #TC1 Tony Stewart
VIP Under the Lights
2000 #UL5 Tony Stewart
VIP Under the Lights Explosives
2000 #UL5 Tony Stewart
VIP Under the Lights Explosives Lasers
2000 #UL5 Tony Stewart
Wheels
1998 #58 Tony Stewart RC
1998 #63 Tony Stewart's Car
1999 #33 Tony Stewart CRC
1999 #68 Tony Stewart's Car
1999 #95 Tony Stewart
Wheels American Thunder
2003 #19 Tony Stewart
2003 #26 Tony Stewart SS
2003 #32 Tony Stewart DT
2004 #24 Tony Stewart
2004 #39 Tony Stewart AS
2004 #78 Tony Stewart CC
2005 #27 Tony Stewart
2005 #43 Tony Stewart AS
2005 #50 Tony Stewart's Car HR
2005 #58 Tony Stewart DT
2005 #73 Tony Stewart RR
2006 #30 Tony Stewart
2006 #35 Tony Stewart DT
2006 #50 Tony Stewart's Car HR
2006 #61 Tony Stewart GR
2006 #71 Tony Stewart SS
2006 #75 Tony Stewart MIA
2006 #88 Tony Stewart NN
2007 #33 Tony Stewart
2007 #44 Tony Stewart's Car DT
2007 #52 Tony Stewart's Car HR
2007 #61 Tony Stewart RW
2007 #68 Tony Stewart BP
2007 #74 Tony Stewart HC
Wheels American Thunder American Dreams
2007 #AD12 Tony Stewart
Wheels American Thunder American Dreams Gold
2007 #ADG12 Tony Stewart
Wheels American Thunder American Eagle
2003 #AE2 Tony Stewart
Wheels American Thunder American Muscle
2003 #AM9 Tony Stewart
2004 #AM6 Tony Stewart
2006 #AM3 Tony Stewart
2007 #AM2 Tony Stewart
Wheels American Thunder American Racing Idol
2006 #RI10 Tony Stewart
Wheels American Thunder American Racing Idol Golden
2006 #RI10 Tony Stewart
Wheels American Thunder Autographed Hat Instant Winner
2007 #AH38 Tony Stewart
Wheels American Thunder Born On
2003 #BO19 Tony Stewart
2003 #BO26 Tony Stewart SS
2003 #BO32 Tony Stewart DT
Wheels American Thunder Cup Quest
2004 #CQ4 Tony Stewart
Wheels American Thunder Double Hat
2006 #DH23 Tony Stewart
2007 #DH7 Tony Stewart
Wheels American Thunder Golden Eagle
2003 #AEG2 Tony Stewart
Wheels American Thunder Grandstand
2006 #GS21 Tony Stewart
Wheels American Thunder Head to Toe
2003 #HT7 Tony Stewart
2005 #HT6 Tony Stewart
2006 #HT4 Tony Stewart
2007 #HT2 Tony Stewart
Wheels American Thunder Heads Up Manufacturer
2003 #HUM21 Tony Stewart
Wheels American Thunder Heads Up Team
2003 #HUT19 Tony Stewart/60
Wheels American Thunder Heads Up Winston
2003 #HUW21 Tony Stewart
Wheels American Thunder Holofoil
2003 #P19 Tony Stewart
2003 #P26 Tony Stewart SS
2003 #P32 Tony Stewart DT
Wheels American Thunder Medallion
2005 #MD11 Tony Stewart
Wheels American Thunder Post Mark
2003 #PM16 Tony Stewart
2004 #PM13 Tony Stewart
Wheels American Thunder Previews
2003 #19 Tony Stewart
2003 #26 Tony Stewart SS
2003 #32 Tony Stewart DT
2004 #EB24 Tony Stewart
2004 #EB39 Tony Stewart AS
2005 #27 Tony Stewart
2006 #EB30 Tony Stewart
2006 #EB75 Tony Stewart MIA
2007 #EB33 Tony Stewart
2007 #EB52 Tony Stewart's Car HR
Wheels American Thunder Pushin Pedal
2003 #PP7 Tony Stewart
2004 #PP15 Tony Stewart
2005 #PP8 Tony Stewart
Wheels American Thunder Pushin' Pedal
2006 #PP4 Tony Stewart
2007 #PP2 Tony Stewart
Wheels American Thunder Rookie Thunder
2003 #RT32 Tony Stewart
Wheels American Thunder Samples
2003 #P19 Tony Stewart
2003 #P26 Tony Stewart SS
2003 #P32 Tony Stewart DT
2004 #24 Tony Stewart
2004 #39 Tony Stewart AS
2004 #78 Tony Stewart CC
2005 #27 Tony Stewart
2005 #43 Tony Stewart AS
2005 #50 Tony Stewart's Car HR
2005 #58 Tony Stewart DT
2005 #73 Tony Stewart RR
Wheels American Thunder Thunder Road
2003 #TR3 Tony Stewart
2004 #TR10 Tony Stewart
2005 #TR10 Tony Stewart
2006 #TR6 Tony Stewart
2007 #TR17 Tony Stewart
Wheels American Thunder Thunder Strokes
2007 #37 Tony Stewart
Wheels American Thunder Thunder Strokes Press Plates Black
2007 #37 Tony Stewart
Wheels American Thunder Thunder Strokes Press Plates Cyan
2007 #37 Tony Stewart
Wheels American Thunder Thunder Strokes Press Plates Magenta
2007 #37 Tony Stewart
Wheels American Thunder Thunder Strokes Press Plates Yellow
2007 #37 Tony Stewart
Wheels American Thunder Triple Hat
2003 #TH12 Tony Stewart
2004 #TH21 Tony Stewart
2005 #TH23 Tony Stewart
Wheels Autographs
1999 #22 Tony Stewart/350
2004 #63 Tony Stewart AT
2005 #56 Tony Stewart
2006 #58 Tony Stewart NC
2007 #38 Tony Stewart NC HG
2008 #31 Tony Stewart NC HG EXCH
Wheels Autographs Chase Edition
2008 #8 Tony Stewart NC EXCH
Wheels Autographs Press Plates Black
2007 #37 Tony Stewart NC
2008 #31 Tony Stewart NC
Wheels Autographs Press Plates Cyan
2007 #37 Tony Stewart NC
2008 #31 Tony Stewart NC
Wheels Autographs Press Plates Magenta
2007 #37 Tony Stewart NC
2008 #31 Tony Stewart NC
Wheels Autographs Press Plates Yellow
2007 #38 Tony Stewart NC
2008 #31 Tony Stewart NC
Wheels Golden
1998 #58 Tony Stewart
1998 #63 Tony Stewart's Car
1999 #33 Tony Stewart
1999 #68 Tony Stewart
1999 #95 Tony Stewart
Wheels High Gear
1999 #45 Tony Stewart
1999 #61 Tony Stewart
2000 #5 Tony Stewart
2000 #32 Tony Stewart's Car
2000 #47 Tony Stewart
2000 #61 Tony Stewart's Car
2000 #2000 T.Stewart High Gear
2001 #5 Tony Stewart
2001 #27 Tony Stewart WCM
2002 #25 Tony Stewart
2002 #32 Tony Stewart's Car
2002 #54 Tony Stewart's Car
2003 #28 Tony Stewart
2003 #34 Tony Stewart's Car
2003 #54 Tony Stewart's Car CM
2003 #64 Tony Stewart NA
2003 #72 Tony Stewart CL
2003 #0 Tony Stewart Champion
2004 #25 Tony Stewart
2005 #13 Tony Stewart
2005 #37 Tony Stewart's Car C
2005 #48 Tony Stewart A
2005 #58 Tony Stewart's Car
2005 #69 Tony Stewart NI
2005 #78 Tony Stewart IF
2006 #1 Tony Stewart
2006 #51 Tony Stewart's Car C
2006 #55 Tony Stewart NA
2006 #60 Tony Stewart NA
2006 #61 Tony Stewart NA
2006 #62 Tony Stewart NA
2006 #65 Tony Stewart CM
2006 #82 Tony Stewart FF
2006 #88 Tony Stewart NI
2006 #0 Tony Stewart Champ
2007 #11 Tony Stewart
2007 #54 Tony Stewart NA
2007 #62 Tony Stewart NA
2007 #63 Tony Stewart NA
2007 #81 Tony Stewart's Car C
2008 #6 Tony Stewart
2008 #47 Tony Stewart's Car C
2008 #75 Tony Stewart NI
2008 #47B Tony Stewart's Car C Purple Top
Wheels High Gear Autographs
2000 #26 Tony Stewart
2001 #31 Tony Stewart
2002 #55 Tony Stewart
Wheels High Gear Blue Hawaii SCDA Promos
2003 #28 Tony Stewart
2003 #34 Tony Stewart's Car
2003 #54 Tony Stewart's Car CM
2003 #64 Tony Stewart WCC
2003 #72 Tony Stewart CL
Wheels High Gear Custom Shop
2000 #CSTS Tony Stewart EXCH
2001 #CSTS Tony Stewart EXCH
2002 #CSTS Tony Stewart EXCH
2003 #CSTS Tony Stewart EXCH
2004 #CSTS Tony Stewart
Wheels High Gear Custom Shop Autograph Redemption
2003 #CSTS Tony Stewart EXCH
Wheels High Gear Custom Shop Autographs
2003 #TSB2 Tony Stewart/10
Wheels High Gear Custom Shop Prizes
2000 #TSA1 Tony Stewart
2000 #TSA2 Tony Stewart
2000 #TSA3 Tony Stewart
2000 #TSB1 Tony Stewart
2000 #TSB2 Tony Stewart
2000 #TSB3 Tony Stewart
2000 #TSC1 Tony Stewart
2000 #TSC2 Tony Stewart
2000 #TSC3 Tony Stewart
2001 #TSA1 Tony Stewart
2001 #TSA2 Tony Stewart
2001 #TSA3 Tony Stewart
2001 #TSB1 Tony Stewart
2001 #TSB2 Tony Stewart
2001 #TSB3 Tony Stewart
2001 #TSC1 Tony Stewart
2001 #TSC2 Tony Stewart
2001 #TSC3 Tony Stewart
2002 #TSA1 Tony Stewart
2002 #TSA2 Tony Stewart
2002 #TSA3 Tony Stewart
2002 #TSB1 Tony Stewart
2002 #TSB2 Tony Stewart
2002 #TSB3 Tony Stewart
2002 #TSC1 Tony Stewart
2002 #TSC2 Tony Stewart
2002 #TSC3 Tony Stewart
2003 #TSA1 Tony Stewart
2003 #TSA2 Tony Stewart
2003 #TSA3 Tony Stewart
2003 #TSB1 Tony Stewart
2003 #TSB2 Tony Stewart
2003 #TSB3 Tony Stewart
2003 #TSC1 Tony Stewart
2003 #TSC2 Tony Stewart
2003 #TSC3 Tony Stewart
Wheels High Gear Driven
2007 #DR12 Tony Stewart
2008 #DR2 Tony Stewart
Wheels High Gear Final Standings
2008 #F6 Tony Stewart/6
Wheels High Gear Final Standings Gold
2007 #FS11 Tony Stewart/11
Wheels High Gear First Gear
1999 #45 Tony Stewart
1999 #61 Tony Stewart
2000 #5 Tony Stewart
2000 #32 Tony Stewart
2000 #47 Tony Stewart
2000 #61 Tony Stewart
2001 #5 Tony Stewart
2001 #27 Tony Stewart WCM
2002 #25 Tony Stewart
2002 #32 Tony Stewart's Car
2002 #54 Tony Stewart's Car
2003 #F28 Tony Stewart
2003 #F34 Tony Stewart's Car
2003 #F54 Tony Stewart's Car CM
2003 #F64 Tony Stewart WCC
2003 #F72 Tony Stewart CL
Wheels High Gear Flag Chasers
2000 #FC5 Tony Stewart
2001 #FC2 Tony Stewart
2002 #FC5 Tony Stewart
Wheels High Gear Flag Chasers Black
2002 #FC5 Tony Stewart
2003 #FC5 Tony Stewart
2004 #FC5 Tony Stewart
2005 #FC3 Tony Stewart
2006 #FC4 Tony Stewart
2007 #FC4 Tony Stewart
2008 #FC2 Tony Stewart
Wheels High Gear Flag Chasers Blue
2004 #FC5 Tony Stewart
Wheels High Gear Flag Chasers Blue-Yellow
2000 #FC5 Tony Stewart
2001 #FC2 Tony Stewart
2002 #FC5 Tony Stewart
2003 #FC5 Tony Stewart
2005 #FC3 Tony Stewart
2006 #FC4 Tony Stewart
2007 #FC4 Tony Stewart
2008 #FC2 Tony Stewart
Wheels High Gear Flag Chasers Checkered
2000 #FC5 Tony Stewart
2001 #FC2 Tony Stewart
2002 #FC5 Tony Stewart
2003 #FC5 Tony Stewart
2004 #FC5 Tony Stewart
2005 #FC3 Tony Stewart
2006 #FC4 Tony Stewart
2007 #FC4 Tony Stewart
2008 #FC2 Tony Stewart
Wheels High Gear Flag Chasers Checkered Blue/Orange
2000 #FC5 Tony Stewart
2001 #FC2 Tony Stewart
2002 #FC5 Tony Stewart
Wheels High Gear Flag Chasers Green
2000 #FC5 Tony Stewart
2001 #FC2 Tony Stewart
2002 #FC5 Tony Stewart
2003 #FC5 Tony Stewart
2004 #FC5 Tony Stewart
2005 #FC3 Tony Stewart
2006 #FC4 Tony Stewart
2007 #FC4 Tony Stewart
2008 #FC2 Tony Stewart
Wheels High Gear Flag Chasers Power Pick
2001 #FCPP Tony Stewart
Wheels High Gear Flag Chasers Red
2000 #FC5 Tony Stewart
2001 #FC2 Tony Stewart
2002 #FC5 Tony Stewart
2003 #FC5 Tony Stewart
2004 #FC5 Tony Stewart
2005 #FC3 Tony Stewart
2006 #FC4 Tony Stewart
2007 #FC4 Tony Stewart
2008 #FC2 Tony Stewart
Wheels High Gear Flag Chasers White
2000 #FC5 Tony Stewart
2001 #FC2 Tony Stewart
2003 #FC5 Tony Stewart
2004 #FC5 Tony Stewart
2005 #FC3 Tony Stewart
2006 #FC4 Tony Stewart
2007 #FC4 Tony Stewart
2008 #FC2 Tony Stewart
Wheels High Gear Flag Chasers Yellow
2000 #FC5 Tony Stewart
2001 #FC2 Tony Stewart
2002 #FC5 Tony Stewart
2003 #FC5 Tony Stewart
2004 #FC5 Tony Stewart
2005 #FC3 Tony Stewart
2006 #FC4 Tony Stewart
2007 #FC4 Tony Stewart
2008 #FC2 Tony Stewart
Wheels High Gear Flag to Flag
2005 #FF24 Tony Stewart
2006 #FF24 Tony Stewart
Wheels High Gear Full Throttle
2003 #FT8 Tony Stewart
2004 #FT4 Tony Stewart
2005 #FT2 Tony Stewart
2006 #FT6 Tony Stewart
2007 #FT8 Tony Stewart
2008 #FT9 Tony Stewart
Wheels High Gear Gear Shifters
2000 #GS4 Tony Stewart
2001 #GS5 Tony Stewart
Wheels High Gear High Groove
2002 #HG25 Tony Stewart
2003 #HG25 Tony Stewart
2004 #HG25 Tony Stewart
Wheels High Gear Hot Streaks
2001 #HS1 Tony Stewart
2002 #HS8 Tony Stewart
Wheels High Gear Hot Treads
2003 #HT16 Tony Stewart
Wheels High Gear Last Lap
2007 #LL5 Tony Stewart
2008 #LL1 Tony Stewart
Wheels High Gear Last Lap Holofoil
2008 #LL1 Tony Stewart
Wheels High Gear Machine
2003 #MM4B Tony Stewart
2004 #MM1B Tony Stewart
2005 #MMB8 Tony Stewart
Wheels High Gear Man
2003 #MM4A Tony Stewart
2004 #MM1A Tony Stewart
2005 #MMA8 Tony Stewart
Wheels High Gear Man & Machine (Machine)
2006 #MMB1 Tony Stewart
Wheels High Gear Man & Machine (Man)
2006 #MMA1 Tony Stewart
Wheels High Gear Man and Machine Cars
2000 #MM1B Tony Stewart's Car
2001 #MM1B Tony Stewart's Car
2002 #MM8B Tony Stewart
Wheels High Gear Man and Machine Drivers
2000 #MM1A Tony Stewart
2001 #MM1A Tony Stewart
2002 #MM8A Tony Stewart
Wheels High Gear MPH
1999 #45 Tony Stewart
1999 #61 Tony Stewart
2000 #5 Tony Stewart
2000 #32 Tony Stewart
2000 #47 Tony Stewart
2000 #61 Tony Stewart
2001 #5 Tony Stewart
2001 #27 Tony Stewart WCM
2002 #25 Tony Stewart
2002 #32 Tony Stewart's Car
2002 #54 Tony Stewart's Car
2003 #M28 Tony Stewart
2003 #M34 Tony Stewart's Car
2003 #M54 Tony Stewart's Car CM
2003 #M64 Tony Stewart WCC
2003 #M72 Tony Stewart CL
2004 #M25 Tony Stewart
2005 #M13 Tony Stewart
2005 #M37 Tony Stewart's Car C
2005 #M48 Tony Stewart A
2005 #M58 Tony Stewart's Car
2005 #M69 Tony Stewart NI
2005 #M78 Tony Stewart IF
2006 #M1 Tony Stewart
2006 #M51 Tony Stewart's Car C
2006 #M55 Tony Stewart NA
2006 #M60 Tony Stewart NA
2006 #M61 Tony Stewart NA
2006 #M62 Tony Stewart NA
2006 #M65 Tony Stewart CM
2006 #M82 Tony Stewart FF
2006 #M88 Tony Stewart NI
2007 #M11 Tony Stewart
2007 #M54 Tony Stewart NA
2007 #M62 Tony Stewart NA
2007 #M63 Tony Stewart NA
2007 #M81 Tony Stewart's Car C
2008 #M6 Tony Stewart
2008 #M47 Tony Stewart's Car C
2008 #M75 Tony Stewart NI
Wheels High Gear Previews
2003 #28 Tony Stewart
2004 #25 Tony Stewart
2007 #EB11 Tony Stewart
2007 #EB54 Tony Stewart NA
2007 #EB62 Tony Stewart NA
2007 #EB63 Tony Stewart NA
2008 #EB6 Tony Stewart
Wheels High Gear Previews Green
2005 #EB13 Tony Stewart
2006 #EB1 Tony Stewart
Wheels High Gear Previews Silver
2005 #EB78 Tony Stewart IF
2006 #EB82 Tony Stewart FF
Wheels High Gear Samples
2003 #28 Tony Stewart
2003 #34 Tony Stewart's Car
2003 #54 Tony Stewart's Car CM
2003 #64 Tony Stewart WCC
2003 #72 Tony Stewart CL
2004 #25 Tony Stewart
2005 #13 Tony Stewart
2005 #37 Tony Stewart's Car C
2005 #48 Tony Stewart A
2005 #58 Tony Stewart's Car
2005 #69 Tony Stewart NI
2005 #78 Tony Stewart IF
Wheels High Gear Sunday Sensation
2000 #OC1 Tony Stewart
2001 #SS5 Tony Stewart
2002 #SS8 Tony Stewart
2003 #SS7 Tony Stewart
2004 #SS5 Tony Stewart
Wheels High Gear The Chase
2008 #TC6 Tony Stewart
Wheels High Gear Top Ten
2004 #TT7 Tony Stewart
Wheels High Gear Top Tier
2000 #TT5 Tony Stewart
2001 #TT6 Tony Stewart
2002 #TT2 Tony Stewart
2003 #TT1 Tony Stewart
2005 #TT6 Tony Stewart
2006 #TT1 Tony Stewart
Wheels High Gear Top Tier Holofoils
2001 #TT6 Tony Stewart
Wheels High Gear Top Tier Numbered
2002 #TT2 Tony Stewart
Wheels High Gear Vintage
2000 #V3 Tony Stewart
Wheels High Gear Winning Edge
2000 #WE4 Tony Stewart
Wheels Runnin and Gunnin
1999 #RG18 Tony Stewart
Wheels Runnin and Gunnin Foils
1999 #RG18 Tony Stewart
Wheels Solos
1999 #33 Tony Stewart

1999 #68 Tony Stewart
1999 #95 Tony Stewart

Truex, Martin Jr.

Bass Pro Shops Racing
2004 #2 Martin Truex Jr.
2004 #3 D.Earnhardt Jr./M.Truex Jr.
McFarlane NASCAR Series 5
2005 #110 Martin Truex Jr. FP
Press Pass
2005 #41 Martin Truex Jr.
2005 #90 Martin Truex Jr. RR
2006 #3 Martin Truex Jr.
2006 #33 Martin Truex Jr. NBS
2006 #102 Martin Truex Jr. U
2007 #22 Martin Truex Jr.
2007 #68 Martin Truex Jr. RR
2008 #11 Martin Truex Jr.
2008 #65 Martin Truex Jr.'s Car BFS
2008 #79 Martin Truex Jr. NS
2008 #90 Martin Truex Jr.'s Car U
2008 #113 Martin Truex Jr. Top 12
Press Pass Autographs
2005 #57 Martin Truex Jr.
2006 #54 Martin Truex Jr. NBS
2007 #45 Martin Truex Jr. NC P
2008 #41 Martin Truex Jr. NC P/E
Press Pass Autographs Press Plates Black
2007 #24 Martin Truex Jr. NC
2008 #33 Martin Truex Jr. NC E
Press Pass Autographs Press Plates Cyan
2007 #25 Martin Truex Jr. NC
2008 #34 Martin Truex Jr. NC E
Press Pass Autographs Press Plates Magenta
2007 #26 Martin Truex Jr. NC
2008 #34 Martin Truex Jr. NC E
Press Pass Autographs Press Plates Yellow
2007 #25 Martin Truex Jr. NC
2008 #33 Martin Truex Jr. NC E
Press Pass Blue
2006 #B3 Martin Truex Jr.
2006 #B33 Martin Truex Jr. NBS
2006 #B102 Martin Truex Jr. U
2007 #B22 Martin Truex Jr.
2007 #B68 Martin Truex Jr. RR
2008 #B11 Martin Truex Jr.
2008 #B65 Martin Truex Jr.'s Car BFS
2008 #B79 Martin Truex Jr. NS
2008 #B90 Martin Truex Jr.'s Car U
2008 #B113 Martin Truex Jr. Top 12
Press Pass Burning Rubber Cars
2006 #BRT17 Martin Truex Jr.
Press Pass Burning Rubber Drivers
2006 #BRD17 Martin Truex Jr.
2008 #BRD12 Martin Truex Jr. Dover
Press Pass Burning Rubber Drivers Gold
2006 #BRD17 Martin Truex Jr.
2008 #BRD12 Martin Truex Jr. Dover
Press Pass Burning Rubber Drivers Prime Cuts
2008 #BRD12 Martin Truex Jr. Dover
Press Pass Burning Rubber Teams
2008 #BRT12 Martin Truex Jr. Dover
Press Pass Burnouts
2006 #HT3 Martin Truex Jr.
2008 #B08 Martin Truex Jr.
Press Pass Burnouts Blue
2008 #B08 Martin Truex Jr.
Press Pass Burnouts Gold
2008 #B08 Martin Truex Jr.
Press Pass Burnouts Holofoil
2006 #HT3 Martin Truex Jr.
Press Pass Collector's Series Box Set
2007 #SB23 Martin Truex Jr.
Press Pass Collectors Series Making the Show
2006 #MS14 Martin Truex Jr.
Press Pass Collectors Series Sunday Best
2007 #CB23 Martin Truex Jr.
Press Pass Cup Chase
2007 #CCR11 Martin Truex Jr. Winner
2008 #CC8 Martin Truex Jr.
Press Pass Cup Chase Prizes
2007 #CC7 Martin Truex Jr.
Press Pass Dale Earnhardt Jr.
2004 #44 Dale Jr./M.Truex Jr. T
2004 #45 Dale Jr.'s Car/M.Truex Jr.'s Car T
2004 #59 Martin Truex Jr.'s Car TO
2004 #60 Martin Truex Jr.'s Car TO
2004 #61 Dale Jr./M.Truex Jr. TO
Press Pass Double Burner Firesuit-Glove
2007 #DB5 Martin Truex Jr.
2008 #DBMT Martin Truex Jr.
Press Pass Double Burner Firesuit-Glove Exchange
2007 #DB5 Martin Truex Jr.
Press Pass Double Burner Metal-Tire
2007 #DB9 Martin Truex Jr.
2008 #DB-MT Martin Truex Jr.
Press Pass Eclipse
2005 #37 Martin Truex Jr.
2005 #89 Martin Truex Jr. SM
2006 #28 Martin Truex Jr. NBS
2006 #41 Martin Truex Jr. WS
2006 #59 Martin Truex Jr. TN
2006 #79 Martin Truex Jr. LL
2006 #86 Martin Truex Jr. SM
2007 #18 Martin Truex Jr.
2008 #10 Martin Truex Jr.
2008 #43 Martin Truex Jr. TO
2008 #59 Martin Truex Jr.'s Car LP
Press Pass Eclipse Escape Velocity
2008 #EV6 Martin Truex Jr.
Press Pass Eclipse Gold
2007 #G18 Martin Truex Jr.
2008 #G10 Martin Truex Jr.
2008 #G43 Martin Truex Jr. TO
2008 #G59 Martin Truex Jr.'s Car LP
Press Pass Eclipse Hyperdrive
2006 #HP8 Martin Truex Jr.
2008 #HP4 Martin Truex Jr.
Press Pass Eclipse Previews
2005 #EB37 Martin Truex Jr.
2005 #EB89 Martin Truex Jr. SM
2006 #EB28 Martin Truex Jr. NBS
2006 #EB59 Martin Truex Jr. TN
2007 #EB18 Martin Truex Jr.
2008 #EB10 Martin Truex Jr.
Press Pass Eclipse Racing Champions
2006 #RC17 Martin Truex Jr. NBS
2007 #RC27 Martin Truex Jr.
Press Pass Eclipse Red
2007 #R18 Martin Truex Jr.
2008 #R10 Martin Truex Jr.
2008 #R43 Martin Truex Jr. TO
2008 #R59 Martin Truex Jr.'s Car LP
Press Pass Eclipse Samples
2005 #37 Martin Truex Jr.
2005 #89 Martin Truex Jr. SM
Press Pass Eclipse Skidmarks
2006 #SM11 Martin Truex Jr.
2007 #SM18 Martin Truex Jr.
Press Pass Eclipse Skidmarks Holofoil
2006 #SM11 Martin Truex Jr.
2007 #SM18 Martin Truex Jr.
Press Pass Eclipse Star Tracks
2008 #ST12 Martin Truex Jr.
Press Pass Eclipse Star Tracks Holofoil
2008 #ST12 Martin Truex Jr.
Press Pass Eclipse Stellar
2008 #ST11 Martin Truex Jr.
Press Pass Eclipse Supernova
2006 #SU4 Martin Truex Jr.
Press Pass Eclipse Teammates Autographs
2007 #1 Dale Jr/Truex Jr/Menard
Press Pass Eclipse Under Cover Autographs
2008 #UC-MT Martin Truex Jr./1
Press Pass Eclipse Under Cover Double Cover Name
2007 #DC6 Dale Jr./Truex Jr.
2008 #DC1 Mark Martin Martin Truex Jr.
Press Pass Eclipse Under Cover Double Cover NASCAR
2007 #DC6 Dale Jr./Truex Jr.
2008 #DC1 Mark Martin Martin Truex Jr.
Press Pass Eclipse Under Cover Drivers
2007 #UCD10 Martin Truex Jr.
2008 #UCD1 Martin Truex Jr.
Press Pass Eclipse Under Cover Drivers Eclipse
2007 #UCD10 Martin Truex Jr.
2008 #UCD1 Martin Truex Jr.
Press Pass Eclipse Under Cover Drivers Name
2007 #UCD10 Martin Truex Jr.
2008 #UCD1 Martin Truex Jr.
Press Pass Eclipse Under Cover Drivers NASCAR
2007 #UCD10 Martin Truex Jr.
2008 #UCD1 Martin Truex Jr.
Press Pass Eclipse Under Cover Teams
2007 #UCT10 Martin Truex Jr.
2008 #UCT1 Martin Truex Jr.
Press Pass Eclipse Under Cover Teams NASCAR
2007 #UCT10 Martin Truex Jr.
2008 #UCT1 Martin Truex Jr.
Press Pass Four Wide
2007 #FW-MT Martin Truex Jr.
2008 #FW-MT Martin Truex Jr.
Press Pass Four Wide Checkered
2007 #FW-MT Martin Truex Jr.
2008 #FW-MT Martin Truex Jr.
Press Pass Four Wide Checkered Exchange
2007 #FW-MT Martin Truex Jr.
Press Pass Four Wide Exchange
2007 #FW-MT Martin Truex Jr.
Press Pass Game Face
2006 #GF8 Martin Truex Jr.
Press Pass Gold
2006 #G3 Martin Truex Jr.
2006 #G33 Martin Truex Jr. NBS
2006 #G102 Martin Truex Jr. U
2007 #G22 Martin Truex Jr.
2007 #G68 Martin Truex Jr. RR
2008 #G11 Martin Truex Jr.
2008 #G65 Martin Truex Jr.'s Car BFS
2008 #G79 Martin Truex Jr. NS
2008 #G90 Martin Truex Jr.'s Car U
2008 #G113 Martin Truex Jr. Top 12
Press Pass Hot Treads
2005 #HTR14 Martin Truex Jr.
2008 #HT4 Martin Truex Jr.
Press Pass Hot Treads Blue
2008 #HT4 Martin Truex Jr.
Press Pass Hot Treads Gold
2008 #HT4 Martin Truex Jr.
Press Pass Hot Treads Holofoil
2005 #HTR14 Martin Truex Jr.
Press Pass Legends Signature Series
2007 #MT Martin Truex Jr.
Press Pass Legends Sunday Swatches Bronze
2007 #MT-SS Martin Truex Jr.
Press Pass Legends Sunday Swatches Gold
2007 #MT-SS Martin Truex Jr.
Press Pass Legends Sunday Swatches Silver
2007 #MT-SS Martin Truex Jr.
Press Pass Legends Triple Threads
2006 #TT-MT Martin Truex Jr.
Press Pass Legends Victory Lane Bronze
2007 #VL9 Martin Truex Jr.
Press Pass Legends Victory Lane Gold
2007 #VL9 Martin Truex Jr.
Press Pass Legends Victory Lane Silver
2007 #VL9 Martin Truex Jr.
Press Pass Optima
2004 #37 Martin Truex Jr. RC
2005 #38 Martin Truex Jr. BGN
2005 #49 Martin Truex Jr. YG
2005 #60 Martin Truex Jr. RR
2006 #3 Martin Truex Jr. CRC
2006 #77 Martin Truex Jr. YG
Press Pass Optima Fan Favorite
2005 #FF25 Martin Truex Jr.
Press Pass Optima G Force
2005 #GF1 Martin Truex Jr.
Press Pass Optima Gold
2004 #G37 Martin Truex Jr.
2005 #G38 Martin Truex Jr. BGN
2005 #G49 Martin Truex Jr. YG
2005 #G60 Martin Truex Jr. RR
2006 #G3 Martin Truex Jr.
2006 #G77 Martin Truex Jr. YG
Press Pass Optima Previews
2004 #EB37 Martin Truex Jr.
2005 #38 Martin Truex Jr. BGN
2005 #49 Martin Truex Jr. YG/1
2006 #EB3 Martin Truex Jr.
2006 #EB77 Martin Truex Jr. YG
Press Pass Optima Q & A
2006 #QA2 Martin Truex Jr.
Press Pass Optima Rookie Relics Cars
2006 #RRT5 Martin Truex Jr.
Press Pass Optima Rookie Relics Drivers
2006 #RRD5 Martin Truex Jr.
Press Pass Optima Samples
2004 #37 Martin Truex Jr.
2005 #38 Martin Truex Jr. BGN
2005 #49 Martin Truex Jr. YG
2005 #60 Martin Truex Jr. RR
Press Pass Panorama
2005 #PPP15 Martin Truex Jr.
2005 #PPP55 Martin Truex Jr.
2005 #PPP65 Martin Truex Jr.
2005 #PPP80 Martin Truex Jr.
Press Pass Platinum
2005 #P41 Martin Truex Jr.
2005 #P90 Martin Truex Jr. RR
2006 #P3 Martin Truex Jr.
2006 #P33 Martin Truex Jr. NBS
2006 #P102 Martin Truex Jr. U
2007 #P22 Martin Truex Jr.
2007 #P68 Martin Truex Jr. RR
2008 #P11 Martin Truex Jr.
2008 #P65 Martin Truex Jr.'s Car BFS
2008 #P79 Martin Truex Jr. NS
2008 #P90 Martin Truex Jr.'s Car U
2008 #P113 Martin Truex Jr. Top 12
Press Pass Premium
2006 #35 Martin Truex Jr. CRC
2006 #52 M.Truex/C.Bowyer/R.Sorenson CL
2006 #74 Martin Truex Jr. PC
2007 #4 Martin Truex Jr.
2007 #43 Martin Truex Jr.'s Car M
2008 #4 Martin Truex Jr.
2008 #40 Martin Truex Jr.'s Car M
2008 #62 Martin Truex Jr. EOP
Press Pass Premium Clean Air
2008 #CA2 Martin Truex Jr.
Press Pass Premium Hot Threads Autographs
2008 #HTMT Martin Truex Jr./1
Press Pass Premium Hot Threads Drivers
2007 #HTD2 Martin Truex Jr.
2008 #HTD2 Martin Truex Jr.
Press Pass Premium Hot Threads Drivers Gold
2007 #HTD2 Martin Truex Jr.
2008 #HTD2 Martin Truex Jr.
Press Pass Premium Hot Threads Patch
2007 #HTP4 Martin Truex Jr. Bass Pro/15
Press Pass Premium Hot Threads Patches
2008 #HTP44 Martin Truex Jr. Bass Pro/3
2008 #HTP45 Martin Truex Jr. DEI logo
Press Pass Premium Hot Threads Team
2007 #HTT2 Martin Truex Jr.
2008 #HTT2 Martin Truex Jr.
Press Pass Premium In the Zone
2006 #IZ9 Martin Truex Jr.
Press Pass Premium In the Zone Red
2006 #IZ9 Martin Truex Jr.
Press Pass Premium Previews
2008 #EB4 Martin Truex Jr.
2008 #EB62 Martin Truex Jr. EOP
Press Pass Premium Red
2007 #R4 Martin Truex Jr.
2007 #R43 Martin Truex Jr.'s Car M
2008 #4 Martin Truex Jr.
2008 #40 Martin Truex Jr.'s Car M
2008 #62 Martin Truex Jr. EOP
Press Pass Premium Wal-Mart
2008 #WM6 Martin Truex Jr.
Press Pass Previews
2006 #EB3 Martin Truex Jr.
2006 #EB33 Martin Truex Jr. NBS
2006 #EB102 Martin Truex Jr. U
2007 #EB22 Martin Truex Jr.
2008 #EB11 Martin Truex Jr.
2008 #EB113 Martin Truex Jr. Top 12
Press Pass Previews Green
2005 #EB41 Martin Truex Jr.
Press Pass Race Day
2007 #RD11 Martin Truex Jr.
2008 #RD3 Martin Truex Jr.
Press Pass Samples
2005 #41 Martin Truex Jr.
2005 #90 Martin Truex Jr. RR
Press Pass Signings
2004 #61 Martin Truex Jr. O
2006 #58 Martin Truex Jr. NC P/S
2007 #71 Martin Truex Jr. NC
2008 #54 Martin Truex Jr.
Press Pass Signings Blue
2007 #32 Martin Truex Jr. NC
Press Pass Signings Gold
2004 #57 Martin Truex Jr. O
2005 #54 Martin Truex Jr.
2006 #52 Martin Truex Jr. NC P/S
2007 #54 Martin Truex Jr. NC
2008 #44 Martin Truex Jr.
Press Pass Signings Press Plates Black
2007 #41 Martin Truex Jr.
Press Pass Signings Press Plates Cyan
2007 #40 Martin Truex Jr.
Press Pass Signings Press Plates Magenta
2007 #43 Martin Truex Jr.
Press Pass Signings Press Plates Yellow
2007 #41 Martin Truex Jr.
Press Pass Signings Red Ink
2006 #19 Martin Truex Jr.
Press Pass Signings Silver
2006 #55 Martin Truex Jr. NC P/S
2007 #53 Martin Truex Jr. NC
2008 #41 Martin Truex Jr.
Press Pass Slideshow
2008 #SS22 Martin Truex Jr.
Press Pass Snapshots
2006 #SN19 Martin Truex Jr.
2006 #SN35 Martin Truex Jr.
2007 #SN27 Martin Truex Jr.
Press Pass Speedway
2008 #11 Martin Truex Jr.
2008 #66 Martin Truex Jr. SH
2008 #74 Martin Truex Jr. UTH
2008 #80 Martin Truex Jr.'s Car RSG
2008 #82 Martin Truex Jr.'s Car WS
Press Pass Speedway Blur
2008 #B6 Martin Truex Jr.
Press Pass Speedway Cockpit
2008 #CP24 Martin Truex Jr.
Press Pass Speedway Corporate Cuts Drivers
2008 #CD-MT Martin Truex Jr.
Press Pass Speedway Corporate Cuts Drivers Patches
2008 #CD-MT Martin Truex Jr./17
Press Pass Speedway Corporate Cuts Team
2008 #CT-MT Martin Truex Jr.
Press Pass Speedway Gold
2008 #G11 Martin Truex Jr.
2008 #G66 Martin Truex Jr. SH
2008 #G74 Martin Truex Jr. UTH
2008 #G80 Martin Truex Jr.'s Car RSG
2008 #G82 Martin Truex Jr.'s Car WS
Press Pass Speedway Holofoil
2008 #H11 Martin Truex Jr.
2008 #H66 Martin Truex Jr. SH
2008 #H74 Martin Truex Jr. UTH
2008 #H80 Martin Truex Jr.'s Car RSG
2008 #H82 Martin Truex Jr.'s Car WS
Press Pass Speedway Previews
2008 #EB11 Martin Truex Jr.
Press Pass Speedway Red
2008 #R11 Martin Truex Jr.
2008 #R66 Martin Truex Jr. SH
2008 #R74 Martin Truex Jr. UTH
2008 #R80 Martin Truex Jr.'s Car RSG
2008 #R82 Martin Truex Jr.'s Car WS
Press Pass Speedway Test Drive
2008 #TD5 Martin Truex Jr.
Press Pass Stealth
2004 #71 Martin Truex Jr. RC
2006 #43 Martin Truex Jr.'s Rig
2006 #52 Truex Jr./Dale Jr. TM
2006 #61 Martin Truex Jr. F
2006 #96 Martin Truex Jr. CRC
2007 #25 Martin Truex Jr.
2007 #55 Martin Truex Jr.'s Crew PC
2007 #71 Truex/Dale Jr./Menard
2008 #33 Martin Truex Jr.
2008 #46 Martin Truex Jr.'s Rig C
2008 #65 Aric Almirola Mark Martin Martin Truex Jr. Paul Menard Regan Smith
2008 #89 Martin Truex Jr. PM
Press Pass Stealth Autographed Hat Entry
2006 #PPH24 Martin Truex Jr.
Press Pass Stealth Battle Armor Drivers
2007 #BAD17 Martin Truex Jr.
2008 #BAD13 Martin Truex Jr.
Press Pass Stealth Battle Armor Teams
2007 #BAT17 Martin Truex Jr.
2008 #BAT13 Martin Truex Jr.
Press Pass Stealth Chrome
2007 #25 Martin Truex Jr.
2007 #55 Martin Truex Jr.'s Crew PC
2007 #71 Truex/Dale Jr./Menard
2008 #33 Martin Truex Jr.
2008 #46 Martin Truex Jr.'s Rig C
2008 #65 Aric Almirola Mark Martin Martin Truex Jr. Paul Menard Regan Smith
2008 #89 Martin Truex Jr. PM
Press Pass Stealth Chrome Exclusives
2007 #X25 Martin Truex Jr.
2007 #X55 Martin Truex Jr.'s Crew PC
2007 #X71 Truex/Dale Jr./Menard
2008 #33 Martin Truex Jr.
2008 #46 Martin Truex Jr.'s Rig C
2008 #65 Aric Almirola Mark Martin Martin Truex Jr. Paul Menard Regan Smith
2008 #89 Martin Truex Jr. PM
Press Pass Stealth Chrome Exclusives Gold
2008 #33 Martin Truex Jr.
2008 #46 Martin Truex Jr.'s Rig C
2008 #65 Aric Almirola Mark Martin Martin Truex Jr. Paul Menard Regan Smith
2008 #89 Martin Truex Jr. PM
Press Pass Stealth Chrome Platinum
2007 #P25 Martin Truex Jr.
2007 #P55 Martin Truex Jr.'s Crew PC
2007 #P71 Truex/Dale Jr./Menard
Press Pass Stealth EFX
2005 #EFX6 Martin Truex Jr.
2006 #EFX5 Martin Truex Jr. 1:48
Press Pass Stealth Gear Grippers Drivers
2006 #GGD16 Martin Truex Jr.
Press Pass Stealth Hot Pass
2006 #HP26 Martin Truex Jr.
Press Pass Stealth Mach 08
2008 #M8-6 Martin Truex Jr.
Press Pass Stealth Maximum Access
2007 #MA26 Martin Truex Jr.
2008 #MA25 Martin Truex Jr.
Press Pass Stealth Maximum Access Autographs
2007 #MA26 Martin Truex Jr.
2008 #MA25 Martin Truex Jr.
Press Pass Stealth No Boundaries
2004 #NB8 Martin Truex Jr.
2005 #NB22 Martin Truex Jr.
Press Pass Stealth Previews
2006 #96 Martin Truex Jr.
2007 #EB25 Martin Truex Jr.
2008 #33 Martin Truex Jr.
2008 #89 Martin Truex Jr. PM
Press Pass Stealth Profile
2006 #P8 Martin Truex Jr.
Press Pass Stealth Retail
2006 #43 Martin Truex Jr.'s Rig
2006 #52 Truex Jr./Dale Jr. TM
2006 #61 Martin Truex Jr. F
2006 #96 Martin Truex Jr. CRC
Press Pass Stealth Retail Gear Grippers Cars
2006 #GGT16 Martin Truex Jr.
Press Pass Stealth Samples
2004 #X71 Martin Truex Jr.
Press Pass Stealth X-Ray
2004 #71 Martin Truex Jr.
2006 #X43 Martin Truex Jr.'s Rig
2006 #X52 Truex Jr./Dale Jr. TM
2006 #X61 Martin Truex Jr. F
2006 #X96 Martin Truex Jr.
Press Pass Target Victory Tires
2008 #TT-MT Martin Truex Jr. Dover
Press Pass Top 25 Drivers & Rides
2006 #C1 Martin Truex Jr.'s Car
2006 #D1 Martin Truex Jr.
Press Pass Top Prospects Memorabilia
2004 #MTT Martin Truex Jr. Tire
2004 #MTSM Martin Truex Jr. Metal
2005 #MT-G Martin Truex Jr. Glove
2005 #MT-S Martin Truex Jr. Shoe
2005 #MT-SM Martin Truex Jr. Metal
2005 #MT-T Martin Truex Jr. Tire
Press Pass Trackside
2004 #39 Martin Truex Jr. RC
2004 #39B Martin Truex Jr. no official
2004 #99 Martin Truex Jr. LD
2005 #43 Martin Truex Jr.
Press Pass Trackside Golden
2004 #G39 Martin Truex Jr.
2004 #G99 Martin Truex Jr. LD
2005 #G43 Martin Truex Jr.
Press Pass Trackside Hat Giveaway
2004 #PPH35 Martin Truex Jr.
2005 #PPH36 Martin Truex Jr.
Press Pass Trackside Hot Pass
2005 #24 Martin Truex Jr.
Press Pass Trackside Hot Pass National
2005 #24 Martin Truex Jr.
Press Pass Trackside Previews
2004 #EB39 Martin Truex Jr.
2005 #43 Martin Truex Jr.
Press Pass Trackside Samples
2004 #39 Martin Truex Jr.
2004 #99 Martin Truex Jr. LD
2005 #43 Martin Truex Jr.
Press Pass Velocity
2006 #VE7 Martin Truex Jr.
Press Pass Wal-Mart Autographs
2007 #MT Martin Truex Jr.
2008 #10 Martin Truex Jr.
Press Pass Weekend Warriors
2008 #WW7 Martin Truex Jr.
TRAKS
2006 #34 Martin Truex Jr. CRC
2006 #37 Martin Truex Jr.'s Car
2006 #100 Martin Truex Jr.'s Car PS
2007 #29 Martin Truex Jr.
2007 #77 Martin Truex Jr. GP
2007 #82 Martin Truex Jr.'s Car NFS
TRAKS Autographs
2006 #37 Martin Truex, Jr. NC
TRAKS Autographs 100
2006 #19 Martin Truex, Jr. NC
TRAKS Autographs 25
2006 #35 Martin Truex, Jr. NC
Traks Driver's Seat
2007 #DS3 Martin Truex Jr.
2007 #DS3B Martin Truex Jr. VAR
Traks Driver's Seat National
2007 #DS3 Martin Truex Jr.
Traks Gold
2007 #G29 Martin Truex Jr.
2007 #G77 Martin Truex Jr. GP
2007 #G82 Martin Truex Jr.'s Car NFS
Traks Holofoil
2007 #H29 Martin Truex Jr.
2007 #H77 Martin Truex Jr. GP
2007 #H82 Martin Truex Jr.'s Car NFS
Traks Hot Pursuit
2007 #HP4 Martin Truex Jr.
Traks Previews
2007 #EB29 Martin Truex Jr.
2007 #EB77 Martin Truex Jr. GP
Traks Red
2007 #R29 Martin Truex Jr.
2007 #R77 Martin Truex Jr. GP
2007 #R82 Martin Truex Jr.'s Car NFS
TRAKS Stickers
2006 #1 Martin Truex Jr.
Traks Track Time
2007 #TT9 Martin Truex Jr.
VIP
2005 #57 Martin Truex Jr. HR
2006 #33 Martin Truex Jr.'s Car R
2006 #73 Martin Truex Jr. AS
2006 #94 Martin Truex Jr. CRC
2007 #1 Martin Truex Jr. CL
2007 #29 Martin Truex Jr.
2007 #49 Martin Truex Jr.'s Car SV
2007 #68 Martin Truex Jr. Red C
2007 #81 Martin Truex Jr. Dover AP
VIP Get A Grip Drivers
2007 #GGD28 Martin Truex Jr.
VIP Get A Grip Teams
2007 #GGT28 Martin Truex Jr.
VIP Making The Show
2005 #4 Martin Truex Jr.
2006 #MS14 Martin Truex Jr.
VIP Previews
2007 #EB1 Martin Truex Jr. CL
2007 #EB29 Martin Truex Jr.
VIP Rookie Stripes
2006 #RS5 Martin Truex Jr.
VIP Samples
2005 #57 Martin Truex Jr. HR
VIP Sunday Best
2007 #SB23 Martin Truex Jr.
Wheels American Thunder
2005 #41 Martin Truex Jr. AS
2005 #75 Martin Truex Jr. RR
2005 #80 Martin Truex Jr. CC
2006 #53 Martin Truex Jr.'s Car HR
2006 #94 Martin Truex Jr. RT AU CRC
2007 #34 Martin Truex Jr.
2007 #38 Martin Truex Jr.'s Car DT
2007 #51 Martin Truex Jr.'s Car HR
Wheels American Thunder American Dreams
2007 #AD8 Martin Truex Jr.
Wheels American Thunder American Dreams Gold
2007 #ADG8 Martin Truex Jr.
Wheels American Thunder American Eagle
2005 #AE6 Martin Truex Jr.
Wheels American Thunder American Muscle
2006 #AM5 Martin Truex Jr.
2007 #AM6 Martin Truex Jr.
Wheels American Thunder American Racing Idol
2006 #RI12 Martin Truex Jr.
Wheels American Thunder American Racing Idol Golden
2006 #RI12 Martin Truex Jr.
Wheels American Thunder Autographed Hat Instant Winner
2007 #AH39 Martin Truex Jr.
Wheels American Thunder Cool Threads
2006 #CT3 Martin Truex Jr.
2007 #CT7 Martin Truex Jr.
Wheels American Thunder Double Hat
2006 #DH25 Martin Truex Jr.
Wheels American Thunder Golden Eagle
2005 #GE6 Martin Truex Jr.
Wheels American Thunder Grandstand
2006 #GS22 Martin Truex Jr.
Wheels American Thunder Head to Toe
2006 #HT7 Martin Truex Jr.
2007 #HT3 Martin Truex Jr.
Wheels American Thunder License to Drive
2005 #5 Martin Truex Jr.
Wheels American Thunder Previews
2005 #80 Martin Truex Jr. CC
2007 #EB34 Martin Truex Jr.
2007 #EB51 Martin Truex Jr.'s Car HR
Wheels American Thunder Pushin' Pedal
2006 #PP10 Martin Truex Jr.
2007 #PP9 Martin Truex Jr.
Wheels American Thunder Samples
2005 #41 Martin Truex Jr. AS
2005 #75 Martin Truex Jr. RR
2005 #80 Martin Truex Jr. CC
Wheels American Thunder Single Hat
2005 #SH2 Martin Truex Jr.
Wheels American Thunder Starting Grid
2007 #SG8 Martin Truex Jr.
Wheels American Thunder Thunder Road
2005 #TR15 Martin Truex Jr.
2006 #TR7 Martin Truex Jr.
2007 #TR3 Martin Truex Jr.
Wheels American Thunder Thunder Strokes
2006 #11 Martin Truex Jr./400
2007 #39 Martin Truex Jr.
Wheels American Thunder Thunder Strokes Press Plates Black
2007 #39 Martin Truex Jr.
Wheels American Thunder Thunder Strokes Press Plates Cyan
2007 #39 Martin Truex Jr.
Wheels American Thunder Thunder Strokes Press Plates Magenta
2007 #39 Martin Truex Jr.
Wheels American Thunder Thunder Strokes Press Plates Yellow
2007 #39 Martin Truex Jr.
Wheels American Thunder Triple Hat
2007 #TH30 Martin Truex Jr.
Wheels Autographs
2004 #64 Martin Truex Jr.
2005 #57 Martin Truex Jr.
2007 #39 Martin Truex Jr. NC HG
2008 #33 Martin Truex Jr. NC HG
Wheels Autographs Chase Edition
2008 #9 Martin Truex Jr. NC
Wheels Autographs Press Plates Black
2007 #38 Martin Truex Jr. NC
2008 #33 Martin Truex Jr. NC
Wheels Autographs Press Plates Cyan
2007 #38 Martin Truex Jr. NC
2008 #33 Martin Truex Jr. NC
Wheels Autographs Press Plates Magenta
2007 #38 Martin Truex Jr. NC
2008 #33 Martin Truex Jr. NC
Wheels Autographs Press Plates Yellow
2007 #40 Martin Truex Jr. NC
2008 #33 Martin Truex Jr. NC
Wheels High Gear
2005 #28 Martin Truex Jr.
2005 #47 Martin Truex Jr. A
2005 #79 Martin Truex Jr. RS
2006 #28 Martin Truex Jr. NBS
2006 #57 Martin Truex Jr. NA
2006 #83 Martin Truex Jr. FF
2007 #18 Martin Truex Jr.
2008 #11 Martin Truex Jr.
2008 #64 Martin Truex Jr.'s Car EL
Wheels High Gear Driven
2007 #DR6 Martin Truex Jr.
2008 #DR15 Martin Truex Jr.
Wheels High Gear Final Standings
2008 #F11 Martin Truex Jr./11
Wheels High Gear Final Standings Gold
2007 #FS18 Martin Truex Jr./19
Wheels High Gear Flag to Flag
2006 #FF25 Martin Truex Jr.
Wheels High Gear Full Throttle
2006 #FT1 Martin Truex Jr.
2007 #FT9 Martin Truex Jr.
2008 #FT8 Martin Truex Jr.
Wheels High Gear Last Lap
2008 #LL5 Martin Truex Jr.
Wheels High Gear Last Lap Holofoil
2008 #LL5 Martin Truex Jr.
Wheels High Gear Man & Machine (Machine)
2006 #MMB7 Martin Truex Jr.
Wheels High Gear Man & Machine (Man)
2006 #MMA7 Martin Truex Jr.
Wheels High Gear MPH
2005 #M28 Martin Truex Jr.
2005 #M47 Martin Truex Jr. A

2005 #M79 Martin Truex Jr. RS
2006 #M28 Martin Truex Jr. NBS
2006 #M57 Martin Truex Jr. NA
2006 #M83 Martin Truex Jr. FF
2007 #M18 Martin Truex Jr.
2008 #M11 Martin Truex Jr.
2008 #M64 Martin Truex Jr.'s Car EL
Wheels High Gear Previews
2007 #EB18 Martin Truex Jr.
2008 #EB11 Martin Truex Jr.
Wheels High Gear Previews Green
2005 #EB28 Martin Truex Jr.
2006 #EB28 Martin Truex Jr. NBS
Wheels High Gear Previews Silver
2006 #EB83 Martin Truex Jr. FF
Wheels High Gear Samples
2005 #28 Martin Truex Jr.
2005 #47 Martin Truex Jr. A
2005 #79 Martin Truex Jr. RS
Wheels High Gear The Chase
2008 #TC11 Martin Truex Jr.

Wallace, Rusty

AC Racing
1991 #2 Rusty Wallace
AC Racing Foldouts
1993 #2 Rusty Wallace
AC Racing Postcards
1992 #7 Rusty Wallace
AC Racing Proven Winners
1990 #1 Rusty Wallace
AC-Delco
1992 #1 Rusty Wallace
Action Packed
1993 #6 Rusty Wallace WIN
1993 #28 Rusty Wallace PW
1993 #83 Rusty Wallace
1993 #84 Rusty Wallace's Car
1993 #107 Rusty Wallace
1993 #108 Rusty Wallace's Car
1993 #163 R.Wallace/Ken.Wallace B
1993 #191 Rusty Wallace RW
1993 #192 Rusty Wallace RW
1993 #193 Rusty Wallace RW
1993 #194 Rusty Wallace's Car RW
1993 #195 Rusty Wallace's Car RW
1993 #196 Rusty Wallace in Pits RW
1993 #197 Rusty Wallace RW
1994 #2 Rusty Wallace
1994 #31 Rusty Wallace's Car WIN
1994 #42 Rusty Wallace's Car
1994 #67 Rusty Wallace
1994 #108 Rusty Wallace's Car
1994 #183 Rusty Wallace WIN
1994 #186 Rusty Wallace WIN
1994 #190 Rusty Wallace WIN
1994 #191 Rusty Wallace WIN
1994 #192 Rusty Wallace WIN
1994 #204 R.Wallace/Kenny/Mike
1994 #206 Rusty Wallace WS
1997 #2 Rusty Wallace
1997 #44 Rusty Wallace's Car
1997 #69 Rusty Wallace
1997 #73 Rusty Wallace's Car
Action Packed 24K Gold
1994 #1G Rusty Wallace
1994 #12G Rusty Wallace's Car
1994 #21G Rusty Wallace
1994 #183G Rusty Wallace WIN
1994 #186G Rusty Wallace WIN
1994 #190G Rusty Wallace WIN
1994 #191G Rusty Wallace WIN
1994 #192G Rusty Wallace WIN
1997 #1 Rusty Wallace
Action Packed Badge of Honor Pins
1994 #4 Rusty Wallace
1995 #9 Rusty Wallace
Action Packed Champ and Challenger
1994 #37 Dale Earnhardt/Rusty Wallace Cars
Action Packed Coastars
1994 #16 Rusty Wallace
Action Packed Country
1995 #12 Rusty Wallace S
1995 #38 Rusty Wallace NT
1995 #39 Rusty Wallace NT
1995 #40 Rusty Wallace NT
1995 #41 Rusty Wallace NT
1995 #42 Rusty Wallace NT
1995 #43 Rusty Wallace NT
Action Packed Country 24K Team
1995 #8 Rusty Wallace
Action Packed Country 2nd Career Choice
1995 #3 Rusty Wallace
Action Packed Country Silver Speed
1995 #12 Rusty Wallace S
1995 #38 Rusty Wallace NT
1995 #39 Rusty Wallace NT
1995 #40 Rusty Wallace NT
1995 #41 Rusty Wallace NT
1995 #42 Rusty Wallace NT
1995 #43 Rusty Wallace NT
Action Packed Credentials
1996 #24 Rusty Wallace
1996 #55 Rusty Wallace SM
Action Packed Credentials Silver Speed
1996 #24 Rusty Wallace
Action Packed Fifth Anniversary
1997 #7 Rusty Wallace
Action Packed First Impressions
1997 #2 Rusty Wallace
1997 #44 Rusty Wallace's Car
1997 #69 Rusty Wallace
1997 #73 Rusty Wallace's Car
Action Packed Mammoth
1994 #2 Rusty Wallace
1995 #MM3 Rusty Wallace
Action Packed Mint
1994 #2 Rusty Wallace
1994 #31 Rusty Wallace's Car WIN
1994 #42 Rusty Wallace's Car
1994 #67 Rusty Wallace
1994 #108 Rusty Wallace's Car
1994 #183 Rusty Wallace WIN
1994 #186 Rusty Wallace WIN
1994 #190 Rusty Wallace WIN
1994 #191 Rusty Wallace WIN
1994 #192 Rusty Wallace WIN
1994 #204 R.Wallace/Kenny/Mike
1994 #206 Rusty Wallace WS
Action Packed Preview
1995 #23 Rusty Wallace
1995 #46 Rusty Wallace PW
1995 #58 Rusty Wallace WIN
1995 #61 Rusty Wallace T10
1995 #77 Rusty Wallace DD
Action Packed Preview 24K Gold
1995 #9G Rusty Wallace
Action Packed Prototypes
1994 #2R945 Rusty Wallace's Car
Action Packed Select 24K Gold
1994 #W5 Rusty Wallace
Action Packed Stars
1995 #25 Rusty Wallace OC
1995 #32 Rusty Wallace's Car
1995 #53 Rusty Wallace RW
1995 #76 Rusty Wallace WW
1995 #77 Rusty Wallace WW
1995 #78 Rusty Wallace WW
1995 #79 Rusty Wallace WW
1995 #80 Rusty Wallace WW
1995 #81 Rusty Wallace WW
Action Packed Stars 24K Gold
1995 #8G Rusty Wallace
1995 #17G Rusty Wallace
1995 #18G Rusty Wallace
Action Packed Stars Silver Speed
1995 #25 Rusty Wallace OC
1995 #32 Rusty Wallace's Car
1995 #53 Rusty Wallace RW
1995 #76 Rusty Wallace WW
1995 #77 Rusty Wallace WW
1995 #78 Rusty Wallace WW
1995 #79 Rusty Wallace WW
1995 #80 Rusty Wallace WW
1995 #81 Rusty Wallace WW
ActionVision
1997 #5 J.Gordon/R.Wall/T.Labonte
1997 #7 Rusty Wallace Pit Stop
Assets
1995 #2 Rusty Wallace
1995 #30 Rusty Wallace
1995 #47 Rusty Wallace's Car
Assets $100 Phone Cards
1995 #5 Rusty Wallace
Assets $1000 Phone Cards
1995 #5 Rusty Wallace
Assets $2 Phone Cards
1995 #18 Rusty Wallace
Assets $2 Phone Cards Gold Signature
1995 #18 Rusty Wallace
Assets $25 Phone Cards
1995 #9 Rusty Wallace
Assets $5 Phone Cards
1995 #9 Rusty Wallace
Assets 1-Minute Phone Cards
1995 #18 Rusty Wallace
Assets 1-Minute Phone Cards Gold Signature
1995 #18 Rusty Wallace
Assets Coca-Cola 600 Die Cut Phone Cards
1995 #2 Rusty Wallace
Assets Gold Signature
1995 #2 Rusty Wallace
1995 #30 Rusty Wallace
1995 #47 Rusty Wallace's Car
Assets Racing $100 Cup Champion Interactive Phone Cards
1996 #10 Rusty Wallace's Car
Assets Racing $1000 Cup Champion Interactive Phone Cards
1996 #17 Rusty Wallace's Car
Assets Racing $2 Phone Cards
1996 #15 Rusty Wallace's Car
Assets Racing Race Day
1996 #RD2 Rusty Wallace's Car
Autographed Racing
1996 #7 Rusty Wallace's Car
1997 #35 Rusty Wallace's Car
1997 #49 D.Earnhardt/R.Wall.Cars
Autographed Racing Front Runners
1996 #77 R.Pemberton/R.Wallace's Car
Autographed Racing Kings of the Circuit $5 Phone Cards
1996 #KC9 Rusty Wallace's Car
Big League Cards Creative Images
1998 #13 Rusty Wallace
Card Dynamics Double Eagle Postcards
1993-95 #2 Rusty Wallace
Card Dynamics Gant Oil
1992 #4 Rusty Wallace/4000
1993 #3 Rusty Wallace
1994 #2 Rusty Wallace
Card Dynamics Montgomery Motors
1994 #3 Rusty Wallace
Card Dynamics Quik Chek
1993 #5 Rusty Wallace/5000
Card Dynamics Rusty Wallace
1992 #4 Rusty Wallace
1992 #5 Rusty Wallace
1992 #3 Rusty Wallace
1992 #2 Rusty Wallace
1992 #1 Rusty Wallace
Classic
1996 #36 Rusty Wallace's Car
Classic Five Sport
1995 #165 Rusty Wallace
Classic Five Sport Printer's Proofs
1995 #165 Rusty Wallace
Classic Five Sport Red Die Cuts
1995 #165 Rusty Wallace
Classic Five Sport Signings
1995-96 #81 Rusty Wallace
Classic Five Sport Signings Blue Signature
1995-96 #81 Rusty Wallace
Classic Five Sport Signings Die Cuts
1995-96 #81 Rusty Wallace
Classic Five Sport Signings Red Signature
1995-96 #81 Rusty Wallace
Classic Five Sport Silver Die Cuts
1995 #165 Rusty Wallace
Classic Five Sport Strive For Five
1995 #RC13 Rusty Wallace
Classic Five-Sport *
1995 #165 Rusty Wallace
Classic Five-Sport Printer's Proofs *
1995 #165 Rusty Wallace
Classic Five-Sport Red Die Cuts *
1995 #165 Rusty Wallace
Classic Five-Sport Silver Die Cuts *
1995 #165 Rusty Wallace
Classic Five-Sport Strive For Five *
1995 #RC13 Rusty Wallace
Classic Mark Martin's Challengers
1996 #MC8 Rusty Wallace's Car
Classic Printer's Proof
1996 #36 Rusty Wallace's Car
Classic Race Chase
1996 #RC2 Rusty Wallace's Car
1996 #RC12 Rusty Wallace's Car
Classic Signings *
1996 #S81 Rusty Wallace
Classic Signings Blue Signature *
1996 #81 Rusty Wallace
Classic Signings Die Cuts *
1996 #81 Rusty Wallace
Classic Signings Red Signature *
1996 #81 Rusty Wallace
Classic Silver
1996 #36 Rusty Wallace's Car
Collector's Choice
1997 #2 Rusty Wallace
1997 #52 Rusty Wallace's Car MM
1997 #102 Rusty Wallace SC
1997 #145 Rusty Wallace TRA
1997 #155 Rusty Wallace CL
1998 #2 Rusty Wallace
1998 #38 Rusty Wallace's Car
1998 #93 Rusty Wallace PP
1998 #111 Rusty Wallace TD
Collector's Choice CC600
1998 #CC7 Rusty Wallace
1998 #CC41 Rusty Wallace's Car
1998 #CC74 Rusty Wallace's Car
Collector's Choice Speedecals
1997 #S3 Rusty Wallace's Car
1997 #S4 Rusty Wallace's Helmet
Collector's Choice Star Quest
1998 #SQ34 Rusty Wallace
1998 #SQ48 Rusty Wallace AUTO
Collector's Choice Triple Force
1997 #H2 Rusty Wallace
1997 #J2 Rusty Wallace
Collector's Choice Upper Deck 500
1997 #UD2 Rusty Wallace
1997 #UD3 Rusty Wallace's Car
Collector's Choice Victory Circle
1997 #VC3 Rusty Wallace
Coyote Rookies
1992 #6 Rusty Wallace
Crown Jewels
1995 #4 Rusty Wallace
Crown Jewels Diamond
1995 #4 Rusty Wallace
Crown Jewels Dual Jewels
1995 #DJ2 R.Wallace/Dale Jarrett
Crown Jewels Dual Jewels Diamond
1995 #DJ2 Rusty Wallace/Dale Jarrett
Crown Jewels Dual Jewels Emerald
1995 #DJ2 Rusty Wallace/Dale Jarrett
Crown Jewels Elite
1996 #6 Rusty Wallace
1996 #32 Rusty Wallace
1996 #34 Rusty Wallace
1996 #54 R.Wallace/Pemberton
1996 #60 Rusty Wallace's Trans.
Crown Jewels Elite Birthstones of the Champions
1996 #BC3 Rusty Wallace
Crown Jewels Elite Birthstones of the Champions Diamond Tribute
1996 #BC3 Rusty Wallace
Crown Jewels Elite Birthstones of the Champions Treasure Chest
1996 #BC3 Rusty Wallace
Crown Jewels Elite Crown Signature Amethyst
1996 #CS3 Rusty Wallace
Crown Jewels Elite Crown Signature Garnet
1996 #CS3 Rusty Wallace
Crown Jewels Elite Crown Signature Peridot
1996 #CS3 Rusty Wallace
Crown Jewels Elite Diamond Tribute
1996 #6 Rusty Wallace
1996 #32 Rusty Wallace
1996 #34 Rusty Wallace
1996 #54 R.Pemberton/R.Wallace
1996 #60 Rusty Wallace's Trans.
Crown Jewels Elite Diamond Tribute Citrine
1996 #6 Rusty Wallace
1996 #32 Rusty Wallace
1996 #34 Rusty Wallace
1996 #54 R.Pemberton/R.Wallace
1996 #60 Rusty Wallace's Trans.
Crown Jewels Elite Dual Jewels Amethyst
1996 #DJ7 R.Wallace/K.Wallace
Crown Jewels Elite Dual Jewels Amethyst Diamond Tribute
1996 #DJ7 R.Wallace/K.Wallace
Crown Jewels Elite Dual Jewels Amethyst Treasure Chest
1996 #DJ7 R.Wallace/K.Wallace
Crown Jewels Elite Dual Jewels Garnet
1996 #DJ7 R.Wallace/K.Wallace
Crown Jewels Elite Dual Jewels Garnet Diamond Tribute
1996 #DJ7 R.Wallace/K.Wallace
Crown Jewels Elite Dual Jewels Garnet Treasure Chest
1996 #DJ7 R.Wallace/K.Wallace
Crown Jewels Elite Dual Jewels Sapphire
1996 #DJ7 R.Wallace/K.Wallace
Crown Jewels Elite Dual Jewels Sapphire Treasure Chest
1996 #DJ7 R.Wallace/K.Wallace
Crown Jewels Elite Emerald
1996 #6 Rusty Wallace
1996 #32 Rusty Wallace
1996 #34 Rusty Wallace
1996 #54 R.Pemberton/R.Wallace
1996 #60 Rusty Wallace's Trans.
Crown Jewels Elite Emerald Treasure Chest
1996 #6 Rusty Wallace
1996 #32 Rusty Wallace
1996 #34 Rusty Wallace
1996 #54 R.Pemberton/R.Wallace
1996 #60 Rusty Wallace's Trans.
Crown Jewels Elite Sapphire
1996 #6 Rusty Wallace
1996 #32 Rusty Wallace
1996 #34 Rusty Wallace
1996 #54 R.Pemberton/R.Wallace
1996 #60 Rusty Wallace's Trans.
Crown Jewels Elite Sapphire Treasure Chest
1996 #6 Rusty Wallace
1996 #32 Rusty Wallace
1996 #34 Rusty Wallace
1996 #54 R.Pemberton/R.Wallace
1996 #60 Rusty Wallace's Trans.
Crown Jewels Elite Treasure Chest
1996 #6 Rusty Wallace
1996 #32 Rusty Wallace
1996 #34 Rusty Wallace
1996 #54 R.Pemberton/R.Wallace
1996 #60 Rusty Wallace's Trans.
Crown Jewels Emerald
1995 #4 Rusty Wallace
Crown Jewels Sapphire
1995 #4 Rusty Wallace
Crown Jewels Signature Gems
1995 #SG2 Rusty Wallace
Dayco Series 1
1992 #2 Rusty Wallace
Dayco Series 2 Rusty Wallace
1993 #11 Rusty Wallace CL
1993 #12 Rusty Wallace/Earnhardt Cars
1993 #13 Rusty Wallace/Rick Mears Cars
1993 #14 Rusty Wallace/Roger Penske
1993 #15 Rusty Wallace
1993 #16 Mike Wallace/Kenny Wallace/Rusty Wallace
1993 #17 Rusty Wallace
1993 #18 Rusty Wallace
1993 #19 Rusty Wallace
1993 #20 Rusty Wallace in Pits
1993 #21 Rusty Wallace/Buddy Parrott
1993 #22 Rusty Wallace
1993 #23 Rusty Wallace/Buddy Parrott/Don Miller
1993 #24 Rusty Wallace FOIL
1993 #25 Rusty Wallace's Car FOIL
Dayco Series 3
1994 #27 Rusty Wallace
eTopps
2003 #7 Rusty Wallace/3126
Finish Line
1993 #5 Rusty Wallace
1993 #45 Rusty Wallace's Car
1993 #122 Rusty Wallace
1994 #29 Rusty Wallace
1994 #74 Rusty Wallace
1994 #90 Rusty Wallace
1994 #104 Rusty Wallace's Car
1995 #2 Rusty Wallace
1995 #34 Rusty Wallace
1995 #70 Rusty Wallace
1996 #3 Rusty Wallace
1996 #27 Rusty Wallace
1996 #28 Rusty Wallace's Car
Finish Line Black Gold
1996 #C2 Rusty Wallace's Car
1996 #D2 Rusty Wallace
Finish Line Coca-Cola 600
1995 #2 Rusty Wallace
1995 #30 Rusty Wallace
1995 #47 Rusty Wallace's Car
Finish Line Coca-Cola 600 Die Cuts
1995 #C2 Rusty Wallace
Finish Line Coca-Cola 600 Winners
1995 #CC6 Rusty Wallace
Finish Line Commemorative Sheets
1993 #2 Rockingham
1993 #9 Talladega
1993 #21 Bristol
Finish Line Diamond Collection $5 Phone Cards
1996 #8 Rusty Wallace
Finish Line Down Home
1994 #10 Rusty Wallace
Finish Line Gold
1994 #10 Rusty Wallace
1994 #16 Rusty Wallace's Car
1994 #24 Rusty Wallace
1994 #59 Rusty Wallace
1994 #68 Rusty Wallace
Finish Line Gold Phone Cards
1994 #8 Rusty Wallace/3000
Finish Line Gold Signature
1994 #5 Rusty Wallace
1995 #GS2 Rusty Wallace
1996 #GS4 Rusty Wallace
Finish Line Gold Teamwork
1994 #TG1 Rusty Wallace/B.Parrott
Finish Line Man and Machine
1996 #MM3 Rusty Wallace
Finish Line Mega-Phone XL Phone Cards
1996 #1 Bill Elliott
Finish Line Phone Card of the Month
1995 #4 Rusty Wallace/1500
Finish Line Phone Cards
1994 #5 Rusty Wallace
1994 #14 Rusty Wallace
Finish Line Phone Pak
1996 #36 Rusty Wallace
1996 #37 Rusty Wallace's Car
Finish Line Phone Pak $10
1996 #11 Rusty Wallace
Finish Line Phone Pak $100
1996 #6 Rusty Wallace
Finish Line Phone Pak $1000
1996 #K4 Rusty Wallace
Finish Line Phone Pak $2 Signature
1996 #36 Rusty Wallace
1996 #37 Rusty Wallace's Car
Finish Line Phone Pak $5
1996 #22 Rusty Wallace
Finish Line Phone Pak $50
1996 #8 Rusty Wallace
Finish Line Phone Pak II
1997 #4 Rusty Wallace
1997 #42 Rusty Wallace $5
1997 #67 Rusty Wallace's Car $10
1997 #90 Rusty Wallace $50
1997 #98 Rusty Wallace $100
Finish Line Platinum 5-Unit Phone Cards
1995 #4 Rusty Wallace
Finish Line Printer's Proof
1995 #2 Rusty Wallace
1995 #34 Rusty Wallace
1995 #70 Rusty Wallace
1996 #3 Rusty Wallace
1996 #27 Rusty Wallace
1996 #28 Rusty Wallace's Car
Finish Line Promos
1994 #P3 Rusty Wallace
Finish Line Silver
1993 #5 Rusty Wallace
1993 #45 Rusty Wallace's Car
1993 #122 Rusty Wallace
1994 #29 Rusty Wallace
1994 #74 Rusty Wallace
1994 #90 Rusty Wallace
1994 #104 Rusty Wallace's Car
1995 #2 Rusty Wallace
1995 #34 Rusty Wallace
1995 #70 Rusty Wallace
1996 #3 Rusty Wallace
1996 #27 Rusty Wallace
1996 #28 Rusty Wallace's Car
Finish Line Standout Cars
1995 #SC3 Rusty Wallace's Car
Finish Line Standout Drivers
1995 #SD3 Rusty Wallace
Finish Line Victory Lane
1994 #VL9 Rusty Wallace
1994 #VL10 Rusty Wallace
Flair
1996 #35 Rusty Wallace
1996 #91 Rusty Wallace's Car
1996 #100 Rusty Wallace CL
Flair Autographs
1996 #12 Rusty Wallace
Flair Center Spotlight
1996 #10 Rusty Wallace
Flair Hot Numbers
1996 #10 Rusty Wallace
Flair Power Performance
1996 #10 Rusty Wallace
High Gear Promos
1994 #P2 Rusty Wallace Silver
1995 #P1 Rusty Wallace
High Gear Promos Gold
1994 #P2 Rusty Wallace Gold
Highland Mint/VIP
1994-95 #6B Rusty Wallace/5000
1994-95 #6S Rusty Wallace/1000
Hi-Tech Brickyard 400
1994 #2 Rusty Wallace's Car
1994 #28 Rusty Wallace's Car
1994 #37 Rusty Wallace
1995 #11 Rusty Wallace's Car
1995 #83 Rusty Wallace
Hi-Tech Brickyard 400 Artist Proofs
1994 #2 Rusty Wallace's Car
1994 #28 Rusty Wallace's Car
1994 #37 Rusty Wallace
Hi-Tech Brickyard 400 Top Ten
1995 #BY4 Rusty Wallace
Hi-Tech Tire Test
1993 #4 Rusty Wallace's Car
1993 #P1 Rusty Wallace's Car Promo
Images
1995 #2 Rusty Wallace
1995 #66 Rusty Wallace
1995 #94 Rusty Wallace
Images Driven
1995 #D8 Rusty Wallace
Images Gold
1995 #2 Rusty Wallace
1995 #66 Rusty Wallace
1995 #94 Rusty Wallace
Images Hard Chargers
1995 #HC6 Rusty Wallace
IROC
1991 #10 Rusty Wallace
Jurassic Park
1997 #5 Rusty Wallace
Jurassic Park Carnivore
1997 #C8 Rusty Wallace
Jurassic Park Pteranodon
1997 #P5 Rusty Wallace
Jurassic Park Raptors
1997 #R11 Rusty Wallace
Jurassic Park Thunder Lizard
1997 #TL4 Rusty Wallace
Jurassic Park T-Rex
1997 #TR6 Rusty Wallace
Jurassic Park Triceratops
1997 #5 Rusty Wallace
KnightQuest
1996 #7 Rusty Wallace K
1996 #23 Rusty Wallace C
KnightQuest Black Knights
1996 #7 Rusty Wallace K
1996 #23 Rusty Wallace C
KnightQuest Knights of the Round Table
1996 #KT8 Rusty Wallace
KnightQuest Protectors of the Crown
1996 #PC4 Rusty Wallace
KnightQuest Red Knight Preview
1996 #7 Rusty Wallace K
1996 #23 Rusty Wallace C
KnightQuest Royalty
1996 #7 Rusty Wallace K
1996 #23 Rusty Wallace C
KnightQuest Santa Claus
1996 #SC3 Rusty Wallace
KnightQuest Santa Claus Green
1996 #SC3 Rusty Wallace
KnightQuest White Knights
1996 #7 Rusty Wallace K
1996 #23 Rusty Wallace C
Mac Tools Winner's Cup
1992 #20 Rusty Wallace
Matchbook Winston Cup Champions
1995 #19 1989 Champion Rusty Wallace
Maxwell House
1993 #10 Rusty Wallace
1993 #19 Rusty Wallace/K.Wallace
Maxx
1989 #27 Rusty Wallace
1989 #54 Rusty Wallace
1989 #114 A.Kulwi/R.Wall Cars YR
1989 #125 Waltrip/Marlin/Elliott/R.Wallace Cars YR
1989 #127 Kul/Elliott/R.Wall/D.Allis/Martin Cars YR
1989 #152 Rusty Wallace VL
1989 #154 Rusty Wallace VL
1989 #165 Rusty Wallace VL
1989 #166 Rusty Wallace VL
1989 #167 Rusty Wallace VL
1989 #169 Rusty Wallace VL
1989 #210 R.Wallace/Ken.Wallace
1990 #27 Rusty Wallace
1990 #168 Rusty Wallace/Darrell Waltrip Cars YR
1990 #187 Rusty Wallace's Car YR
1990 #190 Rusty Wallace YR
1990 #196 Rusty Wallace's Car YR
1990 #197 Rusty Wallace in Pits YR
1990 #198 Rusty Wallace YR
1991 #2 Rusty Wallace
1991 #182 Rusty Wallace YR
1991 #180 Rusty Wallace YR
1993 #2 Rusty Wallace
1993 #286 Rusty Wallace w/Crew YR
1994 #2 Rusty Wallace
1994 #34 Rusty Wallace's Car
1994 #199 Rusty Wallace w/Crew
1994 #206 Rusty Wallace's Car MM
1994 #208 Rusty Wallace YR
1994 #212 Rusty Wallace YR
1994 #213 Rusty Wallace w/Crew YR
1994 #214 Rusty Wallace YR
1994 #223 Rusty Wallace YR
1994 #230 Rusty Wallace w/Crew YR
1994 #231 Rusty Wallace w/Crew YR
1994 #233 Rusty Wallace YR
1994 #235 Rusty Wallace YR
1994 #237 Rusty Wallace YR
1994 #322 Rusty Wallace WS
1994 #335 Gordon/R.Wall/Earn.Cars
1995 #2 Rusty Wallace
1995 #13 Rusty Wallace VL
1995 #51 Rusty Wallace's Car VL
1995 #60 Rusty Wallace VL
1995 #83 Rusty Wallace VL
1995 #87 Rusty Wallace VL
1995 #89 Rusty Wallace VL
1995 #115 Rusty Wallace VL
1995 #127 Rusty Wallace VL
1995 #129 Rusty Wallace VL
1995 #161 Rusty Wallace's Car
1996 #2 Rusty Wallace
1996 #53 Rusty Wallace's Car
1997 #2 Rusty Wallace
1997 #47 Rusty Wallace's Car
1997 #98 Rusty Wallace PS
1997 #101 Rusty Wallace PS
1997 #107 Rusty Wallace MO
1997 #R2 Rusty Wallace Promo
1998 #2 Rusty Wallace
1998 #32 Rusty Wallace's Car
1998 #99 Rusty Wallace's Car FR
1999 #43 Rusty Wallace
1999 #44 Rusty Wallace's Car
1999 #45 Rusty Wallace RR
2000 #2 Rusty Wallace
2000 #42 Rusty Wallace's Car
2000 #78 Rusty Wallace's Car FRF
2000 #85 Rusty Wallace CL
Maxx 10th Anniversary
1998 #1 Rusty Wallace
1998 #46 Rusty Wallace's Car
1998 #101 Rusty Wallace
1998 #117 B.Elliott/R.Wallace
1998 #118 D.Waltrip/R.Wallace
1998 #122 Rusty Wallace
1998 #123 Rusty Wallace
1998 #P1 Rusty Wallace Promo
Maxx 10th Anniversary Buy Back Autographs
1998 #47 Rusty Wallace '88 #14/297
Maxx 10th Anniversary Card of the Year
1998 #CY3 Rusty Wallace
1998 #CY7 Rusty Wallace
Maxx 10th Anniversary Champions Past
1998 #CP5 Rusty Wallace
Maxx 10th Anniversary Champions Past Die Cuts
1998 #CP5 Rusty Wallace
Maxx 10th Anniversary Maxximum Preview
1998 #P2 Rusty Wallace
Maxx 1997 Year In Review
1998 #11 Rusty Wallace
1998 #32 Rusty Wallace's Car
1998 #39 Rusty Wallace
1998 #84 Rusty Wallace's Car
1998 #103 Rusty Wallace's Car
1998 #135 Rusty Wallace's Car
1998 #P09 Rusty Wallace
Maxx Black
1992 #2 Rusty Wallace
1992 #202 Rusty Wallace MM
1992 #269 Rusty Wallace YR
1992 #280 Rusty Wallace YR
Maxx Charlotte
1988 #14 Rusty Wallace RC
1988 #62 R.Wallace/G.Bodine Cars
Maxx Club Sam Bass Chromium
1993 #3 Rusty Wallace
1993 #6 Rusty Wallace
Maxx Collectible Covers
2000 #CCRW Rusty Wallace
Maxx Crisco

1989 #5 Rusty Wallace
Maxx Drive Time
2000 #DT8 Rusty Wallace
Maxx Family Ties
1996 #FT4 R.Wall/M.Wall/K.Wallace
Maxx FANtastic Finishes
1999 #F5 Rusty Wallace's Car
Maxx Flag Firsts
1997 #FF2 Rusty Wallace
Maxx Focus on a Champion
1998 #FC10 Rusty Wallace
1999 #FC7 Rusty Wallace
Maxx Focus on a Champion Cel
1998 #FC10 Rusty Wallace
Maxx Focus on a Champion Gold
1999 #FC7 Rusty Wallace
Maxx Glossy
1990 #27 Rusty Wallace
1990 #168 Rusty Wallace/Darrell Waltrip Cars YR
1990 #187 Rusty Wallace's Car YR
1990 #190 Rusty Wallace YR
1990 #196 Rusty Wallace's Car YR
1990 #197 Rusty Wallace in Pits YR
1990 #198 Rusty Wallace YR
Maxx Holly Farms
1990 #HF4 Rusty Wallace
Maxx Made in America
1996 #2 Rusty Wallace
1996 #53 Rusty Wallace's Car
Maxx Made in America Blue Ribbon
1996 #BR6 Rusty Wallace's Car
Maxx McDonald's
1991 #6 Rusty Wallace
1992 #18 Rusty Wallace
Maxx Medallion
1994 #4 Rusty Wallace
1994 #69 Rusty Wallace
1995 #2 Rusty Wallace
1995 #32 Rusty Wallace's Car
Maxx Medallion Blue
1995 #2 Rusty Wallace
1995 #32 Rusty Wallace's Car
Maxx Motorsport
1994 #2 Rusty Wallace
Maxx Odyssey
1996 #2 Rusty Wallace
1996 #53 Rusty Wallace's Car
Maxx Odyssey Radio Active
1996 #RA6 Rusty Wallace's Car
Maxx On The Road Again
1996 #OTRA3 Rusty Wallace's Trans.
Maxx Premier Plus
1993 #2 Rusty Wallace
1993 #201 Rusty Wallace YR
1994 #2 Rusty Wallace
1994 #34 Rusty Wallace's Car
1994 #99 Rusty Wallace w/Crew
1994 #118 Rusty Wallace's Car
1994 #167 Rusty Wallace YR
1994 #171 Rusty Wallace YR
1994 #172 Rusty Wallace w/Crew YR
1994 #173 Rusty Wallace YR
1994 #182 Rusty Wallace w/Crew YR
1994 #189 Rusty Wallace YR
1994 #190 Rusty Wallace w/Crew YR
1994 #192 Rusty Wallace YR
1994 #194 Rusty Wallace YR
1994 #196 Rusty Wallace YR
1995 #2 Rusty Wallace
1995 #37 Rusty Wallace's Car
1995 #149 Rusty Wallace VL
1995 #153 Rusty Wallace in Pits VL
1995 #155 Rusty Wallace VL
1995 #161 Rusty Wallace VL
1995 #162 Rusty Wallace VL
1995 #163 Rusty Wallace VL
1995 #171 Rusty Wallace VL
1995 #174 Rusty Wallace VL
1995 #175 Rusty Wallace VL
Maxx Premier Plus Crown Chrome
1995 #2 Rusty Wallace
1995 #37 Rusty Wallace's Car
1995 #149 Rusty Wallace VL
1995 #153 Rusty Wallace in Pits VL
1995 #155 Rusty Wallace VL
1995 #161 Rusty Wallace VL
1995 #162 Rusty Wallace VL
1995 #163 Rusty Wallace VL
1995 #171 Rusty Wallace VL
1995 #174 Rusty Wallace VL
1995 #175 Rusty Wallace VL
Maxx Premier Plus PaceSetters
1995 #PS2 Rusty Wallace
Maxx Premier Plus PaceSetters Crown Chrome
1995 #PS2 Rusty Wallace
Maxx Premier Plus Retail Jumbos
1995 #6 Rusty Wallace
Maxx Premier Series
1993 #2 Rusty Wallace
1993 #286 Rusty Wallace w/Crew YR
1994 #258 Rusty Wallace w/Crew
1994 #2 Rusty Wallace
1994 #34 Rusty Wallace's Car
1994 #265 Rusty Wallace's Car MM
1994 #267 Rusty Wallace YR
1994 #271 Rusty Wallace YR
1994 #272 Rusty Wallace YR
1994 #273 Rusty Wallace YR
1994 #282 Rusty Wallace YR
1994 #289 Rusty Wallace YR
1994 #290 Rusty Wallace YR
1994 #292 Rusty Wallace YR
1994 #294 Rusty Wallace YR
1994 #296 Rusty Wallace YR
1995 #2 Rusty Wallace
1995 #37 Rusty Wallace's Car
1995 #264 Rusty Wallace YR
1995 #268 Rusty Wallace in Pits YR
1995 #270 Rusty Wallace YR
1995 #276 Rusty Wallace YR
1995 #277 Rusty Wallace YR
1995 #278 Rusty Wallace YR
1995 #286 Rusty Wallace YR
1995 #289 Rusty Wallace w/ Crew YR
1995 #290 Rusty Wallace YR

1996 #2 Rusty Wallace
1996 #38 Rusty Wallace's Car
Maxx Premier Series Jumbos
1994 #9 Rusty Wallace's Car
Maxx Previews
1989 #7 Rusty Wallace
Maxx Race Ticket
1999 #RT30 Rusty Wallace's Car
Maxx Racer's Ink
1999 #RW Rusty Wallace
2000 #RW Rusty Wallace
Maxx Racing Champions
1994 #3 Rusty Wallace
Maxx Racing for Kids
1991 #3 Sheet 3
Maxx Racing Images
1999 #RI23 Rusty Wallace
Maxx Red
1992 #2 Rusty Wallace
1992 #202 Rusty Wallace MM
1992 #269 Rusty Wallace YR
1992 #280 Rusty Wallace YR
Maxx Rookies of the Year
1994 #6 Rusty Wallace
Maxx Signed, Sealed, and Delivered
1999 #S1 Rusty Wallace/250
Maxx Stand Ups
1995 #5 Rusty Wallace's Car
Maxx Texaco Davey Allison
1993 #8 Dav.Allison/R.Wallace Cars
Maxx The Select 25
1994 #2 Rusty Wallace
Maxx The Winston
1992 #6 Rusty Wallace
1992 #26 Rusty Wallace's Car
1993 #8 Rusty Wallace
1993 #28 Rusty Wallace's Car
Maxx The Winston Acrylics
1991 #19 Rusty Wallace
Maxx Winston 20th Anniversary Foils
1991 #19 Rusty Wallace 1989 Car
Maxximum
1998 #2 Rusty Wallace
1998 #27 Rusty Wallace's Car
1998 #52 Rusty Wallace
1998 #77 Rusty Wallace
2000 #8 Rusty Wallace
Maxximum Battle Proven
1998 #B3 Rusty Wallace
Maxximum Die Cuts
2000 #8 Rusty Wallace
Maxximum Field Generals Four Star Autographs
1998 #1 Rusty Wallace
Maxximum Field Generals One Star
1998 #1 Rusty Wallace
Maxximum Field Generals Three Star Autographs
1998 #1 Rusty Wallace
Maxximum Field Generals Two Star
1998 #1 Rusty Wallace
Maxximum First Class
1998 #F18 Rusty Wallace
Maxximum MPH
2000 #8 Rusty Wallace/2
Maxximum Nifty Fifty
2000 #NF1 Rusty Wallace
2000 #NF2 Rusty Wallace
2000 #NF3 Rusty Wallace
2000 #NF4 Rusty Wallace
2000 #NF5 Rusty Wallace
Maxximum Pure Adrenaline
2000 #PA6 Rusty Wallace
Maxximum Signatures
2000 #RJ2 R.Wallace/J.Mayfield
2000 #RW Rusty Wallace
2000 #RKM3 R.Wal./K.Wal./M.Wal.
McFarlane NASCAR 3-Inch Series 1
2005 #140 Rusty Wallace
McFarlane NASCAR Series 1
2003 #NNO Rusty Wallace R Rusty Suit Rusty Hat
2003 #NNO Rusty Wallace R Rusty Suit Elvis Hat
2003 #NNO Rusty Wallace H Miller Lite Suit
2003 #NNO Rusty Wallace H Miller Lite Suit w/Glasses
McFarlane NASCAR Series 4
2005 #130 Rusty Wallace R
2005 #131 Rusty Wallace R Hat Glasses
2005 #135 Rusty Wallace H Miller Lite
McFarlane NASCAR Series 6
2005 #140 Rusty Wallace
Metallic Impressions 25th Anniversary Winston Cup Champions
1996 #19 Rusty Wallace
Metallic Impressions Avon All-Time Racing Greatest
1996 #5 Rusty Wallace
Metallic Impressions Rusty Wallace
1995 #1 Rusty Wallace
1995 #2 Rusty Wallace
1995 #3 Rusty Wallace
1995 #4 Rusty Wallace
1995 #5 Rusty Wallace
Metallic Impressions Upper Deck Rusty Wallace
1995 #1 Rusty Wallace
1995 #2 Rusty Wallace
1995 #3 Rusty Wallace
1995 #4 Rusty Wallace
1995 #5 Rusty Wallace
1995 #6 Rusty Wallace
1995 #7 Rusty Wallace
1995 #8 Rusty Wallace
1995 #9 Rusty Wallace
1995 #10 Rusty Wallace
1995 #11 Rusty Wallace
1995 #12 Rusty Wallace
1995 #13 Rusty Wallace
1995 #14 Rusty Wallace
1995 #15 Rusty Wallace
1995 #16 Rusty Wallace
1995 #17 Rusty Wallace
1995 #18 Rusty Wallace
1995 #19 Rusty Wallace
1995 #20 Rusty Wallace

Metallic Impressions Winston Cup Champions 10-Card Tin
1995 #9 Rusty Wallace
M-Force
1996 #1 Rusty Wallace
1996 #2 Rusty Wallace's Car
1996 #42 Rusty Wallace
M-Force Black
1996 #B1 Rusty Wallace
1996 #B2 Rusty Wallace's Car
M-Force Sheet Metal
1996 #M1 Rusty Wallace
M-Force Silvers
1996 #S1 Rusty Wallace's Car
1996 #S16 Rusty Wallace
Miller Genuine Draft Rusty Wallace
1992 #NNO Rusty Wallace
1992 #NNO Rusty Wallace
1992 #NNO Rusty Wallace
1992 #NNO Rusty Wallace
1992 #NNO Rusty Wallace
1992 #NNO Rusty Wallace
Miller Genuine Draft Rusty Wallace Post Cards
1993 #NNO Rusty Wallace The Boss
1993 #NNO Rusty Wallace Fire and Ice
1993 #NNO Rusty Wallace Midnight Rider
1993 #NNO Rusty Wallace Pocono Draft '92
Pinnacle
1996 #2 Rusty Wallace
1996 #37 Rusty Wallace's Car
1996 #86 Rusty Wallace W
1996 #89 Rusty Wallace W
1996 #94 Rusty Wallace's Transporter
1997 #2 Rusty Wallace
1997 #31 Rusty Wallace's Car
1997 #62 Rusty Wallace RR
1997 #73 Rusty Wallace TT
1997 #92 Rusty Wallace's Car T4
1997 #96 Rusty Wallace CL
Pinnacle Artist Proofs
1996 #2 Rusty Wallace
1996 #37 Rusty Wallace's Car
1996 #86 Rusty Wallace W
1996 #89 Rusty Wallace W
1996 #94 Rusty Wallace's Transporter
1997 #2 Rusty Wallace P
1997 #31 Rusty Wallace's Car B
1997 #62 Rusty Wallace RR R
1997 #73 Rusty Wallace TT R
1997 #92 Rusty Wallace's Car T4 R
1997 #96 Rusty Wallace CL R
Pinnacle Certified
1997 #2 Rusty Wallace
1997 #36 Rusty Wallace's Car
1997 #95 Rusty Wallace BD
Pinnacle Certified Certified Team
1997 #6 Rusty Wallace
Pinnacle Certified Certified Team Gold
1997 #6 Rusty Wallace
Pinnacle Certified Epix
1997 #E6 Rusty Wallace
Pinnacle Certified Epix Emerald
1997 #E6 Rusty Wallace
Pinnacle Certified Epix Purple
1997 #E6 Rusty Wallace
Pinnacle Certified Mirror Blue
1997 #2 Rusty Wallace
1997 #36 Rusty Wallace's Car
1997 #95 Rusty Wallace BD
Pinnacle Certified Mirror Gold
1997 #2 Rusty Wallace
1997 #36 Rusty Wallace's Car
1997 #95 Rusty Wallace BD
Pinnacle Certified Mirror Red
1997 #2 Rusty Wallace
1997 #36 Rusty Wallace's Car
1997 #95 Rusty Wallace BD
Pinnacle Certified Red
1997 #2 Rusty Wallace
1997 #36 Rusty Wallace's Car
1997 #95 Rusty Wallace BD
Pinnacle Checkered Flag
1996 #2 Rusty Wallace
Pinnacle Cut Above
1996 #8 Rusty Wallace
Pinnacle Foil
1997 #2 Rusty Wallace
1997 #31 Rusty Wallace's Car
1997 #62 Rusty Wallace RR
1997 #73 Rusty Wallace TT
1997 #92 Rusty Wallace's Car T4
1997 #96 Rusty Wallace CL
Pinnacle Mint
1997 #7 Rusty Wallace
1998 #10 Rusty Wallace
1998 #22 Rusty Wallace's Car
1998 #26 Rusty Wallace MM
Pinnacle Mint Bronze
1997 #7 Rusty Wallace
Pinnacle Mint Coins
1997 #7 Rusty Wallace
1998 #10 Rusty Wallace
1998 #22 Rusty Wallace's Car
1998 #2 Rusty Wallace MM
Pinnacle Mint Coins 24K Gold Plated
1997 #7 Rusty Wallace
Pinnacle Mint Coins Bronze Proof
1998 #10 Rusty Wallace
1998 #22 Rusty Wallace's Car
1998 #2 Rusty Wallace MM
Pinnacle Mint Coins Gold Plated
1998 #10 Rusty Wallace
1998 #22 Rusty Wallace's Car
1998 #26 Rusty Wallace MM
Pinnacle Mint Coins Gold Plated Proofs
1998 #10 Rusty Wallace
1998 #22 Rusty Wallace's Car
1998 #26 Rusty Wallace MM
Pinnacle Mint Coins Nickel-Silver
1997 #7 Rusty Wallace
1998 #10 Rusty Wallace
1998 #22 Rusty Wallace's Car
1998 #26 Rusty Wallace MM
Pinnacle Mint Coins Silver Plated Proofs
1998 #10 Rusty Wallace

1998 #22 Rusty Wallace's Car
1998 #26 Rusty Wallace MM
Pinnacle Mint Coins Solid Gold
1998 #10 Rusty Wallace
1998 #22 Rusty Wallace's Car
1998 #26 Rusty Wallace MM
Pinnacle Mint Coins Solid Silver
1998 #10 Rusty Wallace
1998 #22 Rusty Wallace's Car
1998 #26 Rusty Wallace MM
Pinnacle Mint Die Cuts
1998 #10 Rusty Wallace
1998 #22 Rusty Wallace's Car
1998 #26 Rusty Wallace MM
Pinnacle Mint Gold
1997 #7 Rusty Wallace
Pinnacle Mint Gold Team
1998 #10 Rusty Wallace
1998 #22 Rusty Wallace's Car
1998 #26 Rusty Wallace MM
Pinnacle Mint Silver
1997 #7 Rusty Wallace
Pinnacle Mint Silver Team
1998 #10 Rusty Wallace
1998 #22 Rusty Wallace's Car
1998 #26 Rusty Wallace MM
Pinnacle Pole Position
1996 #2 Rusty Wallace
1996 #26 Rusty Wallace's Car
1996 #65 Rusty Wallace WIN
1996 #70 Rusty Wallace WIN
1996 #78 Rusty Wallace EY
Pinnacle Pole Position Certified Strong
1996 #2 Rusty Wallace
Pinnacle Pole Position Lightning Fast
1996 #2 Rusty Wallace
1996 #26 Rusty Wallace's Car
1996 #65 Rusty Wallace
1996 #70 Rusty Wallace
1996 #78 Rusty Wallace
Pinnacle Pole Position No Limit
1996 #2 Rusty Wallace
Pinnacle Pole Position No Limit Gold
1996 #2 Rusty Wallace
Pinnacle Portraits
1997 #18 Rusty Wallace
1997 #38 Rusty Wallace's Car
Pinnacle Precision
1997 #37 Rusty Wallace's Transporter
1997 #39 Rusty Wallace
1997 #40 Rusty Wallace Pit Action
1997 #41 Rusty Wallace's Car
1997 #42 Rusty Wallace
1997 #44 Rusty Wallace's Car
1997 #45 Rusty Wallace
Pinnacle Precision Bronze
1997 #37 Rusty Wallace's Transporter
1997 #39 Rusty Wallace
1997 #40 Rusty Wallace's Car
1997 #41 Rusty Wallace's Car
1997 #42 Rusty Wallace
1997 #44 Rusty Wallace's Car
1997 #45 Rusty Wallace
Pinnacle Precision Gold
1997 #37 Rusty Wallace's Transporter
1997 #39 Rusty Wallace
1997 #40 Rusty Wallace Pit Action
1997 #41 Rusty Wallace's Car
1997 #42 Rusty Wallace
1997 #44 Rusty Wallace's Car
1997 #45 Rusty Wallace
Pinnacle Precision Silver
1997 #37 Rusty Wallace's Transporter
1997 #39 Rusty Wallace
1997 #40 Rusty Wallace Pit Action
1997 #41 Rusty Wallace's Car
1997 #42 Rusty Wallace
1997 #44 Rusty Wallace's Car
1997 #45 Rusty Wallace
Pinnacle Press Plates
1997 #2 Rusty Wallace
1997 #31 Rusty Wallace's Car
1997 #62 Rusty Wallace RR
1997 #73 Rusty Wallace TT
1997 #92 Rusty Wallace's Car T4
1997 #S4-C Rusty Wallace
1997 #TP2A Rusty Wallace
Pinnacle Spellbound
1997 #4C Rusty Wallace
Pinnacle Spellbound Promos
1997 #4C Rusty Wallace
Pinnacle Team Pinnacle
1996 #2 Rusty Wallace
1997 #2 Rusty Wallace
Pinnacle Team Pinnacle Red
1997 #2 Rusty Wallace
Pinnacle Totally Certified Platinum Blue
1997 #2 Rusty Wallace
1997 #36 Rusty Wallace's Car
1997 #95 Rusty Wallace BD
Pinnacle Totally Certified Platinum Gold
1997 #2 Rusty Wallace
1997 #36 Rusty Wallace's Car
1997 #95 Rusty Wallace BD
Pinnacle Totally Certified Platinum Red
1997 #2 Rusty Wallace
1997 #36 Rusty Wallace's Car
1997 #95 Rusty Wallace BD
Pinnacle Trophy Collection
1997 #2 Rusty Wallace
1997 #31 Rusty Wallace's Car
1997 #62 Rusty Wallace RR
1997 #73 Rusty Wallace TT
1997 #92 Rusty Wallace's Car T4
Pinnacle Winston Cup Collection
1996 #2 Rusty Wallace
1996 #37 Rusty Wallace's Car
1996 #86 Rusty Wallace W
1996 #89 Rusty Wallace W
1996 #94 Rusty Wallace's Transporter
Power
1994 #17 Rusty Wallace PW
1994 #39 Rusty Wallace SL
1994 #54 Rusty Wallace in Pits SL
1994 #63 Rusty Wallace's Trans. PR
1994 #122 Rusty Wallace

1994 #123 Rusty Wallace
Power Gold
1994 #17 Rusty Wallace PW
1994 #39 Rusty Wallace SL
1994 #54 Rusty Wallace in Pits SL
1994 #63 Rusty Wallace's Trans. PR
1994 #122 Rusty Wallace
1994 #123 Rusty Wallace
Power Preview
1994 #8 Rusty Wallace
Predator
1997 #6 Rusty Wallace
Predator American Eagle
1997 #AE3 Rusty Wallace
Predator American Eagle First Slash
1997 #AE3 Rusty Wallace
Predator Black Wolf First Strike
1997 #6 Rusty Wallace
Predator Eye of the Tiger
1997 #ET3 Rusty Wallace
Predator Eye of the Tiger First Slash
1997 #ET3 Rusty Wallace
Predator First Slash
1997 #6 Rusty Wallace
Predator Gatorback
1997 #GB5 Rusty Wallace
Predator Gatorback Authentic
1997 #GBA5 Rusty Wallace
Predator Gatorback Authentic First Slash
1997 #GBA5 Rusty Wallace
Predator Gatorback First Slash
1997 #GB5 Rusty Wallace
Predator Golden Eagle
1997 #GE3 Rusty Wallace
Predator Golden Eagle First Slash
1997 #GE3 Rusty Wallace
Predator Grizzly
1997 #6 Rusty Wallace
Predator Grizzly First Slash
1997 #6 Rusty Wallace
Predator Red Wolf
1997 #6 Rusty Wallace
Predator Red Wolf First Slash
1997 #6 Rusty Wallace
Press Pass
1994 #28 Rusty Wallace
1994 #31 Rusty Wallace/K.Wallace
1994 #47 Rusty Wallace's Car
1994 #118 Rusty Wallace DOY
1994 #123 Rusty Wallace TT
1994 #144 Rusty Wallace ART
1995 #34 Rusty Wallace
1995 #47 Rusty Wallace's Car
1995 #135 Rusty Wallace PR
1996 #34 Rusty Wallace
1996 #47 Rusty Wallace's Car
1996 #73 Penske/Miller/Pember/R.Wall TW
1996 #99 Rusty Wallace S
1996 #119 Rusty Wallace's Car PRE
1997 #7 Rusty Wallace
1997 #31 Rusty Wallace's Car
1997 #53 Rusty Wallace
1997 #62 Rusty Wallace's Car
1997 #84 Rusty Wallace
1997 #99 Rusty Wallace's Car
1997 #122 Rusty Wallace's Car
1998 #7 Rusty Wallace
1998 #28 Rusty Wallace's Car
1998 #105 Rusty Wallace RET
1999 #4 Rusty Wallace
1999 #31 Rusty Wallace's Car
1999 #80 Rusty Wallace OTP
1999 #104 Rusty Wallace RET
2000 #8 Rusty Wallace
2000 #54 Rusty Wallace DD
2001 #7 Rusty Wallace
2001 #54 Rusty Wallace's Car
2001 #65 Rusty Wallace REP
2001 #84 Rusty Wallace SO
2002 #35 Rusty Wallace
2002 #76 Rusty Wallace's Car
2003 #32 Rusty Wallace
2003 #91 Rusty Wallace's Car OTW
2004 #32 Rusty Wallace
2004 #64 Rusty Wallace's Car OTW
2004 #76 Penske Power WCS
2005 #3 Rusty Wallace
2005 #68 Rusty Wallace's Car OTW
2005 #79 Rusty Wallace NS
2005 #98 Rusty Wallace Y
2005 #100 Rusty Wallace P
2005 #111 Rusty Wallace's Car
2006 #4 Rusty Wallace
2006 #84 Rusty Wallace's Car OTW
2006 #112 Rusty Wallace TT
2007 #61 Rusty Wallace
2008 #56 Rusty Wallace
Press Pass Authentics
1994 #5 Rusty Wallace
Press Pass Authentics Autographs
1994 #5 Rusty Wallace AUTO
Press Pass Autographs
1997 #7 Rusty Wallace VIP/ACTN
1998 #8 Rusty Wallace
1999 #20 Rusty Wallace/70
2001 #44 Rusty Wallace
2002 #67 Rusty Wallace
2003 #59 Rusty Wallace E/P
2004 #59 Rusty Wallace P
2005 #60 Rusty Wallace E/P
Press Pass Banquet Bound
1997 #BB7 Rusty Wallace
Press Pass Blue
2006 #B4 Rusty Wallace
2006 #B84 Rusty Wallace's Car OTW
2006 #B112 Rusty Wallace TT
2007 #B61 Rusty Wallace
2008 #B56 Rusty Wallace
Press Pass Bryan
1999 #8 Rusty Wallace
Press Pass Burning Rubber
1997 #BR1 Rusty Wallace
1999 #BR8 Rusty Wallace's Car
2000 #BR7 Rusty Wallace
Press Pass Burning Rubber Autographs
2004 #BRRW Rusty Wallace/2

2005 #BR-RW Rusty Wallace/2
2006 #BR-RW Rusty Wallace/2
Press Pass Burning Rubber Cars
2001 #BRC2 Rusty Wallace/105
2002 #BRC2 Rusty Wallace's Car
2003 #BRT5 Rusty Wallace's Car
2004 #BRT9 Rusty Wallace's Car
2005 #BRT6 Rusty Wallace's Car
2006 #BRT18 Rusty Wallace
Press Pass Burning Rubber Cars Autographs
2003 #BRT-RW Rusty Wallace/2
Press Pass Burning Rubber Die Cast Inserts
1996 #3 Rusty Wallace/1996
Press Pass Burning Rubber Drivers
2001 #BRD2 Rusty Wallace/90
2002 #BRD2 Rusty Wallace
2003 #BRD5 Rusty Wallace
2004 #BRD9 Rusty Wallace
2005 #BRD6 Rusty Wallace
2006 #BRD18 Rusty Wallace
Press Pass Burning Rubber Drivers Autographs
2003 #BRD-RW Rusty Wallace/2
Press Pass Burning Rubber Drivers Gold
2005 #BRD6 Rusty Wallace
2006 #BRD18 Rusty Wallace
Press Pass Chase Cars
1999 #18B Rusty Wallace's Car
Press Pass Checkered Flags
1994 #CF4 Rusty Wallace
1995 #CF8 Rusty Wallace
1996 #CF6 Rusty Wallace
Press Pass Clear Cut
1997 #C9 Rusty Wallace
Press Pass Cup Chase
1994 #CC28 Rusty Wallace W3
1995 #34 Rusty Wallace
1996 #34 Rusty Wallace WIN
1997 #CC18 Rusty Wallace WIN
1998 #CC18 Rusty Wallace Win 2
1999 #19 Rusty Wallace WIN
2000 #CC16 Rusty Wallace WIN
2001 #CC2 Rusty Wallace
2002 #CC16 Rusty Wallace
2003 #CCR16 Rusty Wallace
2004 #CCR8 Rusty Wallace
2005 #CCR17 Rusty Wallace
Press Pass Cup Chase Blue Die Cut Prizes
1997 #CC18 Rusty Wallace
Press Pass Cup Chase Die Cut Prizes
1998 #CC18 Rusty Wallace
1999 #19 Rusty Wallace
2000 #CC16 Rusty Wallace
2001 #CC2 Rusty Wallace
Press Pass Cup Chase Foil Prizes
1996 #34 Rusty Wallace
Press Pass Cup Chase Gold Die Cuts
1997 #CC18 Rusty Wallace
Press Pass Cup Chase Prizes
1995 #CCR5 Rusty Wallace
2002 #CC16 Rusty Wallace
2003 #CCR16 Rusty Wallace
2004 #CCR8 Rusty Wallace
2005 #CCP17 Rusty Wallace
Press Pass Double Burner
2001 #DB2 Rusty Wallace
2002 #DB9 Rusty Wallace
2003 #DB5 Rusty Wallace
2004 #DB5 Rusty Wallace
2005 #DB5 Rusty Wallace
Press Pass Double Burner Exchange
2003 #DB5 Rusty Wallace EXCH
2004 #DB5 Rusty Wallace
2005 #DB5 Rusty Wallace
Press Pass Eclipse
2002 #7 Rusty Wallace
2003 #7 Rusty Wallace
2004 #13 Rusty Wallace
2004 #28 Rusty Wallace's Car
2004 #62 Rusty Wallace P
2004 #76 M.Martin/R.Wallace LL
2005 #16 Rusty Wallace
2005 #62 Rusty Wallace P
2005 #82 Rusty Wallace LL
2006 #8 Rusty Wallace
2006 #47 Rusty Wallace P
2006 #65 NCS Top-10 BA
2006 #66 Rusty Wallace BA
2006 #69 Tony Stewart BA
2006 #80 Rusty Wallace LL
2006 #47B Rusty Wallace P Blk Jacket
2007 #62 Rusty Wallace NT
Press Pass Eclipse Destination WIN
2005 #7 Rusty Wallace
Press Pass Eclipse Double Hot Treads
2003 #DT9 R.Newman/R.Wallace
Press Pass Eclipse Gold
2007 #G62 Rusty Wallace NT
Press Pass Eclipse Hyperdrive
2004 #HP2 Rusty Wallace
2006 #HP9 Rusty Wallace
Press Pass Eclipse Maxim
2005 #MX12 Rusty Wallace
Press Pass Eclipse Previews
2003 #7 Rusty Wallace
2004 #13 Rusty Wallace
2005 #EB16 Rusty Wallace
2005 #EB62 Rusty Wallace P
2005 #EB82 Rusty Wallace LL/1
Press Pass Eclipse Racing Champions
2002 #RC10 Rusty Wallace
Press Pass Eclipse Red
2007 #R62 Rusty Wallace NT
Press Pass Eclipse Samples
2002 #7 Rusty Wallace
2003 #7 Rusty Wallace
2004 #13 Rusty Wallace
2004 #28 Rusty Wallace's Car
2004 #62 Rusty Wallace P
2004 #76 M.Martin/R.Wallace LL
2005 #16 Rusty Wallace
2005 #62 Rusty Wallace P
2005 #82 Rusty Wallace LL
Press Pass Eclipse Skidmarks
2002 #SK9 Rusty Wallace

2003 #SM4 Rusty Wallace
2004 #SM15 Rusty Wallace
2005 #SM15 Rusty Wallace
2006 #SM10 Rusty Wallace
Press Pass Eclipse Skidmarks Holofoil
2004 #SM15 Rusty Wallace
2005 #SM15 Rusty Wallace
2006 #SM10 Rusty Wallace
Press Pass Eclipse Solar Eclipse
2002 #S7 Rusty Wallace
2003 #P7 Rusty Wallace
Press Pass Eclipse Supernova
2002 #SN12 Rusty Wallace
2003 #SN12 Rusty Wallace
2006 #SU6 Rusty Wallace
Press Pass Eclipse Supernova Numbered
2002 #SN12 Rusty Wallace
Press Pass Eclipse Teammates Autographs
2003 #RNRW R.Newman/R.Wallace
2004 #7 R.Newman/R.Wallace
2005 #3 R.Newman/R.Wallace
2006 #7 R.Wallace/R.Newman
Press Pass Eclipse Under Cover Autographs
2004 #UCRW Rusty Wallace/2
2005 #UCRW Rusty Wallace/2
2006 #RW Rusty Wallace/2
Press Pass Eclipse Under Cover Cars
2004 #UCD9 Rusty Wallace
2005 #UCT9 Rusty Wallace
2006 #UCT13 Rusty Wallace
Press Pass Eclipse Under Cover Double Cover
2004 #DC2 R.Wallace/R.Newman
2005 #DC2 R.Wallace/R.Newman
2006 #DC4 R.Newman/R.Wallace
Press Pass Eclipse Under Cover Double Cover Holofoil
2006 #DC4 R.Newman/R.Wallace
Press Pass Eclipse Under Cover Driver Gold
2004 #UCD9 Rusty Wallace
Press Pass Eclipse Under Cover Driver Red
2004 #UCD9 Rusty Wallace
2005 #UCD9 Rusty Wallace
Press Pass Eclipse Under Cover Driver Silver
2004 #UCD9 Rusty Wallace
Press Pass Eclipse Under Cover Drivers Gold
2006 #UCD13 Rusty Wallace
Press Pass Eclipse Under Cover Drivers Holofoil
2005 #UCD9 Rusty Wallace
2006 #UCD13 Rusty Wallace
Press Pass Eclipse Under Cover Drivers Silver
2005 #UCD9 Rusty Wallace
2006 #UCD13 Rusty Wallace
Press Pass Eclipse Warp Speed
2002 #WS3 Rusty Wallace
2003 #WS3 Rusty Wallace
Press Pass Focused
1996 #F10 Rusty Wallace
Press Pass Four Wide
2006 #FW-RW Rusty Wallace
Press Pass Four Wide Checkered Flag
2006 #FW-RW Rusty Wallace
Press Pass Gatorade Front Runner Award
2001 #7 Rusty Wallace
Press Pass Gold
2006 #G4 Rusty Wallace
2006 #G84 Rusty Wallace's Car OTW
2006 #G112 Rusty Wallace TT
2007 #G61 Rusty Wallace
2008 #G56 Rusty Wallace
Press Pass Gold Holofoil
2003 #P32 Rusty Wallace
2003 #P91 Rusty Wallace's Car OTW
Press Pass Ground Zero
2001 #GZ2 Rusty Wallace
Press Pass Holofoils
1994 #H6 Rusty Wallace
Press Pass Hot Treads
2001 #HT3 Rusty Wallace/2405
2002 #HT20 Rusty Wallace's Car/2425
2004 #HTR13 Rusty Wallace
2005 #HTR9 Rusty Wallace
Press Pass Hot Treads Holofoil
2004 #HTR13 Rusty Wallace
2005 #HTR9 Rusty Wallace
Press Pass Lasers
1997 #7 Rusty Wallace
1997 #31 Rusty Wallace's Car
1997 #53 Rusty Wallace
1997 #62 Rusty Wallace's Car
1997 #84 Rusty Wallace
1997 #99 Rusty Wallace's Car
1997 #122 Rusty Wallace's Car
Press Pass Legends
2005 #22 Rusty Wallace
2005 #38 Rusty Wallace C
2006 #28 Rusty Wallace
2007 #32 Rusty Wallace
Press Pass Legends Autographs Black
2006 #13 Rusty Wallace/200
Press Pass Legends Autographs Blue
2006 #15 Rusty Wallace/300
Press Pass Legends Blue
2005 #22B Rusty Wallace
2005 #38B Rusty Wallace C
2006 #B28 Rusty Wallace
2007 #B32 Rusty Wallace
Press Pass Legends Bronze
2006 #Z28 Rusty Wallace
2007 #Z32 Rusty Wallace
Press Pass Legends Double Threads Bronze
2005 #DT-NW R.Newman/R.Wallace
Press Pass Legends Double Threads Gold
2005 #DT-NW R.Newman/R.Wallace
Press Pass Legends Double Threads Silver
2005 #DT-NW R.Newman/R.Wallace
Press Pass Legends Father & Son Firesuits Bronze
2007 #RWSW-F R.Wallace/S.Wallace
Press Pass Legends Father & Son Firesuits Gold
2007 #RWSW-F R.Wallace/S.Wallace
Press Pass Legends Father & Son Firesuits Silver
2007 #RWSW-F R.Wallace/S.Wallace
Press Pass Legends Gold
2005 #22G Rusty Wallace
2005 #38G Rusty Wallace C
2006 #G28 Rusty Wallace
2007 #G32 Rusty Wallace
Press Pass Legends Heritage
2005 #HE10 Rusty Wallace
Press Pass Legends Heritage Gold
2006 #HE8 Rusty Wallace
Press Pass Legends Heritage Silver
2006 #HE8 Rusty Wallace
Press Pass Legends Holofoil
2005 #22H Rusty Wallace
2005 #38H Rusty Wallace C
2006 #H28 Rusty Wallace
2007 #H32 Rusty Wallace
Press Pass Legends Legends Gallery Gold
2007 #LG3 Rusty Wallace
Press Pass Legends Legends Gallery Silver
2007 #LG3 Rusty Wallace
Press Pass Legends Memorable Moments Gold
2006 #MM16 Rusty Wallace
2007 #MM5 Rusty Wallace B
Press Pass Legends Memorable Moments Silver
2006 #MM16 Rusty Wallace
2007 #MM5 Rusty Wallace B
Press Pass Legends Press Plates Black
2005 #22 Rusty Wallace
2005 #38 Rusty Wallace C
2006 #PPB28 Rusty Wallace
2007 #PP32 Rusty Wallace
Press Pass Legends Press Plates Black Backs
2006 #PPB28B Rusty Wallace
2007 #PP32 Rusty Wallace
Press Pass Legends Press Plates Cyan
2005 #22 Rusty Wallace
2005 #38 Rusty Wallace C
2006 #PPC28 Rusty Wallace
2007 #PP32 Rusty Wallace
Press Pass Legends Press Plates Cyan Backs
2006 #PPC28B Rusty Wallace
2007 #PP32 Rusty Wallace
Press Pass Legends Press Plates Magenta
2005 #22 Rusty Wallace
2005 #38 Rusty Wallace C
2006 #PPM28 Rusty Wallace
2007 #PP32 Rusty Wallace
Press Pass Legends Press Plates Magenta Backs
2006 #PPM28B Rusty Wallace
2007 #PP32 Rusty Wallace
Press Pass Legends Press Plates Yellow
2005 #22 Rusty Wallace
2005 #38 Rusty Wallace C
2006 #PPY28 Rusty Wallace
2007 #PP32 Rusty Wallace
Press Pass Legends Press Plates Yellow Backs
2006 #PPY28B Rusty Wallace
2007 #PP32 Rusty Wallace
Press Pass Legends Previews
2005 #22 Rusty Wallace
2005 #38 Rusty Wallace C
2006 #EB28 Rusty Wallace
2007 #EB32 Rusty Wallace
Press Pass Legends Racing Artifacts Firesuit Bronze
2006 #RW-F Rusty Wallace
2007 #RW-F Rusty Wallace
Press Pass Legends Racing Artifacts Firesuit Gold
2006 #RW-F Rusty Wallace
2007 #RW-F Rusty Wallace
Press Pass Legends Racing Artifacts Firesuit Patch
2006 #RW-F Rusty Wallace
2007 #RW-F Rusty Wallace
Press Pass Legends Racing Artifacts Firesuit Silver
2006 #RW-F Rusty Wallace
2007 #RW-F Rusty Wallace
Press Pass Legends Racing Artifacts Tire Bronze
2006 #RW-T Rusty Wallace
2007 #RW-T Rusty Wallace
Press Pass Legends Racing Artifacts Tire Gold
2006 #RW-T Rusty Wallace
2007 #RW-T Rusty Wallace
Press Pass Legends Racing Artifacts Tire Silver
2006 #RW-T Rusty Wallace
2007 #RW-T Rusty Wallace
Press Pass Legends Solo
2005 #22S Rusty Wallace
2005 #38S Rusty Wallace C
2006 #S28 Rusty Wallace
2007 #S32 Rusty Wallace
Press Pass Legends Threads & Treads Bronze
2005 #TTRW Rusty Wallace
Press Pass Legends Threads & Treads Gold
2005 #TTRW Rusty Wallace
Press Pass Legends Threads & Treads Silver
2005 #TTRW Rusty Wallace
Press Pass Making the Show Collector's Series
2004 #MS2 Rusty Wallace
Press Pass Millennium
2000 #8 Rusty Wallace
2000 #54 Rusty Wallace
2001 #7 Rusty Wallace
2001 #54 Rusty Wallace's Car
2001 #65 Rusty Wallace REP
2001 #84 Rusty Wallace SO
Press Pass Oil Cans
1998 #OC9 Rusty Wallace
1999 #9 Rusty Wallace
2000 #OC3 Rusty Wallace
Press Pass Oil Slicks
1997 #7 Rusty Wallace
1997 #31 Rusty Wallace's Car
1997 #53 Rusty Wallace
1997 #62 Rusty Wallace's Car
1997 #84 Rusty Wallace
1997 #99 Rusty Wallace's Car
1997 #122 Rusty Wallace's Car
1998 #7 Rusty Wallace
1998 #28 Rusty Wallace's Car
Press Pass Optima
2000 #25 Rusty Wallace
2000 #49 Rusty Wallace WCL
2001 #26 Rusty Wallace
2001 #49 Rusty Wallace WCL
2002 #29 Rusty Wallace
2003 #26 Rusty Wallace
2004 #26 Rusty Wallace
2004 #60 Rusty Wallace's Car RV
2004 #81 Rusty Wallace CP
2005 #29 Rusty Wallace
2005 #29B Rusty Wallace Cup Chase
2005 #73 Rusty Wallace CP
2005 #97 Rusty Wallace R&R
2006 #91 Rusty Wallace 84 ROTY
2006 #92 Rusty Wallace 1st Win '86
2006 #93 Rusty Wallace 89 Champ
2006 #94 Rusty Wallace 50th Win
2006 #95 Rusty Wallace Last Win
2006 #96 Rusty Wallace Short Track
Press Pass Optima Cool Persistence
2000 #CP6 Rusty Wallace
2001 #CP12 Rusty Wallace
2002 #CP12 Rusty Wallace
2003 #CP10 Rusty Wallace
2005 #CP5 Rusty Wallace
Press Pass Optima Encore
2000 #EN9 Rusty Wallace
Press Pass Optima Fan Favorite
2002 #FF26 Rusty Wallace
2003 #FF22 Rusty Wallace
2004 #FF24 Rusty Wallace
2005 #FF26 Rusty Wallace
Press Pass Optima G Force
2000 #GF25 Rusty Wallace
2001 #GF26 Rusty Wallace
2004 #GF6 Rusty Wallace
Press Pass Optima Gold
2001 #26 Rusty Wallace
2001 #49 Rusty Wallace WCL
2002 #29 Rusty Wallace
2003 #G26 Rusty Wallace
2004 #G26 Rusty Wallace
2004 #G60 Rusty Wallace's Car RV
2004 #G81 Rusty Wallace CP
2005 #G29 Rusty Wallace
2005 #G73 Rusty Wallace CP
2005 #G97 Rusty Wallace R&R
2006 #G93 Rusty Wallace 89 Champ
2006 #G94 Rusty Wallace 50th Win
2006 #G95 Rusty Wallace Last Win
2006 #G96 Rusty Wallace Short Track
2006 #G91 Rusty Wallace 84 ROTY
2006 #G92 Rusty Wallace 1st Win '86
Press Pass Optima On the Edge
2001 #OE9 Rusty Wallace
Press Pass Optima Overdrive
2000 #OD9 Rusty Wallace
Press Pass Optima Overdrive Square Cut
2000 #OD9 Rusty Wallace
Press Pass Optima Platinum
2000 #25 Rusty Wallace
2000 #49 Rusty Wallace WCL
Press Pass Optima Previews
2003 #26 Rusty Wallace
2004 #EB26 Rusty Wallace
2005 #29 Rusty Wallace
Press Pass Optima Promos
2002 #29 Rusty Wallace
Press Pass Optima Race Used Lugnuts Autographs
2002 #LNDA18 Rusty Wallace/2
Press Pass Optima Race Used Lugnuts Cars
2000 #LC14 Rusty Wallace's Car
2001 #LNC16 Rusty Wallace's Car
2002 #LNC18 Rusty Wallace's Car
Press Pass Optima Race Used Lugnuts Drivers
2000 #LD14 Rusty Wallace
2001 #LND15 Rusty Wallace
2002 #LND18 Rusty Wallace
Press Pass Optima Samples
2002 #29 Rusty Wallace
2003 #26 Rusty Wallace
2004 #26 Rusty Wallace
2004 #60 Rusty Wallace's Car RV
2004 #81 Rusty Wallace CP
2005 #29 Rusty Wallace
2005 #73 Rusty Wallace CP
2005 #97 Rusty Wallace R&R
Press Pass Optima Thunder Bolts Autographs
2004 #TBRW Rusty Wallace/2
Press Pass Optima Thunder Bolts Cars
2003 #TBT5 Rusty Wallace's Car
2004 #TBT7 Rusty Wallace's Car
Press Pass Optima Thunder Bolts Cars Autographs
2003 #TBT-RW Rusty Wallace/2
Press Pass Optima Thunder Bolts Drivers
2003 #TBD5 Rusty Wallace/60
2004 #TBD7 Rusty Wallace
Press Pass Optima Thunder Bolts Drivers Autographs
2003 #TBD-RW Rusty Wallace/2
Press Pass Optima Up Close
2001 #UC6 Rusty Wallace
2002 #UC5 Rusty Wallace
Press Pass Optima XL
1994 #22 Rusty Wallace
1994 #30 Rusty Wallace
1994 #35 Rusty Wallace DD
1994 #40 Rusty Wallace's Car TC
1994 #51 Rusty Wallace in Pits WCS
1994 #52 E.Irvan/R.Wall./Martin WCS
1995 #22 Rusty Wallace
1995 #45 Rusty Wallace's Car
Press Pass Optima XL Cool Blue
1995 #22 Rusty Wallace
1995 #45 Rusty Wallace's Car
Press Pass Optima XL Die Cut
1995 #22 Rusty Wallace
1995 #45 Rusty Wallace's Car
Press Pass Optima XL Prototypes
1994 #2A R.Wallace DD Name at bottom
1994 #2B R.Wallace DD Name at top
Press Pass Optima XL Red Hot
1994 #22 Rusty Wallace
1994 #30 Rusty Wallace
1994 #35 Rusty Wallace DD
1994 #40 Rusty Wallace's Car TC
1994 #51 Rusty Wallace in Pits WCS
1994 #52 R.Wallace/M.Martin/Irvan WCS
1995 #22 Rusty Wallace
1995 #45 Rusty Wallace's Car
Press Pass Optima XL Stealth
1995 #XLS16 Rusty Wallace
Press Pass Panorama
2005 #PPP16 Rusty Wallace
2005 #PPP34 Rusty Wallace
2005 #PPP45 Rusty Wallace
2005 #PPP61 Rusty Wallace
2005 #PPP64 Rusty Wallace
Press Pass Pit Stop
1998 #PS1 Rusty Wallace's Car
1999 #2 Rusty Wallace's Car
Press Pass Pitstop
2000 #PS2 Rusty Wallace's Car
Press Pass Platinum
2002 #35 Rusty Wallace
2002 #76 Rusty Wallace's Car
2004 #P32 Rusty Wallace
2004 #P64 Rusty Wallace's Car OTW
2004 #P76 Penske Power WCS
2005 #P3 Rusty Wallace
2005 #P68 Rusty Wallace's Car OTW
2005 #P79 Rusty Wallace NS
2005 #P98 Rusty Wallace Y
2005 #P100 Rusty Wallace P
2005 #P111 Rusty Wallace's Car
2006 #P4 Rusty Wallace
2006 #P84 Rusty Wallace's Car OTW
2006 #P112 Rusty Wallace TT
2007 #P61 Rusty Wallace
2008 #P56 Rusty Wallace
Press Pass Premium
1995 #3 Rusty Wallace
1995 #31 Rusty Wallace
1996 #5 Rusty Wallace
1996 #40 Rusty Wallace's Car
1997 #7 Rusty Wallace
1997 #28 Rusty Wallace's Car
1997 #44 Rusty Wallace
1998 #14 Rusty Wallace's Car
1998 #36 Rusty Wallace
1999 #26 Rusty Wallace
1999 #31 Rusty Wallace's Car
2000 #2 Rusty Wallace
2000 #28 Rusty Wallace's Car
2000 #50 Rusty Wallace
2001 #26 Rusty Wallace
2001 #29 Rusty Wallace
2001 #56 Rusty Wallace CC
2001 #81 Rusty Wallace PC
2002 #32 Rusty Wallace
2002 #55 Rusty Wallace CH
2002 #81 Rusty Wallace PC
2003 #29 Rusty Wallace
2003 #52 Rusty Wallace CC
2003 #79 Rusty Wallace PC
2004 #20 Rusty Wallace
2004 #37 Rusty Wallace's Car
2004 #52 Rusty Wallace CC
2004 #71 Rusty Wallace PC
2005 #32 Rusty Wallace
2005 #39 Rusty Wallace's Car M
2005 #52 Rusty Wallace CC
2005 #80 Rusty Wallace PC
Press Pass Premium Asphalt Jungle
2005 #AJ6 Rusty Wallace
Press Pass Premium Badge of Honor
1999 #BH1 Rusty Wallace
Press Pass Premium Badge of Honor Reflectors
1999 #BH1 Rusty Wallace
Press Pass Premium Burning Rubber II
1996 #BR6 Rusty Wallace's Car
Press Pass Premium Crystal Ball
1996 #CB12 Rusty Wallace
1997 #CB12 Rusty Wallace
Press Pass Premium Crystal Ball Die Cut
1997 #CB12 Rusty Wallace
Press Pass Premium Double Burners
1997 #DB4 Rusty Wallace
Press Pass Premium Emerald Proofs
1996 #5 Rusty Wallace
1996 #40 Rusty Wallace's Car
1997 #7 Rusty Wallace
1997 #28 Rusty Wallace's Car
1997 #44 Rusty Wallace
Press Pass Premium Extreme Fire
1999 #FD3A Rusty Wallace 1:144
Press Pass Premium Flag Chasers
1998 #FC6 Rusty Wallace
1998 #FC19 Rusty Wallace's Car
Press Pass Premium Flag Chasers Reflectors
1998 #FC6 Rusty Wallace
1998 #FC19 Rusty Wallace's Car
Press Pass Premium Gold
2001 #26 Rusty Wallace
2001 #29 Rusty Wallace
2001 #56 Rusty Wallace CC
2001 #81 Rusty Wallace PC
Press Pass Premium Holofoil
1995 #3 Rusty Wallace
1995 #31 Rusty Wallace
1996 #5 Rusty Wallace
1996 #40 Rusty Wallace's Car
Press Pass Premium Hot Pursuit
1995 #HP9 Rusty Wallace
1996 #HP8 Rusty Wallace
Press Pass Premium Hot Threads Autographs
2004 #HT-RW Rusty Wallace/2
2005 #HT-RW Rusty Wallace/2
2006 #HT-RW Rusty Wallace/2
Press Pass Premium Hot Threads Cars
2003 #HTT5 Rusty Wallace
2005 #HTT10 Rusty Wallace
Press Pass Premium Hot Threads Cars Autographs
2003 #HTD-RW Rusty Wallace/2
Press Pass Premium Hot Threads Drivers
2003 #HTD5 Rusty Wallace
2005 #HTD10 Rusty Wallace
Press Pass Premium Hot Threads Drivers Autographs
2003 #HTT-RW Rusty Wallace/2
Press Pass Premium Hot Threads Drivers Bronze
2004 #HTD9 Rusty Wallace
Press Pass Premium Hot Threads Drivers Bronze Retail
2004 #HTT9 Rusty Wallace
Press Pass Premium Hot Threads Drivers Gold
2004 #HTD9 Rusty Wallace
2005 #HTD10 Rusty Wallace
Press Pass Premium Hot Threads Drivers Silver
2004 #HTD9 Rusty Wallace
Press Pass Premium In The Zone
2000 #IZ11 Rusty Wallace
2001 #IZ12 Rusty Wallace
2002 #IZ12 Rusty Wallace
2003 #IZ11 Rusty Wallace
2004 #IZ10 Rusty Wallace
2005 #IZ2 Rusty Wallace
Press Pass Premium In the Zone Elite Edition
2004 #IZ10 Rusty Wallace
2005 #IZ2 Rusty Wallace
Press Pass Premium Lap Leaders
1997 #LL11 Rusty Wallace
Press Pass Premium Mirrors
1997 #7 Rusty Wallace
1997 #28 Rusty Wallace's Car
1997 #44 Rusty Wallace CL
Press Pass Premium Oil Slicks
1997 #7 Rusty Wallace
1997 #28 Rusty Wallace's Car
1997 #44 Rusty Wallace
Press Pass Premium Performance Driven
2001 #PD9 Rusty Wallace
2002 #PD9 Rusty Wallace
2003 #PD8 Rusty Wallace
2004 #PD3 Rusty Wallace
2005 #PD8 Rusty Wallace
Press Pass Premium Previews
2003 #29 Rusty Wallace
2004 #20 Rusty Wallace
Press Pass Premium Race Used Firesuit
1999 #F2 Rusty Wallace
2000 #F2 Rusty Wallace
Press Pass Premium Race Used Firesuit Cars
2001 #FC8 Rusty Wallace
2002 #FC7 Rusty Wallace
Press Pass Premium Race Used Firesuit Drivers
2001 #FD8 Rusty Wallace
2002 #FD7 Rusty Wallace
Press Pass Premium Red Hot
1995 #3 Rusty Wallace
1995 #31 Rusty Wallace
Press Pass Premium Red Reflectors
2002 #32 Rusty Wallace
2002 #55 Rusty Wallace CC
2002 #81 Rusty Wallace PC
2003 #29 Rusty Wallace
2003 #52 Rusty Wallace CC
2003 #79 Rusty Wallace PC
Press Pass Premium Reflectors
1998 #14 Rusty Wallace's Car
1998 #36 Rusty Wallace
1999 #R26 Rusty Wallace
1999 #R31 Rusty Wallace's Car
2000 #2 Rusty Wallace
2000 #28 Rusty Wallace
2000 #50 Rusty Wallace
Press Pass Premium Rivalries
1998 #3B Rusty Wallace
Press Pass Premium Samples
2002 #32 Rusty Wallace
2003 #29 Rusty Wallace
2004 #20 Rusty Wallace
2004 #37 Rusty Wallace's Car
2005 #32 Rusty Wallace
2005 #39 Rusty Wallace's Car M
Press Pass Premium Steel Horses
1998 #SH1 Rusty Wallace's Car
1999 #SH1 Rusty Wallace's Car
Press Pass Premium Triple Gear Firesuit
1998 #TGF1 Rusty Wallace
Press Pass Previews
1993 #15 Rusty Wallace
1993 #22 Rusty Wallace
1993 #31 Rusty Wallace's Car
2003 #32 Rusty Wallace
2004 #32 Rusty Wallace
2006 #EB4 Rusty Wallace
Press Pass Previews Green
2005 #EB3 Rusty Wallace
Press Pass Previews Silver
2005 #EB100 Rusty Wallace
Press Pass R and N China
1996 #34 Rusty Wallace
1996 #47 Rusty Wallace's Car
Press Pass Race Day
1994 #RD9 Rusty Wallace
1995 #RD12 Rusty Wallace
Press Pass Red Hot
1995 #34 Rusty Wallace
1995 #47 Rusty Wallace's Car
1995 #135 Rusty Wallace PR
Press Pass Rusty Wallace Fan Club
2003 #RW Rusty Wallace
2004 #RW Rusty Wallace
Press Pass Samples
2003 #32 Rusty Wallace
2003 #91 Rusty Wallace's Car OTW
2004 #32 Rusty Wallace
2004 #64 Rusty Wallace's Car OTW
2004 #76 Penske Power WCS
2005 #3 Rusty Wallace
2005 #68 Rusty Wallace's Car OTW
2005 #79 Rusty Wallace NS
2005 #98 Rusty Wallace Y
2005 #100 Rusty Wallace P
2005 #111 Rusty Wallace's Car
Press Pass Scorchers
1996 #34 Rusty Wallace
1996 #47 Rusty Wallace's Car
1996 #73 Penske/Miller/Pemberton/R.Wall TW
1996 #99 Rusty Wallace S
1996 #119 Rusty Wallace's Car PRE
Press Pass Shockers
1998 #ST7A Rusty Wallace
Press Pass Showcar
2002 #S12A Rusty Wallace's Car
2003 #S12B Rusty Wallace
2005 #SC7 Rusty Wallace
Press Pass Showcar Die Cuts
2000 #SC14 Rusty Wallace's Car
Press Pass Showman
1999 #18A Rusty Wallace
2000 #SM14 Rusty Wallace
2002 #S12A Rusty Wallace
2003 #S12A Rusty Wallace
2005 #SM7 Rusty Wallace
Press Pass Showman Die Cuts
2000 #SM14 Rusty Wallace
Press Pass Showman/Showcar
2001 #S2A Rusty Wallace
2001 #S2B Rusty Wallace's Car
Press Pass Signings
1999 #56 Rusty Wallace
2001 #52 Rusty Wallace P/T/N/S
2002 #68 Rusty Wallace O/P/S/V
2003 #73 Rusty Wallace O/P/S/T/V
2004 #63 Rusty Wallace O/S/T/V
2005 #58 Rusty Wallace
2007 #73 Rusty Wallace
Press Pass Signings Blue Daytona
2007 #7 Rusty Wallace
Press Pass Signings Gold
1999 #28 Rusty Wallace Blue/100
2001 #34 Rusty Wallace P/T/N/S
2002 #64 Rusty Wallace O/P/S/T/V
2003 #74 Rusty Wallace O/S
2004 #59 Rusty Wallace O/P/S/T/V
2005 #57 Rusty Wallace
Press Pass Signings Press Plates Black
2007 #42 Rusty Wallace
Press Pass Signings Press Plates Cyan
2007 #41 Rusty Wallace
Press Pass Signings Press Plates Magenta
2007 #44 Rusty Wallace
Press Pass Signings Press Plates Yellow
2007 #42 Rusty Wallace
Press Pass Signings Transparent
2001 #12 Rusty Wallace P/T/N/S
2002 #10 Rusty Wallace O/P/S/T/V
2004 #10 Rusty Wallace O/P/S/T
Press Pass Skidmarks
1999 #4 Rusty Wallace
1999 #31 Rusty Wallace's Car
1999 #80 Rusty Wallace OTP
2000 #SK7 Rusty Wallace
Press Pass Snapshots
2003 #SN25 Rusty Wallace
2004 #SN26 Rusty Wallace
2005 #SN25 Rusty Wallace
Press Pass Stealth
1998 #31 Rusty Wallace
1998 #32 Rusty Wallace's Car
1998 #50 Rusty Wallace TM
1999 #34 Rusty Wallace
1999 #35 Rusty Wallace's Car
1999 #57 Miller Lite Headphones TT
2000 #4 Rusty Wallace
2000 #5 Rusty Wallace's Car
2000 #71 Rusty Wallace FF
2001 #4 Rusty Wallace
2001 #5 Rusty Wallace's Car
2001 #6 Rusty Wallace
2001 #71 Rusty Wallace SST
2002 #1 Rusty Wallace
2002 #2 Rusty Wallace's Car
2002 #3 Rusty Wallace
2002 #59 Rusty Wallace's Car SST
2002 #72 R.Wallace/R.Newman CL
2003 #1 Rusty Wallace
2003 #2 Rusty Wallace's Car
2003 #3 Rusty Wallace
2003 #55 Rusty Wallace SST
2003 #71 Rusty Wallace SF
2004 #61 Rusty Wallace
2004 #62 Rusty Wallace's Car
2004 #63 Rusty Wallace
2004 #91 Rusty Wallace SF
2005 #11 Rusty Wallace
2005 #14 Rusty Wallace's Car
2005 #17 Rusty Wallace
2005 #82 Rusty Wallace H
2005 #93 Rusty Wallace SF
Press Pass Stealth Behind the Numbers
2000 #BN4 Rusty Wallace
2001 #BN6 Rusty Wallace
2002 #BN6 Rusty Wallace
Press Pass Stealth Big Numbers
1999 #BN17 Rusty Wallace
Press Pass Stealth Big Numbers Die Cuts
1999 #BN17 Rusty Wallace
Press Pass Stealth EFX
2002 #FX3 Rusty Wallace
2003 #FX11 Rusty Wallace
2004 #EF8 Rusty Wallace
2005 #EFX11 Rusty Wallace
Press Pass Stealth Fan Talk
1998 #9 Rusty Wallace
Press Pass Stealth Fan Talk Die Cuts
1998 #9 Rusty Wallace
Press Pass Stealth Fusion
1998 #31 Rusty Wallace
1998 #32 Rusty Wallace's Car
1998 #50 Rusty Wallace TM
1999 #F34 Rusty Wallace
1999 #F35 Rusty Wallace's Car
1999 #F57 Miller Lite Headphones TT
2000 #FS7 Rusty Wallace
2000 #FS8 Rusty Wallace's Car
2000 #FS9 Rusty Wallace

2001 #F9 Rusty Wallace
2002 #F12 Rusty Wallace
2003 #FU11 Rusty Wallace
2004 #FU6 Rusty Wallace
2005 #FU6 Rusty Wallace 1:48
Press Pass Stealth Fusion Green
2000 #FS7 Rusty Wallace
2000 #FS8 Rusty Wallace
2000 #FS9 Rusty Wallace
Press Pass Stealth Fusion Red
2000 #FS7 Rusty Wallace
2000 #FS8 Rusty Wallace
2000 #FS9 Rusty Wallace
Press Pass Stealth Gear Grippers Autographs
2004 #HT-RW Rusty Wallace/2
Press Pass Stealth Gear Grippers Cars
2003 #GGT5 Rusty Wallace
2005 #GGT8 Rusty Wallace
Press Pass Stealth Gear Grippers Cars Autographs
2003 #RW Rusty Wallace/2
Press Pass Stealth Gear Grippers Drivers
2003 #GGD5 Rusty Wallace
2004 #GGD8 Rusty Wallace
2005 #GGD8 Rusty Wallace
Press Pass Stealth Gear Grippers Drivers Autographs
2003 #RW Rusty Wallace/2
Press Pass Stealth Gear Grippers Drivers Retail
2004 #GGT8 Rusty Wallace
Press Pass Stealth Gold
2002 #1 Rusty Wallace
2002 #2 Rusty Wallace's Car
2002 #3 Rusty Wallace
2002 #59 Rusty Wallace's Car SST
2002 #72 R.Wallace/R.Newman CL
Press Pass Stealth Headlines
1999 #SH5 Rusty Wallace
Press Pass Stealth Holofoils
2001 #4 Rusty Wallace
2001 #5 Rusty Wallace's Car
2001 #6 Rusty Wallace
2001 #71 Rusty Wallace SST
Press Pass Stealth Intensity
2000 #IN7 Rusty Wallace
Press Pass Stealth Lap Leaders
2001 #LL2 Rusty Wallace
2001 #LL20 Rusty Wallace's Car
2002 #LL27 Rusty Wallace
Press Pass Stealth Lap Leaders Clear Cars
2001 #LL20 Rusty Wallace's Car
Press Pass Stealth Lap Leaders Clear Drivers
2001 #LL2 Rusty Wallace
Press Pass Stealth No Boundaries
2003 #NB24 Rusty Wallace
2004 #NB25 Rusty Wallace
2005 #NB2 Rusty Wallace
Press Pass Stealth Octane
1998 #35 Rusty Wallace
1998 #36 Rusty Wallace's Car
Press Pass Stealth Octane Die Cuts
1998 #35 Rusty Wallace
1998 #36 Rusty Wallace's Car
Press Pass Stealth Previews
2003 #1 Rusty Wallace
2003 #2 Rusty Wallace's Car
2003 #3 Rusty Wallace
2005 #11 Rusty Wallace
2005 #14 Rusty Wallace's Car
2005 #17 Rusty Wallace
Press Pass Stealth Profile
2000 #PR5 Rusty Wallace
2001 #SP4 Rusty Wallace
2003 #PR8 Rusty Wallace
2005 #PR6 Rusty Wallace
Press Pass Stealth Race Used Glove Cars
2001 #RGC2 Rusty Wallace/120
2002 #GLC2 Rusty Wallace's Car
Press Pass Stealth Race Used Glove Drivers
2001 #RGD2 Rusty Wallace/120
2002 #GLD2 Rusty Wallace
Press Pass Stealth Race Used Gloves
1998 #G1 Rusty Wallace
1999 #G9 Rusty Wallace/150
2000 #G2 Rusty Wallace/100
Press Pass Stealth Red
2003 #P1 Rusty Wallace
2003 #P2 Rusty Wallace's Car
2003 #P3 Rusty Wallace
2003 #P55 Rusty Wallace SST
2003 #P71 Rusty Wallace SF
Press Pass Stealth Samples
2002 #1 Rusty Wallace
2002 #2 Rusty Wallace's Car
2002 #3 Rusty Wallace
2002 #59 Rusty Wallace's Car SST
2002 #72 R.Wallace/R.Newman CL
2003 #1 Rusty Wallace
2003 #2 Rusty Wallace's Car
2003 #3 Rusty Wallace
2003 #55 Rusty Wallace SST
2003 #71 Rusty Wallace SF
2004 #X62 Rusty Wallace's Car
2004 #X61 Rusty Wallace
2004 #X63 Rusty Wallace
2004 #X91 Rusty Wallace SF
2005 #11 Rusty Wallace
2005 #14 Rusty Wallace's Car
2005 #17 Rusty Wallace
2005 #82 Rusty Wallace H
2005 #93 Rusty Wallace SF
Press Pass Stealth SST
2000 #SST8 Rusty Wallace
Press Pass Stealth SST Cars
1999 #SS9 Rusty Wallace's Car
Press Pass Stealth SST Drivers
1999 #SS9 Rusty Wallace
Press Pass Stealth Stars
1998 #17 Rusty Wallace
Press Pass Stealth Stars Die Cuts
1998 #17 Rusty Wallace
Press Pass Stealth Supercharged
2003 #SC4 Rusty Wallace
Press Pass Stealth X-Ray
2004 #61 Rusty Wallace
2004 #62 Rusty Wallace's Car
2004 #63 Rusty Wallace
2004 #91 Rusty Wallace SF
2005 #X11 Rusty Wallace
2005 #X14 Rusty Wallace's Car
2005 #X17 Rusty Wallace
2005 #X82 Rusty Wallace H
2005 #X93 Rusty Wallace SF
Press Pass Techno-Retro
2000 #TR25 Rusty Wallace
Press Pass Top Shelf
2002 #TS9 Rusty Wallace
2003 #TS9 Rusty Wallace
Press Pass Torpedoes
1998 #ST7B Rusty Wallace's Car
Press Pass Torquers
1996 #34 Rusty Wallace
1996 #47 Rusty Wallace's Car
1996 #73 Penske/Miller/Pember/R.Wall TW
1996 #99 Rusty Wallace S
1996 #119 Rusty Wallace's Car PRE
1997 #7 Rusty Wallace
1997 #31 Rusty Wallace's Car
1997 #53 Rusty Wallace
1997 #62 Rusty Wallace's Car
1997 #84 Rusty Wallace
1997 #99 Rusty Wallace's Car
1997 #122 Rusty Wallace's Car
Press Pass Total Memorabilia
2001 #TM2 Rusty Wallace
Press Pass Total Memorabilia Power Pick
2002 #TM9 Rusty Wallace
2003 #TM5 Rusty Wallace
2004 #TM5 Rusty Wallace
2005 #TM5 Rusty Wallace
Press Pass Trackside
2000 #19 Rusty Wallace
2000 #31 Rusty Wallace's Car
2001 #29 Rusty Wallace
2001 #40 Rusty Wallace's Car
2001 #70 Rusty Wallace TM
2001 #89 Rusty Wallace CS
2002 #27 Rusty Wallace
2002 #59 Rusty Wallace RD
2002 #64 Rusty Wallace's Car
2002 #88 Rusty Wallace TM
2003 #18 Rusty Wallace
2003 #55 R.Wallace/K.Wallace FA
2003 #61 Rusty Wallace in Pits
2003 #76 R.Wallace/R.Newman TM
2003 #81 Rusty Wallace CL
2004 #7 Rusty Wallace
2004 #52 Rusty Wallace's Car HS
2004 #52B Rusty Wallace's Car HS SP
2004 #67 Rusty/Gaughan/Newman TM
2004 #114 Rusty Wallace F
2005 #23 Rusty Wallace
2005 #55 Rusty Wallace's Car HS
2005 #77 R.Wallace/K.Wallace FA
2005 #92 Rusty Wallace GP
2005 #98 Rusty Wallace F
Press Pass Trackside Dialed In
2000 #DI8 Rusty Wallace
2001 #D2 Rusty Wallace
2002 #DI12 Rusty Wallace
2003 #DI11 Rusty Wallace
2004 #DI12 Rusty Wallace
2005 #DI9 Rusty Wallace
Press Pass Trackside Die Cuts
2000 #19 Rusty Wallace
2000 #31 Rusty Wallace
2001 #29 Rusty Wallace
2001 #40 Rusty Wallace's Car
2001 #70 Rusty Wallace TM
2001 #89 Rusty Wallace CS
Press Pass Trackside Gold Holofoil
2003 #P18 Rusty Wallace
2003 #P55 R.Wallace/K.Wallace
2003 #P61 Rusty Wallace's Crew
2003 #P76 R.Wallace/R.Newman
2003 #P81 Rusty Wallace CL
Press Pass Trackside Golden
2000 #19 Rusty Wallace
2000 #31 Rusty Wallace
2001 #29 Rusty Wallace
2001 #40 Rusty Wallace's Car
2001 #70 Rusty Wallace TM
2001 #89 Rusty Wallace CS
2001 #90 Checklist
2002 #G27 Rusty Wallace
2003 #G18 Rusty Wallace
2004 #G7 Rusty Wallace
2004 #G52 Rusty Wallace's Car HS
2004 #G67 Wallace/Gaughan/Newman TM
2004 #G114 Rusty Wallace F
2005 #G23 Rusty Wallace
2005 #G55 Rusty Wallace's Car HS
2005 #G77 R.Wallace/K.Wallace FA
2005 #G92 Rusty Wallace GP
2005 #G98 Rusty Wallace F
Press Pass Trackside Hat Giveaway
2003 #PPH29 Rusty Wallace
2004 #PPH32 Rusty Wallace
2005 #PPH33 Rusty Wallace
Press Pass Trackside Hot Pass
2004 #HP17 Rusty Wallace
2005 #17 Rusty Wallace
Press Pass Trackside Hot Pass National
2004 #HP17 Rusty Wallace
2005 #17 Rusty Wallace
Press Pass Trackside Hot Pursuit
2004 #HP5 Rusty Wallace
2005 #HP5 Rusty Wallace
Press Pass Trackside License to Drive
2002 #34 Rusty Wallace
2003 #LD19 Rusty Wallace
Press Pass Trackside License to Drive Die Cuts
2002 #34 Rusty Wallace
Press Pass Trackside Mirror Image
2001 #MI2 Rusty Wallace
2002 #MI9 Rusty Wallace
2003 #MI8 Rusty Wallace
Press Pass Trackside Panorama
2000 #P30 Rusty Wallace
Press Pass Trackside Pit Stoppers
2000 #PS2 Rusty Wallace
Press Pass Trackside Pit Stoppers Autographs
2004 #PS-RW Rusty Wallace/2
2005 #PSRW Rusty Wallace/2
Press Pass Trackside Pit Stoppers Cars
2001 #PSC5 Rusty Wallace's Car
2002 #PSC8 Rusty Wallace's Car/350
2003 #PST5 Rusty Wallace
2004 #PST5 Rusty Wallace
2005 #PST4 Rusty Wallace
Press Pass Trackside Pit Stoppers Cars Autographs
2003 #RW Rusty Wallace/2
Press Pass Trackside Pit Stoppers Drivers
2001 #PSD5 Rusty Wallace/30
2002 #PSD8 Rusty Wallace/175
2003 #PSD5 Rusty Wallace
2004 #PSD5 Rusty Wallace
2005 #PSD4 Rusty Wallace
Press Pass Trackside Pit Stoppers Drivers Autographs
2003 #PSD-RW Rusty Wallace/2
Press Pass Trackside Previews
2003 #18 Rusty Wallace
2004 #EB7 Rusty Wallace
2005 #23 Rusty Wallace
2005 #92 Rusty Wallace GP
Press Pass Trackside Runnin N' Gunnin
2000 #RG3 Rusty Wallace
2001 #RG3 Rusty Wallace
2002 #RG9 Rusty Wallace
2003 #RG8 Rusty Wallace
2004 #RG10 Rusty Wallace
2005 #RG10 Rusty Wallace
Press Pass Trackside Samples
2002 #27 Rusty Wallace
2002 #59 Rusty Wallace RD
2002 #64 Rusty Wallace's Car
2002 #88 Rusty Wallace TM
2003 #18 Rusty Wallace
2003 #55 R.Wallace/K.Wallace FA
2003 #61 Rusty Wallace in Pits
2003 #76 R.Wallace/R.Newman TM
2003 #81 Rusty Wallace CL
2004 #7 Rusty Wallace
2004 #52 Rusty Wallace's Car HS
2004 #67 Wallace/Gaughan/Newman TM
2004 #114 Rusty Wallace F
2005 #23 Rusty Wallace
2005 #55 Rusty Wallace's Car HS
2005 #77 R.Wallace/K.Wallace FA
2005 #92 Rusty Wallace GP
2005 #98 Rusty Wallace F
Press Pass Trackside Too Tough To Tame
2000 #TT7 Rusty Wallace
Press Pass Triple Burner
2001 #TB2 Rusty Wallace
2002 #TB9 Rusty Wallace
2003 #TB5 Rusty Wallace
2004 #TB5 Rusty Wallace
2005 #TB5 Rusty Wallace
Press Pass Triple Burner Exchange
2003 #TB5 Rusty Wallace EXCH
2004 #TB5 Rusty Wallace
2005 #TB5 Rusty Wallace
Press Pass Triple Gear 3 in 1
1998 #STG1 Rusty Wallace
1999 #TG5 Rusty Wallace
Press Pass Triple Gear Burning Rubber
1998 #TG1 Rusty Wallace
Press Pass UMI Cup Chase
2005 #1 Cup Chase Drivers CL
2005 #4 Rusty Wallace
Press Pass Velocity
2001 #VL2 Rusty Wallace
2002 #VL9 Rusty Wallace
2003 #VC9 Rusty Wallace
2004 #VC2 Rusty Wallace
2005 #V9 Rusty Wallace
Press Pass Victory Lane
1997 #VL8A Rusty Wallace
1997 #VL8B Rusty Wallace's Car
Press Pass Victory Lap
2003 #9 Rusty Wallace
Press Pass Vintage
2001 #VN7 Rusty Wallace
2002 #VN25 Rusty Wallace
Pro Set
1991 #5 Rusty Wallace
1991 #6 Rusty Wallace
1991 #8 Rusty Wallace's Car
1992 #12 Rusty Wallace's Transporter
1992 #99 Rusty Wallace
1992 #107 Rusty Wallace's Car
1992 #115 Rusty Wallace
Pro Set Maxwell House
1992 #16 Rusty Wallace
Pro Set Pro Files *
1991 #11 Rusty Wallace
Pro Set Rudy Farms
1992 #9 Rusty Wallace
Race Sharks
1997 #5 Rusty Wallace
1997 #37 Rusty Wallace
1997 #39 Rusty Wallace
1997 #42 Rusty Wallace
Race Sharks First Bite
1997 #5 Rusty Wallace
1997 #37 Rusty Wallace
1997 #39 Rusty Wallace
1997 #42 Rusty Wallace
Race Sharks Great White
1997 #5 Rusty Wallace
1997 #37 Rusty Wallace
1997 #39 Rusty Wallace
1997 #42 Rusty Wallace
Race Sharks Great White Shark's Teeth
1997 #GW5 Rusty Wallace
Race Sharks Great White Shark's Teeth First Bite
1997 #GW5 Rusty Wallace
Race Sharks Hammerhead
1997 #5 Rusty Wallace
1997 #37 Rusty Wallace
1997 #39 Rusty Wallace
1997 #42 Rusty Wallace
Race Sharks Hammerhead First Bite
1997 #5 Rusty Wallace
1997 #37 Rusty Wallace
1997 #39 Rusty Wallace
1997 #42 Rusty Wallace
Race Sharks Shark Attack
1997 #SA4 Rusty Wallace
Race Sharks Shark Attack First Bite
1997 #SA4 Rusty Wallace
Race Sharks Shark Attack First Bite Previews
1997 #4 Rusty Wallace
Race Sharks Tiger Shark
1997 #5 Rusty Wallace
1997 #37 Rusty Wallace
1997 #39 Rusty Wallace
1997 #42 Rusty Wallace
Race Sharks Tiger Shark First Bite
1997 #5 Rusty Wallace
1997 #37 Rusty Wallace
1997 #39 Rusty Wallace
1997 #42 Rusty Wallace
Racer's Choice
1996 #2 Rusty Wallace
1996 #26 Rusty Wallace's Car
1996 #82 Rusty Wallace RW
1997 #2 Rusty Wallace
1997 #37 Rusty Wallace's Car
1997 #91 Rusty Wallace TR
Racer's Choice Artist's Proofs
1996 #2 Rusty Wallace
1996 #26 Rusty Wallace's Car
1996 #82 Rusty Wallace RW
Racer's Choice Busch Clash
1997 #14 Rusty Wallace
Racer's Choice High Octane
1997 #6 Rusty Wallace
Racer's Choice High Octane Glow in the Dark
1997 #6 Rusty Wallace
Racer's Choice Showcase Series
1997 #2 Rusty Wallace
1997 #37 Rusty Wallace's Car
1997 #91 Rusty Wallace TR
Racer's Choice Speedway Collection
1996 #2 Rusty Wallace
1996 #26 Rusty Wallace's Car
1996 #82 Rusty Wallace RW
Racer's Choice Top Ten
1996 #5 Rusty Wallace
SB Motorsports
1997 #46 Rusty Wallace's Car
Score Board IQ
1997 #39 Rusty Wallace's Car
Score Board IQ $10 Phone Cards
1997 #PC2 Rusty Wallace's Car
Score Board IQ Remarques
1997 #SB5 Rusty Wallace's Car
Score Board IQ Remarques Sam Bass Finished
1997 #SB5 Rusty Wallace's Car
Select
1995 #34 Rusty Wallace
1995 #47 Rusty Wallace's Car
1995 #111 R.Wallace/Kenny/Mike IB
1995 #140 Rusty Wallace PS
Select Dream Machines
1995 #DM2 Rusty Wallace's Car
Select Flat Out
1995 #34 Rusty Wallace
1995 #47 Rusty Wallace's Car
1995 #111 Wallace Brothers IB
1995 #140 Rusty Wallace PS
Select Skills
1995 #SS1 Rusty Wallace
SkyBox
1994 #12 Rusty Wallace's Car
SkyBox Profile
1997 #30 Rusty Wallace
1997 #62 Rusty Wallace's Car
SkyBox Profile Autographs
1997 #30 Rusty Wallace
SkyBox Profile Pace Setters
1997 #E8 Rusty Wallace
SkyBox Profile Team
1997 #T9 Rusty Wallace
SLU Racing Winner's Circle
1998 #12A Rusty Wallace FP
1998 #12B R.Wallace FP Elvis
SLU Racing Winner's Circle 12-inch Figures
1999 #3 Rusty Wallace
SP
1995 #2 Rusty Wallace CC
1995 #32 Rusty Wallace
1995 #33 Rusty Wallace
1995 #76 Rusty Wallace's Car
1995 #77 Rusty Wallace's Car
1995 #123 R.Penske/R.Wallace OWN
1996 #2 Rusty Wallace
1996 #46 Rusty Wallace CC
1996 #79 Rusty Wallace RPM
1996 #S1 Rusty Wallace Promo
1997 #2 Rusty Wallace
1997 #44 Rusty Wallace's Car
1997 #85 Rusty Wallace 3F
1997 #113 Rusty Wallace 3F
SP Authentic
1998 #2 Rusty Wallace
1998 #36 Rusty Wallace's Car
1998 #70 Rusty Wallace VL
1998 #SPA2 Rusty Wallace Sample
1999 #16 Rusty Wallace
1999 #41 Rusty Wallace's Car
1999 #64 Rusty Wallace CLASS
1999 #77 Rusty Wallace SP
2000 #6 Rusty Wallace
2000 #81 Rusty Wallace SUP
SP Authentic Behind the Wheel
1998 #BW8 Rusty Wallace
SP Authentic Behind the Wheel Die Cuts
1998 #BW8 Rusty Wallace
SP Authentic Behind the Wheel Gold
1998 #BW8 Rusty Wallace
SP Authentic Cup Challengers
1999 #CC4 Rusty Wallace
SP Authentic Dominance
2000 #D4 Rusty Wallace
SP Authentic Driver's Seat
2000 #DS8 Rusty Wallace
SP Authentic Driving Force
1999 #DF5 Rusty Wallace
SP Authentic In the Driver's Seat
1999 #DS3 Rusty Wallace
SP Authentic Overdrive
1999 #16 Rusty Wallace
1999 #41 Rusty Wallace CAR
1999 #64 Rusty Wallace CLASS
1999 #77 Rusty Wallace SP/2
SP Authentic Overdrive Gold
2000 #6 Rusty Wallace/2
2000 #81 Rusty Wallace SUP/2
SP Authentic Overdrive Silver
2000 #6 Rusty Wallace
2000 #81 Rusty Wallace SUP
SP Authentic Race for the Cup
2000 #R8 Rusty Wallace
SP Authentic Sign of the Times
1998 #S1 Rusty Wallace's Car
1999 #RW Rusty Wallace
2000 #RW Rusty Wallace
SP Authentic Sign of the Times Gold
2000 #RW Rusty Wallace
SP Authentic Traditions
1998 #T5 C.Yarborough/R.Wallace
SP Die Cuts
1995 #2 Rusty Wallace
1995 #32 Rusty Wallace
1995 #33 Rusty Wallace
1995 #76 Rusty Wallace's Car
1995 #77 Rusty Wallace's Car
1995 #123 Roger Penske/R.Wallace
SP Holoview Maximum Effects
1996 #ME2 Rusty Wallace
SP Holoview Maximum Effects Die Cuts
1996 #ME2 Rusty Wallace
SP Race Film
1997 #RD2 Rusty Wallace
SP Racing Legends
1996 #RL21 Rusty Wallace
SP Speed Merchants
1995 #SM2 Rusty Wallace
SP Speed Merchants Die Cuts
1995 #SM2 Rusty Wallace
SP SPx Force Autographs
1997 #SF2 Rusty Wallace
SP Super Series
1997 #2 Rusty Wallace
1997 #44 Rusty Wallace's Car
1997 #85 Rusty Wallace 3F
1997 #113 Rusty Wallace 3F
Speedflix
1996 #1 Rusty Wallace
1996 #18 Rusty Wallace
1996 #36 Rusty Wallace's Car in pits
1996 #71 Rusty Wallace CF
1996 #72 Rusty Wallace CF
1996 #73 Rusty Wallace CF
1996 #74 Rusty Wallace CF
Speedflix Artist Proof's
1996 #1 Rusty Wallace
1996 #18 Rusty Wallace
1996 #36 Rusty Wallace in Pits
1996 #71 Rusty Wallace
1996 #72 Rusty Wallace
1996 #73 Rusty Wallace
1996 #74 Rusty Wallace
Speedflix Clear Shots
1996 #4 Rusty Wallace
Speedflix In Motion
1996 #4 Rusty Wallace's Helmet
Speedflix ProMotion
1996 #4 Rusty Wallace
Sports Legends Rusty Wallace
1992 #1 Rusty Wallace
1992 #2 Rusty Wallace
1992 #3 Rusty Wallace
1992 #4 Rusty Wallace
1992 #5 Rusty Wallace
1992 #6 Rusty Wallace
1992 #7 Rusty Wallace
1992 #8 Rusty Wallace
1992 #9 Rusty Wallace
1992 #10 Rusty Wallace
1992 #11 Rusty Wallace
1992 #12 Rusty Wallace
1992 #13 Rusty Wallace
1992 #14 Rusty Wallace
1992 #15 Rusty Wallace
1992 #16 Rusty Wallace
1992 #17 Rusty Wallace
1992 #18 Rusty Wallace
1992 #19 Rusty Wallace
1992 #20 Rusty Wallace
1992 #21 Rusty Wallace
1992 #22 Rusty Wallace
1992 #23 Rusty Wallace
1992 #24 Rusty Wallace
1992 #25 Rusty Wallace
1992 #26 Rusty Wallace
1992 #27 Rusty Wallace
1992 #28 Rusty Wallace
1992 #29 Rusty Wallace
1992 #30 Rusty Wallace
1992 #P1 Rusty Wallace Prototype
SportsCom FanScan
1997 #12 Rusty Wallace
1998 #8 Rusty Wallace
1999 #8 Rusty Wallace
SPx
1996 #2 Rusty Wallace
1997 #2 Rusty Wallace
1997 #S2 Rusty Wallace Promo
SPx Blue
1997 #2 Rusty Wallace
SPx Elite
1996 #E4 Rusty Wallace
SPx Gold
1996 #2 Rusty Wallace
1997 #2 Rusty Wallace
SPx Silver
1997 #2 Rusty Wallace
SPx SpeedView Autographs
1997 #SV2 Rusty Wallace
Stove Top
1993 #5 Rusty Wallace
Sunbelt Racing Legends
1991 #2 Rusty Wallace
Super Shots California Speedway
2002 #CS5 Rusty Wallace's Car
Super Shots Race-Used Tire Jumbos
2001 #RW1 Rusty Wallace/1000
Traks
1991 #179 Rusty Wallace
1991 #124 Rusty Wallace
1991 #2 Rusty Wallace
1992 #2 Rusty Wallace
1992 #15 Rusty Wallace/Mike/Kenny
1992 #72A Rusty Wallace/Dickerson WL
1992 #72B Rusty Wallace/Dickerson BL
1992 #124A Rusty Wallace
1992 #124B Rusty Wallace
1992 #179A Rusty Wallace BL
1992 #179B Rusty Wallace BL
1992 #P4 Rusty Wallace Prototype
1993 #2 Rusty Wallace Win
1993 #25 Rusty Wallace's Car CL
1993 #58 Rusty Wallace
1993 #145 Rusty Wallace in Pits
1993 #164 Rusty Wallace
1993 #181 Rusty Wallace
1993 #P2 Rusty Wallace Promo
1994 #2 Rusty Wallace
1994 #62 Rusty Wallace
1994 #72 Rusty Wallace's Car
1994 #80 Rusty Wallace
1994 #102 Rusty Wallace
1994 #157 Rusty Wallace
1994 #187 Rusty Wallace's Car
1994 #193 Rusty Wallace
1995 #13 Rusty Wallace
1995 #46 Rusty Wallace
1995 #66 Rusty Wallace
1995 #75 Rusty Wallace
2006 #87 Rusty Wallace
Traks 5th Anniversary
1995 #9 Rusty Wallace
1995 #42 Rusty Wallace
1995 #52 Rusty Wallace's Car
Traks 5th Anniversary Clear Contenders
1995 #C6 Rusty Wallace
Traks 5th Anniversary Gold
1995 #9 Rusty Wallace
1995 #42 Rusty Wallace
1995 #52 Rusty Wallace's Car
Traks 5th Anniversary Jumbos
1995 #E3 Rusty Wallace
Traks 5th Anniversary Jumbos Gold
1995 #E3 Rusty Wallace
Traks 5th Anniversary Retrospective
1995 #R6 Rusty Wallace
Traks ASA
1992 #13 Rusty Wallace w/Car
Traks Auto Value
1994 #21 Rusty Wallace
1994 #49 Rusty Wallace/Ken Schrader Cars
1995 #45 Rusty Wallace
Traks Autographs
1992 #A2 Rusty Wallace
1994 #A12 Rusty Wallace
Traks Cartoons
1994 #C2 Rusty Wallace
Traks Challengers
1995 #C6 Rusty Wallace
Traks Challengers First Run
1995 #C6 Rusty Wallace
Traks First Run
1993 #2 Rusty Wallace Win
1993 #25 Rusty Wallace's Car CL
1993 #58 Rusty Wallace
1993 #145 Rusty Wallace in Pits
1993 #164 Rusty Wallace
1993 #181 Rusty Wallace
1994 #2 Rusty Wallace
1994 #62 Rusty Wallace
1994 #72 Rusty Wallace's Car
1994 #80 Rusty Wallace
1994 #102 Rusty Wallace
1994 #157 Rusty Wallace
1994 #187 Rusty Wallace's Car
1994 #193 Rusty Wallace
1995 #13 Rusty Wallace
1995 #46 Rusty Wallace
1995 #66 Rusty Wallace
1995 #75 Rusty Wallace
Traks Preferred Collector
1993 #11 Rusty Wallace
1994 #21 Rusty Wallace
Traks Racing Machines
1992 #2 Rusty Wallace's Car
1992 #24 Rusty Wallace w/Truck
1992 #58 Rusty Wallace/R.Rudd Cars
1992 #64 Rusty Wallace's Motorhome
1992 #78 Rusty Wallace in Pits
1992 #81 Rusty Wallace's Transp.
1992 #98 B.Lab/T.Lab/R.Wll/Irv Cars CL
1995 #RM10 Rusty Wallace's Car
Traks Racing Machines First Run
1995 #RM10 Rusty Wallace's Car
Traks Series Stars
1995 #SS4 Rusty Wallace
Traks Series Stars First Run
1995 #SS4 Rusty Wallace
Traks Trivia
1993 #3 Rusty Wallace
1993 #11 Rusty Wallace
1993 #29 Rusty Wallace
1993 #39 Rusty Wallace
Traks Valvoline
1995 #97 Rusty Wallace's Car
Traks Winners
1994 #W2 Rusty Wallace
1994 #W6 Rusty Wallace
1994 #W9 Rusty Wallace
1994 #W24 Rusty Wallace
UDA Commemorative Cards
1997 #NNO 199? Rusty Wallace Career/???
Ultra
1996 #17 Rusty Wallace

1996 #18 Rusty Wallace
1996 #19 Rusty Wallace's Car
1996 #161 Rusty Wallace's Helmet
1996 #174 Rusty Wallace's Car RW
1996 #190 Rusty Wallace's Car RW
1996 #200 D.Earn/Gordon/R.Wall.Race Act.
1997 #36 Rusty Wallace
1997 #46 Rusty Wallace's Car
Ultra AKA
1997 #A9 Rusty Wallace
Ultra Autographs
1996 #36 Rusty Wallace
Ultra Boxed Set
1996 #5 Rusty Wallace
Ultra Champions Club
1996 #1 Rusty Wallace
Ultra Flair Preview
1996 #5 Rusty Wallace
Ultra Inside Out
1997 #DC9 Rusty Wallace
Ultra Update
1996 #32 Rusty Wallace
1996 #78 Rusty Wallace's Car
1997 #7 Rusty Wallace
1997 #76 Rusty Wallace's Car
Ultra Update Autographs
1996 #12 Rusty Wallace
1997 #7 Rusty Wallace
Ultra Update Elite Seats
1997 #E9 Rusty Wallace
Ultra Update Proven Power
1996 #15 Rusty Wallace
Ultra Update Winner
1996 #8 Rusty Wallace
Upper Deck
1995 #1 Rusty Wallace
1995 #44 Rusty Wallace w/Car
1995 #69 Rusty Wallace's Car
1995 #137 Rusty Wallace's Car
1995 #161 Rusty Wallace DYK
1995 #182 Rusty Wallace
1995 #183 Rusty Wallace
1995 #229 Rusty Wallace SD
1995 #270 Rusty Wallace's Car
1995 #RW1 Rusty Wallace Promo
1995 #PR1 Rusty Wallace Promo
1995 #PR2 Rusty Wallace Promo
1996 #2 Rusty Wallace
1996 #42 Rusty Wallace SB
1996 #82 Rusty Wallace PP
1996 #136 Rusty Wallace HB
1996 #142 Rusty Wallace HB
1996 #148 Rusty Wallace HB
Upper Deck All-Pro
1996 #AP5 Rusty Wallace
Upper Deck Autographs
1995 #182 Rusty Wallace
Upper Deck Diamond Vision
1998 #2 Rusty Wallace
Upper Deck Diamond Vision Signature Moves
1998 #2 Rusty Wallace
Upper Deck Diamond Vision Vision of a Champion
1998 #VC1 Rusty Wallace
Upper Deck Gold Signature/Electric Gold
1995 #1 Rusty Wallace
1995 #44 Rusty Wallace w/Car
1995 #69 Rusty Wallace's Car
1995 #137 Rusty Wallace's Car
1995 #161 Rusty Wallace DYK
1995 #182 Rusty Wallace
1995 #183 Rusty Wallace
1995 #229 Rusty Wallace SD
1995 #270 Rusty Wallace's Car
Upper Deck Holiday Santa Suit
1999 #NNO Rusty Wallace
Upper Deck Illustrations
1995 #I10 Rusty Wallace
Upper Deck Jumbos
1995 #OS1 Rusty Wallace
Upper Deck MVP
2000 #2 Rusty Wallace
2000 #63 Rusty Wallace's Car
Upper Deck MVP Gold Script
2000 #2 Rusty Wallace
2000 #63 Rusty Wallace
Upper Deck MVP Magic Numbers
2000 #MRW Rusty Wallace's Car
Upper Deck MVP Magic Numbers Autographs
2000 #MARW Rusty Wallace's Car/2
Upper Deck MVP ProSign
2000 #PSRW Rusty Wallace
Upper Deck MVP Silver Script
2000 #2 Rusty Wallace
2000 #63 Rusty Wallace
Upper Deck MVP Super Script
2000 #2 Rusty Wallace/2
2000 #63 Rusty Wallace's Car/2
Upper Deck Pop Weaver
1998 #PW6 Rusty Wallace
Upper Deck Predictor Poles
1996 #RP3 Rusty Wallace
Upper Deck Predictor Poles Prizes
1996 #RP3 Rusty Wallace
Upper Deck Predictor Race Winners
1995 #P1 Rusty Wallace WIN
Upper Deck Predictor Race Winners Coca-Cola 600
1995 #P1 Rusty Wallace
Upper Deck Predictor Race Winners Daytona 500
1995 #P1 Rusty Wallace
Upper Deck Predictor Race Winners Prizes
1995 #P1 Rusty Wallace
Upper Deck Predictor Series Points
1995 #PP1 Rusty Wallace
Upper Deck Predictor Series Points Prizes
1995 #PP1 Rusty Wallace
Upper Deck Predictor Wins
1996 #HP2 Rusty Wallace WIN
Upper Deck Predictor Wins Prizes
1996 #HP2 Rusty Wallace
Upper Deck Racing
2000 #8 Rusty Wallace
Upper Deck Racing Brickyard's Best
2000 #BB1 Rusty Wallace
Upper Deck Racing CHP
2000 #1 Rusty Wallace
Upper Deck Racing Road Signs
2000 #RSRW Rusty Wallace
Upper Deck Racing Tear Aways
2000 #TARW Rusty Wallace
Upper Deck Racing Thunder Road
2000 #TR2 Rusty Wallace
Upper Deck Road To The Cup
1996 #RC4 Rusty Wallace
1996 #RC53 Rusty Wallace's Car
1996 #RC92 Rusty Wallace
1996 #RC127 Rusty Wallace
1997 #7 Rusty Wallace
1997 #49 Rusty Wallace's Car
1997 #91 Rusty Wallace
1997 #124 Rusty Wallace
1998 #2 Rusty Wallace
1998 #46 Rusty Wallace's Car
1998 #63 Rusty Wallace's Car
1998 #86 Rusty Wallace's Car
1999 #22 Rusty Wallace
1999 #59 Rusty Wallace's Car
1999 #75 Rusty Wallace FF
1999 #80 Rusty Wallace HH
Upper Deck Road To The Cup 50th Anniversary
1998 #AN29 Rusty Wallace's Car
1998 #AN40 Rusty Wallace
Upper Deck Road To The Cup 50th Anniversary Autographs
1998 #AN40 Rusty Wallace
Upper Deck Road To The Cup Autographs
1996 #H4 Rusty Wallace
Upper Deck Road To The Cup Cover Story
1998 #CS5 Rusty Wallace
1998 #CS12 Rusty Wallace
Upper Deck Road To The Cup Cup Quest
1997 #CQ5 Rusty Wallace
Upper Deck Road To The Cup Cup Quest Checkered
1997 #CQ5 Rusty Wallace
Upper Deck Road To The Cup Cup Quest Turn 1
1998 #CQ2 Rusty Wallace's Car
Upper Deck Road To The Cup Cup Quest Turn 2
1998 #CQ2 Rusty Wallace's Car
Upper Deck Road To The Cup Cup Quest Turn 3
1998 #CQ2 Rusty Wallace's Car
Upper Deck Road To The Cup Cup Quest Turn 4
1998 #CQ2 Rusty Wallace's Car
Upper Deck Road To The Cup Cup Quest Victory Lane
1998 #CQ2 Rusty Wallace's Car
Upper Deck Road To The Cup Cup Quest White
1997 #CQ5 Rusty Wallace
Upper Deck Road To The Cup Game Face
1996 #GF2 Rusty Wallace
Upper Deck Road To The Cup Jumbos
1996 #WC2 Rusty Wallace
Upper Deck Road To The Cup Leaders of the Pack
1996 #LP2 Rusty Wallace
Upper Deck Road To The Cup Million Dollar Memoirs
1997 #MM9 Rusty Wallace
1997 #MM10Rusty Wallace
1997 #MM11Rusty Wallace
1997 #MM12Rusty Wallace
Upper Deck Road To The Cup Million Dollar Memoirs Autographs
1997 #MM9 Rusty Wallace
1997 #MM10Rusty Wallace
1997 #MM11Rusty Wallace
1997 #MM12Rusty Wallace
Upper Deck Road to the Cup NASCAR Chronicles
1999 #NC3 Rusty Wallace
Upper Deck Road To The Cup Piece of the Action
1997 #7 Rusty Wallace Seat Cover
1997 #8 Rusty Wallace Shoul.Harness
1997 #9 Rusty Wallace Window Net
Upper Deck Road To The Cup Predictor Plus
1997 #7 Rusty Wallace
1997 #14 Rusty Wallace
Upper Deck Road To The Cup Predictor Plus Cel Die Cuts
1997 #7 Rusty Wallace
1997 #14 Rusty Wallace
Upper Deck Road To The Cup Predictor Plus Cels
1997 #7 Rusty Wallace
1997 #14 Rusty Wallace
Upper Deck Road To The Cup Predictor Points
1996 #PP4 Rusty Wallace
Upper Deck Road To The Cup Predictor Points Prizes
1996 #PR4 Rusty Wallace
Upper Deck Road To The Cup Predictor Top 3
1996 #T1 J.Gordon/R.Wallace/T.Labonte
1996 #T4 R.Wall./D.Waltrip/Longshot
1996 #T5 Martin/R.Wallace/B.Labonte
1996 #T10 R.Wallace/T.Lab./K.Petty
Upper Deck Road To The Cup Predictor Top 3 Prizes
1996 #R2 Rusty Wallace
Upper Deck Road To The Cup Premiere Position
1997 #PP8 Rusty Wallace
1997 #PP14 Rusty Wallace
1997 #PP18 Rusty Wallace
1997 #PP26 Rusty Wallace
1997 #PP44 Rusty Wallace
Upper Deck Road to the Cup Road to the Cup Bronze Level 1
1999 #RTTC3Rusty Wallace
Upper Deck Road to the Cup Road to the Cup Gold Level 3
1999 #RTTC3Rusty Wallace
Upper Deck Road to the Cup Road to the Cup Silver Level 2
1999 #RTTC3Rusty Wallace
Upper Deck Road to the Cup Signature Collection
1999 #RW Rusty Wallace
Upper Deck Road to the Cup Signature Collection Checkered Flag
1999 #RW Rusty Wallace
Upper Deck Road to the Cup Tires of Daytona
1999 #T2 Rusty Wallace
Upper Deck Road to the Cup Tires of Daytona Autographed
1999 #TS3 Rusty Wallace/2
Upper Deck Road to the Cup Upper Deck Profiles
1999 #P13 Rusty Wallace
Upper Deck Road To The Cup Winning Materials
1998 #W1 Rusty Wallace
Upper Deck Rusty Wallace Phone Cards
1995 #1 Rusty Wallace
1995 #2 Rusty Wallace
1995 #3 Rusty Wallace
1995 #4 Rusty Wallace
1995 #5 Rusty Wallace
Upper Deck Silver Signature/Electric Silver
1995 #1 Rusty Wallace
1995 #44 Rusty Wallace w/Car
1995 #69 Rusty Wallace's Car
1995 #137 Rusty Wallace's Car
1995 #149 Rusty Wallace CL
1995 #150 Rusty Wallace CL
1995 #161 Rusty Wallace DYK
1995 #182 Rusty Wallace
1995 #183 Rusty Wallace
1995 #229 Rusty Wallace SD
1995 #270 Rusty Wallace's Car
Upper Deck UD Authentics
1998 #RW Rusty Wallace
Upper Deck Victory Circle
1997 #2 Rusty Wallace
1997 #52 Rusty Wallace's Car
1997 #103 Rusty Wallace
1998 #2 Rusty Wallace
1998 #47 Rusty Wallace's Car
1998 #110 Rusty Wallace
1998 #142 Rusty Wallace
1999 #9 Rusty Wallace
1999 #42 Rusty Wallace's Car
1999 #78 Rusty Wallace
1999 #81 Rusty Wallace
1999 #89 Rusty Wallace CL
2000 #4 Rusty Wallace
2000 #62 Rusty Wallace's Car
2000 #71 Rusty Wallace's Car
Upper Deck Victory Circle 32 Days of Speed
1998 #D3 Rusty Wallace
1998 #D7 Rusty Wallace
Upper Deck Victory Circle 32 Days of Speed Gold
1998 #D3 Rusty Wallace
1998 #D7 Rusty Wallace
Upper Deck Victory Circle Championship Reflections
1997 #CR7 Rusty Wallace
Upper Deck Victory Circle Driver's Seat
1997 #DS7 Rusty Wallace
Upper Deck Victory Circle Exclusives Level 1 Silver
2000 #4 Rusty Wallace
2000 #62 Rusty Wallace's Car
2000 #71 Rusty Wallace's Car
Upper Deck Victory Circle Exclusives Level 2 Gold
2000 #4 Rusty Wallace/2
2000 #62 Rusty Wallace's Car/2
2000 #71 Rusty Wallace's Car/2
Upper Deck Victory Circle Income Statement
1999 #IS4 Rusty Wallace
2000 #IS8 Rusty Wallace
Upper Deck Victory Circle Income Statement LTD
2000 #IS8 Rusty Wallace
Upper Deck Victory Circle Magic Numbers
1999 #M4 Rusty Wallace
Upper Deck Victory Circle Magic Numbers Autographs
1999 #M4 Rusty Wallace/2
Upper Deck Victory Circle Piece of the Action
1997 #FS4 Rusty Wallace Firesuit
1997 #FS5 Rusty Wallace Glove
1997 #FS6 Rusty Wallace Shoe
Upper Deck Victory Circle Piece of the Engine
1998 #PE2 Rusty Wallace
1998 #PE7 Rusty Wallace
Upper Deck Victory Circle Point Leaders
1998 #PL9 Rusty Wallace
Upper Deck Victory Circle PowerDeck
2000 #PD3 Rusty Wallace
Upper Deck Victory Circle Predictor
1997 #PE2 Rusty Wallace WIN
Upper Deck Victory Circle Predictor Plus
1998 #2 Rusty Wallace
Upper Deck Victory Circle Predictor Plus Cel Redemption
1998 #2 Rusty Wallace
Upper Deck Victory Circle Predictor Winner Cels
1997 #PH2 Rusty Wallace
Upper Deck Victory Circle Signature Collection
1999 #RW Rusty Wallace
2000 #RW Rusty Wallace
Upper Deck Victory Circle Sparks of Brilliance
1998 #SB2 Rusty Wallace
Upper Deck Victory Circle Speed Zone
1999 #SZ6 Rusty Wallace
Upper Deck Victory Circle Track Masters
1999 #TM5 Rusty Wallace
Upper Deck Victory Circle UD Exclusives
1999 #9 Rusty Wallace
1999 #42 Rusty Wallace
1999 #78 Rusty Wallace
1999 #81 Rusty Wallace
1999 #89 Rusty Wallace CL
Upper Deck Victory Circle Victory Circle
1999 #V9 Rusty Wallace
2000 #V3 Rusty Wallace
Upper Deck Victory Circle Victory Circle LTD
2000 #V3 Rusty Wallace
Upper Deck Victory Circle Victory Lap
1997 #VL10 Rusty Wallace
Upper Deck Victory Circle Winning Material Autographed Victory Hat
2000 #HRW Rusty Wallace
Upper Deck Victory Circle Winning Material Combination
2000 #CRW Rusty Wallace
Upper Deck Victory Circle Winning Material Firesuit
2000 #FSRW Rusty Wallace
Upper Deck Victory Circle Winning Material Tire
2000 #TRW Rusty Wallace
Upper Deck Virtual Velocity
1996 #VV2 Rusty Wallace
Upper Deck Virtual Velocity Gold
1996 #VV2 Rusty Wallace
VIP
1994 #34 Rusty Wallace
1994 #48 Rusty Wallace's Car
1994 #81 Rusty Wallace ART
1994 #P4 Rusty Wallace Prototype
1995 #28 Rusty Wallace
1996 #27 Rusty Wallace
1996 #40 Rusty Wallace's Car
1997 #23 Rusty Wallace
1998 #26 Rusty Wallace
1998 #46 Rusty Wallace's Car
1999 #26 Rusty Wallace
1999 #49 Rusty Wallace's Car
2000 #5 Rusty Wallace
2000 #23 Rusty Wallace V
2000 #31 Rusty Wallace DF
2000 #44 Rusty Wallace 50 W
2001 #5 Rusty Wallace
2001 #26 Rusty Wallace SM
2001 #30 Rusty Wallace RT
2001 #41 Rusty Wallace AS
2002 #2 Rusty Wallace
2002 #31 Rusty Wallace AS
2002 #44 Rusty Wallace PP
2003 #17 Rusty Wallace
2003 #49 Rusty Wallace HR
2004 #17 Rusty Wallace
2004 #31 Rusty Wallace's Car R
2004 #50 Rusty Wallace SG
2004 #61 Rusty Wallace HR
2004 #89 Rusty Wallace ATW
2005 #29 Rusty Wallace
2005 #31 Rusty Wallace's Car R
2005 #70 Rusty Wallace F
2005 #71 Rusty Wallace F
2005 #72 Rusty Wallace F
2005 #79 Rusty Wallace BN
2005 #84 Rusty Wallace ATML
2005 #90 Wallace/Martin/T.Labonte CL
VIP Autographs
1996 #24 Rusty Wallace
VIP Cool Blue
1995 #28 Rusty Wallace
VIP Double Take
1999 #DT2 Rusty Wallace
VIP Driver's Choice
1994 #DC9 Rusty Wallace
2001 #DC6 Rusty Wallace
2002 #DC6 Rusty Wallace
2003 #DC8 Rusty Wallace
2004 #DC4 Rusty Wallace
2005 #DC4 Rusty Wallace
VIP Driver's Choice Die Cuts
2003 #DC8 Rusty Wallace
2004 #DC4 Rusty Wallace
2005 #DC4 Rusty Wallace
VIP Driver's Choice National
2003 #DC8 Rusty Wallace
VIP Driver's Choice Precious Metal
2001 #DC6 Rusty Wallace
VIP Driver's Choice Transparent
2001 #DC6 Rusty Wallace
2002 #DC6 Rusty Wallace
VIP Driver's Choice Transparent LTD
2002 #DC6 Rusty Wallace
VIP Driving Force
1998 #DF18 Rusty Wallace's Car
VIP Driving Force Die Cuts
1998 #DF18 Rusty Wallace's Car
VIP Emerald Proofs
1995 #28 Rusty Wallace
1996 #27 Rusty Wallace
1996 #40 Rusty Wallace's Car
VIP Explosives
1997 #23 Rusty Wallace
1998 #26 Rusty Wallace
1998 #46 Rusty Wallace's Car
1999 #X26 Rusty Wallace
1999 #X49 Rusty Wallace's Car
2000 #X5 Rusty Wallace
2000 #X23 Rusty Wallace V
2000 #X31 Rusty Wallace DF
2000 #X44 Rusty Wallace 50 W
2001 #5 Rusty Wallace
2001 #26 Rusty Wallace SM
2001 #30 Rusty Wallace RT
2001 #41 Rusty Wallace AS
2002 #X2 Rusty Wallace
2002 #X31 Rusty Wallace AS
2002 #X44 Rusty Wallace PP
2003 #X17 Rusty Wallace
2003 #X49 Rusty Wallace HR
VIP Explosives Lasers
1999 #26 Rusty Wallace
1999 #49 Rusty Wallace's Car
2000 #LX5 Rusty Wallace
2000 #LX23 Rusty Wallace V
2000 #LX31 Rusty Wallace DF
2000 #LX44 Rusty Wallace 50 W
2001 #LX5 Rusty Wallace
2001 #LX26 Rusty Wallace SM
2001 #LX30 Rusty Wallace RT
2001 #LX41 Rusty Wallace AS
2002 #LX2 Rusty Wallace
2002 #LX31 Rusty Wallace AS
2002 #LX44 Rusty Wallace PP
VIP Fan's Choice
1995 #FC9 Rusty Wallace
VIP Fan's Choice Gold
1995 #FC9 Rusty Wallace
VIP Gold Signature
1994 #EC7 Rusty Wallace
VIP Head Gear
1996 #HG7 Rusty Wallace
1997 #HG8 Rusty Wallace
1998 #HG9 Rusty Wallace
1999 #HG2 Rusty Wallace
2000 #HG2 Rusty Wallace
2001 #HG2 Rusty Wallace
2002 #HG2 Rusty Wallace
2003 #HG5 Rusty Wallace
2004 #HG11 Rusty Wallace
2005 #11 Rusty Wallace
VIP Head Gear Die Cuts
1996 #HG7 Rusty Wallace
1997 #HG8 Rusty Wallace
1998 #HG9 Rusty Wallace
2001 #HG2 Rusty Wallace
2002 #HG2 Rusty Wallace
2003 #HG5 Rusty Wallace
VIP Head Gear Explosives
2000 #HG2 Rusty Wallace
VIP Head Gear Explosives Laser Die Cuts
2000 #HG2 Rusty Wallace
VIP Head Gear National
2003 #HG5 Rusty Wallace
VIP Head Gear Plastic
1999 #HG2 Rusty Wallace
VIP Head Gear Transparent
2004 #HG11 Rusty Wallace
2005 #11 Rusty Wallace
VIP Knights of Thunder
1997 #KT6 Rusty Wallace
VIP Knights of Thunder Gold
1997 #KT6 Rusty Wallace
VIP Lap Leaders
1998 #LL9 Rusty Wallace's Car
1999 #LL2 Rusty Wallace
2000 #LL6 Rusty Wallace
2003 #LL4 Rusty Wallace
2004 #LL9 Rusty Wallace
2005 #9 Rusty Wallace
VIP Lap Leaders Acetate
1998 #LL9 Rusty Wallace's Car
VIP Lap Leaders Explosives
2000 #LL6 Rusty Wallace
VIP Lap Leaders Explosives Lasers
2000 #LL6 Rusty Wallace
VIP Lap Leaders National
2003 #LL4 Rusty Wallace
VIP Lap Leaders Transparent
2003 #LL4 Rusty Wallace
2004 #LL9 Rusty Wallace
2005 #9 Rusty Wallace
VIP Lap Leaders Transparent LTD
2003 #LL4 Rusty Wallace
VIP Laser Explosive
2003 #LX17 Rusty Wallace
2003 #LX49 Rusty Wallace HR
VIP Making the Show
2000 #MS17 Rusty Wallace
2001 #2 Rusty Wallace
2002 #MS2 Rusty Wallace
2003 #MS1 Rusty Wallace
2004 #MS2 Rusty Wallace
2005 #2 Rusty Wallace
VIP Mile Masters
2001 #MM6 Rusty Wallace
2002 #MM6 Rusty Wallace
2003 #MM11Rusty Wallace
VIP Mile Masters National
2003 #MM11Rusty Wallace
VIP Mile Masters Precious Metal
2001 #MM6 Rusty Wallace
VIP Mile Masters Transparent
2001 #MM6 Rusty Wallace
2002 #MM6 Rusty Wallace
2003 #MM11Rusty Wallace
VIP Mile Masters Transparent LTD
2002 #MM6 Rusty Wallace
2003 #MM11Rusty Wallace
VIP NASCAR Country
1998 #NC9 Rusty Wallace
VIP NASCAR Country Die Cuts
1998 #NC9 Rusty Wallace
VIP Oil Slicks
1997 #23 Rusty Wallace
VIP Out of the Box
1999 #OB10 Rusty Wallace
VIP Precious Metal
1997 #SM5 Rusty Wallace
VIP Previews
2003 #17 Rusty Wallace
2004 #EB31 Rusty Wallace's Car R
2004 #EB50 Rusty Wallace SG
2004 #EB17 Rusty Wallace
2005 #EB29 Rusty Wallace
2005 #EB31 Rusty Wallace's Car R
2005 #EB70 Rusty Wallace F
2005 #EB71 Rusty Wallace F
2005 #EB72 Rusty Wallace F
VIP Race Used Sheet Metal Cars
2002 #SC11 Rusty Wallace's Car
VIP Race Used Sheet Metal Drivers
2002 #SD11 Rusty Wallace
VIP Rear View Mirror
1999 #RM8 Rusty Wallace
2000 #RM2 Rusty Wallace
2001 #RV2 Rusty Wallace
2002 #RM2 Rusty Wallace
VIP Rear View Mirror Die Cuts
2001 #RV2 Rusty Wallace
2002 #RM2 Rusty Wallace
VIP Rear View Mirror Explosives
2000 #RM2 Rusty Wallace
VIP Rear View Mirror Explosives Laser Die Cuts
2000 #RM2 Rusty Wallace
VIP Red Hot
1995 #28 Rusty Wallace
VIP Reflections
1995 #R5 Rusty Wallace
VIP Reflections Gold
1995 #R5 Rusty Wallace
VIP Ring of Honor
1997 #RH1 Rusty Wallace's Car
VIP Ring of Honor Die Cuts
1997 #RH1 Rusty Wallace's Car
VIP Sam Bass Top Flight
1996 #SB5 Rusty Wallace
VIP Sam Bass Top Flight Gold
1996 #SB5 Rusty Wallace
VIP Samples
2002 #2 Rusty Wallace
2002 #31 Rusty Wallace AS
2002 #44 Rusty Wallace PP
2003 #17 Rusty Wallace
2003 #49 Rusty Wallace HR
2004 #17 Rusty Wallace
2004 #61 Rusty Wallace HR
2004 #50 Rusty Wallace SG
2004 #89 Rusty Wallace ATW
2004 #31 Rusty Wallace's Car R
2005 #29 Rusty Wallace
2005 #31 Rusty Wallace's Car R
2005 #70 Rusty Wallace F
2005 #71 Rusty Wallace F
2005 #72 Rusty Wallace F
2005 #79 Rusty Wallace BN
2005 #84 Rusty Wallace ATML
2005 #90 Wallace/Martin/T.Labonte CL
VIP Sheet Metal
1999 #SM1 Rusty Wallace
VIP Solos
1998 #26 Rusty Wallace
1998 #46 Rusty Wallace's Car
VIP Tin
2003 #CT17 Rusty Wallace
2003 #CT49 Rusty Wallace HR
VIP Torquers
1996 #27 Rusty Wallace
1996 #40 Rusty Wallace's Car
VIP Tradin' Paint Bronze
2004 #TPT9 Rusty Wallace
VIP Tradin' Paint Car Autographs
2003 #RW Rusty Wallace/2
VIP Tradin' Paint Cars
2003 #TPT17 Rusty Wallace's Car
2005 #TPT9 Rusty Wallace
VIP Tradin' Paint Driver Autographs
2003 #RW Rusty Wallace/2
VIP Tradin' Paint Drivers
2003 #TPD17 Rusty Wallace
2005 #TPD9 Rusty Wallace
VIP Tradin' Paint Gold
2004 #TPD9 Rusty Wallace
VIP Tradin' Paint Silver
2004 #TPD9 Rusty Wallace
VIP Triple Gear Sheet Metal
1998 #TGS1 Rusty Wallace
VIP Under the Lights
2000 #UL6 Rusty Wallace
VIP Under the Lights Explosives
2000 #UL6 Rusty Wallace
VIP Under the Lights Explosives Lasers
2000 #UL6 Rusty Wallace
VIP Vintage Performance
1999 #2 Rusty Wallace
VIP War Paint
1996 #WP1 Rusty Wallace's Car
VIP War Paint Gold
1996 #WP1 Rusty Wallace's Car
Viper
1996 #6 Rusty Wallace
1996 #41 Rusty Wallace
1997 #5 Rusty Wallace
1997 #52 Rusty Wallace
1997 #67 Rusty Wallace's Car
Viper Anaconda Jumbos
1997 #A6 Rusty Wallace
Viper Black Mamba
1996 #6 Rusty Wallace
1996 #41 Rusty Wallace
Viper Black Mamba First Strike
1996 #6 Rusty Wallace
1996 #41 Rusty Wallace
Viper Black Racer
1997 #5 Rusty Wallace
1997 #52 Rusty Wallace
1997 #67 Rusty Wallace's Car
Viper Black Racer First Strike
1997 #5 Rusty Wallace
1997 #52 Rusty Wallace
1997 #67 Rusty Wallace's Car
Viper Cobra
1996 #C6 Rusty Wallace
1997 #C5 Rusty Wallace
Viper Cobra First Strike
1996 #C6 Rusty Wallace
1997 #C5 Rusty Wallace
Viper Copperhead Die Cuts
1996 #6 Rusty Wallace
1996 #41 Rusty Wallace
Viper Copperhead Die Cuts First Strike
1996 #6 Rusty Wallace
1996 #41 Rusty Wallace
Viper Diamondback
1996 #D6 Rusty Wallace
1997 #DB4 Rusty Wallace
Viper Diamondback Authentic
1996 #DA5 Rusty Wallace
1997 #DBA4 Rusty Wallace
Viper Diamondback Authentic California
1996 #DA5 Rusty Wallace
1997 #DBA4 Rusty Wallace
Viper Diamondback Authentic Eastern
1997 #DBA4 Rusty Wallace
Viper Diamondback Authentic Eastern First Strike
1997 #DBA4 Rusty Wallace
Viper Diamondback Authentic First Strike
1996 #DA5 Rusty Wallace
1997 #DBA4 Rusty Wallace
Viper Diamondback First Strike
1996 #D6 Rusty Wallace
1997 #DB4 Rusty Wallace
Viper First Strike

1996 #6 Rusty Wallace
1996 #41 Rusty Wallace
1997 #5 Rusty Wallace
1997 #52 Rusty Wallace
1997 #67 Rusty Wallace's Car
Viper Green Mamba
1996 #6 Rusty Wallace
1996 #41 Rusty Wallace
Viper King Cobra
1996 #KC7 Rusty Wallace
1997 #KC5 Rusty Wallace
Viper King Cobra First Strike
1996 #KC7 Rusty Wallace
Viper Promos
1996 #P2 Rusty Wallace
Viper Red Cobra
1996 #6 Rusty Wallace
1996 #41 Rusty Wallace
Viper Sidewinder
1997 #S11 Rusty Wallace
Viper Sidewinder First Strike
1997 #S11 Rusty Wallace
Viper Snake Eyes
1997 #SE8 Rusty Wallace
Viper Snake Eyes First Strike
1997 #SE8 Rusty Wallace
Visions
1996 #114 Rusty Wallace's Car
Visions *
1996 #114 Rusty Wallace's Car
Visions Signings
1996 #99 Rusty Wallace's Car
Visions Signings *
1996 #99 Rusty Wallace's Car
Wheels
1998 #29 Rusty Wallace
1998 #45 Rusty Wallace's Car
1999 #34 Rusty Wallace
1999 #55 Rusty Wallace's Car
1999 #74 Rusty Wallace TC
Wheels 50th Anniversary
1998 #A14 Rusty Wallace
1998 #A27 Rusty Wallace's Car
Wheels American Thunder
2003 #20 Rusty Wallace
2003 #27 Rusty Wallace SS
2004 #26 Rusty Wallace
2004 #35 Rusty Wallace's Rig Rt. 66
2004 #45 Rusty Wallace AS
2004 #46 Rusty Wallace's Car HR
2004 #56 Rusty Wallace DT
2004 #79 Rusty Wallace CC
2005 #29 Rusty Wallace
2005 #45 Rusty Wallace AS
2005 #47 Rusty Wallace's Car HR
2005 #56 Rusty Wallace DT
Wheels American Thunder American Eagle
2003 #AE1 Rusty Wallace
2004 #AE11 Rusty Wallace
2005 #AE4 Rusty Wallace
Wheels American Thunder American Muscle
2003 #AM10 Rusty Wallace
2004 #AM5 Rusty Wallace
Wheels American Thunder Born On
2003 #BO20 Rusty Wallace
2003 #BO27 Rusty Wallace SS
Wheels American Thunder Golden Eagle
2003 #AEG1 Rusty Wallace
2004 #AE11 Rusty Wallace
2005 #GE4 Rusty Wallace
Wheels American Thunder Head to Toe
2003 #HT8 Rusty Wallace
Wheels American Thunder Heads Up Goodyear
2003 #HUG8 Rusty Wallace
Wheels American Thunder Heads Up Manufacturer
2003 #HUM19 Rusty Wallace
Wheels American Thunder Heads Up Team
2003 #HUT17 Rusty Wallace/60
Wheels American Thunder Heads Up Winston
2003 #HUW19 Rusty Wallace
Wheels American Thunder Holofoil
2003 #P20 Rusty Wallace
2003 #P27 Rusty Wallace SS
Wheels American Thunder Medallion
2005 #MD3 Rusty Wallace
Wheels American Thunder Post Mark
2003 #PM17 Rusty Wallace
2004 #PM3 Rusty Wallace
Wheels American Thunder Previews
2003 #20 Rusty Wallace
2003 #27 Rusty Wallace SS
2004 #EB26 Rusty Wallace
2004 #EB35 Rusty Wallace Rt. 66
2004 #EB45 Rusty Wallace AS
2005 #29 Rusty Wallace
Wheels American Thunder Pushin Pedal
2003 #PP8 Rusty Wallace
Wheels American Thunder Rookie Thunder
2003 #RT34 Rusty Wallace
Wheels American Thunder Samples
2003 #P20 Rusty Wallace
2003 #P27 Rusty Wallace SS
2004 #26 Rusty Wallace
2004 #35 Rusty Wallace's Rig Rt. 66
2004 #45 Rusty Wallace AS
2004 #46 Rusty Wallace's Car HR
2004 #56 Rusty Wallace DT
2004 #79 Rusty Wallace CC
2005 #29 Rusty Wallace
2005 #45 Rusty Wallace AS
2005 #47 Rusty Wallace's Car HR
2005 #56 Rusty Wallace DT
Wheels American Thunder Thunder Road
2003 #TR4 Rusty Wallace
2004 #TR1 Rusty Wallace
2005 #TR1 Rusty Wallace
Wheels American Thunder Triple Hat
2003 #TH2 Rusty Wallace
2004 #TH23 Rusty Wallace
2005 #TH25 Rusty Wallace
Wheels Autographs
2003 #59 Rusty Wallace AT/HG
2004 #67 Rusty Wallace HG
2005 #60 Rusty Wallace
2006 #60 Rusty Wallace
Wheels Circuit Breaker
1999 #CB7 Rusty Wallace
Wheels Custom Shop
1998 #CSRW Rusty Wallace
1999 #CS5 Rusty Wallace
Wheels Custom Shop Prizes
1998 #RWA1 Rusty Wallace
1998 #RWA2 Rusty Wallace
1998 #RWA3 Rusty Wallace
1998 #RWB1 Rusty Wallace
1998 #RWB2 Rusty Wallace
1998 #RWB3 Rusty Wallace
1998 #RWC1 Rusty Wallace
1998 #RWC2 Rusty Wallace
1998 #RWC3 Rusty Wallace
1999 #RWA1 Rusty Wallace
1999 #RWA2 Rusty Wallace
1999 #RWA3 Rusty Wallace
1999 #RWB1 Rusty Wallace
1999 #RWB2 Rusty Wallace
1999 #RWB3 Rusty Wallace
1999 #RWC1 Rusty Wallace
1999 #RWC2 Rusty Wallace
1999 #RWC3 Rusty Wallace
Wheels Dialed In
1999 #DI2 Rusty Wallace
Wheels Double Take
1998 #E9 Rusty Wallace
Wheels Flag Chasers Daytona Seven
1999 #DS3 Rusty Wallace
Wheels Flag Chasers Daytona Seven Blue-Yellow
1999 #DS3 Rusty Wallace
Wheels Flag Chasers Daytona Seven Checkered
1999 #DS3 Rusty Wallace
Wheels Flag Chasers Daytona Seven Green
1999 #DS3 Rusty Wallace
Wheels Flag Chasers Daytona Seven Red
1999 #DS3 Rusty Wallace
Wheels Flag Chasers Daytona Seven White
1999 #DS3 Rusty Wallace
Wheels Flag Chasers Daytona Seven Yellow
1999 #DS3 Rusty Wallace
Wheels Golden
1998 #29 Rusty Wallace
1998 #45 Rusty Wallace's Car
1999 #34 Rusty Wallace
1999 #55 Rusty Wallace
1999 #74 Rusty Wallace
Wheels Green Flags
1998 #GF17 Rusty Wallace's Car
Wheels Harry Gant
1994 #73 Rusty Wallace
Wheels Harry Gant Gold
1994 #73 Rusty Wallace
Wheels High Gear
1994 #2 Rusty Wallace
1994 #70 Rusty Wallace's Pit Crew
1994 #71 Rusty Wallace DOY
1994 #76 Rusty Wallace WIN
1994 #80 Rusty Wallace WIN
1994 #81 Rusty Wallace WIN
1994 #82 Rusty Wallace WIN
1994 #91 Rusty Wallace BC
1994 #187 Rusty Wallace WIN
1994 #193 Rusty Wallace WIN
1994 #194 Rusty Wallace WIN
1994 #196 Rusty Wallace WIN
1994 #198 Rusty Wallace WIN
1994 #200 Rusty Wallace WIN
1995 #2 Rusty Wallace
1995 #72 Rusty Wallace's Car
1995 #87 Rusty Wallace RW
1998 #9 Rusty Wallace
1998 #28 Rusty Wallace's Car
1999 #4 Rusty Wallace
1999 #28 Rusty Wallace's Car
1999 #68 Rusty Wallace's Car
2000 #8 Rusty Wallace
2000 #28 Rusty Wallace's Car
2000 #55 Rusty Wallace's Car
2001 #6 Rusty Wallace
2001 #32 Rusty Wallace WCM
2001 #52 Rusty Wallace HL
2001 #58 Rusty Wallace CA
2001 #63 Rusty Wallace CA
2002 #26 Rusty Wallace
2002 #33 Rusty Wallace's Car
2003 #29 Rusty Wallace
2003 #55 Rusty Wallace's Car CM
2004 #26 Rusty Wallace
2004 #55 Rusty Wallace's Car
2004 #62 Rusty Wallace HL
2005 #2 Rusty Wallace
2005 #38 Rusty Wallace's Car C
2005 #71 Rusty Wallace NI
2005 #85 Rusty Wallace P
2006 #8 Rusty Wallace
2006 #46 Rusty Wallace's Car C
2006 #84 Rusty Wallace FF
2006 #89 R. Wallace/M. Martin NI
Wheels High Gear Autographs
2001 #33 Rusty Wallace
2002 #56 Rusty Wallace
Wheels High Gear Blue Hawaii SCDA Promos
2003 #29 Rusty Wallace
2003 #55 Rusty Wallace's Car CM
Wheels High Gear Busch Clash
1995 #BC6 Rusty Wallace
Wheels High Gear Busch Clash Gold
1995 #BC6 Rusty Wallace
Wheels High Gear Day One
1994 #187 Rusty Wallace WIN
1994 #193 Rusty Wallace WIN
1994 #194 Rusty Wallace WIN
1994 #196 Rusty Wallace WIN
1994 #198 Rusty Wallace WIN
1994 #200 Rusty Wallace WIN
1995 #2 Rusty Wallace
1995 #72 Rusty Wallace's Car
1995 #87 Rusty Wallace RW
Wheels High Gear Day One Gold
1994 #187 Rusty Wallace WIN
1994 #193 Rusty Wallace WIN
1994 #194 Rusty Wallace WIN
1994 #196 Rusty Wallace WIN
1994 #198 Rusty Wallace WIN
1994 #200 Rusty Wallace WIN
1995 #2 Rusty Wallace
1995 #72 Rusty Wallace's Car
1995 #87 Rusty Wallace RW
Wheels High Gear Dominators
1994 #D2 Rusty Wallace/3000
1995 #D1 Rusty Wallace/1750
Wheels High Gear Dominators Jumbos
1995 #D1 Rusty Wallace/1750
Wheels High Gear First Gear
1998 #7 Rusty Wallace
1998 #28 Rusty Wallace's Car
1999 #4 Rusty Wallace
1999 #28 Rusty Wallace's Car
1999 #68 Rusty Wallace's Car
2000 #8 Rusty Wallace
2000 #28 Rusty Wallace
2000 #55 Rusty Wallace
2001 #6 Rusty Wallace
2001 #32 Rusty Wallace WCM
2001 #52 Rusty Wallace HL
2001 #58 Rusty Wallace CA
2001 #63 Rusty Wallace CA
2002 #26 Rusty Wallace
2002 #33 Rusty Wallace's Car
2003 #F29 Rusty Wallace
2003 #F55 Rusty Wallace's Car CM
Wheels High Gear Flag Chasers
1999 #FC4 Rusty Wallace
Wheels High Gear Flag Chasers Black
2005 #FC2 Rusty Wallace
Wheels High Gear Flag Chasers Blue-Yellow
1999 #FC4 Rusty Wallace
2005 #FC2 Rusty Wallace
Wheels High Gear Flag Chasers Checkered
1999 #FC4 Rusty Wallace
2005 #FC2 Rusty Wallace
Wheels High Gear Flag Chasers Green
1999 #FC4 Rusty Wallace
2005 #FC2 Rusty Wallace
Wheels High Gear Flag Chasers Red
1999 #FC4 Rusty Wallace
2005 #FC2 Rusty Wallace
Wheels High Gear Flag Chasers White
1999 #FC4 Rusty Wallace
2005 #FC2 Rusty Wallace
Wheels High Gear Flag Chasers Yellow
1999 #FC4 Rusty Wallace
2005 #FC2 Rusty Wallace
Wheels High Gear Flag to Flag
2005 #FF26 Rusty Wallace
2006 #FF27 Rusty Wallace
Wheels High Gear Full Throttle
2003 #FT6 Rusty Wallace
Wheels High Gear Gear Jammers
1998 #GJ1 Rusty Wallace
Wheels High Gear Gear Shifters
1999 #GS4 Rusty Wallace
2000 #GS8 Rusty Wallace
2001 #GS6 Rusty Wallace
Wheels High Gear Gold
1994 #2 Rusty Wallace
1994 #70 Rusty Wallace's Pit Crew
1994 #71 Rusty Wallace DOY SP
1994 #76 Rusty Wallace WIN
1994 #80 Rusty Wallace WIN
1994 #81 Rusty Wallace WIN SP
1994 #82 Rusty Wallace WIN
1994 #91 Rusty Wallace BC SP
1994 #187 Rusty Wallace WIN
1994 #193 Rusty Wallace WIN
1994 #194 Rusty Wallace WIN
1994 #196 Rusty Wallace WIN
1994 #198 Rusty Wallace WIN
1994 #200 Rusty Wallace WIN
1995 #2 Rusty Wallace
1995 #72 Rusty Wallace's Car
1995 #87 Rusty Wallace RW
Wheels High Gear High Groove
1998 #HG1 Rusty Wallace's Car
2002 #HG26 Rusty Wallace
2003 #HG26 Rusty Wallace
2004 #HG26 Rusty Wallace
Wheels High Gear Hot Streaks
2002 #HS9 Rusty Wallace
Wheels High Gear Hot Treads
2003 #HT17 Rusty Wallace
Wheels High Gear Machine
2003 #MM3B Rusty Wallace
2005 #MMB9 Rusty Wallace
Wheels High Gear Man
2003 #MM3A Rusty Wallace
2005 #MMA9 Rusty Wallace
Wheels High Gear Man and Machine Cars
1998 #9 Rusty Wallace's Car
1999 #MM9B Rusty Wallace's Car
2000 #MM3B Rusty Wallace's Car
2001 #MM3B Rusty Wallace's Car
2002 #MM9B Rusty Wallace
Wheels High Gear Man and Machine Drivers
1998 #MM9 Rusty Wallace
2000 #MM3A Rusty Wallace
2001 #MM3A Rusty Wallace
2002 #MM9A Rusty Wallace
Wheels High Gear Mega Gold
1994 #MG3 Rusty Wallace
Wheels High Gear MPH
1998 #7 Rusty Wallace
1998 #28 Rusty Wallace's Car
1999 #4 Rusty Wallace
1999 #28 Rusty Wallace's Car
1999 #68 Rusty Wallace's Car
2000 #8 Rusty Wallace
2000 #28 Rusty Wallace
2000 #55 Rusty Wallace
2001 #6 Rusty Wallace
2001 #32 Rusty Wallace WCM
2001 #52 Rusty Wallace HL
2001 #58 Rusty Wallace CA
2001 #63 Rusty Wallace CA
2002 #26 Rusty Wallace
2002 #33 Rusty Wallace's Car
2003 #M29 Rusty Wallace
2003 #M55 Rusty Wallace's Car CM
2004 #M26 Rusty Wallace
2004 #M55 Rusty Wallace's Car
2004 #M62 Rusty Wallace HL
2005 #M2 Rusty Wallace
2005 #M38 Rusty Wallace's Car C
2005 #M71 Rusty Wallace NI
2005 #M85 Rusty Wallace P
2006 #M8 Rusty Wallace
2006 #M46 Rusty Wallace's Car C
2006 #M84 Rusty Wallace FF
2006 #M89 R. Wallace/M. Martin NI
Wheels High Gear Power Pak Teams
1994 #W2 Rusty Wallace
1994 #W34 Rusty Wallace/Buddy Parrott
1994 #W35 Rusty Wallace
1994 #W36 Rusty Wallace in Pits
1994 #W37 Rusty Wallace
1994 #W38 Rusty Wallace w/Car
1994 #W39 Rusty Wallace
1994 #W40 Rusty Wallace's Car
1994 #W41 Rusty Wallace's Car CL
Wheels High Gear Power Pak Teams Gold
1994 #2W Rusty Wallace
1994 #34W Rusty Wallace/Buddy Parrott
1994 #35W Rusty Wallace
1994 #36W Rusty Wallace in Pits
1994 #37W Rusty Wallace
1994 #38W Rusty Wallace w/Car
1994 #39W Rusty Wallace
1994 #40W Rusty Wallace 's Car
Wheels High Gear Previews
2003 #29 Rusty Wallace
2004 #26 Rusty Wallace
2004 #55 Rusty Wallace's Car
Wheels High Gear Previews Green
2005 #EB2 Rusty Wallace
2006 #EB8 Rusty Wallace
Wheels High Gear Previews Silver
2006 #EB84 Rusty Wallace FF
Wheels High Gear Pure Gold
1998 #PG9 Rusty Wallace
Wheels High Gear Samples
2003 #29 Rusty Wallace
2003 #55 Rusty Wallace's Car CM
2004 #26 Rusty Wallace
2004 #55 Rusty Wallace's Car
2004 #62 Rusty Wallace HL
2005 #2 Rusty Wallace
2005 #38 Rusty Wallace's Car C
2005 #71 Rusty Wallace NI
2005 #85 Rusty Wallace P
Wheels High Gear Sunday Sensation
2000 #OC3 Rusty Wallace
2001 #SS2 Rusty Wallace
2002 #SS9 Rusty Wallace
Wheels High Gear Top Tier
1999 #TT4 Rusty Wallace 1:80
2000 #TT8 Rusty Wallace
2006 #TT8 Rusty Wallace
Wheels High Gear Winning Edge
2000 #WE7 Rusty Wallace
Wheels High Groove
1999 #HG6 Rusty Wallace
Wheels Jackpot
1998 #J9 Rusty Wallace
Wheels Rookie Thunder
1993 #25 Rusty Wallace
1993 #46 Rusty Wallace
1993 #60 Rusty Wallace's Car
1993 #63 Rusty Wallace
1993 #65 Rusty Wallace
1993 #66 Rusty Wallace
1993 #67 Rusty Wallace
1993 #68 Rusty Wallace
1993 #87 Rusty Wallace
1993 #90 Rusty Wallace
Wheels Rookie Thunder Platinum
1993 #25 Rusty Wallace
1993 #46 Rusty Wallace
1993 #60 Rusty Wallace's Car
1993 #63 Rusty Wallace
1993 #65 Rusty Wallace
1993 #66 Rusty Wallace
1993 #67 Rusty Wallace
1993 #68 Rusty Wallace
1993 #87 Rusty Wallace
1993 #90 Rusty Wallace
Wheels Runnin and Gunnin
1999 #RG2 Rusty Wallace
Wheels Runnin and Gunnin Foils
1999 #RG2 Rusty Wallace
Wheels Rusty Wallace
1992 #6 Rusty Wallace
1992 #8 Rusty Wallace w/Crew
1992 #9 Rusty Wallace/Mike Wallace/Kenny Wallace
1992 #10 Rusty Wallace
1992 #11 Rusty Wallace
1992 #12 Rusty Wallace
1992 #13 Rusty Wallace
1992 #14 Rusty Wallace Art
1992 #2 Rusty Wallace
1992 #5 Rusty Wallace's Car
Wheels Rusty Wallace Gold
1992 #2 Rusty Wallace
1992 #5 Rusty Wallace's Car
1992 #6 Rusty Wallace
1992 #8 Rusty Wallace w/Crew
1992 #9 Rusty Wallace/Mike Wallace/Kenny Wallace
1992 #10 Rusty Wallace
1992 #11 Rusty Wallace
1992 #12 Rusty Wallace
1992 #13 Rusty Wallace
1992 #14 Rusty Wallace Art
Wheels Solos
1999 #34 Rusty Wallace
1999 #55 Rusty Wallace
1999 #74 Rusty Wallace
Zenith
1995 #2 Rusty Wallace HG
1995 #35 Rusty Wallace's Transporter
1996 #9 Rusty Wallace
1996 #94 Rusty Wallace W
1996 #96 Rusty Wallace W
Zenith Artist Proofs
1996 #9 Rusty Wallace RP
1996 #94 Rusty Wallace W
1996 #96 Rusty Wallace W
Zenith Champion Salute
1996 #7 Rusty Wallace
Zenith Helmets
1995 #2 Rusty Wallace
Zenith Winston Winners
1995 #8 Rusty Wallace
Zenith Z-Team
1995 #11 Rusty Wallace

Waltrip, Darrell

AC Racing
1991 #3 Darrell Waltrip
AC Racing Foldouts
1993 #17 Darrell Waltrip
AC Racing Postcards
1992 #8 Darrell Waltrip
AC Racing Proven Winners
1990 #2 Darrell Waltrip
AC-Delco
1992 #4 Darrell Waltrip
Action Packed
1993 #3 Darrell Waltrip 's Car WIN
1993 #16 Darrell Waltrip
1993 #17 Darrell Waltrip's Car
1993 #24 Darrell Waltrip PW
1993 #41 Darrell Waltrip T10
1993 #103 Darrell Waltrip
1993 #104 Darrell Waltrip's Car
1993 #164 M.Waltrip/D.Waltrip B
1993 #190 Darrell Waltrip
1994 #13 Darrell Waltrip
1994 #70 Darrell Waltrip
1994 #100 Neil Bonnett/Darrell Waltrip
1994 #127 Darrell Waltrip's Car
1994 #166 Darrell Waltrip RR
1997 #17 Darrell Waltrip
1997 #38 Darrell Waltrip's Car
1997 #85 Darrell Waltrip CL
Action Packed 24K Gold
1993 #2G Darrell Waltrip T10
1993 #72G Darrell Waltrip
1994 #24G Darrell Waltrip
Action Packed Chevy Madness
1997 #2 Darrell Waltrip's Car
Action Packed Coastars
1994 #17 Darrell Waltrip
Action Packed Country
1995 #4 Darrell Waltrip RS
1995 #18 Darrell Waltrip S
1995 #21 S.Waltrip/D.Waltrip MRO
1995 #32 Darrell Waltrip NT
1995 #33 Darrell Waltrip NT
1995 #34 Darrell Waltrip NT
1995 #35 Darrell Waltrip NT
1995 #36 Darrell Waltrip NT
1995 #37 Darrell Waltrip NT
Action Packed Country Silver Speed
1995 #4 Darrell Waltrip RS
1995 #18 Darrell Waltrip S
1995 #21 S.Waltrip/D.Waltrip MRO
1995 #32 Darrell Waltrip NT
1995 #33 Darrell Waltrip NT
1995 #34 Darrell Waltrip NT
1995 #35 Darrell Waltrip NT
1995 #36 Darrell Waltrip NT
1995 #37 Darrell Waltrip NT
Action Packed Credentials
1996 #38 Darrell Waltrip
1996 #61 Darrell Waltrip SM
1996 #79 Darrell Waltrip OWN
1996 #90 Stevie Waltrip/Darrell Waltrip BTS
1996 #94 M.Waltrip/D.Waltrip WCA
Action Packed Credentials Silver Speed
1996 #38 Darrell Waltrip
Action Packed First Impressions
1997 #17 Darrell Waltrip
1997 #38 Darrell Waltrip's Car
1997 #85 Darrell Waltrip CL
Action Packed Mint
1994 #13 Darrell Waltrip
1994 #70 Darrell Waltrip
1994 #100 Neil Bonnett/Darrell Waltrip
1994 #127 Darrell Waltrip's Car
1994 #166 Darrell Waltrip RR
Action Packed Preview
1995 #24 Darrell Waltrip
1995 #67 Darrell Waltrip T10
1995 #78 Darrell Waltrip DD
Action Packed Preview 24K Gold
1995 #10G Darrell Waltrip
Action Packed Rolling Thunder
1997 #7 Darrell Waltrip
Action Packed Select 24K Gold
1994 #W1 Darrell Waltrip
Action Packed Stars
1995 #10 Darrell Waltrip OC
1995 #39 Darrell Waltrip's Car
Action Packed Stars Silver Speed
1995 #10 Darrell Waltrip OC
1995 #39 Darrell Waltrip's Car
Assets
1995 #7 Darrell Waltrip
1995 #35 Darrell Waltrip
Assets $2 Phone Cards
1995 #6 Darrell Waltrip
Assets $2 Phone Cards Gold Signature
1995 #6 Darrell Waltrip
Assets $25 Phone Cards
1995 #3 Darrell Waltrip
Assets $5 Phone Cards
1995 #3 Darrell Waltrip
Assets 1-Minute Phone Cards
1995 #6 Darrell Waltrip
Assets 1-Minute Phone Cards Gold Signature
1995 #6 Darrell Waltrip
Assets Gold Signature
1995 #7 Darrell Waltrip
1995 #35 Darrell Waltrip
Assets Racing
1996 #8 Darrell Waltrip
1996 #43 Darrell Waltrip
Assets Racing $100 Cup Champion Interactive Phone Cards
1996 #6 Darrell Waltrip
Assets Racing $1000 Cup Champion Interactive Phone Cards
1996 #11 Darrell Waltrip
Assets Racing $2 Phone Cards
1996 #11 Darrell Waltrip
Assets Racing $5 Phone Cards
1996 #4 Darrell Waltrip
Assets Racing Competitor's License
1996 #CL10 Darrell Waltrip
Autographed Racing
1996 #35 Darrell Waltrip
1997 #15 Darrell Waltrip
1997 #48 D.Waltrip/G.Bodine
Autographed Racing Autographs
1996 #59 Darrell Waltrip
1997 #54 Darrell Waltrip
Autographed Racing Autographs Certified Golds
1996 #59 Darrell Waltrip
Autographed Racing Front Runners
1996 #81 D.Walt.with hel/D.Wal.no hel
1996 #82 D.Wal.with hel/M.Wal.shades
1996 #83 D.Waltrip with hel/M.Waltrip
1996 #84 D.Walt.no hel/M.Walt.shades
1996 #85 D.Waltrip no hel/M.Waltrip
Autographed Racing High Performance
1996 #HP17 Darrell Waltrip
Autographed Racing Mayne Street
1997 #KM15 Darrell Waltrip
Big League Cards Creative Images
1998 #7 Darrell Waltrip
Card Dynamics Darrell Waltrip
1992 #1 Darrell Waltrip
1992 #2 Darrell Waltrip
1992 #3 Darrell Waltrip
1992 #4 Darrell Waltrip
1992 #5 Darrell Waltrip
Card Dynamics Gant Oil
1992 #1 Darrell Waltrip/4000
1994 #6 Darrell Waltrip
Classic
1996 #24 Darrell Waltrip
1996 #60 Darrell Waltrip SP
Classic Five Sport
1995 #176 Darrell Waltrip
Classic Five Sport Autographs Numbered
1995 #176 Darrell Waltrip
Classic Five Sport Printer's Proofs
1995 #176 Darrell Waltrip
Classic Five Sport Red Die Cuts
1995 #176 Darrell Waltrip
Classic Five Sport Signings
1995-96 #89 Darrell Waltrip
Classic Five Sport Signings Blue Signature
1995-96 #89 Darrell Waltrip
Classic Five Sport Signings Die Cuts
1995-96 #89 Darrell Waltrip
Classic Five Sport Signings Red Signature
1995-96 #89 Darrell Waltrip
Classic Five Sport Silver Die Cuts
1995 #176 Darrell Waltrip
Classic Five Sport Strive For Five
1995 #RC6 Darrell Waltrip
Classic Five-Sport *
1995 #176 Darrell Waltrip
Classic Five-Sport Autographs *
1995 #176 Darrell Waltrip/225
Classic Five-Sport Printer's Proofs *
1995 #176 Darrell Waltrip
Classic Five-Sport Red Die Cuts *
1995 #176 Darrell Waltrip
Classic Five-Sport Silver Die Cuts *
1995 #176 Darrell Waltrip
Classic Five-Sport Strive For Five *
1995 #RC6 Darrell Waltrip
Classic Printer's Proof
1996 #24 Darrell Waltrip
Classic Race Chase
1996 #RC15 Darrell Waltrip's Car
Classic Signings *
1996 #S89 Darrell Waltrip
Classic Signings Blue Signature *
1996 #89 Darrell Waltrip
Classic Signings Die Cuts *
1996 #89 Darrell Waltrip
Classic Signings Red Signature *
1996 #89 Darrell Waltrip
Classic Silver
1996 #24 Darrell Waltrip
Collector's Choice
1997 #17 Darrell Waltrip
1997 #67 Darrell Waltrip's Car MM
1997 #119 Darrell Waltrip SC
1997 #151 Darrell Waltrip TRA
1998 #17 Darrell Waltrip
1998 #53 Darrell Waltrip's Car
1998 #112 Darrell Waltrip TD
Collector's Choice CC600
1998 #CC21 Darrell Waltrip
1998 #CC54 Darrell Waltrip
1998 #CC87 Darrell Waltrip
Collector's Choice Speedecals
1997 #S33 Darrell Waltrip's Car
1997 #S34 Darrell Waltrip's Helmet
Collector's Choice Star Quest
1998 #SQ35 Darrell Waltrip
Collector's Choice Upper Deck 500
1997 #UD34 Darrell Waltrip
1997 #UD35 Darrell Waltrip's Car
Collector's Choice Victory Circle
1997 #VC1 Darrell Waltrip
Crown Jewels
1995 #10 Darrell Waltrip
1995 #33 Darrell Waltrip
1995 #51 Darrell Waltrip's Transporter
1995 #64 D.Earn/Waltrip Cars CJT
Crown Jewels Diamond
1995 #10 Darrell Waltrip
1995 #33 Darrell Waltrip
1995 #51 Darrell Waltrip's Transporter
1995 #64 Dale Earnhardt Darrell Waltrip CJT
Crown Jewels Elite
1996 #12 Darrell Waltrip
Crown Jewels Elite Birthstones of the Champions

1996 #BC4 Darrell Waltrip
Crown Jewels Elite Birthstones of the Champions Diamond Tribute
1996 #BC4 Darrell Waltrip
Crown Jewels Elite Birthstones of the Champions Treasure Chest
1996 #BC4 Darrell Waltrip
Crown Jewels Elite Diamond Tribute
1996 #12 Darrell Waltrip
Crown Jewels Elite Diamond Tribute Citrine
1996 #12 Darrell Waltrip
Crown Jewels Elite Dual Jewels Amethyst
1996 #DJ5 D.Waltrip/M.Waltrip
Crown Jewels Elite Dual Jewels Amethyst Diamond Tribute
1996 #DJ5 D.Waltrip/M.Waltrip
Crown Jewels Elite Dual Jewels Amethyst Treasure Chest
1996 #DJ5 D.Waltrip/M.Waltrip
Crown Jewels Elite Dual Jewels Garnet
1996 #DJ5 D.Waltrip/M.Waltrip
Crown Jewels Elite Dual Jewels Garnet Diamond Tribute
1996 #DJ5 D.Waltrip/M.Waltrip
Crown Jewels Elite Dual Jewels Garnet Treasure Chest
1996 #DJ5 D.Waltrip/M.Waltrip
Crown Jewels Elite Dual Jewels Sapphire
1996 #DJ5 D.Waltrip/M.Waltrip
Crown Jewels Elite Dual Jewels Sapphire Treasure Chest
1996 #DJ5 D.Waltrip/M.Waltrip
Crown Jewels Elite Emerald
1996 #12 Darrell Waltrip
Crown Jewels Elite Emerald Treasure Chest
1996 #12 Darrell Waltrip
Crown Jewels Elite Sapphire
1996 #12 Darrell Waltrip
Crown Jewels Elite Sapphire Treasure Chest
1996 #12 Darrell Waltrip
Crown Jewels Elite Treasure Chest
1996 #12 Darrell Waltrip
Crown Jewels Emerald
1995 #10 Darrell Waltrip
1995 #33 Darrell Waltrip
1995 #51 Darrell Waltrip's Transporter
1995 #64 Dale Earnhardt CJT Darrell Waltip
Crown Jewels Sapphire
1995 #10 Darrell Waltrip
1995 #33 Darrell Waltrip
1995 #51 Darrell Waltrip's Transporter
1995 #64 Dale Earnhardt CJT Darrell Waltrip's Cars
Finish Line
1993 #4 Darrell Waltrip
1993 #51 Darrell Waltrip
1993 #95 Darrell Waltrip's Car
1993 #107 Darrell Waltrip
1994 #40 Darrell Waltrip's Car
1994 #102 Darrell Waltrip
1994 #129 Darrell Waltrip
1995 #3 Darrell Waltrip
1995 #17 Darrell Waltrip
1995 #58 Darrell Waltrip
1996 #11 Darrell Waltrip
1996 #56 Darrell Waltrip
1996 #67 Darrell Waltrip's Car
1996 #68 Darrell Waltrip
Finish Line Black Gold
1996 #C12 Darrell Waltrip's Car
1996 #D13 Darrell Waltrip
Finish Line Coca-Cola 600
1995 #7 Darrell Waltrip
1995 #35 Darrell Waltrip
Finish Line Coca-Cola 600 Winners
1995 #CC1 Darrell Waltrip
1995 #CC4 Darrell Waltrip
1995 #CC5 Darrell Waltrip
Finish Line Commemorative Sheets
1993 #8 Martinsville
1993 #18 Talladega
1993 #30 Atlanta
Finish Line Gold
1994 #13 Darrell Waltrip
1994 #30 Darrell Waltrip's Car
1994 #31 Darrell Waltrip
1994 #64 Darrell Waltrip
1994 #66 Darrell Waltrip
Finish Line Gold Phone Cards
1994 #9 Darrell Waltrip/3000
Finish Line Gold Signature
1995 #GS12 Darrell Waltrip
1996 #GS11 Darrell Waltrip
Finish Line Gold Teamwork
1994 #TG10 Darrell Waltrip/Barry Dodson
Finish Line Phone Cards
1994 #15 Darrell Waltrip
Finish Line Phone Pak
1996 #39 Darrell Waltrip
1996 #40 Darrell Waltrip's Car
Finish Line Phone Pak $10
1996 #12 Darrell Waltrip
Finish Line Phone Pak $2 Signature
1996 #39 Darrell Waltrip
1996 #40 Darrell Waltrip's Car
Finish Line Phone Pak $5
1996 #24 Darrell Waltrip
Finish Line Phone Pak II
1997 #10 Darrell Waltrip
1997 #48 Darrell Waltrip $5
1997 #75 Darrell Waltrip's Car $10
Finish Line Printer's Proof
1995 #3 Darrell Waltrip
1995 #17 Darrell Waltrip
1995 #58 Darrell Waltrip
1996 #11 Darrell Waltrip
1996 #56 Darrell Waltrip
1996 #67 Darrell Waltrip's Car
1996 #68 Darrell Waltrip
Finish Line Silver
1993 #4 Darrell Waltrip
1993 #51 Darrell Waltrip
1993 #95 Darrell Waltrip's Car
1993 #107 Darrell Waltrip
1994 #40 Darrell Waltrip's Car
1994 #102 Darrell Waltrip
1994 #129 Darrell Waltrip
1995 #3 Darrell Waltrip
1995 #17 Darrell Waltrip
1995 #58 Darrell Waltrip
1996 #11 Darrell Waltrip
1996 #56 Darrell Waltrip
1996 #67 Darrell Waltrip's Car
1996 #68 Darrell Waltrip
Finish Line Standout Cars
1995 #SC8 Darrell Waltrip's Car
Finish Line Standout Drivers
1995 #SD8 Darrell Waltrip
Hi-Tech Brickyard 400
1994 #18 Darrell Waltrip's Car
1994 #48 Darrell Waltrip
1995 #25 Darrell Waltrip's Car
1995 #78 Darrell Waltrip
Hi-Tech Brickyard 400 Artist Proofs
1994 #18 Darrell Waltrip's Car
1994 #48 Darrell Waltrip
Hi-Tech Brickyard 400 Top Ten
1995 #BY6 Darrell Waltrip
Hi-Tech Tire Test
1993 #2 Darrell Waltrip's Car
Images
1995 #17 Darrell Waltrip
1995 #47 Darrell Waltrip
Images Driven
1995 #D15 Darrell Waltrip
Images Gold
1995 #17 Darrell Waltrip
1995 #47 Darrell Waltrip
Jurassic Park
1997 #17 Darrell Waltrip
Jurassic Park Triceratops
1997 #17 Darrell Waltrip
KnightQuest
1996 #17 Darrell Waltrip K
KnightQuest Black Knights
1996 #17 Darrell Waltrip K
KnightQuest Knights of the Round Table
1996 #KT3 Darrell Waltrip
KnightQuest Protectors of the Crown
1996 #PC1 Darrell Waltrip
KnightQuest Red Knight Preview
1996 #17 Darrell Waltrip K
KnightQuest Royalty
1996 #17 Darrell Waltrip K
KnightQuest White Knights
1996 #17 Darrell Waltrip K
Matchbook Winston Cup Champions
1995 #11 1981 Champion Darrell Waltrip
1995 #12 1982 Champion Darrell Waltrip
1995 #15 1985 Champion Darrell Waltrip
Maxwell House
1993 #8 Darrell Waltrip
1993 #21 Darrell Waltrip/Michael Waltrip
Maxx
1989 #17 Darrell Waltrip
1989 #125 Waltrip/Marlin/Elliott/R.Wallace Cars YR
1989 #140 D.Waltrip/Mich.Waltrip
1989 #150 Darrell Waltrip VL
1989 #164 Darrell Waltrip VL
1990 #17 Darrell Waltrip
1990 #50 Darrell Waltrip Pit Champs
1990 #100 Darrell Waltrip FF
1990 #167 Darrell Waltrip YR
1990 #168 Rusty Wallace/Darrell Waltrip Cars YR
1990 #174 Darrell Waltrip YR
1990 #177 Darrell Waltrip's Car YR
1990 #178 Darrell Waltrip YR
1990 #185 D.Waltrip/T.Labonte/Martin/Jarrett Cars YR
1991 #17 Darrell Waltrip
1991 #150 Darrell Waltrip FF
1993 #17 Darrell Waltrip
1993 #226 Darrell Waltrip MM
1993 #280 Darrell Waltrip YR
1993 #284 Darrell Waltrip YR
1993 #285 Darrell Waltrip YR
1994 #17 Darrell Waltrip
1994 #64 Darrell Waltrip's Car
1995 #17 Darrell Waltrip
1995 #174 Darrell Waltrip's Car
1995 #206 Darrell Waltrip
1995 #207 Darrell Waltrip's Car
1996 #17 Darrell Waltrip
1996 #27 Darrell Waltrip's Car
1997 #17 Darrell Waltrip
1997 #62 Darrell Waltrip's Car
1997 #119 Darrell Waltrip MO
1998 #17 Darrell Waltrip
1998 #47 Darrell Waltrip's Car
1998 #63 Darrell Waltrip's Car HC
1999 #46 Darrell Waltrip
1999 #47 Darrell Waltrip's Car
1999 #48 Darrell Waltrip RR
2000 #35 Darrell Waltrip
Maxx 10th Anniversary
1998 #16 Darrell Waltrip
1998 #61 Darrell Waltrip's Car
1998 #98 Darrell Waltrip
1998 #118 D.Waltrip/R.Wallace
Maxx 10th Anniversary Buy Back Autographs
1998 #48 Darrell Waltrip '88 #10/179
Maxx 10th Anniversary Card of the Year
1998 #CY4 Darrell Waltrip
Maxx 10th Anniversary Champions Past
1998 #CP7 Darrell Waltrip
Maxx 10th Anniversary Champions Past Die Cuts
1998 #CP7 Darrell Waltrip
Maxx 10th Anniversary Maxximum Preview
1998 #P1 Darrell Waltrip
Maxx 1997 Year In Review
1998 #23 Darrell Waltrip
1998 #30 Darrell Waltrip's Car
1998 #48 Darrell Waltrip's Car
1998 #55 Darrell Waltrip's Car
1998 #95 Darrell Waltrip's Car
1998 #140 Darrell Waltrip's Car
1998 #155 Darrell Waltrip's Car
Maxx Black
1992 #17 Darrell Waltrip
1992 #190 Davey Allison/Darrell Waltrip Cars MM
1992 #195 Darrell Waltrip's Car MM
1992 #270 Darrell Waltrip YR
1992 #277 Darrell Waltrip YR
Maxx Charlotte
1988 #10 Darrell Waltrip RC
1988 #27 Darrell Waltrip In Pits
1988 #75 Darrell Waltrip's Car
Maxx Craftsman
1992 #7 Darrell Waltrip
Maxx Crisco
1989 #2 Darrell Waltrip
Maxx Family Ties
1996 #FT5 D.Waltrip/M.Waltrip
Maxx FANtastic Finishes
1999 #F20 Darrell Waltrip's Car
Maxx Flag Firsts
1997 #FF17 Darrell Waltrip
Maxx Glossy
1990 #17 Darrell Waltrip
1990 #50 Darrell Waltrip Pit Champs
1990 #100 Darrell Waltrip FF
1990 #167 Darrell Waltrip YR
1990 #168 Rusty Wallace/Darrell Waltrip Cars YR
1990 #174 Darrell Waltrip YR
1990 #177 Darrell Waltrip's Car YR
1990 #178 Darrell Waltrip YR
1990 #185 D.Walt/T.Lab/Mart/Jarrett Cars YR
Maxx Holly Farms
1990 #HF3 Darrell Waltrip
Maxx IMHOF
1992 #36 Darrell Waltrip's Car
Maxx License to Drive
1995 #12 Darrell Waltrip's Car
Maxx Lowes Foods Stickers
1993 #2 B.Elliott/D.Waltrip/J.Gordon
Maxx Made in America
1996 #17 Darrell Waltrip
1996 #27 Darrell Waltrip's Car
Maxx Made in America Blue Ribbon
1996 #BR11 Darrell Waltrip's Car
Maxx McDonald's
1991 #20 Darrell Waltrip
1992 #16 Darrell Waltrip
Maxx Medallion
1994 #5 Darrell Waltrip
1995 #13 Darrell Waltrip
1995 #43 Darrell Waltrip's Car
Maxx Medallion Blue
1995 #13 Darrell Waltrip
1995 #43 Darrell Waltrip's Car
Maxx Odyssey
1996 #17 Darrell Waltrip
1996 #27 Darrell Waltrip's Car
Maxx Odyssey Radio Active
1996 #RA11 Darrell Waltrip's Car
Maxx On The Road Again
1996 #OTRA4 Darrell Waltrip's Trans.
Maxx Over the Wall
1995 #5 Darrell Waltrip in Pits
Maxx Pepsi 500
1996 #3 Darrell Waltrip
Maxx Premier Plus
1993 #17 Darrell Waltrip
1993 #65 Darrell Waltrip MM
1993 #195 Darrell Waltrip YR
1993 #199 Darrell Waltrip YR
1993 #200 Darrell Waltrip YR
1994 #17 Darrell Waltrip
1994 #64 Darrell Waltrip's Car
1995 #17 Darrell Waltrip
1995 #63 Darrell Waltrip's Car
1995 #P1 Darrell Waltrip Promo
Maxx Premier Plus Crown Chrome
1995 #17 Darrell Waltrip
1995 #63 Darrell Waltrip's Car
Maxx Premier Plus PaceSetters
1995 #PS8 Darrell Waltrip
Maxx Premier Plus PaceSetters Crown Chrome
1995 #PS8 Darrell Waltrip
Maxx Premier Series
1993 #17 Darrell Waltrip
1993 #226 Darrell Waltrip MM
1993 #280 Darrell Waltrip YR
1993 #284 Darrell Waltrip YR
1993 #285 Darrell Waltrip YR
1994 #17 Darrell Waltrip
1994 #64 Darrell Waltrip's Car
1995 #17 Darrell Waltrip
1995 #63 Darrell Waltrip's Car
1996 #17 Darrell Waltrip
1996 #60 Darrell Waltrip's Car
Maxx Premier Series Jumbos
1994 #5 Darrell Waltrip
Maxx Race Ticket
1999 #RT26 Darrell Waltrip's Car
Maxx Racing for Kids
1991 #3 Sheet 3
Maxx Racing Images
1999 #RI1 Darrell Waltrip
Maxx Red
1992 #17 Darrell Waltrip
1992 #190 Davey Allison/Darrell Waltrip Cars MM
1992 #195 Darrell Waltrip's Car MM
1992 #270 Darrell Waltrip YR
1992 #277 Darrell Waltrip YR
Maxx Retail Jumbos
1993 #1 Darrell Waltrip
Maxx SuperTrucks
1996 #ST8 Darrell Waltrip's Truck
Maxx The Select 25
1994 #13 Darrell Waltrip
Maxx The Winston
1992 #11 Darrell Waltrip
1992 #31 Darrell Waltrip's Car
1993 #6 Darrell Waltrip
1993 #26 Darrell Waltrip's Car
Maxx The Winston Acrylics
1991 #20 Darrell Waltrip
Maxx Update
1991 #17 Darrell Waltrip
1991 #150 Darrell Waltrip FF
Maxx Winston 20th Anniversary Foils
1991 #12 Darrell Waltrip 1981 Car
1991 #12 Darrell Waltrip 1982 Car
1991 #15 Darrell Waltrip 1985 Car
Maxximum
1998 #1 Darrell Waltrip
1998 #26 Darrell Waltrip's Car
1998 #51 Darrell Waltrip
1998 #76 Darrell Waltrip's Car
2000 #30 Darrell Waltrip
Maxximum Battle Proven
1998 #B1 Darrell Waltrip
Maxximum Cruise Control
2000 #CC10 Darrell Waltrip
Maxximum Die Cuts
2000 #30 Darrell Waltrip
Maxximum Field Generals Four Star Autographs
1998 #9 Darrell Waltrip
Maxximum Field Generals One Star
1998 #9 Darrell Waltrip
Maxximum Field Generals Three Star Autographs
1998 #9 Darrell Waltrip
Maxximum Field Generals Two Star
1998 #9 Darrell Waltrip
Maxximum First Class
1998 #F19 Darrell Waltrip
Maxximum MPH
2000 #30 Darrell Waltrip/66
Maxximum Signatures
2000 #MD2 M.Waltrip/D.Waltrip
McFarlane NASCAR Series 3
2005 #140 Darrell Waltrip R
2005 #141 Darrell Waltrip R Glasses
2005 #145 Darrell Waltrip H Stooges
Metallic Impressions 25th Anniversary Winston Cup Champions
1996 #11 Darrell Waltrip
1996 #12 Darrell Waltrip
1996 #15 Darrell Waltrip
Metallic Impressions Avon All-Time Racing Greatest
1996 #2 Darrell Waltrip
Metallic Impressions Winston Cup Champions 10-Card Tin
1995 #5 Darrell Waltrip
M-Force
1996 #15 Darrell Waltrip
Pinnacle
1996 #17 Darrell Waltrip
1996 #46 Darrell Waltrip's Car
1997 #17 Darrell Waltrip
1997 #46 Darrell Waltrip's Car
1997 #94 Darrell Waltrip's Car T4
Pinnacle Artist Proofs
1996 #17 Darrell Waltrip
1996 #46 Darrell Waltrip's Car
1997 #17 Darrell Waltrip B
1997 #46 Darrell Waltrip's Car B
1997 #94 Darrell Waltrip's Car T4 R
Pinnacle Certified
1997 #17 Darrell Waltrip
1997 #51 Darrell Waltrip's Car
1997 #69 Darrell Waltrip's Car WP
1997 #70 Darrell Waltrip's Car WP
1997 #71 Darrell Waltrip's Car WP
Pinnacle Certified Epix
1997 #E8 Darrell Waltrip
Pinnacle Certified Epix Emerald
1997 #E8 Darrell Waltrip
Pinnacle Certified Epix Purple
1997 #E8 Darrell Waltrip
Pinnacle Certified Mirror Blue
1997 #17 Darrell Waltrip
1997 #51 Darrell Waltrip's Car
1997 #69 Darrell Waltrip's Car WP
1997 #70 Darrell Waltrip's Car WP
1997 #71 Darrell Waltrip's Car WP
Pinnacle Certified Mirror Gold
1997 #17 Darrell Waltrip
1997 #51 Darrell Waltrip's Car
1997 #69 Darrell Waltrip's Car WP
1997 #70 Darrell Waltrip's Car WP
1997 #71 Darrell Waltrip's Car WP
Pinnacle Certified Mirror Red
1997 #17 Darrell Waltrip
1997 #51 Darrell Waltrip's Car
1997 #69 Darrell Waltrip's Car WP
1997 #70 Darrell Waltrip's Car WP
1997 #71 Darrell Waltrip's Car WP
Pinnacle Certified Red
1997 #17 Darrell Waltrip
1997 #51 Darrell Waltrip's Car
1997 #69 Darrell Waltrip's Car WP
1997 #70 Darrell Waltrip's Car WP
1997 #71 Darrell Waltrip's Car WP
Pinnacle Checkered Flag
1996 #15 Darrell Waltrip
Pinnacle Foil
1997 #17 Darrell Waltrip
1997 #46 Darrell Waltrip's Car
1997 #94 Darrell Waltrip's Car T4
Pinnacle Mint
1997 #4 Darrell Waltrip
Pinnacle Mint Bronze
1997 #4 Darrell Waltrip
Pinnacle Mint Coins
1997 #4 Darrell Waltrip
Pinnacle Mint Coins 24K Gold Plated
1997 #4 Darrell Waltrip
Pinnacle Mint Coins Nickel-Silver
1997 #4 Darrell Waltrip
Pinnacle Mint Gold
1997 #4 Darrell Waltrip
Pinnacle Mint Silver
1997 #4 Darrell Waltrip
Pinnacle Pole Position
1996 #17 Darrell Waltrip
1996 #35 Darrell Waltrip's Car
1996 #81 Darrell Waltrip EY
Pinnacle Pole Position Lightning Fast
1996 #17 Darrell Waltrip
1996 #35 Darrell Waltrip's Car
1996 #81 Darrell Waltrip
Pinnacle Pole Position No Limit
1996 #12 Darrell Waltrip
Pinnacle Pole Position No Limit Gold
1996 #12 Darrell Waltrip
Pinnacle Press Plates
1997 #17 Darrell Waltrip
1997 #46 Darrell Waltrip's Car
1997 #94 Darrell Waltrip's Car T4
1997 #TP4A Darrell Waltrip
Pinnacle Team Pinnacle
1997 #4 Darrell Waltrip
Pinnacle Team Pinnacle Red
1997 #4 Darrell Waltrip
Pinnacle Totally Certified Platinum Blue
1997 #17 Darrell Waltrip
1997 #51 Darrell Waltrip's Car
1997 #69 Darrell Waltrip WP
1997 #70 Darrell Waltrip WP
1997 #71 Darrell Waltrip WP
Pinnacle Totally Certified Platinum Gold
1997 #17 Darrell Waltrip
1997 #51 Darrell Waltrip's Car
1997 #69 Darrell Waltrip WP
1997 #70 Darrell Waltrip WP
1997 #71 Darrell Waltrip WP
Pinnacle Totally Certified Platinum Red
1997 #17 Darrell Waltrip
1997 #51 Darrell Waltrip's Car
1997 #69 Darrell Waltrip WP
1997 #70 Darrell Waltrip WP
1997 #71 Darrell Waltrip WP
Pinnacle Trophy Collection
1997 #17 Darrell Waltrip
1997 #46 Darrell Waltrip's Car
1997 #94 Darrell Waltrip's Car T4
Pinnacle Winston Cup Collection
1996 #17 Darrell Waltrip
1996 #46 Darrell Waltrip's Car
Pioneers of Stock Car Racing
1991-92 #4 D.Waltrip/Walt.Wallace/Fred.Fryar/P.B.Correll
Power
1994 #46 Darrell Waltrip SL
1994 #60 Darrell Waltrip's Trans. PR
1994 #69 Darrell Waltrip PO
1994 #125 Darrell Waltrip
1994 #150 Darrell Waltrip's Car
Power Gold
1994 #46 Darrell Waltrip SL
1994 #60 Darrell Waltrip's Trans. PR
1994 #69 Darrell Waltrip PO
1994 #125 Darrell Waltrip
1994 #150 Darrell Waltrip's Car
Power Preview
1994 #9 Darrell Waltrip
Predator
1997 #18 Darrell Waltrip
Predator American Eagle
1997 #AE10 Darrell Waltrip
Predator American Eagle First Slash
1997 #AE10 Darrell Waltrip
Predator Black Wolf First Strike
1997 #18 Darrell Waltrip
Predator First Slash
1997 #18 Darrell Waltrip
Predator Gatorback
1997 #GB9 Darrell Waltrip
Predator Gatorback Authentic
1997 #GBA9 Darrell Waltrip
Predator Gatorback Authentic First Slash
1997 #GBA9 Darrell Waltrip
Predator Gatorback First Slash
1997 #GB9 Darrell Waltrip
Predator Golden Eagle
1997 #GE10 Darrell Waltrip
Predator Golden Eagle First Slash
1997 #GE10 Darrell Waltrip
Predator Grizzly
1997 #18 Darrell Waltrip
Predator Grizzly First Slash
1997 #18 Darrell Waltrip
Predator Red Wolf
1997 #18 Darrell Waltrip
Predator Red Wolf First Slash
1997 #18 Darrell Waltrip
Press Pass
1994 #29 Darrell Waltrip
1994 #33 Darrell Waltrip/Michael Waltrip
1994 #87 Darrell Waltrip
1995 #35 Darrell Waltrip
1995 #54 Darrell Waltrip's Car
1995 #108 Darrell Waltrip ST
1996 #35 Darrell Waltrip
1996 #54 Darrell Waltrip's Car
1996 #90 Darrell Waltrip DW
1997 #25 Darrell Waltrip
1997 #54 Darrell Waltrip
1998 #22 Darrell Waltrip
1998 #113 Darrell Waltrip RET
1999 #21 Darrell Waltrip
1999 #121 Darrell Waltrip RET
2000 #27 Darrell Waltrip
2001 #31 Darrell Waltrip
Press Pass Autographs
1997 #38 Darrell Waltrip VIP
1998 #13 Darrell Waltrip
2002 #68 Darrell Waltrip
Press Pass Bryan
1999 #10 Darrell Waltrip
Press Pass Cup Chase
1994 #CC29 Darrell Waltrip
1995 #35 Darrell Waltrip
1996 #35 Darrell Waltrip
Press Pass Cup Chase Foil Prizes
1996 #35 Darrell Waltrip
Press Pass Dale The Movie
2007 #7 Dale Earnhardt Darrell Waltrip
2007 #22 Dale Earnhardt Darrell Waltrip Rivalry
Press Pass Daytona 500 50th Anniversary
2008 #26 Darrell Waltrip '89
Press Pass Excedrin Racing
2001 #3 Darrell Waltrip
Press Pass Lasers
1997 #25 Darrell Waltrip
1997 #54 Darrell Waltrip
Press Pass Legends
2006 #21 Darrell Waltrip
2007 #28 Darrell Waltrip
2007 #56 Darrell Waltrip N
2007 #65 Darrell Waltrip Dale Earnhardt R
2007 #67 Cale Yarborough Darrell Waltrip R
Press Pass Legends Autographs Black
2006 #14 Darrell Waltrip/25
2007 #13 Darrell Waltrip/48
Press Pass Legends Autographs Blue
2006 #16 Darrell Waltrip/45
2007 #24 Darrell Waltrip/182
Press Pass Legends Autographs Inscriptions Blue
2007 #15 Darrell Waltrip 11 Jaws/15
Press Pass Legends Blue
2006 #B21 Darrell Waltrip
2007 #B28 Darrell Waltrip
2007 #B56 Darrell Waltrip N
2007 #B65 Darrell Waltrip Dale Earnhardt R
2007 #B67 Cale Yarborough Darrell Waltrip R
Press Pass Legends Bronze
2006 #Z21 Darrell Waltrip
2007 #Z28 Darrell Waltrip
2007 #Z56 Darrell Waltrip N
2007 #Z65 Darrell Waltrip Dale Earnhardt R
2007 #Z67 Cale Yarborough Darrell Waltrip R
Press Pass Legends Gold
2006 #G21 Darrell Waltrip
2007 #G28 Darrell Waltrip
2007 #G56 Darrell Waltrip N
2007 #G65 Darrell Waltrip Dale Earnhardt R
2007 #G67 Cale Yarborough Darrell Waltrip R
Press Pass Legends Heritage Gold
2006 #HE4 Darrell Waltrip
Press Pass Legends Heritage Silver
2006 #HE4 Darrell Waltrip
Press Pass Legends Holofoil
2006 #H21 Darrell Waltrip
2007 #H28 Darrell Waltrip
2007 #H56 Darrell Waltrip N
2007 #H65 Darrell Waltrip Dale Earnhardt R
2007 #H67 Cale Yarborough Darrell Waltrip R
Press Pass Legends Memorable Moments Gold
2007 #MM1 Darrell Waltrip B
2007 #MM9 Darrell Waltrip D
Press Pass Legends Memorable Moments Silver
2007 #MM1 Darrell Waltrip B
2007 #MM9 Darrell Waltrip D
Press Pass Legends Press Plates Black
2006 #PPB21 Darrell Waltrip
2007 #PP28 Darrell Waltrip
2007 #PP56 Darrell Waltrip N
2007 #PP65 Darrell Waltrip Dale Earnhardt R
2007 #PP67 Cale Yarborough Darrell Waltrip R
Press Pass Legends Press Plates Black Backs
2006 #PPB21B Darrell Waltrip
2007 #PP28 Darrell Waltrip
2007 #PP56 Darrell Waltrip N
2007 #PP65 Darrell Waltrip Dale Earnhardt R
2007 #PP67 Cale Yarborough Darrell Waltrip R
Press Pass Legends Press Plates Cyan
2006 #PPC21 Darrell Waltrip
2007 #PP28 Darrell Waltrip
2007 #PP56 Darrell Waltrip N
2007 #PP65 Darrell Waltrip Dale Earnhardt R
2007 #PP67 Cale Yarborough Darrell Waltrip R
Press Pass Legends Press Plates Cyan Backs
2006 #PPC21B Darrell Waltrip
2007 #PP28 Darrell Waltrip
2007 #PP56 Darrell Waltrip N
2007 #PP65 Darrell Waltrip Dale Earnhardt R
2007 #PP67 Cale Yarborough Darrell Waltrip R
Press Pass Legends Press Plates Magenta
2006 #PPM21 Darrell Waltrip
2007 #PP28 Darrell Waltrip
2007 #PP56 Darrell Waltrip N
2007 #PP65 Darrell Waltrip Dale Earnhardt R
2007 #PP67 Cale Yarborough Darrell Waltrip R
Press Pass Legends Press Plates Magenta Backs
2006 #PPM21B Darrell Waltrip
2007 #PP28 Darrell Waltrip
2007 #PP56 Darrell Waltrip N
2007 #PP65 Darrell Waltrip Dale Earnhardt R
2007 #PP67 Cale Yarborough Darrell Waltrip R
Press Pass Legends Press Plates Yellow
2006 #PPY21 Darrell Waltrip
2007 #PP28 Darrell Waltrip
2007 #PP56 Darrell Waltrip N
2007 #PP65 Darrell Waltrip Dale Earnhardt R
2007 #PP67 Cale Yarborough Darrell Waltrip R
Press Pass Legends Press Plates Yellow Backs
2006 #PPY21B Darrell Waltrip
2007 #PP28 Darrell Waltrip
2007 #PP56 Darrell Waltrip N
2007 #PP65 Darrell Waltrip Dale Earnhardt R
2007 #PP67 Cale Yarborough Darrell Waltrip R
Press Pass Legends Previews
2006 #EB21 Darrell Waltrip
2007 #EB28 Darrell Waltrip
2007 #EB65 Darrell Waltrip Dale Earnhardt R
2007 #EB67 Cale Yarborough Darrell Waltrip R
Press Pass Legends Racing Artifacts Firesuit Bronze
2007 #DW-F Darrell Waltrip
Press Pass Legends Racing Artifacts Firesuit Gold
2007 #DW-F Darrell Waltrip
Press Pass Legends Racing Artifacts Firesuit Patch
2007 #DW-F Darrell Waltrip
Press Pass Legends Racing Artifacts Firesuit Silver
2007 #DW-F Darrell Waltrip
Press Pass Legends Solo
2006 #S21 Darrell Waltrip
2007 #S28 Darrell Waltrip
2007 #S56 Darrell Waltrip N
2007 #S65 Darrell Waltrip Dale Earnhardt R
2007 #S67 Cale Yarborough Darrell Waltrip R
Press Pass Millennium
2000 #27 Darrell Waltrip
2001 #31 Darrell Waltrip

Press Pass Oil Slicks
1997 #25 Darrell Waltrip
1997 #54 Darrell Waltrip
1998 #22 Darrell Waltrip
Press Pass Optima
2000 #26 Darrell Waltrip
Press Pass Optima G Force
2000 #GF26 Darrell Waltrip
Press Pass Optima Platinum
2000 #26 Darrell Waltrip
Press Pass Optima XL
1994 #23 Darrell Waltrip
1994 #36 Darrell Waltrip DD
1995 #23 Darrell Waltrip
Press Pass Optima XL Cool Blue
1995 #23 Darrell Waltrip
Press Pass Optima XL Die Cut
1995 #23 Darrell Waltrip
Press Pass Optima XL Prototypes
1995 #XL2 Darrell Waltrip
Press Pass Optima XL Red Hot
1994 #23 Darrell Waltrip
1994 #36 Darrell Waltrip DD
1995 #23 Darrell Waltrip
Press Pass Optima XL Stealth
1995 #XLS17 Darrell Waltrip
Press Pass Pit Stop
1998 #PS8 Darrell Waltrip's Car
Press Pass Premium
1995 #9 Darrell Waltrip
1996 #19 Darrell Waltrip
1997 #25 Darrell Waltrip
2000 #24 Darrell Waltrip
2000 #51 Darrell Waltrip
Press Pass Premium Emerald Proofs
1996 #19 Darrell Waltrip
1997 #25 Darrell Waltrip
Press Pass Premium Holofoil
1995 #9 Darrell Waltrip
1996 #19 Darrell Waltrip
Press Pass Premium Mirrors
1997 #25 Darrell Waltrip
Press Pass Premium Oil Slicks
1997 #25 Darrell Waltrip
Press Pass Premium Red Hot
1995 #9 Darrell Waltrip
Press Pass Premium Reflectors
2000 #24 Darrell Waltrip
2000 #51 Darrell Waltrip
Press Pass R and N China
1996 #35 Darrell Waltrip
Press Pass Red Hot
1995 #35 Darrell Waltrip
1995 #54 Darrell Waltrip's Car
1995 #108 Darrell Waltrip ST
Press Pass Scorchers
1996 #35 Darrell Waltrip
1996 #54 Darrell Waltrip's Car
1996 #90 Darrell Waltrip DW
Press Pass Showman
2000 #SM1 Darrell Waltrip
Press Pass Showman Die Cuts
2000 #SM1 Darrell Waltrip
Press Pass Signings
1999 #57 Darrell Waltrip/175
2000 #61 Darrell Waltrip
2001 #53 Darrell Waltrip P/T/N/S
Press Pass Signings Gold
1999 #29 Darrell Waltrip/100
2000 #32 Darrell Waltrip
2001 #35 Darrell Waltrip P/T/N/S
2002 #65 Darrell Waltrip O/P/S/T/V
Press Pass Signings Transparent
2001 #13 Darrell Waltrip P/T/N/S
Press Pass Skidmarks
1999 #21 Darrell Waltrip
Press Pass Techno-Retro
2000 #TR26 Darrell Waltrip
Press Pass Torquers
1996 #35 Darrell Waltrip
1996 #54 Darrell Waltrip's Car
1996 #90 Darrell Waltrip DW
1997 #25 Darrell Waltrip
1997 #54 Darrell Waltrip
Press Pass Trackside
2000 #25 Darrell Waltrip
2004 #79 B.Parsons/D.Waltrip H
Press Pass Trackside Die Cuts
2000 #25 Darrell Waltrip
Press Pass Trackside Golden
2000 #25 Darrell Waltrip
2004 #G79 B.Parsons/D.Waltrip H
Press Pass Trackside Panorama
2000 #P24 Darrell Waltrip
Press Pass Trackside Samples
2004 #79 B.Parsons/D.Waltrip H
Press Pass Victory Lap
2003 #6 Darrell Waltrip
Press Pass Vintage
2002 #VN34 Darrell Waltrip
Pro Set
1991 #117 Darrell Waltrip
1991 #118 Darrell Waltrip w/Car
1991 #119 Darrell Waltrip's Car
1992 #93 Darrell Waltrip
1992 #97 Darrell Waltrip
1992 #209 Darrell Waltrip's Car
1992 #245 Darrell Waltrip's Transporter
Pro Set Maxwell House
1992 #14 Darrell Waltrip
Pro Set Rudy Farms
1992 #7 Darrell Waltrip
Race Sharks
1997 #11 Darrell Waltrip
Race Sharks First Bite
1997 #11 Darrell Waltrip
Race Sharks Great White
1997 #11 Darrell Waltrip
Race Sharks Hammerhead
1997 #11 Darrell Waltrip
Race Sharks Hammerhead First Bite
1997 #11 Darrell Waltrip
Race Sharks Shark Attack First Bite Previews
1997 #7 Darrell Waltrip
Race Sharks Tiger Shark
1997 #11 Darrell Waltrip
Race Sharks Tiger Shark First Bite
1997 #11 Darrell Waltrip
Racer's Choice
1996 #21 Darrell Waltrip
1996 #37 Darrell Waltrip's Car
1996 #105 Darrell Waltrip BC
1997 #17 Darrell Waltrip
1997 #52 Darrell Waltrip's Car
Racer's Choice Artist's Proofs
1996 #21 Darrell Waltrip
1996 #37 Darrell Waltrip's Car
1996 #105 Darrell Waltrip BC
Racer's Choice Showcase Series
1997 #17 Darrell Waltrip
1997 #52 Darrell Waltrip's Car
Racer's Choice Speedway Collection
1996 #21 Darrell Waltrip
1996 #37 Darrell Waltrip's Car
1996 #105 Darrell Waltrip BC
Redline Standups
1992 #17 Darrell Waltrip
SB Motorsports
1997 #28 Darrell Waltrip
1997 #54 Darrell Waltrip's Car
Score Board IQ
1997 #15 Darrell Waltrip
Score Board IQ Remarques
1997 #SB6 Darrell Waltrip
Score Board IQ Remarques Sam Bass Finished
1997 #SB6 Darrell Waltrip
Select
1995 #35 Darrell Waltrip
1995 #54 Darrell Waltrip's Car
1995 #88 Darrell Waltrip OWN
1995 #113 D.Waltrip/M.Waltrip IB
1995 #133 Junior Johnson/Darrell Waltrip I
Select Dream Machines
1995 #DM10 Darrell Waltrip's Car
Select Flat Out
1995 #35 Darrell Waltrip
1995 #54 Darrell Waltrip's Car
1995 #88 Darrell Waltrip OWN
1995 #113 D.Waltrip/M.Waltrip IB
1995 #133 J.Johnson/D.Waltrip I
Select Skills
1995 #SS16 Darrell Waltrip
SkyBox
1994 #2 Darrell Waltrip's Car
1994 #25 Darrell Waltrip/M.Waltrip Cars
SLU Racing Winner's Circle
1997 #7 Darrell Waltrip
SP
1995 #14 Darrell Waltrip CC
1995 #48 Darrell Waltrip
1995 #90 Darrell Waltrip's Car
1995 #130 Darrell Waltrip OWN
1996 #17 Darrell Waltrip
1996 #60 Darrell Waltrip CC
1997 #17 Darrell Waltrip 3F
1997 #59 Darrell Waltrip's Car
1997 #97 Darrell Waltrip
SP Authentic
1998 #17 Darrell Waltrip
1998 #51 Darrell Waltrip's Car
1998 #69 Darrell Waltrip VL
1999 #26 Darrell Waltrip
1999 #47 Darrell Waltrip's Car
1999 #63 Darrell Waltrip CLASS
2000 #34 Darrell Waltrip
2000 #70 Darrell Waltrip PER
SP Authentic High Velocity
2000 #HV3 Darrell Waltrip
SP Authentic Overdrive
1999 #26 Darrell Waltrip
1999 #47 Darrell Waltrip CAR
1999 #63 Darrell Waltrip CLASS
SP Authentic Overdrive Gold
2000 #34 Darrell Waltrip/66
2000 #70 Darrell Waltrip PER/66
SP Authentic Overdrive Silver
2000 #34 Darrell Waltrip
2000 #70 Darrell Waltrip PER
SP Authentic Sign of the Times
1998 #S7 Darrell Waltrip's Car
SP Die Cuts
1995 #14 Darrell Waltrip
1995 #48 Darrell Waltrip
1995 #90 Darrell Waltrip's Car
1995 #130 Darrell Waltrip
SP Holoview Maximum Effects
1996 #ME17 Darrell Waltrip
SP Holoview Maximum Effects Die Cuts
1996 #ME17 Darrell Waltrip
SP Speed Merchants
1995 #SM17 Darrell Waltrip
SP Speed Merchants Die Cuts
1995 #SM17 Darrell Waltrip
SP Super Series
1997 #17 Darrell Waltrip 3F
1997 #59 Darrell Waltrip's Car
1997 #97 Darrell Waltrip
Speedflix
1996 #7 Darrell Waltrip
1996 #22 Darrell Waltrip
Speedflix Artist Proof's
1996 #7 Darrell Waltrip
1996 #22 Darrell Waltrip
Speedflix In Motion
1996 #7 Darrell Waltrip's Helmet
Speedflix ProMotion
1996 #10 Darrell Waltrip
Sports Illustrated for Kids *
1992-00 #48 Darrell Waltrip
Sports Illustrated for Kids II
1992 #48 Darrell Waltrip Auto Racing
SportsCom FanScan
1998 #9 Darrell Waltrip
1999 #9 Darrell Waltrip
SportStars Photo-Graphics
1986 #12 Darrell Waltrip
SportStars Photo-Graphics Stickers
1985 #NNO Darrell Waltrip
SPx
1996 #17 Darrell Waltrip
1997 #17 Darrell Waltrip
SPx Blue
1997 #17 Darrell Waltrip
SPx Gold
1996 #17 Darrell Waltrip
1997 #17 Darrell Waltrip
SPx Silver
1997 #17 Darrell Waltrip
Sunbelt Racing Legends
1991 #7 Darrell Waltrip
Super Shots Hendrick Motorsports
2001 #H3 Darrell Waltrip w/Michael
2001 #H5 Darrell Waltrip
Super Shots Hendrick Motorsports Autographs
2001 #HSA4 Darrell Waltrip/71
Super Shots Hendrick Motorsports Gold
2001 #HG3 Darrell Waltrip w/Michael
2001 #HG5 Darrell Waltrip
Super Shots Hendrick Motorsports Silver
2001 #HS3 Darrell Waltrip w/Michael
2001 #HS5 Darrell Waltrip
Super Shots Hendrick Motorsports Victory Banners
2001 #HRB5 Darrell Waltrip
Superior Racing Metals
1991 #12 Darrell Waltrip
Texas World Speedway
1991 #9 Darrell Waltrip
Traks
1992 #17 Darrell Waltrip
1992 #56 Darrell Waltrip
1992 #191 S.Marlin/D.Waltrip Crash
1992 #198 Darrell Waltrip's Car CL
2007 #63 Darrell Waltrip CTG
Traks ASA
1992 #42 Darrell Waltrip w/Car
Traks Gold
2007 #G63 Darrell Waltrip CTG
Traks Holofoil
2007 #H63 Darrell Waltrip CTG
Traks Preferred Collector
1993 #9 Darrell Waltrip
Traks Racing Machines
1992 #17 Darrell Waltrip in Pits
1992 #23 Darrell Waltrip's Transp.
1992 #37 Darrell Waltrip's Car
Traks Red
2007 #R63 Darrell Waltrip CTG
Traks Richard Petty
1991 #22 Richard Petty/Earn/D.Waltrip Cars
Traks Team Sets
1992 #127 Darrell Waltrip
1992 #130 Darrell Waltrip's Car
1992 #138 Darrell Waltrip in Pits
1992 #142 Darrell Waltrip
1992 #150 Darrell Waltrip's Transporter CL
UNO Racing
1983 #28 Darrell Waltrip
Upper Deck
1995 #5 Darrell Waltrip
1995 #48 Darrell Waltrip with Car
1995 #73 Darrell Waltrip's Car
1995 #141 Darrell Waltrip's Car
1995 #170 Darrell Waltrip DYK
1995 #197 Darrell Waltrip
1995 #241 Darrell Waltrip SD
1995 #278 Darrell Waltrip's Car
1996 #15 Darrell Waltrip
1996 #55 Darrell Waltrip SB
1996 #95 Darrell Waltrip PP
1996 #130 Darrell Waltrip HB
Upper Deck Autographs
1995 #197 Darrell Waltrip
Upper Deck Gold Signature/Electric Gold
1995 #5 Darrell Waltrip
1995 #48 Darrell Waltrip with Car
1995 #73 Darrell Waltrip's Car
1995 #141 Darrell Waltrip's Car
1995 #170 Darrell Waltrip DYK
1995 #197 Darrell Waltrip
1995 #241 Darrell Waltrip SD
1995 #278 Darrell Waltrip's Car
Upper Deck MVP
2000 #35 Darrell Waltrip
2000 #69 Darrell Waltrip's Car
2000 #96 Darrell Waltrip
Upper Deck MVP Gold Script
2000 #35 Darrell Waltrip
2000 #69 Darrell Waltrip's Car
2000 #96 Darrell Waltrip
Upper Deck MVP ProSign
1999 #DWH Darrell Waltrip Gold
1999 #DWR Darrell Waltrip Silver
2000 #PSDW Darrell Waltrip
Upper Deck MVP Silver Script
2000 #35 Darrell Waltrip
2000 #69 Darrell Waltrip's Car
2000 #96 Darrell Waltrip
Upper Deck MVP Super Script
2000 #35 Darrell Waltrip/66
2000 #69 Darrell Waltrip's Car/66
2000 #96 Darrell Waltrip/66
Upper Deck Racing
2000 #30 Darrell Waltrip
Upper Deck Racing Brickyard's Best
2000 #BB4 Darrell Waltrip
Upper Deck Racing Legends
1996 #RLC9 Darrell Waltrip
Upper Deck Road To The Cup
1996 #RC18 Darrell Waltrip
1996 #RC67 Darrell Waltrip's Car
1996 #RC101 Darrell Waltrip
1996 #RC141 Darrell Waltrip
1997 #30 Darrell Waltrip
1997 #72 Darrell Waltrip's Car
1997 #103 Darrell Waltrip
1997 #117 Darrell Waltrip's Trans.
1997 #139 Darrell Waltrip
1998 #17 Darrell Waltrip
1999 #10 Darrell Waltrip
1999 #35 Darrell Waltrip's Car
1999 #64 Darrell Waltrip FF
Upper Deck Road To The Cup 50th Anniversary
1998 #AN30 Darrell Waltrip's Car
1998 #AN35 Darrell Waltrip
Upper Deck Road To The Cup 50th Anniversary Autographs
1998 #AN35 Darrell Waltrip
Upper Deck Road To The Cup Autographs
1996 #H18 Darrell Waltrip
Upper Deck Road To The Cup Cover Story
1998 #CS3 Darrell Waltrip
1998 #CS16 J.Gordon/D.Waltrip
Upper Deck Road To The Cup Predictor Plus
1997 #20 Darrell Waltrip
Upper Deck Road To The Cup Predictor Plus Cel Die Cuts
1997 #20 Darrell Waltrip
Upper Deck Road To The Cup Predictor Plus Cels
1997 #20 Darrell Waltrip
Upper Deck Road To The Cup Predictor Top 3
1996 #T4 R.Wall./D.Waltrip/Longshot
Upper Deck Road To The Cup Predictor Top 3 Prizes
1996 #R7 Darrell Waltrip
Upper Deck Silver Signature/Electric Silver
1995 #5 Darrell Waltrip
1995 #48 Darrell Waltrip with Car
1995 #73 Darrell Waltrip's Car
1995 #141 Darrell Waltrip's Car
1995 #170 Darrell Waltrip DYK
1995 #197 Darrell Waltrip
1995 #241 Darrell Waltrip SD
1995 #278 Darrell Waltrip's Car
Upper Deck Victory Circle
1997 #17 Darrell Waltrip
1997 #67 Darrell Waltrip's Car
1997 #117 Darrell Waltrip
1998 #17 Darrell Waltrip
1998 #62 Darrell Waltrip's Car
1998 #141 Darrell Waltrip
1999 #19 Darrell Waltrip
1999 #47 Darrell Waltrip's Car
2000 #24 Darrell Waltrip
2000 #79 Darrell Waltrip's Car
Upper Deck Victory Circle Exclusives Level 1 Silver
2000 #24 Darrell Waltrip
2000 #79 Darrell Waltrip's Car
Upper Deck Victory Circle Exclusives Level 2 Gold
2000 #24 Darrell Waltrip/66
2000 #79 Darrell Waltrip's Car/66
Upper Deck Victory Circle Piece of the Engine
1998 #PE1 Darrell Waltrip
1998 #PE6 Darrell Waltrip
Upper Deck Victory Circle Signature Collection
1999 #DW Darrell Waltrip
2000 #DW Darrell Waltrip
Upper Deck Victory Circle Signature Collection Gold
2000 #6 Darrell Waltrip/66
Upper Deck Victory Circle Track Masters
1999 #TM13 Darrell Waltrip
Upper Deck Victory Circle UD Exclusives
1999 #19 Darrell Waltrip
1999 #47 Darrell Waltrip
Upper Deck Virtual Velocity
1996 #VV8 Darrell Waltrip
Upper Deck Virtual Velocity Gold
1996 #VV8 Darrell Waltrip
VIP
1994 #35 Darrell Waltrip
1994 #54 Darrell Waltrip w/Car
1995 #29 Darrell Waltrip
1995 #54 Darrell Waltrip TD
1996 #28 Darrell Waltrip
1997 #24 Darrell Waltrip
2000 #38 Darrell Waltrip 50 W
2000 #47 Darrell Waltrip DT
2004 #85 Darrell Waltrip ATW
VIP Cool Blue
1995 #29 Darrell Waltrip
1995 #54 Darrell Waltrip TD
VIP Emerald Proofs
1995 #29 Darrell Waltrip
1995 #54 Darrell Waltrip TD
1996 #28 Darrell Waltrip
VIP Explosives
1997 #24 Darrell Waltrip
2000 #X38 Darrell Waltrip 50 W
2000 #X47 Darrell Waltrip DT
VIP Explosives Lasers
2000 #LX38 Darrell Waltrip 50 W
2000 #LX47 Darrell Waltrip DT
VIP Head Gear
1996 #HG8 Darrell Waltrip
VIP Head Gear Die Cuts
1996 #HG8 Darrell Waltrip
VIP Oil Slicks
1997 #24 Darrell Waltrip
VIP Red Hot
1995 #29 Darrell Waltrip
1995 #54 Darrell Waltrip TD
VIP Samples
2004 #85 Darrell Waltrip ATW
VIP Torquers
1996 #28 Darrell Waltrip
VIP War Paint
1996 #WP8 Darrell Waltrip's Car
VIP War Paint Gold
1996 #WP8 Darrell Waltrip's Car
Viper
1996 #13 Darrell Waltrip
1997 #17 Darrell Waltrip
Viper Anaconda Jumbos
1997 #A7 Darrell Waltrip
Viper Black Mamba
1996 #13 Darrell Waltrip
Viper Black Mamba First Strike
1996 #13 Darrell Waltrip
Viper Black Racer
1997 #17 Darrell Waltrip
Viper Black Racer First Strike
1997 #17 Darrell Waltrip
Viper Busch Clash
1996 #B6 Darrell Waltrip
Viper Busch Clash First Strike
1996 #B6 Darrell Waltrip
Viper Copperhead Die Cuts
1996 #13 Darrell Waltrip
Viper Copperhead Die Cuts First Strike
1996 #13 Darrell Waltrip
Viper First Strike
1996 #13 Darrell Waltrip
1997 #17 Darrell Waltrip
Viper Green Mamba
1996 #13 Darrell Waltrip
Viper Red Cobra
1996 #13 Darrell Waltrip
Visions
1996 #119 Darrell Waltrip
Visions *
1996 #119 Darrell Waltrip
Visions Signings
1996 #96 Darrell Waltrip
Visions Signings *
1996 #96 Darrell Waltrip
Wheels
1999 #35 Darrell Waltrip
Wheels Golden
1999 #35 Darrell Waltrip
Wheels High Gear
1994 #117 Darrell Waltrip
1995 #7 Darrell Waltrip
1995 #79 Darrell Waltrip's Car
1998 #23 Darrell Waltrip
1998 #70 Darrell Waltrip's Car
1999 #57 Darrell Waltrip
2000 #26 Darrell Waltrip
Wheels High Gear Autographs
1998 #22 Darrell Waltrip/250
2002 #57 Darrell Waltrip
Wheels High Gear Day One
1994 #117 Darrell Waltrip
1995 #7 Darrell Waltrip
1995 #79 Darrell Waltrip's Car
Wheels High Gear Day One Gold
1994 #117 Darrell Waltrip
1995 #7 Darrell Waltrip
1995 #79 Darrell Waltrip's Car
Wheels High Gear First Gear
1998 #21 Darrell Waltrip
1999 #57 Darrell Waltrip
2000 #26 Darrell Waltrip
Wheels High Gear Gear Jammers
1998 #GJ8 Darrell Waltrip
Wheels High Gear Gear Shifters
1999 #GS21 Mike Skinner
2000 #GS21 Darrell Waltrip
Wheels High Gear Gold
1994 #117 Darrell Waltrip
1995 #7 Darrell Waltrip
1995 #79 Darrell Waltrip's Car
Wheels High Gear Mega Gold
1994 #MG11 Darrell Waltrip
Wheels High Gear MPH
1998 #21 Darrell Waltrip
1999 #21 Darrell Waltrip
1999 #57 Darrell Waltrip
2000 #26 Darrell Waltrip
Wheels High Gear Pure Gold
1998 #PG6 Darrell Waltrip
Wheels High Gear Winston Victory Lap Tribute
2004 #WVL5 Darrell Waltrip
Wheels High Gear Winston Victory Lap Tribute Gold
2004 #WVL5 Darrell Waltrip
Wheels Runnin and Gunnin
1999 #RG31 Darrell Waltrip
Wheels Runnin and Gunnin Foils
1999 #RG31 Darrell Waltrip
Wheels Solos
1999 #35 Darrell Waltrip
Zenith
1995 #17 Darrell Waltrip HG
1995 #47 Darrell Waltrip's Transporter
1996 #18 Darrell Waltrip
1996 #41 Darrell Waltrip's Car HV
Zenith Artist Proofs
1996 #18 Darrell Waltrip RP
1996 #41 Darrell Waltrip's Car HV
Zenith Champion Salute
1996 #11 Darrell Waltrip
1996 #14 Darrell Waltrip
1996 #15 Darrell Waltrip
Zenith Highlights
1996 #6 Darrell Waltrip

Waltrip, Michael

Action Packed
1993 #67 Michael Waltrip
1993 #68 Michael Waltrip's Car
1993 #136 Michael Waltrip
1993 #137 Michael Waltrip's Car
1993 #164 M.Waltrip/D.Waltrip B
1993 #179 Michael Waltrip
1993 #206 Michael Waltrip WIN
1994 #17 Michael Waltrip
1994 #88 Michael Waltrip
1994 #97 Kyle Petty w/M.Waltrip KPS
1994 #133 Michael Waltrip's Car
1994 #167 Michael Waltrip RR
1997 #15 Michael Waltrip
1997 #36 Michael Waltrip's Car
1997 #59 Michael Waltrip
1997 #71 Michael Waltrip
1997 #74 Michael Waltrip's Car
Action Packed 24K Gold
1993 #61G Michael Waltrip
1994 #42G Michael Waltrip
1997 #10 Michael Waltrip
Action Packed Coastars
1994 #18 Michael Waltrip
Action Packed Country
1995 #69 Michael Waltrip
Action Packed Country Silver Speed
1995 #69 Michael Waltrip
Action Packed Credentials
1996 #31 Michael Waltrip
1996 #58 Michael Waltrip SM
1996 #96 Michael Waltrip WCA
Action Packed Credentials Silver Speed
1996 #31 Michael Waltrip
Action Packed First Impressions
1997 #15 Michael Waltrip
1997 #36 Michael Waltrip's Car
1997 #59 Michael Waltrip
1997 #71 Michael Waltrip
1997 #74 Michael Waltrip's Car
Action Packed Mint
1994 #17 Michael Waltrip
1994 #88 Michael Waltrip
1994 #97 Kyle Petty w/M.Waltrip KPS
1994 #133 Michael Waltrip's Car
1994 #167 Michael Waltrip RR
Action Packed Preview
1995 #25 Michael Waltrip
Action Packed Stars
1995 #17 Michael Waltrip OC
Action Packed Stars Silver Speed
1995 #17 Michael Waltrip OC
Assets
1995 #19 Michael Waltrip
Assets $2 Phone Cards
1995 #14 Michael Waltrip
Assets $2 Phone Cards Gold Signature
1995 #14 Michael Waltrip
Assets 1-Minute Phone Cards
1995 #14 Michael Waltrip
Assets 1-Minute Phone Cards Gold Signature
1995 #14 Michael Waltrip
Assets Gold Signature
1995 #19 Michael Waltrip
Assets Racing
1996 #28 Michael Waltrip
Assets Racing $100 Cup Champion Interactive Phone Cards
1996 #14 Michael Waltrip
Assets Racing $1000 Cup Champion Interactive Phone Cards
1996 #7 Michael Waltrip
Assets Racing $2 Phone Cards
1996 #18 Michael Waltrip
Assets Racing $5 Phone Cards
1996 #9 Michael Waltrip
Assets Racing Competitor's License
1996 #CL14 Michael Waltrip
Assets Racing Race Day
1996 #RD9 Michael Waltrip's Car
Autographed Racing
1996 #34 Michael Waltrip
1997 #5 Michael Waltrip
1997 #40 Michael Waltrip's Car
1997 #41 D.Earnhardt/J.Gordon
1997 #45 M.Waltrip/B.Labonte
Autographed Racing Autographs
1996 #60 Michael Waltrip
1997 #55 Michael Waltrip
Autographed Racing Autographs Certified Golds
1996 #60 Michael Waltrip
Autographed Racing Front Runners
1996 #82 D.Wal.with hel/M.Wal.shades
1996 #83 D.Waltrip with hel/M.Waltrip
1996 #84 D.Walt.no hel/M.Walt.shades
1996 #85 D.Waltrip no hel/M.Waltrip
1996 #86 M.Waltrip/M.Waltrip shades
1996 #87 M.Waltrip/M.Waltrip's Car
1996 #88 M.Waltrip/Wood Brothers
1996 #89 M.Waltrip's Car/Wood Brothers
Autographed Racing High Performance
1996 #HP9 Michael Waltrip
Autographed Racing Mayne Street
1997 #KM5 Michael Waltrip
Bikers of the Racing Scene
1992 #30 Michael Waltrip
1992 #31
BethBruce/M.Walt/R.Wils/Child./D.Culler/D.Tilley
Card Dynamics Michael Waltrip
1992 #1 Michael Waltrip
1992 #2 Michael Waltrip
1992 #3 Michael Waltrip
1992 #4 Michael Waltrip
1992 #5 Michael Waltrip
Classic
1996 #26 Michael Waltrip
1996 #35 Michael Waltrip's Car
1996 #41 Michael Waltrip
1996 #54 Michael Waltrip SP
Classic Five Sport
1995 #168 Michael Waltrip
Classic Five Sport Printer's Proofs
1995 #168 Michael Waltrip
Classic Five Sport Red Die Cuts
1995 #168 Michael Waltrip
Classic Five Sport Signings
1995-96 #83 Michael Waltrip
Classic Five Sport Signings Blue Signature
1995-96 #83 Michael Waltrip
Classic Five Sport Signings Die Cuts
1995-96 #83 Michael Waltrip
Classic Five Sport Signings Red Signature
1995-96 #83 Michael Waltrip
Classic Five Sport Silver Die Cuts
1995 #168 Michael Waltrip
Classic Five-Sport *
1995 #168 Michael Waltrip
Classic Five-Sport Autographs *
1995 #168 Michael Waltrip/225--Not Confirmed
Classic Five-Sport Printer's Proofs *
1995 #168 Michael Waltrip
Classic Five-Sport Red Die Cuts *
1995 #168 Michael Waltrip
Classic Five-Sport Silver Die Cuts *
1995 #168 Michael Waltrip
Classic Interview
1996 #IV15 Michael Waltrip
Classic Mark Martin's Challengers
1996 #MC2 Michael Waltrip
Classic Printer's Proof

1996 #26 Michael Waltrip
1996 #35 Michael Waltrip's Car
1996 #41 Michael Waltrip
Classic Race Chase
1996 #RC1 Michael Waltrip's Car
1996 #RC11 Michael Waltrip's Car
Classic Signings *
1996 #S83 Michael Waltrip
Classic Signings Blue Signature *
1996 #83 Michael Waltrip
Classic Signings Die Cuts *
1996 #83 Michael Waltrip
Classic Signings Red Signature *
1996 #83 Michael Waltrip
Classic Silver
1996 #26 Michael Waltrip
1996 #35 Michael Waltrip's Car
1996 #41 Michael Waltrip
Collector's Choice
1997 #21 Michael Waltrip
1997 #71 Michael Waltrip's Car MM
1997 #108 Michael Waltrip SC
1998 #21 Michael Waltrip
1998 #57 Michael Waltrip's Car
1998 #106 Michael Waltrip TD
Collector's Choice CC600
1998 #CC25 Michael Waltrip
1998 #CC58 Michael Waltrip
Collector's Choice Speedecals
1997 #S41 Michael Waltrip's Car
1997 #S42 Michael Waltrip's Helmet
Collector's Choice Star Quest
1998 #SQ22 Michael Waltrip
Collector's Choice Triple Force
1997 #E3 Michael Waltrip
Collector's Choice Upper Deck 500
1997 #UD42 Michael Waltrip
1997 #UD43 Michael Waltrip's Car
Crown Jewels
1995 #17 Michael Waltrip
Crown Jewels Diamond
1995 #17 Michael Waltrip
Crown Jewels Elite
1996 #15 Michael Waltrip
Crown Jewels Elite Diamond Tribute
1996 #15 Michael Waltrip
Crown Jewels Elite Diamond Tribute Citrine
1996 #15 Michael Waltrip
Crown Jewels Elite Dual Jewels Amethyst
1996 #DJ5 D.Waltrip/M.Waltrip
Crown Jewels Elite Dual Jewels Amethyst Diamond Tribute
1996 #DJ5 D.Waltrip/M.Waltrip
Crown Jewels Elite Dual Jewels Amethyst Treasure Chest
1996 #DJ5 D.Waltrip/M.Waltrip
Crown Jewels Elite Dual Jewels Garnet
1996 #DJ5 D.Waltrip/M.Waltrip
Crown Jewels Elite Dual Jewels Garnet Diamond Tribute
1996 #DJ5 D.Waltrip/M.Waltrip
Crown Jewels Elite Dual Jewels Garnet Treasure Chest
1996 #DJ5 D.Waltrip/M.Waltrip
Crown Jewels Elite Dual Jewels Sapphire
1996 #DJ5 D.Waltrip/M.Waltrip
Crown Jewels Elite Dual Jewels Sapphire Treasure Chest
1996 #DJ5 D.Waltrip/M.Waltrip
Crown Jewels Elite Emerald
1996 #15 Michael Waltrip
Crown Jewels Elite Emerald Treasure Chest
1996 #15 Michael Waltrip
Crown Jewels Elite Sapphire
1996 #15 Michael Waltrip
Crown Jewels Elite Sapphire Treasure Chest
1996 #15 Michael Waltrip
Crown Jewels Elite Treasure Chest
1996 #15 Michael Waltrip
Crown Jewels Emerald
1995 #17 Michael Waltrip
Crown Jewels Sapphire
1995 #17 Michael Waltrip
Finish Line
1993 #15 Michael Waltrip's Car
1993 #109 Michael Waltrip
1993 #123 Michael Waltrip
1994 #32 Michael Waltrip
1994 #43 Michael Waltrip's Car
1994 #134 Michael Waltrip
1995 #30 Michael Waltrip/Elizabeth Waltrip
1995 #61 Michael Waltrip
1995 #95 Michael Waltrip
1996 #15 Michael Waltrip's Car
1996 #34 Michael Waltrip
1996 #61 Michael Waltrip
Finish Line Black Gold
1996 #C14 Michael Waltrip's Car
1996 #D16 Michael Waltrip
Finish Line Coca-Cola 600
1995 #19 Michael Waltrip
Finish Line Commemorative Sheets
1993 #13 Pocono
1993 #23 Richmond
Finish Line Gold
1994 #12 Michael Waltrip
1994 #62 Michael Waltrip
1994 #74 Michael Waltrip's Car
1994 #84 Michael Waltrip
Finish Line Gold Autographs
1994 #84 Michael Waltrip
Finish Line Gold Signature
1995 #GS11 Michael Waltrip
1996 #GS12 Michael Waltrip
Finish Line Phone Pak
1996 #38 Michael Waltrip
Finish Line Phone Pak $2 Signature
1996 #38 Michael Waltrip
Finish Line Phone Pak $5
1996 #23 Michael Waltrip
Finish Line Phone Pak II
1997 #16 Michael Waltrip

1997 #36 L.Wood/E.Wood/M.Waltrip
1997 #54 Michael Waltrip $5
1997 #65 Michael Waltrip $5
1997 #77 Michael Waltrip's Car $10
Finish Line Printer's Proof
1995 #30 Michael Waltrip/Elizabeth Waltrip
1995 #61 Michael Waltrip
1995 #95 Michael Waltrip
1996 #15 Michael Waltrip's Car
1996 #34 Michael Waltrip
1996 #61 Michael Waltrip
Finish Line Silver
1993 #15 Michael Waltrip's Car
1993 #109 Michael Waltrip
1993 #123 Michael Waltrip
1994 #32 Michael Waltrip
1994 #43 Michael Waltrip's Car
1994 #134 Michael Waltrip
1995 #30 Michael Waltrip/Elizabeth Waltrip
1995 #61 Michael Waltrip
1995 #95 Michael Waltrip
1996 #15 Michael Waltrip's Car
1996 #34 Michael Waltrip
1996 #61 Michael Waltrip
Finish Line Standout Cars
1995 #SC10 Michael Waltrip's Car
Finish Line Standout Drivers
1995 #SD10 Michael Waltrip
Flair
1996 #36 Michael Waltrip
1996 #92 Michael Waltrip's Car
Hi-Tech Brickyard 400
1994 #56 Michael Waltrip
1995 #14 Michael Waltrip's Car
1995 #59 Michael Waltrip
Hi-Tech Brickyard 400 Artist Proofs
1994 #56 Michael Waltrip
Hi-Tech Brickyard 400 Top Ten
1995 #BY8 Michael Waltrip
Images
1995 #30 Michael Waltrip
1995 #70 Michael Waltrip
Images Driven
1995 #D11 Michael Waltrip
Images Gold
1995 #30 Michael Waltrip
1995 #70 Michael Waltrip
Images Hard Chargers
1995 #HC7 Michael Waltrip
Jurassic Park
1997 #10 Michael Waltrip
1997 #36 Michael Waltrip
Jurassic Park Raptors
1997 #R7 Michael Waltrip
Jurassic Park Triceratops
1997 #10 Michael Waltrip
1997 #36 Michael Waltrip
KnightQuest
1996 #19 Michael Waltrip K
KnightQuest Black Knights
1996 #19 Michael Waltrip K
KnightQuest Knights of the Round Table
1996 #KT9 Michael Waltrip
KnightQuest Red Knight Preview
1996 #19 Michael Waltrip K
KnightQuest Royalty
1996 #19 Michael Waltrip K
KnightQuest White Knights
1996 #19 Michael Waltrip K
Maxwell House
1993 #21 Darrell Waltrip/Michael Waltrip
Maxx
1989 #30 Michael Waltrip
1989 #140 D.Waltrip/Mich.Waltrip
1990 #30 Michael Waltrip
1990 #194 Michael Waltrip/Phil Parsons Cars YR
1991 #30 Michael Waltrip
1991 #118 Michael Waltrip Crash MM
1991 #127 Michael Waltrip/D.Cope Cars MM
1993 #30 Michael Waltrip
1994 #30 Michael Waltrip
1994 #70 Michael Waltrip's Car
1994 #260 Michael Waltrip
1994 #261 Michael Waltrip's Car
1995 #30 Michael Waltrip
1995 #167 Michael Waltrip's Car
1995 #244 Michael Waltrip
1995 #245 Michael Waltrip's Car
1995 #246 Michael Waltrip
1995 #247 Michael Waltrip's Car
1996 #30 Michael Waltrip
1996 #39 Michael Waltrip's Car
1997 #21 Michael Waltrip
1997 #66 Michael Waltrip's Car
1997 #113 Michael Waltrip MO
1998 #21 Michael Waltrip
1998 #51 Michael Waltrip's Car
2000 #7 Michael Waltrip
Maxx 10th Anniversary
1998 #19 Michael Waltrip
1998 #64 Michael Waltrip's Car
1998 #99 Michael Waltrip
Maxx 10th Anniversary Buy Back Autographs
1998 #49 M.Waltrip '88 #98/149
Maxx 10th Anniversary Maxximum Preview
1998 #P21 Michael Waltrip
Maxx 1997 Year In Review
1998 #24 Michael Waltrip's Car
1998 #94 Michael Waltrip's Car
Maxx Autographs
1995 #30 Michael Waltrip
Maxx Black
1992 #30 Michael Waltrip
Maxx Charlotte
1988 #23 Michael Waltrip's Car
1988 #98 Michael Waltrip RC
Maxx Chase the Champion
1997 #C8 Michael Waltrip
Maxx Chase the Champion Gold Die Cuts
1997 #C8 Michael Waltrip
Maxx Crisco
1989 #21 Michael Waltrip
Maxx Family Ties

1996 #FT5 D.Waltrip/M.Waltrip
Maxx FANtastic Finishes
1999 #F30 Michael Waltrip's Car
Maxx Glossy
1990 #30 Michael Waltrip
1990 #194 Michael Waltrip/Phil Parsons Cars YR
Maxx Holly Farms
1990 #HF18 Michael Waltrip
Maxx License to Drive
1995 #11 Michael Waltrip's Car
Maxx Made in America
1996 #21 Michael Waltrip
1996 #51 Michael Waltrip's Car
1996 #80 Michael Waltrip
1996 #81 Michael Waltrip's Car
Maxx Made in America Blue Ribbon
1996 #BR5 Michael Waltrip
Maxx McDonald's
1991 #16 Michael Waltrip
1992 #22 Michael Waltrip
Maxx Medallion
1994 #7 Michael Waltrip's Car
1995 #21 Michael Waltrip
1995 #51 Michael Waltrip's Car
Maxx Medallion Blue
1995 #21 Michael Waltrip
1995 #51 Michael Waltrip's Car
Maxx Odyssey
1996 #21 Michael Waltrip
1996 #51 Michael Waltrip's Car
1996 #80 Michael Waltrip
1996 #81 Michael Waltrip's Car
Maxx Odyssey On The Road Again
1996 #OTRA2 Michael Waltrip's Trans.
Maxx Odyssey Radio Active
1996 #RA5 Michael Waltrip
Maxx Premier Plus
1993 #30 Michael Waltrip
1994 #30 Michael Waltrip
1994 #70 Michael Waltrip's Car
1995 #30 Michael Waltrip
1995 #47 Michael Waltrip's Car
Maxx Premier Plus Crown Chrome
1995 #30 Michael Waltrip
1995 #47 Michael Waltrip's Car
Maxx Premier Series
1993 #30 Michael Waltrip
1994 #30 Michael Waltrip
1994 #70 Michael Waltrip
1995 #30 Michael Waltrip
1995 #69 Michael Waltrip's Car
1996 #30 Michael Waltrip
1996 #65 Michael Waltrip's Car
1996 #190 Michael Waltrip BGN
1996 #191 Michael Waltrip's Car
Maxx Previews
1989 #8 Michael Waltrip
Maxx Race Ticket
1999 #RT29 Michael Waltrip's Car
Maxx Racing for Kids
1991 #1 Sheet 1
Maxx Racing Images
1999 #RI20 Michael Waltrip
Maxx Red
1992 #30 Michael Waltrip
Maxx The Select 25
1994 #17 Michael Waltrip
Maxx The Winston
1992 #15 Michael Waltrip
1992 #35 Michael Waltrip's Car
1992 #43 Michael Waltrip Win
1993 #18 Michael Waltrip
1993 #38 Michael Waltrip's Car
Maxx Update
1991 #30 Michael Waltrip
Maxximum
1998 #21 Michael Waltrip
1998 #46 Michael Waltrip's Car
1998 #71 Michael Waltrip
1998 #96 Michael Waltrip's Car
2000 #27 Michael Waltrip
Maxximum Die Cuts
2000 #27 Michael Waltrip
Maxximum First Class
1998 #F4 Michael Waltrip
Maxximum MPH
2000 #27 Michael Waltrip/7
Maxximum Signatures
2000 #MD2 M.Waltrip/D.Waltrip
M-Force
1996 #18 Michael Waltrip
MW Windows
1995 #4 Michael Waltrip
1995 #5 T.Labonte/M.Waltrip/D.Jarrett/D.Green
NAPA
2005 #NNO Michael Waltrip
Nilla Wafers Team Nabisco
2003 #3 Michael Waltrip
2003 #4 Earn.Jr./Green/Harvick/M.Walt
Pinnacle
1996 #21 Michael Waltrip
1996 #48 Michael Waltrip's Car
1997 #21 Michael Waltrip
1997 #50 Michael Waltrip's Car
1997 #83 Michael Waltrip TT
Pinnacle Artist Proofs
1996 #21 Michael Waltrip
1996 #48 Michael Waltrip's Car
1997 #21 Michael Waltrip B
1997 #50 Michael Waltrip's Car B
1997 #83 Michael Waltrip TT R
Pinnacle Certified
1997 #21 Michael Waltrip
1997 #55 Michael Waltrip's Car
1997 #78 Michael Waltrip's Car WP
Pinnacle Certified Mirror Blue
1997 #21 Michael Waltrip
1997 #55 Michael Waltrip's Car
1997 #78 Michael Waltrip's Car WP
Pinnacle Certified Mirror Gold
1997 #21 Michael Waltrip
1997 #55 Michael Waltrip's Car

1997 #78 Michael Waltrip's Car WP
Pinnacle Certified Mirror Red
1997 #21 Michael Waltrip
1997 #55 Michael Waltrip's Car
1997 #78 Michael Waltrip's Car WP
Pinnacle Certified Red
1997 #21 Michael Waltrip
1997 #55 Michael Waltrip's Car
1997 #78 Michael Waltrip's Car WP
Pinnacle Checkered Flag
1996 #11 Michael Waltrip
Pinnacle Foil
1997 #21 Michael Waltrip
1997 #50 Michael Waltrip's Car
1997 #83 Michael Waltrip TT
Pinnacle Mint
1997 #13 Michael Waltrip
1998 #12 Michael Waltrip
1998 #24 Michael Waltrip's Car
Pinnacle Mint Bronze
1997 #13 Michael Waltrip
Pinnacle Mint Coins
1997 #13 Michael Waltrip
1998 #12 Michael Waltrip
1998 #24 Michael Waltrip's Car
Pinnacle Mint Coins 24K Gold Plated
1997 #13 Michael Waltrip
Pinnacle Mint Coins Bronze Proof
1998 #12 Michael Waltrip
1998 #24 Michael Waltrip's Car
Pinnacle Mint Coins Gold Plated
1998 #12 Michael Waltrip
1998 #24 Michael Waltrip's Car
Pinnacle Mint Coins Gold Plated Proofs
1998 #12 Michael Waltrip
1998 #24 Michael Waltrip's Car
Pinnacle Mint Coins Nickel-Silver
1997 #13 Michael Waltrip
1998 #12 Michael Waltrip
1998 #24 Michael Waltrip's Car
Pinnacle Mint Coins Silver Plated Proofs
1998 #12 Michael Waltrip
1998 #24 Michael Waltrip's Car
Pinnacle Mint Coins Solid Gold
1998 #12 Michael Waltrip
1998 #24 Michael Waltrip's Car
Pinnacle Mint Coins Solid Silver
1998 #12 Michael Waltrip
1998 #24 Michael Waltrip's Car
Pinnacle Mint Die Cuts
1998 #12 Michael Waltrip
1998 #24 Michael Waltrip's Car
Pinnacle Mint Gold
1997 #13 Michael Waltrip
Pinnacle Mint Gold Team
1998 #12 Michael Waltrip
1998 #24 Michael Waltrip's Car
Pinnacle Mint Silver
1997 #13 Michael Waltrip
Pinnacle Mint Silver Team
1998 #12 Michael Waltrip
1998 #24 Michael Waltrip's Car
Pinnacle Pole Position
1996 #21 Michael Waltrip
1996 #37 Michael Waltrip's Car
1996 #66 Michael Waltrip WIN
Pinnacle Pole Position Lightning Fast
1996 #21 Michael Waltrip
1996 #37 Michael Waltrip's Car
1996 #66 Michael Waltrip
Pinnacle Portraits
1997 #13 Michael Waltrip
1997 #33 Michael Waltrip's Car
1997 #48 Michael Waltrip SS
Pinnacle Press Plates
1997 #21 Michael Waltrip
1997 #50 Michael Waltrip's Car
1997 #83 Michael Waltrip TT
Pinnacle Totally Certified Platinum Blue
1997 #21 Michael Waltrip
1997 #55 Michael Waltrip's Car
1997 #78 Michael Waltrip WP
Pinnacle Totally Certified Platinum Gold
1997 #21 Michael Waltrip
1997 #55 Michael Waltrip's Car
1997 #78 Michael Waltrip WP
Pinnacle Totally Certified Platinum Red
1997 #21 Michael Waltrip
1997 #55 Michael Waltrip's Car
1997 #78 Michael Waltrip WP
Pinnacle Trophy Collection
1997 #21 Michael Waltrip
1997 #50 Michael Waltrip's Car
1997 #83 Michael Waltrip TT
Pinnacle Winston Cup Collection
1996 #21 Michael Waltrip
1996 #48 Michael Waltrip's Car
Post Cereal
2004 #7 Michael Waltrip
Power
1994 #58 Michael Waltrip in Pits SL
1994 #126 Michael Waltrip
1994 #143 Michael Waltrip's Car
Power Gold
1994 #58 Michael Waltrip in Pits SL
1994 #126 Michael Waltrip
1994 #143 Michael Waltrip's Car
Power Preview
1994 #6 Michael Waltrip
1994 #27 Michael Waltrip's Car FOIL
Predator
1997 #11 Michael Waltrip
1997 #40 Michael Waltrip
Predator Black Wolf First Strike
1997 #11 Michael Waltrip
1997 #40 Michael Waltrip
Predator First Slash
1997 #11 Michael Waltrip
1997 #40 Michael Waltrip
Predator Grizzly
1997 #11 Michael Waltrip
1997 #40 Michael Waltrip

Predator Grizzly First Slash
1997 #11 Michael Waltrip
1997 #40 Michael Waltrip
Predator Red Wolf
1997 #11 Michael Waltrip
1997 #40 Michael Waltrip
Predator Red Wolf First Slash
1997 #11 Michael Waltrip
1997 #40 Michael Waltrip
Press Pass
1994 #30 Michael Waltrip
1994 #33 Darrell Waltrip/Michael Waltrip
1994 #49 Michael Waltrip's Car
1995 #36 Michael Waltrip/Elizabeth Waltrip
1995 #48 Michael Waltrip's Car
1995 #117 Michael Waltrip's Car AW
1996 #36 Michael Waltrip
1996 #48 Michael Waltrip's Car
1996 #118 Michael Waltrip PRE
1997 #14 Michael Waltrip
1997 #38 Michael Waltrip's Car
1997 #63 Michael Waltrip's Car
1997 #78 Michael Waltrip
1997 #79 Michael Waltrip
1997 #93 M.Waltrip/David Pearson
1997 #100 Michael Waltrip
1997 #123 Michael Waltrip
1998 #14 Michael Waltrip
1999 #15 Michael Waltrip
1999 #51 Michael Waltrip
1999 #115 Michael Waltrip RET
2000 #25 Michael Waltrip
2000 #51 Michael Waltrip's Car DD
2000 #98 Michael Waltrip OOP
2002 #36 Michael Waltrip
2002 #64 Michael Waltrip REP
2002 #78 Michael Waltrip's Car
2003 #33 Michael Waltrip
2004 #33 Michael Waltrip
2005 #10 Michael Waltrip
2005 #99 Michael Waltrip Y
2005 #103 Michael Waltrip P
2008 #36 Michael Waltrip
2008 #120 Michael Waltrip CL
Press Pass Autographs
1997 #13 Michael Waltrip PPP/VIP
1998 #9 Michael Waltrip/285
1999 #21 Michael Waltrip/250
2002 #69 Michael Waltrip
2003 #60 Michael Waltrip E/P
2005 #61 Michael Waltrip
2008 #43 Michael Waltrip NC P/E
Press Pass Autographs Press Plates Black
2008 #35 Michael Waltrip NC E
Press Pass Autographs Press Plates Cyan
2008 #36 Michael Waltrip NC P
Press Pass Autographs Press Plates Magenta
2008 #36 Michael Waltrip NC E
Press Pass Autographs Press Plates Yellow
2008 #35 Michael Waltrip NC P
Press Pass Blue
2008 #B36 Michael Waltrip
2008 #B120 Michael Waltrip CL
Press Pass Bryan
1999 #11 Michael Waltrip
Press Pass Burning Rubber
1997 #BR4 Michael Waltrip
Press Pass Burning Rubber Cars
2002 #BRC12 Michael Waltrip's Car
2004 #BRT11 Michael Waltrip's Car
2005 #BRT8 Michael Waltrip's Car
Press Pass Burning Rubber Drivers
2002 #BRD12 Michael Waltrip
2004 #BRD11 Michael Waltrip
2005 #BRD8 Michael Waltrip
Press Pass Burning Rubber Drivers Gold
2005 #BRD8 Michael Waltrip
Press Pass Chase Cars
1999 #10B Michael Waltrip's Car
Press Pass Clear Cut
1997 #C10 Michael Waltrip
Press Pass Coca-Cola Racing Family
2003 #12 Michael Waltrip
Press Pass Coca-Cola Racing Family Scratch-off
2003 #6 Michael Waltrip
Press Pass Collector's Series Box Set
2007 #SB25 Michael Waltrip
Press Pass Collectors Series Sunday Best
2007 #CB25 Michael Waltrip CL
Press Pass Cup Chase
1994 #CC30 Michael Waltrip
1995 #36 Michael Waltrip
1996 #36 Michael Waltrip
1997 #CC19 Michael Waltrip
1998 #CC19 Michael Waltrip
2002 #CC17 Michael Waltrip
2004 #CCR5 Michael Waltrip
2005 #CCR12 Michael Waltrip
Press Pass Cup Chase Blue Die Cut Prizes
1997 #CC19 Michael Waltrip
Press Pass Cup Chase Die Cut Prizes
1998 #CC19 Michael Waltrip
Press Pass Cup Chase Foil Prizes
1996 #36 Michael Waltrip
Press Pass Cup Chase Gold Die Cuts
1997 #CC19 Michael Waltrip
Press Pass Cup Chase Prizes
2002 #CC17 Michael Waltrip
2004 #CCR5 Michael Waltrip
2005 #CCP12 Michael Waltrip
Press Pass Dale Earnhardt Jr.
2004 #42 Dale Jr./M.Waltrip T
Press Pass Dale The Movie
2007 #46 Dale Earnhardt Jr.'s Car Kevin Harvick's Car Michael Waltrip's Car Jimmie Johnson's Car
Press Pass Daytona 500 50th Anniversary
2008 #38 Michael Waltrip '01
2008 #40 Michael Waltrip '03
Press Pass Eclipse
2002 #20 Michael Waltrip
2003 #13 Michael Waltrip
2004 #14 Michael Waltrip

2004 #31 Michael Waltrip's Car
2004 #61 Michael Waltrip P
2004 #80 Michael Waltrip LL
2004 #80B Michael Waltrip LL blue sky
2005 #19 Michael Waltrip
2005 #33 Michael Waltrip's Car S
2005 #61 Michael Waltrip P
2005 #80 Michael Waltrip LL
2008 #27 Michael Waltrip
2008 #36 Michael Waltrip RM
2008 #71 Michael Waltrip BTF
Press Pass Eclipse Destination WIN
2004 #3 Michael Waltrip
2004 #24 Michael Waltrip
Press Pass Eclipse Double Hot Treads
2003 #DT11 S.Park/M.Waltrip
Press Pass Eclipse Escape Velocity
2008 #EV2 Michael Waltrip
Press Pass Eclipse Gold
2008 #G27 Michael Waltrip
2008 #G36 Michael Waltrip RM
2008 #G71 Michael Waltrip BTF
Press Pass Eclipse Hyperdrive
2004 #HP1 Michael Waltrip
2005 #HD1 Michael Waltrip
Press Pass Eclipse Maxim
2004 #MX9 Michael Waltrip
2005 #MX9 Michael Waltrip
Press Pass Eclipse Previews
2003 #13 Michael Waltrip
2004 #14 Michael Waltrip
2005 #EB19 Michael Waltrip
2005 #EB33 Michael Waltrip's Car S
2005 #EB61 Michael Waltrip P
2005 #EB80 Michael Waltrip LL/1
2008 #EB27 Michael Waltrip
2008 #EB36 Michael Waltrip RM
Press Pass Eclipse Racing Champions
2002 #RC1 Michael Waltrip
2003 #RC20 Michael Waltrip
Press Pass Eclipse Red
2008 #R27 Michael Waltrip
2008 #R36 Michael Waltrip RM
2008 #R71 Michael Waltrip BTF
Press Pass Eclipse Samples
2002 #20 Michael Waltrip
2003 #13 Michael Waltrip
2004 #14 Michael Waltrip
2004 #31 Michael Waltrip's Car
2004 #61 Michael Waltrip P
2004 #80 Michael Waltrip LL
2005 #19 Michael Waltrip
2005 #33 Michael Waltrip's Car S
2005 #61 Michael Waltrip P
2005 #80 Michael Waltrip LL
Press Pass Eclipse Skidmarks
2004 #SM17 Michael Waltrip
2005 #SM17 Michael Waltrip
Press Pass Eclipse Skidmarks Holofoil
2004 #SM17 Michael Waltrip
2005 #SM17 Michael Waltrip
Press Pass Eclipse Solar Eclipse
2002 #S20 Michael Waltrip
2003 #P13 Michael Waltrip
Press Pass Eclipse Star Tracks
2008 #ST18 Michael Waltrip
Press Pass Eclipse Star Tracks Holofoil
2008 #ST18 Michael Waltrip
Press Pass Eclipse Supernova
2003 #SN10 Michael Waltrip
Press Pass Eclipse Under Cover Cars
2003 #UCT11 Michael Waltrip
2004 #UCD10 Michael Waltrip
2005 #UCT10 Michael Waltrip
Press Pass Eclipse Under Cover Double Cover
2002 #DC8 D.Earn.Jr./M.Waltrip
2004 #DC1 D.Earnhardt Jr./M.Waltrip
2005 #DC1 D.Earnhardt Jr./M.Waltrip
Press Pass Eclipse Under Cover Driver Gold
2003 #UCD11 Michael Waltrip
2004 #UCD10 Michael Waltrip
Press Pass Eclipse Under Cover Driver Red
2003 #UCD11 Michael Waltrip
2004 #UCD10 Michael Waltrip
2005 #UCD10 Michael Waltrip
Press Pass Eclipse Under Cover Driver Silver
2003 #UCD11 Michael Waltrip
2004 #UCD10 Michael Waltrip
Press Pass Eclipse Under Cover Drivers
2002 #CD11 Michael Waltrip
2008 #UCD13 Michael Waltrip
Press Pass Eclipse Under Cover Drivers Eclipse
2008 #UCD13 Michael Waltrip
Press Pass Eclipse Under Cover Drivers Holofoil
2005 #UCD10 Michael Waltrip
Press Pass Eclipse Under Cover Drivers Name
2008 #UCD13 Michael Waltrip
Press Pass Eclipse Under Cover Drivers NASCAR
2008 #UCD13 Michael Waltrip
Press Pass Eclipse Under Cover Drivers Silver
2005 #UCD10 Michael Waltrip
Press Pass Eclipse Under Cover Gold Cars
2002 #CD11 Michael Waltrip
Press Pass Eclipse Under Cover Gold Drivers
2002 #CD11 Michael Waltrip
Press Pass Eclipse Under Cover Holofoil Drivers
2002 #CD11 Michael Waltrip
Press Pass Eclipse Under Cover Teams
2008 #UCT13 Michael Waltrip
Press Pass Eclipse Under Cover Teams NASCAR
2008 #UCT13 Michael Waltrip
Press Pass Eclipse Warp Speed
2003 #WS8 Michael Waltrip
Press Pass Game Face
2005 #GF8 Michael Waltrip
Press Pass Gold
2008 #G36 Michael Waltrip

2008 #G120 Michael Waltrip CL
Press Pass Gold Holofoil
2003 #P33 Michael Waltrip
Press Pass Hot Treads
2002 #HT7 Michael Waltrip's Car/2300
2002 #HT34 M.Waltrip's Car/900
2004 #HTR16 Michael Waltrip
2005 #HTR15 Michael Waltrip
Press Pass Hot Treads Holofoil
2004 #HTR16 Michael Waltrip
2005 #HTR15 Michael Waltrip
Press Pass Lasers
1997 #14 Michael Waltrip
1997 #38 Michael Waltrip's Car
1997 #63 Michael Waltrip's Car
1997 #78 Michael Waltrip
1997 #79 Michael Waltrip
1997 #93 M.Waltrip/David Pearson
1997 #100 Michael Waltrip
1997 #123 Michael Waltrip
Press Pass Legends Double Threads Bronze
2005 #DT-EW D.Earnhardt Jr./M.Waltrip
Press Pass Legends Double Threads Gold
2005 #DT-EW D.Earnhardt Jr./M.Waltrip
Press Pass Legends Double Threads Silver
2005 #DT-EW D.Earnhardt Jr./M.Waltrip
Press Pass Legends Heritage
2005 #HE11 Michael Waltrip
Press Pass Legends Sunday Swatches Bronze
2007 #MW-SS Michael Waltrip
Press Pass Legends Sunday Swatches Gold
2007 #MW-SS Michael Waltrip
Press Pass Legends Sunday Swatches Silver
2007 #MW-SS Michael Waltrip
Press Pass Making the Show Collector's Series
2004 #MS9 Michael Waltrip
Press Pass Millennium
2000 #25 Michael Waltrip
2000 #51 Michael Waltrip
2000 #98 Michael Waltrip
Press Pass Nabisco Albertsons
2002 #4 Michael Waltrip
2003 #5 Michael Waltrip
Press Pass Nilla Wafers
2004 #4 Michael Waltrip
Press Pass Oil Slicks
1997 #14 Michael Waltrip
1997 #38 Michael Waltrip's Car
1997 #63 Michael Waltrip's Car
1997 #78 Michael Waltrip
1997 #79 Michael Waltrip
1997 #93 M.Waltrip/David Pearson
1997 #100 Michael Waltrip
1997 #123 Michael Waltrip
1998 #14 Michael Waltrip
Press Pass Optima
2000 #27 Michael Waltrip
2001 #27 Michael Waltrip
2002 #30 Michael Waltrip
2003 #27 Michael Waltrip
2004 #27 Michael Waltrip
2004 #92 Michael Waltrip SS
Press Pass Optima Fan Favorite
2003 #FF24 Michael Waltrip
2004 #FF25 Michael Waltrip
Press Pass Optima G Force
2001 #GF27 Michael Waltrip
2004 #GF4 Michael Waltrip
Press Pass Optima Gold
2001 #27 Michael Waltrip
2002 #30 Michael Waltrip
2003 #G27 Michael Waltrip
2004 #G27 Michael Waltrip
2004 #G92 Michael Waltrip SS
Press Pass Optima Platinum
2000 #27 Michael Waltrip
Press Pass Optima Previews
2003 #27 Michael Waltrip
2004 #EB27 Michael Waltrip
Press Pass Optima Promos
2002 #30 Michael Waltrip
Press Pass Optima Q&A
2004 #QA8 Michael Waltrip
Press Pass Optima Samples
2002 #30 Michael Waltrip
2003 #27 Michael Waltrip
2004 #27 Michael Waltrip
2004 #92 Michael Waltrip SS
Press Pass Optima Thunder Bolts Cars
2003 #TBT18 Michael Waltrip's Car
2004 #TBT4 Michael Waltrip's Car
Press Pass Optima Thunder Bolts Drivers
2003 #TBD18 Michael Waltrip/65
2004 #TBD4 Michael Waltrip
Press Pass Optima XL
1994 #24 Michael Waltrip
1995 #24 Michael Waltrip
Press Pass Optima XL Cool Blue
1995 #24 Michael Waltrip
Press Pass Optima XL Die Cut
1995 #24 Michael Waltrip
Press Pass Optima XL Red Hot
1994 #24 Michael Waltrip
1995 #24 Michael Waltrip
Press Pass Optima XL Stealth
1995 #XLS18 Michael Waltrip
Press Pass Panorama
2005 #PPP17 Michael Waltrip
2005 #PPP24 Michael Waltrip
Press Pass Pit Stop
1998 #PS10 Michael Waltrip's Car
1999 #11 Michael Waltrip's Car
Press Pass Platinum
2002 #36 Michael Waltrip
2002 #64 Michael Waltrip REP
2002 #78 Michael Waltrip's Car
2004 #P33 Michael Waltrip
2005 #P10 Michael Waltrip
2005 #P99 Michael Waltrip Y
2005 #P103 Michael Waltrip P
2008 #P36 Michael Waltrip

2008 #P120 Michael Waltrip CL
Press Pass Premium
1995 #10 Michael Waltrip
1996 #12 Michael Waltrip
1996 #33 Michael Waltrip's Car
1997 #14 Michael Waltrip
1998 #7 Michael Waltrip
1998 #45 Michael Waltrip
1999 #27 Michael Waltrip
1999 #50 Michael Waltrip
2000 #6 Michael Waltrip
2001 #27 Michael Waltrip
2001 #33 Michael Waltrip
2001 #69 Michael Waltrip CC
2001 #0 Michael Waltrip Daytona
2002 #33 Michael Waltrip
2002 #47 Michael Waltrip SW
2002 #69 Michael Waltrip CH
2003 #30 Michael Waltrip
2003 #44 Michael Waltrip's Car
2003 #50 Dale Jr./Park/Waltrip CL
2003 #68 Michael Waltrip CC
2003 #80 Michael Waltrip PC
2003 #0 Michael Waltrip
2004 #26 Michael Waltrip
2004 #40 Michael Waltrip's Car
2004 #64 Michael Waltrip CC
2004 #70 Michael Waltrip PC
2005 #33 Michael Waltrip
2005 #42 Michael Waltrip's Car M
2005 #47 Michael Waltrip S
2007 #75 Michael Waltrip DD
2008 #30 Michael Waltrip
2008 #39 Michael Waltrip's Car M
Press Pass Premium $10 Phone Cards
1996 #9 Michael Waltrip
Press Pass Premium $20 Phone Cards
1996 #9 Michael Waltrip
Press Pass Premium $5 Phone Cards
1996 #9 Michael Waltrip
Press Pass Premium Badge of Honor
1999 #BH3A Michael Waltrip
Press Pass Premium Badge of Honor Reflectors
1999 #BH3A Michael Waltrip
Press Pass Premium Clean Air
2008 #CA3 Michael Waltrip
Press Pass Premium Double Burners
1997 #DB5 Michael Waltrip
Press Pass Premium Emerald Proofs
1996 #12 Michael Waltrip
1996 #33 Michael Waltrip's Car
1997 #14 Michael Waltrip
Press Pass Premium Flag Chasers
1998 #FC12 Michael Waltrip
Press Pass Premium Flag Chasers Reflectors
1998 #FC12 Michael Waltrip
Press Pass Premium Gold
2001 #27 Michael Waltrip
2001 #33 Michael Waltrip
2001 #69 Michael Waltrip CC
Press Pass Premium Holofoil
1995 #10 Michael Waltrip
1996 #12 Michael Waltrip
1996 #33 Michael Waltrip's Car
Press Pass Premium Hot Pursuit
1996 #HP9 Michael Waltrip
Press Pass Premium Hot Threads Autographs
2008 #HTMW Michael Waltrip/55
Press Pass Premium Hot Threads Cars
2005 #HTT13 Michael Waltrip
Press Pass Premium Hot Threads Drivers
2005 #HTD13 Michael Waltrip
Press Pass Premium Hot Threads Drivers Bronze
2004 #HTD15 Michael Waltrip
Press Pass Premium Hot Threads Drivers Bronze Retail
2004 #HTT15 Michael Waltrip
Press Pass Premium Hot Threads Drivers Gold
2004 #HTD15 Michael Waltrip
2005 #HTD13 Michael Waltrip
Press Pass Premium Hot Threads Drivers Silver
2004 #HTD15 Michael Waltrip
Press Pass Premium Hot Threads Patches
2008 #HTP50 Michael Waltrip Best Western/14
2008 #HTP51 Michael Waltrip NAPA/14
2008 #HTP52 Michael Waltrip NASCAR bar/6
Press Pass Premium in the Zone
2003 #IZ12 Michael Waltrip
2004 #IZ8 Michael Waltrip
2005 #IZ1 Michael Waltrip
Press Pass Premium in the Zone Elite Edition
2004 #IZ8 Michael Waltrip
2005 #IZ1 Michael Waltrip
Press Pass Premium Lap Leaders
1997 #LL12 Michael Waltrip
Press Pass Premium Mirrors
1997 #14 Michael Waltrip
Press Pass Premium Oil Slicks
1997 #14 Michael Waltrip
Press Pass Premium Performance Driven
2003 #PD9 Michael Waltrip
2007 #PD5 Michael Waltrip
Press Pass Premium Performance Driven Red
2007 #PD5 Michael Waltrip
Press Pass Premium Phone Cards $5
1995 #9 Michael Waltrip
Press Pass Premium Phone Cards $50
1995 #9 Michael Waltrip
Press Pass Premium Previews
2003 #30 Michael Waltrip
2004 #26 Michael Waltrip
2008 #EB30 Michael Waltrip
Press Pass Premium Red
2007 #R75 Michael Waltrip DD
2008 #30 Michael Waltrip
2008 #39 Michael Waltrip's Car M
Press Pass Premium Red Hot
1995 #10 Michael Waltrip
Press Pass Premium Red Reflectors

2002 #33 Michael Waltrip
2002 #47 Michael Waltrip SW
2002 #69 Michael Waltrip CH
2003 #30 Michael Waltrip
2003 #44 Michael Waltrip's Car
2003 #68 Michael Waltrip CC
2003 #80 Michael Waltrip PC
Press Pass Premium Reflectors
1998 #7 Michael Waltrip
1998 #45 Michael Waltrip
1999 #R27 Michael Waltrip
1999 #R50 Michael Waltrip
2000 #6 Michael Waltrip
Press Pass Premium Samples
2002 #33 Michael Waltrip
2002 #47 Michael Waltrip SW
2003 #30 Michael Waltrip
2003 #44 Michael Waltrip's Car
2004 #26 Michael Waltrip
2004 #40 Michael Waltrip's Car
2005 #33 Michael Waltrip
2005 #42 Michael Waltrip's Car M
2005 #47 Michael Waltrip S
Press Pass Previews
2003 #33 Michael Waltrip
2004 #33 Michael Waltrip
2008 #EB36 Michael Waltrip
Press Pass Previews Green
2005 #EB10 Michael Waltrip
Press Pass Previews Silver
2005 #EB103 Michael Waltrip
Press Pass R and N China
1996 #36 Michael Waltrip
Press Pass Race Day
2008 #RD12 Michael Waltrip
Press Pass Race Exclusives
2003 #2 Michael Waltrip
Press Pass Red Hot
1995 #36 Michael Waltrip/Elizabeth Waltrip
1995 #48 Michael Waltrip's Car
1995 #117 Michael Waltrip's Car AW
Press Pass Samples
2003 #33 Michael Waltrip
2004 #33 Michael Waltrip
2005 #10 Michael Waltrip
2005 #99 Michael Waltrip Y
2005 #103 Michael Waltrip P
Press Pass Scorchers
1996 #36 Michael Waltrip
1996 #48 Michael Waltrip's Car
1996 #118 Michael Waltrip PRE
Press Pass Shockers
1998 #ST12A Michael Waltrip
Press Pass Showcar
2002 #S9A Michael Waltrip's Car
2004 #S12B Michael Waltrip's Car
2005 #SC9 Michael Waltrip
Press Pass Showman
1999 #10A Michael Waltrip
2002 #S9A Michael Waltrip
2004 #S12A Michael Waltrip
2005 #SM9 Michael Waltrip
Press Pass Signings
1998 #13 Michael Waltrip PPP/S
1999 #58 Michael Waltrip/500
2000 #62 Michael Waltrip
2001 #54 Michael Waltrip V/S
2002 #69 Michael Waltrip O/P/S/T/V
2003 #74 Michael Waltrip O/P/S/T/V
2004 #64 Michael Waltrip O/P/S/T/V
2005 #59 Michael Waltrip P/S
2007 #75 Michael Waltrip NC
2008 #56 Michael Waltrip
Press Pass Signings Blue
2007 #34 Michael Waltrip NC
2008 #32 Michael Waltrip
Press Pass Signings Gold
1998 #13 Michael Waltrip PPP/VIP
2000 #33 Michael Waltrip
2001 #36 Michael Waltrip V/S
2002 #66 Michael Waltrip O/P/S/T/V
2003 #75 Michael Waltrip O/P/S/T/V
2004 #60 Michael Waltrip O/P/S/T/V
2005 #58 Michael Waltrip P/S
2007 #56 Michael Waltrip NC
Press Pass Signings Platinum
2005 #53 Michael Waltrip P/S
Press Pass Signings Press Plates Black
2007 #43 Michael Waltrip
Press Pass Signings Press Plates Cyan
2007 #42 Michael Waltrip
Press Pass Signings Press Plates Magenta
2007 #45 Michael Waltrip
Press Pass Signings Press Plates Yellow
2007 #43 Michael Waltrip
Press Pass Signings Silver
2007 #54 Michael Waltrip NC
2008 #43 Michael Waltrip
Press Pass Signings Transparent
2004 #11 Michael Waltrip O/P/S/T
Press Pass Skidmarks
1999 #15 Michael Waltrip
1999 #51 Michael Waltrip
Press Pass Slideshow
2008 #SS10 Michael Waltrip
2008 #SS34 Michael Waltrip
Press Pass Snapshots
2004 #SN23 Michael Waltrip
2005 #SN26 Michael Waltrip
Press Pass Speedway
2008 #35 Michael Waltrip
Press Pass Speedway Cockpit
2008 #CP26 Michael Waltrip
Press Pass Speedway Corporate Cuts Drivers
2008 #CD-MW Michael Waltrip
Press Pass Speedway Corporate Cuts Drivers Patches
2008 #CD-MW Michael Waltrip/13
Press Pass Speedway Corporate Cuts Team
2008 #CT-MW Michael Waltrip
Press Pass Speedway Gold
2008 #G35 Michael Waltrip
Press Pass Speedway Holofoil

2008 #H35 Michael Waltrip
Press Pass Speedway Previews
2008 #EB35 Michael Waltrip
Press Pass Speedway Red
2008 #R35 Michael Waltrip
Press Pass Speedway Test Drive
2008 #TD9 Michael Waltrip
Press Pass Stealth
1998 #34 Michael Waltrip
1998 #35 Michael Waltrip's Car
1999 #48 Michael Waltrip
2001 #16 Michael Waltrip
2001 #17 Michael Waltrip's Car
2001 #18 Michael Waltrip
2001 #72 Michael Waltrip SST CL
2003 #13 Michael Waltrip
2003 #14 Michael Waltrip's Car
2003 #15 Michael Waltrip
2003 #59 Michael Waltrip SST
2004 #34 Michael Waltrip
2004 #35 Michael Waltrip's Car
2004 #36 Michael Waltrip
2004 #84 Michael Waltrip SST
2004 #98 Michael Waltrip SF
2005 #56 Michael Waltrip
2005 #59 Michael Waltrip's Car
2005 #62 Michael Waltrip
2005 #84 Michael Waltrip H
2005 #98 Michael Waltrip SF
2007 #28 Michael Waltrip
2008 #35 Michael Waltrip
Press Pass Stealth Battle Armor Drivers
2008 #BAD2 Michael Waltrip
Press Pass Stealth Battle Armor Teams
2008 #BAT2 Michael Waltrip
Press Pass Stealth Big Numbers
1999 #BN18 Michael Waltrip
Press Pass Stealth Big Numbers Die Cuts
1999 #BN18 Michael Waltrip
Press Pass Stealth Chrome
2007 #28 Michael Waltrip
2008 #35 Michael Waltrip
Press Pass Stealth Chrome Exclusives
2007 #X28 Michael Waltrip
2008 #35 Michael Waltrip
Press Pass Stealth Chrome Exclusives Gold
2008 #35 Michael Waltrip
Press Pass Stealth Chrome Platinum
2007 #P28 Michael Waltrip
Press Pass Stealth EFX
2003 #FX12 Michael Waltrip
2004 #EF9 Michael Waltrip
2005 #EFX4 Michael Waltrip
Press Pass Stealth Fusion
1998 #34 Michael Waltrip
1998 #35 Michael Waltrip's Car
1999 #F48 Michael Waltrip
2003 #FU12 Michael Waltrip
2004 #FU4 Michael Waltrip
2005 #FU4 Michael Waltrip 1:112
2007 #F4 Michael Waltrip
Press Pass Stealth Gear Grippers Autographs
2005 #GG-MW Michael Waltrip/15
Press Pass Stealth Gear Grippers Cars
2003 #GGT12 Michael Waltrip/30
2005 #GGT9 Michael Waltrip
Press Pass Stealth Gear Grippers Drivers
2003 #GGD12 Michael Waltrip/30
2004 #GGD10 Michael Waltrip
2005 #GGD9 Michael Waltrip
Press Pass Stealth Gear Grippers Drivers Retail
2004 #GGT10 Michael Waltrip
Press Pass Stealth Holofoils
2001 #16 Michael Waltrip
2001 #17 Michael Waltrip's Car
2001 #18 Michael Waltrip
2001 #72 Michael Waltrip SST CL
Press Pass Stealth Lap Leaders
2001 #LL5 Michael Waltrip
2001 #LL23 Michael Waltrip's Car
Press Pass Stealth Lap Leaders Clear Cars
2001 #LL23 Michael Waltrip's Car
Press Pass Stealth Lap Leaders Clear Drivers
2001 #LL5 Michael Waltrip
Press Pass Stealth Maximum Access
2008 #MA27 Michael Waltrip
Press Pass Stealth Maximum Access Autographs
2008 #MA27 Michael Waltrip
Press Pass Stealth No Boundaries
2003 #NB25 Michael Waltrip
2004 #NB26 Michael Waltrip
2005 #NB1 Michael Waltrip
Press Pass Stealth Octane SLX
1999 #O23 Michael Waltrip
Press Pass Stealth Octane SLX Die Cuts
1999 #O23 Michael Waltrip
Press Pass Stealth Previews
2003 #13 Michael Waltrip
2003 #14 Michael Waltrip's Car
2003 #15 Michael Waltrip
2004 #EB34 Michael Waltrip
2004 #EB35 Michael Waltrip's Car
2004 #EB36 Michael Waltrip
2005 #56 Michael Waltrip
2005 #59 Michael Waltrip's Car
2005 #62 Michael Waltrip
2007 #EB28 Michael Waltrip
2008 #35 Michael Waltrip
Press Pass Stealth Profile
2004 #P11 Michael Waltrip 1:14
Press Pass Stealth Race Used Glove Cars
2001 #RGC3 Michael Waltrip/170
Press Pass Stealth Race Used Glove Drivers
2001 #RGD3 Michael Waltrip/170
Press Pass Stealth Red
2003 #P13 Michael Waltrip
2003 #P14 Michael Waltrip's Car
2003 #P15 Michael Waltrip
2003 #P59 Michael Waltrip SST
Press Pass Stealth Samples
2003 #13 Michael Waltrip
2003 #14 Michael Waltrip's Car
2003 #15 Michael Waltrip

2003 #59 Michael Waltrip SST
2004 #X34 Michael Waltrip
2004 #X35 Michael Waltrip's Car
2004 #X36 Michael Waltrip
2004 #X84 Michael Waltrip SST
2004 #X98 Michael Waltrip SF
2005 #56 Michael Waltrip
2005 #59 Michael Waltrip's Car
2005 #62 Michael Waltrip
2005 #84 Michael Waltrip H
2005 #98 Michael Waltrip SF
Press Pass Stealth Stars
1998 #18 Michael Waltrip
Press Pass Stealth Stars Die Cuts
1998 #18 Michael Waltrip
Press Pass Stealth Supercharged
2003 #SC5 Michael Waltrip
Press Pass Stealth Synthesis
2008 #S8 Michael Waltrip
Press Pass Stealth X-Ray
2004 #34 Michael Waltrip
2004 #35 Michael Waltrip's Car
2004 #36 Michael Waltrip
2004 #84 Michael Waltrip SST
2004 #98 Michael Waltrip SF
2005 #X56 Michael Waltrip
2005 #X59 Michael Waltrip's Car
2005 #X62 Michael Waltrip
2005 #X84 Michael Waltrip H
2005 #X98 Michael Waltrip SF
Press Pass Techno-Retro
2000 #TR27 Michael Waltrip
Press Pass Torpedoes
1998 #ST12B Michael Waltrip's Car
Press Pass Torquers
1996 #36 Michael Waltrip
1996 #48 Michael Waltrip's Car
1996 #118 Michael Waltrip PRE
1997 #14 Michael Waltrip
1997 #38 Michael Waltrip's Car
1997 #63 Michael Waltrip's Car
1997 #78 Michael Waltrip
1997 #79 Michael Waltrip
1997 #93 M.Waltrip/David Pearson
1997 #100 Michael Waltrip
1997 #123 Michael Waltrip
Press Pass Trackside
2000 #5 Michael Waltrip
2001 #11 Michael Waltrip
2001 #44 Michael Waltrip's Car
2002 #12 Michael Waltrip
2002 #68 Michael Waltrip's Car
2002 #74 Michael Waltrip TM
2003 #30 Michael Waltrip
2003 #65 Michael Waltrip in Pits
2004 #30 Michael Waltrip
2004 #56 Michael Waltrip's Car HS
2004 #72 Dale Jr./M.Waltrip TM
2004 #110 Michael Waltrip F
2005 #58 Michael Waltrip's Car HS
2005 #89 Michael Waltrip GP
Press Pass Trackside Dialed In
2001 #D12 Michael Waltrip
2003 #DI12 Michael Waltrip
2004 #DI4 Michael Waltrip
2005 #DI4 Michael Waltrip
Press Pass Trackside Die Cuts
2000 #5 Michael Waltrip
2001 #11 Michael Waltrip
2001 #44 Michael Waltrip's Car
Press Pass Trackside Gold Holofoil
2003 #P30 Michael Waltrip
2003 #P65 Michael Waltrip's Crew
Press Pass Trackside Golden
2000 #5 Michael Waltrip
2001 #11 Michael Waltrip
2001 #44 Michael Waltrip's Car
2002 #G12 Michael Waltrip
2003 #G30 Michael Waltrip
2004 #G30 Michael Waltrip
2004 #G56 Michael Waltrip's Car HS
2004 #G72 D.Earnhardt Jr./M.Waltrip TM
2004 #G110 Michael Waltrip F
2005 #G58 Michael Waltrip's Car HS
2005 #G89 Michael Waltrip GP
Press Pass Trackside Hat Giveaway
2003 #PPH30 Michael Waltrip
2004 #PPH33 Michael Waltrip
2005 #PPH34 Michael Waltrip
Press Pass Trackside Hot Pass
2004 #HP18 Michael Waltrip
2005 #18 Michael Waltrip
Press Pass Trackside Hot Pass National
2004 #HP18 Michael Waltrip
2005 #18 Michael Waltrip
Press Pass Trackside Hot Pursuit
2003 #HP7 Michael Waltrip
2004 #HP3 Michael Waltrip
Press Pass Trackside License to Drive
2002 #35 Michael Waltrip
2003 #LD20 Michael Waltrip
Press Pass Trackside License to Drive Die Cuts
2002 #35 Michael Waltrip
Press Pass Trackside Mirror Image
2003 #MI9 Michael Waltrip
Press Pass Trackside Panorama
2000 #P5 Michael Waltrip
Press Pass Trackside Pit Stoppers Cars
2001 #PSC11 M.Waltrip's Car/200
2003 #PST12 Michael Waltrip
2004 #PST12 Michael Waltrip
2005 #PST8 Michael Waltrip
Press Pass Trackside Pit Stoppers Drivers
2001 #PSD11 Michael Waltrip/75
2003 #PSD12 Michael Waltrip
2004 #PSD12 Michael Waltrip
2005 #PSD8 Michael Waltrip
Press Pass Trackside Previews
2003 #30 Michael Waltrip
2004 #EB30 Michael Waltrip
2005 #89 Michael Waltrip GP
Press Pass Trackside Runnin n' Gunnin
2003 #RG9 Michael Waltrip
2004 #RG4 Michael Waltrip
Press Pass Trackside Samples
2002 #12 Michael Waltrip

2002 #68 Michael Waltrip's Car
2002 #74 Michael Waltrip TM
2003 #30 Michael Waltrip
2003 #65 Michael Waltrip in Pits
2004 #30 Michael Waltrip
2004 #56 Michael Waltrip's Car HS
2004 #72 D.Earnhardt Jr./M.Waltrip TM
2004 #110 Michael Waltrip F
2005 #58 Michael Waltrip's Car HS
2005 #89 Michael Waltrip GP
Press Pass Velocity
2004 #VC1 Michael Waltrip
2005 #V6 Michael Waltrip
Press Pass Victory Lane
1997 #VL9A Michael Waltrip
1997 #VL9B Michael Waltrip's Car
Press Pass Vintage
2002 #VN26 Michael Waltrip
Pro Set
1991 #60 Michael Waltrip's Car
1992 #23 Michael Waltrip
1992 #92 Michael Waltrip's Transporter
1992 #102 Michael Waltrip
1992 #111 Michael Waltrip's Car
1992 #178 Michael Waltrip's Car
Pro Set Maxwell House
1992 #20 Michael Waltrip
Pro Set Rudy Farms
1992 #13 Michael Waltrip
Race Sharks
1997 #12 Michael Waltrip
Race Sharks First Bite
1997 #12 Michael Waltrip
Race Sharks Great White
1997 #12 Michael Waltrip
Race Sharks Hammerhead
1997 #12 Michael Waltrip
Race Sharks Hammerhead First Bite
1997 #12 Michael Waltrip
Race Sharks Shark Attack
1997 #SA7 Michael Waltrip
Race Sharks Shark Attack First Bite
1997 #SA7 Michael Waltrip
Race Sharks Tiger Shark
1997 #12 Michael Waltrip
Race Sharks Tiger Shark First Bite
1997 #12 Michael Waltrip
Racer's Choice
1996 #11 Michael Waltrip
1996 #39 Michael Waltrip w/Car
1996 #78 Michael Waltrip's Car
1997 #21 Michael Waltrip
1997 #56 Michael Waltrip's Car
1997 #100 Michael Waltrip TR
Racer's Choice Artist's Proofs
1996 #11 Michael Waltrip
1996 #39 Michael Waltrip w/Car
1996 #78 Michael Waltrip's Car
Racer's Choice Showcase Series
1997 #21 Michael Waltrip
1997 #56 Michael Waltrip's Car
1997 #100 Michael Waltrip TR
Racer's Choice Speedway Collection
1996 #11 Michael Waltrip
1996 #39 Michael Waltrip w/Car
1996 #78 Michael Waltrip's Car
SB Motorsports
1997 #16 Michael Waltrip
1997 #52 Michael Waltrip's Car
1997 #90 Michael Waltrip
Score Board IQ
1997 #5 Michael Waltrip
1997 #44 Michael Waltrip's Car
Score Board Seven-Eleven Phone Cards
1997 #4 Michael Waltrip
Select
1995 #36 Michael Waltrip
1995 #48 Michael Waltrip's Car
1995 #113 D.Waltrip/M.Waltrip IB
Select Dream Machines
1995 #DM9 Michael Waltrip's Car
Select Flat Out
1995 #36 Michael Waltrip
1995 #48 Michael Waltrip's Car
1995 #113 D.Waltrip/M.Waltrip IB
Select Skills
1995 #SS12 Michael Waltrip
SkyBox
1994 #25 Darrell Waltrip/M.Waltrip Cars
SkyBox Profile
1997 #31 Michael Waltrip
1997 #69 Michael Waltrip's Car
SkyBox Profile Autographs
1997 #31 Michael Waltrip
SkyBox Profile Pace Setters
1997 #E7 Michael Waltrip
SP
1995 #23 Michael Waltrip CC
1995 #62 Michael Waltrip
1995 #103 Michael Waltrip's Car
1996 #21 Michael Waltrip
1996 #53 Michael Waltrip CC
1996 #75 Michael Waltrip RPM
1997 #21 Michael Waltrip 2F
1997 #63 Michael Waltrip's Car
1997 #99 Michael Waltrip
SP Authentic
1998 #21 Michael Waltrip
1998 #55 Michael Waltrip's Car
1999 #21 Michael Waltrip
1999 #59 Michael Waltrip's Car
2000 #26 Michael Waltrip
2000 #53 Michael Waltrip PER
SP Authentic Behind the Wheel
1998 #BW17 Michael Waltrip
SP Authentic Behind the Wheel Die Cuts
1998 #BW17 Michael Waltrip
SP Authentic Behind the Wheel Gold
1998 #BW17 Michael Waltrip
SP Authentic Overdrive
1999 #21 Michael Waltrip
1999 #59 Michael Waltrip CAR
SP Authentic Overdrive Gold
2000 #26 Michael Waltrip/7

2000 #53 Michael Waltrip PER/7

SP Authentic Overdrive Silver

2000 #26 Michael Waltrip
2000 #53 Michael Waltrip PER

SP Authentic Sign of the Times

1998 #S6 Michael Waltrip's Car

SP Die Cuts

1995 #23 Michael Waltrip
1995 #62 Michael Waltrip
1995 #103 Michael Waltrip's Car

SP Speed Merchants

1995 #SM30 Michael Waltrip

SP Speed Merchants Die Cuts

1995 #SM30 Michael Waltrip

SP Super Series

1997 #21 Michael Waltrip 2F
1997 #63 Michael Waltrip's Car
1997 #99 Michael Waltrip

Speedflix

1996 #8 Michael Waltrip
1996 #48 Michael Waltrip DT

Speedflix Artist Proof's

1996 #8 Michael Waltrip
1996 #48 Michael Waltrip DT

Speedflix ProMotion

1996 #5 Michael Waltrip

SPx

1996 #21 Michael Waltrip
1997 #21 Michael Waltrip

SPx Blue

1997 #21 Michael Waltrip

SPx Gold

1996 #21 Michael Waltrip
1997 #21 Michael Waltrip

SPx Silver

1997 #21 Michael Waltrip

Stove Top

1993 #6 Michael Waltrip

Super Shots Hendrick Motorsports

2001 #H3 Darrell Waltrip w/Michael

Super Shots Hendrick Motorsports Gold

2001 #HG3 Darrell Waltrip w/Michael

Super Shots Hendrick Motorsports Silver

2001 #HS3 Darrell Waltrip w/Michael

Traks

1991 #30 Michael Waltrip
1991 #75 Michael Waltrip
1992 #30 Michael Waltrip
1992 #75 Michael Waltrip
1993 #30 Michael Waltrip
1993 #125 Michael Waltrip's Transporter CL
1993 #186 Michael Waltrip
1994 #30 Michael Waltrip
1994 #49 Michael Waltrip's Car
1994 #154 Michael Waltrip
1995 #49 Michael Waltrip
1995 #69 Michael Waltrip
2007 #31 Michael Waltrip

Traks 5th Anniversary

1995 #31 Michael Waltrip
1995 #53 Michael Waltrip's Car

Traks 5th Anniversary Clear Contenders

1995 #C8 Michael Waltrip

Traks 5th Anniversary Gold

1995 #31 Michael Waltrip
1995 #53 Michael Waltrip's Car

Traks 5th Anniversary Jumbos

1995 #E8 Michael Waltrip

Traks 5th Anniversary Jumbos Gold

1995 #E8 Michael Waltrip

Traks Auto Value

1994 #7 Michael Waltrip
1995 #32 Michael Waltrip

Traks Corporate Cuts Driver

2007 #CCD14 Michael Waltrip

Traks Corporate Cuts Patch

2007 #CCD14 Michael Waltrip/12

Traks Corporate Cuts Team

2007 #CCT14 Michael Waltrip

Traks Driver's Seat

2007 #DS19 Michael Waltrip
2007 #DS19B Michael Waltrip VAR

Traks Driver's Seat National

2007 #DS19 Michael Waltrip

Traks First Run

1993 #30 Michael Waltrip
1993 #125 Michael Waltrip's Transporter CL
1993 #186 Michael Waltrip
1994 #30 Michael Waltrip
1994 #49 Michael Waltrip's Car
1994 #154 Michael Waltrip
1995 #49 Mike Waltrip
1995 #69 Michael Waltrip

Traks Gold

2007 #G31 Michael Waltrip

Traks Goody's

1992 #23 Michael Waltrip

Traks Holofoil

2007 #H31 Michael Waltrip

Traks Preferred Collector

1993 #1 Michael Waltrip

Traks Previews

2007 #EB31 Michael Waltrip

Traks Racing Machines

1992 #30 Michael Waltrip's Car
1992 #36 Michael Waltrip's Car
1992 #65 Dav.Allison/M.Waltrip Cars
1992 #72 Michael Waltrip's Transp.
1992 #83 Michael Waltrip's Car
1995 #RM15 Michael Waltrip's Car

Traks Racing Machines First Run

1995 #RM15 Michael Waltrip's Car

Traks Red

2007 #R31 Michael Waltrip

Traks Review and Preview

1996 #28 Michael Waltrip

Traks Review and Preview First Run

1996 #28 Michael Waltrip

Traks Review and Preview Magnets

1996 #28 Michael Waltrip

Traks Review and Preview Triple-Chase

1996 #TC5 Michael Waltrip

Traks Review and Preview Triple-Chase Gold

1996 #TC5 Michael Waltrip

Traks Review and Preview Triple-Chase Holofoil

1996 #TC5 Michael Waltrip

Traks Series Stars

1995 #SS13 Michael Waltrip

Traks Series Stars First Run

1995 #SS13 Michael Waltrip

Traks Team Sets

1992 #76 Michael Waltrip
1992 #77 Michael Waltrip/C.Rider
1992 #79 Michael Waltrip's Car
1992 #82 Michael Waltrip in Pits
1992 #84 Engine Room
1992 #90 Assembly Room
1992 #95 Michael Waltrip
1992 #99 Michael Waltrip's Transporter
1992 #100 Michael Waltrip's Car CL

Traks Trivia

1993 #30 Michael Waltrip

Ultra

1996 #44 Michael Waltrip
1996 #45 Michael Waltrip
1996 #46 Michael Waltrip's Car
1997 #37 Michael Waltrip
1997 #55 Michael Waltrip's Car

Ultra Autographs

1996 #37 Michael Waltrip

Ultra Boxed Set

1996 #12 Michael Waltrip

Ultra Inside Out

1997 #DC15 Michael Waltrip

Ultra Shoney's

1997 #13 Michael Waltrip

Ultra Update

1996 #33 Michael Waltrip
1996 #79 Michael Waltrip's Car
1996 #88 M.Waltrip/E.Wood/L.Wood
1997 #15 Michael Waltrip
1997 #85 Michael Waltrip's Car

Ultra Update Autographs

1997 #15 Michael Waltrip

Ultra Update Double Trouble

1997 #DT5 Michael Waltrip

Upper Deck

1995 #9 Michael Waltrip
1995 #52 Michael Waltrip with Car
1995 #77 Michael Waltrip's Car
1995 #145 Michael Waltrip's Car
1995 #209 Michael Waltrip
1995 #252 Michael Waltrip SD
1996 #28 Michael Waltrip
1996 #68 Michael Waltrip SB
1996 #100 Michael Waltrip PP
1996 #108 Michael Waltrip PP

Upper Deck Autographs

1995 #209 Michael Waltrip

Upper Deck Gold Signature/Electric Gold

1995 #9 Michael Waltrip
1995 #52 Michael Waltrip with Car
1995 #77 Michael Waltrip's Car
1995 #145 Michael Waltrip's Car
1995 #209 Michael Waltrip
1995 #252 Michael Waltrip SD

Upper Deck MVP

2000 #27 Michael Waltrip
2000 #37 Michael Waltrip
2000 #80 Michael Waltrip's Car

Upper Deck MVP Gold Script

2000 #27 Michael Waltrip
2000 #37 Michael Waltrip
2000 #80 Michael Waltrip

Upper Deck MVP Silver Script

2000 #27 Michael Waltrip
2000 #37 Michael Waltrip
2000 #80 Michael Waltrip

Upper Deck MVP Super Script

2000 #27 Michael Waltrip/7
2000 #37 Michael Waltrip/7
2000 #80 Michael Waltrip's Car/7

Upper Deck Racing

2000 #27 Michael Waltrip

Upper Deck Road To The Cup

1996 #RC11 Michael Waltrip
1996 #RC60 Michael Waltrip's Car
1996 #RC96 Michael Waltrip
1997 #16 Michael Waltrip
1997 #58 Michael Waltrip's Car
1997 #113 Michael Waltrip's Trans.
1998 #21 Michael Waltrip
1998 #53 Michael Waltrip's Car
1998 #106 Michael Waltrip

Upper Deck Road To The Cup Autographs

1996 #H11 Michael Waltrip

Upper Deck Silver Signature/Electric Silver

1995 #9 Michael Waltrip
1995 #52 Michael Waltrip with Car
1995 #77 Michael Waltrip's Car
1995 #145 Michael Waltrip's Car
1995 #209 Michael Waltrip
1995 #252 Michael Waltrip SD

Upper Deck Victory Circle

1997 #21 Michael Waltrip
1997 #71 Michael Waltrip's Car
1998 #21 Michael Waltrip
1998 #66 Michael Waltrip's Car
1998 #133 Michael Waltrip
1999 #28 Michael Waltrip
1999 #69 Michael Waltrip's Car
2000 #6 Michael Waltrip

Upper Deck Victory Circle Exclusives Level 1 Silver

2000 #6 Michael Waltrip

Upper Deck Victory Circle Exclusives Level 2 Gold

2000 #6 Michael Waltrip/7

Upper Deck Victory Circle Point Leaders

1998 #PL18 Michael Waltrip

Upper Deck Victory Circle Signature Collection

1999 #MW Michael Waltrip

Upper Deck Victory Circle UD Exclusives

1999 #28 Michael Waltrip
1999 #69 Michael Waltrip

Upper Deck Virtual Velocity

1996 #VV14 Michael Waltrip

Upper Deck Virtual Velocity Gold

1996 #VV14 Michael Waltrip

VIP

1994 #36 Michael Waltrip
1994 #49 Michael Waltrip w/Car
1995 #30 Michael Waltrip
1996 #29 Michael Waltrip
1997 #25 Michael Waltrip
1998 #27 Michael Waltrip
1999 #27 Michael Waltrip
2001 #13 Michael Waltrip
2001 #19 Michael Waltrip SM
2001 #42 Michael Waltrip AS
2003 #18 Michael Waltrip
2003 #19 Michael Waltrip SG
2003 #35 Michael Waltrip AS
2004 #18 Michael Waltrip
2004 #29 Michael Waltrip's Car R
2007 #31 Michael Waltrip
2007 #44 Michael Waltrip Racing AN

VIP Autographs

1996 #25 Michael Waltrip

VIP Cool Blue

1995 #30 Michael Waltrip

VIP Driver's Choice

2001 #DC8 Michael Waltrip
2003 #DC9 Michael Waltrip
2004 #DC6 Michael Waltrip

VIP Driver's Choice Die Cuts

2003 #DC9 Michael Waltrip
2004 #DC6 Michael Waltrip

VIP Driver's Choice National

2003 #DC9 Michael Waltrip

VIP Driver's Choice Precious Metal

2001 #DC8 Michael Waltrip

VIP Driver's Choice Transparent

2001 #DC8 Michael Waltrip

VIP Emerald Proofs

1995 #30 Michael Waltrip
1996 #29 Michael Waltrip

VIP Explosives

1997 #25 Michael Waltrip
1998 #27 Michael Waltrip
1999 #X27 Michael Waltrip
2001 #13 Michael Waltrip
2001 #19 Michael Waltrip SM
2001 #42 Michael Waltrip AS
2003 #X18 Michael Waltrip
2003 #X19 Michael Waltrip SG
2003 #X35 Michael Waltrip AS

VIP Explosives Lasers

1999 #27 Michael Waltrip
2001 #LX13 Michael Waltrip
2001 #LX19 Michael Waltrip SM
2001 #LX42 Michael Waltrip AS

VIP Gear Gallery

2007 #GG8 Michael Waltrip

VIP Gear Gallery Transparent

2007 #GG8 Michael Waltrip

VIP Get A Grip Drivers

2007 #GGD3 Michael Waltrip

VIP Get A Grip Teams

2007 #GGT3 Michael Waltrip

VIP Head Gear

1996 #HG9 Michael Waltrip
1997 #HG9 Michael Waltrip
2004 #HG12 Michael Waltrip

VIP Head Gear Die Cuts

1996 #HG9 Michael Waltrip
1997 #HG9 Michael Waltrip

VIP Head Gear Transparent

2004 #HG12 Michael Waltrip

VIP Lap Leaders

2003 #LL7 Michael Waltrip
2004 #LL5 Michael Waltrip

VIP Lap Leaders National

2003 #LL7 Michael Waltrip

VIP Lap Leaders Transparent

2003 #LL7 Michael Waltrip
2004 #LL5 Michael Waltrip

VIP Lap Leaders Transparent LTD

2003 #LL7 Michael Waltrip

VIP Laser Explosive

2003 #LX18 Michael Waltrip
2003 #LX19 Michael Waltrip SG
2003 #LX35 Michael Waltrip AS

VIP Making the Show

2000 #MS22 Michael Waltrip
2001 #7 Michael Waltrip
2003 #MS6 Michael Waltrip
2004 #MS9 Michael Waltrip

VIP Mile Masters

2001 #MM3 Michael Waltrip
2003 #MM12Michael Waltrip

VIP Mile Masters National

2003 #MM12Michael Waltrip

VIP Mile Masters Precious Metal

2001 #MM3 Michael Waltrip

VIP Mile Masters Transparent

2001 #MM3 Michael Waltrip
2003 #MM12Michael Waltrip

VIP Mile Masters Transparent LTD

2003 #MM12Michael Waltrip

VIP Oil Slicks

1997 #25 Michael Waltrip

VIP Pedal To The Metal

2007 #PM4 Michael Waltrip

VIP Previews

2003 #18 Michael Waltrip
2003 #19 Michael Waltrip SG
2003 #35 Michael Waltrip AS
2004 #EB18 Michael Waltrip
2004 #EB29 Michael Waltrip's Car R
2007 #EB31 Michael Waltrip

VIP Promos

1995 #3G Michael Waltrip Gold
1995 #3R Michael Waltrip Red

VIP Red Hot

1995 #30 Michael Waltrip

VIP Samples

2003 #18 Michael Waltrip
2003 #19 Michael Waltrip SG
2003 #35 Michael Waltrip AS
2004 #18 Michael Waltrip
2004 #29 Michael Waltrip's Car R

VIP Sheet Metal Cars

2001 #SC10 Michael Waltrip's Car

VIP Sheet Metal Drivers

2001 #SD10 Michael Waltrip

VIP Solos

1998 #27 Michael Waltrip

VIP Sunday Best

2007 #SB25 Michael Waltrip

VIP Tin

2003 #CT18 Michael Waltrip
2003 #CT19 Michael Waltrip SG
2003 #CT35 Michael Waltrip AS

VIP Torquers

1996 #29 Michael Waltrip

VIP Tradin' Paint Bronze

2004 #TPT18 Michael Waltrip

VIP Tradin' Paint Cars

2003 #TPT15 Michael Waltrip's Car

VIP Tradin' Paint Drivers

2003 #TPD15 Michael Waltrip

VIP Tradin' Paint Gold

2004 #TPD18 Michael Waltrip

VIP Tradin' Paint Silver

2004 #TPD18 Michael Waltrip

VIP War Paint

1996 #WP10 Michael Waltrip's Car

VIP War Paint Gold

1996 #WP10 Michael Waltrip's Car

Viper

1996 #16 Michael Waltrip
1996 #59 Michael Waltrip
1997 #10 Michael Waltrip
1997 #39 Michael Waltrip

Viper Black Mamba

1996 #16 Michael Waltrip
1996 #59 Michael Waltrip

Viper Black Mamba First Strike

1996 #16 Michael Waltrip
1996 #59 Michael Waltrip

Viper Black Racer

1997 #10 Michael Waltrip
1997 #39 Michael Waltrip

Viper Black Racer First Strike

1997 #10 Michael Waltrip
1997 #39 Michael Waltrip

Viper Copperhead Die Cuts

1996 #16 Michael Waltrip
1996 #59 Michael Waltrip

Viper Copperhead Die Cuts First Strike

1996 #16 Michael Waltrip
1996 #59 Michael Waltrip

Viper First Strike

1996 #16 Michael Waltrip
1996 #59 Michael Waltrip
1997 #10 Michael Waltrip
1997 #39 Michael Waltrip

Viper Green Mamba

1996 #16 Michael Waltrip
1996 #59 Michael Waltrip

Viper Red Cobra

1996 #16 Michael Waltrip
1996 #59 Michael Waltrip

Viper Sidewinder

1997 #S7 Michael Waltrip

Viper Sidewinder First Strike

1997 #S7 Michael Waltrip

Visions

1996 #115 Michael Waltrip

Visions *

1996 #115 Michael Waltrip

Visions Signings

1996 #93 Michael Waltrip

Visions Signings *

1996 #93 Michael Waltrip

Visions Signings Autographs Silver

1996 #77 Michael Waltrip/285

Visions Signings Autographs Silver *

1996 #93A Michael Waltrip/285

Wheels

1998 #30 Michael Waltrip
1998 #59 Michael Waltrip
1999 #36 Michael Waltrip

Wheels 50th Anniversary

1998 #A15 Michael Waltrip

Wheels American Thunder

2003 #21 Michael Waltrip
2003 #33 Michael Waltrip DT
2003 #39 Michael Waltrip CC
2003 #47 M.Waltrip's Transporter
2004 #27 Michael Waltrip
2004 #36 Michael Waltrip's Rig Rt. 66
2004 #40 Michael Waltrip AS
2004 #49 Michael Waltrip's Car HR
2004 #55 Michael Waltrip DT
2004 #67 Michael Waltrip RR
2004 #81 Michael Waltrip CC
2007 #36 Michael Waltrip
2007 #69 Michael Waltrip BP

Wheels American Thunder American Eagle

2004 #AE12 Michael Waltrip

Wheels American Thunder American Muscle

2003 #AM11 Michael Waltrip

Wheels American Thunder Autographed Hat Instant Winner

2007 #AH41 Michael Waltrip

Wheels American Thunder Born On

2003 #BO21 Michael Waltrip
2003 #BO33 Michael Waltrip DT
2003 #BO39 Michael Waltrip CC
2003 #BO47 NAPA Transporter

Wheels American Thunder Cool Threads

2004 #CT15 Michael Waltrip
2007 #CT2 Michael Waltrip

Wheels American Thunder Cup Quest

2004 #CQ9 Michael Waltrip

Wheels American Thunder Golden Eagle

2004 #AE12 Michael Waltrip

Wheels American Thunder Head to Toe

2003 #HT9 Michael Waltrip
2007 #HT1 Michael Waltrip

Wheels American Thunder Heads Up Manufacturer

2003 #HUM23 Michael Waltrip

Wheels American Thunder Heads Up Team

2003 #HUT21 Michael Waltrip/60

Wheels American Thunder Heads Up Winston

2003 #HUW23 Michael Waltrip

Wheels American Thunder Holofoil

2003 #P21 Michael Waltrip
2003 #P33 Michael Waltrip DT
2003 #P39 Michael Waltrip CC
2003 #P47 NAPA Transporter

Wheels American Thunder Post Mark

2003 #PM18 Michael Waltrip
2004 #PM9 Michael Waltrip

Wheels American Thunder Previews

2003 #21 Michael Waltrip
2003 #33 Michael Waltrip DT
2004 #EB27 Michael Waltrip
2004 #EB36 Michael Waltrip Rt. 66
2004 #EB40 Michael Waltrip AS
2007 #EB36 Michael Waltrip

Wheels American Thunder Pushin Pedal

2003 #PP9 Michael Waltrip

Wheels American Thunder Pushin' Pedal

2007 #PP5 Michael Waltrip

Wheels American Thunder Rookie Thunder

2003 #RT35 Michael Waltrip

Wheels American Thunder Samples

2003 #P21 Michael Waltrip
2003 #P33 Michael Waltrip DT
2003 #P39 Michael Waltrip CC
2003 #P47 NAPA Transporter
2004 #27 Michael Waltrip
2004 #36 Michael Waltrip's Rig Rt. 66
2004 #40 Michael Waltrip AS
2004 #49 Michael Waltrip's Car HR
2004 #55 Michael Waltrip DT
2004 #67 Michael Waltrip RR
2004 #81 Michael Waltrip CC

Wheels American Thunder Starting Grid

2007 #SG10 Michael Waltrip

Wheels American Thunder Thunder Road

2003 #TR10 Michael Waltrip
2004 #TR6 Michael Waltrip
2007 #TR2 Michael Waltrip

Wheels American Thunder Thunder Strokes

2007 #42 Michael Waltrip

Wheels American Thunder Thunder Strokes Press Plates Black

2007 #42 Michael Waltrip

Wheels American Thunder Thunder Strokes Press Plates Cyan

2007 #42 Michael Waltrip

Wheels American Thunder Thunder Strokes Press Plates Magenta

2007 #42 Michael Waltrip

Wheels American Thunder Thunder Strokes Press Plates Yellow

2007 #42 Michael Waltrip

Wheels American Thunder Triple Hat

2003 #TH5 Michael Waltrip
2004 #TH24 Michael Waltrip
2007 #TH31 Michael Waltrip

Wheels Autographs

1998 #9 Michael Waltrip
1999 #24 Michael Waltrip/200
2003 #60 Michael Waltrip
2004 #68 Michael Waltrip AT
2005 #61 Michael Waltrip
2008 #35 Michael Waltrip NC HG

Wheels Autographs Press Plates Black

2008 #35 Michael Waltrip NC HG

Wheels Autographs Press Plates Cyan

2008 #35 Michael Waltrip NC HG

Wheels Autographs Press Plates Magenta

2008 #35 Michael Waltrip NC HG

Wheels Autographs Press Plates Yellow

2008 #35 Michael Waltrip NC HG

Wheels Golden

1998 #30 Michael Waltrip
1998 #59 Michael Waltrip
1999 #36 Michael Waltrip

Wheels Green Flags

1998 #GF18 Michael Waltrip's Car

Wheels High Gear

1994 #11 Michael Waltrip
1995 #9 Michael Waltrip
1995 #84 Michael Waltrip's Car
1998 #18 Michael Waltrip
1998 #68 Michael Waltrip's Car
1999 #17 Michael Waltrip
1999 #43 Michael Waltrip
2000 #27 Michael Waltrip
2000 #68 Michael Waltrip
2002 #27 Michael Waltrip
2002 #60 Michael Waltrip HL
2003 #30 Michael Waltrip
2004 #27 Michael Waltrip
2004 #66 Michael Waltrip HL
2005 #8 Michael Waltrip
2005 #60 Michael Waltrip's Car
2005 #76 Michael Waltrip IF
2008 #27 Michael Waltrip

Wheels High Gear Autographs

1998 #23 Michael Waltrip/250
1999 #26 Michael Waltrip/350
2000 #28 Michael Waltrip
2002 #58 Michael Waltrip

Wheels High Gear Blue Hawaii SCDA Promos

2003 #30 Michael Waltrip

Wheels High Gear Day One

1995 #9 Michael Waltrip
1995 #84 Michael Waltrip's Car

Wheels High Gear Day One Gold

1995 #9 Michael Waltrip
1995 #84 Michael Waltrip's Car

Wheels High Gear Driven

2008 #DR16 Michael Waltrip

Wheels High Gear Final Standings

2008 #F27 Michael Waltrip/44

Wheels High Gear First Gear

1998 #14 Michael Waltrip
1998 #68 Michael Waltrip's Car
1999 #17 Michael Waltrip
1999 #43 Michael Waltrip
2000 #27 Michael Waltrip
2000 #68 Michael Waltrip
2002 #27 Michael Waltrip
2002 #60 Michael Waltrip HL
2003 #F30 Michael Waltrip

Wheels High Gear Flag Chasers Black

2004 #FC4 Michael Waltrip

Wheels High Gear Flag Chasers Blue

2004 #FC4 Michael Waltrip

Wheels High Gear Flag Chasers Checkered

2004 #FC4 Michael Waltrip

Wheels High Gear Flag Chasers Green

2004 #FC4 Michael Waltrip

Wheels High Gear Flag Chasers Red

2004 #FC4 Michael Waltrip

Wheels High Gear Flag Chasers White

2004 #FC4 Michael Waltrip

Wheels High Gear Flag Chasers Yellow

2004 #FC4 Michael Waltrip

Wheels High Gear Flag to Flag

2005 #FF27 Michael Waltrip

Wheels High Gear Gear Jammers

1998 #GJ10 Michael Waltrip

Wheels High Gear Gear Shifters

2000 #GS25 Michael Waltrip

Wheels High Gear Gold

1994 #11 Michael Waltrip
1995 #9 Michael Waltrip
1995 #84 Michael Waltrip's Car

Wheels High Gear High Groove

2002 #HG27 Michael Waltrip
2003 #HG27 Michael Waltrip
2004 #HG27 Michael Waltrip

Wheels High Gear Hot Treads

2003 #HT0 Michael Waltrip

Wheels High Gear Machine

2004 #MM4B Michael Waltrip
2005 #MMB1 Michael Waltrip

Wheels High Gear Man

2004 #MM4A Michael Waltrip
2005 #MMA1 Michael Waltrip

Wheels High Gear Mega Gold

1994 #MG12 Michael Waltrip

Wheels High Gear MPH

1998 #14 Michael Waltrip
1998 #68 Michael Waltrip's Car
1999 #15 Michael Waltrip
2000 #27 Michael Waltrip
2000 #68 Michael Waltrip
2002 #27 Michael Waltrip
2002 #60 Michael Waltrip HL
2003 #M30 Michael Waltrip
2004 #M27 Michael Waltrip
2004 #M66 Michael Waltrip HL
2005 #M8 Michael Waltrip
2005 #M60 Michael Waltrip's Car
2005 #M76 Michael Waltrip IF
2008 #M27 Michael Waltrip

Wheels High Gear Previews

2003 #30 Michael Waltrip
2004 #27 Michael Waltrip
2008 #EB27 Michael Waltrip

Wheels High Gear Previews Green

2005 #EB8 Michael Waltrip

Wheels High Gear Previews Silver

2005 #EB76 Michael Waltrip IF

Wheels High Gear Samples

2003 #30 Michael Waltrip
2004 #27 Michael Waltrip
2004 #66 Michael Waltrip HL
2005 #8 Michael Waltrip
2005 #60 Michael Waltrip's Car
2005 #76 Michael Waltrip IF

Wheels High Gear Sunday Sensation

2004 #SS1 Michael Waltrip

Wheels Runnin and Gunnin

1999 #RG10 Michael Waltrip

Wheels Runnin and Gunnin Foils

1999 #RG10 Michael Waltrip

Wheels Solos

1999 #36 Michael Waltrip

Zenith

1995 #29 Michael Waltrip HG
1995 #54 Michael Waltrip's Transporter
1996 #13 Michael Waltrip
1996 #49 Michael Waltrip's Car HV
1996 #62 Michael Waltrip S

Zenith Artist Proofs

1996 #13 Michael Waltrip RP
1996 #49 Michael Waltrip's Car HV
1996 #62 Michael Waltrip S

Zenith Highlights

1996 #10 Michael Waltrip

Zenith Z-Team

1995 #7 Michael Waltrip

Alphabetical Die-Cast Checklist

Biffle, Greg

Action Racing Collectables 1:24
2003 #7 Kleenex Wolfman CW Bank/240
2003 #7 Kleenex Wolfman/1572
Action Racing Collectables 1:64
2008 #16 3M
Action Racing Collectables Platinum 1:2
2008 #16 3M/2928
Action/RCCA 1:24
2003 #7 Kleenex Wolfman/300
2006 #16 National Guard/150
2006 #16 National Guard Color Chrome/100
Action/RCCA Elite 1:24
2003 #7 Kleenex Wolfman/300
2006 #16 National Guard/200
2006 #16 National Guard Color Chrome/100
2006 #16 National Guard Platinum/4
Hot Wheels Alternative Paint Scheme 1:6
2005 #16 Post-It
Hot Wheels Race Day 1:24
2005 #16 National Guard
Hot Wheels Race Day 1:64
2005 #16 National Guard
Hot Wheels Racing 1:24
2001 #60 Grainger
2003 #16 Grainger
Hot Wheels Racing Artist Collection 1:2
2004 #16 Grainger
Hot Wheels Racing Artist Collection 1:6
2004 #16 Grainger
Hot Wheels Racing Goodyear Showcase 1:6
2004 #16 National Guard/15,000
Hot Wheels Racing Justice League 1:24
2004 #16 Flash
2004 #60 Flash
Hot Wheels Racing Justice League 1:64
2004 #16 Flash
2004 #60 Flash
Hot Wheels Racing Justice League Thunde
2004 #16 Flash
Hot Wheels Racing Justice League w/Figu
2004 #16 Flash
Hot Wheels Racing Pit Board 1:64
2001 #60 Grainger
Hot Wheels Racing Pit Cruisers 1:64
2004 #16 Grainger
Hot Wheels Racing Race Day 1:64
2003 #16 Grainger
Hot Wheels Racing Recreational Vehicles
2003 #16 Grainger
Hot Wheels Racing Roush Commemorative 1
2001 #60 Grainger
Hot Wheels Racing Sticker 1:64
2002 #60 Grainger
Hot Wheels Racing Test Track 1:24
2004 #16 Grainger
Hot Wheels Racing Test Track 1:64
2004 #16 Grainger
Hot Wheels Racing Treasure Hunt 1:64
2003 #16 Grainger 7
2003 #21 R.Rudd/Motorcraft 10
Hot Wheels Racing Wrenchin' and Racin'
2003 #16 Grainger
Hot Wheels Team Transporters 1:64
2004 #16 Grainger
2004 #16 National Guard
Hot Wheels Transporters 1:64
2002 #60 Grainger
Hot Wheels Victory Lane Transporters 1:
2004 #16 Grainger
Motorsports Authentics Driver's Select
2007 #16 3M Finishmast/60*
2007 #16 3M Coast Guard American Heroes/2568
2007 #16 3M Blue Tape/600*
2007 #16 3M/2100*
2007 #16 Jackson Hewitt/700*
2007 #16 Dish Network COT/700*
2007 #16 Ameriquest/3000*
2007 #16 Aflac COT/1086*
2007 #16 Ameriquest COT/700*
2007 #16 3M Coast Guard American Heroes
2007 #16 Jackson Hewitt
2007 #16 Ameriquest
Motorsports Authentics Owner's Elite 1:
2007 #16 3M Coast Guard/504*
2007 #16 Ameriquest/708*
2007 #16 3M Coast Guard/504*
Motorsports Authentics Owner's Elite Tr
2007 #16 3M Coast Guard American Heroes/100*
2007 #16 Ameriquest/408*
Motorsports Authentics Pit Stop 1:64
2007 #16 3M Coast Guard American Heroes
2007 #16 3M
2007 #16 Jackson Hewitt
2007 #16 Ameriquest
Motorsports Authentics QVC For Race Fan
2007 #16 Ameriquest Chrome/96
Racing Champions 1:24
1999 #50 Grainger SuperTruck Promo
2000 #50 Grainger SuperTruck Promo
2005 #66 Royal Office Products Promo
2006 #66 Cub Cadet Promo
Racing Champions 1:64
2005 #66 Royal Office Products Promo
Racing Champions 5-Pack 1:64
2000 #NNO 86.SC/43.JH/24.JS/50.GB/2
Racing Champions SuperTrucks 1:24
1998 #50 Grainger
Racing Champions SuperTrucks Gold 1:24
1998 #50 Grainger
Racing Champions Ultra 1:24
2005 #66 Duraflame
Racing Champions Ultra 1:64
2005 #66 Duraflame
RCCA Club 1:24
2008 #16 3M/150
RCCA Elite 1:24
2008 #16 3M/300
2008 #16 3M Platinum/25
2008 #16 3M White Gold/50
Team Caliber First Choice 1:24
2003 #16 Grainger/250
2004 #16 National Guard/250
Team Caliber First Choice Beckett 1:24
2004 #16 Flash AU/1
2004 #60 Flash AU/1
Team Caliber Owners Series 1:24
2001 #60 Grainger/1960
2002 #60 Grainger/3120
2002 #60 Grainger Red Chrome BGN Champ/1200
2003 #9 Oreo/1200
2003 #16 Grainger 1st Win
2003 #16 Grainger/5004
2004 #16 Travelodge
2004 #16 Jackson-Hewitt
2004 #16 Subway
2004 #16 National Guard/3200
2004 #16 Flash/3120
2004 #16 Coke C2/2400
2004 #60 Flash/2400
2004 #60 Charter/2400
2005 #16 Post-It
2005 #16 Subway
2005 #16 Charter Michigan Raced
2005 #16 Jackson-Hewitt
2005 #16 National Guard/600
2005 #66 USPS
Team Caliber Owner's Series 1:24
2006 #16 National Guard/2400
Team Caliber Owners Series 1:64
2002 #60 Grainger/5004
2003 #9 Oreo
2003 #16 Grainger 1st Win
2003 #16 Grainger/5004
2004 #16 National Guard
2004 #60 Charter
Team Caliber Owners Series Banks 1:24
2001 #60 Grainger/756
2002 #60 Grainger/228
2003 #9 Oreo/180
2003 #16 Grainger/300
Team Caliber Owners Series Dark Chrome
2002 #60 Grainger/354
2003 #9 Oreo/180
2003 #16 Grainger 1st Win
2003 #16 Grainger/756
Team Caliber Owners Series Gold 1:24
2001 #60 Grainger/756
Team Caliber Owners Series Pearl Chrome
2004 #16 Jackson-Hewitt
2004 #16 Subway
2004 #16 Travelodge
2004 #16 National Guard/300
2004 #16 Flash/504
2004 #16 Coke C2 Red Chrome/250
2004 #60 Flash
2004 #60 Charter/180
Team Caliber Owners Series Steel 1:24
2001 #60 Grainger/756
Team Caliber Owners Series Transporters
2003 #16 Grainger/1200
2004 #16 National Guard
2004 #16 Flash
2004 #60 Flash
Team Caliber Pit Stop 1:18
2004 #16 National Guard
Team Caliber Pit Stop 1:24
2002 #60 Grainger/2400
2003 #9 Oreo
2003 #16 Grainger 1st Win
2003 #16 Grainger
2004 #16 Travelodge
2004 #16 Subway
2004 #16 National Guard
2004 #16 Jackson-Hewitt
2004 #16 Flash
2004 #16 Coke C2
2004 #60 Flash
2004 #60 Charter
2005 #16 Subway
2005 #16 Post-It
2005 #16 National Guard
2005 #66 USPS promo in window box
2006 #16 Subway
2006 #16 National Guard
2006 #16 Jackson Hewitt
2006 #16 Ameriquest
Team Caliber Pit Stop 1:64
2001 #60 Grainger
2002 #60 Grainger/7560
2003 #9 Oreo
2003 #16 Grainger 1st Win
2003 #16 Grainger
2004 #16 Flash
2004 #16 Coke C2
2004 #16 Travelodge
2004 #16 Subway
2004 #16 National Guard
2004 #16 Jackson-Hewitt
2004 #60 Flash
2004 #60 Charter
2005 #16 Jackson-Hewitt
2005 #16 Subway
2005 #16 Post-It
2005 #16 National Guard
2005 #66 USPS
2006 #16 National Guard
2006 #16 iLevel Weyerhaeuser
2006 #16 Jackson Hewitt
2006 #16 Ameriquest
Team Caliber Pit Stop Transporters 1:64
2003 #16 Grainger
2004 #16 National Guard
2004 #16 Flash
2004 #60 Flash
Team Caliber Preferred 1:24
2001 #60 Grainger Mac Tools/3000
2001 #60 Grainger/5004
2002 #60 Grainger/2340
2003 #9 Oreo/4020
2003 #16 Grainger 1st Win
2003 #16 Grainger/10,008
2004 #16 Jackson-Hewitt
2004 #16 Subway
2004 #16 Travelodge
2004 #16 National Guard/10,080
2004 #16 Flash/3120
2004 #16 Coke C2/10,080
2004 #60 Flash/3120
2004 #60 Charter/10,080
2005 #16 Jackson-Hewitt
2005 #16 Subway
2005 #16 Post-It/3120
2005 #16 National Guard/1800
2005 #16 Charter Michigan Win/1800
2005 #66 USPS/1800
2006 #16 Subway/2508
2006 #16 National Guard
2006 #16 Jackson Hewitt/2700
2006 #16 Ameriquest Soaring Dreams/3000
2006 #16 Ameriquest
Team Caliber Preferred Copper 1:24
2006 #16 Ameriquest
2006 #16 Subway/360
2006 #16 National Guard
Team Caliber Preferred Nickel 1:24
2005 #16 National Guard/180
Team Caliber Promos 1:24
2002 #60 Grainger/1960
Team Caliber Promos 1:64
2004 #16 Jackson Hewitt
2005 #16 National Guard in window box
2005 #66 USPS in window box
2006 #66 Cub Cadet in window box
Team Caliber Pull Backs 1:87
2002 #16 Grainger
Team Caliber/Motorworks Model Kits 1:18
2004 #16 National Guard
Team Caliber/Motorworks Model Kits 1:24
2003 #16 Grainger
Winner's Circle 1:24
2006 #16 National Guard
2007 #16 Ameriquest
Winner's Circle 1:87
2006 #16 National Guard
2007 #16 Ameriquest
Winner's Circle American Heroes 1:87
2007 #16 3M Coast Guard American Heroes
2007 #NNO American Heroes 9-car set
2007 #NNO 8.Dale Jr./Camo/ 16.Biffle/3M National Guard 88.Huffman/Navy 3-car set
Winner's Circle American Heroes Hood 1:
2007 #16 3M Coast Guard AH
Winner's Circle Autographed Hood 1:64
2006 #16 National Guard
Winner's Circle Number Magnet 1:64
2008 #16 3M
Winner's Circle Pit Pass 1:64
2007 #16 Ameriquest
Winner's Circle Schedule Hood 1:64
2007 #16 Ameriquest
Winner's Circle Victory Lane Hoods 1:64
2007 #16 Aflac Kansas Raced

Bowyer, Clint

Action Performance 1:24
2005 #2 Timberland
Action Racing Collectables 1:24
2004 #21 Reese's GM Dealers/144
2004 #21 Reese's/1008
2005 #2 AC Delco CW Bank/144
2005 #2 Timberland/684
2005 #2 AC Delco/2148
2005 #2 AC Delco Chris Cagle/816
2005 #2 AC Delco Chris Cagle GM Dealers/156
2006 #2 AC Delco/2052
2006 #2 AC Delco CW Bank/144
2006 #2 AC Delco GM Dealers/504
2006 #7 Jack Daniel's/4488
2006 #7 Jack Daniel's GM Dealers/760
2006 #7 Jack Daniel's QVC/288
2006 #7 Jack Daniel's Country Cocktails/3504
2006 #7 Jack Daniel's Country Cocktails GM Dealers/504
2006 #7 Jack Daniel's Directv/2328
2006 #7 Jack Daniel's Directv GM Dealers/456
2006 #7 Jack Daniel's Happy B-Day/876
2006 #7 Jack Daniel's Happy B-Day GM Dealers/372
2006 #7 Jack Daniel's Sopranos/2580
2006 #7 Jack Daniel's Texas/600
2006 #7 Jack Daniel's Texas GM Dealers/504
Action Racing Collectables Platinum 1:2
2008 #7 Jack Daniel's/10,740
Action/RCCA 1:24
2004 #21 Reese's/144
2005 #2 AC Delco Chris Cagle/144
2005 #2 AC Delco/288
2006 #2 AC Delco/144
2006 #7 Jack Daniel's Country Cocktails/250
2006 #7 Jack Daniel's Happy B-Day/250
2006 #7 Jack Daniel's Texas/200
2006 #7 Sopranos/277
2006 #7 Directv/277
2006 #7 Jack Daniel's/222
Action/RCCA Elite 1:24
2005 #2 AC Delco Chris Cagle/144
2006 #2 AC Delco Platinum/2
2006 #2 AC Delco/144
2006 #7 Jack Daniel's Country Cocktails/250
2006 #7 Jack Daniel's White Gold/25
2006 #7 Jack Daniel's Platinum/6
2006 #7 Jack Daniel's/333
2006 #7 Directv White Gold/25
2006 #7 Directv Platinum/5
2006 #7 Directv/277
2006 #7 Jack Daniel's Texas White Gold/25
2006 #7 Jack Daniel's Texas Platinum/5
2006 #7 Jack Daniel's Texas/250
2006 #7 Jack Daniel's Sopranos White Gold/25
2006 #7 Jack Daniel's Sopranos Platinum/5
2006 #7 Jack Daniel's Sopranos/277
2006 #7 Jack Daniel's Happy B-Day White Gold/25
2006 #7 Jack Daniel's Happy B-Day Platinum/5
2006 #7 Jack Daniel's Happy B-Day/203
2006 #7 Jack Daniel's Country Cocktails White Gold/25
2006 #7 Jack Daniel's Country Cocktails Platinum/5
Motorsports Authentics Driver's Select
2007 #2 BB&T/2176*
2007 #2 BB&T/72
2007 #7 Jack Daniel's COT New Hamshire Raced/1224*
2007 #7 Jack Daniel's COT/3448*
2007 #7 Jack Daniel's/5412*
2007 #7 Directv/708*
2007 #7 Jack Daniel's COT/696
2007 #7 Jack Daniel's/1200
2007 #7 Directv/180
Motorsports Authentics Owner's Elite 1:
2007 #7 Jack Daniel's COT White Gold/50*
2007 #7 Jack Daniel's COT Platinum/25
2007 #7 Jack Daniel's COT/504
2007 #7 Jack Daniel's White Gold/50*
2007 #7 Jack Daniel's Platinum/25
2007 #7 Jack Daniel's/504*
Motorsports Authentics Owner's Elite Tr
2007 #7 Jack Daniels/1068*
Motorsports Authentics QVC For Race Fan
2007 #7 Jack Daniel's Copper/108
2007 #7 Jack Daniel's Color Chrome/108
Motorsports Authentics Steel 1:16
2006 #7 Jack Daniel's/300
Motorsports Authentics/RCCA Owner's Clu
2007 #7 Jack Daniels/1200
RCCA Club 1:24
2008 #7 Jack Daniel's Salute the Troops/250
2008 #7 Jack Daniel's/150
RCCA Elite 1:24
2008 #7 Jack Daniel's/300
2008 #7 Jack Daniel's Platinum/25
2008 #7 Jack Daniel's White Gold/50
2008 #7 Jack Daniel's Salute the Troops White Gold/50
2008 #7 Jack Daniel's Salute the Troops Platinum/25
2008 #7 Jack Daniel's Salute the Troops/500
Winner's Circle 1:24
2005 #2 AC Delco
2005 #2 Timberland
2007 #7 Directv
Winner's Circle Autographed Hood 1:64
2005 #2 AC Delco Chris Cagle
2005 #2 Timberland
Winner's Circle Driver Photo Hood 1:64
2005 #2 AC Delco

Burton, Jeff

Action Performance 1:24
2005 #31 Cingular black AP box
2005 #31 Cingular
2006 #29 Holiday Inn Promo in split window box
Action Promos 1:64
2005 #31 Cingular in window box
Action Racing Collectables 1:24
1997 #9 Track Gear Bank/3500
1997 #99 Exide Mac Tools/4000
1997 #99 Exide
2000 #8 Baby Ruth '90T-bird/8004
2004 #30 AOL RCR 35th Ann./1848
2005 #31 Cingular Beneficial CW Bank/144
2005 #31 Cingular Big & Rich CW Bank/144
2005 #31 Cingular/2438
2005 #31 Cingular CW Bank/144
2005 #31 Cingular Cingular/30,000
2005 #31 Cingular Beneficial/1164
2005 #31 Cingular GM Dealers/144
2005 #31 Cingular Matco/36
2005 #31 Cingular QVC/144
2005 #31 Cingular Big & Rich/1452
2005 #31 Cingular Big & Rich QVC/120
2006 #21 Coast Guard/804
2006 #21 Coast Guard GM Dealers/288
2006 #29 Holiday Inn/1356
2006 #29 Holiday Inn AU
2006 #31 Cingular/3504
2006 #31 Cingular AU/50
2006 #31 Cingular CW Bank
2006 #31 Cingular QVC/48
2006 #31 Cingular Dover Raced/836
Action Racing Collectables 1:64
1997 #9 Track Gear
1997 #99 Exide
2000 #8 Baby Ruth '90 T-bird/9720
2006 #31 Cingular
Action Racing Collectables Platinum 1:2
2008 #31 AT&T/8396
Action/RCCA 1:24
1996 #99 Exide Bank/3500
1997 #9 Track Gear/3500
1997 #99 Exide Bank/2500
2005 #31 Cingular/288
2005 #31 Cingular Beneficial/144
2005 #31 Cingular Big & Rich/204
2006 #21 Coast Guard/120
2006 #29 Holiday Inn/144
2006 #31 Cingular Dover Raced/131
2006 #31 Cingular/204
Action/RCCA 1:64
1997 #9 Track Gear/3500
1997 #99 Exide/5000
2000 #8 Baby Ruth '90 T-bird/2520
2006 #31 Cingular/336
Action/RCCA Banks 1:24
2000 #8 Baby Ruth '90 T-bird/1500
Action/RCCA Elite 1:24
1997 #9 Track Gear/1500
1997 #99 Exide/2500
2000 #8 Baby Ruth '90 T-bird/804
2005 #31 Cingular Big & Rich/204
2005 #31 Cingular Big & Rich AU/121
2005 #31 Cingular White Gold/25
2005 #31 Cingular AU/150
2005 #31 Cingular/288
2006 #21 Coast Guard AU/50
2006 #31 Cingular Dover Raced/131
2006 #31 Cingular Dover Raced Platinum/2
2006 #31 Cingular White Gold/25
2006 #31 Cingular Platinum/4
2006 #31 Cingular AU/50
2006 #31 Cingular/204
Action/RCCA Elite 1:64
2006 #31 Cingular/144
Brookfield 1:24
2005 #31 Cingular/288
Ertl 1:18
1995 #8 Raybestos
Ertl Proshop 1:18
2000 #99 Exide
Ertl Proshop 1:64
2000 #99 Exide
Ertl White Rose Transporters Promos
1992-94 #1 Baby Ruth '93
Funstuf Trackside 1:64
1992 #8 TIC Financial
Hot Wheels Crew's Choice 1:24
1999 #99 Exide
2000 #99 Exide
Hot Wheels Daytona Set-Up 1:64
2002 #99 Citgo
Hot Wheels Deluxe 1:64
2000 #99 Exide
Hot Wheels Deluxe Black Chrome 1:43
1999 #99 Exide
Hot Wheels Deluxe Go Kart 1:64
2000 #99 Exide
Hot Wheels Deluxe Helicopter 1:64
2000 #99 Exide
Hot Wheels Deluxe Scorchin Scooter 1:64
2000 #99 Exide
Hot Wheels First Edition 1:64
1997 #99 Exide
1998 #99 Exide
Hot Wheels Fresh Paint 1:24
1999 #99 Citgo
Hot Wheels Preview Edition 1:64
1998 #99 Exide
Hot Wheels Pro Racing 1:64
1997 #99 Exide
1999 #99 Exide
Hot Wheels Pro Racing Pit Crew 1:64
1998 #99 Exide
Hot Wheels Pro Racing Pit Crew Gold 1:6
1998 #99 Exide
Hot Wheels Pro Racing Superspeedway 1:6
1997 #99 Exide
Hot Wheels Pro Racing Trading Paint 1:6
1998 #99 Exide
Hot Wheels Race Day Deluxe 1:24
2000 #99 Exide
Hot Wheels Racing 1:24
2001 #99 Citgo
2002 #99 Citgo
2003 #99 Citgo Bass Masters
2003 #99 Citgo
Hot Wheels Racing 1:43
1998 #99 Exide
Hot Wheels Racing 1:64
2000 #99 Exide Batteries
Hot Wheels Racing '33 Roadster 1:64
2002 #99 Citgo 1
Hot Wheels Racing '57 Chevy 1:64
2002 #99 Citgo 2
Hot Wheels Racing '57 T-Bird 1:64
2002 #99 Citgo 2
Hot Wheels Racing Artist Collection 1:2
2004 #99 Citgo
Hot Wheels Racing Blimp 1:64
2001 #99 Citgo 4/4
Hot Wheels Racing Crew's Choice 1:64
2000 #99 Exide
Hot Wheels Racing Daytona 500 1:64
1999 #99 Exide
Hot Wheels Racing Deora 1:64
2001 #99 Citgo 1/4
Hot Wheels Racing Justice League 1:24
2004 #99 Green Lantern
Hot Wheels Racing Justice League 1:64
2004 #99 Green Lantern
Hot Wheels Racing Justice League Thunde
2004 #99 Green Lantern
Hot Wheels Racing Justice League w/Figu
2004 #99 Green Lantern
Hot Wheels Racing Luxury Rides 1:64
2003 #99 Citgo
Hot Wheels Racing NASCAR Rocks 1:24
1999 #99 Exide
Hot Wheels Racing Phaeton 1:64
2002 #99 Citgo 1
Hot Wheels Racing Pit Board 1:64
2001 #99 Exide
2001 #99 Citgo
Hot Wheels Racing Pit Crew 1:64
1999 #99 Exide Gold
1999 #99 Exide
Hot Wheels Racing Promos 1:64
2004 #99 HW Back in Black/10,000
Hot Wheels Racing Radical Rides 1:64
2000 #99 Exide
Hot Wheels Racing Radical Rods 1:43
2001 #99 Citgo
Hot Wheels Racing Record Times 1:64
2002 #99 Citgo
Hot Wheels Racing Recreational Vehicles
2003 #99 Citgo
2003 #99 Citgo
Hot Wheels Racing Roush Commemorative 1
2001 #99 Citgo
Hot Wheels Racing Select 1:24
1999 #99 Exide
Hot Wheels Racing Select 1:64
2001 #99 Citgo
Hot Wheels Racing Special Paint 1:64
2003 #99 Bass Masters
Hot Wheels Racing Sticker 1:64
2002 #99 Citgo
Hot Wheels Racing Tail Draggers 1:64
2001 #99 Exide
Hot Wheels Racing Test Track 1:64
1999 #99 Exide
Hot Wheels Racing Track Edition 1:64
2000 #99 Exide
Hot Wheels Racing Transporters 1:64
2001 #99 Citgo
Hot Wheels Racing Treasure Hunt 1:64
2003 #99 Citgo 3
2004 #99 Hot Wheels/10,000
Hot Wheels Racing Twin Mill 1:64
2001 #99 Citgo 3/4
Hot Wheels Racing Wrenchin' and Racin'
2003 #99 Citgo
Hot Wheels Radical Rides 1:43
1999 #99 Exide
Hot Wheels Select 1:43
1999 #99 Exide
Hot Wheels Select 1:64
2000 #99 Exide
Hot Wheels Select Clear 1:24
1999 #99 Exide
Hot Wheels Select Clear 1:43
1999 #99 Exide
Hot Wheels Short Track 1:64
1997 #99 Exide
Hot Wheels Team Transporters 1:64

2004 #99 Citgo
Hot Wheels Test Track 1:64
1998 #99 Exide
Hot Wheels Thunder Series Motorcycles 1
2002 #99 Citgo
Hot Wheels Track Edition 1:64
1998 #99 Exide
Hot Wheels Trading Paint 1:24
1999 #99 Exide
Hot Wheels Transporters 1:64
2002 #99 Citgo
2003 #99 Citgo
Matchbox White Rose Super Stars 1:64
1993 #8 Baby Ruth BX
1993 #8 TIC Financial BX
1994 #0 TIC Financial FCS BX
1994 #8 Raybestos BX
1995 #8 Raybestos SS Awards
1995 #8 Raybestos
1996 #99 Exide
1990-92 #8 TIC Financial BX 92
Matchbox White Rose Transporters Super
1993 #8 TIC Financial
1993 #8 Baby Ruth
1995 #8 Raybestos
Motorsports Authentics Driver's Select
2007 #29 Holiday Inn/816*
2007 #29 Holiday Inn/144
2007 #31 Prilosec Texas Raced/840
2007 #31 Prilosec/2264*
2007 #31 Lenox/708*
2007 #31 Cingular/3264*
2007 #31 AT&T COT/2135*
2007 #31 Cingular
2007 #31 Prilosec Texas Raced/840
2007 #31 Prilosec/360
2007 #31 Lenox Tools/156
2007 #31 Cingular/360
2007 #31 AT&T COT
Motorsports Authentics Owner's Elite 1:
2007 #31 Prilosec Texas Raced White Gold/50*
2007 #31 Prilosec Texas Raced Platinum/25
2007 #31 Prilosec Texas Raced/504
2007 #31 Cingular/504*
2007 #31 AT&T COT/504*
Motorsports Authentics Owner's Elite Tr
2007 #31 Cingular/300*
Motorsports Authentics Pit Stop 1:64
2007 #31 Cingular
Peachstate/GMP Transporters 1:64
1996-01 #99 Exide/1440
1996-01 #99 Citgo SuperGard/1308 '01
Race Image 1:43
1997 #9 Track Gear
1997 #99 Exide
Racing Champions 1:144
1997 #99 Exide
1998 #99 Exide
Racing Champions 1:24
1994 #8 Raybestos w/Hoosiers
1994 #8 Raybestos w/Goodyears
1995 #8 Raybestos
1996 #99 Exide
1997 #9 Track Gear
1997 #99 Exide
1998 #9 Track Gear
1998 #99 Exide
1999 #99 Exide Bruce Lee
1999 #99 Exide
2000 #9 NorthernLight.com
2000 #99 Exide Chrome/999
2000 #99 Exide
Racing Champions 1:64
1992 #8 TIC Finan.Promo/15,000
1994 #8 Raybestos
1995 #8 Raybestos w/Blue #'s
1995 #8 Raybestos
1996 #99 Exide
1997 #9 Track Gear
1997 #99 Exide Chrome/1997
1997 #99 Exide
1998 #9 Track Gear Chrome/1000
1998 #9 Track Gear
1998 #99 Exide Chrome/5050
1998 #99 Exide
1998 #NNO Roush Racing AUTO Gold/1000 5-car set: 6/16/26/97/99
1998 #NNO Roush Racing 5-Pack 5-cars: 97/6/16/99/26
1999 #99 Exide Bruce Lee
1999 #99 Exide
1999 #NNO Roush Rac.AUTO Platinum/2000 5-car set: 6/16/26/97/99
1999 #NNO Roush Racing AUTO Gold/3000 5-car set: 6/16/26/97/99
2000 #9 Northern Light Promo
2000 #9 Exide Promo in clear box
2000 #99 Exide Chrome/999
2000 #NNO 12-car set/Time Trials/Young Guns and War Paint cars/2500
2000 #NNO 12-car boxed set/2500
Racing Champions 12-Car Sets 1:64
1999 #2 12-Car Set 2
1999 #3 12-Car Set 3
1999 #NNO Intro.Chrome 12-car set/25,000
Racing Champions 24K Gold 1:24
1998 #99 Exide
1999 #9 Track Gear
1999 #99 Exide
Racing Champions 24K Gold 1:64
1998 #9 Track Gear
1998 #99 Exide
1999 #9 Track Gear
1999 #99 Exide
Racing Champions 2-Car Sets 1:24
1999 #99 Bruce Lee/4000
Racing Champions 2-Car Sets 1:64
1999 #99 Exide with Gold car/5000
Racing Champions 5-Pack 1:64
2000 #NNO 99.JB/14.MB/66.DW/97.CL/4.BH
2000 #NNO 6.MM/99.JB/75.WD/7.MW/40.SM
2000 #NNO 6.MM/33.JN/99.JB/2K.Ford/55.KW
2000 #NNO 6.MM/6.MM/99.JB/36.EI/99.JB
Racing Champions 5-Pack Preview 1:144
1997 #NNO 5/24/30/94/99
Racing Champions Authentics 1:24
1998 #99 Exide Bank
1998 #99 Exide/4300
1998 #99 Bruce Lee Bank/500
1998 #99 Bruce Lee
1999 #9 Track Gear/2000
1999 #99 Exide/5000
Racing Champions Banks 1:24
1995 #8 Raybestos
Racing Champions Buss Fuses Promos 1:64
1999 #99 Exide
2000 #99 Exide NAPA
Racing Champions Fan Appreciation 5-Pac
1998 #8 16.KL/30.DC/50/94.BE/99.JB

1999 #1 4.BH/6.MM/36.KS/10/99.JB
1999 #9 30.DC/77.RP/99.JB/10/55.KW
Racing Champions Gold 1:24
1998 #9 Track Gear
1998 #99 Exide Bank
1998 #99 Exide
1999 #99 Exide Bruce Lee
1999 #99 Exide
Racing Champions Gold Hood Open 1:24
1998 #99 Exide Bank
1998 #99 Exide
Racing Champions Gold with Medallion 1:
1998 #9 Track Gear
1998 #99 Exide
1999 #99 Exide
Racing Champions High Octane 1:64
2000 #99 Exide
Racing Champions Hobby Yellow Box 1:64
1994 #8 Raybestos
Racing Champions Model Kits 1:24
2000 #99 Exide
Racing Champions Model Kits 1:64
2000 #99 Exide
2001 #99 Exide
Racing Champions NASCAR Rules 1:64
1999 #9 Track Gear
1999 #99 Bruce Lee
1999 #99 Exide
2000 #99 Exide
Racing Champions Pinnacle Series 1:64
1997 #99 Exide
1998 #9 Track Gear
Racing Champions Pit Crew 1:64
2000 #99 Exide Chrome/999
2000 #99 Exide
Racing Champions Platinum 1:24
1999 #9 Track Gear
1999 #99 Exide
Racing Champions Platinum 1:64
1999 #9 Track Gear
1999 #99 Exide
Racing Champions Premier 1:24
1999 #9 Track Gear Bank/500
1999 #99 Exide Bank/500
1999 #99 Exide/3000
2000 #99 Exide Chrome/999
2000 #99 Exide
Racing Champions Premier 1:64
1994 #8 Raybestos/20,000
1995 #8 Raybestos
2000 #99 Exide No Bull
2000 #99 Exide
Racing Champions Premier Preview 1:24
2000 #99 Exide
Racing Champions Premier Preview 1:64
2000 #99 Exide
Racing Champions Premier Preview Transp
2000 #99 Exide Chrome/999
2000 #99 Exide
Racing Champions Premier Transporters 1
1995 #8 Raybestos/1000
1995 #8 Raybestos
2000 #99 Exide Chrome/999
2000 #99 Exide
Racing Champions Premier with Medallion
1997 #99 Exide
Racing Champions Press Pass Series 1:64
1998 #9 Track Gear
1998 #99 Exide
1999 #9 Track Gear
1999 #99 Exide
Racing Champions Preview 1:144
1997 #99 Exide
Racing Champions Preview 1:24
2000 #99 Exide Chrome/999
2000 #99 Exide
Racing Champions Preview 1:64
1997 #99 Exide
2000 #99 Exide
Racing Champions Preview Transporters 1
2000 #99 Exide
Racing Champions Signature Series 1:24
1998 #9 Track Gear
1999 #99 Exide
Racing Champions Signature Series 1:64
1998 #9 Track Gear
1998 #99 Exide
1999 #99 Exide
Racing Champions Stock Rods 1:24
1998 #18 Exide
1998 #39 Track Gear
1998 #63 Exide Gold
1998 #44 Exide
1999 #74 Exide
1999 #85 Exide
1999 #103 Bruce Lee
2000 #2 Exide '32 Ford
Racing Champions Stock Rods 1:64
1997 #6 Exide
1997 #20 Exide
1997 #44 Exide
1998 #64 Exide
1998 #86 Exide Gold
1998 #90 Exide
1998 #97 Exide Gold
1998 #104 Exide Gold
1998 #109 Track Gear
1998 #137 Track Gear
1999 #157 Exide
1999 #158 Exide Gold
1999 #191 Exide
2000 #2 Exide '69 Cougar
2000 #5 Exide '67 Mustang
Racing Champions Stock Rods 24K Gold 1:
1998 #6 Exide
Racing Champions Stock Rods 5-Pack 1:14
1998 #NNO 50/59/90/99/99
Racing Champions Stock Rods Reflections
1998 #8 Exide
Racing Champions SuperTrucks 1:144
1997 #99 Exide
Racing Champions SuperTrucks 1:24
1997 #99 Exide
Racing Champions SuperTrucks 1:64
1997 #99 Exide
Racing Champions SuperTrucks 5-Pack 1:1
1997 #NNO 99.MM/99.JB/1.MW/15.EI/18.JB
Racing Champions Time Trial 1:64
2000 #99 Exide
Racing Champions Time Trial 2000 1:24
2000 #99 Exide
Racing Champions To the Maxx 1:64

1995 #8 Raybestos
Racing Champions Toys R Us Chrome Chase
1999 #99 Exide
Racing Champions Toys 'R Us Gold 1:64
1998 #99 Exide
Racing Champions Transporters 1:64
1995 #8 Raybestos
1997 #9 Track Gear
1997 #99 Exide
1998 #99 Exide w/car
1998 #99 Exide
1999 #99 Exide
2000 #99 Exide Chrome/999
2000 #99 Exide
Racing Champions Transporters 1:87
1997 #9 Track Gear
1997 #99 Exide
Racing Champions Transporters 24K Gold
1999 #99 Exide
Racing Champions Transporters Gold 1:64
1999 #99 Exide
Racing Champions Transporters Hobby 1:8
1994 #8 Raybestos
Racing Champions Transporters Platinum
1999 #99 Exide
Racing Champions Transporters Retail 1:
1994 #8 Raybestos
Racing Champions Transporters Signature
1999 #99 Exide
Racing Champions Transporters Under the
1999 #99 Exide
Racing Champions Transporters War Paint
2000 #99 Exide
Racing Champions Under the Lights 1:24
1999 #99 Exide
2000 #99 Exide 2-car set/2500
Racing Champions Under the Lights 1:64
1999 #99 Exide 2-cars
1999 #99 Exide
2000 #99 Exide/2596
Racing Champions War Paint 1:24
2000 #99 Exide Hood Open
2000 #99 Exide
Racing Champions War Paint 1:64
2000 #99 Exide 2-cars
2000 #99 Exide
RCCA Club 1:24
2008 #31 AT&T/156
RCCA Elite 1:24
2008 #31 AT&T/300
Revell Collection 1:24
1996 #99 Exide
1997 #99 Exide Texas
1997 #99 Exide/2502
Revell Collection 1:43
1997 #99 Exide/7512
Revell Collection 1:64
1996 #99 Exide
Revell Retail 1:24
1996 #99 Exide
1997 #99 Exide
Revell Retail 1:64
1996 #99 Exide
Revell Select 1:24
1997 #99 Exide
Team Caliber 1:24
1999 #99 Exide No Bull
1999 #99 Exide
Team Caliber 1:64
1999 #99 Exide
Team Caliber First Choice 1:24
2003 #99 Citgo/250
Team Caliber First Choice Beckett 1:24
2004 #99 Green Lantern AU/1
Team Caliber Owners Series 1:24
2000 #9 Northern Light/2340
2000 #99 Exide/3120
2000 #99 Citgo Steel/3120
2000 #99 Citgo Mac Tools/3000
2001 #9 Gain/1500
2001 #99 Citgo Stars&Stripes/1068
2001 #99 Citgo MDA/2250
2001 #99 Citgo/2250
2002 #9 Gain/1200
2002 #99 Citgo Peel Reel Win/2400
2002 #99 Citgo Bass Masters/1800
2002 #99 Citgo/3120
2003 #99 Velveeta/1200
2003 #99 Citgo/7560
2004 #9 Pennzoil/1200
2004 #99 SKF/2400
2004 #99 Green Lantern/3120
2004 #99 Coke C2/2400
Team Caliber Owners Series 1:64
2000 #9 Northern Light/7560
2000 #99 Exide/7560
2001 #99 Citgo
2002 #99 Citgo Peel Reel Win/5004
2002 #99 Citgo/5004
2003 #99 Velveeta
2003 #99 Citgo/5004
Team Caliber Owners Series Banks 1:24
2001 #9 Gain/504
2001 #99 Citgo/426
2002 #9 Gain/180
2002 #99 Citgo Peel Reel Win/180
2002 #99 Citgo Bass Masters/180
2002 #99 Citgo/288
2003 #99 Velveeta/180
2003 #99 Citgo/300
Team Caliber Owners Series Dark Chrome
2002 #9 Gain/504
2002 #99 Citgo Peel Reel Win/504
2002 #99 Citgo Bass Masters/426
2002 #99 Citgo/384
2003 #99 Velveeta/180
2003 #99 Citgo/756
Team Caliber Owners Series Gold 1:24
2000 #99 Exide/1200
2001 #9 Gain/504
2001 #99 Citgo/1008
Team Caliber Owners Series Pearl Chrome
2004 #99 SKF/180
2004 #99 Green Lantern/504
2004 #99 Coke C2 Red Chrome
Team Caliber Owners Series Steel 1:24
2001 #9 Gain/504
2001 #99 Citgo MDA/426
2001 #99 Citgo/1008
Team Caliber Owners Series Transporters
2003 #99 Citgo
Team Caliber Pit Stop 1:24

2001 #99 Citgo
2002 #99 Citgo Peel Reel Win/2400
2002 #99 Citgo/3120
2003 #99 Velveeta
2003 #99 Citgo
2004 #9 Pennzoil
2004 #9 Cottman
2004 #99 TNT NBA All Star Game
2004 #99 SKF
2004 #99 Pennzoil
2004 #99 Green Lantern
2004 #99 Coke C2
Team Caliber Pit Stop 1:64
2001 #99 Citgo
2002 #99 Citgo Peel Reel Win/4128
2002 #99 Citgo Bass Masters/7560
2002 #99 Citgo/10,080
2003 #99 Velveeta
2003 #99 Citgo
2004 #9 Pennzoil
2004 #9 Cottman
2004 #99 TNT NBA All Star Game
2004 #99 SKF
2004 #99 Pennzoil
2004 #99 Green Lantern
2004 #99 Coke C2
Team Caliber Pit Stop Transporters 1:64
2003 #99 Citgo
2004 #99 Green Lantern
Team Caliber Preferred 1:24
2000 #9 Northern Light
2000 #99 Exide/10,008
2001 #9 Gain/1008
2001 #99 Citgo/1908
2001 #99 Citgo MDA Mac Tools/3000
2001 #99 Citgo MDA/5004
2002 #9 Gain/4020
2002 #99 Citgo Peel Reel Win/4128
2002 #99 Citgo Bass Masters/4020
2002 #99 Citgo/2340
2003 #99 Velveeta/4020
2003 #99 Citgo/10,152
2004 #9 Pennzoil/5004
2004 #99 TNT
2004 #99 SKF/5004
2004 #99 Green Lantern/5004
2004 #99 Coke C2/10,080
Team Caliber Preferred Banks 1:24
2000 #9 Northern Light/504
2000 #99 Exide/504
Team Caliber Promos 1:64
2002 #9 Gain
2002 #99 Citgo
Team Caliber Pull Backs 1:87
2002 #99 Citgo
Team Caliber White Knuckle Racing 1:24
2000 #99 Exide
Team Caliber White Knuckle Racing 1:64
2000 #99 Exide Promo
2000 #99 Exide
Winner's Circle 1:24
2006 #31 Cingular
2008 #31 AT&T
Winner's Circle Autographed Hood 1:64
2005 #31 Cingular Big & Rich
Winner's Circle Driver Photo Hood 1:64
2005 #31 Cingular
Winner's Circle Photo Hoods 1:64
2007 #31 Prilosec
Winner's Circle Sam Bass 1:64
2008 #31 AT&T
Winner's Circle Schedule Hood 1:64
2007 #31 Cingular
Winner's Circle Victory Lane Hoods 1:64
2007 #31 Prilosec Texas Raced

Busch, Kurt

Action Racing Collectables 1:24
2003 #2 True Value IROC Lt.Blue AU/5004
2003 #2 True Value IROC Lt.Blue/3540
2004 #97 Crown Royal IROC Chrome/288
2004 #97 Crown Royal IROC/2940
2005 #97 Crown Royal IROC/1152
Action Racing Collectables Platinum 1:2
2008 #2 Miller Lite/3408
Action/RCCA 1:24
2004 #97 Crown Royal IROC Color Chrome/288
2005 #97 Crown Royal IROC Brushed Metal/288
2006 #2 Miller Lite/200
2006 #2 Miller Lite Color Chrome/100
2006 #39 Penske Texas Raced/120
Action/RCCA Elite 1:24
2006 #2 Miller Lite/250
2006 #2 Miller Lite Color Chrome/100
2006 #2 Miller Lite Platinum/5
2006 #39 Penske Texas Raced/120
2006 #39 Penske Texas Raced Platinum/2
Hot Wheels Alternative Paint Scheme 1:2
2005 #97 Irwin Tools
Hot Wheels Alternative Paint Scheme 1:6
2005 #97 Irwin Tools
Hot Wheels Race Day 1:24
2005 #97 Sharpie
Hot Wheels Racing 1:24
2002 #97 Rubbermaid
2003 #97 Rubbermaid Little Tikes
2003 #97 Rubbermaid
Hot Wheels Racing Alternative Paint Sch
2004 #97 Irwin Tools
2004 #97 Irwin Tools
Hot Wheels Racing Artist Collection 1:2
2004 #97 Rubbermaid
Hot Wheels Racing Artist Collection 1:6
2004 #97 Rubbermaid
Hot Wheels Racing Chase for the Cup 1:2
2004 #97 Irwin Tools/6000
Hot Wheels Racing Chase for the Cup 1:6
2004 #97 Sharpie
2004 #97 Irwin Tools
Hot Wheels Racing Color Change 1:64
2004 #97 Irwin Tools
2004 #97 Sharpie
2004 #97 Rubbermaid
Hot Wheels Racing Goodyear Showcase 1:6
2004 #97 Superman/15,000
2004 #97 Sharpie/15,000
2004 #97 Irwin Tools/15,000
Hot Wheels Racing Justice League 1:24
2004 #97 Superman
Hot Wheels Racing Justice League 1:64
2004 #97 Superman
Hot Wheels Racing Justice League Thunde

2004 #97 Superman
Hot Wheels Racing Justice League w/Figu
2004 #97 Superman
Hot Wheels Racing Luxury Rides 1:64
2003 #97 Rubbermaid
Hot Wheels Racing Pit Board 1:64
2001 #97 Sharpie
Hot Wheels Racing Pit Cruisers 1:64
2004 #97 Rubbermaid
Hot Wheels Racing Race Day 1:24
2004 #97 Sharpie
Hot Wheels Racing Race Day 1:64
2003 #97 Rubbermaid
2004 #97 Sharpie
Hot Wheels Racing Recreational Vehicles
2003 #97 Rubbermaid
2003 #97 Rubbermaid
2003 #97 Rubbermaid
2003 #97 Rubbermaid
Hot Wheels Racing Roush Commemorative 1
2001 #97 Sharpie
Hot Wheels Racing Special Paint 1:64
2003 #97 Sharpie
2003 #97 Rubbermaid Little Tikes
Hot Wheels Racing Sticker 1:64
2002 #97 Rubbermaid
Hot Wheels Racing Stock Car Cruisers 1:
2003 #97 Rubbermaid
Hot Wheels Racing Stockerz 1:24
2004 #97 Irwin Tools
2004 #97 Sharpie
2004 #97 Rubbermaid
Hot Wheels Racing Stockerz 1:64
2004 #97 Irwin Tools
2004 #97 Sharpie
2004 #97 Rubbermaid
Hot Wheels Racing Test Track 1:24
2004 #97 Sharpie
Hot Wheels Racing Test Track 1:64
2004 #97 Sharpie
Hot Wheels Racing Treasure Hunt 1:64
2003 #97 Sharpie 4
Hot Wheels Racing Wrenchin' and Racin'
2003 #97 Sharpie
Hot Wheels Team Transporters 1:64
2004 #97 Rubbermaid
Hot Wheels Transporters 1:64
2003 #97 Rubbermaid
Hot Wheels Victory Lane Transporters 1:
2004 #97 Rubbermaid
2004 #97B Rubbermaid
Motorsports Authentics Driver's Select
2007 #2 Miller Lite/4008*
2007 #2 Miller Lite COT/1104*
2007 #2 Miller Lite Wolrd Beer Challenge/1176*
2007 #2 Miller Lite COT
2007 #2 Miller Lite
2007 #12 Penske/1000*
Motorsports Authentics Owner's Elite 1:
2007 #2 Miller Lite COT/504*
2007 #2 Miller Lite AU/504
2007 #2 Miller Lite/1500*
Motorsports Authentics Owner's Elite Tr
2007 #2 Miller Lite/708*
2007 #12 Penske/144*
Motorsports Authentics Pit Stop 1:64
2007 #2 Kurt COT
2007 #2 Kurt
Motorsports Authentics QVC For Race Fan
2007 #2 Miller Lite Color Chrome/96
2007 #2 Miller Lite Chrome/288
Racing Champions 1:24
2000 #99 Exide SuperTruck Promo
RCCA Club 1:24
2008 #2 Miller Lite/150
RCCA Elite 1:24
2008 #2 Miller Lite/300
2008 #2 Miller Lite Platinum/25
2008 #2 Miller Lite White Gold/50
Team Caliber First Choice 1:24
2003 #97 Rubbermaid/504
2004 #97 Sharpie '04 Champ.Employee w/Trophy
2004 #97 Sharpie/250
2004 #97 Irwin Tools/250
2004 #97 Superman/250
Team Caliber First Choice Beckett 1:24
2004 #97 Superman AU/1
Team Caliber Model Kits 1:64
2003 #97 Blue Ice
Team Caliber Owners Series 1:24
2001 #97 Sharpie/2310
2001 #97 100 Years Ford/1800
2002 #97 Rubbermaid Flag/904
2002 #97 Sharpie Million $/2400
2002 #97 Sharpie 500/3120
2002 #97 Rubber.Little Tikes/1800
2002 #97 Rubber.Commercial/2400
2002 #97 Rubbermaid/2400
2003 #97 Sharpie/2400
2003 #97 Irwin Tools2400
2003 #97 Rubbermaid Comm.Products/2400
2003 #97 Blue Ice/2400
2003 #97 Rubbermaid/5004
2004 #97 Superman/5004
2004 #97 Sharpie 40th Ann/3120
2004 #97 Sharpie '04 Champion/2400
2004 #97 Sharpie/2400
2004 #97 Irwin Tools '04 Champion/2400
2004 #97 Irwin Tools/2400
2004 #97 Coke C2/2400
2005 #97 Smirnoff/600
2005 #97 Sharpie AFE/600
2005 #97 Sharpie/804
2005 #97 Irwin Tools/600*
2005 #97 Crown Royal/600*
2005 #97 Crown Royal/756
Team Caliber Owner's Series 1:24
2006 #2 Miller Lite/2400
Team Caliber Owners Series 1:64
2001 #97 Sharpie/5544
2002 #97 Rubber.Commercial/5004
2002 #97 Rubbermaid/5004
2002 #97 Sharpie Million $/5004
2003 #97 Rubbermaid Comm.Products/2400
2003 #97 Irwin Tools
2003 #97 Sharpie
2003 #97 Blue Ice
2003 #97 Rubbermaid/5004
2004 #97 Irwin Tools
Team Caliber Owners Series Banks 1:24
2001 #97 100 Years of Ford/258
2002 #97 Sharpie/504
2002 #97 Sharpie Million $/180

2002 #97 Sharpie 500/180
2002 #97 Rubber.Little Tikes/180
2002 #97 Rubber.Commercial/180
2002 #97 Rubbermaid/252
2003 #97 Blue Ice/180
2003 #97 Sharpie/180
2003 #97 Irwin Tools/180
2003 #97 Rubbermaid Comm.Products/180
2003 #97 Rubbermaid/300

Team Caliber Owners Series Dark Chrome
2002 #97 Sharpie 500/600
2002 #97 Sharpie Million $/540
2002 #97 Rubber.Little Tikes/504
2002 #97 Rubber.Commercial/330
2002 #97 Rubbermaid/288
2003 #97 Sharpie/360
2003 #97 Irwin Tools/240
2003 #97 Rubbermaid Comm.Products/300
2003 #97 Rubbermaid/504
2003 #97 Blue Ice/360

Team Caliber Owners Series Gold 1:24
2001 #97 100 Years of Ford/258
2001 #97 Sharpie/504

Team Caliber Owners Series Pearl Chrome
2004 #97 Coke C2 Red Chrome
2004 #97 Superman/756
2004 #97 Sharpie 40th Ann/504
2004 #97 Sharpie/504
2004 #97 Irwin Tools/300

Team Caliber Owners Series Steel 1:24
2001 #97 100 Years of Ford/258
2001 #97 Sharpie/504

Team Caliber Owners Series Transporters
2003 #97 Rubbermaid/1200
2004 #97 Sharpie
2004 #97 Superman

Team Caliber Pit Stop 1:18
2004 #97 Irwin Tools
2004 #97 Sharpie

Team Caliber Pit Stop 1:24
2001 #97 Sharpie/3132
2002 #97 Sharpie 500/2400
2002 #97 Sharpie Million $/2400
2002 #97 Rubber.Commercial/2400
2002 #97 Rubbermaid/2532
2003 #97 Sharpie
2003 #97 Irwin Tools
2003 #97 Rubber.Commer.Products
2003 #97 Rubbermaid
2003 #97 Blue Ice
2004 #97 Superman
2004 #97 Sharpie 40th Anniversary
2004 #97 Irwin Tools
2004 #97 Coke C2
2005 #97 Sharpie AFE
2005 #97 Sharpie
2005 #97 Irwin Tools
2006 #2 Miller Lite
2006 #39 Penske

Team Caliber Pit Stop 1:64
2001 #97 Sharpie
2002 #97 Sharpie 500/7572
2002 #97 Sharpie Million $/7560
2002 #97 Rubber.Little Tikes
2002 #97 Rubber.Commercial/7560
2002 #97 Rubbermaid/14,120
2003 #97 Sharpie
2003 #97 Irwin Tools
2003 #97 Rubber.Commer.Products
2003 #97 Rubbermaid
2003 #97 Blue Ice
2004 #97 Superman
2004 #97 Sharpie 40th Anniversary
2004 #97 Sharpie '04 Champion
2004 #97 Sharpie
2004 #97 Irwin Tools '04 Champion
2004 #97 Irwin Tools
2004 #97 Coke C2
2005 #97 Sharpie AFE
2005 #97 Sharpie
2005 #97 Irwin Tools
2006 #2 Miller Lite in window box
2006 #2 Kurt
2006 #39 Penske

Team Caliber Pit Stop Transporters 1:64
2003 #97 Rubbermaid
2004 #97 Superman
2004 #97 Sharpie

Team Caliber Preferred 1:24
2001 #97 Sharpie/5220
2001 #97 100 Years of Ford/4020
2002 #97 Sharpie Million $/4668
2002 #97 Sharpie 500/2400
2002 #97 Rubber.Little Tikes/4320
2002 #97 Rubber.Commercial/4116
2002 #97 Rubbermaid/2340
2003 #97 Sharpie/4320
2003 #97 Irwin Tools/6708
2003 #97 Rubbermaid Comm.Products/4128
2003 #97 Blue Ice/2004
2003 #97 Rubbermaid/10,080
2004 #97 Superman Gold Chrome/250
2004 #97 Superman/7560
2004 #97 Sharpie 40th Ann./5004
2004 #97 Sharpie '04 Champion/10,080
2004 #97 Sharpie Chase/1000
2004 #97 Sharpie/10,080
2004 #97 Irwin Tools '04 Champion/2400
2004 #97 Irwin Tools Chase/900
2004 #97 Irwin Tools
2004 #97 Coke C2/10,080
2005 #97 Smirnoff/3120
2005 #97 Sharpie AFE/2400
2005 #97 Sharpie/3120
2005 #97 Irwin Tools/3120
2005 #97 Crown Royal Color Chrome AU/1008
2005 #97 Crown Royal/3120
2006 #2 Miller Lite
2006 #39 Penske/2400

Team Caliber Preferred Copper 1:24
2006 #2 Miller Lite

Team Caliber Preferred Nickel 1:24
2005 #97 Smirnoff/300
2005 #97 Sharpie AFE/180
2005 #97 Sharpie/504
2005 #97 Irwin Tools/504
2005 #97 Crown Royal/756

Team Caliber Promos 1:64
2002 #97 Sharpie

Team Caliber/Motorworks Model Kits 1:24
2003 #97 Rubbermaid
2003 #97 Irwin Tools
2005 #97 Sharpie

Winner's Circle 1:24
2007 #2 Kurt
2008 #2 Kurt

Winner's Circle 1:87
2007 #2 Kurt

Winner's Circle Autographed Hoods 1:64
2008 #2 Kurt

Winner's Circle Limited Edition 1:64
2007 #2 Miller Lite

Winner's Circle Schedule Hood 1:64
2007 #2 Kurt

Winner's Circle Schedule Hoods 1:64
2008 #2 Kurt

Winner's Circle Transporters 1:64
2007 #2 Kurt

Winner's Circle Victory Lane Hoods 1:64
2007 #2 Miller Lite Pocono Raced
2007 #2 Miller Lite Michigan Raced

Busch, Kyle

Action Racing Collectables 1:24
2003 #87 ditech.com AU/2400
2003 #87 ditech.com GM Dealers AU/120
2003 #87 ditech.com Mummy/3372
2003 #87 ditech.com Mummy CW Bank/516
2004 #5 Lowe's/2328
2004 #5 Lowe's CW Bank/264
2004 #5 Lowe's SpongeBob/3396
2004 #5 Lowe's SpongeBob CW Bank
2004 #84 Carquest/3084
2004 #84 Carquest CW Bank/276
2004 #84 Carquest GM Dealers/144
2005 #5 CarQuest CW Bank/156
2005 #5 CarQuest Matco/48
2005 #5 Delphi/3492
2005 #5 Delphi CW Bank/144
2005 #5 Kellogg's Johnny Bravo/3504
2005 #5 Kellogg's Robots/3504
2005 #5 Kellogg's Star Wars GM Dealers
2005 #5 Kellogg's Star Wars QVC/144
2005 #5 Spectrum Ant Killer/2592
2005 #5 CarQuest/1284
2005 #5 Kellogg's/2340
2005 #5 Kellogg's CW Bank/192
2005 #5 Kellogg's GM Dealers/144
2005 #5 Kellogg's Matco/36
2005 #5 Kellogg's QVC/144
2005 #5 Kellogg's California Raced/2508
2005 #5 Kellogg's California Raced QVC/120
2005 #5 Kellogg's ROY Color Chrome/5004
2005 #5 Kellogg's ROY Color Chrome GM Dealers/288
2005 #5 Kellogg's ROY Color Chrome QVC/504
2005 #5 Kellogg's Star Wars/2484
2005 #5 Kellogg's Star Wars CW Bank/204
2005 #15 ditech.com SuperTruck Charlotte Raced w/tire/1956
2005 #15 ditech.com SuperTruck Charlotte Raced w/tire QVC/144
2005 #57 Lowe's Shop-Vac/2472
2006 #5 Kellogg's Ice Age CWB
2006 #5 Kellogg's Ice Age/2556
2006 #5 Kellogg's Cars/3000
2006 #5 Kellogg's QVC/120
2006 #5 Kellogg's GM Dealers/360
2006 #5 Lowe's
2006 #5 Kellogg's Ice Age GM Dealers/288
2006 #5 Carquest/2508
2006 #5 Carquest GM Dealers/72
2006 #5 Delphi/1356
2006 #5 Delphi GM Dealers/96
2006 #5 Kellogg's/3864

Action Racing Collectables 1:64
2004 #5 Lowe's/5040
2004 #84 Carquest/5040
2005 #5 Delphi
2005 #5 Kellogg's Johnny Bravo
2006 #5 Kellogg's Ice Age
2006 #5 Kellogg's Cars
2006 #5 Kellogg's
2008 #18 M&M's

Action Racing Collectables Platinum 1:2
2008 #18 M&M's/5448
2008 #18 Interstate Batteries

Action Racing Collectables Platinum 1:6
2008 #18 M&M's/6192

Action/Funline Muscle Machines 1:24
2005 #5 Kellogg's Hybrid

Action/RCCA 1:24
2003 #87 Ditech.com AU/240
2003 #87 Ditech.com Mummy/300
2004 #5 Lowe's/288
2004 #5 Lowe's SpongeBob/360
2004 #84 CarQuest/360
2005 #5 CarQuest/288
2005 #5 Kellogg's/444
2005 #5 Kellogg's Color Chrome/144
2005 #5 Kellogg's Liquid Metal/144
2005 #5 Kellogg's California Raced/240
2005 #5 Kellogg's Star Wars/408
2005 #15 ditech.com SuperTruck Charlotte Raced w/tire/360
2006 #5 Carquest/120
2006 #5 Delphi/144
2006 #5 Kellogg's Color Chrome/108
2006 #5 Kellogg's Cars/360
2006 #5 Spectracide/144
2006 #5 Kellogg's/120
2006 #5 Kellogg's Ice Age/288
2006 #5 Lowe's/120

Action/RCCA 1:64
2004 #5 Lowe's/576
2004 #84 CarQuest/576
2006 #5 Kellogg's/288
2006 #5 Kellogg's Ice Age/288
2006 #5 Kellogg's Cars/288

Action/RCCA Elite 1:24
2003 #87 Ditech.com Mummy/300
2003 #87 Ditech.com AU/240
2004 #5 Lowe's/288
2004 #5 Lowe's SpongeBob/300
2004 #5 Lowe's SpongeBob White Gold/25
2004 #84 CarQuest/360
2005 #5 CarQuest White Gold/25
2005 #5 Kellogg's White Gold/25
2005 #5 Kellogg's California Raced/240
2005 #5 Kellogg's/444
2005 #5 Kellogg's Color Chrome/144
2005 #5 CarQuest/288
2005 #5 Kellogg's Star Wars White Gold/25
2005 #5 Kellogg's Star Wars/408
2006 #5 Kellogg's Cars Platinum/7
2006 #5 Kellogg's Ice Age 2 AU/144
2006 #5 Kellogg's Cars White Gold/25
2006 #5 Kellogg's White Gold/25
2006 #5 Carquest Platinum/2
2006 #5 Kellogg's Cars AU/144
2006 #5 Kellogg's AU/50
2006 #5 Kellogg's Cars/200
2006 #5 Kellogg's Color Chrome/108
2006 #5 Kellogg's/288
2006 #5 Carquest/120
2006 #5 Kellogg's Ice Age 2 Platinum/5
2006 #5 Kellogg's Platinum/5
2006 #5 Kellogg's Ice Age 2/288

Action/RCCA Elite 1:64
2006 #5 Kellogg's/192
2006 #5 Kellogg's Cars/192
2006 #5 Kellogg's Ice Age 2/144

Brookfield 1:24
2005 #5 Kellogg's/204

Motorsports Authentics Driver's Select
2007 #5 Carquest/1800*
2007 #5 Carquest COT Bristol Raced/1368*
2007 #5 Kellogg's/1800*
2007 #5 Kellogg's COT/1163*
2007 #5 Kellogg's COT
2007 #5 Kellogg's
2007 #5 Kellogg's COT/240
2007 #5 Kellogg's/288
2007 #5 Carquest COT Bristol Raced/1368
2007 #5 Carquest/144

Motorsports Authentics Owner's Elite 1:
2007 #5 Kellogg's COT/504
2007 #5 Kellogg's/504

Motorsports Authentics Owner's Elite Tr
2007 #5 Kellogg's/204*
2007 #5 Carquest/204*

Motorsports Authentics Pit Stop 1:64
2007 #5 Kellogg's

Motorsports Authentics QVC For Race Fan
2007 #5 Kellogg's Color Chrome/96
2007 #5 Kellogg's Chrome/96
2007 #5 Carquest Color Chrome/96
2007 #5 Carquest Chrome/96

Racing Champions 5-Pack 1:64
2004 #NNO 10.SR/22.SW/48.JJ/60.BV/87.KyB
2004 #NNO 01.JN/5.TL/22.SW/38.KK/84.Ky.B in '05 packaging

Racing Champions Ultra 1:24
2004 #5 Lowe's SpongeBob
2004 #5 Lowe's
2005 #5 Kellogg's

Racing Champions Ultra 1:64
2003 #87 Ditech.com
2004 #5 Lowe's SpongeBob
2004 #5 Lowe's
2004 #84 Carquest in '05 packaging
2005 #5 Kellogg's
2005 #5 Delphi

RCCA Club 1:24
2008 #18 M&M's/250

RCCA Elite 1:24
2008 #18 M&M's/408
2008 #18 M&M's Platinum/25
2008 #18 M&M's White Gold/50
2008 #18 M&M's Red White Blue/504
2008 #18 M&M's Red White Blue Platinum/25
2008 #18 M&M's Red White Blue White Gold/50

Team Caliber Model Kits 1:64
2003 #87 Ditech.com

Team Caliber Owners Series 1:24
2003 #87 Ditech.com/1800
2004 #5 Lowe's
2004 #84 Car Quest/2400
2005 #5 CarQuest
2005 #5 Cheez-It
2005 #5 Kellogg's Johnny Bravo
2005 #5 Kellogg's/900

Team Caliber Owners Series 1:64
2004 #84 Car Quest

Team Caliber Owners Series Banks 1:24
2003 #87 Ditech.com/180

Team Caliber Owners Series Dark Chrome
2003 #87 Ditech.com/180

Team Caliber Owners Series Pearl Chrome
2004 #5 Lowe's/180
2004 #5 Lowe's SpongeBob/250
2004 #84 Car Quest/222

Team Caliber Owners Series Transporters
2004 #84 Car Quest

Team Caliber Pit Stop 1:24
2003 #87 Ditech.com
2004 #5 Lowe's SpongeBob
2004 #5 Lowe's
2004 #84 Car Quest
2005 #5 Kellogg's
2005 #5 CarQuest
2005 #5 Kellogg's Johnny Bravo

Team Caliber Pit Stop 1:64
2003 #87 Ditech.com
2004 #5 Lowe's SpongeBob
2004 #5 Lowe's
2004 #84 Car Quest
2005 #5 Kellogg's Johnny Bravo
2005 #5 CarQuest
2005 #5 Cheez-It
2005 #5 Kellogg's

Team Caliber Pit Stop Transporters 1:64
2004 #84 Car Quest

Team Caliber Preferred 1:24
2003 #87 Ditech.com/4020
2004 #5 Lowe's SpongeBob/3120
2004 #5 Lowe's/10,080
2004 #84 Car Quest/10,080
2005 #5 CarQuest
2005 #5 Cheez-It
2005 #5 Kellogg's/1200
2005 #5 Kellogg's Cal. Win/1800
2005 #5 Kellogg's Johnny Bravo/1500

Team Caliber Preferred Nickel 1:24
2005 #5 Kellogg's/504
2005 #5 Kellogg's Johnny Bravo/180

Team Caliber Preferred Trackside 1:24
2006 #5 Kellogg's/48

Team Caliber Promos 1:64
2004 #5 Lowe's SpongeBob

Team Caliber/Motorworks 1:64
2003 #87 ditech.com

Winner's Circle 1:24
2006 #5 Kellogg's
2008 #18 M&M's

Winner's Circle 1:87
2007 #5 Kellogg's
2008 #18 M&M's

Winner's Circle Autographed Hood 1:64
2005 #5 NASCARtoons
2005 #5 Kellogg's Johnny Bravo

Winner's Circle Autographed Hoods 1:64
2008 #18 M&M'S

Winner's Circle Driver Photo Hood 1:64
2005 #5 Kellogg's

Winner's Circle Number Magnet 1:64
2008 #18 M&M'S

Winner's Circle Photo Hoods 1:64
2007 #5 Kellogg's

Winner's Circle Schedule Hood 1:64
2006 #5 Kellogg's
2007 #5 Kellogg's

Winner's Circle Schedule Hoods 1:64
2008 #18 M&M's

Winner's Circle Stickers 1:64
2008 #18 M&M'S

Winner's Circle Transporters 1:64
2008 #18 M&M's

Winner's Circle Victory Lane Hoods 1:64
2007 #5 Carquest COT Bristol Raced

Carpentier, Patrick

Action Indy Cars 1:18
1999 #33 Forsythe Renard/3500
2003 #32 It's Your World

Action Indy Cars 1:43
1999 #33 Forsythe Renard/5000

Hot Wheels First Edition Indy 1:64
1998 #16 Alumax

RCCA Club 1:24
2008 #10 Valvoline/150

Earnhardt, Dale

Action Performance 1:24
1999 #3 Goodwrench
2000 #3 Goodwrench
2001 #3 Goodwrench Promo w/o Sonic logo solid box
2001 #3 Goodwrench w/sonic logo window box
2002 #3 Goodwrench
2003 #3 Goodwrench Forever the Man

Action Performance 1:64
1999 #3 Goodwrench
2000 #3 Goodwrench Red Cell Batteries Promo
2000 #3 Goodwrench
2001 #3 Goodwrench Promo in clear plastic box
2001 #3 Goodwrench w/Sonic decal
2001 #3 Goodwrench BP
2002 #3 Goodwrench
2003 #3 Goodwrench Forever the Man
2005 #3 Goodwrench '00 MC

Action QVC For Race Fans Only 1:24
2000 #3 Goodwrench Peter Max Gold/2000
2000 #3 Goodwrench Taz No Bull Color Chrome/3504
2000 #3 Goodwrench Taz No Bull Gold/2000
2000 #3 Goodwrench No Bull Platinum/2508
2000 #3 Goodwrench No Bull Gold/5000
2000 #3 Goodwrench Gold/2000
2000 #3 Goodwrench Color Chrome/3504
2001 #3 Goodwrench Oreo Platinum/624
2001 #3 Good.Oreo Gold/2000
2001 #3 Goodwrench with Sonic decal
2001 #3 Goodwrench Plat/2508
2001 #3 Goodwren.Gold/10,000
2003 #3 Goodwrench '90 Lumina Platinum/1008
2003 #3 Goodwrench '90 Lumina Pearlized/2508
2003 #3 Goodwrench '90 Lumina Gold/2508
2003 #3 Foundation Plat./1008
2003 #3 Foundation Gold/3333
2003 #NNO Legacy Plat/1008
2003 #NNO Legacy Gold/3333
2004 #3 Goodwrench Peter Max '00 Monte Carlo Color Chrome/504
2004 #3 Goodwrench Crash '97 Daytona Raced Gold/504
2004 #3 Goodwrench Crash '97 Daytona Raced Color Chrome/5004
2004 #3 Goodwrench Olympic '96 Monte Carlo Color Chrome/5004
2005 #3 Goodwrench Plus '98 MC Daytona Win Color Chrome/5004
2005 #12 Budweiser IROC '87 Camaro Color Chrome/504
2006 #NNO HOF Mesma Chrome/1008

Action Racing Collectables 1:18
1998 #3 Wheaties 1997 Monte Carlo/7008
1998 #3 Goodwrench Silver '95MC/7000
1998 #3 Goodwrench Plus Daytona/4008
1998 #3 Goodwrench Plus Bass Pro
1999 #3 Wrangler
1999 #3 Goodwrench Sign Last Lap/2508
1999 #3 Goodwrench Sign/3000
1999 #3 Goodwrench/4008
1999 #3 Coke
2000 #3 Goodwrench Taz No Bull
2000 #3 Goodwrench Peter Max/3000
2000 #3 Goodwrench
2001 #3 Earn/Earn Jr./Pilgrim/Collins C5-R Corvette Platinum/2508
2001 #3 Earn/Earn Jr./Pilgrim/Collins C5-R Color Chrome raced/7500
2001 #3 Earn/Earn Jr./Pilgrim/Collins C5-R Color Chrome/7500
2001 #3 Earn/Earn Jr./Pilgrim/Collins C5-R Corvette 24Kt.Gold/2000
2001 #3 Earn/Earn Jr./Pilgrim/Collins C5-R Corvette raced/1008
2001 #3 Earn/Earn Jr./Pilgrim/Collins C5-R Corvette/16,752
2001 #3 Goodwrench Oreo Daytona/3000
2001 #3 Goodwrench w/sonic decal/20,004
2002 #3 Goodwr.Oreo/2508
2002 #NNO Mon.Carlo SS/11,952
2003 #3 Victory Lap/2508
2003 #3 Foundation/3876
2004 #NNO Monte Carlo SS/5060
2006 #NNO HOF Dale Tribute GM Dealers/180
2006 #NNO HOF Dale Tribute/2508

Action Racing Collectables 1:24
1994 #3 Wrangler '88 MC Aerocoupe Bank/5016
1994 #3 Wrangler 1984 Monte Carlo Bank/5016
1994 #3 Goodwrench 1994 Lumina Bank/5016
1995 #2 Wrangler 1981 Pontiac/5016
1995 #3 Wrangler 1987 Monte Carlo/6000
1995 #3 Wrangler 1985 MC Aerocoupe/6000
1995 #3 Wrangler 1981 Pontiac/5016
1995 #3 Goodwrench Silver Desk Set
1995 #3 Goodwrench Silver Bank GM Parts black wheels
1995 #3 Goodwrench Silver Bank GM red wheels
1995 #3 Goodwrench Silver Bank GM black wheels
1995 #3 Good.Brickyard/10,000
1995 #3 Goodwrench Bank without headlights
1995 #3 Goodwrench Bank '94 Champ w/headlights
1995 #3 Goodwrench Bank Sports Image
1995 #3 Goodwrench black window promo
1995 #3 Goodwrench/6000
1995 #3 Goodwrench Silver Bank GM Parts red wheels
1995 #15 Wrangler 1983 T-bird/5004
1995 #NNO R.Petty 7&7 Champions 2-Bank Set
1995 #NNO J.Gordon Brickyard 2-car set/5000
1996 #3 Olympic Goodwrench Box
1996 #3 Olympic Food City Promo box
1996 #3 Olympic Bank
1996 #3 Goodwrench
1996 #3 AC-Delco Snap-On
1996 #3 AC-Delco
1996 #3 Olympic Sports Image blue box
1996 #3 Olympic Mom-n-Pop's box
1996 #3 Olympic Green Box no tm on Hood
1996 #3 Olympic Green Box
1996 #15 Wrangler '82 T-bird Bank/2508
1997 #3 Wrangler Bank 1984 Monte Carlo Daytona paint
1997 #3 Wheaties Sprt.Image
1997 #3 Wheaties Snap-On Bank
1997 #3 Wheaties mail-In red window netting
1997 #3 Wheaties HO black netting Snap-On Tools
1997 #3 Wheaties HO black window netting
1997 #3 Lowes Food Bank/7992
1997 #3 Goodwrench Brickyard/7500
1997 #3 Goodwrench Plus Bank
1997 #3 Goodwrench Plus
1997 #3 Goodwrench Bank
1997 #3 AC Delco Bank
1998 #3 Dale Jr. Goodwrench/AC Delco Split/624
1998 #3 Goodwr.Plus Gold/500
1998 #3 Goodwrench Plus Daytona Bank/15,000
1998 #3 Goodwr.Plus Daytona
1998 #3 Goodwrench Plus Bass Pro Bank
1998 #3 Goodwr.Plus Bass Pro Black Window Promo
1998 #3 Goodwr.Plus Bass Pro
1998 #3 Goodwrench Plus Bank w/o Coke decal
1998 #3 Goodwrench Plus Bank w/Coke decal
1998 #3 Goodwrench Plus
1998 #3 Coke Bank
1998 #3 Coke
1998 #8 RPM 1975 Dodge Bank/10,000
1998 #8 RPM '75 Dodge/7500
1998 #NNO Jr./Coke Snap-on 2-car set
1998 #K2 Dayvault's '56 Ford Pink Roof
1998 #K2 Dayvault's '56 Ford Dark Roof Bank
1998 #K2 Dayvault's '56 Ford Dark Roof/10,000
1999 #3 Wrangler Bank/5004
1999 #3 Wrangler/5004
1999 #3 Goodwrench Sign Last Lap Bank/2508
1999 #3 Goodwrench Sign Last Lap/15,504
1999 #3 Goodwrench Sign
1999 #3 Goodwrench Crash 1997 Monte Carlo
1999 #3 Goodwr.25th Ann.Bank
1999 #3 Goodwren.25th Ann/2500
1999 #3 Goodwr.Bank/10,008
1999 #3 Goodwrench
1999 #8 Bud Bank/3000
1999 #30 Army '76 Mal.Bank/2508
1999 #30 Army '76 Malibu
1999 #77 Hy-Gain 1976 Malibu Bank
1999 #77 Hy-Gain '76 Malibu
2000 #3 Goodwrench Taz No Bull Bank
2000 #3 Goodwrench Taz No Bull black window/16,008
2000 #3 Goodwrench Taz No Bull/16,008
2000 #3 Goodwrench Talladega Win No Bull/10,003
2000 #3 Goodwrench Platinum 75th Win/25,008
2000 #3 Goodwrench Peter Max Bank/5004
2000 #3 Goodwr.Peter Max Snap-on BW car/7500
2000 #3 Goodwr.Peter Max BW car/100,247
2000 #3 Goodwr.Peter Max/101,916
2000 #3 Goodwrench No Bull Bank raced version/13,333
2000 #3 Goodwrench No Bull raced version
2000 #3 Goodwrench Clear
2000 #3 Goodwren.Brickyard
2000 #3 Goodwrench Bank/3504
2000 #3 Goodwrench/34,992
2001 #3 Goodwrench Talladega Win No Bull Bank/13,333
2001 #3 Good.Clear/5004
2001 #3 Goodwrench Oreo GM Dealers White Gold/5000
2001 #3 Goodwrench Oreo Clear/6000
2001 #3 Goodwrench Oreo Bank/15,000
2001 #3 Goodwrench Oreo/55,008
2001 #3 Goodwr.Bank/2508
2001 #3 Goodwrench White Gold Promo/5000
2001 #3 Goodwrench/33,504
2001 #8 Goodwrench 1987 Nova/10,008
2001 #8 Docs '64 Chev.Bank
2001 #8 Docs '64 Chev/86,924
2001 #2001 DEI Pit Practice Car Snap-on Carolina Run
2001 #2001 DEI Pit Practice Car/2508
2002 #1 True Value '01 IROC Green/28,512
2002 #1 True Value '00 IROC Lt. Blue/39,960
2002 #1 True Value '99 IROC
2002 #2 Coke '80 Pontiac Bank/4044
2002 #2 Coke '80 Pont./64,836
2002 #2 Wrangler 1979 MC Bank/4500
2002 #2 Wrangler '79 MC/68,016
2002 #15 Wrangler '79 Pontiac Ventura Bank/2508
2002 #15 Wrangler '79 Pontiac Ventura GM Dealers/3504
2002 #15 Wrangler '79 Pontiac Ventura/58,716
2002 #NNO Legacy/58,212
2003 #3 Wheaties '97 MC CW Bank/9900
2003 #3 Victory Lap Color Chrome GM Dealers/744
2003 #3 Victory Lap Color Chrome/6012
2003 #3 Victory Lap GM Dealers/3300
2003 #3 Victory Lap CW Bank/1260
2003 #3 Victory Lap/29,628
2003 #3 Goodwrench Bass Pro Bank/16,944
2003 #3 Goodwrench '01 MC Clear GM Dealers/300
2003 #3 Goodwrench '01 Mon.Carlo Clear/6108
2003 #3 Goodwrench '01 MC CW Bank/15,360
2003 #3 Goodwrench No Bull 2000 MC GM Dealers/3504
2003 #3 Goodwrench No Bull 2000 MC CW Bank/1596
2003 #3 Goodwrench No Bull 2000 Monte Carlo/25,244
2003 #3 Goodwrench Silver 1995 MC CW Bank/33,333
2003 #3 Goodwrench '90 Lumina GM Dealers/1908
2003 #3 Goodwrench '90 Lumina/35,664
2003 #3 Foundation CW Bank/2004
2003 #3 Foundation/53,796
2003 #19 Beldon Asphalt '77 Malibu CW Bank/1884
2003 #19 Beldon Asphalt 1977 Malibu/24,716
2006 #NNO Hall of Fame/33,333
2006 #NNO Hall of Fame GM Dealers/2004

Action Racing Collectables 1:32
1998-01 #3 Goodwr.Taz No Bull
1998-01 #3 Goodwrench Silver 1995 Monte Carlo/5000
1998-01 #3 Goodwrench Plus Daytona Win/20,000 '98
1998-01 #3 Goodwrench Plus Bass Pro/5000
1998-01 #3 Goodwren.25th Ann.
1998-01 #3 Goodwrench Sign Last Lap/3504

Action Racing Collectables 1:64
1993 #NNO J.Gordon Kellogg's 2-car promo
1994 #3 16-car set
1994 #3 Wrangler 1984 Monte Carlo
1994 #3 Goodwrench 1988 Monte Carlo Aerocoupe
1994 #3 Goodwrench/16,128
1995 #2 Wrangler/24,912 1981 Pontiac
1995 #3 Goodwrench Silver Race World blister
1995 #3 Goodwrench Silver Winston Select blister
1995 #3 Goodwrench Silver PLS
1995 #3 Goodwrench Brickyard/30,000
1995 #3 Goodwrench
1995 #8 ASA Camaro '85
1995 #NNO R.Petty 7&7 Champ. 2-car blister
1995 #NNO Brickyard 2-car set/25,000
1996 #3 Olympic HO clear windows blue box
1996 #3 Olympic black windows blister
1996 #3 Olympic hood open clear windows blister
1996 #3 Goodwrench Pit Stop blister
1996 #3 Goodwrench Race Day blister
1996 #3 Goodwrench
1996 #3 AC-Delco Japan
1997 #3 Wheaties Mail-In
1997 #3 Wheaties HO SI
1997 #3 Wheaties black window blister

1997 #3 Wheaties
1997 #3 Goodwrench Plus BX
1997 #3 Goodwrench Plus BL
1997 #3 Goodwrench Brickyard/14,256
1997 #3 Goodwrench
1997 #3 AC Delco black window blister
1997 #3 AC Delco
1998 #3 Goodwrench Plus Bass Pro
1998 #3 Goodwrench Plus Daytona Win
1998 #3 Goodwrench Plus BL
1998 #3 Goodwrench Plus
1998 #3 Coke/10,000
1998 #8 RPM '75 Dodge/10,000
1998 #K2 Dayvault's Pink Roof 1956 Ford
1998 #K2 Dayvault's Dark Roof 1956 Ford
1999 #3 Wrangler
1999 #3 Goodwrench Last Lap
1999 #3 Goodwrench Sign
1999 #3 Goodwrench 25th Ann.
1999 #3 Goodwrench
1999 #30 Army '76 Malibu
1999 #77 HyGain '76 Malibu
2000 #3 Goodwr.Taz No Bull
2000 #3 Goodwrench No Bull raced/76,003
2000 #3 Goodwrench/30,024
2001 #3 Goodwrench Talladega No Bull Win
2001 #3 Good.Oreo Tin/34,161
2001 #3 Goodwrench Oreo/55,040
2001 #3 Goodwrench/20,880
2002 #2 Wrangler '79 MC/30,744
2002 #2 Coke '80 Pontiac in a Coke can/61,680
2002 #3 Coke '98 MC in vending machine tin/25,883
2002 #15 Wrangler 1979 Pontiac Ventura/30,744
2002 #NNO Jr./Oreo White Gold 2-car set in tin/7560
2002 #NNO Legacy/29,088
2003 #1 True Value '01 IROC Green/11,736
2003 #1 True Value '00 IROC Lt.Blue/11,736
2003 #1 True Value '99 IROC Blue/12,096
2003 #3 Victory Lap/14,040
2003 #3 Goodwrench No Bull '00 Mon.Carlo/15,264
2003 #3 Foundation/30,888
2003 #19 Beldon Asphalt 1977 Malibu/11,376
2004 #3 9-car set/5040 w/case
2006 #NNO Hall of Fame
Action Racing Collectables AC Racing 1:
1993 #3 Goodwrench
Action Racing Collectables Advanced Pro
2008 #3 Goodwrench '98 Daytona COT/333
2008 #3 Enduring Legends Johnny Cash/333
Action Racing Collectables Ceramic 1
2000-01 #3 Goodwrench Taz '00
2000-01 #3 Goodwrench '97 Monte Carlo Crash/5004 '01
Action Racing Collectables Crystal 1
1998-00 #3 Wrangler/5000 '99
1998-00 #3 Goodwrench Taz/2500 '00
1998-00 #3 Goodwrench '99
1998-00 #3 Coke/9000 '98
Action Racing Collectables Fan Fueler 1
1998 #3 Goodwrench Plus
Action Racing Collectables Historical S
2004 #1 True Value '99 IROC Orange/6372
2004 #2 Mello Yello '79 Pontiac Ventura GM Dealers/984
2004 #2 Mello Yello '79 Pontiac Ventura/11,664
2004 #2 Mello Yello '79 Pontiac Ventura GM Dealers/144
2004 #2 Mello Yello '79 Pontiac Ventura/6960
2004 #3 Wrangler '85 Camaro GM Dealers/1092
2004 #3 Wrangler '85 Camaro/21,000
2004 #3 Goodwrench Olympic '96 Monte Carlo CW Bank/6696
2004 #3 Wheaties '97 MC Mac Tools/288
2004 #3 Wheaties '97 Monte Carlo/2200
2005 #3 True Value IROC Dark Green '00 Firebird/3504
2005 #3 Goodwrench '91 Lumina QVC/1008
2005 #3 Goodwrench '91 Lumina/5004
2005 #3 Goodwrench Daytona Crash '97 Monte Carlo Platinum/300
2005 #3 Goodwrench Daytona Crash '97 Monte Carlo
2005 #12 Budweiser IROC '87 Camaro Liquid Metal QVC/2508
2005 #12 Budweiser IROC '87 Camaro Liquid Metal/6684
2005 #12 Budweiser IROC '87 Camaro GM Dealers Chrome/564
2005 #12 Budweiser IROC '87 Camaro GM Dealers/360
2005 #12 Budweiser IROC '87 Camaro/3276
2005 #14 Budweiser IROC Lime Green '88 Camaro GM Dealers/396
2005 #14 Budweiser IROC Lime Green '88 Camaro QVC/1500
2005 #14 Budweiser IROC Lime Green '88 Camaro/5844
2006 #3 Bud IROC '89 Camaro QVC*
2006 #3 Bud IROC '89 Camaro GM Dealers/792
2006 #3 Bud IROC '89 Camaro/8500*
Action Racing Collectables Pewter 1:64
1996 #3 Wrangler
Action Racing Collectables Pit Wagon
1990-03 #3 Goodwrench 1999
1990-03 #3 Goodwrench Plus Bass Pro '98
1990-03 #3 Goodwrench 7-Time Champ
1990-03 #3 Goodwr.RCCA/2500 '96
1990-03 #3 Goodwrench 1994 Champ/5000 1995
1990-03 #3 Goodwrench/3000 1995
1990-03 #3 Wheaties/3756 '97
1990-03 #3 Wrangler/2508 '99
1990-03 #3 Goodwrench Peter Max paint
1990-03 #3 Goodwrench Taz No Bull
1990-03 #3 Goodwrench 25th Anniversary/2508 '99
1990-03 #NNO Legacy/3333 '03
Action Racing Collectables Platinum Day
2008 #3 Goodwrench Plus '98 Monte Carlo/7104
Action Racing Collectables Transporters
2001 #3 Oreo/2508
2001 #3 Goodwrench/6004
2002 #3 Goodwrench Legacy w/sigs/50,094
2002 #3 Forever the Man/28,672
2003 #NNO Realtree Racing/2712
2004 #NNO Foundation Feed the Children/1764
Action RCR 1:32
2004 #3 AC Delco Japan '97 Monte Carlo QVC/1500
2004 #3 Coca Cola Japan '98 Monte Carlo QVC/1500
2004 #3 Goodwrench '96 MC QVC/1500
2004 #3 Goodwrench Crash '97 Monte Carlo QVC/1500
2004 #3 Goodwr.Plus Daytona Win '98 Monte Carlo QVC/1500
2004 #3 Goodwrench Silver '95 Monte Carlo/2376
2004 #3 Goodwrench Silver '95 Monte Carlo GM Dealers/336
2004 #3 Goodwrench Silver '95 Monte Carlo QVC/1500
2004 #3 Goodwrench Talladega '00 Monte Carlo GM Dealers/528
2004 #3 Goodwrench Talladega '00 Monte Carlo QVC/1500
2004 #3 Goodwrench Peter Max '00 MC QVC/1500
2004 #3 Wrangler '99 Monte Carlo GM Dealers/648
2004 #3 Wrangler '99 Monte Carlo/4380
2004 #3 Goodwrench Taz '00 Monte Carlo
2004 #3 Goodwrench Peter Max '00 MC GM Dealers/888
2004 #3 Goodwrench Peter Max '00 Monte Carlo/5784
2004 #3 Goodwrench Talladega '00 Monte Carlo/3432
2004 #3 Goodwrench Sign '99 Monte Carlo GM Dealers/648
2004 #3 Goodwrench Sign '99 Monte Carlo/4008
2004 #3 Goodwr.Plus Daytona Win '98 MC GM Dealers/264
2004 #3 Goodwr.Plus Daytona Win '98 Monte Carlo/3168
2004 #3 Goodwrench Crash '97 MC GM Dealers/936
2004 #3 Goodwrench Crash '97 Monte Carlo/15,516
2004 #3 Goodwrench Olympics '96 Monte Carlo GM Dealers/408
2004 #3 Goodwrench Olympics '96 Monte Carlo/4344
2004 #3 Goodwrench '96 MC GM Dealers/504
2004 #3 Goodwrench '96 Monte Carlo/4296
2004 #3 Coca Cola Japan '98 MC GM Dealers/528
2004 #3 Coca Cola Japan '98 Monte Carlo/3672
2004 #3 AC Delco Japan '97 MC GM Dealers/624
2004 #3 AC Delco Japan '97 Monte Carlo/4296
2005 #3 Goodwrench 25th Ann. '98 Monte Carlo GM Dealers/312
2005 #3 Goodwrench 25th Ann. '98 Monte Carlo QVC/1500
2005 #3 Wheaties '97 Monte Caro GM Dealers/312
2005 #3 Wheaties '97 Monte Carlo QVC/1500
2005 #3 Wheaties '97 MC/1776
2005 #3 Oreo '01 Monte Carlo QVC/1500
2005 #3 Oreo '01 Monte Carlo GM Dealers/312
2005 #3 Oreo '01 Monte Carlo/1740
2005 #3 Goodwrench Under Lights '00 Monte Carlo QVC/1200
2005 #3 Goodwrench Under Lights '00 Monte Carlo GM Dealers/312
2005 #3 Goodwrench Under Lights '00 Monte Carlo/3504
2005 #3 Goodwrench 25th Ann. '99 Monte Carlo/1728
2005 #3 Bass Pro '98 Monte Carlo/2604
Action Road Racing 1:12
2003 #3 Earn Jr./Pilgrim/Collins '01 C5-R Corvette/6000
2003 #3 Earn Jr./Pilgrim/Collins '01 C5-R Corvette RCCA/100
Action Road Racing 1:43
2000-01 #3 Earn/Earn Jr./Pilgrim/Collins C5-R Corvette raced/2424 '01
2000-01 #3 Earn Jr./Pilgrim/Collins C5-R Corvette/12,024 '01
Action Total Concept 1:64
2000 #3 Goodwrench Peter Max paint/69,480
Action/Funline Muscle Machines 1:18
2004 #3 Goodwrench '69 Camaro
2004 #3 Goodwrench '69 Chevelle
2004 #3 Goodwrench '67 Nova
2005 #3 Goodwrench '69 Chevelle GM Dealers/120
2005 #3 Goodwrench '69 Chevelle QVC/600
2005 #3 Goodwrench '69 Chevelle RCCA/300
2005 #3 Goodwrench '71 Camaro
2005 #3 Goodwrench '69 Chevelle/728
Action/Funline Muscle Machines 1:24
2004 #3 Goodwrench '69 Camaro
2004 #3 Goodwrench '69 Chevelle
2004 #3 Goodwrench '66 Nova
Action/RCCA 1:18
2002 #NNO Monte Carlo SS Color Chrome/1008
2002 #NNO Monte Carlo SS/408
Action/RCCA 1:24
1994 #3 Wrangler '87 Monte Carlo Bank/5016
1994 #3 Wrangler '87 Mon.Carlo
1994 #3 Wrangler '85 Monte Carlo Bank/5016
1994 #3 Wrangler '81 Pontiac Bank/5016
1994 #3 Goodwr.Bank/5016
1994 #3 Goodwrench In Memory of Neil/5016
1995 #2 Wrangler '81 Pontiac Bank/5016
1995 #3 Wrangler 1984 MC yellow deck lid/5016
1995 #3 Wrangler 1984 MC blue deck lid/5016
1995 #3 Goodwrench Silver GM red wheels
1995 #3 Goodwrench Silver GM black wheels
1995 #3 Goodwrench Silver GM Parts red wheels
1995 #3 Goodwrench Silver GM Parts black wheels
1995 #3 Goodwrench Bank without headlights
1995 #3 Goodwrench Bank with headlights
1995 #3 Goodwrench w/SkyBox card/5016
1995 #3 Goodwrench 1986 MC Aerocoupe/5016
1995 #15 Wrangler Bank#1 1983 T-bird/10,008
1995 #NNO R.Petty 7&7 2-cars
1996 #3 Goodwrench Bank
1996 #3 AC Delco Bank
1996 #15 Wrangler 1982 Thunderbird Bank
1996 #15 Wrangler 1982 Thunderbird/10,000
1997 #3 Wrangler '84 Monte Carlo Daytona/10,000
1997 #3 Wheaties Bank
1997 #3 Lowes Food/10,000
1997 #3 Goodwrench Plus Bank/10,000
1997 #3 Goodwrench Plus
1997 #3 Goodwrench/3500
1997 #3 AC Delco/1200
2002 #2 Coke '80 Pont.Bank/5004
2002 #3 Goodwrench Bank '90 Lumina/4008
2002 #8 Docs '64 Chevelle Bank/3504
2002 #15 Wrangler 1979 Pont. Ventura Bank/3000
2002 #NNO Legacy Bank/2004
2003 #3 Victory Lap/2400
2003 #3 Goodwr.Silver '95 Monte Carlo/4800
2003 #3 Goodwrench Bass Pro Shops/4500
2003 #3 Goodwrench '01 Monte Carlo/3333
2003 #3 Goodwrench No Bull '00 Monte Carlo/2508
2003 #3 Goodwrench 1990 Lumina/4008
2003 #3 Foundation/3100
2003 #19 Belden Asphalt '76 Malibu/3600
2006 #NNO Dale Tribute 5-car set/1200
2006 #NNO HOF/1333
Action/RCCA 1:32
2002 #3 4-car set
2002 #3 Goodwrench Gold Peter Max '00MC/960
2002 #3 Goodwrench Peter Max '00MC/3600
2002 #3 Goodwrench Oreo Gold '01MC/600
2002 #3 Goodwrench Oreo '01MC/3000
2002 #3 Goodwrench Gold/720 2001 Monte Carlo
2002 #3 Goodwrench/3600 2001 Monte Carlo
2002 #3 Coke '98 MC in vending machine tin/2004
2002 #NNO Legacy/2004
2003 #3 Goodwrench No Bull '00 Monte Carlo/1008
2003 #3 Goodwr.Silver Select '95 Monte Carlo/1800
2003 #3 Goodwrench Bass Pro Shops
2003 #3 Foundation/1012
1999-00 #3 Wrangler/3500
Action/RCCA 1:64
1994 #3 Wrangler 1985 Monte Carlo notchback
1994 #3 Goodwrench '94 club
1994 #3 Goodwrench/16,128
1994 #3 Wrangler 1987 Monte Carlo fastback
1995 #3 Wrangler 1981 Pontiac/16,128
1995 #3 Goodwrench Silver
1995 #3 Goodwrench 1994 Lumina/16,128
1996 #3 Goodwrench/20,000
1996 #3 AC Delco
1996 #15 Wrangler '82 Thunderbird/20,000
1997 #3 Wheaties
1997 #3 Lowes Foods
1997 #3 Goodwren.Plus/25,000
1997 #3 Goodwrench/5000
1997 #3 AC Delco/20,000
1998 #3 Goodwrench Plus Fan Club box
1998 #3 Goodwr.Plus Bass Pro
1998 #3 Goodwrench Plus
1998 #3 Coke
1998 #8 RPM '75 Dod./12,500
1998 #K2 Dayvault's Pink Roof 1956 Ford
1999 #3 Wrangler/15,192
1999 #3 Goodwrench Sign Last Lap/15,000
1999 #3 Goodwr.Sign/10,000
1999 #3 Goodwrench 25th Anniversary/10,000
1999 #3 Goodwrench/10,000
1999 #30 Army '76 Malibu/5000
1999 #77 Hy-Gain '76 Malibu
2000 #3 Goodwrench Taz No Bull/17,000
2000 #3 Goodwrench Peter Max/5544
2000 #3 Goodwrench/10,008
2000 #NNO D.Earnhardt Jr. No Bull 2-cars in tin/6504
2001 #3 Goodwrench Oreo/3168
2001 #3 Goodwrench Platinum 7-car set/5004
2001 #3 Goodwrench/3024
2002 #2 Coke '80 Pont/6480
2002 #3 Coke '98 MC in vending machine/3000
2002 #3 Goodwrench Plus No Bull 76th Win/6048
2002 #15 Wrangler 1979 Pontiac Ventura/4200
2002 #NNO 7-car set Gold/10,000
2002 #NNO Legacy/3036
2003 #1 True Value '99 IROC Blue/2016
2003 #1 True Value '99 IROC Orange/2016
2003 #1 True Value '00 IROC Lt.Blue/2016
2003 #1 True Value '01 IROC Green/2016
2003 #3 Victory Lap/1500
2003 #3 Foundation/3604
2003 #19 Beldon Asphalt '76 Malibu/3460
2004 #3 RCR Museum 9-car set/1008
2006 #NNO Dale Tribute HOF/1584
Action/RCCA Banks 1:24
1998 #3 Goodwrench Plus Daytona Win
1998 #3 Goodwrench Plus Bass Pro/12,500
1998 #3 Goodwr.Plus/12,500
1998 #3 Coke/15,000
1998 #8 RPM '75 Dodge/12,500
1998 #K2 Dayvault's Pink Roof 1956 Ford
1999 #3 Wrangler/10,020
1999 #3 Goodwrench Sign Last Lap/10,000
1999 #3 Goodwrench Sign
1999 #3 Goodwrench 25th Anniversary/8000
1999 #3 Goodwrench
1999 #30 Army 1976 Malibu Bank/4000
2000 #2 Curb '80 Olds/2004
2000 #3 Wrangler '87MC Aerocoupe/2004
2000 #3 Goodwrench Under the Lights/2304
2000 #3 Goodwrench Taz No Bull/13,500
2000 #3 Goodwrench Peter Max/7500
2000 #3 Goodwrench No Bull/5052
2000 #3 Goodwrench/7000
2001 #3 Goodwrench 1988 Monte Carlo/2005
2001 #3 Goodwr.Oreo/4008
2001 #3 Goodwrench/3996
2001 #8 Goodwrench 1987 Nova Bank/2304
Action/RCCA Dually Trucks 1:24
1994 #3 Goodwrench PLS Bank/5016
1995 #3 Goodwrench 7-Time Champ Bank
1995 #3 Goodwrench PLS Bank/5016
1996 #3 Goodwrench RCCA Bank/3504
1997 #3 Wheaties Bank/5000
Action/RCCA Dually Trucks 1:64
1994-97 #3 Wheaties '97
1994-97 #3 Goodwr./15,000 '96
1994-97 #3 Goodwrench PLS/15,000 '95
1994-97 #3 Goodwrench PLS in blister pack '94
Action/RCCA Dually Trucks with Trailer
1994 #3 Goodwrench PLS/2748
1995 #3 Goodwr.PLS/3492
1996 #3 Goodwrench Silver
1996 #3 Goodwr.RCCA/2500
1997 #3 Wheaties/5000
1998 #3 Goodwr.Bass Pro/5004
1999 #3 Wrangler/3504
1999 #3 Goodwr.Sign/2508
1999 #3 Goodwr.25th/3000
2000 #3 Goodwrench Peter Max/2508
2000 #3 Goodwr.Taz/2508
Action/RCCA Elite 1:24
1997 #3 Wheaties Gold number plate Proto
1997 #3 Wheaties Brass number plate/8618
1997 #3 Wheaties Gold number plate/5000
1997 #3 Goodwr.Plus/12,500
1997 #3 Goodwrench/3500
1997 #3 AC Delco/12,500
1998 #3 Goodwrench 1995 MC Silver/20,000
1998 #3 Goodwrench Plus Daytona Win raced/9996
1998 #3 Goodwrench Plus Bass Pro/10,000
1998 #3 Goodwrench Plus/7500
1998 #3 Coke/12,500
1998 #3 Goodwrench Plus Gold/100
1998 #8 RPM '75 Dod/10,000
1998 #K2 Dayvault's/10,000
1999 #3 Wrangler/7500
1999 #3 Goodwrench Sign Last Lap/8500
1999 #3 Goodwren.Sign/5000
1999 #3 Goodwrench 25th Anniversary/7500
1999 #3 Goodwrench/7500
1999 #30 Army '76 Malibu/2500
1999 #77 Hy-Gain 1976 Malibu/2500
2000 #2 Curb '80 Olds/2700
2000 #3 Wrangler '87MC Aerocoupe/2700
2000 #3 Goodwrench 75th Win Platinum/3504
2000 #3 Goodwrench Under the Lights/1200
2000 #3 Goodwrench Test/3500
2000 #3 Goodwrench Taz No Bull/9504
2000 #3 Goodwrench Peter Max/7500
2000 #3 Goodwrench No Bull/3504
2000 #3 Goodwrench/5000
2000 #2000 DEI Pit Practice/1008
2001 #3 Goodwrench 1988 MC Aerocoupe/3205
2001 #3 Goodwr.Oreo/5004
2001 #3 Good.Test/3504
2001 #3 Goodwr.Metal/7500
2001 #3 Goodwrench Split Clear/3504
2001 #3 Goodwrench/2496
2001 #8 Good.'87 Nova/2304
2001 #2001 DEI Pit Practice Car/2796
2002 #2 Coke '80 Pontiac/5004
2002 #3 Goodwrench Plus No Bull 76th Win/4500
2002 #8 Docs '64 Chevelle/3504
2002 #15 Wrangler 1979 Pontiac Ventura/4008
2002 #NNO Legacy/3000
2003 #3 Victory Lap/3000
2003 #3 Goodwrench No Bull 2000 Monte Carlo/4500
2003 #3 Foundation/4300
2003 #19 Beldon Asphalt '76 Malibu/3600
2006 #NNO HOF White Gold/33
2006 #NNO HOF Platinum/46
2006 #NNO HOF/2333
Action/RCCA Elite 1:32
2003 #3 Goodwr.Silver Select '95 Monte Carlo/1800
2003 #3 Goodwrench Bass Pro Shops/1800
2003 #3 Goodwrench No Bull '00 Monte Carlo/1008
2003 #3 Foundation/1012
Action/RCCA Elite 1:64
2001 #3 Goodwrench Oreo/3168
2001 #3 Good.Metal/7500
2001 #3 Goodwrench/2976
2002 #NNO Legacy/2028
2003 #3 Foundation/2500
2006 #NNO HOF/933
Action/RCCA Elite Historical 1:24
2006 #3 GM Goodwrench '91 Lumina White Gold/33
2006 #3 GM Goodwrench '91 Lumina/1333
Action/RCCA Elite Prototypes 1:24
1998 #3 Coke Proto/12
1998 #3 Goodwrench Plus Daytona Proto
1999 #3 Wrangler Proto
Action/RCCA Gold 1:32
1998 #3 Goodwrench Bass Pro
Action/RCCA Historical 1:24
2006 #3 Budweiser '89 IROC Liquid Color/333
2006 #3 GM Goodwrench '91 Lumina/1333
2006 #3 Budweiser '89 IROC/1333
Action/RCCA Historical Series 1:24
2004 #2 Mello Yello '80 Ventura/1800
2004 #3 Wheaties '97 Monte Carlo/2508
2004 #3 Goodwrench Peter Max '00 Monte Carlo/2400
2004 #3 Goodwrench Olympic '96 Monte Carlo/2700
2004 #3 AC Delco '96 Monte Carlo/1500
2004 #3 Wrangler '85 Camaro/2400
2005 #3 Wrangler '99 Monte Carlo/903
2005 #3 Goodwrench Service Plus '00 Talladega Win/903
2005 #3 Goodwrench Service Plus '98 Daytona Win/903
2005 #3 Coke '98 Monte Carlo/903
2005 #12 Budweiser IROC '87 Camaro/804
2005 #14 Budweiser IROC Lime Green '88 Camaro/1500
2005 #14 Budweiser IROC Lime Green '88 Camaro Color Chrome/504
Action/RCCA Historical Series 1:32
2004 #3 Wheaties '97 Monte Carlo/804
Action/RCCA Historical Series 1:64
2004 #2 Mello Yello '80 Ventura/2160
Action/RCCA Historical Series Elite 1:2
2004 #2 Mello Yello '80 Ventura/2508
2004 #3 Goodwrench Peter Max '00 Monte Carlo Plat./408
2004 #3 Goodwrench Olympic '96 Monte Carlo Plat./408
2004 #3 Goodwrench Olympic '96 Monte Carlo/3996
2004 #3 Goodwrench Crash '97 Daytona Raced Platinum/504
2004 #3 Goodwrench Crash '97 Daytona Raced/10,000
2004 #3 AC Delco '96 Monte Carlo Plat./408
2005 #3 Wrangler '99 Monte Carlo White Gold/33
2005 #3 Wrangler '99 Monte Carlo Platinum/203
2005 #3 Wrangler '99 Monte Carlo Color Chrome/603
2005 #3 Goodwrench Service Plus '00 Talladega Raced White Gold/33
2005 #3 Goodwrench Service Plus '00 Talladega Raced Platinum/203
2005 #3 Goodwrench Service Plus '00 Talladega Raced Color Chrome/603
2005 #3 Goodwrench Service Plus '98 Daytona Raced White Gold/33
2005 #3 Goodwrench Service Plus '98 Daytona Raced Platinum/203
2005 #3 Goodwrench Service Plus '98 Daytona Raced Color Chrome/603
2005 #3 Coke '98 Monte Carlo White Gold/33
2005 #3 Coke '98 Monte Carlo Platinum/203
2005 #3 Coke '98 Monte Carlo Color Chrome/603
Action/RCCA Historical Series Elite 1:3
2004 #3 Wheaties '97 Monte Carlo/804
Action/RCCA Legends, Oldsmobiles and
1991-92 #15 Wrangler
Action/RCCA RCR 1:32
2004 #3 AC Delco Japan '97 Monte Carlo/1500
2004 #3 Goodwr.Plus '98 Daytona Raced/1500
2004 #3 Goodwrench Sign '99 Monte Carlo/1500
2004 #3 Goodwrench Silver '95 Monte Carlo/1500
2004 #3 Goodwrench Talladega '00 Monte Carlo/1500
2004 #3 Wrangler '99 Monte Carlo/1500
2004 #3 Goodwrench Peter Max '00 Monte Carlo/1500
2004 #3 Goodwrench Crash '97 Daytona Raced/1500
2004 #3 Goodwrench Olympics '96 Monte Carlo/1500
2004 #3 Goodwrench '96 Monte Carlo/1500
2004 #3 Coca Cola Japan '98 Monte Carlo/1500
2005 #3 Goodwrench Silver Select '95 Monte Carlo/1500
2005 #3 Goodwrench Service Plus '00 Talladega Raced/1500
2005 #3 Goodwrench Taz '00 Monte Carlo/1500
2005 #3 Goodwrench 25th Ann. '99 Monte Carlo/1500
2005 #3 Oreo '01 Monte Carlo/1008
2005 #3 Wheaties '97 Monte Carlo/1500
2005 #3 Goodwrench Under Lights '00 Monte Carlo/1008
Action/RCCA Revell 1:64
1991-92 #3 Goodwrench
Action/RCCA SelectNet Banks 1:24
1999 #3 Wrangler
Action/RCCA Total View 1:64
2000 #3 Goodwr.Peter Max/5760
2000 #3 Goodwrench No Bull
Action/RCCA Transporters 1:64
1992 #3 Goodwrench DEI
1993 #3 Goodwr.RCCA w/car in black case/10,000
1993 #3 Goodwr.RCCA in wood box w/2-cars/500
1993 #3 Goodwrench RCCA in box with 2-cars
1994 #3 1987 Wrangler yellow RCCA/5016
1994 #3 1985 Wrangler blue RCCA/5016
1994 #3 7-Time Champ Promo Awards Banquet in plastic case
1994 #3 Goodwr.RCCA/2508
1995 #3 Goodwrench Service RCCA/5000
1995 #3 Goodwr.RCCA/5004
1995 #NNO 7&7 Champs RCCA/3000
2002 #3 Goodwrench Plus/33,333
2002 #3 Forever the Man/5004
1996-97 #3 Goodwrench '96
Action/RCCA Transporters 1:96
1994-96 #3 87 Wrangler Yellow
1994-96 #3 85 Wrang.Blue/2508 '94
1994-96 #3 Goodwrench/3000 '96
1994-96 #3 Goodwrench/5000 '95
1994-96 #3 Goodwrench/3000 '94
Brookfield 1:24
1999 #3 Wrangler Silver Incentive/624
1999 #3 Goodwrench/Wrangler/7500 2-car set
2006 #NNO HOF/333
1997-99 #3 AC Delco/15,000 '97
Brookfield Dually with Car and Show
1993-95 #3 Goodwr.Plus/5000 '95
1993-95 #3 Goodwrench without car/5000 '94
1993-95 #3 Goodwr./40,000 '93
1993-95 #NNO 7&7/5000 '95
Brookfield Dually with Car and Show Tra
1997 #3 Wheaties/10,000 '97
1998 #1 Coke Bear/2500
1998 #3 Goodwrench Plus Bass Pro/5000
1998 #3 Coke/2500
1999 #3 Wrangler/3992
1999 #3 Goodwrench Plus Silver/2584
2000 #3 Goodwrench Peter Max/2508
2000 #3 Goodwrench Taz Silver/516
2000 #3 Goodwr.Taz/2164
2000 #3 Goodwrench Taz/2508
2001 #3 Oreo 3-Axle Silver/2892
2001 #3 Oreo 3-Axle/12,198
2001 #3 Oreo 2-Axle Silver/1004
2001 #3 Oreo 2-Axle/6504
2001 #3 Goodwrench Silver/5004
2001 #3 Goodwrench Plus/10,000
Brookfield Sets 1:24
1994-03 #3 Goodwrench/Coke 2-car set/10,000 '96
1994-03 #3 Found.Black/Brushed Metal 2-car set/55,000
1994-03 #NNO Dale Jr./Coke 2-car set/5000 '98
1994-03 #NNO Brickyard 2-car set/5000 '95
Brookfield Sets 1:64
1995 #3 Goodwr./Olympic 3-car set/10,000 '95
Brookfield Suburbans, Blazers, and T
1992-93 #3 Goodwr.Bank/5000 '92
Brookfield Suburbans, Blazers, and Taho
1995 #3 Goodwrench Bank 7-Time Champ Silver/1500
1995 #3 Goodwrench Bank 7-Time Champ/30,000
1995 #3 Goodwrench Silver Tahoe Bank/10,000
1995 #3 Goodwrench Tahoe Bank/10,000
1995 #3 Brickyard/5000
1995 #NNO R.Petty 7-Time Bank split tampos reversed/30,000
1995 #NNO R.Petty 7-Time Bank split paint scheme/30,000
1995 #NNO 7-Time Champ 2-Suburban set/25,000
1996 #3 Olym.Tahoe Silver/832
1996 #3 Olympic Tahoe/10,000
1997 #3 Goodwr.Plus/5000
1998 #3 Goodwrench Bass Pro Tahoe/5000
1999 #3 Wrangler/2508
1999 #3 Goodwrench 25th Anniv.Tahoe/2508
1999 #3 Goodwrench 25th Anniv.Blazer/2508
1999 #3 AC-Delco Bank/5000
2003 #3 Goodwrench Silver Select Suburban/2646
2003 #3 Goodwrench Bass Pro Suburban/3711
Brookfield Trackside 1:25
1995 #3 Goodwrench Silver/10,000
1995 #3 Goodwrench/10,000
1995 #3 AC Delco Silver/800
1996 #3 Goodwr.Olympic/10,000
1996 #3 AC Delco/10,000
1997 #3 Wheaties Suburban/10,000
1997 #3 Wheaties/10,000
1997 #3 Goodwrench Plus Suburban/5000
1998 #3 Goodwrench Plus Bass Pro/10,000
1998 #3 Coke Suburban/3792
1998 #3 Coke/2500
1999 #3 Wrangler Suburban/10,002
1999 #3 Wrangler/2508
1999 #3 Goodwrench Plus/2508
1999 #3 Goodwrench 25th Anniv.Suburban/2748
1999 #3 Goodwr.Silver/5004
2000 #3 Goodwr.Taz/2508
2001 #3 Goodwr.Plus/5004
2001 #3 Goodwr.Silver/960
2001 #3 Goodwrench/3504
Brookfield Trackside 1:64
2004 #3 Goodwrench Peter Max '00 Monte Carlo/5004
Ertl 1:18
1992 #3 Goodwrench/40,000
1995 #3 Goodwrench Silver Buck Fever/15,000
1995 #3 Goodwrench 7-Time Champion/10,000
1996 #3 Goodwrench '95MC Buck Fever/15,000
Ertl 1:64
1986-93 #15 Wrangler Promo
Ertl Pow-R Pull 1:64
1984 #15 Wrangler
Ertl White Rose Transporters Past an
1992-94 #3 1986 Wrangler '92
1992-94 #3 Goodwrench '93
Matchbox White Rose Super Stars 1:64
1994 #3 Gold Lumina SSA BX
1995 #3 Goodwrench
1995 #3 Gold 7-Time SS Aw.
1990-92 #3 MomPop's PBG 92
1990-92 #3 Good. BL 92
1990-92 #3 GM Parts BX 91
1990-92 #3 GM BX 90
Matchbox White Rose Team Convoys 1:6
1990-93 #3 Goodwrench '93
1990-93 #3 Goodwrench 1991 Champ w/Van '92
1990-93 #3 Goodwr.w/van '91
Matchbox White Rose Transporters Pro
1993-94 #3 Goodwr.7-Time Champ in plastic case/4000 '94
1993-94 #3 Goodwr.6-Time Champ in plastic case/5000 '93
Matchbox White Rose Transporters Super
1989 #3 Goodwrench
1990 #3 Goodwrench
1991 #3 Goodwrench
1992 #3 Goodwrench
1994 #3 Goodwrench Snap-on
1995 #3 Snap On
1995 #3 Goodwrench
Motorsports Authentics Dale The Movie 1
2007 #2 Mike Curb '80 Olds 1st Championship/7003
2007 #2 Wrangler '81 Pontiac 1st Wrangler Win/7003
2007 #3 GW Plus '98 MC The 500/7003
2007 #3 Goodwrench '96 MC Starting in Front/7003
2007 #3 Goodwrench '95 MC Bricks/7003
2007 #3 GW Silver '95 MC Silver Select/7003
2007 #3 GW '94 Lumina Number 7/7003
2007 #3 GW '94 Lumina Four Tire Stop/7003
2007 #3 Goodwrench '90 Lumina Engine Change/7003
2007 #3 GW '88 Monte Carlo 1st Goodwrench Win/7003
2007 #3 Wrangler '86 Monte Carlo Muddy Windshield/7003
2007 #3 Wrangler '87 MC#| Pass in the Grass/7003
Motorsports Authentics Steel 1:16
2006 #NNO HOF/1000
Peachstate/GMP Transporters 1:64
1996-01 #3 Goodwren/2500 '96
Racing Champions 1:24
1993 #3 Goodwrench Mom-n-Pop's on fender
1993 #3 Goodwrench Goodyear in Yellow
1993 #3 Goodwrench Goodyear in White
1994 #3 Goodwrench
1991-92 #3 Goodwrench with tampo decals '92
1991-92 #3 Goodwrench with fender stickers '92
Racing Champions 1:43
1992 #3 Goodwrench
1993 #3 Goodwrench
Racing Champions 1:64
1990 #3 GM Perform.Parts
1990 #3 Goodwrench
1990 #NNO 12-car set in case
1991 #3 Lumina PB
1991 #3 Lumina NP
1991 #3 Lumina EB
1992 #3 Goodwrench 5-Time Champion card
1993 #3 Goodwrench 1989 Monte Carlo Promo blister
1993 #3 Goodwrench 1988 Monte Carlo Promo blister
1993 #3 Goodwrench Mom-n-Pop's blister Promo
1993 #3 Goodwrench
1994 #94 McDonald's All-Star Promo
Racing Champions 3-Pack 1:64
1990-92 #NNO M.Shep./R.Petty '90
Racing Champions 5-Pack 1:144
1991 #NNO 3.DE/27.RW/28.DA/30.BH/43.RP
Racing Champions AC Racing Promos 1:64
1992 #3 Goodwrench
Racing Champions Banks 1:24
1992-94 #3 Goodwrench SI '94 Mom-n-Pop's rear fender
1992-94 #3 Goodwrench Snap-On
1992-94 #3 Goodwrench no serial #'d box '92
1992-94 #3 Goodwrench/10,000 with #'d box 1992
1992-94 #3 Goodwrench Western Steer on fender/10,000 '93
1992-94 #3 Goodwrench '93 Mom-n-Pop's rear fender
Racing Champions Flat Bottom 1:64
1989 #3 Goodwrench
Racing Champions Pit Stop 1:24
1992 #3 Goodwrench
Racing Champions Pit Stop 1:43

1992 #3 Goodwrench
1993 #3 Goodwrench
Racing Champions Premier 1:43
1993 #3 Goodwrench/10,000
1994 #3 Goodwrench
Racing Champions Premier 1:64
1992 #3 Goodwrench/40,000
1993 #3 Goodwrench/20,000 DEI on package
1993 #3 Goodwrench/20,000
1994 #3 Goodwrench 6-time champ/10,000
Racing Champions Premier Brickyard 400
1994 #3 Goodwrench
Racing Champions Premier Transporters 1
1993 #3 Goodwrench/7500
1993 #3 Goodwr.DEI/5000
1993 #3 Goodwrench/15,000
1994 #3 Goodwrench
1994 #3 Goodwrench
Racing Champions PVC Box 1:64
1993 #3 Die Hard 500 Win/5000
1993 #3 One Hot Night Win/7500
1993 #3 June 6th Win/5000
1993 #3 Pepsi 400 Win
1993 #3 Coca-Cola 600 Win/7500
1993 #3 Busch Clash/5000
1993 #3 Back in Black/5000
1993 #3 1993 WC Champ with Red Flags in box
1993 #3 1993 WC Champ/5000
Racing Champions Roaring Racers 1:64
1990-91 #3 Goodwrench SW '90
Racing Champions Super Collector's S
1992-94 #3 Goodwrench 3-cars 1:24/43/64 & Transporter
1992-94 #3 Goodwrench 2-cars 1:24/64 & 2-Transporters
Racing Champions Transporters 1:43
1993 #3 Goodwrench
Racing Champions Transporters 1:64
1992 #3 Goodwrench
1993 #3 Winston Win
1993 #3 Goodwrench Promo
1993 #3 Goodwr.Bank/10,000
1993 #3 Goodwrench
Racing Champions Transporters Retail
1993-94 #3 Goodwrench
Racing Champions Transporters Retail 1:
1994 #3 Goodwrench Promo
RCCA Club 1:24
2008 #3 Goodwrench '98 Daytona COT/700
RCCA Elite 1:24
2008 #3 Goodwrench '98 Daytona COT/1000
2008 #3 Goodwrench '98 Daytona COT Platinum/53
2008 #3 Goodwrench '98 Daytona COT White Gold/103
Revell 1:24
1991-95 #3 Goodwrench 6-Time Champion
1991-95 #3 Goodwrench SI '95
1991-95 #3 Goodwrench silver wheels SI '91
1991-95 #3 Goodwrench black wheels SI '93
1991-95 #3 Goodwrench Kellogg's Promo
Revell Club 1:18
1998 #3 Goodwrench Plus Daytona Win/504
1998 #3 Goodwrench Plus Bass Pro/504
1998 #3 Goodwrench Plus
1998 #3 Coke/2004
1999 #3 Goodwrench
2000 #3 Goodwrench Taz No Bull/2508
Revell Club 1:24
1998 #3 Goodwrench Plus Daytona Win/1596
1998 #3 Goodwrench Plus Bass Pro/1002
1998 #3 Goodwrench Plus/1596
1998 #3 Coke/3333
1999 #3 Wrangler/3333
1999 #3 Goodwrench Sign
1999 #3 Goodwrench 25th/1002
1999 #3 Goodwrench/2004
2000 #3 Goodwrench Taz/3333
2000 #3 Goodwrench Peter Max/2004
2000 #3 Goodwrench/2004
2001 #3 Goodwrench Oreo/9996
2001 #3 Goodwrench with Sonic decal/10,000
Revell Collection 1:18
1997 #3 Wheaties/10,008
1998 #3 Goodwrench Plus Brickyard Win
1998 #3 Goodwrench Plus Daytona Win/5004
1998 #3 Goodwrench Plus Bass Pro/8010
1998 #3 Coke/4008
1999 #3 Wrangler/6000
1999 #3 Goodwr.25th Ann./2508
1999 #3 Goodwrench
2000 #3 Goodwr.Taz No Bull/2508
2000 #3 Goodwr.Peter Max/2508
2001 #3 Goodwrench with Sonic decal
Revell Collection 1:24
1996 #3 Olympic
1998 #3 Goodwrench Plus Brickyard Win/10,008
1998 #3 Goodwrench Plus Bass Pro/14,994
1998 #3 Goodwrench Plus Daytona Win/7512
1998 #3 Coke Bank set with 1:64 car/2502
1998 #3 Coke/18,000
1999 #3 Wrangler/14,400
1999 #3 Goodwrench Sign
1999 #3 Goodwrench 25th
1999 #3 Goodwrench/7992
2000 #3 Goodwrench Test/1500
2000 #3 Goodwrench Taz Bank set with 1:64 car/14,400
2000 #3 Goodwrench Peter Max Bank w/1:64 car/1008
2000 #3 Goodwrench Peter Max/5508
2000 #3 Goodwrench/5004
2001 #3 Goodwrench with Sonic decal/10,000
2001 #3 Goodwrench test
2001 #3 Goodwrench Oreo
2001 #3 Goodwrench No Bull
Revell Collection 1:43
1998 #3 Goodwrench Plus Bass Pro
1998 #3 Goodwrench Plus Daytona Win/5004
1998 #3 Coke
1999 #3 Wrangler/5004
1999 #3 Goodwrench
2000 #3 Goodwr.Peter Max/3000
2000 #3 Goodwrench Taz/4000
2001 #3 GW Oreo Daytona
2001 #3 Goodwrench Oreo/48,084
Revell Collection 1:64
1996 #3 Olympic
1998 #3 Goodwrench Plus Brickyard Win/20,016
1998 #3 Goodwrench Plus Bass Pro
1998 #3 Goodwrench Plus Daytona Win/14,400
1998 #3 Coke/27,000
1999 #3 Wrangler/18,000
1999 #3 Goodwrench Sign
1999 #3 Goodwrench 25th
1999 #3 Goodwrench/14,400
2000 #3 Goodwrench Taz No Bull/30,384
2000 #3 Goodwrench Peter Max/1008
2000 #3 Goodwrench/12,024
2001 #3 Goodwrench Oreo Tin
2002 #NNO R.Earnhardt/D.Earnhardt D.Earnhardt Jr. 3-car tin/27,597
Revell Collection Train Sets 1:64
2002 #3 9-car train set/19,504
2003 #3 Foundation/7560
2003 #NNO Earnhardt Legacy/5292
Revell Retail 1:24
1996 #3 Olympic
1996 #3 Goodwrench
Revell Retail 1:64
1996 #3 Olympic Small BX
1996 #3 Olympic blister
1996 #3 Goodwrench
Revell Select 1:24
1998 #3 Goodwr.Plus Bass Pro
1998 #3 Goodwrench Plus
1999 #3 Goodwrench Sign
1999 #3 Goodwren.25th Ann.
2000 #3 Goodwrench Taz
2001 #3 Goodwrench Oreo
2001 #3 Goodwrench
2003 #3 Oreo '01 Monte Carlo
Revell Select Hobby 1:64
1998 #3 Goodwr.Plus Bass Pro
1998 #3 Goodwrench Plus
Revell Select Hobby Transporters 1:64
1998 #3 Goodwrench
Winner's Circle 1:18
2002 #3 Goodwr.Plus No Bull
2002 #3 Goodwr.Peter Max
2002 #3 Goodwrench Oreo
2002 #3 Goodwrench
2002 #3 Gppdwrench Oreo '01
2003 #3 Goodwrench Service Plus '00
2003 #3 Goodwrench Peter Max '00
2003 #3 Goodwrench No Bull '00
2003 #3 Foundation
2004 #3 Goodwrench Service Plus '01 Monte Carlo
2005 #3 Legacy '02
2005 #3 Foundation '03
2005 #3 Goodwrench '00
Winner's Circle 1:24
1996 #3 Goodwrench
1997 #3 Wheaties orange inter.
1997 #3 Wheaties gray interior
1997 #3 Goodwrench Plus
1997 #3 Goodwrench
1997 #3 AC Delco '96 MC
1998 #3 Goodwrench Silver
1998 #3 Goodwr.Daytona
1998 #3 Goodwrench Bass Pro
1998 #3 Goodwrench Plus
1998 #3 Coke
1999 #3 Wrangler
1999 #3 Goodwrench 25th Ann.
1999 #3 Goodwrench
2000 #3 Goodwr.Taz No Bull
2000 #3 Goodwrench Sign
2000 #3 Goodwr.Peter Max
2000 #3 Goodwrench
2001 #3 Goodwrench Oreo
2001 #3 Goodwrench
2002 #3 Goodwr.Oreo
2003 #3 2000 Peter Max
2003 #3 2000 Goodwr.No Bull
2003 #3 Foundation
2003 #NNO Legacy
2004 #3 Goodwrench Olympic '96 Monte Carlo
2004 #3 Coke '98 Monte Carlo
2005 #3 Coke Japan '98 Monte Carlo
2005 #3 Foundation '03
2005 #NNO Legacy '02
2006 #NNO HOF Dale Tribute split window box
Winner's Circle 1:43
1998 #3 Goodwrench Plus
1998 #3 Goodwrench Bass Pro
1998 #3 Coke
1999 #3 Goodwrench 25th Ann. Dale on package
1999 #3 Goodwrench 25th Ann. logo on package
2000 #3 Goodwrench
Winner's Circle 1:64
1996 #3 Goodwrench
1997 #3 Goodwrench
1998 #3 Goodwrench Plus Toy's R Us blister
1998 #3 Goodwrench Plus Daytona 500 blister
1998 #3 Goodwrench Plus 1998 Preview blister
1998 #3 Goodwrench with 25th Anniversary sticker
1998 #3 Goodwrench
1998 #3 Coke
1998 #NNO Goodwrench 25th Wrangler 2-cars
2000 #3 Goodwrench
2000 #3 Goodwrench Sign
2006 #NNO Dale Tribute 5-car set
Winner's Circle 24K Gold 1:64
1999 #3 Goodwrench
Winner's Circle Autographed Hood 1:64
2003 #3 Coke Japan '98
2004 #3 Goodwrench Olympic '96 Monte Carlo
2004 #3 Coke
2006 #NNO HOF Dale Tribute split window box
Winner's Circle Championship with Fi
1998-99 #2 1980 Championship
1998-99 #3 Wrangler '87 Champ.
1998-99 #3 Wrangler '86 Champ.
1998-99 #3 Goodwrench Plus 1998 Daytona 500
1998-99 #3 Goodwrench '94 Champ.
1998-99 #3 Goodwrench '93 Champ.
Winner's Circle Classic Hood 1:64
2001 #3 Goodwrench Silver Select '95
Winner's Circle Cool Customs 1:64
1998-99 #3 GW Silver '57 HT
1998-99 #3 GW '57 Convertible
1998-99 #3 GW '57 Chevy HT
Winner's Circle Dale the Movie Hoods 1:
2007 #2 Wrangler '81 Pontiac
2007 #2 Curb '80 Olds
2007 #3 Goodwrench Plus '98 MC
2007 #3 Goodwrench '96 Monte Carlo
2007 #3 Goodwrench '95 MC
2007 #3 Goodwrench Silver Select '95 MC
2007 #3 Goodwrench '94 MC Clinch
2007 #3 Goodwrench '94 MC
2007 #3 Goodwrench '90 Lumina
2007 #3 Goodwrench '88 MC
2007 #3 Wrangler '87 MC
2007 #3 Wrangler '86 MC
Winner's Circle Decade of Champions 1:6
2003 #3 Goodwrench 1994
2003 #3 Goodwrench 1993
Winner's Circle Deluxe Race Hood 1:64
2000 #3 Taz No Bull
2000 #3 Goodwr.Peter Max
2000 #3 Goodwrench Sign
2000 #3 Goodwrench
Winner's Circle Deluxe Winston Cup Scen
2000 #3 Goodwrench Richmond Win
Winner's Circle Die-Cast Kits 1:64
2003 #3 Goodwrench No Bull '00
Winner's Circle Double Platinum 1:43
2000 #3 R.Childress/Goodwrench
2000 #8 Dale Jr.
2001 #3 R.Childress/Goodwrench
2003 #NNO Legacy
Winner's Circle Driver Hood 1:64
2000-01 #3 Goodwrench '01 car is slanted in package
2000-01 #3 Goodwrench '00 car horizontal in package
Winner's Circle Driver Sticker 1:64
2001 #3 Goodwrench
2003 #1 True Value '01 IROC
2003 #1 True Value '00 IROC
2003 #3 Goodwr.Peter Max '00
2003 #3 Goodwr.No Bull '00
2003 #3 Goodwr.Plus Sign '99
2003 #3 Foundation short package
2003 #3 Foundation
2003 #8 RPM 1975
2003 #30 Army 1976
2003 #77 Hy-Gain 1976
2003 #K-2 Dayvault's '56 Ford
2003 #NNO Legacy short package
2003 #NNO Legacy
Winner's Circle Driver Sticker RCR Muse
2004 #3 Wrangler '99 MC
2004 #3 Goodwrench Peter Max '00 Monte Carlo
2004 #3 Goodwrench '00 Monte Carlo Talladega
2004 #3 Goodwrench Sign '99 Monte Carlo
2004 #3 Goodwrench '97 MC Crash Daytona Raced
2004 #3 Goodwrench Olympic '96 Monte Carlo
2004 #3 Goodwrench '96 Monte Carlo
2004 #3 Coke Japan '98 Monte Carlo
2004 #3 AC Delco '96 Monte Carlo
2005 #3 Wheaties '97 Monte Carlo
2005 #3 Goodwrench Taz '00 MC
2005 #3 Goodwrench Plus '98 MC Daytona Win
2005 #3 Goodwrench 25th Ann.
2005 #3 Goodwrench Silver '95 Monte Carlo
Winner's Circle Fantasy Pack 1:64
1998-99 #3 Wrangler
1998-99 #3 Goodwrench '99
1998-99 #3 Goodwrench Plus '98
Winner's Circle For Kids 1:43
1998 #3 Goodwrench
Winner's Circle Garage Scene 1:43
2000 #3 Goodwrench
Winner's Circle License Plate Series 1:
2001 #3 Goodwrench
Winner's Circle Lifetime Dale Earnha
1996-97 #2 Wrangler '81 Pont. 8/12
1996-97 #2 Curb '80 Olds 4/12 no LTS Logo on backer
1996-97 #2 Curb '80 Olds 4/12 LTS Logo on package
1996-97 #3 Wheat.LTS Logo 5/12 w/gray interior&Wheaties card
1996-97 #3 Wheat.LTS Logo 5/12 with orange interior
1996-97 #3 Wheat.LTS Logo 5/12 with gray interior
1996-97 #3 Wheaties '97 MC 5/12 no LTS Logo on pack.
1996-97 #3 GW '97 MC 1/12 LTS logo on package
1996-97 #3 GW '97 MC 1/12 1997 package
1996-97 #3 AC Delco '96 MC 2/12
1996-97 #3 GW Silver '95 MC 3/12 LTS logo with org.letters
1996-97 #3 GW Silver '95 MC 3/12 LTS logo w/red letters
1996-97 #3 GW Silver '95 MC 3/12 1997 Package
1996-97 #3 GW Silver '95 MC 3/12 1996 package
1996-97 #3 D.Earnhardt/GW '90 Lumina 12/12
1996-97 #3 Lowes '89 Pon. 11/12
1996-97 #3 GW '88 Camaro 7/12 no LTS logo on backer
1996-97 #3 GW '88 Camaro 7/12 LTS logo on package
1996-97 #3 Wrangler '86 MC 10/12
1996-97 #3 Wrangler '84 MC 9/12
1996-97 #8 RPM '75 Charger Bonus
1996-97 #98 1978 MC 6/12 no LTS logo on package
1996-97 #98 1978 MC 6/12 LTS logo on package
2001-02 #2 Hodgdon '79 5/8
2001-02 #3 Goodwrench '01 8/8
2001-02 #3 AC Delco '97 4/8
2001-02 #3 Goodwrench '94 1/8
2001-02 #3 Goodwrench '92 3/8
2001-02 #3 Goodwrench '93 6/8
2001-02 #8 Goodwrench '86 7/8
Winner's Circle Lifetime Dale Earnhardt
1998 #3 GW '88 MC FB 11/11
1998 #3 GW '96 Olympic 10/11
1998 #3 Wrang.'87 Champ. 9/11
1998 #3 GW '93 Champ. 8/11
1998 #3 GW '98 Bass Pro 7/11
1998 #3 Wrangler '85 MC 5/11
1998 #3 GW '94 Champ 4/11
1998 #3 GW '98 MC 2/11
1998 #3 GW '91 Champ 1/11 High Performance card
1998 #3 GW '91 Champ 1/11 Stock Car Ser.card
1998 #15 Wrangler '82 TB 3/11
1998 #K2 Pink '56 Ford 6/11
1999 #2 Wrangler '80 7/13
1999 #2 79 ROY 1/13
1999 #3 GW Wrangler '99 8/13
1999 #3 GW '96 MC 10/13
1999 #3 GW '95 BY Win 2/13
1999 #3 GW '89 Lumina 6/13
1999 #3 Wrangler '87 5/13
1999 #3 Wrangler '84 11/13
1999 #8 GW '88 Daytona 4/13
1999 #30 Army '76 Malibu 12/13
1999 #77 Hi-Gain '76 13/13
2000 #3 GW '00 MC 3/6
2000 #3 GW '99 Brickyard 1/6
2000 #3 GW '99 MC 2/6
2000 #3 GW '92 Lumina 5/6
2000 #15 Wran. '83 T-bird 4/6
Winner's Circle Lifetime Series 1:24
2001 #3 Goodwrench Olympic
2001 #3 AC Delco
Winner's Circle Micro Machines 1:144
1999 #3 Goodwrench 3 Cars, Transporter, helicopter & pit wagon
1999 #3 Goodwrench Car and Transporter
1999 #NNO S.Park/Jr.
1999 #NNO S.Park/D.Earnhardt
1999 #NNO Earnhardt Jr.
Winner's Circle Pit Row 1:64
1998 #3 Goodwr.Plus Daytona Victory Donuts
1998 #3 Goodwr.Plus Daytona Pit Road Celebration
1998 #3 Goodwrench Plus changing tires red inter.
1998 #3 Goodwrench Plus changing tires gray inter.
1998 #3 Goodwrench Plus jumping over wall
1998 #3 Goodwrench Bass Pro
1998 #3 Goodwrench 25th Ann.
1998 #3 Coke
Winner's Circle Pit Scene 1:64
2003 #3 Goodwrench Coming In
Winner's Circle Preview 1:24
2000 #3 Goodwrench Taz No Bull
2000 #3 Goodwrench Sign
Winner's Circle Race Hood 1:43
2003 #NNO Legacy
Winner's Circle Race Hood 1:64
2001-02 #3 Goodwrench Silver
2001-02 #3 Goodwrench Oreo
2001-02 #3 Goodwrench
Winner's Circle Race 'N' Play Transport
1998 #3 Goodwrench
Winner's Circle Sam Bass 1:43
2000 #3 Wrangler '87 MC
2000 #3 Goodwr.Taz No Bull
2000 #3 Goodwr.Peter Max
2000 #3 Goodwrench 2001 Oreo
2000 #3 Goodwr.7-time Champ
2000 #3 Goodwrench
Winner's Circle Sam Bass Gallery 1:64
2001 #3 Wrangler
2001 #3 Goodwrench Plus
2001 #3 Goodwren.Bass Pro
2001 #3 Goodwrench
2001 #3 AC Delco
Winner's Circle Select 1:43
1999 #3 GW Wrangler '99
1999 #3 GW Bass Pro '98
1999 #3 GW Olympic '96
1999 #3 GW Silver '95
Winner's Circle Silver Series 1:64
1999 #2 80 Champ 1/7
1999 #3 94 Champ 7/7
1999 #3 93 Champ 6/7
1999 #3 91 Champ 5/7
1999 #3 90 Champ 4/7
1999 #3 87 Champ 3/7
1999 #3 86 Champ 2/7
Winner's Circle Sneak Previews 1:64
2000 #3 Goodwrench Sign
Winner's Circle Speedweeks 1:43
1999 #3 Goodwrench
Winner's Circle Speedweeks 1:64
1999 #3 Goodwrench
Winner's Circle Stats and Standings 1:6
1999 #3 Goodwrench
Winner's Circle Team Authentics 1:64
2001 #3 Goodwrench Taz Sheetmetal
2001 #3 Goodwrench Firesuit
Winner's Circle Tech Series 1:64
1998 #3 Goodwrench
1999 #3 AC Delco
Winner's Circle Track Support Crew 1:64
1999 #3 Goodwrench
Winner's Circle Transporters 1:64
2000 #3 Goodwrench w/o hat
2000 #3 Goodwrench w/hat with 2000 NASCAR logo
2000 #3 Goodwrench w/hat no 2000 NASCAR logo
2001 #3 Goodwrench
2003 #3 Forever the Man
2004 #NNO Feed the Children
2005 #3 Goodwrench
2006 #NNO HOF Dale Tribute split window box
Winner's Circle Victory Celebration 1:4
1998 #3 Daytona 500 2/15/98
1998 #3 Brickyard 400 8/5/95
Winner's Circle Victory Lane 1:64
1999 #3 Goodwrench Daytona Win 2/15/98
Winner's Circle Victory Lap 1:24
2003 #3 Goodwrench Victory Lap
Winner's Circle Victory Lap 1:64
2003 #3 Goodwrench Victory Lap
Winner's Circle VIP Pass 1:43
2000 #3 Goodwrench Plus
Winner's Circle with Figure 1:24
1998 #3 Coke
Winross Transporters 1:64
1992 #NNO Goodwr.wooden box
1992 #NNO Goodwr.White Rose

Earnhardt, Dale Jr.

Action Performance 1:24
1999 #3 AC Delco
1999 #8 Budweiser
2000 #8 Dale Jr.
2001 #8 Dale Jr.
2002 #8 Dale Jr.
2003 #8 JR
2003 #8 Dale Jr.
Action Performance 1:64
1999 #3 AC Delco Promo Blister
1999 #3 AC Delco box
2002 #8 Dale Jr.
2003 #8 JR
2003 #8 Dale Jr.
2004 #8 Nextel Cup 6-car set
2005 #8 JR
Action QVC For Race Fans Only 1:24
2000 #8 Bud Olympic Gold/2000
2000 #8 Bud Olympic Color Chrome/20,000
2000 #8 Bud Gold/2000
2000 #8 Bud Color Chrome/3504
2001 #8 Bud All-Star Platinum/624
2001 #8 Bud All-Star Gold/2000
2001 #8 Bud Platinum/624
2001 #8 Bud Gold/2500
2001 #8 Bud#(Color Chrome/2508
2002 #3 Oreo Platinum/624
2002 #3 Oreo Gold/2508
2002 #3 Oreo Col.Chrome/2508
2002 #3 Nilla Wafers Platinum/624
2002 #3 Nilla Wafers Gold/2508
2002 #3 Nilla Wafers Color Chrome/7500
2002 #8 Looney Tunes Platinum/624
2002 #8 Looney Tunes Gold/2508
2002 #8 Looney Tunes Color Chrome/5004
2002 #8 Bud All-Star Platinum/624
2002 #8 Bud All-Star Gold/2508
2002 #8 Bud Platinum/624
2002 #8 Bud Gold/2508
2002 #8 Bud Col.Chrome/2508
2003 #8 Oreo Ritz Plat/624
2003 #8 Oreo Ritz Gold/2508
2003 #8 E Concert Platinum/624
2003 #8 E Concert Gold/2508
2003 #8 E Concert Color Chrome/3508
2003 #8 DMP Platinum/624
2003 #8 DMP Gold/2508
2003 #8 Bud StainD Platinum/624
2003 #8 Bud StainD Gold/1000
2003 #8 Bud StainD Color Chrome/3504
2003 #8 Bud StainD Brushed Metal/2508
2003 #8 Bud All-Star Platinum/624
2003 #8 Bud AS Gold/2508
2003 #8 Bud All-Star Color Chrome/2508
2003 #8 Bud Platinum/624
2003 #8 Bud Gold/2508
2004 #8 Oreo Platinum/300
2004 #8 Oreo Gold/504
2004 #8 Oreo Color Chrome/5016
2004 #8 Oreo Brush.Metal/504
2004 #8 Bud World Series Gold/500
2004 #8 Bud World Series Color Chrome/6000
2004 #8 Bud Father's Day Brushed Metal/504
2004 #8 Bud Dave Matthews Color Chrome/6000
2004 #8 Bud Born On Feb.15 Raced Color Chrome/7500
2004 #8 Bud Born On Feb.7 Platinum/300
2004 #8 Bud Born On Feb.7 Gold/504
2004 #8 Bud Born On Feb.7 Color Chrome/5004
2004 #8 Bud Platinum/504
2004 #8 Bud Gold/1008
2004 #8 Bud Color Chr/5016
2004 #8 Earnhardt Jr./Bud Brush.Metal/1008
2004 #81 Chance 2 Taco Bell Color Chrome/5004
2004 #81 Chance 2 KFC Color Chrome/5004
2005 #8 Milestones '04 Daytona 500 Color Chrome/5004
2005 #8 Bud 3 Doors Down Color Chrome/2004
2005 #8 Bud 3 Doors Down Brushed Metal/288
2005 #8 Bud MLB All Star Gold/204
2005 #8 Bud MLB All Star Brushed Metal/288
2005 #8 Bud Born On Feb.20 Color Chrome/3504
2005 #8 Bud Born On Feb.20 Brushed Metal/504
2005 #8 Bud Platinum/300
2005 #8 Bud Color Chrome/3504
2005 #8 Bud Brushed Metal/504
2005 #81 Oreo Ritz Plat./300
2005 #81 Oreo Ritz Color Chrome/3508
2006 #8 Oreo Color Chrome/3504
2006 #8 Bud Father's Day Platinum/288
2006 #8 Bud Dale Tribute Silver/504
2006 #8 Bud Dale Tribute Platinum/411
2006 #8 Bud Richmond Raced Silver/504
2006 #8 Bud Richmond Raced Color Chrome/2508
2006 #8 Bud Gold/504
2006 #8 Bud Color Chrome/3504
Action Racing Collectables 1:18
1998 #31 Wrangler 1997 Monte Carlo/7596
1998 #31 Sikkens Blue 1997 Monte Carlo/7596
1999 #1 Coke
1999 #3 AC Delco Superman
1999 #3 AC Delco
1999 #8 Bud '00/2508
1999 #31 Sikkens White 97MC
1999 #31 Mom 'N' Pop's 1996 Monte Carlo/2508
2000 #8 Bud Olympic
2000 #8 Bud/3504
2001 #3 Earn/Earn Jr./Pilgrim/Collins C5-R Corvette Platinum/2508
2001 #3 Earn/Earn Jr./Pilgrim/Collins C5-R Color Chrome raced/7500
2001 #3 Earn/Earn Jr./Pilgrim/Collins C5-R Color Chrome/7500
2001 #3 Earn/Earn Jr./Pilgrim/Collins C5-R Corvette 24Kt.Gold/2000
2001 #3 Earn/Earn Jr./Pilgrim/Collins C5-R Corvette raced/1008
2001 #3 Earn/Earn Jr./Pilgrim/Collins C5-R Corvette/16,752
2002 #3 Oreo/4008
2002 #3 Nilla Wafers/3504
2002 #3 Oreo Color Chrome/2508
2002 #8 Looney Tunes/3384
2002 #8 Bud All-Star/4512
2002 #8 Bud Color Chrome/2508
2002 #8 Bud/3504
2003 #8 Oreo Ritz/504
2003 #8 E Concert/3024
2003 #8 DMP/4002
2003 #8 Bud StainD/2748
2003 #8 Bud All-Star/3324
2003 #8 Bud/3832
2004 #8 Bud Born On Feb. 15
2004 #8 Bud/1788
2004 #NNO Monte Carlo SS/6840
2005 #3 Milestones '98-'99 Busch Champion/300
2005 #8 Bud MLB All Star Game/1920
2005 #8 Bud 3 Doors Down/1920
2005 #8 Milestones '00 All-Star Win/300
2005 #8 Milestones '01 Daytona Win/504
2005 #8 Milestones '04 Daytona Win/300
2005 #8 Bud Born On Feb.20/1056
2005 #8 Bud Born On Feb.17/630
2005 #8 Bud Born On Feb.12/624
2005 #8 Bud/1194
2006 #8 Bud Father's Day GM Dealers/204
2006 #8 Bud Father's Day/612
2006 #8 Bud Dale Tribute/2437
Action Racing Collectables 1:24
1998 #1 Coke Bear Bank
1998 #1 Coke Bear
1998 #3 AC Delco 1998 BGN Champ Bank
1998 #3 AC Delco 1998 BGN Champ
1998 #3 AC Del.Bank/2500
1998 #3 AC Delco/15,000
1998 #3 Dale Jr. Goodwrench/AC Delco Split/624
1998 #31 Wrangler Bank 1997 Monte Carlo/2508
1998 #31 Wrangler 1997 Monte Carlo/10,008
1998 #31 Sikkens Blue Bank 1997 Monte Carlo/5004
1998 #31 Sikkens Blue 1997 Monte Carlo/5000
1998 #NNO Jr./Coke Snap-on 2-car set
1999 #3 AC Delco Superman Bank
1999 #3 AC Delco Superman
1999 #3 AC Delco Last Lap Bank
1999 #3 AC Delco Last Lap/12,000
1999 #3 AC Delco Bank/5004
1999 #3 AC Delco
1999 #8 Bud Richmond/6708
1999 #8 Bud New Hamp/6708
1999 #8 Bud Michigan/6708
1999 #8 Bud Atlanta/7008
1999 #8 Bud
1999 #31 Sikkens White 1997 Monte Carlo Bank/6000
1999 #31 Sikkens White 1997 Monte Carlo/5000
1999 #31 Mom 'N' Pop's 1996 Monte Carlo Bank/2508
1999 #31 Mom 'N' Pop's 1996 Monte Carlo
1999 #31 Gargoyles 1997 Monte Carlo Bank/2508
1999 #31 Gargoyles 1997 Monte Carlo/8500
2000 #8 Bud Olym./37,440
2000 #8 Bud Brickyard/2508
2000 #8 Bud Bank/3504
2000 #8 Bud/30,000
2001 #3 Mom 'N' Pop's 1994 Camaro/10,008
2001 #7 Church Bros. 1997 Monte Carlo/5028
2001 #8 Bud AS Bank/2508
2001 #8 Bud All-Star/54,408
2001 #8 Bud Talladega Win No Bull w/flag/64,676
2001 #8 Bud Van Camp Promo
2001 #8 Bud Remington on deck lid
2001 #8 Bud Promo in plastic case/3750
2001 #8 Bud Bank/2088
2001 #8 Bud/27,180
2001 #2001 DEI Pit Practice Car Snap-on Carolina Run
2001 #2001 DEI Pit Practice Car/2508
2002 #3 Sun Drop '94 Lumina/24,504
2002 #3 Oreo Snap-On BW Car/21,012
2002 #3 Oreo Clear/7008
2002 #3 Oreo Bank/2508
2002 #3 Oreo/112,996
2002 #3 Nilla Wafers Clear/7008
2002 #3 Nilla Wafers Bank/2508
2002 #3 Nilla Wafers/91,512
2002 #8 Looney Tunes Bank/1980

2002 #8 Looney Tunes/79,992
2002 #8 Bud All-Star White Gold Promo/5004
2002 #8 Bud All-Star Red Clear/5304
2002 #8 Bud All-Star Snap-On BW Car
2002 #8 Bud All-Star Bank/2652
2002 #8 Bud All-Star/103,152
2002 #8 Bud Employee in acrylic case
2002 #8 Bud Champion Spark Plug Promo
2002 #8 Bud Clear/7008
2002 #8 Bud White Gold Promo/5004
2002 #8 Bud Bank/2508
2002 #8 Bud/70,068
2002 #11 True Value 1999 IROC/33,876
2003 #3 Prime Sirloin '95 Monte Carlo brushed metal/3504
2003 #3 Goodwrench '97 Monte Carlo GM Dealers/1416
2003 #3 Goodwrench '97 Monte Carlo/24,396
2003 #8 Oreo Ritz White Gold/2496
2003 #8 Oreo Ritz GM Dealers/5004
2003 #8 Oreo Ritz Clear/6588
2003 #8 Oreo Ritz Bank/2268
2003 #8 Oreo Ritz/77,208
2003 #8 E Concert GM Dealers/5004
2003 #8 E Concert Black Window Bank/2304
2003 #8 E Concert/74,352
2003 #8 DMP GM Deal./3504
2003 #8 DMP Clear/5304
2003 #8 DMP BW Bank/2292
2003 #8 DMP/59,796
2003 #8 Bud StainD GM Dealer/3504
2003 #8 Bud StainD CW Bank/1968
2003 #8 Bud StainD/60,204
2003 #8 Bud All-Star Red Clear GM Dealer/240
2003 #8 Bud All-Star Red Clear/4320
2003 #8 Bud All-Star CW Bank/1475
2003 #8 Bud All-Star/60,456
2003 #8 Bud Talladega/45,024
2003 #8 Bud Talladega '02 CW Bank/1008
2003 #8 Bud Talla.'02/17,052
2003 #8 Bud No Bull '00 Mon.Carlo GM Dealers/3504
2003 #8 Bud No Bull '00 Mon.Carlo CW Bank/1536
2003 #8 Bud No Bull 2000 Monte Carlo/28,764
2003 #8 Bud BW Bank/3300
2003 #8 Bud GM Deal./8504
2003 #8 Bud/105,248
2003 #2003 DEI Pit Practice/2508
2004 #8 Bud Talladega Raced QVC/1008
2004 #8 Bud Born On Feb.12 Raced QVC/2004
2004 #8 Oreo Mac Tools/288
2004 #8 Oreo GM Dealers/2496
2004 #8 Oreo CW Bank/1008
2004 #8 Oreo/34,828
2004 #8 Bud World Series Liquid Metal/4008
2004 #8 Bud World Series CW Bank/900
2004 #8 Bud World Series/21,324
2004 #8 Bud Father's Day GM Dealers/4008
2004 #8 Bud Father's Day CW Bank/1008
2004 #8 Bud Father's Day/41,880
2004 #8 Bud Dave Matthews Band CW Bank/600
2004 #8 Bud Dave Matthews Band/20,700
2004 #8 Bud Born On Feb.15 Raced w/tire CW Bank/5004
2004 #8 Bud Born On Feb.15 Raced/68,808
2004 #8 Bud Born On Feb.15 Raced GM Dealers/4008
2004 #8 Bud Born On Feb.15/5004
2004 #8 Bud Born On Feb.12 Raced GM Dealers/3504
2004 #8 Bud Born On Feb.12 Raced/28,884
2004 #8 Bud Born On Feb.7 GM Dealers/1500
2004 #8 Bud Born On Feb.7 CW Bank/888
2004 #8 Bud Born On Feb.7/16,392
2004 #8 Bud Talladega Raced/7368
2004 #8 Bud Bristol Raced/8808
2004 #8 Bud Mac Tools/288
2004 #8 Bud GM Dealers/7548
2004 #8 Bud CW Bank/1260
2004 #8 Bud/72,072
2004 #81 Taco Bell GM Dealers/1584
2004 #81 Taco Bell CW Bank/1092
2004 #81 Taco Bell/26,656
2004 #81 Menards Bristol Raced/8808
2004 #81 KFC GM Dealers/1944
2004 #81 KFC CW Bank/1068
2004 #81 KFC/24,828
2005 #8 Bud MLB All Star Game Anheuser Busch/156
2005 #8 Bud MLB All Star Game Mac Tools/300
2005 #8 Bud MLB All Star Game GM Dealers Chrome/1992
2005 #8 Bud MLB All Star CW Bank/600
2005 #8 Bud MLB All Star Game/15,804
2005 #8 Bud Born On Feb.20 QVC/2004
2005 #8 Bud Born On Feb.20 Matco/480
2005 #8 Bud Born On Feb.20 Mac Tools/300
2005 #8 Bud Born On Feb.20 GM Dealers/3588
2005 #8 Bud Born On Feb.20 CW Bank/900
2005 #8 Bud Born On Feb.20/22,668
2005 #8 Bud Born On Feb.17 QVC/600
2005 #8 Bud Born On Feb.17 Matco/480
2005 #8 Bud Born On Feb.17 GM Dealers Chrome/1512
2005 #8 Bud Born On Feb.17 GM Dealers/2280
2005 #8 Bud Born On Feb.17 CW Bank/648
2005 #8 Bud Born On Feb.17/13,752
2005 #8 Bud Born On Feb.12 QVC/504
2005 #8 Bud Born On Feb.12 Matco/480
2005 #8 Bud Born On Feb.12 GM Dealers/2640
2005 #8 Bud Born On Feb.12 CW Bank/708
2005 #8 Bud Born On Feb.12/5004
2005 #8 Bud QVC/7500
2005 #8 Bud Matco/492
2005 #8 Bud Mac Tools/300
2005 #8 Bud Liquid Metal/3504
2005 #8 Bud GM Dealers/5004
2005 #8 Bud CW Bank/612
2005 #8 Bud Anheuser Busch/336
2005 #8 Bud/33,960
2005 #8 Bud 3 Doors Down Anhauser Busch/996
2005 #8 Bud 3 Doors Down Mac Tools/348
2005 #8 Bud 3 Doors Down Matco/108
2005 #8 Milestones/5004
2005 #8 Milestones GM Dealers
2005 #8 Bud 3 Doors Down QVC/2004
2005 #8 Bud 3 Doors Down GM Dealers/2160
2005 #8 Bud 3 Doors Down CW Bank/636
2005 #8 Bud 3 Doors Down/15,468
2005 #8 Bud Test w/Tony Eury AU/5016
2005 #8 Bud MLB All Star Chicago Raced QVC/2004
2005 #8 Bud MLB All Star Chicago Raced/2880
2005 #8 Bud MLB All Star Game QVC/2004
2005 #8 Bud MLB All Star Game Matco/96
2005 #81 Menards Matco/72
2005 #81 Oreo Ritz QVC/3000
2005 #81 Oreo Ritz GM Dealers/2016
2005 #81 Oreo Ritz CW Bank/564
2005 #81 Oreo Ritz/15,516
2005 #81 Menards QVC/1508
2005 #81 Menards GM Dealers/1008
2005 #81 Menards/7668
2005 #81 Chance 2 Test QVC/288
2005 #81 Chance 2 Test GM Dealers/288
2005 #81 Chance 2 Test/2616
2006 #8 250 Starts Hamilton*
2006 #8 250 Starts GM Dealers/1980
2006 #8 250 Starts/7812*
2006 #8 Oreo QVC/1008
2006 #8 Oreo Mac Tools/360
2006 #8 Oreo GM Dealers Brushed Metal/504
2006 #8 Oreo CW Bank/480
2006 #8 Oreo/6000
2006 #8 Bud Test QVC*
2006 #8 Bud Test Matco*
2006 #8 Bud Test Mac Tools*
2006 #8 Bud Test GM Dealers/720
2006 #8 Bud Test/5196*
2006 #8 Bud Father's Day Snap-On*
2006 #8 Bud Father's Day QVC*
2006 #8 Bud Father's Day Mac Tools*
2006 #8 Bud Father's Day Hamilton*
2006 #8 Bud Father's Day GM Dealers/3792
2006 #8 Bud Father's Day CW Bank/492
2006 #8 Bud Father's Day Anheuser Busch*
2006 #8 Bud Father's Day/30,456*
2006 #8 Bud Dale Tribute Snap On*
2006 #8 Bud Dale Tribute QVC*
2006 #8 Bud Dale Tribute Mac Tools*
2006 #8 Bud Dale Tribute Hamilton*
2006 #8 Bud Dale Tribute GM Dealers/7392
2006 #8 Bud Dale Tribute Anheuser Busch*
2006 #8 Bud Dale Tribute/44,169*
2006 #8 Bud Richmond Raced GM Dealers/2652
2006 #8 Bud QVC/6500
2006 #8 Bud Matco/228
2006 #8 Bud Mac Tools/504
2006 #8 Bud GM Dealers/2508
2006 #8 Bud CW Bank/504
2006 #8 Bud AB/600
2006 #8 Bud Richmond Raced/8556
2006 #8 Bud/30,000

Action Racing Collectables 1:32
2004 #8 Oreo/1584
2004 #8 Bud Born On Feb.7/1764
2004 #8 Bud/2508
1998-01 #3 AC Del.Last Lap '99
1998-01 #3 AC Delco/12,000 '98
1998-01 #8 Bud/12,000 '99
1998-01 #31 Gargoyles '97MC

Action Racing Collectables 1:43
2005 #81 Menards Promo in wind.box

Action Racing Collectables 1:64
1998 #1 Coke Bear
1998 #3 AC Delco 1998 BGN Champ blister
1998 #3 AC Delco
1998 #31 Sikkens Blue 1997 Monte Carlo
1999 #3 AC Del.Superman
1999 #3 AC Delco Last Lap
1999 #3 AC Delco Promo/10,080
1999 #3 AC Delco
1999 #8 Bud Richmond/10,080
1999 #8 Bud New Hamp/10,080
1999 #8 Bud Michigan/10,080
1999 #8 Bud Atlanta/10,080
1999 #8 Bud
1999 #31 Wrangler '97MC
1999 #31 Sikkens White 1997 Monte Carlo
1999 #31 Gargoyles 1997 Monte Carlo/10,080
2000 #8 Bud
2000 #31 Mom 'N' Pop's 1996 Monte Carlo
2001 #8 Bud All-Star/30,060
2001 #8 Bud in can/30,768
2002 #1 Coke '98 MC in vending machine tin/25,883
2002 #3 Oreo Promo box
2002 #3 Oreo/66,096
2002 #3 Nilla Wafers/Oreo Color Chrome set/8333
2002 #3 Nilla Wafers/57,600
2002 #8 Looney Tunes/41,688
2002 #8 Bud All-Star Color Chrome 2-cars/8888
2002 #8 Bud All-Star/51,984
2002 #8 Bud in bottle/80,016
2002 #NNO Jr./Oreo White Gold 2-car set in tin/7560
2003 #8 Oreo Ritz/46,944
2003 #8 Earnhardt Tribute Concert/35,568
2003 #8 DMP/38,936
2003 #8 Bud StainD/20,520
2003 #8 Bud No Bull '00 Mon.Carlo/15,264
2003 #8 Bud All-Star/12,984
2003 #8 Bud Talladega 4-car raced wins set/5940
2003 #8 Bud/36,288
2003 #11 True Value '99 IROC Orange/10,728
2004 #8 Bud Born On Feb.12 Raced GM Dealers/288
2004 #8 Bud Born On Feb.12 Raced in can
2004 #8 Bud Born On Feb.15 Raced GM Dealers/480
2004 #8 Bud World Series baseball tin/10,000
2004 #8 Oreo/18,288
2004 #8 Bud World Series
2004 #8 Bud Dave Matthews Band
2004 #8 Bud Born On Feb.15 Raced/22,004
2004 #8 Bud Born On Feb.12 Raced/15,000
2004 #8 Bud Born On Feb.7/13,296
2004 #8 Bud/30,480 on a base
2004 #81 Taco Bell GM Dealers/192
2004 #81 Taco Bell/11,664
2004 #81 KFC/12,288
2004 #NNO Father's Day 2-car set/12,288
2004 #NNO Bristol Raced 2-car set
2004 #NNO 3-car Oreo set in tin/7128
2005 #8 Bud MLB All Star Game in baseball tin
2005 #8 Born On Feb.12th Feb.17/Feb.20 3-car set in tin/8000
2005 #8 Bud 3 Doors Down
2005 #8 Bud MLB All Star Game
2005 #8 Bud
2005 #81 Oreo Ritz
2005 #81 Menards
2006 #8 250 Starts
2006 #8 Oreo
2006 #8 Bud Father's Day
2006 #8 Bud Dale Tribute
2006 #8 Bud Richmond Raced
2006 #8 Bud

Action Racing Collectables Advanced Pro
2008 #83 Navy JR Motorsports/383
2008 #88 Mountian Dew Retro/888
2008 #88 National Guard Citizen Soldier/888
2008 #88 National Guard Salute the Troops/888
2008 #88 National Guard Camo/888

Action Racing Collectables Ceramic 1
2000-01 #8 Bud Olympic '00

Action Racing Collectables Crystal 1
1998-00 #1 Coke Bear/9000 '99
1998-00 #3 AC Delco Superman/4008 '99
1998-00 #8 Bud '99

Action Racing Collectables Historical S
2004 #3 AC Delco Last Lap Century '99 Monte Carlo Col.Chrome CW Bank/25,008
2004 #3 Sun Drop '94 Lum. Color Chrome Mac Tools/288
2004 #3 Sun Drop '94 Lum. Color Chrome/11,136
2004 #3 AC Delco Last Lap Color Chrome/1452
2004 #7 Church Bros. '97 MC CW Bank/2008
2004 #7 Church Bros '97 Monte Carlo/2316
2004 #8 Bud '03 Phoenix Raced GM Dealers/324
2004 #8 Bud '03 Phoenix Raced/7116
2004 #8 Bud Olympics '00 Monte Carlo CW Bank/6138
2004 #8 Bud Olympics '00 Monte Carlo QVC/216
2004 #8 Bud Olympics '00 Monte Carlo/1304
2004 #11 True Value '99 IROC Orange/5040

Action Racing Collectables Pit Wagon
1990-03 #3 AC Delco Superman/4308 '99

Action Racing Collectables Platinum 1:2
2008 #5 All Star Test/9204
2008 #88 National Guard/80,488
2008 #88 National Guard Mac Tools/1200
2008 #88 National Guard QVC/22,752
2008 #88 AMP Mac Tools/1200
2008 #88 AMP/108,088

Action Racing Collectables Platinum Day
2008 #8 Bud Born On Feb. 15 '04 Monte Carlo/6180

Action Racing Collectables Transporters
2002 #3 Oreo/5016
2002 #8 Bud/9876
2003 #8 DMP Chance 2/5560
2003 #8 Bud/9876
2004 #8 Bud/2352

Action Road Racing 1:12
2003 #3 Earn Jr./Pilgrim/Collins '01 C5-R Corvette RCCA/100

Action Road Racing 1:18
2004 #2 Dale Jr./A.Wallace Citgo Raced w/tire/6684
2004 #2 Dale Jr./A.Wallace/Citgo GM Dealers/516
2004 #2 Dale Jr./A.Wallace/Citgo Brushed Metal/300
2004 #2 Dale Jr./A.Wallace/Citgo/7188
2004 #8 Dale Jr./B.Said/Corvette C-5R RCCA/600
2004 #8 Dale Jr./B.Said/Corvette C-5R GM Dealers/324
2004 #8 Dale Jr./B.Said/Corvette C-5R/4014

Action Road Racing 1:43
2004 #8 Dale Jr./B.Said/Corvette C-5R/3198
2000-01 #3 Earn/Earn Jr./Pilgrim/Collins C5-R Corvette raced/2424 '01
2000-01 #3 Earn Jr./Pilgrim/Collins C5-R Corvette/12,024 '01

Action Total Concept 1:64
2000 #8 Bud Olympic/26,568

Action/Funline Monster Truck 1:43
2004 #8 JR
2004 #8 DMP

Action/Funline Muscle Machines 1:18
2004 #8 Earnhardt Jr. '69 Camaro
2004 #8 Earnhardt Jr. '69 Chevelle
2004 #8 Earnhardt Jr. '67 Nova
2004 #8 Earnhardt Jr. '66 Nova
2005 #8 Earnhardt Jr '69 Camaro
2005 #8 Earnhardt Jr '69 Chevelle
2005 #8 Earnhardt Jr '71 Camaro

Action/Funline Muscle Machines 1:24
2005 #8 Earnhardt Jr Hybrid/408

Action/Funline Muscle Machines 1:64
2004 #8 Earnhardt Jr. '69 Chevelle

Action/RCCA 1:18
2002 #8 Looney Tunes/504
2002 #8 Bud All-Star/504
2003 #8 Bud All Star/504
2003 #8 DMP/408
2003 #8 E Concert
2003 #8 Bud/600
2005 #8 Bud Born On Feb.20 Color Chrome/200
2005 #8 Bud Born On Feb.17 Color Chrome/88
2005 #8 Bud Born On Feb.12 Color Chrome/140
2005 #8 Bud Color Chrome/288
2006 #8 Bud Father's Day Chrome/408
2006 #8 Bud Dale Tribute Color Chrome/333

Action/RCCA 1:24
2002 #3 Oreo Split Clear/3000
2002 #3 Oreo Bank/5004
2002 #3 Nilla Wafers Split Clear/3000
2002 #3 Nilla Wafers Bank/5004
2002 #8 Looney Tunes Split Clear/2508
2002 #8 Looney Tunes Bank/4008
2002 #8 Bud Talla. April '02 Win Raced Bank/1008
2002 #8 Bud All-Star Split Clear/2508
2002 #8 Bud All-Star Bank/4800
2002 #8 Bud Color Chrome Bank/3600
2002 #8 Bud Split Clear/4500
2002 #8 Bud Bank/3504
2003 #3 Sundrop '94 Lumina/4800
2003 #3 Mom 'n' Pops Prime Sirloin/4800
2003 #8 Bud All-Star Split Clear/1500
2003 #8 E Concert Split Clear/1008
2003 #8 Oreo Ritz#l Split Clear/1008
2003 #8 Oreo Ritz Raced/520
2003 #8 Oreo Ritz CW Bank/3600
2003 #8 E Concert Raced/600
2003 #8 E Con.Bank/3600
2003 #8 DMP Split Clear/1008
2003 #8 DMP Bank/3204
2003 #8 Bud StainD/3100
2003 #8 Bud All-Star/3300
2003 #8 Bud Tall.Oct.'02 Win Raced CW Bank/1008
2003 #8 Bud Talladega Raced/1300
2003 #8 Bud No Bull '00 Monte Carlo/2508
2003 #8 Bud Bank/3300
2004 #8 Bud Bristol Raced/900
2004 #8 Bud Talladega Raced/600
2004 #8 Oreo/3000
2004 #8 Bud World Series/2508
2004 #8 Bud Father's Day/1200
2004 #8 Bud Dave Matthews Band/2388
2004 #8 Bud Born On Feb.15 Raced/4800
2004 #8 Bud Born On Feb.7/3000
2004 #8 Bud Born On Feb.12 Raced/3000
2004 #8 Bud/3600
2004 #81 Taco Bell/1800
2004 #81 Menards Bristol Raced/1008
2004 #81 KFC/3000
2005 #3 Milestones '98-'99 BGN Champ/1500
2005 #8 Bud 3 Doors Down/1200
2005 #8 Milestones '04 Daytona Win/1800
2005 #8 Milestones '01 Daytona Win/1200
2005 #8 Milestones '00 All-Star Win/999
2005 #8 Bud Test/804
2005 #8 Bud MLB All-Star Chicago Raced/444
2005 #8 Bud MLB All-Star/1800
2005 #8 Bud Born On Feb.20/2400
2005 #8 Bud Color Chrome/804
2005 #8 Bud/1500
2005 #81 Menard's/804
2005 #81 Oreo Ritz/1800
2005 #81 Chance 2 Test/408
2006 #8 Goody's/199
2006 #8 Menards Daytona Raced/1008
2006 #8 Oreo/804
2006 #8 Bud/1008
2006 #8 Bud Color Chrome/288
2006 #8 Bud Richmond Raced/888
2006 #8 Bud Dale Tribute/3333
2006 #8 Bud Father's Day/2333
2006 #8 Bud Test/780
2006 #8 250th Start/1008
2006 #NNO Dale Tribute 5-car set/1200

Action/RCCA 1:32
2002 #1 Coke '98 MC in vending machine tin/2004
2002 #3 Nilla Wafers Oreo 2-car set/2016
2002 #8 Looney Tunes Gold/600
2002 #8 Looney Tunes/1416
2002 #8 Bud '02 All-Star Gold/600
2002 #8 Bud '02 All-Star/1416
2002 #8 Bud '01 All-Star Gold/600
2002 #8 Bud '01 All-Star/1416
2002 #8 Bud Gold/652
2002 #8 Bud/3000 with Fan Scan card
2003 #8 Bud No Bull '00 Monte Carlo
2003 #8 E Concert 24K/444
2003 #8 E Concert/1572
2003 #8 DMP 24K/444
2003 #8 DMP/1572
2003 #8 Oreo Ritz Gold/588
2003 #8 Oreo Ritz/2004
2003 #8 Bud StainD/844
2003 #8 Bud All-Star/844
2003 #8 Bud AS 24K/316
2003 #8 Bud 24K/444
2003 #8 Bud/1572
2004 #8 Oreo/600
2004 #8 Bud Born On Feb.15/960
2004 #8 Bud Born On Feb.7/408
2004 #8 Bud/600

Action/RCCA 1:64
1994 #3 Mom 'N' Pop/10,080
1998 #1 Coke Bear
1998 #3 AC Delco/3500
1998 #31 Sikkens Blue 1997 Monte Carlo
1999 #3 AC Delco Superman
1999 #3 AC Delco Last Lap
1999 #3 AC Delco/10,000
1999 #8 Bud Richmond/3500
1999 #8 Bud New Hamp/3500
1999 #8 Bud Michigan/3500
1999 #8 Bud Atlanta/3500
1999 #8 Bud
1999 #31 Wrangler 1997 Monte Carlo/7500
1999 #31 Sikkens White 1997 Monte Carlo/10,000
1999 #31 Gargoyles 1997 Monte Carlo/12,000
2000 #8 Bud Olympic/5040
2000 #8 Bud/10,000
2000 #31 Mom 'N' Pop's 1996 Monte Carlo/10,000
2000 #NNO D.Earnhardt Jr. No Bull 2-cars in tin/6504
2001 #8 Bud All-Star/5040
2001 #8 Bud/2016
2002 #1 Coke '98 MC in vending machine/3000
2002 #3 Oreo Promo
2002 #3 Oreo/6000
2002 #3 Nilla Wafers Promo
2002 #3 Nilla Wafers/6000
2002 #8 Looney Tunes/6000
2002 #8 Bud All-Star/6000
2002 #8 Bud Color Chrome/5040
2003 #8 Bud Talladega raced/2400 4-car set
2003 #8 Oreo Ritz/6060
2003 #8 E Concert/3300
2003 #8 DMP/4670
2003 #8 Bud StainD/4036
2003 #8 Bud All-Star in tin/2340
2003 #8 Bud All-Star/3316
2003 #8 Bud/3748
2004 #8 Oreo/4032
2004 #8 Bud World Series/2448
2004 #8 Bud Dave Matthews Band/2880
2004 #8 Bud Born On Feb.12&15 Raced 2-car set/4008
2004 #8 Bud Born On Feb.7/3024
2004 #8 Bud/3024
2004 #81 Taco Bell/1800
2004 #81 Menards Bristol Raced/720
2004 #81 KFC/3600
2004 #NNO Father's Day/1500 2-car set
2004 #NNO Bristol Raced 2-car set/960
2004 #NNO 3-car set in tin
2005 #8 Bud Born On 3-car set in tin/1500
2005 #8 Bud MLB All-Star in baseball tin/1008
2005 #8 Bud 3 Doors Down/1584
2005 #8 Bud MLB All-Star/2016
2005 #8 Bud/1584
2005 #81 Menards/1008
2005 #81 Oreo Ritz/2016
2006 #8 Menards Daytona Raced/888
2006 #8 Oreo/804
2006 #8 250th Start/1008
2006 #8 Bud Father's Day/2008
2006 #8 Bud Dale Tribute/2133
2006 #8 Bud/936

Action/RCCA Banks 1:24
1998 #1 Coke Bear/12,500
1998 #3 AC Delco/2500
1998 #31 Sikkens Blue 1997 Monte Carlo/3500
1999 #3 AC Delco Last Lap/10,000
1999 #3 AC Delco Superman/15,000
1999 #3 AC Delco/4500
1999 #8 Bud Richmond/2500
1999 #8 Bud New Hamp./2500
1999 #8 Bud Michigan/2500
1999 #8 Bud Atlanta/2500
1999 #8 Bud/5000
1999 #31 Wrangler 1997 Monte Carlo/4500
1999 #31 Sikkens White 1997 Monte Carlo/7500
1999 #31 Mom 'N' Pop's 1996 Monte Carlo/7500
1999 #31 Gargoyles 1997 Monte Carlo/7500
2000 #8 Bud Olympic/7500
2000 #8 Bud No Bull/5052
2000 #8 Bud/7000
2001 #8 Bud All-Star Raced/3504
2001 #8 Bud All-Star/5004
2001 #8 Bud Color Chrome/3600
2001 #8 Bud/1500

Action/RCCA Dually Trucks with Trailer
1994 #NNO Earnhardt Kids/Mom-n-Pop's with 3-cars/3750
1999 #3 AC Delco Superman/3504
2001 #8 Bud All-Star/2640

Action/RCCA Elite 1:24
1998 #1 Coke Bear/10,000
1998 #3 AC Delco Gold Promo/100
1998 #3 AC Delco/1500
1998 #31 Sikkens Blue/2500 1997 Monte Carlo
1999 #3 AC Delco Superman/10,000
1999 #3 AC Del.Platinum/300
1999 #3 AC Delco Last Lap/8500
1999 #3 AC Delco/8500
1999 #8 Bud Richmond/1000
1999 #8 Bud New Hamp/1000
1999 #8 Bud Michigan/1000
1999 #8 Bud Atlanta/1000
1999 #8 Bud/5004
1999 #31 Wrangler 1997 Monte Carlo/3500
1999 #31 Sikkens White 1997 Monte Carlo/4000
1999 #31 Mom 'N' Pop's 1996 Monte Carlo/5000
1999 #31 Gargoyles 1997 Monte Carlo/3500
2000 #8 Bud Olympic/4992
2000 #8 Bud No Bull/3504
2000 #8 Bud Test Gray/3500
2000 #8 Bud/5000
2000 #2000 DEI Pit Practice/1008
2001 #7 Church Bros. 1997 Monte Carlo/1500
2001 #8 Bud All-Star raced version/4008
2001 #8 Bud All-Star/5996
2001 #8 Bud Test/3504
2001 #8 Bud Talladega Win No Bull/2508
2001 #8 Bud Dover Win w/flag/2508
2001 #8 Bud Color Chome/2400
2001 #8 Bud/2004
2001 #2001 DEI Pit Practice Car/2796
2002 #3 Oreo Test Gray/3504
2002 #3 Oreo Raced/2004
2002 #3 Oreo/8988
2002 #3 Nilla Wafers/6504
2002 #8 Looney Tunes Raced/6000
2002 #8 Looney Tunes/6000
2002 #8 Bud All-Star/6996
2002 #8 Bud Test Red/5004
2002 #8 Bud Talladega April '02 Win Raced/1500
2002 #8 Bud Color Chrome/4200
2002 #8 Bud/1200
2002 #2002 DEI Racing Pit Practice/2002
2003 #8 Oreo Ritz Raced/1000
2003 #8 Oreo Ritz/6000
2003 #8 E Concert Raced/1008
2003 #8 E Concert/6300
2003 #8 DMP/5004
2003 #8 Busch Test/1600
2003 #8 Bud StainD/5500
2003 #8 Bud All-Star/5544
2003 #8 Bud Test/4800
2003 #8 Bud Talladega 2003 Win Raced/2200
2003 #8 Bud Talladega October '02 Win Raced/1500
2003 #8 Bud Metal/4000
2003 #8 Bud Col.Chr/2004
2003 #8 Bud/5700
2004 #8 Test/4000
2004 #8 Oreo Platinum/300
2004 #8 Oreo/4800
2004 #8 Bud World Series White Gold/50
2004 #8 Bud World Series Platinum/300
2004 #8 Bud World Series/2888
2004 #8 Bud Father's Day Platinum/300
2004 #8 Bud Father's Day/2200
2004 #8 Bud Dave Matthews Band White Gold/25
2004 #8 Bud Dave Matthews Band Platinum/360
2004 #8 Bud Dave Matthews Band/3888
2004 #8 Bud Born On Feb.15 Raced Platinum/408
2004 #8 Bud Born On Feb.15 Raced/6996
2004 #8 Bud Born On Feb.12 Raced/2400
2004 #8 Bud Born On Feb.7 Platinum/408
2004 #8 Bud Born On Feb.7/4008
2004 #8 Bud Talladega Raced/804
2004 #8 Bud Bristol Raced/1200
2004 #8 Bud Platinum/408
2004 #8 Bud Color Chrome/2400
2004 #8 Bud/5004
2004 #81 Taco Bell Plat/300
2004 #81 Taco Bell/3000
2004 #81 Menards Bristol Raced White Gold/48
2004 #81 Menards Bristol Raced/1500
2004 #81 KFC/4440
2005 #3 Milestones '98-'99 Busch Champion/1500
2005 #8 Milestones '04 Daytona Win/1800
2005 #8 Milestones '01 Daytona Win/1000
2005 #8 Milestones '00 All-Star Win/999
2005 #8 Bud 3 Doors Down White Gold/50
2005 #8 Bud 3 Doors Down Platinum/144
2005 #8 Bud 3 Doors Down/2100
2005 #8 Bud Test/2005
2005 #8 Bud MLB All-Star White Gold/44
2005 #8 Bud MLB All-Star Platinum/144
2005 #8 Bud MLB All-Star/2400
2005 #8 Bud Born On Feb.20 White Gold/50
2005 #8 Bud Born On Feb.20 Platinum/200
2005 #8 Bud Born On Feb.20/3300
2005 #8 Bud Born On Feb.17 White Gold/25
2005 #8 Bud Born On Feb.17 Platinum/88
2005 #8 Bud Born On Feb.12 White Gold/33
2005 #8 Bud Born On Feb.12 Platinum/140
2005 #8 Bud Born On Feb.12/600
2005 #8 Bud White Gold/50
2005 #8 Bud Color Chrome/1200
2005 #8 Bud/2400
2005 #81 Oreo Ritz White Gold/48
2005 #81 Oreo Ritz Platinum/240
2005 #81 Oreo Ritz/2400
2005 #81 Menards White Gold/25
2005 #81 Menards/1200
2005 #81 Chance 2 Test/1008
2006 #8 Goody's/199
2006 #8 Goody's Platinum/3
2006 #8 250th Start White Gold/33
2006 #8 250th Start Platinum/30
2006 #8 250th Start/1500
2006 #8 Oreo White Gold/30
2006 #8 Oreo Platinum/24
2006 #8 Oreo/1200
2006 #8 Menards Daytona Raced Platinum/30
2006 #8 Menards Daytona Raced/1500
2006 #8 Bud Test Platinum/20
2006 #8 Bud Test/1000
2006 #8 Bud Father's Day White Gold/33
2006 #8 Bud Father's Day Platinum/50
2006 #8 Bud Father's Day/3333
2006 #8 Bud Dale Tribute White Gold/33
2006 #8 Bud Dale Tribute Platinum/66
2006 #8 Bud Dale Tribute/3333
2006 #8 Bud Richmond Raced Platinum/27
2006 #8 Bud Richmond Raced/1388
2006 #8 Bud White Gold/30
2006 #8 Bud Platinum/30
2006 #8 Bud Color Chrome/444
2006 #8 Bud/1500

Action/RCCA Elite 1:32
2003 #8 Bud StainD Gold/316
2003 #8 Bud StainD/844
2003 #8 Bud All-Star/844
2003 #8 Bud No Bull '00 Monte Carlo/1008
2003 #8 Bud/1500
2004 #8 Oreo/600
2004 #8 Bud Born On Feb.15/960
2004 #8 Bud Born On Feb.7/408
2004 #8 Bud/600

Action/RCCA Elite 1:64
2001 #8 Bud All-Star/2976
2001 #8 Bud/2016
2002 #3 Oreo/4000
2002 #3 Nilla Wafers/4000
2002 #8 Looney Tunes/4008
2002 #8 Bud All-Star/4612
2002 #8 Bud Color Chrome/3600
2003 #8 Oreo Ritz/4380

2003 #8 E Concert/3300
2003 #8 DMP/2988
2003 #8 Bud StainD/2980
2003 #8 Bud All-Star/3300
2003 #8 Bud/3660
2004 #8 Oreo/2880
2004 #8 Bud World Series/1824
2004 #8 Bud Dave Matthews Band/1968
2004 #8 Bud Born On Feb.7/2016
2004 #8 Bud/2400
2004 #81 Menards Bristol Raced/720
2004 #81 Taco Bell/1200
2004 #81 KFC/2400
2005 #8 Bud 3 Doors Down/1008
2005 #8 Bud MLB All-Star/1440
2005 #8 Bud/1200
2005 #81 Menards/768
2005 #81 Oreo Ritz/1584
2006 #8 Bud/552
2006 #8 Oreo/480
2006 #8 Menards Daytona Raced/528
2006 #8 250th Start/720
2006 #8 Bud Father's Day/1508
2006 #8 Bud Dale Tribute/1533

Action/RCCA Elite Prototypes 1:24
1998 #3 AC Delco Proto
1999 #3 AC Delco Proto/12
1999 #8 Bud Proto/12
1999 #31 Sikk.White Proto 1997 Monte Carlo/12
2000 #8 Bud/12

Action/RCCA Gold 1:32
1998 #3 AC Delco/5000

Action/RCCA Historical Series 1:24
2004 #7 Church Bros. '97 Monte Carlo/2508
2004 #8 Bud '03 Phoenix Raced/504
2004 #8 Bud Olympic '00 Monte Carlo/2508

Action/RCCA Historical Series 1:32
2004 #3 AC Delco Last Lap '99 Monte Carlo/480
2004 #7 Church Bros. '97 Monte Carlo/600
2004 #8 Bud Olympic '00 Monte Carlo/408

Action/RCCA Historical Series Elite 1:2
2004 #8 Bud Olympic '00 Monte Carlo Platinum/408
2004 #8 Bud '03 Phoenix Raced/1008

Action/RCCA Historical Series Elite 1:3
2004 #3 AC Delco Last Lap '99 Monte Carlo/480
2004 #7 Church Bros. '97 Monte Carlo/600
2004 #8 Bud Olympic '00 Monte Carlo/408

Action/RCCA SelectNet 1:64
1999 #3 AC Delco
1999 #31 Wrangler '97MC
1999 #31 Sikkens Wht '97MC

Action/RCCA SelectNet Banks 1:24
1999 #3 AC Delco
1999 #8 Bud
1999 #31 Wrangler '97MC/600
1999 #31 Sikkens White '97MC

Action/RCCA SelectNet Elite 1:24
1999 #8 Bud/1500
1999 #31 Wrangler '97/500
1999 #31 Sikkens White 1997/1000

Action/RCCA Total View 1:64
2000 #8 Bud Olympic/4032
2000 #8 Bud No Bull

Action/RCCA Transporters 1:64
2002 #3 Oreo Color Chr./504
2002 #3 Nilla Wafers/2508
2002 #8 Bud Color Chrome/504
2002 #8 Bud/2508
2003 #8 DMP Chance 2/1800
2003 #8 Bud/2508

Brookfield 1:24
1999 #3 AC Delco Superman Silver/624 '99
2005 #8 Bud Born On Feb.20/900
2005 #8 Bud Born On Feb.17/300
2005 #8 Bud Born On Feb.12/408
2005 #8 Bud/804
2005 #81 Oreo Ritz/804
2006 #8 250th Start/300
2006 #8 Oreo/300
2006 #8 Bud Father's Day/508
2006 #8 Bud Dale Tribute Chrome 2-car set/2004
2006 #8 Bud Dale Tribute/833
2006 #8 Bud/300

Brookfield Dually and Show Trailer 1:25
2003 #8 Bud All-Star 3-axle Silver/2682
2003 #8 Bud StainD 3-axle
2003 #8 Oreo Ritz Silver/572
2003 #8 Oreo Ritz/2804
2003 #8 DMP Silver 3-axle/929
2003 #8 DMP 3-axle/2046
2003 #8 Bud All-Star 3-axle/2682

Brookfield Dually with Car and Show Tra
1999 #3 AC Delco Superman/4244
1999 #3 AC Delco/4224
1999 #8 Bud/2616
2000 #8 Bud Olympic Silver Incentive/380
2000 #8 Bud Olympic/1648
2000 #8 Bud/2048
2002 #3 Oreo Silver/872
2002 #3 Oreo/3608
2002 #3 Nilla Wafers Silver/660
2002 #3 Nilla Wafers/3000
2002 #8 Bud Color Chrome
2002 #8 Bud Silver without car/1052
2002 #8 Bud w/o car/4480

Brookfield Sets 1:24
1994-03 #8 Bud All-Star QVC 2-car set/5004 '01
1994-03 #8 Bud First Win QVC 2-car set/2000 '00
1994-03 #8 Bud Raced E Concert Raced 2-car set/3504
1994-03 #8 Bud All-Star QVC 2-car set/20,004 '02
1994-03 #NNO Dale Jr./Coke 2-car set/5000 '98

Brookfield Suburbans, Blazers, and Taho
1999 #8 Bud/2508
2001 #8 Bud AS Silver/658
2001 #8 Bud All Star/2876
2001 #8 Bud Silver/620
2001 #8 Bud/2464
2002 #3 Oreo Bank/2508

Brookfield Trackside 1:25
1998 #1 Coke Bear Suburban/4086
1998 #3 AC Del.Silver/420
1998 #3 AC Delco
1999 #1 Coke Suburb./1500
1999 #3 AC Delco Suburban/2928
1999 #8 Bud/3072
1999 #31 Sikkens White/3000
1999 #31 Gargoyles/2508
2000 #8 Bud/3072
2001 #8 Bud/2508
2002 #3 Nilla Wafers/2508
2002 #3 Oreo/2508
2002 #8 Bud Color Chrome/600

Brookfield Trackside 1:64
2004 #8 Oreo Ritz/4704
2004 #8 Bud Born On Feb.15/6384

2004 #8 Bud/7624 on a base
2005 #8 Bud Born On Feb.20/4008

Checkered Flag Sports Champions 1:24
2007 #7 JR Motorsports Grand Opening/3883

Checkered Flag Sports Champions Black L
2007 #7 JR Motorsports/833
2007 #7 JR Motorsports AU/833
2007 #7 JR Motorsports 24K/283

Motorsports Authentics Driver's Select
2007 #8 Bud/2004
2007 #8 Veritas/1896*
2007 #8 JM Menards/2232*
2007 #8 Bud '57 Chevy/19,504*
2007 #8 Bud Stars & Stripes/31,272*
2007 #8 Bud Elvis COT/35,816*
2007 #8 Bud Camo American Heroes/41,520
2007 #8 Bud COT/33,934*
2007 #8 Bud/26,904*
2007 #8 Sharpie/13,182*
2007 #8 Bud Stars & Stripes
2007 #8 Bud
2007 #8 Vertis/636
2007 #8 Sharpie/1500
2007 #8 JM Menards/600
2007 #8 Bud Stars & Stripes/31,272
2007 #8 Bud COT/3630
2007 #8 Bud/3792

Motorsports Authentics Owner's Elite 1:
2007 #8 Sharpie White Gold/100
2007 #8 Sharpie Platinum/25
2007 #8 Sharpie/2007
2007 #8 JM Menards/1008*
2007 #8 Bud '57 Chevy White Gold/50
2007 #8 Bud '57 Chevy Platinum/25
2007 #8 Bud '57 Chevy/1008
2007 #8 Bud Test/2007
2007 #8 Bud Stars & Stripes White Gold/50*
2007 #8 Bud Stars & Stripes Platinum/25
2007 #8 Bud Stars & Stripes Color Chrome/2007
2007 #8 Bud Stars & Stripes/2007
2007 #8 Bud Elvis COT White Gold/50*
2007 #8 Bud Elvis COT Platinum/25
2007 #8 Bud Elvis COT/2007
2007 #8 Bud Camo Heroes White Gold/50*
2007 #8 Bud Camo Am.Heroes Platinum/25
2007 #8 Bud Camo Heroes Color Chrome/2007
2007 #8 Bud Camo American Heroes/2007
2007 #8 Bud COT White Gold/50*
2007 #8 Bud COT Platinum/25
2007 #8 Bud COT/2007
2007 #8 Bud White Gold/100
2007 #8 Bud Platinum/25
2007 #8 Bud/2007
2007 #8 Sharpie/2007
2007 #8 Bud Stars & Stripes/2007
2007 #8 Bud Camo American Heroes/1500*
2007 #8 Bud/2007*

Motorsports Authentics Owner's Elite Tr
2007 #8 Sharpie/576*
2007 #8 Bud Camo American Heroes/708*
2007 #8 Bud/2007*

Motorsports Authentics Pit Stop 1:64
2007 #8 Sharpie
2007 #8 JM Menards
2007 #8 DEI '57 Chevy
2007 #8 DEI Stars & Stripes
2007 #8 DEI Elvis COT
2007 #8 DEI Camo Am.Heroes
2007 #8 DEI

Motorsports Authentics Pit Stop Blister
2007 #8 DEI

Motorsports Authentics QVC For Race Fan
2007 #8 Sharpie Platinum/108
2007 #8 Sharpie Mesma Chrome/2508
2007 #8 Sharpie Gold/108
2007 #8 Sharpie Color Chrome/2508
2007 #8 Sharpie Chrome/288
2007 #8 Bud '57 Chevy Platinum/108
2007 #8 Bud '57 Chevy Mesma Chrome/888
2007 #8 Bud '57 Chevy Gold/188
2007 #8 Bud '57 Chevy Color Chrome/3888
2007 #8 Bud '57 Chevy Chrome/504
2007 #8 Bud Stars & Stripes Platinum/108
2007 #8 Bud Stars & Stripes Mesma Chrome/2508
2007 #8 Bud Stars & Stripes Gold Chrome/3888
2007 #8 Bud Stars & Stripes Color Chrome/2508
2007 #8 Bud Stars & Stripes Chrome/504
2007 #8 Bud Elvis COT Platinum/108
2007 #8 Bud Elvis COT Mesma Chrome/888
2007 #8 Bud Elvis COT Mesma Chrome/888
2007 #8 Bud Elvis COT Gold Chrome/3888
2007 #8 Bud Elvis COT Gold/188
2007 #8 Bud Elvis COT Chrome/3888
2007 #8 Bud Camo Heroes Platinum/144
2007 #8 Bud Camo Heroes Mesma Chrome/2508
2007 #8 Bud Camo Heroes Gold/288
2007 #8 Bud Camo Heroes Color Chrome/3888
2007 #8 Bud Camo Heroes Chrome/504
2007 #8 Bud COT Platinum/204
2007 #8 Bud COT Mesma Chrome/2508
2007 #8 Bud COT Gold Chrome/3888
2007 #8 Bud COT Gold/288
2007 #8 Bud COT Color Chrome/2508
2007 #8 Bud COT Chrome/504
2007 #8 Bud Platinum/144
2007 #8 Bud Mesma Chrome/2508
2007 #8 Bud Gold Chrome/3888
2007 #8 Bud Gold/288
2007 #8 Bud Color Chrome/2508
2007 #8 Bud Chrome/2004

Motorsports Authentics Steel 1:16
2006 #8 Bud Father's Day/1800
2006 #8 Bud Dale Tribute/2133
2006 #8 Bud/1100

Motorsports Authentics/RCCA Owner's Clu
2007 #8 Bud '57 Chevy/1008*
2007 #8 Bud Stars & Stripes/3000*
2007 #8 Bud Camo American Heroes/2007*
2007 #8 Bud/3000*

RCCA Club 1:24
2008 #88 Mountian Dew Retro/1200
2008 #88 National Guard/1000
2008 #88 AMP/2100
2008 #88 National Guard Citizen Soldier/1200
2008 #88 National Guard Salute the Troops/500

RCCA Elite 1:24
2008 #5 City Chevrolet Test/1200
2008 #88 Mountain Dew Retro/3000
2008 #88 AMP/5000
2008 #88 National Guard Citizen Soldier/3000
2008 #88 National Guard Citizen Soldier Platinum/25
2008 #88 National Guard Citizen Soldier White Gold/50
2008 #88 AMP Platinum/25
2008 #88 AMP White Gold/50
2008 #88 Mountian Dew Retro Platinum/25

2008 #88 Mountian Dew Retro White Gold/50
2008 #88 National Guard Salute the Troops/1000
2008 #88 National Guard/3000
2008 #88 National Guard Platinum/25
2008 #88 National Guard White Gold/50
2008 #88 National Guard Test/708
2008 #88 AMP Test/504

Revell Club 1:18
1998 #1 Coke Bear/2004
1998 #3 AC Delco/504
1999 #31 Gargoyles '97MC
2000 #8 Bud/2508

Revell Club 1:24
1998 #1 Coke Bear/3330
1998 #3 AC Delco
1999 #3 AC Delco Superman/1500
1999 #3 AC Delco/2004
1999 #8 Bud/1002
1999 #31 Sikkens White 1997 Monte Carlo/2004
1999 #31 Sikkens Blue 1997 Monte Carlo/1002
1999 #31 Mom 'N' Pop's 1996 Monte Carlo/2004
1999 #31 Gargoyles 1997 Monte Carlo/2004
2000 #8 2000 Test
2000 #8 Bud/2004
2001 #8 Bud/2508

Revell Collection 1:18
1998 #1 Coke Bear/4002
1998 #3 AC Delco/3120
1998 #31 Wrangler 1997 Monte Carlo/3120
1998 #31 Sikkens Blue '97MC
1999 #3 AC Delco Superman/4800
1999 #8 Bud/5004
1999 #31 Sikkens White 1997 Monte Carlo/2508
1999 #31 Gargoyles 1997 Monte Carlo/2508
2000 #8 Bud

Revell Collection 1:24
1998 #1 Coke Bear/18,000
1998 #1 Coke Bear Bank
1998 #3 AC Delco Track
1998 #3 AC Delco Dealer/3500
1998 #31 Wrangler Bank 1997 Monte Carlo/2504
1998 #31 Wrangler 1997 Monte Carlo/5004
1999 #3 AC Del.Superman Bank set w/1:64 car/2004
1999 #3 AC Delco Superman/10,530
1999 #3 AC Delco/10,530
1999 #8 Bud Bank set w/1:64 car/2508
1999 #8 Bud/12,024
1999 #31 Sikkens White 1997 Monte Carlo
1999 #31 Sikkens Blue 1997 Monte Carlo/8500
1999 #31 Mom 'N' Pop's 1996 Monte Carlo/3120
1999 #31 Gargoyles 1997 Monte Carlo/5004
2000 #8 Bud Test/1500
2000 #8 Bud Olympic/3120
2000 #8 Bud Bank set with 1:64 car
2000 #8 Bud/5004
2001 #8 Bud Test gray/2508
2001 #8 Bud No Bull Win
2001 #8 Bud All-Star Raced Daytona Win/40,008
2001 #8 Bud All-Star
2001 #8 Bud/22,764
2002 #3 Oreo Test Gray/7776
2002 #3 Oreo Daytona Win w/CD ROM/48,236
2002 #8 Looney Tunes raced version
2002 #8 Bud Test Red/7620
2002 #8 Bud Talla.Win raced version/18,908
2002 #8 Bud Dover Win with Wilson V-ball/38,792
2002 #8 Bud/14,952
2003 #8 Bud Raced Win Phoenix/3504
2003 #8 Test White/4902
2003 #8 Oreo Ritz Raced/3888
2003 #8 E Concert Raced/4872
2003 #8 Bud Test Red/5622
2003 #8 Bud Test/5622
2004 #8 Bud Test Gold/4800
2004 #8 Bud Test Brown/3570
2005 #8 Bud Test/1752
2005 #8 Bud Born On Feb.20/1500

Revell Collection 1:43
1998 #1 Coke Bear/7512
1998 #31 Wrangler '97MC
1999 #3 AC Delco Superman/5508
1999 #3 AC Delco/4008
1999 #8 Bud

Revell Collection 1:64
1998 #1 Coke Bear/27,000
1998 #3 AC Delco
1999 #3 AC Delco Superman/20,016
1999 #3 AC Delco/13,104
1999 #8 Bud
1999 #31 Sikkens White '97MC
1999 #31 Sikkens Blue 1997 Monte Carlo/10,080
1999 #31 Mom 'N' Pop's 1996 Monte Carlo
1999 #31 Gargoyles '97MC
2000 #8 Bud Olympic/9000
2000 #8 Bud/7992
2001 #8 Bud AS Raced/20,016
2001 #8 Bud
2001 #NNO Bud All-Star NAPA SS set in tin/12,000
2002 #3 Oreo in tin/20,016
2002 #3 Nilla Wafers in cookie box/28,608
2002 #8 Bud Talladega Win
2002 #8 Bud/15,336
2002 #NNO R.Earnhardt/D.Earnhardt D.Earnhardt Jr. 3-car tin/27,597

Revell Collection Train Sets 1:64
2002 #8 Looney Tunes 3-car train set/600
2003 #8 Oreo Ritz/5160
2003 #8 E Concert/5688
2003 #8 DMP/5328
2004 #7 Church Bros. '97 Monte Carlo/2556
2004 #8 Oreo/2862

Revell Select 1:24
1998 #3 AC Delco
2001 #8 Bud All-Star
2002 #3 Nilla Wafer
2002 #8 Bud All-Star
2003 #8 DMP
2004 #8 Bud Born On Feb.15

Revell Select Hobby 1:64
1998 #3 AC Delco

Winner's Circle 1:18
2002 #8 Dale Jr.
2002 #8 Looney Tunes '02
2003 #8 MLB All Star '03
2003 #8 E Tribute Concert in '02 package
2003 #8 Dale Jr.
2004 #8 Oreo
2004 #8 JR
2005 #8 DEI
2005 #8 JR
2005 #81 Oreo Ritz
2007 #8 DEI

Winner's Circle 1:24
1998 #1 Coke
1998 #3 AC Delco
1999 #3 AC Del.Superman

1999 #3 AC Delco
1999 #8 Dale Jr.
2001 #8 Dale Jr.
2002 #3 Oreo
2002 #3 Nilla Wafers
2002 #8 Looney Tunes
2002 #8 2002 All-Star Game
2003 #8 Oreo Ritz
2003 #8 MLB All Star '03
2003 #8 Looney Tunes '02
2003 #8 E Tribute Concert
2003 #8 JR thin base
2003 #8 JR
2004 #8 JR Dave Matthews
2004 #8 JR Olympic '00
2004 #8 Oreo
2004 #8 JR
2004 #81 Taco Bell
2004 #81 KFC
2005 #8 JR
2005 #8 DEI
2005 #81 Oreo Ritz
2006 #8 250 Starts
2006 #8 Bud Dale Tribute split window box
2007 #8 DEI
2008 #88 AMP
2008 #88 National Guard

Winner's Circle 1:43
1998 #1 Coke
1998 #3 AC Delco
1998 #31 Sikkens Blue
1999 #3 AC Del.Superman
1999 #3 AC Delco

Winner's Circle 1:64
1998 #1 Coke
1998 #3 AC Delco Champ.
1998 #3 AC Delco
1998 #31 Sikkens Blue
2000 #8 New Stars Red Roof
2000 #8 New Stars Black Roof
2004 #8 Bud Born On Feb.15 Raced
2004 #8 Bud Born On Feb.7
2004 #8 Bud
2005 #8 Bud Born On Feb.17
2005 #8 Bud Born On Feb.20
2005 #8 Bud World Series '04
2005 #8 Bud Test
2005 #8 Bud 3 Doors Down '05
2006 #8 Bud Test
2006 #8 Bud MLB All Star '05
2006 #8 Bud
2006 #NNO Dale Tribute 5-car set

Winner's Circle 1:87
2006 #8 250 Starts
2006 #8 DEI
2007 #8 DEI Stars & Stripes
2007 #8 DEI
2008 #88 AMP
2008 #88 National Guard

Winner's Circle 24K Gold 1:64
1999 #3 AC Delco

Winner's Circle 2-Car Set w/Hood 1:64
2008 #88 AMP/National Guard

Winner's Circle American Heroes 1:24
2007 #8 DEI Camo AH logo
2007 #8 Bud Camo AH logo

Winner's Circle American Heroes 1:87
2007 #8 Bud Camo AH
2007 #NNO American Heroes 9-car set
2007 #NNO 8.Dale Jr./Camo/ 16.Biffle/3M National Guard 88.Huffman/Navy 3-car set

Winner's Circle American Heroes Hood 1:
2007 #8 DEI Camo AH
2007 #8 Bud Camo AH

Winner's Circle Autographed Hood 1:64
2002 #3 Nilla Wafers
2002 #3 Oreo
2003 #1 Coke Japan '98
2003 #8 StainD
2003 #8 Oreo Ritz Dale Jr. Hood
2003 #8 Oreo Ritz Dale Earnhardt Jr. Hood
2003 #8 E Tribute Concert
2003 #8 DMP
2004 #8 StainD
2004 #8 Oreo
2004 #8 JR short package
2004 #8 JR
2004 #8 Dave Matthews Band
2004 #81 Taco Bell
2004 #81 KFC short package
2004 #81 KFC
2005 #8 DEI
2005 #81 Chance 2 Test '98,'99 Champion
2006 #8 Oreo
2006 #8 DEI
2006 #8 Bud Dale Tribute split window box

Winner's Circle Autographed Hoods 1:64
2008 #88 Amp
2008 #88 National Guard

Winner's Circle Championship with Fl
1998-99 #3 AC Delco 1998 BGN Champion

Winner's Circle Cool Customs 1:64
1998-99 #3 AC Delco '57 Chevy
1998-99 #NNO Earnhardt Jr./Earn.Sr./Coke 2-cars

Winner's Circle Daytona 500 1:24
2008 #88 AMP
2008 #88 National Guard

Winner's Circle Daytona 500 1:64
2008 #88 AMP
2008 #88 National Guard

Winner's Circle Daytona 500 1:87
2008 #88 AMP
2008 #88 National Guard

Winner's Circle Daytona 500 2-car sets
2008 #88/08 AMP Daytona 500 Event Car
2008 #88/08 National Guard Daytona 500 Event Car

Winner's Circle Daytona 500 Hoods 1:64
2008 #88 National Guard
2008 #88 AMP

Winner's Circle Daytona 500 Transporter
2008 #88 AMP

Winner's Circle Deluxe Race Hood 1:64
2000 #8 Dale Jr. red roof Remington on deck lid
2000 #8 Dale Jr. red roof no Remington
2000 #8 Dale Jr. black roof Remington on deck lid
2000 #8 Dale Jr. black roof no remington

Winner's Circle Deluxe Winston Cup Scen
2000 #8 Dale Texas Win

Winner's Circle Die-Cast Kits 1:24
2002 #3 Nilla Wafer
2002 #8 Looney Tunes
2002 #8 Dale Jr.
2003 #3 Nilla Wafers '02
2003 #3 Oreo '02

2003 #8 Looney Tunes '02
2004 #8 JR

Winner's Circle Die-Cast Kits 1:64
2002 #8 Looney Tunes
2002 #8 Dale Jr.
2003 #8 Looney Tunes '02

Winner's Circle Double Platinum 1:43
2000 #3 R.Childress/Goodwrench
2000 #8 Dale Jr.
2001 #8 Dale Dale Earnhardt Sr. on card
2002 #3 Oreo
2002 #3 Nilla Wafer
2002 #8 2002 All-Star Game
2002 #8 Looney Tunes
2002 #8 Dale Jr.
2003 #8 Looney Tunes

Winner's Circle Driver Hood 1:64
2000-01 #8 Dale Jr.

Winner's Circle Driver Photo Hood 1:64
2005 #8 DEI

Winner's Circle Driver Sticker 1:64
2001 #8 Dale Jr.
2001 #8 2001 All-Star Game
2001 #8 Dale Jr. July 4th
2002 #8 2002 MLB AS Game
2002 #8 2001 All-Star Game
2002 #8 Looney Tunes
2003 #8 Looney Tunes
2003 #8 DMP
2003 #8 Dale Jr.
2003 #8 JR short package
2003 #8 JR
2003 #11 True Value '99 IROC
2004 #8 Oreo
2004 #8 JR sparkle
2005 #8 DEI

Winner's Circle Dually w/Car on Tracksi
2008 #88 National Guard
2008 #88 AMP

Winner's Circle Event Series 1:64
2005 #8 Bud Born On Feb.15 '04 Daytona Win Feb.7 car
2005 #8 Bud '04 Richmond Win
2005 #8 Bud '04 Atlanta Win

Winner's Circle Fantasy Pack 1:64
1998-99 #3 AC Delco

Winner's Circle Fast Pack 1:64
2002 #15/1/8S.Park/D.Earn Jr.

Winner's Circle Gift Pack 1:64
2002 #8 Dale/Oreo/Nilla Waf.

Winner's Circle Gift Pack With Photo 1:
2002 #8 2001 All-Star 2002 All-Star/Dale Jr.

Winner's Circle Helmets 1:64
2007 #8 DEI

Winner's Circle Hoods 1:64
2007 #8 DEI
2008 #88 AMP

Winner's Circle License Plate 1:64
2007 #8 DEI

Winner's Circle License Plate Series 1:
2001 #8 Dale Jr.

Winner's Circle Lifetime Dale Jr. 1:
2001-02 #3 Goodwrench '96 4/5
2001-02 #8 Dale '01 5/5
2001-02 #8 Dale Jr. '99 1/5
2001-02 #31 Sikkens White '97 2/5
2001-02 #31 Mom 'N' Pops '96 3/5

Winner's Circle Lifetime Series 1:24
2001 #8 Dale Jr.
2001 #31 Mom 'N' Pop's

Winner's Circle Limited Edition 1:24
2007 #8 Sharpie
2007 #8 DEI Stars & Stripes
2007 #8 Bud Test
2007 #8 Bud Stars & Stripes
2007 #8 Bud
2008 #88 AMP

Winner's Circle Limited Edition 1:64
2007 #8 Sharpie
2007 #8 Bud Test
2007 #8 Bud

Winner's Circle Limited Edition 1:87
2007 #8 Bud Stars & Stripes

Winner's Circle Limited Edition Hoods 1
2007 #8 DEI Stars & Stripes
2007 #8 Bud Stars & Stripes

Winner's Circle Medallion 1:64
2007 #8 DEI

Winner's Circle Micro Machines 1:144
1999 #3 AC Delco Car and Transporter
1999 #NNO S.Park/Jr.
1999 #NNO Earnhardt Jr.

Winner's Circle New Stars 1:64
2000 #8 Dale Jr.

Winner's Circle Number Magnet 1:64
2008 #88 Amp
2008 #88 National Guard

Winner's Circle Pit Board 1:64
2008 #88 AMP

Winner's Circle Pit Pass 1:64
2007 #8 DEI

Winner's Circle Pit Pass Preview 1:64
2002 #8 Dale Jr.
2003 #8 JR '03 Preview sticker
2003 #8 JR
2004 #8 JR

Winner's Circle Pit Row 1:64
1998 #1 Coke
1998 #3 AC Delco Fanscan
1998 #3 AC Delco tires off

Winner's Circle Pit Sign 1:64
2006 #8 DEI
2007 #8 DEI

Winner's Circle Preview 1:43
2000 #3 AC Delco Superman 1999
2000 #8 Dale Jr.

Winner's Circle Race Hood 1:43
2002 #3 Oreo
2002 #3 Nilla Wafers
2002 #8 2002 All-Star Game
2003 #8 JR
2003 #8 MLB All Star '02
2003 #8 Oreo Ritz
2003 #8 Looney Tunes '02
2003 #8 E Tribute Concert
2004 #8 Oreo
2004 #8 JR

Winner's Circle Race Hood 1:64
2003 #8 JR
2003 #8 MLB All Star '03
2004 #8 JR
2001-02 #3 Oreo
2001-02 #8 Dale Jr.

Winner's Circle Sam Bass 1:43

2000 #8 Dale Jr.
Winner's Circle Sam Bass 1:64
2008 #88 Amp
2008 #88 National Guard
Winner's Circle Schedule Hood 1:64
2005 #8 JR
2005 #81 Oreo Ritz
2007 #8 DEI
Winner's Circle Schedule Hoods 1:64
2008 #88 National Guard
2008 #88 AMP
Winner's Circle Speedweeks 1:43
1999 #3 AC Delco
Winner's Circle Sticker 1:64
2006 #8 DEI
Winner's Circle Stickers 1:64
2008 #5 All Star Test Car
2008 #88 National Guard
Winner's Circle Team Authentics 1:64
2001 #8 Dale Jr. Sheetmetal
2001 #8 Dale Jr. Firesuit
Winner's Circle Test Hood 1:64
2005 #8 DEI
Winner's Circle Track Support Crew 1:64
1999 #3 AC Delco
Winner's Circle Transporters 1:64
2000 #8 Dale Jr.
2001 #8 Dale Jr.
2002 #3 Oreo
2002 #3 Nilla Wafers
2002 #8 2002 All-Star Game
2002 #8 2001 All-Star Game
2002 #8 Dale Jr.
2003 #8 StainD
2003 #8 Oreo Ritz
2003 #8 Looney Tunes
2003 #8 E Tribute Concert
2003 #8 DMP Chance 2
2003 #8 2003 All-Star
2003 #8 2002 All-Star
2004 #8 StainD
2004 #8 Oreo
2004 #8 MLB All Star '03
2004 #8 JR Souvenir
2004 #8 JR
2005 #8 JR
2005 #81 Oreo Ritz
2007 #8 DEI Stars & Stripes
2007 #8 DEI Camo American Heroes
2007 #8 DEI
2008 #88 3 Doors Down
2008 #88 Amp
2008 #88 Go Daddy
2008 #88 National Guard
Winner's Circle Victory Celebration 1:4
1998 #3 BGN Champ.
1999 #3 Richmond 6/5/98
1999 #3 Co-Cola 300 4/4/98
Winner's Circle with Figure 1:24
1998 #1 Coke
1998 #3 AC Delco

Edwards, Carl

Action Racing Collectables 1:24
2006 #99 Office Depot Holiday QVC*
2006 #99 Office Depot Holiday/1075*
Action Racing Collectables 1:64
2008 #99 Office Depot
Action Racing Collectables Platinum 1:2
2008 #99 Office Depot/7248
Action Racing Collectables Platinum 1:6
2008 #99 Office Depot/3504
Action/RCCA 1:24
2006 #99 Office Depot/150
2006 #99 Office Depot Color Chrome/100
2006 #99 Office Depot Holiday/200
Action/RCCA Elite 1:24
2006 #99 Office Depot/200
2006 #99 Office Depot Color Chrome/100
2006 #99 Office Depot Platinum/4
2006 #99 Office Depot Holiday White Gold/25
2006 #99 Office Depot Holiday Platinum/4
2006 #99 Office Depot Holiday/200
Hot Wheels Alternative Paint Scheme 1:2
2005 #99 Office Depot
Hot Wheels Alternative Paint Scheme 1:6
2005 #99 Office Depot
Hot Wheels Race Day 1:24
2005 #99 AAA
Motorsports Authentics Driver's Select
2007 #60 World Financial/708*
2007 #60 Scotts '07 BGN Champ/1084*
2007 #60 Scotts/1608*
2007 #60 Aflac/1116*
2007 #99 Office Depot Holiday Sam Bass/520*
2007 #99 Office Depot COT/1056*
2007 #99 Office Depot/3756*
2007 #99 Boston Red Sox COT/1764*
2007 #99 Office Depot
Motorsports Authentics Owner's Elite 1:
2007 #99 Office Depot COT/504*
2007 #99 Office Depot White Gold/50*
2007 #99 Office Depot Platinum/25
2007 #99 Office Depot/1008*
2007 #99 Office Depot/2007*
Motorsports Authentics Owner's Elite Tr
2007 #99 Office Depot/708*
Motorsports Authentics Pit Stop 1:64
2007 #60 Scotts
2007 #99 Scotts
2007 #99 Office Depot
Motorsports Authentics QVC For Race Fan
2007 #99 Office Depot Chrome/204
Motorsports Authentics/RCCA Owner's Clu
2007 #99 Office Depot Holiday Sam Bass/96*
2007 #99 Office Depot/1200*
RCCA Elite 1:24
2008 #99 Office Depot/300
2008 #99 Office Depot Platinum/25
2008 #99 Office Depot White Gold/50
Team Caliber First Choice 1:24
2004 #99 World Financial Group/250
Team Caliber Owners Series 1:24
2005 #60 Charter AU/600
2005 #99 Ortho
2005 #99 Round Up
2005 #99 AAA/600
2005 #99 Office Depot/600
2005 #99 World Financial
2005 #99 Stonebridge Life Pocono Raced/600
2005 #99 Scotts 1st Win AU/999
Team Caliber Owner's Series 1:24
2006 #60 Ameriquest
2006 #99 Office Depot/2400
Team Caliber Pit Stop 1:24
2005 #60 Charter
2005 #99 Stonebridge Life Pocono Raced
2005 #99 Office Depot BTS Promo in window box
2005 #99 Office Depot Promo in window box
2005 #99 Office Depot
2005 #99 Round Up
2005 #99 AAA
2006 #60 Ameriquest
2006 #99 Office Depot
Team Caliber Pit Stop 1:64
2005 #60 Charter
2005 #99 Ortho
2005 #99 Round Up
2005 #99 Office Depot
2005 #99 AAA
2005 #99 Stonebridge Life Pocono Raced
2005 #99 World Financial
2005 #99 Scotts 1st Win
2006 #60 iLevel Weyerhaeuser
2006 #60 Ameriquest Soaring Dreams
2006 #60 Ameriquest
2006 #99 Office Depot
Team Caliber Preferred 1:24
2005 #60 Charter/1500
2005 #99 Scotts 1st Win/10,008
2005 #99 Round Up/1800
2005 #99 Ortho/600
2005 #99 Office Depot/5004
2005 #99 AAA/2400
2005 #99 World Financial
2005 #99 World Financial Color Chrome AU/600
2005 #99 Stonebridge Life Pocono Win/3120
2005 #99 Scotts 1st Win AU/999
2005 #99 Scotts 1st Win Color Chrome AU/1008
2006 #60 iLevel Weyerhaeuser/2700
2006 #60 Ameriquest Soaring Dreams/3300
2006 #60 Ameriquest/2400
2006 #99 Office Depot BTS/1800
2006 #99 Office Depot/7500
Team Caliber Preferred Copper 1:24
2006 #60 iLevel Weyerhaeuser/360
2006 #99 Office Depot
Team Caliber Preferred Nickel 1:24
2005 #60 Charter/180
2005 #99 Stonebridge Life Pocono Win/180
2005 #99 Scotts 1st Win
2005 #99 Ortho/180
2005 #99 Office Depot/504
2005 #99 AAA/180
Winner's Circle 1:18
2007 #99 Office Depot
Winner's Circle 1:24
2006 #99 Office Depot
2007 #99 Office Depot
2008 #99 Office Depot
Winner's Circle 1:87
2006 #99 Office Depot
2007 #99 Office Depot
2008 #99 Office Depot
Winner's Circle Autographed Hood 1:64
2006 #99 Office Depot
Winner's Circle Daytona 500 1:24
2008 #99 Office Depot
Winner's Circle Daytona 500 1:87
2008 #99 Office Depot
Winner's Circle Daytona 500 Hoods 1:64
2008 #99 Office Depot
Winner's Circle License Plate 1:64
2007 #99 Office Depot
Winner's Circle Number Magnet 1:64
2008 #99 Office Depot
Winner's Circle Sam Bass Hoods 1:64
2007 #99 Office Depot Holiday
Winner's Circle Schedule Hood 1:64
2007 #99 Office Depot
Winner's Circle Schedule Hoods 1:64
2008 #99 Office Depot
Winner's Circle Stickers 1:64
2008 #99 Office Depot
Winner's Circle Victory Lane Hoods 1:64
2007 #99 Office Depot COT Dover Raced
2007 #99 Office Depot COT Bristol Raced
2007 #99 Office Depot Michigan Raced

Gordon, Jeff

Action Clearly Collectibles 1:24
2005 #24 Daytona Raced Tire/2000
Action Performance 1:24
1999 #24 DuPont
2000 #24 Pepsi
2000 #24 DuPont
2001 #24 DuPont Flames
2002 #24 DuPont Flames
2003 #24 DuPont Flames
2004 #24 DuPont Flames
2005 #24 Milestones 4-Time Brickyard Winner/6000
2005 #24 Milestones 4-Time Champion/6000
2005 #24 Milestones 3-Time Daytona Winner/6000
2005 #24 Milestones '94 Charlotte Win/6000
2005 #24 Halston Z-14 Promo in wind.box
Action Performance 1:64
1999 #24 DuPont
2000 #24 DuPont
2001 #24 DuPont Flames
2002 #24 DuPont Flames
2003 #24 DuPont Flames
2004 #24 Nextel Cup 6-car set
2006 #24 DuPont Flames
Action QVC For Race Fans Only 1:24
1998 #24 Pepsi Gold
2000 #24 DuPont Winston Gold/2000
2000 #24 DuPont Peanuts Gold/2000
2000 #24 DuPont Gold/2000
2000 #67 Outback Steakhouse Gold
2001 #24 Pepsi Platinum/624
2001 #24 Pepsi Gold/2000
2001 #24 Pepsi Color Chr./2508
2001 #24 DuPont Flames Platinum/624
2001 #24 DuPont Flames Color Chrome HMS 100th Win/2508
2001 #24 DuP.Flames Gold/2000
2001 #24 DuPont Flames Color Chrome/2508
2001 #24 DuPont Bugs Bunny Platinum/624
2001 #24 DuPont Bugs Bunny Gold/2000
2002 #24 DuPont Flames 2001 Champ Gold/2508
2002 #24 Pepsi Talladega Platinum/624
2002 #24 Pepsi Talladega Gold/2508
2002 #24 Pepsi Talladega Color Chrome/2508
2002 #24 Pepsi Dayt.Platinum/624
2002 #24 Pepsi Daytona Gold/2508
2002 #24 Pepsi Daytona Color Chrome/7500
2002 #24 DuPont Flames Platinum/624
2002 #24 DuPont Flames Gold/2508
2002 #24 DuPont Flames Color Chrome/22,424
2002 #24 DuP.Bugs Platinum/624
2002 #24 DuPont Bugs Gold/2508
2002 #24 DuPont Bugs Color Chrome/5004
2002 #24 DuPont 200th Ann. Platinum/624
2002 #24 DuPont 200th Ann. Gold/2508
2003 #24 Cookie Monster Color Chrome/2508
2003 #24 Wright Bros.Plat/624
2003 #24 Wright Bros.Gold/1008
2003 #24 Pepsi Billion $ Plat./674
2003 #24 Pepsi Billion $ Gold/1000
2003 #24 Pepsi Billion $ Color Chrome/2508
2003 #24 DuP.Flames Yose.Sam Color Chrome/1008
2003 #24 DuP.Flames Plat/624
2003 #24 DuP.Flames Gold/1000
2004 #24 DuPont Rainbow Color Chrome/504
2004 #24 DuPont Flames Wizard of Oz Platinum/300
2004 #24 DuPont Flames Platinum/300
2004 #24 DuPont Flames Color Chrome/504
2004 #24 DuPont Flames Brushed Metal/1008
2005 #24 Pepsi Star Wars Talladega Raced Silver/624
2005 #24 Pepsi Star Wars Talladega Raced Brushed Copper/288
2005 #24 Pepsi Star Wars Platinum/144
2005 #24 Pepsi Star Wars Gold/300
2005 #24 Pepsi Star Wars Color Chrome/3504
2005 #24 Pepsi Daytona Color Chrome/3504
2005 #24 Mighty Mouse Color Chrome/3504
2005 #24 DuPont Flames Performance Alliance Reverse Color Chrome/3504
2005 #24 DuPont Flames Brushed Metal/504
2006 #24 Superman Silver/288
2006 #24 Superman Platinum/144
2006 #24 Superman Gold/144
2006 #24 Superman Copper/408
2006 #24 Mighty Mouse Copper/288
2006 #24 DuPont Hot Hues Foose Design Gold/108
2006 #24 DuPont Flames Mesma Chrome/408
Action Racing Collectables 1:18
1998 #24 DuPont Chromalusion
1998 #24 Pepsi Star Wars/3000
1999 #24 Pepsi
1999 #24 DuPont NASCAR Racers
1999 #24 DuPont Superman/3000
1999 #24 DuPont
2000 #24 Pepsi
2000 #24 DuPont Winston
2000 #24 DuPont Peanuts
2000 #24 DuPont Millenn./3504
2000 #24 DuPont/3504
2001 #24 DuPont Flames/2508
2001 #24 DuPont 200th Ann./3504
2002 #24 DuPont Bugs/2472
2002 #24 DuPont Flames/4008
2003 #24 DuPont Flames Victory Lap/2508
2003 #24 DuPont Yose.Sam/2508
2003 #24 DuP.Wright Bros./1804
2003 #24 Pepsi Billion $/1996
2003 #24 DuPont Flames/2094
2003 #NNO Monte Carlo SS/4842
2005 #24 Milestones 4X Brickyard Winner/504
2005 #24 Milestones 4X Champion/300
2005 #24 Milestones 4X Daytona Winner/300
2005 #24 Milestones First Win/300
2006 #24 DuPont Hot Hues Foose Design
Action Racing Collectables 1:24
1995 #24 DuPont '95 Champ Bank/20,124
1995 #24 DuPont Bank/9504
1996 #24 DuPont Bank/12,500
1997 #24 Jurassic Park 3 Bank
1997 #24 Jurassic Park 3
1997 #24 DuPont Million $ Date Mac Tools Bank
1997 #24 DuPont Mill.$ Date Bank
1997 #24 DuPont ChromaPrem. Bank/28,000
1997 #24 DuPont ChromaPremier Sports Image/7500
1997 #24 DuPont ChromaPremier Promo
1997 #24 DuPont Brickyard/7500 black windows
1997 #24 DuPont Mac Tools
1997 #24 DuPont
1998 #1 Baby Ruth '92 T-bird Bank/7500
1998 #1 Baby Ruth '92 T-bird
1998 #24 DuPont No Bull Bank
1998 #24 DuPont No Bull
1998 #24 DuPont Chromalusion Mac Tools
1998 #24 DuPont Chromalusion Bank/15,000
1998 #24 DuPont Chromalusion
1998 #24 DuPont Mac Tools
1998 #24 DuPont Brick.Win/2508
1998 #24 DuPont Bank/7500
1998 #24 DuPont
1999 #1 Carol.'91 T-bird Mac Tools
1999 #1 Carolina '91 T-bird Bank
1999 #1 Carolina '91 T-bird
1999 #24 Pepsi Star Wars Mac Tools
1999 #24 Pepsi Star Wars Bank
1999 #24 Pepsi Star Wars
1999 #24 Pepsi Mac Tools
1999 #24 Pepsi Bank/7500
1999 #24 Pepsi
1999 #24 DuPont Superman Bank
1999 #24 DuP.Superman Mac Tools
1999 #24 DuPont Superman
1999 #24 DuPont NASCAR Racers/7800
1999 #24 DuPont Gold 1998 3-Time Champ
1999 #24 DuPont Brickyard/2500
1999 #24 DuPont Bank/7500
1999 #24 DuPont Mac Tools
1999 #24 DuP.Black Window/7500
1999 #24 DuPont
2000 #24 Pepsi Bank/5000
2000 #24 Pepsi/27,282
2000 #24 DuPont Winston
2000 #24 DuPont Peanuts Mac Tools/3000
2000 #24 DuPont Peanuts/48,480
2000 #24 DuPont Sign
2000 #24 DuPont Millen.Bank/5004
2000 #24 DuPont Millennium
2000 #24 DuPont Brickyard/2508
2000 #24 DuPont Bank/3504
2000 #24 DuPont Mac Tools/3000
2000 #24 DuPont/29,220
2000 #67 Outback '90 GP/28,992
2000 #2000 Action Fantasy/1800
2001 #24 DuPont Flames Las Vegas Raced CW Bank/2508
2001 #24 Pepsi Clear/3000
2001 #24 Pepsi Bank/1644
2001 #24 Pepsi/13,032
2001 #24 DuPont Bugs Bunny Clear/6792
2001 #24 DuPont Bugs Bunny Bank/3300
2001 #24 DuPont Bugs Bunny/64,800
2001 #24 Gordon Foundat./36,528
2001 #24 DuPont Flames Brickyard Win/3504
2001 #24 DuPont Flames Mac Tools Promo/3500
2001 #24 DuP.Flames Clear/6996
2001 #24 DuP.Flames Bank/1800
2001 #24 DuPont Flames/38,004
2002 #1 Autolite '89 T-bird Bank/1608
2002 #1 Autolite '89 T-bird/15,036
2002 #24 Pepsi Talladega Color Chrome Bank/1008
2002 #24 Pepsi Talladega Color Chrome/2508
2002 #24 Pepsi Talladega Bank/1800
2002 #24 Pepsi Talladega/19,020
2002 #24 Pepsi Daytona Bank/1800
2002 #24 Pepsi Daytona/37,836
2002 #24 Elmo/26,844
2002 #24 DuP.Flames Clear/7008
2002 #24 DuPont Flames Bank/2508
2002 #24 DuPont Flames/70,224
2002 #24 DuPont Bugs Bank/1644
2002 #24 DuPont Bugs/44,958
2002 #24 DuPont 200th Ann. Clear/7152
2002 #24 DuPont 200th Ann. Bank/3000
2002 #24 DuPont 200th Anniversary/78,180
2003 #6 True Value '98 IROC/12,708
2003 #24 Pepsi Billion $ GM Dealers/648
2003 #24 Pepsi Billion $ CW Bank/1272
2003 #24 Pepsi Billion $/22,692
2003 #24 Pepsi Mac Tools/288
2003 #24 Pepsi GM Dealers/1008
2003 #24 Pepsi DW Bank/864
2003 #24 Pepsi/22,752
2003 #24 DuPont Yose.Sam Bank/1092
2003 #24 DuPont Yose.Sam/19,416
2003 #24 DuPont Wright Bros CW Bank/1440
2003 #24 DuP.Wright Bros./26,520
2003 #24 DuPont Victory Lap CW Bank/672
2003 #24 DuPont Victory Lap/14,592
2003 #24 DuP.Flames GM Dealers
2003 #24 DuPont Flames/34,332
2003 #24 Cookie Monster/21,552
2004 #24 DuPont Flames HMS 20th Hamilton/156
2004 #24 DuPont Flames HMS 20th QVC/2004
2004 #24 DuPont Racing Stripes QVC/1008
2004 #24 400 Career Starts GM Dealers/408
2004 #24 400 Career Starts/3504
2004 #24 Santa QVC
2004 #24 Santa/6132
2004 #24 Pepsi Shards Talladega Raced Mac Tools/468
2004 #24 Pepsi Shards Talladega Raced/4524
2004 #24 Pepsi Shards GM Dealers/504
2004 #24 Pepsi Shards CW Bank/576
2004 #24 Pepsi Shards/11,028
2004 #24 Pepsi Billion Daytona Raced QVC/504
2004 #24 Pepsi Billion Daytona Raced/2892
2004 #24 Pepsi Billion GM Dealers/312
2004 #24 Pepsi Billion CW Bank/1008
2004 #24 Pepsi Billion/9564
2004 #24 DuPont Wizard of Oz CW Bank/528
2004 #24 DuPont Wizard of Oz/14,088
2004 #24 DuPont Rainbow GM Dealers/960
2004 #24 DuPont Rainbow CW Bank/552
2004 #24 DuPont Rainbow/12,900
2004 #24 DuPont Racing Stripes GM Dealers/468
2004 #24 DuPont Racing Stripes/4920
2004 #24 DuPont Flames HMS 20th Mac Tools/468
2004 #24 DuPont Flames HMS 20th GM Dealers/420
2004 #24 DuPont Flames HMS 20th CW Bank/528
2004 #24 DuPont Flames HMS 20th Ann./8232
2004 #24 DuPont Flames California Raced/3012
2004 #24 DuPont Flames Brickyard Raced w/tire/1596
2004 #24 DuPont Flames Brickyard Raced/6612
2004 #24 DuPont Flames Nextel Incentive/4704
2004 #24 DuPont Flames Mac Tools/288
2004 #24 DuPont Flames GM Dealers/2796
2004 #24 DuPont Flames CW Bank/636
2004 #24 DuPont Flames/22,716
2004 #24 Big Bird/9612
2005 #24 DuPont Flames Daytona Raced Color Chrome/3504
2005 #24 Santa Holiday/3504
2005 #24 Pepsi Star Wars Talladega Raced QVC/1008
2005 #24 Pepsi Star Wars Talladega Raced GM Dealers/608
2005 #24 Pepsi Star Wars Talladega Raced/6756
2005 #24 Pepsi Star Wars QVC/2508
2005 #24 Pepsi Star Wars Matco/84
2005 #24 Pepsi Star Wars Mac Tools/300
2005 #24 Pepsi Star Wars GM Dealers/720
2005 #24 Pepsi Star Wars CW Bank/468
2005 #24 Pepsi Star Wars/10,896
2005 #24 Pepsi Daytona QVC/504
2005 #24 Pepsi Daytona Mac Tools/300
2005 #24 Pepsi Daytona GM Dealers/720
2005 #24 Pepsi Daytona CW Bank/360
2005 #24 Pepsi Daytona/8160
2005 #24 Mighty Mouse QVC/1800
2005 #24 Mighty Mouse Liquid Metal/1008
2005 #24 Mighty Mouse GM Dealers/648
2005 #24 Mighty Mouse CW Bank/432
2005 #24 Mighty Mouse/7356
2005 #24 DuPont Test Robbie Loomis AU/2508
2005 #24 DuPont Flames Performance Alliance Reverse QVC/1500
2005 #24 DuPont Flames Performance Alliance Reverse Liquid Metal/1008
2005 #24 DuPont Flames Performance Alliance Reverse GM Dealers/768
2005 #24 DuPont Flames Performance Alliance Reverse CW Bank/402
2005 #24 DuPont Flames Performance Alliance Reverse/10,020
2005 #24 DuPont Flames Martinsville Raced QVC/288
2005 #24 DuPont Flames Martinsville Raced GM Dealers/180
2005 #24 DuPont Flames Martinsville Raced/3528
2005 #24 DuPont Flames Daytona Raced QVC/624
2005 #24 DuPont Flames Daytona Raced GM Dealers/638
2005 #24 DuPont Flames/12,744
2005 #24 DuPont Flames CW Bank/408
2005 #24 DuPont Flames GM Dealers/2700
2005 #24 DuPont Flames Matco/204
2005 #24 DuPont Flames QVC/1500
2005 #24 DuPont Flames Daytona Raced/8856
2006 #24 WSOP JG Foundation GM Dealers/804
2006 #24 WSOP JG Foundation CWB/240
2006 #24 WSOP JG Foundation/9828
2006 #24 Superman QVC*
2006 #24 Superman Matco*
2006 #24 Superman Mac Tools*
2006 #24 Superman GM Dealers Brushed Metal/504
2006 #24 Superman GM Dealers/1356
2006 #24 Superman/9823*
2006 #24 Pepsi QVC*
2006 #24 Pepsi Matco*
2006 #24 Pepsi Mac Tools*
2006 #24 Pepsi GM Dealers/900
2006 #24 Pepsi CW Bank/240
2006 #24 Pepsi/8868*
2006 #24 Nicorette QVC*
2006 #24 Nicorette CW Bank/360
2006 #24 Nicorette/7512*
2006 #24 Mighty Mouse Matco*
2006 #24 Mighty Mouse GM Dealers/708
2006 #24 Mighty Mouse CWB/360
2006 #24 Mighty Mouse/6072*
2006 #24 Holiday JG Foundation QVC*
2006 #24 Holiday JG Foundation GM Dealers/2478
2006 #24 Holiday JG Foundation/3252*
2006 #24 DuPont Hot Hues Foose Design QVC/1500
2006 #24 DuPont Hot Hues Foose Design Matco/84
2006 #24 DuPont Hot Hues Foose Design Mac Tools/504
2006 #24 DuPont Hot Hues Foose Design/18,240
2006 #24 DuPont Flames Test QVC*
2006 #24 DuPont Flames Test Matco*
2006 #24 DuPont Flames Test/4584*
2006 #24 DuPont Flames Sonoma Raced/678
2006 #24 DuPont Flames Performance Alliance QVC*
2006 #24 DuPont Flames Performance Alliance GM Dealers/696
2006 #24 DuPont Flames Performance Alliance CW Bank/240
2006 #24 DuPont Flames Performance Alliance/6528*
2006 #24 DuPont Flames Chicagoland Raced Platinum/125
2006 #24 DuPont Flames Chicagoland Raced Platinum/75
2006 #24 DuPont Flames Chicagoland Raced/2475
2006 #24 DuPont Flames QVC/504
2006 #24 DuPont Flames Matco/216
2006 #24 DuPont Flames Mac Tools/504
2006 #24 DuPont Flames GM Dealers/1008
2006 #24 DuPont Flames/10,008
Action Racing Collectables 1:32
2004 #24 DuPont Flames/1512
1998-01 #24 Pepsi/12,000 w/helmet
1998-01 #24 DuP.Superman/3504 '99
1998-01 #24 DuPont Chroma/3500 '98
Action Racing Collectables 1:64
1993 #NNO J.Gordon Kellogg's 2-car promo
1993 #NNO T.Labonte/J.Gordon Kellogg's Promo 2-car promo
1994 #24 DuPont
1995 #24 DuPont '95 Champ blister
1995 #24 DuPont
1995 #NNO Brickyard 2-car set/25,000
1996 #24 DuPont Race Day blister
1996 #24 DuPont
1997 #24 3-Car Promo blister
1997 #24 Jurassic Park 3 HO SI
1997 #24 Jurassic Park 3 black window blister
1997 #24 Jurassic Park 3
1997 #24 DuPont ChromaPremier/25,000
1997 #24 DuPont Million $ Date black window Mac Tools
1997 #24 DuPont Million $ Date black windows
1997 #24 DuPont Million $ Date
1997 #24 DuPont Bickyard/14,256
1997 #24 DuPont
1998 #24 DuPont No Bull
1998 #24 DuPont Chromalusion
1998 #24 DuPont Brick.Win/10,024
1998 #24 DuPont
1999 #1 Baby Ruth '92 T-bird
1999 #1 Carolina '91 T-bird
1999 #24 Pepsi Star Wars
1999 #24 Pepsi/10,000
1999 #24 DuPont Superman
1999 #24 DuPont NASCAR Racers
1999 #24 DuPont
2000 #24 Pepsi/22,752
2000 #24 DuPont Millennium
2000 #24 DuPont/34,272
2000 #67 Outback Steak.'90 GP
2001 #24 Pepsi in a can
2001 #24 DuPont Flames 2001 Champ.in tin/37,560
2001 #24 DuPont Flames
2001 #24 DuPont Bugs Bunny/50,496
2002 #1 Autolite '89 T-bird/13,464
2002 #24 Pepsi Talladega in a can/23,712
2002 #24 Pepsi Daytona in vending machine/35,952
2002 #24 Elmo/17,424
2002 #24 DuPont Bugs/24,312
2002 #24 DuP.200th Ann./52,056
2002 #24 DuPont 4-cars/2000
2002 #24 DuPont paint can/62,016
2003 #24 Pepsi Billion $/13,752
2003 #24 Pepsi
2003 #24 DuPont Yose.Sam/11,544
2003 #24 DuP.Wright Bros./17,856
2003 #24 DuPont Flames Victory Lap/13,212
2003 #24 DuPont Flames/24,696
2003 #24 Cookie Monster/14,976
2004 #24 Santa/5040
2004 #24 Pepsi Shards/8064
2004 #24 Pepsi Billion/7776
2004 #24 DuPont Wizard of Oz/9024
2004 #24 DuPont Rainbow/8400
2004 #24 DuPont Flames HMS 20th/5952
2004 #24 DuPont Flames Brickyard Raced/5040
2004 #24 DuPont Flames/22,848
2004 #24 Big Bird/7440
2005 #24 Santa Holiday
2005 #24 Pepsi Star Wars
2005 #24 Pepsi Daytona
2005 #24 Mighty Mouse
2005 #24 DuPont Flames Performance Alliance Reverse
2005 #24 DuPont Flames
2006 #24 WSOP JG Foundation
2006 #24 Superman
2006 #24 Pepsi
2006 #24 Nicorette
2006 #24 Mighty Mouse JG Foundation
2006 #24 Holiday JG Foundation
2006 #24 DuPont Hot Hues Foose Design
2006 #24 DuPont Flames Performance Alliance
2006 #24 DuPont Flames
2008 #24 DuPont Flames
Action Racing Collectables AC Racing 1:
1993 #24 DuPont
Action Racing Collectables Ceramic 1
2000-01 #24 DuPont
Action Racing Collectables Crystal 1
1998-00 #1 Baby Ruth 1992T-bird/4008 '99
1998-00 #24 Pepsi/8000 '99
1998-00 #24 DuPont Superman/6000 '99
1998-00 #24 DuPont '99
Action Racing Collectables Fan Fueler 1
1998 #24 DuPont
Action Racing Collectables Historical S
2004 #24 DuPont '96 Monte Carlo 400 Chevy Wins Color Chr./6192
2005 #24 DuPont '93 Lumina ROY/5004
Action Racing Collectables Pit Wagon
1990-03 #24 DuPont 1993 ROY '94
1990-03 #24 DuPont '96 MC/2500
1990-03 #24 Pepsi/2508 '99
1990-03 #24 Jurassic Park 3 '97
1990-03 #24 DuP.Superman/3504 '99
Action Racing Collectables Platinum 1:2
2008 #24 DuPont Flames/37,032
2008 #24 Pepsi
2008 #24 Nicorette/21,468
Action Racing Collectables Platinum 1:6
2008 #24 DuPont Flames/13,824
Action Racing Collectables Platinum Day
2008 #24 DuPont '97 Monte Carlo/2832
Action Racing Collectables Transporters
2001 #24 DuPont Flames/2520
2001 #24 DuPont Bugs/2508
2002 #24 Pepsi Daytona/3132
2002 #24 DuP.4-Time Champ/7404
Action Racing Collectables Valvoline Te
1993 #24 DuPont

Action Total Concept 1:64
2000 #24 DuPont Winston/41,400
2000 #24 DuPont Peanuts/21,456
Action/Funline Monster Truck 1:43
2004 #24 DuPont Flames
2005 #24 Pepsi Star Wars/1896
Action/Funline Muscle Machines 1:18
2004 #24 DuPont Flames '69 Camaro
2004 #24 DuPont Flames '69 Chevelle
2004 #24 DuPont Flames '67 Nova
2005 #24 DuPont Flames '66 Nova
2005 #24 DuPont Flames '69 Camaro
2005 #24 DuPont Flames '69 Chevelle
2005 #24 DuPont Flames '71 Camaro
2005 #24 Mighty Mouse '66 GTO
2005 #24 Mighty Mouse '67 Nova
2005 #24 Pepsi Star Wars '57 Chevy/612
2005 #24 Pepsi Star Wars '69 Camaro/568
2005 #24 Pepsi Star Wars '69 Chevelle/544
Action/Funline Muscle Machines 1:24
2005 #24 DuPont Flames Hybrid408
Action/Funline Muscle Machines 1:64
2004 #24 DuPont Flames '69 Chevelle
Action/RCCA 1:18
2002 #24 DuPont Bugs/504
2003 #NNO Mon.Carlo SS '03/600
Action/RCCA 1:24
1994 #1 Baby Ruth REV/7500
1995 #24 DuPont/5004
1996 #24 DuPont/12,500
1997 #24 Jurassic Park 3
1997 #24 DuPont Million $/15,000
1997 #24 DuPont ChromaPremier/15,000
1997 #24 DuPont Bank/3500
2002 #1 Autolite '89 T-bird Bank/1800
2002 #24 Pepsi Talladega Col.Chrome Bank/1800
2002 #24 Pepsi Talladega Split Clear/2508
2002 #24 Pepsi Daytona Bank/3012
2002 #24 Elmo Bank/2004
2002 #24 DuP.Flames Bank/2800
2002 #24 DuPont Bugs Bank/4008
2002 #24 DuPont 200th Anniv. Clear/7152
2002 #24 DuPont 200th Anniv. Split Clear/2508
2002 #24 DuPont 200th Anniv. Bank/4008
2003 #24 Pepsi Billion $/2224
2003 #24 Pepsi Bank/1524
2003 #24 DuPont Yose.Sam/1900
2003 #24 DuP.Wright Bros./2404
2003 #24 DuPont Victory Lap/1500
2003 #24 DuPont Flames Martinsville Raced/604
2003 #24 DuP.Flames CW Bank/2124
2003 #24 Cookie Monster/1800
2004 #24 Santa/600
2004 #24 400 Career Starts/624
2004 #24 Pepsi Shards Talladega Raced/300
2004 #24 Pepsi Shards/720
2004 #24 Pepsi Billion Daytona Raced/444
2004 #24 Pepsi Billion/1200
2004 #24 DuPont Rainbow/1200
2004 #24 DuPont Racing Stripes/660
2004 #24 DuPont Flames HMS 20th Ann/1500
2004 #24 DuPont Flames Wizard of Oz/1800
2004 #24 DuPont Flames Brickyard Raced/524
2004 #24 DuPont Flames/1800
2004 #24 Big Bird/1500
2004 #24 DuPont Flames Reverse/1200
2005 #24 Foundation Holiday/408
2005 #24 Pepsi/824
2005 #24 Pepsi Star Wars Talladega Raced/424
2005 #24 Pepsi Star Wars/1200
2005 #24 Milestones 4X Daytona/1800
2005 #24 Milestones 4X Champ./1800
2005 #24 Milestones 4X Brickyard/900
2005 #24 Milestones First Win/1008
2005 #24 Mighty Mouse/900
2005 #24 DuPont Test/804
2005 #24 DuPont Flames Martinsville Raced/424
2005 #24 DuPont Flames Daytona Raced/824
2005 #24 DuPont Flames Color Chrome/408
2005 #24 DuPont Flames/1008
2006 #24 DuPont Flames/600
2006 #24 DuPont Flames Chicagoland Raced/375
2006 #24 DuPont Flames Performance Alliance/600
2006 #24 DuPont Flames Test/600
2006 #24 Holiday JG Foundation/408
2006 #24 Mighty Mouse JG Foundation/500
2006 #24 Nicorette/680
2006 #24 Pepsi/700
2006 #24 WSOP JG Foundation/600
2006 #24 Superman/1500
2006 #24 DuPont Flames Color Chrome/288
2006 #24 DuPont Hot Hues Foose Designs/1400
Action/RCCA 1:32
2002 #24 Pepsi Daytona Gold/720
2002 #24 Pepsi Daytona/2280
2002 #24 DuPont Bugs Gold/600
2002 #24 DuPont Bugs/1416
2002 #24 DuPont Flames 2001 WC Champ/3600
2003 #24 Pepsi Billion $ 24K/316
2003 #24 Pepsi Billion $/844
2003 #24 Pepsi in Vending Machine/2004
2003 #24 DuP.Wright Bros.24K/316
2003 #24 DuPont Wright Bros./844
2003 #24 DuPont Flames 24K/444
2003 #24 DuPont Flames/1572
2004 #24 DuPont Flames/600
Action/RCCA 1:64
1993 #24 DuPont gray box
1993 #24 DuPont/15,000
1994 #24 DuPont
1995 #24 DuPont '94 Lum./16,128
1996 #24 DuPont/15,000
1997 #24 Jurassic Park 3 w/card set
1997 #24 Jurassic Park 3
1997 #24 DuPont ChromaPremier/20,000
1997 #24 DuPont Million Dollar Date/25,000
1997 #24 DuPont/5000
1998 #1 Baby Ruth '92 T-bird
1998 #24 DuPont No Bull
1998 #24 DuPont Chroma/15,000
1998 #24 DuPont
1999 #1 Carolina '91 T-bird
1999 #24 Pepsi Star Wars/15,000
1999 #24 Pepsi/10,000
1999 #24 DuPont Superman
1999 #24 DuPont NASCAR Racers/10,000
1999 #24 DuPont/15,000
2000 #24 DuPont Winston/1500
2000 #24 DuPont Peanuts in lunch box/3800
2000 #24 DuPont Millennium/8496
2000 #24 DuPont/10,008
2000 #67 Outback Steak. '90 GP
2001 #24 Pepsi/1584
2001 #24 DuPont Bugs Bunny in lunch box/5004
2001 #24 DuPont/3312
2002 #24 Pepsi Talladega Color Chrome/1584
2002 #24 Pepsi Daytona/3600
2002 #24 Elmo/4032
2002 #24 DuPont Flames/2856
2002 #24 DuPont Bugs/4032
2002 #24 DuPont 200th Ann./3312
2003 #24 Pepsi Billion $/3040
2003 #24 Pepsi/2460
2003 #24 DuPont Yose.Sam/2448
2003 #24 DuP.Wright Bros./3328
2003 #24 DuPont Victory Lap/1008
2003 #24 DuPont Flames/2172
2003 #24 Cookie Monster/2596
2004 #24 Big Bird/1488
2004 #24 DuPont Flames/1872
2004 #24 DuPont Flames Wizard of Oz/2448
2004 #24 DuPont Rainbow/1296
2004 #24 Santa/576
2004 #24 Pepsi Shards/1296
2004 #24 Pepsi Billion/1008
2004 #24 DuPont Flames HMS 20th Ann/1440
2005 #24 DuPont Flames Reverse/1584
2005 #24 Pepsi/1008
2005 #24 Pepsi Star Wars/1584
2005 #24 Mighty Mouse/1296
2005 #24 Foundation Holiday/432
2005 #24 DuPont Flames/1008
2006 #24 WSOP JG Foundation/720
2006 #24 Superman/1296
2006 #24 Pepsi/864
2006 #24 Nicorette/720
2006 #24 Mighty Mouse JG Foundation/576
2006 #24 Holiday JG Foundation/432
2006 #24 DuPont Flames Performance Alliance/600
2006 #24 DuPont Hot Hues Foose/1008
2006 #24 DuPont Flames/720
Action/RCCA Banks 1:24
1998 #1 Baby Ruth '92 T-bird
1998 #24 DuPont Chromal./10,000
1998 #24 DuPont No Bull
1998 #24 DuPont/12,500
1999 #1 Carolina '91 T-bird
1999 #24 Pepsi Star Wars/10,000
1999 #24 Pepsi/5000
1999 #24 DuPont Superman
1999 #24 DuPont NASCAR Racers/8500
1999 #24 DuPont/8500
2000 #24 DuPont Peanuts
2000 #24 DuPont Millenn/10,992
2000 #24 DuPont/7500
2001 #24 Pepsi
2001 #24 DuPont Bugs Bunny/5004
2001 #24 DuPont Flames/3456
Action/RCCA Dually Trucks 1:24
1994 #24 DuPont Coke Bank
1995 #24 DuPont PLS Bank/2508
1995 #24 DuPont RCCA/2008
1996 #24 DuP.RCCA Bank/5000
1998-00 #24 DuPont Millennium Silver Bank/3000 '00
1998-00 #24 DuPont PLS Bank/3000 '98
Action/RCCA Dually Trucks 1:64
1994-97 #24 DuPont/5000 '96
1994-97 #24 DuPont RCCA/2000 '95
1994-97 #24 DuPont PLS/15,000 '95
Action/RCCA Dually Trucks with Trailer
1994 #24 DuPont
1995 #24 DuPont RCCA/2508
1996 #24 DuPont/2500
1998 #24 DuPont Chroma./4500
1998 #24 DuPont PLS/3500
2001 #24 DuPont Bugs/3000
Action/RCCA Elite 1:24
1997 #24 DuPont ChromaPremier Proto
1997 #24 Jurassic Park 3 Proto/12
1997 #24 Jurassic Park 3/7500
1997 #24 DuPont ChromaPremier/5000
1997 #24 DuPont Million Dollar Date/10,000
1997 #24 DuPont/3500
1998 #24 DuP.Chromalusion/7500
1998 #24 DuPont No Bull/1500
1998 #24 DuPont/3500
1999 #1 Carolina '91 T-bird/1500
1999 #1 Baby Ruth '92 T-bird/2500
1999 #24 Pepsi Star Wars/7500
1999 #24 Pepsi/3500
1999 #24 DuP.Superman/10,000
1999 #24 DuPont NASCAR Racers/5500
1999 #24 DuPont/5000
2000 #24 Pepsi/3504
2000 #24 DuPont Winston/1008
2000 #24 DuPont Peanuts/3456
2000 #24 DuPont Millennium/7500
2000 #24 DuPont Test/3000
2000 #24 DuPont/5000
2000 #67 Outback 1990 GP/3000
2001 #24 Pepsi Col.Chrome/3000
2001 #24 Pepsi/1800
2001 #24 Gordon Foundation/3996
2001 #24 DuPont Bugs/7500
2001 #24 DuPont Test/2508
2001 #24 DuPont Flames Platinum HMS 100th Win/1800
2001 #24 DuP.Flames No Bull Las Vegas Raced/3504
2001 #24 DuPont Flames Split Clear/5004
2001 #24 DuPont Flam.Metal/3504
2001 #24 DuPont Flames/3600
2002 #24 Pepsi Talladega/2504
2002 #24 Pepsi Daytona/4500
2002 #24 Elmo/3600
2002 #24 DuPont Bugs/6000
2002 #24 DuPont Test black/4500
2002 #24 DuPont Flames/3204
2002 #24 DuPont 200th Ann./5004
2003 #24 Pepsi Billion $/3724
2003 #24 Pepsi/2724
2003 #24 DuPont Yose.Sam/3000
2003 #24 DuPont Wright Bros./4024
2003 #24 DuPont Victory Lap/2004
2003 #24 DuPont Flames Martinsville Raced/1000
2003 #24 DuPont Flames Color Chrome/804
2003 #24 DuPont Flames/3624
2003 #24 Cookie Monster/3000
2004 #24 400 Career Starts/624
2004 #24 Santa/900
2004 #24 Pepsi Shards Talladega Raced/480
2004 #24 Pepsi Shards/1008
2004 #24 Pepsi Billion Daytona Raced/444
2004 #24 Pepsi Billion/1500
2004 #24 DuPont Rainbow/1800
2004 #24 DuPont Racing Stripes/600
2004 #24 DuPont HMS 20 Years Test/1824
2004 #24 DuPont Flames Wizard of Oz White Gold/25
2004 #24 DuPont Flames Wizard of Oz Platinum/360
2004 #24 DuPont Flames Wizard of Oz/2700
2004 #24 DuPont Flames HMS 20th Ann. Platinum/300
2004 #24 DuPont Flames HMS 20th Ann/1800
2004 #24 DuPont Flames Brickyard Raced/524
2004 #24 DuPont Flames Color Chrome/804
2004 #24 DuPont Flames/2400
2004 #24 Big Bird/2004
2005 #24 Foundation Holiday White Gold/25
2005 #24 Pepsi Star Wars Talladega Raced/624
2005 #24 Pepsi Star Wars White Gold/44
2005 #24 Pepsi Star Wars/2004
2005 #24 Pepsi Daytona White Gold/34
2005 #24 Pepsi Daytona Plat./144
2005 #24 Pepsi Daytona/1224
2005 #24 Milestones 4X Daytona/1800
2005 #24 Milestones 4X Champ/1200
2005 #24 Milestones 4X Brickyard/900
2005 #24 Milestones First Win/1008
2005 #24 Mighty Mouse White Gold/30
2005 #24 Mighty Mouse Plat/144
2005 #24 Mighty Mouse/1500
2005 #24 Foundation Holiday/600
2005 #24 DuPont Test/1200
2005 #24 DuPont Flames Reverse Performance Alliance White Gold/30
2005 #24 DuPont Flames Reverse Performance Alliance/1500
2005 #24 DuPont Flames Martinsville Raced/524
2005 #24 DuPont Flames Daytona Raced White Gold/40
2005 #24 DuPont Flames Daytona Raced/1524
2005 #24 DuPont Flames White Gold/50
2005 #24 DuPont Flames Platinum/144
2005 #24 DuPont Flames Color Chrome/600
2005 #24 DuPont Flames/1500
2006 #24 DuPont Flames Chicagoland Raced/375
2006 #24 DuPont Flames Chicagoland Raced Platinum/7
2006 #24 WSOP JG Foundation White Gold/33
2006 #24 WSOP JG Foundation Platinum/18
2006 #24 WSOP JG Foundation/600
2006 #24 Superman White Gold/40
2006 #24 Superman Platinum/36
2006 #24 Superman/1800
2006 #24 Pepsi White Gold/40
2006 #24 Pepsi Platinum/18
2006 #24 Pepsi/900
2006 #24 Nicorette White Gold/30
2006 #24 Nicorette Platinum/19
2006 #24 Nicorette/999
2006 #24 Mighty Mouse JG Foundation White Gold/30
2006 #24 Mighty Mouse JG Foundation Platinum/18
2006 #24 Mighty Mouse JG Foundation/900
2006 #24 Holiday JG Foundation White Gold/25
2006 #24 Holiday JG Foundation Platinum/10
2006 #24 Holiday JG Foundation Color Chrome/494
2006 #24 DuPont Hot Hues Foose Designs White Gold/40
2006 #24 DuPont Hot Hues Foose Designs Platinum/38
2006 #24 DuPont Hot Hues Foose Designs AU/200
2006 #24 DuPont Hot Hues Chip Foose/1900
2006 #24 DuPont Flames Test Platinum/14
2006 #24 DuPont Flames Test/724
2006 #24 DuPont Flames Performance Alliance Platinum/12
2006 #24 DuPont Flames Performance Alliance/416
2006 #24 DuPont Flames White Gold/30
2006 #24 DuPont Flames Plat./20
2006 #24 DuPont Flames Color Chrome/288
2006 #24 DuPont Flames/1008
Action/RCCA Elite 1:32
2003 #24 Pepsi Billion $/844
2003 #24 DuPont Wright Bros./804
2003 #24 DuPont Flames/1008
2004 #24 DuPont Flames/600
Action/RCCA Elite 1:64
2001 #24 Pepsi/1104
2001 #24 DuPont Bugs Bunny/3960
2001 #24 DuPont Flames/2688
2002 #24 Pepsi Talladega/1200
2002 #24 Pepsi Daytona/3000
2002 #24 Elmo/2016
2002 #24 DuPont Bugs/4008
2002 #24 DuPont Flames/2160
2002 #24 DuPont 200th Ann./3000
2003 #24 Pepsi Billion $/2128
2003 #24 Pepsi/1824
2003 #24 DuPont Yose.Sam/1924
2003 #24 DuP.Wright Bros./2128
2003 #24 DuPont Flames/2124
2003 #24 Cookie Monster/1588
2003 #24 DuPont Flames HMS 20th Ann/1008
2004 #24 Santa/480
2004 #24 Pepsi Shards/1008
2004 #24 Pepsi Billion/1008
2004 #24 DuPont Rainbow/1008
2004 #24 DuPont Flames Wizard of Oz/1200
2004 #24 DuPont Flames/1440
2004 #24 Big Bird/1200
2005 #24 DuPont Flames Reverse/960
2005 #24 Pepsi/720
2005 #24 Pepsi Star Wars/1200
2005 #24 Mighty Mouse/816
2005 #24 Foundation Holiday/288
2005 #24 DuPont Flames/864
2006 #24 Mighty Mouse JG Foundation/336
2006 #24 WSOP JG Foundation/480
2006 #24 Superman/720
2006 #24 Pepsi/528
2006 #24 Nicorette/480
2006 #24 Holiday JG Foundation/288
2006 #24 DuPont Hot Hues Foose Designs/720
2006 #24 DuPont Flames Performance Alliance/240
2006 #24 DuPont Flames/432
Action/RCCA Elite Prototypes 1:24
1998 #24 DuPont No Bull/12
1999 #24 DuPont Proto
2002 #24 Pepsi Daytona/12
Action/RCCA Gold 1:32
1998 #24 DuPont/3500
Action/RCCA Historical Series 1:24
2004 #24 DuPont 300th Chevy Win '96 Monte Carlo Chrome/900
Action/RCCA Historical Series 1:64
2004 #NNO Chevy Wins 4-car tin set
Action/RCCA Historical Series Elite 1:2
2005 #24 DuPont '93 Lumina/1224
Action/RCCA Revell 1:64
1991-92 #1 Baby Ruth Revell
Action/RCCA SelectNet 1:64
1999 #24 Pepsi Daytona
Action/RCCA SelectNet Banks 1:24
1999 #1 Carolina Ford '91
1999 #24 Pepsi/804
Action/RCCA SelectNet Elite 1:24
1999 #24 Pepsi/600
Action/RCCA Sprint 1:24
1995 #20 Hap's RCCA/7500
1996 #40 1987 Stanton RCCA/4008
1999 #4 1990 Diet Pepsi/7500
Action/RCCA Sprint 1:64
1996 #40 1987 Stanton/10,080
Action/RCCA Total View 1:64
2000 #24 Pepsi
2000 #24 DuPont Peanuts/3024
2000 #24 DuPont Millennium
Action/RCCA Transporters 1:64
1993 #24 DuP.GMP in case/2800
1994 #24 DuPont RCCA/5016
1995 #24 DuPont/4008
2001 #24 DuPont Flames Color Chrome RCCA/204
2001 #24 DuPont Bugs Color Chrome RCCA
2002 #24 DuP.4-Time Champ/996
2002 #24 Pepsi Daytona
2002 #24 DuPont 200th Ann./1500
Action/RCCA Transporters 1:96
1994-96 #24 DuPont PLS/4008 '95
Brookfield 1:24
2004 #24 DuPont Racing Stripes/408
2005 #24 Pepsi Star Wars/600
2005 #24 Mighty Mouse/408
2005 #24 DuPont Flames/600
2006 #24 DuPont Flames/240
2006 #24 Holiday JG Foundation/200
2006 #24 Mighty Mouse JG Foundation/204
2006 #24 Pepsi/204
2006 #24 WSOP JG Foundation/200
2006 #24 Superman/300
2006 #24 Nicorette/222
2006 #24 DuPont Hot Hues Foose Designs/300
Brookfield Dually and Show Trailer 1:24
2005 #24 DuPont Flames QVC/400
2005 #24 DuPont Flames GM Dealers/36
2005 #24 DuPont Flames/1668
Brookfield Dually and Show Trailer 1:25
2003 #24 Pepsi Billion $ Silver/333
2003 #24 Pepsi Billion $/2368
Brookfield Dually and Tailgate Set 1:24
2005 #24 DuPont Flames QVC/504
2005 #24 DuPont Flames/1440
Brookfield Dually with Car and Show
1993-95 #24 DuPont without car/10,000 '95
Brookfield Dually with Car and Show Tra
1997 #24 DuP.Lost World Silver without car/400 '97
1997 #24 DuPont Lost World without car/7500 '97
1998 #24 DuPont Chroma./5000
1998 #24 DuP.2-Time Champ/5000
1999 #24 Superman/3168
2000 #24 DuPont Peanuts/2140
2001 #24 DuPont Flames/1788
2002 #24 Pepsi Silver without car/536
2002 #24 Pepsi Daytona without car/2172
2002 #24 DuPont Flames Silver without car/784
2002 #24 DuPont Flames without car/3492
Brookfield Sets 1:24
1994-03 #24 DuPont Peanuts QVC 2-car set/20,000 '00
1994-03 #24 DuPont Charlotte QVC 2-car set/2000 '00
1994-03 #24 DuPont Brickyard 2-car set with Pace Car '94
1994-03 #NNO Brickyard 2-car set/5000 '95
Brookfield Suburbans, Blazers, and T
1992-93 #24 DuP.ROY Bank/25,000
Brookfield Suburbans, Blazers, and Taho
1995 #24 DuPont White Bank/15,000
1995 #24 DuPont Silver Bank/10,000
1995 #24 DuPont Blue Bank/10,000
1996 #24 DuPont Tahoe Bank/5000
1996 #24 DuPont Blazer Silver/150
1996 #24 DuPont Blazer
1997 #24 DuPont Gold 3-time Champ/5000
1998 #24 DuPont Chromalusion Silver Tahoe/250
1998 #24 DuPont Chromalusion Tahoe/5000
1999 #24 Pepsi Blazer/5004
1999 #24 DuPont Superman/2508
2003 #24 Pepsi Delivery Van/600 '03
Brookfield Trackside 1:25
1995 #24 DuPont/10,000
1998 #24 DuPont Chroma/10,000
1999 #24 Superman/2508
1999 #24 Pepsi Suburban/2406
1999 #24 Pepsi/3504
1999 #24 DuPont 24K Gold/3504
1999 #24 DuPont/2508
2001 #24 DuP.Flames '01 Champ w/Suburban/2508
2001 #24 DuP.Flames Silv./960
2001 #24 DuPont Flames/1788
2002 #24 DuPont Flames Color Chrome/960
2002 #24 DuPont Flames/2172
Brookfield Trackside 1:64
2004 #24 DuPont Flames/3504
2005 #24 Pepsi Star Wars/3000
Ertl 1:18
1994 #24 DuP.White Rose Bank w/o serial numbering
1994 #24 DuP.White Rose Bank serial #'d on bottom/5000
1994 #24 DuPont raced/5000
1995 #1 Baby Ruth '92 T-bird Buck Fever/5000
1995 #24 DuPont GMP/3500
1995 #24 DuPont Buck Fever/5000
Ertl White Rose Transporters Past an
1992-94 #24 DuPont '93
Ertl White Rose Transporters Promos
1992-94 #1 Baby Ruth
Funstuf Pit Row 1:43
1992 #1 Baby Ruth
Funstuf Pit Row 1:64
1992 #1 Baby Ruth
GMP Sprint Cars 1:18
1996-01 #6 Molds Unlimit/3672 '97
Hot Wheels Racing Color Change 1:64
2003 #24 Pepsi
2003 #24 DuPont Flames
2004 #24 DuPont Flames
Hot Wheels Racing Power Launchers 1:64
2003 #24 DuPont Flames
Hot Wheels Racing Stockerz 1:24
2004 #24 DuPont Flames
Hot Wheels Racing Stockerz 1:64
2004 #24 DuPont Flames
Hot Wheels Transporters 1:64
2002 #NNO Hendrick 100-Victories Tribute
Matchbox White Rose Super Stars 1:64
1993 #24 DuPont BL
1994 #24 DuPont BX
1995 #24 DuPont
1996 #24 DuPont Gold SS Awards
1996 #24 DuPont
1990-92 #1 Baby Ruth Org/BX 92
1990-92 #1 Baby Ruth Red/BX 92
Matchbox White Rose Team Convoys 1:8
1990-93 #24 DuPont ROY '93
Matchbox White Rose Transporters Super
1992 #1 Baby Ruth
1993 #24 DuPont
1994 #24 DuPont
1995 #24 DuPont
1996 #24 DuPont
Miscellaneous Promos 1:64
1991-04 #1 Baby Ruth First BGN Win blister/20,000 '93
Motorsports Authentics Driver's Select
2007 #24 Underdog JG Found./5180*
2007 #24 Pepsi COT Talladega Raced/3192*
2007 #24 Pepsi COT/5788*
2007 #24 Pepsi/5704*
2007 #24 Nicorette COT/4662*
2007 #24 Nicorette/5704*
2007 #24 Hoiliday Sam Bass Jeff Gordon Foundation/3288*
2007 #24 DuPont Flames '57 Chevy/6180*
2007 #24 DuPont Flames COT Pioneer Employee/711
2007 #24 DuPont Flames COT Phoenix Raced/7676*
2007 #24 DuPont Flames COT Darlington Raced/2892*
2007 #24 DuPont Flames Talladega Raced/7777*
2007 #24 DuPont Flames Pocono Raced/1576*
2007 #24 DuPont Flames Twin 150s Daytona Raced/2256*
2007 #24 DuPont Flames/13,500*
2007 #24 DuPont Dept. of Defense American Heroes/7008
2007 #24 DuPont Flames Cromax Pro Employee/711
2007 #24 DuPont Flames COT/19,228*
2007 #24 Nicorette COT
2007 #24 Pepsi
2007 #24 DuPont Flames '57 Chevy
2007 #24 DuPont Flames COT
2007 #24 DuPont Flames
2007 #24 DuPont Dept. of Defense American Heroes
2007 #24 Pepsi/876
2007 #24 Nicorette COT/876
2007 #24 Nicorette/876
2007 #24 DuPont Flames COT Phoenix Raced/7676
2007 #24 DuPont Flames COT/1200
2007 #24 DuPont Flames Talladega Raced
2007 #24 DuPont Flames/2400
Motorsports Authentics Owner's Elite 1:
2007 #24 Underdog JG Found./708*
2007 #24 Pepsi COT Talladega Raced/504*
2007 #24 Pepsi/1504*
2007 #24 Nicorette COT Platinum/25
2007 #24 Nicorette COT/1142*
2007 #24 Nicorette White Gold/50*
2007 #24 Nicorette Platinum/25
2007 #24 Nicorette/2007
2007 #24 Milestones 77th Win/1200
2007 #24 DuPont Flames '57 Chevy/504
2007 #24 DuPont Flames Test/2007
2007 #24 DuPont Flames COT Phoenix Raced White Gold/50*
2007 #24 DuPont Flames COT Phoenix Raced Platinum/25
2007 #24 DuPont Flames COT Phoenix Raced/1492*
2007 #24 DuPont Flames COT Platinum/25
2007 #24 DuPont Flames COT Platinum/25
2007 #24 DuPont Flames COT/2007
2007 #24 DuPont Flames White Gold/50*
2007 #24 DuPont Flames Platinum/25
2007 #24 DuPont Flames/2007
2007 #24 DuPont Holiday Sam Bass White Gold/50*
2007 #24 DuPont Holiday Sam Bass Platinum/25
2007 #24 DuPont Holiday Sam Bass/504*
2007 #24 DuPont Dept.of Defense Am.Heroes/1200*
2007 #24 Pepsi/2007*
2007 #24 Nicorette/1008*
2007 #24 DuPont Flames/2007*
2007 #24 DuPont Dept.of Defense American Heroes/504*
Motorsports Authentics Owner's Elite Tr
2007 #24 Pepsi/1008*
2007 #24 Nicorette/504*
2007 #24 DuPont Flames/1008*
2007 #24 DuPont Dept. of Defense American Heroes/100*
Motorsports Authentics Pit Stop 1:64
2007 #24 Underdog JG Foundation
2007 #24 Pepsi
2007 #24 Nicorette COT
2007 #24 Nicorette
2007 #24 DuPont Flames COT
2007 #24 DuPont Flames
2007 #24 DuPont Dept.of Defense American Heroes
Motorsports Authentics Pit Stop Blister
2007 #24 DuPont Flames
Motorsports Authentics QVC For Race Fan
2007 #24 Pepsi Mesma Chrome/504
2007 #24 Pepsi Color Chrome/1008
2007 #24 Nicorette COT Mesma Chrome/504
2007 #24 Nicorette COT Copper/504
2007 #24 Nicorette COT Color Chrome/1500
2007 #24 Nicorette Mesma Chrome/504
2007 #24 Nicorette Color Chrome/1008
2007 #24 DuPont Flames '57 Chevy Platinum/144
2007 #24 DuPont Flames '57 Chevy Mesma Chrome/324
2007 #24 DuPont Flames '57 Chevy Gold Chrome/1008
2007 #24 DuPont Flames '57 Chevy Gold/108
2007 #24 DuPont Flames '57 Chevy Copper/504
2007 #24 DuPont Flames '57 Chevy Color Chrome/1500
2007 #24 DuPont Flames Holiday Sam Bass Color Chrome/1500
2007 #24 DuPont Flames COT Phoenix Raced Copper/504
2007 #24 DuPont Flames COT Phoenix Raced Color Chrome/1500
2007 #24 DuPont Flames '57 Chevy Chrome/288
2007 #24 DuPont Flames COT Platinum/108
2007 #24 DuPont Flames COT Mesma Chrome/324
2007 #24 DuPont Flames COT Gold/144
2007 #24 DuPont Flames COT Copper/504
2007 #24 DuPont Flames COT Color Chrome/1008
2007 #24 DuPont Flames COT Chrome/288
2007 #24 DuPont Flames Talladega Raced Mesma Chrome/324
2007 #24 DuPont Flames Talladega Raced Copper/504
2007 #24 DuPont Flames Talladega Raced Color Chrome/1500
2007 #24 DuPont Dept.of Defense Platinum/108
2007 #24 DuPont Dept.of Defense Mesma Chrome/504
2007 #24 DuPont Dept.of Defense Gold/108
2007 #24 DuPont Dept.of Defense Copper/504
2007 #24 DuPont Dept.of Defense Color Chrome/1008
2007 #24 DuPont Dept.of Defense Chrome/504
Motorsports Authentics/RCCA Owner's Clu
2007 #24 Pepsi/1500*
2007 #24 Nicorette/1500*
2007 #24 DuPont Flames '57 Chevy/288
2007 #24 DuPont Flames/1500*
Motorsports Authentics/RCCA Transporter
2007 #24 DuPont Flames/708*
Peachstate/GMP Transporters 1:64
1996-01 #1 Baby Ruth/2800
1996-01 #1 Baby Ruth RCCA/5000
Pole Position 1:64
1991-92 #1 Baby Ruth
Racing Champions 1:144
1996 #24 DuPont
1997 #24 DuPont
Racing Champions 1:24
1993 #24 DuPont
1994 #24 DuPont BYS/10,024
1994 #24 DuPont Coke Win in plastic case/2000
1994 #24 DuP.Snickers on deck lid
1994 #24 DuP.w/plain red deck lid
1995 #24 DuPont Sig.Series HO
1995 #24 DuPont Sig.Series
1995 #24 DuPont
1996 #24 DuPont Pocono Win in plastic case/2424
1996 #24 DuPont The Kid in plastic case/2424
1996 #24 DuPont Darlington in plastic case/2424
1996 #24 DuPont Bristol Win in plastic case/2424

1996 #24 DuPont '95 Champ
1996 #24 DuPont
1997 #24 DuPont Chrome HO
1997 #24 DuPont
1991-92 #1 Baby Ruth '92

Racing Champions 1:43
1992 #1 Baby Ruth
1993 #24 DuPont
1994 #24 DuPont Coca-Cola Win in plastic case
1994 #24 DuPont

Racing Champions 1:64
1992 #1 Baby Ruth Promo black windows
1992 #1 Baby Ruth
1993 #24 DuPont
1993 #NNO Carolina Ford 2-car promo set
1994 #24 DuPont Brickyard
1994 #24 DuPont Coca-Cola 600 Win in plastic case
1994 #24 DuPont
1994 #94 McDonald's All-Star Promo
1994 #NNO Fros.Mini-Wheat Promo 3-cars: Baby Ruth, DuPont, Sprint
1995 #24 DuPont Fan Club/2000 in PVC box
1995 #24 DuPont Coca-Cola
1995 #24 DuPont
1996 #24 DuPont Union 76 Promo
1996 #24 DuPont Fan Club in PVC box/1500
1996 #24 DuPont Chrome/1996
1996 #24 DuPont
1996 #NNO 12-Car set in case
1997 #24 DuPont

Racing Champions 5-Pack 1:144
1997 #NNO 24.JG/32.DJ/40.SM/94.BE/97.CL

Racing Champions 5-Pack Preview 1:144
1997 #NNO 5/24/30/94/99
1997 #NNO 5/6/21/24/28
1997 #NNO 4/5/9/24/29

Racing Champions Banks 1:24
1995 #24 DuPont Sig.Series HO 1995 Champion
1995 #24 DuPont Sig.Series HO
1995 #24 DuPont/10,000
1992-94 #24 DuPont Snickers on deck lid '94
1992-94 #24 DuPont Coke Win '94
1992-94 #24 DuPont BY Win/5024 '94
1992-94 #24 DuPont/10,000 '93

Racing Champions Hobby 1:64
1996 #24 DuPont

Racing Champions Hobby Yellow Box 1:64
1994 #24 DuPont

Racing Champions Matched Serial Numbers
1995 #24 DuPont

Racing Champions Pit Stop 1:24
1993 #24 DuPont
1995 #24 DuPont Sig.Series

Racing Champions Pit Stop 1:43
1993 #24 DuPont

Racing Champions Premier 1:18
1995 #24 DuPont
1996 #24 DuPont '95 WC Champ
1996 #24 DuPont Sig.Series
1996 #24 DuPont

Racing Champions Premier 1:43
1993 #24 DuPont/10,000
1994 #24 DuPont Snickers
1995 #24 Brickyard Win in plastic case

Racing Champions Premier 1:64
1993 #24 DuPont/40,000
1994 #24 DuPont '93 ROY/20,000
1994 #24 DuPont/20,000
1995 #24 DuPont Sig.Series Combo with SuperTruck
1995 #24 DuPont Sig.Series
1995 #24 DuPont/20,000

Racing Champions Premier Banks 1:24
1996 #24 DuPont Chrome/166
1996 #24 DuPont/1830

Racing Champions Premier Brickyard 400
1994 #24 DuPont

Racing Champions Premier Hood Open 1:24
1996 #24 DuPont '95 Champ

Racing Champions Premier Preview with M
1997 #24 DuPont

Racing Champions Premier Transporters 1
1993 #24 DuPont/7500
1993 #24 DuPont/15,000
1994 #24 DuPont Winston Select
1996 #24 DuPont

Racing Champions Premier with Medallion
1996 #24 DuPont '95 Champ
1996 #24 DuPont HO
1996 #24 DuPont

Racing Champions Preview 1:144
1997 #24 DuPont

Racing Champions Preview 1:24
1996 #24 DuPont
1997 #24 DuPont

Racing Champions Preview 1:64
1995 #24 DuPont
1996 #24 DuPont
1997 #24 DuPont

Racing Champions Preview Transporters 1
1995 #24 DuPont
1997 #24 DuPont
1997 #24 DuPont

Racing Champions PVC Box 1:64
1993 #24 DuPont Twin 125 Win/5000
1993 #24 DuPont Daytona/5000
1993 #24 DuPont Fan Club
1993 #24 DuPont/5000
1994 #24 DuPont ROY/5000
1994 #24 DuPont Fan Club/3000

Racing Champions Sprint Cars 1:24
1995 #16 JG Motorsports/5000

Racing Champions Sprint Cars 1:64
1995 #16 JG Motorsp.Promo/10,000
1995 #16 JG Motorsports

Racing Champions SuperTrucks 1:24
1995 #24 DuPont Sig.Ser.
1995 #24 DuPont

Racing Champions SuperTrucks 1:64
1995 #24 NDA/DuPont w/Gordon card

Racing Champions SuperTrucks To the Max
1995 #24 DuPont

Racing Champions To the Maxx 1:64
1994 #24 DuPont
1995 #24 DuPont

Racing Champions Transporters 1:144
1995 #24 DuPont
1996 #24 DuPont
1997 #24 DuPont

Racing Champions Transporters 1:43
1992 #1 Baby Ruth
1993 #24 DuPont

Racing Champions Transporters 1:64
1992 #1 Baby Ruth
1993 #1 Baby Ruth
1993 #24 DuPont Bank/10,000
1993 #24 DuPont
1995 #24 DuPont Sig.Series#(1995 WC Champion
1995 #24 DuPont
1996 #24 DuPont w/car(s)
1997 #24 DuPont

Racing Champions Transporters 1:87
1995 #24 DuPont
1996 #24 DuPont Premier
1997 #24 DuPont

Racing Champions Transporters Hobby 1:8
1994 #24 DuPont

Racing Champions Transporters Retail
1993-94 #24 DuPont '93

Racing Champions Transporters Retail 1:
1994 #24 DuPont Bank
1994 #24 DuPont

RCCA Club 1:24
2008 #24 DuPont Flames/700
2008 #24 Speed Racer/500
2008 #24 DuPont Flames Salute the Troops/500
2008 #24 Nicorette/500
2008 #24 Pepsi/500
2008 #24 Pepsi Stuff/500

RCCA Elite 1:24
2008 #24 DuPont Flames Salute the Troops/1000
2008 #24 DuPont Flames/1200
2008 #24 DuPont Flames Platinum/25
2008 #24 DuPont Flames White Gold/50
2008 #24 Speed Racer/1000
2008 #24 Speed Racer Platinum/25
2008 #24 Speed Racer White Gold/50
2008 #24 Nicorette/700
2008 #24 Nicorette Platinum/25
2008 #24 Nicorette White Gold/50
2008 #24 Pepsi Stuff/1000
2008 #24 Pepsi Stuff Platinum/25
2008 #24 Pepsi Stuff White Gold/50
2008 #24 Pepsi/700
2008 #24 Pepsi Platinum/25
2008 #24 Pepsi White Gold/50
2008 #24 DuPont Test/504

Revell 1:24
1991-95 #1 Baby Ruth RCI

Revell Club 1:18
1998 #24 DuPont Chromalusion
1998 #24 DuPont/1008
1999 #24 Pepsi/1008
1999 #24 DuPont Superman
1999 #24 DuPont/1008
2000 #24 DuPont Millennium/2508

Revell Club 1:24
1998 #24 DuPont Chromalusion/2424
1998 #24 DuPont/1596
1999 #24 Pepsi Star Wars
1999 #24 Pepsi/2004
1999 #24 DuPont Superman/3500
1999 #24 DuPont Daytona
1999 #24 DuPont/2424
2000 #24 DuPont/1002
2000 #24 Pepsi/2508
2000 #24 DuPont Peanuts
2000 #24 DuPont Millennium
2001 #24 Pepsi/1200

Revell Collection 1:18
1997 #24 Jurassic Park 3/5004
1998 #24 DuPont Chromalusion/5004
1998 #24 DuPont Brickyard Win
1998 #24 DuPont/5004
1999 #24 Pepsi Star Wars
1999 #24 Pepsi
1999 #24 DuPont Superman/7500
1999 #24 DuPont NASCAR Racers/2508
1999 #24 DuPont/2508
2000 #24 DuPont Peanuts

Revell Collection 1:24
1996 #24 DuPont/8292
1998 #24 DuPont Chroma/14,400
1998 #24 DuP.Brickyard Win/10,008
1998 #24 DuPont/6000
1999 #24 Pepsi Star Wars/5004
1999 #24 Pepsi set with 1:64 car/3504
1999 #24 Pepsi/10,008
1999 #24 DuPont Superman/16,872
1999 #24 DuPont Daytona/4008
1999 #24 DuPont/7512
2000 #24 Pepsi Bank w/1:64 car
2000 #24 Pepsi
2000 #24 DuPont Winston Bank set with 1:64 car/2508
2000 #24 DuPont Winston/3120
2000 #24 DuPont Test/1500
2000 #24 DuPont Peanuts
2000 #24 DuPont Millennium Bank set with 1:64 car
2000 #24 DuPont Millennium
2000 #24 DuPont/10,080
2001 #24 Pepsi/15,016
2001 #24 DuPont Test black/2508
2001 #24 DuPont No Bull Las Vegas Raced/25,020
2001 #24 DuPont Bugs w/figure
2002 #24 DuPont Test/8058
2002 #24 DuPont Color Chrome 2001 Champion/42,024
2003 #24 DuPont Flames Martinsville Raced/3168
2004 #24 DuPont Test/1848
2005 #24 DuPont Test/1284

Revell Collection 1:43
1998 #24 DuPont Chromalusion
1998 #24 DuP.Brickyard Win/5024
1998 #24 DuPont/5004
1999 #24 Pepsi Star Wars/5508
1999 #24 Pepsi
1999 #24 DuPont Superman
1999 #24 DuPont/4008
2000 #24 DuPont Millennium

Revell Collection 1:64
1998 #24 DuPont Chroma/24,984
1998 #24 DuPont Brickyard Win
1998 #24 DuPont/10,080
1999 #24 Pepsi Star Wars
1999 #24 Pepsi
1999 #24 DuPont Daytona 500
1999 #24 DuP.Superman/23,472
1999 #24 DuPont
2000 #24 Pepsi
2000 #24 DuPont Winston
2000 #24 DuPont Peanuts
2000 #24 DuPont Millennium
2000 #24 DuPont/10,080
2001 #24 Pepsi/17,280
2001 #24 DuPont Flames/24,984

Revell Collection Train Sets 1:64
2003 #24 Pepsi Billion $/4800

Revell Hobby 1:24
1994 #24 DuPont

Revell Retail 1:24
1995 #24 DuPont Dealer Promo DuPont logo on deck lid issued in plain white box
1995 #24 DuPont Dealer Promo Coke logo on deck lid
1995 #24 DuPont Coke deck lid
1995 #24 DuPont
1996 #24 DuPont

Revell Retail 1:64
1996 #24 DuPont

Revell Select 1:24
1998 #24 DuPont
1999 #24 Pepsi Star Wars
1999 #24 Pepsi
2001 #24 DuPont Flames

Revell Select Hobby 1:64
1998 #24 DuPont

Revell Select Hobby Transporters 1:64
1998 #24 DuPont

Road Champs 1:64
1992 #1 Baby Ruth

Road Champs Transporters 1:87
1992 #1 Baby Ruth

Winner's Circle 1:18
2002 #24 DuPont Flames
2003 #24 Pepsi Billion $
2003 #24 Pepsi Talladega '01
2003 #24 DuPont Flames
2004 #24 DuPont Flames HMS 20th Anniversary
2004 #24 Elmo
2004 #24 Pepsi Shards
2004 #24 DuPont Rainbow
2004 #24 DuPont Flames
2005 #24 DuPont Flames
2005 #24 DuPont Refresh
2005 #24 Pepsi Daytona
2007 #24 DuPont Flames

Winner's Circle 1:24
1996 #24 DuPont
1997 #24 Lost World
1997 #24 DuPont ChromaPremier
1997 #24 DuPont Million $ Date
1997 #24 DuPont
1998 #24 DuPont Walmart
1998 #24 DuPont Million $ win
1998 #24 DuPont
1999 #24 Star Wars
1999 #24 Pepsi with figure
1999 #24 Pepsi
1999 #24 DuPont Superman
1999 #24 DuPont No Bull
1999 #24 DuPont Daytona 500
2000 #24 Pepsi
2000 #24 DuPont Millennium
2000 #24 DuPont Peanuts '00
2000 #24 DuPont
2001 #24 DuPont Flames
2002 #24 Pepsi Daytona
2002 #24 DuPont Bugs Rematch
2002 #24 DuPont Bugs '01
2002 #24 DuPont 200th Anniversary
2002 #24 DuPont Flames
2003 #24 Pepsi Billion $
2003 #24 2001 Pepsi Stars&Stripes
2003 #24 2002 Elmo
2003 #24 DuPont Bugs Rematch '02
2003 #24 DuPont Flames
2004 #24 Pepsi Billion
2004 #24 Pepsi
2004 #24 DuPont Wizard of Oz
2004 #24 DuPont Rainbow
2004 #24 DuPont Flames HMS 20th Anniversary
2004 #24 DuPont Flames
2005 #24 DuPont Flames Performance Aliiance Reverse
2005 #24 DuPont Flames Refresh
2005 #24 Pepsi Daytona
2005 #24 DuPont Flames
2006 #24 Holiday JG Foundation
2006 #24 DuPont Hot Hues Foose Design
2006 #24 DuPont Flames
2007 #24 Pepsi
2007 #24 Nicorette
2007 #24 DuPont Flames
2008 #24 DuPont Flames
2008 #24 Nicorette
2008 #24 Pepsi

Winner's Circle 1:43
1998 #24 DuPont Champ.Walmart
1998 #24 DuPont Million $ win
1998 #24 DuPont
1999 #24 Pepsi Star Wars
1999 #24 Pepsi
1999 #24 DuPont Superman
1999 #24 DuPont Daytona 500
1999 #24 DuPont
2000 #24 Pepsi

Winner's Circle 1:64
1997 #24 DuPont
1997 #24 DuPont Million $ Date
1998 #24 DuPont Walmart blister
1998 #24 DuPont Million $ win
1998 #24 DuPont Dayt.500 blister
1998 #24 DuPont '98 WC Champ.
1998 #24 DuPont '98 Prev.blister
1998 #24 DuPont Champ.11/16/97 with figure
2000 #24 DuPont NASCAR Racers

Winner's Circle 1:87
2006 #24 DuPont Hot Hues Foose Design
2006 #24 DuPont Flames
2007 #24 Pepsi
2007 #24 Nicorette
2007 #24 DuPont Flames
2008 #24 DuPont Flames
2008 #24 Nicorette

Winner's Circle 24K Gold 1:64
1999 #24 Pepsi
1999 #24 DuPont

Winner's Circle 2-Car Set w/Hood 1:64
2008 #24 DuPont Flames/Nicorette

Winner's Circle American Heroes 1:24
2007 #24 DuPont D.O.D. AH logo

Winner's Circle American Heroes 1:87
2007 #24 DuPont Dept. of Defense AH
2007 #NNO American Heroes 9-car set
2007 #NNO 4.Burton/AF 24.Gordon/D.O.D. 48.Johnson/P.O.P. 3-car set

Winner's Circle American Heroes Hood 1:
2007 #24 DuPont Dept.of Def. AH

Winner's Circle Autographed Hood 1:64
2002 #24 Pepsi Daytona
2002 #24 DuPont 200th Anniversary
2003 #24 DuPont Flames Yose.Sam
2003 #24 Pepsi Daytona
2003 #24 Pepsi Billion $
2003 #24 DuP.Flames small package
2003 #24 DuPont Flames
2004 #24 Pepsi Billion short package
2004 #24 Pepsi Billion
2004 #24 Pepsi
2004 #24 DuPont Rainbow
2004 #24 DuPont Flames '03 Yose.Sam
2004 #24 DuPont Flames Wizard of Oz
2004 #24 DuPont Flames HMS 20th Anniversary
2005 #24 Pepsi Daytona
2006 #24 Nicorette
2006 #24 DuPont Hot Hues Sam Foose
2006 #24 DuPont Flames Test
2006 #24 DuPont Flames

Winner's Circle Autographed Hoods 1:64
2008 #24 DuPont Flames

Winner's Circle Championship with Fi
1998-99 #24 DuPont '99 Daytona 500
1998-99 #24 DuPont '98 Champ.
1998-99 #24 DuPont '97 Champ.
1998-99 #24 DuPont '95 Champ.

Winner's Circle Classic Hood 1:64
2001 #24 ChromaPremier

Winner's Circle Cool Customs 1:64
2000 #24 Superman '57 Chevy HT
2000 #24 Pepsi '57 Convertible
1998-99 #24 Pepsi Superman 1957 Chevy 1999
1998-99 #24 Pepsi '57 Chevy '99
1998-99 #24 DuPont '63 Impala
1998-99 #24 DuPont '57 Convertible

Winner's Circle Daytona 500 1:24
2008 #24 DuPont Flames

Winner's Circle Daytona 500 1:64
2008 #24 DuPont Flames

Winner's Circle Daytona 500 1:87
2008 #24 DuPont Flames

Winner's Circle Daytona 500 2-car sets
2008 #24/08 DuPont Flames Daytona 500 Event Car

Winner's Circle Daytona 500 Hoods 1:64
2008 #24 DuPont Flames

Winner's Circle Decade of Champions 1:6
2003 #24 DuPont Flames 2001
2003 #24 DuPont 1998
2003 #24 DuPont 1997
2003 #24 DuPont 1995

Winner's Circle Deluxe Driver Sticker 1
2000 #24 DuPont Peanuts
2000 #24 DuPont

Winner's Circle Deluxe Race Hood 1:64
2000 #24 Pepsi
2000 #24 DuPont Silver
2000 #24 DuPont Tyvek deck lid
2000 #24 DuPont Corian deck lid

Winner's Circle Die-Cast Kits 1:24
2002 #24 DuPont Flames
2002 #24 DuPont Bugs Rematch
2003 #24 Dupont
2003 #24 Dupont Bugs Rematch '02
2004 #24 DuPont Rainbow

Winner's Circle Die-Cast Kits 1:64
2002 #24 DuPont Bugs Rematch
2002 #24 DuPont Flames
2003 #24 DuPont Flames
2003 #24 Dupont Bugs Rematch '02

Winner's Circle Double Platinum 1:43
2001 #24 DuPont Bugs
2001 #24 DuPont
2002 #24 DuPont 200th Anniversary
2002 #24 DuPont Bugs 2002
2002 #24 DuPont Flames
2002 #24 DuPont Bugs 2001

Winner's Circle Driver Photo Hood 1:64
2005 #24 DuPont Flames Reverse Performance Alliance
2005 #24 DuPont Flames

Winner's Circle Driver Sticker 1:64
2001 #24 DuPont Peanuts
2001 #24 DuPont Flames
2002 #24 DuPont Flames 2001 WC Champ
2002 #24 DuPont Flames
2002 #24 DuPont Bugs Rematch
2003 #6 True Value '98 IROC
2003 #24 Pepsi Talladega
2003 #24 Elmo '02
2003 #24 Dupont Bugs Rematch '02
2003 #24 Cookie Monster
2004 #24 Pepsi Shards Talladega Raced sparkle
2004 #24 DuPont Flames Fontana Raced sparkle
2004 #24 DuPont Flames sparkle short package
2005 #24 DuPont Flames Daytona Raced
2005 #24 DuPont Flames Performance Alliance Reverse

Winner's Circle Dually w/Car on Tracksi
2008 #24 DuPont Flames

Winner's Circle Event Series 1:64
2005 #24 Pepsi Shards '04 Talladega Win
2005 #24 DuPont Flames '04 California Win

Winner's Circle Fantasy Pack 1:64
1998-99 #24 Pepsi
1998-99 #24 DuPont Superman '99
1998-99 #24 DuPont '99
1998-99 #24 DuPont '98

Winner's Circle For Kids 1:43
1998 #24 DuPont

Winner's Circle Gallery 1:64
2001 #24 DuPont Bugs Bunny
2002 #24 DuPont Flames 2001 WC Champ

Winner's Circle Garage Scene 1:43
2000 #24 DuPont

Winner's Circle Gift Pack 1:64
2002 #24 Pepsi/DuPont Flames DuPont 200th Ann.

Winner's Circle Gift Pack With Photo 1:
2002 #24 DuPont Bugs/DuPont 200th Ann/DuPont Flames

Winner's Circle Helmets 1:64
2007 #24 DuPont Flames

Winner's Circle Hoods 1:64
2007 #24 Pepsi
2007 #24 DuPont Flames

Winner's Circle License Plate 1:64
2007 #24 DuPont Flames

Winner's Circle Lifetime Jeff Gordon
1996-97 #1 Carolina '91 T-bird 5/6
1996-97 #1 Baby Ruth '92 T-bird 4/6
1996-97 #24 Lost World '97 MC 3/6 no LTS logo on package
1996-97 #24 Lost World '97 MC 3/6 LTS logo on package
1996-97 #24 DuPont Chroma 1997 Monte Carlo 2/6
1996-97 #24 DuPont Chroma 1997 Monte Carlo 2/6 '96 Package
1996-97 #24 DuPont '97 Million Doll.Date LTS Bonus
1996-97 #24 DuPont '97 MC 1/6 LTS logo on package
1996-97 #24 DuPont '97 MC 1/6 1997 Package
1996-97 #24 DuPont '97 MC 1/6 1996 Package
1996-97 #24 DuPont '93 Lum. 6/6 w/Gordon card no LTS logo
1996-97 #24 DuPont '93 Lum. 6/6 w/Gordon card LTS logo
1996-97 #24 DuPont '93 Lum. 6/6 with car card
1996-97 #40 1987 Sprint bonus LTS logo in upper right
1996-97 #40 1987 Sprint bonus LTS logo on left edge
2001-02 #6 Sprint Car '89 4/6
2001-02 #24 DuPont Flames '01 5/6
2001-02 #24 DuPont '00 2/6
2001-02 #24 DuPont 50th Win 1/6
2001-02 #24 DuPont Chroma. '98 6/6
2001-02 #24 DuPont Brickyard '94 3/6

Winner's Circle Lifetime Jeff Gordon 1:
1998 #16 1985 Sprint car
1998 #24 DuPont '98 Monte Carlo High Performance card
1998 #24 DuPont '98 Monte Carlo Stock Car Series card
1998 #24 DuPont '94 First Win
1999 #4 Pepsi '90 Midget 8/8
1999 #24 Pepsi '99 MC 2/8
1999 #24 DuPont Superman 5/8
1999 #24 DuPont '99 Test 6/8
1999 #24 DuPont '99 MC 1/8
1999 #24 DuPont '95 Champ 4/8
1999 #24 DuPont '92 Lumina 7/8
1999 #67 Outback '90 GP 3/8
2000 #4 Beast '90 Sprint 2/6
2000 #24 Pepsi '00 MC 1/6
2000 #24 DuPont '00 MC 3/6
2000 #24 DuPont '96 MC 6/6
2000 #24 DuPont '93 MC 5/6
2000 #24 DuPont '92 Lum. 4/6

Winner's Circle Medallion 1:64
2007 #24 DuPont Flames

Winner's Circle Micro Machines 1:144
1999 #24 Pepsi Car and Transporter
1999 #24 DuPont 3 Cars, Transport. tow truck & pit wagon
1999 #NNO J.Gordon
1999 #NNO J.Gordon
1999 #20/24 J.Gordon
1999 #24/28/88 K.Irwin/D.Jarrett
1999 #NNO 7-car Draft Pack
2000 #18/24 J.Gordon

Winner's Circle Number Magnet 1:64
2008 #24 DuPont Flames

Winner's Circle Pit Pass 1:64
2007 #24 Nicorette
2007 #24 DuPont Flames

Winner's Circle Pit Pass Preview 1:64
2002 #24 DuPont Flames
2004 #24 DuPont Flames

Winner's Circle Pit Row 1:64
1998 #24 Pepsi
1998 #24 DuPont right rear tire already changed
1998 #24 DuPont approaching to change right rear tire
1998 #24 DuPont Fanscan pack. four tires on ground
1998 #24 DuPont Fanscan pack. left side raised

Winner's Circle Pit Scene 1:64
2003 #24 DuPont Tires Off
2003 #24 Pepsi Coming In

Winner's Circle Pit Sign 1:64
2006 #24 DuPont Flames
2007 #24 Pepsi
2007 #24 DuPont Flames Test

Winner's Circle Preview 1:24
2000 #24 DuPont

Winner's Circle Preview 1:43
2000 #24 DuPont

Winner's Circle Race Hood 1:43
2002 #24 DuPont 200th Ann.
2002 #24 DuPont Flames
2003 #24 Pepsi
2003 #24 DuPont Flames Yose.Sam

Winner's Circle Race Hood 1:64
2003 #24 DuPont Flames
2001-02 #24 Pepsi '02
2001-02 #24 DuPont 200th Anniv.
2001-02 #24 DuPont Flames
2001-02 #24 DuPont ChromaPremier

Winner's Circle Race 'N' Play Transport
1998 #24 DuPont

Winner's Circle Sam Bass 1:43
2000 #24 DuPont

Winner's Circle Sam Bass 1:64
2008 #24 Foundation Test

Winner's Circle Sam Bass Hoods 1:64
2007 #24 DuPont Flames Holiday

Winner's Circle Schedule Hood 1:64
2005 #24 DuPont Flames
2006 #24 DuPont Flames
2007 #24 DuPont Flames

Winner's Circle Schedule Hoods 1:64
2008 #24 DuPont Flames

Winner's Circle Sneak Previews 1:64
2000 #24 DuPont

Winner's Circle Speedweeks 1:43
1999 #24 DuPont

Winner's Circle Speedweeks 1:64
1999 #24 DuPont

Winner's Circle Stats and Standings 1:6
1999 #24 DuPont

Winner's Circle Sticker 1:64
2006 #24 DuPont Flames

Winner's Circle Stickers 1:64
2008 #24 Pepsi

Winner's Circle Team Authentics 1:64
2001 #24 DuPont Sheetmetal
2001 #24 DuPont Firesuit

Winner's Circle Tech Series 1:64
1998 #24 DuPont
1999 #24 DuPont Superman

Winner's Circle Test Hood 1:64
2005 #24 DuPont

Winner's Circle Track Support Crew 1:64
1999 #24 Pepsi
1999 #24 DuPont

Winner's Circle Transporters 1:64
2000 #24 DuPont with NASCAR 2000 logo on box
2000 #24 DuPont without NASCAR 2000 logo on box
2001 #24 DuPont Flames
2002 #24 Pepsi Daytona
2002 #24 DuPont 200th Ann.
2002 #24 DuPont Flames
2002 #24 DuPont Bugs
2002 #24 DuPont Flames
2003 #24 Pepsi Billion $
2003 #24 Elmo '02
2003 #24 DuPont Bugs Rematch
2003 #24 DuPont Bugs '01
2003 #24 DuPont 4-Time Champ
2004 #24 Pepsi Shards
2004 #24 Pepsi Billion
2004 #24 DuPont Rainbow
2004 #24 DuPont Flames Wizard of Oz
2004 #24 DuPont Flames HMS 20th Ann.
2004 #24 DuPont Flames
2005 #24 Pepsi Daytona
2005 #24 DuPont Flames
2007 #24 Pepsi
2007 #24 DuPont Flames
2007 #24 DuPont Dept.of Defense American Heroes
2008 #24 DuPont Flames

2008 #24 Pepsi

Winner's Circle Victory Celebration 1:4
1996 #24 DuPont Mill.$ win 8/31/97
1998 #24 Charlotte Win
1999 #24 Daytona 500 2/16/97
1999 #24 Daytona 500

Winner's Circle Victory Lane 1:64
1999 #24 DuPont Daytona 2/14/99

Winner's Circle Victory Lane Hoods 1:64
2007 #24 DuPont Flames COT Talladega Raced
2007 #24 DuPont Flames COT Phoenix Raced
2007 #24 DuPont Flames COT Darlington Raced
2007 #24 DuPont Flames Talladega Raced
2007 #24 DuPont Flames Pocono Raced
2007 #24 DuPont Flames Charlotte Raced

Winner's Circle Victory Lap 1:24
2003 #24 DuPont Victory Lap

Winner's Circle Victory Lap 1:64
2003 #24 DuPont Victory Lap

Winner's Circle with Figure 1:24
1998 #24 Pepsi
1998 #24 DuPont No Bull

Winross Transporters 1:64
1993 #NNO DuPont

Hamlin, Denny

Action Promos 1:64
2006 #11 Fed Ex Kinko's in blister
2006 #11 Fed Ex Ground in blister
2006 #11 Fed Ex Freight in blister
2006 #11 Fed Ex Express in blister

Action QVC For Race Fans Only 1:24
2006 #11 Fed Ex Ground Pocono Raced Color Chrome AU/504

Action Racing Collectables 1:24
2006 #11 Fed Ex Express Daytona Shootout Raced GM Dealers/552
2006 #11 Fed Ex Express Daytona Shootout Raced/2208
2006 #11 Fed Ex Express/7728
2006 #11 Fed Ex Kinko's GM Dealers/300
2006 #11 Fed Ex Kinko's CWB/144
2006 #11 Fed Ex Home Delivery QVC*
2006 #11 Fed Ex Home Delivery GM Dealers/648
2006 #11 Fed Ex Home Delivery CWB/300
2006 #11 Fed Ex Home Delivery/2209*
2006 #11 Fed Ex Ground Pocono Raced GM Dealers/636
2006 #11 Fed Ex Ground Pocono Raced/2952
2006 #11 Fed Ex Ground GM Dealers/300
2006 #11 Fed Ex Ground CW Bank/240
2006 #11 Fed Ex Ground/3000
2006 #11 Fed Ex Freight/5208
2006 #11 Fed Ex Express '06 ROY GM Dealers/504
2006 #11 Fed Ex Express '06 ROY/LE
2006 #20 Rockwell Automation/2508

Action Racing Collectables 1:64
2006 #11 Fed Ex Kinko's
2006 #11 Fed Ex Ground
2006 #11 Fed Ex Freight
2006 #11 Fed Ex Express
2006 #20 Rockwell Automation

Action Racing Collectables Platinum 1:2
2008 #11 Fed Ex Express/5148
2008 #11 Fed Ex Freight/2117
2008 #11 Fed Ex Ground/2160
2008 #11 Fed Ex Kinko's/1860

Action/RCCA 1:24
2006 #11 Fed Ex Express/311
2006 #11 Fed Ex Ground Pocono Raced/299
2006 #11 Fed Ex Ground/311
2006 #11 Fed Ex Freight/211
2006 #11 Fed Ex Express Daytona Shootout Raced/311
2006 #11 Fed Ex Kinko's Pocono Raced/299
2006 #11 Fed Ex PGA Cup/211
2006 #11 Fed Ex Kinko's/211
2006 #11 Fed Ex Home Delivery/211
2006 #20 Rockwall Automation/144

Action/RCCA 1:64
2006 #11 Fed Ex Home Delivery/288
2006 #11 Fed Ex Kinko's/288
2006 #11 Fed Ex Ground/360
2006 #11 Fed Ex Freight/288
2006 #11 Fed Ex Express/384
2006 #20 Rockwall Automation/288

Action/RCCA Elite 1:24
2006 #11 Fed Ex Express White Gold/25
2006 #11 Fed Ex Express Platinum/8
2006 #11 FedEx Express/411
2006 #11 Fed Ex Kinko's Pocono Raced Platinum/5
2006 #11 Fed Ex Kinko's Pocono Raced/299
2006 #11 Fed Ex Kinko's Platinum/5
2006 #11 FedEx Kinko's/299
2006 #11 Fed Ex Home Delivery White Gold/25
2006 #11 Fed Ex Home Delivery Platinum/8
2006 #11 Fed Ex Home Delivery/411
2006 #11 Fed Ex Ground Pocono Raced Platinum/5
2006 #11 Fed Ex Ground Pocono Raced/299
2006 #11 FedEx Ground White Gold/25
2006 #11 Fed Ex Ground Platinum/8
2006 #11 FedEx Ground/411
2006 #11 Fed Ex Freight Platinum/5
2006 #11 FedEx Freight/299
2006 #11 Fed Ex Express Daytona Shootout Raced Platinum/4
2006 #11 FedEx Express Daytona Shootout Raced/311
2006 #11 Fed Ex PGA Cup White Gold/25
2006 #11 Fed Ex PGA Cup Platinum/5
2006 #11 Fed Ex PGA Cup/299
2006 #20 Rockwall Automation Platinum/2
2006 #20 Rockwall Automation/144

Action/RCCA Elite 1:64
2006 #11 Fed Ex Freight/144
2006 #11 Fed Ex Ground/144
2006 #11 Fed Ex Home Delivery/144
2006 #11 Fed Ex Kinko's/144
2006 #11 Fed Ex Express/144
2006 #20 Rockwell Automation/288

Motorsports Authentics Driver's Select
2007 #11 Fed Ex Kinko's COT/1372*
2007 #11 Fed Ex Kinko's/3216*
2007 #11 Fed Ex Ground COT New Hampshire Raced/888
2007 #11 Fed Ex Ground COT/1260*
2007 #11 Fed Ex Ground/3756*
2007 #11 Fed Ex Freight Marines American Heroes/3240
2007 #11 Fed Ex Freight COT/1152*
2007 #11 Fed Ex Freight/7008*
2007 #11 Fed Ex Express Sam Bass Holiday/1020*
2007 #11 Fed Ex Express COT/1408*
2007 #11 Fed Ex Express/9000*
2007 #11 Fed Ex Kinko's COT
2007 #11 Fed Ex Kinko's
2007 #11 Fed Ex Ground COT
2007 #11 Fed Ex Ground
2007 #11 Fed Ex Freight Marines American Heroes
2007 #11 Fed Ex Freight COT
2007 #11 Fed Ex Freight
2007 #11 Fed Ex Express COT
2007 #11 Fed Ex Express
2007 #11 Fed Ex Kinko's COT/288
2007 #11 Fed Ex Kinko's/432
2007 #11 Fed Ex Ground COT/288
2007 #11 Fed Ex Ground/432
2007 #11 Fed Ex Freight COT/288
2007 #11 Fed Ex Freight/432
2007 #11 Fed Ex Express COT/360
2007 #11 Fed Ex Express/360

Motorsports Authentics Owner's Elite 1:
2007 #11 Fed Ex Express COT/708
2007 #11 Fed Ex Express White Gold/100
2007 #11 Fed Ex Express Platinum/25
2007 #11 Fed Ex Express/1200*
2007 #11 Fed Ex Test/1200*
2007 #11 Fed Ex Kinko's White Gold/50*
2007 #11 Fed Ex Kinko's Platinum/25
2007 #11 Fed Ex Kinko's/504*
2007 #11 Fed Ex Ground/504*
2007 #11 Fed Ex Freight Marines Heroes White Gold/50*
2007 #11 Fed Ex Freight Marines Heroes Platinum/25
2007 #11 Fed Ex Freight Marines Heroes/1200*
2007 #11 Fed Ex Freight/504*
2007 #11 Fed Ex Express '06 ROY White Gold/100
2007 #11 Fed Ex Express '06 ROY w/tire/111
2007 #11 Fed Ex Express '06 ROY Color Chrome/100
2007 #11 Fed Ex Express '06 ROY/1011
2007 #11 Fed Ex Kinko's/1008*
2007 #11 Fed Ex Freight Marines American Heroes/1507*
2007 #11 Fed Ex Express/2007*

Motorsports Authentics Owner's Elite Tr
2007 #11 Fed Ex Kinko's/404*
2007 #11 Fed Ex Ground/400*
2007 #11 Fed Ex Freight Marines American Heroes/100*
2007 #11 Fed Ex Freight/504*
2007 #11 Fed Ex Express '06 ROY Color Chrome/96*
2007 #11 Fed Ex Express/504*

Motorsports Authentics Pit Stop 1:64
2007 #11 Fed Ex Kinko's COT
2007 #11 Fed Ex Kinko's
2007 #11 Fed Ex Ground COT
2007 #11 Fed Ex Ground
2007 #11 Fed Ex Freight Marines American Heroes
2007 #11 Fed Ex Freight COT
2007 #11 Fed Ex Freight
2007 #11 Fed Ex Express COT
2007 #11 Fed Ex Express

Motorsports Authentics QVC For Race Fan
2007 #11 Fed Ex Express Copper/108
2007 #11 Fed Ex Express Color Chrome/108

Motorsports Authentics Steel 1:18
2006 #11 Fed Ex Express Daytona Shootout Raced/300

Motorsports Authentics/RCCA Owner's Clu
2007 #11 Fed Ex Kinko's/708*
2007 #11 Fed Ex Ground/708*
2007 #11 Fed Ex Freight Marines American Heroes/708*
2007 #11 Fed Ex Freight/708*
2007 #11 Fed Ex Express Holiday Sam Bass/144*
2007 #11 Fed Ex Express/708*

Motorsports Authentics/RCCA Transporter
2007 #11 Fed Ex Express/708*

RCCA Club 1:24
2008 #11 Fed Ex Express/252
2008 #11 Fed Ex Ground/150
2008 #11 Fed Ex Freight/150

RCCA Elite 1:24
2008 #11 Fed Ex Express/408
2008 #11 Fed Ex Express Platinum/25
2008 #11 Fed Ex Express White Gold/50
2008 #11 Fed Ex Ground/300
2008 #11 Fed Ex Kinko's/300
2008 #11 Fed Ex Kinko's Platinum/25
2008 #11 Fed Ex Kinko's White Gold/50

Winner's Circle 1:18
2007 #11 Fed Ex Express

Winner's Circle 1:24
2007 #11 Fed Ex Express
2008 #11 Fed Ex Express

Winner's Circle 1:87
2007 #11 Fed Ex Express
2008 #11 Fed Ex Express

Winner's Circle American Heroes 1:24
2007 #11 Fed Ex Freight Marines American Heroes

Winner's Circle American Heroes 1:87
2007 #11 Fed Ex Freight Marines AH
2007 #NNO American Heroes 9-car set
2007 #NNO 11.Hamlin/Marines 21.Wood/AF 01.Martin/Army 3-car set

Winner's Circle American Heroes Hood 1:
2007 #11 Fed Ex Freight Marines AH

Winner's Circle Autographed Hood 1:64
2006 #11 Fed Ex Express

Winner's Circle Award Winners 1:64
2006 #11 Fed Ex Express ROY

Winner's Circle Helmets 1:64
2007 #11 Fed Ex Express

Winner's Circle License Plate 1:64
2007 #11 Fed Ex Express

Winner's Circle Number Magnet 1:64
2008 #11 FedEx Express

Winner's Circle Pit Pass 1:64
2007 #11 Fed Ex Express

Winner's Circle Sam Bass Hoods 1:64
2007 #11 Fed Ex Express Holiday

Winner's Circle Schedule Hood 1:64
2007 #11 Fed Ex Express

Winner's Circle Stickers 1:64
2008 #11 FedEx Express

Winner's Circle Transporters 1:64
2007 #11 Fed Ex Freight Marines American Heroes
2007 #11 Fed Ex Express

Winner's Circle Victory Lane Hoods 1:64
2007 #11 Fed Ex Express COT New Hampshire Raced

Harvick, Kevin

Action Performance 1:24
2000 #2 AC Delco
2002 #29 Goodwrench
2003 #29 Goodwrench
2005 #29 Goodwrench Hometown

Action Performance 1:64
2001 #29 Goodwrench
2002 #29 Goodwrench
2003 #29 Goodwrench
2004 #29 Goodwrench C2/5040
2004 #29 Nextel Cup 6-car set

Action QVC For Race Fans Only 1:24
2001 #2 AC Delco Gold/1000
2001 #2 AC Delco Color Chr./1000
2001 #29 Goodwrench Oreo Platinum/624
2001 #29 Goodwrench Taz Platinum/624
2001 #29 Goodwrench Taz Gold
2001 #29 Goodwrench Taz Chrome/3504
2001 #29 Goodwrench Oreo Platinum/624
2001 #29 Goodwrench AOL Platinum/624
2001 #29 Goodwr.AOL Gold/1000
2001 #29 Goodwrench Plat/624
2001 #29 Goodwr.Gold/10,000
2002 #29 Goodwrench Taz Gold/1000
2002 #29 Goodwrench Taz Platinum/624
2002 #29 Goodwrench Taz Color Chome/2508
2002 #29 Goodwrench ET Platinum/624
2002 #29 Goodwr.ET Chrome/3504
2002 #29 Goodwren.ET Gold/2508
2002 #29 Goodwr.Platinum/624
2002 #29 Goodwrench Gold/2508
2005 #29 Goodwrench Quicksilver Color Chrome/360
2005 #29 Goodwrench Color Chrome/360

Action Racing Collectables 1:18
2001 #29 Goodwrench Taz/3504
2001 #29 Goodwrench/6000
2002 #29 Goodwrench Taz/1008
2002 #29 Goodwrench ET/3000
2002 #29 Goodwrench/4008
2004 #29 Goodwrench

Action Racing Collectables 1:24
2000 #2 AC Delco/5004
2001 #2 AC Delco '01 BGN Champ GM Dealers/2496
2001 #2 AC Delco Bank/600
2001 #2 AC Delco 2001 Busch Champ/30,000
2001 #2 AC Delco/3300
2001 #29 Goodwrench Rookie of the Year/37,812
2001 #29 Goodwrench White Gold Promo/5000
2001 #29 Goodwrench Clear/8292
2001 #29 Goodwrench/102,432
2001 #29 Goodwrench Taz Clear/7164
2001 #29 Goodwrench Taz/92,748
2001 #29 Goodwrench Oreo Show car/56,196
2001 #29 Goodwrench AOL Color Chrome
2001 #29 Goodwrench AOL Bank/2004
2001 #29 Goodwrench AOL/46,500
2001 #29 Goodwrench Make-a-Wish/6816
2001 #29 Goodwrench Van Camp's box Promo
2001 #NNO AC Delco/Goodwrench dual sponsor split paint/5004
2002 #1 True Value '01 IROC/6996
2002 #29 Snap-On/23,712
2002 #29 Sylvania GM Dealers/1008
2002 #29 Sylvania Bank/504
2002 #29 Sylvania/8016
2002 #29 Sonic Bank/1008
2002 #29 Sonic/21,768
2002 #29 Goodwrench Taz GM Dealers White Gold/2496
2002 #29 Goodwrench Taz GM Dealers/8508
2002 #29 Goodwrench Taz Bank/1056
2002 #29 Goodwrench Taz/21,684
2002 #29 Goodwrench Now Sell Tires GM Dealers/2004
2002 #29 Goodwrench Now Sell Tires/28,896
2002 #29 Goodwrench ET Color Chrome Bank/2700
2002 #29 Goodwrench ET Clear/6288
2002 #29 Goodwrench ET GM Dealers/8508
2002 #29 Goodwrench ET/64,860
2002 #29 Goodwrench GM Dealers/11,616
2002 #29 Goodwrench Clear/4812
2002 #29 Goodwrench Bank/3144
2002 #29 Goodwrench/103,716
2002 #29 Action ET Color Chrome Bank/1284
2002 #29 Action ET/22,860
2002 #29 Reese's Fastbreak/3504
2002 #29 Flag GM Dealers/3420
2003 #6 kevinharvick.com SuperTruck 1st Win/3504
2003 #11 True Value IROC Yellow/7128
2003 #21 Payday BW Bank/720
2003 #21 Payday/12,888
2003 #29 Snap-On GM Deal/1440
2003 #29 Snap-On/20,004
2003 #29 Goodwrench Sugar Ray CW Bank/624
2003 #29 Goodwrench Sugar Ray/8520
2003 #29 Goodwrench Red GM Dealers/12,000
2003 #29 Goodwrench Raced GM Dealers/1644
2003 #29 Goodwrench Raced/8532
2003 #29 Goodwrench GM Dealers/2496
2003 #29 Goodwrench BW Bank/804
2003 #29 Goodwrench/19,416
2004 #21 Reese's Las Vegas Raced QVC/288
2004 #21 Reese's RCR 35th Ann CW Bank/324
2004 #21 Reese's RCR 35th Ann./4812
2004 #21 Reese's Las Vegas Raced/3000
2004 #21 Reese's Mac Tools/288
2004 #21 Reese's GM Dealers/1224
2004 #21 Reese's CW Bank/384
2004 #21 Reese's/11,376
2004 #21 Meijer Reese's White Chocolate CW Bank/228
2004 #21 Meijer Reese's White Chocolate/3744
2004 #21 Hershey's Kisses GM Dealers/1224
2004 #21 Hershey's Kisses CW Bank/408
2004 #21 Hershey's Kisses/8004
2004 #29 Snap-On GM Dealers/1080
2004 #29 Snap-On CW Bank/432
2004 #29 Snap-On/8652
2004 #29 Powerade CW Bank/336
2004 #29 Powerade/3288
2004 #29 Ice Breakers Liquid Ice CW Bank/444
2004 #29 Ice Breakers Liquid Ice/8748
2004 #29 Goodwrench Realtree GM Dealers/1092
2004 #29 Goodwrench Realtree CW Bank/432
2004 #29 Goodwrench Realtree/7572
2004 #29 Goodwrench RCR 35th Ann. CW Bank/444
2004 #29 Goodwrench RCR 35th Ann./7596
2004 #29 Goodwrench KISS CW Bank/420
2004 #29 Goodwrench KISS/8148
2004 #29 Goodwrench Nextel Incentive/2904
2004 #29 Goodwrench Mac Tools/288
2004 #29 Goodwrench GM Dealers/2280
2004 #29 Goodwr.CW Bank/432
2004 #29 Goodwrench/13,884
2004 #29 ESGR Coast Guard CW Bank/348
2004 #29 ESGR Coast Guard/4824
2004 #29 Crown Royal IROC/4776
2004 #29 Coke C2 Mac Tools/468
2004 #29 Coke C2 GM Dealers/288
2004 #29 Coke C2 CW Bank/288
2004 #29 Coke C2/5472
2004 #92 Goodwrench SuperTruck QVC/288
2004 #92 Snap On SuperTruck/4062
2004 #92 Goodwrench SuperTruck/3480
2005 #21 Twizzlers CW Bank/144
2005 #21 Hershey's Take 5/4872
2005 #21 Hershey's Take 5 GM Dealers/468
2005 #21 Hershey's Take 5 QVC/288
2005 #21 Pelon Pelo Rico/2400
2005 #21 Pelon Pelo Rico CW Bank/168
2005 #21 Pelon Pelo Rico GM Dealers/228
2005 #21 Reese's/6144
2005 #21 Reese's GM Dealers/600
2005 #21 Reese's QVC/288
2005 #21 Reese's Honey Roasted/2340
2005 #21 Reese's Honey Roasted Liquid Metal/1164
2005 #21 Twizzlers/1680
2005 #21 Twizzlers GM Dealers/168
2005 #29 Goodwrench Brickyard Mac Tools/300
2005 #29 Goodwrench Gretchen Wilson Matco/48
2005 #29 Goodwrench 20th Anniversary/5004
2005 #29 Goodwrench 20th Ann CW Bank/168
2005 #29 Reese's Big Cup CW Bank/144
2005 #29 Reese's Big Cup Mac Tools/300
2005 #29 Snap-On Snap On/3000
2005 #29 Snap-On/2508
2005 #29 Reese's Big Cup GM Dealers/336
2005 #29 Goodwrench Test Todd Berrier AU/2508
2005 #29 Goodwrench Quicksilver QVC/288
2005 #29 Goodwrench Quicksilver GM Dealers Chrome/1500
2005 #29 Goodwrench Quicksilver CW Bank/168
2005 #29 Goodwrench Quicksilver/5004
2005 #29 Goodwrench Gretchen Wilson QVC/120
2005 #29 Goodwrench Gretchen Wilson GM Dealers/1200
2005 #29 Goodwrench Gretchen Wilson/3480
2005 #29 Goodwrench Daytona QVC/504
2005 #29 Goodwrench Daytona GM Dealers Chrome/2508
2005 #29 Goodwrench Daytona GM Dealers/2004
2005 #29 Goodwrench Daytona CW Bank/216
2005 #29 Goodwrench Daytona/5304
2005 #29 Goodwrench Brickyard QVC/504
2005 #29 Goodwrench Brickyard GM Dealers Chrome/1500
2005 #29 Goodwrench Brickyard GM Dealers/720
2005 #29 Goodwrench Brickyard CW Bank/204
2005 #29 Goodwrench Brickyard/4032
2005 #29 Goodwrench Atlanta GM Dealers Chrome/2508
2005 #29 Goodwrench Atlanta GM Dealers/492
2005 #29 Goodwrench Atlanta CW Bank/240
2005 #29 Goodwrench Atlanta/6000
2005 #29 Goodwrench Bristol Raced GM Dealers/276
2005 #29 Goodwrench Bristol Raced/2400
2005 #29 Goodwrench QVC/504
2005 #29 Goodwrench Matco/120
2005 #29 Goodwrench/6564
2005 #29 Goodwrench CW Bank/216
2005 #29 Goodwrench GM Dealers/1200
2005 #29 Reese's Big Cup/1632
2005 #92 Goodwrench SuperTruck/1452
2005 #92 Yard-Man SuperTruck/1440
2005 #92 Yard-Man SuperTruck GM Dealers/96
2005 #92 Yard-Man SuperTruck Liquid Metal/300
2006 #21 Coast Guard CWB/144
2006 #21 Coast Guard/2004
2006 #21 Coast Guard '06 Busch Champion/LE
2006 #21 Coast Guard '06 Busch Champion GM Dealers/384
2006 #21 Coast Guard Reserve Richmond Raced/1056
2006 #21 Coast Guard Reserve Richmond Raced GM Dealers/72
2006 #29 Reese's Caramel GM Dealers/288
2006 #29 Reese's Caramel/2508
2006 #29 Reese's CW Bank/204
2006 #29 Reese's/5244
2006 #29 Hershey's Kissables CW Bank/204
2006 #29 Hershey's Kissables/4008
2006 #29 Hershey's QVC*
2006 #29 Hershey's Mac Tools*
2006 #29 Hershey's GM Dealers/600
2006 #29 Goodwrench/5004
2006 #29 Goodwrench CW Bank/204
2006 #29 Goodwrench GM Dealers/1200
2006 #29 Goodwrench Mac Tools/504
2006 #29 Goodwrench Matco/72
2006 #29 Goodwrench QVC/144
2006 #29 Goodwrench Holiday/1044*
2006 #29 Goodwrench Holiday GM Dealers/437
2006 #29 Goodwrench Holiday QVC*
2006 #29 Hershey's/2940*
2006 #29 Hershey's CW Bank/204

Action Racing Collectables 1:64
2001 #29 Goodwrench Taz QVC 4-car set in tin/2000
2001 #29 Goodwrench Taz/52,704
2001 #29 Goodwrench AOL/30,456
2001 #29 Goodwrench/44,568
2001 #NNO AC Delco/Goodwrench 2-cars in tin/35,040
2002 #29 Sylvania/9000
2002 #29 Goodwrench Taz/12,024
2002 #29 Goodwrench Now Sell Tires/15,408
2002 #29 Goodwrench ET/40,032
2002 #29 Goodwrench/68,112
2002 #29 Action ET/18,000
2003 #21 Payday/6912
2003 #29 Snap-On/12,528
2003 #29 Goodwrench Sugar Ray/6192
2003 #29 Goodwrench/13,968
2004 #21 Reese's/7248
2004 #21 Hershey's Kisses/6884
2004 #29 Snap-On/5616
2004 #29 Ice Breakers Liquid Ice/5328
2004 #29 Goodwrench Realtree/5568
2004 #29 Goodwrench RCR 35th Ann/5568
2004 #29 Goodwrench KISS/5280
2004 #29 Goodwrench/10,752
2005 #21 Reese's
2005 #21 Pelon Pelo Rico
2005 #21 Hershey's Take 5
2005 #29 Goodwrench 20th Anniversary
2005 #29 Goodwrench Quicksilver
2005 #29 Goodwrench Daytona
2005 #29 Goodwrench Brickyard
2005 #29 Goodwrench Atlanta
2005 #29 Goodwrench
2005 #21/29 Goodwrench/Reese's Chocolate Lovers Bristol Raced
2006 #29 Reese's
2006 #29 Hershey's Kissables
2006 #29 Hershey's
2006 #29 Goodwrench

Action Racing Collectables Advanced Pro
2008 #29 Pennzoil Platinum/144

Action Racing Collectables Historical S
2004 #29 Goodwrench Service Plus '01 Monte Carlo CW Bank/240
2004 #29 Goodwrench Service Plus '01 Monte Carlo blk no./33,000
2004 #29 Goodwrench Service Plus '01 Monte Carlo blk no./10,944

Action Racing Collectables Pit Wagon
1990-03 #29 Snap-On/7494 '02

Action Racing Collectables Platinum 1:2
2008 #29 Shell Pennzoil/11,736

Action Racing Collectables Transporters
2001 #29 Goodwrench/7500
2002 #29 Goodwrench ET/4608
2002 #29 Goodwrench/6000
2003 #29 Snap-On/12,504

Action/Funline Monster Truck 1:43
2004 #29 Goodwrench
2004 #29 KISS
2004 #29 Kid Rock

Action/Funline Muscle Machines 1:18
2004 #29 Goodwrench '69 Camaro
2004 #29 Goodwrench '69 Chevelle
2004 #29 Goodwrench '67 Nova

Action/Funline Muscle Machines 1:24
2004 #29 Goodwrench '69 Camaro
2004 #29 Goodwrench '69 Chevelle
2004 #29 Goodwrench '66 Nova
2005 #29 Goodwrench Hybrid/144

Action/RCCA 1:24
2002 #29 Sylvania Bank/1008
2002 #29 Sonic Bank/1008
2002 #29 Goodwrench Now Sell Tires Bank/1500
2002 #29 Goodwr.ET Bank/2004
2002 #29 Goodwr.Split Clear/2508
2002 #29 Goodwrench Bank/5004
2002 #29 Action ET Bank/1200
2002 #2K2 Childress Racing Pit Practice Bank/1008
2003 #6 Taz SuperTruck
2003 #21 Payday CW Bank/1008
2003 #29 Snap-On CW Bank/1200
2003 #29 Goodwrench Sugar Ray/600
2003 #29 Goodwrench Raced/444
2003 #29 Goodwrench Bank/1300
2004 #21 Reese's Las Vegas Raced/240
2004 #21 Reese's RCR 35th Anniversary/444
2004 #21 Reese's/900
2004 #21 Meijer Reese's White/288
2004 #21 Hershey's Kisses/720
2004 #29 Snap-On/804
2004 #29 Powerade/600
2004 #29 Ice Breakers/504
2004 #29 Goodwrench Realtree/1200
2004 #29 Goodwrench RCR 35th Anniversary/900
2004 #29 Goodwrench KISS/1008
2004 #29 Goodwrench/1008
2004 #29 ESGR Coast Guard/600
2004 #29 Crown Royal IROC Color Chrome/288
2004 #29 Coke C2/600
2004 #92 Goodwrench SuperTruck/444
2005 #21 Twizzlers/144
2005 #21 Reese's/288
2005 #21 Pelon Pelo Rico/360
2005 #21 Hershey's Take 5/504
2005 #29 Goodwrench Atlanta/600
2005 #29 Goodwrench Brickyard/408
2005 #29 Goodwrench Gretchen Wilson/300
2005 #29 Goodwrench Daytona/804
2005 #29 Goodwrench Bristol Raced/204
2005 #29 Goodwrench Color Chrome/288
2005 #29 Goodwrench/600
2005 #29 Goodwrench Hometown Brushed Bronze/144
2005 #29 Goodwrench 20th Anniversary/444
2005 #29 Reese's Big Cup/204
2005 #29 Goodwrench Test/408
2005 #47 KISS Army Color Chrome/300
2005 #47 KISS Army/1200
2005 #92 Goodwrench SuperTruck/144
2005 #92 Yard-Man Color Chrome/300
2006 #21 Coast Guard/120
2006 #21 Coast Guard Reserve Richmond Raced/150
2006 #29 Goodwrench Barenaked Ladies Richmond Raced/250
2006 #29 Goodwrench Holiday/250
2006 #29 Hershey's Kissables/240
2006 #29 Reese's Caramel
2006 #29 Goodwrench/288
2006 #29 Goodwrench Color Chrome/120
2006 #29 Hershey's/360
2006 #29 Reese's/240
2006 #33 Dollar General/100

Action/RCCA 1:32
2002 #29 GW/AC Delco set/3000
2002 #29 Goodwrench Gold/532
2002 #29 Goodwrench with Fan Scan card/2280
2002 #NNO AC Delco/Goodwrench 2-car set/3000

Action/RCCA 1:64
2001 #29 Goodwr.Nilla Wafers Promo
2001 #29 Goodwrench Taz in lunch box/4008
2001 #29 Goodwrench AOL/3888
2001 #29 Goodwrench/4272
2002 #29 Sylvania/1800
2002 #29 Sonic/1584
2002 #29 Goodwrench Taz/1584
2002 #29 Goodwrench Now Sell Tires/2304
2002 #29 Goodwrench ET/4008
2002 #29 Goodwrench/4500
2002 #29 Action ET/2304
2002 #2K2 Childress Racing Pit Practice/2448
2003 #21 Payday/1300
2003 #29 Snap-On/1588
2003 #29 Goodwrench Sugar Ray/1300
2003 #29 Goodwrench/2028
2004 #21 Hershey's Kisses/1008
2004 #21 Reese's/1008
2004 #29 Coke C2/576
2004 #29 Goodwrench/1584
2004 #29 Goodwrench Realtree/1296
2004 #29 Snap-On/1008
2004 #29 Ice Breakers/720
2004 #29 Goodwrench RCR 35th Ann/1008
2004 #29 Goodwrench KISS/1584
2005 #21 Hershey's Take 5/576
2005 #29 Goodwrench Brickyard/576
2005 #29 Goodwrench 20th Anniversary/576
2005 #29 Goodwrench Daytona/864
2005 #29 Goodwrench Atlanta/720
2005 #29 Goodwrench/864
2006 #29 Reese's Caramel
2006 #29 Reese's/288
2006 #29 Hershey's Kissables/432
2006 #29 Hershey's/360
2006 #29 Goodwrench/432

Action/RCCA Banks 1:24
2000 #2 AC Delco/2004
2001 #2 AC Delco/1200
2001 #29 Goodwrench Taz/3200
2001 #29 Goodwrench Oreo Show car Bank/2004
2001 #29 Goodwrench AOL/2504
2001 #29 Goodwrench/3000

Action/RCCA Dually Trucks with Trailer
2001 #29 Goodwrench Taz/2508
2003 #29 Snap-On/8904

Action/RCCA Elite 1:24
2000 #2 AC Delco/1008
2001 #2 AC Delco/804
2001 #2 AC Delco Color Chrome/1200
2001 #29 Goodwrench AOL/4008
2001 #29 Goodwrench Taz/5996
2001 #29 Goodwrench Oreo Show car/4200
2001 #29 Goodwrench Make a Wish Found./2496
2001 #29 Goodwrench Split Clear/5004
2001 #29 Goodwrench/4996
2002 #29 Sylvania/1500
2002 #29 Sonic/1008
2002 #29 Goodwrench Taz/1800
2002 #29 Goodwr.Test Gray/3000
2002 #29 Goodwrench Now Sell Tires/3000
2002 #29 Goodwrench ET/4212
2002 #29 Goodwrench/7500
2002 #29 Action ET/2004
2002 #2K2 Childress Racing Pit Practice/1200
2003 #21 Payday/1500
2003 #29 Goodwrench Sugar Ray/1008
2003 #29 Goodwrench Raced/444
2003 #29 Goodwrench/2500
2003 #29 Snap-On/2004
2004 #21 Reese's RCR 35th Anniversary/444

2004 #21 Reese's Las Vegas Raced/240
2004 #21 Reese's/1200
2004 #21 Meijer Reese's White/288
2004 #21 Hershey's Kisses/1008
2004 #29 Snap-On/1200
2004 #29 Powerade/600
2004 #29 Ice Breakers/804
2004 #29 Goodwrench Realtree/1500
2004 #29 Goodwrench RCR 35th Ann./1200
2004 #29 Goodwrench KISS/1500
2004 #29 Goodwrench Color Chrome/600
2004 #29 Goodwrench/1500
2004 #29 ESGR Coast Guard/600
2004 #29 Coke C2/600
2005 #21 Twizzlers/204
2005 #21 Reese's/288
2005 #21 Pelon Pelo Rico/360
2005 #21 Hershey's Take 5/504
2005 #29 Goodwrench Gretchen Wilson White Gold/25
2005 #29 Goodwrench 20th Anniversary/444
2005 #29 Goodwrench 20th Ann. White Gold/25
2005 #29 Reese's Big Cup/204
2005 #29 Goodwrench Test/600
2005 #29 Goodwrench Quicksilver White Gold/25
2005 #29 Goodwrench Quicksilver
2005 #29 Goodwrench Hometown Brushed Bronze/144
2005 #29 Goodwrench Gretchen Wilson/444
2005 #29 Goodwrench Daytona White Gold/48
2005 #29 Goodwrench Daytona AU/144
2005 #29 Goodwrench Daytona/900
2005 #29 Goodwrench Brickyard White Gold/30
2005 #29 Goodwrench Brickyard/504
2005 #29 Goodwrench Atlanta White Gold/29
2005 #29 Goodwrench Atlanta AU/144
2005 #29 Goodwrench Atlanta/600
2005 #29 Goodwrench Bristol Raced/204
2005 #29 Goodwrench White Gold/30
2005 #29 Goodwrench Color Chrome/360
2005 #29 Goodwrench AU/144
2005 #29 Goodwrench/804
2006 #21 Coast Guard Reserve Richmond Raced Platinum/4
2006 #21 Coast Guard Reserve Richmond Raced/200
2006 #21 Coast Guard Platinum/2
2006 #21 Coast Guard/120
2006 #29 Goodwrench Barenaked Ladies Richmond Raced/250
2006 #29 Goodwrench Barenaked Ladies Richmond Raced Platinum/5
2006 #29 Reese's Caramel White Gold/25
2006 #29 Reese's Caramel Platinum/4
2006 #29 Reese's Caramel/240
2006 #29 Reese's White Gold/25
2006 #29 Reese's Platinum/4
2006 #29 Reese's/240
2006 #29 Hershey's Kissables White Gold/25
2006 #29 Hershey's Kissables Platinum/4
2006 #29 Hershey's Kissables/240
2006 #29 Hershey's White Gold/25
2006 #29 Hershey's Platinum/8
2006 #29 Hershey's/429
2006 #29 Goodwrench Holiday White Gold/25
2006 #29 Goodwrench Holiday Platinum/5
2006 #29 Goodwrench Holiday/250
2006 #29 Goodwrench White Gold/25
2006 #29 Goodwrench Platinum/8
2006 #29 Goodwrench Color Chrome/144
2006 #29 Goodwrench/408
2006 #33 Dollar General/100
2006 #33 Dollar General Platinum/2

Action/RCCA Elite 1:64
2001 #29 Goodwrench Taz/3024
2001 #29 Goodwrench AOL/3000
2001 #29 Goodwrench/2160
2002 #29 Sylvania/1200
2002 #29 Sonic/1536-A
2002 #29 Goodwrench Taz/1200
2002 #29 Goodwrench ET/3400
2002 #29 Goodwrench Now Sell Tires/2004
2002 #29 Goodwrench/4000
2002 #29 Action ET/2016
2002 #2K2 Childress Racing Pit Practice/2160
2003 #21 Payday/1156
2003 #29 Snap-On/1300
2003 #29 Goodwrench Sugar Ray/1012
2003 #29 Goodwrench/1588
2004 #21 Reese's/720
2004 #21 Hershey's Kisses/720
2004 #29 Snap-On/720
2004 #29 Ice Breakers/528
2004 #29 Goodwrench Realtree/1008
2004 #29 Goodwrench RCR 35th Ann./576
2004 #29 Goodwrench KISS/1008
2004 #29 Goodwrench/1008
2005 #21 Hershey's Take 5/480
2005 #29 Goodwrench/576
2005 #29 Goodwrench Atlanta/576
2005 #29 Goodwrench Brickyard/480
2005 #29 Goodwrench Daytona/576
2005 #29 Goodwrench 20th Anniversary/480
2006 #29 Hershey's Kissables/144
2006 #29 Reese's Caramel
2006 #29 Reese's/144
2006 #29 Hershey's/240
2006 #29 Goodwrench/240

Action/RCCA Historical Series 1:24
2004 #29 Goodwrench Service Plus '01 MC black numbers/1008

Action/RCCA Historical Series 1:64
2004 #29 Goodwrench Service Plus '01 MC black numbers/1296

Action/RCCA Historical Series Elite 1:2
2004 #29 Goodwrench Service Plus '01 MC black numbers Plat./300
2004 #29 Goodwrench Service Plus '01 MC black numbers/1500

Action/RCCA Historical Series Elite 1:6
2004 #29 Goodwrench Service Plus '01 MC black numbers/720

Action/RCCA Metal Elite 1:24
2004 #29 Goodwrench/1200

Action/RCCA Transporters 1:64
2003 #29 Snap-On/600

Brookfield 1:24
2005 #29 Goodwrench Daytona/300
2005 #29 Goodwrench 20th Anniversary/204
2005 #29 Goodwrench Atlanta/300
2005 #29 Goodwrench/360

Brookfield Dually with Car and Show Tra
2002 #29 Goodwrench Silver/1192
2002 #29 Goodwrench/4924

Brookfield Sets 1:24
1994-03 #29 Goodwrench QVC 2-cars/2000 '01

Brookfield Suburbans, Blazers, and Taho
2001 #29 Goodwrench Taz/4008
2002 #29 Goodwrench Incentive/386
2002 #29 Goodwrench/4428

Brookfield Trackside 1:25
2001 #29 Goodwrench Taz/2508
2002 #29 Goodwrench Color Chrome/1708
2004 #29 Snap On RCR 35th Ann./2508

Brookfield Trackside 1:64
2004 #21 Hershey's Kisses/3504
2004 #29 Goodwrench/3924

Hot Wheels Racing Color Change 1:64
2003 #29 Snap-On
2003 #29 Goodwrench
2004 #29 Goodwrench

Hot Wheels Racing Power Launchers 1:64
2003 #29 Goodwrench

Hot Wheels Racing Stockerz 1:24
2004 #29 Goodwrench

Hot Wheels Racing Stockerz 1:64
2004 #29 Goodwrench

Motorsports Authentics Driver's Select
2007 #21 Auto Zone Daytona Raced/1908*
2007 #21 Auto Zone/2208*
2007 #21 Auto Zone
2007 #21 Auto Zone/396
2007 #29 Shell Pennzoil Holiday Sam Bass/1129*
2007 #29 Shell Pennzoil COT/10,008*
2007 #29 Shell Pennzoil Daytona Raced Liquid Chrome/729
2007 #29 Shell Pennzoil Daytona Raced/7029*
2007 #29 Shell Pennzoil/13,924*
2007 #29 Reese's/3000*
2007 #29 Pennzoil Platinum COT/2700*
2007 #29 Pennzoil Platinum All Star Charlotte Raced/3255*
2007 #29 Reese's Elvis/723*
2007 #29 Shell Pennzoil COT
2007 #29 Shell Pennzoil
2007 #29 Pennzoil Platinum COT
2007 #29 Shell Pennzoil COT/1500
2007 #29 Shell Pennzoil/2004
2007 #29 Reese's COT/720
2007 #29 Pennzoil Platinum COT/2700
2007 #33 Road Loans/1120*
2007 #33 Road Loans/288
2007 #21/29 Auto Zone Daytona Raced Shell Pennzoil Daytona Raced 2-car set

Motorsports Authentics Owner's Elite 1:
2007 #21 Coast Guard '06 NBS Champion Liquid Color/541
2007 #29 Shell Pennzoil Test/1008*
2007 #29 Shell Pennzoil Holiday Sam Bass/504
2007 #29 Shell Pennzoil COT/1008
2007 #29 Shell Pennzoil Daytona Raced White Gold/50*
2007 #29 Shell Pennzoil Daytona Raced Platinum/25
2007 #29 Shell Pennzoil Daytona Raced/1200*
2007 #29 Shell Pennzoil White Gold/100
2007 #29 Shell Pennzoil Platinum/25
2007 #29 Shell Pennzoil/1008*
2007 #29 Pennzoil Platinum COT/504*
2007 #29 Pennzoil Platinum All Star Win/708*
2007 #29 Shell Pennzoil COT Platinum/25
2007 #29 Shell Pennzoil COT White Gold/50*
2007 #29 Shell Pennzoil/2007*

Motorsports Authentics Owner's Elite Tr
2007 #21 Coast Guard '06 BGN Champ Color Chrome/96*
2007 #29 Shell Pennzoil Daytona Raced/729*
2007 #29 Shell Pennzoil/1500*

Motorsports Authentics Pit Stop 1:64
2007 #21 Auto Zone
2007 #29 Pennzoil Platinum COT
2007 #29 Shell Pennzoil COT
2007 #29 Shell Pennzoil
2007 #29 Reese's

Motorsports Authentics Pit Stop Blister
2007 #29 Shell Pennzoil

Motorsports Authentics QVC For Race Fan
2007 #29 Shell Pennzoil COT Platinum/108
2007 #29 Shell Pennzoil COT Mesma Chrome/288
2007 #29 Shell Pennzoil COT Gold/108
2007 #29 Shell Pennzoil COT Copper/504
2007 #29 Shell Pennzoil COT Color Chrome/1500
2007 #29 Shell Pennzoil COT
2007 #29 Shell Pennzoil Daytona Raced Copper/504
2007 #29 Shell Pennzoil Daytona Raced Color Chrome/1500
2007 #29 Shell Pennzoil Platinum/108
2007 #29 Shell Pennzoil Mesma Chrome/504
2007 #29 Shell Pennzoil Gold/108
2007 #29 Shell Pennzoil Copper/504
2007 #29 Shell Pennzoil Color Chrome/1500
2007 #29 Shell Pennzoil Chrome/504
2007 #29 Reese's Color Chrome/504
2007 #29 Reese's/1008

Motorsports Authentics Steel 1:16
2006 #29 Goodwrench/250

Motorsports Authentics/RCCA Owner's Clu
2007 #29 Shell Pennzoil/1500*

Motorsports Authentics/RCCA Transporter
2007 #29 Shell Pennzoil/708*

Racing Champions 1:24
1999 #98 Porter-Cable SuperTruck Promo

Racing Champions 1:64
1999 #98 Porter-Cable SuperTruck Promo

Racing Champions SuperTrucks 1:64
1998 #75 Spears

RCCA Club 1:24
2008 #29 Pennzoil Platinum/150
2008 #29 Shell/300

RCCA Elite 1:24
2008 #29 Reese's/708
2008 #29 Shell/708
2008 #29 Shell Platinum/25
2008 #29 Shell White Gold/50
2008 #29 Penzoil Platinum/300
2008 #29 Penzoil Platinum Platinum/25
2008 #29 Pennzoil Platinum White Gold/50

Revell Club 1:24
2001 #29 Goodwrench/1500

Revell Collection 1:24
2001 #29 Goodwr.Taz Bank/3504
2001 #29 Goodwrench Taz with figure/10,044
2001 #29 Goodwr.Chicago win
2001 #29 Good.Atlanta Win/17,000
2002 #29 Goodwrench Test/7584
2004 #21 Reese's Raced/3504
2005 #29 Goodwrench Test/816

Revell Select 1:24
2002 #29 Goodwrench Taz
2002 #29 Goodwrench ET
2002 #29 Goodwrench

Winner's Circle 1:18
2002 #29 Goodwrench
2003 #29 Goodwrench
2004 #21 Hershey's Kisses
2004 #29 Goodwrench
2004 #29 Coke C2
2005 #21 Hershey's
2005 #29 Goodwrench
2005 #29 Goodwrench Atlanta
2005 #29 Goodwrench Daytona

Winner's Circle 1:24
2001 #29 Goodwrench White
2001 #29 Goodwrench Taz
2002 #29 Reese's Fast Break
2002 #29 Goodwrench Taz
2002 #29 Goodwrench ET
2002 #29 Goodwrench
2002 #29 Action ET
2003 #29 Goodwrench Taz
2004 #21 Reese's
2004 #21 Hershey's Kisses
2004 #29 Powerade
2004 #29 Goodwrench RCR 35th Anniversary
2004 #29 Goodwrench Realtree
2004 #29 Goodwrench KISS
2004 #29 Goodwrench
2004 #29 Coke C2
2005 #21 Hershey's Take 5
2005 #21 Reese's
2005 #29 Goodwrench Quicksilver
2005 #29 Goodwrench Gretchen Wilson
2005 #29 Goodwrench Brickyard
2005 #29 Goodwrench Daytona
2005 #29 Goodwrench Atlanta
2005 #29 Goodwrench
2006 #29 Goodwrench
2007 #29 Shell Pennzoil
2007 #29 Shell Pennzoil Daytona Raced
2008 #29 Shell

Winner's Circle 1:87
2007 #29 Shell Pennzoil
2008 #29 Shell Pennzoil

Winner's Circle Autographed Hood 1:64
2002 #29 Reese's Fast Break
2002 #29 Goodwrench ET
2002 #29 Action ET
2003 #21 Payday
2004 #21 Reese's 35th Ann. RCR
2004 #21 Reese's
2004 #21 Hershey's Kisses
2004 #29 Powerade
2004 #29 Goodwrench RCR 35th Anniversary
2004 #29 Goodwrench Realtree
2004 #29 Goodwrench KISS
2004 #29 Goodwrench
2004 #29 ESGR Coast Guard short package
2004 #29 Coke C2
2005 #21 Pelon Pelo Rico
2005 #21 Hershey's Take 5
2005 #29 Reese's Big Cup
2005 #29 Goodwrench Gretchen Wilson
2005 #29 Goodwrench Brickyard
2005 #29 Goodwrench

Winner's Circle Award Winners 1:64
2006 #21 Coast Guard '06 Busch Champion

Winner's Circle Daytona 500 1:24
2008 #29 Shell Pennzoil

Winner's Circle Daytona 500 1:87
2008 #29 Shell Pennzoil

Winner's Circle Daytona 500 2-car sets
2008 #29/08 Shell Pennzoil Daytona 500 Event Car

Winner's Circle Daytona 500 Hoods 1:64
2008 #29 Shell Pennzoil

Winner's Circle Daytona 500 Transporter
2008 #29 Shell Pennzoil

Winner's Circle Die-Cast Kits 1:24
2002 #29 Goodwrench

Winner's Circle Die-Cast Kits 1:64
2002 #29 Goodwrench

Winner's Circle Double Platinum 1:43
2001 #29 Goodwrench Taz
2002 #29 Goodwrench Taz
2002 #29 Goodwrench
2002 #29 Reese's Fast Break
2003 #21 Payday
2003 #29 Goodwrench Taz

Winner's Circle Driver Photo Hood 1:64
2005 #29 Goodwrench Quicksilver

Winner's Circle Driver Sticker 1:64
2002 #2 AC Delco '01 BGN Champ
2002 #29 Goodwrench White 2001 Rookie of the Year
2002 #29 Goodwrench Taz
2003 #29 Goodwrench Taz
2004 #29 Goodwrench
2004 #29 Goodwrench '01 black number

Winner's Circle Dually w/Car on Tracksi
2008 #29 Shell

Winner's Circle Fast Pack 1:64
2002 #29/30/31 J.Green/R.Gordon

Winner's Circle Gallery 1:64
2001 #29 Goodwrench Taz
2002 #29 Goodwrench

Winner's Circle Gift Pack 1:64
2002 #29 Goodwrench White/Taz Goodwrench Silver

Winner's Circle License Plate 1:64
2007 #29 Reese's

Winner's Circle Medallion 1:64
2007 #29 Shell Pennzoil

Winner's Circle Number Magnet 1:64
2008 #29 Shell

Winner's Circle Pit Pass Preview 1:64
2002 #29 Goodwrench Silver
2003 #29 Goodwrench
2004 #29 Goodwrench

Winner's Circle Pit Sign 1:64
2007 #29 Shell Pennzoil Test

Winner's Circle Race Hood 1:43
2002 #29 Goodwrench Taz
2002 #29 Goodwrench
2002 #29 Reese's Fast Break
2003 #21 Payday
2003 #29 Goodwrench Taz

Winner's Circle Race Hood 1:64
2001-02 #2 AC Delco
2001-02 #29 Goodwrench White
2001-02 #29 AOL

Winner's Circle Sam Bass Hoods 1:64
2007 #29 Shell Pennzoil Holiday

Winner's Circle Schedule Hood 1:64
2005 #21 Reese's
2005 #21 Hershey's Take 5

Winner's Circle Schedule Hoods 1:64
2008 #29 Shell Pennzoil

Winner's Circle Sticker 1:64
2006 #29 Goodwrench

Winner's Circle Stickers 1:64
2008 #29 Shell

Winner's Circle Test Hood 1:64
2005 #29 Goodwrench

Winner's Circle Transporters 1:64
2001 #29 Goodwrench Taz
2001 #29 Goodwrench White
2002 #29 Goodwrench Taz
2003 #29 Goodwrench Taz
2003 #29 Goodwrench
2004 #21 Hershey's Kisses
2004 #29 Goodwrench
2005 #21 Take 5
2005 #21 Reese's
2005 #29 Goodwrench
2006 #29 Hershey's
2007 #29 Shell Pennzoil
2008 #29 Shell

Winner's Circle Victory Lane Hoods 1:64
2007 #29 Shell Pennzoil Daytona Raced
2007 #29 Pennzoil Platinum Charlotte Raced

Jarrett, Dale

Action Clearly Collectibles 1:24
2005 #88 Raced Sheet Metal/200

Action Performance 1:24
1999 #88 Quality Care
2000 #88 Quality Care
2001 #88 UPS
2002 #88 UPS employee/5004
2002 #88 UPS
2003 #88 UPS
2005 #88 UPS Herbie
2005 #88 UPS Hometown
2006 #88 UPS in AP box

Action Performance 1:64
1999 #88 Quality Care
2000 #88 Quality Care
2001 #88 UPS
2002 #88 UPS
2003 #88 UPS
2005 #88 UPS

Action QVC For Race Fans Only 1:24
2001 #88 UPS Flames Platinum/624
2001 #88 UPS Flames Gold./2000
2001 #88 UPS Flames Color Chrome/2508
2001 #88 UPS Platinum/624
2001 #88 UPS Gold/2000
2002 #88 UPS Muppets Color Chrome/2508
2002 #88 UPS Color Chrome/1000

Action Racing Collectables 1:18
1998 #88 Batman
1999 #88 Quality Care
2000 #88 Qual.Care Air Force
2000 #88 Quality Care/2004
2001 #88 UPS Flames/3000

Action Racing Collectables 1:24
1994 #28 Havoline Bank
1995 #28 Havoline Bank/7992
1996 #88 Quality Care
1997 #32 White Rain Bank/7956
1997 #88 Quality Care Brickyard/7500
1997 #88 Qual.Care Mac Tools/4000
1997 #88 Quality Care/5960
1998 #32 White Rain/6000
1998 #88 Batman Bank
1998 #88 Batman
1998 #88 Quality Care Bank
1998 #88 Quality Care
1999 #11 Rayovac
1999 #11 Green Bay Packers/6084
1999 #88 Qual.Care Mac Tools/5004
1999 #88 Quality Care Bank/2508
1999 #88 Quality Care/14,508
1999 #88 Quality Care Gold QVC Race Fans/2508
1999 #88 Qual.Care Last Lap Bank
1999 #88 Qual.Care Last Lap/12,000
1999 #88 Quality Care White Bank
1999 #88 Quality Care White/8208
2000 #21 Citgo '91 T-bird/3216
2000 #32 Nestle '90 Grand Prix/3000
2000 #88 Qua.Care Last Ride/5008
2000 #88 Quality Care Air Force Bank/2508
2000 #88 Qual.Care Air Force
2000 #88 Quality Care Bank/2508
2000 #88 Quality Care
2001 #88 UPS Flames Clear/7000
2001 #88 UPS Flames/48,780
2001 #88 UPS Split Clear/3500
2001 #88 UPS Flag/12,000
2001 #88 UPS Employee Promo
2001 #88 UPS Clear/6792
2001 #88 UPS Chrome/1020
2001 #88 UPS Bank
2001 #88 UPS Mac Tools/4008
2001 #88 UPS/28,524
2002 #88 UPS Muppet Bank/1200
2002 #88 UPS Muppet/28,140
2002 #88 UPS Color Chrome Bank/2508
2002 #88 UPS Clear/6180
2002 #88 UPS/42,052
2003 #7 True Value '01 IROC AU/3864
2003 #11 True Value IROC Blue/6648
2003 #88 UPS Victory Lap CW Bank/372
2003 #88 UPS Victory Lap/6252
2003 #88 UPS Store Mac Tools/288
2003 #88 UPS Store CW Bank/396
2003 #88 UPS Store/5028
2003 #88 UPS Brn.Yell.Logo Clear/1752
2003 #88 UPS Brown&Yell.Logo BW Bank/790
2003 #88 UPS Brn.Yell.Logo/11,832
2003 #88 UPS Brown Logo BW Bank/780
2003 #88 UPS Brown Logo/11,184
2004 #88 UPS Monsters QVC/288
2004 #88 UPS Monsters Mac Tools/204
2004 #88 UPS Monsters CW Bank/240
2004 #88 UPS Monsters/3000
2004 #88 UPS Bud Shootout Raced w/tire/4188
2004 #88 UPS Arnold Palmer CW Bank/312
2004 #88 UPS Arnold Palmer/6024
2004 #88 UPS Nextel Incentive/2004
2004 #88 UPS CW Bank/324
2004 #88 UPS/7440
2005 #88 UPS Clear/504
2005 #88 UPS Mac Tools/108
2005 #88 UPS Herbie CW Bank/192
2005 #88 UPS Herbie/3624
2005 #88 UPS Talladega Raced w/tire/1500
2005 #88 UPS QVC/360
2005 #88 UPS Matco/96
2005 #88 UPS/2664
2005 #88 UPS Test QVC/144
2005 #88 UPS Test/612
2005 #88 UPS Store Toys for Tots/4008
2005 #88 UPS Star Wars Matco/48
2005 #88 UPS Star Wars CW Bank/192
2005 #88 UPS Star Wars/4908
2005 #88 UPS Mother's Day QVC/288
2005 #88 UPS Mother's Day Matco/24
2005 #88 UPS Mother's Day Mac Tools/108
2005 #88 UPS Mother's Day CW Bank/168
2005 #88 UPS Mother's Day/2664
2005 #88 UPS Herbie QVC/504
2005 #88 UPS Herbie Matco/24
2005 #90 Citifinancial
2006 #88 UPS Freight/3104
2006 #88 UPS QVC/504
2006 #88 UPS Matco/48
2006 #88 UPS Mac Tools/300
2006 #88 UPS/5244

Action Racing Collectables 1:32
1998-01 #88 UPS
1998-01 #88 UPS Flames
1998-01 #88 UPS Flames Van/4008
1998-01 #88 Quality Care '98
1998-01 #88 Batman '98

Action Racing Collectables 1:43
2003 #88 UPS Store promo in window box
2005 #88 UPS Store Toys for Tots Promo in wind.box

Action Racing Collectables 1:64
1995 #28 Havoline/29,808
1996 #88 Quality Care
1997 #32 White Rain/10,080
1997 #88 Quality Care Brickyard/14,256
1997 #88 Quality Care
1998 #32 White Rain Promo blister
1998 #32 White Rain
1998 #88 Batman
1998 #88 Quality Care
1999 #11 Green Bay
1999 #11 Rayovac
1999 #88 Quality Care Last Lap
1999 #88 Quality Care and Quality Care White 2-Car Tin
1999 #88 Quality Care White/14,976
1999 #88 Quality Care/14,876
1999 #28/88 K.Irwin/Batman & Joker
2000 #88 Qual.Care Air Force
2000 #88 Quality Care/20,016
2000 #NNO Armed Forces 5-car set Gold
2000 #NNO Armed Forces 5-car set Promo blister
2001 #88 UPS Flames/37,224
2001 #88 UPS/23,112
2002 #88 UPS Van Color Chrome/22,752
2002 #88 UPS Muppet/22,824
2002 #88 UPS/38,088
2003 #88 UPS Victory Lap/8820
2003 #88 UPS Store/4320
2003 #88 UPS/10,584
2004 #88 UPS Halloween/5040
2004 #88 UPS Arnold Palmer/8400 with golf ball
2004 #88 UPS Arnold Palmer/8400
2004 #88 UPS/6144
2005 #88 UPS Store Toys for Tots
2005 #88 UPS Herbie
2005 #88 UPS
2006 #88 UPS

Action Racing Collectables Advanced Pro
2008 #44 UPS All-Star/144

Action Racing Collectables Ceramic 1
2000-01 #88 Quality Care Air Force '00

Action Racing Collectables Fan Fueler 1
1998 #88 Quality Care

Action Racing Collectables Historical S
2005 #18 Interstate Batteries '93 Lumina/3300

Action Racing Collectables Pit Wagon
1990-03 #18 Interstate Batteries
1990-03 #88 Quality Care Batman

Action Racing Collectables Transporters
2001 #88 UPS/2004
2003 #88 UPS Promo in window box
2003 #88 UPS
2004 #88 UPS

Action Total Concept 1:64
2000 #88 Qual.Care Air Force

Action/Funline Monster Truck 1:43
2004 #88 UPS

Action/Funline Muscle Machines 1:18
2004 #88 Jarrett '49 Mercury
2004 #88 Jarrett '66 Mustang
2005 #88 UPS '66 Mustang
2005 #88 UPS Herbie '49 Mercury
2005 #88 UPS Star Wars '40 Delivery Van/448

Action/Funline Muscle Machines 1:24
2004 #88 UPS '49 Mercury
2004 #88 UPS '66 Mustang
2005 #88 UPS Hybrid/240

Action/RCCA 1:24
1994 #18 Interstate Batteries/2608
1995 #28 Havoline/5016
1996 #88 Quality Care Bank
1997 #32 White Rain
1997 #88 Quality Care Bank/5000
2002 #88 UPS Muppet Bank/1500
2002 #88 UPS Bank/2004
2003 #11 True Value '02 IROC Blue AU/360
2003 #11 True Value '02 IROC Blue/360
2003 #88 UPS Victory Lap/408
2003 #88 UPS Store/504
2003 #88 UPS Br.Yell.Logo Split Clear/504
2003 #88 UPS Brown Logo CW Bank/600
2004 #88 UPS Arnold Palmer/600
2004 #88 UPS Monsters/540
2004 #88 UPS Raced w/tire/240
2004 #88 UPS/300
2005 #88 UPS Herbie/600
2005 #88 UPS Hometown Brushed Bronze/144
2005 #88 UPS Store Toys for Tots/360
2005 #88 UPS Test/360
2005 #88 UPS Star Wars/444
2005 #88 UPS Mother's Day/288
2005 #88 UPS Color Chrome/204
2005 #88 UPS/444
2005 #90 CitiFinancial/240
2006 #88 UPS Color Chrome/120
2006 #88 UPS Freight/200
2006 #88 UPS/288

Action/RCCA 1:32
2003 #88 Race For a Cure

Action/RCCA 1:64
1994 #18 Interstate Batteries/10,000
1995 #28 Havoline
1996 #88 Quality Care
1997 #32 White Rain/3500
1997 #88 Quality Care/5000
1998 #32 White Rain/2500
1998 #88 Batman
1998 #88 Quality Care/5000
1999 #11 Green Bay Packers/2500
1999 #88 Quality Care White
2000 #88 Quality Care
2001 #88 UPS
2002 #88 UPS Muppet/2196
2002 #88 UPS/2880
2003 #88 UPS Store/1008
2003 #88 UPS/1184
2004 #88 UPS Monsters/576
2004 #88 UPS Arnold Palmer with golf ball/720
2004 #88 UPS/504
2005 #88 UPS Store Toys for Tots/408
2005 #88 UPS Herbie/720
2005 #88 UPS/576
2006 #88 UPS/432

Action/RCCA Banks 1:24
1998 #32 White Rain/2000
1998 #88 Quality Care No Bull/2500
1998 #88 Quality Care Batman/7500
1998 #88 Quality Care/5000
1999 #11 Green Bay Packers/1500
1999 #88 Quality Care White/2500
1999 #88 Quality Care Last Lap
1999 #88 Quality Care No Bull
1999 #88 Quality Care/2500
2000 #88 Qual.Care Air Force/4500
2001 #88 UPS Flames/1836
2001 #88 UPS/2700
Action/RCCA Dually Trucks 1:24
1994 #18 Interstate Batteries PLS Bank/4248
1995 #28 Havoline PLS Bank/4248
1996 #88 Qual.Care PLS Bank/3500
Action/RCCA Dually Trucks 1:64
1994-97 #18 Inter.Batt.RCCA/7875 '94
1994-97 #28 Havoline '94
Action/RCCA Dually Trucks with Trailer
1994 #18 Interstate Batteries
1994 #28 Havoline
1998 #88 Batman PLS/3500
Action/RCCA Elite 1:24
1997 #32 White Rain
1997 #88 Quality Care/2000
1998 #88 Qual.Care No Bull/1200
1998 #88 Quality Care
1998 #88 Batman/5000
1998 #88 Quality Care Proto
1999 #11 Green Bay Packers
1999 #88 Qual.Care Last Lap/1000
1999 #88 Quality Care White/1000
1999 #88 Quality Care/1000
2000 #18 Freedlander '87 MC/492
2000 #21 Citgo '91 T-bird/804
2000 #32 Nestle '90 Grand Prix/492
2000 #88 UPS Test/2508
2000 #88 Qua.Care Last Ride/600
2000 #88 Qual.Care Air Force/2004
2000 #88 Quality Care/1500
2001 #88 UPS Flames/3000
2001 #88 UPS Test/2508
2001 #88 UPS Chrome/2004
2001 #88 UPS/3204
2002 #88 UPS Metal/1500
2002 #88 UPS Muppet/2004
2002 #88 UPS/2800
2003 #88 UPS Victory Lap/408
2003 #88 UPS Store/504
2003 #88 UPS Color Chrome/408
2003 #88 UPS/1008
2004 #88 UPS Monsters White Gold/25
2004 #88 UPS Monsters/540
2004 #88 UPS Arnold Palmer/492
2004 #88 UPS Raced w/tire/240
2004 #88 UPS Color Chrome/300
2004 #88 UPS/300
2005 #88 UPS Store Toys for Tots/360
2005 #88 UPS Test/408
2005 #88 UPS Store Toys for Tots White Gold/25
2005 #88 UPS Star Wars White Gold/25
2005 #88 UPS Star Wars/600
2005 #88 UPS Mother's Day/288
2005 #88 UPS Hometown Brushed Bronze/144
2005 #88 UPS Herbie White Gold/28
2005 #88 UPS Herbie AU/144
2005 #88 UPS Herbie/600
2005 #88 UPS White Gold/25
2005 #88 UPS Color Chrome AU/59
2005 #88 UPS Color Chrome/240
2005 #88 UPS/504
2006 #88 UPS/408
2006 #88 UPS Platinum/8
2006 #88 UPS Freight Platinum/4
2006 #88 UPS Freight/200
2006 #88 UPS White Gold/25
2006 #88 UPS Color Chrome/120
Action/RCCA Elite 1:64
2001 #88 UPS Flames/1800
2001 #88 UPS
2002 #88 UPS Muppet/1800
2002 #88 UPS/1584
2003 #88 UPS/1020
2004 #88 UPS Monsters/528
2004 #88 UPS Arnold Palmer/528
2004 #88 UPS/504
2005 #88 UPS/480
2005 #88 UPS Herbie/576
2005 #88 UPS Store Toys for Tots/240
2006 #88 UPS/240
Action/RCCA Gold 1:32
1998 #88 Quality Care/700
Action/RCCA Revell 1:64
1991-92 #18 Interstate Batteries
Action/RCCA SelectNet Banks 1:24
1999 #11 Green Bay Packers/2500
Action/RCCA Total View 1:64
2000 #88 Qual.Care Air Force
Action/RCCA Transporters 1:64
1994 #28 Havoline
1995 #28 Havoline RCCA/4500
2001 #88 UPS Color Chr.RCCA/504
2006 #88 UPS White Pearl/200
Action/RCCA Transporters 1:96
1994-96 #28 Havoline PLS/4008
Brookfield Dually with Car and Show Tra
2000 #88 Quality Care Air Force Silver/628
2000 #88 Quality Care Air Force/1880
2000 #88 Qual.Care Silver/500
2000 #88 Quality Care/2008
2001 #88 UPS Silver/1200
2001 #88 UPS/1308
Brookfield Sets 1:24
1994-03 #88 Quality Care QVC 2-car set/2000 '00
Brookfield Trackside 1:25
1999 #88 Qual.Care White/1932
Brookfield Trackside 1:64
2004 #88 UPS/5004
Ertl 1:18
1992 #18 Interstate Batteries
1995 #28 Havoline/4000
1995 #32 Mac Tools/5000
1996 #88 Quality Care
Ertl 1:64
1986-93 #21 NDA/Citgo '90
Ertl Transporters 1:64
1990 #21 NDA/Citgo Wood Brothers
Ertl White Rose Transporters Past an
1992-94 #18 Interstate Batteries '92
Funstuf Pit Row 1:43
1992 #18 Interstate Batt.
Funstuf Pit Row 1:64
1992 #18 Interstate Batteries
1992 #21 Citgo Winston decal on fender
1992 #21 Citgo
Matchbox White Rose Super Stars 1:64
1993 #32 Pic-N-Pay BX
1994 #32 Pic-N-Pay BX
1995 #28 Havoline
1996 #88 Quality Care
1990-92 #18 Interstate Batt. BL 92
Matchbox White Rose Transporters Super
1992 #18 Interstate Batteries
1994 #32 Pic-N-Pay Shoes
1995 #28 Havoline
1996 #88 Quality Care
Miscellaneous Promos 1:24
1996 #32 Band-Aid DAJ Racing/5000
Motorsports Authentics Driver's Select
2007 #44 UPS 100th Ann.COT/1794*
2007 #44 UPS Toys for Tots/876*
2007 #44 UPS Kentucky Derby/3540*
2007 #44 UPS COT/2208*
2007 #44 UPS/9504*
Motorsports Authentics Owner's Elite 1:
2007 #44 UPS 100th Ann.COT/708*
2007 #44 UPS COT/504
2007 #44 UPS White Gold/50*
2007 #44 UPS Platinum/25
2007 #44 UPS/1008*
2007 #44 UPS/2007*
Motorsports Authentics Owner's Elite Tr
2007 #44 UPS/1000*
Motorsports Authentics Pit Stop 1:64
2007 #44 UPS Kentucky Derby
2007 #44 UPS
Motorsports Authentics QVC For Race Fan
2007 #44 UPS Mesma Chrome/504
2007 #44 UPS Copper/108
2007 #44 UPS Chrome/288
Motorsports Authentics/RCCA Owner's Clu
2007 #44 UPS/504*
Motorsports Authentics/RCCA Transporter
2007 #44 UPS/708*
Racing Champions 1:144
1996 #88 Quality Care
1997 #32 White Rain
Racing Champions 1:24
1993 #18 Interstate Batt.
1994 #18 Interstate Batt.
1995 #28 Havoline
1996 #88 Quality Care
1997 #32 Gillette
1997 #32 White Rain
1991-92 #18 Interstate Batteries
1991-92 #21 Citgo '91
Racing Champions 1:43
1991 #21 Citgo
1992 #18 Interstate Batt.
Racing Champions 1:64
1991 #21 Ford PB
1991 #21 Ford EB
1991 #NNO Daytona 5-car Military set
1992 #18 Interstate Batt.
1992 #21 Citgo
1993 #18 Interstate Batteries
1994 #18 Interstate Batt.
1995 #28 Havoline
1996 #32 Band-Aid Promo
1996 #88 Quality Care Chrome/1996
1996 #88 Quality Care
1996 #NNO 12-Car set in case
1997 #32 White Rain
Racing Champions 2-Car Sets 1:43
1991 #18/21 G.Trammell/D.Jarrett
Racing Champions 5-Pack 1:144
1997 #NNO 24.JG/32.DJ/40.SM/94.BE/97.CL
Racing Champions Banks 1:24
1995 #28 Havoline Hood Open
1995 #32 Mac Tools/4000
1995 #32 Band-Aid
1992-94 #18 Inter.Batt./10,000 '93
Racing Champions Hobby Yellow Box 1:64
1994 #18 Interstate Batt.
Racing Champions Hood Open Banks 1:24
1996 #88 Quality Care
Racing Champions NFL 1:64
1992 #18 Interstate Batteries Seattle Seahawks
1992 #18 Interstate Batteries NY Jets
1992 #18 Interstate Batteries NY Giants
1992 #18 Interstate Batteries Miami Dolphins
1992 #18 Interstate Batteries LA Rams
1992 #18 Interstate Batteries LA Raiders
1992 #18 Interstate Batteries Cleveland Browns
1992 #18 Interstate Batteries Cincinnati Bengals
1992 #18 Interstate Batteries Atlanta Falcons
1992 #18 Interstate Batteries St. Louis Cardinals
Racing Champions Premier 1:18
1996 #88 Quality Care
Racing Champions Premier 1:64
1993 #18 Interstate Batt./20,000
1994 #18 Interstate Batteries
1995 #28 Havoline
Racing Champions Premier Banks 1:24
1996 #88 Quality Care Chrome/166
1996 #88 Quality Care
Racing Champions Premier Brickyard 400
1994 #18 Interstate Batt.
Racing Champions Premier Hood Open 1:24
1996 #88 Quality Care
Racing Champions Premier Transporters 1
1993 #18 Interstate Batt.
1994 #32 Shoe World/2500
1995 #32 Mac Tools/3000
1996 #88 Quality Care
Racing Champions Premier with Medallion
1996 #88 Quality Care
Racing Champions Preview 1:64
1995 #28 Havoline
Racing Champions PVC Box 1:64
1993 #18 Interstate Batteries Daytona Win/10,000
Racing Champions Roaring Racers 1:64
1990-91 #21 Citgo SW '91
1990-91 #21 Citgo BW '91
Racing Champions To the Maxx 1:64
1995 #28 Havoline
Racing Champions Transporters 1:144
1995 #28 Havoline
1997 #32 White Rain
1991-92 #18 Interstate Batteries
Racing Champions Transporters 1:64
1992 #18 Interstate Batt.
1993 #18 Interstate Batt.
1995 #28 E.Irvan/Havoline
1996 #32 Band-Aid w/car(s)
1996 #88 Quality Care w/car(s)
1996 #88 Quality Care
1997 #32 White Rain
1997 #32 Gillette w/car(s)
1997 #32 Gillette
Racing Champions Transporters 1:87
1995 #28 E.Irvan/Havoline
1997 #32 White Rain
1997 #32 Gillette
Racing Champions Transporters Hobby 1:6
1994 #18 Interstate Batt.
Racing Champions Transporters Hobby 1:8
1994 #18 Interstate Batteries
Racing Champions Transporters Retail
1993-94 #18 Interstate Batt.
Racing Champions Transporters Retail 1:
1994 #18 Interstate Batt.
RCCA Club 1:24
2008 #44 UPS/300
2008 #44 UPS All Star/150
RCCA Elite 1:24
2008 #44 UPS/600
2008 #44 UPS All Star/444
2008 #44 UPS All Star Platinum/25
2008 #44 UPS All Star White Gold/50
2008 #44 UPS White Gold/50
2008 #44 UPS Platinum/25
Revell 1:24
1991-95 #18 Interstate Batteries
1991-95 #32 Mac Tools
Revell Club 1:18
1997 #88 Quality Care
1998 #88 Quality Care/504
1998 #88 Batman/1002
Revell Club 1:24
1998 #88 Quality Care
1998 #88 Batman
1999 #11 Green Bay Packers/1002
1999 #88 Quality Care White/1002
1999 #88 Quality Care
2000 #88 Qual.Care Air Force
2000 #88 Quality Care/1500
2001 #88 UPS
Revell Collection 1:18
1997 #88 Quality Care
1998 #88 Quality Care/3120
1998 #88 Batman/3120
Revell Collection 1:24
1996 #88 Quality Care/5004
1997 #32 White Rain
1997 #88 Quality Care
1998 #88 Quality Care
1998 #88 Batman Bank
1998 #88 Batman/6000
1999 #11 Green Bay Packers
1999 #11 Rayovac/2508
1999 #88 Quality Care Last Lap Mac Tools/5004
1999 #88 Quality Care White
1999 #88 Quality Care
2000 #88 Quality Care Air Force Bank set with 1:64 car
2000 #88 Qual.Care Air Force/3120
2000 #88 Quality Care
2001 #88 UPS Test/2508
2001 #88 UPS Darlington Win/14,372
2001 #88 UPS Color Chrome/1500
2001 #88 UPS/12,000
2004 #88 UPS Test/3504
Revell Collection 1:43
1997 #88 Quality Care/10,584
1998 #88 Batman/4008
1998 #88 Quality Care/5004
Revell Collection 1:64
1996 #88 Quality Care/10,574
1998 #88 Quality Care/10,080
1998 #88 Batman
1999 #11 Green Bay Packers/7992
1999 #88 Quality Care/10,080
2000 #88 Qual.Care Air Force/11,088
2000 #88 Quality Care
2001 #88 UPS
Revell Promos 1:64
1993-95 #32 Mac Tools blister '95
Revell Retail 1:24
1995 #32 Mac Tools Promo/5000
1996 #88 Quality Care
1997 #88 Quality Care
Revell Select 1:24
1998 #88 Quality Care
1999 #88 Quality Care Last Lap
Revell Select Hobby 1:24
1997 #32 White Rain
Scaleworks Transporters 1:24
1996-98 #88 Quality Care/2000 '96
Winner's Circle 1:18
2002 #88 UPS
2005 #88 UPS
Winner's Circle 1:24
1997 #88 Quality Care Red Carpet Lease on fender
1997 #88 Qual.Care Ford Credit fender
1998 #88 Quality Care Batman
1998 #88 Quality Care
1999 #88 Quality Care
2000 #88 Quality Care '99 Champ.
2000 #88 Quality Care Air Force
2000 #88 Quality Care
2001 #88 UPS Flames
2001 #88 UPS
2002 #88 UPS Muppets
2002 #88 UPS
2003 #88 UPS
2004 #88 UPS
2005 #88 UPS
2006 #88 UPS
2007 #44 UPS
2008 #44 UPS
Winner's Circle 1:43
1998 #88 Quality Care Batman
1998 #88 Quality Care
1999 #88 Qual.Care No Bull 5 Win
1999 #88 Qual.Care '99 Champ.
Winner's Circle 1:64
1997 #88 Quality Care
1998 #32 White Rain
1998 #88 Quality Care Speedweeks
1998 #88 Quality Care Million $ Win
1998 #88 Quality Care Batman
1998 #88 Quality Care
2000 #88 Qual.Care '99 Champ
Winner's Circle 1:87
2007 #44 UPS
2008 #44 UPS
Winner's Circle Autographed Hood 1:64
2002 #88 UPS Muppets
2004 #88 UPS
2004 #88 UPS Arnold Palmer
2005 #88 UPS Toys for Tots
2005 #88 UPS
Winner's Circle Cool Customs 1:64
1998-99 #88 Qual.Care '65 Galaxie
1998-99 #88 Qual.Care '56 Victoria
Winner's Circle Decade of Champions 1:6
2003 #88 Quality Care 1999
Winner's Circle Deluxe Driver Sticker 1
2000 #88 Qual.Care Air Force
Winner's Circle Deluxe Race Hood 1:64
2000 #88 Quality Care
Winner's Circle Deluxe Winston Cup Scen
2000 #88 Quality Care '99 Champ.
Winner's Circle Die-Cast Kits 1:24
2002 #88 UPS
Winner's Circle Die-Cast Kits 1:64
2002 #88 UPS Flames
2002 #88 UPS
Winner's Circle Double Platinum 1:43
2001 #88 UPS Flames
2002 #88 UPS Muppets
2003 #88 UPS
Winner's Circle Driver Sticker 1:64
2001 #88 UPS
2003 #88 UPS Flames
2003 #88 UPS
Winner's Circle Gallery 1:64
2002 #88 UPS
Winner's Circle Gift Pack 1:64
2002 #88 UPS '01/UPS '02 UPS Flames
Winner's Circle Lifetime Dale Jarrett
2001-02 #28 Havoline '95 1/4
2001-02 #88 Quality Care '96 3/4
Winner's Circle Micro Machines 1:144
1999 #24/28/88 K.Irwin/D.Jarrett
1999 #NNO 7-car Draft Pack
2000 #31/88 M.Skinner/D.Jarrett
Winner's Circle Pit Pass Preview 1:64
2002 #88 UPS
2003 #88 UPS
2004 #88 UPS
Winner's Circle Pit Row 1:64
1998 #88 Quality Care Batman
1998 #88 Qual.Care right side raised
Winner's Circle Pit Sign 1:64
2007 #44 UPS
Winner's Circle Race Hood 1:43
2002 #88 UPS Muppets
2003 #88 UPS brown logo
Winner's Circle Race Hood 1:64
2001-02 #88 UPS Flames '02
2001-02 #88 UPS
Winner's Circle Sam Bass 1:43
2000 #88 Quality Care
Winner's Circle Schedule Hood 1:64
2005 #88 UPS
2006 #88 UPS
Winner's Circle Sneak Previews 1:64
2000 #88 Quality Care
Winner's Circle Speedweeks 1:64
1999 #88 Quality Care
Winner's Circle Stats and Standings 1:6
1999 #88 Quality Care
Winner's Circle Tech Series 1:64
1998 #88 Quality Care
Winner's Circle Test Hood 1:64
2005 #88 UPS
Winner's Circle Transporters 1:64
2000 #88 Quality Care
2001 #88 UPS Flames Truck
2001 #88 UPS
2002 #88 UPS Muppets
2004 #88 UPS
2005 #88 UPS
2006 #88 UPS
2007 #44 UPS
Winner's Circle Victory Celebration 1:4
1999 #88 Quality Care No Bull 5-win 11/11/98
Winner's Circle Victory Lap 1:24
2003 #88 UPS Victory Lap
Winner's Circle Victory Lap 1:64
2003 #88 UPS Victory Lap
Winross Transporters 1:64
1993 #NNO Interstate Batteries
1995 #NNO Mac Tools/2600

Johnson, Jimmie

Action Clearly Collectibles 1:24
2005 #48 Las Vegas Raced Spark Plug/8
2005 #48 Las Vegas Raced Lugnut/100
2005 #48 Daytona Raced Lugnut/100
Action Performance 1:64
2004 #48 Lowe's Tool World/5040
2006 #48 Lowe's
Action QVC For Race Fans Only 1:24
2003 #48 Lowe's SpongeBob Platinum/624
2003 #48 Lowe's SpongeBob Gold/504
2003 #48 Lowe's SpongeBob Color Chrome/1008
2003 #48 Lowe's Power of Pride Platinum/624
2003 #48 Lowe's Power of Pride Gold/504
2006 #48 Lowe's SeaWorld Color Chrome/504
Action Racing Collectables 1:18
2002 #48 Lowe's Sylvester and Tweety/2268
2003 #48 Lowe.Pow.of Pride/1866
Action Racing Collectables 1:24
2000 #92 Alltel/3000
2001 #92 Excedrin/2016
2002 #48 Lowe's Sylvester and Tweety Bank/1140
2002 #48 Lowe's Sylvester and Tweety/25,212
2002 #48 Lowe's Power of Pride Bank
2002 #48 Lowe's Power of Pride/15,552
2002 #48 Lowe's/19,704
2003 #7 True Value IROC AU/3144
2003 #7 True Value IROC/2616
2003 #48 Lowe's SpongeBob CW Bank/948
2003 #48 Lowe's SpongeBob GM Dealer/504
2003 #48 Low.SpongeBob/15,672
2003 #48 Lowe's Power of Pride CW Bank/648
2003 #48 Lowe's Power of Pride/13,728
2003 #48 Lowe's GM Dealers/1008
2003 #48 Lowe's BW Bank/936
2003 #48 Lowe's/30,070
2004 #48 Lowe's Tool World CW Bank/240
2004 #48 Lowe's Tool World/2508
2004 #48 Lowe's SpongeBob CW Bank
2004 #48 Lowe's SpongeBob/2364
2004 #48 Lowe's HMS20th GM Dealers/180
2004 #48 Lowe's HMS20th CW Bank/300
2004 #48 Lowe's HMS20th/10,008
2004 #48 Lowe's Father's Day CW Bank/348
2004 #48 Lowe's Father's Day/3372
2004 #48 Lowe's Atlanta Raced QVC/804
2004 #48 Lowe's Atlanta Raced GM Dealers/852
2004 #48 Lowe's Atlanta Raced CW Bank/432
2004 #48 Lowe's Atlanta Raced/13,788
2004 #48 Lowe's Nextel Incentive/2004
2004 #48 Lowe's Mac Tools/288
2004 #48 Lowe's GM Dealers/1896
2004 #48 Lowe's CW Bank/384
2004 #48 Lowe's/9300
2004 #48 Crown Royal IROC/3792
2005 #48 Lowe's CW Bank/288
2005 #48 Lowe's Las Vegas Raced Mac Tools/300
2005 #48 Lowe's '06 Preview QVC/288
2005 #48 Lowe's '06 Preview GM Dealers/360
2005 #48 Lowe's '06 Preview/6000
2005 #48 Lowe's Test Chad Knaus AU/2508
2005 #48 Lowe's Kobalt GM Dealers/180
2005 #48 Lowe's Kobalt/1848
2005 #48 Lowe's Las Vegas Raced QVC/144
2005 #48 Lowe's Las Vegas Raced/2772
2005 #48 Lowe's QVC/504
2005 #48 Lowe's Matco/84
2005 #48 Lowe's GM Dealers/780
2005 #48 Lowe's/3660
2006 #48 Lowe's '06 Nextel Champ GM Dealers/696
2006 #48 Lowe's '06 Nextel Champion/LE
2006 #48 Lowe's 60th Ann. GM Dealers/564
2006 #48 Lowe's 60th Ann./3036
2006 #48 Lowe's Sea World QVC*
2006 #48 Lowe's Sea World Matco*
2006 #48 Lowe's Sea World GM Dealers/552
2006 #48 Lowe's Sea World/8556*
2006 #48 Lowe's JJ Foundation GM Dealers/1500
2006 #48 Lowe's JJ Foundation/1500*
2006 #48 Lowe's Holiday GM Dealers/288
2006 #48 Lowe's Holiday/840
2006 #48 Lowe's Flames Test Matco*
2006 #48 Lowe's Flames Test GM Dealers/216
2006 #48 Lowe's Flames Test/3552*
2006 #48 Lowe's Daytona Raced w/tire GM Dealers/336
2006 #48 Lowe's Daytona Raced w/tire/1872
2006 #48 Lowe's Matco/120
2006 #48 Lowe's Mac Tools/504
2006 #48 Lowe's/5484
2006 #48 Lowe's QVC/96
2006 #48 Lowe's Daytona Raced Employee/280
Action Racing Collectables 1:64
2002 #48 Lowe's Power of Pride
2002 #48 Lowe's Sylvester and Tweety/19,689
2002 #48 Lowe's/13,608
2003 #6 True Value IROC/7560
2003 #48 Low.SpongeBob/11,532
2003 #48 Lowe's Power of Pride
2003 #48 Lowe's/19,008
2004 #48 Lowe's SpongeBob/3984
2004 #48 Lowe's Power of Pride/11,616
2004 #48 Lowe's HMS 20th/3408
2004 #48 Lowe's/12,960
2005 #48 Lowe's '06 Preview
2005 #48 Lowe's
2006 #48 Lowe's 60th Anniversary
2006 #48 Lowe's SeaWorld
2006 #48 Lowe's Dover Win w/Monster/3948
2006 #48 Lowe's
Action Racing Collectables Historical S
2004 #48 Lowe's '03 Monte Carlo 400 Chevy Wins Color Chr./3204
Action Racing Collectables Platinum 1:2
2008 #48 Lowe's/15,292
2008 #48 Lowe's Kobalt/2237
Action Racing Collectables Platinum 1:6
2008 #48 Lowe's/8208
Action Racing Collectables Platinum Day
2008 #48 Lowe's '06 Monte Carlo/1068
Action Racing Collectables Transporters
2003 #48 Lowe's/2952
Action Road Racing 1:18
2004 #4 B.Leitzinger E.Forbes-Robinson/Boss RCCA/144
2004 #4 B.Leitzinger E.Forbes-Robinson/Boss QVC/504
2004 #4 B.Leitzinger E.Forbes-Robinson/Boss Color Chrome/240
2004 #4 B.Leitzinger E.Forbes-Robinson/Boss/1812
2005 #2 Johnson/Leitzinger/Forbes-Robinson Daytona Prototype/2508
Action/Funline Muscle Machines 1:18
2004 #48 Lowe's '69 Camaro
2004 #48 Lowe's '69 Chevelle
2004 #48 Lowe's '67 Nova
2005 #48 Lowe's '69 Camaro GM Dealers/48
2005 #48 Lowe's '69 Camaro QVC/180
2005 #48 Lowe's '69 Camaro RCCA/120
2005 #48 Lowe's '69 Camaro/368
Action/Funline Muscle Machines 1:24
2005 #48 Lowe's Hybrid/288
Action/RCCA 1:18
2002 #48 Lowe's Syl.&Tweety/504
Action/RCCA 1:24
2002 #48 Lowe's Sylv.&Tweety Bank/1500
2002 #48 Lowe's Power of Pride Bank/900
2002 #48 Lowe's Bank/600
2003 #7 True Value IROC/144
2003 #7 True Value IROC AU/360
2003 #48 Lowe's Split Clear/504
2003 #48 Lowe.SpongeBob/1300
2003 #48 Lowe Pow.of Pride/1444
2003 #48 Lowe's Bank/1500
2004 #48 Lowe's Atlanta Raced/648
2004 #48 Lowe's Tool World/600
2004 #48 Lowe's SpongeBob/504
2004 #48 Lowe's HMS 20th Ann/600
2004 #48 Lowe's Father's Day/240
2004 #48 Lowe's/804
2004 #48 Crown Royal IROC Color Chrome/288
2005 #48 Lowe's Charlotte Raced/240
2005 #48 Lowe's '06 Preview/288
2005 #48 Lowe's Test/408
2005 #48 Lowe's Kobalt/240
2005 #48 Lowe's Las Vegas Raced/144
2005 #48 Lowe's Color Chrome/240
2005 #48 Lowe's/444
2006 #48 Lowe's Flames Test/400
2006 #48 Lowe's Holiday/250
2006 #48 Lowe's JJ Foundation/144
2006 #48 Lowe's Kobalt/144
2006 #48 Lowe's 60th Ann./350
2006 #48 Lowe's Sea World/448
2006 #48 Lowe's Daytona Raced w/tire/248
2006 #48 Lowe's Color Chrome/144
2006 #48 Lowe's/288
Action/RCCA 1:32
2002 #48 Lowe's Gold/480
2002 #48 Lowe's/1536
Action/RCCA 1:64
2002 #48 Lowe's Sylvester and Tweety/2016
2002 #48 Lowe's Power of Pride/5928
2002 #48 Lowe's/1584

2003 #48 Lowe's SpongeBob/1588
2003 #48 Lowe's Pow.of Pride/2460
2003 #48 Lowe's/2460
2003 #48 Lowe's SpongeBob/576
2004 #48 Lowe's HMS 20th Ann/720
2004 #48 Lowe's/1008
2005 #48 Lowe's '06 Preview/288
2005 #48 Lowe's/576
2006 #48 Lowe's 60th Ann./432
2006 #48 Lowe's Sea World/408
2006 #48 Lowe's/528

Action/RCCA Elite 1:24
2000 #92 Alltel/492
2001 #92 Excedrin/492
2002 #48 Lowe's Sylvester and Tweety/2220
2002 #48 Lowe's Power of Pride/1200
2002 #48 Lowe's California Raced/1008
2002 #48 Lowe's/900
2003 #48 Lowe SpongeBob/1648
2003 #48 Lowe Pow.of Pride/2200
2003 #48 Lowe's Test/1900
2003 #48 Lowe's Metal/1600
2003 #48 Lowe's Col.Chrome/804
2003 #48 Lowe's/2400
2004 #48 Lowe's Tool World White Gold/25
2004 #48 Lowe's Tool World/900
2004 #48 Lowe's SpongeBob White Gold/25
2004 #48 Lowe's SpongeBob/504
2004 #48 Lowe's HMS 20th Ann/900
2004 #48 Lowe's Atlanta Raced White Gold/48
2004 #48 Lowe's Atlanta Raced/848
2004 #48 Lowe's Color Chrome/480
2004 #48 Lowe's/1200
2005 #48 Lowe's Charlotte Raced/240
2005 #48 Lowe's Kobalt/240
2005 #48 Lowe's '06 Preview/408
2005 #48 Lowe's '06 Preview White Gold/25
2005 #48 Lowe's Test/504
2005 #48 Lowe's Las Vegas Raced/204
2005 #48 Lowe's White Gold/25
2005 #48 Lowe's Color Chrome/288
2005 #48 Lowe's/504
2006 #48 Lowe's 60th Anniversary White Gold/25
2006 #48 Lowe's 60th Anniversary Platinum/6
2006 #48 Lowe's 60th Anniversary/300
2006 #48 Lowe's SeaWorld White Gold/25
2006 #48 Lowe's SeaWorld Platinum/10
2006 #48 Lowe's SeaWorld AU/100
2006 #48 Lowe's SeaWorld/548
2006 #48 Lowe's JJ Foundation Platinum/2
2006 #48 Lowe's Holiday White Gold/25
2006 #48 Lowe's Holiday Platinum/5
2006 #48 Lowe's Holiday/250
2006 #48 Lowe's Flames Test Platinum/4
2006 #48 Lowe's Flames Test/200
2006 #48 Lowe's Daytona Raced Platinum/4
2006 #48 Lowe's Platinum/8
2006 #48 Lowe's Color Chrome/144
2006 #48 Lowe's Brickyard Raced/240
2006 #48 Lowe's/408
2006 #48 Lowe's White Gold/25
2006 #48 Lowe's JJ Foundation/120
2006 #48 Lowe's Daytona Raced AU/200
2006 #48 Lowe's Daytona Raced w/tire/248

Action/RCCA Elite 1:64
2002 #48 Lowe's Sylvester and Tweety/1584
2002 #48 Lowe's Power of Pride/1584
2002 #48 Lowe's/1584
2003 #48 Lowe SpongeBob/1300
2003 #48 Lowe's Pow.of Pride/1548
2003 #48 Lowe's/1500
2004 #48 Lowe's SpongeBob/480
2004 #48 Lowe's HMS 20th Ann/624
2004 #48 Lowe's/720
2005 #48 Lowe's '06 Preview/240
2005 #48 Lowe's/480
2006 #48 Lowe's 60th Anniversary/240
2006 #48 Lowe's SeaWorld/240
2006 #48 Lowe's/288

Action/RCCA Historical Series 1:24
2004 #48 Lowe's 400th Chevy Win '03 Monte Carlo Chrome/600

Action/RCCA Transporters 1:64
2003 #48 Lowe's/600

Brookfield 1:24
2005 #48 Lowe's/300
2006 #48 Lowe's/144

Hot Wheels Racing Color Change 1:64
2003 #48 Lowe's Power of Pride
2003 #48 Lowe's
2004 #48 Lowe's

Hot Wheels Racing Power Launchers 1:64
2003 #48 Lowe's

Hot Wheels Racing Stockerz 1:24
2004 #48 Lowe's

Hot Wheels Racing Stockerz 1:64
2004 #48 Lowe's

Miscellaneous Promos 1:64
1991-04 #92 Alltel blister/20,000 '00
1991-04 #92 Alltel wind.box/10,000 '00

Motorsports Authentics Driver's Select
2007 #48 Lowe's Las Vegas Raced/1380*
2007 #48 Lowe's/7500*
2007 #48 Lowe's '57 Chevy/1906*
2007 #48 Lowe's Power of Pride American Heroes/4164
2007 #48 Lowe's Kobalt Texas Raced/792*
2007 #48 Lowe's Kobalt Fall Atlanta Raced/853*
2007 #48 Lowe's Kobalt Atlanta RacedLowe's Kobalt Atlanta Raced/1537*
2007 #48 Lowe's Kobalt/1572*
2007 #48 Lowe's JJ Foundation/708*
2007 #48 Lowe's Holiday Sam Bass/1166*
2007 #48 Lowe's COT Richmond Raced/1320*
2007 #48 Lowe's COT Martinsville Raced/1320*
2007 #48 Lowe's COT/6012*
2007 #48 Lowe's Fall Martinsville Raced/792*
2007 #48 Lowe's '06 Nextel Champ
2007 #48 Lowe's '57 Chevy
2007 #48 Lowe's Power of Pride American Heroes
2007 #48 Lowe's COT
2007 #48 Lowe's
2007 #48 Lowe's JJ Foundation/804
2007 #48 Lowe's Kobalt/432
2007 #48 Lowe's COT/840
2007 #48 Lowe's/480

Motorsports Authentics Owner's Elite 1:
2007 #48 Lowe's '57 Chevy/504
2007 #48 Lowe's Test/708
2007 #48 Lowe's Power of Pride American Heroes/708*
2007 #48 Lowe's Kobalt/708
2007 #48 Lowe's Holiday Sam Bass/504*
2007 #48 Lowe's COT/1008
2007 #48 Lowe's White Gold/50*
2007 #48 Lowe's Platinum/25
2007 #48 Lowe's/1200*
2007 #48 Lowe's Power of Pride American Heroes/504*
2007 #48 Lowe's/2007*

Motorsports Authentics Owner's Elite Tr
2007 #48 Lowe's '57 Chevy/100*
2007 #48 Lowe's Power of Pride American Heroes/96*
2007 #48 Lowe's/1008*

Motorsports Authentics Pit Stop 1:64
2007 #48 Lowe's Sam Bass Holiday
2007 #48 Lowe's Power of Pride American Heroes
2007 #48 Lowe's Kobalt
2007 #48 Lowe's COT
2007 #48 Lowe's

Motorsports Authentics Pit Stop Blister
2007 #48 Lowe's

Motorsports Authentics QVC For Race Fan
2007 #48 Lowe's '06 Champ Mesma Chrome/504
2007 #48 Lowe's COT Copper/288
2007 #48 Lowe's COT Copper/288
2007 #48 Lowe's COT Color Chrome/288
2007 #48 Lowe's Platinum/108
2007 #48 Lowe's Mesma Chrome/288
2007 #48 Lowe's Copper/288
2007 #48 Lowe's Gold/108
2007 #48 Lowe's Color Chrome/288

Motorsports Authentics/RCCA Owner's Clu
2007 #48 Lowe's '57 Chevy/288*
2007 #48 Lowe's/1500*

Motorsports Authentics/RCCA Transporter
2007 #48 Lowe's/708*

Racing Champions 1:24
2002 #48 Lowe's/Press Pass card
2002 #48 Lowe's Steel/25
2002 #48 Lowe's Car Cover/500
2002 #48 Lowe's Chrome/1500
2002 #48 Lowe's
2002 #48 Lowe's Power of Pride Car Cover/500
2002 #48 Lowe's Power of Pride with Press Pass card
2002 #48 Lowe's Power of Pride Chrome/1500
2002 #48 Lowe's Power of Pride
2003 #48 Lowe's AU
2003 #48 Lowe's SpongeBob Chrome/1500
2003 #48 Lowe's SpongeBob
2003 #48 Lowe's Power of Pride Steel/50
2003 #48 Lowe's Power of Pride Rain Delay
2003 #48 Lowe's Power of Pride Firesuit/50
2003 #48 Lowe's Power of Pride Chrome/1500
2003 #48 Lowe's Power of Pride with Ultra Series card
2003 #48 Lowe's Steel/50
2003 #48 Lowe's Rain Delay/1500
2003 #48 Lowe's Firesuit/50
2003 #48 Lowe's Chrome/1500 with Press Pass card
2003 #48 Lowe's

Racing Champions 1:64
2001 #92 Excedrin PM Promo BX
2001 #92 Excedrin Cooling Pads Promo BX
2002 #48 Lowe's Power of Pride Chrome/1500
2002 #48 Lowe's Pow.Pride AUTO
2002 #48 Lowe's Power of Pride
2002 #48 Lowe's Promo w/o card
2002 #48 Lowe's First Win Car Cover/500
2002 #48 Lowe's First Win
2002 #48 Lowe's Steel/25
2002 #48 Lowe's Cover/500
2002 #48 Lowe's
2003 #48 Lowe's SpongeBob Promo in Signature Colors box
2003 #48 Lowes Steel/50
2003 #48 Lowe's Rain Delay/1500
2003 #48 Lowe's Firesuit/50
2003 #48 Lowe's Chrome/500
2003 #48 Lowe's '02 Remember
2003 #48 Lowe's

Racing Champions 5-Pack 1:64
2001 #NNO 92.JJ/77.DB/22.WB/25.JN/5.TL
2003 #NNO 48.JJ/23.SW/30.JV/33.PM/45.KP
2003 #NNO 48.JJ/10.JB/11.BB/01.JN/5.TL
2003 #NNO 22.WB/54.TB/7.JS/5.TL/48.JJ
2003 #NNO 5.BV/48.JJ/01.JN/22.WB/10.JB
2004 #NNO 10.SR/22.SW/48.JJ/60.BV/87.KyB
2004 #NNO 10.SR/22.SW/25.BV/27.JS/48.JJ
2004 #NNO 01.JN/22.SW/44.JL/48.JJ/49.KS in '05 packaging

Racing Champions Authentics 1:24
2002 #48 Lowe's Sylvester and Tweety/4167
2002 #48 Lowe's First Win Chrome/511
2002 #48 Lowe's First Win/2555
2002 #48 Lowe's Chrome/199
2002 #48 Lowe's/999
2002 #48 Lowe's Power of Pride Employee/10,000
2002 #48 Lowe's Power of Pride Chrome/199
2002 #48 Lowe's Power of Pride/999
2002 #48 Lowe's 2001 Power of Pride/999
2002 #48 Lowe's Sylvester and Tweety Chrome/833
2003 #48 Lowe's SpongeBob Chrome/404
2003 #48 Low.SpongeBob/2020
2003 #48 Lowe's Power of Pride Chrome/694
2003 #48 Low.Power of Pride/3470
2003 #48 Lowe's Chrome/908
2003 #48 Lowe's Tool World Chrome/500
2004 #48 Lowe's Tool World
2004 #48 Lowe's SpongeBob Chrome/500
2004 #48 Lowe's SpongeBob/2500
2004 #48 Lowe's HMS 20th Ann. Chrome/500
2004 #48 Lowe's HMS 20th Anniversary/2500
2004 #48 Lowe's Chrome
2004 #48 Lowe's/2400
2004 #48 Lowe's Chrome/480
2005 #48 Lowe's/2400

Racing Champions Authentics 1:64
2003 #48 Lowe's/11,028
2003 #48 Lowe's Power of Pride/9814

Racing Champions Bare Metal Previews 1:
2004 #48 Lowe's

Racing Champions Ironman 1:24
2002 #48 Lowe's/504

Racing Champions Premier 1:24
2002 #48 Lowe's Press Pass/2500
2002 #48 Lowe's Power of Pride Chrome/1500
2002 #48 Lowe's Power of Pride
2002 #48 Lowe's First Win Car Cover/500
2002 #48 Lowe's First Win
2002 #48 Lowe's Cover/500
2002 #48 Lowe's

Racing Champions Premier 1:64
2002 #48 Lowe's 3-car set
2002 #48 Lowe's Power of Pride Chrome/1500
2002 #48 Lowe's Power of Pride
2002 #48 Lowe's First Win Car Cover/500
2002 #48 Lowe's First Win
2002 #48 Lowe's Cover/500
2002 #48 Lowe's Chrome/1500
2002 #48 Lowe's
2003 #48 Lowe's Firesuit
2003 #48 Lowe's Steel
2003 #48 Lowe's Firesuit Steel/50
2003 #48 Lowe's Chrome/1500
2003 #48 Lowe's

Racing Champions Premier Preview 1:24
2003 #48 Lowe's 2002 Season to Remember

Racing Champions Premier Preview 1:64
2003 #48 Lowe's 2002 Season to Remember

Racing Champions Preview 1:24
2003 #48 Lowe's 2002 Season to Remember

Racing Champions Preview 1:64
2003 #48 Lowe's '02 Season

Racing Champions Preview Transporters 1
2003 #48 Lowe's 2002 Season to Remember

Racing Champions Real Steel 1:64
2004 #48 Lowe's

Racing Champions Slammers 1:64
2003 #48 Lowe's SpongeBob
2003 #48 Lowe's Power of Pride
2003 #48 Lowe's

Racing Champions Stock Rods 1:18
2002 #48 Lowe's Chrome/199
2002 #48 Lowe's/999
2003 #48 Lowe's '69 Camaro
2003 #48 Lowe's '66 Nova
2003 #48 Lowe's '55 Chevy
2004 #48 Lowe's '64 Impala SS

Racing Champions Stock Rods Preview 1:6
2003 #48 Lowe's '70 Chevelle

Racing Champions Transporters 1:64
2002 #48 Lowe's with 3-cars
2002 #48 Lowe's with Power of Pride car
2002 #48 Lowe's
2003 #48 Lowe's 2003
2003 #48 Lowe's 2002 Season to Remember

Racing Champions Transporters 1:87
2002 #48 Lowe's

Racing Champions Ultra 1:24
2004 #48 Lowe's HMS 20th Ann.
2004 #48 Lowe's Tool World in '05 packaging
2004 #48 Lowe's Tool World
2004 #48 Lowe's SpongeBob
2004 #48 Lowe's HMS 20th Ann. Chrome/500
2004 #48 Lowe's HMS 20th Ann. in '05 packaging
2004 #48 Lowe's
2005 #48 Lowe's Chrome
2005 #48 Lowe's

Racing Champions Ultra 1:64
2003 #48 Lowe's SpongeBob Chrome Promo/1500
2003 #48 Low.SpongeBob Promo
2003 #48 Lowe's Power of Pride Chrome/1500
2003 #48 Lowe's Pow.Pride
2003 #48 Lowe's Steel/50
2003 #48 Lowe's
2004 #48 Lowe's Tool World in '05 packaging
2004 #48 Lowe's Tool World
2004 #48 Lowe's SpongeBob
2004 #48 Lowe's HMS 20th Ann. in '05 packaging
2004 #48 Lowe's HMS 20th Ann.
2004 #48 Lowe's
2005 #48 Lowe's Kobalt
2005 #48 Lowe's Firesuit/50
2005 #48 Lowe's Chrome
2005 #48 Lowe's

Racing Champions Ultra Previews 1:24
2004 #48 Lowe's Chrome/1500
2004 #48 Lowe's

Racing Champions Ultra Previews 1:64
2004 #48 Lowe's Chrome
2004 #48 Lowe's

Racing Champions Ultra Transporters 1:6
2004 #48 Lowe's

Racing Champions Under the Lights 1:24
2002 #48 Lowe's

Racing Champions War Paint 1:24
2002 #48 Lowe's

Racing Champions Window Cling 1:64
2004 #48 Lowe's

RCCA Club 1:24
2008 #48 Lowe's/300

RCCA Elite 1:24
2008 #48 Lowe's/500
2008 #48 Lowe's Platinum/25
2008 #48 Lowe's White Gold/50

Revell Collection 1:24
2002 #48 Lowe's raced California Win/10,844
2003 #48 Lowe's Test Black/4134
2004 #48 Lowe's Darlington Raced/3504
2005 #48 Lowe's Test/744

Team Caliber First Choice 1:24
2003 #48 Lowe's/756

Team Caliber Owners Series 1:24
2002 #48 Lowe's Power of Pride/5004
2002 #48 Lowe's/3120
2003 #48 Lowe's Power of Pride/2400
2003 #48 Lowe's Blue Chr./2400
2003 #48 Lowe's/7560
2004 #48 Lowe's SpongeBob
2004 #48 Lowe's/2400
2005 #48 Lowe's/600

Team Caliber Owners Series 1:64
2002 #48 Lowe's Pow.of Pride/5004
2002 #48 Lowes/5004
2003 #48 Lowe's Power of Pride
2003 #48 Lowe's Blue Chr./7560
2003 #48 Lowe's
2004 #48 Lowe's

Team Caliber Owners Series Banks 1:24
2002 #48 Lowe's Pow.of Pride/390
2002 #48 Lowe's/504
2003 #48 Lowe's/180

Team Caliber Owners Series Dark Chrome
2002 #48 Low.Pow.of Pride/1002
2002 #48 Lowe's/1002
2003 #48 Lowe's Power of Pride Winston/180
2003 #48 Lowe's/684

Team Caliber Owners Series Pearl Chrome
2004 #48 Lowe's SpongeBob/354
2004 #48 Lowe's/222

Team Caliber Owners Series Transporters
2003 #48 Lowe's/800
2004 #48 Lowe's

Team Caliber Pit Stop 1:24
2002 #48 Lowe's Power of Pride
2002 #48 Lowe's
2003 #48 Lowe's Power of Pride
2003 #48 Lowe's
2004 #48 Lowe's SpongeBob
2004 #48 Lowe's
2005 #48 Lowe's

Team Caliber Pit Stop 1:64
2002 #48 Lowe's Power of Pride
2002 #48 Lowe's/1002
2003 #48 Lowe's Power of Pride
2003 #48 Lowe's
2004 #48 Lowe's SpongeBob
2004 #48 Lowe's
2005 #48 Lowe's

Team Caliber Pit Stop Transporters 1:64
2003 #48 Lowe's
2004 #48 Lowe's

Team Caliber Preferred 1:24
2002 #48 Lowe's Power of Pride
2002 #48 Lowe's/10,080
2003 #48 Lowe's Power of Pride/4320
2003 #48 Lowe's/1200
2004 #48 Lowe's SpongeBob/3120
2004 #48 Lowe's Chase/500
2004 #48 Lowe's/10,080
2005 #48 Lowe's/3120

Team Caliber Preferred Nickel 1:24
2005 #48 Lowe's/180

Team Caliber Promos 1:64
2004 #48 Lowe's SpongeBob

Winner's Circle 1:18
2003 #48 Lowe's Sylv.&Tweety
2007 #48 Lowe's

Winner's Circle 1:24
2003 #48 Lowe's Sylvester&Tweety
2003 #48 Lowe's Distributor Exclusive Sticker
2006 #48 Lowe's Sea World
2006 #48 Lowe's
2007 #48 Lowe's
2008 #48 Lowe's

Winner's Circle 1:87
2006 #48 Lowe's Sea World
2006 #48 Lowe's
2007 #48 Lowe's
2008 #48 Lowe's

Winner's Circle American Heroes 1:24
2007 #48 Lowe's Power of Pride American Heroes

Winner's Circle American Heroes 1:87
2007 #48 Lowe's Power of Pride AH
2007 #NNO American Heroes 9-car set
2007 #NNO 4.Burton/AF 24.Gordon/D.O.D. 48.Johnson/P.O.P. 3-car set

Winner's Circle American Heroes Hood 1:
2007 #48 Lowe's Power of Pride AH

Winner's Circle Autographed Hood 1:64
2006 #48 Lowe's Flames Test
2006 #48 Lowe's

Winner's Circle Award Winners 1:64
2006 #48 Lowe's '06 Nextel Champion

Winner's Circle Daytona 500 1:24
2008 #48 Lowe's

Winner's Circle Daytona 500 1:64
2008 #48 Lowe's

Winner's Circle Daytona 500 1:87
2008 #48 Lowe's

Winner's Circle Daytona 500 2-car sets
2008 #48/08 Lowe's Daytona 500 Event Car

Winner's Circle Daytona 500 Hoods 1:64
2008 #48 Lowe's

Winner's Circle Daytona 500 Transporter
2008 #48 Lowe's

Winner's Circle Die-Cast Kits 1:24
2003 #48 Lowe's Sylvester & Tweety '02

Winner's Circle Double Platinum 1:43
2003 #48 Lowe's Sylvester

Winner's Circle Driver Sticker 1:64
2002 #48 Lowe's Sylvester
2003 #48 Lowe's Sylv.&Tweety
2003 #48 Lowe's Distributor Excl.

Winner's Circle Dually w/Car on Tracksi
2008 #48 Lowe's

Winner's Circle Helmets 1:64
2007 #48 Lowe's

Winner's Circle Hoods 1:64
2007 #48 Lowe's

Winner's Circle License Plate 1:64
2007 #48 Lowe's

Winner's Circle Medallion 1:64
2007 #48 Lowe's

Winner's Circle Number Magnet 1:64
2008 #48 Lowe's

Winner's Circle Pit Pass 1:64
2007 #48 Lowe's

Winner's Circle Pit Sign 1:64
2006 #48 Lowe's
2007 #48 Lowe's Test

Winner's Circle Race Hood 1:43
2003 #48 Lowe's Sylv.&Tweety

Winner's Circle Sam Bass 1:64
2008 #48 Lowe's

Winner's Circle Sam Bass Hoods 1:64
2007 #48 Lowe's Holiday

Winner's Circle Schedule Hood 1:64
2006 #48 Lowe's
2007 #48 Lowe's

Winner's Circle Schedule Hoods 1:64
2008 #48 Lowe's

Winner's Circle Sticker 1:64
2006 #48 Lowe's

Winner's Circle Stickers 1:64
2008 #48 Lowe's 2007 Champ

Winner's Circle Transporters 1:64
2002 #48 Lowe's Sylvester
2003 #48 Lowe's Sylvester and Tweety
2007 #48 Lowe's Power of Pride American Heroes
2007 #48 Lowe's
2008 #48 Lowe's

Winner's Circle Victory Lane Hoods 1:64
2007 #48 Lowe's Kobalt Atlanta Raced
2007 #48 Lowe's COT Fall Richmond Raced
2007 #48 Lowe's COT Richmond Raced
2007 #48 Lowe's COT Fall Phoenix Raced
2007 #48 Lowe's COT Fall Martinsville Raced
2007 #48 Lowe's COT Martinsville Raced
2007 #48 Lowe's Texas Raced
2007 #48 Lowe's Las Vegas Raced
2007 #48 Lowe's California Raced
2007 #48 Lowe's Fall Atlanta Raced

Kahne, Kasey

Action Clearly Collectibles 1:24
2005 #9 Richmond Raced Tire/650

Action Performance 1:24
2004 #9 Dodge refresh
2005 #9 Dodge Hometown
2005 #NNO Dodge/STP QVC/504
2005 #NNO Dodge/STP/1896

Action Performance 1:64
2004 #9 Nextel Cup 6-car set
2005 #9 Nextel Cup 6-car set
2005 #9 Dodge
2006 #9 Dodge

Action QVC For Race Fans Only 1:24
2004 #9 Dodge ROY Brushed Metal/504
2004 #9 Dodge Refresh Platinum/300
2004 #9 Dodge Refresh Gold/300
2004 #9 Dodge Refresh Color Chrome/504
2004 #9 Mountain Dew Color Chrome/408
2004 #9 Mopar Color Chrome/1008
2004 #9 Dodge Popeye Color Chrome/504
2004 #9 Dodge Mad Magazine Color Chrome/408
2005 #9 Mopar Color Chrome/1008
2005 #9 Mountain Dew Color Chrome/1008
2005 #9 Mountain Dew Brushed Metal AU/504
2005 #9 Dodge Retro Bud Shootout Platinum/144
2005 #9 Dodge Retro Bud Shootout Gold/288
2005 #9 Dodge Retro Bud Shootout Color Chrome/1008
2005 #9 Dodge Pit Cap Reverse Platinum/144
2005 #9 Dodge Pit Cap Reverse Brushed Metal AU/900
2005 #9 Dodge Gold/300
2005 #9 Dodge Brushed Metal/504
2005 #9 Dodge Pit Cap Reverse Gold/300
2005 #NNO Dodge '75 Charger STP Color Chrome/1008
2006 #9 Dodge Mesma Chrome/288
2006 #9 Dodge Color Chrome/504

Action Racing Collectables 1:24
2002 #98 Channellock/3024
2004 #9 Dodge refresh liquid chrome ROY AU QVC/804
2004 #9 Dodge Mopar Alcone/1008
2004 #9 Dodge Mopar QVC/504
2004 #9 Mountain Dew CW Bank/480
2004 #9 Mountain Dew/6216
2004 #9 Dodge Popeye CW Bank/324
2004 #9 Dodge Popeye/3780
2004 #9 Dodge Pit Cap QVC/504
2004 #9 Dodge Pit Cap CW Bank/384
2004 #9 Dodge Pit Cap/7752
2004 #9 Dodge Mopar Color Chrome/1248
2004 #9 Dodge Mopar/8592
2004 #9 Dodge Mad Magazine CW Bank/456
2004 #9 Dodge Mad Magazine/9024
2004 #9 Dodge refresh QVC/360
2004 #9 Dodge refresh liquid chrome ROY AU/4596
2004 #9 Dodge refresh/12,564
2004 #9 Dodge CW Bank/264
2004 #9 Dodge/3936
2004 #38 Great Clips Shark Tales CW Bank/336
2004 #38 Great Clips Shark Tales/5004
2004 #38 Great Clips/6636
2005 #9 Dodge Longest Yard Mac Tools/300
2005 #9 Mountain Dew Mac Tools/300
2005 #9 Mountain Dew Matco/72
2005 #9 Mopar CW Bank/192
2005 #9 Mountain Dew QVC/600
2005 #9 Mountain Dew CW Bank/348
2005 #9 Mountain Dew/8016
2005 #9 Mopar QVC/288
2005 #9 Mopar/4500
2005 #9 Dodge Test/1452
2005 #9 Dodge Retro Bud Shootout QVC/1008
2005 #9 Dodge Retro Bud Shootout Liquid Metal/1008
2005 #9 Dodge Retro Bud Shootout CW Bank/300
2005 #9 Dodge Retro Bud Shootout/6000
2005 #9 Dodge Pit Cap White QVC/504
2005 #9 Dodge Pit Cap White CW Bank/336
2005 #9 Dodge Pit Cap White/7476
2005 #9 Dodge Mega Cab QVC/288
2005 #9 Dodge Mega Cab/2520
2005 #9 Dodge Longest Yard QVC/288
2005 #9 Dodge Longest Yard/4344
2005 #9 Dodge Richmond Raced QVC/1008
2005 #9 Dodge Richmond Raced Liquid Metal/1056
2005 #9 Dodge Richmond Raced/9420
2005 #9 Dodge QVC/1500
2005 #9 Dodge Matco/108
2005 #9 Dodge Mac Tools/300
2005 #9 Dodge Liquid Metal/2508
2005 #9 Dodge CW Bank/396
2005 #9 Dodge/13,284
2005 #38 Great Clips/2820
2005 #38 Great Clips CW Bank/144
2005 #38 Great Clips QVC/144
2005 #38 Great Clips Spy v. Spy Kids/3504
2005 #38 Great Clips Spy v. Spy Kids QVC/120
2005 #79 Auto Value/2532
2005 #79 Auto Value CW Bank/168
2005 #79 Trus Joist/2004
2006 #9 Ragu/2580
2006 #9 McDonald's CWB/132
2006 #9 McDonald's/1644
2006 #9 Mopar/1980
2006 #9 Dodge UAW Daimler Chrysler 400 CW Bank/144
2006 #9 Dodge UAW Daimler Chrysler 400/1500
2006 #9 Dodge Test/3504
2006 #9 Dodge SRT/1728
2006 #9 Dodge Holiday QVC*
2006 #9 Dodge Holiday/1296*
2006 #9 Dodge QVC/504
2006 #9 Dodge Matco/72
2006 #9 Dodge Mac Tools/504
2006 #9 Dodge CWB/360
2006 #9 Dodge/10,000
2006 #9 Click Michigan Raced/2388
2006 #9 Vitamin Water/2232

Action Racing Collectables 1:64
2004 #9 Mountain Dew in vending tin/5124
2004 #9 Dodge Mopar
2004 #9 Dodge refresh ROY Color Chrome
2004 #9 Dodge refresh/9120
2004 #9 Dodge/4128
2004 #38 Great Clips Shark Tales/4464
2005 #9 Mountain Dew in can
2005 #9 Mountain Dew
2005 #9 Mopar
2005 #9 Dodge Retro Bud Shootout
2005 #9 Dodge Pit Cap White
2005 #9 Dodge
2005 #38 Great Clips
2005 #79 Auto Value
2006 #9 Dodge

Action Racing Collectables Platinum 1:2
2008 #9 Bud/24,600

Action Racing Collectables Transporters
2005 #9 Dodge QVC/288
2005 #9 Dodge/1716

Action/Funline Muscle Machines 1:18
2004 #9 Dodge '68 Dart
2004 #9 Dodge '69 Charger
2005 #9 Dodge '69 Charger
2005 #9 Mopar '69 Charger QVC/504
2005 #9 Mopar '69 Charger RCCA/120
2005 #9 Mopar '69 Charger/616
2005 #9 Mopar '68 Dart QVC/504
2005 #9 Mopar '68 Dart RCCA/60
2005 #9 Mopar '68 Dart/516
2005 #9 Dodge Pit Cap White '69 Charger QVC/504
2005 #9 Dodge Pit Cap White '69 Charger RCCA/144
2005 #9 Dodge Pit Cap White '69 Charger/540
2005 #9 Dodge Pit Cap White '68 Dart QVC/504
2005 #9 Dodge Pit Cap White '68 Dart RCCA/80
2005 #9 Dodge Pit Cap White '68 Dart/504

2005 #9 Dodge '68 Dart QVC/400
2005 #9 Dodge '68 Dart RCCA/120
2005 #9 Dodge '68 Dart/692

Action/Funline Muscle Machines 1:24
2005 #9 Dodge Hybrid/288
2005 #9 Dodge Retro Bud Shootout Hybrid/240

Action/RCCA 1:24
2002 #98 Channellock Bank/408
2004 #9 Mountain Dew/540
2004 #9 Dodge Popeye/576
2004 #9 Dodge Pit Cap/600
2004 #9 Dodge Mopar/444
2004 #9 Dodge Mad Magazine/600
2004 #9 Dodge refresh ROY AU/504
2004 #9 Dodge/288
2004 #38 Great Clips Shark Tale/560
2004 #38 Great Clips/360
2005 #9 Dodge Hometown Brushed Bronze/288
2005 #9 Dodge Ram Mega Cab/240
2005 #9 Mopar/408
2005 #9 Mountain Dew/444
2005 #9 Dodge Test/408
2005 #9 Dodge Retro Bud Shootout/600
2005 #9 Dodge Pit Cap White/504
2005 #9 Dodge Longest Yard/504
2005 #9 Dodge Richmond Raced/499
2005 #9 Dodge Liquid Metal/408
2005 #9 Dodge Color Chrome/408
2005 #9 Dodge/600
2005 #38 Great Clips/240
2005 #79 Trus Joist/204
2005 #79 Auto Value/360
2006 #9 Dodge Color Chrome/144
2006 #9 Dodge Texas Raced/200
2006 #9 Dodge Flames/250
2006 #9 Dodge Holiday/250
2006 #9 Dodge Test/300
2006 #9 Ragu/204
2006 #9 Vitamin Water/100
2006 #9 McDonald's/250
2006 #9 Mopar/200
2006 #9 Dodge UAW Daimler Chrysler 400/250
2006 #9 Dodge SRT/200
2006 #9 Dodge/408
2006 #9 Click Michigan Raced/350

Action/RCCA 1:64
2004 #9 Dodge refresh ROY/576
2004 #9 Mountain Dew in vending tin/600
2004 #9 Dodge Mopar/576
2004 #9 Dodge/576
2004 #38 Great Clips Shark Tale/576
2005 #9 Dodge/720
2005 #9 Mopar/480
2005 #9 Mountain Dew in can/504
2005 #9 Mountain Dew/720
2005 #9 Dodge Retro Bud Shootout/720
2005 #9 Dodge Pit Cap White/576
2006 #9 Dodge/504

Action/RCCA Elite 1:24
2002 #98 Channellock/408
2004 #9 Mountain Dew/540
2004 #9 Dodge Popeye/576
2004 #9 Dodge Pit Cap/600
2004 #9 Dodge Mopar/444
2004 #9 Dodge Mad Magazine White Gold/50
2004 #9 Dodge refresh ROY AU/600
2004 #9 Dodge/288
2004 #9 Dodge Refresh Color Chrome/444
2004 #9 Dodge Pit Cap White Gold/50
2004 #9 Dodge refresh ROY liquid metal/100
2004 #9 Dodge Mad Magazine/600
2004 #38 Great Clips Shark Tale White Gold/25
2004 #38 Great Clips Shark Tale/560
2004 #38 Great Clips/360
2005 #9 Dodge White Gold AU/50
2005 #9 Dodge Ram Mega Cab/288
2005 #9 Dodge Ram Mega Cab White Gold/25
2005 #9 Mountain Dew AU/138
2005 #9 Mountain Dew/804
2005 #9 Mopar White Gold/25
2005 #9 Mopar/480
2005 #9 Dodge Retro Bud Shootout White Gold/50
2005 #9 Dodge Retro Bud Shootout Platinum/144
2005 #9 Dodge Retro Bud Shootout/900
2005 #9 Dodge Pit Cap White/600
2005 #9 Dodge Longest Yard White Gold/25
2005 #9 Dodge Longest Yard/600
2005 #9 Dodge Hometown Brushed Bronze/288
2005 #9 Dodge Richmond Raced Platinum/99
2005 #9 Dodge Richmond Raced AU/144
2005 #9 Dodge Richmond Raced/899
2005 #9 Dodge Platinum/144
2005 #9 Dodge Color Chrome AU/132
2005 #9 Dodge Color Chrome/600
2005 #9 Dodge/900
2005 #9 Dodge White Gold/30
2005 #9 Dodge Pit Cap White White Gold/30
2005 #9 Mountain Dew White Gold/30
2005 #38 Great Clips/240
2005 #79 Trus Joist/204
2005 #79 Auto Value/360
2006 #9 Dodge Texas Raced/200
2006 #9 Dodge Texas Raced Platinum/4
2006 #9 Dodge Test AU/216
2006 #9 Vitamin Water Platinum/3
2006 #9 Vitamin Water/150
2006 #9 Ragu Platinum/4
2006 #9 Ragu/204
2006 #9 McDonald's White Gold/25
2006 #9 McDonald's Platinum/5
2006 #9 McDonald's AU/72
2006 #9 McDonald's/250
2006 #9 Mopar White Gold/25
2006 #9 Mopar Platinum/5
2006 #9 Mopar/250
2006 #9 Dodge UAW Daimler Chrysler 400 Platinum/6
2006 #9 Dodge UAW Daimler Chrysler 400/300
2006 #9 Dodge Test Platinum/8
2006 #9 Dodge Test/400
2006 #9 Dodge SRT Platinum/6
2006 #9 Dodge SRT/250
2006 #9 Dodge Holiday Platinum/5
2006 #9 Dodge Holiday/250
2006 #9 Dodge Flames Platinum/7
2006 #9 Dodge Flames/350
2006 #9 Dodge Color Chrome/144
2006 #9 Dodge AU/216
2006 #9 Dodge/600
2006 #9 Click Michigan Raced Platinum/7
2006 #9 Click Michigan Raced/350
2006 #9 Dodge Platinum/12
2006 #9 Dodge White Gold/25
2006 #9 Dodge SRT White Gold/25
2006 #9 Dodge UAW Daimler Chrysler 400 White Gold/25

Action/RCCA Elite 1:64
2004 #9 Mountain Dew/528

2004 #9 Dodge Mopar/480
2004 #9 Dodge refresh ROY/480
2004 #9 Dodge Refresh Color Chrome/528
2005 #9 Dodge/576
2005 #9 Mopar/408
2005 #9 Mountain Dew/528
2005 #9 Dodge Retro Bud Shootout/528
2005 #9 Dodge Pit Cap White/480
2005 #9 Dodge/576
2006 #9 Dodge/288

Action/RCCA Metal Elite 1:24
2005 #9 Dodge/600

Action/RCCA Sprint 1:24
2001 #91 Wingless Midget/2004
2004 #9 Dodge Curb Records/5004
2005 #9 Valvoline QVC/480
2005 #9 Valvoline Color Chrome/504
2005 #9 Valvoline/4116
2005 #83 Beef Packers '03/3504
2005 #83 Beef Packers '03 Color Chrome/444
2005 #83 Beef Packers '03 QVC/120
2006 #9 Dollar General Color Chrome/400
2006 #9 Sage Fruit Color Chrome/300
2006 #9 Sage Fruit/852

Action/RCCA Transporters 1:64
2005 #9 Dodge Liquid Metal/504

Brookfield 1:24
2005 #9 Dodge/444
2005 #9 Dodge Retro Bud Shootout/240
2005 #9 Mopar/204
2005 #9 Mountain Dew/288
2005 #9 Dodge Pit Cap White/240
2005 #NNO R.Petty Fantasy Charger 2-car set/600
2006 #9 Dodge/144

Brookfield Trackside 1:64
2004 #9 Dodge refresh RCCA/1008
2004 #9 Dodge refresh/4224
2005 #9 Dodge Retro Bud Shootout QVC/288
2005 #9 Dodge Retro Bud Shootout RCCA/600
2005 #9 Dodge Retro Bud Shootout/2760

GMP Sprint Cars 1:18
1996-01 #23 Speed Racer/2004 '01

GMP Sprint Cars 1:50
1998-01 #23 Speed Racer/3600 '01

Motorsports Authentics Driver's Select
2007 #9 Vitamin Water/1674*
2007 #9 Mopar/1608*
2007 #9 McDonald's/1296*
2007 #9 Hellmann's/2208*
2007 #9 Doublemint/1704*
2007 #9 Dodge Dealers Holiday Sam Bass/894*
2007 #9 Dodge Dealers COT/2616*
2007 #9 Dodge Dealers/9504*
2007 #9 McDonald's
2007 #9 Hellmann's
2007 #9 Dodge Dealers COT
2007 #9 Dodge Dealers

Motorsports Authentics Owner's Elite 1:
2007 #9 Doublemint White Gold/50*
2007 #9 Doublemint Platinum/25
2007 #9 Doublemint/504*
2007 #9 Dodge Dealers Test/708*
2007 #9 Dodge Dealers COT/708*
2007 #9 Dodge Dealers/1212*
2007 #9 Dodge Dealers Platinum/25
2007 #9 Dodge Dealers White Gold/100
2007 #9 Dodge Dealers/2007*

Motorsports Authentics Owner's Elite Tr
2007 #9 Doublemint/504*
2007 #9 Dodge Dealers/408*

Motorsports Authentics Pit Stop 1:64
2007 #9 Doublemint
2007 #9 Dodge Dealers

Motorsports Authentics Pit Stop Blister
2007 #9 Dodge Dealers

Motorsports Authentics QVC For Race Fan
2007 #9 Dodge Dealers Mesma Chrome/288
2007 #9 Dodge Dealers Copper/288
2007 #9 Dodge Dealers Color Chrome/288
2007 #9 Dodge Dealers Chrome/288

Motorsports Authentics/RCCA Owner's Clu
2007 #9 Dodge Dealers Holiday Sam Bass/96*
2007 #9 Dodge Dealers/1500*

Motorsports Authentics/RCCA Transporter
2007 #9 Dodge Dealers/708*

Racing Champions 1:24
2004 #38 Great Clips Promo

Racing Champions 5-Pack 1:64
2004 #NNO 01.JN/5.TL/22.SW/38.KK/84.Ky.B in '05 packaging

RCCA Club 1:24
2008 #9 Bud/504

RCCA Elite 1:24
2008 #9 Bud/1500
2008 #9 Bud Platinum/25
2008 #9 Bud White Gold/50

Revell Collection 1:24
2005 #9 Dodge Test/360

Team Caliber Pit Stop 1:64
2003 #38 Great Clips

Team Caliber Promos 1:64
2006 #9 Ultimate Chargers in window box
2006 #9 Ragu in window box

Winner's Circle 1:18
2004 #9 Dodge refresh
2004 #9 Dodge
2005 #9 Dodge
2005 #9 Dodge Mopar
2005 #9 Dodge Pit Cap White
2005 #38 Great Clips
2007 #9 Dodge Dealers

Winner's Circle 1:24
2004 #9 Dodge Popeye
2004 #9 Dodge Refresh
2004 #38 Great Clips Shark Tale
2004 #38 Great Clips
2005 #9 Dodge Pit Cap White
2005 #9 Mountain Dew
2005 #9 Dodge Mopar '04
2005 #9 Dodge '04 ROY
2005 #9 Dodge
2005 #9 Dodge Retro Daytona Shootout
2005 #9 Dodge Longest Yard
2005 #38 Great Clips
2006 #9 Dodge SRT
2006 #9 Dodge Raced
2006 #9 Dodge
2007 #9 Dodge Dealers
2008 #9 KK

Winner's Circle 1:87
2006 #9 Dodge SRT
2006 #9 Dodge
2007 #9 Dodge Dealers
2008 #9 KK

Winner's Circle 2-Car Set w/Pit Board 1
2008 #9 Bud/Bud Color Chrome

Winner's Circle Autographed Hood 1:64
2004 #9 Mountain Dew short package
2004 #9 Dodge Popeye
2004 #9 Dodge Mad Magazine
2004 #9 Dodge
2004 #38 Great Clips Shark Tales
2004 #38 Great Clips
2005 #9 Mountain Dew
2005 #9 Dodge Pit Cap White
2005 #9 Dodge Mopar
2005 #9 Dodge Mopar '04
2005 #9 Dodge Longest Yard
2005 #9 Dodge '04 ROY
2005 #9 Dodge
2005 #9 Dodge Ram Mega Cab
2005 #38 Great Clips
2006 #9 Dodge Test

Winner's Circle Daytona 500 1:24
2008 #9 Bud
2008 #9 KK

Winner's Circle Daytona 500 1:64
2008 #9 KK

Winner's Circle Daytona 500 Hoods 1:64
2008 #9 KK
2008 #9 Bud

Winner's Circle Die-Cast Kits 1:24
2004 #9 Dodge Popeye

Winner's Circle Driver Photo Hood 1:64
2005 #9 Dodge Retro Daytona Shootout

Winner's Circle Driver Sticker 1:64
2004 #9 Dodge Refresh sparkle
2004 #9 Dodge sparkle
2005 #9 Dodge Richmond Raced

Winner's Circle Dually w/Car on Tracks!
2008 #9 KK

Winner's Circle Helmets 1:64
2007 #9 Dodge Dealers

Winner's Circle Hoods 1:64
2007 #9 Dodge Dealers Test

Winner's Circle License Plate 1:64
2007 #9 Dodge Dealers

Winner's Circle Medallion 1:64
2007 #9 Dodge Dealers

Winner's Circle Number Magnet 1:64
2008 #9 KK

Winner's Circle Pit Pass 1:64
2007 #9 Dodge

Winner's Circle Pit Sign 1:64
2006 #9 Dodge
2007 #9 Dodge Dealers

Winner's Circle Sam Bass 1:64
2008 #9 KK

Winner's Circle Sam Bass Hoods 1:64
2007 #9 Dodge Dealers Holiday

Winner's Circle Schedule Hood 1:64
2006 #9 Dodge
2007 #9 Dodge Dealers

Winner's Circle Schedule Hoods 1:64
2008 #9 KK

Winner's Circle Sticker 1:64
2006 #9 Dodge

Winner's Circle Stickers 1:64
2008 #9 KK

Winner's Circle Test Hood 1:64
2005 #9 Dodge

Winner's Circle Transporters 1:64
2004 #9 Dodge Mad Magazine
2004 #9 Dodge Souvenir
2005 #9 Dodge Pit Cap White
2005 #9 Mountain Dew
2005 #9 Dodge
2005 #9 Mopar
2005 #9 Dodge Longest Yard
2005 #38 Great Clips
2007 #9 McDonald's
2007 #9 Dodge Dealers
2008 #9 KK

Kenseth, Matt

Action Racing Collectables 1:24
1999 #17 DeWalt Bank/2508
1999 #17 DeWalt/4008
2004 #17 Crown Royal IROC '04 Champion pearl/1368
2004 #17 Crown Royal IROC/4500
2005 #17 Crown Royal IROC/1272
2006 #17 Crown Royal IROC GM Dealers/132
2006 #17 Crown Royal IROC/1128

Action Racing Collectables 1:64
1999 #17 DeWalt '97 Monte Carlo/7056
2008 #17 DeWalt

Action Racing Collectables Platinum 1:2
2008 #17 Carhartt/3144
2008 #17 DeWalt/6672

Action Racing Collectables Platinum 1:6
2008 #17 DeWalt/3024

Action/RCCA 1:24
2004 #17 Crown Royal IROC '04 Champion Pearl/360
2004 #17 Crown Royal IROC Color Chrome/288
2005 #17 Crown Royal IROC Brushed Metal/288
2006 #17 Crown Royal White Pearl/200
2006 #17 DeWalt/200
2006 #17 DeWalt Color Chrome/100

Action/RCCA 1:64
1999 #17 DeWalt '97MC/3000

Action/RCCA Banks 1:24
1999 #17 DeWalt/2500

Action/RCCA Elite 1:24
1999 #17 DeWalt/1000
2006 #17 DeWalt/250
2006 #17 DeWalt Color Chrome/100
2006 #17 DeWalt Platinum/5
2006 #17 DeWalt White Gold/25

Action/RCCA SelectNet Banks 1:24
1999 #17 DeWalt

Action/RCCA SelectNet Elite 1:24
1999 #17 DeWalt/1000

Ertl Proshop 1:18
2000 #17 DeWalt

Ertl Proshop 1:24
2000 #17 DeWalt

Ertl Proshop 1:64
2000 #17 DeWalt

Hot Wheels Alternative Paint Scheme 1:2
2005 #17 Trex

Hot Wheels Alternative Paint Scheme 1:6
2005 #17 Trex

Hot Wheels Crew's Choice 1:24
1999 #17 DeWalt
2000 #17 DeWalt

Hot Wheels Daytona Set-Up 1:64
2002 #17 DeWalt

Hot Wheels Deluxe 1:24
1999 #17 DeWalt

Hot Wheels Deluxe 1:64
2000 #17 DeWalt

Hot Wheels Deluxe Pit Crew 1:64
2000 #17 DeWalt

Hot Wheels Deluxe Pit Crew Daytona 500
2000 #17 DeWalt

Hot Wheels Race Day 1:64
2005 #17 DeWalt

Hot Wheels Race Day Deluxe 1:24
2000 #17 DeWalt

Hot Wheels Racing 1:24
2001 #17 DeWalt Black
2001 #17 DeWalt Yellow&Black
2002 #17 DeWalt
2003 #17 DeWalt

Hot Wheels Racing Artist Collection 1:2
2004 #17 DeWalt

Hot Wheels Racing Artist Collection 1:6
2004 #17 DeWalt

Hot Wheels Racing Blimp 1:64
2001 #17 DeWalt 2/4

Hot Wheels Racing Chase for the Cup 1:2
2004 #17 DeWalt/6000

Hot Wheels Racing Chase for the Cup 1:6
2004 #17 DeWalt

Hot Wheels Racing Color Change 1:64
2003 #17 DeWalt
2004 #17 DeWalt

Hot Wheels Racing Crew's Choice 1:64
2000 #17 DeWalt

Hot Wheels Racing Deora 1:64
2001 #17 DeWalt 2/4

Hot Wheels Racing Goodyear Showcase 1:6
2004 #17 DeWalt/15,000

Hot Wheels Racing Justice League 1:64
2004 #17 Martian Manhunter

Hot Wheels Racing Justice League Thunde
2004 #17 Martian Manhunter

Hot Wheels Racing Justice League w/Figu
2004 #17 Martian Manhunter

Hot Wheels Racing Luxury Rides 1:64
2003 #17 DeWalt

Hot Wheels Racing Matt Kenseth Champion
2003 #17 DeWalt/10,000
2003 #17 DeWalt
2003 #17 DeWalt Color Change
2003 #17 DeWalt
2003 #17 DeWalt

Hot Wheels Racing Pit Board 1:64
2001 #17 DeWalt

Hot Wheels Racing Pit Crew 1:64
1999 #17 DeWalt

Hot Wheels Racing Pit Cruisers 1:64
2004 #17 DeWalt

Hot Wheels Racing Power Launchers 1:64
2003 #17 DeWalt

Hot Wheels Racing Promos 1:64
2003 #17 DeWalt Wienermobile

Hot Wheels Racing Race Day 1:24
2004 #17 DeWalt

Hot Wheels Racing Race Day 1:64
2003 #17 DeWalt
2004 #17 DeWalt

Hot Wheels Racing Radical Rides 1:64
2000 #17 DeWalt

Hot Wheels Racing Radical Rods 1:43
2001 #17 DeWalt

Hot Wheels Racing Record Times 1:64
2002 #17 DeWalt

Hot Wheels Racing Recreational Vehicles
2003 #17 DeWalt
2003 #17 DeWalt
2003 #17 DeWalt

Hot Wheels Racing Roush Commemorative 1
2001 #17 DeWalt

Hot Wheels Racing Select 1:64
2001 #17 DeWalt Black
2001 #17 DeWalt

Hot Wheels Racing Sticker 1:64
2002 #17 DeWalt

Hot Wheels Racing Stock Car Cruisers 1:
2003 #17 DeWalt

Hot Wheels Racing Stockerz 1:24
2004 #17 DeWalt

Hot Wheels Racing Stockerz 1:64
2004 #17 DeWalt

Hot Wheels Racing Tall Draggers 1:64
2001 #17 DeWalt

Hot Wheels Racing Test Track 1:24
2004 #17 DeWalt

Hot Wheels Racing Test Track 1:64
2004 #17 DeWalt

Hot Wheels Racing Track Edition 1:64
2000 #17 DeWalt

Hot Wheels Racing Transporters 1:64
2001 #17 DeWalt

Hot Wheels Racing Wrenchin' and Racin'
2003 #17 DeWalt

Hot Wheels Radical Rides 1:43
1999 #17 DeWalt

Hot Wheels Select 1:24
2000 #17 DeWalt

Hot Wheels Select 1:64
2000 #17 DeWalt

Hot Wheels Team Transporters 1:64
2004 #17 DeWalt

Hot Wheels Thunder Series Motorcycles 1
2002 #17 DeWalt

Hot Wheels Transporters 1:64
2002 #17 DeWalt
2003 #17 DeWalt

Hot Wheels Victory Lane Transporters 1:
2004 #17 DeWalt

Motorsports Authentics Driver's Select
2007 #17 USG Sheetrock/3434*
2007 #17 R&L Carriers COT/756*
2007 #17 R&L Carriers/1900*
2007 #17 iLevel Wayerhouser/948*
2007 #17 Dish Network/1116*
2007 #17 DeWalt Holiday Sam Bass/780*
2007 #17 DeWalt COT/2182*
2007 #17 DeWalt Homestead-Miami Raced/864*
2007 #17 Carhartt COT/900*
2007 #17 Carhartt for Women/700*
2007 #17 Carhartt California Raced/1200*
2007 #17 Carhartt/1900*
2007 #17 Arby's/2240*
2007 #17 Aflac/1452*
2007 #17 DeWalt/3708*
2007 #17 iLevel Wayerhouser
2007 #17 Carhartt COT

Motorsports Authentics Owner's Elite 1:
2007 #17 DeWalt COT/504
2007 #17 DeWalt/708*
2007 #17 DeWalt/2007*

Motorsports Authentics Owner's Elite Tr
2007 #17 DeWalt/908*
2007 #17 Carhartt/408*

Motorsports Authentics Pit Stop 1:64
2007 #17 USG Sheetrock
2007 #17 R&L Carriers COT
2007 #17 Dish Network
2007 #17 DeWalt COT
2007 #17 DeWalt
2007 #17 Arby's

Motorsports Authentics QVC For Race Fan
2007 #17 R&L Carriers Chrome/96

Motorsports Authentics/RCCA Owner's Clu
2007 #17 DeWalt Holiday Sam Bass/96*
2007 #17 DeWalt/1200*

Peachstate/GMP Transporters 1:64
2002 #17 DeWalt/1200

Race Image Service Kit 1:43
1998 #17 DeWalt

Racing Champions 1:24
1998 #17 Lycos
1999 #17 Luxaire Promo
1999 #17 DeWalt
2000 #17 DeWalt

Racing Champions 1:64
1998 #17 Lycos
1999 #17 Visine Kraft Promo/10,000
1999 #17 DeWalt Kraft Promo
1999 #17 DeWalt Chrome/9999
1999 #17 DeWalt
2000 #17 DeWalt 24 Volt
2000 #17 DeWalt
2000 #NNO 12-car set/Time Trials/Young Guns and War Paint cars/2500
2000 #NNO 12-car boxed set/2500

Racing Champions 12-Car Sets 1:64
1999 #2 12-Car Set 2

Racing Champions 5-Pack 1:64
2000 #NNO 22.WB/17.MK/5.TL/12.JM/40.SM
2001 #NNO 22.WB/17.MK/5.TL/12.JM/40.SM

Racing Champions Gold 1:24
1998 #17 Lycos

Racing Champions Gold with Medallion 1:
1998 #17 Lycos.com

Racing Champions High Octane 1:64
2000 #17 DeWalt

Racing Champions Nascar Rules 1:64
2000 #17 DeWalt

Racing Champions Pit Crew 1:64
2000 #17 DeWalt 24 Volt Chrome/999
2000 #17 DeWalt 24 Volt
2000 #17 DeWalt

Racing Champions Premier 1:24
2000 #17 DeWalt 24 Volt
2000 #17 DeWalt

Racing Champions Premier 1:64
2000 #17 DeWalt 24 Volt
2000 #17 DeWalt
2001 #17 DeWalt Black

Racing Champions Premier Preview 1:24
2000 #17 DeWalt

Racing Champions Premier Preview 1:64
2000 #17 DeWalt
2001 #17 DeWalt '00

Racing Champions Premier Transporters 1
2000 #17 DeWalt

Racing Champions Preview 1:24
2000 #17 DeWalt

Racing Champions Preview 1:64
2000 #17 DeWalt

Racing Champions Signature Series 1:64
1999 #17 DeWalt

Racing Champions Stock Rods 1:64
2000 #3 DeWalt '56 Ford

Racing Champions Time Trial 1:64
2000 #17 DeWalt

Racing Champions Time Trial 2000 1:24
2000 #17 DeWalt

Racing Champions Toys 'R Us Gold 1:64
1998 #17 Lycos

Racing Champions Transporters 1:64
1999 #17 DeWalt
2000 #17 Visine Promo
2000 #17 DeWalt

Racing Champions Transporters Gold 1:64
1999 #17 DeWalt

RCCA Club 1:24
2008 #17 Carhartt/150
2008 #17 DeWalt/150

RCCA Elite 1:24
2008 #17 DeWalt/300

Revell Club 1:24
1999 #17 DeWalt/3508

Team Caliber 1:24
1999 #17 DeWalt Roush/3120
1999 #17 DeWalt/5004

Team Caliber 1:64
1999 #17 DeWalt

Team Caliber First Choice 1:24
2003 #17 Smirnoff Champ/717
2003 #17 DeWalt Victory Lap/717
2003 #17 DeWalt '03 Champ. Employee Promo/2000
2003 #17 DeWalt/756
2004 #17 Smirnoff/504
2004 #17 Martian Manhunter/250
2004 #17 DeWalt/504

Team Caliber First Choice Beckett 1:24
2004 #17 Martian Manhunter AU/1

Team Caliber Model Kits 1:64
2003 #17 DeWalt Million $ Challenge
2003 #17 DeWalt

Team Caliber Owners Series 1:24
2000 #17 DeWalt/5004
2000 #17 Visine/2340
2000 #17 DeW.Emazing.com/5004
2000 #17 DeWalt 24 Volt/5004
2001 #17 Visine-A/2532
2001 #17 DeWalt Saw/1200
2001 #17 DeWalt ROY/2840
2001 #17 DeWalt Flag/804
2001 #17 DeWalt AT&T/2058
2001 #17 DeWalt/5004
2002 #17 DeWalt Million $/2400
2002 #17 DeWalt Flames/3120
2002 #17 AT&T/2400

2002 #17 DeWalt/3120
2003 #17 DeWalt Million $ '03 Champ.
2003 #17 DeWalt Victory Lap/5004
2003 #17 Smirnoff Ice '03 Champ/7500
2003 #17 DeWalt Pearl Gold 2003 Champ/1008
2003 #17 DeWalt Million $ Challenge/2400
2003 #17 DeWalt '03 Champ/6504
2003 #17 DeWalt/7560
2003 #17 Bayer Aleve/1008
2003 #17 Bayer/1008
2003 #17 Alka-Seltzer Morning Relief/1008
2003 #17 Alka-Seltzer Plus/1008
2004 #9 Pennzoil/1200
2004 #17 Express Personnel
2004 #17 Waste Management
2004 #17 Smirnoff/7560
2004 #17 Martian Manhunter/5004
2004 #17 DeWalt/6240
2004 #17 Carhartt/5004
2005 #9 Pennzoil
2005 #17 Waste Management
2005 #17 USG/600
2005 #17 Trex/600
2005 #17 DeWalt/1200
2005 #17 Carhartt/600

Team Caliber Owner's Series 1:24
2006 #17 Carhartt
2006 #17 Trex
2006 #17 DeWalt/2400

Team Caliber Owners Series 1:64
2000 #17 Visine/7560
2000 #17 DeWalt Emazing.com/7560
2000 #17 DeWalt 24 Volt/10,080
2000 #17 DeWalt/10,080
2001 #17 DeWalt ROY
2001 #17 DeWalt/7560
2002 #17 DeWalt/5004
2003 #17 Bayer
2003 #17 DeWalt Million $ Challenge
2003 #17 DeWalt/5004
2004 #17 DeWalt/5004

Team Caliber Owners Series Banks 1:24
2001 #17 Visine-A/504
2001 #17 DeWalt ROY/756
2001 #17 DeWalt Saw/504
2001 #17 DeWalt AT&T/426
2001 #17 DeWalt/1008
2002 #17 DeWalt Million $/198
2002 #17 DeWalt Flames/204
2002 #17 DeWalt/270
2003 #17 Bayer/180
2003 #17 DeWalt Million $ Challenge/180
2003 #17 DeWalt/300

Team Caliber Owners Series Dark Chrome
2002 #17 DeWalt Million Dollar Challenge/588
2002 #17 DeWalt Flames/930
2002 #17 AT&T/504
2002 #17 DeWalt/354
2003 #17 DeWalt '03 Champ.
2003 #17 Victory Lap/600
2003 #17 Smirnoff Ice '03 Champ. Pearl Chrome/1008
2003 #17 DeWalt Million $ Challenge/402
2003 #17 DeWalt/840
2003 #17 Bayer/234

Team Caliber Owners Series Gold 1:24
2000 #17 DeWalt/1200
2001 #17 Visine-A/504
2001 #17 DeWalt/1008

Team Caliber Owners Series Pearl Chrome
2004 #9 Pennzoil/300
2004 #17 Express Personnel
2004 #17 Waste Management
2004 #17 Smirnoff/1008
2004 #17 Martian Manhunter
2004 #17 DeWalt All Star Yellow Chrome AU/1717
2004 #17 DeWalt/600
2004 #17 Carhartt/756

Team Caliber Owners Series Steel 1:24
2001 #17 Visine-A/504
2001 #17 DeWalt/1008

Team Caliber Owners Series Transporters
2003 #17 DeWalt/1200
2004 #17 Martian Manhunter
2004 #17 Smirnoff
2004 #17 DeWalt/600

Team Caliber Pit Stop 1:18
2004 #17 DeWalt

Team Caliber Pit Stop 1:24
2001 #17 DeWalt Saw/3120
2001 #17 DeWalt/3120
2002 #17 DeWalt Million $/3120
2002 #17 AT&T/1800
2002 #17 DeWalt/5520
2003 #17 Smirnoff Ice '03 Champ.
2003 #17 Victory Lap
2003 #17 DeWalt Million $ Challenge
2003 #17 DeWalt '03 Champ.
2003 #17 DeWalt
2003 #17 Bayer
2004 #9 Pennzoil
2004 #17 Martian Manhunter
2004 #17 Express Personnel
2004 #17 DeWalt
2004 #17 Carhartt
2004 #17 Bayer
2005 #9 Pennzoil
2005 #17 Waste Management
2005 #17 USG
2005 #17 Trex
2005 #17 DeWalt
2005 #17 Carhartt
2006 #17 R&L Carriers
2006 #17 Post
2006 #17 Pennzoil
2006 #17 DeWalt
2006 #17 Carhartt
2006 #17 Ameriquest Soaring Dreams
2006 #17 Ameriquest

Team Caliber Pit Stop 1:64
2001 #17 DeWalt Saw/3120
2001 #17 DeWalt Yellow and Black/21168
2001 #17 DeWalt Yellow
2002 #17 DeWalt Million $/7560
2002 #17 DeWalt/7560
2002 #17 AT&T
2003 #17 Bayer
2003 #17 Victory Lap
2003 #17 DeWalt Million $
2003 #17 DeWalt '03 Champ.
2003 #17 DeWalt
2004 #9 Pennzoil
2004 #17 Waste Management
2004 #17 Martian Manhunter
2004 #17 Express Personnel
2004 #17 DeWalt
2004 #17 Carhartt
2004 #17 Bayer
2005 #9 Pennzoil
2005 #17 Waste Management
2005 #17 USG
2005 #17 Trex
2005 #17 DeWalt
2005 #17 Carhartt
2006 #17 Trex
2006 #17 R&L Carriers
2006 #17 Post
2006 #17 Pennzoil
2006 #17 DeWalt
2006 #17 Carhartt
2006 #17 Ameriquest Soaring Dreams
2006 #17 Ameriquest

Team Caliber Pit Stop Transporters 1:64
2003 #17 DeWalt
2004 #17 Martian Manhunter
2004 #17 DeWalt

Team Caliber Preferred 1:24
2000 #17 Visine/5508
2000 #17 DeWalt 24 Volt/20,004
2000 #17 DeWalt/20,004
2001 #17 Visine-A Mac Tools/3000
2001 #17 Visine-A/5136
2001 #17 DeWalt Saw/1896
2001 #17 DeWalt AT&T/1896
2001 #17 DeWalt/2760
2002 #17 DeWalt Million $/1392
2002 #17 DeWalt Flames/1200
2002 #17 AT&T/4128
2002 #17 DeWalt Mac Tools/2400
2002 #17 DeWalt/2448
2003 #17 DeWalt Million $ '03 Champ.
2003 #17 DeWalt Victory Lap Gold/205
2003 #17 DeWalt Victory Lap/10,080
2003 #17 Smirnoff Ice '03 Champ.
2003 #17 DeWalt Million $ Challenge/4128
2003 #17 DeWalt '03 Champ Gold/504
2003 #17 DeWalt '03 Champ/10,080
2003 #17 DeWalt/2400
2003 #17 Bayer/4020
2004 #9 Pennzoil/5004
2004 #17 Express Personnel
2004 #17 Waste Management
2004 #17 Smirnoff Chase/750
2004 #17 Smirnoff/20,080
2004 #17 Martian Manhunter Green Chrome/504
2004 #17 Martian Manhunter Gold/250
2004 #17 Martian Manhunter/7560
2004 #17 DeWalt Chase/1300
2004 #17 DeWalt/20,080
2004 #17 Carhartt/7560
2004 #17 Bayer/4020
2005 #9 Pennzoil/600
2005 #17 Waste Management/3120
2005 #17 USG/1200
2005 #17 Trex/1800
2005 #17 DeWalt/5004
2005 #17 Carhartt/1800
2006 #17 Trex
2006 #17 USG Promo/3210
2006 #17 R&L Carriers/1800
2006 #17 Post/1800
2006 #17 Pennzoil/2700
2006 #17 DeWalt/5004
2006 #17 Carhartt/2016
2006 #17 Ameriquest Soaring Dreams/3000
2006 #17 Ameriquest/1800

Team Caliber Preferred Banks 1:24
2000 #17 Visine/504
2000 #17 DeWalt 24 Volt/756
2000 #17 DeWalt/756

Team Caliber Preferred Copper 1:24
2006 #17 Ameriquest
2006 #17 DeWalt
2006 #17 R&L Carriers
2006 #17 Post
2006 #17 Pennzoil/360

Team Caliber Preferred Nickel 1:24
2005 #9 Pennzoil/252
2005 #17 Waste Management/180
2005 #17 USG/180
2005 #17 Trex/180
2005 #17 DeWalt/1008
2005 #17 Carhartt/300

Team Caliber Promos 1:24
2003 #17 Bayer Yellow
2003 #17 Bayer Blue/400

Team Caliber Promos 1:64
2001 #17 AT&T in PVC box
2003 #17 4-car set
2003 #17 Bayer
2003 #17 Alka-Seltzer Plus
2003 #17 Alka-Seltzer Morning
2003 #17 Aleve
2004 #17 Carhartt in wind.box
2005 #17 Waste Management in window box
2005 #17 USG in window box
2006 #17 USG Sheetrock in window box

Team Caliber Pull Backs 1:87
2002 #17 DeWalt

Team Caliber White Knuckle Racing 1:24
2000 #17 Visine HO
2000 #17 DeWalt

Team Caliber White Knuckle Racing 1:64
2000 #17 Visine Promo
2000 #17 DeWalt

Team Caliber/Motorworks 1:24
2003 #17 DeWalt Victory Lap

Team Caliber/Motorworks 1:64
2003 #17 DeWalt Victory Lap

Team Caliber/Motorworks Model Kits 1:18
2004 #17 DeWalt '03 Champ. w/hat

Team Caliber/Motorworks Model Kits 1:24
2003 #17 DeWalt
2005 #17 DeWalt

Winner's Circle 1:24
2006 #17 DeWalt
2007 #17 DeWalt
2008 #17 DeWalt

Winner's Circle 1:87
2006 #17 DeWalt
2008 #17 DeWalt

Winner's Circle Autographed Hood 1:64
2006 #17 DeWalt

Winner's Circle Autographed Hoods 1:64
2008 #17 DeWalt

Winner's Circle Daytona 500 1:24
2008 #17 DeWalt

Winner's Circle Daytona 500 1:64
2008 #17 DeWalt

Winner's Circle Daytona 500 1:87
2008 #17 DeWalt

Winner's Circle Daytona 500 Hoods 1:64
2008 #17 DeWalt

Winner's Circle License Plate 1:64
2007 #17 DeWalt

Winner's Circle Number Magnet 1:64
2008 #17 DeWalt

Winner's Circle Pit Sign 1:64
2007 #17 DeWalt

Winner's Circle Sam Bass Hoods 1:64
2007 #17 DeWalt Holiday

Winner's Circle Schedule Hood 1:64
2007 #17 DeWalt

Winner's Circle Schedule Hoods 1:64
2008 #17 DeWalt

Winner's Circle Stickers 1:64
2008 #17 Carhartt

Winner's Circle Transporters 1:64
2007 #17 DeWalt

Winner's Circle Victory Lane Hoods 1:64
2007 #17 DeWalt Homestead-Miami Raced
2007 #17 Carhartt California Raced

Keselowski, Brad

RCCA Elite 1:24
2008 #88 Navy Salute the Troops/300
2008 #88 Navy Salute the Troops Platinum/25
2008 #88 Navy Salute the Troops White Gold/50

Winner's Circle Sam Bass 1:64
2008 #88 Navy

Labonte, Bobby

Action Performance 1:24
2000 #18 Interstate Batteries
2002 #18 Interstate Batteries
2003 #18 Interstate Batteries
2005 #18 Interstate Batteries Hometown

Action Performance 1:64
2000 #18 Interstate Batteries
2002 #18 Interstate Batteries
2003 #18 Interstate Batteries
2004 #18 Interstate Batteries
2005 #18 Interstate Batteries

Action QVC For Race Fans Only 1:24
2000 #18 Interstate Batteries Frankenstein Gold/2000
2000 #18 Interstate Batt.All-Star Gold/1000
2000 #18 Interstate Batt.All-Star Color Chrome/1000
2001 #18 Interstate Batteries Jurassic Park 3 Plat./624
2001 #18 Interstate Batteries Jurassic Park 3 Gold/1000
2001 #18 Interstate Batteries Coke Bear Platinum/624
2001 #18 Interstate Batteries Coke Bear Gold/1000
2001 #18 Interstate Batteries Coke Bear Col.Chrome/1000

Action Racing Collectables 1:18
1999 #18 Interstate Batteries NASCAR Racers/2508
2000 #18 Interstate Batteries All Star Game
2001 #18 Interstate Batteries Coke Bear/2508
2001 #18 Interstate Batteries Cal Ripken
2004 #18 Interstate Batteries Shrek 2/2508

Action Racing Collectables 1:24
1996 #18 Inter.Batt.Football HOF
1996 #18 Interstate Batteries
1997 #18 Inter.Batt.Mac Tools
1997 #18 Interstate Batteries
1998 #18 Interstate Batteries Small Soldiers/2508
1998 #18 Interstate Batteries Hot Rod Bank
1998 #18 Interstate Batteries Hot Rod/10,992
1998 #18 Inter.Batt.Bank/2500
1998 #18 Inter.Batteries/5000
1998 #18 Interstate Batteries Small Soldiers Bank
1999 #18 MBNA/4608
1999 #18 Interstate Batteries NASCAR Racers/7500
1999 #18 Interstate Batt.Bank
1999 #18 Interstate Batteries
2000 #18 Interstate Batteries Frankenstein/11,664
2000 #18 Interstate Batteries All Star Game Bank/2808
2000 #18 Interstate Batteries All Star Game/15,482
2000 #18 Inter.Batt.Clear/4008
2000 #18 Inter.Batteries Bank
2000 #18 Interstate Batteries
2001 #18 Interstate Batteries Jur.Park 3 Mac Tools/3000
2001 #18 Interstate Batteries Jurassic Park 3 Clear/6000
2001 #18 Interstate Batteries Jurassic Park 3 Bank/1788
2001 #18 Interstate Batteries Jurassic Park 3/21,096
2001 #18 Interstate Batteries Coke Bear Clear
2001 #18 Interstate Batteries Coke Bear Mac Tools/3000
2001 #18 Interstate Batteries Coke Bear Bank/2004
2001 #18 Interstate Batteries Coke Bear/25,320
2001 #18 Interstate Batteries Cal Ripken/24,636
2001 #18 Inter.Batt.Col.Chrome 2000 WC Champ/19,188
2001 #18 Interstate Batt.Bank
2001 #18 Interstate Batteries
2002 #1 True Value '01 IROC/4668
2002 #18 Let.Roll Mac Tools/1798
2002 #18 Let's Roll Bank/600
2002 #18 Let's Roll/11,158
2002 #18 Inter.Batteries Muppet Bank/960
2002 #18 Inter.Batt.Muppet/17,076
2002 #18 Interstate Batteries Mac Tools/2172
2002 #18 Interstate Batt.Clear/5064
2002 #18 Interstate Batt.Bank/1008
2002 #18 Interstate Batt./19,860
2002 #18 3M 100th Anniv.
2003 #18 Inter.Batteries 3M Employee Promo/2700
2003 #18 Interstate Batteries Victory Lap Mac Tools/288
2003 #18 Interstate Batteries Victory Lap GM Dealers/336
2003 #18 Interstate Batteries Victory Lap CW Bank/420
2003 #18 Interstate Batteries Victory Lap/6876
2003 #18 Inter.Batteries Hulk CW Bank/720
2003 #18 Inter.Batt.Hulk/10,884
2003 #18 Interstate Batteries Advair Purple GM Dealers/300
2003 #18 Interstate Batteries Advair Purple/7068
2003 #18 Interstate Batteries Advair Green/5784
2003 #18 Interstate Batteries GM Dealers/288
2003 #18 Inter.Batt.BW Bank/504
2003 #18 Interstate Batt./11,244
2004 #18 Wellbutrin GM Dealers/108
2004 #18 Wellbutrin CW Bank/288
2004 #18 Wellbutrin/2784
2004 #18 Interstate Batteries Shrek 2 Mac Tools/288
2004 #18 Interstate Batteries Shrek 2 GM Dealers/548
2004 #18 Interstate Batteries Shrek 2 CW Bank/336
2004 #18 Interstate Batteries Shrek 2/8292
2004 #18 Interstate Batteries Father's Day GM Dealers/180
2004 #18 Interstate Batteries Father's Day CW Bank/360
2004 #18 Interstate Batteries Father's Day/3528
2004 #18 Interstate Batteries D-Day GM Dealers/432
2004 #18 Interstate Batteries D-Day CW Bank/360
2004 #18 Interstate Batteries D-Day/6060
2004 #18 Interstate Batteries Nextel Incentive/2304
2004 #18 Interstate Batteries Mac Tools/288
2004 #18 Interstate Batteries GM Dealers/1896
2004 #18 Interstate Batteries CW Bank/372
2004 #18 Interstate Batteries/12,612
2004 #19 Banquet GM Dealers/24
2004 #19 Banquet CW Bank/240
2004 #19 Banquet/1608
2004 #29 ESGR Army GM Dealers/300
2004 #29 ESGR Army CW Bank/300
2004 #29 ESGR Army/4824
2005 #18 Interstate Batteries Madagascar QVC/408
2005 #18 Interstate Batteries Madagascar Matco/84
2005 #18 Interstate Batteries Madagascar GM Dealers/144
2005 #18 Interstate Batteries Madagascar CW Bank/144
2005 #18 Interstate Batteries Madagascar/3864
2005 #18 Interstate Batteries QVC/288
2005 #18 Interstate Batteries Matco/84
2005 #18 Interstate Batteries GM Dealers/360
2005 #18 Interstate Batteries CW Bank/204
2005 #18 Interstate Batteries/4872
2005 #18 FedEx Mac Tools/120
2005 #18 FedEx GM Dealers/180
2005 #18 FedEx/2508
2005 #18 Boniva/996
2005 #46 Silverado Trick Pony SuperTruck/3504
2005 #47 Silverado Trick Pony SuperTruck Martinsville Raced w/tire/1416
2006 #43 STP/2616
2006 #43 Gogurt/1296

Action Racing Collectables 1:32
1998-01 #18/44 T.Stewart Small Soldiers 2-cars/4500 '98

Action Racing Collectables 1:64
1996 #18 Inter.Batt.Football HOF
1996 #18 Interstate Batteries
1997 #18 Interstate Batteries
1998 #18 Interstate Batteries Small Soldiers
1998 #18 Interstate Batt.Hot Rod
1998 #18 Interstate Batteries
1999 #18 MBNA/7488
1999 #18 Interstate Batteries NASCAR Racers
1999 #18 Interstate Batteries
2000 #18 Interstate Batteries Frankenstein/9360
2000 #18 Interstate Batteries
2000 #18/20 T.Stewart Chef Boyardee Promo blister
2001 #18 Interstate Batteries Jurassic Park 3/16,128
2001 #18 Interstate Batteries in a Coke bottle/21,524
2001 #18 Inter.Batteries/10,500
2001 #18/20 Coke Bear 2-car promo blister
2002 #18 Let's Roll in tin/4464
2002 #18 Let's Roll/8856
2002 #18 Interstate Batteries Muppet/14,544
2002 #18 Interstate Batt./18,864
2003 #18 Interstate Batt.Advair
2003 #18 Interstate Batteries Victory Lap/9324
2003 #18 Interstate Batt.Hulk/5256
2003 #18 Interstate Batteries/10,728
2004 #18 Interstate Batteries Shrek 2/5712
2004 #18 Interstate Batteries D-Day/5568
2004 #18 Interstate Batteries/8640
2005 #18 Interstate Batteries Madagascar
2005 #18 Interstate Batteries
2006 #43 STP
2006 #43 Cheerios
2008 #43 Cheerios

Action Racing Collectables Platinum 1:2
2008 #43 Cheerios/3300

Action Racing Collectables Transporters
2001 #18 Interstate Batteries Jurassic Park 3
2001 #18/20 Coke/4008

Action Total Concept 1:64
2000 #18 Interstate Batt.Monsters
2000 #18 Interstate Batteries All Star Game/15,336

Action/Funline Monster Truck 1:43
2004 #18 Interstate Batteries

Action/Funline Muscle Machines 1:18
2004 #18 Interstate Batteries '69 Camaro
2004 #18 Interstate Batteries '69 Chevelle
2004 #18 Interstate Batteries '67 Nova

Action/Funline Muscle Machines 1:24
2004 #18 Interstate Batteries '69 Camaro
2004 #18 Interstate Batteries '69 Chevelle
2004 #18 Interstate Batteries '66 Nova
2005 #18 Interstate Batteries Hybrid

Action/RCCA 1:24
1996 #18 Interstate Batteries Football HOF Bank/10,000
1996 #18 Inter.Batt. Bank/5000
1997 #18 Inter.Batt.Bank/3500
2002 #18 Let's Roll Bank/600
2002 #18 Interstate Batteries Muppet Bank/720
2002 #18 Interstate Batt.Bank/804
2003 #18 Interstate Batteries Victory Lap/600
2003 #18 Interstate Batt. Hulk CW Bank/600
2003 #18 Interstate Batt. Advair Purple/444
2003 #18 Interstate Batt. Advair Green/360
2003 #18 Interstate Batt. CW Bank/504
2004 #18 Wellbutrin/360
2004 #18 Interstate Batteries Shrek 2/600
2004 #18 Interstate Batteries D-Day/504
2004 #18 Interstate Batteries Father's Day/240
2004 #18 Interstate Batteries/504
2004 #19 Banquet/288
2004 #29 ESGR Army/600
2005 #18 Boniva/204
2005 #18 FedEx Freight/240
2005 #18 Interstate Batteries Madagascar/300
2005 #18 Interstate Batteries Test/360
2005 #18 Interstate Batteries Color Chrome/204
2005 #18 Interstate Batteries/288
2005 #47 Silverado Trick Pony Martinsville Raced w/tire/288
2006 #43 Cheerios/200
2006 #43 STP/250
2006 #43 Gogurt/200

Action/RCCA 1:64
1996 #18 Interstate Batt.Football HOF/10,000
1996 #18 Interstate Batt./10,000
1997 #18 Interstate Batt./5000
1998 #18 Interstate Batteries Small Soldiers/10,000
1998 #18 Interstate Batt.Hot Rod
1998 #18 Interstate Batteries
1999 #18 Interstate Batteries
2000 #18 Interstate Batteries NASCAR Racers/4500
2000 #18 Interstate Batteries All Star Game/2880
2000 #18 Interstate Batteries/2520
2001 #18 Interstate Batteries Jurassic Park 3/1484
2001 #18 Interstate Batteries Coke Bear/1800
2001 #18 Inter.Batteries/1584
2002 #18 Let's Roll/1584
2002 #18 Inter.Batt.Muppet/1584
2002 #18 Interstate Batt./1584
2003 #18 Interstate Batt.Hulk/1020
2003 #18 Interstate Batteries/1212
2003 #18 Interstate Batteries/1008
2004 #18 Wellbutrin
2004 #18 Interstate Batteries Shrek 2/1008
2004 #18 Interstate Batteries D-Day/576
2005 #18 Interstate Batteries Madagascar/576
2005 #18 Interstate Batteries/576
2006 #43 Cheerios/144
2006 #43 Gogurt Cars/288
2006 #43 STP/288

Action/RCCA Banks 1:24
1998 #18 Interstate Batteries Small Soldiers/7500
1998 #18 Interstate Batteries/1500
1999 #18 Interstate Batteries NASCAR Racers/3500
1999 #18 Interstate Batteries
2000 #18 Inter.Batteries/1500
2001 #18 Interstate Batteries/1500

Action/RCCA Dually Trucks 1:24
1994 #22 Maxwell House PLS Bank/2508
1996 #18 Interstate Batteries RCCA Bank/2500

Action/RCCA Elite 1:24
1997 #18 Interstate Batt./1500
1998 #18 Interstate Batteries Small Soldiers/5000
1998 #18 Inter.Batt.Hot Rod/1200
1999 #18 MBNA/800
1999 #18 Interstate Batteries NASCAR Racers/2500
1999 #18 Interstate Batteries/1000
2000 #18 Interstate Batteries Frankenstein/696
2000 #18 Inter.Batt.All-Star/1008
2000 #18 Interstate Batteries/1000
2001 #18 Interstate Batteries Jurassic Park 3/804
2001 #18 Inter.Batt.Cal Ripken/1008
2001 #18 Interstate Batteries Coke Bear/1008
2001 #18 Inter.Batt.Test/3504
2001 #18 Interstate Batt./1008
2002 #18 Let's Roll/900
2002 #18 Inter.Batt.Muppet/960
2002 #18 Interstate Batt./1008
2003 #18 Interstate Batteries Victory Lap/600
2003 #18 Interstate Batt.Hulk/900
2003 #18 Interstate Batt. Advair Purple/444
2003 #18 Interstate Batteries/720
2004 #18 Wellbutrin/360
2004 #18 Interstate Batteries Shrek 2/600
2004 #18 Interstate Batteries D-Day/504
2004 #18 Interstate Batteries Color Chrome/300
2004 #18 Interstate Batteries/720
2004 #19 Banquet/288
2004 #29 ESGR Army/600
2005 #18 Boniva/204
2005 #18 Interstate Batteries Test/408
2005 #18 Interstate Batteries Madagascar/408
2005 #18 Interstate Batteries White Gold/25
2005 #18 Interstate Batteries Color Chrome/204
2005 #18 Interstate Batteries/408
2005 #18 FedEx Freight/240
2006 #43 STP White Gold/25
2006 #43 STP Platinum/6
2006 #43 STP/300
2006 #43 Gogurt White Gold/25
2006 #43 Gogurt Platinum/4
2006 #43 Gogurt/200
2006 #43 Cheerios White Gold/25
2006 #43 Cheerios Platinum/4
2006 #43 Cheerios/200

Action/RCCA Elite 1:64
2001 #18 Interstate Batteries Jurassic Park 3/1104
2001 #18 Interstate Batteries Coke Bear/1296
2001 #18 Interstate Batteries
2002 #18 Inter.Batt.Muppet/1200
2002 #18 Interstate Batt./1200
2003 #18 Inter.Batt.Hulk/1200
2003 #18 Interstate Batteries/1212
2004 #18 Interstate Batteries Shrek 2/720
2004 #18 Interstate Batteries D-Day/528
2004 #18 Interstate Batteries/1008
2005 #18 Interstate Batteries/480
2005 #18 Interstate Batteries Madagascar/480
2006 #43 Cheerios/288
2006 #43 Gogurt Cars/192
2006 #43 STP/204

Action/RCCA Gold 1:32
1998 #18 Interstate Batteries

Action/RCCA Legends, Oldsmobiles and
1991-92 #44 Penrose

Action/RCCA Metal Elite 1:24
2005 #18 Interstate Batteries/408

Action/RCCA Transporters 1:64
1992 #44 Penrose Saus.RCCA/5000
2001 #18 Inter.Batt.Color Chrome Jurassic Park 3 RCCA/456

Brookfield 1:24
2005 #18 Interstate Batteries/300
2005 #18 Interstate Batteries Madagascar/144

Brookfield Dually with Car and Show Tra
2001 #18 Inter.Batt.Jurassic Park 3 Silver w/o car/504
2001 #18 Inter.Batt.Jurassic Park 3 w/o car/2004

Brookfield Trackside 1:64
2004 #18 Interstate Batteries Shrek 2/5000

Corgi Race Image Transporters 1:64
1993-95 #22 Maxwell House

Hot Wheels Racing Color Change 1:64
2003 #18 Interstate Batteries
2004 #18 Interstate Batteries

Hot Wheels Racing Power Launchers 1:64
2003 #18 Interstate Batteries

Matchbox White Rose Super Stars 1:64
1993 #22 Maxwell House BL
1995 #18 Interstate Batteries
1990-92 #44 Penrose BX 92
1990-92 #44 Slim Jim BX 92

Matchbox White Rose Transporters Super
1992 #44 Slim Jim
1993 #22 Maxwell House

Miscellaneous Promos 1:24
1996 #44 Shell '96 EPI

Miscellaneous Promos 1:64
1991-04 #18 Inter.Batt.EPI blister '96
1991-04 #18 Banquet in bag '02
1991-04 #44 Shell EPI Motor.blister '96

Motorsports Authentics Driver's Select
2007 #43 General Mills COT/1140*
2007 #43 Cheerios 500 Starts COT/840*
2007 #43 Cheerios Spiderman/2032*
2007 #43 Cheerios Pink Susan G. Komen/1056*
2007 #43 Cheerios COT/960*
2007 #43 Cheerios/4204*
2007 #43 Cheerios

Motorsports Authentics Owner's Elite 1:
2007 #43 Cheerios COT White Gold/50
2007 #43 Cheerios COT Platinum/25
2007 #43 Cheerios COT/504
2007 #43 Cheerios/504*
2007 #43 Cheerios/1008*

Motorsports Authentics Owner's Elite Tr
2007 #43 Cheerios/204*

Motorsports Authentics Pit Stop 1:64
2007 #43 Cheerios

Motorsports Authentics/RCCA Owner's Clu
2007 #43 Cheerios/708*

Peachstate/GMP Transporters 1:64
1996-01 #18 Interstate Batteries '96
1996-01 #22 Max.House RCCA/2500

Press Pass Sets 1:24/64

1996 #18 Inter.Batteries/1008 1:64 car and hauler set
Race Image 1:43
1998 #18 Interstate Batteries
Racing Champions 1:144
1996 #18 Interstate Batteries
1997 #18 Interstate Batteries
Racing Champions 1:24
1993 #22 Maxwell House
1994 #22 Maxwell House
1994 #33 Dentyne
1995 #18 Interstate Batteries
1996 #18 Interstate Batteries
1996 #44 Shell
1997 #18 Interstate Batteries
Racing Champions 1:64
1993 #22 Maxwell House
1994 #22 Maxwell House
1994 #33 Dentyne
1995 #18 Interstate Batteries with roof flaps
1995 #18 Interstate Batteries without roof flaps
1996 #18 Inter.Batt.Chrome/1996
1996 #18 Interstate Batteries
1996 #44 Shell
1997 #18 Interstate Batteries
1997 #NNO 12-Car set in black case
Racing Champions Banks 1:24
1992-94 #22 Maxwell House/7500 '93
1992-94 #33 Dentyne/2500 '94
Racing Champions Hobby 1:64
1996 #18 Interstate Batteries
Racing Champions Matched Serial Numbers
1995 #18 Interstate Batteries
Racing Champions Pinnacle Series 1:64
1997 #18 Interstate Batteries
Racing Champions Premier 1:18
1995 #18 Interstate Batteries
1997 #18 Interstate Batteries Gold
1997 #18 Interstate Batteries
Racing Champions Premier 1:43
1994 #22 Maxwell House/5000
Racing Champions Premier 1:64
1994 #33 Dentyne/10,000
1995 #18 Interstate Batteries
Racing Champions Premier Banks 1:24
1996 #18 Inter.Batt.Chrome/166
1996 #18 Interstate Batteries/1826
1997 #18 Interstate Batt. Gold/166
1997 #18 Interstate Batteries/4992
Racing Champions Premier Gold 1:64
1997 #18 Interstate Batteries
Racing Champions Premier Gold Chrome 1:
1997 #18 Interstate Batteries
Racing Champions Premier Preview with M
1997 #18 Interstate Batteries
Racing Champions Premier Transporters 1
1993 #22 Maxwell House
Racing Champions Premier with Medallion
1996 #18 Inter.Batteries HO
1996 #18 Interstate Batteries
1996 #44 Shell
1997 #18 Interstate Batt.Silver/997
1997 #18 Interstate Batteries
Racing Champions Preview 1:144
1997 #18 Interstate Batteries
Racing Champions Preview 1:24
1996 #18 Interstate Batteries
1997 #18 Interstate Batteries
Racing Champions Preview 1:64
1996 #18 Interstate Batteries
1997 #18 Interstate Batteries
Racing Champions Roaring Racers 1:64
1997 #18 Interstate Batteries
Racing Champions Stock Rods 1:64
1997 #7 Interstate Batteries
Racing Champions To the Maxx 1:64
1995 #18 Interstate Batteries
Racing Champions Transporters 1:144
1997 #18 Interstate Batteries
Racing Champions Transporters 1:64
1993 #22 Maxwell House
1995 #18 Interstate Batteries
1996 #44 Shell
Racing Champions Transporters 1:87
1996 #18 Interstate Batteries
1996 #44 Shell
1997 #18 Interstate Batteries
Racing Champions Transporters Retail
1993-94 #22 Maxwell House
Racing Champions Transporters Retail 1:
1994 #22 Maxwell House
1994 #33 Dentyne
RCCA Club 1:24
2008 #43 Cheerios/150
RCCA Elite 1:24
2008 #43 Cheerios/300
2008 #43 Cheerios Platinum/25
2008 #43 Cheerios White Gold/50
Revell Club 1:18
1998 #18 Intersate Batteries Small Soldiers/1002
1998 #18 Inter.Batt.Hot Rod/504
Revell Club 1:24
1997 #18 Inter.Batt.Texas/1596
1997 #18 Inter.Batteries/1596
1998 #18 Interstate Batteries Small Soldiers/2004
1998 #18 Inter.Batt.Hot Rod
1999 #18 Interstate Batteries
2000 #18 Inter.Batt.All Star
2000 #18 Interstate Batteries/1002
Revell Collection 1:18
1997 #18 Inter.Batt.Texas/3120
1997 #18 Interstate Batteries
1998 #18 Inter.Batt.Small Soldiers
1998 #18 Inter.Batt.Hot Rod/3120
1999 #18 Interstate Batt./2508
2000 #18 Interstate Batteries
Revell Collection 1:24
1996 #18 Interstate Batt./2700
1997 #18 Inter.Batt.TMS Bank
1997 #18 Inter.Batt.Texas/8598
1997 #18 Interstate Batteries/5004
1998 #18 Interstate Batteries Small Soldiers/5598
1998 #18 Inter.Batt.Hot Rod/5598
1998 #18 Interstate Batteries/5598
1999 #18 Interstate Batteries/4000
2000 #18 Interstate Batteries Frankenstein/2508
2000 #18 Interstate Batteries All Star Game w/baseball/3120
2000 #18 Interstate Batteries
2001 #18 Inter.Batt.Juras.Park 3
2005 #18 Interstate Batteries Test/732
Revell Collection 1:43
1998 #18 Interstate Batteries Small Soldiers/5004
1998 #18 Inter.Batt.Hot Rod/5004
1998 #18 Interstate Batteries
Revell Collection 1:64
1996 #18 Interstate Batteries
1997 #NNO Terry 2-car tin
1998 #18 Inter.Batt.Small Soldiers
1998 #18 Interstate Batt.Hot Rod
1998 #18 Interstate Batteries
1999 #18 Interstate Batteries
2000 #18 Interstate Batt./7992
2001 #18 Inter.Batt.'00 Champ 2-car set in tin/6432
2001 #18/20 Jurassic Park 3 in tin/7992
Revell Retail 1:24
1995 #18 Interstate Batteries
1996 #18 Interstate Batteries
Revell Retail 1:64
1996 #18 Interstate Batteries
1997 #18 Interstate Batteries
1997 #18 Interstate Batt.Texas
Revell Select 1:24
1997 #18 Interstate Batt.Texas
1997 #18 Interstate Batteries
1998 #18 Interstate Batt.Hot Rod
1998 #18 Interstate Batteries
Revell Select Hobby 1:64
1997 #18 Interstate Batt.Texas
1997 #18 Interstate Batteries
1998 #18 Interstate Batt.Hot Rod
1998 #18 Interstate Batteries
Team Caliber Owner's Series 1:24
2006 #43 Cheerios
Team Caliber Pit Stop 1:24
2006 #43 Cheerios
Team Caliber Pit Stop 1:64
2006 #43 Cheerios
Team Caliber Preferred 1:24
2006 #43 Cheerios/2400
Team Caliber Preferred Copper 1:24
2006 #43 Cheerios/432
Winner's Circle 1:24
1997 #18 Interstate Batteries
1998 #18 Inter.Batt.Small Soldiers
1998 #18 Interstate Batteries
1999 #18 Interstate Batteries
2000 #18 Interstate Batteries
2001 #18 Inter.Batt.Jur.Park 3
2001 #18 Interstate Batteries
2002 #18 Interstate Batt.Muppets
2002 #18 Inter.Batt.Jurassic Park
2002 #18 Interstate Batteries Coke
2002 #18 Interstate Batteries
2004 #18 Interstate Batteries Shrek 2
2004 #18 Interstate Batteries D-Day
2004 #18 Interstate Batteries
2004 #29 ESGR Army
2005 #18 Interstate Batteries
Winner's Circle 1:43
1999 #18 Interstate Batteries
2000 #18 Interstate Batteries
Winner's Circle 1:64
1997 #18 Interstate Batteries
1998 #18 Inter.Batt.Small Soldiers
1998 #18 Interstate Batt.Hot Rod
1998 #18 Interstate Batteries
2000 #18 Int.Batt.NASCAR Racers
2000 #18 Interstate Batteries
Winner's Circle Autographed Hood 1:64
2002 #18 Inter.Batteries Muppets
2003 #18 Interstate Batteries
2004 #18 Interstate Batteries Shrek 2 small package
2004 #18 Interstate Batteries Shrek 2
2004 #18 Interstate Batteries D-Day short package
2004 #18 Interstate Batteries short package
2004 #29 ESGR Army
2005 #18 Interstate Batteries Madagascar
2005 #18 Interstate Batteries
2005 #18 Boniva
Winner's Circle Autographed Hoods 1:64
2008 #43 Cheerios
Winner's Circle Decade of Champions 1:6
2003 #18 Interstate Batt. 2000
Winner's Circle Deluxe Race Hood 1:64
2000 #18 Interstate Batteries
Winner's Circle Double Platinum 1:43
2000 #18 J.Gibbs/Int.Batteries
2001 #18 Interstate Batteries Coke
2002 #18 Inter.Batt. Muppets
Winner's Circle Driver Hood 1:64
2000-01 #18 Interstate Batteries
Winner's Circle Driver Sticker 1:64
2001 #18 Interstate Batteries
2002 #18 Inter.Batt.Jurassic Park 3
2003 #1 True Value '01 IROC
2004 #18 Interstate Batteries
2005 #18 Interstate Batteries
Winner's Circle Gallery 1:64
2002 #18 Inter.Batt.Coke Bear
Winner's Circle Gift Pack With Photo 1:
2002 #18 Interstate Batt./Muppets Interstate Batt.Coke
Winner's Circle License Plate Series 1:
2001 #18 Interstate Batteries
Winner's Circle Micro Machines 1:144
1999 #NNO J.Gordon
1999 #NNO 7-car Draft Pack
2000 #18/24 J.Gordon
Winner's Circle Photo Hood Spiderman LE
2007 #43 Cheerios Spiderman
Winner's Circle Pit Pass Preview 1:64
2002 #18 Interstate Batteries
2004 #18 Interstate Batteries
Winner's Circle Pit Row 1:64
1999 #18 Inter.Batt.Small Soldiers
1998 #18 Interstate Batteries left side raised
Winner's Circle Preview 1:24
2000 #18 Interstate Batteries
Winner's Circle Preview 1:43
2000 #18 Interstate Batteries
Winner's Circle Race Hood 1:43
2002 #18 Interstate Batt.Muppets
2004 #18 Interstate Batteries Shrek 2
Winner's Circle Race Hood 1:64
2004 #18 Interstate Batteries
2001-02 #18 Inter.Batt.Coke Bear
2001-02 #18 Interstate Batteries
Winner's Circle Schedule Hood 1:64
2005 #18 Interstate Batteries
2006 #18 Interstate Batteries
Winner's Circle Sneak Previews 1:64
2000 #18 Interstate Batteries
Winner's Circle Speedweeks 1:43
1999 #18 Interstate Batteries
Winner's Circle Speedweeks 1:64
1999 #18 Interstate Batteries
Winner's Circle Stickers 1:64
2008 #43 Cheerios
Winner's Circle Team Authentics 1:64
2001 #18 Inter.Batt.Sheetmetal
2001 #18 Inter.Batt.Firesuit
Winner's Circle Tech Series 1:64
1999 #18 Interstate Batteries
Winner's Circle Test Hood 1:64
2005 #18 Interstate Batteries
Winner's Circle Transporters 1:64
2000 #18 Inter.Batt.dark green
2000 #18 Inter.Batt.light green
2002 #18 Interstate Batt.Muppets
2002 #18 Interstate Batt. Jurassic
2002 #18 Interstate Batteries
2004 #18 Interstate Batteries Shrek 2
2004 #18 Interstate Batteries
2005 #18 Interstate Batteries
2005 #18 Interstate Batteries Madagascar
2007 #43 STP
2007 #43 Spiderman
Winner's Circle Winston Cup Scene 1:64
2001 #18 Inter.Batt.No Recount

Logano, Joey

Motorsports Authentics Driver's Select
2007 #20 JG Racing Oil/720*

Martin, Mark

Action QVC For Race Fans Only 1:24
2006 #6 Crown Royal IROC Color Chrome/504
Action Racing Collectables 1:24
1994 #2 Miller American 1984 ASA Bank
1995 #6 Valv.Brickyard Bank/5004
1995 #6 Valvoline Brickyard/8520
1995 #6 Valvoline/5496
1995 #6 Folgers '91 Bank/5004
1996 #2 Miller '85 ASA Bank/6000
1996 #2 Miller '85 ASA
1996 #6 Valvoline Bank
1997 #6 Valvoline Mac Tools
1997 #6 Valvoline
1997 #60 Winn Dixie Bank
2000 #1 Activision '83 MC/6500
2000 #2 Hartley's '79 ASA/5508
2000 #2 G&G Trucking '83 ASA Firebird/5940
2000 #4 Jim Magill Orange 1983 Monte Carlo
2000 #6 Jim Magill Green '83 Monte Carlo Bank/6500
2000 #6 Jim Magill Green 1983 Monte Carlo/7008
2002 #2 Miller '86 ASA/4656
2002 #2 Amsoil '80 ASA/3240
2002 #6 Stroh's Light 1989 T-bird/5004
2002 #31 Fat Boys BBQ 1987 Thunderbird/3444
2003 #1 True Value '98 IROC/5976
2003 #2 SAI Roofing '87 T-bird/3660
2003 #6 Carolina Ford Dealers '86 Thunderbird CWB/600
2003 #6 Carolina Ford Dealers '86 Thunderbird/2736
2003 #8 True Value IROC Grn/6748
2005 #6 Crown Royal IROC QVC/504
2005 #6 Crown Royal IROC GM Dealers/84
2005 #6 Crown Royal IROC Brushed Metal/360
2005 #6 Crown Royal IROC/2232
2006 #6 Crown Royal IROC GM Dealers/192
2006 #6 Crown Royal IROC/2316
2006 #6 AAA Holiday QVC*
2006 #6 AAA Holiday/1584*
Action Racing Collectables 1:64
1995 #6 Valvoline Brickyard blister
1995 #6 Valvoline Brickyard PLS
1995 #6 Valvoline
1995 #6 Folgers/24,912
1996 #2 Miller American 1985 ASA/20,000
1996 #6 Valvoline Race Day
1996 #6 Valvoline
1997 #6 Valvoline
1997 #60 Winn Dixie
2002 #31 Fat Boys BBQ '87 T-bird
2003 #6 Carolina Ford Dealers 1986 Thunderbird
2006 #6 AAA Holiday
Action Racing Collectables Platinum 1:2
2008 #8 U.S. Army/8004
Action Racing Collectables Valvoline Te
1993 #6 Valvoline
Action/RCCA 1:24
1995 #6 Valvoline Brickyard Bank
1995 #6 Valvoline Bank/4500
1995 #6 Folgers '91/2508
1996 #6 Valvoline
1997 #6 Valvoline Bank
1997 #60 Winn Dixie/5500
2002 #2 Miller '86 ASA/120
2002 #31 Fat Boys BBQ 1987 T-bird Bank/600
2003 #2 SAI Roofing '87 T-bird/504
2003 #6 Carolina Ford Dealers Bank '86 Thunderbird/600
2003 #8 True Value IROC Green/460
2005 #6 Crown Royal IROC Brushed Metal/360
2006 #6 AAA/250
2006 #6 AAA Color Chrome/100
2006 #6 AAA Holiday/250
2006 #6 Scotts SuperTruck AU/408
2006 #6 Crown Royal White Pearl/288
Action/RCCA 1:64
1993 #2 Miller Acrylic
1993 #6 Valvoline/15,000
1993 #6 Stroh's Light 2 cars/15,000
1993 #6 Folgers Promo blister
1995 #2 Miller American 1985 ASA/10,000
1995 #6 Valvoline Brickyard
1995 #6 Valvoline/10,080
1996 #6 Valvoline/10,000
1997 #6 Valvoline/5000
1997 #60 Winn Dixie
2000 #6 Jim Magill Green 1983 Monte Carlo/7560
Action/RCCA Banks 1:24
1999 #2 J-Mar Trucking/2500
2000 #1 Activision '83 MC/6500
2000 #4 Jim Magill Orange 1983 Monte Carlo/6500
2000 #6 Jim Magill Green 1983 Monte Carlo/6500
Action/RCCA Dually Trucks 1:24
1996 #6 Valvol.PLS Bank/4512
Action/RCCA Elite 1:24
1997 #6 Valvoline/2500
1997 #60 Winn Dixie/3500
1999 #2 J-Mar Trucking/1000
1999 #6 Jim Magill Green 1983 Monte Carlo/2500
2000 #1 Activision '83 MC/2500
2000 #4 Jim Magill Orange 1983 Monte Carlo/2500
2002 #31 Fat Boys BBQ 1987 T-bird/600
2003 #2 SAI Roofing '87 T-bird/504
2003 #6 Carolina Ford Dealers 1986 Thunderbird/600
2006 #6 AAA/400
2006 #6 AAA Color Chrome/150
2006 #6 AAA Holiday Platinum/5
2006 #6 AAA Holiday/250
Action/RCCA Historical 1:24
2006 #2 True Value '00 IROC/300
Action/RCCA Revell 1:64
1991-92 #6 Valvoline
Action/RCCA Transporters 1:64
1993 #6 Valvoline RCCA with car/2500
1995 #6 Valvoline
Checkered Flag Sports Champion 1:24
2008 #8 U.S. Army
2008 #8 Steak-Umm
Checkered Flag Sports Champions 1:24
2007 #1 U.S. Army COT/10,000
2007 #1 U.S. Army/10,000
Checkered Flag Sports Champions Black L
2007 #1 U.S. Army COT
2007 #1 U.S. Army/1250
Checkered Flag Sports Contender 1:24
2007 #1 U.S. Army COT
2007 #1 U.S. Army
2008 #8 U.S. Army
Checkered Flag Sports Contender 1:64
2007 #1 U.S. Army COT
2007 #1 U.S. Army
Corgi Race Image Transporters 1:64
1993-95 #6 Valvoline '93
Ertl 1:18
1992 #6 Valvoline
1994 #6 Valvoline/30,000
1994 #60 Winn Dixie GMP/3500
1995 #6 Valvoline/15,000
1996 #6 Valvoline/10,000
1997 #6 Valvoline/10,000
Ertl Proshop 1:18
2000 #6 Valvoline
Ertl Proshop 1:24
2000 #6 Valvoline
Ertl Proshop 1:64
2000 #6 Valvoline
Funstuf Pit Row 1:43
1992 #6 Valvoline
Hot Wheels Alternative Paint Scheme 1:6
2005 #6 Kraft
Hot Wheels Batman Begins 1:24
2005 #6 Batman
Hot Wheels Batman Begins 1:64
2005 #6 Batman
Hot Wheels Batman Begins Transporters 1
2005 #6 Batman
Hot Wheels Crew's Choice 1:24
2000 #6 Valvoline
Hot Wheels Crew's Choice 1:43
1999 #6 Valvoline
Hot Wheels Daytona Set-Up 1:64
2002 #6 Pfizer
Hot Wheels Deluxe 1:24
1999 #6 Valvoline Black Chrome
Hot Wheels Deluxe 1:64
2000 #6 Valvoline
Hot Wheels Deluxe Black Chrome 1:43
1999 #6 Valvoline
Hot Wheels Deluxe Go Kart 1:64
2000 #6 Valvoline
Hot Wheels Deluxe Pit Crew 1:64
2000 #6 Valvoline
Hot Wheels Deluxe Pit Crew Daytona 500
2000 #6 Valvoline
Hot Wheels Deluxe Scorchin Scooter 1:64
2000 #6 Valvoline
Hot Wheels First Edition 1:64
1997 #6 Valvoline
1998 #6 Valvoline
1998 #6 Synpower
1998 #6 Eagle One Promo with bottle of car wax
1998 #6 Eagle One
Hot Wheels Fresh Paint 1:24
1999 #6 Zerex
Hot Wheels Preview Edition 1:64
1998 #6 Valvoline
1998 #6 Syntec
1998 #6 Eagle One
Hot Wheels Pro Circuit 1:64
1997 #6 Valvoline
Hot Wheels Pro Racing 1:24
1999 #6 Valvoline
Hot Wheels Pro Racing 1:43
1999 #6 Synpower
1999 #6 Valvoline
Hot Wheels Pro Racing 1:64
1997 #6 Valvoline
1998 #6 Valvoline
1999 #6 Valvoline
Hot Wheels Pro Racing Pit Crew 1:64
1998 #6 Valvoline
Hot Wheels Pro Racing Pit Crew Gold 1:6
1998 #6 Valvoline
Hot Wheels Pro Racing Superspeedway 1:6
1997 #6 Valvoline
Hot Wheels Pro Racing Trading Paint 1:6
1998 #6 Valvoline
Hot Wheels Race Day 1:64
2005 #6 Pfizer
Hot Wheels Race Day Deluxe 1:24
2000 #6 Valvoline
Hot Wheels Racing 1:24
1998 #6 Valvoline
2001 #6 Pfizer
2002 #6 Pfizer
2003 #6 Pfizer
Hot Wheels Racing 1:43
1998 #6 Valvoline
Hot Wheels Racing 1:64
2000 #6 Valvoline
Hot Wheels Racing 2-Car Sets 1:24/1:64
1998 #6 Eagle One w/Valv.1:64
Hot Wheels Racing '57 T-Bird 1:64
2002 #6 Pfizer 1
Hot Wheels Racing Alternative Paint Sch
2004 #6 Viagra White
2004 #6 Oscar Mayer
2004 #6 Viagra Blue
2004 #6 Oscar Mayer
Hot Wheels Racing Anglia 1:64
2001 #6 Pfizer
Hot Wheels Racing Artist Collection 1:2
2004 #6 Pfizer
Hot Wheels Racing Artist Collection 1:6
2004 #6 Pfizer
Hot Wheels Racing Chase for the Cup 1:2
2004 #6 Viagra/6000
Hot Wheels Racing Chase for the Cup 1:6
2004 #6 Viagra
Hot Wheels Racing Color Change 1:64
2004 #6 Pfizer
2004 #6 Oscar Mayer
Hot Wheels Racing Crew's Choice 1:64
2000 #6 Valvoline
Hot Wheels Racing Daytona 500 1:64
1999 #6 Valvoline
Hot Wheels Racing Goodyear Showcase 1:6
2004 #6 Viagra White/15,000
2004 #6 Viagra/15,000
2004 #6 Batman/15,000
Hot Wheels Racing Justice League 1:24
2004 #6 Batman
2004 #9 Batman
Hot Wheels Racing Justice League 1:64
2004 #6 Batman
2004 #9 Batman
Hot Wheels Racing Justice League Thunde
2004 #6 Batman
Hot Wheels Racing Justice League w/Figu
2004 #6 Batman
Hot Wheels Racing Luxury Rides 1:64
2003 #6 Pfizer
Hot Wheels Racing NASCAR Rocks 1:24
1999 #6 Valvoline
Hot Wheels Racing NASCAR Rocks 1:64
1999 #6 Valvoline
Hot Wheels Racing Phaeton 1:64
2002 #6 Pfizer 2
Hot Wheels Racing Pit Board 1:64
2001 #6 Pfizer
Hot Wheels Racing Pit Crew 1:64
1999 #6 Valvoline Gold
1999 #6 Valvoline
1999 #60 Winn Dixie
Hot Wheels Racing Pit Cruisers 1:64
1999 #6 Valvoline
2004 #6 Pfizer
2004 #6 Batman
Hot Wheels Racing Promos 1:64
1999 #6 1999 Valvoline
1999 #6 1997 Valvoline
1999 #6 1995 Valvoline
2002 #6 Kraft blister
Hot Wheels Racing Race Day 1:24
2004 #6 Viagra
Hot Wheels Racing Race Day 1:64
2003 #6 Pfizer
2004 #6 Viagra
Hot Wheels Racing Radical Rides 1:64
2000 #6 Valvoline
Hot Wheels Racing Radical Rods 1:43
2001 #6 Valvoline
Hot Wheels Racing Record Times 1:64
2002 #6 Pfizer
Hot Wheels Racing Recreational Vehicles
2003 #6 Pfizer
2003 #6 Pfizer
2003 #6 Pfizer
2003 #6 Pfizer
Hot Wheels Racing Roush Commemorative 1
2001 #6 Pfizer
Hot Wheels Racing Select 1:24
1999 #6 Valvoline
Hot Wheels Racing Select 1:64
2001 #6 Pfizer
Hot Wheels Racing Special Paint 1:64
2003 #6 Pfizer White
Hot Wheels Racing Speed and Thunder 1:6
1999 #6 Valvoline
Hot Wheels Racing Sticker 1:64
2002 #6 Pfizer
Hot Wheels Racing Stock Car Cruisers 1:
2003 #6 Pfizer
Hot Wheels Racing Stockerz 1:24
2004 #6 Pfizer
2004 #6 Oscar Mayer
Hot Wheels Racing Stockerz 1:64
2004 #6 Pfizer
2004 #6 Oscar Mayer
Hot Wheels Racing Tail Draggers 1:64
2001 #6 Valvoline
Hot Wheels Racing Test Track 1:24
2004 #6 Pfizer
Hot Wheels Racing Test Track 1:64
2004 #6 Pfizer
Hot Wheels Racing The Demon 1:64
2001 #6 Pfizer
Hot Wheels Racing Track Edition 1:64
1999 #6 Valvoline
2000 #6 Valvoline
Hot Wheels Racing Trading Paint 1:64
1999 #6 Valvoline
Hot Wheels Racing Transporters 1:64
2001 #6 Pfizer
Hot Wheels Racing Treasure Hunt 1:64
2003 #6 Pfizer 2
Hot Wheels Racing Wrenchin' and Racin'
2003 #6 Pfizer
Hot Wheels Radical Rides 1:43
1999 #6 Valvoline
Hot Wheels Select 1:24
2000 #6 Valvoline
Hot Wheels Select 1:64
2000 #6 Valvoline
Hot Wheels Select Clear 1:24
1999 #6 Valvoline
Hot Wheels Select Clear 1:43
1999 #6 Valvoline
Hot Wheels Short Track 1:64
1997 #6 Valvoline
Hot Wheels Team Transporters 1:64
2004 #6 Pfizer
Hot Wheels Test Track 1:64
1998 #6 Valvoline
Hot Wheels Thunder Series Motorcycles 1
2002 #6 Pfizer
Hot Wheels Track Edition 1:64
1998 #6 Synpower
1998 #6 Eagle One
1998 #6 Valvoline
Hot Wheels Transporters 1:64
1998 #6 Valvoline
1999 #6 Valvoline
2003 #6 Pfizer
Hot Wheels Valvoline 10 Years Promos 1:
2000 #6 Valvoline 1999
2000 #6 Valvoline 1997
2000 #6 Valvoline 1995
Matchbox White Rose Super Stars 1:64
1993 #6 Valvoline BX
1994 #6 Valvoline BX

1994 #60 Winn Dixie BX
1995 #6 Valvoline
1996 #6 Valvoline

Matchbox White Rose Transporters Super
1990 #6 Folgers
1991 #6 Folgers w/Mack cab
1991 #6 Folgers w/Ford cab
1993 #6 Valvoline
1995 #6 Valvoline
1995 #60 Winn Dixie

Miscellaneous Promos 1:64
1991-04 #6 Stroh Light Tarckside Souv.

Motorsports Authentics Driver's Select
2007 #1 U.S. Army '57 Chevy/1248*
2007 #1 U.S. Army Holiday Sam Bass/912*
2007 #1 U.S. Army Am.Heroes/3204
2007 #1 U.S. Army COT/2508*
2007 #1 U.S. Army/11,340*
2007 #1 Principal Financial/1224*
2007 #1 U.S. Army American Heroes
2007 #1 U.S. Army
2007 #1 U.S. Army Am.Heroes/3204
2007 #1 U.S. Army COT/996
2007 #1 U.S. Army/1008
2007 #5 Autoguard/1152
2007 #6 Dish Network/756*

Motorsports Authentics Owner's Elite 1:
2007 #1 U.S. Army COT/708*
2007 #1 U.S. Army Am.Heroes/708*
2007 #1 U.S. Army White Gold/100
2007 #1 U.S. Army Platinum/25
2007 #1 U.S. Army/1200*
2007 #1 U.S. Army Am.Heroes/1008*
2007 #1 U.S. Army/1008*

Motorsports Authentics Owner's Elite Tr
2007 #1 U.S.Army Am.Heroes/100*
2007 #1 U.S.Army/504*

Motorsports Authentics Pit Stop 1:64
2007 #1 U.S. Army American Heroes
2007 #1 U.S. Army COT
2007 #1 U.S. Army

Motorsports Authentics QVC For Race Fan
2007 #1 U.S. Army American Heroes Mesma Chrome/288
2007 #1 U.S. Army American Heroes Gold/288
2007 #1 U.S. Army American Heroes Copper/504
2007 #1 U.S. Army American Heroes Color Chrome/504
2007 #1 U.S. Army Mesma Chrome AU/504
2007 #1 U.S. Army Gold/288
2007 #1 U.S. Army Copper AU/288
2007 #1 U.S. Army Color Chrome AU/504
2007 #1 U.S. Army Color Chrome/504
2007 #1 U.S. Army Chrome/504

Motorsports Authentics/RCCA Owner's Clu
2007 #1 U.S. Army Holiday Sam Bass/96*
2007 #1 U.S. Army/1200*

Motorsports Authentics/RCCA Transporter
2007 #1 U.S. Army/708*

Peachstate/GMP Transporters 1:64
1996-01 #6 Valvoline '96
1996-01 #60 Winn Dixie RCCA/3500

Race Image 1:43
1997 #6 Valvoline
1998 #6 Valvoline SynPower
1998 #6 Valvoline
1998 #6 Eagle One

Race Image Service Kit 1:43
1998 #6 Eagle One
1998 #6 Valvoline

Raceway Replicas 1:24
1992-97 #6 Valvoline '94

Racing Champions 1:144
1996 #6 Valvoline
1997 #6 Valvoline
1997 #60 Winn Dixie
1998 #6 Valvoline

Racing Champions 1:24
1993 #6 Valvoline
1993 #60 Winn Dixie
1994 #6 Valvoline Reese's
1994 #60 Winn Dixie
1995 #6 Valvoline
1995 #60 Winn Dixie
1996 #6 Valvoline DuraBlend
1996 #6 Valvoline
1996 #60 Winn Dixie
1997 #6 Valvoline
1997 #60 Winn Dixie Promo
1998 #6 3-car set/5000
1998 #6 Valvoline
1998 #6 Synpower
1998 #6 Kosei Promo/2500
1998 #6 Eagle One
1998 #60 Winn Dixie Most BGN Wins Promo/5000
1999 #6 Zerex Chrome/2499
1999 #6 Zerex
1999 #6 Valvoline Chrome/2499
1999 #6 Valvoline
1999 #60 Winn Dixie Beef Promo
1999 #60 Winn Dixie
2000 #6 Valvoline Chrome/999
2000 #6 Valvoline
2002 #2 Cabela's 250 Promo
1991-92 #6 Valvoline
1991-92 #60 Winn Dixie White #'s
1991-92 #60 Winn Dixie Red #'s

Racing Champions 1:43
1991 #6 Valvoline
1993 #6 Valvoline
1993 #60 Winn Dixie
1994 #60 Winn Dixie

Racing Champions 1:64
1992 #6 Valvoline 2-car set
1992 #6 Valvoline
1992 #60 Winn Dixie
1992 #NNO Sears 12-car set
1992 #NNO Collect.Edit.12-car set w/R.Petty
1993 #6 Valvoline
1993 #60 Winn Dixie
1993 #NNO Carolina Ford 2-car promo set
1994 #6 Valvoline
1994 #60 Winn Dixie
1995 #6 Valvoline
1995 #60 Winn Dixie Promo
1995 #60 Winn Dixie
1996 #6 Roush Box Promo
1996 #6 Valv.Dura Blend
1996 #6 Valvoline Chrome/1996
1996 #6 Valvoline
1996 #60 Winn Dixie Promo
1996 #NNO 12-Car set in case
1997 #6 Valvol.Kosei Promo/5000
1997 #6 Valvoline
1997 #60 Winn Dixie Promo
1997 #NNO 12-Car set in black case
1998 #6 Valvoline Chrome/5050
1998 #6 Valvoline
1998 #6 Kosei Promo/5000
1998 #6 Eagle One Chrome/5050
1998 #6 Eagle One
1998 #60 Winn Dixie Promo
1998 #60 Winn Dixie Chrome/1000
1998 #60 Winn Dixie
1998 #NNO Roush Racing AUTO Gold/1000 5-car set: 6/16/26/97/99
1998 #NNO Roush Racing 5-Pack 5-cars: 97/6/16/99/26
1999 #6 Zerex Chrome/9999
1999 #6 Zerex
1999 #6 Valvoline Chrome/9999
1999 #6 Valvoline
1999 #60 Winn Dixie Chrome/9999
1999 #60 Winn Dixie
1999 #NNO Roush Rac.AUTO Platinum/2000 5-car set: 6/16/26/97/99
1999 #NNO Roush Racing AUTO Gold/3000 5-car set: 6/16/26/97/99
2000 #6 Zerex
2000 #6 Valvoline Stars&Stripes
2000 #6 Valvoline Promo in bag
2000 #6 Valvoline No Bull
2000 #6 Valvoline Chrome/999
2000 #6 Valvoline
2000 #6 Eagle One
2000 #60 Winn Dixie Farewell Promo
2000 #60 Winn Dixie Chrome/999
2000 #60 Winn Dixie
2000 #NNO 12-car set/Time Trials/Young Guns and War Paint cars/2500
2000 #NNO 12-car boxed set/2500

Racing Champions 12-Car Sets 1:64
1999 #2 12-Car Set 2
1999 #NNO Intro.Chrome 12-car set/25,000
1999 #NNO Chase Car Collect.12-car set/2000

Racing Champions 24K Gold 1:24
1998 #6 Valvoline
1998 #6 Eagle One
1998 #60 Winn Dixie
1999 #6 Valvoline

Racing Champions 24K Gold 1:64
1998 #6 Valvoline
1998 #60 Winn Dixie
1999 #6 Valvoline

Racing Champions 24K Gold Stock Rods 1:
1999 #3G Valvoline

Racing Champions 2-Car Sets 1:24
1998 #6 Eagle One/5000

Racing Champions 2-Car Sets 1:24/1:64
1999 #6 Zerex Chrome 3-piece set w/Valvoline Transporter
1999 #6 Valvoline/9999

Racing Champions 2-Car Sets 1:64
1999 #6 Zerex with Chrome car/2999
1999 #6 Valvoline with Chrome car/5000
1999 #6 Eagle One with Chrome car/1999

Racing Champions 3-D Originals 1:64
1999 #6 Valvoline

Racing Champions 5-Pack 1:64
2000 #NNO 57.JK/60.GB/36/60.MM/22.WB
2000 #NNO 6.MM/99.JB/75.WD/7.MW/40.SM
2000 #NNO 6.MM/33.JN/99.JB/2K.Ford/55.KW
2000 #NNO 6.MM/33.JN/93.DB/77.RP/75.WD
2000 #NNO 6.MM/6.MM/99.JB/36.EI/99.JB
2000 #NNO 5.TL/40.SM/6.MM/40.SM/6.MM

Racing Champions 5-Pack Preview 1:144
1997 #NNO 5/6/21/24/28

Racing Champions Authentics 1:24
1998 #6 Valvoline Bank
1998 #6 Valvoline/7000
1998 #6 Synpower Bank/2500
1998 #6 Synpower Mac Tools/4000
1998 #6 Synpower/7000
1998 #6 Eagle One Bank
1998 #6 Eagle One/7100
1999 #6 Zerex/8500
1999 #6 Valvoline/8500
1999 #6 Eagle One/8500
1999 #60 Winn Dixie/2000
2000 #6 Valvoline
2000 #6 Eagle One/4000

Racing Champions Banks 1:24
1995 #6 Valvoline
1995 #60 Winn Dixie/10,000
1996 #6 Valvoline
1992-94 #6 Valvoline Reese's
1992-94 #6 Valvoline
1992-94 #60 Winn Dixie/5000 '93
1992-94 #60 Winn Dixie/10,000

Racing Champions Buss Fuses Promos 1:64
1999 #6 Valvoline
2000 #6 Valvoline NAPA

Racing Champions Driver's Choice Banks
1998 #6 Valvoline

Racing Champions Fan Appreciation 5-Pac
1998 #2 6.MM/13.JN/50.JJ/3.LS/94.BE
1999 #1 4.BH/6.MM/36.KS/10/99.JB
1999 #7 00.BJ/6.MM/7.MW/10thA/9.JN
1999 #12 9.JN/6.MM/1.RL/10/5.TL

Racing Champions Gold 1:24
1998 #6 Valvoline Bank
1998 #6 Valvoline
1998 #6 Syntec
1998 #6 Eagle One
1998 #60 Winn Dixie
1999 #6 Valvoline
1999 #60 Winn Dixie

Racing Champions Gold Hood Open 1:24
1998 #6 Valvoline Bank
1998 #6 Valvoline
1998 #6 Synpower Bank
1998 #6 Synpower
1998 #6 Eagle One Bank

Racing Champions Gold NASCAR Fans Hood
1998 #6 Valvoline Synpower

Racing Champions Gold with Medallion 1:
1998 #6 Valvoline
1998 #6 Syntec
1998 #6 Eagle One
1998 #60 Winn Dixie
1999 #6 Valvoline
1999 #60 Winn Dixie

Racing Champions Hobby 1:64
1996 #6 Valvoline

Racing Champions Hobby Yellow Box 1:64
1994 #6 Valvoline

Racing Champions Hood Open Banks 1:24
1996 #60 Winn Dixie Promo/10,000
1997 #6 Valvoline/4992
1997 #60 Winn Dixie Promo/5000

Racing Champions Matched Serial Numbers
1995 #6 Valvoline

Racing Champions Milkhouse Cheese Promo
1992 #6 Valvoline

Racing Champions Model Kits 1:24
2000 #6 Valvoline

Racing Champions Model Kits 1:64
2000 #6 Valvoline

Racing Champions NASCAR Rules 1:64
1999 #6 Zerex
1999 #6 Valvoline
1999 #6 Eagle One
1999 #60 Winn Dixie
2000 #6 Valvoline Preview
2000 #6 Valvoline Chrome/999
2000 #6 Valvoline

Racing Champions Pinnacle Series 1:64
1997 #6 Valvoline
1998 #6 Valvoline

Racing Champions Pit Crew 1:64
2000 #6 Valvoline Chrome/999
2000 #6 Valvoline

Racing Champions Platinum 1:24
1999 #6 Valvoline

Racing Champions Platinum 1:64
1999 #6 Valvoline

Racing Champions Platinum Stock Rods 1:
1999 #3P Valvoline

Racing Champions Precious Metals Team C
1999 #6 Valvoline/9500

Racing Champions Premier 1:18
1997 #6 Valvoline Gold
1997 #6 Valvoline

Racing Champions Premier 1:24
1999 #6 Zerex Mac Tools/5000
1999 #6 Valvoline Bank/500
1999 #6 Valvoline/3000
1999 #6 Eag.One Mac Tools/5000
1999 #60 Winn Dixie Bank/500
1999 #60 Winn Dixie/3000
2000 #6 Valvoline No Bull
2000 #6 Valvoline
2000 #60 Winn Dixie Flag in window box
2000 #60 Winn Dixie Farewell Tour Promo in solid box

Racing Champions Premier 1:43
1993 #6 Valvoline/10,000
1993 #60 Winn Dixie/5000
1994 #6 Valvoline
1994 #60 Winn Dixie
1995 #6 Valvoline
1995 #60 Winn Dixie

Racing Champions Premier 1:64
1993 #6 Valvoline 4 in Row Promo
1993 #6 Valvoline
1993 #60 Winn Dixie
1994 #6 Valvoline 4 in a row
1994 #6 Valvoline
1994 #60 Winn Dixie
1995 #6 Valvoline
1995 #60 Winn Dixie
2000 #6 Zerex
2000 #6 Valvoline No Bull
2000 #6 Valvoline
2001 #6 Zerex '00

Racing Champions Premier Banks 1:24
1996 #6 Valvoline Chrome/166
1996 #6 Valvoline
1997 #6 Valvoline Gold/166
1997 #6 Valvoline

Racing Champions Premier Brickyard 400
1994 #6 Valvoline

Racing Champions Premier Gold 1:64
1997 #6 Valvoline

Racing Champions Premier Gold Chrome 1:
1997 #6 Valvoline

Racing Champions Premier Hood Open 1:24
1996 #6 Valvoline
1996 #60 Winn Dixie

Racing Champions Premier Preview 1:24
2000 #6 Valvoline

Racing Champions Premier Preview 1:64
2000 #6 Valvoline
2001 #6 Zerex '00

Racing Champions Premier Preview Transp
2000 #6 Valvoline

Racing Champions Premier Preview with M
1997 #6 Valvoline

Racing Champions Premier Transporters 1
1993 #6 Valvoline
1993 #60 Winn Dixie/5000
1994 #60 Winn Dixie/7500
1996 #6 Valvoline
1997 #60 Winn Dixie
2000 #6 Valvoline

Racing Champions Premier with Medallion
1996 #6 Valv.Dura Blend HO
1997 #6 Valvoline

Racing Champions Press Pass Series 1:64
1998 #6 Valvoline
1998 #6 Eagle One
1998 #60 Winn Dixie
1999 #6 Valvoline

Racing Champions Preview 1:144
1997 #6 Valvoline

Racing Champions Preview 1:24
1995 #6 Valvoline
1996 #6 Valvoline
1997 #6 Valvoline
2000 #6 Valvoline

Racing Champions Preview 1:64
1995 #6 Valvoline
1996 #6 Valvoline
1997 #6 Valvoline
2000 #6 Valvoline

Racing Champions Preview Transporters 1
1996 #6 Valvoline
1997 #6 Valvoline
1997 #6 Valvoline
2000 #6 Valvoline

Racing Champions PVC Box 1:64
1993 #6 Valvol.Aug.15 Win/5000
1993 #6 Valvol.Aug.8 Win/5000
1993 #60 Winn Dixie

Racing Champions Race Day 1:24
1999 #6 Valvoline

Racing Champions Radio Controled Die Ca
1999 #6 Valvoline

Racing Champions Roaring Racers 1:64
1997 #6 Valvoline

Racing Champions Short Track Champions
1994 #2 RECO

Racing Champions Signature Series 1:24
1998 #6 Valvoline
1999 #6 Valvoline Chrome
1999 #6 Valvoline

Racing Champions Signature Series 1:64
1998 #6 Valvoline
1999 #6 Zerex Chrome/4999
1999 #6 Valvoline Chrome/4999
1999 #6 Valvoline
1999 #60 Winn Dixie

Racing Champions Stock Rods 1:24
1998 #40 Valvoline
1998 #59 Valvoline
1998 #71 Valvoline
1999 #84 Valvoline
2000 #1 Valvoline '37 Ford

Racing Champions Stock Rods 1:64
1997 #3 Valvoline
1997 #17 Valvoline
1997 #37 Valvoline
1997 #47 Valvoline
1998 #62 Valvoline
1998 #85 Winn Dixie
1998 #92 Winn Dixie
1998 #93 Valvoline
1998 #103 Winn Dixie
1998 #108 Valvoline
1998 #124 Valvoline
1998 #136 Valvoline
1999 #154 Valvoline
1999 #186 Valvoline
2000 #1 Valvoline '68 Mustang
2000 #4 Valvoline '40 Ford

Racing Champions Stock Rods 24K Gold 1:
1998 #5 Valvoline

Racing Champions Stock Rods Reflections
1998 #5 Valvoline

Racing Champions SuperTrucks 1:144
1997 #99 Exide

Racing Champions SuperTrucks 1:24
1997 #99 Exide

Racing Champions SuperTrucks 1:64
1997 #99 Exide

Racing Champions SuperTrucks 5-Pack 1:1
1997 #NNO 99.MM/99.JB/1.MW/15.El/18.JB

Racing Champions Time Trial 1:64
2000 #6 Valvoline

Racing Champions Time Trial 2000 1:24
2000 #6 Valvoline

Racing Champions To the Maxx 1:64
1994 #6 Valvoline
1995 #6 Valvoline

Racing Champions Toys R Us Chrome Chase
1999 #6 Valvoline

Racing Champions Toys 'R Us Gold 1:64
1998 #6 Valvoline
1998 #6 Eagle One
1998 #60 Winn Dixie

Racing Champions Transporters 1:144
1997 #6 Valvoline
1997 #60 Winn Dixie
1991-92 #6 Valvoline

Racing Champions Transporters 1:64
1992 #6 Valvoline
1992 #60 Winn Dixie
1993 #6 Valvoline
1993 #60 Winn Dixie
1995 #6 Valvoline
1995 #60 Winn Dixie
1996 #60 Winn Dixie w/car(s)
1996 #60 Winn Dixie
1997 #6 Valvoline w/car(s)
1997 #6 Valvoline
1997 #60 Winn Dixie Promo
1997 #60 Winn Dixie
1998 #6 Eagle One w/car
1998 #6 Eagle One
1998 #60 Winn Dixie P w/car
1998 #60 Winn Dixie w/car
1998 #60 Winn Dixie
1999 #6 Valvoline Chrome/1499
1999 #6 Valvoline
2000 #6 Valvoline Chrome/999
2000 #6 Valvoline

Racing Champions Transporters 1:87
1996 #6 Valvoline
1997 #6 Valvoline
1997 #60 Winn Dixie
1998 #6 Valvoline

Racing Champions Transporters 24K Gold
1998 #6 Valvoline
1998 #60 Winn Dixie
1999 #6 Valvoline

Racing Champions Transporters Gold 1:64
1998 #6 Valvoline
1998 #6 Eagle One
1999 #6 Valvoline

Racing Champions Transporters Hobby 1:8
1994 #6 Valvoline

Racing Champions Transporters Platinum
1999 #6 Valvoline

Racing Champions Transporters Retail
1993-94 #6 Valvoline

Racing Champions Transporters Retail 1:
1994 #6 Valvoline
1994 #60 Winn Dixie

Racing Champions Transporters Signature
1998 #6 Valvoline
1999 #6 Valvoline

Racing Champions Transporters Time Tria
2000 #6 Valvoline

Racing Champions Transporters Under the
1999 #6 Valvoline

Racing Champions Transporters War Paint
2000 #6 Valvoline

Racing Champions Under the Lights 1:24
1999 #6 Zerex/7500
1999 #6 Valvoline
1999 #60 Winn Dixie
2000 #6 Zerex

Racing Champions Under the Lights 1:64
1999 #6 Valvoline Zerex 2-car set
1999 #6 Valvoline Eagle One 2-car set
1999 #6 Valvoline Ames/5000
1999 #6 Valvoline 2-cars
1999 #6 Valvoline
2000 #6 Valvoline/2288

Racing Champions War Paint 1:24
2000 #6 Valvoline Hood Open
2000 #6 Valvoline

Racing Champions War Paint 1:64
2000 #6 Valvoline 2-cars
2000 #6 Valvoline

RCCA Club 1:24
2008 #8 U.S. Army/204
2008 #8 U.S. Army Salute the Troops/150

RCCA Elite 1:24
2008 #8 U.S. Army/408
2008 #8 U.S. Army Platinum/25
2008 #8 U.S. Army White Gold/50
2008 #8 U.S. Army Salute the Troops/300
2008 #8 U.S. Army Salute the Troops Platinum/25
2008 #8 U.S. Army Salute the Troops White Gold/50

Revell 1:24
1991-95 #6 Valvoline
1991-95 #60 Winn Dixie GMP '95

Revell Club 1:24
1997 #6 Valvoline/1596

Revell Collection 1:18
1997 #6 Valvoline
1997 #60 Winn Dixie

Revell Collection 1:24
1996 #6 Valvoline
1997 #6 Valvoline
1997 #60 Winn Dixie

Revell Collection 1:43
1997 #6 Valvoline

Revell Collection 1:64
1996 #6 Valvoline Dura Blend
1996 #6 Valvoline/6912
1997 #NNO Valvoline/WD 2-car tin

Revell Retail 1:24
1995 #6 Valvoline
1996 #6 Valvoline
1997 #6 Valvoline

Revell Retail 1:64
1996 #6 Valvoline
1997 #6 Valvoline

Revell Select 1:24
1997 #6 Valvoline

Revell Select Hobby 1:64
1997 #6 Valvoline

Road Champs 1:43
1992 #6 Valvoline

Road Champs 1:64
1992 #6 Valvoline

Road Champs Transporters 1:64
1992 #6 Valvoline

Road Champs Transporters 1:87
1992 #6 Valvoline

Scaleworks Transporters 1:24
1996-98 #6 Valvoline/2000 '97

Team Caliber 1:24
1999 #6 Eagle One
1999 #6 Valvoline/5004

Team Caliber 1:64
1999 #6 Eagle One
1999 #6 Valvoline/7560

Team Caliber First Choice 1:24
2003 #6 Viagra/756
2004 #6 Viagra White/504
2004 #6 Batman/250

Team Caliber First Choice Beckett 1:24
2004 #6 Batman AU/1
2004 #9 Batman AU/1

Team Caliber Model Kits 1:64
2003 #6 Viagra White
2003 #6 Viagra

Team Caliber Owners Series 1:24
2000 #6 Valvoline Zerex/5004
2000 #6 Valvoline Flag/5004
2000 #6 Valvoline Max Life/5004
2000 #6 Valvoline Eagle One/5004
2000 #6 Valvoline/5004
2000 #60 Winn Dixie Flag/3120
2000 #60 Winn Dixie Flames/3120
2000 #60 Winn Dixie/3120
2001 #6 Viagra Metal Flake/4824
2001 #6 Viagra/7494
2001 #6 Stroh's Lt.'89 T-bird/7998
2001 #6 Pfizer/7494
2001 #6 JR's Garage Promo/200
2001 #6 JR's Garage/3120
2002 #6 Viagra No Bull/6504
2002 #6 Viagra/10008
2002 #6 Pfizer/5004
2002 #6 Kraft/10008
2003 #6 Viagra 500 Starts/1800
2003 #6 Viagra White/1800
2003 #6 Viagra Blue Daytona/1800
2003 #6 Viagra Blue Chrome/10,080
2003 #6 Viagra/10,080
2003 #6 Pfizer/1200
2003 #6 Kraft/1200
2004 #6 Viagra White/3120
2004 #6 Viagra/5004
2004 #6 Pfizer/3120
2004 #6 Oscar Mayer/3120
2004 #6 Batman/7560
2004 #9 Batman/3120
2004 #9 Pennzoil/1200
2005 #6 Viagra Salute to You/1500
2005 #6 Viagra Red, White & Blue Retro Valvoline All Star AU/737
2005 #6 Viagra Red, White & Blue Retro Valvoline/900
2005 #6 Viagra Red Retro Folgers/900
2005 #6 Viagra Orange AU/1800
2005 #6 Viagra Blue Retro Stroh's Light/900
2005 #6 Viagra/600*
2005 #6 Viagra/1200
2005 #6 Kraft/600
2005 #6 Batman/756
2005 #9 Pennzoil

Team Caliber Owner's Series 1:24
2006 #6 Ford The Road Home AU/2400
2006 #6 Ameriquest Soaring Dreams/1800
2006 #6 AAA Last Ride/1080
2006 #6 AAA Insurance/2808
2006 #6 AAA/5004

Team Caliber Owners Series 1:64
2000 #6 Zerex/7560
2000 #6 Valv.Stars&Stripes/7560
2000 #6 Valvoline Max Life
2000 #6 Valvoline/10,080
2000 #6 Eagle One/10,080
2000 #60 Winn Dixie Stars & Stripes/7560
2000 #60 Winn Dixie Flames/7560
2000 #60 Winn Dixie/7560
2001 #6 Viagra Metal Flake/6264
2001 #6 Viagra/7560
2001 #6 Pfizer/7560
2002 #6 Viagra/10080
2002 #6 Pfizer/5004
2002 #6 Kraft/7560
2003 #6 Viagra Blue Daytona
2003 #6 Viagra 500 Starts
2003 #6 Viagra White
2003 #6 Viagra Blue Chr./10,080
2003 #6 Viagra/10,080
2003 #6 Pfizer/5004
2003 #6 Kraft/5004
2004 #6 Kraft
2004 #6 Viagra

Team Caliber Owners Series Banks 1:24
2001 #6 Viagra/1008
2001 #6 Pfizer/1008
2001 #6 JR's Garage/754

2002 #6 Viagra No Bull/372
2002 #6 Viagra/576
2002 #6 Pfizer/372
2002 #6 Kraft/642
2003 #6 Viagra 500 Starts/180
2003 #6 Viagra White/180
2003 #6 Viagra Blue Daytona/180
2003 #6 Viagra/2400
2003 #6 Pfizer/180
2003 #6 Kraft/300

Team Caliber Owners Series Dark Chrome
2002 #6 Viagra No Bull/942
2002 #6 Viagra/1026
2002 #6 Pfizer/426
2002 #6 Kraft/1296
2003 #6 Viagra White/360
2003 #6 Viagra 500 Starts/300
2003 #6 Viagra Blue Daytona/324
2003 #6 Viagra/1002
2003 #6 Pfizer/402
2003 #6 Kraft/300

Team Caliber Owners Series Gold 1:24
2000 #6 Valv. Eagle One/1200
2000 #6 Valvoline/1200
2001 #6 Viagra/1008
2001 #6 Stroh's Light '89 T-bird Mac Tools/5004
2001 #6 Pfizer/1008
2001 #6 JR's Garage

Team Caliber Owners Series Pearl Chrome
2004 #6 Viagra White/504
2004 #6 Viagra/504
2004 #6 Pfizer/402
2004 #6 Oscar Mayer/300
2004 #6 Batman/1008
2004 #9 Batman/504
2004 #9 Pennzoil/252

Team Caliber Owners Series Steel 1:24
2001 #6 Viagra/1008
2001 #6 Pfizer/1008
2001 #6 JR's Garage

Team Caliber Owners Series Transporters
2003 #6 Kraft
2003 #6 Pfizer
2003 #6 Viagra/1800
2004 #6 Batman
2004 #6 Pfizer
2004 #6 Viagra
2004 #9 Batman

Team Caliber Owners Series Vintage 1:24
2002 #6 Stroh's Light '91 T-Bird Dark Chrome/5004
2002 #6 Stroh's Light '91 T-Bird
2002 #6 Folgers '89T-bird/7770

Team Caliber Pit Stop 1:18
2004 #6 Viagra

Team Caliber Pit Stop 1:24
2001 #6 Viagra Metal Flake
2001 #6 Viagra/3120
2001 #6 Pfizer
2002 #6 Viagra/7494
2002 #6 Pfizer/3810
2002 #6 Kraft/5532
2003 #6 Viagra 500 Starts
2003 #6 Viagra White
2003 #6 Viagra Blue Daytona
2003 #6 Viagra
2003 #6 Pfizer
2003 #6 Kraft
2004 #6 Viagra White
2004 #6 Viagra
2004 #6 Pfizer
2004 #6 Oscar Mayer
2004 #6 Batman
2004 #9 Batman
2004 #9 Pennzoil
2005 #6 Viagra Red, White & Blue Retro Valvoline
2005 #6 Viagra Red Retro Folgers
2005 #6 Viagra Orange
2005 #6 Viagra Blue Retro Stroh's Light
2005 #6 Viagra
2005 #6 Kraft
2005 #6 Batman
2005 #9 Pennzoil
2006 #6 Scott's SuperTruck
2006 #6 Pennzoil
2006 #6 Ameriquest
2006 #6 AAA Insurance
2006 #6 AAA

Team Caliber Pit Stop 1:64
2001 #6 Pfizer
2002 #6 Viagra/25,604
2002 #6 Pfizer/8076
2002 #6 Kraft/10,368
2003 #6 Viagra 500 Starts
2003 #6 Viagra White
2003 #6 Viagra Blue Daytona
2003 #6 Viagra
2003 #6 Pfizer
2003 #6 Kraft
2004 #6 Viagra White
2004 #6 Viagra
2004 #6 Pfizer
2004 #6 Oscar Mayer
2004 #6 Batman
2004 #9 Batman
2004 #9 Pennzoil
2005 #6 Viagra Salute to You
2005 #6 Viagra Red, White & Blue Retro Valvoline
2005 #6 Viagra Red Retro Folgers
2005 #6 Viagra Orange
2005 #6 Viagra Blue Retro Stroh's Light
2005 #6 Viagra
2005 #6 Kraft
2005 #6 Batman
2005 #9 Pennzoil
2006 #6 Pennzoil
2006 #6 Ameriquest
2006 #6 AAA Insurance
2006 #6 AAA

Team Caliber Pit Stop Transporters 1:64
2003 #6 Kraft
2003 #6 Pfizer
2003 #6 Viagra
2004 #6 Batman
2004 #6 Pfizer
2004 #6 Viagra
2004 #9 Batman

Team Caliber Preferred 1:24
2000 #6 Zerex/5004
2000 #6 Valv.Max Life/20,004
2000 #6 Valvoline Flag/20,004
2000 #6 Valv.Eagle One/20,004
2000 #6 Valvoline/20,004
2000 #60 Winn Dixie Flag/5508
2000 #60 Winn Dixie Flames/5508
2000 #60 Winn Dixie/20,008
2001 #6 Viagra Metal Flake/10,080
2001 #6 Viagra Dark Chrome Mac Tools/5004
2001 #6 Viagra/4996
2001 #6 Pfizer/10080
2002 #6 Viagra No Bull/1480
2002 #6 Viagra Mac Tools/2400
2002 #6 Viagra/8196
2002 #6 Pfizer/2550
2002 #6 Kraft Mac Tools/2400
2002 #6 Kraft/6196
2003 #6 Viagra 500 Starts
2003 #6 Viagra White/2004
2003 #6 Viagra Blue Daytona/10,080
2003 #6 Viagra/5004
2003 #6 Pfizer/900
2003 #6 Kraft/10,080
2004 #6 Viagra White/10,008
2004 #6 Viagra Chase/1600
2004 #6 Viagra
2004 #6 Pfizer/10,008
2004 #6 Oscar Mayer/10,008
2004 #6 Batman Yellow Chrome/504
2004 #6 Batman Gold/504
2004 #6 Batman/7560
2004 #9 Pennzoil/5004
2004 #9 Batman Gold/504
2004 #9 Batman/5004
2005 #6 Viagra Salute to You
2005 #6 Viagra Red, White & Blue All Star Win/7560
2005 #6 Viagra Red, White & Blue Retro Valvoline/7560
2005 #6 Viagra Red Retro Folgers Color Chrome/Chrome AU set/600
2005 #6 Viagra Red Retro Folgers/2400
2005 #6 Viagra Orange AU/5004
2005 #6 Viagra Blue Retro Stroh's Light/3120
2005 #6 Viagra/5004
2005 #6 Kraft/2400
2005 #6 Batman
2005 #9 Pennzoil/1200
2006 #6 Pennzoil/3000
2006 #6 Folger's '89 t-bird Red Chrome AU/1056
2006 #6 Ameriquest Soaring Dreams/3500
2006 #6 Ameriquest/2400
2006 #6 AAA Insurance/5004
2006 #6 AAA/20,004

Team Caliber Preferred Banks 1:24
2000 #6 Zerex/504
2000 #6 Valvoline Max Life/756
2000 #6 Valvoline/756
2000 #6 Eagle One/756
2000 #60 Winn Dixie Flag/504
2000 #60 Winn Dixie/504

Team Caliber Preferred Copper 1:24
2006 #6 Pennzoil/540
2006 #6 Ameriquest/360
2006 #6 AAA Insurance
2006 #6 AAA

Team Caliber Preferred Nickel 1:24
2005 #6 Viagra Orange AU/756
2005 #6 Viagra/756
2005 #6 Kraft/300
2005 #6 Batman/402
2005 #9 Pennzoil/504

Team Caliber Pull Backs 1:87
2002 #6 Pfizer

Team Caliber White Knuckle Racing 1:24
2000 #6 Eagle One
2000 #6 Valvoline

Team Caliber White Knuckle Racing 1:64
2000 #6 Valvoline
2000 #6 Eagle One Promo

Team Caliber/Motorworks Model Kits 1:24
2003 #6 Viagra
2005 #6 Viagra

Winner's Circle 1:18
2007 #1 U.S. Army

Winner's Circle 1:24
2006 #6 AAA
2007 #1 U.S. Army
2008 #8 U.S. Army

Winner's Circle 1:87
2006 #6 AAA
2007 #1 U.S. Army
2008 #8 U.S. Army

Winner's Circle American Heroes 1:24
2007 #1 Army AH logo

Winner's Circle American Heroes 1:87
2007 #1 U.S. Army AH
2007 #NNO American Heroes 9-car set
2007 #NNO 11.Hamlin/Marines 21.Wood/AF 01.Martin/Army 3-car set

Winner's Circle American Heroes Hood 1:
2007 #1 U.S. Army AH

Winner's Circle Autographed Hood 1:64
2006 #6 AAA

Winner's Circle Driver Sticker 1:64
2003 #1 True Value '98 IROC

Winner's Circle Medallion 1:64
2007 #1 U.S. Army

Winner's Circle Number Magnet 1:64
2008 #8 U.S. Army

Winner's Circle Pit Pass 1:64
2007 #1 U.S. Army

Winner's Circle Sam Bass Hoods 1:64
2007 #1 U.S. Army Holiday

Winner's Circle Stickers 1:64
2008 #8 U.S. Army

Winner's Circle Transporters 1:64
2007 #1 U.S. Army American Heroes

Winross Transporters 1:64
1993 #NNO Valvoline

Montoya, Juan Pablo

Action Racing Collectables Platinum 1:2
2008 #42 Texaco Havoline/3612
2008 #42 Big Red/1092
2008 #42 Texaco Havoline '07 ROY w/tire/708

RCCA Club 1:24
2008 #42 Texaco/252

RCCA Elite 1:24
2008 #42 Texaco/504
2008 #42 Texaco Platinum/25
2008 #42 Texaco White Gold/50

Winner's Circle 1:24
2008 #42 Texaco Havoline
2008 #42 Big Red

Winner's Circle 1:87
2008 #42 Texaco
2008 #42 Big Red

Winner's Circle Autographed Hoods 1:64
2008 #42 Texaco

Winner's Circle Daytona 500 1:24
2008 #42 Texaco

Winner's Circle Number Magnet 1:64
2008 #42 Big Red

Winner's Circle Schedule Hoods 1:64
2008 #42 Texaco Havoline

Winner's Circle Stickers 1:64
2008 #42 Texaco

Winner's Circle Transporters 1:64
2008 #42 Texaco

Newman, Ryan

Action QVC For Race Fans Only 1:24
2002 #12 R.Newman/Alltel ROY Plat./624
2002 #12 R.Newman/Alltel ROY Gold/1008
2003 #12 R.Newman/Alltel Gold/1008

Action Racing Collectables 1:24
2001 #2 R.Newman/Alltel Bank/600
2001 #2 R.Newman/Alltel/2412
2002 #12 R.Newman/Mobil 1 Bank
2002 #12 R.Newman/Mobil 1/11,292
2002 #12 R.Newman/Alltel/10,404
2004 #12 R.Newman/Crown Royal IROC/5004
2006 #12 R.Newman/Crown Royal IROC GM Dealers/132
2006 #12 R.Newman/Crown Royal IROC/1056

Action Racing Collectables 1:64
2002 #12 R.Newman/Mobil 1/9936
2002 #12 R.Newman/Alltel ROY/6640
2002 #12 R.Newman/Alltel/11,664

Action Racing Collectables Platinum 1:2
2002 #12 R.Newman/Alltel/3276

Action/RCCA 1:24
2002 #12 R.Newman/Alltel ROY Color Chrome Bank/780
2002 #12 R.Newman/Mobil 1 Bank/804
2002 #12 R.Newman/Alltel ROY Color Chrome/10,248
2002 #12 R.Newman/Alltel Bank/1008
2004 #12 R.Newman/Crown Royal IROC Color Chrome/288
2006 #12 R.Newman/Alltel/150
2006 #12 R.Newman/Alltel Color Chrome/100
2006 #12 R.Newman/Crown Royal White Pearl/200

Action/RCCA 1:64
2002 #12 R.Newman/Mobil 1/1584
2002 #12 R.Newman/Alltel/1584

Action/RCCA Banks 1:24
2001 #2 R.Newman/Alltel/492

Action/RCCA Elite 1:24
2002 #12 R.Newman/Mobil 1/1008
2002 #12 R.Newman/Alltel ROY Color Chrome/1140
2002 #12 R.Newman/Alltel/1392
2006 #12 R.Newman/Alltel/200
2006 #12 R.Newman/Alltel Color Chrome/100
2006 #12 R.Newman/Alltel Platinum/4

Action/RCCA Elite 1:64
2002 #12 R.Newman/Mobil 1/1584
2002 #12 R.Newman/Alltel/1584

Action/RCCA Sprint 1:24
1999 #39 R.Newman/Gearheads Lewis/2508

Hot Wheels Alternative Paint Scheme 1:6
2005 #12 R.Newman/Mobil 1

Hot Wheels Daytona Set-Up 1:64
2002 #2 R.Newman/Alltel

Hot Wheels Racing 1:24
2001 #2 R.Newman/Alltel
2002 #12 R.Newman/Alltel
2003 #12 R.Newman/Mobil 1 First Win/1212
2003 #12 R.Newman/Mobil 1
2003 #12 R.Newman/Alltel

Hot Wheels Racing '57 T-Bird 1:64
2002 #12 R.Newman/Alltel 3

Hot Wheels Racing Artist Collection 1:2
2004 #12 R.Newman/Alltel

Hot Wheels Racing Artist Collection 1:6
2004 #12 R.Newman/Alltel

Hot Wheels Racing Chase for the Cup 1:2
2004 #12 R.Newman/Alltel/6000

Hot Wheels Racing Color Change 1:64
2003 #12 R.Newman/Sony Wega
2003 #12 R.Newman/Alltel
2004 #12 R.Newman/Alltel

Hot Wheels Racing Goodyear Showcase 1:6
2004 #12 R.Newman/Mobil 1/15,000

Hot Wheels Racing Justice League 1:64
2004 #12 R.Newman/Justice League

Hot Wheels Racing Luxury Rides 1:64
2003 #12 R.Newman/Alltel

Hot Wheels Racing Phaeton 1:64
2002 #2 R.Newman/Alltel 5

Hot Wheels Racing Pit Board 1:64
2001 #2 R.Newman/Alltel

Hot Wheels Racing Pit Cruisers 1:64
2004 #12 R.Newman/Alltel

Hot Wheels Racing Power Launchers 1:64
2003 #12 R.Newman/Alltel

Hot Wheels Racing Race Day 1:24
2004 #12 R.Newman/Alltel

Hot Wheels Racing Race Day 1:64
2003 #12 R.Newman/Alltel
2004 #12 R.Newman/Alltel

Hot Wheels Racing Recreational Vehicles
2003 #12 R.Newman/Alltel
2003 #12 R.Newman/Alltel
2003 #12 R.Newman/Alltel

Hot Wheels Racing Special Paint 1:64
2003 #12 R.Newman/Sony Wega
2003 #12 R.Newman/Mobil 1 First Win/1212
2003 #12 R.Newman/Mobil 1

Hot Wheels Racing Sticker 1:64
2002 #12 R.Newman/Alltel

Hot Wheels Racing Stock Car Cruisers 1:
2003 #12 R.Newman/Alltel

Hot Wheels Racing Stockerz 1:24
2004 #12 R.Newman/Alltel

Hot Wheels Racing Stockerz 1:64
2004 #12 R.Newman/Alltel

Hot Wheels Racing Test Track 1:24
2004 #12 R.Newman/Alltel

Hot Wheels Racing Test Track 1:64
2004 #12 R.Newman/Alltel

Hot Wheels Racing Treasure Hunt 1:64
2003 #12 R.Newman/Alltel 1

Hot Wheels Racing Wrenchin' and Racin'
2003 #12 R.Newman/Alltel

Hot Wheels Team Transporters 1:64
2004 #12 R.Newman/Alltel

Hot Wheels Thunder Series Motorcycles 1
2002 #12 R.Nemwan/Alltel

Hot Wheels Transporters 1:64
2002 #12 R.Newman/Alltel
2003 #12 R.Newman/Alltel

Hot Wheels Victory Lane Transporters 1:
2004 #12 R.Newman/Alltel
2004 #NNO R.Newman/Alltel

Motorsports Authentics Driver's Select
2007 #12 R.Newman/Mobil 1/1400*
2007 #12 R.Newman/Kodak/1852*
2007 #12 R.Newman/Alltel My Circle/800*
2007 #12 R.Newman/Alltel COT/2488*
2007 #12 R.Newman/Alltel/3700*
2007 #12 R.Newman/Alltel My Circle
2007 #12 R.Newman/Alltel
2007 #12 Penske

Motorsports Authentics Owner's Elite 1:
2007 #12 R.Newman/Alltel COT/504*
2007 #12 R.Newman/Alltel/708*

Motorsports Authentics Owner's Elite Tr
2007 #12 R.Newman/Kodak/144*
2007 #12 R.Newman/Alltel/800*
2007 #12 R.Newman/Mobil 1/204*

Motorsports Authentics Pit Stop 1:64
2007 #12 R.Newman/Mobil 1
2007 #12 R.Newman/Kodak
2007 #12 R.Newman/Alltel

Motorsports Authentics QVC For Race Fan
2007 #12 R.Newman/Alltel Chrome/204

Peachstate/GMP Transporters 1:64
2003 #12 R.Newman/Alltel/1200

RCCA Club 1:24
2008 #12 R.Newman/Alltel/150

RCCA Elite 1:24
2008 #12 R.Newman/Alltel/300
2008 #12 R.Newman/Alltel Platinum/25
2008 #12 R.Newman/Alltel White Gold/50
2008 #12 R.Newman/Alltel Mummy 3/400
2008 #12 R.Newman/Alltel Mummy 3 Platinum/25
2008 #12 R.Newman/Alltel Mummy 3 White Gold/50

Team Caliber First Choice 1:24
2003 #12 R.Newman/Alltel/756
2004 #12 R.Newman/Mobil 1 30th Ann./250
2004 #12 R.Newman/Justice League/250

Team Caliber First Choice Beckett 1:24
2004 #12 R.Newman/Justice League AU/1

Team Caliber Model Kits 1:64
2003 #12 R.Newman/Alltel

Team Caliber Owners Series 1:24
2000 #27 R.Newman/Alltel/3500
2001 #2 R.Newman/Alltel/1200
2002 #12 R.Newman/Mobil 1/3120
2002 #12 R.Newman/Alltel Sony WEGA/3120
2002 #12 R.Newman/Alltel Blue Chrome Rookie of the Year/2400
2002 #12 R.Newman/Alltel/5004
2003 #12 R.Newman/Sony Wega/2400
2003 #12 R.Newman/Mobil 1/2400
2003 #12 R.Newman/Alltel 50th Win/1200
2003 #12 R.Newman/Alltel/7560
2004 #12 R.Newman/Sony Wega/3120
2004 #12 R.Newman/Mobil 1 30th Ann./5004
2004 #12 R.Newman/Mobil 1/5004
2004 #12 R.Newman/Justice League/7560
2004 #12 R.Newman/Alltel/5004
2005 #12 R.Newman/Mobil 1 Gold/600
2005 #12 R.Newman/Mobil 1/600
2005 #12 R.Newman/Alltel/1200
2005 #39 R.Newman/Alltel

Team Caliber Owner's Series 1:24
2006 #12 R.Newman/Mobil/1500
2006 #12 R.Newman/Alltel/2400

Team Caliber Owners Series 1:64
2002 #12 R.Newman/Alltel Blue Chrome Rookie of the Year/7560
2002 #12 R.Newman/Alltel/8136
2003 #12 R.Newman/Mobil 1
2003 #12 R.Newman/Alltel/10,080
2004 #12 R.Newman/Alltel

Team Caliber Owners Series Banks 1:24
2001 #2 R.Newman/Alltel/258
2002 #12 R.Newman/Mobil 1/192
2002 #12 R.Newman/Alltel Sony WEGA/198
2002 #12 R.Newman/Alltel/324
2003 #12 R.Newman/Sony Wega/180
2003 #12 R.Newman/Mobil 1/180
2003 #12 R.Newman/Alltel 50th Win/180
2003 #12 R.Newman/Alltel/300

Team Caliber Owners Series Dark Chrome
2002 #12 R.Newman/Mobil 1/378
2002 #12 R.Newman/Alltel Winston/1212
2002 #12 R.Newman/Alltel Sony WEGA/1008
2002 #12 R.Newman/Alltel/558
2003 #12 R.Newman/Sony Wega/220
2003 #12 R.Newman/Alltel '03 DOY Silver Chrome/1200
2003 #12 R.Newman/Mobil 1/324
2003 #12 R.Newman/Alltel 50th Win/180
2003 #12 R.Newman/Alltel/1008

Team Caliber Owners Series Gold 1:24
2001 #2 R.Newman/Alltel/258

Team Caliber Owners Series Pearl Chrome
2004 #12 R.Newman/Sony Wega/756
2004 #12 R.Newman/Mobil 1 30th Ann./504
2004 #12 R.Newman/Mobil 1/600
2004 #12 R.Newman/Justice League/1008
2004 #12 R.Newman/Alltel/504

Team Caliber Owners Series Steel 1:24
2001 #2 R.Newman/Alltel/258

Team Caliber Owners Series Transporters
2003 #12 R.Newman/Alltel/1200
2004 #12 R.Newman/Alltel

Team Caliber Pit Stop 1:18
2004 #12 R.Newman/Alltel

Team Caliber Pit Stop 1:24
2002 #12 R.Newman/Alltel Sony WEGA/2400
2002 #12 R.Newman/Alltel/2724
2003 #12 R.Newman/Sony Wega
2003 #12 R.Newman/Mobil 1
2003 #12 R.Newman/Alltel
2004 #12 R.Newman/Sony Wega
2004 #12 R.Newman/Mobil 1 30th Ann.
2004 #12 R.Newman/Mobil 1
2004 #12 R.Newman/Justice League
2004 #12 R.Newman/Alltel
2005 #12 R.Newman/Sony
2005 #12 R.Newman/Mobil 1 Gold
2005 #12 R.Newman/Mobil 1
2005 #12 R.Newman/Alltel
2006 #12 R.Newman/Sony HDTV
2006 #12 R.Newman/Mobil 1
2006 #12 R.Newman/Alltel Black Brickyard
2006 #12 R.Newman/Alltel

Team Caliber Pit Stop 1:64
2002 #12 R.Newman/Mobil 1/7560
2002 #12 R.Newman/Alltel Sony WEGA/7992
2002 #12 R.Newman/Alltel/17,592
2003 #12 R.Newman/Alltel 50th Win
2003 #12 R.Newman/Sony Wega
2003 #12 R.Newman/Mobil 1
2003 #12 R.Newman/Alltel
2004 #12 R.Newman/Sony Wega
2004 #12 R.Newman/Mobil 1 30th Ann.
2004 #12 R.Newman/Mobil 1
2004 #12 R.Newman/Justice League
2004 #12 R.Newman/Alltel
2005 #12 R.Newman/Sony HDTV
2005 #12 R.Newman/Mobil 1 Gold
2005 #12 R.Newman/Mobil 1
2005 #12 R.Newman/Alltel
2005 #39 R.Newman/Alltel
2006 #12 R.Newman/Sony HDTV
2006 #12 R.Newman/Mobil 1
2006 #12 R.Newman/Alltel Black Brickyard
2006 #12 R.Newman/Alltel

Team Caliber Pit Stop Transporters 1:64
2003 #12 R.Newman/Alltel
2004 #12 R.Newman/Alltel

Team Caliber Preferred 1:24
2001 #2 R.Newman/Alltel AUTO with figurine/1800
2001 #2 R.Newman/Alltel Promo/756
2001 #2 R.Newman/Alltel/3876
2002 #12 R.Newman/Alltel Sony WEGA/5004
2002 #12 R.Newman/Alltel/2820
2002 #12 R.Newman/Mobil 1/1536
2003 #12 R.Newman/Sony Wega/4320
2003 #12 R.Newman/Mobil 1/1200
2003 #12 R.Newman/Alltel 50th Win/4090
2003 #12 R.Newman/Alltel/20,008
2004 #12 R.Newman/Sony Wega/5004
2004 #12 R.Newman/Mobil 1 30th Ann./10,080
2004 #12 R.Newman/Mobil 1/10,080
2004 #12 R.Newman/Justice League Red Chrome/504
2004 #12 R.Newman/Justice League Gold/504
2004 #12 R.Newman/Justice League
2004 #12 R.Newman/Alltel Chase/1100
2004 #12 R.Newman/Alltel/20,080
2005 #12 R.Newman/Sony HDTV/1200
2005 #12 R.Newman/Mobil 1 Gold/2400
2005 #12 R.Newman/Mobil 1/2400
2005 #12 R.Newman/Alltel Gold/624
2005 #12 R.Newman/Alltel/7560
2005 #39 R.Newman/Alltel/1800
2006 #12 R.Newman/Sony HDTV/1800
2006 #12 R.Newman/My Circle/1200
2006 #12 R.Newman/Mobil 1
2006 #12 R.Newman/Alltel Black Brickyard/1800
2006 #12 R.Newman/Alltel

Team Caliber Preferred Copper 1:24
2006 #12 R.Newman/Sony HDTV/180
2006 #12 R.Newman/Mobil 1
2006 #12 R.Newman/Alltel/756

Team Caliber Preferred Nickel 1:24
2005 #12 R.Newman/Sony
2005 #12 R.Newman/Mobil 1/180
2005 #12 R.Newman/Alltel/504

Team Caliber Promos 1:64
2001 #2 R.Newman/Alltel
2002 #2 R.Newman/Alltel with cell.face plate
2002 #12 R.Newman/Alltel Sony WEGA in Sears window box
2003 #12 R.Newman/Alltel

Team Caliber/Motorworks 1:64
2003 #12 R.Newman/Alltel

Team Caliber/Motorworks 4-Packs 1:87
2003 #NNO 10.JB/12.RN/03.Blu.Snow/03.Yel.Rein.
2003 #NNO 5.TL/12.RN/03.R.Santa/03.Yel.Rein.

Team Caliber/Motorworks Model Kits 1:24
2003 #12 R.Newman/Alltel

Winner's Circle 1:24
2006 #12 R.Newman/Alltel
2007 #12 R.Newman/Alltel
2008 #12 R.Newman/Alltel

Winner's Circle 1:87
2006 #12 R.Newman/Alltel
2007 #12 R.Newman/Alltel

Winner's Circle Autographed Hood 1:64
2006 #12 R.Newman/Alltel

Winner's Circle License Plate 1:64
2007 #12 R.Newman/Alltel

Winner's Circle Number Magnet 1:64
2008 #12 R.Newman/Alltel

Winner's Circle Schedule Hood 1:64
2007 #12 R.Newman/Alltel

Winner's Circle Stickers 1:64
2008 #12 R.Newman/Alltel

Winner's Circle Transporters 1:64
2007 #12 R.Newman/Alltel
2008 #12 R.Newman/Daytona 500 Win

Petty, Richard

Action Promos 1:64
2005 #43 STP Fantasy in window box
2005 #43 STP '84 Grand Prix in window box
2005 #43 STP '72 Charger in window box

Action QVC For Race Fans Only 1:24
2003 #43 Yankees 100th Ann. Color Chrome/1008

Action Racing Collectables 1:18
2003 #43 Victory Lap/2508

Action Racing Collectables 1:24
1995 #NNO R.Petty 7&7 Champions 2-Bank Set
2003 #43 STP '75 Charger CW Bank/619
2003 #43 STP '75 Charger/8268
2003 #43 Yankees 100th Ann. AU/6100
2003 #43 Yankees 100th Ann./5700
2003 #43 Victory Lap CW Bank/468
2003 #43 Victory Lap/7440

Action Racing Collectables 1:64
1995 #NNO R.Petty 7&7 Champ. 2-car blister
2003 #43 Victory Lap/10,620
2003 #43 Yankees 100th Ann./6408
2003 #43 STP '75 Charger/6294

Action Racing Collectables Historical S
2004 #43 STP 200th Win 1984 Tribute/3768
2004 #43 STP 200th Win '84 Grand Prix/4992
2004 #43 STP '80 400 Chevy Wins Color Chrome/3924
2005 #43 STP '79 Olds QVC/288
2005 #43 STP '92 Grand Prix AU QVC/504
2005 #43 STP '92 Grand Prix AU/1716
2005 #43 STP '79 Olds/2952

Action/Funline Muscle Machines 1:18
2004 #43 STP '68 Dart
2004 #43 STP '69 Charger
2005 #43 STP '68 Dart
2005 #43 STP '69 Charger QVC/180
2005 #43 STP '69 Charger RCCA/300
2005 #43 STP '69 Charger/316

Action/RCCA 1:24
2003 #43 Yankees 100th AUTO/700
2003 #43 Yankees 100th Ann./500
2003 #43 Victory Lap/804
2003 #43 STP '75 Charger/1000

Action/RCCA 1:64
2003 #43 Yankees 100th Ann./1012
2003 #43 Victory Lap/1008
2003 #43 STP '75 Charger/1444

Action/RCCA Elite 1:24

2003 #43 Yankees 100th AUTO/700
2003 #43 Yankees 100th Ann./520
2003 #43 Victory Lap/1200
2003 #43 STP '75 Charger/1300

Action/RCCA Elite 1:64
2003 #43 Yankees 100th Ann./1012

Action/RCCA Historical Series 1:24
2004 #43 STP 20th Ann. 200th Win/444
2004 #43 STP 200th Win '84 Grand Prix Brushed Metal CW Bank/504
2004 #43 STP 200th Win '84 Grand Prix Brushed Metal/444
2004 #43 STP 200th Win '84 Grand Prix/444
2004 #43 STP 100th Chevy Win '80 Monte Carlo Chrome/600
2005 #43 STP '92 Grand Prix/300
2005 #43 STP '79 Olds/480

Action/RCCA Historical Series 1:64
2004 #43 STP '84 Grand Prix Promo
2004 #43 STP '04 Fantasy Promo
2004 #43 STP '72 Charger Promo

Action/RCCA Historical Series Elite 1:2
2004 #43 STP 20th Ann. 200th Win Platinum/300
2004 #43 STP 20th Ann. 200th Win AU/444
2005 #43 STP '79 Olds Platinum/144
2005 #43 STP '92 Grand Prix AU/408
2005 #43 STP '79 Olds White Gold/25
2005 #43 STP '79 Olds/480

Action/RCCA Revell 1:64
1991-92 #43 STP

Action/RCCA Transporters 1:64
1992 #43 STP RCCA
1995 #NNO 7&7 Champs RCCA/3000

Brookfield 1:24
2005 #NNO R.Petty Fantasy Charger 2-car set/600

Brookfield Dually with Car and Show
1993-95 #NNO 7&7/5000 '95

Brookfield Suburbans, Blazers, and Taho
1995 #NNO R.Petty 7-Time Bank split tampos reversed/30,000
1995 #NNO R.Petty 7-Time Bank split paint scheme/30,000
1995 #NNO 7-Time Champ 2-Suburban set/25,000

Ertl 1:18
1992 #43 STP
1995 #43 STP 7-Time Champ/10,000

Ertl 1:25
1982-84 #43 STP Superstock Package
1982-84 #43 STP Stock Car Package

Ertl 1:64
1986-93 #43 NDA/STP '90

Ertl Motorized Pullback 1:43
1982 #43 STP

Ertl Pow-R Pull 1:64
1984 #43 STP

Ertl Superstock 1:64
1981 #43 STP '80 Chevy blue above and below red stripe on sides
1981 #43 STP Buick red above and blue below on sides

Ertl Transporters 1:64
1990 #43 STP

Ertl White Rose Transporters Promos
1992-94 #43 Petty 35th Anniversary Tour

Funstuf Pit Row 1:64
1992 #43 STP with Winston Decal on Fender
1992 #43 STP
1992 #NNO 6-Car Set

General Mills Hot Wheels Petty Promos 1
2004 #43 STP '74 Charger
2004 #43 STP '64 Plymouth

Hot Wheels Pro Circuit 1:64
1992 #43 STP

Hot Wheels Pro Racing 1:24
1999 #43 STP '81 Buick

Hot Wheels Pro Racing 1:64
1999 #43 STP '72
1999 #43 STP '67
1999 #43 STP '64

Hot Wheels Race Day 1:64
2005 #43 67 Plymouth

Hot Wheels Racing Luxury Rides 1:64
2003 #43 STP

Hot Wheels Racing Pit Cruisers 1:64
2004 #43 STP

Hot Wheels Racing Race Day 1:24
2004 #43 STP

Hot Wheels Racing Radical Rides 1:64
2000 #43 STP

Hot Wheels Racing Radical Rods 1:43
2001 #43 STP

Hot Wheels Racing Select 1:64
2001 #43 70 Plymouth Superbird
2001 #43 68 Plymouth
2001 #43 63 Plymouth
2001 #43 57 Olds

Hot Wheels Racing Test Track 1:24
2004 #43 STP

Hot Wheels Racing Test Track 1:64
2004 #43 STP

Hot Wheels Racing Track Edition 1:64
1999 #43 STP '72
1999 #43 STP '67
1999 #43 STP '64

Hot Wheels Racing Transporters 1:64
2001 #43 STP Tribute

Hot Wheels Racing Treasure Hunt 1:64
2003 #43 STP 9

Hot Wheels Radical Rides 1:43
1999 #43 STP

Hot Wheels Team Transporters 1:64
2004 #43 STP

Hot Wheels Transporters 1:64
2002 #NNO Pettys/Lee/Richard/Kyle/Adam

Matchbox White Rose Super Stars 1:64
1990-92 #43 STP BL 92

Matchbox White Rose Team Convoys 1:6
1990-93 #43 STP w/van '92

Matchbox White Rose Transporters Super
1989 #43 STP
1990 #43 STP
1991 #43 STP 20th Anniversary
1992 #43 STP

Pole Position 1:64
1991-92 #43 STP

Racing Champions 1:24
1991-92 #43 STP '91
1991-92 #43 STP Blue Wheels '92
1991-92 #42/43 K.Petty/Mello Yello/STP 2-cars 1:24

Racing Champions 1:43
1991 #43 STP
1992 #43 STP 1970 Superbird

Racing Champions 1:64
1990 #43 Pontiac
1991 #43 STP PB
1991 #43 STP NP
1991 #43 STP EB
1991 #NNO Sears 13-car set
1991 #NNO Collect.Edit.12-car set w/R.Petty
1992 #43 STP w/Blue wheels
1992 #43 STP w/Black wheels
1992 #NNO Sears 12-car set
1992 #NNO Collect.Edit.12-car set w/R.Petty
1999 #43 STP 7-car set w/transporter
2002 #43 Garfield

Racing Champions 12-Car Sets 1:64
1999 #NNO R.Petty Dodge Motorsports

Racing Champions 24K Gold 1:64
1998 #43 STP 4-cars w/transporter

Racing Champions 2-Car Sets 1:43
1991 #25/43 K.Schrader/R.Petty

Racing Champions 2-Car Sets 1:64
1999 #43 STP '66 Pontiac with Gold car/4343

Racing Champions 3-Pack 1:64
1990-92 #NNO M.Shep./R.Petty '90
1990-92 #NNO D.Cope/M.Shep./R.Petty '90

Racing Champions 5-Pack 1:144
1991 #NNO 3.DE/27.RW/28.DA/30.BH/43.RP

Racing Champions Authentics 1:24
2002 #43 Garfield/999
2004 #43 Blue '57 Olds Chrome/200
2004 #43 Blue '57 Olds/800
2005 #43 70 Superbird Southern Chrysler Silver Chrome/72
2005 #43 70 Superbird Southern Chrysler Black Chrome/72
2005 #43 70 Superbird Southern Chrysler/1002
2005 #43 70 Superbird Marc Times Silver Chrome/72
2005 #43 70 Superbird Marc Times Black Chrome/72
2005 #43 70 Superbird Marc Times/1002
2005 #43 70 Superbird Silver Chrome/72
2005 #43 70 Superbird Black Chrome/72
2005 #43 70 Superbird/1002
2005 #43 64 Plymouth Belvedere Black Chrome/200
2005 #43 64 Plymouth Belvedere/800
2006 #43 64 Belvedere 1st Champ/5004

Racing Champions Banks 1:24
1992-94 #43 STP

Racing Champions Legends 1:64
1991-92 #43 1970 Plym.Superbird Racing Superstars blister
1991-92 #43 1969 Ford Torino

Racing Champions Petty Collection 1:24
1999 #42 57 Oldsmobile
1999 #43 81 Buick
1999 #43 70 Superbird
1999 #43 64 Plymouth

Racing Champions Petty Collection 1:43
1999 #43 70 Superbird 3-car set
1999 #43 70 Superbird

Racing Champions Petty Collection 1:64
1999 #58 1957 Oldsmobile 1958 on package
1999 #59 1959 Plymouth Plaza
1999 #60 1960 Plymouth Fury
1999 #61 1961 Plymouth Fury
1999 #62 1962 Plymouth Savoy
1999 #63 1963 Plymouth Savoy
1999 #64 1964 Plymouth Belvedere
1999 #65 1965 Plymouth Barracuda
1999 #66 1966 Plymouth Belvedere
1999 #67 1967 Plymouth Belvedere GTX
1999 #68 1968 Plymouth Roadrunner
1999 #69 1969 Ford Torino
1999 #70 1970 Plymouth Superbird
1999 #71 Pepsi 1971 Plym.Roadrunner
1999 #72 STP 1972 Plym.Roadrunner
1999 #73 STP 1973 Dodge Charger
1999 #74 STP 1974 Dodge Charger
1999 #75 STP 1975 Dodge Charger
1999 #76 STP 1976 Dodge Charger
1999 #77 STP 1977 Dodge Charger
1999 #78 STP 1977 Monte Carlo 1978 on package
1999 #79 STP 1977 Monte Carlo 1979 on package
1999 #80 STP 1977 Monte Carlo 1980 on package
1999 #81 STP 1981 Buick Regal
1999 #82 STP '82 Pontiac Grand Prix
1999 #83 STP '82 Pontiac Grand Prix 1983 on package
1999 #84 STP '82 Pontiac Grand Prix 1984 on package
1999 #85 STP '85 Pont.Grand Prix
1999 #86 STP '85 Pont.Grand Prix 1986 on package
1999 #87 STP '87 Pont.Grand Prix
1999 #88 STP 1988 Pont.Grand Prix
1999 #89 STP '89 Pont.Grand Prix
1999 #90 STP '90 Pont.Grand Prix
1999 #91 STP '91 Pont.Grand Prix
1999 #92 STP '92 Pont.Grand Prix

Racing Champions Petty Fan Appreciation
1992 #43 Dover Downs Sept.20
1992 #43 Dover Downs May 31
1992 #43 Daytona July 4
1992 #43 Daytona 500 Feb.16
1992 #43 Darlington Sept.6
1992 #43 Darlington March 29
1992 #43 Charlotte Oct.11
1992 #43 Charlotte May 24
1992 #43 Char.One Hot Night May 16
1992 #43 Bristol August 29
1992 #43 Bristol April 3
1992 #43 Atlanta Hooters 500 11/15
1992 #43 Atlanta Motor Speed. 3/15
1992 #43 Watkins Glen Aug.9
1992 #43 Talladega July 26
1992 #43 Talladega May 3
1992 #43 Sears Point June 7
1992 #43 Rockingham Oct.25
1992 #43 Rockingham March 1
1992 #43 Richmond Sept.12
1992 #43 Richmond March 8
1992 #43 Pocono July 19
1992 #43 Pocono Raceway June 14
1992 #43 Phoenix Nov.1
1992 #43 North Wilkesboro Oct.4
1992 #43 North Wilkesboro April 12
1992 #43 Michigan Aug.16
1992 #43 Michigan June 21
1992 #43 Martinsville Sept.27
1992 #43 Martinsville April 26

Racing Champions Pit Stop 1:24
1992 #43 STP

Racing Champions Premier 1:64
1992 #43 STP/20,000

Racing Champions Racing Relatives 1:43
1992 #42/43 K.Petty/Mello Yello/STP

Racing Champions Roaring Racers 1:64
1990-91 #43 STP SW '91
1990-91 #43 STP BW '91

Racing Champions Super Collector's S
1992-94 #43 STP 3-cars:1:24/43/64 and a 1:64 Transporter '92
1992-94 #43 STP Fan Tour 2-cars: 1:24/43 & Transporter '92

Racing Champions Transporters 1:144
1991-92 #43 STP

Racing Champions Transporters 1:64
1992 #43 STP Fan Appreciation Tour
1992 #43 STP
1999 #43 STP w/7-cars

Racing Champions with Figure 1:64
1991 #43 STP

Revell Promos 1:64
1993-95 #43 STP red&blue Pontiac Wisk promo blister
1993-95 #43 STP red&blue '72 Charger Wisk promo blister
1993-95 #43 STP blue Wisk promo blister

Road Champs 1:43
1992 #43 STP

Road Champs 1:64
1992 #43 STP

Road Champs Pull Back Action 1:43
1992 #43 STP

Road Champs Sounds of Power 1:43
1992 #43 STP

Road Champs Transporters 1:64
1992 #43 STP

Road Champs Transporters 1:87
1992 #43 STP

Scaleworks Transporters 1:24
1996-98 #43 STP 25th Anniv/1025 '97

Team Caliber Owners Series 1:24
2002 #43 Garfield/3120

Team Caliber Owners Series Banks 1:24
2002 #43 Garfield/180

Team Caliber Owners Series Dark Chrome
2002 #43 Garfield/396

Team Caliber Owners Series Vintage 1:24
2004 #43 STP '69 Torino

Team Caliber Pit Stop 1:24
2002 #43 Garfield/2400

Team Caliber Pit Stop 1:64
2002 #43 Garfield/7560

Team Caliber Preferred 1:24
2002 #43 Garfield/4428
2006 #43 69 Torino 100th Win Wix Filters
2006 #43 69 Torino AU/5035

Team Caliber Preferred Copper 1:24
2006 #43 69 Torino AU/180

Winner's Circle Driver Sticker 1:64
2005 #43 STP '84 Grand Prix
2005 #43 STP '75 Charger

Winner's Circle Victory Lap 1:24
2003 #43 STP Victory Lap

Winner's Circle Victory Lap 1:64
2003 #43 STP Victory Lap

Winross Transporters 1:64
1991 #NNO STP
1992 #NNO STP Fan Appre. Tour

Ragan, David

Action Racing Collectables 1:64
2008 #6 AAA Travel
2008 #6 AAA Show Your Card
2008 #6 AAA Insurance

Motorsports Authentics Driver's Select
2007 #6 Discount Tire/1200*
2007 #6 AAA Travel/804*
2007 #6 AAA Show Your Card/852*
2007 #6 AAA Insurance/804*
2007 #6 AAA/6624*
2007 #6 AAA COT/708*
2007 #6 Discount Tire
2007 #6 AAA Travel
2007 #6 AAA Show Your Card
2007 #6 AAA Insurance
2007 #6 AAA COT
2007 #6 AAA

Motorsports Authentics Owner's Elite 1:
2007 #6 AAA/504*

Motorsports Authentics Owner's Elite Tr
2007 #6 Discount Tire/144*
2007 #6 AAA/1500*

Motorsports Authentics Pit Stop 1:64
2007 #6 AAA Show Your Card
2007 #6 AAA Insurance
2007 #6 AAA COT
2007 #6 AAA
2007 #6 Discount Tire
2007 #6 AAA Travel

RCCA Club 1:24
2008 #6 AAA/150

Winner's Circle 1:87
2007 #6 AAA

Winner's Circle Number Magnet 1:64
2008 #6 AAA Insurance

Winner's Circle Pit Sign 1:64
2007 #6 AAA

Reutimann, David

Motorsports Authentics Driver's Select
2007 #0 Domino's Pizza/2508*
2007 #0 Burger King COT/708*
2007 #0 Burger King/2200*
2007 #0 Domino's Pizza COT/700*
2007 #99 Aaron's/3488*

Motorsports Authentics Owner's Elite 1:
2007 #0 Domino's COT/504*
2007 #0 Domino's/504*
2007 #0 Burger King COT/504*
2007 #0 Burger King/504*
2007 #0 Domino's/1008*

Motorsports Authentics Owner's Elite Tr
2007 #0 Domino's Pizza/300*
2007 #0 Burger King/300*
2007 #99 Aaron's/144*

Motorsports Authentics Pit Stop 1:64
2007 #0 Domino's Pizza
2007 #0 Burger King
2007 #99 Aaron's

Motorsports Authentics/RCCA Transporter
2007 #0 Domino's/708*

Racing Champions 1:24
2004 #17 NTN Bearings SuperTruck Promo
2005 #17 Toyota TRD SuperTruck Promo

Racing Champions Promos 1:64
2006 #17 Tundra SuperTruck in blister

RCCA Club 1:24
2008 #44 UPS KY Derby/150

RCCA Elite 1:24
2008 #44 UPS KY Derby/300
2008 #44 UPS KY Derby Platinum/25
2008 #44 UPS KY Derby White Gold/50

Winner's Circle 1:24
2007 #0 Burger King

Winner's Circle 1:87
2007 #0 Burger King

Winner's Circle Sam Bass 1:64
2008 #44 UPS

Winner's Circle Transporters 1:64
2007 #0 Burger King

Sadler, Elliott

Action Performance 1:24
2005 #38 E.Sadler/M&M's Hometown

Action Performance 1:64
2005 #38 E.Sadler/M&M's

Action Promos 1:64
2006 #38 E.Sadler/M&M's & Snicker's 2-car set

Action QVC For Race Fans Only 1:24
2005 #38 E.Sadler/M&M's Color Chrome/360

Action Racing Collectables 1:24
1997 #29 E.Sadler/Phillips 66 Bank/3500
1999 #21 E.Sadler/Citgo/4008
2000 #21 E.Sadler/Citgo Virgina Tech/3504
2000 #21 E.Sadler/Citgo '70's Paint/2004 white car w/red roof
2000 #21 E.Sadler/Citgo '50's Paint/2004 red car w/white numbers
2000 #21 E.Sadler/Citgo/3504
2003 #38 E.Sadler/Combos/4932
2003 #38 E.Sadler/M&M's Pedigree/3984
2003 #38 E.Sadler/M&M's Halloween CW Bank/480
2003 #38 E.Sadler/M&M's Halloween/6504
2003 #38 E.Sadler/M&M's Groovy CW Bank/792
2003 #38 E.Sadler/M&M's Groovy/9312
2003 #38 E.Sadler/M&M's Mac Tools/288
2003 #38 E.Sadler/M&M's/8712
2004 #38 E.Sadler/Pedigree Wizard of Oz CW Bank/252
2004 #38 E.Sadler/Pedigree Wizard of Oz/3540
2004 #38 E.Sadler/M&M's July 4th/4644
2004 #38 E.Sadler/M&M's Halloween QVC/288
2004 #38 E.Sadler/M&M's Halloween Mac Tools/204
2004 #38 E.Sadler/M&M's Halloween CW Bank/204
2004 #38 E.Sadler/M&M's Halloween/2556
2004 #38 E.Sadler/M&M's Black&White Raced CW Bank/408
2004 #38 E.Sadler/M&M's Black&White Raced w/tire swatch/2484
2004 #38 E.Sadler/M&M'sBlack&White CW Bank/336
2004 #38 E.Sadler/M&M's Black&White/5880
2004 #38 E.Sadler/M&M's Texas Raced w/tire swatch/3504
2004 #38 E.Sadler/M&M's Mac Tools/288
2004 #38 E.Sadler/M&M's CW Bank/360
2004 #38 E.Sadler/M&M's/9000
2005 #38 E.Sadler/M&M's Clear/504
2005 #38 E.Sadler/Combos CW Bank/144
2005 #38 E.Sadler/Combos/1524
2005 #38 E.Sadler/M&M's/5856
2005 #38 E.Sadler/M&M's Matco/72
2005 #38 E.Sadler/M&M's QVC/504
2005 #38 E.Sadler/M&M's Halloween/4008
2005 #38 E.Sadler/M&M's Halloween QVC/288
2005 #38 E.Sadler/M&M's July 4th/3204
2005 #38 E.Sadler/M&M's July 4th CW Bank/144
2005 #38 E.Sadler/M&M's July 4th QVC/144
2005 #38 E.Sadler/M&M's Star Wars/4332
2005 #38 E.Sadler/M&M's Star Wars CW Bank/204
2005 #38 E.Sadler/M&M's Star Wars Matco/48
2005 #38 E.Sadler/M&M's Star Wars QVC/408
2005 #38 E.Sadler/M&M's Test/792
2005 #38 E.Sadler/M&M's Test QVC/144
2005 #38 E.Sadler/Pedigree/1488
2005 #38 E.Sadler/Pedigree Matco/12
2005 #38 E.Sadler/Pedigree QVC/144
2005 #38 E.Sadler/30th Birthday Fantasy/2640
2005 #38 E.Sadler/30th Birthday Fantasy Matco/12
2005 #90 E.Sadler/Citifinancial/864
2006 #19 E.Sadler/Dodge Holiday QVC*
2006 #19 E.Sadler/Dodge Holiday/576*
2006 #38 E.Sadler/Snickers Mac Tools*
2006 #38 E.Sadler/Snickers CWB/144
2006 #38 E.Sadler/Snickers/2868*
2006 #38 E.Sadler/Pedigree/2508
2006 #38 E.Sadler/M&M's Pirates of the Caribbean Matco*
2006 #38 E.Sadler/M&M's Pirates of the Caribbean Mac Tools*
2006 #38 E.Sadler/M&M's Pirates of the Caribbean CWB/300
2006 #38 E.Sadler/M&M's Pirates of the Caribbean/7560*
2006 #38 E.Sadler/M&M's QVC/96
2006 #38 E.Sadler/M&M's Matco/48
2006 #38 E.Sadler/M&M's Mac Tools/504
2006 #38 E.Sadler/M&M's CW Bank/252
2006 #38 E.Sadler/M&M's/5244
2006 #90 E.Sadler/Citifinancial/2004

Action Racing Collectables 1:64
1997 #29 E.Sadler/Phillips 66
1999 #21 E.Sadler/Citgo
2003 #38 E.Sadler/M&M's Halloween/6696
2003 #38 E.Sadler/M&M's Groovy/8424
2003 #38 E.Sadler/M&M's/9576
2004 #38 E.Sadler/Pedigree Wizard of Oz/4560
2004 #38 E.Sadler/M&M's Halloween
2004 #38 E.Sadler/M&M's Black&White/5184
2004 #38 E.Sadler/M&M's/6576
2005 #38 E.Sadler/Pedigree
2005 #38 E.Sadler/M&M's July 4th
2005 #38 E.Sadler/M&M's Halloween
2005 #38 E.Sadler/M&M's
2006 #38 E.Sadler/Snickers
2006 #38 E.Sadler/M&M's Pirates of the Caribbean
2006 #38 E.Sadler/M&M's
2006 #90 E.Sadler/Citifinancial

Action/Funline Monster Truck 1:43
2004 #38 E.Sadler/M&M's

Action/Funline Muscle Machines 1:18
2004 #38 E.Sadler/M&M's '49 Mercury
2004 #38 E.Sadler/M&M's '66 Mustang
2005 #38 E.Sadler/M&M's '40 Delivery Van/792
2005 #38 E.Sadler/M&M's '66 Mustang/816
2005 #38 E.Sadler/M&M's Star Wars '40 Delivery Van/904

Action/Funline Muscle Machines 1:24
2004 #38 E.Sadler/M&M's '49 Mercury
2004 #38 E.Sadler/M&M's '66 Mustang
2005 #38 E.Sadler/M&M's Hybrid/144

Action/RCCA 1:24
1997 #29 E.Sadler/Phillips 66
2003 #38 E.Sadler/M&M's Halloween/760
2003 #38 E.Sadler/Pedigree/300
2003 #38 E.Sadler/M&M's Groovy/504
2003 #38 E.Sadler/M&M's CW Bank/600
2003 #38 E.Sadler/Combos/604
2004 #38 E.Sadler/Pedigree Wizard of Oz/360
2004 #38 E.Sadler/M&M's July 4/288
2004 #38 E.Sadler/M&M's Halloween/408
2004 #38 E.Sadler/M&M's Black&White Raced w/tire/240
2004 #38 E.Sadler/M&M's Black&White/360
2004 #38 E.Sadler/M&M's Texas Raced/240
2004 #38 E.Sadler/M&M's/300
2005 #8 E.Sadler/M&M's UPS/144
2005 #38 E.Sadler/M&M's Hometown Brushed Bronze/144
2005 #38 E.Sadler/M&M's July 4/288
2005 #38 E.Sadler/30th Birthday Fantasy/300
2005 #38 E.Sadler/Pedigree/288
2005 #38 E.Sadler/M&M's Test/360
2005 #38 E.Sadler/M&M's Star Wars/408
2005 #38 E.Sadler/M&M's Color Chrome/204
2005 #38 E.Sadler/M&M's/408
2005 #38 E.Sadler/Combos/204
2005 #90 E.Sadler/Citi Financial/240
2006 #19 E.Sadler/Dodge Holiday/200
2006 #38 E.Sadler/M&M's Color Chrome/120
2006 #38 E.Sadler/M&M's Mega/180
2006 #38 E.Sadler/Pedigree/120
2006 #38 E.Sadler/Snickers/250
2006 #38 E.Sadler/M&M's Pirates of the Caribbean/300
2006 #38 E.Sadler/M&M's/288
2006 #90 E.Sadler/Citifinancial/100

Action/RCCA 1:64
1997 #29 E.Sadler/Phillips 66/3500
1999 #21 E.Sadler/Citgo/2500
2003 #38 E.Sadler/M&M's Halloween/1012
2003 #38 E.Sadler/M&M's Groovy/1012
2003 #38 E.Sadler/M&M's/1300
2004 #38 E.Sadler/M&M's Halloween/576
2004 #38 E.Sadler/M&M's July 4/576
2004 #38 E.Sadler/Pedigree Wizard of Oz/576
2004 #38 E.Sadler/M&M's Black&White/1008
2004 #38 E.Sadler/M&M's/720
2005 #38 E.Sadler/M&M's July 4/432
2005 #38 E.Sadler/M&M's/576
2006 #38 E.Sadler/M&M's/432
2006 #38 E.Sadler/Snickers/288
2006 #38 E.Sadler/M&M's Pirates of the Caribbean/240

Action/RCCA Banks 1:24
1999 #21 E.Sadler/Citgo/1000

Action/RCCA Elite 1:24
1997 #29 E.Sadler/Phillips 66/1200
2000 #21 E.Sadler/Citgo/804
2003 #38 E.Sadler/M&M's Halloween/504
2003 #38 E.Sadler/M&M's Groovy/720
2003 #38 E.Sadler/M&M's/900
2003 #38 E.Sadler/Combos/400
2004 #38 E.Sadler/Pedigree Wizard of Oz/360
2004 #38 E.Sadler/M&M's July 4/288
2004 #38 E.Sadler/M&M's Halloween/408
2004 #38 E.Sadler/M&M's Black&White Raced w/tire/240
2004 #38 E.Sadler/M&M's Black&White/360
2004 #38 E.Sadler/M&M's Texas Raced/240
2004 #38 E.Sadler/M&M's/300
2005 #8 E.Sadler/M&M's UPS/144
2005 #8 E.Sadler/M&M's UPS White Gold/25
2005 #38 E.Sadler/Combos/204
2005 #38 E.Sadler/M&M's Hometown Brushed Bronze/144
2005 #38 E.Sadler/M&M's Star Wars White Gold/25
2005 #38 E.Sadler/30th Birthday Fantasy/204
2005 #38 E.Sadler/M&M's Test/408
2005 #38 E.Sadler/M&M's Star Wars AU/141
2005 #38 E.Sadler/M&M's Star Wars/480
2005 #38 E.Sadler/M&M's July 4/288
2005 #38 E.Sadler/M&M's Halloween White Gold/25
2005 #38 E.Sadler/M&M White Gold/25
2005 #38 E.Sadler/M&M's Color Chrome/204
2005 #38 E.Sadler/M&M's/408
2006 #19 E.Sadler/Dodge Holiday/200
2006 #19 E.Sadler/Dodge Holiday Platinum/4
2006 #19 E.Sadler/Dodge Holiday White Gold/25
2006 #38 E.Sadler/M&M's/408
2006 #38 E.Sadler/M&M's Platinum/8
2006 #38 E.Sadler/M&M's Mega/180
2006 #38 E.Sadler/M&M's Mega Platinum/3
2006 #38 E.Sadler/Snickers White Gold/25
2006 #38 E.Sadler/Snickers Platinum/5
2006 #38 E.Sadler/Snickers/250
2006 #38 E.Sadler/M&M's Pirates White Gold/25
2006 #38 E.Sadler/M&M's White Gold/25
2006 #38 E.Sadler/M&M's Color Chrome/120
2006 #90 E.Sadler/Citifinancial/100
2006 #90 E.Sadler/Citifinancial Platinum/2

Action/RCCA Elite 1:64
2003 #38 E.Sadler/M&M's Halloween/1012
2003 #38 E.Sadler/M&M's Groovy/1012
2004 #38 E.Sadler/M&M's/504
2005 #38 E.Sadler/M&M's/480
2005 #38 E.Sadler/M&M's July 4/384
2006 #38 E.Sadler/M&M's/240
2006 #38 E.Sadler/Snickers/192
2006 #38 E.Sadler/M&M's Pirates of the Caribbean/240

Action/RCCA Metal Elite 1:24
2005 #38 E.Sadler/M&M's AU/144
2005 #38 E.Sadler/M&M's/408

Brookfield Trackside 1:64
2004 #38 E.Sadler/M&M's/5000
2004 #38 E.Sadler/M&M's black & white/5004
2004 #38 E.Sadler/M&M's Halloween/5004

Hot Wheels Daytona Set-Up 1:64
2002 #21 E.Sadler/Motorcraft

Hot Wheels Deluxe 1:64
2000 #21 E.Sadler/Citgo

Hot Wheels Deluxe Black Chrome 1:43
1999 #21 E.Sadler/Citgo

Hot Wheels Deluxe Hot Rod 1:64
2000 #21 E.Sadler/Citgo

Hot Wheels Deluxe Scorchin Scooter 1:64
2000 #21 E.Sadler/Citgo

Hot Wheels Race Day Deluxe 1:24
2000 #21 E.Sadler/Citgo

Hot Wheels Racing 1:24
2001 #21 E.Sadler/Motorcraft

Hot Wheels Racing Pit Board 1:64
2001 #21 E.Sadler/Motorcraft

Hot Wheels Racing Select 1:64
2001 #21 E.Sadler/Motorcraft

Hot Wheels Racing Sticker 1:64
2002 #21 E.Sadler/Motorcraft

Hot Wheels Racing The Demon 1:64
2001 #21 E.Sadler/Motorcraft

Hot Wheels Racing Track Edition 1:64
1999 #21 E.Sadler/Citgo

Hot Wheels Select 1:64
2000 #21 E.Sadler/Citgo

Hot Wheels Select Clear 1:24
1999 #21 E.Sadler/Citgo

Hot Wheels Select Clear 1:43
1999 #21 E.Sadler/Citgo

Hot Wheels Transporters 1:64
2002 #21 E.Sadler/Motorcraft

Motorsports Authentics Driver's Select
2007 #19 E.Sadler/Dodge Dealers Holiday Sam Bass/387*
2007 #19 E.Sadler/Dodge Dealers/4508*
2007 #19 E.Sadler/Dodge Dealers COT/1104*
2007 #19 E.Sadler/Siemen's COT/1212*
2007 #19 E.Sadler/Siemen's COT
2007 #19 E.Sadler/Dodge Dealers

Motorsports Authentics Owner's Elite 1:
2007 #19 E.Sadler/Dodge Dealers COT/504*
2007 #19 E.Sadler/Dodge Dealers/504*

Motorsports Authentics Owner's Elite Tr
2007 #19 E.Sadler/Dodge Dealers/1716*

Motorsports Authentics Pit Stop 1:64
2007 #19 E.Sadler/Siemen's COT
2007 #19 E.Sadler/Dodge Dealers

Motorsports Authentics Pit Stop Blister

2007 #19 E.Sadler/Dodge Dealers
Motorsports Authentics QVC For Race Fan
2007 #19 E.Sadler/Dodge Dealers Color Chrome/96
Motorsports Authentics/RCCA Owner's Clu
2007 #19 E.Sadler/Dodge Dealers Holiday Sam Bass/96*
Peachstate/GMP Transporters 1:64
2002 #21 E.Sadler/Motorcraft/1400
Racing Champions 1:144
1997 #29 E.Sadler/Phillips 66
1998 #66 E.Sadler/Phillips 66
Racing Champions 1:24
1997 #29 E.Sadler/Phillips 66
1998 #66 E.Sadler/Phillips 66
1999 #21 E.Sadler/Citgo
1999 #21 E.Sadler/Citgo Chrome/2499
2001 #21 E.Sadler/Motorcraft Layin' Rubber
2001 #21 E.Sadler/Motorcraft
2002 #21 E.Sadler/Motorcraft
2004 #38 E.Sadler/M&M's Promo
2004 #38 E.Sadler/Combos Promo
Racing Champions 1:64
1997 #29 E.Sadler/Phillips 66
1998 #66 E.Sadler/Phillips 66
1999 #21 E.Sadler/Citgo Chrome/9999
1999 #21 E.Sadler/Citgo
2000 #NNO 12-car set/Time Trials/Young Guns and War Paint cars/2500
2001 #21 E.Sadler/Motorcraft Layin' Rubber
2001 #21 E.Sadler/Motorcraft
2002 #21 E.Sadler/Motorcraft
2003 #38 E.Sadler/M&M's Groovy Summer Promo in window box
2003 #38 E.Sadler/Combos Promo in wind.box
2004 #38 E.Sadler/M&M's Black&White Promo
2004 #38 E.Sadler/M&M's Yellow Promo
Racing Champions 12-Car Sets 1:64
1999 #3 12-Car Set 3
Racing Champions 5-Pack 1:64
2000 #NNO 42.KI/21.ES/9.SC/34/50.TR
2000 #NNO 21. E.Sadler/Citgo 5-car set
Racing Champions Authentics 1:24
2002 #21 E.Sadler/Motorcraft Chrome/199
2002 #21 E.Sadler/Motorcraft/999
2002 #21 E.Sadler/Air Force Chrome/199
2002 #21 E.Sadler/Air Force/999
Racing Champions Fan Appreciation 5-Pac
1999 #6 21.ES/26.JB/77.RP/99/42.JN
Racing Champions Gold 1:24
1998 #66 E.Sadler/Phillips 66
Racing Champions Gold with Medallion 1:
1998 #66 E.Sadler/Phillips 66
Racing Champions NASCAR Rules 1:64
1999 #21 E.Sadler/Citgo
Racing Champions Premier 1:24
2001 #21 E.Sadler/Motorcraft Layin Rub.
2001 #21 E.Sadler/Motorcraft Chrome/1500
2001 #21 E.Sadler/Motorcraft
Racing Champions Premier 1:64
2001 #21 E.Sadler/Motorcraft
Racing Champions Press Pass Series 1:64
1998 #66 E.Sadler/Phillips 66
1999 #21 E.Sadler/Citgo
Racing Champions Stock Rods 1:24
1998 #33 E.Sadler/Phillips 66
1998 #53 E.Sadler/Phillips 66
Racing Champions Transporters 1:64
1998 #66 E.Sadler/Phillips 66 w/Car
1998 #66 E.Sadler/Phillips 66
Racing Champions Transporters 1:87
1998 #66 E.Sadler/Phillips 66
Racing Champions Transporters Gold 1:64
1998 #66 E.Sadler/Phillips 66
Racing Champions Under the Lights 1:24
1999 #21 E.Sadler/Citgo
Racing Champions Under the Lights 1:64
1999 #21 E.Sadler/Citgo
RCCA Club 1:24
2008 #19 E.Sadler/Best Buy/150
RCCA Elite 1:24
2008 #19 E.Sadler/Best Buy/300
2008 #19 E.Sadler/McDonald's/300
Revell Collection 1:24
2000 #21 E.Sadler/Citgo '60's Red and White/3120
2000 #21 E.Sadler/Citgo MDA Promo
2000 #21 E.Sadler/Citgo MDA/3120
Revell Collection 1:64
1999 #21 E.Sadler/Citgo
2000 #21 E.Sadler/Citgo MDA Promo blister
Team Caliber Owners Series 1:24
2000 #21 E.Sadler/Citgo VT/2340
2000 #21 E.Sadler/Citgo/2340
2001 #21 E.Sadler/Motorcraft/2340
2001 #21 E.Sadler/Air Force/2400
2002 #21 E.Sadler/Motorcraft/1800
2002 #21 E.Sadler/Air Force/2400
Team Caliber Owners Series 1:64
2000 #21 E.Sadler/Citgo/7560
Team Caliber Owners Series Banks 1:24
2001 #21 E.Sadler/Air Force/258
2001 #21 E.Sadler/Motorcraft/756
2002 #21 E.Sadler/Motorcraft/222
2002 #21 E.Sadler/Air Force/180
Team Caliber Owners Series Dark Chrome
2002 #21 E.Sadler/Motorcraft/180
2002 #21 E.Sadler/Air Force/336
Team Caliber Owners Series Gold 1:24
2001 #21 E.Sadler/Motorcraft/504
2001 #21 E.Sadler/Air Force/258
Team Caliber Owners Series Steel 1:24
2001 #21 E.Sadler/Air Force/258
2001 #21 E.Sadler/Motorcraft/504
Team Caliber Pit Stop 1:64
2001 #21 E.Sadler/Motorcraft
2002 #21 E.Sadler/Air Force/5004
Team Caliber Preferred 1:24
2000 #21 E.Sadler/Citgo Virg.Tech/5508
2000 #21 E.Sadler/Citgo/5508
2001 #21 E.Sadler/Air Force/504
2001 #21 E.Sadler/Motorcraft/1500
2002 #21 E.Sadler/Motorcraft/1176
2002 #21 E.Sadler/Air Force/4260
Team Caliber Preferred Banks 1:24
2000 #21 E.Sadler/Citgo Virg.Tech/756
2000 #21 E.Sadler/Citgo/504
Team Caliber Promos 1:64
2000 #21 E.Sadler/Citgo in bag
2002 #21 E.Sadler/Air Force Charlotte Race/Recruiters in box
Team Caliber White Knuckle Racing 1:64
2000 #21 E.Sadler/Citgo Promo
Winner's Circle 1:18
2003 #38 E.Sadler/M&M's
2004 #38 E.Sadler/M&M's
2005 #38 E.Sadler/M&M's
Winner's Circle 1:24
2003 #38 E.Sadler/M&M's Groovy
2003 #38 E.Sadler/M&M's
2004 #38 E.Sadler/Pedigree Wizard of Oz
2004 #38 E.Sadler/M&M's July 4
2004 #38 E.Sadler/M&M's black&white
2004 #38 E.Sadler/M&M's
2005 #38 E.Sadler/M&M's July 4
2005 #38 E.Sadler/M&M's
2005 #38 E.Sadler/Pedigree
2006 #38 E.Sadler/M&M's
Winner's Circle 1:87
2006 #38 E.Sadler/M&M's
2007 #19 E.Sadler/Dodge Dealers
Winner's Circle Autographed Hood 1:24
2003 #38 E.Sadler/M&M's Groovy
2004 #38 E.Sadler/Pedigree Wizard of Oz
2004 #38 E.Sadler/M&M's July 4
2004 #38 E.Sadler/M&M's black&white
2004 #38 E.Sadler/M&M's short package
2004 #38 E.Sadler/M&M's
2005 #38 E.Sadler/M&M's
2005 #38 E.Sadler/Pedigree
2005 #38 E.Sadler/M&M's July 4 Green M&M
2005 #38 E.Sadler/M&M's July 4
2005 #38 E.Sadler/M&M's Halloween
2005 #38 E.Sadler/M&M's
Winner's Circle Die-Cast Kits 1:24
2004 #38 E.Sadler/M&M's July 4
2004 #38 E.Sadler/M&M's
Winner's Circle Driver Sticker 1:64
2004 #38 E.Sadler/M&M's July 4 sparkle
2004 #38 E.Sadler/M&M's Texas Raced sparkle
2005 #38 E.Sadler/M&M's
Winner's Circle Event Series 1:64
2005 #38 E.Sadler/M&M's '04 Texas Win
Winner's Circle Hoods 1:64
2007 #19 E.Sadler/Dodge Dealers
Winner's Circle Medallion 1:64
2007 #19 E.Sadler/Dodge Dealers
Winner's Circle Pit Pass 1:64
2007 #19 E.Sadler/Dodge Dealers
Winner's Circle Race Hood 1:43
2003 #38 E.Sadler/M&M's
Winner's Circle Race Hood 1:64
2003 #38 E.Sadler/M&M's
Winner's Circle Sam Bass 1:64
2008 #19 E.Sadler/Best Buy
Winner's Circle Schedule Hood 1:64
2005 #38 E.Sadler/M&M's
2006 #38 E.Sadler/M&M's
Winner's Circle Test Hood 1:64
2005 #38 E.Sadler/M&M's
Winner's Circle Transporters 1:64
2003 #38 E.Sadler/M&M's Groovy
2004 #38 E.Sadler/M&M's Halloween
2004 #38 E.Sadler/Pedigree Wizard of Oz
2004 #38 E.Sadler/M&M's July 4
2004 #38 E.Sadler/M&M's
2005 #38 E.Sadler/M&M's
2005 #38 E.Sadler/M&M's July 4
2005 #38 E.Sadler/M&M's Halloween
2005 #38 E.Sadler/M&M's
2007 #19 E.Sadler/Dodge Dealers Fantastic 4

Stewart, Tony

Action Indy Cars 1:18
2001 #33 Target Indy 500/7704
Action Performance 1:24
1999 #20 Home Dep.Habitat not/HO
1999 #20 Home Depot Habitat HO
1999 #20 Home Depot not/HO Clear Windows Rookie Stripes
1999 #20 Home Depot HO Clear Windows Rookie Stripes
1999 #20 Home Depot HO Black Windows Rookie Stripes
1999 #20 Home Depot HO Black Windows
2000 #20 Home Depot window box
2000 #20 Home Depot solid box
2002 #20 Home Depot
2003 #20 Home Depot
2004 #20 Home Depot Shrek 2
2005 #20 Home Depot Madagascar Promo
2005 #20 Home Depot Hometown
Action Performance 1:64
1999 #20 Home Depot HO box
2000 #20 Home Depot
2002 #20 Home Depot
2003 #20 Home Depot
2004 #20 Home Depot C2/5040
2004 #20 Nextel Cup 6-car set
2004 #20 Home Depot Shrek 2
2004 #20 Home Depot Olympic
2005 #20 Nextel Cup 6-car set
2005 #20 Home Depot
2006 #20 Home Depot
Action QVC For Race Fans Only 1:24
2000 #20 Home Depot Kids 2-car set/2000
2000 #20 Home Depot Kids Gold/1000
2000 #20 Home Depot Gold/2000
2001 #20 Home Depot Jurassic Park 3 Color Chrome
2001 #20 Home Depot Jurassic Park 3 Platinum/624
2001 #20 Home Depot Jurassic Park 3 Gold/1000
2001 #20 Home Depot Coke Bear Platinum/624
2001 #20 Home Depot Coke Bear Gold/1000
2001 #20 Home Depot Coke Bear Color Chrome/1008
2002 #20 Home Depot Peanuts Orange Platinum/624
2002 #20 Home Depot Peanuts Orange Color Chrome/2508
2002 #20 Home Depot Peanuts Black Platinum/624
2002 #20 Home Depot Peanuts Black Color Chrome/2508
2002 #20 Home Depot Color Chrome/2508
2003 #8 3 Doors Down Platinum/1272
2003 #8 3 Doors Down Gold
2003 #8 3 Doors Down Color Chrome/2508
2003 #20 Home Depot Declaration of Independence Gold/1000
2003 #20 Home Depot Declaration of Independ.Platinum/624
2003 #20 Home Depot Declaration of Independ.Color Chrome/1008
2005 #20 Home Depot Madagascar Color Chrome/300
2005 #20 Home Depot Brickyard Raced Color Chrome/1008
2005 #33 James Dean 50th Ann. Color Chrome/300
2006 #20 Home Depot Platinum/108
2006 #20 Home Depot Color Chrome/504
Action Racing Collectables 1:18
1999 #20 Home Dep.Habitat/10,008
1999 #20 Home Depot/5508
2000 #20 Home Depot ROY/2508
2000 #20 Home Depot
2001 #20 Home Depot Coke Bear/2504
2003 #8 3 Doors Down/1836
2003 #20 Home Depot Victory Lap/2508
2003 #20 Home Depot/2532
2004 #20 Home Depot Reverse Paint
2004 #20 Home Depot Shrek 2/2508
Action Racing Collectables 1:24
1998 #44 Shell Small Soldiers#] Bank/2508
1998 #44 Shell Small Sold./10,992
1998 #44 Shell Bank/2508
1998 #44 Shell/5508
1999 #20 Home Depot Habitat
1999 #20 Home Dep.Fan Club AUTO
1999 #20 Home Depot Gold QVC Race Fans/2508
1999 #20 Home Depot Bank/2508
1999 #20 Home Depot with black windows
1999 #20 Home Depot/5004
2000 #15 Vision3 '96 G.Prix/10,536
2000 #20 Home Dep.Kids Bank/2400
2000 #20 Home Depot Kids Mac Tools/3000
2000 #20 Home Depot Kids/23,676
2000 #20 Home Depot Brickyard
2000 #20 Home Dep.Brushed Metal AUTO Fan Club Promo/4000
2000 #20 Home Depot Bank/2508
2000 #20 Home Depot/29,508
2001 #20 Home Depot Jurassic Park 3 Clear/6000
2001 #20 Home Depot Jurassic Park 3 Bank/1584
2001 #20 Home Depot Jurassic Park 3/22,128
2001 #20 Home Depot Coke Bear Bank/2004
2001 #20 Home Depot Coke Bear/26,280
2001 #20 Home Depot Bank
2001 #20 Home Depot
2002 #11 True Value '01 IROC/8456
2002 #20 Home Depot Mac Tools/2172
2002 #20 Home Depot Clear/4008
2002 #20 Home Depot Bank/1624
2002 #20 Home Depot/26,508
2002 #20 Home Depot Peanuts Orange Mac Tools/1860
2002 #20 Home Depot Peanuts Orange Clear/2508
2002 #20 Home Depot Peanuts Orange Bank/1068
2002 #20 Home Depot Peanuts Orange/20,866
2002 #20 Home Depot Peanuts Black Clear/2508
2002 #20 Home Depot Peanuts Black Bank/984
2002 #20 Home Depot Peanuts Black/22,928
2002 #20 Home Depot Maintenance Warehouse Promo/3504
2002 #20 Home Depot '02 Champ. Color Chrome/17,640
2002 #33 Monaco SuperTruck/8652
2003 #8 3 Doors Down CW Bank/1272
2003 #8 3 Doors Down/26,916
2003 #20 Home Depot Victory Lap Mac Tools/288
2003 #20 Home Depot Victory Lap GM Dealers/588
2003 #20 Home Depot Victory Lap CW Bank/492
2003 #20 Home Depot Victory Lap/10,488
2003 #20 Home Depot Dec.of Indep.CW Bank/1008
2003 #20 Home Depot Declar.of Indep./23,940
2003 #20 Home Depot GM Dealers/1008
2003 #20 Home Depot BW Bank Mac Tools/288
2003 #20 Home Depot BW Bank/1068
2003 #20 Home Depot/29,700
2003 #33 Monaco Diamond Rio SuperTruck Mac Tools/288
2003 #33 Monaco Diamond Rio SuperTruck GM Dealers/360
2003 #33 Monaco Diamond Rio SuperTruck/9424
2004 #20 Home Depot 25th Anniversary/8664
2004 #20 Home Depot Shrek 2 GM Dealers/576
2004 #20 Home Depot Shrek 2 CW Bank/348
2004 #20 Home Depot Shrek 2/10,836
2004 #20 Home Depot Olympics QVC/288
2004 #20 Home Depot Olympics Mac Tools/468
2004 #20 Home Depot Olympics CW Bank/252
2004 #20 Home Depot Olympics/4008
2004 #20 Home Depot Father's Day QVC/504
2004 #20 Home Depot Father's Day Hamilton/156
2004 #20 Home Depot Father's Day CW Bank/420
2004 #20 Home Depot Father's Day/5916
2004 #20 Home Depot Black Mac Tools/288
2004 #20 Home Depot Black CW Bank/432
2004 #20 Home Depot Black/9756
2004 #20 Home Depot Nextel Incentive/3704
2004 #20 Home Depot Mac Tools/288
2004 #20 Home Depot GM Dealers/2244
2004 #20 Home Dep.CW Bank/516
2004 #20 Home Depot/17,460
2004 #20 Coke C2 QVC/504
2004 #20 Coke C2 Mac Tools/468
2004 #20 Coke C2 GM Dealers/456
2004 #20 Coke C2 CW Bank/336
2004 #20 Coke C2/4728
2004 #20 Home Depot 25th Ann. QVC/1200
2004 #20 25 Years of Hard Nosed Racing/3504
2004 #20 Home Depot 25th Ann. CW Bank
2004 #29 Kid Rock GM Dealers/1044
2004 #29 Kid Rock CW Bank/636
2004 #29 Kid Rock/14,076
2004 #29 ESGR Marines GM Dealers/372
2004 #29 ESGR Marines CW Bank/384
2004 #29 ESGR Marines/7308
2004 #47 Sara Evans SuperTruck QVC/504
2004 #47 Sara Evans SuperTruck/4308
2004 #81 Bass Pro Shops CW Bank/408
2004 #81 Bass Pro Shops
2004 #92 McDonald's QVC/444
2004 #92 McDonald's CW Bank/288
2004 #92 McDonald's/3516
2005 #20 Home Depot KaBOOM CW Bank/144
2005 #20 Home Depot Test Greg Zipadelli AU/2508
2005 #20 Home Depot Madagascar QVC/504
2005 #20 Home Depot Madagascar Matco/144
2005 #20 Home Depot Madagascar Mac Tools/300
2005 #20 Home Depot Madagascar Liquid Metal/600
2005 #20 Home Depot Madagascar GM Dealers/204
2005 #20 Home Depot Madagascar CW Bank/216
2005 #20 Home Depot Madagascar/4752
2005 #20 Home Depot KaBOOM QVC/288
2005 #20 Home Depot KaBOOM GM Dealers/168
2005 #20 Home Depot KaBOOM/3000
2005 #20 Home Depot Daytona Raced QVC/288
2005 #20 Home Depot Daytona Raced/2700
2005 #20 Home Depot Brickyard Raced QVC/504
2005 #20 Home Depot Brickyard Raced GM Dealers/288
2005 #20 Home Depot Champion Color Chrome QVC/2508
2005 #20 Home Depot Champion Color Chrome Mac Tools/504
2005 #20 Home Depot Champion Color Chrome/8492
2005 #20 Home Depot Brickyard Raced/3012
2005 #20 Home Depot QVC/720
2005 #20 Home Depot Matco/300
2005 #20 Home Depot GM Dealers/1008
2005 #20 Home Depot CW Bank/264
2005 #20 Home Depot/9000
2005 #33 James Dean 50th Ann.CW Bank/228
2005 #33 Old Spice GM Dealers/144
2005 #33 Old Spice CW Bank/180
2005 #33 Old Spice/2760
2005 #33 Mr.Clean AutoDry Daytona Raced QVC/288
2005 #33 Mr.Clean AutoDry Daytona Raced GM Dealers/240
2005 #33 Mr.Clean AutoDry Daytona Raced/4284
2005 #33 Mr.Clean AutoDry CW Bank/144
2005 #33 Mr.Clean AutoDry/2364
2005 #33 James Dean 50th Anniversary QVC/504
2005 #33 James Dean 50th Ann GM Dealers/432
2005 #33 James Dean 50th Anniversary/5244
2006 #8 Goody's/1644
2006 #20 Powerade QVC*
2006 #20 Powerade Mac Tools*
2006 #20 Powerade GM Dealers/696
2006 #20 Powerade CW Bank/204
2006 #20 Powerade/3852*
2006 #20 Home Depot Test Matco*
2006 #20 Home Depot Test GM Dealers/288
2006 #20 Home Depot Test/3588*
2006 #20 Home Depot Lithium-Ion GM Dealers/504
2006 #20 Home Depot Lithium-Ion/2508
2006 #20 Home Depot Holiday QVC*
2006 #20 Home Depot Holiday GM Dealers/432
2006 #20 Home Depot Holiday/1551*
2006 #20 Home Depot Martinsville Raced QVC*
2006 #20 Home Depot Martinsville Raced GM Dealers/360
2006 #20 Home Depot Martinsville Raced/2520*
2006 #20 Home Depot QVC/504
2006 #20 Home Depot Matco/156
2006 #20 Home Depot Mac Tools/504
2006 #20 Home Depot GM Dealers/1200
2006 #20 Home Depot/9000
2006 #20 Crown Royal IROC GM Dealers/204
2006 #20 Crown Royal IROC/3024
2006 #33 Old Spice GM Dealers/204
2006 #33 Old Spice/3504
Action Racing Collectables 1:32
2004 #20 Home Depot/1488
2004 #29 Kid Rock/1308
Action Racing Collectables 1:64
1998 #44 Shell Small Sold./16,992
1998 #44 Shell/10,080
1999 #20 Home Depot/Habitat 2-car promo set
1999 #20 Home Depot Habitat
1999 #20 Home Depot Promo blister
1999 #20 Home Depot/10,080
2000 #15 Vision3 '96 G.Prix/9720
2000 #20 Home Depot Kids
2000 #20 Home Depot Brickyard/7500
2000 #20 Home Depot
2000 #18/20 T.Stewart Chef Boyardee Promo blister
2001 #20 Home Depot Jurassic Park 3/19,128
2001 #20 Home Depot Coke Bear in Coke bottle/20,516
2001 #20 Home Depot/14,472
2001 #18/20 Coke Bear 2-car promo blister
2002 #20 Old Spice Promo box
2002 #20 Home Depot Peanuts 2-car set promo blister
2002 #20 Home Depot Peanuts Orange/15,048
2002 #20 Home Depot Peanuts Black/15,048
2002 #20 Home Depot Promo Maintenance Ware.blister
2002 #20 Home Depot Promo Old Spice window box
2002 #20 Home Depot '02 Champ. Color Chrome/17,640
2002 #20 Home Depot/23,040
2003 #8 3 Doors Down/14,976
2003 #20 Home Depot Declar.of Indep./16,344
2003 #20 Home Depot/21,384
2003 #33 Monaco Diamond Rio SuperTruck
2004 #20 Home Depot 25th Anniversary/6336
2004 #20 Home Depot Shrek 2/7728
2004 #20 Home Depot Black/6576
2004 #20 Home Dep.tool box/3540
2004 #20 Home Depot/13,584
2004 #29 Kid Rock/7488
2004 #81 Bass Pro/5088
2005 #20 Home Depot Madagascar
2005 #20 Home Depot KaBOOM
2005 #20 Home Depot
2005 #33 James Dean 50th Anniversary
2006 #20 Home Depot
Action Racing Collectables Platinum 1:2
2008 #20 Home Depot/26,880
Action Racing Collectables Transporters
2001 #20 Home Depot Jurassic Park 3 RCCA/456
2001 #20 Home Depot Jurassic Park 3/2052
2002 #20 Home Depot/3000
2003 #20 Home Depot/2848
Action Road Racing 1:18
2004 #20 A.Wallace/Citgo RCCA/204
2004 #20 A.Wallace/Citgo QVC/204
2004 #20 A.Wallace/Citgo Color Chrome/204
2004 #20 A.Wallace/Citgo/936
Action Total Concept 1:64
2000 #20 Home Depot Kids/11,367
Action/Funline Monster Truck 1:43
2004 #20 Smoke
2004 #20 Home Depot
Action/Funline Muscle Machines 1:18
2004 #20 Home Depot '69 Camaro
2004 #20 Home Depot '69 Chevelle
2004 #20 Home Depot '67 Nova
2005 #20 Home Depot '67 Nova/428
2005 #20 Home Depot '67 Nova GM Dealers/48
2005 #20 Home Depot '67 Nova QVC/180
2005 #20 Home Depot '67 Nova RCCA/84
2005 #20 Home Depot '69 Camaro GM Dealers/48
2005 #20 Home Depot '69 Camaro QVC/180
2005 #20 Home Depot '69 Camaro RCCA/84
2005 #20 Home Depot '71 Camaro
2005 #20 Home Depot '69 Camaro/512
Action/Funline Muscle Machines 1:24
2004 #20 Home Depot '69 Camaro
2004 #20 Home Depot '69 Chevelle
2004 #20 Home Depot '66 Nova
2005 #20 Home Depot Hybrid/144
Action/Funline Muscle Machines 1:64
2004 #20 Home Depot '69 Chevelle
Action/RCCA 1:24
2002 #20 Home Depot Peanuts Orange Split Clear/504
2002 #20 Home Depot Peanuts Orange Bank/1008
2002 #20 Home Depot Peanuts Black Split Clear/504
2002 #20 Home Depot Peanuts Black Bank/1008
2002 #20 Home Depot '02 Champ. Color Chrome Bank/1008
2002 #20 Home Depot Split Clear/2508
2002 #20 Home Depot Bank/720
2002 #33 Monaco SuperTruck/600
2003 #8 3 Doors Down/1200
2003 #20 Home Depot Victory Lap/804
2003 #20 Home Depot Declar.of Independence/1600
2003 #20 Home Depot Pocono Raced/504
2003 #20 Home Depot CW Bank/1500
2003 #33 Monaco SuperTruck
2003 #33 Monaco Diamond Rio SuperTruck/600
2004 #20 Home Depot 25th Ann.
2004 #20 Home Depot Shrek 2/1008
2004 #20 Home Depot Olympic/600
2004 #20 Home Depot Father's Day/204
2004 #20 Home Depot Black/1008
2004 #20 Home Depot/1500
2004 #20 Coke C2/600
2004 #29 Kid Rock/1200
2004 #29 ESGR Marines/1008
2004 #47 Sara Evans SuperTruck/504
2004 #81 Bass Pro Shops/600
2004 #92 McDonald's/600
2005 #20 Home Depot KaBOOM/444
2005 #20 Milestones 2X Champion/450
2005 #20 Milestones '05 Brickyard Win/550
2005 #20 Milestones ROY/600
2005 #20 Milestones First Win/600
2005 #20 Home Depot Test/600
2005 #20 Home Depot Madagascar/504
2005 #20 Home Depot Hometown Brushed Bronze/204
2005 #20 Home Depot Daytona Raced/204
2005 #20 Home Depot Brickyard Raced/288
2005 #20 Home Depot Color Chrome/288
2005 #20 Home Depot/600
2005 #33 Old Spice/252
2005 #33 Mr.Clean AutoDry Daytona Raced/288
2005 #33 James Dean 50th Anniversary/504
2006 #20 Home Depot Daytona Raced/250
2006 #20 Home Depot Holiday/250
2006 #20 Home Depot Test/400
2006 #20 Powerade/400
2006 #20 Six Flags/300
2006 #20 Home Depot Martinsville Raced/150
2006 #20 Home Depot Color Chrome/160
2006 #20 Home Depot/600
2006 #20 Crown Royal White Pearl/288
2006 #33 Dollar General/144
2006 #33 Old Spice/288
Action/RCCA 1:32
2003 #8 3 Doors Down/844
2003 #20 Home Depot/Peanuts Orange&Black 3-car set/2004
2003 #20 Home Depot Gold/444
2003 #20 Home Depot/1572
2004 #20 Home Depot/600
2004 #29 Kid Rock/408
1999-00 #20 Home Depot/7500
Action/RCCA 1:64
1998 #44 Shell Small Soldiers/7500
1998 #44 Shell/3500
1999 #20 Home Depot Habitat
1999 #20 Home Depot/3500
2000 #20 Home Depot Kids
2000 #20 Home Depot/10,000
2001 #20 Home Depot Jurassic Park 3/1584
2001 #20 Home Depot Coke Bear/1800
2001 #20 Home Depot/2594
2002 #20 Home Depot Peanuts Orange/1800
2002 #20 Home Depot Peanuts Black/1800
2002 #20 Home Depot '02 Champ. Color Chrome/1212
2002 #20 Home Depot/1584
2003 #8 3 Doors Down/2016
2003 #20 Home Depot Declar.of Independence/2020
2003 #20 Home Depot/2308
2003 #33 Monaco SuperTruck
2003 #33 Monaco Diamond Rio SuperTruck
2004 #20 Home Depot/2016
2004 #20 Home Depot Olympic/720
2004 #20 Home Depot 25th Ann./1008
2004 #20 Home Depot Shrek 2/1008
2004 #20 Home Depot Black/1152
2004 #20 Home Depot in tool box/1500
2004 #20 Coke C2/576
2004 #29 Kid Rock/1200
2004 #81 Bass Pro Shops/720
2005 #20 Home Depot Madagascar/576
2005 #20 Home Depot KaBOOM/480
2005 #20 Home Depot/864
2005 #33 James Dean 50th Anniversary
2006 #20 Powerade/312
2006 #20 Home Depot/600
Action/RCCA Banks 1:24
1998 #44 Shell Small Soldiers/5000
1998 #44 Shell/1500
1999 #20 Home Dep.Habitat/8000
1999 #20 Home Depot/2500
2000 #20 Home Depot Kids/2808
2000 #20 Home Depot/3600
2001 #20 Home Depot/3600
Action/RCCA Dirt Cars 1:24
1999 #98 1998 J.D. Byrider/3000
2000 #20 J.D.Byrider/9000
Action/RCCA Dirt Cars 1:64
1999-00 #20 J.D.Byrider/9072 '00
1999-00 #98 1998 J.D.Byrider/7992 '99
Action/RCCA Elite 1:24
1998 #44 Shell Small Soldiers/3500
1998 #44 Shell/1200
1999 #20 Home Dep.Habitat/5000
1999 #20 Home Depot/1000
2000 #15 Vision 3/1992
2000 #20 Home Depot Kids/1404
2000 #20 Home Depot ROY/5000
2000 #20 Home Depot/5000
2001 #20 Home Depot Jurassic Park 3/1200
2001 #20 Home Depot Coke Bear/1392
2001 #20 Home Depot Test/3504
2001 #20 Home Depot/2004
2002 #20 Home Depot Peanuts Orange/1500
2002 #20 Home Depot Peanuts Black/1500
2002 #20 Home Depot Metal/1800
2002 #20 Home Depot '02 Champ. Color Chrome/2004
2002 #20 Home Depot/1404
2003 #8 3 Doors Down/1800
2003 #20 Home Depot Victory Lap/1200
2003 #20 Home Depot Declar.of Indep./2800
2003 #20 Home Depot Test/1300
2003 #20 Home Depot Pocono Raced/504
2003 #20 Home Depot Color Chrome/1008
2003 #20 Home Depot/1500
2004 #20 Home Depot 25th Ann./1008
2004 #20 Home Depot Test/1200
2004 #20 Home Depot Shrek 2/1500
2004 #20 Home Depot Olympic White Gold/25
2004 #20 Home Depot Olympic/900
2004 #20 Home Depot Black/1500
2004 #20 Home Depot Color Chrome/600
2004 #20 Home Depot/1800
2004 #20 Coke C2/600
2004 #29 Kid Rock/1500
2004 #29 ESGR Marines/1500
2004 #81 Bass Pro Shops/900
2004 #92 McDonald's/600
2005 #20 Milestones 2X Champion/450
2005 #20 Milestones '05 Brickyard/550
2005 #20 Milestones ROY/600
2005 #20 Milestones First Win/600
2005 #20 Home Depot Test/600
2005 #20 Home Depot Madagascar/600
2005 #20 Home Depot Lithium Ion White Gold/25
2005 #20 Home Depot Lithium Ion Platinum/8
2005 #20 Home Depot Lithium Ion/408
2005 #20 Home Depot KaBOOM White Gold/25
2005 #20 Home Depot KaBOOM/504
2005 #20 Home Depot Hometown Brushed Bronze/204
2005 #20 Home Depot '05 Champ Liquid Color/620
2005 #20 Home Depot White Gold/30
2005 #20 Home Depot Color Chrome/360
2005 #20 Home Depot/804
2005 #33 Old Spice/252
2005 #33 Mr.Clean AutoDry Daytona Raced/288
2005 #33 James Dean 50th Ann. White Gold/30
2005 #33 James Dean 50th Anniversary/600
2006 #20 Six Flags Platinum/8
2006 #20 Six Flags White Gold/25
2006 #20 Six Flags/400
2006 #20 Powerade White Gold/25

2006 #20 Powerade Platinum/8
2006 #20 Powerade/400
2006 #20 Home Depot Test Platinum/5
2006 #20 Home Depot Test/600
2006 #20 Home Depot Holiday White Gold/25
2006 #20 Home Depot Holiday Platinum/5
2006 #20 Home Depot Holiday/250
2006 #20 Home Depot Martinsville Raced Platinum/4
2006 #20 Home Depot Martinsville Raced/200
2006 #20 Home Depot Daytona Raced Platinum/5
2006 #20 Home Depot Daytona Raced/250
2006 #20 Home Depot White Gold/30
2006 #20 Home Depot Platinum/16
2006 #20 Home Dep Color Chrome/220
2006 #20 Home Depot/800
2006 #33 Dollar General/144
2006 #33 Dollar General Platinum/2
2006 #33 Old Spice White Gold/25
2006 #33 Old Spice Platinum/5
2006 #33 Old Spice/288

Action/RCCA Elite 1:32
2003 #8 3 Doors Down Gold/316
2003 #8 3 Doors Down/844
2003 #20 Home Depot/1008
2004 #20 Home Depot/844
2004 #29 Kid Rock/408

Action/RCCA Elite 1:64
2001 #20 Home Depot Jurassic Park 3/1104
2001 #20 Home Depot Coke Bear/1296
2001 #20 Home Depot/1824
2002 #20 Home Depot Peanuts Orange/1584
2002 #20 Home Depot Peanuts Black/1584
2002 #20 Home Depot '02 Champ. Color Chrome/1212
2002 #20 Home Depot/1200
2003 #8 3 Doors Down/2028
2003 #20 Home Depot Declar.of Indep./2020
2003 #20 Home Depot/2220
2004 #20 Home Depot Olympic/576
2004 #20 Home Depot 25th Ann./720
2004 #20 Home Depot Shrek 2/1008
2004 #20 Home Depot Black/1008
2004 #20 Home Depot/1440
2004 #29 Kid Rock/1008
2004 #81 Bass Pro Shops/528
2005 #20 Home Depot KaBOOM/480
2005 #20 Home Depot Madagascar/480
2005 #20 Home Depot/576
2005 #33 James Dean 50th Anniversary/528
2006 #20 Powerade/192
2006 #20 Home Depot/384

Action/RCCA Elite Prototypes 1:24
1998 #44 Shell/12

Action/RCCA SelectNet 1:64
1999 #20 Home Depot

Action/RCCA SelectNet Banks 1:24
1999 #20 Home Depot Habitat for Humanity/1600
1999 #20 Home Depot

Action/RCCA SelectNet Elite 1:24
1999 #20 Home Dep.Habitat/1600
1999 #20 Home Depot/1500

Action/RCCA Sprint 1:24
1995 #19 Triple Crown/3500
1996 #20 1995 Triple Crown/5004
1999 #9 1995 Beast/3500
2000 #19 Turkey Night/4800
2001 #19 Performance/8004
2004 #20 American Steelt Michael Ross Foundation/4776
2005 #20 Bass Pro Shops Madagascar QVC/504
2005 #20 Bass Pro Shops Madagascar Matco/144
2005 #20 Bass Pro Shops Madagascar Mac Tools/300
2005 #20 Bass Pro Shops Madagascar/4752
2005 #20 Bass Pro Shops QVC/120
2005 #20 Bass Pro Shops GM Dealers/60
2005 #20 Bass Pro Shops Color Chrome/504
2005 #20 Bass Pro Shops/3276
2005 #20 Artic Cat Michael Ross Foundation/2148
2006 #20 Coca Cola Color Chrome/800

Action/RCCA Transporters 1:64
2002 #20 Home Depot/504
2003 #20 Home Depot/1200

Brookfield 1:24
2005 #20 Home Depot Madagascar/204
2005 #20 Home Depot/360
2005 #33 James Dean 50th Ann./300
2006 #20 Home Depot/250

Brookfield Dually and Tailgate Set 1:24
2005 #20 Home Depot/360

Brookfield Dually with Car and Show Tra
1999 #20 Home Depot/3716
1999 #20 Home Depot Habitat Silver/650
1999 #20 Home Dep.Habitat/2832
1999 #20 Home Depot Silver/799
2000 #20 Home Dep.Kids/1212
2001 #20 Home Depot Jurassic Park 3 w/o car/2004

Brookfield Trackside 1:64
2004 #20 Home Depot Shrek 2/5000
2004 #20 Home Depot Black/3000
2004 #20 Home Depot/4944
2005 #20 Home Depot Madagascar/3000

Ertl American Muscle 1:43
2000 #NNO Glidden

GMP Sprint Cars 1:18
1996-01 #20 Boles 1995 Sprint Champ/3504 '00
1996-01 #20 Boles/3204 '94

Hot Wheels Racing Color Change 1:64
2003 #20 Home Depot
2004 #20 Home Depot

Hot Wheels Racing Power Launchers 1:64
2003 #20 Home Depot

Maisto Indy Racing 1:18
1998 #1 Glidden
1999 #22 Home Depot

Maisto Indy Racing 1:24
1999 #1 Glidden

Maisto Indy Racing 1:64
1999 #1 Glidden

MiniChamps Indy IRL 1:43
1996 #20 Quaker State/4444
1996 #20 Menards Glidden/4444

Motorsports Authentics Driver's Select
2007 #20 Home Depot/8508*
2007 #20 Home Depot Brickyard Raced/3744*
2007 #20 Home Depot Chicagoland Raced/1248*
2007 #20 Home Depot Bud Shootout Daytona Raced/2007*
2007 #20 Home Depot Twin 150s Daytona Raced/2028*
2007 #20 Home Depot Watkins Glen Raced/1116*
2007 #20 Home Depot COT/7392*
2007 #20 Home Depot Holiday Sam Bass/1572*
2007 #20 Home Depot '57 Chevy/300*
2007 #20 Home Depot COT
2007 #20 Home Depot
2007 #20 Home Depot COT/1128
2007 #20 Home Depot/1152
2007 #33 Old Spice/1320*
2007 #33 Old Spice
2007 #33 Old Spice/288

Motorsports Authentics Owner's Elite 1:
2007 #20 Home Depot Test/1200*
2007 #20 Home Depot Holiday Sam Bass White Gold/50*
2007 #20 Home Depot Holiday Sam Bass Platinum/25
2007 #20 Home Depot Holiday Sam Bass/504*
2007 #20 Home Depot COT White Gold/50*
2007 #20 Home Depot COT Platinum/25
2007 #20 Home Depot COT/1212
2007 #20 Home Depot Daytona Shootout Raced/2007
2007 #20 Home Depot Brickyard Raced/504*
2007 #20 Home Depot White Gold/100
2007 #20 Home Depot Platinum/25
2007 #20 Home Depot/1212*
2007 #20 Home Depot/2007*

Motorsports Authentics Owner's Elite Tr
2007 #20 Home Depot/1704*

Motorsports Authentics Pit Stop 1:64
2007 #20 Home Depot COT
2007 #20 Home Depot

Motorsports Authentics Pit Stop Blister
2007 #20 Home Depot

Motorsports Authentics QVC For Race Fan
2007 #20 Home Depot COT Platinum/108
2007 #20 Home Depot COT Mesma Chrome/288
2007 #20 Home Depot COT Copper/504
2007 #20 Home Depot COT Gold/108
2007 #20 Home Depot COT Color Chrome/504
2007 #20 Home Depot Daytona Shootout Raced Copper/288
2007 #20 Home Depot Daytona Shootout Raced Color Chrome/288
2007 #20 Home Depot Brickyard Raced Copper/288
2007 #20 Home Depot Brickyard Raced Color Chrome/288

Motorsports Authentics Steel 1:16
2006 #20 Home Depot/600

Motorsports Authentics/RCCA Owner's Clu
2007 #20 Home Depot/2100*

Motorsports Authentics/RCCA Transporter
2007 #20 Home Depot/Home Depot/706*

Onyx Indy 1:24
1996 #20 Quaker State Menards Indy 500 Pole Win

Peachstate/GMP Transporters 1:64
2002 #20 Home Depot/1500
1996-01 #20 Home Depot/2400 1999 Rookie of the Year '00

Racing Champions 1:24
1999 #20 Arvin Racing Promo/5000

Racing Champions Indy Racing League 1:2
1996 #20 Quaker State
1997 #20 Glidden Menards

Racing Champions Indy Racing League 1:6
1996 #20 Quaker State
1997 #20 Glidden
1999 #22 Home Dep.Promo/12,000

RCCA Club 1:24
2008 #20 Home Depot/408
2008 #20 Home Depot 10th Anniversary/300
2008 #20 Subway/200
2008 #20 Smoke/300

RCCA Elite 1:24
2008 #20 Home Depot/1200
2008 #20 Home Depot Platinum/25
2008 #20 Home Depot White Gold/50
2008 #20 Home Depot 10th Anniversary/1000
2008 #20 Home Depot 10th Anniversary Platinum/25
2008 #20 Home Depot 10th Anniversary White Gold/50
2008 #20 Subway/504
2008 #20 Subway Platinum/25
2008 #20 Subway White Gold/50
2008 #20 Smoke/504

Revell Club 1:18
1998 #44 Shell Small Soldiers/1002
1998 #44 Shell/504
1999 #20 Home Dep.Habitat/2508
2000 #20 Home Depot ROY/2508
2000 #20 Home Depot/2508

Revell Club 1:24
1998 #44 Shell Small Soldiers
1998 #44 Shell/1002
1999 #20 Home Depot Habitat
1999 #20 Home Depot/1002
2000 #20 Home Depot ROY/2508
2000 #20 Home Depot/2004

Revell Collection 1:18
1998 #44 Shell Small Soldiers/3120
1998 #44 Shell/3120
1999 #20 Home Depot
2000 #20 Home Depot ROY
2000 #20 Home Depot/2508

Revell Collection 1:24
1998 #44 Shell Small Soldiers
1998 #44 Shell
1999 #20 Home Depot Habitat Bank set w/1:64 car/4008
1999 #20 Home Depot Habitat
1999 #20 Home Depot/3120
2000 #20 Home Depot '99 ROY Bank set w/1:64 car
2000 #20 Home Depot ROY/7500
2000 #20 Home Depot Kids/2004
2000 #20 Home Depot/5504
2001 #20 Home Depot Jurassic Park 3/3120
2002 #20 Home Depot Atlanta Win w/hula dancer/8358
2003 #20 Home Depot Test Gray
2003 #20 Home Depot Pocono Raced/1888
2004 #20 Home Depot Test/3504
2005 #20 Home Depot Test/972

Revell Collection 1:43
1998 #44 Shell Small Soldiers/5004
1999 #20 Home Dep.Habitat/3000
2000 #20 Home Depot ROY/3000
2000 #20 Home Depot/3000

Revell Collection 1:64
1998 #44 Shell/10,080
1998 #44 Shell Small Sold./10,080
1999 #20 Home Dep.Habitat/10,080
1999 #20 Home Depot/7992
2000 #20 Home Depot Kids
2000 #20 Home Depot ROY/12,080
2000 #20 Home Depot/13,176
2001 #18/20 Jurassic Park 3 in tin/7992

Revell Collection Train Sets 1:64
2003 #20 Home Depot Chevy Rock & Roll/4800

Revell Select 1:24
1998 #44 Shell
2003 #8 3 Doors Down

Revell Select Hobby 1:64
1998 #44 Shell Small Soldiers
1996 #44 Shell

Winner's Circle 1:18
2003 #20 Home Depot Declaration of Independence
2003 #20 Home Depot Declaration of Independence '03
2004 #20 Home Depot Black
2004 #20 Home Depot
2004 #20 Coke C2
2004 #81 Bass Pro Shops
2005 #20 Home Depot
2007 #20 Home Depot

Winner's Circle 1:24
1998 #44 Shell Small Soldiers
1998 #44 Shell
1999 #20 Home Depot
2000 #20 Home Depot ROY
2001 #20 Home Depot Kids '00
2002 #20 Home Depot Peanuts Black
2002 #20 Home Depot Coke
2003 #20 Home Depot Peanuts Orange '02 Champ
2003 #20 Home Depot Peanuts Black
2003 #20 Home Depot thin base
2003 #20 Home Depot
2004 #20 Home Depot 25th Anniversary
2004 #20 Home Depot Shrek 2
2004 #20 Home Depot Black
2004 #20 Home Depot
2004 #20 Coke C2
2004 #81 Bass Pro Shops
2004 #92 McDonald's
2005 #20 Home Depot
2005 #33 Old Spice
2005 #33 Mr. Clean AutoDry
2005 #33 James Dean 50th Ann.
2006 #20 Home Depot
2006 #33 Old Spice
2007 #20 Home Depot Daytona Shootout Raced
2007 #20 Home Depot
2008 #20 Home Depot

Winner's Circle 1:43
1999 #20 Home Depot

Winner's Circle 1:64
1998 #44 Shell Small Soldiers
1998 #44 Shell
2000 #20 Home Dep.3 Win Rookie
2000 #20 Home Depot First Win

Winner's Circle 1:87
2006 #20 Home Depot
2007 #20 Home Depot
2008 #20 Home Depot

Winner's Circle 2-Car Set w/Hood 1:64
2008 #20 Home Depot/HD Color Chrome

Winner's Circle Autographed Hood 1:64
2003 #20 Home Depot Peanuts Orange
2003 #20 Home Depot Declaration of Independence
2004 #20 Home Depot 25th Anniversary
2004 #20 Home Depot Shrek 2 small package
2004 #20 Home Depot Shrek 2
2004 #20 Home Depot Black
2004 #20 Home Depot
2004 #81 Bass Pro Shops
2004 #92 McDonald's
2005 #20 Home Depot Madagascar
2005 #20 Home Depot
2005 #33 Mr.Clean AutoDry
2005 #33 James Dean 50th Ann.
2006 #20 Home Depot Test

Winner's Circle Autographed Hoods 1:64
2008 #20 Home Depot

Winner's Circle Daytona 500 1:24
2008 #20 Home Depot

Winner's Circle Daytona 500 1:64
2008 #20 Home Depot

Winner's Circle Daytona 500 1:87
2008 #20 Home Depot

Winner's Circle Daytona 500 2-car sets
2008 #20/88 Home Depot Daytona 500 Event Car

Winner's Circle Daytona 500 Hoods 1:64
2008 #20 Home Depot

Winner's Circle Decade of Champions 1:6
2003 #20 Home Depot 2002

Winner's Circle Deluxe Race Hood 1:64
2000 #20 Home Depot Kids
2000 #20 Home Depot Habitat
2000 #20 Home Depot

Winner's Circle Die-Cast Kits 1:24
2003 #20 Home Depot
2004 #20 Home Depot

Winner's Circle Die-Cast Kits 1:64
2003 #20 Home Depot '02

Winner's Circle Double Platinum 1:43
2001 #20 Home Depot Coke
2002 #20 Home Depot
2003 #20 Home Dep.Peanuts Orange
2003 #20 Home Depot Peanuts Black

Winner's Circle Driver Hood 1:64
2000-01 #20 Home Depot

Winner's Circle Driver Photo Hood 1:64
2005 #20 Home Depot

Winner's Circle Driver Sticker 1:64
2001 #20 Home Depot
2002 #20 Home Depot Jurassic
2003 #11 True Value '01 IROC '02 Champ. Sticker
2003 #11 True Value '01 IROC
2003 #20 Home Depot Peanuts Orange
2003 #20 Home Depot Peanuts black
2003 #20 Home Depot short package
2003 #20 Home Depot
2004 #20 Home Depot sparkle short package
2004 #29 Kid Rock short package

Winner's Circle Gallery 1:64
2002 #20 Home Depot Coke Bear

Winner's Circle Garage Scene 1:43
2000 #20 Home Depot

Winner's Circle Gift Pack 1:64
2002 #20 Home Depot/Coke Home Depot w/black trim

Winner's Circle Gift Pack With Photo 1:
2002 #20 Black Peanuts/Orange Peanuts/Home Depot

Winner's Circle Helmets 1:64
2007 #20 Home Depot

Winner's Circle Hoods 1:64
2007 #20 Home Depot Test

Winner's Circle License Plate 1:64
2007 #20 Home Depot

Winner's Circle License Plate Series 1:
2001 #20 Home Depot

Winner's Circle Lifetime Series 1:24
2001 #44 Shell

Winner's Circle Lifetime Tony Stewar
2001-02 #9 Beast '95 1/5
2001-02 #15 Vision 3 '96 3/5
2001-02 #20 Home Depot '01 4/5
2001-02 #44 Shell '98 2/5

Winner's Circle Medallion 1:64
2007 #20 Home Depot

Winner's Circle Micro Machines 1:144
1999 #20/24 J.Gordon
1999 #NNO 7-car Draft Pack

Winner's Circle New Stars 1:64
2000 #20 Home Depot

Winner's Circle Number Magnet 1:64
2008 #20 Home Depot

Winner's Circle Pit Pass 1:64
2007 #20 Home Depot

Winner's Circle Pit Pass Preview 1:64
2002 #20 Home Depot
2004 #20 Home Depot

Winner's Circle Pit Scene 1:64
2003 #20 Home Depot Pulling out

Winner's Circle Pit Sign 1:64
2006 #20 Home Depot
2007 #20 Home Depot

Winner's Circle Preview 1:24
2000 #20 Home Depot

Winner's Circle Preview 1:43
2000 #20 Home Depot

Winner's Circle Race Hood 1:43
2003 #20 Home Depot Peanuts Orange
2003 #20 Home Depot Peanuts Black
2003 #20 HD Declaration Independ.
2004 #20 Home Depot
2004 #20 Home Depot Shrek 2

Winner's Circle Race Hood 1:64
2003 #20 Home Depot Peanuts Orange
2003 #20 Declar. of Independence
2003 #20 Home Depot '02 Champ.
2004 #20 Home Depot
2001-02 #20 Home Depot Coke Bear
2001-02 #20 Home Depot

Winner's Circle Sam Bass 1:43
2000 #20 Home Depot

Winner's Circle Sam Bass 1:64
2008 #20 Home Depot

Winner's Circle Sam Bass Hoods 1:64
2007 #20 Home Depot Holiday

Winner's Circle Schedule Hood 1:64
2005 #20 Home Depot
2006 #20 Home Depot
2006 #33 Old Spice
2007 #20 Home Depot

Winner's Circle Schedule Hoods 1:64
2008 #20 Home Depot

Winner's Circle Sneak Previews 1:64
2000 #20 Home Depot first win

Winner's Circle Sticker 1:64
2006 #20 Home Depot

Winner's Circle Stickers 1:64
2008 #20 Home Depot

Winner's Circle Team Authentics 1:64
2001 #20 Home Dep.Sheetmetal
2001 #20 Home Depot Firesuit

Winner's Circle Test Hood 1:64
2005 #20 Home Depot

Winner's Circle Transporters 1:64
2000 #20 Home Depot w/o small logo on side of trailer
2000 #20 Home Depot w/small logo on side of trailer
2002 #20 Home Depot Coca Cola
2002 #20 Jurassic Park III
2002 #20 Home Depot
2003 #8 Chance 2 3 Doors Down
2003 #20 Home Depot
2003 #20 Home Depot Peanuts Orange '02
2003 #20 Home Depot Peanuts Black '02
2004 #20 Home Depot Souvenir
2004 #20 Home Depot Shrek 2
2004 #20 Home Depot
2004 #29 Kid Rock
2005 #20 Home Depot Madagascar
2005 #20 Home Depot
2005 #33 Mr. Clean AutoDry
2006 #20 Home Depot
2007 #20 Home Depot
2008 #20 Home Depot

Winner's Circle Victory Lane Hoods 1:64
2007 #20 Home Depot COT Watkins Glen Raced
2007 #20 Home Depot Daytona Shootout Raced
2007 #20 Home Depot Chicagoland Raced
2007 #20 Home Depot Brickyard Raced

Winner's Circle Victory Lap 1:24
2003 #20 Home Depot Victory Lap

Winner's Circle Victory Lap 1:64
2003 #20 Home Depot Victory Lap

Winner's Circle VIP Pass 1:43
2000 #20 Home Depot

Truex, Martin Jr.

Action Performance 1:24
2004 #1 Bass Pro Shops

Action Performance 1:64
2004 #8 Busch Series 6-car set
2006 #1 Bass Pro Shops

Action QVC For Race Fans Only 1:24
2004 #8 Wrangler Color Chrome AU/408

Action Racing Collectables 1:24
2003 #81 Chance 2/3504
2003 #81 Chance 2 GM Dealers/180
2004 #8 KFC Dover Raced QVC/288
2004 #8 Taco Bell Bristol Raced QVC/288
2004 #8 Wrangler Retro Darlington Raced/5616
2004 #8 Wrangler GM Dealers/456
2004 #8 Wrangler CW Bank/396
2004 #8 Wrangler/5556
2004 #8 Taco Bell Bristol Raced GM Dealers/240
2004 #8 Taco Bell Bristol Raced/6576
2004 #8 Long John Silvers CW Bank/264
2004 #8 Long John Silvers/3948
2004 #8 KFC Dover Raced GM Dealers/348
2004 #8 KFC Dover Raced/1896
2004 #8 Chance 2 Tear Away GM Dealers/144
2004 #8 Chance 2 Tear Away/3216
2004 #8 Chance 2 Richie Evans GM Dealers/144
2004 #8 Chance 2 Richie Evans/2940
2004 #8 Chance 2 Ralph Earnhardt GM Dealers/396
2004 #8 Chance 2 Ralph Earnhardt/5016
2004 #8 Bass Pro Shops '04 Champ. Color Chrome/5004
2004 #8 Bass Pro Shops Talladega Raced GM Dealers/144
2004 #8 Bass Pro Shops Talladega Raced/2904
2004 #8 Bass Pro Shops GM Dealers/360
2004 #8 Bass Pro Shops CW Bank/288
2004 #8 Bass Pro Shops/6384
2004 #8 Wrangler Retro Darlington Raced QVC/288
2004 #81 Chance 2 Robert Gee GM Dealers/144
2004 #81 Chance 2 Robert Gee/2880
2004 #81 Chance 2 GM Dealers/180
2004 #81 Chance 2/4092
2005 #1 Enterprise RAC/5808
2005 #1 Bass Pro Shops Black QVC/288
2005 #1 Bass Pro Shops Black GM Dealers/204
2005 #1 Bass Pro Shops Black/3000
2005 #1 Bass Pro Shops QVC/400
2005 #1 Bass Pro Shops Matco/72
2005 #1 Bass Pro Shops GM Dealers/768
2005 #1 Bass Pro Shops CW Bank/228
2005 #1 Bass Pro Shops/6120
2005 #8 Chance 2 Test QVC/288
2005 #8 Chance 2 Test GM Dealers/252
2005 #8 Chance 2 Test/1848
2005 #8 Crown Royal IROC QVC/288
2005 #8 Crown Royal IROC/2172
2005 #8 Bass Pro Talladega Raced QVC/288
2005 #8 Bass Pro Talladega Raced GM Dealers/444
2005 #8 Bass Pro Talladega Raced/2652
2005 #8 Bass Pro Mexico City Raced GM Dealers/360
2005 #8 Bass Pro Mexico City Raced/2028
2005 #8 Bass Pro Indy Raced QVC/288
2005 #8 Bass Pro Indy Raced/1812
2005 #8 Bass Pro QVC/504
2005 #8 Bass Pro GM Dealers/552
2005 #8 Bass Pro CW Bank/204
2005 #8 Bass Pro/5004
2006 #1 Bass Pro Shops Test GM Dealers/504
2006 #1 Bass Pro Shops Test/3504
2006 #1 Bass Pro Shops Dale Tribute GM Dealers/1488
2006 #1 Bass Pro Shops Dale Tribute/3504
2006 #1 Bass Pro Shops QVC/288
2006 #1 Bass Pro Shops Matco/72
2006 #1 Bass Pro Shops Mac Tools/300
2006 #1 Bass Pro Shops GM Dealers/1008
2006 #1 Bass Pro Shops CWB/204
2006 #1 Bass Pro Shops/6000
2006 #8 Crown Royal IROC GM Dealers/204
2006 #8 Crown Royal IROC/1404
2006 #8 Bass Pro Dale Tribute Talladega Raced GM Dealers/1104
2006 #8 Bass Pro Dale Tribute Talladega Raced/3900
2006 #8 Bass Pro '05 BGN Champ Color Chrome QVC*
2006 #8 Bass Pro '05 BGN Champ Color Chrome GM Dealers/504
2006 #8 Bass Pro '05 BGN Champ Color Chrome/4680*

Action Racing Collectables 1:64
2004 #8 Wrangler/5040
2004 #8 Bass Pro Shops/8496
2005 #1 Bass Pro Shops
2005 #8 Bass Pro
2006 #1 Bass Pro Shops Dale Tribute
2006 #1 Bass Pro Shops
2006 #8 Bass Pro Dale Tribute Talladega Raced
2008 #1 Bass Pro Shops

Action Racing Collectables Platinum 1:2
2008 #1 Bass Pro Shops/4956

Action/RCCA 1:24
2003 #81 Chance 2/400
2004 #8 Bass Pro Shops/444
2004 #8 Chance 2/444
2004 #8 Taco Bell Bristol Raced/540
2004 #8 Long John Silver's/360
2004 #8 KFC Dover Raced/300
2004 #8 Chance 2 Tear Away/444
2004 #8 Chance 2 Richie Evans/360
2004 #8 Chance 2 Ralph Earnhardt/444
2004 #8 Bass Pro Shops '04 Champion Color Chrome/600
2004 #8 Wrangler Retro Raced/408
2004 #8 Wrangler/444
2004 #81 Chance 2 Robert Gee/360
2005 #1 Bass Pro Black/288
2005 #1 Bass Pro Shops/408
2005 #8 Crown Royal IROC Brushed Metal/360
2005 #8 Chance 2 Test/288
2005 #8 Bass Pro Talladega Raced/144
2005 #8 Bass Pro Mexico City Raced/424
2005 #8 Bass Pro/408
2006 #1 Bass Pro Shops/288
2006 #1 Bass Pro Test/250
2006 #1 Bass Pro Dale Tribute/250
2006 #1 Bass Pro Shops Color Chrome/180
2006 #8 Bass Pro Shops Dale Tribute Talladega Raced/250
2006 #8 Crown Royal White Pearl/200
2006 #8 Ritz/200
2006 #NNO Dale Tribute 5-car set/1200

Action/RCCA 1:64
2004 #8 Bass Pro Shops/720
2005 #1 Bass Pro Shops/576
2005 #8 Bass Pro/576
2006 #1 Bass Pro Shops/432

Action/RCCA Elite 1:24
2004 #8 Chance 2/444
2004 #8 Wrangler Retro Raced/408
2004 #8 Wrangler/444
2004 #8 Taco Bell Bristol Raced/540
2004 #8 Long John Silver's/360
2004 #8 KFC Dover Raced/300
2004 #8 Chance 2 Tear Away/360
2004 #8 Chance 2 Richie Evans/360
2004 #8 Chance 2 Ralph Earnhardt/444
2004 #8 Bass Pro Shops '04 Champion Color Chrome/600
2004 #8 Bass Pro Shops/444
2004 #81 Chance 2 Robert Gee/360
2005 #1 Bass Pro Shops White Gold/25
2005 #1 Bass Pro Black White Gold/25
2005 #1 Bass Pro Black/288
2005 #1 Bass Pro Shops/504
2005 #8 Chance 2 Test/408
2005 #8 Bass Pro Talladega Raced/144
2005 #8 Bass Pro Mexico City Raced/200
2005 #8 Bass Pro White Gold/25
2005 #8 Bass Pro/600
2006 #1 Bass Pro Shops Dale Tribute/250
2006 #1 Bass Pro Shops Dale Tribute Platinum/5
2006 #1 Bass Pro Shops Test Platinum/6
2006 #1 Bass Pro Shops Test/300
2006 #1 Bass Pro Shops White Gold/25
2006 #1 Bass Pro Shops Platinum/8
2006 #1 Bass Pro Shops Color Chrome/200
2006 #1 Bass Pro Shops/408
2006 #8 Bass Pro Shops '05 Champ Color Chrome/408
2006 #8 Ritz White Gold/25
2006 #8 Ritz Platinum/6
2006 #8 Ritz/300
2006 #8 Bass Pro Shops Dale Tribute Talladega Raced Platinum/5
2006 #8 Bass Pro Dale Tribute Talladega Raced/250

Action/RCCA Elite 1:64
2005 #1 Bass Pro Shops/480
2005 #8 Bass Pro/480
2006 #1 Bass Pro Shops/240

Brookfield 1:24
2004 #8 Bass Pro '04 Champ Color Chrome/240
2004 #8 Wrangler Retro Raced/240
2005 #1 Bass Pro Shops/204
2005 #8 Bass Pro Shops/204

Brookfield Trackside 1:64
2004 #8 Bass Pro Shops/2400
2004 #8 Bass Pro Shops QVC/504
2004 #8 Bass Pro Shops RCCA/480

Checkered Flag Sports Champion 1:24
2008 #1 Bass Pro Shops

Checkered Flag Sports Contender 1:24
2008 #1 Bass Pro Shops

Checkered Flag Sports Contender 1:64
2008 #1 Bass Pro Shops

Motorsports Authentics Driver's Select
2007 #1 Bass Pro Shops '57 Chevy/1536*
2007 #1 Bass Pro Shops 35th Anniversary/1404*
2007 #1 Bass Pro Shops NWTF/1704*

2007 #1 Bass Pro Shops COT Dover Raced/2248*
2007 #1 Bass Pro Shops COT/1570*
2007 #1 Bass Pro Shops/4800*
2007 #1 Bass Pro Shops COT/360
2007 #1 Bass Pro Shops/600
2007 #8 Ritz Oreo

Motorsports Authentics Owner's Elite 1:
2007 #1 Bass Pro Shops COT Dover Raced/504
2007 #1 Bass Pro Shops COT/504
2007 #1 Bass Pro Shops/708*
2007 #1 Bass Pro Shops/1008*

Motorsports Authentics Owner's Elite Tr
2007 #1 Bass Pro Shops/408*

Motorsports Authentics Pit Stop 1:64
2007 #1 Bass Pro Shops COT
2007 #1 Bass Pro Shops

Motorsports Authentics QVC For Race Fan
2007 #1 Bass Pro Shops '57 Chevy Color Chrome/1500

Motorsports Authentics Steel 1:16
2006 #1 Bass Pro Shops/300

RCCA Club 1:24
2008 #1 Bass Pro Shops/156

RCCA Elite 1:24
2008 #1 Bass Pro Shops/300
2008 #1 Bass Pro Shops Platinum/25
2008 #1 Bass Pro Shops White Gold/50

Team Caliber Preferred Trackside 1:24
2006 #1 Bass Pro/144

Winner's Circle 1:24
2005 #8 Bass Pro
2006 #1 Bass Pro Dale Tribute split window box
2006 #8 Bass Pro Dale Tribute Talladega Raced split window box
2006 #8 Bass Pro
2007 #1 Bass Pro Shops
2008 #1 Bass Pro Shops

Winner's Circle 1:64
2006 #NNO Dale Tribute 5-car set

Winner's Circle 1:87
2007 #1 Bass Pro Shops
2008 #1 Bass Pro Shops

Winner's Circle Autographed Hood 1:64
2005 #8 Chance 2 Test '04 Champ
2006 #1 Bass Pro Shops Test
2006 #1 Bass Pro Dale Tribute split window box
2006 #1 Bass Pro Shops
2006 #8 Bass Pro Dale Tribute Talladega Raced split window box

Winner's Circle Autographed Hoods 1:64
2008 #1 Bass Pro Shops

Winner's Circle Daytona 500 1:24
2008 #1 Bass Pro Shops

Winner's Circle Daytona 500 1:64
2008 #1 Bass Pro Shops

Winner's Circle Daytona 500 1:87
2008 #1 Bass Pro Shops

Winner's Circle Daytona 500 Hoods 1:64
2008 #1 Bass Pro Shops

Winner's Circle Dually w/Car on Tracksi
2008 #1 Bass Pro Shops

Winner's Circle Helmets 1:64
2007 #1 Bass Pro Shops

Winner's Circle Number Magnet 1:64
2008 #1 Bass Pro Shops

Winner's Circle Schedule Hoods 1:64
2008 #1 Bass Pro Shops

Winner's Circle Stickers 1:64
2008 #1 Bass Pro Shops

Winner's Circle Test Hood 1:64
2005 #8 Bass Pro

Winner's Circle Transporters 1:64
2007 #1 Bass Pro Shops

Winner's Circle Victory Lane Hoods 1:64
2007 #1 Bass Pro Shops COT Dover Raced

Wallace, Rusty

Action Clearly Collectibles 1:24
2005 #2 Texas Raced Spark Plug/8
2005 #2 Talladega Raced Spark Plug/8
2005 #2 Daytona Raced Spark Plug/8
2005 #2 Bristol Raced Spark Plug/8
2005 #2 Atlanta Raced Spark Plug/8

Action Performance 1:24
2000 #2 Rusty
2003 #2 Rusty
2004 #2 Miller Lite Last Call
2005 #2 Miller Lite Last Call
2005 #2 Miller Lite Hometown
2005 #27 Milestones '89 Champ/4008

Action Performance 1:64
2000 #2 Rusty Red Cell Batt.Promo
2002 #2 Rusty
2003 #2 Rusty
2005 #NNO Nextel Cup 6-car set 2
2005 #NNO Nextel Cup 6-car set 1

Action President's Platinum Series 1:24
2005 #2 Miller Lite AU/1100

Action QVC For Race Fans Only 1:24
2000 #2 Miller Lite Gold/2000
2001 #2 Mill.Lite Harley Plat/624
2001 #2 Mill.Lite Harley Gold/2000
2001 #2 Miller Lite Harley Color Chrome/2508
2001 #2 Miller Lite Gold/1000
2002 #2 Miller Lite Harley Flames Color Chrome/1008
2003 #2 Mill.Time Live Goo Goo Dolls Color Chrome/1000
2003 #2 Miller Lite 600th Start Col.Chrome/1008
2003 #2 Miller Lite Platinum/624
2003 #2 Miller Lite Gold/1000
2003 #2 Mill.Lite Col.Chrome/1008
2004 #2 Miller Lite Last Call Color Chrome/1500
2004 #2 Miller Lite Martinsville Raced Color Chrome AU/504
2005 #2 700 Starts Color Chrome
2005 #2 Snap On Miller Lite Platinum/108
2005 #2 Snap On Miller Lite Gold/204
2005 #2 Snap On Miller Lite Brushed Metal/288
2005 #2 Mobil Color Chrome/960
2005 #2 Miller Lite Gold/300
2005 #2 Miller Lite Color Chrome/1008
2005 #2 Miller Genuine Draft Platinum/144
2005 #2 Miller Genuine Draft Gold/300
2005 #2 Miller Genuine Draft Color Chrome/Chrome 2-car set/504
2005 #2 Miller Genuine Draft Color Chrome/2004
2005 #2 Miller Genuine Draft Brushed Metal/504
2005 #2 Kodak Color Chrome/2004

Action Racing Collectables 1:18
1999 #2 Miller Lite Harley/3504
1999 #2 Miller Lite/2508
2004 #2 Miller Lite Last Call/1224
2004 #2 Miller Lite/1248

Action Racing Collectables 1:24
1994 #2 Ford Motors Bank/3504
1995 #2 MGD Bank/15,000
1995 #2 MGD7500
1995 #27 Kodiak Bank/6210 1989 Grand Prix in case
1996 #2 Miller Splash Bank
1996 #2 MGD Silver 25th Anniv.
1996 #2 Miller Splash
1997 #2 Miller Lt.Texas Bank/7584
1997 #2 Miller Japan/7500
1997 #2 Miller Lite/10,500
1997 #27 MGD '90GP Bank/6000 in plastic case
1998 #2 Miller Lite TCB Elvis Bank/2508
1998 #2 Miller Lite TCB Elvis
1998 #2 Miller Lite Elvis Bank/15,996
1998 #2 Miller Lite Elvis
1998 #2 Miller Lite Bank/2500
1998 #2 Miller Lite
1998 #2 Adventures of Rusty
1999 #2 Miller Lite Texas
1999 #2 Miller Lite Last Lap Bank
1999 #2 Mill.Lite Last Lap/10,080
1999 #2 Mil.Lite Harley Bank/5004
1999 #2 Miller Lite Harley clear windows
1999 #2 Miller Lite Harley/2508 black windows
1999 #2 Miller Lite Bank/2508
1999 #2 Miller Lite/15,000
2000 #2 Mill.Lite Harley Bank/3276
2000 #2 Mill.Lite Harley/19,704
2000 #2 Miller Lite 10th Ann./6000
2000 #2 Miller Lite Bank/2508
2000 #2 Miller Lite/10,500
2000 #14 Southland '81/3000
2000 #66 Alugard '84 Camaro Red/Yellow/3000
2000 #66 Alugard '84 Camaro Black/3000
2001 #2 Miller Lite Harley Clear/6792
2001 #2 Miller Lite Harley/19,884
2001 #2 Miller Lite Bank/1500
2001 #2 Miller Lite/12,036
2001 #66 Child's '81 Camaro Red
2002 #2 MGD '95 T-bird
2002 #2 MGD '91 T-bird/8940
2002 #2 Miller Lite Flames/8592
2002 #2 Miller Lite Harley Flames Bank/672
2002 #2 Miller Lite Harley Flames/18,072
2002 #2 Miller Lite Elvis Clear/4884
2002 #2 Miller Lite Elvis/23,696
2002 #2 Miller Lite Elvis Bank/1800
2002 #2 Miller Lite Bank/1200
2002 #2 Miller Lite/21,024
2003 #2 Mill.Time Live Goo Goo Dolls CW Bank/856
2003 #2 Miller Time Live Goo Goo Dolls/12,688
2003 #2 Miller Lite 600th CW Bank/504
2003 #2 Miller Lite 600th/9936
2003 #2 Miller Lite Victory Lap CW Bank/420
2003 #2 Miller Lite Victory Lap/7476
2003 #2 Miller Lite BW Bank/708
2003 #2 Miller Lite/18,012
2003 #66 Motion '85T-bird/4356
2004 #2 Miller Lite Penske 50th CW Bank/348
2004 #2 Miller Lite Penske 50th/5628
2004 #2 Miller Lite Puddle Mudd CW Bank/336
2004 #2 Miller Lite Puddle of Mudd/4884
2004 #2 Miller Lite President of Beers CW Bank/384
2004 #2 Miller Lite President of Beers/5412
2004 #2 Miller Lite Last Call Color Chrome/2004
2004 #2 Miller Lite Last Call CW Bank/228
2004 #2 Miller Lite Last Call
2004 #2 Miller Lite Miller Can/2560
2004 #2 Miller Lite Father's Day CW Bank/384
2004 #2 Miller Lite Father's Day/4188
2004 #2 Miller Lite Nextel Incentive/2004
2004 #2 Miller Lite Martinsville Raced w/tire/4188
2004 #2 Miller Lite Mac Tools/288
2004 #2 Miller Lite CW Bank/384
2004 #2 Miller Lite/12,420
2004 #2 Kodak CW Bank/324
2004 #2 Kodak/4836
2004 #66 Duraflame CW Bank/204
2004 #66 Duraflame/2340
2005 #2 Snap-On 85th Ann Matco/48
2005 #2 Snap-On 85th Ann QVC/504
2005 #2 Snap-On 85th Ann Snap On/3504
2005 #2 700 Starts CW Bank/156
2005 #2 700 Starts QVC/504
2005 #2 700 Starts Matco/48
2005 #2 700 Starts/3816
2005 #2 Snap-On 85th Anniversary Pearl Chrome/720
2005 #2 Snap-On 85th Ann CW Bank/252
2005 #2 Snap-On 85th Ann/5508
2005 #2 Mobil QVC/504
2005 #2 Mobil CW Bank/276
2005 #2 Mobil/5676
2005 #2 Miller Lite 500 Consec Starts/2508
2005 #2 Miller Lite Sirius QVC/288
2005 #2 Miller Lite Sirius/2508
2005 #2 Miller Lite Last Race QVC/2004
2005 #2 Miller Lite Last Race Matco/98
2005 #2 Miller Lite Last Race Mac Tools/120
2005 #2 Miller Lite Last Race/3504
2005 #2 Miller Lite Last Call Test QVC/288
2005 #2 Miller Lite Last Call Test/2484
2005 #2 Miller Lite Last Call Daytona Shootout QVC/504
2005 #2 Miller Lite Last Call Daytona Shootout Liquid Metal/2004
2005 #2 Miller Lite Last Call Daytona Shootout CW Bank/204
2005 #2 Miller Lite Last Call Daytona Shootout/4476
2005 #2 Miller Lite Flames Bristol QVC/1008
2005 #2 Miller Lite Flames Bristol/4008
2005 #2 Miller Lite QVC/1008
2005 #2 Miller Lite Matco/180
2005 #2 Miller Lite Mac Tools/108
2005 #2 Miller Lite Liquid Metal/2004
2005 #2 Miller Lite Color Chrome/2004
2005 #2 Miller Lite CW Bank/276
2005 #2 Miller Lite/7584
2005 #2 Miller Genuine Draft QVC/1008
2005 #2 Miller Genuine Draft Pearl Chrome/720
2005 #2 Miller Genuine Draft Matco/72
2005 #2 Miller Genuine Draft CW Bank/264
2005 #2 Miller Genuine Draft/9012
2005 #2 Kodak QVC/504
2005 #2 Kodak Matco/48
2005 #2 Kodak Liquid Metal/708
2005 #2 Kodak CW Bank/228
2005 #2 Kodak/5568
2005 #64 Top Flite CW Bank/144
2005 #64 Top Flite QVC/288
2005 #64 Top Flite/2652
2005 #64 Miller High Life St. Louis Family Trib.QVC/600
2005 #64 Miller High Life St. Louis Family Trib.CW Bank/228
2005 #64 Miller High Life Saint Louis Family Trib/5280
2005 #64 Bell Helicopter QVC/504
2005 #64 Bell Helicopter CW Bank/204
2005 #64 Bell Helicopter/6192
2006 #2 Legendary/4220

Action Racing Collectables 1:32
1998-01 #2 Miller Lite '98

Action Racing Collectables 1:64
1994 #2 Ford Motorsports
1995 #2 MGD in acrylic case
1996 #2 MGD Silver 25th Anniv.
1996 #2 MGD
1997 #2 Miller Lite Texas
1997 #2 Miller Japan/12,000
1997 #2 Miller Lite
1997 #27 MGD '90 GP/10,080
1998 #2 Miller Lite TCB Elvis
1998 #2 Miller Lite Elvis
1998 #2 Miller Lite
1998 #2 Adventures of Rusty
1998 #NNO J.Mayfield/2-car set on pit wall base
1999 #2 Miler Lite Texas
1999 #2 Miller Lite Last Lap
1999 #2 Miller Lite Harley
1999 #2 Miller Lite
2000 #2 Miller Lite/15,048
2001 #2 ML Harley in a can
2001 #2 Miller Lite Harley/14,592
2001 #2 Miller Lite in a can
2002 #2 Miller Lite Flames/9000
2002 #2 Miller Lite Harley Flames/16,680
2002 #2 Miller Lite Elvis/24,864 in a tin box
2002 #2 Miller Lite/39,288 in a bottle
2002 #2 MGD '91 T-bird in a can/16,272
2003 #2 Miller Lite Penske 50th/7536
2003 #2 Miller Time Live Goo Goo Dolls/9360
2003 #2 Miller Lite 600th/9936
2003 #2 Miller Lite Victory Lap/5976
2003 #2 Miller Lite/15,360
2004 #2 Miller Lite Puddle of Mudd/4464
2004 #2 Miller Lite Last Call/3936
2004 #2 Miller Lite in keg
2004 #2 Miller Lite/8496
2004 #2 Kodak/4128
2005 #2 Miller Lite Last Call Daytona Shootout
2005 #2 Miller Lite in a can
2005 #2 Miller Lite
2005 #2 Miller Genuine Draft in can/4068

Action Racing Collectables AC Racing 1:
1993 #2 Pontiac Excitement

Action Racing Collectables Delco Remy 1
1993 #2 Pontiac Excitement

Action Racing Collectables Fan Fueler 1
1998 #2 Ford Motorsports

Action Racing Collectables Historical S
2004 #2 Miller Lite Last Lap Century '99 t-bird Col.Chrome CW Bank/5004
2005 #2 Aluguard '85 Grand Prix QVC/288
2005 #2 Aluguard '85 Grand Prix GM Dealers/144
2005 #2 Aluguard '85 Grand Prix/2376

Action Racing Collectables Pit Wagon
1990-03 #2 Miller Lite in case/3500 '98
1990-03 #2 Miller Lite '97
1990-03 #2 MGD/2508 '95
1990-03 #2 Ford Motor.

Action Racing Collectables Transporters
2002 #2 Miller Lite/2676
2003 #2 Miller Lite Route/2628
2003 #2 Miller Lite/2448
2004 #2 Miller Lite/2508
2005 #2 Miller Lite '00's Trib QVC/504
2005 #2 Miller Lite '00's Trib/1500
2005 #2 Miller Lite '90's Trib QVC/504
2005 #2 Miller Lite '90's Trib/1500
2005 #2 Miller Lite '80's Trib QVC/504
2005 #2 Miller Lite '80's Trib/1500

Action Total Concept 1:64
2000 #2 Miller Lite Harley/20,808

Action/Funline Muscle Machines 1:18
2004 #2 Rusty '69 Charger
2005 #2 700 Starts '68 Charger
2005 #2 700 Starts '68 Dart

Action/Funline Muscle Machines 1:24
2004 #2 Miller Lite '68 Charger
2005 #2 Miller Lite Hybrid/288

Action/RCCA 1:24
1994 #2 MGD '95 T-bird
1994 #2 Ford Motorsports
1995 #27 Kodiak '89 GP/5000
1996 #2 MGD
1996 #2 MGD Silver 25th Ann.Bank
1996 #2 MGD Bank
1997 #2 Miller Lite Texas
1997 #2 Miller Japan Bank/5000
1997 #2 Miller Lite Bank
1997 #27 MGD '90 GP/5000 in plastic case
2002 #2 Miller Lite Flames Bank/804
2002 #2 Miller Lite Harley Flames Bank/1008
2002 #2 Miller Lite Elvis Bank/1200
2002 #2 Mill.Lite Split Clear/2508
2002 #2 Miller Lite Color Chrome Bank/1008
2002 #2 MGD '95 T-bird Bank/600
2003 #2 Miller Lite Penske 50th/804
2003 #2 Miller Time Live Goo Goo Dolls/1204
2003 #2 Mill.Lite 600 Starts/600
2003 #2 Miller Lite Victory Lap/600
2003 #2 Miller Lite CW Bank/1200
2004 #2 Miller Lite Puddle of Mudd/504
2004 #2 Miller Lite President of Beers/600
2004 #2 Miller Lite Penske 50th/504
2004 #2 Miller Lite Martinsville Raced w/Tire/240
2004 #2 Miller Lite Last Call/600
2004 #2 Miller Lite Father's Day/240
2004 #2 Miller Lite Can Promotion/408
2004 #2 Miller Lite/1200
2004 #2 Kodak/600
2004 #66 Duraflame/408
2005 #2 Miller Genuine Draft/600
2005 #2 Miller Lite Bristol/444
2005 #2 Miller Lite Hometown Brushed Bronze/288
2005 #2 Miller Lite Wallace 500/288
2005 #2 700 Starts/360
2005 #2 Snap-On Miller Lite/540
2005 #2 Mobil/444
2005 #2 Miller Lite Last Call Test/360
2005 #2 Miller Lite Last Call Daytona Shootout/600
2005 #2 Miller Lite Color Chrome/288
2005 #2 Miller Lite/480
2005 #2 Milestones 9X Bristol Winner/502
2005 #2 Milestones 700th Start/602
2005 #2 Milestones Last Call/502
2005 #2 Kodak/408
2005 #27 Milestones '89 Champ/802
2005 #64 Miller High Life/504
2005 #64 Top Flite/240
2005 #64 Bell Helicopter/408
2006 #2 Legendary/444

Action/RCCA 1:64
1993 #2 MGD club only
1993 #27 Kodiak '89 Pontiac in plastic case
1995 #2 MGD in acrylic case
1995 #27 Kodiak '89 Grand Prix in plastic case/20,000
1996 #2 MGD Silver 25th Anniv. in plastic case
1996 #2 MGD
1997 #2 Miller Lite Texas
1997 #2 Miller Japan
1997 #2 Miller Lite
1998 #2 Miller Lite TCB Elvis
1998 #2 Miller Lite Elvis
1998 #2 Miller Lite/7500
1998 #2 Adventures of Rusty
1999 #2 Wallace Fan Club
1999 #2 Miller Lite Harley/7500
1999 #2 Mill.Lite Last Lap/3000
1999 #2 Miller Lite/5000
2000 #2 Miller Lite
2001 #2 Miller Lite Harley/3600
2001 #2 Miller Lite/1584
2002 #2 Miller Lite Flames/1596
2002 #2 Miller Lite Harley Flames/1800
2002 #2 Miller Lite Elvis/1800
2002 #2 Miller Lite/1584
2003 #2 Miller Lite Penske 50th/720
2003 #2 Miller Time Live Goo Goo Dolls/1444
2003 #2 Mill.Lite 600 Starts/1012
2003 #2 Miller Lite/1500
2004 #2 Miller Lite Puddle of Mudd/576
2004 #2 Miller Lite Last Call/576
2004 #2 Miller Lite/1588
2004 #2 Kodak/576
2005 #2 Miller Genuine Draft in can/600
2005 #2 Miller Lite in can/600
2005 #2 Miller Lite Last Call Daytona Shootout/576
2005 #2 Miller Lite/576
2005 #2 Miller Genuine Draft/576
2005 #NNO Wallace Family Tribute 3-car set in tin/600

Action/RCCA Banks 1:24
1998 #2 Miller Lite TCB Elvis
1998 #2 Miller Lite Elvis/20,000
1998 #2 Miller Lite/6000
1998 #2 Adventur.of Rusty/3500
1999 #2 Miller Lite True to Texas/1500
1999 #2 Mill.Lite Last Lap/3000
1999 #2 Miller Lite Harley
1999 #2 Miller Lite/3500
2000 #2 Miller Lite Harley/2004
2000 #2 Miller Lite 10th Ann Color Chrome/2196
2000 #2 Miller Lite/2508

Action/RCCA Dually Trucks 1:24
1995 #2 MGD Bank in case
1996 #2 MGD Silver 25th Ann. Bank/2500
1996 #2 Miller Splash Bank/5000
1997 #2 Miller Lite Bank/2500

Action/RCCA Dually Trucks 1:64
1994-97 #2 Miller/10,000 '96

Action/RCCA Dually Trucks with Trailer
1995 #2 Miller Genuine Draft
1996 #2 Miller in case/2500
1997 #2 Miller Lite/3000
2000 #2 Miller Lite in plastic case

Action/RCCA Elite 1:24
1997 #2 Miller Lite Texas/1500
1997 #2 Miller Japan/5000
1997 #2 Miller Lite/5000
1998 #2 Miller Lite TCB Elvis/1000
1998 #2 Miller Lite Elvis/2500
1998 #2 Miller Lite/2500
1998 #2 Adventur.of Rusty/1320
1999 #2 Miller Lite Harley/2500
1999 #2 Miller Lite Last Lap/1500
1999 #2 Miller Lite
2000 #2 Miller Lite Harley/1008
2000 #2 Miller Lite 10th Ann./816
2000 #2 Miller Lite/1000
2001 #2 Miller Lite Harley/3996
2001 #2 Miller Lite Metal/3504
2001 #2 Miller Lite/1008
2002 #2 Miller Lite Flames/1200
2002 #2 Miller Lite Test Flames/1488-A
2002 #2 Miller Lite Harley Flames/1800
2002 #2 Miller Lite Elvis/2004
2002 #2 Miller Lite Color Chrome/1608
2002 #2 MGD '95 T-bird/900
2003 #2 Miller Time Live Goo Goo Dolls/804
2003 #2 Miller Lite 600 Starts/900
2003 #2 Miller Lite Victory Lap/600
2003 #2 Mill.Lite Color Chr./408
2003 #2 Miller Lite/2004
2004 #2 Miller Lite Penske 50th/504
2004 #2 Miller Lite Last Call White Gold/25
2004 #2 Miller Lite Last Call Platinum/204
2004 #2 Miller Lite Last Call/804
2004 #2 Miller Lite Can Promotion/504
2004 #2 Miller Lite Martinsville Raced/240
2004 #2 Miller Lite Color Chrome/408
2004 #2 Miller Lite/1500
2004 #2 Kodak White Gold/25
2004 #2 Kodak/600
2004 #2 Miller Lite President of Beers/600
2004 #2 Miller Lite Puddle of Mudd/504
2004 #66 Duraflame/600
2005 #2 Miller Lite Wallace 500/288
2005 #2 Miller Lite Wallace 500 White Gold/25
2005 #2 700 Starts/360
2005 #2 700 Starts White Gold/25
2005 #2 Snap-On Miller Lite White Gold/25
2005 #2 Snap-On Miller Lite/540
2005 #2 Mobil White Gold/25
2005 #2 Mobil/540
2005 #2 Miller Lite Last Call Test/444
2005 #2 Miller Lite Last Call Daytona Shootout White Gold/25
2005 #2 Miller Lite Last Call Daytona Shootout/600
2005 #2 Miller Lite Hometown Brushed Bronze/288
2005 #2 Miller Lite Bristol White Gold/25
2005 #2 Miller Lite Bristol/600
2005 #2 Miller Lite White Gold/30
2005 #2 Miller Lite Color Chrome/480
2005 #2 Miller Lite/720
2005 #2 Miller Genuine Draft White Gold/30
2005 #2 Miller Genuine Draft/720
2005 #2 Milestones 9X Bristol/502
2005 #2 Milestones 700th Start/602
2005 #2 Milestones Last Call/502
2005 #2 Kodak White Gold/25
2005 #2 Kodak/408
2005 #27 Milestones '89 Champ/802
2005 #64 Top Flite/240
2005 #64 Top Flite White Gold/25
2005 #64 Miller High Life St. Louis#(Family Tribute White Gold/25
2005 #64 Miller High Life St. Louis#(Family Tribute/600
2005 #64 Bell Helicopter White Gold/25
2005 #64 Bell Helicopter/408
2006 #2 Legendary White Gold/25
2006 #2 Legendary Platinum/8
2006 #2 Legendary/444

Action/RCCA Elite 1:64
2001 #2 Miller Lite Harley
2001 #2 Miller Lite/1104
2002 #2 Miller Lite Flames/1212
2002 #2 Miller Lite Harley#(Flames/1800
2002 #2 Miller Lite Elvis/1800
2002 #2 Miller Lite/1584
2003 #2 Miller Lite Penske 50th/504
2003 #2 Miller Time Live Goo Goo Dolls/1204
2003 #2 Mill.Lite 600 Starts/1012
2003 #2 Miller Lite/1500
2004 #2 Miller Lite Puddle of Mudd/528
2004 #2 Miller Lite Last Call/528
2004 #2 Miller Lite/1500
2004 #2 Kodak/576
2005 #2 Miller Lite Last Call Daytona Shootout/480
2005 #2 Miller Lite/480

Action/RCCA Gold 1:32
1998 #2 Miller Lite

Action/RCCA Historical Series 1:24
2005 #2 Alugard '85 Grand Prix/444

Action/RCCA Revell 1:64
1991-92 #2 Pontiac Excite. REV

Action/RCCA Total View 1:64
2000 #2 Miller Lite Harley

Action/RCCA Transporters 1:64
1993 #2 Delco Remy PLS/1000
1994 #2 Miller
1995 #2 MGD RCCA/3000
1995 #2 MGD PLS
2002 #2 Miller Lite/336
2003 #2 Miller Lite/600
2003 #2 Miller Lite Route Color Chrome/1008
2005 #2 Miller Lite Last Call 1980's Tribute Souvenir/504
2005 #2 Miller Lite Last Call 1990's Tribute Souvenir/504
2005 #2 Miller Lite Last Call 2000's Tribute Souvenir/504
2006 #2 Legendary/250

Action/RCCA Transporters 1:96
1994-96 #2 MGD/3000 '95

Brookfield 1:24
2005 #2 Mobil/204
2005 #2 Miller Lite/444

Brookfield Trackside 1:25
2001 #2 Mill.Lite Silver/720
2001 #2 Miller Lite/1788

Brookfield Trackside 1:64
2004 #2 Kodak/5004
2004 #2 Miller Lite/5004
2005 #2 Miller Lite QVC/288
2005 #2 Miller Lite RCCA/504
2005 #2 Miller Lite/2136

Ertl 1:18
1995 #2 MGD/5000
1995 #27 Kodiak '89 GP/3500
1996 #2 Miller Silver/10,000
1996 #27 MGD

Hot Wheels Pro Circuit 1:64
1992 #2 Pontiac

Johnny Lightning Stock Car Legends 1:64
1998 #88 Gatorade '84 GP

Matchbox White Rose Super Stars 1:64
1994 #2 Ford Motor. BX
1997 #2 Miller Lite in a bottle
1990-92 #2 Pontiac Excite.BL 92

Matchbox White Rose Transporters 1:64
1997 #2 Miller Lite

Matchbox White Rose Transporters Super
1992 #2 Penske

Press Pass Sets 1:24/64
1996 #2 Miller 25th Anniv/1996 1:24 Revell Bank & 1:64 car

Racing Champions 1:144
1996 #2 MGD
1997 #2 Penske

Racing Champions 1:24
1993 #2 Pontiac Excitement
1994 #2 Ford w/Blue Ford Oval
1994 #2 Ford w/Blk Ford Oval
1995 #2 Ford Motorsports
1996 #2 Penske Racing
1996 #2 Miller Splash Promo
1996 #2 MGD
1997 #2 Penske
1991-92 #2 Pontiac Excitement
1991-92 #2 AC Delco

Racing Champions 1:43
1991 #2 Pont.Excite.
1993 #2 Pontiac Excitement

Racing Champions 1:64
1990 #27 Old Pontiac MGD
1990 #27 Olds
1990 #27 89 Champ.Promo/30,000
1990 #27 Pontiac w/Silv.Decals
1990 #27 Pontiac Miller
1990 #27 Pontiac MGD
1990 #NNO 12-car set in case
1991 #2 Mobil 1 Promo
1991 #2 Pontiac PB
1991 #2 Pontiac EB
1991 #27 Pontiac Miller EB
1991 #27 Pontiac no MGD EB
1991 #27 Pontiac MGD NP
1991 #27 Pontiac MGD EB
1991 #NNO Sears 13-car set
1992 #2 Pontiac Excite.
1992 #NNO Sears 12-car set
1992 #NNO Collect.Edit.12-car set w/R.Petty
1993 #2 Pontiac Excitement
1994 #2 Ford Motor w/o Blue
1994 #2 Ford Motorsports
1994 #94 McDonald's All-Star Promo
1995 #2 Ford Motor.
1996 #2 Penske
1996 #2 MGD Chrome/1996
1996 #2 MGD
1996 #NNO 12-Car set in case
1997 #2 Penske Racing
1997 #2 Miller Lite Matco Promo/20,000

Racing Champions 5-Pack 1:144
1991 #NNO 9.BE/27.RW/30.BH/33.HG/94.SM
1991 #NNO 3.DE/27.RW/28.DA/30.BH/43.RP

Racing Champions AC Racing Promos 1:64
1992 #2 Pontiac Excitement

Racing Champions Banks 1:24
1995 #2 Ford Motor.
1992-94 #2 Pontiac Excite./2500
1992-94 #2 Ford Motorsports

Racing Champions Hobby Yellow Box 1:64
1994 #2 Ford Motorsports

Racing Champions Hood Open Banks 1:24
1996 #2 MGD
1997 #2 Miller Lite Matco Chrome
1997 #2 Miller Lite Matco

Racing Champions IROC 1:24
1992 #19 True Value IROC Purple

Racing Champions Matched Serial Numbers
1995 #2 Ford

Racing Champions Milkhouse Cheese Promo
1992 #2 MGD

Racing Champions Premier 1:18
1996 #2 MGD
1997 #2 Miller Lite Gold

1997 #2 Miller Lite
Racing Champions Premier 1:43
1994 #2 Ford Motor.
Racing Champions Premier 1:64
1993 #2 Pontiac Excite./40,000
1994 #2 Mac Tools
1994 #2 MGD/20,000
1995 #2 Ford Motor.
Racing Champions Premier Banks 1:24
1996 #2 Penske Chrome/166
1996 #2 Penske
1997 #2 Miller Lite Gold/166
1997 #2 Miller Lite/1992
Racing Champions Premier Gold 1:64
1997 #2 Miller Lite
Racing Champions Premier Gold Chrome 1:
1997 #2 Miller Lite
Racing Champions Premier Hood Open 1:24
1996 #2 MGD
Racing Champions Premier Transporters 1
1993 #2 Ford Motor.
1993 #2 Penske
1994 #2 Penske Mac Tools/7500
1995 #2 Penske Bank
1995 #2 MGD in acrylic case
1996 #2 Penske
Racing Champions Premier with Medallion
1996 #2 MGD HO Miller Pack
1997 #2 Penske
Racing Champions Preview 1:24
1995 #2 Ford Motor.
Racing Champions Preview 1:64
1995 #2 Ford Motor.
Racing Champions Preview Transporters 1
1995 #2 Penske
Racing Champions PVC Box 1:64
1993 #2 Pont.Excitement November 14th Win
1993 #2 Pont.Excitement October 24th Win
1993 #2 Pont.Excitement October 3rd Win
1993 #2 Pont.Excitement September 19th Win
1993 #2 Pont.Excitement September 11th Win
1993 #2 Pont.Excitement July 11th Win
1993 #2 Pont.Excitement April 25th Win/5000
1993 #2 Pont.Excitement April 18th Win/5000
1993 #2 Pont.Excitement April 4th Win/5000
1993 #2 Pont.Excitement Feb.28th Win/5000
Racing Champions Racing Relatives 1:43
1992 #NNO K.Wallace/Pont./Cox
Racing Champions Roaring Racers 1:64
1990-91 #2 NS BW '91
Racing Champions Short Track Champions
1994 #66 Alugard
Racing Champions Stock Rods 1:24
1997 #8 Penske
Racing Champions Stock Rods 1:64
1997 #10 Miller Lite
1997 #18 Penske
1997 #35 Penske
Racing Champions To the Maxx 1:64
1994 #2 Ford Motor.
1995 #2 Ford Motor.
Racing Champions Transporters 1:144
1994 #2 Penske
1996 #2 Penske
1997 #2 Penske
Racing Champions Transporters 1:64
1991 #2 Penske Racing
1992 #2 Penske
1993 #2 Penske
1995 #2 Penske
1996 #2 Penske w/car(s)
1996 #2 Penske
1996 #2 MGD
1997 #2 Penske
Racing Champions Transporters 1:87
1995 #2 MGD in acrylic case
1996 #2 Penske
1997 #2 Penske
Racing Champions Transporters Hobby 1:6
1994 #2 Penske
Racing Champions Transporters Hobby 1:8
1994 #2 Penske
Racing Champions Transporters Retail
1993-94 #2 Penske
Racing Champions Transporters Retail 1:
1994 #2 Penske
Racing Champions with Figure 1:64
1992 #2 Pont.Excitement
Revell Club 1:18
1998 #2 Miller Lite Elvis/1002
1998 #2 Adventures of Rusty
Revell Club 1:24
1997 #2 Miller Lite
1998 #2 Miller Lite Elvis/1596
1998 #2 Adventures of Rusty/1002
1998 #2 Miller Lite/1002
1999 #2 Miller Lite Harley/1002
1999 #2 Miller Lite/504
Revell Collection 1:18
1997 #2 Miller Lite/11,766
1998 #2 Miller Lite TCB Elvis
1998 #2 Miller Lite Elvis/5004
1998 #2 Miller Lite/5004
1998 #2 Advent.of Rusty/5004
1999 #2 Miller Lite Harley/2508
1999 #2 Miller Lite
Revell Collection 1:24
1996 #2 Penske
1996 #2 MGD Silver 25th Anniv.
1996 #22 Miller Splash Truck/2508
1996 #22 MGD Silver 25th Anniversary SuperTruck/2504
1996 #22 MGD Suzuka Thunder/3120
1997 #2 Miller Lite Texas
1997 #2 Miller Lite/25,000
1997 #2 Miller Japan/5496
1998 #2 Miller Lite TCB Elvis Bank/1002
1998 #2 Miller Lite TCB Elvis
1998 #2 Miller Lite Elvis
1998 #2 Miller Lite/5598
1998 #2 Adventures of Rusty
1999 #2 Miller Lite Harley Matco Tools promo
1999 #2 Miller Lite Harley/5004
1999 #2 Miller Lite/5004
2000 #2 Miller Lite Harley
2000 #2 Miller Lite/3120
2001 #2 Miller Lite California win
2002 #2 Miller Lite Test flames/5502
Revell Collection 1:43
1997 #2 Miller Lite
1998 #2 Mill.Lite TCB Elvis/5004
1998 #2 Miller Lite Elvis/7512
1998 #2 Adventur.of Rusty/5004
1999 #2 Miller Lite Harley/3000

Revell Collection 1:64
1996 #2 MGD Silver 25th Anniversary/14,400
1996 #2 MGD/14,400
1997 #2 Miller Lite Texas/10,080
1997 #2 Miller Lite/30,000
1998 #2 Adventures of Rusty
1998 #2 Miller Lite TCB Elvis
1998 #2 Miller Lite Elvis
1998 #2 Miller Lite
1999 #2 Miller Lite Harley
1999 #2 Miller Lite
2000 #2 Miller Lite Harley/7992
2000 #2 Miller Lite
Revell Retail 1:24
1996 #2 Penske
1996 #2 Miller Silver
1997 #2 Penske
Revell Retail 1:64
1996 #2 MGD Silver 25th Anniv. Race Day blister
1996 #2 MGD Silver 25th Anniv.
1996 #2 Penske
1997 #2 Penske
Revell Select 1:24
1997 #2 Miller Lite
1998 #2 Miller Lite Elvis
1998 #2 Miller Lite
1998 #2 Adventures of Rusty
1999 #2 Miller Lite Last Lap
Revell Select Hobby 1:64
1997 #2 Miller Lite
1998 #2 Miller Lite
Road Champs 1:43
1992 #2 Pontiac
Road Champs 1:64
1992 #2 Pontiac
Road Champs Sounds of Power 1:43
1992 #2 Pontiac
Road Champs Transporters 1:87
1992 #2 Pontiac
Winner's Circle 1:18
2005 #2 Rusty
Winner's Circle 1:24
1998 #2 Rusty Elvis
1998 #2 Rusty
1999 #2 Rusty
2001 #2 Rusty Harley
2002 #2 Rusty
2003 #2 Rusty
2004 #2 Rusty
2004 #2 Kodak
2005 #2 Rusty
2006 #64 Bell Helicopter '05
Winner's Circle 1:43
1998 #2 Rusty Elvis
1998 #2 Rusty
1999 #2 Rusty
Winner's Circle 1:64
1998 #2 Rusty
1998 #2 Elvis
1998 #2 Adventures of Rusty
2004 #2 Miller Lite Puddle of Mudd
2004 #2 Miller Lite President of Beers
2004 #2 Miller Lite Last Call
2004 #2 Miller Lite
2005 #2 Miller Lite Last Call Daytona Shootout
2005 #2 Miller Lite Last Call
2005 #2 Miller Lite
2005 #2 Miller Genuine Draft
2006 #2 Miller Lite 700 Starts '05
2006 #2 Miller Lite Bristol '05
Winner's Circle Autographed Hood 1:64
2003 #2 Rusty
2004 #2 Kodak
2005 #2 Mobil Clean 7500
2006 #2 Rusty Bristol Flames
Winner's Circle Cool Customs 1:64
1998-99 #2 Rusty/Adventures of Rusty 2-cars
1998-99 #2 Rusty '65 Galaxie
Winner's Circle Deluxe Winston Cup Scen
2000 #2 Rusty 50th Win
Winner's Circle Die-Cast Kits 1:24
2002 #2 Rusty
Winner's Circle Die-Cast Kits 1:64
2002 #2 Rusty
Winner's Circle Double Platinum 1:43
2001 #2 Pemberton/Rusty
2002 #2 Rusty
2003 #2 Rusty
Winner's Circle Driver Photo Hood 1:64
2005 #2 Rusty
2005 #64 Bell Helicopter
Winner's Circle Driver Sticker 1:64
2003 #2 Rusty Flames
2004 #2 Rusty
Winner's Circle Event Series 1:64
2005 #2 Miller Lite '04 Martinsville Win
Winner's Circle Gallery 1:64
2002 #2 Rusty
Winner's Circle Gift Pack 1:64
2002 #2 Rusty/Rusty Harley Mobil 25th Anniversary
Winner's Circle Micro Machines 1:144
1999 #NNO J.Gordon
1999 #NNO J.Gordon
1999 #NNO 7-car Draft Pack
Winner's Circle Pit Pass Preview 1:64
2002 #2 Rusty
2003 #2 Rusty '03 Preview sticker
2003 #2 Rusty
2004 #2 Rusty
Winner's Circle Pit Row 1:64
1998 #2 Elvis Fanscan package
1998 #2 Rusty no offical
1998 #2 Rusty offical behind car
Winner's Circle Pit Scene 1:64
2003 #2 Rusty Level
Winner's Circle Race Hood 1:43
2002 #2 Rusty
2003 #2 Rusty
Winner's Circle Race Hood 1:64
2003 #2 Rusty
2001-02 #2 Rusty Harley
2001-02 #2 Rusty
Winner's Circle Sneak Previews 1:64
2000 #2 Rusty
Winner's Circle Speedweeks 1:64
1999 #2 Rusty
Winner's Circle Stats and Standings 1:6
1999 #2 Rusty
Winner's Circle Team Authentics 1:64
2001 #2 Rusty Sheetmetal
2001 #2 Rusty Firesuit
Winner's Circle Tech Series 1:64
1999 #2 Penske

Winner's Circle Transporters 1:64
2000 #2 Rusty
2002 #2 Rusty
2004 #2 Kodak
2005 #2 Rusty
Winner's Circle Victory Lap 1:24
2003 #2 Miller Lite Victory Lap
Winner's Circle Victory Lap 1:64
2003 #2 Miller Lite Victory Lap

Waltrip, Darrell

Action Racing Collectables 1:18
2000 #66 Big K Route 66 Flames
2003 #11 Victory Lap/2508
Action Racing Collectables 1:24
1994 #11 Bud Red '86 Monte Carlo Bank
1994 #11 Bud 84 T-bird
1994 #11 Bud '84 Monte Carlo Bank
1995 #11 Mountain Dew/6000
1995 #88 Gatorade Bank 1977 Olds/2508
1997 #17 Parts America Bank Yellow&White
1997 #17 Parts America Bank Red&White
1997 #17 Parts America Bank Orange
1997 #17 Parts America Bank Green w/white no.
1997 #17 Parts America Bank Green w/green number
1997 #17 Parts America Bank Chrome
1997 #17 Parts America Bank Blue&White
1998 #1 Pennzoil Bank
1998 #1 Pennzoil
1998 #300 Flock Special Bank
1998 #300 Flock Special/3500
1999 #66 Big K Route 66 Victory Tour/4008
1999 #66 Big K Route 66/8508
2000 #11 Mountain Dew 1984 Camaro/3000
2000 #11 Pepsi '83 Firebird/4008
2000 #11 Hodgdon '84 Cam./3000
2000 #66 Big K Route 66 Flames Bank/2508
2000 #66 Big K Route 66 Flames/6996
2000 #66 Big K Rte.66 Bank/2508
2000 #66 Big K Route 66
2000 #88 Gatorade '76 Mal./5784
2001 #11 Budweiser 1985 Monte Carlo/8508
2002 #17 Tide SuperTruck/4008
2002 #17 Tide '89 MC/8340
2002 #48 Crowell & Reed 1964 Chevelle Bank/408
2002 #48 Crowell & Reed 1964 Chevelle/3840
2003 #11 Victory Lap CW Bank/348
2003 #11 Victory Lap/6360
2003 #17 Tide Kids SuperTruck/4512
2003 #17 Boogity Boogity GM Dealers AU/240
2003 #17 Boogity Boogity AU/4356
2003 #17 Aaron's 3 Stooges SuperTruck/6108
2003 #88 Gatorade '79 MC/4164
2004 #17 King of Bristol AU/2508
2005 #12 Tundra One & Done BD&A/1752
2005 #12 Tundra One & Done/3504
Action Racing Collectables 1:64
1994 #11 Bud '87 Monte Carlo
1995 #11 Pepsi ASA Camaro/16,128
1995 #11 Mountain Dew 1982 Buick/20,000
1995 #17 Western Auto/24,912
1995 #17 Tide ASA Camaro
1995 #88 Gatorade '80 Olds/16,128
1997 #17 Parts America Yell&White
1997 #17 Parts America Red&White
1997 #17 Parts America Orange
1997 #17 Parts America Green with white number
1997 #17 Parts America Green with green number
1997 #17 Parts America Chrome Box
1997 #17 Parts America Blue&White
1998 #1 Pennzoil
1998 #300 Flock Special
1999 #66 Big K Route 66#1 Victory Tour/10,080
2000 #66 Big K Rte.66 Flame/12,744
2000 #66 Big K Route 66/9000
2001 #11 Bud '85 Monte Carlo in a car/21,000
2003 #11 Victory Lap/8856
2003 #88 Gatorade '79 Monte Carlo
Action Racing Collectables AC Racing 1:
1993 #17 Western Auto
Action Racing Collectables Delco Remy 1
1993 #17 Western Auto
Action Racing Collectables Historical S
2004 #17 Tide '87 400 Chevy Wins Color Chrome/3132
2005 #11 Pepsi '83 Monte Carlo QVC/288
2005 #11 Pepsi '83 Monte Carlo/1332
2005 #88 Gatorade '76
2006 #5 Bud IROC '84 Camaro QVC*
2006 #5 Bud IROC '84 Camaro GM Dealers/228
2006 #5 Bud IROC '84 Camaro/2916*
2006 #11 Mountain Dew '81 Buick Liquid Chrome/1500
Action/RCCA 1:24
1995 #11 Mountain Dew Bank 1981 Buick/5000
1995 #88 Gatorade Bank '80 Monte Carlo/2508
1996 #11 Bud '84 Mon.Carlo Bank
1996 #17 Tide '88 Monte Carlo
1996 #17 Parts America Bank/5000
1996 #17 Parts America
1997 #17 Parts America Yellow&White/6000
1997 #17 Parts America Red&White/6000
1997 #17 Parts Amer.Orange/6000
1997 #17 Parts America Green with white number/6000
1997 #17 Parts America Green with green number/6000
1997 #17 Parts Amer.Chrome/6000
1997 #17 Parts America Blue&White/6000
2002 #17 Tide SuperTruck/504
2002 #48 Crowell&Reed 1964 Chevelle Bank/720
2003 #11 Victory Lap/804
2003 #17 Aaron's Rent 3 Stooges SuperTruck/580
2003 #88 Gatorade Bank 1979 Monte Carlo/600
2004 #17 King of Bristol AU/360
2005 #12 Tundra Last Race/480
2005 #12 Tundra Last Race Color Chrome/99
Action/RCCA 1:64
1993 #11 Bud '84 Monte Carlo notchback/10,080
1993 #11 Superflo ASA Camaro
1993 #88 Gatorade '80 MC/10,080
1994 #17 Western Auto
1995 #17 Western Auto/10,080
1995 #17 Superflo ASA Cam./10,080
1995 #88 Gatorade/10,080
1996 #17 Tide '88 MC/10,080
1997 #17 Parts America Yellow&White/5000
1997 #17 Parts America Red&White/5000
1997 #17 Parts Amer.Orange/5000
1997 #17 Parts America Green with white number/5000
1997 #17 Parts America Green with green number/5000
1997 #17 Parts Amer.Chrome/5000
1997 #17 Parts America Blue&White/5000
1998 #1 Pennzoil
1998 #300 Flock Special
2000 #66 Big K Rte.66 Flames/2520
2000 #66 Big K Route 66/2520
Action/RCCA Banks 1:24
1998 #1 Pennzoil
1998 #300 Flock Special/2000
1999 #66 Big K Route 66/1500
2000 #66 Big K Rte.66 Flames/1008
2000 #66 Big K Route 66/1008
Action/RCCA Dually Trucks 1:24
1997 #17 Parts America Chrome RCCA Bank/2500
Action/RCCA Dually Trucks with Trailer
1997 #17 Parts Amer.Chrome/4000
Action/RCCA Elite 1:24
1997 #17 Parts Amer.Chrome/3500
1997 #17 Parts America/4008
1998 #1 Pennzoil/1200
1998 #300 Flock Special/1200
1999 #66 Big K Route 66/1000
2000 #88 Gatorade '76 Mailbu/600
2001 #11 Budweiser '85 MC/720
2003 #17 Boogity Boogity AU/528
2004 #17 King of Bristol AU/360
2005 #12 Tundra Last Race SuperTruck White Gold/25
Action/RCCA Historical 1:24
2006 #5 Budweiser '84 IROC/300
2006 #5 Budweiser '84 IROC Color Chrome/99
2006 #11 Mountain Dew '81 Buick Regal Liquid Color/288
Action/RCCA Historical Series 1:24
2004 #17 Tide 200th Chevy Win '87 Monte Carlo/600
2005 #11 Pepsi '83 Monte Carlo/444
Action/RCCA Historical Series Elite 1:2
2005 #11 Pepsi '83 Monte Carlo/288
Action/RCCA Revell 1:64
1991-92 #17 Western Auto
Action/RCCA Transporters 1:64
1993 #17 Western Auto RCCA/1392
1993 #17 Delco Remy PLS
Ertl 1:18
1992 #17 Western Auto Parts Amer.
Ertl 1:25
1982-84 #11 Pepsi Challenger Stock Car Package
1982-84 #11 Mountain Dew Caprice Superstock package
1982-84 #88 Gatorade Caprice Superstock package
Ertl Motorized Pullback 1:43
1982 #11 Mountain Dew
Ertl Superstock 1:64
1981 #11 Mountain Dew '80 Chevy issue #1598
1981 #11 Mountain Dew Buick issue #1946
1981 #88 Gatorade '80 Chevy
Ertl White Rose Transporters Past an
1992-94 #11 Mountain Dew
1992-94 #17 Western Auto '94
Hot Wheels Crew's Choice 1:24
2000 #66 Big K Route 66
Hot Wheels Crew's Choice 1:43
1999 #66 Big K
Hot Wheels Deluxe 1:64
2000 #66 Big K
Hot Wheels Deluxe Hot Rod 1:64
2000 #66 Big K
Hot Wheels Deluxe Pit Crew 1:64
2000 #66 Big K
Hot Wheels Deluxe Scorchin Scooter 1:64
2000 #66 Big K
Hot Wheels Pro Racing 1:64
1999 #66 Big K
Hot Wheels Racing Crew's Choice 1:64
2000 #66 Big K
Hot Wheels Racing Daytona 500 1:64
1999 #66 K-Mart
Hot Wheels Racing NASCAR Rocks 1:24
1999 #66 Big K
Hot Wheels Racing NASCAR Rocks 1:64
1999 #66 Big K
Hot Wheels Racing Pit Crew 1:64
1999 #66 Big K
Hot Wheels Racing Radical Rides 1:64
2000 #66 Big K
Hot Wheels Racing Select 1:64
2001 #11 Mountain Dew
Hot Wheels Racing Track Edition 1:64
1999 #66 Big K
2000 #66 Big K
Hot Wheels Racing Transporters 1:64
2001 #11 Darrell Waltrip Tribute
Hot Wheels Radical Rides 1:43
1999 #66 K-Mart Route 66
Hot Wheels Select 1:64
2000 #66 Big K
Hot Wheels Select Clear 1:24
1999 #66 Big K
Hot Wheels Select Clear 1:43
1999 #66 Big K
Hot Wheels Trading Paint 1:24
1999 #66 Big K
Hot Wheels Transporters 1:64
1999 #66 Big K
Johnny Lightning Stock Car Legends 1:64
1998 #11 Pepsi '83 MC
1998 #88 Gatorade '79 MC
Matchbox White Rose Super Stars 1:64
1994 #17 Western Auto BX
Matchbox White Rose Transporters Super
1991 #17 Western Auto
1994 #17 Western Auto
Racing Champions 1:144
1996 #17 Parts America
1997 #17 Parts America Chrome
1997 #17 Parts America
Racing Champions 1:24
1993 #17 Western Auto
1994 #17 Western Auto
1995 #17 Western Auto
1996 #17 Parts America
1997 #17 Part.Amer.Chrome Promo
1997 #17 Parts America Chrome
1997 #17 Parts America
1998 #17 Builders' Square
1998 #300 Flock Special
1999 #66 Big K
2000 #66 Big K 500 Promo in box
2000 #66 Big K Flames
2000 #66 Big K
2004 #11 Toyota TRD SuperTruck Promo
1991-92 #17 Western Auto with tampo decals
1991-92 #17 Western Auto with fender stickers
Racing Champions 1:43
1992 #17 Western Auto Promo
1992 #17 Western Auto
1993 #17 Western Auto
Racing Champions 1:64
1992 #17 Western Auto Promo
1992 #17 Western Auto
1992 #NNO Sears 12-car set
1992 #NNO Collect.Edit.12-car set w/R.Petty

1993 #17 Western Auto
1994 #17 Western Auto
1994 #NNO R.Rudd/Tide 3-car Promo set
1995 #17 Western Auto
1996 #17 Parts America Promo
1996 #17 Parts America Chrome/1996
1996 #17 Parts America
1996 #NNO 12-Car set in case
1997 #17 Parts America Chrome
1997 #17 Parts America
1998 #17 Builder's Square
1998 #300 Flock Special
1998 #NNO Collector's Set 2/5000 12-car set
1999 #66 Big K
Racing Champions 12-Car Sets 1:64
1999 #2 12-Car Set 2
Racing Champions 5-Pack 1:64
2000 #NNO 99.JB/14.MB/66.DW/97.CL/4.BH
Racing Champions AC Racing Promos 1:64
1992 #17 Western Auto
Racing Champions Banks 1:24
1992-94 #17 Tide Primer
1992-94 #17 Tide Orange
1992-94 #17 Western Auto
Racing Champions Craftsman Motorsports
1993 #17 Western Auto
Racing Champions Gold 1:24
1998 #17 HQ Builders' Square
1998 #300 Flock Special
1999 #66 Big K
Racing Champions Gold Hood Open 1:24
1998 #17 Builders' Square
Racing Champions Gold with Medallion 1:
1998 #300 Flock Special
1999 #66 Big K
Racing Champions Hobby Yellow Box 1:64
1994 #17 Western Auto
Racing Champions Milkhouse Cheese Promo
1992 #17 Western Auto
Racing Champions NASCAR Rules 1:64
1999 #66 Big K
Racing Champions Pit Stop 1:24
1992 #17 Western Auto Promo
Racing Champions Premier 1:18
1995 #17 Western Auto
1997 #17 Parts Amer.Chrome
Racing Champions Premier 1:43
1993 #17 Western Auto/10,000
Racing Champions Premier 1:64
1992 #17 Western Auto/20,000
Racing Champions Premier Banks 1:24
1996 #17 Parts Amer.Chrome/166
1996 #17 Parts America
Racing Champions Premier Preview 1:64
2000 #66 Big K Flames
2000 #66 Big K
Racing Champions Premier Transporters 1
1994 #17 Western Auto
Racing Champions Premier with Medallion
1997 #17 Parts America
1997 #17 Parts Amer.Chrome/997
Racing Champions Press Pass Series 1:64
1998 #17 Builders' Square
1999 #66 Big K
Racing Champions Preview 1:24
1996 #17 Western Auto
2000 #66 Big K Flames
Racing Champions Preview 1:64
1996 #17 Western Auto
2000 #66 Big K Flames
Racing Champions Preview Transporters 1
1996 #17 Western Auto
2000 #66 Big K
Racing Champions Stock Rods 1:24
1997 #1 Parts America
Racing Champions Stock Rods 1:64
1997 #9 Parts America
1997 #21 Parts America
1999 #190 Big K
1999 #192 Big K Gold
1999 #197 Big K
Racing Champions SuperTrucks 1:18
1995-96 #17 Western Auto
Racing Champions SuperTrucks 1:64
1996 #5 Die Hard
1996 #17 Western Auto
Racing Champions To the Maxx 1:64
1995 #17 Western Auto
Racing Champions Toys 'R Us Gold 1:64
1998 #17 Builders' Square
1998 #300 Flock Special
Racing Champions Transporters 1:144
1997 #17 Western Auto Chrome
1997 #17 Western Auto
1991-92 #17 Western Auto
Racing Champions Transporters 1:64
1992 #17 Western Auto Promo
1992 #17 Western Auto
1993 #17 Western Auto Promo
1993 #17 Western Auto
1996 #17 Parts America
1997 #17 Parts America w/car(s)
1997 #17 Parts America
2000 #66 Big K
Racing Champions Transporters 1:87
1996 #17 Parts America
1997 #17 Parts America
Racing Champions Transporters Gold 1:64
1999 #66 Big K
Racing Champions Transporters Retail
1993-94 #17 D.Walltrip/Western Auto
Racing Champions Transporters Retail 1:
1994 #17 Western Auto
Racing Champions Under the Lights 1:24
1999 #66 Big K
Revell 1:24
1991-95 #17 Western Auto
Revell Club 1:24
1999 #66 Big K Route 66/1002
2000 #66 Big K Rte.66 Flames/1002
Revell Collection 1:24
1996 #17 Parts America
1997 #17 Parts America
1999 #66 Big K Route 66/2508
2000 #66 Big K Flames
Revell Collection 1:64
1996 #17 Parts America
Revell Retail 1:24
1996 #17 Parts America
1997 #17 Parts Amer.Yellow&White
1997 #17 Parts Amer.Red&White
1997 #17 Parts America Green with white number

1997 #17 Parts America Green with green number
1997 #17 Parts Amer.Chrome Box
1997 #17 Parts Amer.blue&white
Revell Retail 1:64
1996 #17 Parts America
Revell Select 1:24
1997 #17 Parts America
Revell Select Hobby 1:64
1997 #17 Parts Amer.Yellow&White
1997 #17 Parts America Red&White
1997 #17 Parts America Orange
1997 #17 Parts America Green with white number
1997 #17 Parts America Green with green number
1997 #17 Parts America Chrome
1997 #17 Parts America blue&white
Team Caliber Owners Series 1:24
2000 #66 Big K Flames/2340
2000 #66 Big K/2340
Team Caliber Owners Series 1:64
2000 #66 Big K Route 66/7560
Team Caliber Owners Series Vintage 1:24
2003 #11 1987 Pepsi/1800
2003 #11 1985 Budweiser/1800
2003 #17 1992 Western Auto/1200
2003 #17 1995 Parts America/1200
Team Caliber Pit Stop 1:64
2006 #99 Aaron's
Team Caliber Preferred 1:24
2000 #66 Route 66 Flames/5508
2000 #66 Route 66/5508
2006 #99 Aaron's
Team Caliber Preferred Banks 1:24
2000 #66 Route 66 Flames/504
2000 #66 Route 66/504
Team Caliber Preferred Copper 1:24
2006 #99 Aaron's
Winner's Circle 1:24
1997 #17 Parts America
Winner's Circle Lifetime Darrell Waltri
1997 #17 PA Chrome '97 Paint 2/6
1997 #17 PA '90-'97 Paint 3/6
1997 #17 PA '84-'86 Paint 5/6
1997 #17 PA '83 Paint 6/6
1997 #17 PA '81-'82 Paint 4/6
1997 #17 PA '75-'80 Paint 1/6
Winross Transporters 1:64
1992 #NNO Western Auto Red
1992 #NNO Western Auto Black,White&Red

Waltrip, Michael

Action Performance 1:24
2001 #15 NAPA Daytona Win Promo
2003 #15 NAPA Stars&Strip.Promo
2003 #15 NAPA Nilla Wafer Promo
2003 #15 NAPA Dayt.Win Promo
Action Performance 1:64
2005 #15 Napa
Action Racing Collectables 1:24
1996 #21 Citgo Star Trek Bank
1996 #21 Citgo
1998 #21 Citgo Woody/2508
1998 #21 Citgo/4008
2000 #7 Nations Rent Bank
2000 #7 Nations Rent
2001 #15 NAPA Stars&Stripes Bank/1008
2001 #15 NAPA Stars&Stripes/27,348
2001 #15 NAPA Bank
2001 #15 NAPA/6228
2002 #15 NAPA Stars&Stri./9650
2002 #15 NAPA Clear/4548
2002 #15 NAPA Bank/1332
2002 #15 NAPA/17,280
2002 #15 NAPA Stars&Stripes Bank/1008
2003 #15 NAPA Stars&Stripes CW Bank/492
2003 #15 NAPA Stars&Stripes/8652
2003 #15 NAPA Nilla Wafers CW Bank/456
2003 #15 NAPA Nilla Wafers/7164
2003 #15 NAPA Hootie GM Dealers/504
2003 #15 NAPA Hootie CW Bank/684
2003 #15 NAPA Hootie/10,008
2003 #15 NAPA GM Dealer/504
2003 #15 NAPA Bank/480
2003 #15 NAPA/8304
2003 #99 Aaron's Rent T3 GM Dealers/360
2003 #99 Aaron's Rent T3 CW Bank/692
2003 #99 Aaron's Rent T3/8004
2003 #99 Aaron's Rent Three Stooges/7584
2003 #99 Aaron's Rent Cat in the Hat/4968
2003 #99 Aaron's Rent/3504
2003 #2003 DEI Pit Practice/2508
2004 #15 NAPA Stars&Stripes QVC/504
2004 #15 NAPA Stars&Stripes GM Dealers/288
2004 #15 NAPA Stars&Stripes CW Bank/252
2004 #15 NAPA Stars&Stripes/4488
2004 #15 NAPA Father's Day CW Bank/324
2004 #15 NAPA Father's Day/5184
2004 #15 NAPA Nextel Incentive/2304
2004 #15 NAPA Mac Tools/288
2004 #15 NAPA GM Dealers/2004
2004 #15 NAPA CW Bank/396
2004 #15 NAPA/13,596
2004 #47 Sheryl Crow SuperTruck/4344
2004 #99 Aaron's Simpsons/5004
2004 #99 Aaron's Simpsons CW Bank/408
2004 #99 Domino's Pizza/2100
2004 #99 Best Western CW Bank
2004 #99 Best Western/2748
2004 #99 Aaron's Operation Marathon/1296
2004 #99 Aaron's Mad Magazine QVC/288
2004 #99 Aaron's Mad Magazine Mac Tools/204
2004 #99 Aaron's Mad Magazine CW Bank/240
2004 #99 Aaron's Mad Mag/2364
2004 #99 Aaron's LeAnn Rimes GM Dealers/240
2004 #99 Aaron's LeAnn Rimes CW Bank/192
2004 #99 Aaron's LeAnn Rimes/2124
2004 #99 Aaron's Mac Tools/288
2004 #99 Aaron's CW Bank/240
2004 #99 Aaron's/2664
2005 #15 Napa Stars & Stripes CW Bank/144
2005 #15 Napa Stars & Stripes GM Dealers/84
2005 #15 Napa Stars & Stripes/1440
2005 #15 Napa QVC/360
2005 #15 Napa Matco/72
2005 #15 Napa CW Bank/192
2005 #15 Napa/4512
2005 #99 Domino's Pizza GM Dealers/36
2005 #99 Domino's Pizza/2508
2005 #99 Aaron's 50th Ann.Matco/24
2005 #99 Aaron's 50th Ann. GM Dealers/24
2005 #99 Aaron's 50th Anniversary/3660
2005 #99 Aaron's/1200
Action Racing Collectables 1:64
1996 #21 Citgo Star Trek
1996 #21 Citgo

2000 #7 Nations Rent
2000 #15 Nations Rent/7560
2001 #15 NAPA Stars&Strip/22,104
2001 #15 NAPA
2002 #15 NAPA Stars&Stri./10,388
2002 #15 NAPA/16,920
2003 #15 NAPA Stars&Stripes/7992
2003 #15 NAPA Nilla Wafers
2003 #15 NAPA Hootie/7200
2003 #15 NAPA/9072
2003 #99 Aaron's Rent
2003 #99 Aar.Rent 3 Stooges/6408
2003 #99 Aaron's Rent T3/6912
2003 #99 Aaron's Rent Cat in the Hat/3888
2004 #15 NAPA Stars&Stripes/3792
2004 #15 NAPA/8976
2004 #99 Aaron's
2004 #99 Aaron's LeAnn Rimes/5040
2004 #99 Aaron's Simpsons/5040
2005 #15 Napa
2005 #99 Aaron's 50th Anniversary
2005 #99 Aaron's
2005 #99/00 K.Wallace/Aaron's 50th Ann 2-car set in tin
Action Racing Collectables Pit Wagon
1990-03 #30 Pennzoil/2508 '94
Action Racing Collectables Platinum 1:2
2008 #55 Napa/5388
Action/RCCA 1:24
1994 #30 Pennzoil
1996 #21 Citgo Star Trek
1996 #21 Citgo Bank/5000
2002 #15 NAPA Stars&Stripes Bank/504
2002 #15 NAPA Bank/600
2003 #15 NAPA Hootie/496
2003 #15 NAPA Stars&Stripes/504
2003 #15 NAPA Nilla CW Bank/504
2003 #15 NAPA Bank/504
2003 #99 Aaron's Rent Cat in the Hat/444
2003 #99 Aaron's Rent 3 Stooges/460
2003 #99 Aaron's Rent T3/504
2003 #99 Aaron's Rent/444
2004 #15 NAPA Stars & Stripes/288
2004 #15 NAPA Father's Day/240
2004 #15 NAPA/600
2004 #99 Aaron's Dream Machine/300
2004 #99 Best Western/288
2004 #99 Domino's Pizza/360
2004 #99 Aaron's Dream Machine Operation Marathon/360
2004 #99 Aaron's Dream Machine Mad Magazine/288
2004 #99 Aaron's Dream Machine LeAnn Rimes/288
2005 #15 Napa Color Chrome/204
2005 #15 Napa Stars & Stripes/288
2005 #15 Napa/288
2005 #99 Aaron's 50th Anniversary/240
Action/RCCA 1:64
1994 #30 Pennzoil/10,000
1996 #21 Citgo Star Trek/10,000
2000 #7 Nations Rent/2016
2001 #15 NAPA Stars&Stripe/1104
2001 #15 NAPA/1584
2002 #15 NAPA Stars&Stripes/1584
2002 #15 NAPA/1584
2003 #15 NAPA Stars&Stripes/1020
2003 #15 NAPA Nilla Wafers/1020
2003 #15 NAPA Hootie/1012
2003 #15 NAPA/1020
2003 #99 Aaron's Rent T3/1020
2003 #99 Aar.Rent 3 Stooges/1020
2003 #99 Aaron's Rent Cat in the Hat/1020
2004 #15 NAPA Stars & Stripes/720
2004 #15 NAPA/1008
2004 #99 Aaron's Dream Mach.Promo
2005 #15 Napa/576
Action/RCCA Banks 1:24
2000 #7 Nations Rent/1008
2001 #15 NAPA/900
Action/RCCA Dually Trucks 1:64
1994-97 #30 Pennzoil RCCA/7572 '94
Action/RCCA Elite 1:24
2001 #15 NAPA Daytona Raced/2800
2001 #15 NAPA/1008
2002 #15 NAPA Stars&Stripes/540A
2002 #15 NAPA/600
2002 #2002 DEI Racing Pit Practice/2002
2003 #15 NAPA Stars & Stripes/804
2003 #15 NAPA Nilla Wafers/804
2003 #15 NAPA Hootie/496
2003 #15 NAPA Raced/604
2003 #15 NAPA/604
2003 #99 Aaron's Rent T3/804
2003 #99 Aaron's Rent 3 Stooges/460
2003 #99 Aaron's Rent Cat in the Hat/444
2003 #99 Aaron's Rent/444
2004 #15 NAPA Stars & Stripes/288
2004 #15 NAPA Test Daytona/504
2004 #15 NAPA Color Chrome/300
2004 #15 NAPA/800
2004 #99 Best Western/228
2004 #99 Aaron's Dream Machine LeAnn Rimes/288
2005 #15 Napa Stars & Stripes/288
2005 #15 Napa White Gold/25
2005 #15 Napa Color Chrome/204
2005 #15 Napa/408
Action/RCCA Elite 1:64
2001 #15 NAPA Stars&Stripe/1104
2002 #15 NAPA Stars&Strip/1152A
2003 #15 NAPA Stars&Stripes/1020
2003 #15 NAPA Nilla Wafers/1020
2003 #15 NAPA Hootie/1012
2003 #15 NAPA/1020
2003 #99 Aaron's Rent T3/1020
2004 #15 NAPA Stars & Stripes/504
2004 #15 NAPA/720
2005 #15 Napa/480
Action/RCCA Metal Elite 1:24
2004 #15 NAPA/800
Action/RCCA Revell 1:64
1991-92 #30 Pennzoil
Action/RCCA SelectNet 1:64
1999 #15 NAPA Stars& Stripes
Action/RCCA Transporters 1:64
2003 #15 NAPA/600
Brookfield 1:24
2005 #15 Napa/204
Brookfield Dually with Car and Show
1993-95 #30 Pennzoil w/o car Silver/250 '95
1993-95 #30 Pennzoil w/o car/5000 '95
Brookfield Suburbans, Blazers, and Taho
1994 #30 Pennzoil/10,000
Ertl 1:18
1992 #30 Pennzoil
Ertl 1:64
1986-93 #30 NDA/Country Time Max.House '90
Ertl Transporters 1:64
1990 #30 NDA/Country Time

Funstuf Pit Row 1:64
1992 #20 Orkin
Hot Wheels Crew's Choice 1:24
2000 #7 Nations Rent
Hot Wheels Deluxe 1:64
2000 #7 NationsRent
Hot Wheels Deluxe Hydroplane 1:64
2000 #7 Nations Rent
Hot Wheels First Edition 1:64
1997 #21 Citgo
1998 #21 Citgo
Hot Wheels Fresh Paint 1:24
1999 #7 Sealy
Hot Wheels Preview Edition 1:64
1998 #21 Citgo
Hot Wheels Pro Racing 1:64
1997 #21 Citgo
Hot Wheels Pro Racing Pit Crew 1:64
1998 #21 Citgo
Hot Wheels Pro Racing Pit Crew Gold 1:6
1998 #21 Citgo
Hot Wheels Pro Racing Superspeedway 1:6
1997 #21 Citgo
Hot Wheels Pro Racing Trading Paint 1:6
1998 #21 Citgo
Hot Wheels Race Day Deluxe 1:24
2000 #7 NationsRent
Hot Wheels Racing 1:43
1998 #7 Phillips
Hot Wheels Racing Daytona 500 1:64
1999 #7 Phillips
1999 #21 Citgo
Hot Wheels Racing Pit Crew 1:64
1999 #7 Phillips
1999 #21 Citgo
Hot Wheels Racing Radical Rides 1:64
2000 #7 Nations Rent
Hot Wheels Racing Speed and Thunder 1:6
1999 #30 State Fair
Hot Wheels Racing Tall Draggers 1:64
2001 #7 Nations Rent
Hot Wheels Racing Track Edition 1:64
1999 #7 Klaussner/Philips
2000 #7 Nations Rent
Hot Wheels Short Track 1:64
1997 #21 Citgo red top
1997 #21 Citgo
Hot Wheels Test Track 1:64
1998 #21 Citgo
Hot Wheels Track Edition 1:64
1998 #21 Citgo
Hot Wheels Trading Paint 1:24
1999 #7 Phillips
Matchbox White Rose Super Stars 1:64
1994 #30 Pennzoil BX
1996 #21 Citgo
1990-92 #30 Pennzoil BL 92
Matchbox White Rose Team Convoys 1:6
1990-93 #30 Pennzoil w/Van '91
Matchbox White Rose Transporters Super
1992 #30 Pennzoil
1996 #21 Citgo
Motorsports Authentics Driver's Select
2007 #55 NAPA COT/1416*
2007 #55 NAPA/10,404*
Motorsports Authentics Owner's Elite 1:
2007 #55 NAPA COT/504*
2007 #55 NAPA/1008*
2007 #55 NAPA/1008*
Motorsports Authentics Owner's Elite Tr
2007 #55 NAPA/1000*
Motorsports Authentics Pit Stop 1:64
2007 #55 NAPA
Motorsports Authentics/RCCA Owner's Clu
2007 #55 NAPA/708*
Race Image 1:43
1997 #21 Citgo
1998 #21 Citgo
Race Image Service Kit 1:43
1998 #21 Citgo
Racing Champions 1:144
1996 #21 Citgo
1997 #21 Citgo
1998 #21 Citgo
Racing Champions 1:24
1993 #30 Pennzoil
1994 #30 Pennzoil
1996 #21 Citgo
1997 #21 Citgo
1998 #21 Citgo
1999 #7 M.Waltip/Philips
2000 #7 Nations Rent Chrome/999
2000 #7 Nation's Rent
2000 #99 Aaron's Promo
2002 #99 Aaron's Rent
1991-92 #30 Pennzoil
Racing Champions 1:43
1992 #30 Pennzoil
Racing Champions 1:64
1990 #30 Maxwell House Promo
1990 #30 Maxwell House
1990 #30 Country Time Promo
1990 #30 Country Time
1990 #NNO 12-car set in case
1991 #30 Pont.Country Time EB
1991 #30 Pontiac PB
1991 #30 Pontiac NP
1991 #30 Pontiac Pennzoil EB without STP decal
1991 #30 Pontiac Pennzoil EB with STP decal
1992 #30 Pennzoil
1992 #NNO Sears 12-car set
1992 #NNO Collect.Edit.12-car set w/R.Petty
1992 #NNO Collectors Edition 4-car set
1994 #30 Pennzoil
1995 #30 Pennzoil
1996 #12 MW Windows
1996 #21 Citgo Promo
1996 #21 Citgo
1996 #NNO 12-Car set in case
1997 #21 Citgo Chrome/1997
1997 #21 Citgo
1998 #21 Goodwill Games
1998 #21 Citgo
1999 #7 Philips
2000 #7 Nation's Rent
2000 #99 Aaron's Promo
2000 #NNO 12-car boxed set/2500
2002 #99 Aaron's
Racing Champions 24K Gold 1:24
1998 #21 Citgo
Racing Champions 24K Gold 1:64
1998 #21 Citgo

Racing Champions 2-Car Sets 1:24/1:64
1999 #7 Phillips Promo
Racing Champions 3-Pack 1:64
1990-92 #28/30/94 Dav.Allison/M.Waltrip S.Marlin '90
Racing Champions 5-Pack 1:64
2000 #NNO 6.MM/99.JB/75.WD/7.MW/40.SM
Racing Champions 5-Pack Preview 1:144
1997 #NNO 5/6/21/24/28
Racing Champions Authentics 1:24
2000 #7 Nations Rent Matco/3100
Racing Champions Banks 1:24
1992-94 #30 Pennzoil
Racing Champions Fan Appreciation 5-Pac
1998 #6 35.TAB/26.JB/50/21.MW/21.MW
1999 #7 00.BJ/6.MM/7.MW/10thA/9.JN
Racing Champions Flat Bottom 1:64
1989 #30 Country Time
Racing Champions Gold 1:24
1998 #21 Citgo Bank
1998 #21 Citgo
Racing Champions Gold Hood Open 1:24
1998 #21 Goodwill Games
Racing Champions Gold with Medallion 1:
1998 #21 Citgo
Racing Champions Hobby Yellow Box 1:64
1994 #30 Pennzoil
Racing Champions Hood Open Banks 1:24
1996 #21 Citgo
Racing Champions Nascar Rules 1:64
2000 #7 Nation's Rent
Racing Champions Pinnacle Series 1:64
1997 #21 Citgo
1998 #21 Citgo
Racing Champions Pit Crew 1:64
2000 #7 Naions Rent
Racing Champions Premier 1:43
1994 #30 Pennzoil
Racing Champions Premier 1:64
2000 #7 Nation's Rent
2002 #99 Aaron's
Racing Champions Premier Brickyard 400
1994 #30 Pennzoil
Racing Champions Premier Hood Open 1:24
1996 #21 Citgo
Racing Champions Premier with Medallion
1997 #21 Citgo
Racing Champions Press Pass Series 1:64
1998 #21 Goodwill Games
1999 #7 Philips
Racing Champions Preview 1:144
1997 #21 Citgo
Racing Champions Preview 1:24
1997 #21 Citgo
2000 #7 Nation's Rent
Racing Champions Preview 1:64
1995 #30 Pennzoil
1997 #21 Citgo
2000 #7 Nation's Rent
Racing Champions Race Day 1:64
1998 #21 Citgo
Racing Champions Roaring Racers 1:64
1997 #21 Citgo
1990-91 #30 Pennzoil '90
Racing Champions Signature Series 1:64
1998 #21 Citgo
1999 #7 Philips
Racing Champions Stock Rods 1:144
1998 #43 Pennzoil
Racing Champions Stock Rods 1:24
1998 #19 Citgo
1998 #38 Citgo
1998 #64 Citgo
1998 #73 Citgo Gold
Racing Champions Stock Rods 1:64
1998 #65 Citgo
1998 #77 Citgo
1998 #125 Citgo
1998 #128 Citgo
1998 #134 Citgo
1998 #142 Citgo Gold
Racing Champions Stock Rods 24K Gold 1:
1998 #12 Citgo
Racing Champions Super Collector's S
1992-94 #30 Pennzoil 3-cars 1:24/64/87 and 2-Transporters
Racing Champions SuperTrucks 1:144
1997 #1 MW Windows
Racing Champions SuperTrucks 1:24
1997 #1 MW Windows
Racing Champions SuperTrucks 1:64
1997 #1 MW Windows
Racing Champions SuperTrucks 5-Pack 1:1
1997 #NNO 99.MM/99.JB/1.MW/15.EI/18.JB
Racing Champions Toys 'R Us Gold 1:64
1998 #21 Goodwill Games
Racing Champions Transporters 1:144
1995 #30 Pennzoil
1997 #21 Citgo
1991-92 #30 Pennzoil with mini car
Racing Champions Transporters 1:64
1992 #30 Pennzoil
1993 #30 Pennzoil
1996 #21 Citgo w/car(s)
1997 #21 Citgo
1998 #21 Goodwill Games w/car
1998 #21 Goodwill Games
1998 #21 Citgo w/Car
1998 #21 Citgo
2000 #7 Nation's Rent
Racing Champions Transporters 1:87
1996 #12 MW Windows
1996 #21 Citgo
1997 #21 Citgo
1998 #21 Goodwill Games
1998 #21 Citgo
Racing Champions Transporters Gold 1:64
1998 #21 Citgo
Racing Champions Transporters Hobby 1:6
1994 #30 Pennzoil
Racing Champions Transporters Hobby 1:8
1994 #30 Pennzoil
Racing Champions Transporters Retail
1993-94 #30 Pennzoil
Racing Champions Transporters Retail 1:
1994 #30 Pennzoil
Racing Champions Transporters Signature
1998 #21 Citgo
Racing Champions War Paint 1:64
2000 #7 Nations Rent
RCCA Club 1:24
2008 #55 Napa/120
RCCA Elite 1:24

2008 #55 Napa/300
2008 #55 Napa Platinum/25
2008 #55 Napa White Gold/50
Revell 1:24
1991-95 #30 Pennzoil '91
Revell Club 1:24
1997 #21 Citgo Top Dog/1596
1997 #21 Citgo Pearson white/1596
1998 #21 Citgo/1002
Revell Collection 1:18
1997 #21 Citgo Top Dog/3120
Revell Collection 1:24
1997 #21 Citgo Top Dog/5004
1997 #21 Citgo Pearson white&red
1997 #21 Citgo Orange/4122
1997 #55 Sealy
1998 #21 Citgo
2001 #15 NAPA Daytona Win/21.016
2003 #15 NAPA Raced/4824
2004 #15 NAPA Test/1278
Revell Collection 1:43
1997 #21 Citgo Top Dog
1997 #21 Citgo
Revell Collection 1:64
1998 #21 Citgo
2001 #NNO Bud All-Star NAPA SS set in tin/12,000
Revell Retail 1:24
1996 #21 Citgo
1997 #21 Citgo Pearson white&red
1997 #21 Citgo Top Dog
Revell Retail 1:64
1996 #21 Citgo w/Eagle on deck
1996 #21 Citgo
1997 #21 Citgo Top Dog
Revell Select 1:24
1997 #21 Citgo Top Dog
1998 #21 Citgo
Revell Select Hobby 1:64
1997 #21 Citgo Top Dog
1998 #21 Citgo
Team Caliber 1:24
1999 #7 Phillips
Team Caliber 1:64
1999 #7 Phillips
Team Caliber Owners Series 1:24
2000 #7 Nations Rent/2340
Team Caliber Owner's Series 1:24
2006 #55 Napa/2400
Team Caliber Owners Series 1:64
2000 #7 Nations Rent
Team Caliber Pit Stop 1:24
2006 #55 Napa Stars & Stripes
2006 #55 Napa
2006 #55 Domino's
2006 #99 Best Western
2006 #99 Aaron's UT Longhorns
2006 #99 Aaron's
Team Caliber Pit Stop 1:64
2006 #55 Napa Stars & Stripes
2006 #55 Napa
2006 #55 Domino's
2006 #99 Best Western
2006 #99 Aaron's
Team Caliber Preferred 1:24
2000 #7 Nations Rent/5508
2006 #55 Napa Stars & Stripes/2700
2006 #55 Napa/5004
2006 #55 Domino's/3000
2006 #99 Best Western/1800
2006 #99 Aaron's/6504
Team Caliber Preferred Copper 1:24
2006 #55 Napa Stars & Stripes/180
2006 #55 Napa
2006 #99 Best Western/180
2006 #99 Aaron's
Winner's Circle 1:18
2003 #98 Aaron's Cat in the Hat
2004 #15 NAPA
2004 #99 Aaron's Cat in the Hat
Winner's Circle 1:24
2001 #15 NAPA
2004 #15 NAPA
2005 #15 Napa Stars
2005 #99 Domino's Pizza
2007 #55 NAPA
2008 #55 Napa
Winner's Circle 1:87
2007 #55 NAPA
2008 #55 Napa
Winner's Circle Autographed Hood 1:64
2003 #98 Aaron's Cat in the Hat
2004 #99 Aaron's Cat in the Hat
2005 #15 Napa Stars & Stripes
2005 #99 Domino's Pizza
2005 #99 Aaron's
Winner's Circle Double Platinum 1:43
2002 #15 NAPA
Winner's Circle Driver Sticker 1:64
2003 #15 NAPA
2004 #15 NAPA
Winner's Circle Fast Pack 1:64
2002 #15/1/8S.Park/D.Earn Jr.
Winner's Circle Gallery 1:64
2002 #15 NAPA
Winner's Circle Number Magnet 1:64
2008 #55 NAPA
Winner's Circle Pit Pass Preview 1:64
2002 #15 NAPA
2003 #15 NAPA '03 Preview sticker
2003 #15 NAPA
2004 #15 NAPA
Winner's Circle Race Hood 1:43
2002 #15 NAPA
Winner's Circle Race Hood 1:64
2004 #99 Cat in the Hat
2001-02 #15 NAPA
Winner's Circle Schedule Hood 1:64
2005 #15 Napa
2007 #55 NAPA
Winner's Circle Stickers 1:64
2008 #55 NAPA
Winner's Circle Transporters 1:64
2002 #15 NAPA Star&Stripes
2002 #15 NAPA
2003 #98 Aaron's Cat in the Hat
2004 #15 NAPA
2004 #99 Aaron's Cat in the Hat
2005 #15 Napa
2007 #55 NAPA
Winross Transporters 1:64
1994 #NNO Pennzoil
1996 #NNO Citgo

Acknowledgments

When we started this Beckett Guide we were unsure what type of response we would get from dealers when we asked them to play a major role in our price gathering. Most were more than happy to lend a hand. Thanks again to all the contributors nationwide (listed below) as well as our staff here in Dallas.

Those who worked closely with us on this edition and past versions of this book have proven themselves invaluable. We would like to thank the following manufacturers -- Action Performance (Fred & Lisa Wagenhals), Brookfield Collector's Guild and RCCA (Terry Rubritz), Hot Wheels, Peachstate/GMP, Motorsports Authentics (Mark Dyer, Howard Hitchcock, Tara Larson, Cindy Paletsos, Amy Tabor, Scott Warfield), Press Pass (Tom Farrell, Bob Bove & Miles Atkins, and Heather Maillard), Racing Champions (Mary Stevens and Leah Giarritano), Ertl Collectibles (D.J. Kazmierczak & Terri Rehkop), SportCoins (Gregg Yetter), Team Caliber (Mike Brown), Katie Roland & Kevin Davies (GreenLight Toys). Finally we give a special acknowledgment to the late Dennis W. Eckes, "Mr. Sports Americana." The success of the Beckett Price Guides has always been a result of a team effort.

It is very difficult to be "accurate" -- one can only do one's best. But this job is especially difficult since we're shooting at a moving target. Prices are fluctuating all the time. Having several full-time pricing experts has definitely proven to be better than just one, and I thank all of them for working together to provide you, our readers, with the most accurate prices possible.

Many people have provided price input, illustrative material, checklist verifications, errata, and/or background information. We should like to individually thank Red Barnes (Baseline Sports), Mike Otto & John Russo (Bono's of Plano), Mark Dorsey (Hamps Supply), Ed & Lynn Gaffney (North Coast Racing), David Giffert (Victory Lane Race Cards), Jon Hargrove (The Carburetor Shop), Bob Harmon & Dan Talbert (North State Race Cards), Greg Jeffries, Dean & Kathy Knight (Kathy's Kards), Luke Krisher & Anna Schreck (A&L Racing Collectibles), Norm LaBarge, Sandy Larson (Northern Likes Racing), Stewart Lehman (Lehman Racing Collectables), Mike Locotosh (North Coast Racing), Johnny Love (Win Racing), Gene Persinger (G n' G Sports Cards), Scott Polner (Collector's Choice), Mario Raucci (Lane Automotive), Russ Dickey (GoMotorBids), Brian Shepherd (Shepherd's Racing), Richard Schultz (Racing Around), Bono Saunders (Bono's Race Place), Bill Spertzel (Cards Etc.), Danny West (Golden Legacy), Kevin & Trish Wheeler (Sports Cards, Etc.), Tim Legee (Die-Cast Deals), Dave Gaumer (Dave's Pit Stop Race Cards) and Ron Steffe (Brickel's).

Every year we actively solict expert input. We are particularly appreciative of help (however extensive or cursory) provided for this volume. We receive many inquiries, comments and questions regarding material within this book. In fact, each and every one is read and digested. Time constraints, however, prevent us from personally replying. But keep sharing your knowledge. Your letters and input are part of the "big picture" of hobby information we can pass along to readers in our books and magazines. Even though we cannot respond to each letter, you are making significant contributions to the hobby through your interest and comments.

The effort to continually refine and improve this book also involves a growing number of people and types of expertise on our home team. Our company boasts a substantial Sports Data Publishing team, which strengthens our ability to provide comprehensive analysis of the marketplace. Sports Data Publishing capably handled numerous technical details and provided able assistance in the preparation of this edition.

Our racing analyst played a major part in compiling this year's book, traveling thousands of miles during the past year to attend sports card shows, racing events and visit card shops around the United States and Canada. The Beckett racing specialist is Tim Trout (Editor). His pricing analysis and careful proofreading were key contributions to the accuracy of this annual.

Tim Trout's coordination and reconciling of prices as Beckett Racing Editor helped immeasurably. He was ably assisted by the rest of the Price Guide Team: Dan Hitt (Senior Manager), Brian Fleischer, Keith Hower, Grant Sandground, Bryan Hornbeck, Kevin Haake & Matthew Brumley.

The price gathering and analytical talents of this fine group of hobbyists have helped make our Beckett team stronger, while making this guide and its companion Price Guide more widely recognized as the hobby's most reliable and relied upon sources of pricing information.

The Beckett Interactive Department, played a critical role in technology. They spent countless hours programming, testing, and implementing it to simplify the handling of thousands of prices that must be checked and updated for each edition.

In the Production Department, Gean Paul Figari was responsible for the layout and Daniel Moscoso for the photos you see throughout the book.